Profiles
of
Texas

2011
Third Edition

Profiles
of
Texas

A UNIVERSAL REFERENCE BOOK

Grey House
Publishing

PUBLISHER: Leslie Mackenzie
EDITORIAL DIRECTOR: Laura Mars
EDITOR: David Garoogian
MARKETING DIRECTOR: Jessica Moody

Grey House Publishing, Inc.
4919 Route 22
Amenia, NY 12501
518.789.8700
FAX 845.373.6390
www.greyhouse.com
e-mail: books @greyhouse.com

While every effort has been made to ensure the reliability of the information presented in this publication, Grey House Publishing neither guarantees the accuracy of the data contained herein nor assumes any responsibility for errors, omissions or discrepancies. Grey House accepts no payment for listing; inclusion in the publication of any organization, agency, institution, publication, service or individual does not imply endorsement of the editors or publisher.

Errors brought to the attention of the publisher and verified to the satisfaction of the publisher will be corrected in future editions.

First edition published 2005
Printed in Canada

ISBN: 978-1-59237-771-8

Table of Contents

Introduction

Welcome to the third edition of *Profiles of Texas—Facts, Figures & Statistics for 1,784 Populated Places in Texas*. As with the other titles in our *State Profiles* series, we built this work using content from Grey House Publishing's award-winning *Profiles of America*—a 4-volume compilation of data on more than 42,000 places in the United States. We have updated and included the Texas chapter from *Profiles of America*, and added entire fresh chapters of demographic information and ranking sections, so that *Profiles of Texas* is the most comprehensive portrait of the state of Texas ever published.

This third edition provides data on all populated communities and counties in the state of Texas for which the US Census provides individual statistics. It includes seven major sections that cover everything from **Education** to **Ethnic Backgrounds** to **Climate**. All sections include **Comparative Statistics** or **Rankings**, and full-color **Maps** at the back of the book provide valuable information in a quickly processed, visual format. Here's an overview of each section:

1. Profiles

This section, organized by county, gives detailed profiles of 1,784 places plus 254 counties. Based on core Census data, these numbers reflect extensive updates from the U.S. Census Bureau's American Community Survey, and Nielsen Claritas, a trusted source for up-to-date demographic information. In addition, we have added current government statistics and original research, so that these profiles pull together statistical and descriptive information on every Census-recognized place in the state. Major fields of information include:

Geography	*Housing*	*Education*	*Religion*
Ancestry	*Transportation*	*Population*	*Climate*
Economy	*Industry*	*Health*	

In addition to place profiles, this section includes an **Alphabetical Place Index** and **Comparative Statistics** that compare Texas' 100 largest communities by dozens of data points.

2. Education

This section begins with an **Educational State Profile,** summarizing number of schools, students, diplomas granted and educational dollars spent. Following the state profile are **School District Rankings** on 16 topics ranging from *Teacher/Student Ratios* to *High School Drop-Out Rates*. Following these rankings are statewide *National Assessment of Educational Progress (NAEP)* results and data from the *Texas Assessment of Knowledge and Skils (TAKS)*—an overview of student performance by subject, including easy-to-read charts and graphs.

3. Ancestry

This section provides a detailed look at the ancestral and racial makeup of Texas. 217 ethnic categories are ranked three ways: 1) by number, based on all places regardless of population; 2) by percent, based on all places regardless of population; 3) by percent, based on places with populations of 10,000 or more. You will discover, for example, that Austin has the greatest number of *Cypriots* in the state (46), and that 15.2% of the population of Flower Mound are of *Irish* ancestry.

4. Hispanic Population

This section defines Texas' Hispanic population by 23 Hispanic backgrounds from *Argentinian* to *Venezuelan*. It ranks each of 15 categories, from Median Age to Median Home Value, by each Hispanic background. For example, you'll see that Keller has the highest percentage of *Mexicans* who speak English-only at home (63.4%), and that Plano has the highest percentage of *Puerto Ricans* who are four-year college graduates (45.6%).

5. Asian Population

Similar in format to the section on Hispanic Population, this section defines Texas' Asian population by 21 Asian backgrounds from *Bangladeshi* to *Vietnamese*. It ranks each of 14 categories, from Median Age to Median Home Value, by each Asian background. You will learn that *Filipinos* in Sugar Land have a median household income of $91,286 and that 100.0% of *Koreans* in College Station are high-school graduates.

6. Climate
This important topic has been greatly expanded and updated since the last edition. Each state chapter includes a State Summary, two new maps—weather stations and a relief map—and profiles of both National and Cooperative Weather Stations. In addition, you'll find Weather Station Rankings with hundreds of interesting details, such as Amarillo International Airport, Anson, and Penwell reporting the lowest annual extreme minimum temperatures (-12° F).

These sections also include Significant Storm Event data from January 2000 through December 2009. Here you will learn that a hailstorm caused $100 million in property damage in El Paso in September 2009 and that extreme heat was responsible for 49 deaths in Chambers, Harris, Houston, and Montgomery Counties in September 2005.

7. Maps
For a more visual point of view, there are 16 full-color maps of Texas at the back of the book. They provide information on topics such as *Federal Lands and Indian Reservations, Core-Based Statistical Areas and Counties, Hazard Events, Population Demographics, Median Age, Income, Median Home Values, Educational Attainment, Congressional Districts,* and the *2008 Presidential Election.*

Note: The extensive **User's Guide** that follows this Introduction is segmented into six sections and examines, in some detail, each data field in the individual profiles and comparative sections for all chapters. It provides sources for all data points and statistical definitions as necessary.

User's Guide: Profiles

Places Covered

All 254 counties.

1,194 incorporated municipalities. Municipalities are incorporated as either cities, towns or villages.

317 census designated places (CDP). The U.S. Bureau of the Census defines a CDP as "a statistical entity, defined for each decennial census according to Census Bureau guidelines, comprising a densely settled concentration of population that is not within an incorporated place, but is locally identified by a name. CDPs are delineated cooperatively by state and local officials and the Census Bureau, following Census Bureau guidelines. Beginning with Census 2000 there are no size limits."

273 unincorporated communities. The communities included have both their own zip code and statistics for their ZIP Code Tabulation Area (ZCTA) available from the Census Bureau. They are referred to as "postal areas." A ZCTA is a statistical entity developed by the Census Bureau to approximate the delivery area for a US Postal Service 5-digit or 3-digit ZIP Code in the US and Puerto Rico. A ZCTA is an aggregation of census blocks that have the same predominant ZIP Code associated with the mailing addresses in the Census Bureau's Master Address File. Thus, the Postal Service's delivery areas have been adjusted to encompass whole census blocks so that the Census Bureau can tabulate census data for the ZCTAs. ZCTAs do not include all ZIP Codes used for mail delivery and therefore do not precisely depict the area within which mail deliveries associated with that ZIP Code occur. Additionally, some areas that are known by a unique name, although they are part of a larger incorporated place, are also included as "postal areas."

Important Notes

- *Profiles of Texas* uses the term "community" to refer to all places except counties. The term "county" is used to refer to counties and county-equivalents. All places are defined as of the 2000 Census.

- In each community profile, only school districts that have schools that are physically located within the community are shown. In addition, statistics for each school district cover the entire district, regardless of the physical location of the schools within the district.

- Special care should be taken when interpreting certain statistics for communities containing large colleges or universities. College students were counted as residents of the area in which they were living while attending college (as they have been since the 1950 census). One effect this may have is skewing the figures for population, income, housing, and educational attainment.

- Some information (e.g. unemployment rates) is available for both counties and individual communities. Other information is available for just counties (e.g. election results), or just individual communities (e.g. local newspapers).

- Some statistical information is available only for larger communities. In addition, the larger places are more apt to have services such as newspapers, airports, school districts, etc.

- For the most complete information on any community, you should also check the entry for the county in which the community is located. In addition, more information and services will be listed under the larger places in the county.

- For a more in-depth discussion of geographic areas, please refer to the Census Bureau's Geographic Areas Reference Manual at http://www.census.gov/geo/www/garm.html.

Data Sources

CENSUS 2000

The parts of the data which are from the 2000 Decennial Census are from the following sources: *U.S. Bureau of the Census, Census of Population and Housing, 2000: Summary Files 1 and 3.* Summary File 3 (SF 3) consists of 813 detailed tables of Census 2000 social, economic and housing characteristics compiled from a sample of approximately 19 million housing units (about 1 in 6 households) that received the Census 2000 long-form questionnaire. Summary File 1 (SF 1) contains 286 tables focusing on age, sex, households, families, and housing units. This file presents 100-percent population and housing figures for the total population, for 63 race categories, and for many other race and Hispanic or Latino categories.

Comparing SF 3 Estimates with Corresponding Values in SF 1

As in earlier censuses, the responses from the sample of households reporting on long forms must be weighted to reflect the entire population. Specifically, each responding household represents, on average, six or seven other households who reported using short forms.

One consequence of the weighting procedures is that each estimate based on the long form responses has an associated confidence interval. These confidence intervals are wider (as a percentage of the estimate) for geographic areas with smaller populations and for characteristics that occur less frequently in the area being examined (such as the proportion of people in poverty in a middle-income neighborhood).

In order to release as much useful information as possible, statisticians must balance a number of factors. In particular, for Census 2000, the Bureau of the Census created weighting areas—geographic areas from which about two hundred or more long forms were completed—which are large enough to produce good quality estimates. If smaller weighting areas had been used, the confidence intervals around the estimates would have been significantly wider, rendering many estimates less useful due to their lower reliability.

The disadvantage of using weighting areas this large is that, for smaller geographic areas within them, the estimates of characteristics that are also reported on the short form will not match the counts reported in SF 1. Examples of these characteristics are the total number of people, the number of people reporting specific racial categories, and the number of housing units. The official values for items reported on the short form come from SF 1 and SF 2.

The differences between the long form estimates in SF 3 and values in SF 1 are particularly noticeable for the smallest places, tracts, and block groups. The long form estimates of total population and total housing units in SF 3 will, however, match the SF 1 counts for larger geographic areas such as counties and states, and will be essentially the same for medium and large cities.

SF 1 gives exact numbers even for very small groups and areas, whereas SF 3 gives estimates for small groups and areas such as tracts and small places that are less exact. The goal of SF 3 is to identify large differences among areas or large changes over time. Estimates for small areas and small population groups often do exhibit large changes from one census to the next, so having the capability to measure them is worthwhile.

2010 Estimates and 2015 Projections

Most 2000 Census data has been updated with data provided by Nielsen Claritas. Founded in 1971, Nielsen Claritas is the industry leader in applied demography and the preeminent provider of small-area demographic estimates.

Information for Communities

PHYSICAL CHARACTERISTICS

Place Type: Lists the type of place (city, town, village, borough, special city, CDP, township, plantation, gore, district, grant, location, reservation, or postal area). *Source: U.S. Bureau of the Census, Census of Population and Housing, 2000: Summary File 1 and U.S. Postal Service, City State File.*

Land and Water Area: Land and water area in square miles. *Source: U.S. Bureau of the Census, Census of Population and Housing, 2000: Summary File 1.*

Latitude and Longitude: Latitude and longitude in degrees. *Source: U.S. Bureau of the Census, Census of Population and Housing, 2000: Summary File 1.*

Elevation: Elevation in feet. *Source: U.S. Geological Survey, Geographic Names Information System (GNIS).*

HISTORY

History: Historical information. *Source: Columbia University Press, The Columbia Gazetteer of North America; Original research.*

POPULATION

Population: 1990 and 2000 figures are a 100% count of population. 2010 estimates and 2015 projections were provided by Nielsen Claritas. *Source: Nielsen Claritas; U.S. Bureau of the Census, Census of Population and Housing, 2000: Summary File 1.*

Population by Race: 2010 estimates includes the U.S. Bureau of the Census categories of White alone; Black alone; Asian alone; and Hispanic of any race. Alone refers to the fact that these figures are not in combination with any other race. 2010 data for American Indian/Alaska Native and Native Hawaiian/Other Pacific Islander was not available.

The concept of race, as used by the Census Bureau, reflects self-identification by people according to the race or races with which they most closely identify. These categories are socio-political constructs and should not be interpreted as being scientific or anthropological in nature. Furthermore, the race categories include both racial and national-origin groups.

- **White.** A person having origins in any of the original peoples of Europe, the Middle East, or North Africa. It includes people who indicate their race as White or report entries such as Irish, German, Italian, Lebanese, Near Easterner, Arab, or Polish.
- **Black or African American.** A person having origins in any of the Black racial groups of Africa. It includes people who indicate their race as Black, African American, or Negro, or provide written entries such as African American, Afro-American, Kenyan, Nigerian, or Haitian.
- **Asian.** A person having origins in any of the original peoples of the Far East, Southeast Asia, or the Indian subcontinent including, for example, Cambodia, China, India, Japan, Korea, Malaysia, Pakistan, the Philippine Islands, Thailand, and Vietnam. It includes Asian Indian, Chinese, Filipino, Korean, Japanese, Vietnamese, and Other Asian.
- **Hispanic.** The data on the Hispanic or Latino population, which was asked of all people, were derived from answers to long-form questionnaire Item 5, and short-form questionnaire Item 7. The terms Spanish, Hispanic origin, and Latino are used interchangeably. Some respondents identify with all three terms, while others may identify with only one of these three specific terms. Hispanics or Latinos who identify with the terms Spanish, Hispanic, or Latino are those who classify themselves in one of the specific Hispanic or Latino categories listed on the questionnaire—Mexican, Puerto Rican, or Cuban—as well as those who indicate that they are other Spanish, Hispanic, or Latino. People who do not identify with one of the specific origins listed on the questionnaire but indicate that they are other Spanish, Hispanic, or Latino are those whose origins are from Spain, the Spanish-speaking countries of Central or South America, the Dominican Republic, or people identifying themselves generally as Spanish, Spanish-American, Hispanic, Hispano, Latino, and so on. All write-in responses to the other Spanish/Hispanic/ Latino category were coded. Origin can be viewed as the heritage, nationality group, lineage, or country of birth of the person or the person's parents or ancestors before their arrival in the United States. People who identify their origin as Spanish, Hispanic, or Latino may be of any race.

Population Density: 2010 population estimate divided by the land area in square miles. *Source: Nielsen Claritas; U.S. Bureau of the Census, Census of Population and Housing, 2000: Summary File 1.*

Average Household Size: Average household size was calculated by dividing the total population by the total number of households. Figures are 2010 estimates. *Source: Nielsen Claritas.*

Median Age: Figures are 2010 estimates. *Source: Nielsen Claritas.*

Male/Female Ratio: Number of males per 100 females. Figures are 2010 estimates. *Source: Nielsen Claritas.*

Marital Status: Percentage of population never married, now married, widowed, or divorced. *Source: U.S. Census Bureau, American Community Survey, 2005-2009 Five-Year Estimates.*

The marital status classification refers to the status at the time of enumeration. Data on marital status are tabulated only for the population 15 years old and over. Each person was asked whether they were "Now married," "Widowed," "Divorced," or "Never married." Couples who live together (for example, people in common-law marriages) were able to report the marital status they considered to be the most appropriate.

- **Never married**. Never married includes all people who have never been married, including people whose only marriage(s) was annulled.
- **Now married.** All people whose current marriage has not ended by widowhood or divorce. This category includes people defined as "separated."
- **Widowed**. This category includes widows and widowers who have not remarried.
- **Divorced**. This category includes people who are legally divorced and who have not remarried.

Foreign Born: Percentage of population who were not U.S. citizens at birth. Foreign-born people are those who indicated they were either a U.S. citizen by naturalization or they were not a citizen of the United States. *Source: U.S. Census Bureau, American Community Survey, 2005-2009 Five-Year Estimates.*

Ancestry: Largest ancestry groups reported (up to five). Includes multiple ancestries. *Source: U.S. Census Bureau, American Community Survey, 2005-2009 Five-Year Estimates.*

The data represent self-classification by people according to the ancestry group or groups with which they most closely identify. Ancestry refers to a person's ethnic origin or descent, "roots," heritage, or the place of birth of the person, the person's parents, or their ancestors before their arrival in the United States. Some ethnic identities, such as Egyptian or Polish, can be traced to geographic areas outside the United States, while other ethnicities such as Pennsylvania German or Cajun evolved in the United States.

The ancestry question was intended to provide data for groups that were not included in the Hispanic origin and race questions. Therefore, although data on all groups are collected, the ancestry data shown in these tabulations are for non-Hispanic and non-race groups. *See* Population by Race for information on Hispanic and race groups.

The ancestry question allowed respondents to report one or more ancestry groups, although only the first two were coded. If a response was in terms of a dual ancestry, for example, "Irish English," the person was assigned two codes, in this case one for Irish and another for English. However, in certain cases, multiple responses such as "French Canadian," "Greek Cypriote," and "Scotch Irish" were assigned a single code reflecting their status as unique groups. If a person reported one of these unique groups in addition to another group, for example, "Scotch Irish English," resulting in three terms, that person received one code for the unique group (Scotch-Irish) and another one for the remaining group (English). If a person reported "English Irish French," only English and Irish were coded. Certain combinations of ancestries where the ancestry group is a part of another, such as "German-Bavarian," were coded as a single ancestry using the more specific group (Bavarian). Also, responses such as "Polish-American" or "Italian-American" were coded and tabulated as a single entry (Polish or Italian).

The Census Bureau accepted "American" as a unique ethnicity if it was given alone, with an ambiguous response, or with state names. If the respondent listed any other ethnic identity such as "Italian-American," generally the "American" portion of the response was not coded. However, distinct groups such as "American Indian," "Mexican American," and "African American" were coded and identified separately because they represented groups who considered themselves different from those who reported as "Indian," "Mexican," or "African," respectively.

The data is based on the total number of ancestries reported and coded. Thus, the sum of the counts in this type of presentation is not the total population but the total of all responses.

ECONOMY

Unemployment Rate: June 2011. Includes all civilians age 16 or over who were unemployed and looking for work. *Source: U.S. Department of Labor, Bureau of Labor Statistics, Local Area Unemployment Statistics (http://www.bls.gov/lau/home.htm).*

Total Civilian Labor Force: June 2011. Includes all civilians age 16 or over who were either employed, or unemployed and looking for work. *Source: U.S. Department of Labor, Bureau of Labor Statistics, Local Area Unemployment Statistics (http://www.bls.gov/lau/home.htm).*

Single-Family Building Permits Issued: Building permits issued for new single-family housing units in 2010. *Source: U.S. Census Bureau, Manufacturing and Construction Division (http://www.census.gov/const/www/permitsindex.html).*

Multi-Family Building Permits Issued: Building permits issued for new multi-family housing units in 2010. *Source: U.S. Census Bureau, Manufacturing and Construction Division (http://www.census.gov/const/www/permitsindex.html).*

Statistics on housing units authorized by building permits include housing units issued in local permit-issuing jurisdictions by a building or zoning permit. Not all areas of the country require a building or zoning permit. The statistics only represent those areas that do require a permit. Current surveys indicate that construction is undertaken for all but a very small percentage of housing units authorized by building permits. A major portion typically get under way during the month of permit issuance and most of the remainder begin within the three following months. Because of this lag, the housing unit authorization statistics do not represent the number of units actually put into construction for the period shown, and should therefore not be directly interpreted as "housing starts."

Statistics are based upon reports submitted by local building permit officials in response to a mail survey. They are obtained using Form C-404 const/www/c404.pdf, "Report of New Privately-Owned Residential Building or Zoning Permits Issued." When a report is not received, missing data are either (1) obtained from the Survey of Use of Permits (SUP) which is used to collect information on housing starts, or (2) imputed based on the assumption that the ratio of current month authorizations to those of a year ago should be the same for reporting and non-reporting places.

Employment by Occupation: Percentage of the employed civilian population 16 years and over in management, professional, service, sales, farming, construction, and production occupations. *Source: U.S. Census Bureau, American Community Survey, 2005-2009 Five-Year Estimates.*

- **Management** includes management, business, and financial operations occupations:
  Management occupations, except farmers and farm managers
  Farmers and farm managers
  Business and financial operations occupations:
    Business operations specialists
    Financial specialists

- **Professional** includes professional and related occupations:
  Computer and mathematical occupations
  Architecture and engineering occupations:
    Architects, surveyors, cartographers, and engineers
    Drafters, engineering, and mapping technicians
  Life, physical, and social science occupations
  Community and social services occupations
  Legal occupations
  Education, training, and library occupations
  Arts, design, entertainment, sports, and media occupations
  Healthcare practitioners and technical occupations:
    Health diagnosing and treating practitioners and technical occupations
    Health technologists and technicians

- **Service** occupations include:
  Healthcare support occupations
  Protective service occupations:
    Fire fighting, prevention, and law enforcement workers, including supervisors

Other protective service workers, including supervisors
Food preparation and serving related occupations
Building and grounds cleaning and maintenance occupations
Personal care and service occupations

- **Sales** and office occupations include:
  Sales and related occupations
  Office and administrative support occupations

- **Farming,** fishing, and forestry occupations

- **Construction,** extraction, and maintenance occupations include:
  Construction and extraction occupations:
      Supervisors, construction, and extraction workers
      Construction trades workers
      Extraction workers
  Installation, maintenance, and repair occupations

- **Production,** transportation, and material moving occupations include:
  Production occupations
  Transportation and material moving occupations:
      Supervisors, transportation, and material moving workers
      Aircraft and traffic control occupations
      Motor vehicle operators
      Rail, water, and other transportation occupations
      Material moving workers

INCOME

Per Capita Income: Per capita income is the mean income computed for every man, woman, and child in a particular group. It is derived by dividing the total income of a particular group by the total population in that group. Per capita income is rounded to the nearest whole dollar. Figures shown are 2010 estimates. *Source: Nielsen Claritas.*

Median Household Income: Includes the income of the householder and all other individuals 15 years old and over in the household, whether they are related to the householder or not. The median divides the income distribution into two equal parts: one-half of the cases falling below the median income and one-half above the median. For households, the median income is based on the distribution of the total number of households including those with no income. Median income for households is computed on the basis of a standard distribution and is rounded to the nearest whole dollar. Figures shown are 2010 estimates. *Source: Nielsen Claritas.*

Average Household Income: Average household income is obtained by dividing total household income by the total number of households. Figures shown are 2010 estimates. *Source: Nielsen Claritas.*

Percent of Households with Income of $100,000 or more: Figures shown are 2010 estimates. *Source: Nielsen Claritas.*

Poverty Rate: Percentage of population with income below the poverty level. Based on individuals for whom poverty status is determined. Poverty status was determined for all people except institutionalized people, people in military group quarters, people in college dormitories, and unrelated individuals under 15 years old. *Source: U.S. Census Bureau, American Community Survey, 2005-2009 Five-Year Estimates.*

TAXES

Total City Taxes Per Capita: Total city taxes collected divided by the population of the city. *Source: U.S. Bureau of the Census, State and Local Government Finances, 2007 (http://www.census.gov/govs/www/estimate.html).*

Taxes include:
- Property Taxes
- Sales and Gross Receipts Taxes
- Federal Customs Duties
- General Sales and Gross Receipts Taxes

- Selective Sales Taxes (alcoholic beverages; amusements; insurance premiums; motor fuels; pari-mutuels; public utilities; tobacco products; other)
- License Taxes (alcoholic beverages; amusements; corporations in general; hunting and fishing; motor vehicles motor vehicle operators; public utilities; occupation and business, NEC; other)
- Income Taxes (individual income; corporation net income; other)
- Death and Gift
- Documentary & Stock Transfer
- Severance
- Taxes, NEC

Total City Property Taxes Per Capita: Total city property taxes collected divided by the population of the city. *Source: U.S. Bureau of the Census, State and Local Government Finances, 2007 (http://www.census.gov/govs/www/estimate.html).*

Property Taxes include general property taxes, relating to property as a whole, taxed at a single rate or at classified rates according to the class of property. Property refers to real property (e.g. land and structures) as well as personal property; personal property can be either tangible (e.g. automobiles and boats) or intangible (e.g. bank accounts and stocks and bonds). Special property taxes, levied on selected types of property (e.g. oil and gas properties, house trailers, motor vehicles, and intangibles) and subject to rates not directly related to general property tax rates. Taxes based on income produced by property as a measure of its value on the assessment date.

EDUCATION

Educational Attainment: Figures shown are 2010 estimates and show the percent of population age 25 and over with:

- **High school diploma (including GED) or higher:** includes people whose highest degree is a high school diploma or its equivalent, people who attended college but did not receive a degree, and people who received a college, university, or professional degree.
- **Bachelor's degree or higher**
- **Master's degree or higher:** Master's degrees include the traditional MA and MS degrees and field-specific degrees, such as MSW, MEd, MBA, and MLS. *Source: Nielsen Claritas.*

School Districts: Lists the name of each school district, the grade range (PK=pre-kindergarten; KG=kindergarten), the student enrollment, and the district headquarters' phone number. In each community profile, only school districts that have schools that are physically located within the community are shown. In addition, statistics for each school district cover the entire district, regardless of the physical location of the schools within the district. *Source: U.S. Department of Education, National Center for Educational Statistics, Directory of Public Elementary and Secondary Education Agencies, 2009-10.*

Four-year Colleges: Lists the name of each four-year college, the type of institution (private or public; for-profit or non-profit; religious affiliation; historically black), the total student enrollment (Fall 2009), the general telephone number, and the annual tuition and fees for full-time, first-time undergraduate students (in-state and out-of-state). *Source: U.S. Department of Education, National Center for Educational Statistics, IPEDS College Data, 2010-11.*

Two-year Colleges: Lists the name of each two-year college, the type of institution (private or public; for-profit or non-profit; religious affiliation; historically black), the total student enrollment (Fall 2009), the general telephone number, and the annual tuition and fees for full-time, first-time undergraduate students (in-state and out-of-state). *Source: U.S. Department of Education, National Center for Educational Statistics, IPEDS College Data, 2010-11.*

Vocational/Technical Schools: Lists the name of each vocational/technical school, the type of institution (private or public; for-profit or non-profit; religious affiliation; historically black), the total student enrollment (Fall 2009), the general telephone number, and the annual tuition and fees for full-time students. *Source: U.S. Department of Education, National Center for Educational Statistics, IPEDS College Data, 2010-11.*

HOUSING

Homeownership Rate: Percentage of housing units that are owner-occupied. Figures shown are 2010 estimates. *Source: Nielsen Claritas.*

Median Home Value: Median value of all owner-occupied housing units as reported by the owner. Figures shown are 2010 estimates. *Source: Nielsen Claritas.*

Median Rent: Median monthly contract rent on specified renter-occupied and specified vacant-for-rent units. Specified renter-occupied and specified vacant-for-rent units exclude 1-family houses on 10 acres or more. Contract rent is the monthly rent agreed to or contracted for, regardless of any furnishings, utilities, fees, meals, or services that may be included. For vacant units, it is the monthly rent asked for the rental unit at the time of enumeration. *Source: U.S. Census Bureau, American Community Survey, 2005-2009 Five-Year Estimates.*

Median Year Structure Built: Year structure built refers to when the building was first constructed, not when it was remodeled, added to, or converted. For mobile homes, houseboats, RVs, etc, the manufacturer's model year was assumed to be the year built. The data relate to the number of units built during the specified periods that were still in existence at the time of enumeration. *Source: U.S. Census Bureau, American Community Survey, 2005-2009 Five-Year Estimates.*

HOSPITALS

Lists the hospital name and the number of licensed beds. *Source: Grey House Publishing, Directory of Hospital Personnel, 2010.*

SAFETY

Violent Crime Rate: Number of violent crimes reported per 10,000 population. Violent crimes include murder, forcible rape, robbery, and aggravated assault. *Source: Federal Bureau of Investigation, Uniform Crime Reports 2009 (http://www.fbi.gov/ucr/ucr.htm).*

Property Crime Rate: Number of property crimes reported per 10,000 population. Property crimes include burglary, larceny-theft, and motor vehicle theft. *Source: Federal Bureau of Investigation, Uniform Crime Reports 2009 (http://www.fbi.gov/ucr/ucr.htm).*

NEWSPAPERS

Lists the name, circulation and news focus of daily and weekly newspapers. Includes newspapers with offices located in the community profiled. *Source: MediaContactsPro 2009*

TRANSPORTATION

Commute to Work: Percentage of workers 16 years old and over that use the following means of transportation to commute to work: car; public transportation; walk; work from home. *Source: U.S. Census Bureau, American Community Survey, 2005-2009 Five-Year Estimates.*

The means of transportation data for some areas may show workers using modes of public transportation that are not available in those areas (e.g. subway or elevated riders in a metropolitan area where there actually is no subway or elevated service). This result is largely due to people who worked during the reference week at a location that was different from their usual place of work (such as people away from home on business in an area where subway service was available) and people who used more than one means of transportation each day but whose principal means was unavailable where they lived (e.g. residents of non-metropolitan areas who drove to the fringe of a metropolitan area and took the commuter railroad most of the distance to work).

Travel Time to Work: Travel time to work for workers 16 years old and over. Reported for the following intervals: less than 15 minutes; 15 to 30 minutes; 30 to 45 minutes; 45 to 60 minutes; 60 minutes or more. *Source: U.S. Census Bureau, American Community Survey, 2005-2009 Five-Year Estimates.*

Travel time to work refers to the total number of minutes that it usually took the person to get from home to work each day during the reference week. The elapsed time includes time spent waiting for public transportation, picking up passengers in carpools, and time spent in other activities related to getting to work.

Amtrak: Indicates if Amtrak rail or bus service is available. Please note that the cities being served continually change. *Source: National Railroad Passenger Corporation, Amtrak National Timetable, 2011 (www.amtrak.com).*

AIRPORTS

Lists the local airport(s) along with type of service and hub size. *Source: U.S. Department of Transportation, Bureau of Transportation Statistics (http://www.bts.gov).*

ADDITIONAL INFORMATION CONTACTS

The following phone numbers are provided as sources of additional information: Chambers of Commerce; Economic Development Agencies; and Convention & Visitors Bureaus. Efforts have been made to provide the most recent area codes. However, area code changes may have occurred in listed numbers. *Source: Original research.*

Information for Counties

PHYSICAL CHARACTERISTICS

Physical Location: Describes the physical location of the county. *Source: Columbia University Press, The Columbia Gazetteer of North America and original research.*

Land and Water Area: Land and water area in square miles. *Source: U.S. Bureau of the Census, Census of Population and Housing, 2000: Summary File 1.*

Time Zone: Lists the time zone. *Source: Original research.*

Year Organized: Year the county government was organized. *Source: National Association of Counties (www.naco.org).*

County Seat: Lists the county seat. If a county has more than one seat, then both are listed. *Source: National Association of Counties (www.naco.org).*

Metropolitan Area: Indicates the metropolitan area the county is located in. Also lists all the component counties of that metropolitan area. The Office of Management and Budget (OMB) defines metropolitan and micropolitan statistical areas. The most current definitions are as of December 2009. *Source: U.S. Bureau of the Census (http://www.census.gov/population/www/estimates/metrodef.html).*

Climate: Includes all weather stations located within the county. Indicates the station name and elevation as well as the monthly average high and low temperatures, average precipitation, and average snowfall. The period of record is generally 1980-2009, however, certain weather stations contain averages going back as far as 1900. *Source: Grey House Publishing, Weather America: A Thirty-Year Summary of Statistical Weather Data and Rankings, 2010.*

POPULATION

Population: 1990 and 2000 figures are a 100% count of population. 2010 estimates and 2015 projections were provided by Nielsen Claritas. *Source: Nielsen Claritas; U.S. Bureau of the Census, Census of Population and Housing, 2000: Summary File 1.*

Population by Race: 2010 estimates includes the U.S. Bureau of the Census categories of White alone; Black alone; Asian alone; and Hispanic of any race. Alone refers to the fact that these figures are not in combination with any other race. 2010 data for American Indian/Alaska Native and Native Hawaiian/Other Pacific Islander was not available.

The concept of race, as used by the Census Bureau, reflects self-identification by people according to the race or races with which they most closely identify. These categories are socio-political constructs and should not be interpreted as being scientific or anthropological in nature. Furthermore, the race categories include both racial and national-origin groups.

- **White.** A person having origins in any of the original peoples of Europe, the Middle East, or North Africa. It includes people who indicate their race as White or report entries such as Irish, German, Italian, Lebanese, Near Easterner, Arab, or Polish.
- **Black or African American.** A person having origins in any of the Black racial groups of Africa. It includes people who indicate their race as Black, African American, or Negro, or provide written entries such as African American, Afro-American, Kenyan, Nigerian, or Haitian.
- **Asian.** A person having origins in any of the original peoples of the Far East, Southeast Asia, or the Indian subcontinent including, for example, Cambodia, China, India, Japan, Korea, Malaysia, Pakistan, the Philippine Islands, Thailand, and Vietnam. It includes Asian Indian, Chinese, Filipino, Korean, Japanese, Vietnamese, and Other Asian.
- **Hispanic.** The data on the Hispanic or Latino population, which was asked of all people, were derived from answers to long-form questionnaire Item 5, and short-form questionnaire Item 7. The terms Spanish, Hispanic origin, and Latino are used interchangeably. Some respondents identify with all three terms, while others may identify with only one of these three specific terms. Hispanics or Latinos who identify with the terms Spanish, Hispanic, or Latino are those who classify themselves in one of the specific Hispanic or Latino categories listed on the questionnaire—Mexican, Puerto Rican, or Cuban—as well as those who indicate that they are other Spanish, Hispanic, or Latino. People who do not identify with one of the specific origins listed on the questionnaire but indicate that they are other Spanish, Hispanic, or Latino are those whose origins are from Spain, the Spanish-speaking countries of Central or South

America, the Dominican Republic, or people identifying themselves generally as Spanish, Spanish-American, Hispanic, Hispano, Latino, and so on. All write-in responses to the other Spanish/Hispanic/Latino category were coded. Origin can be viewed as the heritage, nationality group, lineage, or country of birth of the person or the person's parents or ancestors before their arrival in the United States. People who identify their origin as Spanish, Hispanic, or Latino may be of any race.

Population Density: 2010 population estimate divided by the land area in square miles. *Source: Nielsen Claritas; U.S. Bureau of the Census, Census of Population and Housing, 2000: Summary File 1.*

Average Household Size: Average household size was calculated by dividing the total population by the total number of households. Figures are 2010 estimates. *Source: Nielsen Claritas.*

Median Age: Figures are 2010 estimates. *Source: Nielsen Claritas.*

Male/Female Ratio: Number of males per 100 females. Figures are 2010 estimates. *Source: Nielsen Claritas.*

RELIGION

Religion: Lists the largest religious groups (up to five) based on the number of adherents divided by the population of the county. Adherents are defined as "all members, including full members, their children and the estimated number of other regular participants who are not considered as communicant, confirmed or full members." The data is based on a study of 149 religious bodies sponsored by the Association of Statisticians of American Religious Bodies. The 149 bodies reported 268,254 congregations and 141,371,963 adherents. *Source: Glenmary Research Center, Religious Congregations & Membership in the United States 2000.*

ECONOMY

Unemployment Rate: June 2011. Includes all civilians age 16 or over who were unemployed and looking for work. *Source: U.S. Department of Labor, Bureau of Labor Statistics, Local Area Unemployment Statistics (http://www.bls.gov/lau/home.htm).*

Total Civilian Labor Force: June 2011. Includes all civilians age 16 or over who were either employed, or unemployed and looking for work. *Source: U.S. Department of Labor, Bureau of Labor Statistics, Local Area Unemployment Statistics (http://www.bls.gov/lau/home.htm).*

Leading Industries: Lists the three largest industries (excluding government) based on the number of employees. *Source: U.S. Bureau of the Census, County Business Patterns 2009 (http://www.census.gov/epcd/cbp/view/cbpview.html).*

Farms: The total number of farms and the total acreage they occupy. *Source: U.S. Department of Agriculture, National Agricultural Statistics Service, 2007 Census of Agriculture (http://www.agcensus.usda.gov).*

Companies that Employ 500 or more persons: The numbers of companies that employ 500 or more persons. Includes private employers only. *Source: U.S. Bureau of the Census, County Business Patterns 2009 (http://www.census.gov/epcd/cbp/view/cbpview.html).*

Companies that Employ 100 - 499 persons: The numbers of companies that employ 100 - 499 persons. Includes private employers only. *Source: U.S. Bureau of the Census, County Business Patterns 2009 (http://www.census.gov/epcd/cbp/view/cbpview.html).*

Companies that Employ 1 - 99 persons: The numbers of companies that employ 1 - 99 persons. Includes private employers only. *Source: U.S. Bureau of the Census, County Business Patterns 2009 (http://www.census.gov/epcd/cbp/view/cbpview.html)*

Black-Owned Businesses: Number of businesses that are majority-owned by a Black or African-American person(s). Majority ownership is defined as having 51 percent or more of the stock or equity in the business. Black or African American is defined as a person having origins in any of the black racial groups of Africa, including those who consider themselves to be "Haitian." *Source: U.S. Bureau of the Census, 2007 Economic Census, Survey of Business Owners: Black-Owned Firms, 2007 (http://www.census.gov/csd/sbo/index.html).*

Asian-Owned Businesses: Number of businesses that are majority-owned by an Asian person(s). Majority ownership is defined as having 51 percent or more of the stock or equity in the business. *Source: U.S. Bureau of the Census, 2007 Economic Census, Survey of Business Owners: Asian-Owned Firms, 2007 (http://www.census.gov/csd/sbo/index.html).*

Hispanic-Owned Businesses: Number of businesses that are majority-owned by a person(s) of Hispanic or Latino origin. Majority ownership is defined as having 51 percent or more of the stock or equity in the business. Hispanic or Latino origin is defined as a person of Cuban, Mexican, Puerto Rican, South or Central American, or other Spanish culture or origin, regardless of race. *Source: U.S. Bureau of the Census, 2007 Economic Census, Survey of Business Owners: Hispanic-Owned Firms, 2007 (http://www.census.gov/csd/sbo/index.html).*

Women-Owned Businesses: Number of businesses that are majority-owned by a woman. Majority ownership is defined as having 51 percent or more of the stock or equity in the business. *Source: U.S. Bureau of the Census, 2007 Economic Census, Survey of Business Owners: Women-Owned Firms, 2007 (http://www.census.gov/csd/sbo/index.html).*

The Survey of Business Owners (SBO) provides statistics that describe the composition of U.S. businesses by gender, Hispanic or Latino origin, and race. Additional statistics include owner's age, education level, veteran status, and primary function in the business; family- and home-based businesses; types of customers and workers; and sources of financing for expansion, capital improvements, or start-up. Economic policymakers in federal, state and local governments use the SBO data to understand conditions of business success and failure by comparing census-to-census changes in business performances and by comparing minority-/nonminority- and women-/men-owned businesses.

Retail Sales per Capita: Total dollar amount of estimated retail sales divided by the population of the county in 2010. *Source: Editor & Publisher Market Guide 2010; U.S. Census Bureau, 2010 Census*

Single-Family Building Permits Issued: Building permits issued for new, single-family housing units in 2010. *Source: U.S. Census Bureau, Manufacturing and Construction Division (http://www.census.gov/const/www/permitsindex.html).*

Multi-Family Building Permits Issued: Building permits issued for new, multi-family housing units in 2010. *Source: U.S. Census Bureau, Manufacturing and Construction Division (http://www.census.gov/const/www/permitsindex.html).*

Statistics on housing units authorized by building permits include housing units issued in local permit-issuing jurisdictions by a building or zoning permit. Not all areas of the country require a building or zoning permit. The statistics only represent those areas that do require a permit. Current surveys indicate that construction is undertaken for all but a very small percentage of housing units authorized by building permits. A major portion typically get under way during the month of permit issuance and most of the remainder begin within the three following months. Because of this lag, the housing unit authorization statistics do not represent the number of units actually put into construction for the period shown, and should therefore not be directly interpreted as "housing starts."

Statistics are based upon reports submitted by local building permit officials in response to a mail survey. They are obtained using Form C-404 const/www/c404.pdf, "Report of New Privately-Owned Residential Building or Zoning Permits Issued." When a report is not received, missing data are either (1) obtained from the Survey of Use of Permits (SUP) which is used to collect information on housing starts, or (2) imputed based on the assumption that the ratio of current month authorizations to those of a year ago should be the same for reporting and non-reporting places.

INCOME

Per Capita Income: Per capita income is the mean income computed for every man, woman, and child in a particular group. It is derived by dividing the total income of a particular group by the total population in that group. Per capita income is rounded to the nearest whole dollar. Figures shown are 2010 estimates. *Source: Nielsen Claritas.*

Median Household Income: Includes the income of the householder and all other individuals 15 years old and over in the household, whether they are related to the householder or not. The median divides the income distribution into two equal parts: one-half of the cases falling below the median income and one-half above the median. For households, the median income is based on the distribution of the total number of households including those with no income. Median income for households is computed on the basis of a standard distribution and is rounded to the nearest whole dollar. Figures shown are 2010 estimates. *Source: Nielsen Claritas.*

Average Household Income: Average household income is obtained by dividing total household income by the total number of households. Figures shown are 2010 estimates. *Source: Nielsen Claritas.*

Percent of Households with Income of $100,000 or more: Figures shown are 2010 estimates. *Source: Nielsen Claritas.*

Poverty Rate: Estimated percentage of population with income in 2009 below the poverty level. *Source: U.S. Bureau of the Census, Small Area Income & Poverty Estimates.*

Bankruptcy Rate: The personal bankruptcy filing rate is the number of bankruptcies per thousand residents in 2010. Personal bankruptcy filings include both Chapter 7 (liquidations) and Chapter 13 (reorganizations) based on the county of residence of the filer. *Source: Federal Deposit Insurance Corporation, Regional Economic Conditions (http://www2.fdic.gov/recon/index.html).*

TAXES

Total County Taxes Per Capita: Total county taxes collected divided by the population of the county. *Source: U.S. Bureau of the Census, State and Local Government Finances, 2007 (http://www.census.gov/govs/www/estimate.html).*

Taxes include:
- Property Taxes
- Sales and Gross Receipts Taxes
- Federal Customs Duties
- General Sales and Gross Receipts Taxes
- Selective Sales Taxes (alcoholic beverages; amusements; insurance premiums; motor fuels; pari-mutuels; public utilities; tobacco products; other)
- License Taxes (alcoholic beverages; amusements; corporations in general; hunting and fishing; motor vehicles motor vehicle operators; public utilities; occupation and business, NEC; other)
- Income Taxes (individual income; corporation net income; other)
- Death and Gift
- Documentary & Stock Transfer
- Severance
- Taxes, NEC

Total County Property Taxes Per Capita: Total county property taxes collected divided by the population of the county. *Source: U.S. Bureau of the Census, State and Local Government Finances, 2007 (http://www.census.gov/govs/www/estimate.html).*

Property Taxes include general property taxes, relating to property as a whole, taxed at a single rate or at classified rates according to the class of property. Property refers to real property (e.g. land and structures) as well as personal property; personal property can be either tangible (e.g. automobiles and boats) or intangible (e.g. bank accounts and stocks and bonds). Special property taxes, levied on selected types of property (e.g. oil and gas properties, house trailers, motor vehicles, and intangibles) and subject to rates not directly related to general property tax rates. Taxes based on income produced by property as a measure of its value on the assessment date.

EDUCATION

Educational Attainment: Figures shown are 2010 estimates and show the percent of population age 25 and over with:

- **High school diploma (including GED) or higher:** includes people whose highest degree was a high school diploma or its equivalent, people who attended college but did not receive a degree, and people who received a college, university, or professional degree.
- **Bachelor's degree or higher**
- **Master's degree or higher:** Master's degrees include the traditional MA and MS degrees and field-specific degrees, such as MSW, MEd, MBA, and MLS. *Source: Nielsen Claritas.*

HOUSING

Homeownership Rate: Percentage of housing units that are owner-occupied. Figures shown are 2010 estimates. *Source: Nielsen Claritas.*

Median Home Value: Median value of all owner-occupied housing units as reported by the owner. Figures shown are 2010 estimates. *Source: Nielsen Claritas.*

Median Rent: Median monthly contract rent on specified renter-occupied and specified vacant-for-rent units. Specified renter-occupied and specified vacant-for-rent units exclude 1-family houses on 10 acres or more. Contract rent is the monthly rent agreed to or contracted for, regardless of any furnishings, utilities, fees, meals, or services that may be included. For vacant units, it is the monthly rent asked for the rental unit at the time of enumeration. *Source: U.S. Census Bureau, American Community Survey, 2005-2009 Five-Year Estimates.*

Median Year Structure Built: Year structure built refers to when the building was first constructed, not when it was remodeled, added to, or converted. For mobile homes, houseboats, RVs, etc, the manufacturer's model year was assumed to be the year built. The data relate to the number of units built during the specified periods that were still in existence at the time of enumeration. *Source: U.S. Census Bureau, American Community Survey, 2005-2009 Five-Year Estimates.*

HEALTH AND VITAL STATISTICS

Birth Rate: Estimated number of births per 10,000 population in 2009. *Source: U.S. Census Bureau, Annual Components of Population Change, July 1, 2008 - July 1 , 2009 (http://www.census.gov/popest/births.html).*

Death Rate: Estimated number of deaths per 10,000 population in 2009. *Source: U.S. Census Bureau, Annual Components of Population Change, July 1, 2008 - July 1 , 2009 (http://www.census.gov/popest/births.html).*

Age-adjusted Cancer Mortality Rate: Number of age-adjusted deaths from cancer per 100,000 population in 2007. Cancer is defined as International Classification of Disease (ICD) codes C00 - D48.9 Neoplasms. *Source: Centers for Disease Control, CDC Wonder (http://wonder.cdc.gov).*

Age-adjusted death rates are weighted averages of the age-specific death rates, where the weights represent a fixed population by age. They are used because the rates of almost all causes of death vary by age. Age adjustment is a technique for "removing" the effects of age from crude rates, so as to allow meaningful comparisons across populations with different underlying age structures. For example, comparing the crude rate of heart disease in New York to that of California is misleading, because the relatively older population in New York will lead to a higher crude death rate, even if the age-specific rates of heart disease in New York and California are the same. For such a comparison, age-adjusted rates would be preferable. Age-adjusted rates should be viewed as relative indexes rather than as direct or actual measures of mortality risk.

Death rates based on counts of twenty or less (≤ 20) are flagged as "Unreliable". Death rates based on fewer than three years of data for counties with populations of less than 100,000 in the 2000 Census counts, are also flagged as "Unreliable" if the number of deaths is five or less (≤ 5).

Number of Physicians: The number of active, non-federal physicians per 10,000 population in 2008. *Source: Area Resource File (ARF) 2009-2010. U.S. Department of Health and Human Services, Health Resources and Services Administration, Bureau of Health Professions, Rockville, MD.*

Number of Hospital Beds: The number of hospital beds per 10,000 population in 2007. *Source: Area Resource File (ARF) 2009-2010. U.S. Department of Health and Human Services, Health Resources and Services Administration, Bureau of Health Professions, Rockville, MD.*

Number of Hospital Admissions: The number of hospital admissions per 10,000 population in 2007. *Source: Area Resource File (ARF) 2009-2010. U.S. Department of Health and Human Services, Health Resources and Services Administration, Bureau of Health Professions, Rockville, MD.*

ENVIRONMENT

Air Quality Index: The percentage of days in 2008 the AQI fell into the Good (0-50), Moderate (51-100), Unhealthy for Sensitive Groups (101-150), and Unhealthy (151+) ranges. Data covers January 2008 through December 2008. Counties with less than 90 days of air quality data were excluded. *Source: AirData: Access to Air Pollution Data , U.S. Environmental Protection Agency, Office of Air and Radiation (http://www.epa.gov/air/data/index.html).*

The AQI is an index for reporting daily air quality. It tells you how clean or polluted your air is, and what associated health concerns you should be aware of. The AQI focuses on health effects that can happen within a few hours or days after breathing polluted air. EPA uses the AQI for five major air pollutants regulated by the Clean Air Act: ground-level ozone, particulate matter, carbon monoxide, sulfur dioxide, and nitrogen dioxide. For each of these pollutants, EPA has established national air quality standards to protect against harmful health effects.

The AQI runs from 0 to 500. The higher the AQI value, the greater the level of air pollution and the greater the health danger. For example, an AQI value of 50 represents good air quality and little potential to affect public health, while an AQI value over 300 represents hazardous air quality. An AQI value of 100 generally corresponds to the national air quality standard for the pollutant, which is the level EPA has set to protect public health. So, AQI values below 100 are generally thought of as satisfactory. When AQI values are above 100, air quality is considered to be unhealthy—at first for certain sensitive groups of people, then for everyone as AQI values get higher. Each category corresponds to a different level of health concern. For example, when the AQI for a pollutant is between 51 and 100, the health concern is "Moderate." Here are the six levels of health concern and what they mean:

- "Good" The AQI value for your community is between 0 and 50. Air quality is considered satisfactory and air pollution poses little or no risk.

- "Moderate" The AQI for your community is between 51 and 100. Air quality is acceptable; however, for some pollutants there may be a moderate health concern for a very small number of individuals. For example, people who are unusually sensitive to ozone may experience respiratory symptoms.

- "Unhealthy for Sensitive Groups" Certain groups of people are particularly sensitive to the harmful effects of certain air pollutants. This means they are likely to be affected at lower levels than the general public. For example, children and adults who are active outdoors and people with respiratory disease are at greater risk from exposure to ozone, while people with heart disease are at greater risk from carbon monoxide. Some people may be sensitive to more than one pollutant. When AQI values are between 101 and 150, members of sensitive groups may experience health effects. The general public is not likely to be affected when the AQI is in this range.

- "Unhealthy" AQI values are between 151 and 200. Everyone may begin to experience health effects. Members of sensitive groups may experience more serious health effects.

- "Very Unhealthy" AQI values between 201 and 300 trigger a health alert, meaning everyone may experience more serious health effects.

- "Hazardous" AQI values over 300 trigger health warnings of emergency conditions. The entire population is more likely to be affected.

ELECTIONS

Elections: 2008 Presidential election results. *Source: Dave Leip's Atlas of U.S. Presidential Elections (http://www.uselectionatlas.org).*

NATIONAL AND STATE PARKS

Lists National and State parks located in the area. *Source: U.S. Geological Survey, Geographic Names Information System.*

ADDITIONAL INFORMATION CONTACTS

The following phone numbers are provided as sources of additional information: Chambers of Commerce; Economic Development Agencies; and Convention & Visitors Bureaus. Efforts have been made to provide the most recent area codes. However, area code changes may have occurred in listed numbers. *Source: Original research.*

User's Guide: Education

School District Rankings

Number of Schools: Total number of schools in the district. *Source: U.S. Department of Education, National Center for Education Statistics, Common Core of Data, Public Elementary/Secondary School Universe Survey: School Year 2009-2010.*

Number of Teachers: Teachers are defined as individuals who provide instruction to pre-kindergarten, kindergarten, grades 1 through 12, or ungraded classes, or individuals who teach in an environment other than a classroom setting, and who maintain daily student attendance records. Numbers reported are full-time equivalents (FTE). *Source: U.S. Department of Education, National Center for Education Statistics, Common Core of Data, Local Education Agency (School District) Universe Survey: School Year 2009-2010.*

Number of Students: A student is an individual for whom instruction is provided in an elementary or secondary education program that is not an adult education program and is under the jurisdiction of a school, school system, or other education institution. *Sources: U.S. Department of Education, National Center for Education Statistics, Common Core of Data, Local Education Agency (School District) Universe Survey: School Year 2009-2010 and Public Elementary/Secondary School Universe Survey: School Year 2009-2010*

Individual Education Program (IEP) Students: A written instructional plan for students with disabilities designated as special education students under IDEA-Part B. The written instructional plan includes a statement of present levels of educational performance of a child; statement of annual goals, including short-term instructional objectives; statement of specific educational services to be provided and the extent to which the child will be able to participate in regular educational programs; the projected date for initiation and anticipated duration of services; the appropriate objectives, criteria and evaluation procedures; and the schedules for determining, on at least an annual basis, whether instructional objectives are being achieved. *Source: U.S. Department of Education, National Center for Education Statistics, Common Core of Data, Local Education Agency (School District) Universe Survey: School Year 2009-2010*

English Language Learner (ELL) Students: Formerly referred to as Limited English Proficient (LEP). Students being served in appropriate programs of language assistance (e.g., English as a Second Language, High Intensity Language Training, bilingual education). Does not include pupils enrolled in a class to learn a language other than English. Also Limited-English-Proficient students are individuals who were not born in the United States or whose native language is a language other than English; or individuals who come from environments where a language other than English is dominant; or individuals who are American Indians and Alaskan Natives and who come from environments where a language other than English has had a significant impact on their level of English language proficiency; and who, by reason thereof, have sufficient difficulty speaking, reading, writing, or understanding the English language, to deny such individuals the opportunity to learn successfully in classrooms where the language of instruction is English or to participate fully in our society. *Source: U.S. Department of Education, National Center for Education Statistics, Common Core of Data, Local Education Agency (School District) Universe Survey: School Year 2009-2010*

Students Eligible for Free Lunch Program: The free lunch program is defined as a program under the National School Lunch Act that provides cash subsidies for free lunches to students based on family size and income criteria. *Source: U.S. Department of Education, National Center for Education Statistics, Common Core of Data, Public Elementary/Secondary School Universe Survey: School Year 2009-2010*

Students Eligible for Reduced-Price Lunch Program: A student who is eligible to participate in the Reduced-Price Lunch Program under the National School Lunch Act. *Source: U.S. Department of Education, National Center for Education Statistics, Common Core of Data, Public Elementary/Secondary School Universe Survey: School Year 2009-2010*

Student/Teacher Ratio: The number of students divided by the number of teachers. Teachers are defined as individuals who provide instruction to pre-kindergarten, kindergarten, grades 1 through 12, or ungraded classes, or individuals who teach in an environment other than a classroom setting, and who maintain daily student attendance records. Numbers are based on full-time equivalents (FTE). *Source: U.S. Department of Education, National Center for Education Statistics, Common Core of Data, Local Education Agency (School District) Universe Survey: School Year 2009-2010.*

Student/Librarian Ratio: The number of students divided by the number of library and media support staff. Library and media support staff are defined as staff members who render other professional library and media services; also includes library aides and those involved in library/media support. Their duties include selecting, preparing, caring for, and making available to instructional staff, equipment, films, filmstrips, transparencies, tapes, TV programs, and similar materials maintained separately or as part of an instructional materials center. Also included are activities in the audio-visual center, TV studio, related-work-study areas, and services provided by audio-visual personnel. Numbers are based on full-time equivalents (FTE). *Source: U.S. Department of Education, National Center for Education Statistics, Common Core of Data, Local Education Agency (School District) Universe Survey: School Year 2009-2010.*

Student/Counselor Ratio: The number of students divided by the number of guidance counselors. Guidance counselors are professional staff assigned specific duties and school time for any of the following activities in an elementary or secondary setting: counseling with students and parents; consulting with other staff members on learning problems; evaluating student abilities; assisting students in making educational and career choices; assisting students in personal and social development; providing referral assistance; and/or working with other staff members in planning and conducting guidance programs for students. The state applies its own standards in apportioning the aggregate of guidance counselors/directors into the elementary and secondary level components. Numbers reported are full-time equivalents (FTE). *Source: U.S. Department of Education, National Center for Education Statistics, Common Core of Data, Local Education Agency (School District) Universe Survey: School Year 2009-2010.*

Total Current Expenditures:
State Profile. The total current expenditures for public elementary and secondary education as reported in the state finance file. Expenditures for equipment, non-public education, school construction, debt financing and community services are excluded. *Source: U.S. Department of Education, National Center for Education Statistics, Common Core of Data, National Public Education Financial Survey, School Year 2007-08 (Fiscal Year 2008)*

District Rankings. The district's total current expenditures for public elementary and secondary education as reported in the district finance file. *Source: U.S. Department of Education, National Center for Education Statistics, Common Core of Data, School District Finance Survey (F-33), Fiscal Year 2008*

Instruction:
State Profile. The total of instructional expenditures as reported in the state finance file. Instruction expenditures are for services and materials directly related to classroom instruction and the interaction between teachers and students. Teacher salaries and benefits, textbooks, classroom supplies and extra curricular activities are included. *Source: U.S. Department of Education, National Center for Education Statistics, Common Core of Data, National Public Education Financial Survey, School Year 2007-08 (Fiscal Year 2008)*

District Rankings. The total current expenditures for instruction for public prekindergarten and kindergarten through grade 12 programs as reported in the district finance file. The expenditures include teacher salaries and benefits and instructional supplies and purchased services. Tuition payments to other school districts are excluded. *Source: U.S. Department of Education, National Center for Education Statistics, Common Core of Data, School District Finance Survey (F-33), Fiscal Year 2008*

Support Services:
State Profile. The total of support services expenditures as reported in the state finance file. *Source: U.S. Department of Education, National Center for Education Statistics, Common Core of Data, National Public Education Financial Survey, School Year 2007-08 (Fiscal Year 2008)*

District Rankings. The total current expenditures for activities that support instruction as reported in the district finance file. Support services include operation and maintenance of buildings, school adminstration, student support services (e.g., nurses, therapists, and guidance counselors), student transportation, instructional staff support (e.g., librarians, instructional specialists), school district administration, business services, research, and data processing. *Source: U.S. Department of Education, National Center for Education Statistics, Common Core of Data, School District Finance Survey (F-33), Fiscal Year 2008*

Total General Revenue:
State Profile. The sum of revenue contributions emerging from local, state, and federal sources as reported in the state finance file. *Source: U.S. Department of Education, National Center for Education Statistics, Common Core of Data, National Public Education Financial Survey, School Year 2007-08 (Fiscal Year 2008)*

District Rankings. The sum of revenue contributions emerging from local, state, and federal sources as reported in the district finance file. *Source: U.S. Department of Education, National Center for Education Statistics, Common Core of Data, School District Finance Survey (F-33), Fiscal Year 2008*

Federal Revenue:
State Profile. Include direct grants-in-aid to schools or agencies, funds distributed through a state or intermediate

agency, and revenues in lieu of taxes to compensate a school district for nontaxable federal institutions within a district's boundary. *Source: U.S. Department of Education, National Center for Education Statistics, Common Core of Data, National Public Education Financial Survey, School Year 2007-08 (Fiscal Year 2008)*

District Rankings. Includes direct revenue and revenue distributed by state governments. Direct Revenue: Aid from project grants for programs such as Impact Aid (P.L. 81- 815 and P.L. 81-874), Indian Education, Bilingual Education, Head Start, Follow Through, Magnet Schools, Dropout Demonstration Assistance, and Gifted/Talented. Revenue Distributed by State Governments: Aid from formula grants distributed through state government agencies. This includes revenue from programs such as the following: Child Nutrition Act; Children with Disabilities-IDEA; Title I; vocational and technical education; other federal aid distributed by the state; and nonspecified federal aid distributed by the state. *Source: U.S. Department of Education, National Center for Education Statistics, Common Core of Data, School District Finance Survey (F-33), Fiscal Year 2008*

State Revenue:
State Profile. Include both direct funds from state governments and funds in lieu of taxation. Revenues in lieu of taxes are paid to compensate a school district for nontaxable state institutions or facilities within the district's boundary. *Source: U.S. Department of Education, National Center for Education Statistics, Common Core of Data, National Public Education Financial Survey, School Year 2007-08 (Fiscal Year 2008)*

District Rankings. Includes state revenue paid to the school system for any purpose, restricted or unrestricted, including the following: capital outlay/debt service; compensatory and basic skills programs; payments on behalf of LEA; special education programs; staff improvement programs; transportation programs; vocational programs; other programs; and nonspecified. *Source: U.S. Department of Education, National Center for Education Statistics, Common Core of Data, School District Finance Survey (F-33), Fiscal Year 2008*

Local Revenue:
State Profile. Include revenues from such sources as local property and nonproperty taxes, investments, and student activities such as textbook sales, transportation and tuition fees, and food service revenues. *Source: U.S. Department of Education, National Center for Education Statistics, Common Core of Data, National Public Education Financial Survey, School Year 2007-08 (Fiscal Year 2008)*

District Rankings. Includes revenue raised within the boundaries of the LEA. These revenues are primarily raised through property taxes, but also come from other types of taxes and fees. *Source: U.S. Department of Education, National Center for Education Statistics, Common Core of Data, School District Finance Survey (F-33), Fiscal Year 2008*

Long-Term Debt:
State Profile. Includes long-term credit obligations of the school system or its parent government and all interest-bearing short-term (repayable within 1 year) credit obligations. Excludes non-interestbearing short-term obligations, interfund obligations, amounts owed in a trust agency capacity, advances and contingent loans from other governments, and rights of individuals to benefits from school system employee retirement funds. *Source: U.S. Department of Education, National Center for Education Statistics, Common Core of Data, National Public Education Financial Survey, School Year 2007-08 (Fiscal Year 2008)*

District Rankings. Includes long-term credit obligations of the school system or its parent government and all interest-bearing short-term (repayable within 1 year) credit obligations. Excludes non-interestbearing short-term obligations, interfund obligations, amounts owed in a trust agency capacity, advances and contingent loans from other governments, and rights of individuals to benefits from school system employee retirement funds. *Source: U.S. Department of Education, National Center for Education Statistics, Common Core of Data, School District Finance Survey (F-33), Fiscal Year 2008*

Note: All financial values shown are dollars per pupil per year. They were calculated by dividing the total dollar amounts by the fall membership. Fall membership is comprised of the total student enrollment on October 1 (or the closest school day to October 1) for all grade levels (including prekindergarten and kindergarten) and ungraded pupils. Membership includes students both present and absent on the measurement day.

Drop-out Rate: A dropout is a student who was enrolled in school at some time during the previous school year; was not enrolled at the beginning of the current school year; has not graduated from high school or completed a state or district approved educational program; and does not meet any of the following exclusionary conditions: has transferred to another public school district, private school, or state- or district-approved educational program; is temporarily absent due to suspension or school-approved illness; or has died. The values shown cover grades 9 through 12. *Note: Drop-out rates are no longer available to the general public disaggregated by grade, race/ethnicity, and gender at the school district level. Beginning with the 2005–06 school year the CCD is reporting dropout data aggregated from the local education agency (district) level to the state level. This allows data users to compare event* *dropout rates across states, regions, and other jurisdictions. Source: U.S. Department of Education, National Center for Education Statistics, Common Core of Data, Local Education Agency (School District) Universe Survey Dropout and Completion Data, 2008-2009; U.S. Department of Education, National Center for Education Statistics, Common Core of Data, State Dropout and Completion Data File, 2008-2009*

Average Freshman Graduation Rate (AFGR): The AFGR is the number of regular diploma recipients in a given year divided by the average of the membership in grades 8, 9, and 10, reported 5, 4, and 3 years earlier, respectively. For example, the denominator of the 2008–09 AFGR is the average of the 8th-grade membership in 2004–05, 9th-grade membership in 2005–06, and 10th-grade membership in 2006–07. Ungraded students are prorated into these grades. Averaging these three grades provides an estimate of the number of first-time freshmen in the class of 2005–06 freshmen in order to estimate the on-time graduation rate for 2008–09.

Caution in interpreting the AFGR. Although the AFGR was selected as the best of the available alternatives, several factors make it fall short of a true on-time graduation rate. First, the AFGR does not take into account any imbalances in the number of students moving in and out of the nation or individual states over the high school years. As a result, the averaged freshman class is at best an approximation of the actual number of freshmen, where differences in the rates of transfers, retention, and dropping out in the three grades affect the average. Second, by including all graduates in a specific year, the graduates may include students who repeated a grade in high school or completed high school early and thus are not on-time graduates in that year. *Source: U.S. Department of Education, National Center for Education Statistics, Common Core of Data, Local Education Agency (School District) Universe Survey Dropout and Completion Data, 2008-2009; U.S. Department of Education, National Center for Education Statistics, Common Core of Data, State Dropout and Completion Data File, 2008-2009*

Number of Diploma Recipients: A student who has received a diploma during the previous school year or subsequent summer school. This category includes regular diploma recipients and other diploma recipients. A High School Diploma is a formal document certifying the successful completion of a secondary school program prescribed by the state education agency or other appropriate body. *Note: Diploma counts are no longer available to the general public disaggregated by grade, race/ethnicity, and gender at the school district level. Source: U.S. Department of Education, National Center for Education Statistics, Common Core of Data, Local Education Agency (School District) Universe Survey Dropout and Completion Data, 2008-2009; U.S. Department of Education, National Center for Education Statistics, Common Core of Data, State Dropout and Completion Data File, 2008-2009*

Note: n/a indicates data not available.

State Educational Profile

Please refer to the District Rankings section in the front of this User's Guide for an explanation of data for all items except for the following:

Average Salary: The average salary for classroom teachers in 2010-2011. *Source: National Education Association, Rankings & Estimates: Rankings of the States 2010 and Estimates of School Statistics 2011*

College Entrance Exam Scores:

Scholastic Aptitude Test (SAT). Note: The College Board strongly discourages the comparison or ranking of states on the basis of SAT scores alone. *Source: The College Board, SAT Trends: Background on the SAT Takers in the Class of 2010*

American College Testing Program (ACT). *Source: ACT, Inc., 2011 ACT National and State Scores*

National Assessment of Educational Progress (NAEP)

The National Assessment of Educational Progress (NAEP), also known as "the Nation's Report Card," is the only nationally representative and continuing assessment of what America's students know and can do in various subject areas. As a result of the "No Child Left Behind" legislation, all states are required to participate in NAEP.

For more information, visit the U.S. Department of Education, National Center for Education Statistics at http://nces.ed.gov/nationsreportcard.

User's Guide: Ancestry

Places Covered

The ranking tables are based on **1,510 places** in Texas. Places include 1,192 municipalities and 318 census designated places (CDP). The U.S. Bureau of the Census defines a CDP as "a statistical entity, defined for each decennial census according to Census Bureau guidelines, comprising a densely settled concentration of population that is not within an incorporated place, but is locally identified by a name. CDPs are delineated cooperatively by state and local officials and the Census Bureau, following Census Bureau guidelines. Beginning with Census 2000 there are no size limits."

Source of Data

The ancestries shown in this chapter were compiled from three different sections of the 2000 Census: Race; Hispanic Origin; and Ancestry. While the ancestries are sorted alphabetically for ease-of-use, it's important to note the origin of each piece of data. Data for Race and Hispanic Origin was taken from Summary File 1 (SF1) while Ancestry data was taken from Summary File 3 (SF3). The distinction is important because SF1 contains the 100-percent data, which is the information compiled from the questions asked of all people and about every housing unit. SF3 was compiled from a sample of approximately 19 million housing units (about 1 in 6 households) that received the Census 2000 long-form questionnaire.

Ancestries Based on Race

The data on race were derived from answers to the question on race that was asked of all people. The concept of race, as used by the Census Bureau, reflects self-identification by people according to the race or races with which they most closely identify. These categories are sociopolitical constructs and should not be interpreted as being scientific or anthropological in nature. Furthermore, the race categories include both racial and national-origin groups.

If an individual did not provide a race response, the race or races of the householder or other household members were assigned using specific rules of precedence of household relationship. For example, if race was missing for a natural-born child in the household, then either the race or races of the householder, another natural-born child, or the spouse of the householder were assigned. If race was not reported for anyone in the household, the race or races of a householder in a previously processed household were assigned.

African-American/Black:
  Not Hispanic
  Hispanic
Alaska Native tribes, specified:
  Alaska Athabascan
  Aleut
  Eskimo
  Tlingit-Haida
  All other tribes
Alaska Native tribes, not specified
American Indian or Alaska Native
  tribes, not specified
American Indian tribes, specified:
  Apache
  Blackfeet
  Cherokee
  Cheyenne
  Chickasaw
  Chippewa
  Choctaw
  Colville
  Comanche
  Cree
  Creek
  Crow

Delaware
Houma
Iroquois
Kiowa
Latin American Indians
Lumbee
Menominee
Navajo
Osage
Ottawa
Paiute
Pima
Potawatomi
Pueblo
Puget Sound Salish
Seminole
Shoshone
Sioux
Tohono O'Odham
Ute
Yakama
Yaqui
Yuman
All other tribes

American Indian tribes,
  not specified
Asian:
  Bangladeshi
  Cambodian
  Chinese, except Taiwanese
  Filipino
  Hmong
  Indian
  Indonesian
  Japanese
  Korean
  Laotian
  Malaysian
  Pakistani
  Sri Lankan
  Taiwanese
  Thai
  Vietnamese
  Other Asian, specified
  Other Asian, not specified
Hawaii Native/Pacific Islander:
  Melanesian:
    Fijian
    Other Melanesian

Micronesian:
  Guamanian/Chamorro
  Other Micronesian
Polynesian:
  Native Hawaiian
  Samoan
  Tongan
  Other Polynesian
Other Pacific Islander, specified
Other Pacific Islander,
  not specified
White:
  Not Hispanic
  Hispanic

African American or Black: A person having origins in any of the Black racial groups of Africa. It includes people who indicate their race as "Black, African Am., or Negro," or provide written entries such as African American, Afro American, Kenyan, Nigerian, or Haitian.

American Indian or Alaska Native: A person having origins in any of the original peoples of North and South America (including Central America) and who maintain tribal affiliation or community attachment. It includes people who classified themselves as described below.

American Indian - Includes people who indicated their race as "American Indian," entered the name of an Indian tribe, or reported such entries as Canadian Indian, French American Indian, or Spanish-American Indian.

Respondents who identified themselves as American Indian were asked to report their enrolled or principal tribe. Therefore, tribal data in tabulations reflect the written entries reported on the questionnaires. Some of the entries (for example, Iroquois, Sioux, Colorado River, and Flathead) represent nations or reservations. The information on tribe is based on self identification and therefore does not reflect any designation of federally or state-recognized tribe. Information on American Indian tribes is presented in summary files. The information for Census 2000 is derived from the American Indian Tribal Classification List for the 1990 census that was updated based on a December 1997 Federal Register Notice, entitled "Indian Entities Recognized and Eligible to Receive Service From the United States Bureau of Indian Affairs," Department of the Interior, Bureau of Indian Affairs, issued by the Office of Management and Budget.

Alaska Native - Includes written responses of Eskimos, Aleuts, and Alaska Indians, as well as entries such as Arctic Slope, Inupiat, Yupik, Alutiiq, Egegik, and Pribilovian. The Alaska tribes are the Alaskan Athabascan, Tlingit, and Haida. The information for Census 2000 is based on the American Indian Tribal Classification List for the 1990 census, which was expanded to list the individual Alaska Native Villages when provided as a written response for race.

Asian: A person having origins in any of the original peoples of the Far East, Southeast Asia, or the Indian subcontinent including, for example, Cambodia, China, India, Japan, Korea, Malaysia, Pakistan, the Philippine Islands, Thailand, and Vietnam. It includes "Asian Indian," "Chinese," "Filipino," "Korean," "Japanese," "Vietnamese," and "Other Asian."

Asian Indian - Includes people who indicated their race as "Asian Indian" or identified themselves as Bengalese, Bharat, Dravidian, East Indian, or Goanese.

Chinese - Includes people who indicate their race as "Chinese" or who identify themselves as Cantonese, or Chinese American.

Filipino - Includes people who indicate their race as "Filipino" or who report entries such as Philipino, Philipine, or Filipino American.

Japanese - Includes people who indicate their race as "Japanese" or who report entries such as Nipponese or Japanese American.

Korean - Includes people who indicate their race as "Korean" or who provide a response of Korean American.

Vietnamese - Includes people who indicate their race as "Vietnamese" or who provide a response of Vietnamese American.

Cambodian - Includes people who provide a response such as Cambodian or Cambodia.

Hmong - Includes people who provide a response such as Hmong, Laohmong, or Mong.

Laotian - Includes people who provide a response such as Laotian, Laos, or Lao.

Thai - Includes people who provide a response such as Thai, Thailand, or Siamese.

Other Asian - Includes people who provide a response of Bangladeshi; Bhutanese; Burmese; Indochinese; Indonesian; Iwo Jiman; Madagascar; Malaysian; Maldivian; Nepalese; Okinawan; Pakistani; Singaporean; Sri Lankan; or Other Asian, specified and Other Asian, not specified.

Native Hawaiian or Other Pacific Islander: A person having origins in any of the original peoples of Hawaii, Guam, Samoa, or other Pacific Islands. It includes people who indicate their race as "Native Hawaiian," "Guamanian or Chamorro," "Samoan," and "Other Pacific Islander."

> *Native Hawaiian* - Includes people who indicate their race as "Native Hawaiian" or who identify themselves as "Part Hawaiian" or "Hawaiian."

> *Guamanian or Chamorro* - Includes people who indicate their race as such, including written entries of Chamorro or Guam.

> *Samoan* - Includes people who indicate their race as "Samoan" or who identify themselves as American Samoan or Western Samoan.

> *Other Pacific Islander* - Includes people who provide a write-in response of a Pacific Islander group, such as Carolinian, Chuukese (Trukese), Fijian, Kosraean, Melanesian, Micronesian, Northern Mariana Islander, Palauan, Papua New Guinean, Pohnpeian, Polynesian, Solomon Islander, Tahitian, Tokelauan, Tongan, Yapese, or Pacific Islander, not specified.

White: A person having origins in any of the original peoples of Europe, the Middle East, or North Africa. It includes people who indicate their race as "White" or report entries such as Irish, German, Italian, Lebanese, Near Easterner, Arab, or Polish.

Ancestries Based on Hispanic Origin

Hispanic or Latino:	Salvadoran	Argentinean	Uruguayan
Central American:	Other Central American	Bolivian	Venezuelan
Costa Rican	Cuban	Chilean	Other South American
Guatemalan	Dominican Republic	Colombian	Other Hispanic/Latino
Honduran	Mexican	Ecuadorian	
Nicaraguan	Puerto Rican	Paraguayan	
Panamanian	South American:	Peruvian	

The data on the Hispanic or Latino population were derived from answers to a question that was asked of all people. The terms "Spanish," "Hispanic origin," and "Latino" are used interchangeably. Some respondents identify with all three terms while others may identify with only one of these three specific terms. Hispanics or Latinos who identify with the terms "Spanish," "Hispanic," or "Latino" are those who classify themselves in one of the specific Spanish, Hispanic, or Latino categories listed on the questionnaire ("Mexican," "Puerto Rican," or "Cuban") as well as those who indicate that they are "other Spanish/Hispanic/Latino." People who do not identify with one of the specific origins listed on the questionnaire but indicate that they are "other Spanish, Hispanic, or Latino" are those whose origins are from Spain, the Spanish-speaking countries of Central or South America, the Dominican Republic, or people identifying themselves generally as Spanish, Spanish-American, Hispanic, Hispano, Latino, and so on. All write-in responses to the "other Spanish/Hispanic/Latino" category were coded.

Origin can be viewed as the heritage, nationality group, lineage, or country of birth of the person or the person's parents or ancestors before their arrival in the United States. People who identify their origin as Spanish, Hispanic, or Latino may be of any race.

In all cases where the origin of households, families, or occupied housing units is classified as Spanish, Hispanic, or Latino, the origin of the householder is used. If an individual could not provide a Hispanic origin response, their origin was assigned using specific rules of precedence of household relationship. For example, if origin was missing for a natural-born daughter in the household, then either the origin of the householder, another natural-born child, or spouse of the householder was assigned. If Hispanic origin was not reported for anyone in the household, the Hispanic origin of a householder in a previously processed household with the same race was assigned.

Other Ancestries

Acadian/Cajun	Moroccan	French, except Basque	Scottish
Afghan	Palestinian	French Canadian	Serbian
African, Subsaharan:	Syrian	German	Slavic
African	Other Arab	German Russian	Slovak
Cape Verdean	Armenian	Greek	Slovene
Ethiopian	Assyrian/Chaldean/Syriac	Guyanese	Soviet Union
Ghanian	Australian	Hungarian	Swedish
Kenyan	Austrian	Icelander	Swiss
Liberian	Basque	Iranian	Turkish
Nigerian	Belgian	Irish	Ukrainian
Senegalese	Brazilian	Israeli	United States or American
Sierra Leonean	British	Italian	Welsh
Somalian	Bulgarian	Latvian	West Indian, excluding Hispanic:
South African	Canadian	Lithuanian	Bahamian
Sudanese	Carpatho Rusyn	Luxemburger	Barbadian
Ugandan	Celtic	Macedonian	Belizean
Zairian	Croatian	Maltese	Bermudan
Zimbabwean	Cypriot	New Zealander	British West Indian
Other Subsaharan African	Czech	Northern European	Dutch West Indian
Albanian	Czechoslovakian	Norwegian	Haitian
Alsatian	Danish	Pennsylvania German	Jamaican
Arab:	Dutch	Polish	Trinidadian and
Arab/Arabic	Eastern European	Portuguese	Tobagonian
Egyptian	English	Romanian	U.S. Virgin Islander
Iraqi	Estonian	Russian	West Indian
Jordanian	European	Scandinavian	Other West Indian
Lebanese	Finnish	Scotch-Irish	Yugoslavian

The data on ancestry were derived from answers to long-form questionnaire Item 10, which was asked of a sample of the population. The data represent self-classification by people according to the ancestry group or groups with which they most closely identify. Ancestry refers to a person's ethnic origin or descent, "roots," heritage, or the place of birth of the person, the person's parents, or their ancestors before their arrival in the United States. Some ethnic identities, such as Egyptian or Polish, can be traced to geographic areas outside the United States, while other ethnicities, such as Pennsylvania German or Cajun, evolved in the United States.

The intent of the ancestry question was not to measure the degree of attachment the respondent had to a particular ethnicity. For example, a response of "Irish" might reflect total involvement in an Irish community or only a memory of ancestors several generations removed from the individual. Also, the question was intended to provide data for groups that were not included in the Hispanic origin and race questions. Official Hispanic origin data come from long-form questionnaire Item 5, and official race data come from long-form questionnaire Item 6. Therefore, although data on all groups are collected, the ancestry data shown in these tabulations are for non-Hispanic and non-race groups.

The ancestry question allowed respondents to report one or more ancestry groups, although only the first two were coded. If a response was in terms of a dual ancestry, for example, "Irish English," the person was assigned two codes, in this case one for Irish and another for English. However, in certain cases, multiple responses such as "French Canadian," "Greek Cypriote," and "Scotch Irish" were assigned a single code reflecting their status as unique groups. If a person reported one of these unique groups in addition to another group, for example, "Scotch Irish English," resulting in three terms, that person received one code for the unique group (Scotch-Irish) and another one for the remaining group (English). If a person reported "English Irish French," only English and Irish were coded. Certain combinations of ancestries where the ancestry group is a part of another, such as "German-Bavarian," were coded as a single ancestry using the more specific group (Bavarian). Also, responses such as "Polish-American" or "Italian-American" were coded and tabulated as a single entry (Polish or Italian).

The Census Bureau accepted "American" as a unique ethnicity if it was given alone, with an ambiguous response, or with state names. If the respondent listed any other ethnic identity such as "Italian-American," generally the "American" portion of the response was not coded. However, distinct groups such as "American Indian," "Mexican American," and "African American" were coded and identified separately because they represented groups who considered themselves different from those who reported as "Indian," "Mexican," or "African," respectively.

Census 2000 tabulations on ancestry are presented using two types of data presentations — one using total people as the base, and the other using total responses as the base. This chapter uses total responses as the base and includes the total number of ancestries reported and coded. If a person reported a multiple ancestry such as "French

Danish," that response was counted twice in the tabulations — once in the French category and again in the Danish category. Thus, the sum of the counts in this type of presentation is not the total population but the total of all responses.

An automated coding system was used for coding ancestry in Census 2000. This greatly reduced the potential for error associated with a clerical review. Specialists with knowledge of the subject matter reviewed, edited, coded, and resolved inconsistent or incomplete responses. The code list used in Census 2000, containing over 1,000 categories, reflects the results of the Census Bureau's experience with the 1990 ancestry question, research, and consultation with many ethnic experts. Many decisions were made to determine the classification of responses. These decisions affected the grouping of the tabulated data. For example, the Italian category includes the responses of Sicilian and Tuscan, as well as a number of other responses.

Although some people consider religious affiliation a component of ethnic identity, the ancestry question was not designed to collect any information concerning religion. Thus, if a religion was given as an answer to the ancestry question, it was listed in the "Other groups" category which is not shown in this chapter.

Ancestry should not be confused with a person's place of birth, although a person's place of birth and ancestry may be the same.

Ranking Section

In the ranking section of this chapter, each ancestry has three tables. The first table shows the top 10 places sorted by number (based on all places, regardless of population), the second table shows the top 10 places sorted by percent (based on all places, regardless of population), the third table shows the top 10 places sorted by percent (based on places with populations of 10,000 or more).

Within each table, column one displays the place name, the state, and the county (if a place spans more than one county, the county that holds the majority of the population is shown). Column two displays the number of people reporting each ancestry, and column three is the percent of the total population reporting each ancestry. For tables representing ancestries based on race or Hispanic origin, the 100-percent population figure from SF1 is used to calculate the value in the "%" column. For all other ancestries the sample population figure from SF3 is used to calculate the value in the "%" column.

Alphabetical Ancestry Cross-Reference Guide

Acadian/Cajun
Afghan
African *See African, sub-Saharan: African*
African American/Black
African American/Black: Hispanic
African American/Black: Not Hispanic
African, sub-Saharan
African, sub-Saharan: African
African, sub-Saharan: Cape Verdean
African, sub-Saharan: Ethiopian
African, sub-Saharan: Ghanian
African, sub-Saharan: Kenyan
African, sub-Saharan: Liberian
African, sub-Saharan: Nigerian
African, sub-Saharan: Other
African, sub-Saharan: Senegalese
African, sub-Saharan: Sierra Leonean
African, sub-Saharan: Somalian
African, sub-Saharan: South African
African, sub-Saharan: Sudanese
African, sub-Saharan: Ugandan
African, sub-Saharan: Zairian
African, sub-Saharan: Zimbabwean
Alaska Athabascan *See Alaska Native: Alaska Athabascan*
Alaska Native tribes, not specified
Alaska Native tribes, specified
Alaska Native: Alaska Athabascan
Alaska Native: Aleut
Alaska Native: All other tribes
Alaska Native: Eskimo
Alaska Native: Tlingit-Haida
Albanian
Aleut *See Alaska Native: Aleut*
Alsatian
American *See United States or American*
American Indian or Alaska Native tribes, not specified
American Indian tribes, not specified
American Indian tribes, specified
American Indian: All other tribes
American Indian: Apache
American Indian: Blackfeet
American Indian: Cherokee
American Indian: Cheyenne
American Indian: Chickasaw
American Indian: Chippewa
American Indian: Choctaw
American Indian: Colville
American Indian: Comanche
American Indian: Cree
American Indian: Creek
American Indian: Crow
American Indian: Delaware
American Indian: Houma
American Indian: Iroquois
American Indian: Kiowa
American Indian: Latin American Indians
American Indian: Lumbee
American Indian: Menominee
American Indian: Navajo
American Indian: Osage
American Indian: Ottawa
American Indian: Paiute
American Indian: Pima
American Indian: Potawatomi

American Indian: Pueblo
American Indian: Puget Sound Salish
American Indian: Seminole
American Indian: Shoshone
American Indian: Sioux
American Indian: Tohono O'Odham
American Indian: Ute
American Indian: Yakama
American Indian: Yaqui
American Indian: Yuman
Apache *See American Indian: Apache*
Arab
Arab/Arabic *See Arab: Arab/Arabic*
Arab: Arab/Arabic
Arab: Egyptian
Arab: Iraqi
Arab: Jordanian
Arab: Lebanese
Arab: Moroccan
Arab: Other
Arab: Palestinian
Arab: Syrian
Argentinean *See Hispanic: Argentinean*
Armenian
Asian
Asian: Bangladeshi
Asian: Cambodian
Asian: Chinese, except Taiwanese
Asian: Filipino
Asian: Hmong
Asian: Indian
Asian: Indonesian
Asian: Japanese
Asian: Korean
Asian: Laotian
Asian: Malaysian
Asian: Other Asian, not specified
Asian: Other Asian, specified
Asian: Pakistani
Asian: Sri Lankan
Asian: Taiwanese
Asian: Thai
Asian: Vietnamese
Assyrian/Chaldean/Syriac
Australian
Austrian
Bahamian *See West Indian: Bahamian, excluding Hispanic*
Bangladeshi *See Asian: Bangladeshi*
Barbadian *See West Indian: Barbadian, excluding Hispanic*
Basque
Belgian
Belizean *See West Indian: Belizean, excluding Hispanic*
Bermudan *See West Indian: Bermudan, excluding Hispanic*
Blackfeet *See American Indian: Blackfeet*
Bolivian *See Hispanic: Bolivian*
Brazilian
British
British West Indian *See West Indian: British West Indian, excluding Hispanic*
Bulgarian
Cambodian *See Asian: Cambodian*
Canadian

Cape Verdean *See African, sub-Saharan: Cape Verdean*
Carpatho Rusyn
Celtic
Central American: *See Hispanic: Central American*
Cherokee *See American Indian: Cherokee*
Cheyenne *See American Indian: Cheyenne*
Chickasaw *See American Indian: Chickasaw*
Chilean *See Hispanic: Chilean*
Chinese, except Taiwanese *See Asian: Chinese, except Taiwanese*
Chippewa *See American Indian: Chippewa*
Choctaw *See American Indian: Choctaw*
Colombian *See Hispanic: Colombian*
Colville *See American Indian: Colville*
Comanche *See American Indian: Comanche*
Costa Rican *See Hispanic: Costa Rican*
Cree *See American Indian: Cree*
Creek *See American Indian: Creek*
Croatian
Crow *See American Indian: Crow*
Cuban *See Hispanic: Cuban*
Cypriot
Czech
Czechoslovakian
Danish
Delaware *See American Indian: Delaware*
Dominican Republic *See Hispanic: Dominican Republic*
Dutch
Dutch West Indian *See West Indian: Dutch West Indian, excluding Hispanic*
Eastern European
Ecuadorian *See Hispanic: Ecuadorian*
Egyptian *See Arab: Egyptian*
English
Eskimo *See Alaska Native: Eskimo*
Estonian
Ethiopian *See African, sub-Saharan: Ethiopian*
European
Fijian *See Hawaii Native/Pacific Islander: Fijian*
Filipino *See Asian: Filipino*
Finnish
French Canadian
French, except Basque
German
German Russian
Ghanian *See African, sub-Saharan: Ghanian*
Greek
Guamanian or Chamorro *See Hawaii Native/Pacific Islander: Guamanian or Chamorro*
Guatemalan *See Hispanic: Guatemalan*
Guyanese
Haitian *See West Indian: Haitian, excluding Hispanic*
Hawaii Native/Pacific Islander
Hawaii Native/Pacific Islander: Fijian
Hawaii Native/Pacific Islander: Guamanian or Chamorro
Hawaii Native/Pacific Islander: Melanesian
Hawaii Native/Pacific Islander: Micronesian
Hawaii Native/Pacific Islander: Native Hawaiian

Hawaii Native/Pacific Islander: Other Melanesian
Hawaii Native/Pacific Islander: Other Micronesian
Hawaii Native/Pacific Islander: Other Pacific
  Islander, not specified
Hawaii Native/Pacific Islander: Other Pacific
  Islander, specified
Hawaii Native/Pacific Islander: Other Polynesian
Hawaii Native/Pacific Islander: Polynesian
Hawaii Native/Pacific Islander: Samoan
Hawaii Native/Pacific Islander: Tongan
Hispanic or Latino
Hispanic: Argentinean
Hispanic: Bolivian
Hispanic: Central American
Hispanic: Chilean
Hispanic: Colombian
Hispanic: Costa Rican
Hispanic: Cuban
Hispanic: Dominican Republic
Hispanic: Ecuadorian
Hispanic: Guatemalan
Hispanic: Honduran
Hispanic: Mexican
Hispanic: Nicaraguan
Hispanic: Other
Hispanic: Other Central American
Hispanic: Other South American
Hispanic: Panamanian
Hispanic: Paraguayan
Hispanic: Peruvian
Hispanic: Puerto Rican
Hispanic: Salvadoran
Hispanic: South American
Hispanic: Uruguayan
Hispanic: Venezuelan
Hmong *See Asian: Hmong*
Honduran *See Hispanic: Honduran*
Houma *See American Indian: Houma*
Hungarian
Icelander
Indian, American *See American Indian*
Indian, Asian *See Asian: Indian*
Indonesian *See Asian: Indonesian*
Iranian
Iraqi *See Arab: Iraqi*
Irish
Iroquois *See American Indian: Iroquois*
Israeli
Italian
Jamaican *See West Indian: Jamaican, excluding
  Hispanic*
Japanese *See Asian: Japanese*
Jordanian *See Arab: Jordanian*
Kenyan *See African, sub-Saharan: Kenyan*
Kiowa *See American Indian: Kiowa*
Korean *See Asian: Korean*
Laotian *See Asian: Laotian*
Latin American Indians *See American Indian: Latin
  American Indians*
Latino *See Hispanic or Latino*
Latvian
Lebanese *See Arab: Lebanese*
Liberian *See African, sub-Saharan: Liberian*
Lithuanian
Lumbee *See American Indian: Lumbee*
Luxemburger
Macedonian
Malaysian *See Asian: Malaysian*
Maltese

Melanesian: *See Hawaii Native/Pacific Islander:
  Melanesian*
Menominee *See American Indian: Menominee*
Mexican *See Hispanic: Mexican*
Micronesian: *See Hawaii Native/Pacific Islander:
  Micronesian*
Moroccan *See Arab: Moroccan*
Native Hawaiian *See Hawaii Native/Pacific
  Islander: Native Hawaiian*
Navajo *See American Indian: Navajo*
New Zealander
Nicaraguan *See Hispanic: Nicaraguan*
Nigerian *See African, sub-Saharan: Nigerian*
Northern European
Norwegian
Osage *See American Indian: Osage*
Ottawa *See American Indian: Ottawa*
Paiute *See American Indian: Paiute*
Pakistani *See Asian: Pakistani*
Palestinian *See Arab: Palestinian*
Panamanian *See Hispanic: Panamanian*
Paraguayan *See Hispanic: Paraguayan*
Pennsylvania German
Peruvian *See Hispanic: Peruvian*
Pima *See American Indian: Pima*
Polish
Polynesian: *See Hawaii Native/Pacific Islander:
  Polynesian*
Portuguese
Potawatomi *See American Indian: Potawatomi*
Pueblo *See American Indian: Pueblo*
Puerto Rican *See Hispanic: Puerto Rican*
Puget Sound Salish *See American Indian: Puget
  Sound Salish*
Romanian
Russian
Salvadoran *See Hispanic: Salvadoran*
Samoan *See Hawaii Native/Pacific Islander:
  Samoan*
Scandinavian
Scotch-Irish
Scottish
Seminole *See American Indian: Seminole*
Senegalese *See African, sub-Saharan: Senegalese*
Serbian
Shoshone *See American Indian: Shoshone*
Sierra Leonean *See African, sub-Saharan: Sierra
  Leonean*
Sioux *See American Indian: Sioux*
Slavic
Slovak
Slovene
Somalian *See African, sub-Saharan: Somalian*
South African *See African, sub-Saharan: South
  African*
South American: *See Hispanic: South American*
Soviet Union
Sri Lankan *See Asian: Sri Lankan*
sub-Saharan African *See African, sub-Saharan*
Sudanese *See African, sub-Saharan: Sudanese*
Swedish
Swiss
Syrian *See Arab: Syrian*
Taiwanese *See Asian: Taiwanese*
Thai *See Asian: Thai*
Tlingit-Haida *See Alaska Native: Tlingit-Haida*
Tohono O'Odham *See American Indian: Tohono
  O'Odham*
Tongan *See Hawaii Native/Pacific Islander: Tongan*

Trinidadian and Tobagonian *See West Indian:
  Trinidadian and Tobagonian, excluding
  Hispanic*
Turkish
U.S. Virgin Islander *See West Indian: U.S.
  Virgin Islander, excluding Hispanic*
Ugandan *See African, sub-Saharan: Ugandan*
Ukrainian
United States or American
Uruguayan *See Hispanic: Uruguayan*
Ute *See American Indian: Ute*
Venezuelan *See Hispanic: Venezuelan*
Vietnamese *See Asian: Vietnamese*
Welsh
West Indian, excluding Hispanic
West Indian: Bahamian, excluding Hispanic
West Indian: Barbadian, excluding Hispanic
West Indian: Belizean, excluding Hispanic
West Indian: Bermudan, excluding Hispanic
West Indian: British West Indian, excluding
  Hispanic
West Indian: Dutch West Indian, excluding
  Hispanic
West Indian: Haitian, excluding Hispanic
West Indian: Jamaican, excluding Hispanic
West Indian: Other, excluding Hispanic
West Indian: Trinidadian and Tobagonian,
  excluding Hispanic
West Indian: U.S. Virgin Islander, excluding
  Hispanic
West Indian: West Indian, excluding Hispanic
White
White: Hispanic
White: Not Hispanic
Yakama *See American Indian: Yakama*
Yaqui *See American Indian: Yaqui*
Yugoslavian
Yuman *See American Indian: Yuman*
Zairian *See African, sub-Saharan: Zairian*
Zimbabwean *See African, sub-Saharan:
  Zimbabwean*

User's Guide: Hispanic Population

Places Covered

Ranking tables cover all counties and all places in Texas with populations of 10,000 or more.

Source of Data

CENSUS 2000

Data for this chapter was derived from following source: *U.S. Bureau of the Census, Census of Population and Housing, 2000: Summary File 4.* Summary File 4 (SF 4) contains sample data, which is the information compiled from the questions asked of a sample (generally 1-in-6) of all people and housing units. Summary File 4 is repeated or iterated for the total population and 335 additional population groups. This chapter focuses on the following 24 population groups:

Hispanic or Latino (of any race)
    Central American
        Costa Rican
        Guatemalan
        Honduran
        Nicaraguan
        Panamanian
        Salvadoran
    Cuban
    Dominican (Dominican Republic)
    Mexican
    Puerto Rican
    South American
        Argentinian
        Bolivian
        Chilean
        Colombian
        Ecuadorian
        Paraguayan
        Peruvian
        Uruguayan
        Venezuelan
    Spaniard
    Other Hispanic or Latino

Please note that the above list only includes Spanish-speaking population groups. Groups such as Brazilian are not classified as Hispanic by the Bureau of the Census because they primarily speak Portugese.

In order for any of the tables for a specific group to be shown in Summary File 4, the data must meet a minimum population threshold. For Summary File 4, all tables are repeated for each race group, American Indian and Alaska Native tribe, and Hispanic or Latino group if the 100-percent count of people of that specific group in a particular geographic area is 100 or more. There also must be 50 or more unweighted people of that specific group in a particular geographic area. For example, if there are 100 or more 100-percent people tabulated as Chilean in County A, and there are 50 or more unweighted people, then all matrices for Chilean are shown in SF 4 for County A.

To maintain confidentiality, the Census Bureau applies statistical procedures that introduce some uncertainty into data for small geographic areas with small population groups. Therefore, tables may contain both sampling and nonsampling error.

In an iterated file such as SF 4, the universes *households, families,* and *occupied housing units* are classified by the race or ethnic group of the householder. In any population table where there is no note, the universe classification is always based on the race or ethnicity of the person. In all housing tables, the universe classification is based on the race or ethnicity of the householder.

Comparing SF 4 Estimates with Corresponding Values in SF 1 and SF 2

As in earlier censuses, the responses from the sample of households reporting on long forms must be weighted to reflect the entire population. Specifically, each responding household represents, on average, six or seven other households who reported using short forms. One consequence of the weighting procedures is that each estimate based on the long form responses has an associated confidence interval. These confidence intervals are wider (as a percentage of the estimate) for geographic areas with smaller populations and for characteristics that occur less frequently in the area being examined (such as the proportion of people in poverty in a middle-income neighborhood). In order to release as much useful information as possible, statisticians must balance a number of factors. In particular, for Census 2000, the Bureau of the Census created weighting areas—geographic areas from which about two hundred or more long forms were completed—which are large enough to produce good quality estimates. If smaller weighting areas had been used, the confidence intervals around the estimates would have been significantly wider, rendering many estimates less useful due to their lower reliability. The disadvantage of using weighting areas this large is that, for smaller geographic areas within them, the estimates of characteristics that are also reported on the short form will not match the counts reported in SF 1 or SF 2. Examples of these characteristics are the total number of people, the number of people reporting specific racial categories, and the number of housing units. The official values for items reported on the short form come from SF 1 and SF 2. The differences between the long form estimates in SF 4 and values in SF 1 or SF 2 are particularly noticeable for the smallest places, tracts, and block groups. The long form estimates of total population and total housing units in SF 4 will, however, match the SF 1 and SF 2 counts for larger geographic areas such as counties and states, and will be essentially the same for medium and large cities. This phenomenon also occurred for the 1990 Census, although in that case, the weighting areas included relatively small places. As a result, the long form estimates matched the short form counts for those places, but the confidence intervals around the estimates of characteristics collected only on the long form were often significantly wider (as a percentage of the estimate). SF 1 gives exact numbers even for very small groups and areas; whereas, SF 4 gives estimates for small groups and areas such as tracts and small places that are less exact. The goal of SF 4 is to identify large differences among areas or large changes over time. Estimates for small areas and small population groups often do exhibit large changes from one census to the next, so having the capability to measure them is worthwhile.

Topics

POPULATION

Total Population: Sample count of total population.

Hispanic Population: The data on the Hispanic or Latino population, which was asked of all people, were derived from answers to long-form questionnaire Item 5, and short-form questionnaire Item 7. The terms "Spanish," "Hispanic origin," and "Latino" are used interchangeably. Some respondents identify with all three terms, while others may identify with only one of these three specific terms. Hispanics or Latinos who identify with the terms "Spanish," "Hispanic," or "Latino" are those who classify themselves in one of the specific Hispanic or Latino categories listed on the questionnaire — "Mexican," "Puerto Rican," or "Cuban" — as well as those who indicate that they are "other Spanish, Hispanic, or Latino." People who do not identify with one of the specific origins listed on the questionnaire but indicate that they are "other Spanish, Hispanic, or Latino" are those whose origins are from Spain, the Spanish-speaking countries of Central or South America, the Dominican Republic, or people identifying themselves generally as Spanish, Spanish-American, Hispanic, Hispano, Latino, and so on. All write-in responses to the "other Spanish/Hispanic/Latino" category were coded. Origin can be viewed as the heritage, nationality group, lineage, or country of birth of the person or the person's parents or ancestors before their arrival in the United States. People who identify their origin as Spanish, Hispanic, or Latino may be of any race.

Population groups whose primary language is not Spanish are not classified as Hispanic by the Bureau of the Census and are not included in this chapter (eg. Brazilian).

AGE

Median Age: Divides the age distribution into two equal parts: one-half of the cases falling below the median age and one-half above the median. Median age is computed on the basis of a single year of age standard distribution.

The data on age, which was asked of all people, were derived from answers to the long-form questionnaire Item 4 and short-form questionnaire Item 6. The age classification is based on the age of the person in complete years as of April 1, 2000. The age of the person usually was derived from their date of birth information. Their reported age was used only when date of birth information was unavailable.

HOUSEHOLD SIZE

Average Household Size: A measure obtained by dividing the number of people in households by the total number of households (or householders). In cases where household members are tabulated by race or Hispanic origin, household members are classified by the race or Hispanic origin of the householder rather than the race or Hispanic origin of each individual. Average household size is rounded to the nearest hundredth.

LANGUAGE SPOKEN AT HOME

English Only: Number and percentage of population 5 years and over who report speaking English-only at home.

Spanish: Number and percentage of population 5 years and over who report speaking Spanish at home.

Language spoken at home data were derived from answers to long-form questionnaire Items 11a and 11b, which were asked of a sample of the population. Data were edited to include in tabulations only the population 5 years old and over. Questions 11a and 11b referred to languages spoken at home in an effort to measure the current use of languages other than English. People who knew languages other than English but did not use them at home or who only used them elsewhere were excluded. Most people who reported speaking a language other than English at home also speak English. The questions did not permit determination of the primary or dominant language of people who spoke both English and another language.

FOREIGN-BORN

Foreign Born: Number and percentage of population who were not U.S. citizens at birth. Foreign-born people are those who indicated they were either a U.S. citizen by naturalization or they were not a citizen of the United States.

Foreign-Born Naturalized Citizens: Number and percentage of population who were not U.S. citizens at birth but became U.S. citizens by naturalization.

The data on place of birth were derived from answers to long-form questionnaire Item 12 which was asked of a sample of the population. Respondents were asked to report the U.S. state, Puerto Rico, U.S. Island Area, or foreign country where they were born. People not reporting a place of birth were assigned the state or country of birth of another family member or their residence 5 years earlier, or were imputed the response of another person with similar characteristics. People born outside the United States were asked to report their place of birth according to current international boundaries. Since numerous changes in boundaries of foreign countries have occurred in the last century, some people may have reported their place of birth in terms of boundaries that existed at the time of their birth or emigration, or in accordance with their own national preference.

EDUCATIONAL ATTAINMENT

High School Graduates: Number and percentage of the population age 25 and over who have a high school diploma or higher. This category includes people whose highest degree was a high school diploma or its equivalent, people who attended college but did not receive a degree, and people who received a college, university, or professional degree. People who reported completing the 12th grade but not receiving a diploma are not high school graduates.

4-Years College Graduates: Number and percentage of the population age 25 and over who have a 4-year college, university, or professional degree.

Data on educational attainment were derived from answers to long-form questionnaire Item 9, which was asked of a sample of the population. Data on attainment are tabulated for the population 25 years old and over.

The order in which degrees were listed on the questionnaire suggested that doctorate degrees were "higher" than professional school degrees, which were "higher" than master's degrees. The question included instructions for people currently enrolled in school to report the level of the previous grade attended or the highest degree received. Respondents who did not report educational attainment or enrollment level were assigned the attainment of a person of the same age, race, Hispanic or Latino origin, occupation and sex, where possible, who resided in the same or a nearby area. Respondents who filled more than one box were edited to the highest level or degree reported.

The question included a response category that allowed respondents to report completing the 12th grade without receiving a high school diploma. It allowed people who received either a high school diploma or the equivalent (Test of General Educational Development—G.E.D.) and did not attend college, to be reported as "high school graduate(s)." The category "Associate degree" included people whose highest degree is an associate degree, which generally requires 2 years of college level work and is either in an occupational program that prepares them for a specific occupation, or an academic program primarily in the arts and sciences. The course work may or may not be transferable to a bachelor's degree. Master's degrees include the traditional MA and MS degrees and field-specific degrees, such as MSW, MEd, MBA, MLS, and MEng. Some examples of professional degrees include medicine, dentistry, chiropractic, optometry, osteopathic medicine, pharmacy, podiatry, veterinary medicine, law, and theology. Vocational and technical training such as barber school training; business, trade, technical, and vocational schools; or other training for a specific trade, are specifically excluded.

INCOME AND POVERTY

Median Household Income (in dollars): Includes the income of the householder and all other individuals 15 years old and over in the household, whether they are related to the householder or not. The median divides the income distribution into two equal parts: one-half of the cases falling below the median income and one-half above the median. For households, the median income is based on the distribution of the total number of households including those with no income. Median income for households is computed on the basis of a standard distribution and is rounded to the nearest whole dollar.

Per Capita Income (in dollars): Per capita income is the mean income computed for every man, woman, and child in a particular group. It is derived by dividing the total income of a particular group by the total population in that group. Per capita income is rounded to the nearest whole dollar.

The data on income in 1999 were derived from answers to long-form questionnaire Items 31 and 32, which were asked of a sample of the population 15 years old and over. "Total income" is the sum of the amounts reported separately for wage or salary income; net self-employment income; interest, dividends, or net rental or royalty income or income from estates and trusts; social security or railroad retirement income; Supplemental Security Income (SSI); public assistance or welfare payments; retirement, survivor, or disability pensions; and all other income.

Receipts from the following sources are not included as income: capital gains, money received from the sale of property (unless the recipient was engaged in the business of selling such property); the value of income "in kind" from food stamps, public housing subsidies, medical care, employer contributions for individuals, etc.; withdrawal of bank deposits; money borrowed; tax refunds; exchange of money between relatives living in the same household; and gifts and lump-sum inheritances, insurance payments, and other types of lump-sum receipts.

The eight types of income reported in the census are defined as follows:

Wage or salary income. Wage or salary income includes total money earnings received for work performed as an employee during the calendar year 1999. It includes wages, salary, armed forces pay, commissions, tips, piece-rate payments, and cash bonuses earned before deductions were made for taxes, bonds, pensions, union dues, etc.

Self-employment income. Self-employment income includes both farm and nonfarm self-employment income. Nonfarm self-employment income includes net money income (gross receipts minus expenses) from one's own business, professional enterprise, or partnership. Gross receipts include the value of all goods sold and services rendered. Expenses include costs of goods purchased, rent, heat, light, power, depreciation charges, wages and salaries paid, business taxes (not personal income taxes), etc. Farm self-employment income includes net money income (gross receipts minus operating expenses) from the operation of a farm by a person on his or her own account, as an owner, renter, or sharecropper. Gross receipts include the value of all products sold, government farm programs, money received from the rental of farm equipment to others, and incidental receipts from the sale of wood, sand, gravel, etc. Operating expenses include cost of feed, fertilizer, seed, and other farming supplies, cash wages paid to farmhands, depreciation charges, cash rent, interest on farm mortgages, farm building repairs, farm taxes (not state and federal personal income taxes), etc. The value of fuel, food, or other farm products used for family living is not included as part of net income.

Interest, dividends, or net rental income. Interest, dividends, or net rental income includes interest on savings or bonds, dividends from stockholdings or membership in associations, net income from rental of property to others and receipts from boarders or lodgers, net royalties, and periodic payments from an estate or trust fund.

Social Security income. Social security income includes social security pensions and survivors benefits, permanent disability insurance payments made by the Social Security Administration prior to deductions for medical insurance, and railroad retirement insurance checks from the U.S. government. Medicare reimbursements are not included.

Supplemental Security Income (SSI). Supplemental Security Income (SSI) is a nationwide U.S. assistance program administered by the Social Security Administration that guarantees a minimum level of income for needy aged, blind, or disabled individuals. The census questionnaire for Puerto Rico asked about the receipt of SSI; however, SSI is not a federally administered program in Puerto Rico. Therefore, it is probably not being interpreted by most respondents as the same as SSI in the United States. The only way a resident of Puerto Rico could have appropriately reported SSI would have been if they lived in the United States at any time during calendar year 1999 and received SSI.

Public assistance income. Public assistance income includes general assistance and Temporary Assistance to Needy Families (TANF). Separate payments received for hospital or other medical care (vendor payments) are excluded. This does not include Supplemental Security Income (SSI).

Retirement income. Retirement income includes: (1) retirement pensions and survivor benefits from a former employer; labor union; or federal, state, or local government; and the U.S. military; (2) income from workers' compensation; disability income from companies or unions; federal, state, or local government; and the U.S. military; (3) periodic receipts from annuities and insurance; and (4) regular income from IRA and KEOGH plans. This does not include social security income.

All other income. All other income includes unemployment compensation, Veterans' Administration (VA) payments, alimony and child support, contributions received periodically from people not living in the household, military family allotments, and other kinds of periodic income other than earnings.

Poverty Status: Number and percentage of population with income in 1999 below the poverty level. Based on individuals for whom poverty status is determined. Poverty status was determined for all people except institutionalized people, people in military group quarters, people in college dormitories, and unrelated individuals under 15 years old.

The poverty status of families and unrelated individuals in 1999 was determined using 48 thresholds (income cutoffs) arranged in a two dimensional matrix. The matrix consists of family size (from 1 person to 9 or more people) cross-classified by presence and number of family members under 18 years old (from no children present to 8 or more children present). Unrelated individuals and 2-person families were further differentiated by the age of the reference person (RP) (under 65 years old and 65 years old and over).

To determine a person's poverty status, one compares the person's total family income with the poverty threshold appropriate for that person's family size and composition. If the total income of that person's family is less than the threshold appropriate for that family, then the person is considered poor, together with every member of his or her family. If a person is not living with anyone related by birth, marriage, or adoption, then the person's own income is compared with his or her poverty threshold.

HOUSING

Homeownership: Number and percentage of housing units that are owner-occupied.

The data on tenure, which was asked at all occupied housing units, were obtained from answers to long-form questionnaire Item 33, and short-form questionnaire Item 2. All occupied housing units are classified as either owner occupied or renter occupied.

A housing unit is owner occupied if the owner or co-owner lives in the unit even if it is mortgaged or not fully paid for. The owner or co-owner must live in the unit and usually is Person 1 on the questionnaire. The unit is "Owned by you or someone in this household with a mortgage or loan" if it is being purchased with a mortgage or some other debt arrangement, such as a deed of trust, trust deed, contract to purchase, land contract, or purchase agreement. The unit is also considered owned with a mortgage if it is built on leased land and there is a mortgage on the unit. Mobile homes occupied by owners with installment loans balances are also included in this category.

Median Gross Rent (in dollars): Median monthly gross rent on specified renter-occupied and specified vacant-for-rent units. Specified renter-occupied and specified vacant-for-rent units exclude 1-family houses on 10 acres or more.

The data on gross rent were obtained from answers to long-form questionnaire Items 45a-d, which were asked on a sample basis. Gross rent is the contract rent plus the estimated average monthly cost of utilities (electricity, gas, water and sewer) and fuels (oil, coal, kerosene, wood, etc.) if these are paid by the renter (or paid for the renter by someone else). Gross rent is intended to eliminate differentials that result from varying practices with respect to the inclusion of utilities and fuels as part of the rental payment. The estimated costs of utilities and fuels are reported on an annual basis but are converted to monthly figures for the tabulations. Renter units occupied without payment of cash rent are shown separately as "No cash rent" in the tabulations.

Housing units that are renter occupied without payment of cash rent are shown separately as "No cash rent" in census data products. The unit may be owned by friends or relatives who live elsewhere and who allow occupancy without charge. Rent-free houses or apartments may be provided to compensate caretakers, ministers, tenant farmers, sharecroppers, or others.

Contract rent is the monthly rent agreed to or contracted for, regardless of any furnishings, utilities, fees, meals, or services that may be included. For vacant units, it is the monthly rent asked for the rental unit at the time of enumeration.

If the contract rent includes rent for a business unit or for living quarters occupied by another household, only that part of the rent estimated to be for the respondent's unit was included. Excluded was any rent paid for additional units or for business premises.

If a renter pays rent to the owner of a condominium or cooperative, and the condominium fee or cooperative carrying charge also is paid by the renter to the owner, the condominium fee or carrying charge was included as rent.

If a renter receives payments from lodgers or roomers who are listed as members of the household, the rent without deduction for any payments received from the lodgers or roomers was to be reported. The respondent was to report the rent agreed to or contracted for even if paid by someone else such as friends or relatives living elsewhere, a church or welfare agency, or the government through subsidies or vouchers.

The median divides the rent distribution into two equal parts: one-half of the cases falling below the median contract rent and one-half above the median. Median contract rents are computed on the basis of a standard distribution and are rounded to the nearest whole dollar. Units reported as "No cash rent" are excluded.

Median Home Value (in dollars): Reported by the owner of specified owner-occupied or specified vacant-for-sale housing units. Specified owner-occupied and specified vacant-for-sale housing units include only 1-family houses on less than 10 acres without a business or medical office on the property. The data for "specified units" exclude mobile homes, houses with a business or medical office, houses on 10 or more acres, and housing units in multi-unit buildings.

The data on value (also referred to as "price asked" for vacant units) were obtained from answers to long-form questionnaire Item 51, which was asked on a sample basis at owner-occupied housing units and units that were being bought, or vacant for sale at the time of enumeration. Value is the respondent's estimate of how much the property (house and lot, mobile home and lot, or condominium unit) would sell for if it were for sale. If the house or mobile home was owned or being bought, but the land on which it sits was not, the respondent was asked to estimate the combined value of the house or mobile home and the land. For vacant units, value was the price asked for the property. Value was tabulated separately for all owner-occupied and vacant-for-sale housing units, owner-occupied and vacant-for-sale mobile homes, and specified owner-occupied and specified vacant-for-sale housing units.

The median divides the value distribution into two equal parts: one-half of the cases falling below the median value of the property (house and lot, mobile home and lot, or condominium unit) and one-half above the median. Median values are computed on the basis of a standard distribution and are rounded to the nearest hundred dollars.

User's Guide: Asian Population

Places Covered

Ranking tables cover all counties and places in Texas with Asian and/or Native Hawaiian and other Pacific Islander residents.

Source of Data

CENSUS 2000

Data for this chapter was derived from following source: *U.S. Bureau of the Census, Census of Population and Housing, 2000: Summary File 4.* Summary File 4 (SF 4) contains sample data, which is the information compiled from the questions asked of a sample (generally 1-in-6) of all people and housing units. Summary File 4 is repeated or iterated for the total population and 335 additional population groups. This chapter focuses on the following 23 population groups:

Asian
    Asian Indian
    Bangladeshi
    Cambodian
    Chinese (except Taiwanese)
    Filipino
    Hmong
    Indonesian
    Japanese
    Korean
    Laotian
    Malaysian
    Pakistani
    Sri Lankan
    Taiwanese
    Thai
    Vietnamese
Native Hawaiian and Other Pacific Islander
    Fijian
    Guamanian or Chamorro
    Hawaiian, Native
    Samoan
    Tongan

Please note that this chapter only includes people who responded to the question on race by indicating only one race. These people are classified by the Census Bureau as the race *alone* population. For example, respondents reporting a single detailed Asian group, such as Korean or Filipino, would be included in the Asian *alone* population. Respondents reporting more than one detailed Asian group, such as Chinese and Japanese or Asian Indian and Chinese and Vietnamese would also be included in the Asian *alone* population. This is because all of the detailed groups in these example combinations are part of the larger Asian race category. The same criteria apply to the Native Hawaiian and Other Pacific Islander groups.

In order for any of the tables for a specific group to be shown in Summary File 4, the data must meet a minimum population threshold. For Summary File 4, all tables are repeated for each race group, American Indian and Alaska Native tribe, and Hispanic or Latino group if the 100-percent count of people of that specific group in a particular geographic area is 100 or more. There also must be 50 or more unweighted people of that specific group in a particular geographic area. For example, if there are 100 or more 100-percent people tabulated as Korean in County A, and there are 50 or more unweighted people, then all matrices for Korean are shown in SF 4 for County A.

To maintain confidentiality, the Census Bureau applies statistical procedures that introduce some uncertainty into data for small geographic areas with small population groups. Therefore, tables may contain both sampling and nonsampling error.

In an iterated file such as SF 4, the universes *households, families,* and *occupied housing units* are classified by the race or ethnic group of the householder. In any population table where there is no note, the universe classification is always based on the race or ethnicity of the person. In all housing tables, the universe classification is based on the race or ethnicity of the householder.

Comparing SF 4 Estimates with Corresponding Values in SF 1 and SF 2

As in earlier censuses, the responses from the sample of households reporting on long forms must be weighted to reflect the entire population. Specifically, each responding household represents, on average, six or seven other households who reported using short forms. One consequence of the weighting procedures is that each estimate based on the long form responses has an associated confidence interval. These confidence intervals are wider (as a percentage of the estimate) for geographic areas with smaller populations and for characteristics that occur less frequently in the area being examined (such as the proportion of people in poverty in a middle-income neighborhood). In order to release as much useful information as possible, statisticians must balance a number of factors. In particular, for Census 2000, the Bureau of the Census created weighting areas—geographic areas from which about two hundred or more long forms were completed—which are large enough to produce good quality estimates. If smaller weighting areas had been used, the confidence intervals around the estimates would have been significantly wider, rendering many estimates less useful due to their lower reliability. The disadvantage of using weighting areas this large is that, for smaller geographic areas within them, the estimates of characteristics that are also reported on the short form will not match the counts reported in SF 1 or SF 2. Examples of these characteristics are the total number of people, the number of people reporting specific racial categories, and the number of housing units. The official values for items reported on the short form come from SF 1 and SF 2. The differences between the long form estimates in SF 4 and values in SF 1 or SF 2 are particularly noticeable for the smallest places, tracts, and block groups. The long form estimates of total population and total housing units in SF 4 will, however, match the SF 1 and SF 2 counts for larger geographic areas such as counties and states, and will be essentially the same for medium and large cities. This phenomenon also occurred for the 1990 Census, although in that case, the weighting areas included relatively small places. As a result, the long form estimates matched the short form counts for those places, but the confidence intervals around the estimates of characteristics collected only on the long form were often significantly wider (as a percentage of the estimate). SF 1 gives exact numbers even for very small groups and areas; whereas, SF 4 gives estimates for small groups and areas such as tracts and small places that are less exact. The goal of SF 4 is to identify large differences among areas or large changes over time. Estimates for small areas and small population groups often do exhibit large changes from one census to the next, so having the capability to measure them is worthwhile.

Topics

POPULATION

Total Population: Sample count of total population of all races.

Asian Population: A person having origins in any of the original peoples of the Far East, Southeast Asia, or the Indian subcontinent including, for example, Cambodia, China, India, Japan, Korea, Malaysia, Pakistan, the Philippine Islands, Thailand, and Vietnam. It includes Asian Indian, Bangladeshi, Cambodian, Chinese (except Taiwanese), Filipino, Hmong, Indonesian, Japanese, Korean, Laotian, Malaysian, Pakistani, Sri Lankan, Taiwanese, Thai, and Vietnamese.

Native Hawaiian or Other Pacific Islander (NHPI) Population: A person having origins in any of the original peoples of Hawaii, Guam, Samoa, or other Pacific Islands. It includes people who indicate their race as Fijian, Guamanian or Chamorro, Native Hawaiian, Samoan, and Tongan.

The data on race, which was asked of all people, were derived from answers to long-form questionnaire Item 6 and short-form questionnaire Item 8. The concept of race, as used by the Census Bureau, reflects self-identification by people according to the race or races with which they most closely identify. These categories are socio-political constructs and should not be interpreted as being scientific or anthropological in nature. Furthermore, the race categories include both racial and national-origin groups.

If an individual did not provide a race response, the race or races of the householder or other household members were assigned using specific rules of precedence of household relationship. For example, if race was missing for a natural-born child in the household, then either the race or races of the householder, another natural-born child, or the spouse of the householder were assigned. If race was not reported for anyone in the household, the race or races of a householder in a previously processed household were assigned.

AGE

Median Age: Divides the age distribution into two equal parts: one-half of the cases falling below the median age and one-half above the median. Median age is computed on the basis of a single year of age standard distribution.

The data on age, which was asked of all people, were derived from answers to the long-form questionnaire Item 4 and short-form questionnaire Item 6. The age classification is based on the age of the person in complete years as of April 1, 2000. The age of the person usually was derived from their date of birth information. Their reported age was used only when date of birth information was unavailable.

HOUSEHOLD SIZE

Average Household Size: A measure obtained by dividing the number of people in households by the total number of households (or householders). In cases where household members are tabulated by race or Hispanic origin, household members are classified by the race or Hispanic origin of the householder rather than the race or Hispanic origin of each individual. Average household size is rounded to the nearest hundredth.

LANGUAGE SPOKEN AT HOME

English Only: Number and percentage of population 5 years and over who report speaking English-only at home.

Language spoken at home data were derived from answers to long-form questionnaire Items 11a and 11b, which were asked of a sample of the population. Data were edited to include in tabulations only the population 5 years old and over. Questions 11a and 11b referred to languages spoken at home in an effort to measure the current use of languages other than English. People who knew languages other than English but did not use them at home or who only used them elsewhere were excluded. Most people who reported speaking a language other than English at home also speak English. The questions did not permit determination of the primary or dominant language of people who spoke both English and another language.

FOREIGN-BORN

Foreign Born: Number and percentage of population who were not U.S. citizens at birth. Foreign-born people are those who indicated they were either a U.S. citizen by naturalization or they were not a citizen of the United States.

Foreign-Born Naturalized Citizens: Number and percentage of population who were not U.S. citizens at birth but became U.S. citizens by naturalization.

The data on place of birth were derived from answers to long-form questionnaire Item 12 which was asked of a sample of the population. Respondents were asked to report the U.S. state, Puerto Rico, U.S. Island Area, or foreign country where they were born. People not reporting a place of birth were assigned the state or country of birth of another family member or their residence 5 years earlier, or were imputed the response of another person with similar characteristics. People born outside the United States were asked to report their place of birth according to current international boundaries. Since numerous changes in boundaries of foreign countries have occurred in the last century, some people may have reported their place of birth in terms of boundaries that existed at the time of their birth or emigration, or in accordance with their own national preference.

EDUCATIONAL ATTAINMENT

High School Graduates: Number and percentage of the population age 25 and over who have a high school diploma or higher. This category includes people whose highest degree was a high school diploma or its equivalent, people who attended college but did not receive a degree, and people who received a college, university, or professional degree. People who reported completing the 12th grade but not receiving a diploma are not high school graduates.

Four-Year College Graduates: Number and percentage of the population age 25 and over who have a 4-year college, university, or professional degree.

Data on educational attainment were derived from answers to long-form questionnaire Item 9, which was asked of a sample of the population. Data on attainment are tabulated for the population 25 years old and over.

The order in which degrees were listed on the questionnaire suggested that doctorate degrees were "higher" than professional school degrees, which were "higher" than master's degrees. The question included instructions for people currently enrolled in school to report the level of the previous grade attended or the highest degree received.

Respondents who did not report educational attainment or enrollment level were assigned the attainment of a person of the same age, race, Hispanic or Latino origin, occupation and sex, where possible, who resided in the same or a nearby area. Respondents who filled more than one box were edited to the highest level or degree reported.

The question included a response category that allowed respondents to report completing the 12th grade without receiving a high school diploma. It allowed people who received either a high school diploma or the equivalent (Test of General Educational Development—G.E.D.) and did not attend college, to be reported as "high school graduate(s)." The category "Associate degree" included people whose highest degree is an associate degree, which generally requires 2 years of college level work and is either in an occupational program that prepares them for a specific occupation, or an academic program primarily in the arts and sciences. The course work may or may not be transferable to a bachelor's degree. Master's degrees include the traditional MA and MS degrees and field-specific degrees, such as MSW, MEd, MBA, MLS, and MEng. Some examples of professional degrees include medicine, dentistry, chiropractic, optometry, osteopathic medicine, pharmacy, podiatry, veterinary medicine, law, and theology. Vocational and technical training such as barber school training; business, trade, technical, and vocational schools; or other training for a specific trade, are specifically excluded.

INCOME AND POVERTY

Median Household Income (in dollars): Includes the income of the householder and all other individuals 15 years old and over in the household, whether they are related to the householder or not. The median divides the income distribution into two equal parts: one-half of the cases falling below the median income and one-half above the median. For households, the median income is based on the distribution of the total number of households including those with no income. Median income for households is computed on the basis of a standard distribution and is rounded to the nearest whole dollar.

Per Capita Income (in dollars): Per capita income is the mean income computed for every man, woman, and child in a particular group. It is derived by dividing the total income of a particular group by the total population in that group. Per capita income is rounded to the nearest whole dollar.

The data on income in 1999 were derived from answers to long-form questionnaire Items 31 and 32, which were asked of a sample of the population 15 years old and over. "Total income" is the sum of the amounts reported separately for wage or salary income; net self-employment income; interest, dividends, or net rental or royalty income or income from estates and trusts; social security or railroad retirement income; Supplemental Security Income (SSI); public assistance or welfare payments; retirement, survivor, or disability pensions; and all other income.

Receipts from the following sources are not included as income: capital gains, money received from the sale of property (unless the recipient was engaged in the business of selling such property); the value of income "in kind" from food stamps, public housing subsidies, medical care, employer contributions for individuals, etc.; withdrawal of bank deposits; money borrowed; tax refunds; exchange of money between relatives living in the same household; and gifts and lump-sum inheritances, insurance payments, and other types of lump-sum receipts.

The eight types of income reported in the census are defined as follows:

Wage or salary income. Wage or salary income includes total money earnings received for work performed as an employee during the calendar year 1999. It includes wages, salary, armed forces pay, commissions, tips, piece-rate payments, and cash bonuses earned before deductions were made for taxes, bonds, pensions, union dues, etc.

Self-employment income. Self-employment income includes both farm and nonfarm self-employment income. Nonfarm self-employment income includes net money income (gross receipts minus expenses) from one's own business, professional enterprise, or partnership. Gross receipts include the value of all goods sold and services rendered. Expenses include costs of goods purchased, rent, heat, light, power, depreciation charges, wages and salaries paid, business taxes (not personal income taxes), etc. Farm self-employment income includes net money income (gross receipts minus operating expenses) from the operation of a farm by a person on his or her own account, as an owner, renter, or sharecropper. Gross receipts include the value of all products sold, government farm programs, money received from the rental of farm equipment to others, and incidental receipts from the sale of wood, sand, gravel, etc. Operating expenses include cost of feed, fertilizer, seed, and other farming supplies, cash wages paid to farmhands, depreciation charges, cash rent, interest on farm mortgages, farm building repairs, farm taxes (not state and federal personal income taxes), etc. The value of fuel, food, or other farm products used for family living is not included as part of net income.

Interest, dividends, or net rental income. Interest, dividends, or net rental income includes interest on savings or bonds, dividends from stockholdings or membership in associations, net income from rental of property to others and receipts from boarders or lodgers, net royalties, and periodic payments from an estate or trust fund.

Social Security income. Social security income includes social security pensions and survivors benefits, permanent disability insurance payments made by the Social Security Administration prior to deductions for medical insurance, and railroad retirement insurance checks from the U.S. government. Medicare reimbursements are not included.

Supplemental Security Income (SSI). Supplemental Security Income (SSI) is a nationwide U.S. assistance program administered by the Social Security Administration that guarantees a minimum level of income for needy aged, blind, or disabled individuals. The census questionnaire for Puerto Rico asked about the receipt of SSI; however, SSI is not a federally administered program in Puerto Rico. Therefore, it is probably not being interpreted by most respondents as the same as SSI in the United States. The only way a resident of Puerto Rico could have appropriately reported SSI would have been if they lived in the United States at any time during calendar year 1999 and received SSI.

Public assistance income. Public assistance income includes general assistance and Temporary Assistance to Needy Families (TANF). Separate payments received for hospital or other medical care (vendor payments) are excluded. This does not include Supplemental Security Income (SSI).

Retirement income. Retirement income includes: (1) retirement pensions and survivor benefits from a former employer; labor union; or federal, state, or local government; and the U.S. military; (2) income from workers' compensation; disability income from companies or unions; federal, state, or local government; and the U.S. military; (3) periodic receipts from annuities and insurance; and (4) regular income from IRA and KEOGH plans. This does not include social security income.

All other income. All other income includes unemployment compensation, Veterans' Administration (VA) payments, alimony and child support, contributions received periodically from people not living in the household, military family allotments, and other kinds of periodic income other than earnings.

Poverty Status: Number and percentage of population with income in 1999 below the poverty level. Based on individuals for whom poverty status is determined. Poverty status was determined for all people except institutionalized people, people in military group quarters, people in college dormitories, and unrelated individuals under 15 years old.

The poverty status of families and unrelated individuals in 1999 was determined using 48 thresholds (income cutoffs) arranged in a two dimensional matrix. The matrix consists of family size (from 1 person to 9 or more people) cross-classified by presence and number of family members under 18 years old (from no children present to 8 or more children present). Unrelated individuals and 2-person families were further differentiated by the age of the reference person (RP) (under 65 years old and 65 years old and over).

To determine a person's poverty status, one compares the person's total family income with the poverty threshold appropriate for that person's family size and composition. If the total income of that person's family is less than the threshold appropriate for that family, then the person is considered poor, together with every member of his or her family. If a person is not living with anyone related by birth, marriage, or adoption, then the person's own income is compared with his or her poverty threshold.

HOUSING

Homeownership: Number and percentage of housing units that are owner-occupied.

The data on tenure, which was asked at all occupied housing units, were obtained from answers to long-form questionnaire Item 33, and short-form questionnaire Item 2. All occupied housing units are classified as either owner occupied or renter occupied.

A housing unit is owner occupied if the owner or co-owner lives in the unit even if it is mortgaged or not fully paid for. The owner or co-owner must live in the unit and usually is Person 1 on the questionnaire. The unit is "Owned by you or someone in this household with a mortgage or loan" if it is being purchased with a mortgage or some other debt arrangement, such as a deed of trust, trust deed, contract to purchase, land contract, or purchase agreement. The unit is also considered owned with a mortgage if it is built on leased land and there is a mortgage on the unit. Mobile homes occupied by owners with installment loans balances are also included in this category.

Median Gross Rent (in dollars): Median monthly gross rent on specified renter-occupied and specified vacant-for-rent units. Specified renter-occupied and specified vacant-for-rent units exclude 1-family houses on 10 acres or more.

The data on gross rent were obtained from answers to long-form questionnaire Items 45a-d, which were asked on a sample basis. Gross rent is the contract rent plus the estimated average monthly cost of utilities (electricity, gas, water and sewer) and fuels (oil, coal, kerosene, wood, etc.) if these are paid by the renter (or paid for the renter by someone else). Gross rent is intended to eliminate differentials that result from varying practices with respect to the inclusion of utilities and fuels as part of the rental payment. The estimated costs of utilities and fuels are reported on an annual basis but are converted to monthly figures for the tabulations. Renter units occupied without payment of cash rent are shown separately as "No cash rent" in the tabulations.

Housing units that are renter occupied without payment of cash rent are shown separately as "No cash rent" in census data products. The unit may be owned by friends or relatives who live elsewhere and who allow occupancy without charge. Rent-free houses or apartments may be provided to compensate caretakers, ministers, tenant farmers, sharecroppers, or others.

Contract rent is the monthly rent agreed to or contracted for, regardless of any furnishings, utilities, fees, meals, or services that may be included. For vacant units, it is the monthly rent asked for the rental unit at the time of enumeration.

If the contract rent includes rent for a business unit or for living quarters occupied by another household, only that part of the rent estimated to be for the respondent's unit was included. Excluded was any rent paid for additional units or for business premises.

If a renter pays rent to the owner of a condominium or cooperative, and the condominium fee or cooperative carrying charge also is paid by the renter to the owner, the condominium fee or carrying charge was included as rent.

If a renter receives payments from lodgers or roomers who are listed as members of the household, the rent without deduction for any payments received from the lodgers or roomers was to be reported. The respondent was to report the rent agreed to or contracted for even if paid by someone else such as friends or relatives living elsewhere, a church or welfare agency, or the government through subsidies or vouchers.

The median divides the rent distribution into two equal parts: one-half of the cases falling below the median contract rent and one-half above the median. Median contract rents are computed on the basis of a standard distribution and are rounded to the nearest whole dollar. Units reported as "No cash rent" are excluded.

Median Home Value (in dollars): Reported by the owner of specified owner-occupied or specified vacant-for-sale housing units. Specified owner-occupied and specified vacant-for-sale housing units include only 1-family houses on less than 10 acres without a business or medical office on the property. The data for "specified units" exclude mobile homes, houses with a business or medical office, houses on 10 or more acres, and housing units in multi-unit buildings.

The data on value (also referred to as "price asked" for vacant units) were obtained from answers to long-form questionnaire Item 51, which was asked on a sample basis at owner-occupied housing units and units that were being bought, or vacant for sale at the time of enumeration. Value is the respondent's estimate of how much the property (house and lot, mobile home and lot, or condominium unit) would sell for if it were for sale. If the house or mobile home was owned or being bought, but the land on which it sits was not, the respondent was asked to estimate the combined value of the house or mobile home and the land. For vacant units, value was the price asked for the property. Value was tabulated separately for all owner-occupied and vacant-for-sale housing units, owner-occupied and vacant-for-sale mobile homes, and specified owner-occupied and specified vacant-for-sale housing units.

The median divides the value distribution into two equal parts: one-half of the cases falling below the median value of the property (house and lot, mobile home and lot, or condominium unit) and one-half above the median. Median values are computed on the basis of a standard distribution and are rounded to the nearest hundred dollars.

User's Guide: Climate

Sources of the Data

The National Climactic Data Center (NCDC) has two main classes or types of weather stations; first-order stations which are staffed by professional meteorologists and cooperative stations which are staffed by volunteers. All 243 National Weather Service (NWS) stations included in this book are first-order stations.

The data in *Weather America** is compiled from several sources. The majority comes from the original NCDC computer tapes (DSI-3220 Summary of Month Cooperative). This data was used to create the entire table for each cooperative station and part of each National Weather Service station. The remainder of the data for each NWS station comes from the International Station Meteorological Climate Summary, Version 4.0, September 1996, which is also available from the NCDC.

Storm events come from the NCDC Storm Events Database which is accessible over the Internet at http://www4.ncdc.noaa.gov/ cgi-win/wwcgi.dll?wwevent~storms.

Weather Station Tables

The weather station tables are grouped by type (National Weather Service and Cooperative) and then arranged alphabetically within each state section. The station name is almost always a place name, and is shown here just as it appears in NCDC data. The station name is followed by the county in which the station is located (or by county equivalent name), the elevation of the station (at the time beginning of the thirty year period) and the latitude and longitude.

The National Weather Service Station tables contain 32 data elements which were compiled from two different sources, the International Station Meteorological Climate Summary (ISMCS) and NCDC DSI-3220 data tapes. The following 13 elements are from the ISMCS: maximum precipitation, minimum precipitation, maximum snowfall, maximum 24-hour snowfall, thunderstorm days, foggy days, predominant sky cover, relative humidity (morning and afternoon), dewpoint, wind speed and direction, and maximum wind gust. The remaining 19 elements come from the DSI-3220 data tapes. The period of record (POR) for data from the DSI-3220 data tapes is 1980-2009. The POR for ISMCS data varies from station to station and appears in a note below each station.

The Cooperative Station tables contain 19 data elements which were all compiled from the DSI-3220 data tapes with a POR of 1980-2009.

Weather Elements (NWS and Cooperative Stations)

The following elements were compiled by the editor from the NCDC DSI-3220 data tapes using a period of record of 1980-2009.

The average temperatures (maximum, minimum, and mean) are the average (see Methodology below) of those temperatures for all available values for a given month. For example, for a given station the average maximum temperature for July is the arithmetic average of all available maximum July temperatures for that station. (Maximum means the highest recorded temperature, minimum means the lowest recorded temperature, and mean means an arithmetic average temperature.)

The extreme maximum temperature is the highest temperature recorded in each month over the period 1980-2009. The extreme minimum temperature is the lowest temperature recorded in each month over the same time period. The extreme maximum daily precipitation is the largest amount of precipitation recorded over a 24-hour period in each month from 1980-2009. The maximum snow depth is the maximum snow depth recorded in each month over the period 1980-2009.

The days for maximum temperature and minimum temperature are the average number of days those criteria were met for all available instances. The symbol ≥ means greater than or equal to, the symbol ≤ means less than or equal to. For example, for a given station, the number of days the maximum temperature was greater than or equal to 90°F in July, is just an arithmetic average of the number of days in all the available Julys for that station.

Heating and cooling degree days are based on the median temperature for a given day and its variance from 65°F. For example, for a given station if the day's high temperature was 50°F and the day's low temperature was 30°F, the median (midpoint) temperature was 40°F. 40°F is 25 degrees below 65°F, hence on this day there would be 25 heating degree days. The also applies for cooling degree days. For example, for a given station if the day's high temperature was 80°F and the day's low temperature was 70°F, the median (midpoint) temperature was 75°F. 75°F is 10 degrees above 65°F, hence on this day there would be 10 cooling degree days. All heating and/or cooling degree days in a month are summed for the month giving respective totals for each element for that month. These sums for a given month for a given station over the past thirty years are again summed and then arithmetically averaged. It should be noted that the heating and cooling degree days do not cancel each other out. It is possible to have both for a given station in the same month.

Precipitation data is computed the same as heating and cooling degree days. Mean precipitation and mean snowfall are arithmetic averages of cumulative totals for the month. All available values for the thirty year period for a given month for a given station are summed and then divided by the number of values. The same is true for days of greater than or equal to 0.1", 0.5",and 1.0" of precipitation, and days of greater than or equal to 1.0" of snow depth on the ground. The word trace appears for precipitation and snowfall amounts that are too small to measure.

Finally, remember that all values presented in the tables and the rankings are averages, maximums, or minimums of available data (see Methodology below) for that specific data element for the last thirty years (1980-2009).

Weather Elements (NWS Stations Only)

The following elements were taken directly from the International Station Meteorological Climate Summary. The periods of records vary per station and are noted at the bottom of each table.

Maximum precipitation, minimum precipitation, maximum snowfall, maximum snow depth, maximum 24-hour snowfall, thunderstorm days, foggy days, relative humidity (morning and afternoon), dewpoint, prevailing wind speed and direction, and maximum wind gust are all self-explanatory.

The word trace appears for precipitation and snowfall amounts that are too small to measure.

Predominant sky cover contains four possible entries: CLR (clear); SCT (scattered); BRK (broken); and OVR (overcast).

Inclusion Criteria—How Stations Were Selected

The basic criteria is that a station must have data for temperature, precipitation, heating and cooling degree days of sufficient quantity in order to create a meaningful average. More specifically, the definition of sufficiency here has two parts. First, there must be 22 values for a given data element, and second, ten of the nineteen elements included in the table must pass this sufficiency test. For example, in regard to mean maximum temperature (the first element on every data table), a given station needs to have a value for every month of at least 22 of the last thirty years in order to meet the criteria, and, in addition, every station included must have at least ten of the nineteen elements at least this minimal level of completeness in order to fulfill the criteria. We then removed stations that were geographicaly close together, giving preference to stations with better data quality. By using this procedure, 1,778 cooperative stations met these requirements and are included here. The 243 National Weather Service stations did not have to meet any minimum requirements.

Methodology

The following discussion applies only to data compiled from the NCDC DSI-3220 data tapes and excludes weather elements that are extreme maximums or minimums.

*Weather America** is based on an arithmetic average of all available data for a specific data element at a given station. For example, the average maximum daily high temperature during July for Alma, Michigan, was abstracted from NCDC source tapes for the thirty Julys, starting in July, 1980 and ending in July, 2009. These thirty figures were then summed and divided by thirty to produce an arithmetic average. As might be expected, there were not thirty values for every data element on every table. For a variety of reasons, NCDC data is sometimes incomplete. Thus the following standards were established.

For those data elements where there were 26-30 values, the data was taken to be essentially complete and an average was computed. For data elements where there were 22-25 values, the data was taken as being partly complete but still valid enough to use to compute an average. Such averages are shown in **bold italic** type to indicate that there was less than 26 values. For the few data elements where there were not even 22 values, no average was computed and 'na' appears in the space. If any of the twelve months for a given data element reported a value of 'na', no annual average was computed and the annual average was reported as 'na' as well.

Thus the basic computational methodology of *Weather America** is to provide an arithmetic average. Because of this, such a pure arithmetic average is somewhat different from the special type of average (called a "normal") which NCDC procedures produces and appears in federal publications.

Perhaps the best outline of the contrasting normalization methodology is found in the following paragraph (which appears as part of an NCDC technical document titled, CLIM81 1961-1990 NORMALS TD-9641 prepared by Lewis France of NCDC in May, 1992):

Normals have been defined as the arithmetic mean of a climatological element computed over a long time period. International agreements eventually led to the decision that the appropriate time period would be three consecutive decades (Guttman, 1989). The data record should be consistent (have no changes in location, instruments, observation practices, etc.; these are identified here as "exposure changes") and have no missing values so a normal will reflect the actual average climatic conditions. If any significant exposure changes have occurred, the data record is said to be "inhomogeneous," and the normal may not reflect a true climatic average. Such data need to be adjusted to remove the nonclimatic inhomogeneities. The resulting (adjusted) record is then said to be "homogeneous." If no exposure changes have occurred at a station, the normal is calculated simply by averaging the appropriate 30 values from the 1961-1990 record.

In the main, there are two "inhomogeneities" that NCDC is correcting for with normalization: adjusting for variances in time of day of observation (at the so-called First Order stations data is based on midnight to midnight observation times and this practice is not necessarily followed at cooperative stations which are staffed by volunteers), and second, estimating data that is either missing or incongruent.

A long discussion of the normalization process is not required here but a short note concerning comparative results of the two methodologies is appropriate.

When the editors first started compiling *Weather America** a concern arose because the normalization process would not be replicated: would our methodology produce strikingly different results than NCDC's? To allay concerns, results of the two processes were compared for the time period normalized results are available (1971-2000). In short, what was found was that the answer to this question is no. Never-the-less, users should be aware that because of both the time period covered (1980-2009) and the methodology used, data in *Weather America** is not compatible with data from other sources.

Potential cautions in using *Weather America**

First, as with any statistical reference work of this type, users need to be aware of the source of the data. The information here comes from NOAA, and it is the most comprehensive and reliable core data available. Although it is the best, it is not perfect. Most weather stations are staffed by volunteers, times of observation sometimes vary, stations occasionally are moved (especially over a thirty year period), equipment is changed or upgraded, and all of these factors affect the uniformity of the data. *Weather America** does not attempt to correct for these factors, and is not intended for either climatologists or atmospheric scientists. Users with concerns about data collection and reporting protocols are both referred to NCDC technical documentation, and also, they are perhaps better served by using the original computer tapes themselves as well.

Second, users need to be aware of the methodology here which is described above. Although this methodology has produced fully satisfactory results, it is not directly compatible with other methodologies, hence variances in the results published here and those which appear in other publications will doubtlessly arise.

Third, is the trap of that informal logical fallacy known as "hasty generalization," and its corollaries. This may involve presuming the future will be like the past (specifically, next year will be an average year), or it may involve misunderstanding the limitations of an arithmetic average, but more interestingly, it may involve those mistakes made most innocently by generalizing informally on too broad a basis. As weather is highly localized, the data should be taken in that context. A weather station collects data about climatic conditions at that spot, and that spot may or may not be an effective paradigm for an entire town or area. For example, the weather station in Burlington, Vermont is located at the airport about 3 miles east of the center of town. Most of Burlington is a lot closer to Lake Champlain, and that should mean to a careful user that there could be a significant difference between the temperature readings gathered at the weather station and readings that might be gathered at City Hall downtown. How much would this difference be? How could it be estimated? There are no answers here for these sorts of questions, but it is important for users of this book to raise them for themselves. (It is interesting to note that similar situations abound across the country. For example, compare different readings for the multiple stations in San Francisco, CA or for those around New York City.)

Our source of data has been consistent, so has our methodology. The data has been computed and reported consistently as well. As a result, the *Weather America** should prove valuable to the careful and informed reader.

Reprinted from *Weather America*, Grey House Publishing, Amenia, NY. Copyright 2011.

Anderson County

Located in east Texas; bounded on the west by the Trinity River, and on the east by the Neches River. Covers a land area of 1,070.79 square miles, a water area of 7.16 square miles, and is located in the Central Time Zone at 31.79° N. Lat., 95.63° W. Long. The county was founded in 1846. County seat is Palestine.

Anderson County is part of the Palestine, TX Micropolitan Statistical Area. The entire metro area includes: Anderson County, TX

Weather Station: Palestine   Elevation: 479 feet

	Jan	Feb	Mar	Apr	May	Jun	Jul	Aug	Sep	Oct	Nov	Dec
High	59	63	70	77	83	89	93	94	88	79	68	60
Low	37	40	47	54	63	69	72	72	65	55	46	38
Precip	3.7	3.9	3.8	3.5	4.3	4.7	2.6	3.3	3.3	4.8	4.3	4.3
Snow	0.2	0.2	tr	0.0	0.0	0.0	0.0	0.0	0.0	0.0	tr	tr

High and Low temperatures in degrees Fahrenheit; Precipitation and Snow in inches

Population: 48,024 (1990); 55,109 (2000); 57,251 (2010); 58,189 (2015 projected); Race: 65.6% White, 22.1% Black, 0.7% Asian, 11.6% Other, 14.6% Hispanic of any race (2010); Density: 53.5 persons per square mile (2010); Average household size: 2.53 (2010); Median age: 35.6 (2010); Males per 100 females: 154.0 (2010).
Religion: Five largest groups: 27.9% Southern Baptist Convention, 8.5% Catholic Church, 4.5% The United Methodist Church, 2.9% Assemblies of God, 2.6% Churches of Christ (2000).
Economy: Unemployment rate: 10.4% (June 2011); Total civilian labor force: 21,182 (June 2011); Leading industries: 17.6% retail trade; 17.1% health care and social assistance; 8.3% accommodation & food services (2009); Farms: 1,771 totaling 346,142 acres (2007); Companies that employ 500 or more persons: 2 (2009); Companies that employ 100 to 499 persons: 12 (2009); Companies that employ less than 100 persons: 905 (2009); Black-owned businesses: n/a (2007); Hispanic-owned businesses: n/a (2007); Asian-owned businesses: 87 (2007); Women-owned businesses: n/a (2007); Retail sales per capita: $6,293 (2010). Single-family building permits issued: 16 (2010); Multi-family building permits issued: 0 (2010).
Income: Per capita income: $17,181 (2010); Median household income: $40,467 (2010); Average household income: $51,903 (2010); Percent of households with income of $100,000 or more: 10.1% (2010); Poverty rate: 24.3% (2009); Bankruptcy rate: 1.28% (2010).
Taxes: Total county taxes per capita: $238 (2007); County property taxes per capita: $178 (2007).
Education: Percent of population age 25 and over with: High school diploma (including GED) or higher: 74.4% (2010); Bachelor's degree or higher: 11.8% (2010); Master's degree or higher: 3.0% (2010).
Housing: Homeownership rate: 73.7% (2010); Median home value: $74,571 (2010); Median contract rent: $429 per month (2005-2009 5-year est.); Median year structure built: 1977 (2005-2009 5-year est.)
Health: Birth rate: 115.1 per 10,000 population (2009); Death rate: 111.6 per 10,000 population (2009); Age-adjusted cancer mortality rate: 270.9 deaths per 100,000 population (2007); Number of physicians: 10.2 per 10,000 population (2008); Hospital beds: 21.1 per 10,000 population (2007); Hospital admissions: 1,115.7 per 10,000 population (2007).
Elections: 2008 Presidential election results: 27.8% Obama, 71.4% McCain, 0.1% Nader
Additional Information Contacts
Anderson County Government . . . . (903) 723-7432
   http://www.co.anderson.tx.us
City of Palestine . . . . (903) 731-8400
   http://www.cityofpalestinetx.com
Palestine Area Chamber of Commerce . . . . (903) 729-6066
   http://www.palestinechamber.org

Anderson County Communities

ELKHART (town). Covers a land area of 1.552 square miles and a water area of 0 square miles. Located at 31.62° N. Lat; 95.57° W. Long. Elevation is 384 feet.
Population: 1,079 (1990); 1,215 (2000); 1,255 (2010); 1,270 (2015 projected); Race: 90.8% White, 6.1% Black, 0.2% Asian, 3.0% Other, 3.4% Hispanic of any race (2010); Density: 808.8 persons per square mile (2010); Average household size: 2.34 (2010); Median age: 41.9 (2010); Males per 100 females: 81.9 (2010); Marriage status: 23.2% never married, 50.8% now married, 14.5% widowed, 11.5% divorced (2005-2009 5-year

est.); Foreign born: 0.4% (2005-2009 5-year est.); Ancestry (includes multiple ancestries): 19.2% English, 17.2% Irish, 6.3% American, 5.4% German, 1.4% French (2005-2009 5-year est.).
Economy: Employment by occupation: 6.3% management, 12.5% professional, 17.8% services, 30.4% sales, 0.0% farming, 7.9% construction, 25.1% production (2005-2009 5-year est.).
Income: Per capita income: $20,020 (2010); Median household income: $37,104 (2010); Average household income: $47,280 (2010); Percent of households with income of $100,000 or more: 11.8% (2010); Poverty rate: 15.4% (2005-2009 5-year est.).
Taxes: Total city taxes per capita: $132 (2007); City property taxes per capita: $60 (2007).
Education: Percent of population age 25 and over with: High school diploma (including GED) or higher: 76.6% (2010); Bachelor's degree or higher: 11.5% (2010); Master's degree or higher: 1.4% (2010).
School District(s)
Elkhart ISD (PK-12)
   2009-10 Enrollment: 1,355 . . . . (903) 764-2952
Housing: Homeownership rate: 70.1% (2010); Median home value: $51,207 (2010); Median contract rent: $403 per month (2005-2009 5-year est.); Median year structure built: 1972 (2005-2009 5-year est.).
Transportation: Commute to work: 93.9% car, 0.0% public transportation, 0.0% walk, 1.2% work from home (2005-2009 5-year est.); Travel time to work: 36.7% less than 15 minutes, 43.8% 15 to 30 minutes, 10.2% 30 to 45 minutes, 4.9% 45 to 60 minutes, 4.4% 60 minutes or more (2005-2009 5-year est.)

FRANKSTON (town). Covers a land area of 2.474 square miles and a water area of 0 square miles. Located at 32.05° N. Lat; 95.50° W. Long. Elevation is 420 feet.
History: Frankston developed around a sawmill, in an area of cultivated fields and wooded tracts.
Population: 1,127 (1990); 1,209 (2000); 1,245 (2010); 1,260 (2015 projected); Race: 86.1% White, 10.4% Black, 0.1% Asian, 3.5% Other, 3.6% Hispanic of any race (2010); Density: 503.2 persons per square mile (2010); Average household size: 2.43 (2010); Median age: 44.6 (2010); Males per 100 females: 81.8 (2010); Marriage status: 14.8% never married, 65.8% now married, 10.5% widowed, 8.8% divorced (2005-2009 5-year est.); Foreign born: 1.3% (2005-2009 5-year est.); Ancestry (includes multiple ancestries): 20.5% Irish, 16.4% English, 11.1% German, 6.4% American, 2.3% Scottish (2005-2009 5-year est.).
Economy: Single-family building permits issued: 5 (2010); Multi-family building permits issued: 0 (2010); Employment by occupation: 2.5% management, 19.1% professional, 23.2% services, 25.0% sales, 1.0% farming, 20.9% construction, 8.4% production (2005-2009 5-year est.).
Income: Per capita income: $19,355 (2010); Median household income: $36,027 (2010); Average household income: $48,010 (2010); Percent of households with income of $100,000 or more: 8.2% (2010); Poverty rate: 10.1% (2005-2009 5-year est.).
Taxes: Total city taxes per capita: $303 (2007); City property taxes per capita: $125 (2007).
Education: Percent of population age 25 and over with: High school diploma (including GED) or higher: 74.6% (2010); Bachelor's degree or higher: 13.3% (2010); Master's degree or higher: 3.5% (2010).
School District(s)
Frankston ISD (PK-12)
   2009-10 Enrollment: 763 . . . . (903) 876-2556
Housing: Homeownership rate: 76.3% (2010); Median home value: $60,656 (2010); Median contract rent: $494 per month (2005-2009 5-year est.); Median year structure built: 1971 (2005-2009 5-year est.).
Safety: Violent crime rate: 8.1 per 10,000 population; Property crime rate: 315.3 per 10,000 population (2009).
Newspapers: Frankston Citizen (Community news; Circulation 1,750)
Transportation: Commute to work: 93.0% car, 0.0% public transportation, 2.6% walk, 4.4% work from home (2005-2009 5-year est.); Travel time to work: 29.7% less than 15 minutes, 22.2% 15 to 30 minutes, 31.0% 30 to 45 minutes, 15.5% 45 to 60 minutes, 1.7% 60 minutes or more (2005-2009 5-year est.)

MONTALBA (unincorporated postal area, zip code 75853). Covers a land area of 62.291 square miles and a water area of 0.235 square miles. Located at 31.93° N. Lat; 95.83° W. Long. Elevation is 427 feet.
Population: 894 (2000); Race: 88.8% White, 8.3% Black, 2.4% Asian, 0.5% Other, 0.7% Hispanic of any race (2000); Density: 14.4 persons per square mile (2000); Age: 30.3% under 18, 13.1% over 64 (2000); Marriage

status: 12.3% never married, 76.0% now married, 5.4% widowed, 6.3% divorced (2000); Foreign born: 1.3% (2000); Ancestry (includes multiple ancestries): 16.5% American, 8.0% English, 6.3% German, 5.8% Irish (2000).
Economy: Employment by occupation: 9.2% management, 18.4% professional, 25.2% services, 17.5% sales, 1.2% farming, 13.4% construction, 15.1% production (2000).
Income: Per capita income: $14,636 (2000); Median household income: $34,659 (2000); Poverty rate: 179.1% (2000).
Education: Percent of population age 25 and over with: High school diploma (including GED) or higher: 72.6% (2000); Bachelor's degree or higher: 13.9% (2000).
Housing: Homeownership rate: 83.2% (2000); Median home value: $50,000 (2000); Median contract rent: $332 per month (2000); Median year structure built: 1976 (2000).
Transportation: Commute to work: 95.5% car, 1.8% public transportation, 0.0% walk, 2.4% work from home (2000); Travel time to work: 14.6% less than 15 minutes, 41.0% 15 to 30 minutes, 26.7% 30 to 45 minutes, 7.8% 45 to 60 minutes, 9.9% 60 minutes or more (2000)

PALESTINE (city). County seat. Covers a land area of 17.699 square miles and a water area of 0.183 square miles. Located at 31.75° N. Lat; 95.63° W. Long. Elevation is 482 feet.
History: Palestine was established in the mid-1800's. Salt, coal, and Orangeburg clay (deteriorated iron ore) were mined here. Oil was discovered nearby in 1929, changing the economic base for Palestine.
Population: 18,292 (1990); 17,598 (2000); 18,297 (2010); 18,581 (2015 projected); Race: 62.4% White, 24.4% Black, 1.1% Asian, 12.1% Other, 17.7% Hispanic of any race (2010); Density: 1,033.8 persons per square mile (2010); Average household size: 2.52 (2010); Median age: 34.9 (2010); Males per 100 females: 85.5 (2010); Marriage status: 30.0% never married, 48.3% now married, 8.8% widowed, 12.9% divorced (2005-2009 5-year est.); Foreign born: 9.2% (2005-2009 5-year est.); Ancestry (includes multiple ancestries): 9.7% Irish, 8.9% German, 8.7% English, 7.7% American, 1.5% Scotch-Irish (2005-2009 5-year est.).
Economy: Single-family building permits issued: 11 (2010); Multi-family building permits issued: 0 (2010); Employment by occupation: 7.0% management, 16.4% professional, 27.6% services, 20.9% sales, 1.5% farming, 9.7% construction, 17.0% production (2005-2009 5-year est.).
Income: Per capita income: $19,510 (2010); Median household income: $38,588 (2010); Average household income: $49,868 (2010); Percent of households with income of $100,000 or more: 9.1% (2010); Poverty rate: 22.0% (2005-2009 5-year est.).
Taxes: Total city taxes per capita: $619 (2007); City property taxes per capita: $249 (2007).
Education: Percent of population age 25 and over with: High school diploma (including GED) or higher: 79.1% (2010); Bachelor's degree or higher: 15.4% (2010); Master's degree or higher: 4.0% (2010).
School District(s)
Azleway Charter School (03-12)
   2009-10 Enrollment: 139 . . . . (903) 566-8444
Elkhart ISD (PK-12)
   2009-10 Enrollment: 1,355 . . . . (903) 764-2952
Honors Academy (KG-12)
   2009-10 Enrollment: 1,068 . . . . (214) 521-6365
Palestine ISD (PK-12)
   2009-10 Enrollment: 3,242 . . . . (903) 731-8001
Westwood ISD (PK-12)
   2009-10 Enrollment: 1,698 . . . . (903) 729-1776
Housing: Homeownership rate: 63.3% (2010); Median home value: $74,564 (2010); Median contract rent: $434 per month (2005-2009 5-year est.); Median year structure built: 1963 (2005-2009 5-year est.).
Hospitals: Palestine Regional Medical Center (258 beds)
Safety: Violent crime rate: 90.4 per 10,000 population; Property crime rate: 500.1 per 10,000 population (2009).
Newspapers: Palestine Herald-Press (Local news; Circulation 10,076)
Transportation: Commute to work: 95.2% car, 0.8% public transportation, 2.4% walk, 0.4% work from home (2005-2009 5-year est.); Travel time to work: 49.8% less than 15 minutes, 32.3% 15 to 30 minutes, 8.2% 30 to 45 minutes, 3.3% 45 to 60 minutes, 6.5% 60 minutes or more (2005-2009 5-year est.)
Airports: Palestine Municipal (general aviation)
Additional Information Contacts
City of Palestine . . . . (903) 731-8400
   http://www.cityofpalestinetx.com

Palestine Area Chamber of Commerce . . . . (903) 729-6066
   http://www.palestinechamber.org

Andrews County

Located in west Texas; bounded on the west by New Mexico. Covers a land area of 1,500.64 square miles, a water area of 0.36 square miles, and is located in the Central Time Zone at 32.33° N. Lat., 102.58° W. Long. The county was founded in 1876. County seat is Andrews.

Andrews County is part of the Andrews, TX Micropolitan Statistical Area. The entire metro area includes: Andrews County, TX

Weather Station: Andrews   Elevation: 3,171 feet

	Jan	Feb	Mar	Apr	May	Jun	Jul	Aug	Sep	Oct	Nov	Dec
High	58	64	72	81	89	94	95	94	88	79	67	59
Low	31	35	41	49	59	66	69	68	61	52	40	32
Precip	0.5	0.7	0.8	0.7	1.5	2.1	1.7	1.7	2.0	1.6	0.7	0.7
Snow	1.3	0.4	tr	0.1	0.0	0.0	0.0	0.0	0.0	tr	0.5	0.9

High and Low temperatures in degrees Fahrenheit; Precipitation and Snow in inches

Population: 14,338 (1990); 13,004 (2000); 13,848 (2010); 14,230 (2015 projected); Race: 72.1% White, 2.2% Black, 0.6% Asian, 25.1% Other, 49.2% Hispanic of any race (2010); Density: 9.2 persons per square mile (2010); Average household size: 2.71 (2010); Median age: 33.9 (2010); Males per 100 females: 98.1 (2010).
Religion: Five largest groups: 43.3% Southern Baptist Convention, 20.3% Catholic Church, 5.3% Churches of Christ, 5.3% The United Methodist Church, 5.1% Assemblies of God (2000).
Economy: Unemployment rate: 6.0% (June 2011); Total civilian labor force: 7,289 (June 2011); Leading industries: 22.7% mining; 16.9% construction; 8.8% other services (except public administration) (2009); Farms: 175 totaling 808,474 acres (2007); Companies that employ 500 or more persons: 0 (2009); Companies that employ 100 to 499 persons: 4 (2009); Companies that employ less than 100 persons: 317 (2009); Black-owned businesses: n/a (2007); Hispanic-owned businesses: 179 (2007); Asian-owned businesses: n/a (2007); Women-owned businesses: 353 (2007); Retail sales per capita: $6,318 (2010). Single-family building permits issued: 31 (2010); Multi-family building permits issued: 40 (2010).
Income: Per capita income: $21,906 (2010); Median household income: $47,628 (2010); Average household income: $59,222 (2010); Percent of households with income of $100,000 or more: 11.9% (2010); Poverty rate: 12.5% (2009); Bankruptcy rate: 0.67% (2010).
Taxes: Total county taxes per capita: $827 (2007); County property taxes per capita: $778 (2007).
Education: Percent of population age 25 and over with: High school diploma (including GED) or higher: 74.0% (2010); Bachelor's degree or higher: 14.0% (2010); Master's degree or higher: 4.3% (2010).
Housing: Homeownership rate: 78.0% (2010); Median home value: $46,589 (2010); Median contract rent: $379 per month (2005-2009 5-year est.); Median year structure built: 1973 (2005-2009 5-year est.)
Health: Birth rate: 182.1 per 10,000 population (2009); Death rate: 80.4 per 10,000 population (2009); Age-adjusted cancer mortality rate: 299.5 deaths per 100,000 population (2007); Number of physicians: 9.5 per 10,000 population (2008); Hospital beds: 33.5 per 10,000 population (2007); Hospital admissions: 946.4 per 10,000 population (2007).
Elections: 2008 Presidential election results: 17.1% Obama, 82.4% McCain, 0.0% Nader
Additional Information Contacts
Andrews County Government . . . . (915) 524-1401
   http://www.co.andrews.tx.us
Andrews Chamber of Commerce . . . . (432) 523-2695
   http://www.andrewstx.com
City of Andrews . . . . (432) 523-4820
   http://www.cityofandrews.org

Andrews County Communities

ANDREWS (city). County seat. Covers a land area of 4.784 square miles and a water area of 0.009 square miles. Located at 32.32° N. Lat; 102.55° W. Long. Elevation is 3,176 feet.
Population: 10,786 (1990); 9,652 (2000); 10,331 (2010); 10,638 (2015 projected); Race: 69.8% White, 2.7% Black, 0.6% Asian, 27.0% Other, 51.3% Hispanic of any race (2010); Density: 2,159.4 persons per square mile (2010); Average household size: 2.65 (2010); Median age: 33.6 (2010); Males per 100 females: 96.5 (2010); Marriage status: 25.2% never

married, 58.3% now married, 6.4% widowed, 10.2% divorced (2005-2009 5-year est.); Foreign born: 11.0% (2005-2009 5-year est.); Ancestry (includes multiple ancestries): 10.7% Irish, 8.2% American, 6.7% English, 6.5% German, 3.2% Scottish (2005-2009 5-year est.).
Economy: Single-family building permits issued: 31 (2010); Multi-family building permits issued: 40 (2010); Employment by occupation: 7.3% management, 12.6% professional, 17.9% services, 22.7% sales, 1.2% farming, 17.2% construction, 21.1% production (2005-2009 5-year est.).
Income: Per capita income: $20,581 (2010); Median household income: $43,841 (2010); Average household income: $54,480 (2010); Percent of households with income of $100,000 or more: 9.9% (2010); Poverty rate: 20.1% (2005-2009 5-year est.).
Taxes: Total city taxes per capita: $363 (2007); City property taxes per capita: $48 (2007).
Education: Percent of population age 25 and over with: High school diploma (including GED) or higher: 73.6% (2010); Bachelor's degree or higher: 12.9% (2010); Master's degree or higher: 4.5% (2010).

School District(s)

Andrews ISD (PK-12)
   2009-10 Enrollment: 3,143 . . . . (432) 523-3640
Housing: Homeownership rate: 75.0% (2010); Median home value: $45,998 (2010); Median contract rent: $378 per month (2005-2009 5-year est.); Median year structure built: 1969 (2005-2009 5-year est.).
Hospitals: Permian General Hospital (85 beds)
Safety: Violent crime rate: 77.4 per 10,000 population; Property crime rate: 342.8 per 10,000 population (2009).
Newspapers: Andrews County News (Regional news; Circulation 3,500)
Transportation: Commute to work: 91.1% car, 0.7% public transportation, 3.6% walk, 2.3% work from home (2005-2009 5-year est.); Travel time to work: 69.4% less than 15 minutes, 9.9% 15 to 30 minutes, 8.8% 30 to 45 minutes, 3.5% 45 to 60 minutes, 8.4% 60 minutes or more (2005-2009 5-year est.)
Additional Information Contacts
Andrews Chamber of Commerce. . . . . (432) 523-2695
   http://www.andrewstx.com
City of Andrews . . . . (432) 523-4820
   http://www.cityofandrews.org

Angelina County

Located in east Texas; bounded on the north and northeast by the Angelina River, and on the south by the Neches River; includes part of Angelina and Davy Crockett National Forests. Covers a land area of 801.56 square miles, a water area of 62.89 square miles, and is located in the Central Time Zone at 31.28° N. Lat., 94.67° W. Long. The county was founded in 1846. County seat is Lufkin.

Angelina County is part of the Lufkin, TX Micropolitan Statistical Area. The entire metro area includes: Angelina County, TX

Weather Station: Lufkin Caa Arpt   Elevation: 275 feet

	Jan	Feb	Mar	Apr	May	Jun	Jul	Aug	Sep	Oct	Nov	Dec
High	60	64	71	78	85	90	94	94	89	80	70	61
Low	39	42	48	55	64	70	72	71	66	56	47	39
Precip	4.2	3.8	3.9	3.1	4.9	4.7	2.9	3.4	3.8	4.5	5.1	4.4
Snow	na	na	na	na	na	na	na	na	na	na	na	na

High and Low temperatures in degrees Fahrenheit; Precipitation and Snow in inches

Population: 69,884 (1990); 80,130 (2000); 84,063 (2010); 85,825 (2015 projected); Race: 72.3% White, 14.6% Black, 0.8% Asian, 12.3% Other, 18.5% Hispanic of any race (2010); Density: 104.9 persons per square mile (2010); Average household size: 2.67 (2010); Median age: 35.6 (2010); Males per 100 females: 96.7 (2010).
Religion: Five largest groups: 27.1% Southern Baptist Convention, 10.4% Catholic Church, 9.8% Baptist Missionary Association of America, 5.5% The United Methodist Church, 4.3% Assemblies of God (2000).
Economy: Unemployment rate: 8.6% (June 2011); Total civilian labor force: 39,809 (June 2011); Leading industries: 25.0% health care and social assistance; 17.5% retail trade; 15.4% manufacturing (2009); Farms: 1,109 totaling 115,258 acres (2007); Companies that employ 500 or more persons: 5 (2009); Companies that employ 100 to 499 persons: 36 (2009); Companies that employ less than 100 persons: 1,815 (2009); Black-owned businesses: n/a (2007); Hispanic-owned businesses: n/a (2007); Asian-owned businesses: n/a (2007); Women-owned businesses: 1,487 (2007); Retail sales per capita: $16,392 (2010). Single-family building permits issued: 43 (2010); Multi-family building permits issued: 80 (2010).

Income: Per capita income: $18,403 (2010); Median household income: $38,705 (2010); Average household income: $49,660 (2010); Percent of households with income of $100,000 or more: 9.0% (2010); Poverty rate: 17.0% (2009); Bankruptcy rate: 1.83% (2010).
Taxes: Total county taxes per capita: $209 (2007); County property taxes per capita: $136 (2007).
Education: Percent of population age 25 and over with: High school diploma (including GED) or higher: 77.5% (2010); Bachelor's degree or higher: 15.3% (2010); Master's degree or higher: 3.6% (2010).
Housing: Homeownership rate: 67.0% (2010); Median home value: $74,354 (2010); Median contract rent: $455 per month (2005-2009 5-year est.); Median year structure built: 1978 (2005-2009 5-year est.)
Health: Birth rate: 158.8 per 10,000 population (2009); Death rate: 96.9 per 10,000 population (2009); Age-adjusted cancer mortality rate: 157.1 deaths per 100,000 population (2007); Number of physicians: 17.0 per 10,000 population (2008); Hospital beds: 41.8 per 10,000 population (2007); Hospital admissions: 1,846.3 per 10,000 population (2007).
Elections: 2008 Presidential election results: 32.2% Obama, 67.1% McCain, 0.0% Nader
Additional Information Contacts
Angelina County Government . . . . (936) 634-5413
   http://www.angelinacounty.net
City of Diboll . . . . (936) 829-4757
   http://cityofdiboll.com
City of Lufkin . . . . (936) 634-8881
   http://www.ci.lufkin.tx.us
Lufkin/Angelina County Chamber of Commerce . . . . (936) 634-6644
   http://www.lufkintexas.org

Angelina County Communities

BURKE (city). Covers a land area of 0.628 square miles and a water area of 0 square miles. Located at 31.22° N. Lat; 94.76° W. Long. Elevation is 272 feet.
Population: 314 (1990); 315 (2000); 291 (2010); 279 (2015 projected); Race: 88.0% White, 1.0% Black, 0.3% Asian, 10.7% Other, 30.2% Hispanic of any race (2010); Density: 463.3 persons per square mile (2010); Average household size: 2.88 (2010); Median age: 31.6 (2010); Males per 100 females: 103.5 (2010); Marriage status: 17.1% never married, 52.8% now married, 9.6% widowed, 20.5% divorced (2005-2009 5-year est.); Foreign born: 2.4% (2005-2009 5-year est.); Ancestry (includes multiple ancestries): 21.0% American, 19.5% Scotch-Irish, 18.2% Irish, 16.9% Norwegian, 16.1% French (2005-2009 5-year est.).
Economy: Employment by occupation: 10.6% management, 2.4% professional, 7.9% services, 34.0% sales, 12.2% farming, 12.2% construction, 20.7% production (2005-2009 5-year est.).
Income: Per capita income: $16,355 (2010); Median household income: $41,786 (2010); Average household income: $47,574 (2010); Percent of households with income of $100,000 or more: 5.9% (2010); Poverty rate: 9.4% (2005-2009 5-year est.).
Taxes: Total city taxes per capita: $22 (2007); City property taxes per capita: $0 (2007).
Education: Percent of population age 25 and over with: High school diploma (including GED) or higher: 63.4% (2010); Bachelor's degree or higher: 6.4% (2010); Master's degree or higher: 1.2% (2010).
Housing: Homeownership rate: 78.2% (2010); Median home value: $55,217 (2010); Median contract rent: $198 per month (2005-2009 5-year est.); Median year structure built: 1974 (2005-2009 5-year est.).
Transportation: Commute to work: 72.3% car, 12.8% public transportation, 0.9% walk, 0.6% work from home (2005-2009 5-year est.); Travel time to work: 42.2% less than 15 minutes, 37.9% 15 to 30 minutes, 5.2% 30 to 45 minutes, 0.6% 45 to 60 minutes, 14.1% 60 minutes or more (2005-2009 5-year est.)

DIBOLL (city). Covers a land area of 4.790 square miles and a water area of 0.025 square miles. Located at 31.18° N. Lat; 94.78° W. Long. Elevation is 210 feet.
History: Diboll developed around a lumber mill.
Population: 4,645 (1990); 5,470 (2000); 5,455 (2010); 5,493 (2015 projected); Race: 54.8% White, 22.5% Black, 0.1% Asian, 22.7% Other, 40.6% Hispanic of any race (2010); Density: 1,138.8 persons per square mile (2010); Average household size: 3.01 (2010); Median age: 34.3 (2010); Males per 100 females: 133.6 (2010); Marriage status: 34.8% never married, 48.2% now married, 4.2% widowed, 12.8% divorced (2005-2009 5-year est.); Foreign born: 16.0% (2005-2009 5-year est.);

Ancestry (includes multiple ancestries): 8.0% Irish, 7.1% English, 5.1% German, 1.9% American, 1.7% Dutch (2005-2009 5-year est.).
Economy: Single-family building permits issued: 3 (2010); Multi-family building permits issued: 0 (2010); Employment by occupation: 7.7% management, 8.4% professional, 22.8% services, 23.1% sales, 0.0% farming, 8.9% construction, 29.2% production (2005-2009 5-year est.).
Income: Per capita income: $12,446 (2010); Median household income: $32,578 (2010); Average household income: $39,119 (2010); Percent of households with income of $100,000 or more: 5.1% (2010); Poverty rate: 35.0% (2005-2009 5-year est.).
Taxes: Total city taxes per capita: $388 (2007); City property taxes per capita: $156 (2007).
Education: Percent of population age 25 and over with: High school diploma (including GED) or higher: 61.0% (2010); Bachelor's degree or higher: 7.9% (2010); Master's degree or higher: 1.4% (2010).

School District(s)
Diboll ISD (PK-12)
   2009-10 Enrollment: 1,962 . . . . (936) 829-4718
Housing: Homeownership rate: 53.2% (2010); Median home value: $60,561 (2010); Median contract rent: $335 per month (2005-2009 5-year est.); Median year structure built: 1975 (2005-2009 5-year est.).
Safety: Violent crime rate: 18.0 per 10,000 population; Property crime rate: 250.7 per 10,000 population (2009).
Newspapers: Free Press (Local news; Circulation 4,000)
Transportation: Commute to work: 94.3% car, 0.0% public transportation, 3.9% walk, 0.5% work from home (2005-2009 5-year est.); Travel time to work: 24.4% less than 15 minutes, 41.6% 15 to 30 minutes, 24.8% 30 to 45 minutes, 3.6% 45 to 60 minutes, 5.6% 60 minutes or more (2005-2009 5-year est.)
Additional Information Contacts
City of Diboll. . . . . (936) 829-4757
   http://cityofdiboll.com

HUDSON (city). Covers a land area of 4.580 square miles and a water area of 0 square miles. Located at 31.33° N. Lat; 94.79° W. Long. Elevation is 335 feet.
Population: 2,586 (1990); 3,792 (2000); 4,467 (2010); 4,778 (2015 projected); Race: 82.1% White, 4.3% Black, 0.3% Asian, 13.3% Other, 21.2% Hispanic of any race (2010); Density: 975.3 persons per square mile (2010); Average household size: 2.92 (2010); Median age: 33.2 (2010); Males per 100 females: 98.6 (2010); Marriage status: 16.0% never married, 64.5% now married, 6.5% widowed, 13.1% divorced (2005-2009 5-year est.); Foreign born: 7.9% (2005-2009 5-year est.); Ancestry (includes multiple ancestries): 17.5% German, 13.1% English, 10.7% Irish, 6.7% American, 3.5% Dutch (2005-2009 5-year est.).
Economy: Single-family building permits issued: 14 (2010); Multi-family building permits issued: 0 (2010); Employment by occupation: 10.5% management, 11.4% professional, 24.8% services, 21.3% sales, 0.8% farming, 14.9% construction, 16.2% production (2005-2009 5-year est.).
Income: Per capita income: $16,533 (2010); Median household income: $39,207 (2010); Average household income: $48,381 (2010); Percent of households with income of $100,000 or more: 7.6% (2010); Poverty rate: 12.3% (2005-2009 5-year est.).
Taxes: Total city taxes per capita: $118 (2007); City property taxes per capita: $45 (2007).
Education: Percent of population age 25 and over with: High school diploma (including GED) or higher: 80.9% (2010); Bachelor's degree or higher: 11.4% (2010); Master's degree or higher: 3.1% (2010).
Housing: Homeownership rate: 72.9% (2010); Median home value: $71,239 (2010); Median contract rent: $555 per month (2005-2009 5-year est.); Median year structure built: 1984 (2005-2009 5-year est.).
Safety: Violent crime rate: 39.0 per 10,000 population; Property crime rate: 220.3 per 10,000 population (2009).
Transportation: Commute to work: 96.9% car, 2.1% public transportation, 0.0% walk, 1.0% work from home (2005-2009 5-year est.); Travel time to work: 50.5% less than 15 minutes, 31.9% 15 to 30 minutes, 8.9% 30 to 45 minutes, 2.2% 45 to 60 minutes, 6.5% 60 minutes or more (2005-2009 5-year est.)

HUNTINGTON (city). Covers a land area of 2.728 square miles and a water area of 0 square miles. Located at 31.27° N. Lat; 94.57° W. Long. Elevation is 325 feet.
History: Incorporated 1938.
Population: 1,794 (1990); 2,068 (2000); 2,125 (2010); 2,144 (2015 projected); Race: 87.1% White, 7.2% Black, 0.1% Asian, 5.6% Other, 4.8%

Hispanic of any race (2010); Density: 778.9 persons per square mile (2010); Average household size: 2.70 (2010); Median age: 32.7 (2010); Males per 100 females: 92.8 (2010); Marriage status: 23.9% never married, 52.1% now married, 8.1% widowed, 15.9% divorced (2005-2009 5-year est.); Foreign born: 1.1% (2005-2009 5-year est.); Ancestry (includes multiple ancestries): 20.6% German, 19.6% Irish, 12.3% American, 9.4% English, 5.1% Hungarian (2005-2009 5-year est.).
Economy: Employment by occupation: 9.5% management, 14.5% professional, 28.5% services, 20.7% sales, 0.0% farming, 7.9% construction, 18.8% production (2005-2009 5-year est.).
Income: Per capita income: $17,577 (2010); Median household income: $38,263 (2010); Average household income: $47,344 (2010); Percent of households with income of $100,000 or more: 9.4% (2010); Poverty rate: 31.8% (2005-2009 5-year est.).
Taxes: Total city taxes per capita: $310 (2007); City property taxes per capita: $148 (2007).
Education: Percent of population age 25 and over with: High school diploma (including GED) or higher: 78.4% (2010); Bachelor's degree or higher: 12.3% (2010); Master's degree or higher: 2.0% (2010).

School District(s)
Huntington ISD (PK-12)
   2009-10 Enrollment: 1,750 . . . . (936) 876-4287
Housing: Homeownership rate: 63.4% (2010); Median home value: $64,177 (2010); Median contract rent: $417 per month (2005-2009 5-year est.); Median year structure built: 1976 (2005-2009 5-year est.).
Safety: Violent crime rate: 19.0 per 10,000 population; Property crime rate: 146.9 per 10,000 population (2009).
Transportation: Commute to work: 90.8% car, 0.0% public transportation, 4.6% walk, 3.1% work from home (2005-2009 5-year est.); Travel time to work: 35.1% less than 15 minutes, 42.9% 15 to 30 minutes, 14.8% 30 to 45 minutes, 3.0% 45 to 60 minutes, 4.2% 60 minutes or more (2005-2009 5-year est.)

LUFKIN (city). County seat. Covers a land area of 26.699 square miles and a water area of 0.131 square miles. Located at 31.33° N. Lat; 94.73° W. Long. Elevation is 312 feet.
History: Lufkin was established in a forested area where pine, cypress, hickory, oak and magnolia trees produce timber and pulpwood.
Population: 30,721 (1990); 32,709 (2000); 34,425 (2010); 35,216 (2015 projected); Race: 56.9% White, 25.0% Black, 1.7% Asian, 16.4% Other, 24.1% Hispanic of any race (2010); Density: 1,289.4 persons per square mile (2010); Average household size: 2.56 (2010); Median age: 35.4 (2010); Males per 100 females: 90.8 (2010); Marriage status: 27.7% never married, 50.9% now married, 9.8% widowed, 11.7% divorced (2005-2009 5-year est.); Foreign born: 11.5% (2005-2009 5-year est.); Ancestry (includes multiple ancestries): 9.8% German, 9.1% English, 8.2% American, 7.2% Irish, 2.7% African (2005-2009 5-year est.).
Economy: Unemployment rate: 8.7% (June 2011); Total civilian labor force: 16,411 (June 2011); Single-family building permits issued: 26 (2010); Multi-family building permits issued: 80 (2010); Employment by occupation: 10.3% management, 21.2% professional, 17.4% services, 22.1% sales, 0.6% farming, 8.6% construction, 19.7% production (2005-2009 5-year est.).
Income: Per capita income: $19,570 (2010); Median household income: $36,543 (2010); Average household income: $50,305 (2010); Percent of households with income of $100,000 or more: 10.2% (2010); Poverty rate: 19.0% (2005-2009 5-year est.).
Taxes: Total city taxes per capita: $684 (2007); City property taxes per capita: $262 (2007).
Education: Percent of population age 25 and over with: High school diploma (including GED) or higher: 77.8% (2010); Bachelor's degree or higher: 20.2% (2010); Master's degree or higher: 4.8% (2010).

School District(s)
Central ISD (PK-12)
   2009-10 Enrollment: 1,530 . . . . (936) 853-2216
Diboll ISD (PK-12)
   2009-10 Enrollment: 1,962 . . . . (936) 829-4718
Hudson ISD (PK-12)
   2009-10 Enrollment: 2,597 . . . . (936) 875-3351
Lufkin ISD (PK-12)
   2009-10 Enrollment: 8,630 . . . . (936) 634-6696
Pineywoods Community Academy (PK-09)
   2009-10 Enrollment: 336 . . . . (936) 634-5515
Zavalla ISD (PK-12)
   2009-10 Enrollment: 480 . . . . (936) 897-2271

Two-year College(s)

Angelina College (Public)

Fall 2009 Enrollment: 5,422 . . . . (936) 639-1301

  2010-11 Tuition: In-state $2,220; Out-of-state $3,030

Vocational/Technical School(s)

Academy of Hair Design (Private, For-profit)

Fall 2009 Enrollment: 78 . . . . (936) 634-8440

  2010-11 Tuition: $8,500

Housing: Homeownership rate: 54.4% (2010); Median home value: $86,891 (2010); Median contract rent: $473 per month (2005-2009 5-year est.); Median year structure built: 1975 (2005-2009 5-year est.).

Hospitals: Memorial Health System of East Texas (234 beds); Woodland Heights Medical Center (146 beds)

Safety: Violent crime rate: 48.2 per 10,000 population; Property crime rate: 739.3 per 10,000 population (2009).

Newspapers: The Lufkin Daily News (Local news)

Transportation: Commute to work: 95.5% car, 0.5% public transportation, 1.0% walk, 1.1% work from home (2005-2009 5-year est.); Travel time to work: 56.7% less than 15 minutes, 27.6% 15 to 30 minutes, 7.9% 30 to 45 minutes, 2.5% 45 to 60 minutes, 5.4% 60 minutes or more (2005-2009 5-year est.)

Additional Information Contacts

City of Lufkin . . . . (936) 634-8881

  http://www.ci.lufkin.tx.us

Lufkin/Angelina County Chamber of Commerce . . . . (936) 634-6644

  http://www.lufkintexas.org

POLLOK (unincorporated postal area, zip code 75969). Covers a land area of 80.522 square miles and a water area of 0.033 square miles. Located at 31.43° N. Lat; 94.87° W. Long. Elevation is 305 feet.

Population: 4,256 (2000); Race: 92.3% White, 4.1% Black, 0.0% Asian, 3.6% Other, 3.2% Hispanic of any race (2000); Density: 52.9 persons per square mile (2000); Age: 27.2% under 18, 9.6% over 64 (2000); Marriage status: 23.9% never married, 61.4% now married, 4.4% widowed, 10.2% divorced (2000); Foreign born: 1.2% (2000); Ancestry (includes multiple ancestries): 16.1% American, 8.9% Irish, 5.6% German, 3.4% English (2000).

Economy: Employment by occupation: 10.3% management, 16.7% professional, 15.1% services, 21.6% sales, 2.3% farming, 13.1% construction, 20.9% production (2000).

Income: Per capita income: $15,381 (2000); Median household income: $37,981 (2000); Poverty rate: 179.1% (2000).

Education: Percent of population age 25 and over with: High school diploma (including GED) or higher: 62.8% (2000); Bachelor's degree or higher: 8.4% (2000).

School District(s)

Central ISD (PK-12)

  2009-10 Enrollment: 1,530 . . . . (936) 853-2216

Lufkin ISD (PK-12)

  2009-10 Enrollment: 8,630 . . . . (936) 634-6696

Housing: Homeownership rate: 85.6% (2000); Median home value: $50,500 (2000); Median contract rent: $265 per month (2000); Median year structure built: 1979 (2000).

Transportation: Commute to work: 93.3% car, 0.0% public transportation, 2.2% walk, 3.6% work from home (2000); Travel time to work: 23.6% less than 15 minutes, 51.5% 15 to 30 minutes, 16.0% 30 to 45 minutes, 3.8% 45 to 60 minutes, 5.1% 60 minutes or more (2000)

ZAVALLA (city). Covers a land area of 2.110 square miles and a water area of 0 square miles. Located at 31.15° N. Lat; 94.41° W. Long. Elevation is 223 feet.

History: Zavalla was named for the settlement near Jasper that was the seat of government for the De Zavala colony in 1829. The second "l" was added to the name much later.

Population: 701 (1990); 647 (2000); 642 (2010); 637 (2015 projected); Race: 97.4% White, 0.2% Black, 0.0% Asian, 2.5% Other, 2.8% Hispanic of any race (2010); Density: 304.3 persons per square mile (2010); Average household size: 2.40 (2010); Median age: 40.5 (2010); Males per 100 females: 95.1 (2010); Marriage status: 14.5% never married, 56.3% now married, 12.3% widowed, 16.9% divorced (2005-2009 5-year est.); Foreign born: 0.7% (2005-2009 5-year est.); Ancestry (includes multiple ancestries): 28.3% Irish, 27.6% English, 16.1% American, 11.3% French, 10.5% German (2005-2009 5-year est.).

Economy: Employment by occupation: 14.6% management, 6.7% professional, 27.6% services, 22.2% sales, 0.0% farming, 15.9% construction, 13.0% production (2005-2009 5-year est.).

Income: Per capita income: $20,080 (2010); Median household income: $36,029 (2010); Average household income: $47,790 (2010); Percent of households with income of $100,000 or more: 9.0% (2010); Poverty rate: 27.5% (2005-2009 5-year est.).

Taxes: Total city taxes per capita: $175 (2007); City property taxes per capita: $23 (2007).

Education: Percent of population age 25 and over with: High school diploma (including GED) or higher: 77.6% (2010); Bachelor's degree or higher: 7.8% (2010); Master's degree or higher: 1.6% (2010).

School District(s)

Zavalla ISD (PK-12)

  2009-10 Enrollment: 480 . . . . (936) 897-2271

Housing: Homeownership rate: 80.9% (2010); Median home value: $58,000 (2010); Median contract rent: $364 per month (2005-2009 5-year est.); Median year structure built: 1979 (2005-2009 5-year est.).

Transportation: Commute to work: 88.8% car, 0.0% public transportation, 5.6% walk, 0.0% work from home (2005-2009 5-year est.); Travel time to work: 34.3% less than 15 minutes, 15.0% 15 to 30 minutes, 19.7% 30 to 45 minutes, 8.2% 45 to 60 minutes, 22.7% 60 minutes or more (2005-2009 5-year est.)

Aransas County

Located in south Texas, on the Gulf Coast; includes St. Joseph Island. Covers a land area of 251.86 square miles, a water area of 276.09 square miles, and is located in the Central Time Zone at 28.04° N. Lat., 97.04° W. Long. The county was founded in 1871. County seat is Rockport.

Aransas County is part of the Corpus Christi, TX Metropolitan Statistical Area. The entire metro area includes: Aransas County, TX; Nueces County, TX; San Patricio County, TX

Weather Station: Aransas Wildlife Refuge   Elevation: 15 feet

	Jan	Feb	Mar	Apr	May	Jun	Jul	Aug	Sep	Oct	Nov	Dec
High	64	67	73	78	83	88	90	91	88	82	74	65
Low	46	50	56	63	71	76	77	77	73	65	57	47
Precip	3.1	2.6	2.7	1.8	4.3	3.8	3.8	3.4	4.2	4.5	3.5	2.1
Snow	tr	tr	tr	0.0	0.0	0.0	0.0	0.0	0.0	0.0	0.0	0.2

High and Low temperatures in degrees Fahrenheit; Precipitation and Snow in inches

Weather Station: Rockport   Elevation: 8 feet

	Jan	Feb	Mar	Apr	May	Jun	Jul	Aug	Sep	Oct	Nov	Dec
High	66	68	73	79	84	89	91	92	89	83	75	67
Low	47	51	57	64	72	77	78	78	74	66	57	48
Precip	2.4	2.1	2.4	1.7	3.5	3.1	3.1	2.8	4.6	4.2	3.1	1.8
Snow	0.0	0.0	0.0	0.0	0.0	0.0	0.0	0.0	0.0	0.0	0.0	0.2

High and Low temperatures in degrees Fahrenheit; Precipitation and Snow in inches

Population: 17,892 (1990); 22,497 (2000); 25,794 (2010); 27,347 (2015 projected); Race: 86.7% White, 1.7% Black, 2.4% Asian, 9.2% Other, 22.9% Hispanic of any race (2010); Density: 102.4 persons per square mile (2010); Average household size: 2.36 (2010); Median age: 43.9 (2010); Males per 100 females: 96.6 (2010).

Religion: Five largest groups: 15.0% Catholic Church, 12.1% Southern Baptist Convention, 2.3% The United Methodist Church, 1.7% Presbyterian Church (U.S.A.), 1.2% Lutheran Church—Missouri Synod (2000).

Economy: Unemployment rate: 8.3% (June 2011); Total civilian labor force: 12,074 (June 2011); Leading industries: 28.5% retail trade; 22.9% accommodation & food services; 12.6% health care and social assistance (2009); Farms: 94 totaling 50,951 acres (2007); Companies that employ 500 or more persons: 0 (2009); Companies that employ 100 to 499 persons: 5 (2009); Companies that employ less than 100 persons: 478 (2009); Black-owned businesses: n/a (2007); Hispanic-owned businesses: n/a (2007); Asian-owned businesses: n/a (2007); Women-owned businesses: n/a (2007); Retail sales per capita: $12,819 (2010). Single-family building permits issued: 100 (2010); Multi-family building permits issued: 0 (2010).

Income: Per capita income: $24,772 (2010); Median household income: $41,796 (2010); Average household income: $58,781 (2010); Percent of households with income of $100,000 or more: 14.3% (2010); Poverty rate: 19.2% (2009); Bankruptcy rate: 2.64% (2010).

Taxes: Total county taxes per capita: $347 (2007); County property taxes per capita: $253 (2007).

Education: Percent of population age 25 and over with: High school diploma (including GED) or higher: 81.3% (2010); Bachelor's degree or higher: 23.6% (2010); Master's degree or higher: 7.1% (2010).
Housing: Homeownership rate: 75.4% (2010); Median home value: $114,710 (2010); Median contract rent: $527 per month (2005-2009 5-year est.); Median year structure built: 1979 (2005-2009 5-year est.)
Health: Birth rate: 112.8 per 10,000 population (2009); Death rate: 119.6 per 10,000 population (2009); Age-adjusted cancer mortality rate: 160.8 deaths per 100,000 population (2007); Number of physicians: 7.3 per 10,000 population (2008); Hospital beds: 0.0 per 10,000 population (2007); Hospital admissions: 0.0 per 10,000 population (2007).
Elections: 2008 Presidential election results: 30.7% Obama, 68.4% McCain, 0.0% Nader
National and State Parks: Aransas National Wildlife Refuge; Copano Bay Causeway State Park; Goose Island State Park
Additional Information Contacts
Aransas County Government. . . . . (361) 790-0100
   http://www.aransascountytx.gov
City of Rockport. . . . . (361) 729-2213
   http://www.cityofrockport.com
Rockport-Fulton Chamber of Commerce. . . . . (361) 729-6445
   http://www.1rockport.org

Aransas County Communities

FULTON (town). Covers a land area of 1.351 square miles and a water area of 0.841 square miles. Located at 28.06° N. Lat; 97.04° W. Long. Elevation is 10 feet.
History: Fulton was named for George W. Fulton, who built a house here in 1872. The town developed around a meat packing plant.
Population: 1,199 (1990); 1,553 (2000); 1,680 (2010); 1,758 (2015 projected); Race: 87.1% White, 1.3% Black, 6.0% Asian, 5.6% Other, 11.4% Hispanic of any race (2010); Density: 1,244.0 persons per square mile (2010); Average household size: 2.13 (2010); Median age: 52.8 (2010); Males per 100 females: 98.8 (2010); Marriage status: 18.3% never married, 61.6% now married, 10.1% widowed, 10.0% divorced (2005-2009 5-year est.); Foreign born: 6.3% (2005-2009 5-year est.); Ancestry (includes multiple ancestries): 20.9% German, 19.9% Irish, 9.9% English, 6.0% Scotch-Irish, 4.9% French (2005-2009 5-year est.).
Economy: Single-family building permits issued: 9 (2010); Multi-family building permits issued: 0 (2010); Employment by occupation: 7.0% management, 8.6% professional, 16.8% services, 27.1% sales, 0.0% farming, 24.0% construction, 16.5% production (2005-2009 5-year est.).
Income: Per capita income: $27,043 (2010); Median household income: $40,990 (2010); Average household income: $57,668 (2010); Percent of households with income of $100,000 or more: 11.9% (2010); Poverty rate: 22.8% (2005-2009 5-year est.).
Taxes: Total city taxes per capita: $388 (2007); City property taxes per capita: $93 (2007).
Education: Percent of population age 25 and over with: High school diploma (including GED) or higher: 81.4% (2010); Bachelor's degree or higher: 23.1% (2010); Master's degree or higher: 7.1% (2010).
School District(s)
Aransas County ISD (PK-12)
   2009-10 Enrollment: 3,156 . . . . (361) 790-2212
Housing: Homeownership rate: 76.2% (2010); Median home value: $87,073 (2010); Median contract rent: $439 per month (2005-2009 5-year est.); Median year structure built: 1981 (2005-2009 5-year est.).
Transportation: Commute to work: 80.7% car, 0.0% public transportation, 11.9% walk, 1.9% work from home (2005-2009 5-year est.); Travel time to work: 62.0% less than 15 minutes, 17.4% 15 to 30 minutes, 9.5% 30 to 45 minutes, 9.1% 45 to 60 minutes, 2.1% 60 minutes or more (2005-2009 5-year est.)

ROCKPORT (city). County seat. Covers a land area of 9.391 square miles and a water area of 5.122 square miles. Located at 28.03° N. Lat; 97.05° W. Long. Elevation is 7 feet.
History: Rockport was founded in 1868 by the Morgan Steamship Company of New York, and became a leading Texas seaport shipping hides, tallow, and bone fertilizer.
Population: 6,268 (1990); 7,385 (2000); 9,402 (2010); 10,269 (2015 projected); Race: 87.3% White, 2.1% Black, 2.4% Asian, 8.2% Other, 22.9% Hispanic of any race (2010); Density: 1,001.2 persons per square mile (2010); Average household size: 2.26 (2010); Median age: 45.5 (2010); Males per 100 females: 93.4 (2010); Marriage status: 19.4% never

married, 60.9% now married, 8.6% widowed, 11.1% divorced (2005-2009 5-year est.); Foreign born: 4.2% (2005-2009 5-year est.); Ancestry (includes multiple ancestries): 21.3% German, 15.1% English, 11.4% Irish, 6.2% American, 5.9% French (2005-2009 5-year est.).
Economy: Single-family building permits issued: 83 (2010); Multi-family building permits issued: 0 (2010); Employment by occupation: 17.8% management, 14.6% professional, 18.4% services, 27.5% sales, 2.7% farming, 11.4% construction, 7.6% production (2005-2009 5-year est.).
Income: Per capita income: $26,551 (2010); Median household income: $40,151 (2010); Average household income: $60,465 (2010); Percent of households with income of $100,000 or more: 15.7% (2010); Poverty rate: 15.1% (2005-2009 5-year est.).
Taxes: Total city taxes per capita: $585 (2007); City property taxes per capita: $258 (2007).
Education: Percent of population age 25 and over with: High school diploma (including GED) or higher: 84.7% (2010); Bachelor's degree or higher: 29.0% (2010); Master's degree or higher: 8.7% (2010).
School District(s)
Aransas County ISD (PK-12)
   2009-10 Enrollment: 3,156 . . . . (361) 790-2212
Housing: Homeownership rate: 67.4% (2010); Median home value: $142,716 (2010); Median contract rent: $553 per month (2005-2009 5-year est.); Median year structure built: 1979 (2005-2009 5-year est.).
Safety: Violent crime rate: 18.0 per 10,000 population; Property crime rate: 520.6 per 10,000 population (2009).
Newspapers: The Coastal Bend Herald (Local news; Circulation 5,000); Pilot (Community news; Circulation 5,300)
Transportation: Commute to work: 86.0% car, 0.0% public transportation, 4.6% walk, 8.1% work from home (2005-2009 5-year est.); Travel time to work: 64.1% less than 15 minutes, 19.4% 15 to 30 minutes, 6.6% 30 to 45 minutes, 4.9% 45 to 60 minutes, 5.0% 60 minutes or more (2005-2009 5-year est.)
Airports: Aransas County (general aviation)
Additional Information Contacts
City of Rockport. . . . . (361) 729-2213
   http://www.cityofrockport.com
Rockport-Fulton Chamber of Commerce. . . . . (361) 729-6445
   http://www.1rockport.org

Archer County

Located in north Texas; drained by the West Fork of the Trinity River; includes Lake Kickapoo, and parts of Diversion and Wichita Lakes. Covers a land area of 909.70 square miles, a water area of 16.09 square miles, and is located in the Central Time Zone at 33.65° N. Lat., 98.69° W. Long. The county was founded in 1858. County seat is Archer City.

Archer County is part of the Wichita Falls, TX Metropolitan Statistical Area. The entire metro area includes: Archer County, TX; Clay County, TX; Wichita County, TX

Weather Station: Archer City   Elevation: 1,044 feet

	Jan	Feb	Mar	Apr	May	Jun	Jul	Aug	Sep	Oct	Nov	Dec
High	57	60	69	78	85	92	97	98	89	79	67	57
Low	31	34	42	50	60	68	72	72	63	53	42	32
Precip	1.2	2.0	2.2	2.3	4.2	3.7	1.8	2.5	2.7	3.7	2.0	1.8
Snow	1.1	0.8	0.4	0.0	0.0	0.0	0.0	0.0	0.0	tr	0.4	1.0

High and Low temperatures in degrees Fahrenheit; Precipitation and Snow in inches

Population: 7,973 (1990); 8,854 (2000); 9,281 (2010); 9,472 (2015 projected); Race: 92.1% White, 1.6% Black, 0.1% Asian, 6.2% Other, 7.6% Hispanic of any race (2010); Density: 10.2 persons per square mile (2010); Average household size: 2.61 (2010); Median age: 39.3 (2010); Males per 100 females: 100.1 (2010).
Religion: Five largest groups: 44.7% Southern Baptist Convention, 15.4% Catholic Church, 5.7% The United Methodist Church, 3.0% Churches of Christ, 2.0% Assemblies of God (2000).
Economy: Unemployment rate: 6.4% (June 2011); Total civilian labor force: 4,967 (June 2011); Leading industries: 12.7% mining; 10.7% health care and social assistance; 9.9% construction (2009); Farms: 513 totaling 507,607 acres (2007); Companies that employ 500 or more persons: 0 (2009); Companies that employ 100 to 499 persons: 0 (2009); Companies that employ less than 100 persons: 189 (2009); Black-owned businesses: n/a (2007); Hispanic-owned businesses: n/a (2007); Asian-owned businesses: n/a (2007); Women-owned businesses: n/a (2007); Retail

sales per capita: $7,109 (2010). Single-family building permits issued: 12 (2010); Multi-family building permits issued: 0 (2010).
Income: Per capita income: $24,643 (2010); Median household income: $49,401 (2010); Average household income: $64,339 (2010); Percent of households with income of $100,000 or more: 15.1% (2010); Poverty rate: 10.7% (2009); Bankruptcy rate: 2.70% (2010).
Taxes: Total county taxes per capita: $398 (2007); County property taxes per capita: $319 (2007).
Education: Percent of population age 25 and over with: High school diploma (including GED) or higher: 84.9% (2010); Bachelor's degree or higher: 17.3% (2010); Master's degree or higher: 4.1% (2010).
Housing: Homeownership rate: 79.7% (2010); Median home value: $87,193 (2010); Median contract rent: $306 per month (2005-2009 5-year est.); Median year structure built: 1973 (2005-2009 5-year est.)
Health: Birth rate: 141.4 per 10,000 population (2009); Death rate: 93.1 per 10,000 population (2009); Age-adjusted cancer mortality rate: 145.4 (Unreliable) deaths per 100,000 population (2007); Number of physicians: 4.5 per 10,000 population (2008); Hospital beds: 0.0 per 10,000 population (2007); Hospital admissions: 0.0 per 10,000 population (2007).
Elections: 2008 Presidential election results: 17.0% Obama, 82.4% McCain, 0.1% Nader
Additional Information Contacts
Archer County Government . . . . (940) 574-4811
    http://www.co.archer.tx.us/ips/cms
Archer City Chamber of Commerce . . . . (940) 574-2489
    http://www.archercity.org

Archer County Communities

ARCHER CITY (city). County seat. Covers a land area of 2.207 square miles and a water area of 0.015 square miles. Located at 33.59° N. Lat; 98.62° W. Long. Elevation is 1,063 feet.
History: Archer City experienced a boom from oil in 1931, when the first deep well in the county began producing near here.
Population: 1,782 (1990); 1,848 (2000); 1,891 (2010); 1,910 (2015 projected); Race: 95.9% White, 0.0% Black, 0.0% Asian, 4.1% Other, 4.5% Hispanic of any race (2010); Density: 856.8 persons per square mile (2010); Average household size: 2.43 (2010); Median age: 40.0 (2010); Males per 100 females: 94.3 (2010); Marriage status: 21.9% never married, 62.4% now married, 8.1% widowed, 7.7% divorced (2005-2009 5-year est.); Foreign born: 2.5% (2005-2009 5-year est.); Ancestry (includes multiple ancestries): 17.7% German, 15.5% Irish, 10.9% English, 4.2% Scottish, 3.9% Dutch (2005-2009 5-year est.).
Economy: Single-family building permits issued: 1 (2010); Multi-family building permits issued: 0 (2010); Employment by occupation: 10.2% management, 13.4% professional, 24.2% services, 19.0% sales, 0.0% farming, 21.8% construction, 11.4% production (2005-2009 5-year est.).
Income: Per capita income: $22,234 (2010); Median household income: $40,726 (2010); Average household income: $53,982 (2010); Percent of households with income of $100,000 or more: 9.9% (2010); Poverty rate: 11.3% (2005-2009 5-year est.).
Taxes: Total city taxes per capita: $259 (2007); City property taxes per capita: $122 (2007).
Education: Percent of population age 25 and over with: High school diploma (including GED) or higher: 79.8% (2010); Bachelor's degree or higher: 14.4% (2010); Master's degree or higher: 4.2% (2010).
School District(s)
Archer City ISD (PK-12)
    2009-10 Enrollment: 483 . . . . (940) 574-4536
Housing: Homeownership rate: 72.7% (2010); Median home value: $58,051 (2010); Median contract rent: $249 per month (2005-2009 5-year est.); Median year structure built: 1964 (2005-2009 5-year est.).
Newspapers: Archer County News (Community news; Circulation 1,588)
Transportation: Commute to work: 95.3% car, 0.0% public transportation, 2.3% walk, 2.3% work from home (2005-2009 5-year est.); Travel time to work: 54.1% less than 15 minutes, 21.3% 15 to 30 minutes, 18.5% 30 to 45 minutes, 2.2% 45 to 60 minutes, 3.9% 60 minutes or more (2005-2009 5-year est.)
Additional Information Contacts
Archer City Chamber of Commerce . . . . (940) 574-2489
    http://www.archercity.org

HOLLIDAY (city). Covers a land area of 1.951 square miles and a water area of 0 square miles. Located at 33.81° N. Lat; 98.69° W. Long. Elevation is 1,053 feet.

History: Oil was discovered in Holliday in 1920, adding to the economy based on agriculture.
Population: 1,475 (1990); 1,632 (2000); 1,748 (2010); 1,800 (2015 projected); Race: 94.7% White, 0.1% Black, 0.3% Asian, 5.0% Other, 5.7% Hispanic of any race (2010); Density: 895.9 persons per square mile (2010); Average household size: 2.61 (2010); Median age: 36.2 (2010); Males per 100 females: 93.6 (2010); Marriage status: 20.3% never married, 67.5% now married, 2.0% widowed, 10.2% divorced (2005-2009 5-year est.); Foreign born: 0.3% (2005-2009 5-year est.); Ancestry (includes multiple ancestries): 19.4% German, 14.4% Irish, 12.0% English, 5.6% Dutch, 5.0% American (2005-2009 5-year est.).
Economy: Single-family building permits issued: 8 (2010); Multi-family building permits issued: 0 (2010); Employment by occupation: 15.5% management, 15.4% professional, 20.4% services, 16.2% sales, 1.2% farming, 17.4% construction, 13.9% production (2005-2009 5-year est.).
Income: Per capita income: $21,207 (2010); Median household income: $42,368 (2010); Average household income: $55,299 (2010); Percent of households with income of $100,000 or more: 11.2% (2010); Poverty rate: 7.5% (2005-2009 5-year est.).
Taxes: Total city taxes per capita: $293 (2007); City property taxes per capita: $96 (2007).
Education: Percent of population age 25 and over with: High school diploma (including GED) or higher: 84.7% (2010); Bachelor's degree or higher: 15.5% (2010); Master's degree or higher: 3.0% (2010).
School District(s)
Holliday ISD (PK-12)
    2009-10 Enrollment: 874 . . . . (940) 586-1281
Housing: Homeownership rate: 73.1% (2010); Median home value: $69,873 (2010); Median contract rent: $424 per month (2005-2009 5-year est.); Median year structure built: 1970 (2005-2009 5-year est.).
Safety: Violent crime rate: 0.0 per 10,000 population; Property crime rate: 60.8 per 10,000 population (2009).
Transportation: Commute to work: 94.3% car, 0.0% public transportation, 0.7% walk, 3.8% work from home (2005-2009 5-year est.); Travel time to work: 33.6% less than 15 minutes, 51.4% 15 to 30 minutes, 12.0% 30 to 45 minutes, 1.3% 45 to 60 minutes, 1.6% 60 minutes or more (2005-2009 5-year est.)

LAKESIDE CITY (town). Covers a land area of 0.626 square miles and a water area of 0 square miles. Located at 33.82° N. Lat; 98.54° W. Long. Elevation is 1,004 feet.
Population: 864 (1990); 984 (2000); 1,008 (2010); 1,061 (2015 projected); Race: 92.4% White, 5.7% Black, 0.0% Asian, 2.0% Other, 1.9% Hispanic of any race (2010); Density: 1,611.0 persons per square mile (2010); Average household size: 2.72 (2010); Median age: 47.0 (2010); Males per 100 females: 102.0 (2010); Marriage status: 16.8% never married, 65.9% now married, 5.7% widowed, 11.6% divorced (2005-2009 5-year est.); Foreign born: 1.6% (2005-2009 5-year est.); Ancestry (includes multiple ancestries): 18.8% German, 16.6% American, 10.9% Irish, 9.8% English, 4.7% Czech (2005-2009 5-year est.).
Economy: Single-family building permits issued: 3 (2010); Multi-family building permits issued: 0 (2010); Employment by occupation: 6.5% management, 28.3% professional, 9.8% services, 33.8% sales, 0.0% farming, 7.7% construction, 13.8% production (2005-2009 5-year est.).
Income: Per capita income: $31,372 (2010); Median household income: $71,837 (2010); Average household income: $85,202 (2010); Percent of households with income of $100,000 or more: 26.4% (2010); Poverty rate: 4.1% (2005-2009 5-year est.).
Taxes: Total city taxes per capita: $122 (2007); City property taxes per capita: $99 (2007).
Education: Percent of population age 25 and over with: High school diploma (including GED) or higher: 92.8% (2010); Bachelor's degree or higher: 26.9% (2010); Master's degree or higher: 6.8% (2010).
Housing: Homeownership rate: 93.8% (2010); Median home value: $140,461 (2010); Median contract rent: $815 per month (2005-2009 5-year est.); Median year structure built: 1979 (2005-2009 5-year est.).
Transportation: Commute to work: 98.5% car, 0.0% public transportation, 0.7% walk, 0.8% work from home (2005-2009 5-year est.); Travel time to work: 37.5% less than 15 minutes, 53.4% 15 to 30 minutes, 5.3% 30 to 45 minutes, 0.0% 45 to 60 minutes, 3.8% 60 minutes or more (2005-2009 5-year est.)

MEGARGEL (town). Covers a land area of 0.613 square miles and a water area of 0 square miles. Located at 33.45° N. Lat; 98.92° W. Long. Elevation is 1,286 feet.

Population: 237 (1990); 248 (2000); 256 (2010); 258 (2015 projected); **Race:** 91.8% White, 3.5% Black, 0.4% Asian, 4.3% Other, 3.9% Hispanic of any race (2010); **Density:** 417.5 persons per square mile (2010); Average household size: 2.31 (2010); Median age: 44.3 (2010); Males per 100 females: 101.6 (2010); Marriage status: 21.5% never married, 42.9% now married, 20.1% widowed, 15.5% divorced (2005-2009 5-year est.); Foreign born: 1.5% (2005-2009 5-year est.); Ancestry (includes multiple ancestries): 33.3% Irish, 17.8% English, 12.9% German, 8.0% Hungarian, 6.8% Czech (2005-2009 5-year est.).
Economy: Employment by occupation: 7.3% management, 9.1% professional, 15.5% services, 12.7% sales, 8.2% farming, 23.6% construction, 23.6% production (2005-2009 5-year est.).
Income: Per capita income: $21,776 (2010); Median household income: $38,281 (2010); Average household income: $49,932 (2010); Percent of households with income of $100,000 or more: 9.0% (2010); Poverty rate: 26.1% (2005-2009 5-year est.).
Taxes: Total city taxes per capita: $221 (2007); City property taxes per capita: $202 (2007).
Education: Percent of population age 25 and over with: High school diploma (including GED) or higher: 83.0% (2010); Bachelor's degree or higher: 14.8% (2010); Master's degree or higher: 2.2% (2010).
Housing: Homeownership rate: 79.3% (2010); Median home value: $54,286 (2010); Median contract rent: $284 per month (2005-2009 5-year est.); Median year structure built: 1957 (2005-2009 5-year est.).
Transportation: Commute to work: 83.0% car, 0.0% public transportation, 0.0% walk, 9.4% work from home (2005-2009 5-year est.); Travel time to work: 27.1% less than 15 minutes, 60.4% 15 to 30 minutes, 6.3% 30 to 45 minutes, 0.0% 45 to 60 minutes, 6.3% 60 minutes or more (2005-2009 5-year est.)

SCOTLAND (city). Covers a land area of 11.214 square miles and a water area of 0.053 square miles. Located at 33.64° N. Lat; 98.44° W. Long. Elevation is 961 feet.
Population: 490 (1990); 438 (2000); 444 (2010); 448 (2015 projected); **Race:** 82.4% White, 0.0% Black, 0.0% Asian, 17.6% Other, 26.4% Hispanic of any race (2010); **Density:** 39.6 persons per square mile (2010); Average household size: 2.88 (2010); Median age: 31.6 (2010); Males per 100 females: 108.5 (2010); Marriage status: 16.8% never married, 59.6% now married, 10.2% widowed, 13.5% divorced (2005-2009 5-year est.); Foreign born: 8.0% (2005-2009 5-year est.); Ancestry (includes multiple ancestries): 40.1% German, 15.7% Irish, 7.7% English, 3.0% American, 2.7% French (2005-2009 5-year est.).
Economy: Employment by occupation: 5.0% management, 11.7% professional, 25.7% services, 20.7% sales, 2.7% farming, 23.4% construction, 10.8% production (2005-2009 5-year est.).
Income: Per capita income: $20,493 (2010); Median household income: $48,966 (2010); Average household income: $58,506 (2010); Percent of households with income of $100,000 or more: 13.6% (2010); Poverty rate: 8.9% (2005-2009 5-year est.).
Taxes: Total city taxes per capita: $39 (2007); City property taxes per capita: $0 (2007).
Education: Percent of population age 25 and over with: High school diploma (including GED) or higher: 82.2% (2010); Bachelor's degree or higher: 14.7% (2010); Master's degree or higher: 3.5% (2010).
Housing: Homeownership rate: 79.9% (2010); Median home value: $94,211 (2010); Median contract rent: $336 per month (2005-2009 5-year est.); Median year structure built: 1977 (2005-2009 5-year est.).
Transportation: Commute to work: 94.1% car, 0.9% public transportation, 0.5% walk, 4.5% work from home (2005-2009 5-year est.); Travel time to work: 22.2% less than 15 minutes, 46.7% 15 to 30 minutes, 27.8% 30 to 45 minutes, 0.0% 45 to 60 minutes, 3.3% 60 minutes or more (2005-2009 5-year est.)

WINDTHORST (town). Covers a land area of 2.502 square miles and a water area of 0.030 square miles. Located at 33.57° N. Lat; 98.43° W. Long. Elevation is 1,033 feet.
History: Windthorst was founded in 1891 by immigrants from Germany.
Population: 367 (1990); 440 (2000); 441 (2010); 444 (2015 projected); **Race:** 83.0% White, 0.0% Black, 0.0% Asian, 17.0% Other, 26.1% Hispanic of any race (2010); **Density:** 176.3 persons per square mile (2010); Average household size: 2.88 (2010); Median age: 32.9 (2010); Males per 100 females: 104.2 (2010); Marriage status: 24.8% never married, 60.4% now married, 4.2% widowed, 10.5% divorced (2005-2009 5-year est.); Foreign born: 24.2% (2005-2009 5-year est.); Ancestry

(includes multiple ancestries): 35.1% German, 5.7% Irish, 3.3% American, 2.7% Dutch, 1.9% English (2005-2009 5-year est.).
Economy: Employment by occupation: 5.3% management, 13.3% professional, 7.6% services, 22.0% sales, 20.1% farming, 13.6% construction, 18.2% production (2005-2009 5-year est.).
Income: Per capita income: $20,454 (2010); Median household income: $48,707 (2010); Average household income: $57,598 (2010); Percent of households with income of $100,000 or more: 13.1% (2010); Poverty rate: 23.2% (2005-2009 5-year est.).
Taxes: Total city taxes per capita: $346 (2007); City property taxes per capita: $0 (2007).
Education: Percent of population age 25 and over with: High school diploma (including GED) or higher: 83.3% (2010); Bachelor's degree or higher: 16.0% (2010); Master's degree or higher: 4.6% (2010).

School District(s)
Windthorst ISD (PK-12)
   2009-10 Enrollment: 490 . . . . (940) 423-6688
Housing: Homeownership rate: 80.4% (2010); Median home value: $92,500 (2010); Median contract rent: $351 per month (2005-2009 5-year est.); Median year structure built: 1971 (2005-2009 5-year est.).
Transportation: Commute to work: 72.0% car, 1.1% public transportation, 9.8% walk, 14.0% work from home (2005-2009 5-year est.); Travel time to work: 58.6% less than 15 minutes, 12.3% 15 to 30 minutes, 23.8% 30 to 45 minutes, 0.0% 45 to 60 minutes, 5.3% 60 minutes or more (2005-2009 5-year est.)

Armstrong County

Located in north Texas, on the Panhandle. Covers a land area of 913.63 square miles, a water area of 0.18 square miles, and is located in the Central Time Zone at 35.00° N. Lat., 101.37° W. Long. The county was founded in 1876. County seat is Claude.

Armstrong County is part of the Amarillo, TX Metropolitan Statistical Area. The entire metro area includes: Armstrong County, TX; Carson County, TX; Potter County, TX; Randall County, TX

Population: 2,021 (1990); 2,148 (2000); 2,182 (2010); 2,195 (2015 projected); **Race:** 90.7% White, 1.1% Black, 0.0% Asian, 8.2% Other, 11.2% Hispanic of any race (2010); **Density:** 2.4 persons per square mile (2010); Average household size: 2.59 (2010); Median age: 43.3 (2010); Males per 100 females: 93.8 (2010).
Religion: Four largest groups: 50.6% Southern Baptist Convention, 18.0% The United Methodist Church, 3.0% Churches of Christ, 0.8% Christian Church (Disciples of Christ) (2000).
Economy: Unemployment rate: 4.7% (June 2011); Total civilian labor force: 1,058 (June 2011); Leading industries: Farms: 291 totaling 516,299 acres (2007); Companies that employ 500 or more persons: 0 (2009); Companies that employ 100 to 499 persons: 0 (2009); Companies that employ less than 100 persons: 30 (2009); Black-owned businesses: n/a (2007); Hispanic-owned businesses: n/a (2007); Asian-owned businesses: n/a (2007); Women-owned businesses: n/a (2007); Retail sales per capita: $1,790 (2010). Single-family building permits issued: 0 (2010); Multi-family building permits issued: 0 (2010).
Income: Per capita income: $22,791 (2010); Median household income: $50,786 (2010); Average household income: $61,001 (2010); Percent of households with income of $100,000 or more: 15.5% (2010); Poverty rate: 10.2% (2009); Bankruptcy rate: 1.55% (2010).
Taxes: Total county taxes per capita: $194 (2007); County property taxes per capita: $102 (2007).
Education: Percent of population age 25 and over with: High school diploma (including GED) or higher: 86.3% (2010); Bachelor's degree or higher: 22.0% (2010); Master's degree or higher: 4.6% (2010).
Housing: Homeownership rate: 77.4% (2010); Median home value: $91,692 (2010); Median contract rent: $406 per month (2005-2009 5-year est.); Median year structure built: 1957 (2005-2009 5-year est.)
Health: Birth rate: 135.6 per 10,000 population (2009); Death rate: 67.8 per 10,000 population (2009); Age-adjusted cancer mortality rate: 303.5 (Unreliable) deaths per 100,000 population (2007); Number of physicians: 0.0 per 10,000 population (2008); Hospital beds: 0.0 per 10,000 population (2007); Hospital admissions: 0.0 per 10,000 population (2007).
Elections: 2008 Presidential election results: 12.9% Obama, 86.5% McCain, 0.0% Nader
Additional Information Contacts
Armstrong County Government . . . . (806) 226-3221
   http://www.co.armstrong.tx.us/ips/cms

Armstrong County Communities

CLAUDE (city). County seat. Covers a land area of 1.713 square miles and a water area of 0 square miles. Located at 35.10° N. Lat; 101.36° W. Long. Elevation is 3,406 feet.
History: Unlike so many Texan towns, where lawlessness and carousing were early problems, the town of Claude was so law-abiding that the Armstrong County Jail, erected here in the 1890's, was used as a parsonage by the local Methodist minister.
Population: 1,199 (1990); 1,313 (2000); 1,299 (2010); 1,290 (2015 projected); Race: 93.5% White, 0.8% Black, 0.0% Asian, 5.7% Other, 10.1% Hispanic of any race (2010); Density: 758.3 persons per square mile (2010); Average household size: 2.57 (2010); Median age: 43.3 (2010); Males per 100 females: 93.0 (2010); Marriage status: 11.9% never married, 70.3% now married, 10.5% widowed, 7.3% divorced (2005-2009 5-year est.); Foreign born: 1.2% (2005-2009 5-year est.); Ancestry (includes multiple ancestries): 18.1% Irish, 16.8% German, 8.9% English, 4.0% Polish, 3.1% Scotch-Irish (2005-2009 5-year est.).
Economy: Single-family building permits issued: 0 (2010); Multi-family building permits issued: 0 (2010); Employment by occupation: 14.4% management, 20.7% professional, 26.0% services, 16.6% sales, 0.9% farming, 9.2% construction, 12.3% production (2005-2009 5-year est.).
Income: Per capita income: $22,514 (2010); Median household income: $52,434 (2010); Average household income: $59,525 (2010); Percent of households with income of $100,000 or more: 14.5% (2010); Poverty rate: 14.8% (2005-2009 5-year est.).
Taxes: Total city taxes per capita: $199 (2007); City property taxes per capita: $163 (2007).
Education: Percent of population age 25 and over with: High school diploma (including GED) or higher: 86.9% (2010); Bachelor's degree or higher: 23.5% (2010); Master's degree or higher: 5.3% (2010).

School District(s)
Claude ISD (KG-12)
    2009-10 Enrollment: 321 . . . . (806) 226-7331
Housing: Homeownership rate: 78.7% (2010); Median home value: $88,298 (2010); Median contract rent: $345 per month (2005-2009 5-year est.); Median year structure built: 1961 (2005-2009 5-year est.).
Newspapers: Claude News (Local news; Circulation 1,500)
Transportation: Commute to work: 95.7% car, 0.0% public transportation, 0.0% walk, 0.3% work from home (2005-2009 5-year est.); Travel time to work: 31.3% less than 15 minutes, 17.7% 15 to 30 minutes, 38.3% 30 to 45 minutes, 7.5% 45 to 60 minutes, 5.1% 60 minutes or more (2005-2009 5-year est.)

Atascosa County

Located in southwestern Texas; drained by the Atascosa River. Covers a land area of 1,232.12 square miles, a water area of 3.49 square miles, and is located in the Central Time Zone at 28.92° N. Lat., 98.52° W. Long. The county was founded in 1856. County seat is Jourdanton.

Atascosa County is part of the San Antonio-New Braunfels, TX Metropolitan Statistical Area. The entire metro area includes: Atascosa County, TX; Bandera County, TX; Bexar County, TX; Comal County, TX; Guadalupe County, TX; Kendall County, TX; Medina County, TX; Wilson County, TX

Weather Station: Charlotte 5 NNW   Elevation: 440 feet

	Jan	Feb	Mar	Apr	May	Jun	Jul	Aug	Sep	Oct	Nov	Dec
High	68	72	78	85	90	95	97	97	92	85	76	68
Low	42	46	52	59	67	72	73	73	69	61	51	43
Precip	1.3	1.6	2.0	1.9	3.0	3.3	2.2	2.2	2.8	3.1	1.9	1.5
Snow	0.0	0.0	0.0	0.0	0.0	0.0	0.0	0.0	0.0	tr	0.0	tr

High and Low temperatures in degrees Fahrenheit; Precipitation and Snow in inches

Weather Station: Poteet   Elevation: 479 feet

	Jan	Feb	Mar	Apr	May	Jun	Jul	Aug	Sep	Oct	Nov	Dec
High	65	68	75	82	88	94	95	97	92	84	74	65
Low	40	43	50	57	66	71	72	73	69	60	50	41
Precip	1.4	1.8	2.1	1.9	3.4	3.8	2.6	2.3	2.6	3.0	1.8	1.7
Snow	0.0	tr	0.0	0.0	0.0	0.0	0.0	0.0	0.0	0.0	0.0	0.0

High and Low temperatures in degrees Fahrenheit; Precipitation and Snow in inches

Population: 30,533 (1990); 38,628 (2000); 44,710 (2010); 47,594 (2015 projected); Race: 71.6% White, 1.1% Black, 0.5% Asian, 26.8% Other, 60.7% Hispanic of any race (2010); Density: 36.3 persons per square mile (2010); Average household size: 2.96 (2010); Median age: 33.8 (2010); Males per 100 females: 97.4 (2010).
Religion: Five largest groups: 40.6% Catholic Church, 13.5% Southern Baptist Convention, 3.7% The United Methodist Church, 1.6% Churches of Christ, 1.2% Evangelical Lutheran Church in America (2000).
Economy: Unemployment rate: 9.0% (June 2011); Total civilian labor force: 20,332 (June 2011); Leading industries: 23.8% retail trade; 19.4% health care and social assistance; 13.3% accommodation & food services (2009); Farms: 1,810 totaling 643,594 acres (2007); Companies that employ 500 or more persons: 0 (2009); Companies that employ 100 to 499 persons: 6 (2009); Companies that employ less than 100 persons: 617 (2009); Black-owned businesses: n/a (2007); Hispanic-owned businesses: 1,355 (2007); Asian-owned businesses: n/a (2007); Women-owned businesses: n/a (2007); Retail sales per capita: $9,653 (2010). Single-family building permits issued: 34 (2010); Multi-family building permits issued: 2 (2010).
Income: Per capita income: $18,638 (2010); Median household income: $43,637 (2010); Average household income: $55,043 (2010); Percent of households with income of $100,000 or more: 10.9% (2010); Poverty rate: 18.5% (2009); Bankruptcy rate: 1.59% (2010).
Taxes: Total county taxes per capita: $271 (2007); County property taxes per capita: $222 (2007).
Education: Percent of population age 25 and over with: High school diploma (including GED) or higher: 74.3% (2010); Bachelor's degree or higher: 10.3% (2010); Master's degree or higher: 3.5% (2010).
Housing: Homeownership rate: 75.1% (2010); Median home value: $77,465 (2010); Median contract rent: $409 per month (2005-2009 5-year est.); Median year structure built: 1982 (2005-2009 5-year est.)
Health: Birth rate: 155.5 per 10,000 population (2009); Death rate: 83.1 per 10,000 population (2009); Age-adjusted cancer mortality rate: 191.8 deaths per 100,000 population (2007); Number of physicians: 6.6 per 10,000 population (2008); Hospital beds: 15.4 per 10,000 population (2007); Hospital admissions: 721.7 per 10,000 population (2007).
Elections: 2008 Presidential election results: 44.4% Obama, 55.0% McCain, 0.1% Nader
Additional Information Contacts
Atascosa County Government . . . . (830) 767-2511
    http://www.co.atascosa.tx.us/ips/cms
City of Pleasanton . . . . (830) 569-3867
    http://www.pleasantontx.org
Lytle Chamber of Commerce . . . . (830) 772-5843
    http://www.lytlechamber.com
Pleasanton Chamber of Commerce. . . . . (830) 569-2163
    http://www.pleasantoncofc.com

Atascosa County Communities

CAMPBELLTON (unincorporated postal area, zip code 78008). Covers a land area of 133.600 square miles and a water area of 0.473 square miles. Located at 28.75° N. Lat; 98.21° W. Long. Elevation is 240 feet.
Population: 412 (2000); Race: 73.0% White, 0.0% Black, 0.0% Asian, 27.0% Other, 61.4% Hispanic of any race (2000); Density: 3.1 persons per square mile (2000); Age: 29.1% under 18, 21.6% over 64 (2000); Marriage status: 17.0% never married, 63.0% now married, 13.8% widowed, 6.2% divorced (2000); Foreign born: 1.1% (2000); Ancestry (includes multiple ancestries): 13.9% German, 9.5% American, 4.8% English, 3.4% Irish (2000).
Economy: Employment by occupation: 14.7% management, 13.5% professional, 22.1% services, 9.8% sales, 6.7% farming, 16.6% construction, 16.6% production (2000).
Income: Per capita income: $13,622 (2000); Median household income: $24,097 (2000); Poverty rate: 179.1% (2000).
Education: Percent of population age 25 and over with: High school diploma (including GED) or higher: 79.0% (2000); Bachelor's degree or higher: 14.4% (2000).
Housing: Homeownership rate: 87.6% (2000); Median home value: $27,700 (2000); Median contract rent: n/a per month (2000); Median year structure built: 1965 (2000).
Transportation: Commute to work: 88.3% car, 0.0% public transportation, 0.0% walk, 3.7% work from home (2000); Travel time to work: 23.6% less than 15 minutes, 15.3% 15 to 30 minutes, 50.3% 30 to 45 minutes, 0.0% 45 to 60 minutes, 10.8% 60 minutes or more (2000)

CHARLOTTE (city). Covers a land area of 1.988 square miles and a water area of 0 square miles. Located at 28.86° N. Lat; 98.70° W. Long. Elevation is 541 feet.
History: Incorporated 1940.
Population: 1,469 (1990); 1,637 (2000); 1,662 (2010); 1,682 (2015 projected); Race: 70.3% White, 0.2% Black, 0.0% Asian, 29.5% Other, 74.3% Hispanic of any race (2010); Density: 836.0 persons per square mile (2010); Average household size: 2.92 (2010); Median age: 32.9 (2010); Males per 100 females: 101.9 (2010); Marriage status: 30.7% never married, 57.2% now married, 5.4% widowed, 6.7% divorced (2005-2009 5-year est.); Foreign born: 9.7% (2005-2009 5-year est.); Ancestry (includes multiple ancestries): 5.9% Irish, 5.3% English, 3.0% German, 2.2% French, 1.1% Italian (2005-2009 5-year est.).
Economy: Single-family building permits issued: 1 (2010); Multi-family building permits issued: 0 (2010); Employment by occupation: 6.8% management, 4.2% professional, 23.4% services, 21.4% sales, 5.4% farming, 26.4% construction, 12.4% production (2005-2009 5-year est.).
Income: Per capita income: $13,942 (2010); Median household income: $31,711 (2010); Average household income: $41,320 (2010); Percent of households with income of $100,000 or more: 5.6% (2010); Poverty rate: 34.7% (2005-2009 5-year est.).
Taxes: Total city taxes per capita: $81 (2007); City property taxes per capita: $44 (2007).
Education: Percent of population age 25 and over with: High school diploma (including GED) or higher: 62.8% (2010); Bachelor's degree or higher: 7.4% (2010); Master's degree or higher: 1.3% (2010).

School District(s)
Charlotte ISD (PK-12)
   2009-10 Enrollment: 548 . . . . (830) 277-1431
Housing: Homeownership rate: 78.2% (2010); Median home value: $46,000 (2010); Median contract rent: $285 per month (2005-2009 5-year est.); Median year structure built: 1968 (2005-2009 5-year est.).
Transportation: Commute to work: 95.5% car, 0.0% public transportation, 3.8% walk, 0.7% work from home (2005-2009 5-year est.); Travel time to work: 43.6% less than 15 minutes, 20.5% 15 to 30 minutes, 9.2% 30 to 45 minutes, 12.1% 45 to 60 minutes, 14.6% 60 minutes or more (2005-2009 5-year est.)

CHRISTINE (town). Covers a land area of 1.758 square miles and a water area of 0 square miles. Located at 28.79° N. Lat; 98.49° W. Long. Elevation is 331 feet.
Population: 377 (1990); 436 (2000); 403 (2010); 392 (2015 projected); Race: 84.9% White, 2.7% Black, 0.5% Asian, 11.9% Other, 50.9% Hispanic of any race (2010); Density: 229.2 persons per square mile (2010); Average household size: 2.69 (2010); Median age: 38.5 (2010); Males per 100 females: 105.6 (2010); Marriage status: 36.0% never married, 42.4% now married, 3.2% widowed, 18.4% divorced (2005-2009 5-year est.); Foreign born: 8.6% (2005-2009 5-year est.); Ancestry (includes multiple ancestries): 12.2% German, 8.9% English, 5.8% American, 4.9% Irish, 3.1% Scotch-Irish (2005-2009 5-year est.).
Economy: Employment by occupation: 1.1% management, 11.9% professional, 22.2% services, 25.0% sales, 3.4% farming, 22.7% construction, 13.6% production (2005-2009 5-year est.).
Income: Per capita income: $20,448 (2010); Median household income: $44,130 (2010); Average household income: $52,467 (2010); Percent of households with income of $100,000 or more: 10.7% (2010); Poverty rate: 21.7% (2005-2009 5-year est.).
Taxes: Total city taxes per capita: $286 (2007); City property taxes per capita: $286 (2007).
Education: Percent of population age 25 and over with: High school diploma (including GED) or higher: 77.5% (2010); Bachelor's degree or higher: 8.2% (2010); Master's degree or higher: 0.0% (2010).
Housing: Homeownership rate: 80.0% (2010); Median home value: $61,333 (2010); Median contract rent: $492 per month (2005-2009 5-year est.); Median year structure built: 1982 (2005-2009 5-year est.).
Transportation: Commute to work: 90.0% car, 0.0% public transportation, 0.0% walk, 8.8% work from home (2005-2009 5-year est.); Travel time to work: 12.3% less than 15 minutes, 35.5% 15 to 30 minutes, 29.7% 30 to 45 minutes, 11.6% 45 to 60 minutes, 11.0% 60 minutes or more (2005-2009 5-year est.)

JOURDANTON (city). County seat. Covers a land area of 3.484 square miles and a water area of 0 square miles. Located at 28.92° N. Lat; 98.54° W. Long. Elevation is 459 feet.

Population: 3,250 (1990); 3,732 (2000); 4,278 (2010); 4,550 (2015 projected); Race: 74.2% White, 2.1% Black, 0.5% Asian, 23.2% Other, 49.0% Hispanic of any race (2010); Density: 1,227.8 persons per square mile (2010); Average household size: 2.90 (2010); Median age: 34.1 (2010); Males per 100 females: 98.2 (2010); Marriage status: 30.9% never married, 55.3% now married, 4.6% widowed, 9.2% divorced (2005-2009 5-year est.); Foreign born: 1.6% (2005-2009 5-year est.); Ancestry (includes multiple ancestries): 14.7% German, 11.1% Irish, 5.6% Polish, 4.8% English, 2.7% Italian (2005-2009 5-year est.).
Economy: Single-family building permits issued: 6 (2010); Multi-family building permits issued: 0 (2010); Employment by occupation: 9.7% management, 15.7% professional, 14.8% services, 27.3% sales, 0.0% farming, 22.3% construction, 10.1% production (2005-2009 5-year est.).
Income: Per capita income: $20,425 (2010); Median household income: $43,969 (2010); Average household income: $57,917 (2010); Percent of households with income of $100,000 or more: 7.4% (2010); Poverty rate: 17.0% (2005-2009 5-year est.).
Taxes: Total city taxes per capita: $196 (2007); City property taxes per capita: $88 (2007).
Education: Percent of population age 25 and over with: High school diploma (including GED) or higher: 78.0% (2010); Bachelor's degree or higher: 8.4% (2010); Master's degree or higher: 4.8% (2010).

School District(s)
Charlotte ISD (PK-12)
   2009-10 Enrollment: 548 . . . . (830) 277-1431
Devine ISD (PK-12)
   2009-10 Enrollment: 1,913 . . . . (830) 851-0795
Jourdanton ISD (PK-12)
   2009-10 Enrollment: 1,276 . . . . (830) 769-3548
McMullen County ISD (PK-12)
   2009-10 Enrollment: 170 . . . . (361) 274-3315
Pearsall ISD (PK-12)
   2009-10 Enrollment: 2,275 . . . . (830) 334-8001
Pleasanton ISD (PK-12)
   2009-10 Enrollment: 3,440 . . . . (830) 569-1200
Somerset ISD (PK-12)
   2009-10 Enrollment: 3,726 . . . . (866) 852-9858
Housing: Homeownership rate: 76.5% (2010); Median home value: $71,535 (2010); Median contract rent: $444 per month (2005-2009 5-year est.); Median year structure built: 1976 (2005-2009 5-year est.).
Hospitals: South Texas Regional Medical Center (47 beds)
Safety: Violent crime rate: 4.6 per 10,000 population; Property crime rate: 73.0 per 10,000 population (2009).
Transportation: Commute to work: 90.4% car, 2.7% public transportation, 4.5% walk, 0.4% work from home (2005-2009 5-year est.); Travel time to work: 42.5% less than 15 minutes, 19.1% 15 to 30 minutes, 12.5% 30 to 45 minutes, 15.1% 45 to 60 minutes, 10.8% 60 minutes or more (2005-2009 5-year est.)

LYTLE (city). Covers a land area of 4.016 square miles and a water area of 0.048 square miles. Located at 29.23° N. Lat; 98.80° W. Long. Elevation is 722 feet.
Population: 2,255 (1990); 2,383 (2000); 2,870 (2010); 3,059 (2015 projected); Race: 68.2% White, 1.0% Black, 0.7% Asian, 30.1% Other, 66.1% Hispanic of any race (2010); Density: 714.7 persons per square mile (2010); Average household size: 3.06 (2010); Median age: 34.2 (2010); Males per 100 females: 95.0 (2010); Marriage status: 32.9% never married, 47.5% now married, 7.2% widowed, 12.4% divorced (2005-2009 5-year est.); Foreign born: 5.0% (2005-2009 5-year est.); Ancestry (includes multiple ancestries): 22.6% German, 7.2% English, 4.9% Irish, 4.6% French, 4.2% Scottish (2005-2009 5-year est.).
Economy: Single-family building permits issued: 10 (2010); Multi-family building permits issued: 2 (2010); Employment by occupation: 8.5% management, 21.1% professional, 18.1% services, 37.0% sales, 0.0% farming, 8.7% construction, 6.6% production (2005-2009 5-year est.).
Income: Per capita income: $17,360 (2010); Median household income: $43,258 (2010); Average household income: $53,196 (2010); Percent of households with income of $100,000 or more: 12.2% (2010); Poverty rate: 15.6% (2005-2009 5-year est.).
Taxes: Total city taxes per capita: $328 (2007); City property taxes per capita: $115 (2007).
Education: Percent of population age 25 and over with: High school diploma (including GED) or higher: 77.8% (2010); Bachelor's degree or higher: 12.1% (2010); Master's degree or higher: 3.8% (2010).

School District(s)

Lytle ISD (PK-12)

2009-10 Enrollment: 1,712 . . . . (830) 709-5100

Housing: Homeownership rate: 72.8% (2010); Median home value: $89,870 (2010); Median contract rent: $454 per month (2005-2009 5-year est.); Median year structure built: 1975 (2005-2009 5-year est.).

Safety: Violent crime rate: 7.0 per 10,000 population; Property crime rate: 386.9 per 10,000 population (2009).

Transportation: Commute to work: 96.0% car, 0.0% public transportation, 1.8% walk, 0.7% work from home (2005-2009 5-year est.); Travel time to work: 32.5% less than 15 minutes, 28.1% 15 to 30 minutes, 20.2% 30 to 45 minutes, 14.4% 45 to 60 minutes, 4.8% 60 minutes or more (2005-2009 5-year est.)

Additional Information Contacts

Lytle Chamber of Commerce . . . . (830) 772-5843
http://www.lytlechamber.com

MCCOY (unincorporated postal area, zip code 78053). Covers a land area of 84.373 square miles and a water area of 0.382 square miles. Located at 28.90° N. Lat; 98.28° W. Long. Elevation is 299 feet.

Population: 151 (2000); Race: 100.0% White, 0.0% Black, 0.0% Asian, 0.0% Other, 0.0% Hispanic of any race (2000); Density: 1.8 persons per square mile (2000); Age: 21.0% under 18, 27.2% over 64 (2000); Marriage status: 25.0% never married, 67.2% now married, 7.8% widowed, 0.0% divorced (2000); Foreign born: 0.0% (2000); Ancestry (includes multiple ancestries): 59.3% German, 14.8% Irish, 11.1% Czech (2000).

Economy: Employment by occupation: 36.8% management, 44.7% professional, 0.0% services, 18.4% sales, 0.0% farming, 0.0% construction, 0.0% production (2000).

Income: Per capita income: $11,796 (2000); Median household income: $16,813 (2000); Poverty rate: 179.1% (2000).

Education: Percent of population age 25 and over with: High school diploma (including GED) or higher: 40.6% (2000); Bachelor's degree or higher: 26.6% (2000).

Housing: Homeownership rate: 65.0% (2000); Median home value: $162,500 (2000); Median contract rent: $225 per month (2000); Median year structure built: 1943 (2000).

Transportation: Commute to work: 100.0% car, 0.0% public transportation, 0.0% walk, 0.0% work from home (2000); Travel time to work: 23.7% less than 15 minutes, 18.4% 15 to 30 minutes, 44.7% 30 to 45 minutes, 0.0% 45 to 60 minutes, 13.2% 60 minutes or more (2000)

PLEASANTON (city). Covers a land area of 6.390 square miles and a water area of 0 square miles. Located at 28.96° N. Lat; 98.48° W. Long. Elevation is 361 feet.

History: Pleasanton was settled in the 1850's as a cattle round-up point on the old Western Trail to Dodge City, Kansas.

Population: 7,629 (1990); 8,266 (2000); 9,757 (2010); 10,417 (2015 projected); Race: 82.3% White, 1.3% Black, 0.8% Asian, 15.6% Other, 50.8% Hispanic of any race (2010); Density: 1,526.8 persons per square mile (2010); Average household size: 2.76 (2010); Median age: 34.6 (2010); Males per 100 females: 94.8 (2010); Marriage status: 29.3% never married, 49.3% now married, 10.0% widowed, 11.5% divorced (2005-2009 5-year est.); Foreign born: 3.4% (2005-2009 5-year est.); Ancestry (includes multiple ancestries): 13.3% Irish, 12.9% English, 9.6% German, 6.3% American, 2.5% Czech (2005-2009 5-year est.).

Economy: Single-family building permits issued: 17 (2010); Multi-family building permits issued: 0 (2010); Employment by occupation: 10.4% management, 14.9% professional, 23.2% services, 17.9% sales, 0.2% farming, 17.8% construction, 15.7% production (2005-2009 5-year est.).

Income: Per capita income: $19,065 (2010); Median household income: $41,648 (2010); Average household income: $52,668 (2010); Percent of households with income of $100,000 or more: 10.5% (2010); Poverty rate: 18.4% (2005-2009 5-year est.).

Taxes: Total city taxes per capita: $386 (2007); City property taxes per capita: $134 (2007).

Education: Percent of population age 25 and over with: High school diploma (including GED) or higher: 79.2% (2010); Bachelor's degree or higher: 14.8% (2010); Master's degree or higher: 5.2% (2010).

School District(s)

Pleasanton ISD (PK-12)

2009-10 Enrollment: 3,440 . . . . (830) 569-1200

Housing: Homeownership rate: 64.4% (2010); Median home value: $94,844 (2010); Median contract rent: $415 per month (2005-2009 5-year est.); Median year structure built: 1981 (2005-2009 5-year est.).

Safety: Violent crime rate: 42.7 per 10,000 population; Property crime rate: 378.9 per 10,000 population (2009).

Newspapers: Pleasanton Express (Community news; Circulation 8,600)

Transportation: Commute to work: 92.1% car, 0.0% public transportation, 4.8% walk, 2.7% work from home (2005-2009 5-year est.); Travel time to work: 39.8% less than 15 minutes, 21.2% 15 to 30 minutes, 12.5% 30 to 45 minutes, 14.6% 45 to 60 minutes, 11.9% 60 minutes or more (2005-2009 5-year est.)

Additional Information Contacts

City of Pleasanton . . . . (830) 569-3867
http://www.pleasantontx.org

Pleasanton Chamber of Commerce . . . . (830) 569-2163
http://www.pleasantoncofc.com

POTEET (city). Covers a land area of 1.486 square miles and a water area of 0 square miles. Located at 29.04° N. Lat; 98.57° W. Long. Elevation is 446 feet.

Population: 3,137 (1990); 3,305 (2000); 3,616 (2010); 3,770 (2015 projected); Race: 66.4% White, 0.6% Black, 0.5% Asian, 32.5% Other, 87.1% Hispanic of any race (2010); Density: 2,433.5 persons per square mile (2010); Average household size: 3.03 (2010); Median age: 31.6 (2010); Males per 100 females: 92.9 (2010); Marriage status: 41.1% never married, 38.1% now married, 10.4% widowed, 10.4% divorced (2005-2009 5-year est.); Foreign born: 4.6% (2005-2009 5-year est.); Ancestry (includes multiple ancestries): 4.9% Irish, 4.0% English, 3.3% German, 3.2% French, 1.1% Swedish (2005-2009 5-year est.).

Economy: Single-family building permits issued: 0 (2010); Multi-family building permits issued: 0 (2010); Employment by occupation: 6.1% management, 10.0% professional, 25.0% services, 19.7% sales, 1.1% farming, 18.0% construction, 20.2% production (2005-2009 5-year est.).

Income: Per capita income: $14,809 (2010); Median household income: $38,026 (2010); Average household income: $45,265 (2010); Percent of households with income of $100,000 or more: 5.9% (2010); Poverty rate: 45.0% (2005-2009 5-year est.).

Taxes: Total city taxes per capita: $177 (2007); City property taxes per capita: $90 (2007).

Education: Percent of population age 25 and over with: High school diploma (including GED) or higher: 63.6% (2010); Bachelor's degree or higher: 7.0% (2010); Master's degree or higher: 2.0% (2010).

School District(s)

Poteet ISD (PK-12)

2009-10 Enrollment: 1,785 . . . . (830) 742-3567

Housing: Homeownership rate: 67.0% (2010); Median home value: $50,000 (2010); Median contract rent: $271 per month (2005-2009 5-year est.); Median year structure built: 1971 (2005-2009 5-year est.).

Safety: Violent crime rate: 38.1 per 10,000 population; Property crime rate: 274.7 per 10,000 population (2009).

Transportation: Commute to work: 95.9% car, 0.0% public transportation, 2.6% walk, 1.5% work from home (2005-2009 5-year est.); Travel time to work: 31.0% less than 15 minutes, 20.7% 15 to 30 minutes, 18.6% 30 to 45 minutes, 14.9% 45 to 60 minutes, 14.8% 60 minutes or more (2005-2009 5-year est.)

Austin County

Located in south Texas; bounded on the east by the Brazos River. Covers a land area of 652.59 square miles, a water area of 3.78 square miles, and is located in the Central Time Zone at 29.85° N. Lat., 96.23° W. Long. The county was founded in 1836. County seat is Bellville.

Austin County is part of the Houston-Sugar Land-Baytown, TX Metropolitan Statistical Area. The entire metro area includes: Austin County, TX; Brazoria County, TX; Chambers County, TX; Fort Bend County, TX; Galveston County, TX; Harris County, TX; Liberty County, TX; Montgomery County, TX; San Jacinto County, TX; Waller County, TX

Population: 19,832 (1990); 23,590 (2000); 27,789 (2010); 29,781 (2015 projected); Race: 78.0% White, 9.3% Black, 0.5% Asian, 12.2% Other, 22.6% Hispanic of any race (2010); Density: 42.6 persons per square mile (2010); Average household size: 2.69 (2010); Median age: 37.0 (2010); Males per 100 females: 98.8 (2010).

Religion: Five largest groups: 20.7% Catholic Church, 9.4% Southern Baptist Convention, 7.5% The United Methodist Church, 5.8% Evangelical Lutheran Church in America, 3.6% Lutheran Church—Missouri Synod (2000).

Economy: Unemployment rate: 8.6% (June 2011); Total civilian labor force: 13,711 (June 2011); Leading industries: 36.4% manufacturing; 10.3% retail trade; 8.3% construction (2009); Farms: 2,112 totaling 333,928 acres (2007); Companies that employ 500 or more persons: 2 (2009); Companies that employ 100 to 499 persons: 9 (2009); Companies that employ less than 100 persons: 565 (2009); Black-owned businesses: n/a (2007); Hispanic-owned businesses: n/a (2007); Asian-owned businesses: n/a (2007); Women-owned businesses: 644 (2007); Retail sales per capita: $14,652 (2010). Single-family building permits issued: 18 (2010); Multi-family building permits issued: 3 (2010).
Income: Per capita income: $23,948 (2010); Median household income: $51,006 (2010); Average household income: $64,770 (2010); Percent of households with income of $100,000 or more: 16.7% (2010); Poverty rate: 11.0% (2009); Bankruptcy rate: 1.44% (2010).
Taxes: Total county taxes per capita: $357 (2007); County property taxes per capita: $286 (2007).
Education: Percent of population age 25 and over with: High school diploma (including GED) or higher: 81.2% (2010); Bachelor's degree or higher: 16.3% (2010); Master's degree or higher: 4.8% (2010).
Housing: Homeownership rate: 79.4% (2010); Median home value: $131,675 (2010); Median contract rent: $477 per month (2005-2009 5-year est.); Median year structure built: 1978 (2005-2009 5-year est.)
Health: Birth rate: 136.5 per 10,000 population (2009); Death rate: 94.7 per 10,000 population (2009); Age-adjusted cancer mortality rate: 135.3 deaths per 100,000 population (2007); Number of physicians: 3.3 per 10,000 population (2008); Hospital beds: 9.4 per 10,000 population (2007); Hospital admissions: 273.1 per 10,000 population (2007).
Elections: 2008 Presidential election results: 24.1% Obama, 75.0% McCain, 0.1% Nader
National and State Parks: Stephen F Austin State Park
Additional Information Contacts
Austin County Government . . . . (979) 865-5911
  http://www.austincounty.com/ips/cms
Bellville Chamber of Commerce . . . . (979) 865-3407
  http://www.bellville.com
City of Sealy . . . . (979) 885-3511
  http://www.ci.sealy.tx.us
Sealy Chamber of Commerce . . . . (979) 885-3222
  http://www.sealychamber.com

Austin County Communities

BELLVILLE (city). County seat. Covers a land area of 2.613 square miles and a water area of 0 square miles. Located at 29.94° N. Lat; 96.25° W. Long. Elevation is 292 feet.
History: Settled 1847, incorporated 1927.
Population: 3,634 (1990); 3,794 (2000); 4,546 (2010); 4,926 (2015 projected); Race: 82.4% White, 8.8% Black, 0.5% Asian, 8.4% Other, 19.4% Hispanic of any race (2010); Density: 1,739.8 persons per square mile (2010); Average household size: 2.57 (2010); Median age: 38.0 (2010); Males per 100 females: 97.0 (2010); Marriage status: 26.7% never married, 54.8% now married, 7.7% widowed, 10.8% divorced (2005-2009 5-year est.); Foreign born: 7.1% (2005-2009 5-year est.); Ancestry (includes multiple ancestries): 32.0% German, 7.7% Irish, 7.4% English, 7.2% Czech, 4.4% Dutch West Indian (2005-2009 5-year est.).
Economy: Single-family building permits issued: 4 (2010); Multi-family building permits issued: 3 (2010); Employment by occupation: 13.1% management, 16.8% professional, 25.6% services, 8.8% sales, 0.5% farming, 13.5% construction, 21.7% production (2005-2009 5-year est.).
Income: Per capita income: $22,575 (2010); Median household income: $47,783 (2010); Average household income: $59,064 (2010); Percent of households with income of $100,000 or more: 14.9% (2010); Poverty rate: 8.7% (2005-2009 5-year est.).
Taxes: Total city taxes per capita: $244 (2007); City property taxes per capita: $141 (2007).
Education: Percent of population age 25 and over with: High school diploma (including GED) or higher: 80.7% (2010); Bachelor's degree or higher: 20.9% (2010); Master's degree or higher: 4.9% (2010).
School District(s)
Bellville ISD (PK-12)
  2009-10 Enrollment: 2,167 . . . . (979) 865-3133
Housing: Homeownership rate: 71.9% (2010); Median home value: $132,364 (2010); Median contract rent: $427 per month (2005-2009 5-year est.); Median year structure built: 1975 (2005-2009 5-year est.).
Hospitals: Bellville General Hospital (32 beds)

Safety: Violent crime rate: 24.5 per 10,000 population; Property crime rate: 227.4 per 10,000 population (2009).
Transportation: Commute to work: 91.5% car, 0.0% public transportation, 0.8% walk, 5.3% work from home (2005-2009 5-year est.); Travel time to work: 46.2% less than 15 minutes, 31.0% 15 to 30 minutes, 4.8% 30 to 45 minutes, 7.5% 45 to 60 minutes, 10.4% 60 minutes or more (2005-2009 5-year est.)
Additional Information Contacts
Bellville Chamber of Commerce . . . . (979) 865-3407
  http://www.bellville.com

CAT SPRING (unincorporated postal area, zip code 78933). Covers a land area of 78.109 square miles and a water area of 0.195 square miles. Located at 29.77° N. Lat; 96.39° W. Long. Elevation is 308 feet.
Population: 766 (2000); Race: 95.4% White, 3.3% Black, 0.0% Asian, 1.3% Other, 2.0% Hispanic of any race (2000); Density: 9.8 persons per square mile (2000); Age: 34.1% under 18, 19.4% over 64 (2000); Marriage status: 13.5% never married, 72.2% now married, 9.7% widowed, 4.5% divorced (2000); Foreign born: 0.0% (2000); Ancestry (includes multiple ancestries): 42.6% German, 12.8% Irish, 10.2% American, 7.7% Czech (2000).
Economy: Employment by occupation: 18.1% management, 18.1% professional, 14.1% services, 21.3% sales, 0.0% farming, 14.6% construction, 13.8% production (2000).
Income: Per capita income: $18,193 (2000); Median household income: $45,417 (2000); Poverty rate: 179.1% (2000).
Education: Percent of population age 25 and over with: High school diploma (including GED) or higher: 85.1% (2000); Bachelor's degree or higher: 13.9% (2000).
Housing: Homeownership rate: 78.2% (2000); Median home value: $97,600 (2000); Median contract rent: $342 per month (2000); Median year structure built: 1977 (2000).
Transportation: Commute to work: 91.1% car, 0.0% public transportation, 0.0% walk, 8.1% work from home (2000); Travel time to work: 12.1% less than 15 minutes, 34.5% 15 to 30 minutes, 22.1% 30 to 45 minutes, 8.2% 45 to 60 minutes, 23.0% 60 minutes or more (2000)

INDUSTRY (city). Covers a land area of 1.045 square miles and a water area of 0.022 square miles. Located at 29.97° N. Lat; 96.50° W. Long. Elevation is 312 feet.
Population: 233 (1990); 304 (2000); 353 (2010); 373 (2015 projected); Race: 88.1% White, 5.1% Black, 0.6% Asian, 6.2% Other, 12.7% Hispanic of any race (2010); Density: 337.9 persons per square mile (2010); Average household size: 2.43 (2010); Median age: 41.2 (2010); Males per 100 females: 104.0 (2010); Marriage status: 32.7% never married, 58.3% now married, 4.9% widowed, 4.0% divorced (2005-2009 5-year est.); Foreign born: 5.0% (2005-2009 5-year est.); Ancestry (includes multiple ancestries): 26.6% German, 17.0% Czech, 9.6% English, 1.4% Scottish, 1.1% Italian (2005-2009 5-year est.).
Economy: Employment by occupation: 6.6% management, 14.8% professional, 13.9% services, 20.5% sales, 13.9% farming, 21.3% construction, 9.0% production (2005-2009 5-year est.).
Income: Per capita income: $26,797 (2010); Median household income: $54,167 (2010); Average household income: $67,362 (2010); Percent of households with income of $100,000 or more: 17.2% (2010); Poverty rate: 13.1% (2005-2009 5-year est.).
Taxes: Total city taxes per capita: $321 (2007); City property taxes per capita: $0 (2007).
Education: Percent of population age 25 and over with: High school diploma (including GED) or higher: 80.2% (2010); Bachelor's degree or higher: 18.5% (2010); Master's degree or higher: 7.7% (2010).
School District(s)
Bellville ISD (PK-12)
  2009-10 Enrollment: 2,167 . . . . (979) 865-3133
Housing: Homeownership rate: 83.4% (2010); Median home value: $134,375 (2010); Median contract rent: n/a per month (2005-2009 5-year est.); Median year structure built: 1972 (2005-2009 5-year est.).
Transportation: Commute to work: 100.0% car, 0.0% public transportation, 0.0% walk, 0.0% work from home (2005-2009 5-year est.); Travel time to work: 43.4% less than 15 minutes, 23.8% 15 to 30 minutes, 26.2% 30 to 45 minutes, 0.0% 45 to 60 minutes, 6.6% 60 minutes or more (2005-2009 5-year est.)

NEW ULM (unincorporated postal area, zip code 78950). Covers a land area of 80.305 square miles and a water area of 0.055 square miles. Located at 29.90° N. Lat; 96.49° W. Long. Elevation is 404 feet.
Population: 1,559 (2000); Race: 88.4% White, 8.6% Black, 0.0% Asian, 4.0% Other, 4.0% Hispanic of any race (2000); Density: 19.4 persons per square mile (2000); Age: 20.2% under 18, 19.6% over 64 (2000); Marriage status: 13.3% never married, 72.3% now married, 9.1% widowed, 5.3% divorced (2000); Foreign born: 3.7% (2000); Ancestry (includes multiple ancestries): 42.4% German, 8.9% Czech, 5.7% English, 4.8% American (2000).
Economy: Employment by occupation: 21.8% management, 14.3% professional, 7.1% services, 20.2% sales, 2.5% farming, 11.3% construction, 22.7% production (2000).
Income: Per capita income: $25,009 (2000); Median household income: $40,938 (2000); Poverty rate: 179.1% (2000).
Education: Percent of population age 25 and over with: High school diploma (including GED) or higher: 74.4% (2000); Bachelor's degree or higher: 18.7% (2000).
Housing: Homeownership rate: 88.9% (2000); Median home value: $84,500 (2000); Median contract rent: $320 per month (2000); Median year structure built: 1978 (2000).
Transportation: Commute to work: 87.5% car, 0.0% public transportation, 1.9% walk, 9.8% work from home (2000); Travel time to work: 20.9% less than 15 minutes, 24.7% 15 to 30 minutes, 28.5% 30 to 45 minutes, 4.5% 45 to 60 minutes, 21.5% 60 minutes or more (2000)

SAN FELIPE (town). Covers a land area of 8.371 square miles and a water area of 0.273 square miles. Located at 29.79° N. Lat; 96.10° W. Long. Elevation is 154 feet.
History: San Felipe was established in 1823 as the headquarters of the Austin colony, and was the first unofficial capital of American settlement in what was then a Mexican province. As such, it was the scene of many "firsts" in Texas history, including the first protest against Mexican rule at a meeting in 1832.
Population: 725 (1990); 868 (2000); 973 (2010); 1,021 (2015 projected); Race: 70.6% White, 19.6% Black, 0.2% Asian, 9.6% Other, 24.3% Hispanic of any race (2010); Density: 116.2 persons per square mile (2010); Average household size: 2.77 (2010); Median age: 34.9 (2010); Males per 100 females: 101.4 (2010); Marriage status: 24.9% never married, 57.5% now married, 9.7% widowed, 8.0% divorced (2005-2009 5-year est.); Foreign born: 6.3% (2005-2009 5-year est.); Ancestry (includes multiple ancestries): 32.3% German, 13.9% Czech, 9.3% Irish, 8.4% English, 6.5% American (2005-2009 5-year est.).
Economy: Single-family building permits issued: 1 (2010); Multi-family building permits issued: 0 (2010); Employment by occupation: 15.4% management, 22.5% professional, 8.4% services, 20.6% sales, 1.4% farming, 8.4% construction, 23.3% production (2005-2009 5-year est.).
Income: Per capita income: $25,213 (2010); Median household income: $57,292 (2010); Average household income: $69,779 (2010); Percent of households with income of $100,000 or more: 21.4% (2010); Poverty rate: 9.7% (2005-2009 5-year est.).
Taxes: Total city taxes per capita: $284 (2007); City property taxes per capita: $204 (2007).
Education: Percent of population age 25 and over with: High school diploma (including GED) or higher: 80.1% (2010); Bachelor's degree or higher: 8.3% (2010); Master's degree or higher: 2.7% (2010).
Housing: Homeownership rate: 81.8% (2010); Median home value: $87,941 (2010); Median contract rent: $442 per month (2005-2009 5-year est.); Median year structure built: 1974 (2005-2009 5-year est.).
Safety: Violent crime rate: 40.6 per 10,000 population; Property crime rate: 121.8 per 10,000 population (2009).
Transportation: Commute to work: 90.8% car, 0.0% public transportation, 2.6% walk, 1.4% work from home (2005-2009 5-year est.); Travel time to work: 31.9% less than 15 minutes, 35.7% 15 to 30 minutes, 14.0% 30 to 45 minutes, 2.9% 45 to 60 minutes, 15.5% 60 minutes or more (2005-2009 5-year est.)

SEALY (city). Covers a land area of 6.912 square miles and a water area of 0.017 square miles. Located at 29.77° N. Lat; 96.15° W. Long. Elevation is 200 feet.
History: Incorporated after 1940.
Population: 4,835 (1990); 5,248 (2000); 6,276 (2010); 6,682 (2015 projected); Race: 70.1% White, 10.4% Black, 0.6% Asian, 18.9% Other, 34.8% Hispanic of any race (2010); Density: 908.0 persons per square mile

(2010); Average household size: 2.76 (2010); Median age: 33.7 (2010); Males per 100 females: 96.8 (2010); Marriage status: 29.3% never married, 53.2% now married, 5.8% widowed, 11.6% divorced (2005-2009 5-year est.); Foreign born: 14.2% (2005-2009 5-year est.); Ancestry (includes multiple ancestries): 23.1% German, 7.3% Czech, 5.5% Irish, 3.7% English, 2.9% French (2005-2009 5-year est.).
Economy: Single-family building permits issued: 10 (2010); Multi-family building permits issued: 0 (2010); Employment by occupation: 8.5% management, 15.0% professional, 21.4% services, 24.9% sales, 0.5% farming, 9.1% construction, 20.6% production (2005-2009 5-year est.).
Income: Per capita income: $23,639 (2010); Median household income: $49,953 (2010); Average household income: $65,026 (2010); Percent of households with income of $100,000 or more: 15.1% (2010); Poverty rate: 7.4% (2005-2009 5-year est.).
Taxes: Total city taxes per capita: $509 (2007); City property taxes per capita: $172 (2007).
Education: Percent of population age 25 and over with: High school diploma (including GED) or higher: 79.9% (2010); Bachelor's degree or higher: 12.6% (2010); Master's degree or higher: 3.2% (2010).
School District(s)
Sealy ISD (PK-12)
    2009-10 Enrollment: 2,612 . . . . (979) 885-3516
Housing: Homeownership rate: 72.6% (2010); Median home value: $117,881 (2010); Median contract rent: $513 per month (2005-2009 5-year est.); Median year structure built: 1975 (2005-2009 5-year est.).
Safety: Violent crime rate: 65.8 per 10,000 population; Property crime rate: 227.2 per 10,000 population (2009).
Newspapers: The Sealy News (Local news; Circulation 5,600)
Transportation: Commute to work: 88.2% car, 0.4% public transportation, 4.4% walk, 5.8% work from home (2005-2009 5-year est.); Travel time to work: 46.5% less than 15 minutes, 22.2% 15 to 30 minutes, 17.0% 30 to 45 minutes, 4.6% 45 to 60 minutes, 9.6% 60 minutes or more (2005-2009 5-year est.)
Additional Information Contacts
City of Sealy . . . . (979) 885-3511
    http://www.ci.sealy.tx.us
Sealy Chamber of Commerce . . . . (979) 885-3222
    http://www.sealychamber.com

WALLIS (city). Covers a land area of 1.527 square miles and a water area of 0.012 square miles. Located at 29.63° N. Lat; 96.06° W. Long. Elevation is 128 feet.
Population: 1,072 (1990); 1,172 (2000); 1,361 (2010); 1,455 (2015 projected); Race: 70.0% White, 12.9% Black, 0.0% Asian, 17.1% Other, 32.2% Hispanic of any race (2010); Density: 891.5 persons per square mile (2010); Average household size: 2.86 (2010); Median age: 34.6 (2010); Males per 100 females: 97.2 (2010); Marriage status: 21.1% never married, 50.1% now married, 11.4% widowed, 17.3% divorced (2005-2009 5-year est.); Foreign born: 9.5% (2005-2009 5-year est.); Ancestry (includes multiple ancestries): 18.1% German, 15.6% Czech, 11.0% Irish, 5.3% Scotch-Irish, 3.3% Polish (2005-2009 5-year est.).
Economy: Single-family building permits issued: 3 (2010); Multi-family building permits issued: 0 (2010); Employment by occupation: 15.7% management, 23.1% professional, 9.8% services, 16.9% sales, 0.0% farming, 9.5% construction, 25.0% production (2005-2009 5-year est.).
Income: Per capita income: $17,020 (2010); Median household income: $38,952 (2010); Average household income: $48,174 (2010); Percent of households with income of $100,000 or more: 6.5% (2010); Poverty rate: 7.7% (2005-2009 5-year est.).
Taxes: Total city taxes per capita: $257 (2007); City property taxes per capita: $165 (2007).
Education: Percent of population age 25 and over with: High school diploma (including GED) or higher: 75.5% (2010); Bachelor's degree or higher: 7.7% (2010); Master's degree or higher: 2.9% (2010).
School District(s)
Brazos ISD (PK-12)
    2009-10 Enrollment: 822 . . . . (979) 478-6551
Paradigm Accelerated Charter School (07-12)
    2009-10 Enrollment: 219 . . . . (254) 445-4844
Housing: Homeownership rate: 82.5% (2010); Median home value: $84,286 (2010); Median contract rent: $484 per month (2005-2009 5-year est.); Median year structure built: 1965 (2005-2009 5-year est.).
Safety: Violent crime rate: 37.2 per 10,000 population; Property crime rate: 126.6 per 10,000 population (2009).
Newspapers: Wallis News-Review (Local news; Circulation 1,300)

Transportation: Commute to work: 94.5% car, 0.0% public transportation, 1.5% walk, 1.0% work from home (2005-2009 5-year est.); Travel time to work: 27.4% less than 15 minutes, 34.7% 15 to 30 minutes, 26.9% 30 to 45 minutes, 3.3% 45 to 60 minutes, 7.8% 60 minutes or more (2005-2009 5-year est.)

Bailey County

Located in northwest Texas; bounded on the west by New Mexico. Covers a land area of 826.69 square miles, a water area of 0.68 square miles, and is located in the Central Time Zone at 34.11° N. Lat., 102.81° W. Long. The county was founded in 1876. County seat is Muleshoe.

Weather Station: Muleshoe 1   Elevation: 3,825 feet

	Jan	Feb	Mar	Apr	May	Jun	Jul	Aug	Sep	Oct	Nov	Dec
High	53	58	65	73	82	90	92	90	83	74	62	53
Low	21	24	30	38	49	59	63	62	54	41	29	21
Precip	0.5	0.4	0.9	1.0	2.1	2.7	2.1	3.1	2.5	1.7	0.8	0.7
Snow	1.7	1.2	0.7	0.3	0.0	0.0	0.0	0.0	0.0	tr	1.1	2.8

High and Low temperatures in degrees Fahrenheit; Precipitation and Snow in inches

Weather Station: Muleshoe Natl Wdlf Ref   Elevation: 3,740 feet

	Jan	Feb	Mar	Apr	May	Jun	Jul	Aug	Sep	Oct	Nov	Dec
High	54	59	66	74	83	91	93	91	84	75	63	54
Low	22	25	32	39	50	59	62	61	54	42	31	23
Precip	0.5	0.4	0.9	0.8	2.3	2.7	2.0	2.8	2.6	1.7	0.7	0.7
Snow	1.0	0.7	0.2	0.2	0.0	0.0	0.0	0.0	0.0	tr	0.5	1.7

High and Low temperatures in degrees Fahrenheit; Precipitation and Snow in inches

Population: 7,064 (1990); 6,594 (2000); 6,174 (2010); 5,957 (2015 projected); Race: 60.6% White, 1.6% Black, 0.1% Asian, 37.7% Other, 55.9% Hispanic of any race (2010); Density: 7.5 persons per square mile (2010); Average household size: 2.74 (2010); Median age: 34.4 (2010); Males per 100 females: 97.7 (2010).
Religion: Five largest groups: 38.8% Southern Baptist Convention, 23.5% Catholic Church, 12.4% The United Methodist Church, 6.2% Churches of Christ, 2.7% Assemblies of God (2000).
Economy: Unemployment rate: 7.9% (June 2011); Total civilian labor force: 3,337 (June 2011); Leading industries: 18.0% retail trade; 15.9% accommodation & food services; 11.3% wholesale trade (2009); Farms: 564 totaling 476,176 acres (2007); Companies that employ 500 or more persons: 0 (2009); Companies that employ 100 to 499 persons: 2 (2009); Companies that employ less than 100 persons: 165 (2009); Black-owned businesses: n/a (2007); Hispanic-owned businesses: n/a (2007); Asian-owned businesses: n/a (2007); Women-owned businesses: n/a (2007); Retail sales per capita: $8,955 (2010). Single-family building permits issued: 0 (2010); Multi-family building permits issued: 0 (2010).
Income: Per capita income: $16,000 (2010); Median household income: $33,904 (2010); Average household income: $43,887 (2010); Percent of households with income of $100,000 or more: 7.2% (2010); Poverty rate: 17.9% (2009); Bankruptcy rate: 1.39% (2010).
Taxes: Total county taxes per capita: $346 (2007); County property taxes per capita: $265 (2007).
Education: Percent of population age 25 and over with: High school diploma (including GED) or higher: 67.2% (2010); Bachelor's degree or higher: 10.5% (2010); Master's degree or higher: 2.9% (2010).
Housing: Homeownership rate: 69.4% (2010); Median home value: $42,305 (2010); Median contract rent: $244 per month (2005-2009 5-year est.); Median year structure built: 1967 (2005-2009 5-year est.)
Health: Birth rate: 207.2 per 10,000 population (2009); Death rate: 70.1 per 10,000 population (2009); Age-adjusted cancer mortality rate: 180.6 (Unreliable) deaths per 100,000 population (2007); Number of physicians: 14.3 per 10,000 population (2008); Hospital beds: 39.8 per 10,000 population (2007); Hospital admissions: 1,491.6 per 10,000 population (2007).
Elections: 2008 Presidential election results: 29.4% Obama, 69.9% McCain, 0.0% Nader
National and State Parks: Muleshoe National Wildlife Refuge
Additional Information Contacts
Bailey County Government . . . . (806) 272-3077
   http://www.co.bailey.tx.us/ips/cms
City of Muleshoe . . . . (806) 272-4528
   http://www.city-of-muleshoe.com
Muleshoe Chamber of Commerce . . . . (806) 272-4248
   http://muleshoechamber.com

Bailey County Communities

BULA (unincorporated postal area, zip code 79320). Covers a land area of 56.778 square miles and a water area of 0 square miles. Located at 33.86° N. Lat; 102.67° W. Long. Elevation is 3,793 feet.
Population: 92 (2000); Race: 55.8% White, 0.0% Black, 0.0% Asian, 44.2% Other, 51.9% Hispanic of any race (2000); Density: 1.6 persons per square mile (2000); Age: 37.5% under 18, 12.5% over 64 (2000); Marriage status: 38.2% never married, 56.6% now married, 5.3% widowed, 0.0% divorced (2000); Foreign born: 11.5% (2000); Ancestry (includes multiple ancestries): 7.7% German, 4.8% Irish, 3.8% English, 2.9% American (2000).
Economy: Employment by occupation: 8.6% management, 17.1% professional, 5.7% services, 25.7% sales, 28.6% farming, 14.3% construction, 0.0% production (2000).
Income: Per capita income: $10,367 (2000); Median household income: $24,688 (2000); Poverty rate: 179.1% (2000).
Education: Percent of population age 25 and over with: High school diploma (including GED) or higher: 52.0% (2000); Bachelor's degree or higher: 12.0% (2000).
Housing: Homeownership rate: 36.4% (2000); Median home value: $15,000 (2000); Median contract rent: $225 per month (2000); Median year structure built: 1956 (2000).
Transportation: Commute to work: 100.0% car, 0.0% public transportation, 0.0% walk, 0.0% work from home (2000); Travel time to work: 20.0% less than 15 minutes, 54.3% 15 to 30 minutes, 20.0% 30 to 45 minutes, 0.0% 45 to 60 minutes, 5.7% 60 minutes or more (2000)

ENOCHS (unincorporated postal area, zip code 79324). Covers a land area of 81.112 square miles and a water area of 0.097 square miles. Located at 33.89° N. Lat; 102.78° W. Long. Elevation is 3,789 feet.
Population: 86 (2000); Race: 90.2% White, 0.0% Black, 0.0% Asian, 9.8% Other, 19.6% Hispanic of any race (2000); Density: 1.1 persons per square mile (2000); Age: 28.3% under 18, 20.7% over 64 (2000); Marriage status: 15.1% never married, 80.8% now married, 0.0% widowed, 4.1% divorced (2000); Foreign born: 7.6% (2000); Ancestry (includes multiple ancestries): 7.6% English, 6.5% Irish, 6.5% American, 5.4% German (2000).
Economy: Employment by occupation: 16.7% management, 30.0% professional, 0.0% services, 16.7% sales, 33.3% farming, 0.0% construction, 3.3% production (2000).
Income: Per capita income: $14,138 (2000); Median household income: $21,875 (2000); Poverty rate: 179.1% (2000).
Education: Percent of population age 25 and over with: High school diploma (including GED) or higher: 72.6% (2000); Bachelor's degree or higher: 17.7% (2000).
Housing: Homeownership rate: 60.0% (2000); Median home value: $23,100 (2000); Median contract rent: $463 per month (2000); Median year structure built: 1965 (2000).
Transportation: Commute to work: 90.0% car, 3.3% public transportation, 0.0% walk, 6.7% work from home (2000); Travel time to work: 53.6% less than 15 minutes, 32.1% 15 to 30 minutes, 0.0% 30 to 45 minutes, 0.0% 45 to 60 minutes, 14.3% 60 minutes or more (2000)

MAPLE (unincorporated postal area, zip code 79344). Covers a land area of 67.097 square miles and a water area of 0 square miles. Located at 33.85° N. Lat; 102.95° W. Long. Elevation is 3,875 feet.
Population: 182 (2000); Race: 91.1% White, 0.0% Black, 0.0% Asian, 8.9% Other, 12.0% Hispanic of any race (2000); Density: 2.7 persons per square mile (2000); Age: 24.7% under 18, 12.0% over 64 (2000); Marriage status: 21.7% never married, 63.3% now married, 5.0% widowed, 10.0% divorced (2000); Foreign born: 4.4% (2000); Ancestry (includes multiple ancestries): 25.9% English, 14.6% American, 8.9% Irish, 8.2% German (2000).
Economy: Employment by occupation: 26.6% management, 26.6% professional, 9.4% services, 10.9% sales, 12.5% farming, 6.3% construction, 7.8% production (2000).
Income: Per capita income: $18,596 (2000); Median household income: $48,438 (2000); Poverty rate: 179.1% (2000).
Education: Percent of population age 25 and over with: High school diploma (including GED) or higher: 77.1% (2000); Bachelor's degree or higher: 17.7% (2000).
Housing: Homeownership rate: 55.0% (2000); Median home value: $47,000 (2000); Median contract rent: $142 per month (2000); Median year structure built: 1961 (2000).

Transportation: Commute to work: 85.5% car, 0.0% public transportation, 12.9% walk, 1.6% work from home (2000); Travel time to work: 60.7% less than 15 minutes, 16.4% 15 to 30 minutes, 6.6% 30 to 45 minutes, 0.0% 45 to 60 minutes, 16.4% 60 minutes or more (2000)

MULESHOE (city). County seat. Covers a land area of 3.422 square miles and a water area of 0 square miles. Located at 34.22° N. Lat; 102.72° W. Long. Elevation is 3,793 feet.

History: Muleshoe grew up on the site of the Muleshoe Ranch, for which it was named. Irrigation enabled the area to produce cotton, grain sorghum, and alfalfa.

Population: 4,571 (1990); 4,530 (2000); 4,169 (2010); 3,986 (2015 projected); Race: 58.2% White, 1.7% Black, 0.2% Asian, 40.0% Other, 61.6% Hispanic of any race (2010); Density: 1,218.4 persons per square mile (2010); Average household size: 2.74 (2010); Median age: 32.9 (2010); Males per 100 females: 95.5 (2010); Marriage status: 17.8% never married, 62.5% now married, 8.7% widowed, 11.0% divorced (2005-2009 5-year est.); Foreign born: 17.4% (2005-2009 5-year est.); Ancestry (includes multiple ancestries): 5.8% American, 5.4% English, 4.9% Irish, 4.4% German, 2.8% African (2005-2009 5-year est.).

Economy: Single-family building permits issued: 0 (2010); Multi-family building permits issued: 0 (2010); Employment by occupation: 14.1% management, 11.3% professional, 22.3% services, 20.5% sales, 10.1% farming, 5.1% construction, 16.8% production (2005-2009 5-year est.).

Income: Per capita income: $15,157 (2010); Median household income: $30,514 (2010); Average household income: $41,657 (2010); Percent of households with income of $100,000 or more: 6.6% (2010); Poverty rate: 18.4% (2005-2009 5-year est.).

Taxes: Total city taxes per capita: $224 (2007); City property taxes per capita: $149 (2007).

Education: Percent of population age 25 and over with: High school diploma (including GED) or higher: 64.3% (2010); Bachelor's degree or higher: 10.4% (2010); Master's degree or higher: 3.1% (2010).

School District(s)
Muleshoe ISD (PK-12)
    2009-10 Enrollment: 1,446 . . . . (806) 272-7404

Housing: Homeownership rate: 70.3% (2010); Median home value: $37,994 (2010); Median contract rent: $241 per month (2005-2009 5-year est.); Median year structure built: 1969 (2005-2009 5-year est.).

Hospitals: Muleshoe Area Medical Center (31 beds)

Safety: Violent crime rate: 35.4 per 10,000 population; Property crime rate: 262.2 per 10,000 population (2009).

Newspapers: Muleshoe & Bailey County Journal (Community news; Circulation 2,000)

Transportation: Commute to work: 94.1% car, 0.0% public transportation, 0.0% walk, 3.1% work from home (2005-2009 5-year est.); Travel time to work: 62.1% less than 15 minutes, 18.7% 15 to 30 minutes, 16.7% 30 to 45 minutes, 0.0% 45 to 60 minutes, 2.4% 60 minutes or more (2005-2009 5-year est.)

Additional Information Contacts
City of Muleshoe . . . . (806) 272-4528
    http://www.city-of-muleshoe.com
Muleshoe Chamber of Commerce . . . . (806) 272-4248
    http://muleshoechamber.com

Bandera County

Located in southwestern Texas, on the Edwards Plateau; includes part of Medina Lake. Covers a land area of 791.73 square miles, a water area of 5.81 square miles, and is located in the Central Time Zone at 29.72° N. Lat; 99.11° W. Long. The county was founded in 1856. County seat is Bandera.

Bandera County is part of the San Antonio-New Braunfels, TX Metropolitan Statistical Area. The entire metro area includes: Atascosa County, TX; Bandera County, TX; Bexar County, TX; Comal County, TX; Guadalupe County, TX; Kendall County, TX; Medina County, TX; Wilson County, TX

Weather Station: Medina 2 W										Elevation: 1,705 feet	
	Jan	Feb	Mar	Apr	May	Jun	Jul	Aug	Sep	Oct	Nov	Dec
High	63	67	73	80	86	92	94	95	90	81	71	63
Low	34	38	45	51	62	68	69	69	64	54	44	36
Precip	1.9	1.8	3.4	2.3	4.4	4.4	2.9	2.2	3.7	4.3	2.5	2.2
Snow	1.0	0.1	tr	0.0	0.0	0.0	0.0	0.0	0.0	tr	0.1	tr

High and Low temperatures in degrees Fahrenheit; Precipitation and Snow in inches

Population: 10,562 (1990); 17,645 (2000); 20,984 (2010); 22,570 (2015 projected); Race: 92.3% White, 1.0% Black, 0.4% Asian, 6.3% Other, 17.2% Hispanic of any race (2010); Density: 26.5 persons per square mile (2010); Average household size: 2.51 (2010); Median age: 41.8 (2010); Males per 100 females: 98.1 (2010).

Religion: Five largest groups: 17.4% Catholic Church, 11.1% Southern Baptist Convention, 5.6% The United Methodist Church, 1.9% Churches of Christ, 1.8% Evangelical Lutheran Church in America (2000).

Economy: Unemployment rate: 7.1% (June 2011); Total civilian labor force: 10,165 (June 2011); Leading industries: 26.0% accommodation & food services; 17.3% retail trade; 10.3% health care and social assistance (2009); Farms: 972 totaling 329,416 acres (2007); Companies that employ 500 or more persons: 0 (2009); Companies that employ 100 to 499 persons: 0 (2009); Companies that employ less than 100 persons: 374 (2009); Black-owned businesses: n/a (2007); Hispanic-owned businesses: n/a (2007); Asian-owned businesses: n/a (2007); Women-owned businesses: n/a (2007); Retail sales per capita: $5,590 (2010). Single-family building permits issued: 0 (2010); Multi-family building permits issued: 0 (2010).

Income: Per capita income: $23,795 (2010); Median household income: $47,370 (2010); Average household income: $60,093 (2010); Percent of households with income of $100,000 or more: 14.8% (2010); Poverty rate: 14.2% (2009); Bankruptcy rate: 1.77% (2010).

Taxes: Total county taxes per capita: $444 (2007); County property taxes per capita: $336 (2007).

Education: Percent of population age 25 and over with: High school diploma (including GED) or higher: 88.5% (2010); Bachelor's degree or higher: 25.2% (2010); Master's degree or higher: 6.6% (2010).

Housing: Homeownership rate: 77.8% (2010); Median home value: $140,287 (2010); Median contract rent: $454 per month (2005-2009 5-year est.); Median year structure built: 1982 (2005-2009 5-year est.)

Health: Birth rate: 98.7 per 10,000 population (2009); Death rate: 91.0 per 10,000 population (2009); Age-adjusted cancer mortality rate: 198.8 deaths per 100,000 population (2007); Number of physicians: 6.3 per 10,000 population (2008); Hospital beds: 0.0 per 10,000 population (2007); Hospital admissions: 0.0 per 10,000 population (2007).

Elections: 2008 Presidential election results: 24.2% Obama, 74.6% McCain, 0.1% Nader

National and State Parks: Avalon State Park

Additional Information Contacts
Bandera County Government . . . . (830) 796-3781
    http://www.banderacounty.org
Bandera County Chamber of Commerce. . . . . (830) 796-3280
    http://www.banderatex.com

Bandera County Communities

BANDERA (city). County seat. Covers a land area of 1.167 square miles and a water area of 0 square miles. Located at 29.72° N. Lat; 99.07° W. Long. Elevation is 1,243 feet.

History: Bandera was founded in the 1850's as a shingle camp. Later, many people of Polish descent moved to this location on the Medina River.

Population: 903 (1990); 957 (2000); 1,032 (2010); 1,069 (2015 projected); Race: 95.2% White, 0.3% Black, 0.0% Asian, 4.6% Other, 21.2% Hispanic of any race (2010); Density: 884.4 persons per square mile (2010); Average household size: 2.14 (2010); Median age: 44.2 (2010); Males per 100 females: 93.6 (2010); Marriage status: 17.3% never married, 48.3% now married, 12.0% widowed, 22.4% divorced (2005-2009 5-year est.); Foreign born: 3.9% (2005-2009 5-year est.); Ancestry (includes multiple ancestries): 27.4% German, 15.1% Italian, 10.8% Irish, 8.9% English, 7.0% French (2005-2009 5-year est.).

Economy: Single-family building permits issued: 0 (2010); Multi-family building permits issued: 0 (2010); Employment by occupation: 15.0% management, 18.5% professional, 38.3% services, 15.9% sales, 0.0% farming, 7.0% construction, 5.2% production (2005-2009 5-year est.).

Income: Per capita income: $24,837 (2010); Median household income: $38,918 (2010); Average household income: $54,057 (2010); Percent of households with income of $100,000 or more: 10.7% (2010); Poverty rate: 20.7% (2005-2009 5-year est.).

Taxes: Total city taxes per capita: $555 (2007); City property taxes per capita: $198 (2007).

Education: Percent of population age 25 and over with: High school diploma (including GED) or higher: 84.2% (2010); Bachelor's degree or higher: 22.2% (2010); Master's degree or higher: 8.2% (2010).

Bandera ISD (PK-12)
  2009-10 Enrollment: 2,539 . . . . (830) 796-3313
Housing: Homeownership rate: 63.5% (2010); Median home value: $114,899 (2010); Median contract rent: $521 per month (2005-2009 5-year est.); Median year structure built: 1972 (2005-2009 5-year est.).
Newspapers: Bandera Bulletin (Community news; Circulation 5,500)
Transportation: Commute to work: 89.6% car, 0.0% public transportation, 5.4% walk, 4.4% work from home (2005-2009 5-year est.); Travel time to work: 65.9% less than 15 minutes, 8.9% 15 to 30 minutes, 6.6% 30 to 45 minutes, 4.5% 45 to 60 minutes, 14.1% 60 minutes or more (2005-2009 5-year est.)
Additional Information Contacts
Bandera County Chamber of Commerce . . . . (830) 796-3280
  http://www.banderatex.com

LAKEHILLS (CDP). Aka North Lake. Covers a land area of 30.294 square miles and a water area of 4.079 square miles. Located at 29.59° N. Lat; 98.94° W. Long. Elevation is 1,348 feet.
Population: 2,578 (1990); 4,668 (2000); 5,813 (2010); 6,355 (2015 projected); Race: 90.5% White, 1.1% Black, 0.4% Asian, 8.0% Other, 18.3% Hispanic of any race (2010); Density: 191.9 persons per square mile (2010); Average household size: 2.54 (2010); Median age: 41.6 (2010); Males per 100 females: 100.4 (2010); Marriage status: 20.9% never married, 57.8% now married, 3.5% widowed, 17.8% divorced (2005-2009 5-year est.); Foreign born: 4.0% (2005-2009 5-year est.); Ancestry (includes multiple ancestries): 22.9% German, 19.1% Irish, 16.4% English, 7.6% Scottish, 7.5% French (2005-2009 5-year est.).
Economy: Employment by occupation: 20.3% management, 18.0% professional, 18.2% services, 24.9% sales, 0.0% farming, 14.6% construction, 3.9% production (2005-2009 5-year est.).
Income: Per capita income: $22,754 (2010); Median household income: $47,813 (2010); Average household income: $57,822 (2010); Percent of households with income of $100,000 or more: 13.2% (2010); Poverty rate: 11.2% (2005-2009 5-year est.).
Education: Percent of population age 25 and over with: High school diploma (including GED) or higher: 89.8% (2010); Bachelor's degree or higher: 20.4% (2010); Master's degree or higher: 4.3% (2010).
Housing: Homeownership rate: 80.3% (2010); Median home value: $133,559 (2010); Median contract rent: $386 per month (2005-2009 5-year est.); Median year structure built: 1983 (2005-2009 5-year est.).
Transportation: Commute to work: 92.9% car, 0.0% public transportation, 0.7% walk, 6.4% work from home (2005-2009 5-year est.); Travel time to work: 18.8% less than 15 minutes, 13.5% 15 to 30 minutes, 19.7% 30 to 45 minutes, 31.3% 45 to 60 minutes, 16.7% 60 minutes or more (2005-2009 5-year est.)

PIPE CREEK (unincorporated postal area, zip code 78063). Aka Pipecreek. Covers a land area of 111.851 square miles and a water area of 0.012 square miles. Located at 29.64° N. Lat; 98.93° W. Long. Elevation is 1,362 feet.
Population: 7,851 (2000); Race: 93.7% White, 0.2% Black, 0.2% Asian, 5.9% Other, 14.0% Hispanic of any race (2000); Density: 70.2 persons per square mile (2000); Age: 24.8% under 18, 12.1% over 64 (2000); Marriage status: 15.9% never married, 67.2% now married, 5.3% widowed, 11.6% divorced (2000); Foreign born: 3.7% (2000); Ancestry (includes multiple ancestries): 23.7% German, 12.4% Irish, 12.3% English, 7.9% American (2000).
Economy: Employment by occupation: 16.4% management, 15.8% professional, 14.0% services, 27.9% sales, 1.1% farming, 15.7% construction, 9.1% production (2000).
Income: Per capita income: $20,487 (2000); Median household income: $46,012 (2000); Poverty rate: 179.1% (2000).
Education: Percent of population age 25 and over with: High school diploma (including GED) or higher: 87.8% (2000); Bachelor's degree or higher: 16.9% (2000).
School District(s)
Bandera ISD (PK-12)
  2009-10 Enrollment: 2,539 . . . . (830) 796-3313
Housing: Homeownership rate: 85.4% (2000); Median home value: $100,600 (2000); Median contract rent: $426 per month (2000); Median year structure built: 1985 (2000).
Transportation: Commute to work: 92.7% car, 0.1% public transportation, 2.1% walk, 4.2% work from home (2000); Travel time to work: 14.6% less

than 15 minutes, 15.9% 15 to 30 minutes, 23.5% 30 to 45 minutes, 32.0% 45 to 60 minutes, 14.0% 60 minutes or more (2000)

TARPLEY (unincorporated postal area, zip code 78883). Covers a land area of 40.360 square miles and a water area of 0.055 square miles. Located at 29.67° N. Lat; 99.34° W. Long. Elevation is 1,322 feet.
Population: 261 (2000); Race: 96.1% White, 0.0% Black, 0.0% Asian, 3.9% Other, 5.4% Hispanic of any race (2000); Density: 6.5 persons per square mile (2000); Age: 21.4% under 18, 20.2% over 64 (2000); Marriage status: 6.7% never married, 79.8% now married, 5.8% widowed, 7.7% divorced (2000); Foreign born: 0.8% (2000); Ancestry (includes multiple ancestries): 30.4% German, 14.0% English, 10.1% Irish, 8.9% French (2000).
Economy: Employment by occupation: 28.6% management, 11.6% professional, 3.6% services, 33.0% sales, 7.1% farming, 14.3% construction, 1.8% production (2000).
Income: Per capita income: $21,383 (2000); Median household income: $45,341 (2000); Poverty rate: 179.1% (2000).
Education: Percent of population age 25 and over with: High school diploma (including GED) or higher: 89.4% (2000); Bachelor's degree or higher: 41.7% (2000).
Housing: Homeownership rate: 89.4% (2000); Median home value: $98,800 (2000); Median contract rent: $350 per month (2000); Median year structure built: 1980 (2000).
Transportation: Commute to work: 84.8% car, 0.0% public transportation, 0.0% walk, 9.8% work from home (2000); Travel time to work: 8.9% less than 15 minutes, 28.7% 15 to 30 minutes, 16.8% 30 to 45 minutes, 5.0% 45 to 60 minutes, 40.6% 60 minutes or more (2000)

VANDERPOOL (unincorporated postal area, zip code 78885). Covers a land area of 96.839 square miles and a water area of 0.010 square miles. Located at 29.78° N. Lat; 99.55° W. Long. Elevation is 1,578 feet.
Population: 203 (2000); Race: 100.0% White, 0.0% Black, 0.0% Asian, 0.0% Other, 2.4% Hispanic of any race (2000); Density: 2.1 persons per square mile (2000); Age: 16.0% under 18, 22.8% over 64 (2000); Marriage status: 7.4% never married, 78.4% now married, 10.8% widowed, 3.4% divorced (2000); Foreign born: 1.0% (2000); Ancestry (includes multiple ancestries): 32.5% English, 23.8% German, 19.9% Irish, 16.0% French, 9.2% American (2000).
Economy: Employment by occupation: 31.6% management, 5.1% professional, 17.7% services, 22.8% sales, 7.6% farming, 11.4% construction, 3.8% production (2000).
Income: Per capita income: $25,634 (2000); Median household income: $40,536 (2000); Poverty rate: 179.1% (2000).
Education: Percent of population age 25 and over with: High school diploma (including GED) or higher: 86.4% (2000); Bachelor's degree or higher: 23.7% (2000).
Housing: Homeownership rate: 78.4% (2000); Median home value: $85,000 (2000); Median contract rent: $250 per month (2000); Median year structure built: 1984 (2000).
Transportation: Commute to work: 62.3% car, 0.0% public transportation, 5.2% walk, 27.3% work from home (2000); Travel time to work: 39.3% less than 15 minutes, 26.8% 15 to 30 minutes, 10.7% 30 to 45 minutes, 5.4% 45 to 60 minutes, 17.9% 60 minutes or more (2000)

Bastrop County

Located in south central Texas; drained by the Colorado River. Covers a land area of 888.35 square miles, a water area of 7.57 square miles, and is located in the Central Time Zone at 30.12° N. Lat., 97.29° W. Long. The county was founded in 1836. County seat is Bastrop.

Bastrop County is part of the Austin-Round Rock-San Marcos, TX Metropolitan Statistical Area. The entire metro area includes: Bastrop County, TX; Caldwell County, TX; Hays County, TX; Travis County, TX; Williamson County, TX

Weather Station: Elgin										Elevation: 579 feet		
	Jan	Feb	Mar	Apr	May	Jun	Jul	Aug	Sep	Oct	Nov	Dec
High	62	66	73	80	86	92	96	96	90	82	72	63
Low	41	44	51	57	66	71	73	73	68	59	50	42
Precip	2.4	2.2	2.8	2.1	4.4	3.9	1.9	2.0	2.7	4.1	3.2	2.5
Snow	0.1	tr	tr	0.0	0.0	0.0	0.0	0.0	0.0	0.0	0.0	0.0

High and Low temperatures in degrees Fahrenheit; Precipitation and Snow in inches

Weather Station: Smithville Elevation: 339 feet

	Jan	Feb	Mar	Apr	May	Jun	Jul	Aug	Sep	Oct	Nov	Dec
High	62	66	73	80	86	93	96	97	91	83	73	64
Low	37	40	48	55	64	70	72	71	66	56	47	39
Precip	2.7	2.4	2.8	2.5	4.5	3.4	2.1	2.1	3.6	4.8	3.5	2.8
Snow	0.0	0.0	0.0	0.0	0.0	0.0	0.0	0.0	0.0	0.0	0.0	tr

High and Low temperatures in degrees Fahrenheit; Precipitation and Snow in inches

Population: 38,263 (1990); 57,733 (2000); 76,050 (2010); 84,836 (2015 projected); Race: 78.2% White, 8.2% Black, 0.7% Asian, 12.8% Other, 29.7% Hispanic of any race (2010); Density: 85.6 persons per square mile (2010); Average household size: 2.82 (2010); Median age: 35.5 (2010); Males per 100 females: 103.0 (2010).

Religion: Five largest groups: 14.5% Southern Baptist Convention, 13.2% Catholic Church, 3.5% The United Methodist Church, 1.9% Evangelical Lutheran Church in America, 1.8% Lutheran Church—Missouri Synod (2000).

Economy: Unemployment rate: 9.1% (June 2011); Total civilian labor force: 35,579 (June 2011); Leading industries: 20.8% retail trade; 19.7% accommodation & food services; 15.6% health care and social assistance (2009); Farms: 2,207 totaling 402,079 acres (2007); Companies that employ 500 or more persons: 1 (2009); Companies that employ 100 to 499 persons: 13 (2009); Companies that employ less than 100 persons: 1,015 (2009); Black-owned businesses: n/a (2007); Hispanic-owned businesses: 780 (2007); Asian-owned businesses: n/a (2007); Women-owned businesses: 1,395 (2007); Retail sales per capita: $12,870 (2010). Single-family building permits issued: 31 (2010); Multi-family building permits issued: 2 (2010).

Income: Per capita income: $22,169 (2010); Median household income: $53,183 (2010); Average household income: $63,602 (2010); Percent of households with income of $100,000 or more: 16.0% (2010); Poverty rate: 14.6% (2009); Bankruptcy rate: 2.00% (2010).

Taxes: Total county taxes per capita: $349 (2007); County property taxes per capita: $294 (2007).

Education: Percent of population age 25 and over with: High school diploma (including GED) or higher: 78.8% (2010); Bachelor's degree or higher: 16.6% (2010); Master's degree or higher: 5.2% (2010).

Housing: Homeownership rate: 79.6% (2010); Median home value: $122,362 (2010); Median contract rent: $599 per month (2005-2009 5-year est.); Median year structure built: 1988 (2005-2009 5-year est.)

Health: Birth rate: 126.7 per 10,000 population (2009); Death rate: 73.5 per 10,000 population (2009); Age-adjusted cancer mortality rate: 230.0 deaths per 100,000 population (2007); Number of physicians: 5.0 per 10,000 population (2008); Hospital beds: 6.6 per 10,000 population (2007); Hospital admissions: 282.5 per 10,000 population (2007).

Elections: 2008 Presidential election results: 45.1% Obama, 53.3% McCain, 0.1% Nader

National and State Parks: Bastrop State Park; Buescher State Park

Additional Information Contacts
Bastrop County Government . . . . (512) 332-7200
  http://www.co.bastrop.tx.us
Bastrop Chamber of Commerce . . . . (512) 303-0558
  http://www.bastropchamber.com
City of Bastrop . . . . (512) 332-8800
  http://www.cityofbastrop.org
City of Elgin . . . . (512) 281-5724
  http://www.elgintx.com
City of Smithville . . . . (512) 237-3282
  http://www.ci.smithville.tx.us
Greater Elgin Chamber of Commerce . . . . (512) 285-4515
  http://www.elgintxchamber.com
Smithville Area Chamber of Commerce. . . . . (512) 237-2313
  http://www.smithvilletx.org

Bastrop County Communities

BASTROP (city). County seat. Covers a land area of 7.268 square miles and a water area of 0.046 square miles. Located at 30.11° N. Lat; 97.31° W. Long. Elevation is 367 feet.

History: Bastrop was incorporated in 1837, and named for Baron de Bastrop, a friend of Moses Austin. Bastrop's early economy was based on cotton, pecans, turkeys, lumber, and lignite.

Population: 4,281 (1990); 5,340 (2000); 7,516 (2010); 8,523 (2015 projected); Race: 75.3% White, 12.8% Black, 1.8% Asian, 10.0% Other, 18.9% Hispanic of any race (2010); Density: 1,034.2 persons per square mile (2010); Average household size: 2.56 (2010); Median age: 36.0

(2010); Males per 100 females: 97.8 (2010); Marriage status: 29.0% never married, 46.8% now married, 7.4% widowed, 16.7% divorced (2005-2009 5-year est.); Foreign born: 5.0% (2005-2009 5-year est.); Ancestry (includes multiple ancestries): 21.3% German, 10.2% Irish, 9.1% English, 5.0% Danish, 4.6% American (2005-2009 5-year est.).

Economy: Single-family building permits issued: 22 (2010); Multi-family building permits issued: 2 (2010); Employment by occupation: 18.5% management, 19.7% professional, 15.7% services, 24.6% sales, 0.0% farming, 15.4% construction, 6.1% production (2005-2009 5-year est.).

Income: Per capita income: $24,488 (2010); Median household income: $50,482 (2010); Average household income: $63,427 (2010); Percent of households with income of $100,000 or more: 16.9% (2010); Poverty rate: 8.0% (2005-2009 5-year est.).

Taxes: Total city taxes per capita: $844 (2007); City property taxes per capita: $312 (2007).

Education: Percent of population age 25 and over with: High school diploma (including GED) or higher: 85.2% (2010); Bachelor's degree or higher: 26.1% (2010); Master's degree or higher: 11.0% (2010).

School District(s)
Bastrop ISD (PK-12)
  2009-10 Enrollment: 8,936 . . . . (512) 321-2292
Fruit of Excellence (PK-12)
  2009-10 Enrollment: 27 . . . . (512) 303-5550
Smithville ISD (PK-12)
  2009-10 Enrollment: 1,709 . . . . (512) 237-2487

Housing: Homeownership rate: 66.0% (2010); Median home value: $141,972 (2010); Median contract rent: $792 per month (2005-2009 5-year est.); Median year structure built: 1988 (2005-2009 5-year est.).

Hospitals: Lakeside Hospital at Bastrop

Safety: Violent crime rate: 20.5 per 10,000 population; Property crime rate: 490.2 per 10,000 population (2009).

Newspapers: Bastrop Advertiser (Community news; Circulation 5,120)

Transportation: Commute to work: 87.4% car, 0.0% public transportation, 0.6% walk, 2.7% work from home (2005-2009 5-year est.); Travel time to work: 39.8% less than 15 minutes, 12.8% 15 to 30 minutes, 17.4% 30 to 45 minutes, 21.3% 45 to 60 minutes, 8.7% 60 minutes or more (2005-2009 5-year est.)

Additional Information Contacts
Bastrop Chamber of Commerce . . . . (512) 303-0558
  http://www.bastropchamber.com
City of Bastrop . . . . (512) 332-8800
  http://www.cityofbastrop.org

CAMP SWIFT (CDP). Covers a land area of 11.941 square miles and a water area of 0.146 square miles. Located at 30.18° N. Lat; 97.29° W. Long. Elevation is 440 feet.

Population: 2,795 (1990); 4,731 (2000); 5,529 (2010); 6,020 (2015 projected); Race: 72.7% White, 7.9% Black, 0.2% Asian, 19.2% Other, 36.7% Hispanic of any race (2010); Density: 463.0 persons per square mile (2010); Average household size: 2.80 (2010); Median age: 35.5 (2010); Males per 100 females: 133.0 (2010); Marriage status: 25.9% never married, 52.9% now married, 2.4% widowed, 18.9% divorced (2005-2009 5-year est.); Foreign born: 7.0% (2005-2009 5-year est.); Ancestry (includes multiple ancestries): 16.0% German, 8.5% English, 6.5% Irish, 4.8% American, 3.3% Polish (2005-2009 5-year est.).

Economy: Employment by occupation: 6.8% management, 20.5% professional, 30.0% services, 26.6% sales, 0.0% farming, 9.7% construction, 6.4% production (2005-2009 5-year est.).

Income: Per capita income: $22,260 (2010); Median household income: $61,029 (2010); Average household income: $69,827 (2010); Percent of households with income of $100,000 or more: 18.1% (2010); Poverty rate: 10.3% (2005-2009 5-year est.).

Education: Percent of population age 25 and over with: High school diploma (including GED) or higher: 79.8% (2010); Bachelor's degree or higher: 12.8% (2010); Master's degree or higher: 2.1% (2010).

Housing: Homeownership rate: 85.7% (2010); Median home value: $110,768 (2010); Median contract rent: $702 per month (2005-2009 5-year est.); Median year structure built: 1989 (2005-2009 5-year est.).

Transportation: Commute to work: 96.3% car, 0.0% public transportation, 1.2% walk, 1.4% work from home (2005-2009 5-year est.); Travel time to work: 31.2% less than 15 minutes, 32.8% 15 to 30 minutes, 8.2% 30 to 45 minutes, 6.4% 45 to 60 minutes, 21.4% 60 minutes or more (2005-2009 5-year est.)

CEDAR CREEK (unincorporated postal area, zip code 78612).
Covers a land area of 103.407 square miles and a water area of 0.232 square miles. Located at 30.13° N. Lat; 97.49° W. Long. Elevation is 433 feet.
Population: 9,063 (2000); Race: 78.0% White, 7.4% Black, 1.0% Asian, 13.6% Other, 27.0% Hispanic of any race (2000); Density: 87.6 persons per square mile (2000); Age: 29.8% under 18, 6.7% over 64 (2000); Marriage status: 22.9% never married, 60.5% now married, 4.4% widowed, 12.1% divorced (2000); Foreign born: 9.9% (2000); Ancestry (includes multiple ancestries): 14.2% German, 9.4% Irish, 8.5% American, 6.5% English (2000).
Economy: Employment by occupation: 10.4% management, 16.4% professional, 12.0% services, 26.6% sales, 0.0% farming, 18.3% construction, 16.3% production (2000).
Income: Per capita income: $18,395 (2000); Median household income: $47,601 (2000); Poverty rate: 179.1% (2000).
Education: Percent of population age 25 and over with: High school diploma (including GED) or higher: 77.0% (2000); Bachelor's degree or higher: 14.8% (2000).

School District(s)
Bastrop ISD (PK-12)
    2009-10 Enrollment: 8,936 . . . . (512) 321-2292
Housing: Homeownership rate: 85.9% (2000); Median home value: $99,800 (2000); Median contract rent: $460 per month (2000); Median year structure built: 1987 (2000).
Transportation: Commute to work: 95.4% car, 0.0% public transportation, 1.0% walk, 3.2% work from home (2000); Travel time to work: 8.1% less than 15 minutes, 15.6% 15 to 30 minutes, 40.2% 30 to 45 minutes, 21.9% 45 to 60 minutes, 14.2% 60 minutes or more (2000)

CIRCLE D-KC ESTATES (CDP). Covers a land area of 9.275 square miles and a water area of 0.035 square miles. Located at 30.16° N. Lat; 97.23° W. Long.
Population: 1,278 (1990); 2,010 (2000); 2,501 (2010); 2,729 (2015 projected); Race: 76.2% White, 6.7% Black, 0.2% Asian, 16.8% Other, 32.5% Hispanic of any race (2010); Density: 269.7 persons per square mile (2010); Average household size: 2.77 (2010); Median age: 35.9 (2010); Males per 100 females: 124.1 (2010); Marriage status: 18.5% never married, 59.9% now married, 10.5% widowed, 11.1% divorced (2005-2009 5-year est.); Foreign born: 0.0% (2005-2009 5-year est.); Ancestry (includes multiple ancestries): 20.4% Irish, 19.9% German, 11.5% English, 9.0% American, 3.3% Hungarian (2005-2009 5-year est.).
Economy: Employment by occupation: 17.7% management, 23.4% professional, 10.9% services, 28.3% sales, 0.0% farming, 8.0% construction, 11.8% production (2005-2009 5-year est.).
Income: Per capita income: $23,549 (2010); Median household income: $61,334 (2010); Average household income: $70,577 (2010); Percent of households with income of $100,000 or more: 18.7% (2010); Poverty rate: 10.8% (2005-2009 5-year est.).
Education: Percent of population age 25 and over with: High school diploma (including GED) or higher: 80.6% (2010); Bachelor's degree or higher: 14.1% (2010); Master's degree or higher: 2.6% (2010).
Housing: Homeownership rate: 85.7% (2010); Median home value: $112,297 (2010); Median contract rent: $470 per month (2005-2009 5-year est.); Median year structure built: 1993 (2005-2009 5-year est.).
Transportation: Commute to work: 93.1% car, 0.0% public transportation, 1.0% walk, 4.6% work from home (2005-2009 5-year est.); Travel time to work: 21.8% less than 15 minutes, 36.6% 15 to 30 minutes, 11.3% 30 to 45 minutes, 22.8% 45 to 60 minutes, 7.5% 60 minutes or more (2005-2009 5-year est.)

ELGIN (city). Covers a land area of 4.695 square miles and a water area of 0 square miles. Located at 30.34° N. Lat; 97.37° W. Long. Elevation is 581 feet.
History: Settled 1867, incorporated 1890.
Population: 5,035 (1990); 5,700 (2000); 9,544 (2010); 11,030 (2015 projected); Race: 71.2% White, 12.3% Black, 0.9% Asian, 15.6% Other, 49.3% Hispanic of any race (2010); Density: 2,032.7 persons per square mile (2010); Average household size: 3.04 (2010); Median age: 32.9 (2010); Males per 100 females: 97.3 (2010); Marriage status: 27.0% never married, 48.8% now married, 8.0% widowed, 16.2% divorced (2005-2009 5-year est.); Foreign born: 11.0% (2005-2009 5-year est.); Ancestry (includes multiple ancestries): 14.1% German, 6.5% Irish, 5.4% English, 2.5% French, 2.1% Swedish (2005-2009 5-year est.).

Economy: Single-family building permits issued: 1 (2010); Multi-family building permits issued: 0 (2010); Employment by occupation: 10.6% management, 14.4% professional, 22.8% services, 24.0% sales, 1.3% farming, 12.4% construction, 14.6% production (2005-2009 5-year est.).
Income: Per capita income: $20,981 (2010); Median household income: $49,919 (2010); Average household income: $64,524 (2010); Percent of households with income of $100,000 or more: 14.5% (2010); Poverty rate: 17.5% (2005-2009 5-year est.).
Taxes: Total city taxes per capita: $383 (2007); City property taxes per capita: $209 (2007).
Education: Percent of population age 25 and over with: High school diploma (including GED) or higher: 69.1% (2010); Bachelor's degree or higher: 16.3% (2010); Master's degree or higher: 5.7% (2010).

School District(s)
Elgin ISD (PK-12)
    2009-10 Enrollment: 3,995 . . . . (512) 281-3434
Housing: Homeownership rate: 70.2% (2010); Median home value: $106,063 (2010); Median contract rent: $640 per month (2005-2009 5-year est.); Median year structure built: 1989 (2005-2009 5-year est.).
Safety: Violent crime rate: 19.0 per 10,000 population; Property crime rate: 305.0 per 10,000 population (2009).
Newspapers: Elgin Courier (Community news; Circulation 3,500)
Transportation: Commute to work: 95.5% car, 0.0% public transportation, 0.5% walk, 2.2% work from home (2005-2009 5-year est.); Travel time to work: 26.5% less than 15 minutes, 16.3% 15 to 30 minutes, 36.2% 30 to 45 minutes, 14.0% 45 to 60 minutes, 7.0% 60 minutes or more (2005-2009 5-year est.)
Additional Information Contacts
City of Elgin . . . . (512) 281-5724
    http://www.elgintx.com
Greater Elgin Chamber of Commerce . . . . (512) 285-4515
    http://www.elgintxchamber.com

MCDADE (unincorporated postal area, zip code 78650). Covers a land area of 49.689 square miles and a water area of 0.146 square miles. Located at 30.28° N. Lat; 97.23° W. Long. Elevation is 551 feet.
Population: 1,050 (2000); Race: 71.1% White, 3.7% Black, 0.0% Asian, 25.2% Other, 33.0% Hispanic of any race (2000); Density: 21.1 persons per square mile (2000); Age: 27.2% under 18, 11.4% over 64 (2000); Marriage status: 17.8% never married, 65.0% now married, 5.3% widowed, 11.9% divorced (2000); Foreign born: 13.0% (2000); Ancestry (includes multiple ancestries): 19.8% German, 6.6% Irish, 6.2% English, 5.1% American (2000).
Economy: Employment by occupation: 7.9% management, 13.1% professional, 16.4% services, 20.1% sales, 1.7% farming, 19.2% construction, 21.6% production (2000).
Income: Per capita income: $17,962 (2000); Median household income: $39,107 (2000); Poverty rate: 179.1% (2000).
Education: Percent of population age 25 and over with: High school diploma (including GED) or higher: 72.4% (2000); Bachelor's degree or higher: 13.6% (2000).

School District(s)
McDade ISD (PK-08)
    2009-10 Enrollment: 183 . . . . (512) 273-0292
Housing: Homeownership rate: 75.8% (2000); Median home value: $74,200 (2000); Median contract rent: $316 per month (2000); Median year structure built: 1972 (2000).
Transportation: Commute to work: 92.8% car, 0.0% public transportation, 0.9% walk, 3.9% work from home (2000); Travel time to work: 7.7% less than 15 minutes, 20.7% 15 to 30 minutes, 21.3% 30 to 45 minutes, 36.3% 45 to 60 minutes, 14.0% 60 minutes or more (2000)

PAIGE (unincorporated postal area, zip code 78659). Covers a land area of 123.407 square miles and a water area of 0.326 square miles. Located at 30.21° N. Lat; 97.11° W. Long. Elevation is 538 feet.
Population: 2,623 (2000); Race: 96.3% White, 0.2% Black, 0.2% Asian, 3.3% Other, 8.0% Hispanic of any race (2000); Density: 21.3 persons per square mile (2000); Age: 26.1% under 18, 9.1% over 64 (2000); Marriage status: 17.0% never married, 66.5% now married, 4.3% widowed, 12.2% divorced (2000); Foreign born: 3.4% (2000); Ancestry (includes multiple ancestries): 30.9% German, 12.3% Irish, 9.1% English, 7.6% American (2000).
Economy: Employment by occupation: 15.2% management, 18.5% professional, 12.5% services, 22.6% sales, 1.2% farming, 19.8% construction, 10.1% production (2000).

Income: Per capita income: $20,262 (2000); Median household income: $43,083 (2000); Poverty rate: 179.1% (2000).
Education: Percent of population age 25 and over with: High school diploma (including GED) or higher: 82.9% (2000); Bachelor's degree or higher: 17.5% (2000).
Housing: Homeownership rate: 86.0% (2000); Median home value: $95,900 (2000); Median contract rent: $432 per month (2000); Median year structure built: 1988 (2000).
Transportation: Commute to work: 94.4% car, 0.6% public transportation, 1.1% walk, 3.0% work from home (2000); Travel time to work: 14.8% less than 15 minutes, 26.1% 15 to 30 minutes, 9.8% 30 to 45 minutes, 18.0% 45 to 60 minutes, 31.3% 60 minutes or more (2000)

RED ROCK (unincorporated postal area, zip code 78662). Covers a land area of 75.583 square miles and a water area of 0.037 square miles. Located at 29.95° N. Lat; 97.42° W. Long. Elevation is 489 feet.
Population: 2,078 (2000); Race: 93.9% White, 3.1% Black, 0.3% Asian, 2.7% Other, 6.8% Hispanic of any race (2000); Density: 27.5 persons per square mile (2000); Age: 28.2% under 18, 10.3% over 64 (2000); Marriage status: 20.6% never married, 59.6% now married, 8.2% widowed, 11.6% divorced (2000); Foreign born: 2.1% (2000); Ancestry (includes multiple ancestries): 37.4% German, 13.0% Irish, 11.5% English, 5.2% American (2000).
Economy: Employment by occupation: 14.4% management, 19.5% professional, 9.7% services, 25.9% sales, 0.0% farming, 15.0% construction, 15.7% production (2000).
Income: Per capita income: $18,722 (2000); Median household income: $46,078 (2000); Poverty rate: 179.1% (2000).
Education: Percent of population age 25 and over with: High school diploma (including GED) or higher: 85.8% (2000); Bachelor's degree or higher: 13.6% (2000).

School District(s)
Bastrop ISD (PK-12)
   2009-10 Enrollment: 8,936 . . . . (512) 321-2292
Housing: Homeownership rate: 86.8% (2000); Median home value: $83,800 (2000); Median contract rent: $467 per month (2000); Median year structure built: 1984 (2000).
Transportation: Commute to work: 93.0% car, 0.0% public transportation, 0.7% walk, 3.9% work from home (2000); Travel time to work: 10.1% less than 15 minutes, 17.2% 15 to 30 minutes, 25.6% 30 to 45 minutes, 19.3% 45 to 60 minutes, 27.7% 60 minutes or more (2000)

ROSANKY (unincorporated postal area, zip code 78953). Covers a land area of 98.219 square miles and a water area of 0.084 square miles. Located at 29.84° N. Lat; 97.33° W. Long. Elevation is 505 feet.
Population: 679 (2000); Race: 93.0% White, 3.4% Black, 0.0% Asian, 3.6% Other, 6.6% Hispanic of any race (2000); Density: 6.9 persons per square mile (2000); Age: 10.9% under 18, 19.4% over 64 (2000); Marriage status: 11.5% never married, 64.8% now married, 6.9% widowed, 16.8% divorced (2000); Foreign born: 0.0% (2000); Ancestry (includes multiple ancestries): 33.1% German, 12.0% English, 9.9% Irish, 4.2% American (2000).
Economy: Employment by occupation: 15.1% management, 22.8% professional, 10.3% services, 18.3% sales, 6.7% farming, 13.5% construction, 13.5% production (2000).
Income: Per capita income: $21,326 (2000); Median household income: $41,111 (2000); Poverty rate: 179.1% (2000).
Education: Percent of population age 25 and over with: High school diploma (including GED) or higher: 87.4% (2000); Bachelor's degree or higher: 22.7% (2000).
Housing: Homeownership rate: 79.2% (2000); Median home value: $94,600 (2000); Median contract rent: $346 per month (2000); Median year structure built: 1980 (2000).
Transportation: Commute to work: 90.9% car, 0.0% public transportation, 2.3% walk, 6.8% work from home (2000); Travel time to work: 10.1% less than 15 minutes, 10.5% 15 to 30 minutes, 27.2% 30 to 45 minutes, 17.1% 45 to 60 minutes, 35.2% 60 minutes or more (2000)

SMITHVILLE (city). Covers a land area of 3.506 square miles and a water area of 0.027 square miles. Located at 30.00° N. Lat; 97.15° W. Long. Elevation is 325 feet.
History: Settled 1827, incorporated 1895.
Population: 3,275 (1990); 3,901 (2000); 4,793 (2010); 5,307 (2015 projected); Race: 79.8% White, 12.0% Black, 0.7% Asian, 7.4% Other, 16.3% Hispanic of any race (2010); Density: 1,367.1 persons per square

mile (2010); Average household size: 2.64 (2010); Median age: 36.8 (2010); Males per 100 females: 90.5 (2010); Marriage status: 28.7% never married, 41.1% now married, 11.6% widowed, 18.6% divorced (2005-2009 5-year est.); Foreign born: 3.9% (2005-2009 5-year est.); Ancestry (includes multiple ancestries): 20.2% German, 9.1% Irish, 9.1% English, 6.1% American, 5.2% Italian (2005-2009 5-year est.).
Economy: Single-family building permits issued: 8 (2010); Multi-family building permits issued: 0 (2010); Employment by occupation: 14.3% management, 22.8% professional, 17.1% services, 25.0% sales, 0.0% farming, 11.4% construction, 9.4% production (2005-2009 5-year est.).
Income: Per capita income: $18,533 (2010); Median household income: $40,526 (2010); Average household income: $50,085 (2010); Percent of households with income of $100,000 or more: 11.6% (2010); Poverty rate: 19.5% (2005-2009 5-year est.).
Taxes: Total city taxes per capita: $170 (2007); City property taxes per capita: $81 (2007).
Education: Percent of population age 25 and over with: High school diploma (including GED) or higher: 75.1% (2010); Bachelor's degree or higher: 15.9% (2010); Master's degree or higher: 4.9% (2010).

School District(s)
Smithville ISD (PK-12)
   2009-10 Enrollment: 1,709 . . . . (512) 237-2487
Housing: Homeownership rate: 66.3% (2010); Median home value: $109,626 (2010); Median contract rent: $383 per month (2005-2009 5-year est.); Median year structure built: 1965 (2005-2009 5-year est.).
Hospitals: Smithville Regional Hospital
Safety: Violent crime rate: 24.3 per 10,000 population; Property crime rate: 187.5 per 10,000 population (2009).
Newspapers: Smithville Times (Local news; Circulation 3,000)
Transportation: Commute to work: 84.3% car, 0.0% public transportation, 8.0% walk, 5.6% work from home (2005-2009 5-year est.); Travel time to work: 31.9% less than 15 minutes, 30.2% 15 to 30 minutes, 11.5% 30 to 45 minutes, 5.7% 45 to 60 minutes, 20.6% 60 minutes or more (2005-2009 5-year est.)
Additional Information Contacts
City of Smithville . . . . (512) 237-3282
   http://www.ci.smithville.tx.us
Smithville Area Chamber of Commerce. . . . . (512) 237-2313
   http://www.smithvilletx.org

WYLDWOOD (CDP). Covers a land area of 12.052 square miles and a water area of 0.065 square miles. Located at 30.13° N. Lat; 97.45° W. Long. Elevation is 512 feet.
Population: 1,819 (1990); 2,310 (2000); 2,273 (2010); 2,510 (2015 projected); Race: 79.4% White, 9.0% Black, 0.7% Asian, 10.9% Other, 19.4% Hispanic of any race (2010); Density: 188.6 persons per square mile (2010); Average household size: 2.78 (2010); Median age: 36.8 (2010); Males per 100 females: 98.5 (2010); Marriage status: 27.0% never married, 59.0% now married, 7.1% widowed, 6.9% divorced (2005-2009 5-year est.); Foreign born: 7.5% (2005-2009 5-year est.); Ancestry (includes multiple ancestries): 24.3% German, 13.7% Irish, 6.9% English, 6.7% American, 5.3% Norwegian (2005-2009 5-year est.).
Economy: Employment by occupation: 7.5% management, 25.2% professional, 17.1% services, 18.6% sales, 1.1% farming, 26.7% construction, 3.8% production (2005-2009 5-year est.).
Income: Per capita income: $24,976 (2010); Median household income: $62,091 (2010); Average household income: $70,046 (2010); Percent of households with income of $100,000 or more: 18.7% (2010); Poverty rate: 29.3% (2005-2009 5-year est.).
Education: Percent of population age 25 and over with: High school diploma (including GED) or higher: 86.0% (2010); Bachelor's degree or higher: 16.6% (2010); Master's degree or higher: 5.5% (2010).
Housing: Homeownership rate: 80.6% (2010); Median home value: $131,335 (2010); Median contract rent: $586 per month (2005-2009 5-year est.); Median year structure built: 1986 (2005-2009 5-year est.).
Transportation: Commute to work: 98.8% car, 0.0% public transportation, 0.0% walk, 1.2% work from home (2005-2009 5-year est.); Travel time to work: 6.3% less than 15 minutes, 28.1% 15 to 30 minutes, 44.9% 30 to 45 minutes, 15.8% 45 to 60 minutes, 4.9% 60 minutes or more (2005-2009 5-year est.)

Baylor County

Located in north Texas, in prairie region; drained by the Wichita River and Kemp and Diversion Lakes. Covers a land area of 870.77 square miles, a water area of 30.24 square miles, and is located in the Central Time Zone at 33.60° N. Lat., 99.25° W. Long. The county was founded in 1858. County seat is Seymour.

Weather Station: Lake Kemp | | | | | | | | | Elevation: 1,166 feet

	Jan	Feb	Mar	Apr	May	Jun	Jul	Aug	Sep	Oct	Nov	Dec
High	54	58	67	77	85	92	98	97	89	78	65	55
Low	30	33	41	50	60	68	72	72	63	52	41	31
Precip	1.0	1.7	1.9	1.7	3.5	4.0	1.5	1.9	2.9	2.6	1.6	1.3
Snow	0.5	0.8	0.0	0.0	0.0	0.0	0.0	0.0	0.0	0.0	0.5	0.6

High and Low temperatures in degrees Fahrenheit; Precipitation and Snow in inches

Weather Station: Seymour | | | | | | | | | Elevation: 1,285 feet

	Jan	Feb	Mar	Apr	May	Jun	Jul	Aug	Sep	Oct	Nov	Dec
High	55	58	66	76	84	91	97	96	88	77	65	55
Low	29	32	40	48	59	67	72	71	63	51	39	29
Precip	1.1	1.9	2.1	1.8	4.2	3.8	2.1	2.4	3.1	2.7	2.0	1.5
Snow	0.9	0.4	tr	0.0	0.0	0.0	0.0	0.0	0.0	0.0	0.8	0.4

High and Low temperatures in degrees Fahrenheit; Precipitation and Snow in inches

Population: 4,385 (1990); 4,093 (2000); 3,870 (2010); 3,755 (2015 projected); Race: 88.2% White, 3.9% Black, 1.0% Asian, 7.0% Other, 12.0% Hispanic of any race (2010); Density: 4.4 persons per square mile (2010); Average household size: 2.26 (2010); Median age: 45.3 (2010); Males per 100 females: 91.9 (2010).
Religion: Five largest groups: 66.8% Southern Baptist Convention, 13.9% Catholic Church, 9.6% The United Methodist Church, 5.3% Churches of Christ, 2.7% Presbyterian Church (U.S.A.) (2000).
Economy: Unemployment rate: 7.1% (June 2011); Total civilian labor force: 1,865 (June 2011); Leading industries: Farms: 268 totaling 547,029 acres (2007); Companies that employ 500 or more persons: 0 (2009); Companies that employ 100 to 499 persons: 2 (2009); Companies that employ less than 100 persons: 117 (2009); Black-owned businesses: n/a (2007); Hispanic-owned businesses: n/a (2007); Asian-owned businesses: n/a (2007); Women-owned businesses: n/a (2007); Retail sales per capita: $8,072 (2010). Single-family building permits issued: 0 (2010); Multi-family building permits issued: 0 (2010).
Income: Per capita income: $18,656 (2010); Median household income: $31,948 (2010); Average household income: $42,605 (2010); Percent of households with income of $100,000 or more: 6.7% (2010); Poverty rate: 18.9% (2009); Bankruptcy rate: 2.36% (2010).
Taxes: Total county taxes per capita: $259 (2007); County property taxes per capita: $194 (2007).
Education: Percent of population age 25 and over with: High school diploma (including GED) or higher: 75.3% (2010); Bachelor's degree or higher: 13.4% (2010); Master's degree or higher: 3.4% (2010).
Housing: Homeownership rate: 70.5% (2010); Median home value: $39,589 (2010); Median contract rent: $258 per month (2005-2009 5-year est.); Median year structure built: 1962 (2005-2009 5-year est.)
Health: Birth rate: 146.9 per 10,000 population (2009); Death rate: 149.6 per 10,000 population (2009); Age-adjusted cancer mortality rate: 124.6 (Unreliable) deaths per 100,000 population (2007); Number of physicians: 8.1 per 10,000 population (2008); Hospital beds: 98.4 per 10,000 population (2007); Hospital admissions: 1,795.3 per 10,000 population (2007).
Elections: 2008 Presidential election results: 22.3% Obama, 76.8% McCain, 0.0% Nader
Additional Information Contacts
Baylor County Government . . . . (940) 889-3322
http://www.baylorcountytexas.us
City of Seymour
http://www.cityofseymour.org
Seymour Chamber of Commerce . . . . (940) 888-2921
http://www.seymourtxchamber.org

Baylor County Communities

SEYMOUR (city). County seat. Covers a land area of 2.724 square miles and a water area of 0 square miles. Located at 33.59° N. Lat; 99.26° W. Long. Elevation is 1,289 feet.
History: Seymour, on the Salt Fork of the Brazos River, was settled in 1878 by a group from Oregon. Cotton was the mainstay of the economy, with a cotton oil mill, compress, and cotton gins operating here.
Population: 3,247 (1990); 2,908 (2000); 2,671 (2010); 2,568 (2015 projected); Race: 86.8% White, 4.9% Black, 1.3% Asian, 7.0% Other, 12.9% Hispanic of any race (2010); Density: 980.5 persons per square mile

(2010); Average household size: 2.27 (2010); Median age: 42.0 (2010); Males per 100 females: 88.5 (2010); Marriage status: 21.7% never married, 50.6% now married, 12.1% widowed, 15.6% divorced (2005-2009 5-year est.); Foreign born: 4.8% (2005-2009 5-year est.); Ancestry (includes multiple ancestries): 18.1% German, 12.4% Irish, 9.8% English, 7.2% American, 6.8% Czech (2005-2009 5-year est.).
Economy: Single-family building permits issued: 0 (2010); Multi-family building permits issued: 0 (2010); Employment by occupation: 9.4% management, 17.4% professional, 15.5% services, 27.8% sales, 1.4% farming, 18.6% construction, 9.9% production (2005-2009 5-year est.).
Income: Per capita income: $17,976 (2010); Median household income: $29,615 (2010); Average household income: $41,241 (2010); Percent of households with income of $100,000 or more: 6.7% (2010); Poverty rate: 18.0% (2005-2009 5-year est.).
Taxes: Total city taxes per capita: $150 (2007); City property taxes per capita: $91 (2007).
Education: Percent of population age 25 and over with: High school diploma (including GED) or higher: 74.0% (2010); Bachelor's degree or higher: 12.2% (2010); Master's degree or higher: 2.9% (2010).
School District(s)
Seymour ISD (PK-12)
2009-10 Enrollment: 580 . . . . (940) 889-3525
Housing: Homeownership rate: 68.1% (2010); Median home value: $39,106 (2010); Median contract rent: $242 per month (2005-2009 5-year est.); Median year structure built: 1961 (2005-2009 5-year est.).
Hospitals: Seymour Hospital (49 beds)
Safety: Violent crime rate: 50.2 per 10,000 population; Property crime rate: 127.4 per 10,000 population (2009).
Newspapers: Baylor County Banner (Community news; Circulation 2,500)
Transportation: Commute to work: 97.8% car, 0.0% public transportation, 0.0% walk, 0.8% work from home (2005-2009 5-year est.); Travel time to work: 65.2% less than 15 minutes, 20.1% 15 to 30 minutes, 2.4% 30 to 45 minutes, 3.0% 45 to 60 minutes, 9.4% 60 minutes or more (2005-2009 5-year est.)
Additional Information Contacts
City of Seymour . . . .
http://www.cityofseymour.org
Seymour Chamber of Commerce . . . . (940) 888-2921
http://www.seymourtxchamber.org

Bee County

Located in south Texas; drained by the Aransas River. Covers a land area of 880.14 square miles, a water area of 0.17 square miles, and is located in the Central Time Zone at 28.41° N. Lat., 97.74° W. Long. The county was founded in 1857. County seat is Beeville.

Bee County is part of the Beeville, TX Micropolitan Statistical Area. The entire metro area includes: Bee County, TX

Weather Station: Beeville 5 NE | | | | | | | | | Elevation: 254 feet

	Jan	Feb	Mar	Apr	May	Jun	Jul	Aug	Sep	Oct	Nov	Dec
High	65	69	74	81	87	92	95	95	91	84	75	67
Low	43	47	53	59	67	72	73	73	69	61	53	45
Precip	2.1	1.7	2.6	2.5	3.1	3.7	3.4	2.8	3.6	3.5	2.2	1.7
Snow	0.0	0.0	0.0	0.0	0.0	0.0	0.0	0.0	0.0	0.0	0.0	0.2

High and Low temperatures in degrees Fahrenheit; Precipitation and Snow in inches

Population: 25,135 (1990); 32,359 (2000); 33,143 (2010); 33,466 (2015 projected); Race: 66.2% White, 10.6% Black, 0.5% Asian, 22.6% Other, 55.9% Hispanic of any race (2010); Density: 37.7 persons per square mile (2010); Average household size: 2.67 (2010); Median age: 32.3 (2010); Males per 100 females: 156.7 (2010).
Religion: Five largest groups: 21.3% Catholic Church, 11.8% Southern Baptist Convention, 2.5% The United Methodist Church, 1.3% Evangelical Lutheran Church in America, 1.1% Churches of Christ (2000).
Economy: Unemployment rate: 10.0% (June 2011); Total civilian labor force: 12,659 (June 2011); Leading industries: 25.4% health care and social assistance; 22.4% retail trade; 13.0% accommodation & food services (2009); Farms: 952 totaling 548,400 acres (2007); Companies that employ 500 or more persons: 0 (2009); Companies that employ 100 to 499 persons: 5 (2009); Companies that employ less than 100 persons: 444 (2009); Black-owned businesses: 41 (2007); Hispanic-owned businesses: n/a (2007); Asian-owned businesses: n/a (2007); Women-owned businesses: n/a (2007); Retail sales per capita: $8,621 (2010).

Single-family building permits issued: 9 (2010); Multi-family building permits issued: 0 (2010).
Income: Per capita income: $13,130 (2010); Median household income: $36,223 (2010); Average household income: $45,348 (2010); Percent of households with income of $100,000 or more: 7.1% (2010); Poverty rate: 28.6% (2009); Bankruptcy rate: 0.62% (2010).
Taxes: Total county taxes per capita: $168 (2007); County property taxes per capita: $119 (2007).
Education: Percent of population age 25 and over with: High school diploma (including GED) or higher: 70.4% (2010); Bachelor's degree or higher: 10.2% (2010); Master's degree or higher: 3.6% (2010).
Housing: Homeownership rate: 63.4% (2010); Median home value: $65,593 (2010); Median contract rent: $407 per month (2005-2009 5-year est.); Median year structure built: 1971 (2005-2009 5-year est.)
Health: Birth rate: 114.2 per 10,000 population (2009); Death rate: 71.1 per 10,000 population (2009); Age-adjusted cancer mortality rate: 153.4 deaths per 100,000 population (2007); Number of physicians: 5.3 per 10,000 population (2008); Hospital beds: 19.4 per 10,000 population (2007); Hospital admissions: 796.3 per 10,000 population (2007).
Elections: 2008 Presidential election results: 44.7% Obama, 54.8% McCain, 0.0% Nader
Additional Information Contacts
Bee County Government . . . . (361) 362-3200
   http://www.co.bee.tx.us/ips/cms
Bee County Chamber of Commerce . . . . (361) 358-3267
   http://www.beecountychamber.org
City of Beeville . . . . (361) 358-4641
   http://beevilletx.org

Bee County Communities

BEEVILLE (city). Aka Chase. County seat. Covers a land area of 6.107 square miles and a water area of 0 square miles. Located at 28.40° N. Lat; 97.75° W. Long. Elevation is 210 feet.
History: Beeville was settled in the 1830's by Irish immigrants. It was first a cattle and cotton town, but oil wells brought an added prosperity to the community.
Population: 13,547 (1990); 13,129 (2000); 12,549 (2010); 12,314 (2015 projected); Race: 78.1% White, 1.4% Black, 0.7% Asian, 19.8% Other, 71.8% Hispanic of any race (2010); Density: 2,054.7 persons per square mile (2010); Average household size: 2.67 (2010); Median age: 32.7 (2010); Males per 100 females: 92.5 (2010); Marriage status: 32.0% never married, 48.7% now married, 9.3% widowed, 10.0% divorced (2005-2009 5-year est.); Foreign born: 3.2% (2005-2009 5-year est.); Ancestry (includes multiple ancestries): 11.8% German, 7.6% Irish, 6.2% English, 2.6% Scotch-Irish, 2.2% American (2005-2009 5-year est.).
Economy: Single-family building permits issued: 9 (2010); Multi-family building permits issued: 0 (2010); Employment by occupation: 6.9% management, 16.2% professional, 35.7% services, 20.7% sales, 1.0% farming, 11.2% construction, 8.4% production (2005-2009 5-year est.).
Income: Per capita income: $13,921 (2010); Median household income: $29,814 (2010); Average household income: $37,571 (2010); Percent of households with income of $100,000 or more: 3.7% (2010); Poverty rate: 24.9% (2005-2009 5-year est.).
Taxes: Total city taxes per capita: $399 (2007); City property taxes per capita: $176 (2007).
Education: Percent of population age 25 and over with: High school diploma (including GED) or higher: 64.0% (2010); Bachelor's degree or higher: 11.2% (2010); Master's degree or higher: 3.9% (2010).
School District(s)
Beeville ISD (PK-12)
   2009-10 Enrollment: 3,535 . . . . (361) 358-7111
St Mary's Academy Charter School (KG-06)
   2009-10 Enrollment: 333 . . . . (361) 358-5601
Two-year College(s)
Coastal Bend College (Public)
   Fall 2009 Enrollment: 4,196 . . . . (361) 358-2838
   2010-11 Tuition: In-state $2,400; Out-of-state $2,400
Housing: Homeownership rate: 52.4% (2010); Median home value: $60,363 (2010); Median contract rent: $356 per month (2005-2009 5-year est.); Median year structure built: 1967 (2005-2009 5-year est.).
Hospitals: Christus Spohn Hospital Beeville (69 beds)
Safety: Violent crime rate: 60.9 per 10,000 population; Property crime rate: 337.0 per 10,000 population (2009).
Newspapers: The Bee-Picayune (Local news)

Transportation: Commute to work: 84.7% car, 1.2% public transportation, 4.0% walk, 2.3% work from home (2005-2009 5-year est.); Travel time to work: 63.9% less than 15 minutes, 17.9% 15 to 30 minutes, 6.5% 30 to 45 minutes, 2.1% 45 to 60 minutes, 9.6% 60 minutes or more (2005-2009 5-year est.)
Additional Information Contacts
Bee County Chamber of Commerce . . . . (361) 358-3267
   http://www.beecountychamber.org
City of Beeville . . . . (361) 358-4641
   http://beevilletx.org

BLUE BERRY HILL (CDP). Covers a land area of 2.926 square miles and a water area of 0 square miles. Located at 28.38° N. Lat; 97.78° W. Long. Elevation is 272 feet.
Population: 947 (1990); 982 (2000); 1,024 (2010); 1,040 (2015 projected); Race: 71.6% White, 0.3% Black, 0.5% Asian, 27.6% Other, 63.4% Hispanic of any race (2010); Density: 349.9 persons per square mile (2010); Average household size: 2.72 (2010); Median age: 35.9 (2010); Males per 100 females: 99.2 (2010); Marriage status: 51.9% never married, 35.9% now married, 5.7% widowed, 6.5% divorced (2005-2009 5-year est.); Foreign born: 0.0% (2005-2009 5-year est.); Ancestry (includes multiple ancestries): 25.0% Irish, 25.0% Dutch, 21.4% German, 2.0% French, 0.7% English (2005-2009 5-year est.).
Economy: Employment by occupation: 4.9% management, 3.0% professional, 65.3% services, 19.7% sales, 0.0% farming, 7.2% construction, 0.0% production (2005-2009 5-year est.).
Income: Per capita income: $17,197 (2010); Median household income: $42,279 (2010); Average household income: $47,081 (2010); Percent of households with income of $100,000 or more: 8.0% (2010); Poverty rate: 0.0% (2005-2009 5-year est.).
Education: Percent of population age 25 and over with: High school diploma (including GED) or higher: 59.7% (2010); Bachelor's degree or higher: 6.1% (2010); Master's degree or higher: 3.0% (2010).
Housing: Homeownership rate: 79.0% (2010); Median home value: $58,125 (2010); Median contract rent: n/a per month (2005-2009 5-year est.); Median year structure built: 1983 (2005-2009 5-year est.).
Transportation: Commute to work: 97.9% car, 0.0% public transportation, 0.0% walk, 2.1% work from home (2005-2009 5-year est.); Travel time to work: 42.4% less than 15 minutes, 54.5% 15 to 30 minutes, 0.0% 30 to 45 minutes, 0.0% 45 to 60 minutes, 3.1% 60 minutes or more (2005-2009 5-year est.)

NORMANNA (CDP). Covers a land area of 1.329 square miles and a water area of 0 square miles. Located at 28.52° N. Lat; 97.78° W. Long. Elevation is 269 feet.
Population: 122 (1990); 121 (2000); 118 (2010); 117 (2015 projected); Race: 78.8% White, 0.8% Black, 0.0% Asian, 20.3% Other, 40.7% Hispanic of any race (2010); Density: 88.8 persons per square mile (2010); Average household size: 2.43 (2010); Median age: 43.0 (2010); Males per 100 females: 107.0 (2010); Marriage status: 6.1% never married, 63.6% now married, 27.3% widowed, 3.0% divorced (2005-2009 5-year est.); Foreign born: 0.0% (2005-2009 5-year est.); Ancestry (includes multiple ancestries): 56.1% Irish, 9.8% German, 7.3% English (2005-2009 5-year est.).
Economy: Employment by occupation: 0.0% management, 0.0% professional, 0.0% services, 0.0% sales, 0.0% farming, 100.0% construction, 0.0% production (2005-2009 5-year est.).
Income: Per capita income: $20,158 (2010); Median household income: $42,500 (2010); Average household income: $49,728 (2010); Percent of households with income of $100,000 or more: 9.8% (2005-2009 5-year est.).
Education: Percent of population age 25 and over with: High school diploma (including GED) or higher: 63.0% (2010); Bachelor's degree or higher: 13.6% (2010); Master's degree or higher: 8.6% (2010).
Housing: Homeownership rate: 80.4% (2010); Median home value: $58,333 (2010); Median contract rent: n/a per month (2005-2009 5-year est.); Median year structure built: 1980 (2005-2009 5-year est.).
Transportation: Commute to work: 100.0% car, 0.0% public transportation, 0.0% walk, 0.0% work from home (2005-2009 5-year est.); Travel time to work: 0.0% less than 15 minutes, 0.0% 15 to 30 minutes, 0.0% 30 to 45 minutes, 0.0% 45 to 60 minutes, 100.0% 60 minutes or more (2005-2009 5-year est.)

PAWNEE (CDP). Covers a land area of 5.217 square miles and a water area of 0 square miles. Located at 28.64° N. Lat; 98.00° W. Long. Elevation is 384 feet.
Population: 211 (1990); 201 (2000); 194 (2010); 192 (2015 projected); Race: 82.5% White, 1.0% Black, 0.0% Asian, 16.5% Other, 37.1% Hispanic of any race (2010); Density: 37.2 persons per square mile (2010); Average household size: 2.37 (2010); Median age: 42.6 (2010); Males per 100 females: 115.6 (2010); Marriage status: 21.1% never married, 69.5% now married, 9.5% widowed, 0.0% divorced (2005-2009 5-year est.); Foreign born: 1.6% (2005-2009 5-year est.); Ancestry (includes multiple ancestries): 4.1% Irish, 4.1% German, 4.1% French, 4.1% English (2005-2009 5-year est.).
Economy: Employment by occupation: 0.0% management, 7.5% professional, 17.0% services, 22.6% sales, 3.8% farming, 22.6% construction, 26.4% production (2005-2009 5-year est.).
Income: Per capita income: $20,244 (2010); Median household income: $40,357 (2010); Average household income: $49,441 (2010); Percent of households with income of $100,000 or more: 9.2% (2010); Poverty rate: 12.2% (2005-2009 5-year est.).
Education: Percent of population age 25 and over with: High school diploma (including GED) or higher: 58.9% (2010); Bachelor's degree or higher: 12.4% (2010); Master's degree or higher: 6.2% (2010).
School District(s)
Pawnee ISD (PK-08)
    2009-10 Enrollment: 137 . . . . (361) 456-7256
Housing: Homeownership rate: 80.3% (2010); Median home value: $66,000 (2010); Median contract rent: n/a per month (2005-2009 5-year est.); Median year structure built: 1953 (2005-2009 5-year est.).
Transportation: Commute to work: 100.0% car, 0.0% public transportation, 0.0% walk, 0.0% work from home (2005-2009 5-year est.); Travel time to work: 50.9% less than 15 minutes, 13.2% 15 to 30 minutes, 35.8% 30 to 45 minutes, 0.0% 45 to 60 minutes, 0.0% 60 minutes or more (2005-2009 5-year est.)

PETTUS (CDP). Covers a land area of 5.802 square miles and a water area of 0 square miles. Located at 28.61° N. Lat; 97.80° W. Long. Elevation is 299 feet.
Population: 581 (1990); 608 (2000); 596 (2010); 591 (2015 projected); Race: 73.5% White, 0.8% Black, 0.0% Asian, 25.7% Other, 46.6% Hispanic of any race (2010); Density: 102.7 persons per square mile (2010); Average household size: 2.48 (2010); Median age: 40.2 (2010); Males per 100 females: 98.0 (2010); Marriage status: 32.8% never married, 50.5% now married, 10.0% widowed, 6.8% divorced (2005-2009 5-year est.); Foreign born: 1.4% (2005-2009 5-year est.); Ancestry (includes multiple ancestries): 26.9% Irish, 24.4% German, 11.4% English, 4.7% Scotch-Irish, 3.2% French (2005-2009 5-year est.).
Economy: Employment by occupation: 10.3% management, 31.3% professional, 35.3% services, 16.1% sales, 0.0% farming, 3.6% construction, 3.6% production (2005-2009 5-year est.).
Income: Per capita income: $20,046 (2010); Median household income: $40,577 (2010); Average household income: $48,809 (2010); Percent of households with income of $100,000 or more: 9.4% (2010); Poverty rate: 11.7% (2005-2009 5-year est.).
Education: Percent of population age 25 and over with: High school diploma (including GED) or higher: 61.4% (2010); Bachelor's degree or higher: 11.4% (2010); Master's degree or higher: 5.6% (2010).
School District(s)
Pettus ISD (PK-12)
    2009-10 Enrollment: 405 . . . . (361) 375-2296
Housing: Homeownership rate: 77.4% (2010); Median home value: $55,897 (2010); Median contract rent: $521 per month (2005-2009 5-year est.); Median year structure built: 1961 (2005-2009 5-year est.).
Transportation: Commute to work: 93.6% car, 0.0% public transportation, 6.4% walk, 0.0% work from home (2005-2009 5-year est.); Travel time to work: 49.3% less than 15 minutes, 45.8% 15 to 30 minutes, 4.4% 30 to 45 minutes, 0.0% 45 to 60 minutes, 0.5% 60 minutes or more (2005-2009 5-year est.)

SKIDMORE (CDP). Covers a land area of 10.512 square miles and a water area of 0.009 square miles. Located at 28.25° N. Lat; 97.68° W. Long. Elevation is 154 feet.
Population: 804 (1990); 1,013 (2000); 1,103 (2010); 1,139 (2015 projected); Race: 87.0% White, 0.8% Black, 0.5% Asian, 11.6% Other, 51.8% Hispanic of any race (2010); Density: 104.9 persons per square mile

(2010); Average household size: 2.84 (2010); Median age: 36.3 (2010); Males per 100 females: 109.7 (2010); Marriage status: 30.4% never married, 53.7% now married, 7.3% widowed, 8.6% divorced (2005-2009 5-year est.); Foreign born: 1.9% (2005-2009 5-year est.); Ancestry (includes multiple ancestries): 18.8% German, 7.2% Irish, 1.4% Czech, 1.1% Dutch West Indian (2005-2009 5-year est.).
Economy: Employment by occupation: 6.8% management, 28.4% professional, 14.8% services, 3.2% sales, 8.4% farming, 15.2% construction, 23.2% production (2005-2009 5-year est.).
Income: Per capita income: $12,926 (2010); Median household income: $28,971 (2010); Average household income: $36,169 (2010); Percent of households with income of $100,000 or more: 3.1% (2010); Poverty rate: 27.9% (2005-2009 5-year est.).
Education: Percent of population age 25 and over with: High school diploma (including GED) or higher: 58.6% (2010); Bachelor's degree or higher: 5.8% (2010); Master's degree or higher: 3.3% (2010).
School District(s)
Skidmore-Tynan ISD (PK-12)
    2009-10 Enrollment: 821 . . . . (361) 287-3426
Housing: Homeownership rate: 81.9% (2010); Median home value: $50,755 (2010); Median contract rent: $307 per month (2005-2009 5-year est.); Median year structure built: 1959 (2005-2009 5-year est.).
Transportation: Commute to work: 88.8% car, 0.0% public transportation, 2.8% walk, 8.4% work from home (2005-2009 5-year est.); Travel time to work: 8.3% less than 15 minutes, 16.6% 15 to 30 minutes, 0.0% 30 to 45 minutes, 21.4% 45 to 60 minutes, 53.7% 60 minutes or more (2005-2009 5-year est.)

TULETA (CDP). Covers a land area of 4.479 square miles and a water area of 0 square miles. Located at 28.57° N. Lat; 97.79° W. Long. Elevation is 325 feet.
Population: 272 (1990); 292 (2000); 284 (2010); 282 (2015 projected); Race: 71.1% White, 0.7% Black, 0.0% Asian, 28.2% Other, 49.3% Hispanic of any race (2010); Density: 63.4 persons per square mile (2010); Average household size: 2.51 (2010); Median age: 41.0 (2010); Males per 100 females: 94.5 (2010); Marriage status: 27.1% never married, 49.2% now married, 11.6% widowed, 12.1% divorced (2005-2009 5-year est.); Foreign born: 0.0% (2005-2009 5-year est.); Ancestry (includes multiple ancestries): 46.9% Irish, 17.4% American, 15.6% English, 7.6% German, 3.6% Scotch-Irish (2005-2009 5-year est.).
Economy: Employment by occupation: 0.0% management, 15.3% professional, 22.4% services, 23.5% sales, 0.0% farming, 24.5% construction, 14.3% production (2005-2009 5-year est.).
Income: Per capita income: $19,994 (2010); Median household income: $40,000 (2010); Average household income: $47,612 (2010); Percent of households with income of $100,000 or more: 8.9% (2010); Poverty rate: 12.9% (2005-2009 5-year est.).
Education: Percent of population age 25 and over with: High school diploma (including GED) or higher: 61.6% (2010); Bachelor's degree or higher: 11.1% (2010); Master's degree or higher: 5.8% (2010).
Housing: Homeownership rate: 76.8% (2010); Median home value: $53,684 (2010); Median contract rent: n/a per month (2005-2009 5-year est.); Median year structure built: 1959 (2005-2009 5-year est.).
Transportation: Commute to work: 100.0% car, 0.0% public transportation, 0.0% walk, 0.0% work from home (2005-2009 5-year est.); Travel time to work: 6.9% less than 15 minutes, 49.4% 15 to 30 minutes, 0.0% 30 to 45 minutes, 0.0% 45 to 60 minutes, 43.7% 60 minutes or more (2005-2009 5-year est.)

TULSITA (CDP). Covers a land area of 1.991 square miles and a water area of 0 square miles. Located at 28.64° N. Lat; 97.81° W. Long. Elevation is 318 feet.
Population: 21 (1990); 20 (2000); 20 (2010); 20 (2015 projected); Race: 85.0% White, 0.0% Black, 0.0% Asian, 15.0% Other, 35.0% Hispanic of any race (2010); Density: 10.0 persons per square mile (2010); Average household size: 2.38 (2010); Median age: 40.0 (2010); Males per 100 females: 122.2 (2010); Marriage status: n/a never married, n/a now married, n/a widowed, n/a divorced (2005-2009 5-year est.); Foreign born: n/a (2005-2009 5-year est.); Ancestry (includes multiple ancestries): n/a (2005-2009 5-year est.).
Economy: Employment by occupation: n/a management, n/a professional, n/a services, n/a sales, n/a farming, n/a construction, n/a production (2005-2009 5-year est.).
Income: Per capita income: $20,243 (2010); Median household income: $35,000 (2010); Average household income: $41,250 (2010); Percent of

households with income of $100,000 or more: 0.0% (2010); Poverty rate: n/a (2005-2009 5-year est.).
Education: Percent of population age 25 and over with: High school diploma (including GED) or higher: 60.0% (2010); Bachelor's degree or higher: 6.7% (2010); Master's degree or higher: 6.7% (2010).
Housing: Homeownership rate: 75.0% (2010); Median home value: $80,000 (2010); Median contract rent: n/a per month (2005-2009 5-year est.); Median year structure built: 1971 (2005-2009 5-year est.).
Transportation: Commute to work: n/a car, n/a public transportation, n/a walk, n/a work from home (2005-2009 5-year est.); Travel time to work: n/a less than 15 minutes, n/a 15 to 30 minutes, n/a 30 to 45 minutes, n/a 45 to 60 minutes, n/a 60 minutes or more (2005-2009 5-year est.)

TYNAN (CDP). Covers a land area of 3.435 square miles and a water area of 0 square miles. Located at 28.16° N. Lat; 97.75° W. Long. Elevation is 167 feet.
Population: 276 (1990); 301 (2000); 304 (2010); 308 (2015 projected); Race: 87.8% White, 0.7% Black, 0.0% Asian, 11.5% Other, 39.1% Hispanic of any race (2010); Density: 88.5 persons per square mile (2010); Average household size: 2.81 (2010); Median age: 39.3 (2010); Males per 100 females: 101.3 (2010); Marriage status: 50.8% never married, 33.0% now married, 12.4% widowed, 3.8% divorced (2005-2009 5-year est.); Foreign born: 0.0% (2005-2009 5-year est.); Ancestry (includes multiple ancestries): 13.4% German, 1.7% Irish (2005-2009 5-year est.).
Economy: Employment by occupation: 3.7% management, 0.0% professional, 54.2% services, 34.6% sales, 0.0% farming, 0.0% construction, 7.5% production (2005-2009 5-year est.).
Income: Per capita income: $14,755 (2010); Median household income: $30,833 (2010); Average household income: $41,435 (2010); Percent of households with income of $100,000 or more: 10.2% (2010); Poverty rate: 5.4% (2005-2009 5-year est.).
Education: Percent of population age 25 and over with: High school diploma (including GED) or higher: 63.5% (2010); Bachelor's degree or higher: 11.0% (2010); Master's degree or higher: 3.0% (2010).
Housing: Homeownership rate: 82.4% (2010); Median home value: $71,538 (2010); Median contract rent: n/a per month (2005-2009 5-year est.); Median year structure built: 1976 (2005-2009 5-year est.).
Transportation: Commute to work: 100.0% car, 0.0% public transportation, 0.0% walk, 0.0% work from home (2005-2009 5-year est.); Travel time to work: 53.9% less than 15 minutes, 24.7% 15 to 30 minutes, 9.0% 30 to 45 minutes, 0.0% 45 to 60 minutes, 12.4% 60 minutes or more (2005-2009 5-year est.)

Bell County

Located in central Texas; drained by the Little, Leon, and Lampasas Rivers. Covers a land area of 1,059.72 square miles, a water area of 28.21 square miles, and is located in the Central Time Zone at 31.07° N. Lat., 97.52° W. Long. The county was founded in 1850. County seat is Belton.

Bell County is part of the Killeen-Temple-Fort Hood, TX Metropolitan Statistical Area. The entire metro area includes: Bell County, TX; Coryell County, TX; Lampasas County, TX

Weather Station: Stillhouse Hollow Dam   Elevation: 706 feet

	Jan	Feb	Mar	Apr	May	Jun	Jul	Aug	Sep	Oct	Nov	Dec
High	60	65	71	79	85	91	96	96	90	81	70	61
Low	35	39	46	54	63	69	72	72	66	56	46	37
Precip	2.2	2.5	3.1	2.6	4.9	4.0	1.8	2.3	3.5	3.8	3.0	2.6
Snow	0.0	0.0	tr	0.0	0.0	0.0	0.0	0.0	0.0	0.0	tr	tr

High and Low temperatures in degrees Fahrenheit; Precipitation and Snow in inches

Population: 191,088 (1990); 237,974 (2000); 292,165 (2010); 318,006 (2015 projected); Race: 60.2% White, 20.1% Black, 2.8% Asian, 16.9% Other, 20.0% Hispanic of any race (2010); Density: 275.7 persons per square mile (2010); Average household size: 2.72 (2010); Median age: 32.0 (2010); Males per 100 females: 100.8 (2010).
Religion: Five largest groups: 22.5% Southern Baptist Convention, 10.5% Catholic Church, 4.7% The United Methodist Church, 2.0% Churches of Christ, 1.2% Assemblies of God (2000).
Economy: Unemployment rate: 8.7% (June 2011); Total civilian labor force: 131,977 (June 2011); Leading industries: 23.7% health care and social assistance; 16.4% retail trade; 13.4% accommodation & food services (2009); Farms: 2,384 totaling 431,945 acres (2007); Companies that employ 500 or more persons: 17 (2009); Companies that employ 100 to 499 persons: 102 (2009); Companies that employ less than 100

persons: 4,579 (2009); Black-owned businesses: 1,485 (2007); Hispanic-owned businesses: 1,418 (2007); Asian-owned businesses: n/a (2007); Women-owned businesses: n/a (2007); Retail sales per capita: $9,592 (2010); Single-family building permits issued: 1,750 (2010); Multi-family building permits issued: 164 (2010).
Income: Per capita income: $22,705 (2010); Median household income: $49,037 (2010); Average household income: $62,731 (2010); Percent of households with income of $100,000 or more: 14.5% (2010); Poverty rate: 15.3% (2009); Bankruptcy rate: 2.21% (2010).
Taxes: Total county taxes per capita: $184 (2007); County property taxes per capita: $129 (2007).
Education: Percent of population age 25 and over with: High school diploma (including GED) or higher: 88.5% (2010); Bachelor's degree or higher: 21.9% (2010); Master's degree or higher: 7.1% (2010).
Housing: Homeownership rate: 59.5% (2010); Median home value: $111,422 (2010); Median contract rent: $593 per month (2005-2009 5-year est.); Median year structure built: 1985 (2005-2009 5-year est.)
Health: Birth rate: 199.3 per 10,000 population (2009); Death rate: 64.7 per 10,000 population (2009); Age-adjusted cancer mortality rate: 202.3 deaths per 100,000 population (2007); Number of physicians: 39.1 per 10,000 population (2008); Hospital beds: 101.2 per 10,000 population (2007); Hospital admissions: 2,662.4 per 10,000 population (2007).
Elections: 2008 Presidential election results: 44.7% Obama, 54.5% McCain, 0.1% Nader
Additional Information Contacts

Bell County Government . . . . (254) 939-3521
  http://www.bellcountytx.com
Belton Area Chamber of Commerce . . . . (254) 939-3551
  http://www.beltonchamber.com
City of Belton . . . . (254) 933-5800
  http://www.ci.belton.tx.us
City of Harker Heights . . . . (254) 953-5600
  http://www.ci.harker-heights.tx.us
City of Killeen . . . . (254) 501-7600
  http://www.ci.killeen.tx.us/
City of Temple . . . . (254) 298-5561
  http://www.ci.temple.tx.us
Greater Killeen Chamber of Commerce. . . . . (254) 526-9551
  http://www.killeenchamber.com/chamber
Harker Heights Chamber of Commerce. . . . . (254) 699-4999
  http://www.hhchamber.com
Salado Chamber of Commerce . . . . (254) 947-5040
  http://www.saladochamber.com
Temple Chamber of Commerce. (254) 773-2105
  http://www.templetx.org

Bell County Communities

BELTON (city). County seat. Covers a land area of 12.485 square miles and a water area of 0.671 square miles. Located at 31.05° N. Lat; 97.46° W. Long. Elevation is 509 feet.
History: Belton was established along Nolan Creek. In 1886, the Primary and Female Department of Baylor University was moved to Belton, where it became Mary Hardin-Baylor College.
Population: 12,730 (1990); 14,623 (2000); 15,920 (2010); 17,027 (2015 projected); Race: 74.8% White, 6.0% Black, 1.0% Asian, 18.2% Other, 27.0% Hispanic of any race (2010); Density: 1,275.1 persons per square mile (2010); Average household size: 2.69 (2010); Median age: 30.9 (2010); Males per 100 females: 97.2 (2010); Marriage status: 36.0% never married, 46.8% now married, 7.1% widowed, 10.1% divorced (2005-2009 5-year est.); Foreign born: 7.3% (2005-2009 5-year est.); Ancestry (includes multiple ancestries): 15.6% German, 14.3% English, 10.3% Irish, 6.5% American, 2.6% French (2005-2009 5-year est.).
Economy: Single-family building permits issued: 78 (2010); Multi-family building permits issued: 76 (2010); Employment by occupation: 13.1% management, 20.9% professional, 15.8% services, 24.4% sales, 0.6% farming, 9.2% construction, 16.0% production (2005-2009 5-year est.).
Income: Per capita income: $19,820 (2010); Median household income: $44,407 (2010); Average household income: $58,242 (2010); Percent of households with income of $100,000 or more: 13.5% (2010); Poverty rate: 18.5% (2005-2009 5-year est.).
Taxes: Total city taxes per capita: $462 (2007); City property taxes per capita: $209 (2007).

Education: Percent of population age 25 and over with: High school diploma (including GED) or higher: 76.8% (2010); Bachelor's degree or higher: 21.4% (2010); Master's degree or higher: 7.4% (2010).

School District(s)

Belton ISD (PK-12)

   2009-10 Enrollment: 8,859 . . . . (254) 215-2000

Trinity Charter School (KG-12)

   2009-10 Enrollment: 277 . . . . (512) 706-7564

Four-year College(s)

University of Mary Hardin-Baylor (Private, Not-for-profit, Baptist)

   Fall 2009 Enrollment: 2,689 . . . . (800) 727-8642

   2010-11 Tuition: In-state $21,600; Out-of-state $21,600

Housing: Homeownership rate: 60.7% (2010); Median home value: $94,318 (2010); Median contract rent: $476 per month (2005-2009 5-year est.); Median year structure built: 1974 (2005-2009 5-year est.).

Safety: Violent crime rate: 19.3 per 10,000 population; Property crime rate: 400.4 per 10,000 population (2009).

Newspapers: Belton Journal (Local news; Circulation 4,000); Temple Daily Telegram - Belton Bureau (Local news)

Transportation: Commute to work: 91.0% car, 0.3% public transportation, 4.0% walk, 3.6% work from home (2005-2009 5-year est.); Travel time to work: 39.5% less than 15 minutes, 41.5% 15 to 30 minutes, 14.5% 30 to 45 minutes, 2.1% 45 to 60 minutes, 2.4% 60 minutes or more (2005-2009 5-year est.)

Additional Information Contacts

Belton Area Chamber of Commerce . . . . (254) 939-3551

   http://www.beltonchamber.com

City of Belton . . . . (254) 933-5800

   http://www.ci.belton.tx.us

FORT HOOD (CDP). Covers a land area of 14.945 square miles and a water area of 0.053 square miles. Located at 31.13° N. Lat; 97.78° W. Long.

Population: 35,513 (1990); 33,711 (2000); 31,532 (2010); 31,551 (2015 projected); Race: 54.5% White, 24.6% Black, 2.1% Asian, 18.8% Other, 20.0% Hispanic of any race (2010); Density: 2,109.9 persons per square mile (2010); Average household size: 4.04 (2010); Median age: 22.1 (2010); Males per 100 females: 165.0 (2010); Marriage status: 41.2% never married, 53.4% now married, 0.7% widowed, 4.8% divorced (2005-2009 5-year est.); Foreign born: 4.8% (2005-2009 5-year est.); Ancestry (includes multiple ancestries): 15.6% German, 10.6% Irish, 4.4% English, 3.9% Italian, 3.0% American (2005-2009 5-year est.).

Economy: Employment by occupation: 7.1% management, 14.4% professional, 21.1% services, 39.2% sales, 0.5% farming, 9.8% construction, 7.9% production (2005-2009 5-year est.).

Income: Per capita income: $12,754 (2010); Median household income: $42,456 (2010); Average household income: $46,901 (2010); Percent of households with income of $100,000 or more: 3.5% (2010); Poverty rate: 19.9% (2005-2009 5-year est.).

Education: Percent of population age 25 and over with: High school diploma (including GED) or higher: 97.3% (2010); Bachelor's degree or higher: 13.5% (2010); Master's degree or higher: 3.2% (2010).

School District(s)

Killeen ISD (PK-12)

   2009-10 Enrollment: 39,603 . . . . (254) 336-0006

Housing: Homeownership rate: 2.0% (2010); Median home value: $112,281 (2010); Median contract rent: $939 per month (2005-2009 5-year est.); Median year structure built: 1980 (2005-2009 5-year est.).

Transportation: Commute to work: 73.2% car, 0.1% public transportation, 18.6% walk, 6.9% work from home (2005-2009 5-year est.); Travel time to work: 66.2% less than 15 minutes, 29.4% 15 to 30 minutes, 3.1% 30 to 45 minutes, 1.0% 45 to 60 minutes, 0.3% 60 minutes or more (2005-2009 5-year est.)

HARKER HEIGHTS (city). Covers a land area of 12.760 square miles and a water area of 0 square miles. Located at 31.06° N. Lat; 97.65° W. Long. Elevation is 764 feet.

Population: 12,708 (1990); 17,308 (2000); 25,567 (2010); 29,098 (2015 projected); Race: 66.0% White, 16.1% Black, 4.1% Asian, 13.8% Other, 15.5% Hispanic of any race (2010); Density: 2,003.6 persons per square mile (2010); Average household size: 2.84 (2010); Median age: 33.6 (2010); Males per 100 females: 100.2 (2010); Marriage status: 23.0% never married, 58.7% now married, 5.4% widowed, 12.9% divorced (2005-2009 5-year est.); Foreign born: 7.2% (2005-2009 5-year est.);

Ancestry (includes multiple ancestries): 13.1% German, 7.1% Irish, 5.4% English, 4.0% American, 2.3% Italian (2005-2009 5-year est.).

Economy: Unemployment rate: 7.6% (June 2011); Total civilian labor force: 12,400 (June 2011); Single-family building permits issued: 176 (2010); Multi-family building permits issued: 4 (2010); Employment by occupation: 11.9% management, 23.5% professional, 19.5% services, 28.9% sales, 0.0% farming, 6.8% construction, 9.2% production (2005-2009 5-year est.).

Income: Per capita income: $27,869 (2010); Median household income: $63,149 (2010); Average household income: $79,403 (2010); Percent of households with income of $100,000 or more: 25.7% (2010); Poverty rate: 11.6% (2005-2009 5-year est.).

Taxes: Total city taxes per capita: $392 (2007); City property taxes per capita: $207 (2007).

Education: Percent of population age 25 and over with: High school diploma (including GED) or higher: 91.6% (2010); Bachelor's degree or higher: 31.0% (2010); Master's degree or higher: 12.1% (2010).

School District(s)

Killeen ISD (PK-12)

   2009-10 Enrollment: 39,603 . . . . (254) 336-0006

Housing: Homeownership rate: 60.5% (2010); Median home value: $148,985 (2010); Median contract rent: $550 per month (2005-2009 5-year est.); Median year structure built: 1992 (2005-2009 5-year est.).

Safety: Violent crime rate: 21.2 per 10,000 population; Property crime rate: 291.3 per 10,000 population (2009).

Transportation: Commute to work: 94.1% car, 0.4% public transportation, 2.5% walk, 2.0% work from home (2005-2009 5-year est.); Travel time to work: 29.4% less than 15 minutes, 48.1% 15 to 30 minutes, 14.5% 30 to 45 minutes, 3.2% 45 to 60 minutes, 4.8% 60 minutes or more (2005-2009 5-year est.)

Additional Information Contacts

City of Harker Heights . . . . (254) 953-5600

   http://www.ci.harker-heights.tx.us

Harker Heights Chamber of Commerce. . . . . (254) 699-4999

   http://www.hhchamber.com

HOLLAND (town). Covers a land area of 1.763 square miles and a water area of 0 square miles. Located at 30.88° N. Lat; 97.40° W. Long. Elevation is 525 feet.

Population: 1,118 (1990); 1,102 (2000); 1,055 (2010); 1,073 (2015 projected); Race: 88.3% White, 2.7% Black, 0.7% Asian, 8.2% Other, 22.0% Hispanic of any race (2010); Density: 598.4 persons per square mile (2010); Average household size: 2.77 (2010); Median age: 29.8 (2010); Males per 100 females: 91.8 (2010); Marriage status: 16.6% never married, 41.3% now married, 11.8% widowed, 30.3% divorced (2005-2009 5-year est.); Foreign born: 2.0% (2005-2009 5-year est.); Ancestry (includes multiple ancestries): 24.8% German, 20.4% English, 8.2% Czech, 7.7% Irish, 7.1% Scottish (2005-2009 5-year est.).

Economy: Single-family building permits issued: 1 (2010); Multi-family building permits issued: 0 (2010); Employment by occupation: 6.4% management, 8.1% professional, 23.4% services, 24.3% sales, 0.0% farming, 16.2% construction, 21.7% production (2005-2009 5-year est.).

Income: Per capita income: $16,754 (2010); Median household income: $36,587 (2010); Average household income: $46,312 (2010); Percent of households with income of $100,000 or more: 7.3% (2010); Poverty rate: 16.6% (2005-2009 5-year est.).

Taxes: Total city taxes per capita: $184 (2007); City property taxes per capita: $88 (2007).

Education: Percent of population age 25 and over with: High school diploma (including GED) or higher: 77.2% (2010); Bachelor's degree or higher: 9.1% (2010); Master's degree or higher: 1.9% (2010).

School District(s)

Holland ISD (PK-12)

   2009-10 Enrollment: 540 . . . . (254) 657-0175

Housing: Homeownership rate: 71.7% (2010); Median home value: $65,294 (2010); Median contract rent: $456 per month (2005-2009 5-year est.); Median year structure built: 1971 (2005-2009 5-year est.).

Safety: Violent crime rate: 17.5 per 10,000 population; Property crime rate: 96.2 per 10,000 population (2009).

Transportation: Commute to work: 96.6% car, 0.0% public transportation, 0.0% walk, 2.1% work from home (2005-2009 5-year est.); Travel time to work: 17.3% less than 15 minutes, 37.7% 15 to 30 minutes, 19.0% 30 to 45 minutes, 11.7% 45 to 60 minutes, 14.3% 60 minutes or more (2005-2009 5-year est.)

KILLEEN (city). Covers a land area of 35.346 square miles and a water area of 0.053 square miles. Located at 31.10° N. Lat; 97.72° W. Long. Elevation is 827 feet.

History: Killeen was a small farm village until 1942, when Fort Hood was established nearby. Oveta Culp Hobby, U.S. secretary of health, education, and welfare from 1953 to 1955, was born in Killeen in 1905.

Population: 64,711 (1990); 86,911 (2000); 116,488 (2010); 127,959 (2015 projected); Race: 42.0% White, 32.6% Black, 4.1% Asian, 21.3% Other, 21.7% Hispanic of any race (2010); Density: 3,295.7 persons per square mile (2010); Average household size: 2.74 (2010); Median age: 30.0 (2010); Males per 100 females: 100.7 (2010); Marriage status: 27.6% never married, 55.8% now married, 3.7% widowed, 13.0% divorced (2005-2009 5-year est.); Foreign born: 9.3% (2005-2009 5-year est.); Ancestry (includes multiple ancestries): 9.1% German, 4.6% Irish, 3.4% English, 3.1% American, 2.4% Italian (2005-2009 5-year est.).

Economy: Unemployment rate: 9.4% (June 2011); Total civilian labor force: 50,596 (June 2011); Single-family building permits issued: 1,044 (2010); Multi-family building permits issued: 66 (2010); Employment by occupation: 8.7% management, 16.5% professional, 24.3% services, 29.7% sales, 0.1% farming, 10.8% construction, 9.8% production (2005-2009 5-year est.).

Income: Per capita income: $19,644 (2010); Median household income: $45,587 (2010); Average household income: $53,881 (2010); Percent of households with income of $100,000 or more: 9.3% (2010); Poverty rate: 16.4% (2005-2009 5-year est.).

Taxes: Total city taxes per capita: $463 (2007); City property taxes per capita: $202 (2007).

Education: Percent of population age 25 and over with: High school diploma (including GED) or higher: 92.2% (2010); Bachelor's degree or higher: 17.6% (2010); Master's degree or higher: 4.0% (2010).

School District(s)

Belton ISD (PK-12)
    2009-10 Enrollment: 8,859 . . . . (254) 215-2000
Florence ISD (PK-12)
    2009-10 Enrollment: 1,020 . . . . (254) 793-2850
Honors Academy (KG-12)
    2009-10 Enrollment: 1,068 . . . . (214) 521-6365
Killeen ISD (PK-12)
    2009-10 Enrollment: 39,603 . . . . (254) 336-0006
Richard Milburn Alter High School (Killeen) (09-12)
    2009-10 Enrollment: 161 . . . . (830) 557-6181
Transformative Charter Academy (09-12)
    2009-10 Enrollment: 80 . . . . (254) 628-8989
Troy ISD (PK-12)
    2009-10 Enrollment: 1,274 . . . . (254) 938-2595

Two-year College(s)

Central Texas College (Public)
    Fall 2009 Enrollment: 24,133 . . . . (254) 526-7161
    2010-11 Tuition: In-state $2,310; Out-of-state $4,890

Housing: Homeownership rate: 52.6% (2010); Median home value: $102,881 (2010); Median contract rent: $596 per month (2005-2009 5-year est.); Median year structure built: 1988 (2005-2009 5-year est.).

Hospitals: Darnall Army Community Hospital (264 beds); Metroplex Hospital (213 beds)

Safety: Violent crime rate: 62.2 per 10,000 population; Property crime rate: 456.9 per 10,000 population (2009).

Newspapers: Fort Hood Sentinel (Local news; Circulation 22,500); Killeen Daily Herald (Regional news; Circulation 26,000); Temple Daily Telegram - Killeen Bureau (Local news)

Transportation: Commute to work: 94.7% car, 0.4% public transportation, 1.4% walk, 1.6% work from home (2005-2009 5-year est.); Travel time to work: 35.8% less than 15 minutes, 47.8% 15 to 30 minutes, 10.2% 30 to 45 minutes, 3.0% 45 to 60 minutes, 3.2% 60 minutes or more (2005-2009 5-year est.); Amtrak: train and bus service available.

Airports: Robert Gray AAF (primary service); Skylark Field (general aviation)

Additional Information Contacts

City of Killeen . . . . (254) 501-7600
    http://www.ci.killeen.tx.us/
Greater Killeen Chamber of Commerce . . . . (254) 526-9551
    http://www.killeenchamber.com/chamber

LITTLE RIVER-ACADEMY (city). Covers a land area of 2.745 square miles and a water area of 0 square miles. Located at 30.98° N. Lat; 97.35° W. Long. Elevation is 486 feet.

Population: 1,360 (1990); 1,645 (2000); 1,716 (2010); 1,807 (2015 projected); Race: 88.2% White, 0.5% Black, 0.3% Asian, 11.0% Other, 14.8% Hispanic of any race (2010); Density: 625.1 persons per square mile (2010); Average household size: 2.89 (2010); Median age: 36.4 (2010); Males per 100 females: 97.7 (2010); Marriage status: 22.7% never married, 62.9% now married, 5.3% widowed, 9.2% divorced (2005-2009 5-year est.); Foreign born: 3.1% (2005-2009 5-year est.); Ancestry (includes multiple ancestries): 27.4% English, 25.5% German, 12.1% Irish, 4.7% American, 4.0% Czech (2005-2009 5-year est.).

Economy: Employment by occupation: 8.6% management, 22.7% professional, 12.0% services, 25.8% sales, 0.0% farming, 9.8% construction, 21.1% production (2005-2009 5-year est.).

Income: Per capita income: $23,920 (2010); Median household income: $59,859 (2010); Average household income: $68,981 (2010); Percent of households with income of $100,000 or more: 15.7% (2010); Poverty rate: 6.6% (2005-2009 5-year est.).

Taxes: Total city taxes per capita: $80 (2007); City property taxes per capita: $0 (2007).

Education: Percent of population age 25 and over with: High school diploma (including GED) or higher: 82.5% (2010); Bachelor's degree or higher: 19.1% (2010); Master's degree or higher: 10.1% (2010).

School District(s)

Academy ISD (PK-12)
    2009-10 Enrollment: 1,075 . . . . (254) 982-4304
Holland ISD (PK-12)
    2009-10 Enrollment: 540 . . . . (254) 657-0175
Salado ISD (PK-12)
    2009-10 Enrollment: 1,350 . . . . (254) 947-6900
Troy ISD (PK-12)
    2009-10 Enrollment: 1,274 . . . . (254) 938-2595

Housing: Homeownership rate: 80.5% (2010); Median home value: $104,167 (2010); Median contract rent: $475 per month (2005-2009 5-year est.); Median year structure built: 1981 (2005-2009 5-year est.).

Transportation: Commute to work: 97.6% car, 0.8% public transportation, 0.4% walk, 0.9% work from home (2005-2009 5-year est.); Travel time to work: 24.3% less than 15 minutes, 58.2% 15 to 30 minutes, 8.4% 30 to 45 minutes, 4.6% 45 to 60 minutes, 4.5% 60 minutes or more (2005-2009 5-year est.)

MORGAN'S POINT RESORT (city). Covers a land area of 2.555 square miles and a water area of 0 square miles. Located at 31.15° N. Lat; 97.45° W. Long.

Population: 1,759 (1990); 2,989 (2000); 4,372 (2010); 5,123 (2015 projected); Race: 89.9% White, 0.4% Black, 0.6% Asian, 9.0% Other, 8.9% Hispanic of any race (2010); Density: 1,710.9 persons per square mile (2010); Average household size: 2.70 (2010); Median age: 38.6 (2010); Males per 100 females: 94.9 (2010); Marriage status: 17.4% never married, 61.9% now married, 5.6% widowed, 15.0% divorced (2005-2009 5-year est.); Foreign born: 4.0% (2005-2009 5-year est.); Ancestry (includes multiple ancestries): 28.1% German, 17.8% English, 7.5% Irish, 7.3% American, 4.7% Scotch-Irish (2005-2009 5-year est.).

Economy: Single-family building permits issued: 7 (2010); Multi-family building permits issued: 0 (2010); Employment by occupation: 16.9% management, 19.2% professional, 21.8% services, 30.0% sales, 0.0% farming, 3.4% construction, 8.8% production (2005-2009 5-year est.).

Income: Per capita income: $30,791 (2010); Median household income: $68,204 (2010); Average household income: $83,542 (2010); Percent of households with income of $100,000 or more: 24.7% (2010); Poverty rate: 5.6% (2005-2009 5-year est.).

Taxes: Total city taxes per capita: $344 (2007); City property taxes per capita: $275 (2007).

Education: Percent of population age 25 and over with: High school diploma (including GED) or higher: 88.2% (2010); Bachelor's degree or higher: 26.0% (2010); Master's degree or higher: 9.0% (2010).

Housing: Homeownership rate: 89.5% (2010); Median home value: $129,265 (2010); Median contract rent: $713 per month (2005-2009 5-year est.); Median year structure built: 1991 (2005-2009 5-year est.).

Safety: Violent crime rate: 4.3 per 10,000 population; Property crime rate: 123.8 per 10,000 population (2009).

Transportation: Commute to work: 91.3% car, 0.0% public transportation, 1.0% walk, 7.7% work from home (2005-2009 5-year est.); Travel time to

work: 16.9% less than 15 minutes, 50.7% 15 to 30 minutes, 18.0% 30 to 45 minutes, 7.5% 45 to 60 minutes, 7.0% 60 minutes or more (2005-2009 5-year est.)

NOLANVILLE (city). Covers a land area of 2.529 square miles and a water area of 0 square miles. Located at 31.07° N. Lat; 97.60° W. Long. Elevation is 709 feet.
Population: 1,840 (1990); 2,150 (2000); 3,005 (2010); 3,464 (2015 projected); Race: 79.1% White, 6.4% Black, 0.6% Asian, 13.8% Other, 20.4% Hispanic of any race (2010); Density: 1,188.0 persons per square mile (2010); Average household size: 2.72 (2010); Median age: 33.6 (2010); Males per 100 females: 102.8 (2010); Marriage status: 24.6% never married, 59.2% now married, 4.2% widowed, 12.0% divorced (2005-2009 5-year est.); Foreign born: 7.5% (2005-2009 5-year est.); Ancestry (includes multiple ancestries): 19.0% German, 9.5% Irish, 8.4% English, 2.4% French, 2.2% Scotch-Irish (2005-2009 5-year est.).
Economy: Single-family building permits issued: 24 (2010); Multi-family building permits issued: 0 (2010); Employment by occupation: 5.4% management, 21.0% professional, 17.0% services, 16.3% sales, 4.6% farming, 21.9% construction, 13.7% production (2005-2009 5-year est.).
Income: Per capita income: $21,096 (2010); Median household income: $48,179 (2010); Average household income: $57,344 (2010); Percent of households with income of $100,000 or more: 10.3% (2010); Poverty rate: 14.0% (2005-2009 5-year est.).
Taxes: Total city taxes per capita: $11 (2007); City property taxes per capita: $0 (2007).
Education: Percent of population age 25 and over with: High school diploma (including GED) or higher: 84.3% (2010); Bachelor's degree or higher: 12.8% (2010); Master's degree or higher: 3.2% (2010).
School District(s)
Killeen ISD (PK-12)
    2009-10 Enrollment: 39,603 . . . . (254) 336-0006
Housing: Homeownership rate: 70.8% (2010); Median home value: $85,370 (2010); Median contract rent: $551 per month (2005-2009 5-year est.); Median year structure built: 1990 (2005-2009 5-year est.).
Safety: Violent crime rate: 43.1 per 10,000 population; Property crime rate: 235.5 per 10,000 population (2009).
Transportation: Commute to work: 92.3% car, 2.0% public transportation, 0.8% walk, 2.3% work from home (2005-2009 5-year est.); Travel time to work: 13.0% less than 15 minutes, 58.3% 15 to 30 minutes, 18.6% 30 to 45 minutes, 2.9% 45 to 60 minutes, 7.3% 60 minutes or more (2005-2009 5-year est.)

ROGERS (town). Covers a land area of 0.756 square miles and a water area of 0 square miles. Located at 30.93° N. Lat; 97.22° W. Long. Elevation is 545 feet.
Population: 1,131 (1990); 1,117 (2000); 1,041 (2010); 1,052 (2015 projected); Race: 75.4% White, 2.8% Black, 0.1% Asian, 21.7% Other, 25.8% Hispanic of any race (2010); Density: 1,377.3 persons per square mile (2010); Average household size: 2.66 (2010); Median age: 33.5 (2010); Males per 100 females: 92.1 (2010); Marriage status: 23.4% never married, 48.3% now married, 11.8% widowed, 16.5% divorced (2005-2009 5-year est.); Foreign born: 1.2% (2005-2009 5-year est.); Ancestry (includes multiple ancestries): 28.9% English, 18.5% German, 7.6% Irish, 4.6% Scottish, 3.9% Czech (2005-2009 5-year est.).
Economy: Single-family building permits issued: 0 (2010); Multi-family building permits issued: 0 (2010); Employment by occupation: 5.4% management, 21.0% professional, 17.3% services, 31.8% sales, 2.4% farming, 11.9% construction, 10.1% production (2005-2009 5-year est.).
Income: Per capita income: $19,329 (2010); Median household income: $40,156 (2010); Average household income: $51,362 (2010); Percent of households with income of $100,000 or more: 10.0% (2010); Poverty rate: 14.8% (2005-2009 5-year est.).
Taxes: Total city taxes per capita: $217 (2007); City property taxes per capita: $115 (2007).
Education: Percent of population age 25 and over with: High school diploma (including GED) or higher: 70.7% (2010); Bachelor's degree or higher: 8.3% (2010); Master's degree or higher: 2.2% (2010).
School District(s)
Rogers ISD (PK-12)
    2009-10 Enrollment: 827 . . . . (254) 642-3802
Housing: Homeownership rate: 75.7% (2010); Median home value: $54,773 (2010); Median contract rent: $247 per month (2005-2009 5-year est.); Median year structure built: 1965 (2005-2009 5-year est.).

Transportation: Commute to work: 96.8% car, 0.0% public transportation, 0.6% walk, 1.9% work from home (2005-2009 5-year est.); Travel time to work: 21.0% less than 15 minutes, 50.1% 15 to 30 minutes, 17.4% 30 to 45 minutes, 8.2% 45 to 60 minutes, 3.3% 60 minutes or more (2005-2009 5-year est.)

SALADO (village). Covers a land area of 17.021 square miles and a water area of 0 square miles. Located at 30.95° N. Lat; 97.53° W. Long. Elevation is 600 feet.
History: Salado was founded in 1859 by General Sterling C. Robertson. It was the site of the Scottish Clans of Texas' Tartan Banner Parade each November.
Population: 2,009 (1990); 3,475 (2000); 4,035 (2010); 4,484 (2015 projected); Race: 90.3% White, 0.3% Black, 0.5% Asian, 8.8% Other, 9.5% Hispanic of any race (2010); Density: 237.1 persons per square mile (2010); Average household size: 2.59 (2010); Median age: 45.9 (2010); Males per 100 females: 99.5 (2010); Marriage status: 16.2% never married, 69.3% now married, 7.4% widowed, 7.1% divorced (2005-2009 5-year est.); Foreign born: 1.4% (2005-2009 5-year est.); Ancestry (includes multiple ancestries): 31.1% English, 19.8% German, 15.0% Irish, 10.4% American, 8.5% Scottish (2005-2009 5-year est.).
Economy: Single-family building permits issued: 2 (2010); Multi-family building permits issued: 0 (2010); Employment by occupation: 24.1% management, 29.1% professional, 14.3% services, 22.4% sales, 0.0% farming, 7.0% construction, 3.0% production (2005-2009 5-year est.).
Income: Per capita income: $43,374 (2010); Median household income: $87,700 (2010); Average household income: $112,174 (2010); Percent of households with income of $100,000 or more: 42.1% (2010); Poverty rate: 4.3% (2005-2009 5-year est.).
Taxes: Total city taxes per capita: $278 (2007); City property taxes per capita: $0 (2007).
Education: Percent of population age 25 and over with: High school diploma (including GED) or higher: 91.2% (2010); Bachelor's degree or higher: 40.4% (2010); Master's degree or higher: 16.5% (2010).
School District(s)
Salado ISD (PK-12)
    2009-10 Enrollment: 1,350 . . . . (254) 947-6900
Housing: Homeownership rate: 87.5% (2010); Median home value: $223,784 (2010); Median contract rent: $747 per month (2005-2009 5-year est.); Median year structure built: 1988 (2005-2009 5-year est.).
Safety: Violent crime rate: 0.0 per 10,000 population; Property crime rate: 96.6 per 10,000 population (2009).
Newspapers: Salado Village Voice (Local news; Circulation 2,500)
Transportation: Commute to work: 89.9% car, 0.0% public transportation, 0.0% walk, 10.1% work from home (2005-2009 5-year est.); Travel time to work: 27.7% less than 15 minutes, 43.0% 15 to 30 minutes, 15.5% 30 to 45 minutes, 8.2% 45 to 60 minutes, 5.5% 60 minutes or more (2005-2009 5-year est.)
Additional Information Contacts
Salado Chamber of Commerce . . . . (254) 947-5040
    http://www.saladochamber.com

TEMPLE (city). Covers a land area of 65.351 square miles and a water area of 0.092 square miles. Located at 31.09° N. Lat; 97.36° W. Long. Elevation is 719 feet.
History: Temple was founded in 1880 by the Gulf, Colorado & Santa Fe Railroad, and named for a railroad construction engineer. The climate in Temple, considered especially beneficial for respiratory ailments, led to the establishment of several large hospitals.
Population: 48,442 (1990); 54,514 (2000); 59,269 (2010); 62,887 (2015 projected); Race: 71.1% White, 13.6% Black, 1.7% Asian, 13.5% Other, 21.7% Hispanic of any race (2010); Density: 906.9 persons per square mile (2010); Average household size: 2.45 (2010); Median age: 37.0 (2010); Males per 100 females: 93.2 (2010); Marriage status: 25.7% never married, 54.2% now married, 8.3% widowed, 11.8% divorced (2005-2009 5-year est.); Foreign born: 8.1% (2005-2009 5-year est.); Ancestry (includes multiple ancestries): 16.5% German, 12.3% English, 8.6% Irish, 5.5% American, 3.2% Scotch-Irish (2005-2009 5-year est.).
Economy: Unemployment rate: 7.5% (June 2011); Total civilian labor force: 31,799 (June 2011); Single-family building permits issued: 408 (2010); Multi-family building permits issued: 18 (2010); Employment by occupation: 11.2% management, 24.8% professional, 18.7% services, 23.6% sales, 0.1% farming, 7.8% construction, 13.7% production (2005-2009 5-year est.).

Income: Per capita income: $25,204 (2010); Median household income: $45,840 (2010); Average household income: $62,860 (2010); Percent of households with income of $100,000 or more: 14.6% (2010); Poverty rate: 13.0% (2005-2009 5-year est.).

Taxes: Total city taxes per capita: $694 (2007); City property taxes per capita: $312 (2007).

Education: Percent of population age 25 and over with: High school diploma (including GED) or higher: 83.9% (2010); Bachelor's degree or higher: 26.2% (2010); Master's degree or higher: 9.8% (2010).

School District(s)

Belton ISD (PK-12)
  2009-10 Enrollment: 8,859 . . . . (254) 215-2000
Temple Education Center (PK-12)
  2009-10 Enrollment: 179 . . . . (254) 778-8682
Temple ISD (PK-12)
  2009-10 Enrollment: 8,783 . . . . (254) 215-6760

Two-year College(s)

Temple College (Public)
  Fall 2009 Enrollment: 5,659 . . . . (254) 298-8282
  2010-11 Tuition: In-state $3,120; Out-of-state $4,704

Vocational/Technical School(s)

Central Texas Beauty College (Private, For-profit)
  Fall 2009 Enrollment: 74 . . . . (254) 773-9911
  2010-11 Tuition: $7,295

Housing: Homeownership rate: 59.5% (2010); Median home value: $108,356 (2010); Median contract rent: $536 per month (2005-2009 5-year est.); Median year structure built: 1977 (2005-2009 5-year est.).

Hospitals: Central Texas Veterans Health Care System (1063 beds); Kings Daughters Hospital (150 beds); Scott and White Memorial Hospital (625 beds)

Newspapers: Temple Daily Telegram (Local news; Circulation 22,587)

Transportation: Commute to work: 95.4% car, 0.2% public transportation, 1.7% walk, 1.7% work from home (2005-2009 5-year est.); Travel time to work: 50.8% less than 15 minutes, 35.0% 15 to 30 minutes, 8.1% 30 to 45 minutes, 4.0% 45 to 60 minutes, 2.0% 60 minutes or more (2005-2009 5-year est.); Amtrak: train service available.

Airports: Draughon-Miller Central Texas Regional (general aviation)

Additional Information Contacts

City of Temple . . . . (254) 298-5561
  http://www.ci.temple.tx.us
Temple Chamber of Commerce . . . . (254) 773-2105
  http://www.templetx.org

TROY (city). Covers a land area of 3.556 square miles and a water area of 0 square miles. Located at 31.20° N. Lat; 97.30° W. Long. Elevation is 679 feet.

Population: 1,212 (1990); 1,378 (2000); 1,398 (2010); 1,447 (2015 projected); Race: 89.8% White, 0.6% Black, 0.4% Asian, 9.2% Other, 15.9% Hispanic of any race (2010); Density: 393.1 persons per square mile (2010); Average household size: 2.70 (2010); Median age: 37.3 (2010); Males per 100 females: 92.6 (2010); Marriage status: 22.1% never married, 55.5% now married, 6.0% widowed, 16.4% divorced (2005-2009 5-year est.); Foreign born: 3.0% (2005-2009 5-year est.); Ancestry (includes multiple ancestries): 22.4% English, 17.5% German, 8.1% Irish, 7.1% American, 4.3% Scottish (2005-2009 5-year est.).

Economy: Single-family building permits issued: 10 (2010); Multi-family building permits issued: 0 (2010); Employment by occupation: 10.7% management, 22.0% professional, 13.1% services, 25.8% sales, 0.4% farming, 8.6% construction, 19.4% production (2005-2009 5-year est.).

Income: Per capita income: $24,318 (2010); Median household income: $56,305 (2010); Average household income: $65,609 (2010); Percent of households with income of $100,000 or more: 18.2% (2010); Poverty rate: 11.6% (2005-2009 5-year est.).

Taxes: Total city taxes per capita: $275 (2007); City property taxes per capita: $132 (2007).

Education: Percent of population age 25 and over with: High school diploma (including GED) or higher: 86.2% (2010); Bachelor's degree or higher: 17.4% (2010); Master's degree or higher: 5.8% (2010).

School District(s)

Troy ISD (PK-12)
  2009-10 Enrollment: 1,274 . . . . (254) 938-2595

Housing: Homeownership rate: 79.7% (2010); Median home value: $95,000 (2010); Median contract rent: $510 per month (2005-2009 5-year est.); Median year structure built: 1977 (2005-2009 5-year est.).

Safety: Violent crime rate: 7.0 per 10,000 population; Property crime rate: 175.1 per 10,000 population (2009).

Transportation: Commute to work: 94.4% car, 0.0% public transportation, 0.3% walk, 4.6% work from home (2005-2009 5-year est.); Travel time to work: 37.0% less than 15 minutes, 50.6% 15 to 30 minutes, 8.9% 30 to 45 minutes, 2.2% 45 to 60 minutes, 1.4% 60 minutes or more (2005-2009 5-year est.)

Bexar County

Located in southwest central Texas; drained by the Medina and San Antonio Rivers. Covers a land area of 1,246.82 square miles, a water area of 9.84 square miles, and is located in the Central Time Zone at 29.45° N. Lat., 98.50° W. Long. The county was founded in 1835. County seat is San Antonio.

Bexar County is part of the San Antonio-New Braunfels, TX Metropolitan Statistical Area. The entire metro area includes: Atascosa County, TX; Bandera County, TX; Bexar County, TX; Comal County, TX; Guadalupe County, TX; Kendall County, TX; Medina County, TX; Wilson County, TX

Weather Station: San Antonio Intl Arpt   Elevation: 809 feet

	Jan	Feb	Mar	Apr	May	Jun	Jul	Aug	Sep	Oct	Nov	Dec
High	63	67	74	81	87	93	95	96	91	82	72	64
Low	41	44	51	58	67	73	75	75	69	60	50	42
Precip	1.6	1.7	2.3	2.0	4.1	4.0	2.6	2.2	2.9	4.1	2.4	1.9
Snow	0.7	0.1	tr	tr	tr	tr	0.0	0.0	0.0	tr	tr	tr

High and Low temperatures in degrees Fahrenheit; Precipitation and Snow in inches

Population: 1,185,394 (1990); 1,392,931 (2000); 1,660,756 (2010); 1,788,089 (2015 projected); Race: 66.6% White, 7.0% Black, 2.0% Asian, 24.4% Other, 58.2% Hispanic of any race (2010); Density: 1,332.0 persons per square mile (2010); Average household size: 2.79 (2010); Median age: 33.1 (2010); Males per 100 females: 95.6 (2010).

Religion: Five largest groups: 41.2% Catholic Church, 8.6% Southern Baptist Convention, 3.2% Independent, Charismatic Churches, 3.0% The United Methodist Church, 0.9% Evangelical Lutheran Church in America (2000).

Economy: Unemployment rate: 8.3% (June 2011); Total civilian labor force: 799,087 (June 2011); Leading industries: 16.1% health care and social assistance; 12.9% retail trade; 12.9% accommodation & food services (2009); Farms: 2,496 totaling 425,909 acres (2007); Companies that employ 500 or more persons: 112 (2009); Companies that employ 100 to 499 persons: 863 (2009); Companies that employ less than 100 persons: 31,436 (2009); Black-owned businesses: 5,019 (2007); Hispanic-owned businesses: 49,564 (2007); Asian-owned businesses: 4,584 (2007); Women-owned businesses: 37,734 (2007); Retail sales per capita: $13,835 (2010); Single-family building permits issued: 3,151 (2010); Multi-family building permits issued: 1,502 (2010).

Income: Per capita income: $22,221 (2010); Median household income: $46,722 (2010); Average household income: $62,513 (2010); Percent of households with income of $100,000 or more: 15.8% (2010); Poverty rate: 17.7% (2009); Bankruptcy rate: 2.28% (2010).

Taxes: Total county taxes per capita: $273 (2007); County property taxes per capita: $250 (2007).

Education: Percent of population age 25 and over with: High school diploma (including GED) or higher: 80.6% (2010); Bachelor's degree or higher: 24.2% (2010); Master's degree or higher: 8.5% (2010).

Housing: Homeownership rate: 62.9% (2010); Median home value: $110,000 (2010); Median contract rent: $609 per month (2005-2009 5-year est.); Median year structure built: 1980 (2005-2009 5-year est.).

Health: Birth rate: 167.5 per 10,000 population (2009); Death rate: 66.5 per 10,000 population (2009); Age-adjusted cancer mortality rate: 166.4 deaths per 100,000 population (2007); Number of physicians: 33.0 per 10,000 population (2008); Hospital beds: 44.3 per 10,000 population (2007); Hospital admissions: 1,746.1 per 10,000 population (2007).

Environment: Air Quality Index: 71.2% good, 25.5% moderate, 3.3% unhealthy for sensitive individuals, 0.0% unhealthy (percent of days in 2008)

Elections: 2008 Presidential election results: 52.2% Obama, 46.7% McCain, 0.0% Nader

National and State Parks: Martinez State Park; San Antonio Missions National Historical Park

Additional Information Contacts

Bexar County Government . . . . (210) 335-2011
  http://www.bexar.org

African American Chamber of Commerce of San Antonio. . (210) 490-1624
　http://www.aaccsa.com
Alamo City Black Chamber of Commerce . . . . (210) 226-9055
　http://www.alamocitychamber.org
City of Alamo Heights . . . . (210) 822-3331
　http://www.alamoheightstx.gov
City of Converse . . . . (210) 658-5356
　http://www.conversetx.net
City of Hill Country Village . . . . (210) 494-3671
　http://www.hcv.org
City of Kirby . . . . (210) 661-3198
　http://www.kirbytx.org
City of Leon Valley . . . . (210) 684-1391
　http://www.leonvalleytexas.gov
City of Live Oak . . . . (210) 653-9140
　http://www.liveoaktx.net
City of San Antonio . . . . (210) 207-7080
　http://www.sanantonio.gov
City of Selma . . . . (210) 651-6661
　http://www.ci.selma.tx.us
City of Terrell Hills . . . . (210) 824-7401
　http://www.terrell-hills.com
City of Universal City . . . . (210) 659-0333
　http://www.universalcitytexas.com
City of Windcrest . . . . (210) 655-0022
　http://www.ci.windcrest.tx.us
Greater San Antonio Chamber of Commerce . . . . (210) 229-2100
　http://www.sachamber.org
North San Antonio Chamber of Commerce . . . . (210) 344-4848
　http://www.northsachamber.com
Randolph Metrocom Chamber of Commerce . . . . (210) 658-8322
　http://www.randolphmetrocomchamber.org
San Antonio Hispanic Chamber of Commerce . . . . (210) 225-0462
　http://www.sahcc.org
San Antonio Women's Chamber of Commerce . . . . (210) 299-2636
　http://sanantoniowomenschamberofcommerce.memberlodge.org
South San Antonio Chamber . . . . (210) 533-1600
　http://www.southsachamber.org
Westside Development Corporation . . . . (210) 207-0039
　http://www.sanantonio.gov/wdc

Bexar County Communities

ADKINS (unincorporated postal area, zip code 78101). Aka Sayors. Covers a land area of 51.720 square miles and a water area of 0.004 square miles. Located at 29.32° N. Lat; 98.21° W. Long. Elevation is 558 feet.
Population: 6,203 (2000); Race: 85.2% White, 3.4% Black, 0.6% Asian, 10.8% Other, 22.3% Hispanic of any race (2000); Density: 119.9 persons per square mile (2000); Age: 28.6% under 18, 10.2% over 64 (2000); Marriage status: 21.3% never married, 65.0% now married, 4.5% widowed, 9.1% divorced (2000); Foreign born: 2.2% (2000); Ancestry (includes multiple ancestries): 25.2% German, 13.4% Polish, 10.2% Irish, 7.1% American (2000).
Economy: Employment by occupation: 12.3% management, 13.4% professional, 9.2% services, 28.7% sales, 1.0% farming, 20.7% construction, 14.7% production (2000).
Income: Per capita income: $20,134 (2000); Median household income: $48,636 (2000); Poverty rate: 179.1% (2000).
Education: Percent of population age 25 and over with: High school diploma (including GED) or higher: 81.2% (2000); Bachelor's degree or higher: 13.5% (2000).
Housing: Homeownership rate: 90.0% (2000); Median home value: $93,800 (2000); Median contract rent: $422 per month (2000); Median year structure built: 1986 (2000).
Transportation: Commute to work: 93.5% car, 0.4% public transportation, 2.0% walk, 3.4% work from home (2000); Travel time to work: 12.9% less than 15 minutes, 31.2% 15 to 30 minutes, 37.3% 30 to 45 minutes, 11.4% 45 to 60 minutes, 7.1% 60 minutes or more (2000)

ALAMO HEIGHTS (city). Covers a land area of 1.846 square miles and a water area of 0 square miles. Located at 29.48° N. Lat; 98.46° W. Long. Elevation is 801 feet.
History: Fort Sam Houston to SE. Incorporated 1926.

Population: 6,502 (1990); 7,319 (2000); 7,638 (2010); 7,968 (2015 projected); Race: 92.2% White, 0.8% Black, 1.2% Asian, 5.9% Other, 17.3% Hispanic of any race (2010); Density: 4,137.7 persons per square mile (2010); Average household size: 2.22 (2010); Median age: 42.6 (2010); Males per 100 females: 83.7 (2010); Marriage status: 24.6% never married, 59.2% now married, 5.1% widowed, 11.1% divorced (2005-2009 5-year est.); Foreign born: 3.6% (2005-2009 5-year est.); Ancestry (includes multiple ancestries): 19.9% German, 19.0% English, 14.6% Irish, 8.7% American, 6.9% Scotch-Irish (2005-2009 5-year est.).
Economy: Single-family building permits issued: 4 (2010); Multi-family building permits issued: 25 (2010); Employment by occupation: 21.5% management, 42.4% professional, 6.1% services, 22.2% sales, 0.0% farming, 4.7% construction, 3.1% production (2005-2009 5-year est.).
Income: Per capita income: $47,317 (2010); Median household income: $74,658 (2010); Average household income: $110,412 (2010); Percent of households with income of $100,000 or more: 35.5% (2010); Poverty rate: 4.5% (2005-2009 5-year est.).
Taxes: Total city taxes per capita: $794 (2007); City property taxes per capita: $520 (2007).
Education: Percent of population age 25 and over with: High school diploma (including GED) or higher: 97.3% (2010); Bachelor's degree or higher: 66.1% (2010); Master's degree or higher: 30.6% (2010).
Housing: Homeownership rate: 66.6% (2010); Median home value: $318,429 (2010); Median contract rent: $768 per month (2005-2009 5-year est.); Median year structure built: 1948 (2005-2009 5-year est.).
Safety: Violent crime rate: 9.5 per 10,000 population; Property crime rate: 364.6 per 10,000 population (2009).
Transportation: Commute to work: 89.5% car, 1.1% public transportation, 3.7% walk, 4.3% work from home (2005-2009 5-year est.); Travel time to work: 41.2% less than 15 minutes, 39.8% 15 to 30 minutes, 16.3% 30 to 45 minutes, 0.9% 45 to 60 minutes, 1.9% 60 minutes or more (2005-2009 5-year est.)
Additional Information Contacts
City of Alamo Heights . . . . (210) 822-3331
　http://www.alamoheightstx.gov

ATASCOSA (unincorporated postal area, zip code 78002). Covers a land area of 41.814 square miles and a water area of 0.098 square miles. Located at 29.28° N. Lat; 98.72° W. Long. Elevation is 650 feet.
Population: 6,691 (2000); Race: 69.6% White, 0.8% Black, 0.1% Asian, 29.5% Other, 68.6% Hispanic of any race (2000); Density: 160.0 persons per square mile (2000); Age: 28.9% under 18, 11.3% over 64 (2000); Marriage status: 24.7% never married, 57.4% now married, 7.6% widowed, 10.3% divorced (2000); Foreign born: 10.7% (2000); Ancestry (includes multiple ancestries): 10.3% German, 5.6% Irish, 5.4% American, 2.6% English (2000).
Economy: Employment by occupation: 8.7% management, 10.8% professional, 13.4% services, 27.5% sales, 2.0% farming, 22.8% construction, 14.8% production (2000).
Income: Per capita income: $12,923 (2000); Median household income: $29,855 (2000); Poverty rate: 179.1% (2000).
Education: Percent of population age 25 and over with: High school diploma (including GED) or higher: 60.8% (2000); Bachelor's degree or higher: 6.9% (2000).
School District(s)
Southwest ISD (PK-12)
　2009-10 Enrollment: 11,531 . . . . (210) 622-4731
Housing: Homeownership rate: 77.0% (2000); Median home value: $57,500 (2000); Median contract rent: $294 per month (2000); Median year structure built: 1980 (2000).
Transportation: Commute to work: 91.0% car, 0.0% public transportation, 0.8% walk, 5.3% work from home (2000); Travel time to work: 12.8% less than 15 minutes, 24.4% 15 to 30 minutes, 41.4% 30 to 45 minutes, 12.0% 45 to 60 minutes, 9.4% 60 minutes or more (2000)

BALCONES HEIGHTS (city). Covers a land area of 0.645 square miles and a water area of 0 square miles. Located at 29.49° N. Lat; 98.54° W. Long. Elevation is 830 feet.
Population: 3,022 (1990); 3,016 (2000); 2,947 (2010); 2,992 (2015 projected); Race: 68.2% White, 3.8% Black, 1.5% Asian, 26.5% Other, 76.6% Hispanic of any race (2010); Density: 4,567.7 persons per square mile (2010); Average household size: 2.09 (2010); Median age: 33.4 (2010); Males per 100 females: 106.4 (2010); Marriage status: 38.5% never married, 38.1% now married, 3.6% widowed, 19.7% divorced (2005-2009 5-year est.); Foreign born: 13.3% (2005-2009 5-year est.);

Ancestry (includes multiple ancestries): 8.2% German, 4.9% Irish, 4.8% English, 2.0% Scotch-Irish, 1.5% Italian (2005-2009 5-year est.).
Economy: Single-family building permits issued: 0 (2010); Multi-family building permits issued: 0 (2010); Employment by occupation: 8.3% management, 6.5% professional, 32.3% services, 22.8% sales, 1.0% farming, 18.8% construction, 10.3% production (2005-2009 5-year est.).
Income: Per capita income: $14,219 (2010); Median household income: $22,784 (2010); Average household income: $29,760 (2010); Percent of households with income of $100,000 or more: 3.5% (2010); Poverty rate: 36.6% (2005-2009 5-year est.).
Taxes: Total city taxes per capita: $889 (2007); City property taxes per capita: $326 (2007).
Education: Percent of population age 25 and over with: High school diploma (including GED) or higher: 78.4% (2010); Bachelor's degree or higher: 13.0% (2010); Master's degree or higher: 4.6% (2010).
Housing: Homeownership rate: 17.0% (2010); Median home value: $86,346 (2010); Median contract rent: $489 per month (2005-2009 5-year est.); Median year structure built: 1968 (2005-2009 5-year est.).
Safety: Violent crime rate: 130.8 per 10,000 population; Property crime rate: 1,519.6 per 10,000 population (2009).
Transportation: Commute to work: 73.7% car, 17.3% public transportation, 2.8% walk, 0.7% work from home (2005-2009 5-year est.); Travel time to work: 20.5% less than 15 minutes, 35.7% 15 to 30 minutes, 30.3% 30 to 45 minutes, 1.6% 45 to 60 minutes, 11.9% 60 minutes or more (2005-2009 5-year est.)

CASTLE HILLS (city).
Covers a land area of 2.480 square miles and a water area of 0 square miles. Located at 29.52° N. Lat; 98.51° W. Long. Elevation is 840 feet.
History: The area was originally settled in the early 1920's by a handful of families attracted by the plentiful water supply provided by the Olmos Creek. Perhaps most notable the Slimp Family, whose house was set atop a hill for which the city was named.
Population: 4,198 (1990); 4,202 (2000); 4,146 (2010); 4,224 (2015 projected); Race: 90.6% White, 0.6% Black, 1.8% Asian, 6.9% Other, 38.6% Hispanic of any race (2010); Density: 1,671.5 persons per square mile (2010); Average household size: 2.24 (2010); Median age: 51.8 (2010); Males per 100 females: 84.9 (2010); Marriage status: 21.7% never married, 60.2% now married, 10.4% widowed, 7.7% divorced (2005-2009 5-year est.); Foreign born: 6.0% (2005-2009 5-year est.); Ancestry (includes multiple ancestries): 13.0% English, 11.8% German, 6.8% Irish, 5.1% Scotch-Irish, 5.0% American (2005-2009 5-year est.).
Economy: Single-family building permits issued: 6 (2010); Multi-family building permits issued: 0 (2010); Employment by occupation: 17.5% management, 36.8% professional, 6.5% services, 31.3% sales, 0.0% farming, 2.9% construction, 4.9% production (2005-2009 5-year est.).
Income: Per capita income: $38,496 (2010); Median household income: $57,454 (2010); Average household income: $85,776 (2010); Percent of households with income of $100,000 or more: 27.4% (2010); Poverty rate: 6.9% (2005-2009 5-year est.).
Taxes: Total city taxes per capita: $760 (2007); City property taxes per capita: $415 (2007).
Education: Percent of population age 25 and over with: High school diploma (including GED) or higher: 93.8% (2010); Bachelor's degree or higher: 42.3% (2010); Master's degree or higher: 16.5% (2010).
Housing: Homeownership rate: 74.6% (2010); Median home value: $201,408 (2010); Median contract rent: $764 per month (2005-2009 5-year est.); Median year structure built: 1964 (2005-2009 5-year est.).
Safety: Violent crime rate: 19.0 per 10,000 population; Property crime rate: 739.4 per 10,000 population (2009).
Transportation: Commute to work: 87.7% car, 4.4% public transportation, 0.4% walk, 5.5% work from home (2005-2009 5-year est.); Travel time to work: 36.2% less than 15 minutes, 46.2% 15 to 30 minutes, 10.1% 30 to 45 minutes, 6.2% 45 to 60 minutes, 1.3% 60 minutes or more (2005-2009 5-year est.)

CHINA GROVE (town).
Covers a land area of 4.116 square miles and a water area of 0 square miles. Located at 29.39° N. Lat; 98.34° W. Long. Elevation is 653 feet.
Population: 878 (1990); 1,247 (2000); 1,236 (2010); 1,259 (2015 projected); Race: 82.7% White, 9.4% Black, 0.1% Asian, 7.8% Other, 25.7% Hispanic of any race (2010); Density: 300.3 persons per square mile (2010); Average household size: 2.90 (2010); Median age: 39.6 (2010); Males per 100 females: 95.6 (2010); Marriage status: 21.2% never married, 68.3% now married, 2.3% widowed, 8.1% divorced (2005-2009 5-year

est.); Foreign born: 1.8% (2005-2009 5-year est.); Ancestry (includes multiple ancestries): 28.0% German, 13.7% Polish, 7.3% Irish, 4.3% Scottish, 4.3% Scotch-Irish (2005-2009 5-year est.).
Economy: Single-family building permits issued: 0 (2010); Multi-family building permits issued: 0 (2010); Employment by occupation: 17.8% management, 24.2% professional, 3.8% services, 29.1% sales, 0.0% farming, 11.6% construction, 13.5% production (2005-2009 5-year est.).
Income: Per capita income: $27,359 (2010); Median household income: $72,727 (2010); Average household income: $79,501 (2010); Percent of households with income of $100,000 or more: 25.8% (2010); Poverty rate: 1.9% (2005-2009 5-year est.).
Taxes: Total city taxes per capita: $153 (2007); City property taxes per capita: $18 (2007).
Education: Percent of population age 25 and over with: High school diploma (including GED) or higher: 87.2% (2010); Bachelor's degree or higher: 19.9% (2010); Master's degree or higher: 6.7% (2010).
Housing: Homeownership rate: 92.0% (2010); Median home value: $131,863 (2010); Median contract rent: n/a per month (2005-2009 5-year est.); Median year structure built: 1985 (2005-2009 5-year est.).
Transportation: Commute to work: 98.3% car, 0.0% public transportation, 1.0% walk, 0.8% work from home (2005-2009 5-year est.); Travel time to work: 32.6% less than 15 minutes, 39.0% 15 to 30 minutes, 21.1% 30 to 45 minutes, 6.2% 45 to 60 minutes, 1.2% 60 minutes or more (2005-2009 5-year est.)

CONVERSE (city).
Covers a land area of 6.329 square miles and a water area of 0 square miles. Located at 29.51° N. Lat; 98.31° W. Long. Elevation is 719 feet.
Population: 8,893 (1990); 11,508 (2000); 15,602 (2010); 17,514 (2015 projected); Race: 59.5% White, 17.9% Black, 2.3% Asian, 20.3% Other, 37.7% Hispanic of any race (2010); Density: 2,465.2 persons per square mile (2010); Average household size: 2.91 (2010); Median age: 34.0 (2010); Males per 100 females: 97.4 (2010); Marriage status: 24.4% never married, 53.1% now married, 5.1% widowed, 17.4% divorced (2005-2009 5-year est.); Foreign born: 6.4% (2005-2009 5-year est.); Ancestry (includes multiple ancestries): 17.9% German, 10.3% Irish, 5.2% English, 4.3% Dutch, 3.4% Italian (2005-2009 5-year est.).
Economy: Single-family building permits issued: 142 (2010); Multi-family building permits issued: 0 (2010); Employment by occupation: 11.9% management, 18.9% professional, 15.9% services, 31.2% sales, 0.8% farming, 9.0% construction, 12.4% production (2005-2009 5-year est.).
Income: Per capita income: $20,982 (2010); Median household income: $53,947 (2010); Average household income: $61,271 (2010); Percent of households with income of $100,000 or more: 13.3% (2010); Poverty rate: 10.0% (2005-2009 5-year est.).
Taxes: Total city taxes per capita: $356 (2007); City property taxes per capita: $179 (2007).
Education: Percent of population age 25 and over with: High school diploma (including GED) or higher: 90.5% (2010); Bachelor's degree or higher: 18.2% (2010); Master's degree or higher: 5.2% (2010).

School District(s)
Judson ISD (PK-12)
   2009-10 Enrollment: 21,750 . . . . (210) 945-5100
Housing: Homeownership rate: 69.5% (2010); Median home value: $106,632 (2010); Median contract rent: $713 per month (2005-2009 5-year est.); Median year structure built: 1989 (2005-2009 5-year est.).
Safety: Violent crime rate: 18.5 per 10,000 population; Property crime rate: 253.9 per 10,000 population (2009).
Transportation: Commute to work: 96.6% car, 0.0% public transportation, 0.0% walk, 1.9% work from home (2005-2009 5-year est.); Travel time to work: 21.2% less than 15 minutes, 48.5% 15 to 30 minutes, 22.5% 30 to 45 minutes, 5.1% 45 to 60 minutes, 2.7% 60 minutes or more (2005-2009 5-year est.)
Additional Information Contacts
City of Converse . . . . (210) 658-5356
  http://www.conversetx.net

CROSS MOUNTAIN (CDP).
Covers a land area of 7.341 square miles and a water area of 0 square miles. Located at 29.65° N. Lat; 98.65° W. Long. Elevation is 1,398 feet.
Population: 1,009 (1990); 1,524 (2000); 3,151 (2010); 3,617 (2015 projected); Race: 85.6% White, 3.3% Black, 2.5% Asian, 8.7% Other, 27.5% Hispanic of any race (2010); Density: 429.3 persons per square mile (2010); Average household size: 2.80 (2010); Median age: 40.7 (2010); Males per 100 females: 98.7 (2010); Marriage status: 16.1% never married,

75.0% now married, 3.2% widowed, 5.7% divorced (2005-2009 5-year est.); Foreign born: 9.6% (2005-2009 5-year est.); Ancestry (includes multiple ancestries): 15.6% German, 10.3% Irish, 8.3% English, 6.3% American, 5.4% Italian (2005-2009 5-year est.).

Economy: Employment by occupation: 28.2% management, 38.2% professional, 6.3% services, 18.4% sales, 0.0% farming, 4.3% construction, 4.6% production (2005-2009 5-year est.).

Income: Per capita income: $49,447 (2010); Median household income: $114,221 (2010); Average household income: $139,277 (2010); Percent of households with income of $100,000 or more: 57.0% (2010); Poverty rate: 2.3% (2005-2009 5-year est.).

Education: Percent of population age 25 and over with: High school diploma (including GED) or higher: 98.5% (2010); Bachelor's degree or higher: 56.4% (2010); Master's degree or higher: 29.2% (2010).

Housing: Homeownership rate: 93.0% (2010); Median home value: $287,299 (2010); Median contract rent: $1,303 per month (2005-2009 5-year est.); Median year structure built: 2002 (2005-2009 5-year est.).

Transportation: Commute to work: 88.9% car, 0.0% public transportation, 0.0% walk, 9.4% work from home (2005-2009 5-year est.); Travel time to work: 11.8% less than 15 minutes, 49.9% 15 to 30 minutes, 28.1% 30 to 45 minutes, 7.7% 45 to 60 minutes, 2.6% 60 minutes or more (2005-2009 5-year est.)

ELMENDORF (city).

ELMENDORF (city). Covers a land area of 1.235 square miles and a water area of 0 square miles. Located at 29.26° N. Lat; 98.33° W. Long. Elevation is 499 feet.

Population: 568 (1990); 664 (2000); 673 (2010); 693 (2015 projected); Race: 65.2% White, 1.6% Black, 0.1% Asian, 33.0% Other, 64.0% Hispanic of any race (2010); Density: 544.7 persons per square mile (2010); Average household size: 3.15 (2010); Median age: 32.5 (2010); Males per 100 females: 92.8 (2010); Marriage status: 29.9% never married, 47.6% now married, 4.3% widowed, 18.2% divorced (2005-2009 5-year est.); Foreign born: 9.0% (2005-2009 5-year est.); Ancestry (includes multiple ancestries): 14.0% French, 13.8% German, 8.3% Irish, 2.5% Polish, 2.1% English (2005-2009 5-year est.).

Economy: Single-family building permits issued: 4 (2010); Multi-family building permits issued: 0 (2010); Employment by occupation: 6.9% management, 24.4% professional, 19.3% services, 17.0% sales, 0.0% farming, 16.6% construction, 15.8% production (2005-2009 5-year est.).

Income: Per capita income: $19,686 (2010); Median household income: $52,083 (2010); Average household income: $63,603 (2010); Percent of households with income of $100,000 or more: 16.0% (2010); Poverty rate: 27.8% (2005-2009 5-year est.).

Taxes: Total city taxes per capita: $124 (2007); City property taxes per capita: $47 (2007).

Education: Percent of population age 25 and over with: High school diploma (including GED) or higher: 72.4% (2010); Bachelor's degree or higher: 6.8% (2010); Master's degree or higher: 1.8% (2010).

Housing: Homeownership rate: 85.4% (2010); Median home value: $84,706 (2010); Median contract rent: $500 per month (2005-2009 5-year est.); Median year structure built: 1991 (2005-2009 5-year est.).

Transportation: Commute to work: 98.5% car, 0.7% public transportation, 0.4% walk, 0.0% work from home (2005-2009 5-year est.); Travel time to work: 5.2% less than 15 minutes, 35.7% 15 to 30 minutes, 35.9% 30 to 45 minutes, 21.4% 45 to 60 minutes, 1.7% 60 minutes or more (2005-2009 5-year est.)

FAIR OAKS RANCH (city).

FAIR OAKS RANCH (city). Covers a land area of 7.153 square miles and a water area of 0 square miles. Located at 29.73° N. Lat; 98.64° W. Long. Elevation is 1,270 feet.

History: During the 1930s Ralph E. Fair, Sr., a successful oilman and rancher, purchased several land tracts that became the 5000-acre Fair Oaks Ranch. He originally focused his efforts on raising racehorses, but in the 1940s Fair began cattle ranching and developed his own Hereford strain.

Population: 2,196 (1990); 4,695 (2000); 5,691 (2010); 6,598 (2015 projected); Race: 94.6% White, 0.8% Black, 0.8% Asian, 3.8% Other, 11.8% Hispanic of any race (2010); Density: 795.6 persons per square mile (2010); Average household size: 2.79 (2010); Median age: 46.8 (2010); Males per 100 females: 101.3 (2010); Marriage status: 14.7% never married, 78.9% now married, 3.4% widowed, 3.0% divorced (2005-2009 5-year est.); Foreign born: 2.4% (2005-2009 5-year est.); Ancestry (includes multiple ancestries): 28.0% German, 25.1% English, 17.0% Irish, 7.7% American, 4.4% Polish (2005-2009 5-year est.).

Economy: Single-family building permits issued: 30 (2010); Multi-family building permits issued: 0 (2010); Employment by occupation: 31.7% management, 30.6% professional, 7.7% services, 23.9% sales, 0.9% farming, 2.5% construction, 2.7% production (2005-2009 5-year est.).

Income: Per capita income: $51,113 (2010); Median household income: $109,760 (2010); Average household income: $142,811 (2010); Percent of households with income of $100,000 or more: 55.0% (2010); Poverty rate: 0.9% (2005-2009 5-year est.).

Taxes: Total city taxes per capita: $342 (2007); City property taxes per capita: $276 (2007).

Education: Percent of population age 25 and over with: High school diploma (including GED) or higher: 96.7% (2010); Bachelor's degree or higher: 54.3% (2010); Master's degree or higher: 21.7% (2010).

School District(s)

Boerne ISD (PK-12)
    2009-10 Enrollment: 6,392 . . . . (830) 357-2000

Housing: Homeownership rate: 93.7% (2010); Median home value: $362,554 (2010); Median contract rent: $2,000+ per month (2005-2009 5-year est.); Median year structure built: 1994 (2005-2009 5-year est.).

Safety: Violent crime rate: 7.6 per 10,000 population; Property crime rate: 77.7 per 10,000 population (2009).

Transportation: Commute to work: 87.5% car, 0.0% public transportation, 1.5% walk, 8.3% work from home (2005-2009 5-year est.); Travel time to work: 13.1% less than 15 minutes, 30.3% 15 to 30 minutes, 42.3% 30 to 45 minutes, 8.9% 45 to 60 minutes, 5.4% 60 minutes or more (2005-2009 5-year est.)

GREY FOREST (city).

GREY FOREST (city). Covers a land area of 0.739 square miles and a water area of 0 square miles. Located at 29.61° N. Lat; 98.68° W. Long. Elevation is 1,142 feet.

Population: 365 (1990); 418 (2000); 302 (2010); 343 (2015 projected); Race: 94.7% White, 0.3% Black, 1.3% Asian, 3.6% Other, 23.5% Hispanic of any race (2010); Density: 408.8 persons per square mile (2010); Average household size: 2.67 (2010); Median age: 46.8 (2010); Males per 100 females: 96.1 (2010); Marriage status: 18.4% never married, 67.0% now married, 4.1% widowed, 10.5% divorced (2005-2009 5-year est.); Foreign born: 3.3% (2005-2009 5-year est.); Ancestry (includes multiple ancestries): 29.7% German, 19.8% Irish, 11.1% English, 10.5% American, 8.4% French (2005-2009 5-year est.).

Economy: Single-family building permits issued: 0 (2010); Multi-family building permits issued: 0 (2010); Employment by occupation: 12.4% management, 28.4% professional, 18.3% services, 26.6% sales, 0.0% farming, 11.8% construction, 2.4% production (2005-2009 5-year est.).

Income: Per capita income: $41,767 (2010); Median household income: $89,167 (2010); Average household income: $111,748 (2010); Percent of households with income of $100,000 or more: 44.2% (2010); Poverty rate: 4.2% (2005-2009 5-year est.).

Taxes: Total city taxes per capita: $174 (2007); City property taxes per capita: $0 (2007).

Education: Percent of population age 25 and over with: High school diploma (including GED) or higher: 93.2% (2010); Bachelor's degree or higher: 42.3% (2010); Master's degree or higher: 19.1% (2010).

Housing: Homeownership rate: 90.3% (2010); Median home value: $243,750 (2010); Median contract rent: $375 per month (2005-2009 5-year est.); Median year structure built: 1946 (2005-2009 5-year est.).

Transportation: Commute to work: 92.1% car, 1.8% public transportation, 1.8% walk, 2.4% work from home (2005-2009 5-year est.); Travel time to work: 13.8% less than 15 minutes, 26.3% 15 to 30 minutes, 41.9% 30 to 45 minutes, 12.5% 45 to 60 minutes, 5.6% 60 minutes or more (2005-2009 5-year est.)

HELOTES (city).

HELOTES (city). Covers a land area of 4.225 square miles and a water area of 0 square miles. Located at 29.56° N. Lat; 98.68° W. Long. Elevation is 1,037 feet.

History: The town name is derived from the Spanish word helote, which means "green maize" but exactly how the town came to be called Helotes is still a subject of debate.

Population: 2,193 (1990); 4,285 (2000); 4,025 (2010); 4,633 (2015 projected); Race: 80.5% White, 3.5% Black, 3.3% Asian, 12.7% Other, 32.4% Hispanic of any race (2010); Density: 952.7 persons per square mile (2010); Average household size: 2.92 (2010); Median age: 39.5 (2010); Males per 100 females: 95.3 (2010); Marriage status: 21.4% never married, 66.0% now married, 3.5% widowed, 9.2% divorced (2005-2009 5-year est.); Foreign born: 4.9% (2005-2009 5-year est.); Ancestry (includes

multiple ancestries): 18.3% German, 12.0% Irish, 7.3% English, 4.9% French, 4.7% American (2005-2009 5-year est.).
Economy: Single-family building permits issued: 57 (2010); Multi-family building permits issued: 0 (2010); Employment by occupation: 24.9% management, 27.7% professional, 11.6% services, 23.0% sales, 0.0% farming, 9.2% construction, 3.7% production (2005-2009 5-year est.).
Income: Per capita income: $37,442 (2010); Median household income: $91,804 (2010); Average household income: $109,371 (2010); Percent of households with income of $100,000 or more: 43.5% (2010); Poverty rate: 3.3% (2005-2009 5-year est.).
Taxes: Total city taxes per capita: $396 (2007); City property taxes per capita: $216 (2007).
Education: Percent of population age 25 and over with: High school diploma (including GED) or higher: 94.2% (2010); Bachelor's degree or higher: 43.0% (2010); Master's degree or higher: 16.3% (2010).

School District(s)
Northside ISD (PK-12)
    2009-10 Enrollment: 92,335 . . . . (210) 397-8500
Housing: Homeownership rate: 93.4% (2010); Median home value: $224,946 (2010); Median contract rent: $880 per month (2005-2009 5-year est.); Median year structure built: 1998 (2005-2009 5-year est.).
Safety: Violent crime rate: 2.4 per 10,000 population; Property crime rate: 84.4 per 10,000 population (2009).
Newspapers: Helotes Echo (Community news; Circulation 3,500)
Transportation: Commute to work: 94.0% car, 0.0% public transportation, 0.2% walk, 5.3% work from home (2005-2009 5-year est.); Travel time to work: 9.5% less than 15 minutes, 36.9% 15 to 30 minutes, 33.4% 30 to 45 minutes, 12.4% 45 to 60 minutes, 7.8% 60 minutes or more (2005-2009 5-year est.)

HILL COUNTRY VILLAGE (city). Covers a land area of 2.180 square miles and a water area of 0 square miles. Located at 29.58° N. Lat; 98.48° W. Long. Elevation is 945 feet.
Population: 1,046 (1990); 1,028 (2000); 1,037 (2010); 1,048 (2015 projected); Race: 91.5% White, 2.0% Black, 0.6% Asian, 5.9% Other, 22.9% Hispanic of any race (2010); Density: 475.6 persons per square mile (2010); Average household size: 2.67 (2010); Median age: 45.7 (2010); Males per 100 females: 92.0 (2010); Marriage status: 18.4% never married, 71.0% now married, 2.5% widowed, 8.1% divorced (2005-2009 5-year est.); Foreign born: 7.3% (2005-2009 5-year est.); Ancestry (includes multiple ancestries): 26.5% German, 18.1% Irish, 17.1% English, 7.0% Italian, 5.6% Scottish (2005-2009 5-year est.).
Economy: Single-family building permits issued: 0 (2010); Multi-family building permits issued: 0 (2010); Employment by occupation: 26.4% management, 40.1% professional, 2.6% services, 29.4% sales, 0.0% farming, 0.0% construction, 1.5% production (2005-2009 5-year est.).
Income: Per capita income: $54,098 (2010); Median household income: $90,250 (2010); Average household income: $143,469 (2010); Percent of households with income of $100,000 or more: 45.0% (2010); Poverty rate: 1.3% (2005-2009 5-year est.).
Taxes: Total city taxes per capita: $1,563 (2007); City property taxes per capita: $192 (2007).
Education: Percent of population age 25 and over with: High school diploma (including GED) or higher: 97.3% (2010); Bachelor's degree or higher: 59.7% (2010); Master's degree or higher: 27.1% (2010).
Housing: Homeownership rate: 89.9% (2010); Median home value: $277,660 (2010); Median contract rent: n/a per month (2005-2009 5-year est.); Median year structure built: 1977 (2005-2009 5-year est.).
Safety: Violent crime rate: 8.9 per 10,000 population; Property crime rate: 373.7 per 10,000 population (2009).
Transportation: Commute to work: 92.2% car, 0.0% public transportation, 0.7% walk, 7.1% work from home (2005-2009 5-year est.); Travel time to work: 30.8% less than 15 minutes, 42.0% 15 to 30 minutes, 23.2% 30 to 45 minutes, 0.8% 45 to 60 minutes, 3.2% 60 minutes or more (2005-2009 5-year est.)
Additional Information Contacts
City of Hill Country Village . . . . (210) 494-3671
    http://www.hcv.org

HOLLYWOOD PARK (town). Covers a land area of 1.471 square miles and a water area of 0 square miles. Located at 29.59° N. Lat; 98.48° W. Long. Elevation is 961 feet.
History: The Town of Hollywood Park was incorporated December 7, 1955, following an election held in October, 1955, under Title 28 Revised Civil Statutes of the State of Texas, as a General Law City.

Population: 2,881 (1990); 2,983 (2000); 3,278 (2010); 3,487 (2015 projected); Race: 92.8% White, 2.3% Black, 0.7% Asian, 4.2% Other, 15.9% Hispanic of any race (2010); Density: 2,227.8 persons per square mile (2010); Average household size: 2.47 (2010); Median age: 47.5 (2010); Males per 100 females: 90.9 (2010); Marriage status: 17.0% never married, 69.7% now married, 8.2% widowed, 5.1% divorced (2005-2009 5-year est.); Foreign born: 3.2% (2005-2009 5-year est.); Ancestry (includes multiple ancestries): 33.7% German, 15.1% Irish, 11.9% English, 7.2% Polish, 6.4% Scotch-Irish (2005-2009 5-year est.).
Economy: Single-family building permits issued: 0 (2010); Multi-family building permits issued: 0 (2010); Employment by occupation: 29.5% management, 35.7% professional, 2.0% services, 18.6% sales, 0.0% farming, 10.9% construction, 3.3% production (2005-2009 5-year est.).
Income: Per capita income: $36,223 (2010); Median household income: $72,672 (2010); Average household income: $94,056 (2010); Percent of households with income of $100,000 or more: 33.8% (2010); Poverty rate: 0.9% (2005-2009 5-year est.).
Taxes: Total city taxes per capita: $627 (2007); City property taxes per capita: $361 (2007).
Education: Percent of population age 25 and over with: High school diploma (including GED) or higher: 97.0% (2010); Bachelor's degree or higher: 48.0% (2010); Master's degree or higher: 17.7% (2010).
Housing: Homeownership rate: 85.5% (2010); Median home value: $234,029 (2010); Median contract rent: $948 per month (2005-2009 5-year est.); Median year structure built: 1968 (2005-2009 5-year est.).
Safety: Violent crime rate: 14.9 per 10,000 population; Property crime rate: 304.9 per 10,000 population (2009).
Transportation: Commute to work: 90.5% car, 1.0% public transportation, 1.3% walk, 7.2% work from home (2005-2009 5-year est.); Travel time to work: 20.5% less than 15 minutes, 43.8% 15 to 30 minutes, 31.7% 30 to 45 minutes, 1.9% 45 to 60 minutes, 2.1% 60 minutes or more (2005-2009 5-year est.)

KIRBY (city). Covers a land area of 1.869 square miles and a water area of 0.033 square miles. Located at 29.46° N. Lat; 98.38° W. Long. Elevation is 686 feet.
Population: 8,326 (1990); 8,673 (2000); 8,516 (2010); 8,709 (2015 projected); Race: 60.0% White, 14.2% Black, 2.6% Asian, 23.2% Other, 50.6% Hispanic of any race (2010); Density: 4,557.1 persons per square mile (2010); Average household size: 2.88 (2010); Median age: 33.9 (2010); Males per 100 females: 96.8 (2010); Marriage status: 27.4% never married, 50.2% now married, 4.5% widowed, 17.9% divorced (2005-2009 5-year est.); Foreign born: 14.7% (2005-2009 5-year est.); Ancestry (includes multiple ancestries): 16.3% German, 5.3% Irish, 4.3% Polish, 3.9% English, 3.2% American (2005-2009 5-year est.).
Economy: Single-family building permits issued: 0 (2010); Multi-family building permits issued: 0 (2010); Employment by occupation: 8.9% management, 11.2% professional, 15.0% services, 32.9% sales, 0.5% farming, 12.1% construction, 19.4% production (2005-2009 5-year est.).
Income: Per capita income: $18,046 (2010); Median household income: $44,573 (2010); Average household income: $52,039 (2010); Percent of households with income of $100,000 or more: 7.9% (2010); Poverty rate: 14.2% (2005-2009 5-year est.).
Taxes: Total city taxes per capita: $191 (2007); City property taxes per capita: $124 (2007).
Education: Percent of population age 25 and over with: High school diploma (including GED) or higher: 79.8% (2010); Bachelor's degree or higher: 10.1% (2010); Master's degree or higher: 2.5% (2010).
Housing: Homeownership rate: 76.5% (2010); Median home value: $74,371 (2010); Median contract rent: $491 per month (2005-2009 5-year est.); Median year structure built: 1974 (2005-2009 5-year est.).
Safety: Violent crime rate: 16.3 per 10,000 population; Property crime rate: 189.6 per 10,000 population (2009).
Transportation: Commute to work: 94.3% car, 0.0% public transportation, 0.8% walk, 1.9% work from home (2005-2009 5-year est.); Travel time to work: 29.1% less than 15 minutes, 42.5% 15 to 30 minutes, 24.0% 30 to 45 minutes, 1.7% 45 to 60 minutes, 2.8% 60 minutes or more (2005-2009 5-year est.)
Additional Information Contacts
City of Kirby . . . . (210) 661-3198
    http://www.kirbytx.org

LACKLAND AFB (CDP). Covers a land area of 4.284 square miles and a water area of 0 square miles. Located at 29.39° N. Lat; 98.61° W. Long.

Population: 8,707 (1990); 7,123 (2000); 6,857 (2010); 7,010 (2015 projected); Race: 59.2% White, 20.2% Black, 5.0% Asian, 15.7% Other, 18.2% Hispanic of any race (2010); Density: 1,600.5 persons per square mile (2010); Average household size: 3.53 (2010); Median age: 20.4 (2010); Males per 100 females: 260.3 (2010); Marriage status: 71.7% never married, 23.8% now married, 0.0% widowed, 4.6% divorced (2005-2009 5-year est.); Foreign born: 8.6% (2005-2009 5-year est.); Ancestry (includes multiple ancestries): 23.7% German, 14.3% Irish, 9.6% English, 5.6% Italian, 4.5% Scottish (2005-2009 5-year est.).
Economy: Employment by occupation: 25.1% management, 24.1% professional, 13.8% services, 19.0% sales, 0.0% farming, 11.6% construction, 6.5% production (2005-2009 5-year est.).
Income: Per capita income: $10,377 (2010); Median household income: $41,409 (2010); Average household income: $46,355 (2010); Percent of households with income of $100,000 or more: 3.4% (2010); Poverty rate: 34.6% (2005-2009 5-year est.).
Education: Percent of population age 25 and over with: High school diploma (including GED) or higher: 98.7% (2010); Bachelor's degree or higher: 17.4% (2010); Master's degree or higher: 2.9% (2010).
Housing: Homeownership rate: 4.4% (2010); Median home value: $82,000 (2010); Median contract rent: $1,087 per month (2005-2009 5-year est.); Median year structure built: 1999 (2005-2009 5-year est.).
Hospitals: 59th Medical Wing - Wilford Hall Medical Center (1000 beds)
Newspapers: Lackland Talespinner (Local news; Circulation 20,000)
Transportation: Commute to work: 17.5% car, 3.1% public transportation, 38.0% walk, 41.0% work from home (2005-2009 5-year est.); Travel time to work: 80.7% less than 15 minutes, 15.1% 15 to 30 minutes, 3.6% 30 to 45 minutes, 0.7% 45 to 60 minutes, 0.0% 60 minutes or more (2005-2009 5-year est.)

LEON VALLEY (city). Covers a land area of 3.412 square miles and a water area of 0 square miles. Located at 29.49° N. Lat; 98.61° W. Long. Elevation is 827 feet.
Population: 9,421 (1990); 9,239 (2000); 10,093 (2010); 10,617 (2015 projected); Race: 69.7% White, 3.3% Black, 3.3% Asian, 23.7% Other, 54.9% Hispanic of any race (2010); Density: 2,958.3 persons per square mile (2010); Average household size: 2.52 (2010); Median age: 37.6 (2010); Males per 100 females: 94.4 (2010); Marriage status: 24.6% never married, 53.8% now married, 7.3% widowed, 14.3% divorced (2005-2009 5-year est.); Foreign born: 11.5% (2005-2009 5-year est.); Ancestry (includes multiple ancestries): 10.6% German, 7.3% English, 6.1% American, 4.7% Irish, 2.8% Italian (2005-2009 5-year est.).
Economy: Single-family building permits issued: 64 (2010); Multi-family building permits issued: 0 (2010); Employment by occupation: 10.9% management, 25.9% professional, 16.4% services, 30.0% sales, 0.1% farming, 9.5% construction, 7.2% production (2005-2009 5-year est.).
Income: Per capita income: $24,826 (2010); Median household income: $51,922 (2010); Average household income: $62,552 (2010); Percent of households with income of $100,000 or more: 15.8% (2010); Poverty rate: 10.2% (2005-2009 5-year est.).
Taxes: Total city taxes per capita: $557 (2007); City property taxes per capita: $299 (2007).
Education: Percent of population age 25 and over with: High school diploma (including GED) or higher: 88.4% (2010); Bachelor's degree or higher: 29.0% (2010); Master's degree or higher: 9.9% (2010).
Housing: Homeownership rate: 65.8% (2010); Median home value: $122,884 (2010); Median contract rent: $616 per month (2005-2009 5-year est.); Median year structure built: 1976 (2005-2009 5-year est.).
Safety: Violent crime rate: 39.5 per 10,000 population; Property crime rate: 736.3 per 10,000 population (2009).
Transportation: Commute to work: 93.5% car, 1.2% public transportation, 0.0% walk, 3.2% work from home (2005-2009 5-year est.); Travel time to work: 23.5% less than 15 minutes, 46.6% 15 to 30 minutes, 22.7% 30 to 45 minutes, 4.1% 45 to 60 minutes, 3.1% 60 minutes or more (2005-2009 5-year est.)
Additional Information Contacts
City of Leon Valley. . . . . (210) 684-1391
http://www.leonvalleytexas.gov

LIVE OAK (city). Covers a land area of 4.679 square miles and a water area of 0.034 square miles. Located at 29.55° N. Lat; 98.33° W. Long. Elevation is 912 feet.
Population: 10,023 (1990); 9,156 (2000); 12,376 (2010); 13,822 (2015 projected); Race: 73.5% White, 10.0% Black, 2.6% Asian, 13.9% Other, 34.7% Hispanic of any race (2010); Density: 2,644.9 persons per square

mile (2010); Average household size: 2.63 (2010); Median age: 38.1 (2010); Males per 100 females: 92.7 (2010); Marriage status: 20.6% never married, 55.9% now married, 6.4% widowed, 17.1% divorced (2005-2009 5-year est.); Foreign born: 7.5% (2005-2009 5-year est.); Ancestry (includes multiple ancestries): 15.2% German, 10.5% Irish, 9.6% English, 4.5% Italian, 3.3% American (2005-2009 5-year est.).
Economy: Single-family building permits issued: 146 (2010); Multi-family building permits issued: 0 (2010); Employment by occupation: 15.4% management, 18.6% professional, 20.7% services, 28.2% sales, 0.0% farming, 6.5% construction, 10.5% production (2005-2009 5-year est.).
Income: Per capita income: $24,102 (2010); Median household income: $54,351 (2010); Average household income: $63,195 (2010); Percent of households with income of $100,000 or more: 14.9% (2010); Poverty rate: 5.2% (2005-2009 5-year est.).
Taxes: Total city taxes per capita: $681 (2007); City property taxes per capita: $198 (2007).
Education: Percent of population age 25 and over with: High school diploma (including GED) or higher: 91.1% (2010); Bachelor's degree or higher: 22.3% (2010); Master's degree or higher: 4.8% (2010).
School District(s)
Judson ISD (PK-12)
   2009-10 Enrollment: 21,750 . . . . (210) 945-5100
Radiance Academy of Learning (PK-12)
   2009-10 Enrollment: 740 . . . . (210) 658-6848
Housing: Homeownership rate: 71.4% (2010); Median home value: $105,872 (2010); Median contract rent: $709 per month (2005-2009 5-year est.); Median year structure built: 1979 (2005-2009 5-year est.).
Safety: Violent crime rate: 22.7 per 10,000 population; Property crime rate: 458.4 per 10,000 population (2009).
Transportation: Commute to work: 93.4% car, 0.2% public transportation, 0.4% walk, 4.5% work from home (2005-2009 5-year est.); Travel time to work: 28.0% less than 15 minutes, 38.3% 15 to 30 minutes, 25.2% 30 to 45 minutes, 5.7% 45 to 60 minutes, 2.8% 60 minutes or more (2005-2009 5-year est.)
Additional Information Contacts
City of Live Oak . . . . (210) 653-9140
http://www.liveoaktx.net

OLMOS PARK (city). Covers a land area of 0.607 square miles and a water area of 0 square miles. Located at 29.47° N. Lat; 98.48° W. Long. Elevation is 807 feet.
History: Olmos Dam (flood control) built here across small Olmos Creek (tributary of San Antonio River) after 1921 flood. Trinity University in South. Incorporated 1939.
Population: 2,161 (1990); 2,343 (2000); 2,299 (2010); 2,338 (2015 projected); Race: 94.0% White, 1.4% Black, 1.0% Asian, 3.6% Other, 17.4% Hispanic of any race (2010); Density: 3,787.6 persons per square mile (2010); Average household size: 2.26 (2010); Median age: 43.8 (2010); Males per 100 females: 89.4 (2010); Marriage status: 20.9% never married, 67.8% now married, 5.8% widowed, 5.5% divorced (2005-2009 5-year est.); Foreign born: 3.7% (2005-2009 5-year est.); Ancestry (includes multiple ancestries): 26.8% German, 17.5% English, 12.1% Irish, 8.7% American, 4.8% Scottish (2005-2009 5-year est.).
Economy: Single-family building permits issued: 2 (2010); Multi-family building permits issued: 0 (2010); Employment by occupation: 27.9% management, 42.1% professional, 11.2% services, 15.9% sales, 0.0% farming, 2.0% construction, 0.9% production (2005-2009 5-year est.).
Income: Per capita income: $67,833 (2010); Median household income: $107,883 (2010); Average household income: $153,642 (2010); Percent of households with income of $100,000 or more: 53.5% (2010); Poverty rate: 6.0% (2005-2009 5-year est.).
Taxes: Total city taxes per capita: $1,236 (2007); City property taxes per capita: $971 (2007).
Education: Percent of population age 25 and over with: High school diploma (including GED) or higher: 96.8% (2010); Bachelor's degree or higher: 67.2% (2010); Master's degree or higher: 31.6% (2010).
Housing: Homeownership rate: 67.7% (2010); Median home value: $526,471 (2010); Median contract rent: $573 per month (2005-2009 5-year est.); Median year structure built: 1942 (2005-2009 5-year est.).
Safety: Violent crime rate: 4.3 per 10,000 population; Property crime rate: 407.1 per 10,000 population (2009).
Transportation: Commute to work: 89.4% car, 1.1% public transportation, 0.5% walk, 9.0% work from home (2005-2009 5-year est.); Travel time to work: 50.0% less than 15 minutes, 43.1% 15 to 30 minutes, 2.5% 30 to 45

minutes, 1.8% 45 to 60 minutes, 2.6% 60 minutes or more (2005-2009 5-year est.)

SAINT HEDWIG (town). Covers a land area of 30.086 square miles and a water area of 0 square miles. Located at 29.42° N. Lat; 98.21° W. Long. Elevation is 577 feet.
Population: 1,443 (1990); 1,875 (2000); 1,862 (2010); 1,950 (2015 projected); Race: 89.0% White, 2.8% Black, 0.2% Asian, 8.0% Other, 18.2% Hispanic of any race (2010); Density: 61.9 persons per square mile (2010); Average household size: 2.80 (2010); Median age: 38.4 (2010); Males per 100 females: 105.3 (2010); Marriage status: 24.5% never married, 60.9% now married, 6.7% widowed, 7.9% divorced (2005-2009 5-year est.); Foreign born: 5.0% (2005-2009 5-year est.); Ancestry (includes multiple ancestries): 28.5% German, 26.3% Polish, 12.5% Irish, 4.0% American, 3.3% French (2005-2009 5-year est.).
Economy: Single-family building permits issued: 7 (2010); Multi-family building permits issued: 0 (2010); Employment by occupation: 15.7% management, 13.8% professional, 12.7% services, 31.4% sales, 0.3% farming, 13.2% construction, 12.9% production (2005-2009 5-year est.).
Income: Per capita income: $25,879 (2010); Median household income: $63,654 (2010); Average household income: $72,280 (2010); Percent of households with income of $100,000 or more: 23.3% (2010); Poverty rate: 9.1% (2005-2009 5-year est.).
Taxes: Total city taxes per capita: $201 (2007); City property taxes per capita: $176 (2007).
Education: Percent of population age 25 and over with: High school diploma (including GED) or higher: 83.3% (2010); Bachelor's degree or higher: 15.0% (2010); Master's degree or higher: 3.7% (2010).
Housing: Homeownership rate: 90.8% (2010); Median home value: $118,784 (2010); Median contract rent: $538 per month (2005-2009 5-year est.); Median year structure built: 1989 (2005-2009 5-year est.).
Transportation: Commute to work: 92.5% car, 0.0% public transportation, 0.9% walk, 5.2% work from home (2005-2009 5-year est.); Travel time to work: 9.7% less than 15 minutes, 33.5% 15 to 30 minutes, 36.5% 30 to 45 minutes, 11.6% 45 to 60 minutes, 8.8% 60 minutes or more (2005-2009 5-year est.)

SAN ANTONIO (city). County seat. Covers a land area of 407.559 square miles and a water area of 4.514 square miles. Located at 29.45° N. Lat; 98.51° W. Long. Elevation is 650 feet.
History: The name of San Antonio was given to the village on the river by Father Damian Massanet, who came in 1691 to set up a cross and say mass for the Payayas who lived here. Mission San Antonio was founded in 1718 by Father Antonio de San Buenaventura Olivares, and Governor Martin de Alarcon founded the Villa de Bejar (Bexar) nearby. Several other missions and settlements sprang up, and in 1794 they were consolidated into San Antonio de Bexar, the capital of the Province of Texas. San Antonio's famous defense of the Alamo came in 1836 when the Mexican dictator Santa Anna took the fortress after every defender had died. After the Civil War, when San Antonio contributed heavily to the Confederate cause, the beginning of the cattle drives and the coming of the railroad made San Antonio a livestock center with meat packing, flour mills, cement plants and breweries.
Population: 997,258 (1990); 1,144,646 (2000); 1,323,124 (2010); 1,420,762 (2015 projected); Race: 65.5% White, 6.5% Black, 1.9% Asian, 26.1% Other, 62.8% Hispanic of any race (2010); Density: 3,246.5 persons per square mile (2010); Average household size: 2.77 (2010); Median age: 32.8 (2010); Males per 100 females: 94.7 (2010); Marriage status: 33.6% never married, 48.7% now married, 5.7% widowed, 12.0% divorced (2005-2009 5-year est.); Foreign born: 13.4% (2005-2009 5-year est.); Ancestry (includes multiple ancestries): 9.4% German, 5.3% Irish, 4.9% English, 4.0% American, 1.9% Italian (2005-2009 5-year est.).
Economy: Unemployment rate: 7.9% (June 2011); Total civilian labor force: 660,936 (June 2011); Single-family building permits issued: 2,337 (2010); Multi-family building permits issued: 1,237 (2010); Employment by occupation: 12.7% management, 19.2% professional, 18.9% services, 28.3% sales, 0.2% farming, 10.7% construction, 10.1% production (2005-2009 5-year est.).
Income: Per capita income: $20,873 (2010); Median household income: $43,723 (2010); Average household income: $58,165 (2010); Percent of households with income of $100,000 or more: 13.7% (2010); Poverty rate: 18.6% (2005-2009 5-year est.).
Taxes: Total city taxes per capita: $472 (2007); City property taxes per capita: $225 (2007).

Education: Percent of population age 25 and over with: High school diploma (including GED) or higher: 78.6% (2010); Bachelor's degree or higher: 23.1% (2010); Master's degree or higher: 8.1% (2010).
School District(s)
Academy of Careers and Technologies Charter School (09-12)
  2009-10 Enrollment: 145 . . . . (210) 534-9690
Alamo Heights ISD (PK-12)
  2009-10 Enrollment: 4,762 . . . . (210) 824-2483
Bexar County Academy (PK-08)
  2009-10 Enrollment: 482 . . . . (210) 432-8600
Brooks Academy of Science and Engineering (06-12)
  2009-10 Enrollment: 686 . . . . (210) 633-9006
City Center Health Careers (06-09)
  2009-10 Enrollment: 67 . . . . (210) 255-8265
Comal ISD (PK-12)
  2009-10 Enrollment: 16,700 . . . . (830) 221-2000
East Central ISD (PK-12)
  2009-10 Enrollment: 9,292 . . . . (210) 648-7861
Edgewood ISD (PK-12)
  2009-10 Enrollment: 12,392 . . . . (210) 444-4500
Ft Sam Houston ISD (PK-12)
  2009-10 Enrollment: 1,472 . . . . (210) 368-8701
George Gervin Academy (PK-12)
  2009-10 Enrollment: 779 . . . . (210) 568-8800
George I Sanchez Charter HS San Antonio Branch (08-12)
  2009-10 Enrollment: 168 . . . . (210) 270-8567
Guardian Angel Performance Arts Academy (KG-08)
  2009-10 Enrollment: 17 . . . . (210) 253-9064
Harlandale ISD (PK-12)
  2009-10 Enrollment: 14,521 . . . . (210) 989-4300
Harmony Science Academy (San Antonio) (KG-11)
  2009-10 Enrollment: 768 . . . . (210) 674-7788
Henry Ford Academy Alameda School for Art + Design (09-09)
  2009-10 Enrollment: 74 . . . . (210) 226-4031
Higgs Carter King Gifted & Talented Charter Academy (PK-12)
  2009-10 Enrollment: 498 . . . . (210) 735-2341
John H Wood Jr Public Charter District (05-12)
  2009-10 Enrollment: 348 . . . . (210) 638-5003
Jubilee Academic Center (PK-12)
  2009-10 Enrollment: 701 . . . . (210) 333-6227
Judson ISD (PK-12)
  2009-10 Enrollment: 21,750 . . . . (210) 945-5100
Kipp Aspire Academy (05-09)
  2009-10 Enrollment: 496 . . . . (210) 735-7300
La Escuela de Las Americas (PK-02)
  2009-10 Enrollment: 98 . . . . (210) 978-0515
Lackland ISD (PK-12)
  2009-10 Enrollment: 936 . . . . (210) 357-5000
Lighthouse Charter School (PK-08)
  2009-10 Enrollment: 207 . . . . (210) 674-4100
Medina Valley ISD (PK-12)
  2009-10 Enrollment: 3,382 . . . . (830) 931-2243
New Frontiers Charter School (KG-08)
  2009-10 Enrollment: 609 . . . . (210) 533-3655
North East ISD (PK-12)
  2009-10 Enrollment: 65,498 . . . . (210) 804-7000
Northside ISD (PK-12)
  2009-10 Enrollment: 92,335 . . . . (210) 397-8500
Por Vida Academy (09-12)
  2009-10 Enrollment: 305 . . . . (210) 532-8816
Positive Solutions Charter School (09-12)
  2009-10 Enrollment: 224 . . . . (210) 299-1025
Radiance Academy of Learning (PK-12)
  2009-10 Enrollment: 740 . . . . (210) 658-6848
Responsive Education Solutions (KG-12)
  2009-10 Enrollment: 5,022 . . . . (972) 316-3663
San Antonio Can High School (09-12)
  2009-10 Enrollment: 377 . . . . (214) 943-2244
San Antonio ISD (PK-12)
  2009-10 Enrollment: 55,327 . . . . (210) 554-2200
San Antonio Preparatory Academy (PK-12)
  2009-10 Enrollment: 755 . . . . (210) 593-0111
San Antonio School for Inquiry & Creativity (KG-12)
  2009-10 Enrollment: 373 . . . . (210) 738-0020

San Antonio Technology Academy (09-12)
  2009-10 Enrollment: 85 . . . . (210) 733-8100
School of Excellence in Education (PK-12)
  2009-10 Enrollment: 2,087 . . . . (210) 431-9881
School of Science and Technology (KG-12)
  2009-10 Enrollment: 694 . . . . (210) 804-0222
School of Science and Technology Discovery (KG-09)
  2009-10 Enrollment: 345 . . . . (210) 804-0222
Shekinah Radiance Academy (PK-12)
  2009-10 Enrollment: 1,125 . . . . (210) 658-6848
Somerset ISD (PK-12)
  2009-10 Enrollment: 3,726 . . . . (866) 852-9858
South San Antonio ISD (PK-12)
  2009-10 Enrollment: 9,974 . . . . (210) 977-7000
Southside ISD (PK-12)
  2009-10 Enrollment: 5,216 . . . . (210) 882-1600
Southwest ISD (PK-12)
  2009-10 Enrollment: 11,531 . . . . (210) 622-4731
Southwest Preparatory School (09-12)
  2009-10 Enrollment: 805 . . . . (210) 829-8017
University of Texas University Charter School (KG-12)
  2009-10 Enrollment: 907 . . . . (512) 471-5652

Four-year College(s)
Baptist University of the Americas (Private, Not-for-profit, Baptist)
  Fall 2009 Enrollment: 208 . . . . (210) 924-4338
  2010-11 Tuition: In-state $6,000; Out-of-state $6,000
Hallmark College of Technology/Hallmark College of Aeronautics (Private, For-profit)
  Fall 2009 Enrollment: 835 . . . . (210) 690-9000
ITT Technical Institute-San Antonio (Private, For-profit)
  Fall 2009 Enrollment: 729 . . . . (210) 694-4612
  2010-11 Tuition: In-state $18,048; Out-of-state $18,048
International Academy of Design and Technology (Private, For-profit)
  Fall 2009 Enrollment: 476 . . . . (210) 530-9449
  2010-11 Tuition: In-state $11,900; Out-of-state $11,900
Oblate School of Theology (Private, Not-for-profit, Roman Catholic)
  Fall 2009 Enrollment: 190 . . . . (210) 341-1366
Our Lady of the Lake University-San Antonio (Private, Not-for-profit, Roman Catholic)
  Fall 2009 Enrollment: 2,660 . . . . (210) 434-6711
  2010-11 Tuition: In-state $21,900; Out-of-state $21,900
St Marys University (Private, Not-for-profit, Roman Catholic)
  Fall 2009 Enrollment: 3,893 . . . . (210) 436-3011
  2010-11 Tuition: In-state $22,576; Out-of-state $22,576
The University of Texas Health Science Center at San Antonio (Public)
  Fall 2009 Enrollment: 3,223 . . . . (210) 567-2621
  2010-11 Tuition: In-state $4,979; Out-of-state $14,279
The University of Texas at San Antonio (Public)
  Fall 2009 Enrollment: 28,955 . . . . (210) 458-4011
  2010-11 Tuition: In-state $6,718; Out-of-state $14,158
Trinity University (Private, Not-for-profit, Presbyterian Church (USA))
  Fall 2009 Enrollment: 2,693 . . . . (210) 999-7011
  2010-11 Tuition: In-state $30,015; Out-of-state $30,015
University of Phoenix-San Antonio Campus (Private, For-profit)
  Fall 2009 Enrollment: 942 . . . . (210) 524-2100
  2010-11 Tuition: In-state $11,640; Out-of-state $11,640
University of the Incarnate Word (Private, Not-for-profit, Roman Catholic)
  Fall 2009 Enrollment: 6,756 . . . . (210) 829-6000
  2010-11 Tuition: In-state $21,890; Out-of-state $21,890

Two-year College(s)
Baptist Health System School of Health Professions (Private, For-profit)
  Fall 2009 Enrollment: 458 . . . . (210) 297-9636
  2010-11 Tuition: In-state $6,692; Out-of-state $6,692
Career Point College (Private, For-profit)
  Fall 2009 Enrollment: 1,802 . . . . (210) 732-3000
  2010-11 Tuition: In-state $17,918; Out-of-state $17,918
Galen College of Nursing-San Antonio (Private, For-profit)
  Fall 2009 Enrollment: 639 . . . . (210) 733-3056
Kaplan Career Institute-San Antonio Campus (Private, For-profit)
  Fall 2009 Enrollment: 1,082 . . . . (210) 366-5500
Northwest Vista College (Public)
  Fall 2009 Enrollment: 14,587 . . . . (210) 486-4000
  2010-11 Tuition: In-state $2,846; Out-of-state $5,414

Palo Alto College (Public)
  Fall 2009 Enrollment: 8,335 . . . . (210) 486-3000
  2010-11 Tuition: In-state $2,846; Out-of-state $5,414
San Antonio College (Public)
  Fall 2009 Enrollment: 24,135 . . . . (210) 486-0000
  2010-11 Tuition: In-state $2,846; Out-of-state $5,414
Sanford-Brown College (Private, For-profit)
  Fall 2009 Enrollment: 221 . . . . (210) 246-7700
  2010-11 Tuition: In-state $13,068; Out-of-state $13,068
St Philips College (Public, Historically black)
  Fall 2009 Enrollment: 11,008 . . . . (210) 486-2000
  2010-11 Tuition: In-state $2,846; Out-of-state $5,414
Texas Careers (Private, For-profit)
  Fall 2009 Enrollment: 1,058 . . . . (210) 308-8584
The Academy of Health Care Professions (Private, For-profit)
  Fall 2009 Enrollment: 163 . . . . (210) 298-3600

Vocational/Technical School(s)
Aveda Institute San Antonio (Private, For-profit)
  Fall 2009 Enrollment: 204 . . . . (210) 222-0023
  2010-11 Tuition: $15,200
Career Quest (Private, For-profit)
  Fall 2009 Enrollment: 356 . . . . (210) 366-2701
  2010-11 Tuition: $14,229
Everest Institute-San Antonio (Private, For-profit)
  Fall 2009 Enrollment: 1,374 . . . . (210) 732-7800
  2010-11 Tuition: $14,810
Lamson Institute (Private, For-profit)
  Fall 2009 Enrollment: 353 . . . . (2.1) 052-E+12
  2010-11 Tuition: $14,707
Milan Institute (Private, For-profit)
  Fall 2009 Enrollment: 281 . . . . (210) 647-5100
  2010-11 Tuition: $15,446
Milan Institute of Cosmetology (Private, For-profit)
  Fall 2009 Enrollment: 205 . . . . (210) 656-1991
  2010-11 Tuition: $15,446
Milan Institute of Cosmetology (Private, For-profit)
  Fall 2009 Enrollment: 227 . . . . (210) 922-5900
  2010-11 Tuition: $15,446
Mims Classic Beauty College (Private, For-profit)
  Fall 2009 Enrollment: 60 . . . . (210) 344-2041
  2010-11 Tuition: $10,100
Paul Mitchell the School-San Antonio (Private, For-profit)
  Fall 2009 Enrollment: 249 . . . . (210) 523-8333
  2010-11 Tuition: $16,000
SW School of Business and Technical Careers-Cosmetology (Private, For-profit)
  Fall 2009 Enrollment: 51 . . . . (830) 626-7007
  2010-11 Tuition: $10,600
San Antonio Beauty College 3 (Private, For-profit)
  Fall 2009 Enrollment: 81 . . . . (210) 654-9734
  2010-11 Tuition: $14,905
San Antonio Beauty College 4 (Private, For-profit)
  Fall 2009 Enrollment: 72 . . . . (210) 433-7222
  2010-11 Tuition: $14,905
Southern Careers Institute1 Inc. (Private, For-profit)
  Fall 2009 Enrollment: 169 . . . . (512) 437-7507
  2010-11 Tuition: $13,600
Southwest School of Business and Technical Careers-San Antonio (Private, For-profit)
  Fall 2009 Enrollment: 395 . . . . (830) 626-7007
  2010-11 Tuition: $12,550

Housing: Homeownership rate: 59.2% (2010); Median home value: $102,257 (2010); Median contract rent: $603 per month (2005-2009 5-year est.); Median year structure built: 1978 (2005-2009 5-year est.).
Hospitals: Baptist Medical Center (375 beds); Brooke Army Medical Center (450 beds); Christus Santa Rosa Hospital - City Centre (1034 beds); HealthSouth Rehabilitation Institute of San Antonio (108 beds); Laurel Ridge Treatment Center (196 beds); Methodist Ambulatory Surgery Hospital NW; Methodist Children's Hospital (150 beds); Methodist Healthcare System; Methodist Hospital (683 beds); Methodist Specialty and Transplant Hospital (382 beds); Nix Healthcare System (244 beds); North Central Baptist Hospital (120 beds); Northeast Baptist Hospital (275 beds); Northeast Methodist Hospital (117 beds); San Antonio State Hospital (292 beds); San Antonio Warm Springs Rehabilitation Hospital (64 beds); South Texas Veterans Health Care System (268 beds); Southeast

Baptist Hospital (181 beds); Southwest General Hospital (327 beds); Southwest Mental Health Center (52 beds); Southwest Texas Methodist Hospital (700 beds); Spine Hospital of South Texas; St. Luke's Baptist Hospital (252 beds); Texas Center for Infectious Disease (150 beds); Texsan Heart Hospital (60 beds); University Hospital (604 beds)
Safety: Violent crime rate: 57.1 per 10,000 population; Property crime rate: 667.1 per 10,000 population (2009).
Newspapers: Conexión (Local news; Circulation 10,000); Daily Commercial Recorder (Local news; Circulation 1,000); The Dallas Morning News - San Antonio Bureau (Local news); The Herald - Northeast (Local news; Circulation 39,600); Houston Chronicle - San Antonio Bureau (Local news); Kelly Observer (Local news; Circulation 18,500); La Prensa (Local news; Circulation 20,000); Medical Patriot (Local news; Circulation 5,500); North San Antonio Times (Community news; Circulation 5,500); Northside Recorder-Times (Community news; Circulation 90,600); Rumbo de San Antonio (Local news; Circulation 25,000); San Antonio Current (Local news; Circulation 41,000); San Antonio Express-News (Regional news; Circulation 349,280); San Antonio Informer (Local news; Circulation 7,500); The San Antonio Observer (Local news); Southside Reporter (Community news; Circulation 77,500); Today's Catholic (Regional news; Circulation 20,000)
Transportation: Commute to work: 90.1% car, 3.3% public transportation, 2.1% walk, 2.6% work from home (2005-2009 5-year est.); Travel time to work: 23.3% less than 15 minutes, 44.4% 15 to 30 minutes, 22.8% 30 to 45 minutes, 5.1% 45 to 60 minutes, 4.4% 60 minutes or more (2005-2009 5-year est.); Amtrak: train service available.
Airports: Lackland AFB (Kelly Field Annex) (general aviation); San Antonio International (primary service/medium hub); Stinson Municipal (general aviation)
Additional Information Contacts
African American Chamber of Commerce of San Antonio. . (210) 490-1624
  http://www.aaccsa.com
Alamo City Black Chamber of Commerce . . . . (210) 226-9055
  http://www.alamocitychamber.org
City of San Antonio . . . . (210) 207-7080
  http://www.sanantonio.gov
Greater San Antonio Chamber of Commerce . . . . (210) 229-2100
  http://www.sachamber.org
North San Antonio Chamber of Commerce . . . . (210) 344-4848
  http://www.northsachamber.com
Randolph Metrocom Chamber of Commerce . . . . (210) 658-8322
  http://www.randolphmetrocomchamber.org
San Antonio Hispanic Chamber of Commerce . . . . (210) 225-0462
  http://www.sahcc.org
San Antonio Women's Chamber of Commerce . . . . (210) 299-2636
  http://sanantoniowomenschamberofcommerce.memberlodge.org
South San Antonio Chamber . . . . (210) 533-1600
  http://www.southsachamber.org
Westside Development Corporation . . . . (210) 207-0039
  http://www.sanantonio.gov/wdc

SCENIC OAKS (CDP). Covers a land area of 8.328 square miles and a water area of 0.011 square miles. Located at 29.70° N. Lat; 98.66° W. Long. Elevation is 1,325 feet.
History: Scenic Oaks is adjacent to Campp Bullis. Established in 1917, Camp Bullis was originally used as one of many training sites for the American Expeditionary Force soon to be sent to Europe. Used as a small arms and rifle range for Fort Sam Houston, no units were stationed at the Camp.
Population: 2,340 (1990); 3,279 (2000); 4,224 (2010); 4,740 (2015 projected); Race: 91.7% White, 0.2% Black, 1.3% Asian, 6.8% Other, 18.6% Hispanic of any race (2010); Density: 507.2 persons per square mile (2010); Average household size: 2.73 (2010); Median age: 45.6 (2010); Males per 100 females: 96.4 (2010); Marriage status: 24.1% never married, 64.7% now married, 3.4% widowed, 7.8% divorced (2005-2009 5-year est.); Foreign born: 9.6% (2005-2009 5-year est.); Ancestry (includes multiple ancestries): 22.6% German, 13.2% Irish, 10.7% English, 8.3% American, 6.2% Italian (2005-2009 5-year est.).
Economy: Employment by occupation: 21.7% management, 29.6% professional, 8.9% services, 25.3% sales, 0.0% farming, 6.7% construction, 7.8% production (2005-2009 5-year est.).
Income: Per capita income: $48,062 (2010); Median household income: $109,583 (2010); Average household income: $131,329 (2010); Percent of households with income of $100,000 or more: 54.5% (2010); Poverty rate: 1.6% (2005-2009 5-year est.).

Education: Percent of population age 25 and over with: High school diploma (including GED) or higher: 94.6% (2010); Bachelor's degree or higher: 53.1% (2010); Master's degree or higher: 22.3% (2010).
Housing: Homeownership rate: 93.1% (2010); Median home value: $267,337 (2010); Median contract rent: $683 per month (2005-2009 5-year est.); Median year structure built: 1990 (2005-2009 5-year est.).
Transportation: Commute to work: 93.4% car, 0.0% public transportation, 1.8% walk, 4.1% work from home (2005-2009 5-year est.); Travel time to work: 11.1% less than 15 minutes, 42.8% 15 to 30 minutes, 30.2% 30 to 45 minutes, 5.8% 45 to 60 minutes, 10.1% 60 minutes or more (2005-2009 5-year est.)

SELMA (city). Covers a land area of 4.866 square miles and a water area of 0 square miles. Located at 29.58° N. Lat; 98.31° W. Long. Elevation is 755 feet.
Population: 482 (1990); 788 (2000); 3,259 (2010); 3,682 (2015 projected); Race: 84.0% White, 5.8% Black, 1.6% Asian, 8.6% Other, 42.4% Hispanic of any race (2010); Density: 669.7 persons per square mile (2010); Average household size: 2.68 (2010); Median age: 37.8 (2010); Males per 100 females: 106.4 (2010); Marriage status: 25.8% never married, 60.7% now married, 5.3% widowed, 8.2% divorced (2005-2009 5-year est.); Foreign born: 5.9% (2005-2009 5-year est.); Ancestry (includes multiple ancestries): 17.2% German, 8.4% Irish, 5.0% English, 3.5% Polish, 2.6% Italian (2005-2009 5-year est.).
Economy: Single-family building permits issued: 111 (2010); Multi-family building permits issued: 240 (2010); Employment by occupation: 18.8% management, 30.4% professional, 12.3% services, 21.8% sales, 0.0% farming, 8.0% construction, 8.8% production (2005-2009 5-year est.).
Income: Per capita income: $24,796 (2010); Median household income: $53,480 (2010); Average household income: $66,893 (2010); Percent of households with income of $100,000 or more: 16.8% (2010); Poverty rate: 7.4% (2005-2009 5-year est.).
Taxes: Total city taxes per capita: $1,727 (2007); City property taxes per capita: $393 (2007).
Education: Percent of population age 25 and over with: High school diploma (including GED) or higher: 84.7% (2010); Bachelor's degree or higher: 25.9% (2010); Master's degree or higher: 7.6% (2010).
Housing: Homeownership rate: 70.2% (2010); Median home value: $135,056 (2010); Median contract rent: $1,121 per month (2005-2009 5-year est.); Median year structure built: 2001 (2005-2009 5-year est.).
Safety: Violent crime rate: 10.7 per 10,000 population; Property crime rate: 396.4 per 10,000 population (2009).
Transportation: Commute to work: 96.0% car, 0.0% public transportation, 0.0% walk, 2.8% work from home (2005-2009 5-year est.); Travel time to work: 22.6% less than 15 minutes, 35.4% 15 to 30 minutes, 24.3% 30 to 45 minutes, 13.5% 45 to 60 minutes, 4.2% 60 minutes or more (2005-2009 5-year est.)
Additional Information Contacts
City of Selma . . . . (210) 651-6661
  http://www.ci.selma.tx.us

SHAVANO PARK (city). Covers a land area of 1.770 square miles and a water area of 0 square miles. Located at 29.58° N. Lat; 98.55° W. Long. Elevation is 978 feet.
Population: 1,697 (1990); 1,754 (2000); 1,839 (2010); 1,997 (2015 projected); Race: 88.2% White, 1.7% Black, 4.1% Asian, 5.9% Other, 22.3% Hispanic of any race (2010); Density: 1,038.9 persons per square mile (2010); Average household size: 2.80 (2010); Median age: 45.6 (2010); Males per 100 females: 95.6 (2010); Marriage status: 17.8% never married, 70.9% now married, 5.0% widowed, 6.3% divorced (2005-2009 5-year est.); Foreign born: 6.7% (2005-2009 5-year est.); Ancestry (includes multiple ancestries): 25.6% German, 19.3% English, 11.4% Irish, 9.3% American, 5.8% Italian (2005-2009 5-year est.).
Economy: Single-family building permits issued: 14 (2010); Multi-family building permits issued: 0 (2010); Employment by occupation: 27.7% management, 43.9% professional, 7.6% services, 15.8% sales, 0.0% farming, 3.2% construction, 1.8% production (2005-2009 5-year est.).
Income: Per capita income: $51,808 (2010); Median household income: $110,972 (2010); Average household income: $145,672 (2010); Percent of households with income of $100,000 or more: 56.0% (2010); Poverty rate: 0.4% (2005-2009 5-year est.).
Taxes: Total city taxes per capita: $252 (2007); City property taxes per capita: $111 (2007).

Education: Percent of population age 25 and over with: High school diploma (including GED) or higher: 97.0% (2010); Bachelor's degree or higher: 59.1% (2010); Master's degree or higher: 24.6% (2010).
Housing: Homeownership rate: 93.6% (2010); Median home value: $264,559 (2010); Median contract rent: $620 per month (2005-2009 5-year est.); Median year structure built: 1984 (2005-2009 5-year est.).
Safety: Violent crime rate: 0.0 per 10,000 population; Property crime rate: 180.1 per 10,000 population (2009).
Transportation: Commute to work: 87.8% car, 0.3% public transportation, 0.9% walk, 11.0% work from home (2005-2009 5-year est.); Travel time to work: 21.5% less than 15 minutes, 56.5% 15 to 30 minutes, 16.5% 30 to 45 minutes, 2.2% 45 to 60 minutes, 3.2% 60 minutes or more (2005-2009 5-year est.)

SOMERSET (city).
Covers a land area of 2.003 square miles and a water area of 0 square miles. Located at 29.22° N. Lat; 98.65° W. Long. Elevation is 646 feet.
Population: 1,144 (1990); 1,550 (2000); 1,744 (2010); 1,878 (2015 projected); Race: 75.2% White, 0.3% Black, 0.0% Asian, 24.4% Other, 79.1% Hispanic of any race (2010); Density: 870.5 persons per square mile (2010); Average household size: 2.98 (2010); Median age: 30.2 (2010); Males per 100 females: 100.5 (2010); Marriage status: 26.0% never married, 57.2% now married, 3.7% widowed, 13.1% divorced (2005-2009 5-year est.); Foreign born: 3.5% (2005-2009 5-year est.); Ancestry (includes multiple ancestries): 8.6% German, 4.9% Irish, 3.4% English, 2.0% Italian, 1.9% French (2005-2009 5-year est.).
Economy: Single-family building permits issued: 1 (2010); Multi-family building permits issued: 0 (2010); Employment by occupation: 7.4% management, 23.2% professional, 9.8% services, 26.5% sales, 0.0% farming, 19.4% construction, 13.6% production (2005-2009 5-year est.).
Income: Per capita income: $14,496 (2010); Median household income: $35,163 (2010); Average household income: $43,176 (2010); Percent of households with income of $100,000 or more: 7.5% (2010); Poverty rate: 17.0% (2005-2009 5-year est.).
Taxes: Total city taxes per capita: $182 (2007); City property taxes per capita: $114 (2007).
Education: Percent of population age 25 and over with: High school diploma (including GED) or higher: 66.6% (2010); Bachelor's degree or higher: 5.8% (2010); Master's degree or higher: 2.4% (2010).

School District(s)
Somerset ISD (PK-12)
    2009-10 Enrollment: 3,726 . . . . (866) 852-9858
Housing: Homeownership rate: 75.5% (2010); Median home value: $62,698 (2010); Median contract rent: $432 per month (2005-2009 5-year est.); Median year structure built: 1969 (2005-2009 5-year est.).
Safety: Violent crime rate: 26.7 per 10,000 population; Property crime rate: 272.1 per 10,000 population (2009).
Transportation: Commute to work: 93.3% car, 0.6% public transportation, 1.4% walk, 1.2% work from home (2005-2009 5-year est.); Travel time to work: 21.8% less than 15 minutes, 22.8% 15 to 30 minutes, 35.8% 30 to 45 minutes, 13.6% 45 to 60 minutes, 6.0% 60 minutes or more (2005-2009 5-year est.)

TERRELL HILLS (city).
Covers a land area of 1.655 square miles and a water area of 0 square miles. Located at 29.48° N. Lat; 98.44° W. Long. Elevation is 801 feet.
History: Fort Sam Houston and National Cemetery to Southeast. Incorporated 1939.
Population: 4,592 (1990); 5,019 (2000); 5,209 (2010); 5,441 (2015 projected); Race: 94.5% White, 0.4% Black, 0.2% Asian, 5.0% Other, 15.1% Hispanic of any race (2010); Density: 3,147.4 persons per square mile (2010); Average household size: 2.70 (2010); Median age: 40.4 (2010); Males per 100 females: 89.6 (2010); Marriage status: 23.2% never married, 61.0% now married, 5.1% widowed, 10.7% divorced (2005-2009 5-year est.); Foreign born: 2.9% (2005-2009 5-year est.); Ancestry (includes multiple ancestries): 20.5% German, 20.4% English, 17.1% Irish, 9.9% American, 5.7% Scottish (2005-2009 5-year est.).
Economy: Single-family building permits issued: 1 (2010); Multi-family building permits issued: 0 (2010); Employment by occupation: 35.3% management, 32.6% professional, 7.1% services, 22.2% sales, 0.0% farming, 0.7% construction, 2.1% production (2005-2009 5-year est.).
Income: Per capita income: $44,863 (2010); Median household income: $88,029 (2010); Average household income: $121,147 (2010); Percent of households with income of $100,000 or more: 43.5% (2010); Poverty rate: 2.7% (2005-2009 5-year est.).

Taxes: Total city taxes per capita: $799 (2007); City property taxes per capita: $714 (2007).
Education: Percent of population age 25 and over with: High school diploma (including GED) or higher: 96.5% (2010); Bachelor's degree or higher: 66.4% (2010); Master's degree or higher: 23.9% (2010).
Housing: Homeownership rate: 89.0% (2010); Median home value: $315,094 (2010); Median contract rent: $1,641 per month (2005-2009 5-year est.); Median year structure built: 1954 (2005-2009 5-year est.).
Safety: Violent crime rate: 5.7 per 10,000 population; Property crime rate: 224.1 per 10,000 population (2009).
Transportation: Commute to work: 90.5% car, 1.2% public transportation, 0.6% walk, 6.3% work from home (2005-2009 5-year est.); Travel time to work: 36.2% less than 15 minutes, 48.9% 15 to 30 minutes, 12.3% 30 to 45 minutes, 0.8% 45 to 60 minutes, 1.8% 60 minutes or more (2005-2009 5-year est.)
Additional Information Contacts
City of Terrell Hills . . . . (210) 824-7401
    http://www.terrell-hills.com

TIMBERWOOD PARK (CDP).
Covers a land area of 19.029 square miles and a water area of 0.014 square miles. Located at 29.69° N. Lat; 98.49° W. Long. Elevation is 1,234 feet.
History: Timberwood Park, also known as Timberwood, is a suburban residential community located west of U. S. Highway 281 about twenty miles north of San Antonio in northern Bexar County. Development had begun by the 1980s, and in 1990 Timberwood Park had a population of 2,578.
Population: 2,578 (1990); 5,889 (2000); 13,980 (2010); 15,497 (2015 projected); Race: 86.8% White, 1.8% Black, 1.1% Asian, 10.2% Other, 25.9% Hispanic of any race (2010); Density: 734.7 persons per square mile (2010); Average household size: 2.95 (2010); Median age: 36.3 (2010); Males per 100 females: 98.4 (2010); Marriage status: 18.3% never married, 67.4% now married, 3.8% widowed, 10.4% divorced (2005-2009 5-year est.); Foreign born: 12.7% (2005-2009 5-year est.); Ancestry (includes multiple ancestries): 17.6% German, 15.1% English, 9.2% Irish, 7.0% French, 7.0% American (2005-2009 5-year est.).
Economy: Employment by occupation: 23.9% management, 22.9% professional, 10.4% services, 34.0% sales, 0.0% farming, 5.1% construction, 3.7% production (2005-2009 5-year est.).
Income: Per capita income: $43,689 (2010); Median household income: $99,264 (2010); Average household income: $129,027 (2010); Percent of households with income of $100,000 or more: 49.6% (2010); Poverty rate: 1.8% (2005-2009 5-year est.).
Education: Percent of population age 25 and over with: High school diploma (including GED) or higher: 92.0% (2010); Bachelor's degree or higher: 40.2% (2010); Master's degree or higher: 12.5% (2010).
Housing: Homeownership rate: 92.9% (2010); Median home value: $237,760 (2010); Median contract rent: $982 per month (2005-2009 5-year est.); Median year structure built: 2003 (2005-2009 5-year est.).
Transportation: Commute to work: 91.5% car, 0.4% public transportation, 0.0% walk, 5.7% work from home (2005-2009 5-year est.); Travel time to work: 6.4% less than 15 minutes, 30.3% 15 to 30 minutes, 38.4% 30 to 45 minutes, 14.6% 45 to 60 minutes, 10.2% 60 minutes or more (2005-2009 5-year est.)

UNIVERSAL CITY (city).
Covers a land area of 5.650 square miles and a water area of 0 square miles. Located at 29.55° N. Lat; 98.30° W. Long. Elevation is 764 feet.
Population: 13,098 (1990); 14,849 (2000); 18,658 (2010); 20,491 (2015 projected); Race: 77.5% White, 6.8% Black, 3.1% Asian, 12.6% Other, 27.5% Hispanic of any race (2010); Density: 3,302.3 persons per square mile (2010); Average household size: 2.47 (2010); Median age: 38.2 (2010); Males per 100 females: 96.4 (2010); Marriage status: 26.9% never married, 52.9% now married, 5.8% widowed, 14.4% divorced (2005-2009 5-year est.); Foreign born: 6.2% (2005-2009 5-year est.); Ancestry (includes multiple ancestries): 19.7% German, 10.0% Irish, 9.8% English, 4.8% American, 3.9% Italian (2005-2009 5-year est.).
Economy: Single-family building permits issued: 23 (2010); Multi-family building permits issued: 0 (2010); Employment by occupation: 15.7% management, 21.5% professional, 16.0% services, 27.4% sales, 0.0% farming, 8.6% construction, 10.7% production (2005-2009 5-year est.).
Income: Per capita income: $28,143 (2010); Median household income: $58,812 (2010); Average household income: $69,642 (2010); Percent of households with income of $100,000 or more: 19.7% (2010); Poverty rate: 8.5% (2005-2009 5-year est.).

Taxes: Total city taxes per capita: $377 (2007); City property taxes per capita: $167 (2007).
Education: Percent of population age 25 and over with: High school diploma (including GED) or higher: 91.6% (2010); Bachelor's degree or higher: 30.2% (2010); Master's degree or higher: 10.9% (2010).

School District(s)

Judson ISD (PK-12)
    2009-10 Enrollment: 21,750 . . . . (210) 945-5100
Radiance Academy of Learning (PK-12)
    2009-10 Enrollment: 740 . . . . (210) 658-6848
Schertz-Cibolo-Univarsal City ISD (PK-12)
    2009-10 Enrollment: 11,718 . . . . (210) 945-6200

Housing: Homeownership rate: 62.1% (2010); Median home value: $124,395 (2010); Median contract rent: $661 per month (2005-2009 5-year est.); Median year structure built: 1981 (2005-2009 5-year est.).
Safety: Violent crime rate: 27.1 per 10,000 population; Property crime rate: 249.7 per 10,000 population (2009).
Transportation: Commute to work: 94.4% car, 0.4% public transportation, 1.6% walk, 2.0% work from home (2005-2009 5-year est.); Travel time to work: 29.0% less than 15 minutes, 37.3% 15 to 30 minutes, 22.0% 30 to 45 minutes, 6.3% 45 to 60 minutes, 5.3% 60 minutes or more (2005-2009 5-year est.)
Additional Information Contacts
City of Universal City . . . . (210) 659-0333
    http://www.universalcitytexas.com

VON ORMY (unincorporated postal area, zip code 78073). Covers a land area of 51.850 square miles and a water area of 0.160 square miles. Located at 29.22° N. Lat; 98.60° W. Long. Elevation is 591 feet.
Population: 7,106 (2000); Race: 69.3% White, 0.0% Black, 0.1% Asian, 30.6% Other, 75.9% Hispanic of any race (2000); Density: 137.0 persons per square mile (2000); Age: 33.8% under 18, 7.8% over 64 (2000); Marriage status: 26.5% never married, 60.5% now married, 5.3% widowed, 7.7% divorced (2000); Foreign born: 8.2% (2000); Ancestry (includes multiple ancestries): 6.3% German, 3.9% American, 3.0% Irish, 2.5% English (2000).
Economy: Employment by occupation: 11.1% management, 6.8% professional, 16.9% services, 26.3% sales, 1.2% farming, 20.3% construction, 17.4% production (2000).
Income: Per capita income: $11,651 (2000); Median household income: $32,621 (2000); Poverty rate: 179.1% (2000).
Education: Percent of population age 25 and over with: High school diploma (including GED) or higher: 59.2% (2000); Bachelor's degree or higher: 8.3% (2000).

School District(s)

Somerset ISD (PK-12)
    2009-10 Enrollment: 3,726 . . . . (866) 852-9858

Housing: Homeownership rate: 85.5% (2000); Median home value: $46,000 (2000); Median contract rent: $327 per month (2000); Median year structure built: 1982 (2000).
Transportation: Commute to work: 92.6% car, 0.0% public transportation, 2.5% walk, 2.4% work from home (2000); Travel time to work: 12.7% less than 15 minutes, 31.8% 15 to 30 minutes, 29.3% 30 to 45 minutes, 10.9% 45 to 60 minutes, 15.3% 60 minutes or more (2000)

WINDCREST (city). Covers a land area of 1.817 square miles and a water area of 0 square miles. Located at 29.51° N. Lat; 98.38° W. Long. Elevation is 787 feet.
History: In 1959, a group of 51 qualified electors petitioned Bexar County Commissioners' Court for incorporation of the about two square miles known as Windcrest. The petition won approval and on September 15, 1959, an election was held which resulted in a unanimous vote for incorporation of the proposed city, which was so ordered by Charles W. Anderson, County Judge of Bexar County, on September 18, 1959.
Population: 5,326 (1990); 5,105 (2000); 5,348 (2010); 5,580 (2015 projected); Race: 76.9% White, 10.7% Black, 2.7% Asian, 9.7% Other, 25.5% Hispanic of any race (2010); Density: 2,942.6 persons per square mile (2010); Average household size: 2.25 (2010); Median age: 53.8 (2010); Males per 100 females: 85.3 (2010); Marriage status: 18.4% never married, 58.0% now married, 9.7% widowed, 13.8% divorced (2005-2009 5-year est.); Foreign born: 10.8% (2005-2009 5-year est.); Ancestry (includes multiple ancestries): 18.2% English, 18.0% German, 7.0% Irish, 5.6% American, 4.8% Scotch-Irish (2005-2009 5-year est.).
Economy: Single-family building permits issued: 19 (2010); Multi-family building permits issued: 0 (2010); Employment by occupation: 23.7%

management, 29.7% professional, 13.7% services, 24.7% sales, 1.7% farming, 2.9% construction, 3.5% production (2005-2009 5-year est.).
Income: Per capita income: $30,874 (2010); Median household income: $59,948 (2010); Average household income: $70,732 (2010); Percent of households with income of $100,000 or more: 23.3% (2010); Poverty rate: 6.2% (2005-2009 5-year est.).
Taxes: Total city taxes per capita: $868 (2007); City property taxes per capita: $298 (2007).
Education: Percent of population age 25 and over with: High school diploma (including GED) or higher: 94.0% (2010); Bachelor's degree or higher: 36.3% (2010); Master's degree or higher: 16.1% (2010).
Housing: Homeownership rate: 80.0% (2010); Median home value: $153,843 (2010); Median contract rent: $741 per month (2005-2009 5-year est.); Median year structure built: 1973 (2005-2009 5-year est.).
Safety: Violent crime rate: 29.7 per 10,000 population; Property crime rate: 731.5 per 10,000 population (2009).
Transportation: Commute to work: 93.0% car, 1.8% public transportation, 0.5% walk, 3.2% work from home (2005-2009 5-year est.); Travel time to work: 27.4% less than 15 minutes, 41.3% 15 to 30 minutes, 22.5% 30 to 45 minutes, 2.6% 45 to 60 minutes, 6.2% 60 minutes or more (2005-2009 5-year est.)
Additional Information Contacts
City of Windcrest . . . . (210) 655-0022
    http://www.ci.windcrest.tx.us

Blanco County

Located in south central Texas, on the Edwards Plateau; drained by the Pedernales and Blanco Rivers. Covers a land area of 711.24 square miles, a water area of 2.16 square miles, and is located in the Central Time Zone at 30.24° N. Lat., 98.38° W. Long. The county was founded in 1858. County seat is Johnson City.

Weather Station: Blanco									Elevation: 1,370 feet			
	Jan	Feb	Mar	Apr	May	Jun	Jul	Aug	Sep	Oct	Nov	Dec
High	60	64	70	78	84	90	93	95	89	79	69	61
Low	35	38	45	52	62	68	70	70	64	55	45	36
Precip	1.9	2.0	2.9	2.3	4.2	4.2	2.3	2.0	3.1	4.4	2.9	2.3
Snow	0.3	0.1	tr	0.0	0.0	0.0	0.0	0.0	0.0	0.0	tr	tr

High and Low temperatures in degrees Fahrenheit; Precipitation and Snow in inches

Weather Station: Johnson City									Elevation: 1,231 feet			
	Jan	Feb	Mar	Apr	May	Jun	Jul	Aug	Sep	Oct	Nov	Dec
High	61	65	71	79	86	91	95	96	89	81	70	62
Low	35	39	47	53	63	69	71	71	64	55	45	37
Precip	2.0	2.2	2.7	2.4	4.0	4.0	2.3	2.2	3.1	4.0	3.1	2.0
Snow	0.4	0.2	0.0	0.0	0.0	0.0	0.0	0.0	0.0	0.0	tr	tr

High and Low temperatures in degrees Fahrenheit; Precipitation and Snow in inches

Population: 5,972 (1990); 8,418 (2000); 9,449 (2010); 9,932 (2015 projected); Race: 87.9% White, 1.6% Black, 0.2% Asian, 10.4% Other, 20.4% Hispanic of any race (2010); Density: 13.3 persons per square mile (2010); Average household size: 2.52 (2010); Median age: 37.8 (2010); Males per 100 females: 100.2 (2010).
Religion: Five largest groups: 19.0% Southern Baptist Convention, 10.9% The United Methodist Church, 9.1% Catholic Church, 5.6% Evangelical Lutheran Church in America, 2.9% Churches of Christ (2000).
Economy: Unemployment rate: 6.4% (June 2011); Total civilian labor force: 5,131 (June 2011); Leading industries: 14.7% construction; 13.0% accommodation & food services; 12.5% retail trade (2009); Farms: 888 totaling 395,667 acres (2007); Companies that employ 500 or more persons: 0 (2009); Companies that employ 100 to 499 persons: 2 (2009); Companies that employ less than 100 persons: 255 (2009); Black-owned businesses: n/a (2007); Hispanic-owned businesses: n/a (2007); Asian-owned businesses: n/a (2007); Women-owned businesses: n/a (2007); Retail sales per capita: $9,209 (2010). Single-family building permits issued: 5 (2010); Multi-family building permits issued: 16 (2010).
Income: Per capita income: $28,580 (2010); Median household income: $56,990 (2010); Average household income: $72,738 (2010); Percent of households with income of $100,000 or more: 21.3% (2010); Poverty rate: 12.2% (2009); Bankruptcy rate: 1.30% (2010).
Taxes: Total county taxes per capita: $361 (2007); County property taxes per capita: $270 (2007).
Education: Percent of population age 25 and over with: High school diploma (including GED) or higher: 84.7% (2010); Bachelor's degree or higher: 24.3% (2010); Master's degree or higher: 7.2% (2010).

Housing: Homeownership rate: 77.1% (2010); Median home value: $146,703 (2010); Median contract rent: $443 per month (2005-2009 5-year est.); Median year structure built: 1982 (2005-2009 5-year est.)
Health: Birth rate: 127.2 per 10,000 population (2009); Death rate: 104.4 per 10,000 population (2009); Age-adjusted cancer mortality rate: 225.8 (Unreliable) deaths per 100,000 population (2007); Number of physicians: 7.7 per 10,000 population (2008); Hospital beds: 0.0 per 10,000 population (2007); Hospital admissions: 0.0 per 10,000 population (2007).
Elections: 2008 Presidential election results: 29.7% Obama, 69.2% McCain, 0.1% Nader
National and State Parks: Blanco State Park
Additional Information Contacts
Blanco County Government. . . . . (830) 868-4266
 http://www.co.blanco.tx.us/ips/cms
Blanco Chamber of Commerce . . . . (830) 833-5101
 http://www.blancochamber.com
Johnson City Chamber of Commerce . . . . (830) 868-7684
 http://www.johnsoncity-texas.com

Blanco County Communities

BLANCO (city). Covers a land area of 1.673 square miles and a water area of 0.049 square miles. Located at 30.10° N. Lat; 98.42° W. Long. Elevation is 1,329 feet.
History: At one time, Blanco served as the seat of Blanco County. Its name, which came from the Blanco River, is Spanish for "white."
Population: 1,238 (1990); 1,505 (2000); 1,565 (2010); 1,597 (2015 projected); Race: 85.3% White, 2.2% Black, 0.3% Asian, 12.1% Other, 31.1% Hispanic of any race (2010); Density: 935.5 persons per square mile (2010); Average household size: 2.47 (2010); Median age: 34.6 (2010); Males per 100 females: 95.4 (2010); Marriage status: 26.2% never married, 57.6% now married, 5.9% widowed, 10.3% divorced (2005-2009 5-year est.); Foreign born: 12.7% (2005-2009 5-year est.); Ancestry (includes multiple ancestries): 42.1% German, 8.6% English, 7.7% Irish, 3.3% French, 3.1% Italian (2005-2009 5-year est.).
Economy: Single-family building permits issued: 2 (2010); Multi-family building permits issued: 0 (2010); Employment by occupation: 9.8% management, 13.7% professional, 23.9% services, 17.9% sales, 4.5% farming, 22.8% construction, 7.5% production (2005-2009 5-year est.).
Income: Per capita income: $21,078 (2010); Median household income: $43,304 (2010); Average household income: $53,641 (2010); Percent of households with income of $100,000 or more: 9.2% (2010); Poverty rate: 14.6% (2005-2009 5-year est.).
Taxes: Total city taxes per capita: $357 (2007); City property taxes per capita: $92 (2007).
Education: Percent of population age 25 and over with: High school diploma (including GED) or higher: 80.8% (2010); Bachelor's degree or higher: 19.2% (2010); Master's degree or higher: 6.0% (2010).
School District(s)
Blanco ISD (PK-12)
 2009-10 Enrollment: 973 . . . . (830) 833-4414
Housing: Homeownership rate: 63.5% (2010); Median home value: $114,549 (2010); Median contract rent: $419 per month (2005-2009 5-year est.); Median year structure built: 1975 (2005-2009 5-year est.).
Safety: Violent crime rate: 44.8 per 10,000 population; Property crime rate: 332.9 per 10,000 population (2009).
Newspapers: Blanco County News (Community news; Circulation 3,200)
Transportation: Commute to work: 86.9% car, 0.0% public transportation, 4.1% walk, 8.2% work from home (2005-2009 5-year est.); Travel time to work: 56.2% less than 15 minutes, 23.2% 15 to 30 minutes, 8.8% 30 to 45 minutes, 3.8% 45 to 60 minutes, 8.0% 60 minutes or more (2005-2009 5-year est.)
Additional Information Contacts
Blanco Chamber of Commerce . . . . (830) 833-5101
 http://www.blancochamber.com

HYE (unincorporated postal area, zip code 78635). Covers a land area of 15.975 square miles and a water area of 0 square miles. Located at 30.21° N. Lat; 98.53° W. Long. Elevation is 1,453 feet.
Population: 96 (2000); Race: 100.0% White, 0.0% Black, 0.0% Asian, 0.0% Other, 0.0% Hispanic of any race (2000); Density: 6.0 persons per square mile (2000); Age: 17.1% under 18, 18.3% over 64 (2000); Marriage status: 18.9% never married, 81.1% now married, 0.0% widowed, 0.0% divorced (2000); Foreign born: 0.0% (2000); Ancestry (includes multiple

ancestries): 62.2% German, 11.0% French, 8.5% English, 6.1% American (2000).
Economy: Employment by occupation: 9.5% management, 0.0% professional, 16.7% services, 23.8% sales, 9.5% farming, 9.5% construction, 31.0% production (2000).
Income: Per capita income: $18,406 (2000); Median household income: $43,393 (2000); Poverty rate: 179.1% (2000).
Education: Percent of population age 25 and over with: High school diploma (including GED) or higher: 89.4% (2000); Bachelor's degree or higher: 6.1% (2000).
Housing: Homeownership rate: 90.2% (2000); Median home value: $137,500 (2000); Median contract rent: $525 per month (2000); Median year structure built: 1979 (2000).
Transportation: Commute to work: 78.6% car, 0.0% public transportation, 0.0% walk, 21.4% work from home (2000); Travel time to work: 24.2% less than 15 minutes, 21.2% 15 to 30 minutes, 24.2% 30 to 45 minutes, 0.0% 45 to 60 minutes, 30.3% 60 minutes or more (2000)

JOHNSON CITY (city). County seat. Covers a land area of 1.336 square miles and a water area of 0 square miles. Located at 30.27° N. Lat; 98.40° W. Long. Elevation is 1,198 feet.
History: Johnson City was named for the family of President Lyndon B. Johnson (1908-1973), who came to live here in 1913 when Lyndon was five years old. LBJ Ranch, home of Lyndon Johnson, was established nearby.
Population: 962 (1990); 1,191 (2000); 1,367 (2010); 1,451 (2015 projected); Race: 86.2% White, 0.5% Black, 0.5% Asian, 12.8% Other, 27.2% Hispanic of any race (2010); Density: 1,023.5 persons per square mile (2010); Average household size: 2.61 (2010); Median age: 34.4 (2010); Males per 100 females: 95.8 (2010); Marriage status: 28.4% never married, 55.1% now married, 5.1% widowed, 11.3% divorced (2005-2009 5-year est.); Foreign born: 4.5% (2005-2009 5-year est.); Ancestry (includes multiple ancestries): 26.1% German, 19.3% Irish, 13.2% English, 5.2% Swedish, 5.2% Polish (2005-2009 5-year est.).
Economy: Single-family building permits issued: 3 (2010); Multi-family building permits issued: 16 (2010); Employment by occupation: 8.9% management, 13.9% professional, 21.1% services, 28.4% sales, 1.1% farming, 14.8% construction, 11.8% production (2005-2009 5-year est.).
Income: Per capita income: $25,673 (2010); Median household income: $56,644 (2010); Average household income: $69,198 (2010); Percent of households with income of $100,000 or more: 18.8% (2010); Poverty rate: 16.6% (2005-2009 5-year est.).
Taxes: Total city taxes per capita: $372 (2007); City property taxes per capita: $204 (2007).
Education: Percent of population age 25 and over with: High school diploma (including GED) or higher: 80.7% (2010); Bachelor's degree or higher: 21.0% (2010); Master's degree or higher: 7.0% (2010).
School District(s)
Johnson City ISD (PK-12)
 2009-10 Enrollment: 684 . . . . (830) 868-7410
Housing: Homeownership rate: 72.0% (2010); Median home value: $114,835 (2010); Median contract rent: $349 per month (2005-2009 5-year est.); Median year structure built: 1978 (2005-2009 5-year est.).
Safety: Violent crime rate: 0.0 per 10,000 population; Property crime rate: 199.3 per 10,000 population (2009).
Newspapers: Record-Courier (Local news; Circulation 2,100)
Transportation: Commute to work: 91.7% car, 0.0% public transportation, 2.6% walk, 2.6% work from home (2005-2009 5-year est.); Travel time to work: 50.1% less than 15 minutes, 20.4% 15 to 30 minutes, 12.3% 30 to 45 minutes, 6.8% 45 to 60 minutes, 10.4% 60 minutes or more (2005-2009 5-year est.)
Additional Information Contacts
Johnson City Chamber of Commerce . . . . (830) 868-7684
 http://www.johnsoncity-texas.com

ROUND MOUNTAIN (town). Covers a land area of 2.300 square miles and a water area of 0 square miles. Located at 30.43° N. Lat; 98.35° W. Long. Elevation is 1,280 feet.
Population: 46 (1990); 111 (2000); 129 (2010); 139 (2015 projected); Race: 89.1% White, 0.0% Black, 0.0% Asian, 10.9% Other, 12.4% Hispanic of any race (2010); Density: 56.1 persons per square mile (2010); Average household size: 2.43 (2010); Median age: 39.3 (2010); Males per 100 females: 98.5 (2010); Marriage status: 20.1% never married, 44.4% now married, 5.9% widowed, 29.6% divorced (2005-2009 5-year est.); Foreign born: 9.2% (2005-2009 5-year est.); Ancestry (includes multiple

ancestries): 36.4% German, 3.1% English, 2.1% Irish, 1.0% French, 1.0% Scotch-Irish (2005-2009 5-year est.).

Economy: Employment by occupation: 15.1% management, 8.4% professional, 15.1% services, 33.6% sales, 15.1% farming, 12.6% construction, 0.0% production (2005-2009 5-year est.).

Income: Per capita income: $40,894 (2010); Median household income: $79,688 (2010); Average household income: $100,849 (2010); Percent of households with income of $100,000 or more: 37.7% (2010); Poverty rate: 30.8% (2005-2009 5-year est.).

Taxes: Total city taxes per capita: $8 (2007); City property taxes per capita: $0 (2007).

Education: Percent of population age 25 and over with: High school diploma (including GED) or higher: 85.2% (2010); Bachelor's degree or higher: 29.5% (2010); Master's degree or higher: 6.8% (2010).

Housing: Homeownership rate: 84.9% (2010); Median home value: $231,250 (2010); Median contract rent: n/a per month (2005-2009 5-year est.); Median year structure built: 1981 (2005-2009 5-year est.).

Transportation: Commute to work: 100.0% car, 0.0% public transportation, 0.0% walk, 0.0% work from home (2005-2009 5-year est.); Travel time to work: 27.6% less than 15 minutes, 61.2% 15 to 30 minutes, 6.9% 30 to 45 minutes, 2.6% 45 to 60 minutes, 1.7% 60 minutes or more (2005-2009 5-year est.)

Airports: West Ranch (general aviation)

Borden County

Located in northwestern Texas; drained by the Colorado River. Covers a land area of 898.80 square miles, a water area of 7.24 square miles, and is located in the Central Time Zone at 32.72° N. Lat., 101.43° W. Long. The county was founded in 1876. County seat is Gail.

Weather Station: Gail   Elevation: 2,528 feet

	Jan	Feb	Mar	Apr	May	Jun	Jul	Aug	Sep	Oct	Nov	Dec
High	58	63	71	80	87	92	95	94	87	78	66	58
Low	32	35	42	50	59	66	70	69	62	52	40	32
Precip	0.6	0.7	1.0	1.3	2.8	2.7	1.8	2.3	2.7	2.0	0.9	0.8
Snow	0.1	0.2	tr	tr	0.0	0.0	0.0	0.0	0.0	0.0	0.1	0.3

High and Low temperatures in degrees Fahrenheit; Precipitation and Snow in inches

Population: 799 (1990); 729 (2000); 637 (2010); 592 (2015 projected); Race: 87.3% White, 0.2% Black, 0.0% Asian, 12.6% Other, 16.3% Hispanic of any race (2010); Density: 0.7 persons per square mile (2010); Average household size: 2.38 (2010); Median age: 43.9 (2010); Males per 100 females: 100.9 (2010).

Religion: Largest group: 35.4% Southern Baptist Convention (2000).

Economy: Unemployment rate: 4.2% (June 2011); Total civilian labor force: 479 (June 2011); Leading industries: Farms: 116 totaling 435,166 acres (2007); Companies that employ 500 or more persons: 0 (2009); Companies that employ 100 to 499 persons: 0 (2009); Companies that employ less than 100 persons: 3 (2009); Black-owned businesses: n/a (2007); Hispanic-owned businesses: n/a (2007); Asian-owned businesses: n/a (2007); Women-owned businesses: n/a (2007); Retail sales per capita: $2,340 (2010). Single-family building permits issued: n/a (2010); Multi-family building permits issued: n/a (2010).

Income: Per capita income: $26,221 (2010); Median household income: $40,833 (2010); Average household income: $62,323 (2010); Percent of households with income of $100,000 or more: 15.7% (2010); Poverty rate: 11.3% (2009); Bankruptcy rate: n/a (2010).

Taxes: Total county taxes per capita: $2,378 (2007); County property taxes per capita: $2,316 (2007).

Education: Percent of population age 25 and over with: High school diploma (including GED) or higher: 86.5% (2010); Bachelor's degree or higher: 23.4% (2010); Master's degree or higher: 4.8% (2010).

Housing: Homeownership rate: 72.0% (2010); Median home value: $78,846 (2010); Median contract rent: $412 per month (2005-2009 5-year est.); Median year structure built: 1957 (2005-2009 5-year est.)

Health: Birth rate: 33.6 per 10,000 population (2009); Death rate: 16.8 per 10,000 population (2009); Age-adjusted cancer mortality rate: Suppressed deaths per 100,000 population (2007); Number of physicians: 0.0 per 10,000 population (2008); Hospital beds: 0.0 per 10,000 population (2007); Hospital admissions: 0.0 per 10,000 population (2007).

Elections: 2008 Presidential election results: 11.1% Obama, 87.5% McCain, 0.0% Nader

Additional Information Contacts

Borden County Government . . . . (806) 856-4391
   http://www.co.borden.tx.us/ips/cms

Borden County Communities

GAIL (unincorporated postal area, zip code 79738). County seat. Covers a land area of 170.626 square miles and a water area of 0.104 square miles. Located at 32.72° N. Lat; 101.45° W. Long. Elevation is 2,556 feet.

History: Both the town of Gail and the county of Borden were named for Gail Borden, Texas pioneer and inventor of the process for condensing milk. Gail developed as a range town, serving the surrounding ranches.

Population: 238 (2000); Race: 84.0% White, 0.0% Black, 4.2% Asian, 11.8% Other, 14.2% Hispanic of any race (2000); Density: 1.4 persons per square mile (2000); Age: 26.4% under 18, 11.8% over 64 (2000); Marriage status: 16.4% never married, 63.6% now married, 6.1% widowed, 13.9% divorced (2000); Foreign born: 4.2% (2000); Ancestry (includes multiple ancestries): 15.1% Irish, 9.4% American, 9.0% German, 6.6% English (2000).

Economy: Employment by occupation: 25.8% management, 20.2% professional, 14.5% services, 10.5% sales, 8.9% farming, 8.9% construction, 11.3% production (2000).

Income: Per capita income: $17,716 (2000); Median household income: $35,208 (2000); Poverty rate: 179.1% (2000).

Education: Percent of population age 25 and over with: High school diploma (including GED) or higher: 88.2% (2000); Bachelor's degree or higher: 22.2% (2000).

School District(s)

Borden County ISD (PK-12)
   2009-10 Enrollment: 222 . . . . (806) 756-4313

Housing: Homeownership rate: 71.3% (2000); Median home value: $46,000 (2000); Median contract rent: <$101 per month (2000); Median year structure built: 1972 (2000).

Newspapers: Borden Star (Community news; Circulation 600)

Transportation: Commute to work: 84.7% car, 0.0% public transportation, 12.9% walk, 0.0% work from home (2000); Travel time to work: 60.5% less than 15 minutes, 10.5% 15 to 30 minutes, 16.1% 30 to 45 minutes, 6.5% 45 to 60 minutes, 6.5% 60 minutes or more (2000)

Bosque County

Located in central Texas; bounded on the northeast and east by the Brazos River. Covers a land area of 989.18 square miles, a water area of 13.46 square miles, and is located in the Central Time Zone at 31.88° N. Lat., 97.61° W. Long. The county was founded in 1854. County seat is Meridian.

Weather Station: Whitney Dam   Elevation: 574 feet

	Jan	Feb	Mar	Apr	May	Jun	Jul	Aug	Sep	Oct	Nov	Dec
High	59	62	69	77	85	92	97	97	90	80	69	59
Low	35	38	46	53	63	69	72	71	65	54	45	35
Precip	2.0	2.4	3.5	2.8	4.2	4.5	1.6	2.1	2.7	4.0	2.8	2.8
Snow	0.0	tr	0.0	0.0	0.0	0.0	0.0	0.0	0.0	0.0	0.0	0.1

High and Low temperatures in degrees Fahrenheit; Precipitation and Snow in inches

Population: 15,125 (1990); 17,204 (2000); 18,312 (2010); 18,816 (2015 projected); Race: 88.3% White, 2.7% Black, 0.1% Asian, 8.9% Other, 15.1% Hispanic of any race (2010); Density: 18.5 persons per square mile (2010); Average household size: 2.49 (2010); Median age: 41.7 (2010); Males per 100 females: 96.9 (2010).

Religion: Five largest groups: 36.7% Southern Baptist Convention, 10.8% The United Methodist Church, 7.3% Catholic Church, 6.8% Evangelical Lutheran Church in America, 3.2% Churches of Christ (2000).

Economy: Unemployment rate: 9.2% (June 2011); Total civilian labor force: 8,273 (June 2011); Leading industries: 22.1% health care and social assistance; 19.1% manufacturing; 16.8% retail trade (2009); Farms: 1,399 totaling 550,995 acres (2007); Companies that employ 500 or more persons: 0 (2009); Companies that employ 100 to 499 persons: 3 (2009); Companies that employ less than 100 persons: 296 (2009); Black-owned businesses: n/a (2007); Hispanic-owned businesses: n/a (2007); Asian-owned businesses: n/a (2007); Women-owned businesses: n/a (2007); Retail sales per capita: $6,934 (2010). Single-family building permits issued: 2 (2010); Multi-family building permits issued: 4 (2010).

Income: Per capita income: $21,666 (2010); Median household income: $42,752 (2010); Average household income: $54,781 (2010); Percent of households with income of $100,000 or more: 11.4% (2010); Poverty rate: 14.5% (2009); Bankruptcy rate: 2.00% (2010).

Taxes: Total county taxes per capita: $260 (2007); County property taxes per capita: $192 (2007).

Education: Percent of population age 25 and over with: High school diploma (including GED) or higher: 80.7% (2010); Bachelor's degree or higher: 17.0% (2010); Master's degree or higher: 4.7% (2010).
Housing: Homeownership rate: 76.0% (2010); Median home value: $82,393 (2010); Median contract rent: $389 per month (2005-2009 5-year est.); Median year structure built: 1973 (2005-2009 5-year est.).
Health: Birth rate: 124.8 per 10,000 population (2009); Death rate: 134.4 per 10,000 population (2009); Age-adjusted cancer mortality rate: 249.7 deaths per 100,000 population (2007); Number of physicians: 7.4 per 10,000 population (2008); Hospital beds: 22.5 per 10,000 population (2007); Hospital admissions: 860.3 per 10,000 population (2007).
Elections: 2008 Presidential election results: 23.5% Obama, 75.4% McCain, 0.0% Nader
Additional Information Contacts
Bosque County Government . . . . (254) 435-2382
   http://www.bosquecounty.us
Clifton Chamber of Commerce . . . . (254) 675-3720
   http://www.cliftontexas.org
Meridian Chamber of Commerce . . . . (254) 435-2966
   http://www.meridian-chamber.com

Bosque County Communities

CLIFTON (city). Covers a land area of 1.912 square miles and a water area of 0 square miles. Located at 31.78° N. Lat; 97.58° W. Long. Elevation is 673 feet.
History: Settled 1880, incorporated 1902.
Population: 3,208 (1990); 3,542 (2000); 3,691 (2010); 3,770 (2015 projected); Race: 81.1% White, 3.0% Black, 0.2% Asian, 15.7% Other, 26.3% Hispanic of any race (2010); Density: 1,930.2 persons per square mile (2010); Average household size: 2.54 (2010); Median age: 39.2 (2010); Males per 100 females: 87.1 (2010); Marriage status: 20.9% never married, 48.2% now married, 16.8% widowed, 14.1% divorced (2005-2009 5-year est.); Foreign born: 9.3% (2005-2009 5-year est.); Ancestry (includes multiple ancestries): 19.5% German, 11.7% American, 9.7% English, 7.8% Norwegian, 6.9% Irish (2005-2009 5-year est.).
Economy: Single-family building permits issued: 1 (2010); Multi-family building permits issued: 4 (2010); Employment by occupation: 11.9% management, 15.5% professional, 28.4% services, 17.9% sales, 1.3% farming, 6.9% construction, 18.1% production (2005-2009 5-year est.).
Income: Per capita income: $16,881 (2010); Median household income: $33,325 (2010); Average household income: $45,392 (2010); Percent of households with income of $100,000 or more: 8.8% (2010); Poverty rate: 14.0% (2005-2009 5-year est.).
Taxes: Total city taxes per capita: $327 (2007); City property taxes per capita: $123 (2007).
Education: Percent of population age 25 and over with: High school diploma (including GED) or higher: 72.7% (2010); Bachelor's degree or higher: 18.1% (2010); Master's degree or higher: 4.7% (2010).
School District(s)
Clifton ISD (PK-12)
   2009-10 Enrollment: 1,142 . . . . (254) 675-2827
Housing: Homeownership rate: 63.6% (2010); Median home value: $68,639 (2010); Median contract rent: $352 per month (2005-2009 5-year est.); Median year structure built: 1970 (2005-2009 5-year est.).
Hospitals: Goodall-Witcher Healthcare Foundation (72 beds)
Safety: Violent crime rate: 8.4 per 10,000 population; Property crime rate: 86.9 per 10,000 population (2009).
Newspapers: Clifton Record (Local news; Circulation 3,560)
Transportation: Commute to work: 96.1% car, 0.0% public transportation, 3.1% walk, 0.9% work from home (2005-2009 5-year est.); Travel time to work: 56.1% less than 15 minutes, 19.6% 15 to 30 minutes, 14.5% 30 to 45 minutes, 6.2% 45 to 60 minutes, 3.7% 60 minutes or more (2005-2009 5-year est.)
Additional Information Contacts
Clifton Chamber of Commerce . . . . (254) 675-3720
   http://www.cliftontexas.org

CRANFILLS GAP (city). Covers a land area of 0.728 square miles and a water area of 0 square miles. Located at 31.77° N. Lat; 97.82° W. Long. Elevation is 968 feet.
Population: 269 (1990); 335 (2000); 382 (2010); 398 (2015 projected); Race: 91.1% White, 3.7% Black, 0.3% Asian, 5.0% Other, 6.0% Hispanic of any race (2010); Density: 524.5 persons per square mile (2010); Average household size: 2.51 (2010); Median age: 41.5 (2010); Males per

100 females: 95.9 (2010); Marriage status: 12.9% never married, 62.6% now married, 10.1% widowed, 14.4% divorced (2005-2009 5-year est.); Foreign born: 5.3% (2005-2009 5-year est.); Ancestry (includes multiple ancestries): 26.9% American, 19.1% German, 11.3% Norwegian, 11.3% Irish, 6.6% English (2005-2009 5-year est.).
Economy: Employment by occupation: 7.6% management, 15.3% professional, 11.2% services, 21.8% sales, 2.9% farming, 5.9% construction, 35.3% production (2005-2009 5-year est.).
Income: Per capita income: $28,434 (2010); Median household income: $58,333 (2010); Average household income: $70,313 (2010); Percent of households with income of $100,000 or more: 17.8% (2010); Poverty rate: 23.1% (2005-2009 5-year est.).
Taxes: Total city taxes per capita: $90 (2007); City property taxes per capita: $51 (2007).
Education: Percent of population age 25 and over with: High school diploma (including GED) or higher: 88.7% (2010); Bachelor's degree or higher: 27.1% (2010); Master's degree or higher: 5.6% (2010).
School District(s)
Cranfills Gap ISD (PK-12)
   2009-10 Enrollment: 108 . . . . (254) 597-2505
Housing: Homeownership rate: 80.9% (2010); Median home value: $104,167 (2010); Median contract rent: $255 per month (2005-2009 5-year est.); Median year structure built: 1958 (2005-2009 5-year est.).
Transportation: Commute to work: 93.7% car, 0.0% public transportation, 6.3% walk, 0.0% work from home (2005-2009 5-year est.); Travel time to work: 29.7% less than 15 minutes, 34.2% 15 to 30 minutes, 18.4% 30 to 45 minutes, 1.9% 45 to 60 minutes, 15.8% 60 minutes or more (2005-2009 5-year est.)

IREDELL (city). Covers a land area of 0.459 square miles and a water area of 0 square miles. Located at 31.98° N. Lat; 97.87° W. Long. Elevation is 902 feet.
Population: 332 (1990); 360 (2000); 381 (2010); 391 (2015 projected); Race: 95.8% White, 0.0% Black, 0.0% Asian, 4.2% Other, 6.0% Hispanic of any race (2010); Density: 829.5 persons per square mile (2010); Average household size: 2.35 (2010); Median age: 43.6 (2010); Males per 100 females: 105.9 (2010); Marriage status: 17.5% never married, 53.4% now married, 11.7% widowed, 17.5% divorced (2005-2009 5-year est.); Foreign born: 6.5% (2005-2009 5-year est.); Ancestry (includes multiple ancestries): 20.6% German, 19.9% American, 18.8% Irish, 12.3% Dutch, 10.8% English (2005-2009 5-year est.).
Economy: Employment by occupation: 14.1% management, 22.2% professional, 23.2% services, 8.1% sales, 0.0% farming, 18.2% construction, 14.1% production (2005-2009 5-year est.).
Income: Per capita income: $18,873 (2010); Median household income: $33,696 (2010); Average household income: $44,691 (2010); Percent of households with income of $100,000 or more: 6.8% (2010); Poverty rate: 25.0% (2005-2009 5-year est.).
Taxes: Total city taxes per capita: $85 (2007); City property taxes per capita: $39 (2007).
Education: Percent of population age 25 and over with: High school diploma (including GED) or higher: 83.4% (2010); Bachelor's degree or higher: 16.2% (2010); Master's degree or higher: 5.3% (2010).
School District(s)
Iredell ISD (PK-12)
   2009-10 Enrollment: 132 . . . . (254) 364-2411
Housing: Homeownership rate: 78.4% (2010); Median home value: $92,857 (2010); Median contract rent: $382 per month (2005-2009 5-year est.); Median year structure built: 1943 (2005-2009 5-year est.).
Transportation: Commute to work: 85.7% car, 0.0% public transportation, 12.1% walk, 2.2% work from home (2005-2009 5-year est.); Travel time to work: 33.7% less than 15 minutes, 15.7% 15 to 30 minutes, 32.6% 30 to 45 minutes, 5.6% 45 to 60 minutes, 12.4% 60 minutes or more (2005-2009 5-year est.)

KOPPERL (unincorporated postal area, zip code 76652). Covers a land area of 64.832 square miles and a water area of 0.044 square miles. Located at 32.11° N. Lat; 97.54° W. Long. Elevation is 577 feet.
Population: 959 (2000); Race: 98.0% White, 0.0% Black, 0.0% Asian, 2.0% Other, 5.9% Hispanic of any race (2000); Density: 14.8 persons per square mile (2000); Age: 23.5% under 18, 13.6% over 64 (2000); Marriage status: 11.7% never married, 72.2% now married, 8.6% widowed, 7.4% divorced (2000); Foreign born: 2.1% (2000); Ancestry (includes multiple ancestries): 21.1% American, 14.7% German, 9.9% Irish, 5.5% English (2000).

Economy: Employment by occupation: 16.5% management, 12.3% professional, 10.7% services, 23.5% sales, 1.6% farming, 17.2% construction, 18.1% production (2000).
Income: Per capita income: $16,401 (2000); Median household income: $32,083 (2000); Poverty rate: 179.1% (2000).
Education: Percent of population age 25 and over with: High school diploma (including GED) or higher: 74.2% (2000); Bachelor's degree or higher: 10.0% (2000).

School District(s)

Kopperl ISD (PK-12)
  2009-10 Enrollment: 250 . . . . (254) 889-3502
Housing: Homeownership rate: 81.4% (2000); Median home value: $47,900 (2000); Median contract rent: $325 per month (2000); Median year structure built: 1978 (2000).
Transportation: Commute to work: 91.0% car, 0.0% public transportation, 2.8% walk, 6.1% work from home (2000); Travel time to work: 16.6% less than 15 minutes, 18.1% 15 to 30 minutes, 28.2% 30 to 45 minutes, 11.8% 45 to 60 minutes, 25.2% 60 minutes or more (2000)

MERIDIAN (city). County seat. Covers a land area of 2.163 square miles and a water area of 0.005 square miles. Located at 31.92° N. Lat; 97.65° W. Long. Elevation is 761 feet.
History: Settled 1854, incorporated 1886.
Population: 1,393 (1990); 1,491 (2000); 1,562 (2010); 1,596 (2015 projected); Race: 80.2% White, 8.5% Black, 0.1% Asian, 11.3% Other, 28.0% Hispanic of any race (2010); Density: 722.1 persons per square mile (2010); Average household size: 2.76 (2010); Median age: 35.0 (2010); Males per 100 females: 90.0 (2010); Marriage status: 19.4% never married, 50.0% now married, 21.7% widowed, 8.8% divorced (2005-2009 5-year est.); Foreign born: 6.5% (2005-2009 5-year est.); Ancestry (includes multiple ancestries): 20.7% American, 14.1% Irish, 11.8% German, 6.3% English, 2.4% Norwegian (2005-2009 5-year est.).
Economy: Single-family building permits issued: 1 (2010); Multi-family building permits issued: 0 (2010); Employment by occupation: 3.9% management, 10.0% professional, 23.9% services, 20.4% sales, 2.3% farming, 12.7% construction, 26.8% production (2005-2009 5-year est.).
Income: Per capita income: $21,039 (2010); Median household income: $49,907 (2010); Average household income: $58,918 (2010); Percent of households with income of $100,000 or more: 14.4% (2010); Poverty rate: 45.9% (2005-2009 5-year est.).
Taxes: Total city taxes per capita: $246 (2007); City property taxes per capita: $118 (2007).
Education: Percent of population age 25 and over with: High school diploma (including GED) or higher: 75.7% (2010); Bachelor's degree or higher: 17.1% (2010); Master's degree or higher: 6.8% (2010).

School District(s)

Kopperl ISD (PK-12)
  2009-10 Enrollment: 250 . . . . (254) 889-3502
Meridian ISD (PK-12)
  2009-10 Enrollment: 518 . . . . (254) 435-2081
Housing: Homeownership rate: 65.2% (2010); Median home value: $56,349 (2010); Median contract rent: $366 per month (2005-2009 5-year est.); Median year structure built: 1962 (2005-2009 5-year est.).
Safety: Violent crime rate: 6.7 per 10,000 population; Property crime rate: 53.5 per 10,000 population (2009).
Newspapers: Bosque County News (Community news; Circulation 1,400)
Transportation: Commute to work: 93.0% car, 0.0% public transportation, 2.5% walk, 0.8% work from home (2005-2009 5-year est.); Travel time to work: 50.6% less than 15 minutes, 25.8% 15 to 30 minutes, 9.5% 30 to 45 minutes, 7.2% 45 to 60 minutes, 6.8% 60 minutes or more (2005-2009 5-year est.)
Additional Information Contacts
Meridian Chamber of Commerce. . . . . (254) 435-2966
  http://www.meridian-chamber.com

MORGAN (city). Covers a land area of 0.747 square miles and a water area of 0 square miles. Located at 32.01° N. Lat; 97.60° W. Long. Elevation is 761 feet.
Population: 461 (1990); 485 (2000); 479 (2010); 475 (2015 projected); Race: 71.0% White, 2.1% Black, 0.0% Asian, 26.9% Other, 43.4% Hispanic of any race (2010); Density: 641.3 persons per square mile (2010); Average household size: 2.98 (2010); Median age: 30.0 (2010); Males per 100 females: 111.9 (2010); Marriage status: 14.8% never married, 63.3% now married, 4.9% widowed, 17.0% divorced (2005-2009 5-year est.); Foreign born: 13.2% (2005-2009 5-year est.); Ancestry

(includes multiple ancestries): 15.2% Scotch-Irish, 9.6% German, 7.1% American, 6.6% African, 4.4% Swedish (2005-2009 5-year est.).
Economy: Employment by occupation: 2.0% management, 3.3% professional, 25.7% services, 25.3% sales, 0.4% farming, 7.8% construction, 35.5% production (2005-2009 5-year est.).
Income: Per capita income: $11,103 (2010); Median household income: $26,607 (2010); Average household income: $32,997 (2010); Percent of households with income of $100,000 or more: 1.9% (2010); Poverty rate: 16.0% (2005-2009 5-year est.).
Taxes: Total city taxes per capita: $71 (2007); City property taxes per capita: $27 (2007).
Education: Percent of population age 25 and over with: High school diploma (including GED) or higher: 52.6% (2010); Bachelor's degree or higher: 3.0% (2010); Master's degree or higher: 2.6% (2010).

School District(s)

Morgan ISD (PK-12)
  2009-10 Enrollment: 131 . . . . (254) 635-2311
Housing: Homeownership rate: 83.9% (2010); Median home value: $26,471 (2010); Median contract rent: $462 per month (2005-2009 5-year est.); Median year structure built: 1964 (2005-2009 5-year est.).
Transportation: Commute to work: 93.9% car, 0.0% public transportation, 5.3% walk, 0.0% work from home (2005-2009 5-year est.); Travel time to work: 26.5% less than 15 minutes, 10.2% 15 to 30 minutes, 19.6% 30 to 45 minutes, 22.4% 45 to 60 minutes, 21.2% 60 minutes or more (2005-2009 5-year est.)

VALLEY MILLS (city). Covers a land area of 0.701 square miles and a water area of 0 square miles. Located at 31.65° N. Lat; 97.47° W. Long. Elevation is 594 feet.
Population: 1,085 (1990); 1,123 (2000); 1,114 (2010); 1,108 (2015 projected); Race: 83.0% White, 5.0% Black, 0.4% Asian, 11.5% Other, 12.3% Hispanic of any race (2010); Density: 1,588.4 persons per square mile (2010); Average household size: 2.47 (2010); Median age: 37.2 (2010); Males per 100 females: 88.8 (2010); Marriage status: 19.7% never married, 67.0% now married, 2.8% widowed, 10.5% divorced (2005-2009 5-year est.); Foreign born: 11.2% (2005-2009 5-year est.); Ancestry (includes multiple ancestries): 21.6% German, 18.7% American, 11.6% Irish, 5.8% English, 2.2% Dutch (2005-2009 5-year est.).
Economy: Single-family building permits issued: 0 (2010); Multi-family building permits issued: 0 (2010); Employment by occupation: 9.0% management, 12.1% professional, 22.2% services, 23.1% sales, 1.3% farming, 20.0% construction, 12.4% production (2005-2009 5-year est.).
Income: Per capita income: $18,353 (2010); Median household income: $38,524 (2010); Average household income: $46,848 (2010); Percent of households with income of $100,000 or more: 6.2% (2010); Poverty rate: 11.1% (2005-2009 5-year est.).
Taxes: Total city taxes per capita: $177 (2007); City property taxes per capita: $128 (2007).
Education: Percent of population age 25 and over with: High school diploma (including GED) or higher: 79.7% (2010); Bachelor's degree or higher: 12.6% (2010); Master's degree or higher: 3.7% (2010).

School District(s)

Valley Mills ISD (PK-12)
  2009-10 Enrollment: 629 . . . . (254) 932-5210
Housing: Homeownership rate: 67.9% (2010); Median home value: $78,182 (2010); Median contract rent: $484 per month (2005-2009 5-year est.); Median year structure built: 1962 (2005-2009 5-year est.).
Newspapers: Valley Mills Progress (Community news; Circulation 750)
Transportation: Commute to work: 93.1% car, 0.0% public transportation, 2.4% walk, 1.2% work from home (2005-2009 5-year est.); Travel time to work: 25.6% less than 15 minutes, 29.5% 15 to 30 minutes, 34.4% 30 to 45 minutes, 3.2% 45 to 60 minutes, 7.3% 60 minutes or more (2005-2009 5-year est.)

WALNUT SPRINGS (city). Covers a land area of 1.333 square miles and a water area of 0 square miles. Located at 32.05° N. Lat; 97.74° W. Long. Elevation is 912 feet.
Population: 716 (1990); 755 (2000); 801 (2010); 817 (2015 projected); Race: 85.8% White, 0.1% Black, 0.0% Asian, 14.1% Other, 36.7% Hispanic of any race (2010); Density: 600.9 persons per square mile (2010); Average household size: 2.82 (2010); Median age: 32.2 (2010); Males per 100 females: 105.9 (2010); Marriage status: 17.8% never married, 52.5% now married, 3.4% widowed, 26.4% divorced (2005-2009 5-year est.); Foreign born: 13.3% (2005-2009 5-year est.); Ancestry

(includes multiple ancestries): 25.9% American, 11.1% Irish, 6.0% German, 4.7% English, 1.7% Italian (2005-2009 5-year est.).
Economy: Employment by occupation: 6.6% management, 13.6% professional, 27.4% services, 26.7% sales, 1.6% farming, 6.1% construction, 18.1% production (2005-2009 5-year est.).
Income: Per capita income: $14,476 (2010); Median household income: $30,833 (2010); Average household income: $41,523 (2010); Percent of households with income of $100,000 or more: 5.6% (2010); Poverty rate: 31.2% (2005-2009 5-year est.).
Taxes: Total city taxes per capita: $102 (2007); City property taxes per capita: $46 (2007).
Education: Percent of population age 25 and over with: High school diploma (including GED) or higher: 73.5% (2010); Bachelor's degree or higher: 7.2% (2010); Master's degree or higher: 1.9% (2010).

School District(s)
Walnut Springs ISD (PK-12)
2009-10 Enrollment: 212 . . . . (254) 797-2133
Housing: Homeownership rate: 78.2% (2010); Median home value: $40,000 (2010); Median contract rent: $467 per month (2005-2009 5-year est.); Median year structure built: 1972 (2005-2009 5-year est.).
Transportation: Commute to work: 95.6% car, 3.0% public transportation, 0.0% walk, 1.4% work from home (2005-2009 5-year est.); Travel time to work: 25.5% less than 15 minutes, 26.7% 15 to 30 minutes, 16.7% 30 to 45 minutes, 21.5% 45 to 60 minutes, 9.7% 60 minutes or more (2005-2009 5-year est.)

Bowie County

Located in northeastern Texas; bounded on the north by the Red River and the Oklahoma and Arkansas borders, on the east by the Arkansas border, and on the south by the Sulphur River. Covers a land area of 887.87 square miles, a water area of 34.90 square miles, and is located in the Central Time Zone at 33.43° N. Lat., 94.25° W. Long. The county was founded in 1840. County seat is New Boston.

Bowie County is part of the Texarkana, TX-Texarkana, AR Metropolitan Statistical Area. The entire metro area includes: Miller County, AR; Bowie County, TX

Weather Station: Texarkana										Elevation: 390 feet		
	Jan	Feb	Mar	Apr	May	Jun	Jul	Aug	Sep	Oct	Nov	Dec
High	54	59	67	75	82	89	93	94	87	76	65	56
Low	33	36	44	52	62	69	73	72	65	53	43	35
Precip	4.0	4.2	4.8	4.3	5.2	4.8	3.6	2.2	3.7	5.2	5.0	5.1
Snow	0.5	0.5	tr	0.0	0.0	0.0	0.0	0.0	0.0	0.0	0.0	0.1

High and Low temperatures in degrees Fahrenheit; Precipitation and Snow in inches

Population: 81,665 (1990); 89,306 (2000); 94,159 (2010); 96,345 (2015 projected); Race: 70.6% White, 24.6% Black, 0.7% Asian, 4.0% Other, 5.9% Hispanic of any race (2010); Density: 106.1 persons per square mile (2010); Average household size: 2.52 (2010); Median age: 36.5 (2010); Males per 100 females: 102.0 (2010).
Religion: Five largest groups: 33.2% Southern Baptist Convention, 7.2% The United Methodist Church, 3.7% The American Baptist Association, 3.3% Churches of Christ, 3.2% Catholic Church (2000).
Economy: Unemployment rate: 9.0% (June 2011); Total civilian labor force: 45,589 (June 2011); Leading industries: 21.6% health care and social assistance; 19.6% retail trade; 13.1% accommodation & food services (2009); Farms: 1,610 totaling 291,674 acres (2007); Companies that employ 500 or more persons: 4 (2009); Companies that employ 100 to 499 persons: 38 (2009); Companies that employ less than 100 persons: 2,137 (2009); Black-owned businesses: 733 (2007); Hispanic-owned businesses: n/a (2007); Asian-owned businesses: n/a (2007); Women-owned businesses: 1,823 (2007); Retail sales per capita: $16,413 (2010). Single-family building permits issued: 61 (2010); Multi-family building permits issued: 131 (2010).
Income: Per capita income: $21,142 (2010); Median household income: $41,636 (2010); Average household income: $55,609 (2010); Percent of households with income of $100,000 or more: 12.5% (2010); Poverty rate: 19.8% (2009); Bankruptcy rate: 2.34% (2010).
Taxes: Total county taxes per capita: $174 (2007); County property taxes per capita: $119 (2007).
Education: Percent of population age 25 and over with: High school diploma (including GED) or higher: 83.2% (2010); Bachelor's degree or higher: 17.2% (2010); Master's degree or higher: 5.0% (2010).

Housing: Homeownership rate: 63.0% (2010); Median home value: $83,373 (2010); Median contract rent: $443 per month (2005-2009 5-year est.); Median year structure built: 1976 (2005-2009 5-year est.)
Health: Birth rate: 126.0 per 10,000 population (2009); Death rate: 99.7 per 10,000 population (2009); Age-adjusted cancer mortality rate: 199.4 deaths per 10,000 population (2007); Number of physicians: 26.6 per 10,000 population (2008); Hospital beds: 67.2 per 10,000 population (2007); Hospital admissions: 3,334.5 per 10,000 population (2007).
Elections: 2008 Presidential election results: 30.7% Obama, 68.7% McCain, 0.0% Nader
Additional Information Contacts
Bowie County Government . . . . (903) 628-2571
   http://www.co.bowie.tx.us/ips/cms
City of Texarkana . . . . (903) 798-3900
   http://www.ci.texarkana.tx.us
De Kalb Chamber of Commerce . . . . (903) 667-3706
   http://www.dekalbtexas.org
New Boston Chamber of Commerce . . . . (903) 628-2581
   http://www.newbostontx.org
Texarkana Chamber of Commerce . . . . (903) 792-7191
   http://texarkana.wliinc2.com

Bowie County Communities

DE KALB (city). Covers a land area of 1.311 square miles and a water area of 0 square miles. Located at 33.50° N. Lat; 94.61° W. Long. Elevation is 410 feet.
History: De Kalb was named for Baron de Kalb, a German general in the American Revolutionary Army. Cotton was the principal crop of the area.
Population: 1,976 (1990); 1,769 (2000); 1,710 (2010); 1,689 (2015 projected); Race: 69.1% White, 27.7% Black, 0.1% Asian, 3.1% Other, 3.9% Hispanic of any race (2010); Density: 1,304.1 persons per square mile (2010); Average household size: 2.27 (2010); Median age: 41.0 (2010); Males per 100 females: 83.9 (2010); Marriage status: 27.1% never married, 52.1% now married, 14.2% widowed, 6.7% divorced (2005-2009 5-year est.); Foreign born: 1.6% (2005-2009 5-year est.); Ancestry (includes multiple ancestries): 13.2% Irish, 7.9% African, 7.2% German, 6.4% American, 6.0% English (2005-2009 5-year est.).
Economy: Employment by occupation: 3.7% management, 13.4% professional, 18.7% services, 20.1% sales, 8.8% farming, 15.7% construction, 19.6% production (2005-2009 5-year est.).
Income: Per capita income: $16,602 (2010); Median household income: $25,747 (2010); Average household income: $38,387 (2010); Percent of households with income of $100,000 or more: 4.3% (2010); Poverty rate: 32.0% (2005-2009 5-year est.).
Taxes: Total city taxes per capita: $392 (2007); City property taxes per capita: $331 (2007).
Education: Percent of population age 25 and over with: High school diploma (including GED) or higher: 74.7% (2010); Bachelor's degree or higher: 14.3% (2010); Master's degree or higher: 4.8% (2010).

School District(s)
Dekalb ISD (PK-12)
2009-10 Enrollment: 813 . . . . (903) 667-2566
Hubbard ISD (PK-08)
2009-10 Enrollment: 123 . . . . (903) 667-2645
Housing: Homeownership rate: 54.1% (2010); Median home value: $58,030 (2010); Median contract rent: $323 per month (2005-2009 5-year est.); Median year structure built: 1959 (2005-2009 5-year est.).
Safety: Violent crime rate: 22.2 per 10,000 population; Property crime rate: 260.5 per 10,000 population (2009).
Transportation: Commute to work: 100.0% car, 0.0% public transportation, 0.0% walk, 0.0% work from home (2005-2009 5-year est.); Travel time to work: 37.0% less than 15 minutes, 22.6% 15 to 30 minutes, 28.8% 30 to 45 minutes, 6.3% 45 to 60 minutes, 5.3% 60 minutes or more (2005-2009 5-year est.)
Additional Information Contacts
De Kalb Chamber of Commerce . . . . (903) 667-3706
   http://www.dekalbtexas.org

HOOKS (city). Covers a land area of 2.058 square miles and a water area of 0 square miles. Located at 33.46° N. Lat; 94.28° W. Long. Elevation is 374 feet.
History: Hooks was established as a supply center in 1836, in an area of lignite deposits.

Population: 2,673 (1990); 2,973 (2000); 2,976 (2010); 2,970 (2015 projected); Race: 79.4% White, 13.0% Black, 0.4% Asian, 7.1% Other, 3.5% Hispanic of any race (2010); Density: 1,446.0 persons per square mile (2010); Average household size: 2.45 (2010); Median age: 35.5 (2010); Males per 100 females: 87.2 (2010); Marriage status: 25.7% never married, 50.0% now married, 9.8% widowed, 14.5% divorced (2005-2009 5-year est.); Foreign born: 0.0% (2005-2009 5-year est.); Ancestry (includes multiple ancestries): 16.6% German, 11.5% Irish, 10.3% American, 4.9% French, 3.5% English (2005-2009 5-year est.).
Economy: Single-family building permits issued: 1 (2010); Multi-family building permits issued: 0 (2010); Employment by occupation: 6.0% management, 16.4% professional, 21.1% services, 22.0% sales, 0.0% farming, 18.6% construction, 15.9% production (2005-2009 5-year est.).
Income: Per capita income: $20,138 (2010); Median household income: $41,207 (2010); Average household income: $49,304 (2010); Percent of households with income of $100,000 or more: 6.7% (2010); Poverty rate: 19.7% (2005-2009 5-year est.).
Taxes: Total city taxes per capita: $6 (2007); City property taxes per capita: $0 (2007).
Education: Percent of population age 25 and over with: High school diploma (including GED) or higher: 85.7% (2010); Bachelor's degree or higher: 11.0% (2010); Master's degree or higher: 2.6% (2010).

School District(s)
Hooks ISD (PK-12)
    2009-10 Enrollment: 1,034 . . . . (903) 547-6077
Leary ISD (PK-08)
    2009-10 Enrollment: 115 . . . . (903) 838-8960
Housing: Homeownership rate: 61.0% (2010); Median home value: $59,634 (2010); Median contract rent: $386 per month (2005-2009 5-year est.); Median year structure built: 1973 (2005-2009 5-year est.).
Safety: Violent crime rate: 30.5 per 10,000 population; Property crime rate: 115.1 per 10,000 population (2009).
Transportation: Commute to work: 98.4% car, 0.0% public transportation, 0.0% walk, 1.6% work from home (2005-2009 5-year est.); Travel time to work: 45.0% less than 15 minutes, 40.8% 15 to 30 minutes, 4.6% 30 to 45 minutes, 3.5% 45 to 60 minutes, 6.2% 60 minutes or more (2005-2009 5-year est.)

LEARY (city). Covers a land area of 2.585 square miles and a water area of 0 square miles. Located at 33.46° N. Lat; 94.22° W. Long. Elevation is 377 feet.
Population: 592 (1990); 555 (2000); 582 (2010); 593 (2015 projected); Race: 91.8% White, 2.7% Black, 0.3% Asian, 5.2% Other, 4.3% Hispanic of any race (2010); Density: 225.2 persons per square mile (2010); Average household size: 2.65 (2010); Median age: 38.4 (2010); Males per 100 females: 93.4 (2010); Marriage status: 23.2% never married, 45.1% now married, 6.5% widowed, 25.2% divorced (2005-2009 5-year est.); Foreign born: 0.0% (2005-2009 5-year est.); Ancestry (includes multiple ancestries): 14.3% English, 13.6% Irish, 10.0% American, 6.7% German, 6.0% French (2005-2009 5-year est.).
Economy: Employment by occupation: 8.0% management, 16.3% professional, 9.7% services, 47.3% sales, 3.2% farming, 4.9% construction, 10.7% production (2005-2009 5-year est.).
Income: Per capita income: $25,224 (2010); Median household income: $55,804 (2010); Average household income: $68,193 (2010); Percent of households with income of $100,000 or more: 18.6% (2010); Poverty rate: 13.3% (2005-2009 5-year est.).
Taxes: Total city taxes per capita: $29 (2007); City property taxes per capita: $2 (2007).
Education: Percent of population age 25 and over with: High school diploma (including GED) or higher: 84.0% (2010); Bachelor's degree or higher: 12.4% (2010); Master's degree or higher: 3.6% (2010).
Housing: Homeownership rate: 80.9% (2010); Median home value: $70,000 (2010); Median contract rent: $408 per month (2005-2009 5-year est.); Median year structure built: 1972 (2005-2009 5-year est.).
Transportation: Commute to work: 90.6% car, 0.0% public transportation, 2.2% walk, 7.2% work from home (2005-2009 5-year est.); Travel time to work: 31.8% less than 15 minutes, 57.8% 15 to 30 minutes, 4.5% 30 to 45 minutes, 5.9% 45 to 60 minutes, 0.0% 60 minutes or more (2005-2009 5-year est.)

MAUD (city). Covers a land area of 1.487 square miles and a water area of 0 square miles. Located at 33.33° N. Lat; 94.34° W. Long. Elevation is 289 feet.

Population: 1,082 (1990); 1,028 (2000); 1,076 (2010); 1,099 (2015 projected); Race: 87.3% White, 9.8% Black, 0.2% Asian, 2.8% Other, 1.7% Hispanic of any race (2010); Density: 723.6 persons per square mile (2010); Average household size: 2.55 (2010); Median age: 38.3 (2010); Males per 100 females: 101.1 (2010); Marriage status: 21.8% never married, 48.7% now married, 7.5% widowed, 22.0% divorced (2005-2009 5-year est.); Foreign born: 0.6% (2005-2009 5-year est.); Ancestry (includes multiple ancestries): 16.0% Irish, 7.2% English, 6.9% American, 6.8% German, 4.1% French (2005-2009 5-year est.).
Economy: Single-family building permits issued: 1 (2010); Multi-family building permits issued: 4 (2010); Employment by occupation: 5.1% management, 15.0% professional, 13.5% services, 30.3% sales, 1.0% farming, 17.0% construction, 18.1% production (2005-2009 5-year est.).
Income: Per capita income: $21,574 (2010); Median household income: $45,982 (2010); Average household income: $55,827 (2010); Percent of households with income of $100,000 or more: 14.7% (2010); Poverty rate: 15.9% (2005-2009 5-year est.).
Taxes: Total city taxes per capita: $160 (2007); City property taxes per capita: $73 (2007).
Education: Percent of population age 25 and over with: High school diploma (including GED) or higher: 80.6% (2010); Bachelor's degree or higher: 11.0% (2010); Master's degree or higher: 2.8% (2010).

School District(s)
Maud ISD (PK-12)
    2009-10 Enrollment: 513 . . . . (903) 585-2219
Housing: Homeownership rate: 77.3% (2010); Median home value: $62,000 (2010); Median contract rent: $340 per month (2005-2009 5-year est.); Median year structure built: 1972 (2005-2009 5-year est.).
Transportation: Commute to work: 90.9% car, 0.0% public transportation, 0.6% walk, 6.3% work from home (2005-2009 5-year est.); Travel time to work: 25.0% less than 15 minutes, 39.0% 15 to 30 minutes, 29.9% 30 to 45 minutes, 5.5% 45 to 60 minutes, 0.6% 60 minutes or more (2005-2009 5-year est.)

NASH (city). Covers a land area of 2.823 square miles and a water area of 0.012 square miles. Located at 33.44° N. Lat; 94.12° W. Long. Elevation is 351 feet.
Population: 1,965 (1990); 2,169 (2000); 2,506 (2010); 2,647 (2015 projected); Race: 76.3% White, 17.8% Black, 0.7% Asian, 5.2% Other, 4.7% Hispanic of any race (2010); Density: 887.8 persons per square mile (2010); Average household size: 2.53 (2010); Median age: 35.8 (2010); Males per 100 females: 92.8 (2010); Marriage status: 41.4% never married, 36.5% now married, 5.5% widowed, 16.5% divorced (2005-2009 5-year est.); Foreign born: 19.6% (2005-2009 5-year est.); Ancestry (includes multiple ancestries): 9.8% German, 6.9% Irish, 6.6% American, 5.0% African, 4.6% English (2005-2009 5-year est.).
Economy: Single-family building permits issued: 12 (2010); Multi-family building permits issued: 16 (2010); Employment by occupation: 6.8% management, 13.8% professional, 26.3% services, 24.5% sales, 0.0% farming, 14.2% construction, 14.4% production (2005-2009 5-year est.).
Income: Per capita income: $18,345 (2010); Median household income: $38,750 (2010); Average household income: $46,640 (2010); Percent of households with income of $100,000 or more: 6.7% (2010); Poverty rate: 17.8% (2005-2009 5-year est.).
Taxes: Total city taxes per capita: $112 (2007); City property taxes per capita: $63 (2007).
Education: Percent of population age 25 and over with: High school diploma (including GED) or higher: 85.8% (2010); Bachelor's degree or higher: 15.7% (2010); Master's degree or higher: 4.6% (2010).

School District(s)
Texarkana ISD (PK-12)
    2009-10 Enrollment: 6,849 . . . . (903) 794-3651
Housing: Homeownership rate: 61.4% (2010); Median home value: $63,276 (2010); Median contract rent: $509 per month (2005-2009 5-year est.); Median year structure built: 1983 (2005-2009 5-year est.).
Safety: Violent crime rate: 12.3 per 10,000 population; Property crime rate: 234.6 per 10,000 population (2009).
Transportation: Commute to work: 95.7% car, 0.7% public transportation, 0.0% walk, 3.6% work from home (2005-2009 5-year est.); Travel time to work: 48.2% less than 15 minutes, 40.6% 15 to 30 minutes, 8.0% 30 to 45 minutes, 1.2% 45 to 60 minutes, 1.9% 60 minutes or more (2005-2009 5-year est.)

NEW BOSTON (city). County seat. Covers a land area of 3.491 square miles and a water area of 0 square miles. Located at 33.46° N. Lat; 94.41° W. Long. Elevation is 358 feet.

History: New Boston was the outgrowth of the pioneer town of Old Boston, as was Boston, which became the seat of Bowie County. In the early 1800's there was a ferry across the Red River at Pecan Point, just north of New Boston.

Population: 5,133 (1990); 4,808 (2000); 4,831 (2010); 4,782 (2015 projected); Race: 75.6% White, 20.3% Black, 0.7% Asian, 3.4% Other, 2.3% Hispanic of any race (2010); Density: 1,383.7 persons per square mile (2010); Average household size: 2.42 (2010); Median age: 36.1 (2010); Males per 100 females: 82.9 (2010); Marriage status: 23.5% never married, 55.0% now married, 8.4% widowed, 13.0% divorced (2005-2009 5-year est.); Foreign born: 4.8% (2005-2009 5-year est.); Ancestry (includes multiple ancestries): 20.4% American, 12.7% Irish, 7.0% English, 4.6% Dutch, 4.2% African (2005-2009 5-year est.).

Economy: Single-family building permits issued: 3 (2010); Multi-family building permits issued: 0 (2010); Employment by occupation: 8.4% management, 15.8% professional, 14.5% services, 18.4% sales, 2.6% farming, 15.1% construction, 25.3% production (2005-2009 5-year est.).

Income: Per capita income: $18,744 (2010); Median household income: $34,922 (2010); Average household income: $45,993 (2010); Percent of households with income of $100,000 or more: 6.1% (2010); Poverty rate: 21.8% (2005-2009 5-year est.).

Taxes: Total city taxes per capita: $251 (2007); City property taxes per capita: $113 (2007).

Education: Percent of population age 25 and over with: High school diploma (including GED) or higher: 85.5% (2010); Bachelor's degree or higher: 12.1% (2010); Master's degree or higher: 4.5% (2010).

School District(s)

Dekalb ISD (PK-12)
    2009-10 Enrollment: 813 . . . . (903) 667-2566
Malta ISD (PK-06)
    2009-10 Enrollment: 114 . . . . (903) 667-2950
Maud ISD (PK-12)
    2009-10 Enrollment: 513 . . . . (903) 585-2219
New Boston ISD (PK-12)
    2009-10 Enrollment: 1,397 . . . . (903) 628-2521
Red Lick ISD (PK-08)
    2009-10 Enrollment: 434 . . . . (903) 838-8230
Simms ISD (PK-12)
    2009-10 Enrollment: 581 . . . . (903) 543-2219

Housing: Homeownership rate: 57.5% (2010); Median home value: $68,705 (2010); Median contract rent: $383 per month (2005-2009 est.); Median year structure built: 1969 (2005-2009 5-year est.).

Safety: Violent crime rate: 45.2 per 10,000 population; Property crime rate: 437.3 per 10,000 population (2009).

Newspapers: Bowie County Citizens Tribune (Local news; Circulation 12,500)

Transportation: Commute to work: 96.9% car, 0.0% public transportation, 1.7% walk, 1.5% work from home (2005-2009 5-year est.); Travel time to work: 45.0% less than 15 minutes, 34.3% 15 to 30 minutes, 15.5% 30 to 45 minutes, 2.0% 45 to 60 minutes, 3.2% 60 minutes or more (2005-2009 5-year est.)

Additional Information Contacts
New Boston Chamber of Commerce . . . . (903) 628-2581
    http://www.newbostontx.org

RED LICK (city). Covers a land area of 1.926 square miles and a water area of 0 square miles. Located at 33.47° N. Lat; 94.17° W. Long. Elevation is 361 feet.

Population: 681 (1990); 853 (2000); 1,069 (2010); 1,168 (2015 projected); Race: 92.3% White, 4.8% Black, 0.7% Asian, 2.2% Other, 1.5% Hispanic of any race (2010); Density: 554.9 persons per square mile (2010); Average household size: 2.74 (2010); Median age: 40.5 (2010); Males per 100 females: 94.7 (2010); Marriage status: 11.2% never married, 75.5% now married, 4.5% widowed, 8.7% divorced (2005-2009 5-year est.); Foreign born: 2.4% (2005-2009 5-year est.); Ancestry (includes multiple ancestries): 13.7% American, 13.1% Irish, 10.9% German, 7.1% English, 5.9% Scotch-Irish (2005-2009 5-year est.).

Economy: Employment by occupation: 15.9% management, 30.8% professional, 13.6% services, 21.6% sales, 0.0% farming, 12.7% construction, 5.4% production (2005-2009 5-year est.).

Income: Per capita income: $37,754 (2010); Median household income: $77,193 (2010); Average household income: $103,628 (2010); Percent of households with income of $100,000 or more: 36.7% (2010); Poverty rate: 8.4% (2005-2009 5-year est.).

Taxes: Total city taxes per capita: $84 (2007); City property taxes per capita: $60 (2007).

Education: Percent of population age 25 and over with: High school diploma (including GED) or higher: 88.9% (2010); Bachelor's degree or higher: 31.1% (2010); Master's degree or higher: 10.8% (2010).

Housing: Homeownership rate: 84.9% (2010); Median home value: $163,596 (2010); Median contract rent: $391 per month (2005-2009 5-year est.); Median year structure built: 1993 (2005-2009 5-year est.).

Transportation: Commute to work: 96.7% car, 0.0% public transportation, 0.0% walk, 1.7% work from home (2005-2009 5-year est.); Travel time to work: 44.2% less than 15 minutes, 51.9% 15 to 30 minutes, 2.4% 30 to 45 minutes, 0.0% 45 to 60 minutes, 1.5% 60 minutes or more (2005-2009 5-year est.)

REDWATER (city). Covers a land area of 1.952 square miles and a water area of 0.002 square miles. Located at 33.36° N. Lat; 94.25° W. Long. Elevation is 295 feet.

History: Redwater was the home of the Page family, who in 1890 produced the first American quadruplets on record.

Population: 824 (1990); 872 (2000); 900 (2010); 916 (2015 projected); Race: 93.6% White, 3.4% Black, 0.1% Asian, 2.9% Other, 0.9% Hispanic of any race (2010); Density: 461.0 persons per square mile (2010); Average household size: 2.70 (2010); Median age: 36.2 (2010); Males per 100 females: 101.3 (2010); Marriage status: 26.2% never married, 48.1% now married, 4.5% widowed, 21.2% divorced (2005-2009 5-year est.); Foreign born: 0.0% (2005-2009 5-year est.); Ancestry (includes multiple ancestries): 14.2% American, 13.4% German, 7.7% Irish, 5.4% French, 4.2% English (2005-2009 5-year est.).

Economy: Employment by occupation: 9.0% management, 15.9% professional, 14.5% services, 29.2% sales, 0.0% farming, 15.9% construction, 15.5% production (2005-2009 5-year est.).

Income: Per capita income: $21,043 (2010); Median household income: $46,400 (2010); Average household income: $57,349 (2010); Percent of households with income of $100,000 or more: 11.7% (2010); Poverty rate: 14.3% (2005-2009 5-year est.).

Taxes: Total city taxes per capita: $104 (2007); City property taxes per capita: $34 (2007).

Education: Percent of population age 25 and over with: High school diploma (including GED) or higher: 86.1% (2010); Bachelor's degree or higher: 11.0% (2010); Master's degree or higher: 2.4% (2010).

School District(s)

Redwater ISD (PK-12)
    2009-10 Enrollment: 1,102 . . . . (903) 671-3481

Housing: Homeownership rate: 72.3% (2010); Median home value: $77,619 (2010); Median contract rent: $353 per month (2005-2009 5-year est.); Median year structure built: 1980 (2005-2009 5-year est.).

Transportation: Commute to work: 93.0% car, 0.0% public transportation, 5.8% walk, 1.2% work from home (2005-2009 5-year est.); Travel time to work: 25.4% less than 15 minutes, 40.8% 15 to 30 minutes, 29.6% 30 to 45 minutes, 0.6% 45 to 60 minutes, 3.5% 60 minutes or more (2005-2009 5-year est.)

SIMMS (unincorporated postal area, zip code 75574). Covers a land area of 106.637 square miles and a water area of 0.398 square miles. Located at 33.32° N. Lat; 94.53° W. Long. Elevation is 351 feet.

Population: 1,863 (2000); Race: 97.0% White, 0.0% Black, 0.0% Asian, 3.0% Other, 0.9% Hispanic of any race (2000); Density: 17.5 persons per square mile (2000); Age: 26.6% under 18, 14.3% over 64 (2000); Marriage status: 15.9% never married, 66.5% now married, 9.6% widowed, 8.0% divorced (2000); Foreign born: 0.3% (2000); Ancestry (includes multiple ancestries): 12.7% American, 12.0% Irish, 8.3% German, 6.5% English (2000).

Economy: Employment by occupation: 5.1% management, 12.4% professional, 14.9% services, 23.1% sales, 2.9% farming, 18.9% construction, 22.7% production (2000).

Income: Per capita income: $13,573 (2000); Median household income: $29,647 (2000); Poverty rate: 179.1% (2000).

Education: Percent of population age 25 and over with: High school diploma (including GED) or higher: 68.6% (2000); Bachelor's degree or higher: 7.2% (2000).

Texarkana Chamber of Commerce . . . . (903) 792-7191
    http://texarkana.wliinc2.com

School District(s)

Simms ISD (PK-12)
    2009-10 Enrollment: 581 . . . . (903) 543-2219
Housing: Homeownership rate: 83.1% (2000); Median home value:
$59,600 (2000); Median contract rent: $241 per month (2000); Median year
structure built: 1978 (2000).
Transportation: Commute to work: 95.8% car, 0.0% public transportation,
2.0% walk, 1.1% work from home (2000); Travel time to work: 15.5% less
than 15 minutes, 35.9% 15 to 30 minutes, 28.4% 30 to 45 minutes, 13.1%
45 to 60 minutes, 7.1% 60 minutes or more (2000)

TEXARKANA (city). Covers a land area of 25.626 square miles and a
water area of 0.102 square miles. Located at 33.43° N. Lat; 94.06° W.
Long. Elevation is 299 feet.
History: Texarkana was founded in 1873 on the border, its twin city in
Arkansas having the same name. Texarkana developed as an industrial
and shipping center with diversified industry.
Population: 34,438 (1990); 34,782 (2000); 37,653 (2010); 38,771 (2015
projected); Race: 56.5% White, 38.0% Black, 1.2% Asian, 4.3% Other,
4.3% Hispanic of any race (2010); Density: 1,469.3 persons per square
mile (2010); Average household size: 2.45 (2010); Median age: 36.3
(2010); Males per 100 females: 92.5 (2010); Marriage status: 33.3% never
married, 44.7% now married, 8.0% widowed, 14.0% divorced (2005-2009
5-year est.); Foreign born: 3.4% (2005-2009 5-year est.); Ancestry
(includes multiple ancestries): 11.7% Irish, 11.0% American, 10.6%
German, 7.6% English, 4.6% African (2005-2009 5-year est.).
Economy: Unemployment rate: 8.8% (June 2011); Total civilian labor
force: 17,374 (June 2011); Single-family building permits issued: 38 (2010);
Multi-family building permits issued: 111 (2010); Employment by
occupation: 9.1% management, 25.6% professional, 19.8% services,
25.2% sales, 0.1% farming, 8.1% construction, 12.2% production
(2005-2009 5-year est.).
Income: Per capita income: $21,187 (2010); Median household income:
$35,812 (2010); Average household income: $53,587 (2010); Percent of
households with income of $100,000 or more: 12.9% (2010); Poverty rate:
20.4% (2005-2009 5-year est.).
Taxes: Total city taxes per capita: $705 (2007); City property taxes per
capita: $274 (2007).
Education: Percent of population age 25 and over with: High school
diploma (including GED) or higher: 84.2% (2010); Bachelor's degree or
higher: 21.2% (2010); Master's degree or higher: 6.3% (2010).

School District(s)

Liberty-Eylau ISD (PK-12)
    2009-10 Enrollment: 2,893 . . . . (903) 832-1535
Pleasant Grove ISD (PK-12)
    2009-10 Enrollment: 1,971 . . . . (903) 831-4086
Red Lick ISD (PK-08)
    2009-10 Enrollment: 434 . . . . (903) 838-8230
Texarkana ISD (PK-12)
    2009-10 Enrollment: 6,849 . . . . (903) 794-3651

Four-year College(s)

Texas A & M University-Texarkana (Public)
    Fall 2009 Enrollment: 1,653. . . . . (903) 223-3000
    2010-11 Tuition: In-state $4,467; Out-of-state $11,907

Two-year College(s)

Texarkana College (Public)
    Fall 2009 Enrollment: 5,018. . . . . (903) 838-4541
    2010-11 Tuition: In-state $2,470; Out-of-state $2,970
Housing: Homeownership rate: 50.7% (2010); Median home value:
$90,662 (2010); Median contract rent: $463 per month (2005-2009 5-year
est.); Median year structure built: 1971 (2005-2009 5-year est.).
Hospitals: Christus St. Michael Health System (278 beds); HealthSouth
Rehabilitation Hospital of Texarkana (60 beds); Wadley Regional Medical
Center (407 beds)
Safety: Violent crime rate: 150.8 per 10,000 population; Property crime
rate: 691.1 per 10,000 population (2009).
Newspapers: Texarkana Gazette (Local news; Circulation 33,133)
Transportation: Commute to work: 90.2% car, 0.7% public transportation,
2.4% walk, 3.1% work from home (2005-2009 5-year est.); Travel time to
work: 57.1% less than 15 minutes, 30.8% 15 to 30 minutes, 8.2% 30 to 45
minutes, 1.6% 45 to 60 minutes, 2.3% 60 minutes or more (2005-2009
5-year est.)
Additional Information Contacts
City of Texarkana. . . . . (903) 798-3900
    http://www.ci.texarkana.tx.us

Texarkana Chamber of Commerce . . . . (903) 792-7191
    http://texarkana.wliinc2.com

WAKE VILLAGE (city). Covers a land area of 1.658 square miles
and a water area of 0 square miles. Located at 33.42° N. Lat; 94.11° W.
Long. Elevation is 341 feet.
History: Incorporated 1944. Also called Wake.
Population: 4,991 (1990); 5,129 (2000); 5,478 (2010); 5,607 (2015
projected); Race: 73.9% White, 21.4% Black, 0.8% Asian, 3.9% Other,
4.1% Hispanic of any race (2010); Density: 3,303.4 persons per square
mile (2010); Average household size: 2.50 (2010); Median age: 37.1
(2010); Males per 100 females: 91.7 (2010); Marriage status: 28.5% never
married, 52.1% now married, 6.3% widowed, 13.1% divorced (2005-2009
5-year est.); Foreign born: 3.3% (2005-2009 5-year est.); Ancestry
(includes multiple ancestries): 17.3% American, 10.9% Irish, 9.3% German,
7.3% English, 4.9% Italian (2005-2009 5-year est.).
Economy: Single-family building permits issued: 6 (2010); Multi-family
building permits issued: 0 (2010); Employment by occupation: 9.9%
management, 15.8% professional, 19.9% services, 32.7% sales, 0.0%
farming, 8.2% construction, 13.5% production (2005-2009 5-year est.).
Income: Per capita income: $22,799 (2010); Median household income:
$45,951 (2010); Average household income: $57,138 (2010); Percent of
households with income of $100,000 or more: 13.5% (2010); Poverty rate:
13.8% (2005-2009 5-year est.).
Taxes: Total city taxes per capita: $169 (2007); City property taxes per
capita: $121 (2007).
Education: Percent of population age 25 and over with: High school
diploma (including GED) or higher: 90.9% (2010); Bachelor's degree or
higher: 25.7% (2010); Master's degree or higher: 8.1% (2010).

School District(s)

Texarkana ISD (PK-12)
    2009-10 Enrollment: 6,849 . . . . (903) 794-3651
Housing: Homeownership rate: 62.4% (2010); Median home value:
$92,222 (2010); Median contract rent: $443 per month (2005-2009 5-year
est.); Median year structure built: 1977 (2005-2009 5-year est.).
Safety: Violent crime rate: 0.0 per 10,000 population; Property crime rate:
121.9 per 10,000 population (2009).
Transportation: Commute to work: 96.7% car, 0.0% public transportation,
1.7% walk, 1.3% work from home (2005-2009 5-year est.); Travel time to
work: 46.8% less than 15 minutes, 39.9% 15 to 30 minutes, 11.1% 30 to 45
minutes, 0.4% 45 to 60 minutes, 1.8% 60 minutes or more (2005-2009
5-year est.)

Brazoria County

Located in south Texas, on the Gulf of Mexico. Covers a land area of
1,386.40 square miles, a water area of 211.04 square miles, and is located
in the Central Time Zone at 29.20° N. Lat., 95.39° W. Long. The county
was founded in 1836. County seat is Angleton.

Brazoria County is part of the Houston-Sugar Land-Baytown, TX
Metropolitan Statistical Area. The entire metro area includes: Austin
County, TX; Brazoria County, TX; Chambers County, TX; Fort Bend
County, TX; Galveston County, TX; Harris County, TX; Liberty County, TX;
Montgomery County, TX; San Jacinto County, TX; Waller County, TX

Weather Station: Angleton 2 W   Elevation: 26 feet

	Jan	Feb	Mar	Apr	May	Jun	Jul	Aug	Sep	Oct	Nov	Dec
High	64	66	72	78	84	89	91	92	88	81	73	65
Low	44	48	53	59	67	72	74	73	70	61	53	46
Precip	4.7	3.3	3.8	3.5	4.6	6.1	4.4	5.2	6.9	5.4	4.7	4.4
Snow	0.0	tr	0.0	0.0	0.0	0.0	0.0	0.0	0.0	0.0	0.0	tr

High and Low temperatures in degrees Fahrenheit; Precipitation and Snow in inches

Weather Station: Freeport 2 NW   Elevation: 7 feet

	Jan	Feb	Mar	Apr	May	Jun	Jul	Aug	Sep	Oct	Nov	Dec
High	64	66	72	78	84	89	91	92	88	81	73	66
Low	46	49	55	62	70	76	78	77	73	64	55	48
Precip	4.2	2.7	3.1	2.8	3.5	4.9	4.5	3.9	6.8	5.0	4.4	3.5
Snow	0.0	tr	0.0	0.0	0.0	0.0	0.0	0.0	0.0	0.0	0.0	0.0

High and Low temperatures in degrees Fahrenheit; Precipitation and Snow in inches

Population: 191,707 (1990); 241,767 (2000); 311,758 (2010); 345,252
(2015 projected); Race: 69.2% White, 11.1% Black, 4.8% Asian, 14.9%
Other, 26.8% Hispanic of any race (2010); Density: 224.9 persons per

square mile (2010); Average household size: 2.82 (2010); Median age: 33.7 (2010); Males per 100 females: 103.7 (2010).

Religion: Five largest groups: 20.0% Catholic Church, 18.1% Southern Baptist Convention, 5.0% The United Methodist Church, 1.5% Assemblies of God, 1.5% Churches of Christ (2000).

Economy: Unemployment rate: 9.5% (June 2011); Total civilian labor force: 151,907 (June 2011); Leading industries: 18.3% retail trade; 16.9% manufacturing; 15.2% construction (2009); Farms: 2,580 totaling 528,957 acres (2007); Companies that employ 500 or more persons: 10 (2009); Companies that employ 100 to 499 persons: 83 (2009); Companies that employ less than 100 persons: 4,659 (2009); Black-owned businesses: 2,120 (2007); Hispanic-owned businesses: 3,322 (2007); Asian-owned businesses: 1,322 (2007); Women-owned businesses: 6,514 (2007); Retail sales per capita: $10,030 (2010). Single-family building permits issued: 1,647 (2010); Multi-family building permits issued: 332 (2010).

Income: Per capita income: $26,525 (2010); Median household income: $63,196 (2010); Average household income: $77,141 (2010); Percent of households with income of $100,000 or more: 25.6% (2010); Poverty rate: 10.0% (2009); Bankruptcy rate: 1.85% (2010).

Taxes: Total county taxes per capita: $293 (2007); County property taxes per capita: $221 (2007).

Education: Percent of population age 25 and over with: High school diploma (including GED) or higher: 84.9% (2010); Bachelor's degree or higher: 25.2% (2010); Master's degree or higher: 8.1% (2010).

Housing: Homeownership rate: 74.7% (2010); Median home value: $131,046 (2010); Median contract rent: $575 per month (2005-2009 5-year est.); Median year structure built: 1984 (2005-2009 5-year est.)

Health: Birth rate: 160.9 per 10,000 population (2009); Death rate: 64.7 per 10,000 population (2009); Age-adjusted cancer mortality rate: 196.6 deaths per 100,000 population (2007); Number of physicians: 25.0 per 10,000 population (2008); Hospital beds: 7.5 per 10,000 population (2007); Hospital admissions: 339.7 per 10,000 population (2007).

Environment: Air Quality Index: 87.4% good, 10.6% moderate, 2.0% unhealthy for sensitive individuals, 0.0% unhealthy (percent of days in 2008)

Elections: 2008 Presidential election results: 34.8% Obama, 64.3% McCain, 0.1% Nader

National and State Parks: Brazoria National Wildlife Refuge; San Bernard National Wildlife Refuge

Additional Information Contacts

Brazoria County Government . . . . (979) 849-5711
  http://www.brazoria-county.com
Alvin Manvel Area Chamber of Commerce . . . . (281) 331-3944
  http://www.alvinmanvelchamber.org
Brazoria Chamber of Commerce . . . . (979) 798-6100
  http://www.brazoriachamber.net
Brazosport Area Chamber of Commerce . . . . (979) 285-2501
  http://www.brazosport.org
City of Alvin . . . . (281) 388-4200
  http://www.alvin-tx.gov
City of Angleton . . . . (979) 849-4364
  http://www.angleton.tx.us
City of Clute . . . . (979) 265-2541
  http://www.ci.clute.tx.us
City of Freeport . . . . (979) 233-3526
  http://www.freeport.tx.us
City of Lake Jackson . . . . (979) 415-2400
  http://www.lakejackson-tx.gov
City of Manvel . . . . (281) 489-0630
  http://www.cityofmanvel.com
City of Pearland . . . . (281) 652-1600
  http://www.cityofpearland.com
City of Sweeny . . . . (979) 548-3321
  http://www.ci.sweeny.tx.us
City of West Columbia . . . . (979) 345-3123
  http://westcolumbiatx.org
Greater Angleton Chamber of Commerce . . . . (979) 849-6443
  http://www.angletonchamber.org
Pearland Chamber of Commerce . . . . (281) 485-3634
  http://www.pearlandchamber.com
Sweeny Chamber of Commerce . . . . (979) 548-3249
  http://www.mysweeny.com/chamber
Town of Quintana . . . . (979) 233-0848
  http://www.quintana-tx.org

Brazoria County Communities

ALVIN (city). Covers a land area of 16.435 square miles and a water area of 0.906 square miles. Located at 29.39° N. Lat; 95.27° W. Long. Elevation is 43 feet.

Population: 18,712 (1990); 21,413 (2000); 23,759 (2010); 25,908 (2015 projected); Race: 76.7% White, 2.4% Black, 1.5% Asian, 19.5% Other, 36.0% Hispanic of any race (2010); Density: 1,445.6 persons per square mile (2010); Average household size: 2.75 (2010); Median age: 31.7 (2010); Males per 100 females: 98.2 (2010); Marriage status: 24.0% never married, 56.0% now married, 8.8% widowed, 11.2% divorced (2005-2009 5-year est.); Foreign born: 10.7% (2005-2009 5-year est.); Ancestry (includes multiple ancestries): 13.1% German, 11.7% Irish, 10.1% American, 7.2% English, 4.7% French (2005-2009 5-year est.).

Economy: Single-family building permits issued: 53 (2010); Multi-family building permits issued: 110 (2010); Employment by occupation: 10.4% management, 17.2% professional, 18.0% services, 21.0% sales, 0.0% farming, 16.2% construction, 17.2% production (2005-2009 5-year est.).

Income: Per capita income: $20,697 (2010); Median household income: $47,174 (2010); Average household income: $57,200 (2010); Percent of households with income of $100,000 or more: 12.1% (2010); Poverty rate: 13.8% (2005-2009 5-year est.).

Taxes: Total city taxes per capita: $539 (2007); City property taxes per capita: $262 (2007).

Education: Percent of population age 25 and over with: High school diploma (including GED) or higher: 82.9% (2010); Bachelor's degree or higher: 18.3% (2010); Master's degree or higher: 5.7% (2010).

School District(s)
Alvin ISD (PK-12)
  2009-10 Enrollment: 16,788 . . . . (281) 388-1130
Two-year College(s)
Alvin Community College (Public)
  Fall 2009 Enrollment: 5,240 . . . . (281) 756-3500
  2010-11 Tuition: In-state $2,084; Out-of-state $3,476

Housing: Homeownership rate: 58.1% (2010); Median home value: $102,037 (2010); Median contract rent: $588 per month (2005-2009 5-year est.); Median year structure built: 1975 (2005-2009 5-year est.).

Safety: Violent crime rate: 23.0 per 10,000 population; Property crime rate: 300.7 per 10,000 population (2009).

Newspapers: Alvin Sun & Advertiser (Community news; Circulation 17,000)

Transportation: Commute to work: 92.2% car, 0.6% public transportation, 2.8% walk, 1.8% work from home (2005-2009 5-year est.); Travel time to work: 32.5% less than 15 minutes, 21.9% 15 to 30 minutes, 23.2% 30 to 45 minutes, 12.7% 45 to 60 minutes, 9.7% 60 minutes or more (2005-2009 5-year est.)

Additional Information Contacts
Alvin Manvel Area Chamber of Commerce . . . . (281) 331-3944
  http://www.alvinmanvelchamber.org
City of Alvin . . . . (281) 388-4200
  http://www.alvin-tx.gov

ANGLETON (city). County seat. Covers a land area of 10.564 square miles and a water area of 0.021 square miles. Located at 29.16° N. Lat; 95.42° W. Long. Elevation is 30 feet.

History: Named for the wife of George W. Angle, a member of the Boston Syndicate. Angleton was settled in the old plantation area of Texas. General Albert Sidney Johnston was one of the early planters here.

Population: 17,352 (1990); 18,130 (2000); 19,220 (2010); 20,331 (2015 projected); Race: 69.9% White, 14.5% Black, 1.6% Asian, 14.0% Other, 29.2% Hispanic of any race (2010); Density: 1,819.5 persons per square mile (2010); Average household size: 2.73 (2010); Median age: 32.6 (2010); Males per 100 females: 100.1 (2010); Marriage status: 28.9% never married, 53.8% now married, 6.9% widowed, 10.4% divorced (2005-2009 5-year est.); Foreign born: 7.3% (2005-2009 5-year est.); Ancestry (includes multiple ancestries): 16.3% German, 9.7% Irish, 7.9% English, 7.5% American, 4.9% French (2005-2009 5-year est.).

Economy: Single-family building permits issued: 22 (2010); Multi-family building permits issued: 0 (2010); Employment by occupation: 8.3% management, 14.8% professional, 22.1% services, 20.7% sales, 1.3% farming, 13.2% construction, 19.7% production (2005-2009 5-year est.).

Income: Per capita income: $21,957 (2010); Median household income: $51,208 (2010); Average household income: $61,044 (2010); Percent of households with income of $100,000 or more: 15.6% (2010); Poverty rate: 14.7% (2005-2009 5-year est.).

Taxes: Total city taxes per capita: $386 (2007); City property taxes per capita: $232 (2007).
Education: Percent of population age 25 and over with: High school diploma (including GED) or higher: 84.4% (2010); Bachelor's degree or higher: 21.6% (2010); Master's degree or higher: 6.0% (2010).

School District(s)

Angleton ISD (PK-12)
   2009-10 Enrollment: 6,338 . . . . (979) 864-8000
Pearland ISD (PK-12)
   2009-10 Enrollment: 18,308 . . . . (281) 485-3203
Housing: Homeownership rate: 68.6% (2010); Median home value: $95,955 (2010); Median contract rent: $527 per month (2005-2009 5-year est.); Median year structure built: 1976 (2005-2009 5-year est.).
Hospitals: Angleton-Danbury Medical Center (48 beds)
Safety: Violent crime rate: 55.7 per 10,000 population; Property crime rate: 309.1 per 10,000 population (2009).
Newspapers: The Bulletin (Local news; Circulation 8,000)
Transportation: Commute to work: 94.7% car, 0.0% public transportation, 2.4% walk, 1.5% work from home (2005-2009 5-year est.); Travel time to work: 31.9% less than 15 minutes, 34.3% 15 to 30 minutes, 18.5% 30 to 45 minutes, 6.0% 45 to 60 minutes, 9.3% 60 minutes or more (2005-2009 5-year est.)
Airports: Brazoria County (general aviation)
Additional Information Contacts
City of Angleton . . . . (979) 849-4364
   http://www.angleton.tx.us
Greater Angleton Chamber of Commerce . . . . (979) 849-6443
   http://www.angletonchamber.org

BAILEY'S PRAIRIE (village). Covers a land area of 7.507 square miles and a water area of 0.185 square miles. Located at 29.15° N. Lat; 95.49° W. Long.

Population: 634 (1990); 694 (2000); 681 (2010); 793 (2015 projected); Race: 83.6% White, 9.5% Black, 0.1% Asian, 6.8% Other, 20.6% Hispanic of any race (2010); Density: 90.7 persons per square mile (2010); Average household size: 2.95 (2010); Median age: 39.3 (2010); Males per 100 females: 99.1 (2010); Marriage status: 16.6% never married, 77.6% now married, 1.1% widowed, 4.6% divorced (2005-2009 5-year est.); Foreign born: 0.6% (2005-2009 5-year est.); Ancestry (includes multiple ancestries): 18.4% German, 12.8% English, 11.9% Irish, 8.7% French, 8.1% Czech (2005-2009 5-year est.).
Economy: Employment by occupation: 11.5% management, 40.3% professional, 8.6% services, 22.7% sales, 0.0% farming, 5.1% construction, 11.8% production (2005-2009 5-year est.).
Income: Per capita income: $29,204 (2010); Median household income: $75,298 (2010); Average household income: $88,824 (2010); Percent of households with income of $100,000 or more: 31.1% (2010); Poverty rate: 3.8% (2005-2009 5-year est.).
Taxes: Total city taxes per capita: $62 (2007); City property taxes per capita: $62 (2007).
Education: Percent of population age 25 and over with: High school diploma (including GED) or higher: 89.4% (2010); Bachelor's degree or higher: 26.6% (2010); Master's degree or higher: 8.8% (2010).
Housing: Homeownership rate: 91.8% (2010); Median home value: $149,490 (2010); Median contract rent: n/a per month (2005-2009 5-year est.); Median year structure built: 1981 (2005-2009 5-year est.).
Transportation: Commute to work: 88.6% car, 4.9% public transportation, 0.0% walk, 5.6% work from home (2005-2009 5-year est.); Travel time to work: 20.8% less than 15 minutes, 43.6% 15 to 30 minutes, 14.5% 30 to 45 minutes, 12.1% 45 to 60 minutes, 9.0% 60 minutes or more (2005-2009 5-year est.)

BONNEY (village). Covers a land area of 1.657 square miles and a water area of 0 square miles. Located at 29.31° N. Lat; 95.45° W. Long. Elevation is 46 feet.

Population: 326 (1990); 384 (2000); 439 (2010); 460 (2015 projected); Race: 45.8% White, 35.8% Black, 0.2% Asian, 18.2% Other, 25.7% Hispanic of any race (2010); Density: 265.0 persons per square mile (2010); Average household size: 2.92 (2010); Median age: 42.0 (2010); Males per 100 females: 372.0 (2010); Marriage status: 29.5% never married, 52.5% now married, 1.6% widowed, 16.4% divorced (2005-2009 5-year est.); Foreign born: 7.8% (2005-2009 5-year est.); Ancestry (includes multiple ancestries): 21.6% Irish, 16.0% German, 10.0% French, 3.9% Scottish, 2.2% Scotch-Irish (2005-2009 5-year est.).

Economy: Employment by occupation: 2.3% management, 19.8% professional, 51.9% services, 11.5% sales, 0.0% farming, 14.5% construction, 0.0% production (2005-2009 5-year est.).
Income: Per capita income: $9,891 (2010); Median household income: $54,167 (2010); Average household income: $66,048 (2010); Percent of households with income of $100,000 or more: 17.7% (2010); Poverty rate: 6.1% (2005-2009 5-year est.).
Education: Percent of population age 25 and over with: High school diploma (including GED) or higher: 77.2% (2010); Bachelor's degree or higher: 11.8% (2010); Master's degree or higher: 3.8% (2010).
Housing: Homeownership rate: 77.4% (2010); Median home value: $70,000 (2010); Median contract rent: n/a per month (2005-2009 5-year est.); Median year structure built: 1975 (2005-2009 5-year est.).
Transportation: Commute to work: 91.6% car, 0.0% public transportation, 0.0% walk, 2.3% work from home (2005-2009 5-year est.); Travel time to work: 58.6% less than 15 minutes, 14.1% 15 to 30 minutes, 7.0% 30 to 45 minutes, 11.7% 45 to 60 minutes, 8.6% 60 minutes or more (2005-2009 5-year est.)

BRAZORIA (city). Covers a land area of 1.871 square miles and a water area of 0 square miles. Located at 29.04° N. Lat; 95.56° W. Long. Elevation is 30 feet.

History: Brazoria was established along the railroad. Old Brazoria, founded in 1826, was located a half mile away, and had been an important port for the Austin colony.
Population: 2,805 (1990); 2,787 (2000); 2,890 (2010); 3,064 (2015 projected); Race: 79.4% White, 9.2% Black, 0.7% Asian, 10.7% Other, 16.2% Hispanic of any race (2010); Density: 1,544.4 persons per square mile (2010); Average household size: 2.65 (2010); Median age: 32.8 (2010); Males per 100 females: 93.7 (2010); Marriage status: 20.9% never married, 49.3% now married, 8.7% widowed, 21.1% divorced (2005-2009 5-year est.); Foreign born: 2.1% (2005-2009 5-year est.); Ancestry (includes multiple ancestries): 19.6% German, 13.6% Irish, 12.1% English, 6.3% American, 4.8% Scottish (2005-2009 5-year est.).
Economy: Single-family building permits issued: 9 (2010); Multi-family building permits issued: 0 (2010); Employment by occupation: 8.8% management, 14.7% professional, 14.4% services, 24.5% sales, 0.0% farming, 24.9% construction, 12.6% production (2005-2009 5-year est.).
Income: Per capita income: $21,149 (2010); Median household income: $47,534 (2010); Average household income: $55,718 (2010); Percent of households with income of $100,000 or more: 13.2% (2010); Poverty rate: 16.0% (2005-2009 5-year est.).
Taxes: Total city taxes per capita: $450 (2007); City property taxes per capita: $194 (2007).
Education: Percent of population age 25 and over with: High school diploma (including GED) or higher: 83.7% (2010); Bachelor's degree or higher: 10.6% (2010); Master's degree or higher: 4.7% (2010).

School District(s)

Columbia-Brazoria ISD (PK-12)
   2009-10 Enrollment: 3,081 . . . . (979) 345-5147
Housing: Homeownership rate: 71.4% (2010); Median home value: $79,645 (2010); Median contract rent: $390 per month (2005-2009 5-year est.); Median year structure built: 1972 (2005-2009 5-year est.).
Safety: Violent crime rate: 80.8 per 10,000 population; Property crime rate: 343.4 per 10,000 population (2009).
Transportation: Commute to work: 93.3% car, 0.6% public transportation, 3.6% walk, 1.2% work from home (2005-2009 5-year est.); Travel time to work: 19.3% less than 15 minutes, 46.5% 15 to 30 minutes, 22.3% 30 to 45 minutes, 3.2% 45 to 60 minutes, 8.7% 60 minutes or more (2005-2009 5-year est.)
Additional Information Contacts
Brazoria Chamber of Commerce . . . . (979) 798-6100
   http://www.brazoriachamber.net

BROOKSIDE VILLAGE (city). Covers a land area of 2.106 square miles and a water area of 0 square miles. Located at 29.58° N. Lat; 95.31° W. Long. Elevation is 52 feet.

Population: 1,462 (1990); 1,960 (2000); 1,880 (2010); 2,109 (2015 projected); Race: 67.9% White, 7.0% Black, 1.3% Asian, 23.8% Other, 36.0% Hispanic of any race (2010); Density: 892.8 persons per square mile (2010); Average household size: 2.89 (2010); Median age: 38.9 (2010); Males per 100 females: 103.5 (2010); Marriage status: 25.8% never married, 61.5% now married, 4.4% widowed, 8.3% divorced (2005-2009 5-year est.); Foreign born: 10.5% (2005-2009 5-year est.); Ancestry

(includes multiple ancestries): 16.1% German, 10.2% American, 9.3% English, 9.0% Irish, 6.1% Czech (2005-2009 5-year est.).
Economy: Single-family building permits issued: 2 (2010); Multi-family building permits issued: 0 (2010); Employment by occupation: 11.1% management, 18.2% professional, 18.4% services, 26.6% sales, 0.0% farming, 8.4% construction, 17.3% production (2005-2009 5-year est.).
Income: Per capita income: $26,386 (2010); Median household income: $65,140 (2010); Average household income: $76,225 (2010); Percent of households with income of $100,000 or more: 23.0% (2010); Poverty rate: 6.3% (2005-2009 5-year est.).
Taxes: Total city taxes per capita: $225 (2007); City property taxes per capita: $179 (2007).
Education: Percent of population age 25 and over with: High school diploma (including GED) or higher: 83.8% (2010); Bachelor's degree or higher: 21.2% (2010); Master's degree or higher: 7.3% (2010).
Housing: Homeownership rate: 85.9% (2010); Median home value: $142,914 (2010); Median contract rent: $514 per month (2005-2009 5-year est.); Median year structure built: 1971 (2005-2009 5-year est.).
Safety: Violent crime rate: 15.1 per 10,000 population; Property crime rate: 115.8 per 10,000 population (2009).
Transportation: Commute to work: 96.3% car, 0.5% public transportation, 2.5% walk, 0.7% work from home (2005-2009 5-year est.); Travel time to work: 21.7% less than 15 minutes, 30.3% 15 to 30 minutes, 29.8% 30 to 45 minutes, 11.5% 45 to 60 minutes, 6.7% 60 minutes or more (2005-2009 5-year est.).

CLUTE (city). Aka Clute City. Covers a land area of 5.348 square miles and a water area of 0.288 square miles. Located at 29.02° N. Lat; 95.39° W. Long. Elevation is 13 feet.
Population: 9,576 (1990); 10,424 (2000); 11,211 (2010); 12,037 (2015 projected); Race: 59.0% White, 8.6% Black, 1.7% Asian, 30.8% Other, 57.3% Hispanic of any race (2010); Density: 2,096.2 persons per square mile (2010); Average household size: 2.82 (2010); Median age: 29.7 (2010); Males per 100 females: 100.7 (2010); Marriage status: 30.5% never married, 54.8% now married, 5.1% widowed, 9.6% divorced (2005-2009 5-year est.); Foreign born: 14.5% (2005-2009 5-year est.); Ancestry (includes multiple ancestries): 8.2% German, 7.8% Irish, 4.1% American, 3.7% English, 2.0% French (2005-2009 5-year est.).
Economy: Single-family building permits issued: 14 (2010); Multi-family building permits issued: 0 (2010); Employment by occupation: 6.5% management, 11.1% professional, 22.9% services, 22.6% sales, 0.0% farming, 19.3% construction, 17.6% production (2005-2009 5-year est.).
Income: Per capita income: $16,799 (2010); Median household income: $38,826 (2010); Average household income: $47,594 (2010); Percent of households with income of $100,000 or more: 8.1% (2010); Poverty rate: 17.1% (2005-2009 5-year est.).
Taxes: Total city taxes per capita: $406 (2007); City property taxes per capita: $163 (2007).
Education: Percent of population age 25 and over with: High school diploma (including GED) or higher: 72.9% (2010); Bachelor's degree or higher: 12.4% (2010); Master's degree or higher: 3.0% (2010).
School District(s)
Brazosport ISD (PK-12)
    2009-10 Enrollment: 12,861 . . . . (979) 730-7000
Housing: Homeownership rate: 43.7% (2010); Median home value: $69,418 (2010); Median contract rent: $455 per month (2005-2009 5-year est.); Median year structure built: 1977 (2005-2009 5-year est.).
Safety: Violent crime rate: 42.6 per 10,000 population; Property crime rate: 349.9 per 10,000 population (2009).
Newspapers: The Facts (Community news; Circulation 16,821)
Transportation: Commute to work: 93.7% car, 0.0% public transportation, 0.8% walk, 2.9% work from home (2005-2009 5-year est.); Travel time to work: 43.6% less than 15 minutes, 39.9% 15 to 30 minutes, 7.1% 30 to 45 minutes, 3.1% 45 to 60 minutes, 6.3% 60 minutes or more (2005-2009 5-year est.)
Additional Information Contacts
Brazosport Area Chamber of Commerce. . . . . (979) 285-2501
    http://www.brazosport.org
City of Clute . . . . (979) 265-2541
    http://www.ci.clute.tx.us

DAMON (CDP). Covers a land area of 1.387 square miles and a water area of 0 square miles. Located at 29.29° N. Lat; 95.73° W. Long. Elevation is 79 feet.

Population: 468 (1990); 535 (2000); 515 (2010); 523 (2015 projected); Race: 77.9% White, 0.2% Black, 0.4% Asian, 21.6% Other, 28.0% Hispanic of any race (2010); Density: 371.3 persons per square mile (2010); Average household size: 2.54 (2010); Median age: 35.4 (2010); Males per 100 females: 101.2 (2010); Marriage status: 32.6% never married, 39.7% now married, 9.6% widowed, 18.0% divorced (2005-2009 5-year est.); Foreign born: 3.7% (2005-2009 5-year est.); Ancestry (includes multiple ancestries): 47.4% German, 9.6% English, 8.7% Irish, 6.2% French, 5.9% Czech (2005-2009 5-year est.).
Economy: Employment by occupation: 15.0% management, 7.8% professional, 11.1% services, 26.8% sales, 0.0% farming, 23.5% construction, 15.7% production (2005-2009 5-year est.).
Income: Per capita income: $19,259 (2010); Median household income: $41,689 (2010); Average household income: $48,879 (2010); Percent of households with income of $100,000 or more: 8.9% (2010); Poverty rate: 29.4% (2005-2009 5-year est.).
Education: Percent of population age 25 and over with: High school diploma (including GED) or higher: 74.0% (2010); Bachelor's degree or higher: 10.1% (2010); Master's degree or higher: 3.3% (2010).
School District(s)
Damon ISD (PK-08)
    2009-10 Enrollment: 168 . . . . (979) 742-3457
Housing: Homeownership rate: 76.8% (2010); Median home value: $56,429 (2010); Median contract rent: n/a per month (2005-2009 5-year est.); Median year structure built: 1975 (2005-2009 5-year est.).
Transportation: Commute to work: 90.2% car, 0.0% public transportation, 0.0% walk, 2.0% work from home (2005-2009 5-year est.); Travel time to work: 22.0% less than 15 minutes, 10.0% 15 to 30 minutes, 34.7% 30 to 45 minutes, 12.7% 45 to 60 minutes, 20.7% 60 minutes or more (2005-2009 5-year est.)

DANBURY (city). Covers a land area of 0.960 square miles and a water area of 0 square miles. Located at 29.22° N. Lat; 95.34° W. Long. Elevation is 23 feet.
Population: 1,514 (1990); 1,611 (2000); 1,771 (2010); 1,927 (2015 projected); Race: 87.1% White, 1.2% Black, 0.3% Asian, 11.4% Other, 19.3% Hispanic of any race (2010); Density: 1,844.7 persons per square mile (2010); Average household size: 2.93 (2010); Median age: 32.2 (2010); Males per 100 females: 98.5 (2010); Marriage status: 23.7% never married, 59.7% now married, 4.5% widowed, 12.2% divorced (2005-2009 5-year est.); Foreign born: 5.1% (2005-2009 5-year est.); Ancestry (includes multiple ancestries): 20.8% German, 14.0% Irish, 11.8% Czech, 8.2% English, 6.9% American (2005-2009 5-year est.).
Economy: Single-family building permits issued: 2 (2010); Multi-family building permits issued: 0 (2010); Employment by occupation: 14.2% management, 15.4% professional, 9.4% services, 25.3% sales, 0.5% farming, 16.8% construction, 18.3% production (2005-2009 5-year est.).
Income: Per capita income: $22,529 (2010); Median household income: $57,906 (2010); Average household income: $66,635 (2010); Percent of households with income of $100,000 or more: 21.1% (2010); Poverty rate: 17.4% (2005-2009 5-year est.).
Taxes: Total city taxes per capita: $280 (2007); City property taxes per capita: $214 (2007).
Education: Percent of population age 25 and over with: High school diploma (including GED) or higher: 87.4% (2010); Bachelor's degree or higher: 18.9% (2010); Master's degree or higher: 5.1% (2010).
School District(s)
Danbury ISD (PK-12)
    2009-10 Enrollment: 773 . . . . (979) 922-1218
Housing: Homeownership rate: 79.9% (2010); Median home value: $100,654 (2010); Median contract rent: $534 per month (2005-2009 5-year est.); Median year structure built: 1973 (2005-2009 5-year est.).
Safety: Violent crime rate: 0.0 per 10,000 population; Property crime rate: 29.6 per 10,000 population (2009).
Transportation: Commute to work: 98.1% car, 0.0% public transportation, 0.8% walk, 0.0% work from home (2005-2009 5-year est.); Travel time to work: 22.8% less than 15 minutes, 30.5% 15 to 30 minutes, 20.6% 30 to 45 minutes, 8.1% 45 to 60 minutes, 17.9% 60 minutes or more (2005-2009 5-year est.)
Airports: Salaika Aviation (general aviation)

FREEPORT (city). Aka Brazosport. Covers a land area of 11.881 square miles and a water area of 1.395 square miles. Located at 28.96° N. Lat; 95.35° W. Long. Elevation is 3 feet.

History: Named for its location at the mouth of the Brazos River. Freeport developed as a major Texas port, shipping chiefly sulphur and petrochemicals. It was also home to a shrimp fleet numbering 300 vessels. Sulphur production started near here in 1913.

Population: 11,393 (1990); 12,708 (2000); 12,829 (2010); 13,569 (2015 projected); Race: 59.0% White, 13.4% Black, 0.5% Asian, 27.1% Other, 62.4% Hispanic of any race (2010); Density: 1,079.8 persons per square mile (2010); Average household size: 3.09 (2010); Median age: 28.3 (2010); Males per 100 females: 99.3 (2010); Marriage status: 31.4% never married, 52.0% now married, 3.9% widowed, 12.8% divorced (2005-2009 5-year est.); Foreign born: 24.5% (2005-2009 5-year est.); Ancestry (includes multiple ancestries): 8.4% German, 5.4% English, 4.1% Irish, 3.2% American, 3.1% French (2005-2009 5-year est.).

Economy: Single-family building permits issued: 9 (2010); Multi-family building permits issued: 0 (2010); Employment by occupation: 8.0% management, 8.9% professional, 23.0% services, 17.7% sales, 1.9% farming, 21.9% construction, 18.6% production (2005-2009 5-year est.).

Income: Per capita income: $14,360 (2010); Median household income: $35,429 (2010); Average household income: $44,383 (2010); Percent of households with income of $100,000 or more: 6.9% (2010); Poverty rate: 19.6% (2005-2009 5-year est.).

Taxes: Total city taxes per capita: $373 (2007); City property taxes per capita: $172 (2007).

Education: Percent of population age 25 and over with: High school diploma (including GED) or higher: 62.7% (2010); Bachelor's degree or higher: 7.3% (2010); Master's degree or higher: 2.8% (2010).

School District(s)

Brazosport ISD (PK-12)
    2009-10 Enrollment: 12,861 . . . . (979) 730-7000

Housing: Homeownership rate: 55.1% (2010); Median home value: $55,348 (2010); Median contract rent: $436 per month (2005-2009 5-year est.); Median year structure built: 1960 (2005-2009 5-year est.).

Safety: Violent crime rate: 22.5 per 10,000 population; Property crime rate: 387.3 per 10,000 population (2009).

Transportation: Commute to work: 95.5% car, 0.0% public transportation, 1.4% walk, 2.7% work from home (2005-2009 5-year est.); Travel time to work: 45.2% less than 15 minutes, 32.6% 15 to 30 minutes, 10.4% 30 to 45 minutes, 6.6% 45 to 60 minutes, 5.2% 60 minutes or more (2005-2009 5-year est.)

Additional Information Contacts

Brazosport Area Chamber of Commerce. . . . . (979) 285-2501
    http://www.brazosport.org
City of Freeport . . . . (979) 233-3526
    http://www.freeport.tx.us

HILLCREST (village). Covers a land area of 0.436 square miles and a water area of 0 square miles. Located at 29.39° N. Lat; 95.22° W. Long. Elevation is 33 feet.

Population: 695 (1990); 722 (2000); 761 (2010); 824 (2015 projected); Race: 84.2% White, 1.3% Black, 0.8% Asian, 13.7% Other, 24.7% Hispanic of any race (2010); Density: 1,745.1 persons per square mile (2010); Average household size: 2.48 (2010); Median age: 35.2 (2010); Males per 100 females: 94.6 (2010); Marriage status: 18.8% never married, 71.1% now married, 4.3% widowed, 5.8% divorced (2005-2009 5-year est.); Foreign born: 1.3% (2005-2009 5-year est.); Ancestry (includes multiple ancestries): 28.3% German, 17.1% Irish, 11.1% American, 10.0% English, 5.6% French (2005-2009 5-year est.).

Economy: Single-family building permits issued: 0 (2010); Multi-family building permits issued: 0 (2010); Employment by occupation: 13.0% management, 26.7% professional, 10.4% services, 23.9% sales, 0.0% farming, 9.0% construction, 17.1% production (2005-2009 5-year est.).

Income: Per capita income: $29,189 (2010); Median household income: $60,142 (2010); Average household income: $71,327 (2010); Percent of households with income of $100,000 or more: 20.8% (2010); Poverty rate: 1.9% (2005-2009 5-year est.).

Taxes: Total city taxes per capita: $164 (2007); City property taxes per capita: $99 (2007).

Education: Percent of population age 25 and over with: High school diploma (including GED) or higher: 95.3% (2010); Bachelor's degree or higher: 36.6% (2010); Master's degree or higher: 13.6% (2010).

Housing: Homeownership rate: 57.7% (2010); Median home value: $174,457 (2010); Median contract rent: n/a per month (2005-2009 5-year est.); Median year structure built: 1973 (2005-2009 5-year est.).

Transportation: Commute to work: 91.4% car, 0.0% public transportation, 0.0% walk, 3.7% work from home (2005-2009 5-year est.); Travel time to work: 22.2% less than 15 minutes, 23.8% 15 to 30 minutes, 24.4% 30 to 45 minutes, 16.4% 45 to 60 minutes, 13.2% 60 minutes or more (2005-2009 5-year est.)

HOLIDAY LAKES (town). Covers a land area of 0.974 square miles and a water area of 0.139 square miles. Located at 29.20° N. Lat; 95.51° W. Long. Elevation is 36 feet.

Population: 1,039 (1990); 1,095 (2000); 1,151 (2010); 1,234 (2015 projected); Race: 67.8% White, 12.9% Black, 0.0% Asian, 19.3% Other, 39.7% Hispanic of any race (2010); Density: 1,182.2 persons per square mile (2010); Average household size: 2.92 (2010); Median age: 31.4 (2010); Males per 100 females: 104.4 (2010); Marriage status: 25.6% never married, 53.2% now married, 3.7% widowed, 17.5% divorced (2005-2009 5-year est.); Foreign born: 25.2% (2005-2009 5-year est.); Ancestry (includes multiple ancestries): 17.5% Irish, 15.6% German, 7.9% French, 3.9% American, 3.0% Scotch-Irish (2005-2009 5-year est.).

Economy: Single-family building permits issued: 4 (2010); Multi-family building permits issued: 0 (2010); Employment by occupation: 2.8% management, 7.2% professional, 23.7% services, 5.2% sales, 0.0% farming, 39.2% construction, 21.9% production (2005-2009 5-year est.).

Income: Per capita income: $20,983 (2010); Median household income: $51,333 (2010); Average household income: $61,783 (2010); Percent of households with income of $100,000 or more: 14.2% (2010); Poverty rate: 39.6% (2005-2009 5-year est.).

Taxes: Total city taxes per capita: $51 (2007); City property taxes per capita: $48 (2007).

Education: Percent of population age 25 and over with: High school diploma (including GED) or higher: 73.2% (2010); Bachelor's degree or higher: 7.1% (2010); Master's degree or higher: 3.1% (2010).

Housing: Homeownership rate: 86.0% (2010); Median home value: $50,241 (2010); Median contract rent: $393 per month (2005-2009 5-year est.); Median year structure built: 1984 (2005-2009 5-year est.).

Transportation: Commute to work: 100.0% car, 0.0% public transportation, 0.0% walk, 0.0% work from home (2005-2009 5-year est.); Travel time to work: 5.3% less than 15 minutes, 51.6% 15 to 30 minutes, 29.8% 30 to 45 minutes, 6.4% 45 to 60 minutes, 6.9% 60 minutes or more (2005-2009 5-year est.)

IOWA COLONY (village). Covers a land area of 5.755 square miles and a water area of 0.014 square miles. Located at 29.44° N. Lat; 95.41° W. Long. Elevation is 59 feet.

Population: 675 (1990); 804 (2000); 1,109 (2010); 1,278 (2015 projected); Race: 69.9% White, 11.4% Black, 4.9% Asian, 13.9% Other, 26.1% Hispanic of any race (2010); Density: 192.7 persons per square mile (2010); Average household size: 2.93 (2010); Median age: 35.7 (2010); Males per 100 females: 98.7 (2010); Marriage status: 25.5% never married, 59.7% now married, 5.9% widowed, 8.9% divorced (2005-2009 5-year est.); Foreign born: 19.2% (2005-2009 5-year est.); Ancestry (includes multiple ancestries): 11.8% Irish, 6.2% German, 4.6% English, 4.4% American, 2.8% Czech (2005-2009 5-year est.).

Economy: Employment by occupation: 13.4% management, 8.8% professional, 20.6% services, 20.6% sales, 0.8% farming, 15.3% construction, 20.6% production (2005-2009 5-year est.).

Income: Per capita income: $27,552 (2010); Median household income: $68,344 (2010); Average household income: $80,191 (2010); Percent of households with income of $100,000 or more: 25.3% (2010); Poverty rate: 14.9% (2005-2009 5-year est.).

Taxes: Total city taxes per capita: $51 (2007); City property taxes per capita: $36 (2007).

Education: Percent of population age 25 and over with: High school diploma (including GED) or higher: 82.9% (2010); Bachelor's degree or higher: 17.4% (2010); Master's degree or higher: 5.1% (2010).

Housing: Homeownership rate: 87.3% (2010); Median home value: $136,856 (2010); Median contract rent: $558 per month (2005-2009 5-year est.); Median year structure built: 1988 (2005-2009 5-year est.).

Transportation: Commute to work: 98.6% car, 0.0% public transportation, 0.0% walk, 0.6% work from home (2005-2009 5-year est.); Travel time to work: 3.3% less than 15 minutes, 28.3% 15 to 30 minutes, 34.3% 30 to 45 minutes, 18.6% 45 to 60 minutes, 15.5% 60 minutes or more (2005-2009 5-year est.)

JONES CREEK (village). Covers a land area of 2.623 square miles and a water area of 0 square miles. Located at 28.97° N. Lat; 95.47° W. Long. Elevation is 13 feet.

Population: 2,160 (1990); 2,130 (2000); 2,128 (2010); 2,211 (2015 projected); Race: 81.4% White, 2.3% Black, 1.4% Asian, 14.9% Other, 24.5% Hispanic of any race (2010); Density: 811.2 persons per square mile (2010); Average household size: 2.70 (2010); Median age: 34.7 (2010); Males per 100 females: 106.2 (2010); Marriage status: 21.4% never married, 64.3% now married, 6.2% widowed, 8.1% divorced (2005-2009 5-year est.); Foreign born: 8.4% (2005-2009 5-year est.); Ancestry (includes multiple ancestries): 20.8% German, 14.2% Irish, 11.1% American, 7.7% English, 3.1% Czech (2005-2009 5-year est.).
Economy: Single-family building permits issued: 2 (2010); Multi-family building permits issued: 0 (2010); Employment by occupation: 9.3% management, 13.8% professional, 8.7% services, 28.2% sales, 0.4% farming, 26.5% construction, 13.2% production (2005-2009 5-year est.).
Income: Per capita income: $22,554 (2010); Median household income: $50,929 (2010); Average household income: $61,033 (2010); Percent of households with income of $100,000 or more: 15.6% (2010); Poverty rate: 8.9% (2005-2009 5-year est.).
Taxes: Total city taxes per capita: $119 (2007); City property taxes per capita: $66 (2007).
Education: Percent of population age 25 and over with: High school diploma (including GED) or higher: 85.3% (2010); Bachelor's degree or higher: 13.3% (2010); Master's degree or higher: 2.3% (2010).
Housing: Homeownership rate: 78.3% (2010); Median home value: $91,304 (2010); Median contract rent: $404 per month (2005-2009 5-year est.); Median year structure built: 1969 (2005-2009 5-year est.).
Safety: Violent crime rate: 9.5 per 10,000 population; Property crime rate: 61.9 per 10,000 population (2009).
Transportation: Commute to work: 97.8% car, 0.0% public transportation, 0.5% walk, 0.7% work from home (2005-2009 5-year est.); Travel time to work: 20.4% less than 15 minutes, 62.1% 15 to 30 minutes, 7.1% 30 to 45 minutes, 0.4% 45 to 60 minutes, 9.9% 60 minutes or more (2005-2009 5-year est.)
Additional Information Contacts
Brazosport Area Chamber of Commerce. . . . . (979) 285-2501
   http://www.brazosport.org

LAKE JACKSON (city). Covers a land area of 19.038 square miles and a water area of 0.760 square miles. Located at 29.03° N. Lat; 95.43° W. Long. Elevation is 13 feet.
History: Named for the Jackson brothers, who owned a plantation here. Founded 1941.
Population: 22,942 (1990); 26,386 (2000); 27,823 (2010); 29,607 (2015 projected); Race: 81.0% White, 5.5% Black, 3.5% Asian, 10.0% Other, 19.3% Hispanic of any race (2010); Density: 1,461.4 persons per square mile (2010); Average household size: 2.73 (2010); Median age: 33.5 (2010); Males per 100 females: 94.9 (2010); Marriage status: 21.7% never married, 64.9% now married, 5.3% widowed, 8.2% divorced (2005-2009 5-year est.); Foreign born: 6.6% (2005-2009 5-year est.); Ancestry (includes multiple ancestries): 17.1% German, 13.0% Irish, 12.7% English, 7.0% American, 5.4% French (2005-2009 5-year est.).
Economy: Unemployment rate: 8.7% (June 2011); Total civilian labor force: 14,502 (June 2011); Single-family building permits issued: 19 (2010); Multi-family building permits issued: 96 (2010); Employment by occupation: 13.0% management, 28.0% professional, 11.8% services, 24.7% sales, 0.0% farming, 11.4% construction, 11.0% production (2005-2009 5-year est.).
Income: Per capita income: $31,414 (2010); Median household income: $70,757 (2010); Average household income: $85,817 (2010); Percent of households with income of $100,000 or more: 31.1% (2010); Poverty rate: 8.2% (2005-2009 5-year est.).
Taxes: Total city taxes per capita: $407 (2007); City property taxes per capita: $176 (2007).
Education: Percent of population age 25 and over with: High school diploma (including GED) or higher: 94.5% (2010); Bachelor's degree or higher: 40.7% (2010); Master's degree or higher: 12.5% (2010).

School District(s)
Brazosport ISD (PK-12)
   2009-10 Enrollment: 12,861 . . . . (979) 730-7000

Four-year College(s)
Brazosport College (Public)
   Fall 2009 Enrollment: 3,908. (979) 230-3000
   2010-11 Tuition: In-state $2,412; Out-of-state $3,822
Housing: Homeownership rate: 69.5% (2010); Median home value: $134,235 (2010); Median contract rent: $647 per month (2005-2009 5-year est.); Median year structure built: 1978 (2005-2009 5-year est.).

Hospitals: Brazosport Memorial Hospital (165 beds)
Safety: Violent crime rate: 14.5 per 10,000 population; Property crime rate: 270.6 per 10,000 population (2009).
Transportation: Commute to work: 97.4% car, 0.0% public transportation, 0.6% walk, 1.7% work from home (2005-2009 5-year est.); Travel time to work: 41.0% less than 15 minutes, 40.2% 15 to 30 minutes, 6.9% 30 to 45 minutes, 3.5% 45 to 60 minutes, 8.4% 60 minutes or more (2005-2009 5-year est.)
Additional Information Contacts
Brazosport Area Chamber of Commerce. . . . . (979) 285-2501
   http://www.brazosport.org
City of Lake Jackson . . . . (979) 415-2400
   http://www.lakejackson-tx.gov

LIVERPOOL (city). Covers a land area of 0.950 square miles and a water area of 0 square miles. Located at 29.29° N. Lat; 95.27° W. Long. Elevation is 20 feet.
Population: 396 (1990); 404 (2000); 464 (2010); 520 (2015 projected); Race: 79.3% White, 0.4% Black, 0.2% Asian, 20.0% Other, 16.2% Hispanic of any race (2010); Density: 488.6 persons per square mile (2010); Average household size: 2.56 (2010); Median age: 35.9 (2010); Males per 100 females: 107.1 (2010); Marriage status: 17.8% never married, 55.0% now married, 12.4% widowed, 14.8% divorced (2005-2009 5-year est.); Foreign born: 0.6% (2005-2009 5-year est.); Ancestry (includes multiple ancestries): 39.5% German, 10.6% English, 8.1% Irish, 7.0% Czech, 5.9% French (2005-2009 5-year est.).
Economy: Single-family building permits issued: 1 (2010); Multi-family building permits issued: 0 (2010); Employment by occupation: 2.0% management, 19.7% professional, 23.8% services, 21.8% sales, 0.0% farming, 14.3% construction, 18.4% production (2005-2009 5-year est.).
Income: Per capita income: $28,269 (2010); Median household income: $64,423 (2010); Average household income: $71,865 (2010); Percent of households with income of $100,000 or more: 14.4% (2010); Poverty rate: 17.6% (2005-2009 5-year est.).
Taxes: Total city taxes per capita: $97 (2007); City property taxes per capita: $54 (2007).
Education: Percent of population age 25 and over with: High school diploma (including GED) or higher: 86.5% (2010); Bachelor's degree or higher: 15.8% (2010); Master's degree or higher: 7.1% (2010).
Housing: Homeownership rate: 81.8% (2010); Median home value: $111,538 (2010); Median contract rent: $429 per month (2005-2009 5-year est.); Median year structure built: 1979 (2005-2009 5-year est.).
Transportation: Commute to work: 100.0% car, 0.0% public transportation, 0.0% walk, 0.0% work from home (2005-2009 5-year est.); Travel time to work: 10.3% less than 15 minutes, 31.0% 15 to 30 minutes, 20.7% 30 to 45 minutes, 25.5% 45 to 60 minutes, 12.4% 60 minutes or more (2005-2009 5-year est.)

MANVEL (city). Covers a land area of 23.300 square miles and a water area of 0.002 square miles. Located at 29.47° N. Lat; 95.35° W. Long. Elevation is 52 feet.
Population: 2,880 (1990); 3,046 (2000); 6,172 (2010); 7,182 (2015 projected); Race: 76.8% White, 6.2% Black, 3.6% Asian, 13.3% Other, 25.2% Hispanic of any race (2010); Density: 264.9 persons per square mile (2010); Average household size: 2.98 (2010); Median age: 35.1 (2010); Males per 100 females: 100.4 (2010); Marriage status: 20.5% never married, 66.6% now married, 4.2% widowed, 8.7% divorced (2005-2009 5-year est.); Foreign born: 11.0% (2005-2009 5-year est.); Ancestry (includes multiple ancestries): 15.4% German, 12.5% English, 9.3% Irish, 9.2% Italian, 4.3% American (2005-2009 5-year est.).
Economy: Single-family building permits issued: 178 (2010); Multi-family building permits issued: 0 (2010); Employment by occupation: 5.4% management, 13.1% professional, 15.4% services, 31.0% sales, 0.0% farming, 22.8% construction, 12.2% production (2005-2009 5-year est.).
Income: Per capita income: $27,413 (2010); Median household income: $68,989 (2010); Average household income: $81,486 (2010); Percent of households with income of $100,000 or more: 28.3% (2010); Poverty rate: 10.6% (2005-2009 5-year est.).
Taxes: Total city taxes per capita: $558 (2007); City property taxes per capita: $258 (2007).
Education: Percent of population age 25 and over with: High school diploma (including GED) or higher: 81.4% (2010); Bachelor's degree or higher: 15.3% (2010); Master's degree or higher: 3.7% (2010).

School District(s)

Alvin ISD (PK-12)

    2009-10 Enrollment: 16,788 . . . . (281) 388-1130

Housing: Homeownership rate: 84.9% (2010); Median home value: $139,024 (2010); Median contract rent: $532 per month (2005-2009 5-year est.); Median year structure built: 1986 (2005-2009 5-year est.).

Safety: Violent crime rate: 21.3 per 10,000 population; Property crime rate: 121.8 per 10,000 population (2009).

Transportation: Commute to work: 95.7% car, 0.0% public transportation, 0.4% walk, 3.9% work from home (2005-2009 5-year est.); Travel time to work: 13.3% less than 15 minutes, 26.9% 15 to 30 minutes, 29.1% 30 to 45 minutes, 21.1% 45 to 60 minutes, 9.5% 60 minutes or more (2005-2009 5-year est.)

Additional Information Contacts

City of Manvel . . . . (281) 489-0630
    http://www.cityofmanvel.com

OLD OCEAN (unincorporated postal area, zip code 77463). Covers a land area of 4.915 square miles and a water area of 0.067 square miles. Located at 29.13° N. Lat; 95.79° W. Long. Elevation is 39 feet.

Population: 109 (2000); Race: 76.8% White, 15.9% Black, 0.0% Asian, 7.3% Other, 7.3% Hispanic of any race (2000); Density: 22.2 persons per square mile (2000); Age: 19.5% under 18, 0.0% over 64 (2000); Marriage status: 0.0% never married, 71.2% now married, 18.2% widowed, 10.6% divorced (2000); Foreign born: 0.0% (2000); Ancestry (includes multiple ancestries): 31.7% American (2000).

Economy: Employment by occupation: 27.3% management, 0.0% professional, 0.0% services, 42.4% sales, 0.0% farming, 0.0% construction, 30.3% production (2000).

Income: Per capita income: $16,702 (2000); Median household income: $15,893 (2000); Poverty rate: 179.1% (2000).

Education: Percent of population age 25 and over with: High school diploma (including GED) or higher: 89.5% (2000); Bachelor's degree or higher: 0.0% (2000).

Housing: Homeownership rate: 76.5% (2000); Median home value: $95,000 (2000); Median contract rent: $275 per month (2000); Median year structure built: 1979 (2000).

Transportation: Commute to work: 100.0% car, 0.0% public transportation, 0.0% walk, 0.0% work from home (2000); Travel time to work: 0.0% less than 15 minutes, 51.5% 15 to 30 minutes, 18.2% 30 to 45 minutes, 30.3% 45 to 60 minutes, 0.0% 60 minutes or more (2000)

OYSTER CREEK (city). Covers a land area of 1.895 square miles and a water area of 0.108 square miles. Located at 28.99° N. Lat; 95.32° W. Long. Elevation is 7 feet.

Population: 1,102 (1990); 1,192 (2000); 1,225 (2010); 1,294 (2015 projected); Race: 81.5% White, 6.5% Black, 1.6% Asian, 10.4% Other, 21.3% Hispanic of any race (2010); Density: 646.5 persons per square mile (2010); Average household size: 2.49 (2010); Median age: 33.4 (2010); Males per 100 females: 105.9 (2010); Marriage status: 13.8% never married, 62.3% now married, 5.0% widowed, 18.9% divorced (2005-2009 5-year est.); Foreign born: 6.0% (2005-2009 5-year est.); Ancestry (includes multiple ancestries): 14.1% German, 12.3% American, 10.9% Irish, 8.8% French, 5.9% English (2005-2009 5-year est.).

Economy: Single-family building permits issued: 2 (2010); Multi-family building permits issued: 0 (2010); Employment by occupation: 2.1% management, 8.7% professional, 18.4% services, 17.9% sales, 1.5% farming, 34.2% construction, 17.1% production (2005-2009 5-year est.).

Income: Per capita income: $24,828 (2010); Median household income: $44,716 (2010); Average household income: $61,522 (2010); Percent of households with income of $100,000 or more: 13.4% (2010); Poverty rate: 15.4% (2005-2009 5-year est.).

Taxes: Total city taxes per capita: $714 (2007); City property taxes per capita: $175 (2007).

Education: Percent of population age 25 and over with: High school diploma (including GED) or higher: 75.3% (2010); Bachelor's degree or higher: 13.4% (2010); Master's degree or higher: 6.2% (2010).

Housing: Homeownership rate: 67.2% (2010); Median home value: $61,087 (2010); Median contract rent: $465 per month (2005-2009 5-year est.); Median year structure built: 1981 (2005-2009 5-year est.).

Safety: Violent crime rate: 88.4 per 10,000 population; Property crime rate: 345.7 per 10,000 population (2009).

Transportation: Commute to work: 89.6% car, 0.0% public transportation, 3.3% walk, 4.1% work from home (2005-2009 5-year est.); Travel time to work: 39.5% less than 15 minutes, 39.7% 15 to 30 minutes, 5.7% 30 to 45

minutes, 4.3% 45 to 60 minutes, 10.8% 60 minutes or more (2005-2009 5-year est.)

Additional Information Contacts

Brazosport Area Chamber of Commerce. . . . . (979) 285-2501
    http://www.brazosport.org

PEARLAND (city). Covers a land area of 39.330 square miles and a water area of 0.033 square miles. Located at 29.55° N. Lat; 95.29° W. Long. Elevation is 49 feet.

Population: 23,788 (1990); 37,640 (2000); 68,888 (2010); 79,381 (2015 projected); Race: 70.5% White, 10.0% Black, 7.2% Asian, 12.3% Other, 21.7% Hispanic of any race (2010); Density: 1,751.5 persons per square mile (2010); Average household size: 2.88 (2010); Median age: 34.2 (2010); Males per 100 females: 96.4 (2010); Marriage status: 21.8% never married, 65.1% now married, 4.1% widowed, 9.1% divorced (2005-2009 5-year est.); Foreign born: 12.9% (2005-2009 5-year est.); Ancestry (includes multiple ancestries): 14.3% German, 8.9% English, 8.7% American, 8.6% Irish, 3.6% Italian (2005-2009 5-year est.).

Economy: Unemployment rate: 7.4% (June 2011); Total civilian labor force: 47,380 (June 2011); Single-family building permits issued: 722 (2010); Multi-family building permits issued: 126 (2010); Employment by occupation: 19.3% management, 32.4% professional, 9.0% services, 24.4% sales, 0.0% farming, 6.3% construction, 8.6% production (2005-2009 5-year est.).

Income: Per capita income: $31,033 (2010); Median household income: $75,898 (2010); Average household income: $89,405 (2010); Percent of households with income of $100,000 or more: 33.6% (2010); Poverty rate: 4.2% (2005-2009 5-year est.).

Taxes: Total city taxes per capita: $727 (2007); City property taxes per capita: $403 (2007).

Education: Percent of population age 25 and over with: High school diploma (including GED) or higher: 88.1% (2010); Bachelor's degree or higher: 31.3% (2010); Master's degree or higher: 9.2% (2010).

School District(s)

Alvin ISD (PK-12)

    2009-10 Enrollment: 16,788 . . . . (281) 388-1130

Pearland ISD (PK-12)

    2009-10 Enrollment: 18,308 . . . . (281) 485-3203

Housing: Homeownership rate: 79.5% (2010); Median home value: $169,240 (2010); Median contract rent: $813 per month (2005-2009 5-year est.); Median year structure built: 1997 (2005-2009 5-year est.).

Safety: Violent crime rate: 14.7 per 10,000 population; Property crime rate: 226.6 per 10,000 population (2009).

Newspapers: Friendswood Journal (Community news; Circulation 3,750); Pearland Journal (Community news; Circulation 52,000); Reporter-News (Community news; Circulation 12,500)

Transportation: Commute to work: 94.9% car, 0.4% public transportation, 0.5% walk, 2.7% work from home (2005-2009 5-year est.); Travel time to work: 13.7% less than 15 minutes, 28.6% 15 to 30 minutes, 32.8% 30 to 45 minutes, 16.8% 45 to 60 minutes, 8.1% 60 minutes or more (2005-2009 5-year est.)

Additional Information Contacts

City of Pearland . . . . (281) 652-1600
    http://www.cityofpearland.com

Pearland Chamber of Commerce . . . . (281) 485-3634
    http://www.pearlandchamber.com

QUINTANA (town). Covers a land area of 0.607 square miles and a water area of 1.222 square miles. Located at 28.92° N. Lat; 95.31° W. Long. Elevation is 7 feet.

Population: 40 (1990); 38 (2000); 87 (2010); 92 (2015 projected); Race: 67.8% White, 19.5% Black, 1.1% Asian, 11.5% Other, 36.8% Hispanic of any race (2010); Density: 143.4 persons per square mile (2010); Average household size: 2.56 (2010); Median age: 28.7 (2010); Males per 100 females: 97.7 (2010); Marriage status: 5.9% never married, 55.9% now married, 20.6% widowed, 17.6% divorced (2005-2009 5-year est.); Foreign born: 0.0% (2005-2009 5-year est.); Ancestry (includes multiple ancestries): 29.3% German, 17.1% French, 12.2% Scotch-Irish, 12.2% Lithuanian, 9.8% Irish (2005-2009 5-year est.).

Economy: Single-family building permits issued: 1 (2010); Multi-family building permits issued: 0 (2010); Employment by occupation: 18.5% management, 18.5% professional, 37.0% services, 11.1% sales, 0.0% farming, 7.4% construction, 7.4% production (2005-2009 5-year est.).

Income: Per capita income: $15,789 (2010); Median household income: $30,000 (2010); Average household income: $51,397 (2010); Percent of

households with income of $100,000 or more: 5.9% (2010); Poverty rate: 39.0% (2005-2009 5-year est.).
Taxes: Total city taxes per capita: $340 (2007); City property taxes per capita: $43 (2007).
Education: Percent of population age 25 and over with: High school diploma (including GED) or higher: 81.3% (2010); Bachelor's degree or higher: 8.3% (2010); Master's degree or higher: 2.1% (2010).
Housing: Homeownership rate: 41.2% (2010); Median home value: $100,000 (2010); Median contract rent: $436 per month (2005-2009 5-year est.); Median year structure built: 1955 (2005-2009 5-year est.).
Transportation: Commute to work: 70.4% car, 0.0% public transportation, 29.6% walk, 0.0% work from home (2005-2009 5-year est.); Travel time to work: 81.5% less than 15 minutes, 11.1% 15 to 30 minutes, 7.4% 30 to 45 minutes, 0.0% 45 to 60 minutes, 0.0% 60 minutes or more (2005-2009 5-year est.)
Additional Information Contacts
Brazosport Area Chamber of Commerce. . . . . (979) 285-2501
  http://www.brazosport.org
Town of Quintana. . . . . (979) 233-0848
  http://www.quintana-tx.org

RICHWOOD (city). Aka Richwood Village. Covers a land area of 1.567 square miles and a water area of 0.069 square miles. Located at 29.06° N. Lat; 95.41° W. Long. Elevation is 16 feet.
Population: 2,761 (1990); 3,012 (2000); 3,519 (2010); 3,863 (2015 projected); Race: 69.7% White, 13.9% Black, 0.5% Asian, 15.9% Other, 31.4% Hispanic of any race (2010); Density: 2,246.1 persons per square mile (2010); Average household size: 2.61 (2010); Median age: 31.4 (2010); Males per 100 females: 98.0 (2010); Marriage status: 28.2% never married, 56.2% now married, 1.7% widowed, 13.9% divorced (2005-2009 5-year est.); Foreign born: 11.8% (2005-2009 5-year est.); Ancestry (includes multiple ancestries): 17.6% German, 11.9% Irish, 7.4% English, 7.0% Polish, 5.2% American (2005-2009 5-year est.).
Economy: Single-family building permits issued: 26 (2010); Multi-family building permits issued: 0 (2010); Employment by occupation: 10.0% management, 12.0% professional, 16.2% services, 30.5% sales, 0.0% farming, 20.0% construction, 11.3% production (2005-2009 5-year est.).
Income: Per capita income: $24,774 (2010); Median household income: $57,219 (2010); Average household income: $64,675 (2010); Percent of households with income of $100,000 or more: 14.8% (2010); Poverty rate: 14.3% (2005-2009 5-year est.).
Taxes: Total city taxes per capita: $342 (2007); City property taxes per capita: $209 (2007).
Education: Percent of population age 25 and over with: High school diploma (including GED) or higher: 90.8% (2010); Bachelor's degree or higher: 23.3% (2010); Master's degree or higher: 8.2% (2010).
School District(s)
Brazosport ISD (PK-12)
  2009-10 Enrollment: 12,861 . . . . (979) 730-7000
Housing: Homeownership rate: 56.3% (2010); Median home value: $110,838 (2010); Median contract rent: $550 per month (2005-2009 5-year est.); Median year structure built: 1982 (2005-2009 5-year est.).
Safety: Violent crime rate: 2.9 per 10,000 population; Property crime rate: 162.8 per 10,000 population (2009).
Transportation: Commute to work: 97.0% car, 0.0% public transportation, 0.4% walk, 1.9% work from home (2005-2009 5-year est.); Travel time to work: 44.8% less than 15 minutes, 33.0% 15 to 30 minutes, 10.4% 30 to 45 minutes, 4.9% 45 to 60 minutes, 6.9% 60 minutes or more (2005-2009 5-year est.)
Additional Information Contacts
Brazosport Area Chamber of Commerce. . . . . (979) 285-2501
  http://www.brazosport.org

ROSHARON (unincorporated postal area, zip code 77583). Covers a land area of 185.855 square miles and a water area of 1.847 square miles. Located at 29.42° N. Lat; 95.45° W. Long. Elevation is 49 feet.
Population: 16,851 (2000); Race: 52.0% White, 26.7% Black, 2.8% Asian, 18.5% Other, 29.3% Hispanic of any race (2000); Density: 90.7 persons per square mile (2000); Age: 20.0% under 18, 4.7% over 64 (2000); Marriage status: 28.6% never married, 48.3% now married, 4.0% widowed, 19.2% divorced (2000); Foreign born: 10.8% (2000); Ancestry (includes multiple ancestries): 7.3% German, 6.4% Irish, 5.3% American, 3.5% English (2000).

Economy: Employment by occupation: 9.9% management, 12.2% professional, 17.8% services, 24.6% sales, 0.5% farming, 17.6% construction, 17.4% production (2000).
Income: Per capita income: $11,320 (2000); Median household income: $43,718 (2000); Poverty rate: 179.1% (2000).
Education: Percent of population age 25 and over with: High school diploma (including GED) or higher: 69.0% (2000); Bachelor's degree or higher: 7.7% (2000).
School District(s)
Alvin ISD (PK-12)
  2009-10 Enrollment: 16,788 . . . . (281) 388-1130
Fort Bend ISD (PK-12)
  2009-10 Enrollment: 69,374 . . . . (281) 634-1000
Housing: Homeownership rate: 83.2% (2000); Median home value: $79,200 (2000); Median contract rent: $385 per month (2000); Median year structure built: 1984 (2000).
Transportation: Commute to work: 94.1% car, 0.2% public transportation, 1.6% walk, 3.0% work from home (2000); Travel time to work: 12.9% less than 15 minutes, 25.0% 15 to 30 minutes, 30.6% 30 to 45 minutes, 19.6% 45 to 60 minutes, 11.9% 60 minutes or more (2000)

SURFSIDE BEACH (city). Covers a land area of 1.784 square miles and a water area of 0.451 square miles. Located at 28.95° N. Lat; 95.28° W. Long. Elevation is 7 feet.
History: Includes Velasco, historic port.
Population: 611 (1990); 763 (2000); 900 (2010); 1,003 (2015 projected); Race: 89.4% White, 3.8% Black, 0.6% Asian, 6.2% Other, 3.0% Hispanic of any race (2010); Density: 504.5 persons per square mile (2010); Average household size: 2.12 (2010); Median age: 45.3 (2010); Males per 100 females: 109.8 (2010); Marriage status: 18.3% never married, 51.0% now married, 6.5% widowed, 24.1% divorced (2005-2009 5-year est.); Foreign born: 2.2% (2005-2009 5-year est.); Ancestry (includes multiple ancestries): 20.2% Irish, 19.2% English, 18.4% German, 10.4% French, 8.0% American (2005-2009 5-year est.).
Economy: Single-family building permits issued: 12 (2010); Multi-family building permits issued: 0 (2010); Employment by occupation: 11.8% management, 21.4% professional, 5.8% services, 28.0% sales, 0.0% farming, 15.9% construction, 17.1% production (2005-2009 5-year est.).
Income: Per capita income: $33,811 (2010); Median household income: $51,786 (2010); Average household income: $70,427 (2010); Percent of households with income of $100,000 or more: 19.9% (2010); Poverty rate: 14.5% (2005-2009 5-year est.).
Taxes: Total city taxes per capita: $726 (2007); City property taxes per capita: $570 (2007).
Education: Percent of population age 25 and over with: High school diploma (including GED) or higher: 89.6% (2010); Bachelor's degree or higher: 24.8% (2010); Master's degree or higher: 11.4% (2010).
Housing: Homeownership rate: 60.4% (2010); Median home value: $116,745 (2010); Median contract rent: $567 per month (2005-2009 5-year est.); Median year structure built: 1975 (2005-2009 5-year est.).
Safety: Violent crime rate: 78.1 per 10,000 population; Property crime rate: 312.5 per 10,000 population (2009).
Transportation: Commute to work: 94.8% car, 0.0% public transportation, 3.5% walk, 0.9% work from home (2005-2009 5-year est.); Travel time to work: 33.8% less than 15 minutes, 30.0% 15 to 30 minutes, 9.3% 30 to 45 minutes, 3.8% 45 to 60 minutes, 23.0% 60 minutes or more (2005-2009 5-year est.)
Additional Information Contacts
Brazosport Area Chamber of Commerce. . . . . (979) 285-2501
  http://www.brazosport.org

SWEENY (city). Covers a land area of 1.862 square miles and a water area of 0 square miles. Located at 29.04° N. Lat; 95.70° W. Long. Elevation is 30 feet.
History: Sweeny was named for John Sweeny, on whose plantation land the town was established. A refinery of the Phillips Petroleum Company and a gasoline plant of the Pan American Petroleum Corporation chose Sweeny as a location.
Population: 3,305 (1990); 3,624 (2000); 3,732 (2010); 3,901 (2015 projected); Race: 71.0% White, 18.4% Black, 0.7% Asian, 9.9% Other, 16.1% Hispanic of any race (2010); Density: 2,004.6 persons per square mile (2010); Average household size: 2.65 (2010); Median age: 33.9 (2010); Males per 100 females: 93.6 (2010); Marriage status: 20.6% never married, 58.0% now married, 9.3% widowed, 12.1% divorced (2005-2009 5-year est.); Foreign born: 5.5% (2005-2009 5-year est.); Ancestry

(includes multiple ancestries): 18.7% Irish, 8.7% German, 5.5% American, 4.3% Scottish, 4.3% English (2005-2009 5-year est.).

Economy: Single-family building permits issued: 4 (2010); Multi-family building permits issued: 0 (2010); Employment by occupation: 7.7% management, 13.6% professional, 22.1% services, 27.1% sales, 0.0% farming, 15.0% construction, 14.4% production (2005-2009 5-year est.).

Income: Per capita income: $20,379 (2010); Median household income: $45,071 (2010); Average household income: $54,292 (2010); Percent of households with income of $100,000 or more: 13.5% (2010); Poverty rate: 4.1% (2005-2009 5-year est.).

Taxes: Total city taxes per capita: $292 (2007); City property taxes per capita: $150 (2007).

Education: Percent of population age 25 and over with: High school diploma (including GED) or higher: 83.5% (2010); Bachelor's degree or higher: 15.5% (2010); Master's degree or higher: 3.7% (2010).

School District(s)

Sweeny ISD (PK-12)
    2009-10 Enrollment: 1,934 . . . . (979) 491-8000

Housing: Homeownership rate: 71.4% (2010); Median home value: $92,695 (2010); Median contract rent: $505 per month (2005-2009 5-year est.); Median year structure built: 1968 (2005-2009 5-year est.).

Hospitals: Sweeny Community Hospital (20 beds)

Safety: Violent crime rate: 22.1 per 10,000 population; Property crime rate: 199.3 per 10,000 population (2009).

Transportation: Commute to work: 96.4% car, 0.0% public transportation, 1.1% walk, 1.0% work from home (2005-2009 5-year est.); Travel time to work: 24.9% less than 15 minutes, 27.7% 15 to 30 minutes, 25.5% 30 to 45 minutes, 8.7% 45 to 60 minutes, 13.3% 60 minutes or more (2005-2009 5-year est.)

Additional Information Contacts

City of Sweeny. . . . . (979) 548-3321
    http://www.ci.sweeny.tx.us
Sweeny Chamber of Commerce . . . . (979) 548-3249
    http://www.mysweeny.com/chamber

WEST COLUMBIA (city).

Covers a land area of 2.560 square miles and a water area of 0 square miles. Located at 29.14° N. Lat; 95.64° W. Long. Elevation is 36 feet.

History: West Columbia was founded by Josiah Bell in 1826, two miles west of another town he founded on the Brazos River in 1824. West Columbia served as the capital of the Republic of Texas in 1836, when Sam Houston was inaugurated as president.

Population: 4,415 (1990); 4,255 (2000); 4,061 (2010); 4,225 (2015 projected); Race: 71.9% White, 16.3% Black, 0.7% Asian, 11.1% Other, 21.3% Hispanic of any race (2010); Density: 1,586.1 persons per square mile (2010); Average household size: 2.53 (2010); Median age: 34.5 (2010); Males per 100 females: 92.6 (2010); Marriage status: 26.8% never married, 54.3% now married, 7.8% widowed, 11.1% divorced (2005-2009 5-year est.); Foreign born: 5.3% (2005-2009 5-year est.); Ancestry (includes multiple ancestries): 14.2% German, 10.2% Irish, 8.0% English, 5.9% American, 2.8% Scotch-Irish (2005-2009 5-year est.).

Economy: Single-family building permits issued: 1 (2010); Multi-family building permits issued: 0 (2010); Employment by occupation: 9.1% management, 11.4% professional, 27.0% services, 21.6% sales, 0.9% farming, 18.2% construction, 11.7% production (2005-2009 5-year est.).

Income: Per capita income: $22,197 (2010); Median household income: $43,644 (2010); Average household income: $57,337 (2010); Percent of households with income of $100,000 or more: 14.1% (2010); Poverty rate: 27.4% (2005-2009 5-year est.).

Taxes: Total city taxes per capita: $347 (2007); City property taxes per capita: $217 (2007).

Education: Percent of population age 25 and over with: High school diploma (including GED) or higher: 82.3% (2010); Bachelor's degree or higher: 19.2% (2010); Master's degree or higher: 5.8% (2010).

School District(s)

Columbia-Brazoria ISD (PK-12)
    2009-10 Enrollment: 3,081 . . . . (979) 345-5147
Shekinah Radiance Academy (PK-12)
    2009-10 Enrollment: 1,125 . . . . (210) 658-6848

Housing: Homeownership rate: 65.9% (2010); Median home value: $88,662 (2010); Median contract rent: $410 per month (2005-2009 5-year est.); Median year structure built: 1969 (2005-2009 5-year est.).

Safety: Violent crime rate: 67.1 per 10,000 population; Property crime rate: 150.9 per 10,000 population (2009).

Newspapers: Brazoria County News (Local news; Circulation 11,000)

Transportation: Commute to work: 93.3% car, 0.0% public transportation, 5.1% walk, 1.6% work from home (2005-2009 5-year est.); Travel time to work: 31.1% less than 15 minutes, 20.4% 15 to 30 minutes, 31.8% 30 to 45 minutes, 4.0% 45 to 60 minutes, 12.6% 60 minutes or more (2005-2009 5-year est.)

Additional Information Contacts

City of West Columbia . . . . (979) 345-3123
    http://westcolumbiatx.org

WILD PEACH VILLAGE (CDP).

Covers a land area of 10.052 square miles and a water area of 0 square miles. Located at 29.07° N. Lat; 95.62° W. Long. Elevation is 26 feet.

Population: 2,440 (1990); 2,498 (2000); 2,382 (2010); 2,433 (2015 projected); Race: 81.2% White, 9.5% Black, 0.4% Asian, 8.9% Other, 13.1% Hispanic of any race (2010); Density: 237.0 persons per square mile (2010); Average household size: 2.79 (2010); Median age: 32.5 (2010); Males per 100 females: 95.1 (2010); Marriage status: 21.0% never married, 63.9% now married, 4.0% widowed, 11.2% divorced (2005-2009 5-year est.); Foreign born: 7.6% (2005-2009 5-year est.); Ancestry (includes multiple ancestries): 26.8% German, 16.7% Irish, 11.7% American, 9.9% French, 4.6% Scottish (2005-2009 5-year est.).

Economy: Employment by occupation: 17.8% management, 10.8% professional, 21.5% services, 9.9% sales, 0.0% farming, 24.8% construction, 15.2% production (2005-2009 5-year est.).

Income: Per capita income: $19,616 (2010); Median household income: $47,715 (2010); Average household income: $54,777 (2010); Percent of households with income of $100,000 or more: 12.5% (2010); Poverty rate: 7.7% (2005-2009 5-year est.).

Education: Percent of population age 25 and over with: High school diploma (including GED) or higher: 80.5% (2010); Bachelor's degree or higher: 8.8% (2010); Master's degree or higher: 2.8% (2010).

Housing: Homeownership rate: 84.6% (2010); Median home value: $95,000 (2010); Median contract rent: $427 per month (2005-2009 5-year est.); Median year structure built: 1976 (2005-2009 5-year est.).

Transportation: Commute to work: 90.2% car, 0.0% public transportation, 0.0% walk, 8.4% work from home (2005-2009 5-year est.); Travel time to work: 28.0% less than 15 minutes, 14.5% 15 to 30 minutes, 40.4% 30 to 45 minutes, 5.1% 45 to 60 minutes, 11.9% 60 minutes or more (2005-2009 5-year est.)

Brazos County

Located in east central Texas; bounded on the east by the Navasota River, and on the west and southwest by the Brazos River. Covers a land area of 585.78 square miles, a water area of 4.51 square miles, and is located in the Central Time Zone at 30.63° N. Lat., 96.34° W. Long. The county was founded in 1841. County seat is Bryan.

Brazos County is part of the College Station-Bryan, TX Metropolitan Statistical Area. The entire metro area includes: Brazos County, TX; Burleson County, TX; Robertson County, TX

Weather Station: College Station Easterwood									Elevation: 313 feet			
	Jan	Feb	Mar	Apr	May	Jun	Jul	Aug	Sep	Oct	Nov	Dec
High	61	65	72	79	86	92	95	96	91	81	71	62
Low	41	44	51	58	66	72	74	74	69	59	50	42
Precip	3.2	2.8	3.3	2.5	4.6	4.3	2.2	2.7	3.3	4.5	3.2	3.2
Snow	na	na	na	na	na	na	na	na	na	na	na	na

High and Low temperatures in degrees Fahrenheit; Precipitation and Snow in inches

Population: 121,862 (1990); 152,415 (2000); 177,768 (2010); 189,786 (2015 projected); Race: 72.2% White, 10.5% Black, 4.4% Asian, 13.0% Other, 21.4% Hispanic of any race (2010); Density: 303.5 persons per square mile (2010); Average household size: 2.53 (2010); Median age: 24.9 (2010); Males per 100 females: 104.4 (2010).

Religion: Five largest groups: 24.6% Catholic Church, 10.2% Southern Baptist Convention, 4.7% The United Methodist Church, 1.8% Churches of Christ, 1.6% Independent, Non-Charismatic Churches (2000).

Economy: Unemployment rate: 7.2% (June 2011); Total civilian labor force: 98,367 (June 2011); Leading industries: 17.5% retail trade; 16.5% accommodation & food services; 14.5% health care and social assistance (2009); Farms: 1,350 totaling 275,752 acres (2007); Companies that employ 500 or more persons: 6 (2009); Companies that employ 100 to 499 persons: 70 (2009); Companies that employ less than 100 persons: 3,678 (2009); Black-owned businesses: 799 (2007); Hispanic-owned businesses: 1,352 (2007); Asian-owned businesses: n/a (2007); Women-owned

businesses: n/a (2007); Retail sales per capita: $13,125 (2010).
Single-family building permits issued: 760 (2010); Multi-family building permits issued: 218 (2010).

Income: Per capita income: $21,508 (2010); Median household income: $38,103 (2010); Average household income: $57,812 (2010); Percent of households with income of $100,000 or more: 15.2% (2010); Poverty rate: 29.8% (2009); Bankruptcy rate: 0.59% (2010).

Taxes: Total county taxes per capita: $297 (2007); County property taxes per capita: $220 (2007).

Education: Percent of population age 25 and over with: High school diploma (including GED) or higher: 84.2% (2010); Bachelor's degree or higher: 40.1% (2010); Master's degree or higher: 15.6% (2010).

Housing: Homeownership rate: 47.1% (2010); Median home value: $134,126 (2010); Median contract rent: $595 per month (2005-2009 5-year est.); Median year structure built: 1985 (2005-2009 5-year est.)

Health: Birth rate: 149.1 per 10,000 population (2009); Death rate: 49.5 per 10,000 population (2009); Age-adjusted cancer mortality rate: 165.4 deaths per 100,000 population (2007); Number of physicians: 26.1 per 10,000 population (2008); Hospital beds: 24.0 per 10,000 population (2007); Hospital admissions: 1,349.5 per 10,000 population (2007).

Elections: 2008 Presidential election results: 34.9% Obama, 63.9% McCain, 0.1% Nader

Additional Information Contacts
Brazos County Government........................ (979) 361-4102
http://www.co.brazos.tx.us
Bryan-College Station Chamber of Commerce .... (979) 260-5200
http://www.bcschamber.org
City of Bryan .... (979) 209-5100
http://www.bryantx.gov
City of College Station .... (979) 764-3500
http://www.cstx.gov

Brazos County Communities

BRYAN (city). County seat. Covers a land area of 43.335 square miles and a water area of 0.085 square miles. Located at 30.66° N. Lat; 96.36° W. Long. Elevation is 374 feet.

History: Bryan was established as the center of a plantation area, where the main crop of cotton was replaced by alfalfa. Bryan has benefited from the proximity of Texas Agricultural & Mechanical University in nearby College Station.

Population: 55,759 (1990); 65,660 (2000); 71,783 (2010); 75,758 (2015 projected); Race: 61.5% White, 17.7% Black, 1.4% Asian, 19.4% Other, 34.6% Hispanic of any race (2010); Density: 1,656.5 persons per square mile (2010); Average household size: 2.66 (2010); Median age: 28.7 (2010); Males per 100 females: 100.8 (2010); Marriage status: 40.2% never married, 46.1% now married, 5.3% widowed, 8.4% divorced (2005-2009 5-year est.); Foreign born: 12.1% (2005-2009 5-year est.); Ancestry (includes multiple ancestries): 13.2% German, 7.8% English, 7.5% Irish, 3.9% American, 2.9% Italian (2005-2009 5-year est.).

Economy: Unemployment rate: 6.9% (June 2011); Total civilian labor force: 40,166 (June 2011); Single-family building permits issued: 269 (2010); Multi-family building permits issued: 4 (2010); Employment by occupation: 10.6% management, 19.8% professional, 21.0% services, 24.3% sales, 0.5% farming, 12.7% construction, 11.2% production (2005-2009 5-year est.).

Income: Per capita income: $19,493 (2010); Median household income: $39,949 (2010); Average household income: $52,596 (2010); Percent of households with income of $100,000 or more: 10.9% (2010); Poverty rate: 26.9% (2005-2009 5-year est.).

Taxes: Total city taxes per capita: $558 (2007); City property taxes per capita: $256 (2007).

Education: Percent of population age 25 and over with: High school diploma (including GED) or higher: 75.2% (2010); Bachelor's degree or higher: 26.7% (2010); Master's degree or higher: 9.6% (2010).

School District(s)
Brazos School for Inquiry & Creativity (PK-12)
    2009-10 Enrollment: 490 .... (979) 268-8884
Bryan ISD (PK-12)
    2009-10 Enrollment: 15,579 .... (979) 209-1000
Harmony Science Academy (College Station) (KG-11)
    2009-10 Enrollment: 274 .... (979) 779-2100

Vocational/Technical School(s)
Charles and Sues School of Hair Design (Private, For-profit)
    Fall 2009 Enrollment: 25 .... (979) 776-4375
    2010-11 Tuition: $17,000
Manuel and Theresa's School of Hair Design (Private, For-profit)
    Fall 2009 Enrollment: 56 .... (979) 821-2050
    2010-11 Tuition: $12,900

Housing: Homeownership rate: 51.5% (2010); Median home value: $105,391 (2010); Median contract rent: $543 per month (2005-2009 5-year est.); Median year structure built: 1979 (2005-2009 5-year est.).

Hospitals: St. Joseph Regional Health Center (210 beds); The Physicians Centre Hospital

Safety: Violent crime rate: 77.6 per 10,000 population; Property crime rate: 565.4 per 10,000 population (2009).

Newspapers: The Bryan-College Station Eagle (Local news; Circulation 24,000)

Transportation: Commute to work: 92.2% car, 1.3% public transportation, 1.4% walk, 2.3% work from home (2005-2009 5-year est.); Travel time to work: 45.0% less than 15 minutes, 44.5% 15 to 30 minutes, 5.2% 30 to 45 minutes, 2.7% 45 to 60 minutes, 2.6% 60 minutes or more (2005-2009 5-year est.)

Additional Information Contacts
Bryan-College Station Chamber of Commerce .... (979) 260-5200
http://www.bcschamber.org
City of Bryan .... (979) 209-5100
http://www.bryantx.gov

COLLEGE STATION (city). Covers a land area of 40.255 square miles and a water area of 0.039 square miles. Located at 30.60° N. Lat; 96.31° W. Long. Elevation is 338 feet.

History: College Station is the home of Texas Agricultural & Mechanical University, which had a major role in the improvement of Texan agriculture after 1871.

Population: 53,318 (1990); 67,890 (2000); 84,952 (2010); 91,594 (2015 projected); Race: 78.6% White, 5.4% Black, 7.8% Asian, 8.1% Other, 11.5% Hispanic of any race (2010); Density: 2,110.3 persons per square mile (2010); Average household size: 2.37 (2010); Median age: 23.4 (2010); Males per 100 females: 106.6 (2010); Marriage status: 65.3% never married, 29.1% now married, 1.8% widowed, 3.8% divorced (2005-2009 5-year est.); Foreign born: 12.4% (2005-2009 5-year est.); Ancestry (includes multiple ancestries): 18.2% German, 10.4% English, 8.8% Irish, 4.0% American, 2.9% French (2005-2009 5-year est.).

Economy: Unemployment rate: 7.3% (June 2011); Total civilian labor force: 47,076 (June 2011); Single-family building permits issued: 491 (2010); Multi-family building permits issued: 214 (2010); Employment by occupation: 10.6% management, 34.9% professional, 17.0% services, 24.7% sales, 0.3% farming, 6.1% construction, 6.4% production (2005-2009 5-year est.).

Income: Per capita income: $21,810 (2010); Median household income: $31,132 (2010); Average household income: $57,713 (2010); Percent of households with income of $100,000 or more: 17.2% (2010); Poverty rate: 39.4% (2005-2009 5-year est.).

Taxes: Total city taxes per capita: $528 (2007); City property taxes per capita: $225 (2007).

Education: Percent of population age 25 and over with: High school diploma (including GED) or higher: 94.0% (2010); Bachelor's degree or higher: 58.7% (2010); Master's degree or higher: 24.5% (2010).

School District(s)
College Station ISD (PK-12)
    2009-10 Enrollment: 10,102 .... (979) 764-5400

Four-year College(s)
Texas A & M University (Public)
    Fall 2009 Enrollment: 48,702..................... (979) 845-3211
    2010-11 Tuition: In-state $8,387; Out-of-state $22,817
Texas A&M Health Science Center (Public)
    Fall 2009 Enrollment: 1,828 .... (979) 458-7200

Housing: Homeownership rate: 36.3% (2010); Median home value: $181,040 (2010); Median contract rent: $621 per month (2005-2009 5-year est.); Median year structure built: 1988 (2005-2009 5-year est.).

Hospitals: College Station Medical Center (119 beds)

Safety: Violent crime rate: 19.8 per 10,000 population; Property crime rate: 379.6 per 10,000 population (2009).

Transportation: Commute to work: 86.3% car, 3.6% public transportation, 3.5% walk, 2.9% work from home (2005-2009 5-year est.); Travel time to work: 48.6% less than 15 minutes, 42.4% 15 to 30 minutes, 5.0% 30 to 45

minutes, 0.9% 45 to 60 minutes, 3.1% 60 minutes or more (2005-2009 5-year est.)

Airports: Easterwood Field (primary service)

Additional Information Contacts

Bryan-College Station Chamber of Commerce . . . . (979) 260-5200
http://www.bcschamber.org

City of College Station . . . . (979) 764-3500
http://www.cstx.gov

MILLICAN (town). Covers a land area of 4.013 square miles and a water area of 0.004 square miles. Located at 30.46° N. Lat; 96.20° W. Long. Elevation is 312 feet.

Population: 84 (1990); 108 (2000); 102 (2010); 106 (2015 projected); Race: 81.4% White, 3.9% Black, 0.0% Asian, 14.7% Other, 15.7% Hispanic of any race (2010); Density: 25.4 persons per square mile (2010); Average household size: 2.91 (2010); Median age: 30.8 (2010); Males per 100 females: 104.0 (2010); Marriage status: 0.0% never married, 77.3% now married, 22.7% widowed, 0.0% divorced (2005-2009 5-year est.); Foreign born: 0.0% (2005-2009 5-year est.); Ancestry (includes multiple ancestries): 38.7% German, 25.8% American, 22.6% Irish (2005-2009 5-year est.).

Economy: Employment by occupation: 22.2% management, 33.3% professional, 0.0% services, 22.2% sales, 0.0% farming, 22.2% construction, 0.0% production (2005-2009 5-year est.).

Income: Per capita income: $27,172 (2010); Median household income: $59,722 (2010); Average household income: $74,214 (2010); Percent of households with income of $100,000 or more: 20.0% (2010); Poverty rate: 0.0% (2005-2009 5-year est.).

Education: Percent of population age 25 and over with: High school diploma (including GED) or higher: 72.4% (2010); Bachelor's degree or higher: 27.6% (2010); Master's degree or higher: 10.3% (2010).

Housing: Homeownership rate: 82.9% (2010); Median home value: $118,750 (2010); Median contract rent: n/a per month (2005-2009 5-year est.); Median year structure built: 1983 (2005-2009 5-year est.).

Transportation: Commute to work: 100.0% car, 0.0% public transportation, 0.0% walk, 0.0% work from home (2005-2009 5-year est.); Travel time to work: 44.4% less than 15 minutes, 33.3% 15 to 30 minutes, 22.2% 30 to 45 minutes, 0.0% 45 to 60 minutes, 0.0% 60 minutes or more (2005-2009 5-year est.)

WIXON VALLEY (city). Covers a land area of 1.794 square miles and a water area of 0.020 square miles. Located at 30.76° N. Lat; 96.32° W. Long. Elevation is 335 feet.

Population: 186 (1990); 235 (2000); 206 (2010); 218 (2015 projected); Race: 91.3% White, 2.9% Black, 0.0% Asian, 5.8% Other, 12.6% Hispanic of any race (2010); Density: 114.8 persons per square mile (2010); Average household size: 2.71 (2010); Median age: 35.4 (2010); Males per 100 females: 92.5 (2010); Marriage status: 10.7% never married, 79.3% now married, 7.1% widowed, 2.9% divorced (2005-2009 5-year est.); Foreign born: 1.1% (2005-2009 5-year est.); Ancestry (includes multiple ancestries): 34.1% German, 31.9% English, 12.1% Scotch-Irish, 7.7% Irish, 7.1% Polish (2005-2009 5-year est.).

Economy: Employment by occupation: 14.6% management, 24.0% professional, 11.5% services, 28.1% sales, 0.0% farming, 8.3% construction, 13.5% production (2005-2009 5-year est.).

Income: Per capita income: $27,640 (2010); Median household income: $62,500 (2010); Average household income: $80,625 (2010); Percent of households with income of $100,000 or more: 22.4% (2010); Poverty rate: 5.5% (2005-2009 5-year est.).

Taxes: Total city taxes per capita: $92 (2007); City property taxes per capita: $0 (2007).

Education: Percent of population age 25 and over with: High school diploma (including GED) or higher: 82.8% (2010); Bachelor's degree or higher: 23.1% (2010); Master's degree or higher: 3.7% (2010).

Housing: Homeownership rate: 81.6% (2010); Median home value: $114,286 (2010); Median contract rent: $943 per month (2005-2009 5-year est.); Median year structure built: 1976 (2005-2009 5-year est.).

Transportation: Commute to work: 94.7% car, 0.0% public transportation, 1.1% walk, 4.3% work from home (2005-2009 5-year est.); Travel time to work: 12.2% less than 15 minutes, 68.9% 15 to 30 minutes, 15.6% 30 to 45 minutes, 2.2% 45 to 60 minutes, 1.1% 60 minutes or more (2005-2009 5-year est.)

Brewster County

Located in west Texas, in mountainous area; bounded on the south by the Big Bend of the Rio Grande and the Mexican border; includes the Chisos Mountains and Santa Elena, Mariscal, and Boquillas Canyons in the south, and the Santiago Mountains in the central part. Covers a land area of 6,192.61 square miles, a water area of 0.18 square miles, and is located in the Central Time Zone at 29.99° N. Lat., 103.40° W. Long. The county was founded in 1887. County seat is Alpine.

Weather Station: Alpine   **Elevation: 4,529 feet**

	Jan	Feb	Mar	Apr	May	Jun	Jul	Aug	Sep	Oct	Nov	Dec
High	62	65	72	79	86	91	89	88	84	78	69	62
Low	32	35	39	46	56	62	64	63	57	49	39	33
Precip	0.5	0.6	0.5	0.6	1.3	2.7	2.7	3.1	2.8	1.6	0.5	0.6
Snow	0.4	0.1	tr	tr	0.0	0.0	0.0	0.0	0.0	tr	0.4	0.3

High and Low temperatures in degrees Fahrenheit; Precipitation and Snow in inches

Weather Station: Boquillas Ranger Stn   **Elevation: 1,879 feet**

	Jan	Feb	Mar	Apr	May	Jun	Jul	Aug	Sep	Oct	Nov	Dec
High	70	75	83	92	99	104	103	101	97	88	78	69
Low	31	36	44	52	64	71	72	71	66	54	41	32
Precip	0.4	0.4	0.3	0.4	1.2	1.3	1.1	1.2	1.0	1.4	0.6	0.4
Snow	tr	0.0	0.0	0.0	0.0	0.0	0.0	0.0	0.0	0.0	0.0	tr

High and Low temperatures in degrees Fahrenheit; Precipitation and Snow in inches

Weather Station: Castolon   **Elevation: 2,167 feet**

	Jan	Feb	Mar	Apr	May	Jun	Jul	Aug	Sep	Oct	Nov	Dec
High	68	74	83	91	100	104	102	101	96	88	77	68
Low	35	40	48	56	66	73	74	73	68	57	44	35
Precip	0.4	0.3	0.3	0.4	1.0	1.5	1.7	1.7	1.4	1.2	0.4	0.3
Snow	0.1	tr	tr	0.0	0.0	0.0	0.0	0.0	0.0	0.0	tr	tr

High and Low temperatures in degrees Fahrenheit; Precipitation and Snow in inches

Weather Station: Chisos Basin   **Elevation: 5,298 feet**

	Jan	Feb	Mar	Apr	May	Jun	Jul	Aug	Sep	Oct	Nov	Dec
High	57	61	67	75	82	85	84	82	78	72	65	58
Low	37	39	44	51	59	64	64	63	59	52	44	38
Precip	0.7	0.7	0.5	0.6	1.7	2.7	3.4	3.8	2.4	1.8	0.7	0.6
Snow	1.1	0.1	tr	0.1	0.0	0.0	0.0	0.0	0.0	0.0	0.5	0.2

High and Low temperatures in degrees Fahrenheit; Precipitation and Snow in inches

Weather Station: Lajitas   **Elevation: 2,439 feet**

	Jan	Feb	Mar	Apr	May	Jun	Jul	Aug	Sep	Oct	Nov	Dec
High	69	75	83	91	98	102	100	99	95	87	77	69
Low	35	40	46	54	64	73	74	73	68	56	43	35
Precip	0.4	0.3	0.3	0.4	0.9	1.4	2.2	1.3	1.5	1.4	0.3	0.3
Snow	0.1	0.0	0.0	0.0	0.0	0.0	0.0	0.0	0.0	0.0	0.0	tr

High and Low temperatures in degrees Fahrenheit; Precipitation and Snow in inches

Weather Station: Marathon   **Elevation: 4,089 feet**

	Jan	Feb	Mar	Apr	May	Jun	Jul	Aug	Sep	Oct	Nov	Dec
High	62	66	73	81	88	91	91	90	85	79	70	64
Low	30	33	39	46	55	61	63	62	58	48	37	31
Precip	0.5	0.4	0.4	0.7	1.5	2.1	2.4	2.2	2.0	1.8	0.4	0.5
Snow	0.6	tr	tr	tr	0.0	0.0	0.0	0.0	0.0	tr	0.2	0.1

High and Low temperatures in degrees Fahrenheit; Precipitation and Snow in inches

Weather Station: Panther Junction   **Elevation: 3,740 feet**

	Jan	Feb	Mar	Apr	May	Jun	Jul	Aug	Sep	Oct	Nov	Dec
High	62	66	74	82	90	94	93	91	87	79	70	62
Low	36	40	46	53	62	67	69	68	62	54	44	37
Precip	0.6	0.5	0.4	0.6	1.4	1.9	2.2	2.3	1.5	1.5	0.6	0.5
Snow	0.8	tr	0.0	0.1	0.0	0.0	0.0	0.0	0.0	0.0	0.2	tr

High and Low temperatures in degrees Fahrenheit; Precipitation and Snow in inches

Population: 8,681 (1990); 8,866 (2000); 9,443 (2010); 9,706 (2015 projected); Race: 80.3% White, 2.1% Black, 0.4% Asian, 17.2% Other, 42.7% Hispanic of any race (2010); Density: 1.5 persons per square mile (2010); Average household size: 2.24 (2010); Median age: 34.8 (2010); Males per 100 females: 101.2 (2010).

Religion: Five largest groups: 28.6% Catholic Church, 15.5% Southern Baptist Convention, 4.9% The United Methodist Church, 1.6% Assemblies of God, 1.5% Presbyterian Church (U.S.A.) (2000).

Economy: Unemployment rate: 6.6% (June 2011); Total civilian labor force: 5,261 (June 2011); Leading industries: 27.4% accommodation & food services; 20.6% health care and social assistance; 16.2% retail trade (2009); Farms: 158 totaling 1,747,087 acres (2007); Companies that employ 500 or more persons: 0 (2009); Companies that employ 100 to 499 persons: 5 (2009); Companies that employ less than 100 persons: 294 (2009); Black-owned businesses: n/a (2007); Hispanic-owned businesses: n/a (2007); Asian-owned businesses: n/a (2007); Women-owned businesses: 344 (2007); Retail sales per capita: $14,476 (2010). Single-family building permits issued: 18 (2010); Multi-family building permits issued: 0 (2010).

Income: Per capita income: $20,586 (2010); Median household income: $35,851 (2010); Average household income: $47,884 (2010); Percent of households with income of $100,000 or more: 9.2% (2010); Poverty rate: 17.3% (2009); Bankruptcy rate: 0.32% (2010).

Taxes: Total county taxes per capita: $284 (2007); County property taxes per capita: $168 (2007).

Education: Percent of population age 25 and over with: High school diploma (including GED) or higher: 83.4% (2010); Bachelor's degree or higher: 30.2% (2010); Master's degree or higher: 10.8% (2010).

Housing: Homeownership rate: 57.1% (2010); Median home value: $89,549 (2010); Median contract rent: $418 per month (2005-2009 5-year est.); Median year structure built: 1972 (2005-2009 5-year est.)

Health: Birth rate: 128.7 per 10,000 population (2009); Death rate: 74.9 per 10,000 population (2009); Age-adjusted cancer mortality rate: 164.0 (Unreliable) deaths per 100,000 population (2007); Number of physicians: 11.9 per 10,000 population (2008); Hospital beds: 27.2 per 10,000 population (2007); Hospital admissions: 1,288.1 per 10,000 population (2007).

Environment: Air Quality Index: 91.4% good, 8.6% moderate, 0.0% unhealthy for sensitive individuals, 0.0% unhealthy (percent of days in 2008)

Elections: 2008 Presidential election results: 50.5% Obama, 47.6% McCain, 0.4% Nader

National and State Parks: Big Bend National Park

Additional Information Contacts

Brewster County Government . . . . (432) 837-2412
    http://brewstercountytx.com
Alpine Chamber of Commerce . . . . (432) 837-2326
    http://www.alpinetexas.com
Big Bend Chamber of Commerce . . . . (432) 371-2320
    http://bigbendchamber.homestead.com
City of Alpine . . . . (432) 837-3301
    http://www.ci.alpine.tx.us
Marathon Chamber of Commerce . . . . (432) 386-4516
    http://www.marathontexas.com

Brewster County Communities

ALPINE (city). County seat. Covers a land area of 4.085 square miles and a water area of 0 square miles. Located at 30.36° N. Lat; 103.66° W. Long. Elevation is 4,475 feet.

History: Alpine was founded in 1882 when the railroad was built through the district. Ranchers who lived in Alpine operated large spreads where they raised Highland Herefords. Mining also played a role in Alpine's history, with gold, silver, copper, lead, quicksilver, marble, zinc, coal, and potash all found in the region.

Population: 5,843 (1990); 5,786 (2000); 6,153 (2010); 6,317 (2015 projected); Race: 78.9% White, 1.9% Black, 0.5% Asian, 18.8% Other, 47.4% Hispanic of any race (2010); Density: 1,506.3 persons per square mile (2010); Average household size: 2.25 (2010); Median age: 33.8 (2010); Males per 100 females: 97.3 (2010); Marriage status: 42.1% never married, 37.3% now married, 6.9% widowed, 13.6% divorced (2005-2009 5-year est.); Foreign born: 5.9% (2005-2009 5-year est.); Ancestry (includes multiple ancestries): 14.1% German, 10.8% English, 7.2% Irish, 4.6% American, 4.4% French (2005-2009 5-year est.).

Economy: Single-family building permits issued: 18 (2010); Multi-family building permits issued: 0 (2010); Employment by occupation: 7.5% management, 16.0% professional, 28.3% services, 20.3% sales, 0.6% farming, 15.9% construction, 11.4% production (2005-2009 5-year est.).

Income: Per capita income: $18,295 (2010); Median household income: $31,390 (2010); Average household income: $41,418 (2010); Percent of households with income of $100,000 or more: 5.9% (2010); Poverty rate: 21.2% (2005-2009 5-year est.).

Taxes: Total city taxes per capita: $329 (2007); City property taxes per capita: $137 (2007).

Education: Percent of population age 25 and over with: High school diploma (including GED) or higher: 82.8% (2010); Bachelor's degree or higher: 29.1% (2010); Master's degree or higher: 12.0% (2010).

Alpine ISD (PK-12)
    2009-10 Enrollment: 1,062 . . . . (432) 837-7700
Sul Ross State University (Public)
    Fall 2009 Enrollment: 3,047 . . . . (432) 837-8011
    2010-11 Tuition: In-state $4,568; Out-of-state $12,008

Housing: Homeownership rate: 53.4% (2010); Median home value: $78,821 (2010); Median contract rent: $428 per month (2005-2009 5-year est.); Median year structure built: 1972 (2005-2009 5-year est.).

Hospitals: Big Bend Regional Medical Center (40 beds)

Safety: Violent crime rate: 25.3 per 10,000 population; Property crime rate: 142.4 per 10,000 population (2009).

Newspapers: Alpine Avalanche (Community news; Circulation 4,250)

Transportation: Commute to work: 88.6% car, 0.0% public transportation, 5.9% walk, 1.7% work from home (2005-2009 5-year est.); Travel time to work: 79.7% less than 15 minutes, 10.5% 15 to 30 minutes, 4.8% 30 to 45 minutes, 2.7% 45 to 60 minutes, 2.3% 60 minutes or more (2005-2009 5-year est.); Amtrak: train service available.

Airports: Alpine-Casparis Municipal (general aviation)

Additional Information Contacts

Alpine Chamber of Commerce . . . . (432) 837-2326
    http://www.alpinetexas.com
City of Alpine . . . . (432) 837-3301
    http://www.ci.alpine.tx.us

MARATHON (CDP). Covers a land area of 5.255 square miles and a water area of 0 square miles. Located at 30.20° N. Lat; 103.24° W. Long. Elevation is 4,055 feet.

History: Marathon developed as a supply center for the ranching country of Brewster County, the Big Bend country of the Rio Grande.

Population: 595 (1990); 455 (2000); 383 (2010); 357 (2015 projected); Race: 86.9% White, 2.1% Black, 0.0% Asian, 11.0% Other, 43.1% Hispanic of any race (2010); Density: 72.9 persons per square mile (2010); Average household size: 2.27 (2010); Median age: 45.3 (2010); Males per 100 females: 103.7 (2010); Marriage status: 17.0% never married, 61.4% now married, 8.0% widowed, 13.6% divorced (2005-2009 5-year est.); Foreign born: 7.7% (2005-2009 5-year est.); Ancestry (includes multiple ancestries): 13.2% German, 11.9% English, 7.0% Irish, 5.0% Scotch-Irish, 4.0% French (2005-2009 5-year est.).

Economy: Employment by occupation: 12.8% management, 10.8% professional, 29.7% services, 9.2% sales, 2.6% farming, 12.3% construction, 22.6% production (2005-2009 5-year est.).

Income: Per capita income: $28,058 (2010); Median household income: $38,214 (2010); Average household income: $62,811 (2010); Percent of households with income of $100,000 or more: 18.9% (2010); Poverty rate: 24.9% (2005-2009 5-year est.).

Education: Percent of population age 25 and over with: High school diploma (including GED) or higher: 75.7% (2010); Bachelor's degree or higher: 26.5% (2010); Master's degree or higher: 7.0% (2010).

Marathon ISD (PK-12)
    2009-10 Enrollment: 51 . . . . (432) 386-4431

Housing: Homeownership rate: 70.4% (2010); Median home value: $78,333 (2010); Median contract rent: $383 per month (2005-2009 5-year est.); Median year structure built: 1949 (2005-2009 5-year est.).

Transportation: Commute to work: 90.3% car, 0.0% public transportation, 3.1% walk, 5.1% work from home (2005-2009 5-year est.); Travel time to work: 85.9% less than 15 minutes, 4.9% 15 to 30 minutes, 7.6% 30 to 45 minutes, 0.0% 45 to 60 minutes, 1.6% 60 minutes or more (2005-2009 5-year est.)

Additional Information Contacts

Marathon Chamber of Commerce . . . . (432) 386-4516
    http://www.marathontexas.com

STUDY BUTTE-TERLINGUA (CDP). Covers a land area of 15.953 square miles and a water area of 0 square miles. Located at 29.32° N. Lat; 103.56° W. Long.

Population: 262 (1990); 267 (2000); 315 (2010); 332 (2015 projected); Race: 84.4% White, 1.0% Black, 0.3% Asian, 14.3% Other, 38.1% Hispanic of any race (2010); Density: 19.7 persons per square mile (2010); Average household size: 2.20 (2010); Median age: 44.1 (2010); Males per 100 females: 108.6 (2010); Marriage status: 32.8% never married, 39.7% now married, 9.5% widowed, 18.1% divorced (2005-2009 5-year est.); Foreign born: 21.2% (2005-2009 5-year est.); Ancestry (includes multiple

ancestries): 26.7% German, 11.0% English, 8.2% Irish, 5.5% French Canadian, 4.1% Dutch (2005-2009 5-year est.).

Economy: Employment by occupation: 11.0% management, 7.3% professional, 63.4% services, 18.3% sales, 0.0% farming, 0.0% construction, 0.0% production (2005-2009 5-year est.).

Income: Per capita income: $24,896 (2010); Median household income: $44,773 (2010); Average household income: $55,437 (2010); Percent of households with income of $100,000 or more: 13.3% (2010); Poverty rate: 18.5% (2005-2009 5-year est.).

Education: Percent of population age 25 and over with: High school diploma (including GED) or higher: 80.5% (2010); Bachelor's degree or higher: 33.6% (2010); Master's degree or higher: 10.5% (2010).

Housing: Homeownership rate: 57.3% (2010); Median home value: $125,000 (2010); Median contract rent: $271 per month (2005-2009 5-year est.); Median year structure built: 1988 (2005-2009 5-year est.).

Transportation: Commute to work: 91.5% car, 0.0% public transportation, 8.5% walk, 0.0% work from home (2005-2009 5-year est.); Travel time to work: 58.5% less than 15 minutes, 22.0% 15 to 30 minutes, 7.3% 30 to 45 minutes, 12.2% 45 to 60 minutes, 0.0% 60 minutes or more (2005-2009 5-year est.)

TERLINGUA (unincorporated postal area, zip code 79852). Covers a land area of 427.987 square miles and a water area of 0.036 square miles. Located at 29.44° N. Lat; 103.63° W. Long. Elevation is 2,897 feet.

History: Mercury mines active in late 19th century. For most of 20th century it has been a ghost town. Site of annual Chili Cookoff since 1967.

Population: 621 (2000); Race: 84.4% White, 0.0% Black, 3.3% Asian, 12.3% Other, 42.8% Hispanic of any race (2000); Density: 1.5 persons per square mile (2000); Age: 25.0% under 18, 11.0% over 64 (2000); Marriage status: 21.6% never married, 62.1% now married, 1.1% widowed, 15.2% divorced (2000); Foreign born: 24.3% (2000); Ancestry (includes multiple ancestries): 8.4% English, 6.4% Scotch-Irish, 5.7% German, 4.0% Scottish (2000).

Economy: Employment by occupation: 12.5% management, 9.8% professional, 20.1% services, 28.0% sales, 1.6% farming, 18.8% construction, 9.2% production (2000).

Income: Per capita income: $17,714 (2000); Median household income: $35,259 (2000); Poverty rate: 179.1% (2000).

Education: Percent of population age 25 and over with: High school diploma (including GED) or higher: 80.7% (2000); Bachelor's degree or higher: 25.5% (2000).

School District(s)

Terlingua Csd (KG-12)
    2009-10 Enrollment: 123 . . . . (432) 371-2281

Housing: Homeownership rate: 55.7% (2000); Median home value: $56,400 (2000); Median contract rent: $264 per month (2000); Median year structure built: 1984 (2000).

Transportation: Commute to work: 72.0% car, 0.0% public transportation, 20.9% walk, 5.4% work from home (2000); Travel time to work: 59.5% less than 15 minutes, 20.7% 15 to 30 minutes, 13.5% 30 to 45 minutes, 4.0% 45 to 60 minutes, 2.3% 60 minutes or more (2000)

Additional Information Contacts
Big Bend Chamber of Commerce . . . . (432) 371-2320
    http://bigbendchamber.homestead.com

Briscoe County

Located in northwestern Texas; drained by Tule Creek and Prairie Dog Town Fork of the Red River. Covers a land area of 900.25 square miles, a water area of 1.33 square miles, and is located in the Central Time Zone at 34.48° N. Lat., 101.27° W. Long. The county was founded in 1876. County seat is Silverton.

Weather Station: Silverton										Elevation: 3,279 feet		
	Jan	Feb	Mar	Apr	May	Jun	Jul	Aug	Sep	Oct	Nov	Dec
High	51	55	63	72	80	87	91	90	83	73	61	51
Low	23	26	33	41	52	61	65	64	56	44	32	24
Precip	0.7	0.8	1.3	1.5	2.9	4.1	2.2	2.7	2.3	1.8	0.9	0.9
Snow	2.6	2.3	1.1	0.2	0.0	0.0	0.0	0.0	0.0	0.1	1.9	2.7

High and Low temperatures in degrees Fahrenheit; Precipitation and Snow in inches

Population: 1,971 (1990); 1,790 (2000); 1,480 (2010); 1,403 (2015 projected); Race: 80.7% White, 3.1% Black, 0.1% Asian, 16.1% Other, 25.7% Hispanic of any race (2010); Density: 1.6 persons per square mile (2010); Average household size: 2.46 (2010); Median age: 46.6 (2010); Males per 100 females: 96.3 (2010).

Religion: Five largest groups: 61.1% Southern Baptist Convention, 15.5% Catholic Church, 15.3% The United Methodist Church, 11.6% Churches of Christ, 1.5% Assemblies of God (2000).

Economy: Unemployment rate: 7.0% (June 2011); Total civilian labor force: 672 (June 2011); Leading industries: Farms: 333 totaling 546,734 acres (2007); Companies that employ 500 or more persons: 0 (2009); Companies that employ 100 to 499 persons: 0 (2009); Companies that employ less than 100 persons: 36 (2009); Black-owned businesses: n/a (2007); Hispanic-owned businesses: n/a (2007); Asian-owned businesses: n/a (2007); Women-owned businesses: n/a (2007); Retail sales per capita: $5,842 (2010). Single-family building permits issued: n/a (2010); Multi-family building permits issued: n/a (2010).

Income: Per capita income: $19,014 (2010); Median household income: $38,549 (2010); Average household income: $46,822 (2010); Percent of households with income of $100,000 or more: 7.2% (2010); Poverty rate: 15.2% (2009); Bankruptcy rate: n/a (2010).

Taxes: Total county taxes per capita: $446 (2007); County property taxes per capita: $367 (2007).

Education: Percent of population age 25 and over with: High school diploma (including GED) or higher: 80.2% (2010); Bachelor's degree or higher: 20.0% (2010); Master's degree or higher: 3.9% (2010).

Housing: Homeownership rate: 75.2% (2010); Median home value: $47,013 (2010); Median contract rent: $376 per month (2005-2009 5-year est.); Median year structure built: 1954 (2005-2009 5-year est.).

Health: Birth rate: 98.0 per 10,000 population (2009); Death rate: 126.1 per 10,000 population (2009); Age-adjusted cancer mortality rate: Suppressed deaths per 100,000 population (2007); Number of physicians: 6.8 per 10,000 population (2008); Hospital beds: 0.0 per 10,000 population (2007); Hospital admissions: 0.0 per 10,000 population (2007).

Elections: 2008 Presidential election results: 24.7% Obama, 74.3% McCain, 0.1% Nader

Additional Information Contacts
Briscoe County Government . . . . (806) 823-2131
    http://www.co.briscoe.tx.us/ips/cms

Briscoe County Communities

QUITAQUE (city). Covers a land area of 0.719 square miles and a water area of 0 square miles. Located at 34.36° N. Lat; 101.05° W. Long. Elevation is 2,572 feet.

Population: 513 (1990); 432 (2000); 341 (2010); 321 (2015 projected); Race: 77.4% White, 6.7% Black, 0.0% Asian, 15.8% Other, 29.3% Hispanic of any race (2010); Density: 474.3 persons per square mile (2010); Average household size: 2.40 (2010); Median age: 49.6 (2010); Males per 100 females: 101.8 (2010); Marriage status: 15.1% never married, 70.9% now married, 10.9% widowed, 3.0% divorced (2005-2009 5-year est.); Foreign born: 10.5% (2005-2009 5-year est.); Ancestry (includes multiple ancestries): 22.9% German, 20.1% Irish, 6.5% American, 5.7% Dutch, 4.8% English (2005-2009 5-year est.).

Economy: Employment by occupation: 9.8% management, 9.1% professional, 16.7% services, 33.3% sales, 8.3% farming, 14.4% construction, 8.3% production (2005-2009 5-year est.).

Income: Per capita income: $19,267 (2010); Median household income: $40,870 (2010); Average household income: $47,764 (2010); Percent of households with income of $100,000 or more: 8.5% (2010); Poverty rate: 25.9% (2005-2009 5-year est.).

Taxes: Total city taxes per capita: $145 (2007); City property taxes per capita: $145 (2007).

Education: Percent of population age 25 and over with: High school diploma (including GED) or higher: 76.6% (2010); Bachelor's degree or higher: 17.7% (2010); Master's degree or higher: 3.6% (2010).

Housing: Homeownership rate: 72.5% (2010); Median home value: $45,789 (2010); Median contract rent: $375 per month (2005-2009 5-year est.); Median year structure built: 1951 (2005-2009 5-year est.).

Newspapers: Quitaque Valley Tribune (Community news; Circulation 900)

Transportation: Commute to work: 85.6% car, 0.0% public transportation, 6.8% walk, 7.6% work from home (2005-2009 5-year est.); Travel time to work: 82.8% less than 15 minutes, 0.0% 15 to 30 minutes, 5.7% 30 to 45 minutes, 0.0% 45 to 60 minutes, 11.5% 60 minutes or more (2005-2009 5-year est.)

SILVERTON (city). County seat. Covers a land area of 1.006 square miles and a water area of 0 square miles. Located at 34.47° N. Lat; 101.30° W. Long. Elevation is 3,278 feet.

Population: 779 (1990); 771 (2000); 637 (2010); 605 (2015 projected); Race: 82.3% White, 1.6% Black, 0.0% Asian, 16.2% Other, 24.3% Hispanic of any race (2010); Density: 633.2 persons per square mile (2010); Average household size: 2.49 (2010); Median age: 44.9 (2010); Males per 100 females: 100.3 (2010); Marriage status: 18.6% never married, 56.4% now married, 16.0% widowed, 9.0% divorced (2005-2009 5-year est.); Foreign born: 14.4% (2005-2009 5-year est.); Ancestry (includes multiple ancestries): 24.1% Irish, 9.3% German, 9.2% Scottish, 5.7% English, 5.4% Dutch West Indian (2005-2009 5-year est.).
Economy: Employment by occupation: 5.0% management, 13.9% professional, 33.2% services, 18.2% sales, 8.9% farming, 8.2% construction, 12.5% production (2005-2009 5-year est.).
Income: Per capita income: $18,903 (2010); Median household income: $37,941 (2010); Average household income: $45,508 (2010); Percent of households with income of $100,000 or more: 6.6% (2010); Poverty rate: 28.9% (2005-2009 5-year est.).
Taxes: Total city taxes per capita: $241 (2007); City property taxes per capita: $125 (2007).
Education: Percent of population age 25 and over with: High school diploma (including GED) or higher: 81.4% (2010); Bachelor's degree or higher: 20.9% (2010); Master's degree or higher: 4.1% (2010).

School District(s)

Silverton ISD (PK-12)
    2009-10 Enrollment: 163 . . . . (806) 823-2476
Housing: Homeownership rate: 76.6% (2010); Median home value: $48,485 (2010); Median contract rent: $368 per month (2005-2009 5-year est.); Median year structure built: 1956 (2005-2009 5-year est.).
Newspapers: Briscoe County News (Community news; Circulation 900)
Transportation: Commute to work: 87.3% car, 0.0% public transportation, 1.5% walk, 11.2% work from home (2005-2009 5-year est.); Travel time to work: 46.8% less than 15 minutes, 13.5% 15 to 30 minutes, 20.7% 30 to 45 minutes, 13.1% 45 to 60 minutes, 5.9% 60 minutes or more (2005-2009 5-year est.)

Brooks County

Located in southeastern Texas. Covers a land area of 943.28 square miles, a water area of 0.33 square miles, and is located in the Central Time Zone at 27.09° N. Lat., 98.20° W. Long. The county was founded in 1911. County seat is Falfurrias.

Weather Station: Falfurrias   Elevation: 120 feet

	Jan	Feb	Mar	Apr	May	Jun	Jul	Aug	Sep	Oct	Nov	Dec
High	69	72	79	85	91	95	97	97	92	86	77	69
Low	45	48	54	61	69	73	74	74	70	62	54	46
Precip	1.1	1.5	1.2	1.1	2.7	2.7	2.4	2.7	3.7	3.4	1.4	1.3
Snow	0.0	0.0	0.0	0.0	0.0	0.0	0.0	0.0	0.0	0.0	0.0	0.0

High and Low temperatures in degrees Fahrenheit; Precipitation and Snow in inches

Population: 8,204 (1990); 7,976 (2000); 7,628 (2010); 7,444 (2015 projected); Race: 75.9% White, 0.3% Black, 0.1% Asian, 23.7% Other, 90.9% Hispanic of any race (2010); Density: 8.1 persons per square mile (2010); Average household size: 2.85 (2010); Median age: 34.8 (2010); Males per 100 females: 91.9 (2010).
Religion: Five largest groups: 43.9% Catholic Church, 5.9% Southern Baptist Convention, 1.5% The United Methodist Church, 1.0% Presbyterian Church (U.S.A.), 1.0% Seventh-day Adventist Church (2000).
Economy: Unemployment rate: 11.1% (June 2011); Total civilian labor force: 3,221 (June 2011); Leading industries: 21.6% accommodation & food services; 20.9% retail trade; 9.6% mining (2009); Farms: 494 totaling 548,619 acres (2007); Companies that employ 500 or more persons: 0 (2009); Companies that employ 100 to 499 persons: 2 (2009); Companies that employ less than 100 persons: 130 (2009); Black-owned businesses: n/a (2007); Hispanic-owned businesses: n/a (2007); Asian-owned businesses: n/a (2007); Women-owned businesses: n/a (2007); Retail sales per capita: $8,980 (2010). Single-family building permits issued: 3 (2010); Multi-family building permits issued: 0 (2010).
Income: Per capita income: $14,212 (2010); Median household income: $25,845 (2010); Average household income: $40,498 (2010); Percent of households with income of $100,000 or more: 5.7% (2010); Poverty rate: 33.0% (2009); Bankruptcy rate: 0.55% (2010).
Taxes: Total county taxes per capita: $750 (2007); County property taxes per capita: $671 (2007).
Education: Percent of population age 25 and over with: High school diploma (including GED) or higher: 55.7% (2010); Bachelor's degree or higher: 8.2% (2010); Master's degree or higher: 4.3% (2010).

Housing: Homeownership rate: 71.1% (2010); Median home value: $43,690 (2010); Median contract rent: $139 per month (2005-2009 5-year est.); Median year structure built: 1964 (2005-2009 5-year est.)
Health: Birth rate: 196.6 per 10,000 population (2009); Death rate: 82.7 per 10,000 population (2009); Age-adjusted cancer mortality rate: 174.8 (Unreliable) deaths per 100,000 population (2007); Number of physicians: 0.0 per 10,000 population (2008); Hospital beds: 0.0 per 10,000 population (2007); Hospital admissions: 0.0 per 10,000 population (2007).
Elections: 2008 Presidential election results: 75.7% Obama, 24.1% McCain, 0.0% Nader
Additional Information Contacts
Brooks County Government . . . . (361) 325-5604
    http://www.co.brooks.tx.us/ips/cms
City of Falfurrias . . . . (361) 325-2420
    http://www.falfurrias-tx.com
Falfurrias Chamber of Commerce . . . . (361) 325-3333

Brooks County Communities

AIRPORT ROAD ADDITION (CDP). Covers a land area of 2.112 square miles and a water area of 0 square miles. Located at 27.22° N. Lat; 98.10° W. Long. Elevation is 102 feet.
Population: 115 (1990); 132 (2000); 134 (2010); 135 (2015 projected); Race: 80.6% White, 0.0% Black, 0.0% Asian, 19.4% Other, 84.3% Hispanic of any race (2010); Density: 63.4 persons per square mile (2010); Average household size: 2.98 (2010); Median age: 36.5 (2010); Males per 100 females: 112.7 (2010); Marriage status: 16.4% never married, 52.5% now married, 13.1% widowed, 18.0% divorced (2005-2009 5-year est.); Foreign born: 0.0% (2005-2009 5-year est.); Ancestry (includes multiple ancestries): 13.3% American (2005-2009 5-year est.).
Economy: Employment by occupation: 0.0% management, 58.1% professional, 41.9% services, 0.0% sales, 0.0% farming, 0.0% construction, 0.0% production (2005-2009 5-year est.).
Income: Per capita income: $14,490 (2010); Median household income: $32,222 (2010); Average household income: $41,889 (2010); Percent of households with income of $100,000 or more: 4.4% (2010); Poverty rate: 0.0% (2005-2009 5-year est.).
Education: Percent of population age 25 and over with: High school diploma (including GED) or higher: 68.2% (2010); Bachelor's degree or higher: 10.6% (2010); Master's degree or higher: 4.7% (2010).
Housing: Homeownership rate: 77.8% (2010); Median home value: $76,250 (2010); Median contract rent: n/a per month (2005-2009 5-year est.); Median year structure built: 1962 (2005-2009 5-year est.).
Transportation: Commute to work: 100.0% car, 0.0% public transportation, 0.0% walk, 0.0% work from home (2005-2009 5-year est.); Travel time to work: 32.6% less than 15 minutes, 0.0% 15 to 30 minutes, 41.9% 30 to 45 minutes, 0.0% 45 to 60 minutes, 25.6% 60 minutes or more (2005-2009 5-year est.)

CANTU ADDITION (CDP). Covers a land area of 0.300 square miles and a water area of 0 square miles. Located at 27.20° N. Lat; 98.15° W. Long. Elevation is 112 feet.
Population: 134 (1990); 217 (2000); 186 (2010); 172 (2015 projected); Race: 73.1% White, 0.5% Black, 0.5% Asian, 25.8% Other, 93.0% Hispanic of any race (2010); Density: 619.8 persons per square mile (2010); Average household size: 2.76 (2010); Median age: 35.6 (2010); Males per 100 females: 91.8 (2010); Marriage status: 51.8% never married, 0.0% now married, 0.0% widowed, 48.2% divorced (2005-2009 5-year est.); Foreign born: 0.0% (2005-2009 5-year est.); Ancestry (includes multiple ancestries): n/a (2005-2009 5-year est.).
Economy: Employment by occupation: n/a management, n/a professional, n/a services, n/a sales, n/a farming, n/a construction, n/a production (2005-2009 5-year est.).
Income: Per capita income: $18,441 (2010); Median household income: $36,364 (2010); Average household income: $54,545 (2010); Percent of households with income of $100,000 or more: 13.6% (2010); Poverty rate: 100.0% (2005-2009 5-year est.).
Education: Percent of population age 25 and over with: High school diploma (including GED) or higher: 54.7% (2010); Bachelor's degree or higher: 12.0% (2010); Master's degree or higher: 7.7% (2010).
Housing: Homeownership rate: 63.6% (2010); Median home value: $56,667 (2010); Median contract rent: n/a per month (2005-2009 5-year est.); Median year structure built: 1976 (2005-2009 5-year est.).
Transportation: Commute to work: n/a car, n/a public transportation, n/a walk, n/a work from home (2005-2009 5-year est.); Travel time to work: n/a

less than 15 minutes, n/a 15 to 30 minutes, n/a 30 to 45 minutes, n/a 45 to 60 minutes, n/a 60 minutes or more (2005-2009 5-year est.)

ENCINO (CDP). Covers a land area of 6.752 square miles and a water area of 0 square miles. Located at 26.94° N. Lat; 98.11° W. Long. Elevation is 125 feet.

Population: 183 (1990); 177 (2000); 162 (2010); 155 (2015 projected); Race: 91.4% White, 0.6% Black, 0.0% Asian, 8.0% Other, 92.0% Hispanic of any race (2010); Density: 24.0 persons per square mile (2010); Average household size: 2.66 (2010); Median age: 46.7 (2010); Males per 100 females: 95.2 (2010); Marriage status: 51.3% never married, 23.1% now married, 25.6% widowed, 0.0% divorced (2005-2009 5-year est.); Foreign born: 0.0% (2005-2009 5-year est.); Ancestry (includes multiple ancestries): n/a (2005-2009 5-year est.).
Economy: Employment by occupation: 0.0% management, 0.0% professional, 8.0% services, 54.0% sales, 38.0% farming, 0.0% construction, 0.0% production (2005-2009 5-year est.).
Income: Per capita income: $19,069 (2010); Median household income: $39,375 (2010); Average household income: $55,697 (2010); Percent of households with income of $100,000 or more: 6.6% (2010); Poverty rate: 38.1% (2005-2009 5-year est.).
Education: Percent of population age 25 and over with: High school diploma (including GED) or higher: 47.0% (2010); Bachelor's degree or higher: 7.0% (2010); Master's degree or higher: 1.7% (2010).

School District(s)
Encino School (PK-08)
    2009-10 Enrollment: 40 . . . . (361) 568-3375
Housing: Homeownership rate: 78.7% (2010); Median home value: $40,000 (2010); Median contract rent: n/a per month (2005-2009 5-year est.); Median year structure built: 1971 (2005-2009 5-year est.).
Transportation: Commute to work: 100.0% car, 0.0% public transportation, 0.0% walk, 0.0% work from home (2005-2009 5-year est.); Travel time to work: 8.0% less than 15 minutes, 92.0% 15 to 30 minutes, 0.0% 30 to 45 minutes, 0.0% 45 to 60 minutes, 0.0% 60 minutes or more (2005-2009 5-year est.)
Airports: El Coyote Ranch (general aviation)

FALFURRIAS (city). County seat. Covers a land area of 2.750 square miles and a water area of 0 square miles. Located at 27.22° N. Lat; 98.14° W. Long. Elevation is 115 feet.

History: Falfurrias became the center of a dairying industry when Edward C. Lasater brought Jersey cows here in 1908. Early industries also included citrus fruit packing plants and cotton processing plants.
Population: 5,925 (1990); 5,297 (2000); 4,980 (2010); 4,831 (2015 projected); Race: 72.9% White, 0.3% Black, 0.1% Asian, 26.7% Other, 92.6% Hispanic of any race (2010); Density: 1,811.1 persons per square mile (2010); Average household size: 2.84 (2010); Median age: 33.7 (2010); Males per 100 females: 89.2 (2010); Marriage status: 26.3% never married, 51.5% now married, 16.9% widowed, 5.2% divorced (2005-2009 5-year est.); Foreign born: 5.5% (2005-2009 5-year est.); Ancestry (includes multiple ancestries): 2.5% Polish, 0.9% Swedish, 0.9% Norwegian, 0.8% German, 0.8% American (2005-2009 5-year est.).
Economy: Single-family building permits issued: 3 (2010); Multi-family building permits issued: 0 (2010); Employment by occupation: 4.5% management, 18.5% professional, 34.8% services, 23.6% sales, 0.6% farming, 12.0% construction, 6.0% production (2005-2009 5-year est.).
Income: Per capita income: $13,422 (2010); Median household income: $21,378 (2010); Average household income: $38,184 (2010); Percent of households with income of $100,000 or more: 5.7% (2010); Poverty rate: 35.1% (2005-2009 5-year est.).
Taxes: Total city taxes per capita: $239 (2007); City property taxes per capita: $58 (2007).
Education: Percent of population age 25 and over with: High school diploma (including GED) or higher: 53.0% (2010); Bachelor's degree or higher: 7.7% (2010); Master's degree or higher: 4.4% (2010).

School District(s)
Brooks County ISD (PK-12)
    2009-10 Enrollment: 1,495 . . . . (361) 325-8000
La Gloria ISD (PK-06)
    2009-10 Enrollment: 116 . . . . (361) 325-2330
Housing: Homeownership rate: 68.6% (2010); Median home value: $37,841 (2010); Median contract rent: $122 per month (2005-2009 5-year est.); Median year structure built: 1963 (2005-2009 5-year est.).
Safety: Violent crime rate: 71.3 per 10,000 population; Property crime rate: 517.7 per 10,000 population (2009).

Newspapers: Falfurrias Facts (Community news; Circulation 2,500)
Transportation: Commute to work: 88.8% car, 0.0% public transportation, 1.5% walk, 9.7% work from home (2005-2009 5-year est.); Travel time to work: 55.0% less than 15 minutes, 17.5% 15 to 30 minutes, 11.7% 30 to 45 minutes, 10.6% 45 to 60 minutes, 5.3% 60 minutes or more (2005-2009 5-year est.)
Airports: Brooks County (general aviation)
Additional Information Contacts
City of Falfurrias. . . . . (361) 325-2420
    http://www.falfurrias-tx.com
Falfurrias Chamber of Commerce . . . . (361) 325-3333

FLOWELLA (CDP). Covers a land area of 1.027 square miles and a water area of 0 square miles. Located at 27.21° N. Lat; 98.06° W. Long. Elevation is 95 feet.

Population: 94 (1990); 134 (2000); 141 (2010); 142 (2015 projected); Race: 80.9% White, 0.0% Black, 0.0% Asian, 19.1% Other, 84.4% Hispanic of any race (2010); Density: 137.4 persons per square mile (2010); Average household size: 2.94 (2010); Median age: 40.7 (2010); Males per 100 females: 110.4 (2010); Marriage status: 26.7% never married, 51.2% now married, 22.1% widowed, 0.0% divorced (2005-2009 5-year est.); Foreign born: 0.0% (2005-2009 5-year est.); Ancestry (includes multiple ancestries): n/a (2005-2009 5-year est.).
Economy: Employment by occupation: 17.6% management, 41.2% professional, 0.0% services, 41.2% sales, 0.0% farming, 0.0% construction, 0.0% production (2005-2009 5-year est.).
Income: Per capita income: $14,490 (2010); Median household income: $32,000 (2010); Average household income: $41,719 (2010); Percent of households with income of $100,000 or more: 4.2% (2010); Poverty rate: 58.1% (2005-2009 5-year est.).
Education: Percent of population age 25 and over with: High school diploma (including GED) or higher: 67.7% (2010); Bachelor's degree or higher: 10.8% (2010); Master's degree or higher: 5.4% (2010).
Housing: Homeownership rate: 77.1% (2010); Median home value: $71,250 (2010); Median contract rent: n/a per month (2005-2009 5-year est.); Median year structure built: 1968 (2005-2009 5-year est.).
Transportation: Commute to work: 100.0% car, 0.0% public transportation, 0.0% walk, 0.0% work from home (2005-2009 5-year est.); Travel time to work: 82.4% less than 15 minutes, 17.6% 15 to 30 minutes, 0.0% 30 to 45 minutes, 0.0% 45 to 60 minutes, 0.0% 60 minutes or more (2005-2009 5-year est.)

Brown County

Located in central Texas; bounded on the south by the Colorado River; includes Lake Brownwood. Covers a land area of 943.85 square miles, a water area of 13.08 square miles, and is located in the Central Time Zone at 31.77° N. Lat., 98.99° W. Long. The county was founded in 1856. County seat is Brownwood.

Brown County is part of the Brownwood, TX Micropolitan Statistical Area. The entire metro area includes: Brown County, TX

Weather Station: Brownwood									Elevation: 1,384 feet			
	Jan	Feb	Mar	Apr	May	Jun	Jul	Aug	Sep	Oct	Nov	Dec
High	60	64	71	80	86	92	96	97	90	80	69	61
Low	32	36	43	51	61	67	70	70	63	52	42	33
Precip	1.3	2.4	2.6	2.2	4.0	4.7	1.8	2.4	3.0	3.0	1.8	1.6
Snow	0.4	tr	tr	0.1	0.0	0.0	0.0	0.0	0.0	0.0	0.1	0.4

High and Low temperatures in degrees Fahrenheit; Precipitation and Snow in inches

Population: 34,371 (1990); 37,674 (2000); 38,917 (2010); 39,452 (2015 projected); Race: 85.1% White, 4.0% Black, 0.7% Asian, 10.2% Other, 18.6% Hispanic of any race (2010); Density: 41.2 persons per square mile (2010); Average household size: 2.46 (2010); Median age: 37.1 (2010); Males per 100 females: 97.8 (2010).
Religion: Five largest groups: 45.8% Southern Baptist Convention, 8.9% The United Methodist Church, 6.1% Catholic Church, 5.0% Churches of Christ, 1.1% Independent, Charismatic Churches (2000).
Economy: Unemployment rate: 8.0% (June 2011); Total civilian labor force: 18,477 (June 2011); Leading industries: 23.7% health care and social assistance; 21.9% manufacturing; 15.7% retail trade (2009); Farms: 1,726 totaling 560,065 acres (2007); Companies that employ 500 or more persons: 5 (2009); Companies that employ 100 to 499 persons: 6 (2009); Companies that employ less than 100 persons: 894 (2009); Black-owned businesses: n/a (2007); Hispanic-owned businesses: n/a (2007);

Asian-owned businesses: n/a (2007); Women-owned businesses: 740 (2007); Retail sales per capita: $13,583 (2010). Single-family building permits issued: 17 (2010); Multi-family building permits issued: 4 (2010).
Income: Per capita income: $20,289 (2010); Median household income: $40,495 (2010); Average household income: $51,841 (2010); Percent of households with income of $100,000 or more: 10.3% (2010); Poverty rate: 17.9% (2009); Bankruptcy rate: 1.42% (2010).
Taxes: Total county taxes per capita: $226 (2007); County property taxes per capita: $194 (2007).
Education: Percent of population age 25 and over with: High school diploma (including GED) or higher: 80.8% (2010); Bachelor's degree or higher: 15.5% (2010); Master's degree or higher: 4.6% (2010).
Housing: Homeownership rate: 72.5% (2010); Median home value: $66,801 (2010); Median contract rent: $399 per month (2005-2009 5-year est.); Median year structure built: 1972 (2005-2009 5-year est.)
Health: Birth rate: 126.3 per 10,000 population (2009); Death rate: 123.1 per 10,000 population (2009); Age-adjusted cancer mortality rate: 211.9 deaths per 100,000 population (2007); Number of physicians: 16.5 per 10,000 population (2008); Hospital beds: 43.9 per 10,000 population (2007); Hospital admissions: 1,632.3 per 10,000 population (2007).
Elections: 2008 Presidential election results: 18.8% Obama, 80.3% McCain, 0.1% Nader
National and State Parks: Lake Brownwood State Park
Additional Information Contacts
Brown County Government . . . . (325) 643-2828
    http://www.browncountytx.org/ips/cms
Brownwood Area Chamber of Commerce . . . . (325) 646-9535
    http://www.brownwoodchamber.org
City of Brownwood . . . . (325) 646-5775
    http://www.ci.brownwood.tx.us

Brown County Communities

BANGS (city). Covers a land area of 1.382 square miles and a water area of 0 square miles. Located at 31.71° N. Lat; 99.13° W. Long. Elevation is 1,608 feet.
Population: 1,555 (1990); 1,620 (2000); 1,560 (2010); 1,533 (2015 projected); Race: 84.0% White, 3.7% Black, 0.0% Asian, 12.2% Other, 13.9% Hispanic of any race (2010); Density: 1,128.5 persons per square mile (2010); Average household size: 2.41 (2010); Median age: 39.2 (2010); Males per 100 females: 87.7 (2010); Marriage status: 23.4% never married, 44.6% now married, 15.8% widowed, 16.2% divorced (2005-2009 5-year est.); Foreign born: 0.6% (2005-2009 5-year est.); Ancestry (includes multiple ancestries): 29.9% English, 10.8% German, 10.5% Irish, 9.1% American, 2.6% Dutch (2005-2009 5-year est.).
Economy: Single-family building permits issued: 2 (2010); Multi-family building permits issued: 0 (2010); Employment by occupation: 4.6% management, 21.3% professional, 25.8% services, 24.5% sales, 0.8% farming, 6.9% construction, 16.0% production (2005-2009 5-year est.).
Income: Per capita income: $19,178 (2010); Median household income: $36,026 (2010); Average household income: $46,397 (2010); Percent of households with income of $100,000 or more: 6.0% (2010); Poverty rate: 14.3% (2005-2009 5-year est.).
Taxes: Total city taxes per capita: $187 (2007); City property taxes per capita: $92 (2007).
Education: Percent of population age 25 and over with: High school diploma (including GED) or higher: 76.1% (2010); Bachelor's degree or higher: 11.6% (2010); Master's degree or higher: 3.7% (2010).
School District(s)
Bangs ISD (PK-12)
    2009-10 Enrollment: 1,098 . . . . (325) 752-6612
Housing: Homeownership rate: 70.4% (2010); Median home value: $46,635 (2010); Median contract rent: $226 per month (2005-2009 5-year est.); Median year structure built: 1965 (2005-2009 5-year est.).
Safety: Violent crime rate: 25.6 per 10,000 population; Property crime rate: 70.5 per 10,000 population (2009).
Transportation: Commute to work: 93.2% car, 0.0% public transportation, 3.0% walk, 2.3% work from home (2005-2009 5-year est.); Travel time to work: 21.6% less than 15 minutes, 63.1% 15 to 30 minutes, 13.5% 30 to 45 minutes, 0.0% 45 to 60 minutes, 1.9% 60 minutes or more (2005-2009 5-year est.)

BLANKET (town). Covers a land area of 0.575 square miles and a water area of 0 square miles. Located at 31.82° N. Lat; 98.78° W. Long. Elevation is 1,621 feet.

Population: 383 (1990); 402 (2000); 473 (2010); 499 (2015 projected); Race: 91.5% White, 0.8% Black, 0.4% Asian, 7.2% Other, 6.1% Hispanic of any race (2010); Density: 823.0 persons per square mile (2010); Average household size: 2.58 (2010); Median age: 40.3 (2010); Males per 100 females: 101.3 (2010); Marriage status: 31.7% never married, 57.9% now married, 5.0% widowed, 5.3% divorced (2005-2009 5-year est.); Foreign born: 7.6% (2005-2009 5-year est.); Ancestry (includes multiple ancestries): 25.2% English, 13.8% German, 8.0% Irish, 5.8% American, 2.3% Dutch (2005-2009 5-year est.).
Economy: Single-family building permits issued: 0 (2010); Multi-family building permits issued: 0 (2010); Employment by occupation: 7.1% management, 3.2% professional, 3.2% services, 29.4% sales, 1.6% farming, 20.6% construction, 34.9% production (2005-2009 5-year est.).
Income: Per capita income: $23,099 (2010); Median household income: $52,926 (2010); Average household income: $57,377 (2010); Percent of households with income of $100,000 or more: 11.5% (2010); Poverty rate: 26.5% (2005-2009 5-year est.).
Taxes: Total city taxes per capita: $59 (2007); City property taxes per capita: $34 (2007).
Education: Percent of population age 25 and over with: High school diploma (including GED) or higher: 87.6% (2010); Bachelor's degree or higher: 15.2% (2010); Master's degree or higher: 3.4% (2010).
School District(s)
Blanket ISD (PK-12)
    2009-10 Enrollment: 227 . . . . (325) 748-5311
Housing: Homeownership rate: 85.2% (2010); Median home value: $88,000 (2010); Median contract rent: $473 per month (2005-2009 5-year est.); Median year structure built: 1944 (2005-2009 5-year est.).
Transportation: Commute to work: 97.6% car, 0.0% public transportation, 2.4% walk, 0.0% work from home (2005-2009 5-year est.); Travel time to work: 5.6% less than 15 minutes, 49.2% 15 to 30 minutes, 38.9% 30 to 45 minutes, 4.0% 45 to 60 minutes, 2.4% 60 minutes or more (2005-2009 5-year est.)

BROOKESMITH (unincorporated postal area, zip code 76827). Covers a land area of 85.985 square miles and a water area of 0.352 square miles. Located at 31.54° N. Lat; 99.13° W. Long. Elevation is 1,348 feet.
Population: 478 (2000); Race: 99.2% White, 0.8% Black, 0.0% Asian, 0.0% Other, 5.8% Hispanic of any race (2000); Density: 5.6 persons per square mile (2000); Age: 33.3% under 18, 7.9% over 64 (2000); Marriage status: 20.3% never married, 67.1% now married, 5.3% widowed, 7.2% divorced (2000); Foreign born: 2.3% (2000); Ancestry (includes multiple ancestries): 18.3% American, 11.9% German, 9.6% English, 7.7% Irish (2000).
Economy: Employment by occupation: 16.1% management, 20.3% professional, 10.6% services, 18.9% sales, 0.5% farming, 10.1% construction, 23.5% production (2000).
Income: Per capita income: $22,577 (2000); Median household income: $43,125 (2000); Poverty rate: 179.1% (2000).
Education: Percent of population age 25 and over with: High school diploma (including GED) or higher: 89.2% (2000); Bachelor's degree or higher: 18.2% (2000).
School District(s)
Brookesmith ISD (PK-12)
    2009-10 Enrollment: 183 . . . . (325) 643-3023
Housing: Homeownership rate: 89.9% (2000); Median home value: $31,700 (2000); Median contract rent: $425 per month (2000); Median year structure built: 1981 (2000).
Transportation: Commute to work: 94.5% car, 0.0% public transportation, 0.9% walk, 4.6% work from home (2000); Travel time to work: 15.9% less than 15 minutes, 57.0% 15 to 30 minutes, 14.0% 30 to 45 minutes, 2.9% 45 to 60 minutes, 10.1% 60 minutes or more (2000)

BROWNWOOD (city). County seat. Covers a land area of 12.599 square miles and a water area of 0 square miles. Located at 31.70° N. Lat; 98.98° W. Long. Elevation is 1,365 feet.
History: Brownwood developed as a shipping center of cotton, farm products, and oil.
Population: 18,657 (1990); 18,813 (2000); 18,841 (2010); 18,802 (2015 projected); Race: 80.7% White, 5.5% Black, 1.0% Asian, 12.8% Other, 26.5% Hispanic of any race (2010); Density: 1,495.5 persons per square mile (2010); Average household size: 2.46 (2010); Median age: 33.4 (2010); Males per 100 females: 93.7 (2010); Marriage status: 24.6% never married, 51.4% now married, 11.2% widowed, 12.8% divorced (2005-2009

5-year est.); Foreign born: 4.9% (2005-2009 5-year est.); Ancestry (includes multiple ancestries): 18.2% English, 12.3% German, 10.7% Irish, 10.4% American, 2.6% Scotch-Irish (2005-2009 5-year est.).
Economy: Single-family building permits issued: 9 (2010); Multi-family building permits issued: 4 (2010); Employment by occupation: 7.9% management, 17.3% professional, 19.2% services, 24.0% sales, 1.2% farming, 8.3% construction, 22.0% production (2005-2009 5-year est.).
Income: Per capita income: $17,964 (2010); Median household income: $35,609 (2010); Average household income: $46,551 (2010); Percent of households with income of $100,000 or more: 9.1% (2010); Poverty rate: 23.0% (2005-2009 5-year est.).
Taxes: Total city taxes per capita: $636 (2007); City property taxes per capita: $212 (2007).
Education: Percent of population age 25 and over with: High school diploma (including GED) or higher: 78.1% (2010); Bachelor's degree or higher: 16.5% (2010); Master's degree or higher: 5.0% (2010).

School District(s)
Brownwood ISD (PK-12)
   2009-10 Enrollment: 3,525 . . . . (325) 643-5644
Ron Jackson State Juvenile Corr Complex Unit I (07-12)
   2009-10 Enrollment: 142 . . . . (325) 641-4200
Ron Jackson State Juvenile Corr Complex Unit II (09-12)
   2009-10 Enrollment: 38 . . . . (325) 641-4277

Four-year College(s)
Howard Payne University (Private, Not-for-profit, Baptist)
   Fall 2009 Enrollment: 1,232 . . . . (325) 646-2502
   2010-11 Tuition: In-state $19,950; Out-of-state $19,950
Housing: Homeownership rate: 62.0% (2010); Median home value: $55,321 (2010); Median contract rent: $410 per month (2005-2009 5-year est.); Median year structure built: 1966 (2005-2009 5-year est.).
Hospitals: Brownwood Regional Medical Center (196 beds)
Safety: Violent crime rate: 46.0 per 10,000 population; Property crime rate: 425.8 per 10,000 population (2009).
Newspapers: Brownwood Bulletin (Regional news)
Transportation: Commute to work: 92.5% car, 0.2% public transportation, 2.2% walk, 1.3% work from home (2005-2009 5-year est.); Travel time to work: 70.5% less than 15 minutes, 21.1% 15 to 30 minutes, 4.7% 30 to 45 minutes, 1.3% 45 to 60 minutes, 2.4% 60 minutes or more (2005-2009 5-year est.)
Airports: Brownwood Regional (general aviation)
Additional Information Contacts
Brownwood Area Chamber of Commerce . . . . (325) 646-9535
   http://www.brownwoodchamber.org
City of Brownwood . . . . (325) 646-5775
   http://www.ci.brownwood.tx.us

EARLY (city).
Covers a land area of 2.567 square miles and a water area of 0 square miles. Located at 31.74° N. Lat; 98.94° W. Long. Elevation is 1,414 feet.
Population: 2,707 (1990); 2,588 (2000); 2,737 (2010); 2,807 (2015 projected); Race: 92.8% White, 0.7% Black, 0.7% Asian, 5.8% Other, 11.4% Hispanic of any race (2010); Density: 1,066.2 persons per square mile (2010); Average household size: 2.64 (2010); Median age: 37.3 (2010); Males per 100 females: 92.6 (2010); Marriage status: 19.7% never married, 68.6% now married, 2.6% widowed, 9.1% divorced (2005-2009 5-year est.); Foreign born: 5.2% (2005-2009 5-year est.); Ancestry (includes multiple ancestries): 17.9% English, 16.6% German, 11.0% Irish, 5.4% American, 2.9% Italian (2005-2009 5-year est.).
Economy: Single-family building permits issued: 6 (2010); Multi-family building permits issued: 0 (2010); Employment by occupation: 8.5% management, 26.6% professional, 20.5% services, 19.8% sales, 0.0% farming, 7.2% construction, 17.3% production (2005-2009 5-year est.).
Income: Per capita income: $22,093 (2010); Median household income: $45,119 (2010); Average household income: $59,456 (2010); Percent of households with income of $100,000 or more: 12.8% (2010); Poverty rate: 13.6% (2005-2009 5-year est.).
Taxes: Total city taxes per capita: $425 (2007); City property taxes per capita: $46 (2007).
Education: Percent of population age 25 and over with: High school diploma (including GED) or higher: 85.1% (2010); Bachelor's degree or higher: 15.2% (2010); Master's degree or higher: 4.6% (2010).

School District(s)
Bangs ISD (PK-12)
   2009-10 Enrollment: 1,098 . . . . (325) 752-6612

Early ISD (PK-12)
   2009-10 Enrollment: 1,258 . . . . (325) 646-7934
Novice ISD (PK-12)
   2009-10 Enrollment: 107 . . . . (325) 625-4069
Paradigm Accelerated Charter School (07-12)
   2009-10 Enrollment: 219 . . . . (254) 445-4844
Housing: Homeownership rate: 76.8% (2010); Median home value: $75,238 (2010); Median contract rent: $444 per month (2005-2009 5-year est.); Median year structure built: 1974 (2005-2009 5-year est.).
Safety: Violent crime rate: 3.6 per 10,000 population; Property crime rate: 234.3 per 10,000 population (2009).
Transportation: Commute to work: 93.5% car, 0.0% public transportation, 2.3% walk, 4.1% work from home (2005-2009 5-year est.); Travel time to work: 55.3% less than 15 minutes, 38.9% 15 to 30 minutes, 2.4% 30 to 45 minutes, 0.0% 45 to 60 minutes, 3.3% 60 minutes or more (2005-2009 5-year est.)

LAKE BROWNWOOD (CDP).
Covers a land area of 5.725 square miles and a water area of 0.010 square miles. Located at 31.82° N. Lat; 99.09° W. Long. Elevation is 1,444 feet.
Population: 1,221 (1990); 1,694 (2000); 1,808 (2010); 1,859 (2015 projected); Race: 81.8% White, 1.6% Black, 0.0% Asian, 16.6% Other, 14.0% Hispanic of any race (2010); Density: 315.8 persons per square mile (2010); Average household size: 2.32 (2010); Median age: 42.7 (2010); Males per 100 females: 102.2 (2010); Marriage status: 13.9% never married, 72.7% now married, 2.1% widowed, 11.4% divorced (2005-2009 5-year est.); Foreign born: 1.1% (2005-2009 5-year est.); Ancestry (includes multiple ancestries): 28.4% English, 8.3% German, 8.1% Irish, 7.8% Scottish, 6.0% Austrian (2005-2009 5-year est.).
Economy: Employment by occupation: 5.2% management, 19.9% professional, 15.4% services, 25.1% sales, 3.9% farming, 6.3% construction, 24.3% production (2005-2009 5-year est.).
Income: Per capita income: $15,195 (2010); Median household income: $30,866 (2010); Average household income: $35,283 (2010); Percent of households with income of $100,000 or more: 1.0% (2010); Poverty rate: 11.7% (2005-2009 5-year est.).
Education: Percent of population age 25 and over with: High school diploma (including GED) or higher: 80.7% (2010); Bachelor's degree or higher: 5.5% (2010); Master's degree or higher: 1.5% (2010).
Housing: Homeownership rate: 82.3% (2010); Median home value: $54,557 (2010); Median contract rent: $193 per month (2005-2009 5-year est.); Median year structure built: 1974 (2005-2009 5-year est.).
Transportation: Commute to work: 91.3% car, 0.0% public transportation, 5.6% walk, 1.8% work from home (2005-2009 5-year est.); Travel time to work: 16.8% less than 15 minutes, 65.0% 15 to 30 minutes, 11.5% 30 to 45 minutes, 0.0% 45 to 60 minutes, 6.7% 60 minutes or more (2005-2009 5-year est.)

MAY (unincorporated postal area, zip code 76857).
Covers a land area of 128.833 square miles and a water area of 0.176 square miles. Located at 31.91° N. Lat; 98.95° W. Long. Elevation is 1,667 feet.
Population: 1,611 (2000); Race: 96.7% White, 0.0% Black, 0.2% Asian, 3.1% Other, 4.0% Hispanic of any race (2000); Density: 12.5 persons per square mile (2000); Age: 21.6% under 18, 21.9% over 64 (2000); Marriage status: 14.2% never married, 69.3% now married, 6.7% widowed, 9.8% divorced (2000); Foreign born: 2.8% (2000); Ancestry (includes multiple ancestries): 25.1% American, 12.2% Irish, 8.9% English, 8.9% German (2000).
Economy: Employment by occupation: 15.0% management, 11.8% professional, 11.1% services, 26.8% sales, 2.2% farming, 12.7% construction, 20.5% production (2000).
Income: Per capita income: $16,621 (2000); Median household income: $32,188 (2000); Poverty rate: 179.1% (2000).
Education: Percent of population age 25 and over with: High school diploma (including GED) or higher: 75.5% (2000); Bachelor's degree or higher: 15.2% (2000).

School District(s)
May ISD (PK-12)
   2009-10 Enrollment: 253 . . . . (254) 259-2091
Housing: Homeownership rate: 86.7% (2000); Median home value: $38,300 (2000); Median contract rent: $167 per month (2000); Median year structure built: 1981 (2000).
Transportation: Commute to work: 93.0% car, 0.0% public transportation, 0.6% walk, 4.7% work from home (2000); Travel time to work: 21.4% less

than 15 minutes, 27.3% 15 to 30 minutes, 38.9% 30 to 45 minutes, 4.3% 45 to 60 minutes, 8.1% 60 minutes or more (2000)

ZEPHYR (unincorporated postal area, zip code 76890). Covers a land area of 96.118 square miles and a water area of 0.323 square miles. Located at 31.68° N. Lat; 98.77° W. Long. Elevation is 1,519 feet.
Population: 972 (2000); Race: 92.6% White, 0.6% Black, 0.0% Asian, 6.8% Other, 9.1% Hispanic of any race (2000); Density: 10.1 persons per square mile (2000); Age: 26.0% under 18, 17.1% over 64 (2000); Marriage status: 16.7% never married, 69.7% now married, 7.2% widowed, 6.4% divorced (2000); Foreign born: 5.0% (2000); Ancestry (includes multiple ancestries): 13.8% American, 11.1% German, 8.2% Irish, 7.6% English (2000).
Economy: Employment by occupation: 12.1% management, 15.9% professional, 15.1% services, 24.7% sales, 2.5% farming, 10.1% construction, 19.6% production (2000).
Income: Per capita income: $19,278 (2000); Median household income: $35,852 (2000); Poverty rate: 179.1% (2000).
Education: Percent of population age 25 and over with: High school diploma (including GED) or higher: 79.5% (2000); Bachelor's degree or higher: 17.1% (2000).

School District(s)
Zephyr ISD (PK-12)
　2009-10 Enrollment: 211 . . . . (325) 739-5331
Housing: Homeownership rate: 85.1% (2000); Median home value: $40,000 (2000); Median contract rent: $300 per month (2000); Median year structure built: 1976 (2000).
Transportation: Commute to work: 88.3% car, 0.0% public transportation, 1.8% walk, 8.7% work from home (2000); Travel time to work: 18.7% less than 15 minutes, 53.9% 15 to 30 minutes, 18.4% 30 to 45 minutes, 0.3% 45 to 60 minutes, 8.7% 60 minutes or more (2000)

Burleson County

Located in south central Texas; bounded on the northeast and east by the Brazos River, and on the south by Yegua Creek. Covers a land area of 665.54 square miles, a water area of 12.24 square miles, and is located in the Central Time Zone at 30.44° N. Lat., 96.61° W. Long. The county was founded in 1846. County seat is Caldwell.

Burleson County is part of the College Station-Bryan, TX Metropolitan Statistical Area. The entire metro area includes: Brazos County, TX; Burleson County, TX; Robertson County, TX

Weather Station: Somerville Dam											Elevation: 263 feet	
	Jan	Feb	Mar	Apr	May	Jun	Jul	Aug	Sep	Oct	Nov	Dec
High	61	64	71	78	85	92	95	96	91	82	71	63
Low	37	41	48	55	64	71	73	72	66	56	47	38
Precip	2.9	2.9	3.1	2.8	4.2	4.3	1.8	2.5	3.2	4.6	3.6	3.1
Snow	0.0	tr	0.0	0.0	0.0	0.0	0.0	0.0	0.0	0.0	0.0	0.0

High and Low temperatures in degrees Fahrenheit; Precipitation and Snow in inches

Population: 13,625 (1990); 16,470 (2000); 17,657 (2010); 18,202 (2015 projected); Race: 73.7% White, 13.5% Black, 0.2% Asian, 12.6% Other, 17.1% Hispanic of any race (2010); Density: 26.5 persons per square mile (2010); Average household size: 2.57 (2010); Median age: 40.0 (2010); Males per 100 females: 95.4 (2010).
Religion: Five largest groups: 23.0% Southern Baptist Convention, 9.2% Catholic Church, 5.6% The United Methodist Church, 3.2% Evangelical Lutheran Church in America, 1.4% United Church of Christ (2000).
Economy: Unemployment rate: 7.1% (June 2011); Total civilian labor force: 8,152 (June 2011); Leading industries: 19.6% retail trade; 13.1% accommodation & food services; 11.2% manufacturing (2009); Farms: 1,582 totaling 361,022 acres (2007); Companies that employ 500 or more persons: 0 (2009); Companies that employ 100 to 499 persons: 2 (2009); Companies that employ less than 100 persons: 303 (2009); Black-owned businesses: n/a (2007); Hispanic-owned businesses: n/a (2007); Asian-owned businesses: n/a (2007); Women-owned businesses: 391 (2007); Retail sales per capita: $9,034 (2010). Single-family building permits issued: 11 (2010); Multi-family building permits issued: 0 (2010).
Income: Per capita income: $22,339 (2010); Median household income: $44,868 (2010); Average household income: $57,560 (2010); Percent of households with income of $100,000 or more: 13.3% (2010); Poverty rate: 15.6% (2009); Bankruptcy rate: 0.57% (2010).
Taxes: Total county taxes per capita: $382 (2007); County property taxes per capita: $308 (2007).

Education: Percent of population age 25 and over with: High school diploma (including GED) or higher: 76.7% (2010); Bachelor's degree or higher: 14.8% (2010); Master's degree or higher: 3.9% (2010).
Housing: Homeownership rate: 78.1% (2010); Median home value: $77,895 (2010); Median contract rent: $385 per month (2005-2009 5-year est.); Median year structure built: 1980 (2005-2009 5-year est.)
Health: Birth rate: 136.4 per 10,000 population (2009); Death rate: 92.9 per 10,000 population (2009); Age-adjusted cancer mortality rate: 176.1 deaths per 100,000 population (2007); Number of physicians: 4.2 per 10,000 population (2008); Hospital beds: 15.1 per 10,000 population (2007); Hospital admissions: 210.7 per 10,000 population (2007).
Elections: 2008 Presidential election results: 30.8% Obama, 68.2% McCain, 0.0% Nader
National and State Parks: Birch Creek State Park
Additional Information Contacts
Burleson County Government . . . . (979) 567-2329
　http://www.co.burleson.tx.us
Burleson County Chamber of Commerce . . . . (979) 567-0000
　http://www.burlesoncountytx.com
Burleson County Chamber of Commerce . . . . (979) 596-2383
　http://www.burlesoncountytx.com

Burleson County Communities

CALDWELL (city). County seat. Covers a land area of 3.377 square miles and a water area of 0 square miles. Located at 30.52° N. Lat; 96.70° W. Long. Elevation is 384 feet.
Population: 3,181 (1990); 3,449 (2000); 3,909 (2010); 4,118 (2015 projected); Race: 67.5% White, 14.1% Black, 0.4% Asian, 18.0% Other, 25.7% Hispanic of any race (2010); Density: 1,157.7 persons per square mile (2010); Average household size: 2.67 (2010); Median age: 36.3 (2010); Males per 100 females: 90.6 (2010); Marriage status: 26.1% never married, 53.2% now married, 12.1% widowed, 8.7% divorced (2005-2009 5-year est.); Foreign born: 14.6% (2005-2009 5-year est.); Ancestry (includes multiple ancestries): 18.6% German, 11.0% Czech, 9.4% Irish, 6.5% English, 4.2% American (2005-2009 5-year est.).
Economy: Single-family building permits issued: 11 (2010); Multi-family building permits issued: 0 (2010); Employment by occupation: 7.7% management, 18.9% professional, 18.9% services, 15.1% sales, 3.9% farming, 21.5% construction, 14.0% production (2005-2009 5-year est.).
Income: Per capita income: $17,466 (2010); Median household income: $39,938 (2010); Average household income: $47,135 (2010); Percent of households with income of $100,000 or more: 8.2% (2010); Poverty rate: 20.7% (2005-2009 5-year est.).
Taxes: Total city taxes per capita: $387 (2007); City property taxes per capita: $169 (2007).
Education: Percent of population age 25 and over with: High school diploma (including GED) or higher: 75.3% (2010); Bachelor's degree or higher: 18.9% (2010); Master's degree or higher: 5.2% (2010).

School District(s)
Caldwell ISD (PK-12)
　2009-10 Enrollment: 1,887 . . . . (979) 567-9000
Dime Box ISD (PK-12)
　2009-10 Enrollment: 178 . . . . (979) 884-2324
Snook ISD (PK-12)
　2009-10 Enrollment: 517 . . . . (979) 272-8307
Somerville ISD (PK-12)
　2009-10 Enrollment: 462 . . . . (979) 596-2153
Housing: Homeownership rate: 64.2% (2010); Median home value: $72,688 (2010); Median contract rent: $416 per month (2005-2009 5-year est.); Median year structure built: 1970 (2005-2009 5-year est.).
Hospitals: Burleson St. Joseph Health Center
Safety: Violent crime rate: 8.0 per 10,000 population; Property crime rate: 72.1 per 10,000 population (2009).
Newspapers: Burleson County Citizen-Tribune (Local news; Circulation 4,200)
Transportation: Commute to work: 93.0% car, 0.0% public transportation, 0.7% walk, 6.3% work from home (2005-2009 5-year est.); Travel time to work: 42.8% less than 15 minutes, 13.5% 15 to 30 minutes, 35.1% 30 to 45 minutes, 4.2% 45 to 60 minutes, 4.4% 60 minutes or more (2005-2009 5-year est.)
Additional Information Contacts
Burleson County Chamber of Commerce . . . . (979) 567-0000
　http://www.burlesoncountytx.com

SNOOK (city). Covers a land area of 2.010 square miles and a water area of 0.003 square miles. Located at 30.49° N. Lat; 96.47° W. Long. Elevation is 240 feet.
Population: 489 (1990); 568 (2000); 594 (2010); 605 (2015 projected); Race: 72.7% White, 18.2% Black, 0.3% Asian, 8.8% Other, 13.0% Hispanic of any race (2010); Density: 295.5 persons per square mile (2010); Average household size: 2.58 (2010); Median age: 37.0 (2010); Males per 100 females: 100.0 (2010); Marriage status: 27.7% never married, 52.3% now married, 7.7% widowed, 12.3% divorced (2005-2009 5-year est.); Foreign born: 3.5% (2005-2009 5-year est.); Ancestry (includes multiple ancestries): 19.6% Czech, 18.0% German, 5.7% Polish, 4.2% Czechoslovakian, 3.3% African (2005-2009 5-year est.).
Economy: Employment by occupation: 17.4% management, 7.7% professional, 30.0% services, 17.9% sales, 0.0% farming, 22.2% construction, 4.8% production (2005-2009 5-year est.).
Income: Per capita income: $26,635 (2010); Median household income: $50,521 (2010); Average household income: $67,989 (2010); Percent of households with income of $100,000 or more: 17.8% (2010); Poverty rate: 31.0% (2005-2009 5-year est.).
Taxes: Total city taxes per capita: $339 (2007); City property taxes per capita: $98 (2007).
Education: Percent of population age 25 and over with: High school diploma (including GED) or higher: 78.6% (2010); Bachelor's degree or higher: 15.2% (2010); Master's degree or higher: 3.9% (2010).
School District(s)
Snook ISD (PK-12)
    2009-10 Enrollment: 517 . . . . (979) 272-8307
Housing: Homeownership rate: 75.7% (2010); Median home value: $80,000 (2010); Median contract rent: $285 per month (2005-2009 5-year est.); Median year structure built: 1969 (2005-2009 5-year est.).
Transportation: Commute to work: 99.5% car, 0.0% public transportation, 0.0% walk, 0.0% work from home (2005-2009 5-year est.); Travel time to work: 19.9% less than 15 minutes, 36.4% 15 to 30 minutes, 39.8% 30 to 45 minutes, 0.0% 45 to 60 minutes, 3.9% 60 minutes or more (2005-2009 5-year est.)

SOMERVILLE (city). Covers a land area of 2.984 square miles and a water area of 0.003 square miles. Located at 30.34° N. Lat; 96.53° W. Long. Elevation is 249 feet.
History: Established 1883.
Population: 1,542 (1990); 1,704 (2000); 1,741 (2010); 1,756 (2015 projected); Race: 60.1% White, 27.7% Black, 0.1% Asian, 12.1% Other, 19.7% Hispanic of any race (2010); Density: 583.5 persons per square mile (2010); Average household size: 2.62 (2010); Median age: 35.6 (2010); Males per 100 females: 94.5 (2010); Marriage status: 26.9% never married, 53.1% now married, 9.6% widowed, 10.4% divorced (2005-2009 5-year est.); Foreign born: 7.5% (2005-2009 5-year est.); Ancestry (includes multiple ancestries): 11.4% German, 4.2% English, 3.4% French, 2.9% Czech, 2.5% Scotch-Irish (2005-2009 5-year est.).
Economy: Single-family building permits issued: 0 (2010); Multi-family building permits issued: 0 (2010); Employment by occupation: 13.8% management, 13.5% professional, 24.3% services, 16.0% sales, 0.6% farming, 13.3% construction, 18.6% production (2005-2009 5-year est.).
Income: Per capita income: $16,785 (2010); Median household income: $32,000 (2010); Average household income: $44,109 (2010); Percent of households with income of $100,000 or more: 5.7% (2010); Poverty rate: 19.2% (2005-2009 5-year est.).
Taxes: Total city taxes per capita: $387 (2007); City property taxes per capita: $200 (2007).
Education: Percent of population age 25 and over with: High school diploma (including GED) or higher: 75.2% (2010); Bachelor's degree or higher: 11.6% (2010); Master's degree or higher: 4.7% (2010).
School District(s)
Somerville ISD (PK-12)
    2009-10 Enrollment: 462 . . . . (979) 596-2153
Housing: Homeownership rate: 74.4% (2010); Median home value: $64,699 (2010); Median contract rent: $371 per month (2005-2009 5-year est.); Median year structure built: 1968 (2005-2009 5-year est.).
Safety: Violent crime rate: 29.7 per 10,000 population; Property crime rate: 237.7 per 10,000 population (2009).
Transportation: Commute to work: 92.9% car, 0.0% public transportation, 2.6% walk, 0.0% work from home (2005-2009 5-year est.); Travel time to work: 34.0% less than 15 minutes, 21.2% 15 to 30 minutes, 32.8% 30 to 45

minutes, 6.0% 45 to 60 minutes, 6.0% 60 minutes or more (2005-2009 5-year est.)
Additional Information Contacts
Burleson County Chamber of Commerce . . . . (979) 596-2383
    http://www.burlesoncountytx.com

Burnet County

Located in central Texas; bounded on the west by the Colorado River. Covers a land area of 996.04 square miles, a water area of 24.93 square miles, and is located in the Central Time Zone at 30.71° N. Lat., 98.22° W. Long. The county was founded in 1852. County seat is Burnet.

Burnet County is part of the Marble Falls, TX Micropolitan Statistical Area. The entire metro area includes: Burnet County, TX

Weather Station: Burnet   Elevation: 1,274 feet

	Jan	Feb	Mar	Apr	May	Jun	Jul	Aug	Sep	Oct	Nov	Dec
High	60	63	70	78	84	89	93	94	88	79	69	60
Low	35	38	45	53	62	68	71	71	65	55	45	36
Precip	1.7	2.1	2.8	2.1	4.3	4.6	2.0	1.8	3.4	3.7	2.8	2.1
Snow	tr	tr	0.0	0.0	0.0	0.0	0.0	0.0	0.0	0.0	0.1	0.0

High and Low temperatures in degrees Fahrenheit; Precipitation and Snow in inches

Population: 22,687 (1990); 34,147 (2000); 45,925 (2010); 51,571 (2015 projected); Race: 87.5% White, 2.2% Black, 0.5% Asian, 9.8% Other, 17.4% Hispanic of any race (2010); Density: 46.1 persons per square mile (2010); Average household size: 2.57 (2010); Median age: 41.5 (2010); Males per 100 females: 93.5 (2010).
Religion: Five largest groups: 24.5% Southern Baptist Convention, 11.8% Catholic Church, 5.6% The United Methodist Church, 3.8% Churches of Christ, 2.5% Evangelical Lutheran Church in America (2000).
Economy: Unemployment rate: 7.5% (June 2011); Total civilian labor force: 22,789 (June 2011); Leading industries: 23.1% retail trade; 14.1% accommodation & food services; 13.3% health care and social assistance (2009); Farms: 1,531 totaling 482,149 acres (2007); Companies that employ 500 or more persons: 0 (2009); Companies that employ 100 to 499 persons: 9 (2009); Companies that employ less than 100 persons: 1,065 (2009); Black-owned businesses: n/a (2007); Hispanic-owned businesses: n/a (2007); Asian-owned businesses: n/a (2007); Women-owned businesses: 1,295 (2007); Retail sales per capita: $14,429 (2010). Single-family building permits issued: 189 (2010); Multi-family building permits issued: 0 (2010).
Income: Per capita income: $24,199 (2010); Median household income: $48,433 (2010); Average household income: $63,300 (2010); Percent of households with income of $100,000 or more: 15.8% (2010); Poverty rate: 13.0% (2009); Bankruptcy rate: 1.98% (2010).
Taxes: Total county taxes per capita: $301 (2007); County property taxes per capita: $266 (2007).
Education: Percent of population age 25 and over with: High school diploma (including GED) or higher: 81.3% (2010); Bachelor's degree or higher: 20.0% (2010); Master's degree or higher: 6.2% (2010).
Housing: Homeownership rate: 77.2% (2010); Median home value: $133,459 (2010); Median contract rent: $465 per month (2005-2009 5-year est.); Median year structure built: 1980 (2005-2009 5-year est.)
Health: Birth rate: 120.0 per 10,000 population (2009); Death rate: 106.5 per 10,000 population (2009); Age-adjusted cancer mortality rate: 146.0 deaths per 100,000 population (2007); Number of physicians: 10.1 per 10,000 population (2008); Hospital beds: 5.7 per 10,000 population (2007); Hospital admissions: 298.1 per 10,000 population (2007).
Elections: 2008 Presidential election results: 27.3% Obama, 71.4% McCain, 0.1% Nader
National and State Parks: Inks Lake State Park; Longhorn Cavern State Park
Additional Information Contacts
Burnet County Government . . . . (512) 756-5420
    http://www.burnetcountytexas.org
Burnet Chamber of Commerce . . . . (512) 756-4297
    http://www.burnetchamber.org
City of Burnet . . . . (512) 756-6093
    http://www.cityofburnet.com
City of Granite Shoals . . . . (830) 598-2424
    http://www.graniteshoals.org
City of Marble Falls . . . . (830) 693-3615
    http://www.ci.marble-falls.tx.us

Marble Falls/Lake LBJ Chamber of Commerce . . . . (830) 693-2815
http://www.marblefalls.org

Burnet County Communities

BERTRAM (city). Covers a land area of 1.088 square miles and a water area of 0 square miles. Located at 30.74° N. Lat; 98.05° W. Long. Elevation is 1,263 feet.
Population: 861 (1990); 1,122 (2000); 1,481 (2010); 1,667 (2015 projected); Race: 91.7% White, 1.6% Black, 0.3% Asian, 6.4% Other, 12.5% Hispanic of any race (2010); Density: 1,361.3 persons per square mile (2010); Average household size: 2.66 (2010); Median age: 41.7 (2010); Males per 100 females: 94.1 (2010); Marriage status: 24.6% never married, 53.3% now married, 10.7% widowed, 11.4% divorced (2005-2009 5-year est.); Foreign born: 6.1% (2005-2009 5-year est.); Ancestry (includes multiple ancestries): 19.6% English, 19.3% German, 18.3% Irish, 2.9% European, 2.5% Norwegian (2005-2009 5-year est.).
Economy: Single-family building permits issued: 2 (2010); Multi-family building permits issued: 0 (2010); Employment by occupation: 7.5% management, 5.1% professional, 25.0% services, 36.6% sales, 0.0% farming, 19.6% construction, 6.2% production (2005-2009 5-year est.).
Income: Per capita income: $27,640 (2010); Median household income: $59,852 (2010); Average household income: $75,568 (2010); Percent of households with income of $100,000 or more: 23.8% (2010); Poverty rate: 12.7% (2005-2009 5-year est.).
Taxes: Total city taxes per capita: $278 (2007); City property taxes per capita: $146 (2007).
Education: Percent of population age 25 and over with: High school diploma (including GED) or higher: 77.6% (2010); Bachelor's degree or higher: 13.5% (2010); Master's degree or higher: 5.0% (2010).
School District(s)
Burnet CISD (PK-12)
    2009-10 Enrollment: 3,366 . . . . (512) 756-2124
Housing: Homeownership rate: 83.2% (2010); Median home value: $131,151 (2010); Median contract rent: $628 per month (2005-2009 5-year est.); Median year structure built: 1968 (2005-2009 5-year est.).
Safety: Violent crime rate: 34.6 per 10,000 population; Property crime rate: 97.0 per 10,000 population (2009).
Transportation: Commute to work: 87.5% car, 0.0% public transportation, 0.5% walk, 6.1% work from home (2005-2009 5-year est.); Travel time to work: 17.9% less than 15 minutes, 35.4% 15 to 30 minutes, 25.4% 30 to 45 minutes, 15.0% 45 to 60 minutes, 6.3% 60 minutes or more (2005-2009 5-year est.)
Additional Information Contacts
Burnet Chamber of Commerce . . . . (512) 756-4297
    http://www.burnetchamber.org

BRIGGS (unincorporated postal area, zip code 78608). Covers a land area of 32.019 square miles and a water area of 0.014 square miles. Located at 30.93° N. Lat; 97.90° W. Long. Elevation is 1,102 feet.
Population: 279 (2000); Race: 94.4% White, 0.0% Black, 0.0% Asian, 5.6% Other, 5.0% Hispanic of any race (2000); Density: 8.7 persons per square mile (2000); Age: 27.6% under 18, 12.9% over 64 (2000); Marriage status: 15.5% never married, 80.1% now married, 4.4% widowed, 0.0% divorced (2000); Foreign born: 0.0% (2000); Ancestry (includes multiple ancestries): 15.4% German, 14.1% English, 7.8% Scotch-Irish, 7.8% American (2000).
Economy: Employment by occupation: 25.2% management, 0.0% professional, 4.9% services, 25.2% sales, 0.0% farming, 37.9% construction, 6.8% production (2000).
Income: Per capita income: $13,692 (2000); Median household income: $40,469 (2000); Poverty rate: 179.1% (2000).
Education: Percent of population age 25 and over with: High school diploma (including GED) or higher: 68.3% (2000); Bachelor's degree or higher: 11.9% (2000).
Housing: Homeownership rate: 89.2% (2000); Median home value: $63,300 (2000); Median contract rent: $375 per month (2000); Median year structure built: 1992 (2000).
Transportation: Commute to work: 94.5% car, 0.0% public transportation, 0.0% walk, 5.5% work from home (2000); Travel time to work: 16.3% less than 15 minutes, 17.4% 15 to 30 minutes, 8.1% 30 to 45 minutes, 14.0% 45 to 60 minutes, 44.2% 60 minutes or more (2000)

BURNET (city). County seat. Covers a land area of 6.832 square miles and a water area of 0 square miles. Located at 30.75° N. Lat; 98.22° W. Long. Elevation is 1,286 feet.
History: Burnet grew up near Fort Croghan, established in 1849 at the foot of Post Mountain. Burnet became a center for crushed stone, graphite, and farm products.
Population: 3,608 (1990); 4,735 (2000); 6,056 (2010); 6,673 (2015 projected); Race: 80.6% White, 7.8% Black, 0.7% Asian, 10.9% Other, 19.2% Hispanic of any race (2010); Density: 886.4 persons per square mile (2010); Average household size: 2.53 (2010); Median age: 37.8 (2010); Males per 100 females: 77.4 (2010); Marriage status: 28.9% never married, 47.7% now married, 11.9% widowed, 11.5% divorced (2005-2009 5-year est.); Foreign born: 3.7% (2005-2009 5-year est.); Ancestry (includes multiple ancestries): 20.6% German, 18.1% Irish, 13.3% English, 9.0% American, 3.5% French (2005-2009 5-year est.).
Economy: Single-family building permits issued: 19 (2010); Multi-family building permits issued: 0 (2010); Employment by occupation: 13.1% management, 17.5% professional, 13.1% services, 26.4% sales, 3.1% farming, 17.1% construction, 9.7% production (2005-2009 5-year est.).
Income: Per capita income: $18,275 (2010); Median household income: $38,919 (2010); Average household income: $50,535 (2010); Percent of households with income of $100,000 or more: 10.2% (2010); Poverty rate: 17.2% (2005-2009 5-year est.).
Taxes: Total city taxes per capita: $512 (2007); City property taxes per capita: $201 (2007).
Education: Percent of population age 25 and over with: High school diploma (including GED) or higher: 72.0% (2010); Bachelor's degree or higher: 12.2% (2010); Master's degree or higher: 4.4% (2010).
School District(s)
Burnet CISD (PK-12)
    2009-10 Enrollment: 3,366 . . . . (512) 756-2124
Housing: Homeownership rate: 64.0% (2010); Median home value: $106,980 (2010); Median contract rent: $431 per month (2005-2009 5-year est.); Median year structure built: 1973 (2005-2009 5-year est.).
Hospitals: Seton Highland Lakes (42 beds)
Safety: Violent crime rate: 19.7 per 10,000 population; Property crime rate: 137.6 per 10,000 population (2009).
Newspapers: Burnet Bulletin (Community news; Circulation 3,900)
Transportation: Commute to work: 90.6% car, 0.0% public transportation, 1.7% walk, 4.0% work from home (2005-2009 5-year est.); Travel time to work: 44.6% less than 15 minutes, 37.1% 15 to 30 minutes, 8.1% 30 to 45 minutes, 0.0% 45 to 60 minutes, 10.1% 60 minutes or more (2005-2009 5-year est.)
Airports: Burnet Municipal Kate Craddock Field (general aviation)
Additional Information Contacts
Burnet Chamber of Commerce . . . . (512) 756-4297
    http://www.burnetchamber.org
City of Burnet . . . . (512) 756-6093
    http://www.cityofburnet.com

COTTONWOOD SHORES (city). Covers a land area of 0.940 square miles and a water area of 0 square miles. Located at 30.55° N. Lat; 98.32° W. Long. Elevation is 830 feet.
Population: 585 (1990); 877 (2000); 1,195 (2010); 1,354 (2015 projected); Race: 86.9% White, 0.3% Black, 0.0% Asian, 12.7% Other, 20.7% Hispanic of any race (2010); Density: 1,271.2 persons per square mile (2010); Average household size: 2.77 (2010); Median age: 37.0 (2010); Males per 100 females: 99.5 (2010); Marriage status: 25.5% never married, 54.7% now married, 3.3% widowed, 16.5% divorced (2005-2009 5-year est.); Foreign born: 8.7% (2005-2009 5-year est.); Ancestry (includes multiple ancestries): 16.4% German, 9.3% Irish, 7.8% English, 4.9% American, 3.4% Scotch-Irish (2005-2009 5-year est.).
Economy: Single-family building permits issued: 2 (2010); Multi-family building permits issued: 0 (2010); Employment by occupation: 5.8% management, 11.7% professional, 19.5% services, 17.5% sales, 0.0% farming, 24.6% construction, 20.9% production (2005-2009 5-year est.).
Income: Per capita income: $24,444 (2010); Median household income: $52,987 (2010); Average household income: $67,459 (2010); Percent of households with income of $100,000 or more: 14.6% (2010); Poverty rate: 22.1% (2005-2009 5-year est.).
Taxes: Total city taxes per capita: $149 (2007); City property taxes per capita: $111 (2007).

Education: Percent of population age 25 and over with: High school diploma (including GED) or higher: 83.5% (2010); Bachelor's degree or higher: 22.3% (2010); Master's degree or higher: 7.7% (2010).
Housing: Homeownership rate: 81.0% (2010); Median home value: $97,442 (2010); Median contract rent: $530 per month (2005-2009 5-year est.); Median year structure built: 1981 (2005-2009 5-year est.).
Safety: Violent crime rate: 0.0 per 10,000 population; Property crime rate: 16.4 per 10,000 population (2009).
Transportation: Commute to work: 93.8% car, 0.0% public transportation, 0.0% walk, 5.0% work from home (2005-2009 5-year est.); Travel time to work: 39.4% less than 15 minutes, 35.5% 15 to 30 minutes, 13.1% 30 to 45 minutes, 2.8% 45 to 60 minutes, 9.2% 60 minutes or more (2005-2009 5-year est.)

GRANITE SHOALS (city). Covers a land area of 2.463 square miles and a water area of 0.779 square miles. Located at 30.58° N. Lat; 98.38° W. Long. Elevation is 879 feet.

Population: 1,423 (1990); 2,040 (2000); 2,582 (2010); 2,870 (2015 projected); Race: 74.8% White, 1.4% Black, 0.3% Asian, 23.5% Other, 40.3% Hispanic of any race (2010); Density: 1,048.3 persons per square mile (2010); Average household size: 2.71 (2010); Median age: 36.7 (2010); Males per 100 females: 101.6 (2010); Marriage status: 24.0% never married, 49.1% now married, 15.0% widowed, 11.9% divorced (2005-2009 5-year est.); Foreign born: 9.4% (2005-2009 5-year est.); Ancestry (includes multiple ancestries): 30.8% English, 17.7% German, 11.5% American, 7.5% Irish, 3.3% Scotch-Irish (2005-2009 5-year est.).
Economy: Single-family building permits issued: 11 (2010); Multi-family building permits issued: 0 (2010); Employment by occupation: 9.7% management, 8.3% professional, 15.9% services, 20.0% sales, 0.0% farming, 25.2% construction, 21.0% production (2005-2009 5-year est.).
Income: Per capita income: $18,054 (2010); Median household income: $35,368 (2010); Average household income: $48,758 (2010); Percent of households with income of $100,000 or more: 8.2% (2010); Poverty rate: 14.5% (2005-2009 5-year est.).
Taxes: Total city taxes per capita: $472 (2007); City property taxes per capita: $387 (2007).
Education: Percent of population age 25 and over with: High school diploma (including GED) or higher: 70.3% (2010); Bachelor's degree or higher: 13.6% (2010); Master's degree or higher: 5.0% (2010).

School District(s)

Marble Falls ISD (PK-12)
   2009-10 Enrollment: 4,011 . . . . (830) 693-4357
Housing: Homeownership rate: 79.6% (2010); Median home value: $85,524 (2010); Median contract rent: $393 per month (2005-2009 5-year est.); Median year structure built: 1975 (2005-2009 5-year est.).
Safety: Violent crime rate: 38.2 per 10,000 population; Property crime rate: 236.4 per 10,000 population (2009).
Transportation: Commute to work: 83.9% car, 0.0% public transportation, 0.7% walk, 12.9% work from home (2005-2009 5-year est.); Travel time to work: 21.6% less than 15 minutes, 26.7% 15 to 30 minutes, 17.2% 30 to 45 minutes, 0.0% 45 to 60 minutes, 34.5% 60 minutes or more (2005-2009 5-year est.)
Additional Information Contacts
City of Granite Shoals . . . . (830) 598-2424
   http://www.graniteshoals.org

HIGHLAND HAVEN (city). Covers a land area of 0.424 square miles and a water area of 0.116 square miles. Located at 30.60° N. Lat; 98.39° W. Long. Elevation is 843 feet.

Population: 313 (1990); 450 (2000); 511 (2010); 548 (2015 projected); Race: 94.1% White, 0.6% Black, 0.2% Asian, 5.1% Other, 10.0% Hispanic of any race (2010); Density: 1,204.9 persons per square mile (2010); Average household size: 2.17 (2010); Median age: 61.2 (2010); Males per 100 females: 98.1 (2010); Marriage status: 13.9% never married, 61.1% now married, 12.7% widowed, 12.3% divorced (2005-2009 5-year est.); Foreign born: 0.0% (2005-2009 5-year est.); Ancestry (includes multiple ancestries): 21.7% German, 19.7% English, 11.4% Irish, 8.1% Swiss, 7.0% American (2005-2009 5-year est.).
Economy: Single-family building permits issued: 3 (2010); Multi-family building permits issued: 0 (2010); Employment by occupation: 23.2% management, 18.1% professional, 5.2% services, 41.3% sales, 0.0% farming, 7.7% construction, 4.5% production (2005-2009 5-year est.).
Income: Per capita income: $31,728 (2010); Median household income: $56,154 (2010); Average household income: $67,797 (2010); Percent of

households with income of $100,000 or more: 16.5% (2010); Poverty rate: 4.6% (2005-2009 5-year est.).
Taxes: Total city taxes per capita: $144 (2007); City property taxes per capita: $111 (2007).
Education: Percent of population age 25 and over with: High school diploma (including GED) or higher: 86.5% (2010); Bachelor's degree or higher: 23.9% (2010); Master's degree or higher: 5.9% (2010).
Housing: Homeownership rate: 91.5% (2010); Median home value: $187,500 (2010); Median contract rent: $945 per month (2005-2009 5-year est.); Median year structure built: 1981 (2005-2009 5-year est.).
Transportation: Commute to work: 95.5% car, 0.0% public transportation, 0.0% walk, 4.5% work from home (2005-2009 5-year est.); Travel time to work: 6.8% less than 15 minutes, 52.0% 15 to 30 minutes, 15.5% 30 to 45 minutes, 2.7% 45 to 60 minutes, 23.0% 60 minutes or more (2005-2009 5-year est.)

MARBLE FALLS (city). Covers a land area of 6.144 square miles and a water area of 0.555 square miles. Located at 30.57° N. Lat; 98.27° W. Long. Elevation is 823 feet.

History: Marble Falls was established along the Colorado River, where the falls were formed by large rocks in the river. The town's early industry was the quarrying of granite.
Population: 4,055 (1990); 4,959 (2000); 7,115 (2010); 8,075 (2015 projected); Race: 86.4% White, 2.6% Black, 1.0% Asian, 10.0% Other, 22.9% Hispanic of any race (2010); Density: 1,158.0 persons per square mile (2010); Average household size: 2.50 (2010); Median age: 37.1 (2010); Males per 100 females: 91.6 (2010); Marriage status: 22.1% never married, 47.4% now married, 14.5% widowed, 15.9% divorced (2005-2009 5-year est.); Foreign born: 13.1% (2005-2009 5-year est.); Ancestry (includes multiple ancestries): 16.4% German, 14.3% English, 13.8% Irish, 3.5% French, 3.1% Scotch-Irish (2005-2009 5-year est.).
Economy: Single-family building permits issued: 10 (2010); Multi-family building permits issued: 0 (2010); Employment by occupation: 13.2% management, 9.9% professional, 20.6% services, 23.3% sales, 0.5% farming, 21.1% construction, 11.4% production (2005-2009 5-year est.).
Income: Per capita income: $20,799 (2010); Median household income: $39,749 (2010); Average household income: $52,496 (2010); Percent of households with income of $100,000 or more: 11.8% (2010); Poverty rate: 10.8% (2005-2009 5-year est.).
Taxes: Total city taxes per capita: $1,179 (2007); City property taxes per capita: $255 (2007).
Education: Percent of population age 25 and over with: High school diploma (including GED) or higher: 82.7% (2010); Bachelor's degree or higher: 19.3% (2010); Master's degree or higher: 6.5% (2010).

School District(s)

Marble Falls ISD (PK-12)
   2009-10 Enrollment: 4,011 . . . . (830) 693-4357
Housing: Homeownership rate: 59.1% (2010); Median home value: $127,530 (2010); Median contract rent: $518 per month (2005-2009 5-year est.); Median year structure built: 1978 (2005-2009 5-year est.).
Safety: Violent crime rate: 18.0 per 10,000 population; Property crime rate: 484.3 per 10,000 population (2009).
Newspapers: The Highlander (Local news; Circulation 6,800); Kingsland Current (Community news); Marble Falls Highlander (Local news; Circulation 6,800)
Transportation: Commute to work: 95.3% car, 0.0% public transportation, 1.8% walk, 2.4% work from home (2005-2009 5-year est.); Travel time to work: 46.8% less than 15 minutes, 32.2% 15 to 30 minutes, 14.8% 30 to 45 minutes, 2.6% 45 to 60 minutes, 3.7% 60 minutes or more (2005-2009 5-year est.)
Additional Information Contacts
City of Marble Falls . . . . (830) 693-3615
   http://www.ci.marble-falls.tx.us
Marble Falls/Lake LBJ Chamber of Commerce . . . . (830) 693-2815
   http://www.marblefalls.org

MEADOWLAKES (city). Covers a land area of 0.773 square miles and a water area of 0.012 square miles. Located at 30.56° N. Lat; 98.29° W. Long. Elevation is 804 feet.

Population: 514 (1990); 1,293 (2000); 2,176 (2010); 2,492 (2015 projected); Race: 96.5% White, 0.6% Black, 0.7% Asian, 2.2% Other, 7.4% Hispanic of any race (2010); Density: 2,815.9 persons per square mile (2010); Average household size: 2.34 (2010); Median age: 55.9 (2010); Males per 100 females: 92.1 (2010); Marriage status: 6.3% never married, 72.3% now married, 12.0% widowed, 9.4% divorced (2005-2009 5-year est.); Foreign born: 2.1% (2005-2009 5-year est.); Ancestry (includes multiple ancestries): 25.0% German, 21.4% English, 12.3% American, 11.4% Irish, 10.0% Scotch-Irish (2005-2009 5-year est.).

Economy: Single-family building permits issued: 5 (2010); Multi-family building permits issued: 0 (2010); Employment by occupation: 18.1% management, 26.8% professional, 13.5% services, 32.5% sales, 0.0% farming, 3.4% construction, 5.7% production (2005-2009 5-year est.).

Income: Per capita income: $32,513 (2010); Median household income: $59,424 (2010); Average household income: $76,258 (2010); Percent of households with income of $100,000 or more: 23.4% (2010); Poverty rate: 2.7% (2005-2009 5-year est.).

Taxes: Total city taxes per capita: $90 (2007); City property taxes per capita: $56 (2007).

Education: Percent of population age 25 and over with: High school diploma (including GED) or higher: 93.8% (2010); Bachelor's degree or higher: 41.6% (2010); Master's degree or higher: 15.2% (2010).

Housing: Homeownership rate: 82.1% (2010); Median home value: $218,266 (2010); Median contract rent: $1,121 per month (2005-2009 5-year est.); Median year structure built: 1993 (2005-2009 5-year est.).

Transportation: Commute to work: 88.4% car, 0.0% public transportation, 0.5% walk, 9.2% work from home (2005-2009 5-year est.); Travel time to work: 56.7% less than 15 minutes, 27.0% 15 to 30 minutes, 3.0% 30 to 45 minutes, 4.1% 45 to 60 minutes, 9.3% 60 minutes or more (2005-2009 5-year est.)

SPICEWOOD (unincorporated postal area, zip code 78669). Covers a land area of 74.259 square miles and a water area of 0.130 square miles. Located at 30.42° N. Lat; 98.08° W. Long. Elevation is 768 feet.

Population: 5,527 (2000); Race: 96.5% White, 0.0% Black, 0.1% Asian, 3.4% Other, 6.9% Hispanic of any race (2000); Density: 74.4 persons per square mile (2000); Age: 22.4% under 18, 11.6% over 64 (2000); Marriage status: 16.6% never married, 68.8% now married, 4.5% widowed, 10.1% divorced (2000); Foreign born: 2.6% (2000); Ancestry (includes multiple ancestries): 24.2% German, 16.5% English, 13.3% Irish, 10.8% American (2000).

Economy: Employment by occupation: 21.2% management, 24.0% professional, 8.5% services, 28.8% sales, 0.1% farming, 12.5% construction, 4.9% production (2000).

Income: Per capita income: $32,624 (2000); Median household income: $61,672 (2000); Poverty rate: 179.1% (2000).

Education: Percent of population age 25 and over with: High school diploma (including GED) or higher: 90.2% (2000); Bachelor's degree or higher: 34.9% (2000).

School District(s)

Marble Falls ISD (PK-12)
    2009-10 Enrollment: 4,011 . . . . (830) 693-4357
Housing: Homeownership rate: 89.5% (2000); Median home value: $162,500 (2000); Median contract rent: $528 per month (2000); Median year structure built: 1986 (2000).

Transportation: Commute to work: 91.2% car, 0.1% public transportation, 0.9% walk, 5.5% work from home (2000); Travel time to work: 9.5% less than 15 minutes, 17.0% 15 to 30 minutes, 31.4% 30 to 45 minutes, 26.1% 45 to 60 minutes, 16.0% 60 minutes or more (2000)

Caldwell County

Located in south central Texas; bounded on the southwest by the San Marcos River. Covers a land area of 545.73 square miles, a water area of 1.69 square miles, and is located in the Central Time Zone at 29.81° N. Lat., 97.66° W. Long. The county was founded in 1848. County seat is Lockhart.

Caldwell County is part of the Austin-Round Rock-San Marcos, TX Metropolitan Statistical Area. The entire metro area includes: Bastrop County, TX; Caldwell County, TX; Hays County, TX; Travis County, TX; Williamson County, TX

Weather Station: Luling   Elevation: 399 feet

	Jan	Feb	Mar	Apr	May	Jun	Jul	Aug	Sep	Oct	Nov	Dec
High	62	66	73	80	86	92	96	97	91	83	72	64
Low	38	42	49	55	64	71	72	72	66	57	48	39
Precip	2.2	2.2	2.5	2.7	4.3	4.1	2.0	2.2	3.5	4.6	2.9	2.6
Snow	0.4	tr	0.0	0.0	0.0	0.0	0.0	0.0	0.0	0.0	tr	tr

High and Low temperatures in degrees Fahrenheit; Precipitation and Snow in inches

Population: 26,392 (1990); 32,194 (2000); 37,183 (2010); 39,547 (2015 projected); Race: 69.5% White, 6.9% Black, 0.5% Asian, 23.1% Other, 44.5% Hispanic of any race (2010); Density: 68.1 persons per square mile (2010); Average household size: 2.82 (2010); Median age: 35.2 (2010); Males per 100 females: 97.6 (2010).

Religion: Five largest groups: 20.6% Catholic Church, 17.1% Southern Baptist Convention, 4.7% The United Methodist Church, 1.5% Evangelical Lutheran Church in America, 1.3% Christian Church (Disciples of Christ) (2000).

Economy: Unemployment rate: 10.0% (June 2011); Total civilian labor force: 16,442 (June 2011); Leading industries: 20.6% retail trade; 20.2% health care and social assistance; 13.3% manufacturing (2009); Farms: 1,421 totaling 304,737 acres (2007); Companies that employ 500 or more persons: 0 (2009); Companies that employ 100 to 499 persons: 10 (2009); Companies that employ less than 100 persons: 514 (2009); Black-owned businesses: n/a (2007); Hispanic-owned businesses: 583 (2007); Asian-owned businesses: n/a (2007); Women-owned businesses: 682 (2007); Retail sales per capita: $7,622 (2010). Single-family building permits issued: 10 (2010); Multi-family building permits issued: 29 (2010).

Income: Per capita income: $19,343 (2010); Median household income: $46,005 (2010); Average household income: $56,209 (2010); Percent of households with income of $100,000 or more: 12.0% (2010); Poverty rate: 16.8% (2009); Bankruptcy rate: 1.11% (2010).

Taxes: Total county taxes per capita: $257 (2007); County property taxes per capita: $212 (2007).

Education: Percent of population age 25 and over with: High school diploma (including GED) or higher: 75.0% (2010); Bachelor's degree or higher: 15.1% (2010); Master's degree or higher: 3.9% (2010).

Housing: Homeownership rate: 68.5% (2010); Median home value: $98,365 (2010); Median contract rent: $492 per month (2005-2009 5-year est.); Median year structure built: 1980 (2005-2009 5-year est.)

Health: Birth rate: 138.6 per 10,000 population (2009); Death rate: 69.3 per 10,000 population (2009); Age-adjusted cancer mortality rate: 194.4 deaths per 100,000 population (2007); Number of physicians: 5.3 per 10,000 population (2008); Hospital beds: 16.1 per 10,000 population (2007); Hospital admissions: 534.8 per 10,000 population (2007).

Elections: 2008 Presidential election results: 46.4% Obama, 52.4% McCain, 0.1% Nader

National and State Parks: Lockhart State Park

Additional Information Contacts
Caldwell County Government . . . . (512) 398-1800
    http://www.co.caldwell.tx.us/ips/cms
City of Lockhart . . . . (512) 398-3461
    http://www.lockhart-tx.org
City of Luling . . . . (830) 875-2481
    http://www.cityofluling.net
Greater Caldwell Hispanic Chamber of Commerce . . . . (512) 398-9600
    http://www.lockharthispanicchamber.org
Lockhart Chamber of Commerce . . . . (512) 398-2818
    http://www.lockhartchamber.com
Luling Area Chamber of Commerce . . . . (830) 875-3214
    http://www.lulingcc.org

Caldwell County Communities

DALE (unincorporated postal area, zip code 78616). Covers a land area of 122.754 square miles and a water area of 0.221 square miles. Located at 29.92° N. Lat; 97.56° W. Long. Elevation is 522 feet.

Population: 4,369 (2000); Race: 75.9% White, 5.7% Black, 0.8% Asian, 17.6% Other, 27.7% Hispanic of any race (2000); Density: 35.6 persons per square mile (2000); Age: 30.8% under 18, 8.5% over 64 (2000); Marriage status: 19.2% never married, 63.5% now married, 5.1% widowed, 12.2% divorced (2000); Foreign born: 5.8% (2000); Ancestry (includes multiple ancestries): 14.8% German, 8.9% American, 7.3% English, 7.1% Irish (2000).

Economy: Employment by occupation: 16.9% management, 11.3% professional, 12.5% services, 26.6% sales, 0.7% farming, 19.6% construction, 12.4% production (2000).

Income: Per capita income: $18,613 (2000); Median household income: $43,396 (2000); Poverty rate: 179.1% (2000).

Education: Percent of population age 25 and over with: High school diploma (including GED) or higher: 75.9% (2000); Bachelor's degree or higher: 13.1% (2000).

Housing: Homeownership rate: 86.6% (2000); Median home value: $77,100 (2000); Median contract rent: $397 per month (2000); Median year structure built: 1987 (2000).
Transportation: Commute to work: 94.7% car, 0.0% public transportation, 0.3% walk, 4.7% work from home (2000); Travel time to work: 5.1% less than 15 minutes, 18.6% 15 to 30 minutes, 20.6% 30 to 45 minutes, 31.9% 45 to 60 minutes, 23.7% 60 minutes or more (2000)

LOCKHART (city). County seat. Covers a land area of 11.247 square miles and a water area of 0.016 square miles. Located at 29.88° N. Lat; 97.67° W. Long. Elevation is 515 feet.
History: Lockhart State Park to Southeast is on site of battle of Plum Creek (1840), Texan defeat of Comanche Indians after they swept through the area's settlements. Founded 1848, incorporated 1870.
Population: 9,383 (1990); 11,615 (2000); 13,255 (2010); 13,963 (2015 projected); Race: 67.6% White, 11.6% Black, 0.6% Asian, 20.2% Other, 47.0% Hispanic of any race (2010); Density: 1,178.5 persons per square mile (2010); Average household size: 2.74 (2010); Median age: 34.8 (2010); Males per 100 females: 95.1 (2010); Marriage status: 31.1% never married, 47.0% now married, 6.4% widowed, 15.6% divorced (2005-2009 5-year est.); Foreign born: 4.2% (2005-2009 5-year est.); Ancestry (includes multiple ancestries): 13.1% German, 10.5% Irish, 5.0% English, 2.6% French, 2.6% American (2005-2009 5-year est.).
Economy: Single-family building permits issued: 5 (2010); Multi-family building permits issued: 0 (2010); Employment by occupation: 11.3% management, 15.4% professional, 22.0% services, 26.0% sales, 0.2% farming, 12.3% construction, 12.8% production (2005-2009 5-year est.).
Income: Per capita income: $18,694 (2010); Median household income: $48,759 (2010); Average household income: $55,348 (2010); Percent of households with income of $100,000 or more: 11.8% (2010); Poverty rate: 20.1% (2005-2009 5-year est.).
Taxes: Total city taxes per capita: $310 (2007); City property taxes per capita: $178 (2007).
Education: Percent of population age 25 and over with: High school diploma (including GED) or higher: 74.1% (2010); Bachelor's degree or higher: 14.7% (2010); Master's degree or higher: 4.2% (2010).

School District(s)

Lockhart ISD (PK-12)
    2009-10 Enrollment: 4,636 . . . . (512) 398-0000
University of Texas University Charter School (KG-12)
    2009-10 Enrollment: 907 . . . . (512) 471-5652
Housing: Homeownership rate: 58.8% (2010); Median home value: $99,231 (2010); Median contract rent: $597 per month (2005-2009 5-year est.); Median year structure built: 1977 (2005-2009 5-year est.).
Safety: Violent crime rate: 55.4 per 10,000 population; Property crime rate: 253.4 per 10,000 population (2009).
Newspapers: The Lockhart Post-Register (Local news; Circulation 4,100)
Transportation: Commute to work: 93.4% car, 0.6% public transportation, 0.8% walk, 3.1% work from home (2005-2009 5-year est.); Travel time to work: 37.4% less than 15 minutes, 15.4% 15 to 30 minutes, 14.5% 30 to 45 minutes, 19.6% 45 to 60 minutes, 13.1% 60 minutes or more (2005-2009 5-year est.)
Airports: Lockhart Municipal (general aviation)
Additional Information Contacts
City of Lockhart . . . . (512) 398-3461
    http://www.lockhart-tx.org
Greater Caldwell Hispanic Chamber of Commerce . . . . (512) 398-9600
    http://www.lockharthispanicchamber.org
Lockhart Chamber of Commerce . . . . (512) 398-2818
    http://www.lockhartchamber.com

LULING (city). Covers a land area of 3.837 square miles and a water area of 0.007 square miles. Located at 29.68° N. Lat; 97.64° W. Long. Elevation is 410 feet.
History: Luling was founded in 1874. After an unruly beginning, with local residents such as Rowdy Joe, Texas Jack, and Monte Joe, Luling became a cattle center. Oil was discovered in 1922 by Edgar B. Davis, who later sold his oil interests and established the Luling Foundation Farm, a demonstration farm that boosted agriculture in the area.
Population: 4,836 (1990); 5,080 (2000); 5,473 (2010); 5,701 (2015 projected); Race: 64.3% White, 6.8% Black, 0.8% Asian, 28.0% Other, 52.9% Hispanic of any race (2010); Density: 1,426.5 persons per square mile (2010); Average household size: 2.77 (2010); Median age: 33.7 (2010); Males per 100 females: 89.4 (2010); Marriage status: 24.8% never married, 51.6% now married, 10.8% widowed, 12.8% divorced (2005-2009

5-year est.); Foreign born: 14.9% (2005-2009 5-year est.); Ancestry (includes multiple ancestries): 8.4% Irish, 8.1% German, 7.4% English, 3.4% Scotch-Irish, 2.7% American (2005-2009 5-year est.).
Economy: Single-family building permits issued: 5 (2010); Multi-family building permits issued: 29 (2010); Employment by occupation: 10.6% management, 8.1% professional, 17.1% services, 33.7% sales, 0.0% farming, 15.6% construction, 15.0% production (2005-2009 5-year est.).
Income: Per capita income: $15,371 (2010); Median household income: $32,708 (2010); Average household income: $42,696 (2010); Percent of households with income of $100,000 or more: 7.0% (2010); Poverty rate: 29.3% (2005-2009 5-year est.).
Taxes: Total city taxes per capita: $257 (2007); City property taxes per capita: $115 (2007).
Education: Percent of population age 25 and over with: High school diploma (including GED) or higher: 62.9% (2010); Bachelor's degree or higher: 13.6% (2010); Master's degree or higher: 4.4% (2010).

School District(s)

Luling ISD (PK-12)
    2009-10 Enrollment: 1,472 . . . . (830) 875-3191
Housing: Homeownership rate: 60.4% (2010); Median home value: $70,881 (2010); Median contract rent: $360 per month (2005-2009 5-year est.); Median year structure built: 1963 (2005-2009 5-year est.).
Hospitals: Seton Edgar B Davis Hospital; Warm Springs Specialty Hospital at Luling (42 beds)
Safety: Violent crime rate: 89.1 per 10,000 population; Property crime rate: 414.6 per 10,000 population (2009).
Newspapers: Newsboy & Signal (Community news; Circulation 2,500)
Transportation: Commute to work: 88.8% car, 3.1% public transportation, 0.8% walk, 5.9% work from home (2005-2009 5-year est.); Travel time to work: 47.0% less than 15 minutes, 21.5% 15 to 30 minutes, 12.6% 30 to 45 minutes, 11.6% 45 to 60 minutes, 7.3% 60 minutes or more (2005-2009 5-year est.)
Additional Information Contacts
City of Luling . . . . (830) 875-2481
    http://www.cityofluling.net
Luling Area Chamber of Commerce . . . . (830) 875-3214
    http://www.lulingcc.org

MARTINDALE (city). Covers a land area of 2.017 square miles and a water area of 0 square miles. Located at 29.84° N. Lat; 97.84° W. Long. Elevation is 525 feet.
Population: 948 (1990); 953 (2000); 1,114 (2010); 1,191 (2015 projected); Race: 58.0% White, 1.3% Black, 0.4% Asian, 40.3% Other, 60.1% Hispanic of any race (2010); Density: 552.2 persons per square mile (2010); Average household size: 2.89 (2010); Median age: 34.0 (2010); Males per 100 females: 97.9 (2010); Marriage status: 27.4% never married, 60.6% now married, 3.8% widowed, 8.2% divorced (2005-2009 5-year est.); Foreign born: 2.7% (2005-2009 5-year est.); Ancestry (includes multiple ancestries): 7.1% German, 6.8% Irish, 4.3% English, 3.0% Cajun, 2.4% French (2005-2009 5-year est.).
Economy: Single-family building permits issued: 0 (2010); Multi-family building permits issued: 0 (2010); Employment by occupation: 16.1% management, 20.2% professional, 28.9% services, 17.1% sales, 0.9% farming, 7.5% construction, 9.2% production (2005-2009 5-year est.).
Income: Per capita income: $20,060 (2010); Median household income: $47,684 (2010); Average household income: $56,864 (2010); Percent of households with income of $100,000 or more: 16.1% (2010); Poverty rate: 13.9% (2005-2009 5-year est.).
Taxes: Total city taxes per capita: $513 (2007); City property taxes per capita: $229 (2007).
Education: Percent of population age 25 and over with: High school diploma (including GED) or higher: 74.5% (2010); Bachelor's degree or higher: 18.6% (2010); Master's degree or higher: 4.9% (2010).
Housing: Homeownership rate: 70.1% (2010); Median home value: $97,391 (2010); Median contract rent: $475 per month (2005-2009 5-year est.); Median year structure built: 1970 (2005-2009 5-year est.).
Safety: Violent crime rate: 25.6 per 10,000 population; Property crime rate: 162.3 per 10,000 population (2009).
Transportation: Commute to work: 96.4% car, 0.7% public transportation, 0.0% walk, 2.9% work from home (2005-2009 5-year est.); Travel time to work: 31.0% less than 15 minutes, 33.0% 15 to 30 minutes, 12.5% 30 to 45 minutes, 11.3% 45 to 60 minutes, 12.2% 60 minutes or more (2005-2009 5-year est.)

MAXWELL (unincorporated postal area, zip code 78656). Covers a land area of 27.785 square miles and a water area of 0.031 square miles. Located at 29.88° N. Lat; 97.83° W. Long. Elevation is 597 feet.
Population: 2,133 (2000); Race: 66.9% White, 1.9% Black, 0.3% Asian, 30.9% Other, 60.1% Hispanic of any race (2000); Density: 76.8 persons per square mile (2000); Age: 33.3% under 18, 6.5% over 64 (2000); Marriage status: 24.7% never married, 60.3% now married, 4.1% widowed, 10.9% divorced (2000); Foreign born: 4.7% (2000); Ancestry (includes multiple ancestries): 10.5% German, 6.8% English, 5.7% Irish, 4.1% American (2000).
Economy: Employment by occupation: 9.2% management, 13.3% professional, 15.3% services, 31.0% sales, 1.7% farming, 14.7% construction, 14.8% production (2000).
Income: Per capita income: $13,939 (2000); Median household income: $39,149 (2000); Poverty rate: 179.1% (2000).
Education: Percent of population age 25 and over with: High school diploma (including GED) or higher: 72.8% (2000); Bachelor's degree or higher: 9.9% (2000).
Housing: Homeownership rate: 75.2% (2000); Median home value: $73,300 (2000); Median contract rent: $375 per month (2000); Median year structure built: 1987 (2000).
Transportation: Commute to work: 97.5% car, 0.0% public transportation, 0.9% walk, 1.6% work from home (2000); Travel time to work: 22.5% less than 15 minutes, 35.0% 15 to 30 minutes, 18.8% 30 to 45 minutes, 10.3% 45 to 60 minutes, 13.4% 60 minutes or more (2000)

MUSTANG RIDGE (city). Covers a land area of 3.793 square miles and a water area of 0 square miles. Located at 30.04° N. Lat; 97.69° W. Long. Elevation is 623 feet.
Population: 576 (1990); 785 (2000); 918 (2010); 1,017 (2015 projected); Race: 65.1% White, 4.5% Black, 0.1% Asian, 30.3% Other, 54.2% Hispanic of any race (2010); Density: 242.0 persons per square mile (2010); Average household size: 3.15 (2010); Median age: 34.2 (2010); Males per 100 females: 100.0 (2010); Marriage status: 29.8% never married, 57.3% now married, 5.2% widowed, 7.8% divorced (2005-2009 5-year est.); Foreign born: 8.9% (2005-2009 5-year est.); Ancestry (includes multiple ancestries): 15.3% German, 12.8% Irish, 5.0% English, 2.0% Scottish, 1.4% American (2005-2009 5-year est.).
Economy: Employment by occupation: 7.3% management, 12.2% professional, 29.8% services, 19.7% sales, 2.6% farming, 16.8% construction, 11.5% production (2005-2009 5-year est.).
Income: Per capita income: $19,440 (2010); Median household income: $51,480 (2010); Average household income: $60,361 (2010); Percent of households with income of $100,000 or more: 12.7% (2010); Poverty rate: 22.6% (2005-2009 5-year est.).
Education: Percent of population age 25 and over with: High school diploma (including GED) or higher: 73.4% (2010); Bachelor's degree or higher: 9.5% (2010); Master's degree or higher: 1.8% (2010).
Housing: Homeownership rate: 85.2% (2010); Median home value: $115,854 (2010); Median contract rent: $1,277 per month (2005-2009 5-year est.); Median year structure built: 1985 (2005-2009 5-year est.).
Safety: Violent crime rate: 10.5 per 10,000 population; Property crime rate: 105.3 per 10,000 population (2009).
Transportation: Commute to work: 89.7% car, 0.0% public transportation, 1.3% walk, 8.4% work from home (2005-2009 5-year est.); Travel time to work: 4.6% less than 15 minutes, 20.4% 15 to 30 minutes, 43.1% 30 to 45 minutes, 14.0% 45 to 60 minutes, 17.8% 60 minutes or more (2005-2009 5-year est.)

Calhoun County

Located in south Texas, on the Gulf of Mexico. Covers a land area of 512.31 square miles, a water area of 519.84 square miles, and is located in the Central Time Zone at 28.53° N. Lat., 96.62° W. Long. The county was founded in 1846. County seat is Port Lavaca.

Calhoun County is part of the Victoria, TX Metropolitan Statistical Area. The entire metro area includes: Calhoun County, TX; Goliad County, TX; Victoria County, TX

Weather Station: Point Comfort — Elevation: 20 feet

	Jan	Feb	Mar	Apr	May	Jun	Jul	Aug	Sep	Oct	Nov	Dec
High	65	68	73	79	85	90	91	92	89	82	74	66
Low	47	50	56	63	70	76	78	78	72	65	56	48
Precip	3.1	2.4	3.2	2.4	4.5	4.4	3.6	2.8	4.4	5.0	3.9	2.5
Snow	0.0	0.0	0.0	0.0	0.0	0.0	0.0	0.0	0.0	0.0	0.0	0.0

High and Low temperatures in degrees Fahrenheit; Precipitation and Snow in inches

Population: 19,053 (1990); 20,647 (2000); 20,852 (2010); 20,914 (2015 projected); Race: 75.8% White, 2.7% Black, 3.9% Asian, 17.6% Other, 44.7% Hispanic of any race (2010); Density: 40.7 persons per square mile (2010); Average household size: 2.73 (2010); Median age: 37.4 (2010); Males per 100 females: 100.2 (2010).
Religion: Five largest groups: 24.0% Southern Baptist Convention, 15.7% Catholic Church, 6.2% The United Methodist Church, 4.1% Assemblies of God, 2.0% Evangelical Lutheran Church in America (2000).
Economy: Unemployment rate: 10.1% (June 2011); Total civilian labor force: 9,875 (June 2011); Leading industries: 33.9% manufacturing; 23.0% construction; 10.8% retail trade (2009); Farms: 291 totaling 230,400 acres (2007); Companies that employ 500 or more persons: 4 (2009); Companies that employ 100 to 499 persons: 10 (2009); Companies that employ less than 100 persons: 394 (2009); Black-owned businesses: n/a (2007); Hispanic-owned businesses: n/a (2007); Asian-owned businesses: n/a (2007); Women-owned businesses: 445 (2007); Retail sales per capita: $11,293 (2010). Single-family building permits issued: 56 (2010); Multi-family building permits issued: 0 (2010).
Income: Per capita income: $20,545 (2010); Median household income: $43,952 (2010); Average household income: $56,410 (2010); Percent of households with income of $100,000 or more: 12.8% (2010); Poverty rate: 16.0% (2009); Bankruptcy rate: 0.88% (2010).
Taxes: Total county taxes per capita: $823 (2007); County property taxes per capita: $745 (2007).
Education: Percent of population age 25 and over with: High school diploma (including GED) or higher: 73.9% (2010); Bachelor's degree or higher: 12.7% (2010); Master's degree or higher: 2.4% (2010).
Housing: Homeownership rate: 67.8% (2010); Median home value: $80,147 (2010); Median contract rent: $420 per month (2005-2009 5-year est.); Median year structure built: 1972 (2005-2009 5-year est.)
Health: Birth rate: 151.2 per 10,000 population (2009); Death rate: 87.5 per 10,000 population (2009); Age-adjusted cancer mortality rate: 198.1 deaths per 100,000 population (2007); Number of physicians: 8.3 per 10,000 population (2008); Hospital beds: 12.3 per 10,000 population (2007); Hospital admissions: 696.2 per 10,000 population (2007).
Elections: 2008 Presidential election results: 39.7% Obama, 59.7% McCain, 0.0% Nader
Additional Information Contacts
Calhoun County Government . . . . (361) 553-4600
  http://www.calhouncotx.org
City of Port Lavaca . . . . (361) 552-9793
  http://www.portlavaca.org
Port Lavaca Chamber of Commerce . . . . (361) 552-2959
  http://portlavacatx.org

Calhoun County Communities

POINT COMFORT (city). Covers a land area of 1.309 square miles and a water area of 0 square miles. Located at 28.67° N. Lat; 96.55° W. Long. Elevation is 16 feet.
Population: 965 (1990); 781 (2000); 738 (2010); 714 (2015 projected); Race: 87.3% White, 2.3% Black, 1.6% Asian, 8.8% Other, 24.0% Hispanic of any race (2010); Density: 563.9 persons per square mile (2010); Average household size: 2.79 (2010); Median age: 36.7 (2010); Males per 100 females: 97.3 (2010); Marriage status: 23.0% never married, 63.3% now married, 8.8% widowed, 4.9% divorced (2005-2009 5-year est.); Foreign born: 4.7% (2005-2009 5-year est.); Ancestry (includes multiple ancestries): 24.9% Irish, 20.2% German, 17.7% Czech, 13.6% English, 11.9% French (2005-2009 5-year est.).
Economy: Single-family building permits issued: 0 (2010); Multi-family building permits issued: 0 (2010); Employment by occupation: 7.8% management, 15.4% professional, 8.1% services, 29.5% sales, 1.2% farming, 21.7% construction, 16.3% production (2005-2009 5-year est.).
Income: Per capita income: $22,962 (2010); Median household income: $54,667 (2010); Average household income: $64,828 (2010); Percent of households with income of $100,000 or more: 13.0% (2010); Poverty rate: 9.6% (2005-2009 5-year est.).

Taxes: Total city taxes per capita: $512 (2007); City property taxes per capita: $419 (2007).
Education: Percent of population age 25 and over with: High school diploma (including GED) or higher: 88.2% (2010); Bachelor's degree or higher: 8.8% (2010); Master's degree or higher: 1.9% (2010).

School District(s)
Calhoun County ISD (PK-12)
   2009-10 Enrollment: 4,276 . . . . (361) 552-9728
Housing: Homeownership rate: 47.3% (2010); Median home value: $70,303 (2010); Median contract rent: $580 per month (2005-2009 5-year est.); Median year structure built: 1956 (2005-2009 5-year est.).
Safety: Violent crime rate: 14.2 per 10,000 population; Property crime rate: 212.5 per 10,000 population (2009).
Transportation: Commute to work: 93.7% car, 0.0% public transportation, 3.1% walk, 2.2% work from home (2005-2009 5-year est.); Travel time to work: 55.0% less than 15 minutes, 25.1% 15 to 30 minutes, 15.1% 30 to 45 minutes, 4.8% 45 to 60 minutes, 0.0% 60 minutes or more (2005-2009 5-year est.)

PORT LAVACA (city). County seat. Covers a land area of 9.786 square miles and a water area of 3.851 square miles. Located at 28.61° N. Lat; 96.63° W. Long. Elevation is 16 feet.
History: Port Lavaca was founded by the Spanish in 1815 and called La Vaca (Spanish for "the cow") although the river had been named Lavaca by La Salle. In between the Spanish La Vaca and the present Port Lavaca, the town was called Linnville. Port Lavaca was once a shipping center, then turned to commercial and sport fishing.
Population: 11,231 (1990); 12,035 (2000); 11,735 (2010); 11,589 (2015 projected); Race: 69.6% White, 3.7% Black, 5.2% Asian, 21.5% Other, 56.1% Hispanic of any race (2010); Density: 1,199.2 persons per square mile (2010); Average household size: 2.83 (2010); Median age: 35.1 (2010); Males per 100 females: 99.0 (2010); Marriage status: 24.5% never married, 58.4% now married, 6.3% widowed, 10.8% divorced (2005-2009 5-year est.); Foreign born: 16.1% (2005-2009 5-year est.); Ancestry (includes multiple ancestries): 10.6% German, 8.6% Irish, 7.2% English, 3.4% American, 2.6% Czech (2005-2009 5-year est.).
Economy: Single-family building permits issued: 6 (2010); Multi-family building permits issued: 0 (2010); Employment by occupation: 9.8% management, 15.5% professional, 18.5% services, 17.5% sales, 0.3% farming, 18.0% construction, 20.4% production (2005-2009 5-year est.).
Income: Per capita income: $19,135 (2010); Median household income: $41,269 (2010); Average household income: $54,597 (2010); Percent of households with income of $100,000 or more: 13.8% (2010); Poverty rate: 17.2% (2005-2009 5-year est.).
Taxes: Total city taxes per capita: $447 (2007); City property taxes per capita: $233 (2007).
Education: Percent of population age 25 and over with: High school diploma (including GED) or higher: 73.6% (2010); Bachelor's degree or higher: 13.6% (2010); Master's degree or higher: 2.4% (2010).

School District(s)
Calhoun County ISD (PK-12)
   2009-10 Enrollment: 4,276 . . . . (361) 552-9728
Edna ISD (PK-12)
   2009-10 Enrollment: 1,470 . . . . (361) 782-3573
Housing: Homeownership rate: 60.4% (2010); Median home value: $80,799 (2010); Median contract rent: $399 per month (2005-2009 5-year est.); Median year structure built: 1970 (2005-2009 5-year est.).
Hospitals: Memorial Medical Center (49 beds)
Safety: Violent crime rate: 56.3 per 10,000 population; Property crime rate: 254.1 per 10,000 population (2009).
Newspapers: The Port Lavaca Wave (Community news; Circulation 4,500)
Transportation: Commute to work: 95.0% car, 1.4% public transportation, 1.6% walk, 0.1% work from home (2005-2009 5-year est.); Travel time to work: 50.7% less than 15 minutes, 28.6% 15 to 30 minutes, 9.4% 30 to 45 minutes, 6.6% 45 to 60 minutes, 4.7% 60 minutes or more (2005-2009 5-year est.)
Additional Information Contacts
City of Port Lavaca. . . . . (361) 552-9793
   http://www.portlavaca.org
Port Lavaca Chamber of Commerce . . . . (361) 552-2959
   http://portlavacatx.org

SEADRIFT (city). Covers a land area of 1.248 square miles and a water area of 0.007 square miles. Located at 28.41° N. Lat; 96.71° W. Long. Elevation is 10 feet.

Population: 1,280 (1990); 1,352 (2000); 1,407 (2010); 1,432 (2015 projected); Race: 79.4% White, 0.9% Black, 8.8% Asian, 10.9% Other, 25.2% Hispanic of any race (2010); Density: 1,127.1 persons per square mile (2010); Average household size: 2.63 (2010); Median age: 36.6 (2010); Males per 100 females: 97.9 (2010); Marriage status: 31.1% never married, 51.5% now married, 8.8% widowed, 8.6% divorced (2005-2009 5-year est.); Foreign born: 10.5% (2005-2009 5-year est.); Ancestry (includes multiple ancestries): 25.1% Irish, 22.1% German, 9.2% English, 5.2% Czech, 3.1% Czechoslovakian (2005-2009 5-year est.).
Economy: Single-family building permits issued: 13 (2010); Multi-family building permits issued: 0 (2010); Employment by occupation: 6.7% management, 16.4% professional, 28.4% services, 12.1% sales, 6.9% farming, 17.5% construction, 12.1% production (2005-2009 5-year est.).
Income: Per capita income: $17,691 (2010); Median household income: $37,708 (2010); Average household income: $46,738 (2010); Percent of households with income of $100,000 or more: 5.8% (2010); Poverty rate: 14.4% (2005-2009 5-year est.).
Education: Percent of population age 25 and over with: High school diploma (including GED) or higher: 67.5% (2010); Bachelor's degree or higher: 9.5% (2010); Master's degree or higher: 1.7% (2010).

School District(s)
Calhoun County ISD (PK-12)
   2009-10 Enrollment: 4,276 . . . . (361) 552-9728
Housing: Homeownership rate: 77.6% (2010); Median home value: $53,553 (2010); Median contract rent: $459 per month (2005-2009 5-year est.); Median year structure built: 1968 (2005-2009 5-year est.).
Safety: Violent crime rate: 13.9 per 10,000 population; Property crime rate: 201.1 per 10,000 population (2009).
Transportation: Commute to work: 96.3% car, 0.0% public transportation, 1.1% walk, 2.0% work from home (2005-2009 5-year est.); Travel time to work: 42.0% less than 15 minutes, 11.3% 15 to 30 minutes, 25.4% 30 to 45 minutes, 11.9% 45 to 60 minutes, 9.3% 60 minutes or more (2005-2009 5-year est.)

Callahan County

Located in central Texas; drained to the north by tributaries of the Brazos River, and to the south by tributaries of the Colorado River. Covers a land area of 898.62 square miles, a water area of 2.64 square miles, and is located in the Central Time Zone at 32.32° N. Lat., 99.37° W. Long. The county was founded in 1877. County seat is Baird.

Callahan County is part of the Abilene, TX Metropolitan Statistical Area. The entire metro area includes: Callahan County, TX; Jones County, TX; Taylor County, TX

Weather Station: Putnam									Elevation: 1,590 feet			
	Jan	Feb	Mar	Apr	May	Jun	Jul	Aug	Sep	Oct	Nov	Dec
High	58	62	70	79	85	91	96	96	88	79	68	58
Low	34	37	44	52	61	68	72	71	64	54	44	34
Precip	1.1	1.8	2.4	1.7	3.3	4.1	2.0	2.0	2.6	3.0	2.0	1.4
Snow	1.4	0.8	0.5	0.2	0.0	0.0	0.0	0.0	0.0	0.0	0.6	1.3

High and Low temperatures in degrees Fahrenheit; Precipitation and Snow in inches

Population: 11,859 (1990); 12,905 (2000); 13,957 (2010); 14,443 (2015 projected); Race: 91.8% White, 1.9% Black, 0.3% Asian, 6.0% Other, 8.3% Hispanic of any race (2010); Density: 15.5 persons per square mile (2010); Average household size: 2.50 (2010); Median age: 40.5 (2010); Males per 100 females: 93.7 (2010).
Religion: Five largest groups: 39.6% Southern Baptist Convention, 8.8% The United Methodist Church, 6.2% Churches of Christ, 1.5% Catholic Church, 0.5% The Church of Jesus Christ of Latter-day Saints (2000).
Economy: Unemployment rate: 7.8% (June 2011); Total civilian labor force: 6,868 (June 2011); Leading industries: 17.0% retail trade; 10.8% accommodation & food services; 7.4% manufacturing (2009); Farms: 1,058 totaling 532,595 acres (2007); Companies that employ 500 or more persons: 0 (2009); Companies that employ 100 to 499 persons: 1 (2009); Companies that employ less than 100 persons: 223 (2009); Black-owned businesses: n/a (2007); Hispanic-owned businesses: n/a (2007); Asian-owned businesses: n/a (2007); Women-owned businesses: n/a (2007); Retail sales per capita: $9,234 (2010). Single-family building permits issued: 2 (2010); Multi-family building permits issued: 0 (2010).
Income: Per capita income: $19,744 (2010); Median household income: $40,958 (2010); Average household income: $49,547 (2010); Percent of households with income of $100,000 or more: 8.3% (2010); Poverty rate: 14.3% (2009); Bankruptcy rate: 2.04% (2010).

Taxes: Total county taxes per capita: $160 (2007); County property taxes per capita: $91 (2007).

Education: Percent of population age 25 and over with: High school diploma (including GED) or higher: 83.9% (2010); Bachelor's degree or higher: 13.7% (2010); Master's degree or higher: 3.5% (2010).

Housing: Homeownership rate: 79.1% (2010); Median home value: $75,172 (2010); Median contract rent: $415 per month (2005-2009 5-year est.); Median year structure built: 1975 (2005-2009 5-year est.)

Health: Birth rate: 121.4 per 10,000 population (2009); Death rate: 104.3 per 10,000 population (2009); Age-adjusted cancer mortality rate: 203.4 deaths per 100,000 population (2007); Number of physicians: 3.0 per 10,000 population (2008); Hospital beds: 0.0 per 10,000 population (2007); Hospital admissions: 0.0 per 10,000 population (2007).

Elections: 2008 Presidential election results: 18.6% Obama, 80.3% McCain, 0.0% Nader

Additional Information Contacts

Callahan County Government . . . . (325) 854-1155
    http://www.co.callahan.tx.us/ips/cms
Clyde Chamber of Commerce . . . . (915) 893-4221
Cross Plains Chamber of Commerce . . . . (254) 725-7251
    http://www.crossplains.com/COC.htm
Development Corporation of Baird. . . . . (325) 854-1165
    http://bairdtexas.com

Callahan County Communities

BAIRD (city). County seat. Covers a land area of 2.622 square miles and a water area of 0.066 square miles. Located at 32.39° N. Lat; 99.39° W. Long. Elevation is 1,722 feet.

History: Settled 1880, incorporated 1891.

Population: 1,658 (1990); 1,623 (2000); 1,731 (2010); 1,792 (2015 projected); Race: 91.3% White, 0.8% Black, 0.5% Asian, 7.3% Other, 13.6% Hispanic of any race (2010); Density: 660.2 persons per square mile (2010); Average household size: 2.36 (2010); Median age: 43.7 (2010); Males per 100 females: 96.3 (2010); Marriage status: 17.9% never married, 57.5% now married, 12.8% widowed, 11.8% divorced (2005-2009 5-year est.); Foreign born: 3.4% (2005-2009 5-year est.); Ancestry (includes multiple ancestries): 16.6% Irish, 12.7% American, 10.7% German, 7.9% English, 4.5% Scotch-Irish (2005-2009 5-year est.).

Economy: Employment by occupation: 6.2% management, 17.1% professional, 20.4% services, 26.5% sales, 3.9% farming, 16.4% construction, 9.6% production (2005-2009 5-year est.).

Income: Per capita income: $19,190 (2010); Median household income: $36,540 (2010); Average household income: $45,584 (2010); Percent of households with income of $100,000 or more: 7.4% (2010); Poverty rate: 12.7% (2005-2009 5-year est.).

Taxes: Total city taxes per capita: $115 (2007); City property taxes per capita: $115 (2007).

Education: Percent of population age 25 and over with: High school diploma (including GED) or higher: 81.5% (2010); Bachelor's degree or higher: 13.6% (2010); Master's degree or higher: 2.6% (2010).

School District(s)

Baird ISD (PK-12)
    2009-10 Enrollment: 329 . . . . (325) 854-1400

Housing: Homeownership rate: 73.3% (2010); Median home value: $68,495 (2010); Median contract rent: $262 per month (2005-2009 5-year est.); Median year structure built: 1956 (2005-2009 5-year est.).

Safety: Violent crime rate: 23.9 per 10,000 population; Property crime rate: 83.5 per 10,000 population (2009).

Transportation: Commute to work: 86.7% car, 0.0% public transportation, 3.9% walk, 0.0% work from home (2005-2009 5-year est.); Travel time to work: 34.7% less than 15 minutes, 27.5% 15 to 30 minutes, 24.3% 30 to 45 minutes, 5.9% 45 to 60 minutes, 7.5% 60 minutes or more (2005-2009 5-year est.)

Additional Information Contacts

Development Corporation of Baird. . . . . (325) 854-1165
    http://bairdtexas.com

CLYDE (city). Covers a land area of 2.388 square miles and a water area of 0 square miles. Located at 32.40° N. Lat; 99.49° W. Long. Elevation is 1,991 feet.

Population: 3,245 (1990); 3,345 (2000); 3,563 (2010); 3,667 (2015 projected); Race: 92.1% White, 3.2% Black, 0.4% Asian, 4.2% Other, 6.7% Hispanic of any race (2010); Density: 1,492.3 persons per square mile (2010); Average household size: 2.49 (2010); Median age: 37.4 (2010);

Males per 100 females: 89.1 (2010); Marriage status: 21.1% never married, 59.6% now married, 3.8% widowed, 15.5% divorced (2005-2009 5-year est.); Foreign born: 1.7% (2005-2009 5-year est.); Ancestry (includes multiple ancestries): 19.5% Irish, 19.1% German, 9.8% English, 5.3% Scotch-Irish, 3.7% American (2005-2009 5-year est.).

Economy: Single-family building permits issued: 2 (2010); Multi-family building permits issued: 0 (2010); Employment by occupation: 4.0% management, 27.7% professional, 15.1% services, 23.1% sales, 0.0% farming, 18.2% construction, 11.9% production (2005-2009 5-year est.).

Income: Per capita income: $20,241 (2010); Median household income: $41,812 (2010); Average household income: $50,517 (2010); Percent of households with income of $100,000 or more: 8.2% (2010); Poverty rate: 7.7% (2005-2009 5-year est.).

Taxes: Total city taxes per capita: $325 (2007); City property taxes per capita: $154 (2007).

Education: Percent of population age 25 and over with: High school diploma (including GED) or higher: 86.9% (2010); Bachelor's degree or higher: 13.6% (2010); Master's degree or higher: 4.4% (2010).

School District(s)

Clyde CISD (PK-12)
    2009-10 Enrollment: 1,443 . . . . (325) 893-4222
Eula ISD (PK-12)
    2009-10 Enrollment: 382 . . . . (325) 529-3186

Housing: Homeownership rate: 76.5% (2010); Median home value: $78,281 (2010); Median contract rent: $438 per month (2005-2009 5-year est.); Median year structure built: 1973 (2005-2009 5-year est.).

Safety: Violent crime rate: 20.9 per 10,000 population; Property crime rate: 227.0 per 10,000 population (2009).

Newspapers: Clyde Journal (Community news; Circulation 2,500)

Transportation: Commute to work: 92.3% car, 0.0% public transportation, 2.5% walk, 3.4% work from home (2005-2009 5-year est.); Travel time to work: 33.7% less than 15 minutes, 30.3% 15 to 30 minutes, 28.4% 30 to 45 minutes, 5.0% 45 to 60 minutes, 2.6% 60 minutes or more (2005-2009 5-year est.)

Additional Information Contacts

Clyde Chamber of Commerce . . . . (915) 893-4221

CROSS PLAINS (town). Covers a land area of 1.196 square miles and a water area of 0 square miles. Located at 32.12° N. Lat; 99.16° W. Long. Elevation is 1,742 feet.

History: Settled c.1876, incorporated 1911.

Population: 1,063 (1990); 1,068 (2000); 1,065 (2010); 1,065 (2015 projected); Race: 95.8% White, 0.4% Black, 0.0% Asian, 3.8% Other, 5.4% Hispanic of any race (2010); Density: 890.6 persons per square mile (2010); Average household size: 2.36 (2010); Median age: 47.3 (2010); Males per 100 females: 90.5 (2010); Marriage status: 19.9% never married, 47.9% now married, 12.5% widowed, 19.7% divorced (2005-2009 5-year est.); Foreign born: 2.7% (2005-2009 5-year est.); Ancestry (includes multiple ancestries): 9.9% Irish, 9.5% German, 6.3% English, 6.2% American, 3.2% French (2005-2009 5-year est.).

Economy: Employment by occupation: 6.8% management, 8.2% professional, 16.9% services, 22.3% sales, 2.3% farming, 24.8% construction, 18.9% production (2005-2009 5-year est.).

Income: Per capita income: $17,407 (2010); Median household income: $33,333 (2010); Average household income: $41,723 (2010); Percent of households with income of $100,000 or more: 5.9% (2010); Poverty rate: 24.3% (2005-2009 5-year est.).

Taxes: Total city taxes per capita: $135 (2007); City property taxes per capita: $0 (2007).

Education: Percent of population age 25 and over with: High school diploma (including GED) or higher: 79.9% (2010); Bachelor's degree or higher: 15.4% (2010); Master's degree or higher: 5.8% (2010).

School District(s)

Cross Plains ISD (PK-12)
    2009-10 Enrollment: 377 . . . . (254) 725-6121

Housing: Homeownership rate: 77.9% (2010); Median home value: $68,947 (2010); Median contract rent: $208 per month (2005-2009 5-year est.); Median year structure built: 1969 (2005-2009 5-year est.).

Newspapers: Cross Plains Review (Community news; Circulation 1,600)

Transportation: Commute to work: 86.5% car, 0.0% public transportation, 4.6% walk, 8.3% work from home (2005-2009 5-year est.); Travel time to work: 47.0% less than 15 minutes, 25.2% 15 to 30 minutes, 10.1% 30 to 45 minutes, 12.4% 45 to 60 minutes, 5.4% 60 minutes or more (2005-2009 5-year est.)

Additional Information Contacts

Cross Plains Chamber of Commerce .... (254) 725-7251
http://www.crossplains.com/COC.htm

PUTNAM (town). Covers a land area of 1.013 square miles and a water area of 0 square miles. Located at 32.37° N. Lat; 99.19° W. Long. Elevation is 1,608 feet.
Population: 103 (1990); 88 (2000); 108 (2010); 114 (2015 projected); Race: 91.7% White, 0.9% Black, 0.0% Asian, 7.4% Other, 14.8% Hispanic of any race (2010); Density: 106.6 persons per square mile (2010); Average household size: 2.40 (2010); Median age: 43.0 (2010); Males per 100 females: 100.0 (2010); Marriage status: 5.1% never married, 64.1% now married, 11.5% widowed, 19.2% divorced (2005-2009 5-year est.); Foreign born: 0.0% (2005-2009 5-year est.); Ancestry (includes multiple ancestries): 35.8% Irish, 11.6% English, 7.4% Dutch, 6.3% German, 2.1% Scotch-Irish (2005-2009 5-year est.).
Economy: Employment by occupation: 15.6% management, 0.0% professional, 0.0% services, 6.3% sales, 0.0% farming, 40.6% construction, 37.5% production (2005-2009 5-year est.).
Income: Per capita income: $19,628 (2010); Median household income: $35,938 (2010); Average household income: $47,222 (2010); Percent of households with income of $100,000 or more: 6.7% (2010); Poverty rate: 16.8% (2005-2009 5-year est.).
Taxes: Total city taxes per capita: $286 (2007); City property taxes per capita: $33 (2007).
Education: Percent of population age 25 and over with: High school diploma (including GED) or higher: 82.9% (2010); Bachelor's degree or higher: 14.5% (2010); Master's degree or higher: 2.6% (2010).
Housing: Homeownership rate: 75.6% (2010); Median home value: $70,000 (2010); Median contract rent: n/a per month (2005-2009 5-year est.); Median year structure built: 1950 (2005-2009 5-year est.).
Transportation: Commute to work: 100.0% car, 0.0% public transportation, 0.0% walk, 0.0% work from home (2005-2009 5-year est.); Travel time to work: 84.4% less than 15 minutes, 15.6% 15 to 30 minutes, 0.0% 30 to 45 minutes, 0.0% 45 to 60 minutes, 0.0% 60 minutes or more (2005-2009 5-year est.)

Cameron County

Located in south Texas; bounded on the south by the Mexican border, and on the east by Laguna Madre (inlet of the Gulf of Mexico). Covers a land area of 905.76 square miles, a water area of 370.58 square miles, and is located in the Central Time Zone at 26.08° N. Lat., 97.55° W. Long. The county was founded in 1848. County seat is Brownsville.

Cameron County is part of the Brownsville-Harlingen, TX Metropolitan Statistical Area. The entire metro area includes: Cameron County, TX

Weather Station: Brownsville Intl Arpt   Elevation: 19 feet

	Jan	Feb	Mar	Apr	May	Jun	Jul	Aug	Sep	Oct	Nov	Dec
High	71	74	79	84	89	92	94	94	91	86	79	72
Low	52	55	60	66	72	76	76	76	73	67	59	53
Precip	1.3	1.0	1.2	1.5	2.6	2.3	1.9	2.7	5.5	3.8	1.9	1.2
Snow	tr	0.0	tr	0.0	0.0	0.0	0.0	tr	0.0	0.0	tr	tr

High and Low temperatures in degrees Fahrenheit; Precipitation and Snow in inches

Weather Station: Harlingen   Elevation: 38 feet

	Jan	Feb	Mar	Apr	May	Jun	Jul	Aug	Sep	Oct	Nov	Dec
High	70	74	79	84	89	94	95	96	92	86	79	71
Low	50	53	58	64	71	75	75	75	72	66	58	51
Precip	1.3	1.6	1.4	1.9	3.1	2.3	2.1	2.5	5.1	3.3	1.5	1.6
Snow	0.0	0.0	0.0	0.0	0.0	0.0	0.0	0.0	0.0	0.0	0.0	0.1

High and Low temperatures in degrees Fahrenheit; Precipitation and Snow in inches

Weather Station: Port Isabel   Elevation: 17 feet

	Jan	Feb	Mar	Apr	May	Jun	Jul	Aug	Sep	Oct	Nov	Dec
High	69	71	76	80	85	89	90	91	89	84	77	70
Low	53	56	61	67	74	77	78	78	75	70	63	54
Precip	1.8	1.5	1.4	1.4	2.2	2.1	1.7	1.9	5.8	4.1	2.6	1.5
Snow	0.0	0.0	0.0	0.0	0.0	0.0	0.0	0.0	0.0	0.0	0.0	0.1

High and Low temperatures in degrees Fahrenheit; Precipitation and Snow in inches

Population: 260,120 (1990); 335,227 (2000); 405,301 (2010); 438,655 (2015 projected); Race: 79.5% White, 0.7% Black, 0.5% Asian, 19.3% Other, 86.5% Hispanic of any race (2010); Density: 447.5 persons per square mile (2010); Average household size: 3.34 (2010); Median age: 29.3 (2010); Males per 100 females: 92.0 (2010).

Religion: Five largest groups: 40.0% Catholic Church, 5.2% Southern Baptist Convention, 1.4% The United Methodist Church, 1.2% Assemblies of God, 0.8% The Church of Jesus Christ of Latter-day Saints (2000).
Economy: Unemployment rate: 12.9% (June 2011); Total civilian labor force: 156,815 (June 2011); Leading industries: 28.6% health care and social assistance; 17.9% retail trade; 11.9% accommodation & food services (2009); Farms: 1,241 totaling 349,479 acres (2007); Companies that employ 500 or more persons: 20 (2009); Companies that employ 100 to 499 persons: 129 (2009); Companies that employ less than 100 persons: 6,171 (2009); Black-owned businesses: 343 (2007); Hispanic-owned businesses: 18,653 (2007); Asian-owned businesses: 505 (2007); Women-owned businesses: 8,593 (2007); Retail sales per capita: $8,961 (2010). Single-family building permits issued: 1,062 (2010); Multi-family building permits issued: 196 (2010).
Income: Per capita income: $13,157 (2010); Median household income: $31,260 (2010); Average household income: $43,959 (2010); Percent of households with income of $100,000 or more: 8.0% (2010); Poverty rate: 34.0% (2009); Bankruptcy rate: 1.87% (2010).
Taxes: Total county taxes per capita: $115 (2007); County property taxes per capita: $107 (2007).
Education: Percent of population age 25 and over with: High school diploma (including GED) or higher: 62.8% (2010); Bachelor's degree or higher: 15.2% (2010); Master's degree or higher: 5.2% (2010).
Housing: Homeownership rate: 67.8% (2010); Median home value: $70,751 (2010); Median contract rent: $403 per month (2005-2009 5-year est.); Median year structure built: 1983 (2005-2009 5-year est.)
Health: Birth rate: 225.5 per 10,000 population (2009); Death rate: 57.8 per 10,000 population (2009); Age-adjusted cancer mortality rate: 147.0 deaths per 100,000 population (2007); Number of physicians: 13.3 per 10,000 population (2008); Hospital beds: 32.6 per 10,000 population (2007); Hospital admissions: 1,347.7 per 10,000 population (2007).
Environment: Air Quality Index: 74.9% good, 25.1% moderate, 0.0% unhealthy for sensitive individuals, 0.0% unhealthy (percent of days in 2008)
Elections: 2008 Presidential election results: 63.8% Obama, 35.1% McCain, 0.0% Nader
National and State Parks: Laguna Atascosa National Wildlife Refuge; Palo Alto Battlefield National Historic Site; Texas State Park
Additional Information Contacts
Cameron County Government .... (956) 544-0830
http://www.co.cameron.tx.us
Brownsville Chamber of Commerce .... (956) 542-4341
http://www.brownsvillechamber.com
City of Brownsville .... (956) 548-6007
http://www.cob.us
City of Harlingen .... (956) 216-5001
http://www.myharlingen.us
City of La Feria.................................. (956) 797-2261
http://www.cityoflaferia.com
City of San Benito .... (956) 361-3800
http://www.cityofsanbenito.com
Harlingen Area Chamber of Commerce............... (956) 423-5440
http://www.harlingen.com
Harlingen Hispanic Chamber of Commerce .... (956) 421-2400
http://www.harlingenchamber.com
Los Fresnos Area Chamber of Commerce .... (956) 233-4488
http://www.losfresnoschamber.com
Port Isabel Chamber of Commerce .... (956) 943-2262
http://www.portisabel.org
San Benito Chamber of Commerce................... (956) 399-5321
http://www.cityofsanbenito.com
South Padre Island Chamber of Commerce .... (956) 761-4412
http://www.spichamber.com
Town of South Padre Island....................... (956) 761-6456
http://myspi.org

Cameron County Communities

ARROYO ALTO (CDP). Covers a land area of 0.056 square miles and a water area of 0 square miles. Located at 26.13° N. Lat; 97.82° W. Long. Elevation is 52 feet.
Population: 182 (1990); 320 (2000); 322 (2010); 333 (2015 projected); Race: 67.1% White, 0.3% Black, 0.0% Asian, 32.6% Other, 73.3% Hispanic of any race (2010); Density: 5,766.1 persons per square mile (2010); Average household size: 2.80 (2010); Median age: 40.0 (2010);

Males per 100 females: 97.5 (2010); Marriage status: n/a never married, n/a now married, n/a widowed, n/a divorced (2005-2009 5-year est.); Foreign born: n/a (2005-2009 5-year est.); Ancestry (includes multiple ancestries): n/a (2005-2009 5-year est.).

Economy: Employment by occupation: n/a management, n/a professional, n/a services, n/a sales, n/a farming, n/a construction, n/a production (2005-2009 5-year est.).

Income: Per capita income: $16,286 (2010); Median household income: $36,389 (2010); Average household income: $43,587 (2010); Percent of households with income of $100,000 or more: 5.2% (2010); Poverty rate: n/a (2005-2009 5-year est.).

Education: Percent of population age 25 and over with: High school diploma (including GED) or higher: 65.4% (2010); Bachelor's degree or higher: 10.7% (2010); Master's degree or higher: 5.1% (2010).

Housing: Homeownership rate: 86.1% (2010); Median home value: $82,500 (2010); Median contract rent: n/a per month (2005-2009 5-year est.); Median year structure built: n/a (2005-2009 5-year est.).

Transportation: Commute to work: n/a car, n/a public transportation, n/a walk, n/a work from home (2005-2009 5-year est.); Travel time to work: n/a less than 15 minutes, n/a 15 to 30 minutes, n/a 30 to 45 minutes, n/a 45 to 60 minutes, n/a 60 minutes or more (2005-2009 5-year est.)

ARROYO COLORADO ESTATES (CDP). Covers a land area of 1.096 square miles and a water area of 0 square miles. Located at 26.18° N. Lat; 97.61° W. Long.

Population: 450 (1990); 755 (2000); 1,129 (2010); 1,303 (2015 projected); Race: 91.0% White, 0.3% Black, 0.6% Asian, 8.1% Other, 87.6% Hispanic of any race (2010); Density: 1,030.2 persons per square mile (2010); Average household size: 3.63 (2010); Median age: 27.5 (2010); Males per 100 females: 102.7 (2010); Marriage status: 49.4% never married, 47.3% now married, 0.0% widowed, 3.3% divorced (2005-2009 5-year est.); Foreign born: 37.8% (2005-2009 5-year est.); Ancestry (includes multiple ancestries): n/a (2005-2009 5-year est.).

Economy: Employment by occupation: 13.2% management, 0.0% professional, 18.2% services, 36.8% sales, 1.7% farming, 22.2% construction, 7.9% production (2005-2009 5-year est.).

Income: Per capita income: $16,630 (2010); Median household income: $40,236 (2010); Average household income: $60,410 (2010); Percent of households with income of $100,000 or more: 17.7% (2010); Poverty rate: 24.5% (2005-2009 5-year est.).

Education: Percent of population age 25 and over with: High school diploma (including GED) or higher: 69.2% (2010); Bachelor's degree or higher: 24.2% (2010); Master's degree or higher: 11.4% (2010).

Housing: Homeownership rate: 88.7% (2010); Median home value: $90,000 (2010); Median contract rent: n/a per month (2005-2009 5-year est.); Median year structure built: 1987 (2005-2009 5-year est.).

Transportation: Commute to work: 86.8% car, 0.0% public transportation, 9.9% walk, 0.0% work from home (2005-2009 5-year est.); Travel time to work: 25.8% less than 15 minutes, 48.3% 15 to 30 minutes, 15.2% 30 to 45 minutes, 0.0% 45 to 60 minutes, 10.6% 60 minutes or more (2005-2009 5-year est.)

ARROYO GARDENS-LA TINA RANCH (CDP). Covers a land area of 16.277 square miles and a water area of 0.203 square miles. Located at 26.21° N. Lat; 97.49° W. Long.

Population: 542 (1990); 732 (2000); 754 (2010); 781 (2015 projected); Race: 85.5% White, 0.1% Black, 0.1% Asian, 14.2% Other, 92.8% Hispanic of any race (2010); Density: 46.3 persons per square mile (2010); Average household size: 3.46 (2010); Median age: 29.8 (2010); Males per 100 females: 91.9 (2010); Marriage status: 34.9% never married, 61.2% now married, 4.0% widowed, 0.0% divorced (2005-2009 5-year est.); Foreign born: 20.4% (2005-2009 5-year est.); Ancestry (includes multiple ancestries): 4.4% German (2005-2009 5-year est.).

Economy: Employment by occupation: 0.0% management, 0.0% professional, 26.7% services, 25.2% sales, 12.9% farming, 0.0% construction, 35.1% production (2005-2009 5-year est.).

Income: Per capita income: $10,202 (2010); Median household income: $24,000 (2010); Average household income: $34,610 (2010); Percent of households with income of $100,000 or more: 5.0% (2010); Poverty rate: 30.4% (2005-2009 5-year est.).

Education: Percent of population age 25 and over with: High school diploma (including GED) or higher: 58.8% (2010); Bachelor's degree or higher: 14.0% (2010); Master's degree or higher: 3.0% (2010).

Housing: Homeownership rate: 89.4% (2010); Median home value: $52,708 (2010); Median contract rent: n/a per month (2005-2009 5-year est.); Median year structure built: 1987 (2005-2009 5-year est.).

Transportation: Commute to work: 87.8% car, 0.0% public transportation, 0.0% walk, 12.2% work from home (2005-2009 5-year est.); Travel time to work: 0.0% less than 15 minutes, 48.1% 15 to 30 minutes, 32.3% 30 to 45 minutes, 0.0% 45 to 60 minutes, 19.6% 60 minutes or more (2005-2009 5-year est.)

BAYVIEW (town). Covers a land area of 2.803 square miles and a water area of 0.468 square miles. Located at 26.13° N. Lat; 97.40° W. Long. Elevation is 26 feet.

Population: 230 (1990); 323 (2000); 496 (2010); 546 (2015 projected); Race: 70.4% White, 1.2% Black, 0.8% Asian, 27.6% Other, 76.0% Hispanic of any race (2010); Density: 177.0 persons per square mile (2010); Average household size: 3.64 (2010); Median age: 29.7 (2010); Males per 100 females: 125.5 (2010); Marriage status: 8.6% never married, 67.5% now married, 7.2% widowed, 16.8% divorced (2005-2009 5-year est.); Foreign born: 6.7% (2005-2009 5-year est.); Ancestry (includes multiple ancestries): 22.0% English, 13.3% German, 10.9% Irish, 9.4% American, 3.7% Italian (2005-2009 5-year est.).

Economy: Single-family building permits issued: 0 (2010); Multi-family building permits issued: 0 (2010); Employment by occupation: 14.6% management, 29.9% professional, 6.1% services, 25.6% sales, 0.0% farming, 14.6% construction, 9.1% production (2005-2009 5-year est.).

Income: Per capita income: $11,425 (2010); Median household income: $30,769 (2010); Average household income: $41,757 (2010); Percent of households with income of $100,000 or more: 9.0% (2010); Poverty rate: 4.5% (2005-2009 5-year est.).

Taxes: Total city taxes per capita: $196 (2007); City property taxes per capita: $151 (2007).

Education: Percent of population age 25 and over with: High school diploma (including GED) or higher: 56.6% (2010); Bachelor's degree or higher: 16.0% (2010); Master's degree or higher: 7.6% (2010).

Housing: Homeownership rate: 82.9% (2010); Median home value: $83,333 (2010); Median contract rent: $578 per month (2005-2009 5-year est.); Median year structure built: 1978 (2005-2009 5-year est.).

Transportation: Commute to work: 75.0% car, 6.1% public transportation, 0.0% walk, 18.9% work from home (2005-2009 5-year est.); Travel time to work: 25.6% less than 15 minutes, 36.1% 15 to 30 minutes, 35.3% 30 to 45 minutes, 1.5% 45 to 60 minutes, 1.5% 60 minutes or more (2005-2009 5-year est.)

BIXBY (CDP). Covers a land area of 1.645 square miles and a water area of 0 square miles. Located at 26.14° N. Lat; 97.85° W. Long. Elevation is 59 feet.

Population: 227 (1990); 356 (2000); 407 (2010); 443 (2015 projected); Race: 83.3% White, 0.0% Black, 0.0% Asian, 16.7% Other, 79.1% Hispanic of any race (2010); Density: 247.4 persons per square mile (2010); Average household size: 3.08 (2010); Median age: 29.0 (2010); Males per 100 females: 92.9 (2010); Marriage status: 7.1% never married, 75.8% now married, 6.0% widowed, 11.0% divorced (2005-2009 5-year est.); Foreign born: 29.6% (2005-2009 5-year est.); Ancestry (includes multiple ancestries): n/a (2005-2009 5-year est.).

Economy: Employment by occupation: 0.0% management, 0.0% professional, 21.4% services, 40.7% sales, 0.0% farming, 24.8% construction, 13.1% production (2005-2009 5-year est.).

Income: Per capita income: $9,296 (2010); Median household income: $23,182 (2010); Average household income: $29,015 (2010); Percent of households with income of $100,000 or more: 3.0% (2010); Poverty rate: 34.7% (2005-2009 5-year est.).

Education: Percent of population age 25 and over with: High school diploma (including GED) or higher: 48.2% (2010); Bachelor's degree or higher: 6.7% (2010); Master's degree or higher: 2.7% (2010).

Housing: Homeownership rate: 76.5% (2010); Median home value: $44,737 (2010); Median contract rent: $353 per month (2005-2009 5-year est.); Median year structure built: 1975 (2005-2009 5-year est.).

Transportation: Commute to work: 100.0% car, 0.0% public transportation, 0.0% walk, 0.0% work from home (2005-2009 5-year est.); Travel time to work: 40.0% less than 15 minutes, 60.0% 15 to 30 minutes, 0.0% 30 to 45 minutes, 0.0% 45 to 60 minutes, 0.0% 60 minutes or more (2005-2009 5-year est.)

BLUETOWN-IGLESIA ANTIGUA (CDP). Covers a land area of 5.086 square miles and a water area of 0.057 square miles. Located at 26.07° N. Lat; 97.82° W. Long.

Population: 543 (1990); 692 (2000); 670 (2010); 677 (2015 projected); Race: 67.0% White, 0.0% Black, 0.0% Asian, 33.0% Other, 95.1% Hispanic of any race (2010); Density: 131.7 persons per square mile (2010); Average household size: 3.83 (2010); Median age: 26.6 (2010); Males per 100 females: 92.0 (2010); Marriage status: 27.8% never married, 66.6% now married, 4.4% widowed, 1.3% divorced (2005-2009 5-year est.); Foreign born: 35.1% (2005-2009 5-year est.); Ancestry (includes multiple ancestries): 2.6% German (2005-2009 5-year est.).
Economy: Employment by occupation: 10.6% management, 0.0% professional, 19.1% services, 25.5% sales, 4.3% farming, 13.8% construction, 26.6% production (2005-2009 5-year est.).
Income: Per capita income: $7,109 (2010); Median household income: $20,119 (2010); Average household income: $28,143 (2010); Percent of households with income of $100,000 or more: 2.9% (2010); Poverty rate: 41.8% (2005-2009 5-year est.).
Education: Percent of population age 25 and over with: High school diploma (including GED) or higher: 36.0% (2010); Bachelor's degree or higher: 4.0% (2010); Master's degree or higher: 1.4% (2010).
Housing: Homeownership rate: 76.6% (2010); Median home value: $41,579 (2010); Median contract rent: $320 per month (2005-2009 5-year est.); Median year structure built: 1978 (2005-2009 5-year est.).
Transportation: Commute to work: 95.6% car, 0.0% public transportation, 4.4% walk, 0.0% work from home (2005-2009 5-year est.); Travel time to work: 28.9% less than 15 minutes, 46.7% 15 to 30 minutes, 4.4% 30 to 45 minutes, 15.6% 45 to 60 minutes, 4.4% 60 minutes or more (2005-2009 5-year est.)

BROWNSVILLE (city). County seat. Covers a land area of 80.400 square miles and a water area of 2.619 square miles. Located at 25.93° N. Lat; 97.48° W. Long. Elevation is 33 feet.

History: Fort Taylor, named for Zachary Taylor, was built in 1846 by the U.S. Army. The name was later changed to Fort Brown, to honor Major Jacob Brown who had died in defense of the fort. In 1848 the Brownsville Town Company, under the leadership of Charles Stillman of Connecticut, platted the town. Brownsville prospered immediately as a supply center for west-bound gold seekers. Large cattle ranches were developed in the area, and the town's position on the Rio Grande with access to the Gulf of Mexico made it an important seaport. During the Civil War, Brownsville was a Confederate port, held for a time by Union forces. Periods of peace after the Civil War were interrupted by political strife across the Mexican border, which impacted on Brownsville. By the 1920's, developers were promoting Brownsville as a place to locate, and in 1930 a plan to improve the port with a 17-mile channel from the Gulf was begun.
Population: 114,025 (1990); 139,722 (2000); 179,334 (2010); 195,419 (2015 projected); Race: 81.3% White, 0.6% Black, 0.6% Asian, 17.5% Other, 92.2% Hispanic of any race (2010); Density: 2,230.5 persons per square mile (2010); Average household size: 3.55 (2010); Median age: 28.4 (2010); Males per 100 females: 89.8 (2010); Marriage status: 29.9% never married, 57.3% now married, 5.8% widowed, 7.0% divorced (2005-2009 5-year est.); Foreign born: 30.0% (2005-2009 5-year est.); Ancestry (includes multiple ancestries): 1.5% German, 1.3% American, 1.0% Irish, 0.9% English, 0.5% French (2005-2009 5-year est.).
Economy: Unemployment rate: 13.2% (June 2011); Total civilian labor force: 68,106 (June 2011); Single-family building permits issued: 578 (2010); Multi-family building permits issued: 22 (2010); Employment by occupation: 7.7% management, 17.0% professional, 23.3% services, 27.7% sales, 0.7% farming, 10.4% construction, 13.3% production (2005-2009 5-year est.).
Income: Per capita income: $11,780 (2010); Median household income: $30,276 (2010); Average household income: $41,815 (2010); Percent of households with income of $100,000 or more: 7.3% (2010); Poverty rate: 37.0% (2005-2009 5-year est.).
Taxes: Total city taxes per capita: $378 (2007); City property taxes per capita: $164 (2007).
Education: Percent of population age 25 and over with: High school diploma (including GED) or higher: 60.4% (2010); Bachelor's degree or higher: 16.2% (2010); Master's degree or higher: 5.7% (2010).

School District(s)
Brownsville ISD (PK-12)
   2009-10 Enrollment: 49,121 . . . . (956) 548-8000

Harmony Science Academy (Brownsville) (KG-09)
   2009-10 Enrollment: 381 . . . . (956) 574-9555
Idea Public Schools (PK-12)
   2009-10 Enrollment: 5,515 . . . . (956) 377-8000
Los Fresnos CISD (PK-12)
   2009-10 Enrollment: 9,734 . . . . (956) 254-5000
One Stop Multiservice Charter School (PK-12)
   2009-10 Enrollment: 746 . . . . (956) 393-2227
Raul Yzaguirre School for Success (PK-12)
   2009-10 Enrollment: 1,145 . . . . (713) 649-6201
Responsive Education Solutions (KG-12)
   2009-10 Enrollment: 5,022 . . . . (972) 316-3663

Four-year College(s)
The University of Texas at Brownsville (Public)
   Fall 2009 Enrollment: 6,174 . . . . (956) 882-8200
   2010-11 Tuition: In-state $5,109; Out-of-state $13,169

Two-year College(s)
Career Centers of Texas-Brownsville (Private, For-profit)
   Fall 2009 Enrollment: 628 . . . . (956) 547-8200

Vocational/Technical School(s)
South Texas Vocational Technical Institute (Private, For-profit)
   Fall 2009 Enrollment: 653 . . . . (956) 554-3515
   2010-11 Tuition: $16,700

Housing: Homeownership rate: 62.6% (2010); Median home value: $73,086 (2010); Median contract rent: $389 per month (2005-2009 5-year est.); Median year structure built: 1984 (2005-2009 5-year est.).
Hospitals: Brownsville Medical Center (243 beds); Brownsville Surgical Hospital; Valley Regional Medical Center (214 beds)
Safety: Violent crime rate: 25.3 per 10,000 population; Property crime rate: 544.8 per 10,000 population (2009).
Newspapers: Brownsville Herald (Local news; Circulation 17,519); El Bravo - Brownsville Edition (Local news); El Heraldo De Brownsville (Regional news; Circulation 18,200)
Transportation: Commute to work: 91.2% car, 1.3% public transportation, 2.3% walk, 2.3% work from home (2005-2009 5-year est.); Travel time to work: 33.7% less than 15 minutes, 46.8% 15 to 30 minutes, 13.3% 30 to 45 minutes, 3.2% 45 to 60 minutes, 3.0% 60 minutes or more (2005-2009 5-year est.)
Airports: Brownsville/South Padre Island International (primary service)
Additional Information Contacts
Brownsville Chamber of Commerce . . . . (956) 542-4341
   http://www.brownsvillechamber.com
City of Brownsville . . . . (956) 548-6007
   http://www.cob.us

CAMERON PARK (CDP). Covers a land area of 0.598 square miles and a water area of 0.013 square miles. Located at 25.97° N. Lat; 97.47° W. Long. Elevation is 16 feet.

Population: 3,274 (1990); 5,961 (2000); 7,019 (2010); 7,656 (2015 projected); Race: 89.9% White, 0.1% Black, 0.1% Asian, 9.9% Other, 99.4% Hispanic of any race (2010); Density: 11,730.5 persons per square mile (2010); Average household size: 4.52 (2010); Median age: 22.6 (2010); Males per 100 females: 100.0 (2010); Marriage status: 34.0% never married, 59.8% now married, 3.5% widowed, 2.7% divorced (2005-2009 5-year est.); Foreign born: 37.2% (2005-2009 5-year est.); Ancestry (includes multiple ancestries): n/a (2005-2009 5-year est.).
Economy: Employment by occupation: 4.6% management, 8.4% professional, 35.5% services, 12.4% sales, 0.0% farming, 25.4% construction, 13.6% production (2005-2009 5-year est.).
Income: Per capita income: $6,010 (2010); Median household income: $22,697 (2010); Average household income: $27,113 (2010); Percent of households with income of $100,000 or more: 1.9% (2010); Poverty rate: 56.4% (2005-2009 5-year est.).
Education: Percent of population age 25 and over with: High school diploma (including GED) or higher: 24.9% (2010); Bachelor's degree or higher: 3.7% (2010); Master's degree or higher: 0.7% (2010).
Housing: Homeownership rate: 70.9% (2010); Median home value: $42,725 (2010); Median contract rent: $354 per month (2005-2009 5-year est.); Median year structure built: 1987 (2005-2009 5-year est.).
Transportation: Commute to work: 84.9% car, 1.6% public transportation, 3.7% walk, 4.5% work from home (2005-2009 5-year est.); Travel time to work: 30.1% less than 15 minutes, 53.0% 15 to 30 minutes, 11.1% 30 to 45 minutes, 2.8% 45 to 60 minutes, 3.0% 60 minutes or more (2005-2009 5-year est.)

CHULA VISTA-ORASON (CDP). Covers a land area of 0.506 square miles and a water area of 0 square miles. Located at 26.07° N. Lat; 97.44° W. Long.
Population: 247 (1990); 394 (2000); 455 (2010); 495 (2015 projected); Race: 88.4% White, 1.1% Black, 0.0% Asian, 10.5% Other, 83.3% Hispanic of any race (2010); Density: 899.1 persons per square mile (2010); Average household size: 3.76 (2010); Median age: 26.9 (2010); Males per 100 females: 102.2 (2010); Marriage status: 12.1% never married, 77.9% now married, 0.0% widowed, 10.0% divorced (2005-2009 5-year est.); Foreign born: 22.1% (2005-2009 5-year est.); Ancestry (includes multiple ancestries): 3.0% German, 3.0% Scotch-Irish, 2.5% English (2005-2009 5-year est.).
Economy: Employment by occupation: 11.5% management, 0.0% professional, 33.8% services, 15.2% sales, 0.0% farming, 23.0% construction, 16.4% production (2005-2009 5-year est.).
Income: Per capita income: $10,985 (2010); Median household income: $29,500 (2010); Average household income: $42,128 (2010); Percent of households with income of $100,000 or more: 9.9% (2010); Poverty rate: 25.3% (2005-2009 5-year est.).
Education: Percent of population age 25 and over with: High school diploma (including GED) or higher: 64.3% (2010); Bachelor's degree or higher: 12.2% (2010); Master's degree or higher: 7.1% (2010).
Housing: Homeownership rate: 81.0% (2010); Median home value: $84,000 (2010); Median contract rent: n/a per month (2005-2009 5-year est.); Median year structure built: 1999 (2005-2009 5-year est.).
Transportation: Commute to work: 100.0% car, 0.0% public transportation, 0.0% walk, 0.0% work from home (2005-2009 5-year est.); Travel time to work: 19.0% less than 15 minutes, 21.2% 15 to 30 minutes, 47.2% 30 to 45 minutes, 12.6% 45 to 60 minutes, 0.0% 60 minutes or more (2005-2009 5-year est.)

COMBES (town). Covers a land area of 2.468 square miles and a water area of 0.014 square miles. Located at 26.24° N. Lat; 97.72° W. Long. Elevation is 39 feet.
Population: 2,204 (1990); 2,553 (2000); 2,677 (2010); 2,798 (2015 projected); Race: 79.0% White, 0.6% Black, 0.2% Asian, 20.2% Other, 79.3% Hispanic of any race (2010); Density: 1,084.8 persons per square mile (2010); Average household size: 3.08 (2010); Median age: 32.0 (2010); Males per 100 females: 94.0 (2010); Marriage status: 19.2% never married, 67.5% now married, 5.6% widowed, 7.7% divorced (2005-2009 5-year est.); Foreign born: 20.4% (2005-2009 5-year est.); Ancestry (includes multiple ancestries): 3.8% German, 2.9% Irish, 1.7% French, 1.7% English, 0.5% American (2005-2009 5-year est.).
Economy: Single-family building permits issued: 21 (2010); Multi-family building permits issued: 0 (2010); Employment by occupation: 9.8% management, 7.3% professional, 28.2% services, 27.4% sales, 1.4% farming, 12.9% construction, 13.1% production (2005-2009 5-year est.).
Income: Per capita income: $11,835 (2010); Median household income: $31,250 (2010); Average household income: $36,260 (2010); Percent of households with income of $100,000 or more: 3.0% (2010); Poverty rate: 39.1% (2005-2009 5-year est.).
Taxes: Total city taxes per capita: $135 (2007); City property taxes per capita: $93 (2007).
Education: Percent of population age 25 and over with: High school diploma (including GED) or higher: 68.3% (2010); Bachelor's degree or higher: 6.8% (2010); Master's degree or higher: 1.5% (2010).

School District(s)
Harlingen CISD (PK-12)
    2009-10 Enrollment: 18,205 . . . . (956) 430-9503
Housing: Homeownership rate: 84.3% (2010); Median home value: $71,752 (2010); Median contract rent: $418 per month (2005-2009 5-year est.); Median year structure built: 1987 (2005-2009 5-year est.).
Safety: Violent crime rate: 35.1 per 10,000 population; Property crime rate: 193.0 per 10,000 population (2009).
Transportation: Commute to work: 98.6% car, 0.0% public transportation, 0.0% walk, 1.4% work from home (2005-2009 5-year est.); Travel time to work: 32.7% less than 15 minutes, 55.0% 15 to 30 minutes, 5.8% 30 to 45 minutes, 3.7% 45 to 60 minutes, 2.7% 60 minutes or more (2005-2009 5-year est.)

DEL MAR HEIGHTS (CDP). Covers a land area of 0.394 square miles and a water area of 0 square miles. Located at 26.05° N. Lat; 97.42° W. Long. Elevation is 10 feet.

Population: 172 (1990); 259 (2000); 306 (2010); 335 (2015 projected); Race: 77.8% White, 1.6% Black, 0.0% Asian, 20.6% Other, 96.7% Hispanic of any race (2010); Density: 777.4 persons per square mile (2010); Average household size: 4.14 (2010); Median age: 23.0 (2010); Males per 100 females: 100.0 (2010); Marriage status: 0.0% never married, 74.5% now married, 0.0% widowed, 25.5% divorced (2005-2009 5-year est.); Foreign born: 73.3% (2005-2009 5-year est.); Ancestry (includes multiple ancestries): n/a (2005-2009 5-year est.).
Economy: Employment by occupation: n/a management, n/a professional, n/a services, n/a sales, n/a farming, n/a construction, n/a production (2005-2009 5-year est.).
Income: Per capita income: $5,073 (2010); Median household income: $19,000 (2010); Average household income: $21,318 (2010); Percent of households with income of $100,000 or more: 0.0% (2010); Poverty rate: 100.0% (2005-2009 5-year est.).
Education: Percent of population age 25 and over with: High school diploma (including GED) or higher: 45.1% (2010); Bachelor's degree or higher: 0.0% (2010); Master's degree or higher: 0.0% (2010).
Housing: Homeownership rate: 79.7% (2010); Median home value: $33,000 (2010); Median contract rent: n/a per month (2005-2009 5-year est.); Median year structure built: 1980 (2005-2009 5-year est.).
Transportation: Commute to work: n/a car, n/a public transportation, n/a walk, n/a work from home (2005-2009 5-year est.); Travel time to work: n/a less than 15 minutes, n/a 15 to 30 minutes, n/a 30 to 45 minutes, n/a 45 to 60 minutes, n/a 60 minutes or more (2005-2009 5-year est.)

EL CAMINO ANGOSTO (CDP). Covers a land area of 0.371 square miles and a water area of 0 square miles. Located at 26.11° N. Lat; 97.64° W. Long. Elevation is 36 feet.
Population: 124 (1990); 254 (2000); 293 (2010); 316 (2015 projected); Race: 59.7% White, 0.0% Black, 0.0% Asian, 40.3% Other, 94.2% Hispanic of any race (2010); Density: 788.8 persons per square mile (2010); Average household size: 4.01 (2010); Median age: 24.6 (2010); Males per 100 females: 99.3 (2010); Marriage status: 16.1% never married, 83.9% now married, 0.0% widowed, 0.0% divorced (2005-2009 5-year est.); Foreign born: 28.8% (2005-2009 5-year est.); Ancestry (includes multiple ancestries): n/a (2005-2009 5-year est.).
Economy: Employment by occupation: 0.0% management, 0.0% professional, 42.0% services, 0.0% sales, 0.0% farming, 58.0% construction, 0.0% production (2005-2009 5-year est.).
Income: Per capita income: $7,960 (2010); Median household income: $24,250 (2010); Average household income: $31,199 (2010); Percent of households with income of $100,000 or more: 4.1% (2010); Poverty rate: 70.8% (2005-2009 5-year est.).
Education: Percent of population age 25 and over with: High school diploma (including GED) or higher: 42.1% (2010); Bachelor's degree or higher: 4.1% (2010); Master's degree or higher: 2.1% (2010).
Housing: Homeownership rate: 87.7% (2010); Median home value: $49,333 (2010); Median contract rent: n/a per month (2005-2009 5-year est.); Median year structure built: 1985 (2005-2009 5-year est.).
Transportation: Commute to work: 100.0% car, 0.0% public transportation, 0.0% walk, 0.0% work from home (2005-2009 5-year est.); Travel time to work: 100.0% less than 15 minutes, 0.0% 15 to 30 minutes, 0.0% 30 to 45 minutes, 0.0% 45 to 60 minutes, 0.0% 60 minutes or more (2005-2009 5-year est.)

ENCANTADA-RANCHITO EL CALABOZ (CDP). Covers a land area of 4.169 square miles and a water area of 0.053 square miles. Located at 26.02° N. Lat; 97.63° W. Long. Elevation is 46 feet.
Population: 1,125 (1990); 2,100 (2000); 2,526 (2010); 2,761 (2015 projected); Race: 76.9% White, 0.1% Black, 0.0% Asian, 23.0% Other, 96.9% Hispanic of any race (2010); Density: 605.9 persons per square mile (2010); Average household size: 4.17 (2010); Median age: 25.3 (2010); Males per 100 females: 96.9 (2010); Marriage status: 35.1% never married, 61.4% now married, 2.6% widowed, 0.9% divorced (2005-2009 5-year est.); Foreign born: 31.4% (2005-2009 5-year est.); Ancestry (includes multiple ancestries): 2.3% American, 0.4% Irish (2005-2009 5-year est.).
Economy: Employment by occupation: 2.4% management, 2.7% professional, 33.4% services, 18.7% sales, 0.0% farming, 19.0% construction, 23.9% production (2005-2009 5-year est.).
Income: Per capita income: $10,838 (2010); Median household income: $33,209 (2010); Average household income: $44,315 (2010); Percent of households with income of $100,000 or more: 6.4% (2010); Poverty rate: 53.9% (2005-2009 5-year est.).

Education: Percent of population age 25 and over with: High school diploma (including GED) or higher: 48.3% (2010); Bachelor's degree or higher: 7.2% (2010); Master's degree or higher: 2.3% (2010).

Housing: Homeownership rate: 87.5% (2010); Median home value: $56,522 (2010); Median contract rent: n/a per month (2005-2009 5-year est.); Median year structure built: 1992 (2005-2009 5-year est.).

Transportation: Commute to work: 94.8% car, 0.0% public transportation, 2.0% walk, 3.2% work from home (2005-2009 5-year est.); Travel time to work: 8.9% less than 15 minutes, 26.7% 15 to 30 minutes, 48.8% 30 to 45 minutes, 8.0% 45 to 60 minutes, 7.7% 60 minutes or more (2005-2009 5-year est.)

GRAND ACRES (CDP). Covers a land area of 0.481 square miles and a water area of 0 square miles. Located at 26.24° N. Lat; 97.82° W. Long. Elevation is 49 feet.

Population: 175 (1990); 203 (2000); 192 (2010); 190 (2015 projected); Race: 59.4% White, 0.0% Black, 0.0% Asian, 40.6% Other, 94.8% Hispanic of any race (2010); Density: 398.9 persons per square mile (2010); Average household size: 3.56 (2010); Median age: 28.3 (2010); Males per 100 females: 88.2 (2010); Marriage status: n/a never married, n/a now married, n/a widowed, n/a divorced (2005-2009 5-year est.); Foreign born: n/a (2005-2009 5-year est.); Ancestry (includes multiple ancestries): n/a (2005-2009 5-year est.).

Economy: Employment by occupation: n/a management, n/a professional, n/a services, n/a sales, n/a farming, n/a construction, n/a production (2005-2009 5-year est.).

Income: Per capita income: $9,225 (2010); Median household income: $25,000 (2010); Average household income: $31,250 (2010); Percent of households with income of $100,000 or more: 3.7% (2010); Poverty rate: n/a (2005-2009 5-year est.).

Education: Percent of population age 25 and over with: High school diploma (including GED) or higher: 49.1% (2010); Bachelor's degree or higher: 6.6% (2010); Master's degree or higher: 2.8% (2010).

Housing: Homeownership rate: 72.2% (2010); Median home value: $54,167 (2010); Median contract rent: n/a per month (2005-2009 5-year est.); Median year structure built: n/a (2005-2009 5-year est.).

Transportation: Commute to work: n/a car, n/a public transportation, n/a walk, n/a work from home (2005-2009 5-year est.); Travel time to work: n/a less than 15 minutes, n/a 15 to 30 minutes, n/a 30 to 45 minutes, n/a 45 to 60 minutes, n/a 60 minutes or more (2005-2009 5-year est.)

GREEN VALLEY FARMS (CDP). Covers a land area of 3.949 square miles and a water area of 0 square miles. Located at 26.12° N. Lat; 97.56° W. Long. Elevation is 20 feet.

Population: 404 (1990); 720 (2000); 998 (2010); 1,146 (2015 projected); Race: 85.9% White, 0.5% Black, 0.0% Asian, 13.6% Other, 96.0% Hispanic of any race (2010); Density: 252.7 persons per square mile (2010); Average household size: 4.12 (2010); Median age: 25.3 (2010); Males per 100 females: 93.8 (2010); Marriage status: 17.1% never married, 72.3% now married, 10.7% widowed, 0.0% divorced (2005-2009 5-year est.); Foreign born: 30.5% (2005-2009 5-year est.); Ancestry (includes multiple ancestries): n/a (2005-2009 5-year est.).

Economy: Employment by occupation: 18.0% management, 5.9% professional, 32.0% services, 22.2% sales, 0.0% farming, 0.0% construction, 21.9% production (2005-2009 5-year est.).

Income: Per capita income: $7,301 (2010); Median household income: $21,825 (2010); Average household income: $30,124 (2010); Percent of households with income of $100,000 or more: 3.7% (2010); Poverty rate: 52.9% (2005-2009 5-year est.).

Education: Percent of population age 25 and over with: High school diploma (including GED) or higher: 48.3% (2010); Bachelor's degree or higher: 9.1% (2010); Master's degree or higher: 3.2% (2010).

Housing: Homeownership rate: 86.8% (2010); Median home value: $52,542 (2010); Median contract rent: $400 per month (2005-2009 5-year est.); Median year structure built: 1990 (2005-2009 5-year est.).

Transportation: Commute to work: 100.0% car, 0.0% public transportation, 0.0% walk, 0.0% work from home (2005-2009 5-year est.); Travel time to work: 5.9% less than 15 minutes, 59.5% 15 to 30 minutes, 34.6% 30 to 45 minutes, 0.0% 45 to 60 minutes, 0.0% 60 minutes or more (2005-2009 5-year est.)

HARLINGEN (city). Covers a land area of 34.070 square miles and a water area of 0.255 square miles. Located at 26.19° N. Lat; 97.69° W. Long. Elevation is 39 feet.

History: Harlingen was founded by Lon C. Hill. It was once known as Six-Shooter Junction because of the company of Texas Rangers stationed here, as well as the U.S. customs and immigration inspectors.

Population: 50,040 (1990); 57,564 (2000); 65,547 (2010); 70,116 (2015 projected); Race: 77.6% White, 1.2% Black, 1.0% Asian, 20.2% Other, 78.1% Hispanic of any race (2010); Density: 1,923.9 persons per square mile (2010); Average household size: 2.90 (2010); Median age: 31.6 (2010); Males per 100 females: 91.1 (2010); Marriage status: 26.0% never married, 58.5% now married, 7.2% widowed, 8.3% divorced (2005-2009 5-year est.); Foreign born: 14.1% (2005-2009 5-year est.); Ancestry (includes multiple ancestries): 6.3% German, 4.1% English, 3.3% Irish, 2.4% American, 1.2% French (2005-2009 5-year est.).

Economy: Unemployment rate: 11.6% (June 2011); Total civilian labor force: 26,962 (June 2011); Single-family building permits issued: 106 (2010); Multi-family building permits issued: 0 (2010); Employment by occupation: 12.4% management, 22.7% professional, 20.4% services, 28.5% sales, 0.6% farming, 6.2% construction, 9.3% production (2005-2009 5-year est.).

Income: Per capita income: $16,528 (2010); Median household income: $34,002 (2010); Average household income: $48,348 (2010); Percent of households with income of $100,000 or more: 9.7% (2010); Poverty rate: 30.4% (2005-2009 5-year est.).

Taxes: Total city taxes per capita: $558 (2007); City property taxes per capita: $200 (2007).

Education: Percent of population age 25 and over with: High school diploma (including GED) or higher: 72.2% (2010); Bachelor's degree or higher: 18.0% (2010); Master's degree or higher: 5.7% (2010).

School District(s)
Harlingen CISD (PK-12)
　　2009-10 Enrollment: 18,205 . . . . (956) 430-9503
Jubilee Academic Center (PK-12)
　　2009-10 Enrollment: 701 . . . . (210) 333-6227
South Texas Educational Technologies Inc (PK-06)
　　2009-10 Enrollment: 620 . . . . (956) 969-3092

Two-year College(s)
Texas State Technical College Harlingen (Public)
　　Fall 2009 Enrollment: 5,988. . . . . (956) 364-4000
　　2010-11 Tuition: In-state $5,205; Out-of-state $11,640

Vocational/Technical School(s)
University of Cosmetology Arts and Sciences (Private, For-profit)
　　Fall 2009 Enrollment: 139 . . . . (956) 412-1212
　　2010-11 Tuition: $14,905

Housing: Homeownership rate: 59.8% (2010); Median home value: $76,585 (2010); Median contract rent: $455 per month (2005-2009 5-year est.); Median year structure built: 1979 (2005-2009 5-year est.).

Hospitals: Harlingen Medical Center (80 beds); Rio Grande State Center (150 beds); Valley Baptist Medical Center (588 beds)

Safety: Violent crime rate: 45.8 per 10,000 population; Property crime rate: 676.3 per 10,000 population (2009).

Newspapers: Valley Morning Star (Local news; Circulation 32,000)

Transportation: Commute to work: 95.1% car, 0.1% public transportation, 1.5% walk, 1.6% work from home (2005-2009 5-year est.); Travel time to work: 49.9% less than 15 minutes, 31.6% 15 to 30 minutes, 12.9% 30 to 45 minutes, 4.1% 45 to 60 minutes, 1.4% 60 minutes or more (2005-2009 5-year est.)

Airports: Valley International (primary service/small hub)

Additional Information Contacts
City of Harlingen . . . . (956) 216-5001
　　http://www.myharlingen.us
Harlingen Area Chamber of Commerce. . . . . (956) 423-5440
　　http://www.harlingen.com
Harlingen Hispanic Chamber of Commerce . . . . (956) 421-2400
　　http://www.harlingenchamber.com

INDIAN LAKE (town). Covers a land area of 0.208 square miles and a water area of 0.048 square miles. Located at 26.08° N. Lat; 97.50° W. Long. Elevation is 30 feet.

Population: 390 (1990); 541 (2000); 671 (2010); 743 (2015 projected); Race: 80.9% White, 0.1% Black, 0.1% Asian, 18.8% Other, 71.7% Hispanic of any race (2010); Density: 3,228.0 persons per square mile (2010); Average household size: 2.72 (2010); Median age: 38.1 (2010); Males per 100 females: 93.9 (2010); Marriage status: 12.3% never married, 70.1% now married, 8.0% widowed, 9.7% divorced (2005-2009 5-year est.); Foreign born: 20.6% (2005-2009 5-year est.); Ancestry (includes

multiple ancestries): 15.5% Irish, 12.3% German, 7.6% English, 3.2% American, 1.9% Scotch-Irish (2005-2009 5-year est.).
Economy: Employment by occupation: 5.7% management, 27.0% professional, 24.3% services, 16.5% sales, 0.0% farming, 18.3% construction, 8.3% production (2005-2009 5-year est.).
Income: Per capita income: $12,231 (2010); Median household income: $28,000 (2010); Average household income: $33,664 (2010); Percent of households with income of $100,000 or more: 4.0% (2010); Poverty rate: 16.3% (2005-2009 5-year est.).
Taxes: Total city taxes per capita: $149 (2007); City property taxes per capita: $144 (2007).
Education: Percent of population age 25 and over with: High school diploma (including GED) or higher: 74.0% (2010); Bachelor's degree or higher: 15.6% (2010); Master's degree or higher: 2.6% (2010).
Housing: Homeownership rate: 81.4% (2010); Median home value: $55,246 (2010); Median contract rent: $475 per month (2005-2009 5-year est.); Median year structure built: 1981 (2005-2009 5-year est.).
Transportation: Commute to work: 91.2% car, 5.9% public transportation, 0.0% walk, 2.9% work from home (2005-2009 5-year est.); Travel time to work: 22.2% less than 15 minutes, 22.7% 15 to 30 minutes, 41.9% 30 to 45 minutes, 0.0% 45 to 60 minutes, 13.1% 60 minutes or more (2005-2009 5-year est.)

LA FERIA (city). Covers a land area of 1.989 square miles and a water area of 0 square miles. Located at 26.15° N. Lat; 97.82° W. Long. Elevation is 56 feet.
Population: 5,168 (1990); 6,115 (2000); 5,604 (2010); 5,532 (2015 projected); Race: 71.6% White, 0.4% Black, 0.4% Asian, 27.6% Other, 78.5% Hispanic of any race (2010); Density: 2,818.1 persons per square mile (2010); Average household size: 2.96 (2010); Median age: 30.9 (2010); Males per 100 females: 88.4 (2010); Marriage status: 26.3% never married, 57.6% now married, 6.3% widowed, 9.8% divorced (2005-2009 5-year est.); Foreign born: 15.2% (2005-2009 5-year est.); Ancestry (includes multiple ancestries): 5.5% German, 2.9% English, 2.2% American, 1.2% Irish, 1.1% Dutch (2005-2009 5-year est.).
Economy: Single-family building permits issued: 6 (2010); Multi-family building permits issued: 0 (2010); Employment by occupation: 10.3% management, 13.7% professional, 20.4% services, 25.2% sales, 6.6% farming, 13.3% construction, 10.4% production (2005-2009 5-year est.).
Income: Per capita income: $15,277 (2010); Median household income: $33,460 (2010); Average household income: $45,320 (2010); Percent of households with income of $100,000 or more: 9.6% (2010); Poverty rate: 36.1% (2005-2009 5-year est.).
Taxes: Total city taxes per capita: $300 (2007); City property taxes per capita: $139 (2007).
Education: Percent of population age 25 and over with: High school diploma (including GED) or higher: 66.1% (2010); Bachelor's degree or higher: 12.7% (2010); Master's degree or higher: 3.6% (2010).

School District(s)
La Feria ISD (PK-12)
    2009-10 Enrollment: 3,468 . . . . (956) 797-2612
Housing: Homeownership rate: 74.9% (2010); Median home value: $61,822 (2010); Median contract rent: $241 per month (2005-2009 5-year est.); Median year structure built: 1984 (2005-2009 5-year est.).
Safety: Violent crime rate: 9.9 per 10,000 population; Property crime rate: 474.3 per 10,000 population (2009).
Transportation: Commute to work: 91.1% car, 0.0% public transportation, 1.0% walk, 2.7% work from home (2005-2009 5-year est.); Travel time to work: 33.7% less than 15 minutes, 44.9% 15 to 30 minutes, 14.6% 30 to 45 minutes, 4.3% 45 to 60 minutes, 2.5% 60 minutes or more (2005-2009 5-year est.)

Additional Information Contacts
City of La Feria. . . . . (956) 797-2261
   http://www.cityoflaferia.com

LA FERIA NORTH (CDP). Covers a land area of 1.166 square miles and a water area of 0.047 square miles. Located at 26.18° N. Lat; 97.82° W. Long. Elevation is 56 feet.
Population: 89 (1990); 168 (2000); 178 (2010); 186 (2015 projected); Race: 78.1% White, 0.0% Black, 0.0% Asian, 21.9% Other, 63.5% Hispanic of any race (2010); Density: 152.6 persons per square mile (2010); Average household size: 2.78 (2010); Median age: 34.1 (2010); Males per 100 females: 87.4 (2010); Marriage status: 0.0% never married, 100.0% now married, 0.0% widowed, 0.0% divorced (2005-2009 5-year

est.); Foreign born: 30.4% (2005-2009 5-year est.); Ancestry (includes multiple ancestries): n/a (2005-2009 5-year est.).
Economy: Employment by occupation: 0.0% management, 50.0% professional, 0.0% services, 0.0% sales, 0.0% farming, 0.0% construction, 50.0% production (2005-2009 5-year est.).
Income: Per capita income: $15,377 (2010); Median household income: $33,889 (2010); Average household income: $43,008 (2010); Percent of households with income of $100,000 or more: 7.8% (2010); Poverty rate: 0.0% (2005-2009 5-year est.).
Education: Percent of population age 25 and over with: High school diploma (including GED) or higher: 67.9% (2010); Bachelor's degree or higher: 10.1% (2010); Master's degree or higher: 4.6% (2010).
Housing: Homeownership rate: 81.3% (2010); Median home value: $45,000 (2010); Median contract rent: n/a per month (2005-2009 5-year est.); Median year structure built: 2005 (2005-2009 5-year est.).
Transportation: Commute to work: 100.0% car, 0.0% public transportation, 0.0% walk, 0.0% work from home (2005-2009 5-year est.); Travel time to work: 0.0% less than 15 minutes, 0.0% 15 to 30 minutes, 100.0% 30 to 45 minutes, 0.0% 45 to 60 minutes, 0.0% 60 minutes or more (2005-2009 5-year est.)

LA PALOMA (CDP). Covers a land area of 0.258 square miles and a water area of 0 square miles. Located at 26.04° N. Lat; 97.66° W. Long. Elevation is 49 feet.
Population: 173 (1990); 354 (2000); 402 (2010); 434 (2015 projected); Race: 60.0% White, 0.0% Black, 0.0% Asian, 40.0% Other, 94.5% Hispanic of any race (2010); Density: 1,557.3 persons per square mile (2010); Average household size: 4.02 (2010); Median age: 24.5 (2010); Males per 100 females: 100.0 (2010); Marriage status: 48.8% never married, 41.3% now married, 10.0% widowed, 0.0% divorced (2005-2009 5-year est.); Foreign born: 29.4% (2005-2009 5-year est.); Ancestry (includes multiple ancestries): n/a (2005-2009 5-year est.).
Economy: Employment by occupation: 7.2% management, 0.0% professional, 8.4% services, 16.9% sales, 0.0% farming, 22.9% construction, 44.6% production (2005-2009 5-year est.).
Income: Per capita income: $7,960 (2010); Median household income: $24,286 (2010); Average household income: $30,975 (2010); Percent of households with income of $100,000 or more: 4.0% (2010); Poverty rate: 3.6% (2005-2009 5-year est.).
Education: Percent of population age 25 and over with: High school diploma (including GED) or higher: 42.4% (2010); Bachelor's degree or higher: 4.5% (2010); Master's degree or higher: 1.5% (2010).
Housing: Homeownership rate: 88.0% (2010); Median home value: $48,889 (2010); Median contract rent: n/a per month (2005-2009 5-year est.); Median year structure built: 1996 (2005-2009 5-year est.).
Transportation: Commute to work: 83.1% car, 0.0% public transportation, 16.9% walk, 0.0% work from home (2005-2009 5-year est.); Travel time to work: 55.4% less than 15 minutes, 7.2% 15 to 30 minutes, 37.3% 30 to 45 minutes, 0.0% 45 to 60 minutes, 0.0% 60 minutes or more (2005-2009 5-year est.)

LAGO (CDP). Covers a land area of 0.043 square miles and a water area of 0.007 square miles. Located at 26.08° N. Lat; 97.61° W. Long. Elevation is 39 feet.
Population: 109 (1990); 246 (2000); 268 (2010); 284 (2015 projected); Race: 66.4% White, 0.0% Black, 0.0% Asian, 33.6% Other, 97.0% Hispanic of any race (2010); Density: 6,230.2 persons per square mile (2010); Average household size: 4.12 (2010); Median age: 25.6 (2010); Males per 100 females: 95.6 (2010); Marriage status: 37.3% never married, 15.7% now married, 0.0% widowed, 47.1% divorced (2005-2009 5-year est.); Foreign born: 14.8% (2005-2009 5-year est.); Ancestry (includes multiple ancestries): n/a (2005-2009 5-year est.).
Economy: Employment by occupation: 0.0% management, 0.0% professional, 72.7% services, 27.3% sales, 0.0% farming, 0.0% construction, 0.0% production (2005-2009 5-year est.).
Income: Per capita income: $8,624 (2010); Median household income: $23,438 (2010); Average household income: $34,500 (2010); Percent of households with income of $100,000 or more: 4.6% (2010); Poverty rate: 44.4% (2005-2009 5-year est.).
Education: Percent of population age 25 and over with: High school diploma (including GED) or higher: 41.2% (2010); Bachelor's degree or higher: 6.6% (2010); Master's degree or higher: 1.5% (2010).
Housing: Homeownership rate: 84.6% (2010); Median home value: $65,556 (2010); Median contract rent: n/a per month (2005-2009 5-year est.); Median year structure built: n/a (2005-2009 5-year est.).

Transportation: Commute to work: 100.0% car, 0.0% public transportation, 0.0% walk, 0.0% work from home (2005-2009 5-year est.); Travel time to work: 0.0% less than 15 minutes, 0.0% 15 to 30 minutes, 100.0% 30 to 45 minutes, 0.0% 45 to 60 minutes, 0.0% 60 minutes or more (2005-2009 5-year est.)

LAGUNA HEIGHTS (CDP). Aka Bayside. Covers a land area of 0.276 square miles and a water area of 0 square miles. Located at 26.08° N. Lat; 97.25° W. Long. Elevation is 10 feet.

Population: 1,671 (1990); 1,990 (2000); 1,905 (2010); 1,912 (2015 projected); Race: 52.8% White, 0.9% Black, 0.0% Asian, 46.2% Other, 95.0% Hispanic of any race (2010); Density: 6,894.7 persons per square mile (2010); Average household size: 3.77 (2010); Median age: 26.8 (2010); Males per 100 females: 98.4 (2010); Marriage status: 31.2% never married, 60.2% now married, 6.1% widowed, 2.4% divorced (2005-2009 5-year est.); Foreign born: 51.8% (2005-2009 5-year est.); Ancestry (includes multiple ancestries): 5.8% English (2005-2009 5-year est.).
Economy: Employment by occupation: 0.0% management, 0.7% professional, 49.0% services, 22.0% sales, 3.9% farming, 19.4% construction, 5.1% production (2005-2009 5-year est.).
Income: Per capita income: $6,360 (2010); Median household income: $19,852 (2010); Average household income: $23,936 (2010); Percent of households with income of $100,000 or more: 2.4% (2010); Poverty rate: 57.7% (2005-2009 5-year est.).
Education: Percent of population age 25 and over with: High school diploma (including GED) or higher: 47.7% (2010); Bachelor's degree or higher: 5.7% (2010); Master's degree or higher: 3.8% (2010).
Housing: Homeownership rate: 54.1% (2010); Median home value: $41,957 (2010); Median contract rent: $326 per month (2005-2009 5-year est.); Median year structure built: 1981 (2005-2009 5-year est.).
Transportation: Commute to work: 91.5% car, 0.0% public transportation, 0.0% walk, 0.8% work from home (2005-2009 5-year est.); Travel time to work: 56.4% less than 15 minutes, 34.0% 15 to 30 minutes, 6.7% 30 to 45 minutes, 3.0% 45 to 60 minutes, 0.0% 60 minutes or more (2005-2009 5-year est.)

LAGUNA VISTA (town). Covers a land area of 2.181 square miles and a water area of 0 square miles. Located at 26.10° N. Lat; 97.29° W. Long. Elevation is 10 feet.

Population: 1,216 (1990); 1,658 (2000); 2,703 (2010); 3,147 (2015 projected); Race: 75.5% White, 0.7% Black, 0.4% Asian, 23.4% Other, 58.6% Hispanic of any race (2010); Density: 1,239.2 persons per square mile (2010); Average household size: 2.93 (2010); Median age: 29.9 (2010); Males per 100 females: 87.6 (2010); Marriage status: 23.5% never married, 60.0% now married, 6.9% widowed, 9.6% divorced (2005-2009 5-year est.); Foreign born: 10.3% (2005-2009 5-year est.); Ancestry (includes multiple ancestries): 14.2% German, 9.3% Irish, 6.1% English, 2.3% Scotch-Irish, 2.0% Polish (2005-2009 5-year est.).
Economy: Single-family building permits issued: 14 (2010); Multi-family building permits issued: 0 (2010); Employment by occupation: 18.6% management, 31.5% professional, 11.2% services, 24.7% sales, 2.4% farming, 5.6% construction, 6.1% production (2005-2009 5-year est.).
Income: Per capita income: $21,062 (2010); Median household income: $43,495 (2010); Average household income: $61,559 (2010); Percent of households with income of $100,000 or more: 14.9% (2010); Poverty rate: 8.6% (2005-2009 5-year est.).
Taxes: Total city taxes per capita: $176 (2007); City property taxes per capita: $135 (2007).
Education: Percent of population age 25 and over with: High school diploma (including GED) or higher: 85.6% (2010); Bachelor's degree or higher: 27.3% (2010); Master's degree or higher: 10.7% (2010).
Housing: Homeownership rate: 65.0% (2010); Median home value: $133,798 (2010); Median contract rent: $766 per month (2005-2009 5-year est.); Median year structure built: 1991 (2005-2009 5-year est.).
Safety: Violent crime rate: 11.7 per 10,000 population; Property crime rate: 172.5 per 10,000 population (2009).
Transportation: Commute to work: 84.0% car, 0.0% public transportation, 0.4% walk, 9.8% work from home (2005-2009 5-year est.); Travel time to work: 28.5% less than 15 minutes, 39.6% 15 to 30 minutes, 27.6% 30 to 45 minutes, 2.0% 45 to 60 minutes, 2.3% 60 minutes or more (2005-2009 5-year est.)

LAS PALMAS-JUAREZ (CDP). Covers a land area of 0.399 square miles and a water area of 0 square miles. Located at 26.20° N. Lat; 97.73° W. Long. Elevation is 39 feet.

Population: 1,370 (1990); 1,666 (2000); 1,968 (2010); 2,153 (2015 projected); Race: 94.2% White, 0.9% Black, 0.2% Asian, 4.7% Other, 77.0% Hispanic of any race (2010); Density: 4,926.4 persons per square mile (2010); Average household size: 3.07 (2010); Median age: 30.0 (2010); Males per 100 females: 91.4 (2010); Marriage status: 15.7% never married, 73.8% now married, 8.1% widowed, 2.5% divorced (2005-2009 5-year est.); Foreign born: 21.0% (2005-2009 5-year est.); Ancestry (includes multiple ancestries): 2.2% American (2005-2009 5-year est.).
Economy: Employment by occupation: 3.9% management, 2.3% professional, 38.3% services, 12.9% sales, 0.0% farming, 42.6% construction, 0.0% production (2005-2009 5-year est.).
Income: Per capita income: $12,636 (2010); Median household income: $30,405 (2010); Average household income: $38,657 (2010); Percent of households with income of $100,000 or more: 5.5% (2010); Poverty rate: 76.6% (2005-2009 5-year est.).
Education: Percent of population age 25 and over with: High school diploma (including GED) or higher: 67.1% (2010); Bachelor's degree or higher: 11.0% (2010); Master's degree or higher: 3.5% (2010).
Housing: Homeownership rate: 80.8% (2010); Median home value: $54,063 (2010); Median contract rent: n/a per month (2005-2009 5-year est.); Median year structure built: 1979 (2005-2009 5-year est.).
Transportation: Commute to work: 95.7% car, 0.0% public transportation, 0.0% walk, 4.3% work from home (2005-2009 5-year est.); Travel time to work: 38.8% less than 15 minutes, 53.9% 15 to 30 minutes, 0.0% 30 to 45 minutes, 0.0% 45 to 60 minutes, 7.3% 60 minutes or more (2005-2009 5-year est.)

LASANA (CDP). Covers a land area of 0.902 square miles and a water area of 0 square miles. Located at 26.25° N. Lat; 97.69° W. Long. Elevation is 36 feet.

Population: 94 (1990); 135 (2000); 137 (2010); 142 (2015 projected); Race: 60.6% White, 0.0% Black, 0.7% Asian, 38.7% Other, 89.1% Hispanic of any race (2010); Density: 152.0 persons per square mile (2010); Average household size: 3.51 (2010); Median age: 30.8 (2010); Males per 100 females: 101.5 (2010); Marriage status: n/a never married, n/a now married, n/a widowed, n/a divorced (2005-2009 5-year est.); Foreign born: n/a (2005-2009 5-year est.); Ancestry (includes multiple ancestries): n/a (2005-2009 5-year est.).
Economy: Employment by occupation: n/a management, n/a professional, n/a services, n/a sales, n/a farming, n/a construction, n/a production (2005-2009 5-year est.).
Income: Per capita income: $10,237 (2010); Median household income: $28,750 (2010); Average household income: $37,628 (2010); Percent of households with income of $100,000 or more: 5.1% (2010); Poverty rate: n/a (2005-2009 5-year est.).
Education: Percent of population age 25 and over with: High school diploma (including GED) or higher: 62.5% (2010); Bachelor's degree or higher: 6.3% (2010); Master's degree or higher: 1.3% (2010).
Housing: Homeownership rate: 84.6% (2010); Median home value: $68,750 (2010); Median contract rent: n/a per month (2005-2009 5-year est.); Median year structure built: n/a (2005-2009 5-year est.).
Transportation: Commute to work: n/a car, n/a public transportation, n/a walk, n/a work from home (2005-2009 5-year est.); Travel time to work: n/a less than 15 minutes, n/a 15 to 30 minutes, n/a 30 to 45 minutes, n/a 45 to 60 minutes, n/a 60 minutes or more (2005-2009 5-year est.)

LAURELES (CDP). Covers a land area of 4.855 square miles and a water area of 0 square miles. Located at 26.11° N. Lat; 97.49° W. Long. Elevation is 20 feet.

Population: 1,453 (1990); 3,285 (2000); 4,358 (2010); 4,940 (2015 projected); Race: 90.1% White, 0.3% Black, 0.0% Asian, 9.5% Other, 93.7% Hispanic of any race (2010); Density: 897.6 persons per square mile (2010); Average household size: 3.99 (2010); Median age: 25.2 (2010); Males per 100 females: 96.5 (2010); Marriage status: 27.5% never married, 64.0% now married, 1.5% widowed, 7.0% divorced (2005-2009 5-year est.); Foreign born: 28.7% (2005-2009 5-year est.); Ancestry (includes multiple ancestries): 2.9% American, 0.5% German, 0.4% Italian (2005-2009 5-year est.).
Economy: Employment by occupation: 5.2% management, 11.2% professional, 32.7% services, 16.8% sales, 0.0% farming, 10.4% construction, 23.6% production (2005-2009 5-year est.).
Income: Per capita income: $7,617 (2010); Median household income: $22,151 (2010); Average household income: $30,344 (2010); Percent of households with income of $100,000 or more: 2.8% (2010); Poverty rate: 42.2% (2005-2009 5-year est.).

Education: Percent of population age 25 and over with: High school diploma (including GED) or higher: 51.1% (2010); Bachelor's degree or higher: 8.0% (2010); Master's degree or higher: 2.2% (2010).
Housing: Homeownership rate: 85.3% (2010); Median home value: $51,733 (2010); Median contract rent: $185 per month (2005-2009 5-year est.); Median year structure built: 1994 (2005-2009 5-year est.).
Transportation: Commute to work: 96.5% car, 0.0% public transportation, 0.0% walk, 3.5% work from home (2005-2009 5-year est.); Travel time to work: 25.3% less than 15 minutes, 40.6% 15 to 30 minutes, 25.5% 30 to 45 minutes, 6.8% 45 to 60 minutes, 1.7% 60 minutes or more (2005-2009 5-year est.)

LOS FRESNOS (city). Covers a land area of 2.414 square miles and a water area of 0.104 square miles. Located at 26.07° N. Lat; 97.47° W. Long. Elevation is 23 feet.
History: Palo Alto Battlefield National Historic Site to South; Laguna Atacosca National Wildlife Refuge to Northeast. Incorporated after 1940.
Population: 2,630 (1990); 4,512 (2000); 5,773 (2010); 6,424 (2015 projected); Race: 82.5% White, 0.7% Black, 0.2% Asian, 16.6% Other, 88.6% Hispanic of any race (2010); Density: 2,391.2 persons per square mile (2010); Average household size: 3.48 (2010); Median age: 28.5 (2010); Males per 100 females: 94.5 (2010); Marriage status: 27.7% never married, 58.6% now married, 8.2% widowed, 5.5% divorced (2005-2009 5-year est.); Foreign born: 19.8% (2005-2009 5-year est.); Ancestry (includes multiple ancestries): 2.9% Welsh, 2.5% English, 2.3% Irish, 2.2% German, 1.7% Italian (2005-2009 5-year est.).
Economy: Single-family building permits issued: 20 (2010); Multi-family building permits issued: 0 (2010); Employment by occupation: 10.1% management, 12.3% professional, 22.4% services, 33.2% sales, 0.0% farming, 4.0% construction, 18.0% production (2005-2009 5-year est.).
Income: Per capita income: $11,144 (2010); Median household income: $29,080 (2010); Average household income: $38,532 (2010); Percent of households with income of $100,000 or more: 5.3% (2010); Poverty rate: 32.3% (2005-2009 5-year est.).
Taxes: Total city taxes per capita: $279 (2007); City property taxes per capita: $149 (2007).
Education: Percent of population age 25 and over with: High school diploma (including GED) or higher: 67.6% (2010); Bachelor's degree or higher: 14.9% (2010); Master's degree or higher: 4.4% (2010).

School District(s)
Los Fresnos CISD (PK-12)
    2009-10 Enrollment: 9,734 . . . . (956) 254-5000
Housing: Homeownership rate: 78.7% (2010); Median home value: $70,328 (2010); Median contract rent: $456 per month (2005-2009 5-year est.); Median year structure built: 1985 (2005-2009 5-year est.).
Safety: Violent crime rate: 26.5 per 10,000 population; Property crime rate: 228.0 per 10,000 population (2009).
Transportation: Commute to work: 92.1% car, 0.0% public transportation, 0.5% walk, 5.3% work from home (2005-2009 5-year est.); Travel time to work: 25.6% less than 15 minutes, 43.3% 15 to 30 minutes, 25.2% 30 to 45 minutes, 2.0% 45 to 60 minutes, 3.8% 60 minutes or more (2005-2009 5-year est.)
Additional Information Contacts
Los Fresnos Area Chamber of Commerce . . . . (956) 233-4488
    http://www.losfresnoschamber.com

LOS INDIOS (town). Covers a land area of 1.720 square miles and a water area of <.001 square miles. Located at 26.05° N. Lat; 97.74° W. Long. Elevation is 56 feet.
Population: 858 (1990); 1,149 (2000); 1,201 (2010); 1,247 (2015 projected); Race: 58.4% White, 0.3% Black, 0.1% Asian, 41.2% Other, 91.2% Hispanic of any race (2010); Density: 698.2 persons per square mile (2010); Average household size: 3.86 (2010); Median age: 25.7 (2010); Males per 100 females: 94.0 (2010); Marriage status: 17.1% never married, 61.5% now married, 17.1% widowed, 4.3% divorced (2005-2009 5-year est.); Foreign born: 25.8% (2005-2009 5-year est.); Ancestry (includes multiple ancestries): 1.9% American, 0.3% German (2005-2009 5-year est.).
Economy: Single-family building permits issued: 3 (2010); Multi-family building permits issued: 0 (2010); Employment by occupation: 9.8% management, 7.9% professional, 18.2% services, 26.3% sales, 10.0% farming, 13.0% construction, 14.9% production (2005-2009 5-year est.).
Income: Per capita income: $9,074 (2010); Median household income: $24,922 (2010); Average household income: $34,767 (2010); Percent of

households with income of $100,000 or more: 3.2% (2010); Poverty rate: 42.1% (2005-2009 5-year est.).
Taxes: Total city taxes per capita: $89 (2007); City property taxes per capita: $0 (2007).
Education: Percent of population age 25 and over with: High school diploma (including GED) or higher: 47.0% (2010); Bachelor's degree or higher: 3.8% (2010); Master's degree or higher: 1.6% (2010).
Housing: Homeownership rate: 84.6% (2010); Median home value: $56,094 (2010); Median contract rent: $223 per month (2005-2009 5-year est.); Median year structure built: 1981 (2005-2009 5-year est.).
Transportation: Commute to work: 91.3% car, 0.0% public transportation, 3.2% walk, 2.0% work from home (2005-2009 5-year est.); Travel time to work: 22.0% less than 15 minutes, 36.6% 15 to 30 minutes, 23.8% 30 to 45 minutes, 10.7% 45 to 60 minutes, 6.8% 60 minutes or more (2005-2009 5-year est.)

LOZANO (CDP). Covers a land area of 0.115 square miles and a water area of 0 square miles. Located at 26.19° N. Lat; 97.54° W. Long. Elevation is 26 feet.
Population: 243 (1990); 324 (2000); 326 (2010); 331 (2015 projected); Race: 89.9% White, 0.0% Black, 0.0% Asian, 10.1% Other, 96.0% Hispanic of any race (2010); Density: 2,822.5 persons per square mile (2010); Average household size: 3.47 (2010); Median age: 30.2 (2010); Males per 100 females: 96.4 (2010); Marriage status: 45.8% never married, 33.3% now married, 0.0% widowed, 20.8% divorced (2005-2009 5-year est.); Foreign born: 0.0% (2005-2009 5-year est.); Ancestry (includes multiple ancestries): n/a (2005-2009 5-year est.).
Economy: Employment by occupation: 0.0% management, 0.0% professional, 0.0% services, 0.0% sales, 0.0% farming, 0.0% construction, 100.0% production (2005-2009 5-year est.).
Income: Per capita income: $8,833 (2010); Median household income: $20,600 (2010); Average household income: $30,319 (2010); Percent of households with income of $100,000 or more: 5.3% (2010); Poverty rate: 100.0% (2005-2009 5-year est.).
Education: Percent of population age 25 and over with: High school diploma (including GED) or higher: 56.4% (2010); Bachelor's degree or higher: 13.3% (2010); Master's degree or higher: 1.6% (2010).
Housing: Homeownership rate: 89.4% (2010); Median home value: $52,632 (2010); Median contract rent: n/a per month (2005-2009 5-year est.); Median year structure built: 1985 (2005-2009 5-year est.).
Transportation: Commute to work: 100.0% car, 0.0% public transportation, 0.0% walk, 0.0% work from home (2005-2009 5-year est.); Travel time to work: 0.0% less than 15 minutes, 0.0% 15 to 30 minutes, 0.0% 30 to 45 minutes, 0.0% 45 to 60 minutes, 100.0% 60 minutes or more (2005-2009 5-year est.)

OLMITO (CDP). Covers a land area of 0.670 square miles and a water area of 0.024 square miles. Located at 26.02° N. Lat; 97.53° W. Long. Elevation is 30 feet.
Population: 925 (1990); 1,198 (2000); 1,438 (2010); 1,571 (2015 projected); Race: 94.5% White, 0.0% Black, 0.7% Asian, 4.8% Other, 83.9% Hispanic of any race (2010); Density: 2,146.1 persons per square mile (2010); Average household size: 3.17 (2010); Median age: 30.3 (2010); Males per 100 females: 97.0 (2010); Marriage status: 37.5% never married, 51.3% now married, 8.4% widowed, 2.7% divorced (2005-2009 5-year est.); Foreign born: 39.4% (2005-2009 5-year est.); Ancestry (includes multiple ancestries): 5.6% German, 4.3% English, 1.2% Scotch-Irish, 1.1% Austrian (2005-2009 5-year est.).
Economy: Employment by occupation: 0.0% management, 15.9% professional, 41.3% services, 16.6% sales, 0.0% farming, 17.7% construction, 8.5% production (2005-2009 5-year est.).
Income: Per capita income: $13,395 (2010); Median household income: $24,451 (2010); Average household income: $42,279 (2010); Percent of households with income of $100,000 or more: 8.4% (2010); Poverty rate: 62.1% (2005-2009 5-year est.).
Education: Percent of population age 25 and over with: High school diploma (including GED) or higher: 59.9% (2010); Bachelor's degree or higher: 21.7% (2010); Master's degree or higher: 7.6% (2010).
School District(s)
Los Fresnos CISD (PK-12)
    2009-10 Enrollment: 9,734 . . . . (956) 254-5000
Housing: Homeownership rate: 74.6% (2010); Median home value: $79,048 (2010); Median contract rent: $272 per month (2005-2009 5-year est.); Median year structure built: 1974 (2005-2009 5-year est.).

Transportation: Commute to work: 80.1% car, 0.0% public transportation, 4.1% walk, 15.9% work from home (2005-2009 5-year est.); Travel time to work: 19.3% less than 15 minutes, 52.2% 15 to 30 minutes, 28.5% 30 to 45 minutes, 0.0% 45 to 60 minutes, 0.0% 60 minutes or more (2005-2009 5-year est.)

PALM VALLEY (city). Covers a land area of 0.624 square miles and a water area of 0 square miles. Located at 26.20° N. Lat; 97.75° W. Long. Elevation is 43 feet.

Population: 978 (1990); 1,298 (2000); 1,172 (2010); 1,227 (2015 projected); Race: 93.3% White, 0.9% Black, 0.9% Asian, 4.9% Other, 32.0% Hispanic of any race (2010); Density: 1,879.3 persons per square mile (2010); Average household size: 2.18 (2010); Median age: 57.6 (2010); Males per 100 females: 90.6 (2010); Marriage status: 19.9% never married, 57.6% now married, 10.2% widowed, 12.3% divorced (2005-2009 5-year est.); Foreign born: 7.3% (2005-2009 5-year est.); Ancestry (includes multiple ancestries): 22.6% German, 20.8% English, 20.5% Irish, 4.7% Italian, 4.1% American (2005-2009 5-year est.).
Economy: Single-family building permits issued: 0 (2010); Multi-family building permits issued: 0 (2010); Employment by occupation: 25.3% management, 26.2% professional, 3.1% services, 37.5% sales, 0.0% farming, 3.3% construction, 4.6% production (2005-2009 5-year est.).
Income: Per capita income: $44,832 (2010); Median household income: $70,089 (2010); Average household income: $97,751 (2010); Percent of households with income of $100,000 or more: 32.7% (2010); Poverty rate: 14.8% (2005-2009 5-year est.).
Taxes: Total city taxes per capita: $349 (2007); City property taxes per capita: $308 (2007).
Education: Percent of population age 25 and over with: High school diploma (including GED) or higher: 97.0% (2010); Bachelor's degree or higher: 46.7% (2010); Master's degree or higher: 18.6% (2010).
Housing: Homeownership rate: 87.5% (2010); Median home value: $182,813 (2010); Median contract rent: $926 per month (2005-2009 5-year est.); Median year structure built: 1979 (2005-2009 5-year est.).
Transportation: Commute to work: 90.4% car, 0.0% public transportation, 0.6% walk, 6.7% work from home (2005-2009 5-year est.); Travel time to work: 38.4% less than 15 minutes, 46.2% 15 to 30 minutes, 9.2% 30 to 45 minutes, 3.2% 45 to 60 minutes, 3.0% 60 minutes or more (2005-2009 5-year est.)

PORT ISABEL (city). Covers a land area of 2.196 square miles and a water area of 0.713 square miles. Located at 26.07° N. Lat; 97.21° W. Long. Elevation is 7 feet.

History: Port Isabel Lighthouse (1835) State Historic Site. Formerly called Point Isabel. In Mexican War was supply base for General Zachary Taylor. Incorporated 1928.
Population: 4,474 (1990); 4,865 (2000); 5,069 (2010); 5,280 (2015 projected); Race: 73.4% White, 1.2% Black, 0.2% Asian, 25.2% Other, 74.4% Hispanic of any race (2010); Density: 2,308.4 persons per square mile (2010); Average household size: 2.81 (2010); Median age: 31.6 (2010); Males per 100 females: 93.7 (2010); Marriage status: 29.1% never married, 54.5% now married, 7.3% widowed, 9.1% divorced (2005-2009 5-year est.); Foreign born: 22.4% (2005-2009 5-year est.); Ancestry (includes multiple ancestries): 6.1% German, 4.3% Irish, 3.5% French, 2.2% English, 1.9% American (2005-2009 5-year est.).
Economy: Single-family building permits issued: 3 (2010); Multi-family building permits issued: 0 (2010); Employment by occupation: 7.8% management, 8.8% professional, 42.4% services, 19.8% sales, 0.9% farming, 13.5% construction, 6.7% production (2005-2009 5-year est.).
Income: Per capita income: $15,013 (2010); Median household income: $30,095 (2010); Average household income: $41,200 (2010); Percent of households with income of $100,000 or more: 5.7% (2010); Poverty rate: 37.3% (2005-2009 5-year est.).
Taxes: Total city taxes per capita: $665 (2007); City property taxes per capita: $263 (2007).
Education: Percent of population age 25 and over with: High school diploma (including GED) or higher: 66.2% (2010); Bachelor's degree or higher: 13.2% (2010); Master's degree or higher: 3.6% (2010).
School District(s)
Point Isabel ISD (PK-12)
   2009-10 Enrollment: 2,538 . . . . (956) 943-0005
Housing: Homeownership rate: 58.7% (2010); Median home value: $84,438 (2010); Median contract rent: $352 per month (2005-2009 5-year est.); Median year structure built: 1977 (2005-2009 5-year est.).

Safety: Violent crime rate: 43.2 per 10,000 population; Property crime rate: 612.6 per 10,000 population (2009).
Newspapers: Port Isabel/South Padre Press (Local news; Circulation 4,692)
Transportation: Commute to work: 77.7% car, 3.7% public transportation, 4.7% walk, 0.8% work from home (2005-2009 5-year est.); Travel time to work: 60.7% less than 15 minutes, 28.8% 15 to 30 minutes, 6.7% 30 to 45 minutes, 1.1% 45 to 60 minutes, 2.7% 60 minutes or more (2005-2009 5-year est.)
Airports: Port Isabel-Cameron County (general aviation)
Additional Information Contacts
Port Isabel Chamber of Commerce . . . . (956) 943-2262
  http://www.portisabel.org

PRIMERA (town). Covers a land area of 1.536 square miles and a water area of 0 square miles. Located at 26.22° N. Lat; 97.75° W. Long. Elevation is 43 feet.

Population: 2,030 (1990); 2,723 (2000); 3,216 (2010); 3,497 (2015 projected); Race: 84.1% White, 0.9% Black, 0.1% Asian, 15.0% Other, 80.6% Hispanic of any race (2010); Density: 2,093.2 persons per square mile (2010); Average household size: 3.33 (2010); Median age: 29.1 (2010); Males per 100 females: 94.7 (2010); Marriage status: 34.9% never married, 56.6% now married, 3.8% widowed, 4.7% divorced (2005-2009 5-year est.); Foreign born: 13.8% (2005-2009 5-year est.); Ancestry (includes multiple ancestries): 4.9% German, 3.0% English, 2.6% American, 1.0% French, 1.0% European (2005-2009 5-year est.).
Economy: Single-family building permits issued: 8 (2010); Multi-family building permits issued: 0 (2010); Employment by occupation: 9.2% management, 15.0% professional, 28.7% services, 31.3% sales, 0.0% farming, 8.3% construction, 7.4% production (2005-2009 5-year est.).
Income: Per capita income: $12,011 (2010); Median household income: $34,248 (2010); Average household income: $40,163 (2010); Percent of households with income of $100,000 or more: 3.0% (2010); Poverty rate: 29.7% (2005-2009 5-year est.).
Taxes: Total city taxes per capita: $192 (2007); City property taxes per capita: $125 (2007).
Education: Percent of population age 25 and over with: High school diploma (including GED) or higher: 64.8% (2010); Bachelor's degree or higher: 6.5% (2010); Master's degree or higher: 1.7% (2010).
Housing: Homeownership rate: 82.6% (2010); Median home value: $76,194 (2010); Median contract rent: $510 per month (2005-2009 5-year est.); Median year structure built: 1990 (2005-2009 5-year est.).
Safety: Violent crime rate: 4.6 per 10,000 population; Property crime rate: 115.8 per 10,000 population (2009).
Transportation: Commute to work: 96.8% car, 0.0% public transportation, 1.3% walk, 1.4% work from home (2005-2009 5-year est.); Travel time to work: 32.7% less than 15 minutes, 53.6% 15 to 30 minutes, 9.2% 30 to 45 minutes, 3.9% 45 to 60 minutes, 0.5% 60 minutes or more (2005-2009 5-year est.)

RANCHO VIEJO (town). Covers a land area of 2.107 square miles and a water area of 0.162 square miles. Located at 26.03° N. Lat; 97.55° W. Long. Elevation is 30 feet.

Population: 880 (1990); 1,754 (2000); 2,010 (2010); 2,162 (2015 projected); Race: 90.2% White, 0.9% Black, 4.0% Asian, 4.9% Other, 69.5% Hispanic of any race (2010); Density: 954.1 persons per square mile (2010); Average household size: 2.66 (2010); Median age: 37.3 (2010); Males per 100 females: 94.6 (2010); Marriage status: 21.5% never married, 64.1% now married, 4.1% widowed, 10.4% divorced (2005-2009 5-year est.); Foreign born: 23.3% (2005-2009 5-year est.); Ancestry (includes multiple ancestries): 9.9% German, 7.5% English, 4.7% Scotch-Irish, 3.5% American, 3.4% Danish (2005-2009 5-year est.).
Economy: Single-family building permits issued: 11 (2010); Multi-family building permits issued: 0 (2010); Employment by occupation: 23.8% management, 42.5% professional, 9.3% services, 18.6% sales, 0.0% farming, 2.5% construction, 3.4% production (2005-2009 5-year est.).
Income: Per capita income: $31,422 (2010); Median household income: $56,351 (2010); Average household income: $83,550 (2010); Percent of households with income of $100,000 or more: 26.4% (2010); Poverty rate: 10.2% (2005-2009 5-year est.).
Taxes: Total city taxes per capita: $459 (2007); City property taxes per capita: $359 (2007).
Education: Percent of population age 25 and over with: High school diploma (including GED) or higher: 82.7% (2010); Bachelor's degree or higher: 41.7% (2010); Master's degree or higher: 18.7% (2010).

Housing: Homeownership rate: 77.7% (2010); Median home value: $148,723 (2010); Median contract rent: $677 per month (2005-2009 5-year est.); Median year structure built: 1981 (2005-2009 5-year est.).
Safety: Violent crime rate: 32.4 per 10,000 population; Property crime rate: 178.0 per 10,000 population (2009).
Transportation: Commute to work: 93.5% car, 0.0% public transportation, 0.0% walk, 4.0% work from home (2005-2009 5-year est.); Travel time to work: 19.0% less than 15 minutes, 62.4% 15 to 30 minutes, 13.3% 30 to 45 minutes, 2.8% 45 to 60 minutes, 2.5% 60 minutes or more (2005-2009 5-year est.)

RANGERVILLE (village). Covers a land area of 3.527 square miles and a water area of 0.021 square miles. Located at 26.10° N. Lat; 97.73° W. Long. Elevation is 52 feet.
Population: 280 (1990); 203 (2000); 223 (2010); 234 (2015 projected); Race: 58.3% White, 0.4% Black, 0.0% Asian, 41.3% Other, 90.6% Hispanic of any race (2010); Density: 63.2 persons per square mile (2010); Average household size: 3.84 (2010); Median age: 26.4 (2010); Males per 100 females: 92.2 (2010); Marriage status: 0.0% never married, 0.0% now married, 0.0% widowed, 100.0% divorced (2005-2009 5-year est.); Foreign born: 0.0% (2005-2009 5-year est.); Ancestry (includes multiple ancestries): 30.4% American (2005-2009 5-year est.).
Economy: Employment by occupation: 0.0% management, 100.0% professional, 0.0% services, 0.0% sales, 0.0% farming, 0.0% construction, 0.0% production (2005-2009 5-year est.).
Income: Per capita income: $9,590 (2010); Median household income: $25,000 (2010); Average household income: $32,241 (2010); Percent of households with income of $100,000 or more: 1.7% (2010); Poverty rate: 100.0% (2005-2009 5-year est.).
Education: Percent of population age 25 and over with: High school diploma (including GED) or higher: 48.3% (2010); Bachelor's degree or higher: 3.4% (2010); Master's degree or higher: 1.7% (2010).
Housing: Homeownership rate: 84.5% (2010); Median home value: $53,636 (2010); Median contract rent: n/a per month (2005-2009 5-year est.); Median year structure built: 1989 (2005-2009 5-year est.).
Transportation: Commute to work: 0.0% car, 0.0% public transportation, 100.0% walk, 0.0% work from home (2005-2009 5-year est.); Travel time to work: 100.0% less than 15 minutes, 0.0% 15 to 30 minutes, 0.0% 30 to 45 minutes, 0.0% 45 to 60 minutes, 0.0% 60 minutes or more (2005-2009 5-year est.)

RATAMOSA (CDP). Covers a land area of 2.009 square miles and a water area of 0 square miles. Located at 26.20° N. Lat; 97.85° W. Long. Elevation is 52 feet.
Population: 168 (1990); 218 (2000); 220 (2010); 226 (2015 projected); Race: 67.7% White, 0.9% Black, 0.0% Asian, 31.4% Other, 88.2% Hispanic of any race (2010); Density: 109.5 persons per square mile (2010); Average household size: 3.55 (2010); Median age: 29.7 (2010); Males per 100 females: 96.4 (2010); Marriage status: 0.0% never married, 100.0% now married, 0.0% widowed, 0.0% divorced (2005-2009 5-year est.); Foreign born: 0.0% (2005-2009 5-year est.); Ancestry (includes multiple ancestries): 51.4% English (2005-2009 5-year est.).
Economy: Employment by occupation: 0.0% management, 100.0% professional, 0.0% services, 0.0% sales, 0.0% farming, 0.0% construction, 0.0% production (2005-2009 5-year est.).
Income: Per capita income: $17,171 (2010); Median household income: $40,000 (2010); Average household income: $58,790 (2010); Percent of households with income of $100,000 or more: 14.5% (2010); Poverty rate: 0.0% (2005-2009 5-year est.).
Education: Percent of population age 25 and over with: High school diploma (including GED) or higher: 62.9% (2010); Bachelor's degree or higher: 12.1% (2010); Master's degree or higher: 4.0% (2010).
Housing: Homeownership rate: 83.9% (2010); Median home value: $77,778 (2010); Median contract rent: n/a per month (2005-2009 5-year est.); Median year structure built: n/a (2005-2009 5-year est.).
Transportation: Commute to work: 100.0% car, 0.0% public transportation, 0.0% walk, 0.0% work from home (2005-2009 5-year est.); Travel time to work: 0.0% less than 15 minutes, 100.0% 15 to 30 minutes, 0.0% 30 to 45 minutes, 0.0% 45 to 60 minutes, 0.0% 60 minutes or more (2005-2009 5-year est.)

REID HOPE KING (CDP). Covers a land area of 0.296 square miles and a water area of 0 square miles. Located at 25.92° N. Lat; 97.41° W. Long. Elevation is 16 feet.

Population: 378 (1990); 802 (2000); 1,026 (2010); 1,142 (2015 projected); Race: 79.3% White, 1.6% Black, 0.1% Asian, 19.0% Other, 82.7% Hispanic of any race (2010); Density: 3,468.0 persons per square mile (2010); Average household size: 3.29 (2010); Median age: 29.7 (2010); Males per 100 females: 89.3 (2010); Marriage status: 12.8% never married, 59.2% now married, 16.4% widowed, 11.6% divorced (2005-2009 5-year est.); Foreign born: 19.8% (2005-2009 5-year est.); Ancestry (includes multiple ancestries): n/a (2005-2009 5-year est.).
Economy: Employment by occupation: 13.5% management, 7.2% professional, 28.4% services, 44.2% sales, 0.0% farming, 0.0% construction, 6.7% production (2005-2009 5-year est.).
Income: Per capita income: $12,585 (2010); Median household income: $26,935 (2010); Average household income: $41,450 (2010); Percent of households with income of $100,000 or more: 8.3% (2010); Poverty rate: 43.8% (2005-2009 5-year est.).
Education: Percent of population age 25 and over with: High school diploma (including GED) or higher: 50.8% (2010); Bachelor's degree or higher: 10.2% (2010); Master's degree or higher: 3.5% (2010).
Housing: Homeownership rate: 74.0% (2010); Median home value: $45,179 (2010); Median contract rent: n/a per month (2005-2009 5-year est.); Median year structure built: 1965 (2005-2009 5-year est.).
Transportation: Commute to work: 91.9% car, 3.6% public transportation, 4.6% walk, 0.0% work from home (2005-2009 5-year est.); Travel time to work: 5.6% less than 15 minutes, 68.5% 15 to 30 minutes, 25.9% 30 to 45 minutes, 0.0% 45 to 60 minutes, 0.0% 60 minutes or more (2005-2009 5-year est.)

RIO HONDO (city). Covers a land area of 1.393 square miles and a water area of 0.087 square miles. Located at 26.23° N. Lat; 97.58° W. Long. Elevation is 26 feet.
Population: 1,718 (1990); 1,942 (2000); 1,957 (2010); 2,005 (2015 projected); Race: 71.9% White, 0.1% Black, 0.5% Asian, 27.5% Other, 86.1% Hispanic of any race (2010); Density: 1,405.1 persons per square mile (2010); Average household size: 3.10 (2010); Median age: 30.9 (2010); Males per 100 females: 93.0 (2010); Marriage status: 24.2% never married, 58.8% now married, 7.4% widowed, 9.6% divorced (2005-2009 5-year est.); Foreign born: 12.1% (2005-2009 5-year est.); Ancestry (includes multiple ancestries): 5.6% German, 4.5% English, 2.7% American, 2.6% Italian, 2.1% Irish (2005-2009 5-year est.).
Economy: Single-family building permits issued: 4 (2010); Multi-family building permits issued: 0 (2010); Employment by occupation: 6.1% management, 23.8% professional, 17.3% services, 30.7% sales, 0.5% farming, 9.4% construction, 12.2% production (2005-2009 5-year est.).
Income: Per capita income: $11,253 (2010); Median household income: $27,172 (2010); Average household income: $34,489 (2010); Percent of households with income of $100,000 or more: 4.1% (2010); Poverty rate: 37.9% (2005-2009 5-year est.).
Taxes: Total city taxes per capita: $253 (2007); City property taxes per capita: $143 (2007).
Education: Percent of population age 25 and over with: High school diploma (including GED) or higher: 61.9% (2010); Bachelor's degree or higher: 11.5% (2010); Master's degree or higher: 3.5% (2010).

School District(s)
Rio Hondo ISD (PK-12)
    2009-10 Enrollment: 2,310 . . . . (956) 748-1000
Housing: Homeownership rate: 75.9% (2010); Median home value: $58,879 (2010); Median contract rent: $331 per month (2005-2009 5-year est.); Median year structure built: 1977 (2005-2009 5-year est.).
Transportation: Commute to work: 91.6% car, 0.0% public transportation, 2.0% walk, 3.8% work from home (2005-2009 5-year est.); Travel time to work: 35.5% less than 15 minutes, 52.5% 15 to 30 minutes, 7.9% 30 to 45 minutes, 2.7% 45 to 60 minutes, 1.4% 60 minutes or more (2005-2009 5-year est.)

SAN BENITO (city). Covers a land area of 11.005 square miles and a water area of 0.208 square miles. Located at 26.13° N. Lat; 97.63° W. Long. Elevation is 36 feet.
History: Incorporated 1911.
Population: 20,834 (1990); 23,444 (2000); 25,112 (2010); 26,410 (2015 projected); Race: 76.0% White, 0.3% Black, 0.3% Asian, 23.4% Other, 91.3% Hispanic of any race (2010); Density: 2,281.8 persons per square mile (2010); Average household size: 3.29 (2010); Median age: 29.1 (2010); Males per 100 females: 91.2 (2010); Marriage status: 26.9% never married, 58.3% now married, 6.2% widowed, 8.6% divorced (2005-2009 5-year est.); Foreign born: 20.2% (2005-2009 5-year est.); Ancestry

(includes multiple ancestries): 2.9% German, 2.5% American, 2.0% Irish, 1.9% English, 1.2% Norwegian (2005-2009 5-year est.).
Economy: Unemployment rate: 11.6% (June 2011); Total civilian labor force: 9,786 (June 2011); Single-family building permits issued: 30 (2010); Multi-family building permits issued: 0 (2010); Employment by occupation: 6.3% management, 16.1% professional, 27.5% services, 28.7% sales, 0.7% farming, 10.2% construction, 10.5% production (2005-2009 5-year est.).
Income: Per capita income: $11,786 (2010); Median household income: $27,342 (2010); Average household income: $38,672 (2010); Percent of households with income of $100,000 or more: 6.3% (2010); Poverty rate: 33.9% (2005-2009 5-year est.).
Taxes: Total city taxes per capita: $350 (2007); City property taxes per capita: $138 (2007).
Education: Percent of population age 25 and over with: High school diploma (including GED) or higher: 58.2% (2010); Bachelor's degree or higher: 10.2% (2010); Master's degree or higher: 2.7% (2010).

School District(s)

Brownsville ISD (PK-12)
   2009-10 Enrollment: 49,121 . . . . (956) 548-8000
Idea Public Schools (PK-12)
   2009-10 Enrollment: 5,515 . . . . (956) 377-8000
Los Fresnos CISD (PK-12)
   2009-10 Enrollment: 9,734 . . . . (956) 254-5000
Mid-Valley Academy (09-12)
   2009-10 Enrollment: 380 . . . . (210) 227-0295
San Benito CISD (PK-12)
   2009-10 Enrollment: 11,209 . . . . (956) 361-6110
Santa Rosa ISD (PK-12)
   2009-10 Enrollment: 1,177 . . . . (956) 636-9800
South Texas ISD (07-12)
   2009-10 Enrollment: 3,023 . . . . (956) 514-4216

Vocational/Technical School(s)

South Texas Training Center (Private, For-profit)
   Fall 2009 Enrollment: 42 . . . . (956) 399-9698
   2010-11 Tuition: In-state $5,080; Out-of-state $5,080
Housing: Homeownership rate: 68.4% (2010); Median home value: $49,641 (2010); Median contract rent: $386 per month (2005-2009 5-year est.); Median year structure built: 1978 (2005-2009 5-year est.).
Hospitals: Dolly Vinsant Memorial Hospital (81 beds)
Safety: Violent crime rate: 25.4 per 10,000 population; Property crime rate: 469.9 per 10,000 population (2009).
Newspapers: NEWS (Local news; Circulation 5,000); San Benito News (Local news)
Transportation: Commute to work: 92.4% car, 0.0% public transportation, 3.2% walk, 2.0% work from home (2005-2009 5-year est.); Travel time to work: 33.7% less than 15 minutes, 43.5% 15 to 30 minutes, 12.1% 30 to 45 minutes, 5.1% 45 to 60 minutes, 5.6% 60 minutes or more (2005-2009 5-year est.)
Additional Information Contacts
City of San Benito . . . . (956) 361-3800
   http://www.cityofsanbenito.com
San Benito Chamber of Commerce. . . . . (956) 399-5321
   http://www.cityofsanbenito.com

SAN PEDRO (CDP).
Covers a land area of 2.475 square miles and a water area of 0 square miles. Located at 25.98° N. Lat; 97.59° W. Long. Elevation is 46 feet.
Population: 444 (1990); 668 (2000); 774 (2010); 841 (2015 projected); Race: 62.3% White, 0.1% Black, 0.0% Asian, 37.6% Other, 77.4% Hispanic of any race (2010); Density: 312.7 persons per square mile (2010); Average household size: 3.39 (2010); Median age: 31.5 (2010); Males per 100 females: 91.6 (2010); Marriage status: 18.2% never married, 66.5% now married, 0.0% widowed, 15.4% divorced (2005-2009 5-year est.); Foreign born: 9.3% (2005-2009 5-year est.); Ancestry (includes multiple ancestries): 14.7% American (2005-2009 5-year est.).
Economy: Employment by occupation: 6.3% management, 0.0% professional, 71.7% services, 0.0% sales, 0.0% farming, 8.2% construction, 13.8% production (2005-2009 5-year est.).
Income: Per capita income: $13,693 (2010); Median household income: $44,457 (2010); Average household income: $46,239 (2010); Percent of households with income of $100,000 or more: 4.4% (2010); Poverty rate: 34.8% (2005-2009 5-year est.).

Education: Percent of population age 25 and over with: High school diploma (including GED) or higher: 66.7% (2010); Bachelor's degree or higher: 8.6% (2010); Master's degree or higher: 4.3% (2010).
Housing: Homeownership rate: 90.8% (2010); Median home value: $60,345 (2010); Median contract rent: n/a per month (2005-2009 5-year est.); Median year structure built: 1982 (2005-2009 5-year est.).
Transportation: Commute to work: 78.6% car, 0.0% public transportation, 0.0% walk, 21.4% work from home (2005-2009 5-year est.); Travel time to work: 0.0% less than 15 minutes, 81.6% 15 to 30 minutes, 0.0% 30 to 45 minutes, 18.4% 45 to 60 minutes, 0.0% 60 minutes or more (2005-2009 5-year est.)

SANTA MARIA (CDP).
Covers a land area of 0.234 square miles and a water area of 0 square miles. Located at 26.07° N. Lat; 97.84° W. Long. Elevation is 66 feet.
Population: 815 (1990); 846 (2000); 816 (2010); 825 (2015 projected); Race: 67.2% White, 0.0% Black, 0.0% Asian, 32.8% Other, 95.2% Hispanic of any race (2010); Density: 3,493.7 persons per square mile (2010); Average household size: 3.83 (2010); Median age: 26.7 (2010); Males per 100 females: 89.8 (2010); Marriage status: 31.8% never married, 53.8% now married, 5.7% widowed, 8.7% divorced (2005-2009 5-year est.); Foreign born: 27.6% (2005-2009 5-year est.); Ancestry (includes multiple ancestries): n/a (2005-2009 5-year est.).
Economy: Employment by occupation: 0.0% management, 3.3% professional, 33.6% services, 25.4% sales, 7.4% farming, 9.8% construction, 20.5% production (2005-2009 5-year est.).
Income: Per capita income: $7,109 (2010); Median household income: $20,196 (2010); Average household income: $27,547 (2010); Percent of households with income of $100,000 or more: 2.3% (2010); Poverty rate: 61.9% (2005-2009 5-year est.).
Education: Percent of population age 25 and over with: High school diploma (including GED) or higher: 35.7% (2010); Bachelor's degree or higher: 3.5% (2010); Master's degree or higher: 0.9% (2010).

School District(s)

Santa Maria ISD (PK-12)
   2009-10 Enrollment: 666 . . . . (956) 565-6308
Housing: Homeownership rate: 77.0% (2010); Median home value: $42,500 (2010); Median contract rent: $225 per month (2005-2009 5-year est.); Median year structure built: 1968 (2005-2009 5-year est.).
Transportation: Commute to work: 92.6% car, 0.0% public transportation, 7.4% walk, 0.0% work from home (2005-2009 5-year est.); Travel time to work: 41.8% less than 15 minutes, 40.2% 15 to 30 minutes, 7.4% 30 to 45 minutes, 10.7% 45 to 60 minutes, 0.0% 60 minutes or more (2005-2009 5-year est.)

SANTA ROSA (town).
Covers a land area of 0.588 square miles and a water area of 0 square miles. Located at 26.25° N. Lat; 97.82° W. Long. Elevation is 49 feet.
Population: 2,241 (1990); 2,833 (2000); 2,724 (2010); 2,734 (2015 projected); Race: 58.0% White, 0.6% Black, 0.1% Asian, 41.4% Other, 94.0% Hispanic of any race (2010); Density: 4,629.5 persons per square mile (2010); Average household size: 3.59 (2010); Median age: 26.6 (2010); Males per 100 females: 92.5 (2010); Marriage status: 24.5% never married, 69.7% now married, 3.0% widowed, 2.8% divorced (2005-2009 5-year est.); Foreign born: 38.8% (2005-2009 5-year est.); Ancestry (includes multiple ancestries): 0.4% Polish, 0.3% English, 0.3% German, 0.3% American, 0.3% Irish (2005-2009 5-year est.).
Economy: Single-family building permits issued: 2 (2010); Multi-family building permits issued: 0 (2010); Employment by occupation: 2.7% management, 9.3% professional, 30.6% services, 27.5% sales, 5.0% farming, 12.6% construction, 12.2% production (2005-2009 5-year est.).
Income: Per capita income: $10,011 (2010); Median household income: $27,673 (2010); Average household income: $35,950 (2010); Percent of households with income of $100,000 or more: 4.4% (2010); Poverty rate: 67.5% (2005-2009 5-year est.).
Taxes: Total city taxes per capita: $68 (2007); City property taxes per capita: $55 (2007).
Education: Percent of population age 25 and over with: High school diploma (including GED) or higher: 49.7% (2010); Bachelor's degree or higher: 6.6% (2010); Master's degree or higher: 1.8% (2010).

School District(s)

Santa Rosa ISD (PK-12)
   2009-10 Enrollment: 1,177 . . . . (956) 636-9800

Housing: Homeownership rate: 76.8% (2010); Median home value: $57,197 (2010); Median contract rent: $254 per month (2005-2009 5-year est.); Median year structure built: 1974 (2005-2009 5-year est.).
Safety: Violent crime rate: 44.3 per 10,000 population; Property crime rate: 202.3 per 10,000 population (2009).
Transportation: Commute to work: 94.9% car, 0.0% public transportation, 2.7% walk, 0.6% work from home (2005-2009 5-year est.); Travel time to work: 30.3% less than 15 minutes, 46.0% 15 to 30 minutes, 15.9% 30 to 45 minutes, 4.9% 45 to 60 minutes, 2.9% 60 minutes or more (2005-2009 5-year est.)

SOLIS (CDP).
Covers a land area of 2.102 square miles and a water area of 0 square miles. Located at 26.16° N. Lat; 97.84° W. Long. Elevation is 59 feet.
Population: 367 (1990); 545 (2000); 604 (2010); 648 (2015 projected); Race: 79.5% White, 0.0% Black, 0.0% Asian, 20.5% Other, 81.3% Hispanic of any race (2010); Density: 287.4 persons per square mile (2010); Average household size: 3.18 (2010); Median age: 29.3 (2010); Males per 100 females: 93.0 (2010); Marriage status: 23.6% never married, 31.9% now married, 19.8% widowed, 24.7% divorced (2005-2009 5-year est.); Foreign born: 9.2% (2005-2009 5-year est.); Ancestry (includes multiple ancestries): 17.0% Irish, 8.9% English, 6.3% Scottish, 5.5% French, 2.3% American (2005-2009 5-year est.).
Economy: Employment by occupation: 0.0% management, 0.0% professional, 29.6% services, 52.0% sales, 0.0% farming, 18.4% construction, 0.0% production (2005-2009 5-year est.).
Income: Per capita income: $11,212 (2010); Median household income: $25,690 (2010); Average household income: $35,763 (2010); Percent of households with income of $100,000 or more: 6.3% (2010); Poverty rate: 13.5% (2005-2009 5-year est.).
Education: Percent of population age 25 and over with: High school diploma (including GED) or higher: 52.1% (2010); Bachelor's degree or higher: 8.6% (2010); Master's degree or higher: 3.6% (2010).
Housing: Homeownership rate: 77.9% (2010); Median home value: $50,000 (2010); Median contract rent: n/a per month (2005-2009 5-year est.); Median year structure built: 1972 (2005-2009 5-year est.).
Transportation: Commute to work: 100.0% car, 0.0% public transportation, 0.0% walk, 0.0% work from home (2005-2009 5-year est.); Travel time to work: 42.9% less than 15 minutes, 29.6% 15 to 30 minutes, 0.0% 30 to 45 minutes, 9.2% 45 to 60 minutes, 18.4% 60 minutes or more (2005-2009 5-year est.)

SOUTH PADRE ISLAND (town).
Covers a land area of 1.813 square miles and a water area of 0.082 square miles. Located at 26.11° N. Lat; 97.17° W. Long. Elevation is 7 feet.
Population: 1,716 (1990); 2,422 (2000); 2,890 (2010); 3,146 (2015 projected); Race: 95.5% White, 0.7% Black, 0.1% Asian, 3.7% Other, 23.2% Hispanic of any race (2010); Density: 1,594.0 persons per square mile (2010); Average household size: 1.90 (2010); Median age: 58.1 (2010); Males per 100 females: 105.0 (2010); Marriage status: 21.0% never married, 61.6% now married, 4.2% widowed, 13.2% divorced (2005-2009 5-year est.); Foreign born: 10.8% (2005-2009 5-year est.); Ancestry (includes multiple ancestries): 17.6% German, 16.7% English, 8.3% Irish, 4.7% Scottish, 4.1% Polish (2005-2009 5-year est.).
Economy: Single-family building permits issued: 5 (2010); Multi-family building permits issued: 128 (2010); Employment by occupation: 17.4% management, 33.3% professional, 9.6% services, 19.0% sales, 0.0% farming, 17.7% construction, 3.0% production (2005-2009 5-year est.).
Income: Per capita income: $37,248 (2010); Median household income: $47,326 (2010); Average household income: $70,434 (2010); Percent of households with income of $100,000 or more: 17.0% (2010); Poverty rate: 10.5% (2005-2009 5-year est.).
Taxes: Total city taxes per capita: $4,913 (2007); City property taxes per capita: $1,540 (2007).
Education: Percent of population age 25 and over with: High school diploma (including GED) or higher: 94.5% (2010); Bachelor's degree or higher: 33.7% (2010); Master's degree or higher: 14.4% (2010).
Housing: Homeownership rate: 72.9% (2010); Median home value: $204,310 (2010); Median contract rent: $828 per month (2005-2009 5-year est.); Median year structure built: 1981 (2005-2009 5-year est.).
Safety: Violent crime rate: 242.7 per 10,000 population; Property crime rate: 2,479.2 per 10,000 population (2009).
Newspapers: Island Breeze (Local news)
Transportation: Commute to work: 80.3% car, 1.1% public transportation, 7.2% walk, 7.2% work from home (2005-2009 5-year est.); Travel time to

work: 53.6% less than 15 minutes, 19.9% 15 to 30 minutes, 11.7% 30 to 45 minutes, 0.0% 45 to 60 minutes, 14.8% 60 minutes or more (2005-2009 5-year est.)
Additional Information Contacts
South Padre Island Chamber of Commerce . . . . (956) 761-4412
  http://www.spichamber.com
Town of South Padre Island. . . . . (956) 761-6456
  http://myspi.org

SOUTH POINT (CDP).
Covers a land area of 1.285 square miles and a water area of 0.050 square miles. Located at 25.87° N. Lat; 97.38° W. Long. Elevation is 16 feet.
Population: 682 (1990); 1,118 (2000); 1,197 (2010); 1,259 (2015 projected); Race: 92.1% White, 0.2% Black, 0.0% Asian, 7.8% Other, 97.2% Hispanic of any race (2010); Density: 931.6 persons per square mile (2010); Average household size: 3.94 (2010); Median age: 27.6 (2010); Males per 100 females: 94.6 (2010); Marriage status: 32.2% never married, 50.8% now married, 13.1% widowed, 3.9% divorced (2005-2009 5-year est.); Foreign born: 25.7% (2005-2009 5-year est.); Ancestry (includes multiple ancestries): 0.7% American, 0.7% German (2005-2009 5-year est.).
Economy: Employment by occupation: 7.3% management, 3.3% professional, 28.0% services, 24.0% sales, 0.0% farming, 19.6% construction, 17.8% production (2005-2009 5-year est.).
Income: Per capita income: $9,007 (2010); Median household income: $27,750 (2010); Average household income: $34,811 (2010); Percent of households with income of $100,000 or more: 3.9% (2010); Poverty rate: 52.6% (2005-2009 5-year est.).
Education: Percent of population age 25 and over with: High school diploma (including GED) or higher: 52.5% (2010); Bachelor's degree or higher: 3.3% (2010); Master's degree or higher: 0.0% (2010).
Housing: Homeownership rate: 79.6% (2010); Median home value: $53,333 (2010); Median contract rent: $553 per month (2005-2009 5-year est.); Median year structure built: 1986 (2005-2009 5-year est.).
Transportation: Commute to work: 85.2% car, 0.0% public transportation, 0.0% walk, 3.5% work from home (2005-2009 5-year est.); Travel time to work: 25.5% less than 15 minutes, 43.7% 15 to 30 minutes, 20.2% 30 to 45 minutes, 0.0% 45 to 60 minutes, 10.5% 60 minutes or more (2005-2009 5-year est.)

TIERRA BONITA (CDP).
Covers a land area of 1.031 square miles and a water area of 0 square miles. Located at 26.26° N. Lat; 97.82° W. Long. Elevation is 46 feet.
Population: 125 (1990); 160 (2000); 159 (2010); 162 (2015 projected); Race: 56.0% White, 1.3% Black, 0.0% Asian, 42.8% Other, 92.5% Hispanic of any race (2010); Density: 154.3 persons per square mile (2010); Average household size: 3.70 (2010); Median age: 26.1 (2010); Males per 100 females: 96.3 (2010); Marriage status: n/a never married, n/a now married, n/a widowed, n/a divorced (2005-2009 5-year est.); Foreign born: n/a (2005-2009 5-year est.); Ancestry (includes multiple ancestries): n/a (2005-2009 5-year est.).
Economy: Employment by occupation: n/a management, n/a professional, n/a services, n/a sales, n/a farming, n/a construction, n/a production (2005-2009 5-year est.).
Income: Per capita income: $11,164 (2010); Median household income: $28,750 (2010); Average household income: $34,012 (2010); Percent of households with income of $100,000 or more: 2.3% (2010); Poverty rate: n/a (2005-2009 5-year est.).
Education: Percent of population age 25 and over with: High school diploma (including GED) or higher: 52.4% (2010); Bachelor's degree or higher: 8.5% (2010); Master's degree or higher: 2.4% (2010).
Housing: Homeownership rate: 83.7% (2010); Median home value: $66,667 (2010); Median contract rent: n/a per month (2005-2009 5-year est.); Median year structure built: n/a (2005-2009 5-year est.).
Transportation: Commute to work: n/a car, n/a public transportation, n/a walk, n/a work from home (2005-2009 5-year est.); Travel time to work: n/a less than 15 minutes, n/a 15 to 30 minutes, n/a 30 to 45 minutes, n/a 45 to 60 minutes, n/a 60 minutes or more (2005-2009 5-year est.)

VILLA DEL SOL (CDP).
Covers a land area of 0.185 square miles and a water area of 0 square miles. Located at 26.19° N. Lat; 97.57° W. Long. Elevation is 30 feet.
Population: 99 (1990); 132 (2000); 133 (2010); 135 (2015 projected); Race: 90.2% White, 0.0% Black, 0.0% Asian, 9.8% Other, 96.2% Hispanic of any race (2010); Density: 720.8 persons per square mile (2010);

Average household size: 3.50 (2010); Median age: 28.8 (2010); Males per 100 females: 104.6 (2010); Marriage status: 27.3% never married, 72.7% now married, 0.0% widowed, 0.0% divorced (2005-2009 5-year est.); Foreign born: 0.0% (2005-2009 5-year est.); Ancestry (includes multiple ancestries): 22.0% Scottish, 22.0% English (2005-2009 5-year est.).
Economy: Employment by occupation: 28.1% management, 21.9% professional, 0.0% services, 0.0% sales, 0.0% farming, 50.0% construction, 0.0% production (2005-2009 5-year est.).
Income: Per capita income: $8,853 (2010); Median household income: $21,000 (2010); Average household income: $32,303 (2010); Percent of households with income of $100,000 or more: 7.9% (2010); Poverty rate: 0.0% (2005-2009 5-year est.).
Education: Percent of population age 25 and over with: High school diploma (including GED) or higher: 56.2% (2010); Bachelor's degree or higher: 13.7% (2010); Master's degree or higher: 2.7% (2010).
Housing: Homeownership rate: 89.5% (2010); Median home value: $57,500 (2010); Median contract rent: n/a per month (2005-2009 5-year est.); Median year structure built: 1998 (2005-2009 5-year est.).
Transportation: Commute to work: 100.0% car, 0.0% public transportation, 0.0% walk, 0.0% work from home (2005-2009 5-year est.); Travel time to work: 0.0% less than 15 minutes, 100.0% 15 to 30 minutes, 0.0% 30 to 45 minutes, 0.0% 45 to 60 minutes, 0.0% 60 minutes or more (2005-2009 5-year est.)

VILLA PANCHO (CDP). Covers a land area of 0.302 square miles and a water area of 0 square miles. Located at 25.88° N. Lat; 97.41° W. Long. Elevation is 13 feet.
Population: 228 (1990); 386 (2000); 119 (2010); 136 (2015 projected); Race: 76.5% White, 0.0% Black, 0.0% Asian, 23.5% Other, 97.5% Hispanic of any race (2010); Density: 393.8 persons per square mile (2010); Average household size: 4.10 (2010); Median age: 23.3 (2010); Males per 100 females: 85.9 (2010); Marriage status: 23.0% never married, 77.0% now married, 0.0% widowed, 0.0% divorced (2005-2009 5-year est.); Foreign born: 37.8% (2005-2009 5-year est.); Ancestry (includes multiple ancestries): n/a (2005-2009 5-year est.).
Economy: Employment by occupation: 0.0% management, 0.0% professional, 20.3% services, 61.0% sales, 0.0% farming, 0.0% construction, 18.6% production (2005-2009 5-year est.).
Income: Per capita income: $5,612 (2010); Median household income: $21,250 (2010); Average household income: $23,621 (2010); Percent of households with income of $100,000 or more: 0.0% (2010); Poverty rate: 0.0% (2005-2009 5-year est.).
Education: Percent of population age 25 and over with: High school diploma (including GED) or higher: 33.9% (2010); Bachelor's degree or higher: 0.0% (2010); Master's degree or higher: 0.0% (2010).
Housing: Homeownership rate: 75.9% (2010); Median home value: $51,429 (2010); Median contract rent: n/a per month (2005-2009 5-year est.); Median year structure built: 1985 (2005-2009 5-year est.).
Transportation: Commute to work: 100.0% car, 0.0% public transportation, 0.0% walk, 0.0% work from home (2005-2009 5-year est.); Travel time to work: 22.9% less than 15 minutes, 77.1% 15 to 30 minutes, 0.0% 30 to 45 minutes, 0.0% 45 to 60 minutes, 0.0% 60 minutes or more (2005-2009 5-year est.)

YZNAGA (CDP). Covers a land area of 5.431 square miles and a water area of 0 square miles. Located at 26.31° N. Lat; 97.81° W. Long. Elevation is 43 feet.
Population: 80 (1990); 103 (2000); 103 (2010); 105 (2015 projected); Race: 56.3% White, 1.9% Black, 0.0% Asian, 41.7% Other, 91.3% Hispanic of any race (2010); Density: 19.0 persons per square mile (2010); Average household size: 3.68 (2010); Median age: 25.4 (2010); Males per 100 females: 102.0 (2010); Marriage status: 0.0% never married, 100.0% now married, 0.0% widowed, 0.0% divorced (2005-2009 5-year est.); Foreign born: 61.3% (2005-2009 5-year est.); Ancestry (includes multiple ancestries): n/a (2005-2009 5-year est.).
Economy: Employment by occupation: 0.0% management, 0.0% professional, 0.0% services, 0.0% sales, 0.0% farming, 100.0% construction, 0.0% production (2005-2009 5-year est.).
Income: Per capita income: $11,164 (2010); Median household income: $31,667 (2010); Average household income: $35,179 (2010); Percent of households with income of $100,000 or more: 3.6% (2010); Poverty rate: 100.0% (2005-2009 5-year est.).
Education: Percent of population age 25 and over with: High school diploma (including GED) or higher: 53.8% (2010); Bachelor's degree or higher: 9.6% (2010); Master's degree or higher: 1.9% (2010).

Housing: Homeownership rate: 82.1% (2010); Median home value: $62,500 (2010); Median contract rent: n/a per month (2005-2009 5-year est.); Median year structure built: before 1940 (2005-2009 5-year est.).
Transportation: Commute to work: 100.0% car, 0.0% public transportation, 0.0% walk, 0.0% work from home (2005-2009 5-year est.); Travel time to work: 0.0% less than 15 minutes, 0.0% 15 to 30 minutes, 100.0% 30 to 45 minutes, 0.0% 45 to 60 minutes, 0.0% 60 minutes or more (2005-2009 5-year est.)

Camp County

Located in northeastern Texas; includes Lake Bob Sandlin. Covers a land area of 197.51 square miles, a water area of 5.69 square miles, and is located in the Central Time Zone at 32.98° N. Lat., 95.00° W. Long. The county was founded in 1874. County seat is Pittsburg.
Population: 9,904 (1990); 11,549 (2000); 13,084 (2010); 13,807 (2015 projected); Race: 65.6% White, 17.1% Black, 0.8% Asian, 16.5% Other, 22.2% Hispanic of any race (2010); Density: 66.2 persons per square mile (2010); Average household size: 2.65 (2010); Median age: 35.2 (2010); Males per 100 females: 96.0 (2010).
Religion: Five largest groups: 37.2% Southern Baptist Convention, 13.8% Baptist Missionary Association of America, 11.1% Catholic Church, 5.9% The United Methodist Church, 4.0% Churches of Christ (2000).
Economy: Unemployment rate: 9.7% (June 2011); Total civilian labor force: 6,097 (June 2011); Leading industries: 12.4% health care and social assistance; 11.3% retail trade; 7.7% accommodation & food services (2009); Farms: 482 totaling 68,552 acres (2007); Companies that employ 500 or more persons: 1 (2009); Companies that employ 100 to 499 persons: 3 (2009); Companies that employ less than 100 persons: 223 (2009); Black-owned businesses: n/a (2007); Hispanic-owned businesses: 102 (2007); Asian-owned businesses: n/a (2007); Women-owned businesses: n/a (2007); Retail sales per capita: $13,491 (2010). Single-family building permits issued: 2 (2010); Multi-family building permits issued: 2 (2010).
Income: Per capita income: $18,696 (2010); Median household income: $37,279 (2010); Average household income: $49,536 (2010); Percent of households with income of $100,000 or more: 9.5% (2010); Poverty rate: 20.1% (2009); Bankruptcy rate: 1.04% (2010).
Taxes: Total county taxes per capita: $281 (2007); County property taxes per capita: $200 (2007).
Education: Percent of population age 25 and over with: High school diploma (including GED) or higher: 75.5% (2010); Bachelor's degree or higher: 14.0% (2010); Master's degree or higher: 4.2% (2010).
Housing: Homeownership rate: 72.8% (2010); Median home value: $80,943 (2010); Median contract rent: $397 per month (2005-2009 5-year est.); Median year structure built: 1982 (2005-2009 5-year est.)
Health: Birth rate: 177.4 per 10,000 population (2009); Death rate: 107.9 per 10,000 population (2009); Age-adjusted cancer mortality rate: 193.3 deaths per 100,000 population (2007); Number of physicians: 8.7 per 10,000 population (2008); Hospital beds: 20.0 per 10,000 population (2007); Hospital admissions: 1,028.9 per 10,000 population (2007).
Elections: 2008 Presidential election results: 38.0% Obama, 61.3% McCain, 0.0% Nader
Additional Information Contacts
Camp County Government . . . . (903) 856-2731
   http://www.co.camp.tx.us/ips/cms
Camp County Chamber of Commerce. . . . . (903) 856-3442
   http://www.pittsburgchamber.com

Camp County Communities

LEESBURG (unincorporated postal area, zip code 75451). Covers a land area of 38.557 square miles and a water area of 0.157 square miles. Located at 32.97° N. Lat; 95.11° W. Long. Elevation is 397 feet.
Population: 1,265 (2000); Race: 75.3% White, 6.9% Black, 2.9% Asian, 14.9% Other, 13.1% Hispanic of any race (2000); Density: 32.8 persons per square mile (2000); Age: 31.1% under 18, 13.1% over 64 (2000); Marriage status: 10.2% never married, 76.3% now married, 5.4% widowed, 8.1% divorced (2000); Foreign born: 10.2% (2000); Ancestry (includes multiple ancestries): 22.4% American, 13.0% Irish, 10.8% English, 1.9% German (2000).
Economy: Employment by occupation: 11.0% management, 12.0% professional, 15.4% services, 16.5% sales, 7.5% farming, 16.7% construction, 20.8% production (2000).

Income: Per capita income: $12,532 (2000); Median household income: $32,393 (2000); Poverty rate: 179.1% (2000).
Education: Percent of population age 25 and over with: High school diploma (including GED) or higher: 64.6% (2000); Bachelor's degree or higher: 4.5% (2000).
Housing: Homeownership rate: 89.0% (2000); Median home value: $43,900 (2000); Median contract rent: $338 per month (2000); Median year structure built: 1982 (2000).
Transportation: Commute to work: 93.5% car, 0.0% public transportation, 4.8% walk, 1.6% work from home (2000); Travel time to work: 16.2% less than 15 minutes, 61.5% 15 to 30 minutes, 14.8% 30 to 45 minutes, 1.8% 45 to 60 minutes, 5.7% 60 minutes or more (2000)

PITTSBURG (city). County seat. Covers a land area of 3.339 square miles and a water area of 0.004 square miles. Located at 32.99° N. Lat; 94.96° W. Long. Elevation is 394 feet.
History: Pittsburg developed as the seat of Camp County, where oil, beef cattle, farm products and fruit orchards provided the basis of the economy.
Population: 4,124 (1990); 4,347 (2000); 4,844 (2010); 5,073 (2015 projected); Race: 49.4% White, 25.8% Black, 0.9% Asian, 23.9% Other, 33.7% Hispanic of any race (2010); Density: 1,450.7 persons per square mile (2010); Average household size: 2.71 (2010); Median age: 31.6 (2010); Males per 100 females: 90.5 (2010); Marriage status: 32.1% never married, 48.1% now married, 9.4% widowed, 10.4% divorced (2005-2009 5-year est.); Foreign born: 18.5% (2005-2009 5-year est.); Ancestry (includes multiple ancestries): 6.5% English, 6.5% German, 6.2% African, 5.8% Irish, 3.9% American (2005-2009 5-year est.).
Economy: Single-family building permits issued: 2 (2010); Multi-family building permits issued: 2 (2010); Employment by occupation: 6.1% management, 12.8% professional, 22.3% services, 20.2% sales, 2.4% farming, 6.6% construction, 29.6% production (2005-2009 5-year est.).
Income: Per capita income: $16,221 (2010); Median household income: $30,915 (2010); Average household income: $44,479 (2010); Percent of households with income of $100,000 or more: 10.0% (2010); Poverty rate: 29.2% (2005-2009 5-year est.).
Taxes: Total city taxes per capita: $361 (2007); City property taxes per capita: $158 (2007).
Education: Percent of population age 25 and over with: High school diploma (including GED) or higher: 73.3% (2010); Bachelor's degree or higher: 16.0% (2010); Master's degree or higher: 6.0% (2010).
School District(s)
Pittsburg ISD (PK-12)
    2009-10 Enrollment: 2,437 . . . . (903) 856-3628
Housing: Homeownership rate: 58.6% (2010); Median home value: $80,114 (2010); Median contract rent: $371 per month (2005-2009 5-year est.); Median year structure built: 1973 (2005-2009 5-year est.).
Hospitals: E Texas Medical Center - Pittsburg (49 beds)
Safety: Violent crime rate: 59.5 per 10,000 population; Property crime rate: 289.2 per 10,000 population (2009).
Newspapers: Pittsburg Gazette (Community news; Circulation 3,300)
Transportation: Commute to work: 86.4% car, 0.7% public transportation, 5.8% walk, 3.3% work from home (2005-2009 5-year est.); Travel time to work: 47.1% less than 15 minutes, 34.2% 15 to 30 minutes, 10.7% 30 to 45 minutes, 1.3% 45 to 60 minutes, 6.7% 60 minutes or more (2005-2009 5-year est.)
Additional Information Contacts
Camp County Chamber of Commerce. . . . . (903) 856-3442
    http://www.pittsburgchamber.com

ROCKY MOUND (town). Covers a land area of 0.407 square miles and a water area of 0 square miles. Located at 33.03° N. Lat; 95.03° W. Long. Elevation is 430 feet.
Population: 51 (1990); 93 (2000); 114 (2010); 122 (2015 projected); Race: 79.8% White, 8.8% Black, 1.8% Asian, 9.6% Other, 11.4% Hispanic of any race (2010); Density: 279.9 persons per square mile (2010); Average household size: 2.48 (2010); Median age: 39.7 (2010); Males per 100 females: 83.9 (2010); Marriage status: 15.0% never married, 67.5% now married, 2.5% widowed, 15.0% divorced (2005-2009 5-year est.); Foreign born: 0.0% (2005-2009 5-year est.); Ancestry (includes multiple ancestries): 36.4% African, 18.2% English, 13.6% Irish, 9.1% Scotch-Irish, 2.3% German (2005-2009 5-year est.).
Economy: Employment by occupation: 0.0% management, 20.7% professional, 0.0% services, 17.2% sales, 0.0% farming, 13.8% construction, 48.3% production (2005-2009 5-year est.).

Income: Per capita income: $21,397 (2010); Median household income: $37,500 (2010); Average household income: $47,935 (2010); Percent of households with income of $100,000 or more: 6.5% (2010); Poverty rate: 6.8% (2005-2009 5-year est.).
Taxes: Total city taxes per capita: $178 (2007); City property taxes per capita: $0 (2007).
Education: Percent of population age 25 and over with: High school diploma (including GED) or higher: 77.9% (2010); Bachelor's degree or higher: 10.4% (2010); Master's degree or higher: 1.3% (2010).
Housing: Homeownership rate: 82.6% (2010); Median home value: $93,333 (2010); Median contract rent: n/a per month (2005-2009 5-year est.); Median year structure built: 1968 (2005-2009 5-year est.).
Transportation: Commute to work: 100.0% car, 0.0% public transportation, 0.0% walk, 0.0% work from home (2005-2009 5-year est.); Travel time to work: 10.3% less than 15 minutes, 48.3% 15 to 30 minutes, 41.4% 30 to 45 minutes, 0.0% 45 to 60 minutes, 0.0% 60 minutes or more (2005-2009 5-year est.)

Carson County

Located in north Texas, in the high plains of the Panhandle. Covers a land area of 923.19 square miles, a water area of 0.91 square miles, and is located in the Central Time Zone at 35.40° N. Lat., 101.26° W. Long. The county was founded in 1876. County seat is Panhandle.

Carson County is part of the Amarillo, TX Metropolitan Statistical Area. The entire metro area includes: Armstrong County, TX; Carson County, TX; Potter County, TX; Randall County, TX

Weather Station: Panhandle   Elevation: 3,532 feet

	Jan	Feb	Mar	Apr	May	Jun	Jul	Aug	Sep	Oct	Nov	Dec
High	50	54	63	72	80	88	93	91	84	73	60	49
Low	22	25	32	40	50	60	64	63	55	44	32	23
Precip	0.6	0.7	1.4	1.7	2.9	3.6	2.3	2.8	2.1	1.9	0.9	0.8
Snow	3.7	3.2	2.0	0.5	0.1	0.0	0.0	0.0	0.0	0.3	1.8	4.1

High and Low temperatures in degrees Fahrenheit; Precipitation and Snow in inches

Population: 6,576 (1990); 6,516 (2000); 6,320 (2010); 6,214 (2015 projected); Race: 92.1% White, 1.2% Black, 0.1% Asian, 6.5% Other, 8.5% Hispanic of any race (2010); Density: 6.8 persons per square mile (2010); Average household size: 2.54 (2010); Median age: 41.7 (2010); Males per 100 females: 95.8 (2010).
Religion: Five largest groups: 48.1% Southern Baptist Convention, 15.4% Catholic Church, 13.9% The United Methodist Church, 5.2% Christian Church (Disciples of Christ), 4.5% Churches of Christ (2000).
Economy: Unemployment rate: 6.1% (June 2011); Total civilian labor force: 3,257 (June 2011); Leading industries: Farms: 422 totaling 537,445 acres (2007); Companies that employ 500 or more persons: 1 (2009); Companies that employ 100 to 499 persons: 0 (2009); Companies that employ less than 100 persons: 112 (2009); Black-owned businesses: n/a (2007); Hispanic-owned businesses: n/a (2007); Asian-owned businesses: n/a (2007); Women-owned businesses: 88 (2007); Retail sales per capita: $6,790 (2010). Single-family building permits issued: 1 (2010); Multi-family building permits issued: 0 (2010).
Income: Per capita income: $23,327 (2010); Median household income: $48,389 (2010); Average household income: $60,026 (2010); Percent of households with income of $100,000 or more: 13.0% (2010); Poverty rate: 8.8% (2009); Bankruptcy rate: 1.77% (2010).
Taxes: Total county taxes per capita: $176 (2007); County property taxes per capita: $168 (2007).
Education: Percent of population age 25 and over with: High school diploma (including GED) or higher: 86.5% (2010); Bachelor's degree or higher: 17.1% (2010); Master's degree or higher: 4.5% (2010).
Housing: Homeownership rate: 82.3% (2010); Median home value: $74,379 (2010); Median contract rent: $504 per month (2005-2009 5-year est.); Median year structure built: 1966 (2005-2009 5-year est.).
Health: Birth rate: 126.0 per 10,000 population (2009); Death rate: 109.7 per 10,000 population (2009); Age-adjusted cancer mortality rate: 190.6 (Unreliable) deaths per 100,000 population (2007); Number of physicians: 0.0 per 10,000 population (2008); Hospital beds: 0.0 per 10,000 population (2007); Hospital admissions: 0.0 per 10,000 population (2007).
Elections: 2008 Presidential election results: 13.6% Obama, 85.5% McCain, 0.0% Nader
Additional Information Contacts
Carson County Government . . . . (806) 537-3622
    http://www.co.carson.tx.us/ips/cms

Carson County Communities

GROOM (town). Covers a land area of 0.754 square miles and a water area of 0 square miles. Located at 35.20° N. Lat; 101.10° W. Long. Elevation is 3,255 feet.

Population: 613 (1990); 587 (2000); 582 (2010); 578 (2015 projected); Race: 91.9% White, 0.0% Black, 0.2% Asian, 7.9% Other, 9.6% Hispanic of any race (2010); Density: 772.1 persons per square mile (2010); Average household size: 2.48 (2010); Median age: 41.9 (2010); Males per 100 females: 104.2 (2010); Marriage status: 32.0% never married, 56.6% now married, 5.2% widowed, 6.2% divorced (2005-2009 5-year est.); Foreign born: 1.6% (2005-2009 5-year est.); Ancestry (includes multiple ancestries): 21.1% German, 9.0% Irish, 8.9% American, 7.5% Scotch-Irish, 6.6% English (2005-2009 5-year est.).

Economy: Single-family building permits issued: 1 (2010); Multi-family building permits issued: 0 (2010); Employment by occupation: 15.3% management, 23.0% professional, 7.3% services, 25.1% sales, 1.4% farming, 19.9% construction, 8.0% production (2005-2009 5-year est.).

Income: Per capita income: $22,497 (2010); Median household income: $46,731 (2010); Average household income: $56,851 (2010); Percent of households with income of $100,000 or more: 11.1% (2010); Poverty rate: 14.1% (2005-2009 5-year est.).

Taxes: Total city taxes per capita: $238 (2007); City property taxes per capita: $112 (2007).

Education: Percent of population age 25 and over with: High school diploma (including GED) or higher: 87.5% (2010); Bachelor's degree or higher: 21.8% (2010); Master's degree or higher: 6.8% (2010).

School District(s)
Grandview-Hopkins ISD (KG-06)
    2009-10 Enrollment: 29 . . . . (806) 669-3831
Groom ISD (PK-12)
    2009-10 Enrollment: 135 . . . . (806) 248-7557

Housing: Homeownership rate: 82.6% (2010); Median home value: $80,606 (2010); Median contract rent: $317 per month (2005-2009 5-year est.); Median year structure built: 1952 (2005-2009 5-year est.).

Newspapers: The Groom/McLean News (Community news; Circulation 1,400)

Transportation: Commute to work: 89.2% car, 0.0% public transportation, 3.5% walk, 1.0% work from home (2005-2009 5-year est.); Travel time to work: 62.7% less than 15 minutes, 1.4% 15 to 30 minutes, 22.2% 30 to 45 minutes, 10.6% 45 to 60 minutes, 3.2% 60 minutes or more (2005-2009 5-year est.)

PANHANDLE (town). County seat. Covers a land area of 2.128 square miles and a water area of 0 square miles. Located at 35.34° N. Lat; 101.38° W. Long. Elevation is 3,458 feet.

History: Alibates Flint Quarries National Monument to Northwest. Became county seat 1888, incorporated 1909.

Population: 2,353 (1990); 2,589 (2000); 2,453 (2010); 2,383 (2015 projected); Race: 91.6% White, 1.3% Black, 0.0% Asian, 7.1% Other, 10.5% Hispanic of any race (2010); Density: 1,152.7 persons per square mile (2010); Average household size: 2.58 (2010); Median age: 38.2 (2010); Males per 100 females: 93.6 (2010); Marriage status: 10.1% never married, 75.8% now married, 10.9% widowed, 3.2% divorced (2005-2009 5-year est.); Foreign born: 1.6% (2005-2009 5-year est.); Ancestry (includes multiple ancestries): 25.5% German, 16.5% Irish, 14.3% English, 8.4% Scottish, 5.1% Scotch-Irish (2005-2009 5-year est.).

Economy: Single-family building permits issued: 0 (2010); Multi-family building permits issued: 0 (2010); Employment by occupation: 15.3% management, 15.8% professional, 6.4% services, 27.6% sales, 0.6% farming, 14.6% construction, 19.6% production (2005-2009 5-year est.).

Income: Per capita income: $23,614 (2010); Median household income: $49,784 (2010); Average household income: $61,736 (2010); Percent of households with income of $100,000 or more: 14.3% (2010); Poverty rate: 3.2% (2005-2009 5-year est.).

Taxes: Total city taxes per capita: $229 (2007); City property taxes per capita: $166 (2007).

Education: Percent of population age 25 and over with: High school diploma (including GED) or higher: 88.2% (2010); Bachelor's degree or higher: 19.7% (2010); Master's degree or higher: 4.7% (2010).

School District(s)
Panhandle ISD (PK-12)
    2009-10 Enrollment: 696 . . . . (806) 537-3568

Housing: Homeownership rate: 82.9% (2010); Median home value: $76,752 (2010); Median contract rent: $927 per month (2005-2009 5-year est.); Median year structure built: 1967 (2005-2009 5-year est.).

Safety: Violent crime rate: 12.1 per 10,000 population; Property crime rate: 101.1 per 10,000 population (2009).

Newspapers: Herald (Local news; Circulation 1,300)

Transportation: Commute to work: 93.7% car, 0.0% public transportation, 0.7% walk, 2.8% work from home (2005-2009 5-year est.); Travel time to work: 38.3% less than 15 minutes, 17.2% 15 to 30 minutes, 36.1% 30 to 45 minutes, 6.8% 45 to 60 minutes, 1.5% 60 minutes or more (2005-2009 5-year est.)

SKELLYTOWN (town). Covers a land area of 0.431 square miles and a water area of 0 square miles. Located at 35.57° N. Lat; 101.17° W. Long. Elevation is 3,235 feet.

Population: 664 (1990); 610 (2000); 571 (2010); 554 (2015 projected); Race: 89.7% White, 1.1% Black, 0.4% Asian, 8.9% Other, 8.2% Hispanic of any race (2010); Density: 1,325.9 persons per square mile (2010); Average household size: 2.52 (2010); Median age: 45.3 (2010); Males per 100 females: 94.2 (2010); Marriage status: 20.1% never married, 60.4% now married, 10.6% widowed, 8.8% divorced (2005-2009 5-year est.); Foreign born: 0.0% (2005-2009 5-year est.); Ancestry (includes multiple ancestries): 21.9% German, 11.0% English, 9.4% Irish, 5.2% Scottish, 3.0% Dutch (2005-2009 5-year est.).

Economy: Single-family building permits issued: 0 (2010); Multi-family building permits issued: 0 (2010); Employment by occupation: 6.0% management, 16.8% professional, 3.8% services, 27.2% sales, 0.0% farming, 13.6% construction, 32.6% production (2005-2009 5-year est.).

Income: Per capita income: $19,148 (2010); Median household income: $39,167 (2010); Average household income: $48,326 (2010); Percent of households with income of $100,000 or more: 7.9% (2010); Poverty rate: 8.2% (2005-2009 5-year est.).

Taxes: Total city taxes per capita: $153 (2007); City property taxes per capita: $130 (2007).

Education: Percent of population age 25 and over with: High school diploma (including GED) or higher: 80.4% (2010); Bachelor's degree or higher: 9.1% (2010); Master's degree or higher: 2.5% (2010).

School District(s)
Spring Creek ISD (PK-06)
    2009-10 Enrollment: 105 . . . . (806) 273-6791

Housing: Homeownership rate: 85.9% (2010); Median home value: $39,839 (2010); Median contract rent: $543 per month (2005-2009 5-year est.); Median year structure built: 1961 (2005-2009 5-year est.).

Transportation: Commute to work: 100.0% car, 0.0% public transportation, 0.0% walk, 0.0% work from home (2005-2009 5-year est.); Travel time to work: 31.4% less than 15 minutes, 41.3% 15 to 30 minutes, 7.6% 30 to 45 minutes, 1.2% 45 to 60 minutes, 18.6% 60 minutes or more (2005-2009 5-year est.)

WHITE DEER (town). Covers a land area of 1.743 square miles and a water area of 0 square miles. Located at 35.43° N. Lat; 101.17° W. Long. Elevation is 3,366 feet.

Population: 1,125 (1990); 1,060 (2000); 1,026 (2010); 1,011 (2015 projected); Race: 96.2% White, 0.2% Black, 0.0% Asian, 3.6% Other, 4.7% Hispanic of any race (2010); Density: 588.5 persons per square mile (2010); Average household size: 2.47 (2010); Median age: 41.7 (2010); Males per 100 females: 92.1 (2010); Marriage status: 21.2% never married, 66.4% now married, 5.8% widowed, 6.5% divorced (2005-2009 5-year est.); Foreign born: 4.0% (2005-2009 5-year est.); Ancestry (includes multiple ancestries): 16.5% German, 14.7% Irish, 11.9% English, 8.1% French, 4.2% Norwegian (2005-2009 5-year est.).

Economy: Single-family building permits issued: 0 (2010); Multi-family building permits issued: 0 (2010); Employment by occupation: 14.4% management, 21.7% professional, 13.6% services, 18.6% sales, 1.8% farming, 12.8% construction, 17.2% production (2005-2009 5-year est.).

Income: Per capita income: $21,914 (2010); Median household income: $43,404 (2010); Average household income: $53,819 (2010); Percent of households with income of $100,000 or more: 7.7% (2010); Poverty rate: 11.2% (2005-2009 5-year est.).

Taxes: Total city taxes per capita: $266 (2007); City property taxes per capita: $168 (2007).

Education: Percent of population age 25 and over with: High school diploma (including GED) or higher: 86.9% (2010); Bachelor's degree or higher: 14.7% (2010); Master's degree or higher: 3.7% (2010).

White Deer ISD (PK-12)
    2009-10 Enrollment: 385 . . . . (806) 883-2311
Housing: Homeownership rate: 81.2% (2010); Median home value: $72,833 (2010); Median contract rent: $418 per month (2005-2009 5-year est.); Median year structure built: 1966 (2005-2009 5-year est.).
Newspapers: White Deer News (Community news; Circulation 750)
Transportation: Commute to work: 95.2% car, 0.0% public transportation, 3.5% walk, 0.0% work from home (2005-2009 5-year est.); Travel time to work: 47.9% less than 15 minutes, 30.1% 15 to 30 minutes, 14.2% 30 to 45 minutes, 0.0% 45 to 60 minutes, 7.8% 60 minutes or more (2005-2009 5-year est.)

Cass County

Located in northeastern Texas; bounded on the east by the Arkansas and Louisiana borders, and on the north by the Sulphur River. Covers a land area of 937.35 square miles, a water area of 22.99 square miles, and is located in the Central Time Zone at 33.07° N. Lat., 94.32° W. Long. The county was founded in 1846. County seat is Linden.

Weather Station: Wright Patman Dam & Lock   Elevation: 282 feet

	Jan	Feb	Mar	Apr	May	Jun	Jul	Aug	Sep	Oct	Nov	Dec
High	54	59	67	74	82	89	93	93	86	76	65	56
Low	33	37	45	52	61	68	72	70	63	51	43	35
Precip	3.7	4.0	4.5	3.9	4.7	4.6	3.2	2.5	3.2	5.1	4.6	4.6
Snow	0.1	0.4	0.0	0.0	0.0	0.0	0.0	0.0	0.0	0.0	tr	0.1

High and Low temperatures in degrees Fahrenheit; Precipitation and Snow in inches

Population: 29,982 (1990); 30,438 (2000); 30,030 (2010); 29,777 (2015 projected); Race: 77.9% White, 18.8% Black, 0.1% Asian, 3.2% Other, 2.8% Hispanic of any race (2010); Density: 32.0 persons per square mile (2010); Average household size: 2.37 (2010); Median age: 41.9 (2010); Males per 100 females: 92.9 (2010).
Religion: Five largest groups: 42.0% Southern Baptist Convention, 8.8% The American Baptist Association, 8.2% The United Methodist Church, 2.0% Churches of Christ, 1.3% Assemblies of God (2000).
Economy: Unemployment rate: 11.4% (June 2011); Total civilian labor force: 13,550 (June 2011); Leading industries: 20.8% health care and social assistance; 20.2% manufacturing; 17.0% retail trade (2009); Farms: 1,067 totaling 176,645 acres (2007); Companies that employ 500 or more persons: 1 (2009); Companies that employ 100 to 499 persons: 4 (2009); Companies that employ less than 100 persons: 512 (2009); Black-owned businesses: n/a (2007); Hispanic-owned businesses: n/a (2007); Asian-owned businesses: n/a (2007); Women-owned businesses: 580 (2007); Retail sales per capita: $7,522 (2010). Single-family building permits issued: 0 (2010); Multi-family building permits issued: 0 (2010).
Income: Per capita income: $20,484 (2010); Median household income: $37,083 (2010); Average household income: $49,047 (2010); Percent of households with income of $100,000 or more: 9.2% (2010); Poverty rate: 19.3% (2009); Bankruptcy rate: 2.92% (2010).
Taxes: Total county taxes per capita: $221 (2007); County property taxes per capita: $196 (2007).
Education: Percent of population age 25 and over with: High school diploma (including GED) or higher: 79.8% (2010); Bachelor's degree or higher: 12.3% (2010); Master's degree or higher: 3.7% (2010).
Housing: Homeownership rate: 74.8% (2010); Median home value: $67,105 (2010); Median contract rent: $332 per month (2005-2009 5-year est.); Median year structure built: 1976 (2005-2009 5-year est.)
Health: Birth rate: 116.8 per 10,000 population (2009); Death rate: 135.3 per 10,000 population (2009); Age-adjusted cancer mortality rate: 216.9 deaths per 100,000 population (2007); Number of physicians: 4.4 per 10,000 population (2008); Hospital beds: 27.6 per 10,000 population (2007); Hospital admissions: 957.4 per 10,000 population (2007).
Elections: 2008 Presidential election results: 29.5% Obama, 69.9% McCain, 0.0% Nader
National and State Parks: Atlanta State Park
Additional Information Contacts
Cass County Government . . . . (903) 756-5181
    http://www.co.cass.tx.us/ips/cms
Atlanta Area Chamber of Commerce . . . . (903) 796-3296
    http://www.atlantatexas.org/chamber
City of Atlanta . . . . (903) 796-2192
    http://www.atlantatexas.org
Hughes Springs Chamber of Commerce . . . . (903) 639-2351
    http://www.hughesspringstx.net

Lake O' The Pines Chamber of Commerce . . . . (903) 755-2597
    http://www.lakeothepines.com
Linden Economic Development Corporation . . . . (903) 756-7774
    http://www.lindentexas.org

Cass County Communities

ATLANTA (city). Covers a land area of 10.934 square miles and a water area of 0.133 square miles. Located at 33.11° N. Lat; 94.16° W. Long. Elevation is 259 feet.
History: Atlanta developed around a brick factory and a canning plant that processed tomatoes, beans, and other vegetables from the surrounding truck-farming area.
Population: 6,102 (1990); 5,745 (2000); 5,521 (2010); 5,414 (2015 projected); Race: 65.0% White, 31.6% Black, 0.3% Asian, 3.1% Other, 2.2% Hispanic of any race (2010); Density: 504.9 persons per square mile (2010); Average household size: 2.37 (2010); Median age: 38.1 (2010); Males per 100 females: 86.3 (2010); Marriage status: 23.3% never married, 49.8% now married, 14.1% widowed, 12.8% divorced (2005-2009 5-year est.); Foreign born: 2.1% (2005-2009 5-year est.); Ancestry (includes multiple ancestries): 16.0% American, 9.6% English, 7.9% Irish, 3.0% German, 1.9% African (2005-2009 5-year est.).
Economy: Single-family building permits issued: 0 (2010); Multi-family building permits issued: 0 (2010); Employment by occupation: 14.9% management, 20.1% professional, 18.7% services, 20.3% sales, 0.0% farming, 6.6% construction, 19.5% production (2005-2009 5-year est.).
Income: Per capita income: $18,502 (2010); Median household income: $33,227 (2010); Average household income: $44,471 (2010); Percent of households with income of $100,000 or more: 7.8% (2010); Poverty rate: 21.5% (2005-2009 5-year est.).
Taxes: Total city taxes per capita: $438 (2007); City property taxes per capita: $220 (2007).
Education: Percent of population age 25 and over with: High school diploma (including GED) or higher: 80.4% (2010); Bachelor's degree or higher: 14.8% (2010); Master's degree or higher: 5.1% (2010).
School District(s)
Atlanta ISD (PK-12)
    2009-10 Enrollment: 1,813 . . . . (903) 796-4194
Housing: Homeownership rate: 64.1% (2010); Median home value: $68,788 (2010); Median contract rent: $352 per month (2005-2009 5-year est.); Median year structure built: 1974 (2005-2009 5-year est.).
Hospitals: Atlanta Memorial Hospital (65 beds)
Safety: Violent crime rate: 69.8 per 10,000 population; Property crime rate: 437.2 per 10,000 population (2009).
Newspapers: Citizens Journal (Local news; Circulation 4,000)
Transportation: Commute to work: 96.3% car, 0.0% public transportation, 1.6% walk, 1.6% work from home (2005-2009 5-year est.); Travel time to work: 53.0% less than 15 minutes, 21.3% 15 to 30 minutes, 16.1% 30 to 45 minutes, 3.5% 45 to 60 minutes, 6.1% 60 minutes or more (2005-2009 5-year est.)
Additional Information Contacts
Atlanta Area Chamber of Commerce . . . . (903) 796-3296
    http://www.atlantatexas.org/chamber
City of Atlanta . . . . (903) 796-2192
    http://www.atlantatexas.org

AVINGER (town). Covers a land area of 1.869 square miles and a water area of 0.001 square miles. Located at 32.89° N. Lat; 94.55° W. Long. Elevation is 394 feet.
Population: 478 (1990); 464 (2000); 450 (2010); 441 (2015 projected); Race: 74.0% White, 21.3% Black, 0.0% Asian, 4.7% Other, 2.4% Hispanic of any race (2010); Density: 240.8 persons per square mile (2010); Average household size: 2.20 (2010); Median age: 41.7 (2010); Males per 100 females: 88.3 (2010); Marriage status: 13.6% never married, 58.0% now married, 16.1% widowed, 12.3% divorced (2005-2009 5-year est.); Foreign born: 0.5% (2005-2009 5-year est.); Ancestry (includes multiple ancestries): 20.4% German, 17.4% Irish, 10.4% American, 6.7% English, 4.6% French (2005-2009 5-year est.).
Economy: Employment by occupation: 6.3% management, 11.1% professional, 27.8% services, 22.2% sales, 0.0% farming, 7.1% construction, 25.4% production (2005-2009 5-year est.).
Income: Per capita income: $19,920 (2010); Median household income: $28,438 (2010); Average household income: $44,154 (2010); Percent of households with income of $100,000 or more: 6.9% (2010); Poverty rate: 29.9% (2005-2009 5-year est.).

Taxes: Total city taxes per capita: $157 (2007); City property taxes per capita: $102 (2007).
Education: Percent of population age 25 and over with: High school diploma (including GED) or higher: 78.5% (2010); Bachelor's degree or higher: 13.5% (2010); Master's degree or higher: 5.4% (2010).

School District(s)
Avinger ISD (KG-12)
    2009-10 Enrollment: 129 . . . . (903) 562-1271
Housing: Homeownership rate: 68.6% (2010); Median home value: $47,778 (2010); Median contract rent: $188 per month (2005-2009 5-year est.); Median year structure built: 1953 (2005-2009 5-year est.).
Transportation: Commute to work: 90.5% car, 0.0% public transportation, 2.9% walk, 6.7% work from home (2005-2009 5-year est.); Travel time to work: 24.5% less than 15 minutes, 24.5% 15 to 30 minutes, 10.2% 30 to 45 minutes, 33.7% 45 to 60 minutes, 7.1% 60 minutes or more (2005-2009 5-year est.)
Additional Information Contacts
Lake O' The Pines Chamber of Commerce . . . . (903) 755-2597
    http://www.lakeothepines.com

BIVINS (unincorporated postal area, zip code 75555). Covers a land area of 109.827 square miles and a water area of 0.134 square miles. Located at 32.93° N. Lat; 94.13° W. Long. Elevation is 318 feet.
Population: 1,446 (2000); Race: 84.5% White, 14.6% Black, 0.1% Asian, 0.8% Other, 0.3% Hispanic of any race (2000); Density: 13.2 persons per square mile (2000); Age: 26.8% under 18, 19.1% over 64 (2000); Marriage status: 15.7% never married, 67.0% now married, 6.6% widowed, 10.6% divorced (2000); Foreign born: 0.3% (2000); Ancestry (includes multiple ancestries): 24.0% American, 12.7% Irish, 7.2% English, 6.8% German (2000).
Economy: Employment by occupation: 5.4% management, 20.9% professional, 10.6% services, 16.8% sales, 0.7% farming, 17.7% construction, 27.9% production (2000).
Income: Per capita income: $13,749 (2000); Median household income: $30,718 (2000); Poverty rate: 179.1% (2000).
Education: Percent of population age 25 and over with: High school diploma (including GED) or higher: 75.2% (2000); Bachelor's degree or higher: 10.7% (2000).
Housing: Homeownership rate: 87.9% (2000); Median home value: $57,000 (2000); Median contract rent: $368 per month (2000); Median year structure built: 1981 (2000).
Transportation: Commute to work: 95.9% car, 2.1% public transportation, 0.4% walk, 1.1% work from home (2000); Travel time to work: 20.4% less than 15 minutes, 30.9% 15 to 30 minutes, 14.3% 30 to 45 minutes, 16.2% 45 to 60 minutes, 18.3% 60 minutes or more (2000)

BLOOMBURG (town). Covers a land area of 1.006 square miles and a water area of 0 square miles. Located at 33.13° N. Lat; 94.05° W. Long. Elevation is 315 feet.
Population: 376 (1990); 375 (2000); 397 (2010); 405 (2015 projected); Race: 90.7% White, 6.8% Black, 0.3% Asian, 2.3% Other, 3.3% Hispanic of any race (2010); Density: 394.5 persons per square mile (2010); Average household size: 2.38 (2010); Median age: 41.6 (2010); Males per 100 females: 94.6 (2010); Marriage status: 20.6% never married, 56.0% now married, 9.4% widowed, 14.0% divorced (2005-2009 5-year est.); Foreign born: 0.0% (2005-2009 5-year est.); Ancestry (includes multiple ancestries): 24.3% English, 18.7% American, 10.4% Irish, 6.8% German, 2.8% Italian (2005-2009 5-year est.).
Economy: Employment by occupation: 3.4% management, 30.9% professional, 8.1% services, 16.1% sales, 5.4% farming, 13.4% construction, 22.8% production (2005-2009 5-year est.).
Income: Per capita income: $23,053 (2010); Median household income: $41,058 (2010); Average household income: $54,266 (2010); Percent of households with income of $100,000 or more: 12.0% (2010); Poverty rate: 24.7% (2005-2009 5-year est.).
Taxes: Total city taxes per capita: $114 (2007); City property taxes per capita: $43 (2007).
Education: Percent of population age 25 and over with: High school diploma (including GED) or higher: 82.0% (2010); Bachelor's degree or higher: 11.7% (2010); Master's degree or higher: 3.5% (2010).

School District(s)
Bloomburg ISD (PK-12)
    2009-10 Enrollment: 282 . . . . (903) 728-5216

Housing: Homeownership rate: 73.7% (2010); Median home value: $75,625 (2010); Median contract rent: $363 per month (2005-2009 5-year est.); Median year structure built: 1958 (2005-2009 5-year est.).
Safety: Violent crime rate: 0.0 per 10,000 population; Property crime rate: 0.0 per 10,000 population (2009).
Transportation: Commute to work: 86.0% car, 0.0% public transportation, 4.1% walk, 9.9% work from home (2005-2009 5-year est.); Travel time to work: 44.0% less than 15 minutes, 17.4% 15 to 30 minutes, 19.3% 30 to 45 minutes, 4.6% 45 to 60 minutes, 14.7% 60 minutes or more (2005-2009 5-year est.)

DOMINO (town). Covers a land area of 0.343 square miles and a water area of 0 square miles. Located at 33.25° N. Lat; 94.11° W. Long. Elevation is 249 feet.
Population: 101 (1990); 52 (2000); 53 (2010); 53 (2015 projected); Race: 77.4% White, 20.8% Black, 0.0% Asian, 1.9% Other, 1.9% Hispanic of any race (2010); Density: 154.3 persons per square mile (2010); Average household size: 2.52 (2010); Median age: 42.5 (2010); Males per 100 females: 71.0 (2010); Marriage status: 43.4% never married, 30.2% now married, 0.0% widowed, 26.4% divorced (2005-2009 5-year est.); Foreign born: 0.0% (2005-2009 5-year est.); Ancestry (includes multiple ancestries): n/a (2005-2009 5-year est.).
Economy: Employment by occupation: 0.0% management, 0.0% professional, 69.2% services, 0.0% sales, 0.0% farming, 30.8% construction, 0.0% production (2005-2009 5-year est.).
Income: Per capita income: $19,465 (2010); Median household income: $37,500 (2010); Average household income: $46,429 (2010); Percent of households with income of $100,000 or more: 9.5% (2010); Poverty rate: 85.9% (2005-2009 5-year est.).
Taxes: Total city taxes per capita: $510 (2007); City property taxes per capita: $0 (2007).
Education: Percent of population age 25 and over with: High school diploma (including GED) or higher: 77.1% (2010); Bachelor's degree or higher: 5.7% (2010); Master's degree or higher: 0.0% (2010).
Housing: Homeownership rate: 85.7% (2010); Median home value: $48,000 (2010); Median contract rent: n/a per month (2005-2009 5-year est.); Median year structure built: 1984 (2005-2009 5-year est.).
Transportation: Commute to work: 100.0% car, 0.0% public transportation, 0.0% walk, 0.0% work from home (2005-2009 5-year est.); Travel time to work: 30.8% less than 15 minutes, 50.0% 15 to 30 minutes, 19.2% 30 to 45 minutes, 0.0% 45 to 60 minutes, 0.0% 60 minutes or more (2005-2009 5-year est.)

DOUGLASSVILLE (town). Covers a land area of 6.323 square miles and a water area of 0 square miles. Located at 33.19° N. Lat; 94.35° W. Long. Elevation is 394 feet.
History: Douglassville was founded in 1853 as the center of a plantation area. The town was named for John Douglass, who built a cabin here in 1854.
Population: 192 (1990); 175 (2000); 169 (2010); 167 (2015 projected); Race: 63.3% White, 33.7% Black, 0.0% Asian, 3.0% Other, 0.6% Hispanic of any race (2010); Density: 26.7 persons per square mile (2010); Average household size: 2.35 (2010); Median age: 43.2 (2010); Males per 100 females: 96.5 (2010); Marriage status: 15.3% never married, 44.1% now married, 8.5% widowed, 32.2% divorced (2005-2009 5-year est.); Foreign born: 0.0% (2005-2009 5-year est.); Ancestry (includes multiple ancestries): 33.7% American, 21.5% Cajun, 10.4% English, 9.1% Irish, 6.1% French (2005-2009 5-year est.).
Economy: Single-family building permits issued: 0 (2010); Multi-family building permits issued: 0 (2010); Employment by occupation: 12.2% management, 16.3% professional, 5.1% services, 15.3% sales, 0.0% farming, 37.8% construction, 13.3% production (2005-2009 5-year est.).
Income: Per capita income: $18,990 (2010); Median household income: $31,923 (2010); Average household income: $44,549 (2010); Percent of households with income of $100,000 or more: 8.3% (2010); Poverty rate: 16.5% (2005-2009 5-year est.).
Taxes: Total city taxes per capita: $166 (2007); City property taxes per capita: $0 (2007).
Education: Percent of population age 25 and over with: High school diploma (including GED) or higher: 81.1% (2010); Bachelor's degree or higher: 5.7% (2010); Master's degree or higher: 1.6% (2010).
Housing: Homeownership rate: 81.9% (2010); Median home value: $68,750 (2010); Median contract rent: $421 per month (2005-2009 5-year est.); Median year structure built: 1949 (2005-2009 5-year est.).

Transportation: Commute to work: 96.9% car, 0.0% public transportation, 0.0% walk, 3.1% work from home (2005-2009 5-year est.); Travel time to work: 12.6% less than 15 minutes, 24.2% 15 to 30 minutes, 48.4% 30 to 45 minutes, 2.1% 45 to 60 minutes, 12.6% 60 minutes or more (2005-2009 5-year est.)

HUGHES SPRINGS (city). Covers a land area of 2.437 square miles and a water area of 0 square miles. Located at 32.99° N. Lat; 94.63° W. Long. Elevation is 377 feet.

Population: 1,956 (1990); 1,856 (2000); 1,868 (2010); 1,872 (2015 projected); Race: 76.6% White, 19.6% Black, 0.0% Asian, 3.8% Other, 6.0% Hispanic of any race (2010); Density: 766.6 persons per square mile (2010); Average household size: 2.29 (2010); Median age: 35.7 (2010); Males per 100 females: 86.4 (2010); Marriage status: 24.2% never married, 54.5% now married, 8.0% widowed, 13.3% divorced (2005-2009 5-year est.); Foreign born: 3.8% (2005-2009 5-year est.); Ancestry (includes multiple ancestries): 17.3% American, 8.2% German, 6.8% Irish, 4.8% English, 3.4% African (2005-2009 5-year est.).

Economy: Single-family building permits issued: 0 (2010); Multi-family building permits issued: 0 (2010); Employment by occupation: 7.9% management, 18.5% professional, 19.3% services, 28.4% sales, 1.8% farming, 7.9% construction, 16.4% production (2005-2009 5-year est.).

Income: Per capita income: $17,401 (2010); Median household income: $31,364 (2010); Average household income: $39,969 (2010); Percent of households with income of $100,000 or more: 5.5% (2010); Poverty rate: 28.1% (2005-2009 5-year est.).

Taxes: Total city taxes per capita: $245 (2007); City property taxes per capita: $135 (2007).

Education: Percent of population age 25 and over with: High school diploma (including GED) or higher: 76.9% (2010); Bachelor's degree or higher: 9.8% (2010); Master's degree or higher: 2.5% (2010).

School District(s)
Hughes Springs ISD (PK-12)
　　2009-10 Enrollment: 1,096 . . . . (903) 639-3802

Housing: Homeownership rate: 54.6% (2010); Median home value: $57,985 (2010); Median contract rent: $291 per month (2005-2009 5-year est.); Median year structure built: 1964 (2005-2009 5-year est.).

Transportation: Commute to work: 95.5% car, 0.0% public transportation, 0.5% walk, 3.9% work from home (2005-2009 5-year est.); Travel time to work: 48.3% less than 15 minutes, 23.2% 15 to 30 minutes, 16.4% 30 to 45 minutes, 7.1% 45 to 60 minutes, 5.0% 60 minutes or more (2005-2009 5-year est.)

Additional Information Contacts
Hughes Springs Chamber of Commerce . . . . (903) 639-2351
　　http://www.hughesspringstx.net

LINDEN (city). County seat. Covers a land area of 3.523 square miles and a water area of 0 square miles. Located at 33.00° N. Lat; 94.36° W. Long. Elevation is 381 feet.

History: Linden developed as a shipping center for livestock and dairy products. The printing press used by the newspaper in Linden after 1875 had been recovered from the bottom of the Red River. Formerly used in Shreveport, Louisiana, it had been thrown in the river to keep it from being confiscated by Federal troops in 1864.

Population: 2,375 (1990); 2,256 (2000); 2,160 (2010); 2,116 (2015 projected); Race: 74.8% White, 22.0% Black, 0.2% Asian, 2.9% Other, 2.7% Hispanic of any race (2010); Density: 613.1 persons per square mile (2010); Average household size: 2.15 (2010); Median age: 45.0 (2010); Males per 100 females: 87.3 (2010); Marriage status: 21.0% never married, 50.8% now married, 8.7% widowed, 19.5% divorced (2005-2009 5-year est.); Foreign born: 7.6% (2005-2009 5-year est.); Ancestry (includes multiple ancestries): 28.4% American, 7.0% Irish, 6.9% English, 5.1% German, 3.3% African (2005-2009 5-year est.).

Economy: Employment by occupation: 4.8% management, 17.9% professional, 29.5% services, 18.2% sales, 4.8% farming, 12.8% construction, 12.0% production (2005-2009 5-year est.).

Income: Per capita income: $20,289 (2010); Median household income: $33,333 (2010); Average household income: $46,095 (2010); Percent of households with income of $100,000 or more: 9.4% (2010); Poverty rate: 24.7% (2005-2009 5-year est.).

Taxes: Total city taxes per capita: $216 (2007); City property taxes per capita: $123 (2007).

Education: Percent of population age 25 and over with: High school diploma (including GED) or higher: 76.0% (2010); Bachelor's degree or higher: 14.9% (2010); Master's degree or higher: 3.5% (2010).

School District(s)
Linden-Kildare CISD (PK-12)
　　2009-10 Enrollment: 802 . . . . (903) 756-5027

Housing: Homeownership rate: 61.7% (2010); Median home value: $59,580 (2010); Median contract rent: $328 per month (2005-2009 5-year est.); Median year structure built: 1969 (2005-2009 5-year est.).

Hospitals: Good Shepherd Medical Center-Linden (25 beds); Good Shepherd Medical Center-Linden

Safety: Violent crime rate: 66.2 per 10,000 population; Property crime rate: 297.7 per 10,000 population (2009).

Newspapers: Cass County Sun (Community news; Circulation 2,000)

Transportation: Commute to work: 92.0% car, 0.6% public transportation, 5.8% walk, 1.0% work from home (2005-2009 5-year est.); Travel time to work: 38.8% less than 15 minutes, 25.6% 15 to 30 minutes, 17.2% 30 to 45 minutes, 7.7% 45 to 60 minutes, 10.8% 60 minutes or more (2005-2009 5-year est.)

Additional Information Contacts
Linden Economic Development Corporation . . . . (903) 756-7774
　　http://www.lindentexas.org

MARIETTA (town). Covers a land area of 0.577 square miles and a water area of 0 square miles. Located at 33.17° N. Lat; 94.54° W. Long. Elevation is 351 feet.

Population: 161 (1990); 112 (2000); 106 (2010); 102 (2015 projected); Race: 77.4% White, 22.6% Black, 0.0% Asian, 0.0% Other, 0.9% Hispanic of any race (2010); Density: 183.6 persons per square mile (2010); Average household size: 2.30 (2010); Median age: 51.9 (2010); Males per 100 females: 89.3 (2010); Marriage status: 18.7% never married, 54.7% now married, 12.0% widowed, 14.7% divorced (2005-2009 5-year est.); Foreign born: 0.0% (2005-2009 5-year est.); Ancestry (includes multiple ancestries): 19.5% American, 18.3% Irish, 17.1% German, 4.9% Scotch-Irish, 2.4% Scottish (2005-2009 5-year est.).

Economy: Employment by occupation: 0.0% management, 20.8% professional, 16.7% services, 16.7% sales, 0.0% farming, 25.0% construction, 20.8% production (2005-2009 5-year est.).

Income: Per capita income: $15,596 (2010); Median household income: $25,000 (2010); Average household income: $28,859 (2010); Percent of households with income of $100,000 or more: 0.0% (2010); Poverty rate: 7.3% (2005-2009 5-year est.).

Education: Percent of population age 25 and over with: High school diploma (including GED) or higher: 79.7% (2010); Bachelor's degree or higher: 8.9% (2010); Master's degree or higher: 1.3% (2010).

Housing: Homeownership rate: 84.8% (2010); Median home value: $55,000 (2010); Median contract rent: $508 per month (2005-2009 5-year est.); Median year structure built: 1949 (2005-2009 5-year est.).

Transportation: Commute to work: 81.8% car, 0.0% public transportation, 9.1% walk, 9.1% work from home (2005-2009 5-year est.); Travel time to work: 30.0% less than 15 minutes, 50.0% 15 to 30 minutes, 5.0% 30 to 45 minutes, 0.0% 45 to 60 minutes, 15.0% 60 minutes or more (2005-2009 5-year est.)

QUEEN CITY (city). Covers a land area of 3.576 square miles and a water area of 0.020 square miles. Located at 33.15° N. Lat; 94.15° W. Long. Elevation is 358 feet.

Population: 1,731 (1990); 1,613 (2000); 1,636 (2010); 1,642 (2015 projected); Race: 81.7% White, 14.5% Black, 0.2% Asian, 3.5% Other, 3.6% Hispanic of any race (2010); Density: 457.5 persons per square mile (2010); Average household size: 2.43 (2010); Median age: 38.3 (2010); Males per 100 females: 88.0 (2010); Marriage status: 20.0% never married, 59.7% now married, 11.3% widowed, 9.0% divorced (2005-2009 5-year est.); Foreign born: 1.2% (2005-2009 5-year est.); Ancestry (includes multiple ancestries): 14.4% American, 12.5% German, 10.8% Irish, 5.3% English, 3.1% Scottish (2005-2009 5-year est.).

Economy: Employment by occupation: 3.9% management, 15.4% professional, 24.4% services, 16.9% sales, 1.3% farming, 18.7% construction, 19.3% production (2005-2009 5-year est.).

Income: Per capita income: $18,092 (2010); Median household income: $33,750 (2010); Average household income: $44,266 (2010); Percent of households with income of $100,000 or more: 7.6% (2010); Poverty rate: 16.7% (2005-2009 5-year est.).

Taxes: Total city taxes per capita: $258 (2007); City property taxes per capita: $141 (2007).

Education: Percent of population age 25 and over with: High school diploma (including GED) or higher: 77.9% (2010); Bachelor's degree or higher: 9.3% (2010); Master's degree or higher: 3.0% (2010).

School District(s)
Queen City ISD (PK-12)
    2009-10 Enrollment: 1,088 . . . . (903) 796-8256
Housing: Homeownership rate: 64.1% (2010); Median home value: $66,957 (2010); Median contract rent: $349 per month (2005-2009 5-year est.); Median year structure built: 1982 (2005-2009 5-year est.).
Safety: Violent crime rate: 71.4 per 10,000 population; Property crime rate: 259.6 per 10,000 population (2009).
Transportation: Commute to work: 97.7% car, 0.0% public transportation, 0.0% walk, 0.5% work from home (2005-2009 5-year est.); Travel time to work: 24.7% less than 15 minutes, 38.8% 15 to 30 minutes, 22.4% 30 to 45 minutes, 5.1% 45 to 60 minutes, 9.0% 60 minutes or more (2005-2009 5-year est.)

Castro County

Located in northwestern Texas. Covers a land area of 898.31 square miles, a water area of 1.00 square miles, and is located in the Central Time Zone at 34.53° N. Lat., 102.28° W. Long. The county was founded in 1876. County seat is Dimmitt.

Weather Station: Dimmitt 2 N   Elevation: 3,850 feet

	Jan	Feb	Mar	Apr	May	Jun	Jul	Aug	Sep	Oct	Nov	Dec
High	51	55	63	72	81	88	91	89	83	72	60	50
Low	21	24	30	38	48	58	62	61	53	41	30	22
Precip	0.6	0.5	1.0	1.0	2.8	3.8	2.1	3.3	2.6	1.8	0.7	0.8
Snow	3.2	1.5	1.0	0.4	0.0	0.0	0.0	0.0	0.0	0.1	1.3	3.4

High and Low temperatures in degrees Fahrenheit; Precipitation and Snow in inches

Weather Station: Hart   Elevation: 3,640 feet

	Jan	Feb	Mar	Apr	May	Jun	Jul	Aug	Sep	Oct	Nov	Dec
High	52	57	64	72	81	88	90	88	82	73	61	51
Low	22	25	32	40	51	60	63	62	54	43	31	23
Precip	0.5	0.6	1.0	1.2	2.6	2.9	1.8	2.7	1.9	1.3	0.8	0.7
Snow	0.5	0.8	0.5	tr	0.0	0.0	0.0	0.0	0.0	0.0	0.9	1.0

High and Low temperatures in degrees Fahrenheit; Precipitation and Snow in inches

Population: 9,070 (1990); 8,285 (2000); 7,230 (2010); 6,704 (2015 projected); Race: 73.4% White, 2.8% Black, 0.0% Asian, 23.7% Other, 54.5% Hispanic of any race (2010); Density: 8.0 persons per square mile (2010); Average household size: 2.90 (2010); Median age: 35.6 (2010); Males per 100 females: 101.4 (2010).
Religion: Five largest groups: 36.7% Southern Baptist Convention, 26.9% Catholic Church, 8.5% The United Methodist Church, 4.4% Churches of Christ, 1.0% Christian Churches and Churches of Christ (2000).
Economy: Unemployment rate: 5.9% (June 2011); Total civilian labor force: 3,604 (June 2011); Leading industries: 18.6% retail trade; 10.3% wholesale trade; 9.1% other services (except public administration) (2009); Farms: 485 totaling 567,255 acres (2007); Companies that employ 500 or more persons: 0 (2009); Companies that employ 100 to 499 persons: 1 (2009); Companies that employ less than 100 persons: 178 (2009); Black-owned businesses: n/a (2007); Hispanic-owned businesses: 43 (2007); Asian-owned businesses: n/a (2007); Women-owned businesses: n/a (2007); Retail sales per capita: $8,270 (2010). Single-family building permits issued: 0 (2010); Multi-family building permits issued: 0 (2010).
Income: Per capita income: $17,862 (2010); Median household income: $38,956 (2010); Average household income: $51,742 (2010); Percent of households with income of $100,000 or more: 10.1% (2010); Poverty rate: 21.0% (2009); Bankruptcy rate: 0.74% (2010).
Taxes: Total county taxes per capita: $399 (2007); County property taxes per capita: $316 (2007).
Education: Percent of population age 25 and over with: High school diploma (including GED) or higher: 70.9% (2010); Bachelor's degree or higher: 16.9% (2010); Master's degree or higher: 4.0% (2010).
Housing: Homeownership rate: 69.1% (2010); Median home value: $64,866 (2010); Median contract rent: $415 per month (2005-2009 5-year est.); Median year structure built: 1961 (2005-2009 5-year est.)
Health: Birth rate: 173.9 per 10,000 population (2009); Death rate: 77.1 per 10,000 population (2009); Age-adjusted cancer mortality rate: 153.5 (Unreliable) deaths per 100,000 population (2007); Number of physicians: 4.2 per 10,000 population (2008); Hospital beds: 34.9 per 10,000 population (2007); Hospital admissions: 1,137.9 per 10,000 population (2007).
Elections: 2008 Presidential election results: 31.4% Obama, 68.2% McCain, 0.0% Nader
Additional Information Contacts

Castro County Government . . . . (806) 647-4451
    http://www.co.castro.tx.us/ips/cms
Dimmitt Chamber of Commerce . . . . (806) 647-2524
    http://www.dimmittchamber.com

Castro County Communities

DIMMITT (city). County seat. Covers a land area of 2.067 square miles and a water area of 0 square miles. Located at 34.54° N. Lat; 102.31° W. Long. Elevation is 3,875 feet.
History: Established 1891.
Population: 4,655 (1990); 4,375 (2000); 3,749 (2010); 3,443 (2015 projected); Race: 73.4% White, 3.3% Black, 0.0% Asian, 23.2% Other, 60.2% Hispanic of any race (2010); Density: 1,813.6 persons per square mile (2010); Average household size: 2.87 (2010); Median age: 34.8 (2010); Males per 100 females: 95.6 (2010); Marriage status: 18.0% never married, 64.8% now married, 9.7% widowed, 7.5% divorced (2005-2009 5-year est.); Foreign born: 25.3% (2005-2009 5-year est.); Ancestry (includes multiple ancestries): 10.1% German, 8.2% Irish, 6.8% English, 4.0% Scottish, 2.4% American (2005-2009 5-year est.).
Economy: Single-family building permits issued: 0 (2010); Multi-family building permits issued: 0 (2010); Employment by occupation: 9.4% management, 17.8% professional, 19.9% services, 19.7% sales, 7.2% farming, 5.4% construction, 20.5% production (2005-2009 5-year est.).
Income: Per capita income: $16,974 (2010); Median household income: $36,344 (2010); Average household income: $48,542 (2010); Percent of households with income of $100,000 or more: 9.5% (2010); Poverty rate: 26.7% (2005-2009 5-year est.).
Taxes: Total city taxes per capita: $191 (2007); City property taxes per capita: $88 (2007).
Education: Percent of population age 25 and over with: High school diploma (including GED) or higher: 68.2% (2010); Bachelor's degree or higher: 17.5% (2010); Master's degree or higher: 4.1% (2010).
School District(s)
Dimmitt ISD (PK-12)
    2009-10 Enrollment: 1,197 . . . . (806) 647-3101
Housing: Homeownership rate: 69.4% (2010); Median home value: $61,258 (2010); Median contract rent: $424 per month (2005-2009 5-year est.); Median year structure built: 1961 (2005-2009 5-year est.).
Hospitals: Plains Memorial Hospital
Safety: Violent crime rate: 13.8 per 10,000 population; Property crime rate: 310.8 per 10,000 population (2009).
Newspapers: Castro County News (Community news; Circulation 2,357)
Transportation: Commute to work: 94.4% car, 1.6% public transportation, 0.5% walk, 2.1% work from home (2005-2009 5-year est.); Travel time to work: 68.5% less than 15 minutes, 13.8% 15 to 30 minutes, 11.5% 30 to 45 minutes, 2.8% 45 to 60 minutes, 3.4% 60 minutes or more (2005-2009 5-year est.)
Additional Information Contacts
Dimmitt Chamber of Commerce . . . . (806) 647-2524
    http://www.dimmittchamber.com

HART (city). Covers a land area of 0.751 square miles and a water area of 0 square miles. Located at 34.38° N. Lat; 102.11° W. Long. Elevation is 3,671 feet.
Population: 1,221 (1990); 1,198 (2000); 1,022 (2010); 946 (2015 projected); Race: 58.4% White, 5.4% Black, 0.0% Asian, 36.2% Other, 73.9% Hispanic of any race (2010); Density: 1,360.2 persons per square mile (2010); Average household size: 3.08 (2010); Median age: 32.1 (2010); Males per 100 females: 105.2 (2010); Marriage status: 16.6% never married, 66.9% now married, 8.4% widowed, 8.1% divorced (2005-2009 5-year est.); Foreign born: 24.6% (2005-2009 5-year est.); Ancestry (includes multiple ancestries): 4.3% American, 3.0% German, 2.9% English, 2.1% Irish, 0.9% Italian (2005-2009 5-year est.).
Economy: Single-family building permits issued: 0 (2010); Multi-family building permits issued: 0 (2010); Employment by occupation: 9.5% management, 11.7% professional, 15.9% services, 18.1% sales, 4.8% farming, 10.2% construction, 29.8% production (2005-2009 5-year est.).
Income: Per capita income: $13,641 (2010); Median household income: $33,696 (2010); Average household income: $41,250 (2010); Percent of households with income of $100,000 or more: 2.7% (2010); Poverty rate: 31.6% (2005-2009 5-year est.).
Taxes: Total city taxes per capita: $133 (2007); City property taxes per capita: $80 (2007).

Education: Percent of population age 25 and over with: High school diploma (including GED) or higher: 61.9% (2010); Bachelor's degree or higher: 9.2% (2010); Master's degree or higher: 2.5% (2010).

School District(s)

Hart ISD (PK-12)

    2009-10 Enrollment: 301 . . . . (806) 938-2143

Housing: Homeownership rate: 69.6% (2010); Median home value: $47,500 (2010); Median contract rent: $306 per month (2005-2009 5-year est.); Median year structure built: 1961 (2005-2009 5-year est.).

Newspapers: Hart Beat (Community news; Circulation 400)

Transportation: Commute to work: 91.6% car, 0.7% public transportation, 4.3% walk, 3.3% work from home (2005-2009 5-year est.); Travel time to work: 65.1% less than 15 minutes, 20.8% 15 to 30 minutes, 12.1% 30 to 45 minutes, 0.0% 45 to 60 minutes, 2.1% 60 minutes or more (2005-2009 5-year est.)

NAZARETH (city). Covers a land area of 0.348 square miles and a water area of 0 square miles. Located at 34.54° N. Lat; 102.10° W. Long. Elevation is 3,760 feet.

Population: 309 (1990); 356 (2000); 334 (2010); 324 (2015 projected); Race: 91.3% White, 0.3% Black, 0.0% Asian, 8.4% Other, 19.2% Hispanic of any race (2010); Density: 959.0 persons per square mile (2010); Average household size: 2.76 (2010); Median age: 43.2 (2010); Males per 100 females: 111.4 (2010); Marriage status: 24.3% never married, 66.3% now married, 4.1% widowed, 5.3% divorced (2005-2009 5-year est.); Foreign born: 0.0% (2005-2009 5-year est.); Ancestry (includes multiple ancestries): 37.7% German, 10.9% English, 6.3% Dutch, 3.9% Lebanese, 1.8% Swedish (2005-2009 5-year est.).

Economy: Employment by occupation: 32.8% management, 17.5% professional, 10.9% services, 13.1% sales, 0.0% farming, 16.8% construction, 8.8% production (2005-2009 5-year est.).

Income: Per capita income: $27,480 (2010); Median household income: $56,250 (2010); Average household income: $77,624 (2010); Percent of households with income of $100,000 or more: 19.8% (2010); Poverty rate: 11.6% (2005-2009 5-year est.).

Taxes: Total city taxes per capita: $128 (2007); City property taxes per capita: $52 (2007).

Education: Percent of population age 25 and over with: High school diploma (including GED) or higher: 90.7% (2010); Bachelor's degree or higher: 24.4% (2010); Master's degree or higher: 5.3% (2010).

School District(s)

Nazareth ISD (PK-12)

    2009-10 Enrollment: 236 . . . . (806) 945-2231

Housing: Homeownership rate: 76.9% (2010); Median home value: $86,429 (2010); Median contract rent: n/a per month (2005-2009 5-year est.); Median year structure built: 1963 (2005-2009 5-year est.).

Transportation: Commute to work: 74.3% car, 0.0% public transportation, 0.0% walk, 25.7% work from home (2005-2009 5-year est.); Travel time to work: 49.5% less than 15 minutes, 37.4% 15 to 30 minutes, 8.4% 30 to 45 minutes, 0.0% 45 to 60 minutes, 4.7% 60 minutes or more (2005-2009 5-year est.)

Chambers County

Located in southeastern Texas, on Gulf coastal plains; bounded on the south by East Bay. Covers a land area of 599.31 square miles, a water area of 272.68 square miles, and is located in the Central Time Zone at 29.75° N. Lat., 94.67° W. Long. The county was founded in 1858. County seat is Anahuac.

Chambers County is part of the Houston-Sugar Land-Baytown, TX Metropolitan Statistical Area. The entire metro area includes: Austin County, TX; Brazoria County, TX; Chambers County, TX; Fort Bend County, TX; Galveston County, TX; Harris County, TX; Liberty County, TX; Montgomery County, TX; San Jacinto County, TX; Waller County, TX

Weather Station: Anahuac										Elevation: 23 feet	
	Jan	Feb	Mar	Apr	May	Jun	Jul	Aug	Sep	Oct	Nov	Dec
High	62	65	71	77	84	89	92	92	88	81	72	63
Low	43	46	52	58	67	73	75	74	69	59	51	44
Precip	4.7	3.0	3.6	3.6	5.3	6.5	5.2	5.1	6.4	5.1	4.1	4.5
Snow	0.0	tr	0.0	0.0	0.0	0.0	0.0	0.0	0.0	0.0	0.0	tr

High and Low temperatures in degrees Fahrenheit; Precipitation and Snow in inches

Population: 20,088 (1990); 26,031 (2000); 32,519 (2010); 35,618 (2015 projected); Race: 76.2% White, 10.9% Black, 1.0% Asian, 12.0% Other,

17.6% Hispanic of any race (2010); Density: 54.3 persons per square mile (2010); Average household size: 2.81 (2010); Median age: 35.7 (2010); Males per 100 females: 100.9 (2010).

Religion: Five largest groups: 25.5% Southern Baptist Convention, 14.3% Catholic Church, 8.0% The United Methodist Church, 2.8% The American Baptist Association, 1.9% Assemblies of God (2000).

Economy: Unemployment rate: 11.1% (June 2011); Total civilian labor force: 16,057 (June 2011); Leading industries: 19.2% manufacturing; 17.8% transportation & warehousing; 9.8% accommodation & food services (2009); Farms: 650 totaling 267,343 acres (2007); Companies that employ 500 or more persons: 2 (2009); Companies that employ 100 to 499 persons: 11 (2009); Companies that employ less than 100 persons: 480 (2009); Black-owned businesses: n/a (2007); Hispanic-owned businesses: n/a (2007); Asian-owned businesses: n/a (2007); Women-owned businesses: 706 (2007); Retail sales per capita: $8,732 (2010). Single-family building permits issued: 226 (2010); Multi-family building permits issued: 0 (2010).

Income: Per capita income: $26,446 (2010); Median household income: $63,599 (2010); Average household income: $74,753 (2010); Percent of households with income of $100,000 or more: 25.4% (2010); Poverty rate: 8.7% (2009); Bankruptcy rate: 1.12% (2010).

Taxes: Total county taxes per capita: $833 (2007); County property taxes per capita: $769 (2007).

Education: Percent of population age 25 and over with: High school diploma (including GED) or higher: 83.5% (2010); Bachelor's degree or higher: 14.8% (2010); Master's degree or higher: 3.7% (2010).

Housing: Homeownership rate: 82.1% (2010); Median home value: $116,167 (2010); Median contract rent: $436 per month (2005-2009 5-year est.); Median year structure built: 1986 (2005-2009 5-year est.)

Health: Birth rate: 124.1 per 10,000 population (2009); Death rate: 63.0 per 10,000 population (2009); Age-adjusted cancer mortality rate: 128.8 deaths per 100,000 population (2007); Number of physicians: 3.7 per 10,000 population (2008); Hospital beds: 13.5 per 10,000 population (2007); Hospital admissions: 329.3 per 10,000 population (2007).

Elections: 2008 Presidential election results: 24.0% Obama, 75.1% McCain, 0.1% Nader

National and State Parks: Anahuac National Wildlife Refuge

Additional Information Contacts

Chambers County Government . . . . (409) 267-2895
    http://co.chambers.tx.us
Anahuac Area Chamber of Commerce . . . . (409) 267-4190
    http://www.anahuacchamber.com
West Chambers County Chamber of Commerce . . . . (281) 576-5440
    http://www.westchamberscoc.com
Winnie Area Chamber of Commerce . . . . (409) 296-2231
    http://www.winnietexas.org

Chambers County Communities

ANAHUAC (city). County seat. Covers a land area of 2.115 square miles and a water area of 0 square miles. Located at 29.76° N. Lat; 94.67° W. Long. Elevation is 30 feet.

History: In 1832 Anahuac was an important port of entry on Trinity Bay, and the Mexican government placed a heavy duty on imports to discourage Anglo-American immigration. This met with strong protest from the colonists, whose retaliation was later called "The Boston Tea Party of Texas."

Population: 1,993 (1990); 2,210 (2000); 2,070 (2010); 2,079 (2015 projected); Race: 53.8% White, 25.2% Black, 1.5% Asian, 19.5% Other, 22.7% Hispanic of any race (2010); Density: 978.6 persons per square mile (2010); Average household size: 2.73 (2010); Median age: 33.6 (2010); Males per 100 females: 90.8 (2010); Marriage status: 27.4% never married, 55.4% now married, 7.5% widowed, 9.7% divorced (2005-2009 5-year est.); Foreign born: 7.6% (2005-2009 5-year est.); Ancestry (includes multiple ancestries): 11.7% German, 10.5% Irish, 7.1% American, 6.2% English, 4.9% French (2005-2009 5-year est.).

Economy: Single-family building permits issued: 6 (2010); Multi-family building permits issued: 0 (2010); Employment by occupation: 9.4% management, 14.1% professional, 22.8% services, 22.3% sales, 3.3% farming, 19.4% construction, 8.7% production (2005-2009 5-year est.).

Income: Per capita income: $21,742 (2010); Median household income: $49,400 (2010); Average household income: $59,441 (2010); Percent of households with income of $100,000 or more: 15.9% (2010); Poverty rate: 18.3% (2005-2009 5-year est.).

Taxes: Total city taxes per capita: $185 (2007); City property taxes per capita: $107 (2007).
Education: Percent of population age 25 and over with: High school diploma (including GED) or higher: 80.8% (2010); Bachelor's degree or higher: 16.8% (2010); Master's degree or higher: 4.5% (2010).

School District(s)
Anahuac ISD (PK-12)
    2009-10 Enrollment: 1,289 . . . . (409) 267-3600
Housing: Homeownership rate: 72.4% (2010); Median home value: $81,264 (2010); Median contract rent: $335 per month (2005-2009 5-year est.); Median year structure built: 1973 (2005-2009 5-year est.).
Hospitals: Bayside Community Hospital (30 beds)
Newspapers: The Progress (Local news; Circulation 2,500)
Transportation: Commute to work: 93.6% car, 0.0% public transportation, 2.3% walk, 2.2% work from home (2005-2009 5-year est.); Travel time to work: 49.7% less than 15 minutes, 18.2% 15 to 30 minutes, 10.4% 30 to 45 minutes, 8.7% 45 to 60 minutes, 12.9% 60 minutes or more (2005-2009 5-year est.)

Additional Information Contacts
Anahuac Area Chamber of Commerce . . . . (409) 267-4190
    http://www.anahuacchamber.com

BEACH CITY (city). Aka Sea Crest Park. Covers a land area of 4.436 square miles and a water area of 0 square miles. Located at 29.70° N. Lat; 94.86° W. Long. Elevation is 20 feet.
Population: 852 (1990); 1,645 (2000); 2,156 (2010); 2,449 (2015 projected); Race: 89.1% White, 6.3% Black, 0.6% Asian, 3.9% Other, 6.3% Hispanic of any race (2010); Density: 486.1 persons per square mile (2010); Average household size: 2.66 (2010); Median age: 39.9 (2010); Males per 100 females: 99.6 (2010); Marriage status: 12.7% never married, 75.7% now married, 3.4% widowed, 8.3% divorced (2005-2009 5-year est.); Foreign born: 2.2% (2005-2009 5-year est.); Ancestry (includes multiple ancestries): 19.3% American, 15.1% German, 12.4% English, 7.0% Irish, 4.0% Dutch (2005-2009 5-year est.).
Economy: Single-family building permits issued: 27 (2010); Multi-family building permits issued: 0 (2010); Employment by occupation: 13.3% management, 22.8% professional, 5.8% services, 24.8% sales, 0.0% farming, 18.7% construction, 14.5% production (2005-2009 5-year est.).
Income: Per capita income: $39,675 (2010); Median household income: $90,299 (2010); Average household income: $105,713 (2010); Percent of households with income of $100,000 or more: 43.6% (2010); Poverty rate: 5.2% (2005-2009 5-year est.).
Education: Percent of population age 25 and over with: High school diploma (including GED) or higher: 92.1% (2010); Bachelor's degree or higher: 19.9% (2010); Master's degree or higher: 5.4% (2010).
Housing: Homeownership rate: 82.1% (2010); Median home value: $150,781 (2010); Median contract rent: $614 per month (2005-2009 5-year est.); Median year structure built: 1991 (2005-2009 5-year est.).
Transportation: Commute to work: 98.7% car, 0.0% public transportation, 0.0% walk, 1.0% work from home (2005-2009 5-year est.); Travel time to work: 18.5% less than 15 minutes, 40.0% 15 to 30 minutes, 22.5% 30 to 45 minutes, 8.3% 45 to 60 minutes, 10.6% 60 minutes or more (2005-2009 5-year est.)

COVE (city). Covers a land area of 1.217 square miles and a water area of 0.046 square miles. Located at 29.81° N. Lat; 94.82° W. Long. Elevation is 23 feet.
Population: 402 (1990); 323 (2000); 458 (2010); 523 (2015 projected); Race: 86.0% White, 3.3% Black, 0.0% Asian, 10.7% Other, 16.2% Hispanic of any race (2010); Density: 376.2 persons per square mile (2010); Average household size: 3.01 (2010); Median age: 35.4 (2010); Males per 100 females: 104.5 (2010); Marriage status: 2.8% never married, 77.9% now married, 2.8% widowed, 16.4% divorced (2005-2009 5-year est.); Foreign born: 0.0% (2005-2009 5-year est.); Ancestry (includes multiple ancestries): 17.2% American, 12.9% German, 9.5% Irish, 7.2% Czech, 7.0% European (2005-2009 5-year est.).
Economy: Employment by occupation: 24.4% management, 10.4% professional, 11.9% services, 15.9% sales, 0.0% farming, 12.9% construction, 24.4% production (2005-2009 5-year est.).
Income: Per capita income: $31,997 (2010); Median household income: $90,152 (2010); Average household income: $97,895 (2010); Percent of households with income of $100,000 or more: 41.4% (2010); Poverty rate: 5.7% (2005-2009 5-year est.).
Taxes: Total city taxes per capita: $87 (2007); City property taxes per capita: $0 (2007).

Education: Percent of population age 25 and over with: High school diploma (including GED) or higher: 92.8% (2010); Bachelor's degree or higher: 21.4% (2010); Master's degree or higher: 5.5% (2010).
Housing: Homeownership rate: 90.1% (2010); Median home value: $199,219 (2010); Median contract rent: $621 per month (2005-2009 5-year est.); Median year structure built: 1994 (2005-2009 5-year est.).
Transportation: Commute to work: 99.5% car, 0.0% public transportation, 0.0% walk, 0.0% work from home (2005-2009 5-year est.); Travel time to work: 19.6% less than 15 minutes, 34.7% 15 to 30 minutes, 17.1% 30 to 45 minutes, 19.1% 45 to 60 minutes, 9.5% 60 minutes or more (2005-2009 5-year est.)

HANKAMER (unincorporated postal area, zip code 77560). Covers a land area of 29.517 square miles and a water area of 0.359 square miles. Located at 29.86° N. Lat; 94.58° W. Long. Elevation is 33 feet.
Population: 1,065 (2000); Race: 57.0% White, 38.9% Black, 0.0% Asian, 4.1% Other, 6.7% Hispanic of any race (2000); Density: 36.1 persons per square mile (2000); Age: 30.6% under 18, 10.2% over 64 (2000); Marriage status: 33.5% never married, 49.2% now married, 7.9% widowed, 9.4% divorced (2000); Foreign born: 4.0% (2000); Ancestry (includes multiple ancestries): 16.7% American, 5.3% English, 4.1% Irish, 2.1% German (2000).
Economy: Employment by occupation: 3.7% management, 18.4% professional, 14.7% services, 19.9% sales, 2.6% farming, 15.0% construction, 25.7% production (2000).
Income: Per capita income: $14,344 (2000); Median household income: $38,173 (2000); Poverty rate: 179.1% (2000).
Education: Percent of population age 25 and over with: High school diploma (including GED) or higher: 62.6% (2000); Bachelor's degree or higher: 6.7% (2000).
Housing: Homeownership rate: 91.6% (2000); Median home value: $42,100 (2000); Median contract rent: $287 per month (2000); Median year structure built: 1975 (2000).
Transportation: Commute to work: 98.1% car, 0.0% public transportation, 0.0% walk, 1.9% work from home (2000); Travel time to work: 20.4% less than 15 minutes, 40.2% 15 to 30 minutes, 14.2% 30 to 45 minutes, 11.5% 45 to 60 minutes, 13.7% 60 minutes or more (2000)

MONT BELVIEU (city). Covers a land area of 14.526 square miles and a water area of 0.360 square miles. Located at 29.86° N. Lat; 94.87° W. Long. Elevation is 69 feet.
Population: 1,638 (1990); 2,324 (2000); 2,702 (2010); 2,933 (2015 projected); Race: 87.5% White, 5.1% Black, 0.6% Asian, 6.7% Other, 11.4% Hispanic of any race (2010); Density: 186.0 persons per square mile (2010); Average household size: 2.83 (2010); Median age: 34.3 (2010); Males per 100 females: 99.0 (2010); Marriage status: 18.9% never married, 74.6% now married, 2.8% widowed, 3.7% divorced (2005-2009 5-year est.); Foreign born: 2.1% (2005-2009 5-year est.); Ancestry (includes multiple ancestries): 16.6% German, 15.0% Irish, 9.3% French, 9.0% American, 8.6% English (2005-2009 5-year est.).
Economy: Single-family building permits issued: 58 (2010); Multi-family building permits issued: 0 (2010); Employment by occupation: 8.4% management, 22.4% professional, 10.9% services, 16.1% sales, 0.0% farming, 16.6% construction, 25.6% production (2005-2009 5-year est.).
Income: Per capita income: $28,427 (2010); Median household income: $68,269 (2010); Average household income: $80,335 (2010); Percent of households with income of $100,000 or more: 26.9% (2010); Poverty rate: 10.6% (2005-2009 5-year est.).
Taxes: Total city taxes per capita: $4,048 (2007); City property taxes per capita: $2,747 (2007).
Education: Percent of population age 25 and over with: High school diploma (including GED) or higher: 86.8% (2010); Bachelor's degree or higher: 11.2% (2010); Master's degree or higher: 1.6% (2010).
School District(s)
Barbers Hill ISD (PK-12)
    2009-10 Enrollment: 4,121 . . . . (281) 576-2221
Housing: Homeownership rate: 70.1% (2010); Median home value: $139,448 (2010); Median contract rent: $558 per month (2005-2009 5-year est.); Median year structure built: 1987 (2005-2009 5-year est.).
Safety: Violent crime rate: 21.9 per 10,000 population; Property crime rate: 390.9 per 10,000 population (2009).
Transportation: Commute to work: 98.6% car, 0.0% public transportation, 1.3% walk, 0.1% work from home (2005-2009 5-year est.); Travel time to work: 20.8% less than 15 minutes, 46.1% 15 to 30 minutes, 22.0% 30 to 45

minutes, 4.5% 45 to 60 minutes, 6.5% 60 minutes or more (2005-2009 5-year est.)

Additional Information Contacts

West Chambers County Chamber of Commerce .... (281) 576-5440
http://www.westchamberscoc.com

OLD RIVER-WINFREE (city). Aka Winfree. Covers a land area of 1.255 square miles and a water area of 0 square miles. Located at 29.87° N. Lat; 94.82° W. Long. Elevation is 36 feet.
Population: 1,233 (1990); 1,364 (2000); 1,482 (2010); 1,575 (2015 projected); Race: 93.8% White, 2.6% Black, 0.2% Asian, 3.4% Other, 6.9% Hispanic of any race (2010); Density: 1,180.5 persons per square mile (2010); Average household size: 2.95 (2010); Median age: 35.3 (2010); Males per 100 females: 100.0 (2010); Marriage status: 22.5% never married, 60.9% now married, 5.3% widowed, 11.3% divorced (2005-2009 5-year est.); Foreign born: 2.5% (2005-2009 5-year est.); Ancestry (includes multiple ancestries): 19.4% American, 12.1% Irish, 10.7% German, 9.7% English, 7.7% French (2005-2009 5-year est.).
Economy: Employment by occupation: 7.9% management, 12.5% professional, 9.8% services, 28.7% sales, 0.0% farming, 14.5% construction, 26.6% production (2005-2009 5-year est.).
Income: Per capita income: $30,656 (2010); Median household income: $80,097 (2010); Average household income: $90,742 (2010); Percent of households with income of $100,000 or more: 33.7% (2010); Poverty rate: 13.9% (2005-2009 5-year est.).
Taxes: Total city taxes per capita: $44 (2007); City property taxes per capita: $0 (2007).
Education: Percent of population age 25 and over with: High school diploma (including GED) or higher: 88.4% (2010); Bachelor's degree or higher: 12.4% (2010); Master's degree or higher: 2.3% (2010).
Housing: Homeownership rate: 86.3% (2010); Median home value: $157,394 (2010); Median contract rent: $625 per month (2005-2009 5-year est.); Median year structure built: 1989 (2005-2009 5-year est.).
Transportation: Commute to work: 98.7% car, 0.0% public transportation, 1.2% walk, 0.1% work from home (2005-2009 5-year est.); Travel time to work: 11.9% less than 15 minutes, 36.2% 15 to 30 minutes, 19.5% 30 to 45 minutes, 15.5% 45 to 60 minutes, 17.0% 60 minutes or more (2005-2009 5-year est.)

STOWELL (CDP). Covers a land area of 9.904 square miles and a water area of 0.383 square miles. Located at 29.78° N. Lat; 94.37° W. Long. Elevation is 23 feet.
Population: 1,419 (1990); 1,572 (2000); 1,630 (2010); 1,708 (2015 projected); Race: 46.9% White, 38.0% Black, 0.0% Asian, 15.1% Other, 16.8% Hispanic of any race (2010); Density: 164.6 persons per square mile (2010); Average household size: 2.73 (2010); Median age: 34.2 (2010); Males per 100 females: 104.0 (2010); Marriage status: 33.0% never married, 41.4% now married, 10.0% widowed, 15.7% divorced (2005-2009 5-year est.); Foreign born: 6.2% (2005-2009 5-year est.); Ancestry (includes multiple ancestries): 10.2% Irish, 7.0% English, 6.2% American, 5.8% African, 4.5% European (2005-2009 5-year est.).
Economy: Employment by occupation: 9.0% management, 6.1% professional, 13.8% services, 24.2% sales, 0.0% farming, 29.9% construction, 17.1% production (2005-2009 5-year est.).
Income: Per capita income: $18,262 (2010); Median household income: $38,214 (2010); Average household income: $49,945 (2010); Percent of households with income of $100,000 or more: 11.7% (2010); Poverty rate: 25.0% (2005-2009 5-year est.).
Education: Percent of population age 25 and over with: High school diploma (including GED) or higher: 73.9% (2010); Bachelor's degree or higher: 10.3% (2010); Master's degree or higher: 2.9% (2010).
Housing: Homeownership rate: 79.0% (2010); Median home value: $65,658 (2010); Median contract rent: $402 per month (2005-2009 5-year est.); Median year structure built: 1975 (2005-2009 5-year est.).
Transportation: Commute to work: 100.0% car, 0.0% public transportation, 0.0% walk, 0.0% work from home (2005-2009 5-year est.); Travel time to work: 23.8% less than 15 minutes, 11.0% 15 to 30 minutes, 25.4% 30 to 45 minutes, 25.9% 45 to 60 minutes, 13.9% 60 minutes or more (2005-2009 5-year est.)
Airports: Chambers County-Winnie Stowell Airport (general aviation)

WALLISVILLE (unincorporated postal area, zip code 77597). Covers a land area of 24.676 square miles and a water area of 2.213 square miles. Located at 29.84° N. Lat; 94.70° W. Long. Elevation is 7 feet.

Population: 824 (2000); Race: 84.2% White, 13.8% Black, 0.0% Asian, 2.0% Other, 2.4% Hispanic of any race (2000); Density: 33.4 persons per square mile (2000); Age: 22.8% under 18, 10.9% over 64 (2000); Marriage status: 19.9% never married, 63.9% now married, 7.1% widowed, 9.1% divorced (2000); Foreign born: 1.2% (2000); Ancestry (includes multiple ancestries): 21.6% German, 14.4% French, 10.7% American, 6.3% English (2000).
Economy: Employment by occupation: 8.6% management, 18.5% professional, 9.9% services, 24.5% sales, 0.0% farming, 14.2% construction, 24.2% production (2000).
Income: Per capita income: $23,367 (2000); Median household income: $38,922 (2000); Poverty rate: 179.1% (2000).
Education: Percent of population age 25 and over with: High school diploma (including GED) or higher: 73.4% (2000); Bachelor's degree or higher: 11.8% (2000).
Housing: Homeownership rate: 84.3% (2000); Median home value: $89,000 (2000); Median contract rent: $386 per month (2000); Median year structure built: 1985 (2000).
Transportation: Commute to work: 98.6% car, 0.0% public transportation, 1.4% walk, 0.0% work from home (2000); Travel time to work: 19.0% less than 15 minutes, 34.5% 15 to 30 minutes, 14.9% 30 to 45 minutes, 22.3% 45 to 60 minutes, 9.2% 60 minutes or more (2000)

WINNIE (CDP). Covers a land area of 3.976 square miles and a water area of 0 square miles. Located at 29.81° N. Lat; 94.38° W. Long. Elevation is 26 feet.
Population: 2,238 (1990); 2,914 (2000); 3,227 (2010); 3,459 (2015 projected); Race: 74.6% White, 11.7% Black, 0.3% Asian, 13.4% Other, 18.1% Hispanic of any race (2010); Density: 811.7 persons per square mile (2010); Average household size: 2.59 (2010); Median age: 35.0 (2010); Males per 100 females: 103.9 (2010); Marriage status: 14.7% never married, 63.4% now married, 11.7% widowed, 10.3% divorced (2005-2009 5-year est.); Foreign born: 15.1% (2005-2009 5-year est.); Ancestry (includes multiple ancestries): 24.1% American, 14.3% French, 7.2% German, 4.5% Irish, 4.2% French Canadian (2005-2009 5-year est.).
Economy: Employment by occupation: 8.9% management, 9.7% professional, 23.7% services, 17.0% sales, 0.0% farming, 21.0% construction, 19.7% production (2005-2009 5-year est.).
Income: Per capita income: $15,847 (2010); Median household income: $35,774 (2010); Average household income: $43,017 (2010); Percent of households with income of $100,000 or more: 7.0% (2010); Poverty rate: 15.0% (2005-2009 5-year est.).
Education: Percent of population age 25 and over with: High school diploma (including GED) or higher: 69.0% (2010); Bachelor's degree or higher: 8.6% (2010); Master's degree or higher: 1.7% (2010).

School District(s)

East Chambers ISD (PK-12)
    2009-10 Enrollment: 1,297 .... (409) 296-6100
Housing: Homeownership rate: 66.7% (2010); Median home value: $69,423 (2010); Median contract rent: $247 per month (2005-2009 5-year est.); Median year structure built: 1979 (2005-2009 5-year est.).
Newspapers: The Hometown Press (Community news; Circulation 2,000)
Transportation: Commute to work: 87.3% car, 0.0% public transportation, 0.0% walk, 2.3% work from home (2005-2009 5-year est.); Travel time to work: 42.3% less than 15 minutes, 9.3% 15 to 30 minutes, 37.2% 30 to 45 minutes, 3.8% 45 to 60 minutes, 7.4% 60 minutes or more (2005-2009 5-year est.)
Airports: Chambers County-Winnie Stowell Airport (general aviation)
Additional Information Contacts
Winnie Area Chamber of Commerce.................. (409) 296-2231
http://www.winnietexas.org

Cherokee County

Located in east Texas; bounded on the west by the Neches River, and partly bounded on the east by the Angelina River. Covers a land area of 1,052.22 square miles, a water area of 9.72 square miles, and is located in the Central Time Zone at 31.89° N. Lat., 95.19° W. Long. The county was founded in 1846. County seat is Rusk.

Cherokee County is part of the Jacksonville, TX Micropolitan Statistical Area. The entire metro area includes: Cherokee County, TX

Weather Station: Rusk   Elevation: 720 feet

	Jan	Feb	Mar	Apr	May	Jun	Jul	Aug	Sep	Oct	Nov	Dec
High	56	60	68	75	82	88	92	93	87	77	67	58
Low	37	40	47	54	63	69	72	71	66	56	47	38
Precip	4.3	4.0	4.4	3.5	4.5	4.6	3.1	2.9	3.5	5.3	4.6	4.5
Snow	0.1	tr	0.1	0.0	0.0	0.0	0.0	0.0	0.0	0.0	tr	tr

High and Low temperatures in degrees Fahrenheit; Precipitation and Snow in inches

Population: 41,049 (1990); 46,659 (2000); 49,397 (2010); 50,636 (2015 projected); Race: 71.3% White, 14.6% Black, 0.4% Asian, 13.6% Other, 19.8% Hispanic of any race (2010); Density: 46.9 persons per square mile (2010); Average household size: 2.65 (2010); Median age: 35.7 (2010); Males per 100 females: 103.0 (2010).
Religion: Five largest groups: 22.5% Southern Baptist Convention, 12.2% Baptist Missionary Association of America, 7.1% The American Baptist Association, 6.4% The United Methodist Church, 3.8% Catholic Church (2000).
Economy: Unemployment rate: 9.5% (June 2011); Total civilian labor force: 20,939 (June 2011); Leading industries: 25.4% manufacturing; 21.8% health care and social assistance; 14.0% retail trade (2009); Farms: 1,625 totaling 294,383 acres (2007); Companies that employ 500 or more persons: 1 (2009); Companies that employ 100 to 499 persons: 12 (2009); Companies that employ less than 100 persons: 775 (2009); Black-owned businesses: n/a (2007); Hispanic-owned businesses: n/a (2007); Asian-owned businesses: n/a (2007); Women-owned businesses: 782 (2007); Retail sales per capita: $6,392 (2010). Single-family building permits issued: 16 (2010); Multi-family building permits issued: 14 (2010).
Income: Per capita income: $17,504 (2010); Median household income: $36,384 (2010); Average household income: $48,049 (2010); Percent of households with income of $100,000 or more: 8.1% (2010); Poverty rate: 22.5% (2009); Bankruptcy rate: 2.01% (2010).
Taxes: Total county taxes per capita: $244 (2007); County property taxes per capita: $198 (2007).
Education: Percent of population age 25 and over with: High school diploma (including GED) or higher: 72.8% (2010); Bachelor's degree or higher: 10.9% (2010); Master's degree or higher: 4.0% (2010).
Housing: Homeownership rate: 73.4% (2010); Median home value: $66,522 (2010); Median contract rent: $366 per month (2005-2009 5-year est.); Median year structure built: 1977 (2005-2009 5-year est.)
Health: Birth rate: 154.1 per 10,000 population (2009); Death rate: 105.4 per 10,000 population (2009); Age-adjusted cancer mortality rate: 191.7 deaths per 100,000 population (2007); Number of physicians: 12.4 per 10,000 population (2008); Hospital beds: 85.8 per 10,000 population (2007); Hospital admissions: 1,022.3 per 10,000 population (2007).
Elections: 2008 Presidential election results: 28.1% Obama, 71.2% McCain, 0.1% Nader
National and State Parks: Fairchild State Forest; Jim Hogg State Park
Additional Information Contacts
Cherokee County Government . . . . (903) 683-2324
    http://www.co.cherokee.tx.us/ips/cms
City of Jacksonville . . . . (903) 586-3510
    http://jacksonville-texas.com
City of Rusk . . . . (903) 683-2213
    http://www.rusktx.com
Jacksonville Chamber of Commerce . . . . (903) 586-2217
    http://www.jacksonvilletexas.com
Rusk Chamber of Commerce . . . . (903) 683-4242
    http://www.ruskchamber.com

Cherokee County Communities

ALTO (town). Covers a land area of 1.683 square miles and a water area of 0 square miles. Located at 31.65° N. Lat; 95.07° W. Long. Elevation is 436 feet.
History: Alto developed around a tomato cannery and a cotton gin.
Population: 1,073 (1990); 1,190 (2000); 1,184 (2010); 1,178 (2015 projected); Race: 66.6% White, 19.2% Black, 0.3% Asian, 13.9% Other, 16.4% Hispanic of any race (2010); Density: 703.5 persons per square mile (2010); Average household size: 2.54 (2010); Median age: 36.5 (2010); Males per 100 females: 93.8 (2010); Marriage status: 17.1% never married, 59.0% now married, 12.0% widowed, 11.9% divorced (2005-2009 est.); Foreign born: 8.3% (2005-2009 5-year est.); Ancestry (includes multiple ancestries): 17.1% English, 14.6% Irish, 7.5% German, 1.8% Scotch-Irish, 1.6% American (2005-2009 5-year est.).
Economy: Single-family building permits issued: 0 (2010); Multi-family building permits issued: 0 (2010); Employment by occupation: 4.1%

management, 13.7% professional, 36.1% services, 10.1% sales, 2.7% farming, 17.0% construction, 16.2% production (2005-2009 5-year est.).
Income: Per capita income: $18,688 (2010); Median household income: $36,130 (2010); Average household income: $48,213 (2010); Percent of households with income of $100,000 or more: 8.2% (2010); Poverty rate: 21.9% (2005-2009 5-year est.).
Taxes: Total city taxes per capita: $170 (2007); City property taxes per capita: $63 (2007).
Education: Percent of population age 25 and over with: High school diploma (including GED) or higher: 72.9% (2010); Bachelor's degree or higher: 8.0% (2010); Master's degree or higher: 3.3% (2010).
School District(s)
Alto ISD (PK-12)
    2009-10 Enrollment: 698 . . . . (936) 858-7101
Housing: Homeownership rate: 71.0% (2010); Median home value: $55,000 (2010); Median contract rent: $284 per month (2005-2009 5-year est.); Median year structure built: 1964 (2005-2009 5-year est.).
Safety: Violent crime rate: 42.6 per 10,000 population; Property crime rate: 391.5 per 10,000 population (2009).
Transportation: Commute to work: 97.4% car, 0.0% public transportation, 1.8% walk, 0.0% work from home (2005-2009 5-year est.); Travel time to work: 40.3% less than 15 minutes, 22.8% 15 to 30 minutes, 18.6% 30 to 45 minutes, 11.4% 45 to 60 minutes, 7.0% 60 minutes or more (2005-2009 5-year est.)

CUNEY (town). Covers a land area of 1.636 square miles and a water area of 0 square miles. Located at 32.03° N. Lat; 95.41° W. Long. Elevation is 374 feet.
Population: 170 (1990); 145 (2000); 171 (2010); 181 (2015 projected); Race: 72.5% White, 24.0% Black, 0.0% Asian, 3.5% Other, 4.1% Hispanic of any race (2010); Density: 104.5 persons per square mile (2010); Average household size: 2.55 (2010); Median age: 38.3 (2010); Males per 100 females: 90.0 (2010); Marriage status: 25.7% never married, 34.5% now married, 15.9% widowed, 23.9% divorced (2005-2009 5-year est.); Foreign born: 0.0% (2005-2009 5-year est.); Ancestry (includes multiple ancestries): 8.6% Irish, 5.5% English (2005-2009 5-year est.).
Economy: Single-family building permits issued: 0 (2010); Multi-family building permits issued: 0 (2010); Employment by occupation: 0.0% management, 7.0% professional, 53.5% services, 9.3% sales, 0.0% farming, 18.6% construction, 11.6% production (2005-2009 5-year est.).
Income: Per capita income: $17,266 (2010); Median household income: $36,250 (2010); Average household income: $41,530 (2010); Percent of households with income of $100,000 or more: 4.5% (2010); Poverty rate: 28.1% (2005-2009 5-year est.).
Taxes: Total city taxes per capita: $570 (2007); City property taxes per capita: $0 (2007).
Education: Percent of population age 25 and over with: High school diploma (including GED) or higher: 71.1% (2010); Bachelor's degree or higher: 5.3% (2010); Master's degree or higher: 3.5% (2010).
Housing: Homeownership rate: 83.6% (2010); Median home value: $80,000 (2010); Median contract rent: n/a per month (2005-2009 5-year est.); Median year structure built: 1969 (2005-2009 5-year est.).
Transportation: Commute to work: 95.3% car, 0.0% public transportation, 0.0% walk, 4.7% work from home (2005-2009 5-year est.); Travel time to work: 9.8% less than 15 minutes, 68.3% 15 to 30 minutes, 7.3% 30 to 45 minutes, 9.8% 45 to 60 minutes, 4.9% 60 minutes or more (2005-2009 5-year est.)

GALLATIN (city). Covers a land area of 4.595 square miles and a water area of 0 square miles. Located at 31.90° N. Lat; 95.15° W. Long. Elevation is 404 feet.
Population: 368 (1990); 378 (2000); 392 (2010); 398 (2015 projected); Race: 82.9% White, 10.7% Black, 0.5% Asian, 5.9% Other, 9.7% Hispanic of any race (2010); Density: 85.3 persons per square mile (2010); Average household size: 2.73 (2010); Median age: 35.8 (2010); Males per 100 females: 101.0 (2010); Marriage status: 28.2% never married, 58.3% now married, 3.4% widowed, 10.2% divorced (2005-2009 5-year est.); Foreign born: 9.3% (2005-2009 5-year est.); Ancestry (includes multiple ancestries): 30.6% Irish, 26.4% English, 3.7% Italian, 3.7% French, 3.2% Dutch (2005-2009 5-year est.).
Economy: Employment by occupation: 11.3% management, 2.8% professional, 18.9% services, 13.2% sales, 0.0% farming, 20.8% construction, 33.0% production (2005-2009 5-year est.).
Income: Per capita income: $14,713 (2010); Median household income: $34,808 (2010); Average household income: $41,541 (2010); Percent of

households with income of $100,000 or more: 4.5% (2010); Poverty rate: 18.1% (2005-2009 5-year est.).
Taxes: Total city taxes per capita: $280 (2007); City property taxes per capita: $116 (2007).
Education: Percent of population age 25 and over with: High school diploma (including GED) or higher: 75.4% (2010); Bachelor's degree or higher: 10.7% (2010); Master's degree or higher: 3.6% (2010).
Housing: Homeownership rate: 78.9% (2010); Median home value: $83,125 (2010); Median contract rent: $311 per month (2005-2009 5-year est.); Median year structure built: 1972 (2005-2009 5-year est.).
Transportation: Commute to work: 100.0% car, 0.0% public transportation, 0.0% walk, 0.0% work from home (2005-2009 5-year est.); Travel time to work: 26.4% less than 15 minutes, 67.9% 15 to 30 minutes, 2.8% 30 to 45 minutes, 0.0% 45 to 60 minutes, 2.8% 60 minutes or more (2005-2009 5-year est.)

JACKSONVILLE (city). Covers a land area of 14.137 square miles and a water area of 0.013 square miles. Located at 31.96° N. Lat; 95.26° W. Long. Elevation is 522 feet.
History: Jacksonville developed as the trading and shipping center for tomato farms.
Population: 13,143 (1990); 13,868 (2000); 14,640 (2010); 15,010 (2015 projected); Race: 60.3% White, 18.1% Black, 0.7% Asian, 21.0% Other, 33.4% Hispanic of any race (2010); Density: 1,035.6 persons per square mile (2010); Average household size: 2.72 (2010); Median age: 32.5 (2010); Males per 100 females: 93.6 (2010); Marriage status: 34.0% never married, 47.1% now married, 9.3% widowed, 9.7% divorced (2005-2009 5-year est.); Foreign born: 18.0% (2005-2009 5-year est.); Ancestry (includes multiple ancestries): 10.3% English, 8.6% American, 7.1% German, 6.8% Irish, 1.1% African (2005-2009 5-year est.).
Economy: Single-family building permits issued: 9 (2010); Multi-family building permits issued: 14 (2010); Employment by occupation: 7.2% management, 10.3% professional, 20.6% services, 16.6% sales, 2.1% farming, 11.7% construction, 31.4% production (2005-2009 5-year est.).
Income: Per capita income: $16,349 (2010); Median household income: $31,356 (2010); Average household income: $45,585 (2010); Percent of households with income of $100,000 or more: 8.0% (2010); Poverty rate: 26.0% (2005-2009 5-year est.).
Taxes: Total city taxes per capita: $409 (2007); City property taxes per capita: $208 (2007).
Education: Percent of population age 25 and over with: High school diploma (including GED) or higher: 67.9% (2010); Bachelor's degree or higher: 14.8% (2010); Master's degree or higher: 5.6% (2010).

School District(s)
Jacksonville ISD (PK-12)
    2009-10 Enrollment: 4,902 . . . . (903) 586-6511
Four-year College(s)
Baptist Missionary Association Theological Seminary (Private, Not-for-profit, Baptist)
    Fall 2009 Enrollment: 128 . . . . (903) 586-2501
    2010-11 Tuition: In-state $3,800; Out-of-state $3,800
Two-year College(s)
Jacksonville College-Main Campus (Private, Not-for-profit, Baptist)
    Fall 2009 Enrollment: 327 . . . . (903) 586-2518
    2010-11 Tuition: In-state $7,036; Out-of-state $7,036
Lon Morris College (Private, Not-for-profit, United Methodist)
    Fall 2009 Enrollment: 817 . . . . (903) 589-4000
    2010-11 Tuition: In-state $13,572; Out-of-state $13,572
Housing: Homeownership rate: 57.8% (2010); Median home value: $62,070 (2010); Median contract rent: $407 per month (2005-2009 5-year est.); Median year structure built: 1973 (2005-2009 5-year est.).
Hospitals: East Texas Medical Center - Jacksonville (94 beds); Mother Frances Hospital Jacksonville
Safety: Violent crime rate: 83.2 per 10,000 population; Property crime rate: 594.8 per 10,000 population (2009).
Newspapers: Jacksonville Daily Progress (Local news; Circulation 4,699)
Transportation: Commute to work: 95.3% car, 0.0% public transportation, 1.8% walk, 1.5% work from home (2005-2009 5-year est.); Travel time to work: 62.7% less than 15 minutes, 21.0% 15 to 30 minutes, 7.9% 30 to 45 minutes, 3.8% 45 to 60 minutes, 4.6% 60 minutes or more (2005-2009 5-year est.)
Additional Information Contacts
City of Jacksonville . . . . (903) 586-3510
    http://jacksonville-texas.com

Jacksonville Chamber of Commerce . . . . (903) 586-2217
    http://www.jacksonvilletexas.com

NEW SUMMERFIELD (city). Aka Summerfield. Covers a land area of 4.688 square miles and a water area of 0 square miles. Located at 31.97° N. Lat; 95.11° W. Long. Elevation is 472 feet.
Population: 731 (1990); 998 (2000); 1,000 (2010); 999 (2015 projected); Race: 66.5% White, 3.3% Black, 0.0% Asian, 30.2% Other, 57.4% Hispanic of any race (2010); Density: 213.3 persons per square mile (2010); Average household size: 3.08 (2010); Median age: 31.3 (2010); Males per 100 females: 112.8 (2010); Marriage status: 31.4% never married, 52.4% now married, 3.5% widowed, 12.7% divorced (2005-2009 5-year est.); Foreign born: 39.6% (2005-2009 5-year est.); Ancestry (includes multiple ancestries): 7.2% Irish, 4.7% English, 4.1% Lebanese, 3.4% Scottish, 2.4% German (2005-2009 5-year est.).
Economy: Single-family building permits issued: 0 (2010); Multi-family building permits issued: 0 (2010); Employment by occupation: 3.6% management, 6.7% professional, 8.8% services, 19.5% sales, 24.7% farming, 14.0% construction, 22.8% production (2005-2009 5-year est.).
Income: Per capita income: $15,029 (2010); Median household income: $36,940 (2010); Average household income: $45,885 (2010); Percent of households with income of $100,000 or more: 6.2% (2010); Poverty rate: 33.5% (2005-2009 5-year est.).
Taxes: Total city taxes per capita: $20 (2007); City property taxes per capita: $0 (2007).
Education: Percent of population age 25 and over with: High school diploma (including GED) or higher: 64.5% (2010); Bachelor's degree or higher: 8.4% (2010); Master's degree or higher: 4.7% (2010).
School District(s)
New Summerfield ISD (PK-12)
    2009-10 Enrollment: 479 . . . . (903) 726-3306
Housing: Homeownership rate: 72.0% (2010); Median home value: $45,366 (2010); Median contract rent: $313 per month (2005-2009 5-year est.); Median year structure built: 1984 (2005-2009 5-year est.).
Transportation: Commute to work: 90.4% car, 0.0% public transportation, 4.2% walk, 5.4% work from home (2005-2009 5-year est.); Travel time to work: 48.2% less than 15 minutes, 24.1% 15 to 30 minutes, 11.3% 30 to 45 minutes, 4.2% 45 to 60 minutes, 12.2% 60 minutes or more (2005-2009 5-year est.)

REKLAW (city). Covers a land area of 2.938 square miles and a water area of 0.005 square miles. Located at 31.86° N. Lat; 94.98° W. Long.
Population: 266 (1990); 327 (2000); 344 (2010); 351 (2015 projected); Race: 67.7% White, 11.6% Black, 0.0% Asian, 20.6% Other, 22.1% Hispanic of any race (2010); Density: 117.1 persons per square mile (2010); Average household size: 2.59 (2010); Median age: 34.8 (2010); Males per 100 females: 107.2 (2010); Marriage status: 22.5% never married, 53.7% now married, 13.0% widowed, 10.7% divorced (2005-2009 5-year est.); Foreign born: 10.6% (2005-2009 5-year est.); Ancestry (includes multiple ancestries): 23.9% Irish, 11.6% English, 10.9% French, 8.7% American, 5.2% Polish (2005-2009 5-year est.).
Economy: Employment by occupation: 4.5% management, 12.1% professional, 7.6% services, 15.2% sales, 7.6% farming, 16.7% construction, 36.4% production (2005-2009 5-year est.).
Income: Per capita income: $20,392 (2010); Median household income: $42,500 (2010); Average household income: $51,617 (2010); Percent of households with income of $100,000 or more: 10.5% (2010); Poverty rate: 32.2% (2005-2009 5-year est.).
Taxes: Total city taxes per capita: $12 (2007); City property taxes per capita: $0 (2007).
Education: Percent of population age 25 and over with: High school diploma (including GED) or higher: 73.4% (2010); Bachelor's degree or higher: 8.6% (2010); Master's degree or higher: 2.7% (2010).
Housing: Homeownership rate: 81.2% (2010); Median home value: $51,818 (2010); Median contract rent: $270 per month (2005-2009 5-year est.); Median year structure built: 1973 (2005-2009 5-year est.).
Transportation: Commute to work: 95.5% car, 0.0% public transportation, 4.5% walk, 0.0% work from home (2005-2009 5-year est.); Travel time to work: 4.5% less than 15 minutes, 68.2% 15 to 30 minutes, 6.1% 30 to 45 minutes, 16.7% 45 to 60 minutes, 4.5% 60 minutes or more (2005-2009 5-year est.)

RUSK (city). County seat. Covers a land area of 6.822 square miles and a water area of 0.023 square miles. Located at 31.79° N. Lat; 95.15° W. Long. Elevation is 518 feet.

History: Rusk was named for General Thomas J. Rusk, a lawyer who lived here from 1829 to 1856. During the Civil War, Rusk was a supply center for salt, iron ore, and lumber.
Population: 4,402 (1990); 5,085 (2000); 5,253 (2010); 5,301 (2015 projected); Race: 53.9% White, 35.6% Black, 1.0% Asian, 9.5% Other, 11.1% Hispanic of any race (2010); Density: 770.0 persons per square mile (2010); Average household size: 2.43 (2010); Median age: 37.2 (2010); Males per 100 females: 171.5 (2010); Marriage status: 37.8% never married, 38.5% now married, 9.7% widowed, 14.0% divorced (2005-2009 5-year est.); Foreign born: 5.4% (2005-2009 5-year est.); Ancestry (includes multiple ancestries): 18.5% Irish, 15.8% English, 7.8% American, 7.3% German, 3.1% Italian (2005-2009 5-year est.).
Economy: Single-family building permits issued: 7 (2010); Multi-family building permits issued: 0 (2010); Employment by occupation: 7.7% management, 25.8% professional, 31.9% services, 22.1% sales, 0.1% farming, 3.9% construction, 8.6% production (2005-2009 5-year est.).
Income: Per capita income: $14,913 (2010); Median household income: $36,829 (2010); Average household income: $47,333 (2010); Percent of households with income of $100,000 or more: 8.1% (2010); Poverty rate: 12.0% (2005-2009 5-year est.).
Taxes: Total city taxes per capita: $230 (2007); City property taxes per capita: $86 (2007).
Education: Percent of population age 25 and over with: High school diploma (including GED) or higher: 71.9% (2010); Bachelor's degree or higher: 7.1% (2010); Master's degree or higher: 2.3% (2010).

School District(s)

Rusk ISD (PK-12)
    2009-10 Enrollment: 2,141 . . . . (903) 683-5592
Housing: Homeownership rate: 64.9% (2010); Median home value: $66,959 (2010); Median contract rent: $363 per month (2005-2009 5-year est.); Median year structure built: 1971 (2005-2009 5-year est.).
Hospitals: Rusk State Hospital (166 beds)
Safety: Violent crime rate: 18.8 per 10,000 population; Property crime rate: 243.9 per 10,000 population (2009).
Newspapers: Cherokeean/Herald (Community news; Circulation 4,200)
Transportation: Commute to work: 97.8% car, 0.0% public transportation, 1.1% walk, 0.0% work from home (2005-2009 5-year est.); Travel time to work: 72.6% less than 15 minutes, 17.9% 15 to 30 minutes, 4.5% 30 to 45 minutes, 0.2% 45 to 60 minutes, 4.8% 60 minutes or more (2005-2009 5-year est.)
Additional Information Contacts
City of Rusk . . . . (903) 683-2213
    http://www.rusktx.com
Rusk Chamber of Commerce . . . . (903) 683-4242
    http://www.ruskchamber.com

WELLS (town). Covers a land area of 1.914 square miles and a water area of 0 square miles. Located at 31.49° N. Lat; 94.94° W. Long. Elevation is 325 feet.
Population: 761 (1990); 769 (2000); 772 (2010); 772 (2015 projected); Race: 80.3% White, 9.5% Black, 0.0% Asian, 10.2% Other, 10.1% Hispanic of any race (2010); Density: 403.4 persons per square mile (2010); Average household size: 2.59 (2010); Median age: 38.0 (2010); Males per 100 females: 96.4 (2010); Marriage status: 31.4% never married, 37.9% now married, 16.9% widowed, 13.7% divorced (2005-2009 5-year est.); Foreign born: 3.1% (2005-2009 5-year est.); Ancestry (includes multiple ancestries): 19.2% English, 12.3% Irish, 3.4% German, 1.7% Italian, 0.8% Scotch-Irish (2005-2009 5-year est.).
Economy: Employment by occupation: 1.9% management, 11.9% professional, 52.1% services, 14.6% sales, 6.1% farming, 9.2% construction, 4.2% production (2005-2009 5-year est.).
Income: Per capita income: $17,570 (2010); Median household income: $36,528 (2010); Average household income: $45,767 (2010); Percent of households with income of $100,000 or more: 7.3% (2010); Poverty rate: 36.6% (2005-2009 5-year est.).
Taxes: Total city taxes per capita: $141 (2007); City property taxes per capita: $74 (2007).
Education: Percent of population age 25 and over with: High school diploma (including GED) or higher: 70.6% (2010); Bachelor's degree or higher: 8.6% (2010); Master's degree or higher: 2.7% (2010).

School District(s)

Wells ISD (PK-12)
    2009-10 Enrollment: 316 . . . . (936) 867-4466

Housing: Homeownership rate: 76.3% (2010); Median home value: $56,061 (2010); Median contract rent: $241 per month (2005-2009 5-year est.); Median year structure built: 1964 (2005-2009 5-year est.).
Safety: Violent crime rate: 100.1 per 10,000 population; Property crime rate: 262.8 per 10,000 population (2009).
Transportation: Commute to work: 92.6% car, 0.0% public transportation, 4.7% walk, 2.7% work from home (2005-2009 5-year est.); Travel time to work: 40.0% less than 15 minutes, 31.6% 15 to 30 minutes, 20.0% 30 to 45 minutes, 6.0% 45 to 60 minutes, 2.4% 60 minutes or more (2005-2009 5-year est.)

Childress County

Located in north Texas, in a prairie area; drained by Prairie Dog Town Fork of the Red River. Covers a land area of 710.34 square miles, a water area of 3.27 square miles, and is located in the Central Time Zone at 34.47° N. Lat., 100.20° W. Long. The county was founded in 1887. County seat is Childress.

Weather Station: Childress Municipal Arpt   Elevation: 1,951 feet

	Jan	Feb	Mar	Apr	May	Jun	Jul	Aug	Sep	Oct	Nov	Dec
High	54	58	66	76	83	90	95	94	86	76	64	54
Low	28	31	39	48	58	66	71	69	61	49	38	29
Precip	0.7	0.9	1.6	1.8	3.2	4.1	1.9	2.5	2.4	2.1	1.3	0.9
Snow	na	na	na	na	na	na	na	na	na	na	na	na

High and Low temperatures in degrees Fahrenheit; Precipitation and Snow in inches

Population: 5,953 (1990); 7,688 (2000); 7,661 (2010); 7,636 (2015 projected); Race: 62.2% White, 15.9% Black, 0.7% Asian, 21.2% Other, 24.1% Hispanic of any race (2010); Density: 10.8 persons per square mile (2010); Average household size: 2.40 (2010); Median age: 35.8 (2010); Males per 100 females: 154.3 (2010).
Religion: Five largest groups: 40.4% Southern Baptist Convention, 9.8% The United Methodist Church, 6.1% Churches of Christ, 4.4% Catholic Church, 1.9% Christian Church (Disciples of Christ) (2000).
Economy: Unemployment rate: 7.7% (June 2011); Total civilian labor force: 3,283 (June 2011); Leading industries: 27.1% retail trade; 27.1% health care and social assistance; 22.1% accommodation & food services (2009); Farms: 374 totaling 399,383 acres (2007); Companies that employ 500 or more persons: 0 (2009); Companies that employ 100 to 499 persons: 2 (2009); Companies that employ less than 100 persons: 164 (2009); Black-owned businesses: n/a (2007); Hispanic-owned businesses: n/a (2007); Asian-owned businesses: n/a (2007); Women-owned businesses: n/a (2007); Retail sales per capita: $9,785 (2010). Single-family building permits issued: 3 (2010); Multi-family building permits issued: 0 (2010).
Income: Per capita income: $14,234 (2010); Median household income: $34,309 (2010); Average household income: $44,103 (2010); Percent of households with income of $100,000 or more: 5.4% (2010); Poverty rate: 25.4% (2009); Bankruptcy rate: 1.12% (2010).
Taxes: Total county taxes per capita: $178 (2007); County property taxes per capita: $90 (2007).
Education: Percent of population age 25 and over with: High school diploma (including GED) or higher: 70.3% (2010); Bachelor's degree or higher: 9.6% (2010); Master's degree or higher: 2.9% (2010).
Housing: Homeownership rate: 68.5% (2010); Median home value: $62,490 (2010); Median contract rent: $412 per month (2005-2009 5-year est.); Median year structure built: 1959 (2005-2009 5-year est.)
Health: Birth rate: 111.3 per 10,000 population (2009); Death rate: 96.7 per 10,000 population (2009); Age-adjusted cancer mortality rate: 321.0 deaths per 100,000 population (2007); Number of physicians: 11.9 per 10,000 population (2008); Hospital beds: 51.7 per 10,000 population (2007); Hospital admissions: 1,881.4 per 10,000 population (2007).
Elections: 2008 Presidential election results: 21.6% Obama, 77.6% McCain, 0.0% Nader
Additional Information Contacts
Childress County Government . . . . (940) 937-6143
    http://www.co.childress.tx.us/ips/cms
Childress Chamber of Commerce . . . . (940) 937-2567
    http://biz.childresstexas.net/chamberofcommerce
City of Childress . . . . (940) 937-3684
    http://www.childresstexas.net

Childress County Communities

CHILDRESS (city). County seat. Covers a land area of 8.247 square miles and a water area of 0.044 square miles. Located at 34.42° N. Lat; 100.21° W. Long. Elevation is 1,870 feet.
History: Childress was established on land that was once part of the great OX Ranch. The town developed as a railroad division point and shipping center for a cattle and agricultural area.
Population: 5,057 (1990); 6,778 (2000); 6,510 (2010); 6,426 (2015 projected); Race: 66.3% White, 13.1% Black, 0.7% Asian, 20.0% Other, 23.3% Hispanic of any race (2010); Density: 789.3 persons per square mile (2010); Average household size: 2.40 (2010); Median age: 36.2 (2010); Males per 100 females: 135.1 (2010); Marriage status: 33.1% never married, 46.5% now married, 8.2% widowed, 12.3% divorced (2005-2009 5-year est.); Foreign born: 6.4% (2005-2009 5-year est.); Ancestry (includes multiple ancestries): 10.1% German, 8.7% Irish, 8.0% American, 5.9% English, 1.8% Scotch-Irish (2005-2009 5-year est.).
Economy: Single-family building permits issued: 3 (2010); Multi-family building permits issued: 0 (2010); Employment by occupation: 7.3% management, 14.5% professional, 34.2% services, 22.6% sales, 1.2% farming, 12.1% construction, 8.1% production (2005-2009 5-year est.).
Income: Per capita income: $15,261 (2010); Median household income: $34,060 (2010); Average household income: $44,124 (2010); Percent of households with income of $100,000 or more: 5.5% (2010); Poverty rate: 31.6% (2005-2009 5-year est.).
Taxes: Total city taxes per capita: $179 (2007); City property taxes per capita: $92 (2007).
Education: Percent of population age 25 and over with: High school diploma (including GED) or higher: 71.0% (2010); Bachelor's degree or higher: 10.2% (2010); Master's degree or higher: 2.9% (2010).
School District(s)
Childress ISD (PK-12)
    2009-10 Enrollment: 1,127 . . . . (940) 937-2501
Housing: Homeownership rate: 67.8% (2010); Median home value: $62,094 (2010); Median contract rent: $423 per month (2005-2009 5-year est.); Median year structure built: 1961 (2005-2009 5-year est.).
Hospitals: Childress Regional Medical Center (60 beds)
Safety: Violent crime rate: 33.9 per 10,000 population; Property crime rate: 148.1 per 10,000 population (2009).
Newspapers: Childress Index (Community news; Circulation 3,000)
Transportation: Commute to work: 90.8% car, 0.0% public transportation, 4.6% walk, 1.5% work from home (2005-2009 5-year est.); Travel time to work: 83.5% less than 15 minutes, 11.5% 15 to 30 minutes, 4.4% 30 to 45 minutes, 0.6% 45 to 60 minutes, 0.0% 60 minutes or more (2005-2009 5-year est.)
Additional Information Contacts
Childress Chamber of Commerce . . . . (940) 937-2567
    http://biz.childresstexas.net/chamberofcommerce
City of Childress . . . . (940) 937-3684
    http://www.childresstexas.net

TELL (unincorporated postal area, zip code 79259). Covers a land area of 34.689 square miles and a water area of 0.059 square miles. Located at 34.39° N. Lat; 100.40° W. Long. Elevation is 1,903 feet.
Population: 60 (2000); Race: 100.0% White, 0.0% Black, 0.0% Asian, 0.0% Other, 0.0% Hispanic of any race (2000); Density: 1.7 persons per square mile (2000); Age: 0.0% under 18, 64.3% over 64 (2000); Marriage status: 35.7% never married, 46.4% now married, 17.9% widowed, 0.0% divorced (2000); Foreign born: 0.0% (2000); Ancestry (includes multiple ancestries): 35.7% Irish, 35.7% English, 17.9% German (2000).
Economy: Employment by occupation: 100.0% management, 0.0% professional, 0.0% services, 0.0% sales, 0.0% farming, 0.0% construction, 0.0% production (2000).
Income: Per capita income: $15,982 (2000); Median household income: $16,250 (2000); Poverty rate: 179.1% (2000).
Education: Percent of population age 25 and over with: High school diploma (including GED) or higher: 53.6% (2000); Bachelor's degree or higher: 0.0% (2000).
Housing: Homeownership rate: 100.0% (2000); Median home value: $25,400 (2000); Median contract rent: n/a per month (2000); Median year structure built: before 1940 (2000).
Transportation: Commute to work: 100.0% car, 0.0% public transportation, 0.0% walk, 0.0% work from home (2000); Travel time to work: 0.0% less than 15 minutes, 50.0% 15 to 30 minutes, 50.0% 30 to 45 minutes, 0.0% 45 to 60 minutes, 0.0% 60 minutes or more (2000)

Clay County

Located in north Texas; bounded on the north by the Red River and the Oklahoma border; drained by the Wichita and Little Wichita Rivers. Covers a land area of 1,097.82 square miles, a water area of 18.36 square miles, and is located in the Central Time Zone at 33.77° N. Lat., 98.19° W. Long. The county was founded in 1857. County seat is Henrietta.

Clay County is part of the Wichita Falls, TX Metropolitan Statistical Area. The entire metro area includes: Archer County, TX; Clay County, TX; Wichita County, TX

Weather Station: Henrietta   Elevation: 930 feet

	Jan	Feb	Mar	Apr	May	Jun	Jul	Aug	Sep	Oct	Nov	Dec
High	54	58	66	75	83	90	97	97	89	77	65	55
Low	28	32	40	48	58	66	71	70	62	51	39	30
Precip	1.6	2.2	2.6	2.7	4.3	4.0	1.7	2.5	2.8	3.5	2.0	2.3
Snow	0.2	0.1	tr	0.0	0.0	0.0	0.0	0.0	0.0	tr	0.1	0.2

High and Low temperatures in degrees Fahrenheit; Precipitation and Snow in inches

Population: 10,024 (1990); 11,006 (2000); 10,956 (2010); 10,911 (2015 projected); Race: 93.3% White, 1.1% Black, 0.1% Asian, 5.4% Other, 5.1% Hispanic of any race (2010); Density: 10.0 persons per square mile (2010); Average household size: 2.48 (2010); Median age: 41.7 (2010); Males per 100 females: 95.3 (2010).
Religion: Five largest groups: 51.4% Southern Baptist Convention, 7.4% The United Methodist Church, 4.8% Churches of Christ, 2.3% Church of God (Cleveland, Tennessee), 2.1% Catholic Church (2000).
Economy: Unemployment rate: 6.5% (June 2011); Total civilian labor force: 5,974 (June 2011); Leading industries: 24.6% retail trade; 18.5% health care and social assistance; 8.8% other services (except public administration) (2009); Farms: 931 totaling 661,617 acres (2007); Companies that employ 500 or more persons: 0 (2009); Companies that employ 100 to 499 persons: 0 (2009); Companies that employ less than 100 persons: 133 (2009); Black-owned businesses: n/a (2007); Hispanic-owned businesses: n/a (2007); Asian-owned businesses: n/a (2007); Women-owned businesses: n/a (2007); Retail sales per capita: $9,517 (2010). Single-family building permits issued: 0 (2010); Multi-family building permits issued: 0 (2010).
Income: Per capita income: $22,918 (2010); Median household income: $47,964 (2010); Average household income: $57,248 (2010); Percent of households with income of $100,000 or more: 11.8% (2010); Poverty rate: 9.8% (2009); Bankruptcy rate: 3.48% (2010).
Taxes: Total county taxes per capita: $385 (2007); County property taxes per capita: $334 (2007).
Education: Percent of population age 25 and over with: High school diploma (including GED) or higher: 84.3% (2010); Bachelor's degree or higher: 15.2% (2010); Master's degree or higher: 2.7% (2010).
Housing: Homeownership rate: 81.6% (2010); Median home value: $74,220 (2010); Median contract rent: $432 per month (2005-2009 5-year est.); Median year structure built: 1974 (2005-2009 5-year est.)
Health: Birth rate: 94.6 per 10,000 population (2009); Death rate: 97.3 per 10,000 population (2009); Age-adjusted cancer mortality rate: 182.4 deaths per 100,000 population (2007); Number of physicians: 5.5 per 10,000 population (2008); Hospital beds: 22.5 per 10,000 population (2007); Hospital admissions: 402.1 per 10,000 population (2007).
Elections: 2008 Presidential election results: 20.3% Obama, 78.9% McCain, 0.1% Nader
Additional Information Contacts
Clay County Government. . . . . (940) 538-4631
    http://www.co.clay.tx.us/ips/cms
Henrietta & Clay County Chamber of Commerce . . . . (940) 538-5261
    http://www.hccchamber.org

Clay County Communities

BELLEVUE (city). Covers a land area of 0.846 square miles and a water area of 0 square miles. Located at 33.63° N. Lat; 98.01° W. Long. Elevation is 1,037 feet.
Population: 333 (1990); 386 (2000); 373 (2010); 366 (2015 projected); Race: 95.2% White, 0.0% Black, 0.3% Asian, 4.6% Other, 3.5% Hispanic of any race (2010); Density: 440.7 persons per square mile (2010); Average household size: 2.50 (2010); Median age: 42.0 (2010); Males per 100 females: 103.8 (2010); Marriage status: 13.8% never married, 63.9% now married, 3.1% widowed, 19.2% divorced (2005-2009 5-year est.); Foreign born: 0.7% (2005-2009 5-year est.); Ancestry (includes multiple

ancestries): 13.7% Irish, 9.4% German, 3.9% American, 3.7% French, 2.8% English (2005-2009 5-year est.).
Economy: Employment by occupation: 6.8% management, 22.3% professional, 9.2% services, 35.4% sales, 0.0% farming, 12.6% construction, 13.6% production (2005-2009 5-year est.).
Income: Per capita income: $28,148 (2010); Median household income: $49,022 (2010); Average household income: $69,883 (2010); Percent of households with income of $100,000 or more: 16.1% (2010); Poverty rate: 1.3% (2005-2009 5-year est.).
Taxes: Total city taxes per capita: $91 (2007); City property taxes per capita: $55 (2007).
Education: Percent of population age 25 and over with: High school diploma (including GED) or higher: 84.6% (2010); Bachelor's degree or higher: 17.6% (2010); Master's degree or higher: 4.1% (2010).
School District(s)
Bellevue ISD (KG-12)
  2009-10 Enrollment: 159 . . . . (940) 928-2104
Housing: Homeownership rate: 83.2% (2010); Median home value: $73,750 (2010); Median contract rent: n/a per month (2005-2009 5-year est.); Median year structure built: 1956 (2005-2009 5-year est.).
Transportation: Commute to work: 90.5% car, 0.0% public transportation, 7.4% walk, 0.0% work from home (2005-2009 5-year est.); Travel time to work: 36.0% less than 15 minutes, 20.6% 15 to 30 minutes, 25.9% 30 to 45 minutes, 13.2% 45 to 60 minutes, 4.2% 60 minutes or more (2005-2009 5-year est.)

BYERS (city). Covers a land area of 0.978 square miles and a water area of 0.022 square miles. Located at 34.07° N. Lat; 98.19° W. Long. Elevation is 1,010 feet.
Population: 513 (1990); 517 (2000); 515 (2010); 512 (2015 projected); Race: 91.1% White, 0.2% Black, 0.0% Asian, 8.7% Other, 8.2% Hispanic of any race (2010); Density: 526.6 persons per square mile (2010); Average household size: 2.55 (2010); Median age: 42.0 (2010); Males per 100 females: 98.1 (2010); Marriage status: 20.9% never married, 63.8% now married, 7.4% widowed, 7.9% divorced (2005-2009 5-year est.); Foreign born: 0.0% (2005-2009 5-year est.); Ancestry (includes multiple ancestries): 24.4% German, 11.0% English, 8.6% Irish, 2.6% Russian, 2.4% American (2005-2009 5-year est.).
Economy: Employment by occupation: 9.1% management, 21.3% professional, 20.5% services, 22.0% sales, 0.0% farming, 12.2% construction, 15.0% production (2005-2009 5-year est.).
Income: Per capita income: $22,900 (2010); Median household income: $50,000 (2010); Average household income: $59,530 (2010); Percent of households with income of $100,000 or more: 10.9% (2010); Poverty rate: 19.8% (2005-2009 5-year est.).
Taxes: Total city taxes per capita: $102 (2007); City property taxes per capita: $81 (2007).
Education: Percent of population age 25 and over with: High school diploma (including GED) or higher: 83.1% (2010); Bachelor's degree or higher: 18.3% (2010); Master's degree or higher: 3.8% (2010).
School District(s)
Byers ISD (PK-12)
  2009-10 Enrollment: 101 . . . . (940) 529-6102
Housing: Homeownership rate: 78.7% (2010); Median home value: $80,500 (2010); Median contract rent: $453 per month (2005-2009 5-year est.); Median year structure built: 1960 (2005-2009 5-year est.).
Transportation: Commute to work: 94.3% car, 0.0% public transportation, 0.0% walk, 5.7% work from home (2005-2009 5-year est.); Travel time to work: 32.9% less than 15 minutes, 28.6% 15 to 30 minutes, 31.2% 30 to 45 minutes, 4.3% 45 to 60 minutes, 3.0% 60 minutes or more (2005-2009 5-year est.)

DEAN (city). Aka Dean Dale. Covers a land area of 2.142 square miles and a water area of 0.002 square miles. Located at 33.92° N. Lat; 98.37° W. Long. Elevation is 961 feet.
Population: 277 (1990); 341 (2000); 347 (2010); 351 (2015 projected); Race: 93.4% White, 0.9% Black, 0.0% Asian, 5.8% Other, 6.1% Hispanic of any race (2010); Density: 162.0 persons per square mile (2010); Average household size: 2.59 (2010); Median age: 43.8 (2010); Males per 100 females: 102.9 (2010); Marriage status: 14.3% never married, 63.1% now married, 5.0% widowed, 17.6% divorced (2005-2009 5-year est.); Foreign born: 4.1% (2005-2009 5-year est.); Ancestry (includes multiple ancestries): 13.1% German, 11.4% American, 6.1% Irish, 3.4% Italian, 1.7% English (2005-2009 5-year est.).

Economy: Employment by occupation: 6.2% management, 29.4% professional, 17.5% services, 15.8% sales, 0.0% farming, 16.4% construction, 14.7% production (2005-2009 5-year est.).
Income: Per capita income: $23,758 (2010); Median household income: $53,676 (2010); Average household income: $60,690 (2010); Percent of households with income of $100,000 or more: 13.4% (2010); Poverty rate: 5.2% (2005-2009 5-year est.).
Taxes: Total city taxes per capita: $185 (2007); City property taxes per capita: $95 (2007).
Education: Percent of population age 25 and over with: High school diploma (including GED) or higher: 86.3% (2010); Bachelor's degree or higher: 12.9% (2010); Master's degree or higher: 2.7% (2010).
Housing: Homeownership rate: 85.1% (2010); Median home value: $107,576 (2010); Median contract rent: $295 per month (2005-2009 5-year est.); Median year structure built: 1983 (2005-2009 5-year est.).
Transportation: Commute to work: 90.8% car, 0.0% public transportation, 1.6% walk, 7.6% work from home (2005-2009 5-year est.); Travel time to work: 24.6% less than 15 minutes, 64.3% 15 to 30 minutes, 8.8% 30 to 45 minutes, 0.0% 45 to 60 minutes, 2.3% 60 minutes or more (2005-2009 5-year est.)

HENRIETTA (city). County seat. Covers a land area of 4.697 square miles and a water area of 0.049 square miles. Located at 33.81° N. Lat; 98.19° W. Long. Elevation is 912 feet.
History: Henrietta was first founded in 1857 but abandoned in 1861. Resettled in 1873, it was named for the wife of Henry Clay. In its early days, Henrietta was a supply center for Fort Sill.
Population: 2,956 (1990); 3,264 (2000); 3,236 (2010); 3,229 (2015 projected); Race: 93.3% White, 1.9% Black, 0.0% Asian, 4.8% Other, 4.4% Hispanic of any race (2010); Density: 688.9 persons per square mile (2010); Average household size: 2.43 (2010); Median age: 39.7 (2010); Males per 100 females: 91.0 (2010); Marriage status: 17.2% never married, 64.3% now married, 7.5% widowed, 10.9% divorced (2005-2009 5-year est.); Foreign born: 3.0% (2005-2009 5-year est.); Ancestry (includes multiple ancestries): 13.9% German, 10.4% American, 9.3% English, 8.6% Irish, 4.2% Dutch (2005-2009 5-year est.).
Economy: Single-family building permits issued: 0 (2010); Multi-family building permits issued: 0 (2010); Employment by occupation: 10.0% management, 23.1% professional, 16.2% services, 25.7% sales, 0.0% farming, 9.1% construction, 15.9% production (2005-2009 5-year est.).
Income: Per capita income: $22,210 (2010); Median household income: $46,427 (2010); Average household income: $54,885 (2010); Percent of households with income of $100,000 or more: 12.7% (2010); Poverty rate: 12.2% (2005-2009 5-year est.).
Taxes: Total city taxes per capita: $348 (2007); City property taxes per capita: $157 (2007).
Education: Percent of population age 25 and over with: High school diploma (including GED) or higher: 82.9% (2010); Bachelor's degree or higher: 16.6% (2010); Master's degree or higher: 2.2% (2010).
School District(s)
Henrietta ISD (PK-12)
  2009-10 Enrollment: 907 . . . . (940) 720-7900
Midway ISD (PK-12)
  2009-10 Enrollment: 112 . . . . (940) 476-2215
Housing: Homeownership rate: 76.6% (2010); Median home value: $61,208 (2010); Median contract rent: $412 per month (2005-2009 5-year est.); Median year structure built: 1964 (2005-2009 5-year est.).
Hospitals: Clay County Memorial Hospital (32 beds)
Newspapers: Clay County Leader (Community news; Circulation 3,000)
Transportation: Commute to work: 95.0% car, 0.0% public transportation, 3.6% walk, 1.4% work from home (2005-2009 5-year est.); Travel time to work: 44.0% less than 15 minutes, 31.6% 15 to 30 minutes, 17.1% 30 to 45 minutes, 0.4% 45 to 60 minutes, 6.9% 60 minutes or more (2005-2009 5-year est.)
Additional Information Contacts
Henrietta & Clay County Chamber of Commerce . . . . (940) 538-5261
  http://www.hccchamber.org

JOLLY (city). Covers a land area of 0.986 square miles and a water area of 0 square miles. Located at 33.87° N. Lat; 98.34° W. Long. Elevation is 984 feet.
Population: 201 (1990); 188 (2000); 191 (2010); 193 (2015 projected); Race: 94.2% White, 1.0% Black, 0.0% Asian, 4.7% Other, 5.8% Hispanic of any race (2010); Density: 193.8 persons per square mile (2010); Average household size: 2.58 (2010); Median age: 41.3 (2010); Males per

100 females: 89.1 (2010); Marriage status: 6.6% never married, 79.8% now married, 2.9% widowed, 10.7% divorced (2005-2009 5-year est.); Foreign born: 0.0% (2005-2009 5-year est.); Ancestry (includes multiple ancestries): 14.4% German, 13.8% American, 8.4% Irish, 8.1% English, 2.7% French (2005-2009 5-year est.).

Economy: Employment by occupation: 12.8% management, 19.3% professional, 15.5% services, 30.5% sales, 0.0% farming, 12.3% construction, 9.6% production (2005-2009 5-year est.).

Income: Per capita income: $23,774 (2010); Median household income: $55,263 (2010); Average household income: $62,973 (2010); Percent of households with income of $100,000 or more: 14.9% (2010); Poverty rate: 0.0% (2005-2009 5-year est.).

Taxes: Total city taxes per capita: $175 (2007); City property taxes per capita: $0 (2007).

Education: Percent of population age 25 and over with: High school diploma (including GED) or higher: 87.4% (2010); Bachelor's degree or higher: 12.6% (2010); Master's degree or higher: 2.2% (2010).

Housing: Homeownership rate: 85.1% (2010); Median home value: $106,579 (2010); Median contract rent: n/a per month (2005-2009 5-year est.); Median year structure built: 1984 (2005-2009 5-year est.).

Transportation: Commute to work: 95.5% car, 0.0% public transportation, 1.1% walk, 3.4% work from home (2005-2009 5-year est.); Travel time to work: 17.5% less than 15 minutes, 67.3% 15 to 30 minutes, 13.5% 30 to 45 minutes, 1.8% 45 to 60 minutes, 0.0% 60 minutes or more (2005-2009 5-year est.)

PETROLIA (city). Covers a land area of 0.744 square miles and a water area of 0 square miles. Located at 34.01° N. Lat; 98.23° W. Long. Elevation is 997 feet.

History: Petrolia, near Wichita Falls, was established when oil and natural gas were found in 1907. In 1910, the Dorthukia Dunn well at Petrolia became the first gusher of North Texas.

Population: 762 (1990); 782 (2000); 763 (2010); 753 (2015 projected); Race: 91.1% White, 3.0% Black, 0.0% Asian, 5.9% Other, 5.2% Hispanic of any race (2010); Density: 1,025.6 persons per square mile (2010); Average household size: 2.47 (2010); Median age: 36.6 (2010); Males per 100 females: 81.2 (2010); Marriage status: 22.7% never married, 60.3% now married, 3.9% widowed, 13.0% divorced (2005-2009 5-year est.); Foreign born: 0.0% (2005-2009 5-year est.); Ancestry (includes multiple ancestries): 17.6% German, 16.4% Irish, 7.1% American, 4.2% English, 4.0% Polish (2005-2009 5-year est.).

Economy: Employment by occupation: 13.5% management, 16.4% professional, 11.3% services, 34.8% sales, 0.7% farming, 6.6% construction, 16.7% production (2005-2009 5-year est.).

Income: Per capita income: $17,262 (2010); Median household income: $34,674 (2010); Average household income: $42,961 (2010); Percent of households with income of $100,000 or more: 4.2% (2010); Poverty rate: 13.2% (2005-2009 5-year est.).

Taxes: Total city taxes per capita: $178 (2007); City property taxes per capita: $67 (2007).

Education: Percent of population age 25 and over with: High school diploma (including GED) or higher: 78.5% (2010); Bachelor's degree or higher: 10.6% (2010); Master's degree or higher: 0.8% (2010).

School District(s)

Petrolia ISD (PK-12)

   2009-10 Enrollment: 485 . . . . (940) 524-3555

Housing: Homeownership rate: 80.3% (2010); Median home value: $46,563 (2010); Median contract rent: $475 per month (2005-2009 5-year est.); Median year structure built: 1974 (2005-2009 5-year est.).

Transportation: Commute to work: 99.0% car, 0.0% public transportation, 0.5% walk, 0.0% work from home (2005-2009 5-year est.); Travel time to work: 40.7% less than 15 minutes, 23.5% 15 to 30 minutes, 32.1% 30 to 45 minutes, 1.7% 45 to 60 minutes, 2.0% 60 minutes or more (2005-2009 5-year est.)

Cochran County

Located in northwestern Texas; bounded on the west by New Mexico. Covers a land area of 775.22 square miles, a water area of 0.09 square miles, and is located in the Central Time Zone at 33.65° N. Lat., 102.78° W. Long. The county was founded in 1876. County seat is Morton.

Weather Station: Morton   Elevation: 3,759 feet

	Jan	Feb	Mar	Apr	May	Jun	Jul	Aug	Sep	Oct	Nov	Dec
High	54	59	66	74	83	90	92	90	84	74	63	54
Low	24	27	33	41	52	61	64	63	56	45	33	25
Precip	0.6	0.6	1.1	0.9	2.2	2.5	2.6	2.7	2.5	1.8	0.9	0.8
Snow	2.2	1.3	0.4	0.3	0.0	0.0	0.0	0.0	0.0	0.1	1.4	2.9

High and Low temperatures in degrees Fahrenheit; Precipitation and Snow in inches

Population: 4,377 (1990); 3,730 (2000); 3,139 (2010); 2,845 (2015 projected); Race: 59.6% White, 5.9% Black, 0.3% Asian, 34.2% Other, 48.3% Hispanic of any race (2010); Density: 4.0 persons per square mile (2010); Average household size: 2.68 (2010); Median age: 37.5 (2010); Males per 100 females: 89.9 (2010).

Religion: Five largest groups: 52.9% Southern Baptist Convention, 15.1% Catholic Church, 11.9% Baptist Missionary Association of America, 7.3% Churches of Christ, 6.2% The United Methodist Church (2000).

Economy: Unemployment rate: 9.7% (June 2011); Total civilian labor force: 1,340 (June 2011); Leading industries: 21.7% retail trade (2009); Farms: 341 totaling 489,051 acres (2007); Companies that employ 500 or more persons: 0 (2009); Companies that employ 100 to 499 persons: 0 (2009); Companies that employ less than 100 persons: 61 (2009); Black-owned businesses: n/a (2007); Hispanic-owned businesses: n/a (2007); Asian-owned businesses: n/a (2007); Women-owned businesses: n/a (2007); Retail sales per capita: $6,378 (2010). Single-family building permits issued: 0 (2010); Multi-family building permits issued: 0 (2010).

Income: Per capita income: $18,156 (2010); Median household income: $35,702 (2010); Average household income: $48,957 (2010); Percent of households with income of $100,000 or more: 8.5% (2010); Poverty rate: 21.5% (2009); Bankruptcy rate: 0.64% (2010).

Taxes: Total county taxes per capita: $680 (2007); County property taxes per capita: $629 (2007).

Education: Percent of population age 25 and over with: High school diploma (including GED) or higher: 68.9% (2010); Bachelor's degree or higher: 11.5% (2010); Master's degree or higher: 4.8% (2010).

Housing: Homeownership rate: 71.6% (2010); Median home value: $33,365 (2010); Median contract rent: $247 per month (2005-2009 5-year est.); Median year structure built: 1960 (2005-2009 5-year est.)

Health: Birth rate: 187.9 per 10,000 population (2009); Death rate: 44.4 per 10,000 population (2009); Age-adjusted cancer mortality rate: Suppressed deaths per 100,000 population (2007); Number of physicians: 6.7 per 10,000 population (2008); Hospital beds: 58.3 per 10,000 population (2007); Hospital admissions: 275.3 per 10,000 population (2007).

Elections: 2008 Presidential election results: 26.9% Obama, 71.7% McCain, 0.0% Nader

Additional Information Contacts

Cochran County Government . . . . (806) 266-5508
  http://www.co.cochran.tx.us/ips/cms
Morton Area Chamber of Commerce. . . . . (806) 266-5200

Cochran County Communities

MORTON (city). County seat. Covers a land area of 1.411 square miles and a water area of 0 square miles. Located at 33.72° N. Lat; 102.75° W. Long. Elevation is 3,760 feet.

History: Incorporated 1934.

Population: 2,594 (1990); 2,249 (2000); 1,887 (2010); 1,706 (2015 projected); Race: 50.7% White, 7.2% Black, 0.2% Asian, 41.9% Other, 55.5% Hispanic of any race (2010); Density: 1,337.2 persons per square mile (2010); Average household size: 2.76 (2010); Median age: 35.3 (2010); Males per 100 females: 92.0 (2010); Marriage status: 13.3% never married, 71.0% now married, 8.0% widowed, 7.7% divorced (2005-2009 5-year est.); Foreign born: 18.2% (2005-2009 5-year est.); Ancestry (includes multiple ancestries): 7.8% American, 4.7% German, 4.0% English, 3.8% Irish, 3.0% Albanian (2005-2009 5-year est.).

Economy: Single-family building permits issued: 0 (2010); Multi-family building permits issued: 0 (2010); Employment by occupation: 8.9% management, 13.7% professional, 19.6% services, 19.5% sales, 13.1% farming, 11.8% construction, 13.5% production (2005-2009 5-year est.).

Income: Per capita income: $16,259 (2010); Median household income: $33,318 (2010); Average household income: $44,885 (2010); Percent of households with income of $100,000 or more: 6.5% (2010); Poverty rate: 33.9% (2005-2009 5-year est.).

Taxes: Total city taxes per capita: $78 (2007); City property taxes per capita: $25 (2007).

Education: Percent of population age 25 and over with: High school diploma (including GED) or higher: 63.5% (2010); Bachelor's degree or higher: 9.0% (2010); Master's degree or higher: 4.9% (2010).

School District(s)

Anton ISD (PK-12)
    2009-10 Enrollment: 271 . . . . (806) 997-2301
Morton ISD (PK-12)
    2009-10 Enrollment: 470 . . . . (806) 266-5505
Housing: Homeownership rate: 74.6% (2010); Median home value: $26,978 (2010); Median contract rent: $199 per month (2005-2009 5-year est.); Median year structure built: 1958 (2005-2009 5-year est.).
Hospitals: Cochran Memorial Hospital (30 beds)
Newspapers: Morton Tribune (Community news; Circulation 1,300)
Transportation: Commute to work: 94.9% car, 0.5% public transportation, 0.0% walk, 2.7% work from home (2005-2009 5-year est.); Travel time to work: 47.5% less than 15 minutes, 20.6% 15 to 30 minutes, 15.3% 30 to 45 minutes, 2.3% 45 to 60 minutes, 14.2% 60 minutes or more (2005-2009 5-year est.)

Additional Information Contacts
Morton Area Chamber of Commerce . . . . (806) 266-5200

WHITEFACE (town). Covers a land area of 0.581 square miles and a water area of 0 square miles. Located at 33.60° N. Lat; 102.61° W. Long. Elevation is 3,678 feet.

Population: 513 (1990); 465 (2000); 397 (2010); 363 (2015 projected); Race: 64.7% White, 3.3% Black, 0.0% Asian, 32.0% Other, 48.4% Hispanic of any race (2010); Density: 682.9 persons per square mile (2010); Average household size: 2.68 (2010); Median age: 40.1 (2010); Males per 100 females: 88.2 (2010); Marriage status: 12.2% never married, 67.3% now married, 11.6% widowed, 8.8% divorced (2005-2009 5-year est.); Foreign born: 4.7% (2005-2009 5-year est.); Ancestry (includes multiple ancestries): 24.4% German, 15.5% English, 15.5% Irish, 4.7% Scotch-Irish, 3.1% Norwegian (2005-2009 5-year est.).
Economy: Single-family building permits issued: 0 (2010); Multi-family building permits issued: 0 (2010); Employment by occupation: 8.8% management, 9.4% professional, 13.8% services, 28.2% sales, 17.7% farming, 3.3% construction, 18.8% production (2005-2009 5-year est.).
Income: Per capita income: $20,677 (2010); Median household income: $41,964 (2010); Average household income: $55,929 (2010); Percent of households with income of $100,000 or more: 8.8% (2010); Poverty rate: 8.3% (2005-2009 5-year est.).
Taxes: Total city taxes per capita: $154 (2007); City property taxes per capita: $121 (2007).
Education: Percent of population age 25 and over with: High school diploma (including GED) or higher: 72.3% (2010); Bachelor's degree or higher: 18.4% (2010); Master's degree or higher: 6.6% (2010).

School District(s)

Whiteface CISD (PK-12)
    2009-10 Enrollment: 310 . . . . (806) 287-1154
Housing: Homeownership rate: 70.9% (2010); Median home value: $34,063 (2010); Median contract rent: $403 per month (2005-2009 5-year est.); Median year structure built: 1959 (2005-2009 5-year est.).
Transportation: Commute to work: 82.1% car, 0.0% public transportation, 13.1% walk, 2.4% work from home (2005-2009 5-year est.); Travel time to work: 39.0% less than 15 minutes, 42.7% 15 to 30 minutes, 4.9% 30 to 45 minutes, 0.0% 45 to 60 minutes, 13.4% 60 minutes or more (2005-2009 5-year est.)

Coke County

Located in west Texas; intersected by the Colorado River. Covers a land area of 898.81 square miles, a water area of 29.17 square miles, and is located in the Central Time Zone at 31.90° N. Lat., 100.50° W. Long. The county was founded in 1889. County seat is Robert Lee.

Weather Station: Robert Lee   Elevation: 1,779 feet

	Jan	Feb	Mar	Apr	May	Jun	Jul	Aug	Sep	Oct	Nov	Dec
High	59	63	71	80	88	93	97	96	89	80	68	59
Low	31	34	42	50	60	68	71	70	63	52	41	31
Precip	0.8	1.3	1.5	1.5	3.1	2.8	1.3	2.8	2.9	2.7	1.3	1.0
Snow	0.1	tr	0.0	0.1	0.0	0.0	0.0	0.0	0.0	0.0	tr	0.1

High and Low temperatures in degrees Fahrenheit; Precipitation and Snow in inches

Population: 3,424 (1990); 3,864 (2000); 3,614 (2010); 3,488 (2015 projected); Race: 87.6% White, 1.6% Black, 0.1% Asian, 10.7% Other, 19.8% Hispanic of any race (2010); Density: 4.0 persons per square mile

(2010); Average household size: 2.27 (2010); Median age: 48.7 (2010); Males per 100 females: 96.1 (2010).
Religion: Five largest groups: 46.0% Southern Baptist Convention, 8.7% Baptist Missionary Association of America, 8.6% The United Methodist Church, 7.6% Churches of Christ, 1.5% Catholic Church (2000).
Economy: Unemployment rate: 9.0% (June 2011); Total civilian labor force: 1,313 (June 2011); Leading industries: 25.3% retail trade; 16.8% mining; 10.6% other services (except public administration) (2009); Farms: 430 totaling 491,211 acres (2007); Companies that employ 500 or more persons: 0 (2009); Companies that employ 100 to 499 persons: 0 (2009); Companies that employ less than 100 persons: 68 (2009); Black-owned businesses: n/a (2007); Hispanic-owned businesses: n/a (2007); Asian-owned businesses: n/a (2007); Women-owned businesses: n/a (2007); Retail sales per capita: $8,386 (2010). Single-family building permits issued: 0 (2010); Multi-family building permits issued: 0 (2010).
Income: Per capita income: $20,994 (2010); Median household income: $35,531 (2010); Average household income: $50,207 (2010); Percent of households with income of $100,000 or more: 10.8% (2010); Poverty rate: 17.1% (2009); Bankruptcy rate: 0.90% (2010).
Taxes: Total county taxes per capita: $441 (2007); County property taxes per capita: $367 (2007).
Education: Percent of population age 25 and over with: High school diploma (including GED) or higher: 78.7% (2010); Bachelor's degree or higher: 16.2% (2010); Master's degree or higher: 3.8% (2010).
Housing: Homeownership rate: 77.1% (2010); Median home value: $61,361 (2010); Median contract rent: $268 per month (2005-2009 5-year est.); Median year structure built: 1973 (2005-2009 5-year est.)
Health: Birth rate: 87.6 per 10,000 population (2009); Death rate: 142.0 per 10,000 population (2009); Age-adjusted cancer mortality rate: 146.1 (Unreliable) deaths per 100,000 population (2007); Number of physicians: 8.9 per 10,000 population (2008); Hospital beds: 0.0 per 10,000 population (2007); Hospital admissions: 0.0 per 10,000 population (2007).
Elections: 2008 Presidential election results: 19.1% Obama, 79.8% McCain, 0.1% Nader
Additional Information Contacts
Coke County Government . . . . (325) 453-2641
    http://www.co.coke.tx.us/ips/cms

Coke County Communities

BRONTE (town). Covers a land area of 1.439 square miles and a water area of 0 square miles. Located at 31.88° N. Lat; 100.29° W. Long. Elevation is 1,795 feet.

History: Old Fort Chadbourne to North.
Population: 962 (1990); 1,076 (2000); 1,112 (2010); 1,114 (2015 projected); Race: 84.5% White, 4.2% Black, 0.1% Asian, 11.2% Other, 28.1% Hispanic of any race (2010); Density: 773.0 persons per square mile (2010); Average household size: 2.37 (2010); Median age: 40.5 (2010); Males per 100 females: 110.6 (2010); Marriage status: 23.5% never married, 52.2% now married, 11.7% widowed, 12.6% divorced (2005-2009 5-year est.); Foreign born: 11.8% (2005-2009 5-year est.); Ancestry (includes multiple ancestries): 20.5% German, 19.7% Irish, 9.1% English, 7.0% American, 4.8% Scottish (2005-2009 5-year est.).
Economy: Single-family building permits issued: 0 (2010); Multi-family building permits issued: 0 (2010); Employment by occupation: 8.7% management, 27.4% professional, 18.7% services, 19.4% sales, 10.3% farming, 6.6% construction, 8.9% production (2005-2009 5-year est.).
Income: Per capita income: $18,660 (2010); Median household income: $32,016 (2010); Average household income: $49,411 (2010); Percent of households with income of $100,000 or more: 10.5% (2010); Poverty rate: 20.6% (2005-2009 5-year est.).
Taxes: Total city taxes per capita: $169 (2007); City property taxes per capita: $79 (2007).
Education: Percent of population age 25 and over with: High school diploma (including GED) or higher: 78.4% (2010); Bachelor's degree or higher: 17.9% (2010); Master's degree or higher: 4.0% (2010).

School District(s)

Bronte ISD (PK-12)
    2009-10 Enrollment: 321 . . . . (325) 473-2511
Housing: Homeownership rate: 72.9% (2010); Median home value: $57,069 (2010); Median contract rent: $297 per month (2005-2009 5-year est.); Median year structure built: 1969 (2005-2009 5-year est.).
Transportation: Commute to work: 85.5% car, 0.0% public transportation, 5.3% walk, 8.3% work from home (2005-2009 5-year est.); Travel time to work: 55.2% less than 15 minutes, 18.3% 15 to 30 minutes, 19.9% 30 to 45

minutes, 5.7% 45 to 60 minutes, 0.8% 60 minutes or more (2005-2009 5-year est.)

ROBERT LEE (city). County seat. Covers a land area of 1.140 square miles and a water area of 0 square miles. Located at 31.89° N. Lat; 100.48° W. Long. Elevation is 1,827 feet.
History: Old Fort Chadbourne is 12 miles Northeast.
Population: 1,289 (1990); 1,171 (2000); 1,046 (2010); 988 (2015 projected); Race: 89.1% White, 0.1% Black, 0.2% Asian, 10.6% Other, 20.8% Hispanic of any race (2010); Density: 917.1 persons per square mile (2010); Average household size: 2.21 (2010); Median age: 50.2 (2010); Males per 100 females: 83.8 (2010); Marriage status: 20.1% never married, 47.4% now married, 16.9% widowed, 15.6% divorced (2005-2009 5-year est.); Foreign born: 5.9% (2005-2009 5-year est.); Ancestry (includes multiple ancestries): 17.7% Irish, 12.0% American, 10.7% German, 10.3% English, 2.7% French (2005-2009 5-year est.).
Economy: Single-family building permits issued: 0 (2010); Multi-family building permits issued: 0 (2010); Employment by occupation: 6.9% management, 11.0% professional, 23.1% services, 23.1% sales, 0.0% farming, 15.7% construction, 20.2% production (2005-2009 5-year est.).
Income: Per capita income: $19,055 (2010); Median household income: $31,940 (2010); Average household income: $42,890 (2010); Percent of households with income of $100,000 or more: 8.4% (2010); Poverty rate: 22.7% (2005-2009 5-year est.).
Taxes: Total city taxes per capita: $168 (2007); City property taxes per capita: $92 (2007).
Education: Percent of population age 25 and over with: High school diploma (including GED) or higher: 73.4% (2010); Bachelor's degree or higher: 13.9% (2010); Master's degree or higher: 2.3% (2010).

School District(s)

Robert Lee ISD (PK-12)
    2009-10 Enrollment: 251 . . . . (325) 453-4555
Housing: Homeownership rate: 74.9% (2010); Median home value: $51,098 (2010); Median contract rent: $230 per month (2005-2009 5-year est.); Median year structure built: 1959 (2005-2009 5-year est.).
Newspapers: Observer Enterprise (Community news; Circulation 2,000)
Transportation: Commute to work: 85.0% car, 0.0% public transportation, 4.8% walk, 6.7% work from home (2005-2009 5-year est.); Travel time to work: 44.8% less than 15 minutes, 12.7% 15 to 30 minutes, 13.7% 30 to 45 minutes, 18.4% 45 to 60 minutes, 10.5% 60 minutes or more (2005-2009 5-year est.)

SILVER (unincorporated postal area, zip code 76949). Covers a land area of 27.099 square miles and a water area of 0.006 square miles. Located at 32.04° N. Lat; 100.69° W. Long. Elevation is 2,100 feet.
Population: 30 (2000); Race: 100.0% White, 0.0% Black, 0.0% Asian, 0.0% Other, 0.0% Hispanic of any race (2000); Density: 1.1 persons per square mile (2000); Age: 0.0% under 18, 37.5% over 64 (2000); Marriage status: 12.5% never married, 81.3% now married, 6.3% widowed, 0.0% divorced (2000); Foreign born: 0.0% (2000); Ancestry (includes multiple ancestries): 46.9% American, 12.5% European (2000).
Economy: Employment by occupation: 15.8% management, 10.5% professional, 0.0% services, 31.6% sales, 10.5% farming, 0.0% construction, 31.6% production (2000).
Income: Per capita income: $21,394 (2000); Median household income: $37,500 (2000); Poverty rate: 179.1% (2000).
Education: Percent of population age 25 and over with: High school diploma (including GED) or higher: 83.3% (2000); Bachelor's degree or higher: 20.0% (2000).
Housing: Homeownership rate: 100.0% (2000); Median home value: $37,500 (2000); Median contract rent: n/a per month (2000); Median year structure built: 1970 (2000).
Transportation: Commute to work: 100.0% car, 0.0% public transportation, 0.0% walk, 0.0% work from home (2000); Travel time to work: 21.1% less than 15 minutes, 26.3% 15 to 30 minutes, 31.6% 30 to 45 minutes, 21.1% 45 to 60 minutes, 0.0% 60 minutes or more (2000)

Coleman County

Located in central Texas; bounded on the south by the Colorado River and drained by its tributaries. Covers a land area of 1,260.20 square miles, a water area of 21.25 square miles, and is located in the Central Time Zone at 31.82° N. Lat., 99.44° W. Long. The county was founded in 1858. County seat is Coleman.

Weather Station: Coleman   Elevation: 1,727 feet

	Jan	Feb	Mar	Apr	May	Jun	Jul	Aug	Sep	Oct	Nov	Dec
High	59	63	71	79	86	91	95	95	88	79	68	59
Low	34	38	44	52	61	67	70	70	63	54	43	35
Precip	1.1	2.0	2.4	1.9	3.8	4.5	1.8	2.5	2.9	3.0	1.9	1.4
Snow	0.6	0.5	0.2	0.1	0.0	0.0	0.0	0.0	0.0	tr	0.2	0.5

High and Low temperatures in degrees Fahrenheit; Precipitation and Snow in inches

Weather Station: Hords Creek Dam   Elevation: 1,941 feet

	Jan	Feb	Mar	Apr	May	Jun	Jul	Aug	Sep	Oct	Nov	Dec
High	57	61	69	77	84	90	94	94	87	78	67	58
Low	30	34	42	49	58	65	69	68	61	51	40	31
Precip	1.0	1.8	2.1	1.6	3.6	4.2	1.7	2.2	2.7	2.7	1.8	1.1
Snow	0.0	0.1	tr	0.0	0.0	0.0	0.0	0.0	0.0	0.0	0.0	tr

High and Low temperatures in degrees Fahrenheit; Precipitation and Snow in inches

Population: 9,710 (1990); 9,235 (2000); 8,566 (2010); 8,225 (2015 projected); Race: 87.0% White, 2.7% Black, 0.3% Asian, 10.0% Other, 14.9% Hispanic of any race (2010); Density: 6.8 persons per square mile (2010); Average household size: 2.32 (2010); Median age: 43.7 (2010); Males per 100 females: 92.9 (2010).
Religion: Five largest groups: 33.3% Southern Baptist Convention, 9.6% The United Methodist Church, 9.0% Catholic Church, 4.9% Churches of Christ, 3.3% Christian Church (Disciples of Christ) (2000).
Economy: Unemployment rate: 7.7% (June 2011); Total civilian labor force: 4,319 (June 2011); Leading industries: 20.6% health care and social assistance; 15.6% retail trade; 14.1% manufacturing (2009); Farms: 1,003 totaling 699,452 acres (2007); Companies that employ 500 or more persons: 0 (2009); Companies that employ 100 to 499 persons: 2 (2009); Companies that employ less than 100 persons: 217 (2009); Black-owned businesses: n/a (2007); Hispanic-owned businesses: n/a (2007); Asian-owned businesses: n/a (2007); Women-owned businesses: 309 (2007); Retail sales per capita: $9,198 (2010). Single-family building permits issued: 1 (2010); Multi-family building permits issued: 0 (2010).
Income: Per capita income: $20,010 (2010); Median household income: $34,025 (2010); Average household income: $47,155 (2010); Percent of households with income of $100,000 or more: 8.3% (2010); Poverty rate: 27.1% (2009); Bankruptcy rate: 1.34% (2010).
Taxes: Total county taxes per capita: $255 (2007); County property taxes per capita: $203 (2007).
Education: Percent of population age 25 and over with: High school diploma (including GED) or higher: 76.1% (2010); Bachelor's degree or higher: 13.1% (2010); Master's degree or higher: 3.8% (2010).
Housing: Homeownership rate: 72.5% (2010); Median home value: $48,013 (2010); Median contract rent: $254 per month (2005-2009 5-year est.); Median year structure built: 1958 (2005-2009 5-year est.)
Health: Birth rate: 127.4 per 10,000 population (2009); Death rate: 171.0 per 10,000 population (2009); Age-adjusted cancer mortality rate: 157.5 (Unreliable) deaths per 100,000 population (2007); Number of physicians: 7.0 per 10,000 population (2008); Hospital beds: 29.4 per 10,000 population (2007); Hospital admissions: 786.6 per 10,000 population (2007).
Elections: 2008 Presidential election results: 17.4% Obama, 81.3% McCain, 0.0% Nader
Additional Information Contacts
Coleman County Government . . . . (325) 625-4218
    http://www.co.coleman.tx.us/ips/cms
City of Coleman . . . . (325) 625-4116
    http://www.cityofcolemantx.us
Coleman County Chamber of Commerce . . . . (325) 625-2163
    http://www.colemantexas.org
Santa Anna Economic Development Corporation . . . . (325) 348-3511
    http://www.santaannaedc.org

Coleman County Communities

BURKETT (unincorporated postal area, zip code 76828). Covers a land area of 74.778 square miles and a water area of 0.307 square miles. Located at 32.02° N. Lat; 99.23° W. Long. Elevation is 1,558 feet.
Population: 214 (2000); Race: 88.7% White, 0.0% Black, 0.0% Asian, 11.3% Other, 8.4% Hispanic of any race (2000); Density: 2.9 persons per square mile (2000); Age: 14.6% under 18, 20.9% over 64 (2000); Marriage status: 19.6% never married, 53.1% now married, 11.6% widowed, 15.6% divorced (2000); Foreign born: 0.0% (2000); Ancestry (includes multiple ancestries): 15.1% American, 7.1% German, 6.7% French, 5.9% Irish (2000).

Economy: Employment by occupation: 30.7% management, 12.5% professional, 0.0% services, 8.0% sales, 3.4% farming, 19.3% construction, 26.1% production (2000).
Income: Per capita income: $12,018 (2000); Median household income: $22,375 (2000); Poverty rate: 179.1% (2000).
Education: Percent of population age 25 and over with: High school diploma (including GED) or higher: 69.8% (2000); Bachelor's degree or higher: 3.1% (2000).
Housing: Homeownership rate: 81.6% (2000); Median home value: $26,500 (2000); Median contract rent: $137 per month (2000); Median year structure built: 1960 (2000).
Transportation: Commute to work: 87.5% car, 0.0% public transportation, 0.0% walk, 12.5% work from home (2000); Travel time to work: 23.4% less than 15 minutes, 27.3% 15 to 30 minutes, 40.3% 30 to 45 minutes, 9.1% 45 to 60 minutes, 0.0% 60 minutes or more (2000)

COLEMAN (city). County seat. Covers a land area of 6.163 square miles and a water area of 0.042 square miles. Located at 31.82° N. Lat; 99.42° W. Long. Elevation is 1,703 feet.
History: Coleman was established at the geographic center of Texas. It became a major oil producer. Nearby, Camp Colorado was built as a U.S. military post on Jim Ned Creek, but was abandoned at the start of the Civil War.
Population: 5,416 (1990); 5,127 (2000); 4,720 (2010); 4,515 (2015 projected); Race: 82.4% White, 3.3% Black, 0.3% Asian, 14.0% Other, 18.4% Hispanic of any race (2010); Density: 765.9 persons per square mile (2010); Average household size: 2.35 (2010); Median age: 40.2 (2010); Males per 100 females: 88.1 (2010); Marriage status: 17.2% never married, 58.1% now married, 15.7% widowed, 9.1% divorced (2005-2009 5-year est.); Foreign born: 1.7% (2005-2009 5-year est.); Ancestry (includes multiple ancestries): 15.0% English, 14.4% Irish, 11.7% German, 7.4% American, 1.2% French (2005-2009 5-year est.).
Economy: Single-family building permits issued: 1 (2010); Multi-family building permits issued: 0 (2010); Employment by occupation: 7.0% management, 21.2% professional, 19.9% services, 16.1% sales, 0.0% farming, 8.7% construction, 27.1% production (2005-2009 5-year est.).
Income: Per capita income: $19,103 (2010); Median household income: $31,997 (2010); Average household income: $45,116 (2010); Percent of households with income of $100,000 or more: 7.4% (2010); Poverty rate: 36.0% (2005-2009 5-year est.).
Taxes: Total city taxes per capita: $320 (2007); City property taxes per capita: $37 (2007).
Education: Percent of population age 25 and over with: High school diploma (including GED) or higher: 73.4% (2010); Bachelor's degree or higher: 10.4% (2010); Master's degree or higher: 3.1% (2010).
School District(s)
Coleman ISD (PK-12)
    2009-10 Enrollment: 959 . . . . (325) 625-3575
Housing: Homeownership rate: 67.5% (2010); Median home value: $40,414 (2010); Median contract rent: $287 per month (2005-2009 5-year est.); Median year structure built: 1953 (2005-2009 5-year est.).
Hospitals: Coleman County Medical Center (46 beds)
Safety: Violent crime rate: 2.2 per 10,000 population; Property crime rate: 370.1 per 10,000 population (2009).
Newspapers: Chronicle & Democrat Voice (Community news; Circulation 3,318)
Transportation: Commute to work: 97.7% car, 0.0% public transportation, 0.7% walk, 1.6% work from home (2005-2009 5-year est.); Travel time to work: 65.5% less than 15 minutes, 8.8% 15 to 30 minutes, 15.5% 30 to 45 minutes, 3.8% 45 to 60 minutes, 6.4% 60 minutes or more (2005-2009 5-year est.)
Additional Information Contacts
City of Coleman . . . . (325) 625-4116
    http://www.cityofcolemantx.us
Coleman County Chamber of Commerce . . . . (325) 625-2163
    http://www.colemantexas.org

GOLDSBORO (unincorporated postal area, zip code 79519). Covers a land area of 27.780 square miles and a water area of 0.139 square miles. Located at 32.04° N. Lat; 99.70° W. Long. Elevation is 1,942 feet.
Population: 46 (2000); Race: 100.0% White, 0.0% Black, 0.0% Asian, 0.0% Other, 0.0% Hispanic of any race (2000); Density: 1.7 persons per square mile (2000); Age: 0.0% under 18, 45.5% over 64 (2000); Marriage status: 40.9% never married, 36.4% now married, 13.6% widowed, 9.1% divorced (2000); Foreign born: 0.0% (2000); Ancestry (includes multiple

ancestries): 31.8% American, 27.3% Irish, 18.2% German, 9.1% French (2000).
Economy: Employment by occupation: 25.0% management, 0.0% professional, 50.0% services, 25.0% sales, 0.0% farming, 0.0% construction, 0.0% production (2000).
Income: Per capita income: $12,409 (2000); Median household income: $4,444 (2000); Poverty rate: 179.1% (2000).
Education: Percent of population age 25 and over with: High school diploma (including GED) or higher: 80.0% (2000); Bachelor's degree or higher: 10.0% (2000).
Housing: Homeownership rate: 100.0% (2000); Median home value: n/a (2000); Median contract rent: n/a per month (2000); Median year structure built: 1959 (2000).
Transportation: Commute to work: 25.0% car, 0.0% public transportation, 25.0% walk, 25.0% work from home (2000); Travel time to work: 0.0% less than 15 minutes, 0.0% 15 to 30 minutes, 100.0% 30 to 45 minutes, 0.0% 45 to 60 minutes, 0.0% 60 minutes or more (2000)

GOULDBUSK (unincorporated postal area, zip code 76845). Covers a land area of 91.902 square miles and a water area of 0.186 square miles. Located at 31.54° N. Lat; 99.47° W. Long. Elevation is 1,512 feet.
Population: 159 (2000); Race: 95.8% White, 0.0% Black, 0.0% Asian, 4.2% Other, 3.4% Hispanic of any race (2000); Density: 1.7 persons per square mile (2000); Age: 26.3% under 18, 27.1% over 64 (2000); Marriage status: 16.1% never married, 68.8% now married, 7.5% widowed, 7.5% divorced (2000); Foreign born: 1.7% (2000); Ancestry (includes multiple ancestries): 19.5% Irish, 16.1% English, 12.7% German, 7.6% Welsh (2000).
Economy: Employment by occupation: 27.5% management, 10.0% professional, 25.0% services, 10.0% sales, 2.5% farming, 17.5% construction, 7.5% production (2000).
Income: Per capita income: $15,054 (2000); Median household income: $23,333 (2000); Poverty rate: 179.1% (2000).
Education: Percent of population age 25 and over with: High school diploma (including GED) or higher: 74.1% (2000); Bachelor's degree or higher: 15.3% (2000).
Housing: Homeownership rate: 89.3% (2000); Median home value: $55,000 (2000); Median contract rent: $125 per month (2000); Median year structure built: 1974 (2000).
Transportation: Commute to work: 82.5% car, 0.0% public transportation, 2.5% walk, 15.0% work from home (2000); Travel time to work: 23.5% less than 15 minutes, 50.0% 15 to 30 minutes, 14.7% 30 to 45 minutes, 0.0% 45 to 60 minutes, 11.8% 60 minutes or more (2000)

NOVICE (city). Covers a land area of 0.452 square miles and a water area of 0 square miles. Located at 31.98° N. Lat; 99.62° W. Long. Elevation is 1,988 feet.
Population: 183 (1990); 142 (2000); 135 (2010); 131 (2015 projected); Race: 93.3% White, 0.0% Black, 1.5% Asian, 5.2% Other, 4.4% Hispanic of any race (2010); Density: 298.7 persons per square mile (2010); Average household size: 2.33 (2010); Median age: 49.0 (2010); Males per 100 females: 110.9 (2010); Marriage status: 24.4% never married, 51.3% now married, 17.9% widowed, 6.4% divorced (2005-2009 5-year est.); Foreign born: 0.0% (2005-2009 5-year est.); Ancestry (includes multiple ancestries): 50.0% English, 22.5% Irish, 13.7% German, 2.0% French, 2.0% Scotch-Irish (2005-2009 5-year est.).
Economy: Employment by occupation: 16.7% management, 13.9% professional, 8.3% services, 19.4% sales, 11.1% farming, 22.2% construction, 8.3% production (2005-2009 5-year est.).
Income: Per capita income: $23,110 (2010); Median household income: $40,455 (2010); Average household income: $51,552 (2010); Percent of households with income of $100,000 or more: 8.6% (2010); Poverty rate: 2.0% (2005-2009 5-year est.).
Taxes: Total city taxes per capita: $58 (2007); City property taxes per capita: $58 (2007).
Education: Percent of population age 25 and over with: High school diploma (including GED) or higher: 80.6% (2010); Bachelor's degree or higher: 19.4% (2010); Master's degree or higher: 5.1% (2010).
School District(s)
Novice ISD (PK-12)
    2009-10 Enrollment: 107 . . . . (325) 625-4069
Housing: Homeownership rate: 82.8% (2010); Median home value: $60,000 (2010); Median contract rent: n/a per month (2005-2009 5-year est.); Median year structure built: 1945 (2005-2009 5-year est.).

Transportation: Commute to work: 100.0% car, 0.0% public transportation, 0.0% walk, 0.0% work from home (2005-2009 5-year est.); Travel time to work: 27.8% less than 15 minutes, 22.2% 15 to 30 minutes, 36.1% 30 to 45 minutes, 13.9% 45 to 60 minutes, 0.0% 60 minutes or more (2005-2009 5-year est.)

ROCKWOOD (unincorporated postal area, zip code 76873). Covers a land area of 49.227 square miles and a water area of 0.182 square miles. Located at 31.51° N. Lat; 99.37° W. Long. Elevation is 1,483 feet.
Population: 58 (2000); Race: 100.0% White, 0.0% Black, 0.0% Asian, 0.0% Other, 0.0% Hispanic of any race (2000); Density: 1.2 persons per square mile (2000); Age: 8.5% under 18, 42.4% over 64 (2000); Marriage status: 5.6% never married, 75.9% now married, 11.1% widowed, 7.4% divorced (2000); Foreign born: 0.0% (2000); Ancestry (includes multiple ancestries): 22.0% Irish, 16.9% American, 16.9% English, 6.8% Scotch-Irish (2000).
Economy: Employment by occupation: 40.0% management, 20.0% professional, 5.0% services, 0.0% sales, 5.0% farming, 10.0% construction, 20.0% production (2000).
Income: Per capita income: $19,561 (2000); Median household income: $20,000 (2000); Poverty rate: 179.1% (2000).
Education: Percent of population age 25 and over with: High school diploma (including GED) or higher: 74.1% (2000); Bachelor's degree or higher: 24.1% (2000).
Housing: Homeownership rate: 87.9% (2000); Median home value: <$10,000 (2000); Median contract rent: $175 per month (2000); Median year structure built: 1964 (2000).
Transportation: Commute to work: 90.0% car, 0.0% public transportation, 10.0% walk, 0.0% work from home (2000); Travel time to work: 65.0% less than 15 minutes, 10.0% 15 to 30 minutes, 25.0% 30 to 45 minutes, 0.0% 45 to 60 minutes, 0.0% 60 minutes or more (2000)

SANTA ANNA (town). Covers a land area of 1.937 square miles and a water area of 0 square miles. Located at 31.74° N. Lat; 99.32° W. Long. Elevation is 1,755 feet.
Population: 1,249 (1990); 1,081 (2000); 1,000 (2010); 960 (2015 projected); Race: 90.5% White, 5.0% Black, 0.0% Asian, 4.5% Other, 19.5% Hispanic of any race (2010); Density: 516.2 persons per square mile (2010); Average household size: 2.32 (2010); Median age: 39.4 (2010); Males per 100 females: 96.9 (2010); Marriage status: 14.8% never married, 52.7% now married, 9.2% widowed, 23.3% divorced (2005-2009 5-year est.); Foreign born: 5.8% (2005-2009 5-year est.); Ancestry (includes multiple ancestries): 26.1% English, 12.9% Irish, 9.3% German, 3.7% American, 2.8% Scottish (2005-2009 5-year est.).
Economy: Employment by occupation: 3.3% management, 17.5% professional, 20.8% services, 10.5% sales, 3.1% farming, 18.4% construction, 26.3% production (2005-2009 5-year est.).
Income: Per capita income: $15,618 (2010); Median household income: $30,943 (2010); Average household income: $37,118 (2010); Percent of households with income of $100,000 or more: 2.6% (2010); Poverty rate: 23.4% (2005-2009 5-year est.).
Taxes: Total city taxes per capita: $262 (2007); City property taxes per capita: $126 (2007).
Education: Percent of population age 25 and over with: High school diploma (including GED) or higher: 75.4% (2010); Bachelor's degree or higher: 10.9% (2010); Master's degree or higher: 3.4% (2010).

School District(s)
Santa Anna ISD (PK-12)
   2009-10 Enrollment: 270 . . . . (325) 348-3136
Housing: Homeownership rate: 67.8% (2010); Median home value: $43,662 (2010); Median contract rent: $166 per month (2005-2009 5-year est.); Median year structure built: 1954 (2005-2009 5-year est.).
Safety: Violent crime rate: 49.5 per 10,000 population; Property crime rate: 148.5 per 10,000 population (2009).
Transportation: Commute to work: 95.8% car, 0.0% public transportation, 0.0% walk, 4.2% work from home (2005-2009 5-year est.); Travel time to work: 28.4% less than 15 minutes, 37.3% 15 to 30 minutes, 24.0% 30 to 45 minutes, 1.4% 45 to 60 minutes, 8.9% 60 minutes or more (2005-2009 5-year est.)
Additional Information Contacts
Santa Anna Economic Development Corporation . . . . (325) 348-3511
   http://www.santaannaedc.org

TALPA (unincorporated postal area, zip code 76882). Covers a land area of 63.953 square miles and a water area of 0.133 square miles. Located at 31.80° N. Lat; 99.68° W. Long. Elevation is 1,962 feet.
Population: 197 (2000); Race: 96.5% White, 0.0% Black, 0.4% Asian, 3.1% Other, 10.6% Hispanic of any race (2000); Density: 3.1 persons per square mile (2000); Age: 31.3% under 18, 21.6% over 64 (2000); Marriage status: 11.0% never married, 57.6% now married, 13.4% widowed, 18.0% divorced (2000); Foreign born: 4.0% (2000); Ancestry (includes multiple ancestries): 30.8% American, 16.3% German, 11.0% Irish, 2.2% Dutch (2000).
Economy: Employment by occupation: 9.8% management, 16.3% professional, 16.3% services, 20.7% sales, 12.0% farming, 8.7% construction, 16.3% production (2000).
Income: Per capita income: $14,163 (2000); Median household income: $22,083 (2000); Poverty rate: 179.1% (2000).
Education: Percent of population age 25 and over with: High school diploma (including GED) or higher: 81.2% (2000); Bachelor's degree or higher: 11.7% (2000).
Housing: Homeownership rate: 74.7% (2000); Median home value: $29,400 (2000); Median contract rent: $258 per month (2000); Median year structure built: 1953 (2000).
Transportation: Commute to work: 87.0% car, 0.0% public transportation, 2.2% walk, 8.7% work from home (2000); Travel time to work: 17.9% less than 15 minutes, 33.3% 15 to 30 minutes, 25.0% 30 to 45 minutes, 14.3% 45 to 60 minutes, 9.5% 60 minutes or more (2000)

VALERA (unincorporated postal area, zip code 76884). Covers a land area of 31.494 square miles and a water area of 0.173 square miles. Located at 31.75° N. Lat; 99.54° W. Long. Elevation is 1,818 feet.
Population: 147 (2000); Race: 94.6% White, 0.0% Black, 0.0% Asian, 5.4% Other, 13.7% Hispanic of any race (2000); Density: 4.7 persons per square mile (2000); Age: 16.7% under 18, 18.5% over 64 (2000); Marriage status: 12.7% never married, 80.3% now married, 5.6% widowed, 1.4% divorced (2000); Foreign born: 7.1% (2000); Ancestry (includes multiple ancestries): 15.5% American, 9.5% Irish, 8.9% European, 6.5% French (2000).
Economy: Employment by occupation: 28.7% management, 24.5% professional, 17.0% services, 9.6% sales, 0.0% farming, 11.7% construction, 8.5% production (2000).
Income: Per capita income: $17,013 (2000); Median household income: $33,438 (2000); Poverty rate: 179.1% (2000).
Education: Percent of population age 25 and over with: High school diploma (including GED) or higher: 81.0% (2000); Bachelor's degree or higher: 19.8% (2000).

School District(s)
Novice ISD (PK-12)
   2009-10 Enrollment: 107 . . . . (325) 625-4069
Panther Creek CISD (PK-12)
   2009-10 Enrollment: 166 . . . . (325) 357-4506
Housing: Homeownership rate: 85.5% (2000); Median home value: $18,000 (2000); Median contract rent: $225 per month (2000); Median year structure built: 1961 (2000).
Transportation: Commute to work: 86.2% car, 0.0% public transportation, 9.6% walk, 4.3% work from home (2000); Travel time to work: 34.4% less than 15 minutes, 33.3% 15 to 30 minutes, 4.4% 30 to 45 minutes, 12.2% 45 to 60 minutes, 15.6% 60 minutes or more (2000)

VOSS (unincorporated postal area, zip code 76888). Covers a land area of 76.582 square miles and a water area of 12.725 square miles. Located at 31.58° N. Lat; 99.62° W. Long. Elevation is 1,634 feet.
Population: 71 (2000); Race: 98.4% White, 0.0% Black, 0.0% Asian, 1.6% Other, 6.5% Hispanic of any race (2000); Density: 0.9 persons per square mile (2000); Age: 11.3% under 18, 22.6% over 64 (2000); Marriage status: 16.1% never married, 67.9% now married, 3.6% widowed, 12.5% divorced (2000); Foreign born: 0.0% (2000); Ancestry (includes multiple ancestries): 24.2% German, 12.9% American, 11.3% Irish, 9.7% Scotch-Irish (2000).
Economy: Employment by occupation: 29.0% management, 19.4% professional, 22.6% services, 12.9% sales, 0.0% farming, 6.5% construction, 9.7% production (2000).
Income: Per capita income: $39,113 (2000); Median household income: $41,250 (2000); Poverty rate: 179.1% (2000).
Education: Percent of population age 25 and over with: High school diploma (including GED) or higher: 60.4% (2000); Bachelor's degree or higher: 24.5% (2000).

Housing: Homeownership rate: 93.8% (2000); Median home value: $21,700 (2000); Median contract rent: n/a per month (2000); Median year structure built: 1992 (2000).
Transportation: Commute to work: 87.1% car, 12.9% public transportation, 0.0% walk, 0.0% work from home (2000); Travel time to work: 35.5% less than 15 minutes, 29.0% 15 to 30 minutes, 6.5% 30 to 45 minutes, 22.6% 45 to 60 minutes, 6.5% 60 minutes or more (2000)

Collin County

Located in north Texas; drained by the East Fork of the Trinity River. Covers a land area of 847.56 square miles, a water area of 38.29 square miles, and is located in the Central Time Zone at 33.13° N. Lat., 96.64° W. Long. The county was founded in 1846. County seat is McKinney.

Collin County is part of the Dallas-Fort Worth-Arlington, TX Metropolitan Statistical Area. The entire metro area includes: Dallas-Plano-Irving, TX Metropolitan Division (Collin County, TX; Dallas County, TX; Delta County, TX; Denton County, TX; Ellis County, TX; Hunt County, TX; Kaufman County, TX; Rockwall County, TX); Fort Worth-Arlington, TX Metropolitan Division (Johnson County, TX; Parker County, TX; Tarrant County, TX; Wise County, TX)

Weather Station: Lavon Dam — Elevation: 509 feet

	Jan	Feb	Mar	Apr	May	Jun	Jul	Aug	Sep	Oct	Nov	Dec
High	56	60	67	75	82	90	95	96	89	78	67	57
Low	32	37	44	52	62	69	72	72	64	53	44	35
Precip	2.6	2.9	3.6	3.5	5.2	4.5	2.0	1.8	3.2	4.4	3.6	3.2
Snow	0.0	0.1	0.1	0.0	0.0	0.0	0.0	0.0	0.0	0.0	0.0	0.2

High and Low temperatures in degrees Fahrenheit; Precipitation and Snow in inches

Weather Station: McKinney 3 S — Elevation: 595 feet

	Jan	Feb	Mar	Apr	May	Jun	Jul	Aug	Sep	Oct	Nov	Dec
High	56	60	68	76	83	90	95	96	88	78	66	57
Low	34	37	45	52	62	69	73	72	64	54	44	36
Precip	2.8	3.2	3.7	3.5	5.9	4.3	2.3	1.9	2.9	4.2	3.8	3.4
Snow	0.3	0.5	0.2	0.0	0.0	0.0	0.0	0.0	0.0	0.0	0.1	0.2

High and Low temperatures in degrees Fahrenheit; Precipitation and Snow in inches

Weather Station: Wellington — Elevation: 2,040 feet

	Jan	Feb	Mar	Apr	May	Jun	Jul	Aug	Sep	Oct	Nov	Dec
High	55	59	67	77	84	92	97	96	88	77	65	54
Low	27	31	38	46	56	64	69	69	61	49	37	29
Precip	0.7	0.7	1.4	1.8	3.4	3.5	2.1	1.9	2.4	2.6	1.1	0.8
Snow	1.5	0.8	0.1	tr	0.0	0.0	0.0	0.0	0.0	0.0	0.6	1.3

High and Low temperatures in degrees Fahrenheit; Precipitation and Snow in inches

Population: 264,036 (1990); 491,675 (2000); 808,727 (2010); 961,458 (2015 projected); Race: 72.3% White, 8.0% Black, 9.9% Asian, 9.8% Other, 14.7% Hispanic of any race (2010); Density: 954.2 persons per square mile (2010); Average household size: 2.72 (2010); Median age: 34.3 (2010); Males per 100 females: 100.8 (2010).
Religion: Five largest groups: 18.3% Catholic Church, 16.0% Southern Baptist Convention, 6.1% The United Methodist Church, 1.7% Independent, Non-Charismatic Churches, 1.4% Jewish Estimate (2000).
Economy: Unemployment rate: 8.0% (June 2011); Total civilian labor force: 428,962 (June 2011); Leading industries: 14.5% retail trade; 11.7% finance & insurance; 10.4% accommodation & food services (2009); Farms: 2,235 totaling 290,831 acres (2007); Companies that employ 500 or more persons: 58 (2009); Companies that employ 100 to 499 persons: 361 (2009); Companies that employ less than 100 persons: 16,834 (2009); Black-owned businesses: 3,632 (2007); Hispanic-owned businesses: 5,650 (2007); Asian-owned businesses: 7,834 (2007); Women-owned businesses: 22,023 (2007); Retail sales per capita: $15,731 (2010). Single-family building permits issued: 4,171 (2010); Multi-family building permits issued: 362 (2010).
Income: Per capita income: $39,023 (2010); Median household income: $83,040 (2010); Average household income: $106,309 (2010); Percent of households with income of $100,000 or more: 39.2% (2010); Poverty rate: 7.1% (2009); Bankruptcy rate: 3.75% (2010).
Taxes: Total county taxes per capita: $221 (2007); County property taxes per capita: $204 (2007).
Education: Percent of population age 25 and over with: High school diploma (including GED) or higher: 92.2% (2010); Bachelor's degree or higher: 47.1% (2010); Master's degree or higher: 15.1% (2010).

Housing: Homeownership rate: 70.5% (2010); Median home value: $193,372 (2010); Median contract rent: $779 per month (2005-2009 5-year est.); Median year structure built: 1994 (2005-2009 5-year est.)
Health: Birth rate: 152.6 per 10,000 population (2009); Death rate: 39.8 per 10,000 population (2009); Age-adjusted cancer mortality rate: 139.7 deaths per 100,000 population (2007); Number of physicians: 23.6 per 10,000 population (2008); Hospital beds: 20.7 per 10,000 population (2007); Hospital admissions: 861.9 per 10,000 population (2007).
Environment: Air Quality Index: 80.7% good, 17.7% moderate, 1.6% unhealthy for sensitive individuals, 0.0% unhealthy (percent of days in 2008)
Elections: 2008 Presidential election results: 36.7% Obama, 62.2% McCain, 0.1% Nader
Additional Information Contacts

Collin County Government . . . . (972) 548-4100
    http://www.co.collin.tx.us
Allen Fairview Chamber of Commerce . . . . (972) 727-5585
    http://www.allenchamber.com
City of Allen . . . . (214) 509-4100
    http://www.cityofallen.org
City of Frisco . . . . (972) 292-5000
    http://www.ci.frisco.tx.us
City of Lowry Crossing . . . . (972) 542-8678
    http://www.lowrycrossingtexas.org
City of Lucas . . . . (972) 727-8999
    http://www.lucastexas.us
City of McKinney . . . . (972) 547-7500
    http://www.mckinneytexas.org
City of Murphy . . . . (972) 468-4000
    http://www.murphytx.org
City of Plano . . . . (972) 941-7000
    http://www.plano.gov
City of Weston . . . . (972) 382-1001
    http://westontexas.com
City of Wylie . . . . (972) 516-6000
    http://www.ci.wylie.tx.us
Farmersville Chamber of Commerce . . . . (972) 782-6533
    http://www.farmersvilletx.com/chamber
Frisco Chamber of Commerce . . . . (972) 335-9522
    http://www.friscochamber.com
McKinney Chamber of Commerce . . . . (972) 542-0163
    http://www.mckinneytx.org
Plano Chamber of Commerce . . . . (972) 424-7547
    http://www.planochamber.org
Princeton Area Chamber of Commerce . . . . (972) 736-6462
    http://www.princetontxchamber.com
Town of Fairview . . . . (972) 886-4234
    http://www.fairviewtexas.org
Town of Prosper . . . . (972) 346-2640
    http://www.prospertx.gov
Wylie Chamber of Commerce . . . . (972) 442-2804
    http://www.wyliechamber.org

Collin County Communities

ALLEN (city). Covers a land area of 26.339 square miles and a water area of 0 square miles. Located at 33.10° N. Lat; 96.66° W. Long. Elevation is 659 feet.
Population: 19,208 (1990); 43,554 (2000); 85,603 (2010); 104,900 (2015 projected); Race: 78.5% White, 7.2% Black, 7.2% Asian, 7.1% Other, 10.4% Hispanic of any race (2010); Density: 3,250.1 persons per square mile (2010); Average household size: 3.07 (2010); Median age: 33.5 (2010); Males per 100 females: 100.3 (2010); Marriage status: 21.8% never married, 64.8% now married, 3.4% widowed, 10.0% divorced (2005-2009 5-year est.); Foreign born: 14.6% (2005-2009 5-year est.); Ancestry (includes multiple ancestries): 17.5% German, 11.7% Irish, 11.1% English, 5.4% American, 3.9% Italian (2005-2009 5-year est.).
Economy: Unemployment rate: 7.2% (June 2011); Total civilian labor force: 44,148 (June 2011); Single-family building permits issued: 444 (2010); Multi-family building permits issued: 0 (2010); Employment by occupation: 22.4% management, 30.0% professional, 9.9% services, 27.5% sales, 0.1% farming, 5.7% construction, 4.3% production (2005-2009 5-year est.).
Income: Per capita income: $37,472 (2010); Median household income: $94,840 (2010); Average household income: $115,069 (2010); Percent of

households with income of $100,000 or more: 46.2% (2010); Poverty rate: 3.6% (2005-2009 5-year est.).
Taxes: Total city taxes per capita: $767 (2007); City property taxes per capita: $400 (2007).
Education: Percent of population age 25 and over with: High school diploma (including GED) or higher: 95.9% (2010); Bachelor's degree or higher: 50.0% (2010); Master's degree or higher: 14.4% (2010).

School District(s)
Allen ISD (PK-12)
    2009-10 Enrollment: 18,242 . . . . (972) 727-0511
Lovejoy ISD (PK-12)
    2009-10 Enrollment: 3,230 . . . . (469) 742-8000
Plano ISD (PK-12)
    2009-10 Enrollment: 54,939 . . . . (469) 752-8100
Housing: Homeownership rate: 85.6% (2010); Median home value: $190,876 (2010); Median contract rent: $904 per month (2005-2009 5-year est.); Median year structure built: 1998 (2005-2009 5-year est.).
Hospitals: Texas Health Presbyterian Hospital Allen
Safety: Violent crime rate: 9.0 per 10,000 population; Property crime rate: 176.6 per 10,000 population (2009).
Newspapers: Allen American (Community news; Circulation 5,200)
Transportation: Commute to work: 89.9% car, 1.3% public transportation, 0.4% walk, 7.1% work from home (2005-2009 5-year est.); Travel time to work: 20.3% less than 15 minutes, 34.4% 15 to 30 minutes, 25.2% 30 to 45 minutes, 12.0% 45 to 60 minutes, 8.0% 60 minutes or more (2005-2009 5-year est.)
Additional Information Contacts
Allen Fairview Chamber of Commerce . . . . (972) 727-5585
    http://www.allenchamber.com
City of Allen . . . . (214) 509-4100
    http://www.cityofallen.org

ANNA (city). Covers a land area of 1.673 square miles and a water area of 0 square miles. Located at 33.35° N. Lat; 96.55° W. Long. Elevation is 712 feet.
Population: 996 (1990); 1,225 (2000); 2,963 (2010); 3,648 (2015 projected); Race: 77.4% White, 1.6% Black, 1.0% Asian, 20.0% Other, 29.5% Hispanic of any race (2010); Density: 1,770.9 persons per square mile (2010); Average household size: 2.98 (2010); Median age: 35.6 (2010); Males per 100 females: 109.4 (2010); Marriage status: 22.3% never married, 60.1% now married, 4.3% widowed, 13.4% divorced (2005-2009 5-year est.); Foreign born: 14.1% (2005-2009 5-year est.); Ancestry (includes multiple ancestries): 14.2% German, 11.0% Irish, 9.7% American, 7.6% English, 3.3% Italian (2005-2009 5-year est.).
Economy: Employment by occupation: 14.9% management, 21.0% professional, 18.6% services, 22.2% sales, 0.4% farming, 7.6% construction, 15.4% production (2005-2009 5-year est.).
Income: Per capita income: $24,742 (2010); Median household income: $60,729 (2010); Average household income: $73,886 (2010); Percent of households with income of $100,000 or more: 22.4% (2010); Poverty rate: 11.4% (2005-2009 5-year est.).
Taxes: Total city taxes per capita: $2,155 (2007); City property taxes per capita: $672 (2007).
Education: Percent of population age 25 and over with: High school diploma (including GED) or higher: 76.1% (2010); Bachelor's degree or higher: 12.2% (2010); Master's degree or higher: 2.8% (2010).

School District(s)
Anna ISD (PK-12)
    2009-10 Enrollment: 2,246 . . . . (972) 924-1000
Housing: Homeownership rate: 73.3% (2010); Median home value: $111,441 (2010); Median contract rent: $789 per month (2005-2009 5-year est.); Median year structure built: 2002 (2005-2009 5-year est.).
Safety: Violent crime rate: 36.7 per 10,000 population; Property crime rate: 598.1 per 10,000 population (2009).
Transportation: Commute to work: 89.1% car, 0.0% public transportation, 0.6% walk, 4.3% work from home (2005-2009 5-year est.); Travel time to work: 17.8% less than 15 minutes, 28.9% 15 to 30 minutes, 21.4% 30 to 45 minutes, 17.9% 45 to 60 minutes, 14.0% 60 minutes or more (2005-2009 5-year est.)

BLUE RIDGE (city). Covers a land area of 0.659 square miles and a water area of 0 square miles. Located at 33.29° N. Lat; 96.40° W. Long. Elevation is 614 feet.
Population: 523 (1990); 672 (2000); 704 (2010); 790 (2015 projected); Race: 90.9% White, 0.0% Black, 0.3% Asian, 8.8% Other, 10.8% Hispanic

of any race (2010); Density: 1,067.8 persons per square mile (2010); Average household size: 2.82 (2010); Median age: 36.1 (2010); Males per 100 females: 99.4 (2010); Marriage status: 22.1% never married, 48.7% now married, 11.0% widowed, 18.2% divorced (2005-2009 5-year est.); Foreign born: 4.2% (2005-2009 5-year est.); Ancestry (includes multiple ancestries): 24.8% German, 9.3% Irish, 8.6% English, 6.6% Italian, 5.0% American (2005-2009 5-year est.).
Economy: Single-family building permits issued: 0 (2010); Multi-family building permits issued: 0 (2010); Employment by occupation: 2.6% management, 13.4% professional, 23.3% services, 42.6% sales, 0.0% farming, 9.5% construction, 8.5% production (2005-2009 5-year est.).
Income: Per capita income: $22,846 (2010); Median household income: $54,902 (2010); Average household income: $64,730 (2010); Percent of households with income of $100,000 or more: 18.0% (2010); Poverty rate: 11.7% (2005-2009 5-year est.).
Taxes: Total city taxes per capita: $226 (2007); City property taxes per capita: $100 (2007).
Education: Percent of population age 25 and over with: High school diploma (including GED) or higher: 79.9% (2010); Bachelor's degree or higher: 13.7% (2010); Master's degree or higher: 5.5% (2010).

School District(s)
Blue Ridge ISD (PK-12)
    2009-10 Enrollment: 673 . . . . (972) 752-5554
Housing: Homeownership rate: 81.6% (2010); Median home value: $96,774 (2010); Median contract rent: $610 per month (2005-2009 5-year est.); Median year structure built: 1983 (2005-2009 5-year est.).
Transportation: Commute to work: 83.4% car, 0.0% public transportation, 0.0% walk, 7.0% work from home (2005-2009 5-year est.); Travel time to work: 11.1% less than 15 minutes, 17.1% 15 to 30 minutes, 40.7% 30 to 45 minutes, 16.8% 45 to 60 minutes, 14.3% 60 minutes or more (2005-2009 5-year est.)

CELINA (town). Covers a land area of 1.686 square miles and a water area of 0 square miles. Located at 33.32° N. Lat; 96.78° W. Long. Elevation is 692 feet.
Population: 1,729 (1990); 1,861 (2000); 1,991 (2010); 2,256 (2015 projected); Race: 67.6% White, 11.8% Black, 0.2% Asian, 20.5% Other, 32.5% Hispanic of any race (2010); Density: 1,181.1 persons per square mile (2010); Average household size: 2.87 (2010); Median age: 34.2 (2010); Males per 100 females: 102.3 (2010); Marriage status: 21.6% never married, 65.2% now married, 3.3% widowed, 9.9% divorced (2005-2009 5-year est.); Foreign born: 12.5% (2005-2009 5-year est.); Ancestry (includes multiple ancestries): 16.0% German, 15.1% Irish, 11.7% English, 9.6% American, 2.0% Scotch-Irish (2005-2009 5-year est.).
Economy: Single-family building permits issued: 56 (2010); Multi-family building permits issued: 0 (2010); Employment by occupation: 20.5% management, 16.3% professional, 21.8% services, 20.2% sales, 2.4% farming, 12.9% construction, 5.9% production (2005-2009 5-year est.).
Income: Per capita income: $24,518 (2010); Median household income: $48,591 (2010); Average household income: $69,435 (2010); Percent of households with income of $100,000 or more: 17.9% (2010); Poverty rate: 4.9% (2005-2009 5-year est.).
Taxes: Total city taxes per capita: $228 (2007); City property taxes per capita: $197 (2007).
Education: Percent of population age 25 and over with: High school diploma (including GED) or higher: 72.8% (2010); Bachelor's degree or higher: 15.8% (2010); Master's degree or higher: 5.4% (2010).

School District(s)
Celina ISD (PK-12)
    2009-10 Enrollment: 1,904 . . . . (469) 742-9100
Housing: Homeownership rate: 70.2% (2010); Median home value: $99,079 (2010); Median contract rent: $510 per month (2005-2009 5-year est.); Median year structure built: 1996 (2005-2009 5-year est.).
Safety: Violent crime rate: 21.6 per 10,000 population; Property crime rate: 113.0 per 10,000 population (2009).
Newspapers: Celina Record (Community news)
Transportation: Commute to work: 88.1% car, 3.1% public transportation, 0.3% walk, 7.5% work from home (2005-2009 5-year est.); Travel time to work: 24.1% less than 15 minutes, 19.0% 15 to 30 minutes, 27.2% 30 to 45 minutes, 20.8% 45 to 60 minutes, 8.9% 60 minutes or more (2005-2009 5-year est.)

FAIRVIEW (town). Covers a land area of 8.806 square miles and a water area of 0.003 square miles. Located at 33.14° N. Lat; 96.62° W. Long. Elevation is 630 feet.

History: The town was incorporated in 1958 with a population of 50. The town is adjacent to the 289-acre Heard Wildlife Sanctuary.
Population: 1,728 (1990); 2,644 (2000); 9,072 (2010); 11,108 (2015 projected); Race: 81.0% White, 4.0% Black, 6.3% Asian, 8.7% Other, 10.9% Hispanic of any race (2010); Density: 1,030.2 persons per square mile (2010); Average household size: 3.19 (2010); Median age: 34.0 (2010); Males per 100 females: 101.6 (2010); Marriage status: 16.7% never married, 71.1% now married, 3.7% widowed, 8.4% divorced (2005-2009 5-year est.); Foreign born: 6.5% (2005-2009 5-year est.); Ancestry (includes multiple ancestries): 25.1% German, 20.6% English, 13.1% Irish, 8.9% American, 5.6% Scottish (2005-2009 5-year est.).
Economy: Single-family building permits issued: 41 (2010); Multi-family building permits issued: 41 (2010); Employment by occupation: 25.6% management, 34.3% professional, 4.3% services, 28.0% sales, 0.0% farming, 5.6% construction, 2.3% production (2005-2009 5-year est.).
Income: Per capita income: $46,195 (2010); Median household income: $117,222 (2010); Average household income: $147,369 (2010); Percent of households with income of $100,000 or more: 59.8% (2010); Poverty rate: 1.5% (2005-2009 5-year est.).
Taxes: Total city taxes per capita: $479 (2007); City property taxes per capita: $294 (2007).
Education: Percent of population age 25 and over with: High school diploma (including GED) or higher: 94.0% (2010); Bachelor's degree or higher: 53.6% (2010); Master's degree or higher: 18.3% (2010).
School District(s)
Lovejoy ISD (PK-12)
    2009-10 Enrollment: 3,230 . . . . (469) 742-8000
Housing: Homeownership rate: 87.5% (2010); Median home value: $274,862 (2010); Median contract rent: $747 per month (2005-2009 5-year est.); Median year structure built: 2002 (2005-2009 5-year est.).
Transportation: Commute to work: 81.9% car, 1.2% public transportation, 1.1% walk, 12.5% work from home (2005-2009 5-year est.); Travel time to work: 20.8% less than 15 minutes, 17.8% 15 to 30 minutes, 27.0% 30 to 45 minutes, 20.2% 45 to 60 minutes, 14.2% 60 minutes or more (2005-2009 5-year est.)
Additional Information Contacts
Town of Fairview . . . . (972) 886-4234
    http://www.fairviewtexas.org

FARMERSVILLE (city). Covers a land area of 3.240 square miles and a water area of 0.172 square miles. Located at 33.16° N. Lat; 96.36° W. Long. Elevation is 653 feet.
Population: 2,704 (1990); 3,118 (2000); 3,495 (2010); 4,023 (2015 projected); Race: 83.2% White, 9.4% Black, 0.1% Asian, 7.3% Other, 22.8% Hispanic of any race (2010); Density: 1,078.6 persons per square mile (2010); Average household size: 2.71 (2010); Median age: 34.3 (2010); Males per 100 females: 93.2 (2010); Marriage status: 23.5% never married, 46.2% now married, 13.6% widowed, 16.7% divorced (2005-2009 5-year est.); Foreign born: 8.2% (2005-2009 5-year est.); Ancestry (includes multiple ancestries): 15.5% German, 10.0% American, 8.9% Irish, 7.7% French, 6.3% English (2005-2009 5-year est.).
Economy: Single-family building permits issued: 7 (2010); Multi-family building permits issued: 0 (2010); Employment by occupation: 9.1% management, 11.5% professional, 27.9% services, 25.0% sales, 0.0% farming, 9.5% construction, 15.2% production (2005-2009 5-year est.).
Income: Per capita income: $20,939 (2010); Median household income: $44,581 (2010); Average household income: $57,601 (2010); Percent of households with income of $100,000 or more: 13.0% (2010); Poverty rate: 15.0% (2005-2009 5-year est.).
Taxes: Total city taxes per capita: $350 (2007); City property taxes per capita: $190 (2007).
Education: Percent of population age 25 and over with: High school diploma (including GED) or higher: 73.3% (2010); Bachelor's degree or higher: 12.3% (2010); Master's degree or higher: 5.5% (2010).
School District(s)
Farmersville ISD (PK-12)
    2009-10 Enrollment: 1,457 . . . . (972) 782-6601
Housing: Homeownership rate: 64.6% (2010); Median home value: $80,419 (2010); Median contract rent: $492 per month (2005-2009 5-year est.); Median year structure built: 1972 (2005-2009 5-year est.).
Safety: Violent crime rate: 2.8 per 10,000 population; Property crime rate: 145.1 per 10,000 population (2009).
Newspapers: The Farmersville Times (Local news; Circulation 2,450); The Princeton Herald (Community news; Circulation 3,600)

Transportation: Commute to work: 96.7% car, 0.0% public transportation, 0.0% walk, 1.4% work from home (2005-2009 5-year est.); Travel time to work: 32.3% less than 15 minutes, 30.7% 15 to 30 minutes, 9.1% 30 to 45 minutes, 11.4% 45 to 60 minutes, 16.5% 60 minutes or more (2005-2009 5-year est.)
Additional Information Contacts
Farmersville Chamber of Commerce . . . . (972) 782-6533
    http://www.farmersvilletx.com/chamber

FRISCO (city). Covers a land area of 69.881 square miles and a water area of 0.163 square miles. Located at 33.14° N. Lat; 96.81° W. Long. Elevation is 696 feet.
Population: 6,767 (1990); 33,714 (2000); 114,030 (2010); 137,258 (2015 projected); Race: 79.7% White, 8.1% Black, 3.7% Asian, 8.5% Other, 13.7% Hispanic of any race (2010); Density: 1,631.8 persons per square mile (2010); Average household size: 2.86 (2010); Median age: 32.2 (2010); Males per 100 females: 100.3 (2010); Marriage status: 21.2% never married, 66.9% now married, 2.5% widowed, 9.4% divorced (2005-2009 5-year est.); Foreign born: 15.1% (2005-2009 5-year est.); Ancestry (includes multiple ancestries): 17.2% German, 12.5% Irish, 12.2% English, 6.1% American, 5.3% Italian (2005-2009 5-year est.).
Economy: Unemployment rate: 7.5% (June 2011); Total civilian labor force: 55,197 (June 2011); Single-family building permits issued: 1,284 (2010); Multi-family building permits issued: 0 (2010); Employment by occupation: 27.7% management, 25.7% professional, 10.4% services, 28.1% sales, 0.0% farming, 4.3% construction, 3.8% production (2005-2009 5-year est.).
Income: Per capita income: $40,083 (2010); Median household income: $95,132 (2010); Average household income: $114,642 (2010); Percent of households with income of $100,000 or more: 46.3% (2010); Poverty rate: 3.7% (2005-2009 5-year est.).
Taxes: Total city taxes per capita: $1,279 (2007); City property taxes per capita: $498 (2007).
Education: Percent of population age 25 and over with: High school diploma (including GED) or higher: 92.6% (2010); Bachelor's degree or higher: 46.2% (2010); Master's degree or higher: 12.5% (2010).
School District(s)
Frisco ISD (PK-12)
    2009-10 Enrollment: 33,973 . . . . (469) 633-6000
Lewisville ISD (PK-12)
    2009-10 Enrollment: 50,840 . . . . (469) 713-5200
Little Elm ISD (PK-12)
    2009-10 Enrollment: 6,112 . . . . (972) 292-1847
Housing: Homeownership rate: 83.4% (2010); Median home value: $201,643 (2010); Median contract rent: $897 per month (2005-2009 5-year est.); Median year structure built: 2001 (2005-2009 5-year est.).
Hospitals: Centennial Medical Center
Safety: Violent crime rate: 10.0 per 10,000 population; Property crime rate: 190.1 per 10,000 population (2009).
Newspapers: All About Frisco Monthly (Local news; Circulation 13,500); Frisco Enterprise (Local news; Circulation 4,500)
Transportation: Commute to work: 87.4% car, 0.3% public transportation, 0.9% walk, 9.0% work from home (2005-2009 5-year est.); Travel time to work: 21.9% less than 15 minutes, 30.7% 15 to 30 minutes, 25.6% 30 to 45 minutes, 12.4% 45 to 60 minutes, 9.4% 60 minutes or more (2005-2009 5-year est.)
Additional Information Contacts
City of Frisco . . . . (972) 292-5000
    http://www.ci.frisco.tx.us
Frisco Chamber of Commerce . . . . (972) 335-9522
    http://www.friscochamber.com

JOSEPHINE (city). Covers a land area of 1.630 square miles and a water area of 0 square miles. Located at 33.06° N. Lat; 96.31° W. Long. Elevation is 581 feet.
Population: 524 (1990); 594 (2000); 815 (2010); 993 (2015 projected); Race: 81.2% White, 1.3% Black, 0.2% Asian, 17.2% Other, 26.0% Hispanic of any race (2010); Density: 500.1 persons per square mile (2010); Average household size: 3.08 (2010); Median age: 33.8 (2010); Males per 100 females: 102.7 (2010); Marriage status: 13.3% never married, 67.2% now married, 2.1% widowed, 17.5% divorced (2005-2009 5-year est.); Foreign born: 0.0% (2005-2009 5-year est.); Ancestry (includes multiple ancestries): 22.5% Irish, 11.9% Dutch, 10.1% German, 9.4% American, 8.8% English (2005-2009 5-year est.).

Economy: Single-family building permits issued: 9 (2010); Multi-family building permits issued: 0 (2010); Employment by occupation: 26.8% management, 6.4% professional, 9.1% services, 33.6% sales, 1.3% farming, 10.7% construction, 12.1% production (2005-2009 5-year est.).
Income: Per capita income: $21,702 (2010); Median household income: $54,957 (2010); Average household income: $66,226 (2010); Percent of households with income of $100,000 or more: 15.8% (2010); Poverty rate: 0.0% (2005-2009 5-year est.).
Taxes: Total city taxes per capita: $318 (2007); City property taxes per capita: $122 (2007).
Education: Percent of population age 25 and over with: High school diploma (including GED) or higher: 80.2% (2010); Bachelor's degree or higher: 11.3% (2010); Master's degree or higher: 4.0% (2010).
Housing: Homeownership rate: 87.2% (2010); Median home value: $103,947 (2010); Median contract rent: $664 per month (2005-2009 5-year est.); Median year structure built: 1978 (2005-2009 5-year est.).
Transportation: Commute to work: 94.6% car, 0.0% public transportation, 5.4% walk, 0.0% work from home (2005-2009 5-year est.); Travel time to work: 27.5% less than 15 minutes, 24.8% 15 to 30 minutes, 8.4% 30 to 45 minutes, 21.1% 45 to 60 minutes, 18.1% 60 minutes or more (2005-2009 5-year est.)

LAVON (town). Covers a land area of 1.261 square miles and a water area of 0 square miles. Located at 33.02° N. Lat; 96.43° W. Long. Elevation is 525 feet.
Population: 309 (1990); 387 (2000); 541 (2010); 662 (2015 projected); Race: 87.8% White, 1.8% Black, 0.9% Asian, 9.4% Other, 15.9% Hispanic of any race (2010); Density: 429.0 persons per square mile (2010); Average household size: 2.92 (2010); Median age: 36.4 (2010); Males per 100 females: 104.2 (2010); Marriage status: 26.9% never married, 60.2% now married, 8.9% widowed, 4.1% divorced (2005-2009 5-year est.); Foreign born: 2.0% (2005-2009 5-year est.); Ancestry (includes multiple ancestries): 18.5% German, 13.9% American, 12.0% Irish, 10.5% Czech, 7.1% English (2005-2009 5-year est.).
Economy: Employment by occupation: 19.6% management, 24.6% professional, 4.7% services, 34.3% sales, 0.0% farming, 9.5% construction, 7.2% production (2005-2009 5-year est.).
Income: Per capita income: $23,706 (2010); Median household income: $57,108 (2010); Average household income: $70,297 (2010); Percent of households with income of $100,000 or more: 16.8% (2010); Poverty rate: 3.9% (2005-2009 5-year est.).
Taxes: Total city taxes per capita: $869 (2007); City property taxes per capita: $688 (2007).
Education: Percent of population age 25 and over with: High school diploma (including GED) or higher: 81.6% (2010); Bachelor's degree or higher: 15.3% (2010); Master's degree or higher: 3.1% (2010).

School District(s)
Community ISD (PK-12)
   2009-10 Enrollment: 1,633 . . . . (972) 843-8400
Housing: Homeownership rate: 88.6% (2010); Median home value: $124,468 (2010); Median contract rent: $975 per month (2005-2009 5-year est.); Median year structure built: 2002 (2005-2009 5-year est.).
Safety: Violent crime rate: 70.4 per 10,000 population; Property crime rate: 868.5 per 10,000 population (2009).
Transportation: Commute to work: 91.0% car, 2.3% public transportation, 0.0% walk, 5.0% work from home (2005-2009 5-year est.); Travel time to work: 10.9% less than 15 minutes, 18.2% 15 to 30 minutes, 23.2% 30 to 45 minutes, 29.5% 45 to 60 minutes, 18.2% 60 minutes or more (2005-2009 5-year est.)

LOWRY CROSSING (city). Covers a land area of 2.788 square miles and a water area of 0 square miles. Located at 33.16° N. Lat; 96.54° W. Long. Elevation is 512 feet.
Population: 907 (1990); 1,229 (2000); 1,895 (2010); 2,279 (2015 projected); Race: 79.5% White, 1.9% Black, 0.7% Asian, 17.9% Other, 25.1% Hispanic of any race (2010); Density: 679.6 persons per square mile (2010); Average household size: 2.89 (2010); Median age: 34.8 (2010); Males per 100 females: 103.1 (2010); Marriage status: 20.6% never married, 69.4% now married, 2.3% widowed, 7.7% divorced (2005-2009 5-year est.); Foreign born: 7.9% (2005-2009 5-year est.); Ancestry (includes multiple ancestries): 15.3% English, 15.1% German, 11.2% American, 10.2% Irish, 4.4% Scottish (2005-2009 5-year est.).
Economy: Single-family building permits issued: 1 (2010); Multi-family building permits issued: 0 (2010); Employment by occupation: 11.2%

management, 26.7% professional, 9.7% services, 22.8% sales, 0.0% farming, 11.9% construction, 17.8% production (2005-2009 5-year est.).
Income: Per capita income: $27,639 (2010); Median household income: $63,908 (2010); Average household income: $79,790 (2010); Percent of households with income of $100,000 or more: 25.8% (2010); Poverty rate: 5.6% (2005-2009 5-year est.).
Taxes: Total city taxes per capita: $69 (2007); City property taxes per capita: $0 (2007).
Education: Percent of population age 25 and over with: High school diploma (including GED) or higher: 78.6% (2010); Bachelor's degree or higher: 16.0% (2010); Master's degree or higher: 4.8% (2010).
Housing: Homeownership rate: 86.3% (2010); Median home value: $111,677 (2010); Median contract rent: $930 per month (2005-2009 5-year est.); Median year structure built: 1991 (2005-2009 5-year est.).
Transportation: Commute to work: 88.7% car, 0.0% public transportation, 0.0% walk, 9.1% work from home (2005-2009 5-year est.); Travel time to work: 18.7% less than 15 minutes, 30.1% 15 to 30 minutes, 18.7% 30 to 45 minutes, 15.2% 45 to 60 minutes, 17.2% 60 minutes or more (2005-2009 5-year est.)

Additional Information Contacts
City of Lowry Crossing . . . . (972) 542-8678
   http://www.lowrycrossingtexas.org

LUCAS (city). Covers a land area of 9.195 square miles and a water area of 0.004 square miles. Located at 33.10° N. Lat; 96.57° W. Long. Elevation is 568 feet.
History: Before 1841, there were no white people in Collin County. Just prior to settlement by the white man, Lucas was inhabited by Indians, mainly Caddo, Kickapoo, Cherokee, Delaware and Tonkawa who were peaceful farming/hunting tribes. The Delaware had a village in the vicinity of Fitzhugh Mills. Beginning with one of the earliest men, the Clovis man, ten thousand years ago, many different Indian tribes have inhabited the region over the centuries, changing and morphing as tribes conquered or integrated with other tribes.
Population: 2,550 (1990); 2,890 (2000); 5,984 (2010); 7,379 (2015 projected); Race: 90.4% White, 1.9% Black, 1.5% Asian, 6.2% Other, 5.7% Hispanic of any race (2010); Density: 650.8 persons per square mile (2010); Average household size: 3.03 (2010); Median age: 40.1 (2010); Males per 100 females: 102.2 (2010); Marriage status: 18.3% never married, 71.5% now married, 2.8% widowed, 7.4% divorced (2005-2009 5-year est.); Foreign born: 7.8% (2005-2009 5-year est.); Ancestry (includes multiple ancestries): 19.9% German, 17.3% Irish, 12.9% American, 10.8% English, 8.9% French (2005-2009 5-year est.).
Economy: Single-family building permits issued: 75 (2010); Multi-family building permits issued: 0 (2010); Employment by occupation: 28.1% management, 32.9% professional, 7.9% services, 22.3% sales, 0.7% farming, 5.6% construction, 2.6% production (2005-2009 5-year est.).
Income: Per capita income: $43,557 (2010); Median household income: $109,302 (2010); Average household income: $132,108 (2010); Percent of households with income of $100,000 or more: 54.9% (2010); Poverty rate: 6.0% (2005-2009 5-year est.).
Taxes: Total city taxes per capita: $455 (2007); City property taxes per capita: $318 (2007).
Education: Percent of population age 25 and over with: High school diploma (including GED) or higher: 94.9% (2010); Bachelor's degree or higher: 42.1% (2010); Master's degree or higher: 13.2% (2010).

School District(s)
Lovejoy ISD (PK-12)
   2009-10 Enrollment: 3,230 . . . . (469) 742-8000
Housing: Homeownership rate: 92.5% (2010); Median home value: $247,505 (2010); Median contract rent: $971 per month (2005-2009 5-year est.); Median year structure built: 1991 (2005-2009 5-year est.).
Transportation: Commute to work: 85.3% car, 1.1% public transportation, 1.1% walk, 11.2% work from home (2005-2009 5-year est.); Travel time to work: 12.9% less than 15 minutes, 32.3% 15 to 30 minutes, 33.2% 30 to 45 minutes, 13.7% 45 to 60 minutes, 7.9% 60 minutes or more (2005-2009 5-year est.)

Additional Information Contacts
City of Lucas . . . . (972) 727-8999
   http://www.lucastexas.us

MCKINNEY (city). County seat. Covers a land area of 58.027 square miles and a water area of 0.476 square miles. Located at 33.19° N. Lat; 96.64° W. Long. Elevation is 630 feet.

History: McKinney was named for Collin McKinney, Texas founder, for whom Collin County also is named. McKinney developed around a cotton textile plant.
Population: 21,807 (1990); 54,369 (2000); 130,459 (2010); 158,661 (2015 projected); Race: 75.9% White, 8.3% Black, 2.8% Asian, 13.0% Other, 18.1% Hispanic of any race (2010); Density: 2,248.3 persons per square mile (2010); Average household size: 2.96 (2010); Median age: 31.8 (2010); Males per 100 females: 101.2 (2010); Marriage status: 25.1% never married, 61.0% now married, 3.7% widowed, 10.3% divorced (2005-2009 5-year est.); Foreign born: 12.4% (2005-2009 5-year est.); Ancestry (includes multiple ancestries): 16.1% German, 11.2% Irish, 11.1% English, 10.1% American, 3.8% Italian (2005-2009 5-year est.).
Economy: Unemployment rate: 9.0% (June 2011); Total civilian labor force: 63,515 (June 2011); Single-family building permits issued: 1,051 (2010); Multi-family building permits issued: 0 (2010); Employment by occupation: 21.4% management, 24.2% professional, 12.6% services, 28.7% sales, 0.5% farming, 6.0% construction, 6.6% production (2005-2009 5-year est.).
Income: Per capita income: $36,765 (2010); Median household income: $86,813 (2010); Average household income: $109,865 (2010); Percent of households with income of $100,000 or more: 41.0% (2010); Poverty rate: 9.7% (2005-2009 5-year est.).
Taxes: Total city taxes per capita: $815 (2007); City property taxes per capita: $402 (2007).
Education: Percent of population age 25 and over with: High school diploma (including GED) or higher: 89.1% (2010); Bachelor's degree or higher: 45.9% (2010); Master's degree or higher: 12.8% (2010).

School District(s)

Celina ISD (PK-12)
    2009-10 Enrollment: 1,904 . . . . (469) 742-9100
Frisco ISD (PK-12)
    2009-10 Enrollment: 33,973 . . . . (469) 633-6000
Life School (KG-12)
    2009-10 Enrollment: 3,434 . . . . (972) 274-7900
Lovejoy ISD (PK-12)
    2009-10 Enrollment: 3,230 . . . . (469) 742-8000
McKinney ISD (PK-12)
    2009-10 Enrollment: 23,933 . . . . (469) 742-4070
Melissa ISD (PK-12)
    2009-10 Enrollment: 1,378 . . . . (972) 837-2411
Prosper ISD (PK-12)
    2009-10 Enrollment: 3,637 . . . . (469) 219-2000
Responsive Education Solutions (KG-12)
    2009-10 Enrollment: 5,022 . . . . (972) 316-3663

Two-year College(s)

Collin County Community College District (Public)
    Fall 2009 Enrollment: 24,872. (972) 881-5790
    2010-11 Tuition: In-state $1,864; Out-of-state $3,514
Housing: Homeownership rate: 77.1% (2010); Median home value: $197,258 (2010); Median contract rent: $708 per month (2005-2009 5-year est.); Median year structure built: 2000 (2005-2009 5-year est.).
Hospitals: Medical Center of McKinney (259 beds); Medical Center of McKinney (200 beds)
Safety: Violent crime rate: 18.5 per 10,000 population; Property crime rate: 252.7 per 10,000 population (2009).
Newspapers: McKinney Courier-Gazette (Local news; Circulation 8,500)
Transportation: Commute to work: 88.9% car, 1.0% public transportation, 1.2% walk, 6.0% work from home (2005-2009 5-year est.); Travel time to work: 23.4% less than 15 minutes, 26.6% 15 to 30 minutes, 24.4% 30 to 45 minutes, 14.1% 45 to 60 minutes, 11.5% 60 minutes or more (2005-2009 5-year est.)
Airports: Collin County Regional at McKinney (general aviation)
Additional Information Contacts
City of McKinney . . . . (972) 547-7500
    http://www.mckinneytexas.org
McKinney Chamber of Commerce. . . . . (972) 542-0163
    http://www.mckinneytx.org

MELISSA (city). Covers a land area of 4.586 square miles and a water area of 0 square miles. Located at 33.28° N. Lat; 96.57° W. Long. Elevation is 679 feet.
Population: 868 (1990); 1,350 (2000); 3,056 (2010); 3,746 (2015 projected); Race: 83.9% White, 1.0% Black, 0.1% Asian, 14.9% Other, 20.6% Hispanic of any race (2010); Density: 666.4 persons per square mile (2010); Average household size: 2.87 (2010); Median age: 35.1 (2010);

Males per 100 females: 102.5 (2010); Marriage status: 15.0% never married, 68.3% now married, 4.5% widowed, 12.2% divorced (2005-2009 5-year est.); Foreign born: 3.9% (2005-2009 5-year est.); Ancestry (includes multiple ancestries): 27.9% German, 14.2% Irish, 13.1% American, 5.2% English, 5.0% Italian (2005-2009 5-year est.).
Economy: Single-family building permits issued: 121 (2010); Multi-family building permits issued: 0 (2010); Employment by occupation: 18.5% management, 21.5% professional, 13.5% services, 27.5% sales, 0.0% farming, 9.5% construction, 9.5% production (2005-2009 5-year est.).
Income: Per capita income: $36,234 (2010); Median household income: $75,342 (2010); Average household income: $104,136 (2010); Percent of households with income of $100,000 or more: 33.1% (2010); Poverty rate: 7.3% (2005-2009 5-year est.).
Taxes: Total city taxes per capita: $783 (2007); City property taxes per capita: $339 (2007).
Education: Percent of population age 25 and over with: High school diploma (including GED) or higher: 81.7% (2010); Bachelor's degree or higher: 22.7% (2010); Master's degree or higher: 7.4% (2010).

School District(s)

Melissa ISD (PK-12)
    2009-10 Enrollment: 1,378 . . . . (972) 837-2411
Housing: Homeownership rate: 78.8% (2010); Median home value: $117,448 (2010); Median contract rent: $920 per month (2005-2009 5-year est.); Median year structure built: 2003 (2005-2009 5-year est.).
Safety: Violent crime rate: 8.2 per 10,000 population; Property crime rate: 162.6 per 10,000 population (2009).
Transportation: Commute to work: 90.3% car, 0.2% public transportation, 2.1% walk, 7.2% work from home (2005-2009 5-year est.); Travel time to work: 18.7% less than 15 minutes, 24.1% 15 to 30 minutes, 22.9% 30 to 45 minutes, 17.5% 45 to 60 minutes, 16.7% 60 minutes or more (2005-2009 5-year est.)

MURPHY (city). Covers a land area of 5.255 square miles and a water area of 0 square miles. Located at 33.01° N. Lat; 96.60° W. Long. Elevation is 581 feet.
History: The original townsite, located on land owned by C. A. McMillen, was first called Old Decator, after McMillen's hometown, and later, Maxwell's Branch. When the St. Louis Southwestern Railway reached the area in 1888, the residents renamed the town Murphy, in honor of William Murphy, who provided land for the tracks and the construction of a depot.
Population: 1,620 (1990); 3,099 (2000); 13,383 (2010); 16,122 (2015 projected); Race: 65.0% White, 12.9% Black, 13.5% Asian, 8.6% Other, 12.7% Hispanic of any race (2010); Density: 2,546.8 persons per square mile (2010); Average household size: 2.93 (2010); Median age: 35.8 (2010); Males per 100 females: 98.9 (2010); Marriage status: 17.6% never married, 75.8% now married, 1.9% widowed, 4.6% divorced (2005-2009 5-year est.); Foreign born: 23.2% (2005-2009 5-year est.); Ancestry (includes multiple ancestries): 17.8% German, 8.7% English, 8.0% Irish, 5.1% American, 2.5% Scottish (2005-2009 5-year est.).
Economy: Single-family building permits issued: 113 (2010); Multi-family building permits issued: 0 (2010); Employment by occupation: 27.0% management, 34.3% professional, 9.0% services, 20.3% sales, 0.0% farming, 2.4% construction, 7.0% production (2005-2009 5-year est.).
Income: Per capita income: $37,230 (2010); Median household income: $91,167 (2010); Average household income: $109,045 (2010); Percent of households with income of $100,000 or more: 43.4% (2010); Poverty rate: 3.9% (2005-2009 5-year est.).
Taxes: Total city taxes per capita: $759 (2007); City property taxes per capita: $354 (2007).
Education: Percent of population age 25 and over with: High school diploma (including GED) or higher: 93.4% (2010); Bachelor's degree or higher: 44.9% (2010); Master's degree or higher: 15.2% (2010).

School District(s)

Plano ISD (PK-12)
    2009-10 Enrollment: 54,939 . . . . (469) 752-8100
Housing: Homeownership rate: 90.9% (2010); Median home value: $224,684 (2010); Median contract rent: $1,571 per month (2005-2009 5-year est.); Median year structure built: 2003 (2005-2009 5-year est.).
Safety: Violent crime rate: 5.7 per 10,000 population; Property crime rate: 81.9 per 10,000 population (2009).
Transportation: Commute to work: 88.8% car, 2.4% public transportation, 0.2% walk, 7.7% work from home (2005-2009 5-year est.); Travel time to work: 13.6% less than 15 minutes, 34.6% 15 to 30 minutes, 29.7% 30 to 45 minutes, 16.5% 45 to 60 minutes, 5.6% 60 minutes or more (2005-2009 5-year est.)

Additional Information Contacts
City of Murphy . . . . (972) 468-4000
   http://www.murphytx.org

NEVADA (city). Covers a land area of 1.158 square miles and a water area of 0 square miles. Located at 33.04° N. Lat; 96.37° W. Long. Elevation is 643 feet.
Population: 486 (1990); 563 (2000); 787 (2010); 962 (2015 projected); Race: 86.9% White, 1.8% Black, 0.8% Asian, 10.5% Other, 17.3% Hispanic of any race (2010); Density: 679.4 persons per square mile (2010); Average household size: 2.95 (2010); Median age: 35.7 (2010); Males per 100 females: 106.6 (2010); Marriage status: 23.0% never married, 58.7% now married, 4.7% widowed, 13.7% divorced (2005-2009 5-year est.); Foreign born: 2.0% (2005-2009 5-year est.); Ancestry (includes multiple ancestries): 16.1% Irish, 12.8% German, 5.8% American, 4.8% Scotch-Irish, 4.4% French (2005-2009 5-year est.).
Economy: Single-family building permits issued: 2 (2010); Multi-family building permits issued: 0 (2010); Employment by occupation: 12.5% management, 22.6% professional, 7.8% services, 29.6% sales, 0.0% farming, 16.1% construction, 11.4% production (2005-2009 5-year est.).
Income: Per capita income: $23,461 (2010); Median household income: $56,514 (2010); Average household income: $68,361 (2010); Percent of households with income of $100,000 or more: 16.1% (2010); Poverty rate: 3.7% (2005-2009 5-year est.).
Taxes: Total city taxes per capita: $175 (2007); City property taxes per capita: $68 (2007).
Education: Percent of population age 25 and over with: High school diploma (including GED) or higher: 82.0% (2010); Bachelor's degree or higher: 15.1% (2010); Master's degree or higher: 3.7% (2010).
School District(s)
Community ISD (PK-12)
   2009-10 Enrollment: 1,633 . . . . (972) 843-8400
Housing: Homeownership rate: 88.4% (2010); Median home value: $121,970 (2010); Median contract rent: $664 per month (2005-2009 5-year est.); Median year structure built: 1987 (2005-2009 5-year est.).
Transportation: Commute to work: 93.0% car, 0.0% public transportation, 0.0% walk, 7.0% work from home (2005-2009 5-year est.); Travel time to work: 13.2% less than 15 minutes, 16.5% 15 to 30 minutes, 23.7% 30 to 45 minutes, 27.9% 45 to 60 minutes, 18.6% 60 minutes or more (2005-2009 5-year est.)

NEW HOPE (town). Covers a land area of 1.437 square miles and a water area of <.001 square miles. Located at 33.21° N. Lat; 96.56° W. Long. Elevation is 600 feet.
Population: 601 (1990); 662 (2000); 956 (2010); 1,165 (2015 projected); Race: 89.9% White, 0.2% Black, 0.5% Asian, 9.4% Other, 13.4% Hispanic of any race (2010); Density: 665.4 persons per square mile (2010); Average household size: 2.83 (2010); Median age: 37.5 (2010); Males per 100 females: 104.7 (2010); Marriage status: 22.1% never married, 63.3% now married, 4.7% widowed, 9.8% divorced (2005-2009 5-year est.); Foreign born: 7.1% (2005-2009 5-year est.); Ancestry (includes multiple ancestries): 14.8% English, 12.5% German, 12.4% American, 11.8% Scottish, 9.4% Irish (2005-2009 5-year est.).
Economy: Employment by occupation: 11.6% management, 21.0% professional, 9.8% services, 31.1% sales, 0.0% farming, 9.1% construction, 17.4% production (2005-2009 5-year est.).
Income: Per capita income: $25,938 (2010); Median household income: $62,209 (2010); Average household income: $73,521 (2010); Percent of households with income of $100,000 or more: 21.3% (2010); Poverty rate: 10.4% (2005-2009 5-year est.).
Taxes: Total city taxes per capita: $503 (2007); City property taxes per capita: $160 (2007).
Education: Percent of population age 25 and over with: High school diploma (including GED) or higher: 81.5% (2010); Bachelor's degree or higher: 16.5% (2010); Master's degree or higher: 3.9% (2010).
Housing: Homeownership rate: 84.6% (2010); Median home value: $120,000 (2010); Median contract rent: $644 per month (2005-2009 5-year est.); Median year structure built: 1983 (2005-2009 5-year est.).
Transportation: Commute to work: 95.8% car, 0.0% public transportation, 0.0% walk, 4.2% work from home (2005-2009 5-year est.); Travel time to work: 24.2% less than 15 minutes, 22.6% 15 to 30 minutes, 23.2% 30 to 45 minutes, 20.5% 45 to 60 minutes, 9.4% 60 minutes or more (2005-2009 5-year est.)

PARKER (city). Covers a land area of 5.187 square miles and a water area of 0 square miles. Located at 33.05° N. Lat; 96.62° W. Long. Elevation is 604 feet.
History: Some of the families that came to farm and raise their children were the Dillehays, Gregorys, Hogges, McCrearys, and Parkers. John C. Parker was the first known settler. Our community was named for his son, William C. Parker. Southfork Ranch, known around the world as the home of J.R Ewing in the TV show "Dallas" is located in Parker.
Population: 1,058 (1990); 1,379 (2000); 1,883 (2010); 2,314 (2015 projected); Race: 66.6% White, 13.5% Black, 9.5% Asian, 10.4% Other, 14.7% Hispanic of any race (2010); Density: 363.0 persons per square mile (2010); Average household size: 3.01 (2010); Median age: 35.7 (2010); Males per 100 females: 101.6 (2010); Marriage status: 16.9% never married, 74.4% now married, 4.9% widowed, 3.9% divorced (2005-2009 5-year est.); Foreign born: 16.7% (2005-2009 5-year est.); Ancestry (includes multiple ancestries): 15.1% German, 14.3% Irish, 11.8% English, 6.3% American, 5.5% French (2005-2009 5-year est.).
Economy: Single-family building permits issued: 25 (2010); Multi-family building permits issued: 0 (2010); Employment by occupation: 21.0% management, 35.1% professional, 9.3% services, 21.8% sales, 0.0% farming, 4.5% construction, 8.3% production (2005-2009 5-year est.).
Income: Per capita income: $40,754 (2010); Median household income: $99,496 (2010); Average household income: $122,772 (2010); Percent of households with income of $100,000 or more: 49.6% (2010); Poverty rate: 4.7% (2005-2009 5-year est.).
Taxes: Total city taxes per capita: $682 (2007); City property taxes per capita: $451 (2007).
Education: Percent of population age 25 and over with: High school diploma (including GED) or higher: 95.1% (2010); Bachelor's degree or higher: 48.7% (2010); Master's degree or higher: 14.6% (2010).
School District(s)
Allen ISD (PK-12)
   2009-10 Enrollment: 18,242 . . . . (972) 727-0511
Housing: Homeownership rate: 94.9% (2010); Median home value: $226,359 (2010); Median contract rent: $343 per month (2005-2009 5-year est.); Median year structure built: 1996 (2005-2009 5-year est.).
Safety: Violent crime rate: 0.0 per 10,000 population; Property crime rate: 78.3 per 10,000 population (2009).
Transportation: Commute to work: 89.8% car, 0.8% public transportation, 0.1% walk, 8.4% work from home (2005-2009 5-year est.); Travel time to work: 12.2% less than 15 minutes, 46.3% 15 to 30 minutes, 22.2% 30 to 45 minutes, 14.3% 45 to 60 minutes, 4.9% 60 minutes or more (2005-2009 5-year est.)

PLANO (city). Covers a land area of 71.566 square miles and a water area of 0.062 square miles. Located at 33.05° N. Lat; 96.74° W. Long. Elevation is 666 feet.
Population: 128,507 (1990); 222,030 (2000); 280,422 (2010); 325,345 (2015 projected); Race: 64.0% White, 8.7% Black, 17.4% Asian, 9.9% Other, 14.9% Hispanic of any race (2010); Density: 3,918.4 persons per square mile (2010); Average household size: 2.65 (2010); Median age: 35.5 (2010); Males per 100 females: 100.4 (2010); Marriage status: 26.2% never married, 60.4% now married, 3.8% widowed, 9.6% divorced (2005-2009 5-year est.); Foreign born: 21.8% (2005-2009 5-year est.); Ancestry (includes multiple ancestries): 14.9% German, 10.9% Irish, 10.2% English, 7.6% American, 3.7% Italian (2005-2009 5-year est.).
Economy: Unemployment rate: 7.5% (June 2011); Total civilian labor force: 149,182 (June 2011); Single-family building permits issued: 311 (2010); Multi-family building permits issued: 303 (2010); Employment by occupation: 22.9% management, 28.0% professional, 10.8% services, 28.2% sales, 0.0% farming, 5.2% construction, 4.9% production (2005-2009 5-year est.).
Income: Per capita income: $42,764 (2010); Median household income: $86,954 (2010); Average household income: $113,481 (2010); Percent of households with income of $100,000 or more: 42.3% (2010); Poverty rate: 6.0% (2005-2009 5-year est.).
Taxes: Total city taxes per capita: $798 (2007); City property taxes per capita: $413 (2007).
Education: Percent of population age 25 and over with: High school diploma (including GED) or higher: 94.2% (2010); Bachelor's degree or higher: 54.1% (2010); Master's degree or higher: 18.9% (2010).
School District(s)
Anna ISD (PK-12)
   2009-10 Enrollment: 2,246 . . . . (972) 924-1000

Frisco ISD (PK-12)
    2009-10 Enrollment: 33,973 . . . . (469) 633-6000
Plano ISD (PK-12)
    2009-10 Enrollment: 54,939 . . . . (469) 752-8100
Housing: Homeownership rate: 65.0% (2010); Median home value: $205,917 (2010); Median contract rent: $798 per month (2005-2009 5-year est.); Median year structure built: 1990 (2005-2009 5-year est.).
Hospitals: Baylor Regional Medical Center at Plano; Medical Center of Plano (427 beds); Presbyterian Hospital of Plano (370 beds); Presbyterian Plano Center for Diagnostics & Surgery
Safety: Violent crime rate: 17.0 per 10,000 population; Property crime rate: 293.1 per 10,000 population (2009).
Newspapers: The Dallas Morning News Collin County Edition (Local news); Inside Collin County Business (Regional news; Circulation 10,000); Plano Insider (Community news); Plano Star Courier (Local news; Circulation 11,000)
Transportation: Commute to work: 89.3% car, 1.8% public transportation, 0.9% walk, 6.1% work from home (2005-2009 5-year est.); Travel time to work: 20.9% less than 15 minutes, 38.9% 15 to 30 minutes, 24.0% 30 to 45 minutes, 9.4% 45 to 60 minutes, 6.8% 60 minutes or more (2005-2009 5-year est.)
Additional Information Contacts
City of Plano. . . . . (972) 941-7000
    http://www.plano.gov
Plano Chamber of Commerce . . . . (972) 424-7547
    http://www.planochamber.org

PRINCETON (city).
Covers a land area of 4.338 square miles and a water area of 0.005 square miles. Located at 33.18° N. Lat; 96.50° W. Long. Elevation is 574 feet.
Population: 2,562 (1990); 3,477 (2000); 4,129 (2010); 4,993 (2015 projected); Race: 85.1% White, 1.3% Black, 0.3% Asian, 13.4% Other, 18.3% Hispanic of any race (2010); Density: 951.7 persons per square mile (2010); Average household size: 2.66 (2010); Median age: 35.2 (2010); Males per 100 females: 97.7 (2010); Marriage status: 23.1% never married, 59.2% now married, 8.1% widowed, 9.7% divorced (2005-2009 5-year est.); Foreign born: 7.2% (2005-2009 5-year est.); Ancestry (includes multiple ancestries): 17.9% American, 17.0% German, 13.6% Irish, 6.1% English, 4.4% Italian (2005-2009 5-year est.).
Economy: Single-family building permits issued: 84 (2010); Multi-family building permits issued: 14 (2010); Employment by occupation: 9.6% management, 14.5% professional, 14.5% services, 31.3% sales, 0.0% farming, 17.2% construction, 12.9% production (2005-2009 5-year est.).
Income: Per capita income: $19,576 (2010); Median household income: $44,730 (2010); Average household income: $52,033 (2010); Percent of households with income of $100,000 or more: 9.9% (2010); Poverty rate: 5.9% (2005-2009 5-year est.).
Taxes: Total city taxes per capita: $529 (2007); City property taxes per capita: $287 (2007).
Education: Percent of population age 25 and over with: High school diploma (including GED) or higher: 73.9% (2010); Bachelor's degree or higher: 12.2% (2010); Master's degree or higher: 5.1% (2010).
School District(s)
Princeton ISD (PK-12)
    2009-10 Enrollment: 2,996 . . . . (469) 952-5400
Housing: Homeownership rate: 63.2% (2010); Median home value: $84,979 (2010); Median contract rent: $711 per month (2005-2009 5-year est.); Median year structure built: 1993 (2005-2009 5-year est.).
Safety: Violent crime rate: 27.6 per 10,000 population; Property crime rate: 191.7 per 10,000 population (2009).
Transportation: Commute to work: 95.2% car, 0.9% public transportation, 0.6% walk, 2.8% work from home (2005-2009 5-year est.); Travel time to work: 13.3% less than 15 minutes, 34.8% 15 to 30 minutes, 22.3% 30 to 45 minutes, 19.4% 45 to 60 minutes, 10.2% 60 minutes or more (2005-2009 5-year est.)
Additional Information Contacts
Princeton Area Chamber of Commerce. . . . . (972) 736-6462
    http://www.princetontxchamber.com

PROSPER (town).
Covers a land area of 4.950 square miles and a water area of 0 square miles. Located at 33.23° N. Lat; 96.79° W. Long. Elevation is 682 feet.
Population: 1,259 (1990); 2,097 (2000); 5,970 (2010); 7,398 (2015 projected); Race: 91.5% White, 0.7% Black, 0.6% Asian, 7.2% Other, 24.7% Hispanic of any race (2010); Density: 1,206.0 persons per square

mile (2010); Average household size: 3.13 (2010); Median age: 32.4 (2010); Males per 100 females: 103.7 (2010); Marriage status: 20.8% never married, 71.2% now married, 1.8% widowed, 6.3% divorced (2005-2009 5-year est.); Foreign born: 6.7% (2005-2009 5-year est.); Ancestry (includes multiple ancestries): 22.3% German, 15.0% English, 12.1% Irish, 9.5% American, 4.8% French (2005-2009 5-year est.).
Economy: Single-family building permits issued: 280 (2010); Multi-family building permits issued: 0 (2010); Employment by occupation: 29.2% management, 20.2% professional, 9.4% services, 26.6% sales, 1.0% farming, 6.0% construction, 7.6% production (2005-2009 5-year est.).
Income: Per capita income: $34,343 (2010); Median household income: $81,591 (2010); Average household income: $107,600 (2010); Percent of households with income of $100,000 or more: 39.4% (2010); Poverty rate: 4.1% (2005-2009 5-year est.).
Taxes: Total city taxes per capita: $1,224 (2007); City property taxes per capita: $325 (2007).
Education: Percent of population age 25 and over with: High school diploma (including GED) or higher: 85.5% (2010); Bachelor's degree or higher: 30.9% (2010); Master's degree or higher: 9.8% (2010).
School District(s)
Prosper ISD (PK-12)
    2009-10 Enrollment: 3,637 . . . . (469) 219-2000
Housing: Homeownership rate: 82.3% (2010); Median home value: $182,949 (2010); Median contract rent: $1,177 per month (2005-2009 5-year est.); Median year structure built: 2003 (2005-2009 5-year est.).
Safety: Violent crime rate: 2.5 per 10,000 population; Property crime rate: 114.9 per 10,000 population (2009).
Transportation: Commute to work: 91.4% car, 0.1% public transportation, 0.0% walk, 7.5% work from home (2005-2009 5-year est.); Travel time to work: 17.9% less than 15 minutes, 25.7% 15 to 30 minutes, 24.6% 30 to 45 minutes, 20.6% 45 to 60 minutes, 11.2% 60 minutes or more (2005-2009 5-year est.)
Additional Information Contacts
Town of Prosper. . . . . (972) 346-2640
    http://www.prospertx.gov

SAINT PAUL (town).
Covers a land area of 1.608 square miles and a water area of 0 square miles. Located at 33.04° N. Lat; 96.54° W. Long. Elevation is 564 feet.
Population: 574 (1990); 630 (2000); 1,489 (2010); 1,822 (2015 projected); Race: 81.1% White, 7.1% Black, 1.9% Asian, 9.9% Other, 16.1% Hispanic of any race (2010); Density: 926.3 persons per square mile (2010); Average household size: 3.04 (2010); Median age: 35.7 (2010); Males per 100 females: 101.8 (2010); Marriage status: 18.2% never married, 71.1% now married, 1.7% widowed, 9.0% divorced (2005-2009 5-year est.); Foreign born: 4.3% (2005-2009 5-year est.); Ancestry (includes multiple ancestries): 16.0% German, 9.2% Irish, 7.7% English, 7.6% American, 2.5% Scotch-Irish (2005-2009 5-year est.).
Economy: Single-family building permits issued: 0 (2010); Multi-family building permits issued: 0 (2010); Employment by occupation: 18.5% management, 28.2% professional, 4.7% services, 32.9% sales, 0.0% farming, 6.2% construction, 9.4% production (2005-2009 5-year est.).
Income: Per capita income: $28,765 (2010); Median household income: $72,524 (2010); Average household income: $87,771 (2010); Percent of households with income of $100,000 or more: 29.7% (2010); Poverty rate: 4.9% (2005-2009 5-year est.).
Taxes: Total city taxes per capita: $369 (2007); City property taxes per capita: $284 (2007).
Education: Percent of population age 25 and over with: High school diploma (including GED) or higher: 89.5% (2010); Bachelor's degree or higher: 22.7% (2010); Master's degree or higher: 5.4% (2010).
Housing: Homeownership rate: 91.8% (2010); Median home value: $136,328 (2010); Median contract rent: $837 per month (2005-2009 5-year est.); Median year structure built: 1993 (2005-2009 5-year est.).
Transportation: Commute to work: 84.4% car, 9.3% public transportation, 0.0% walk, 6.3% work from home (2005-2009 5-year est.); Travel time to work: 11.8% less than 15 minutes, 31.6% 15 to 30 minutes, 33.2% 30 to 45 minutes, 14.4% 45 to 60 minutes, 8.9% 60 minutes or more (2005-2009 5-year est.)

WESTMINSTER (city).
Covers a land area of 1.816 square miles and a water area of 0.010 square miles. Located at 33.35° N. Lat; 96.44° W. Long. Elevation is 699 feet.
Population: 368 (1990); 390 (2000); 373 (2010); 399 (2015 projected); Race: 92.2% White, 0.8% Black, 0.5% Asian, 6.4% Other, 10.7% Hispanic

of any race (2010); Density: 205.4 persons per square mile (2010); Average household size: 2.76 (2010); Median age: 38.4 (2010); Males per 100 females: 96.3 (2010); Marriage status: n/a never married, n/a now married, n/a widowed, n/a divorced (2005-2009 5-year est.); Foreign born: n/a (2005-2009 5-year est.); Ancestry (includes multiple ancestries): n/a (2005-2009 5-year est.).
Economy: Employment by occupation: n/a management, n/a professional, n/a services, n/a sales, n/a farming, n/a construction, n/a production (2005-2009 5-year est.).
Income: Per capita income: $26,214 (2010); Median household income: $55,093 (2010); Average household income: $73,685 (2010); Percent of households with income of $100,000 or more: 20.0% (2010); Poverty rate: n/a (2005-2009 5-year est.).
Education: Percent of population age 25 and over with: High school diploma (including GED) or higher: 81.9% (2010); Bachelor's degree or higher: 12.9% (2010); Master's degree or higher: 3.6% (2010).
Housing: Homeownership rate: 85.9% (2010); Median home value: $97,500 (2010); Median contract rent: n/a per month (2005-2009 5-year est.); Median year structure built: n/a (2005-2009 5-year est.).
Transportation: Commute to work: n/a car, n/a public transportation, n/a walk, n/a work from home (2005-2009 5-year est.); Travel time to work: n/a less than 15 minutes, n/a 15 to 30 minutes, n/a 30 to 45 minutes, n/a 45 to 60 minutes, n/a 60 minutes or more (2005-2009 5-year est.)

WESTON (city). Covers a land area of 4.640 square miles and a water area of 0 square miles. Located at 33.32° N. Lat; 96.64° W. Long. Elevation is 748 feet.
Population: 485 (1990); 635 (2000); 708 (2010); 819 (2015 projected); Race: 88.4% White, 2.0% Black, 0.4% Asian, 9.2% Other, 10.5% Hispanic of any race (2010); Density: 152.6 persons per square mile (2010); Average household size: 2.75 (2010); Median age: 41.1 (2010); Males per 100 females: 101.7 (2010); Marriage status: 14.9% never married, 73.6% now married, 3.1% widowed, 8.4% divorced (2005-2009 5-year est.); Foreign born: 2.6% (2005-2009 5-year est.); Ancestry (includes multiple ancestries): 30.9% Irish, 15.1% American, 13.4% German, 9.8% English, 3.8% Polish (2005-2009 5-year est.).
Economy: Single-family building permits issued: 0 (2010); Multi-family building permits issued: 0 (2010); Employment by occupation: 22.6% management, 26.4% professional, 7.2% services, 23.1% sales, 0.0% farming, 13.0% construction, 7.7% production (2005-2009 5-year est.).
Income: Per capita income: $33,835 (2010); Median household income: $74,279 (2010); Average household income: $93,307 (2010); Percent of households with income of $100,000 or more: 33.9% (2010); Poverty rate: 4.1% (2005-2009 5-year est.).
Taxes: Total city taxes per capita: $162 (2007); City property taxes per capita: $117 (2007).
Education: Percent of population age 25 and over with: High school diploma (including GED) or higher: 86.8% (2010); Bachelor's degree or higher: 26.1% (2010); Master's degree or higher: 6.9% (2010).
Housing: Homeownership rate: 81.7% (2010); Median home value: $170,000 (2010); Median contract rent: $525 per month (2005-2009 5-year est.); Median year structure built: 1985 (2005-2009 5-year est.).
Transportation: Commute to work: 88.0% car, 0.0% public transportation, 0.0% walk, 11.1% work from home (2005-2009 5-year est.); Travel time to work: 14.1% less than 15 minutes, 37.8% 15 to 30 minutes, 11.4% 30 to 45 minutes, 17.3% 45 to 60 minutes, 19.5% 60 minutes or more (2005-2009 5-year est.)
Additional Information Contacts
City of Weston . . . . (972) 382-1001
    http://westontexas.com

WYLIE (city). Covers a land area of 19.369 square miles and a water area of 13.932 square miles. Located at 33.01° N. Lat; 96.52° W. Long. Elevation is 558 feet.
Population: 8,930 (1990); 15,132 (2000); 37,980 (2010); 45,891 (2015 projected); Race: 83.7% White, 4.6% Black, 1.2% Asian, 10.5% Other, 17.6% Hispanic of any race (2010); Density: 1,960.8 persons per square mile (2010); Average household size: 2.95 (2010); Median age: 33.7 (2010); Males per 100 females: 99.8 (2010); Marriage status: 20.9% never married, 62.5% now married, 3.5% widowed, 13.1% divorced (2005-2009 5-year est.); Foreign born: 12.7% (2005-2009 5-year est.); Ancestry (includes multiple ancestries): 12.5% German, 8.3% Irish, 7.3% American, 6.6% English, 4.0% French (2005-2009 5-year est.).
Economy: Unemployment rate: 7.9% (June 2011); Total civilian labor force: 20,658 (June 2011); Single-family building permits issued: 267

(2010); Multi-family building permits issued: 4 (2010); Employment by occupation: 16.3% management, 23.2% professional, 12.2% services, 30.4% sales, 0.0% farming, 9.7% construction, 8.2% production (2005-2009 5-year est.).
Income: Per capita income: $28,346 (2010); Median household income: $70,201 (2010); Average household income: $83,698 (2010); Percent of households with income of $100,000 or more: 26.0% (2010); Poverty rate: 6.3% (2005-2009 5-year est.).
Taxes: Total city taxes per capita: $542 (2007); City property taxes per capita: $376 (2007).
Education: Percent of population age 25 and over with: High school diploma (including GED) or higher: 88.0% (2010); Bachelor's degree or higher: 24.1% (2010); Master's degree or higher: 5.7% (2010).
School District(s)
Wylie ISD (PK-12)
    2009-10 Enrollment: 12,063 . . . . (972) 429-3000
Housing: Homeownership rate: 84.7% (2010); Median home value: $129,066 (2010); Median contract rent: $766 per month (2005-2009 5-year est.); Median year structure built: 2000 (2005-2009 5-year est.).
Safety: Violent crime rate: 6.2 per 10,000 population; Property crime rate: 166.4 per 10,000 population (2009).
Newspapers: Wylie News (Community news; Circulation 4,200)
Transportation: Commute to work: 92.8% car, 0.9% public transportation, 0.7% walk, 3.5% work from home (2005-2009 5-year est.); Travel time to work: 16.3% less than 15 minutes, 25.0% 15 to 30 minutes, 28.5% 30 to 45 minutes, 19.2% 45 to 60 minutes, 10.9% 60 minutes or more (2005-2009 5-year est.)
Additional Information Contacts
City of Wylie . . . . (972) 516-6000
    http://www.ci.wylie.tx.us
Wylie Chamber of Commerce . . . . (972) 442-2804
    http://www.wyliechamber.org

Collingsworth County

Located in north Texas, in the Panhandle; bounded on the east by Oklahoma; drained by the Salt Fork of the Red River. Covers a land area of 918.80 square miles, a water area of 0.64 square miles, and is located in the Central Time Zone at 34.92° N. Lat., 100.24° W. Long. The county was founded in 1876. County seat is Wellington.

Weather Station: Wellington									Elevation: 2,040 feet			
	Jan	Feb	Mar	Apr	May	Jun	Jul	Aug	Sep	Oct	Nov	Dec
High	55	59	67	77	84	92	97	96	88	77	65	54
Low	27	31	38	46	56	64	69	69	61	49	37	29
Precip	0.7	0.7	1.4	1.8	3.4	3.5	2.1	1.9	2.4	2.6	1.1	0.8
Snow	1.5	0.8	0.1	tr	0.0	0.0	0.0	0.0	0.0	0.0	0.6	1.3

High and Low temperatures in degrees Fahrenheit; Precipitation and Snow in inches

Population: 3,573 (1990); 3,206 (2000); 3,026 (2010); 2,932 (2015 projected); Race: 74.8% White, 6.6% Black, 0.2% Asian, 18.4% Other, 25.9% Hispanic of any race (2010); Density: 3.3 persons per square mile (2010); Average household size: 2.45 (2010); Median age: 39.4 (2010); Males per 100 females: 96.1 (2010).
Religion: Five largest groups: 54.4% Southern Baptist Convention, 14.9% The United Methodist Church, 9.9% Churches of Christ, 6.8% Church of the Nazarene, 2.9% Christian Churches and Churches of Christ (2000).
Economy: Unemployment rate: 6.6% (June 2011); Total civilian labor force: 1,417 (June 2011); Leading industries: 18.8% retail trade; 7.1% other services (except public administration); 4.0% arts, entertainment & recreation (2009); Farms: 442 totaling 512,537 acres (2007); Companies that employ 500 or more persons: 0 (2009); Companies that employ 100 to 499 persons: 0 (2009); Companies that employ less than 100 persons: 67 (2009); Black-owned businesses: n/a (2007); Hispanic-owned businesses: n/a (2007); Asian-owned businesses: n/a (2007); Women-owned businesses: n/a (2007); Retail sales per capita: $7,585 (2010). Single-family building permits issued: 1 (2010); Multi-family building permits issued: 0 (2010).
Income: Per capita income: $20,606 (2010); Median household income: $35,232 (2010); Average household income: $51,223 (2010); Percent of households with income of $100,000 or more: 11.4% (2010); Poverty rate: 18.8% (2009); Bankruptcy rate: 0.98% (2010).
Taxes: Total county taxes per capita: $421 (2007); County property taxes per capita: $353 (2007).

Education: Percent of population age 25 and over with: High school diploma (including GED) or higher: 76.5% (2010); Bachelor's degree or higher: 17.2% (2010); Master's degree or higher: 5.7% (2010).
Housing: Homeownership rate: 77.2% (2010); Median home value: $52,622 (2010); Median contract rent: $280 per month (2005-2009 5-year est.); Median year structure built: 1958 (2005-2009 5-year est.)
Health: Birth rate: 179.9 per 10,000 population (2009); Death rate: 94.8 per 10,000 population (2009); Age-adjusted cancer mortality rate: 183.6 (Unreliable) deaths per 100,000 population (2007); Number of physicians: 6.6 per 10,000 population (2008); Hospital beds: 53.9 per 10,000 population (2007); Hospital admissions: 1,374.2 per 10,000 population (2007).
Elections: 2008 Presidential election results: 19.6% Obama, 78.9% McCain, 0.0% Nader
Additional Information Contacts
Collingsworth County Government . . . . (806) 447-5408
 http://www.co.collingsworth.tx.us/ips/cms
Wellington Chamber of Commerce . . . . (806) 447-2544
 http://www.wellingtontx.com

Collingsworth County Communities

DODSON (town). Aka Dodsonville. Covers a land area of 0.606 square miles and a water area of 0 square miles. Located at 34.76° N. Lat; 100.02° W. Long. Elevation is 1,791 feet.
Population: 113 (1990); 115 (2000); 110 (2010); 108 (2015 projected); Race: 86.4% White, 0.9% Black, 0.0% Asian, 12.7% Other, 11.8% Hispanic of any race (2010); Density: 181.5 persons per square mile (2010); Average household size: 2.34 (2010); Median age: 48.5 (2010); Males per 100 females: 103.7 (2010); Marriage status: 15.9% never married, 41.3% now married, 12.7% widowed, 30.2% divorced (2005-2009 5-year est.); Foreign born: 17.4% (2005-2009 5-year est.); Ancestry (includes multiple ancestries): 21.7% German, 15.2% Irish, 8.7% English, 2.2% Scottish, 2.2% American (2005-2009 5-year est.).
Economy: Employment by occupation: 16.7% management, 0.0% professional, 25.0% services, 20.8% sales, 12.5% farming, 25.0% construction, 0.0% production (2005-2009 5-year est.).
Income: Per capita income: $25,025 (2010); Median household income: $45,833 (2010); Average household income: $57,128 (2010); Percent of households with income of $100,000 or more: 14.9% (2010); Poverty rate: 53.3% (2005-2009 5-year est.).
Taxes: Total city taxes per capita: $65 (2007); City property taxes per capita: $19 (2007).
Education: Percent of population age 25 and over with: High school diploma (including GED) or higher: 82.9% (2010); Bachelor's degree or higher: 23.2% (2010); Master's degree or higher: 8.5% (2010).
Housing: Homeownership rate: 83.0% (2010); Median home value: $61,250 (2010); Median contract rent: n/a per month (2005-2009 5-year est.); Median year structure built: 1972 (2005-2009 5-year est.).
Transportation: Commute to work: 100.0% car, 0.0% public transportation, 0.0% walk, 0.0% work from home (2005-2009 5-year est.); Travel time to work: 66.7% less than 15 minutes, 33.3% 15 to 30 minutes, 0.0% 30 to 45 minutes, 0.0% 45 to 60 minutes, 0.0% 60 minutes or more (2005-2009 5-year est.)

QUAIL (CDP). Covers a land area of 3.169 square miles and a water area of 0 square miles. Located at 34.91° N. Lat; 100.38° W. Long. Elevation is 2,234 feet.
Population: 37 (1990); 33 (2000); 31 (2010); 31 (2015 projected); Race: 87.1% White, 0.0% Black, 0.0% Asian, 12.9% Other, 9.7% Hispanic of any race (2010); Density: 9.8 persons per square mile (2010); Average household size: 2.38 (2010); Median age: 31.3 (2010); Males per 100 females: 106.7 (2010); Marriage status: 0.0% never married, 100.0% now married, 0.0% widowed, 0.0% divorced (2005-2009 5-year est.); Foreign born: 0.0% (2005-2009 5-year est.); Ancestry (includes multiple ancestries): 20.0% Norwegian (2005-2009 5-year est.).
Economy: Employment by occupation: 20.0% management, 0.0% professional, 0.0% services, 30.0% sales, 20.0% farming, 30.0% construction, 0.0% production (2005-2009 5-year est.).
Income: Per capita income: $25,025 (2010); Median household income: $42,500 (2010); Average household income: $49,038 (2010); Percent of households with income of $100,000 or more: 7.7% (2010); Poverty rate: 0.0% (2005-2009 5-year est.).

Education: Percent of population age 25 and over with: High school diploma (including GED) or higher: 83.3% (2010); Bachelor's degree or higher: 22.2% (2010); Master's degree or higher: 5.6% (2010).
Housing: Homeownership rate: 84.6% (2010); Median home value: $75,000 (2010); Median contract rent: n/a per month (2005-2009 5-year est.); Median year structure built: 1962 (2005-2009 5-year est.).
Transportation: Commute to work: 100.0% car, 0.0% public transportation, 0.0% walk, 0.0% work from home (2005-2009 5-year est.); Travel time to work: 30.0% less than 15 minutes, 30.0% 15 to 30 minutes, 40.0% 30 to 45 minutes, 0.0% 45 to 60 minutes, 0.0% 60 minutes or more (2005-2009 5-year est.)

SAMNORWOOD (CDP). Covers a land area of 1.626 square miles and a water area of 0 square miles. Located at 35.05° N. Lat; 100.28° W. Long. Elevation is 2,198 feet.
Population: 52 (1990); 39 (2000); 37 (2010); 36 (2015 projected); Race: 86.5% White, 0.0% Black, 0.0% Asian, 13.5% Other, 10.8% Hispanic of any race (2010); Density: 22.8 persons per square mile (2010); Average household size: 2.31 (2010); Median age: 45.8 (2010); Males per 100 females: 117.6 (2010); Marriage status: 38.1% never married, 61.9% now married, 0.0% widowed, 0.0% divorced (2005-2009 5-year est.); Foreign born: 0.0% (2005-2009 5-year est.); Ancestry (includes multiple ancestries): 16.7% American (2005-2009 5-year est.).
Economy: Employment by occupation: 0.0% management, 0.0% professional, 37.5% services, 37.5% sales, 0.0% farming, 25.0% construction, 0.0% production (2005-2009 5-year est.).
Income: Per capita income: $25,025 (2010); Median household income: $45,000 (2010); Average household income: $52,969 (2010); Percent of households with income of $100,000 or more: 12.5% (2010); Poverty rate: 0.0% (2005-2009 5-year est.).
Education: Percent of population age 25 and over with: High school diploma (including GED) or higher: 88.9% (2010); Bachelor's degree or higher: 25.9% (2010); Master's degree or higher: 11.1% (2010).
School District(s)
Samnorwood ISD (PK-12)
 2009-10 Enrollment: 101 . . . . (806) 256-2039
Housing: Homeownership rate: 81.3% (2010); Median home value: $65,000 (2010); Median contract rent: n/a per month (2005-2009 5-year est.); Median year structure built: 1944 (2005-2009 5-year est.).
Transportation: Commute to work: 62.5% car, 0.0% public transportation, 37.5% walk, 0.0% work from home (2005-2009 5-year est.); Travel time to work: 75.0% less than 15 minutes, 25.0% 15 to 30 minutes, 0.0% 30 to 45 minutes, 0.0% 45 to 60 minutes, 0.0% 60 minutes or more (2005-2009 5-year est.)

WELLINGTON (city). County seat. Covers a land area of 1.362 square miles and a water area of 0 square miles. Located at 34.85° N. Lat; 100.21° W. Long. Elevation is 2,031 feet.
History: Incorporated 1909.
Population: 2,490 (1990); 2,275 (2000); 2,131 (2010); 2,055 (2015 projected); Race: 71.4% White, 8.2% Black, 0.2% Asian, 20.2% Other, 30.5% Hispanic of any race (2010); Density: 1,564.7 persons per square mile (2010); Average household size: 2.47 (2010); Median age: 36.4 (2010); Males per 100 females: 93.0 (2010); Marriage status: 19.1% never married, 60.0% now married, 10.8% widowed, 10.1% divorced (2005-2009 5-year est.); Foreign born: 4.7% (2005-2009 5-year est.); Ancestry (includes multiple ancestries): 14.5% Irish, 10.4% German, 5.6% American, 5.5% English, 2.6% Dutch (2005-2009 5-year est.).
Economy: Single-family building permits issued: 1 (2010); Multi-family building permits issued: 0 (2010); Employment by occupation: 17.0% management, 18.2% professional, 17.0% services, 24.2% sales, 5.1% farming, 5.2% construction, 13.2% production (2005-2009 5-year est.).
Income: Per capita income: $19,403 (2010); Median household income: $32,679 (2010); Average household income: $49,267 (2010); Percent of households with income of $100,000 or more: 10.7% (2010); Poverty rate: 23.4% (2005-2009 5-year est.).
Taxes: Total city taxes per capita: $184 (2007); City property taxes per capita: $53 (2007).
Education: Percent of population age 25 and over with: High school diploma (including GED) or higher: 74.0% (2010); Bachelor's degree or higher: 15.2% (2010); Master's degree or higher: 4.4% (2010).
School District(s)
Wellington ISD (PK-12)
 2009-10 Enrollment: 548 . . . . (806) 447-2512

Housing: Homeownership rate: 75.2% (2010); Median home value: $48,641 (2010); Median contract rent: $285 per month (2005-2009 5-year est.); Median year structure built: 1958 (2005-2009 5-year est.).
Hospitals: Collingsworth General Hospital (25 beds)
Newspapers: Wellington Leader (Community news; Circulation 2,100)
Transportation: Commute to work: 86.9% car, 0.0% public transportation, 5.2% walk, 7.9% work from home (2005-2009 5-year est.); Travel time to work: 75.6% less than 15 minutes, 11.5% 15 to 30 minutes, 6.8% 30 to 45 minutes, 4.5% 45 to 60 minutes, 1.5% 60 minutes or more (2005-2009 5-year est.)
Additional Information Contacts
Wellington Chamber of Commerce . . . . (806) 447-2544
  http://www.wellingtontx.com

Colorado County

Located in south Texas; drained by the Colorado and San Bernard Rivers; includes Eagle Lake. Covers a land area of 962.95 square miles, a water area of 10.64 square miles, and is located in the Central Time Zone at 29.63° N. Lat., 96.54° W. Long. The county was founded in 1836. County seat is Columbus.

Weather Station: Columbus   Elevation: 199 feet

	Jan	Feb	Mar	Apr	May	Jun	Jul	Aug	Sep	Oct	Nov	Dec
High	65	68	75	81	87	93	96	98	93	85	74	66
Low	38	41	48	55	63	68	69	69	64	54	46	38
Precip	3.6	2.8	3.2	3.1	4.8	4.9	3.1	2.9	3.1	4.8	4.5	3.2
Snow	0.0	0.0	tr	0.0	0.0	0.0	0.0	0.0	0.0	0.0	0.0	tr

High and Low temperatures in degrees Fahrenheit; Precipitation and Snow in inches

Population: 18,383 (1990); 20,390 (2000); 21,559 (2010); 22,096 (2015 projected); Race: 70.4% White, 13.9% Black, 0.4% Asian, 15.2% Other, 24.7% Hispanic of any race (2010); Density: 22.4 persons per square mile (2010); Average household size: 2.55 (2010); Median age: 39.6 (2010); Males per 100 females: 96.2 (2010).
Religion: Five largest groups: 33.0% Catholic Church, 11.0% Southern Baptist Convention, 8.5% Evangelical Lutheran Church in America, 5.6% The United Methodist Church, 2.6% United Church of Christ (2000).
Economy: Unemployment rate: 8.1% (June 2011); Total civilian labor force: 10,708 (June 2011); Leading industries: 23.5% manufacturing; 15.6% retail trade; 14.9% health care and social assistance (2009); Farms: 1,790 totaling 527,393 acres (2007); Companies that employ 500 or more persons: 0 (2009); Companies that employ 100 to 499 persons: 10 (2009); Companies that employ less than 100 persons: 541 (2009); Black-owned businesses: n/a (2007); Hispanic-owned businesses: n/a (2007); Asian-owned businesses: n/a (2007); Women-owned businesses: 531 (2007); Retail sales per capita: $13,235 (2010). Single-family building permits issued: 7 (2010); Multi-family building permits issued: 0 (2010).
Income: Per capita income: $21,639 (2010); Median household income: $41,977 (2010); Average household income: $56,850 (2010); Percent of households with income of $100,000 or more: 12.2% (2010); Poverty rate: 16.0% (2009); Bankruptcy rate: 0.90% (2010).
Taxes: Total county taxes per capita: $341 (2007); County property taxes per capita: $265 (2007).
Education: Percent of population age 25 and over with: High school diploma (including GED) or higher: 76.4% (2010); Bachelor's degree or higher: 16.8% (2010); Master's degree or higher: 4.7% (2010).
Housing: Homeownership rate: 75.3% (2010); Median home value: $88,338 (2010); Median contract rent: $409 per month (2005-2009 5-year est.); Median year structure built: 1971 (2005-2009 5-year est.)
Health: Birth rate: 139.0 per 10,000 population (2009); Death rate: 103.1 per 10,000 population (2009); Age-adjusted cancer mortality rate: 175.5 deaths per 100,000 population (2007); Number of physicians: 14.0 per 10,000 population (2008); Hospital beds: 43.4 per 10,000 population (2007); Hospital admissions: 1,284.4 per 10,000 population (2007).
Elections: 2008 Presidential election results: 30.0% Obama, 69.4% McCain, 0.0% Nader
Additional Information Contacts
Colorado County Government . . . . (979) 732-2604
  http://www.co.colorado.tx.us/ips/cms
City of Columbus . . . . (979) 732-2366
  http://www.columbustexas.net
Eagle Lake Chamber of Commerce . . . . (979) 234-2780
  http://www.visiteaglelake.com

Colorado County Communities

ALLEYTON (unincorporated postal area, zip code 78935). Covers a land area of 45.048 square miles and a water area of 0.337 square miles. Located at 29.69° N. Lat; 96.45° W. Long. Elevation is 187 feet.
History: Alleyton was founded in 1824. Near the town, Santa Anna and his army crossed the Colorado River in pursuit of the Texans in 1836.
Population: 578 (2000); Race: 75.2% White, 15.8% Black, 0.0% Asian, 9.0% Other, 18.5% Hispanic of any race (2000); Density: 12.8 persons per square mile (2000); Age: 36.5% under 18, 12.3% over 64 (2000); Marriage status: 19.3% never married, 69.8% now married, 6.3% widowed, 4.6% divorced (2000); Foreign born: 8.6% (2000); Ancestry (includes multiple ancestries): 29.1% German, 16.3% Irish, 11.1% American, 7.5% Welsh (2000).
Economy: Employment by occupation: 12.2% management, 13.2% professional, 19.9% services, 16.4% sales, 2.1% farming, 13.2% construction, 23.0% production (2000).
Income: Per capita income: $17,430 (2000); Median household income: $42,083 (2000); Poverty rate: 179.1% (2000).
Education: Percent of population age 25 and over with: High school diploma (including GED) or higher: 71.5% (2000); Bachelor's degree or higher: 21.3% (2000).
Housing: Homeownership rate: 87.1% (2000); Median home value: $64,600 (2000); Median contract rent: $338 per month (2000); Median year structure built: 1964 (2000).
Transportation: Commute to work: 92.6% car, 0.0% public transportation, 0.0% walk, 7.4% work from home (2000); Travel time to work: 29.9% less than 15 minutes, 33.0% 15 to 30 minutes, 4.6% 30 to 45 minutes, 6.5% 45 to 60 minutes, 26.1% 60 minutes or more (2000)

ALTAIR (unincorporated postal area, zip code 77412). Covers a land area of 30.797 square miles and a water area of 0.265 square miles. Located at 29.60° N. Lat; 96.52° W. Long. Elevation is 207 feet.
Population: 172 (2000); Race: 48.4% White, 51.6% Black, 0.0% Asian, 0.0% Other, 0.0% Hispanic of any race (2000); Density: 5.6 persons per square mile (2000); Age: 42.7% under 18, 6.9% over 64 (2000); Marriage status: 38.8% never married, 44.8% now married, 3.0% widowed, 13.3% divorced (2000); Foreign born: 0.0% (2000); Ancestry (includes multiple ancestries): 22.2% Czech, 9.7% English, 8.9% German, 7.3% American (2000).
Economy: Employment by occupation: 0.0% management, 17.6% professional, 25.9% services, 23.5% sales, 0.0% farming, 0.0% construction, 32.9% production (2000).
Income: Per capita income: $8,840 (2000); Median household income: $17,391 (2000); Poverty rate: 179.1% (2000).
Education: Percent of population age 25 and over with: High school diploma (including GED) or higher: 85.3% (2000); Bachelor's degree or higher: 0.0% (2000).
School District(s)
Rice CISD (PK-12)
  2009-10 Enrollment: 1,324 . . . . (979) 234-3531
Housing: Homeownership rate: 62.2% (2000); Median home value: $24,600 (2000); Median contract rent: $125 per month (2000); Median year structure built: 1981 (2000).
Transportation: Commute to work: 100.0% car, 0.0% public transportation, 0.0% walk, 0.0% work from home (2000); Travel time to work: 42.4% less than 15 minutes, 32.9% 15 to 30 minutes, 16.5% 30 to 45 minutes, 8.2% 45 to 60 minutes, 0.0% 60 minutes or more (2000)

COLUMBUS (city). County seat. Covers a land area of 2.822 square miles and a water area of 0 square miles. Located at 29.70° N. Lat; 96.54° W. Long. Elevation is 203 feet.
History: Columbus was founded in 1823 by members of Austin's colony, with Baron de Bastrop assisting. The first civil court of Colorado County was held under the County Court Live Oak, a giant tree that stood in Columbus.
Population: 3,429 (1990); 3,916 (2000); 4,182 (2010); 4,277 (2015 projected); Race: 62.4% White, 19.5% Black, 0.5% Asian, 17.6% Other, 23.5% Hispanic of any race (2010); Density: 1,481.7 persons per square mile (2010); Average household size: 2.42 (2010); Median age: 40.8 (2010); Males per 100 females: 90.4 (2010); Marriage status: 29.9% never married, 45.3% now married, 17.4% widowed, 7.4% divorced (2005-2009 5-year est.); Foreign born: 8.0% (2005-2009 5-year est.); Ancestry (includes multiple ancestries): 26.9% German, 9.1% Irish, 7.3% Czech, 5.9% English, 4.6% French (2005-2009 5-year est.).

Economy: Single-family building permits issued: 3 (2010); Multi-family building permits issued: 0 (2010); Employment by occupation: 8.8% management, 12.6% professional, 26.5% services, 14.9% sales, 2.2% farming, 13.7% construction, 21.2% production (2005-2009 5-year est.).
Income: Per capita income: $19,012 (2010); Median household income: $36,890 (2010); Average household income: $49,402 (2010); Percent of households with income of $100,000 or more: 10.7% (2010); Poverty rate: 22.1% (2005-2009 5-year est.).
Taxes: Total city taxes per capita: $460 (2007); City property taxes per capita: $108 (2007).
Education: Percent of population age 25 and over with: High school diploma (including GED) or higher: 75.0% (2010); Bachelor's degree or higher: 19.9% (2010); Master's degree or higher: 4.8% (2010).

School District(s)
Columbus ISD (PK-12)
   2009-10 Enrollment: 1,538 . . . . (979) 732-5704
Housing: Homeownership rate: 61.4% (2010); Median home value: $102,626 (2010); Median contract rent: $458 per month (2005-2009 5-year est.); Median year structure built: 1959 (2005-2009 5-year est.).
Hospitals: Columbus Community Hospital (40 beds)
Safety: Violent crime rate: 110.7 per 10,000 population; Property crime rate: 254.8 per 10,000 population (2009).
Newspapers: Banner Press (Community news; Circulation 4,500); Colorado County Citizen (Community news; Circulation 4,200)
Transportation: Commute to work: 89.2% car, 0.0% public transportation, 5.0% walk, 4.8% work from home (2005-2009 5-year est.); Travel time to work: 57.5% less than 15 minutes, 24.0% 15 to 30 minutes, 4.7% 30 to 45 minutes, 2.1% 45 to 60 minutes, 11.8% 60 minutes or more (2005-2009 5-year est.)
Additional Information Contacts
City of Columbus . . . . (979) 732-2366
   http://www.columbustexas.net

EAGLE LAKE (city). Covers a land area of 2.725 square miles and a water area of 0 square miles. Located at 29.58° N. Lat; 96.33° W. Long. Elevation is 174 feet.
History: The town of Eagle Lake was founded by the Austin colonists, and grew as a center for rice milling. Game birds on the nearby lake gave the town the nickname of the "Goose Hunting Capital of the World."
Population: 3,551 (1990); 3,664 (2000); 3,743 (2010); 3,772 (2015 projected); Race: 52.9% White, 24.7% Black, 0.0% Asian, 22.5% Other, 47.4% Hispanic of any race (2010); Density: 1,373.6 persons per square mile (2010); Average household size: 2.73 (2010); Median age: 34.4 (2010); Males per 100 females: 97.0 (2010); Marriage status: 32.2% never married, 49.3% now married, 9.9% widowed, 8.6% divorced (2005-2009 5-year est.); Foreign born: 13.4% (2005-2009 5-year est.); Ancestry (includes multiple ancestries): 6.9% German, 3.9% American, 2.8% English, 2.0% Irish, 2.0% Czech (2005-2009 5-year est.).
Economy: Single-family building permits issued: 2 (2010); Multi-family building permits issued: 0 (2010); Employment by occupation: 4.4% management, 17.1% professional, 20.3% services, 16.9% sales, 0.0% farming, 9.8% construction, 31.5% production (2005-2009 5-year est.).
Income: Per capita income: $16,713 (2010); Median household income: $33,691 (2010); Average household income: $45,627 (2010); Percent of households with income of $100,000 or more: 7.0% (2010); Poverty rate: 32.7% (2005-2009 5-year est.).
Taxes: Total city taxes per capita: $210 (2007); City property taxes per capita: $95 (2007).
Education: Percent of population age 25 and over with: High school diploma (including GED) or higher: 66.7% (2010); Bachelor's degree or higher: 11.9% (2010); Master's degree or higher: 3.6% (2010).

School District(s)
Rice CISD (PK-12)
   2009-10 Enrollment: 1,324 . . . . (979) 234-3531
Housing: Homeownership rate: 67.2% (2010); Median home value: $49,688 (2010); Median contract rent: $337 per month (2005-2009 5-year est.); Median year structure built: 1968 (2005-2009 5-year est.).
Hospitals: Rice Medical Center (25 beds)
Safety: Violent crime rate: 38.0 per 10,000 population; Property crime rate: 133.1 per 10,000 population (2009).
Transportation: Commute to work: 96.1% car, 1.0% public transportation, 0.6% walk, 2.3% work from home (2005-2009 5-year est.); Travel time to work: 43.5% less than 15 minutes, 19.6% 15 to 30 minutes, 17.8% 30 to 45 minutes, 5.2% 45 to 60 minutes, 13.9% 60 minutes or more (2005-2009 5-year est.)

Additional Information Contacts
Eagle Lake Chamber of Commerce. . . . . (979) 234-2780
   http://www.visiteaglelake.com

GARWOOD (unincorporated postal area, zip code 77442). Covers a land area of 176.676 square miles and a water area of 1.254 square miles. Located at 29.42° N. Lat; 96.45° W. Long. Elevation is 161 feet.
Population: 1,256 (2000); Race: 78.2% White, 12.1% Black, 0.0% Asian, 9.7% Other, 18.5% Hispanic of any race (2000); Density: 7.1 persons per square mile (2000); Age: 22.8% under 18, 19.6% over 64 (2000); Marriage status: 27.7% never married, 56.2% now married, 9.8% widowed, 6.3% divorced (2000); Foreign born: 9.0% (2000); Ancestry (includes multiple ancestries): 24.0% German, 15.0% Czech, 4.8% American, 3.5% African (2000).
Economy: Employment by occupation: 23.0% management, 7.5% professional, 7.5% services, 21.4% sales, 10.8% farming, 11.3% construction, 18.6% production (2000).
Income: Per capita income: $21,537 (2000); Median household income: $29,821 (2000); Poverty rate: 179.1% (2000).
Education: Percent of population age 25 and over with: High school diploma (including GED) or higher: 72.1% (2000); Bachelor's degree or higher: 13.3% (2000).

School District(s)
Rice CISD (PK-12)
   2009-10 Enrollment: 1,324 . . . . (979) 234-3531
Housing: Homeownership rate: 80.3% (2000); Median home value: $59,600 (2000); Median contract rent: $244 per month (2000); Median year structure built: 1960 (2000).
Transportation: Commute to work: 81.2% car, 0.0% public transportation, 6.0% walk, 6.4% work from home (2000); Travel time to work: 43.3% less than 15 minutes, 31.8% 15 to 30 minutes, 8.6% 30 to 45 minutes, 0.0% 45 to 60 minutes, 16.4% 60 minutes or more (2000)

GLIDDEN (unincorporated postal area, zip code 78943). Covers a land area of 0.584 square miles and a water area of 0.003 square miles. Located at 29.69° N. Lat; 96.59° W. Long. Elevation is 236 feet.
Population: 318 (2000); Race: 40.0% White, 23.2% Black, 0.0% Asian, 36.8% Other, 43.5% Hispanic of any race (2000); Density: 544.5 persons per square mile (2000); Age: 33.9% under 18, 23.2% over 64 (2000); Marriage status: 28.5% never married, 44.7% now married, 22.1% widowed, 4.7% divorced (2000); Foreign born: 22.3% (2000); Ancestry (includes multiple ancestries): 10.1% German, 8.4% Irish, 3.5% French, 2.3% Scottish (2000).
Economy: Employment by occupation: 0.0% management, 13.2% professional, 53.8% services, 7.5% sales, 0.0% farming, 5.7% construction, 19.8% production (2000).
Income: Per capita income: $11,006 (2000); Median household income: $34,375 (2000); Poverty rate: 179.1% (2000).
Education: Percent of population age 25 and over with: High school diploma (including GED) or higher: 54.9% (2000); Bachelor's degree or higher: 10.3% (2000).
Housing: Homeownership rate: 85.2% (2000); Median home value: $33,200 (2000); Median contract rent: $311 per month (2000); Median year structure built: 1958 (2000).
Transportation: Commute to work: 100.0% car, 0.0% public transportation, 0.0% walk, 0.0% work from home (2000); Travel time to work: 32.0% less than 15 minutes, 38.1% 15 to 30 minutes, 0.0% 30 to 45 minutes, 0.0% 45 to 60 minutes, 29.9% 60 minutes or more (2000)

ROCK ISLAND (unincorporated postal area, zip code 77470). Covers a land area of 17.548 square miles and a water area of 0.016 square miles. Located at 29.60° N. Lat; 96.52° W. Long. Elevation is 246 feet.
Population: 315 (2000); Race: 82.4% White, 0.0% Black, 0.0% Asian, 17.6% Other, 36.5% Hispanic of any race (2000); Density: 18.0 persons per square mile (2000); Age: 21.2% under 18, 25.9% over 64 (2000); Marriage status: 2.4% never married, 78.6% now married, 14.1% widowed, 4.9% divorced (2000); Foreign born: 22.4% (2000); Ancestry (includes multiple ancestries): 18.0% German, 13.7% American, 8.2% Czech, 6.7% Irish (2000).
Economy: Employment by occupation: 22.2% management, 11.1% professional, 14.4% services, 11.1% sales, 10.0% farming, 18.9% construction, 12.2% production (2000).
Income: Per capita income: $12,096 (2000); Median household income: $25,446 (2000); Poverty rate: 179.1% (2000).

Education: Percent of population age 25 and over with: High school diploma (including GED) or higher: 64.2% (2000); Bachelor's degree or higher: 9.0% (2000).
Housing: Homeownership rate: 71.3% (2000); Median home value: $36,900 (2000); Median contract rent: $225 per month (2000); Median year structure built: 1969 (2000).
Transportation: Commute to work: 82.6% car, 0.0% public transportation, 0.0% walk, 0.0% work from home (2000); Travel time to work: 17.4% less than 15 minutes, 36.0% 15 to 30 minutes, 29.1% 30 to 45 minutes, 10.5% 45 to 60 minutes, 7.0% 60 minutes or more (2000)

SHERIDAN (unincorporated postal area, zip code 77475). Covers a land area of 49.220 square miles and a water area of 0.244 square miles. Located at 29.60° N. Lat; 96.52° W. Long. Elevation is 276 feet.
Population: 794 (2000); Race: 92.0% White, 2.4% Black, 0.0% Asian, 5.6% Other, 11.3% Hispanic of any race (2000); Density: 16.1 persons per square mile (2000); Age: 17.5% under 18, 24.7% over 64 (2000); Marriage status: 13.6% never married, 71.7% now married, 3.4% widowed, 11.2% divorced (2000); Foreign born: 6.6% (2000); Ancestry (includes multiple ancestries): 18.4% Irish, 16.8% German, 12.7% English, 11.2% American (2000).
Economy: Employment by occupation: 13.0% management, 8.7% professional, 17.8% services, 21.0% sales, 1.1% farming, 14.1% construction, 24.3% production (2000).
Income: Per capita income: $12,616 (2000); Median household income: $24,803 (2000); Poverty rate: 179.1% (2000).
Education: Percent of population age 25 and over with: High school diploma (including GED) or higher: 75.8% (2000); Bachelor's degree or higher: 7.8% (2000).

School District(s)
Rice CISD (PK-12)
    2009-10 Enrollment: 1,324 . . . . (979) 234-3531
Housing: Homeownership rate: 93.9% (2000); Median home value: $50,000 (2000); Median contract rent: $275 per month (2000); Median year structure built: 1976 (2000).
Transportation: Commute to work: 91.3% car, 0.0% public transportation, 4.5% walk, 4.2% work from home (2000); Travel time to work: 22.4% less than 15 minutes, 15.7% 15 to 30 minutes, 29.5% 30 to 45 minutes, 5.1% 45 to 60 minutes, 27.2% 60 minutes or more (2000)

WEIMAR (city). Covers a land area of 2.258 square miles and a water area of 0 square miles. Located at 29.70° N. Lat; 96.78° W. Long. Elevation is 410 feet.
Population: 2,059 (1990); 1,981 (2000); 2,173 (2010); 2,272 (2015 projected); Race: 70.0% White, 18.4% Black, 1.9% Asian, 9.7% Other, 17.1% Hispanic of any race (2010); Density: 962.3 persons per square mile (2010); Average household size: 2.42 (2010); Median age: 43.5 (2010); Males per 100 females: 86.8 (2010); Marriage status: 26.9% never married, 55.8% now married, 10.8% widowed, 6.4% divorced (2005-2009 5-year est.); Foreign born: 5.4% (2005-2009 5-year est.); Ancestry (includes multiple ancestries): 23.9% German, 9.9% Czech, 6.2% Irish, 6.1% American, 4.5% English (2005-2009 5-year est.).
Economy: Single-family building permits issued: 2 (2010); Multi-family building permits issued: 0 (2010); Employment by occupation: 9.9% management, 19.4% professional, 24.8% services, 22.5% sales, 0.0% farming, 7.5% construction, 15.9% production (2005-2009 5-year est.).
Income: Per capita income: $18,789 (2010); Median household income: $35,693 (2010); Average household income: $46,309 (2010); Percent of households with income of $100,000 or more: 6.6% (2010); Poverty rate: 14.9% (2005-2009 5-year est.).
Taxes: Total city taxes per capita: $242 (2007); City property taxes per capita: $112 (2007).
Education: Percent of population age 25 and over with: High school diploma (including GED) or higher: 73.5% (2010); Bachelor's degree or higher: 15.6% (2010); Master's degree or higher: 4.5% (2010).

School District(s)
Weimar ISD (PK-12)
    2009-10 Enrollment: 602 . . . . (979) 725-9506
Housing: Homeownership rate: 75.4% (2010); Median home value: $82,439 (2010); Median contract rent: $362 per month (2005-2009 5-year est.); Median year structure built: 1961 (2005-2009 5-year est.).
Hospitals: Colorado Fayette Medical Center (38 beds)
Safety: Violent crime rate: 19.8 per 10,000 population; Property crime rate: 163.3 per 10,000 population (2009).
Newspapers: Weimar Mercury (Local news; Circulation 3,500)

Transportation: Commute to work: 88.0% car, 0.0% public transportation, 7.1% walk, 2.6% work from home (2005-2009 5-year est.); Travel time to work: 64.9% less than 15 minutes, 21.1% 15 to 30 minutes, 5.0% 30 to 45 minutes, 1.0% 45 to 60 minutes, 8.0% 60 minutes or more (2005-2009 5-year est.)

Comal County

Located in south central Texas; drained by the Guadalupe River. Covers a land area of 561.45 square miles, a water area of 13.15 square miles, and is located in the Central Time Zone at 29.77° N. Lat., 98.22° W. Long. The county was founded in 1846. County seat is New Braunfels.

Comal County is part of the San Antonio-New Braunfels, TX Metropolitan Statistical Area. The entire metro area includes: Atascosa County, TX; Bandera County, TX; Bexar County, TX; Comal County, TX; Guadalupe County, TX; Kendall County, TX; Medina County, TX; Wilson County, TX

Weather Station: Canyon Dam   Elevation: 1,000 feet

	Jan	Feb	Mar	Apr	May	Jun	Jul	Aug	Sep	Oct	Nov	Dec
High	61	65	71	78	85	91	94	95	89	80	71	62
Low	39	42	49	56	64	70	72	72	68	59	49	40
Precip	2.3	2.0	2.8	2.5	4.1	4.6	2.9	2.3	3.4	4.6	3.2	2.2
Snow	0.4	tr	tr	0.0	0.0	0.0	0.0	0.0	0.0	0.0	0.0	0.0

High and Low temperatures in degrees Fahrenheit; Precipitation and Snow in inches

Weather Station: New Braunfels   Elevation: 709 feet

	Jan	Feb	Mar	Apr	May	Jun	Jul	Aug	Sep	Oct	Nov	Dec
High	63	66	73	80	86	92	95	96	90	82	72	63
Low	38	41	48	55	64	70	72	72	66	57	48	39
Precip	1.9	1.9	2.4	2.1	4.0	4.7	2.5	2.3	3.0	4.4	2.5	2.4
Snow	0.3	0.0	0.0	0.0	0.0	0.0	0.0	0.0	0.0	0.0	0.0	0.0

High and Low temperatures in degrees Fahrenheit; Precipitation and Snow in inches

Population: 51,832 (1990); 78,021 (2000); 115,775 (2010); 133,932 (2015 projected); Race: 85.9% White, 2.3% Black, 0.9% Asian, 10.9% Other, 25.4% Hispanic of any race (2010); Density: 206.2 persons per square mile (2010); Average household size: 2.64 (2010); Median age: 36.2 (2010); Males per 100 females: 97.9 (2010).
Religion: Five largest groups: 22.1% Catholic Church, 11.4% Southern Baptist Convention, 4.9% Evangelical Lutheran Church in America, 4.2% The United Methodist Church, 3.3% Independent, Non-Charismatic Churches (2000).
Economy: Unemployment rate: 7.4% (June 2011); Total civilian labor force: 59,756 (June 2011); Leading industries: 14.8% retail trade; 13.0% accommodation & food services; 11.6% health care and social assistance (2009); Farms: 939 totaling 192,454 acres (2007); Companies that employ 500 or more persons: 4 (2009); Companies that employ 100 to 499 persons: 46 (2009); Companies that employ less than 100 persons: 2,739 (2009); Black-owned businesses: n/a (2007); Hispanic-owned businesses: 1,272 (2007); Asian-owned businesses: n/a (2007); Women-owned businesses: 3,190 (2007); Retail sales per capita: $12,687 (2010). Single-family building permits issued: 846 (2010); Multi-family building permits issued: 0 (2010).
Income: Per capita income: $29,472 (2010); Median household income: $61,666 (2010); Average household income: $78,134 (2010); Percent of households with income of $100,000 or more: 23.4% (2010); Poverty rate: 8.8% (2009); Bankruptcy rate: 2.41% (2010).
Taxes: Total county taxes per capita: $303 (2007); County property taxes per capita: $218 (2007).
Education: Percent of population age 25 and over with: High school diploma (including GED) or higher: 89.1% (2010); Bachelor's degree or higher: 30.6% (2010); Master's degree or higher: 9.8% (2010).
Housing: Homeownership rate: 74.1% (2010); Median home value: $162,823 (2010); Median contract rent: $656 per month (2005-2009 5-year est.); Median year structure built: 1990 (2005-2009 5-year est.)
Health: Birth rate: 141.1 per 10,000 population (2009); Death rate: 77.3 per 10,000 population (2009); Age-adjusted cancer mortality rate: 178.0 deaths per 100,000 population (2007); Number of physicians: 16.9 per 10,000 population (2008); Hospital beds: 16.3 per 10,000 population (2007); Hospital admissions: 697.1 per 10,000 population (2007).
Elections: 2008 Presidential election results: 25.7% Obama, 73.0% McCain, 0.1% Nader
Additional Information Contacts
Comal County Government . . . . (830) 620-5501
    http://www.co.comal.tx.us

Bulverde/Spring Branch Area Chamber of Commerce .... (830) 438-4285
  http://www.bulverdechamber.com
Canyon Lake Chamber of Commerce .... (830) 964-2223
  http://www.canyonlakechamber.com
City of Bulverde .... (830) 438-3612
  http://www.ci.bulverde.tx.us
City of Garden Ridge .... (210) 651-6632
  http://www.ci.garden-ridge.tx.us
City of New Braunfels .... (830) 221-4000
  http://www.ci.new-braunfels.tx.us
Greater New Braunfels Chamber of Commerce .... (830) 625-2385
  http://www.nbcham.org
New Braunfels Women's Chamber of Commerce
  http://nbwcc.net

Comal County Communities

BULVERDE (city). Aka Bulverde East. Covers a land area of 7.588 square miles and a water area of 0 square miles. Located at 29.74° N. Lat; 98.41° W. Long. Elevation is 1,093 feet.

History: For many years the closest post office to Bulverde was at Smithson Valley. A local post office that operated from 1879 to 1919 was named for Luciano Bulverdo, an early area landowner.

Population: 1,921 (1990); 3,761 (2000); 5,454 (2010); 6,399 (2015 projected); Race: 90.8% White, 0.7% Black, 1.0% Asian, 7.6% Other, 15.6% Hispanic of any race (2010); Density: 718.8 persons per square mile (2010); Average household size: 2.89 (2010); Median age: 37.1 (2010); Males per 100 females: 102.7 (2010); Marriage status: 18.5% never married, 70.4% now married, 3.6% widowed, 7.5% divorced (2005-2009 5-year est.); Foreign born: 3.2% (2005-2009 5-year est.); Ancestry (includes multiple ancestries): 28.2% German, 16.8% English, 14.0% Irish, 11.6% American, 5.2% French (2005-2009 5-year est.).

Economy: Single-family building permits issued: 9 (2010); Multi-family building permits issued: 0 (2010); Employment by occupation: 21.4% management, 19.6% professional, 17.7% services, 24.1% sales, 0.0% farming, 12.6% construction, 4.6% production (2005-2009 5-year est.).

Income: Per capita income: $37,069 (2010); Median household income: $86,372 (2010); Average household income: $107,114 (2010); Percent of households with income of $100,000 or more: 38.8% (2010); Poverty rate: 1.7% (2005-2009 5-year est.).

Taxes: Total city taxes per capita: $405 (2007); City property taxes per capita: $145 (2007).

Education: Percent of population age 25 and over with: High school diploma (including GED) or higher: 94.4% (2010); Bachelor's degree or higher: 35.3% (2010); Master's degree or higher: 11.5% (2010).

School District(s)
Comal ISD (PK-12)
  2009-10 Enrollment: 16,700 .... (830) 221-2000
Housing: Homeownership rate: 90.0% (2010); Median home value: $259,002 (2010); Median contract rent: $979 per month (2005-2009 5-year est.); Median year structure built: 1992 (2005-2009 5-year est.).
Safety: Violent crime rate: 10.6 per 10,000 population; Property crime rate: 174.3 per 10,000 population (2009).
Newspapers: Bulverde Community News (Local news; Circulation 6,000)
Transportation: Commute to work: 88.3% car, 0.0% public transportation, 0.0% walk, 9.8% work from home (2005-2009 5-year est.); Travel time to work: 12.6% less than 15 minutes, 24.0% 15 to 30 minutes, 29.3% 30 to 45 minutes, 26.7% 45 to 60 minutes, 7.3% 60 minutes or more (2005-2009 5-year est.)
Additional Information Contacts
Bulverde/Spring Branch Area Chamber of Commerce .... (830) 438-4285
  http://www.bulverdechamber.com
City of Bulverde .... (830) 438-3612
  http://www.ci.bulverde.tx.us

CANYON LAKE (CDP). Aka Canyon City. Covers a land area of 144.255 square miles and a water area of 12.617 square miles. Located at 29.88° N. Lat; 98.26° W. Long. Elevation is 965 feet.
Population: 9,973 (1990); 16,870 (2000); 22,123 (2010); 25,459 (2015 projected); Race: 92.2% White, 1.1% Black, 0.3% Asian, 6.4% Other, 14.0% Hispanic of any race (2010); Density: 153.4 persons per square mile (2010); Average household size: 2.48 (2010); Median age: 41.2 (2010); Males per 100 females: 99.6 (2010); Marriage status: 16.9% never married, 65.7% now married, 5.1% widowed, 12.3% divorced (2005-2009 5-year est.); Foreign born: 4.2% (2005-2009 5-year est.); Ancestry (includes multiple ancestries): 25.1% German, 15.9% English, 15.8% Irish, 8.2% American, 5.1% French (2005-2009 5-year est.).

Economy: Employment by occupation: 11.6% management, 20.9% professional, 11.8% services, 28.8% sales, 0.0% farming, 17.3% construction, 9.5% production (2005-2009 5-year est.).

Income: Per capita income: $28,053 (2010); Median household income: $57,201 (2010); Average household income: $69,608 (2010); Percent of households with income of $100,000 or more: 18.2% (2010); Poverty rate: 11.4% (2005-2009 5-year est.).

Education: Percent of population age 25 and over with: High school diploma (including GED) or higher: 90.2% (2010); Bachelor's degree or higher: 25.6% (2010); Master's degree or higher: 8.0% (2010).

School District(s)
Comal ISD (PK-12)
  2009-10 Enrollment: 16,700 .... (830) 221-2000
Trinity Charter School (KG-12)
  2009-10 Enrollment: 277 .... (512) 706-7564
Housing: Homeownership rate: 81.6% (2010); Median home value: $131,323 (2010); Median contract rent: $619 per month (2005-2009 5-year est.); Median year structure built: 1986 (2005-2009 5-year est.).
Newspapers: Bulverde Standard (Community news; Circulation 2,000); Canyon Lake Week (Community news; Circulation 2,000); Comal County Beacon (Community news; Circulation 2,000); Times Guardian (Community news; Circulation 3,000)
Transportation: Commute to work: 89.4% car, 0.2% public transportation, 1.0% walk, 6.5% work from home (2005-2009 5-year est.); Travel time to work: 16.6% less than 15 minutes, 22.1% 15 to 30 minutes, 22.9% 30 to 45 minutes, 19.2% 45 to 60 minutes, 19.1% 60 minutes or more (2005-2009 5-year est.)
Additional Information Contacts
Canyon Lake Chamber of Commerce .... (830) 964-2223
  http://www.canyonlakechamber.com

FISCHER (unincorporated postal area, zip code 78623). Covers a land area of 10.532 square miles and a water area of 0 square miles. Located at 29.96° N. Lat; 98.21° W. Long. Elevation is 1,148 feet.
Population: 310 (2000); Race: 100.0% White, 0.0% Black, 0.0% Asian, 0.0% Other, 0.0% Hispanic of any race (2000); Density: 29.4 persons per square mile (2000); Age: 14.7% under 18, 24.6% over 64 (2000); Marriage status: 7.4% never married, 88.3% now married, 4.3% widowed, 0.0% divorced (2000); Foreign born: 0.0% (2000); Ancestry (includes multiple ancestries): 25.7% German, 24.6% English, 16.8% Scottish, 15.2% French, 12.6% Hungarian (2000).
Economy: Employment by occupation: 49.1% management, 19.8% professional, 11.3% services, 11.3% sales, 8.5% farming, 0.0% construction, 0.0% production (2000).
Income: Per capita income: $27,058 (2000); Median household income: $66,042 (2000); Poverty rate: 179.1% (2000).
Education: Percent of population age 25 and over with: High school diploma (including GED) or higher: 100.0% (2000); Bachelor's degree or higher: 48.3% (2000).

School District(s)
Comal ISD (PK-12)
  2009-10 Enrollment: 16,700 .... (830) 221-2000
Housing: Homeownership rate: 100.0% (2000); Median home value: $135,000 (2000); Median contract rent: n/a per month (2000); Median year structure built: 1991 (2000).
Transportation: Commute to work: 79.2% car, 0.0% public transportation, 0.0% walk, 20.8% work from home (2000); Travel time to work: 0.0% less than 15 minutes, 25.0% 15 to 30 minutes, 39.3% 30 to 45 minutes, 35.7% 45 to 60 minutes, 0.0% 60 minutes or more (2000)

GARDEN RIDGE (city). Covers a land area of 7.877 square miles and a water area of 0.173 square miles. Located at 29.63° N. Lat; 98.29° W. Long. Elevation is 892 feet.
Population: 1,476 (1990); 1,882 (2000); 2,896 (2010); 3,392 (2015 projected); Race: 87.4% White, 6.9% Black, 1.8% Asian, 3.9% Other, 10.8% Hispanic of any race (2010); Density: 367.6 persons per square mile (2010); Average household size: 2.67 (2010); Median age: 45.8 (2010); Males per 100 females: 97.5 (2010); Marriage status: 14.0% never married, 77.4% now married, 4.4% widowed, 4.1% divorced (2005-2009 5-year est.); Foreign born: 7.5% (2005-2009 5-year est.); Ancestry (includes multiple ancestries): 31.3% German, 17.0% English, 7.6% Irish, 5.3% American, 4.6% French (2005-2009 5-year est.).

Economy: Single-family building permits issued: 33 (2010); Multi-family building permits issued: 0 (2010); Employment by occupation: 23.2% management, 24.0% professional, 4.3% services, 38.1% sales, 0.0% farming, 3.8% construction, 6.6% production (2005-2009 5-year est.).
Income: Per capita income: $49,480 (2010); Median household income: $108,604 (2010); Average household income: $132,057 (2010); Percent of households with income of $100,000 or more: 54.9% (2010); Poverty rate: 2.4% (2005-2009 5-year est.).
Taxes: Total city taxes per capita: $576 (2007); City property taxes per capita: $289 (2007).
Education: Percent of population age 25 and over with: High school diploma (including GED) or higher: 96.3% (2010); Bachelor's degree or higher: 48.6% (2010); Master's degree or higher: 20.0% (2010).
Housing: Homeownership rate: 92.4% (2010); Median home value: $309,350 (2010); Median contract rent: $1,477 per month (2005-2009 5-year est.); Median year structure built: 1995 (2005-2009 5-year est.).
Transportation: Commute to work: 93.0% car, 0.0% public transportation, 1.2% walk, 3.9% work from home (2005-2009 5-year est.); Travel time to work: 17.0% less than 15 minutes, 25.1% 15 to 30 minutes, 38.0% 30 to 45 minutes, 15.6% 45 to 60 minutes, 4.4% 60 minutes or more (2005-2009 5-year est.)
Additional Information Contacts
City of Garden Ridge . . . . (210) 651-6632
http://www.ci.garden-ridge.tx.us

NEW BRAUNFELS (city). County seat. Covers a land area of
29.248 square miles and a water area of 0.149 square miles. Located at 29.70° N. Lat; 98.12° W. Long. Elevation is 630 feet.
History: Many immigrants from Germany settled in New Braunfels after 1845. The town has advertised itself as the Sausage Capital of the World, celebrating its meat industry with Wurst Week in November. New Braunfels was named for Prince Carl Zu Solms-Braunfels, who founded the town on the Comal River.
Population: 27,952 (1990); 36,494 (2000); 52,163 (2010); 59,607 (2015 projected); Race: 81.4% White, 2.9% Black, 1.1% Asian, 14.6% Other, 37.0% Hispanic of any race (2010); Density: 1,783.4 persons per square mile (2010); Average household size: 2.57 (2010); Median age: 34.2 (2010); Males per 100 females: 95.6 (2010); Marriage status: 25.1% never married, 57.6% now married, 7.4% widowed, 9.9% divorced (2005-2009 5-year est.); Foreign born: 7.0% (2005-2009 5-year est.); Ancestry (includes multiple ancestries): 24.6% German, 11.1% Irish, 9.7% English, 4.7% American, 2.9% Italian (2005-2009 5-year est.).
Economy: Unemployment rate: 7.0% (June 2011); Total civilian labor force: 28,952 (June 2011); Single-family building permits issued: 356 (2010); Multi-family building permits issued: 0 (2010); Employment by occupation: 15.4% management, 19.1% professional, 17.4% services, 27.9% sales, 0.3% farming, 9.3% construction, 10.7% production (2005-2009 5-year est.).
Income: Per capita income: $24,785 (2010); Median household income: $51,694 (2010); Average household income: $64,140 (2010); Percent of households with income of $100,000 or more: 15.6% (2010); Poverty rate: 11.0% (2005-2009 5-year est.).
Taxes: Total city taxes per capita: $677 (2007); City property taxes per capita: $211 (2007).
Education: Percent of population age 25 and over with: High school diploma (including GED) or higher: 84.3% (2010); Bachelor's degree or higher: 29.1% (2010); Master's degree or higher: 9.2% (2010).
School District(s)
Comal ISD (PK-12)
    2009-10 Enrollment: 16,700 . . . . (830) 221-2000
New Braunfels ISD (PK-12)
    2009-10 Enrollment: 7,856 . . . . (830) 643-5700
Responsive Education Solutions (KG-12)
    2009-10 Enrollment: 5,022 . . . . (972) 316-3663
Vocational/Technical School(s)
Seguin Beauty School (Private, For-profit)
    Fall 2009 Enrollment: 46 . . . . (830) 372-0935
    2010-11 Tuition: $13,500
Housing: Homeownership rate: 60.6% (2010); Median home value: $134,081 (2010); Median contract rent: $677 per month (2005-2009 5-year est.); Median year structure built: 1988 (2005-2009 5-year est.).
Hospitals: McKenna Memorial Hospital (132 beds)
Safety: Violent crime rate: 25.5 per 10,000 population; Property crime rate: 386.6 per 10,000 population (2009).

Newspapers: Canyon Lake Times Guardian (Community news; Circulation 2,500); New Braunfels Herald-Zeitung (Local news; Circulation 8,500)
Transportation: Commute to work: 93.1% car, 0.0% public transportation, 2.0% walk, 3.0% work from home (2005-2009 5-year est.); Travel time to work: 43.1% less than 15 minutes, 29.3% 15 to 30 minutes, 12.5% 30 to 45 minutes, 8.3% 45 to 60 minutes, 6.7% 60 minutes or more (2005-2009 5-year est.)
Airports: New Braunfels Municipal (general aviation)
Additional Information Contacts
City of New Braunfels . . . . (830) 221-4000
http://www.ci.new-braunfels.tx.us
Greater New Braunfels Chamber of Commerce . . . . (830) 625-2385
http://www.nbcham.org
New Braunfels Women's Chamber of Commerce . . . .
http://nbwcc.net

SPRING BRANCH (unincorporated postal area, zip code 78070).
Covers a land area of 111.632 square miles and a water area of 0.015 square miles. Located at 29.89° N. Lat; 98.40° W. Long. Elevation is 1,115 feet.
Population: 7,283 (2000); Race: 93.0% White, 0.5% Black, 0.7% Asian, 5.8% Other, 11.7% Hispanic of any race (2000); Density: 65.2 persons per square mile (2000); Age: 29.8% under 18, 7.7% over 64 (2000); Marriage status: 16.9% never married, 68.5% now married, 4.4% widowed, 10.1% divorced (2000); Foreign born: 3.2% (2000); Ancestry (includes multiple ancestries): 28.1% German, 11.7% Irish, 10.4% English, 7.6% American (2000).
Economy: Employment by occupation: 16.4% management, 21.8% professional, 9.6% services, 26.8% sales, 0.3% farming, 14.6% construction, 10.5% production (2000).
Income: Per capita income: $22,096 (2000); Median household income: $51,227 (2000); Poverty rate: 179.1% (2000).
Education: Percent of population age 25 and over with: High school diploma (including GED) or higher: 90.6% (2000); Bachelor's degree or higher: 23.7% (2000).
School District(s)
Comal ISD (PK-12)
    2009-10 Enrollment: 16,700 . . . . (830) 221-2000
Housing: Homeownership rate: 90.1% (2000); Median home value: $136,200 (2000); Median contract rent: $501 per month (2000); Median year structure built: 1990 (2000).
Transportation: Commute to work: 95.1% car, 0.0% public transportation, 0.8% walk, 3.2% work from home (2000); Travel time to work: 6.9% less than 15 minutes, 17.4% 15 to 30 minutes, 28.8% 30 to 45 minutes, 28.8% 45 to 60 minutes, 18.0% 60 minutes or more (2000)

Comanche County

Located in central Texas; drained by the Leon and South Leon Rivers. Covers a land area of 937.69 square miles, a water area of 9.98 square miles, and is located in the Central Time Zone at 31.97° N. Lat., 98.56° W. Long. The county was founded in 1856. County seat is Comanche.

Weather Station: Proctor Reservoir								Elevation: 1,221 feet			
	Jan	Feb	Mar	Apr	May	Jun	Jul	Aug	Sep	Oct	Nov	Dec
High	59	62	69	78	84	91	95	96	89	79	68	59
Low	31	35	43	51	60	67	70	70	62	52	42	33
Precip	1.3	2.2	2.7	2.5	4.7	4.9	1.8	2.0	3.0	3.3	2.2	1.6
Snow	tr	tr	0.0	0.0	0.0	0.0	0.0	0.0	0.0	0.0	0.0	tr

High and Low temperatures in degrees Fahrenheit; Precipitation and Snow in inches

Population: 13,381 (1990); 14,026 (2000); 13,936 (2010); 13,866 (2015 projected); Race: 84.2% White, 0.8% Black, 0.5% Asian, 14.4% Other, 24.9% Hispanic of any race (2010); Density: 14.9 persons per square mile (2010); Average household size: 2.49 (2010); Median age: 40.6 (2010); Males per 100 females: 96.2 (2010).
Religion: Five largest groups: 42.0% Southern Baptist Convention, 9.2% The United Methodist Church, 5.1% Catholic Church, 4.4% Churches of Christ, 0.7% National Association of Free Will Baptists (2000).
Economy: Unemployment rate: 7.6% (June 2011); Total civilian labor force: 6,912 (June 2011); Leading industries: 23.2% health care and social assistance; 19.3% retail trade; 9.5% accommodation & food services (2009); Farms: 1,451 totaling 578,943 acres (2007); Companies that employ 500 or more persons: 0 (2009); Companies that employ 100 to 499 persons: 2 (2009); Companies that employ less than 100 persons: 276 (2009); Black-owned businesses: n/a (2007); Hispanic-owned businesses:

n/a (2007); Asian-owned businesses: n/a (2007); Women-owned businesses: n/a (2007); Retail sales per capita: $9,647 (2010).
Single-family building permits issued: 1 (2010); Multi-family building permits issued: 0 (2010).
Income: Per capita income: $19,051 (2010); Median household income: $37,289 (2010); Average household income: $48,125 (2010); Percent of households with income of $100,000 or more: 7.8% (2010); Poverty rate: 21.7% (2009); Bankruptcy rate: 0.99% (2010).
Taxes: Total county taxes per capita: $240 (2007); County property taxes per capita: $217 (2007).
Education: Percent of population age 25 and over with: High school diploma (including GED) or higher: 75.5% (2010); Bachelor's degree or higher: 14.5% (2010); Master's degree or higher: 4.2% (2010).
Housing: Homeownership rate: 74.4% (2010); Median home value: $67,134 (2010); Median contract rent: $293 per month (2005-2009 5-year est.); Median year structure built: 1973 (2005-2009 5-year est.)
Health: Birth rate: 144.6 per 10,000 population (2009); Death rate: 124.6 per 10,000 population (2009); Age-adjusted cancer mortality rate: 201.5 deaths per 100,000 population (2007); Number of physicians: 7.4 per 10,000 population (2008); Hospital beds: 28.2 per 10,000 population (2007); Hospital admissions: 1,293.1 per 10,000 population (2007).
Elections: 2008 Presidential election results: 25.6% Obama, 73.1% McCain, 0.1% Nader
Additional Information Contacts
Comanche County Government . . . . (325) 356-2466
    http://www.comanchecountytexas.us
Comanche Chamber of Commerce . . . . (325) 356-3233
    http://www.comanchechamber.org
De Leon Chamber of Commerce . . . . (254) 893-2083
    http://www.deleontexas.com/chamber

Comanche County Communities

COMANCHE (city). County seat. Covers a land area of 4.490 square miles and a water area of 0 square miles. Located at 31.90° N. Lat; 98.60° W. Long. Elevation is 1,381 feet.
History: Comanche was once a congregating point for buffalo hunters and trail drivers. It grew as a ranching center, producing peanuts, pecans, fruits, grains, cotton, and cattle.
Population: 4,128 (1990); 4,482 (2000); 4,351 (2010); 4,271 (2015 projected); Race: 73.5% White, 2.2% Black, 1.1% Asian, 23.2% Other, 32.9% Hispanic of any race (2010); Density: 969.1 persons per square mile (2010); Average household size: 2.59 (2010); Median age: 36.1 (2010); Males per 100 females: 91.3 (2010); Marriage status: 23.1% never married, 52.1% now married, 15.9% widowed, 8.9% divorced (2005-2009 5-year est.); Foreign born: 16.6% (2005-2009 5-year est.); Ancestry (includes multiple ancestries): 8.8% English, 7.4% Irish, 6.6% American, 6.5% German, 3.5% Scottish (2005-2009 5-year est.).
Economy: Single-family building permits issued: 1 (2010); Multi-family building permits issued: 0 (2010); Employment by occupation: 8.8% management, 11.2% professional, 21.7% services, 16.6% sales, 8.9% farming, 11.9% construction, 20.8% production (2005-2009 5-year est.).
Income: Per capita income: $16,496 (2010); Median household income: $36,215 (2010); Average household income: $44,023 (2010); Percent of households with income of $100,000 or more: 6.6% (2010); Poverty rate: 26.0% (2005-2009 5-year est.).
Taxes: Total city taxes per capita: $279 (2007); City property taxes per capita: $146 (2007).
Education: Percent of population age 25 and over with: High school diploma (including GED) or higher: 73.9% (2010); Bachelor's degree or higher: 11.3% (2010); Master's degree or higher: 3.6% (2010).
School District(s)
Comanche ISD (PK-12)
    2009-10 Enrollment: 1,210 . . . . (325) 356-2727
Paradigm Accelerated Charter School (07-12)
    2009-10 Enrollment: 219 . . . . (254) 445-4844
Housing: Homeownership rate: 67.7% (2010); Median home value: $49,735 (2010); Median contract rent: $288 per month (2005-2009 5-year est.); Median year structure built: 1964 (2005-2009 5-year est.).
Hospitals: Comanche County Medical Center (25 beds)
Safety: Violent crime rate: 35.9 per 10,000 population; Property crime rate: 376.2 per 10,000 population (2009).
Transportation: Commute to work: 93.0% car, 0.0% public transportation, 4.6% walk, 2.0% work from home (2005-2009 5-year est.); Travel time to work: 61.5% less than 15 minutes, 12.4% 15 to 30 minutes, 12.4% 30 to 45

minutes, 7.1% 45 to 60 minutes, 6.7% 60 minutes or more (2005-2009 5-year est.)
Airports: Comanche County-City (general aviation)
Additional Information Contacts
Comanche Chamber of Commerce . . . . (325) 356-3233
    http://www.comanchechamber.org

DE LEON (city). Covers a land area of 2.070 square miles and a water area of 0 square miles. Located at 32.11° N. Lat; 98.53° W. Long. Elevation is 1,280 feet.
History: Founded 1887, incorporated as city 1919.
Population: 2,190 (1990); 2,433 (2000); 2,375 (2010); 2,335 (2015 projected); Race: 89.5% White, 0.3% Black, 0.0% Asian, 10.3% Other, 30.5% Hispanic of any race (2010); Density: 1,147.1 persons per square mile (2010); Average household size: 2.47 (2010); Median age: 37.4 (2010); Males per 100 females: 90.9 (2010); Marriage status: 25.3% never married, 50.8% now married, 10.0% widowed, 13.9% divorced (2005-2009 5-year est.); Foreign born: 1.6% (2005-2009 5-year est.); Ancestry (includes multiple ancestries): 16.1% Irish, 9.9% German, 7.3% English, 6.2% American, 2.1% French (2005-2009 5-year est.).
Economy: Employment by occupation: 6.8% management, 14.1% professional, 15.8% services, 36.5% sales, 1.2% farming, 8.2% construction, 17.3% production (2005-2009 5-year est.).
Income: Per capita income: $15,607 (2010); Median household income: $26,835 (2010); Average household income: $38,620 (2010); Percent of households with income of $100,000 or more: 5.0% (2010); Poverty rate: 26.3% (2005-2009 5-year est.).
Taxes: Total city taxes per capita: $255 (2007); City property taxes per capita: $128 (2007).
Education: Percent of population age 25 and over with: High school diploma (including GED) or higher: 64.2% (2010); Bachelor's degree or higher: 12.4% (2010); Master's degree or higher: 3.4% (2010).
School District(s)
De Leon ISD (PK-12)
    2009-10 Enrollment: 704 . . . . (254) 893-5095
Housing: Homeownership rate: 68.2% (2010); Median home value: $48,369 (2010); Median contract rent: $288 per month (2005-2009 5-year est.); Median year structure built: 1964 (2005-2009 5-year est.).
Safety: Violent crime rate: 12.9 per 10,000 population; Property crime rate: 167.7 per 10,000 population (2009).
Newspapers: Deleon Free Press (Community news; Circulation 2,000)
Transportation: Commute to work: 86.2% car, 0.0% public transportation, 0.8% walk, 1.6% work from home (2005-2009 5-year est.); Travel time to work: 53.4% less than 15 minutes, 11.0% 15 to 30 minutes, 28.6% 30 to 45 minutes, 2.8% 45 to 60 minutes, 4.2% 60 minutes or more (2005-2009 5-year est.)
Additional Information Contacts
De Leon Chamber of Commerce . . . . (254) 893-2083
    http://www.deleontexas.com/chamber

GUSTINE (town). Covers a land area of 0.913 square miles and a water area of 0 square miles. Located at 31.84° N. Lat; 98.40° W. Long. Elevation is 1,191 feet.
Population: 430 (1990); 457 (2000); 489 (2010); 505 (2015 projected); Race: 82.4% White, 0.0% Black, 0.0% Asian, 17.6% Other, 31.7% Hispanic of any race (2010); Density: 535.7 persons per square mile (2010); Average household size: 2.52 (2010); Median age: 41.3 (2010); Males per 100 females: 104.6 (2010); Marriage status: 14.2% never married, 72.9% now married, 7.6% widowed, 5.3% divorced (2005-2009 5-year est.); Foreign born: 6.6% (2005-2009 5-year est.); Ancestry (includes multiple ancestries): 17.8% German, 15.1% English, 11.5% Irish, 7.8% Scotch-Irish, 7.1% American (2005-2009 5-year est.).
Economy: Employment by occupation: 20.7% management, 6.0% professional, 22.8% services, 10.3% sales, 10.3% farming, 10.3% construction, 19.6% production (2005-2009 5-year est.).
Income: Per capita income: $20,397 (2010); Median household income: $35,000 (2010); Average household income: $50,773 (2010); Percent of households with income of $100,000 or more: 8.2% (2010); Poverty rate: 22.4% (2005-2009 5-year est.).
Taxes: Total city taxes per capita: $93 (2007); City property taxes per capita: $27 (2007).
Education: Percent of population age 25 and over with: High school diploma (including GED) or higher: 73.2% (2010); Bachelor's degree or higher: 13.0% (2010); Master's degree or higher: 3.5% (2010).

School District(s)

Gustine ISD (PK-12)

    2009-10 Enrollment: 232 . . . . (325) 667-7981

Housing: Homeownership rate: 75.8% (2010); Median home value: $74,211 (2010); Median contract rent: $260 per month (2005-2009 5-year est.); Median year structure built: 1969 (2005-2009 5-year est.).

Transportation: Commute to work: 86.8% car, 0.0% public transportation, 10.4% walk, 0.5% work from home (2005-2009 5-year est.); Travel time to work: 34.8% less than 15 minutes, 33.1% 15 to 30 minutes, 17.1% 30 to 45 minutes, 5.5% 45 to 60 minutes, 9.4% 60 minutes or more (2005-2009 5-year est.)

SIDNEY (unincorporated postal area, zip code 76474). Covers a land area of 37.989 square miles and a water area of 0.108 square miles. Located at 31.96° N. Lat; 98.78° W. Long. Elevation is 1,430 feet.

Population: 331 (2000); Race: 92.5% White, 0.0% Black, 0.0% Asian, 7.5% Other, 8.1% Hispanic of any race (2000); Density: 8.7 persons per square mile (2000); Age: 22.2% under 18, 18.4% over 64 (2000); Marriage status: 19.6% never married, 62.6% now married, 9.6% widowed, 8.1% divorced (2000); Foreign born: 4.1% (2000); Ancestry (includes multiple ancestries): 22.8% American, 13.1% Irish, 12.8% English, 10.3% German (2000).

Economy: Employment by occupation: 13.6% management, 17.8% professional, 14.8% services, 23.7% sales, 5.9% farming, 11.2% construction, 13.0% production (2000).

Income: Per capita income: $17,137 (2000); Median household income: $38,182 (2000); Poverty rate: 179.1% (2000).

Education: Percent of population age 25 and over with: High school diploma (including GED) or higher: 76.1% (2000); Bachelor's degree or higher: 13.8% (2000).

School District(s)

Sidney ISD (KG-12)

    2009-10 Enrollment: 122 . . . . (254) 842-5500

Housing: Homeownership rate: 78.9% (2000); Median home value: $51,400 (2000); Median contract rent: $200 per month (2000); Median year structure built: 1963 (2000).

Transportation: Commute to work: 89.6% car, 0.0% public transportation, 4.9% walk, 4.3% work from home (2000); Travel time to work: 27.4% less than 15 minutes, 33.1% 15 to 30 minutes, 14.6% 30 to 45 minutes, 14.0% 45 to 60 minutes, 10.8% 60 minutes or more (2000)

Concho County

Located in west central Texas, on the North Edwards Plateau; bounded on the northeast by the Colorado River. Covers a land area of 991.45 square miles, a water area of 2.23 square miles, and is located in the Central Time Zone at 31.33° N. Lat., 99.87° W. Long. The county was founded in 1858. County seat is Paint Rock.

Weather Station: Paint Rock										Elevation: 1,625 feet		
	Jan	Feb	Mar	Apr	May	Jun	Jul	Aug	Sep	Oct	Nov	Dec
High	62	66	73	82	89	94	97	96	90	81	70	62
Low	32	36	44	51	61	68	70	70	63	53	41	32
Precip	1.0	1.6	2.0	1.3	3.4	3.9	1.7	2.1	3.2	2.6	1.7	1.2
Snow	1.2	0.5	0.1	0.1	0.0	0.0	0.0	0.0	0.0	0.0	0.3	0.5

High and Low temperatures in degrees Fahrenheit; Precipitation and Snow in inches

Population: 3,044 (1990); 3,966 (2000); 3,648 (2010); 3,487 (2015 projected); Race: 87.4% White, 1.1% Black, 0.1% Asian, 11.5% Other, 43.6% Hispanic of any race (2010); Density: 3.7 persons per square mile (2010); Average household size: 2.43 (2010); Median age: 36.2 (2010); Males per 100 females: 208.1 (2010).

Religion: Five largest groups: 18.2% Southern Baptist Convention, 12.5% Catholic Church, 5.0% Churches of Christ, 3.9% The United Methodist Church, 3.3% Lutheran Church—Missouri Synod (2000).

Economy: Unemployment rate: 8.8% (June 2011); Total civilian labor force: 1,279 (June 2011); Leading industries: 19.9% health care and social assistance; 12.5% retail trade; 9.7% accommodation & food services (2009); Farms: 418 totaling 551,371 acres (2007); Companies that employ 500 or more persons: 0 (2009); Companies that employ 100 to 499 persons: 1 (2009); Companies that employ less than 100 persons: 49 (2009); Black-owned businesses: n/a (2007); Hispanic-owned businesses: n/a (2007); Asian-owned businesses: n/a (2007); Women-owned businesses: n/a (2007); Retail sales per capita: $5,177 (2010). Single-family building permits issued: n/a (2010); Multi-family building permits issued: n/a (2010).

Income: Per capita income: $17,394 (2010); Median household income: $41,161 (2010); Average household income: $56,648 (2010); Percent of households with income of $100,000 or more: 10.8% (2010); Poverty rate: 29.5% (2009); Bankruptcy rate: 0.97% (2010).

Taxes: Total county taxes per capita: $418 (2007); County property taxes per capita: $339 (2007).

Education: Percent of population age 25 and over with: High school diploma (including GED) or higher: 64.9% (2010); Bachelor's degree or higher: 15.9% (2010); Master's degree or higher: 3.3% (2010).

Housing: Homeownership rate: 73.2% (2010); Median home value: $61,759 (2010); Median contract rent: $316 per month (2005-2009 5-year est.); Median year structure built: 1966 (2005-2009 5-year est.)

Health: Birth rate: 100.6 per 10,000 population (2009); Death rate: 72.6 per 10,000 population (2009); Age-adjusted cancer mortality rate: Suppressed deaths per 100,000 population (2007); Number of physicians: 8.3 per 10,000 population (2008); Hospital beds: 44.6 per 10,000 population (2007); Hospital admissions: 265.1 per 10,000 population (2007).

Elections: 2008 Presidential election results: 23.9% Obama, 74.9% McCain, 0.0% Nader

Additional Information Contacts

Concho County Government . . . . (325) 732-4321
    http://www.co.concho.tx.us/ips/cms
Eden Chamber of Commerce . . . . (325) 869-3336
    http://www.edentexas.com

Concho County Communities

EDEN (city). Covers a land area of 2.427 square miles and a water area of 0 square miles. Located at 31.21° N. Lat; 99.84° W. Long. Elevation is 2,054 feet.

Population: 1,676 (1990); 2,561 (2000); 2,288 (2010); 2,151 (2015 projected); Race: 91.4% White, 1.5% Black, 0.1% Asian, 7.0% Other, 49.8% Hispanic of any race (2010); Density: 942.7 persons per square mile (2010); Average household size: 2.39 (2010); Median age: 34.2 (2010); Males per 100 females: 267.8 (2010); Marriage status: 29.5% never married, 55.2% now married, 5.1% widowed, 10.2% divorced (2005-2009 5-year est.); Foreign born: 51.6% (2005-2009 5-year est.); Ancestry (includes multiple ancestries): 17.0% American, 8.2% German, 6.6% English, 3.7% Irish, 2.2% French (2005-2009 5-year est.).

Economy: Single-family building permits issued: 0 (2010); Multi-family building permits issued: 0 (2010); Employment by occupation: 8.9% management, 20.6% professional, 25.4% services, 13.0% sales, 0.2% farming, 24.7% construction, 7.1% production (2005-2009 5-year est.).

Income: Per capita income: $14,889 (2010); Median household income: $39,712 (2010); Average household income: $54,326 (2010); Percent of households with income of $100,000 or more: 10.0% (2010); Poverty rate: 15.2% (2005-2009 5-year est.).

Taxes: Total city taxes per capita: $184 (2007); City property taxes per capita: $100 (2007).

Education: Percent of population age 25 and over with: High school diploma (including GED) or higher: 60.3% (2010); Bachelor's degree or higher: 13.9% (2010); Master's degree or higher: 2.7% (2010).

School District(s)

Eden CISD (PK-12)

    2009-10 Enrollment: 266 . . . . (325) 869-4121

Housing: Homeownership rate: 68.2% (2010); Median home value: $59,833 (2010); Median contract rent: $305 per month (2005-2009 5-year est.); Median year structure built: 1963 (2005-2009 5-year est.).

Hospitals: Concho County Hospital (20 beds)

Safety: Violent crime rate: 4.2 per 10,000 population; Property crime rate: 173.6 per 10,000 population (2009).

Newspapers: The Eden Echo (Community news; Circulation 1,100)

Transportation: Commute to work: 91.2% car, 0.0% public transportation, 4.9% walk, 2.6% work from home (2005-2009 5-year est.); Travel time to work: 68.8% less than 15 minutes, 5.6% 15 to 30 minutes, 5.8% 30 to 45 minutes, 3.8% 45 to 60 minutes, 15.9% 60 minutes or more (2005-2009 5-year est.)

Additional Information Contacts

Eden Chamber of Commerce . . . . (325) 869-3336
    http://www.edentexas.com

EOLA (unincorporated postal area, zip code 76937). Covers a land area of 34.204 square miles and a water area of 0 square miles. Located at 31.37° N. Lat; 100.10° W. Long. Elevation is 1,808 feet.

Population: 281 (2000); Race: 72.1% White, 0.0% Black, 0.0% Asian, 27.9% Other, 50.0% Hispanic of any race (2000); Density: 8.2 persons per square mile (2000); Age: 32.1% under 18, 10.9% over 64 (2000); Marriage status: 23.5% never married, 64.7% now married, 3.8% widowed, 8.0% divorced (2000); Foreign born: 8.0% (2000); Ancestry (includes multiple ancestries): 19.6% German, 18.6% Czech, 5.1% Irish, 2.6% Scottish (2000).
Economy: Employment by occupation: 15.1% management, 9.4% professional, 21.7% services, 25.5% sales, 3.8% farming, 10.4% construction, 14.2% production (2000).
Income: Per capita income: $18,500 (2000); Median household income: $22,917 (2000); Poverty rate: 179.1% (2000).
Education: Percent of population age 25 and over with: High school diploma (including GED) or higher: 61.9% (2000); Bachelor's degree or higher: 7.2% (2000).
Housing: Homeownership rate: 78.3% (2000); Median home value: $22,800 (2000); Median contract rent: $318 per month (2000); Median year structure built: 1962 (2000).
Transportation: Commute to work: 99.1% car, 0.0% public transportation, 0.0% walk, 0.0% work from home (2000); Travel time to work: 17.0% less than 15 minutes, 27.4% 15 to 30 minutes, 41.5% 30 to 45 minutes, 8.5% 45 to 60 minutes, 5.7% 60 minutes or more (2000)

MILLERSVIEW (unincorporated postal area, zip code 76862). Covers a land area of 132.777 square miles and a water area of 0.236 square miles. Located at 31.44° N. Lat; 99.70° W. Long. Elevation is 1,644 feet.
Population: 168 (2000); Race: 98.1% White, 0.0% Black, 0.0% Asian, 1.9% Other, 0.6% Hispanic of any race (2000); Density: 1.3 persons per square mile (2000); Age: 14.8% under 18, 21.6% over 64 (2000); Marriage status: 13.5% never married, 75.7% now married, 5.4% widowed, 5.4% divorced (2000); Foreign born: 0.6% (2000); Ancestry (includes multiple ancestries): 19.8% German, 14.8% American, 11.1% English, 8.0% Scotch-Irish, 5.6% Czech (2000).
Economy: Employment by occupation: 39.5% management, 16.3% professional, 5.8% services, 12.8% sales, 7.0% farming, 5.8% construction, 12.8% production (2000).
Income: Per capita income: $17,998 (2000); Median household income: $33,281 (2000); Poverty rate: 179.1% (2000).
Education: Percent of population age 25 and over with: High school diploma (including GED) or higher: 84.8% (2000); Bachelor's degree or higher: 15.2% (2000).
Housing: Homeownership rate: 73.9% (2000); Median home value: $75,000 (2000); Median contract rent: $350 per month (2000); Median year structure built: 1982 (2000).
Transportation: Commute to work: 83.7% car, 0.0% public transportation, 3.5% walk, 12.8% work from home (2000); Travel time to work: 65.3% less than 15 minutes, 18.7% 15 to 30 minutes, 4.0% 30 to 45 minutes, 2.7% 45 to 60 minutes, 9.3% 60 minutes or more (2000)

PAINT ROCK (town). County seat. Covers a land area of 1.661 square miles and a water area of 0 square miles. Located at 31.50° N. Lat; 99.92° W. Long. Elevation is 1,631 feet.
History: Paint Rock was named for the rock paintings along the Concho River near the town. The town developed as a shipping center for wool.
Population: 227 (1990); 320 (2000); 330 (2010); 325 (2015 projected); Race: 77.0% White, 0.0% Black, 0.3% Asian, 22.7% Other, 27.0% Hispanic of any race (2010); Density: 198.7 persons per square mile (2010); Average household size: 2.48 (2010); Median age: 46.0 (2010); Males per 100 females: 107.5 (2010); Marriage status: 24.8% never married, 63.7% now married, 4.9% widowed, 6.6% divorced (2005-2009 5-year est.); Foreign born: 4.8% (2005-2009 5-year est.); Ancestry (includes multiple ancestries): 27.2% American, 11.7% German, 9.6% English, 9.0% Scotch-Irish, 3.0% Welsh (2005-2009 5-year est.).
Economy: Employment by occupation: 23.5% management, 20.9% professional, 13.1% services, 19.0% sales, 0.0% farming, 6.5% construction, 17.0% production (2005-2009 5-year est.).
Income: Per capita income: $23,917 (2010); Median household income: $43,365 (2010); Average household income: $59,850 (2010); Percent of households with income of $100,000 or more: 12.0% (2010); Poverty rate: 35.9% (2005-2009 5-year est.).
Taxes: Total city taxes per capita: $120 (2007); City property taxes per capita: $49 (2007).
Education: Percent of population age 25 and over with: High school diploma (including GED) or higher: 77.5% (2010); Bachelor's degree or higher: 20.5% (2010); Master's degree or higher: 4.5% (2010).

School District(s)
Eden CISD (PK-12)
    2009-10 Enrollment: 266 . . . . (325) 869-4121
Paint Rock ISD (PK-12)
    2009-10 Enrollment: 139 . . . . (325) 732-4314
Housing: Homeownership rate: 78.9% (2010); Median home value: $62,500 (2010); Median contract rent: n/a per month (2005-2009 5-year est.); Median year structure built: 1945 (2005-2009 5-year est.).
Transportation: Commute to work: 83.0% car, 0.0% public transportation, 17.0% walk, 0.0% work from home (2005-2009 5-year est.); Travel time to work: 34.6% less than 15 minutes, 10.5% 15 to 30 minutes, 53.6% 30 to 45 minutes, 1.3% 45 to 60 minutes, 0.0% 60 minutes or more (2005-2009 5-year est.)

Cooke County

Located in north Texas; bounded on the north by the Red River, Lake Texoma, and the Oklahoma border; drained by the Elm Fork of Trinity River. Covers a land area of 873.64 square miles, a water area of 25.17 square miles, and is located in the Central Time Zone at 33.62° N. Lat., 97.16° W. Long. The county was founded in 1848. County seat is Gainesville.

Cooke County is part of the Gainesville, TX Micropolitan Statistical Area. The entire metro area includes: Cooke County, TX

Population: 30,777 (1990); 36,363 (2000); 39,976 (2010); 41,658 (2015 projected); Race: 84.8% White, 3.4% Black, 0.7% Asian, 11.1% Other, 15.0% Hispanic of any race (2010); Density: 45.8 persons per square mile (2010); Average household size: 2.60 (2010); Median age: 36.5 (2010); Males per 100 females: 98.4 (2010).
Religion: Five largest groups: 24.1% Southern Baptist Convention, 22.5% Catholic Church, 4.6% The United Methodist Church, 3.2% Churches of Christ, 1.3% The American Baptist Association (2000).
Economy: Unemployment rate: 6.5% (June 2011); Total civilian labor force: 22,048 (June 2011); Leading industries: 27.1% manufacturing; 16.0% retail trade; 11.3% accommodation & food services (2009); Farms: 1,956 totaling 455,393 acres (2007); Companies that employ 500 or more persons: 3 (2009); Companies that employ 100 to 499 persons: 7 (2009); Companies that employ less than 100 persons: 862 (2009); Black-owned businesses: n/a (2007); Hispanic-owned businesses: 222 (2007); Asian-owned businesses: n/a (2007); Women-owned businesses: n/a (2007); Retail sales per capita: $16,374 (2010). Single-family building permits issued: 26 (2010); Multi-family building permits issued: 0 (2010).
Income: Per capita income: $24,269 (2010); Median household income: $50,410 (2010); Average household income: $63,956 (2010); Percent of households with income of $100,000 or more: 16.4% (2010); Poverty rate: 14.8% (2009); Bankruptcy rate: 1.61% (2010).
Taxes: Total county taxes per capita: $337 (2007); County property taxes per capita: $262 (2007).
Education: Percent of population age 25 and over with: High school diploma (including GED) or higher: 82.9% (2010); Bachelor's degree or higher: 19.7% (2010); Master's degree or higher: 4.8% (2010).
Housing: Homeownership rate: 72.1% (2010); Median home value: $108,252 (2010); Median contract rent: $474 per month (2005-2009 5-year est.); Median year structure built: 1976 (2005-2009 5-year est.)
Health: Birth rate: 143.1 per 10,000 population (2009); Death rate: 100.6 per 10,000 population (2009); Age-adjusted cancer mortality rate: 189.5 deaths per 100,000 population (2007); Number of physicians: 7.0 per 10,000 population (2008); Hospital beds: 20.3 per 10,000 population (2007); Hospital admissions: 758.9 per 10,000 population (2007).
Elections: 2008 Presidential election results: 20.3% Obama, 79.0% McCain, 0.0% Nader
Additional Information Contacts
Cooke County Government . . . . (940) 668-5435
    http://www.co.cooke.tx.us/ips/cms
City of Gainesville . . . . (940) 668-4500
    http://www.gainesville.tx.us
Gainesville Chamber of Commerce . . . . (940) 665-5241
    http://www.gogainesville.net
Muenster Chamber of Commerce . . . . (940) 759-2227
    http://www.muensterchamber.com
Valley View Chamber of Commerce . . . . (940) 726-3281

Cooke County Communities

CALLISBURG (city). Covers a land area of 2.345 square miles and a water area of 0 square miles. Located at 33.70° N. Lat; 97.01° W. Long. Elevation is 804 feet.

Population: 344 (1990); 365 (2000); 356 (2010); 363 (2015 projected); Race: 94.9% White, 0.0% Black, 0.3% Asian, 4.8% Other, 6.5% Hispanic of any race (2010); Density: 151.8 persons per square mile (2010); Average household size: 2.74 (2010); Median age: 38.0 (2010); Males per 100 females: 109.4 (2010); Marriage status: 18.9% never married, 55.0% now married, 7.5% widowed, 18.6% divorced (2005-2009 5-year est.); Foreign born: 1.8% (2005-2009 5-year est.); Ancestry (includes multiple ancestries): 16.2% American, 14.1% German, 8.9% Irish, 8.1% English, 4.5% Dutch (2005-2009 5-year est.).

Economy: Employment by occupation: 10.6% management, 13.1% professional, 14.4% services, 16.9% sales, 0.0% farming, 21.9% construction, 23.1% production (2005-2009 5-year est.).

Income: Per capita income: $24,252 (2010); Median household income: $58,553 (2010); Average household income: $68,000 (2010); Percent of households with income of $100,000 or more: 15.4% (2010); Poverty rate: 14.2% (2005-2009 5-year est.).

Taxes: Total city taxes per capita: $71 (2007); City property taxes per capita: $33 (2007).

Education: Percent of population age 25 and over with: High school diploma (including GED) or higher: 89.7% (2010); Bachelor's degree or higher: 15.5% (2010); Master's degree or higher: 5.6% (2010).

School District(s)
Callisburg ISD (PK-12)
    2009-10 Enrollment: 1,240 . . . . (940) 665-0540
Housing: Homeownership rate: 80.8% (2010); Median home value: $121,296 (2010); Median contract rent: $294 per month (2005-2009 5-year est.); Median year structure built: 1978 (2005-2009 5-year est.).
Transportation: Commute to work: 95.0% car, 0.0% public transportation, 1.3% walk, 3.8% work from home (2005-2009 5-year est.); Travel time to work: 6.5% less than 15 minutes, 33.8% 15 to 30 minutes, 33.1% 30 to 45 minutes, 10.4% 45 to 60 minutes, 16.2% 60 minutes or more (2005-2009 5-year est.)

ERA (unincorporated postal area, zip code 76238). Covers a land area of 22.531 square miles and a water area of 0.056 square miles. Located at 33.49° N. Lat; 97.39° W. Long. Elevation is 909 feet.

Population: 99 (2000); Race: 92.5% White, 0.0% Black, 0.0% Asian, 7.5% Other, 7.5% Hispanic of any race (2000); Density: 4.4 persons per square mile (2000); Age: 36.6% under 18, 4.3% over 64 (2000); Marriage status: 11.5% never married, 72.1% now married, 9.8% widowed, 6.6% divorced (2000); Foreign born: 0.0% (2000); Ancestry (includes multiple ancestries): 20.4% German, 12.9% American, 7.5% Irish, 7.5% French (2000).

Economy: Employment by occupation: 14.3% management, 11.4% professional, 2.9% services, 28.6% sales, 0.0% farming, 14.3% construction, 28.6% production (2000).

Income: Per capita income: $18,089 (2000); Median household income: $34,375 (2000); Poverty rate: 179.1% (2000).

Education: Percent of population age 25 and over with: High school diploma (including GED) or higher: 91.5% (2000); Bachelor's degree or higher: 33.9% (2000).

School District(s)
Era ISD (PK-12)
    2009-10 Enrollment: 440 . . . . (940) 665-2007
Housing: Homeownership rate: 78.8% (2000); Median home value: $75,000 (2000); Median contract rent: n/a per month (2000); Median year structure built: 1969 (2000).
Transportation: Commute to work: 100.0% car, 0.0% public transportation, 0.0% walk, 0.0% work from home (2000); Travel time to work: 5.7% less than 15 minutes, 28.6% 15 to 30 minutes, 28.6% 30 to 45 minutes, 28.6% 45 to 60 minutes, 8.6% 60 minutes or more (2000)

GAINESVILLE (city). County seat. Covers a land area of 16.998 square miles and a water area of 0.027 square miles. Located at 33.63° N. Lat; 97.14° W. Long. Elevation is 751 feet.

History: Gainesville was a stop on the Butterfield Stage Line after 1858, and before that was on the route of gold seekers heading west. The town also served as a supply point for cattle drovers on the Dodge City trail. The early economy of Gainesville was supported by cotton, grain, livestock, and poultry. Oil production and a natural gas refinery were added later.

Population: 14,551 (1990); 15,538 (2000); 17,443 (2010); 18,275 (2015 projected); Race: 74.0% White, 6.4% Black, 0.9% Asian, 18.7% Other, 26.9% Hispanic of any race (2010); Density: 1,026.2 persons per square mile (2010); Average household size: 2.58 (2010); Median age: 33.9 (2010); Males per 100 females: 91.9 (2010); Marriage status: 23.1% never married, 56.0% now married, 9.3% widowed, 11.5% divorced (2005-2009 5-year est.); Foreign born: 14.1% (2005-2009 5-year est.); Ancestry (includes multiple ancestries): 12.1% German, 12.0% Irish, 8.2% English, 6.9% American, 2.8% Scotch-Irish (2005-2009 5-year est.).

Economy: Single-family building permits issued: 10 (2010); Multi-family building permits issued: 0 (2010); Employment by occupation: 9.0% management, 14.0% professional, 20.6% services, 23.0% sales, 0.3% farming, 15.0% construction, 18.2% production (2005-2009 5-year est.).

Income: Per capita income: $19,434 (2010); Median household income: $39,813 (2010); Average household income: $51,050 (2010); Percent of households with income of $100,000 or more: 10.9% (2010); Poverty rate: 22.4% (2005-2009 5-year est.).

Taxes: Total city taxes per capita: $628 (2007); City property taxes per capita: $268 (2007).

Education: Percent of population age 25 and over with: High school diploma (including GED) or higher: 77.2% (2010); Bachelor's degree or higher: 17.6% (2010); Master's degree or higher: 4.6% (2010).

School District(s)
Callisburg ISD (PK-12)
    2009-10 Enrollment: 1,240 . . . . (940) 665-0540
Gainesville ISD (PK-12)
    2009-10 Enrollment: 2,636 . . . . (940) 665-4362
Gainesville State School (09-12)
    2009-10 Enrollment: 264 . . . . (940) 665-0701
Sivells Bend ISD (PK-08)
    2009-10 Enrollment: 70 . . . . (940) 665-6411
Walnut Bend ISD (PK-08)
    2009-10 Enrollment: 68 . . . . (940) 665-5990

Two-year College(s)
North Central Texas College (Public)
    Fall 2009 Enrollment: 9,156 . . . . (940) 668-7731
    2010-11 Tuition: In-state $1,968; Out-of-state $3,000
Housing: Homeownership rate: 58.5% (2010); Median home value: $76,318 (2010); Median contract rent: $490 per month (2005-2009 5-year est.); Median year structure built: 1966 (2005-2009 5-year est.).
Hospitals: North Texas Medical Centertal (60 beds)
Safety: Violent crime rate: 54.4 per 10,000 population; Property crime rate: 497.4 per 10,000 population (2009).
Newspapers: Gainesville Daily Register (Local news; Circulation 20,000)
Transportation: Commute to work: 92.1% car, 0.7% public transportation, 1.1% walk, 4.4% work from home (2005-2009 5-year est.); Travel time to work: 54.7% less than 15 minutes, 16.4% 15 to 30 minutes, 13.1% 30 to 45 minutes, 4.6% 45 to 60 minutes, 11.2% 60 minutes or more (2005-2009 5-year est.); Amtrak: train service available.
Airports: Gainesville Municipal (general aviation)
Additional Information Contacts
City of Gainesville . . . . (940) 668-4500
    http://www.gainesville.tx.us
Gainesville Chamber of Commerce . . . . (940) 665-5241
    http://www.gogainesville.net

LAKE KIOWA (CDP). Covers a land area of 2.998 square miles and a water area of 0.784 square miles. Located at 33.56° N. Lat; 97.00° W. Long. Elevation is 709 feet.

Population: 1,236 (1990); 1,883 (2000); 2,084 (2010); 2,172 (2015 projected); Race: 95.1% White, 0.0% Black, 0.7% Asian, 4.2% Other, 3.2% Hispanic of any race (2010); Density: 695.1 persons per square mile (2010); Average household size: 2.24 (2010); Median age: 56.3 (2010); Males per 100 females: 95.3 (2010); Marriage status: 9.0% never married, 70.8% now married, 11.8% widowed, 8.4% divorced (2005-2009 5-year est.); Foreign born: 2.9% (2005-2009 5-year est.); Ancestry (includes multiple ancestries): 26.0% English, 20.2% German, 16.9% Irish, 8.9% American, 7.2% Scotch-Irish (2005-2009 5-year est.).

Economy: Employment by occupation: 18.6% management, 33.2% professional, 19.5% services, 23.2% sales, 0.0% farming, 3.9% construction, 1.6% production (2005-2009 5-year est.).

Income: Per capita income: $37,723 (2010); Median household income: $67,824 (2010); Average household income: $84,614 (2010); Percent of households with income of $100,000 or more: 26.5% (2010); Poverty rate: 1.2% (2005-2009 5-year est.).

Education: Percent of population age 25 and over with: High school diploma (including GED) or higher: 93.4% (2010); Bachelor's degree or higher: 28.6% (2010); Master's degree or higher: 6.3% (2010).
Housing: Homeownership rate: 91.8% (2010); Median home value: $190,136 (2010); Median contract rent: $779 per month (2005-2009 5-year est.); Median year structure built: 1990 (2005-2009 5-year est.).
Transportation: Commute to work: 85.5% car, 0.0% public transportation, 2.2% walk, 12.3% work from home (2005-2009 5-year est.); Travel time to work: 19.6% less than 15 minutes, 27.7% 15 to 30 minutes, 18.7% 30 to 45 minutes, 7.6% 45 to 60 minutes, 26.4% 60 minutes or more (2005-2009 5-year est.)

LINDSAY (town). Covers a land area of 1.113 square miles and a water area of 0 square miles. Located at 33.63° N. Lat; 97.22° W. Long. Elevation is 794 feet.
Population: 629 (1990); 788 (2000); 893 (2010); 940 (2015 projected); Race: 97.9% White, 0.4% Black, 0.2% Asian, 1.5% Other, 1.7% Hispanic of any race (2010); Density: 802.6 persons per square mile (2010); Average household size: 2.91 (2010); Median age: 34.0 (2010); Males per 100 females: 99.3 (2010); Marriage status: 20.4% never married, 70.2% now married, 7.0% widowed, 2.5% divorced (2005-2009 5-year est.); Foreign born: 1.3% (2005-2009 5-year est.); Ancestry (includes multiple ancestries): 69.9% German, 18.7% Irish, 12.0% English, 5.1% French, 3.2% American (2005-2009 5-year est.).
Economy: Single-family building permits issued: 4 (2010); Multi-family building permits issued: 0 (2010); Employment by occupation: 10.7% management, 27.7% professional, 14.4% services, 21.1% sales, 0.0% farming, 1.6% construction, 24.5% production (2005-2009 5-year est.).
Income: Per capita income: $27,302 (2010); Median household income: $73,007 (2010); Average household income: $79,275 (2010); Percent of households with income of $100,000 or more: 26.4% (2010); Poverty rate: 0.6% (2005-2009 5-year est.).
Taxes: Total city taxes per capita: $331 (2007); City property taxes per capita: $96 (2007).
Education: Percent of population age 25 and over with: High school diploma (including GED) or higher: 87.6% (2010); Bachelor's degree or higher: 25.6% (2010); Master's degree or higher: 3.1% (2010).

School District(s)
Lindsay ISD (PK-12)
    2009-10 Enrollment: 533 . . . . (940) 668-8923
Housing: Homeownership rate: 83.4% (2010); Median home value: $123,944 (2010); Median contract rent: $298 per month (2005-2009 5-year est.); Median year structure built: 1978 (2005-2009 5-year est.).
Transportation: Commute to work: 92.2% car, 2.9% public transportation, 0.0% walk, 4.2% work from home (2005-2009 5-year est.); Travel time to work: 69.8% less than 15 minutes, 8.2% 15 to 30 minutes, 13.1% 30 to 45 minutes, 4.6% 45 to 60 minutes, 4.4% 60 minutes or more (2005-2009 5-year est.)

MUENSTER (city). Covers a land area of 1.287 square miles and a water area of 0.013 square miles. Located at 33.65° N. Lat; 97.37° W. Long. Elevation is 1,001 feet.
History: Muenster was founded in 1889 by two German brothers, and named for a city in their former country. The town developed as a market and supply center for farmers, and later for oil workers.
Population: 1,402 (1990); 1,556 (2000); 1,650 (2010); 1,692 (2015 projected); Race: 96.5% White, 0.0% Black, 1.3% Asian, 2.1% Other, 2.1% Hispanic of any race (2010); Density: 1,282.4 persons per square mile (2010); Average household size: 2.56 (2010); Median age: 35.9 (2010); Males per 100 females: 88.8 (2010); Marriage status: 28.4% never married, 53.0% now married, 10.1% widowed, 8.5% divorced (2005-2009 5-year est.); Foreign born: 1.6% (2005-2009 5-year est.); Ancestry (includes multiple ancestries): 61.7% German, 9.4% Irish, 5.7% English, 4.2% American, 2.6% French (2005-2009 5-year est.).
Economy: Single-family building permits issued: 3 (2010); Multi-family building permits issued: 0 (2010); Employment by occupation: 11.7% management, 15.9% professional, 13.5% services, 19.3% sales, 1.5% farming, 12.7% construction, 25.4% production (2005-2009 5-year est.).
Income: Per capita income: $28,619 (2010); Median household income: $57,016 (2010); Average household income: $72,229 (2010); Percent of households with income of $100,000 or more: 16.4% (2010); Poverty rate: 4.3% (2005-2009 5-year est.).
Taxes: Total city taxes per capita: $403 (2007); City property taxes per capita: $166 (2007).

Education: Percent of population age 25 and over with: High school diploma (including GED) or higher: 86.2% (2010); Bachelor's degree or higher: 21.1% (2010); Master's degree or higher: 5.7% (2010).
School District(s)
Muenster ISD (PK-12)
    2009-10 Enrollment: 487 . . . . (940) 759-2281
Housing: Homeownership rate: 79.1% (2010); Median home value: $117,892 (2010); Median contract rent: $505 per month (2005-2009 5-year est.); Median year structure built: 1966 (2005-2009 5-year est.).
Hospitals: Muenster Memorial Hospital (18 beds)
Newspapers: Muenster Enterprise (Community news; Circulation 1,900)
Transportation: Commute to work: 92.1% car, 0.0% public transportation, 3.8% walk, 2.9% work from home (2005-2009 5-year est.); Travel time to work: 58.8% less than 15 minutes, 18.8% 15 to 30 minutes, 9.4% 30 to 45 minutes, 6.1% 45 to 60 minutes, 6.9% 60 minutes or more (2005-2009 5-year est.)
Additional Information Contacts
Muenster Chamber of Commerce . . . . (940) 759-2227
    http://www.muensterchamber.com

OAK RIDGE (town). Covers a land area of 0.133 square miles and a water area of 0 square miles. Located at 33.64° N. Lat; 97.04° W. Long. Elevation is 860 feet.
Population: 180 (1990); 224 (2000); 232 (2010); 236 (2015 projected); Race: 83.2% White, 6.9% Black, 0.4% Asian, 9.5% Other, 10.8% Hispanic of any race (2010); Density: 1,743.0 persons per square mile (2010); Average household size: 2.68 (2010); Median age: 30.6 (2010); Males per 100 females: 132.0 (2010); Marriage status: 22.8% never married, 67.5% now married, 2.6% widowed, 7.0% divorced (2005-2009 5-year est.); Foreign born: 2.7% (2005-2009 5-year est.); Ancestry (includes multiple ancestries): 10.6% German, 9.0% Irish, 2.7% Norwegian, 2.7% Danish, 2.1% Pennsylvania German (2005-2009 5-year est.).
Economy: Single-family building permits issued: 6 (2010); Multi-family building permits issued: 0 (2010); Employment by occupation: 0.0% management, 12.2% professional, 25.6% services, 35.4% sales, 3.7% farming, 9.8% construction, 13.4% production (2005-2009 5-year est.).
Income: Per capita income: $20,131 (2010); Median household income: $46,250 (2010); Average household income: $55,433 (2010); Percent of households with income of $100,000 or more: 10.7% (2010); Poverty rate: 24.9% (2005-2009 5-year est.).
Taxes: Total city taxes per capita: $333 (2007); City property taxes per capita: $39 (2007).
Education: Percent of population age 25 and over with: High school diploma (including GED) or higher: 82.1% (2010); Bachelor's degree or higher: 19.4% (2010); Master's degree or higher: 3.0% (2010).
Housing: Homeownership rate: 81.3% (2010); Median home value: $112,500 (2010); Median contract rent: $500 per month (2005-2009 5-year est.); Median year structure built: 1985 (2005-2009 5-year est.).
Safety: Violent crime rate: 40.2 per 10,000 population; Property crime rate: 401.6 per 10,000 population (2009).
Transportation: Commute to work: 91.4% car, 0.0% public transportation, 0.0% walk, 4.3% work from home (2005-2009 5-year est.); Travel time to work: 28.4% less than 15 minutes, 61.2% 15 to 30 minutes, 6.0% 30 to 45 minutes, 0.0% 45 to 60 minutes, 4.5% 60 minutes or more (2005-2009 5-year est.)

VALLEY VIEW (town). Covers a land area of 2.311 square miles and a water area of 0.004 square miles. Located at 33.49° N. Lat; 97.16° W. Long. Elevation is 722 feet.
Population: 642 (1990); 737 (2000); 803 (2010); 834 (2015 projected); Race: 93.4% White, 0.5% Black, 3.1% Asian, 3.0% Other, 3.5% Hispanic of any race (2010); Density: 347.5 persons per square mile (2010); Average household size: 2.69 (2010); Median age: 33.7 (2010); Males per 100 females: 95.9 (2010); Marriage status: 17.5% never married, 67.6% now married, 7.7% widowed, 7.3% divorced (2005-2009 5-year est.); Foreign born: 3.6% (2005-2009 5-year est.); Ancestry (includes multiple ancestries): 29.9% German, 16.0% English, 15.8% Irish, 3.3% Scotch-Irish, 3.1% Italian (2005-2009 5-year est.).
Economy: Single-family building permits issued: 3 (2010); Multi-family building permits issued: 0 (2010); Employment by occupation: 8.4% management, 17.5% professional, 15.2% services, 27.4% sales, 1.1% farming, 7.8% construction, 22.7% production (2005-2009 5-year est.).
Income: Per capita income: $28,401 (2010); Median household income: $71,528 (2010); Average household income: $76,463 (2010); Percent of

households with income of $100,000 or more: 24.7% (2010); Poverty rate: 4.5% (2005-2009 5-year est.).
Taxes: Total city taxes per capita: $231 (2007); City property taxes per capita: $83 (2007).
Education: Percent of population age 25 and over with: High school diploma (including GED) or higher: 89.7% (2010); Bachelor's degree or higher: 22.1% (2010); Master's degree or higher: 4.3% (2010).

School District(s)
Valley View ISD (PK-12)
   2009-10 Enrollment: 642 . . . . (940) 726-3659
Housing: Homeownership rate: 66.6% (2010); Median home value: $105,078 (2010); Median contract rent: $475 per month (2005-2009 5-year est.); Median year structure built: 1968 (2005-2009 5-year est.).
Safety: Violent crime rate: 25.2 per 10,000 population; Property crime rate: 50.4 per 10,000 population (2009).
Transportation: Commute to work: 94.3% car, 0.0% public transportation, 0.0% walk, 4.5% work from home (2005-2009 5-year est.); Travel time to work: 31.4% less than 15 minutes, 33.6% 15 to 30 minutes, 22.7% 30 to 45 minutes, 8.2% 45 to 60 minutes, 4.0% 60 minutes or more (2005-2009 5-year est.)
Additional Information Contacts
Valley View Chamber of Commerce . . . . (940) 726-3281

Coryell County

Located in central Texas; drained by the Leon River. Covers a land area of 1,051.76 square miles, a water area of 4.97 square miles, and is located in the Central Time Zone at 31.30° N. Lat., 97.80° W. Long. The county was founded in 1854. County seat is Gatesville.

Coryell County is part of the Killeen-Temple-Fort Hood, TX Metropolitan Statistical Area. The entire metro area includes: Bell County, TX; Coryell County, TX; Lampasas County, TX

Weather Station: Evant 1 SSW   Elevation: 1,245 feet

	Jan	Feb	Mar	Apr	May	Jun	Jul	Aug	Sep	Oct	Nov	Dec
High	59	62	69	77	84	90	94	95	88	79	68	59
Low	34	38	45	52	61	68	71	71	64	55	44	35
Precip	1.7	2.3	2.7	2.5	4.2	4.6	2.1	2.4	2.6	2.9	2.3	1.7
Snow	0.5	0.1	tr	0.1	0.0	0.0	0.0	0.0	0.0	0.0	tr	tr

High and Low temperatures in degrees Fahrenheit; Precipitation and Snow in inches

Weather Station: Gatesville 4 SSE   Elevation: 759 feet

	Jan	Feb	Mar	Apr	May	Jun	Jul	Aug	Sep	Oct	Nov	Dec
High	61	64	71	79	85	90	95	96	90	80	70	61
Low	35	38	46	53	62	68	71	71	64	55	45	36
Precip	2.0	2.5	2.9	2.6	4.1	3.8	2.2	2.5	2.5	3.4	3.0	2.6
Snow	0.1	0.1	tr	tr	0.0	0.0	0.0	0.0	0.0	0.0	0.0	0.1

High and Low temperatures in degrees Fahrenheit; Precipitation and Snow in inches

Population: 64,213 (1990); 74,978 (2000); 75,399 (2010); 75,472 (2015 projected); Race: 66.3% White, 19.0% Black, 1.7% Asian, 13.0% Other, 13.6% Hispanic of any race (2010); Density: 71.7 persons per square mile (2010); Average household size: 2.97 (2010); Median age: 30.1 (2010); Males per 100 females: 102.2 (2010).
Religion: Five largest groups: 20.3% Southern Baptist Convention, 6.7% Independent, Charismatic Churches, 3.6% The United Methodist Church, 2.5% Catholic Church, 1.3% Churches of Christ (2000).
Economy: Unemployment rate: 10.6% (June 2011); Total civilian labor force: 25,379 (June 2011); Leading industries: 17.0% retail trade; 15.1% professional, scientific & technical services; 11.5% accommodation & food services (2009); Farms: 1,339 totaling 488,358 acres (2007); Companies that employ 500 or more persons: 2 (2009); Companies that employ 100 to 499 persons: 12 (2009); Companies that employ less than 100 persons: 722 (2009); Black-owned businesses: 147 (2007); Hispanic-owned businesses: 190 (2007); Asian-owned businesses: 107 (2007); Women-owned businesses: 789 (2007); Retail sales per capita: $6,711 (2010). Single-family building permits issued: 194 (2010); Multi-family building permits issued: 119 (2010).
Income: Per capita income: $17,978 (2010); Median household income: $48,243 (2010); Average household income: $58,742 (2010); Percent of households with income of $100,000 or more: 11.3% (2010); Poverty rate: 16.4% (2009); Bankruptcy rate: 1.60% (2010).
Taxes: Total county taxes per capita: $119 (2007); County property taxes per capita: $87 (2007).

Education: Percent of population age 25 and over with: High school diploma (including GED) or higher: 89.4% (2010); Bachelor's degree or higher: 14.6% (2010); Master's degree or higher: 3.8% (2010).
Housing: Homeownership rate: 56.9% (2010); Median home value: $93,967 (2010); Median contract rent: $544 per month (2005-2009 5-year est.); Median year structure built: 1981 (2005-2009 5-year est.)
Health: Birth rate: 116.9 per 10,000 population (2009); Death rate: 45.9 per 10,000 population (2009); Age-adjusted cancer mortality rate: 199.4 deaths per 100,000 population (2007); Number of physicians: 3.8 per 10,000 population (2008); Hospital beds: 19.0 per 10,000 population (2007); Hospital admissions: 194.8 per 10,000 population (2007).
Elections: 2008 Presidential election results: 36.1% Obama, 63.0% McCain, 0.1% Nader
National and State Parks: Mother Neff State Park
Additional Information Contacts
Coryell County Government. . . . . (254) 865-5911
   http://www.coryellcounty.org
City of Copperas Cove. . . . . (254) 547-4221
   http://www.ci.copperas-cove.tx.us
City of Gatesville . . . . (254) 865-8951
   http://www.ci.gatesville.tx.us
Copperas Cove Chamber of Commerce . . . . (254) 547-7571
   http://www.copperascove.com
Gatesville Chamber of Commerce. . . . . (254) 865-2617
   http://www.gatesvilletx.info

Coryell County Communities

COPPERAS COVE (city). Covers a land area of 13.926 square miles and a water area of 0 square miles. Located at 31.12° N. Lat; 97.90° W. Long. Elevation is 1,093 feet.
History: Adjoins large Fort Hood Military Reservation on its West side, to which it owes much of its existence since established in 1942.
Population: 24,297 (1990); 29,592 (2000); 30,607 (2010); 31,005 (2015 projected); Race: 65.8% White, 18.1% Black, 2.4% Asian, 13.6% Other, 12.5% Hispanic of any race (2010); Density: 2,197.8 persons per square mile (2010); Average household size: 2.88 (2010); Median age: 30.5 (2010); Males per 100 females: 96.5 (2010); Marriage status: 31.5% never married, 53.9% now married, 4.3% widowed, 10.4% divorced (2005-2009 5-year est.); Foreign born: 6.6% (2005-2009 5-year est.); Ancestry (includes multiple ancestries): 18.4% German, 8.8% Irish, 8.6% English, 4.8% American, 3.1% Italian (2005-2009 5-year est.).
Economy: Unemployment rate: 8.7% (June 2011); Total civilian labor force: 13,709 (June 2011); Single-family building permits issued: 182 (2010); Multi-family building permits issued: 111 (2010); Employment by occupation: 7.7% management, 18.2% professional, 21.9% services, 26.9% sales, 0.0% farming, 15.4% construction, 9.9% production (2005-2009 5-year est.).
Income: Per capita income: $21,217 (2010); Median household income: $51,032 (2010); Average household income: $61,418 (2010); Percent of households with income of $100,000 or more: 12.6% (2010); Poverty rate: 17.2% (2005-2009 5-year est.).
Taxes: Total city taxes per capita: $330 (2007); City property taxes per capita: $202 (2007).
Education: Percent of population age 25 and over with: High school diploma (including GED) or higher: 95.5% (2010); Bachelor's degree or higher: 18.7% (2010); Master's degree or higher: 5.4% (2010).

School District(s)
Copperas Cove ISD (PK-12)
   2009-10 Enrollment: 8,258 . . . . (254) 547-1227
Lampasas ISD (PK-12)
   2009-10 Enrollment: 3,372 . . . . (512) 556-6224
Housing: Homeownership rate: 56.2% (2010); Median home value: $95,520 (2010); Median contract rent: $560 per month (2005-2009 5-year est.); Median year structure built: 1984 (2005-2009 5-year est.).
Safety: Violent crime rate: 35.7 per 10,000 population; Property crime rate: 312.4 per 10,000 population (2009).
Newspapers: The Leader-Press (Local news; Circulation 3,100)
Transportation: Commute to work: 93.9% car, 0.5% public transportation, 2.5% walk, 1.1% work from home (2005-2009 5-year est.); Travel time to work: 31.3% less than 15 minutes, 45.2% 15 to 30 minutes, 14.4% 30 to 45 minutes, 4.9% 45 to 60 minutes, 4.1% 60 minutes or more (2005-2009 5-year est.)
Additional Information Contacts

City of Copperas Cove............................(254) 547-4221
http://www.ci.copperas-cove.tx.us
Copperas Cove Chamber of Commerce..............(254) 547-7571
http://www.copperascove.com

EVANT (town). Covers a land area of 0.609 square miles and a water
area of 0 square miles. Located at 31.47° N. Lat; 98.15° W. Long.
Elevation is 1,253 feet.
Population: 444 (1990); 393 (2000); 380 (2010); 371 (2015 projected);
Race: 90.8% White, 2.1% Black, 0.3% Asian, 6.8% Other, 7.9% Hispanic
of any race (2010); Density: 623.6 persons per square mile (2010);
Average household size: 2.44 (2010); Median age: 49.4 (2010); Males per
100 females: 95.9 (2010); Marriage status: 39.6% never married, 38.5%
now married, 4.7% widowed, 17.2% divorced (2005-2009 5-year est.);
Foreign born: 11.6% (2005-2009 5-year est.); Ancestry (includes multiple
ancestries): 23.0% English, 9.5% American, 6.8% Irish, 5.6% German,
1.4% Scotch-Irish (2005-2009 5-year est.).
Economy: Employment by occupation: 17.5% management, 15.7%
professional, 10.0% services, 35.4% sales, 0.9% farming, 6.1%
construction, 14.4% production (2005-2009 5-year est.).
Income: Per capita income: $22,358 (2010); Median household income:
$43,077 (2010); Average household income: $53,830 (2010); Percent of
households with income of $100,000 or more: 12.2% (2010); Poverty rate:
19.2% (2005-2009 5-year est.).
Taxes: Total city taxes per capita: $167 (2007); City property taxes per
capita: $69 (2007).
Education: Percent of population age 25 and over with: High school
diploma (including GED) or higher: 85.9% (2010); Bachelor's degree or
higher: 18.1% (2010); Master's degree or higher: 6.1% (2010).
School District(s)
Evant ISD (PK-12)
2009-10 Enrollment: 240 ....(254) 471-5536
Housing: Homeownership rate: 80.8% (2010); Median home value:
$92,941 (2010); Median contract rent: $378 per month (2005-2009 5-year
est.); Median year structure built: 1969 (2005-2009 5-year est.).
Transportation: Commute to work: 100.0% car, 0.0% public
transportation, 0.0% walk, 0.0% work from home (2005-2009 5-year est.);
Travel time to work: 40.7% less than 15 minutes, 17.7% 15 to 30 minutes,
37.2% 30 to 45 minutes, 1.8% 45 to 60 minutes, 2.7% 60 minutes or more
(2005-2009 5-year est.)

GATESVILLE (city). County seat. Covers a land area of 8.690 square
miles and a water area of 0.008 square miles. Located at 31.43° N. Lat;
97.73° W. Long. Elevation is 807 feet.
History: Gatesville was named for Fort Gates, a frontier post built in 1849
on the Leon River. Gatesville became an industrial town with cotton
processing, plastics and livestock feed mills.
Population: 11,633 (1990); 15,591 (2000); 15,391 (2010); 15,191 (2015
projected); Race: 67.2% White, 22.6% Black, 0.4% Asian, 9.7% Other,
14.9% Hispanic of any race (2010); Density: 1,771.1 persons per square
mile (2010); Average household size: 2.64 (2010); Median age: 36.5
(2010); Males per 100 females: 57.6 (2010); Marriage status: 31.4% never
married, 42.6% now married, 10.0% widowed, 15.9% divorced (2005-2009
5-year est.); Foreign born: 5.9% (2005-2009 5-year est.); Ancestry
(includes multiple ancestries): 15.9% German, 11.6% Irish, 11.2% English,
7.9% American, 3.8% Scotch-Irish (2005-2009 5-year est.).
Economy: Single-family building permits issued: 12 (2010); Multi-family
building permits issued: 8 (2010); Employment by occupation: 6.1%
management, 11.7% professional, 22.2% services, 19.7% sales, 1.4%
farming, 25.7% construction, 13.2% production (2005-2009 5-year est.).
Income: Per capita income: $13,748 (2010); Median household income:
$42,803 (2010); Average household income: $53,134 (2010); Percent of
households with income of $100,000 or more: 10.3% (2010); Poverty rate:
14.5% (2005-2009 5-year est.).
Taxes: Total city taxes per capita: $176 (2007); City property taxes per
capita: $57 (2007).
Education: Percent of population age 25 and over with: High school
diploma (including GED) or higher: 76.6% (2010); Bachelor's degree or
higher: 10.6% (2010); Master's degree or higher: 2.2% (2010).
School District(s)
Gatesville ISD (PK-12)
2009-10 Enrollment: 2,816 ....(254) 865-7251

Vocational/Technical School(s)
Coryell Cosmetology College (Private, For-profit)
Fall 2009 Enrollment: 35 ....(254) 248-1716
2010-11 Tuition: $7,800
Housing: Homeownership rate: 69.6% (2010); Median home value:
$78,594 (2010); Median contract rent: $344 per month (2005-2009 5-year
est.); Median year structure built: 1964 (2005-2009 5-year est.).
Hospitals: Coryell Memorial Hospital (55 beds)
Safety: Violent crime rate: 13.2 per 10,000 population; Property crime rate:
161.2 per 10,000 population (2009).
Newspapers: Messenger & Star Forum (Local news; Circulation 4,500)
Transportation: Commute to work: 95.1% car, 0.0% public transportation,
1.6% walk, 2.9% work from home (2005-2009 5-year est.); Travel time to
work: 63.4% less than 15 minutes, 15.5% 15 to 30 minutes, 9.7% 30 to 45
minutes, 9.6% 45 to 60 minutes, 1.8% 60 minutes or more (2005-2009
5-year est.)
Additional Information Contacts
City of Gatesville ....(254) 865-8951
http://www.ci.gatesville.tx.us
Gatesville Chamber of Commerce...................(254) 865-2617
http://www.gatesvilletx.info

JONESBORO (unincorporated postal area, zip code 76538). Covers a
land area of 157.358 square miles and a water area of 0.075 square miles.
Located at 31.63° N. Lat; 97.90° W. Long. Elevation is 965 feet.
Population: 2,053 (2000); Race: 69.6% White, 21.3% Black, 2.6% Asian,
6.5% Other, 9.4% Hispanic of any race (2000); Density: 13.0 persons per
square mile (2000); Age: 11.6% under 18, 6.5% over 64 (2000); Marriage
status: 52.8% never married, 40.4% now married, 1.7% widowed, 5.1%
divorced (2000); Foreign born: 4.3% (2000); Ancestry (includes multiple
ancestries): 11.8% German, 6.4% English, 6.4% Irish, 4.8% American
(2000).
Economy: Employment by occupation: 19.9% management, 15.0%
professional, 16.3% services, 21.4% sales, 5.8% farming, 11.4%
construction, 10.3% production (2000).
Income: Per capita income: $15,995 (2000); Median household income:
$42,546 (2000); Poverty rate: 179.1% (2000).
Education: Percent of population age 25 and over with: High school
diploma (including GED) or higher: 88.7% (2000); Bachelor's degree or
higher: 14.5% (2000).
School District(s)
Jonesboro ISD (KG-12)
2009-10 Enrollment: 133 ....(254) 463-2111
Housing: Homeownership rate: 81.1% (2000); Median home value:
$44,700 (2000); Median contract rent: $406 per month (2000); Median year
structure built: 1972 (2000).
Transportation: Commute to work: 82.1% car, 0.5% public transportation,
11.3% walk, 3.0% work from home (2000); Travel time to work: 45.2% less
than 15 minutes, 42.5% 15 to 30 minutes, 7.3% 30 to 45 minutes, 1.5% 45
to 60 minutes, 3.5% 60 minutes or more (2000)

OGLESBY (city). Covers a land area of 0.492 square miles and a water
area of 0 square miles. Located at 31.41° N. Lat; 97.51° W. Long.
Elevation is 846 feet.
Population: 452 (1990); 458 (2000); 476 (2010); 486 (2015 projected);
Race: 88.9% White, 2.3% Black, 0.2% Asian, 8.6% Other, 7.6% Hispanic
of any race (2010); Density: 966.6 persons per square mile (2010);
Average household size: 2.74 (2010); Median age: 35.9 (2010); Males per
100 females: 108.8 (2010); Marriage status: 25.7% never married, 54.4%
now married, 6.0% widowed, 13.9% divorced (2005-2009 5-year est.);
Foreign born: 1.9% (2005-2009 5-year est.); Ancestry (includes multiple
ancestries): 22.1% Irish, 10.3% German, 8.5% Dutch, 8.5% American,
4.2% English (2005-2009 5-year est.).
Economy: Employment by occupation: 7.0% management, 16.7%
professional, 18.6% services, 21.4% sales, 0.9% farming, 13.5%
construction, 21.9% production (2005-2009 5-year est.).
Income: Per capita income: $24,037 (2010); Median household income:
$54,276 (2010); Average household income: $66,121 (2010); Percent of
households with income of $100,000 or more: 15.2% (2010); Poverty rate:
7.6% (2005-2009 5-year est.).
Taxes: Total city taxes per capita: $101 (2007); City property taxes per
capita: $35 (2007).
Education: Percent of population age 25 and over with: High school
diploma (including GED) or higher: 87.7% (2010); Bachelor's degree or
higher: 13.9% (2010); Master's degree or higher: 5.2% (2010).

School District(s)

Oglesby ISD (PK-12)

2009-10 Enrollment: 172 . . . . (254) 456-2271

Housing: Homeownership rate: 80.0% (2010); Median home value: $78,824 (2010); Median contract rent: $271 per month (2005-2009 5-year est.); Median year structure built: 1952 (2005-2009 5-year est.).

Transportation: Commute to work: 95.7% car, 0.0% public transportation, 1.4% walk, 1.4% work from home (2005-2009 5-year est.); Travel time to work: 27.0% less than 15 minutes, 27.5% 15 to 30 minutes, 28.4% 30 to 45 minutes, 12.7% 45 to 60 minutes, 4.4% 60 minutes or more (2005-2009 5-year est.)

PURMELA (unincorporated postal area, zip code 76566). Covers a land area of 58.618 square miles and a water area of 0.039 square miles. Located at 31.50° N. Lat; 97.99° W. Long. Elevation is 1,047 feet.

Population: 303 (2000); Race: 92.2% White, 2.4% Black, 0.0% Asian, 5.4% Other, 4.4% Hispanic of any race (2000); Density: 5.2 persons per square mile (2000); Age: 22.4% under 18, 11.9% over 64 (2000); Marriage status: 15.7% never married, 72.3% now married, 5.1% widowed, 6.8% divorced (2000); Foreign born: 4.4% (2000); Ancestry (includes multiple ancestries): 23.4% American, 18.6% Irish, 15.9% German, 6.1% English (2000).

Economy: Employment by occupation: 6.1% management, 19.8% professional, 19.1% services, 21.4% sales, 3.8% farming, 13.0% construction, 16.8% production (2000).

Income: Per capita income: $16,220 (2000); Median household income: $25,909 (2000); Poverty rate: 179.1% (2000).

Education: Percent of population age 25 and over with: High school diploma (including GED) or higher: 75.2% (2000); Bachelor's degree or higher: 12.8% (2000).

Housing: Homeownership rate: 80.8% (2000); Median home value: $49,000 (2000); Median contract rent: $555 per month (2000); Median year structure built: 1972 (2000).

Transportation: Commute to work: 93.9% car, 0.0% public transportation, 0.8% walk, 5.3% work from home (2000); Travel time to work: 11.3% less than 15 minutes, 29.8% 15 to 30 minutes, 25.0% 30 to 45 minutes, 10.5% 45 to 60 minutes, 23.4% 60 minutes or more (2000)

SOUTH MOUNTAIN (town). Covers a land area of 1.629 square miles and a water area of 0 square miles. Located at 31.43° N. Lat; 97.67° W. Long. Elevation is 1,020 feet.

Population: 301 (1990); 412 (2000); 376 (2010); 371 (2015 projected); Race: 75.0% White, 13.3% Black, 0.8% Asian, 10.9% Other, 13.0% Hispanic of any race (2010); Density: 230.8 persons per square mile (2010); Average household size: 2.64 (2010); Median age: 35.5 (2010); Males per 100 females: 170.5 (2010); Marriage status: 11.7% never married, 65.6% now married, 14.5% widowed, 8.2% divorced (2005-2009 5-year est.); Foreign born: 1.0% (2005-2009 5-year est.); Ancestry (includes multiple ancestries): 29.8% English, 28.5% American, 10.0% German, 7.8% Irish, 5.8% French (2005-2009 5-year est.).

Economy: Employment by occupation: 10.0% management, 16.9% professional, 22.3% services, 23.8% sales, 0.0% farming, 22.3% construction, 4.6% production (2005-2009 5-year est.).

Income: Per capita income: $14,432 (2010); Median household income: $44,545 (2010); Average household income: $50,417 (2010); Percent of households with income of $100,000 or more: 6.9% (2010); Poverty rate: 0.0% (2005-2009 5-year est.).

Taxes: Total city taxes per capita: $265 (2007); City property taxes per capita: $66 (2007).

Education: Percent of population age 25 and over with: High school diploma (including GED) or higher: 79.4% (2010); Bachelor's degree or higher: 11.0% (2010); Master's degree or higher: 1.1% (2010).

Housing: Homeownership rate: 70.8% (2010); Median home value: $86,250 (2010); Median contract rent: $195 per month (2005-2009 5-year est.); Median year structure built: 1971 (2005-2009 5-year est.).

Transportation: Commute to work: 96.2% car, 0.0% public transportation, 2.3% walk, 1.5% work from home (2005-2009 5-year est.); Travel time to work: 39.1% less than 15 minutes, 36.7% 15 to 30 minutes, 8.6% 30 to 45 minutes, 10.2% 45 to 60 minutes, 5.5% 60 minutes or more (2005-2009 5-year est.)

Cottle County

Located in northwestern Texas; drained by the Pease and Wichita Rivers. Covers a land area of 901.18 square miles, a water area of 0.42 square miles, and is located in the Central Time Zone at 34.05° N. Lat., 100.26° W. Long. The county was founded in 1892. County seat is Paducah.

Weather Station: Paducah — Elevation: 1,899 feet

	Jan	Feb	Mar	Apr	May	Jun	Jul	Aug	Sep	Oct	Nov	Dec
High	55	59	67	76	84	91	97	95	87	77	65	55
Low	28	32	39	47	57	66	70	69	61	49	38	29
Precip	0.9	1.1	1.5	1.8	3.8	3.8	1.6	2.3	2.8	2.3	1.3	1.1
Snow	2.0	1.1	0.3	0.2	0.0	0.0	0.0	0.0	0.0	tr	0.8	1.5

High and Low temperatures in degrees Fahrenheit; Precipitation and Snow in inches

Population: 2,247 (1990); 1,904 (2000); 1,610 (2010); 1,465 (2015 projected); Race: 78.0% White, 11.4% Black, 0.0% Asian, 10.7% Other, 23.5% Hispanic of any race (2010); Density: 1.8 persons per square mile (2010); Average household size: 2.20 (2010); Median age: 48.2 (2010); Males per 100 females: 92.8 (2010).

Religion: Five largest groups: 58.7% Southern Baptist Convention, 12.1% The United Methodist Church, 10.3% Catholic Church, 9.0% Christian Church (Disciples of Christ), 7.6% Baptist Missionary Association of America (2000).

Economy: Unemployment rate: 6.8% (June 2011); Total civilian labor force: 746 (June 2011); Leading industries: 30.0% retail trade (2009); Farms: 299 totaling 534,519 acres (2007); Companies that employ 500 or more persons: 0 (2009); Companies that employ 100 to 499 persons: 0 (2009); Companies that employ less than 100 persons: 36 (2009); Black-owned businesses: n/a (2007); Hispanic-owned businesses: n/a (2007); Asian-owned businesses: n/a (2007); Women-owned businesses: n/a (2007); Retail sales per capita: $12,703 (2010). Single-family building permits issued: 0 (2010); Multi-family building permits issued: 0 (2010).

Income: Per capita income: $20,600 (2010); Median household income: $33,416 (2010); Average household income: $44,920 (2010); Percent of households with income of $100,000 or more: 6.9% (2010); Poverty rate: 22.7% (2009); Bankruptcy rate: 1.34% (2010).

Taxes: Total county taxes per capita: $637 (2007); County property taxes per capita: $525 (2007).

Education: Percent of population age 25 and over with: High school diploma (including GED) or higher: 71.5% (2010); Bachelor's degree or higher: 17.4% (2010); Master's degree or higher: 3.9% (2010).

Housing: Homeownership rate: 69.7% (2010); Median home value: $32,439 (2010); Median contract rent: $193 per month (2005-2009 5-year est.); Median year structure built: 1952 (2005-2009 5-year est.)

Health: Birth rate: 146.9 per 10,000 population (2009); Death rate: 51.1 per 10,000 population (2009); Age-adjusted cancer mortality rate: 244.1 (Unreliable) deaths per 100,000 population (2007); Number of physicians: 0.0 per 10,000 population (2008); Hospital beds: 0.0 per 10,000 population (2007); Hospital admissions: 0.0 per 10,000 population (2007).

Elections: 2008 Presidential election results: 26.5% Obama, 72.2% McCain, 0.0% Nader

Additional Information Contacts

Cottle County Government . . . . (806) 492-3613
  http://www.co.cottle.tx.us/ips/cms
Paducah Chamber of Commerce . . . . (806) 492-2044
  http://www.paducahtx.com

Cottle County Communities

PADUCAH (town). County seat. Covers a land area of 1.521 square miles and a water area of 0 square miles. Located at 34.01° N. Lat; 100.30° W. Long. Elevation is 1,860 feet.

History: Paducah developed as the center of a cotton, grain, and livestock area. Early industries here were cotton gins and a farm equipment plant.

Population: 1,788 (1990); 1,498 (2000); 1,236 (2010); 1,118 (2015 projected); Race: 81.3% White, 7.9% Black, 0.0% Asian, 10.8% Other, 22.8% Hispanic of any race (2010); Density: 812.8 persons per square mile (2010); Average household size: 2.15 (2010); Median age: 49.8 (2010); Males per 100 females: 90.2 (2010); Marriage status: 24.2% never married, 58.4% now married, 12.8% widowed, 4.6% divorced (2005-2009 5-year est.); Foreign born: 3.6% (2005-2009 5-year est.); Ancestry (includes multiple ancestries): 13.3% English, 12.0% Irish, 10.1% African, 9.8% German, 4.5% French (2005-2009 5-year est.).

Economy: Single-family building permits issued: 0 (2010); Multi-family building permits issued: 0 (2010); Employment by occupation: 9.5% management, 13.8% professional, 28.5% services, 22.1% sales, 4.1% farming, 5.9% construction, 16.0% production (2005-2009 5-year est.).

Income: Per capita income: $20,424 (2010); Median household income: $32,470 (2010); Average household income: $43,532 (2010); Percent of

households with income of $100,000 or more: 6.6% (2010); Poverty rate: 12.4% (2005-2009 5-year est.).

Taxes: Total city taxes per capita: $154 (2007); City property taxes per capita: $112 (2007).

Education: Percent of population age 25 and over with: High school diploma (including GED) or higher: 68.8% (2010); Bachelor's degree or higher: 15.9% (2010); Master's degree or higher: 3.8% (2010).

School District(s)

Paducah ISD (PK-12)

    2009-10 Enrollment: 235 . . . . (806) 492-3524

Housing: Homeownership rate: 73.8% (2010); Median home value: $29,470 (2010); Median contract rent: $182 per month (2005-2009 5-year est.); Median year structure built: 1953 (2005-2009 5-year est.).

Safety: Violent crime rate: 8.1 per 10,000 population; Property crime rate: 89.1 per 10,000 population (2009).

Newspapers: Post (Community news; Circulation 1,550)

Transportation: Commute to work: 93.1% car, 0.4% public transportation, 4.4% walk, 1.5% work from home (2005-2009 5-year est.); Travel time to work: 64.1% less than 15 minutes, 5.9% 15 to 30 minutes, 22.2% 30 to 45 minutes, 0.4% 45 to 60 minutes, 7.5% 60 minutes or more (2005-2009 5-year est.)

Additional Information Contacts

Paducah Chamber of Commerce . . . . (806) 492-2044
    http://www.paducahtx.com

Crane County

Located in west Texas, on the western edge of Edwards Plateau; bounded on the south by the Pecos River. Covers a land area of 785.56 square miles, a water area of 0.03 square miles, and is located in the Central Time Zone at 31.44° N. Lat., 102.45° W. Long. The county was founded in 1927. County seat is Crane.

Weather Station: Crane									Elevation: 2,629 feet		
	Jan	Feb	Mar	Apr	May	Jun	Jul	Aug	Sep	Oct	Nov	Dec
High	62	66	74	83	90	94	96	95	88	80	69	62
Low	33	37	44	52	62	69	72	71	64	54	42	34
Precip	0.6	0.7	0.5	0.8	1.5	1.7	1.2	2.0	2.7	1.8	0.8	0.7
Snow	0.9	0.0	0.1	tr	0.0	0.0	0.0	0.0	0.0	tr	0.6	0.8

High and Low temperatures in degrees Fahrenheit; Precipitation and Snow in inches

Population: 4,652 (1990); 3,996 (2000); 4,047 (2010); 4,066 (2015 projected); Race: 68.5% White, 3.2% Black, 0.3% Asian, 28.0% Other, 53.4% Hispanic of any race (2010); Density: 5.2 persons per square mile (2010); Average household size: 2.85 (2010); Median age: 35.0 (2010); Males per 100 females: 96.6 (2010).

Religion: Five largest groups: 33.4% Southern Baptist Convention, 8.2% Christian Churches and Churches of Christ, 6.3% Catholic Church, 5.8% The United Methodist Church, 4.3% Churches of Christ (2000).

Economy: Unemployment rate: 8.8% (June 2011); Total civilian labor force: 1,617 (June 2011); Leading industries: 46.7% mining; 9.5% retail trade; 8.8% construction (2009); Farms: 37 totaling 375,177 acres (2007); Companies that employ 500 or more persons: 0 (2009); Companies that employ 100 to 499 persons: 1 (2009); Companies that employ less than 100 persons: 77 (2009); Black-owned businesses: n/a (2007); Hispanic-owned businesses: n/a (2007); Asian-owned businesses: n/a (2007); Women-owned businesses: 161 (2007); Retail sales per capita: $6,849 (2010). Single-family building permits issued: 2 (2010); Multi-family building permits issued: 24 (2010).

Income: Per capita income: $20,847 (2010); Median household income: $45,438 (2010); Average household income: $59,923 (2010); Percent of households with income of $100,000 or more: 14.5% (2010); Poverty rate: 12.1% (2009); Bankruptcy rate: 0.46% (2010).

Taxes: Total county taxes per capita: $1,721 (2007); County property taxes per capita: $1,629 (2007).

Education: Percent of population age 25 and over with: High school diploma (including GED) or higher: 73.8% (2010); Bachelor's degree or higher: 13.8% (2010); Master's degree or higher: 5.4% (2010).

Housing: Homeownership rate: 83.8% (2010); Median home value: $41,395 (2010); Median contract rent: $343 per month (2005-2009 5-year est.); Median year structure built: 1967 (2005-2009 5-year est.)

Health: Birth rate: 170.5 per 10,000 population (2009); Death rate: 40.8 per 10,000 population (2009); Age-adjusted cancer mortality rate: 177.9 (Unreliable) deaths per 100,000 population (2007); Number of physicians: 9.9 per 10,000 population (2008); Hospital beds: 64.7 per 10,000

population (2007); Hospital admissions: 512.7 per 10,000 population (2007).

Elections: 2008 Presidential election results: 21.9% Obama, 77.0% McCain, 0.0% Nader

Additional Information Contacts

Crane County Government . . . . (325) 558-3581
    http://www.co.crane.tx.us/ips/cms
Crane County Chamber of Commerce . . . . (432) 558-2311
    http://www.cranechamber.net

Crane County Communities

CRANE (city). County seat. Covers a land area of 1.020 square miles and a water area of 0 square miles. Located at 31.39° N. Lat; 102.35° W. Long. Elevation is 2,575 feet.

History: Founded 1926, incorporated 1933.

Population: 3,530 (1990); 3,191 (2000); 3,208 (2010); 3,237 (2015 projected); Race: 67.8% White, 3.0% Black, 0.3% Asian, 28.9% Other, 55.6% Hispanic of any race (2010); Density: 3,146.4 persons per square mile (2010); Average household size: 2.86 (2010); Median age: 33.9 (2010); Males per 100 females: 95.3 (2010); Marriage status: 15.7% never married, 67.6% now married, 4.7% widowed, 11.9% divorced (2005-2009 5-year est.); Foreign born: 10.7% (2005-2009 5-year est.); Ancestry (includes multiple ancestries): 13.1% Irish, 11.0% German, 3.9% American, 3.8% English, 3.2% French (2005-2009 5-year est.).

Economy: Single-family building permits issued: 2 (2010); Multi-family building permits issued: 24 (2010); Employment by occupation: 5.7% management, 12.3% professional, 18.0% services, 23.6% sales, 0.0% farming, 19.6% construction, 20.8% production (2005-2009 5-year est.).

Income: Per capita income: $20,087 (2010); Median household income: $43,691 (2010); Average household income: $57,489 (2010); Percent of households with income of $100,000 or more: 13.0% (2010); Poverty rate: 26.6% (2005-2009 5-year est.).

Taxes: Total city taxes per capita: $321 (2007); City property taxes per capita: $106 (2007).

Education: Percent of population age 25 and over with: High school diploma (including GED) or higher: 72.6% (2010); Bachelor's degree or higher: 13.9% (2010); Master's degree or higher: 5.9% (2010).

School District(s)

Crane ISD (PK-12)

    2009-10 Enrollment: 1,006 . . . . (432) 558-1022

Housing: Homeownership rate: 83.3% (2010); Median home value: $39,712 (2010); Median contract rent: $299 per month (2005-2009 5-year est.); Median year structure built: 1964 (2005-2009 5-year est.).

Hospitals: Crane Memorial Hospital (28 beds)

Safety: Violent crime rate: 15.6 per 10,000 population; Property crime rate: 87.5 per 10,000 population (2009).

Newspapers: Crane News (Local news; Circulation 1,700)

Transportation: Commute to work: 94.6% car, 0.0% public transportation, 0.0% walk, 3.3% work from home (2005-2009 5-year est.); Travel time to work: 60.5% less than 15 minutes, 8.0% 15 to 30 minutes, 17.0% 30 to 45 minutes, 5.5% 45 to 60 minutes, 8.9% 60 minutes or more (2005-2009 5-year est.)

Additional Information Contacts

Crane County Chamber of Commerce . . . . (432) 558-2311
    http://www.cranechamber.net

Crockett County

Located in west Texas, on the Edwards Plateau; bounded on the west by the Pecos River. Covers a land area of 2,807.42 square miles, a water area of 0.01 square miles, and is located in the Central Time Zone at 30.74° N. Lat., 101.35° W. Long. The county was founded in 1875. County seat is Ozona.

Weather Station: Ozona 1 SSW									Elevation: 2,339 feet		
	Jan	Feb	Mar	Apr	May	Jun	Jul	Aug	Sep	Oct	Nov	Dec
High	59	64	71	79	87	91	93	93	87	78	68	60
Low	30	34	42	50	60	67	69	68	61	51	40	31
Precip	0.9	1.0	1.6	1.3	2.3	2.1	1.0	2.1	2.2	2.3	1.1	0.7
Snow	0.1	0.0	tr	0.0	0.0	0.0	0.0	0.0	0.0	0.1	0.3	tr

High and Low temperatures in degrees Fahrenheit; Precipitation and Snow in inches

Population: 4,078 (1990); 4,099 (2000); 4,087 (2010); 4,074 (2015 projected); Race: 73.8% White, 1.0% Black, 0.3% Asian, 25.0% Other, 60.0% Hispanic of any race (2010); Density: 1.5 persons per square mile

(2010); Average household size: 2.59 (2010); Median age: 39.3 (2010); Males per 100 females: 97.1 (2010).
Religion: Five largest groups: 33.8% Southern Baptist Convention, 29.3% Catholic Church, 11.2% The United Methodist Church, 6.7% Churches of Christ, 2.5% Assemblies of God (2000).
Economy: Unemployment rate: 6.2% (June 2011); Total civilian labor force: 2,099 (June 2011); Leading industries: 25.7% retail trade; 20.3% mining; 16.4% accommodation & food services (2009); Farms: 183 totaling 1,602,485 acres (2007); Companies that employ 500 or more persons: 0 (2009); Companies that employ 100 to 499 persons: 0 (2009); Companies that employ less than 100 persons: 133 (2009); Black-owned businesses: n/a (2007); Hispanic-owned businesses: n/a (2007); Asian-owned businesses: n/a (2007); Women-owned businesses: n/a (2007); Retail sales per capita: $12,672 (2010). Single-family building permits issued: n/a (2010); Multi-family building permits issued: n/a (2010).
Income: Per capita income: $20,849 (2010); Median household income: $41,087 (2010); Average household income: $54,626 (2010); Percent of households with income of $100,000 or more: 11.5% (2010); Poverty rate: 14.1% (2009); Bankruptcy rate: 0.27% (2010).
Taxes: Total county taxes per capita: $2,430 (2007); County property taxes per capita: $2,336 (2007).
Education: Percent of population age 25 and over with: High school diploma (including GED) or higher: 67.3% (2010); Bachelor's degree or higher: 11.6% (2010); Master's degree or higher: 3.5% (2010).
Housing: Homeownership rate: 69.3% (2010); Median home value: $61,027 (2010); Median contract rent: $360 per month (2005-2009 5-year est.); Median year structure built: 1968 (2005-2009 5-year est.)
Health: Birth rate: 168.4 per 10,000 population (2009); Death rate: 34.8 per 10,000 population (2009); Age-adjusted cancer mortality rate: 370.7 (Unreliable) deaths per 100,000 population (2007); Number of physicians: 2.6 per 10,000 population (2008); Hospital beds: 0.0 per 10,000 population (2007); Hospital admissions: 0.0 per 10,000 population (2007).
Elections: 2008 Presidential election results: 33.1% Obama, 66.4% McCain, 0.0% Nader
Additional Information Contacts
Crockett County Government . . . . (325) 392-2022
    http://www.co.crockett.tx.us/ips/cms
Ozona Chamber of Commerce . . . . (325) 392-3737
    http://www.ozona.com

Crockett County Communities

OZONA (CDP). County seat. Covers a land area of 4.678 square miles and a water area of 0 square miles. Located at 30.70° N. Lat; 101.20° W. Long. Elevation is 2,349 feet.
History: Ozona was established with a lot of space around it, as the only town in a county larger than the state of Delaware. The spot chosen for the town was at the only water hole in a semidesert range land.
Population: 3,181 (1990); 3,436 (2000); 3,449 (2010); 3,454 (2015 projected); Race: 73.1% White, 1.0% Black, 0.3% Asian, 25.5% Other, 63.2% Hispanic of any race (2010); Density: 737.3 persons per square mile (2010); Average household size: 2.62 (2010); Median age: 38.3 (2010); Males per 100 females: 95.6 (2010); Marriage status: 14.7% never married, 65.9% now married, 3.6% widowed, 15.7% divorced (2005-2009 5-year est.); Foreign born: 14.3% (2005-2009 5-year est.); Ancestry (includes multiple ancestries): 15.6% American, 4.2% Dutch West Indian, 3.6% Irish, 1.6% German, 1.6% Scottish (2005-2009 5-year est.).
Economy: Employment by occupation: 10.1% management, 5.6% professional, 15.8% services, 23.7% sales, 0.0% farming, 20.5% construction, 24.3% production (2005-2009 5-year est.).
Income: Per capita income: $19,541 (2010); Median household income: $39,402 (2010); Average household income: $52,146 (2010); Percent of households with income of $100,000 or more: 10.8% (2010); Poverty rate: 12.9% (2005-2009 5-year est.).
Education: Percent of population age 25 and over with: High school diploma (including GED) or higher: 64.2% (2010); Bachelor's degree or higher: 11.2% (2010); Master's degree or higher: 3.6% (2010).
School District(s)
Crockett County Consolidated CSD (PK-12)
    2009-10 Enrollment: 745 . . . . (325) 392-5501
Housing: Homeownership rate: 71.7% (2010); Median home value: $57,670 (2010); Median contract rent: $347 per month (2005-2009 5-year est.); Median year structure built: 1969 (2005-2009 5-year est.).
Newspapers: Ozona Stockman (Community news; Circulation 1,800)

Transportation: Commute to work: 90.4% car, 0.0% public transportation, 1.6% walk, 4.1% work from home (2005-2009 5-year est.); Travel time to work: 60.1% less than 15 minutes, 19.7% 15 to 30 minutes, 3.8% 30 to 45 minutes, 4.3% 45 to 60 minutes, 12.0% 60 minutes or more (2005-2009 5-year est.)
Airports: Ozona Municipal (general aviation)
Additional Information Contacts
Ozona Chamber of Commerce . . . . (325) 392-3737
    http://www.ozona.com

Crosby County

Located in northwestern Texas; drained by the White River and Double Mountain Fork of the Brazos River. Covers a land area of 899.51 square miles, a water area of 2.17 square miles, and is located in the Central Time Zone at 33.62° N. Lat., 101.31° W. Long. The county was founded in 1876. County seat is Crosbyton.

Crosby County is part of the Lubbock, TX Metropolitan Statistical Area. The entire metro area includes: Crosby County, TX; Lubbock County, TX

Weather Station: Crosbyton										Elevation: 3,009 feet		
	Jan	Feb	Mar	Apr	May	Jun	Jul	Aug	Sep	Oct	Nov	Dec
High	54	58	66	75	83	89	93	91	84	75	64	54
Low	26	29	36	44	55	63	67	66	58	48	36	27
Precip	0.8	0.9	1.3	1.9	2.8	3.1	2.1	2.6	3.0	2.1	1.1	1.0
Snow	2.2	1.3	0.6	0.1	0.0	0.0	0.0	0.0	0.0	tr	1.2	1.6

High and Low temperatures in degrees Fahrenheit; Precipitation and Snow in inches

Population: 7,304 (1990); 7,072 (2000); 6,184 (2010); 5,739 (2015 projected); Race: 60.5% White, 4.3% Black, 0.1% Asian, 35.0% Other, 52.8% Hispanic of any race (2010); Density: 6.9 persons per square mile (2010); Average household size: 2.73 (2010); Median age: 36.4 (2010); Males per 100 females: 92.4 (2010).
Religion: Five largest groups: 40.3% Southern Baptist Convention, 23.2% Catholic Church, 11.1% The United Methodist Church, 7.1% Churches of Christ, 1.9% Assemblies of God (2000).
Economy: Unemployment rate: 8.8% (June 2011); Total civilian labor force: 2,639 (June 2011); Leading industries: 22.3% health care and social assistance; 21.7% wholesale trade; 6.6% manufacturing (2009); Farms: 371 totaling 552,628 acres (2007); Companies that employ 500 or more persons: 0 (2009); Companies that employ 100 to 499 persons: 0 (2009); Companies that employ less than 100 persons: 112 (2009); Black-owned businesses: n/a (2007); Hispanic-owned businesses: n/a (2007); Asian-owned businesses: n/a (2007); Women-owned businesses: 141 (2007); Retail sales per capita: $11,385 (2010). Single-family building permits issued: 0 (2010); Multi-family building permits issued: 0 (2010).
Income: Per capita income: $18,527 (2010); Median household income: $34,635 (2010); Average household income: $50,289 (2010); Percent of households with income of $100,000 or more: 9.7% (2010); Poverty rate: 28.7% (2009); Bankruptcy rate: 0.33% (2010).
Taxes: Total county taxes per capita: $334 (2007); County property taxes per capita: $292 (2007).
Education: Percent of population age 25 and over with: High school diploma (including GED) or higher: 67.9% (2010); Bachelor's degree or higher: 12.2% (2010); Master's degree or higher: 3.3% (2010).
Housing: Homeownership rate: 67.1% (2010); Median home value: $50,410 (2010); Median contract rent: $304 per month (2005-2009 5-year est.); Median year structure built: 1962 (2005-2009 5-year est.)
Health: Birth rate: 180.1 per 10,000 population (2009); Death rate: 93.3 per 10,000 population (2009); Age-adjusted cancer mortality rate: 208.1 (Unreliable) deaths per 100,000 population (2007); Number of physicians: 3.2 per 10,000 population (2008); Hospital beds: 40.0 per 10,000 population (2007); Hospital admissions: 1,025.8 per 10,000 population (2007).
Elections: 2008 Presidential election results: 35.7% Obama, 63.8% McCain, 0.0% Nader
Additional Information Contacts
Crosby County Government . . . . (806) 675-2011
    http://www.co.crosby.tx.us/ips/cms
Crosbyton Chamber of Commerce . . . . (806) 675-2261
    http://www.crosbytoncoc.com
Ralls Chamber of Commerce. . . . . (806) 253-2342

Crosby County Communities

CROSBYTON (city). County seat. Covers a land area of 2.113 square miles and a water area of 0 square miles. Located at 33.65° N. Lat; 101.23° W. Long. Elevation is 3,022 feet.

History: Crosbyton was founded in 1908 on the lands of the Two Buckle Ranch. The town became a shipping point for grain, cattle, and cotton products.

Population: 2,009 (1990); 1,874 (2000); 1,609 (2010); 1,481 (2015 projected); Race: 56.6% White, 5.3% Black, 0.2% Asian, 37.9% Other, 51.8% Hispanic of any race (2010); Density: 761.5 persons per square mile (2010); Average household size: 2.63 (2010); Median age: 38.7 (2010); Males per 100 females: 88.8 (2010); Marriage status: 22.0% never married, 64.6% now married, 7.8% widowed, 5.6% divorced (2005-2009 5-year est.); Foreign born: 0.7% (2005-2009 5-year est.); Ancestry (includes multiple ancestries): 8.5% English, 7.3% American, 5.1% Irish, 4.8% German, 2.2% French (2005-2009 5-year est.).

Economy: Single-family building permits issued: 0 (2010); Multi-family building permits issued: 0 (2010); Employment by occupation: 8.5% management, 20.4% professional, 22.4% services, 24.7% sales, 5.1% farming, 10.3% construction, 8.5% production (2005-2009 5-year est.).

Income: Per capita income: $20,146 (2010); Median household income: $33,521 (2010); Average household income: $51,834 (2010); Percent of households with income of $100,000 or more: 9.8% (2010); Poverty rate: 22.2% (2005-2009 5-year est.).

Taxes: Total city taxes per capita: $120 (2007); City property taxes per capita: $70 (2007).

Education: Percent of population age 25 and over with: High school diploma (including GED) or higher: 69.6% (2010); Bachelor's degree or higher: 15.4% (2010); Master's degree or higher: 3.8% (2010).

School District(s)

Crosbyton CISD (PK-12)
    2009-10 Enrollment: 425 . . . . (806) 675-7331

Housing: Homeownership rate: 69.5% (2010); Median home value: $49,655 (2010); Median contract rent: $237 per month (2005-2009 5-year est.); Median year structure built: 1963 (2005-2009 5-year est.).

Hospitals: Crosbyton Clinic Hospital

Newspapers: Crosby County News & Chronicle (Local news; Circulation 1,600)

Transportation: Commute to work: 84.5% car, 0.0% public transportation, 9.4% walk, 5.6% work from home (2005-2009 5-year est.); Travel time to work: 67.3% less than 15 minutes, 9.4% 15 to 30 minutes, 6.4% 30 to 45 minutes, 14.1% 45 to 60 minutes, 2.8% 60 minutes or more (2005-2009 5-year est.)

Additional Information Contacts

Crosbyton Chamber of Commerce . . . . (806) 675-2261
    http://www.crosbytoncoc.com

LORENZO (city). Covers a land area of 1.032 square miles and a water area of 0 square miles. Located at 33.67° N. Lat; 101.53° W. Long. Elevation is 3,166 feet.

Population: 1,208 (1990); 1,372 (2000); 1,167 (2010); 1,066 (2015 projected); Race: 66.4% White, 7.1% Black, 0.4% Asian, 26.0% Other, 57.6% Hispanic of any race (2010); Density: 1,130.7 persons per square mile (2010); Average household size: 2.82 (2010); Median age: 34.3 (2010); Males per 100 females: 97.1 (2010); Marriage status: 15.0% never married, 69.9% now married, 4.3% widowed, 10.9% divorced (2005-2009 5-year est.); Foreign born: 7.7% (2005-2009 5-year est.); Ancestry (includes multiple ancestries): 8.0% American, 7.6% English, 3.9% German, 3.6% Irish, 1.6% French (2005-2009 5-year est.).

Economy: Single-family building permits issued: 0 (2010); Multi-family building permits issued: 0 (2010); Employment by occupation: 10.8% management, 23.0% professional, 20.4% services, 15.3% sales, 6.5% farming, 7.0% construction, 17.0% production (2005-2009 5-year est.).

Income: Per capita income: $15,399 (2010); Median household income: $30,375 (2010); Average household income: $43,438 (2010); Percent of households with income of $100,000 or more: 7.5% (2010); Poverty rate: 14.1% (2005-2009 5-year est.).

Taxes: Total city taxes per capita: $154 (2007); City property taxes per capita: $100 (2007).

Education: Percent of population age 25 and over with: High school diploma (including GED) or higher: 65.0% (2010); Bachelor's degree or higher: 11.9% (2010); Master's degree or higher: 4.0% (2010).

School District(s)

Lorenzo ISD (PK-12)
    2009-10 Enrollment: 317 . . . . (806) 634-5591

Housing: Homeownership rate: 68.5% (2010); Median home value: $47,215 (2010); Median contract rent: $400 per month (2005-2009 5-year est.); Median year structure built: 1965 (2005-2009 5-year est.).

Safety: Violent crime rate: 8.6 per 10,000 population; Property crime rate: 60.0 per 10,000 population (2009).

Transportation: Commute to work: 94.6% car, 0.0% public transportation, 5.2% walk, 0.2% work from home (2005-2009 5-year est.); Travel time to work: 48.5% less than 15 minutes, 14.9% 15 to 30 minutes, 26.0% 30 to 45 minutes, 7.5% 45 to 60 minutes, 3.1% 60 minutes or more (2005-2009 5-year est.)

RALLS (city). Covers a land area of 1.340 square miles and a water area of 0 square miles. Located at 33.67° N. Lat; 101.38° W. Long. Elevation is 3,107 feet.

History: Founded 1911; incorporated 1921.

Population: 2,172 (1990); 2,252 (2000); 2,009 (2010); 1,884 (2015 projected); Race: 54.6% White, 2.0% Black, 0.0% Asian, 43.4% Other, 59.5% Hispanic of any race (2010); Density: 1,499.1 persons per square mile (2010); Average household size: 2.87 (2010); Median age: 35.2 (2010); Males per 100 females: 90.2 (2010); Marriage status: 20.9% never married, 54.2% now married, 15.2% widowed, 9.7% divorced (2005-2009 5-year est.); Foreign born: 5.8% (2005-2009 5-year est.); Ancestry (includes multiple ancestries): 11.8% German, 6.7% Irish, 2.8% American, 2.4% English, 1.6% Dutch (2005-2009 5-year est.).

Economy: Single-family building permits issued: 0 (2010); Multi-family building permits issued: 0 (2010); Employment by occupation: 7.2% management, 13.1% professional, 21.8% services, 23.2% sales, 6.8% farming, 15.1% construction, 12.8% production (2005-2009 5-year est.).

Income: Per capita income: $17,102 (2010); Median household income: $36,736 (2010); Average household income: $49,286 (2010); Percent of households with income of $100,000 or more: 10.5% (2010); Poverty rate: 37.5% (2005-2009 5-year est.).

Taxes: Total city taxes per capita: $198 (2007); City property taxes per capita: $118 (2007).

Education: Percent of population age 25 and over with: High school diploma (including GED) or higher: 65.1% (2010); Bachelor's degree or higher: 9.0% (2010); Master's degree or higher: 2.8% (2010).

School District(s)

Ralls ISD (PK-12)
    2009-10 Enrollment: 542 . . . . (806) 253-2509

Housing: Homeownership rate: 72.9% (2010); Median home value: $45,413 (2010); Median contract rent: $290 per month (2005-2009 5-year est.); Median year structure built: 1957 (2005-2009 5-year est.).

Safety: Violent crime rate: 25.7 per 10,000 population; Property crime rate: 221.0 per 10,000 population (2009).

Transportation: Commute to work: 93.7% car, 0.0% public transportation, 2.7% walk, 3.4% work from home (2005-2009 5-year est.); Travel time to work: 52.1% less than 15 minutes, 11.8% 15 to 30 minutes, 21.2% 30 to 45 minutes, 14.9% 45 to 60 minutes, 0.0% 60 minutes or more (2005-2009 5-year est.)

Additional Information Contacts

Ralls Chamber of Commerce. . . . . (806) 253-2342

Culberson County

Located in west Texas; mountain and plateau area, bounded on the north by New Mexico; includes the Guadalupe Mountains and Guadalupe Peak, the highest point in the state (8,751 ft). Covers a land area of 3,812.46 square miles, a water area of 0.25 square miles, and is located in the Central/Mountain Time Zone at 31.30° N. Lat., 104.58° W. Long. The county was founded in 1911. County seat is Van Horn.

Weather Station: Van Horn										Elevation: 3,955 feet	
	Jan	Feb	Mar	Apr	May	Jun	Jul	Aug	Sep	Oct	Nov	Dec
High	59	63	70	79	87	94	93	91	86	78	67	58
Low	29	33	38	46	56	64	66	65	58	48	37	29
Precip	0.4	0.5	0.2	0.3	0.6	1.1	2.2	2.2	1.6	1.2	0.5	0.6
Snow	0.8	0.4	0.2	0.0	0.0	0.0	0.0	0.0	0.0	0.1	0.4	1.0

High and Low temperatures in degrees Fahrenheit; Precipitation and Snow in inches

Population: 3,407 (1990); 2,975 (2000); 2,405 (2010); 2,264 (2015 projected); Race: 69.8% White, 1.0% Black, 0.6% Asian, 28.6% Other, 68.8% Hispanic of any race (2010); Density: 0.6 persons per square mile

(2010); Average household size: 2.66 (2010); Median age: 41.9 (2010); Males per 100 females: 97.0 (2010).

Religion: Five largest groups: 47.4% Catholic Church, 37.0% Southern Baptist Convention, 4.2% Churches of Christ, 3.5% The United Methodist Church, 2.3% Seventh-day Adventist Church (2000).

Economy: Unemployment rate: 4.7% (June 2011); Total civilian labor force: 1,647 (June 2011); Leading industries: 40.2% retail trade; 33.2% accommodation & food services (2009); Farms: 55 totaling 1,374,032 acres (2007); Companies that employ 500 or more persons: 0 (2009); Companies that employ 100 to 499 persons: 0 (2009); Companies that employ less than 100 persons: 52 (2009); Black-owned businesses: n/a (2007); Hispanic-owned businesses: n/a (2007); Asian-owned businesses: n/a (2007); Women-owned businesses: n/a (2007); Retail sales per capita: $27,761 (2010). Single-family building permits issued: 3 (2010); Multi-family building permits issued: 0 (2010).

Income: Per capita income: $16,049 (2010); Median household income: $33,504 (2010); Average household income: $41,820 (2010); Percent of households with income of $100,000 or more: 5.0% (2010); Poverty rate: 22.9% (2009); Bankruptcy rate: 0.42% (2010).

Taxes: Total county taxes per capita: $773 (2007); County property taxes per capita: $722 (2007).

Education: Percent of population age 25 and over with: High school diploma (including GED) or higher: 62.4% (2010); Bachelor's degree or higher: 15.7% (2010); Master's degree or higher: 3.6% (2010).

Housing: Homeownership rate: 68.6% (2010); Median home value: $39,570 (2010); Median contract rent: $281 per month (2005-2009 5-year est.); Median year structure built: 1970 (2005-2009 5-year est.)

Health: Birth rate: 126.1 per 10,000 population (2009); Death rate: 13.0 per 10,000 population (2009); Age-adjusted cancer mortality rate: Suppressed deaths per 100,000 population (2007); Number of physicians: 4.1 per 10,000 population (2008); Hospital beds: 56.2 per 10,000 population (2007); Hospital admissions: 1,003.6 per 10,000 population (2007).

Elections: 2008 Presidential election results: 64.8% Obama, 33.9% McCain, 0.0% Nader

National and State Parks: Guadalupe Mountains National Park

Additional Information Contacts

Culberson County Government . . . . (432) 238-2115
    http://www.co.culberson.tx.us/ips/cms
Van Horn Chamber of Commerce . . . . (915) 283-2043
    http://www.vanhorntexas.org

Culberson County Communities

VAN HORN (town). County seat. Covers a land area of 2.875 square miles and a water area of 0 square miles. Located at 31.04° N. Lat; 104.83° W. Long. Elevation is 4,042 feet.

History: The town of Van Horn was named for Van Horn Wells, a frontier watering place to the south.

Population: 2,936 (1990); 2,435 (2000); 1,944 (2010); 1,821 (2015 projected); Race: 66.1% White, 1.0% Black, 0.5% Asian, 32.5% Other, 76.2% Hispanic of any race (2010); Density: 676.1 persons per square mile (2010); Average household size: 2.76 (2010); Median age: 40.2 (2010); Males per 100 females: 93.6 (2010); Marriage status: 38.1% never married, 44.8% now married, 9.4% widowed, 7.7% divorced (2005-2009 5-year est.); Foreign born: 14.6% (2005-2009 5-year est.); Ancestry (includes multiple ancestries): 8.8% American, 7.4% English, 6.8% German, 6.3% Irish, 1.2% Scottish (2005-2009 5-year est.).

Economy: Single-family building permits issued: 3 (2010); Multi-family building permits issued: 0 (2010); Employment by occupation: 9.3% management, 29.2% professional, 27.8% services, 14.8% sales, 1.4% farming, 11.3% construction, 6.2% production (2005-2009 5-year est.).

Income: Per capita income: $15,520 (2010); Median household income: $32,500 (2010); Average household income: $42,031 (2010); Percent of households with income of $100,000 or more: 5.8% (2010); Poverty rate: 29.8% (2005-2009 5-year est.).

Taxes: Total city taxes per capita: $462 (2007); City property taxes per capita: $82 (2007).

Education: Percent of population age 25 and over with: High school diploma (including GED) or higher: 60.2% (2010); Bachelor's degree or higher: 14.1% (2010); Master's degree or higher: 3.7% (2010).

School District(s)
Culberson County-Allamoore ISD (PK-12)
    2009-10 Enrollment: 487 . . . . (432) 283-2245

Housing: Homeownership rate: 72.4% (2010); Median home value: $38,210 (2010); Median contract rent: $267 per month (2005-2009 5-year est.); Median year structure built: 1969 (2005-2009 5-year est.).

Hospitals: Culberson Hospital (25 beds)

Newspapers: Van Horn Advocate (Community news; Circulation 1,000)

Transportation: Commute to work: 94.3% car, 0.6% public transportation, 0.0% walk, 0.9% work from home (2005-2009 5-year est.); Travel time to work: 89.5% less than 15 minutes, 8.4% 15 to 30 minutes, 1.4% 30 to 45 minutes, 0.0% 45 to 60 minutes, 0.6% 60 minutes or more (2005-2009 5-year est.)

Airports: Culberson County (general aviation)

Additional Information Contacts

Van Horn Chamber of Commerce . . . . (915) 283-2043
    http://www.vanhorntexas.org

Dallam County

Located in north Texas, in the Panhandle; bounded on the north by Oklahoma, and on the west by New Mexico. Covers a land area of 1,504.69 square miles, a water area of 0.56 square miles, and is located in the Central Time Zone at 36.19° N. Lat., 102.66° W. Long. The county was founded in 1876. County seat is Dalhart.

Weather Station: Dalhart Municipal Arpt									Elevation: 3,990 feet		
	Jan	Feb	Mar	Apr	May	Jun	Jul	Aug	Sep	Oct	Nov	Dec
High	50	54	62	70	79	88	92	89	82	71	59	49
Low	21	24	30	39	49	59	63	62	54	41	29	21
Precip	0.5	0.4	1.2	1.2	2.3	2.2	2.9	2.8	1.7	1.5	0.6	0.6
Snow	na	na	na	na	na	na	na	na	na	na	na	na

High and Low temperatures in degrees Fahrenheit; Precipitation and Snow in inches

Population: 5,461 (1990); 6,222 (2000); 6,349 (2010); 6,399 (2015 projected); Race: 77.9% White, 2.3% Black, 0.7% Asian, 19.0% Other, 34.9% Hispanic of any race (2010); Density: 4.2 persons per square mile (2010); Average household size: 2.74 (2010); Median age: 33.5 (2010); Males per 100 females: 102.1 (2010).

Religion: Five largest groups: 17.9% Catholic Church, 11.7% The United Methodist Church, 8.5% Southern Baptist Convention, 6.6% Churches of Christ, 5.9% Christian Churches and Churches of Christ (2000).

Economy: Unemployment rate: 5.1% (June 2011); Total civilian labor force: 3,845 (June 2011); Leading industries: 22.0% wholesale trade; 17.0% accommodation & food services; 12.1% retail trade (2009); Farms: 452 totaling 936,886 acres (2007); Companies that employ 500 or more persons: 0 (2009); Companies that employ 100 to 499 persons: 1 (2009); Companies that employ less than 100 persons: 221 (2009); Black-owned businesses: n/a (2007); Hispanic-owned businesses: n/a (2007); Asian-owned businesses: n/a (2007); Women-owned businesses: n/a (2007); Retail sales per capita: $15,751 (2010). Single-family building permits issued: 7 (2010); Multi-family building permits issued: 76 (2010).

Income: Per capita income: $16,157 (2010); Median household income: $32,593 (2010); Average household income: $42,540 (2010); Percent of households with income of $100,000 or more: 5.6% (2010); Poverty rate: 14.5% (2009); Bankruptcy rate: 2.81% (2010).

Taxes: Total county taxes per capita: $294 (2007); County property taxes per capita: $225 (2007).

Education: Percent of population age 25 and over with: High school diploma (including GED) or higher: 70.5% (2010); Bachelor's degree or higher: 10.8% (2010); Master's degree or higher: 3.0% (2010).

Housing: Homeownership rate: 60.9% (2010); Median home value: $65,621 (2010); Median contract rent: $505 per month (2005-2009 5-year est.); Median year structure built: 1957 (2005-2009 5-year est.).

Health: Birth rate: 181.2 per 10,000 population (2009); Death rate: 66.7 per 10,000 population (2009); Age-adjusted cancer mortality rate: 141.4 (Unreliable) deaths per 100,000 population (2007); Number of physicians: 11.2 per 10,000 population (2008); Hospital beds: 34.2 per 10,000 population (2007); Hospital admissions: 963.0 per 10,000 population (2007).

Elections: 2008 Presidential election results: 19.0% Obama, 79.9% McCain, 0.1% Nader

National and State Parks: Rita Blanca National Grassland

Additional Information Contacts

Dallam County Government . . . . (806) 249-2450
    http://www.dallam.org/county
City of Dalhart . . . . (806) 244-5511
    http://www.dallam.org/city/dalhart.html

Dalhart Area Chamber of Commerce . . . . (806) 244-5646
http://www.dalhart.org

Dallam County Communities

DALHART (city). County seat. Covers a land area of 4.292 square
miles and a water area of 0 square miles. Located at 36.06° N. Lat;
102.51° W. Long. Elevation is 3,983 feet.
History: Dalhart began as a frontier town of cowboys, land speculators,
and railroad construction workers. It became the seat of Dalhart County in
1903, and developed around the railroad shops, grain elevators, and
shipping pens for cattle.
Population: 6,266 (1990); 7,237 (2000); 7,217 (2010); 7,189 (2015
projected); Race: 82.7% White, 2.1% Black, 0.8% Asian, 14.4% Other,
28.5% Hispanic of any race (2010); Density: 1,681.5 persons per square
mile (2010); Average household size: 2.60 (2010); Median age: 34.2
(2010); Males per 100 females: 99.8 (2010); Marriage status: 20.0% never
married, 59.7% now married, 6.9% widowed, 13.4% divorced (2005-2009
5-year est.); Foreign born: 8.5% (2005-2009 5-year est.); Ancestry
(includes multiple ancestries): 22.3% German, 13.9% Irish, 10.7% English,
5.6% American, 3.2% Scotch-Irish (2005-2009 5-year est.).
Economy: Single-family building permits issued: 7 (2010); Multi-family
building permits issued: 76 (2010); Employment by occupation: 11.4%
management, 11.5% professional, 15.5% services, 22.0% sales, 2.8%
farming, 16.4% construction, 20.4% production (2005-2009 5-year est.).
Income: Per capita income: $19,895 (2010); Median household income:
$36,214 (2010); Average household income: $50,822 (2010); Percent of
households with income of $100,000 or more: 9.2% (2010); Poverty rate:
10.1% (2005-2009 5-year est.).
Taxes: Total city taxes per capita: $323 (2007); City property taxes per
capita: $102 (2007).
Education: Percent of population age 25 and over with: High school
diploma (including GED) or higher: 76.4% (2010); Bachelor's degree or
higher: 14.8% (2010); Master's degree or higher: 3.7% (2010).
School District(s)
Dalhart ISD (PK-12)
    2009-10 Enrollment: 1,683 . . . . (806) 244-7810
Stratford ISD (PK-12)
    2009-10 Enrollment: 595 . . . . (806) 366-3300
Housing: Homeownership rate: 68.1% (2010); Median home value:
$83,207 (2010); Median contract rent: $498 per month (2005-2009 5-year
est.); Median year structure built: 1963 (2005-2009 5-year est.).
Hospitals: Coon Memorial Hospital (23 beds)
Safety: Violent crime rate: 24.3 per 10,000 population; Property crime rate:
209.8 per 10,000 population (2009).
Newspapers: Dalhart Daily Texan (Local news; Circulation 2,076)
Transportation: Commute to work: 80.6% car, 0.3% public transportation,
2.6% walk, 4.8% work from home (2005-2009 5-year est.); Travel time to
work: 78.2% less than 15 minutes, 15.5% 15 to 30 minutes, 4.2% 30 to 45
minutes, 1.1% 45 to 60 minutes, 1.0% 60 minutes or more (2005-2009
5-year est.)
Airports: Dalhart Municipal (general aviation)
Additional Information Contacts
City of Dalhart . . . . (806) 244-5511
http://www.dallam.org/city/dalhart.html
Dalhart Area Chamber of Commerce . . . . (806) 244-5646
http://www.dalhart.org

TEXLINE (town). Covers a land area of 1.014 square miles and a water
area of 0 square miles. Located at 36.37° N. Lat; 103.02° W. Long.
Elevation is 4,692 feet.
Population: 425 (1990); 511 (2000); 524 (2010); 532 (2015 projected);
Race: 88.2% White, 0.0% Black, 0.0% Asian, 11.8% Other, 27.3%
Hispanic of any race (2010); Density: 517.0 persons per square mile
(2010); Average household size: 2.76 (2010); Median age: 34.6 (2010);
Males per 100 females: 96.3 (2010); Marriage status: 21.4% never married,
56.6% now married, 8.2% widowed, 13.8% divorced (2005-2009 5-year
est.); Foreign born: 18.1% (2005-2009 5-year est.); Ancestry (includes
multiple ancestries): 23.4% Irish, 18.5% German, 9.6% English, 7.5%
Hungarian, 4.4% American (2005-2009 5-year est.).
Economy: Employment by occupation: 13.1% management, 7.8%
professional, 12.7% services, 12.3% sales, 29.9% farming, 9.8%
construction, 14.3% production (2005-2009 5-year est.).
Income: Per capita income: $19,230 (2010); Median household income:
$41,977 (2010); Average household income: $55,132 (2010); Percent of

households with income of $100,000 or more: 10.5% (2010); Poverty rate:
29.3% (2005-2009 5-year est.).
Taxes: Total city taxes per capita: $257 (2007); City property taxes per
capita: $156 (2007).
Education: Percent of population age 25 and over with: High school
diploma (including GED) or higher: 74.5% (2010); Bachelor's degree or
higher: 19.4% (2010); Master's degree or higher: 4.5% (2010).
School District(s)
Texline ISD (PK-12)
    2009-10 Enrollment: 168 . . . . (806) 362-4667
Housing: Homeownership rate: 59.5% (2010); Median home value:
$72,778 (2010); Median contract rent: $323 per month (2005-2009 5-year
est.); Median year structure built: 1970 (2005-2009 5-year est.).
Transportation: Commute to work: 88.5% car, 0.0% public transportation,
4.9% walk, 4.5% work from home (2005-2009 5-year est.); Travel time to
work: 51.3% less than 15 minutes, 31.0% 15 to 30 minutes, 6.9% 30 to 45
minutes, 3.0% 45 to 60 minutes, 7.8% 60 minutes or more (2005-2009
5-year est.)

Dallas County

Located in northeastern Texas; drained by the Trinity River. Covers a land
area of 879.60 square miles, a water area of 28.96 square miles, and is
located in the Central Time Zone at 32.80° N. Lat., 96.78° W. Long. The
county was founded in 1846. County seat is Dallas.

Dallas County is part of the Dallas-Fort Worth-Arlington, TX Metropolitan
Statistical Area. The entire metro area includes: Dallas-Plano-Irving, TX
Metropolitan Division (Collin County, TX; Dallas County, TX; Delta County,
TX; Denton County, TX; Ellis County, TX; Hunt County, TX; Kaufman
County, TX; Rockwall County, TX); Fort Worth-Arlington, TX Metropolitan
Division (Johnson County, TX; Parker County, TX; Tarrant County, TX;
Wise County, TX)

Weather Station: Dallas Love Field   Elevation: 439 feet

	Jan	Feb	Mar	Apr	May	Jun	Jul	Aug	Sep	Oct	Nov	Dec
High	57	61	69	77	84	92	96	96	89	78	67	58
Low	37	41	49	56	65	73	77	77	69	58	47	38
Precip	2.0	2.6	3.4	3.1	5.1	4.1	2.2	1.9	2.7	4.7	2.8	2.5
Snow	0.5	0.3	tr	tr	tr	tr	0.0	0.0	0.0	tr	0.1	0.4

High and Low temperatures in degrees Fahrenheit; Precipitation and Snow in inches

Population: 1,852,162 (1990); 2,218,899 (2000); 2,443,619 (2010);
2,548,608 (2015 projected); Race: 52.5% White, 20.1% Black, 4.4% Asian,
22.9% Other, 40.0% Hispanic of any race (2010); Density: 2,778.1 persons
per square mile (2010); Average household size: 2.78 (2010); Median age:
33.8 (2010); Males per 100 females: 103.0 (2010).
Religion: Five largest groups: 21.7% Catholic Church, 12.7% Southern
Baptist Convention, 4.8% The United Methodist Church, 2.0% Churches of
Christ, 1.7% Jewish Estimate (2000).
Economy: Unemployment rate: 9.2% (June 2011); Total civilian labor
force: 1,184,259 (June 2011); Leading industries: 11.1% health care and
social assistance; 9.2% retail trade; 9.1% administration, support, waste
management, remediation services (2009); Farms: 755 totaling 88,010
acres (2007); Companies that employ 500 or more persons: 248 (2009);
Companies that employ 100 to 499 persons: 1,977 (2009); Companies that
employ less than 100 persons: 59,134 (2009); Black-owned businesses:
31,079 (2007); Hispanic-owned businesses: 35,056 (2007); Asian-owned
businesses: 15,800 (2007); Women-owned businesses: 64,173 (2007);
Retail sales per capita: $20,402 (2010). Single-family building permits
issued: 2,742 (2010); Multi-family building permits issued: 2,743 (2010).
Income: Per capita income: $24,508 (2010); Median household income:
$48,606 (2010); Average household income: $68,553 (2010); Percent of
households with income of $100,000 or more: 17.8% (2010); Poverty rate:
18.7% (2009); Bankruptcy rate: 2.82% (2010).
Taxes: Total county taxes per capita: $288 (2007); County property taxes
per capita: $269 (2007).
Education: Percent of population age 25 and over with: High school
diploma (including GED) or higher: 74.3% (2010); Bachelor's degree or
higher: 26.2% (2010); Master's degree or higher: 9.0% (2010).
Housing: Homeownership rate: 55.8% (2010); Median home value:
$128,882 (2010); Median contract rent: $663 per month (2005-2009 5-year
est.); Median year structure built: 1976 (2005-2009 5-year est.)
Health: Birth rate: 171.3 per 10,000 population (2009); Death rate: 57.8 per
10,000 population (2009); Age-adjusted cancer mortality rate: 170.7 deaths
per 100,000 population (2007); Number of physicians: 30.0 per 10,000

population (2008); Hospital beds: 34.2 per 10,000 population (2007); Hospital admissions: 1,297.2 per 10,000 population (2007).

Environment: Air Quality Index: 71.6% good, 26.1% moderate, 2.3% unhealthy for sensitive individuals, 0.0% unhealthy (percent of days in 2008)

Elections: 2008 Presidential election results: 57.2% Obama, 41.9% McCain, 0.1% Nader

Additional Information Contacts

Dallas County Government . . . . (214) 653-7555
  http://www.dallascounty.org
Balch Springs Chamber of Commerce . . . . (972) 557-0988
  http://www.balchspringschamber.org
Cedar Hill Chamber of Commerce. . . . . (972) 291-7817
  http://www.cedarhillchamber.org
City of Balch Springs . . . . (972) 557-6070
  http://www.cityofbalchsprings.com
City of Cedar Hill . . . . (972) 291-5100
  http://www.cedarhilltxgov.org
City of Coppell . . . . (972) 304-3618
  http://www.ci.coppell.tx.us
City of Dallas . . . . (214) 670-5111
  http://www.dallascityhall.com
City of De Soto. . . . . (972) 274-2489
  http://www.ci.desoto.tx.us
City of Duncanville . . . . (972) 780-5000
  http://www.ci.duncanville.tx.us
City of Farmers Branch . . . . (972) 247-3131
  http://www.ci.farmers-branch.tx.us
City of Garland. . . . . (972) 205-2000
  http://www.ci.garland.tx.us
City of Glenn Heights . . . . (972) 223-1690
  http://www.glennheights.com
City of Grand Prairie . . . . (972) 237-8000
  http://gptx.org
City of Highland Park . . . . (214) 521-4161
  http://www.hptx.org
City of Irving . . . . (972) 721-2600
  http://www.ci.irving.tx.us
City of Lancaster . . . . (972) 218-1300
  http://www.lancaster-tx.com
City of Mesquite . . . . (972) 288-7711
  http://www.cityofmesquite.com
City of Richardson . . . . (972) 744-4100
  http://www.cor.net
City of Rowlett . . . . (972) 412-6116
  http://www.ci.rowlett.tx.us
City of Sachse . . . . (972) 495-1212
  http://www.cityofsachse.com
City of Seagoville . . . . (972) 287-2050
  http://www.seagoville.us
City of University Park . . . . (214) 363-1644
  http://www.uptexas.org
Dallas Regional Chamber of Commerce . . . . (214) 746-6600
  http://www.dallaschamber.org
De Soto Chamber of Commerce . . . . (972) 224-3565
  http://www.desotochamber.org
Duncanville Chamber of Commerce . . . . (972) 780-4990
  http://www.duncanvillechamber.org
Farmers Branch Chamber of Commerce. . . . . (972) 243-8966
  http://www.fbchamber.com
French American Chamber of Commerce Dallas/Fort Worth . . . . (972) 241-0111
  http://www.faccdallas.com
Garland Chamber of Commerce . . . . (972) 272-7551
  http://www.garlandchamber.com
Grand Prairie Chamber of Commerce . . . . (972) 264-1558
  http://www.grandprairiechamber.org
Greater East Dallas Chamber of Commerce . . . . (214) 328-4100
  http://www.dallasnortheastchamber.net
Greater Grand Prairie Hispanic Chamber of Commerce . . . (817) 881-4734
  http://ggphcc.com
Lancaster Chamber of Commerce. . . . . (972) 227-2579
  http://www.lancastertx.org
Mesquite Chamber of Commerce . . . . (972) 285-0211
  http://www.mesquitechamber.com

Richardson Economic Development Partnership . . . . (972) 792-2800
  http://www.telecomcorridor.com
Rowlett Chamber of Commerce. . . . . (972) 475-3200
  http://www.rowlettchamber.com
Sachse Chamber of Commerce. . . . . (972) 496-1212
  http://www.sachsechamber.com
Seagoville Chamber of Commerce . . . . (972) 287-5184
  http://www.seagovillecoc.org
Southeast Dallas Chamber of Commerce . . . . (214) 398-9590
  http://www.sedcc.org
Swedish American Chamber of Commerce. . . . . (214) 707-0200
  http://www.sacctx.com
Town of Addison . . . . (972) 450-7001
  http://www.addisontx.gov
Town of Sunnyvale . . . . (972) 226-7177
  http://www.townofsunnyvale.org
US-Mexico Chamber of Commerce. . . . . (214) 651-4300
  http://www.usmcoc.org
United States Chamber of Commerce. . . . . (972) 387-1099
Wilmer Chamber of Commerce . . . . (972) 525-3668

Dallas County Communities

ADDISON (town). Covers a land area of 4.427 square miles and a water area of 0 square miles. Located at 32.95° N. Lat; 96.83° W. Long. Elevation is 636 feet.

History: The land occupied by the town of Addison was settled as early as 1846 when Preston Witt built a house near White Rock Creek.

Population: 8,847 (1990); 14,166 (2000); 13,394 (2010); 13,952 (2015 projected); Race: 64.8% White, 7.2% Black, 7.7% Asian, 20.2% Other, 30.8% Hispanic of any race (2010); Density: 3,025.6 persons per square mile (2010); Average household size: 1.80 (2010); Median age: 36.2 (2010); Males per 100 females: 111.7 (2010); Marriage status: 40.7% never married, 40.7% now married, 2.2% widowed, 16.5% divorced (2005-2009 5-year est.); Foreign born: 26.5% (2005-2009 5-year est.); Ancestry (includes multiple ancestries): 9.3% American, 8.0% German, 7.0% Irish, 6.1% English, 3.5% Scottish (2005-2009 5-year est.).

Economy: Single-family building permits issued: 2 (2010); Multi-family building permits issued: 367 (2010); Employment by occupation: 18.1% management, 23.7% professional, 12.1% services, 26.8% sales, 0.4% farming, 8.5% construction, 10.4% production (2005-2009 5-year est.).

Income: Per capita income: $45,939 (2010); Median household income: $59,143 (2010); Average household income: $82,598 (2010); Percent of households with income of $100,000 or more: 24.6% (2010); Poverty rate: 10.6% (2005-2009 5-year est.).

Taxes: Total city taxes per capita: $2,265 (2007); City property taxes per capita: $962 (2007).

Education: Percent of population age 25 and over with: High school diploma (including GED) or higher: 93.1% (2010); Bachelor's degree or higher: 48.6% (2010); Master's degree or higher: 17.0% (2010).

Housing: Homeownership rate: 23.3% (2010); Median home value: $262,812 (2010); Median contract rent: $712 per month (2005-2009 5-year est.); Median year structure built: 1986 (2005-2009 5-year est.).

Safety: Violent crime rate: 59.7 per 10,000 population; Property crime rate: 676.5 per 10,000 population (2009).

Transportation: Commute to work: 92.0% car, 0.3% public transportation, 2.2% walk, 4.6% work from home (2005-2009 5-year est.); Travel time to work: 26.6% less than 15 minutes, 45.0% 15 to 30 minutes, 23.1% 30 to 45 minutes, 3.0% 45 to 60 minutes, 2.3% 60 minutes or more (2005-2009 5-year est.)

Additional Information Contacts

Metrocrest Chamber of Commerce . . . . (469) 587-0420
  http://www.metrocrestchamber.com
Town of Addison . . . . (972) 450-7001
  http://www.addisontx.gov

BALCH SPRINGS (city). Covers a land area of 8.057 square miles and a water area of 0.007 square miles. Located at 32.71° N. Lat; 96.61° W. Long. Elevation is 499 feet.

Population: 17,409 (1990); 19,375 (2000); 20,300 (2010); 20,628 (2015 projected); Race: 48.8% White, 22.5% Black, 0.6% Asian, 28.2% Other, 40.3% Hispanic of any race (2010); Density: 2,519.5 persons per square mile (2010); Average household size: 3.24 (2010); Median age: 30.5 (2010); Males per 100 females: 98.6 (2010); Marriage status: 31.2% never married, 51.5% now married, 6.4% widowed, 10.9% divorced (2005-2009

5-year est.); Foreign born: 15.4% (2005-2009 5-year est.); Ancestry (includes multiple ancestries): 16.8% American, 3.8% German, 3.6% Irish, 2.9% English, 0.7% French (2005-2009 5-year est.).

Economy: Single-family building permits issued: 77 (2010); Multi-family building permits issued: 0 (2010); Employment by occupation: 8.0% management, 9.5% professional, 17.5% services, 27.3% sales, 0.2% farming, 20.9% construction, 16.5% production (2005-2009 5-year est.).

Income: Per capita income: $14,232 (2010); Median household income: $39,272 (2010); Average household income: $46,230 (2010); Percent of households with income of $100,000 or more: 4.2% (2010); Poverty rate: 22.6% (2005-2009 5-year est.).

Taxes: Total city taxes per capita: $486 (2007); City property taxes per capita: $226 (2007).

Education: Percent of population age 25 and over with: High school diploma (including GED) or higher: 66.6% (2010); Bachelor's degree or higher: 6.1% (2010); Master's degree or higher: 2.1% (2010).

School District(s)

Mesquite ISD (PK-12)
    2009-10 Enrollment: 37,272 . . . . (972) 288-6411

Housing: Homeownership rate: 63.6% (2010); Median home value: $79,204 (2010); Median contract rent: $606 per month (2005-2009 5-year est.); Median year structure built: 1976 (2005-2009 5-year est.).

Safety: Violent crime rate: 77.3 per 10,000 population; Property crime rate: 840.8 per 10,000 population (2009).

Transportation: Commute to work: 95.9% car, 0.5% public transportation, 0.1% walk, 1.7% work from home (2005-2009 5-year est.); Travel time to work: 19.8% less than 15 minutes, 29.7% 15 to 30 minutes, 27.3% 30 to 45 minutes, 12.0% 45 to 60 minutes, 11.1% 60 minutes or more (2005-2009 5-year est.)

Additional Information Contacts

Balch Springs Chamber of Commerce . . . . (972) 557-0988
    http://www.balchspringschamber.org
City of Balch Springs . . . . (972) 557-6070
    http://www.cityofbalchsprings.com

CEDAR HILL (city). Covers a land area of 35.153 square miles and a water area of 0.089 square miles. Located at 32.58° N. Lat; 96.94° W. Long. Elevation is 830 feet.

Population: 20,267 (1990); 32,093 (2000); 45,294 (2010); 50,263 (2015 projected); Race: 44.8% White, 40.9% Black, 1.9% Asian, 12.4% Other, 18.2% Hispanic of any race (2010); Density: 1,288.5 persons per square mile (2010); Average household size: 3.01 (2010); Median age: 34.1 (2010); Males per 100 females: 94.6 (2010); Marriage status: 31.0% never married, 53.6% now married, 4.3% widowed, 11.1% divorced (2005-2009 5-year est.); Foreign born: 7.0% (2005-2009 5-year est.); Ancestry (includes multiple ancestries): 6.3% German, 5.3% Irish, 4.9% English, 4.0% American, 2.5% French (2005-2009 5-year est.).

Economy: Unemployment rate: 9.6% (June 2011); Total civilian labor force: 24,117 (June 2011); Single-family building permits issued: 85 (2010); Multi-family building permits issued: 0 (2010); Employment by occupation: 17.6% management, 22.1% professional, 12.3% services, 29.5% sales, 0.1% farming, 6.5% construction, 11.8% production (2005-2009 5-year est.).

Income: Per capita income: $25,667 (2010); Median household income: $66,655 (2010); Average household income: $77,553 (2010); Percent of households with income of $100,000 or more: 22.8% (2010); Poverty rate: 6.0% (2005-2009 5-year est.).

Taxes: Total city taxes per capita: $752 (2007); City property taxes per capita: $399 (2007).

Education: Percent of population age 25 and over with: High school diploma (including GED) or higher: 90.3% (2010); Bachelor's degree or higher: 27.6% (2010); Master's degree or higher: 7.7% (2010).

School District(s)

Cedar Hill ISD (PK-12)
    2009-10 Enrollment: 8,284 . . . . (972) 291-1581

Four-year College(s)

Northwood University (Private, Not-for-profit)
    Fall 2009 Enrollment: 930 . . . . (972) 291-1541
    2010-11 Tuition: In-state $19,272; Out-of-state $19,272

Housing: Homeownership rate: 84.2% (2010); Median home value: $132,651 (2010); Median contract rent: $843 per month (2005-2009 5-year est.); Median year structure built: 1992 (2005-2009 5-year est.).

Safety: Violent crime rate: 26.0 per 10,000 population; Property crime rate: 364.2 per 10,000 population (2009).

Transportation: Commute to work: 92.5% car, 1.9% public transportation, 1.7% walk, 3.2% work from home (2005-2009 5-year est.); Travel time to work: 18.9% less than 15 minutes, 27.8% 15 to 30 minutes, 30.0% 30 to 45 minutes, 13.2% 45 to 60 minutes, 10.2% 60 minutes or more (2005-2009 5-year est.)

Additional Information Contacts

Cedar Hill Chamber of Commerce. . . . . (972) 291-7817
    http://www.cedarhillchamber.org
City of Cedar Hill . . . . (972) 291-5100
    http://www.cedarhilltxgov.org

COCKRELL HILL (city). Covers a land area of 0.580 square miles and a water area of 0 square miles. Located at 32.73° N. Lat; 96.88° W. Long. Elevation is 640 feet.

Population: 3,746 (1990); 4,443 (2000); 4,338 (2010); 4,306 (2015 projected); Race: 43.5% White, 1.2% Black, 0.1% Asian, 55.2% Other, 91.2% Hispanic of any race (2010); Density: 7,483.5 persons per square mile (2010); Average household size: 4.04 (2010); Median age: 27.1 (2010); Males per 100 females: 107.5 (2010); Marriage status: 29.6% never married, 57.4% now married, 4.8% widowed, 8.2% divorced (2005-2009 5-year est.); Foreign born: 43.6% (2005-2009 5-year est.); Ancestry (includes multiple ancestries): 2.7% German, 2.6% Irish, 1.9% English, 0.9% Polish, 0.5% Scottish (2005-2009 5-year est.).

Economy: Single-family building permits issued: 2 (2010); Multi-family building permits issued: 0 (2010); Employment by occupation: 2.8% management, 4.0% professional, 16.7% services, 20.0% sales, 0.0% farming, 30.1% construction, 26.4% production (2005-2009 5-year est.).

Income: Per capita income: $11,662 (2010); Median household income: $39,640 (2010); Average household income: $47,148 (2010); Percent of households with income of $100,000 or more: 7.5% (2010); Poverty rate: 27.8% (2005-2009 5-year est.).

Taxes: Total city taxes per capita: $190 (2007); City property taxes per capita: $97 (2007).

Education: Percent of population age 25 and over with: High school diploma (including GED) or higher: 36.7% (2010); Bachelor's degree or higher: 4.6% (2010); Master's degree or higher: 2.0% (2010).

Housing: Homeownership rate: 58.4% (2010); Median home value: $71,232 (2010); Median contract rent: $485 per month (2005-2009 5-year est.); Median year structure built: 1952 (2005-2009 5-year est.).

Safety: Violent crime rate: 44.7 per 10,000 population; Property crime rate: 336.2 per 10,000 population (2009).

Transportation: Commute to work: 95.0% car, 2.9% public transportation, 0.0% walk, 1.4% work from home (2005-2009 5-year est.); Travel time to work: 14.9% less than 15 minutes, 41.2% 15 to 30 minutes, 23.1% 30 to 45 minutes, 12.5% 45 to 60 minutes, 8.4% 60 minutes or more (2005-2009 5-year est.)

COPPELL (city). Covers a land area of 14.868 square miles and a water area of 0.027 square miles. Located at 32.96° N. Lat; 96.98° W. Long. Elevation is 518 feet.

Population: 16,881 (1990); 35,958 (2000); 39,175 (2010); 41,250 (2015 projected); Race: 78.3% White, 4.2% Black, 11.6% Asian, 5.9% Other, 9.7% Hispanic of any race (2010); Density: 2,634.9 persons per square mile (2010); Average household size: 2.99 (2010); Median age: 33.7 (2010); Males per 100 females: 99.8 (2010); Marriage status: 23.5% never married, 64.6% now married, 2.6% widowed, 9.3% divorced (2005-2009 5-year est.); Foreign born: 14.9% (2005-2009 5-year est.); Ancestry (includes multiple ancestries): 17.2% German, 15.9% English, 12.1% Irish, 6.8% American, 5.9% Italian (2005-2009 5-year est.).

Economy: Unemployment rate: 7.3% (June 2011); Total civilian labor force: 20,605 (June 2011); Single-family building permits issued: 83 (2010); Multi-family building permits issued: 0 (2010); Employment by occupation: 32.2% management, 27.8% professional, 7.9% services, 25.6% sales, 0.1% farming, 2.9% construction, 3.6% production (2005-2009 5-year est.).

Income: Per capita income: $48,538 (2010); Median household income: $112,822 (2010); Average household income: $145,039 (2010); Percent of households with income of $100,000 or more: 55.9% (2010); Poverty rate: 2.4% (2005-2009 5-year est.).

Taxes: Total city taxes per capita: $1,085 (2007); City property taxes per capita: $670 (2007).

Education: Percent of population age 25 and over with: High school diploma (including GED) or higher: 96.6% (2010); Bachelor's degree or higher: 61.9% (2010); Master's degree or higher: 19.7% (2010).

School District(s)

Carrollton-Farmers Branch ISD (PK-12)
  2009-10 Enrollment: 25,920 . . . . (972) 968-6100
Coppell ISD (PK-12)
  2009-10 Enrollment: 9,982 . . . . (214) 496-6000
Manara Academy (KG-05)
  2009-10 Enrollment: 250 . . . . (972) 304-1155
Housing: Homeownership rate: 75.8% (2010); Median home value: $276,634 (2010); Median contract rent: $856 per month (2005-2009 5-year est.); Median year structure built: 1991 (2005-2009 5-year est.).
Safety: Violent crime rate: 10.9 per 10,000 population; Property crime rate: 167.2 per 10,000 population (2009).
Newspapers: Citizens' Advocate (Local news; Circulation 5,000)
Transportation: Commute to work: 90.3% car, 0.4% public transportation, 1.2% walk, 7.3% work from home (2005-2009 5-year est.); Travel time to work: 25.1% less than 15 minutes, 40.0% 15 to 30 minutes, 26.5% 30 to 45 minutes, 5.9% 45 to 60 minutes, 2.6% 60 minutes or more (2005-2009 5-year est.)
Additional Information Contacts
City of Coppell . . . . (972) 304-3618
  http://www.ci.coppell.tx.us

DALLAS (city). County seat. Covers a land area of 342.544 square miles and a water area of 42.456 square miles. Located at 32.80° N. Lat; 96.78° W. Long. Elevation is 420 feet.
History: Dallas was begun by John Neely Bryan, who came to Texas from Arkansas and settled along the Trinity River on a military route that the Republic of Texas had made between Austin and the Red River. In 1842 other settlers joined Bryan. Their village was called Dallas, probably named for George Mifflin Dallas, U.S. Vice President under James Polk, as was Dallas County when it was formed in 1846. Dallas developed steadily and calmly, becoming the seat of Dallas County in 1850. The population was augmented in 1855 by several hundred European immigrants who, after giving up on a cooperative community that they had established nearby, moved to Dallas. Dallas was incorporated in 1856. Cotton growing commenced after the Civil War, and when the railroad brought easier shipping in 1872, Dallas experienced a boom time. Wheat, wool, cotton, hides, sheep and cattle moved through Dallas to market.
Population: 1,006,971 (1990); 1,188,580 (2000); 1,297,289 (2010); 1,357,127 (2015 projected); Race: 48.1% White, 23.0% Black, 3.0% Asian, 25.9% Other, 45.8% Hispanic of any race (2010); Density: 3,787.2 persons per square mile (2010); Average household size: 2.64 (2010); Median age: 33.3 (2010); Males per 100 females: 105.2 (2010); Marriage status: 38.5% never married, 45.3% now married, 5.2% widowed, 11.0% divorced (2005-2009 5-year est.); Foreign born: 25.4% (2005-2009 5-year est.); Ancestry (includes multiple ancestries): 6.4% German, 5.7% English, 5.1% Irish, 3.0% American, 1.6% French (2005-2009 5-year est.).
Economy: Unemployment rate: 9.2% (June 2011); Total civilian labor force: 608,602 (June 2011); Single-family building permits issued: 865 (2010); Multi-family building permits issued: 1,744 (2010); Employment by occupation: 13.7% management, 16.8% professional, 18.1% services, 24.3% sales, 0.2% farming, 13.9% construction, 12.9% production (2005-2009 5-year est.).
Income: Per capita income: $24,273 (2010); Median household income: $43,066 (2010); Average household income: $64,560 (2010); Percent of households with income of $100,000 or more: 16.0% (2010); Poverty rate: 21.8% (2005-2009 5-year est.).
Taxes: Total city taxes per capita: $761 (2007); City property taxes per capita: $431 (2007).
Education: Percent of population age 25 and over with: High school diploma (including GED) or higher: 69.4% (2010); Bachelor's degree or higher: 26.7% (2010); Master's degree or higher: 9.5% (2010).

School District(s)

A+ Academy (PK-12)
  2009-10 Enrollment: 1,033 . . . . (214) 381-2208
Academy of Dallas (PK-08)
  2009-10 Enrollment: 535 . . . . (214) 371-9600
Advantage Academy (KG-12)
  2009-10 Enrollment: 1,507 . . . . (214) 276-5800
Aw Brown-Fellowship Charter School (PK-06)
  2009-10 Enrollment: 1,352 . . . . (972) 709-4700
Carrollton-Farmers Branch ISD (PK-12)
  2009-10 Enrollment: 25,920 . . . . (972) 968-6100
Children First Academy of Dallas (PK-07)
  2009-10 Enrollment: 318 . . . . (214) 371-2545

Coppell ISD (PK-12)
  2009-10 Enrollment: 9,982 . . . . (214) 496-6000
Dallas Can Academy Charter (09-12)
  2009-10 Enrollment: 2,137 . . . . (214) 943-2244
Dallas Community Charter School (PK-03)
  2009-10 Enrollment: 208 . . . . (214) 824-8950
Dallas County Juvenile Justice (05-12)
  2009-10 Enrollment: 497 . . . . (214) 698-4257
Dallas ISD (PK-12)
  2009-10 Enrollment: 157,111 . . . . (972) 925-3700
Desoto ISD (PK-12)
  2009-10 Enrollment: 9,069 . . . . (972) 223-6666
Duncanville ISD (PK-12)
  2009-10 Enrollment: 12,903 . . . . (972) 708-2000
Faith Family Academy of Oak Cliff (PK-12)
  2009-10 Enrollment: 1,262 . . . . (972) 224-4110
Focus Learning Academy (PK-08)
  2009-10 Enrollment: 555 . . . . (214) 467-7751
Gateway Charter Academy (PK-12)
  2009-10 Enrollment: 797 . . . . (214) 375-2039
Golden Rule Charter School (PK-08)
  2009-10 Enrollment: 755 . . . . (214) 333-9330
Grand Prairie ISD (PK-12)
  2009-10 Enrollment: 26,395 . . . . (972) 264-6141
Hampton Preparatory (04-11)
  2009-10 Enrollment: 485 . . . . (972) 421-1982
Harmony Science Academy (KG-12)
  2009-10 Enrollment: 1,804 . . . . (713) 343-3333
Highland Park ISD (PK-12)
  2009-10 Enrollment: 6,448 . . . . (214) 780-3000
Inspired Vision Academy (PK-08)
  2009-10 Enrollment: 971 . . . . (214) 381-2208
Irving ISD (PK-12)
  2009-10 Enrollment: 33,679 . . . . (972) 600-5000
Kipp Truth Academy (05-08)
  2009-10 Enrollment: 264 . . . . (214) 375-8326
La Academia de Estrellas (KG-05)
  2009-10 Enrollment: 354 . . . . (214) 946-8908
Life School (KG-12)
  2009-10 Enrollment: 3,434 . . . . (972) 274-7900
Mesquite ISD (PK-12)
  2009-10 Enrollment: 37,272 . . . . (972) 288-6411
Nova Academy (KG-06)
  2009-10 Enrollment: 179 . . . . (214) 391-3088
Nova Academy (Southeast) (KG-06)
  2009-10 Enrollment: 275 . . . . (214) 391-5952
Peak Preparatory School (KG-12)
  2009-10 Enrollment: 898 . . . . (214) 821-7325
Pegasus School of Liberal Arts and Sciences (04-12)
  2009-10 Enrollment: 470 . . . . (214) 740-9991
Plano ISD (PK-12)
  2009-10 Enrollment: 54,939 . . . . (469) 752-8100
Reconciliation Academy (PK-02)
  2009-10 Enrollment: 160 . . . . (214) 824-4747
Responsive Education Solutions (KG-12)
  2009-10 Enrollment: 5,022 . . . . (972) 316-3663
Richardson ISD (PK-12)
  2009-10 Enrollment: 34,843 . . . . (469) 593-0000
Richland Collegiate HS of Math Science Engineering (11-12)
  2009-10 Enrollment: 380 . . . . (972) 761-6888
Shekinah Radiance Academy (PK-12)
  2009-10 Enrollment: 1,125 . . . . (210) 658-6848
St Anthony School (KG-08)
  2009-10 Enrollment: 288 . . . . (214) 421-3645
Sunnyvale ISD (PK-11)
  2009-10 Enrollment: 1,010 . . . . (972) 226-7601
The School of Liberal Arts and Science (PK-10)
  2009-10 Enrollment: 714 . . . . (214) 946-9100
Trinity Basin Preparatory (PK-08)
  2009-10 Enrollment: 618 . . . . (214) 946-9100
Williams Preparatory (KG-11)
  2009-10 Enrollment: 653 . . . . (214) 276-0352

Four-year College(s)

Dallas Baptist University (Private, Not-for-profit, Baptist)
    Fall 2009 Enrollment: 5,400. . . . . (214) 333-7100
    2010-11 Tuition: In-state $18,690; Out-of-state $18,690

Dallas Christian College (Private, Not-for-profit, Christian Churches and Churches of Christ)
    Fall 2009 Enrollment: 329 . . . . (972) 241-3371
    2010-11 Tuition: In-state $12,188; Out-of-state $12,188

Dallas Theological Seminary (Private, Not-for-profit, Undenominational)
    Fall 2009 Enrollment: 1,974. . . . . (214) 824-3094

Parker College of Chiropractic (Private, Not-for-profit)
    Fall 2009 Enrollment: 976 . . . . (972) 438-6932

Paul Quinn College (Private, Not-for-profit, Historically black, African Methodist Episcopal)
    Fall 2009 Enrollment: 171 . . . . (214) 379-5577
    2010-11 Tuition: In-state $12,350; Out-of-state $12,350

Southern Methodist University (Private, Not-for-profit, United Methodist)
    Fall 2009 Enrollment: 10,891 . . . . (214) 768-2000
    2010-11 Tuition: In-state $37,230; Out-of-state $37,230

The Art Institute of Dallas (Private, For-profit)
    Fall 2009 Enrollment: 2,067. . . . . (214) 692-8080
    2010-11 Tuition: In-state $17,618; Out-of-state $17,618

University of Phoenix-Dallas Fort Worth Campus (Private, For-profit)
    Fall 2009 Enrollment: 1,410. . . . . (972) 385-1055
    2010-11 Tuition: In-state $11,640; Out-of-state $11,640

University of Texas Southwestern Medical Center at Dallas (Public)
    Fall 2009 Enrollment: 2,459. . . . . (214) 648-3606

Westwood College-Dallas (Private, For-profit)
    Fall 2009 Enrollment: 611 . . . . (214) 570-0100
    2010-11 Tuition: In-state $13,825; Out-of-state $13,825

Two-year College(s)

ATI Career Training Center (Private, For-profit)
    Fall 2009 Enrollment: 1,172. . . . . (214) 902-8191

Aviation Institute of Maintenance-Dallas (Private, For-profit)
    Fall 2009 Enrollment: 493 . . . . (214) 333-9711
    2010-11 Tuition: In-state $13,167; Out-of-state $13,167

Central Texas Commercial College (Private, For-profit)
    Fall 2009 Enrollment: 50 . . . . (214) 368-3680
    2010-11 Tuition: In-state $19,368; Out-of-state $19,368

Court Reporting Institute-Wheeler Institute of Texas (Private, For-profit)
    Fall 2009 Enrollment: 969 . . . . (214) 350-9722
    2010-11 Tuition: In-state $10,075; Out-of-state $10,075

Dallas Institute of Funeral Service (Private, Not-for-profit)
    Fall 2009 Enrollment: 107 . . . . (214) 388-5466
    2010-11 Tuition: In-state $12,000; Out-of-state $12,000

Dallas Nursing Institute (Private, For-profit)
    Fall 2009 Enrollment: 134 . . . . (214) 613-3770

El Centro College (Public)
    Fall 2009 Enrollment: 9,072. . . . . (214) 860-2037
    2010-11 Tuition: In-state $2,280; Out-of-state $3,630

Everest College-Dallas (Private, For-profit)
    Fall 2009 Enrollment: 1,261. . . . . (214) 234-4850
    2010-11 Tuition: In-state $13,599; Out-of-state $13,599

K D Studio (Private, For-profit)
    Fall 2009 Enrollment: 161 . . . . (214) 638-0484
    2010-11 Tuition: In-state $15,215; Out-of-state $15,215

Kaplan College (Private, For-profit)
    Fall 2009 Enrollment: 368 . . . . (972) 385-1446

Le Cordon Bleu Institute of Culinary Arts-Dallas (Private, For-profit)
    Fall 2009 Enrollment: 886 . . . . (214) 647-8500
    2010-11 Tuition: In-state $34,500; Out-of-state $34,500

Mountain View College (Public)
    Fall 2009 Enrollment: 8,203. . . . . (214) 860-8680
    2010-11 Tuition: In-state $2,280; Out-of-state $3,630

Richland College (Public)
    Fall 2009 Enrollment: 18,201. . . . . (972) 238-6100
    2010-11 Tuition: In-state $2,280; Out-of-state $3,630

Sanford-Brown College (Private, For-profit)
    Fall 2009 Enrollment: 1,183. . . . . (214) 459-8490
    2010-11 Tuition: In-state $15,306; Out-of-state $15,306

Wade College (Private, For-profit)
    Fall 2009 Enrollment: 236 . . . . (214) 637-3530
    2010-11 Tuition: In-state $10,445; Out-of-state $10,445

Vocational/Technical School(s)

ATI Career Training Center (Private, For-profit)
    Fall 2009 Enrollment: 549 . . . . (214) 989-3001
    2010-11 Tuition: $16,700

ATI Technical Training Center (Private, For-profit)
    Fall 2009 Enrollment: 1,005. . . . . (214) 352-2222
    2010-11 Tuition: $22,850

Dallas Barber & Stylist College (Private, For-profit)
    Fall 2009 Enrollment: 140 . . . . (214) 575-2168
    2010-11 Tuition: $9,300

MJ's Beauty Academy Inc (Private, For-profit)
    Fall 2009 Enrollment: 52 . . . . (214) 374-7500
    2010-11 Tuition: $12,950

Neilson Beauty College (Private, For-profit)
    Fall 2009 Enrollment: 73 . . . . (214) 946-0458
    2010-11 Tuition: $10,150

Ogle School Hair Skin Nails (Private, For-profit)
    Fall 2009 Enrollment: 323 . . . . (214) 461-9838
    2010-11 Tuition: $15,600

PCI Health Training Center (Private, For-profit)
    Fall 2009 Enrollment: 908 . . . . (214) 630-0568
    2010-11 Tuition: $13,295

Platt College (Private, For-profit)
    Fall 2009 Enrollment: 260 . . . . (972) 243-0900
    2010-11 Tuition: $31,000

Ronny J's Barber Styling (Private, For-profit)
    Fall 2009 Enrollment: 39 . . . . (214) 275-7151
    2010-11 Tuition: $12,800

Tint School of Makeup and Cosmetology (Private, For-profit)
    Fall 2009 Enrollment: 167 . . . . (214) 956-0088
    2010-11 Tuition: $11,275

Vatterott Education Center (Private, For-profit)
    Fall 2009 Enrollment: 303 . . . . (214) 352-8288
    2010-11 Tuition: $8,100

Housing: Homeownership rate: 45.3% (2010); Median home value: $125,526 (2010); Median contract rent: $637 per month (2005-2009 5-year est.); Median year structure built: 1974 (2005-2009 5-year est.).

Hospitals: Baylor Heart and Vascular Center; Baylor Institute for Rehabilitation (116 beds); Baylor University Medical Center at Dallas (1025 beds); Children's Medical Center (406 beds); Doctors Hospital of Dallas (222 beds); Doctors Hospital of Dallas (222 beds); Green Oaks Hospital (106 beds); Mary Shiels Hospital (28 beds); Medical City Dallas (598 beds); Methodist Charlton Medical Center (245 beds); Methodist Medical Center (478 beds); Parkland Health & Hospital System (997 beds); Pine Creek Medical Center; Presbyterian Hospital of Dallas (866 beds); RHD Memorial Medical Center (155 beds); Texas Institute for Surgery at Presbyterian Hospital; Texas Scottish Rite Hospital for Children (100 beds); Timberlawn Mental Health System (124 beds); UT Southwestern University Hospital; Veterans Affairs North Texas Health Care System (VANTHCS); Zale-Lipshy University Hospital (151 beds)

Safety: Violent crime rate: 79.2 per 10,000 population; Property crime rate: 553.1 per 10,000 population (2009).

Newspapers: Al Día (Local news; Circulation 40,000); Black Economic Times (Local news); Dallas Chinese Times (Local news; Circulation 10,000); Dallas Examiner (Local news; Circulation 30,000); The Dallas Morning News (Regional news; Circulation 411,919); Dallas Observer (Local news; Circulation 110,000); Dallas Post Tribune (Community news; Circulation 18,000); The Dallas Weekly (Local news; Circulation 20,300); El Católico de Texas (Regional news; Circulation 10,000); El Extra (Local news; Circulation 29,310); El Heraldo News (Regional news; Circulation 30,000); El Hispano News (Local news; Circulation 28,447); El Lider USA (Local news; Circulation 51,200); Elite News (Community news; Circulation 50,000); House & Garden - The Dallas Morning News; Korea Times Dallas Edition (Local news; Circulation 3,500); Latino Times (Local news; Circulation 40,000); Lewisville Leader (Local news; Circulation 24,700); The Movies-The Dallas Morning News; The National Christian Reporter (International news; Circulation 15,000); North Dallas People (Community news; Circulation 20,000); Novedades News (Regional news; Circulation 38,000); Oak Cliff Tribune (Community news; Circulation 4,000); Park Cities News (Community news; Circulation 10,000); Park Cities People (Community news; Circulation 9,000); Quick (Regional news); Senior News Source (Local news; Circulation 200,000); Southlake Times (Local news); Texas Catholic (Local news; Circulation 50,000); Texas Jewish Post (Local news; Circulation 4,200); Travel - The Dallas Morning News; Turtle Creek News (Local news; Circulation 11,000); The United Methodist Reporter (International news; Circulation 110,000); United Methodist Review

(National news; Circulation 140,000); The Wall Street Journal - Dallas Bureau (Regional news); West Plano People (Circulation 4,000); White Rocker News (Community news; Circulation 4,900)

Transportation: Commute to work: 89.0% car, 4.3% public transportation, 1.9% walk, 3.4% work from home (2005-2009 5-year est.); Travel time to work: 22.0% less than 15 minutes, 40.6% 15 to 30 minutes, 24.0% 30 to 45 minutes, 6.9% 45 to 60 minutes, 6.5% 60 minutes or more (2005-2009 5-year est.); Amtrak: train service available.

Airports: Addison (general aviation); Dallas Executive (general aviation); Dallas Love Field (primary service/medium hub)

Additional Information Contacts

City of Dallas . . . . (214) 670-5111
   http://www.dallascityhall.com
Dallas Regional Chamber of Commerce . . . . (214) 746-6600
   http://www.dallaschamber.org
French American Chamber of Commerce Dallas/Fort Worth . . . . (972) 241-0111
   http://www.faccdallas.com
Greater East Dallas Chamber of Commerce . . . . (214) 328-4100
   http://www.dallasnortheastchamber.net
Southeast Dallas Chamber of Commerce . . . . (214) 398-9590
   http://www.sedcc.org
Swedish American Chamber of Commerce . . . . (214) 707-0200
   http://www.sacctx.com
US-Mexico Chamber of Commerce . . . . (214) 651-4300
   http://www.usmcoc.org
United States Chamber of Commerce . . . . (972) 387-1099

DESOTO (city).
Covers a land area of 21.580 square miles and a water area of 0 square miles. Located at 32.59° N. Lat; 96.85° W. Long. Elevation is 650 feet.

Population: 30,543 (1990); 37,646 (2000); 49,765 (2010); 54,574 (2015 projected); Race: 37.5% White, 54.0% Black, 1.3% Asian, 7.2% Other, 12.4% Hispanic of any race (2010); Density: 2,306.1 persons per square mile (2010); Average household size: 2.84 (2010); Median age: 36.9 (2010); Males per 100 females: 93.7 (2010); Marriage status: 27.7% never married, 52.4% now married, 7.6% widowed, 12.3% divorced (2005-2009 5-year est.); Foreign born: 4.9% (2005-2009 5-year est.); Ancestry (includes multiple ancestries): 5.1% German, 4.1% English, 3.9% Irish, 3.0% American, 1.4% African (2005-2009 5-year est.).

Economy: Unemployment rate: 10.0% (June 2011); Total civilian labor force: 25,753 (June 2011); Single-family building permits issued: 114 (2010); Multi-family building permits issued: 0 (2010); Employment by occupation: 16.8% management, 24.1% professional, 12.0% services, 31.2% sales, 0.0% farming, 5.8% construction, 10.2% production (2005-2009 5-year est.).

Income: Per capita income: $26,054 (2010); Median household income: $62,054 (2010); Average household income: $74,318 (2010); Percent of households with income of $100,000 or more: 21.7% (2010); Poverty rate: 8.1% (2005-2009 5-year est.).

Taxes: Total city taxes per capita: $646 (2007); City property taxes per capita: $398 (2007).

Education: Percent of population age 25 and over with: High school diploma (including GED) or higher: 89.1% (2010); Bachelor's degree or higher: 30.1% (2010); Master's degree or higher: 10.3% (2010).

School District(s)

Desoto ISD (PK-12)
   2009-10 Enrollment: 9,069 . . . . (972) 223-6666
Golden Rule Charter School (PK-08)
   2009-10 Enrollment: 755 . . . . (214) 333-9330

Vocational/Technical School(s)

PCCenter (Private, For-profit)
   Fall 2009 Enrollment: 43 . . . . (972) 224-9800
   2010-11 Tuition: $13,300

Housing: Homeownership rate: 78.3% (2010); Median home value: $142,329 (2010); Median contract rent: $680 per month (2005-2009 5-year est.); Median year structure built: 1987 (2005-2009 5-year est.).

Safety: Violent crime rate: 36.5 per 10,000 population; Property crime rate: 357.0 per 10,000 population (2009).

Newspapers: Cedar Hill Today (Community news; Circulation 5,500); The Dallas/Fort Worth Heritage (Local news); DeSoto Today (Community news); Duncanville Today (Community news; Circulation 10,500); Focus Daily News (Community news; Circulation 26,374); Lancaster Today (Community news; Circulation 4,300); Midlothian Today (Community news; Circulation 1,673)

Transportation: Commute to work: 95.0% car, 1.1% public transportation, 0.5% walk, 3.0% work from home (2005-2009 5-year est.); Travel time to work: 16.3% less than 15 minutes, 30.7% 15 to 30 minutes, 30.6% 30 to 45 minutes, 14.9% 45 to 60 minutes, 7.6% 60 minutes or more (2005-2009 5-year est.)

Additional Information Contacts

City of De Soto . . . . (972) 274-2489
   http://www.ci.desoto.tx.us
De Soto Chamber of Commerce . . . . (972) 224-3565
   http://www.desotochamber.org

DUNCANVILLE (city).
Covers a land area of 11.287 square miles and a water area of 0.003 square miles. Located at 32.64° N. Lat; 96.91° W. Long. Elevation is 725 feet.

History: Named for John Duncan, who helped in the building of the railroad. Established 1882. Incorporated 1947.

Population: 35,609 (1990); 36,081 (2000); 35,634 (2010); 35,786 (2015 projected); Race: 51.0% White, 31.3% Black, 1.8% Asian, 15.9% Other, 26.3% Hispanic of any race (2010); Density: 3,157.0 persons per square mile (2010); Average household size: 2.79 (2010); Median age: 37.4 (2010); Males per 100 females: 92.9 (2010); Marriage status: 29.6% never married, 55.3% now married, 5.5% widowed, 9.6% divorced (2005-2009 5-year est.); Foreign born: 11.4% (2005-2009 5-year est.); Ancestry (includes multiple ancestries): 7.4% German, 6.8% English, 5.5% Irish, 5.2% American, 2.0% French (2005-2009 5-year est.).

Economy: Unemployment rate: 9.7% (June 2011); Total civilian labor force: 18,541 (June 2011); Single-family building permits issued: 8 (2010); Multi-family building permits issued: 0 (2010); Employment by occupation: 12.1% management, 18.3% professional, 14.8% services, 30.4% sales, 0.1% farming, 10.4% construction, 13.9% production (2005-2009 5-year est.).

Income: Per capita income: $24,247 (2010); Median household income: $54,760 (2010); Average household income: $67,550 (2010); Percent of households with income of $100,000 or more: 17.8% (2010); Poverty rate: 12.5% (2005-2009 5-year est.).

Taxes: Total city taxes per capita: $647 (2007); City property taxes per capita: $343 (2007).

Education: Percent of population age 25 and over with: High school diploma (including GED) or higher: 85.8% (2010); Bachelor's degree or higher: 27.2% (2010); Master's degree or higher: 9.0% (2010).

School District(s)

Duncanville ISD (PK-12)
   2009-10 Enrollment: 12,903 . . . . (972) 708-2000
Zoe Learning Academy (PK-06)
   2009-10 Enrollment: 553 . . . . (713) 748-4228

Vocational/Technical School(s)

State Beauty Academy (Private, For-profit)
   Fall 2009 Enrollment: 50 . . . . (972) 298-0100
   2010-11 Tuition: $14,385

Housing: Homeownership rate: 73.1% (2010); Median home value: $119,408 (2010); Median contract rent: $760 per month (2005-2009 5-year est.); Median year structure built: 1977 (2005-2009 5-year est.).

Safety: Violent crime rate: 50.7 per 10,000 population; Property crime rate: 452.2 per 10,000 population (2009).

Transportation: Commute to work: 93.1% car, 1.8% public transportation, 0.9% walk, 2.9% work from home (2005-2009 5-year est.); Travel time to work: 20.7% less than 15 minutes, 35.8% 15 to 30 minutes, 26.2% 30 to 45 minutes, 10.5% 45 to 60 minutes, 6.8% 60 minutes or more (2005-2009 5-year est.)

Additional Information Contacts

City of Duncanville . . . . (972) 780-5000
   http://www.ci.duncanville.tx.us
Duncanville Chamber of Commerce . . . . (972) 780-4990
   http://www.duncanvillechamber.org

FARMERS BRANCH (city).
Covers a land area of 12.002 square miles and a water area of 0.011 square miles. Located at 32.92° N. Lat; 96.87° W. Long. Elevation is 463 feet.

History: Named for a branch of the Trinity River, along which early settlers established farms. Has local Historical Park. Settled 1841. Incorporated 1946

Population: 24,250 (1990); 27,508 (2000); 28,307 (2010); 28,090 (2015 projected); Race: 70.7% White, 2.8% Black, 3.6% Asian, 22.8% Other, 53.3% Hispanic of any race (2010); Density: 2,358.5 persons per square mile (2010); Average household size: 2.87 (2010); Median age: 36.1

(2010); Males per 100 females: 104.7 (2010); Marriage status: 30.7% never married, 53.9% now married, 5.8% widowed, 9.6% divorced (2005-2009 5-year est.); Foreign born: 26.7% (2005-2009 5-year est.); Ancestry (includes multiple ancestries): 11.9% English, 8.3% American, 8.1% German, 6.2% Irish, 2.2% French (2005-2009 5-year est.).
Economy: Unemployment rate: 8.6% (June 2011); Total civilian labor force: 14,048 (June 2011); Single-family building permits issued: 8 (2010); Multi-family building permits issued: 0 (2010); Employment by occupation: 16.1% management, 13.4% professional, 15.3% services, 26.2% sales, 0.1% farming, 14.9% construction, 14.0% production (2005-2009 5-year est.).
Income: Per capita income: $27,707 (2010); Median household income: $60,013 (2010); Average household income: $79,774 (2010); Percent of households with income of $100,000 or more: 23.3% (2010); Poverty rate: 9.1% (2005-2009 5-year est.).
Taxes: Total city taxes per capita: $1,390 (2007); City property taxes per capita: $626 (2007).
Education: Percent of population age 25 and over with: High school diploma (including GED) or higher: 74.1% (2010); Bachelor's degree or higher: 24.7% (2010); Master's degree or higher: 7.1% (2010).
School District(s)
Carrollton-Farmers Branch ISD (PK-12)
    2009-10 Enrollment: 25,920 . . . . (972) 968-6100
Dallas Can Academy Charter (09-12)
    2009-10 Enrollment: 2,137 . . . . (214) 943-2244
Four-year College(s)
Argosy University-Dallas (Private, For-profit)
    Fall 2009 Enrollment: 534 . . . . (214) 890-9900
    2010-11 Tuition: In-state $19,812; Out-of-state $19,812
Two-year College(s)
Brookhaven College (Public)
    Fall 2009 Enrollment: 11,814 . . . . (972) 860-4700
    2010-11 Tuition: In-state $2,280; Out-of-state $3,630
Housing: Homeownership rate: 65.3% (2010); Median home value: $138,675 (2010); Median contract rent: $749 per month (2005-2009 5-year est.); Median year structure built: 1967 (2005-2009 5-year est.).
Safety: Violent crime rate: 27.0 per 10,000 population; Property crime rate: 583.8 per 10,000 population (2009).
Transportation: Commute to work: 91.9% car, 1.6% public transportation, 2.2% walk, 3.4% work from home (2005-2009 5-year est.); Travel time to work: 28.5% less than 15 minutes, 46.4% 15 to 30 minutes, 18.7% 30 to 45 minutes, 3.2% 45 to 60 minutes, 3.3% 60 minutes or more (2005-2009 5-year est.)
Additional Information Contacts
City of Farmers Branch . . . . (972) 247-3131
    http://www.ci.farmers-branch.tx.us
Farmers Branch Chamber of Commerce . . . . (972) 243-8966
    http://www.fbchamber.com

GARLAND (city).
Covers a land area of 57.110 square miles and a water area of 0.002 square miles. Located at 32.90° N. Lat; 96.63° W. Long. Elevation is 551 feet.
History: Named for Augustus Hill Garland (1832-1899), U.S. senator and attorney general. Garland developed as an industrial center, and as a residential area for commuters to Dallas.
Population: 180,940 (1990); 215,768 (2000); 217,620 (2010); 220,083 (2015 projected); Race: 56.4% White, 13.2% Black, 8.3% Asian, 22.1% Other, 37.1% Hispanic of any race (2010); Density: 3,810.5 persons per square mile (2010); Average household size: 2.98 (2010); Median age: 34.6 (2010); Males per 100 females: 100.5 (2010); Marriage status: 30.7% never married, 54.2% now married, 4.6% widowed, 10.6% divorced (2005-2009 5-year est.); Foreign born: 27.9% (2005-2009 5-year est.); Ancestry (includes multiple ancestries): 8.0% German, 7.1% Irish, 6.4% English, 3.9% American, 2.5% French (2005-2009 5-year est.).
Economy: Unemployment rate: 9.0% (June 2011); Total civilian labor force: 110,544 (June 2011); Single-family building permits issued: 147 (2010); Multi-family building permits issued: 0 (2010); Employment by occupation: 11.3% management, 16.2% professional, 16.9% services, 26.0% sales, 0.4% farming, 14.4% construction, 14.8% production (2005-2009 5-year est.).
Income: Per capita income: $22,448 (2010); Median household income: $54,066 (2010); Average household income: $66,731 (2010); Percent of households with income of $100,000 or more: 17.2% (2010); Poverty rate: 13.4% (2005-2009 5-year est.).

Taxes: Total city taxes per capita: $459 (2007); City property taxes per capita: $306 (2007).
Education: Percent of population age 25 and over with: High school diploma (including GED) or higher: 78.4% (2010); Bachelor's degree or higher: 21.4% (2010); Master's degree or higher: 6.1% (2010).
School District(s)
Alpha Charter School (KG-12)
    2009-10 Enrollment: 202 . . . . (972) 272-2173
Garland ISD (PK-12)
    2009-10 Enrollment: 57,861 . . . . (972) 494-8201
Mesquite ISD (PK-12)
    2009-10 Enrollment: 37,272 . . . . (972) 288-6411
Responsive Education Solutions (KG-12)
    2009-10 Enrollment: 5,022 . . . . (972) 316-3663
Richardson ISD (PK-12)
    2009-10 Enrollment: 34,843 . . . . (469) 593-0000
Four-year College(s)
Amberton University (Private, Not-for-profit, Undenominational)
    Fall 2009 Enrollment: 1,533 . . . . (972) 279-6511
Two-year College(s)
Remington College-Dallas Campus (Private, For-profit)
    Fall 2009 Enrollment: 1,446 . . . . (972) 686-7878
    2010-11 Tuition: In-state $14,745; Out-of-state $14,745
Vocational/Technical School(s)
ATI Career Training Center (Private, For-profit)
    Fall 2009 Enrollment: 284 . . . . (972) 535-5525
    2010-11 Tuition: $22,850
International Beauty College 3 (Private, For-profit)
    Fall 2009 Enrollment: 63 . . . . (972) 530-1103
    2010-11 Tuition: $9,588
National Beauty College (Private, For-profit)
    Fall 2009 Enrollment: 47 . . . . (972) 226-6900
    2010-11 Tuition: $14,100
Housing: Homeownership rate: 68.5% (2010); Median home value: $121,794 (2010); Median contract rent: $701 per month (2005-2009 5-year est.); Median year structure built: 1977 (2005-2009 5-year est.).
Hospitals: Baylor Medical Center at Garland (223 beds); Baylor Medical Center at Garland (223 beds)
Safety: Violent crime rate: 27.8 per 10,000 population; Property crime rate: 415.7 per 10,000 population (2009).
Newspapers: The Dallas Morning News - Garland Bureau (Community news)
Transportation: Commute to work: 92.4% car, 2.8% public transportation, 1.4% walk, 2.4% work from home (2005-2009 5-year est.); Travel time to work: 19.1% less than 15 minutes, 36.1% 15 to 30 minutes, 26.0% 30 to 45 minutes, 10.9% 45 to 60 minutes, 7.9% 60 minutes or more (2005-2009 5-year est.)
Airports: Garland/DFW Heloplex (general aviation)
Additional Information Contacts
City of Garland . . . . (972) 205-2000
    http://www.ci.garland.tx.us
Garland Chamber of Commerce . . . . (972) 272-7551
    http://www.garlandchamber.com

GLENN HEIGHTS (city).
Covers a land area of 7.019 square miles and a water area of 0 square miles. Located at 32.54° N. Lat; 96.85° W. Long. Elevation is 676 feet.
Population: 4,564 (1990); 7,224 (2000); 10,938 (2010); 12,517 (2015 projected); Race: 52.4% White, 37.0% Black, 0.6% Asian, 9.9% Other, 21.3% Hispanic of any race (2010); Density: 1,558.4 persons per square mile (2010); Average household size: 3.11 (2010); Median age: 31.8 (2010); Males per 100 females: 97.2 (2010); Marriage status: 33.7% never married, 49.3% now married, 2.1% widowed, 14.9% divorced (2005-2009 5-year est.); Foreign born: 5.4% (2005-2009 5-year est.); Ancestry (includes multiple ancestries): 7.6% Irish, 7.5% German, 4.9% English, 4.7% American, 0.9% Dutch (2005-2009 5-year est.).
Economy: Single-family building permits issued: 30 (2010); Multi-family building permits issued: 0 (2010); Employment by occupation: 17.3% management, 12.7% professional, 7.7% services, 31.3% sales, 0.0% farming, 11.9% construction, 19.1% production (2005-2009 5-year est.).
Income: Per capita income: $20,793 (2010); Median household income: $54,860 (2010); Average household income: $64,663 (2010); Percent of households with income of $100,000 or more: 13.5% (2010); Poverty rate: 13.2% (2005-2009 5-year est.).

Taxes: Total city taxes per capita: $242 (2007); City property taxes per capita: $215 (2007).

Education: Percent of population age 25 and over with: High school diploma (including GED) or higher: 86.1% (2010); Bachelor's degree or higher: 19.4% (2010); Master's degree or higher: 4.4% (2010).

School District(s)

Desoto ISD (PK-12)
2009-10 Enrollment: 9,069 . . . . (972) 223-6666
Red Oak ISD (PK-12)
2009-10 Enrollment: 5,408 . . . . (972) 617-2941

Housing: Homeownership rate: 78.8% (2010); Median home value: $119,367 (2010); Median contract rent: $713 per month (2005-2009 5-year est.); Median year structure built: 1992 (2005-2009 5-year est.).

Safety: Violent crime rate: 28.5 per 10,000 population; Property crime rate: 202.7 per 10,000 population (2009).

Transportation: Commute to work: 91.7% car, 1.3% public transportation, 0.3% walk, 4.7% work from home (2005-2009 5-year est.); Travel time to work: 17.0% less than 15 minutes, 28.9% 15 to 30 minutes, 29.1% 30 to 45 minutes, 13.1% 45 to 60 minutes, 12.0% 60 minutes or more (2005-2009 5-year est.)

Additional Information Contacts

City of Glenn Heights. . . . . (972) 223-1690
http://www.glennheights.com

GRAND PRAIRIE (city).
Covers a land area of 71.403 square miles and a water area of 10.136 square miles. Located at 32.71° N. Lat; 97.01° W. Long. Elevation is 515 feet.

Population: 99,814 (1990); 127,427 (2000); 172,438 (2010); 189,180 (2015 projected); Race: 50.6% White, 16.6% Black, 5.1% Asian, 27.7% Other, 44.4% Hispanic of any race (2010); Density: 2,415.0 persons per square mile (2010); Average household size: 3.00 (2010); Median age: 32.6 (2010); Males per 100 females: 100.7 (2010); Marriage status: 30.4% never married, 54.5% now married, 4.3% widowed, 10.8% divorced (2005-2009 5-year est.); Foreign born: 20.0% (2005-2009 5-year est.); Ancestry (includes multiple ancestries): 7.0% German, 5.9% Irish, 5.4% American, 5.2% English, 1.7% French (2005-2009 5-year est.).

Economy: Unemployment rate: 8.9% (June 2011); Total civilian labor force: 79,863 (June 2011); Single-family building permits issued: 387 (2010); Multi-family building permits issued: 0 (2010); Employment by occupation: 12.4% management, 15.7% professional, 15.1% services, 27.6% sales, 0.1% farming, 12.2% construction, 16.7% production (2005-2009 5-year est.).

Income: Per capita income: $21,545 (2010); Median household income: $53,995 (2010); Average household income: $64,578 (2010); Percent of households with income of $100,000 or more: 16.4% (2010); Poverty rate: 14.4% (2005-2009 5-year est.).

Taxes: Total city taxes per capita: $753 (2007); City property taxes per capita: $354 (2007).

Education: Percent of population age 25 and over with: High school diploma (including GED) or higher: 75.8% (2010); Bachelor's degree or higher: 20.3% (2010); Master's degree or higher: 5.2% (2010).

School District(s)

Arlington ISD (PK-12)
2009-10 Enrollment: 63,487 . . . . (682) 867-4611
Grand Prairie ISD (PK-12)
2009-10 Enrollment: 26,395 . . . . (972) 264-6141
Harmony Science Academy (Fort Worth) (KG-11)
2009-10 Enrollment: 1,948 . . . . (817) 263-0700
Mansfield ISD (PK-12)
2009-10 Enrollment: 31,662 . . . . (817) 299-6300

Two-year College(s)

Arlington Career Institute (Private, For-profit)
Fall 2009 Enrollment: 332 . . . . (972) 647-1607
Lincoln College of Technology (Private, For-profit)
Fall 2009 Enrollment: 2,018. . . . . (972) 660-5701
2010-11 Tuition: In-state $19,341; Out-of-state $19,341

Vocational/Technical School(s)

Mid-Cities Barber College (Private, For-profit)
Fall 2009 Enrollment: 24 . . . . (972) 642-1892
2010-11 Tuition: $8,375

Housing: Homeownership rate: 67.5% (2010); Median home value: $121,427 (2010); Median contract rent: $663 per month (2005-2009 5-year est.); Median year structure built: 1983 (2005-2009 5-year est.).

Safety: Violent crime rate: 31.8 per 10,000 population; Property crime rate: 482.4 per 10,000 population (2009).

Transportation: Commute to work: 94.7% car, 0.4% public transportation, 0.8% walk, 2.7% work from home (2005-2009 5-year est.); Travel time to work: 18.4% less than 15 minutes, 36.0% 15 to 30 minutes, 28.0% 30 to 45 minutes, 9.7% 45 to 60 minutes, 7.9% 60 minutes or more (2005-2009 5-year est.)

Airports: Grand Prairie Municipal (general aviation)

Additional Information Contacts

City of Grand Prairie . . . . (972) 237-8000
http://gptx.org
Grand Prairie Chamber of Commerce . . . . (972) 264-1558
http://www.grandprairiechamber.org
Greater Grand Prairie Hispanic Chamber of Commerce . . . (817) 881-4734
http://ggphcc.com

HIGHLAND PARK (town).
Covers a land area of 2.240 square miles and a water area of 0 square miles. Located at 32.83° N. Lat; 96.80° W. Long. Elevation is 528 feet.

History: In 1916 V.C. Prather set aside land to build one of the first planned shopping centers; construction actually began in 1931 (Spanish architectural style). Settled 1907, incorporated 1913.

Population: 8,739 (1990); 8,842 (2000); 9,437 (2010); 9,760 (2015 projected); Race: 96.3% White, 0.4% Black, 0.9% Asian, 2.3% Other, 3.8% Hispanic of any race (2010); Density: 4,213.6 persons per square mile (2010); Average household size: 2.56 (2010); Median age: 43.1 (2010); Males per 100 females: 90.4 (2010); Marriage status: 20.6% never married, 65.9% now married, 6.4% widowed, 7.2% divorced (2005-2009 5-year est.); Foreign born: 8.3% (2005-2009 5-year est.); Ancestry (includes multiple ancestries): 27.1% English, 17.2% German, 16.1% Irish, 7.5% American, 5.9% French (2005-2009 5-year est.).

Economy: Single-family building permits issued: 14 (2010); Multi-family building permits issued: 0 (2010); Employment by occupation: 33.4% management, 36.5% professional, 3.4% services, 23.1% sales, 0.0% farming, 2.3% construction, 1.4% production (2005-2009 5-year est.).

Income: Per capita income: $82,775 (2010); Median household income: $162,269 (2010); Average household income: $212,586 (2010); Percent of households with income of $100,000 or more: 64.3% (2010); Poverty rate: 3.1% (2005-2009 5-year est.).

Taxes: Total city taxes per capita: $1,253 (2007); City property taxes per capita: $801 (2007).

Education: Percent of population age 25 and over with: High school diploma (including GED) or higher: 98.7% (2010); Bachelor's degree or higher: 74.1% (2010); Master's degree or higher: 30.1% (2010).

Housing: Homeownership rate: 83.3% (2010); Median home value: $887,044 (2010); Median contract rent: $943 per month (2005-2009 5-year est.); Median year structure built: 1952 (2005-2009 5-year est.).

Safety: Violent crime rate: 9.8 per 10,000 population; Property crime rate: 271.1 per 10,000 population (2009).

Transportation: Commute to work: 88.8% car, 0.4% public transportation, 2.5% walk, 6.5% work from home (2005-2009 5-year est.); Travel time to work: 46.7% less than 15 minutes, 42.7% 15 to 30 minutes, 8.7% 30 to 45 minutes, 1.3% 45 to 60 minutes, 0.6% 60 minutes or more (2005-2009 5-year est.)

Additional Information Contacts

City of Highland Park. . . . . (214) 521-4161
http://www.hptx.org

HUTCHINS (city).
Covers a land area of 8.487 square miles and a water area of 0.131 square miles. Located at 32.64° N. Lat; 96.70° W. Long. Elevation is 466 feet.

History: Hutchins was established in an area where cotton and corn were grown.

Population: 2,719 (1990); 2,805 (2000); 3,560 (2010); 3,877 (2015 projected); Race: 35.0% White, 41.7% Black, 0.1% Asian, 23.1% Other, 31.3% Hispanic of any race (2010); Density: 419.4 persons per square mile (2010); Average household size: 2.94 (2010); Median age: 33.6 (2010); Males per 100 females: 146.9 (2010); Marriage status: 31.2% never married, 54.2% now married, 4.4% widowed, 10.3% divorced (2005-2009 5-year est.); Foreign born: 21.6% (2005-2009 5-year est.); Ancestry (includes multiple ancestries): 3.5% Irish, 3.3% Nigerian, 3.2% American, 2.2% English, 2.2% German (2005-2009 5-year est.).

Economy: Single-family building permits issued: 1 (2010); Multi-family building permits issued: 0 (2010); Employment by occupation: 5.2% management, 10.6% professional, 17.0% services, 23.7% sales, 0.0% farming, 16.4% construction, 27.2% production (2005-2009 5-year est.).

Income: Per capita income: $13,962 (2010); Median household income: $38,409 (2010); Average household income: $44,848 (2010); Percent of households with income of $100,000 or more: 5.2% (2010); Poverty rate: 16.7% (2005-2009 5-year est.).

Taxes: Total city taxes per capita: $904 (2007); City property taxes per capita: $303 (2007).

Education: Percent of population age 25 and over with: High school diploma (including GED) or higher: 66.0% (2010); Bachelor's degree or higher: 4.0% (2010); Master's degree or higher: 1.1% (2010).

Housing: Homeownership rate: 87.1% (2010); Median home value: $60,593 (2010); Median contract rent: $680 per month (2005-2009 5-year est.); Median year structure built: 1984 (2005-2009 5-year est.).

Safety: Violent crime rate: 51.1 per 10,000 population; Property crime rate: 728.7 per 10,000 population (2009).

Transportation: Commute to work: 95.3% car, 0.3% public transportation, 0.0% walk, 3.3% work from home (2005-2009 5-year est.); Travel time to work: 20.1% less than 15 minutes, 27.0% 15 to 30 minutes, 28.1% 30 to 45 minutes, 15.3% 45 to 60 minutes, 9.5% 60 minutes or more (2005-2009 5-year est.)

IRVING (city). Covers a land area of 67.228 square miles and a water area of 0.443 square miles. Located at 32.84° N. Lat; 96.96° W. Long. Elevation is 482 feet.

History: Named for the sound of the word, by one of its founders. Irving was platted in 1902 along the Rock Island Railroad tracks. The town developed as a residential center for Dallas workers, as well as an industrial town.

Population: 155,037 (1990); 191,615 (2000); 201,484 (2010); 206,713 (2015 projected); Race: 54.7% White, 10.9% Black, 10.8% Asian, 23.6% Other, 43.2% Hispanic of any race (2010); Density: 2,997.0 persons per square mile (2010); Average household size: 2.53 (2010); Median age: 33.4 (2010); Males per 100 females: 107.3 (2010); Marriage status: 34.9% never married, 50.5% now married, 4.0% widowed, 10.7% divorced (2005-2009 5-year est.); Foreign born: 32.1% (2005-2009 5-year est.); Ancestry (includes multiple ancestries): 8.4% German, 6.8% Irish, 6.1% English, 4.8% American, 1.9% Italian (2005-2009 5-year est.).

Economy: Unemployment rate: 8.2% (June 2011); Total civilian labor force: 112,255 (June 2011); Single-family building permits issued: 338 (2010); Multi-family building permits issued: 0 (2010); Employment by occupation: 14.1% management, 18.7% professional, 14.9% services, 26.4% sales, 0.3% farming, 12.6% construction, 13.1% production (2005-2009 5-year est.).

Income: Per capita income: $26,328 (2010); Median household income: $49,609 (2010); Average household income: $66,820 (2010); Percent of households with income of $100,000 or more: 16.2% (2010); Poverty rate: 15.1% (2005-2009 5-year est.).

Taxes: Total city taxes per capita: $818 (2007); City property taxes per capita: $390 (2007).

Education: Percent of population age 25 and over with: High school diploma (including GED) or higher: 78.3% (2010); Bachelor's degree or higher: 31.6% (2010); Master's degree or higher: 11.3% (2010).

School District(s)

Carrollton-Farmers Branch ISD (PK-12)
    2009-10 Enrollment: 25,920 . . . . (972) 968-6100
Coppell ISD (PK-12)
    2009-10 Enrollment: 9,982 . . . . (214) 496-6000
Honors Academy (KG-12)
    2009-10 Enrollment: 1,068 . . . . (214) 521-6365
Irving ISD (PK-12)
    2009-10 Enrollment: 33,679 . . . . (972) 600-5000
North Hills Preparatory School (KG-12)
    2009-10 Enrollment: 1,335 . . . . (972) 501-0645
Peak Preparatory School (KG-12)
    2009-10 Enrollment: 898 . . . . (214) 821-7325
Universal Academy (PK-12)
    2009-10 Enrollment: 1,397 . . . . (972) 255-1800
Winfree Academy Charter Schools (09-12)
    2009-10 Enrollment: 1,862 . . . . (972) 869-3250

Four-year College(s)

DeVry University-Texas (Private, For-profit)
    Fall 2009 Enrollment: 5,058. . . . . (972) 929-6777
    2010-11 Tuition: In-state $14,826; Out-of-state $14,826
University of Dallas (Private, Not-for-profit, Roman Catholic)
    Fall 2009 Enrollment: 2,883 . . . . (972) 721-5000
    2010-11 Tuition: In-state $29,463; Out-of-state $29,463

Two-year College(s)

High-Tech Institute-Dallas (Private, For-profit)
    Fall 2009 Enrollment: 746 . . . . (972) 871-2824
North Lake College (Public)
    Fall 2009 Enrollment: 11,644. (972) 273-3000
    2010-11 Tuition: In-state $2,280; Out-of-state $3,630

Vocational/Technical School(s)

MediaTech Institute-Irving (Private, For-profit)
    Fall 2009 Enrollment: 202 . . . . (972) 869-1122
Tint School of Makeup and Cosmetology (Private, For-profit)
    Fall 2009 Enrollment: 53 . . . . (972) 513-1176
    2010-11 Tuition: $11,275

Housing: Homeownership rate: 39.1% (2010); Median home value: $136,188 (2010); Median contract rent: $683 per month (2005-2009 5-year est.); Median year structure built: 1981 (2005-2009 5-year est.).

Hospitals: Las Colinas Medical Center (70 beds)

Safety: Violent crime rate: 29.8 per 10,000 population; Property crime rate: 416.3 per 10,000 population (2009).

Transportation: Commute to work: 92.2% car, 1.8% public transportation, 1.3% walk, 2.8% work from home (2005-2009 5-year est.); Travel time to work: 27.7% less than 15 minutes, 41.7% 15 to 30 minutes, 21.7% 30 to 45 minutes, 5.2% 45 to 60 minutes, 3.7% 60 minutes or more (2005-2009 5-year est.)

Additional Information Contacts
City of Irving. . . . . (972) 721-2600
    http://www.ci.irving.tx.us

LANCASTER (city). Covers a land area of 29.293 square miles and a water area of 0.011 square miles. Located at 32.60° N. Lat; 96.77° W. Long. Elevation is 522 feet.

History: Named for Lancaster, Kentucky, which was named for Lancaster in England. Has grown significantly as part of the expanding Dallas—Fort Worth metropolitan area. Town destroyed by 1994 tornado. Settled 1846. Incorporated 1886.

Population: 22,156 (1990); 25,894 (2000); 37,674 (2010); 41,550 (2015 projected); Race: 27.8% White, 55.9% Black, 0.3% Asian, 16.0% Other, 19.7% Hispanic of any race (2010); Density: 1,286.1 persons per square mile (2010); Average household size: 2.84 (2010); Median age: 34.2 (2010); Males per 100 females: 91.0 (2010); Marriage status: 32.0% never married, 48.9% now married, 5.0% widowed, 14.1% divorced (2005-2009 5-year est.); Foreign born: 7.2% (2005-2009 5-year est.); Ancestry (includes multiple ancestries): 4.3% Irish, 2.9% English, 2.5% German, 2.3% American, 0.9% Scotch-Irish (2005-2009 5-year est.).

Economy: Unemployment rate: 11.3% (June 2011); Total civilian labor force: 17,260 (June 2011); Single-family building permits issued: 54 (2010); Multi-family building permits issued: 0 (2010); Employment by occupation: 11.2% management, 14.6% professional, 14.4% services, 33.1% sales, 0.0% farming, 8.5% construction, 18.2% production (2005-2009 5-year est.).

Income: Per capita income: $19,301 (2010); Median household income: $46,805 (2010); Average household income: $55,275 (2010); Percent of households with income of $100,000 or more: 11.0% (2010); Poverty rate: 13.4% (2005-2009 5-year est.).

Taxes: Total city taxes per capita: $524 (2007); City property taxes per capita: $273 (2007).

Education: Percent of population age 25 and over with: High school diploma (including GED) or higher: 79.8% (2010); Bachelor's degree or higher: 18.4% (2010); Master's degree or higher: 6.6% (2010).

School District(s)

Accelerated Intermediate Academy (PK-08)
    2009-10 Enrollment: 454 . . . . (713) 283-6298
Lancaster ISD (PK-12)
    2009-10 Enrollment: 6,176 . . . . (972) 218-1400
Life School (KG-12)
    2009-10 Enrollment: 3,434 . . . . (972) 274-7900
Responsive Education Solutions (KG-12)
    2009-10 Enrollment: 5,022 . . . . (972) 316-3663
Texas Serenity Academy (KG-08)
    2009-10 Enrollment: 390 . . . . (281) 931-8887

Two-year College(s)

Cedar Valley College (Public)
    Fall 2009 Enrollment: 5,886. (972) 860-8201
    2010-11 Tuition: In-state $2,280; Out-of-state $3,630

Housing: Homeownership rate: 69.8% (2010); Median home value: $104,077 (2010); Median contract rent: $671 per month (2005-2009 5-year est.); Median year structure built: 1986 (2005-2009 5-year est.).

Hospitals: Medical Center at Lancaster (90 beds)

Transportation: Commute to work: 94.2% car, 1.0% public transportation, 1.3% walk, 2.5% work from home (2005-2009 5-year est.); Travel time to work: 12.0% less than 15 minutes, 32.8% 15 to 30 minutes, 34.5% 30 to 45 minutes, 14.0% 45 to 60 minutes, 6.6% 60 minutes or more (2005-2009 5-year est.)

Additional Information Contacts

City of Lancaster . . . . (972) 218-1300
    http://www.lancaster-tx.com
Lancaster Chamber of Commerce. . . . . (972) 227-2579
    http://www.lancastertx.org

MESQUITE (city). Covers a land area of 43.416 square miles and a water area of 0.048 square miles. Located at 32.78° N. Lat; 96.61° W. Long. Elevation is 495 feet.

History: Named for the mesquite plant found in the area. Mesquite was settled in 1872 and incorporated in 1882.

Population: 101,507 (1990); 124,523 (2000); 134,426 (2010); 139,286 (2015 projected); Race: 60.8% White, 19.5% Black, 4.6% Asian, 15.1% Other, 25.2% Hispanic of any race (2010); Density: 3,096.2 persons per square mile (2010); Average household size: 2.93 (2010); Median age: 34.4 (2010); Males per 100 females: 96.7 (2010); Marriage status: 28.8% never married, 53.8% now married, 5.5% widowed, 12.0% divorced (2005-2009 5-year est.); Foreign born: 15.2% (2005-2009 5-year est.); Ancestry (includes multiple ancestries): 14.6% American, 7.6% German, 6.1% Irish, 6.1% English, 1.7% French (2005-2009 5-year est.).

Economy: Unemployment rate: 8.9% (June 2011); Total civilian labor force: 69,666 (June 2011); Single-family building permits issued: 42 (2010); Multi-family building permits issued: 0 (2010); Employment by occupation: 12.4% management, 16.7% professional, 14.2% services, 30.1% sales, 0.3% farming, 13.0% construction, 13.3% production (2005-2009 5-year est.).

Income: Per capita income: $22,105 (2010); Median household income: $55,187 (2010); Average household income: $64,658 (2010); Percent of households with income of $100,000 or more: 15.4% (2010); Poverty rate: 9.9% (2005-2009 5-year est.).

Taxes: Total city taxes per capita: $618 (2007); City property taxes per capita: $269 (2007).

Education: Percent of population age 25 and over with: High school diploma (including GED) or higher: 83.4% (2010); Bachelor's degree or higher: 18.8% (2010); Master's degree or higher: 5.9% (2010).

School District(s)

Dallas ISD (PK-12)
    2009-10 Enrollment: 157,111 . . . . (972) 925-3700
Education Center International Academy (KG-12)
    2009-10 Enrollment: 201 . . . . (972) 530-6157
Mesquite ISD (PK-12)
    2009-10 Enrollment: 37,272 . . . . (972) 288-6411

Two-year College(s)

Eastfield College (Public)
    Fall 2009 Enrollment: 11,944. (972) 860-7100
    2010-11 Tuition: In-state $2,280; Out-of-state $3,630

Vocational/Technical School(s)

Hands on Therapy (Private, For-profit)
    Fall 2009 Enrollment: 27 . . . . (972) 285-6133
    2010-11 Tuition: $4,924
Metroplex Beauty School (Private, For-profit)
    Fall 2009 Enrollment: 108 . . . . (972) 288-5485
    2010-11 Tuition: $8,925

Housing: Homeownership rate: 69.8% (2010); Median home value: $118,449 (2010); Median contract rent: $701 per month (2005-2009 5-year est.); Median year structure built: 1982 (2005-2009 5-year est.).

Hospitals: Dallas Regional Medical Cetner (176 beds); Mesquite Community Hospital (172 beds)

Safety: Violent crime rate: 40.2 per 10,000 population; Property crime rate: 506.9 per 10,000 population (2009).

Newspapers: Mesquite News (Community news; Circulation 24,000); The Rowlett Lakeshore Times (Local news; Circulation 4,200)

Transportation: Commute to work: 95.7% car, 0.4% public transportation, 0.8% walk, 2.2% work from home (2005-2009 5-year est.); Travel time to work: 20.3% less than 15 minutes, 29.2% 15 to 30 minutes, 29.7% 30 to 45

minutes, 12.5% 45 to 60 minutes, 8.2% 60 minutes or more (2005-2009 5-year est.)

Airports: Mesquite Metro (general aviation)

Additional Information Contacts

City of Mesquite . . . . (972) 288-7711
    http://www.cityofmesquite.com
Mesquite Chamber of Commerce . . . . (972) 285-0211
    http://www.mesquitechamber.com

RICHARDSON (city). Covers a land area of 28.564 square miles and a water area of 0.003 square miles. Located at 32.96° N. Lat; 96.71° W. Long. Elevation is 630 feet.

Population: 74,717 (1990); 91,802 (2000); 101,892 (2010); 108,805 (2015 projected); Race: 64.7% White, 8.2% Black, 15.7% Asian, 11.4% Other, 18.3% Hispanic of any race (2010); Density: 3,567.1 persons per square mile (2010); Average household size: 2.61 (2010); Median age: 38.1 (2010); Males per 100 females: 100.0 (2010); Marriage status: 29.3% never married, 56.2% now married, 5.5% widowed, 8.9% divorced (2005-2009 5-year est.); Foreign born: 20.6% (2005-2009 5-year est.); Ancestry (includes multiple ancestries): 12.5% German, 11.4% American, 10.8% English, 8.6% Irish, 3.0% French (2005-2009 5-year est.).

Economy: Unemployment rate: 7.5% (June 2011); Total civilian labor force: 55,591 (June 2011); Single-family building permits issued: 56 (2010); Multi-family building permits issued: 140 (2010); Employment by occupation: 19.8% management, 28.1% professional, 13.5% services, 26.2% sales, 0.1% farming, 6.1% construction, 6.2% production (2005-2009 5-year est.).

Income: Per capita income: $32,098 (2010); Median household income: $67,112 (2010); Average household income: $84,067 (2010); Percent of households with income of $100,000 or more: 27.9% (2010); Poverty rate: 9.1% (2005-2009 5-year est.).

Taxes: Total city taxes per capita: $896 (2007); City property taxes per capita: $466 (2007).

Education: Percent of population age 25 and over with: High school diploma (including GED) or higher: 90.9% (2010); Bachelor's degree or higher: 46.8% (2010); Master's degree or higher: 16.9% (2010).

School District(s)

Cedar Hill ISD (PK-12)
    2009-10 Enrollment: 8,284 . . . . (972) 291-1581
Evolution Academy Charter School (09-12)
    2009-10 Enrollment: 379 . . . . (972) 907-3755
Garland ISD (PK-12)
    2009-10 Enrollment: 57,861 . . . . (972) 494-8201
Plano ISD (PK-12)
    2009-10 Enrollment: 54,939 . . . . (469) 752-8100
Richardson ISD (PK-12)
    2009-10 Enrollment: 34,843 . . . . (469) 593-0000
Winfree Academy Charter Schools (09-12)
    2009-10 Enrollment: 1,862 . . . . (972) 869-3250

Four-year College(s)

ITT Technical Institute-Richardson (Private, For-profit)
    Fall 2009 Enrollment: 744 . . . . (972) 690-9100
    2010-11 Tuition: In-state $18,048; Out-of-state $18,048
The University of Texas at Dallas (Public)
    Fall 2009 Enrollment: 15,783 . . . . (972) 883-2111
    2010-11 Tuition: In-state $9,886; Out-of-state $22,170

Vocational/Technical School(s)

ATI Career Training Center (Private, For-profit)
    Fall 2009 Enrollment: 461 . . . . (214) 646-8460
    2010-11 Tuition: $16,700

Housing: Homeownership rate: 65.8% (2010); Median home value: $171,531 (2010); Median contract rent: $831 per month (2005-2009 5-year est.); Median year structure built: 1976 (2005-2009 5-year est.).

Hospitals: Richardson Medical Center (205 beds)

Safety: Violent crime rate: 22.4 per 10,000 population; Property crime rate: 348.2 per 10,000 population (2009).

Newspapers: The Dallas Morning News - Richardson Bureau (Community news)

Transportation: Commute to work: 88.7% car, 2.8% public transportation, 2.5% walk, 4.9% work from home (2005-2009 5-year est.); Travel time to work: 26.8% less than 15 minutes, 39.7% 15 to 30 minutes, 23.9% 30 to 45 minutes, 6.4% 45 to 60 minutes, 3.1% 60 minutes or more (2005-2009 5-year est.)

Additional Information Contacts

City of Richardson . . . . (972) 744-4100
  http://www.cor.net
Richardson Economic Development Partnership . . . . (972) 792-2800
  http://www.telecomcorridor.com

ROWLETT (city). Covers a land area of 20.227 square miles and a
water area of 0.018 square miles. Located at 32.90° N. Lat; 96.54° W.
Long. Elevation is 505 feet.
Population: 23,880 (1990); 44,503 (2000); 57,187 (2010); 62,811 (2015
projected); Race: 72.9% White, 13.0% Black, 4.5% Asian, 9.7% Other,
14.1% Hispanic of any race (2010); Density: 2,827.3 persons per square
mile (2010); Average household size: 3.18 (2010); Median age: 34.2
(2010); Males per 100 females: 99.5 (2010); Marriage status: 24.6% never
married, 62.8% now married, 4.5% widowed, 8.2% divorced (2005-2009
5-year est.); Foreign born: 10.4% (2005-2009 5-year est.); Ancestry
(includes multiple ancestries): 12.1% German, 9.7% English, 8.0% Irish,
6.7% American, 3.0% French (2005-2009 5-year est.).
Economy: Unemployment rate: 8.2% (June 2011); Total civilian labor
force: 29,349 (June 2011); Single-family building permits issued: 24 (2010);
Multi-family building permits issued: 0 (2010); Employment by occupation:
15.0% management, 26.7% professional, 12.0% services, 30.0% sales,
0.1% farming, 8.4% construction, 8.0% production (2005-2009 5-year est.).
Income: Per capita income: $29,896 (2010); Median household income:
$82,415 (2010); Average household income: $95,205 (2010); Percent of
households with income of $100,000 or more: 34.7% (2010); Poverty rate:
5.2% (2005-2009 5-year est.).
Taxes: Total city taxes per capita: $622 (2007); City property taxes per
capita: $409 (2007).
Education: Percent of population age 25 and over with: High school
diploma (including GED) or higher: 93.0% (2010); Bachelor's degree or
higher: 31.9% (2010); Master's degree or higher: 9.5% (2010).
School District(s)
Garland ISD (PK-12)
  2009-10 Enrollment: 57,861 . . . . (972) 494-8201
Rockwall ISD (PK-12)
  2009-10 Enrollment: 13,843 . . . . (972) 771-0605
Housing: Homeownership rate: 93.4% (2010); Median home value:
$160,057 (2010); Median contract rent: $933 per month (2005-2009 5-year
est.); Median year structure built: 1991 (2005-2009 5-year est.).
Hospitals: Lake Pointe Medical Center (99 beds)
Safety: Violent crime rate: 10.7 per 10,000 population; Property crime rate:
189.6 per 10,000 population (2009).
Transportation: Commute to work: 92.7% car, 1.5% public transportation,
0.6% walk, 4.7% work from home (2005-2009 5-year est.); Travel time to
work: 14.8% less than 15 minutes, 28.8% 15 to 30 minutes, 30.7% 30 to 45
minutes, 15.4% 45 to 60 minutes, 10.4% 60 minutes or more (2005-2009
5-year est.)
Additional Information Contacts
City of Rowlett . . . . (972) 412-6116
  http://www.ci.rowlett.tx.us
Rowlett Chamber of Commerce. . . . . (972) 475-3200
  http://www.rowlettchamber.com

SACHSE (city). Covers a land area of 9.733 square miles and a water
area of 0.159 square miles. Located at 32.97° N. Lat; 96.58° W. Long.
Elevation is 548 feet.
Population: 5,506 (1990); 9,751 (2000); 18,987 (2010); 22,113 (2015
projected); Race: 77.8% White, 7.7% Black, 4.3% Asian, 10.2% Other,
14.5% Hispanic of any race (2010); Density: 1,950.7 persons per square
mile (2010); Average household size: 3.06 (2010); Median age: 34.7
(2010); Males per 100 females: 100.6 (2010); Marriage status: 21.4%
never married, 67.3% now married, 3.3% widowed, 8.0% divorced
(2005-2009 5-year est.); Foreign born: 12.8% (2005-2009 5-year est.);
Ancestry (includes multiple ancestries): 15.1% German, 10.4% Irish, 10.4%
English, 5.3% American, 2.7% Italian (2005-2009 5-year est.).
Economy: Single-family building permits issued: 118 (2010); Multi-family
building permits issued: 0 (2010); Employment by occupation: 21.9%
management, 23.0% professional, 12.8% services, 27.4% sales, 0.0%
farming, 5.8% construction, 9.1% production (2005-2009 5-year est.).
Income: Per capita income: $30,404 (2010); Median household income:
$82,173 (2010); Average household income: $93,100 (2010); Percent of
households with income of $100,000 or more: 34.4% (2010); Poverty rate:
5.4% (2005-2009 5-year est.).
Taxes: Total city taxes per capita: $502 (2007); City property taxes per
capita: $301 (2007).

Education: Percent of population age 25 and over with: High school
diploma (including GED) or higher: 91.8% (2010); Bachelor's degree or
higher: 27.7% (2010); Master's degree or higher: 8.3% (2010).
School District(s)
Garland ISD (PK-12)
  2009-10 Enrollment: 57,861 . . . . (972) 494-8201
Wylie ISD (PK-12)
  2009-10 Enrollment: 12,063 . . . . (972) 429-3000
Housing: Homeownership rate: 88.8% (2010); Median home value:
$163,527 (2010); Median contract rent: $729 per month (2005-2009 5-year
est.); Median year structure built: 1999 (2005-2009 5-year est.).
Safety: Violent crime rate: 6.5 per 10,000 population; Property crime rate:
110.0 per 10,000 population (2009).
Transportation: Commute to work: 91.5% car, 2.9% public transportation,
0.0% walk, 4.6% work from home (2005-2009 5-year est.); Travel time to
work: 14.1% less than 15 minutes, 30.9% 15 to 30 minutes, 32.2% 30 to 45
minutes, 13.1% 45 to 60 minutes, 9.7% 60 minutes or more (2005-2009
5-year est.)
Additional Information Contacts
City of Sachse . . . . (972) 495-1212
  http://www.cityofsachse.com
Sachse Chamber of Commerce. . . . . (972) 496-1212
  http://www.sachsechamber.com

SEAGOVILLE (city). Covers a land area of 16.244 square miles and a
water area of 0.048 square miles. Located at 32.65° N. Lat; 96.55° W.
Long. Elevation is 440 feet.
Population: 8,969 (1990); 10,823 (2000); 12,623 (2010); 13,422 (2015
projected); Race: 70.0% White, 10.3% Black, 0.5% Asian, 19.1% Other,
31.2% Hispanic of any race (2010); Density: 777.1 persons per square mile
(2010); Average household size: 2.99 (2010); Median age: 34.7 (2010);
Males per 100 females: 122.6 (2010); Marriage status: 27.5% never
married, 54.0% now married, 5.2% widowed, 13.3% divorced (2005-2009
5-year est.); Foreign born: 11.5% (2005-2009 5-year est.); Ancestry
(includes multiple ancestries): 16.6% American, 8.3% German, 6.6% Irish,
4.6% English, 2.3% Scotch-Irish (2005-2009 5-year est.).
Economy: Single-family building permits issued: 55 (2010); Multi-family
building permits issued: 0 (2010); Employment by occupation: 7.7%
management, 17.6% professional, 11.1% services, 25.1% sales, 0.0%
farming, 22.2% construction, 16.2% production (2005-2009 5-year est.).
Income: Per capita income: $18,041 (2010); Median household income:
$46,804 (2010); Average household income: $56,713 (2010); Percent of
households with income of $100,000 or more: 12.8% (2010); Poverty rate:
11.3% (2005-2009 5-year est.).
Taxes: Total city taxes per capita: $457 (2007); City property taxes per
capita: $223 (2007).
Education: Percent of population age 25 and over with: High school
diploma (including GED) or higher: 66.7% (2010); Bachelor's degree or
higher: 6.3% (2010); Master's degree or higher: 2.3% (2010).
School District(s)
Dallas ISD (PK-12)
  2009-10 Enrollment: 157,111 . . . . (972) 925-3700
Shekinah Radiance Academy (PK-12)
  2009-10 Enrollment: 1,125 . . . . (210) 658-6848
Housing: Homeownership rate: 80.7% (2010); Median home value:
$76,688 (2010); Median contract rent: $654 per month (2005-2009 5-year
est.); Median year structure built: 1982 (2005-2009 5-year est.).
Safety: Violent crime rate: 27.2 per 10,000 population; Property crime rate:
497.0 per 10,000 population (2009).
Newspapers: Seagoville Suburbia News (Local news; Circulation 2,000)
Transportation: Commute to work: 97.3% car, 0.0% public transportation,
0.0% walk, 1.9% work from home (2005-2009 5-year est.); Travel time to
work: 15.6% less than 15 minutes, 20.4% 15 to 30 minutes, 38.7% 30 to 45
minutes, 13.6% 45 to 60 minutes, 11.7% 60 minutes or more (2005-2009
5-year est.)
Additional Information Contacts
City of Seagoville . . . . (972) 287-2050
  http://www.seagoville.us
Seagoville Chamber of Commerce . . . . (972) 287-5184
  http://www.seagovillecoc.org

SUNNYVALE (town). Covers a land area of 16.745 square miles and
a water area of 0 square miles. Located at 32.80° N. Lat; 96.57° W. Long.
Elevation is 486 feet.

History: In the year 1953, the hamlets of Hatterville, New Hope, Long Creek, and Tripp merged under the name Sunnyvale. The name was chosen in a contest from a local school. Today, there are many reminders of Sunnyvale's rich history, like the old New Hope School; the Tripp First Baptist Church, built in 1882; and many antique houses.
Population: 2,230 (1990); 2,693 (2000); 4,302 (2010); 4,830 (2015 projected); Race: 81.3% White, 8.6% Black, 3.2% Asian, 6.9% Other, 10.4% Hispanic of any race (2010); Density: 256.9 persons per square mile (2010); Average household size: 2.88 (2010); Median age: 39.8 (2010); Males per 100 females: 97.3 (2010); Marriage status: 24.6% never married, 69.4% now married, 2.9% widowed, 3.1% divorced (2005-2009 5-year est.); Foreign born: 12.1% (2005-2009 5-year est.); Ancestry (includes multiple ancestries): 19.1% American, 9.2% English, 5.8% German, 4.9% Irish, 4.1% Scotch-Irish (2005-2009 5-year est.).
Economy: Single-family building permits issued: 52 (2010); Multi-family building permits issued: 0 (2010); Employment by occupation: 33.6% management, 29.4% professional, 6.5% services, 21.6% sales, 0.4% farming, 5.7% construction, 2.8% production (2005-2009 5-year est.).
Income: Per capita income: $37,431 (2010); Median household income: $74,196 (2010); Average household income: $107,373 (2010); Percent of households with income of $100,000 or more: 37.2% (2010); Poverty rate: 4.8% (2005-2009 5-year est.).
Taxes: Total city taxes per capita: $1,209 (2007); City property taxes per capita: $494 (2007).
Education: Percent of population age 25 and over with: High school diploma (including GED) or higher: 92.1% (2010); Bachelor's degree or higher: 28.9% (2010); Master's degree or higher: 10.4% (2010).

School District(s)

Sunnyvale ISD (PK-11)
    2009-10 Enrollment: 1,010 . . . . (972) 226-7601
Housing: Homeownership rate: 86.1% (2010); Median home value: $239,276 (2010); Median contract rent: $393 per month (2005-2009 5-year est.); Median year structure built: 1995 (2005-2009 5-year est.).
Transportation: Commute to work: 95.3% car, 0.8% public transportation, 0.4% walk, 3.5% work from home (2005-2009 5-year est.); Travel time to work: 27.9% less than 15 minutes, 26.1% 15 to 30 minutes, 36.3% 30 to 45 minutes, 5.1% 45 to 60 minutes, 4.6% 60 minutes or more (2005-2009 5-year est.)
Additional Information Contacts
Town of Sunnyvale . . . . (972) 226-7177
    http://www.townofsunnyvale.org

UNIVERSITY PARK (city).
Covers a land area of 3.720 square miles and a water area of 0.006 square miles. Located at 32.85° N. Lat; 96.79° W. Long. Elevation is 548 feet.
History: Named for it being home to Southern Methodist University. Seat of Southern Methodist University. Incorporated 1924.
Population: 22,259 (1990); 23,324 (2000); 26,315 (2010); 27,915 (2015 projected); Race: 93.0% White, 1.7% Black, 2.3% Asian, 3.0% Other, 4.6% Hispanic of any race (2010); Density: 7,073.1 persons per square mile (2010); Average household size: 2.73 (2010); Median age: 29.7 (2010); Males per 100 females: 91.4 (2010); Marriage status: 36.9% never married, 52.9% now married, 3.3% widowed, 6.9% divorced (2005-2009 5-year est.); Foreign born: 4.7% (2005-2009 5-year est.); Ancestry (includes multiple ancestries): 21.8% German, 21.6% English, 13.9% Irish, 7.5% American, 7.0% Scottish (2005-2009 5-year est.).
Economy: Unemployment rate: 7.6% (June 2011); Total civilian labor force: 10,840 (June 2011); Single-family building permits issued: 44 (2010); Multi-family building permits issued: 0 (2010); Employment by occupation: 29.0% management, 33.1% professional, 6.5% services, 27.9% sales, 0.0% farming, 1.4% construction, 2.2% production (2005-2009 5-year est.).
Income: Per capita income: $57,293 (2010); Median household income: $110,789 (2010); Average household income: $176,046 (2010); Percent of households with income of $100,000 or more: 53.4% (2010); Poverty rate: 5.3% (2005-2009 5-year est.).
Taxes: Total city taxes per capita: $861 (2007); City property taxes per capita: $551 (2007).
Education: Percent of population age 25 and over with: High school diploma (including GED) or higher: 98.2% (2010); Bachelor's degree or higher: 80.1% (2010); Master's degree or higher: 33.6% (2010).
Housing: Homeownership rate: 72.9% (2010); Median home value: $739,861 (2010); Median contract rent: $1,161 per month (2005-2009 5-year est.); Median year structure built: 1957 (2005-2009 5-year est.).
Safety: Violent crime rate: 4.8 per 10,000 population; Property crime rate: 166.2 per 10,000 population (2009).

Transportation: Commute to work: 83.9% car, 0.8% public transportation, 5.8% walk, 8.6% work from home (2005-2009 5-year est.); Travel time to work: 45.5% less than 15 minutes, 38.3% 15 to 30 minutes, 13.6% 30 to 45 minutes, 1.8% 45 to 60 minutes, 0.8% 60 minutes or more (2005-2009 5-year est.)
Additional Information Contacts
City of University Park . . . . (214) 363-1644
    http://www.uptexas.org

WILMER (city).
Covers a land area of 6.296 square miles and a water area of 0 square miles. Located at 32.59° N. Lat; 96.68° W. Long. Elevation is 466 feet.
Population: 2,408 (1990); 3,393 (2000); 3,342 (2010); 3,311 (2015 projected); Race: 43.8% White, 20.1% Black, 0.0% Asian, 36.1% Other, 57.5% Hispanic of any race (2010); Density: 530.8 persons per square mile (2010); Average household size: 3.23 (2010); Median age: 31.4 (2010); Males per 100 females: 113.5 (2010); Marriage status: 37.3% never married, 46.7% now married, 3.8% widowed, 12.1% divorced (2005-2009 5-year est.); Foreign born: 27.4% (2005-2009 5-year est.); Ancestry (includes multiple ancestries): 3.6% Irish, 3.5% American, 3.0% English, 2.9% German, 1.5% French (2005-2009 5-year est.).
Economy: Single-family building permits issued: 5 (2010); Multi-family building permits issued: 0 (2010); Employment by occupation: 7.8% management, 7.3% professional, 18.1% services, 16.8% sales, 0.0% farming, 11.6% construction, 38.5% production (2005-2009 5-year est.).
Income: Per capita income: $13,713 (2010); Median household income: $37,199 (2010); Average household income: $45,567 (2010); Percent of households with income of $100,000 or more: 6.1% (2010); Poverty rate: 26.2% (2005-2009 5-year est.).
Taxes: Total city taxes per capita: $284 (2007); City property taxes per capita: $135 (2007).
Education: Percent of population age 25 and over with: High school diploma (including GED) or higher: 52.2% (2010); Bachelor's degree or higher: 5.2% (2010); Master's degree or higher: 1.0% (2010).

School District(s)

Honors Academy (KG-12)
    2009-10 Enrollment: 1,068 . . . . (214) 521-6365
Housing: Homeownership rate: 73.6% (2010); Median home value: $44,740 (2010); Median contract rent: $502 per month (2005-2009 5-year est.); Median year structure built: 1975 (2005-2009 5-year est.).
Safety: Violent crime rate: 19.5 per 10,000 population; Property crime rate: 233.7 per 10,000 population (2009).
Transportation: Commute to work: 97.2% car, 0.0% public transportation, 0.7% walk, 0.7% work from home (2005-2009 5-year est.); Travel time to work: 24.5% less than 15 minutes, 27.6% 15 to 30 minutes, 23.8% 30 to 45 minutes, 16.1% 45 to 60 minutes, 8.1% 60 minutes or more (2005-2009 5-year est.)
Additional Information Contacts
Wilmer Chamber of Commerce . . . . (972) 525-3668

Dawson County

Located in northwestern Texas; in high plains area, drained by intermittent Sulphur Springs Creek. Covers a land area of 902.06 square miles, a water area of 0.06 square miles, and is located in the Central Time Zone at 32.74° N. Lat., 101.93° W. Long. The county was founded in 1858. County seat is Lamesa.

Dawson County is part of the Lamesa, TX Micropolitan Statistical Area. The entire metro area includes: Dawson County, TX

Weather Station: Lamesa 1 SSE									Elevation: 2,964 feet		
	Jan	Feb	Mar	Apr	May	Jun	Jul	Aug	Sep	Oct	Nov	Dec
High	55	60	68	77	86	92	94	93	86	77	65	56
Low	26	30	36	44	55	63	66	65	58	47	36	27
Precip	0.6	0.8	1.0	0.9	2.4	2.9	1.7	1.7	3.4	1.9	1.0	0.9
Snow	1.7	0.8	0.1	tr	0.0	0.0	0.0	0.0	0.0	0.0	0.8	1.0

High and Low temperatures in degrees Fahrenheit; Precipitation and Snow in inches

Population: 14,349 (1990); 14,985 (2000); 13,700 (2010); 13,055 (2015 projected); Race: 69.9% White, 9.4% Black, 0.5% Asian, 20.2% Other, 52.0% Hispanic of any race (2010); Density: 15.2 persons per square mile (2010); Average household size: 2.63 (2010); Median age: 36.0 (2010); Males per 100 females: 130.4 (2010).

Religion: Five largest groups: 40.6% Southern Baptist Convention, 18.1% Catholic Church, 7.5% The United Methodist Church, 5.2% Churches of Christ, 2.3% International Church of the Foursquare Gospel (2000).
Economy: Unemployment rate: 9.2% (June 2011); Total civilian labor force: 5,341 (June 2011); Leading industries: 18.9% retail trade; 18.4% accommodation & food services; 13.5% health care and social assistance (2009); Farms: 555 totaling 568,036 acres (2007); Companies that employ 500 or more persons: 0 (2009); Companies that employ 100 to 499 persons: 2 (2009); Companies that employ less than 100 persons: 283 (2009); Black-owned businesses: n/a (2007); Hispanic-owned businesses: n/a (2007); Asian-owned businesses: n/a (2007); Women-owned businesses: n/a (2007); Retail sales per capita: $11,283 (2010). Single-family building permits issued: 1 (2010); Multi-family building permits issued: 0 (2010).
Income: Per capita income: $17,419 (2010); Median household income: $35,926 (2010); Average household income: $51,297 (2010); Percent of households with income of $100,000 or more: 9.8% (2010); Poverty rate: 23.6% (2009); Bankruptcy rate: 0.93% (2010).
Taxes: Total county taxes per capita: $439 (2007); County property taxes per capita: $359 (2007).
Education: Percent of population age 25 and over with: High school diploma (including GED) or higher: 70.5% (2010); Bachelor's degree or higher: 12.0% (2010); Master's degree or higher: 2.7% (2010).
Housing: Homeownership rate: 71.5% (2010); Median home value: $49,498 (2010); Median contract rent: $276 per month (2005-2009 5-year est.); Median year structure built: 1961 (2005-2009 5-year est.)
Health: Birth rate: 149.4 per 10,000 population (2009); Death rate: 93.0 per 10,000 population (2009); Age-adjusted cancer mortality rate: 195.2 deaths per 100,000 population (2007); Number of physicians: 4.4 per 10,000 population (2008); Hospital beds: 21.0 per 10,000 population (2007); Hospital admissions: 374.5 per 10,000 population (2007).
Elections: 2008 Presidential election results: 28.1% Obama, 70.9% McCain, 0.0% Nader
Additional Information Contacts
Dawson County Government . . . . (806) 872-7544
   http://www.co.dawson.tx.us/ips/cms
City of Lamesa . . . . (806) 872-2124
   http://www.ci.lamesa.tx.us
Lamesa Area Chamber of Commerce . . . . (806) 872-2181
   http://growlamesa.com

Dawson County Communities

ACKERLY (city). Covers a land area of 0.309 square miles and a water area of 0 square miles. Located at 32.52° N. Lat; 101.71° W. Long. Elevation is 2,802 feet.
Population: 243 (1990); 245 (2000); 240 (2010); 236 (2015 projected); Race: 75.4% White, 0.0% Black, 0.8% Asian, 23.8% Other, 34.6% Hispanic of any race (2010); Density: 776.3 persons per square mile (2010); Average household size: 2.67 (2010); Median age: 42.1 (2010); Males per 100 females: 101.7 (2010); Marriage status: 20.9% never married, 75.3% now married, 1.1% widowed, 2.7% divorced (2005-2009 5-year est.); Foreign born: 10.4% (2005-2009 5-year est.); Ancestry (includes multiple ancestries): 11.7% Italian, 10.7% Irish, 10.4% German, 3.0% English, 2.3% Scottish (2005-2009 5-year est.).
Economy: Employment by occupation: 27.5% management, 17.6% professional, 31.3% services, 0.0% sales, 7.6% farming, 6.1% construction, 9.9% production (2005-2009 5-year est.).
Income: Per capita income: $27,675 (2010); Median household income: $48,750 (2010); Average household income: $72,472 (2010); Percent of households with income of $100,000 or more: 21.1% (2010); Poverty rate: 19.8% (2005-2009 5-year est.).
Taxes: Total city taxes per capita: $204 (2007); City property taxes per capita: $113 (2007).
Education: Percent of population age 25 and over with: High school diploma (including GED) or higher: 75.8% (2010); Bachelor's degree or higher: 9.9% (2010); Master's degree or higher: 1.2% (2010).
School District(s)
Sands CISD (PK-12)
   2009-10 Enrollment: 224 . . . . (432) 353-4888
Housing: Homeownership rate: 70.0% (2010); Median home value: $85,000 (2010); Median contract rent: $450 per month (2005-2009 5-year est.); Median year structure built: 1958 (2005-2009 5-year est.).
Transportation: Commute to work: 86.3% car, 0.0% public transportation, 12.2% walk, 0.0% work from home (2005-2009 5-year est.); Travel time to

work: 62.6% less than 15 minutes, 22.9% 15 to 30 minutes, 14.5% 30 to 45 minutes, 0.0% 45 to 60 minutes, 0.0% 60 minutes or more (2005-2009 5-year est.)

LAMESA (city). County seat. Covers a land area of 4.783 square miles and a water area of 0 square miles. Located at 32.73° N. Lat; 101.95° W. Long. Elevation is 2,992 feet.
History: Lamesa's name is the Spanish "la mesa" (the table), for its location on the plains at the edge of Cap Rock. Cotton and cattle were the basis of Lamesa's early economy, followed by oil.
Population: 10,843 (1990); 9,952 (2000); 9,033 (2010); 8,598 (2015 projected); Race: 70.6% White, 4.3% Black, 0.4% Asian, 24.7% Other, 57.4% Hispanic of any race (2010); Density: 1,888.7 persons per square mile (2010); Average household size: 2.62 (2010); Median age: 35.9 (2010); Males per 100 females: 99.8 (2010); Marriage status: 16.1% never married, 64.0% now married, 9.0% widowed, 11.0% divorced (2005-2009 5-year est.); Foreign born: 5.6% (2005-2009 5-year est.); Ancestry (includes multiple ancestries): 6.6% German, 6.1% Irish, 5.6% English, 5.4% American, 0.8% Welsh (2005-2009 5-year est.).
Economy: Single-family building permits issued: 1 (2010); Multi-family building permits issued: 0 (2010); Employment by occupation: 14.1% management, 14.1% professional, 19.3% services, 24.0% sales, 6.2% farming, 11.1% construction, 11.3% production (2005-2009 5-year est.).
Income: Per capita income: $18,212 (2010); Median household income: $34,624 (2010); Average household income: $48,550 (2010); Percent of households with income of $100,000 or more: 8.4% (2010); Poverty rate: 23.5% (2005-2009 5-year est.).
Taxes: Total city taxes per capita: $307 (2007); City property taxes per capita: $136 (2007).
Education: Percent of population age 25 and over with: High school diploma (including GED) or higher: 67.3% (2010); Bachelor's degree or higher: 14.4% (2010); Master's degree or higher: 3.4% (2010).
School District(s)
Borden County ISD (PK-12)
   2009-10 Enrollment: 222 . . . . (806) 756-4313
Klondike ISD (PK-12)
   2009-10 Enrollment: 208 . . . . (806) 462-7334
Lamesa ISD (PK-12)
   2009-10 Enrollment: 1,933 . . . . (806) 872-5461
Housing: Homeownership rate: 74.1% (2010); Median home value: $45,171 (2010); Median contract rent: $273 per month (2005-2009 5-year est.); Median year structure built: 1959 (2005-2009 5-year est.).
Hospitals: Medical Arts Hospital (44 beds)
Safety: Violent crime rate: 41.0 per 10,000 population; Property crime rate: 380.8 per 10,000 population (2009).
Newspapers: Lamesa Press-Reporter (Local news; Circulation 3,850)
Transportation: Commute to work: 93.3% car, 0.0% public transportation, 0.7% walk, 2.0% work from home (2005-2009 5-year est.); Travel time to work: 76.0% less than 15 minutes, 15.9% 15 to 30 minutes, 3.8% 30 to 45 minutes, 0.6% 45 to 60 minutes, 3.7% 60 minutes or more (2005-2009 5-year est.)
Additional Information Contacts
City of Lamesa . . . . (806) 872-2124
   http://www.ci.lamesa.tx.us
Lamesa Area Chamber of Commerce . . . . (806) 872-2181
   http://growlamesa.com

LOS YBANEZ (city). Covers a land area of 0.088 square miles and a water area of 0 square miles. Located at 32.71° N. Lat; 101.91° W. Long. Elevation is 2,972 feet.
Population: 83 (1990); 32 (2000); 25 (2010); 24 (2015 projected); Race: 56.0% White, 36.0% Black, 0.0% Asian, 8.0% Other, 48.0% Hispanic of any race (2010); Density: 285.2 persons per square mile (2010); Average household size: 2.33 (2010); Median age: 32.9 (2010); Males per 100 females: ***.* (2010); Marriage status: 100.0% never married, 0.0% now married, 0.0% widowed, 0.0% divorced (2005-2009 5-year est.); Foreign born: 0.0% (2005-2009 5-year est.); Ancestry (includes multiple ancestries): n/a (2005-2009 5-year est.).
Economy: Employment by occupation: n/a management, n/a professional, n/a services, n/a sales, n/a farming, n/a construction, n/a production (2005-2009 5-year est.).
Income: Per capita income: $9,418 (2010); Median household income: $30,000 (2010); Average household income: $30,833 (2010); Percent of households with income of $100,000 or more: 0.0% (2010); Poverty rate: 100.0% (2005-2009 5-year est.).

Taxes: Total city taxes per capita: $533 (2007); City property taxes per capita: $0 (2007).
Education: Percent of population age 25 and over with: High school diploma (including GED) or higher: 72.2% (2010); Bachelor's degree or higher: 0.0% (2010); Master's degree or higher: 0.0% (2010).
Housing: Homeownership rate: 33.3% (2010); Median home value: $90,000 (2010); Median contract rent: n/a per month (2005-2009 5-year est.); Median year structure built: 1947 (2005-2009 5-year est.).
Transportation: Commute to work: n/a car, n/a public transportation, n/a walk, n/a work from home (2005-2009 5-year est.); Travel time to work: n/a less than 15 minutes, n/a 15 to 30 minutes, n/a 30 to 45 minutes, n/a 45 to 60 minutes, n/a 60 minutes or more (2005-2009 5-year est.)

WELCH (unincorporated postal area, zip code 79377). Covers a land area of 45.195 square miles and a water area of 0 square miles. Located at 32.93° N. Lat; 102.14° W. Long. Elevation is 3,110 feet.
Population: 367 (2000); Race: 85.8% White, 0.0% Black, 0.0% Asian, 14.2% Other, 44.1% Hispanic of any race (2000); Density: 8.1 persons per square mile (2000); Age: 35.1% under 18, 8.7% over 64 (2000); Marriage status: 19.4% never married, 70.4% now married, 8.5% widowed, 1.7% divorced (2000); Foreign born: 15.8% (2000); Ancestry (includes multiple ancestries): 7.8% Irish, 5.7% American, 5.4% English, 4.5% Scotch-Irish (2000).
Economy: Employment by occupation: 20.5% management, 16.4% professional, 21.9% services, 13.0% sales, 21.2% farming, 4.8% construction, 2.1% production (2000).
Income: Per capita income: $11,896 (2000); Median household income: $31,923 (2000); Poverty rate: 179.1% (2000).
Education: Percent of population age 25 and over with: High school diploma (including GED) or higher: 66.1% (2000); Bachelor's degree or higher: 11.3% (2000).

School District(s)
Dawson ISD (PK-12)
   2009-10 Enrollment: 168 . . . . (806) 489-7568
Housing: Homeownership rate: 70.6% (2000); Median home value: $40,000 (2000); Median contract rent: $261 per month (2000); Median year structure built: 1963 (2000).
Transportation: Commute to work: 95.9% car, 0.0% public transportation, 2.7% walk, 0.0% work from home (2000); Travel time to work: 56.2% less than 15 minutes, 24.7% 15 to 30 minutes, 17.1% 30 to 45 minutes, 0.0% 45 to 60 minutes, 2.1% 60 minutes or more (2000)

DeWitt County

Located in south Texas; drained by the Guadalupe River. Covers a land area of 909.18 square miles, a water area of 1.29 square miles, and is located in the Central Time Zone at 29.09° N. Lat., 97.33° W. Long. The county was founded in 1846. County seat is Cuero.
Population: 18,840 (1990); 20,013 (2000); 19,990 (2010); 19,944 (2015 projected); Race: 74.7% White, 11.2% Black, 0.2% Asian, 13.8% Other, 30.2% Hispanic of any race (2010); Density: 22.0 persons per square mile (2010); Average household size: 2.52 (2010); Median age: 40.7 (2010); Males per 100 females: 108.1 (2010).
Religion: Five largest groups: 26.6% Catholic Church, 13.2% Evangelical Lutheran Church in America, 9.7% Southern Baptist Convention, 2.2% The United Methodist Church, 1.7% Presbyterian Church (U.S.A.) (2000).
Economy: Unemployment rate: 8.0% (June 2011); Total civilian labor force: 9,244 (June 2011); Leading industries: 24.7% health care and social assistance; 18.1% manufacturing; 16.6% retail trade (2009); Farms: 1,811 totaling 549,237 acres (2007); Companies that employ 500 or more persons: 0 (2009); Companies that employ 100 to 499 persons: 6 (2009); Companies that employ less than 100 persons: 419 (2009); Black-owned businesses: n/a (2007); Hispanic-owned businesses: n/a (2007); Asian-owned businesses: n/a (2007); Women-owned businesses: 402 (2007); Retail sales per capita: $7,396 (2010). Single-family building permits issued: 7 (2010); Multi-family building permits issued: 0 (2010).
Income: Per capita income: $18,631 (2010); Median household income: $37,620 (2010); Average household income: $49,958 (2010); Percent of households with income of $100,000 or more: 10.1% (2010); Poverty rate: 19.3% (2009); Bankruptcy rate: 1.33% (2010).
Taxes: Total county taxes per capita: $266 (2007); County property taxes per capita: $235 (2007).
Education: Percent of population age 25 and over with: High school diploma (including GED) or higher: 73.2% (2010); Bachelor's degree or higher: 13.3% (2010); Master's degree or higher: 4.0% (2010).

Housing: Homeownership rate: 74.7% (2010); Median home value: $67,029 (2010); Median contract rent: $327 per month (2005-2009 5-year est.); Median year structure built: 1966 (2005-2009 5-year est.)
Health: Birth rate: 116.7 per 10,000 population (2009); Death rate: 117.2 per 10,000 population (2009); Age-adjusted cancer mortality rate: 212.3 deaths per 100,000 population (2007); Number of physicians: 5.1 per 10,000 population (2008); Hospital beds: 24.8 per 10,000 population (2007); Hospital admissions: 1,409.8 per 10,000 population (2007).
Elections: 2008 Presidential election results: 25.9% Obama, 73.8% McCain, 0.0% Nader
Additional Information Contacts
DeWitt County Government . . . . (361) 275-2116
   http://www.co.dewitt.tx.us/ips/cms

DeWitt County Communities

CUERO (city). County seat. Covers a land area of 4.937 square miles and a water area of 0.018 square miles. Located at 29.09° N. Lat; 97.29° W. Long. Elevation is 184 feet.
History: Cuero was named for the creek on which it was located, called Arroyo del Cuero (Creek of the Rawhide) because wild cattle and buffalo often were stuck in the boggy banks of the creek. Cuero may have been the beginning point of the Chisholm Trail. Cotton was the leading crop here, but Cuero was also known for its turkeys.
Population: 6,700 (1990); 6,571 (2000); 6,893 (2010); 6,974 (2015 projected); Race: 66.2% White, 16.2% Black, 0.5% Asian, 17.2% Other, 35.0% Hispanic of any race (2010); Density: 1,396.3 persons per square mile (2010); Average household size: 2.54 (2010); Median age: 38.6 (2010); Males per 100 females: 103.0 (2010); Marriage status: 30.9% never married, 44.0% now married, 7.0% widowed, 18.1% divorced (2005-2009 5-year est.); Foreign born: 3.2% (2005-2009 5-year est.); Ancestry (includes multiple ancestries): 17.5% German, 7.8% English, 6.0% Irish, 3.4% American, 2.5% Polish (2005-2009 5-year est.).
Economy: Single-family building permits issued: 6 (2010); Multi-family building permits issued: 0 (2010); Employment by occupation: 6.4% management, 14.0% professional, 28.5% services, 26.1% sales, 0.3% farming, 11.4% construction, 13.4% production (2005-2009 5-year est.).
Income: Per capita income: $16,871 (2010); Median household income: $32,087 (2010); Average household income: $45,263 (2010); Percent of households with income of $100,000 or more: 8.3% (2010); Poverty rate: 17.5% (2005-2009 5-year est.).
Taxes: Total city taxes per capita: $288 (2007); City property taxes per capita: $75 (2007).
Education: Percent of population age 25 and over with: High school diploma (including GED) or higher: 70.5% (2010); Bachelor's degree or higher: 11.9% (2010); Master's degree or higher: 3.5% (2010).

School District(s)
Cuero ISD (PK-12)
   2009-10 Enrollment: 1,879 . . . . (361) 275-3832
Ezzell ISD (KG-08)
   2009-10 Enrollment: 59 . . . . (361) 798-4448
Hallettsville ISD (PK-12)
   2009-10 Enrollment: 867 . . . . (361) 798-2242
Meyersville ISD (KG-08)
   2009-10 Enrollment: 163 . . . . (361) 277-5817
Moulton ISD (PK-12)
   2009-10 Enrollment: 311 . . . . (361) 596-4609
Nordheim ISD (PK-12)
   2009-10 Enrollment: 96 . . . . (361) 938-5211
Shiner ISD (PK-12)
   2009-10 Enrollment: 559 . . . . (361) 594-3121
Sweet Home ISD (PK-08)
   2009-10 Enrollment: 121 . . . . (361) 293-3221
Vysehrad ISD (KG-08)
   2009-10 Enrollment: 95 . . . . (361) 798-4118
Westhoff ISD (PK-08)
   2009-10 Enrollment: 42 . . . . (830) 236-5519
Yoakum ISD (PK-12)
   2009-10 Enrollment: 1,544 . . . . (361) 293-3162
Yorktown ISD (PK-12)
   2009-10 Enrollment: 539 . . . . (361) 564-2252
Housing: Homeownership rate: 71.2% (2010); Median home value: $57,363 (2010); Median contract rent: $374 per month (2005-2009 5-year est.); Median year structure built: 1964 (2005-2009 5-year est.).
Hospitals: Cuero Community Hospital (60 beds)

Safety: Violent crime rate: 20.3 per 10,000 population; Property crime rate: 165.6 per 10,000 population (2009).

Transportation: Commute to work: 94.7% car, 0.0% public transportation, 1.5% walk, 2.4% work from home (2005-2009 5-year est.); Travel time to work: 64.5% less than 15 minutes, 17.3% 15 to 30 minutes, 12.5% 30 to 45 minutes, 2.3% 45 to 60 minutes, 3.4% 60 minutes or more (2005-2009 5-year est.)

Additional Information Contacts

City of Cuero . . . . (361) 275-3476
   http://www.cityofcuero.net
Cuero Chamber of Commerce. . . . . (361) 275-2112
   http://www.cuero.org

MEYERSVILLE (unincorporated postal area, zip code 77974). Covers a land area of 29.597 square miles and a water area of 0.015 square miles. Located at 28.89° N. Lat; 97.29° W. Long. Elevation is 230 feet.

Population: 381 (2000); Race: 100.0% White, 0.0% Black, 0.0% Asian, 0.0% Other, 2.9% Hispanic of any race (2000); Density: 12.9 persons per square mile (2000); Age: 25.4% under 18, 17.9% over 64 (2000); Marriage status: 22.4% never married, 65.3% now married, 5.7% widowed, 6.5% divorced (2000); Foreign born: 1.0% (2000); Ancestry (includes multiple ancestries): 56.7% German, 8.8% Polish, 5.5% Irish, 3.9% Dutch (2000).

Economy: Employment by occupation: 13.1% management, 21.4% professional, 16.6% services, 16.6% sales, 2.1% farming, 13.1% construction, 17.2% production (2000).

Income: Per capita income: $15,480 (2000); Median household income: $34,375 (2000); Poverty rate: 179.1% (2000).

Education: Percent of population age 25 and over with: High school diploma (including GED) or higher: 81.5% (2000); Bachelor's degree or higher: 13.5% (2000).

School District(s)

Meyersville ISD (KG-08)
   2009-10 Enrollment: 163 . . . . (361) 277-5817

Housing: Homeownership rate: 87.9% (2000); Median home value: $85,000 (2000); Median contract rent: $238 per month (2000); Median year structure built: 1970 (2000).

Transportation: Commute to work: 92.4% car, 0.0% public transportation, 0.0% walk, 7.6% work from home (2000); Travel time to work: 11.9% less than 15 minutes, 32.8% 15 to 30 minutes, 33.6% 30 to 45 minutes, 10.4% 45 to 60 minutes, 11.2% 60 minutes or more (2000)

NORDHEIM (city). Covers a land area of 0.475 square miles and a water area of 0 square miles. Located at 28.92° N. Lat; 97.61° W. Long. Elevation is 404 feet.

Population: 344 (1990); 323 (2000); 331 (2010); 331 (2015 projected); Race: 84.3% White, 0.0% Black, 0.0% Asian, 0.0% Other, 25.7% Hispanic of any race (2010); Density: 697.6 persons per square mile (2010); Average household size: 2.36 (2010); Median age: 45.8 (2010); Males per 100 females: 92.4 (2010); Marriage status: 23.2% never married, 52.7% now married, 16.2% widowed, 7.9% divorced (2005-2009 5-year est.); Foreign born: 4.3% (2005-2009 5-year est.); Ancestry (includes multiple ancestries): 39.2% German, 6.3% Polish, 5.5% American, 5.5% Irish, 4.1% Scotch-Irish (2005-2009 5-year est.).

Economy: Employment by occupation: 3.9% management, 28.8% professional, 28.1% services, 20.3% sales, 2.6% farming, 9.8% construction, 6.5% production (2005-2009 5-year est.).

Income: Per capita income: $22,074 (2010); Median household income: $46,429 (2010); Average household income: $51,786 (2010); Percent of households with income of $100,000 or more: 10.0% (2010); Poverty rate: 23.8% (2005-2009 5-year est.).

Taxes: Total city taxes per capita: $147 (2007); City property taxes per capita: $70 (2007).

Education: Percent of population age 25 and over with: High school diploma (including GED) or higher: 77.1% (2010); Bachelor's degree or higher: 15.5% (2010); Master's degree or higher: 5.3% (2010).

School District(s)

Nordheim ISD (PK-12)
   2009-10 Enrollment: 96 . . . . (361) 938-5211

Housing: Homeownership rate: 84.3% (2010); Median home value: $70,000 (2010); Median contract rent: $134 per month (2005-2009 5-year est.); Median year structure built: before 1940 (2005-2009 5-year est.).

Transportation: Commute to work: 83.7% car, 2.0% public transportation, 5.9% walk, 7.2% work from home (2005-2009 5-year est.); Travel time to work: 28.9% less than 15 minutes, 28.2% 15 to 30 minutes, 16.9% 30 to 45

minutes, 7.0% 45 to 60 minutes, 19.0% 60 minutes or more (2005-2009 5-year est.)

WESTHOFF (unincorporated postal area, zip code 77994). Covers a land area of 69.855 square miles and a water area of 0.167 square miles. Located at 29.19° N. Lat; 97.47° W. Long. Elevation is 262 feet.

Population: 438 (2000); Race: 84.1% White, 6.5% Black, 0.0% Asian, 9.4% Other, 22.4% Hispanic of any race (2000); Density: 6.3 persons per square mile (2000); Age: 19.9% under 18, 27.4% over 64 (2000); Marriage status: 15.8% never married, 58.9% now married, 13.1% widowed, 12.2% divorced (2000); Foreign born: 3.2% (2000); Ancestry (includes multiple ancestries): 29.1% German, 5.5% Czech, 5.2% Irish, 4.7% American (2000).

Economy: Employment by occupation: 18.0% management, 14.8% professional, 18.0% services, 17.5% sales, 3.3% farming, 19.7% construction, 8.7% production (2000).

Income: Per capita income: $15,838 (2000); Median household income: $26,774 (2000); Poverty rate: 179.1% (2000).

Education: Percent of population age 25 and over with: High school diploma (including GED) or higher: 68.1% (2000); Bachelor's degree or higher: 13.2% (2000).

School District(s)

Westhoff ISD (PK-08)
   2009-10 Enrollment: 42 . . . . (830) 236-5519

Housing: Homeownership rate: 88.2% (2000); Median home value: $36,500 (2000); Median contract rent: $292 per month (2000); Median year structure built: 1952 (2000).

Transportation: Commute to work: 86.3% car, 0.0% public transportation, 6.6% walk, 6.0% work from home (2000); Travel time to work: 20.3% less than 15 minutes, 37.2% 15 to 30 minutes, 18.6% 30 to 45 minutes, 7.6% 45 to 60 minutes, 16.3% 60 minutes or more (2000)

YORKTOWN (city). Covers a land area of 1.723 square miles and a water area of 0 square miles. Located at 28.98° N. Lat; 97.50° W. Long. Elevation is 276 feet.

Population: 2,258 (1990); 2,271 (2000); 2,098 (2010); 2,020 (2015 projected); Race: 82.8% White, 2.7% Black, 0.0% Asian, 14.5% Other, 33.5% Hispanic of any race (2010); Density: 1,217.7 persons per square mile (2010); Average household size: 2.47 (2010); Median age: 42.9 (2010); Males per 100 females: 94.8 (2010); Marriage status: 25.6% never married, 55.7% now married, 8.9% widowed, 9.9% divorced (2005-2009 5-year est.); Foreign born: 4.7% (2005-2009 5-year est.); Ancestry (includes multiple ancestries): 35.5% German, 11.2% Irish, 10.9% Polish, 3.9% French, 3.5% Italian (2005-2009 5-year est.).

Economy: Single-family building permits issued: 1 (2010); Multi-family building permits issued: 0 (2010); Employment by occupation: 10.6% management, 15.2% professional, 14.9% services, 13.0% sales, 1.6% farming, 27.8% construction, 16.9% production (2005-2009 5-year est.).

Income: Per capita income: $19,356 (2010); Median household income: $36,966 (2010); Average household income: $48,729 (2010); Percent of households with income of $100,000 or more: 9.8% (2010); Poverty rate: 16.5% (2005-2009 5-year est.).

Taxes: Total city taxes per capita: $173 (2007); City property taxes per capita: $70 (2007).

Education: Percent of population age 25 and over with: High school diploma (including GED) or higher: 71.1% (2010); Bachelor's degree or higher: 12.2% (2010); Master's degree or higher: 4.5% (2010).

School District(s)

Yorktown ISD (PK-12)
   2009-10 Enrollment: 539 . . . . (361) 564-2252

Housing: Homeownership rate: 75.6% (2010); Median home value: $57,460 (2010); Median contract rent: $340 per month (2005-2009 5-year est.); Median year structure built: 1957 (2005-2009 5-year est.).

Safety: Violent crime rate: 23.3 per 10,000 population; Property crime rate: 139.9 per 10,000 population (2009).

Newspapers: Yorktown News-View (Local news; Circulation 2,800)

Transportation: Commute to work: 91.4% car, 0.0% public transportation, 2.7% walk, 2.5% work from home (2005-2009 5-year est.); Travel time to work: 46.5% less than 15 minutes, 17.9% 15 to 30 minutes, 12.1% 30 to 45 minutes, 11.9% 45 to 60 minutes, 11.5% 60 minutes or more (2005-2009 5-year est.)

Additional Information Contacts

Yorktown Chamber of Commerce . . . . (361) 564-2661
   http://www.yorktowntx.com/cofc-board.htm

Deaf Smith County

Located in north Texas, in the Panhandle; bounded on the west by New Mexico; drained by Palo Duro and Tierra Blanca Creeks. Covers a land area of 1,497.34 square miles, a water area of 0.92 square miles, and is located in the Central Time Zone at 34.89° N. Lat., 102.50° W. Long. The county was founded in 1876. County seat is Hereford.

Deaf Smith County is part of the Hereford, TX Micropolitan Statistical Area. The entire metro area includes: Deaf Smith County, TX

Weather Station: Hereford   Elevation: 3,819 feet

	Jan	Feb	Mar	Apr	May	Jun	Jul	Aug	Sep	Oct	Nov	Dec
High	51	55	63	72	80	89	92	90	83	72	60	50
Low	23	26	32	40	50	60	64	63	55	43	31	23
Precip	0.6	0.5	1.2	1.0	2.0	3.4	2.1	3.4	2.1	1.7	0.8	0.8
Snow	4.0	2.5	1.9	0.7	tr	0.0	0.0	0.0	0.0	0.2	2.1	4.4

High and Low temperatures in degrees Fahrenheit; Precipitation and Snow in inches

Population: 19,153 (1990); 18,561 (2000); 18,764 (2010); 18,829 (2015 projected); Race: 68.9% White, 1.6% Black, 0.3% Asian, 29.2% Other, 64.7% Hispanic of any race (2010); Density: 12.5 persons per square mile (2010); Average household size: 2.91 (2010); Median age: 31.7 (2010); Males per 100 females: 96.4 (2010).
Religion: Five largest groups: 40.3% Catholic Church, 22.1% Southern Baptist Convention, 9.1% The United Methodist Church, 4.1% Church of the Nazarene, 2.5% Churches of Christ (2000).
Economy: Unemployment rate: 6.4% (June 2011); Total civilian labor force: 9,204 (June 2011); Leading industries: 26.9% manufacturing; 15.3% retail trade; 9.8% health care and social assistance (2009); Farms: 637 totaling 945,814 acres (2007); Companies that employ 500 or more persons: 1 (2009); Companies that employ 100 to 499 persons: 4 (2009); Companies that employ less than 100 persons: 403 (2009); Black-owned businesses: n/a (2007); Hispanic-owned businesses: n/a (2007); Asian-owned businesses: n/a (2007); Women-owned businesses: 384 (2007); Retail sales per capita: $10,203 (2010). Single-family building permits issued: 1 (2010); Multi-family building permits issued: 0 (2010).
Income: Per capita income: $15,239 (2010); Median household income: $33,649 (2010); Average household income: $44,589 (2010); Percent of households with income of $100,000 or more: 6.9% (2010); Poverty rate: 19.3% (2009); Bankruptcy rate: 1.70% (2010).
Taxes: Total county taxes per capita: $325 (2007); County property taxes per capita: $224 (2007).
Education: Percent of population age 25 and over with: High school diploma (including GED) or higher: 66.7% (2010); Bachelor's degree or higher: 13.5% (2010); Master's degree or higher: 3.9% (2010).
Housing: Homeownership rate: 65.2% (2010); Median home value: $55,969 (2010); Median contract rent: $436 per month (2005-2009 5-year est.); Median year structure built: 1966 (2005-2009 5-year est.)
Health: Birth rate: 202.1 per 10,000 population (2009); Death rate: 79.0 per 10,000 population (2009); Age-adjusted cancer mortality rate: 171.1 deaths per 100,000 population (2007); Number of physicians: 5.4 per 10,000 population (2008); Hospital beds: 19.1 per 10,000 population (2007); Hospital admissions: 455.9 per 10,000 population (2007).
Elections: 2008 Presidential election results: 26.3% Obama, 73.1% McCain, 0.1% Nader
Additional Information Contacts
Deaf Smith County Government . . . . (806) 363-7000
  http://www.co.deaf-smith.tx.us/ips/cms
City of Hereford . . . . (806) 363-7100
  http://www.hereford-tx.gov
Deaf Smith County Chamber of Commerce . . . . (806) 364-3333
  http://www.herefordtx.org

Deaf Smith County Communities

HEREFORD (city). County seat. Covers a land area of 5.613 square miles and a water area of 0 square miles. Located at 34.82° N. Lat; 102.39° W. Long. Elevation is 3,816 feet.
History: Hereford was named for the cattle that formed the economic base of the community. Grain and vegetables were grown in Hereford after an irrigation project provided water. The Holly Sugar Company located a refinery here in 1964.
Population: 14,796 (1990); 14,597 (2000); 14,522 (2010); 14,489 (2015 projected); Race: 68.8% White, 1.8% Black, 0.3% Asian, 29.1% Other, 69.3% Hispanic of any race (2010); Density: 2,587.4 persons per square

mile (2010); Average household size: 2.91 (2010); Median age: 30.7 (2010); Males per 100 females: 94.8 (2010); Marriage status: 26.5% never married, 58.7% now married, 7.2% widowed, 7.6% divorced (2005-2009 5-year est.); Foreign born: 19.2% (2005-2009 5-year est.); Ancestry (includes multiple ancestries): 10.1% German, 6.0% Irish, 3.4% American, 3.2% English, 1.7% French (2005-2009 5-year est.).
Economy: Single-family building permits issued: 1 (2010); Multi-family building permits issued: 0 (2010); Employment by occupation: 8.5% management, 10.7% professional, 15.9% services, 26.0% sales, 5.5% farming, 12.8% construction, 20.5% production (2005-2009 5-year est.).
Income: Per capita income: $14,905 (2010); Median household income: $33,501 (2010); Average household income: $43,682 (2010); Percent of households with income of $100,000 or more: 6.5% (2010); Poverty rate: 18.7% (2005-2009 5-year est.).
Taxes: Total city taxes per capita: $157 (2007); City property taxes per capita: $87 (2007).
Education: Percent of population age 25 and over with: High school diploma (including GED) or higher: 66.3% (2010); Bachelor's degree or higher: 14.2% (2010); Master's degree or higher: 4.4% (2010).

School District(s)
Hereford ISD (PK-12)
  2009-10 Enrollment: 4,282 . . . . (806) 364-0606
Walcott ISD (PK-06)
  2009-10 Enrollment: 138 . . . . (806) 289-5222
Housing: Homeownership rate: 63.1% (2010); Median home value: $53,978 (2010); Median contract rent: $434 per month (2005-2009 5-year est.); Median year structure built: 1967 (2005-2009 5-year est.).
Hospitals: Hereford Regional Medical Center (40 beds)
Safety: Violent crime rate: 49.7 per 10,000 population; Property crime rate: 320.1 per 10,000 population (2010).
Newspapers: Hereford Brand (Local news; Circulation 3,700)
Transportation: Commute to work: 97.0% car, 0.8% public transportation, 0.7% walk, 1.3% work from home (2005-2009 5-year est.); Travel time to work: 61.5% less than 15 minutes, 18.4% 15 to 30 minutes, 11.5% 30 to 45 minutes, 5.1% 45 to 60 minutes, 3.6% 60 minutes or more (2005-2009 5-year est.)
Airports: Hereford Municipal (general aviation)
Additional Information Contacts
City of Hereford . . . . (806) 363-7100
  http://www.hereford-tx.gov
Deaf Smith County Chamber of Commerce . . . . (806) 364-3333
  http://www.herefordtx.org

Delta County

Located in northeastern Texas; bounded by the North and South Forks of the Sulphur River. Covers a land area of 277.08 square miles, a water area of 0.84 square miles, and is located in the Central Time Zone at 33.38° N. Lat., 95.71° W. Long. The county was founded in 1870. County seat is Cooper.

Delta County is part of the Dallas-Fort Worth-Arlington, TX Metropolitan Statistical Area. The entire metro area includes: Dallas-Plano-Irving, TX Metropolitan Division (Collin County, TX; Dallas County, TX; Delta County, TX; Denton County, TX; Ellis County, TX; Hunt County, TX; Kaufman County, TX; Rockwall County, TX); Fort Worth-Arlington, TX Metropolitan Division (Johnson County, TX; Parker County, TX; Tarrant County, TX; Wise County, TX)

Population: 4,857 (1990); 5,327 (2000); 5,470 (2010); 5,530 (2015 projected); Race: 86.7% White, 7.3% Black, 0.1% Asian, 5.9% Other, 6.1% Hispanic of any race (2010); Density: 19.7 persons per square mile (2010); Average household size: 2.50 (2010); Median age: 39.1 (2010); Males per 100 females: 95.9 (2010).
Religion: Five largest groups: 39.6% Southern Baptist Convention, 10.8% The United Methodist Church, 2.2% Churches of Christ, 1.7% Baptist Missionary Association of America, 0.9% Assemblies of God (2000).
Economy: Unemployment rate: 10.6% (June 2011); Total civilian labor force: 2,362 (June 2011); Leading industries: 65.5% health care and social assistance; 5.4% retail trade; 1.9% professional, scientific & technical services (2009); Farms: 538 totaling 132,841 acres (2007); Companies that employ 500 or more persons: 0 (2009); Companies that employ 100 to 499 persons: 1 (2009); Companies that employ less than 100 persons: 56 (2009); Black-owned businesses: n/a (2007); Hispanic-owned businesses: n/a (2007); Asian-owned businesses: n/a (2007); Women-owned businesses: n/a (2007); Retail sales per capita: $4,991 (2010).

Single-family building permits issued: 3 (2010); Multi-family building permits issued: 0 (2010).
Income: Per capita income: $18,828 (2010); Median household income: $36,065 (2010); Average household income: $47,313 (2010); Percent of households with income of $100,000 or more: 8.6% (2010); Poverty rate: 18.8% (2009); Bankruptcy rate: 3.04% (2010).
Taxes: Total county taxes per capita: $332 (2007); County property taxes per capita: $266 (2007).
Education: Percent of population age 25 and over with: High school diploma (including GED) or higher: 80.4% (2010); Bachelor's degree or higher: 15.6% (2010); Master's degree or higher: 6.0% (2010).
Housing: Homeownership rate: 75.5% (2010); Median home value: $57,150 (2010); Median contract rent: $369 per month (2005-2009 5-year est.); Median year structure built: 1968 (2005-2009 5-year est.)
Health: Birth rate: 114.6 per 10,000 population (2009); Death rate: 116.5 per 10,000 population (2009); Age-adjusted cancer mortality rate: 186.9 (Unreliable) deaths per 100,000 population (2007); Number of physicians: 1.8 per 10,000 population (2008); Hospital beds: 0.0 per 10,000 population (2007); Hospital admissions: 0.0 per 10,000 population (2007).
Elections: 2008 Presidential election results: 26.9% Obama, 72.2% McCain, 0.0% Nader
Additional Information Contacts
Delta County Government . . . . (903) 395-2211
    http://www.co.delta.tx.us/ips/cms
Delta County Chamber of Commerce . . . . (903) 395-4314
    http://www.deltacounty.org

Delta County Communities

BEN FRANKLIN (unincorporated postal area, zip code 75415). Covers a land area of 22.323 square miles and a water area of 0.048 square miles. Located at 33.46° N. Lat; 95.75° W. Long. Elevation is 486 feet.
Population: 214 (2000); Race: 72.9% White, 26.3% Black, 0.0% Asian, 0.8% Other, 0.0% Hispanic of any race (2000); Density: 9.6 persons per square mile (2000); Age: 23.5% under 18, 14.1% over 64 (2000); Marriage status: 22.5% never married, 62.0% now married, 8.0% widowed, 7.5% divorced (2000); Foreign born: 0.0% (2000); Ancestry (includes multiple ancestries): 18.0% Scotch-Irish, 9.0% English, 8.2% Irish, 4.7% American (2000).
Economy: Employment by occupation: 8.3% management, 10.0% professional, 16.7% services, 20.0% sales, 7.5% farming, 27.5% construction, 10.0% production (2000).
Income: Per capita income: $12,904 (2000); Median household income: $39,375 (2000); Poverty rate: 179.1% (2000).
Education: Percent of population age 25 and over with: High school diploma (including GED) or higher: 76.7% (2000); Bachelor's degree or higher: 7.6% (2000).
Housing: Homeownership rate: 93.9% (2000); Median home value: $46,000 (2000); Median contract rent: $263 per month (2000); Median year structure built: 1950 (2000).
Transportation: Commute to work: 90.0% car, 0.8% public transportation, 0.0% walk, 4.2% work from home (2000); Travel time to work: 20.0% less than 15 minutes, 57.4% 15 to 30 minutes, 12.2% 30 to 45 minutes, 7.0% 45 to 60 minutes, 3.5% 60 minutes or more (2000)

COOPER (city). County seat. Covers a land area of 1.438 square miles and a water area of 0.007 square miles. Located at 33.37° N. Lat; 95.68° W. Long. Elevation is 482 feet.
History: Settled in 1870s.
Population: 2,172 (1990); 2,150 (2000); 2,184 (2010); 2,195 (2015 projected); Race: 79.1% White, 13.8% Black, 0.0% Asian, 7.1% Other, 8.2% Hispanic of any race (2010); Density: 1,518.5 persons per square mile (2010); Average household size: 2.45 (2010); Median age: 36.8 (2010); Males per 100 females: 84.8 (2010); Marriage status: 31.1% never married, 51.4% now married, 9.0% widowed, 8.5% divorced (2005-2009 5-year est.); Foreign born: 4.0% (2005-2009 5-year est.); Ancestry (includes multiple ancestries): 20.4% American, 14.3% Irish, 8.4% English, 4.9% German, 4.1% French (2005-2009 5-year est.).
Economy: Single-family building permits issued: 3 (2010); Multi-family building permits issued: 0 (2010); Employment by occupation: 7.7% management, 16.1% professional, 21.1% services, 14.8% sales, 0.0% farming, 18.9% construction, 21.5% production (2005-2009 5-year est.).
Income: Per capita income: $16,786 (2010); Median household income: $27,698 (2010); Average household income: $41,395 (2010); Percent of

households with income of $100,000 or more: 6.4% (2010); Poverty rate: 20.8% (2005-2009 5-year est.).
Taxes: Total city taxes per capita: $274 (2007); City property taxes per capita: $185 (2007).
Education: Percent of population age 25 and over with: High school diploma (including GED) or higher: 75.6% (2010); Bachelor's degree or higher: 15.2% (2010); Master's degree or higher: 5.7% (2010).
School District(s)
Cooper ISD (PK-12)
    2009-10 Enrollment: 851 . . . . (903) 395-2112
Housing: Homeownership rate: 64.4% (2010); Median home value: $51,985 (2010); Median contract rent: $346 per month (2005-2009 5-year est.); Median year structure built: 1966 (2005-2009 5-year est.).
Newspapers: Review (Community news; Circulation 2,500)
Transportation: Commute to work: 89.3% car, 0.0% public transportation, 1.3% walk, 8.3% work from home (2005-2009 5-year est.); Travel time to work: 34.5% less than 15 minutes, 28.0% 15 to 30 minutes, 17.8% 30 to 45 minutes, 9.8% 45 to 60 minutes, 9.9% 60 minutes or more (2005-2009 5-year est.)
Additional Information Contacts
Delta County Chamber of Commerce . . . . (903) 395-4314
    http://www.deltacounty.org

KLONDIKE (unincorporated postal area, zip code 75448). Covers a land area of 49.423 square miles and a water area of 0.087 square miles. Located at 33.31° N. Lat; 95.81° W. Long. Elevation is 478 feet.
Population: 844 (2000); Race: 97.8% White, 0.0% Black, 0.0% Asian, 2.2% Other, 0.0% Hispanic of any race (2000); Density: 17.1 persons per square mile (2000); Age: 14.0% under 18, 23.0% over 64 (2000); Marriage status: 12.4% never married, 66.4% now married, 14.6% widowed, 6.7% divorced (2000); Foreign born: 0.0% (2000); Ancestry (includes multiple ancestries): 32.4% American, 13.4% Irish, 5.5% English, 3.0% Scottish (2000).
Economy: Employment by occupation: 14.4% management, 9.3% professional, 22.0% services, 19.2% sales, 0.6% farming, 12.5% construction, 22.0% production (2000).
Income: Per capita income: $18,609 (2000); Median household income: $26,597 (2000); Poverty rate: 179.1% (2000).
Education: Percent of population age 25 and over with: High school diploma (including GED) or higher: 82.5% (2000); Bachelor's degree or higher: 11.8% (2000).
Housing: Homeownership rate: 84.7% (2000); Median home value: $36,700 (2000); Median contract rent: $525 per month (2000); Median year structure built: 1969 (2000).
Transportation: Commute to work: 90.7% car, 0.0% public transportation, 0.0% walk, 6.0% work from home (2000); Travel time to work: 40.8% less than 15 minutes, 29.6% 15 to 30 minutes, 17.3% 30 to 45 minutes, 0.0% 45 to 60 minutes, 12.3% 60 minutes or more (2000)

LAKE CREEK (unincorporated postal area, zip code 75450). Covers a land area of 67.236 square miles and a water area of 0.447 square miles. Located at 33.40° N. Lat; 95.52° W. Long. Elevation is 443 feet.
Population: 464 (2000); Race: 86.7% White, 0.0% Black, 2.4% Asian, 10.9% Other, 0.0% Hispanic of any race (2000); Density: 6.9 persons per square mile (2000); Age: 21.9% under 18, 21.4% over 64 (2000); Marriage status: 17.7% never married, 71.2% now married, 3.1% widowed, 8.0% divorced (2000); Foreign born: 2.9% (2000); Ancestry (includes multiple ancestries): 23.9% American, 11.6% English, 6.7% Scotch-Irish, 4.3% Irish (2000).
Economy: Employment by occupation: 8.7% management, 16.9% professional, 18.6% services, 18.6% sales, 0.0% farming, 9.3% construction, 27.9% production (2000).
Income: Per capita income: $13,681 (2000); Median household income: $37,813 (2000); Poverty rate: 179.1% (2000).
Education: Percent of population age 25 and over with: High school diploma (including GED) or higher: 78.2% (2000); Bachelor's degree or higher: 11.1% (2000).
Housing: Homeownership rate: 87.1% (2000); Median home value: $39,100 (2000); Median contract rent: $275 per month (2000); Median year structure built: 1977 (2000).
Transportation: Commute to work: 83.7% car, 3.5% public transportation, 0.0% walk, 9.3% work from home (2000); Travel time to work: 11.5% less than 15 minutes, 38.5% 15 to 30 minutes, 14.7% 30 to 45 minutes, 18.6% 45 to 60 minutes, 16.7% 60 minutes or more (2000)

PECAN GAP (city). Covers a land area of 0.623 square miles and a water area of 0 square miles. Located at 33.43° N. Lat; 95.84° W. Long. Elevation is 571 feet.
Population: 256 (1990); 214 (2000); 219 (2010); 221 (2015 projected); Race: 90.9% White, 2.7% Black, 0.0% Asian, 6.4% Other, 7.3% Hispanic of any race (2010); Density: 351.6 persons per square mile (2010); Average household size: 2.46 (2010); Median age: 41.1 (2010); Males per 100 females: 104.7 (2010); Marriage status: 57.9% never married, 35.0% now married, 5.6% widowed, 1.5% divorced (2005-2009 5-year est.); Foreign born: 13.9% (2005-2009 5-year est.); Ancestry (includes multiple ancestries): 29.6% German, 19.0% Irish, 9.5% American, 4.4% English, 1.5% Scottish (2005-2009 5-year est.).
Economy: Employment by occupation: 0.0% management, 6.6% professional, 23.4% services, 13.9% sales, 0.0% farming, 27.7% construction, 28.5% production (2005-2009 5-year est.).
Income: Per capita income: $18,347 (2010); Median household income: $36,974 (2010); Average household income: $43,202 (2010); Percent of households with income of $100,000 or more: 6.7% (2010); Poverty rate: 25.9% (2005-2009 5-year est.).
Taxes: Total city taxes per capita: $94 (2007); City property taxes per capita: $22 (2007).
Education: Percent of population age 25 and over with: High school diploma (including GED) or higher: 85.4% (2010); Bachelor's degree or higher: 14.6% (2010); Master's degree or higher: 5.7% (2010).

School District(s)

Fannindel ISD (PK-12)
    2009-10 Enrollment: 196 . . . . (903) 367-7251
Housing: Homeownership rate: 83.1% (2010); Median home value: $51,429 (2010); Median contract rent: n/a per month (2005-2009 5-year est.); Median year structure built: 1961 (2005-2009 5-year est.).
Transportation: Commute to work: 82.2% car, 0.0% public transportation, 8.1% walk, 9.6% work from home (2005-2009 5-year est.); Travel time to work: 16.4% less than 15 minutes, 28.7% 15 to 30 minutes, 1.6% 30 to 45 minutes, 13.1% 45 to 60 minutes, 40.2% 60 minutes or more (2005-2009 5-year est.)

Denton County

Located in north Texas; drained by the Elm Fork of the Trinity River. Covers a land area of 888.54 square miles, a water area of 69.34 square miles, and is located in the Central Time Zone at 33.13° N. Lat., 97.06° W. Long. The county was founded in 1846. County seat is Denton.

Denton County is part of the Dallas-Fort Worth-Arlington, TX Metropolitan Statistical Area. The entire metro area includes: Dallas-Plano-Irving, TX Metropolitan Division (Collin County, TX; Dallas County, TX; Delta County, TX; Denton County, TX; Ellis County, TX; Hunt County, TX; Kaufman County, TX; Rockwall County, TX); Fort Worth-Arlington, TX Metropolitan Division (Johnson County, TX; Parker County, TX; Tarrant County, TX; Wise County, TX)

Weather Station: Denton 2 SE										Elevation: 629 feet		
	Jan	Feb	Mar	Apr	May	Jun	Jul	Aug	Sep	Oct	Nov	Dec
High	56	60	68	76	83	90	95	95	87	77	66	56
Low	35	38	46	53	62	70	74	73	66	55	45	36
Precip	2.1	2.8	3.2	3.2	5.4	3.7	2.3	2.1	3.1	4.8	2.9	2.5
Snow	0.1	0.2	0.1	0.0	0.0	0.0	0.0	0.0	0.0	0.0	tr	0.2

High and Low temperatures in degrees Fahrenheit; Precipitation and Snow in inches

Weather Station: Pilot Point										Elevation: 689 feet		
	Jan	Feb	Mar	Apr	May	Jun	Jul	Aug	Sep	Oct	Nov	Dec
High	54	59	67	76	83	90	97	97	89	78	65	56
Low	31	35	42	50	60	69	74	73	65	54	42	33
Precip	2.4	3.6	3.9	3.2	6.7	4.3	2.3	2.7	3.6	5.2	3.7	3.6
Snow	0.1	0.5	tr	0.0	0.0	0.0	0.0	0.0	0.0	0.0	tr	0.1

High and Low temperatures in degrees Fahrenheit; Precipitation and Snow in inches

Population: 274,173 (1990); 432,976 (2000); 672,413 (2010); 787,694 (2015 projected); Race: 74.5% White, 8.0% Black, 5.6% Asian, 11.8% Other, 17.6% Hispanic of any race (2010); Density: 756.8 persons per square mile (2010); Average household size: 2.71 (2010); Median age: 32.6 (2010); Males per 100 females: 100.2 (2010).
Religion: Five largest groups: 12.4% Southern Baptist Convention, 6.4% Catholic Church, 4.6% The United Methodist Church, 1.5% The Church of Jesus Christ of Latter-day Saints, 1.4% Assemblies of God (2000).

Economy: Unemployment rate: 7.9% (June 2011); Total civilian labor force: 362,725 (June 2011); Leading industries: 16.3% retail trade; 12.4% health care and social assistance; 12.4% accommodation & food services (2009); Farms: 2,575 totaling 350,274 acres (2007); Companies that employ 500 or more persons: 25 (2009); Companies that employ 100 to 499 persons: 232 (2009); Companies that employ less than 100 persons: 10,968 (2009); Black-owned businesses: 3,126 (2007); Hispanic-owned businesses: 5,076 (2007); Asian-owned businesses: 3,649 (2007); Women-owned businesses: 17,709 (2007); Retail sales per capita: $12,059 (2010). Single-family building permits issued: 1,495 (2010); Multi-family building permits issued: 601 (2010).
Income: Per capita income: $34,016 (2010); Median household income: $72,873 (2010); Average household income: $93,245 (2010); Percent of households with income of $100,000 or more: 33.2% (2010); Poverty rate: 8.7% (2009); Bankruptcy rate: 0.69% (2010).
Taxes: Total county taxes per capita: $181 (2007); County property taxes per capita: $168 (2007).
Education: Percent of population age 25 and over with: High school diploma (including GED) or higher: 89.9% (2010); Bachelor's degree or higher: 37.9% (2010); Master's degree or higher: 11.0% (2010).
Housing: Homeownership rate: 66.9% (2010); Median home value: $172,797 (2010); Median contract rent: $713 per month (2005-2009 5-year est.); Median year structure built: 1992 (2005-2009 5-year est.)
Health: Birth rate: 156.9 per 10,000 population (2009); Death rate: 39.2 per 10,000 population (2009); Age-adjusted cancer mortality rate: 179.3 deaths per 100,000 population (2007); Number of physicians: 17.7 per 10,000 population (2008); Hospital beds: 15.6 per 10,000 population (2007); Hospital admissions: 659.1 per 10,000 population (2007).
Environment: Air Quality Index: 70.8% good, 25.9% moderate, 3.3% unhealthy for sensitive individuals, 0.0% unhealthy (percent of days in 2008)
Elections: 2008 Presidential election results: 37.5% Obama, 61.6% McCain, 0.1% Nader

Additional Information Contacts

Denton County Government . . . . (972) 349-2820
   http://www.co.denton.tx.us
Aubrey Chamber of Commerce . . . . (940) 365-9781
   http://aubreycoc.org
City of Argyle . . . . (940) 464-7273
   http://www.argyletx.com
City of Carrollton . . . . (972) 466-3000
   http://www.cityofcarrollton.com
City of Corinth . . . . (940) 498-3200
   http://cityofcorinth.com
City of Denton . . . . (940) 349-8200
   http://www.cityofdenton.com
City of Highland Village . . . . (972) 899-5131
   http://www.highlandvillage.org
City of Krum . . . . (940) 482-3491
   http://www.ci.krum.tx.us
City of Lake Dallas . . . . (940) 497-2226
   http://www.lakedallas.com
City of Lewisville . . . . (972) 219-3400
   http://www.cityoflewisville.com
City of The Colony . . . . (972) 625-1756
   http://www.ci.the-colony.tx.us
Denton Black Chamber of Commerce . . . . (940) 391-1536
   http://dentonblackchamberonline.org
Denton Chamber of Commerce . . . . (940) 382-9693
   http://www.denton-chamber.org
Denton Hispanic Chamber of Commerce . . . . (940) 565-1919
   http://dentonhispanicchamber.org
Flower Mound Chamber of Commerce . . . . (972) 539-0500
   http://www.flowermoundchamber.com
Lake Cities Chamber of Commerce . . . . (940) 497-3097
   http://www.lakecitieschamber.com
Little Elm Chamber of Commerce . . . . (972) 292-3777
   http://www.littleelmchamber.org
Metrocrest Chamber of Commerce . . . . (469) 587-0420
   http://www.metrocrestchamber.com
Sanger Area Chamber of Commerce . . . . (940) 458-7702
   http://www.sangertexas.com
The Colony Chamber of Commerce . . . . (214) 705-3075
   http://www.thecolonychamber.com
Town of Bartonville . . . . (817) 430-4052
   http://townofbartonville.com

Town of Double Oak . . . . (972) 539-9464
   http://www.double-oak.com
Town of Flower Mound . . . . (972) 874-6076
   http://www.flower-mound.com
Town of Shady Shores. . . . . (940) 498-0044
   http://www.shady-shores.com
Town of Trophy Club . . . . (682) 831-4600
   http://www.trophyclub.org

Denton County Communities

ARGYLE (city). Covers a land area of 11.139 square miles and a water area of 0.008 square miles. Located at 33.11° N. Lat; 97.18° W. Long. Elevation is 699 feet.

Population: 1,729 (1990); 2,365 (2000); 3,938 (2010); 4,735 (2015 projected); Race: 91.6% White, 1.0% Black, 0.4% Asian, 7.0% Other, 8.5% Hispanic of any race (2010); Density: 353.5 persons per square mile (2010); Average household size: 2.93 (2010); Median age: 38.7 (2010); Males per 100 females: 99.9 (2010); Marriage status: 21.9% never married, 67.2% now married, 1.3% widowed, 9.6% divorced (2005-2009 5-year est.); Foreign born: 2.6% (2005-2009 5-year est.); Ancestry (includes multiple ancestries): 22.2% German, 18.8% Irish, 15.1% English, 9.1% Scottish, 5.3% American (2005-2009 5-year est.).

Economy: Single-family building permits issued: 16 (2010); Multi-family building permits issued: 0 (2010); Employment by occupation: 17.0% management, 20.2% professional, 15.8% services, 32.1% sales, 1.4% farming, 6.3% construction, 7.2% production (2005-2009 5-year est.).

Income: Per capita income: $44,662 (2010); Median household income: $101,150 (2010); Average household income: $130,604 (2010); Percent of households with income of $100,000 or more: 50.6% (2010); Poverty rate: 5.6% (2005-2009 5-year est.).

Taxes: Total city taxes per capita: $612 (2007); City property taxes per capita: $388 (2007).

Education: Percent of population age 25 and over with: High school diploma (including GED) or higher: 94.4% (2010); Bachelor's degree or higher: 44.9% (2010); Master's degree or higher: 14.3% (2010).

School District(s)
Argyle ISD (PK-12)
   2009-10 Enrollment: 1,790 . . . . (940) 464-7241
Denton ISD (PK-12)
   2009-10 Enrollment: 22,825 . . . . (940) 369-0000

Housing: Homeownership rate: 89.4% (2010); Median home value: $304,582 (2010); Median contract rent: $1,650 per month (2005-2009 5-year est.); Median year structure built: 1992 (2005-2009 5-year est.).

Safety: Violent crime rate: 2.7 per 10,000 population; Property crime rate: 65.2 per 10,000 population (2009).

Transportation: Commute to work: 89.5% car, 0.4% public transportation, 1.4% walk, 7.8% work from home (2005-2009 5-year est.); Travel time to work: 17.1% less than 15 minutes, 35.0% 15 to 30 minutes, 23.1% 30 to 45 minutes, 15.2% 45 to 60 minutes, 9.6% 60 minutes or more (2005-2009 5-year est.)

Additional Information Contacts
City of Argyle . . . . (940) 464-7273
   http://www.argyletx.com

AUBREY (city). Covers a land area of 2.082 square miles and a water area of 0 square miles. Located at 33.30° N. Lat; 96.98° W. Long. Elevation is 689 feet.

Population: 1,267 (1990); 1,500 (2000); 2,321 (2010); 2,794 (2015 projected); Race: 91.2% White, 1.6% Black, 0.4% Asian, 6.8% Other, 7.2% Hispanic of any race (2010); Density: 1,114.6 persons per square mile (2010); Average household size: 2.73 (2010); Median age: 35.6 (2010); Males per 100 females: 97.0 (2010); Marriage status: 22.5% never married, 54.0% now married, 5.8% widowed, 17.7% divorced (2005-2009 5-year est.); Foreign born: 1.3% (2005-2009 5-year est.); Ancestry (includes multiple ancestries): 16.3% American, 13.7% Irish, 13.0% German, 10.7% English, 3.9% Dutch (2005-2009 5-year est.).

Economy: Single-family building permits issued: 9 (2010); Multi-family building permits issued: 0 (2010); Employment by occupation: 13.2% management, 13.8% professional, 17.3% services, 27.6% sales, 0.4% farming, 16.5% construction, 11.2% production (2005-2009 5-year est.).

Income: Per capita income: $30,990 (2010); Median household income: $66,307 (2010); Average household income: $84,480 (2010); Percent of households with income of $100,000 or more: 26.1% (2010); Poverty rate: 8.7% (2005-2009 5-year est.).

Taxes: Total city taxes per capita: $387 (2007); City property taxes per capita: $232 (2007).

Education: Percent of population age 25 and over with: High school diploma (including GED) or higher: 87.1% (2010); Bachelor's degree or higher: 23.5% (2010); Master's degree or higher: 6.9% (2010).

School District(s)
Aubrey ISD (PK-12)
   2009-10 Enrollment: 1,784 . . . . (940) 668-0060
Denton ISD (PK-12)
   2009-10 Enrollment: 22,825 . . . . (940) 369-0000
Education Center (KG-12)
   2009-10 Enrollment: 765 . . . . (972) 292-2405

Housing: Homeownership rate: 83.3% (2010); Median home value: $154,433 (2010); Median contract rent: $659 per month (2005-2009 5-year est.); Median year structure built: 1982 (2005-2009 5-year est.).

Transportation: Commute to work: 93.0% car, 0.3% public transportation, 2.8% walk, 3.2% work from home (2005-2009 5-year est.); Travel time to work: 22.6% less than 15 minutes, 35.3% 15 to 30 minutes, 20.8% 30 to 45 minutes, 7.0% 45 to 60 minutes, 14.3% 60 minutes or more (2005-2009 5-year est.)

Additional Information Contacts
Aubrey Chamber of Commerce . . . . (940) 365-9781
   http://aubreycoc.org

BARTONVILLE (town). Covers a land area of 6.030 square miles and a water area of 0.021 square miles. Located at 33.07° N. Lat; 97.15° W. Long. Elevation is 640 feet.

Population: 852 (1990); 1,093 (2000); 1,358 (2010); 1,602 (2015 projected); Race: 86.4% White, 0.4% Black, 1.5% Asian, 11.7% Other, 16.9% Hispanic of any race (2010); Density: 225.2 persons per square mile (2010); Average household size: 2.82 (2010); Median age: 39.9 (2010); Males per 100 females: 103.3 (2010); Marriage status: 20.7% never married, 56.7% now married, 5.4% widowed, 17.2% divorced (2005-2009 5-year est.); Foreign born: 6.7% (2005-2009 5-year est.); Ancestry (includes multiple ancestries): 17.7% German, 17.0% English, 14.5% American, 9.7% Irish, 5.9% Italian (2005-2009 5-year est.).

Economy: Single-family building permits issued: 5 (2010); Multi-family building permits issued: 0 (2010); Employment by occupation: 15.3% management, 20.4% professional, 13.0% services, 39.3% sales, 0.3% farming, 8.4% construction, 3.2% production (2005-2009 5-year est.).

Income: Per capita income: $53,148 (2010); Median household income: $111,890 (2010); Average household income: $151,076 (2010); Percent of households with income of $100,000 or more: 54.1% (2010); Poverty rate: 2.8% (2005-2009 5-year est.).

Taxes: Total city taxes per capita: $408 (2007); City property taxes per capita: $189 (2007).

Education: Percent of population age 25 and over with: High school diploma (including GED) or higher: 91.2% (2010); Bachelor's degree or higher: 40.5% (2010); Master's degree or higher: 9.7% (2010).

Housing: Homeownership rate: 86.7% (2010); Median home value: $292,949 (2010); Median contract rent: $781 per month (2005-2009 5-year est.); Median year structure built: 1988 (2005-2009 5-year est.).

Transportation: Commute to work: 89.2% car, 0.0% public transportation, 0.3% walk, 7.0% work from home (2005-2009 5-year est.); Travel time to work: 14.6% less than 15 minutes, 31.1% 15 to 30 minutes, 23.1% 30 to 45 minutes, 16.3% 45 to 60 minutes, 14.8% 60 minutes or more (2005-2009 5-year est.)

Additional Information Contacts
Town of Bartonville . . . . (817) 430-4052
   http://townofbartonville.com

CARROLLTON (city). Covers a land area of 36.469 square miles and a water area of 0.176 square miles. Located at 32.99° N. Lat; 96.89° W. Long.

Population: 82,359 (1990); 109,576 (2000); 128,767 (2010); 140,963 (2015 projected); Race: 60.3% White, 9.1% Black, 15.0% Asian, 15.6% Other, 27.6% Hispanic of any race (2010); Density: 3,530.9 persons per square mile (2010); Average household size: 2.82 (2010); Median age: 35.1 (2010); Males per 100 females: 99.8 (2010); Marriage status: 29.1% never married, 57.6% now married, 3.5% widowed, 9.8% divorced (2005-2009 5-year est.); Foreign born: 24.4% (2005-2009 5-year est.); Ancestry (includes multiple ancestries): 12.7% German, 10.0% Irish, 9.7% English, 5.5% American, 2.8% French (2005-2009 5-year est.).

Economy: Unemployment rate: 7.4% (June 2011); Total civilian labor force: 72,439 (June 2011); Employment by occupation: 18.5%

management, 19.2% professional, 13.2% services, 29.4% sales, 0.0% farming, 8.5% construction, 11.2% production (2005-2009 5-year est.).
Income: Per capita income: $30,654 (2010); Median household income: $70,349 (2010); Average household income: $86,457 (2010); Percent of households with income of $100,000 or more: 29.6% (2010); Poverty rate: 8.2% (2005-2009 5-year est.).
Taxes: Total city taxes per capita: $686 (2007); City property taxes per capita: $421 (2007).
Education: Percent of population age 25 and over with: High school diploma (including GED) or higher: 86.5% (2010); Bachelor's degree or higher: 37.6% (2010); Master's degree or higher: 10.3% (2010).

School District(s)
Carrollton-Farmers Branch ISD (PK-12)
   2009-10 Enrollment: 25,920 . . . . (972) 968-6100
Dallas ISD (PK-12)
   2009-10 Enrollment: 157,111 . . . . (972) 925-3700
Harmony Science Academy (Fort Worth) (KG-11)
   2009-10 Enrollment: 1,948 . . . . (817) 263-0700
Lewisville ISD (PK-12)
   2009-10 Enrollment: 50,840 . . . . (469) 713-5200
Responsive Education Solutions (KG-12)
   2009-10 Enrollment: 5,022 . . . . (972) 316-3663

Vocational/Technical School(s)
Cosmetology Career Center LLC (Private, For-profit)
   Fall 2009 Enrollment: 331 . . . . (972) 669-0494
   2010-11 Tuition: $17,000
Toni & Guy Hairdressing Academy (Private, For-profit)
   Fall 2009 Enrollment: 152 . . . . (972) 416-8396
   2010-11 Tuition: $15,000
Housing: Homeownership rate: 65.9% (2010); Median home value: $164,752 (2010); Median contract rent: $756 per month (2005-2009 5-year est.); Median year structure built: 1985 (2005-2009 5-year est.).
Hospitals: Regency Hospital of North Dallas; Trinity Medical Center (149 beds)
Safety: Violent crime rate: 19.6 per 10,000 population; Property crime rate: 318.7 per 10,000 population (2009).
Newspapers: El Sol De Texas (Local news; Circulation 25,000)
Transportation: Commute to work: 91.9% car, 0.9% public transportation, 1.8% walk, 4.0% work from home (2005-2009 5-year est.); Travel time to work: 21.7% less than 15 minutes, 43.6% 15 to 30 minutes, 25.5% 30 to 45 minutes, 5.8% 45 to 60 minutes, 3.4% 60 minutes or more (2005-2009 5-year est.)

Additional Information Contacts
City of Carrollton . . . . (972) 466-3000
   http://www.cityofcarrollton.com
Metrocrest Chamber of Commerce . . . . (469) 587-0420
   http://www.metrocrestchamber.com

COPPER CANYON (town). Covers a land area of 4.455 square miles and a water area of 0.009 square miles. Located at 33.09° N. Lat; 97.09° W. Long. Elevation is 623 feet.
Population: 1,074 (1990); 1,216 (2000); 1,053 (2010); 1,251 (2015 projected); Race: 94.3% White, 1.3% Black, 1.2% Asian, 3.1% Other, 6.2% Hispanic of any race (2010); Density: 236.4 persons per square mile (2010); Average household size: 3.03 (2010); Median age: 37.8 (2010); Males per 100 females: 99.4 (2010); Marriage status: 20.8% never married, 64.9% now married, 4.5% widowed, 9.8% divorced (2005-2009 5-year est.); Foreign born: 3.2% (2005-2009 5-year est.); Ancestry (includes multiple ancestries): 20.7% German, 15.9% English, 12.3% Irish, 9.2% French, 7.3% American (2005-2009 5-year est.).
Economy: Single-family building permits issued: 3 (2010); Multi-family building permits issued: 0 (2010); Employment by occupation: 31.1% management, 21.3% professional, 7.9% services, 29.5% sales, 0.0% farming, 4.7% construction, 5.5% production (2005-2009 5-year est.).
Income: Per capita income: $55,199 (2010); Median household income: $127,976 (2010); Average household income: $167,277 (2010); Percent of households with income of $100,000 or more: 66.7% (2010); Poverty rate: 1.8% (2005-2009 5-year est.).
Taxes: Total city taxes per capita: $348 (2007); City property taxes per capita: $170 (2007).
Education: Percent of population age 25 and over with: High school diploma (including GED) or higher: 96.9% (2010); Bachelor's degree or higher: 54.4% (2010); Master's degree or higher: 14.9% (2010).

Housing: Homeownership rate: 94.5% (2010); Median home value: $304,023 (2010); Median contract rent: $763 per month (2005-2009 5-year est.); Median year structure built: 1986 (2005-2009 5-year est.).
Transportation: Commute to work: 86.6% car, 0.0% public transportation, 2.7% walk, 6.5% work from home (2005-2009 5-year est.); Travel time to work: 17.2% less than 15 minutes, 34.9% 15 to 30 minutes, 25.7% 30 to 45 minutes, 16.8% 45 to 60 minutes, 5.4% 60 minutes or more (2005-2009 5-year est.)

CORINTH (city). Covers a land area of 7.858 square miles and a water area of 0.045 square miles. Located at 33.14° N. Lat; 97.07° W. Long. Elevation is 607 feet.
Population: 3,982 (1990); 11,325 (2000); 21,441 (2010); 26,054 (2015 projected); Race: 80.2% White, 9.2% Black, 3.9% Asian, 6.7% Other, 10.2% Hispanic of any race (2010); Density: 2,728.7 persons per square mile (2010); Average household size: 2.99 (2010); Median age: 33.2 (2010); Males per 100 females: 99.4 (2010); Marriage status: 23.0% never married, 64.6% now married, 4.1% widowed, 8.2% divorced (2005-2009 5-year est.); Foreign born: 5.3% (2005-2009 5-year est.); Ancestry (includes multiple ancestries): 23.3% German, 15.9% English, 13.6% Irish, 7.3% American, 3.9% Italian (2005-2009 5-year est.).
Economy: Single-family building permits issued: 40 (2010); Multi-family building permits issued: 0 (2010); Employment by occupation: 24.7% management, 23.2% professional, 8.3% services, 28.2% sales, 0.0% farming, 7.8% construction, 7.8% production (2005-2009 5-year est.).
Income: Per capita income: $38,288 (2010); Median household income: $98,642 (2010); Average household income: $114,410 (2010); Percent of households with income of $100,000 or more: 48.7% (2010); Poverty rate: 2.2% (2005-2009 5-year est.).
Taxes: Total city taxes per capita: $536 (2007); City property taxes per capita: $372 (2007).
Education: Percent of population age 25 and over with: High school diploma (including GED) or higher: 95.5% (2010); Bachelor's degree or higher: 37.8% (2010); Master's degree or higher: 10.8% (2010).

School District(s)
Denton ISD (PK-12)
   2009-10 Enrollment: 22,825 . . . . (940) 369-0000
Lake Dallas ISD (PK-12)
   2009-10 Enrollment: 4,090 . . . . (940) 497-4039
Housing: Homeownership rate: 93.7% (2010); Median home value: $180,362 (2010); Median contract rent: $930 per month (2005-2009 5-year est.); Median year structure built: 1998 (2005-2009 5-year est.).
Safety: Violent crime rate: 13.1 per 10,000 population; Property crime rate: 137.2 per 10,000 population (2009).
Transportation: Commute to work: 91.7% car, 0.4% public transportation, 1.8% walk, 4.5% work from home (2005-2009 5-year est.); Travel time to work: 18.3% less than 15 minutes, 26.6% 15 to 30 minutes, 29.0% 30 to 45 minutes, 16.0% 45 to 60 minutes, 10.0% 60 minutes or more (2005-2009 5-year est.)

Additional Information Contacts
City of Corinth . . . . (940) 498-3200
   http://cityofcorinth.com
Lake Cities Chamber of Commerce . . . . (940) 497-3097
   http://www.lakecitieschamber.com

CORRAL CITY (town). Covers a land area of 0.044 square miles and a water area of 0 square miles. Located at 33.10° N. Lat; 97.22° W. Long. Elevation is 692 feet.
Population: 46 (1990); 89 (2000); 200 (2010); 240 (2015 projected); Race: 92.5% White, 1.0% Black, 0.0% Asian, 6.5% Other, 5.5% Hispanic of any race (2010); Density: 4,544.8 persons per square mile (2010); Average household size: 2.80 (2010); Median age: 34.7 (2010); Males per 100 females: 96.1 (2010); Marriage status: 11.5% never married, 36.5% now married, 0.0% widowed, 51.9% divorced (2005-2009 5-year est.); Foreign born: 0.0% (2005-2009 5-year est.); Ancestry (includes multiple ancestries): 43.9% English, 10.5% American, 1.8% Polish (2005-2009 5-year est.).
Economy: Employment by occupation: 5.1% management, 35.9% professional, 2.6% services, 17.9% sales, 0.0% farming, 33.3% construction, 5.1% production (2005-2009 5-year est.).
Income: Per capita income: $33,402 (2010); Median household income: $74,038 (2010); Average household income: $87,359 (2010); Percent of households with income of $100,000 or more: 31.0% (2010); Poverty rate: 0.0% (2005-2009 5-year est.).

Taxes: Total city taxes per capita: $1,029 (2007); City property taxes per capita: $0 (2007).

Education: Percent of population age 25 and over with: High school diploma (including GED) or higher: 88.4% (2010); Bachelor's degree or higher: 22.5% (2010); Master's degree or higher: 8.5% (2010).

Housing: Homeownership rate: 80.3% (2010); Median home value: $167,500 (2010); Median contract rent: $379 per month (2005-2009 5-year est.); Median year structure built: 2001 (2005-2009 5-year est.).

Transportation: Commute to work: 94.9% car, 0.0% public transportation, 5.1% walk, 0.0% work from home (2005-2009 5-year est.); Travel time to work: 12.8% less than 15 minutes, 28.2% 15 to 30 minutes, 53.8% 30 to 45 minutes, 0.0% 45 to 60 minutes, 5.1% 60 minutes or more (2005-2009 5-year est.)

CROSS ROADS (town). Aka New Hope. Covers a land area of 6.877 square miles and a water area of 0 square miles. Located at 33.23° N. Lat; 97.00° W. Long.

Population: 391 (1990); 603 (2000); 984 (2010); 1,185 (2015 projected); Race: 89.7% White, 1.6% Black, 0.5% Asian, 8.1% Other, 9.6% Hispanic of any race (2010); Density: 143.1 persons per square mile (2010); Average household size: 2.78 (2010); Median age: 37.5 (2010); Males per 100 females: 100.4 (2010); Marriage status: 12.4% never married, 75.6% now married, 1.0% widowed, 11.0% divorced (2005-2009 5-year est.); Foreign born: 2.7% (2005-2009 5-year est.); Ancestry (includes multiple ancestries): 24.1% German, 16.3% Irish, 12.0% English, 8.2% French, 7.8% Scottish (2005-2009 5-year est.).

Economy: Employment by occupation: 19.2% management, 29.4% professional, 9.3% services, 31.0% sales, 0.9% farming, 7.7% construction, 2.5% production (2005-2009 5-year est.).

Income: Per capita income: $41,148 (2010); Median household income: $82,813 (2010); Average household income: $113,475 (2010); Percent of households with income of $100,000 or more: 40.7% (2010); Poverty rate: 2.2% (2005-2009 5-year est.).

Taxes: Total city taxes per capita: $174 (2007); City property taxes per capita: $94 (2007).

Education: Percent of population age 25 and over with: High school diploma (including GED) or higher: 87.8% (2010); Bachelor's degree or higher: 26.9% (2010); Master's degree or higher: 7.7% (2010).

Housing: Homeownership rate: 85.6% (2010); Median home value: $199,375 (2010); Median contract rent: $1,000 per month (2005-2009 5-year est.); Median year structure built: 2001 (2005-2009 5-year est.).

Transportation: Commute to work: 95.1% car, 0.0% public transportation, 0.0% walk, 4.5% work from home (2005-2009 5-year est.); Travel time to work: 18.3% less than 15 minutes, 24.8% 15 to 30 minutes, 19.4% 30 to 45 minutes, 19.8% 45 to 60 minutes, 17.7% 60 minutes or more (2005-2009 5-year est.)

DENTON (city). County seat. Covers a land area of 61.494 square miles and a water area of 0.831 square miles. Located at 33.21° N. Lat; 97.12° W. Long. Elevation is 659 feet.

History: Named for John B. Denton (1806-1841), military officer. Denton Normal School, which became North Texas State University, was opened in 1890 in Denton. It was joined by Texas Woman's University, formerly the State College for Women, and the Texas Agricultural Experiment Station, a part of the Texas A&M University system.

Population: 65,296 (1990); 80,537 (2000); 117,420 (2010); 137,087 (2015 projected); Race: 68.5% White, 10.3% Black, 4.1% Asian, 17.1% Other, 24.2% Hispanic of any race (2010); Density: 1,909.4 persons per square mile (2010); Average household size: 2.40 (2010); Median age: 30.3 (2010); Males per 100 females: 99.0 (2010); Marriage status: 45.3% never married, 40.6% now married, 3.9% widowed, 10.2% divorced (2005-2009 5-year est.); Foreign born: 12.0% (2005-2009 5-year est.); Ancestry (includes multiple ancestries): 16.8% German, 11.7% Irish, 10.6% English, 4.9% American, 2.8% Italian (2005-2009 5-year est.).

Economy: Unemployment rate: 7.4% (June 2011); Total civilian labor force: 65,713 (June 2011); Single-family building permits issued: 381 (2010); Multi-family building permits issued: 477 (2010); Employment by occupation: 12.1% management, 22.3% professional, 21.4% services, 26.2% sales, 0.1% farming, 7.4% construction, 10.5% production (2005-2009 5-year est.).

Income: Per capita income: $24,302 (2010); Median household income: $44,680 (2010); Average household income: $61,693 (2010); Percent of households with income of $100,000 or more: 16.2% (2010); Poverty rate: 18.5% (2005-2009 5-year est.).

Taxes: Total city taxes per capita: $684 (2007); City property taxes per capita: $274 (2007).

Education: Percent of population age 25 and over with: High school diploma (including GED) or higher: 84.0% (2010); Bachelor's degree or higher: 36.2% (2010); Master's degree or higher: 14.3% (2010).

School District(s)

Carrollton-Farmers Branch ISD (PK-12)
2009-10 Enrollment: 25,920 . . . . (972) 968-6100
Denton ISD (PK-12)
2009-10 Enrollment: 22,825 . . . . (940) 369-0000
Education Center (KG-12)
2009-10 Enrollment: 765 . . . . (972) 292-2405
Krum ISD (PK-12)
2009-10 Enrollment: 1,613 . . . . (940) 482-6000
Lake Dallas ISD (PK-12)
2009-10 Enrollment: 4,090 . . . . (940) 497-4039
Lewisville ISD (PK-12)
2009-10 Enrollment: 50,840 . . . . (469) 713-5200
Ponder ISD (PK-12)
2009-10 Enrollment: 1,233 . . . . (940) 479-8200
Sanger ISD (PK-12)
2009-10 Enrollment: 2,594 . . . . (940) 458-7438
The Legends Academy (07-10)
2009-10 Enrollment: 33 . . . . (940) 387-6021
Trinity Charter School (KG-12)
2009-10 Enrollment: 277 . . . . (512) 706-7564
Winfree Academy Charter Schools (09-12)
2009-10 Enrollment: 1,862 . . . . (972) 869-3250

Four-year College(s)

Texas Woman's University (Public)
Fall 2009 Enrollment: 13,338 . . . . (940) 898-2000
2010-11 Tuition: In-state $5,428; Out-of-state $12,868
University of North Texas (Public)
Fall 2009 Enrollment: 35,003 . . . . (940) 565-2000
2010-11 Tuition: In-state $7,306; Out-of-state $14,746

Housing: Homeownership rate: 45.5% (2010); Median home value: $126,228 (2010); Median contract rent: $642 per month (2005-2009 5-year est.); Median year structure built: 1986 (2005-2009 5-year est.).

Hospitals: Denton Regional Medical Center (200 beds)

Safety: Violent crime rate: 24.6 per 10,000 population; Property crime rate: 263.1 per 10,000 population (2009).

Newspapers: Denton Record-Chronicle (Local news; Circulation 17,500); La Crónica (Local news; Circulation 5,000)

Transportation: Commute to work: 87.3% car, 1.1% public transportation, 4.7% walk, 4.0% work from home (2005-2009 5-year est.); Travel time to work: 37.8% less than 15 minutes, 30.3% 15 to 30 minutes, 13.8% 30 to 45 minutes, 9.8% 45 to 60 minutes, 8.2% 60 minutes or more (2005-2009 5-year est.)

Airports: Denton Municipal (general aviation)

Additional Information Contacts

City of Denton . . . . (940) 349-8200
http://www.cityofdenton.com
Denton Black Chamber of Commerce . . . . (940) 391-1536
http://dentonblackchamberonline.org
Denton Chamber of Commerce . . . . (940) 382-9693
http://www.denton-chamber.org
Denton Hispanic Chamber of Commerce . . . . (940) 565-1919
http://dentonhispanicchamber.org

DOUBLE OAK (town). Covers a land area of 2.176 square miles and a water area of 0.005 square miles. Located at 33.06° N. Lat; 97.11° W. Long. Elevation is 659 feet.

Population: 1,710 (1990); 2,179 (2000); 3,144 (2010); 3,710 (2015 projected); Race: 92.5% White, 1.8% Black, 1.1% Asian, 4.6% Other, 5.7% Hispanic of any race (2010); Density: 1,444.9 persons per square mile (2010); Average household size: 3.22 (2010); Median age: 38.0 (2010); Males per 100 females: 97.5 (2010); Marriage status: 16.1% never married, 77.8% now married, 3.3% widowed, 2.9% divorced (2005-2009 5-year est.); Foreign born: 1.9% (2005-2009 5-year est.); Ancestry (includes multiple ancestries): 26.9% German, 21.9% Irish, 17.6% English, 8.2% Norwegian, 7.6% Scottish (2005-2009 5-year est.).

Economy: Single-family building permits issued: 4 (2010); Multi-family building permits issued: 0 (2010); Employment by occupation: 24.5% management, 23.3% professional, 14.3% services, 34.3% sales, 0.0% farming, 1.2% construction, 2.4% production (2005-2009 5-year est.).

Income: Per capita income: $53,723 (2010); Median household income: $145,551 (2010); Average household income: $173,529 (2010); Percent of households with income of $100,000 or more: 71.9% (2010); Poverty rate: 0.4% (2005-2009 5-year est.).

Taxes: Total city taxes per capita: $359 (2007); City property taxes per capita: $262 (2007).

Education: Percent of population age 25 and over with: High school diploma (including GED) or higher: 96.7% (2010); Bachelor's degree or higher: 53.3% (2010); Master's degree or higher: 17.5% (2010).

Housing: Homeownership rate: 97.5% (2010); Median home value: $344,578 (2010); Median contract rent: $1,708 per month (2005-2009 5-year est.); Median year structure built: 1988 (2005-2009 5-year est.).

Safety: Violent crime rate: 8.8 per 10,000 population; Property crime rate: 46.7 per 10,000 population (2009).

Transportation: Commute to work: 87.2% car, 0.0% public transportation, 0.2% walk, 11.6% work from home (2005-2009 5-year est.); Travel time to work: 16.8% less than 15 minutes, 31.5% 15 to 30 minutes, 34.6% 30 to 45 minutes, 12.4% 45 to 60 minutes, 4.7% 60 minutes or more (2005-2009 5-year est.)

Additional Information Contacts

Town of Double Oak . . . . (972) 539-9464
  http://www.double-oak.com

FLOWER MOUND (town). Covers a land area of 40.875 square miles and a water area of 2.499 square miles. Located at 33.03° N. Lat; 97.07° W. Long. Elevation is 604 feet.

Population: 15,788 (1990); 50,702 (2000); 72,350 (2010); 86,064 (2015 projected); Race: 84.9% White, 5.0% Black, 5.3% Asian, 4.8% Other, 7.7% Hispanic of any race (2010); Density: 1,770.0 persons per square mile (2010); Average household size: 3.15 (2010); Median age: 33.3 (2010); Males per 100 females: 98.4 (2010); Marriage status: 21.0% never married, 68.7% now married, 3.0% widowed, 7.2% divorced (2005-2009 5-year est.); Foreign born: 8.2% (2005-2009 5-year est.); Ancestry (includes multiple ancestries): 23.8% German, 15.3% English, 13.5% Irish, 5.9% American, 5.2% Italian (2005-2009 5-year est.).

Economy: Unemployment rate: 6.7% (June 2011); Total civilian labor force: 36,455 (June 2011); Single-family building permits issued: 100 (2010); Multi-family building permits issued: 0 (2010); Employment by occupation: 27.8% management, 23.4% professional, 7.9% services, 30.5% sales, 0.1% farming, 4.4% construction, 5.8% production (2005-2009 5-year est.).

Income: Per capita income: $45,729 (2010); Median household income: $119,773 (2010); Average household income: $143,913 (2010); Percent of households with income of $100,000 or more: 63.2% (2010); Poverty rate: 3.1% (2005-2009 5-year est.).

Taxes: Total city taxes per capita: $566 (2007); City property taxes per capita: $368 (2007).

Education: Percent of population age 25 and over with: High school diploma (including GED) or higher: 97.6% (2010); Bachelor's degree or higher: 54.0% (2010); Master's degree or higher: 14.3% (2010).

School District(s)

Lewisville ISD (PK-12)
  2009-10 Enrollment: 50,840 . . . . (469) 713-5200

Housing: Homeownership rate: 93.5% (2010); Median home value: $232,044 (2010); Median contract rent: $1,154 per month (2005-2009 5-year est.); Median year structure built: 1995 (2005-2009 5-year est.).

Safety: Violent crime rate: 6.6 per 10,000 population; Property crime rate: 79.0 per 10,000 population (2009).

Newspapers: The Flower Mound Messenger (Local news; Circulation 40,000)

Transportation: Commute to work: 89.5% car, 0.3% public transportation, 0.4% walk, 8.3% work from home (2005-2009 5-year est.); Travel time to work: 19.6% less than 15 minutes, 30.8% 15 to 30 minutes, 31.8% 30 to 45 minutes, 12.6% 45 to 60 minutes, 5.2% 60 minutes or more (2005-2009 5-year est.)

Additional Information Contacts

Flower Mound Chamber of Commerce . . . . (972) 539-0500
  http://www.flowermoundchamber.com
Town of Flower Mound . . . . (972) 874-6076
  http://www.flower-mound.com

HACKBERRY (town). Covers a land area of 0.537 square miles and a water area of 0.002 square miles. Located at 33.15° N. Lat; 96.91° W. Long. Elevation is 551 feet.

Population: 371 (1990); 544 (2000); 1,195 (2010); 1,434 (2015 projected); Race: 71.0% White, 3.0% Black, 2.2% Asian, 23.8% Other, 32.5% Hispanic of any race (2010); Density: 2,225.1 persons per square mile (2010); Average household size: 3.11 (2010); Median age: 33.2 (2010); Males per 100 females: 106.0 (2010); Marriage status: 30.3% never married, 59.5% now married, 5.3% widowed, 4.9% divorced (2005-2009 5-year est.); Foreign born: 24.0% (2005-2009 5-year est.); Ancestry (includes multiple ancestries): 6.0% Irish, 5.5% American, 4.7% German, 3.1% English, 1.6% Scandinavian (2005-2009 5-year est.).

Economy: Single-family building permits issued: 0 (2010); Multi-family building permits issued: 0 (2010); Employment by occupation: 3.3% management, 2.0% professional, 17.6% services, 24.8% sales, 0.0% farming, 30.7% construction, 21.6% production (2005-2009 5-year est.).

Income: Per capita income: $28,278 (2010); Median household income: $71,307 (2010); Average household income: $88,053 (2010); Percent of households with income of $100,000 or more: 28.6% (2010); Poverty rate: 23.8% (2005-2009 5-year est.).

Taxes: Total city taxes per capita: $224 (2007); City property taxes per capita: $158 (2007).

Education: Percent of population age 25 and over with: High school diploma (including GED) or higher: 71.6% (2010); Bachelor's degree or higher: 21.1% (2010); Master's degree or higher: 5.1% (2010).

Housing: Homeownership rate: 88.5% (2010); Median home value: $137,681 (2010); Median contract rent: $533 per month (2005-2009 5-year est.); Median year structure built: 1990 (2005-2009 5-year est.).

Transportation: Commute to work: 97.0% car, 0.0% public transportation, 0.0% walk, 3.0% work from home (2005-2009 5-year est.); Travel time to work: 20.6% less than 15 minutes, 35.9% 15 to 30 minutes, 17.6% 30 to 45 minutes, 14.5% 45 to 60 minutes, 11.5% 60 minutes or more (2005-2009 5-year est.)

HEBRON (town). Covers a land area of 4.068 square miles and a water area of 0.022 square miles. Located at 33.02° N. Lat; 96.89° W. Long. Elevation is 577 feet.

Population: 570 (1990); 874 (2000); 3,523 (2010); 4,162 (2015 projected); Race: 74.8% White, 4.7% Black, 16.0% Asian, 4.4% Other, 5.3% Hispanic of any race (2010); Density: 866.0 persons per square mile (2010); Average household size: 2.64 (2010); Median age: 35.0 (2010); Males per 100 females: 103.9 (2010); Marriage status: 22.2% never married, 73.0% now married, 1.6% widowed, 3.2% divorced (2005-2009 5-year est.); Foreign born: 5.2% (2005-2009 5-year est.); Ancestry (includes multiple ancestries): 50.0% English, 29.7% German, 11.5% Swedish, 8.0% French, 4.9% Irish (2005-2009 5-year est.).

Economy: Employment by occupation: 32.2% management, 25.0% professional, 3.3% services, 38.2% sales, 0.0% farming, 1.3% construction, 0.0% production (2005-2009 5-year est.).

Income: Per capita income: $38,836 (2010); Median household income: $83,494 (2010); Average household income: $105,724 (2010); Percent of households with income of $100,000 or more: 40.7% (2010); Poverty rate: 4.9% (2005-2009 5-year est.).

Taxes: Total city taxes per capita: $215 (2007); City property taxes per capita: $0 (2007).

Education: Percent of population age 25 and over with: High school diploma (including GED) or higher: 88.8% (2010); Bachelor's degree or higher: 50.1% (2010); Master's degree or higher: 15.0% (2010).

Housing: Homeownership rate: 66.1% (2010); Median home value: $203,951 (2010); Median contract rent: $2,000+ per month (2005-2009 5-year est.); Median year structure built: 1993 (2005-2009 5-year est.).

Transportation: Commute to work: 77.6% car, 0.0% public transportation, 17.9% walk, 4.5% work from home (2005-2009 5-year est.); Travel time to work: 30.5% less than 15 minutes, 26.6% 15 to 30 minutes, 39.1% 30 to 45 minutes, 2.3% 45 to 60 minutes, 1.6% 60 minutes or more (2005-2009 5-year est.)

HICKORY CREEK (town). Covers a land area of 4.537 square miles and a water area of 0.060 square miles. Located at 33.11° N. Lat; 97.03° W. Long. Elevation is 577 feet.

Population: 1,893 (1990); 2,078 (2000); 3,085 (2010); 3,557 (2015 projected); Race: 87.3% White, 2.1% Black, 1.7% Asian, 8.9% Other, 9.5% Hispanic of any race (2010); Density: 680.0 persons per square mile (2010); Average household size: 2.62 (2010); Median age: 39.2 (2010); Males per 100 females: 101.1 (2010); Marriage status: 22.2% never married, 65.5% now married, 2.4% widowed, 9.9% divorced (2005-2009 5-year est.); Foreign born: 11.1% (2005-2009 5-year est.); Ancestry

(includes multiple ancestries): 19.9% German, 16.0% Irish, 9.8% English, 7.9% American, 3.9% French (2005-2009 5-year est.).
Economy: Single-family building permits issued: 20 (2010); Multi-family building permits issued: 0 (2010); Employment by occupation: 22.8% management, 25.9% professional, 7.7% services, 31.3% sales, 0.0% farming, 5.8% construction, 6.5% production (2005-2009 5-year est.).
Income: Per capita income: $44,164 (2010); Median household income: $87,281 (2010); Average household income: $115,649 (2010); Percent of households with income of $100,000 or more: 42.6% (2010); Poverty rate: 2.8% (2005-2009 5-year est.).
Taxes: Total city taxes per capita: $117 (2007); City property taxes per capita: $30 (2007).
Education: Percent of population age 25 and over with: High school diploma (including GED) or higher: 93.2% (2010); Bachelor's degree or higher: 29.4% (2010); Master's degree or higher: 8.5% (2010).

School District(s)
Responsive Education Solutions (KG-12)
    2009-10 Enrollment: 5,022 . . . . (972) 316-3663
Housing: Homeownership rate: 89.0% (2010); Median home value: $168,612 (2010); Median contract rent: $1,556 per month (2005-2009 5-year est.); Median year structure built: 1990 (2005-2009 5-year est.).
Safety: Violent crime rate: 5.0 per 10,000 population; Property crime rate: 225.7 per 10,000 population (2009).
Transportation: Commute to work: 87.6% car, 0.0% public transportation, 0.0% walk, 11.8% work from home (2005-2009 5-year est.); Travel time to work: 22.9% less than 15 minutes, 30.1% 15 to 30 minutes, 28.3% 30 to 45 minutes, 10.5% 45 to 60 minutes, 8.2% 60 minutes or more (2005-2009 5-year est.)
Additional Information Contacts
Lake Cities Chamber of Commerce. . . . . (940) 497-3097
   http://www.lakecitieschamber.com

HIGHLAND VILLAGE (city). Covers a land area of 5.517 square
miles and a water area of 0.893 square miles. Located at 33.08° N. Lat; 97.05° W. Long. Elevation is 554 feet.
History: Highland Village incorporated as a city in the early 1960s, though it only registered 516 residents in the 1970 census. The opening of the Dallas-Fort Worth International Airport helped spur massive growth in cities north of the airport, including Highland Village.
Population: 7,212 (1990); 12,173 (2000); 16,925 (2010); 19,772 (2015 projected); Race: 90.9% White, 2.4% Black, 3.2% Asian, 3.4% Other, 4.9% Hispanic of any race (2010); Density: 3,067.9 persons per square mile (2010); Average household size: 3.10 (2010); Median age: 35.8 (2010); Males per 100 females: 99.6 (2010); Marriage status: 21.1% never married, 71.8% now married, 3.1% widowed, 4.1% divorced (2005-2009 5-year est.); Foreign born: 8.7% (2005-2009 5-year est.); Ancestry (includes multiple ancestries): 23.7% German, 19.6% English, 16.0% Irish, 8.7% American, 5.4% French (2005-2009 5-year est.).
Economy: Single-family building permits issued: 22 (2010); Multi-family building permits issued: 0 (2010); Employment by occupation: 28.6% management, 22.4% professional, 9.8% services, 30.0% sales, 0.1% farming, 4.1% construction, 5.1% production (2005-2009 5-year est.).
Income: Per capita income: $50,465 (2010); Median household income: $124,087 (2010); Average household income: $156,416 (2010); Percent of households with income of $100,000 or more: 65.7% (2010); Poverty rate: 1.4% (2005-2009 5-year est.).
Taxes: Total city taxes per capita: $591 (2007); City property taxes per capita: $389 (2007).
Education: Percent of population age 25 and over with: High school diploma (including GED) or higher: 97.6% (2010); Bachelor's degree or higher: 56.4% (2010); Master's degree or higher: 18.7% (2010).

School District(s)
Lewisville ISD (PK-12)
    2009-10 Enrollment: 50,840 . . . . (469) 713-5200
Housing: Homeownership rate: 96.7% (2010); Median home value: $251,003 (2010); Median contract rent: $2,000+ per month (2005-2009 5-year est.); Median year structure built: 1991 (2005-2009 5-year est.).
Safety: Violent crime rate: 3.5 per 10,000 population; Property crime rate: 60.6 per 10,000 population (2009).
Newspapers: The News Connection (Community news; Circulation 30,000)
Transportation: Commute to work: 88.7% car, 0.3% public transportation, 0.9% walk, 8.6% work from home (2005-2009 5-year est.); Travel time to work: 18.2% less than 15 minutes, 26.5% 15 to 30 minutes, 30.0% 30 to 45

minutes, 16.3% 45 to 60 minutes, 8.9% 60 minutes or more (2005-2009 5-year est.)
Additional Information Contacts
City of Highland Village . . . . (972) 899-5131
   http://www.highlandvillage.org

JUSTIN (city). Covers a land area of 2.373 square miles and a water
area of 0 square miles. Located at 33.08° N. Lat; 97.29° W. Long. Elevation is 643 feet.
Population: 1,234 (1990); 1,891 (2000); 2,922 (2010); 3,536 (2015 projected); Race: 91.1% White, 1.5% Black, 1.2% Asian, 6.2% Other, 8.7% Hispanic of any race (2010); Density: 1,231.3 persons per square mile (2010); Average household size: 2.85 (2010); Median age: 36.1 (2010); Males per 100 females: 101.0 (2010); Marriage status: 20.3% never married, 66.3% now married, 2.7% widowed, 10.7% divorced (2005-2009 5-year est.); Foreign born: 1.3% (2005-2009 5-year est.); Ancestry (includes multiple ancestries): 19.7% German, 16.1% Irish, 13.2% English, 7.8% American, 5.4% Dutch (2005-2009 5-year est.).
Economy: Single-family building permits issued: 0 (2010); Multi-family building permits issued: 0 (2010); Employment by occupation: 14.8% management, 19.1% professional, 11.5% services, 30.5% sales, 0.0% farming, 12.9% construction, 11.1% production (2005-2009 5-year est.).
Income: Per capita income: $27,752 (2010); Median household income: $68,989 (2010); Average household income: $79,890 (2010); Percent of households with income of $100,000 or more: 26.0% (2010); Poverty rate: 6.7% (2005-2009 5-year est.).
Taxes: Total city taxes per capita: $686 (2007); City property taxes per capita: $217 (2007).
Education: Percent of population age 25 and over with: High school diploma (including GED) or higher: 83.8% (2010); Bachelor's degree or higher: 20.1% (2010); Master's degree or higher: 6.5% (2010).

School District(s)
Northwest ISD (PK-12)
    2009-10 Enrollment: 14,164 . . . . (817) 215-0000
Housing: Homeownership rate: 81.6% (2010); Median home value: $146,752 (2010); Median contract rent: $148 per month (2005-2009 5-year est.); Median year structure built: 1994 (2005-2009 5-year est.).
Transportation: Commute to work: 90.6% car, 0.0% public transportation, 0.2% walk, 8.0% work from home (2005-2009 5-year est.); Travel time to work: 14.0% less than 15 minutes, 24.1% 15 to 30 minutes, 28.7% 30 to 45 minutes, 17.3% 45 to 60 minutes, 15.9% 60 minutes or more (2005-2009 5-year est.)

KRUGERVILLE (city). Covers a land area of 0.722 square miles and
a water area of 0 square miles. Located at 33.28° N. Lat; 96.99° W. Long. Elevation is 692 feet.
Population: 765 (1990); 903 (2000); 1,477 (2010); 1,776 (2015 projected); Race: 90.9% White, 1.6% Black, 0.4% Asian, 7.1% Other, 7.7% Hispanic of any race (2010); Density: 2,046.1 persons per square mile (2010); Average household size: 2.74 (2010); Median age: 35.4 (2010); Males per 100 females: 96.1 (2010); Marriage status: 26.8% never married, 62.7% now married, 3.3% widowed, 7.2% divorced (2005-2009 5-year est.); Foreign born: 2.2% (2005-2009 5-year est.); Ancestry (includes multiple ancestries): 30.2% German, 17.9% English, 15.1% Irish, 6.4% American, 5.0% French (2005-2009 5-year est.).
Economy: Single-family building permits issued: 1 (2010); Multi-family building permits issued: 0 (2010); Employment by occupation: 8.9% management, 31.2% professional, 12.9% services, 30.3% sales, 0.0% farming, 6.7% construction, 10.0% production (2005-2009 5-year est.).
Income: Per capita income: $30,843 (2010); Median household income: $66,260 (2010); Average household income: $84,259 (2010); Percent of households with income of $100,000 or more: 26.1% (2010); Poverty rate: 0.9% (2005-2009 5-year est.).
Taxes: Total city taxes per capita: $114 (2007); City property taxes per capita: $73 (2007).
Education: Percent of population age 25 and over with: High school diploma (including GED) or higher: 86.9% (2010); Bachelor's degree or higher: 23.2% (2010); Master's degree or higher: 7.0% (2010).
Housing: Homeownership rate: 83.1% (2010); Median home value: $154,775 (2010); Median contract rent: $1,094 per month (2005-2009 5-year est.); Median year structure built: 1988 (2005-2009 5-year est.).
Transportation: Commute to work: 93.6% car, 0.0% public transportation, 0.0% walk, 6.0% work from home (2005-2009 5-year est.); Travel time to work: 14.3% less than 15 minutes, 43.7% 15 to 30 minutes, 12.0% 30 to 45

minutes, 12.8% 45 to 60 minutes, 17.2% 60 minutes or more (2005-2009 5-year est.)

KRUM (city). Covers a land area of 1.964 square miles and a water area of 0 square miles. Located at 33.26° N. Lat; 97.23° W. Long. Elevation is 738 feet.
Population: 1,586 (1990); 1,979 (2000); 3,460 (2010); 4,118 (2015 projected); Race: 87.6% White, 1.3% Black, 0.9% Asian, 10.3% Other, 11.0% Hispanic of any race (2010); Density: 1,761.9 persons per square mile (2010); Average household size: 2.92 (2010); Median age: 33.8 (2010); Males per 100 females: 94.9 (2010); Marriage status: 17.8% never married, 61.9% now married, 5.2% widowed, 15.0% divorced (2005-2009 5-year est.); Foreign born: 4.2% (2005-2009 5-year est.); Ancestry (includes multiple ancestries): 16.1% English, 15.3% German, 15.0% Irish, 10.6% American, 3.9% Scotch-Irish (2005-2009 5-year est.).
Economy: Single-family building permits issued: 36 (2010); Multi-family building permits issued: 0 (2010); Employment by occupation: 11.6% management, 16.0% professional, 16.2% services, 34.1% sales, 0.0% farming, 13.2% construction, 8.9% production (2005-2009 5-year est.).
Income: Per capita income: $26,773 (2010); Median household income: $66,460 (2010); Average household income: $77,903 (2010); Percent of households with income of $100,000 or more: 23.3% (2010); Poverty rate: 2.6% (2005-2009 5-year est.).
Taxes: Total city taxes per capita: $142 (2007); City property taxes per capita: $122 (2007).
Education: Percent of population age 25 and over with: High school diploma (including GED) or higher: 88.0% (2010); Bachelor's degree or higher: 27.4% (2010); Master's degree or higher: 7.9% (2010).
School District(s)
Krum ISD (PK-12)
    2009-10 Enrollment: 1,613 . . . . (940) 482-6000
Housing: Homeownership rate: 85.0% (2010); Median home value: $128,667 (2010); Median contract rent: $809 per month (2005-2009 5-year est.); Median year structure built: 1990 (2005-2009 5-year est.).
Transportation: Commute to work: 95.1% car, 0.5% public transportation, 1.2% walk, 2.8% work from home (2005-2009 5-year est.); Travel time to work: 21.5% less than 15 minutes, 51.3% 15 to 30 minutes, 12.8% 30 to 45 minutes, 9.4% 45 to 60 minutes, 5.1% 60 minutes or more (2005-2009 5-year est.)
Additional Information Contacts
City of Krum . . . . (940) 482-3491
    http://www.ci.krum.tx.us

LAKE DALLAS (city). Covers a land area of 2.289 square miles and a water area of 0.332 square miles. Located at 33.12° N. Lat; 97.02° W. Long. Elevation is 574 feet.
History: Lake Dallas developed as a recreational community on the western shore of Lake Garza-Little Elm, later known as Lake Lewisville.
Population: 3,829 (1990); 6,166 (2000); 8,656 (2010); 10,177 (2015 projected); Race: 84.1% White, 5.6% Black, 1.3% Asian, 9.0% Other, 16.5% Hispanic of any race (2010); Density: 3,781.2 persons per square mile (2010); Average household size: 2.70 (2010); Median age: 34.7 (2010); Males per 100 females: 101.7 (2010); Marriage status: 33.2% never married, 49.4% now married, 4.8% widowed, 12.5% divorced (2005-2009 5-year est.); Foreign born: 5.5% (2005-2009 5-year est.); Ancestry (includes multiple ancestries): 15.5% Irish, 15.0% German, 10.3% English, 8.3% American, 4.4% French (2005-2009 5-year est.).
Economy: Single-family building permits issued: 9 (2010); Multi-family building permits issued: 0 (2010); Employment by occupation: 14.2% management, 14.4% professional, 11.2% services, 33.0% sales, 0.0% farming, 18.9% construction, 8.3% production (2005-2009 5-year est.).
Income: Per capita income: $30,633 (2010); Median household income: $68,124 (2010); Average household income: $81,668 (2010); Percent of households with income of $100,000 or more: 27.7% (2010); Poverty rate: 6.6% (2005-2009 5-year est.).
Taxes: Total city taxes per capita: $345 (2007); City property taxes per capita: $208 (2007).
Education: Percent of population age 25 and over with: High school diploma (including GED) or higher: 86.7% (2010); Bachelor's degree or higher: 23.2% (2010); Master's degree or higher: 6.4% (2010).
School District(s)
Lake Dallas ISD (PK-12)
    2009-10 Enrollment: 4,090 . . . . (940) 497-4039

Housing: Homeownership rate: 74.2% (2010); Median home value: $157,726 (2010); Median contract rent: $645 per month (2005-2009 5-year est.); Median year structure built: 1990 (2005-2009 5-year est.).
Safety: Violent crime rate: 38.7 per 10,000 population; Property crime rate: 245.9 per 10,000 population (2009).
Newspapers: Argyle Sun (Community news; Circulation 4,000); Lake Cities Sun (Local news; Circulation 4,000)
Transportation: Commute to work: 93.2% car, 0.0% public transportation, 0.0% walk, 5.5% work from home (2005-2009 5-year est.); Travel time to work: 24.4% less than 15 minutes, 31.9% 15 to 30 minutes, 22.4% 30 to 45 minutes, 15.8% 45 to 60 minutes, 5.6% 60 minutes or more (2005-2009 5-year est.)
Additional Information Contacts
City of Lake Dallas . . . . (940) 497-2226
    http://www.lakedallas.com
Lake Cities Chamber of Commerce . . . . (940) 497-3097
    http://www.lakecitieschamber.com

LAKEWOOD VILLAGE (city). Covers a land area of 0.735 square miles and a water area of 0.009 square miles. Located at 33.14° N. Lat; 96.97° W. Long. Elevation is 548 feet.
Population: 165 (1990); 342 (2000); 672 (2010); 811 (2015 projected); Race: 89.0% White, 1.8% Black, 0.4% Asian, 8.8% Other, 10.7% Hispanic of any race (2010); Density: 914.4 persons per square mile (2010); Average household size: 2.81 (2010); Median age: 40.6 (2010); Males per 100 females: 103.6 (2010); Marriage status: 16.6% never married, 59.9% now married, 8.9% widowed, 14.6% divorced (2005-2009 5-year est.); Foreign born: 7.4% (2005-2009 5-year est.); Ancestry (includes multiple ancestries): 26.4% German, 15.9% English, 13.5% American, 10.8% Irish, 5.1% Italian (2005-2009 5-year est.).
Economy: Employment by occupation: 20.1% management, 24.7% professional, 6.5% services, 28.6% sales, 0.0% farming, 6.5% construction, 13.6% production (2005-2009 5-year est.).
Income: Per capita income: $50,380 (2010); Median household income: $110,326 (2010); Average household income: $141,412 (2010); Percent of households with income of $100,000 or more: 54.0% (2010); Poverty rate: 2.4% (2005-2009 5-year est.).
Taxes: Total city taxes per capita: $616 (2007); City property taxes per capita: $365 (2007).
Education: Percent of population age 25 and over with: High school diploma (including GED) or higher: 88.4% (2010); Bachelor's degree or higher: 30.0% (2010); Master's degree or higher: 8.3% (2010).
Housing: Homeownership rate: 88.3% (2010); Median home value: $298,485 (2010); Median contract rent: $883 per month (2005-2009 5-year est.); Median year structure built: 1996 (2005-2009 5-year est.).
Transportation: Commute to work: 88.7% car, 0.0% public transportation, 0.0% walk, 9.3% work from home (2005-2009 5-year est.); Travel time to work: 11.0% less than 15 minutes, 16.2% 15 to 30 minutes, 39.7% 30 to 45 minutes, 19.1% 45 to 60 minutes, 14.0% 60 minutes or more (2005-2009 5-year est.)

LEWISVILLE (city). Covers a land area of 36.794 square miles and a water area of 5.544 square miles. Located at 33.03° N. Lat; 97.00° W. Long. Elevation is 525 feet.
Population: 46,533 (1990); 77,737 (2000); 105,466 (2010); 123,647 (2015 projected); Race: 66.6% White, 11.3% Black, 7.0% Asian, 15.1% Other, 23.8% Hispanic of any race (2010); Density: 2,866.4 persons per square mile (2010); Average household size: 2.58 (2010); Median age: 31.9 (2010); Males per 100 females: 101.7 (2010); Marriage status: 34.0% never married, 49.9% now married, 2.6% widowed, 13.4% divorced (2005-2009 5-year est.); Foreign born: 20.6% (2005-2009 5-year est.); Ancestry (includes multiple ancestries): 14.4% German, 10.5% Irish, 10.1% English, 5.7% American, 2.7% French (2005-2009 5-year est.).
Economy: Unemployment rate: 7.4% (June 2011); Total civilian labor force: 61,703 (June 2011); Single-family building permits issued: 79 (2010); Multi-family building permits issued: 120 (2010); Employment by occupation: 14.6% management, 19.8% professional, 17.4% services, 30.5% sales, 0.0% farming, 8.4% construction, 9.4% production (2005-2009 5-year est.).
Income: Per capita income: $30,480 (2010); Median household income: $66,500 (2010); Average household income: $78,650 (2010); Percent of households with income of $100,000 or more: 25.5% (2010); Poverty rate: 8.5% (2005-2009 5-year est.).
Taxes: Total city taxes per capita: $604 (2007); City property taxes per capita: $270 (2007).

Education: Percent of population age 25 and over with: High school diploma (including GED) or higher: 89.3% (2010); Bachelor's degree or higher: 37.2% (2010); Master's degree or higher: 8.8% (2010).

School District(s)

Education Center (KG-12)
    2009-10 Enrollment: 765 . . . . (972) 292-2405
Lewisville ISD (PK-12)
    2009-10 Enrollment: 50,840 . . . . (469) 713-5200
Metro Academy of Math and Science (PK-12)
    2009-10 Enrollment: 359 . . . . (817) 229-5200
Responsive Education Solutions (KG-12)
    2009-10 Enrollment: 5,022 . . . . (972) 316-3663
Universal Academy (PK-12)
    2009-10 Enrollment: 1,397 . . . . (972) 255-1800
Winfree Academy Charter Schools (09-12)
    2009-10 Enrollment: 1,862 . . . . (972) 869-3250

Housing: Homeownership rate: 52.1% (2010); Median home value: $153,630 (2010); Median contract rent: $737 per month (2005-2009 5-year est.); Median year structure built: 1991 (2005-2009 5-year est.).
Hospitals: Medical Center of Lewisville (202 beds)
Safety: Violent crime rate: 18.8 per 10,000 population; Property crime rate: 346.0 per 10,000 population (2009).
Newspapers: The Colony Courier-Leader (Local news; Circulation 10,000); Coppell Gazette (Community news; Circulation 8,500); The Dallas Morning News - Denton County Bureau (Local news); Flower Mound Leader; Lewisville News (Local news; Circulation 20,950).
Transportation: Commute to work: 94.4% car, 0.6% public transportation, 0.9% walk, 3.0% work from home (2005-2009 5-year est.); Travel time to work: 25.1% less than 15 minutes, 31.7% 15 to 30 minutes, 29.3% 30 to 45 minutes, 9.1% 45 to 60 minutes, 4.7% 60 minutes or more (2005-2009 5-year est.)
Additional Information Contacts
City of Lewisville . . . . (972) 219-3400
    http://www.cityoflewisville.com

LINCOLN PARK (town). Covers a land area of 0.152 square miles and a water area of 0 square miles. Located at 33.22° N. Lat; 96.97° W. Long. Elevation is 591 feet.
Population: 287 (1990); 517 (2000); 463 (2010); 540 (2015 projected); Race: 78.0% White, 2.2% Black, 0.0% Asian, 19.9% Other, 27.4% Hispanic of any race (2010); Density: 3,038.1 persons per square mile (2010); Average household size: 2.95 (2010); Median age: 33.8 (2010); Males per 100 females: 103.1 (2010); Marriage status: 22.4% never married, 41.8% now married, 6.0% widowed, 29.9% divorced (2005-2009 5-year est.); Foreign born: 2.5% (2005-2009 5-year est.); Ancestry (includes multiple ancestries): 12.9% English, 12.5% German, 12.5% American, 10.4% Swedish, 9.6% Irish (2005-2009 5-year est.).
Economy: Employment by occupation: 12.2% management, 14.3% professional, 26.5% services, 19.0% sales, 0.0% farming, 7.5% construction, 20.4% production (2005-2009 5-year est.).
Income: Per capita income: $29,777 (2010); Median household income: $68,403 (2010); Average household income: $88,408 (2010); Percent of households with income of $100,000 or more: 26.8% (2010); Poverty rate: 4.2% (2005-2009 5-year est.).
Taxes: Total city taxes per capita: $75 (2007); City property taxes per capita: $0 (2007).
Education: Percent of population age 25 and over with: High school diploma (including GED) or higher: 81.7% (2010); Bachelor's degree or higher: 19.4% (2010); Master's degree or higher: 7.3% (2010).
Housing: Homeownership rate: 80.9% (2010); Median home value: $121,324 (2010); Median contract rent: $589 per month (2005-2009 5-year est.); Median year structure built: 1995 (2005-2009 5-year est.).
Transportation: Commute to work: 97.3% car, 0.0% public transportation, 1.4% walk, 1.4% work from home (2005-2009 5-year est.); Travel time to work: 18.6% less than 15 minutes, 12.4% 15 to 30 minutes, 26.9% 30 to 45 minutes, 37.9% 45 to 60 minutes, 4.1% 60 minutes or more (2005-2009 5-year est.)

LITTLE ELM (town). Covers a land area of 4.852 square miles and a water area of 0.024 square miles. Located at 33.16° N. Lat; 96.93° W. Long. Elevation is 545 feet.
Population: 1,388 (1990); 3,646 (2000); 20,712 (2010); 24,018 (2015 projected); Race: 73.2% White, 5.4% Black, 0.7% Asian, 20.7% Other, 29.6% Hispanic of any race (2010); Density: 4,269.1 persons per square mile (2010); Average household size: 3.04 (2010); Median age: 30.5

(2010); Males per 100 females: 104.6 (2010); Marriage status: 26.0% never married, 60.1% now married, 2.8% widowed, 11.1% divorced (2005-2009 5-year est.); Foreign born: 15.5% (2005-2009 5-year est.); Ancestry (includes multiple ancestries): 17.2% German, 9.6% English, 9.2% Irish, 4.4% Italian, 4.4% American (2005-2009 5-year est.).
Economy: Unemployment rate: 6.4% (June 2011); Total civilian labor force: 13,452 (June 2011); Single-family building permits issued: 389 (2010); Multi-family building permits issued: 0 (2010); Employment by occupation: 18.6% management, 21.2% professional, 14.1% services, 30.0% sales, 0.2% farming, 9.7% construction, 6.1% production (2005-2009 5-year est.).
Income: Per capita income: $26,037 (2010); Median household income: $68,449 (2010); Average household income: $79,079 (2010); Percent of households with income of $100,000 or more: 26.2% (2010); Poverty rate: 5.8% (2005-2009 5-year est.).
Taxes: Total city taxes per capita: $396 (2007); City property taxes per capita: $186 (2007).
Education: Percent of population age 25 and over with: High school diploma (including GED) or higher: 77.3% (2010); Bachelor's degree or higher: 16.8% (2010); Master's degree or higher: 2.7% (2010).

School District(s)

Education Center (KG-12)
    2009-10 Enrollment: 765 . . . . (972) 292-2405
Frisco ISD (PK-12)
    2009-10 Enrollment: 33,973 . . . . (469) 633-6000
Little Elm ISD (PK-12)
    2009-10 Enrollment: 6,112 . . . . (972) 292-1847

Housing: Homeownership rate: 82.7% (2010); Median home value: $153,068 (2010); Median contract rent: $1,070 per month (2005-2009 5-year est.); Median year structure built: 2003 (2005-2009 5-year est.).
Safety: Violent crime rate: 7.2 per 10,000 population; Property crime rate: 83.2 per 10,000 population (2009).
Newspapers: The Little Elm Journal (Community news)
Transportation: Commute to work: 95.9% car, 0.0% public transportation, 0.2% walk, 3.2% work from home (2005-2009 5-year est.); Travel time to work: 14.6% less than 15 minutes, 16.7% 15 to 30 minutes, 30.7% 30 to 45 minutes, 20.5% 45 to 60 minutes, 17.5% 60 minutes or more (2005-2009 5-year est.)
Additional Information Contacts
Little Elm Chamber of Commerce . . . . (972) 292-3777
    http://www.littleelmchamber.org

MARSHALL CREEK (town). Covers a land area of 0.231 square miles and a water area of 0 square miles. Located at 33.01° N. Lat; 97.20° W. Long. Elevation is 610 feet.
Population: 320 (1990); 431 (2000); 560 (2010); 658 (2015 projected); Race: 89.6% White, 3.0% Black, 1.1% Asian, 6.3% Other, 12.5% Hispanic of any race (2010); Density: 2,422.5 persons per square mile (2010); Average household size: 2.89 (2010); Median age: 34.0 (2010); Males per 100 females: 104.4 (2010); Marriage status: n/a never married, n/a now married, n/a widowed, n/a divorced (2005-2009 5-year est.); Foreign born: n/a (2005-2009 5-year est.); Ancestry (includes multiple ancestries): n/a (2005-2009 5-year est.).
Economy: Employment by occupation: n/a management, n/a professional, n/a services, n/a sales, n/a farming, n/a construction, n/a production (2005-2009 5-year est.).
Income: Per capita income: $32,853 (2010); Median household income: $82,857 (2010); Average household income: $93,203 (2010); Percent of households with income of $100,000 or more: 37.5% (2010); Poverty rate: n/a (2005-2009 5-year est.).
Taxes: Total city taxes per capita: $72 (2007); City property taxes per capita: $62 (2007).
Education: Percent of population age 25 and over with: High school diploma (including GED) or higher: 90.7% (2010); Bachelor's degree or higher: 31.0% (2010); Master's degree or higher: 9.0% (2010).
Housing: Homeownership rate: 88.0% (2010); Median home value: $179,861 (2010); Median contract rent: n/a per month (2005-2009 5-year est.); Median year structure built: n/a (2005-2009 5-year est.).
Transportation: Commute to work: n/a car, n/a public transportation, n/a walk, n/a work from home (2005-2009 5-year est.); Travel time to work: n/a less than 15 minutes, n/a 15 to 30 minutes, n/a 30 to 45 minutes, n/a 45 to 60 minutes, n/a 60 minutes or more (2005-2009 5-year est.)

NORTHLAKE (town). Covers a land area of 15.223 square miles and a water area of 0.006 square miles. Located at 33.08° N. Lat; 97.25° W. Long. Elevation is 689 feet.
Population: 523 (1990); 921 (2000); 1,374 (2010); 1,648 (2015 projected); Race: 90.2% White, 1.7% Black, 0.5% Asian, 7.6% Other, 8.5% Hispanic of any race (2010); Density: 90.3 persons per square mile (2010); Average household size: 2.72 (2010); Median age: 34.6 (2010); Males per 100 females: 100.0 (2010); Marriage status: 33.2% never married, 44.2% now married, 4.6% widowed, 18.1% divorced (2005-2009 5-year est.); Foreign born: 6.5% (2005-2009 5-year est.); Ancestry (includes multiple ancestries): 18.6% German, 10.6% Irish, 8.3% American, 6.3% Scotch-Irish, 6.0% English (2005-2009 5-year est.).
Economy: Single-family building permits issued: 1 (2010); Multi-family building permits issued: 0 (2010); Employment by occupation: 15.0% management, 18.4% professional, 10.5% services, 26.3% sales, 0.0% farming, 14.1% construction, 15.8% production (2005-2009 5-year est.).
Income: Per capita income: $29,142 (2010); Median household income: $63,107 (2010); Average household income: $79,559 (2010); Percent of households with income of $100,000 or more: 27.0% (2010); Poverty rate: 4.9% (2005-2009 5-year est.).
Taxes: Total city taxes per capita: $274 (2007); City property taxes per capita: $112 (2007).
Education: Percent of population age 25 and over with: High school diploma (including GED) or higher: 88.4% (2010); Bachelor's degree or higher: 22.7% (2010); Master's degree or higher: 6.7% (2010).
Housing: Homeownership rate: 70.4% (2010); Median home value: $147,866 (2010); Median contract rent: $713 per month (2005-2009 5-year est.); Median year structure built: 1996 (2005-2009 5-year est.).
Safety: Violent crime rate: 4.4 per 10,000 population; Property crime rate: 190.3 per 10,000 population (2009).
Transportation: Commute to work: 96.0% car, 0.0% public transportation, 0.0% walk, 4.0% work from home (2005-2009 5-year est.); Travel time to work: 27.8% less than 15 minutes, 24.1% 15 to 30 minutes, 27.5% 30 to 45 minutes, 14.1% 45 to 60 minutes, 6.5% 60 minutes or more (2005-2009 5-year est.)

OAK POINT (city). Covers a land area of 5.697 square miles and a water area of 0.243 square miles. Located at 33.18° N. Lat; 96.99° W. Long. Elevation is 600 feet.
History: The City of Oak Point, incorporated in 1976, operates under a Council-Manager form of government. Oak Point is a General Law City.
Population: 753 (1990); 1,747 (2000); 3,912 (2010); 4,696 (2015 projected); Race: 87.3% White, 1.7% Black, 0.4% Asian, 10.5% Other, 13.3% Hispanic of any race (2010); Density: 686.7 persons per square mile (2010); Average household size: 2.83 (2010); Median age: 39.1 (2010); Males per 100 females: 103.4 (2010); Marriage status: 17.6% never married, 62.5% now married, 4.0% widowed, 15.9% divorced (2005-2009 5-year est.); Foreign born: 4.1% (2005-2009 5-year est.); Ancestry (includes multiple ancestries): 30.8% German, 15.7% English, 13.6% Irish, 6.7% American, 5.4% French (2005-2009 5-year est.).
Economy: Single-family building permits issued: 28 (2010); Multi-family building permits issued: 0 (2010); Employment by occupation: 21.5% management, 22.0% professional, 22.2% services, 24.7% sales, 0.0% farming, 6.3% construction, 13.3% production (2005-2009 5-year est.).
Income: Per capita income: $47,156 (2010); Median household income: $99,782 (2010); Average household income: $133,462 (2010); Percent of households with income of $100,000 or more: 49.9% (2010); Poverty rate: 5.1% (2005-2009 5-year est.).
Taxes: Total city taxes per capita: $642 (2007); City property taxes per capita: $431 (2007).
Education: Percent of population age 25 and over with: High school diploma (including GED) or higher: 87.4% (2010); Bachelor's degree or higher: 28.4% (2010); Master's degree or higher: 8.1% (2010).
School District(s)
Little Elm ISD (PK-12)
   2009-10 Enrollment: 6,112 . . . . (972) 292-1847
Housing: Homeownership rate: 87.1% (2010); Median home value: $263,429 (2010); Median contract rent: $789 per month (2005-2009 5-year est.); Median year structure built: 1997 (2005-2009 5-year est.).
Transportation: Commute to work: 87.6% car, 0.0% public transportation, 0.6% walk, 10.8% work from home (2005-2009 5-year est.); Travel time to work: 14.2% less than 15 minutes, 18.2% 15 to 30 minutes, 30.1% 30 to 45 minutes, 17.6% 45 to 60 minutes, 20.0% 60 minutes or more (2005-2009 5-year est.)

PILOT POINT (city). Covers a land area of 3.048 square miles and a water area of 0 square miles. Located at 33.39° N. Lat; 96.95° W. Long. Elevation is 722 feet.
History: Settled 1835, incorporated 1906.
Population: 2,574 (1990); 3,538 (2000); 3,930 (2010); 4,376 (2015 projected); Race: 76.7% White, 6.3% Black, 0.4% Asian, 16.5% Other, 20.6% Hispanic of any race (2010); Density: 1,289.3 persons per square mile (2010); Average household size: 2.74 (2010); Median age: 33.9 (2010); Males per 100 females: 99.5 (2010); Marriage status: 29.3% never married, 51.5% now married, 5.9% widowed, 13.3% divorced (2005-2009 5-year est.); Foreign born: 23.0% (2005-2009 5-year est.); Ancestry (includes multiple ancestries): 20.2% German, 15.9% Irish, 10.0% English, 5.0% American, 4.9% French (2005-2009 5-year est.).
Economy: Single-family building permits issued: 5 (2010); Multi-family building permits issued: 4 (2010); Employment by occupation: 14.2% management, 10.4% professional, 20.6% services, 23.0% sales, 2.9% farming, 19.2% construction, 9.9% production (2005-2009 5-year est.).
Income: Per capita income: $24,855 (2010); Median household income: $57,011 (2010); Average household income: $68,544 (2010); Percent of households with income of $100,000 or more: 15.6% (2010); Poverty rate: 9.9% (2005-2009 5-year est.).
Taxes: Total city taxes per capita: $471 (2007); City property taxes per capita: $255 (2007).
Education: Percent of population age 25 and over with: High school diploma (including GED) or higher: 77.3% (2010); Bachelor's degree or higher: 19.1% (2010); Master's degree or higher: 6.0% (2010).
School District(s)
Pilot Point ISD (PK-12)
   2009-10 Enrollment: 1,528 . . . . (940) 686-8700
Housing: Homeownership rate: 71.9% (2010); Median home value: $118,297 (2010); Median contract rent: $492 per month (2005-2009 5-year est.); Median year structure built: 1980 (2005-2009 5-year est.).
Safety: Violent crime rate: 11.1 per 10,000 population; Property crime rate: 75.3 per 10,000 population (2009).
Newspapers: Pilot Point Post-Signal (Community news; Circulation 2,000)
Transportation: Commute to work: 97.2% car, 0.0% public transportation, 0.0% walk, 2.8% work from home (2005-2009 5-year est.); Travel time to work: 23.3% less than 15 minutes, 9.3% 15 to 30 minutes, 32.8% 30 to 45 minutes, 11.0% 45 to 60 minutes, 23.6% 60 minutes or more (2005-2009 5-year est.)

PONDER (town). Covers a land area of 3.175 square miles and a water area of 0 square miles. Located at 33.18° N. Lat; 97.28° W. Long. Elevation is 732 feet.
Population: 459 (1990); 507 (2000); 1,017 (2010); 1,231 (2015 projected); Race: 89.4% White, 1.6% Black, 0.8% Asian, 8.3% Other, 8.3% Hispanic of any race (2010); Density: 320.4 persons per square mile (2010); Average household size: 2.96 (2010); Median age: 34.6 (2010); Males per 100 females: 98.6 (2010); Marriage status: 19.9% never married, 72.3% now married, 5.0% widowed, 2.9% divorced (2005-2009 5-year est.); Foreign born: 1.5% (2005-2009 5-year est.); Ancestry (includes multiple ancestries): 24.8% German, 8.1% English, 7.9% Scottish, 6.9% French, 6.5% American (2005-2009 5-year est.).
Economy: Single-family building permits issued: 3 (2010); Multi-family building permits issued: 0 (2010); Employment by occupation: 12.4% management, 18.2% professional, 14.7% services, 26.6% sales, 0.0% farming, 10.7% construction, 17.5% production (2005-2009 5-year est.).
Income: Per capita income: $29,280 (2010); Median household income: $71,546 (2010); Average household income: $87,223 (2010); Percent of households with income of $100,000 or more: 28.9% (2010); Poverty rate: 0.4% (2005-2009 5-year est.).
Taxes: Total city taxes per capita: $225 (2007); City property taxes per capita: $78 (2007).
Education: Percent of population age 25 and over with: High school diploma (including GED) or higher: 85.8% (2010); Bachelor's degree or higher: 18.1% (2010); Master's degree or higher: 6.6% (2010).
School District(s)
Ponder ISD (PK-12)
   2009-10 Enrollment: 1,233 . . . . (940) 479-8200
Housing: Homeownership rate: 82.8% (2010); Median home value: $147,333 (2010); Median contract rent: $875 per month (2005-2009 5-year est.); Median year structure built: 1989 (2005-2009 5-year est.).
Safety: Violent crime rate: 0.0 per 10,000 population; Property crime rate: 49.1 per 10,000 population (2009).

Transportation: Commute to work: 98.6% car, 0.0% public transportation, 0.0% walk, 0.7% work from home (2005-2009 5-year est.); Travel time to work: 5.7% less than 15 minutes, 44.0% 15 to 30 minutes, 31.2% 30 to 45 minutes, 7.9% 45 to 60 minutes, 11.2% 60 minutes or more (2005-2009 5-year est.)

ROANOKE (city). Covers a land area of 6.027 square miles and a water area of 0.010 square miles. Located at 33.00° N. Lat; 97.22° W. Long. Elevation is 633 feet.
Population: 1,858 (1990); 2,810 (2000); 5,836 (2010); 6,983 (2015 projected); Race: 86.2% White, 2.9% Black, 1.7% Asian, 9.2% Other, 13.2% Hispanic of any race (2010); Density: 968.3 persons per square mile (2010); Average household size: 2.65 (2010); Median age: 33.3 (2010); Males per 100 females: 102.7 (2010); Marriage status: 28.0% never married, 49.9% now married, 4.2% widowed, 18.0% divorced (2005-2009 5-year est.); Foreign born: 6.4% (2005-2009 5-year est.); Ancestry (includes multiple ancestries): 19.6% German, 17.6% English, 14.4% Irish, 7.5% American, 7.0% French (2005-2009 5-year est.).
Economy: Single-family building permits issued: 76 (2010); Multi-family building permits issued: 0 (2010); Employment by occupation: 18.5% management, 22.5% professional, 11.6% services, 28.6% sales, 1.4% farming, 9.4% construction, 8.0% production (2005-2009 5-year est.).
Income: Per capita income: $29,133 (2010); Median household income: $66,193 (2010); Average household income: $77,349 (2010); Percent of households with income of $100,000 or more: 27.8% (2010); Poverty rate: 5.5% (2005-2009 5-year est.).
Taxes: Total city taxes per capita: $223 (2007); City property taxes per capita: $90 (2007).
Education: Percent of population age 25 and over with: High school diploma (including GED) or higher: 89.2% (2010); Bachelor's degree or higher: 27.9% (2010); Master's degree or higher: 5.7% (2010).
School District(s)
Northwest ISD (PK-12)
    2009-10 Enrollment: 14,164 . . . . (817) 215-0000
Housing: Homeownership rate: 64.8% (2010); Median home value: $162,869 (2010); Median contract rent: $790 per month (2005-2009 5-year est.); Median year structure built: 1995 (2005-2009 5-year est.).
Safety: Violent crime rate: 24.8 per 10,000 population; Property crime rate: 316.1 per 10,000 population (2009).
Transportation: Commute to work: 94.2% car, 0.0% public transportation, 1.3% walk, 4.0% work from home (2005-2009 5-year est.); Travel time to work: 25.6% less than 15 minutes, 33.0% 15 to 30 minutes, 24.0% 30 to 45 minutes, 12.2% 45 to 60 minutes, 5.2% 60 minutes or more (2005-2009 5-year est.)

SANGER (city). Covers a land area of 3.144 square miles and a water area of 0.007 square miles. Located at 33.36° N. Lat; 97.17° W. Long. Elevation is 676 feet.
Population: 3,681 (1990); 4,534 (2000); 6,211 (2010); 7,281 (2015 projected); Race: 89.5% White, 1.8% Black, 0.4% Asian, 8.3% Other, 12.8% Hispanic of any race (2010); Density: 1,975.3 persons per square mile (2010); Average household size: 2.67 (2010); Median age: 34.1 (2010); Males per 100 females: 96.9 (2010); Marriage status: 29.1% never married, 46.1% now married, 4.8% widowed, 20.0% divorced (2005-2009 5-year est.); Foreign born: 2.7% (2005-2009 5-year est.); Ancestry (includes multiple ancestries): 21.1% German, 16.2% Irish, 15.2% English, 7.7% American, 3.9% French (2005-2009 5-year est.).
Economy: Single-family building permits issued: 9 (2010); Multi-family building permits issued: 0 (2010); Employment by occupation: 13.4% management, 15.6% professional, 18.1% services, 18.8% sales, 1.0% farming, 15.0% construction, 18.0% production (2005-2009 5-year est.).
Income: Per capita income: $24,384 (2010); Median household income: $55,125 (2010); Average household income: $65,723 (2010); Percent of households with income of $100,000 or more: 16.6% (2010); Poverty rate: 15.2% (2005-2009 5-year est.).
Taxes: Total city taxes per capita: $387 (2007); City property taxes per capita: $263 (2007).
Education: Percent of population age 25 and over with: High school diploma (including GED) or higher: 81.9% (2010); Bachelor's degree or higher: 18.1% (2010); Master's degree or higher: 6.6% (2010).
School District(s)
Sanger ISD (PK-12)
    2009-10 Enrollment: 2,594 . . . . (940) 458-7438

Housing: Homeownership rate: 71.6% (2010); Median home value: $105,058 (2010); Median contract rent: $588 per month (2005-2009 5-year est.); Median year structure built: 1991 (2005-2009 5-year est.).
Safety: Violent crime rate: 21.9 per 10,000 population; Property crime rate: 181.5 per 10,000 population (2009).
Newspapers: Lewisville/Flower Mound Business (Local news; Circulation 5,300); Sanger Courier (Community news; Circulation 3,000)
Transportation: Commute to work: 97.0% car, 0.0% public transportation, 0.5% walk, 1.5% work from home (2005-2009 5-year est.); Travel time to work: 25.0% less than 15 minutes, 49.7% 15 to 30 minutes, 11.3% 30 to 45 minutes, 7.8% 45 to 60 minutes, 6.2% 60 minutes or more (2005-2009 5-year est.)
Additional Information Contacts
Sanger Area Chamber of Commerce . . . . (940) 458-7702
    http://www.sangertexas.com

SHADY SHORES (town). Covers a land area of 2.898 square miles and a water area of 0.005 square miles. Located at 33.16° N. Lat; 97.03° W. Long. Elevation is 538 feet.
Population: 1,118 (1990); 1,461 (2000); 2,622 (2010); 3,213 (2015 projected); Race: 87.3% White, 6.0% Black, 1.1% Asian, 5.6% Other, 13.0% Hispanic of any race (2010); Density: 904.7 persons per square mile (2010); Average household size: 3.02 (2010); Median age: 34.9 (2010); Males per 100 females: 105.6 (2010); Marriage status: 19.5% never married, 68.5% now married, 4.3% widowed, 7.7% divorced (2005-2009 5-year est.); Foreign born: 3.6% (2005-2009 5-year est.); Ancestry (includes multiple ancestries): 20.7% German, 19.9% Irish, 17.0% English, 6.8% Scottish, 4.2% American (2005-2009 5-year est.).
Economy: Single-family building permits issued: 3 (2010); Multi-family building permits issued: 0 (2010); Employment by occupation: 20.8% management, 22.1% professional, 10.6% services, 30.0% sales, 0.3% farming, 8.5% construction, 7.7% production (2005-2009 5-year est.).
Income: Per capita income: $35,823 (2010); Median household income: $96,242 (2010); Average household income: $108,330 (2010); Percent of households with income of $100,000 or more: 47.2% (2010); Poverty rate: 1.4% (2005-2009 5-year est.).
Taxes: Total city taxes per capita: $284 (2007); City property taxes per capita: $253 (2007).
Education: Percent of population age 25 and over with: High school diploma (including GED) or higher: 93.7% (2010); Bachelor's degree or higher: 31.6% (2010); Master's degree or higher: 7.5% (2010).
School District(s)
Denton ISD (PK-12)
    2009-10 Enrollment: 22,825 . . . . (940) 369-0000
Lake Dallas ISD (PK-12)
    2009-10 Enrollment: 4,090 . . . . (940) 497-4039
Housing: Homeownership rate: 90.5% (2010); Median home value: $214,505 (2010); Median contract rent: $729 per month (2005-2009 5-year est.); Median year structure built: 1993 (2005-2009 5-year est.).
Transportation: Commute to work: 93.8% car, 0.0% public transportation, 0.0% walk, 5.9% work from home (2005-2009 5-year est.); Travel time to work: 20.2% less than 15 minutes, 33.4% 15 to 30 minutes, 25.3% 30 to 45 minutes, 10.2% 45 to 60 minutes, 10.9% 60 minutes or more (2005-2009 5-year est.)
Additional Information Contacts
Lake Cities Chamber of Commerce . . . . (940) 497-3097
    http://www.lakecitieschamber.com
Town of Shady Shores . . . . (940) 498-0044
    http://www.shady-shores.com

THE COLONY (city). Covers a land area of 13.661 square miles and a water area of 2.074 square miles. Located at 33.09° N. Lat; 96.88° W. Long. Elevation is 591 feet.
Population: 22,178 (1990); 26,531 (2000); 38,796 (2010); 45,698 (2015 projected); Race: 80.7% White, 7.1% Black, 2.3% Asian, 9.9% Other, 17.3% Hispanic of any race (2010); Density: 2,839.9 persons per square mile (2010); Average household size: 2.96 (2010); Median age: 33.0 (2010); Males per 100 females: 99.5 (2010); Marriage status: 30.4% never married, 56.4% now married, 2.3% widowed, 10.9% divorced (2005-2009 5-year est.); Foreign born: 13.1% (2005-2009 5-year est.); Ancestry (includes multiple ancestries): 17.2% German, 13.6% Irish, 10.9% English, 5.2% American, 3.6% Italian (2005-2009 5-year est.).
Economy: Unemployment rate: 8.0% (June 2011); Total civilian labor force: 24,445 (June 2011); Single-family building permits issued: 37 (2010); Multi-family building permits issued: 0 (2010); Employment by occupation:

16.7% management, 23.5% professional, 12.3% services, 31.8% sales, 0.1% farming, 8.0% construction, 7.8% production (2005-2009 5-year est.).
Income: Per capita income: $35,379 (2010); Median household income: $86,623 (2010); Average household income: $104,808 (2010); Percent of households with income of $100,000 or more: 39.6% (2010); Poverty rate: 4.7% (2005-2009 5-year est.).
Taxes: Total city taxes per capita: $537 (2007); City property taxes per capita: $321 (2007).
Education: Percent of population age 25 and over with: High school diploma (including GED) or higher: 93.2% (2010); Bachelor's degree or higher: 31.5% (2010); Master's degree or higher: 8.9% (2010).

School District(s)
Education Center (KG-12)
    2009-10 Enrollment: 765 . . . . (972) 292-2405
Lewisville ISD (PK-12)
    2009-10 Enrollment: 50,840 . . . . (469) 713-5200
Housing: Homeownership rate: 79.2% (2010); Median home value: $147,869 (2010); Median contract rent: $948 per month (2005-2009 5-year est.); Median year structure built: 1989 (2005-2009 5-year est.).
Safety: Violent crime rate: 11.9 per 10,000 population; Property crime rate: 155.9 per 10,000 population (2009).
Transportation: Commute to work: 94.3% car, 0.6% public transportation, 0.4% walk, 3.8% work from home (2005-2009 5-year est.); Travel time to work: 13.6% less than 15 minutes, 34.2% 15 to 30 minutes, 33.2% 30 to 45 minutes, 12.5% 45 to 60 minutes, 6.5% 60 minutes or more (2005-2009 5-year est.)
Additional Information Contacts
City of The Colony . . . . (972) 625-1756
    http://www.ci.the-colony.tx.us
The Colony Chamber of Commerce . . . . (214) 705-3075
    http://www.thecolonychamber.com

TROPHY CLUB (town). Covers a land area of 4.050 square miles and a water area of 0.011 square miles. Located at 33.00° N. Lat; 97.19° W. Long. Elevation is 607 feet.
History: Trophy Club became a Town in 1985, giving it the right to govern itselves and move along the path to where it is today. 2010 will be its 25th year (SILVER) Anniversary.
Population: 3,951 (1990); 6,350 (2000); 7,866 (2010); 9,079 (2015 projected); Race: 92.3% White, 1.8% Black, 1.5% Asian, 4.4% Other, 7.2% Hispanic of any race (2010); Density: 1,942.3 persons per square mile (2010); Average household size: 2.80 (2010); Median age: 38.3 (2010); Males per 100 females: 103.7 (2010); Marriage status: 15.0% never married, 70.4% now married, 2.8% widowed, 11.7% divorced (2005-2009 5-year est.); Foreign born: 8.5% (2005-2009 5-year est.); Ancestry (includes multiple ancestries): 19.5% German, 18.8% English, 17.9% Irish, 6.7% Italian, 5.6% American (2005-2009 5-year est.).
Economy: Single-family building permits issued: 211 (2010); Multi-family building permits issued: 0 (2010); Employment by occupation: 28.3% management, 26.1% professional, 10.5% services, 27.0% sales, 0.0% farming, 4.0% construction, 4.1% production (2005-2009 5-year est.).
Income: Per capita income: $47,570 (2010); Median household income: $108,166 (2010); Average household income: $133,259 (2010); Percent of households with income of $100,000 or more: 55.8% (2010); Poverty rate: 2.7% (2005-2009 5-year est.).
Taxes: Total city taxes per capita: $484 (2007); City property taxes per capita: $344 (2007).
Education: Percent of population age 25 and over with: High school diploma (including GED) or higher: 96.2% (2010); Bachelor's degree or higher: 46.1% (2010); Master's degree or higher: 13.1% (2010).

School District(s)
Northwest ISD (PK-12)
    2009-10 Enrollment: 14,164 . . . . (817) 215-0000
Housing: Homeownership rate: 89.7% (2010); Median home value: $240,659 (2010); Median contract rent: $976 per month (2005-2009 5-year est.); Median year structure built: 1990 (2005-2009 5-year est.).
Hospitals: Baylor Medical Center at Trophy Club
Safety: Violent crime rate: 7.3 per 10,000 population; Property crime rate: 100.3 per 10,000 population (2009).
Transportation: Commute to work: 87.7% car, 1.7% public transportation, 0.0% walk, 9.9% work from home (2005-2009 5-year est.); Travel time to work: 21.4% less than 15 minutes, 25.1% 15 to 30 minutes, 31.8% 30 to 45 minutes, 12.6% 45 to 60 minutes, 9.1% 60 minutes or more (2005-2009 5-year est.)
Additional Information Contacts

Town of Trophy Club . . . . (682) 831-4600
    http://www.trophyclub.org

Dickens County

Located in northwestern Texas; rolling plains area. Covers a land area of 904.21 square miles, a water area of 1.00 square miles, and is located in the Central Time Zone at 33.59° N. Lat., 100.81° W. Long. The county was founded in 1876. County seat is Dickens.

Weather Station: Spur   Elevation: 2,296 feet

	Jan	Feb	Mar	Apr	May	Jun	Jul	Aug	Sep	Oct	Nov	Dec
High	56	60	68	77	84	91	95	93	86	77	65	56
Low	27	30	37	45	56	64	67	67	59	48	36	27
Precip	0.7	0.9	1.4	1.8	2.9	3.4	2.1	2.9	2.5	2.1	1.1	1.0
Snow	0.5	0.4	tr	0.1	0.0	0.0	0.0	0.0	0.0	0.0	0.4	0.5

High and Low temperatures in degrees Fahrenheit; Precipitation and Snow in inches

Population: 2,571 (1990); 2,762 (2000); 2,530 (2010); 2,411 (2015 projected); Race: 72.5% White, 9.2% Black, 0.2% Asian, 18.1% Other, 30.6% Hispanic of any race (2010); Density: 2.8 persons per square mile (2010); Average household size: 2.25 (2010); Median age: 38.5 (2010); Males per 100 females: 142.1 (2010).
Religion: Five largest groups: 50.2% Southern Baptist Convention, 10.8% Catholic Church, 9.5% The United Methodist Church, 9.4% Churches of Christ, 3.0% Assemblies of God (2000).
Economy: Unemployment rate: 15.2% (June 2011); Total civilian labor force: 953 (June 2011); Leading industries: 17.2% retail trade; 13.9% accommodation & food services; 8.0% health care and social assistance (2009); Farms: 446 totaling 574,273 acres (2007); Companies that employ 500 or more persons: 0 (2009); Companies that employ 100 to 499 persons: 0 (2009); Companies that employ less than 100 persons: 48 (2009); Black-owned businesses: n/a (2007); Hispanic-owned businesses: n/a (2007); Asian-owned businesses: n/a (2007); Women-owned businesses: n/a (2007); Retail sales per capita: $4,148 (2010). Single-family building permits issued: n/a (2010); Multi-family building permits issued: n/a (2010).
Income: Per capita income: $15,927 (2010); Median household income: $32,667 (2010); Average household income: $42,565 (2010); Percent of households with income of $100,000 or more: 5.7% (2010); Poverty rate: 25.4% (2009); Bankruptcy rate: 1.65% (2010).
Taxes: Total county taxes per capita: $560 (2007); County property taxes per capita: $276 (2007).
Education: Percent of population age 25 and over with: High school diploma (including GED) or higher: 77.0% (2010); Bachelor's degree or higher: 9.7% (2010); Master's degree or higher: 1.8% (2010).
Housing: Homeownership rate: 76.0% (2010); Median home value: $35,146 (2010); Median contract rent: $146 per month (2005-2009 5-year est.); Median year structure built: 1957 (2005-2009 5-year est.).
Health: Birth rate: 82.0 per 10,000 population (2009); Death rate: 36.9 per 10,000 population (2009); Age-adjusted cancer mortality rate: 173.7 (Unreliable) deaths per 100,000 population (2007); Number of physicians: 0.0 per 10,000 population (2008); Hospital beds: 0.0 per 10,000 population (2007); Hospital admissions: 0.0 per 10,000 population (2007).
Elections: 2008 Presidential election results: 24.1% Obama, 75.1% McCain, 0.0% Nader
Additional Information Contacts
Dickens County Government . . . . (806) 623-5532
    http://www.co.dickens.tx.us/ips/cms
Spur Area Chamber of Commerce . . . . (806) 271-3363
    http://www.spurchamber.com

Dickens County Communities

AFTON (unincorporated postal area, zip code 79220). Covers a land area of 104.405 square miles and a water area of 0.026 square miles. Located at 33.74° N. Lat; 100.76° W. Long. Elevation is 2,536 feet.
Population: 193 (2000); Race: 72.6% White, 1.8% Black, 0.0% Asian, 25.6% Other, 23.2% Hispanic of any race (2000); Density: 1.8 persons per square mile (2000); Age: 20.8% under 18, 25.6% over 64 (2000); Marriage status: 11.4% never married, 62.9% now married, 9.3% widowed, 16.4% divorced (2000); Foreign born: 9.5% (2000); Ancestry (includes multiple ancestries): 19.6% American, 14.3% English, 8.3% Irish, 7.7% German (2000).

Economy: Employment by occupation: 19.3% management, 17.0% professional, 10.2% services, 15.9% sales, 14.8% farming, 11.4% construction, 11.4% production (2000).
Income: Per capita income: $13,822 (2000); Median household income: $19,688 (2000); Poverty rate: 179.1% (2000).
Education: Percent of population age 25 and over with: High school diploma (including GED) or higher: 87.6% (2000); Bachelor's degree or higher: 17.8% (2000).

School District(s)
Patton Springs ISD (PK-12)
   2009-10 Enrollment: 92 . . . . (806) 689-2220
Housing: Homeownership rate: 72.9% (2000); Median home value: $22,000 (2000); Median contract rent: $225 per month (2000); Median year structure built: 1956 (2000).
Transportation: Commute to work: 84.9% car, 5.8% public transportation, 2.3% walk, 3.5% work from home (2000); Travel time to work: 56.6% less than 15 minutes, 15.7% 15 to 30 minutes, 9.6% 30 to 45 minutes, 2.4% 45 to 60 minutes, 15.7% 60 minutes or more (2000)

DICKENS (city). County seat. Covers a land area of 0.976 square miles and a water area of 0 square miles. Located at 33.62° N. Lat; 100.83° W. Long. Elevation is 2,546 feet.
Population: 318 (1990); 332 (2000); 300 (2010); 291 (2015 projected); Race: 74.0% White, 15.0% Black, 0.0% Asian, 11.0% Other, 30.0% Hispanic of any race (2010); Density: 307.3 persons per square mile (2010); Average household size: 2.29 (2010); Median age: 34.3 (2010); Males per 100 females: 200.0 (2010); Marriage status: 11.5% never married, 71.0% now married, 12.6% widowed, 4.9% divorced (2005-2009 5-year est.); Foreign born: 0.0% (2005-2009 5-year est.); Ancestry (includes multiple ancestries): 12.4% English, 11.0% Irish, 9.6% German, 7.7% Italian, 6.7% Scotch-Irish (2005-2009 5-year est.).
Economy: Employment by occupation: 31.4% management, 14.0% professional, 10.5% services, 14.0% sales, 2.3% farming, 27.9% construction, 0.0% production (2005-2009 5-year est.).
Income: Per capita income: $13,870 (2010); Median household income: $26,875 (2010); Average household income: $40,706 (2010); Percent of households with income of $100,000 or more: 7.1% (2010); Poverty rate: 16.3% (2005-2009 5-year est.).
Taxes: Total city taxes per capita: $236 (2007); City property taxes per capita: $52 (2007).
Education: Percent of population age 25 and over with: High school diploma (including GED) or higher: 78.7% (2010); Bachelor's degree or higher: 8.8% (2010); Master's degree or higher: 2.3% (2010).
Housing: Homeownership rate: 75.3% (2010); Median home value: $45,000 (2010); Median contract rent: $410 per month (2005-2009 5-year est.); Median year structure built: 1965 (2005-2009 5-year est.).
Transportation: Commute to work: 74.4% car, 0.0% public transportation, 17.1% walk, 8.5% work from home (2005-2009 5-year est.); Travel time to work: 73.3% less than 15 minutes, 13.3% 15 to 30 minutes, 6.7% 30 to 45 minutes, 6.7% 45 to 60 minutes, 0.0% 60 minutes or more (2005-2009 5-year est.)

MCADOO (unincorporated postal area, zip code 79243). Covers a land area of 85.481 square miles and a water area of 0.036 square miles. Located at 33.78° N. Lat; 100.98° W. Long. Elevation is 2,982 feet.
Population: 102 (2000); Race: 93.6% White, 0.0% Black, 0.0% Asian, 6.4% Other, 6.4% Hispanic of any race (2000); Density: 1.2 persons per square mile (2000); Age: 12.8% under 18, 42.6% over 64 (2000); Marriage status: 7.9% never married, 71.9% now married, 10.1% widowed, 10.1% divorced (2000); Foreign born: 0.0% (2000); Ancestry (includes multiple ancestries): 37.2% American, 9.6% Irish, 5.3% German, 4.3% Swedish (2000).
Economy: Employment by occupation: 34.0% management, 0.0% professional, 0.0% services, 38.3% sales, 27.7% farming, 0.0% construction, 0.0% production (2000).
Income: Per capita income: $34,332 (2000); Median household income: $34,500 (2000); Poverty rate: 179.1% (2000).
Education: Percent of population age 25 and over with: High school diploma (including GED) or higher: 58.5% (2000); Bachelor's degree or higher: 8.5% (2000).
Housing: Homeownership rate: 92.5% (2000); Median home value: $50,800 (2000); Median contract rent: n/a per month (2000); Median year structure built: 1957 (2000).
Transportation: Commute to work: 100.0% car, 0.0% public transportation, 0.0% walk, 0.0% work from home (2000); Travel time to

work: 61.7% less than 15 minutes, 38.3% 15 to 30 minutes, 0.0% 30 to 45 minutes, 0.0% 45 to 60 minutes, 0.0% 60 minutes or more (2000)

SPUR (city). Covers a land area of 1.616 square miles and a water area of 0 square miles. Located at 33.47° N. Lat; 100.85° W. Long. Elevation is 2,287 feet.
History: Spur was founded in 1909 on the route of the Mackenzie Trail, and named for the Spur Ranch.
Population: 1,312 (1990); 1,088 (2000); 959 (2010); 895 (2015 projected); Race: 70.9% White, 2.0% Black, 0.4% Asian, 26.7% Other, 31.6% Hispanic of any race (2010); Density: 593.5 persons per square mile (2010); Average household size: 2.21 (2010); Median age: 46.5 (2010); Males per 100 females: 87.7 (2010); Marriage status: 23.8% never married, 49.0% now married, 10.8% widowed, 16.5% divorced (2005-2009 5-year est.); Foreign born: 6.1% (2005-2009 5-year est.); Ancestry (includes multiple ancestries): 12.2% American, 10.1% Irish, 8.1% English, 3.7% German, 3.7% French (2005-2009 5-year est.).
Economy: Employment by occupation: 8.8% management, 10.9% professional, 30.7% services, 20.3% sales, 4.8% farming, 10.9% construction, 13.6% production (2005-2009 5-year est.).
Income: Per capita income: $18,526 (2010); Median household income: $34,167 (2010); Average household income: $40,867 (2010); Percent of households with income of $100,000 or more: 3.6% (2010); Poverty rate: 37.8% (2005-2009 5-year est.).
Taxes: Total city taxes per capita: $267 (2007); City property taxes per capita: $191 (2007).
Education: Percent of population age 25 and over with: High school diploma (including GED) or higher: 75.4% (2010); Bachelor's degree or higher: 10.8% (2010); Master's degree or higher: 1.3% (2010).

School District(s)
Spur ISD (PK-12)
   2009-10 Enrollment: 311 . . . . (806) 271-3272
Housing: Homeownership rate: 76.3% (2010); Median home value: $29,706 (2010); Median contract rent: $137 per month (2005-2009 5-year est.); Median year structure built: 1956 (2005-2009 5-year est.).
Safety: Violent crime rate: 32.5 per 10,000 population; Property crime rate: 54.2 per 10,000 population (2009).
Newspapers: Texas Spur (Local news; Circulation 1,987)
Transportation: Commute to work: 99.3% car, 0.0% public transportation, 0.7% walk, 0.0% work from home (2005-2009 5-year est.); Travel time to work: 77.8% less than 15 minutes, 6.0% 15 to 30 minutes, 5.5% 30 to 45 minutes, 4.6% 45 to 60 minutes, 6.0% 60 minutes or more (2005-2009 5-year est.)
Additional Information Contacts
Spur Area Chamber of Commerce . . . . (806) 271-3363
   http://www.spurchamber.com

Dimmit County

Located in southwestern Texas, on the plains of the Rio Grande; drained by the Nueces River. Covers a land area of 1,330.91 square miles, a water area of 3.57 square miles, and is located in the Central Time Zone at 28.46° N. Lat., 99.75° W. Long. The county was founded in 1858. County seat is Carrizo Springs.

Weather Station: Carrizo Springs								Elevation: 612 feet			
	Jan	Feb	Mar	Apr	May	Jun	Jul	Aug	Sep	Oct	Nov	Dec
High	67	71	78	86	92	97	99	99	93	85	75	66
Low	41	45	52	60	68	73	74	75	70	61	50	41
Precip	1.1	1.0	1.2	1.4	2.9	2.1	1.9	1.7	2.3	2.1	1.3	0.8
Snow	0.0	0.0	0.0	0.0	0.0	0.0	0.0	0.0	0.0	0.0	0.0	0.0

High and Low temperatures in degrees Fahrenheit; Precipitation and Snow in inches

Population: 10,433 (1990); 10,248 (2000); 9,784 (2010); 9,542 (2015 projected); Race: 76.8% White, 1.1% Black, 0.9% Asian, 21.2% Other, 83.7% Hispanic of any race (2010); Density: 7.4 persons per square mile (2010); Average household size: 2.90 (2010); Median age: 33.6 (2010); Males per 100 females: 93.3 (2010).
Religion: Five largest groups: 94.7% Catholic Church, 12.9% Southern Baptist Convention, 2.3% The United Methodist Church, 0.5% Episcopal Church, 0.5% Churches of Christ (2000).
Economy: Unemployment rate: 10.2% (June 2011); Total civilian labor force: 4,354 (June 2011); Leading industries: 25.1% health care and social assistance; 14.2% accommodation & food services; 11.9% mining (2009); Farms: 388 totaling 708,015 acres (2007); Companies that employ 500 or more persons: 0 (2009); Companies that employ 100 to 499 persons: 1

(2009); Companies that employ less than 100 persons: 163 (2009); Black-owned businesses: n/a (2007); Hispanic-owned businesses: n/a (2007); Asian-owned businesses: n/a (2007); Women-owned businesses: n/a (2007); Retail sales per capita: $8,840 (2010). Single-family building permits issued: 5 (2010); Multi-family building permits issued: 0 (2010).

Income: Per capita income: $14,880 (2010); Median household income: $32,811 (2010); Average household income: $42,510 (2010); Percent of households with income of $100,000 or more: 7.9% (2010); Poverty rate: 30.6% (2009); Bankruptcy rate: 0.40% (2010).

Taxes: Total county taxes per capita: $332 (2007); County property taxes per capita: $258 (2007).

Education: Percent of population age 25 and over with: High school diploma (including GED) or higher: 61.6% (2010); Bachelor's degree or higher: 11.8% (2010); Master's degree or higher: 2.3% (2010).

Housing: Homeownership rate: 72.0% (2010); Median home value: $39,164 (2010); Median contract rent: $196 per month (2005-2009 5-year est.); Median year structure built: 1976 (2005-2009 5-year est.)

Health: Birth rate: 177.0 per 10,000 population (2009); Death rate: 64.5 per 10,000 population (2009); Age-adjusted cancer mortality rate: 149.9 (Unreliable) deaths per 100,000 population (2007); Number of physicians: 6.2 per 10,000 population (2008); Hospital beds: 35.8 per 10,000 population (2007); Hospital admissions: 1,542.4 per 10,000 population (2007).

Elections: 2008 Presidential election results: 75.0% Obama, 24.4% McCain, 0.1% Nader

Additional Information Contacts
Dimmit County Government. . . . . (830) 876-2323
  http://www.dimmitcountytx.com
City of Carrizo Springs. . . . . (830) 876-2476
Dimmit County Chamber of Commerce. . . . . (830) 876-5205
  http://dimmitcountytx.com

Dimmit County Communities

ASHERTON (city). Covers a land area of 0.834 square miles and a water area of 0 square miles. Located at 28.44° N. Lat; 99.76° W. Long. Elevation is 535 feet.

History: Incorporated 1925.

Population: 1,608 (1990); 1,342 (2000); 1,238 (2010); 1,193 (2015 projected); Race: 64.6% White, 0.2% Black, 0.2% Asian, 35.0% Other, 84.9% Hispanic of any race (2010); Density: 1,484.9 persons per square mile (2010); Average household size: 2.92 (2010); Median age: 34.4 (2010); Males per 100 females: 91.3 (2010); Marriage status: 28.1% never married, 58.3% now married, 5.9% widowed, 7.7% divorced (2005-2009 5-year est.); Foreign born: 15.5% (2005-2009 5-year est.); Ancestry (includes multiple ancestries): 5.8% German, 4.6% American, 2.9% Italian, 0.7% English (2005-2009 5-year est.).

Economy: Single-family building permits issued: 0 (2010); Multi-family building permits issued: 0 (2010); Employment by occupation: 5.7% management, 11.5% professional, 44.5% services, 9.2% sales, 2.8% farming, 9.0% construction, 17.2% production (2005-2009 5-year est.).

Income: Per capita income: $16,335 (2010); Median household income: $37,641 (2010); Average household income: $47,535 (2010); Percent of households with income of $100,000 or more: 7.1% (2010); Poverty rate: 46.8% (2005-2009 5-year est.).

Taxes: Total city taxes per capita: $309 (2007); City property taxes per capita: $92 (2007).

Education: Percent of population age 25 and over with: High school diploma (including GED) or higher: 61.7% (2010); Bachelor's degree or higher: 12.8% (2010); Master's degree or higher: 2.7% (2010).

School District(s)
Carrizo Springs CISD (PK-12)
  2009-10 Enrollment: 2,395 . . . . (830) 876-2473

Housing: Homeownership rate: 79.7% (2010); Median home value: $27,204 (2010); Median contract rent: $196 per month (2005-2009 5-year est.); Median year structure built: 1976 (2005-2009 5-year est.).

Transportation: Commute to work: 93.8% car, 2.6% public transportation, 2.4% walk, 1.3% work from home (2005-2009 5-year est.); Travel time to work: 25.0% less than 15 minutes, 40.6% 15 to 30 minutes, 13.2% 30 to 45 minutes, 3.7% 45 to 60 minutes, 17.4% 60 minutes or more (2005-2009 5-year est.)

Additional Information Contacts
Dimmit County Chamber of Commerce. . . . . (830) 876-5205
  http://dimmitcountytx.com

BIG WELLS (city). Covers a land area of 0.555 square miles and a water area of 0 square miles. Located at 28.57° N. Lat; 99.57° W. Long. Elevation is 538 feet.

History: Incorporated 1933.

Population: 756 (1990); 704 (2000); 710 (2010); 711 (2015 projected); Race: 72.0% White, 0.6% Black, 0.4% Asian, 27.0% Other, 88.5% Hispanic of any race (2010); Density: 1,278.9 persons per square mile (2010); Average household size: 2.75 (2010); Median age: 38.7 (2010); Males per 100 females: 97.8 (2010); Marriage status: 30.4% never married, 50.7% now married, 7.4% widowed, 11.5% divorced (2005-2009 5-year est.); Foreign born: 0.0% (2005-2009 5-year est.); Ancestry (includes multiple ancestries): 3.7% German, 1.9% English, 1.6% Polish (2005-2009 5-year est.).

Economy: Single-family building permits issued: 0 (2010); Multi-family building permits issued: 0 (2010); Employment by occupation: 3.0% management, 20.8% professional, 27.5% services, 11.4% sales, 0.8% farming, 23.3% construction, 13.1% production (2005-2009 5-year est.).

Income: Per capita income: $8,831 (2010); Median household income: $20,391 (2010); Average household income: $24,329 (2010); Percent of households with income of $100,000 or more: 0.4% (2010); Poverty rate: 41.1% (2005-2009 5-year est.).

Taxes: Total city taxes per capita: $55 (2007); City property taxes per capita: $40 (2007).

Education: Percent of population age 25 and over with: High school diploma (including GED) or higher: 42.5% (2010); Bachelor's degree or higher: 1.8% (2010); Master's degree or higher: 0.0% (2010).

School District(s)
Carrizo Springs CISD (PK-12)
  2009-10 Enrollment: 2,395 . . . . (830) 876-2473

Housing: Homeownership rate: 82.1% (2010); Median home value: $24,568 (2010); Median contract rent: $237 per month (2005-2009 5-year est.); Median year structure built: 1977 (2005-2009 5-year est.).

Transportation: Commute to work: 81.8% car, 0.0% public transportation, 16.4% walk, 0.0% work from home (2005-2009 5-year est.); Travel time to work: 60.9% less than 15 minutes, 11.6% 15 to 30 minutes, 15.6% 30 to 45 minutes, 9.3% 45 to 60 minutes, 2.7% 60 minutes or more (2005-2009 5-year est.)

Additional Information Contacts
Dimmit County Chamber of Commerce. . . . . (830) 876-5205
  http://dimmitcountytx.com

BRUNDAGE (CDP). Covers a land area of 23.402 square miles and a water area of 0.102 square miles. Located at 28.59° N. Lat; 99.66° W. Long. Elevation is 535 feet.

Population: 31 (1990); 31 (2000); 29 (2010); 29 (2015 projected); Race: 72.4% White, 0.0% Black, 0.0% Asian, 27.6% Other, 89.7% Hispanic of any race (2010); Density: 1.2 persons per square mile (2010); Average household size: 2.64 (2010); Median age: 30.0 (2010); Males per 100 females: 81.3 (2010); Marriage status: n/a never married, n/a now married, n/a widowed, n/a divorced (2005-2009 5-year est.); Foreign born: n/a (2005-2009 5-year est.); Ancestry (includes multiple ancestries): n/a (2005-2009 5-year est.).

Economy: Employment by occupation: n/a management, n/a professional, n/a services, n/a sales, n/a farming, n/a construction, n/a production (2005-2009 5-year est.).

Income: Per capita income: $8,831 (2010); Median household income: $16,667 (2010); Average household income: $18,182 (2010); Percent of households with income of $100,000 or more: 0.0% (2010); Poverty rate: n/a (2005-2009 5-year est.).

Education: Percent of population age 25 and over with: High school diploma (including GED) or higher: 31.3% (2010); Bachelor's degree or higher: 0.0% (2010); Master's degree or higher: 0.0% (2010).

Housing: Homeownership rate: 81.8% (2010); Median home value: $22,500 (2010); Median contract rent: n/a per month (2005-2009 5-year est.); Median year structure built: n/a (2005-2009 5-year est.).

Transportation: Commute to work: n/a car, n/a public transportation, n/a walk, n/a work from home (2005-2009 5-year est.); Travel time to work: n/a less than 15 minutes, n/a 15 to 30 minutes, n/a 30 to 45 minutes, n/a 45 to 60 minutes, n/a 60 minutes or more (2005-2009 5-year est.)

CARRIZO HILL (CDP). Covers a land area of 0.484 square miles and a water area of 0 square miles. Located at 28.50° N. Lat; 99.82° W. Long. Elevation is 630 feet.

Population: 506 (1990); 548 (2000); 513 (2010); 500 (2015 projected); Race: 85.4% White, 0.6% Black, 0.8% Asian, 13.3% Other, 77.8% Hispanic of any race (2010); Density: 1,058.9 persons per square mile (2010); Average household size: 2.93 (2010); Median age: 33.9 (2010); Males per 100 females: 97.3 (2010); Marriage status: 13.0% never married, 87.0% now married, 0.0% widowed, 0.0% divorced (2005-2009 5-year est.); Foreign born: 3.6% (2005-2009 5-year est.); Ancestry (includes multiple ancestries): 10.5% Dutch, 5.6% German (2005-2009 5-year est.).
Economy: Employment by occupation: 0.0% management, 13.3% professional, 17.2% services, 20.0% sales, 0.0% farming, 19.6% construction, 29.8% production (2005-2009 5-year est.).
Income: Per capita income: $18,897 (2010); Median household income: $40,323 (2010); Average household income: $50,345 (2010); Percent of households with income of $100,000 or more: 13.8% (2010); Poverty rate: 36.2% (2005-2009 5-year est.).
Education: Percent of population age 25 and over with: High school diploma (including GED) or higher: 79.1% (2010); Bachelor's degree or higher: 15.2% (2010); Master's degree or higher: 3.6% (2010).
Housing: Homeownership rate: 76.4% (2010); Median home value: $41,500 (2010); Median contract rent: $200 per month (2005-2009 5-year est.); Median year structure built: 1996 (2005-2009 5-year est.).
Transportation: Commute to work: 85.3% car, 0.0% public transportation, 0.0% walk, 14.7% work from home (2005-2009 5-year est.); Travel time to work: 70.0% less than 15 minutes, 0.0% 15 to 30 minutes, 14.4% 30 to 45 minutes, 0.0% 45 to 60 minutes, 15.6% 60 minutes or more (2005-2009 5-year est.)

CARRIZO SPRINGS (city). County seat. Covers a land area of 3.119 square miles and a water area of 0.010 square miles. Located at 28.52° N. Lat; 99.86° W. Long. Elevation is 604 feet.
History: Carrizo Springs called itself "The Hub of the Winter Garden of Texas" to attract residents. Irrigation from artesian wells made the surrounding land productive.
Population: 5,745 (1990); 5,655 (2000); 5,392 (2010); 5,228 (2015 projected); Race: 78.0% White, 1.7% Black, 1.2% Asian, 19.1% Other, 85.4% Hispanic of any race (2010); Density: 1,728.5 persons per square mile (2010); Average household size: 2.90 (2010); Median age: 32.9 (2010); Males per 100 females: 92.5 (2010); Marriage status: 34.5% never married, 49.5% now married, 8.2% widowed, 7.8% divorced (2005-2009 5-year est.); Foreign born: 9.4% (2005-2009 5-year est.); Ancestry (includes multiple ancestries): 2.9% French, 1.0% German, 0.9% American, 0.5% Irish, 0.2% Scotch-Irish (2005-2009 5-year est.).
Economy: Single-family building permits issued: 5 (2010); Multi-family building permits issued: 0 (2010); Employment by occupation: 7.7% management, 23.0% professional, 31.3% services, 19.7% sales, 0.0% farming, 9.4% construction, 8.9% production (2005-2009 5-year est.).
Income: Per capita income: $13,799 (2010); Median household income: $31,889 (2010); Average household income: $40,134 (2010); Percent of households with income of $100,000 or more: 6.6% (2010); Poverty rate: 43.0% (2005-2009 5-year est.).
Taxes: Total city taxes per capita: $255 (2007); City property taxes per capita: $62 (2007).
Education: Percent of population age 25 and over with: High school diploma (including GED) or higher: 58.3% (2010); Bachelor's degree or higher: 11.5% (2010); Master's degree or higher: 2.0% (2010).
School District(s)
Carrizo Springs CISD (PK-12)
    2009-10 Enrollment: 2,395 . . . . (830) 876-2473
Housing: Homeownership rate: 67.7% (2010); Median home value: $46,983 (2010); Median contract rent: $185 per month (2005-2009 5-year est.); Median year structure built: 1972 (2005-2009 5-year est.).
Hospitals: Dimmit County Memorial Hospital (35 beds)
Newspapers: Carrizo Springs Javelin (Community news; Circulation 2,000)
Transportation: Commute to work: 95.1% car, 1.2% public transportation, 3.7% walk, 0.0% work from home (2005-2009 5-year est.); Travel time to work: 74.5% less than 15 minutes, 8.9% 15 to 30 minutes, 6.2% 30 to 45 minutes, 2.2% 45 to 60 minutes, 8.2% 60 minutes or more (2005-2009 5-year est.)
Airports: Dimmit County (general aviation); Faith Ranch (general aviation)
Additional Information Contacts
City of Carrizo Springs. . . . . (830) 876-2476
Dimmit County Chamber of Commerce . . . . (830) 876-5205
    http://dimmitcountytx.com

CATARINA (CDP). Covers a land area of 3.782 square miles and a water area of 0 square miles. Located at 28.34° N. Lat; 99.61° W. Long. Elevation is 551 feet.
Population: 92 (1990); 135 (2000); 153 (2010); 160 (2015 projected); Race: 68.0% White, 0.0% Black, 0.0% Asian, 32.0% Other, 75.2% Hispanic of any race (2010); Density: 40.5 persons per square mile (2010); Average household size: 3.00 (2010); Median age: 32.7 (2010); Males per 100 females: 86.6 (2010); Marriage status: 0.0% never married, 91.3% now married, 8.7% widowed, 0.0% divorced (2005-2009 5-year est.); Foreign born: 0.0% (2005-2009 5-year est.); Ancestry (includes multiple ancestries): 30.1% Irish, 25.4% English, 19.1% French, 14.5% German (2005-2009 5-year est.).
Economy: Employment by occupation: 43.9% management, 0.0% professional, 12.3% services, 28.9% sales, 14.9% farming, 0.0% construction, 0.0% production (2005-2009 5-year est.).
Income: Per capita income: $18,319 (2010); Median household income: $40,250 (2010); Average household income: $57,647 (2010); Percent of households with income of $100,000 or more: 13.7% (2010); Poverty rate: 0.0% (2005-2009 5-year est.).
Education: Percent of population age 25 and over with: High school diploma (including GED) or higher: 64.8% (2010); Bachelor's degree or higher: 17.0% (2010); Master's degree or higher: 6.8% (2010).
Housing: Homeownership rate: 60.8% (2010); Median home value: $42,000 (2010); Median contract rent: n/a per month (2005-2009 5-year est.); Median year structure built: 1971 (2005-2009 5-year est.).
Transportation: Commute to work: 100.0% car, 0.0% public transportation, 0.0% walk, 0.0% work from home (2005-2009 5-year est.); Travel time to work: 28.9% less than 15 minutes, 21.9% 15 to 30 minutes, 12.3% 30 to 45 minutes, 0.0% 45 to 60 minutes, 36.8% 60 minutes or more (2005-2009 5-year est.)

Donley County

Located in north Texas, in the Panhandle; crossed by the Salt Fork of the Red River. Covers a land area of 929.77 square miles, a water area of 3.28 square miles, and is located in the Central Time Zone at 34.97° N. Lat., 100.81° W. Long. The county was founded in 1876. County seat is Clarendon.

Weather Station: Clarendon Municipal Arpt									Elevation: 2,871 feet			
	Jan	Feb	Mar	Apr	May	Jun	Jul	Aug	Sep	Oct	Nov	Dec
High	53	57	64	73	81	89	95	93	85	75	63	53
Low	24	27	34	43	53	62	66	65	57	45	33	25
Precip	0.7	0.8	1.5	2.2	3.3	3.6	2.0	3.1	2.5	2.1	1.1	1.0
Snow	1.7	0.6	0.7	0.3	0.0	0.0	0.0	0.0	0.0	0.0	0.7	2.3

High and Low temperatures in degrees Fahrenheit; Precipitation and Snow in inches

Population: 3,696 (1990); 3,828 (2000); 3,957 (2010); 4,013 (2015 projected); Race: 88.0% White, 6.0% Black, 0.2% Asian, 5.9% Other, 8.3% Hispanic of any race (2010); Density: 4.3 persons per square mile (2010); Average household size: 2.28 (2010); Median age: 41.9 (2010); Males per 100 females: 95.9 (2010).
Religion: Five largest groups: 41.4% Southern Baptist Convention, 13.7% The United Methodist Church, 6.8% Churches of Christ, 3.1% Catholic Church, 2.2% Assemblies of God (2000).
Economy: Unemployment rate: 7.3% (June 2011); Total civilian labor force: 1,964 (June 2011); Leading industries: 31.9% retail trade; 19.5% accommodation & food services; 8.6% other services (except public administration) (2009); Farms: 392 totaling 588,947 acres (2007); Companies that employ 500 or more persons: 0 (2009); Companies that employ 100 to 499 persons: 0 (2009); Companies that employ less than 100 persons: 82 (2009); Black-owned businesses: n/a (2007); Hispanic-owned businesses: n/a (2007); Asian-owned businesses: n/a (2007); Women-owned businesses: n/a (2007); Retail sales per capita: $10,237 (2010). Single-family building permits issued: 1 (2010); Multi-family building permits issued: 0 (2010).
Income: Per capita income: $20,401 (2010); Median household income: $37,397 (2010); Average household income: $48,773 (2010); Percent of households with income of $100,000 or more: 9.2% (2010); Poverty rate: 20.1% (2009); Bankruptcy rate: 1.35% (2010).
Taxes: Total county taxes per capita: $306 (2007); County property taxes per capita: $167 (2007).
Education: Percent of population age 25 and over with: High school diploma (including GED) or higher: 83.1% (2010); Bachelor's degree or higher: 17.3% (2010); Master's degree or higher: 5.1% (2010).

Housing: Homeownership rate: 72.8% (2010); Median home value: $65,686 (2010); Median contract rent: $375 per month (2005-2009 5-year est.); Median year structure built: 1961 (2005-2009 5-year est.)
Health: Birth rate: 98.3 per 10,000 population (2009); Death rate: 106.4 per 10,000 population (2009); Age-adjusted cancer mortality rate: 151.1 (Unreliable) deaths per 100,000 population (2007); Number of physicians: 2.7 per 10,000 population (2008); Hospital beds: 0.0 per 10,000 population (2007); Hospital admissions: 0.0 per 10,000 population (2007).
Elections: 2008 Presidential election results: 17.2% Obama, 81.3% McCain, 0.0% Nader
National and State Parks: Lake McClellan National Grassland
Additional Information Contacts
Donley County Government . . . . (806) 874-3625
   http://www.co.donley.tx.us/ips/cms
Clarendon Chamber of Commerce . . . . (806) 874-2421
   http://www.donleytx.com

Donley County Communities

CLARENDON (city). County seat. Covers a land area of 2.907 square miles and a water area of 0.099 square miles. Located at 34.93° N. Lat; 100.89° W. Long. Elevation is 2,733 feet.
History: Old Clarendon was founded in 1878 by a Methodist minister, and populated largely by graduates of Harvard, Yale, Princeton, and the University of Virginia. When the railroad line was laid a few miles away in 1887, the town moved to the tracks.
Population: 2,067 (1990); 1,974 (2000); 2,117 (2010); 2,169 (2015 projected); Race: 83.6% White, 9.9% Black, 0.2% Asian, 6.3% Other, 8.5% Hispanic of any race (2010); Density: 728.2 persons per square mile (2010); Average household size: 2.32 (2010); Median age: 35.5 (2010); Males per 100 females: 92.8 (2010); Marriage status: 37.0% never married, 53.7% now married, 6.1% widowed, 3.2% divorced (2005-2009 5-year est.); Foreign born: 4.8% (2005-2009 5-year est.); Ancestry (includes multiple ancestries): 22.5% German, 18.2% Irish, 8.5% English, 3.4% French, 2.7% Scottish (2005-2009 5-year est.).
Economy: Single-family building permits issued: 0 (2010); Multi-family building permits issued: 0 (2010); Employment by occupation: 11.6% management, 23.4% professional, 19.4% services, 15.8% sales, 2.1% farming, 14.3% construction, 13.4% production (2005-2009 5-year est.).
Income: Per capita income: $19,868 (2010); Median household income: $35,366 (2010); Average household income: $50,308 (2010); Percent of households with income of $100,000 or more: 9.1% (2010); Poverty rate: 17.1% (2005-2009 5-year est.).
Taxes: Total city taxes per capita: $133 (2007); City property taxes per capita: $123 (2007).
Education: Percent of population age 25 and over with: High school diploma (including GED) or higher: 83.6% (2010); Bachelor's degree or higher: 19.6% (2010); Master's degree or higher: 7.1% (2010).
School District(s)
Clarendon ISD (PK-12)
   2009-10 Enrollment: 533 . . . . (806) 874-2062
Two-year College(s)
Clarendon College (Public)
   Fall 2009 Enrollment: 1,427 . . . . (806) 874-3571
   2010-11 Tuition: In-state $2,448; Out-of-state $3,192
Housing: Homeownership rate: 68.4% (2010); Median home value: $65,067 (2010); Median contract rent: $369 per month (2005-2009 5-year est.); Median year structure built: 1944 (2005-2009 5-year est.).
Newspapers: Clarendon Enterprise (Community news; Circulation 1,225)
Transportation: Commute to work: 94.6% car, 0.0% public transportation, 0.8% walk, 3.8% work from home (2005-2009 5-year est.); Travel time to work: 71.9% less than 15 minutes, 7.3% 15 to 30 minutes, 4.9% 30 to 45 minutes, 3.3% 45 to 60 minutes, 12.6% 60 minutes or more (2005-2009 5-year est.)
Additional Information Contacts
Clarendon Chamber of Commerce . . . . (806) 874-2421
   http://www.donleytx.com

HEDLEY (city). Covers a land area of 0.729 square miles and a water area of 0 square miles. Located at 34.86° N. Lat; 100.66° W. Long. Elevation is 2,621 feet.
Population: 391 (1990); 379 (2000); 339 (2010); 326 (2015 projected); Race: 89.7% White, 1.8% Black, 0.0% Asian, 8.6% Other, 9.1% Hispanic of any race (2010); Density: 465.2 persons per square mile (2010); Average household size: 2.32 (2010); Median age: 41.3 (2010); Males per

100 females: 93.7 (2010); Marriage status: 16.5% never married, 68.2% now married, 10.3% widowed, 5.0% divorced (2005-2009 5-year est.); Foreign born: 0.0% (2005-2009 5-year est.); Ancestry (includes multiple ancestries): 21.9% Irish, 10.1% German, 9.0% English, 6.8% Scotch-Irish, 4.1% Dutch (2005-2009 5-year est.).
Economy: Employment by occupation: 8.6% management, 7.4% professional, 35.4% services, 13.1% sales, 10.3% farming, 9.7% construction, 15.4% production (2005-2009 5-year est.).
Income: Per capita income: $20,110 (2010); Median household income: $38,333 (2010); Average household income: $45,257 (2010); Percent of households with income of $100,000 or more: 6.8% (2010); Poverty rate: 16.4% (2005-2009 5-year est.).
Taxes: Total city taxes per capita: $102 (2007); City property taxes per capita: $51 (2007).
Education: Percent of population age 25 and over with: High school diploma (including GED) or higher: 72.8% (2010); Bachelor's degree or higher: 15.5% (2010); Master's degree or higher: 1.7% (2010).
School District(s)
Hedley ISD (PK-12)
   2009-10 Enrollment: 137 . . . . (806) 856-5323
Housing: Homeownership rate: 76.7% (2010); Median home value: $48,750 (2010); Median contract rent: $268 per month (2005-2009 5-year est.); Median year structure built: before 1940 (2005-2009 5-year est.).
Transportation: Commute to work: 89.0% car, 0.0% public transportation, 4.0% walk, 2.3% work from home (2005-2009 5-year est.); Travel time to work: 42.0% less than 15 minutes, 32.0% 15 to 30 minutes, 12.4% 30 to 45 minutes, 5.9% 45 to 60 minutes, 7.7% 60 minutes or more (2005-2009 5-year est.)

HOWARDWICK (city). Covers a land area of 1.816 square miles and a water area of 0 square miles. Located at 35.03° N. Lat; 100.90° W. Long. Elevation is 2,769 feet.
Population: 211 (1990); 437 (2000); 456 (2010); 469 (2015 projected); Race: 96.1% White, 0.7% Black, 0.2% Asian, 3.1% Other, 7.7% Hispanic of any race (2010); Density: 251.1 persons per square mile (2010); Average household size: 2.20 (2010); Median age: 53.4 (2010); Males per 100 females: 108.2 (2010); Marriage status: 7.6% never married, 66.6% now married, 10.0% widowed, 15.9% divorced (2005-2009 5-year est.); Foreign born: 1.5% (2005-2009 5-year est.); Ancestry (includes multiple ancestries): 22.2% German, 12.0% English, 10.8% Irish, 6.4% French, 4.4% Scotch-Irish (2005-2009 5-year est.).
Economy: Single-family building permits issued: 1 (2010); Multi-family building permits issued: 0 (2010); Employment by occupation: 27.8% management, 19.1% professional, 24.3% services, 20.0% sales, 3.5% farming, 2.6% construction, 2.6% production (2005-2009 5-year est.).
Income: Per capita income: $21,755 (2010); Median household income: $39,929 (2010); Average household income: $46,292 (2010); Percent of households with income of $100,000 or more: 10.1% (2010); Poverty rate: 19.3% (2005-2009 5-year est.).
Taxes: Total city taxes per capita: $301 (2007); City property taxes per capita: $166 (2007).
Education: Percent of population age 25 and over with: High school diploma (including GED) or higher: 88.6% (2010); Bachelor's degree or higher: 14.6% (2010); Master's degree or higher: 3.7% (2010).
Housing: Homeownership rate: 78.3% (2010); Median home value: $81,250 (2010); Median contract rent: $420 per month (2005-2009 5-year est.); Median year structure built: 1981 (2005-2009 5-year est.).
Transportation: Commute to work: 97.4% car, 0.0% public transportation, 0.0% walk, 0.0% work from home (2005-2009 5-year est.); Travel time to work: 42.6% less than 15 minutes, 33.9% 15 to 30 minutes, 6.1% 30 to 45 minutes, 2.6% 45 to 60 minutes, 14.8% 60 minutes or more (2005-2009 5-year est.)

Duval County

Located in south Texas. Covers a land area of 1,792.71 square miles, a water area of 2.97 square miles, and is located in the Central Time Zone at 27.71° N. Lat., 98.51° W. Long. The county was founded in 1858. County seat is San Diego.

Weather Station: Benavides 2   Elevation: 379 feet

	Jan	Feb	Mar	Apr	May	Jun	Jul	Aug	Sep	Oct	Nov	Dec
High	68	72	79	85	91	95	96	97	92	85	77	69
Low	45	48	54	61	69	73	74	74	70	61	53	44
Precip	1.3	1.4	1.1	1.4	3.4	2.6	2.4	2.0	3.0	2.0	1.3	1.1
Snow	0.0	0.0	0.0	0.0	0.0	0.0	0.0	0.0	0.0	0.0	0.0	0.2

High and Low temperatures in degrees Fahrenheit; Precipitation and Snow in inches

Population: 12,918 (1990); 13,120 (2000); 12,049 (2010); 11,510 (2015 projected); Race: 80.0% White, 0.9% Black, 0.2% Asian, 19.0% Other, 87.1% Hispanic of any race (2010); Density: 6.7 persons per square mile (2010); Average household size: 2.76 (2010); Median age: 36.2 (2010); Males per 100 females: 105.6 (2010).
Religion: Five largest groups: 59.5% Catholic Church, 10.2% Southern Baptist Convention, 1.0% The United Methodist Church, 0.4% Churches of Christ, 0.3% Assemblies of God (2000).
Economy: Unemployment rate: 10.1% (June 2011); Total civilian labor force: 5,457 (June 2011); Leading industries: 32.2% mining; 27.3% health care and social assistance; 11.1% retail trade (2009); Farms: 1,507 totaling 1,021,206 acres (2007); Companies that employ 500 or more persons: 0 (2009); Companies that employ 100 to 499 persons: 3 (2009); Companies that employ less than 100 persons: 132 (2009); Black-owned businesses: n/a (2007); Hispanic-owned businesses: 615 (2007); Asian-owned businesses: n/a (2007); Women-owned businesses: 221 (2007); Retail sales per capita: $4,755 (2010). Single-family building permits issued: n/a (2010); Multi-family building permits issued: n/a (2010).
Income: Per capita income: $17,747 (2010); Median household income: $33,988 (2010); Average household income: $49,464 (2010); Percent of households with income of $100,000 or more: 10.1% (2010); Poverty rate: 25.5% (2009); Bankruptcy rate: 0.51% (2010).
Taxes: Total county taxes per capita: $644 (2007); County property taxes per capita: $606 (2007).
Education: Percent of population age 25 and over with: High school diploma (including GED) or higher: 66.1% (2010); Bachelor's degree or higher: 10.5% (2010); Master's degree or higher: 3.8% (2010).
Housing: Homeownership rate: 79.4% (2010); Median home value: $36,974 (2010); Median contract rent: $264 per month (2005-2009 5-year est.); Median year structure built: 1971 (2005-2009 5-year est.)
Health: Birth rate: 172.4 per 10,000 population (2009); Death rate: 94.9 per 10,000 population (2009); Age-adjusted cancer mortality rate: 169.3 deaths per 100,000 population (2007); Number of physicians: 0.0 per 10,000 population (2008); Hospital beds: 0.0 per 10,000 population (2007); Hospital admissions: 0.0 per 10,000 population (2007).
Elections: 2008 Presidential election results: 74.8% Obama, 24.4% McCain, 0.0% Nader
Additional Information Contacts
Duval County Government . . . . (361) 279-3322

Freer Chamber of Commerce . . . . (361) 394-6891
    http://www.visitfreer.com

Duval County Communities

BENAVIDES (city). Covers a land area of 1.805 square miles and a water area of 0 square miles. Located at 27.59° N. Lat; 98.41° W. Long. Elevation is 371 feet.
History: Incorporated 1936.
Population: 1,788 (1990); 1,686 (2000); 1,506 (2010); 1,420 (2015 projected); Race: 78.9% White, 0.0% Black, 0.2% Asian, 20.9% Other, 95.3% Hispanic of any race (2010); Density: 834.3 persons per square mile (2010); Average household size: 2.61 (2010); Median age: 40.7 (2010); Males per 100 females: 92.8 (2010); Marriage status: 27.1% never married, 54.9% now married, 12.9% widowed, 5.2% divorced (2005-2009 5-year est.); Foreign born: 2.7% (2005-2009 5-year est.); Ancestry (includes multiple ancestries): 2.4% American, 0.9% English, 0.7% Portuguese, 0.0% Italian (2005-2009 5-year est.).
Economy: Employment by occupation: 8.8% management, 14.9% professional, 34.6% services, 10.2% sales, 0.0% farming, 23.1% construction, 8.4% production (2005-2009 5-year est.).
Income: Per capita income: $18,352 (2010); Median household income: $33,311 (2010); Average household income: $48,241 (2010); Percent of households with income of $100,000 or more: 11.8% (2010); Poverty rate: 35.7% (2005-2009 5-year est.).
Taxes: Total city taxes per capita: $335 (2007); City property taxes per capita: $78 (2007).

Education: Percent of population age 25 and over with: High school diploma (including GED) or higher: 69.8% (2010); Bachelor's degree or higher: 15.9% (2010); Master's degree or higher: 6.7% (2010).
School District(s)
Benavides ISD (PK-12)
    2009-10 Enrollment: 408 . . . . (361) 256-3000
Housing: Homeownership rate: 83.0% (2010); Median home value: $33,660 (2010); Median contract rent: $328 per month (2005-2009 5-year est.); Median year structure built: 1960 (2005-2009 5-year est.).
Transportation: Commute to work: 89.1% car, 0.0% public transportation, 4.6% walk, 5.4% work from home (2005-2009 5-year est.); Travel time to work: 48.3% less than 15 minutes, 16.4% 15 to 30 minutes, 8.8% 30 to 45 minutes, 9.7% 45 to 60 minutes, 16.8% 60 minutes or more (2005-2009 5-year est.)

CONCEPCION (CDP). Covers a land area of 0.080 square miles and a water area of 0 square miles. Located at 27.39° N. Lat; 98.35° W. Long. Elevation is 292 feet.
Population: 77 (1990); 61 (2000); 61 (2010); 58 (2015 projected); Race: 78.7% White, 0.0% Black, 0.0% Asian, 21.3% Other, 83.6% Hispanic of any race (2010); Density: 760.8 persons per square mile (2010); Average household size: 2.61 (2010); Median age: 40.6 (2010); Males per 100 females: 84.8 (2010); Marriage status: 32.6% never married, 56.5% now married, 0.0% widowed, 10.9% divorced (2005-2009 5-year est.); Foreign born: 18.0% (2005-2009 5-year est.); Ancestry (includes multiple ancestries): n/a (2005-2009 5-year est.).
Economy: Employment by occupation: 0.0% management, 11.1% professional, 0.0% services, 0.0% sales, 0.0% farming, 61.1% construction, 27.8% production (2005-2009 5-year est.).
Income: Per capita income: $14,065 (2010); Median household income: $26,667 (2010); Average household income: $33,043 (2010); Percent of households with income of $100,000 or more: 0.0% (2010); Poverty rate: 0.0% (2005-2009 5-year est.).
Education: Percent of population age 25 and over with: High school diploma (including GED) or higher: 52.5% (2010); Bachelor's degree or higher: 5.0% (2010); Master's degree or higher: 0.0% (2010).
Housing: Homeownership rate: 87.0% (2010); Median home value: $30,000 (2010); Median contract rent: n/a per month (2005-2009 5-year est.); Median year structure built: 1987 (2005-2009 5-year est.).
Transportation: Commute to work: 100.0% car, 0.0% public transportation, 0.0% walk, 0.0% work from home (2005-2009 5-year est.); Travel time to work: 61.1% less than 15 minutes, 0.0% 15 to 30 minutes, 11.1% 30 to 45 minutes, 0.0% 45 to 60 minutes, 27.8% 60 minutes or more (2005-2009 5-year est.)

FREER (city). Covers a land area of 4.029 square miles and a water area of 0.037 square miles. Located at 27.87° N. Lat; 98.61° W. Long. Elevation is 518 feet.
History: Incorporated 1938.
Population: 3,271 (1990); 3,241 (2000); 2,910 (2010); 2,745 (2015 projected); Race: 82.3% White, 0.4% Black, 0.2% Asian, 17.0% Other, 75.5% Hispanic of any race (2010); Density: 722.2 persons per square mile (2010); Average household size: 2.80 (2010); Median age: 34.0 (2010); Males per 100 females: 97.3 (2010); Marriage status: 23.0% never married, 59.7% now married, 9.3% widowed, 8.0% divorced (2005-2009 5-year est.); Foreign born: 8.0% (2005-2009 5-year est.); Ancestry (includes multiple ancestries): 5.3% English, 4.9% German, 3.0% Irish, 2.3% French, 1.6% American (2005-2009 5-year est.).
Economy: Employment by occupation: 6.9% management, 16.2% professional, 17.8% services, 16.0% sales, 3.0% farming, 26.6% construction, 13.5% production (2005-2009 5-year est.).
Income: Per capita income: $20,339 (2010); Median household income: $39,365 (2010); Average household income: $57,112 (2010); Percent of households with income of $100,000 or more: 12.3% (2010); Poverty rate: 33.4% (2005-2009 5-year est.).
Taxes: Total city taxes per capita: $266 (2007); City property taxes per capita: $0 (2007).
Education: Percent of population age 25 and over with: High school diploma (including GED) or higher: 67.7% (2010); Bachelor's degree or higher: 7.5% (2010); Master's degree or higher: 2.2% (2010).
School District(s)
Freer ISD (PK-12)
    2009-10 Enrollment: 846 . . . . (361) 394-6025

Housing: Homeownership rate: 77.5% (2010); Median home value: $36,600 (2010); Median contract rent: $356 per month (2005-2009 5-year est.); Median year structure built: 1975 (2005-2009 5-year est.).
Safety: Violent crime rate: 48.2 per 10,000 population; Property crime rate: 196.1 per 10,000 population (2009).
Newspapers: Freer Press (Local news; Circulation 856)
Transportation: Commute to work: 82.1% car, 0.0% public transportation, 3.6% walk, 7.7% work from home (2005-2009 5-year est.); Travel time to work: 65.2% less than 15 minutes, 0.7% 15 to 30 minutes, 12.6% 30 to 45 minutes, 8.2% 45 to 60 minutes, 13.3% 60 minutes or more (2005-2009 5-year est.)
Additional Information Contacts
Freer Chamber of Commerce . . . . (361) 394-6891
   http://www.visitfreer.com

REALITOS (CDP). Covers a land area of 0.271 square miles and a water area of 0 square miles. Located at 27.44° N. Lat; 98.52° W. Long. Elevation is 443 feet.
Population: 262 (1990); 209 (2000); 186 (2010); 176 (2015 projected); Race: 78.5% White, 0.0% Black, 0.0% Asian, 21.5% Other, 82.8% Hispanic of any race (2010); Density: 686.1 persons per square mile (2010); Average household size: 2.58 (2010); Median age: 45.0 (2010); Males per 100 females: 102.2 (2010); Marriage status: 21.3% never married, 59.0% now married, 19.7% widowed, 0.0% divorced (2005-2009 5-year est.); Foreign born: 11.5% (2005-2009 5-year est.); Ancestry (includes multiple ancestries): 7.9% German (2005-2009 5-year est.).
Economy: Employment by occupation: 0.0% management, 0.0% professional, 0.0% services, 0.0% sales, 0.0% farming, 41.5% construction, 58.5% production (2005-2009 5-year est.).
Income: Per capita income: $14,065 (2010); Median household income: $25,556 (2010); Average household income: $37,711 (2010); Percent of households with income of $100,000 or more: 5.6% (2010); Poverty rate: 40.9% (2005-2009 5-year est.).
Education: Percent of population age 25 and over with: High school diploma (including GED) or higher: 53.5% (2010); Bachelor's degree or higher: 7.9% (2010); Master's degree or higher: 2.4% (2010).
Housing: Homeownership rate: 85.9% (2010); Median home value: $35,625 (2010); Median contract rent: n/a per month (2005-2009 5-year est.); Median year structure built: 1968 (2005-2009 5-year est.).
Transportation: Commute to work: 100.0% car, 0.0% public transportation, 0.0% walk, 0.0% work from home (2005-2009 5-year est.); Travel time to work: 0.0% less than 15 minutes, 32.3% 15 to 30 minutes, 16.9% 30 to 45 minutes, 0.0% 45 to 60 minutes, 50.8% 60 minutes or more (2005-2009 5-year est.)

SAN DIEGO (city). County seat. Covers a land area of 1.629 square miles and a water area of 0 square miles. Located at 27.76° N. Lat; 98.23° W. Long. Elevation is 308 feet.
History: San Diego was once a lively cattle shipping town, where a detachment of Texas Rangers were sent to cope with the gun-toting cowboys and the bands of rustlers. A scheme was hatched in San Diego in 1914 for the reannexation of Texas, New Mexico, Arizona, and California to Mexico, but the plan was never carried out.
Population: 4,983 (1990); 4,753 (2000); 4,483 (2010); 4,344 (2015 projected); Race: 76.7% White, 0.4% Black, 0.0% Asian, 22.9% Other, 96.6% Hispanic of any race (2010); Density: 2,751.3 persons per square mile (2010); Average household size: 2.92 (2010); Median age: 31.8 (2010); Males per 100 females: 92.7 (2010); Marriage status: 34.0% never married, 45.1% now married, 7.9% widowed, 13.0% divorced (2005-2009 5-year est.); Foreign born: 0.6% (2005-2009 5-year est.); Ancestry (includes multiple ancestries): 2.3% American, 1.9% Irish, 0.4% French, 0.3% German, 0.3% English (2005-2009 5-year est.).
Economy: Employment by occupation: 4.8% management, 13.1% professional, 25.0% services, 26.9% sales, 3.3% farming, 10.4% construction, 16.5% production (2005-2009 5-year est.).
Income: Per capita income: $14,178 (2010); Median household income: $27,951 (2010); Average household income: $41,248 (2010); Percent of households with income of $100,000 or more: 7.0% (2010); Poverty rate: 25.8% (2005-2009 5-year est.).
Taxes: Total city taxes per capita: $70 (2007); City property taxes per capita: $0 (2007).
Education: Percent of population age 25 and over with: High school diploma (including GED) or higher: 62.4% (2010); Bachelor's degree or higher: 8.8% (2010); Master's degree or higher: 4.3% (2010).

School District(s)
San Diego ISD (PK-12)
   2009-10 Enrollment: 1,369 . . . . (361) 279-3382
Housing: Homeownership rate: 74.9% (2010); Median home value: $33,072 (2010); Median contract rent: $267 per month (2005-2009 5-year est.); Median year structure built: 1973 (2005-2009 5-year est.).
Safety: Violent crime rate: 59.1 per 10,000 population; Property crime rate: 334.0 per 10,000 population (2009).
Newspapers: Duval County Picture (Local news; Circulation 2,500)
Transportation: Commute to work: 90.3% car, 0.0% public transportation, 3.8% walk, 5.1% work from home (2005-2009 5-year est.); Travel time to work: 45.3% less than 15 minutes, 30.5% 15 to 30 minutes, 13.2% 30 to 45 minutes, 2.9% 45 to 60 minutes, 8.2% 60 minutes or more (2005-2009 5-year est.)

Eastland County

Located in north central Texas; drained by the Leon River; includes Lake Cisco. Covers a land area of 926.01 square miles, a water area of 5.89 square miles, and is located in the Central Time Zone at 32.34° N. Lat., 98.82° W. Long. The county was founded in 1858. County seat is Eastland.

Weather Station: Eastland   Elevation: 1,433 feet

	Jan	Feb	Mar	Apr	May	Jun	Jul	Aug	Sep	Oct	Nov	Dec
High	57	60	68	77	84	90	95	95	87	78	66	57
Low	30	34	41	49	59	66	69	68	61	50	40	31
Precip	1.2	2.1	2.2	1.9	3.4	3.9	1.6	2.5	2.6	3.3	1.9	1.9
Snow	0.6	0.4	0.5	tr	0.0	0.0	0.0	0.0	0.0	tr	0.2	0.6

High and Low temperatures in degrees Fahrenheit; Precipitation and Snow in inches

Weather Station: Rising Star 1 S   Elevation: 1,632 feet

	Jan	Feb	Mar	Apr	May	Jun	Jul	Aug	Sep	Oct	Nov	Dec
High	56	60	68	77	83	89	94	94	87	77	66	57
Low	31	35	41	49	60	67	70	69	63	52	41	32
Precip	1.2	2.2	2.5	2.1	4.7	5.2	2.0	2.5	2.6	3.3	2.1	1.6
Snow	1.2	0.6	0.4	0.0	0.0	0.0	0.0	0.0	0.0	0.0	0.1	0.7

High and Low temperatures in degrees Fahrenheit; Precipitation and Snow in inches

Population: 18,488 (1990); 18,297 (2000); 18,298 (2010); 18,264 (2015 projected); Race: 87.7% White, 3.0% Black, 0.4% Asian, 8.9% Other, 14.6% Hispanic of any race (2010); Density: 19.8 persons per square mile (2010); Average household size: 2.39 (2010); Median age: 39.2 (2010); Males per 100 females: 93.5 (2010).
Religion: Five largest groups: 48.6% Southern Baptist Convention, 9.2% The United Methodist Church, 8.5% Churches of Christ, 2.8% Catholic Church, 2.6% Christian Church (Disciples of Christ) (2000).
Economy: Unemployment rate: 8.6% (June 2011); Total civilian labor force: 8,841 (June 2011); Leading industries: 20.0% mining; 16.1% health care and social assistance; 14.4% retail trade (2009); Farms: 1,324 totaling 520,132 acres (2007); Companies that employ 500 or more persons: 1 (2009); Companies that employ 100 to 499 persons: 6 (2009); Companies that employ less than 100 persons: 456 (2009); Black-owned businesses: n/a (2007); Hispanic-owned businesses: n/a (2007); Asian-owned businesses: n/a (2007); Women-owned businesses: 408 (2007); Retail sales per capita: $11,926 (2010). Single-family building permits issued: 1 (2010); Multi-family building permits issued: 0 (2010).
Income: Per capita income: $20,496 (2010); Median household income: $38,007 (2010); Average household income: $51,037 (2010); Percent of households with income of $100,000 or more: 10.3% (2010); Poverty rate: 19.7% (2009); Bankruptcy rate: 1.70% (2010).
Taxes: Total county taxes per capita: $234 (2007); County property taxes per capita: $191 (2007).
Education: Percent of population age 25 and over with: High school diploma (including GED) or higher: 77.7% (2010); Bachelor's degree or higher: 14.1% (2010); Master's degree or higher: 3.8% (2010).
Housing: Homeownership rate: 74.9% (2010); Median home value: $46,370 (2010); Median contract rent: $280 per month (2005-2009 5-year est.); Median year structure built: 1964 (2005-2009 5-year est.).
Health: Birth rate: 134.3 per 10,000 population (2009); Death rate: 136.0 per 10,000 population (2009); Age-adjusted cancer mortality rate: 265.8 deaths per 100,000 population (2007); Number of physicians: 6.6 per 10,000 population (2008); Hospital beds: 19.6 per 10,000 population (2007); Hospital admissions: 748.7 per 10,000 population (2007).
Elections: 2008 Presidential election results: 19.5% Obama, 79.4% McCain, 0.1% Nader
Additional Information Contacts

Eastland County Government .... (254) 629-1263
   http://county.eastlandcountytexas.com
Cisco Chamber of Commerce .... (254) 442-2537
   http://ciscotx.com
Eastland Chamber of Commerce.................... (254) 629-2332
   http://www.eastlandchamber.com
Gorman Economic Development Corporation .... (254) 734-3933
   http://www.gormantx.com
Ranger Chamber of Commerce..................... (254) 647-3091

Eastland County Communities

CARBON (town). Covers a land area of 1.020 square miles and a water area of 0 square miles. Located at 32.27° N. Lat; 98.82° W. Long. Elevation is 1,601 feet.
Population: 255 (1990); 224 (2000); 244 (2010); 248 (2015 projected); Race: 89.8% White, 0.0% Black, 0.0% Asian, 10.2% Other, 14.8% Hispanic of any race (2010); Density: 239.2 persons per square mile (2010); Average household size: 2.35 (2010); Median age: 43.4 (2010); Males per 100 females: 100.0 (2010); Marriage status: 15.4% never married, 71.4% now married, 5.0% widowed, 8.2% divorced (2005-2009 5-year est.); Foreign born: 2.6% (2005-2009 5-year est.); Ancestry (includes multiple ancestries): 16.1% German, 14.6% Irish, 10.2% American, 9.6% English, 2.3% French (2005-2009 5-year est.).
Economy: Employment by occupation: 11.2% management, 8.0% professional, 16.0% services, 25.7% sales, 1.1% farming, 14.4% construction, 23.5% production (2005-2009 5-year est.).
Income: Per capita income: $24,031 (2010); Median household income: $45,500 (2010); Average household income: $54,760 (2010); Percent of households with income of $100,000 or more: 8.7% (2010); Poverty rate: 6.8% (2005-2009 5-year est.).
Taxes: Total city taxes per capita: $36 (2007); City property taxes per capita: $0 (2007).
Education: Percent of population age 25 and over with: High school diploma (including GED) or higher: 83.3% (2010); Bachelor's degree or higher: 23.5% (2010); Master's degree or higher: 4.9% (2010).
Housing: Homeownership rate: 81.7% (2010); Median home value: $62,727 (2010); Median contract rent: $182 per month (2005-2009 5-year est.); Median year structure built: 1971 (2005-2009 5-year est.).
Transportation: Commute to work: 100.0% car, 0.0% public transportation, 0.0% walk, 0.0% work from home (2005-2009 5-year est.); Travel time to work: 24.6% less than 15 minutes, 46.5% 15 to 30 minutes, 5.3% 30 to 45 minutes, 20.3% 45 to 60 minutes, 3.2% 60 minutes or more (2005-2009 5-year est.)

CISCO (city). Covers a land area of 4.849 square miles and a water area of 0.008 square miles. Located at 32.38° N. Lat; 98.98° W. Long. Elevation is 1,634 feet.
History: Mobley Astell (1916), Conrad Hilton's 1st hotel, purchased in 1919. Had oil boom, 1918. Settled 1851, incorporated 1919.
Population: 3,813 (1990); 3,851 (2000); 3,707 (2010); 3,643 (2015 projected); Race: 87.5% White, 5.2% Black, 0.3% Asian, 7.0% Other, 12.5% Hispanic of any race (2010); Density: 764.4 persons per square mile (2010); Average household size: 2.40 (2010); Median age: 34.6 (2010); Males per 100 females: 88.9 (2010); Marriage status: 34.8% never married, 43.8% now married, 11.5% widowed, 9.9% divorced (2005-2009 5-year est.); Foreign born: 9.8% (2005-2009 5-year est.); Ancestry (includes multiple ancestries): 11.7% American, 10.5% German, 7.8% English, 6.2% Scotch-Irish, 5.5% Irish (2005-2009 5-year est.).
Economy: Single-family building permits issued: 1 (2010); Multi-family building permits issued: 0 (2010); Employment by occupation: 7.3% management, 12.6% professional, 31.3% services, 24.8% sales, 0.8% farming, 14.8% construction, 8.4% production (2005-2009 5-year est.).
Income: Per capita income: $17,764 (2010); Median household income: $33,486 (2010); Average household income: $45,504 (2010); Percent of households with income of $100,000 or more: 7.6% (2010); Poverty rate: 23.5% (2005-2009 5-year est.).
Taxes: Total city taxes per capita: $136 (2007); City property taxes per capita: $88 (2007).
Education: Percent of population age 25 and over with: High school diploma (including GED) or higher: 77.4% (2010); Bachelor's degree or higher: 13.5% (2010); Master's degree or higher: 5.0% (2010).
School District(s)
Cisco ISD (PK-12)
   2009-10 Enrollment: 849 .... (254) 442-3056

Two-year College(s)
Cisco College (Public)
   Fall 2009 Enrollment: 4,260. .... (254) 442-5000
   2010-11 Tuition: In-state $2,568; Out-of-state $2,874
Housing: Homeownership rate: 73.1% (2010); Median home value: $35,402 (2010); Median contract rent: $251 per month (2005-2009 5-year est.); Median year structure built: 1960 (2005-2009 5-year est.).
Safety: Violent crime rate: 18.9 per 10,000 population; Property crime rate: 137.4 per 10,000 population (2009).
Newspapers: Press (Local news; Circulation 2,575)
Transportation: Commute to work: 85.9% car, 0.0% public transportation, 9.6% walk, 3.3% work from home (2005-2009 5-year est.); Travel time to work: 64.0% less than 15 minutes, 15.4% 15 to 30 minutes, 10.0% 30 to 45 minutes, 4.1% 45 to 60 minutes, 6.5% 60 minutes or more (2005-2009 5-year est.)
Additional Information Contacts
Cisco Chamber of Commerce .... (254) 442-2537
   http://ciscotx.com

DESDEMONA (unincorporated postal area, zip code 76445). Covers a land area of 60.179 square miles and a water area of 0.097 square miles. Located at 32.29° N. Lat; 98.55° W. Long. Elevation is 1,358 feet.
Population: 331 (2000); Race: 91.9% White, 1.2% Black, 0.0% Asian, 6.9% Other, 19.7% Hispanic of any race (2000); Density: 5.5 persons per square mile (2000); Age: 25.2% under 18, 27.8% over 64 (2000); Marriage status: 19.5% never married, 71.1% now married, 7.2% widowed, 2.2% divorced (2000); Foreign born: 11.0% (2000); Ancestry (includes multiple ancestries): 15.9% English, 14.5% American, 4.6% German, 2.9% French (2000).
Economy: Employment by occupation: 23.5% management, 9.6% professional, 14.0% services, 14.7% sales, 8.1% farming, 11.0% construction, 19.1% production (2000).
Income: Per capita income: $10,453 (2000); Median household income: $21,016 (2000); Poverty rate: 179.1% (2000).
Education: Percent of population age 25 and over with: High school diploma (including GED) or higher: 65.3% (2000); Bachelor's degree or higher: 14.4% (2000).
Housing: Homeownership rate: 69.6% (2000); Median home value: $51,200 (2000); Median contract rent: $195 per month (2000); Median year structure built: 1963 (2000).
Transportation: Commute to work: 87.5% car, 0.0% public transportation, 0.0% walk, 12.5% work from home (2000); Travel time to work: 29.4% less than 15 minutes, 44.5% 15 to 30 minutes, 21.8% 30 to 45 minutes, 4.2% 45 to 60 minutes, 0.0% 60 minutes or more (2000)

EASTLAND (city). County seat. Covers a land area of 2.827 square miles and a water area of 0 square miles. Located at 32.39° N. Lat; 98.82° W. Long. Elevation is 1,440 feet.
History: Eastland, a booming oil town between 1917 and 1922, gained dubious notice when the cornerstone of the old courthouse was dug out in 1928. It contained the embalmed remains of a horned toad, placed there in 1897. The toad, known as Old Rip, revived and lived for eleven months.
Population: 3,749 (1990); 3,769 (2000); 3,825 (2010); 3,870 (2015 projected); Race: 90.6% White, 1.9% Black, 0.1% Asian, 7.3% Other, 17.4% Hispanic of any race (2010); Density: 1,352.9 persons per square mile (2010); Average household size: 2.47 (2010); Median age: 36.3 (2010); Males per 100 females: 91.9 (2010); Marriage status: 22.1% never married, 48.2% now married, 9.5% widowed, 20.2% divorced (2005-2009 5-year est.); Foreign born: 5.5% (2005-2009 5-year est.); Ancestry (includes multiple ancestries): 14.7% American, 9.1% English, 8.0% Irish, 6.8% German, 3.3% Dutch (2005-2009 5-year est.).
Economy: Employment by occupation: 10.6% management, 15.8% professional, 22.0% services, 25.5% sales, 0.0% farming, 9.3% construction, 16.8% production (2005-2009 5-year est.).
Income: Per capita income: $22,245 (2010); Median household income: $40,967 (2010); Average household income: $56,400 (2010); Percent of households with income of $100,000 or more: 12.0% (2010); Poverty rate: 31.8% (2005-2009 5-year est.).
Taxes: Total city taxes per capita: $453 (2007); City property taxes per capita: $161 (2007).
Education: Percent of population age 25 and over with: High school diploma (including GED) or higher: 76.0% (2010); Bachelor's degree or higher: 11.2% (2010); Master's degree or higher: 2.9% (2010).

School District(s)
Eastland ISD (PK-12)
    2009-10 Enrollment: 1,173 . . . . (254) 631-5120
Housing: Homeownership rate: 68.8% (2010); Median home value: $47,847 (2010); Median contract rent: $414 per month (2005-2009 5-year est.); Median year structure built: 1960 (2005-2009 5-year est.).
Hospitals: Eastland Memorial Hospital (83 beds)
Safety: Violent crime rate: 36.0 per 10,000 population; Property crime rate: 354.9 per 10,000 population (2009).
Newspapers: Callahan County Star (Community news; Circulation 75); Eastland Telegram (Local news; Circulation 2,200); Rising Star (Community news; Circulation 750)
Transportation: Commute to work: 96.9% car, 0.0% public transportation, 1.4% walk, 1.0% work from home (2005-2009 5-year est.); Travel time to work: 80.6% less than 15 minutes, 11.8% 15 to 30 minutes, 3.7% 30 to 45 minutes, 2.5% 45 to 60 minutes, 1.4% 60 minutes or more (2005-2009 5-year est.)
Airports: Eastland Municipal (general aviation)
Additional Information Contacts
Eastland Chamber of Commerce. (254) 629-2332
    http://www.eastlandchamber.com

GORMAN (city). Covers a land area of 1.647 square miles and a water area of 0 square miles. Located at 32.21° N. Lat; 98.67° W. Long. Elevation is 1,453 feet.
History: Founded 1890, incorporated 1902.
Population: 1,290 (1990); 1,236 (2000); 1,206 (2010); 1,188 (2015 projected); Race: 71.0% White, 0.2% Black, 0.2% Asian, 28.6% Other, 33.8% Hispanic of any race (2010); Density: 732.5 persons per square mile (2010); Average household size: 2.52 (2010); Median age: 37.4 (2010); Males per 100 females: 88.4 (2010); Marriage status: 17.1% never married, 58.8% now married, 15.5% widowed, 8.6% divorced (2005-2009 5-year est.); Foreign born: 14.1% (2005-2009 5-year est.); Ancestry (includes multiple ancestries): 11.6% English, 11.1% Irish, 11.1% German, 3.7% American, 2.5% French (2005-2009 5-year est.).
Economy: Employment by occupation: 4.8% management, 23.4% professional, 13.6% services, 20.1% sales, 4.0% farming, 4.0% construction, 30.2% production (2005-2009 5-year est.).
Income: Per capita income: $16,503 (2010); Median household income: $33,806 (2010); Average household income: $42,700 (2010); Percent of households with income of $100,000 or more: 6.9% (2010); Poverty rate: 23.8% (2005-2009 5-year est.).
Taxes: Total city taxes per capita: $254 (2007); City property taxes per capita: $157 (2007).
Education: Percent of population age 25 and over with: High school diploma (including GED) or higher: 69.5% (2010); Bachelor's degree or higher: 11.8% (2010); Master's degree or higher: 3.6% (2010).
School District(s)
Gorman ISD (PK-12)
    2009-10 Enrollment: 344 . . . . (254) 734-3171
Housing: Homeownership rate: 72.3% (2010); Median home value: $40,678 (2010); Median contract rent: $273 per month (2005-2009 5-year est.); Median year structure built: 1959 (2005-2009 5-year est.).
Safety: Violent crime rate: 32.5 per 10,000 population; Property crime rate: 81.3 per 10,000 population (2009).
Newspapers: Gorman Progress (Community news; Circulation 1,000)
Transportation: Commute to work: 94.3% car, 0.0% public transportation, 2.3% walk, 0.0% work from home (2005-2009 5-year est.); Travel time to work: 49.7% less than 15 minutes, 19.3% 15 to 30 minutes, 26.0% 30 to 45 minutes, 2.1% 45 to 60 minutes, 2.9% 60 minutes or more (2005-2009 5-year est.)
Additional Information Contacts
Gorman Economic Development Corporation . . . . (254) 734-3933
    http://www.gormantx.com

RANGER (city). Covers a land area of 7.002 square miles and a water area of 0.133 square miles. Located at 32.47° N. Lat; 98.67° W. Long. Elevation is 1,437 feet.
History: Ranger was founded in 1881 and named for a camp of Texas Rangers nearby. Until 1917, when the McCleskey well began producing, Ranger was a cattle and cotton shipping point of the Central Plains.
Population: 2,803 (1990); 2,584 (2000); 2,571 (2010); 2,548 (2015 projected); Race: 79.8% White, 8.6% Black, 1.3% Asian, 10.3% Other, 16.3% Hispanic of any race (2010); Density: 367.2 persons per square mile (2010); Average household size: 2.33 (2010); Median age: 33.6 (2010);

Males per 100 females: 98.1 (2010); Marriage status: 44.1% never married, 35.1% now married, 8.2% widowed, 12.6% divorced (2005-2009 5-year est.); Foreign born: 1.5% (2005-2009 5-year est.); Ancestry (includes multiple ancestries): 21.5% Irish, 14.6% German, 11.4% English, 6.6% American, 4.8% Dutch West Indian (2005-2009 5-year est.).
Economy: Employment by occupation: 3.5% management, 11.4% professional, 31.2% services, 19.4% sales, 4.8% farming, 15.5% construction, 14.2% production (2005-2009 5-year est.).
Income: Per capita income: $15,963 (2010); Median household income: $33,345 (2010); Average household income: $41,121 (2010); Percent of households with income of $100,000 or more: 6.1% (2010); Poverty rate: 22.1% (2005-2009 5-year est.).
Taxes: Total city taxes per capita: $35 (2007); City property taxes per capita: $0 (2007).
Education: Percent of population age 25 and over with: High school diploma (including GED) or higher: 74.9% (2010); Bachelor's degree or higher: 15.1% (2010); Master's degree or higher: 4.9% (2010).
School District(s)
Ranger ISD (PK-12)
    2009-10 Enrollment: 466 . . . . (254) 647-1187
Two-year College(s)
Ranger College (Public)
    Fall 2009 Enrollment: 1,000. . . . . (254) 647-3234
    2010-11 Tuition: In-state $2,470; Out-of-state $2,830
Housing: Homeownership rate: 69.9% (2010); Median home value: $32,526 (2010); Median contract rent: $187 per month (2005-2009 5-year est.); Median year structure built: 1956 (2005-2009 5-year est.).
Safety: Violent crime rate: 46.9 per 10,000 population; Property crime rate: 265.9 per 10,000 population (2009).
Newspapers: Ranger Times (Local news; Circulation 2,000)
Transportation: Commute to work: 90.7% car, 0.0% public transportation, 4.0% walk, 2.4% work from home (2005-2009 5-year est.); Travel time to work: 49.9% less than 15 minutes, 23.6% 15 to 30 minutes, 13.5% 30 to 45 minutes, 3.2% 45 to 60 minutes, 9.8% 60 minutes or more (2005-2009 5-year est.)
Additional Information Contacts
Ranger Chamber of Commerce. (254) 647-3091

RISING STAR (town). Covers a land area of 1.677 square miles and a water area of 0 square miles. Located at 32.09° N. Lat; 98.96° W. Long. Elevation is 1,624 feet.
History: Settled 1880; incorporated 1905.
Population: 859 (1990); 835 (2000); 832 (2010); 828 (2015 projected); Race: 91.0% White, 0.6% Black, 0.1% Asian, 8.3% Other, 9.0% Hispanic of any race (2010); Density: 496.1 persons per square mile (2010); Average household size: 2.32 (2010); Median age: 42.8 (2010); Males per 100 females: 90.0 (2010); Marriage status: 16.3% never married, 49.7% now married, 28.0% widowed, 6.0% divorced (2005-2009 5-year est.); Foreign born: 0.3% (2005-2009 5-year est.); Ancestry (includes multiple ancestries): 17.1% Irish, 13.9% German, 11.1% English, 10.3% American, 2.6% Scotch-Irish (2005-2009 5-year est.).
Economy: Employment by occupation: 12.1% management, 17.9% professional, 15.6% services, 11.6% sales, 2.2% farming, 18.3% construction, 22.3% production (2005-2009 5-year est.).
Income: Per capita income: $19,931 (2010); Median household income: $30,854 (2010); Average household income: $47,515 (2010); Percent of households with income of $100,000 or more: 11.1% (2010); Poverty rate: 34.9% (2005-2009 5-year est.).
Taxes: Total city taxes per capita: $145 (2007); City property taxes per capita: $104 (2007).
Education: Percent of population age 25 and over with: High school diploma (including GED) or higher: 75.0% (2010); Bachelor's degree or higher: 14.8% (2010); Master's degree or higher: 4.6% (2010).
School District(s)
Rising Star ISD (PK-12)
    2009-10 Enrollment: 229 . . . . (254) 643-2717
Housing: Homeownership rate: 74.6% (2010); Median home value: $35,417 (2010); Median contract rent: $183 per month (2005-2009 5-year est.); Median year structure built: 1958 (2005-2009 5-year est.).
Safety: Violent crime rate: 48.4 per 10,000 population; Property crime rate: 0.0 per 10,000 population (2009).
Transportation: Commute to work: 90.9% car, 0.0% public transportation, 1.4% walk, 7.8% work from home (2005-2009 5-year est.); Travel time to work: 36.1% less than 15 minutes, 4.0% 15 to 30 minutes, 30.7% 30 to 45

minutes, 12.4% 45 to 60 minutes, 16.8% 60 minutes or more (2005-2009 5-year est.)

Ector County

Located in west Texas, on the Edwards Plateau; includes sand dunes in the southwest. Covers a land area of 901.06 square miles, a water area of 0.62 square miles, and is located in the Central Time Zone at 31.86° N. Lat., 102.43° W. Long. The county was founded in 1887. County seat is Odessa.

Ector County is part of the Odessa, TX Metropolitan Statistical Area. The entire metro area includes: Ector County, TX

Weather Station: Penwell   Elevation: 2,939 feet

	Jan	Feb	Mar	Apr	May	Jun	Jul	Aug	Sep	Oct	Nov	Dec
High	59	63	71	79	88	94	96	94	88	79	68	58
Low	30	34	41	49	59	67	70	69	62	51	39	30
Precip	0.6	0.7	0.6	0.6	2.2	1.6	1.2	1.5	2.1	1.4	0.7	0.6
Snow	0.6	0.3	0.1	0.0	0.0	0.0	0.0	0.0	0.0	0.0	tr	0.5

High and Low temperatures in degrees Fahrenheit; Precipitation and Snow in inches

Population: 118,934 (1990); 121,123 (2000); 133,402 (2010); 139,140 (2015 projected); Race: 69.3% White, 4.4% Black, 0.8% Asian, 25.5% Other, 51.6% Hispanic of any race (2010); Density: 148.1 persons per square mile (2010); Average household size: 2.72 (2010); Median age: 32.0 (2010); Males per 100 females: 96.2 (2010).
Religion: Five largest groups: 23.0% Southern Baptist Convention, 12.6% Catholic Church, 4.4% Independent, Non-Charismatic Churches, 3.1% The United Methodist Church, 2.4% Churches of Christ (2000).
Economy: Unemployment rate: 6.9% (June 2011); Total civilian labor force: 73,580 (June 2011); Leading industries: 14.9% health care and social assistance; 14.1% retail trade; 10.1% accommodation & food services (2009); Farms: 301 totaling 423,919 acres (2007); Companies that employ 500 or more persons: 4 (2009); Companies that employ 100 to 499 persons: 61 (2009); Companies that employ less than 100 persons: 3,183 (2009); Black-owned businesses: 233 (2007); Hispanic-owned businesses: 3,587 (2007); Asian-owned businesses: 193 (2007); Women-owned businesses: 3,094 (2007); Retail sales per capita: $15,231 (2010). Single-family building permits issued: 268 (2010); Multi-family building permits issued: 440 (2010).
Income: Per capita income: $22,080 (2010); Median household income: $45,982 (2010); Average household income: $60,441 (2010); Percent of households with income of $100,000 or more: 14.3% (2010); Poverty rate: 16.9% (2009); Bankruptcy rate: 1.01% (2010).
Taxes: Total county taxes per capita: $209 (2007); County property taxes per capita: $206 (2007).
Education: Percent of population age 25 and over with: High school diploma (including GED) or higher: 73.7% (2010); Bachelor's degree or higher: 11.8% (2010); Master's degree or higher: 3.5% (2010).
Housing: Homeownership rate: 68.5% (2010); Median home value: $74,688 (2010); Median contract rent: $461 per month (2005-2009 5-year est.); Median year structure built: 1972 (2005-2009 5-year est.)
Health: Birth rate: 186.3 per 10,000 population (2009); Death rate: 81.6 per 10,000 population (2009); Age-adjusted cancer mortality rate: 179.9 deaths per 100,000 population (2007); Number of physicians: 19.6 per 10,000 population (2008); Hospital beds: 45.0 per 10,000 population (2007); Hospital admissions: 1,810.6 per 10,000 population (2007).
Environment: Air Quality Index: 93.4% good, 6.2% moderate, 0.3% unhealthy for sensitive individuals, 0.0% unhealthy (percent of days in 2008)
Elections: 2008 Presidential election results: 25.6% Obama, 73.5% McCain, 0.1% Nader
Additional Information Contacts
Ector County Government . . . . (432) 335-3030
  http://www.co.ector.tx.us
City of Odessa . . . . (432) 335-3200
  http://www.odessa-tx.gov
Odessa Chamber of Commerce . . . . (432) 332-9111
  http://www.odessachamber.com

Ector County Communities

GARDENDALE (CDP). Covers a land area of 11.408 square miles and a water area of 0 square miles. Located at 32.02° N. Lat; 102.37° W. Long. Elevation is 2,966 feet.

Population: 1,163 (1990); 1,197 (2000); 1,638 (2010); 1,800 (2015 projected); Race: 83.6% White, 0.8% Black, 0.2% Asian, 15.4% Other, 22.5% Hispanic of any race (2010); Density: 143.6 persons per square mile (2010); Average household size: 2.60 (2010); Median age: 40.7 (2010); Males per 100 females: 102.5 (2010); Marriage status: 12.2% never married, 78.9% now married, 1.3% widowed, 7.6% divorced (2005-2009 5-year est.); Foreign born: 0.0% (2005-2009 5-year est.); Ancestry (includes multiple ancestries): 12.5% Irish, 11.8% English, 11.0% German, 5.7% American, 4.3% Scotch-Irish (2005-2009 5-year est.).
Economy: Employment by occupation: 11.8% management, 15.8% professional, 0.0% services, 38.9% sales, 0.0% farming, 24.1% construction, 9.4% production (2005-2009 5-year est.).
Income: Per capita income: $37,488 (2010); Median household income: $85,025 (2010); Average household income: $97,579 (2010); Percent of households with income of $100,000 or more: 40.4% (2010); Poverty rate: 11.8% (2005-2009 5-year est.).
Education: Percent of population age 25 and over with: High school diploma (including GED) or higher: 88.6% (2010); Bachelor's degree or higher: 13.4% (2010); Master's degree or higher: 5.6% (2010).
Housing: Homeownership rate: 90.8% (2010); Median home value: $135,682 (2010); Median contract rent: $429 per month (2005-2009 5-year est.); Median year structure built: 1977 (2005-2009 5-year est.).
Transportation: Commute to work: 91.3% car, 0.0% public transportation, 2.1% walk, 6.6% work from home (2005-2009 5-year est.); Travel time to work: 15.9% less than 15 minutes, 67.9% 15 to 30 minutes, 13.5% 30 to 45 minutes, 0.0% 45 to 60 minutes, 2.7% 60 minutes or more (2005-2009 5-year est.)

GOLDSMITH (city). Covers a land area of 0.318 square miles and a water area of 0 square miles. Located at 31.98° N. Lat; 102.61° W. Long. Elevation is 3,140 feet.
Population: 297 (1990); 253 (2000); 330 (2010); 359 (2015 projected); Race: 83.6% White, 0.6% Black, 0.0% Asian, 15.8% Other, 43.3% Hispanic of any race (2010); Density: 1,038.0 persons per square mile (2010); Average household size: 2.77 (2010); Median age: 32.2 (2010); Males per 100 females: 106.3 (2010); Marriage status: 17.0% never married, 55.6% now married, 8.2% widowed, 19.3% divorced (2005-2009 5-year est.); Foreign born: 5.6% (2005-2009 5-year est.); Ancestry (includes multiple ancestries): 20.4% Irish, 12.8% English, 9.7% American, 5.6% French, 4.6% Scottish (2005-2009 5-year est.).
Economy: Employment by occupation: 0.0% management, 29.5% professional, 3.8% services, 19.2% sales, 0.0% farming, 25.6% construction, 21.8% production (2005-2009 5-year est.).
Income: Per capita income: $26,965 (2010); Median household income: $63,021 (2010); Average household income: $80,189 (2010); Percent of households with income of $100,000 or more: 25.2% (2010); Poverty rate: 36.7% (2005-2009 5-year est.).
Taxes: Total city taxes per capita: $237 (2007); City property taxes per capita: $53 (2007).
Education: Percent of population age 25 and over with: High school diploma (including GED) or higher: 72.4% (2010); Bachelor's degree or higher: 9.7% (2010); Master's degree or higher: 3.6% (2010).
Housing: Homeownership rate: 83.2% (2010); Median home value: $54,211 (2010); Median contract rent: $333 per month (2005-2009 5-year est.); Median year structure built: 1951 (2005-2009 5-year est.).
Transportation: Commute to work: 96.2% car, 0.0% public transportation, 3.8% walk, 0.0% work from home (2005-2009 5-year est.); Travel time to work: 19.2% less than 15 minutes, 19.2% 15 to 30 minutes, 29.5% 30 to 45 minutes, 21.8% 45 to 60 minutes, 10.3% 60 minutes or more (2005-2009 5-year est.)

ODESSA (city). County seat. Covers a land area of 36.798 square miles and a water area of 0.073 square miles. Located at 31.86° N. Lat; 102.36° W. Long. Elevation is 2,900 feet.
History: Odessa began as a cow town established along the Texas & Pacific Railway in 1881. After oil was discovered, Odessa became the shipping and refining center of the Permian Basin.
Population: 90,079 (1990); 90,943 (2000); 99,493 (2010); 103,753 (2015 projected); Race: 69.8% White, 5.5% Black, 1.0% Asian, 23.7% Other, 50.6% Hispanic of any race (2010); Density: 2,703.8 persons per square mile (2010); Average household size: 2.64 (2010); Median age: 32.2 (2010); Males per 100 females: 94.6 (2010); Marriage status: 27.4% never married, 54.5% now married, 7.0% widowed, 11.1% divorced (2005-2009 5-year est.); Foreign born: 10.6% (2005-2009 5-year est.); Ancestry

(includes multiple ancestries): 8.5% German, 6.7% Irish, 6.2% American, 6.2% English, 2.1% French (2005-2009 5-year est.).
Economy: Unemployment rate: 6.9% (June 2011); Total civilian labor force: 55,328 (June 2011); Single-family building permits issued: 268 (2010); Multi-family building permits issued: 440 (2010); Employment by occupation: 9.5% management, 15.7% professional, 15.8% services, 28.4% sales, 0.1% farming, 14.7% construction, 15.8% production (2005-2009 5-year est.).
Income: Per capita income: $22,973 (2010); Median household income: $45,426 (2010); Average household income: $61,174 (2010); Percent of households with income of $100,000 or more: 14.3% (2010); Poverty rate: 16.1% (2005-2009 5-year est.).
Taxes: Total city taxes per capita: $414 (2007); City property taxes per capita: $173 (2007).
Education: Percent of population age 25 and over with: High school diploma (including GED) or higher: 75.7% (2010); Bachelor's degree or higher: 14.0% (2010); Master's degree or higher: 4.2% (2010).

School District(s)

Ector County ISD (PK-12)
    2009-10 Enrollment: 27,435 . . . . (432) 334-7100
Richard Milburn Academy (Ector County) (09-12)
    2009-10 Enrollment: 481 . . . . (830) 557-6181

Four-year College(s)

The University of Texas of the Permian Basin (Public)
    Fall 2009 Enrollment: 3,546 . . . . (432) 552-2020
    2010-11 Tuition: In-state $4,900; Out-of-state $12,340

Two-year College(s)

Odessa College (Public)
    Fall 2009 Enrollment: 5,132 . . . . (432) 335-6400
    2010-11 Tuition: In-state $2,640; Out-of-state $3,690

Vocational/Technical School(s)

American Commercial College-Odessa (Private, For-profit)
    Fall 2009 Enrollment: 181 . . . . (432) 362-6768
    2010-11 Tuition: $12,600

Housing: Homeownership rate: 63.8% (2010); Median home value: $79,434 (2010); Median contract rent: $476 per month (2005-2009 5-year est.); Median year structure built: 1968 (2005-2009 5-year est.).
Hospitals: Alliance Hospital (70 beds); Medical Center Hospital (307 beds); Odessa Regional Hospital (146 beds)
Safety: Violent crime rate: 78.9 per 10,000 population; Property crime rate: 411.8 per 10,000 population (2009).
Newspapers: Odessa American (Community news; Circulation 26,548)
Transportation: Commute to work: 95.4% car, 0.3% public transportation, 1.1% walk, 1.9% work from home (2005-2009 5-year est.); Travel time to work: 46.1% less than 15 minutes, 39.9% 15 to 30 minutes, 8.3% 30 to 45 minutes, 1.7% 45 to 60 minutes, 4.1% 60 minutes or more (2005-2009 5-year est.)
Airports: Odessa-Schlemeyer Field (general aviation)
Additional Information Contacts
City of Odessa . . . . (432) 335-3200
    http://www.odessa-tx.gov
Odessa Chamber of Commerce . . . . (432) 332-9111
    http://www.odessachamber.com

WEST ODESSA (CDP).

Covers a land area of 62.450 square miles and a water area of 0 square miles. Located at 31.84° N. Lat; 102.48° W. Long. Elevation is 2,986 feet.
Population: 16,557 (1990); 17,799 (2000); 19,152 (2010); 19,832 (2015 projected); Race: 61.8% White, 0.7% Black, 0.1% Asian, 37.4% Other, 61.7% Hispanic of any race (2010); Density: 306.7 persons per square mile (2010); Average household size: 3.11 (2010); Median age: 30.6 (2010); Males per 100 females: 99.2 (2010); Marriage status: 24.5% never married, 60.5% now married, 4.9% widowed, 10.1% divorced (2005-2009 5-year est.); Foreign born: 15.1% (2005-2009 5-year est.); Ancestry (includes multiple ancestries): 8.0% German, 7.1% Irish, 4.5% English, 3.6% American, 1.4% Scotch-Irish (2005-2009 5-year est.).
Economy: Employment by occupation: 5.0% management, 8.2% professional, 16.0% services, 27.3% sales, 0.7% farming, 20.1% construction, 22.7% production (2005-2009 5-year est.).
Income: Per capita income: $17,749 (2010); Median household income: $45,893 (2010); Average household income: $54,883 (2010); Percent of households with income of $100,000 or more: 11.3% (2010); Poverty rate: 17.8% (2005-2009 5-year est.).

Education: Percent of population age 25 and over with: High school diploma (including GED) or higher: 67.3% (2010); Bachelor's degree or higher: 5.1% (2010); Master's degree or higher: 1.6% (2010).
Housing: Homeownership rate: 86.1% (2010); Median home value: $54,463 (2010); Median contract rent: $413 per month (2005-2009 5-year est.); Median year structure built: 1982 (2005-2009 5-year est.).
Transportation: Commute to work: 93.0% car, 0.5% public transportation, 0.2% walk, 3.5% work from home (2005-2009 5-year est.); Travel time to work: 23.1% less than 15 minutes, 47.9% 15 to 30 minutes, 16.6% 30 to 45 minutes, 3.8% 45 to 60 minutes, 8.5% 60 minutes or more (2005-2009 5-year est.)

Edwards County

Located in southwestern Texas, on the Edwards Plateau; drained by the South Llano and Nueces Rivers. Covers a land area of 2,119.75 square miles, a water area of 0.19 square miles, and is located in the Central Time Zone at 30.02° N. Lat., 100.24° W. Long. The county was founded in 1858. County seat is Rocksprings.

Weather Station: Rocksprings										Elevation: 2,411 feet		
	Jan	Feb	Mar	Apr	May	Jun	Jul	Aug	Sep	Oct	Nov	Dec
High	59	64	70	78	84	89	92	92	86	78	68	60
Low	37	40	47	53	62	67	69	69	64	56	46	38
Precip	1.0	1.1	1.8	1.7	3.1	3.1	2.0	2.6	2.8	3.4	1.8	1.1
Snow	0.1	0.1	tr	0.0	0.0	0.0	0.0	0.0	0.0	0.0	0.3	tr

High and Low temperatures in degrees Fahrenheit; Precipitation and Snow in inches

Population: 2,266 (1990); 2,162 (2000); 1,900 (2010); 1,771 (2015 projected); Race: 80.6% White, 1.9% Black, 0.2% Asian, 17.4% Other, 49.4% Hispanic of any race (2010); Density: 0.9 persons per square mile (2010); Average household size: 2.56 (2010); Median age: 34.1 (2010); Males per 100 females: 104.5 (2010).
Religion: Five largest groups: 35.2% Catholic Church, 24.4% Southern Baptist Convention, 8.0% The United Methodist Church, 7.8% Churches of Christ, 3.8% Presbyterian Church (U.S.A.) (2000).
Economy: Unemployment rate: 8.0% (June 2011); Total civilian labor force: 1,003 (June 2011); Leading industries: 30.4% retail trade (2009); Farms: 480 totaling 996,471 acres (2007); Companies that employ 500 or more persons: 0 (2009); Companies that employ 100 to 499 persons: 0 (2009); Companies that employ less than 100 persons: 35 (2009); Black-owned businesses: n/a (2007); Hispanic-owned businesses: n/a (2007); Asian-owned businesses: n/a (2007); Women-owned businesses: n/a (2007); Retail sales per capita: $5,757 (2010). Single-family building permits issued: n/a (2010); Multi-family building permits issued: n/a (2010).
Income: Per capita income: $18,976 (2010); Median household income: $35,129 (2010); Average household income: $48,795 (2010); Percent of households with income of $100,000 or more: 9.7% (2010); Poverty rate: 25.0% (2009); Bankruptcy rate: 0.50% (2010).
Taxes: Total county taxes per capita: $922 (2007); County property taxes per capita: $839 (2007).
Education: Percent of population age 25 and over with: High school diploma (including GED) or higher: 73.1% (2010); Bachelor's degree or higher: 19.7% (2010); Master's degree or higher: 5.0% (2010).
Housing: Homeownership rate: 78.2% (2010); Median home value: $55,437 (2010); Median contract rent: $271 per month (2005-2009 5-year est.); Median year structure built: 1961 (2005-2009 5-year est.).
Health: Birth rate: 177.1 per 10,000 population (2009); Death rate: 5.4 per 10,000 population (2009); Age-adjusted cancer mortality rate: Suppressed deaths per 100,000 population (2007); Number of physicians: 5.1 per 10,000 population (2008); Hospital beds: 0.0 per 10,000 population (2007); Hospital admissions: 0.0 per 10,000 population (2007).
Elections: 2008 Presidential election results: 33.4% Obama, 65.0% McCain, 0.1% Nader
Additional Information Contacts
Edwards County Government . . . . (830) 683-2235
    http://www.edwardscountytexas.us
Rocksprings Chamber of Commerce . . . . (830) 683-6466

Edwards County Communities

BARKSDALE (unincorporated postal area, zip code 78828). Covers a land area of 452.252 square miles and a water area of 0.035 square miles. Located at 29.78° N. Lat; 100.08° W. Long. Elevation is 1,499 feet.
Population: 389 (2000); Race: 98.1% White, 0.0% Black, 0.0% Asian, 1.9% Other, 3.8% Hispanic of any race (2000); Density: 0.9 persons per

square mile (2000); Age: 19.9% under 18, 25.1% over 64 (2000); Marriage status: 12.6% never married, 72.1% now married, 8.4% widowed, 7.0% divorced (2000); Foreign born: 2.4% (2000); Ancestry (includes multiple ancestries): 21.0% English, 14.4% German, 13.0% American, 11.6% Irish (2000).

Economy: Employment by occupation: 23.0% management, 24.8% professional, 9.7% services, 12.7% sales, 9.1% farming, 6.7% construction, 13.9% production (2000).

Income: Per capita income: $20,547 (2000); Median household income: $35,625 (2000); Poverty rate: 179.1% (2000).

Education: Percent of population age 25 and over with: High school diploma (including GED) or higher: 78.0% (2000); Bachelor's degree or higher: 19.6% (2000).

School District(s)
Nueces Canyon CISD (KG-12)
    2009-10 Enrollment: 282 . . . . (830) 234-3514

Housing: Homeownership rate: 75.9% (2000); Median home value: $48,100 (2000); Median contract rent: $330 per month (2000); Median year structure built: 1972 (2000).

Transportation: Commute to work: 84.2% car, 1.2% public transportation, 3.0% walk, 9.7% work from home (2000); Travel time to work: 46.3% less than 15 minutes, 16.8% 15 to 30 minutes, 11.4% 30 to 45 minutes, 13.4% 45 to 60 minutes, 12.1% 60 minutes or more (2000)

Additional Information Contacts
Nueces Canyon Chamber of Commerce . . . . (830) 597-6241
    http://www.mycampwood.com

ROCKSPRINGS (town). County seat. Covers a land area of 1.208 square miles and a water area of 0 square miles. Located at 30.01° N. Lat; 100.20° W. Long. Elevation is 2,402 feet.

History: Rocksprings developed as the center of an Angora goat and sheep raising area.

Population: 1,339 (1990); 1,285 (2000); 1,121 (2010); 1,041 (2015 projected); Race: 73.9% White, 1.9% Black, 0.3% Asian, 24.0% Other, 71.4% Hispanic of any race (2010); Density: 928.3 persons per square mile (2010); Average household size: 2.85 (2010); Median age: 29.5 (2010); Males per 100 females: 111.1 (2010); Marriage status: 28.9% never married, 46.0% now married, 7.3% widowed, 17.7% divorced (2005-2009 5-year est.); Foreign born: 9.1% (2005-2009 5-year est.); Ancestry (includes multiple ancestries): 21.0% American, 10.7% English, 6.4% Irish, 3.4% German, 2.0% Scotch-Irish (2005-2009 5-year est.).

Economy: Employment by occupation: 10.0% management, 14.7% professional, 11.8% services, 20.0% sales, 1.9% farming, 28.4% construction, 13.2% production (2005-2009 5-year est.).

Income: Per capita income: $12,623 (2010); Median household income: $28,047 (2010); Average household income: $35,855 (2010); Percent of households with income of $100,000 or more: 3.7% (2010); Poverty rate: 27.0% (2005-2009 5-year est.).

Taxes: Total city taxes per capita: $142 (2007); City property taxes per capita: $53 (2007).

Education: Percent of population age 25 and over with: High school diploma (including GED) or higher: 64.3% (2010); Bachelor's degree or higher: 12.3% (2010); Master's degree or higher: 3.1% (2010).

School District(s)
Rocksprings ISD (PK-12)
    2009-10 Enrollment: 299 . . . . (830) 683-4137

Housing: Homeownership rate: 80.2% (2010); Median home value: $38,774 (2010); Median contract rent: $263 per month (2005-2009 5-year est.); Median year structure built: 1963 (2005-2009 5-year est.).

Newspapers: Texas Mohair Weekly (Local news; Circulation 1,200)

Transportation: Commute to work: 91.8% car, 0.0% public transportation, 2.7% walk, 1.3% work from home (2005-2009 5-year est.); Travel time to work: 63.2% less than 15 minutes, 4.9% 15 to 30 minutes, 4.0% 30 to 45 minutes, 11.0% 45 to 60 minutes, 16.9% 60 minutes or more (2005-2009 5-year est.)

Airports: Edwards County (general aviation)

Additional Information Contacts
Rocksprings Chamber of Commerce . . . . (830) 683-6466

El Paso County

Located in west Texas; bounded on the north by New Mexico, and on the west and the south by the Rio Grande and the Mexican border; includes the Hueco Mountains in the northeast, and the Franklin Mountains in the northwest. Covers a land area of 1,013.11 square miles, a water area of

1.57 square miles, and is located in the Mountain Time Zone at 31.77° N. Lat., 106.35° W. Long. The county was founded in 1850. County seat is El Paso.

El Paso County is part of the El Paso, TX Metropolitan Statistical Area. The entire metro area includes: El Paso County, TX

Weather Station: El Paso Intl Arpt   Elevation: 3,917 feet

	Jan	Feb	Mar	Apr	May	Jun	Jul	Aug	Sep	Oct	Nov	Dec
High	58	64	71	79	88	96	96	93	88	79	67	58
Low	32	37	42	50	59	67	70	69	63	51	39	32
Precip	0.4	0.4	0.3	0.2	0.5	0.9	1.5	2.1	1.5	0.6	0.5	0.8
Snow	na	na	na	na	na	na	na	na	na	na	na	na

High and Low temperatures in degrees Fahrenheit; Precipitation and Snow in inches

Weather Station: La Tuna 1 S   Elevation: 3,799 feet

	Jan	Feb	Mar	Apr	May	Jun	Jul	Aug	Sep	Oct	Nov	Dec
High	59	65	72	80	89	97	96	94	89	80	67	58
Low	30	35	40	48	57	65	69	67	61	49	37	30
Precip	0.5	0.4	0.2	0.1	0.4	0.9	1.7	2.1	1.2	0.7	0.4	0.7
Snow	0.0	tr	0.0	0.0	0.0	0.0	0.0	0.0	0.0	0.0	tr	0.0

High and Low temperatures in degrees Fahrenheit; Precipitation and Snow in inches

Weather Station: Tornillo 2 SSE   Elevation: 3,525 feet

	Jan	Feb	Mar	Apr	May	Jun	Jul	Aug	Sep	Oct	Nov	Dec
High	60	66	73	81	90	96	95	92	88	80	69	59
Low	28	33	38	45	54	62	66	65	59	47	35	28
Precip	0.4	0.4	0.3	0.2	0.5	0.9	1.6	1.5	1.3	0.8	0.5	0.6
Snow	0.3	tr	0.0	0.0	0.0	0.0	0.0	0.0	0.0	0.0	0.3	0.3

High and Low temperatures in degrees Fahrenheit; Precipitation and Snow in inches

Population: 591,610 (1990); 679,622 (2000); 764,048 (2010); 803,756 (2015 projected); Race: 72.9% White, 2.7% Black, 1.1% Asian, 23.3% Other, 82.2% Hispanic of any race (2010); Density: 754.2 persons per square mile (2010); Average household size: 3.12 (2010); Median age: 31.4 (2010); Males per 100 females: 92.6 (2010).

Religion: Five largest groups: 51.5% Catholic Church, 3.6% Southern Baptist Convention, 1.3% The United Methodist Church, 0.9% Assemblies of God, 0.8% The Church of Jesus Christ of Latter-day Saints (2000).

Economy: Unemployment rate: 10.9% (June 2011); Total civilian labor force: 323,513 (June 2011); Leading industries: 17.4% health care and social assistance; 16.4% retail trade; 12.5% accommodation & food services (2009); Farms: 590 totaling 168,556 acres (2007); Companies that employ 500 or more persons: 28 (2009); Companies that employ 100 to 499 persons: 277 (2009); Companies that employ less than 100 persons: 12,874 (2009); Black-owned businesses: 1,365 (2007); Hispanic-owned businesses: 38,791 (2007); Asian-owned businesses: 1,234 (2007); Women-owned businesses: 17,127 (2007); Retail sales per capita: $11,241 (2010). Single-family building permits issued: 2,961 (2010); Multi-family building permits issued: 1,588 (2010).

Income: Per capita income: $16,178 (2010); Median household income: $36,981 (2010); Average household income: $50,645 (2010); Percent of households with income of $100,000 or more: 10.3% (2010); Poverty rate: 23.7% (2009); Bankruptcy rate: 3.37% (2010).

Taxes: Total county taxes per capita: $253 (2007); County property taxes per capita: $196 (2007).

Education: Percent of population age 25 and over with: High school diploma (including GED) or higher: 71.0% (2010); Bachelor's degree or higher: 19.2% (2010); Master's degree or higher: 6.5% (2010).

Housing: Homeownership rate: 65.3% (2010); Median home value: $97,312 (2010); Median contract rent: $495 per month (2005-2009 5-year est.); Median year structure built: 1978 (2005-2009 5-year est.)

Health: Birth rate: 200.3 per 10,000 population (2009); Death rate: 61.6 per 10,000 population (2009); Age-adjusted cancer mortality rate: 145.5 deaths per 100,000 population (2007); Number of physicians: 18.6 per 10,000 population (2008); Hospital beds: 28.0 per 10,000 population (2007); Hospital admissions: 1,236.2 per 10,000 population (2007).

Environment: Air Quality Index: 47.7% good, 47.1% moderate, 5.2% unhealthy for sensitive individuals, 0.0% unhealthy (percent of days in 2008)

Elections: 2008 Presidential election results: 65.7% Obama, 33.3% McCain, 0.1% Nader

National and State Parks: Chamizal National Memorial

Additional Information Contacts
El Paso County Government . . . . (915) 546-2000
    http://www.co.el-paso.tx.us

Anthony Chamber of Commerce . . . . (915) 886-2815
   http://www.anthonychamberofcommerce.com
City of El Paso . . . . (915) 541-4000
   http://www.elpasotexas.gov
City of Horizon City . . . . (915) 852-1046
   http://www.horizoncity-tx.gov
City of Socorro . . . . (915) 858-2915
   http://www.socorrotexas.org
El Paso Hispanic Chamber of Commerce . . . . (915) 566-4066
   http://www.ephcc.org
Greater El Paso Chamber of Commerce . . . . (915) 534-0500
   http://www.elpaso.org

El Paso County Communities

AGUA DULCE (CDP). Covers a land area of 8.086 square miles and a water area of 0 square miles. Located at 31.64° N. Lat; 106.13° W. Long. Elevation is 4,032 feet.
Population: 99 (1990); 738 (2000); 1,484 (2010); 1,716 (2015 projected); Race: 72.8% White, 1.1% Black, 0.0% Asian, 26.1% Other, 94.2% Hispanic of any race (2010); Density: 183.5 persons per square mile (2010); Average household size: 4.10 (2010); Median age: 24.9 (2010); Males per 100 females: 98.4 (2010); Marriage status: 47.5% never married, 45.3% now married, 1.1% widowed, 6.1% divorced (2005-2009 5-year est.); Foreign born: 36.5% (2005-2009 5-year est.); Ancestry (includes multiple ancestries): n/a (2005-2009 5-year est.).
Economy: Employment by occupation: 2.1% management, 9.7% professional, 18.6% services, 35.5% sales, 1.7% farming, 13.6% construction, 18.9% production (2005-2009 5-year est.).
Income: Per capita income: $8,211 (2010); Median household income: $25,000 (2010); Average household income: $32,905 (2010); Percent of households with income of $100,000 or more: 2.0% (2010); Poverty rate: 46.1% (2005-2009 5-year est.).
Education: Percent of population age 25 and over with: High school diploma (including GED) or higher: 59.5% (2010); Bachelor's degree or higher: 3.2% (2010); Master's degree or higher: 0.0% (2010).
School District(s)
Agua Dulce ISD (PK-12)
   2009-10 Enrollment: 344 . . . . (361) 998-2542
Housing: Homeownership rate: 88.9% (2010); Median home value: $72,469 (2010); Median contract rent: n/a per month (2005-2009 5-year est.); Median year structure built: 1992 (2005-2009 5-year est.).
Transportation: Commute to work: 95.0% car, 0.0% public transportation, 0.0% walk, 2.3% work from home (2005-2009 5-year est.); Travel time to work: 7.0% less than 15 minutes, 53.3% 15 to 30 minutes, 28.3% 30 to 45 minutes, 2.4% 45 to 60 minutes, 9.0% 60 minutes or more (2005-2009 5-year est.)

ANTHONY (town). Covers a land area of 6.497 square miles and a water area of 0.023 square miles. Located at 31.99° N. Lat; 106.59° W. Long. Elevation is 3,806 feet.
History: Incorporated 1952.
Population: 3,328 (1990); 3,850 (2000); 4,455 (2010); 4,748 (2015 projected); Race: 83.3% White, 3.3% Black, 0.1% Asian, 13.2% Other, 86.7% Hispanic of any race (2010); Density: 685.7 persons per square mile (2010); Average household size: 3.39 (2010); Median age: 33.1 (2010); Males per 100 females: 199.0 (2010); Marriage status: 29.8% never married, 49.0% now married, 7.0% widowed, 14.3% divorced (2005-2009 5-year est.); Foreign born: 29.4% (2005-2009 5-year est.); Ancestry (includes multiple ancestries): 2.7% Irish, 2.6% English, 2.6% German, 2.0% American, 1.0% French Canadian (2005-2009 5-year est.).
Economy: Single-family building permits issued: 18 (2010); Multi-family building permits issued: 0 (2010); Employment by occupation: 11.3% management, 8.8% professional, 27.2% services, 24.6% sales, 0.0% farming, 8.7% construction, 19.3% production (2005-2009 5-year est.).
Income: Per capita income: $11,671 (2010); Median household income: $27,815 (2010); Average household income: $39,264 (2010); Percent of households with income of $100,000 or more: 4.9% (2010); Poverty rate: 37.5% (2005-2009 5-year est.).
Taxes: Total city taxes per capita: $259 (2007); City property taxes per capita: $102 (2007).
Education: Percent of population age 25 and over with: High school diploma (including GED) or higher: 63.2% (2010); Bachelor's degree or higher: 7.3% (2010); Master's degree or higher: 2.3% (2010).

School District(s)
Anthony ISD (PK-12)
   2009-10 Enrollment: 833 . . . . (915) 886-6500
Housing: Homeownership rate: 74.8% (2010); Median home value: $80,231 (2010); Median contract rent: $413 per month (2005-2009 5-year est.); Median year structure built: 1977 (2005-2009 5-year est.).
Safety: Violent crime rate: 45.4 per 10,000 population; Property crime rate: 447.6 per 10,000 population (2009).
Transportation: Commute to work: 84.9% car, 0.3% public transportation, 3.6% walk, 3.0% work from home (2005-2009 5-year est.); Travel time to work: 32.5% less than 15 minutes, 37.6% 15 to 30 minutes, 16.9% 30 to 45 minutes, 9.4% 45 to 60 minutes, 3.6% 60 minutes or more (2005-2009 5-year est.)
Additional Information Contacts
Anthony Chamber of Commerce . . . . (915) 886-2815
   http://www.anthonychamberofcommerce.com

BUTTERFIELD (CDP). Covers a land area of 3.161 square miles and a water area of 0 square miles. Located at 31.83° N. Lat; 106.09° W. Long. Elevation is 4,219 feet.
Population: 5 (1990); 61 (2000); 79 (2010); 87 (2015 projected); Race: 68.4% White, 2.5% Black, 1.3% Asian, 27.8% Other, 73.4% Hispanic of any race (2010); Density: 25.0 persons per square mile (2010); Average household size: 3.16 (2010); Median age: 33.6 (2010); Males per 100 females: 97.5 (2010); Marriage status: 0.0% never married, 100.0% now married, 0.0% widowed, 0.0% divorced (2005-2009 5-year est.); Foreign born: 0.0% (2005-2009 5-year est.); Ancestry (includes multiple ancestries): n/a (2005-2009 5-year est.).
Economy: Employment by occupation: 0.0% management, 48.4% professional, 0.0% services, 0.0% sales, 0.0% farming, 0.0% construction, 51.6% production (2005-2009 5-year est.).
Income: Per capita income: $11,210 (2010); Median household income: $28,000 (2010); Average household income: $33,000 (2010); Percent of households with income of $100,000 or more: 4.0% (2010); Poverty rate: 0.0% (2005-2009 5-year est.).
Education: Percent of population age 25 and over with: High school diploma (including GED) or higher: 55.1% (2010); Bachelor's degree or higher: 10.2% (2010); Master's degree or higher: 0.0% (2010).
Housing: Homeownership rate: 92.0% (2010); Median home value: $52,857 (2010); Median contract rent: n/a per month (2005-2009 5-year est.); Median year structure built: n/a (2005-2009 5-year est.).
Transportation: Commute to work: 100.0% car, 0.0% public transportation, 0.0% walk, 0.0% work from home (2005-2009 5-year est.); Travel time to work: 0.0% less than 15 minutes, 48.4% 15 to 30 minutes, 0.0% 30 to 45 minutes, 51.6% 45 to 60 minutes, 0.0% 60 minutes or more (2005-2009 5-year est.)

CANUTILLO (CDP). Covers a land area of 3.029 square miles and a water area of 0 square miles. Located at 31.91° N. Lat; 106.60° W. Long. Elevation is 3,773 feet.
Population: 4,454 (1990); 5,129 (2000); 5,737 (2010); 6,063 (2015 projected); Race: 92.5% White, 0.5% Black, 0.0% Asian, 7.0% Other, 90.8% Hispanic of any race (2010); Density: 1,893.9 persons per square mile (2010); Average household size: 3.31 (2010); Median age: 30.1 (2010); Males per 100 females: 94.3 (2010); Marriage status: 29.9% never married, 62.9% now married, 2.7% widowed, 4.5% divorced (2005-2009 5-year est.); Foreign born: 20.8% (2005-2009 5-year est.); Ancestry (includes multiple ancestries): 3.3% American, 2.2% German, 1.3% English, 0.5% Irish, 0.4% French (2005-2009 5-year est.).
Economy: Employment by occupation: 10.0% management, 9.4% professional, 21.8% services, 22.5% sales, 3.3% farming, 12.5% construction, 20.5% production (2005-2009 5-year est.).
Income: Per capita income: $11,322 (2010); Median household income: $27,983 (2010); Average household income: $37,394 (2010); Percent of households with income of $100,000 or more: 6.2% (2010); Poverty rate: 31.6% (2005-2009 5-year est.).
Education: Percent of population age 25 and over with: High school diploma (including GED) or higher: 46.4% (2010); Bachelor's degree or higher: 8.0% (2010); Master's degree or higher: 1.6% (2010).
School District(s)
Canutillo ISD (PK-12)
   2009-10 Enrollment: 5,867 . . . . (915) 877-7444
Housing: Homeownership rate: 76.1% (2010); Median home value: $61,867 (2010); Median contract rent: $379 per month (2005-2009 5-year est.); Median year structure built: 1983 (2005-2009 5-year est.).

Transportation: Commute to work: 86.6% car, 0.0% public transportation, 2.0% walk, 9.4% work from home (2005-2009 5-year est.); Travel time to work: 28.7% less than 15 minutes, 44.2% 15 to 30 minutes, 15.4% 30 to 45 minutes, 7.1% 45 to 60 minutes, 4.6% 60 minutes or more (2005-2009 5-year est.)

CLINT (town). Covers a land area of 1.951 square miles and a water area of 0.008 square miles. Located at 31.59° N. Lat; 106.22° W. Long. Elevation is 3,638 feet.

Population: 1,035 (1990); 980 (2000); 961 (2010); 984 (2015 projected); Race: 77.7% White, 0.1% Black, 0.2% Asian, 22.0% Other, 90.9% Hispanic of any race (2010); Density: 492.6 persons per square mile (2010); Average household size: 3.33 (2010); Median age: 32.5 (2010); Males per 100 females: 97.7 (2010); Marriage status: 23.8% never married, 47.0% now married, 7.3% widowed, 21.9% divorced (2005-2009 5-year est.); Foreign born: 12.8% (2005-2009 5-year est.); Ancestry (includes multiple ancestries): 23.2% American, 5.2% Irish, 3.7% German, 0.9% Dutch, 0.9% Swedish (2005-2009 5-year est.).

Economy: Single-family building permits issued: 0 (2010); Multi-family building permits issued: 0 (2010); Employment by occupation: 10.9% management, 35.8% professional, 15.6% services, 25.1% sales, 2.5% farming, 0.8% construction, 9.2% production (2005-2009 5-year est.).

Income: Per capita income: $14,599 (2010); Median household income: $36,375 (2010); Average household income: $47,232 (2010); Percent of households with income of $100,000 or more: 9.7% (2010); Poverty rate: 20.6% (2005-2009 5-year est.).

Taxes: Total city taxes per capita: $217 (2007); City property taxes per capita: $133 (2007).

Education: Percent of population age 25 and over with: High school diploma (including GED) or higher: 64.7% (2010); Bachelor's degree or higher: 11.8% (2010); Master's degree or higher: 2.3% (2010).

School District(s)

Clint ISD (PK-12)
    2009-10 Enrollment: 11,295 . . . . (915) 926-4000
Housing: Homeownership rate: 82.7% (2010); Median home value: $85,319 (2010); Median contract rent: $357 per month (2005-2009 5-year est.); Median year structure built: 1960 (2005-2009 5-year est.).
Safety: Violent crime rate: 10.3 per 10,000 population; Property crime rate: 195.7 per 10,000 population (2009).
Transportation: Commute to work: 87.3% car, 0.0% public transportation, 0.0% walk, 7.7% work from home (2005-2009 5-year est.); Travel time to work: 14.7% less than 15 minutes, 40.3% 15 to 30 minutes, 27.2% 30 to 45 minutes, 13.1% 45 to 60 minutes, 4.8% 60 minutes or more (2005-2009 5-year est.)

EL PASO (city). County seat. Covers a land area of 249.076 square miles and a water area of 1.456 square miles. Located at 31.79° N. Lat; 106.42° W. Long. Elevation is 3,717 feet.

History: El Paso began as the village of El Paso del Norte, the Pass of the North on the Rio Grande, first named by explorer Juan de Onate in 1598. For a time in the 1600's it was the seat of government for northern Mexico. A ranch established by Juan Maria Ponce de Leon in 1827 became the nucleus for the present El Paso. Several smaller communities were established nearby in the 1850's; one called Franklin, founded by Benjamin F. Coontz, received a post office in 1852 and became a station on the Butterfield Stage Line. In 1859, Franklin and El Paso became one, and the Franklin name was no longer used. When El Paso was incorporated in 1873, the population was 173. The ensuing decades brought the railroads, population booms, and outlaws. El Paso emerged as a major port of entry to the U.S. from Mexico, and as a processor of the products of the surrounding area, evident in the city's slogan of "Copper, Cotton, Cattle, Clothing and Climate."

Population: 515,541 (1990); 563,662 (2000); 614,938 (2010); 640,686 (2015 projected); Race: 72.2% White, 2.8% Black, 1.2% Asian, 23.7% Other, 80.4% Hispanic of any race (2010); Density: 2,468.9 persons per square mile (2010); Average household size: 3.00 (2010); Median age: 32.6 (2010); Males per 100 females: 90.2 (2010); Marriage status: 30.3% never married, 53.1% now married, 6.2% widowed, 10.4% divorced (2005-2009 5-year est.); Foreign born: 25.7% (2005-2009 5-year est.); Ancestry (includes multiple ancestries): 4.0% German, 3.5% American, 2.8% Irish, 2.4% English, 1.0% Italian (2005-2009 5-year est.).

Economy: Unemployment rate: 10.0% (June 2011); Total civilian labor force: 274,948 (June 2011); Single-family building permits issued: 2,478 (2010); Multi-family building permits issued: 1,584 (2010); Employment by occupation: 11.3% management, 19.3% professional, 19.6% services,

28.5% sales, 0.2% farming, 8.7% construction, 12.4% production (2005-2009 5-year est.).

Income: Per capita income: $17,492 (2010); Median household income: $38,566 (2010); Average household income: $52,557 (2010); Percent of households with income of $100,000 or more: 11.1% (2010); Poverty rate: 25.3% (2005-2009 5-year est.).

Taxes: Total city taxes per capita: $488 (2007); City property taxes per capita: $246 (2007).

Education: Percent of population age 25 and over with: High school diploma (including GED) or higher: 74.2% (2010); Bachelor's degree or higher: 21.6% (2010); Master's degree or higher: 7.4% (2010).

School District(s)

Burnham Wood Charter School District (KG-10)
    2009-10 Enrollment: 782 . . . . (915) 584-9499
Canutillo ISD (PK-12)
    2009-10 Enrollment: 5,867 . . . . (915) 877-7444
Clint ISD (PK-12)
    2009-10 Enrollment: 11,295 . . . . (915) 926-4000
El Paso Academy (09-12)
    2009-10 Enrollment: 474 . . . . (915) 590-8589
El Paso ISD (PK-12)
    2009-10 Enrollment: 63,378 . . . . (915) 779-3781
El Paso School of Excellence (PK-08)
    2009-10 Enrollment: 456 . . . . (214) 381-2208
Fabens ISD (PK-12)
    2009-10 Enrollment: 2,491 . . . . (915) 765-2600
Harmony Science Academy (El Paso) (KG-11)
    2009-10 Enrollment: 1,112 . . . . (713) 343-3333
La Fe Preparatory School (PK-03)
    2009-10 Enrollment: 156 . . . . (915) 533-4690
Paso Del Norte (09-12)
    2009-10 Enrollment: 413 . . . . (210) 227-0295
Responsive Education Solutions (KG-12)
    2009-10 Enrollment: 5,022 . . . . (972) 316-3663
Socorro ISD (PK-12)
    2009-10 Enrollment: 41,357 . . . . (915) 937-0000
Somerset Charter School
    2009-10 Enrollment: n/a . . . . (915) 584-9499
Vista Del Futuro Charter School
    2009-10 Enrollment: n/a . . . . (915) 584-9499
Ysleta ISD (PK-12)
    2009-10 Enrollment: 44,620 . . . . (915) 434-0000

Four-year College(s)

The University of Texas at El Paso (Public)
    Fall 2009 Enrollment: 21,011. . . . . (915) 747-5000
    2010-11 Tuition: In-state $8,020; Out-of-state $19,255

Two-year College(s)

Anamarc Educational Institute (Private, For-profit)
    Fall 2009 Enrollment: 715 . . . . (915) 351-8100
Career Centers of Texas-El Paso (Private, For-profit)
    Fall 2009 Enrollment: 701 . . . . (915) 595-1935
Computer Career Center (Private, For-profit)
    Fall 2009 Enrollment: 994 . . . . (915) 779-8031
    2010-11 Tuition: In-state $18,563; Out-of-state $18,563
El Paso Community College (Public)
    Fall 2009 Enrollment: 28,168. . . . . (915) 831-2000
    2010-11 Tuition: In-state $1,690; Out-of-state $2,242
International Business College (Private, For-profit)
    Fall 2009 Enrollment: 214 . . . . (915) 842-0422
International Business College (Private, For-profit)
    Fall 2009 Enrollment: 300 . . . . (915) 859-0422
Southwest Career College (Private, For-profit)
    Fall 2009 Enrollment: 650 . . . . (915) 778-4001
    2010-11 Tuition: In-state $12,500; Out-of-state $12,500
Western Technical College (Private, For-profit)
    Fall 2009 Enrollment: 958 . . . . (915) 532-3737
Western Technical College (Private, For-profit)
    Fall 2009 Enrollment: 549 . . . . (915) 566-9621

Vocational/Technical School(s)

CET-El Paso (Private, Not-for-profit)
    Fall 2009 Enrollment: 138 . . . . (408) 287-7924
    2010-11 Tuition: $8,779
Pipo Academy of Hair Design (Private, For-profit)
    Fall 2009 Enrollment: 46 . . . . (915) 565-3491
    2010-11 Tuition: $9,500

Tri-State Cosmetology Institute 1 (Private, For-profit)
Fall 2009 Enrollment: 331 . . . . (915) 533-8274
2010-11 Tuition: $10,500
Housing: Homeownership rate: 62.4% (2010); Median home value: $102,897 (2010); Median contract rent: $499 per month (2005-2009 5-year est.); Median year structure built: 1976 (2005-2009 5-year est.).
Hospitals: Columbia Medical Center - West (255 beds); Del Sol Medical Center (336 beds); El Paso Specialty Hospital (31 beds); NCED Mental Health Center; Physicians Specialty Hospital of El Paso; Providence Memorial Hospital (508 beds); Sierra Medical Center (365 beds); Sierra Providence Physical Rehabilitation Hospital (87 beds); Southwestern General Hospital (120 beds); Thomason General Hospital (346 beds); William Beaumont Army Medical Center (200 beds)
Safety: Violent crime rate: 45.7 per 10,000 population; Property crime rate: 299.4 per 10,000 population (2009).
Newspapers: El Conquistador (Regional news; Circulation 15,000); El Diario - El Paso Edition (Local news; Circulation 20,000); El Paso Internet Courier (Local news; Circulation 600); El Paso Times (Local news; Circulation 77,212); The Fort Bliss Monitor (Local news; Circulation 20,000); Rio Grande Catholic (Regional news; Circulation 30,000); Texas Treasures (Community news; Circulation 290,000); Vecinos (Local news; Circulation 38,500)
Transportation: Commute to work: 90.9% car, 2.2% public transportation, 2.1% walk, 2.4% work from home (2005-2009 5-year est.); Travel time to work: 25.9% less than 15 minutes, 47.0% 15 to 30 minutes, 20.6% 30 to 45 minutes, 3.8% 45 to 60 minutes, 2.8% 60 minutes or more (2005-2009 5-year est.); Amtrak: train service available.
Airports: Biggs AAF (Fort Bliss) (general aviation); El Paso International (primary service/small hub)
Additional Information Contacts
City of El Paso . . . . (915) 541-4000
http://www.elpasotexas.gov
El Paso Hispanic Chamber of Commerce . . . . (915) 566-4066
http://www.ephcc.org
Greater El Paso Chamber of Commerce . . . . (915) 534-0500
http://www.elpaso.org

FABENS (CDP). Covers a land area of 3.690 square miles and a water area of 0.002 square miles. Located at 31.50° N. Lat; 106.15° W. Long. Elevation is 3,615 feet.
Population: 5,589 (1990); 8,043 (2000); 8,282 (2010); 8,568 (2015 projected); Race: 74.3% White, 0.7% Black, 0.0% Asian, 24.9% Other, 96.9% Hispanic of any race (2010); Density: 2,244.6 persons per square mile (2010); Average household size: 3.62 (2010); Median age: 26.6 (2010); Males per 100 females: 90.6 (2010); Marriage status: 30.5% never married, 55.6% now married, 6.2% widowed, 7.7% divorced (2005-2009 5-year est.); Foreign born: 31.7% (2005-2009 5-year est.); Ancestry (includes multiple ancestries): 7.9% American, 0.3% German, 0.3% Danish, 0.3% English, 0.3% Swiss (2005-2009 5-year est.).
Economy: Employment by occupation: 5.9% management, 7.2% professional, 20.4% services, 23.7% sales, 1.4% farming, 15.1% construction, 26.3% production (2005-2009 5-year est.).
Income: Per capita income: $7,982 (2010); Median household income: $21,746 (2010); Average household income: $28,730 (2010); Percent of households with income of $100,000 or more: 2.6% (2010); Poverty rate: 43.2% (2005-2009 5-year est.).
Education: Percent of population age 25 and over with: High school diploma (including GED) or higher: 48.1% (2010); Bachelor's degree or higher: 4.5% (2010); Master's degree or higher: 1.5% (2010).

School District(s)

Fabens ISD (PK-12)
2009-10 Enrollment: 2,491 . . . . (915) 765-2600
Housing: Homeownership rate: 70.1% (2010); Median home value: $59,968 (2010); Median contract rent: $263 per month (2005-2009 5-year est.); Median year structure built: 1984 (2005-2009 5-year est.).
Transportation: Commute to work: 86.6% car, 0.9% public transportation, 2.9% walk, 2.6% work from home (2005-2009 5-year est.); Travel time to work: 26.3% less than 15 minutes, 21.8% 15 to 30 minutes, 35.9% 30 to 45 minutes, 9.8% 45 to 60 minutes, 6.1% 60 minutes or more (2005-2009 5-year est.)

FORT BLISS (CDP). Covers a land area of 6.167 square miles and a water area of 0 square miles. Located at 31.80° N. Lat; 106.42° W. Long.
Population: 13,915 (1990); 8,264 (2000); 6,648 (2010); 6,385 (2015 projected); Race: 57.6% White, 21.3% Black, 2.5% Asian, 18.6% Other,

22.3% Hispanic of any race (2010); Density: 1,078.1 persons per square mile (2010); Average household size: 3.50 (2010); Median age: 22.5 (2010); Males per 100 females: 187.8 (2010); Marriage status: 45.1% never married, 51.2% now married, 0.0% widowed, 3.7% divorced (2005-2009 5-year est.); Foreign born: 3.9% (2005-2009 5-year est.); Ancestry (includes multiple ancestries): 15.1% German, 12.8% Irish, 6.9% American, 4.7% English, 3.3% Dutch (2005-2009 5-year est.).
Economy: Employment by occupation: 9.7% management, 21.2% professional, 16.2% services, 20.5% sales, 0.0% farming, 19.0% construction, 13.4% production (2005-2009 5-year est.).
Income: Per capita income: $15,042 (2010); Median household income: $43,213 (2010); Average household income: $54,751 (2010); Percent of households with income of $100,000 or more: 7.6% (2010); Poverty rate: 11.3% (2005-2009 5-year est.).
Education: Percent of population age 25 and over with: High school diploma (including GED) or higher: 94.8% (2010); Bachelor's degree or higher: 29.3% (2010); Master's degree or higher: 6.4% (2010).
Housing: Homeownership rate: 1.5% (2010); Median home value: $80,000 (2010); Median contract rent: $882 per month (2005-2009 5-year est.); Median year structure built: 1970 (2005-2009 5-year est.).
Transportation: Commute to work: 51.6% car, 2.3% public transportation, 20.2% walk, 22.9% work from home (2005-2009 5-year est.); Travel time to work: 75.6% less than 15 minutes, 17.8% 15 to 30 minutes, 5.6% 30 to 45 minutes, 0.6% 45 to 60 minutes, 0.5% 60 minutes or more (2005-2009 5-year est.)
Airports: Biggs AAF (Fort Bliss) (general aviation)

HOMESTEAD MEADOWS NORTH (CDP). Covers a land area of 16.634 square miles and a water area of 0 square miles. Located at 31.84° N. Lat; 106.17° W. Long. Elevation is 4,075 feet.
Population: 1,760 (1990); 4,232 (2000); 5,285 (2010); 5,771 (2015 projected); Race: 76.1% White, 6.5% Black, 0.3% Asian, 17.1% Other, 80.4% Hispanic of any race (2010); Density: 317.7 persons per square mile (2010); Average household size: 3.69 (2010); Median age: 25.0 (2010); Males per 100 females: 146.3 (2010); Marriage status: 26.5% never married, 55.6% now married, 8.1% widowed, 9.8% divorced (2005-2009 5-year est.); Foreign born: 33.8% (2005-2009 5-year est.); Ancestry (includes multiple ancestries): 3.9% American, 1.7% Irish, 1.6% English, 1.3% German, 1.3% Swedish (2005-2009 5-year est.).
Economy: Employment by occupation: 6.8% management, 10.8% professional, 20.1% services, 27.1% sales, 1.4% farming, 15.8% construction, 17.9% production (2005-2009 5-year est.).
Income: Per capita income: $11,253 (2010); Median household income: $33,042 (2010); Average household income: $41,126 (2010); Percent of households with income of $100,000 or more: 4.7% (2010); Poverty rate: 37.1% (2005-2009 5-year est.).
Education: Percent of population age 25 and over with: High school diploma (including GED) or higher: 67.9% (2010); Bachelor's degree or higher: 7.1% (2010); Master's degree or higher: 2.7% (2010).
Housing: Homeownership rate: 85.9% (2010); Median home value: $73,984 (2010); Median contract rent: $372 per month (2005-2009 5-year est.); Median year structure built: 1990 (2005-2009 5-year est.).
Transportation: Commute to work: 90.6% car, 0.0% public transportation, 0.4% walk, 4.7% work from home (2005-2009 5-year est.); Travel time to work: 10.3% less than 15 minutes, 41.2% 15 to 30 minutes, 29.8% 30 to 45 minutes, 14.0% 45 to 60 minutes, 4.7% 60 minutes or more (2005-2009 5-year est.)

HOMESTEAD MEADOWS SOUTH (CDP). Covers a land area of 3.348 square miles and a water area of 0 square miles. Located at 31.80° N. Lat; 106.17° W. Long. Elevation is 4,068 feet.
Population: 3,258 (1990); 6,807 (2000); 11,895 (2010); 13,670 (2015 projected); Race: 63.6% White, 0.9% Black, 0.6% Asian, 34.9% Other, 93.8% Hispanic of any race (2010); Density: 3,552.5 persons per square mile (2010); Average household size: 4.13 (2010); Median age: 25.6 (2010); Males per 100 females: 94.0 (2010); Marriage status: 34.2% never married, 58.7% now married, 3.5% widowed, 3.5% divorced (2005-2009 5-year est.); Foreign born: 42.2% (2005-2009 5-year est.); Ancestry (includes multiple ancestries): 1.1% German, 0.6% American, 0.4% Scotch-Irish, 0.3% Irish, 0.2% English (2005-2009 5-year est.).
Economy: Employment by occupation: 7.7% management, 4.5% professional, 25.5% services, 22.2% sales, 1.7% farming, 20.1% construction, 18.2% production (2005-2009 5-year est.).
Income: Per capita income: $11,436 (2010); Median household income: $38,092 (2010); Average household income: $47,329 (2010); Percent of

households with income of $100,000 or more: 9.5% (2010); Poverty rate: 38.1% (2005-2009 5-year est.).

Education: Percent of population age 25 and over with: High school diploma (including GED) or higher: 55.6% (2010); Bachelor's degree or higher: 9.1% (2010); Master's degree or higher: 1.5% (2010).

Housing: Homeownership rate: 90.3% (2010); Median home value: $84,532 (2010); Median contract rent: $473 per month (2005-2009 5-year est.); Median year structure built: 1991 (2005-2009 5-year est.).

Transportation: Commute to work: 95.8% car, 0.5% public transportation, 1.9% walk, 1.4% work from home (2005-2009 5-year est.); Travel time to work: 21.9% less than 15 minutes, 28.3% 15 to 30 minutes, 33.9% 30 to 45 minutes, 12.9% 45 to 60 minutes, 3.0% 60 minutes or more (2005-2009 5-year est.)

HORIZON CITY (city).
Covers a land area of 5.732 square miles and a water area of 0 square miles. Located at 31.68° N. Lat; 106.19° W. Long. Elevation is 4,022 feet.

Population: 2,338 (1990); 5,233 (2000); 9,653 (2010); 11,207 (2015 projected); Race: 76.1% White, 1.1% Black, 0.2% Asian, 22.7% Other, 80.7% Hispanic of any race (2010); Density: 1,683.9 persons per square mile (2010); Average household size: 3.31 (2010); Median age: 31.3 (2010); Males per 100 females: 93.2 (2010); Marriage status: 26.4% never married, 63.9% now married, 2.0% widowed, 7.6% divorced (2005-2009 5-year est.); Foreign born: 21.2% (2005-2009 5-year est.); Ancestry (includes multiple ancestries): 5.8% American, 3.4% German, 2.3% English, 2.1% Irish, 1.2% French (2005-2009 5-year est.).

Economy: Single-family building permits issued: 386 (2010); Multi-family building permits issued: 4 (2010); Employment by occupation: 9.1% management, 16.2% professional, 17.3% services, 31.2% sales, 0.5% farming, 9.7% construction, 16.1% production (2005-2009 5-year est.).

Income: Per capita income: $19,652 (2010); Median household income: $53,222 (2010); Average household income: $65,199 (2010); Percent of households with income of $100,000 or more: 19.8% (2010); Poverty rate: 15.9% (2005-2009 5-year est.).

Taxes: Total city taxes per capita: $184 (2007); City property taxes per capita: $85 (2007).

Education: Percent of population age 25 and over with: High school diploma (including GED) or higher: 82.8% (2010); Bachelor's degree or higher: 21.0% (2010); Master's degree or higher: 6.0% (2010).

Housing: Homeownership rate: 89.1% (2010); Median home value: $122,141 (2010); Median contract rent: $687 per month (2005-2009 5-year est.); Median year structure built: 1999 (2005-2009 5-year est.).

Safety: Violent crime rate: 11.1 per 10,000 population; Property crime rate: 175.6 per 10,000 population (2009).

Transportation: Commute to work: 94.8% car, 0.5% public transportation, 0.6% walk, 3.0% work from home (2005-2009 5-year est.); Travel time to work: 13.0% less than 15 minutes, 38.5% 15 to 30 minutes, 31.9% 30 to 45 minutes, 12.4% 45 to 60 minutes, 4.3% 60 minutes or more (2005-2009 5-year est.)

Additional Information Contacts

City of Horizon City . . . . (915) 852-1046
http://www.horizoncity-tx.gov

MORNING GLORY (CDP).
Covers a land area of 1.072 square miles and a water area of 0 square miles. Located at 31.56° N. Lat; 106.21° W. Long. Elevation is 3,632 feet.

Population: 509 (1990); 627 (2000); 680 (2010); 717 (2015 projected); Race: 91.2% White, 0.3% Black, 0.0% Asian, 8.5% Other, 95.4% Hispanic of any race (2010); Density: 634.6 persons per square mile (2010); Average household size: 3.70 (2010); Median age: 25.5 (2010); Males per 100 females: 96.5 (2010); Marriage status: 31.3% never married, 66.4% now married, 0.0% widowed, 2.3% divorced (2005-2009 5-year est.); Foreign born: 35.2% (2005-2009 5-year est.); Ancestry (includes multiple ancestries): n/a (2005-2009 5-year est.).

Economy: Employment by occupation: 0.0% management, 4.9% professional, 31.1% services, 28.2% sales, 0.0% farming, 13.6% construction, 22.3% production (2005-2009 5-year est.).

Income: Per capita income: $8,939 (2010); Median household income: $23,023 (2010); Average household income: $31,585 (2010); Percent of households with income of $100,000 or more: 2.7% (2010); Poverty rate: 39.0% (2005-2009 5-year est.).

Education: Percent of population age 25 and over with: High school diploma (including GED) or higher: 42.7% (2010); Bachelor's degree or higher: 8.1% (2010); Master's degree or higher: 0.6% (2010).

Housing: Homeownership rate: 75.4% (2010); Median home value: $60,833 (2010); Median contract rent: n/a per month (2005-2009 5-year est.); Median year structure built: 1987 (2005-2009 5-year est.).

Transportation: Commute to work: 86.4% car, 0.0% public transportation, 13.6% walk, 0.0% work from home (2005-2009 5-year est.); Travel time to work: 13.6% less than 15 minutes, 35.9% 15 to 30 minutes, 8.7% 30 to 45 minutes, 15.5% 45 to 60 minutes, 26.2% 60 minutes or more (2005-2009 5-year est.)

PRADO VERDE (CDP).
Covers a land area of 0.128 square miles and a water area of 0 square miles. Located at 31.89° N. Lat; 106.61° W. Long. Elevation is 3,763 feet.

Population: 173 (1990); 200 (2000); 206 (2010); 216 (2015 projected); Race: 95.6% White, 0.0% Black, 0.0% Asian, 4.4% Other, 63.1% Hispanic of any race (2010); Density: 1,604.4 persons per square mile (2010); Average household size: 2.94 (2010); Median age: 36.9 (2010); Males per 100 females: 100.0 (2010); Marriage status: 46.1% never married, 30.7% now married, 18.5% widowed, 4.7% divorced (2005-2009 5-year est.); Foreign born: 10.4% (2005-2009 5-year est.); Ancestry (includes multiple ancestries): 22.5% Dutch, 15.2% Danish, 7.3% Scotch-Irish, 3.2% American (2005-2009 5-year est.).

Economy: Employment by occupation: 7.4% management, 54.4% professional, 0.0% services, 38.3% sales, 0.0% farming, 0.0% construction, 0.0% production (2005-2009 5-year est.).

Income: Per capita income: $39,040 (2010); Median household income: $77,083 (2010); Average household income: $115,071 (2010); Percent of households with income of $100,000 or more: 34.3% (2010); Poverty rate: 0.0% (2005-2009 5-year est.).

Education: Percent of population age 25 and over with: High school diploma (including GED) or higher: 87.1% (2010); Bachelor's degree or higher: 46.2% (2010); Master's degree or higher: 19.7% (2010).

Housing: Homeownership rate: 84.3% (2010); Median home value: $181,250 (2010); Median contract rent: n/a per month (2005-2009 5-year est.); Median year structure built: 1979 (2005-2009 5-year est.).

Transportation: Commute to work: 100.0% car, 0.0% public transportation, 0.0% walk, 0.0% work from home (2005-2009 5-year est.); Travel time to work: 11.4% less than 15 minutes, 73.2% 15 to 30 minutes, 7.4% 30 to 45 minutes, 8.1% 45 to 60 minutes, 0.0% 60 minutes or more (2005-2009 5-year est.)

SAN ELIZARIO (CDP).
Covers a land area of 9.927 square miles and a water area of 0 square miles. Located at 31.58° N. Lat; 106.26° W. Long. Elevation is 3,642 feet.

History: San Elizario began as a presidio town, founded by the Spanish in 1680. U.S. troops were garrisoned at San Elizario in 1850, and the California Volunteers had their headquarters here in 1862.

Population: 4,397 (1990); 11,046 (2000); 12,982 (2010); 14,155 (2015 projected); Race: 95.0% White, 0.2% Black, 0.0% Asian, 4.9% Other, 97.7% Hispanic of any race (2010); Density: 1,307.8 persons per square mile (2010); Average household size: 4.08 (2010); Median age: 24.8 (2010); Males per 100 females: 95.9 (2010); Marriage status: 30.4% never married, 59.1% now married, 5.5% widowed, 4.9% divorced (2005-2009 5-year est.); Foreign born: 38.9% (2005-2009 5-year est.); Ancestry (includes multiple ancestries): 3.1% American, 0.4% Irish, 0.1% English, 0.1% German (2005-2009 5-year est.).

Economy: Employment by occupation: 3.7% management, 8.8% professional, 16.9% services, 16.2% sales, 1.5% farming, 22.9% construction, 30.0% production (2005-2009 5-year est.).

Income: Per capita income: $7,760 (2010); Median household income: $24,526 (2010); Average household income: $31,484 (2010); Percent of households with income of $100,000 or more: 1.8% (2010); Poverty rate: 50.1% (2005-2009 5-year est.).

Education: Percent of population age 25 and over with: High school diploma (including GED) or higher: 36.6% (2010); Bachelor's degree or higher: 3.6% (2010); Master's degree or higher: 0.7% (2010).

School District(s)

San Elizario ISD (PK-12)
2009-10 Enrollment: 4,044 . . . . (915) 872-3900

Housing: Homeownership rate: 85.4% (2010); Median home value: $65,485 (2010); Median contract rent: $391 per month (2005-2009 5-year est.); Median year structure built: 1987 (2005-2009 5-year est.).

Transportation: Commute to work: 90.7% car, 0.8% public transportation, 0.4% walk, 4.3% work from home (2005-2009 5-year est.); Travel time to work: 13.6% less than 15 minutes, 36.1% 15 to 30 minutes, 37.8% 30 to 45

minutes, 9.9% 45 to 60 minutes, 2.5% 60 minutes or more (2005-2009 5-year est.)

SOCORRO (city). Covers a land area of 17.507 square miles and a water area of 0 square miles. Located at 31.64° N. Lat; 106.27° W. Long. Elevation is 3,661 feet.

History: The first mission on the site of Socorro was probably built in 1683. In 1766 a mission here was named Mission de la Purisima Concepcion del Socorro (Mission of the Most Pure Conception of the Socorro).

Population: 22,995 (1990); 27,152 (2000); 32,215 (2010); 34,817 (2015 projected); Race: 72.3% White, 0.5% Black, 0.1% Asian, 27.2% Other, 96.6% Hispanic of any race (2010); Density: 1,840.2 persons per square mile (2010); Average household size: 3.89 (2010); Median age: 28.3 (2010); Males per 100 females: 92.4 (2010); Marriage status: 31.7% never married, 55.8% now married, 5.4% widowed, 7.2% divorced (2005-2009 5-year est.); Foreign born: 33.7% (2005-2009 5-year est.); Ancestry (includes multiple ancestries): 2.8% American, 0.4% German, 0.4% French, 0.4% Irish, 0.2% Italian (2005-2009 5-year est.).

Economy: Unemployment rate: 12.9% (June 2011); Total civilian labor force: 12,598 (June 2011); Single-family building permits issued: 76 (2010); Multi-family building permits issued: 0 (2010); Employment by occupation: 4.7% management, 12.4% professional, 19.7% services, 22.9% sales, 0.3% farming, 17.0% construction, 22.9% production (2005-2009 5-year est.).

Income: Per capita income: $9,338 (2010); Median household income: $29,720 (2010); Average household income: $36,303 (2010); Percent of households with income of $100,000 or more: 3.3% (2010); Poverty rate: 27.3% (2005-2009 5-year est.).

Taxes: Total city taxes per capita: $120 (2007); City property taxes per capita: $88 (2007).

Education: Percent of population age 25 and over with: High school diploma (including GED) or higher: 49.9% (2010); Bachelor's degree or higher: 5.3% (2010); Master's degree or higher: 2.0% (2010).

Housing: Homeownership rate: 80.9% (2010); Median home value: $75,246 (2010); Median contract rent: $368 per month (2005-2009 5-year est.); Median year structure built: 1987 (2005-2009 5-year est.).

Safety: Violent crime rate: 32.0 per 10,000 population; Property crime rate: 217.4 per 10,000 population (2009).

Transportation: Commute to work: 90.3% car, 0.0% public transportation, 1.7% walk, 2.9% work from home (2005-2009 5-year est.); Travel time to work: 18.1% less than 15 minutes, 39.9% 15 to 30 minutes, 32.3% 30 to 45 minutes, 6.6% 45 to 60 minutes, 3.0% 60 minutes or more (2005-2009 5-year est.)

Additional Information Contacts
City of Socorro . . . . (915) 858-2915
    http://www.socorrotexas.org

SPARKS (CDP). Covers a land area of 1.343 square miles and a water area of 0 square miles. Located at 31.67° N. Lat; 106.23° W. Long. Elevation is 3,812 feet.

Population: 1,276 (1990); 2,974 (2000); 4,695 (2010); 5,459 (2015 projected); Race: 68.2% White, 0.0% Black, 0.1% Asian, 31.7% Other, 96.5% Hispanic of any race (2010); Density: 3,495.2 persons per square mile (2010); Average household size: 3.86 (2010); Median age: 25.4 (2010); Males per 100 females: 92.0 (2010); Marriage status: 30.6% never married, 63.7% now married, 2.9% widowed, 2.9% divorced (2005-2009 5-year est.); Foreign born: 42.6% (2005-2009 5-year est.); Ancestry (includes multiple ancestries): 3.1% American, 0.2% Irish (2005-2009 5-year est.).

Economy: Employment by occupation: 5.4% management, 4.6% professional, 21.1% services, 21.6% sales, 0.0% farming, 20.2% construction, 27.1% production (2005-2009 5-year est.).

Income: Per capita income: $9,435 (2010); Median household income: $31,684 (2010); Average household income: $36,417 (2010); Percent of households with income of $100,000 or more: 2.1% (2010); Poverty rate: 48.3% (2005-2009 5-year est.).

Education: Percent of population age 25 and over with: High school diploma (including GED) or higher: 46.6% (2010); Bachelor's degree or higher: 2.1% (2010); Master's degree or higher: 0.8% (2010).

Housing: Homeownership rate: 86.5% (2010); Median home value: $50,511 (2010); Median contract rent: $378 per month (2005-2009 5-year est.); Median year structure built: 1994 (2005-2009 5-year est.).

Transportation: Commute to work: 91.2% car, 0.0% public transportation, 0.0% walk, 4.1% work from home (2005-2009 5-year est.); Travel time to work: 5.2% less than 15 minutes, 36.7% 15 to 30 minutes, 53.7% 30 to 45

minutes, 2.4% 45 to 60 minutes, 2.0% 60 minutes or more (2005-2009 5-year est.)

TORNILLO (CDP). Covers a land area of 3.421 square miles and a water area of 0 square miles. Located at 31.43° N. Lat; 106.09° W. Long. Elevation is 3,586 feet.

Population: 728 (1990); 1,609 (2000); 1,900 (2010); 2,068 (2015 projected); Race: 94.2% White, 0.1% Black, 0.0% Asian, 5.7% Other, 98.3% Hispanic of any race (2010); Density: 555.5 persons per square mile (2010); Average household size: 3.89 (2010); Median age: 23.6 (2010); Males per 100 females: 94.3 (2010); Marriage status: 30.5% never married, 60.0% now married, 5.8% widowed, 3.6% divorced (2005-2009 5-year est.); Foreign born: 44.9% (2005-2009 5-year est.); Ancestry (includes multiple ancestries): n/a (2005-2009 5-year est.).

Economy: Employment by occupation: 5.8% management, 8.4% professional, 25.8% services, 14.2% sales, 14.8% farming, 10.9% construction, 20.2% production (2005-2009 5-year est.).

Income: Per capita income: $7,136 (2010); Median household income: $21,493 (2010); Average household income: $28,303 (2010); Percent of households with income of $100,000 or more: 2.2% (2010); Poverty rate: 45.9% (2005-2009 5-year est.).

Education: Percent of population age 25 and over with: High school diploma (including GED) or higher: 34.8% (2010); Bachelor's degree or higher: 2.6% (2010); Master's degree or higher: 0.3% (2010).

School District(s)
Tornillo ISD (PK-12)
    2009-10 Enrollment: 1,324 . . . . (915) 765-3000

Housing: Homeownership rate: 84.3% (2010); Median home value: $44,762 (2010); Median contract rent: $290 per month (2005-2009 5-year est.); Median year structure built: 1982 (2005-2009 5-year est.).

Transportation: Commute to work: 93.6% car, 0.0% public transportation, 0.5% walk, 3.1% work from home (2005-2009 5-year est.); Travel time to work: 29.7% less than 15 minutes, 23.8% 15 to 30 minutes, 26.3% 30 to 45 minutes, 12.8% 45 to 60 minutes, 7.4% 60 minutes or more (2005-2009 5-year est.)

VINTON (village). Covers a land area of 2.426 square miles and a water area of 0 square miles. Located at 31.95° N. Lat; 106.59° W. Long. Elevation is 3,796 feet.

Population: 605 (1990); 1,892 (2000); 2,064 (2010); 2,186 (2015 projected); Race: 89.5% White, 0.6% Black, 0.0% Asian, 9.9% Other, 96.4% Hispanic of any race (2010); Density: 850.8 persons per square mile (2010); Average household size: 3.78 (2010); Median age: 24.5 (2010); Males per 100 females: 98.5 (2010); Marriage status: 32.5% never married, 57.7% now married, 4.9% widowed, 4.9% divorced (2005-2009 5-year est.); Foreign born: 36.7% (2005-2009 5-year est.); Ancestry (includes multiple ancestries): 2.8% American, 0.9% English, 0.8% German, 0.3% Irish, 0.2% Polish (2005-2009 5-year est.).

Economy: Single-family building permits issued: 3 (2010); Multi-family building permits issued: 0 (2010); Employment by occupation: 2.3% management, 14.9% professional, 10.5% services, 27.7% sales, 0.4% farming, 7.9% construction, 36.3% production (2005-2009 5-year est.).

Income: Per capita income: $10,370 (2010); Median household income: $29,554 (2010); Average household income: $38,494 (2010); Percent of households with income of $100,000 or more: 4.4% (2010); Poverty rate: 21.7% (2005-2009 5-year est.).

Taxes: Total city taxes per capita: $229 (2007); City property taxes per capita: $81 (2007).

Education: Percent of population age 25 and over with: High school diploma (including GED) or higher: 44.7% (2010); Bachelor's degree or higher: 4.6% (2010); Master's degree or higher: 1.3% (2010).

School District(s)
Canutillo ISD (PK-12)
    2009-10 Enrollment: 5,867 . . . . (915) 877-7444

Housing: Homeownership rate: 81.5% (2010); Median home value: $68,252 (2010); Median contract rent: $465 per month (2005-2009 5-year est.); Median year structure built: 1989 (2005-2009 5-year est.).

Transportation: Commute to work: 86.6% car, 1.1% public transportation, 1.1% walk, 1.4% work from home (2005-2009 5-year est.); Travel time to work: 33.6% less than 15 minutes, 38.1% 15 to 30 minutes, 14.0% 30 to 45 minutes, 10.5% 45 to 60 minutes, 3.8% 60 minutes or more (2005-2009 5-year est.)

WESTWAY (CDP). Covers a land area of 1.321 square miles and a water area of 0 square miles. Located at 31.95° N. Lat; 106.57° W. Long. Elevation is 3,960 feet.

Population: 2,381 (1990); 3,829 (2000); 4,231 (2010); 4,504 (2015 projected); Race: 98.6% White, 0.5% Black, 0.0% Asian, 0.9% Other, 98.2% Hispanic of any race (2010); Density: 3,203.4 persons per square mile (2010); Average household size: 4.05 (2010); Median age: 25.4 (2010); Males per 100 females: 94.9 (2010); Marriage status: 32.0% never married, 54.1% now married, 3.9% widowed, 10.0% divorced (2005-2009 5-year est.); Foreign born: 44.8% (2005-2009 5-year est.); Ancestry (includes multiple ancestries): 1.8% German, 1.5% American, 1.0% Greek, 1.0% Irish, 0.9% English (2005-2009 5-year est.).

Economy: Employment by occupation: 4.0% management, 2.9% professional, 30.1% services, 18.6% sales, 3.7% farming, 19.1% construction, 21.6% production (2005-2009 5-year est.).

Income: Per capita income: $8,666 (2010); Median household income: $27,940 (2010); Average household income: $35,086 (2010); Percent of households with income of $100,000 or more: 1.7% (2010); Poverty rate: 52.9% (2005-2009 5-year est.).

Education: Percent of population age 25 and over with: High school diploma (including GED) or higher: 37.7% (2010); Bachelor's degree or higher: 0.8% (2010); Master's degree or higher: 0.1% (2010).

Housing: Homeownership rate: 82.5% (2010); Median home value: $56,585 (2010); Median contract rent: $335 per month (2005-2009 5-year est.); Median year structure built: 1983 (2005-2009 5-year est.).

Transportation: Commute to work: 88.2% car, 0.0% public transportation, 0.0% walk, 1.4% work from home (2005-2009 5-year est.); Travel time to work: 37.7% less than 15 minutes, 38.0% 15 to 30 minutes, 14.4% 30 to 45 minutes, 5.6% 45 to 60 minutes, 4.3% 60 minutes or more (2005-2009 5-year est.)

Ellis County

Located in north Texas; bounded on the east by the Trinity River. Covers a land area of 939.91 square miles, a water area of 11.75 square miles, and is located in the Central Time Zone at 32.39° N. Lat., 96.79° W. Long. The county was founded in 1849. County seat is Waxahachie.

Ellis County is part of the Dallas-Fort Worth-Arlington, TX Metropolitan Statistical Area. The entire metro area includes: Dallas-Plano-Irving, TX Metropolitan Division (Collin County, TX; Dallas County, TX; Delta County, TX; Denton County, TX; Ellis County, TX; Hunt County, TX; Kaufman County, TX; Rockwall County, TX); Fort Worth-Arlington, TX Metropolitan Division (Johnson County, TX; Parker County, TX; Tarrant County, TX; Wise County, TX)

Weather Station: Bardwell Dam											Elevation: 460 feet	
	Jan	Feb	Mar	Apr	May	Jun	Jul	Aug	Sep	Oct	Nov	Dec
High	57	61	68	76	83	91	95	96	89	79	68	58
Low	33	37	45	53	62	69	72	72	64	53	43	34
Precip	2.7	2.9	3.6	3.0	4.5	4.0	1.8	2.2	2.9	4.2	3.2	3.2
Snow	0.1	tr	0.0	0.0	0.0	0.0	0.0	0.0	0.0	0.0	0.0	0.1

High and Low temperatures in degrees Fahrenheit; Precipitation and Snow in inches

Weather Station: Ferris											Elevation: 470 feet	
	Jan	Feb	Mar	Apr	May	Jun	Jul	Aug	Sep	Oct	Nov	Dec
High	57	62	69	77	84	91	96	97	90	79	68	58
Low	35	39	45	53	62	69	72	72	65	55	45	36
Precip	2.9	3.0	3.9	3.1	4.6	4.0	1.9	2.4	2.6	4.6	3.0	3.4
Snow	0.1	0.3	tr	0.0	0.0	0.0	0.0	0.0	0.0	0.0	tr	0.3

High and Low temperatures in degrees Fahrenheit; Precipitation and Snow in inches

Weather Station: Waxahachie											Elevation: 629 feet	
	Jan	Feb	Mar	Apr	May	Jun	Jul	Aug	Sep	Oct	Nov	Dec
High	57	62	69	77	84	91	95	96	89	79	67	58
Low	36	39	47	54	63	70	73	73	66	56	46	37
Precip	2.2	3.0	3.7	3.3	4.2	4.0	2.4	2.4	3.3	4.6	3.1	3.2
Snow	tr	0.2	0.0	0.0	0.0	0.0	0.0	0.0	0.0	0.0	tr	tr

High and Low temperatures in degrees Fahrenheit; Precipitation and Snow in inches

Population: 85,167 (1990); 111,360 (2000); 153,990 (2010); 174,450 (2015 projected); Race: 76.1% White, 9.9% Black, 0.6% Asian, 13.4% Other, 23.6% Hispanic of any race (2010); Density: 163.8 persons per square mile (2010); Average household size: 3.00 (2010); Median age: 33.1 (2010); Males per 100 females: 99.5 (2010).

Religion: Five largest groups: 19.5% Southern Baptist Convention, 14.5% Catholic Church, 7.1% The United Methodist Church, 6.4% Baptist Missionary Association of America, 2.7% Churches of Christ (2000).

Economy: Unemployment rate: 9.8% (June 2011); Total civilian labor force: 74,196 (June 2011); Leading industries: 25.4% manufacturing; 15.8% retail trade; 10.8% accommodation & food services (2009); Farms: 2,415 totaling 442,656 acres (2007); Companies that employ 500 or more persons: 6 (2009); Companies that employ 100 to 499 persons: 47 (2009); Companies that employ less than 100 persons: 2,393 (2009); Black-owned businesses: n/a (2007); Hispanic-owned businesses: 1,462 (2007); Asian-owned businesses: n/a (2007); Women-owned businesses: 3,769 (2007); Retail sales per capita: $8,525 (2010). Single-family building permits issued: 487 (2010); Multi-family building permits issued: 10 (2010).

Income: Per capita income: $24,093 (2010); Median household income: $60,345 (2010); Average household income: $72,863 (2010); Percent of households with income of $100,000 or more: 21.0% (2010); Poverty rate: 10.9% (2009); Bankruptcy rate: 3.31% (2010).

Taxes: Total county taxes per capita: $211 (2007); County property taxes per capita: $195 (2007).

Education: Percent of population age 25 and over with: High school diploma (including GED) or higher: 83.4% (2010); Bachelor's degree or higher: 20.4% (2010); Master's degree or higher: 5.7% (2010).

Housing: Homeownership rate: 75.3% (2010); Median home value: $129,198 (2010); Median contract rent: $614 per month (2005-2009 5-year est.); Median year structure built: 1988 (2005-2009 5-year est.)

Health: Birth rate: 161.9 per 10,000 population (2009); Death rate: 66.0 per 10,000 population (2009); Age-adjusted cancer mortality rate: 183.5 deaths per 100,000 population (2007); Number of physicians: 8.7 per 10,000 population (2008); Hospital beds: 7.8 per 10,000 population (2007); Hospital admissions: 426.0 per 10,000 population (2007).

Environment: Air Quality Index: 74.8% good, 23.3% moderate, 2.0% unhealthy for sensitive individuals, 0.0% unhealthy (percent of days in 2008)

Elections: 2008 Presidential election results: 28.5% Obama, 70.7% McCain, 0.1% Nader

Additional Information Contacts

Ellis County Government	(972) 825-5000
http://www.co.ellis.tx.us	
City of Ennis	(972) 878-1234
http://www.ennis-texas.com	
City of Midlothian	(972) 775-3481
http://www.midlothian.tx.us	
City of Red Oak	(972) 617-3638
http://www.redoaktx.org	
City of Waxahachie	(972) 937-7330
http://www.waxahachie.com	
Ennis Chamber of Commerce	(972) 878-2625
http://www.ennis-chamber.com	
Ennis Negro Chamber of Commerce	(972) 875-9222
Glenn Heights Chamber of Commerce	(972) 274-5100
http://www.glennheights.com	
Midlothian Chamber of Commerce	(972) 723-8600
http://www.midlothianchamber.org	
Red Oak Area Chamber of Commerce	(972) 617-0906
http://www.redoakareachamber.org	
Waxahachie Chamber of Commerce	(972) 937-2390
http://www.waxahachiechamber.com	

Ellis County Communities

ALMA (town). Covers a land area of 5.031 square miles and a water area of 0 square miles. Located at 32.28° N. Lat; 96.54° W. Long. Elevation is 469 feet.

Population: 210 (1990); 302 (2000); 463 (2010); 541 (2015 projected); Race: 79.5% White, 2.6% Black, 0.2% Asian, 17.7% Other, 24.6% Hispanic of any race (2010); Density: 92.0 persons per square mile (2010); Average household size: 2.97 (2010); Median age: 33.4 (2010); Males per 100 females: 98.7 (2010); Marriage status: 23.1% never married, 63.9% now married, 8.8% widowed, 4.2% divorced (2005-2009 5-year est.); Foreign born: 1.1% (2005-2009 5-year est.); Ancestry (includes multiple ancestries): 20.4% English, 20.1% Irish, 13.3% German, 10.8% Czech, 9.0% European (2005-2009 5-year est.).

Economy: Employment by occupation: 3.8% management, 27.4% professional, 13.2% services, 15.1% sales, 1.9% farming, 15.1% construction, 23.6% production (2005-2009 5-year est.).

Income: Per capita income: $21,308 (2010); Median household income: $51,515 (2010); Average household income: $62,869 (2010); Percent of households with income of $100,000 or more: 14.1% (2010); Poverty rate: 7.2% (2005-2009 5-year est.).
Taxes: Total city taxes per capita: $132 (2007); City property taxes per capita: $0 (2007).
Education: Percent of population age 25 and over with: High school diploma (including GED) or higher: 78.9% (2010); Bachelor's degree or higher: 10.7% (2010); Master's degree or higher: 1.7% (2010).
Housing: Homeownership rate: 85.9% (2010); Median home value: $119,355 (2010); Median contract rent: n/a per month (2005-2009 5-year est.); Median year structure built: 1981 (2005-2009 5-year est.).
Transportation: Commute to work: 91.0% car, 0.0% public transportation, 3.0% walk, 4.0% work from home (2005-2009 5-year est.); Travel time to work: 57.3% less than 15 minutes, 10.4% 15 to 30 minutes, 11.5% 30 to 45 minutes, 14.6% 45 to 60 minutes, 6.3% 60 minutes or more (2005-2009 5-year est.)

BARDWELL (city). Covers a land area of 0.278 square miles and a water area of 0 square miles. Located at 32.26° N. Lat; 96.69° W. Long. Elevation is 482 feet.
Population: 451 (1990); 583 (2000); 682 (2010); 749 (2015 projected); Race: 69.8% White, 13.3% Black, 0.0% Asian, 16.9% Other, 37.7% Hispanic of any race (2010); Density: 2,449.3 persons per square mile (2010); Average household size: 3.31 (2010); Median age: 30.8 (2010); Males per 100 females: 101.8 (2010); Marriage status: 36.8% never married, 51.3% now married, 5.5% widowed, 6.5% divorced (2005-2009 5-year est.); Foreign born: 16.3% (2005-2009 5-year est.); Ancestry (includes multiple ancestries): 9.4% Irish, 4.6% American, 3.3% Czech, 1.6% Dutch West Indian, 1.3% Scotch-Irish (2005-2009 5-year est.).
Economy: Single-family building permits issued: 0 (2010); Multi-family building permits issued: 0 (2010); Employment by occupation: 7.5% management, 7.5% professional, 16.4% services, 19.3% sales, 3.2% farming, 20.7% construction, 25.4% production (2005-2009 5-year est.).
Income: Per capita income: $20,226 (2010); Median household income: $61,170 (2010); Average household income: $66,626 (2010); Percent of households with income of $100,000 or more: 19.4% (2010); Poverty rate: 16.8% (2005-2009 5-year est.).
Taxes: Total city taxes per capita: $97 (2007); City property taxes per capita: $27 (2007).
Education: Percent of population age 25 and over with: High school diploma (including GED) or higher: 66.9% (2010); Bachelor's degree or higher: 11.6% (2010); Master's degree or higher: 6.2% (2010).
Housing: Homeownership rate: 76.2% (2010); Median home value: $74,167 (2010); Median contract rent: $388 per month (2005-2009 5-year est.); Median year structure built: 1985 (2005-2009 5-year est.).
Transportation: Commute to work: 91.5% car, 0.0% public transportation, 2.8% walk, 4.0% work from home (2005-2009 5-year est.); Travel time to work: 29.4% less than 15 minutes, 27.7% 15 to 30 minutes, 18.9% 30 to 45 minutes, 12.6% 45 to 60 minutes, 11.3% 60 minutes or more (2005-2009 5-year est.)

ENNIS (city). Covers a land area of 17.993 square miles and a water area of 0.404 square miles. Located at 32.33° N. Lat; 96.62° W. Long. Elevation is 538 feet.
History: Named for Cornelius Ennis, an officer of the Houston and Texas Central railroad. Ennis was established along the railroad line, and became a commercial and industrial center, as well as the site of the Ellis County Fair.
Population: 14,004 (1990); 16,045 (2000); 19,617 (2010); 21,836 (2015 projected); Race: 58.7% White, 14.6% Black, 0.4% Asian, 26.3% Other, 45.3% Hispanic of any race (2010); Density: 1,090.2 persons per square mile (2010); Average household size: 3.02 (2010); Median age: 31.4 (2010); Males per 100 females: 99.4 (2010); Marriage status: 26.4% never married, 54.2% now married, 8.2% widowed, 11.2% divorced (2005-2009 5-year est.); Foreign born: 12.8% (2005-2009 5-year est.); Ancestry (includes multiple ancestries): 8.3% German, 8.2% Irish, 6.4% English, 5.4% Czech, 4.3% American (2005-2009 5-year est.).
Economy: Single-family building permits issued: 7 (2010); Multi-family building permits issued: 6 (2010); Employment by occupation: 12.5% management, 12.0% professional, 15.3% services, 24.7% sales, 0.2% farming, 15.3% construction, 20.2% production (2005-2009 5-year est.).
Income: Per capita income: $17,505 (2010); Median household income: $43,527 (2010); Average household income: $52,969 (2010); Percent of

households with income of $100,000 or more: 10.8% (2010); Poverty rate: 20.5% (2005-2009 5-year est.).
Taxes: Total city taxes per capita: $696 (2007); City property taxes per capita: $383 (2007).
Education: Percent of population age 25 and over with: High school diploma (including GED) or higher: 72.3% (2010); Bachelor's degree or higher: 13.8% (2010); Master's degree or higher: 4.4% (2010).
School District(s)
Ennis ISD (PK-12)
   2009-10 Enrollment: 5,829 . . . . (972) 872-7000
Housing: Homeownership rate: 58.7% (2010); Median home value: $97,154 (2010); Median contract rent: $574 per month (2005-2009 5-year est.); Median year structure built: 1976 (2005-2009 5-year est.).
Hospitals: Ennis Regional Medical Center
Safety: Violent crime rate: 45.8 per 10,000 population; Property crime rate: 447.5 per 10,000 population (2009).
Newspapers: The Ennis Daily News (Community news; Circulation 4,500)
Transportation: Commute to work: 96.4% car, 0.2% public transportation, 1.2% walk, 1.1% work from home (2005-2009 5-year est.); Travel time to work: 49.9% less than 15 minutes, 20.0% 15 to 30 minutes, 13.1% 30 to 45 minutes, 7.9% 45 to 60 minutes, 9.0% 60 minutes or more (2005-2009 5-year est.)
Additional Information Contacts
City of Ennis. . . . . (972) 878-1234
   http://www.ennis-texas.com
Ennis Chamber of Commerce . . . . (972) 878-2625
   http://www.ennis-chamber.com
Ennis Negro Chamber of Commerce. . . . . (972) 875-9222

FERRIS (city). Covers a land area of 3.108 square miles and a water area of 0 square miles. Located at 32.53° N. Lat; 96.66° W. Long. Elevation is 466 feet.
History: Settled 1870, incorporated 1874.
Population: 2,214 (1990); 2,175 (2000); 2,882 (2010); 3,218 (2015 projected); Race: 72.2% White, 17.8% Black, 0.5% Asian, 9.5% Other, 37.1% Hispanic of any race (2010); Density: 927.3 persons per square mile (2010); Average household size: 3.25 (2010); Median age: 31.6 (2010); Males per 100 females: 94.2 (2010); Marriage status: 30.8% never married, 48.1% now married, 7.6% widowed, 13.5% divorced (2005-2009 5-year est.); Foreign born: 12.2% (2005-2009 5-year est.); Ancestry (includes multiple ancestries): 9.8% American, 7.9% Irish, 7.8% German, 3.2% English, 1.6% European (2005-2009 5-year est.).
Economy: Single-family building permits issued: 4 (2010); Multi-family building permits issued: 4 (2010); Employment by occupation: 9.0% management, 12.4% professional, 21.9% services, 27.8% sales, 0.5% farming, 11.6% construction, 16.8% production (2005-2009 5-year est.).
Income: Per capita income: $22,339 (2010); Median household income: $50,636 (2010); Average household income: $71,845 (2010); Percent of households with income of $100,000 or more: 18.6% (2010); Poverty rate: 21.2% (2005-2009 5-year est.).
Taxes: Total city taxes per capita: $411 (2007); City property taxes per capita: $198 (2007).
Education: Percent of population age 25 and over with: High school diploma (including GED) or higher: 70.6% (2010); Bachelor's degree or higher: 16.2% (2010); Master's degree or higher: 4.6% (2010).
School District(s)
Ferris ISD (PK-12)
   2009-10 Enrollment: 2,423 . . . . (972) 544-3858
Housing: Homeownership rate: 70.0% (2010); Median home value: $72,038 (2010); Median contract rent: $526 per month (2005-2009 5-year est.); Median year structure built: 1972 (2005-2009 5-year est.).
Safety: Violent crime rate: 34.5 per 10,000 population; Property crime rate: 321.7 per 10,000 population (2009).
Transportation: Commute to work: 95.1% car, 0.0% public transportation, 1.2% walk, 3.7% work from home (2005-2009 5-year est.); Travel time to work: 18.6% less than 15 minutes, 34.2% 15 to 30 minutes, 24.0% 30 to 45 minutes, 12.8% 45 to 60 minutes, 10.3% 60 minutes or more (2005-2009 5-year est.)

FORRESTON (unincorporated postal area, zip code 76041). Covers a land area of 12.133 square miles and a water area of 0.055 square miles. Located at 32.24° N. Lat; 96.86° W. Long. Elevation is 541 feet.
Population: 366 (2000); Race: 82.0% White, 13.9% Black, 0.0% Asian, 4.1% Other, 0.0% Hispanic of any race (2000); Density: 30.2 persons per square mile (2000); Age: 16.9% under 18, 10.5% over 64 (2000); Marriage

status: 0.5% never married, 74.3% now married, 12.2% widowed, 13.1% divorced (2000); Foreign born: 1.5% (2000); Ancestry (includes multiple ancestries): 10.1% Irish, 6.4% American, 6.0% English, 5.6% Scottish (2000).

Economy: Employment by occupation: 22.0% management, 7.3% professional, 1.1% services, 33.3% sales, 0.6% farming, 16.4% construction, 19.2% production (2000).

Income: Per capita income: $27,323 (2000); Median household income: $56,500 (2000); Poverty rate: 179.1% (2000).

Education: Percent of population age 25 and over with: High school diploma (including GED) or higher: 90.2% (2000); Bachelor's degree or higher: 12.3% (2000).

Housing: Homeownership rate: 71.1% (2000); Median home value: $48,100 (2000); Median contract rent: $472 per month (2000); Median year structure built: 1960 (2000).

Transportation: Commute to work: 97.0% car, 0.0% public transportation, 0.0% walk, 0.6% work from home (2000); Travel time to work: 18.8% less than 15 minutes, 28.5% 15 to 30 minutes, 13.9% 30 to 45 minutes, 18.2% 45 to 60 minutes, 20.6% 60 minutes or more (2000)

GARRETT (town). Covers a land area of 0.335 square miles and a water area of 0 square miles. Located at 32.36° N. Lat; 96.65° W. Long. Elevation is 554 feet.

Population: 340 (1990); 448 (2000); 477 (2010); 532 (2015 projected); Race: 75.9% White, 2.5% Black, 0.0% Asian, 21.6% Other, 31.2% Hispanic of any race (2010); Density: 1,425.6 persons per square mile (2010); Average household size: 2.96 (2010); Median age: 31.9 (2010); Males per 100 females: 96.3 (2010); Marriage status: 27.3% never married, 58.3% now married, 5.8% widowed, 8.8% divorced (2005-2009 5-year est.); Foreign born: 28.9% (2005-2009 5-year est.); Ancestry (includes multiple ancestries): 6.4% English, 5.3% German, 4.8% American, 4.6% Irish, 3.8% Czech (2005-2009 5-year est.).

Economy: Single-family building permits issued: 0 (2010); Multi-family building permits issued: 0 (2010); Employment by occupation: 6.4% management, 3.6% professional, 19.6% services, 29.9% sales, 5.7% farming, 6.4% construction, 28.5% production (2005-2009 5-year est.).

Income: Per capita income: $23,054 (2010); Median household income: $58,036 (2010); Average household income: $67,919 (2010); Percent of households with income of $100,000 or more: 17.4% (2010); Poverty rate: 22.6% (2005-2009 5-year est.).

Taxes: Total city taxes per capita: $78 (2007); City property taxes per capita: $71 (2007).

Education: Percent of population age 25 and over with: High school diploma (including GED) or higher: 86.3% (2010); Bachelor's degree or higher: 21.2% (2010); Master's degree or higher: 4.8% (2010).

Housing: Homeownership rate: 79.5% (2010); Median home value: $109,756 (2010); Median contract rent: $531 per month (2005-2009 5-year est.); Median year structure built: 1975 (2005-2009 5-year est.).

Transportation: Commute to work: 97.8% car, 0.0% public transportation, 0.0% walk, 2.2% work from home (2005-2009 5-year est.); Travel time to work: 34.8% less than 15 minutes, 38.6% 15 to 30 minutes, 18.0% 30 to 45 minutes, 5.6% 45 to 60 minutes, 3.0% 60 minutes or more (2005-2009 5-year est.)

ITALY (town). Covers a land area of 1.794 square miles and a water area of 0 square miles. Located at 32.18° N. Lat; 96.88° W. Long. Elevation is 571 feet.

History: The town of Italy was established near the site where the Confederate government operated a hat factory during the Civil War.

Population: 1,707 (1990); 1,993 (2000); 2,157 (2010); 2,288 (2015 projected); Race: 70.0% White, 21.1% Black, 0.2% Asian, 8.7% Other, 16.9% Hispanic of any race (2010); Density: 1,202.6 persons per square mile (2010); Average household size: 3.00 (2010); Median age: 32.1 (2010); Males per 100 females: 94.7 (2010); Marriage status: 29.5% never married, 50.4% now married, 7.9% widowed, 12.2% divorced (2005-2009 5-year est.); Foreign born: 2.1% (2005-2009 5-year est.); Ancestry (includes multiple ancestries): 12.9% German, 12.9% Irish, 7.1% American, 6.0% English, 4.9% Scotch-Irish (2005-2009 5-year est.).

Economy: Single-family building permits issued: 0 (2010); Multi-family building permits issued: 0 (2010); Employment by occupation: 15.0% management, 14.1% professional, 7.8% services, 24.6% sales, 1.5% farming, 15.5% construction, 21.3% production (2005-2009 5-year est.).

Income: Per capita income: $22,428 (2010); Median household income: $58,377 (2010); Average household income: $66,836 (2010); Percent of

households with income of $100,000 or more: 16.2% (2010); Poverty rate: 19.0% (2005-2009 5-year est.).

Taxes: Total city taxes per capita: $206 (2007); City property taxes per capita: $155 (2007).

Education: Percent of population age 25 and over with: High school diploma (including GED) or higher: 83.0% (2010); Bachelor's degree or higher: 17.8% (2010); Master's degree or higher: 4.4% (2010).

School District(s)

Italy ISD (PK-12)

    2009-10 Enrollment: 638 . . . . (972) 483-1815

Housing: Homeownership rate: 71.6% (2010); Median home value: $77,692 (2010); Median contract rent: $533 per month (2005-2009 5-year est.); Median year structure built: 1976 (2005-2009 5-year est.).

Safety: Violent crime rate: 41.6 per 10,000 population; Property crime rate: 226.7 per 10,000 population (2009).

Transportation: Commute to work: 90.9% car, 0.0% public transportation, 3.0% walk, 4.5% work from home (2005-2009 5-year est.); Travel time to work: 23.0% less than 15 minutes, 26.2% 15 to 30 minutes, 21.1% 30 to 45 minutes, 15.4% 45 to 60 minutes, 14.2% 60 minutes or more (2005-2009 5-year est.)

MAYPEARL (city). Covers a land area of 0.469 square miles and a water area of 0 square miles. Located at 32.31° N. Lat; 97.00° W. Long. Elevation is 531 feet.

Population: 781 (1990); 746 (2000); 886 (2010); 973 (2015 projected); Race: 82.8% White, 6.1% Black, 1.9% Asian, 9.1% Other, 21.7% Hispanic of any race (2010); Density: 1,888.6 persons per square mile (2010); Average household size: 3.09 (2010); Median age: 31.8 (2010); Males per 100 females: 100.5 (2010); Marriage status: 21.2% never married, 61.6% now married, 7.2% widowed, 10.0% divorced (2005-2009 5-year est.); Foreign born: 4.3% (2005-2009 5-year est.); Ancestry (includes multiple ancestries): 24.7% German, 16.8% Irish, 6.6% English, 4.6% American, 2.4% Polish (2005-2009 5-year est.).

Economy: Single-family building permits issued: 4 (2010); Multi-family building permits issued: 0 (2010); Employment by occupation: 15.6% management, 19.0% professional, 12.8% services, 18.0% sales, 0.0% farming, 14.1% construction, 20.5% production (2005-2009 5-year est.).

Income: Per capita income: $20,845 (2010); Median household income: $55,577 (2010); Average household income: $64,199 (2010); Percent of households with income of $100,000 or more: 16.7% (2010); Poverty rate: 2.7% (2005-2009 5-year est.).

Taxes: Total city taxes per capita: $283 (2007); City property taxes per capita: $196 (2007).

Education: Percent of population age 25 and over with: High school diploma (including GED) or higher: 80.2% (2010); Bachelor's degree or higher: 13.0% (2010); Master's degree or higher: 3.8% (2010).

School District(s)

Maypearl ISD (PK-12)

    2009-10 Enrollment: 1,102 . . . . (972) 435-1000

Housing: Homeownership rate: 67.9% (2010); Median home value: $123,438 (2010); Median contract rent: $438 per month (2005-2009 5-year est.); Median year structure built: 1963 (2005-2009 5-year est.).

Transportation: Commute to work: 88.1% car, 4.9% public transportation, 0.0% walk, 4.3% work from home (2005-2009 5-year est.); Travel time to work: 12.8% less than 15 minutes, 21.7% 15 to 30 minutes, 15.0% 30 to 45 minutes, 28.1% 45 to 60 minutes, 22.4% 60 minutes or more (2005-2009 5-year est.)

MIDLOTHIAN (city). Covers a land area of 37.708 square miles and a water area of 0.187 square miles. Located at 32.48° N. Lat; 96.98° W. Long. Elevation is 755 feet.

History: Settled 1880; incorporated 1898.

Population: 5,644 (1990); 7,480 (2000); 13,647 (2010); 15,691 (2015 projected); Race: 89.5% White, 3.3% Black, 0.7% Asian, 6.5% Other, 13.5% Hispanic of any race (2010); Density: 361.9 persons per square mile (2010); Average household size: 2.96 (2010); Median age: 34.1 (2010); Males per 100 females: 101.1 (2010); Marriage status: 23.5% never married, 61.0% now married, 4.1% widowed, 11.3% divorced (2005-2009 5-year est.); Foreign born: 6.8% (2005-2009 5-year est.); Ancestry (includes multiple ancestries): 16.5% German, 13.0% Irish, 11.1% English, 8.9% American, 2.7% Scotch-Irish (2005-2009 5-year est.).

Economy: Single-family building permits issued: 159 (2010); Multi-family building permits issued: 0 (2010); Employment by occupation: 15.9% management, 19.4% professional, 13.6% services, 27.9% sales, 0.0% farming, 13.1% construction, 10.0% production (2005-2009 5-year est.).

Income: Per capita income: $25,488 (2010); Median household income: $67,134 (2010); Average household income: $75,278 (2010); Percent of households with income of $100,000 or more: 22.8% (2010); Poverty rate: 6.4% (2005-2009 5-year est.).

Taxes: Total city taxes per capita: $1,947 (2007); City property taxes per capita: $1,317 (2007).

Education: Percent of population age 25 and over with: High school diploma (including GED) or higher: 89.2% (2010); Bachelor's degree or higher: 25.7% (2010); Master's degree or higher: 5.9% (2010).

School District(s)

Midlothian ISD (PK-12)

   2009-10 Enrollment: 7,329 . . . . (972) 775-8296

Housing: Homeownership rate: 77.5% (2010); Median home value: $146,747 (2010); Median contract rent: $690 per month (2005-2009 5-year est.); Median year structure built: 1996 (2005-2009 5-year est.).

Safety: Violent crime rate: 27.1 per 10,000 population; Property crime rate: 227.5 per 10,000 population (2009).

Newspapers: Midlothian Mirror (Local news; Circulation 2,300)

Transportation: Commute to work: 95.6% car, 0.9% public transportation, 0.8% walk, 2.3% work from home (2005-2009 5-year est.); Travel time to work: 24.7% less than 15 minutes, 27.5% 15 to 30 minutes, 21.9% 30 to 45 minutes, 14.8% 45 to 60 minutes, 11.2% 60 minutes or more (2005-2009 5-year est.)

Airports: Mid-Way Regional (general aviation)

Additional Information Contacts

City of Midlothian . . . . (972) 775-3481
   http://www.midlothian.tx.us

Midlothian Chamber of Commerce . . . . (972) 723-8600
   http://www.midlothianchamber.org

MILFORD (town). Covers a land area of 1.829 square miles and a water area of 0 square miles. Located at 32.12° N. Lat; 96.94° W. Long. Elevation is 617 feet.

Population: 697 (1990); 685 (2000); 733 (2010); 778 (2015 projected); Race: 53.8% White, 30.0% Black, 1.5% Asian, 14.7% Other, 22.9% Hispanic of any race (2010); Density: 400.8 persons per square mile (2010); Average household size: 2.68 (2010); Median age: 32.5 (2010); Males per 100 females: 98.1 (2010); Marriage status: 23.0% never married, 50.6% now married, 9.9% widowed, 16.5% divorced (2005-2009 5-year est.); Foreign born: 0.0% (2005-2009 5-year est.); Ancestry (includes multiple ancestries): 17.3% German, 16.8% American, 14.0% Irish, 3.4% Dutch, 2.9% Scotch-Irish (2005-2009 5-year est.).

Economy: Single-family building permits issued: 0 (2010); Multi-family building permits issued: 0 (2010); Employment by occupation: 9.1% management, 7.5% professional, 12.9% services, 25.8% sales, 0.0% farming, 7.5% construction, 37.1% production (2005-2009 5-year est.).

Income: Per capita income: $18,104 (2010); Median household income: $31,111 (2010); Average household income: $48,221 (2010); Percent of households with income of $100,000 or more: 12.8% (2010); Poverty rate: 29.9% (2005-2009 5-year est.).

Taxes: Total city taxes per capita: $158 (2007); City property taxes per capita: $97 (2007).

Education: Percent of population age 25 and over with: High school diploma (including GED) or higher: 77.4% (2010); Bachelor's degree or higher: 10.5% (2010); Master's degree or higher: 1.9% (2010).

School District(s)

Milford ISD (PK-12)

   2009-10 Enrollment: 254 . . . . (972) 493-2911

Housing: Homeownership rate: 72.3% (2010); Median home value: $54,359 (2010); Median contract rent: $364 per month (2005-2009 5-year est.); Median year structure built: 1971 (2005-2009 5-year est.).

Safety: Violent crime rate: 13.3 per 10,000 population; Property crime rate: 159.2 per 10,000 population (2009).

Transportation: Commute to work: 89.2% car, 0.0% public transportation, 1.6% walk, 5.4% work from home (2005-2009 5-year est.); Travel time to work: 18.2% less than 15 minutes, 45.5% 15 to 30 minutes, 25.0% 30 to 45 minutes, 8.0% 45 to 60 minutes, 3.4% 60 minutes or more (2005-2009 5-year est.)

OAK LEAF (town). Covers a land area of 2.303 square miles and a water area of 0 square miles. Located at 32.52° N. Lat; 96.85° W. Long. Elevation is 604 feet.

Population: 1,093 (1990); 1,209 (2000); 1,471 (2010); 1,681 (2015 projected); Race: 89.2% White, 4.8% Black, 0.3% Asian, 5.7% Other, 7.3% Hispanic of any race (2010); Density: 638.6 persons per square mile

(2010); Average household size: 2.95 (2010); Median age: 41.6 (2010); Males per 100 females: 103.2 (2010); Marriage status: 29.7% never married, 60.5% now married, 3.7% widowed, 6.1% divorced (2005-2009 5-year est.); Foreign born: 2.9% (2005-2009 5-year est.); Ancestry (includes multiple ancestries): 17.5% English, 12.9% Irish, 11.8% German, 8.9% American, 5.2% Italian (2005-2009 5-year est.).

Economy: Single-family building permits issued: 1 (2010); Multi-family building permits issued: 0 (2010); Employment by occupation: 15.0% management, 14.7% professional, 14.6% services, 30.9% sales, 0.2% farming, 7.3% construction, 17.2% production (2005-2009 5-year est.).

Income: Per capita income: $36,578 (2010); Median household income: $91,346 (2010); Average household income: $107,871 (2010); Percent of households with income of $100,000 or more: 42.8% (2010); Poverty rate: 0.8% (2005-2009 5-year est.).

Taxes: Total city taxes per capita: $267 (2007); City property taxes per capita: $193 (2007).

Education: Percent of population age 25 and over with: High school diploma (including GED) or higher: 94.6% (2010); Bachelor's degree or higher: 36.8% (2010); Master's degree or higher: 13.9% (2010).

Housing: Homeownership rate: 95.8% (2010); Median home value: $198,975 (2010); Median contract rent: $900 per month (2005-2009 5-year est.); Median year structure built: 1985 (2005-2009 5-year est.).

Transportation: Commute to work: 86.9% car, 2.7% public transportation, 0.0% walk, 9.8% work from home (2005-2009 5-year est.); Travel time to work: 14.5% less than 15 minutes, 33.3% 15 to 30 minutes, 26.2% 30 to 45 minutes, 12.8% 45 to 60 minutes, 13.2% 60 minutes or more (2005-2009 5-year est.)

OVILLA (city). Covers a land area of 5.706 square miles and a water area of 0 square miles. Located at 32.53° N. Lat; 96.89° W. Long. Elevation is 610 feet.

History: To escape annexation by DeSoto or any other neighboring city, the town of Ovilla was incorporated in 1963. In the first census after incorporation its population was 339; by 2000 the census showed a population of 3,405. Boxcar Willie was born in the area surrounding Ovilla; the overpass at Interstate 35E and FM 664 in Red Oak is named in his memory.

Population: 2,032 (1990); 3,405 (2000); 4,166 (2010); 4,634 (2015 projected); Race: 80.6% White, 13.3% Black, 1.2% Asian, 4.9% Other, 6.0% Hispanic of any race (2010); Density: 730.1 persons per square mile (2010); Average household size: 3.12 (2010); Median age: 35.6 (2010); Males per 100 females: 98.2 (2010); Marriage status: 18.2% never married, 70.8% now married, 5.4% widowed, 5.6% divorced (2005-2009 5-year est.); Foreign born: 8.0% (2005-2009 5-year est.); Ancestry (includes multiple ancestries): 15.5% German, 10.3% English, 9.9% Irish, 4.9% American, 3.3% Lebanese (2005-2009 5-year est.).

Economy: Single-family building permits issued: 1 (2010); Multi-family building permits issued: 0 (2010); Employment by occupation: 15.5% management, 21.6% professional, 12.5% services, 33.7% sales, 0.0% farming, 9.6% construction, 7.0% production (2005-2009 5-year est.).

Income: Per capita income: $33,673 (2010); Median household income: $88,900 (2010); Average household income: $105,071 (2010); Percent of households with income of $100,000 or more: 41.7% (2010); Poverty rate: 3.2% (2005-2009 5-year est.).

Taxes: Total city taxes per capita: $495 (2007); City property taxes per capita: $408 (2007).

Education: Percent of population age 25 and over with: High school diploma (including GED) or higher: 94.3% (2010); Bachelor's degree or higher: 42.9% (2010); Master's degree or higher: 12.6% (2010).

Housing: Homeownership rate: 94.8% (2010); Median home value: $196,487 (2010); Median contract rent: $681 per month (2005-2009 5-year est.); Median year structure built: 1989 (2005-2009 5-year est.).

Safety: Violent crime rate: 9.9 per 10,000 population; Property crime rate: 49.7 per 10,000 population (2009).

Transportation: Commute to work: 83.8% car, 2.2% public transportation, 0.0% walk, 14.0% work from home (2005-2009 5-year est.); Travel time to work: 13.8% less than 15 minutes, 36.0% 15 to 30 minutes, 22.5% 30 to 45 minutes, 13.0% 45 to 60 minutes, 14.7% 60 minutes or more (2005-2009 5-year est.)

PALMER (town). Covers a land area of 2.826 square miles and a water area of 0 square miles. Located at 32.42° N. Lat; 96.66° W. Long. Elevation is 463 feet.

History: Palmer was founded in 1845, and named for Martin Palmer, a participant in the Battle of San Jacinto.

Population: 1,671 (1990); 1,774 (2000); 2,307 (2010); 2,622 (2015 projected); Race: 85.5% White, 3.3% Black, 0.5% Asian, 10.8% Other, 32.6% Hispanic of any race (2010); Density: 816.3 persons per square mile (2010); Average household size: 3.23 (2010); Median age: 32.3 (2010); Males per 100 females: 99.4 (2010); Marriage status: 21.8% never married, 57.5% now married, 10.8% widowed, 9.9% divorced (2005-2009 5-year est.); Foreign born: 13.8% (2005-2009 5-year est.); Ancestry (includes multiple ancestries): 17.5% Irish, 12.1% German, 10.5% English, 4.8% American, 2.3% Dutch West Indian (2005-2009 5-year est.).
Economy: Single-family building permits issued: 1 (2010); Multi-family building permits issued: 0 (2010); Employment by occupation: 5.3% management, 11.7% professional, 17.5% services, 26.4% sales, 0.0% farming, 17.8% construction, 21.3% production (2005-2009 5-year est.).
Income: Per capita income: $21,531 (2010); Median household income: $55,114 (2010); Average household income: $69,335 (2010); Percent of households with income of $100,000 or more: 16.7% (2010); Poverty rate: 14.6% (2005-2009 5-year est.).
Taxes: Total city taxes per capita: $233 (2007); City property taxes per capita: $143 (2007).
Education: Percent of population age 25 and over with: High school diploma (including GED) or higher: 76.6% (2010); Bachelor's degree or higher: 12.7% (2010); Master's degree or higher: 4.8% (2010).

School District(s)

Palmer ISD (PK-12)
　2009-10 Enrollment: 1,126 . . . . (972) 449-3389
Housing: Homeownership rate: 80.7% (2010); Median home value: $90,566 (2010); Median contract rent: $557 per month (2005-2009 5-year est.); Median year structure built: 1979 (2005-2009 5-year est.).
Safety: Violent crime rate: 8.6 per 10,000 population; Property crime rate: 142.5 per 10,000 population (2009).
Transportation: Commute to work: 95.6% car, 0.0% public transportation, 1.3% walk, 2.3% work from home (2005-2009 5-year est.); Travel time to work: 19.4% less than 15 minutes, 39.4% 15 to 30 minutes, 18.7% 30 to 45 minutes, 15.4% 45 to 60 minutes, 7.2% 60 minutes or more (2005-2009 5-year est.)

PECAN HILL (city). Covers a land area of 1.948 square miles and a water area of 0 square miles. Located at 32.48° N. Lat; 96.78° W. Long. Elevation is 541 feet.

Population: 564 (1990); 672 (2000); 837 (2010); 922 (2015 projected); Race: 77.4% White, 9.7% Black, 0.1% Asian, 12.8% Other, 19.4% Hispanic of any race (2010); Density: 429.7 persons per square mile (2010); Average household size: 3.18 (2010); Median age: 32.5 (2010); Males per 100 females: 105.7 (2010); Marriage status: 19.0% never married, 60.1% now married, 3.8% widowed, 17.1% divorced (2005-2009 5-year est.); Foreign born: 4.9% (2005-2009 5-year est.); Ancestry (includes multiple ancestries): 20.9% English, 15.3% Irish, 11.1% American, 7.0% German, 5.2% Scotch-Irish (2005-2009 5-year est.).
Economy: Single-family building permits issued: 0 (2010); Multi-family building permits issued: 0 (2010); Employment by occupation: 16.6% management, 12.5% professional, 9.4% services, 31.3% sales, 0.0% farming, 16.9% construction, 13.4% production (2005-2009 5-year est.).
Income: Per capita income: $26,846 (2010); Median household income: $73,611 (2010); Average household income: $85,309 (2010); Percent of households with income of $100,000 or more: 26.3% (2010); Poverty rate: 7.1% (2005-2009 5-year est.).
Taxes: Total city taxes per capita: $131 (2007); City property taxes per capita: $122 (2007).
Education: Percent of population age 25 and over with: High school diploma (including GED) or higher: 90.4% (2010); Bachelor's degree or higher: 20.3% (2010); Master's degree or higher: 4.5% (2010).
Housing: Homeownership rate: 93.1% (2010); Median home value: $145,250 (2010); Median contract rent: $255 per month (2005-2009 5-year est.); Median year structure built: 1987 (2005-2009 5-year est.).
Transportation: Commute to work: 97.8% car, 0.0% public transportation, 0.0% walk, 0.0% work from home (2005-2009 5-year est.); Travel time to work: 11.5% less than 15 minutes, 28.7% 15 to 30 minutes, 27.4% 30 to 45 minutes, 15.9% 45 to 60 minutes, 16.6% 60 minutes or more (2005-2009 5-year est.)

RED OAK (city). Covers a land area of 7.820 square miles and a water area of 0 square miles. Located at 32.52° N. Lat; 96.80° W. Long. Elevation is 607 feet.

Population: 3,556 (1990); 4,301 (2000); 7,177 (2010); 8,191 (2015 projected); Race: 76.3% White, 8.2% Black, 1.7% Asian, 13.8% Other,

22.8% Hispanic of any race (2010); Density: 917.7 persons per square mile (2010); Average household size: 2.86 (2010); Median age: 33.0 (2010); Males per 100 females: 96.9 (2010); Marriage status: 27.3% never married, 60.0% now married, 3.8% widowed, 8.9% divorced (2005-2009 5-year est.); Foreign born: 5.1% (2005-2009 5-year est.); Ancestry (includes multiple ancestries): 11.2% German, 10.3% American, 9.4% English, 8.8% Irish, 4.7% Italian (2005-2009 5-year est.).
Economy: Single-family building permits issued: 40 (2010); Multi-family building permits issued: 0 (2010); Employment by occupation: 12.2% management, 21.4% professional, 17.8% services, 24.8% sales, 0.0% farming, 10.3% construction, 13.5% production (2005-2009 5-year est.).
Income: Per capita income: $21,078 (2010); Median household income: $47,938 (2010); Average household income: $60,012 (2010); Percent of households with income of $100,000 or more: 15.2% (2010); Poverty rate: 5.2% (2005-2009 5-year est.).
Taxes: Total city taxes per capita: $597 (2007); City property taxes per capita: $279 (2007).
Education: Percent of population age 25 and over with: High school diploma (including GED) or higher: 82.4% (2010); Bachelor's degree or higher: 13.2% (2010); Master's degree or higher: 5.3% (2010).

School District(s)

Life School (KG-12)
　2009-10 Enrollment: 3,434 . . . . (972) 274-7900
Red Oak ISD (PK-12)
　2009-10 Enrollment: 5,408 . . . . (972) 617-2941
Housing: Homeownership rate: 66.1% (2010); Median home value: $122,397 (2010); Median contract rent: $694 per month (2005-2009 5-year est.); Median year structure built: 1994 (2005-2009 5-year est.).
Safety: Violent crime rate: 8.1 per 10,000 population; Property crime rate: 240.6 per 10,000 population (2009).
Transportation: Commute to work: 95.2% car, 1.2% public transportation, 0.8% walk, 2.6% work from home (2005-2009 5-year est.); Travel time to work: 21.2% less than 15 minutes, 29.5% 15 to 30 minutes, 27.8% 30 to 45 minutes, 11.4% 45 to 60 minutes, 10.1% 60 minutes or more (2005-2009 5-year est.)
Additional Information Contacts
City of Red Oak . . . . (972) 617-3638
　http://www.redoaktx.org
Glenn Heights Chamber of Commerce . . . . (972) 274-5100
　http://www.glennheights.com
Red Oak Area Chamber of Commerce . . . . (972) 617-0906
　http://www.redoakareachamber.org

WAXAHACHIE (city). County seat. Covers a land area of 39.965 square miles and a water area of 1.203 square miles. Located at 32.40° N. Lat; 96.84° W. Long. Elevation is 558 feet.

History: Named for the Indian translation of "cow creek". Waxahachie became one of the largest primary cotton markets in Texas, with a textile mill, cottonseed oil mills, and other industries. A powder mill operated by the Confederate government in Waxahachie during the Civil War exploded in 1863.
Population: 18,112 (1990); 21,426 (2000); 29,971 (2010); 33,781 (2015 projected); Race: 65.2% White, 18.8% Black, 0.7% Asian, 15.3% Other, 24.4% Hispanic of any race (2010); Density: 749.9 persons per square mile (2010); Average household size: 2.78 (2010); Median age: 32.6 (2010); Males per 100 females: 96.4 (2010); Marriage status: 27.4% never married, 54.1% now married, 7.0% widowed, 11.6% divorced (2005-2009 5-year est.); Foreign born: 6.5% (2005-2009 5-year est.); Ancestry (includes multiple ancestries): 12.3% German, 11.1% Irish, 9.5% English, 6.3% American, 2.9% French (2005-2009 5-year est.).
Economy: Unemployment rate: 10.4% (June 2011); Total civilian labor force: 14,083 (June 2011); Single-family building permits issued: 150 (2010); Multi-family building permits issued: 0 (2010); Employment by occupation: 10.9% management, 18.5% professional, 18.9% services, 26.1% sales, 0.5% farming, 9.2% construction, 15.9% production (2005-2009 5-year est.).
Income: Per capita income: $22,575 (2010); Median household income: $52,176 (2010); Average household income: $64,548 (2010); Percent of households with income of $100,000 or more: 16.5% (2010); Poverty rate: 15.6% (2005-2009 5-year est.).
Taxes: Total city taxes per capita: $892 (2007); City property taxes per capita: $404 (2007).
Education: Percent of population age 25 and over with: High school diploma (including GED) or higher: 83.2% (2010); Bachelor's degree or higher: 22.3% (2010); Master's degree or higher: 7.4% (2010).

School District(s)
Waxahachie Faith Family Academy (PK-12)
 2009-10 Enrollment: 260 . . . . (972) 224-4110
Waxahachie ISD (PK-12)
 2009-10 Enrollment: 6,924 . . . . (972) 923-4631
Four-year College(s)
Southwestern Assemblies of God University (Private, Not-for-profit, Assemblies of God Church)
 Fall 2009 Enrollment: 2,018 . . . . (888) 937-4010
 2010-11 Tuition: In-state $14,830; Out-of-state $14,830
Housing: Homeownership rate: 61.2% (2010); Median home value: $120,238 (2010); Median contract rent: $622 per month (2005-2009 5-year est.); Median year structure built: 1981 (2005-2009 5-year est.).
Hospitals: Baylor Medical Center-Ellis County (69 beds)
Safety: Violent crime rate: 35.8 per 10,000 population; Property crime rate: 335.4 per 10,000 population (2009).
Newspapers: Ellis County Chronicle (Local news; Circulation 3,500); Waxahachie Daily Light (Local news; Circulation 5,000)
Transportation: Commute to work: 93.6% car, 0.4% public transportation, 1.6% walk, 3.4% work from home (2005-2009 5-year est.); Travel time to work: 46.2% less than 15 minutes, 22.5% 15 to 30 minutes, 13.9% 30 to 45 minutes, 8.4% 45 to 60 minutes, 9.0% 60 minutes or more (2005-2009 5-year est.)
Airports: Mid-Way Regional (general aviation)
Additional Information Contacts
City of Waxahachie . . . . (972) 937-7330
 http://www.waxahachie.com
Waxahachie Chamber of Commerce . . . . (972) 937-2390
 http://www.waxahachiechamber.com

Erath County

Located in north central Texas; drained by the Bosque River. Covers a land area of 1,086.33 square miles, a water area of 3.47 square miles, and is located in the Central Time Zone at 32.21° N. Lat., 98.23° W. Long. The county was founded in 1856. County seat is Stephenville.

Erath County is part of the Stephenville, TX Micropolitan Statistical Area. The entire metro area includes: Erath County, TX

Weather Station: Dublin — Elevation: 1,501 feet

	Jan	Feb	Mar	Apr	May	Jun	Jul	Aug	Sep	Oct	Nov	Dec
High	55	60	67	76	82	89	93	94	87	77	65	56
Low	33	36	43	51	60	67	70	70	63	54	43	34
Precip	1.6	2.7	3.0	2.8	5.1	5.1	1.9	2.9	3.5	3.6	2.6	2.2
Snow	0.3	0.2	tr	0.1	0.0	0.0	0.0	0.0	0.0	tr	0.1	0.4

High and Low temperatures in degrees Fahrenheit; Precipitation and Snow in inches

Weather Station: Stephenville Clark Field — Elevation: 1,308 feet

	Jan	Feb	Mar	Apr	May	Jun	Jul	Aug	Sep	Oct	Nov	Dec
High	57	60	68	76	83	89	94	94	87	78	66	57
Low	32	36	44	51	61	68	71	70	63	53	43	33
Precip	1.4	2.2	2.9	2.5	4.4	3.9	1.5	2.3	2.8	2.9	2.2	2.0
Snow	0.6	0.2	0.1	tr	tr	tr	0.0	0.0	0.0	tr	tr	0.5

High and Low temperatures in degrees Fahrenheit; Precipitation and Snow in inches

Population: 27,991 (1990); 33,001 (2000); 36,445 (2010); 38,058 (2015 projected); Race: 87.1% White, 1.3% Black, 0.7% Asian, 10.9% Other, 18.1% Hispanic of any race (2010); Density: 33.5 persons per square mile (2010); Average household size: 2.51 (2010); Median age: 31.6 (2010); Males per 100 females: 98.4 (2010).
Religion: Five largest groups: 32.6% Southern Baptist Convention, 8.0% The United Methodist Church, 5.4% Churches of Christ, 5.4% Catholic Church, 1.1% Assemblies of God (2000).
Economy: Unemployment rate: 7.1% (June 2011); Total civilian labor force: 19,184 (June 2011); Leading industries: 17.2% manufacturing; 17.1% retail trade; 15.6% health care and social assistance (2009); Farms: 2,189 totaling 622,923 acres (2007); Companies that employ 500 or more persons: 0 (2009); Companies that employ 100 to 499 persons: 16 (2009); Companies that employ less than 100 persons: 911 (2009); Black-owned businesses: n/a (2007); Hispanic-owned businesses: n/a (2007); Asian-owned businesses: n/a (2007); Women-owned businesses: n/a (2007); Retail sales per capita: $13,107 (2010). Single-family building permits issued: 45 (2010); Multi-family building permits issued: 0 (2010).
Income: Per capita income: $20,483 (2010); Median household income: $38,897 (2010); Average household income: $53,519 (2010); Percent of

households with income of $100,000 or more: 12.2% (2010); Poverty rate: 20.7% (2009); Bankruptcy rate: 1.51% (2010).
Taxes: Total county taxes per capita: $283 (2007); County property taxes per capita: $227 (2007).
Education: Percent of population age 25 and over with: High school diploma (including GED) or higher: 79.6% (2010); Bachelor's degree or higher: 25.4% (2010); Master's degree or higher: 7.6% (2010).
Housing: Homeownership rate: 63.4% (2010); Median home value: $106,702 (2010); Median contract rent: $435 per month (2005-2009 5-year est.); Median year structure built: 1979 (2005-2009 5-year est.)
Health: Birth rate: 144.5 per 10,000 population (2009); Death rate: 81.0 per 10,000 population (2009); Age-adjusted cancer mortality rate: 205.9 deaths per 100,000 population (2007); Number of physicians: 11.2 per 10,000 population (2008); Hospital beds: 16.1 per 10,000 population (2007); Hospital admissions: 783.8 per 10,000 population (2007).
Elections: 2008 Presidential election results: 22.3% Obama, 76.8% McCain, 0.1% Nader
Additional Information Contacts
Erath County Government . . . . (254) 965-1452
 http://co.erath.tx.us
City of Stephenville . . . . (254) 918-1220
 http://www.ci.stephenville.tx.us
Dublin Chamber of Commerce . . . . (254) 445-3422
 http://www.dublintxchamber.com
Stephenville Chamber of Commerce . . . . (254) 965-5313
 http://www.stephenvilletexas.org

Erath County Communities

BLUFF DALE (unincorporated postal area, zip code 76433). Aka Bluffdale. Covers a land area of 115.772 square miles and a water area of 0.095 square miles. Located at 32.31° N. Lat; 98.03° W. Long. Elevation is 896 feet.
Population: 850 (2000); Race: 98.6% White, 0.0% Black, 0.0% Asian, 1.4% Other, 3.2% Hispanic of any race (2000); Density: 7.3 persons per square mile (2000); Age: 20.5% under 18, 15.3% over 64 (2000); Marriage status: 14.6% never married, 74.0% now married, 4.7% widowed, 6.7% divorced (2000); Foreign born: 2.5% (2000); Ancestry (includes multiple ancestries): 20.2% American, 10.8% English, 10.2% Irish, 7.4% German (2000).
Economy: Employment by occupation: 20.6% management, 15.5% professional, 16.6% services, 20.3% sales, 5.8% farming, 9.5% construction, 11.8% production (2000).
Income: Per capita income: $21,288 (2000); Median household income: $39,688 (2000); Poverty rate: 179.1% (2000).
Education: Percent of population age 25 and over with: High school diploma (including GED) or higher: 80.3% (2000); Bachelor's degree or higher: 24.3% (2000).
School District(s)
Bluff Dale ISD (KG-08)
 2009-10 Enrollment: 100 . . . . (254) 728-3277
Housing: Homeownership rate: 77.4% (2000); Median home value: $43,800 (2000); Median contract rent: $338 per month (2000); Median year structure built: 1971 (2000).
Transportation: Commute to work: 92.5% car, 0.0% public transportation, 1.6% walk, 5.8% work from home (2000); Travel time to work: 17.9% less than 15 minutes, 42.9% 15 to 30 minutes, 21.1% 30 to 45 minutes, 3.5% 45 to 60 minutes, 14.6% 60 minutes or more (2000)

DUBLIN (city). Covers a land area of 3.405 square miles and a water area of <.001 square miles. Located at 32.08° N. Lat; 98.34° W. Long. Elevation is 1,463 feet.
History: The name of Dublin came from the term "doublin' in," referring to the practice of early residents to gather in one double-size cabin when they feared an attack.
Population: 3,287 (1990); 3,754 (2000); 4,151 (2010); 4,336 (2015 projected); Race: 73.0% White, 0.3% Black, 0.1% Asian, 26.5% Other, 38.5% Hispanic of any race (2010); Density: 1,219.0 persons per square mile (2010); Average household size: 2.87 (2010); Median age: 30.5 (2010); Males per 100 females: 93.3 (2010); Marriage status: 20.7% never married, 62.2% now married, 8.1% widowed, 9.0% divorced (2005-2009 5-year est.); Foreign born: 13.9% (2005-2009 5-year est.); Ancestry (includes multiple ancestries): 15.3% German, 8.2% Irish, 7.5% American, 4.8% English, 4.5% French (2005-2009 5-year est.).

Economy: Single-family building permits issued: 2 (2010); Multi-family building permits issued: 0 (2010); Employment by occupation: 7.0% management, 15.8% professional, 8.4% services, 22.1% sales, 4.9% farming, 9.7% construction, 32.0% production (2005-2009 5-year est.).
Income: Per capita income: $14,075 (2010); Median household income: $31,567 (2010); Average household income: $40,350 (2010); Percent of households with income of $100,000 or more: 6.1% (2010); Poverty rate: 19.0% (2005-2009 5-year est.).
Taxes: Total city taxes per capita: $257 (2007); City property taxes per capita: $112 (2007).
Education: Percent of population age 25 and over with: High school diploma (including GED) or higher: 68.3% (2010); Bachelor's degree or higher: 18.3% (2010); Master's degree or higher: 4.5% (2010).

School District(s)
Dublin ISD (PK-12)
   2009-10 Enrollment: 1,287 . . . . (254) 445-3341
Paradigm Accelerated Charter School (07-12)
   2009-10 Enrollment: 219 . . . . (254) 445-4844
Housing: Homeownership rate: 64.5% (2010); Median home value: $66,124 (2010); Median contract rent: $287 per month (2005-2009 5-year est.); Median year structure built: 1968 (2005-2009 5-year est.).
Safety: Violent crime rate: 2.6 per 10,000 population; Property crime rate: 107.7 per 10,000 population (2009).
Newspapers: Dublin Citizen (Community news; Circulation 2,000)
Transportation: Commute to work: 97.1% car, 0.0% public transportation, 1.8% walk, 0.0% work from home (2005-2009 5-year est.); Travel time to work: 28.6% less than 15 minutes, 59.1% 15 to 30 minutes, 5.7% 30 to 45 minutes, 1.2% 45 to 60 minutes, 5.3% 60 minutes or more (2005-2009 5-year est.)
Additional Information Contacts
Dublin Chamber of Commerce . . . . (254) 445-3422
   http://www.dublintxchamber.com

STEPHENVILLE (city). County seat. Covers a land area of 10.026 square miles and a water area of 0.019 square miles. Located at 32.22° N. Lat; 98.21° W. Long. Elevation is 1,273 feet.
History: Tarleton State College began in Stephenville in 1899 as John Tarleton Agricultural College.
Population: 13,643 (1990); 14,921 (2000); 16,998 (2010); 17,906 (2015 projected); Race: 89.3% White, 2.3% Black, 1.1% Asian, 7.3% Other, 13.5% Hispanic of any race (2010); Density: 1,695.5 persons per square mile (2010); Average household size: 2.27 (2010); Median age: 29.0 (2010); Males per 100 females: 93.7 (2010); Marriage status: 45.8% never married, 38.4% now married, 7.2% widowed, 8.6% divorced (2005-2009 5-year est.); Foreign born: 5.2% (2005-2009 5-year est.); Ancestry (includes multiple ancestries): 13.8% German, 13.0% Irish, 9.1% American, 8.3% English, 2.2% Scotch-Irish (2005-2009 5-year est.).
Economy: Single-family building permits issued: 43 (2010); Multi-family building permits issued: 0 (2010); Employment by occupation: 10.6% management, 16.7% professional, 17.2% services, 29.7% sales, 2.6% farming, 10.2% construction, 13.0% production (2005-2009 5-year est.).
Income: Per capita income: $18,877 (2010); Median household income: $34,704 (2010); Average household income: $46,534 (2010); Percent of households with income of $100,000 or more: 9.0% (2010); Poverty rate: 29.5% (2005-2009 5-year est.).
Taxes: Total city taxes per capita: $537 (2007); City property taxes per capita: $166 (2007).
Education: Percent of population age 25 and over with: High school diploma (including GED) or higher: 80.2% (2010); Bachelor's degree or higher: 28.2% (2010); Master's degree or higher: 10.0% (2010).

School District(s)
Erath Excels Academy Inc (07-12)
   2009-10 Enrollment: 159 . . . . (254) 965-8883
Huckabay ISD (KG-12)
   2009-10 Enrollment: 191 . . . . (254) 968-8476
Stephenville (PK-12)
   2009-10 Enrollment: 3,553 . . . . (254) 968-7990
Three Way ISD (PK-08)
   2009-10 Enrollment: 57 . . . . (254) 965-6496

Four-year College(s)
Tarleton State University (Public)
   Fall 2009 Enrollment: 10,424 . . . . (254) 968-9000
   2010-11 Tuition: In-state $5,195; Out-of-state $12,635

Housing: Homeownership rate: 52.4% (2010); Median home value: $97,292 (2010); Median contract rent: $448 per month (2005-2009 5-year est.); Median year structure built: 1976 (2005-2009 5-year est.).
Hospitals: Harris Methodist Erath County (98 beds)
Safety: Violent crime rate: 30.9 per 10,000 population; Property crime rate: 340.5 per 10,000 population (2009).
Newspapers: Stephenville Empire Tribune (Local news; Circulation 5,500)
Transportation: Commute to work: 92.5% car, 0.0% public transportation, 2.7% walk, 4.3% work from home (2005-2009 5-year est.); Travel time to work: 71.1% less than 15 minutes, 18.4% 15 to 30 minutes, 6.1% 30 to 45 minutes, 1.5% 45 to 60 minutes, 2.9% 60 minutes or more (2005-2009 5-year est.)
Airports: Clark Field Municipal (general aviation)
Additional Information Contacts
City of Stephenville . . . . (254) 918-1220
   http://www.ci.stephenville.tx.us
Stephenville Chamber of Commerce . . . . (254) 965-5313
   http://www.stephenvilletexas.org

Falls County

Located in east central Texas; prairie area, drained by the Brazos River. Covers a land area of 769.09 square miles, a water area of 4.72 square miles, and is located in the Central Time Zone at 31.26° N. Lat., 96.96° W. Long. The county was founded in 1850. County seat is Marlin.

Weather Station: Marlin 3 NE   Elevation: 388 feet

	Jan	Feb	Mar	Apr	May	Jun	Jul	Aug	Sep	Oct	Nov	Dec
High	60	65	71	78	84	91	94	95	90	80	70	61
Low	37	41	48	55	64	70	73	73	67	57	47	38
Precip	2.8	2.7	3.5	2.6	5.1	3.8	1.9	2.3	2.8	4.2	3.2	3.3
Snow	0.1	0.1	tr	tr	0.0	0.0	0.0	0.0	0.0	0.0	tr	tr

High and Low temperatures in degrees Fahrenheit; Precipitation and Snow in inches

Population: 17,712 (1990); 18,576 (2000); 17,262 (2010); 16,588 (2015 projected); Race: 59.9% White, 26.6% Black, 0.1% Asian, 13.4% Other, 19.3% Hispanic of any race (2010); Density: 22.4 persons per square mile (2010); Average household size: 2.54 (2010); Median age: 37.6 (2010); Males per 100 females: 84.8 (2010).
Religion: Five largest groups: 23.2% Southern Baptist Convention, 16.0% Catholic Church, 6.4% The United Methodist Church, 3.2% Lutheran Church—Missouri Synod, 2.3% Churches of Christ (2000).
Economy: Unemployment rate: 10.7% (June 2011); Total civilian labor force: 6,769 (June 2011); Leading industries: 27.9% health care and social assistance; 7.8% other services (except public administration); 7.3% accommodation & food services (2009); Farms: 1,295 totaling 445,217 acres (2007); Companies that employ 500 or more persons: 0 (2009); Companies that employ 100 to 499 persons: 2 (2009); Companies that employ less than 100 persons: 228 (2009); Black-owned businesses: n/a (2007); Hispanic-owned businesses: n/a (2007); Asian-owned businesses: n/a (2007); Women-owned businesses: n/a (2007); Retail sales per capita: $5,457 (2010). Single-family building permits issued: 5 (2010); Multi-family building permits issued: 0 (2010).
Income: Per capita income: $16,538 (2010); Median household income: $32,642 (2010); Average household income: $44,709 (2010); Percent of households with income of $100,000 or more: 7.6% (2010); Poverty rate: 23.2% (2009); Bankruptcy rate: 1.67% (2010).
Taxes: Total county taxes per capita: $246 (2007); County property taxes per capita: $201 (2007).
Education: Percent of population age 25 and over with: High school diploma (including GED) or higher: 72.3% (2010); Bachelor's degree or higher: 10.8% (2010); Master's degree or higher: 3.5% (2010).
Housing: Homeownership rate: 69.4% (2010); Median home value: $54,123 (2010); Median contract rent: $326 per month (2005-2009 5-year est.); Median year structure built: 1967 (2005-2009 5-year est.)
Health: Birth rate: 125.7 per 10,000 population (2009); Death rate: 98.9 per 10,000 population (2009); Age-adjusted cancer mortality rate: 206.2 deaths per 100,000 population (2007); Number of physicians: 4.8 per 10,000 population (2008); Hospital beds: 19.0 per 10,000 population (2007); Hospital admissions: 672.1 per 10,000 population (2007).
Elections: 2008 Presidential election results: 39.7% Obama, 59.4% McCain, 0.1% Nader
Additional Information Contacts
Falls County Government . . . . (254) 883-1408

City of Marlin . . . . (254) 883-1474

Marlin Chamber of Commerce . . . . (254) 803-3301
  http://www.marlintexas.com
Rosebud Chamber of Commerce . . . . (254) 583-7979

Falls County Communities

CHILTON (unincorporated postal area, zip code 76632). Covers a land area of 66.138 square miles and a water area of 0.195 square miles. Located at 31.28° N. Lat; 97.06° W. Long. Elevation is 430 feet.
History: Chilton developed as an agricultural supply center and shipping point. In 1924, as a resident named Myrin was drilling for oil, hot artesian water was struck. The water was piped and distributed throughout the town.
Population: 1,789 (2000); Race: 72.6% White, 12.8% Black, 0.0% Asian, 14.6% Other, 27.9% Hispanic of any race (2000); Density: 27.0 persons per square mile (2000); Age: 29.3% under 18, 15.2% over 64 (2000); Marriage status: 20.5% never married, 60.4% now married, 8.5% widowed, 10.5% divorced (2000); Foreign born: 13.1% (2000); Ancestry (includes multiple ancestries): 12.5% German, 9.7% Irish, 7.6% English, 7.3% American (2000).
Economy: Employment by occupation: 12.4% management, 10.1% professional, 17.6% services, 14.6% sales, 5.1% farming, 16.3% construction, 24.0% production (2000).
Income: Per capita income: $15,080 (2000); Median household income: $30,156 (2000); Poverty rate: 179.1% (2000).
Education: Percent of population age 25 and over with: High school diploma (including GED) or higher: 65.9% (2000); Bachelor's degree or higher: 7.5% (2000).
School District(s)
Chilton ISD (PK-12)
  2009-10 Enrollment: 495 . . . . (254) 546-1200
Housing: Homeownership rate: 82.6% (2000); Median home value: $38,100 (2000); Median contract rent: $300 per month (2000); Median year structure built: 1970 (2000).
Transportation: Commute to work: 92.3% car, 0.3% public transportation, 1.6% walk, 5.2% work from home (2000); Travel time to work: 18.9% less than 15 minutes, 28.2% 15 to 30 minutes, 35.8% 30 to 45 minutes, 8.2% 45 to 60 minutes, 8.9% 60 minutes or more (2000)

GOLINDA (city). Covers a land area of 4.154 square miles and a water area of 0 square miles. Located at 31.37° N. Lat; 97.07° W. Long. Elevation is 482 feet.
Population: 377 (1990); 423 (2000); 453 (2010); 451 (2015 projected); Race: 86.3% White, 8.2% Black, 0.2% Asian, 5.3% Other, 8.6% Hispanic of any race (2010); Density: 109.1 persons per square mile (2010); Average household size: 2.64 (2010); Median age: 40.5 (2010); Males per 100 females: 94.4 (2010); Marriage status: 22.7% never married, 64.3% now married, 4.2% widowed, 8.7% divorced (2005-2009 5-year est.); Foreign born: 1.2% (2005-2009 5-year est.); Ancestry (includes multiple ancestries): 19.7% Czech, 19.6% German, 18.0% Irish, 15.8% English, 4.0% American (2005-2009 5-year est.).
Economy: Employment by occupation: 12.5% management, 27.6% professional, 4.4% services, 26.2% sales, 1.2% farming, 22.1% construction, 6.1% production (2005-2009 5-year est.).
Income: Per capita income: $24,501 (2010); Median household income: $53,354 (2010); Average household income: $67,618 (2010); Percent of households with income of $100,000 or more: 15.4% (2010); Poverty rate: 9.2% (2005-2009 5-year est.).
Taxes: Total city taxes per capita: $86 (2007); City property taxes per capita: $0 (2007).
Education: Percent of population age 25 and over with: High school diploma (including GED) or higher: 85.2% (2010); Bachelor's degree or higher: 16.5% (2010); Master's degree or higher: 4.8% (2010).
Housing: Homeownership rate: 82.2% (2010); Median home value: $70,800 (2010); Median contract rent: $642 per month (2005-2009 5-year est.); Median year structure built: 1984 (2005-2009 5-year est.).
Transportation: Commute to work: 95.9% car, 0.0% public transportation, 2.3% walk, 0.0% work from home (2005-2009 5-year est.); Travel time to work: 14.6% less than 15 minutes, 46.8% 15 to 30 minutes, 32.5% 30 to 45 minutes, 0.6% 45 to 60 minutes, 5.6% 60 minutes or more (2005-2009 5-year est.)

LOTT (city). Covers a land area of 1.035 square miles and a water area of 0.013 square miles. Located at 31.20° N. Lat; 97.03° W. Long. Elevation is 522 feet.

Population: 775 (1990); 724 (2000); 697 (2010); 675 (2015 projected); Race: 70.4% White, 17.8% Black, 0.1% Asian, 11.6% Other, 12.2% Hispanic of any race (2010); Density: 673.3 persons per square mile (2010); Average household size: 2.52 (2010); Median age: 38.9 (2010); Males per 100 females: 89.4 (2010); Marriage status: 32.5% never married, 47.1% now married, 4.5% widowed, 15.9% divorced (2005-2009 5-year est.); Foreign born: 1.5% (2005-2009 5-year est.); Ancestry (includes multiple ancestries): 19.5% German, 12.0% Irish, 11.4% English, 5.5% French, 5.2% American (2005-2009 5-year est.).
Economy: Single-family building permits issued: 0 (2010); Multi-family building permits issued: 0 (2010); Employment by occupation: 4.2% management, 8.5% professional, 30.5% services, 12.1% sales, 4.5% farming, 20.3% construction, 19.8% production (2005-2009 5-year est.).
Income: Per capita income: $16,624 (2010); Median household income: $31,548 (2010); Average household income: $41,083 (2010); Percent of households with income of $100,000 or more: 5.1% (2010); Poverty rate: 27.6% (2005-2009 5-year est.).
Taxes: Total city taxes per capita: $449 (2007); City property taxes per capita: $240 (2007).
Education: Percent of population age 25 and over with: High school diploma (including GED) or higher: 72.7% (2010); Bachelor's degree or higher: 10.5% (2010); Master's degree or higher: 2.6% (2010).
School District(s)
Rosebud-Lott ISD (PK-12)
  2009-10 Enrollment: 799 . . . . (254) 583-4510
Housing: Homeownership rate: 73.3% (2010); Median home value: $50,000 (2010); Median contract rent: $194 per month (2005-2009 5-year est.); Median year structure built: 1959 (2005-2009 5-year est.).
Safety: Violent crime rate: 74.6 per 10,000 population; Property crime rate: 313.4 per 10,000 population (2009).
Transportation: Commute to work: 97.4% car, 1.4% public transportation, 0.0% walk, 1.1% work from home (2005-2009 5-year est.); Travel time to work: 21.9% less than 15 minutes, 35.2% 15 to 30 minutes, 33.4% 30 to 45 minutes, 9.5% 45 to 60 minutes, 0.0% 60 minutes or more (2005-2009 5-year est.)

MARLIN (city). County seat. Covers a land area of 4.523 square miles and a water area of 0.051 square miles. Located at 31.30° N. Lat; 96.89° W. Long. Elevation is 390 feet.
History: Drillers looking for water in 1891 struck a pool of hot water. Reports of the therapeutic qualities of the water later led to the town of Marlin becoming a health spa.
Population: 6,386 (1990); 6,628 (2000); 6,142 (2010); 5,901 (2015 projected); Race: 37.5% White, 43.6% Black, 0.2% Asian, 18.6% Other, 25.0% Hispanic of any race (2010); Density: 1,357.9 persons per square mile (2010); Average household size: 2.53 (2010); Median age: 34.8 (2010); Males per 100 females: 90.6 (2010); Marriage status: 42.0% never married, 38.1% now married, 9.9% widowed, 10.1% divorced (2005-2009 5-year est.); Foreign born: 5.9% (2005-2009 5-year est.); Ancestry (includes multiple ancestries): 7.3% German, 6.8% English, 4.4% Irish, 3.6% American, 2.5% French (2005-2009 5-year est.).
Economy: Single-family building permits issued: 3 (2010); Multi-family building permits issued: 0 (2010); Employment by occupation: 3.6% management, 20.0% professional, 42.9% services, 9.9% sales, 1.1% farming, 13.2% construction, 9.3% production (2005-2009 5-year est.).
Income: Per capita income: $14,076 (2010); Median household income: $24,974 (2010); Average household income: $37,822 (2010); Percent of households with income of $100,000 or more: 5.2% (2010); Poverty rate: 36.4% (2005-2009 5-year est.).
Taxes: Total city taxes per capita: $310 (2007); City property taxes per capita: $178 (2007).
Education: Percent of population age 25 and over with: High school diploma (including GED) or higher: 69.0% (2010); Bachelor's degree or higher: 9.9% (2010); Master's degree or higher: 3.4% (2010).
School District(s)
Chilton ISD (PK-12)
  2009-10 Enrollment: 495 . . . . (254) 546-1200
Marlin ISD (PK-12)
  2009-10 Enrollment: 1,116 . . . . (254) 883-3585
Riesel ISD (PK-12)
  2009-10 Enrollment: 581 . . . . (254) 896-6411
Rosebud-Lott ISD (PK-12)
  2009-10 Enrollment: 799 . . . . (254) 583-4510

Housing: Homeownership rate: 58.8% (2010); Median home value: $44,337 (2010); Median contract rent: $328 per month (2005-2009 5-year est.); Median year structure built: 1960 (2005-2009 5-year est.).
Hospitals: Falls Community Hospital (44 beds)
Safety: Violent crime rate: 48.8 per 10,000 population; Property crime rate: 165.6 per 10,000 population (2009).
Newspapers: Marlin Democrat (Local news; Circulation 3,200)
Transportation: Commute to work: 88.1% car, 0.0% public transportation, 5.7% walk, 1.9% work from home (2005-2009 5-year est.); Travel time to work: 40.3% less than 15 minutes, 24.6% 15 to 30 minutes, 22.0% 30 to 45 minutes, 3.6% 45 to 60 minutes, 9.5% 60 minutes or more (2005-2009 5-year est.)

Additional Information Contacts

City of Marlin . . . . (254) 883-1474
Marlin Chamber of Commerce. . . . . (254) 803-3301
   http://www.marlintexas.com

OTTO (unincorporated postal area, zip code 76675). Covers a land area of 17.276 square miles and a water area of 0 square miles. Located at 31.41° N. Lat; 96.81° W. Long. Elevation is 466 feet.
Population: 116 (2000); Race: 95.9% White, 4.1% Black, 0.0% Asian, 0.0% Other, 34.1% Hispanic of any race (2000); Density: 6.7 persons per square mile (2000); Age: 21.1% under 18, 14.6% over 64 (2000); Marriage status: 10.3% never married, 80.4% now married, 9.3% widowed, 0.0% divorced (2000); Foreign born: 0.0% (2000); Ancestry (includes multiple ancestries): 57.7% German, 18.7% Irish, 4.1% Czechoslovakian, 4.1% Norwegian (2000).
Economy: Employment by occupation: 9.6% management, 9.6% professional, 0.0% services, 44.2% sales, 0.0% farming, 21.2% construction, 15.4% production (2000).
Income: Per capita income: $16,027 (2000); Median household income: $58,929 (2000); Poverty rate: 179.1% (2000).
Education: Percent of population age 25 and over with: High school diploma (including GED) or higher: 60.9% (2000); Bachelor's degree or higher: 5.7% (2000).
Housing: Homeownership rate: 72.1% (2000); Median home value: $84,400 (2000); Median contract rent: $213 per month (2000); Median year structure built: 1971 (2000).
Transportation: Commute to work: 100.0% car, 0.0% public transportation, 0.0% walk, 0.0% work from home (2000); Travel time to work: 44.2% less than 15 minutes, 13.5% 15 to 30 minutes, 7.7% 30 to 45 minutes, 19.2% 45 to 60 minutes, 15.4% 60 minutes or more (2000)

REAGAN (unincorporated postal area, zip code 76680). Covers a land area of 50.415 square miles and a water area of 0.064 square miles. Located at 31.19° N. Lat; 96.81° W. Long. Elevation is 381 feet.
Population: 241 (2000); Race: 91.0% White, 9.0% Black, 0.0% Asian, 0.0% Other, 0.0% Hispanic of any race (2000); Density: 4.8 persons per square mile (2000); Age: 15.4% under 18, 24.5% over 64 (2000); Marriage status: 3.8% never married, 72.3% now married, 7.5% widowed, 16.4% divorced (2000); Foreign born: 0.0% (2000); Ancestry (includes multiple ancestries): 23.9% Irish, 18.1% German, 8.5% Polish, 8.5% English (2000).
Economy: Employment by occupation: 18.9% management, 24.4% professional, 7.8% services, 5.6% sales, 0.0% farming, 27.8% construction, 15.6% production (2000).
Income: Per capita income: $14,754 (2000); Median household income: $29,500 (2000); Poverty rate: 179.1% (2000).
Education: Percent of population age 25 and over with: High school diploma (including GED) or higher: 81.4% (2000); Bachelor's degree or higher: 14.1% (2000).
Housing: Homeownership rate: 89.7% (2000); Median home value: $35,400 (2000); Median contract rent: $275 per month (2000); Median year structure built: 1959 (2000).
Transportation: Commute to work: 100.0% car, 0.0% public transportation, 0.0% walk, 0.0% work from home (2000); Travel time to work: 23.3% less than 15 minutes, 37.8% 15 to 30 minutes, 17.8% 30 to 45 minutes, 21.1% 45 to 60 minutes, 0.0% 60 minutes or more (2000)

ROSEBUD (city). Covers a land area of 0.778 square miles and a water area of 0 square miles. Located at 31.07° N. Lat; 96.97° W. Long. Elevation is 397 feet.
History: At one time, Rosebud claimed to have at least one rose bush in each yard. Many of the early residents of Rosebud were of Czechoslovakian and German descent.

Population: 1,638 (1990); 1,493 (2000); 1,369 (2010); 1,310 (2015 projected); Race: 59.8% White, 17.4% Black, 0.1% Asian, 22.8% Other, 31.5% Hispanic of any race (2010); Density: 1,759.8 persons per square mile (2010); Average household size: 2.56 (2010); Median age: 38.9 (2010); Males per 100 females: 93.4 (2010); Marriage status: 19.0% never married, 58.4% now married, 14.1% widowed, 8.5% divorced (2005-2009 5-year est.); Foreign born: 5.6% (2005-2009 5-year est.); Ancestry (includes multiple ancestries): 29.0% German, 11.3% Czech, 7.3% English, 6.0% Irish, 4.5% Scottish (2005-2009 5-year est.).
Economy: Single-family building permits issued: 2 (2010); Multi-family building permits issued: 0 (2010); Employment by occupation: 16.8% management, 17.5% professional, 13.7% services, 18.2% sales, 1.4% farming, 10.7% construction, 21.6% production (2005-2009 5-year est.).
Income: Per capita income: $16,839 (2010); Median household income: $31,810 (2010); Average household income: $43,325 (2010); Percent of households with income of $100,000 or more: 8.4% (2010); Poverty rate: 23.4% (2005-2009 5-year est.).
Taxes: Total city taxes per capita: $104 (2007); City property taxes per capita: $104 (2007).
Education: Percent of population age 25 and over with: High school diploma (including GED) or higher: 71.3% (2010); Bachelor's degree or higher: 11.5% (2010); Master's degree or higher: 5.5% (2010).

School District(s)
Rosebud-Lott ISD (PK-12)
   2009-10 Enrollment: 799 . . . . (254) 583-4510
Housing: Homeownership rate: 67.0% (2010); Median home value: $47,846 (2010); Median contract rent: $244 per month (2005-2009 5-year est.); Median year structure built: 1961 (2005-2009 5-year est.).
Safety: Violent crime rate: 22.7 per 10,000 population; Property crime rate: 68.2 per 10,000 population (2009).
Newspapers: Rosebud News (Community news; Circulation 2,074)
Transportation: Commute to work: 91.5% car, 1.7% public transportation, 1.9% walk, 1.9% work from home (2005-2009 5-year est.); Travel time to work: 38.4% less than 15 minutes, 20.5% 15 to 30 minutes, 22.7% 30 to 45 minutes, 10.4% 45 to 60 minutes, 8.0% 60 minutes or more (2005-2009 5-year est.)

Additional Information Contacts
Rosebud Chamber of Commerce . . . . (254) 583-7979

Fannin County

Located in northeastern Texas; bounded on the north by the Red River and the Oklahoma border; drained by the South Sulphur and North Sulphur Rivers. Covers a land area of 891.45 square miles, a water area of 7.71 square miles, and is located in the Central Time Zone at 33.55° N. Lat., 96.15° W. Long. The county was founded in 1837. County seat is Bonham.

Fannin County is part of the Bonham, TX Micropolitan Statistical Area. The entire metro area includes: Fannin County, TX

Weather Station: Bonham 3 NNE								Elevation: 600 feet			
	Jan	Feb	Mar	Apr	May	Jun	Jul	Aug	Sep	Oct	Nov	Dec
High	53	58	66	74	81	88	93	94	87	76	64	55
Low	32	35	43	50	60	67	71	71	63	52	42	33
Precip	2.7	3.3	4.1	3.6	5.5	4.9	3.5	2.2	3.3	5.4	3.8	3.6
Snow	0.4	0.8	0.2	0.0	0.0	0.0	0.0	0.0	0.0	0.0	tr	0.6

High and Low temperatures in degrees Fahrenheit; Precipitation and Snow in inches

Population: 24,804 (1990); 31,242 (2000); 34,607 (2010); 36,176 (2015 projected); Race: 85.0% White, 7.6% Black, 0.4% Asian, 7.0% Other, 7.9% Hispanic of any race (2010); Density: 38.8 persons per square mile (2010); Average household size: 2.53 (2010); Median age: 38.3 (2010); Males per 100 females: 111.7 (2010).
Religion: Five largest groups: 47.0% Southern Baptist Convention, 10.3% Catholic Church, 6.6% The United Methodist Church, 4.5% Churches of Christ, 1.4% Church of God (Cleveland, Tennessee) (2000).
Economy: Unemployment rate: 10.7% (June 2011); Total civilian labor force: 13,964 (June 2011); Leading industries: 28.7% health care and social assistance; 17.7% retail trade; 12.7% accommodation & food services (2009); Farms: 2,110 totaling 473,853 acres (2007); Companies that employ 500 or more persons: 0 (2009); Companies that employ 100 to 499 persons: 8 (2009); Companies that employ less than 100 persons: 482 (2009); Black-owned businesses: n/a (2007); Hispanic-owned businesses: n/a (2007); Asian-owned businesses: n/a (2007); Women-owned businesses: n/a (2007); Retail sales per capita: $8,578 (2010).

Single-family building permits issued: 1 (2010); Multi-family building permits issued: 0 (2010).
Income: Per capita income: $19,733 (2010); Median household income: $43,113 (2010); Average household income: $54,142 (2010); Percent of households with income of $100,000 or more: 11.3% (2010); Poverty rate: 17.3% (2009); Bankruptcy rate: 2.26% (2010).
Taxes: Total county taxes per capita: $202 (2007); County property taxes per capita: $181 (2007).
Education: Percent of population age 25 and over with: High school diploma (including GED) or higher: 80.9% (2010); Bachelor's degree or higher: 14.8% (2010); Master's degree or higher: 4.3% (2010).
Housing: Homeownership rate: 73.0% (2010); Median home value: $78,015 (2010); Median contract rent: $405 per month (2005-2009 5-year est.); Median year structure built: 1976 (2005-2009 5-year est.)
Health: Birth rate: 125.5 per 10,000 population (2009); Death rate: 118.8 per 10,000 population (2009); Age-adjusted cancer mortality rate: 198.5 deaths per 100,000 population (2007); Number of physicians: 3.0 per 10,000 population (2008); Hospital beds: 7.6 per 10,000 population (2007); Hospital admissions: 379.4 per 10,000 population (2007).
Elections: 2008 Presidential election results: 29.6% Obama, 69.2% McCain, 0.1% Nader
National and State Parks: Bonham State Park; Caddo National Grassland
Additional Information Contacts
Fannin County Government . . . . (903) 583-7486
   http://www.co.fannin.tx.us/ips/cms
Bonham Area Chamber of Commerce . . . . (903) 583-4811
   http://www.bonhamchamber.com
City of Bonham . . . . (903) 583-7555
   http://www.cobon.net
Honey Grove Chamber of Commerce . . . . (903) 378-7211
   http://www.honeygrovechamber.com

Fannin County Communities

BAILEY (city). Covers a land area of 0.400 square miles and a water area of 0 square miles. Located at 33.43° N. Lat; 96.16° W. Long. Elevation is 712 feet.
Population: 187 (1990); 213 (2000); 240 (2010); 251 (2015 projected); Race: 93.8% White, 1.3% Black, 0.0% Asian, 5.0% Other, 5.0% Hispanic of any race (2010); Density: 599.7 persons per square mile (2010); Average household size: 2.58 (2010); Median age: 38.8 (2010); Males per 100 females: 90.5 (2010); Marriage status: 6.2% never married, 75.3% now married, 1.4% widowed, 17.1% divorced (2005-2009 5-year est.); Foreign born: 0.0% (2005-2009 5-year est.); Ancestry (includes multiple ancestries): 13.3% German, 11.8% Irish, 9.7% Scandinavian, 9.2% Italian, 8.7% Scotch-Irish (2005-2009 5-year est.).
Economy: Employment by occupation: 14.3% management, 26.9% professional, 15.1% services, 12.6% sales, 0.0% farming, 9.2% construction, 21.8% production (2005-2009 5-year est.).
Income: Per capita income: $23,108 (2010); Median household income: $52,315 (2010); Average household income: $64,866 (2010); Percent of households with income of $100,000 or more: 11.8% (2010); Poverty rate: 1.5% (2005-2009 5-year est.).
Taxes: Total city taxes per capita: $338 (2007); City property taxes per capita: $191 (2007).
Education: Percent of population age 25 and over with: High school diploma (including GED) or higher: 87.0% (2010); Bachelor's degree or higher: 17.9% (2010); Master's degree or higher: 3.1% (2010).
Housing: Homeownership rate: 81.7% (2010); Median home value: $85,000 (2010); Median contract rent: $458 per month (2005-2009 5-year est.); Median year structure built: 1964 (2005-2009 5-year est.).
Transportation: Commute to work: 93.9% car, 0.0% public transportation, 6.1% walk, 0.0% work from home (2005-2009 5-year est.); Travel time to work: 27.8% less than 15 minutes, 20.9% 15 to 30 minutes, 28.7% 30 to 45 minutes, 7.8% 45 to 60 minutes, 14.8% 60 minutes or more (2005-2009 5-year est.)

BONHAM (city). County seat. Covers a land area of 9.362 square miles and a water area of 0 square miles. Located at 33.58° N. Lat; 96.18° W. Long. Elevation is 610 feet.
History: Bonham was named for James Butler Bonham, who died at the Alamo.
Population: 7,352 (1990); 9,990 (2000); 11,091 (2010); 11,579 (2015 projected); Race: 71.8% White, 18.5% Black, 0.7% Asian, 9.1% Other,

13.1% Hispanic of any race (2010); Density: 1,184.7 persons per square mile (2010); Average household size: 2.39 (2010); Median age: 35.8 (2010); Males per 100 females: 159.5 (2010); Marriage status: 26.1% never married, 43.6% now married, 13.8% widowed, 16.5% divorced (2005-2009 5-year est.); Foreign born: 7.1% (2005-2009 5-year est.); Ancestry (includes multiple ancestries): 12.5% German, 9.8% Irish, 8.2% American, 7.1% English, 2.3% French (2005-2009 5-year est.).
Economy: Single-family building permits issued: 1 (2010); Multi-family building permits issued: 0 (2010); Employment by occupation: 11.1% management, 10.6% professional, 25.2% services, 18.9% sales, 0.6% farming, 15.1% construction, 18.6% production (2005-2009 5-year est.).
Income: Per capita income: $14,009 (2010); Median household income: $31,853 (2010); Average household income: $43,184 (2010); Percent of households with income of $100,000 or more: 7.3% (2010); Poverty rate: 24.8% (2005-2009 5-year est.).
Taxes: Total city taxes per capita: $340 (2007); City property taxes per capita: $146 (2007).
Education: Percent of population age 25 and over with: High school diploma (including GED) or higher: 74.6% (2010); Bachelor's degree or higher: 12.6% (2010); Master's degree or higher: 5.1% (2010).
School District(s)
Bonham ISD (PK-12)
   2009-10 Enrollment: 1,955 . . . . (903) 583-5526
Housing: Homeownership rate: 59.2% (2010); Median home value: $64,385 (2010); Median contract rent: $403 per month (2005-2009 5-year est.); Median year structure built: 1968 (2005-2009 5-year est.).
Hospitals: Northeast Medical Center (75 beds)
Safety: Violent crime rate: 21.4 per 10,000 population; Property crime rate: 328.8 per 10,000 population (2009).
Newspapers: Fannin County Special (Community news; Circulation 14,462)
Transportation: Commute to work: 95.8% car, 0.0% public transportation, 2.2% walk, 2.0% work from home (2005-2009 5-year est.); Travel time to work: 61.8% less than 15 minutes, 11.8% 15 to 30 minutes, 10.6% 30 to 45 minutes, 3.7% 45 to 60 minutes, 12.0% 60 minutes or more (2005-2009 5-year est.)
Additional Information Contacts
Bonham Area Chamber of Commerce . . . . (903) 583-4811
   http://www.bonhamchamber.com
City of Bonham . . . . (903) 583-7555
   http://www.cobon.net

DODD CITY (town). Aka Dodds. Covers a land area of 1.693 square miles and a water area of 0 square miles. Located at 33.57° N. Lat; 96.07° W. Long. Elevation is 673 feet.
Population: 350 (1990); 419 (2000); 435 (2010); 442 (2015 projected); Race: 95.2% White, 1.8% Black, 0.0% Asian, 3.0% Other, 0.2% Hispanic of any race (2010); Density: 257.0 persons per square mile (2010); Average household size: 2.59 (2010); Median age: 40.5 (2010); Males per 100 females: 98.6 (2010); Marriage status: 17.9% never married, 70.4% now married, 5.6% widowed, 6.0% divorced (2005-2009 5-year est.); Foreign born: 7.8% (2005-2009 5-year est.); Ancestry (includes multiple ancestries): 42.0% Irish, 23.7% German, 9.5% American, 5.7% English, 1.9% French (2005-2009 5-year est.).
Economy: Employment by occupation: 7.1% management, 15.6% professional, 12.4% services, 19.1% sales, 0.0% farming, 26.2% construction, 19.6% production (2005-2009 5-year est.).
Income: Per capita income: $29,291 (2010); Median household income: $54,167 (2010); Average household income: $75,476 (2010); Percent of households with income of $100,000 or more: 20.2% (2010); Poverty rate: 12.6% (2005-2009 5-year est.).
Taxes: Total city taxes per capita: $124 (2007); City property taxes per capita: $77 (2007).
Education: Percent of population age 25 and over with: High school diploma (including GED) or higher: 83.2% (2010); Bachelor's degree or higher: 14.8% (2010); Master's degree or higher: 2.7% (2010).
School District(s)
Dodd City ISD (PK-12)
   2009-10 Enrollment: 318 . . . . (903) 583-7585
Housing: Homeownership rate: 75.6% (2010); Median home value: $67,222 (2010); Median contract rent: $381 per month (2005-2009 5-year est.); Median year structure built: 1980 (2005-2009 5-year est.).
Transportation: Commute to work: 100.0% car, 0.0% public transportation, 0.0% walk, 0.0% work from home (2005-2009 5-year est.); Travel time to work: 35.6% less than 15 minutes, 22.0% 15 to 30 minutes,

22.4% 30 to 45 minutes, 13.7% 45 to 60 minutes, 6.3% 60 minutes or more (2005-2009 5-year est.)

ECTOR (city).
Covers a land area of 1.183 square miles and a water area of 0 square miles. Located at 33.57° N. Lat; 96.27° W. Long. Elevation is 650 feet.

Population: 581 (1990); 600 (2000); 636 (2010); 656 (2015 projected); Race: 94.7% White, 0.0% Black, 0.3% Asian, 5.0% Other, 1.4% Hispanic of any race (2010); Density: 537.8 persons per square mile (2010); Average household size: 2.48 (2010); Median age: 37.9 (2010); Males per 100 females: 93.3 (2010); Marriage status: 22.6% never married, 52.2% now married, 9.8% widowed, 15.4% divorced (2005-2009 5-year est.); Foreign born: 0.0% (2005-2009 5-year est.); Ancestry (includes multiple ancestries): 26.5% German, 19.1% Irish, 15.9% English, 6.0% American, 3.4% Welsh (2005-2009 5-year est.).

Economy: Employment by occupation: 3.3% management, 19.0% professional, 12.7% services, 31.7% sales, 1.0% farming, 14.4% construction, 18.0% production (2005-2009 5-year est.).

Income: Per capita income: $22,151 (2010); Median household income: $52,083 (2010); Average household income: $55,410 (2010); Percent of households with income of $100,000 or more: 10.5% (2010); Poverty rate: 7.1% (2005-2009 5-year est.).

Education: Percent of population age 25 and over with: High school diploma (including GED) or higher: 85.0% (2010); Bachelor's degree or higher: 16.3% (2010); Master's degree or higher: 3.4% (2010).

School District(s)
Ector ISD (KG-12)
   2009-10 Enrollment: 251 . . . . (903) 961-2355

Housing: Homeownership rate: 70.3% (2010); Median home value: $73,000 (2010); Median contract rent: $433 per month (2005-2009 5-year est.); Median year structure built: 1957 (2005-2009 5-year est.).

Transportation: Commute to work: 88.7% car, 0.0% public transportation, 11.3% walk, 0.0% work from home (2005-2009 5-year est.); Travel time to work: 39.1% less than 15 minutes, 28.1% 15 to 30 minutes, 18.9% 30 to 45 minutes, 9.3% 45 to 60 minutes, 4.6% 60 minutes or more (2005-2009 5-year est.)

HONEY GROVE (city).
Covers a land area of 2.639 square miles and a water area of 0.039 square miles. Located at 33.58° N. Lat; 95.90° W. Long. Elevation is 673 feet.

History: Honey Grove developed as the center of a dairy farming region.

Population: 1,806 (1990); 1,746 (2000); 1,933 (2010); 2,030 (2015 projected); Race: 82.7% White, 9.6% Black, 0.7% Asian, 7.0% Other, 8.7% Hispanic of any race (2010); Density: 732.4 persons per square mile (2010); Average household size: 2.45 (2010); Median age: 41.0 (2010); Males per 100 females: 86.6 (2010); Marriage status: 25.9% never married, 54.2% now married, 7.7% widowed, 12.2% divorced (2005-2009 5-year est.); Foreign born: 8.5% (2005-2009 5-year est.); Ancestry (includes multiple ancestries): 18.6% Irish, 11.4% German, 6.9% American, 6.1% English, 5.1% African (2005-2009 5-year est.).

Economy: Single-family building permits issued: 0 (2010); Multi-family building permits issued: 0 (2010); Employment by occupation: 5.1% management, 14.0% professional, 11.1% services, 18.3% sales, 7.3% farming, 15.6% construction, 28.6% production (2005-2009 5-year est.).

Income: Per capita income: $18,389 (2010); Median household income: $36,648 (2010); Average household income: $46,079 (2010); Percent of households with income of $100,000 or more: 9.5% (2010); Poverty rate: 26.2% (2005-2009 5-year est.).

Taxes: Total city taxes per capita: $284 (2007); City property taxes per capita: $140 (2007).

Education: Percent of population age 25 and over with: High school diploma (including GED) or higher: 78.0% (2010); Bachelor's degree or higher: 13.5% (2010); Master's degree or higher: 4.9% (2010).

School District(s)
Honey Grove ISD (PK-12)
   2009-10 Enrollment: 612 . . . . (903) 378-2264

Housing: Homeownership rate: 63.7% (2010); Median home value: $72,268 (2010); Median contract rent: $350 per month (2005-2009 5-year est.); Median year structure built: 1960 (2005-2009 5-year est.).

Newspapers: Ladonia News (Local news; Circulation 3,000)

Transportation: Commute to work: 87.5% car, 0.0% public transportation, 2.6% walk, 3.3% work from home (2005-2009 5-year est.); Travel time to work: 27.7% less than 15 minutes, 36.4% 15 to 30 minutes, 19.6% 30 to 45 minutes, 7.4% 45 to 60 minutes, 8.9% 60 minutes or more (2005-2009 5-year est.)

Additional Information Contacts
Honey Grove Chamber of Commerce . . . . (903) 378-7211
   http://www.honeygrovechamber.com

IVANHOE (unincorporated postal area, zip code 75447).
Covers a land area of 59.805 square miles and a water area of 0.715 square miles. Located at 33.77° N. Lat; 96.12° W. Long. Elevation is 610 feet.

Population: 1,044 (2000); Race: 95.0% White, 0.0% Black, 0.0% Asian, 5.0% Other, 4.0% Hispanic of any race (2000); Density: 17.5 persons per square mile (2000); Age: 24.6% under 18, 14.6% over 64 (2000); Marriage status: 17.3% never married, 68.1% now married, 5.8% widowed, 8.8% divorced (2000); Foreign born: 3.8% (2000); Ancestry (includes multiple ancestries): 33.6% American, 8.0% Irish, 7.7% German, 5.6% English (2000).

Economy: Employment by occupation: 12.3% management, 15.7% professional, 9.3% services, 21.6% sales, 3.6% farming, 16.1% construction, 21.4% production (2000).

Income: Per capita income: $19,071 (2000); Median household income: $42,308 (2000); Poverty rate: 179.1% (2000).

Education: Percent of population age 25 and over with: High school diploma (including GED) or higher: 77.8% (2000); Bachelor's degree or higher: 13.9% (2000).

School District(s)
Sam Rayburn ISD (PK-12)
   2009-10 Enrollment: 444 . . . . (903) 664-2255

Housing: Homeownership rate: 84.4% (2000); Median home value: $65,900 (2000); Median contract rent: $260 per month (2000); Median year structure built: 1983 (2000).

Transportation: Commute to work: 94.6% car, 0.6% public transportation, 0.4% walk, 3.9% work from home (2000); Travel time to work: 14.1% less than 15 minutes, 40.0% 15 to 30 minutes, 17.4% 30 to 45 minutes, 8.9% 45 to 60 minutes, 19.5% 60 minutes or more (2000)

LADONIA (town).
Covers a land area of 1.835 square miles and a water area of 0 square miles. Located at 33.42° N. Lat; 95.94° W. Long. Elevation is 627 feet.

History: Historic downtown restored.

Population: 685 (1990); 667 (2000); 721 (2010); 750 (2015 projected); Race: 83.6% White, 10.4% Black, 1.0% Asian, 5.0% Other, 2.6% Hispanic of any race (2010); Density: 393.0 persons per square mile (2010); Average household size: 2.57 (2010); Median age: 36.7 (2010); Males per 100 females: 91.2 (2010); Marriage status: 27.4% never married, 50.9% now married, 12.2% widowed, 9.5% divorced (2005-2009 5-year est.); Foreign born: 4.7% (2005-2009 5-year est.); Ancestry (includes multiple ancestries): 15.8% German, 15.5% Irish, 9.5% Italian, 8.4% American, 7.5% English (2005-2009 5-year est.).

Economy: Employment by occupation: 14.5% management, 5.0% professional, 7.4% services, 45.0% sales, 0.0% farming, 2.5% construction, 25.6% production (2005-2009 5-year est.).

Income: Per capita income: $18,670 (2010); Median household income: $39,227 (2010); Average household income: $48,639 (2010); Percent of households with income of $100,000 or more: 8.2% (2010); Poverty rate: 22.7% (2005-2009 5-year est.).

Taxes: Total city taxes per capita: $173 (2007); City property taxes per capita: $96 (2007).

Education: Percent of population age 25 and over with: High school diploma (including GED) or higher: 80.6% (2010); Bachelor's degree or higher: 9.7% (2010); Master's degree or higher: 3.2% (2010).

School District(s)
Fannindel ISD (PK-12)
   2009-10 Enrollment: 196 . . . . (903) 367-7251

Housing: Homeownership rate: 76.2% (2010); Median home value: $56,296 (2010); Median contract rent: $346 per month (2005-2009 5-year est.); Median year structure built: 1955 (2005-2009 5-year est.).

Transportation: Commute to work: 88.8% car, 1.2% public transportation, 6.6% walk, 3.3% work from home (2005-2009 5-year est.); Travel time to work: 17.9% less than 15 minutes, 27.8% 15 to 30 minutes, 26.1% 30 to 45 minutes, 5.1% 45 to 60 minutes, 23.1% 60 minutes or more (2005-2009 5-year est.)

LEONARD (city).
Covers a land area of 1.971 square miles and a water area of 0 square miles. Located at 33.38° N. Lat; 96.24° W. Long. Elevation is 719 feet.

History: Settled c.1880.

Population: 1,790 (1990); 1,846 (2000); 2,121 (2010); 2,254 (2015 projected); Race: 85.0% White, 3.2% Black, 0.1% Asian, 11.7% Other, 9.5% Hispanic of any race (2010); Density: 1,076.3 persons per square mile (2010); Average household size: 2.63 (2010); Median age: 34.0 (2010); Males per 100 females: 93.9 (2010); Marriage status: 26.3% never married, 54.0% now married, 5.9% widowed, 13.8% divorced (2005-2009 5-year est.); Foreign born: 2.0% (2005-2009 5-year est.); Ancestry (includes multiple ancestries): 23.4% Irish, 20.8% German, 10.9% English, 7.9% American, 5.9% Dutch (2005-2009 5-year est.).
Economy: Single-family building permits issued: 0 (2010); Multi-family building permits issued: 0 (2010); Employment by occupation: 11.5% management, 10.9% professional, 22.3% services, 20.1% sales, 3.3% farming, 14.2% construction, 17.8% production (2005-2009 5-year est.).
Income: Per capita income: $20,328 (2010); Median household income: $44,624 (2010); Average household income: $54,190 (2010); Percent of households with income of $100,000 or more: 11.7% (2010); Poverty rate: 18.1% (2005-2009 5-year est.).
Taxes: Total city taxes per capita: $326 (2007); City property taxes per capita: $183 (2007).
Education: Percent of population age 25 and over with: High school diploma (including GED) or higher: 81.5% (2010); Bachelor's degree or higher: 17.0% (2010); Master's degree or higher: 2.0% (2010).

School District(s)

Leonard ISD (PK-12)
    2009-10 Enrollment: 896 . . . . (903) 587-2318
Housing: Homeownership rate: 63.7% (2010); Median home value: $84,133 (2010); Median contract rent: $375 per month (2005-2009 5-year est.); Median year structure built: 1973 (2005-2009 5-year est.).
Newspapers: Leonard Graphic (Community news; Circulation 1,400)
Transportation: Commute to work: 95.3% car, 0.0% public transportation, 1.5% walk, 2.9% work from home (2005-2009 5-year est.); Travel time to work: 35.0% less than 15 minutes, 9.4% 15 to 30 minutes, 28.1% 30 to 45 minutes, 12.2% 45 to 60 minutes, 15.3% 60 minutes or more (2005-2009 5-year est.)

RAVENNA (city). Covers a land area of 1.211 square miles and a water area of 0 square miles. Located at 33.67° N. Lat; 96.24° W. Long. Elevation is 597 feet.
Population: 188 (1990); 215 (2000); 227 (2010); 231 (2015 projected); Race: 93.4% White, 1.3% Black, 0.0% Asian, 5.3% Other, 4.4% Hispanic of any race (2010); Density: 187.5 persons per square mile (2010); Average household size: 2.58 (2010); Median age: 42.4 (2010); Males per 100 females: 102.7 (2010); Marriage status: 13.1% never married, 69.4% now married, 13.5% widowed, 3.9% divorced (2005-2009 5-year est.); Foreign born: 0.8% (2005-2009 5-year est.); Ancestry (includes multiple ancestries): 14.8% Irish, 12.7% English, 10.2% German, 4.5% Dutch, 3.7% American (2005-2009 5-year est.).
Economy: Employment by occupation: 20.6% management, 13.7% professional, 16.0% services, 23.7% sales, 0.0% farming, 15.3% construction, 10.7% production (2005-2009 5-year est.).
Income: Per capita income: $23,838 (2010); Median household income: $45,714 (2010); Average household income: $63,977 (2010); Percent of households with income of $100,000 or more: 14.8% (2010); Poverty rate: 4.9% (2005-2009 5-year est.).
Taxes: Total city taxes per capita: $35 (2007); City property taxes per capita: $0 (2007).
Education: Percent of population age 25 and over with: High school diploma (including GED) or higher: 84.8% (2010); Bachelor's degree or higher: 12.7% (2010); Master's degree or higher: 1.9% (2010).
Housing: Homeownership rate: 86.4% (2010); Median home value: $81,818 (2010); Median contract rent: n/a per month (2005-2009 5-year est.); Median year structure built: 1974 (2005-2009 5-year est.).
Transportation: Commute to work: 98.5% car, 0.0% public transportation, 1.5% walk, 0.0% work from home (2005-2009 5-year est.); Travel time to work: 22.1% less than 15 minutes, 60.3% 15 to 30 minutes, 12.2% 30 to 45 minutes, 1.5% 45 to 60 minutes, 3.8% 60 minutes or more (2005-2009 5-year est.)

SAVOY (city). Covers a land area of 0.723 square miles and a water area of 0 square miles. Located at 33.60° N. Lat; 96.36° W. Long. Elevation is 679 feet.
Population: 865 (1990); 850 (2000); 909 (2010); 937 (2015 projected); Race: 95.4% White, 0.1% Black, 0.6% Asian, 4.0% Other, 1.7% Hispanic of any race (2010); Density: 1,257.7 persons per square mile (2010); Average household size: 2.50 (2010); Median age: 42.1 (2010); Males per

100 females: 87.4 (2010); Marriage status: 13.1% never married, 63.3% now married, 9.5% widowed, 14.2% divorced (2005-2009 5-year est.); Foreign born: 0.2% (2005-2009 5-year est.); Ancestry (includes multiple ancestries): 25.5% German, 16.0% Irish, 8.0% American, 5.5% African, 5.1% English (2005-2009 5-year est.).
Economy: Single-family building permits issued: 0 (2010); Multi-family building permits issued: 0 (2010); Employment by occupation: 2.4% management, 22.2% professional, 14.4% services, 20.2% sales, 1.5% farming, 18.5% construction, 20.7% production (2005-2009 5-year est.).
Income: Per capita income: $20,104 (2010); Median household income: $45,582 (2010); Average household income: $53,891 (2010); Percent of households with income of $100,000 or more: 8.8% (2010); Poverty rate: 13.3% (2005-2009 5-year est.).
Taxes: Total city taxes per capita: $200 (2007); City property taxes per capita: $116 (2007).
Education: Percent of population age 25 and over with: High school diploma (including GED) or higher: 80.5% (2010); Bachelor's degree or higher: 9.5% (2010); Master's degree or higher: 2.5% (2010).

School District(s)

Savoy ISD (PK-12)
    2009-10 Enrollment: 302 . . . . (903) 965-5262
Housing: Homeownership rate: 68.4% (2010); Median home value: $62,683 (2010); Median contract rent: $514 per month (2005-2009 5-year est.); Median year structure built: 1969 (2005-2009 5-year est.).
Transportation: Commute to work: 97.1% car, 0.0% public transportation, 1.7% walk, 0.7% work from home (2005-2009 5-year est.); Travel time to work: 20.8% less than 15 minutes, 36.9% 15 to 30 minutes, 15.3% 30 to 45 minutes, 11.4% 45 to 60 minutes, 15.6% 60 minutes or more (2005-2009 5-year est.)

TELEPHONE (unincorporated postal area, zip code 75488). Covers a land area of 107.486 square miles and a water area of 1.239 square miles. Located at 33.76° N. Lat; 96.00° W. Long. Elevation is 568 feet.
Population: 981 (2000); Race: 97.2% White, 0.6% Black, 0.0% Asian, 2.2% Other, 1.3% Hispanic of any race (2000); Density: 9.1 persons per square mile (2000); Age: 23.0% under 18, 15.3% over 64 (2000); Marriage status: 16.2% never married, 65.2% now married, 10.0% widowed, 8.6% divorced (2000); Foreign born: 2.6% (2000); Ancestry (includes multiple ancestries): 28.7% American, 8.7% Irish, 7.6% German, 5.8% English (2000).
Economy: Employment by occupation: 13.4% management, 11.5% professional, 16.1% services, 19.4% sales, 1.5% farming, 13.0% construction, 25.1% production (2000).
Income: Per capita income: $15,938 (2000); Median household income: $32,361 (2000); Poverty rate: 179.1% (2000).
Education: Percent of population age 25 and over with: High school diploma (including GED) or higher: 71.0% (2000); Bachelor's degree or higher: 11.0% (2000).
Housing: Homeownership rate: 84.6% (2000); Median home value: $38,900 (2000); Median contract rent: $296 per month (2000); Median year structure built: 1980 (2000).
Transportation: Commute to work: 90.9% car, 0.0% public transportation, 0.7% walk, 7.5% work from home (2000); Travel time to work: 13.2% less than 15 minutes, 37.6% 15 to 30 minutes, 20.6% 30 to 45 minutes, 7.9% 45 to 60 minutes, 20.6% 60 minutes or more (2000)

TRENTON (city). Covers a land area of 1.588 square miles and a water area of 0 square miles. Located at 33.43° N. Lat; 96.34° W. Long. Elevation is 761 feet.
Population: 681 (1990); 662 (2000); 773 (2010); 828 (2015 projected); Race: 86.5% White, 2.5% Black, 0.0% Asian, 11.0% Other, 11.8% Hispanic of any race (2010); Density: 486.7 persons per square mile (2010); Average household size: 2.51 (2010); Median age: 35.4 (2010); Males per 100 females: 92.3 (2010); Marriage status: 23.1% never married, 63.8% now married, 4.2% widowed, 8.8% divorced (2005-2009 5-year est.); Foreign born: 5.2% (2005-2009 5-year est.); Ancestry (includes multiple ancestries): 15.4% Irish, 15.0% German, 10.9% American, 4.6% Dutch, 4.4% English (2005-2009 5-year est.).
Economy: Single-family building permits issued: 0 (2010); Multi-family building permits issued: 0 (2010); Employment by occupation: 8.0% management, 17.6% professional, 19.8% services, 25.7% sales, 0.0% farming, 9.9% construction, 19.0% production (2005-2009 5-year est.).
Income: Per capita income: $27,107 (2010); Median household income: $52,966 (2010); Average household income: $69,156 (2010); Percent of

households with income of $100,000 or more: 21.8% (2010); Poverty rate: 15.7% (2005-2009 5-year est.).
Taxes: Total city taxes per capita: $266 (2007); City property taxes per capita: $168 (2007).
Education: Percent of population age 25 and over with: High school diploma (including GED) or higher: 81.7% (2010); Bachelor's degree or higher: 16.5% (2010); Master's degree or higher: 4.3% (2010).

School District(s)

Trenton ISD (PK-12)
    2009-10 Enrollment: 574 . . . . (903) 989-2245
Housing: Homeownership rate: 66.2% (2010); Median home value: $71,053 (2010); Median contract rent: $449 per month (2005-2009 5-year est.); Median year structure built: 1956 (2005-2009 5-year est.).
Newspapers: Trenton Tribune (Local news; Circulation 1,300)
Transportation: Commute to work: 95.5% car, 0.0% public transportation, 0.0% walk, 3.4% work from home (2005-2009 5-year est.); Travel time to work: 22.8% less than 15 minutes, 12.6% 15 to 30 minutes, 30.1% 30 to 45 minutes, 4.1% 45 to 60 minutes, 30.4% 60 minutes or more (2005-2009 5-year est.)

WINDOM (town). Covers a land area of 0.549 square miles and a water area of 0 square miles. Located at 33.56° N. Lat; 96.00° W. Long. Elevation is 696 feet.
Population: 269 (1990); 245 (2000); 250 (2010); 254 (2015 projected); Race: 95.2% White, 1.6% Black, 0.0% Asian, 3.2% Other, 0.0% Hispanic of any race (2010); Density: 455.7 persons per square mile (2010); Average household size: 2.58 (2010); Median age: 38.6 (2010); Males per 100 females: 92.3 (2010); Marriage status: 31.1% never married, 53.0% now married, 2.4% widowed, 13.5% divorced (2005-2009 5-year est.); Foreign born: 0.0% (2005-2009 5-year est.); Ancestry (includes multiple ancestries): 29.4% Irish, 18.4% English, 12.2% German, 6.4% Scotch-Irish, 4.1% American (2005-2009 5-year est.).
Economy: Employment by occupation: 15.2% management, 24.8% professional, 3.6% services, 13.9% sales, 0.0% farming, 15.2% construction, 27.3% production (2005-2009 5-year est.).
Income: Per capita income: $29,291 (2010); Median household income: $56,618 (2010); Average household income: $76,933 (2010); Percent of households with income of $100,000 or more: 21.6% (2010); Poverty rate: 6.4% (2005-2009 5-year est.).
Taxes: Total city taxes per capita: $132 (2007); City property taxes per capita: $47 (2007).
Education: Percent of population age 25 and over with: High school diploma (including GED) or higher: 83.6% (2010); Bachelor's degree or higher: 15.8% (2010); Master's degree or higher: 3.0% (2010).
Housing: Homeownership rate: 75.3% (2010); Median home value: $66,364 (2010); Median contract rent: n/a per month (2005-2009 5-year est.); Median year structure built: 1982 (2005-2009 5-year est.).
Transportation: Commute to work: 87.8% car, 8.3% public transportation, 0.0% walk, 0.0% work from home (2005-2009 5-year est.); Travel time to work: 32.1% less than 15 minutes, 26.3% 15 to 30 minutes, 18.6% 30 to 45 minutes, 7.1% 45 to 60 minutes, 16.0% 60 minutes or more (2005-2009 5-year est.)

Fayette County

Located in south central Texas; drained by the Colorado River and the headwaters of the Lavaca and Navidad Rivers. Covers a land area of 950.03 square miles, a water area of 9.81 square miles, and is located in the Central Time Zone at 29.85° N. Lat., 96.91° W. Long. The county was founded in 1837. County seat is La Grange.

Weather Station: Flatonia — Elevation: 520 feet

	Jan	Feb	Mar	Apr	May	Jun	Jul	Aug	Sep	Oct	Nov	Dec
High	62	66	72	79	85	91	94	95	89	81	71	63
Low	43	46	52	59	67	72	73	73	69	61	52	44
Precip	2.5	2.3	2.7	2.5	4.6	4.2	2.3	2.6	3.4	4.5	3.5	2.6
Snow	0.2	tr	tr	0.0	0.0	0.0	0.0	0.0	0.0	0.0	0.0	tr

High and Low temperatures in degrees Fahrenheit; Precipitation and Snow in inches

Weather Station: La Grange — Elevation: 356 feet

	Jan	Feb	Mar	Apr	May	Jun	Jul	Aug	Sep	Oct	Nov	Dec
High	63	67	73	81	87	92	96	97	91	83	72	64
Low	41	44	51	58	66	72	74	73	68	59	51	42
Precip	3.0	3.0	2.9	2.6	4.3	4.2	2.4	2.6	3.5	4.9	3.6	3.2
Snow	tr	tr	0.0	0.0	0.0	0.0	0.0	0.0	0.0	0.0	0.0	tr

High and Low temperatures in degrees Fahrenheit; Precipitation and Snow in inches

Population: 20,095 (1990); 21,804 (2000); 23,828 (2010); 24,762 (2015 projected); Race: 81.8% White, 7.2% Black, 0.4% Asian, 10.7% Other, 16.8% Hispanic of any race (2010); Density: 25.1 persons per square mile (2010); Average household size: 2.44 (2010); Median age: 43.1 (2010); Males per 100 females: 95.6 (2010).
Religion: Five largest groups: 41.5% Catholic Church, 12.8% Evangelical Lutheran Church in America, 11.2% Southern Baptist Convention, 6.7% Lutheran Church—Missouri Synod, 4.2% The United Methodist Church (2000).
Economy: Unemployment rate: 6.7% (June 2011); Total civilian labor force: 12,214 (June 2011); Leading industries: 17.6% health care and social assistance; 17.3% retail trade; 14.2% manufacturing (2009); Farms: 2,991 totaling 565,708 acres (2007); Companies that employ 500 or more persons: 0 (2009); Companies that employ 100 to 499 persons: 7 (2009); Companies that employ less than 100 persons: 738 (2009); Black-owned businesses: n/a (2007); Hispanic-owned businesses: n/a (2007); Asian-owned businesses: n/a (2007); Women-owned businesses: 632 (2007); Retail sales per capita: $13,325 (2010). Single-family building permits issued: 5 (2010); Multi-family building permits issued: 0 (2010).
Income: Per capita income: $23,833 (2010); Median household income: $44,981 (2010); Average household income: $58,977 (2010); Percent of households with income of $100,000 or more: 13.7% (2010); Poverty rate: 12.1% (2009); Bankruptcy rate: 0.96% (2010).
Taxes: Total county taxes per capita: $391 (2007); County property taxes per capita: $293 (2007).
Education: Percent of population age 25 and over with: High school diploma (including GED) or higher: 75.6% (2010); Bachelor's degree or higher: 15.4% (2010); Master's degree or higher: 3.4% (2010).
Housing: Homeownership rate: 74.1% (2010); Median home value: $108,106 (2010); Median contract rent: $438 per month (2005-2009 5-year est.); Median year structure built: 1973 (2005-2009 5-year est.)
Health: Birth rate: 117.5 per 10,000 population (2009); Death rate: 128.9 per 10,000 population (2009); Age-adjusted cancer mortality rate: 194.1 deaths per 100,000 population (2007); Number of physicians: 9.6 per 10,000 population (2008); Hospital beds: 21.3 per 10,000 population (2007); Hospital admissions: 992.2 per 10,000 population (2007).
Environment: Air Quality Index: 90.4% good, 9.6% moderate, 0.0% unhealthy for sensitive individuals, 0.0% unhealthy (percent of days in 2008)
Elections: 2008 Presidential election results: 28.1% Obama, 70.8% McCain, 0.1% Nader
National and State Parks: Monument Hill State Park
Additional Information Contacts
Fayette County Government . . . . (979) 968-3055
    http://www.co.fayette.tx.us
City of La Grange. . . . . (979) 968-5805
    http://www.cityoflg.com
Ellinger Chamber of Commerce. . . . . (979) 378-2311
Fayetteville Chamber of Commerce . . . . (979) 378-4021
    http://www.fayettevilletx.com
Flatonia Chamber of Commerce . . . . (361) 865-3920
    http://www.flatonia-tx.com
Greater Schulenburg Chamber of Commerce . . . . (979) 743-4514
    http://www.schulenburgchamber.org
La Grange Area Chamber of Commerce. . . . . (979) 968-5756
    http://www.lagrangetx.org
Town of Flatonia . . . . (361) 865-3548
    http://www.ci.flatonia.tx.us

Fayette County Communities

CARMINE (city). Covers a land area of 1.647 square miles and a water area of 0 square miles. Located at 30.14° N. Lat; 96.68° W. Long. Elevation is 433 feet.
Population: 192 (1990); 228 (2000); 231 (2010); 232 (2015 projected); Race: 92.6% White, 3.9% Black, 0.0% Asian, 3.5% Other, 6.1% Hispanic of any race (2010); Density: 140.2 persons per square mile (2010); Average household size: 2.33 (2010); Median age: 47.3 (2010); Males per 100 females: 99.1 (2010); Marriage status: 36.1% never married, 29.0% now married, 15.4% widowed, 19.5% divorced (2005-2009 5-year est.); Foreign born: 4.0% (2005-2009 5-year est.); Ancestry (includes multiple ancestries): 49.4% German, 12.6% Polish, 5.7% English, 5.2% American (2005-2009 5-year est.).
Economy: Single-family building permits issued: 0 (2010); Multi-family building permits issued: 0 (2010); Employment by occupation: 17.4%

management, 20.7% professional, 15.2% services, 21.7% sales, 0.0% farming, 0.0% construction, 25.0% production (2005-2009 5-year est.).
Income: Per capita income: $28,457 (2010); Median household income: $47,000 (2010); Average household income: $65,102 (2010); Percent of households with income of $100,000 or more: 14.3% (2010); Poverty rate: 21.3% (2005-2009 5-year est.).
Taxes: Total city taxes per capita: $226 (2007); City property taxes per capita: $130 (2007).
Education: Percent of population age 25 and over with: High school diploma (including GED) or higher: 83.0% (2010); Bachelor's degree or higher: 24.8% (2010); Master's degree or higher: 9.7% (2010).

School District(s)
Round Top-Carmine ISD (PK-12)
   2009-10 Enrollment: 240 . . . . (979) 278-4250
Housing: Homeownership rate: 84.7% (2010); Median home value: $159,615 (2010); Median contract rent: n/a per month (2005-2009 5-year est.); Median year structure built: 1956 (2005-2009 5-year est.).
Transportation: Commute to work: 93.3% car, 0.0% public transportation, 0.0% walk, 6.7% work from home (2005-2009 5-year est.); Travel time to work: 14.3% less than 15 minutes, 36.9% 15 to 30 minutes, 13.1% 30 to 45 minutes, 10.7% 45 to 60 minutes, 25.0% 60 minutes or more (2005-2009 5-year est.)

ELLINGER (unincorporated postal area, zip code 78938). Covers a land area of 5.977 square miles and a water area of 0 square miles. Located at 29.83° N. Lat; 96.70° W. Long. Elevation is 295 feet.
Population: 336 (2000); Race: 99.4% White, 0.0% Black, 0.0% Asian, 0.6% Other, 10.1% Hispanic of any race (2000); Density: 56.2 persons per square mile (2000); Age: 21.2% under 18, 16.7% over 64 (2000); Marriage status: 12.6% never married, 72.2% now married, 12.2% widowed, 3.0% divorced (2000); Foreign born: 4.2% (2000); Ancestry (includes multiple ancestries): 37.9% German, 22.4% Czech, 7.5% English, 6.0% Russian (2000).
Economy: Employment by occupation: 8.4% management, 9.0% professional, 4.8% services, 28.3% sales, 1.2% farming, 19.3% construction, 28.9% production (2000).
Income: Per capita income: $15,724 (2000); Median household income: $21,667 (2000); Poverty rate: 179.1% (2000).
Education: Percent of population age 25 and over with: High school diploma (including GED) or higher: 66.1% (2000); Bachelor's degree or higher: 7.9% (2000).
Housing: Homeownership rate: 83.9% (2000); Median home value: $53,700 (2000); Median contract rent: $213 per month (2000); Median year structure built: 1962 (2000).
Transportation: Commute to work: 95.2% car, 0.0% public transportation, 3.6% walk, 1.2% work from home (2000); Travel time to work: 25.6% less than 15 minutes, 43.9% 15 to 30 minutes, 13.4% 30 to 45 minutes, 0.0% 45 to 60 minutes, 17.1% 60 minutes or more (2000)
Additional Information Contacts
Ellinger Chamber of Commerce. . . . . (979) 378-2311

FAYETTEVILLE (city). Covers a land area of 0.433 square miles and a water area of 0 square miles. Located at 29.90° N. Lat; 96.67° W. Long. Elevation is 394 feet.
Population: 283 (1990); 261 (2000); 274 (2010); 281 (2015 projected); Race: 92.3% White, 2.9% Black, 0.7% Asian, 4.0% Other, 2.9% Hispanic of any race (2010); Density: 632.4 persons per square mile (2010); Average household size: 2.34 (2010); Median age: 45.7 (2010); Males per 100 females: 100.0 (2010); Marriage status: 24.2% never married, 54.2% now married, 12.5% widowed, 9.2% divorced (2005-2009 5-year est.); Foreign born: 0.0% (2005-2009 5-year est.); Ancestry (includes multiple ancestries): 38.8% Czech, 35.6% German, 8.6% English, 8.3% Irish, 8.3% American (2005-2009 5-year est.).
Economy: Single-family building permits issued: 1 (2010); Multi-family building permits issued: 0 (2010); Employment by occupation: 12.5% management, 16.9% professional, 25.6% services, 24.4% sales, 0.0% farming, 8.8% construction, 11.9% production (2005-2009 5-year est.).
Income: Per capita income: $19,531 (2010); Median household income: $36,023 (2010); Average household income: $45,406 (2010); Percent of households with income of $100,000 or more: 6.8% (2010); Poverty rate: 5.8% (2005-2009 5-year est.).
Taxes: Total city taxes per capita: $339 (2007); City property taxes per capita: $190 (2007).

Education: Percent of population age 25 and over with: High school diploma (including GED) or higher: 76.6% (2010); Bachelor's degree or higher: 12.7% (2010); Master's degree or higher: 3.0% (2010).

School District(s)
Fayetteville ISD (PK-12)
   2009-10 Enrollment: 223 . . . . (979) 378-4242
Housing: Homeownership rate: 79.5% (2010); Median home value: $89,167 (2010); Median contract rent: $510 per month (2005-2009 5-year est.); Median year structure built: 1945 (2005-2009 5-year est.).
Transportation: Commute to work: 82.5% car, 2.5% public transportation, 11.3% walk, 2.5% work from home (2005-2009 5-year est.); Travel time to work: 31.4% less than 15 minutes, 34.6% 15 to 30 minutes, 17.3% 30 to 45 minutes, 1.3% 45 to 60 minutes, 15.4% 60 minutes or more (2005-2009 5-year est.)
Additional Information Contacts
Fayetteville Chamber of Commerce . . . . (979) 378-4021
   http://www.fayettevilletx.com

FLATONIA (town). Covers a land area of 1.619 square miles and a water area of 0.017 square miles. Located at 29.68° N. Lat; 97.10° W. Long. Elevation is 456 feet.
History: Founded 1874, incorporated 1875.
Population: 1,405 (1990); 1,377 (2000); 1,378 (2010); 1,378 (2015 projected); Race: 78.0% White, 6.1% Black, 0.0% Asian, 15.9% Other, 42.8% Hispanic of any race (2010); Density: 851.4 persons per square mile (2010); Average household size: 2.66 (2010); Median age: 37.3 (2010); Males per 100 females: 100.0 (2010); Marriage status: 18.6% never married, 64.3% now married, 12.5% widowed, 4.6% divorced (2005-2009 5-year est.); Foreign born: 19.7% (2005-2009 5-year est.); Ancestry (includes multiple ancestries): 18.8% Czech, 18.2% German, 6.7% Irish, 6.7% English, 2.1% French (2005-2009 5-year est.).
Economy: Single-family building permits issued: 2 (2010); Multi-family building permits issued: 0 (2010); Employment by occupation: 8.8% management, 8.1% professional, 20.6% services, 20.1% sales, 4.2% farming, 10.0% construction, 28.1% production (2005-2009 5-year est.).
Income: Per capita income: $17,038 (2010); Median household income: $35,227 (2010); Average household income: $45,561 (2010); Percent of households with income of $100,000 or more: 8.8% (2010); Poverty rate: 15.8% (2005-2009 5-year est.).
Taxes: Total city taxes per capita: $341 (2007); City property taxes per capita: $129 (2007).
Education: Percent of population age 25 and over with: High school diploma (including GED) or higher: 58.2% (2010); Bachelor's degree or higher: 10.5% (2010); Master's degree or higher: 2.3% (2010).

School District(s)
Flatonia ISD (PK-12)
   2009-10 Enrollment: 560 . . . . (361) 865-2941
Housing: Homeownership rate: 69.7% (2010); Median home value: $55,522 (2010); Median contract rent: $282 per month (2005-2009 5-year est.); Median year structure built: 1971 (2005-2009 5-year est.).
Safety: Violent crime rate: 13.9 per 10,000 population; Property crime rate: 118.3 per 10,000 population (2009).
Newspapers: Argus (Community news; Circulation 1,391)
Transportation: Commute to work: 96.0% car, 0.2% public transportation, 1.3% walk, 0.5% work from home (2005-2009 5-year est.); Travel time to work: 64.1% less than 15 minutes, 24.5% 15 to 30 minutes, 8.2% 30 to 45 minutes, 0.4% 45 to 60 minutes, 2.9% 60 minutes or more (2005-2009 5-year est.)
Additional Information Contacts
Flatonia Chamber of Commerce . . . . (361) 865-3920
   http://www.flatonia-tx.com
Town of Flatonia . . . . (361) 865-3548
   http://www.ci.flatonia.tx.us

LA GRANGE (city). County seat. Covers a land area of 3.568 square miles and a water area of 0.011 square miles. Located at 29.90° N. Lat; 96.87° W. Long. Elevation is 266 feet.
History: The first settlers in La Grange were cotton plantation owners. La Grange contributed soldiers to the Texas Revolution as well as to the Confederate cause during the Civil War.
Population: 4,107 (1990); 4,478 (2000); 5,002 (2010); 5,298 (2015 projected); Race: 68.1% White, 11.3% Black, 0.8% Asian, 19.8% Other, 28.4% Hispanic of any race (2010); Density: 1,402.0 persons per square mile (2010); Average household size: 2.51 (2010); Median age: 37.1 (2010); Males per 100 females: 91.9 (2010); Marriage status: 26.5% never

married, 49.4% now married, 14.8% widowed, 9.3% divorced (2005-2009 5-year est.); Foreign born: 9.7% (2005-2009 5-year est.); Ancestry (includes multiple ancestries): 27.7% German, 9.2% Czech, 6.7% Irish, 4.2% English, 3.1% American (2005-2009 5-year est.).
Economy: Single-family building permits issued: 0 (2010); Multi-family building permits issued: 0 (2010); Employment by occupation: 7.5% management, 15.6% professional, 28.9% services, 20.9% sales, 0.0% farming, 10.8% construction, 16.3% production (2005-2009 5-year est.).
Income: Per capita income: $19,972 (2010); Median household income: $40,619 (2010); Average household income: $50,763 (2010); Percent of households with income of $100,000 or more: 10.8% (2010); Poverty rate: 18.9% (2005-2009 5-year est.).
Taxes: Total city taxes per capita: $468 (2007); City property taxes per capita: $102 (2007).
Education: Percent of population age 25 and over with: High school diploma (including GED) or higher: 73.4% (2010); Bachelor's degree or higher: 13.1% (2010); Master's degree or higher: 2.6% (2010).
School District(s)
La Grange ISD (PK-12)
   2009-10 Enrollment: 1,905 . . . . (979) 968-7000
Housing: Homeownership rate: 59.8% (2010); Median home value: $91,786 (2010); Median contract rent: $470 per month (2005-2009 5-year est.); Median year structure built: 1972 (2005-2009 5-year est.).
Hospitals: Saint Mark's Medical Center
Safety: Violent crime rate: 6.3 per 10,000 population; Property crime rate: 103.5 per 10,000 population (2009).
Newspapers: Fayette County Record (Local news; Circulation 6,500)
Transportation: Commute to work: 95.0% car, 0.0% public transportation, 0.9% walk, 2.0% work from home (2005-2009 5-year est.); Travel time to work: 51.3% less than 15 minutes, 38.5% 15 to 30 minutes, 4.9% 30 to 45 minutes, 0.0% 45 to 60 minutes, 5.3% 60 minutes or more (2005-2009 5-year est.)
Additional Information Contacts
City of La Grange. . . . . (979) 968-5805
  http://www.cityoflg.com
La Grange Area Chamber of Commerce. . . . . (979) 968-5756
  http://www.lagrangetx.org

LEDBETTER (unincorporated postal area, zip code 78946). Covers a land area of 124.718 square miles and a water area of 1.285 square miles. Located at 30.18° N. Lat; 96.78° W. Long. Elevation is 433 feet.
Population: 1,024 (2000); Race: 69.8% White, 23.4% Black, 0.0% Asian, 6.8% Other, 5.6% Hispanic of any race (2000); Density: 8.2 persons per square mile (2000); Age: 23.8% under 18, 23.3% over 64 (2000); Marriage status: 19.8% never married, 62.3% now married, 8.6% widowed, 9.3% divorced (2000); Foreign born: 0.3% (2000); Ancestry (includes multiple ancestries): 23.4% German, 10.8% English, 5.5% American, 5.5% Irish (2000).
Economy: Employment by occupation: 14.4% management, 8.5% professional, 22.2% services, 19.1% sales, 3.8% farming, 14.9% construction, 17.2% production (2000).
Income: Per capita income: $17,466 (2000); Median household income: $24,890 (2000); Poverty rate: 179.1% (2000).
Education: Percent of population age 25 and over with: High school diploma (including GED) or higher: 71.3% (2000); Bachelor's degree or higher: 14.4% (2000).
Housing: Homeownership rate: 77.1% (2000); Median home value: $72,800 (2000); Median contract rent: $298 per month (2000); Median year structure built: 1975 (2000).
Transportation: Commute to work: 85.4% car, 0.0% public transportation, 2.4% walk, 11.2% work from home (2000); Travel time to work: 18.5% less than 15 minutes, 40.6% 15 to 30 minutes, 29.6% 30 to 45 minutes, 2.7% 45 to 60 minutes, 8.6% 60 minutes or more (2000)

MULDOON (unincorporated postal area, zip code 78949). Covers a land area of 106.792 square miles and a water area of 0.137 square miles. Located at 29.84° N. Lat; 97.08° W. Long. Elevation is 341 feet.
Population: 529 (2000); Race: 93.9% White, 1.5% Black, 0.0% Asian, 4.6% Other, 9.6% Hispanic of any race (2000); Density: 5.0 persons per square mile (2000); Age: 15.1% under 18, 26.8% over 64 (2000); Marriage status: 11.9% never married, 75.7% now married, 9.1% widowed, 3.3% divorced (2000); Foreign born: 4.6% (2000); Ancestry (includes multiple ancestries): 23.8% German, 12.3% Czech, 12.1% American, 7.7% English (2000).

Economy: Employment by occupation: 16.6% management, 13.4% professional, 15.2% services, 22.1% sales, 2.8% farming, 14.7% construction, 15.2% production (2000).
Income: Per capita income: $19,019 (2000); Median household income: $35,556 (2000); Poverty rate: 179.1% (2000).
Education: Percent of population age 25 and over with: High school diploma (including GED) or higher: 75.5% (2000); Bachelor's degree or higher: 13.9% (2000).
Housing: Homeownership rate: 83.6% (2000); Median home value: $83,200 (2000); Median contract rent: $209 per month (2000); Median year structure built: 1977 (2000).
Transportation: Commute to work: 96.3% car, 0.0% public transportation, 2.3% walk, 1.4% work from home (2000); Travel time to work: 20.6% less than 15 minutes, 32.7% 15 to 30 minutes, 14.0% 30 to 45 minutes, 9.3% 45 to 60 minutes, 23.4% 60 minutes or more (2000)

ROUND TOP (town). Covers a land area of 0.956 square miles and a water area of 0 square miles. Located at 30.06° N. Lat; 96.69° W. Long. Elevation is 440 feet.
History: Round Top Academy (1854-1861). Established 1835.
Population: 81 (1990); 77 (2000); 80 (2010); 80 (2015 projected); Race: 92.5% White, 3.8% Black, 0.0% Asian, 3.8% Other, 6.3% Hispanic of any race (2010); Density: 83.7 persons per square mile (2010); Average household size: 2.32 (2010); Median age: 51.4 (2010); Males per 100 females: 86.0 (2010); Marriage status: 0.0% never married, 60.3% now married, 31.0% widowed, 8.6% divorced (2005-2009 5-year est.); Foreign born: 14.8% (2005-2009 5-year est.); Ancestry (includes multiple ancestries): 47.5% German, 31.1% English, 27.9% Irish, 14.8% Swedish, 9.8% Scotch-Irish (2005-2009 5-year est.).
Economy: Single-family building permits issued: 0 (2010); Multi-family building permits issued: 0 (2010); Employment by occupation: 13.6% management, 63.6% professional, 0.0% services, 22.7% sales, 0.0% farming, 0.0% construction, 0.0% production (2005-2009 5-year est.).
Income: Per capita income: $28,457 (2010); Median household income: $47,500 (2010); Average household income: $60,809 (2010); Percent of households with income of $100,000 or more: 11.8% (2010); Poverty rate: 9.8% (2005-2009 5-year est.).
Taxes: Total city taxes per capita: $377 (2007); City property taxes per capita: $143 (2007).
Education: Percent of population age 25 and over with: High school diploma (including GED) or higher: 82.0% (2010); Bachelor's degree or higher: 26.2% (2010); Master's degree or higher: 11.5% (2010).
School District(s)
Round Top-Carmine ISD (PK-12)
   2009-10 Enrollment: 240 . . . . (979) 278-4250
Housing: Homeownership rate: 85.3% (2010); Median home value: $175,000 (2010); Median contract rent: n/a per month (2005-2009 5-year est.); Median year structure built: before 1940 (2005-2009 5-year est.).
Transportation: Commute to work: 100.0% car, 0.0% public transportation, 0.0% walk, 0.0% work from home (2005-2009 5-year est.); Travel time to work: 59.1% less than 15 minutes, 25.0% 15 to 30 minutes, 15.9% 30 to 45 minutes, 0.0% 45 to 60 minutes, 0.0% 60 minutes or more (2005-2009 5-year est.)

SCHULENBURG (city). Covers a land area of 2.436 square miles and a water area of 0 square miles. Located at 29.68° N. Lat; 96.90° W. Long. Elevation is 367 feet.
History: Schulenburg was founded by German and Bohemian colonists. A mill here made flour from cottonseed.
Population: 2,487 (1990); 2,699 (2000); 2,736 (2010); 2,743 (2015 projected); Race: 73.2% White, 15.2% Black, 0.5% Asian, 11.0% Other, 18.5% Hispanic of any race (2010); Density: 1,123.0 persons per square mile (2010); Average household size: 2.29 (2010); Median age: 45.0 (2010); Males per 100 females: 85.2 (2010); Marriage status: 25.7% never married, 45.2% now married, 23.0% widowed, 6.1% divorced (2005-2009 5-year est.); Foreign born: 5.5% (2005-2009 5-year est.); Ancestry (includes multiple ancestries): 30.6% German, 22.8% Czech, 3.7% English, 3.6% Irish, 2.6% American (2005-2009 5-year est.).
Economy: Single-family building permits issued: 2 (2010); Multi-family building permits issued: 0 (2010); Employment by occupation: 10.3% management, 16.7% professional, 18.1% services, 13.1% sales, 0.0% farming, 13.8% construction, 27.9% production (2005-2009 5-year est.).
Income: Per capita income: $20,928 (2010); Median household income: $36,697 (2010); Average household income: $50,102 (2010); Percent of

households with income of $100,000 or more: 10.1% (2010); Poverty rate: 19.3% (2005-2009 5-year est.).

Taxes: Total city taxes per capita: $294 (2007); City property taxes per capita: $100 (2007).

Education: Percent of population age 25 and over with: High school diploma (including GED) or higher: 76.6% (2010); Bachelor's degree or higher: 14.5% (2010); Master's degree or higher: 1.8% (2010).

School District(s)

Schulenburg ISD (PK-12)

    2009-10 Enrollment: 745 . . . . (979) 743-3448

Housing: Homeownership rate: 61.2% (2010); Median home value: $80,530 (2010); Median contract rent: $339 per month (2005-2009 5-year est.); Median year structure built: 1964 (2005-2009 5-year est.).

Safety: Violent crime rate: 55.8 per 10,000 population; Property crime rate: 223.0 per 10,000 population (2009).

Newspapers: Sticker (Local news; Circulation 2,823)

Transportation: Commute to work: 87.5% car, 0.0% public transportation, 7.7% walk, 0.4% work from home (2005-2009 5-year est.); Travel time to work: 58.5% less than 15 minutes, 23.4% 15 to 30 minutes, 8.2% 30 to 45 minutes, 0.5% 45 to 60 minutes, 9.4% 60 minutes or more (2005-2009 5-year est.)

Additional Information Contacts

Greater Schulenburg Chamber of Commerce . . . . (979) 743-4514
    http://www.schulenburgchamber.org

WEST POINT (unincorporated postal area, zip code 78963). Covers a land area of 31.047 square miles and a water area of 0.052 square miles. Located at 29.93° N. Lat; 97.02° W. Long. Elevation is 341 feet.

Population: 541 (2000); Race: 94.4% White, 5.6% Black, 0.0% Asian, 0.0% Other, 0.0% Hispanic of any race (2000); Density: 17.4 persons per square mile (2000); Age: 18.5% under 18, 14.2% over 64 (2000); Marriage status: 17.0% never married, 70.2% now married, 7.8% widowed, 5.0% divorced (2000); Foreign born: 0.0% (2000); Ancestry (includes multiple ancestries): 28.6% German, 18.5% French, 16.3% Czech, 12.5% American (2000).

Economy: Employment by occupation: 14.6% management, 14.2% professional, 2.2% services, 32.3% sales, 0.0% farming, 22.6% construction, 14.2% production (2000).

Income: Per capita income: $17,228 (2000); Median household income: $41,250 (2000); Poverty rate: 179.1% (2000).

Education: Percent of population age 25 and over with: High school diploma (including GED) or higher: 78.5% (2000); Bachelor's degree or higher: 12.2% (2000).

Housing: Homeownership rate: 84.9% (2000); Median home value: $72,300 (2000); Median contract rent: $329 per month (2000); Median year structure built: 1975 (2000).

Transportation: Commute to work: 94.6% car, 0.0% public transportation, 0.0% walk, 5.4% work from home (2000); Travel time to work: 29.7% less than 15 minutes, 44.0% 15 to 30 minutes, 12.4% 30 to 45 minutes, 8.1% 45 to 60 minutes, 5.7% 60 minutes or more (2000)

Fisher County

Located in northwest central Texas; rolling plains, drained by the Double Mountain and Clear Forks of the Brazos River. Covers a land area of 901.16 square miles, a water area of 0.58 square miles, and is located in the Central Time Zone at 32.76° N. Lat., 100.40° W. Long. The county was founded in 1876. County seat is Roby.

Weather Station: Rotan   Elevation: 1,935 feet

	Jan	Feb	Mar	Apr	May	Jun	Jul	Aug	Sep	Oct	Nov	Dec
High	58	62	70	80	87	93	96	95	88	79	67	58
Low	31	35	42	50	60	67	71	70	63	52	41	32
Precip	0.8	1.4	1.6	1.6	3.7	3.0	2.0	2.6	2.8	2.3	1.3	1.1
Snow	0.9	1.2	tr	0.3	0.0	0.0	0.0	0.0	0.0	0.0	0.6	1.2

High and Low temperatures in degrees Fahrenheit; Precipitation and Snow in inches

Population: 4,842 (1990); 4,344 (2000); 4,005 (2010); 3,834 (2015 projected); Race: 80.8% White, 3.9% Black, 0.2% Asian, 15.1% Other, 24.0% Hispanic of any race (2010); Density: 4.4 persons per square mile (2010); Average household size: 2.32 (2010); Median age: 45.2 (2010); Males per 100 females: 95.4 (2010).

Religion: Five largest groups: 68.8% Southern Baptist Convention, 12.8% The United Methodist Church, 12.4% Catholic Church, 5.9% Churches of Christ, 5.4% International Church of the Foursquare Gospel (2000).

Economy: Unemployment rate: 7.3% (June 2011); Total civilian labor force: 2,011 (June 2011); Leading industries: 24.3% health care and social assistance; 8.5% finance & insurance; 7.7% other services (except public administration) (2009); Farms: 661 totaling 544,989 acres (2007); Companies that employ 500 or more persons: 0 (2009); Companies that employ 100 to 499 persons: 0 (2009); Companies that employ less than 100 persons: 63 (2009); Black-owned businesses: n/a (2007); Hispanic-owned businesses: n/a (2007); Asian-owned businesses: n/a (2007); Women-owned businesses: n/a (2007); Retail sales per capita: $3,605 (2010). Single-family building permits issued: 0 (2010); Multi-family building permits issued: 0 (2010).

Income: Per capita income: $19,616 (2010); Median household income: $35,057 (2010); Average household income: $45,915 (2010); Percent of households with income of $100,000 or more: 6.8% (2010); Poverty rate: 19.2% (2009); Bankruptcy rate: 1.50% (2010).

Taxes: Total county taxes per capita: $544 (2007); County property taxes per capita: $490 (2007).

Education: Percent of population age 25 and over with: High school diploma (including GED) or higher: 78.0% (2010); Bachelor's degree or higher: 13.8% (2010); Master's degree or higher: 3.3% (2010).

Housing: Homeownership rate: 75.0% (2010); Median home value: $40,864 (2010); Median contract rent: $236 per month (2005-2009 5-year est.); Median year structure built: 1959 (2005-2009 5-year est.).

Health: Birth rate: 100.9 per 10,000 population (2009); Death rate: 113.8 per 10,000 population (2009); Age-adjusted cancer mortality rate: 185.9 (Unreliable) deaths per 100,000 population (2007); Number of physicians: 10.2 per 10,000 population (2008); Hospital beds: 25.3 per 10,000 population (2007); Hospital admissions: 618.0 per 10,000 population (2007).

Elections: 2008 Presidential election results: 38.5% Obama, 60.7% McCain, 0.0% Nader

Additional Information Contacts

Fisher County Government . . . . (325) 776-2151
    http://www.co.fisher.tx.us/ips/cms

Fisher County Communities

MCCAULLEY (unincorporated postal area, zip code 79534). Covers a land area of 58.794 square miles and a water area of 0 square miles. Located at 32.76° N. Lat; 100.21° W. Long. Elevation is 1,883 feet.

Population: 220 (2000); Race: 97.2% White, 1.4% Black, 0.0% Asian, 1.4% Other, 4.6% Hispanic of any race (2000); Density: 3.7 persons per square mile (2000); Age: 25.0% under 18, 23.6% over 64 (2000); Marriage status: 14.7% never married, 74.1% now married, 5.3% widowed, 5.9% divorced (2000); Foreign born: 2.3% (2000); Ancestry (includes multiple ancestries): 14.8% American, 10.2% English, 9.7% Irish, 5.1% German (2000).

Economy: Employment by occupation: 21.7% management, 15.7% professional, 15.7% services, 9.6% sales, 3.6% farming, 15.7% construction, 18.1% production (2000).

Income: Per capita income: $12,855 (2000); Median household income: $26,719 (2000); Poverty rate: 179.1% (2000).

Education: Percent of population age 25 and over with: High school diploma (including GED) or higher: 76.2% (2000); Bachelor's degree or higher: 10.6% (2000).

Housing: Homeownership rate: 89.7% (2000); Median home value: $13,300 (2000); Median contract rent: $138 per month (2000); Median year structure built: 1958 (2000).

Transportation: Commute to work: 90.4% car, 0.0% public transportation, 0.0% walk, 7.2% work from home (2000); Travel time to work: 45.5% less than 15 minutes, 28.6% 15 to 30 minutes, 15.6% 30 to 45 minutes, 5.2% 45 to 60 minutes, 5.2% 60 minutes or more (2000)

ROBY (city). County seat. Covers a land area of 0.719 square miles and a water area of 0 square miles. Located at 32.74° N. Lat; 100.38° W. Long. Elevation is 1,962 feet.

Population: 616 (1990); 673 (2000); 604 (2010); 571 (2015 projected); Race: 84.9% White, 5.8% Black, 0.0% Asian, 9.3% Other, 21.4% Hispanic of any race (2010); Density: 840.1 persons per square mile (2010); Average household size: 2.36 (2010); Median age: 40.4 (2010); Males per 100 females: 86.4 (2010); Marriage status: 20.4% never married, 54.5% now married, 15.3% widowed, 9.8% divorced (2005-2009 5-year est.); Foreign born: 5.4% (2005-2009 5-year est.); Ancestry (includes multiple ancestries): 12.1% German, 9.8% American, 7.6% Irish, 3.8% English, 3.0% Dutch (2005-2009 5-year est.).

Economy: Employment by occupation: 12.0% management, 18.2% professional, 18.2% services, 10.2% sales, 8.0% farming, 18.9% construction, 14.5% production (2005-2009 5-year est.).
Income: Per capita income: $19,844 (2010); Median household income: $38,649 (2010); Average household income: $48,135 (2010); Percent of households with income of $100,000 or more: 6.9% (2010); Poverty rate: 14.4% (2005-2009 5-year est.).
Taxes: Total city taxes per capita: $199 (2007); City property taxes per capita: $94 (2007).
Education: Percent of population age 25 and over with: High school diploma (including GED) or higher: 82.3% (2010); Bachelor's degree or higher: 11.4% (2010); Master's degree or higher: 1.2% (2010).

School District(s)

Roby CISD (PK-12)
　　2009-10 Enrollment: 303 . . . . (325) 776-2222
Housing: Homeownership rate: 74.6% (2010); Median home value: $41,316 (2010); Median contract rent: $208 per month (2005-2009 5-year est.); Median year structure built: 1954 (2005-2009 5-year est.).
Transportation: Commute to work: 91.6% car, 0.0% public transportation, 8.4% walk, 0.0% work from home (2005-2009 5-year est.); Travel time to work: 57.8% less than 15 minutes, 25.9% 15 to 30 minutes, 12.4% 30 to 45 minutes, 1.2% 45 to 60 minutes, 2.8% 60 minutes or more (2005-2009 5-year est.)

ROTAN (city). Covers a land area of 2.036 square miles and a water area of 0 square miles. Located at 32.85° N. Lat; 100.46° W. Long. Elevation is 1,949 feet.

History: Incorporated 1908.
Population: 1,913 (1990); 1,611 (2000); 1,467 (2010); 1,395 (2015 projected); Race: 68.6% White, 6.8% Black, 0.3% Asian, 24.3% Other, 36.4% Hispanic of any race (2010); Density: 720.5 persons per square mile (2010); Average household size: 2.28 (2010); Median age: 43.3 (2010); Males per 100 females: 89.8 (2010); Marriage status: 17.6% never married, 63.2% now married, 8.8% widowed, 10.4% divorced (2005-2009 5-year est.); Foreign born: 3.7% (2005-2009 5-year est.); Ancestry (includes multiple ancestries): 15.9% German, 12.8% American, 10.0% Irish, 4.9% English, 2.8% French (2005-2009 5-year est.).
Economy: Single-family building permits issued: 0 (2010); Multi-family building permits issued: 0 (2010); Employment by occupation: 9.4% management, 21.3% professional, 18.1% services, 14.8% sales, 6.1% farming, 13.8% construction, 16.3% production (2005-2009 5-year est.).
Income: Per capita income: $15,200 (2010); Median household income: $25,108 (2010); Average household income: $34,924 (2010); Percent of households with income of $100,000 or more: 3.0% (2010); Poverty rate: 24.1% (2005-2009 5-year est.).
Taxes: Total city taxes per capita: $127 (2007); City property taxes per capita: $66 (2007).
Education: Percent of population age 25 and over with: High school diploma (including GED) or higher: 70.9% (2010); Bachelor's degree or higher: 11.9% (2010); Master's degree or higher: 2.7% (2010).

School District(s)

Blackwell CISD (PK-12)
　　2009-10 Enrollment: 164 . . . . (325) 282-2311
Highland ISD (PK-12)
　　2009-10 Enrollment: 227 . . . . (325) 766-3652
Roby CISD (PK-12)
　　2009-10 Enrollment: 303 . . . . (325) 776-2222
Roscoe ISD (PK-12)
　　2009-10 Enrollment: 365 . . . . (325) 766-3629
Rotan ISD (PK-12)
　　2009-10 Enrollment: 338 . . . . (325) 735-2332
Sweetwater ISD (PK-12)
　　2009-10 Enrollment: 2,320 . . . . (325) 235-8601
Trent ISD (PK-12)
　　2009-10 Enrollment: 198 . . . . (325) 862-6400
Housing: Homeownership rate: 65.7% (2010); Median home value: $32,177 (2010); Median contract rent: $233 per month (2005-2009 5-year est.); Median year structure built: 1958 (2005-2009 5-year est.).
Hospitals: Fisher County Hospital (30 beds)
Transportation: Commute to work: 93.9% car, 0.0% public transportation, 1.4% walk, 1.9% work from home (2005-2009 5-year est.); Travel time to work: 65.3% less than 15 minutes, 10.8% 15 to 30 minutes, 9.7% 30 to 45 minutes, 2.7% 45 to 60 minutes, 11.6% 60 minutes or more (2005-2009 5-year est.)

SYLVESTER (unincorporated postal area, zip code 79560). Covers a land area of 76.979 square miles and a water area of 0.014 square miles. Located at 32.68° N. Lat; 100.20° W. Long. Elevation is 1,854 feet.

Population: 185 (2000); Race: 97.3% White, 0.0% Black, 0.0% Asian, 2.7% Other, 3.3% Hispanic of any race (2000); Density: 2.4 persons per square mile (2000); Age: 24.0% under 18, 27.9% over 64 (2000); Marriage status: 14.3% never married, 61.0% now married, 14.9% widowed, 9.7% divorced (2000); Foreign born: 0.0% (2000); Ancestry (includes multiple ancestries): 19.7% German, 13.1% American, 13.1% Irish, 4.9% Scotch-Irish (2000).
Economy: Employment by occupation: 15.0% management, 16.7% professional, 11.7% services, 20.0% sales, 1.7% farming, 10.0% construction, 25.0% production (2000).
Income: Per capita income: $16,701 (2000); Median household income: $28,750 (2000); Poverty rate: 179.1% (2000).
Education: Percent of population age 25 and over with: High school diploma (including GED) or higher: 70.4% (2000); Bachelor's degree or higher: 20.8% (2000).
Housing: Homeownership rate: 82.4% (2000); Median home value: $22,900 (2000); Median contract rent: $185 per month (2000); Median year structure built: 1954 (2000).
Transportation: Commute to work: 90.0% car, 0.0% public transportation, 3.3% walk, 5.0% work from home (2000); Travel time to work: 17.5% less than 15 minutes, 42.1% 15 to 30 minutes, 15.8% 30 to 45 minutes, 8.8% 45 to 60 minutes, 15.8% 60 minutes or more (2000)

Floyd County

Located in northwestern Texas; drained by the White River. Covers a land area of 992.19 square miles, a water area of 0.32 square miles, and is located in the Central Time Zone at 34.10° N. Lat., 101.34° W. Long. The county was founded in 1876. County seat is Floydada.

Weather Station: Floydada										Elevation: 3,219 feet		
	Jan	Feb	Mar	Apr	May	Jun	Jul	Aug	Sep	Oct	Nov	Dec
High	51	56	64	73	81	89	93	91	83	73	61	51
Low	25	28	35	43	54	63	67	66	58	47	35	26
Precip	0.6	0.7	1.2	1.5	2.9	3.7	1.9	2.3	2.9	1.7	0.9	0.7
Snow	2.2	1.5	0.4	0.2	0.0	0.0	0.0	0.0	0.0	tr	1.4	1.6

High and Low temperatures in degrees Fahrenheit; Precipitation and Snow in inches

Population: 8,497 (1990); 7,771 (2000); 6,719 (2010); 6,196 (2015 projected); Race: 70.7% White, 4.5% Black, 0.2% Asian, 24.6% Other, 50.3% Hispanic of any race (2010); Density: 6.8 persons per square mile (2010); Average household size: 2.79 (2010); Median age: 39.3 (2010); Males per 100 females: 94.2 (2010).
Religion: Five largest groups: 41.3% Southern Baptist Convention, 14.7% Catholic Church, 14.2% The United Methodist Church, 6.0% Churches of Christ, 3.3% Assemblies of God (2000).
Economy: Unemployment rate: 9.2% (June 2011); Total civilian labor force: 3,032 (June 2011); Leading industries: 14.0% wholesale trade; 12.0% retail trade; 6.2% other services (except public administration) (2009); Farms: 650 totaling 627,686 acres (2007); Companies that employ 500 or more persons: 0 (2009); Companies that employ 100 to 499 persons: 1 (2009); Companies that employ less than 100 persons: 159 (2009); Black-owned businesses: n/a (2007); Hispanic-owned businesses: n/a (2007); Asian-owned businesses: n/a (2007); Women-owned businesses: 86 (2007); Retail sales per capita: $10,257 (2010). Single-family building permits issued: 0 (2010); Multi-family building permits issued: 0 (2010).
Income: Per capita income: $16,618 (2010); Median household income: $32,137 (2010); Average household income: $46,759 (2010); Percent of households with income of $100,000 or more: 9.9% (2010); Poverty rate: 23.2% (2009); Bankruptcy rate: 0.31% (2010).
Taxes: Total county taxes per capita: $263 (2007); County property taxes per capita: $189 (2007).
Education: Percent of population age 25 and over with: High school diploma (including GED) or higher: 69.4% (2010); Bachelor's degree or higher: 14.1% (2010); Master's degree or higher: 2.3% (2010).
Housing: Homeownership rate: 71.9% (2010); Median home value: $51,229 (2010); Median contract rent: $294 per month (2005-2009 5-year est.); Median year structure built: 1955 (2005-2009 5-year est.)
Health: Birth rate: 142.1 per 10,000 population (2009); Death rate: 89.6 per 10,000 population (2009); Age-adjusted cancer mortality rate: 204.6 (Unreliable) deaths per 100,000 population (2007); Number of physicians:

10.8 per 10,000 population (2008); Hospital beds: 37.7 per 10,000 population (2007); Hospital admissions: 772.6 per 10,000 population (2007).
Elections: 2008 Presidential election results: 29.0% Obama, 70.8% McCain, 0.0% Nader
Additional Information Contacts
Floyd County Government . . . . (806) 983-2244

Floydada Chamber of Commerce . . . . (806) 983-3434
    http://www.floydadachamber.com

Floyd County Communities

FLOYDADA (city). County seat. Covers a land area of 2.030 square miles and a water area of 0 square miles. Located at 33.98° N. Lat; 101.33° W. Long. Elevation is 3,182 feet.
History: Floydada, as well as Floyd County, were named for a defender of the Alamo. The town grew as the center of a large agricultural area, with grain elevators to store the wheat produced in the vicinity.
Population: 3,897 (1990); 3,676 (2000); 3,234 (2010); 2,996 (2015 projected); Race: 68.3% White, 4.3% Black, 0.2% Asian, 27.2% Other, 55.7% Hispanic of any race (2010); Density: 1,593.0 persons per square mile (2010); Average household size: 2.76 (2010); Median age: 38.4 (2010); Males per 100 females: 91.7 (2010); Marriage status: 14.7% never married, 71.3% now married, 8.0% widowed, 5.9% divorced (2005-2009 5-year est.); Foreign born: 0.8% (2005-2009 5-year est.); Ancestry (includes multiple ancestries): 6.3% German, 5.8% Irish, 5.3% English, 5.2% American, 2.4% African (2005-2009 5-year est.).
Economy: Single-family building permits issued: 0 (2010); Multi-family building permits issued: 0 (2010); Employment by occupation: 8.3% management, 12.2% professional, 19.2% services, 23.9% sales, 15.4% farming, 8.3% construction, 12.8% production (2005-2009 5-year est.).
Income: Per capita income: $14,756 (2010); Median household income: $28,769 (2010); Average household income: $41,181 (2010); Percent of households with income of $100,000 or more: 7.6% (2010); Poverty rate: 31.5% (2005-2009 5-year est.).
Taxes: Total city taxes per capita: $120 (2007); City property taxes per capita: $78 (2007).
Education: Percent of population age 25 and over with: High school diploma (including GED) or higher: 65.1% (2010); Bachelor's degree or higher: 12.7% (2010); Master's degree or higher: 2.1% (2010).
School District(s)
Floydada ISD (PK-12)
    2009-10 Enrollment: 881 . . . . (806) 983-3498
Housing: Homeownership rate: 73.4% (2010); Median home value: $41,399 (2010); Median contract rent: $280 per month (2005-2009 5-year est.); Median year structure built: 1956 (2005-2009 5-year est.).
Safety: Violent crime rate: 56.7 per 10,000 population; Property crime rate: 340.1 per 10,000 population (2009).
Newspapers: Floyd County Hesperian-Beacon (Community news; Circulation 2,600)
Transportation: Commute to work: 94.9% car, 0.0% public transportation, 3.3% walk, 1.9% work from home (2005-2009 5-year est.); Travel time to work: 68.3% less than 15 minutes, 9.2% 15 to 30 minutes, 11.3% 30 to 45 minutes, 4.2% 45 to 60 minutes, 7.0% 60 minutes or more (2005-2009 5-year est.)
Additional Information Contacts
Floydada Chamber of Commerce . . . . (806) 983-3434
    http://www.floydadachamber.com

LOCKNEY (town). Covers a land area of 1.550 square miles and a water area of 0 square miles. Located at 34.12° N. Lat; 101.44° W. Long. Elevation is 3,278 feet.
History: Settled 1894, incorporated 1907.
Population: 2,207 (1990); 2,056 (2000); 1,720 (2010); 1,565 (2015 projected); Race: 71.4% White, 2.8% Black, 0.1% Asian, 25.7% Other, 56.2% Hispanic of any race (2010); Density: 1,109.5 persons per square mile (2010); Average household size: 2.90 (2010); Median age: 37.2 (2010); Males per 100 females: 89.8 (2010); Marriage status: 14.8% never married, 74.0% now married, 6.4% widowed, 4.9% divorced (2005-2009 5-year est.); Foreign born: 9.2% (2005-2009 5-year est.); Ancestry (includes multiple ancestries): 9.5% English, 9.1% Irish, 8.3% German, 2.2% Dutch, 1.9% African (2005-2009 5-year est.).
Economy: Single-family building permits issued: 0 (2010); Multi-family building permits issued: 0 (2010); Employment by occupation: 8.8%

management, 16.2% professional, 12.6% services, 22.9% sales, 6.2% farming, 15.5% construction, 17.7% production (2005-2009 5-year est.).
Income: Per capita income: $16,942 (2010); Median household income: $36,238 (2010); Average household income: $49,402 (2010); Percent of households with income of $100,000 or more: 10.0% (2010); Poverty rate: 16.6% (2005-2009 5-year est.).
Taxes: Total city taxes per capita: $127 (2007); City property taxes per capita: $92 (2007).
Education: Percent of population age 25 and over with: High school diploma (including GED) or higher: 68.4% (2010); Bachelor's degree or higher: 13.1% (2010); Master's degree or higher: 2.8% (2010).
School District(s)
Lockney ISD (PK-12)
    2009-10 Enrollment: 552 . . . . (806) 652-2115
Housing: Homeownership rate: 73.7% (2010); Median home value: $52,346 (2010); Median contract rent: $241 per month (2005-2009 5-year est.); Median year structure built: 1953 (2005-2009 5-year est.).
Hospitals: WJ Mangold Memorial Hospital (27 beds)
Safety: Violent crime rate: 18.4 per 10,000 population; Property crime rate: 269.8 per 10,000 population (2009).
Transportation: Commute to work: 93.8% car, 0.0% public transportation, 4.2% walk, 2.0% work from home (2005-2009 5-year est.); Travel time to work: 44.2% less than 15 minutes, 29.8% 15 to 30 minutes, 16.7% 30 to 45 minutes, 0.1% 45 to 60 minutes, 9.2% 60 minutes or more (2005-2009 5-year est.)

Foard County

Located in north Texas; bounded on the north by the Pease River, and on the south by the Wichita River. Covers a land area of 706.68 square miles, a water area of 1.01 square miles, and is located in the Central Time Zone at 33.98° N. Lat., 99.75° W. Long. The county was founded in 1891. County seat is Crowell.
Population: 1,794 (1990); 1,622 (2000); 1,373 (2010); 1,249 (2015 projected); Race: 81.6% White, 4.3% Black, 0.1% Asian, 13.9% Other, 17.8% Hispanic of any race (2010); Density: 1.9 persons per square mile (2010); Average household size: 2.38 (2010); Median age: 45.0 (2010); Males per 100 females: 93.7 (2010).
Religion: Five largest groups: 40.8% Southern Baptist Convention, 22.1% The United Methodist Church, 9.6% Christian Churches and Churches of Christ, 7.7% Churches of Christ, 6.0% Catholic Church (2000).
Economy: Unemployment rate: 7.9% (June 2011); Total civilian labor force: 721 (June 2011); Leading industries: 28.5% health care and social assistance; 16.6% other services (except public administration) (2009); Farms: 212 totaling 375,790 acres (2007); Companies that employ 500 or more persons: 0 (2009); Companies that employ 100 to 499 persons: 0 (2009); Companies that employ less than 100 persons: 33 (2009); Black-owned businesses: n/a (2007); Hispanic-owned businesses: n/a (2007); Asian-owned businesses: n/a (2007); Women-owned businesses: n/a (2007); Retail sales per capita: $5,537 (2010). Single-family building permits issued: n/a (2010); Multi-family building permits issued: n/a (2010).
Income: Per capita income: $16,553 (2010); Median household income: $29,539 (2010); Average household income: $39,783 (2010); Percent of households with income of $100,000 or more: 5.1% (2010); Poverty rate: 19.9% (2009); Bankruptcy rate: 1.51% (2010).
Taxes: Total county taxes per capita: $460 (2007); County property taxes per capita: $410 (2007).
Education: Percent of population age 25 and over with: High school diploma (including GED) or higher: 75.2% (2010); Bachelor's degree or higher: 11.8% (2010); Master's degree or higher: 3.2% (2010).
Housing: Homeownership rate: 73.3% (2010); Median home value: $34,783 (2010); Median contract rent: $195 per month (2005-2009 5-year est.); Median year structure built: 1953 (2005-2009 5-year est.)
Health: Birth rate: 90.0 per 10,000 population (2009); Death rate: 75.0 per 10,000 population (2009); Age-adjusted cancer mortality rate: Suppressed deaths per 100,000 population (2007); Number of physicians: 0.0 per 10,000 population (2008); Hospital beds: 0.0 per 10,000 population (2007); Hospital admissions: 0.0 per 10,000 population (2007).
Elections: 2008 Presidential election results: 36.8% Obama, 60.8% McCain, 0.0% Nader
Additional Information Contacts
Foard County Government . . . . (940) 684-1424

Crowell Chamber of Commerce . . . . (940) 684-1310
    http://www.crowelltex.com

Foard County Communities

CROWELL (city). County seat. Covers a land area of 1.887 square miles and a water area of 0 square miles. Located at 33.98° N. Lat; 99.72° W. Long. Elevation is 1,473 feet.

History: Settled 1887, incorporated 1908; rebuilt after destructive tornado in 1942.

Population: 1,230 (1990); 1,141 (2000); 950 (2010); 860 (2015 projected); Race: 79.4% White, 3.2% Black, 0.0% Asian, 17.5% Other, 20.6% Hispanic of any race (2010); Density: 503.4 persons per square mile (2010); Average household size: 2.34 (2010); Median age: 43.5 (2010); Males per 100 females: 92.7 (2010); Marriage status: 27.7% never married, 52.0% now married, 14.2% widowed, 6.1% divorced (2005-2009 5-year est.); Foreign born: 3.9% (2005-2009 5-year est.); Ancestry (includes multiple ancestries): 14.8% German, 14.4% Irish, 13.7% American, 7.4% Dutch, 4.8% English (2005-2009 5-year est.).

Economy: Employment by occupation: 14.5% management, 8.3% professional, 27.1% services, 15.1% sales, 9.1% farming, 8.3% construction, 17.8% production (2005-2009 5-year est.).

Income: Per capita income: $14,111 (2010); Median household income: $25,877 (2010); Average household income: $33,204 (2010); Percent of households with income of $100,000 or more: 2.5% (2010); Poverty rate: 32.5% (2005-2009 5-year est.).

Taxes: Total city taxes per capita: $216 (2007); City property taxes per capita: $87 (2007).

Education: Percent of population age 25 and over with: High school diploma (including GED) or higher: 71.7% (2010); Bachelor's degree or higher: 10.5% (2010); Master's degree or higher: 3.6% (2010).

School District(s)

Crowell ISD (PK-12)
  2009-10 Enrollment: 217 . . . . (940) 684-1403

Housing: Homeownership rate: 70.6% (2010); Median home value: $32,143 (2010); Median contract rent: $191 per month (2005-2009 5-year est.); Median year structure built: 1954 (2005-2009 5-year est.).

Safety: Violent crime rate: 0.0 per 10,000 population; Property crime rate: 10.7 per 10,000 population (2009).

Newspapers: Foard County News (Community news; Circulation 1,100)

Transportation: Commute to work: 90.1% car, 0.0% public transportation, 7.8% walk, 2.1% work from home (2005-2009 5-year est.); Travel time to work: 72.0% less than 15 minutes, 5.2% 15 to 30 minutes, 19.0% 30 to 45 minutes, 1.1% 45 to 60 minutes, 2.8% 60 minutes or more (2005-2009 5-year est.)

Additional Information Contacts
Crowell Chamber of Commerce . . . . (940) 684-1310
  http://www.crowelltex.com

Fort Bend County

Located in south Texas; drained by the Brazos and San Bernard Rivers. Covers a land area of 874.64 square miles, a water area of 11.41 square miles, and is located in the Central Time Zone at 29.57° N. Lat., 95.69° W. Long. The county was founded in 1837. County seat is Richmond.

Fort Bend County is part of the Houston-Sugar Land-Baytown, TX Metropolitan Statistical Area. The entire metro area includes: Austin County, TX; Brazoria County, TX; Chambers County, TX; Fort Bend County, TX; Galveston County, TX; Harris County, TX; Liberty County, TX; Montgomery County, TX; San Jacinto County, TX; Waller County, TX

Weather Station: Sugar Land										Elevation: 82 feet		
	Jan	Feb	Mar	Apr	May	Jun	Jul	Aug	Sep	Oct	Nov	Dec
High	63	66	73	79	86	91	94	94	90	82	72	64
Low	43	46	52	59	67	73	75	75	70	61	51	44
Precip	3.8	3.0	3.6	3.4	4.5	5.6	3.7	4.3	4.8	5.0	4.4	3.2
Snow	tr	tr	tr	0.0	0.0	0.0	0.0	0.0	0.0	0.0	0.0	tr

High and Low temperatures in degrees Fahrenheit; Precipitation and Snow in inches

Weather Station: Thompsons 3 WSW										Elevation: 71 feet		
	Jan	Feb	Mar	Apr	May	Jun	Jul	Aug	Sep	Oct	Nov	Dec
High	64	67	73	80	87	92	94	95	90	83	74	65
Low	44	47	53	59	67	72	74	74	69	60	53	45
Precip	4.0	2.8	3.4	3.4	4.0	4.8	3.9	4.4	4.5	4.8	4.3	3.6
Snow	tr	tr	0.0	0.0	0.0	0.0	0.0	0.0	0.0	0.0	0.0	0.1

High and Low temperatures in degrees Fahrenheit; Precipitation and Snow in inches

Population: 225,421 (1990); 354,452 (2000); 564,152 (2010); 665,167 (2015 projected); Race: 50.7% White, 20.4% Black, 14.7% Asian, 14.2% Other, 24.1% Hispanic of any race (2010); Density: 645.0 persons per square mile (2010); Average household size: 3.13 (2010); Median age: 33.4 (2010); Males per 100 females: 98.6 (2010).

Religion: Five largest groups: 24.8% Catholic Church, 8.7% Southern Baptist Convention, 4.4% The United Methodist Church, 1.0% Churches of Christ, 0.8% The Church of Jesus Christ of Latter-day Saints (2000).

Economy: Unemployment rate: 8.2% (June 2011); Total civilian labor force: 286,629 (June 2011); Leading industries: 18.9% retail trade; 12.7% accommodation & food services; 11.8% health care and social assistance (2009); Farms: 1,404 totaling 382,740 acres (2007); Companies that employ 500 or more persons: 8 (2009); Companies that employ 100 to 499 persons: 180 (2009); Companies that employ less than 100 persons: 8,744 (2009); Black-owned businesses: 8,339 (2007); Hispanic-owned businesses: 8,039 (2007); Asian-owned businesses: 8,295 (2007); Women-owned businesses: 16,125 (2007); Retail sales per capita: $10,977 (2010). Single-family building permits issued: 4,724 (2010); Multi-family building permits issued: 230 (2010).

Income: Per capita income: $32,647 (2010); Median household income: $80,993 (2010); Average household income: $102,833 (2010); Percent of households with income of $100,000 or more: 38.2% (2010); Poverty rate: 7.5% (2009); Bankruptcy rate: 2.30% (2010).

Taxes: Total county taxes per capita: $275 (2007); County property taxes per capita: $275 (2007).

Education: Percent of population age 25 and over with: High school diploma (including GED) or higher: 87.4% (2010); Bachelor's degree or higher: 39.6% (2010); Master's degree or higher: 12.9% (2010).

Housing: Homeownership rate: 81.3% (2010); Median home value: $166,139 (2010); Median contract rent: $824 per month (2005-2009 5-year est.); Median year structure built: 1993 (2005-2009 5-year est.)

Health: Birth rate: 143.1 per 10,000 population (2009); Death rate: 39.2 per 10,000 population (2009); Age-adjusted cancer mortality rate: 147.2 deaths per 100,000 population (2007); Number of physicians: 20.6 per 10,000 population (2008); Hospital beds: 12.0 per 10,000 population (2007); Hospital admissions: 461.9 per 10,000 population (2007).

Elections: 2008 Presidential election results: 48.5% Obama, 50.9% McCain, 0.1% Nader

Additional Information Contacts
Fort Bend County Government . . . . (281) 342-3411
  http://www.co.fort-bend.tx.us
Central Fort Bend Chamber Alliance . . . . (281) 342-5464
  http://www.roserichchamber.org
City of Missouri City . . . . (281) 403-8500
  http://www.missouricitytx.gov
City of Richmond . . . . (281) 342-5456
  http://www.ci.richmond.tx.us
City of Rosenberg . . . . (832) 595-3300
  http://www.ci.rosenberg.tx.us
City of Stafford . . . . (281) 261-3900
  http://www.cityofstafford.com
City of Sugar Land . . . . (281) 275-2700
  http://www.sugarlandtx.gov
Fort Bend Chamber of Commerce . . . . (281) 491-0800
  http://www.fortbendchamber.org
Needville Area Chamber of Commerce . . . . (979) 793-5700
  http://www.needville.org

Fort Bend County Communities

ARCOLA (city). Covers a land area of 1.911 square miles and a water area of 0 square miles. Located at 29.50° N. Lat; 95.46° W. Long. Elevation is 66 feet.

Population: 666 (1990); 1,048 (2000); 1,997 (2010); 2,422 (2015 projected); Race: 55.6% White, 18.6% Black, 9.5% Asian, 16.3% Other, 32.9% Hispanic of any race (2010); Density: 1,045.2 persons per square mile (2010); Average household size: 3.37 (2010); Median age: 32.7 (2010); Males per 100 females: 100.1 (2010); Marriage status: 38.4% never married, 54.4% now married, 3.3% widowed, 4.0% divorced (2005-2009 5-year est.); Foreign born: 26.9% (2005-2009 5-year est.); Ancestry (includes multiple ancestries): 3.2% American, 2.7% Irish, 2.6% English, 2.1% French, 1.2% Haitian (2005-2009 5-year est.).

Economy: Employment by occupation: 4.4% management, 5.6% professional, 25.1% services, 27.7% sales, 0.4% farming, 31.3% construction, 5.6% production (2005-2009 5-year est.).

Income: Per capita income: $37,959 (2010); Median household income: $96,914 (2010); Average household income: $127,538 (2010); Percent of households with income of $100,000 or more: 48.3% (2010); Poverty rate: 18.1% (2005-2009 5-year est.).
Taxes: Total city taxes per capita: $600 (2007); City property taxes per capita: $269 (2007).
Education: Percent of population age 25 and over with: High school diploma (including GED) or higher: 84.8% (2010); Bachelor's degree or higher: 36.7% (2010); Master's degree or higher: 12.3% (2010).
Housing: Homeownership rate: 89.9% (2010); Median home value: $221,538 (2010); Median contract rent: $467 per month (2005-2009 5-year est.); Median year structure built: 1992 (2005-2009 5-year est.).
Safety: Violent crime rate: 79.9 per 10,000 population; Property crime rate: 303.8 per 10,000 population (2009).
Transportation: Commute to work: 94.8% car, 0.0% public transportation, 1.9% walk, 3.3% work from home (2005-2009 5-year est.); Travel time to work: 19.6% less than 15 minutes, 24.9% 15 to 30 minutes, 42.1% 30 to 45 minutes, 6.3% 45 to 60 minutes, 7.1% 60 minutes or more (2005-2009 5-year est.)

BEASLEY (city). Covers a land area of 1.004 square miles and a water area of 0 square miles. Located at 29.49° N. Lat; 95.91° W. Long. Elevation is 108 feet.

Population: 515 (1990); 590 (2000); 719 (2010); 840 (2015 projected); Race: 73.4% White, 6.4% Black, 0.6% Asian, 19.6% Other, 50.3% Hispanic of any race (2010); Density: 716.5 persons per square mile (2010); Average household size: 3.11 (2010); Median age: 32.0 (2010); Males per 100 females: 102.0 (2010); Marriage status: 29.9% never married, 50.5% now married, 6.5% widowed, 13.0% divorced (2005-2009 5-year est.); Foreign born: 7.5% (2005-2009 5-year est.); Ancestry (includes multiple ancestries): 23.3% German, 16.1% Czech, 10.8% Irish, 6.3% Polish, 4.1% Italian (2005-2009 5-year est.).
Economy: Single-family building permits issued: 0 (2010); Multi-family building permits issued: 0 (2010); Employment by occupation: 11.8% management, 11.4% professional, 24.0% services, 23.6% sales, 0.0% farming, 8.9% construction, 20.3% production (2005-2009 5-year est.).
Income: Per capita income: $19,135 (2010); Median household income: $52,664 (2010); Average household income: $59,610 (2010); Percent of households with income of $100,000 or more: 13.4% (2010); Poverty rate: 2.7% (2005-2009 5-year est.).
Taxes: Total city taxes per capita: $139 (2007); City property taxes per capita: $82 (2007).
Education: Percent of population age 25 and over with: High school diploma (including GED) or higher: 71.3% (2010); Bachelor's degree or higher: 7.7% (2010); Master's degree or higher: 1.4% (2010).

School District(s)

Lamar CISD (PK-12)
    2009-10 Enrollment: 23,864 . . . . (832) 223-0000
Housing: Homeownership rate: 77.1% (2010); Median home value: $85,556 (2010); Median contract rent: $522 per month (2005-2009 5-year est.); Median year structure built: 1978 (2005-2009 5-year est.).
Transportation: Commute to work: 92.6% car, 0.0% public transportation, 0.0% walk, 3.7% work from home (2005-2009 5-year est.); Travel time to work: 10.7% less than 15 minutes, 37.9% 15 to 30 minutes, 19.2% 30 to 45 minutes, 24.9% 45 to 60 minutes, 7.3% 60 minutes or more (2005-2009 5-year est.)

CINCO RANCH (CDP). Covers a land area of 4.932 square miles and a water area of 0 square miles. Located at 29.74° N. Lat; 95.75° W. Long. Elevation is 112 feet.

History: The Cinco Ranch community goes back to before Texas became a republic. In the 1820s, pioneer Moses Austin was granted by the Spanish government the authority to settle 300 families in the valleys of the Brazos and Colorado rivers.
Population: 1,433 (1990); 11,196 (2000); 21,128 (2010); 25,653 (2015 projected); Race: 82.4% White, 2.8% Black, 10.8% Asian, 3.9% Other, 7.1% Hispanic of any race (2010); Density: 4,283.8 persons per square mile (2010); Average household size: 3.40 (2010); Median age: 32.3 (2010); Males per 100 females: 97.8 (2010); Marriage status: 23.7% never married, 68.7% now married, 2.2% widowed, 5.5% divorced (2005-2009 5-year est.); Foreign born: 20.1% (2005-2009 5-year est.); Ancestry (includes multiple ancestries): 13.4% German, 12.8% English, 11.6% Irish, 8.0% American, 5.7% Italian (2005-2009 5-year est.).

Economy: Employment by occupation: 32.0% management, 32.1% professional, 7.3% services, 24.1% sales, 0.0% farming, 1.2% construction, 3.3% production (2005-2009 5-year est.).
Income: Per capita income: $49,453 (2010); Median household income: $138,202 (2010); Average household income: $168,086 (2010); Percent of households with income of $100,000 or more: 73.4% (2010); Poverty rate: 2.6% (2005-2009 5-year est.).
Education: Percent of population age 25 and over with: High school diploma (including GED) or higher: 98.4% (2010); Bachelor's degree or higher: 66.2% (2010); Master's degree or higher: 21.5% (2010).
Housing: Homeownership rate: 94.2% (2010); Median home value: $274,100 (2010); Median contract rent: $940 per month (2005-2009 5-year est.); Median year structure built: 1997 (2005-2009 5-year est.).
Transportation: Commute to work: 90.0% car, 4.1% public transportation, 0.7% walk, 4.7% work from home (2005-2009 5-year est.); Travel time to work: 17.6% less than 15 minutes, 24.8% 15 to 30 minutes, 28.0% 30 to 45 minutes, 15.3% 45 to 60 minutes, 14.3% 60 minutes or more (2005-2009 5-year est.)

CUMINGS (CDP). Covers a land area of 3.027 square miles and a water area of 0.074 square miles. Located at 29.57° N. Lat; 95.80° W. Long. Elevation is 85 feet.

Population: 385 (1990); 683 (2000); 889 (2010); 1,063 (2015 projected); Race: 77.1% White, 0.6% Black, 0.9% Asian, 21.5% Other, 66.8% Hispanic of any race (2010); Density: 293.6 persons per square mile (2010); Average household size: 3.26 (2010); Median age: 32.9 (2010); Males per 100 females: 95.0 (2010); Marriage status: 45.4% never married, 47.4% now married, 1.3% widowed, 5.8% divorced (2005-2009 5-year est.); Foreign born: 14.8% (2005-2009 5-year est.); Ancestry (includes multiple ancestries): 1.2% American (2005-2009 5-year est.).
Economy: Employment by occupation: 0.0% management, 13.8% professional, 20.9% services, 32.0% sales, 0.0% farming, 21.3% construction, 12.0% production (2005-2009 5-year est.).
Income: Per capita income: $32,615 (2010); Median household income: $73,491 (2010); Average household income: $105,614 (2010); Percent of households with income of $100,000 or more: 35.9% (2010); Poverty rate: 31.3% (2005-2009 5-year est.).
Education: Percent of population age 25 and over with: High school diploma (including GED) or higher: 75.8% (2010); Bachelor's degree or higher: 33.3% (2010); Master's degree or higher: 8.7% (2010).
Housing: Homeownership rate: 86.4% (2010); Median home value: $160,000 (2010); Median contract rent: $553 per month (2005-2009 5-year est.); Median year structure built: 1993 (2005-2009 5-year est.).
Transportation: Commute to work: 100.0% car, 0.0% public transportation, 0.0% walk, 0.0% work from home (2005-2009 5-year est.); Travel time to work: 23.6% less than 15 minutes, 37.3% 15 to 30 minutes, 16.4% 30 to 45 minutes, 18.2% 45 to 60 minutes, 4.4% 60 minutes or more (2005-2009 5-year est.)

FAIRCHILDS (village). Covers a land area of 2.215 square miles and a water area of 0 square miles. Located at 29.44° N. Lat; 95.77° W. Long. Elevation is 79 feet.

Population: 505 (1990); 678 (2000); 907 (2010); 1,074 (2015 projected); Race: 74.5% White, 3.3% Black, 0.7% Asian, 21.5% Other, 38.5% Hispanic of any race (2010); Density: 409.6 persons per square mile (2010); Average household size: 3.05 (2010); Median age: 34.2 (2010); Males per 100 females: 102.9 (2010); Marriage status: 22.4% never married, 60.6% now married, 8.2% widowed, 8.9% divorced (2005-2009 5-year est.); Foreign born: 7.4% (2005-2009 5-year est.); Ancestry (includes multiple ancestries): 23.3% German, 22.9% Czech, 5.8% English, 4.9% Irish, 2.5% Polish (2005-2009 5-year est.).
Economy: Employment by occupation: 10.5% management, 9.4% professional, 11.7% services, 25.4% sales, 0.0% farming, 15.2% construction, 27.7% production (2005-2009 5-year est.).
Income: Per capita income: $23,116 (2010); Median household income: $61,581 (2010); Average household income: $70,471 (2010); Percent of households with income of $100,000 or more: 19.9% (2010); Poverty rate: 6.3% (2005-2009 5-year est.).
Taxes: Total city taxes per capita: $356 (2007); City property taxes per capita: $194 (2007).
Education: Percent of population age 25 and over with: High school diploma (including GED) or higher: 82.0% (2010); Bachelor's degree or higher: 11.6% (2010); Master's degree or higher: 4.0% (2010).

Housing: Homeownership rate: 81.8% (2010); Median home value: $109,539 (2010); Median contract rent: $621 per month (2005-2009 5-year est.); Median year structure built: 1993 (2005-2009 5-year est.).
Transportation: Commute to work: 96.1% car, 0.0% public transportation, 0.0% walk, 2.0% work from home (2005-2009 5-year est.); Travel time to work: 15.5% less than 15 minutes, 29.5% 15 to 30 minutes, 35.1% 30 to 45 minutes, 8.8% 45 to 60 minutes, 11.2% 60 minutes or more (2005-2009 5-year est.)

FIFTH STREET (CDP).
Covers a land area of 0.812 square miles and a water area of 0 square miles. Located at 29.59° N. Lat; 95.54° W. Long. Elevation is 75 feet.
Population: 1,599 (1990); 2,059 (2000); 2,118 (2010); 2,458 (2015 projected); Race: 41.2% White, 19.1% Black, 0.7% Asian, 39.0% Other, 66.8% Hispanic of any race (2010); Density: 2,609.5 persons per square mile (2010); Average household size: 3.32 (2010); Median age: 32.3 (2010); Males per 100 females: 112.7 (2010); Marriage status: 37.6% never married, 52.7% now married, 0.6% widowed, 9.1% divorced (2005-2009 5-year est.); Foreign born: 34.7% (2005-2009 5-year est.); Ancestry (includes multiple ancestries): 9.8% German, 4.7% Irish, 4.3% American, 1.8% Czech, 1.3% French (2005-2009 5-year est.).
Economy: Employment by occupation: 0.0% management, 6.5% professional, 23.1% services, 37.9% sales, 0.0% farming, 13.0% construction, 19.5% production (2005-2009 5-year est.).
Income: Per capita income: $18,891 (2010); Median household income: $53,463 (2010); Average household income: $61,925 (2010); Percent of households with income of $100,000 or more: 18.9% (2010); Poverty rate: 26.1% (2005-2009 5-year est.).
Education: Percent of population age 25 and over with: High school diploma (including GED) or higher: 57.3% (2010); Bachelor's degree or higher: 16.8% (2010); Master's degree or higher: 3.3% (2010).
Housing: Homeownership rate: 70.9% (2010); Median home value: $102,174 (2010); Median contract rent: $314 per month (2005-2009 5-year est.); Median year structure built: 1965 (2005-2009 5-year est.).
Transportation: Commute to work: 81.1% car, 2.0% public transportation, 0.0% walk, 17.0% work from home (2005-2009 5-year est.); Travel time to work: 29.9% less than 15 minutes, 42.3% 15 to 30 minutes, 19.7% 30 to 45 minutes, 5.7% 45 to 60 minutes, 2.4% 60 minutes or more (2005-2009 5-year est.)

FOUR CORNERS (CDP).
Covers a land area of 2.845 square miles and a water area of 0 square miles. Located at 29.66° N. Lat; 95.65° W. Long. Elevation is 92 feet.
Population: 1,138 (1990); 2,954 (2000); 8,693 (2010); 10,589 (2015 projected); Race: 36.9% White, 20.1% Black, 27.6% Asian, 15.4% Other, 28.4% Hispanic of any race (2010); Density: 3,055.2 persons per square mile (2010); Average household size: 3.76 (2010); Median age: 30.7 (2010); Males per 100 females: 97.7 (2010); Marriage status: 31.9% never married, 52.6% now married, 3.1% widowed, 12.4% divorced (2005-2009 5-year est.); Foreign born: 36.7% (2005-2009 5-year est.); Ancestry (includes multiple ancestries): 6.4% American, 6.1% English, 5.5% Nigerian, 4.2% German, 2.0% African (2005-2009 5-year est.).
Economy: Employment by occupation: 14.1% management, 20.5% professional, 18.2% services, 25.4% sales, 0.3% farming, 11.4% construction, 10.1% production (2005-2009 5-year est.).
Income: Per capita income: $26,228 (2010); Median household income: $86,579 (2010); Average household income: $98,510 (2010); Percent of households with income of $100,000 or more: 39.6% (2010); Poverty rate: 6.3% (2005-2009 5-year est.).
Education: Percent of population age 25 and over with: High school diploma (including GED) or higher: 83.1% (2010); Bachelor's degree or higher: 44.9% (2010); Master's degree or higher: 14.8% (2010).
Housing: Homeownership rate: 84.9% (2010); Median home value: $181,775 (2010); Median contract rent: $1,174 per month (2005-2009 5-year est.); Median year structure built: 2001 (2005-2009 5-year est.).
Transportation: Commute to work: 96.5% car, 1.3% public transportation, 0.6% walk, 1.6% work from home (2005-2009 5-year est.); Travel time to work: 7.5% less than 15 minutes, 40.0% 15 to 30 minutes, 26.9% 30 to 45 minutes, 18.3% 45 to 60 minutes, 7.3% 60 minutes or more (2005-2009 5-year est.)

FRESNO (CDP).
Covers a land area of 8.986 square miles and a water area of 0.007 square miles. Located at 29.52° N. Lat; 95.46° W. Long. Elevation is 72 feet.

Population: 3,004 (1990); 6,603 (2000); 18,168 (2010); 22,216 (2015 projected); Race: 38.4% White, 39.0% Black, 3.2% Asian, 19.4% Other, 40.5% Hispanic of any race (2010); Density: 2,021.9 persons per square mile (2010); Average household size: 3.57 (2010); Median age: 30.6 (2010); Males per 100 females: 99.2 (2010); Marriage status: 35.6% never married, 48.0% now married, 5.2% widowed, 11.2% divorced (2005-2009 5-year est.); Foreign born: 14.6% (2005-2009 5-year est.); Ancestry (includes multiple ancestries): 2.2% American, 1.6% Irish, 1.6% German, 1.5% English, 1.1% Nigerian (2005-2009 5-year est.).
Economy: Employment by occupation: 11.0% management, 20.6% professional, 14.3% services, 25.6% sales, 0.0% farming, 14.7% construction, 13.8% production (2005-2009 5-year est.).
Income: Per capita income: $21,989 (2010); Median household income: $68,873 (2010); Average household income: $78,471 (2010); Percent of households with income of $100,000 or more: 25.3% (2010); Poverty rate: 9.0% (2005-2009 5-year est.).
Education: Percent of population age 25 and over with: High school diploma (including GED) or higher: 74.4% (2010); Bachelor's degree or higher: 27.3% (2010); Master's degree or higher: 9.6% (2010).
School District(s)
Fort Bend ISD (PK-12)
   2009-10 Enrollment: 69,374 . . . . (281) 634-1000
Housing: Homeownership rate: 88.2% (2010); Median home value: $142,635 (2010); Median contract rent: $662 per month (2005-2009 5-year est.); Median year structure built: 2000 (2005-2009 5-year est.).
Transportation: Commute to work: 92.1% car, 1.5% public transportation, 1.1% walk, 1.3% work from home (2005-2009 5-year est.); Travel time to work: 10.6% less than 15 minutes, 29.6% 15 to 30 minutes, 34.5% 30 to 45 minutes, 16.1% 45 to 60 minutes, 9.2% 60 minutes or more (2005-2009 5-year est.)

FULSHEAR (city).
Covers a land area of 8.164 square miles and a water area of 0.004 square miles. Located at 29.69° N. Lat; 95.89° W. Long. Elevation is 131 feet.
Population: 557 (1990); 716 (2000); 827 (2010); 990 (2015 projected); Race: 63.2% White, 19.1% Black, 0.7% Asian, 16.9% Other, 22.4% Hispanic of any race (2010); Density: 101.3 persons per square mile (2010); Average household size: 2.83 (2010); Median age: 37.2 (2010); Males per 100 females: 96.9 (2010); Marriage status: 23.6% never married, 56.3% now married, 7.1% widowed, 12.9% divorced (2005-2009 5-year est.); Foreign born: 4.3% (2005-2009 5-year est.); Ancestry (includes multiple ancestries): 23.1% German, 14.4% Irish, 14.2% American, 10.8% Czech, 7.9% English (2005-2009 5-year est.).
Economy: Single-family building permits issued: 0 (2010); Multi-family building permits issued: 0 (2010); Employment by occupation: 18.3% management, 22.5% professional, 11.7% services, 25.4% sales, 0.0% farming, 10.4% construction, 11.7% production (2005-2009 5-year est.).
Income: Per capita income: $41,550 (2010); Median household income: $84,028 (2010); Average household income: $117,106 (2010); Percent of households with income of $100,000 or more: 42.1% (2010); Poverty rate: 9.1% (2005-2009 5-year est.).
Taxes: Total city taxes per capita: $555 (2007); City property taxes per capita: $152 (2007).
Education: Percent of population age 25 and over with: High school diploma (including GED) or higher: 86.5% (2010); Bachelor's degree or higher: 36.3% (2010); Master's degree or higher: 13.6% (2010).
School District(s)
Lamar CISD (PK-12)
   2009-10 Enrollment: 23,864 . . . . (832) 223-0000
Housing: Homeownership rate: 82.2% (2010); Median home value: $216,279 (2010); Median contract rent: $675 per month (2005-2009 5-year est.); Median year structure built: 1979 (2005-2009 5-year est.).
Transportation: Commute to work: 94.2% car, 0.0% public transportation, 0.0% walk, 1.7% work from home (2005-2009 5-year est.); Travel time to work: 16.9% less than 15 minutes, 27.1% 15 to 30 minutes, 28.8% 30 to 45 minutes, 12.3% 45 to 60 minutes, 14.8% 60 minutes or more (2005-2009 5-year est.)
Additional Information Contacts
West I-10 Chamber of Commerce . . . . (281) 375-8100
   http://www.westi10chamber.org

GREATWOOD (CDP).
Covers a land area of 3.893 square miles and a water area of 0.040 square miles. Located at 29.55° N. Lat; 95.67° W. Long. Elevation is 69 feet.

History: The planned community of 2,050 acres began about the late 1980s or early 1990s and is a project of developer Newland Communities. Amenities include a civic center, country club, golf course, and other recreation facilities.
Population: 2,153 (1990); 6,640 (2000); 9,297 (2010); 11,211 (2015 projected); Race: 80.0% White, 4.3% Black, 11.2% Asian, 4.5% Other, 4.9% Hispanic of any race (2010); Density: 2,388.1 persons per square mile (2010); Average household size: 2.93 (2010); Median age: 36.4 (2010); Males per 100 females: 97.6 (2010); Marriage status: 16.3% never married, 72.3% now married, 4.8% widowed, 6.6% divorced (2005-2009 5-year est.); Foreign born: 11.9% (2005-2009 5-year est.); Ancestry (includes multiple ancestries): 23.5% German, 13.6% Irish, 12.5% English, 7.2% French, 5.1% Italian (2005-2009 5-year est.).
Economy: Employment by occupation: 26.6% management, 33.2% professional, 4.1% services, 26.2% sales, 0.0% farming, 4.7% construction, 5.3% production (2005-2009 5-year est.).
Income: Per capita income: $57,348 (2010); Median household income: $141,055 (2010); Average household income: $168,276 (2010); Percent of households with income of $100,000 or more: 71.0% (2010); Poverty rate: 1.4% (2005-2009 5-year est.).
Education: Percent of population age 25 and over with: High school diploma (including GED) or higher: 97.8% (2010); Bachelor's degree or higher: 62.9% (2010); Master's degree or higher: 20.0% (2010).
Housing: Homeownership rate: 97.8% (2010); Median home value: $256,060 (2010); Median contract rent: $2,000+ per month (2005-2009 5-year est.); Median year structure built: 1996 (2005-2009 5-year est.).
Transportation: Commute to work: 91.7% car, 0.2% public transportation, 0.7% walk, 7.0% work from home (2005-2009 5-year est.); Travel time to work: 12.1% less than 15 minutes, 25.1% 15 to 30 minutes, 32.1% 30 to 45 minutes, 15.6% 45 to 60 minutes, 15.1% 60 minutes or more (2005-2009 5-year est.)

GUY (unincorporated postal area, zip code 77444). Covers a land area of 24.791 square miles and a water area of 0.268 square miles. Located at 29.30° N. Lat; 95.79° W. Long. Elevation is 75 feet.
Population: 668 (2000); Race: 89.7% White, 0.0% Black, 0.0% Asian, 10.3% Other, 15.3% Hispanic of any race (2000); Density: 26.9 persons per square mile (2000); Age: 33.1% under 18, 10.1% over 64 (2000); Marriage status: 22.2% never married, 56.4% now married, 8.1% widowed, 13.3% divorced (2000); Foreign born: 1.5% (2000); Ancestry (includes multiple ancestries): 22.4% German, 21.6% Czech, 6.1% English, 5.1% American (2000).
Economy: Employment by occupation: 13.1% management, 8.2% professional, 9.4% services, 25.3% sales, 0.8% farming, 24.9% construction, 18.4% production (2000).
Income: Per capita income: $16,311 (2000); Median household income: $34,063 (2000); Poverty rate: 179.1% (2000).
Education: Percent of population age 25 and over with: High school diploma (including GED) or higher: 74.3% (2000); Bachelor's degree or higher: 6.7% (2000).
Housing: Homeownership rate: 78.9% (2000); Median home value: $66,100 (2000); Median contract rent: $420 per month (2000); Median year structure built: 1974 (2000).
Transportation: Commute to work: 99.6% car, 0.0% public transportation, 0.0% walk, 0.0% work from home (2000); Travel time to work: 12.0% less than 15 minutes, 13.7% 15 to 30 minutes, 26.2% 30 to 45 minutes, 25.8% 45 to 60 minutes, 22.3% 60 minutes or more (2000)

KENDLETON (city). Covers a land area of 1.064 square miles and a water area of 0 square miles. Located at 29.44° N. Lat; 96.00° W. Long. Elevation is 95 feet.
Population: 496 (1990); 466 (2000); 396 (2010); 399 (2015 projected); Race: 14.6% White, 63.4% Black, 0.0% Asian, 22.0% Other, 29.3% Hispanic of any race (2010); Density: 372.1 persons per square mile (2010); Average household size: 2.59 (2010); Median age: 31.9 (2010); Males per 100 females: 88.6 (2010); Marriage status: 29.7% never married, 44.6% now married, 9.9% widowed, 15.9% divorced (2005-2009 5-year est.); Foreign born: 5.6% (2005-2009 5-year est.); Ancestry (includes multiple ancestries): 7.7% Irish, 0.6% Danish (2005-2009 5-year est.).
Economy: Single-family building permits issued: 0 (2010); Multi-family building permits issued: 0 (2010); Employment by occupation: 6.7% management, 30.6% professional, 13.1% services, 29.4% sales, 0.0% farming, 17.9% construction, 2.4% production (2005-2009 5-year est.).
Income: Per capita income: $18,984 (2010); Median household income: $36,071 (2010); Average household income: $45,833 (2010); Percent of

households with income of $100,000 or more: 11.1% (2010); Poverty rate: 13.2% (2005-2009 5-year est.).
Taxes: Total city taxes per capita: $63 (2007); City property taxes per capita: $63 (2007).
Education: Percent of population age 25 and over with: High school diploma (including GED) or higher: 67.5% (2010); Bachelor's degree or higher: 8.3% (2010); Master's degree or higher: 2.1% (2010).
School District(s)
Kendleton ISD (PK-06)
    2009-10 Enrollment: 78 . . . . (979) 532-2855
Housing: Homeownership rate: 75.2% (2010); Median home value: $59,063 (2010); Median contract rent: $425 per month (2005-2009 5-year est.); Median year structure built: 1978 (2005-2009 5-year est.).
Transportation: Commute to work: 98.4% car, 0.0% public transportation, 1.6% walk, 0.0% work from home (2005-2009 5-year est.); Travel time to work: 10.7% less than 15 minutes, 28.2% 15 to 30 minutes, 45.2% 30 to 45 minutes, 11.5% 45 to 60 minutes, 4.4% 60 minutes or more (2005-2009 5-year est.)

MEADOWS PLACE (city). Aka Meadows. Covers a land area of 0.936 square miles and a water area of 0 square miles. Located at 29.65° N. Lat; 95.58° W. Long. Elevation is 85 feet.
History: Meadows Place was part of Stafford's extraterritorial jurisdiction prior to incorporation on November 14, 1983. Meadows Place was incorporated as Meadows, but this was changed to "Meadows Place" in 1997 due to postal conflicts with a city of a similar name, Meadow.
Population: 4,632 (1990); 4,912 (2000); 6,365 (2010); 6,966 (2015 projected); Race: 52.7% White, 14.1% Black, 23.0% Asian, 10.2% Other, 16.9% Hispanic of any race (2010); Density: 6,800.2 persons per square mile (2010); Average household size: 2.60 (2010); Median age: 35.1 (2010); Males per 100 females: 93.1 (2010); Marriage status: n/a never married, n/a now married, n/a widowed, n/a divorced (2005-2009 5-year est.); Foreign born: n/a (2005-2009 5-year est.); Ancestry (includes multiple ancestries): n/a (2005-2009 5-year est.).
Economy: Employment by occupation: n/a management, n/a professional, n/a services, n/a sales, n/a farming, n/a construction, n/a production (2005-2009 5-year est.).
Income: Per capita income: $32,098 (2010); Median household income: $72,575 (2010); Average household income: $83,540 (2010); Percent of households with income of $100,000 or more: 29.6% (2010); Poverty rate: n/a (2005-2009 5-year est.).
Taxes: Total city taxes per capita: $447 (2007); City property taxes per capita: $233 (2007).
Education: Percent of population age 25 and over with: High school diploma (including GED) or higher: 94.4% (2010); Bachelor's degree or higher: 49.9% (2010); Master's degree or higher: 17.9% (2010).
School District(s)
Fort Bend ISD (PK-12)
    2009-10 Enrollment: 69,374 . . . . (281) 634-1000
Housing: Homeownership rate: 63.1% (2010); Median home value: $139,086 (2010); Median contract rent: n/a per month (2005-2009 5-year est.); Median year structure built: n/a (2005-2009 5-year est.).
Safety: Violent crime rate: 12.1 per 10,000 population; Property crime rate: 208.3 per 10,000 population (2009).
Transportation: Commute to work: n/a car, n/a public transportation, n/a walk, n/a work from home (2005-2009 5-year est.); Travel time to work: n/a less than 15 minutes, n/a 15 to 30 minutes, n/a 30 to 45 minutes, n/a 45 to 60 minutes, n/a 60 minutes or more (2005-2009 5-year est.)

MISSION BEND (CDP). Covers a land area of 5.225 square miles and a water area of 0.032 square miles. Located at 29.69° N. Lat; 95.66° W. Long. Elevation is 95 feet.
Population: 24,945 (1990); 30,831 (2000); 34,307 (2010); 38,008 (2015 projected); Race: 35.0% White, 29.2% Black, 16.1% Asian, 19.7% Other, 34.5% Hispanic of any race (2010); Density: 6,565.3 persons per square mile (2010); Average household size: 3.48 (2010); Median age: 32.8 (2010); Males per 100 females: 97.1 (2010); Marriage status: 32.7% never married, 54.3% now married, 3.9% widowed, 9.1% divorced (2005-2009 5-year est.); Foreign born: 35.1% (2005-2009 5-year est.); Ancestry (includes multiple ancestries): 4.2% German, 3.9% Nigerian, 3.6% Irish, 2.6% English, 2.5% American (2005-2009 5-year est.).
Economy: Employment by occupation: 11.6% management, 17.8% professional, 21.3% services, 29.2% sales, 0.0% farming, 9.2% construction, 10.9% production (2005-2009 5-year est.).

Income: Per capita income: $22,506 (2010); Median household income: $67,202 (2010); Average household income: $78,056 (2010); Percent of households with income of $100,000 or more: 23.1% (2010); Poverty rate: 9.3% (2005-2009 5-year est.).

Education: Percent of population age 25 and over with: High school diploma (including GED) or higher: 87.8% (2010); Bachelor's degree or higher: 33.0% (2010); Master's degree or higher: 8.9% (2010).

Housing: Homeownership rate: 85.2% (2010); Median home value: $124,095 (2010); Median contract rent: $903 per month (2005-2009 5-year est.); Median year structure built: 1985 (2005-2009 5-year est.).

Transportation: Commute to work: 93.7% car, 2.1% public transportation, 0.4% walk, 2.5% work from home (2005-2009 5-year est.); Travel time to work: 10.9% less than 15 minutes, 31.9% 15 to 30 minutes, 31.7% 30 to 45 minutes, 14.2% 45 to 60 minutes, 11.3% 60 minutes or more (2005-2009 5-year est.)

MISSOURI CITY (city).
Covers a land area of 29.698 square miles and a water area of 0.717 square miles. Located at 29.58° N. Lat; 95.53° W. Long. Elevation is 79 feet.

Population: 36,681 (1990); 52,913 (2000); 78,314 (2010); 92,673 (2015 projected); Race: 33.2% White, 41.3% Black, 15.5% Asian, 10.0% Other, 15.5% Hispanic of any race (2010); Density: 2,637.0 persons per square mile (2010); Average household size: 3.16 (2010); Median age: 34.6 (2010); Males per 100 females: 95.4 (2010); Marriage status: 31.4% never married, 54.6% now married, 4.9% widowed, 9.1% divorced (2005-2009 5-year est.); Foreign born: 21.0% (2005-2009 5-year est.); Ancestry (includes multiple ancestries): 8.1% German, 5.8% English, 4.8% Irish, 3.1% American, 2.9% Nigerian (2005-2009 5-year est.).

Economy: Unemployment rate: 8.2% (June 2011); Total civilian labor force: 41,813 (June 2011); Single-family building permits issued: 138 (2010); Multi-family building permits issued: 0 (2010); Employment by occupation: 17.7% management, 28.0% professional, 12.2% services, 28.2% sales, 0.0% farming, 5.4% construction, 8.4% production (2005-2009 5-year est.).

Income: Per capita income: $32,387 (2010); Median household income: $83,792 (2010); Average household income: $102,042 (2010); Percent of households with income of $100,000 or more: 39.2% (2010); Poverty rate: 8.6% (2005-2009 5-year est.).

Taxes: Total city taxes per capita: $445 (2007); City property taxes per capita: $274 (2007).

Education: Percent of population age 25 and over with: High school diploma (including GED) or higher: 91.7% (2010); Bachelor's degree or higher: 46.1% (2010); Master's degree or higher: 16.6% (2010).

School District(s)
Fort Bend ISD (PK-12)
   2009-10 Enrollment: 69,374 . . . . (281) 634-1000
La Amistad Love & Learning Academy (PK-05)
   2009-10 Enrollment: 347 . . . . (281) 988-9231

Housing: Homeownership rate: 89.0% (2010); Median home value: $153,948 (2010); Median contract rent: $1,022 per month (2005-2009 5-year est.); Median year structure built: 1989 (2005-2009 5-year est.).

Hospitals: Memorial Hermann Fort Bend Hospital (84 beds)

Safety: Violent crime rate: 15.9 per 10,000 population; Property crime rate: 167.6 per 10,000 population (2009).

Transportation: Commute to work: 93.1% car, 1.6% public transportation, 0.3% walk, 3.8% work from home (2005-2009 5-year est.); Travel time to work: 13.5% less than 15 minutes, 28.7% 15 to 30 minutes, 36.9% 30 to 45 minutes, 13.5% 45 to 60 minutes, 7.4% 60 minutes or more (2005-2009 5-year est.)

Additional Information Contacts
City of Missouri City . . . . (281) 403-8500
   http://www.missouricitytx.gov

NEEDVILLE (city).
Covers a land area of 1.702 square miles and a water area of 0 square miles. Located at 29.39° N. Lat; 95.84° W. Long. Elevation is 89 feet.

Population: 2,335 (1990); 2,609 (2000); 3,478 (2010); 4,095 (2015 projected); Race: 74.8% White, 10.3% Black, 0.4% Asian, 14.5% Other, 30.3% Hispanic of any race (2010); Density: 2,042.9 persons per square mile (2010); Average household size: 2.71 (2010); Median age: 34.2 (2010); Males per 100 females: 91.9 (2010); Marriage status: 28.4% never married, 49.7% now married, 7.9% widowed, 14.0% divorced (2005-2009 5-year est.); Foreign born: 12.3% (2005-2009 5-year est.); Ancestry (includes multiple ancestries): 24.9% German, 13.0% Czech, 8.7% English, 4.8% Irish, 4.2% Italian (2005-2009 5-year est.).

Economy: Single-family building permits issued: 6 (2010); Multi-family building permits issued: 0 (2010); Employment by occupation: 12.7% management, 16.4% professional, 26.0% services, 19.4% sales, 0.8% farming, 17.6% construction, 7.1% production (2005-2009 5-year est.).

Income: Per capita income: $24,762 (2010); Median household income: $57,832 (2010); Average household income: $67,548 (2010); Percent of households with income of $100,000 or more: 19.5% (2010); Poverty rate: 4.5% (2005-2009 5-year est.).

Taxes: Total city taxes per capita: $182 (2007); City property taxes per capita: $142 (2007).

Education: Percent of population age 25 and over with: High school diploma (including GED) or higher: 78.4% (2010); Bachelor's degree or higher: 13.3% (2010); Master's degree or higher: 4.3% (2010).

School District(s)
Needville ISD (PK-12)
   2009-10 Enrollment: 2,602 . . . . (979) 793-4308

Housing: Homeownership rate: 71.8% (2010); Median home value: $99,853 (2010); Median contract rent: $478 per month (2005-2009 5-year est.); Median year structure built: 1977 (2005-2009 5-year est.).

Safety: Violent crime rate: 14.0 per 10,000 population; Property crime rate: 33.7 per 10,000 population (2009).

Newspapers: Gulf Coast Tribune (Community news; Circulation 1,600)

Transportation: Commute to work: 90.3% car, 0.5% public transportation, 2.6% walk, 3.1% work from home (2005-2009 5-year est.); Travel time to work: 30.3% less than 15 minutes, 28.0% 15 to 30 minutes, 17.0% 30 to 45 minutes, 8.6% 45 to 60 minutes, 16.1% 60 minutes or more (2005-2009 5-year est.)

Additional Information Contacts
Needville Area Chamber of Commerce . . . . (979) 793-5700
   http://www.needville.org

NEW TERRITORY (CDP).
Covers a land area of 5.047 square miles and a water area of 0.045 square miles. Located at 29.59° N. Lat; 95.67° W. Long. Elevation is 75 feet.

History: New Territory opened in 1989. The City of Sugar Land plans to annex New Territory in 2017.

Population: 933 (1990); 13,861 (2000); 19,154 (2010); 22,929 (2015 projected); Race: 35.6% White, 12.1% Black, 45.3% Asian, 6.9% Other, 6.1% Hispanic of any race (2010); Density: 3,794.8 persons per square mile (2010); Average household size: 3.63 (2010); Median age: 29.0 (2010); Males per 100 females: 107.9 (2010); Marriage status: 29.6% never married, 57.1% now married, 6.7% widowed, 6.6% divorced (2005-2009 5-year est.); Foreign born: 33.2% (2005-2009 5-year est.); Ancestry (includes multiple ancestries): 12.0% German, 8.3% Irish, 5.9% English, 3.3% Italian, 3.2% American (2005-2009 5-year est.).

Economy: Employment by occupation: 23.7% management, 37.2% professional, 9.7% services, 23.8% sales, 0.0% farming, 3.3% construction, 2.3% production (2005-2009 5-year est.).

Income: Per capita income: $40,511 (2010); Median household income: $130,178 (2010); Average household income: $153,667 (2010); Percent of households with income of $100,000 or more: 69.2% (2010); Poverty rate: 4.9% (2005-2009 5-year est.).

Education: Percent of population age 25 and over with: High school diploma (including GED) or higher: 93.3% (2010); Bachelor's degree or higher: 60.4% (2010); Master's degree or higher: 20.5% (2010).

Housing: Homeownership rate: 93.0% (2010); Median home value: $249,834 (2010); Median contract rent: $1,308 per month (2005-2009 5-year est.); Median year structure built: 1995 (2005-2009 5-year est.).

Transportation: Commute to work: 90.4% car, 1.0% public transportation, 3.5% walk, 4.4% work from home (2005-2009 5-year est.); Travel time to work: 14.4% less than 15 minutes, 31.4% 15 to 30 minutes, 27.3% 30 to 45 minutes, 18.2% 45 to 60 minutes, 8.7% 60 minutes or more (2005-2009 5-year est.)

ORCHARD (city).
Covers a land area of 0.378 square miles and a water area of 0 square miles. Located at 29.60° N. Lat; 95.96° W. Long. Elevation is 125 feet.

Population: 391 (1990); 408 (2000); 370 (2010); 381 (2015 projected); Race: 62.7% White, 13.8% Black, 0.0% Asian, 23.5% Other, 28.6% Hispanic of any race (2010); Density: 978.5 persons per square mile (2010); Average household size: 2.82 (2010); Median age: 32.3 (2010); Males per 100 females: 100.0 (2010); Marriage status: 8.9% never married, 82.7% now married, 4.8% widowed, 3.6% divorced (2005-2009 5-year est.); Foreign born: 4.5% (2005-2009 5-year est.); Ancestry (includes

multiple ancestries): 13.1% Irish, 9.7% German, 6.4% Czech, 5.0% American, 4.0% Scotch-Irish (2005-2009 5-year est.).
Economy: Employment by occupation: 9.2% management, 11.7% professional, 13.8% services, 25.5% sales, 2.6% farming, 26.5% construction, 10.7% production (2005-2009 5-year est.).
Income: Per capita income: $23,857 (2010); Median household income: $59,274 (2010); Average household income: $66,870 (2010); Percent of households with income of $100,000 or more: 22.9% (2010); Poverty rate: 2.7% (2005-2009 5-year est.).
Taxes: Total city taxes per capita: $166 (2007); City property taxes per capita: $84 (2007).
Education: Percent of population age 25 and over with: High school diploma (including GED) or higher: 78.6% (2010); Bachelor's degree or higher: 12.6% (2010); Master's degree or higher: 2.5% (2010).

School District(s)

Brazos ISD (PK-12)
  2009-10 Enrollment: 822 . . . . (979) 478-6551
Housing: Homeownership rate: 72.5% (2010); Median home value: $107,258 (2010); Median contract rent: $600 per month (2005-2009 5-year est.); Median year structure built: 1972 (2005-2009 5-year est.).
Transportation: Commute to work: 92.3% car, 0.0% public transportation, 5.1% walk, 0.0% work from home (2005-2009 5-year est.); Travel time to work: 15.3% less than 15 minutes, 43.4% 15 to 30 minutes, 21.9% 30 to 45 minutes, 3.1% 45 to 60 minutes, 16.3% 60 minutes or more (2005-2009 5-year est.)

PECAN GROVE (CDP). Covers a land area of 8.730 square miles and a water area of 0.025 square miles. Located at 29.62° N. Lat; 95.73° W. Long. Elevation is 82 feet.

History: Bruce Belin and Associates purchased approximately 1,450 acres in 1973 and by 1978 began construction of the development. Named for the stately pecan trees growing in the area, the community was originally referred to as Pecan Grove Plantation and later simply Pecan Grove.
Population: 9,648 (1990); 13,551 (2000); 15,266 (2010); 17,220 (2015 projected); Race: 88.2% White, 3.3% Black, 1.8% Asian, 6.7% Other, 16.3% Hispanic of any race (2010); Density: 1,748.7 persons per square mile (2010); Average household size: 2.97 (2010); Median age: 34.8 (2010); Males per 100 females: 97.8 (2010); Marriage status: 24.8% never married, 62.9% now married, 3.1% widowed, 9.2% divorced (2005-2009 5-year est.); Foreign born: 3.5% (2005-2009 5-year est.); Ancestry (includes multiple ancestries): 19.1% German, 14.7% English, 12.2% Irish, 9.6% American, 6.2% French (2005-2009 5-year est.).
Economy: Employment by occupation: 23.7% management, 27.9% professional, 10.1% services, 31.4% sales, 0.0% farming, 3.0% construction, 3.9% production (2005-2009 5-year est.).
Income: Per capita income: $42,228 (2010); Median household income: $95,100 (2010); Average household income: $125,533 (2010); Percent of households with income of $100,000 or more: 47.0% (2010); Poverty rate: 4.4% (2005-2009 5-year est.).
Education: Percent of population age 25 and over with: High school diploma (including GED) or higher: 95.7% (2010); Bachelor's degree or higher: 49.3% (2010); Master's degree or higher: 10.9% (2010).
Housing: Homeownership rate: 81.1% (2010); Median home value: $186,738 (2010); Median contract rent: $794 per month (2005-2009 5-year est.); Median year structure built: 1987 (2005-2009 5-year est.).
Transportation: Commute to work: 93.0% car, 1.5% public transportation, 0.1% walk, 4.6% work from home (2005-2009 5-year est.); Travel time to work: 14.5% less than 15 minutes, 27.1% 15 to 30 minutes, 25.3% 30 to 45 minutes, 19.0% 45 to 60 minutes, 14.0% 60 minutes or more (2005-2009 5-year est.)

PLEAK (village). Covers a land area of 1.999 square miles and a water area of 0 square miles. Located at 29.48° N. Lat; 95.81° W. Long. Elevation is 85 feet.

Population: 827 (1990); 947 (2000); 1,506 (2010); 1,812 (2015 projected); Race: 59.6% White, 3.9% Black, 0.3% Asian, 36.3% Other, 66.2% Hispanic of any race (2010); Density: 753.4 persons per square mile (2010); Average household size: 3.20 (2010); Median age: 32.6 (2010); Males per 100 females: 101.3 (2010); Marriage status: 26.4% never married, 56.8% now married, 5.8% widowed, 11.1% divorced (2005-2009 5-year est.); Foreign born: 7.4% (2005-2009 5-year est.); Ancestry (includes multiple ancestries): 21.2% German, 9.1% Czech, 7.3% Irish, 7.0% American, 5.9% English (2005-2009 5-year est.).

Economy: Employment by occupation: 10.9% management, 15.3% professional, 22.6% services, 24.1% sales, 1.1% farming, 8.2% construction, 17.8% production (2005-2009 5-year est.).
Income: Per capita income: $20,013 (2010); Median household income: $55,724 (2010); Average household income: $64,735 (2010); Percent of households with income of $100,000 or more: 17.0% (2010); Poverty rate: 17.0% (2005-2009 5-year est.).
Taxes: Total city taxes per capita: $59 (2007); City property taxes per capita: $0 (2007).
Education: Percent of population age 25 and over with: High school diploma (including GED) or higher: 73.1% (2010); Bachelor's degree or higher: 11.4% (2010); Master's degree or higher: 5.4% (2010).
Housing: Homeownership rate: 80.0% (2010); Median home value: $104,646 (2010); Median contract rent: $699 per month (2005-2009 5-year est.); Median year structure built: 1984 (2005-2009 5-year est.).
Transportation: Commute to work: 96.3% car, 0.6% public transportation, 0.0% walk, 3.1% work from home (2005-2009 5-year est.); Travel time to work: 17.7% less than 15 minutes, 29.8% 15 to 30 minutes, 15.7% 30 to 45 minutes, 20.3% 45 to 60 minutes, 16.5% 60 minutes or more (2005-2009 5-year est.)

RICHMOND (city). County seat. Covers a land area of 3.724 square miles and a water area of 0.218 square miles. Located at 29.58° N. Lat; 95.76° W. Long. Elevation is 92 feet.

History: Named for Richmond, Virginia, which was named for Richmond in Surrey, England. Richmond was settled in 1822 by Austin's colonists, at a bend in the Brazos River. Richmond was the burial place of several Texas patriots, including Erastus (Deaf) Smith (scout for General Sam Houston), Mirabeau B. Lamar (commander of Houston's cavalry at San Jacinto and second President of the Republic of Texas), and Jane Long (called the Mother of Texas).
Population: 9,843 (1990); 11,081 (2000); 13,308 (2010); 15,405 (2015 projected); Race: 45.6% White, 13.0% Black, 1.5% Asian, 39.9% Other, 66.0% Hispanic of any race (2010); Density: 3,573.4 persons per square mile (2010); Average household size: 3.19 (2010); Median age: 31.1 (2010); Males per 100 females: 104.0 (2010); Marriage status: 36.9% never married, 46.9% now married, 5.0% widowed, 11.2% divorced (2005-2009 5-year est.); Foreign born: 22.0% (2005-2009 5-year est.); Ancestry (includes multiple ancestries): 5.8% German, 3.2% American, 3.1% Irish, 2.7% Czech, 2.0% Polish (2005-2009 5-year est.).
Economy: Single-family building permits issued: 4 (2010); Multi-family building permits issued: 0 (2010); Employment by occupation: 7.7% management, 10.8% professional, 21.2% services, 23.2% sales, 1.6% farming, 17.7% construction, 17.8% production (2005-2009 5-year est.).
Income: Per capita income: $18,747 (2010); Median household income: $44,755 (2010); Average household income: $60,934 (2010); Percent of households with income of $100,000 or more: 15.2% (2010); Poverty rate: 24.3% (2005-2009 5-year est.).
Taxes: Total city taxes per capita: $496 (2007); City property taxes per capita: $178 (2007).
Education: Percent of population age 25 and over with: High school diploma (including GED) or higher: 59.5% (2010); Bachelor's degree or higher: 15.1% (2010); Master's degree or higher: 5.5% (2010).

School District(s)

Fort Bend ISD (PK-12)
  2009-10 Enrollment: 69,374 . . . . (281) 634-1000
Lamar CISD (PK-12)
  2009-10 Enrollment: 23,864 . . . . (832) 223-0000
University of Texas University Charter School (KG-12)
  2009-10 Enrollment: 907 . . . . (512) 471-5652
Housing: Homeownership rate: 56.0% (2010); Median home value: $85,586 (2010); Median contract rent: $486 per month (2005-2009 5-year est.); Median year structure built: 1978 (2005-2009 5-year est.).
Hospitals: Oakbend Medical Center (185 beds); Polly Ryon Memorial Hospital (185 beds)
Safety: Violent crime rate: 43.8 per 10,000 population; Property crime rate: 238.6 per 10,000 population (2009).
Transportation: Commute to work: 95.6% car, 0.2% public transportation, 0.7% walk, 1.9% work from home (2005-2009 5-year est.); Travel time to work: 34.0% less than 15 minutes, 29.5% 15 to 30 minutes, 13.3% 30 to 45 minutes, 8.9% 45 to 60 minutes, 14.2% 60 minutes or more (2005-2009 5-year est.)
Additional Information Contacts
City of Richmond . . . . (281) 342-5456
  http://www.ci.richmond.tx.us

ROSENBERG

ROSENBERG (city). Covers a land area of 21.245 square miles and a water area of 0.010 square miles. Located at 29.55° N. Lat; 95.80° W. Long. Elevation is 105 feet.

History: Named for Henry Rosenberg, railroad president. Rosenberg was founded in 1883 when the railroad was constructed, and became a shipping center for the cotton, rice, and sugar grown in the area.

Population: 20,420 (1990); 24,043 (2000); 34,922 (2010); 42,061 (2015 projected); Race: 61.9% White, 10.7% Black, 0.4% Asian, 27.0% Other, 65.6% Hispanic of any race (2010); Density: 1,643.8 persons per square mile (2010); Average household size: 3.02 (2010); Median age: 31.8 (2010); Males per 100 females: 98.7 (2010); Marriage status: 31.1% never married, 50.4% now married, 6.3% widowed, 12.2% divorced (2005-2009 5-year est.); Foreign born: 16.1% (2005-2009 5-year est.); Ancestry (includes multiple ancestries): 9.1% German, 3.7% American, 3.4% English, 3.4% Czech, 3.2% Irish (2005-2009 5-year est.).

Economy: Unemployment rate: 8.4% (June 2011); Total civilian labor force: 16,344 (June 2011); Single-family building permits issued: 135 (2010); Multi-family building permits issued: 0 (2010); Employment by occupation: 10.7% management, 12.1% professional, 19.2% services, 26.4% sales, 0.5% farming, 13.5% construction, 17.5% production (2005-2009 5-year est.).

Income: Per capita income: $17,621 (2010); Median household income: $43,363 (2010); Average household income: $53,060 (2010); Percent of households with income of $100,000 or more: 10.3% (2010); Poverty rate: 19.4% (2005-2009 5-year est.).

Taxes: Total city taxes per capita: $478 (2007); City property taxes per capita: $157 (2007).

Education: Percent of population age 25 and over with: High school diploma (including GED) or higher: 67.7% (2010); Bachelor's degree or higher: 12.4% (2010); Master's degree or higher: 3.5% (2010).

School District(s)

Lamar CISD (PK-12)

    2009-10 Enrollment: 23,864 . . . . (832) 223-0000

Housing: Homeownership rate: 57.5% (2010); Median home value: $96,129 (2010); Median contract rent: $569 per month (2005-2009 5-year est.); Median year structure built: 1978 (2005-2009 5-year est.).

Safety: Violent crime rate: 18.7 per 10,000 population; Property crime rate: 193.2 per 10,000 population (2009).

Newspapers: Rosenberg Herald-Coaster (Local news; Circulation 7,500)

Transportation: Commute to work: 94.0% car, 1.2% public transportation, 1.7% walk, 1.6% work from home (2005-2009 5-year est.); Travel time to work: 33.1% less than 15 minutes, 29.4% 15 to 30 minutes, 15.2% 30 to 45 minutes, 10.0% 45 to 60 minutes, 12.4% 60 minutes or more (2005-2009 5-year est.)

Additional Information Contacts

Central Fort Bend Chamber Alliance . . . . (281) 342-5464
   http://www.roserichchamber.org

City of Rosenberg . . . . (832) 595-3300
   http://www.ci.rosenberg.tx.us

SIENNA PLANTATION

SIENNA PLANTATION (CDP). Covers a land area of 16.154 square miles and a water area of 0.295 square miles. Located at 29.49° N. Lat; 95.50° W. Long. Elevation is 59 feet.

History: Originally part of Stephen F. Austin's "Old Three Hundred" colony settlement, the land that has become Sienna Plantation was first settled by Captain William Hall and Captain David Fitzgerald, who, in 1824, located their farms on the east bank of the Brazos River.

Population: 532 (1990); 1,896 (2000); 10,060 (2010); 12,102 (2015 projected); Race: 57.0% White, 21.5% Black, 5.0% Asian, 16.4% Other, 25.4% Hispanic of any race (2010); Density: 622.8 persons per square mile (2010); Average household size: 3.42 (2010); Median age: 31.3 (2010); Males per 100 females: 104.9 (2010); Marriage status: 23.4% never married, 67.5% now married, 1.3% widowed, 7.8% divorced (2005-2009 5-year est.); Foreign born: 11.2% (2005-2009 5-year est.); Ancestry (includes multiple ancestries): 18.2% German, 8.2% Irish, 8.0% English, 4.3% French, 4.2% American (2005-2009 5-year est.).

Economy: Employment by occupation: 30.9% management, 29.1% professional, 6.6% services, 21.6% sales, 0.0% farming, 5.6% construction, 6.3% production (2005-2009 5-year est.).

Income: Per capita income: $40,774 (2010); Median household income: $112,966 (2010); Average household income: $139,356 (2010); Percent of households with income of $100,000 or more: 56.1% (2010); Poverty rate: 3.3% (2005-2009 5-year est.).

Education: Percent of population age 25 and over with: High school diploma (including GED) or higher: 84.6% (2010); Bachelor's degree or higher: 41.2% (2010); Master's degree or higher: 12.1% (2010).

Housing: Homeownership rate: 90.2% (2010); Median home value: $238,036 (2010); Median contract rent: $1,300 per month (2005-2009 5-year est.); Median year structure built: n/a (2005-2009 5-year est.).

Transportation: Commute to work: 93.3% car, 1.2% public transportation, 0.5% walk, 4.7% work from home (2005-2009 5-year est.); Travel time to work: 4.5% less than 15 minutes, 21.5% 15 to 30 minutes, 37.1% 30 to 45 minutes, 21.5% 45 to 60 minutes, 15.4% 60 minutes or more (2005-2009 5-year est.)

SIMONTON

SIMONTON (city). Covers a land area of 2.026 square miles and a water area of 0 square miles. Located at 29.68° N. Lat; 95.99° W. Long. Elevation is 115 feet.

Population: 731 (1990); 718 (2000); 813 (2010); 915 (2015 projected); Race: 86.6% White, 4.1% Black, 0.9% Asian, 8.5% Other, 12.7% Hispanic of any race (2010); Density: 401.3 persons per square mile (2010); Average household size: 2.62 (2010); Median age: 44.8 (2010); Males per 100 females: 100.2 (2010); Marriage status: 20.0% never married, 64.2% now married, 5.2% widowed, 10.6% divorced (2005-2009 5-year est.); Foreign born: 11.8% (2005-2009 5-year est.); Ancestry (includes multiple ancestries): 16.8% German, 15.3% American, 11.8% English, 8.6% Irish, 5.6% Italian (2005-2009 5-year est.).

Economy: Single-family building permits issued: 1 (2010); Multi-family building permits issued: 0 (2010); Employment by occupation: 24.2% management, 17.1% professional, 16.8% services, 24.2% sales, 1.9% farming, 8.2% construction, 7.6% production (2005-2009 5-year est.).

Income: Per capita income: $48,380 (2010); Median household income: $102,778 (2010); Average household income: $127,056 (2010); Percent of households with income of $100,000 or more: 51.3% (2010); Poverty rate: 0.5% (2005-2009 5-year est.).

Taxes: Total city taxes per capita: $208 (2007); City property taxes per capita: $113 (2007).

Education: Percent of population age 25 and over with: High school diploma (including GED) or higher: 92.2% (2010); Bachelor's degree or higher: 37.6% (2010); Master's degree or higher: 11.2% (2010).

Housing: Homeownership rate: 90.0% (2010); Median home value: $231,667 (2010); Median contract rent: $925 per month (2005-2009 5-year est.); Median year structure built: 1975 (2005-2009 5-year est.).

Transportation: Commute to work: 92.1% car, 0.0% public transportation, 0.0% walk, 6.3% work from home (2005-2009 5-year est.); Travel time to work: 1.7% less than 15 minutes, 38.3% 15 to 30 minutes, 18.6% 30 to 45 minutes, 24.6% 45 to 60 minutes, 16.8% 60 minutes or more (2005-2009 5-year est.)

Additional Information Contacts

West I-10 Chamber of Commerce . . . . (281) 375-8100
   http://www.westi10chamber.org

STAFFORD

STAFFORD (city). Covers a land area of 6.978 square miles and a water area of 0 square miles. Located at 29.62° N. Lat; 95.56° W. Long. Elevation is 85 feet.

Population: 8,604 (1990); 15,681 (2000); 18,830 (2010); 22,465 (2015 projected); Race: 30.8% White, 27.8% Black, 24.6% Asian, 16.8% Other, 23.6% Hispanic of any race (2010); Density: 2,698.3 persons per square mile (2010); Average household size: 2.64 (2010); Median age: 33.7 (2010); Males per 100 females: 97.0 (2010); Marriage status: 38.6% never married, 46.2% now married, 4.2% widowed, 11.0% divorced (2005-2009 5-year est.); Foreign born: 30.6% (2005-2009 5-year est.); Ancestry (includes multiple ancestries): 7.3% German, 5.5% Irish, 3.5% Nigerian, 3.0% English, 3.0% French (2005-2009 5-year est.).

Economy: Single-family building permits issued: 20 (2010); Multi-family building permits issued: 0 (2010); Employment by occupation: 15.1% management, 23.1% professional, 13.5% services, 27.8% sales, 0.0% farming, 9.7% construction, 10.7% production (2005-2009 5-year est.).

Income: Per capita income: $26,716 (2010); Median household income: $59,069 (2010); Average household income: $70,503 (2010); Percent of households with income of $100,000 or more: 20.4% (2010); Poverty rate: 7.9% (2005-2009 5-year est.).

Taxes: Total city taxes per capita: $809 (2007); City property taxes per capita: $0 (2007).

Education: Percent of population age 25 and over with: High school diploma (including GED) or higher: 88.3% (2010); Bachelor's degree or higher: 36.8% (2010); Master's degree or higher: 12.2% (2010).

School District(s)
Stafford Msd (PK-12)

2009-10 Enrollment: 3,162 . . . . (281) 261-9200

Housing: Homeownership rate: 47.4% (2010); Median home value: $136,247 (2010); Median contract rent: $833 per month (2005-2009 5-year est.); Median year structure built: 1990 (2005-2009 5-year est.).

Safety: Violent crime rate: 39.0 per 10,000 population; Property crime rate: 424.7 per 10,000 population (2009).

Newspapers: Fort Bend Star (Local news)

Transportation: Commute to work: 94.9% car, 1.4% public transportation, 1.7% walk, 1.2% work from home (2005-2009 5-year est.); Travel time to work: 25.1% less than 15 minutes, 33.6% 15 to 30 minutes, 26.5% 30 to 45 minutes, 8.5% 45 to 60 minutes, 6.3% 60 minutes or more (2005-2009 5-year est.)

Additional Information Contacts

City of Stafford . . . . (281) 261-3900
http://www.cityofstafford.com

SUGAR LAND (city). Covers a land area of 24.087 square miles and a water area of 0.832 square miles. Located at 29.60° N. Lat; 95.61° W. Long. Elevation is 75 feet.

Population: 44,150 (1990); 63,328 (2000); 78,697 (2010); 91,114 (2015 projected); Race: 51.9% White, 7.7% Black, 32.3% Asian, 8.1% Other, 11.0% Hispanic of any race (2010); Density: 3,267.2 persons per square mile (2010); Average household size: 2.98 (2010); Median age: 36.7 (2010); Males per 100 females: 95.5 (2010); Marriage status: 25.4% never married, 61.8% now married, 4.6% widowed, 8.2% divorced (2005-2009 5-year est.); Foreign born: 31.0% (2005-2009 5-year est.); Ancestry (includes multiple ancestries): 11.5% German, 9.1% English, 7.6% Irish, 5.5% American, 3.7% French (2005-2009 5-year est.).

Economy: Unemployment rate: 6.6% (June 2011); Total civilian labor force: 42,993 (June 2011); Single-family building permits issued: 437 (2010); Multi-family building permits issued: 0 (2010); Employment by occupation: 23.2% management, 32.9% professional, 7.9% services, 27.7% sales, 0.2% farming, 2.5% construction, 5.5% production (2005-2009 5-year est.).

Income: Per capita income: $39,680 (2010); Median household income: $93,025 (2010); Average household income: $118,590 (2010); Percent of households with income of $100,000 or more: 45.7% (2010); Poverty rate: 5.8% (2005-2009 5-year est.).

Taxes: Total city taxes per capita: $808 (2007); City property taxes per capita: $271 (2007).

Education: Percent of population age 25 and over with: High school diploma (including GED) or higher: 94.4% (2010); Bachelor's degree or higher: 55.1% (2010); Master's degree or higher: 20.6% (2010).

School District(s)
Fort Bend ISD (PK-12)

2009-10 Enrollment: 69,374 . . . . (281) 634-1000

Harmony School of Science (Houston) (KG-09)

2009-10 Enrollment: 620 . . . . (281) 265-2525

Lamar CISD (PK-12)

2009-10 Enrollment: 23,864 . . . . (832) 223-0000

Housing: Homeownership rate: 81.6% (2010); Median home value: $206,621 (2010); Median contract rent: $1,028 per month (2005-2009 5-year est.); Median year structure built: 1989 (2005-2009 5-year est.).

Hospitals: Methodist Sugar Land Hospital; Surgical Specialty Hospital of Sugar Land

Safety: Violent crime rate: 13.7 per 10,000 population; Property crime rate: 224.2 per 10,000 population (2009).

Newspapers: First Colony Monthly (Community news; Circulation 40,000); Fort Bend/Southwest Sun (Community news; Circulation 30,000)

Transportation: Commute to work: 91.4% car, 2.1% public transportation, 0.5% walk, 5.3% work from home (2005-2009 5-year est.); Travel time to work: 19.3% less than 15 minutes, 30.2% 15 to 30 minutes, 31.6% 30 to 45 minutes, 12.9% 45 to 60 minutes, 6.0% 60 minutes or more (2005-2009 5-year est.)

Additional Information Contacts

City of Sugar Land . . . . (281) 275-2700
http://www.sugarlandtx.gov

Fort Bend Chamber of Commerce . . . . (281) 491-0800
http://www.fortbendchamber.org

THOMPSONS (town). Covers a land area of 6.191 square miles and a water area of 2.175 square miles. Located at 29.48° N. Lat; 95.60° W. Long. Elevation is 66 feet.

Population: 171 (1990); 236 (2000); 743 (2010); 890 (2015 projected); Race: 67.7% White, 12.5% Black, 4.6% Asian, 15.2% Other, 28.7% Hispanic of any race (2010); Density: 120.0 persons per square mile (2010); Average household size: 3.00 (2010); Median age: 34.6 (2010); Males per 100 females: 99.7 (2010); Marriage status: 46.3% never married, 50.2% now married, 3.1% widowed, 0.4% divorced (2005-2009 5-year est.); Foreign born: 5.7% (2005-2009 5-year est.); Ancestry (includes multiple ancestries): 14.0% Arab, 12.5% German, 9.7% Czech, 7.5% Swedish, 5.0% American (2005-2009 5-year est.).

Economy: Employment by occupation: 20.9% management, 10.1% professional, 25.0% services, 23.6% sales, 4.1% farming, 12.2% construction, 4.1% production (2005-2009 5-year est.).

Income: Per capita income: $35,318 (2010); Median household income: $80,814 (2010); Average household income: $107,208 (2010); Percent of households with income of $100,000 or more: 36.7% (2010); Poverty rate: 9.7% (2005-2009 5-year est.).

Taxes: Total city taxes per capita: $2,349 (2007); City property taxes per capita: $0 (2007).

Education: Percent of population age 25 and over with: High school diploma (including GED) or higher: 82.8% (2010); Bachelor's degree or higher: 32.6% (2010); Master's degree or higher: 10.2% (2010).

Housing: Homeownership rate: 82.3% (2010); Median home value: $132,432 (2010); Median contract rent: $614 per month (2005-2009 5-year est.); Median year structure built: 1974 (2005-2009 5-year est.).

Transportation: Commute to work: 95.6% car, 0.0% public transportation, 4.4% walk, 0.0% work from home (2005-2009 5-year est.); Travel time to work: 32.1% less than 15 minutes, 26.3% 15 to 30 minutes, 10.2% 30 to 45 minutes, 14.6% 45 to 60 minutes, 16.8% 60 minutes or more (2005-2009 5-year est.)

Franklin County

Located in northeastern Texas; bounded on the north by the Sulphur River; drained by White Oak and Cypress Bayous. Covers a land area of 285.66 square miles, a water area of 9.12 square miles, and is located in the Central Time Zone at 33.09° N. Lat., 95.21° W. Long. The county was founded in 1875. County seat is Mount Vernon.

Weather Station: Mount Vernon											Elevation: 479 feet	
	Jan	Feb	Mar	Apr	May	Jun	Jul	Aug	Sep	Oct	Nov	Dec
High	55	59	67	75	81	89	93	94	87	76	65	56
Low	34	37	45	52	61	69	72	72	64	53	44	35
Precip	2.9	3.5	4.4	3.4	5.3	4.6	3.6	2.4	3.4	5.2	4.6	4.3
Snow	0.5	0.5	tr	0.1	0.0	0.0	0.0	0.0	0.0	0.0	tr	0.5

High and Low temperatures in degrees Fahrenheit; Precipitation and Snow in inches

Population: 7,802 (1990); 9,458 (2000); 11,146 (2010); 11,946 (2015 projected); Race: 84.0% White, 5.8% Black, 0.2% Asian, 10.0% Other, 14.0% Hispanic of any race (2010); Density: 39.0 persons per square mile (2010); Average household size: 2.44 (2010); Median age: 38.8 (2010); Males per 100 females: 95.9 (2010).

Religion: Five largest groups: 48.6% Southern Baptist Convention, 7.0% The United Methodist Church, 6.1% Baptist Missionary Association of America, 5.2% Catholic Church, 2.6% Churches of Christ (2000).

Economy: Unemployment rate: 8.4% (June 2011); Total civilian labor force: 5,311 (June 2011); Leading industries: 18.1% transportation & warehousing; 2.8% accommodation & food services; 2.7% other services (except public administration) (2009); Farms: 564 totaling 133,528 acres (2007); Companies that employ 500 or more persons: 2 (2009); Companies that employ 100 to 499 persons: 1 (2009); Companies that employ less than 100 persons: 181 (2009); Black-owned businesses: n/a (2007); Hispanic-owned businesses: n/a (2007); Asian-owned businesses: n/a (2007); Women-owned businesses: n/a (2007); Retail sales per capita: $9,043 (2010). Single-family building permits issued: 2 (2010); Multi-family building permits issued: 0 (2010).

Income: Per capita income: $21,471 (2010); Median household income: $38,851 (2010); Average household income: $53,057 (2010); Percent of households with income of $100,000 or more: 11.3% (2010); Poverty rate: 15.5% (2009); Bankruptcy rate: 1.02% (2010).

Taxes: Total county taxes per capita: $400 (2007); County property taxes per capita: $363 (2007).

Education: Percent of population age 25 and over with: High school diploma (including GED) or higher: 82.2% (2010); Bachelor's degree or higher: 17.8% (2010); Master's degree or higher: 5.6% (2010).

Housing: Homeownership rate: 77.3% (2010); Median home value: $88,869 (2010); Median contract rent: $425 per month (2005-2009 5-year est.); Median year structure built: 1983 (2005-2009 5-year est.)
Health: Birth rate: 124.5 per 10,000 population (2009); Death rate: 106.1 per 10,000 population (2009); Age-adjusted cancer mortality rate: 147.3 deaths per 100,000 population (2007); Number of physicians: 6.4 per 10,000 population (2008); Hospital beds: 27.2 per 10,000 population (2007); Hospital admissions: 516.0 per 10,000 population (2007).
Elections: 2008 Presidential election results: 23.1% Obama, 75.5% McCain, 0.2% Nader
Additional Information Contacts
Franklin County Government . . . . (903) 537-2342
   http://www.co.franklin.tx.us/ips/cms
Franklin County Chamber of Commerce . . . . (903) 537-4365
   http://franklincountytx.com

Franklin County Communities

MOUNT VERNON (town). County seat. Covers a land area of 3.695 square miles and a water area of 0 square miles. Located at 33.18° N. Lat; 95.22° W. Long. Elevation is 492 feet.
History: Mount Vernon developed around cotton gins and a sawmill.
Population: 2,252 (1990); 2,286 (2000); 2,844 (2010); 3,101 (2015 projected); Race: 67.9% White, 17.1% Black, 0.3% Asian, 14.7% Other, 18.5% Hispanic of any race (2010); Density: 769.7 persons per square mile (2010); Average household size: 2.43 (2010); Median age: 34.1 (2010); Males per 100 females: 89.3 (2010); Marriage status: 33.6% never married, 44.1% now married, 5.2% widowed, 17.2% divorced (2005-2009 5-year est.); Foreign born: 9.1% (2005-2009 5-year est.); Ancestry (includes multiple ancestries): 10.0% Irish, 9.1% English, 8.3% Italian, 7.7% German, 4.3% French (2005-2009 5-year est.).
Economy: Single-family building permits issued: 2 (2010); Multi-family building permits issued: 0 (2010); Employment by occupation: 9.7% management, 14.7% professional, 22.3% services, 27.1% sales, 0.8% farming, 4.8% construction, 20.6% production (2005-2009 5-year est.).
Income: Per capita income: $19,377 (2010); Median household income: $34,909 (2010); Average household income: $48,522 (2010); Percent of households with income of $100,000 or more: 8.6% (2010); Poverty rate: 25.5% (2005-2009 5-year est.).
Taxes: Total city taxes per capita: $393 (2007); City property taxes per capita: $214 (2007).
Education: Percent of population age 25 and over with: High school diploma (including GED) or higher: 81.2% (2010); Bachelor's degree or higher: 18.6% (2010); Master's degree or higher: 6.2% (2010).
School District(s)
Mount Vernon ISD (PK-12)
   2009-10 Enrollment: 1,541 . . . . (903) 537-2546
Housing: Homeownership rate: 62.2% (2010); Median home value: $71,721 (2010); Median contract rent: $407 per month (2005-2009 5-year est.); Median year structure built: 1973 (2005-2009 5-year est.).
Hospitals: East Texas Medical Center - Mt. Vernon (49 beds)
Newspapers: Mt. Vernon Optic-Herald (Community news; Circulation 3,000)
Transportation: Commute to work: 98.1% car, 0.0% public transportation, 1.0% walk, 1.0% work from home (2005-2009 5-year est.); Travel time to work: 43.8% less than 15 minutes, 34.4% 15 to 30 minutes, 17.1% 30 to 45 minutes, 2.1% 45 to 60 minutes, 2.5% 60 minutes or more (2005-2009 5-year est.)
Additional Information Contacts
Franklin County Chamber of Commerce . . . . (903) 537-4365
   http://franklincountytx.com

SCROGGINS (unincorporated postal area, zip code 75480). Covers a land area of 30.117 square miles and a water area of 2.352 square miles. Located at 33.04° N. Lat; 95.19° W. Long. Elevation is 361 feet.
Population: 1,427 (2000); Race: 91.2% White, 0.0% Black, 0.0% Asian, 8.8% Other, 8.4% Hispanic of any race (2000); Density: 47.4 persons per square mile (2000); Age: 18.4% under 18, 25.1% over 64 (2000); Marriage status: 9.1% never married, 75.0% now married, 6.4% widowed, 9.6% divorced (2000); Foreign born: 7.4% (2000); Ancestry (includes multiple ancestries): 21.7% German, 13.0% American, 12.6% English, 10.6% Irish (2000).
Economy: Employment by occupation: 13.5% management, 20.5% professional, 3.8% services, 22.0% sales, 9.7% farming, 15.4% construction, 15.0% production (2000).

Income: Per capita income: $19,833 (2000); Median household income: $34,663 (2000); Poverty rate: 179.1% (2000).
Education: Percent of population age 25 and over with: High school diploma (including GED) or higher: 86.7% (2000); Bachelor's degree or higher: 18.4% (2000).
Housing: Homeownership rate: 88.3% (2000); Median home value: $132,400 (2000); Median contract rent: $277 per month (2000); Median year structure built: 1984 (2000).
Transportation: Commute to work: 83.4% car, 0.0% public transportation, 6.6% walk, 10.0% work from home (2000); Travel time to work: 24.3% less than 15 minutes, 48.1% 15 to 30 minutes, 13.3% 30 to 45 minutes, 7.3% 45 to 60 minutes, 7.0% 60 minutes or more (2000)

Freestone County

Located in east central Texas; bounded on the northeast and east by the Trinity River. Covers a land area of 877.43 square miles, a water area of 14.70 square miles, and is located in the Central Time Zone at 31.70° N. Lat., 96.19° W. Long. The county was founded in 1850. County seat is Fairfield.

Weather Station: Fairfield 3 W											Elevation: 432 feet	
	Jan	Feb	Mar	Apr	May	Jun	Jul	Aug	Sep	Oct	Nov	Dec
High	60	63	71	78	84	90	95	96	90	80	69	60
Low	38	41	47	54	63	69	72	71	65	56	48	38
Precip	3.1	3.9	3.7	2.9	5.1	4.1	2.2	2.4	2.9	4.3	4.4	4.1
Snow	0.1	0.1	tr	tr	0.0	0.0	0.0	0.0	0.0	0.0	tr	0.1

High and Low temperatures in degrees Fahrenheit; Precipitation and Snow in inches

Population: 15,818 (1990); 17,867 (2000); 19,657 (2010); 20,493 (2015 projected); Race: 74.7% White, 17.4% Black, 0.3% Asian, 7.6% Other, 11.9% Hispanic of any race (2010); Density: 22.4 persons per square mile (2010); Average household size: 2.44 (2010); Median age: 37.0 (2010); Males per 100 females: 109.7 (2010).
Religion: Five largest groups: 21.4% Southern Baptist Convention, 15.9% Baptist Missionary Association of America, 9.8% The United Methodist Church, 4.2% Catholic Church, 2.0% Churches of Christ (2000).
Economy: Unemployment rate: 7.3% (June 2011); Total civilian labor force: 10,441 (June 2011); Leading industries: 18.3% mining; 15.3% health care and social assistance; 14.6% retail trade (2009); Farms: 1,473 totaling 399,584 acres (2007); Companies that employ 500 or more persons: 0 (2009); Companies that employ 100 to 499 persons: 7 (2009); Companies that employ less than 100 persons: 350 (2009); Black-owned businesses: n/a (2007); Hispanic-owned businesses: n/a (2007); Asian-owned businesses: n/a (2007); Women-owned businesses: n/a (2007); Retail sales per capita: $9,026 (2010). Single-family building permits issued: 9 (2010); Multi-family building permits issued: 0 (2010).
Income: Per capita income: $21,883 (2010); Median household income: $43,478 (2010); Average household income: $56,103 (2010); Percent of households with income of $100,000 or more: 12.6% (2010); Poverty rate: 14.9% (2009); Bankruptcy rate: 1.04% (2010).
Taxes: Total county taxes per capita: $220 (2007); County property taxes per capita: $218 (2007).
Education: Percent of population age 25 and over with: High school diploma (including GED) or higher: 81.4% (2010); Bachelor's degree or higher: 12.0% (2010); Master's degree or higher: 3.2% (2010).
Housing: Homeownership rate: 77.1% (2010); Median home value: $70,767 (2010); Median contract rent: $398 per month (2005-2009 5-year est.); Median year structure built: 1977 (2005-2009 5-year est.)
Health: Birth rate: 131.5 per 10,000 population (2009); Death rate: 103.1 per 10,000 population (2009); Age-adjusted cancer mortality rate: 284.3 deaths per 100,000 population (2007); Number of physicians: 4.2 per 10,000 population (2008); Hospital beds: 10.6 per 10,000 population (2007); Hospital admissions: 386.8 per 10,000 population (2007).
Elections: 2008 Presidential election results: 27.9% Obama, 71.4% McCain, 0.1% Nader
Additional Information Contacts
Freestone County Government . . . . (254) 389-2635
   http://www.co.freestone.tx.us/ips/cms
Fairfield Chamber of Commerce . . . . (903) 389-5792
   http://www.fairfieldtxchamber.com
Teague Chamber of Commerce . . . . (254) 739-2061
   http://www.teaguetexas.net

Freestone County Communities

DONIE (unincorporated postal area, zip code 75838). Covers a land area of 69.864 square miles and a water area of 0.227 square miles. Located at 31.47° N. Lat; 96.22° W. Long. Elevation is 489 feet.
Population: 509 (2000); Race: 96.2% White, 1.0% Black, 0.0% Asian, 2.8% Other, 16.7% Hispanic of any race (2000); Density: 7.3 persons per square mile (2000); Age: 26.0% under 18, 25.4% over 64 (2000); Marriage status: 20.1% never married, 62.7% now married, 10.6% widowed, 6.6% divorced (2000); Foreign born: 0.0% (2000); Ancestry (includes multiple ancestries): 26.5% American, 7.5% English, 5.2% Irish, 4.2% German (2000).
Economy: Employment by occupation: 11.8% management, 11.0% professional, 17.6% services, 24.1% sales, 8.2% farming, 12.2% construction, 15.1% production (2000).
Income: Per capita income: $19,431 (2000); Median household income: $29,375 (2000); Poverty rate: 179.1% (2000).
Education: Percent of population age 25 and over with: High school diploma (including GED) or higher: 77.6% (2000); Bachelor's degree or higher: 10.0% (2000).
Housing: Homeownership rate: 78.3% (2000); Median home value: $67,500 (2000); Median contract rent: $350 per month (2000); Median year structure built: 1973 (2000).
Transportation: Commute to work: 82.0% car, 0.0% public transportation, 3.3% walk, 12.2% work from home (2000); Travel time to work: 33.5% less than 15 minutes, 29.8% 15 to 30 minutes, 36.7% 30 to 45 minutes, 0.0% 45 to 60 minutes, 0.0% 60 minutes or more (2000)

FAIRFIELD (city). County seat. Covers a land area of 4.513 square miles and a water area of 0 square miles. Located at 31.72° N. Lat; 96.15° W. Long. Elevation is 463 feet.
History: Incorporated 1933.
Population: 3,249 (1990); 3,094 (2000); 3,694 (2010); 3,951 (2015 projected); Race: 72.0% White, 16.6% Black, 0.6% Asian, 10.8% Other, 16.7% Hispanic of any race (2010); Density: 818.6 persons per square mile (2010); Average household size: 2.37 (2010); Median age: 36.5 (2010); Males per 100 females: 98.4 (2010); Marriage status: 31.5% never married, 51.9% now married, 9.1% widowed, 7.5% divorced (2005-2009 5-year est.); Foreign born: 2.3% (2005-2009 5-year est.); Ancestry (includes multiple ancestries): 16.5% German, 12.4% Irish, 10.0% American, 7.6% English, 3.5% Dutch (2005-2009 5-year est.).
Economy: Single-family building permits issued: 0 (2010); Multi-family building permits issued: 0 (2010); Employment by occupation: 7.2% management, 35.6% professional, 8.2% services, 26.1% sales, 2.1% farming, 7.9% construction, 13.0% production (2005-2009 5-year est.).
Income: Per capita income: $21,016 (2010); Median household income: $39,080 (2010); Average household income: $50,947 (2010); Percent of households with income of $100,000 or more: 9.3% (2010); Poverty rate: 15.0% (2005-2009 5-year est.).
Taxes: Total city taxes per capita: $473 (2007); City property taxes per capita: $127 (2007).
Education: Percent of population age 25 and over with: High school diploma (including GED) or higher: 80.6% (2010); Bachelor's degree or higher: 10.6% (2010); Master's degree or higher: 3.5% (2010).
School District(s)
Dew ISD (PK-08)
   2009-10 Enrollment: 149 . . . . (903) 389-2828
Fairfield ISD (PK-12)
   2009-10 Enrollment: 1,811 . . . . (903) 389-2532
Teague ISD (PK-12)
   2009-10 Enrollment: 1,220 . . . . (254) 739-3071
Housing: Homeownership rate: 67.8% (2010); Median home value: $65,953 (2010); Median contract rent: $450 per month (2005-2009 5-year est.); Median year structure built: 1974 (2005-2009 5-year est.).
Hospitals: East Texas Medical Center - Fairfield (48 beds)
Safety: Violent crime rate: 16.3 per 10,000 population; Property crime rate: 116.9 per 10,000 population (2009).
Newspapers: Recorder (Community news; Circulation 4,000)
Transportation: Commute to work: 99.1% car, 0.0% public transportation, 0.0% walk, 0.9% work from home (2005-2009 5-year est.); Travel time to work: 46.4% less than 15 minutes, 21.1% 15 to 30 minutes, 25.6% 30 to 45 minutes, 1.6% 45 to 60 minutes, 5.3% 60 minutes or more (2005-2009 5-year est.)
Additional Information Contacts

Fairfield Chamber of Commerce . . . . (903) 389-5792
   http://www.fairfieldtxchamber.com

KIRVIN (town). Covers a land area of 0.403 square miles and a water area of 0 square miles. Located at 31.76° N. Lat; 96.33° W. Long. Elevation is 463 feet.
Population: 107 (1990); 122 (2000); 137 (2010); 145 (2015 projected); Race: 79.6% White, 14.6% Black, 0.0% Asian, 5.8% Other, 5.8% Hispanic of any race (2010); Density: 340.2 persons per square mile (2010); Average household size: 2.66 (2010); Median age: 36.8 (2010); Males per 100 females: 85.1 (2010); Marriage status: 11.1% never married, 72.2% now married, 5.6% widowed, 11.1% divorced (2005-2009 5-year est.); Foreign born: 0.0% (2005-2009 5-year est.); Ancestry (includes multiple ancestries): 62.6% English, 10.4% Irish (2005-2009 5-year est.).
Economy: Employment by occupation: 6.5% management, 0.0% professional, 10.9% services, 23.9% sales, 0.0% farming, 58.7% construction, 0.0% production (2005-2009 5-year est.).
Income: Per capita income: $25,786 (2010); Median household income: $61,538 (2010); Average household income: $68,400 (2010); Percent of households with income of $100,000 or more: 16.0% (2010); Poverty rate: 12.2% (2005-2009 5-year est.).
Education: Percent of population age 25 and over with: High school diploma (including GED) or higher: 78.3% (2010); Bachelor's degree or higher: 9.8% (2010); Master's degree or higher: 4.3% (2010).
Housing: Homeownership rate: 86.0% (2010); Median home value: $61,667 (2010); Median contract rent: n/a per month (2005-2009 5-year est.); Median year structure built: 1966 (2005-2009 5-year est.).
Transportation: Commute to work: 73.9% car, 0.0% public transportation, 13.0% walk, 13.0% work from home (2005-2009 5-year est.); Travel time to work: 60.0% less than 15 minutes, 0.0% 15 to 30 minutes, 40.0% 30 to 45 minutes, 0.0% 45 to 60 minutes, 0.0% 60 minutes or more (2005-2009 5-year est.)

STREETMAN (town). Covers a land area of 0.482 square miles and a water area of 0.004 square miles. Located at 31.87° N. Lat; 96.32° W. Long. Elevation is 371 feet.
Population: 260 (1990); 203 (2000); 189 (2010); 183 (2015 projected); Race: 88.9% White, 8.5% Black, 0.0% Asian, 2.6% Other, 7.4% Hispanic of any race (2010); Density: 392.5 persons per square mile (2010); Average household size: 2.01 (2010); Median age: 49.1 (2010); Males per 100 females: 96.9 (2010); Marriage status: 13.3% never married, 63.3% now married, 14.4% widowed, 8.9% divorced (2005-2009 5-year est.); Foreign born: 0.0% (2005-2009 5-year est.); Ancestry (includes multiple ancestries): 24.8% German, 8.8% Irish, 5.6% English, 3.2% Dutch, 2.4% American (2005-2009 5-year est.).
Economy: Employment by occupation: 16.0% management, 20.0% professional, 0.0% services, 60.0% sales, 0.0% farming, 0.0% construction, 4.0% production (2005-2009 5-year est.).
Income: Per capita income: $22,833 (2010); Median household income: $32,143 (2010); Average household income: $45,426 (2010); Percent of households with income of $100,000 or more: 9.6% (2010); Poverty rate: 14.4% (2005-2009 5-year est.).
Taxes: Total city taxes per capita: $48 (2007); City property taxes per capita: $0 (2007).
Education: Percent of population age 25 and over with: High school diploma (including GED) or higher: 79.6% (2010); Bachelor's degree or higher: 4.8% (2010); Master's degree or higher: 0.0% (2010).
Housing: Homeownership rate: 74.5% (2010); Median home value: $35,714 (2010); Median contract rent: n/a per month (2005-2009 5-year est.); Median year structure built: 1961 (2005-2009 5-year est.).
Transportation: Commute to work: 100.0% car, 0.0% public transportation, 0.0% walk, 0.0% work from home (2005-2009 5-year est.); Travel time to work: 10.0% less than 15 minutes, 90.0% 15 to 30 minutes, 0.0% 30 to 45 minutes, 0.0% 45 to 60 minutes, 0.0% 60 minutes or more (2005-2009 5-year est.)

TEAGUE (city). Covers a land area of 3.438 square miles and a water area of 0 square miles. Located at 31.62° N. Lat; 96.28° W. Long. Elevation is 495 feet.
History: From Teague was shipped the freestone (soft stone such as sandstone or limestone which can be cut without shattering) which gave Freestone County its name. Teague's early industries also included cotton gins and a cottonseed oil mill.
Population: 3,237 (1990); 4,557 (2000); 4,766 (2010); 4,882 (2015 projected); Race: 58.9% White, 31.9% Black, 0.2% Asian, 9.0% Other,

19.4% Hispanic of any race (2010); Density: 1,386.2 persons per square mile (2010); Average household size: 2.48 (2010); Median age: 31.9 (2010); Males per 100 females: 163.3 (2010); Marriage status: 27.8% never married, 56.4% now married, 8.8% widowed, 7.0% divorced (2005-2009 5-year est.); Foreign born: 7.9% (2005-2009 5-year est.); Ancestry (includes multiple ancestries): 15.0% English, 10.8% Irish, 10.2% German, 6.6% American, 5.4% French (2005-2009 5-year est.).

Economy: Single-family building permits issued: 9 (2010); Multi-family building permits issued: 0 (2010); Employment by occupation: 7.3% management, 20.9% professional, 17.8% services, 20.9% sales, 0.3% farming, 15.9% construction, 16.9% production (2005-2009 5-year est.).

Income: Per capita income: $17,991 (2010); Median household income: $41,705 (2010); Average household income: $53,275 (2010); Percent of households with income of $100,000 or more: 11.1% (2010); Poverty rate: 18.1% (2005-2009 5-year est.).

Taxes: Total city taxes per capita: $204 (2007); City property taxes per capita: $123 (2007).

Education: Percent of population age 25 and over with: High school diploma (including GED) or higher: 79.5% (2010); Bachelor's degree or higher: 10.7% (2010); Master's degree or higher: 2.8% (2010).

School District(s)

Teague ISD (PK-12)

2009-10 Enrollment: 1,220 . . . . (254) 739-3071

Housing: Homeownership rate: 70.9% (2010); Median home value: $48,995 (2010); Median contract rent: $341 per month (2005-2009 5-year est.); Median year structure built: 1970 (2005-2009 5-year est.).

Safety: Violent crime rate: 58.9 per 10,000 population; Property crime rate: 225.1 per 10,000 population (2009).

Newspapers: Teague Chronicle (Local news; Circulation 2,500)

Transportation: Commute to work: 90.6% car, 0.0% public transportation, 0.0% walk, 4.2% work from home (2005-2009 5-year est.); Travel time to work: 43.7% less than 15 minutes, 22.8% 15 to 30 minutes, 7.4% 30 to 45 minutes, 11.8% 45 to 60 minutes, 14.3% 60 minutes or more (2005-2009 5-year est.)

Additional Information Contacts

Teague Chamber of Commerce . . . . (254) 739-2061
http://www.teaguetexas.net

WORTHAM (town). Covers a land area of 1.982 square miles and a water area of 0.005 square miles. Located at 31.78° N. Lat; 96.46° W. Long. Elevation is 476 feet.

History: Confederate Reunion Grounds State Historical Site to Southwest. Incorporated 1910.

Population: 1,025 (1990); 1,082 (2000); 1,114 (2010); 1,144 (2015 projected); Race: 82.0% White, 12.9% Black, 0.0% Asian, 5.0% Other, 5.0% Hispanic of any race (2010); Density: 562.1 persons per square mile (2010); Average household size: 2.48 (2010); Median age: 34.7 (2010); Males per 100 females: 87.9 (2010); Marriage status: 24.0% never married, 50.4% now married, 12.9% widowed, 12.7% divorced (2005-2009 5-year est.); Foreign born: 6.9% (2005-2009 5-year est.); Ancestry (includes multiple ancestries): 14.3% English, 10.2% Irish, 8.9% German, 5.8% French, 5.2% American (2005-2009 5-year est.).

Economy: Single-family building permits issued: 0 (2010); Multi-family building permits issued: 0 (2010); Employment by occupation: 13.9% management, 24.1% professional, 21.6% services, 19.2% sales, 0.0% farming, 13.0% construction, 8.2% production (2005-2009 5-year est.).

Income: Per capita income: $20,873 (2010); Median household income: $39,674 (2010); Average household income: $51,980 (2010); Percent of households with income of $100,000 or more: 9.6% (2010); Poverty rate: 37.0% (2005-2009 5-year est.).

Taxes: Total city taxes per capita: $344 (2007); City property taxes per capita: $173 (2007).

Education: Percent of population age 25 and over with: High school diploma (including GED) or higher: 81.3% (2010); Bachelor's degree or higher: 11.9% (2010); Master's degree or higher: 3.3% (2010).

School District(s)

Wortham ISD (PK-12)

2009-10 Enrollment: 504 . . . . (254) 765-3095

Housing: Homeownership rate: 66.0% (2010); Median home value: $48,545 (2010); Median contract rent: $221 per month (2005-2009 5-year est.); Median year structure built: 1965 (2005-2009 5-year est.).

Safety: Violent crime rate: 73.4 per 10,000 population; Property crime rate: 293.6 per 10,000 population (2009).

Transportation: Commute to work: 90.1% car, 0.0% public transportation, 0.0% walk, 9.9% work from home (2005-2009 5-year est.); Travel time to work: 23.4% less than 15 minutes, 46.6% 15 to 30 minutes, 14.4% 30 to 45 minutes, 7.7% 45 to 60 minutes, 7.9% 60 minutes or more (2005-2009 5-year est.)

Frio County

Located in southwestern Texas; drained by the Frio River. Covers a land area of 1,133.02 square miles, a water area of 1.26 square miles, and is located in the Central Time Zone at 28.88° N. Lat., 99.11° W. Long. The county was founded in 1858. County seat is Pearsall.

Weather Station: Dilley   Elevation: 549 feet

	Jan	Feb	Mar	Apr	May	Jun	Jul	Aug	Sep	Oct	Nov	Dec
High	65	70	76	84	89	94	97	98	92	84	74	67
Low	42	45	52	59	67	72	73	73	69	61	51	43
Precip	1.3	1.3	1.9	1.4	3.6	3.1	2.4	2.2	2.8	3.2	1.7	1.2
Snow	tr	0.0	0.0	0.0	0.0	0.0	0.0	0.0	0.0	tr	0.0	0.1

High and Low temperatures in degrees Fahrenheit; Precipitation and Snow in inches

Weather Station: Pearsall   Elevation: 634 feet

	Jan	Feb	Mar	Apr	May	Jun	Jul	Aug	Sep	Oct	Nov	Dec
High	66	70	77	84	91	96	98	98	93	85	75	66
Low	38	42	49	55	63	68	69	69	65	56	47	39
Precip	1.4	1.5	1.8	1.8	3.1	3.5	2.5	1.8	2.5	3.0	1.5	1.1
Snow	0.0	0.0	0.0	0.0	0.0	0.0	0.0	0.0	0.0	tr	0.0	0.0

High and Low temperatures in degrees Fahrenheit; Precipitation and Snow in inches

Population: 13,472 (1990); 16,252 (2000); 16,408 (2010); 16,454 (2015 projected); Race: 71.3% White, 5.2% Black, 0.7% Asian, 22.9% Other, 73.9% Hispanic of any race (2010); Density: 14.5 persons per square mile (2010); Average household size: 2.86 (2010); Median age: 32.3 (2010); Males per 100 females: 121.3 (2010).

Religion: Five largest groups: 60.4% Catholic Church, 12.7% Southern Baptist Convention, 6.7% The United Methodist Church, 1.2% Assemblies of God, 1.1% Churches of Christ (2000).

Economy: Unemployment rate: 8.1% (June 2011); Total civilian labor force: 7,861 (June 2011); Leading industries: 18.7% health care and social assistance; 17.8% retail trade; 10.0% accommodation & food services (2009); Farms: 724 totaling 645,429 acres (2007); Companies that employ 500 or more persons: 1 (2009); Companies that employ 100 to 499 persons: 0 (2009); Companies that employ less than 100 persons: 242 (2009); Black-owned businesses: n/a (2007); Hispanic-owned businesses: 653 (2007); Asian-owned businesses: n/a (2007); Women-owned businesses: 385 (2007); Retail sales per capita: $8,685 (2010). Single-family building permits issued: 11 (2010); Multi-family building permits issued: 0 (2010).

Income: Per capita income: $19,890 (2010); Median household income: $32,894 (2010); Average household income: $44,083 (2010); Percent of households with income of $100,000 or more: 7.3% (2010); Poverty rate: 32.4% (2009); Bankruptcy rate: 0.23% (2010).

Taxes: Total county taxes per capita: $256 (2007); County property taxes per capita: $208 (2007).

Education: Percent of population age 25 and over with: High school diploma (including GED) or higher: 63.2% (2010); Bachelor's degree or higher: 9.7% (2010); Master's degree or higher: 2.0% (2010).

Housing: Homeownership rate: 66.8% (2010); Median home value: $43,911 (2010); Median contract rent: $288 per month (2005-2009 5-year est.); Median year structure built: 1973 (2005-2009 5-year est.)

Health: Birth rate: 158.5 per 10,000 population (2009); Death rate: 63.8 per 10,000 population (2009); Age-adjusted cancer mortality rate: 150.2 deaths per 100,000 population (2007); Number of physicians: 5.0 per 10,000 population (2008); Hospital beds: 24.8 per 10,000 population (2007); Hospital admissions: 1,068.1 per 10,000 population (2007).

Elections: 2008 Presidential election results: 59.2% Obama, 40.5% McCain, 0.0% Nader

Additional Information Contacts

Frio County Government . . . . (830) 334-3100
http://www.co.frio.tx.us/ips/cms
City of Pearsall. . . . . (830) 334-3676
Pearsall Chamber of Commerce . . . . (830) 334-9414
http://www.pearsalltexas.com

Frio County Communities

BIGFOOT (CDP). Covers a land area of 23.882 square miles and a water area of 0.025 square miles. Located at 29.05° N. Lat; 98.84° W. Long. Elevation is 650 feet.
Population: 301 (1990); 304 (2000); 314 (2010); 318 (2015 projected); Race: 87.3% White, 0.6% Black, 0.3% Asian, 11.8% Other, 41.4% Hispanic of any race (2010); Density: 13.1 persons per square mile (2010); Average household size: 2.51 (2010); Median age: 41.6 (2010); Males per 100 females: 97.5 (2010); Marriage status: 14.5% never married, 61.0% now married, 0.0% widowed, 24.5% divorced (2005-2009 5-year est.); Foreign born: 0.0% (2005-2009 5-year est.); Ancestry (includes multiple ancestries): 27.1% Irish, 20.5% German, 16.7% Cajun, 10.8% Scotch-Irish, 9.8% American (2005-2009 5-year est.).
Economy: Employment by occupation: 0.0% management, 8.0% professional, 25.7% services, 0.0% sales, 16.5% farming, 0.0% construction, 49.8% production (2005-2009 5-year est.).
Income: Per capita income: $21,885 (2010); Median household income: $45,227 (2010); Average household income: $55,907 (2010); Percent of households with income of $100,000 or more: 18.5% (2010); Poverty rate: 0.0% (2005-2009 5-year est.).
Education: Percent of population age 25 and over with: High school diploma (including GED) or higher: 68.9% (2010); Bachelor's degree or higher: 12.4% (2010); Master's degree or higher: 2.9% (2010).
School District(s)
Cotulla ISD (PK-12)
   2009-10 Enrollment: 1,178 . . . . (830) 879-3073
Devine ISD (PK-12)
   2009-10 Enrollment: 1,913 . . . . (830) 851-0795
Jourdanton ISD (PK-12)
   2009-10 Enrollment: 1,276 . . . . (830) 769-3548
Medina Valley ISD (PK-12)
   2009-10 Enrollment: 3,382 . . . . (830) 931-2243
Housing: Homeownership rate: 83.1% (2010); Median home value: $59,500 (2010); Median contract rent: n/a per month (2005-2009 5-year est.); Median year structure built: 1985 (2005-2009 5-year est.).
Transportation: Commute to work: 100.0% car, 0.0% public transportation, 0.0% walk, 0.0% work from home (2005-2009 5-year est.); Travel time to work: 8.0% less than 15 minutes, 13.7% 15 to 30 minutes, 16.5% 30 to 45 minutes, 39.0% 45 to 60 minutes, 22.9% 60 minutes or more (2005-2009 5-year est.)

DILLEY (city). Covers a land area of 2.334 square miles and a water area of 0 square miles. Located at 28.67° N. Lat; 99.17° W. Long. Elevation is 561 feet.
History: Settled 1880, incorporated 1920.
Population: 2,795 (1990); 3,674 (2000); 3,732 (2010); 3,745 (2015 projected); Race: 66.3% White, 12.4% Black, 1.2% Asian, 20.2% Other, 69.2% Hispanic of any race (2010); Density: 1,599.1 persons per square mile (2010); Average household size: 2.90 (2010); Median age: 30.3 (2010); Males per 100 females: 157.2 (2010); Marriage status: 41.0% never married, 46.5% now married, 5.7% widowed, 6.9% divorced (2005-2009 5-year est.); Foreign born: 5.4% (2005-2009 5-year est.); Ancestry (includes multiple ancestries): 9.3% English, 4.9% Polish, 3.6% German, 3.2% French, 2.5% American (2005-2009 5-year est.).
Economy: Single-family building permits issued: 2 (2010); Multi-family building permits issued: 0 (2010); Employment by occupation: 7.1% management, 25.2% professional, 26.4% services, 18.0% sales, 2.3% farming, 10.8% construction, 10.2% production (2005-2009 5-year est.).
Income: Per capita income: $21,908 (2010); Median household income: $28,528 (2010); Average household income: $37,270 (2010); Percent of households with income of $100,000 or more: 3.9% (2010); Poverty rate: 24.8% (2005-2009 5-year est.).
Taxes: Total city taxes per capita: $143 (2007); City property taxes per capita: $51 (2007).
Education: Percent of population age 25 and over with: High school diploma (including GED) or higher: 64.6% (2010); Bachelor's degree or higher: 8.7% (2010); Master's degree or higher: 1.9% (2010).
School District(s)
Dilley ISD (PK-12)
   2009-10 Enrollment: 917 . . . . (830) 965-1912
Housing: Homeownership rate: 67.6% (2010); Median home value: $29,386 (2010); Median contract rent: $265 per month (2005-2009 5-year est.); Median year structure built: 1968 (2005-2009 5-year est.).
Hospitals: Community General Hospital

Safety: Violent crime rate: 25.0 per 10,000 population; Property crime rate: 80.6 per 10,000 population (2009).
Transportation: Commute to work: 90.5% car, 0.0% public transportation, 2.9% walk, 4.7% work from home (2005-2009 5-year est.); Travel time to work: 66.8% less than 15 minutes, 17.2% 15 to 30 minutes, 6.1% 30 to 45 minutes, 2.1% 45 to 60 minutes, 7.8% 60 minutes or more (2005-2009 5-year est.)

HILLTOP (CDP). Covers a land area of 1.193 square miles and a water area of 0 square miles. Located at 28.69° N. Lat; 99.17° W. Long. Elevation is 522 feet.
Population: 91 (1990); 300 (2000); 309 (2010); 313 (2015 projected); Race: 62.5% White, 24.6% Black, 1.6% Asian, 11.3% Other, 52.4% Hispanic of any race (2010); Density: 259.0 persons per square mile (2010); Average household size: 2.73 (2010); Median age: 30.3 (2010); Males per 100 females: 263.5 (2010); Marriage status: 47.7% never married, 52.3% now married, 0.0% widowed, 0.0% divorced (2005-2009 5-year est.); Foreign born: 0.0% (2005-2009 5-year est.); Ancestry (includes multiple ancestries): 16.9% English (2005-2009 5-year est.).
Economy: Employment by occupation: 0.0% management, 27.0% professional, 0.0% services, 52.0% sales, 0.0% farming, 0.0% construction, 21.0% production (2005-2009 5-year est.).
Income: Per capita income: $32,532 (2010); Median household income: $35,000 (2010); Average household income: $45,292 (2010); Percent of households with income of $100,000 or more: 5.0% (2010); Poverty rate: 0.0% (2005-2009 5-year est.).
Education: Percent of population age 25 and over with: High school diploma (including GED) or higher: 76.0% (2010); Bachelor's degree or higher: 9.8% (2010); Master's degree or higher: 1.5% (2010).
Housing: Homeownership rate: 53.3% (2010); Median home value: $34,286 (2010); Median contract rent: n/a per month (2005-2009 5-year est.); Median year structure built: 1991 (2005-2009 5-year est.).
Transportation: Commute to work: 100.0% car, 0.0% public transportation, 0.0% walk, 0.0% work from home (2005-2009 5-year est.); Travel time to work: 35.0% less than 15 minutes, 65.0% 15 to 30 minutes, 0.0% 30 to 45 minutes, 0.0% 45 to 60 minutes, 0.0% 60 minutes or more (2005-2009 5-year est.)

MOORE (CDP). Covers a land area of 31.223 square miles and a water area of 0.019 square miles. Located at 29.06° N. Lat; 99.01° W. Long. Elevation is 663 feet.
Population: 584 (1990); 644 (2000); 664 (2010); 672 (2015 projected); Race: 87.5% White, 0.3% Black, 0.2% Asian, 12.0% Other, 41.4% Hispanic of any race (2010); Density: 21.3 persons per square mile (2010); Average household size: 2.52 (2010); Median age: 42.1 (2010); Males per 100 females: 108.2 (2010); Marriage status: 16.9% never married, 57.5% now married, 11.0% widowed, 14.6% divorced (2005-2009 5-year est.); Foreign born: 0.0% (2005-2009 5-year est.); Ancestry (includes multiple ancestries): 49.7% American, 14.4% English, 6.8% German, 4.6% Scotch-Irish (2005-2009 5-year est.).
Economy: Employment by occupation: 0.0% management, 0.0% professional, 0.0% services, 25.0% sales, 0.0% farming, 38.6% construction, 36.4% production (2005-2009 5-year est.).
Income: Per capita income: $21,885 (2010); Median household income: $44,667 (2010); Average household income: $55,200 (2010); Percent of households with income of $100,000 or more: 17.9% (2010); Poverty rate: 7.5% (2005-2009 5-year est.).
Education: Percent of population age 25 and over with: High school diploma (including GED) or higher: 69.4% (2010); Bachelor's degree or higher: 12.4% (2010); Master's degree or higher: 3.4% (2010).
Housing: Homeownership rate: 82.8% (2010); Median home value: $57,955 (2010); Median contract rent: n/a per month (2005-2009 5-year est.); Median year structure built: 1976 (2005-2009 5-year est.).
Transportation: Commute to work: 100.0% car, 0.0% public transportation, 0.0% walk, 0.0% work from home (2005-2009 5-year est.); Travel time to work: 0.0% less than 15 minutes, 48.5% 15 to 30 minutes, 31.8% 30 to 45 minutes, 19.7% 45 to 60 minutes, 0.0% 60 minutes or more (2005-2009 5-year est.)

NORTH PEARSALL (CDP). Covers a land area of 1.335 square miles and a water area of 0 square miles. Located at 28.91° N. Lat; 99.09° W. Long. Elevation is 623 feet.
Population: 399 (1990); 561 (2000); 567 (2010); 569 (2015 projected); Race: 64.0% White, 0.5% Black, 0.7% Asian, 34.7% Other, 90.1% Hispanic of any race (2010); Density: 424.8 persons per square mile

(2010); Average household size: 3.19 (2010); Median age: 31.5 (2010); Males per 100 females: 103.2 (2010); Marriage status: 0.0% never married, 78.5% now married, 7.6% widowed, 13.9% divorced (2005-2009 5-year est.); Foreign born: 10.0% (2005-2009 5-year est.); Ancestry (includes multiple ancestries): 32.0% German, 22.4% Irish, 10.0% Russian, 5.0% English (2005-2009 5-year est.).

Economy: Employment by occupation: 0.0% management, 9.4% professional, 52.0% services, 0.0% sales, 0.0% farming, 9.9% construction, 28.7% production (2005-2009 5-year est.).

Income: Per capita income: $16,903 (2010); Median household income: $42,241 (2010); Average household income: $53,441 (2010); Percent of households with income of $100,000 or more: 9.0% (2010); Poverty rate: 0.0% (2005-2009 5-year est.).

Education: Percent of population age 25 and over with: High school diploma (including GED) or higher: 57.6% (2010); Bachelor's degree or higher: 9.4% (2010); Master's degree or higher: 1.5% (2010).

Housing: Homeownership rate: 67.4% (2010); Median home value: $50,909 (2010); Median contract rent: $139 per month (2005-2009 5-year est.); Median year structure built: 1987 (2005-2009 5-year est.).

Transportation: Commute to work: 100.0% car, 0.0% public transportation, 0.0% walk, 0.0% work from home (2005-2009 5-year est.); Travel time to work: 50.0% less than 15 minutes, 36.1% 15 to 30 minutes, 0.0% 30 to 45 minutes, 0.0% 45 to 60 minutes, 13.9% 60 minutes or more (2005-2009 5-year est.)

PEARSALL (city). County seat. Covers a land area of 4.223 square miles and a water area of 0.011 square miles. Located at 28.89° N. Lat; 99.09° W. Long. Elevation is 633 feet.

History: Pearsall developed as a market town for the northern Winter Garden district, producing watermelon, vegetables, grains, peanuts and pecans.

Population: 6,924 (1990); 7,157 (2000); 7,190 (2010); 7,197 (2015 projected); Race: 72.8% White, 0.3% Black, 0.3% Asian, 26.6% Other, 83.8% Hispanic of any race (2010); Density: 1,702.5 persons per square mile (2010); Average household size: 2.91 (2010); Median age: 33.2 (2010); Males per 100 females: 103.2 (2010); Marriage status: 27.3% never married, 56.2% now married, 9.3% widowed, 7.2% divorced (2005-2009 5-year est.); Foreign born: 9.9% (2005-2009 5-year est.); Ancestry (includes multiple ancestries): 3.8% American, 3.2% German, 2.7% English, 1.1% Czech, 0.9% Italian (2005-2009 5-year est.).

Economy: Single-family building permits issued: 9 (2010); Multi-family building permits issued: 0 (2010); Employment by occupation: 9.4% management, 8.8% professional, 24.0% services, 26.2% sales, 6.1% farming, 17.2% construction, 8.3% production (2005-2009 5-year est.).

Income: Per capita income: $17,016 (2010); Median household income: $31,567 (2010); Average household income: $41,799 (2010); Percent of households with income of $100,000 or more: 6.0% (2010); Poverty rate: 26.4% (2005-2009 5-year est.).

Taxes: Total city taxes per capita: $300 (2007); City property taxes per capita: $139 (2007).

Education: Percent of population age 25 and over with: High school diploma (including GED) or higher: 59.0% (2010); Bachelor's degree or higher: 8.8% (2010); Master's degree or higher: 2.0% (2010).

School District(s)

Pearsall ISD (PK-12)

   2009-10 Enrollment: 2,275 . . . . (830) 334-8001

Housing: Homeownership rate: 64.0% (2010); Median home value: $46,050 (2010); Median contract rent: $208 per month (2005-2009 5-year est.); Median year structure built: 1971 (2005-2009 5-year est.).

Hospitals: Frio Regional Hospital (22 beds)

Safety: Violent crime rate: 35.2 per 10,000 population; Property crime rate: 251.9 per 10,000 population (2009).

Newspapers: Frio Nueces Current (Community news; Circulation 3,600)

Transportation: Commute to work: 90.6% car, 0.3% public transportation, 2.9% walk, 2.3% work from home (2005-2009 5-year est.); Travel time to work: 65.0% less than 15 minutes, 12.7% 15 to 30 minutes, 6.7% 30 to 45 minutes, 0.2% 45 to 60 minutes, 15.4% 60 minutes or more (2005-2009 5-year est.)

Additional Information Contacts

City of Pearsall. . . . . (830) 334-3676

Pearsall Chamber of Commerce . . . . (830) 334-9414

  http://www.pearsalltexas.com

WEST PEARSALL (CDP). Covers a land area of 0.077 square miles and a water area of 0 square miles. Located at 28.89° N. Lat; 99.10° W. Long. Elevation is 617 feet.

Population: 306 (1990); 349 (2000); 347 (2010); 341 (2015 projected); Race: 66.3% White, 0.0% Black, 0.3% Asian, 33.4% Other, 92.8% Hispanic of any race (2010); Density: 4,527.5 persons per square mile (2010); Average household size: 3.07 (2010); Median age: 32.6 (2010); Males per 100 females: 98.3 (2010); Marriage status: n/a never married, n/a now married, n/a widowed, n/a divorced (2005-2009 5-year est.); Foreign born: n/a (2005-2009 5-year est.); Ancestry (includes multiple ancestries): n/a (2005-2009 5-year est.).

Economy: Employment by occupation: n/a management, n/a professional, n/a services, n/a sales, n/a farming, n/a construction, n/a production (2005-2009 5-year est.).

Income: Per capita income: $13,811 (2010); Median household income: $30,833 (2010); Average household income: $40,265 (2010); Percent of households with income of $100,000 or more: 6.2% (2010); Poverty rate: n/a (2005-2009 5-year est.).

Education: Percent of population age 25 and over with: High school diploma (including GED) or higher: 48.5% (2010); Bachelor's degree or higher: 4.4% (2010); Master's degree or higher: 0.5% (2010).

Housing: Homeownership rate: 65.5% (2010); Median home value: $37,500 (2010); Median contract rent: n/a per month (2005-2009 5-year est.); Median year structure built: n/a (2005-2009 5-year est.).

Transportation: Commute to work: n/a car, n/a public transportation, n/a walk, n/a work from home (2005-2009 5-year est.); Travel time to work: n/a less than 15 minutes, n/a 15 to 30 minutes, n/a 30 to 45 minutes, n/a 45 to 60 minutes, n/a 60 minutes or more (2005-2009 5-year est.)

Gaines County

Located in northwestern Texas; bounded on the west by New Mexico. Covers a land area of 1,502.35 square miles, a water area of 0.49 square miles, and is located in the Central Time Zone at 32.77° N. Lat., 102.66° W. Long. The county was founded in 1876. County seat is Seminole.

Weather Station: Seminole   Elevation: 3,339 feet

	Jan	Feb	Mar	Apr	May	Jun	Jul	Aug	Sep	Oct	Nov	Dec
High	56	60	68	77	86	92	94	92	86	77	65	56
Low	28	31	37	45	55	64	67	65	58	48	36	28
Precip	0.7	0.8	1.0	0.9	2.6	2.3	2.3	1.9	2.7	1.5	1.0	0.8
Snow	2.8	1.4	0.4	0.3	0.0	0.0	0.0	0.0	0.0	tr	1.2	1.9

High and Low temperatures in degrees Fahrenheit; Precipitation and Snow in inches

Population: 14,123 (1990); 14,467 (2000); 15,449 (2010); 15,899 (2015 projected); Race: 78.1% White, 2.6% Black, 0.2% Asian, 19.1% Other, 39.7% Hispanic of any race (2010); Density: 10.3 persons per square mile (2010); Average household size: 3.03 (2010); Median age: 31.1 (2010); Males per 100 females: 98.5 (2010).

Religion: Five largest groups: 38.0% Southern Baptist Convention, 16.2% Catholic Church, 11.1% Mennonite; Other Groups, 4.9% Churches of Christ, 4.6% The United Methodist Church (2000).

Economy: Unemployment rate: 6.4% (June 2011); Total civilian labor force: 7,208 (June 2011); Leading industries: 16.1% mining; 15.2% retail trade; 11.5% other services (except public administration) (2009); Farms: 825 totaling 947,728 acres (2007); Companies that employ 500 or more persons: 0 (2009); Companies that employ 100 to 499 persons: 4 (2009); Companies that employ less than 100 persons: 334 (2009); Black-owned businesses: n/a (2007); Hispanic-owned businesses: n/a (2007); Asian-owned businesses: n/a (2007); Women-owned businesses: 286 (2007); Retail sales per capita: $8,790 (2010). Single-family building permits issued: 7 (2010); Multi-family building permits issued: 0 (2010).

Income: Per capita income: $16,864 (2010); Median household income: $38,632 (2010); Average household income: $51,229 (2010); Percent of households with income of $100,000 or more: 9.5% (2010); Poverty rate: 16.5% (2009); Bankruptcy rate: 0.96% (2010).

Taxes: Total county taxes per capita: $683 (2007); County property taxes per capita: $656 (2007).

Education: Percent of population age 25 and over with: High school diploma (including GED) or higher: 62.4% (2010); Bachelor's degree or higher: 12.3% (2010); Master's degree or higher: 3.0% (2010).

Housing: Homeownership rate: 76.9% (2010); Median home value: $51,955 (2010); Median contract rent: $348 per month (2005-2009 5-year est.); Median year structure built: 1973 (2005-2009 5-year est.)

Health: Birth rate: 213.2 per 10,000 population (2009); Death rate: 54.6 per 10,000 population (2009); Age-adjusted cancer mortality rate: 175.6 deaths per 100,000 population (2007); Number of physicians: 2.7 per 10,000 population (2008); Hospital beds: 16.9 per 10,000 population (2007); Hospital admissions: 445.1 per 10,000 population (2007).
Elections: 2008 Presidential election results: 16.0% Obama, 83.2% McCain, 0.0% Nader
Additional Information Contacts
Gaines County Government . . . . (432) 758-5411
    http://www.co.gaines.tx.us/ips/cms
City of Seminole. . . . . (432) 758-3676
Seagraves Chamber of Commerce . . . . (806) 546-2609
Seminole Area Chamber of Commerce . . . . (432) 758-2352
    http://www.seminoletxchamber.org

Gaines County Communities

LOOP (unincorporated postal area, zip code 79342). Covers a land area of 107.904 square miles and a water area of 0 square miles. Located at 32.89° N. Lat; 102.31° W. Long. Elevation is 3,258 feet.
Population: 450 (2000); Race: 70.8% White, 0.7% Black, 0.0% Asian, 28.5% Other, 43.5% Hispanic of any race (2000); Density: 4.2 persons per square mile (2000); Age: 33.9% under 18, 9.6% over 64 (2000); Marriage status: 22.0% never married, 68.6% now married, 6.1% widowed, 3.2% divorced (2000); Foreign born: 22.7% (2000); Ancestry (includes multiple ancestries): 20.3% American, 7.2% Irish, 4.7% English, 3.7% German (2000).
Economy: Employment by occupation: 12.6% management, 20.0% professional, 20.0% services, 15.4% sales, 13.7% farming, 3.4% construction, 14.9% production (2000).
Income: Per capita income: $11,941 (2000); Median household income: $31,000 (2000); Poverty rate: 179.1% (2000).
Education: Percent of population age 25 and over with: High school diploma (including GED) or higher: 62.5% (2000); Bachelor's degree or higher: 12.5% (2000).
School District(s)
Loop ISD (PK-12)
    2009-10 Enrollment: 137 . . . . (806) 487-6412
Housing: Homeownership rate: 73.9% (2000); Median home value: $37,800 (2000); Median contract rent: $200 per month (2000); Median year structure built: 1970 (2000).
Transportation: Commute to work: 84.7% car, 0.0% public transportation, 8.8% walk, 5.3% work from home (2000); Travel time to work: 57.1% less than 15 minutes, 21.7% 15 to 30 minutes, 15.5% 30 to 45 minutes, 1.2% 45 to 60 minutes, 4.3% 60 minutes or more (2000)

SEAGRAVES (city). Covers a land area of 1.450 square miles and a water area of 0 square miles. Located at 32.94° N. Lat; 102.56° W. Long. Elevation is 3,353 feet.
History: Incorporated 1928.
Population: 2,398 (1990); 2,334 (2000); 2,406 (2010); 2,445 (2015 projected); Race: 64.3% White, 6.0% Black, 0.1% Asian, 29.6% Other, 63.3% Hispanic of any race (2010); Density: 1,659.5 persons per square mile (2010); Average household size: 2.86 (2010); Median age: 32.0 (2010); Males per 100 females: 98.7 (2010); Marriage status: 24.1% never married, 61.1% now married, 8.1% widowed, 6.7% divorced (2005-2009 5-year est.); Foreign born: 19.0% (2005-2009 5-year est.); Ancestry (includes multiple ancestries): 15.2% German, 7.5% Irish, 2.5% French, 2.0% English, 1.0% Scotch-Irish (2005-2009 5-year est.).
Economy: Single-family building permits issued: 0 (2010); Multi-family building permits issued: 0 (2010); Employment by occupation: 10.6% management, 12.5% professional, 15.6% services, 19.6% sales, 8.4% farming, 16.1% construction, 17.1% production (2005-2009 5-year est.).
Income: Per capita income: $14,670 (2010); Median household income: $32,632 (2010); Average household income: $41,977 (2010); Percent of households with income of $100,000 or more: 5.4% (2010); Poverty rate: 20.0% (2005-2009 5-year est.).
Taxes: Total city taxes per capita: $220 (2007); City property taxes per capita: $149 (2007).
Education: Percent of population age 25 and over with: High school diploma (including GED) or higher: 58.9% (2010); Bachelor's degree or higher: 9.8% (2010); Master's degree or higher: 3.5% (2010).
School District(s)
Seagraves ISD (PK-12)
    2009-10 Enrollment: 606 . . . . (806) 387-2035

Smyer ISD (PK-12)
    2009-10 Enrollment: 369 . . . . (806) 234-2935
Housing: Homeownership rate: 70.3% (2010); Median home value: $36,228 (2010); Median contract rent: $243 per month (2005-2009 5-year est.); Median year structure built: 1971 (2005-2009 5-year est.).
Safety: Violent crime rate: 17.0 per 10,000 population; Property crime rate: 144.6 per 10,000 population (2009).
Transportation: Commute to work: 92.8% car, 0.0% public transportation, 3.6% walk, 0.6% work from home (2005-2009 5-year est.); Travel time to work: 58.6% less than 15 minutes, 22.1% 15 to 30 minutes, 6.4% 30 to 45 minutes, 3.8% 45 to 60 minutes, 9.1% 60 minutes or more (2005-2009 5-year est.)
Additional Information Contacts
Seagraves Chamber of Commerce . . . . (806) 546-2609

SEMINOLE (city). County seat. Covers a land area of 3.354 square miles and a water area of 0 square miles. Located at 32.71° N. Lat; 102.65° W. Long. Elevation is 3,297 feet.
History: Founded 1908, incorporated 1936.
Population: 6,465 (1990); 5,910 (2000); 6,406 (2010); 6,614 (2015 projected); Race: 78.0% White, 2.6% Black, 0.3% Asian, 19.0% Other, 41.6% Hispanic of any race (2010); Density: 1,910.2 persons per square mile (2010); Average household size: 2.84 (2010); Median age: 32.2 (2010); Males per 100 females: 96.6 (2010); Marriage status: 23.0% never married, 62.1% now married, 6.1% widowed, 8.8% divorced (2005-2009 5-year est.); Foreign born: 10.5% (2005-2009 5-year est.); Ancestry (includes multiple ancestries): 13.9% German, 7.9% Irish, 6.6% American, 6.0% English, 2.1% Dutch (2005-2009 5-year est.).
Economy: Single-family building permits issued: 7 (2010); Multi-family building permits issued: 0 (2010); Employment by occupation: 10.2% management, 17.1% professional, 17.7% services, 19.7% sales, 1.1% farming, 21.8% construction, 12.4% production (2005-2009 5-year est.).
Income: Per capita income: $16,698 (2010); Median household income: $37,317 (2010); Average household income: $47,552 (2010); Percent of households with income of $100,000 or more: 7.7% (2010); Poverty rate: 18.2% (2005-2009 5-year est.).
Taxes: Total city taxes per capita: $368 (2007); City property taxes per capita: $180 (2007).
Education: Percent of population age 25 and over with: High school diploma (including GED) or higher: 65.2% (2010); Bachelor's degree or higher: 13.8% (2010); Master's degree or higher: 3.1% (2010).
School District(s)
Seminole ISD (PK-12)
    2009-10 Enrollment: 2,380 . . . . (432) 758-3662
Housing: Homeownership rate: 78.4% (2010); Median home value: $52,208 (2010); Median contract rent: $350 per month (2005-2009 5-year est.); Median year structure built: 1967 (2005-2009 5-year est.).
Hospitals: Memorial Hospital
Safety: Violent crime rate: 8.1 per 10,000 population; Property crime rate: 165.9 per 10,000 population (2009).
Newspapers: Seminole Sentinel (Local news; Circulation 2,100)
Transportation: Commute to work: 95.1% car, 0.0% public transportation, 0.8% walk, 3.8% work from home (2005-2009 5-year est.); Travel time to work: 70.3% less than 15 minutes, 11.4% 15 to 30 minutes, 12.3% 30 to 45 minutes, 1.7% 45 to 60 minutes, 4.3% 60 minutes or more (2005-2009 5-year est.)
Additional Information Contacts
City of Seminole. . . . . (432) 758-3676
Seminole Area Chamber of Commerce . . . . (432) 758-2352
    http://www.seminoletxchamber.org

Galveston County

Located in south Texas; bounded on the east by Galveston Bay, and on the south by the Gulf of Mexico and West Bay; includes the Bolivar Peninsula and Galveston Island. Covers a land area of 398.47 square miles, a water area of 474.46 square miles, and is located in the Central Time Zone at 29.38° N. Lat., 94.93° W. Long. The county was founded in 1838. County seat is Galveston.

Galveston County is part of the Houston-Sugar Land-Baytown, TX Metropolitan Statistical Area. The entire metro area includes: Austin County, TX; Brazoria County, TX; Chambers County, TX; Fort Bend County, TX; Galveston County, TX; Harris County, TX; Liberty County, TX; Montgomery County, TX; San Jacinto County, TX; Waller County, TX

Population: 217,399 (1990); 250,158 (2000); 296,295 (2010); 318,199 (2015 projected); Race: 71.2% White, 13.9% Black, 2.8% Asian, 12.1% Other, 21.8% Hispanic of any race (2010); Density: 743.6 persons per square mile (2010); Average household size: 2.58 (2010); Median age: 35.9 (2010); Males per 100 females: 96.5 (2010).
Religion: Five largest groups: 16.8% Catholic Church, 13.3% Southern Baptist Convention, 5.3% The United Methodist Church, 1.4% Episcopal Church, 1.2% Evangelical Lutheran Church in America (2000).
Economy: Unemployment rate: 10.0% (June 2011); Total civilian labor force: 146,661 (June 2011); Leading industries: 19.6% health care and social assistance; 16.5% accommodation & food services; 15.7% retail trade (2009); Farms: 692 totaling 103,387 acres (2007); Companies that employ 500 or more persons: 7 (2009); Companies that employ 100 to 499 persons: 87 (2009); Companies that employ less than 100 persons: 4,979 (2009); Black-owned businesses: 1,731 (2007); Hispanic-owned businesses: 2,366 (2007); Asian-owned businesses: 1,352 (2007); Women-owned businesses: 6,852 (2007); Retail sales per capita: $11,435 (2010); Single-family building permits issued: 1,731 (2010); Multi-family building permits issued: 240 (2010).
Income: Per capita income: $28,461 (2010); Median household income: $56,502 (2010); Average household income: $74,232 (2010); Percent of households with income of $100,000 or more: 24.0% (2010); Poverty rate: 14.7% (2009); Bankruptcy rate: 2.27% (2010).
Taxes: Total county taxes per capita: $352 (2007); County property taxes per capita: $344 (2007).
Education: Percent of population age 25 and over with: High school diploma (including GED) or higher: 85.9% (2010); Bachelor's degree or higher: 26.0% (2010); Master's degree or higher: 8.6% (2010).
Housing: Homeownership rate: 66.7% (2010); Median home value: $132,845 (2010); Median contract rent: $630 per month (2005-2009 5-year est.); Median year structure built: 1978 (2005-2009 5-year est.)
Health: Birth rate: 151.1 per 10,000 population (2009); Death rate: 85.6 per 10,000 population (2009); Age-adjusted cancer mortality rate: 219.1 deaths per 100,000 population (2007); Number of physicians: 48.3 per 10,000 population (2008); Hospital beds: 35.2 per 10,000 population (2007); Hospital admissions: 1,564.8 per 10,000 population (2007).
Environment: Air Quality Index: 86.8% good, 12.5% moderate, 0.3% unhealthy for sensitive individuals, 0.3% unhealthy (percent of days in 2008)
Elections: 2008 Presidential election results: 39.8% Obama, 59.3% McCain, 0.1% Nader
National and State Parks: Galveston Island State Park
Additional Information Contacts

Galveston County Government . . . . (281) 766-2244
  http://www.co.galveston.tx.us
City of Dickinson . . . . (281) 337-2489
  http://www.ci.dickinson.tx.us
City of Friendswood . . . . (281) 996-3200
  http://www.ci.friendswood.tx.us
City of Galveston . . . . (409) 797-3500
  http://www.cityofgalveston.org
City of Hitchcock . . . . (409) 986-5591
  http://hitchcockidc.us
City of Kemah . . . . (281) 334-1611
  http://www.kemah-tx.gov
City of La Marque. . . . . (409) 938-9200
  http://www.ci.la-marque.tx.us
City of League City . . . . (281) 554-1000
  http://www.leaguecity.com
City of Santa Fe . . . . (409) 925-6412
  http://www.ci.santa-fe.tx.us
City of Texas City. . . . . (409) 948-3111
  http://www.texas-city-tx.org
Friendswood Chamber of Commerce . . . . (281) 482-3329
  http://www.friendswood-chamber.com
Galveston Chamber of Commerce . . . . (409) 763-5326
  http://www.galvestoncc.com
League City Chamber of Commerce . . . . (281) 338-7339
  http://www.leaguecitychamber.com
North Galveston County Chamber of Commerce . . . . (281) 534-4380
  http://www.northgalvestoncountychamber.com
Texas City-La Marque Chamber of Commerce . . . . (409) 935-1408
  http://www.texascitychamber.com

Galveston County Communities

BACLIFF (CDP). Covers a land area of 2.518 square miles and a water area of 0.005 square miles. Located at 29.50° N. Lat; 94.98° W. Long. Elevation is 16 feet.
Population: 5,479 (1990); 6,962 (2000); 8,170 (2010); 8,958 (2015 projected); Race: 75.6% White, 2.3% Black, 3.8% Asian, 18.2% Other, 36.1% Hispanic of any race (2010); Density: 3,244.3 persons per square mile (2010); Average household size: 2.65 (2010); Median age: 34.3 (2010); Males per 100 females: 107.8 (2010); Marriage status: 26.7% never married, 59.2% now married, 3.3% widowed, 10.8% divorced (2005-2009 5-year est.); Foreign born: 15.2% (2005-2009 5-year est.); Ancestry (includes multiple ancestries): 15.5% Irish, 13.7% German, 10.1% American, 7.7% English, 6.9% French (2005-2009 5-year est.).
Economy: Employment by occupation: 9.8% management, 16.0% professional, 23.4% services, 20.3% sales, 1.5% farming, 20.3% construction, 8.8% production (2005-2009 5-year est.).
Income: Per capita income: $18,721 (2010); Median household income: $38,225 (2010); Average household income: $49,651 (2010); Percent of households with income of $100,000 or more: 9.7% (2010); Poverty rate: 24.1% (2005-2009 5-year est.).
Education: Percent of population age 25 and over with: High school diploma (including GED) or higher: 75.5% (2010); Bachelor's degree or higher: 11.2% (2010); Master's degree or higher: 3.6% (2010).
School District(s)
Dickinson ISD (PK-12)
  2009-10 Enrollment: 8,878 . . . . (281) 229-6000
Housing: Homeownership rate: 65.7% (2010); Median home value: $72,904 (2010); Median contract rent: $644 per month (2005-2009 5-year est.); Median year structure built: 1975 (2005-2009 5-year est.).
Transportation: Commute to work: 85.7% car, 0.0% public transportation, 4.6% walk, 1.0% work from home (2005-2009 5-year est.); Travel time to work: 23.9% less than 15 minutes, 25.4% 15 to 30 minutes, 23.3% 30 to 45 minutes, 13.7% 45 to 60 minutes, 13.7% 60 minutes or more (2005-2009 5-year est.)

BAYOU VISTA (city). Aka Highland Bayou. Covers a land area of 0.495 square miles and a water area of 0 square miles. Located at 29.32° N. Lat; 94.93° W. Long. Elevation is 3 feet.
Population: 1,320 (1990); 1,644 (2000); 1,766 (2010); 1,865 (2015 projected); Race: 93.8% White, 0.6% Black, 1.1% Asian, 4.5% Other, 5.3% Hispanic of any race (2010); Density: 3,570.2 persons per square mile (2010); Average household size: 2.03 (2010); Median age: 49.4 (2010); Males per 100 females: 112.0 (2010); Marriage status: 12.3% never married, 60.7% now married, 4.7% widowed, 22.3% divorced (2005-2009 5-year est.); Foreign born: 5.8% (2005-2009 5-year est.); Ancestry (includes multiple ancestries): 21.3% German, 17.2% English, 13.7% Irish, 7.3% Scotch-Irish, 5.1% Italian (2005-2009 5-year est.).
Economy: Single-family building permits issued: 4 (2010); Multi-family building permits issued: 0 (2010); Employment by occupation: 15.0% management, 16.3% professional, 7.9% services, 37.4% sales, 0.5% farming, 13.8% construction, 9.1% production (2005-2009 5-year est.).
Income: Per capita income: $46,698 (2010); Median household income: $80,382 (2010); Average household income: $95,297 (2010); Percent of households with income of $100,000 or more: 37.0% (2010); Poverty rate: 7.3% (2005-2009 5-year est.).
Taxes: Total city taxes per capita: $338 (2007); City property taxes per capita: $251 (2007).
Education: Percent of population age 25 and over with: High school diploma (including GED) or higher: 94.6% (2010); Bachelor's degree or higher: 23.4% (2010); Master's degree or higher: 7.5% (2010).
Housing: Homeownership rate: 81.8% (2010); Median home value: $170,052 (2010); Median contract rent: $979 per month (2005-2009 5-year est.); Median year structure built: 1978 (2005-2009 5-year est.).
Safety: Violent crime rate: 0.0 per 10,000 population; Property crime rate: 35.5 per 10,000 population (2009).
Transportation: Commute to work: 93.1% car, 0.0% public transportation, 0.0% walk, 4.6% work from home (2005-2009 5-year est.); Travel time to work: 18.5% less than 15 minutes, 36.9% 15 to 30 minutes, 17.8% 30 to 45 minutes, 9.7% 45 to 60 minutes, 17.1% 60 minutes or more (2005-2009 5-year est.)

BOLIVAR PENINSULA (CDP). Covers a land area of 45.191 square miles and a water area of 1.481 square miles. Located at 29.46° N. Lat; 94.60° W. Long. Elevation is 10 feet.

Population: 2,807 (1990); 3,853 (2000); 988 (2010); 783 (2015 projected); Race: 91.3% White, 0.7% Black, 0.6% Asian, 7.4% Other, 10.1% Hispanic of any race (2010); Density: 21.9 persons per square mile (2010); Average household size: 2.07 (2010); Median age: 52.1 (2010); Males per 100 females: 103.7 (2010); Marriage status: 18.3% never married, 60.0% now married, 7.2% widowed, 14.5% divorced (2005-2009 5-year est.); Foreign born: 8.5% (2005-2009 5-year est.); Ancestry (includes multiple ancestries): 20.7% Irish, 17.1% English, 13.2% French, 12.6% German, 9.1% American (2005-2009 5-year est.).
Economy: Employment by occupation: 6.0% management, 13.9% professional, 9.4% services, 19.8% sales, 0.0% farming, 30.7% construction, 20.1% production (2005-2009 5-year est.).
Income: Per capita income: $39,162 (2010); Median household income: $55,519 (2010); Average household income: $80,947 (2010); Percent of households with income of $100,000 or more: 24.7% (2010); Poverty rate: 23.2% (2005-2009 5-year est.).
Education: Percent of population age 25 and over with: High school diploma (including GED) or higher: 82.6% (2010); Bachelor's degree or higher: 18.0% (2010); Master's degree or higher: 6.3% (2010).
Housing: Homeownership rate: 82.6% (2010); Median home value: $84,655 (2010); Median contract rent: $439 per month (2005-2009 5-year est.); Median year structure built: 1970 (2005-2009 5-year est.).
Transportation: Commute to work: 91.2% car, 0.0% public transportation, 7.5% walk, 1.0% work from home (2005-2009 5-year est.); Travel time to work: 39.5% less than 15 minutes, 22.2% 15 to 30 minutes, 8.4% 30 to 45 minutes, 3.9% 45 to 60 minutes, 26.0% 60 minutes or more (2005-2009 5-year est.)

CLEAR LAKE SHORES (city). Covers a land area of 0.467 square miles and a water area of 0.184 square miles. Located at 29.54° N. Lat; 95.03° W. Long. Elevation is 10 feet.
Population: 1,081 (1990); 1,205 (2000); 1,350 (2010); 1,463 (2015 projected); Race: 95.0% White, 0.5% Black, 0.7% Asian, 3.9% Other, 3.8% Hispanic of any race (2010); Density: 2,892.6 persons per square mile (2010); Average household size: 2.01 (2010); Median age: 47.8 (2010); Males per 100 females: 102.4 (2010); Marriage status: 20.2% never married, 56.6% now married, 4.0% widowed, 19.1% divorced (2005-2009 5-year est.); Foreign born: 4.7% (2005-2009 5-year est.); Ancestry (includes multiple ancestries): 22.0% German, 17.4% English, 13.3% Irish, 6.6% Dutch, 6.3% French (2005-2009 5-year est.).
Economy: Single-family building permits issued: 9 (2010); Multi-family building permits issued: 0 (2010); Employment by occupation: 17.4% management, 26.0% professional, 7.5% services, 27.9% sales, 0.0% farming, 11.2% construction, 9.9% production (2005-2009 5-year est.).
Income: Per capita income: $62,582 (2010); Median household income: $96,389 (2010); Average household income: $126,124 (2010); Percent of households with income of $100,000 or more: 48.1% (2010); Poverty rate: 9.0% (2005-2009 5-year est.).
Taxes: Total city taxes per capita: $1,470 (2007); City property taxes per capita: $633 (2007).
Education: Percent of population age 25 and over with: High school diploma (including GED) or higher: 95.0% (2010); Bachelor's degree or higher: 43.8% (2010); Master's degree or higher: 16.9% (2010).
Housing: Homeownership rate: 74.4% (2010); Median home value: $222,609 (2010); Median contract rent: $1,118 per month (2005-2009 5-year est.); Median year structure built: 1979 (2005-2009 5-year est.).
Transportation: Commute to work: 89.9% car, 1.2% public transportation, 0.0% walk, 5.2% work from home (2005-2009 5-year est.); Travel time to work: 23.9% less than 15 minutes, 37.1% 15 to 30 minutes, 10.6% 30 to 45 minutes, 14.0% 45 to 60 minutes, 14.4% 60 minutes or more (2005-2009 5-year est.)

DICKINSON (city). Covers a land area of 9.653 square miles and a water area of 0.148 square miles. Located at 29.46° N. Lat; 95.05° W. Long. Elevation is 16 feet.
Population: 15,262 (1990); 17,093 (2000); 19,166 (2010); 20,437 (2015 projected); Race: 66.9% White, 11.4% Black, 2.0% Asian, 19.6% Other, 31.1% Hispanic of any race (2010); Density: 1,985.4 persons per square mile (2010); Average household size: 2.71 (2010); Median age: 34.5 (2010); Males per 100 females: 97.7 (2010); Marriage status: 27.2% never married, 52.6% now married, 7.7% widowed, 12.4% divorced (2005-2009 5-year est.); Foreign born: 10.8% (2005-2009 5-year est.); Ancestry (includes multiple ancestries): 15.1% German, 8.4% Irish, 7.1% English, 6.7% American, 4.8% Italian (2005-2009 5-year est.).

Economy: Single-family building permits issued: 64 (2010); Multi-family building permits issued: 0 (2010); Employment by occupation: 12.7% management, 18.6% professional, 19.8% services, 23.2% sales, 0.3% farming, 12.4% construction, 13.1% production (2005-2009 5-year est.).
Income: Per capita income: $24,457 (2010); Median household income: $51,676 (2010); Average household income: $66,610 (2010); Percent of households with income of $100,000 or more: 19.8% (2010); Poverty rate: 13.3% (2005-2009 5-year est.).
Taxes: Total city taxes per capita: $509 (2007); City property taxes per capita: $151 (2007).
Education: Percent of population age 25 and over with: High school diploma (including GED) or higher: 85.2% (2010); Bachelor's degree or higher: 23.5% (2010); Master's degree or higher: 6.9% (2010).
School District(s)
Bay Area Charter Inc (PK-12)
   2009-10 Enrollment: 369 . . . . (281) 316-0001
Clear Creek ISD (PK-12)
   2009-10 Enrollment: 37,611 . . . . (281) 284-0079
Dickinson ISD (PK-12)
   2009-10 Enrollment: 8,878 . . . . (281) 229-6000
Housing: Homeownership rate: 67.3% (2010); Median home value: $119,375 (2010); Median contract rent: $614 per month (2005-2009 5-year est.); Median year structure built: 1978 (2005-2009 5-year est.).
Safety: Violent crime rate: 35.6 per 10,000 population; Property crime rate: 388.3 per 10,000 population (2009).
Transportation: Commute to work: 92.2% car, 0.3% public transportation, 3.3% walk, 0.8% work from home (2005-2009 5-year est.); Travel time to work: 22.5% less than 15 minutes, 37.6% 15 to 30 minutes, 23.5% 30 to 45 minutes, 9.2% 45 to 60 minutes, 7.1% 60 minutes or more (2005-2009 5-year est.)
Additional Information Contacts
City of Dickinson . . . . (281) 337-2489
   http://www.ci.dickinson.tx.us
North Galveston County Chamber of Commerce . . . . (281) 534-4380
   http://www.northgalvestoncountychamber.com

FRIENDSWOOD (city). Covers a land area of 21.022 square miles and a water area of 0 square miles. Located at 29.51° N. Lat; 95.19° W. Long. Elevation is 33 feet.
Population: 23,020 (1990); 29,037 (2000); 35,622 (2010); 38,938 (2015 projected); Race: 86.0% White, 3.2% Black, 3.7% Asian, 7.1% Other, 12.1% Hispanic of any race (2010); Density: 1,694.5 persons per square mile (2010); Average household size: 2.84 (2010); Median age: 36.4 (2010); Males per 100 females: 95.1 (2010); Marriage status: 21.0% never married, 64.9% now married, 6.5% widowed, 7.7% divorced (2005-2009 5-year est.); Foreign born: 8.5% (2005-2009 5-year est.); Ancestry (includes multiple ancestries): 22.8% German, 14.5% English, 14.0% Irish, 7.3% American, 5.0% French (2005-2009 5-year est.).
Economy: Unemployment rate: 7.5% (June 2011); Total civilian labor force: 18,141 (June 2011); Single-family building permits issued: 148 (2010); Multi-family building permits issued: 0 (2010); Employment by occupation: 21.0% management, 29.7% professional, 12.0% services, 23.8% sales, 0.1% farming, 6.4% construction, 7.0% production (2005-2009 5-year est.).
Income: Per capita income: $36,324 (2010); Median household income: $84,175 (2010); Average household income: $103,782 (2010); Percent of households with income of $100,000 or more: 39.8% (2010); Poverty rate: 5.1% (2005-2009 5-year est.).
Taxes: Total city taxes per capita: $500 (2007); City property taxes per capita: $338 (2007).
Education: Percent of population age 25 and over with: High school diploma (including GED) or higher: 94.6% (2010); Bachelor's degree or higher: 41.9% (2010); Master's degree or higher: 12.1% (2010).
School District(s)
Clear Creek ISD (PK-12)
   2009-10 Enrollment: 37,611 . . . . (281) 284-0079
Friendswood ISD (PK-12)
   2009-10 Enrollment: 5,970 . . . . (281) 482-1267
Two-year College(s)
Texas School of Business-Friendswood Inc (Private, For-profit)
   Fall 2009 Enrollment: 388 . . . . (281) 648-0880
Housing: Homeownership rate: 79.9% (2010); Median home value: $196,880 (2010); Median contract rent: $810 per month (2005-2009 5-year est.); Median year structure built: 1984 (2005-2009 5-year est.).

Safety: Violent crime rate: 7.8 per 10,000 population; Property crime rate: 129.3 per 10,000 population (2009).
Transportation: Commute to work: 93.5% car, 1.2% public transportation, 1.0% walk, 3.6% work from home (2005-2009 5-year est.); Travel time to work: 20.4% less than 15 minutes, 32.4% 15 to 30 minutes, 25.2% 30 to 45 minutes, 12.4% 45 to 60 minutes, 9.5% 60 minutes or more (2005-2009 5-year est.)

Additional Information Contacts
City of Friendswood . . . . (281) 996-3200
   http://www.ci.friendswood.tx.us
Friendswood Chamber of Commerce . . . . (281) 482-3329
   http://www.friendswood-chamber.com

GALVESTON (city). County seat. Covers a land area of 46.151 square miles and a water area of 162.194 square miles. Located at 29.28° N. Lat; 94.82° W. Long. Elevation is 7 feet.

History: Named for Bernardo de Galvez (1746-1786), Spanish colonial leader and statesman. Galveston's location on a long, narrow island two miles off the coast in the Gulf of Mexico shaped its history as a seaport, a pirate haven, and the victim of hurricanes. Though explorers, including Cabeza de Vaca in 1528, came this way, settlement began in 1816 when Don Luis Aury claimed the island for Mexico and set up a government. The pirate Jean Lafitte followed in 1817, taking over the settlement, naming it Campeachy, and using it for the next four years as his base of operations and the site of his fortified house known as Maison Rouge. Galveston became a U.S. port in 1825, and was incorporated as a city in 1839. In June of 1865 Major General Gordon Granger freed all slaves in Texas, thus creating "Juneteenth" as Emancipation Day. Galveston grew as an exporter of cotton, sulphur, and grain. The most devastating of many hurricanes struck in 1900, referred to as the year of The Storm, when an estimated 6,000 people died and 1500 acres of houses were destroyed.
Population: 59,070 (1990); 57,247 (2000); 52,974 (2010); 49,030 (2015 projected); Race: 58.6% White, 21.8% Black, 4.4% Asian, 15.2% Other, 30.8% Hispanic of any race (2010); Density: 1,147.8 persons per square mile (2010); Average household size: 2.25 (2010); Median age: 35.7 (2010); Males per 100 females: 95.6 (2010); Marriage status: 35.5% never married, 43.6% now married, 7.0% widowed, 13.9% divorced (2005-2009 5-year est.); Foreign born: 12.5% (2005-2009 5-year est.); Ancestry (includes multiple ancestries): 11.8% German, 9.6% Irish, 7.9% English, 4.1% American, 3.8% Italian (2005-2009 5-year est.).
Economy: Unemployment rate: 9.5% (June 2011); Total civilian labor force: 26,153 (June 2011); Single-family building permits issued: 105 (2010); Multi-family building permits issued: 0 (2010); Employment by occupation: 10.4% management, 23.5% professional, 24.5% services, 22.0% sales, 0.4% farming, 9.2% construction, 10.1% production (2005-2009 5-year est.).
Income: Per capita income: $23,414 (2010); Median household income: $36,294 (2010); Average household income: $54,205 (2010); Percent of households with income of $100,000 or more: 12.5% (2010); Poverty rate: 21.9% (2005-2009 5-year est.).
Taxes: Total city taxes per capita: $881 (2007); City property taxes per capita: $281 (2007).
Education: Percent of population age 25 and over with: High school diploma (including GED) or higher: 79.1% (2010); Bachelor's degree or higher: 26.5% (2010); Master's degree or higher: 11.6% (2010).

School District(s)
Ambassadors Preparatory Academy (PK-06)
   2009-10 Enrollment: 183 . . . . (409) 762-1115
Galveston ISD (PK-12)
   2009-10 Enrollment: 6,358 . . . . (409) 766-5121
Odyssey Academy Inc (PK-08)
   2009-10 Enrollment: 506 . . . . (409) 750-9289

Four-year College(s)
Texas A & M University at Galveston (Public)
   Fall 2009 Enrollment: 1,774 . . . . (409) 740-4414
   2010-11 Tuition: In-state $7,158; Out-of-state $16,458
The University of Texas Medical Branch (Public)
   Fall 2009 Enrollment: 2,430 . . . . (409) 772-1011

Two-year College(s)
Galveston College (Public)
   Fall 2009 Enrollment: 2,167 . . . . (409) 944-1220
   2010-11 Tuition: In-state $1,414; Out-of-state $2,314
Housing: Homeownership rate: 41.7% (2010); Median home value: $115,379 (2010); Median contract rent: $594 per month (2005-2009 5-year est.); Median year structure built: 1965 (2005-2009 5-year est.).

Hospitals: Shriners Burns Hospital for Children (30 beds); University of Texas Medical Branch Hospitals
Safety: Violent crime rate: 72.2 per 10,000 population; Property crime rate: 573.6 per 10,000 population (2009).
Newspapers: The Daily News (Regional news; Circulation 26,765)
Transportation: Commute to work: 82.4% car, 2.4% public transportation, 5.9% walk, 3.0% work from home (2005-2009 5-year est.); Travel time to work: 52.2% less than 15 minutes, 31.5% 15 to 30 minutes, 7.9% 30 to 45 minutes, 2.9% 45 to 60 minutes, 5.4% 60 minutes or more (2005-2009 5-year est.); Amtrak: bus service available.
Airports: Scholes International at Galveston (general aviation)

Additional Information Contacts
City of Galveston . . . . (409) 797-3500
   http://www.cityofgalveston.org
Galveston Chamber of Commerce . . . . (409) 763-5326
   http://www.galvestoncc.com

GILCHRIST (unincorporated postal area, zip code 77617). Covers a land area of 6.767 square miles and a water area of 0.026 square miles. Located at 29.52° N. Lat; 94.47° W. Long. Elevation is 7 feet.

Population: 508 (2000); Race: 94.5% White, 1.1% Black, 0.0% Asian, 4.4% Other, 5.8% Hispanic of any race (2000); Density: 75.1 persons per square mile (2000); Age: 19.0% under 18, 15.8% over 64 (2000); Marriage status: 17.2% never married, 53.7% now married, 9.2% widowed, 19.9% divorced (2000); Foreign born: 1.3% (2000); Ancestry (includes multiple ancestries): 17.9% American, 13.7% German, 12.8% Irish, 8.3% French (2000).
Economy: Employment by occupation: 4.7% management, 14.2% professional, 18.0% services, 28.4% sales, 1.4% farming, 18.0% construction, 15.2% production (2000).
Income: Per capita income: $19,303 (2000); Median household income: $30,114 (2000); Poverty rate: 179.1% (2000).
Education: Percent of population age 25 and over with: High school diploma (including GED) or higher: 74.6% (2000); Bachelor's degree or higher: 11.1% (2000).
Housing: Homeownership rate: 80.6% (2000); Median home value: $49,500 (2000); Median contract rent: $415 per month (2000); Median year structure built: 1971 (2000).
Transportation: Commute to work: 84.4% car, 2.0% public transportation, 0.0% walk, 11.7% work from home (2000); Travel time to work: 23.2% less than 15 minutes, 21.0% 15 to 30 minutes, 13.3% 30 to 45 minutes, 11.6% 45 to 60 minutes, 30.9% 60 minutes or more (2000)

HIGH ISLAND (unincorporated postal area, zip code 77623). Covers a land area of 16.190 square miles and a water area of 0.491 square miles. Located at 29.54° N. Lat; 94.42° W. Long. Elevation is 23 feet.

Population: 474 (2000); Race: 93.4% White, 0.0% Black, 4.2% Asian, 2.4% Other, 4.2% Hispanic of any race (2000); Density: 29.3 persons per square mile (2000); Age: 22.5% under 18, 24.5% over 64 (2000); Marriage status: 17.6% never married, 58.8% now married, 11.5% widowed, 12.1% divorced (2000); Foreign born: 2.0% (2000); Ancestry (includes multiple ancestries): 29.3% American, 14.0% French, 11.8% Irish, 11.8% German (2000).
Economy: Employment by occupation: 11.5% management, 16.5% professional, 22.5% services, 13.7% sales, 0.5% farming, 28.0% construction, 7.1% production (2000).
Income: Per capita income: $19,746 (2000); Median household income: $29,444 (2000); Poverty rate: 179.1% (2000).
Education: Percent of population age 25 and over with: High school diploma (including GED) or higher: 70.2% (2000); Bachelor's degree or higher: 8.1% (2000).

School District(s)
High Island ISD (PK-12)
   2009-10 Enrollment: 186 . . . . (409) 286-5317
Housing: Homeownership rate: 80.7% (2000); Median home value: $46,800 (2000); Median contract rent: $283 per month (2000); Median year structure built: 1963 (2000).
Transportation: Commute to work: 90.1% car, 0.0% public transportation, 2.2% walk, 4.4% work from home (2000); Travel time to work: 38.5% less than 15 minutes, 17.2% 15 to 30 minutes, 16.7% 30 to 45 minutes, 10.3% 45 to 60 minutes, 17.2% 60 minutes or more (2000)

HITCHCOCK (city). Covers a land area of 66.463 square miles and a water area of 25.546 square miles. Located at 29.33° N. Lat; 95.01° W. Long. Elevation is 16 feet.

Population: 5,853 (1990); 6,386 (2000); 7,516 (2010); 8,274 (2015 projected); Race: 61.7% White, 28.1% Black, 0.3% Asian, 9.9% Other, 17.6% Hispanic of any race (2010); Density: 113.1 persons per square mile (2010); Average household size: 2.59 (2010); Median age: 35.6 (2010); Males per 100 females: 92.9 (2010); Marriage status: 32.1% never married, 51.4% now married, 6.4% widowed, 10.0% divorced (2005-2009 5-year est.); Foreign born: 6.5% (2005-2009 5-year est.); Ancestry (includes multiple ancestries): 11.8% German, 9.3% Irish, 6.6% English, 2.6% African, 2.3% French (2005-2009 5-year est.).
Economy: Single-family building permits issued: 29 (2010); Multi-family building permits issued: 0 (2010); Employment by occupation: 7.9% management, 11.0% professional, 27.9% services, 25.9% sales, 0.0% farming, 17.5% construction, 9.8% production (2005-2009 5-year est.).
Income: Per capita income: $18,498 (2010); Median household income: $37,195 (2010); Average household income: $48,081 (2010); Percent of households with income of $100,000 or more: 9.8% (2010); Poverty rate: 24.0% (2005-2009 5-year est.).
Taxes: Total city taxes per capita: $320 (2007); City property taxes per capita: $182 (2007).
Education: Percent of population age 25 and over with: High school diploma (including GED) or higher: 78.9% (2010); Bachelor's degree or higher: 9.6% (2010); Master's degree or higher: 3.7% (2010).

School District(s)

Hitchcock ISD (PK-12)
    2009-10 Enrollment: 1,200 . . . . (409) 986-5514
Housing: Homeownership rate: 67.9% (2010); Median home value: $78,650 (2010); Median contract rent: $593 per month (2005-2009 5-year est.); Median year structure built: 1976 (2005-2009 5-year est.).
Safety: Violent crime rate: 41.2 per 10,000 population; Property crime rate: 277.1 per 10,000 population (2009).
Transportation: Commute to work: 89.9% car, 0.0% public transportation, 3.5% walk, 1.1% work from home (2005-2009 5-year est.); Travel time to work: 32.7% less than 15 minutes, 33.3% 15 to 30 minutes, 17.4% 30 to 45 minutes, 10.1% 45 to 60 minutes, 6.5% 60 minutes or more (2005-2009 5-year est.)

Additional Information Contacts
City of Hitchcock . . . . (409) 986-5591
    http://hitchcockidc.us

JAMAICA BEACH (city). Covers a land area of 0.723 square miles and a water area of 0.063 square miles. Located at 29.19° N. Lat; 94.98° W. Long. Elevation is 3 feet.
Population: 624 (1990); 1,075 (2000); 1,090 (2010); 1,132 (2015 projected); Race: 93.7% White, 0.2% Black, 1.0% Asian, 5.1% Other, 11.4% Hispanic of any race (2010); Density: 1,508.4 persons per square mile (2010); Average household size: 2.13 (2010); Median age: 47.3 (2010); Males per 100 females: 100.4 (2010); Marriage status: 22.8% never married, 52.5% now married, 4.3% widowed, 20.4% divorced (2005-2009 5-year est.); Foreign born: 2.6% (2005-2009 5-year est.); Ancestry (includes multiple ancestries): 21.8% English, 14.8% German, 14.2% Irish, 7.4% Scottish, 6.7% Czech (2005-2009 5-year est.).
Economy: Single-family building permits issued: 11 (2010); Multi-family building permits issued: 0 (2010); Employment by occupation: 33.3% management, 17.3% professional, 9.2% services, 25.7% sales, 0.0% farming, 11.7% construction, 2.7% production (2005-2009 5-year est.).
Income: Per capita income: $57,709 (2010); Median household income: $85,096 (2010); Average household income: $122,642 (2010); Percent of households with income of $100,000 or more: 40.9% (2010); Poverty rate: 6.0% (2005-2009 5-year est.).
Taxes: Total city taxes per capita: $600 (2007); City property taxes per capita: $528 (2007).
Education: Percent of population age 25 and over with: High school diploma (including GED) or higher: 96.0% (2010); Bachelor's degree or higher: 50.4% (2010); Master's degree or higher: 20.2% (2010).
Housing: Homeownership rate: 81.4% (2010); Median home value: $216,393 (2010); Median contract rent: $865 per month (2005-2009 5-year est.); Median year structure built: 1977 (2005-2009 5-year est.).
Safety: Violent crime rate: 18.1 per 10,000 population; Property crime rate: 181.3 per 10,000 population (2009).
Transportation: Commute to work: 92.3% car, 0.0% public transportation, 0.0% walk, 7.7% work from home (2005-2009 5-year est.); Travel time to work: 21.4% less than 15 minutes, 30.1% 15 to 30 minutes, 27.1% 30 to 45 minutes, 8.3% 45 to 60 minutes, 13.1% 60 minutes or more (2005-2009 5-year est.)

KEMAH (city). Covers a land area of 1.791 square miles and a water area of 0.030 square miles. Located at 29.53° N. Lat; 95.01° W. Long. Elevation is 7 feet.
History: In area referred to as Clear Lake City.
Population: 1,107 (1990); 2,330 (2000); 2,625 (2010); 2,971 (2015 projected); Race: 68.5% White, 3.9% Black, 3.3% Asian, 24.3% Other, 34.5% Hispanic of any race (2010); Density: 1,465.5 persons per square mile (2010); Average household size: 2.77 (2010); Median age: 34.6 (2010); Males per 100 females: 106.2 (2010); Marriage status: 26.1% never married, 60.1% now married, 2.9% widowed, 10.8% divorced (2005-2009 5-year est.); Foreign born: 19.5% (2005-2009 5-year est.); Ancestry (includes multiple ancestries): 19.0% German, 9.1% Italian, 8.2% Irish, 7.1% English, 6.3% American (2005-2009 5-year est.).
Economy: Single-family building permits issued: 23 (2010); Multi-family building permits issued: 3 (2010); Employment by occupation: 21.3% management, 19.7% professional, 16.2% services, 18.7% sales, 0.0% farming, 10.7% construction, 13.5% production (2005-2009 5-year est.).
Income: Per capita income: $34,535 (2010); Median household income: $72,104 (2010); Average household income: $95,928 (2010); Percent of households with income of $100,000 or more: 32.4% (2010); Poverty rate: 8.3% (2005-2009 5-year est.).
Taxes: Total city taxes per capita: $1,135 (2007); City property taxes per capita: $139 (2007).
Education: Percent of population age 25 and over with: High school diploma (including GED) or higher: 87.9% (2010); Bachelor's degree or higher: 31.8% (2010); Master's degree or higher: 10.4% (2010).

School District(s)

Clear Creek ISD (PK-12)
    2009-10 Enrollment: 37,611 . . . . (281) 284-0079
Housing: Homeownership rate: 66.8% (2010); Median home value: $198,529 (2010); Median contract rent: $675 per month (2005-2009 5-year est.); Median year structure built: 1992 (2005-2009 5-year est.).
Safety: Violent crime rate: 23.8 per 10,000 population; Property crime rate: 389.2 per 10,000 population (2009).
Transportation: Commute to work: 89.8% car, 0.9% public transportation, 2.1% walk, 4.5% work from home (2005-2009 5-year est.); Travel time to work: 24.6% less than 15 minutes, 22.9% 15 to 30 minutes, 25.8% 30 to 45 minutes, 8.9% 45 to 60 minutes, 17.8% 60 minutes or more (2005-2009 5-year est.)
Additional Information Contacts
City of Kemah . . . . (281) 334-1611
    http://www.kemah-tx.gov

LA MARQUE (city). Covers a land area of 14.223 square miles and a water area of 0.039 square miles. Located at 29.36° N. Lat; 94.97° W. Long. Elevation is 16 feet.
History: La Marque was named in 1882, and was first a marketing center for fruit raised in the area. It grew with the development of oil refineries here.
Population: 14,099 (1990); 13,682 (2000); 15,375 (2010); 16,495 (2015 projected); Race: 53.5% White, 34.2% Black, 0.5% Asian, 11.8% Other, 21.1% Hispanic of any race (2010); Density: 1,081.0 persons per square mile (2010); Average household size: 2.51 (2010); Median age: 36.3 (2010); Males per 100 females: 91.6 (2010); Marriage status: 31.5% never married, 49.5% now married, 7.9% widowed, 11.1% divorced (2005-2009 5-year est.); Foreign born: 6.0% (2005-2009 5-year est.); Ancestry (includes multiple ancestries): 10.0% German, 9.3% Irish, 5.8% English, 5.1% French, 4.1% American (2005-2009 5-year est.).
Economy: Single-family building permits issued: 69 (2010); Multi-family building permits issued: 0 (2010); Employment by occupation: 8.8% management, 18.9% professional, 18.3% services, 29.6% sales, 0.4% farming, 10.5% construction, 13.4% production (2005-2009 5-year est.).
Income: Per capita income: $21,466 (2010); Median household income: $41,953 (2010); Average household income: $54,019 (2010); Percent of households with income of $100,000 or more: 13.2% (2010); Poverty rate: 16.1% (2005-2009 5-year est.).
Taxes: Total city taxes per capita: $472 (2007); City property taxes per capita: $211 (2007).
Education: Percent of population age 25 and over with: High school diploma (including GED) or higher: 83.5% (2010); Bachelor's degree or higher: 15.2% (2010); Master's degree or higher: 4.6% (2010).

School District(s)

La Marque ISD (PK-12)
    2009-10 Enrollment: 3,398 . . . . (409) 938-4251

Mainland Preparatory Academy (PK-08)
  2009-10 Enrollment: 481 . . . . (409) 934-9100
Shekinah Radiance Academy (PK-12)
  2009-10 Enrollment: 1,125 . . . . (210) 658-6848
Housing: Homeownership rate: 70.9% (2010); Median home value:
$89,556 (2010); Median contract rent: $511 per month (2005-2009 5-year
est.); Median year structure built: 1964 (2005-2009 5-year est.).
Safety: Violent crime rate: 105.6 per 10,000 population; Property crime
rate: 470.0 per 10,000 population (2009).
Transportation: Commute to work: 91.4% car, 0.0% public transportation,
0.8% walk, 2.8% work from home (2005-2009 5-year est.); Travel time to
work: 23.5% less than 15 minutes, 41.8% 15 to 30 minutes, 21.1% 30 to 45
minutes, 5.7% 45 to 60 minutes, 8.0% 60 minutes or more (2005-2009
5-year est.); Amtrak: bus service available.
Additional Information Contacts
City of La Marque. . . . . (409) 938-9200
  http://www.ci.la-marque.tx.us

LEAGUE CITY (city). Covers a land area of 51.240 square miles and
a water area of 1.113 square miles. Located at 29.50° N. Lat; 95.09° W.
Long. Elevation is 20 feet.
History: Incorporated 1961.
Population: 30,247 (1990); 45,444 (2000); 72,973 (2010); 83,055 (2015
projected); Race: 80.5% White, 5.7% Black, 4.1% Asian, 9.8% Other,
16.3% Hispanic of any race (2010); Density: 1,424.1 persons per square
mile (2010); Average household size: 2.74 (2010); Median age: 35.7
(2010); Males per 100 females: 98.4 (2010); Marriage status: 23.1% never
married, 64.0% now married, 2.9% widowed, 10.0% divorced (2005-2009
5-year est.); Foreign born: 10.5% (2005-2009 5-year est.); Ancestry
(includes multiple ancestries): 17.6% German, 11.8% Irish, 10.7% English,
5.3% Italian, 5.0% French (2005-2009 5-year est.).
Economy: Unemployment rate: 8.3% (June 2011); Total civilian labor
force: 40,037 (June 2011); Single-family building permits issued: 770
(2010); Multi-family building permits issued: 206 (2010); Employment by
occupation: 16.8% management, 33.0% professional, 10.2% services,
24.1% sales, 0.1% farming, 7.7% construction, 8.2% production
(2005-2009 5-year est.).
Income: Per capita income: $35,388 (2010); Median household income:
$83,450 (2010); Average household income: $97,181 (2010); Percent of
households with income of $100,000 or more: 37.2% (2010); Poverty rate:
5.8% (2005-2009 5-year est.).
Taxes: Total city taxes per capita: $540 (2007); City property taxes per
capita: $354 (2007).
Education: Percent of population age 25 and over with: High school
diploma (including GED) or higher: 93.4% (2010); Bachelor's degree or
higher: 37.8% (2010); Master's degree or higher: 11.5% (2010).
School District(s)
Bay Area Charter Inc (PK-12)
  2009-10 Enrollment: 369 . . . . (281) 316-0001
Clear Creek ISD (PK-12)
  2009-10 Enrollment: 37,611 . . . . (281) 284-0079
Dickinson ISD (PK-12)
  2009-10 Enrollment: 8,878 . . . . (281) 229-6000
Housing: Homeownership rate: 75.8% (2010); Median home value:
$180,119 (2010); Median contract rent: $801 per month (2005-2009 5-year
est.); Median year structure built: 1995 (2005-2009 5-year est.).
Safety: Violent crime rate: 16.3 per 10,000 population; Property crime rate:
278.9 per 10,000 population (2009).
Newspapers: Bay Area Advertiser (Community news; Circulation 21,000);
Galveston County Advertiser (Local news; Circulation 14,000)
Transportation: Commute to work: 93.6% car, 0.6% public transportation,
0.7% walk, 2.3% work from home (2005-2009 5-year est.); Travel time to
work: 20.4% less than 15 minutes, 35.7% 15 to 30 minutes, 23.6% 30 to 45
minutes, 10.4% 45 to 60 minutes, 9.8% 60 minutes or more (2005-2009
5-year est.)
Additional Information Contacts
City of League City. . . . . (281) 554-1000
  http://www.leaguecity.com
League City Chamber of Commerce . . . . (281) 338-7339
  http://www.leaguecitychamber.com

PORT BOLIVAR (unincorporated postal area, zip code 77650).
Covers a land area of 33.627 square miles and a water area of 0.473
square miles. Located at 29.43° N. Lat; 94.68° W. Long. Elevation is 7 feet.

Population: 2,871 (2000); Race: 92.5% White, 0.7% Black, 0.2% Asian,
6.6% Other, 7.7% Hispanic of any race (2000); Density: 85.4 persons per
square mile (2000); Age: 16.5% under 18, 22.4% over 64 (2000); Marriage
status: 13.8% never married, 61.7% now married, 8.1% widowed, 16.3%
divorced (2000); Foreign born: 4.7% (2000); Ancestry (includes multiple
ancestries): 14.2% Irish, 13.0% German, 12.8% American, 7.6% English
(2000).
Economy: Employment by occupation: 5.1% management, 17.0%
professional, 14.3% services, 21.5% sales, 2.4% farming, 19.8%
construction, 19.9% production (2000).
Income: Per capita income: $28,423 (2000); Median household income:
$36,080 (2000); Poverty rate: 179.1% (2000).
Education: Percent of population age 25 and over with: High school
diploma (including GED) or higher: 79.4% (2000); Bachelor's degree or
higher: 17.2% (2000).
School District(s)
Galveston ISD (PK-12)
  2009-10 Enrollment: 6,358 . . . . (409) 766-5121
Housing: Homeownership rate: 85.0% (2000); Median home value:
$58,900 (2000); Median contract rent: $382 per month (2000); Median year
structure built: 1978 (2000).
Transportation: Commute to work: 93.5% car, 4.0% public transportation,
0.0% walk, 0.8% work from home (2000); Travel time to work: 30.4% less
than 15 minutes, 14.3% 15 to 30 minutes, 9.1% 30 to 45 minutes, 17.1%
45 to 60 minutes, 29.1% 60 minutes or more (2000)

SAN LEON (CDP). Covers a land area of 4.882 square miles and a
water area of 0.287 square miles. Located at 29.48° N. Lat; 94.92° W.
Long. Elevation is 10 feet.
Population: 3,328 (1990); 4,365 (2000); 5,413 (2010); 6,026 (2015
projected); Race: 74.7% White, 1.6% Black, 5.8% Asian, 17.9% Other,
24.4% Hispanic of any race (2010); Density: 1,108.8 persons per square
mile (2010); Average household size: 2.33 (2010); Median age: 40.4
(2010); Males per 100 females: 108.6 (2010); Marriage status: 23.3%
never married, 55.7% now married, 8.9% widowed, 12.1% divorced
(2005-2009 5-year est.); Foreign born: 14.0% (2005-2009 5-year est.);
Ancestry (includes multiple ancestries): 14.5% German, 13.2% Irish, 7.7%
English, 6.4% French, 5.6% American (2005-2009 5-year est.).
Economy: Employment by occupation: 7.6% management, 11.3%
professional, 15.0% services, 20.2% sales, 0.5% farming, 19.7%
construction, 25.7% production (2005-2009 5-year est.).
Income: Per capita income: $21,605 (2010); Median household income:
$39,068 (2010); Average household income: $50,266 (2010); Percent of
households with income of $100,000 or more: 10.5% (2010); Poverty rate:
17.1% (2005-2009 5-year est.).
Education: Percent of population age 25 and over with: High school
diploma (including GED) or higher: 81.5% (2010); Bachelor's degree or
higher: 13.6% (2010); Master's degree or higher: 4.9% (2010).
Housing: Homeownership rate: 70.3% (2010); Median home value:
$91,930 (2010); Median contract rent: $599 per month (2005-2009 5-year
est.); Median year structure built: 1978 (2005-2009 5-year est.).
Transportation: Commute to work: 94.3% car, 0.5% public transportation,
2.5% walk, 2.7% work from home (2005-2009 5-year est.); Travel time to
work: 17.0% less than 15 minutes, 35.2% 15 to 30 minutes, 26.4% 30 to 45
minutes, 7.0% 45 to 60 minutes, 14.5% 60 minutes or more (2005-2009
5-year est.)

SANTA FE (city). Covers a land area of 13.990 square miles and a
water area of <.001 square miles. Located at 29.38° N. Lat; 95.10° W.
Long. Elevation is 30 feet.
Population: 8,624 (1990); 9,548 (2000); 10,679 (2010); 11,742 (2015
projected); Race: 93.9% White, 0.5% Black, 0.3% Asian, 5.4% Other,
12.8% Hispanic of any race (2010); Density: 763.3 persons per square mile
(2010); Average household size: 2.69 (2010); Median age: 35.8 (2010);
Males per 100 females: 96.7 (2010); Marriage status: 22.6% never married,
60.0% now married, 5.9% widowed, 11.6% divorced (2005-2009 5-year
est.); Foreign born: 4.2% (2005-2009 5-year est.); Ancestry (includes
multiple ancestries): 18.0% German, 17.9% Irish, 10.7% Italian, 9.6%
English, 7.7% French (2005-2009 5-year est.).
Economy: Single-family building permits issued: 33 (2010); Multi-family
building permits issued: 0 (2010); Employment by occupation: 14.5%
management, 18.6% professional, 11.7% services, 23.4% sales, 0.0%
farming, 15.4% construction, 16.3% production (2005-2009 5-year est.).
Income: Per capita income: $29,425 (2010); Median household income:
$66,089 (2010); Average household income: $78,963 (2010); Percent of

households with income of $100,000 or more: 27.0% (2010); Poverty rate: 8.0% (2005-2009 5-year est.).
Taxes: Total city taxes per capita: $337 (2007); City property taxes per capita: $106 (2007).
Education: Percent of population age 25 and over with: High school diploma (including GED) or higher: 85.3% (2010); Bachelor's degree or higher: 13.2% (2010); Master's degree or higher: 4.8% (2010).

School District(s)

Santa Fe ISD (PK-12)
    2009-10 Enrollment: 4,505 . . . . (409) 925-3526
Housing: Homeownership rate: 79.6% (2010); Median home value: $119,696 (2010); Median contract rent: $667 per month (2005-2009 5-year est.); Median year structure built: 1985 (2005-2009 5-year est.).
Safety: Violent crime rate: 29.3 per 10,000 population; Property crime rate: 281.7 per 10,000 population (2009).
Newspapers: La Marque Times (Local news; Circulation 4,200)
Transportation: Commute to work: 93.8% car, 0.5% public transportation, 0.4% walk, 2.9% work from home (2005-2009 5-year est.); Travel time to work: 20.5% less than 15 minutes, 35.3% 15 to 30 minutes, 21.5% 30 to 45 minutes, 14.5% 45 to 60 minutes, 8.2% 60 minutes or more (2005-2009 5-year est.)

Additional Information Contacts
City of Santa Fe . . . . (409) 925-6412
    http://www.ci.santa-fe.tx.us

TEXAS CITY (city).
Covers a land area of 62.370 square miles and a water area of 104.864 square miles. Located at 29.40° N. Lat; 94.93° W. Long. Elevation is 10 feet.
History: Named for the Indian translation of "friends". Texas City developed as a major oil refining and shipping port on Galveston Bay.
Population: 40,735 (1990); 41,521 (2000); 46,177 (2010); 49,864 (2015 projected); Race: 56.2% White, 29.7% Black, 1.0% Asian, 13.1% Other, 25.3% Hispanic of any race (2010); Density: 740.4 persons per square mile (2010); Average household size: 2.56 (2010); Median age: 34.9 (2010); Males per 100 females: 90.5 (2010); Marriage status: 28.0% never married, 51.6% now married, 7.6% widowed, 12.9% divorced (2005-2009 5-year est.); Foreign born: 8.6% (2005-2009 5-year est.); Ancestry (includes multiple ancestries): 10.3% German, 9.0% Irish, 5.9% English, 3.9% American, 2.5% French (2005-2009 5-year est.).
Economy: Unemployment rate: 12.9% (June 2011); Total civilian labor force: 20,844 (June 2011); Single-family building permits issued: 35 (2010); Multi-family building permits issued: 31 (2010); Employment by occupation: 9.2% management, 16.2% professional, 22.1% services, 26.3% sales, 0.1% farming, 12.3% construction, 13.9% production (2005-2009 5-year est.).
Income: Per capita income: $21,430 (2010); Median household income: $42,753 (2010); Average household income: $55,583 (2010); Percent of households with income of $100,000 or more: 14.1% (2010); Poverty rate: 15.8% (2005-2009 5-year est.).
Taxes: Total city taxes per capita: $885 (2007); City property taxes per capita: $440 (2007).
Education: Percent of population age 25 and over with: High school diploma (including GED) or higher: 82.1% (2010); Bachelor's degree or higher: 13.4% (2010); Master's degree or higher: 3.7% (2010).

School District(s)

La Marque ISD (PK-12)
    2009-10 Enrollment: 3,398 . . . . (409) 938-4251
Texas City ISD (PK-12)
    2009-10 Enrollment: 5,984 . . . . (409) 916-0100

Two-year College(s)

College of the Mainland (Public)
    Fall 2009 Enrollment: 3,916 . . . . (409) 938-1211
    2010-11 Tuition: In-state $1,727; Out-of-state $2,927
Housing: Homeownership rate: 61.2% (2010); Median home value: $91,350 (2010); Median contract rent: $566 per month (2005-2009 5-year est.); Median year structure built: 1972 (2005-2009 5-year est.).
Hospitals: Mainland Medical Center (223 beds)
Safety: Violent crime rate: 56.0 per 10,000 population; Property crime rate: 424.3 per 10,000 population (2009).
Newspapers: Texas City Sun (Local news; Circulation 14,000)
Transportation: Commute to work: 92.0% car, 0.0% public transportation, 1.6% walk, 1.0% work from home (2005-2009 5-year est.); Travel time to work: 39.6% less than 15 minutes, 32.1% 15 to 30 minutes, 15.5% 30 to 45 minutes, 6.1% 45 to 60 minutes, 6.7% 60 minutes or more (2005-2009 5-year est.)

Additional Information Contacts
City of Texas City . . . . (409) 948-3111
    http://www.texas-city-tx.org
Texas City-La Marque Chamber of Commerce . . . . (409) 935-1408
    http://www.texascitychamber.com

TIKI ISLAND (village).
Covers a land area of 0.648 square miles and a water area of 0.700 square miles. Located at 29.29° N. Lat; 94.91° W. Long.
Population: 537 (1990); 1,016 (2000); 1,432 (2010); 1,642 (2015 projected); Race: 95.1% White, 0.2% Black, 1.4% Asian, 3.3% Other, 3.6% Hispanic of any race (2010); Density: 2,209.6 persons per square mile (2010); Average household size: 2.05 (2010); Median age: 52.8 (2010); Males per 100 females: 105.5 (2010); Marriage status: 12.9% never married, 69.2% now married, 7.2% widowed, 10.7% divorced (2005-2009 5-year est.); Foreign born: 6.0% (2005-2009 5-year est.); Ancestry (includes multiple ancestries): 19.8% German, 16.2% English, 12.8% Irish, 8.4% American, 6.2% Italian (2005-2009 5-year est.).
Economy: Single-family building permits issued: 6 (2010); Multi-family building permits issued: 0 (2010); Employment by occupation: 38.7% management, 28.6% professional, 2.4% services, 19.9% sales, 0.0% farming, 5.0% construction, 5.5% production (2005-2009 5-year est.).
Income: Per capita income: $72,125 (2010); Median household income: $116,951 (2010); Average household income: $148,181 (2010); Percent of households with income of $100,000 or more: 62.8% (2010); Poverty rate: 1.4% (2005-2009 5-year est.).
Taxes: Total city taxes per capita: $95 (2007); City property taxes per capita: $0 (2007).
Education: Percent of population age 25 and over with: High school diploma (including GED) or higher: 97.1% (2010); Bachelor's degree or higher: 42.3% (2010); Master's degree or higher: 13.8% (2010).
Housing: Homeownership rate: 92.3% (2010); Median home value: $357,879 (2010); Median contract rent: $883 per month (2005-2009 5-year est.); Median year structure built: 1991 (2005-2009 5-year est.).
Transportation: Commute to work: 91.6% car, 0.7% public transportation, 0.5% walk, 6.4% work from home (2005-2009 5-year est.); Travel time to work: 13.5% less than 15 minutes, 39.0% 15 to 30 minutes, 8.9% 30 to 45 minutes, 18.4% 45 to 60 minutes, 20.2% 60 minutes or more (2005-2009 5-year est.)

Garza County

Located in northwestern Texas; in rolling plains, drained by the Salt and Double Mountain Forks of the Brazos River. Covers a land area of 895.56 square miles, a water area of 0.63 square miles, and is located in the Central Time Zone at 33.18° N. Lat., 101.32° W. Long. The county was founded in 1876. County seat is Post.

Weather Station: Post										Elevation: 2,620 feet		
	Jan	Feb	Mar	Apr	May	Jun	Jul	Aug	Sep	Oct	Nov	Dec
High	55	60	67	77	84	91	94	93	86	76	65	56
Low	29	32	39	47	57	66	70	69	61	51	39	30
Precip	0.6	1.0	0.9	1.4	2.9	3.0	1.8	2.8	2.7	2.4	1.3	0.9
Snow	0.9	0.9	0.2	0.1	0.0	0.0	0.0	0.0	0.0	tr	1.2	1.1

High and Low temperatures in degrees Fahrenheit; Precipitation and Snow in inches

Population: 5,143 (1990); 4,872 (2000); 4,838 (2010); 4,814 (2015 projected); Race: 71.7% White, 5.6% Black, 0.1% Asian, 22.5% Other, 40.2% Hispanic of any race (2010); Density: 5.4 persons per square mile (2010); Average household size: 2.59 (2010); Median age: 36.3 (2010); Males per 100 females: 115.5 (2010).
Religion: Five largest groups: 34.6% Southern Baptist Convention, 22.5% Catholic Church, 10.6% The United Methodist Church, 7.1% Churches of Christ, 3.3% Presbyterian Church (U.S.A.) (2000).
Economy: Unemployment rate: 6.6% (June 2011); Total civilian labor force: 2,522 (June 2011); Leading industries: 15.8% mining; 13.4% retail trade; 13.3% accommodation & food services (2009); Farms: 300 totaling 512,460 acres (2007); Companies that employ 500 or more persons: 0 (2009); Companies that employ 100 to 499 persons: 1 (2009); Companies that employ less than 100 persons: 124 (2009); Black-owned businesses: n/a (2007); Hispanic-owned businesses: n/a (2007); Asian-owned businesses: n/a (2007); Women-owned businesses: n/a (2007); Retail sales per capita: $4,321 (2010). Single-family building permits issued: 1 (2010); Multi-family building permits issued: 0 (2010).
Income: Per capita income: $18,556 (2010); Median household income: $39,634 (2010); Average household income: $52,162 (2010); Percent of

households with income of $100,000 or more: 11.3% (2010); Poverty rate: 21.9% (2009); Bankruptcy rate: 0.46% (2010).
Taxes: Total county taxes per capita: $505 (2007); County property taxes per capita: $435 (2007).
Education: Percent of population age 25 and over with: High school diploma (including GED) or higher: 74.8% (2010); Bachelor's degree or higher: 11.2% (2010); Master's degree or higher: 3.4% (2010).
Housing: Homeownership rate: 68.6% (2010); Median home value: $53,942 (2010); Median contract rent: $324 per month (2005-2009 5-year est.); Median year structure built: 1965 (2005-2009 5-year est.)
Health: Birth rate: 111.6 per 10,000 population (2009); Death rate: 79.4 per 10,000 population (2009); Age-adjusted cancer mortality rate: 208.2 (Unreliable) deaths per 100,000 population (2007); Number of physicians: 4.3 per 10,000 population (2008); Hospital beds: 0.0 per 10,000 population (2007); Hospital admissions: 0.0 per 10,000 population (2007).
Elections: 2008 Presidential election results: 21.4% Obama, 77.5% McCain, 0.1% Nader
Additional Information Contacts
Garza County Government . . . . (806) 495-4407
  http://www.garzacounty.net
Post Chamber of Commerce . . . . (806) 495-3461
  http://www.postcitytexas.com

Garza County Communities

POST (city). County seat. Covers a land area of 3.750 square miles and a water area of 0.019 square miles. Located at 33.19° N. Lat; 101.38° W. Long. Elevation is 2,605 feet.
History: Post was founded in 1907 by the cereal king C.W. Post of Battle Creek, Michigan, who wanted to build a model town here. He established a cotton textile mill, but died before completing his plan.
Population: 3,768 (1990); 3,708 (2000); 3,651 (2010); 3,621 (2015 projected); Race: 70.9% White, 5.3% Black, 0.1% Asian, 23.6% Other, 45.5% Hispanic of any race (2010); Density: 973.6 persons per square mile (2010); Average household size: 2.55 (2010); Median age: 35.6 (2010); Males per 100 females: 119.0 (2010); Marriage status: 19.8% never married, 63.2% now married, 4.6% widowed, 12.4% divorced (2005-2009 5-year est.); Foreign born: 39.4% (2005-2009 5-year est.); Ancestry (includes multiple ancestries): 5.8% English, 4.9% American, 4.6% German, 3.7% Irish, 1.1% French (2005-2009 5-year est.).
Economy: Single-family building permits issued: 1 (2010); Multi-family building permits issued: 0 (2010); Employment by occupation: 9.3% management, 13.2% professional, 17.4% services, 27.3% sales, 0.0% farming, 16.9% construction, 15.9% production (2005-2009 5-year est.).
Income: Per capita income: $17,035 (2010); Median household income: $36,205 (2010); Average household income: $47,995 (2010); Percent of households with income of $100,000 or more: 8.7% (2010); Poverty rate: 23.5% (2005-2009 5-year est.).
Education: Percent of population age 25 and over with: High school diploma (including GED) or higher: 73.7% (2010); Bachelor's degree or higher: 10.0% (2010); Master's degree or higher: 2.9% (2010).

School District(s)

Post ISD (PK-12)
    2009-10 Enrollment: 836 . . . . (806) 495-3343
Housing: Homeownership rate: 69.7% (2010); Median home value: $49,646 (2010); Median contract rent: $321 per month (2005-2009 5-year est.); Median year structure built: 1965 (2005-2009 5-year est.).
Newspapers: Post Dispatch (Community news; Circulation 1,800)
Transportation: Commute to work: 96.9% car, 0.0% public transportation, 0.0% walk, 2.8% work from home (2005-2009 5-year est.); Travel time to work: 79.6% less than 15 minutes, 3.9% 15 to 30 minutes, 4.0% 30 to 45 minutes, 7.8% 45 to 60 minutes, 4.7% 60 minutes or more (2005-2009 5-year est.)
Additional Information Contacts
Post Chamber of Commerce . . . . (806) 495-3461
  http://www.postcitytexas.com

Gillespie County

Located in south central Texas, on the Edwards Plateau; drained by the Pedernales River. Covers a land area of 1,061.06 square miles, a water area of 0.42 square miles, and is located in the Central Time Zone at 30.28° N. Lat., 98.92° W. Long. The county was founded in 1846. County seat is Fredericksburg.

Gillespie County is part of the Fredericksburg, TX Micropolitan Statistical Area. The entire metro area includes: Gillespie County, TX

Weather Station: Fredericksburg   Elevation: 1,685 feet

	Jan	Feb	Mar	Apr	May	Jun	Jul	Aug	Sep	Oct	Nov	Dec
High	61	65	72	79	85	91	93	94	88	80	70	62
Low	36	40	47	53	63	68	70	69	64	55	45	37
Precip	1.5	1.8	2.5	2.3	4.0	3.8	2.3	2.2	3.0	3.8	2.4	2.0
Snow	0.1	0.1	tr	0.0	0.0	0.0	0.0	0.0	0.0	0.0	0.1	tr

High and Low temperatures in degrees Fahrenheit; Precipitation and Snow in inches

Population: 17,204 (1990); 20,814 (2000); 24,779 (2010); 26,666 (2015 projected); Race: 91.3% White, 0.8% Black, 0.3% Asian, 7.7% Other, 18.1% Hispanic of any race (2010); Density: 23.4 persons per square mile (2010); Average household size: 2.33 (2010); Median age: 44.8 (2010); Males per 100 females: 92.3 (2010).
Religion: Five largest groups: 34.7% Catholic Church, 20.1% Evangelical Lutheran Church in America, 7.6% Southern Baptist Convention, 6.1% The United Methodist Church, 1.9% Episcopal Church (2000).
Economy: Unemployment rate: 5.5% (June 2011); Total civilian labor force: 13,740 (June 2011); Leading industries: 19.8% retail trade; 18.1% health care and social assistance; 15.9% accommodation & food services (2009); Farms: 1,853 totaling 652,940 acres (2007); Companies that employ 500 or more persons: 1 (2009); Companies that employ 100 to 499 persons: 5 (2009); Companies that employ less than 100 persons: 884 (2009); Black-owned businesses: n/a (2007); Hispanic-owned businesses: n/a (2007); Asian-owned businesses: n/a (2007); Women-owned businesses: 1,258 (2007); Retail sales per capita: $13,211 (2010). Single-family building permits issued: 34 (2010); Multi-family building permits issued: 0 (2010).
Income: Per capita income: $29,612 (2010); Median household income: $54,180 (2010); Average household income: $69,914 (2010); Percent of households with income of $100,000 or more: 17.8% (2010); Poverty rate: 11.0% (2009); Bankruptcy rate: 1.42% (2010).
Taxes: Total county taxes per capita: $298 (2007); County property taxes per capita: $200 (2007).
Education: Percent of population age 25 and over with: High school diploma (including GED) or higher: 84.7% (2010); Bachelor's degree or higher: 26.1% (2010); Master's degree or higher: 10.1% (2010).
Housing: Homeownership rate: 76.4% (2010); Median home value: $170,760 (2010); Median contract rent: $628 per month (2005-2009 5-year est.); Median year structure built: 1980 (2005-2009 5-year est.)
Health: Birth rate: 118.3 per 10,000 population (2009); Death rate: 134.0 per 10,000 population (2009); Age-adjusted cancer mortality rate: 137.2 deaths per 100,000 population (2007); Number of physicians: 33.1 per 10,000 population (2008); Hospital beds: 33.2 per 10,000 population (2007); Hospital admissions: 1,656.0 per 10,000 population (2007).
Elections: 2008 Presidential election results: 20.9% Obama, 77.5% McCain, 0.1% Nader
National and State Parks: Lyndon B Johnson National Historical Park
Additional Information Contacts
Gillespie County Government . . . . (830) 997-7502
  http://www.gillespiecounty.org
City of Fredericksburg . . . . (830) 997-7521
  http://www.fbgtx.org
Fredericksburg Chamber of Commerce . . . . (830) 997-6523
  http://www.fredericksburg-texas.com
Harper Chamber of Commerce . . . . (830) 864-5656
  http://harpertexas.com
Stonewall Chamber of Commerce . . . . (830) 644-2735
  http://www.stonewalltexas.com

Gillespie County Communities

DOSS (unincorporated postal area, zip code 78618). Covers a land area of 148.109 square miles and a water area of 0 square miles. Located at 30.48° N. Lat; 99.17° W. Long. Elevation is 1,729 feet.
Population: 225 (2000); Race: 100.0% White, 0.0% Black, 0.0% Asian, 0.0% Other, 0.0% Hispanic of any race (2000); Density: 1.5 persons per square mile (2000); Age: 17.2% under 18, 30.6% over 64 (2000); Marriage status: 11.4% never married, 82.2% now married, 4.0% widowed, 2.5% divorced (2000); Foreign born: 0.0% (2000); Ancestry (includes multiple ancestries): 63.8% German, 12.9% English, 8.6% American, 3.4% Irish, 2.2% Swiss (2000).

Economy: Employment by occupation: 37.9% management, 21.0% professional, 12.9% services, 7.3% sales, 1.6% farming, 8.9% construction, 10.5% production (2000).
Income: Per capita income: $17,078 (2000); Median household income: $35,625 (2000); Poverty rate: 179.1% (2000).
Education: Percent of population age 25 and over with: High school diploma (including GED) or higher: 87.2% (2000); Bachelor's degree or higher: 27.8% (2000).

School District(s)
Doss Consolidated Csd (KG-08)
    2009-10 Enrollment: 20 . . . . (830) 669-2411
Housing: Homeownership rate: 81.1% (2000); Median home value: $83,300 (2000); Median contract rent: $225 per month (2000); Median year structure built: 1956 (2000).
Transportation: Commute to work: 75.8% car, 1.6% public transportation, 0.0% walk, 22.6% work from home (2000); Travel time to work: 20.8% less than 15 minutes, 26.0% 15 to 30 minutes, 38.5% 30 to 45 minutes, 5.2% 45 to 60 minutes, 9.4% 60 minutes or more (2000)

FREDERICKSBURG (city). County seat. Covers a land area of 6.640 square miles and a water area of 0 square miles. Located at 30.27° N. Lat; 98.87° W. Long. Elevation is 1,693 feet.
History: Fredericksburg's first residents were German immigrants, who built their homes of stone quarried from the hillsides. These settlers came in 1846, encouraged by the Society for the Protection of German Immigrants in Texas. They named the village for Frederick the Great of Prussia. The residents of Fredericksburg generally did not support the Confederacy during the Civil War, and remained isolated until 1912, when they built their own railroad connection with the San Antonio & Aransas Pass line.
Population: 8,169 (1990); 8,911 (2000); 11,127 (2010); 12,135 (2015 projected); Race: 92.0% White, 1.0% Black, 0.3% Asian, 6.8% Other, 18.8% Hispanic of any race (2010); Density: 1,675.9 persons per square mile (2010); Average household size: 2.26 (2010); Median age: 44.5 (2010); Males per 100 females: 88.1 (2010); Marriage status: 16.6% never married, 59.0% now married, 12.4% widowed, 12.0% divorced (2005-2009 5-year est.); Foreign born: 6.8% (2005-2009 5-year est.); Ancestry (includes multiple ancestries): 41.5% German, 14.1% English, 13.8% Irish, 4.6% Scottish, 4.6% American (2005-2009 5-year est.).
Economy: Single-family building permits issued: 34 (2010); Multi-family building permits issued: 0 (2010); Employment by occupation: 15.4% management, 18.9% professional, 16.1% services, 26.7% sales, 1.2% farming, 14.6% construction, 7.0% production (2005-2009 5-year est.).
Income: Per capita income: $28,485 (2010); Median household income: $50,399 (2010); Average household income: $65,833 (2010); Percent of households with income of $100,000 or more: 16.0% (2010); Poverty rate: 5.6% (2005-2009 5-year est.).
Taxes: Total city taxes per capita: $662 (2007); City property taxes per capita: $191 (2007).
Education: Percent of population age 25 and over with: High school diploma (including GED) or higher: 85.6% (2010); Bachelor's degree or higher: 26.7% (2010); Master's degree or higher: 10.1% (2010).

School District(s)
Fredericksburg ISD (PK-12)
    2009-10 Enrollment: 2,941 . . . . (830) 997-9551
Housing: Homeownership rate: 72.4% (2010); Median home value: $157,756 (2010); Median contract rent: $636 per month (2005-2009 5-year est.); Median year structure built: 1974 (2005-2009 5-year est.).
Hospitals: Hill Country Memorial Hospital (84 beds)
Safety: Violent crime rate: 6.2 per 10,000 population; Property crime rate: 180.8 per 10,000 population (2009).
Newspapers: Fredericksburg Standard - Radio Post (Community news; Circulation 9,900)
Transportation: Commute to work: 89.2% car, 0.0% public transportation, 3.3% walk, 6.9% work from home (2005-2009 5-year est.); Travel time to work: 69.6% less than 15 minutes, 18.2% 15 to 30 minutes, 5.3% 30 to 45 minutes, 1.4% 45 to 60 minutes, 5.6% 60 minutes or more (2005-2009 5-year est.)
Airports: Gillespie County (general aviation)
Additional Information Contacts
City of Fredericksburg . . . . (830) 997-7521
    http://www.fbgtx.org
Fredericksburg Chamber of Commerce . . . . (830) 997-6523
    http://www.fredericksburg-texas.com

HARPER (CDP). Covers a land area of 56.583 square miles and a water area of 0 square miles. Located at 30.30° N. Lat; 99.24° W. Long. Elevation is 2,054 feet.
Population: 778 (1990); 1,006 (2000); 1,003 (2010); 1,014 (2015 projected); Race: 93.6% White, 0.1% Black, 0.3% Asian, 6.0% Other, 9.8% Hispanic of any race (2010); Density: 17.7 persons per square mile (2010); Average household size: 2.35 (2010); Median age: 43.5 (2010); Males per 100 females: 97.8 (2010); Marriage status: 19.5% never married, 53.3% now married, 6.2% widowed, 21.0% divorced (2005-2009 5-year est.); Foreign born: 1.6% (2005-2009 5-year est.); Ancestry (includes multiple ancestries): 55.9% German, 15.4% Irish, 12.8% English, 4.8% Czech, 4.7% American (2005-2009 5-year est.).
Economy: Employment by occupation: 12.1% management, 10.5% professional, 5.0% services, 23.9% sales, 2.0% farming, 25.4% construction, 21.1% production (2005-2009 5-year est.).
Income: Per capita income: $32,004 (2010); Median household income: $55,035 (2010); Average household income: $74,660 (2010); Percent of households with income of $100,000 or more: 21.1% (2010); Poverty rate: 12.4% (2005-2009 5-year est.).
Education: Percent of population age 25 and over with: High school diploma (including GED) or higher: 85.4% (2010); Bachelor's degree or higher: 21.2% (2010); Master's degree or higher: 8.0% (2010).

School District(s)
Harper ISD (PK-12)
    2009-10 Enrollment: 627 . . . . (830) 864-4044
Housing: Homeownership rate: 81.3% (2010); Median home value: $131,024 (2010); Median contract rent: $712 per month (2005-2009 5-year est.); Median year structure built: 1976 (2005-2009 5-year est.).
Transportation: Commute to work: 79.7% car, 0.0% public transportation, 14.0% walk, 6.3% work from home (2005-2009 5-year est.); Travel time to work: 36.8% less than 15 minutes, 17.5% 15 to 30 minutes, 39.2% 30 to 45 minutes, 2.6% 45 to 60 minutes, 3.9% 60 minutes or more (2005-2009 5-year est.)
Additional Information Contacts
Harper Chamber of Commerce . . . . (830) 864-5656
    http://harpertexas.com

STONEWALL (CDP). Covers a land area of 15.175 square miles and a water area of 0 square miles. Located at 30.24° N. Lat; 98.66° W. Long. Elevation is 1,467 feet.
History: Stonewall was named in 1870 for Stonewall Jackson.
Population: 377 (1990); 469 (2000); 523 (2010); 551 (2015 projected); Race: 91.0% White, 0.4% Black, 0.2% Asian, 8.4% Other, 17.0% Hispanic of any race (2010); Density: 34.5 persons per square mile (2010); Average household size: 2.35 (2010); Median age: 43.7 (2010); Males per 100 females: 101.9 (2010); Marriage status: 23.1% never married, 63.2% now married, 0.0% widowed, 13.7% divorced (2005-2009 5-year est.); Foreign born: 16.5% (2005-2009 5-year est.); Ancestry (includes multiple ancestries): 34.9% German, 17.9% English, 9.2% American, 4.4% Lithuanian, 3.6% Irish (2005-2009 5-year est.).
Economy: Employment by occupation: 23.1% management, 2.6% professional, 20.6% services, 23.7% sales, 24.6% farming, 0.0% construction, 5.4% production (2005-2009 5-year est.).
Income: Per capita income: $28,699 (2010); Median household income: $54,423 (2010); Average household income: $65,258 (2010); Percent of households with income of $100,000 or more: 17.9% (2010); Poverty rate: 32.4% (2005-2009 5-year est.).
Education: Percent of population age 25 and over with: High school diploma (including GED) or higher: 78.8% (2010); Bachelor's degree or higher: 23.0% (2010); Master's degree or higher: 8.5% (2010).

School District(s)
Fredericksburg ISD (PK-12)
    2009-10 Enrollment: 2,941 . . . . (830) 997-9551
Housing: Homeownership rate: 81.2% (2010); Median home value: $162,500 (2010); Median contract rent: n/a per month (2005-2009 5-year est.); Median year structure built: 1970 (2005-2009 5-year est.).
Transportation: Commute to work: 51.4% car, 0.0% public transportation, 16.0% walk, 32.6% work from home (2005-2009 5-year est.); Travel time to work: 47.9% less than 15 minutes, 44.9% 15 to 30 minutes, 0.0% 30 to 45 minutes, 3.4% 45 to 60 minutes, 3.8% 60 minutes or more (2005-2009 5-year est.)
Additional Information Contacts
Stonewall Chamber of Commerce . . . . (830) 644-2735
    http://www.stonewalltexas.com

WILLOW CITY (unincorporated postal area, zip code 78675). Covers a land area of 48.391 square miles and a water area of 0.010 square miles. Located at 30.46° N. Lat; 98.71° W. Long. Elevation is 1,713 feet.
Population: 168 (2000); Race: 81.3% White, 0.0% Black, 0.0% Asian, 18.7% Other, 38.2% Hispanic of any race (2000); Density: 3.5 persons per square mile (2000); Age: 21.5% under 18, 26.4% over 64 (2000); Marriage status: 4.4% never married, 92.0% now married, 0.0% widowed, 3.5% divorced (2000); Foreign born: 4.9% (2000); Ancestry (includes multiple ancestries): 19.4% German, 8.3% French, 4.9% Hungarian, 4.9% Irish (2000).
Economy: Employment by occupation: 20.0% management, 16.4% professional, 0.0% services, 30.9% sales, 21.8% farming, 0.0% construction, 10.9% production (2000).
Income: Per capita income: $17,088 (2000); Median household income: $43,214 (2000); Poverty rate: 179.1% (2000).
Education: Percent of population age 25 and over with: High school diploma (including GED) or higher: 80.0% (2000); Bachelor's degree or higher: 31.8% (2000).
Housing: Homeownership rate: 82.1% (2000); Median home value: $65,000 (2000); Median contract rent: n/a per month (2000); Median year structure built: 1975 (2000).
Transportation: Commute to work: 100.0% car, 0.0% public transportation, 0.0% walk, 0.0% work from home (2000); Travel time to work: 29.1% less than 15 minutes, 34.5% 15 to 30 minutes, 23.6% 30 to 45 minutes, 12.7% 45 to 60 minutes, 0.0% 60 minutes or more (2000)

Glasscock County

Located in west Texas; rolling prairie and woodland area, drained by tributaries of the Colorado River. Covers a land area of 900.75 square miles, a water area of 0.19 square miles, and is located in the Central Time Zone at 31.85° N. Lat., 101.54° W. Long. The county was founded in 1887. County seat is Garden City.
Population: 1,447 (1990); 1,406 (2000); 1,195 (2010); 1,090 (2015 projected); Race: 75.9% White, 0.8% Black, 0.0% Asian, 23.3% Other, 31.9% Hispanic of any race (2010); Density: 1.3 persons per square mile (2010); Average household size: 2.77 (2010); Median age: 41.3 (2010); Males per 100 females: 110.8 (2010).
Religion: Four largest groups: 38.8% Catholic Church, 13.7% Southern Baptist Convention, 3.8% The United Methodist Church, 3.1% Churches of Christ (2000).
Economy: Unemployment rate: 6.0% (June 2011); Total civilian labor force: 613 (June 2011); Leading industries: Farms: 185 totaling 479,785 acres (2007); Companies that employ 500 or more persons: 0 (2009); Companies that employ 100 to 499 persons: 0 (2009); Companies that employ less than 100 persons: 15 (2009); Black-owned businesses: n/a (2007); Hispanic-owned businesses: n/a (2007); Asian-owned businesses: n/a (2007); Women-owned businesses: n/a (2007); Retail sales per capita: $4,935 (2010). Single-family building permits issued: n/a (2010); Multi-family building permits issued: n/a (2010).
Income: Per capita income: $27,462 (2010); Median household income: $49,683 (2010); Average household income: $76,143 (2010); Percent of households with income of $100,000 or more: 17.4% (2010); Poverty rate: 10.8% (2009); Bankruptcy rate: n/a (2010).
Taxes: Total county taxes per capita: $368 (2007); County property taxes per capita: $313 (2007).
Education: Percent of population age 25 and over with: High school diploma (including GED) or higher: 74.3% (2010); Bachelor's degree or higher: 21.0% (2010); Master's degree or higher: 3.7% (2010).
Housing: Homeownership rate: 65.2% (2010); Median home value: $80,938 (2010); Median contract rent: $329 per month (2005-2009 5-year est.); Median year structure built: 1972 (2005-2009 5-year est.)
Health: Birth rate: 114.7 per 10,000 population (2009); Death rate: 8.2 per 10,000 population (2009); Age-adjusted cancer mortality rate: n/a deaths per 100,000 population (2007); Number of physicians: 0.0 per 10,000 population (2008); Hospital beds: 0.0 per 10,000 population (2007); Hospital admissions: 0.0 per 10,000 population (2007).
Elections: 2008 Presidential election results: 9.3% Obama, 90.1% McCain, 0.0% Nader
Additional Information Contacts
Glasscock County Government . . . . (432) 354-2382
   http://www.co.glasscock.tx.us/ips/cms

Glasscock County Communities

GARDEN CITY (unincorporated postal area, zip code 79739). County seat. Covers a land area of 523.910 square miles and a water area of 0.109 square miles. Located at 31.80° N. Lat; 101.51° W. Long. Elevation is 2,638 feet.
Population: 1,020 (2000); Race: 72.8% White, 0.0% Black, 0.0% Asian, 27.2% Other, 33.6% Hispanic of any race (2000); Density: 1.9 persons per square mile (2000); Age: 37.1% under 18, 6.7% over 64 (2000); Marriage status: 25.1% never married, 68.0% now married, 3.0% widowed, 3.8% divorced (2000); Foreign born: 16.9% (2000); Ancestry (includes multiple ancestries): 33.3% German, 4.9% English, 4.9% Irish, 4.6% Czech (2000).
Economy: Employment by occupation: 24.0% management, 16.7% professional, 6.8% services, 14.7% sales, 14.7% farming, 9.5% construction, 13.6% production (2000).
Income: Per capita income: $18,172 (2000); Median household income: $36,250 (2000); Poverty rate: 179.1% (2000).
Education: Percent of population age 25 and over with: High school diploma (including GED) or higher: 68.4% (2000); Bachelor's degree or higher: 19.7% (2000).

School District(s)
Glasscock County ISD (PK-12)
   2009-10 Enrollment: 275 . . . . (432) 354-2230
Housing: Homeownership rate: 59.5% (2000); Median home value: $52,000 (2000); Median contract rent: $146 per month (2000); Median year structure built: 1975 (2000).
Transportation: Commute to work: 82.4% car, 0.0% public transportation, 8.4% walk, 8.9% work from home (2000); Travel time to work: 58.5% less than 15 minutes, 18.5% 15 to 30 minutes, 11.0% 30 to 45 minutes, 8.0% 45 to 60 minutes, 3.9% 60 minutes or more (2000)

Goliad County

Located in south Texas; drained by the San Antonio River. Covers a land area of 853.52 square miles, a water area of 5.83 square miles, and is located in the Central Time Zone at 28.68° N. Lat., 97.39° W. Long. The county was founded in 1836. County seat is Goliad.

Goliad County is part of the Victoria, TX Metropolitan Statistical Area. The entire metro area includes: Calhoun County, TX; Goliad County, TX; Victoria County, TX

Weather Station: Goliad   Elevation: 142 feet

	Jan	Feb	Mar	Apr	May	Jun	Jul	Aug	Sep	Oct	Nov	Dec
High	69	72	77	83	89	94	96	97	93	86	77	69
Low	44	47	53	60	68	72	73	73	69	61	53	45
Precip	2.5	1.9	2.6	2.6	4.1	3.8	3.6	3.4	4.3	3.9	2.5	1.8
Snow	0.1	tr	0.0	0.0	0.0	0.0	0.0	0.0	0.0	0.0	0.0	0.4

High and Low temperatures in degrees Fahrenheit; Precipitation and Snow in inches

Population: 5,980 (1990); 6,928 (2000); 7,324 (2010); 7,502 (2015 projected); Race: 82.0% White, 5.2% Black, 0.2% Asian, 12.6% Other, 35.6% Hispanic of any race (2010); Density: 8.6 persons per square mile (2010); Average household size: 2.52 (2010); Median age: 41.6 (2010); Males per 100 females: 98.4 (2010).
Religion: Five largest groups: 33.4% Catholic Church, 12.9% Southern Baptist Convention, 11.4% Evangelical Lutheran Church in America, 4.8% The United Methodist Church, 2.0% The Church of Jesus Christ of Latter-day Saints (2000).
Economy: Unemployment rate: 7.2% (June 2011); Total civilian labor force: 3,483 (June 2011); Leading industries: 19.4% retail trade; 13.6% accommodation & food services; 2.9% professional, scientific & technical services (2009); Farms: 1,083 totaling 469,513 acres (2007); Companies that employ 500 or more persons: 0 (2009); Companies that employ 100 to 499 persons: 0 (2009); Companies that employ less than 100 persons: 115 (2009); Black-owned businesses: n/a (2007); Hispanic-owned businesses: n/a (2007); Asian-owned businesses: n/a (2007); Women-owned businesses: 160 (2007); Retail sales per capita: $5,195 (2010). Single-family building permits issued: n/a (2010); Multi-family building permits issued: n/a (2010).
Income: Per capita income: $22,010 (2010); Median household income: $42,666 (2010); Average household income: $55,788 (2010); Percent of households with income of $100,000 or more: 12.5% (2010); Poverty rate: 15.6% (2009); Bankruptcy rate: 1.90% (2010).

Taxes: Total county taxes per capita: $724 (2007); County property taxes per capita: $621 (2007).

Education: Percent of population age 25 and over with: High school diploma (including GED) or higher: 77.3% (2010); Bachelor's degree or higher: 13.8% (2010); Master's degree or higher: 4.2% (2010).

Housing: Homeownership rate: 78.5% (2010); Median home value: $92,815 (2010); Median contract rent: $338 per month (2005-2009 5-year est.); Median year structure built: 1974 (2005-2009 5-year est.)

Health: Birth rate: 115.2 per 10,000 population (2009); Death rate: 78.2 per 10,000 population (2009); Age-adjusted cancer mortality rate: 186.3 (Unreliable) deaths per 100,000 population (2007); Number of physicians: 2.8 per 10,000 population (2008); Hospital beds: 0.0 per 10,000 population (2007); Hospital admissions: 0.0 per 10,000 population (2007).

Elections: 2008 Presidential election results: 36.4% Obama, 62.9% McCain, 0.1% Nader

National and State Parks: Fannin State Park; Goliad State Park

Additional Information Contacts

Goliad County Government . . . . (361) 645-3627
   http://www.co.goliad.tx.us/ips/cms

Goliad County Chamber of Commerce . . . . (361) 645-3563
   http://www.GoliadCC.org

Goliad County Communities

GOLIAD (city). County seat. Covers a land area of 1.526 square miles and a water area of 0 square miles. Located at 28.66° N. Lat; 97.39° W. Long. Elevation is 164 feet.

History: Goliad grew up around a mission and a presidio built here by the Spaniards in 1749. The presidio was captured in 1812 when Mexico revolted against Spain, and then the Mexicans were forced out at the beginning of the Texas Revolution in 1835.

Population: 1,981 (1990); 1,975 (2000); 1,976 (2010); 1,987 (2015 projected); Race: 74.3% White, 6.8% Black, 0.6% Asian, 18.2% Other, 52.9% Hispanic of any race (2010); Density: 1,294.9 persons per square mile (2010); Average household size: 2.44 (2010); Median age: 39.2 (2010); Males per 100 females: 96.8 (2010); Marriage status: 25.4% never married, 55.3% now married, 6.7% widowed, 12.5% divorced (2005-2009 5-year est.); Foreign born: 3.8% (2005-2009 5-year est.); Ancestry (includes multiple ancestries): 20.7% German, 7.7% Irish, 5.1% English, 2.6% French, 2.4% Scottish (2005-2009 5-year est.).

Economy: Employment by occupation: 7.1% management, 12.1% professional, 25.4% services, 27.6% sales, 15.3% farming, 10.6% production (2005-2009 5-year est.).

Income: Per capita income: $18,634 (2010); Median household income: $33,713 (2010); Average household income: $46,132 (2010); Percent of households with income of $100,000 or more: 9.1% (2010); Poverty rate: 16.0% (2005-2009 5-year est.).

Taxes: Total city taxes per capita: $324 (2007); City property taxes per capita: $128 (2007).

Education: Percent of population age 25 and over with: High school diploma (including GED) or higher: 73.0% (2010); Bachelor's degree or higher: 13.3% (2010); Master's degree or higher: 4.4% (2010).

School District(s)

Goliad ISD (PK-12)
   2009-10 Enrollment: 1,349 . . . . (361) 645-3259

Housing: Homeownership rate: 68.3% (2010); Median home value: $80,294 (2010); Median contract rent: $418 per month (2005-2009 5-year est.); Median year structure built: 1962 (2005-2009 5-year est.).

Newspapers: Goliad Texan Express (Local news; Circulation 2,198)

Transportation: Commute to work: 85.1% car, 0.0% public transportation, 9.4% walk, 4.2% work from home (2005-2009 5-year est.); Travel time to work: 59.8% less than 15 minutes, 5.6% 15 to 30 minutes, 23.1% 30 to 45 minutes, 4.0% 45 to 60 minutes, 7.6% 60 minutes or more (2005-2009 5-year est.)

Additional Information Contacts

Goliad County Chamber of Commerce . . . . (361) 645-3563
   http://www.GoliadCC.org

Gonzales County

Located in south central Texas; drained by the Guadalupe and San Marcos Rivers. Covers a land area of 1,067.75 square miles, a water area of 2.07 square miles, and is located in the Central Time Zone at 29.45° N. Lat., 97.50° W. Long. The county was founded in 1836. County seat is Gonzales.

Weather Station: Gonzales 1 N										Elevation: 379 feet		
	Jan	Feb	Mar	Apr	May	Jun	Jul	Aug	Sep	Oct	Nov	Dec
High	62	66	72	80	86	92	95	96	90	82	72	63
Low	40	43	50	57	66	71	73	73	68	59	49	41
Precip	2.3	1.9	2.4	2.5	4.3	4.0	2.1	2.7	3.0	4.0	3.0	2.6
Snow	tr	0.0	0.0	0.0	0.0	0.0	0.0	0.0	0.0	0.0	0.0	tr

High and Low temperatures in degrees Fahrenheit; Precipitation and Snow in inches

Weather Station: Nixon										Elevation: 399 feet		
	Jan	Feb	Mar	Apr	May	Jun	Jul	Aug	Sep	Oct	Nov	Dec
High	64	68	74	81	87	92	95	96	91	83	73	64
Low	42	45	51	58	66	71	73	73	68	59	51	42
Precip	2.1	2.3	2.5	2.3	4.3	3.5	2.5	2.9	3.2	3.4	2.8	2.1
Snow	0.4	tr	0.0	0.0	0.0	0.0	0.0	0.0	0.0	0.0	0.0	0.0

High and Low temperatures in degrees Fahrenheit; Precipitation and Snow in inches

Population: 17,205 (1990); 18,628 (2000); 19,357 (2010); 19,673 (2015 projected); Race: 69.8% White, 8.0% Black, 0.3% Asian, 21.9% Other, 45.2% Hispanic of any race (2010); Density: 18.1 persons per square mile (2010); Average household size: 2.68 (2010); Median age: 35.0 (2010); Males per 100 females: 99.5 (2010).

Religion: Five largest groups: 21.1% Catholic Church, 21.1% Southern Baptist Convention, 10.2% The United Methodist Church, 2.2% Evangelical Lutheran Church in America, 1.3% Presbyterian Church (U.S.A.) (2000).

Economy: Unemployment rate: 6.7% (June 2011); Total civilian labor force: 9,939 (June 2011); Leading industries: 29.2% manufacturing; 16.0% health care and social assistance; 15.7% retail trade (2009); Farms: 1,861 totaling 654,077 acres (2007); Companies that employ 500 or more persons: 0 (2009); Companies that employ 100 to 499 persons: 9 (2009); Companies that employ less than 100 persons: 379 (2009); Black-owned businesses: n/a (2007); Hispanic-owned businesses: n/a (2007); Asian-owned businesses: n/a (2007); Women-owned businesses: 421 (2007); Retail sales per capita: $9,480 (2010). Single-family building permits issued: 1 (2010); Multi-family building permits issued: 0 (2010).

Income: Per capita income: $17,789 (2010); Median household income: $35,279 (2010); Average household income: $47,812 (2010); Percent of households with income of $100,000 or more: 8.9% (2010); Poverty rate: 19.8% (2009); Bankruptcy rate: 0.85% (2010).

Taxes: Total county taxes per capita: $222 (2007); County property taxes per capita: $163 (2007).

Education: Percent of population age 25 and over with: High school diploma (including GED) or higher: 67.9% (2010); Bachelor's degree or higher: 12.5% (2010); Master's degree or higher: 2.6% (2010).

Housing: Homeownership rate: 67.0% (2010); Median home value: $67,561 (2010); Median contract rent: $317 per month (2005-2009 5-year est.); Median year structure built: 1972 (2005-2009 5-year est.)

Health: Birth rate: 194.3 per 10,000 population (2009); Death rate: 94.3 per 10,000 population (2009); Age-adjusted cancer mortality rate: 225.9 deaths per 100,000 population (2007); Number of physicians: 5.6 per 10,000 population (2008); Hospital beds: 17.6 per 10,000 population (2007); Hospital admissions: 599.3 per 10,000 population (2007).

Elections: 2008 Presidential election results: 34.5% Obama, 64.8% McCain, 0.1% Nader

National and State Parks: Palmetto State Park

Additional Information Contacts

Gonzales County Government. . . . . (830) 672-2327
   http://www.co.gonzales.tx.us/ips/cms

City of Gonzales. . . . . (830) 672-2815
   http://www.cityofgonzales.org

Gonzales Chamber of Commerce . . . . (830) 672-6532
   http://www.gonzalestexas.com

Gonzales County Communities

COST (unincorporated postal area, zip code 78614). Covers a land area of 65.671 square miles and a water area of 0.003 square miles. Located at 29.40° N. Lat; 97.58° W. Long. Elevation is 371 feet.

Population: 444 (2000); Race: 90.5% White, 4.0% Black, 0.0% Asian, 5.5% Other, 17.4% Hispanic of any race (2000); Density: 6.8 persons per square mile (2000); Age: 32.1% under 18, 10.5% over 64 (2000); Marriage status: 15.0% never married, 71.0% now married, 10.5% widowed, 3.5% divorced (2000); Foreign born: 9.5% (2000); Ancestry (includes multiple ancestries): 46.7% German, 13.8% American, 10.2% English, 9.0% Irish (2000).

Economy: Employment by occupation: 13.5% management, 16.6% professional, 2.1% services, 27.5% sales, 9.3% farming, 9.8% construction, 21.2% production (2000).
Income: Per capita income: $16,966 (2000); Median household income: $34,107 (2000); Poverty rate: 179.1% (2000).
Education: Percent of population age 25 and over with: High school diploma (including GED) or higher: 73.7% (2000); Bachelor's degree or higher: 14.7% (2000).
Housing: Homeownership rate: 74.6% (2000); Median home value: $83,200 (2000); Median contract rent: $506 per month (2000); Median year structure built: 1967 (2000).
Transportation: Commute to work: 87.5% car, 0.0% public transportation, 9.5% walk, 3.0% work from home (2000); Travel time to work: 42.8% less than 15 minutes, 29.4% 15 to 30 minutes, 4.1% 30 to 45 minutes, 3.6% 45 to 60 minutes, 20.1% 60 minutes or more (2000)

GONZALES (city). County seat. Covers a land area of 5.098 square miles and a water area of 0 square miles. Located at 29.50° N. Lat; 97.44° W. Long. Elevation is 285 feet.

History: Gonzales was settled in 1825 by James Kerr, and was named for Don Rafael Gonzales, provisional governor of the Mexican province of Coahuila and Texas. Gonzales claims the first shots of the Texas Revolution were fired here in 1835, when the Mexican government demanded the return of a cannon they had earlier given to the town.
Population: 7,041 (1990); 7,202 (2000); 7,256 (2010); 7,257 (2015 projected); Race: 61.8% White, 11.2% Black, 0.5% Asian, 26.5% Other, 49.8% Hispanic of any race (2010); Density: 1,423.4 persons per square mile (2010); Average household size: 2.69 (2010); Median age: 33.1 (2010); Males per 100 females: 96.4 (2010); Marriage status: 34.5% never married, 44.6% now married, 10.4% widowed, 10.5% divorced (2005-2009 5-year est.); Foreign born: 11.8% (2005-2009 5-year est.); Ancestry (includes multiple ancestries): 12.0% German, 10.5% Irish, 5.4% Czech, 4.0% English, 2.5% French (2005-2009 5-year est.).
Economy: Single-family building permits issued: 1 (2010); Multi-family building permits issued: 0 (2010); Employment by occupation: 10.6% management, 12.8% professional, 16.8% services, 22.8% sales, 10.9% farming, 8.6% construction, 17.4% production (2005-2009 5-year est.).
Income: Per capita income: $16,775 (2010); Median household income: $34,698 (2010); Average household income: $45,261 (2010); Percent of households with income of $100,000 or more: 7.5% (2010); Poverty rate: 18.3% (2005-2009 5-year est.).
Taxes: Total city taxes per capita: $344 (2007); City property taxes per capita: $93 (2007).
Education: Percent of population age 25 and over with: High school diploma (including GED) or higher: 65.5% (2010); Bachelor's degree or higher: 11.2% (2010); Master's degree or higher: 1.7% (2010).

School District(s)
Gonzales ISD (PK-12)
    2009-10 Enrollment: 2,532 . . . . (830) 672-9551
Housing: Homeownership rate: 59.1% (2010); Median home value: $59,601 (2010); Median contract rent: $330 per month (2005-2009 5-year est.); Median year structure built: 1968 (2005-2009 5-year est.).
Hospitals: Gonzales Memorial Hospital (35 beds)
Safety: Violent crime rate: 132.8 per 10,000 population; Property crime rate: 446.3 per 10,000 population (2009).
Newspapers: Gonzales Inquirer (Local news; Circulation 3,800)
Transportation: Commute to work: 96.2% car, 0.0% public transportation, 2.1% walk, 1.1% work from home (2005-2009 5-year est.); Travel time to work: 61.2% less than 15 minutes, 19.9% 15 to 30 minutes, 7.2% 30 to 45 minutes, 2.7% 45 to 60 minutes, 9.0% 60 minutes or more (2005-2009 5-year est.)
Additional Information Contacts
City of Gonzales. . . . . (830) 672-2815
    http://www.cityofgonzales.org
Gonzales Chamber of Commerce . . . . (830) 672-6532
    http://www.gonzalestexas.com

HARWOOD (unincorporated postal area, zip code 78632). Covers a land area of 78.592 square miles and a water area of 0.031 square miles. Located at 29.69° N. Lat; 97.45° W. Long. Elevation is 463 feet.
Population: 634 (2000); Race: 93.0% White, 0.8% Black, 0.0% Asian, 6.2% Other, 15.7% Hispanic of any race (2000); Density: 8.1 persons per square mile (2000); Age: 24.7% under 18, 25.1% over 64 (2000); Marriage status: 14.9% never married, 72.5% now married, 5.3% widowed, 7.3% divorced (2000); Foreign born: 5.6% (2000); Ancestry (includes multiple

ancestries): 16.8% German, 8.8% English, 6.5% Irish, 5.1% Scotch-Irish (2000).
Economy: Employment by occupation: 27.6% management, 13.6% professional, 7.5% services, 19.7% sales, 4.4% farming, 5.7% construction, 21.5% production (2000).
Income: Per capita income: $17,738 (2000); Median household income: $30,948 (2000); Poverty rate: 179.1% (2000).
Education: Percent of population age 25 and over with: High school diploma (including GED) or higher: 68.5% (2000); Bachelor's degree or higher: 11.8% (2000).
Housing: Homeownership rate: 93.6% (2000); Median home value: $57,500 (2000); Median contract rent: $325 per month (2000); Median year structure built: 1976 (2000).
Transportation: Commute to work: 81.1% car, 1.8% public transportation, 0.0% walk, 17.1% work from home (2000); Travel time to work: 25.4% less than 15 minutes, 24.3% 15 to 30 minutes, 13.8% 30 to 45 minutes, 13.2% 45 to 60 minutes, 23.3% 60 minutes or more (2000)

LEESVILLE (unincorporated postal area, zip code 78122). Covers a land area of 51.239 square miles and a water area of 0.122 square miles. Located at 29.42° N. Lat; 97.73° W. Long. Elevation is 377 feet.
Population: 419 (2000); Race: 71.9% White, 12.7% Black, 0.0% Asian, 15.4% Other, 18.6% Hispanic of any race (2000); Density: 8.2 persons per square mile (2000); Age: 20.9% under 18, 17.4% over 64 (2000); Marriage status: 13.5% never married, 68.7% now married, 7.3% widowed, 10.5% divorced (2000); Foreign born: 0.0% (2000); Ancestry (includes multiple ancestries): 27.7% German, 15.8% Irish, 7.0% American, 5.7% French (2000).
Economy: Employment by occupation: 31.0% management, 15.3% professional, 9.4% services, 13.3% sales, 6.4% farming, 21.7% construction, 3.0% production (2000).
Income: Per capita income: $15,426 (2000); Median household income: $31,458 (2000); Poverty rate: 179.1% (2000).
Education: Percent of population age 25 and over with: High school diploma (including GED) or higher: 81.9% (2000); Bachelor's degree or higher: 19.4% (2000).
Housing: Homeownership rate: 94.8% (2000); Median home value: $37,500 (2000); Median contract rent: $225 per month (2000); Median year structure built: 1981 (2000).
Transportation: Commute to work: 92.1% car, 0.0% public transportation, 0.0% walk, 7.9% work from home (2000); Travel time to work: 16.0% less than 15 minutes, 14.4% 15 to 30 minutes, 45.5% 30 to 45 minutes, 9.6% 45 to 60 minutes, 14.4% 60 minutes or more (2000)

NIXON (city). Covers a land area of 1.134 square miles and a water area of 0 square miles. Located at 29.27° N. Lat; 97.76° W. Long. Elevation is 390 feet.
Population: 1,995 (1990); 2,186 (2000); 2,239 (2010); 2,282 (2015 projected); Race: 78.2% White, 2.3% Black, 0.1% Asian, 19.3% Other, 62.8% Hispanic of any race (2010); Density: 1,974.9 persons per square mile (2010); Average household size: 3.01 (2010); Median age: 30.9 (2010); Males per 100 females: 96.7 (2010); Marriage status: 25.1% never married, 61.9% now married, 6.8% widowed, 6.2% divorced (2005-2009 5-year est.); Foreign born: 22.1% (2005-2009 5-year est.); Ancestry (includes multiple ancestries): 6.6% Irish, 5.6% German, 3.9% English, 1.2% Scotch-Irish, 1.1% Polish (2005-2009 5-year est.).
Economy: Single-family building permits issued: 0 (2010); Multi-family building permits issued: 0 (2010); Employment by occupation: 9.6% management, 12.0% professional, 26.5% services, 12.4% sales, 2.6% farming, 7.0% construction, 29.9% production (2005-2009 5-year est.).
Income: Per capita income: $13,363 (2010); Median household income: $30,076 (2010); Average household income: $40,967 (2010); Percent of households with income of $100,000 or more: 6.6% (2010); Poverty rate: 23.0% (2005-2009 5-year est.).
Taxes: Total city taxes per capita: $240 (2007); City property taxes per capita: $44 (2007).
Education: Percent of population age 25 and over with: High school diploma (including GED) or higher: 60.5% (2010); Bachelor's degree or higher: 9.0% (2010); Master's degree or higher: 3.2% (2010).

School District(s)
Nixon-Smiley CISD (PK-12)
    2009-10 Enrollment: 1,060 . . . . (830) 582-1536
Housing: Homeownership rate: 62.6% (2010); Median home value: $34,695 (2010); Median contract rent: $286 per month (2005-2009 5-year est.); Median year structure built: 1965 (2005-2009 5-year est.).

Safety: Violent crime rate: 36.6 per 10,000 population; Property crime rate: 105.1 per 10,000 population (2009).
Transportation: Commute to work: 87.1% car, 0.0% public transportation, 12.2% walk, 0.4% work from home (2005-2009 5-year est.); Travel time to work: 51.2% less than 15 minutes, 5.9% 15 to 30 minutes, 13.5% 30 to 45 minutes, 10.9% 45 to 60 minutes, 18.5% 60 minutes or more (2005-2009 5-year est.)

SMILEY (city). Covers a land area of 0.521 square miles and a water area of 0 square miles. Located at 29.26° N. Lat; 97.63° W. Long. Elevation is 312 feet.
Population: 432 (1990); 453 (2000); 428 (2010); 415 (2015 projected); Race: 88.6% White, 0.2% Black, 0.0% Asian, 11.2% Other, 42.3% Hispanic of any race (2010); Density: 821.8 persons per square mile (2010); Average household size: 2.49 (2010); Median age: 37.8 (2010); Males per 100 females: 97.2 (2010); Marriage status: 33.6% never married, 56.9% now married, 7.2% widowed, 2.2% divorced (2005-2009 5-year est.); Foreign born: 3.4% (2005-2009 5-year est.); Ancestry (includes multiple ancestries): 9.6% German, 8.0% Irish, 6.6% English, 1.8% French, 1.6% Dutch (2005-2009 5-year est.).
Economy: Employment by occupation: 13.8% management, 4.8% professional, 5.8% services, 21.7% sales, 0.0% farming, 15.3% construction, 38.6% production (2005-2009 5-year est.).
Income: Per capita income: $14,995 (2010); Median household income: $25,500 (2010); Average household income: $36,441 (2010); Percent of households with income of $100,000 or more: 5.9% (2010); Poverty rate: 45.0% (2005-2009 5-year est.).
Taxes: Total city taxes per capita: $193 (2007); City property taxes per capita: $85 (2007).
Education: Percent of population age 25 and over with: High school diploma (including GED) or higher: 59.6% (2010); Bachelor's degree or higher: 11.5% (2010); Master's degree or higher: 2.4% (2010).
School District(s)
Nixon-Smiley CISD (PK-12)
    2009-10 Enrollment: 1,060 . . . . (830) 582-1536
Housing: Homeownership rate: 75.3% (2010); Median home value: $53,125 (2010); Median contract rent: $275 per month (2005-2009 5-year est.); Median year structure built: 1969 (2005-2009 5-year est.).
Transportation: Commute to work: 92.2% car, 0.0% public transportation, 0.0% walk, 7.8% work from home (2005-2009 5-year est.); Travel time to work: 38.2% less than 15 minutes, 10.3% 15 to 30 minutes, 9.1% 30 to 45 minutes, 12.1% 45 to 60 minutes, 30.3% 60 minutes or more (2005-2009 5-year est.)

WAELDER (city). Aka Cranz. Covers a land area of 1.279 square miles and a water area of 0.007 square miles. Located at 29.69° N. Lat; 97.29° W. Long. Elevation is 381 feet.
Population: 745 (1990); 947 (2000); 1,004 (2010); 1,037 (2015 projected); Race: 48.3% White, 18.8% Black, 0.2% Asian, 32.7% Other, 61.3% Hispanic of any race (2010); Density: 784.9 persons per square mile (2010); Average household size: 2.74 (2010); Median age: 36.4 (2010); Males per 100 females: 100.8 (2010); Marriage status: 31.6% never married, 43.1% now married, 15.1% widowed, 10.2% divorced (2005-2009 5-year est.); Foreign born: 9.9% (2005-2009 5-year est.); Ancestry (includes multiple ancestries): 3.6% Irish, 2.2% American, 2.0% German, 1.3% Czech, 1.3% African (2005-2009 5-year est.).
Economy: Employment by occupation: 0.8% management, 10.7% professional, 12.8% services, 25.6% sales, 7.0% farming, 3.7% construction, 39.3% production (2005-2009 5-year est.).
Income: Per capita income: $15,931 (2010); Median household income: $29,352 (2010); Average household income: $43,794 (2010); Percent of households with income of $100,000 or more: 6.3% (2010); Poverty rate: 31.5% (2005-2009 5-year est.).
Taxes: Total city taxes per capita: $7 (2007); City property taxes per capita: $0 (2007).
Education: Percent of population age 25 and over with: High school diploma (including GED) or higher: 54.4% (2010); Bachelor's degree or higher: 7.8% (2010); Master's degree or higher: 2.9% (2010).
School District(s)
Waelder ISD (PK-12)
    2009-10 Enrollment: 264 . . . . (830) 788-7161
Housing: Homeownership rate: 69.5% (2010); Median home value: $40,256 (2010); Median contract rent: $204 per month (2005-2009 5-year est.); Median year structure built: 1970 (2005-2009 5-year est.).

Safety: Violent crime rate: 50.2 per 10,000 population; Property crime rate: 120.4 per 10,000 population (2009).
Transportation: Commute to work: 81.0% car, 0.0% public transportation, 15.3% walk, 3.7% work from home (2005-2009 5-year est.); Travel time to work: 63.5% less than 15 minutes, 15.0% 15 to 30 minutes, 13.7% 30 to 45 minutes, 5.6% 45 to 60 minutes, 2.1% 60 minutes or more (2005-2009 5-year est.)

Gray County

Located in north Texas, in the Panhandle; drained by the North Fork of the Red River Covers a land area of 928.28 square miles, a water area of 0.97 square miles, and is located in the Central Time Zone at 35.43° N. Lat., 100.85° W. Long. The county was founded in 1876. County seat is Pampa.

Gray County is part of the Pampa, TX Micropolitan Statistical Area. The entire metro area includes: Gray County, TX; Roberts County, TX

Weather Station: Mc Lean   Elevation: 2,859 feet

	Jan	Feb	Mar	Apr	May	Jun	Jul	Aug	Sep	Oct	Nov	Dec
High	52	56	64	74	81	87	92	91	84	74	62	51
Low	27	30	36	45	54	63	67	66	59	48	37	28
Precip	0.8	1.1	1.8	2.1	3.8	3.8	2.9	2.9	2.6	2.6	1.3	1.1
Snow	2.1	1.0	1.0	0.1	0.0	0.0	0.0	0.0	0.0	0.0	0.9	2.6

High and Low temperatures in degrees Fahrenheit; Precipitation and Snow in inches

Weather Station: Pampa 2   Elevation: 3,149 feet

	Jan	Feb	Mar	Apr	May	Jun	Jul	Aug	Sep	Oct	Nov	Dec
High	49	53	61	70	78	87	92	90	82	71	59	49
Low	23	26	33	41	52	61	66	65	57	45	33	24
Precip	0.7	0.7	1.6	2.0	3.0	3.7	2.6	2.7	2.2	2.0	1.0	0.9
Snow	3.7	3.3	3.6	0.9	0.2	0.0	0.0	0.0	tr	0.1	1.6	5.0

High and Low temperatures in degrees Fahrenheit; Precipitation and Snow in inches

Weather Station: Sherman   Elevation: 759 feet

	Jan	Feb	Mar	Apr	May	Jun	Jul	Aug	Sep	Oct	Nov	Dec
High	53	57	65	73	81	88	93	94	86	75	64	54
Low	33	36	44	52	61	69	73	72	65	54	44	35
Precip	2.5	2.9	3.9	3.5	5.3	5.0	2.5	2.1	3.7	5.4	3.5	3.0
Snow	0.3	0.8	tr	0.0	0.0	0.0	0.0	0.0	0.0	0.0	0.2	0.3

High and Low temperatures in degrees Fahrenheit; Precipitation and Snow in inches

Population: 23,967 (1990); 22,744 (2000); 22,655 (2010); 22,572 (2015 projected); Race: 75.6% White, 6.2% Black, 0.5% Asian, 17.7% Other, 21.1% Hispanic of any race (2010); Density: 24.4 persons per square mile (2010); Average household size: 2.34 (2010); Median age: 37.6 (2010); Males per 100 females: 104.4 (2010).
Religion: Five largest groups: 50.0% Southern Baptist Convention, 7.3% Catholic Church, 6.4% The United Methodist Church, 6.2% Churches of Christ, 3.2% Christian Church (Disciples of Christ) (2000).
Economy: Unemployment rate: 7.3% (June 2011); Total civilian labor force: 10,839 (June 2011); Leading industries: 17.8% retail trade; 13.3% health care and social assistance; 10.2% accommodation & food services (2009); Farms: 391 totaling 509,367 acres (2007); Companies that employ 500 or more persons: 0 (2009); Companies that employ 100 to 499 persons: 5 (2009); Companies that employ less than 100 persons: 628 (2009); Black-owned businesses: n/a (2007); Hispanic-owned businesses: n/a (2007); Asian-owned businesses: n/a (2007); Women-owned businesses: n/a (2007); Retail sales per capita: $10,905 (2010). Single-family building permits issued: 3 (2010); Multi-family building permits issued: 0 (2010).
Income: Per capita income: $21,988 (2010); Median household income: $42,207 (2010); Average household income: $55,105 (2010); Percent of households with income of $100,000 or more: 12.5% (2010); Poverty rate: 15.1% (2009); Bankruptcy rate: 1.37% (2010).
Taxes: Total county taxes per capita: $279 (2007); County property taxes per capita: $257 (2007).
Education: Percent of population age 25 and over with: High school diploma (including GED) or higher: 78.0% (2010); Bachelor's degree or higher: 11.0% (2010); Master's degree or higher: 2.3% (2010).
Housing: Homeownership rate: 75.2% (2010); Median home value: $51,617 (2010); Median contract rent: $399 per month (2005-2009 5-year est.); Median year structure built: 1957 (2005-2009 5-year est.)
Health: Birth rate: 165.4 per 10,000 population (2009); Death rate: 112.3 per 10,000 population (2009); Age-adjusted cancer mortality rate: 186.5 deaths per 100,000 population (2007); Number of physicians: 10.9 per

10,000 population (2008); Hospital beds: 41.7 per 10,000 population (2007); Hospital admissions: 1,425.6 per 10,000 population (2007).
Elections: 2008 Presidential election results: 14.2% Obama, 85.1% McCain, 0.0% Nader
Additional Information Contacts
Gray County Government . . . . (806) 669-8004
 http://www.co.gray.tx.us/ips/cms
City of Pampa . . . . (806) 669-5750
 http://www.cityofpampa.org
Greater Pampa Area Chamber of Commerce . . . . (806) 669-3241
 http://www.pampachamber.com
Mc Lean Chamber of Commerce. . . . . (806) 779-0000

Gray County Communities

LEFORS (town). Covers a land area of 0.395 square miles and a water area of 0 square miles. Located at 35.43° N. Lat; 100.80° W. Long. Elevation is 2,805 feet.
Population: 659 (1990); 559 (2000); 573 (2010); 578 (2015 projected); Race: 94.8% White, 0.2% Black, 0.0% Asian, 5.1% Other, 7.9% Hispanic of any race (2010); Density: 1,452.0 persons per square mile (2010); Average household size: 2.37 (2010); Median age: 37.1 (2010); Males per 100 females: 85.4 (2010); Marriage status: 11.3% never married, 78.0% now married, 6.6% widowed, 4.1% divorced (2005-2009 5-year est.); Foreign born: 0.5% (2005-2009 5-year est.); Ancestry (includes multiple ancestries): 25.9% Irish, 25.7% English, 14.9% German, 6.5% American, 5.0% Scottish (2005-2009 5-year est.).
Economy: Employment by occupation: 9.9% management, 3.9% professional, 10.5% services, 27.6% sales, 0.0% farming, 13.8% construction, 34.2% production (2005-2009 5-year est.).
Income: Per capita income: $18,224 (2010); Median household income: $35,909 (2010); Average household income: $43,254 (2010); Percent of households with income of $100,000 or more: 4.1% (2010); Poverty rate: 13.4% (2005-2009 5-year est.).
Taxes: Total city taxes per capita: $63 (2007); City property taxes per capita: $25 (2007).
Education: Percent of population age 25 and over with: High school diploma (including GED) or higher: 80.8% (2010); Bachelor's degree or higher: 5.4% (2010); Master's degree or higher: 0.6% (2010).
School District(s)
Lefors ISD (PK-12)
 2009-10 Enrollment: 161 . . . . (806) 835-2533
Housing: Homeownership rate: 85.1% (2010); Median home value: $34,231 (2010); Median contract rent: $319 per month (2005-2009 5-year est.); Median year structure built: 1958 (2005-2009 5-year est.).
Transportation: Commute to work: 100.0% car, 0.0% public transportation, 0.0% walk, 0.0% work from home (2005-2009 5-year est.); Travel time to work: 38.2% less than 15 minutes, 48.0% 15 to 30 minutes, 7.9% 30 to 45 minutes, 1.3% 45 to 60 minutes, 4.6% 60 minutes or more (2005-2009 5-year est.)

MCLEAN (town). Covers a land area of 1.175 square miles and a water area of 0 square miles. Located at 35.23° N. Lat; 100.60° W. Long. Elevation is 2,861 feet.
History: Settled 1901, incorporated 1909.
Population: 849 (1990); 830 (2000); 853 (2010); 857 (2015 projected); Race: 92.8% White, 0.6% Black, 0.4% Asian, 6.2% Other, 7.2% Hispanic of any race (2010); Density: 725.8 persons per square mile (2010); Average household size: 2.18 (2010); Median age: 48.6 (2010); Males per 100 females: 81.1 (2010); Marriage status: 25.8% never married, 52.7% now married, 11.7% widowed, 9.7% divorced (2005-2009 5-year est.); Foreign born: 0.5% (2005-2009 5-year est.); Ancestry (includes multiple ancestries): 20.8% English, 19.7% Irish, 17.3% German, 10.0% Scotch-Irish, 4.7% American (2005-2009 5-year est.).
Economy: Employment by occupation: 10.4% management, 22.1% professional, 26.1% services, 10.0% sales, 4.0% farming, 12.0% construction, 15.3% production (2005-2009 5-year est.).
Income: Per capita income: $22,779 (2010); Median household income: $40,333 (2010); Average household income: $51,721 (2010); Percent of households with income of $100,000 or more: 11.5% (2010); Poverty rate: 19.5% (2005-2009 5-year est.).
Taxes: Total city taxes per capita: $165 (2007); City property taxes per capita: $105 (2007).

Education: Percent of population age 25 and over with: High school diploma (including GED) or higher: 74.0% (2010); Bachelor's degree or higher: 10.4% (2010); Master's degree or higher: 2.6% (2010).
School District(s)
Mclean ISD (PK-12)
 2009-10 Enrollment: 220 . . . . (806) 779-2301
Housing: Homeownership rate: 78.9% (2010); Median home value: $40,222 (2010); Median contract rent: $274 per month (2005-2009 5-year est.); Median year structure built: 1947 (2005-2009 5-year est.).
Transportation: Commute to work: 93.7% car, 0.0% public transportation, 6.3% walk, 0.0% work from home (2005-2009 5-year est.); Travel time to work: 79.0% less than 15 minutes, 10.9% 15 to 30 minutes, 5.9% 30 to 45 minutes, 3.4% 45 to 60 minutes, 0.8% 60 minutes or more (2005-2009 5-year est.)
Additional Information Contacts
Mc Lean Chamber of Commerce. . . . . (806) 779-0000

PAMPA (city). County seat. Covers a land area of 8.725 square miles and a water area of 0 square miles. Located at 35.54° N. Lat; 100.96° W. Long. Elevation is 3,238 feet.
History: Pampa was named for its resemblance to the Argentine pampas, treeless grassland areas. The town owed its growth to the many oil wells, though cattle feeding pens continued to serve the surrounding ranches even after the oil derricks were dotting the landscape.
Population: 19,959 (1990); 17,887 (2000); 17,778 (2010); 17,687 (2015 projected); Race: 80.2% White, 2.6% Black, 0.4% Asian, 16.8% Other, 20.9% Hispanic of any race (2010); Density: 2,037.5 persons per square mile (2010); Average household size: 2.35 (2010); Median age: 38.3 (2010); Males per 100 females: 91.9 (2010); Marriage status: 18.0% never married, 63.0% now married, 9.3% widowed, 9.7% divorced (2005-2009 5-year est.); Foreign born: 7.5% (2005-2009 5-year est.); Ancestry (includes multiple ancestries): 13.6% English, 12.8% American, 11.6% German, 8.6% Irish, 2.0% Scotch-Irish (2005-2009 5-year est.).
Economy: Single-family building permits issued: 3 (2010); Multi-family building permits issued: 0 (2010); Employment by occupation: 8.0% management, 12.6% professional, 17.8% services, 27.5% sales, 2.4% farming, 16.2% construction, 15.5% production (2005-2009 5-year est.).
Income: Per capita income: $23,144 (2010); Median household income: $42,172 (2010); Average household income: $54,812 (2010); Percent of households with income of $100,000 or more: 12.4% (2010); Poverty rate: 18.1% (2005-2009 5-year est.).
Taxes: Total city taxes per capita: $444 (2007); City property taxes per capita: $170 (2007).
Education: Percent of population age 25 and over with: High school diploma (including GED) or higher: 78.5% (2010); Bachelor's degree or higher: 11.5% (2010); Master's degree or higher: 2.6% (2010).
School District(s)
Pampa ISD (PK-12)
 2009-10 Enrollment: 3,474 . . . . (806) 669-4700
Housing: Homeownership rate: 75.0% (2010); Median home value: $51,174 (2010); Median contract rent: $409 per month (2005-2009 5-year est.); Median year structure built: 1957 (2005-2009 5-year est.).
Hospitals: Pampa Regional Medical Center (115 beds)
Safety: Violent crime rate: 68.6 per 10,000 population; Property crime rate: 490.1 per 10,000 population (2009).
Newspapers: Pampa News (Community news; Circulation 7,200)
Transportation: Commute to work: 93.5% car, 0.2% public transportation, 3.0% walk, 1.4% work from home (2005-2009 5-year est.); Travel time to work: 67.6% less than 15 minutes, 16.2% 15 to 30 minutes, 5.0% 30 to 45 minutes, 2.9% 45 to 60 minutes, 8.3% 60 minutes or more (2005-2009 5-year est.)
Airports: Perry Lefors Field (general aviation)
Additional Information Contacts
City of Pampa . . . . (806) 669-5750
 http://www.cityofpampa.org
Greater Pampa Area Chamber of Commerce . . . . (806) 669-3241
 http://www.pampachamber.com

Grayson County

Located in north Texas; bounded on the north by the Red River, Lake Texoma, and the Oklahoma border. Covers a land area of 933.51 square miles, a water area of 45.68 square miles, and is located in the Central Time Zone at 33.65° N. Lat., 96.64° W. Long. The county was founded in 1846. County seat is Sherman.

Grayson County is part of the Sherman-Denison, TX Metropolitan Statistical Area. The entire metro area includes: Grayson County, TX

Weather Station: Sherman   Elevation: 759 feet

	Jan	Feb	Mar	Apr	May	Jun	Jul	Aug	Sep	Oct	Nov	Dec
High	53	57	65	73	81	88	93	94	86	75	64	54
Low	33	36	44	52	61	69	73	72	65	54	44	35
Precip	2.5	2.9	3.9	3.5	5.3	5.0	2.5	2.1	3.7	5.4	3.5	3.0
Snow	0.3	0.8	tr	0.0	0.0	0.0	0.0	0.0	0.0	0.0	0.2	0.3

High and Low temperatures in degrees Fahrenheit; Precipitation and Snow in inches

Population: 95,021 (1990); 110,595 (2000); 120,896 (2010); 125,689 (2015 projected); Race: 84.7% White, 5.7% Black, 0.8% Asian, 8.8% Other, 10.5% Hispanic of any race (2010); Density: 129.5 persons per square mile (2010); Average household size: 2.55 (2010); Median age: 37.3 (2010); Males per 100 females: 95.5 (2010).
Religion: Five largest groups: 35.0% Southern Baptist Convention, 7.3% The United Methodist Church, 4.2% Catholic Church, 4.0% Churches of Christ, 2.1% Assemblies of God (2000).
Economy: Unemployment rate: 9.2% (June 2011); Total civilian labor force: 58,109 (June 2011); Leading industries: 19.8% health care and social assistance; 17.6% manufacturing; 16.4% retail trade (2009); Farms: 2,723 totaling 400,414 acres (2007); Companies that employ 500 or more persons: 9 (2009); Companies that employ 100 to 499 persons: 46 (2009); Companies that employ less than 100 persons: 2,527 (2009); Black-owned businesses: 208 (2007); Hispanic-owned businesses: n/a (2007); Asian-owned businesses: 178 (2007); Women-owned businesses: 3,480 (2007); Retail sales per capita: $15,992 (2010). Single-family building permits issued: 75 (2010); Multi-family building permits issued: 252 (2010).
Income: Per capita income: $22,906 (2010); Median household income: $46,001 (2010); Average household income: $59,235 (2010); Percent of households with income of $100,000 or more: 14.1% (2010); Poverty rate: 14.1% (2009); Bankruptcy rate: 2.75% (2010).
Taxes: Total county taxes per capita: $238 (2007); County property taxes per capita: $218 (2007).
Education: Percent of population age 25 and over with: High school diploma (including GED) or higher: 85.1% (2010); Bachelor's degree or higher: 17.0% (2010); Master's degree or higher: 5.4% (2010).
Housing: Homeownership rate: 71.8% (2010); Median home value: $92,076 (2010); Median contract rent: $517 per month (2005-2009 5-year est.); Median year structure built: 1975 (2005-2009 5-year est.)
Health: Birth rate: 138.7 per 10,000 population (2009); Death rate: 103.1 per 10,000 population (2009); Age-adjusted cancer mortality rate: 186.9 deaths per 100,000 population (2007); Number of physicians: 18.0 per 10,000 population (2008); Hospital beds: 45.6 per 10,000 population (2007); Hospital admissions: 1,434.4 per 10,000 population (2007).
Elections: 2008 Presidential election results: 30.5% Obama, 68.3% McCain, 0.1% Nader
National and State Parks: Eisenhower State Park; Hagerman National Wildlife Refuge
Additional Information Contacts

Grayson County Government . . . . (903) 813-4228
   http://www.co.grayson.tx.us
City of Denison. . . . . (903) 465-2720
   http://www.cityofdenison.com
City of Sherman . . . . (903) 892-7205
   http://www.ci.sherman.tx.us
Denison Area Chamber of Commerce. . . . . (903) 465-1551
   http://www.denisontexas.us
Pottsboro Chamber of Commerce . . . . (903) 786-6371
   http://www.pottsborochamber.com
Sherman Chamber of Commerce . . . . (903) 893-1184
   http://www.shermanchamber.us
Van Alstyne Chamber of Commerce . . . . (903) 482-6066
   http://vanalstynechamber.org
Whitesboro Chamber of Commerce . . . . (903) 564-3331
   http://www.whitesborotx.com
Whitewright Area Chamber of Commerce . . . . (903) 364-2000
   http://www.whitewright.org

Grayson County Communities

BELLS (town). Covers a land area of 2.286 square miles and a water area of 0 square miles. Located at 33.61° N. Lat; 96.41° W. Long. Elevation is 689 feet.

Population: 970 (1990); 1,190 (2000); 1,302 (2010); 1,345 (2015 projected); Race: 94.2% White, 0.2% Black, 0.3% Asian, 5.3% Other, 2.7% Hispanic of any race (2010); Density: 569.7 persons per square mile (2010); Average household size: 2.49 (2010); Median age: 36.5 (2010); Males per 100 females: 92.6 (2010); Marriage status: 15.9% never married, 65.9% now married, 5.0% widowed, 13.3% divorced (2005-2009 5-year est.); Foreign born: 0.3% (2005-2009 5-year est.); Ancestry (includes multiple ancestries): 13.6% Irish, 11.5% American, 11.0% English, 5.5% Scotch-Irish, 5.1% German (2005-2009 5-year est.).
Economy: Single-family building permits issued: 0 (2010); Multi-family building permits issued: 0 (2010); Employment by occupation: 11.1% management, 19.5% professional, 11.6% services, 28.6% sales, 0.0% farming, 11.2% construction, 18.0% production (2005-2009 5-year est.).
Income: Per capita income: $22,781 (2010); Median household income: $47,425 (2010); Average household income: $57,118 (2010); Percent of households with income of $100,000 or more: 13.8% (2010); Poverty rate: 16.9% (2005-2009 5-year est.).
Taxes: Total city taxes per capita: $275 (2007); City property taxes per capita: $119 (2007).
Education: Percent of population age 25 and over with: High school diploma (including GED) or higher: 85.9% (2010); Bachelor's degree or higher: 11.9% (2010); Master's degree or higher: 3.5% (2010).

School District(s)

Bells ISD (PK-12)
   2009-10 Enrollment: 790 . . . . (903) 965-7721
Housing: Homeownership rate: 75.1% (2010); Median home value: $88,909 (2010); Median contract rent: $435 per month (2005-2009 5-year est.); Median year structure built: 1979 (2005-2009 5-year est.).
Transportation: Commute to work: 97.9% car, 0.0% public transportation, 0.6% walk, 0.9% work from home (2005-2009 5-year est.); Travel time to work: 14.6% less than 15 minutes, 63.0% 15 to 30 minutes, 11.4% 30 to 45 minutes, 2.9% 45 to 60 minutes, 8.2% 60 minutes or more (2005-2009 5-year est.)

COLLINSVILLE (town). Covers a land area of 0.718 square miles and a water area of 0 square miles. Located at 33.56° N. Lat; 96.91° W. Long. Elevation is 751 feet.
Population: 1,129 (1990); 1,235 (2000); 1,502 (2010); 1,635 (2015 projected); Race: 90.4% White, 0.3% Black, 0.1% Asian, 9.1% Other, 9.2% Hispanic of any race (2010); Density: 2,092.5 persons per square mile (2010); Average household size: 2.65 (2010); Median age: 36.7 (2010); Males per 100 females: 94.6 (2010); Marriage status: 25.2% never married, 47.2% now married, 21.5% widowed, 6.1% divorced (2005-2009 5-year est.); Foreign born: 0.0% (2005-2009 5-year est.); Ancestry (includes multiple ancestries): 18.9% American, 16.2% Irish, 10.7% English, 5.4% German, 3.6% Scottish (2005-2009 5-year est.).
Economy: Single-family building permits issued: 1 (2010); Multi-family building permits issued: 0 (2010); Employment by occupation: 6.6% management, 24.8% professional, 9.1% services, 28.0% sales, 1.5% farming, 19.8% construction, 10.2% production (2005-2009 5-year est.).
Income: Per capita income: $20,922 (2010); Median household income: $46,168 (2010); Average household income: $56,015 (2010); Percent of households with income of $100,000 or more: 11.4% (2010); Poverty rate: 6.3% (2005-2009 5-year est.).
Taxes: Total city taxes per capita: $155 (2007); City property taxes per capita: $72 (2007).
Education: Percent of population age 25 and over with: High school diploma (including GED) or higher: 85.2% (2010); Bachelor's degree or higher: 10.2% (2010); Master's degree or higher: 2.5% (2010).

School District(s)

Collinsville ISD (PK-12)
   2009-10 Enrollment: 543 . . . . (903) 429-6272
Housing: Homeownership rate: 76.4% (2010); Median home value: $93,297 (2010); Median contract rent: $550 per month (2005-2009 5-year est.); Median year structure built: 1985 (2005-2009 5-year est.).
Safety: Violent crime rate: 13.1 per 10,000 population; Property crime rate: 177.2 per 10,000 population (2009).
Transportation: Commute to work: 93.9% car, 0.0% public transportation, 1.2% walk, 4.2% work from home (2005-2009 5-year est.); Travel time to work: 32.4% less than 15 minutes, 11.2% 15 to 30 minutes, 22.3% 30 to 45 minutes, 19.6% 45 to 60 minutes, 14.5% 60 minutes or more (2005-2009 5-year est.)

DENISON (city).

Covers a land area of 22.591 square miles and a water area of 0.323 square miles. Located at 33.75° N. Lat; 96.55° W. Long. Elevation is 728 feet.

History: Denison was the birthplace of Dwight D. Eisenhower (1890-1969), 34th president of the United States. Eisenhower's father, employed in the railroad shops in Denison, moved his family to Abilene, Kansas, when Dwight was one year old.

Population: 21,587 (1990); 22,773 (2000); 24,260 (2010); 24,873 (2015 projected); Race: 82.6% White, 7.9% Black, 0.6% Asian, 8.9% Other, 7.9% Hispanic of any race (2010); Density: 1,073.9 persons per square mile (2010); Average household size: 2.47 (2010); Median age: 38.7 (2010); Males per 100 females: 92.0 (2010); Marriage status: 22.7% never married, 48.9% now married, 10.3% widowed, 18.1% divorced (2005-2009 5-year est.); Foreign born: 4.0% (2005-2009 5-year est.); Ancestry (includes multiple ancestries): 14.4% Irish, 12.3% English, 11.7% German, 9.9% American, 4.0% French (2005-2009 5-year est.).

Economy: Single-family building permits issued: 14 (2010); Multi-family building permits issued: 0 (2010); Employment by occupation: 9.9% management, 15.5% professional, 20.0% services, 29.1% sales, 0.0% farming, 10.9% construction, 14.7% production (2005-2009 5-year est.).

Income: Per capita income: $22,146 (2010); Median household income: $40,607 (2010); Average household income: $55,174 (2010); Percent of households with income of $100,000 or more: 13.2% (2010); Poverty rate: 18.5% (2005-2009 5-year est.).

Taxes: Total city taxes per capita: $442 (2007); City property taxes per capita: $148 (2007).

Education: Percent of population age 25 and over with: High school diploma (including GED) or higher: 82.9% (2010); Bachelor's degree or higher: 14.0% (2010); Master's degree or higher: 4.6% (2010).

School District(s)

Denison ISD (PK-12)
2009-10 Enrollment: 4,492 . . . . (903) 462-7000
Sherman ISD (PK-12)
2009-10 Enrollment: 6,714 . . . . (903) 891-6400
Whitesboro ISD (PK-12)
2009-10 Enrollment: 1,554 . . . . (903) 564-4200

Two-year College(s)

Grayson County College (Public)
Fall 2009 Enrollment: 4,856. (903) 465-6030
2010-11 Tuition: In-state $1,776; Out-of-state $2,952

Housing: Homeownership rate: 69.5% (2010); Median home value: $72,464 (2010); Median contract rent: $468 per month (2005-2009 5-year est.); Median year structure built: 1963 (2005-2009 5-year est.).

Hospitals: Texoma Medical Center (267 beds)

Safety: Violent crime rate: 38.1 per 10,000 population; Property crime rate: 487.9 per 10,000 population (2009).

Transportation: Commute to work: 93.8% car, 0.4% public transportation, 1.6% walk, 3.1% work from home (2005-2009 5-year est.); Travel time to work: 48.6% less than 15 minutes, 35.6% 15 to 30 minutes, 5.6% 30 to 45 minutes, 3.7% 45 to 60 minutes, 6.5% 60 minutes or more (2005-2009 5-year est.)

Additional Information Contacts

City of Denison. . . . . (903) 465-2720
http://www.cityofdenison.com
Denison Area Chamber of Commerce. . . . . (903) 465-1551
http://www.denisontexas.us

DORCHESTER (town).

Covers a land area of 1.001 square miles and a water area of 0 square miles. Located at 33.53° N. Lat; 96.69° W. Long. Elevation is 866 feet.

Population: 137 (1990); 109 (2000); 150 (2010); 168 (2015 projected); Race: 91.3% White, 1.3% Black, 0.0% Asian, 7.3% Other, 6.0% Hispanic of any race (2010); Density: 149.9 persons per square mile (2010); Average household size: 3.00 (2010); Median age: 37.8 (2010); Males per 100 females: 97.4 (2010); Marriage status: 40.4% never married, 52.1% now married, 0.0% widowed, 7.4% divorced (2005-2009 5-year est.); Foreign born: 0.0% (2005-2009 5-year est.); Ancestry (includes multiple ancestries): 37.7% Czech, 18.4% German, 14.0% English, 8.8% Czechoslovakian, 7.0% American (2005-2009 5-year est.).

Economy: Employment by occupation: 10.0% management, 6.0% professional, 12.0% services, 50.0% sales, 0.0% farming, 0.0% construction, 22.0% production (2005-2009 5-year est.).

Income: Per capita income: $27,994 (2010); Median household income: $73,077 (2010); Average household income: $80,950 (2010); Percent of households with income of $100,000 or more: 30.0% (2010); Poverty rate: 3.5% (2005-2009 5-year est.).

Taxes: Total city taxes per capita: $73 (2007); City property taxes per capita: $0 (2007).

Education: Percent of population age 25 and over with: High school diploma (including GED) or higher: 92.9% (2010); Bachelor's degree or higher: 17.3% (2010); Master's degree or higher: 7.1% (2010).

Housing: Homeownership rate: 92.0% (2010); Median home value: $138,235 (2010); Median contract rent: $275 per month (2005-2009 5-year est.); Median year structure built: 1975 (2005-2009 5-year est.).

Transportation: Commute to work: 100.0% car, 0.0% public transportation, 0.0% walk, 0.0% work from home (2005-2009 5-year est.); Travel time to work: 12.8% less than 15 minutes, 34.0% 15 to 30 minutes, 34.0% 30 to 45 minutes, 12.8% 45 to 60 minutes, 6.4% 60 minutes or more (2005-2009 5-year est.)

GORDONVILLE (unincorporated postal area, zip code 76245).

Covers a land area of 19.316 square miles and a water area of 0.009 square miles. Located at 33.84° N. Lat; 96.82° W. Long. Elevation is 722 feet.

Population: 1,576 (2000); Race: 98.0% White, 0.0% Black, 0.0% Asian, 2.0% Other, 4.5% Hispanic of any race (2000); Density: 81.6 persons per square mile (2000); Age: 13.5% under 18, 23.2% over 64 (2000); Marriage status: 8.5% never married, 72.8% now married, 8.2% widowed, 10.4% divorced (2000); Foreign born: 0.7% (2000); Ancestry (includes multiple ancestries): 14.5% English, 14.3% American, 10.7% German, 8.8% Irish (2000).

Economy: Employment by occupation: 11.7% management, 2.4% professional, 16.4% services, 22.4% sales, 1.4% farming, 31.1% construction, 14.5% production (2000).

Income: Per capita income: $23,426 (2000); Median household income: $28,491 (2000); Poverty rate: 179.1% (2000).

Education: Percent of population age 25 and over with: High school diploma (including GED) or higher: 69.0% (2000); Bachelor's degree or higher: 7.0% (2000).

Housing: Homeownership rate: 88.1% (2000); Median home value: $48,600 (2000); Median contract rent: $385 per month (2000); Median year structure built: 1976 (2000).

Transportation: Commute to work: 93.9% car, 0.0% public transportation, 0.0% walk, 4.8% work from home (2000); Travel time to work: 31.2% less than 15 minutes, 7.2% 15 to 30 minutes, 22.7% 30 to 45 minutes, 18.7% 45 to 60 minutes, 20.2% 60 minutes or more (2000)

GUNTER (city).

Covers a land area of 1.502 square miles and a water area of 0 square miles. Located at 33.45° N. Lat; 96.74° W. Long. Elevation is 705 feet.

Population: 891 (1990); 1,230 (2000); 1,219 (2010); 1,225 (2015 projected); Race: 74.0% White, 1.0% Black, 0.8% Asian, 24.2% Other, 36.7% Hispanic of any race (2010); Density: 811.4 persons per square mile (2010); Average household size: 3.12 (2010); Median age: 37.1 (2010); Males per 100 females: 85.3 (2010); Marriage status: 17.7% never married, 70.1% now married, 4.1% widowed, 8.1% divorced (2005-2009 5-year est.); Foreign born: 17.8% (2005-2009 5-year est.); Ancestry (includes multiple ancestries): 19.7% English, 12.4% German, 8.2% Irish, 5.9% Scotch-Irish, 3.9% American (2005-2009 5-year est.).

Economy: Single-family building permits issued: 3 (2010); Multi-family building permits issued: 0 (2010); Employment by occupation: 6.7% management, 18.0% professional, 18.8% services, 23.8% sales, 0.8% farming, 10.6% construction, 21.3% production (2005-2009 5-year est.).

Income: Per capita income: $19,216 (2010); Median household income: $56,743 (2010); Average household income: $63,944 (2010); Percent of households with income of $100,000 or more: 17.0% (2010); Poverty rate: 5.7% (2005-2009 5-year est.).

Taxes: Total city taxes per capita: $282 (2007); City property taxes per capita: $156 (2007).

Education: Percent of population age 25 and over with: High school diploma (including GED) or higher: 78.8% (2010); Bachelor's degree or higher: 13.4% (2010); Master's degree or higher: 2.8% (2010).

School District(s)

Gunter ISD (PK-12)
2009-10 Enrollment: 780 . . . . (903) 433-4750

Housing: Homeownership rate: 70.2% (2010); Median home value: $97,200 (2010); Median contract rent: $519 per month (2005-2009 5-year est.); Median year structure built: 1973 (2005-2009 5-year est.).

Transportation: Commute to work: 92.4% car, 0.0% public transportation, 3.3% walk, 0.7% work from home (2005-2009 5-year est.); Travel time to work: 26.0% less than 15 minutes, 27.1% 15 to 30 minutes, 22.4% 30 to 45 minutes, 9.3% 45 to 60 minutes, 15.2% 60 minutes or more (2005-2009 5-year est.)

HOWE (town).
Covers a land area of 3.865 square miles and a water area of 0 square miles. Located at 33.50° N. Lat; 96.61° W. Long. Elevation is 840 feet.
Population: 2,181 (1990); 2,478 (2000); 2,649 (2010); 2,750 (2015 projected); Race: 94.0% White, 0.7% Black, 0.2% Asian, 5.2% Other, 6.1% Hispanic of any race (2010); Density: 685.4 persons per square mile (2010); Average household size: 2.71 (2010); Median age: 32.7 (2010); Males per 100 females: 93.4 (2010); Marriage status: 18.9% never married, 64.6% now married, 5.3% widowed, 11.3% divorced (2005-2009 5-year est.); Foreign born: 4.5% (2005-2009 5-year est.); Ancestry (includes multiple ancestries): 17.4% German, 15.8% English, 10.7% Irish, 8.0% American, 4.4% Italian (2005-2009 5-year est.).
Economy: Single-family building permits issued: 1 (2010); Multi-family building permits issued: 0 (2010); Employment by occupation: 7.7% management, 25.4% professional, 16.7% services, 20.7% sales, 0.0% farming, 11.5% construction, 18.0% production (2005-2009 5-year est.).
Income: Per capita income: $19,844 (2010); Median household income: $44,101 (2010); Average household income: $54,041 (2010); Percent of households with income of $100,000 or more: 11.1% (2010); Poverty rate: 14.0% (2005-2009 5-year est.).
Taxes: Total city taxes per capita: $240 (2007); City property taxes per capita: $121 (2007).
Education: Percent of population age 25 and over with: High school diploma (including GED) or higher: 91.2% (2010); Bachelor's degree or higher: 11.6% (2010); Master's degree or higher: 2.9% (2010).
School District(s)
Howe ISD (PK-12)
    2009-10 Enrollment: 982 . . . . (903) 532-5518
Housing: Homeownership rate: 76.1% (2010); Median home value: $85,769 (2010); Median contract rent: $402 per month (2005-2009 5-year est.); Median year structure built: 1975 (2005-2009 5-year est.).
Safety: Violent crime rate: 14.7 per 10,000 population; Property crime rate: 103.1 per 10,000 population (2009).
Transportation: Commute to work: 94.6% car, 0.0% public transportation, 1.8% walk, 3.7% work from home (2005-2009 5-year est.); Travel time to work: 23.6% less than 15 minutes, 34.4% 15 to 30 minutes, 24.0% 30 to 45 minutes, 7.8% 45 to 60 minutes, 10.2% 60 minutes or more (2005-2009 5-year est.)

KNOLLWOOD (village).
Covers a land area of 0.313 square miles and a water area of 0 square miles. Located at 33.68° N. Lat; 96.61° W. Long. Elevation is 827 feet.
Population: 205 (1990); 375 (2000); 448 (2010); 480 (2015 projected); Race: 85.0% White, 7.1% Black, 2.9% Asian, 4.9% Other, 6.5% Hispanic of any race (2010); Density: 1,429.3 persons per square mile (2010); Average household size: 2.19 (2010); Median age: 36.4 (2010); Males per 100 females: 89.8 (2010); Marriage status: 29.3% never married, 27.6% now married, 13.4% widowed, 29.7% divorced (2005-2009 5-year est.); Foreign born: 4.5% (2005-2009 5-year est.); Ancestry (includes multiple ancestries): 19.2% German, 12.9% Scotch-Irish, 12.6% English, 9.0% American, 8.4% Irish (2005-2009 5-year est.).
Economy: Employment by occupation: 4.5% management, 15.4% professional, 18.6% services, 34.0% sales, 0.0% farming, 11.5% construction, 16.0% production (2005-2009 5-year est.).
Income: Per capita income: $23,304 (2010); Median household income: $34,861 (2010); Average household income: $50,579 (2010); Percent of households with income of $100,000 or more: 9.4% (2010); Poverty rate: 14.7% (2005-2009 5-year est.).
Taxes: Total city taxes per capita: $66 (2007); City property taxes per capita: $0 (2007).
Education: Percent of population age 25 and over with: High school diploma (including GED) or higher: 86.7% (2010); Bachelor's degree or higher: 21.8% (2010); Master's degree or higher: 5.1% (2010).
Housing: Homeownership rate: 70.9% (2010); Median home value: $82,727 (2010); Median contract rent: $561 per month (2005-2009 5-year est.); Median year structure built: 1994 (2005-2009 5-year est.).
Transportation: Commute to work: 98.7% car, 0.0% public transportation, 0.0% walk, 1.3% work from home (2005-2009 5-year est.); Travel time to work: 54.6% less than 15 minutes, 41.4% 15 to 30 minutes, 2.0% 30 to 45

minutes, 2.0% 45 to 60 minutes, 0.0% 60 minutes or more (2005-2009 5-year est.)

POTTSBORO (town).
Covers a land area of 2.849 square miles and a water area of 0 square miles. Located at 33.78° N. Lat; 96.67° W. Long. Elevation is 761 feet.
Population: 1,177 (1990); 1,579 (2000); 1,851 (2010); 1,978 (2015 projected); Race: 94.7% White, 0.1% Black, 0.3% Asian, 4.9% Other, 2.5% Hispanic of any race (2010); Density: 649.8 persons per square mile (2010); Average household size: 2.69 (2010); Median age: 38.8 (2010); Males per 100 females: 95.0 (2010); Marriage status: 21.2% never married, 59.5% now married, 5.3% widowed, 14.1% divorced (2005-2009 5-year est.); Foreign born: 1.1% (2005-2009 5-year est.); Ancestry (includes multiple ancestries): 17.9% German, 11.8% Irish, 11.5% American, 10.4% English, 3.6% Italian (2005-2009 5-year est.).
Economy: Single-family building permits issued: 5 (2010); Multi-family building permits issued: 0 (2010); Employment by occupation: 13.6% management, 21.3% professional, 11.6% services, 36.1% sales, 0.0% farming, 5.9% construction, 11.5% production (2005-2009 5-year est.).
Income: Per capita income: $23,955 (2010); Median household income: $55,122 (2010); Average household income: $63,788 (2010); Percent of households with income of $100,000 or more: 14.9% (2010); Poverty rate: 8.8% (2005-2009 5-year est.).
Taxes: Total city taxes per capita: $412 (2007); City property taxes per capita: $208 (2007).
Education: Percent of population age 25 and over with: High school diploma (including GED) or higher: 90.5% (2010); Bachelor's degree or higher: 19.4% (2010); Master's degree or higher: 4.9% (2010).
School District(s)
Pottsboro ISD (PK-12)
    2009-10 Enrollment: 1,255 . . . . (903) 786-3051
Housing: Homeownership rate: 77.1% (2010); Median home value: $108,413 (2010); Median contract rent: $532 per month (2005-2009 5-year est.); Median year structure built: 1990 (2005-2009 5-year est.).
Safety: Violent crime rate: 4.6 per 10,000 population; Property crime rate: 296.0 per 10,000 population (2009).
Newspapers: Pottsboro Press (Community news; Circulation 1,315)
Transportation: Commute to work: 94.5% car, 0.0% public transportation, 0.7% walk, 4.1% work from home (2005-2009 5-year est.); Travel time to work: 31.1% less than 15 minutes, 44.7% 15 to 30 minutes, 7.0% 30 to 45 minutes, 6.8% 45 to 60 minutes, 10.3% 60 minutes or more (2005-2009 5-year est.)
Additional Information Contacts
Pottsboro Chamber of Commerce . . . . (903) 786-6371
    http://www.pottsborochamber.com

SADLER (city).
Covers a land area of 0.600 square miles and a water area of 0 square miles. Located at 33.68° N. Lat; 96.84° W. Long. Elevation is 719 feet.
Population: 316 (1990); 404 (2000); 412 (2010); 425 (2015 projected); Race: 93.9% White, 0.2% Black, 0.0% Asian, 5.8% Other, 5.3% Hispanic of any race (2010); Density: 686.7 persons per square mile (2010); Average household size: 2.78 (2010); Median age: 38.5 (2010); Males per 100 females: 99.0 (2010); Marriage status: 13.5% never married, 52.5% now married, 12.5% widowed, 21.5% divorced (2005-2009 5-year est.); Foreign born: 0.0% (2005-2009 5-year est.); Ancestry (includes multiple ancestries): 23.6% Irish, 9.5% German, 7.9% American, 3.3% Dutch West Indian, 2.9% English (2005-2009 5-year est.).
Economy: Employment by occupation: 7.8% management, 10.8% professional, 4.9% services, 52.0% sales, 2.0% farming, 5.9% construction, 16.7% production (2005-2009 5-year est.).
Income: Per capita income: $23,534 (2010); Median household income: $53,289 (2010); Average household income: $64,307 (2010); Percent of households with income of $100,000 or more: 15.5% (2010); Poverty rate: 7.8% (2005-2009 5-year est.).
Taxes: Total city taxes per capita: $70 (2007); City property taxes per capita: $0 (2007).
Education: Percent of population age 25 and over with: High school diploma (including GED) or higher: 86.6% (2010); Bachelor's degree or higher: 17.0% (2010); Master's degree or higher: 4.7% (2010).
School District(s)
S and S CISD (PK-12)
    2009-10 Enrollment: 842 . . . . (903) 564-6051

Housing: Homeownership rate: 88.5% (2010); Median home value: $106,481 (2010); Median contract rent: $446 per month (2005-2009 5-year est.); Median year structure built: 1960 (2005-2009 5-year est.).
Transportation: Commute to work: 96.1% car, 0.0% public transportation, 3.9% walk, 0.0% work from home (2005-2009 5-year est.); Travel time to work: 9.8% less than 15 minutes, 52.9% 15 to 30 minutes, 35.3% 30 to 45 minutes, 0.0% 45 to 60 minutes, 2.0% 60 minutes or more (2005-2009 5-year est.)

SHERMAN (city). County seat. Covers a land area of 38.550 square miles and a water area of 0.068 square miles. Located at 33.64° N. Lat; 96.61° W. Long. Elevation is 735 feet.

History: Sherman developed as a transportation center when the Butterfield stage route from St. Louis to San Francisco was charted through the town in 1857. Later, the railroads kept Sherman strategically situated as a shipping center.
Population: 32,235 (1990); 35,082 (2000); 38,670 (2010); 40,318 (2015 projected); Race: 74.8% White, 10.8% Black, 1.3% Asian, 13.1% Other, 18.9% Hispanic of any race (2010); Density: 1,003.1 persons per square mile (2010); Average household size: 2.47 (2010); Median age: 34.2 (2010); Males per 100 females: 94.8 (2010); Marriage status: 28.3% never married, 48.8% now married, 8.0% widowed, 14.9% divorced (2005-2009 5-year est.); Foreign born: 9.9% (2005-2009 5-year est.); Ancestry (includes multiple ancestries): 13.1% Irish, 12.2% German, 9.8% English, 7.2% American, 2.7% French (2005-2009 5-year est.).
Economy: Unemployment rate: 9.3% (June 2011); Total civilian labor force: 17,936 (June 2011); Single-family building permits issued: 35 (2010); Multi-family building permits issued: 252 (2010); Employment by occupation: 9.4% management, 18.6% professional, 19.3% services, 25.6% sales, 0.3% farming, 10.1% construction, 16.7% production (2005-2009 5-year est.).
Income: Per capita income: $20,921 (2010); Median household income: $40,360 (2010); Average household income: $53,334 (2010); Percent of households with income of $100,000 or more: 10.8% (2010); Poverty rate: 17.8% (2005-2009 5-year est.).
Taxes: Total city taxes per capita: $575 (2007); City property taxes per capita: $190 (2007).
Education: Percent of population age 25 and over with: High school diploma (including GED) or higher: 83.3% (2010); Bachelor's degree or higher: 19.7% (2010); Master's degree or higher: 6.7% (2010).

School District(s)
Sherman ISD (PK-12)
    2009-10 Enrollment: 6,714 . . . . (903) 891-6400
Four-year College(s)
Austin College (Private, Not-for-profit, Presbyterian Church (USA))
    Fall 2009 Enrollment: 1,364 . . . . (903) 813-2000
    2010-11 Tuition: In-state $29,235; Out-of-state $29,235
Housing: Homeownership rate: 59.1% (2010); Median home value: $89,524 (2010); Median contract rent: $536 per month (2005-2009 5-year est.); Median year structure built: 1971 (2005-2009 5-year est.).
Hospitals: Willson N Jones (160 beds); Wilson N. Jones Medical Center (241 beds)
Safety: Violent crime rate: 48.7 per 10,000 population; Property crime rate: 415.5 per 10,000 population (2009).
Newspapers: Herald Democrat (Local news; Circulation 26,000)
Transportation: Commute to work: 92.9% car, 0.2% public transportation, 2.0% walk, 3.3% work from home (2005-2009 5-year est.); Travel time to work: 51.1% less than 15 minutes, 30.5% 15 to 30 minutes, 8.9% 30 to 45 minutes, 3.0% 45 to 60 minutes, 6.4% 60 minutes or more (2005-2009 5-year est.)
Airports: North Texas Regional Airport (general aviation)
Additional Information Contacts
City of Sherman . . . . (903) 892-7205
    http://www.ci.sherman.tx.us
Sherman Chamber of Commerce . . . . (903) 893-1184
    http://www.shermanchamber.us

SOUTHMAYD (city). Covers a land area of 2.295 square miles and a water area of 0.004 square miles. Located at 33.62° N. Lat; 96.71° W. Long. Elevation is 735 feet.

Population: 721 (1990); 992 (2000); 1,013 (2010); 1,025 (2015 projected); Race: 91.4% White, 1.5% Black, 0.5% Asian, 6.6% Other, 2.4% Hispanic of any race (2010); Density: 441.3 persons per square mile (2010); Average household size: 2.79 (2010); Median age: 37.0 (2010); Males per 100 females: 99.0 (2010); Marriage status: 18.1% never married, 68.4%

now married, 5.1% widowed, 8.4% divorced (2005-2009 5-year est.); Foreign born: 2.9% (2005-2009 5-year est.); Ancestry (includes multiple ancestries): 16.7% German, 13.0% Irish, 9.4% American, 6.5% English, 3.3% Dutch (2005-2009 5-year est.).
Economy: Employment by occupation: 7.5% management, 9.8% professional, 19.8% services, 19.8% sales, 0.0% farming, 16.4% construction, 26.7% production (2005-2009 5-year est.).
Income: Per capita income: $26,945 (2010); Median household income: $62,005 (2010); Average household income: $74,442 (2010); Percent of households with income of $100,000 or more: 20.4% (2010); Poverty rate: 5.4% (2005-2009 5-year est.).
Taxes: Total city taxes per capita: $125 (2007); City property taxes per capita: $0 (2007).
Education: Percent of population age 25 and over with: High school diploma (including GED) or higher: 91.4% (2010); Bachelor's degree or higher: 16.5% (2010); Master's degree or higher: 5.5% (2010).

School District(s)
S and S CISD (PK-12)
    2009-10 Enrollment: 842 . . . . (903) 564-6051
Housing: Homeownership rate: 89.3% (2010); Median home value: $69,231 (2010); Median contract rent: $384 per month (2005-2009 5-year est.); Median year structure built: 1984 (2005-2009 5-year est.).
Transportation: Commute to work: 87.0% car, 2.3% public transportation, 0.0% walk, 10.2% work from home (2005-2009 5-year est.); Travel time to work: 25.9% less than 15 minutes, 50.1% 15 to 30 minutes, 17.3% 30 to 45 minutes, 4.5% 45 to 60 minutes, 2.1% 60 minutes or more (2005-2009 5-year est.)

TIOGA (town). Covers a land area of 1.233 square miles and a water area of 0.011 square miles. Located at 33.46° N. Lat; 96.91° W. Long. Elevation is 673 feet.

Population: 642 (1990); 754 (2000); 943 (2010); 1,033 (2015 projected); Race: 89.9% White, 0.7% Black, 2.1% Asian, 7.2% Other, 22.7% Hispanic of any race (2010); Density: 765.1 persons per square mile (2010); Average household size: 2.66 (2010); Median age: 35.6 (2010); Males per 100 females: 103.2 (2010); Marriage status: 15.2% never married, 66.4% now married, 7.5% widowed, 11.0% divorced (2005-2009 5-year est.); Foreign born: 11.3% (2005-2009 5-year est.); Ancestry (includes multiple ancestries): 25.9% German, 13.8% Irish, 12.7% English, 9.9% American, 5.6% French (2005-2009 5-year est.).
Economy: Single-family building permits issued: 4 (2010); Multi-family building permits issued: 0 (2010); Employment by occupation: 12.8% management, 20.8% professional, 17.0% services, 21.2% sales, 0.0% farming, 10.3% construction, 17.9% production (2005-2009 5-year est.).
Income: Per capita income: $25,501 (2010); Median household income: $57,500 (2010); Average household income: $67,620 (2010); Percent of households with income of $100,000 or more: 18.1% (2010); Poverty rate: 13.1% (2005-2009 5-year est.).
Taxes: Total city taxes per capita: $302 (2007); City property taxes per capita: $160 (2007).
Education: Percent of population age 25 and over with: High school diploma (including GED) or higher: 81.1% (2010); Bachelor's degree or higher: 12.3% (2010); Master's degree or higher: 5.1% (2010).

School District(s)
Tioga ISD (PK-08)
    2009-10 Enrollment: 159 . . . . (940) 437-2366
Housing: Homeownership rate: 74.3% (2010); Median home value: $97,347 (2010); Median contract rent: $528 per month (2005-2009 5-year est.); Median year structure built: 1977 (2005-2009 5-year est.).
Safety: Violent crime rate: 10.6 per 10,000 population; Property crime rate: 242.9 per 10,000 population (2009).
Transportation: Commute to work: 95.1% car, 0.0% public transportation, 0.0% walk, 1.6% work from home (2005-2009 5-year est.); Travel time to work: 37.6% less than 15 minutes, 26.4% 15 to 30 minutes, 7.3% 30 to 45 minutes, 5.3% 45 to 60 minutes, 23.4% 60 minutes or more (2005-2009 5-year est.)

TOM BEAN (city). Covers a land area of 1.411 square miles and a water area of 0 square miles. Located at 33.52° N. Lat; 96.48° W. Long. Elevation is 820 feet.

Population: 890 (1990); 941 (2000); 1,020 (2010); 1,058 (2015 projected); Race: 93.0% White, 1.2% Black, 0.3% Asian, 5.5% Other, 6.1% Hispanic of any race (2010); Density: 723.0 persons per square mile (2010); Average household size: 2.76 (2010); Median age: 35.7 (2010); Males per 100 females: 98.8 (2010); Marriage status: 29.3% never married, 50.7%

now married, 7.3% widowed, 12.7% divorced (2005-2009 5-year est.); Foreign born: 0.0% (2005-2009 5-year est.); Ancestry (includes multiple ancestries): 26.8% Irish, 19.3% German, 11.2% English, 7.7% Dutch, 7.6% French (2005-2009 5-year est.).

Economy: Single-family building permits issued: 0 (2010); Multi-family building permits issued: 0 (2010); Employment by occupation: 5.7% management, 15.7% professional, 7.0% services, 34.9% sales, 0.0% farming, 10.5% construction, 26.2% production (2005-2009 5-year est.).

Income: Per capita income: $21,885 (2010); Median household income: $53,516 (2010); Average household income: $60,203 (2010); Percent of households with income of $100,000 or more: 13.0% (2010); Poverty rate: 19.4% (2005-2009 5-year est.).

Taxes: Total city taxes per capita: $146 (2007); City property taxes per capita: $146 (2007).

Education: Percent of population age 25 and over with: High school diploma (including GED) or higher: 92.9% (2010); Bachelor's degree or higher: 12.0% (2010); Master's degree or higher: 3.6% (2010).

School District(s)
Tom Bean ISD (PK-12)
  2009-10 Enrollment: 795 . . . . (903) 546-6076

Housing: Homeownership rate: 76.4% (2010); Median home value: $90,400 (2010); Median contract rent: $485 per month (2005-2009 5-year est.); Median year structure built: 1974 (2005-2009 5-year est.).

Transportation: Commute to work: 96.2% car, 0.0% public transportation, 2.7% walk, 0.0% work from home (2005-2009 5-year est.); Travel time to work: 22.4% less than 15 minutes, 40.8% 15 to 30 minutes, 21.9% 30 to 45 minutes, 7.3% 45 to 60 minutes, 7.6% 60 minutes or more (2005-2009 5-year est.)

VAN ALSTYNE (city). Covers a land area of 3.411 square miles and a water area of 0 square miles. Located at 33.42° N. Lat; 96.57° W. Long. Elevation is 784 feet.

History: Established 1853.

Population: 2,144 (1990); 2,502 (2000); 3,048 (2010); 3,312 (2015 projected); Race: 90.4% White, 1.9% Black, 0.3% Asian, 7.3% Other, 11.5% Hispanic of any race (2010); Density: 893.6 persons per square mile (2010); Average household size: 2.71 (2010); Median age: 36.7 (2010); Males per 100 females: 99.9 (2010); Marriage status: 11.6% never married, 63.5% now married, 12.0% widowed, 12.9% divorced (2005-2009 5-year est.); Foreign born: 4.8% (2005-2009 5-year est.); Ancestry (includes multiple ancestries): 22.1% Irish, 12.5% German, 10.5% English, 4.5% American, 3.4% Scottish (2005-2009 5-year est.).

Economy: Single-family building permits issued: 6 (2010); Multi-family building permits issued: 0 (2010); Employment by occupation: 9.0% management, 27.6% professional, 25.7% services, 18.4% sales, 0.0% farming, 10.7% construction, 8.6% production (2005-2009 5-year est.).

Income: Per capita income: $24,838 (2010); Median household income: $56,784 (2010); Average household income: $67,317 (2010); Percent of households with income of $100,000 or more: 18.6% (2010); Poverty rate: 6.2% (2005-2009 5-year est.).

Taxes: Total city taxes per capita: $66 (2007); City property taxes per capita: $0 (2007).

Education: Percent of population age 25 and over with: High school diploma (including GED) or higher: 85.3% (2010); Bachelor's degree or higher: 19.0% (2010); Master's degree or higher: 4.4% (2010).

School District(s)
Van Alstyne ISD (PK-12)
  2009-10 Enrollment: 1,360 . . . . (903) 482-8802

Housing: Homeownership rate: 76.2% (2010); Median home value: $121,547 (2010); Median contract rent: $570 per month (2005-2009 5-year est.); Median year structure built: 1974 (2005-2009 5-year est.).

Safety: Violent crime rate: 26.6 per 10,000 population; Property crime rate: 136.1 per 10,000 population (2009).

Newspapers: Leader (Community news; Circulation 1,500)

Transportation: Commute to work: 95.5% car, 0.6% public transportation, 0.0% walk, 3.8% work from home (2005-2009 5-year est.); Travel time to work: 29.9% less than 15 minutes, 31.1% 15 to 30 minutes, 9.5% 30 to 45 minutes, 8.9% 45 to 60 minutes, 20.6% 60 minutes or more (2005-2009 5-year est.)

Additional Information Contacts
Van Alstyne Chamber of Commerce . . . . (903) 482-6066
  http://vanalstynechamber.org

WHITESBORO (city). Covers a land area of 3.187 square miles and a water area of 0.004 square miles. Located at 33.66° N. Lat; 96.90° W. Long. Elevation is 820 feet.

History: Whitesboro developed around cotton gins and cottonseed, feed, and flour mills.

Population: 3,339 (1990); 3,760 (2000); 4,087 (2010); 4,261 (2015 projected); Race: 95.1% White, 0.2% Black, 0.5% Asian, 4.2% Other, 4.5% Hispanic of any race (2010); Density: 1,282.5 persons per square mile (2010); Average household size: 2.54 (2010); Median age: 38.2 (2010); Males per 100 females: 90.3 (2010); Marriage status: 26.3% never married, 42.5% now married, 13.3% widowed, 17.9% divorced (2005-2009 5-year est.); Foreign born: 2.5% (2005-2009 5-year est.); Ancestry (includes multiple ancestries): 19.3% American, 13.7% German, 13.5% Irish, 4.7% English, 3.9% French (2005-2009 5-year est.).

Economy: Single-family building permits issued: 6 (2010); Multi-family building permits issued: 0 (2010); Employment by occupation: 13.6% management, 12.4% professional, 25.7% services, 28.9% sales, 0.9% farming, 10.2% construction, 8.3% production (2005-2009 5-year est.).

Income: Per capita income: $20,579 (2010); Median household income: $44,593 (2010); Average household income: $52,457 (2010); Percent of households with income of $100,000 or more: 10.2% (2010); Poverty rate: 17.4% (2005-2009 5-year est.).

Taxes: Total city taxes per capita: $264 (2007); City property taxes per capita: $125 (2007).

Education: Percent of population age 25 and over with: High school diploma (including GED) or higher: 80.4% (2010); Bachelor's degree or higher: 11.0% (2010); Master's degree or higher: 4.5% (2010).

School District(s)
Whitesboro ISD (PK-12)
  2009-10 Enrollment: 1,554 . . . . (903) 564-4200

Housing: Homeownership rate: 74.2% (2010); Median home value: $79,398 (2010); Median contract rent: $429 per month (2005-2009 5-year est.); Median year structure built: 1973 (2005-2009 5-year est.).

Safety: Violent crime rate: 17.3 per 10,000 population; Property crime rate: 278.6 per 10,000 population (2009).

Newspapers: Whitesboro News-Record (Community news; Circulation 3,000)

Transportation: Commute to work: 91.1% car, 0.5% public transportation, 3.2% walk, 3.7% work from home (2005-2009 5-year est.); Travel time to work: 39.3% less than 15 minutes, 30.2% 15 to 30 minutes, 23.5% 30 to 45 minutes, 4.0% 45 to 60 minutes, 3.1% 60 minutes or more (2005-2009 5-year est.)

Additional Information Contacts
Whitesboro Chamber of Commerce . . . . (903) 564-3331
  http://www.whitesborotx.com

WHITEWRIGHT (town). Covers a land area of 2.096 square miles and a water area of 0.010 square miles. Located at 33.51° N. Lat; 96.39° W. Long. Elevation is 751 feet.

History: Settled 1877, incorporated 1888.

Population: 1,714 (1990); 1,740 (2000); 1,716 (2010); 1,709 (2015 projected); Race: 86.4% White, 7.4% Black, 1.5% Asian, 4.7% Other, 3.4% Hispanic of any race (2010); Density: 818.6 persons per square mile (2010); Average household size: 2.63 (2010); Median age: 38.5 (2010); Males per 100 females: 87.5 (2010); Marriage status: 24.5% never married, 51.3% now married, 9.2% widowed, 15.0% divorced (2005-2009 5-year est.); Foreign born: 1.7% (2005-2009 5-year est.); Ancestry (includes multiple ancestries): 30.3% English, 17.3% German, 14.6% Irish, 5.2% American, 4.7% Italian (2005-2009 5-year est.).

Economy: Employment by occupation: 11.3% management, 15.2% professional, 20.7% services, 35.1% sales, 0.5% farming, 6.7% construction, 10.5% production (2005-2009 5-year est.).

Income: Per capita income: $22,646 (2010); Median household income: $50,663 (2010); Average household income: $61,103 (2010); Percent of households with income of $100,000 or more: 16.1% (2010); Poverty rate: 9.7% (2005-2009 5-year est.).

Taxes: Total city taxes per capita: $293 (2007); City property taxes per capita: $119 (2007).

Education: Percent of population age 25 and over with: High school diploma (including GED) or higher: 81.3% (2010); Bachelor's degree or higher: 15.2% (2010); Master's degree or higher: 4.1% (2010).

School District(s)
Whitewright ISD (PK-12)
  2009-10 Enrollment: 770 . . . . (903) 364-2155

Housing: Homeownership rate: 72.6% (2010); Median home value: $77,222 (2010); Median contract rent: $518 per month (2005-2009 5-year est.); Median year structure built: 1964 (2005-2009 5-year est.).
Newspapers: Whitewright Sun (Local news; Circulation 1,000)
Transportation: Commute to work: 95.1% car, 0.0% public transportation, 0.2% walk, 4.4% work from home (2005-2009 5-year est.); Travel time to work: 31.1% less than 15 minutes, 28.9% 15 to 30 minutes, 19.5% 30 to 45 minutes, 4.1% 45 to 60 minutes, 16.4% 60 minutes or more (2005-2009 5-year est.)
Additional Information Contacts
Whitewright Area Chamber of Commerce . . . . (903) 364-2000
   http://www.whitewright.org

Gregg County

Located in east Texas; drained by the Sabine River. Covers a land area of 274.03 square miles, a water area of 2.34 square miles, and is located in the Central Time Zone at 32.49° N. Lat., 94.80° W. Long. The county was founded in 1873. County seat is Longview.

Gregg County is part of the Longview, TX Metropolitan Statistical Area. The entire metro area includes: Gregg County, TX; Rusk County, TX; Upshur County, TX

Population: 104,948 (1990); 111,379 (2000); 119,893 (2010); 123,816 (2015 projected); Race: 69.3% White, 20.0% Black, 0.9% Asian, 9.8% Other, 13.9% Hispanic of any race (2010); Density: 437.5 persons per square mile (2010); Average household size: 2.53 (2010); Median age: 35.1 (2010); Males per 100 females: 95.2 (2010).
Religion: Five largest groups: 35.7% Southern Baptist Convention, 8.2% The United Methodist Church, 7.6% Catholic Church, 5.0% Churches of Christ, 2.0% Christian Church (Disciples of Christ) (2000).
Economy: Unemployment rate: 7.1% (June 2011); Total civilian labor force: 68,501 (June 2011); Leading industries: 15.2% health care and social assistance; 14.4% retail trade; 14.1% manufacturing (2009); Farms: 486 totaling 45,192 acres (2007); Companies that employ 500 or more persons: 8 (2009); Companies that employ 100 to 499 persons: 97 (2009); Companies that employ less than 100 persons: 3,886 (2009); Black-owned businesses: 1,166 (2007); Hispanic-owned businesses: 515 (2007); Asian-owned businesses: n/a (2007); Women-owned businesses: 3,377 (2007); Retail sales per capita: $21,685 (2010). Single-family building permits issued: 198 (2010); Multi-family building permits issued: 278 (2010).
Income: Per capita income: $23,316 (2010); Median household income: $44,368 (2010); Average household income: $59,728 (2010); Percent of households with income of $100,000 or more: 14.3% (2010); Poverty rate: 15.0% (2009); Bankruptcy rate: 1.69% (2010).
Taxes: Total county taxes per capita: $282 (2007); County property taxes per capita: $142 (2007).
Education: Percent of population age 25 and over with: High school diploma (including GED) or higher: 83.5% (2010); Bachelor's degree or higher: 21.5% (2010); Master's degree or higher: 6.6% (2010).
Housing: Homeownership rate: 62.0% (2010); Median home value: $107,163 (2010); Median contract rent: $519 per month (2005-2009 5-year est.); Median year structure built: 1975 (2005-2009 5-year est.)
Health: Birth rate: 156.6 per 10,000 population (2009); Death rate: 99.0 per 10,000 population (2009); Age-adjusted cancer mortality rate: 210.7 deaths per 100,000 population (2007); Number of physicians: 24.3 per 10,000 population (2008); Hospital beds: 54.2 per 10,000 population (2007); Hospital admissions: 2,299.5 per 10,000 population (2007).
Environment: Air Quality Index: 91.8% good, 7.9% moderate, 0.3% unhealthy for sensitive individuals, 0.0% unhealthy (percent of days in 2008)
Elections: 2008 Presidential election results: 30.9% Obama, 68.5% McCain, 0.0% Nader
Additional Information Contacts
Gregg County Government . . . . (903) 236-8420
   http://www.co.gregg.tx.us
City of Gladewater . . . . (903) 845-2196
   http://www.cityofgladewater.com
City of Kilgore . . . . (903) 984-5081
   http://www.cityofkilgore.com
City of Longview . . . . (903) 237-1000
   http://longviewtexas.gov
Gladewater Chamber of Commerce . . . . (903) 845-5501
   http://www.gladewaterchamber.com

Kilgore Chamber of Commerce . . . . (903) 984-5022
   http://www.kilgorechamber.com
Liberty City Chamber of Commerce. . . . . (903) 981-5222
   http://www.libertycitychamber.com
Longview Chamber of Commerce . . . . (903) 237-4000
   http://www.longviewchamber.com
Town of White Oak . . . . (903) 759-3936
   http://www.cityofwhiteoak.com
White Oak Economic Development Corporation . . . . (903) 759-3936
   http://www.cityofwhiteoak.com/edc.htm

Gregg County Communities

CLARKSVILLE CITY (city). Covers a land area of 6.303 square miles and a water area of 0.163 square miles. Located at 32.52° N. Lat; 94.89° W. Long. Elevation is 361 feet.
Population: 725 (1990); 806 (2000); 852 (2010); 874 (2015 projected); Race: 90.0% White, 5.4% Black, 0.0% Asian, 4.6% Other, 2.2% Hispanic of any race (2010); Density: 135.2 persons per square mile (2010); Average household size: 2.62 (2010); Median age: 40.3 (2010); Males per 100 females: 95.4 (2010); Marriage status: 23.0% never married, 59.9% now married, 6.8% widowed, 10.3% divorced (2005-2009 5-year est.); Foreign born: 2.5% (2005-2009 5-year est.); Ancestry (includes multiple ancestries): 16.1% American, 10.7% English, 9.4% French, 9.4% German, 6.7% Irish (2005-2009 5-year est.).
Economy: Single-family building permits issued: 2 (2010); Multi-family building permits issued: 0 (2010); Employment by occupation: 10.3% management, 17.2% professional, 13.5% services, 31.9% sales, 0.0% farming, 9.1% construction, 18.1% production (2005-2009 5-year est.).
Income: Per capita income: $21,435 (2010); Median household income: $43,250 (2010); Average household income: $58,032 (2010); Percent of households with income of $100,000 or more: 12.6% (2010); Poverty rate: 8.2% (2005-2009 5-year est.).
Taxes: Total city taxes per capita: $269 (2007); City property taxes per capita: $227 (2007).
Education: Percent of population age 25 and over with: High school diploma (including GED) or higher: 82.3% (2010); Bachelor's degree or higher: 10.9% (2010); Master's degree or higher: 3.6% (2010).
Housing: Homeownership rate: 73.2% (2010); Median home value: $87,500 (2010); Median contract rent: $381 per month (2005-2009 5-year est.); Median year structure built: 1979 (2005-2009 5-year est.).
Transportation: Commute to work: 93.5% car, 0.0% public transportation, 0.0% walk, 2.0% work from home (2005-2009 5-year est.); Travel time to work: 25.9% less than 15 minutes, 50.3% 15 to 30 minutes, 12.4% 30 to 45 minutes, 3.8% 45 to 60 minutes, 7.6% 60 minutes or more (2005-2009 5-year est.)

EASTON (city). Covers a land area of 2.491 square miles and a water area of 0 square miles. Located at 32.38° N. Lat; 94.58° W. Long.
Population: 401 (1990); 524 (2000); 470 (2010); 447 (2015 projected); Race: 56.0% White, 30.6% Black, 0.6% Asian, 12.8% Other, 18.7% Hispanic of any race (2010); Density: 188.7 persons per square mile (2010); Average household size: 2.51 (2010); Median age: 38.2 (2010); Males per 100 females: 98.3 (2010); Marriage status: 22.8% never married, 65.8% now married, 5.7% widowed, 5.7% divorced (2005-2009 5-year est.); Foreign born: 18.0% (2005-2009 5-year est.); Ancestry (includes multiple ancestries): 13.3% American, 2.2% African, 0.9% German, 0.8% French Canadian (2005-2009 5-year est.).
Economy: Employment by occupation: 3.3% management, 7.6% professional, 15.6% services, 9.8% sales, 0.0% farming, 12.0% construction, 51.8% production (2005-2009 5-year est.).
Income: Per capita income: $23,929 (2010); Median household income: $43,214 (2010); Average household income: $59,853 (2010); Percent of households with income of $100,000 or more: 15.5% (2010); Poverty rate: 43.9% (2005-2009 5-year est.).
Taxes: Total city taxes per capita: $34 (2007); City property taxes per capita: $0 (2007).
Education: Percent of population age 25 and over with: High school diploma (including GED) or higher: 78.3% (2010); Bachelor's degree or higher: 19.1% (2010); Master's degree or higher: 8.6% (2010).
Housing: Homeownership rate: 88.8% (2010); Median home value: $96,154 (2010); Median contract rent: $328 per month (2005-2009 5-year est.); Median year structure built: 1981 (2005-2009 5-year est.).
Transportation: Commute to work: 92.8% car, 0.0% public transportation, 0.0% walk, 0.0% work from home (2005-2009 5-year est.); Travel time to

work: 3.4% less than 15 minutes, 43.0% 15 to 30 minutes, 45.6% 30 to 45 minutes, 8.0% 45 to 60 minutes, 0.0% 60 minutes or more (2005-2009 5-year est.)

GLADEWATER (city). Covers a land area of 11.606 square miles and a water area of 0.527 square miles. Located at 32.54° N. Lat; 94.94° W. Long. Elevation is 364 feet.
Population: 6,006 (1990); 6,078 (2000); 6,287 (2010); 6,395 (2015 projected); Race: 79.8% White, 14.3% Black, 0.9% Asian, 4.9% Other, 4.6% Hispanic of any race (2010); Density: 541.7 persons per square mile (2010); Average household size: 2.56 (2010); Median age: 35.7 (2010); Males per 100 females: 90.0 (2010); Marriage status: 24.2% never married, 52.3% now married, 12.1% widowed, 11.4% divorced (2005-2009 5-year est.); Foreign born: 0.7% (2005-2009 5-year est.); Ancestry (includes multiple ancestries): 24.7% American, 12.1% Irish, 10.6% German, 10.2% English, 5.0% Scottish (2005-2009 5-year est.).
Economy: Single-family building permits issued: 18 (2010); Multi-family building permits issued: 0 (2010); Employment by occupation: 9.3% management, 15.4% professional, 13.9% services, 27.6% sales, 3.0% farming, 10.7% construction, 20.2% production (2005-2009 5-year est.).
Income: Per capita income: $17,885 (2010); Median household income: $38,102 (2010); Average household income: $47,087 (2010); Percent of households with income of $100,000 or more: 7.4% (2010); Poverty rate: 21.7% (2005-2009 5-year est.).
Taxes: Total city taxes per capita: $453 (2007); City property taxes per capita: $275 (2007).
Education: Percent of population age 25 and over with: High school diploma (including GED) or higher: 81.5% (2010); Bachelor's degree or higher: 14.6% (2010); Master's degree or higher: 5.2% (2010).
School District(s)
Gladewater ISD (PK-12)
    2009-10 Enrollment: 2,067 . . . . (903) 845-6991
Sabine ISD (PK-12)
    2009-10 Enrollment: 1,298 . . . . (903) 984-8564
Union Grove ISD (PK-12)
    2009-10 Enrollment: 738 . . . . (903) 845-5509
Housing: Homeownership rate: 64.7% (2010); Median home value: $83,913 (2010); Median contract rent: $482 per month (2005-2009 5-year est.); Median year structure built: 1967 (2005-2009 5-year est.).
Safety: Violent crime rate: 82.6 per 10,000 population; Property crime rate: 609.7 per 10,000 population (2009).
Newspapers: Gladewater Mirror (Community news; Circulation 2,000)
Transportation: Commute to work: 90.5% car, 0.0% public transportation, 1.1% walk, 4.1% work from home (2005-2009 5-year est.); Travel time to work: 30.2% less than 15 minutes, 41.6% 15 to 30 minutes, 21.0% 30 to 45 minutes, 3.3% 45 to 60 minutes, 4.0% 60 minutes or more (2005-2009 5-year est.)
Additional Information Contacts
City of Gladewater . . . . (903) 845-2196
    http://www.cityofgladewater.com
Gladewater Chamber of Commerce . . . . (903) 845-5501
    http://www.gladewaterchamber.com

KILGORE (city). Covers a land area of 15.391 square miles and a water area of 0.035 square miles. Located at 32.38° N. Lat; 94.86° W. Long. Elevation is 358 feet.
History: Kilgore developed as a major oil production center, with offices of the oil industry.
Population: 11,386 (1990); 11,301 (2000); 12,271 (2010); 12,729 (2015 projected); Race: 73.0% White, 12.2% Black, 1.1% Asian, 13.7% Other, 17.1% Hispanic of any race (2010); Density: 797.3 persons per square mile (2010); Average household size: 2.50 (2010); Median age: 35.3 (2010); Males per 100 females: 94.9 (2010); Marriage status: 25.2% never married, 54.4% now married, 8.7% widowed, 11.7% divorced (2005-2009 5-year est.); Foreign born: 8.8% (2005-2009 5-year est.); Ancestry (includes multiple ancestries): 19.5% American, 15.8% Irish, 11.6% German, 10.1% English, 4.8% French (2005-2009 5-year est.).
Economy: Single-family building permits issued: 11 (2010); Multi-family building permits issued: 114 (2010); Employment by occupation: 8.8% management, 14.8% professional, 17.8% services, 31.0% sales, 1.1% farming, 12.0% construction, 14.5% production (2005-2009 5-year est.).
Income: Per capita income: $22,367 (2010); Median household income: $45,219 (2010); Average household income: $57,479 (2010); Percent of households with income of $100,000 or more: 13.2% (2010); Poverty rate: 11.9% (2005-2009 5-year est.).

Taxes: Total city taxes per capita: $820 (2007); City property taxes per capita: $283 (2007).
Education: Percent of population age 25 and over with: High school diploma (including GED) or higher: 80.6% (2010); Bachelor's degree or higher: 19.1% (2010); Master's degree or higher: 6.1% (2010).
School District(s)
Kilgore ISD (PK-12)
    2009-10 Enrollment: 3,811 . . . . (903) 988-3900
Sabine ISD (PK-12)
    2009-10 Enrollment: 1,298 . . . . (903) 984-8564
White Oak ISD (PK-12)
    2009-10 Enrollment: 1,397 . . . . (903) 291-2200
Two-year College(s)
Kilgore College (Public)
    Fall 2009 Enrollment: 6,375 . . . . (903) 984-8531
    2010-11 Tuition: In-state $2,496; Out-of-state $3,456
Housing: Homeownership rate: 66.8% (2010); Median home value: $81,053 (2010); Median contract rent: $477 per month (2005-2009 5-year est.); Median year structure built: 1970 (2005-2009 5-year est.).
Hospitals: Allegiance Specialty Hospital (60 beds)
Safety: Violent crime rate: 35.6 per 10,000 population; Property crime rate: 668.9 per 10,000 population (2009).
Newspapers: Kilgore News Herald (Local news; Circulation 6,000)
Transportation: Commute to work: 91.4% car, 0.0% public transportation, 2.1% walk, 2.9% work from home (2005-2009 5-year est.); Travel time to work: 44.5% less than 15 minutes, 34.7% 15 to 30 minutes, 14.0% 30 to 45 minutes, 2.3% 45 to 60 minutes, 4.5% 60 minutes or more (2005-2009 5-year est.)
Additional Information Contacts
City of Kilgore . . . . (903) 984-5081
    http://www.cityofkilgore.com
Kilgore Chamber of Commerce . . . . (903) 984-5022
    http://www.kilgorechamber.com
Liberty City Chamber of Commerce . . . . (903) 981-5222
    http://www.libertycitychamber.com

LAKEPORT (city). Aka Elderville. Covers a land area of 1.551 square miles and a water area of 0 square miles. Located at 32.41° N. Lat; 94.70° W. Long. Elevation is 295 feet.
Population: 712 (1990); 861 (2000); 918 (2010); 943 (2015 projected); Race: 36.7% White, 58.1% Black, 0.3% Asian, 4.9% Other, 7.5% Hispanic of any race (2010); Density: 591.8 persons per square mile (2010); Average household size: 2.52 (2010); Median age: 42.3 (2010); Males per 100 females: 96.6 (2010); Marriage status: 25.5% never married, 47.4% now married, 7.6% widowed, 19.5% divorced (2005-2009 5-year est.); Foreign born: 6.7% (2005-2009 5-year est.); Ancestry (includes multiple ancestries): 15.2% American, 9.3% English, 8.4% Irish, 6.6% German, 2.4% Swiss (2005-2009 5-year est.).
Economy: Single-family building permits issued: 0 (2010); Multi-family building permits issued: 0 (2010); Employment by occupation: 5.3% management, 20.7% professional, 17.5% services, 22.8% sales, 0.0% farming, 5.3% construction, 28.5% production (2005-2009 5-year est.).
Income: Per capita income: $25,284 (2010); Median household income: $52,206 (2010); Average household income: $64,021 (2010); Percent of households with income of $100,000 or more: 16.7% (2010); Poverty rate: 17.6% (2005-2009 5-year est.).
Taxes: Total city taxes per capita: $212 (2007); City property taxes per capita: $78 (2007).
Education: Percent of population age 25 and over with: High school diploma (including GED) or higher: 83.8% (2010); Bachelor's degree or higher: 21.4% (2010); Master's degree or higher: 4.6% (2010).
Housing: Homeownership rate: 88.8% (2010); Median home value: $82,388 (2010); Median contract rent: $600 per month (2005-2009 5-year est.); Median year structure built: 1976 (2005-2009 5-year est.).
Transportation: Commute to work: 99.0% car, 0.0% public transportation, 0.0% walk, 1.0% work from home (2005-2009 5-year est.); Travel time to work: 27.1% less than 15 minutes, 52.0% 15 to 30 minutes, 13.5% 30 to 45 minutes, 0.0% 45 to 60 minutes, 7.5% 60 minutes or more (2005-2009 5-year est.)

LIBERTY CITY (CDP). Covers a land area of 3.925 square miles and a water area of 0 square miles. Located at 32.45° N. Lat; 94.94° W. Long. Elevation is 390 feet.
Population: 1,658 (1990); 1,935 (2000); 2,175 (2010); 2,283 (2015 projected); Race: 87.3% White, 9.0% Black, 0.1% Asian, 3.5% Other, 4.0%

Hispanic of any race (2010); Density: 554.2 persons per square mile (2010); Average household size: 2.74 (2010); Median age: 35.3 (2010); Males per 100 females: 94.7 (2010); Marriage status: 14.8% never married, 63.7% now married, 3.3% widowed, 18.2% divorced (2005-2009 5-year est.); Foreign born: 1.0% (2005-2009 5-year est.); Ancestry (includes multiple ancestries): 39.0% American, 15.1% Irish, 15.0% German, 9.7% English, 6.5% Norwegian (2005-2009 5-year est.).

Economy: Employment by occupation: 10.4% management, 14.8% professional, 13.9% services, 25.9% sales, 2.0% farming, 20.4% construction, 12.5% production (2005-2009 5-year est.).

Income: Per capita income: $29,119 (2010); Median household income: $66,071 (2010); Average household income: $79,192 (2010); Percent of households with income of $100,000 or more: 29.0% (2010); Poverty rate: 7.0% (2005-2009 5-year est.).

Education: Percent of population age 25 and over with: High school diploma (including GED) or higher: 87.6% (2010); Bachelor's degree or higher: 18.2% (2010); Master's degree or higher: 6.8% (2010).

Housing: Homeownership rate: 75.0% (2010); Median home value: $118,912 (2010); Median contract rent: $534 per month (2005-2009 5-year est.); Median year structure built: 1981 (2005-2009 5-year est.).

Transportation: Commute to work: 93.0% car, 0.0% public transportation, 0.0% walk, 7.0% work from home (2005-2009 5-year est.); Travel time to work: 35.7% less than 15 minutes, 42.9% 15 to 30 minutes, 12.0% 30 to 45 minutes, 3.6% 45 to 60 minutes, 5.8% 60 minutes or more (2005-2009 5-year est.)

LONGVIEW (city). County seat. Covers a land area of 54.660 square miles and a water area of 0.101 square miles. Located at 32.50° N. Lat; 94.75° W. Long. Elevation is 371 feet.

History: Longview's population swelled in 1930 when the East Texas oil boom prompted industrial expansion.

Population: 70,346 (1990); 73,344 (2000); 78,836 (2010); 81,369 (2015 projected); Race: 66.0% White, 22.8% Black, 1.1% Asian, 10.0% Other, 15.4% Hispanic of any race (2010); Density: 1,442.3 persons per square mile (2010); Average household size: 2.49 (2010); Median age: 34.6 (2010); Males per 100 females: 94.9 (2010); Marriage status: 26.6% never married, 52.6% now married, 8.0% widowed, 12.7% divorced (2005-2009 5-year est.); Foreign born: 8.7% (2005-2009 5-year est.); Ancestry (includes multiple ancestries): 12.9% American, 11.0% Irish, 10.1% German, 9.7% English, 3.4% French (2005-2009 5-year est.).

Economy: Unemployment rate: 7.5% (June 2011); Total civilian labor force: 43,828 (June 2011); Single-family building permits issued: 167 (2010); Multi-family building permits issued: 164 (2010); Employment by occupation: 10.7% management, 18.8% professional, 17.6% services, 25.2% sales, 0.1% farming, 10.7% construction, 16.8% production (2005-2009 5-year est.).

Income: Per capita income: $23,185 (2010); Median household income: $42,778 (2010); Average household income: $58,508 (2010); Percent of households with income of $100,000 or more: 13.4% (2010); Poverty rate: 16.4% (2005-2009 5-year est.).

Taxes: Total city taxes per capita: $698 (2007); City property taxes per capita: $261 (2007).

Education: Percent of population age 25 and over with: High school diploma (including GED) or higher: 84.6% (2010); Bachelor's degree or higher: 22.7% (2010); Master's degree or higher: 6.8% (2010).

School District(s)
East Texas Charter Schools (09-12)
  2009-10 Enrollment: 157 . . . . (903) 753-9400
Longview ISD (PK-12)
  2009-10 Enrollment: 8,348 . . . . (903) 381-2200
Pine Tree ISD (PK-12)
  2009-10 Enrollment: 4,746 . . . . (903) 295-5000
Spring Hill ISD (PK-12)
  2009-10 Enrollment: 1,849 . . . . (903) 759-4404

Four-year College(s)
LeTourneau University (Private, Not-for-profit, Interdenominational)
  Fall 2009 Enrollment: 3,386. (903) 233-3000
  2010-11 Tuition: In-state $21,980; Out-of-state $21,980

Housing: Homeownership rate: 56.4% (2010); Median home value: $110,569 (2010); Median contract rent: $526 per month (2005-2009 5-year est.); Median year structure built: 1974 (2005-2009 5-year est.).

Hospitals: Good Shepherd Medical Center (412 beds); Longview Regional Medical Center (164 beds)

Safety: Violent crime rate: 91.2 per 10,000 population; Property crime rate: 707.9 per 10,000 population (2009).

Newspapers: Longview News-Journal (Local news; Circulation 34,000)

Transportation: Commute to work: 93.0% car, 0.4% public transportation, 0.7% walk, 2.6% work from home (2005-2009 5-year est.); Travel time to work: 42.9% less than 15 minutes, 40.4% 15 to 30 minutes, 8.6% 30 to 45 minutes, 3.7% 45 to 60 minutes, 4.4% 60 minutes or more (2005-2009 5-year est.); Amtrak: train service available.

Airports: East Texas Regional (primary service)

Additional Information Contacts
City of Longview. . . . . (903) 237-1000
  http://longviewtexas.gov
Longview Chamber of Commerce . . . . (903) 237-4000
  http://www.longviewchamber.com

WARREN CITY (city). Covers a land area of 1.768 square miles and a water area of 0 square miles. Located at 32.55° N. Lat; 94.90° W. Long. Elevation is 371 feet.

Population: 264 (1990); 343 (2000); 343 (2010); 344 (2015 projected); Race: 87.8% White, 7.0% Black, 0.0% Asian, 5.2% Other, 2.6% Hispanic of any race (2010); Density: 194.0 persons per square mile (2010); Average household size: 2.48 (2010); Median age: 42.6 (2010); Males per 100 females: 93.8 (2010); Marriage status: 21.0% never married, 56.6% now married, 6.8% widowed, 15.5% divorced (2005-2009 5-year est.); Foreign born: 0.0% (2005-2009 5-year est.); Ancestry (includes multiple ancestries): 35.2% American, 8.2% English, 7.7% Irish, 2.6% German, 1.2% French (2005-2009 5-year est.).

Economy: Employment by occupation: 11.3% management, 26.3% professional, 17.0% services, 13.9% sales, 0.0% farming, 11.9% construction, 19.6% production (2005-2009 5-year est.).

Income: Per capita income: $21,034 (2010); Median household income: $40,192 (2010); Average household income: $54,413 (2010); Percent of households with income of $100,000 or more: 9.8% (2010); Poverty rate: 11.3% (2005-2009 5-year est.).

Taxes: Total city taxes per capita: $282 (2007); City property taxes per capita: $256 (2007).

Education: Percent of population age 25 and over with: High school diploma (including GED) or higher: 80.5% (2010); Bachelor's degree or higher: 6.2% (2010); Master's degree or higher: 2.9% (2010).

Housing: Homeownership rate: 70.5% (2010); Median home value: $61,111 (2010); Median contract rent: $753 per month (2005-2009 5-year est.); Median year structure built: 1974 (2005-2009 5-year est.).

Transportation: Commute to work: 98.9% car, 0.0% public transportation, 0.0% walk, 1.1% work from home (2005-2009 5-year est.); Travel time to work: 12.4% less than 15 minutes, 57.1% 15 to 30 minutes, 22.6% 30 to 45 minutes, 5.1% 45 to 60 minutes, 2.8% 60 minutes or more (2005-2009 5-year est.)

WHITE OAK (city). Covers a land area of 9.087 square miles and a water area of 0.049 square miles. Located at 32.53° N. Lat; 94.85° W. Long. Elevation is 413 feet.

Population: 5,136 (1990); 5,624 (2000); 6,442 (2010); 6,831 (2015 projected); Race: 91.3% White, 2.4% Black, 0.0% Asian, 6.3% Other, 6.6% Hispanic of any race (2010); Density: 709.0 persons per square mile (2010); Average household size: 2.82 (2010); Median age: 34.2 (2010); Males per 100 females: 97.5 (2010); Marriage status: 19.7% never married, 63.3% now married, 3.4% widowed, 13.6% divorced (2005-2009 5-year est.); Foreign born: 3.6% (2005-2009 5-year est.); Ancestry (includes multiple ancestries): 16.4% American, 15.6% English, 14.3% German, 13.8% Irish, 2.7% French (2005-2009 5-year est.).

Economy: Single-family building permits issued: 0 (2010); Multi-family building permits issued: 0 (2010); Employment by occupation: 10.0% management, 20.5% professional, 16.4% services, 32.0% sales, 0.0% farming, 10.9% construction, 10.2% production (2005-2009 5-year est.).

Income: Per capita income: $22,844 (2010); Median household income: $52,340 (2010); Average household income: $64,634 (2010); Percent of households with income of $100,000 or more: 16.1% (2010); Poverty rate: 12.3% (2005-2009 5-year est.).

Taxes: Total city taxes per capita: $365 (2007); City property taxes per capita: $238 (2007).

Education: Percent of population age 25 and over with: High school diploma (including GED) or higher: 84.3% (2010); Bachelor's degree or higher: 22.2% (2010); Master's degree or higher: 7.7% (2010).

School District(s)
White Oak ISD (PK-12)
  2009-10 Enrollment: 1,397 . . . . (903) 291-2200

Housing: Homeownership rate: 72.9% (2010); Median home value: $122,837 (2010); Median contract rent: $508 per month (2005-2009 5-year est.); Median year structure built: 1978 (2005-2009 5-year est.).
Safety: Violent crime rate: 4.7 per 10,000 population; Property crime rate: 221.1 per 10,000 population (2009).
Newspapers: White Oak Independent (Community news; Circulation 1,200)
Transportation: Commute to work: 95.1% car, 1.4% public transportation, 0.3% walk, 1.7% work from home (2005-2009 5-year est.); Travel time to work: 32.0% less than 15 minutes, 46.2% 15 to 30 minutes, 17.8% 30 to 45 minutes, 2.5% 45 to 60 minutes, 1.5% 60 minutes or more (2005-2009 5-year est.)
Additional Information Contacts
Town of White Oak .... (903) 759-3936
   http://www.cityofwhiteoak.com
White Oak Economic Development Corporation .... (903) 759-3936
   http://www.cityofwhiteoak.com/edc.htm

Grimes County

Located in east central Texas; bounded on the west by the Navasota and Brazos Rivers. Covers a land area of 793.60 square miles, a water area of 7.56 square miles, and is located in the Central Time Zone at 30.48° N. Lat., 95.99° W. Long. The county was founded in 1846. County seat is Anderson.
Population: 18,828 (1990); 23,552 (2000); 25,856 (2010); 26,930 (2015 projected); Race: 72.5% White, 17.5% Black, 0.5% Asian, 9.5% Other, 18.9% Hispanic of any race (2010); Density: 32.6 persons per square mile (2010); Average household size: 2.67 (2010); Median age: 38.1 (2010); Males per 100 females: 113.0 (2010).
Religion: Five largest groups: 19.2% Catholic Church, 13.4% Southern Baptist Convention, 4.3% The United Methodist Church, 4.0% Lutheran Church—Missouri Synod, 1.6% Baptist Missionary Association of America (2000).
Economy: Unemployment rate: 8.9% (June 2011); Total civilian labor force: 12,069 (June 2011); Leading industries: 39.5% manufacturing; 11.6% retail trade; 10.6% wholesale trade (2009); Farms: 1,853 totaling 437,140 acres (2007); Companies that employ 500 or more persons: 1 (2009); Companies that employ 100 to 499 persons: 9 (2009); Companies that employ less than 100 persons: 352 (2009); Black-owned businesses: n/a (2007); Hispanic-owned businesses: n/a (2007); Asian-owned businesses: n/a (2007); Women-owned businesses: n/a (2007); Retail sales per capita: $6,815 (2010). Single-family building permits issued: 3 (2010); Multi-family building permits issued: 0 (2010).
Income: Per capita income: $19,358 (2010); Median household income: $43,620 (2010); Average household income: $56,473 (2010); Percent of households with income of $100,000 or more: 11.4% (2010); Poverty rate: 18.1% (2009); Bankruptcy rate: 1.04% (2010).
Taxes: Total county taxes per capita: $327 (2007); County property taxes per capita: $263 (2007).
Education: Percent of population age 25 and over with: High school diploma (including GED) or higher: 73.5% (2010); Bachelor's degree or higher: 12.3% (2010); Master's degree or higher: 3.1% (2010).
Housing: Homeownership rate: 69.6% (2010); Median home value: $94,640 (2010); Median contract rent: $402 per month (2005-2009 5-year est.); Median year structure built: 1982 (2005-2009 5-year est.)
Health: Birth rate: 136.9 per 10,000 population (2009); Death rate: 94.2 per 10,000 population (2009); Age-adjusted cancer mortality rate: 148.9 deaths per 100,000 population (2007); Number of physicians: 3.9 per 10,000 population (2008); Hospital beds: 9.7 per 10,000 population (2007); Hospital admissions: 257.5 per 10,000 population (2007).
Elections: 2008 Presidential election results: 32.5% Obama, 66.8% McCain, 0.0% Nader
Additional Information Contacts
Grimes County Government .... (936) 873-2662
   http://www.co.grimes.tx.us/ips/cms
City of Navasota .... (936) 825-6408
   http://www.navasotatx.gov
Navasota-Grimes County Chamber of Commerce .... (936) 825-6600
   http://www.navasotagrimeschamber.com

Grimes County Communities

ANDERSON (city). County seat. Covers a land area of 0.515 square miles and a water area of 0 square miles. Located at 30.48° N. Lat; 95.98° W. Long. Elevation is 344 feet.
History: Fanthorp Inn State Historic Site is here, a log structure (1834) where many Texas notables are purported to have stayed.
Population: 281 (1990); 257 (2000); 234 (2010); 226 (2015 projected); Race: 81.6% White, 13.7% Black, 0.0% Asian, 4.7% Other, 5.1% Hispanic of any race (2010); Density: 453.9 persons per square mile (2010); Average household size: 2.31 (2010); Median age: 43.2 (2010); Males per 100 females: 93.4 (2010); Marriage status: 28.7% never married, 36.8% now married, 18.4% widowed, 16.2% divorced (2005-2009 5-year est.); Foreign born: 0.0% (2005-2009 5-year est.); Ancestry (includes multiple ancestries): 12.5% German, 12.5% Irish, 6.8% Polish, 4.1% English, 2.7% Scottish (2005-2009 5-year est.).
Economy: Employment by occupation: 9.2% management, 9.2% professional, 38.7% services, 26.6% sales, 11.0% farming, 1.2% construction, 4.0% production (2005-2009 5-year est.).
Income: Per capita income: $25,173 (2010); Median household income: $44,474 (2010); Average household income: $54,525 (2010); Percent of households with income of $100,000 or more: 12.0% (2010); Poverty rate: 11.7% (2005-2009 5-year est.).
Taxes: Total city taxes per capita: $242 (2007); City property taxes per capita: $58 (2007).
Education: Percent of population age 25 and over with: High school diploma (including GED) or higher: 82.0% (2010); Bachelor's degree or higher: 12.9% (2010); Master's degree or higher: 2.2% (2010).
School District(s)
Anderson-Shiro CISD (PK-12)
   2009-10 Enrollment: 686 .... (936) 873-2802
Housing: Homeownership rate: 74.0% (2010); Median home value: $88,571 (2010); Median contract rent: n/a per month (2005-2009 5-year est.); Median year structure built: 1955 (2005-2009 5-year est.).
Transportation: Commute to work: 100.0% car, 0.0% public transportation, 0.0% walk, 0.0% work from home (2005-2009 5-year est.); Travel time to work: 34.1% less than 15 minutes, 34.7% 15 to 30 minutes, 17.9% 30 to 45 minutes, 10.4% 45 to 60 minutes, 2.9% 60 minutes or more (2005-2009 5-year est.)

BEDIAS (unincorporated postal area, zip code 77831). Covers a land area of 170.076 square miles and a water area of 0.955 square miles. Located at 30.74° N. Lat; 95.91° W. Long. Elevation is 338 feet.
Population: 2,755 (2000); Race: 89.4% White, 7.9% Black, 0.0% Asian, 2.7% Other, 4.8% Hispanic of any race (2000); Density: 16.2 persons per square mile (2000); Age: 27.5% under 18, 15.3% over 64 (2000); Marriage status: 17.5% never married, 65.3% now married, 6.8% widowed, 10.3% divorced (2000); Foreign born: 2.6% (2000); Ancestry (includes multiple ancestries): 22.4% American, 13.4% German, 12.2% English, 10.2% Irish (2000).
Economy: Employment by occupation: 18.2% management, 8.0% professional, 16.0% services, 18.9% sales, 2.5% farming, 16.7% construction, 19.6% production (2000).
Income: Per capita income: $14,798 (2000); Median household income: $31,280 (2000); Poverty rate: 179.1% (2000).
Education: Percent of population age 25 and over with: High school diploma (including GED) or higher: 67.1% (2000); Bachelor's degree or higher: 8.5% (2000).
Housing: Homeownership rate: 89.7% (2000); Median home value: $53,400 (2000); Median contract rent: $335 per month (2000); Median year structure built: 1986 (2000).
Transportation: Commute to work: 91.0% car, 0.5% public transportation, 1.6% walk, 5.1% work from home (2000); Travel time to work: 9.9% less than 15 minutes, 16.3% 15 to 30 minutes, 24.4% 30 to 45 minutes, 24.6% 45 to 60 minutes, 24.9% 60 minutes or more (2000)

IOLA (unincorporated postal area, zip code 77861). Covers a land area of 119.357 square miles and a water area of 0.618 square miles. Located at 30.75° N. Lat; 96.09° W. Long. Elevation is 338 feet.
Population: 1,866 (2000); Race: 94.9% White, 0.6% Black, 0.0% Asian, 4.5% Other, 7.4% Hispanic of any race (2000); Density: 15.6 persons per square mile (2000); Age: 28.6% under 18, 13.0% over 64 (2000); Marriage status: 16.7% never married, 68.9% now married, 5.6% widowed, 8.8% divorced (2000); Foreign born: 1.8% (2000); Ancestry (includes multiple

ancestries): 18.5% American, 14.1% German, 13.8% Irish, 12.3% English (2000).

Economy: Employment by occupation: 12.0% management, 12.8% professional, 15.3% services, 23.1% sales, 1.7% farming, 18.3% construction, 16.8% production (2000).

Income: Per capita income: $14,682 (2000); Median household income: $33,558 (2000); Poverty rate: 179.1% (2000).

Education: Percent of population age 25 and over with: High school diploma (including GED) or higher: 80.1% (2000); Bachelor's degree or higher: 11.8% (2000).

School District(s)

Iola ISD (PK-12)

2009-10 Enrollment: 509 . . . . (936) 394-2361

Housing: Homeownership rate: 88.1% (2000); Median home value: $55,600 (2000); Median contract rent: $342 per month (2000); Median year structure built: 1984 (2000).

Newspapers: Iola Register (Regional news; Circulation 42,000)

Transportation: Commute to work: 91.7% car, 0.4% public transportation, 0.9% walk, 7.0% work from home (2000); Travel time to work: 19.5% less than 15 minutes, 11.4% 15 to 30 minutes, 32.8% 30 to 45 minutes, 23.0% 45 to 60 minutes, 13.4% 60 minutes or more (2000)

NAVASOTA (city). Covers a land area of 6.118 square miles and a water area of 0.015 square miles. Located at 30.38° N. Lat; 96.08° W. Long. Elevation is 217 feet.

History: The settlement at the junction of the LaBahia San Antonio and Nacogdoches Roads was first called Nolansville for James Nolan, who built a log cabin here that served as a stage stop. The town was established as Navasota in 1858.

Population: 6,306 (1990); 6,789 (2000); 7,605 (2010); 7,995 (2015 projected); Race: 55.6% White, 30.5% Black, 0.9% Asian, 13.0% Other, 32.7% Hispanic of any race (2010); Density: 1,243.1 persons per square mile (2010); Average household size: 2.72 (2010); Median age: 32.4 (2010); Males per 100 females: 88.1 (2010); Marriage status: 43.8% never married, 35.3% now married, 8.6% widowed, 12.3% divorced (2005-2009 5-year est.); Foreign born: 12.3% (2005-2009 5-year est.); Ancestry (includes multiple ancestries): 5.8% German, 5.0% American, 4.7% Irish, 3.6% English, 1.6% Scotch-Irish (2005-2009 5-year est.).

Economy: Single-family building permits issued: 3 (2010); Multi-family building permits issued: 0 (2010); Employment by occupation: 6.0% management, 7.3% professional, 27.1% services, 19.3% sales, 2.2% farming, 12.0% construction, 26.1% production (2005-2009 5-year est.).

Income: Per capita income: $16,878 (2010); Median household income: $35,963 (2010); Average household income: $47,172 (2010); Percent of households with income of $100,000 or more: 6.5% (2010); Poverty rate: 18.4% (2005-2009 5-year est.).

Taxes: Total city taxes per capita: $347 (2007); City property taxes per capita: $120 (2007).

Education: Percent of population age 25 and over with: High school diploma (including GED) or higher: 72.0% (2010); Bachelor's degree or higher: 14.8% (2010); Master's degree or higher: 3.6% (2010).

School District(s)

Navasota ISD (PK-12)

2009-10 Enrollment: 2,883 . . . . (936) 825-4200

Housing: Homeownership rate: 48.7% (2010); Median home value: $88,981 (2010); Median contract rent: $321 per month (2005-2009 5-year est.); Median year structure built: 1973 (2005-2009 5-year est.).

Hospitals: Grimes/St. Joseph's Health Center (47 beds)

Safety: Violent crime rate: 60.2 per 10,000 population; Property crime rate: 349.2 per 10,000 population (2009).

Newspapers: The Navasota Examiner (Community news; Circulation 623)

Transportation: Commute to work: 96.5% car, 0.0% public transportation, 0.9% walk, 1.8% work from home (2005-2009 5-year est.); Travel time to work: 55.2% less than 15 minutes, 27.3% 15 to 30 minutes, 9.9% 30 to 45 minutes, 5.4% 45 to 60 minutes, 2.2% 60 minutes or more (2005-2009 5-year est.)

Additional Information Contacts

City of Navasota. . . . . (936) 825-6408
http://www.navasotatx.gov

Navasota-Grimes County Chamber of Commerce . . . . (936) 825-6600
http://www.navasotagrimeschamber.com

PLANTERSVILLE (unincorporated postal area, zip code 77363). Covers a land area of 51.814 square miles and a water area of 0.091

square miles. Located at 30.28° N. Lat; 95.85° W. Long. Elevation is 358 feet.

Population: 2,092 (2000); Race: 85.1% White, 7.2% Black, 0.3% Asian, 7.4% Other, 10.2% Hispanic of any race (2000); Density: 40.4 persons per square mile (2000); Age: 26.6% under 18, 8.1% over 64 (2000); Marriage status: 24.8% never married, 56.7% now married, 5.9% widowed, 12.6% divorced (2000); Foreign born: 2.7% (2000); Ancestry (includes multiple ancestries): 10.5% Polish, 9.7% American, 9.7% German, 5.8% Irish (2000).

Economy: Employment by occupation: 9.0% management, 10.7% professional, 15.3% services, 25.2% sales, 1.3% farming, 19.3% construction, 19.1% production (2000).

Income: Per capita income: $16,167 (2000); Median household income: $34,018 (2000); Poverty rate: 179.1% (2000).

Education: Percent of population age 25 and over with: High school diploma (including GED) or higher: 68.1% (2000); Bachelor's degree or higher: 9.9% (2000).

Housing: Homeownership rate: 91.2% (2000); Median home value: $73,900 (2000); Median contract rent: $351 per month (2000); Median year structure built: 1986 (2000).

Transportation: Commute to work: 94.0% car, 0.0% public transportation, 1.0% walk, 2.4% work from home (2000); Travel time to work: 6.8% less than 15 minutes, 22.2% 15 to 30 minutes, 16.1% 30 to 45 minutes, 13.9% 45 to 60 minutes, 41.1% 60 minutes or more (2000)

RICHARDS (unincorporated postal area, zip code 77873). Covers a land area of 91.215 square miles and a water area of 0.225 square miles. Located at 30.56° N. Lat; 95.83° W. Long. Elevation is 305 feet.

Population: 999 (2000); Race: 85.2% White, 9.5% Black, 1.7% Asian, 3.6% Other, 8.7% Hispanic of any race (2000); Density: 11.0 persons per square mile (2000); Age: 24.6% under 18, 15.4% over 64 (2000); Marriage status: 16.6% never married, 62.9% now married, 7.6% widowed, 12.9% divorced (2000); Foreign born: 3.6% (2000); Ancestry (includes multiple ancestries): 15.8% German, 12.6% Irish, 11.6% American, 9.1% English (2000).

Economy: Employment by occupation: 11.1% management, 18.7% professional, 20.3% services, 20.3% sales, 3.1% farming, 10.9% construction, 15.6% production (2000).

Income: Per capita income: $18,862 (2000); Median household income: $33,750 (2000); Poverty rate: 179.1% (2000).

Education: Percent of population age 25 and over with: High school diploma (including GED) or higher: 77.6% (2000); Bachelor's degree or higher: 20.1% (2000).

School District(s)

Richards ISD (PK-12)

2009-10 Enrollment: 140 . . . . (936) 851-2364

Housing: Homeownership rate: 81.4% (2000); Median home value: $51,500 (2000); Median contract rent: $388 per month (2000); Median year structure built: 1980 (2000).

Transportation: Commute to work: 91.1% car, 0.0% public transportation, 1.7% walk, 6.5% work from home (2000); Travel time to work: 15.6% less than 15 minutes, 23.3% 15 to 30 minutes, 27.1% 30 to 45 minutes, 21.5% 45 to 60 minutes, 12.5% 60 minutes or more (2000)

TODD MISSION (city). Covers a land area of 2.095 square miles and a water area of 0.012 square miles. Located at 30.26° N. Lat; 95.82° W. Long. Elevation is 282 feet.

Population: 54 (1990); 146 (2000); 192 (2010); 211 (2015 projected); Race: 87.0% White, 4.2% Black, 0.0% Asian, 8.9% Other, 10.4% Hispanic of any race (2010); Density: 91.6 persons per square mile (2010); Average household size: 2.67 (2010); Median age: 38.5 (2010); Males per 100 females: 95.9 (2010); Marriage status: 6.5% never married, 93.5% now married, 0.0% widowed, 0.0% divorced (2005-2009 5-year est.); Foreign born: 0.0% (2005-2009 5-year est.); Ancestry (includes multiple ancestries): 36.8% German, 15.9% Italian, 12.1% Irish, 4.4% American, 2.7% English (2005-2009 5-year est.).

Economy: Employment by occupation: 5.1% management, 3.0% professional, 0.0% services, 43.4% sales, 0.0% farming, 48.5% construction, 0.0% production (2005-2009 5-year est.).

Income: Per capita income: $19,192 (2010); Median household income: $41,923 (2010); Average household income: $50,660 (2010); Percent of households with income of $100,000 or more: 9.7% (2010); Poverty rate: 13.2% (2005-2009 5-year est.).

Taxes: Total city taxes per capita: $830 (2007); City property taxes per capita: $75 (2007).

Education: Percent of population age 25 and over with: High school diploma (including GED) or higher: 75.8% (2010); Bachelor's degree or higher: 9.1% (2010); Master's degree or higher: 0.8% (2010).
Housing: Homeownership rate: 84.7% (2010); Median home value: $83,333 (2010); Median contract rent: n/a per month (2005-2009 5-year est.); Median year structure built: 1994 (2005-2009 5-year est.).
Transportation: Commute to work: 90.9% car, 0.0% public transportation, 0.0% walk, 9.1% work from home (2005-2009 5-year est.); Travel time to work: 0.0% less than 15 minutes, 0.0% 15 to 30 minutes, 0.0% 30 to 45 minutes, 0.0% 45 to 60 minutes, 100.0% 60 minutes or more (2005-2009 5-year est.)

Guadalupe County

Located in south central Texas; drained by the San Marcos and Guadalupe Rivers. Covers a land area of 711.14 square miles, a water area of 3.03 square miles, and is located in the Central Time Zone at 29.59° N. Lat., 97.99° W. Long. The county was founded in 1846. County seat is Seguin.

Guadalupe County is part of the San Antonio-New Braunfels, TX Metropolitan Statistical Area. The entire metro area includes: Atascosa County, TX; Bandera County, TX; Bexar County, TX; Comal County, TX; Guadalupe County, TX; Kendall County, TX; Medina County, TX; Wilson County, TX

Population: 64,873 (1990); 89,023 (2000); 124,904 (2010); 142,127 (2015 projected); Race: 74.7% White, 6.2% Black, 1.4% Asian, 17.7% Other, 35.0% Hispanic of any race (2010); Density: 175.6 persons per square mile (2010); Average household size: 2.88 (2010); Median age: 34.5 (2010); Males per 100 females: 97.6 (2010).
Religion: Five largest groups: 15.4% Catholic Church, 8.5% Southern Baptist Convention, 4.2% Evangelical Lutheran Church in America, 3.6% The United Methodist Church, 2.4% United Church of Christ (2000).
Economy: Unemployment rate: 7.5% (June 2011); Total civilian labor force: 62,473 (June 2011); Leading industries: 19.7% manufacturing; 16.1% retail trade; 11.6% health care and social assistance (2009); Farms: 2,462 totaling 385,015 acres (2007); Companies that employ 500 or more persons: 6 (2009); Companies that employ 100 to 499 persons: 32 (2009); Companies that employ less than 100 persons: 1,746 (2009); Black-owned businesses: n/a (2007); Hispanic-owned businesses: 2,117 (2007); Asian-owned businesses: n/a (2007); Women-owned businesses: 2,891 (2007); Retail sales per capita: $6,987 (2010). Single-family building permits issued: 868 (2010); Multi-family building permits issued: 187 (2010).
Income: Per capita income: $24,545 (2010); Median household income: $59,037 (2010); Average household income: $71,153 (2010); Percent of households with income of $100,000 or more: 19.7% (2010); Poverty rate: 11.2% (2009); Bankruptcy rate: 1.85% (2010).
Taxes: Total county taxes per capita: $250 (2007); County property taxes per capita: $192 (2007).
Education: Percent of population age 25 and over with: High school diploma (including GED) or higher: 83.6% (2010); Bachelor's degree or higher: 23.8% (2010); Master's degree or higher: 8.6% (2010).
Housing: Homeownership rate: 76.7% (2010); Median home value: $131,108 (2010); Median contract rent: $580 per month (2005-2009 5-year est.); Median year structure built: 1989 (2005-2009 5-year est.).
Health: Birth rate: 142.5 per 10,000 population (2009); Death rate: 69.9 per 10,000 population (2009); Age-adjusted cancer mortality rate: 166.1 deaths per 100,000 population (2007); Number of physicians: 8.7 per 10,000 population (2008); Hospital beds: 8.7 per 10,000 population (2007); Hospital admissions: 465.3 per 10,000 population (2007).
Elections: 2008 Presidential election results: 34.0% Obama, 64.9% McCain, 0.0% Nader
Additional Information Contacts
Guadalupe County Government . . . . (830) 303-4188
  http://www.co.guadalupe.tx.us
City of Schertz . . . . (210) 619-1000
  http://www.schertz.com
City of Seguin. . . . . (830) 401-2468
  http://www.seguintexas.gov
Seguin Area Chamber of Commerce. . . . . (830) 379-6382
  http://www.seguinchamber.com

Guadalupe County Communities

CIBOLO (city). Covers a land area of 5.329 square miles and a water area of 0 square miles. Located at 29.56° N. Lat; 98.23° W. Long. Elevation is 699 feet.
Population: 1,879 (1990); 3,035 (2000); 9,692 (2010); 11,441 (2015 projected); Race: 75.3% White, 10.0% Black, 2.0% Asian, 12.6% Other, 17.6% Hispanic of any race (2010); Density: 1,818.8 persons per square mile (2010); Average household size: 2.89 (2010); Median age: 35.8 (2010); Males per 100 females: 95.4 (2010); Marriage status: 24.3% never married, 65.1% now married, 4.0% widowed, 6.6% divorced (2005-2009 5-year est.); Foreign born: 4.6% (2005-2009 5-year est.); Ancestry (includes multiple ancestries): 21.3% German, 13.6% Irish, 11.1% English, 6.2% French, 4.8% American (2005-2009 5-year est.).
Economy: Single-family building permits issued: 360 (2010); Multi-family building permits issued: 0 (2010); Employment by occupation: 18.5% management, 27.7% professional, 14.2% services, 28.6% sales, 0.0% farming, 6.3% construction, 4.6% production (2005-2009 5-year est.).
Income: Per capita income: $32,808 (2010); Median household income: $82,867 (2010); Average household income: $94,851 (2010); Percent of households with income of $100,000 or more: 37.0% (2010); Poverty rate: 2.7% (2005-2009 5-year est.).
Taxes: Total city taxes per capita: $473 (2007); City property taxes per capita: $144 (2007).
Education: Percent of population age 25 and over with: High school diploma (including GED) or higher: 92.7% (2010); Bachelor's degree or higher: 36.0% (2010); Master's degree or higher: 15.0% (2010).
School District(s)
Schertz-Cibolo-Universal City ISD (PK-12)
  2009-10 Enrollment: 11,718 . . . . (210) 945-6200
Housing: Homeownership rate: 86.5% (2010); Median home value: $175,483 (2010); Median contract rent: $915 per month (2005-2009 5-year est.); Median year structure built: 2002 (2005-2009 5-year est.).
Safety: Violent crime rate: 10.4 per 10,000 population; Property crime rate: 104.1 per 10,000 population (2009).
Transportation: Commute to work: 94.8% car, 0.0% public transportation, 0.2% walk, 3.7% work from home (2005-2009 5-year est.); Travel time to work: 20.9% less than 15 minutes, 38.5% 15 to 30 minutes, 25.9% 30 to 45 minutes, 9.2% 45 to 60 minutes, 5.5% 60 minutes or more (2005-2009 5-year est.)

GERONIMO (CDP). Covers a land area of 9.173 square miles and a water area of 0 square miles. Located at 29.66° N. Lat; 97.96° W. Long. Elevation is 581 feet.
Population: 441 (1990); 619 (2000); 680 (2010); 774 (2015 projected); Race: 66.6% White, 2.1% Black, 0.7% Asian, 30.6% Other, 48.8% Hispanic of any race (2010); Density: 74.1 persons per square mile (2010); Average household size: 3.15 (2010); Median age: 32.6 (2010); Males per 100 females: 102.4 (2010); Marriage status: 26.5% never married, 51.3% now married, 14.7% widowed, 7.5% divorced (2005-2009 5-year est.); Foreign born: 6.1% (2005-2009 5-year est.); Ancestry (includes multiple ancestries): 13.6% German, 3.7% English, 2.2% Irish (2005-2009 5-year est.).
Economy: Employment by occupation: 7.2% management, 0.0% professional, 4.8% services, 60.8% sales, 0.0% farming, 5.8% construction, 21.3% production (2005-2009 5-year est.).
Income: Per capita income: $19,933 (2010); Median household income: $51,862 (2010); Average household income: $60,070 (2010); Percent of households with income of $100,000 or more: 12.1% (2010); Poverty rate: 7.2% (2005-2009 5-year est.).
Education: Percent of population age 25 and over with: High school diploma (including GED) or higher: 78.9% (2010); Bachelor's degree or higher: 17.1% (2010); Master's degree or higher: 5.4% (2010).
Housing: Homeownership rate: 81.9% (2010); Median home value: $108,772 (2010); Median contract rent: $622 per month (2005-2009 5-year est.); Median year structure built: 1992 (2005-2009 5-year est.).
Transportation: Commute to work: 100.0% car, 0.0% public transportation, 0.0% walk, 0.0% work from home (2005-2009 5-year est.); Travel time to work: 30.7% less than 15 minutes, 37.6% 15 to 30 minutes, 11.3% 30 to 45 minutes, 9.9% 45 to 60 minutes, 10.6% 60 minutes or more (2005-2009 5-year est.)

KINGSBURY (CDP). Covers a land area of 28.770 square miles and a water area of 0.067 square miles. Located at 29.64° N. Lat; 97.81° W. Long. Elevation is 604 feet.

Population: 482 (1990); 652 (2000); 681 (2010); 739 (2015 projected); Race: 87.8% White, 2.1% Black, 0.0% Asian, 10.1% Other, 24.7% Hispanic of any race (2010); Density: 23.7 persons per square mile (2010); Average household size: 2.67 (2010); Median age: 38.7 (2010); Males per 100 females: 104.5 (2010); Marriage status: 19.5% never married, 62.2% now married, 7.7% widowed, 10.6% divorced (2005-2009 5-year est.); Foreign born: 3.5% (2005-2009 5-year est.); Ancestry (includes multiple ancestries): 35.8% German, 20.7% English, 17.7% Irish, 4.8% Scottish, 4.6% American (2005-2009 5-year est.).
Economy: Employment by occupation: 14.5% management, 6.6% professional, 14.5% services, 46.7% sales, 0.0% farming, 0.0% construction, 17.8% production (2005-2009 5-year est.).
Income: Per capita income: $26,394 (2010); Median household income: $59,280 (2010); Average household income: $70,716 (2010); Percent of households with income of $100,000 or more: 18.4% (2010); Poverty rate: 15.6% (2005-2009 5-year est.).
Education: Percent of population age 25 and over with: High school diploma (including GED) or higher: 83.5% (2010); Bachelor's degree or higher: 15.7% (2010); Master's degree or higher: 7.1% (2010).
Housing: Homeownership rate: 79.2% (2010); Median home value: $118,182 (2010); Median contract rent: n/a per month (2005-2009 5-year est.); Median year structure built: 1991 (2005-2009 5-year est.).
Transportation: Commute to work: 93.4% car, 0.0% public transportation, 0.0% walk, 6.6% work from home (2005-2009 5-year est.); Travel time to work: 0.0% less than 15 minutes, 57.7% 15 to 30 minutes, 0.0% 30 to 45 minutes, 28.9% 45 to 60 minutes, 13.4% 60 minutes or more (2005-2009 5-year est.)

MARION (city). Covers a land area of 0.712 square miles and a water area of 0 square miles. Located at 29.57° N. Lat; 98.13° W. Long. Elevation is 646 feet.
Population: 912 (1990); 1,099 (2000); 1,188 (2010); 1,300 (2015 projected); Race: 80.7% White, 3.0% Black, 1.3% Asian, 14.9% Other, 34.9% Hispanic of any race (2010); Density: 1,669.0 persons per square mile (2010); Average household size: 3.04 (2010); Median age: 33.9 (2010); Males per 100 females: 97.7 (2010); Marriage status: 31.0% never married, 46.6% now married, 9.0% widowed, 13.5% divorced (2005-2009 5-year est.); Foreign born: 9.5% (2005-2009 5-year est.); Ancestry (includes multiple ancestries): 28.2% German, 8.2% Irish, 6.3% English, 3.8% Polish, 3.7% American (2005-2009 5-year est.).
Economy: Single-family building permits issued: 0 (2010); Multi-family building permits issued: 0 (2010); Employment by occupation: 8.4% management, 10.9% professional, 19.6% services, 24.5% sales, 2.5% farming, 10.1% construction, 24.0% production (2005-2009 5-year est.).
Income: Per capita income: $21,020 (2010); Median household income: $48,286 (2010); Average household income: $60,801 (2010); Percent of households with income of $100,000 or more: 11.3% (2010); Poverty rate: 13.7% (2005-2009 5-year est.).
Taxes: Total city taxes per capita: $342 (2007); City property taxes per capita: $276 (2007).
Education: Percent of population age 25 and over with: High school diploma (including GED) or higher: 82.7% (2010); Bachelor's degree or higher: 15.9% (2010); Master's degree or higher: 7.7% (2010).
School District(s)
Marion ISD (PK-12)
    2009-10 Enrollment: 1,358 . . . . (830) 914-2803
Housing: Homeownership rate: 79.7% (2010); Median home value: $96,531 (2010); Median contract rent: $481 per month (2005-2009 5-year est.); Median year structure built: 1974 (2005-2009 5-year est.).
Transportation: Commute to work: 96.2% car, 0.0% public transportation, 0.5% walk, 0.5% work from home (2005-2009 5-year est.); Travel time to work: 28.3% less than 15 minutes, 44.2% 15 to 30 minutes, 13.9% 30 to 45 minutes, 7.6% 45 to 60 minutes, 6.1% 60 minutes or more (2005-2009 5-year est.)

MCQUEENEY (CDP). Covers a land area of 4.151 square miles and a water area of 0.438 square miles. Located at 29.59° N. Lat; 98.04° W. Long. Elevation is 548 feet.
Population: 2,122 (1990); 2,527 (2000); 2,591 (2010); 2,817 (2015 projected); Race: 82.7% White, 1.0% Black, 0.4% Asian, 15.8% Other, 27.1% Hispanic of any race (2010); Density: 624.2 persons per square mile (2010); Average household size: 2.55 (2010); Median age: 36.7 (2010); Males per 100 females: 99.8 (2010); Marriage status: 22.3% never married, 58.3% now married, 5.4% widowed, 14.1% divorced (2005-2009 5-year est.); Foreign born: 2.7% (2005-2009 5-year est.); Ancestry (includes

multiple ancestries): 35.9% German, 27.4% Irish, 10.7% English, 2.3% American, 2.3% Czech (2005-2009 5-year est.).
Economy: Employment by occupation: 10.5% management, 15.4% professional, 11.2% services, 33.4% sales, 0.0% farming, 21.8% construction, 7.8% production (2005-2009 5-year est.).
Income: Per capita income: $25,561 (2010); Median household income: $51,721 (2010); Average household income: $65,076 (2010); Percent of households with income of $100,000 or more: 12.5% (2010); Poverty rate: 16.3% (2005-2009 5-year est.).
Education: Percent of population age 25 and over with: High school diploma (including GED) or higher: 87.5% (2010); Bachelor's degree or higher: 21.2% (2010); Master's degree or higher: 3.9% (2010).
School District(s)
Seguin ISD (PK-12)
    2009-10 Enrollment: 7,562 . . . . (830) 372-5771
Housing: Homeownership rate: 74.6% (2010); Median home value: $126,685 (2010); Median contract rent: $466 per month (2005-2009 5-year est.); Median year structure built: 1985 (2005-2009 5-year est.).
Transportation: Commute to work: 91.9% car, 0.0% public transportation, 0.9% walk, 4.7% work from home (2005-2009 5-year est.); Travel time to work: 11.5% less than 15 minutes, 56.8% 15 to 30 minutes, 15.4% 30 to 45 minutes, 11.9% 45 to 60 minutes, 4.4% 60 minutes or more (2005-2009 5-year est.)

NEW BERLIN (city). Covers a land area of 2.845 square miles and a water area of 0 square miles. Located at 29.46° N. Lat; 98.10° W. Long. Elevation is 571 feet.
Population: 236 (1990); 467 (2000); 415 (2010); 449 (2015 projected); Race: 90.8% White, 2.4% Black, 0.0% Asian, 6.7% Other, 18.3% Hispanic of any race (2010); Density: 145.9 persons per square mile (2010); Average household size: 2.77 (2010); Median age: 39.3 (2010); Males per 100 females: 97.6 (2010); Marriage status: 19.6% never married, 63.9% now married, 6.1% widowed, 10.3% divorced (2005-2009 5-year est.); Foreign born: 0.6% (2005-2009 5-year est.); Ancestry (includes multiple ancestries): 45.2% German, 17.1% Irish, 8.4% American, 8.1% Polish, 6.1% English (2005-2009 5-year est.).
Economy: Employment by occupation: 17.8% management, 17.8% professional, 10.2% services, 29.3% sales, 3.6% farming, 8.4% construction, 12.9% production (2005-2009 5-year est.).
Income: Per capita income: $23,275 (2010); Median household income: $48,448 (2010); Average household income: $62,950 (2010); Percent of households with income of $100,000 or more: 17.3% (2010); Poverty rate: 6.8% (2005-2009 5-year est.).
Taxes: Total city taxes per capita: $173 (2007); City property taxes per capita: $119 (2007).
Education: Percent of population age 25 and over with: High school diploma (including GED) or higher: 87.6% (2010); Bachelor's degree or higher: 23.0% (2010); Master's degree or higher: 8.9% (2010).
Housing: Homeownership rate: 88.0% (2010); Median home value: $120,833 (2010); Median contract rent: $528 per month (2005-2009 5-year est.); Median year structure built: 1988 (2005-2009 5-year est.).
Transportation: Commute to work: 85.0% car, 0.0% public transportation, 0.0% walk, 15.0% work from home (2005-2009 5-year est.); Travel time to work: 16.0% less than 15 minutes, 30.5% 15 to 30 minutes, 32.6% 30 to 45 minutes, 16.0% 45 to 60 minutes, 4.8% 60 minutes or more (2005-2009 5-year est.)

NORTHCLIFF (CDP). Covers a land area of 1.671 square miles and a water area of 0 square miles. Located at 29.62° N. Lat; 98.22° W. Long. Elevation is 827 feet.
Population: 1,392 (1990); 1,819 (2000); 2,895 (2010); 3,481 (2015 projected); Race: 80.2% White, 5.3% Black, 1.9% Asian, 12.5% Other, 18.5% Hispanic of any race (2010); Density: 1,732.6 persons per square mile (2010); Average household size: 2.60 (2010); Median age: 40.4 (2010); Males per 100 females: 97.2 (2010); Marriage status: n/a never married, n/a now married, n/a widowed, n/a divorced (2005-2009 5-year est.); Foreign born: n/a (2005-2009 5-year est.); Ancestry (includes multiple ancestries): n/a (2005-2009 5-year est.).
Economy: Employment by occupation: n/a management, n/a professional, n/a services, n/a sales, n/a farming, n/a construction, n/a production (2005-2009 5-year est.).
Income: Per capita income: $23,756 (2010); Median household income: $57,836 (2010); Average household income: $61,598 (2010); Percent of households with income of $100,000 or more: 10.5% (2010); Poverty rate: n/a (2005-2009 5-year est.).

Education: Percent of population age 25 and over with: High school diploma (including GED) or higher: 93.1% (2010); Bachelor's degree or higher: 15.1% (2010); Master's degree or higher: 5.5% (2010).
Housing: Homeownership rate: 82.2% (2010); Median home value: $127,640 (2010); Median contract rent: n/a per month (2005-2009 5-year est.); Median year structure built: n/a (2005-2009 5-year est.).
Transportation: Commute to work: n/a car, n/a public transportation, n/a walk, n/a work from home (2005-2009 5-year est.); Travel time to work: n/a less than 15 minutes, n/a 15 to 30 minutes, n/a 30 to 45 minutes, n/a 45 to 60 minutes, n/a 60 minutes or more (2005-2009 5-year est.)

REDWOOD (CDP). Covers a land area of 5.873 square miles and a water area of 0.069 square miles. Located at 29.81° N. Lat; 97.91° W. Long. Elevation is 554 feet.
Population: 2,191 (1990); 3,586 (2000); 3,615 (2010); 3,893 (2015 projected); Race: 45.4% White, 1.1% Black, 0.1% Asian, 53.4% Other, 82.5% Hispanic of any race (2010); Density: 615.6 persons per square mile (2010); Average household size: 3.70 (2010); Median age: 29.4 (2010); Males per 100 females: 107.9 (2010); Marriage status: 31.3% never married, 48.7% now married, 3.7% widowed, 16.4% divorced (2005-2009 5-year est.); Foreign born: 21.6% (2005-2009 5-year est.); Ancestry (includes multiple ancestries): 6.1% American, 4.2% English, 4.1% Scotch-Irish, 3.5% Polish, 3.4% German (2005-2009 5-year est.).
Economy: Employment by occupation: 2.4% management, 7.8% professional, 21.3% services, 16.3% sales, 0.0% farming, 33.7% construction, 18.4% production (2005-2009 5-year est.).
Income: Per capita income: $15,420 (2010); Median household income: $47,865 (2010); Average household income: $56,263 (2010); Percent of households with income of $100,000 or more: 11.3% (2010); Poverty rate: 22.6% (2005-2009 5-year est.).
Education: Percent of population age 25 and over with: High school diploma (including GED) or higher: 70.1% (2010); Bachelor's degree or higher: 11.6% (2010); Master's degree or higher: 3.1% (2010).
Housing: Homeownership rate: 78.9% (2010); Median home value: $68,390 (2010); Median contract rent: $513 per month (2005-2009 5-year est.); Median year structure built: 1990 (2005-2009 5-year est.).
Transportation: Commute to work: 96.7% car, 0.0% public transportation, 0.6% walk, 2.2% work from home (2005-2009 5-year est.); Travel time to work: 22.3% less than 15 minutes, 41.5% 15 to 30 minutes, 17.3% 30 to 45 minutes, 5.8% 45 to 60 minutes, 13.2% 60 minutes or more (2005-2009 5-year est.)

SANTA CLARA (city). Covers a land area of 2.077 square miles and a water area of 0 square miles. Located at 29.58° N. Lat; 98.16° W. Long. Elevation is 594 feet.
Population: 678 (1990); 889 (2000); 946 (2010); 1,058 (2015 projected); Race: 79.3% White, 3.2% Black, 0.8% Asian, 16.7% Other, 30.5% Hispanic of any race (2010); Density: 455.4 persons per square mile (2010); Average household size: 3.04 (2010); Median age: 33.8 (2010); Males per 100 females: 100.0 (2010); Marriage status: 25.7% never married, 59.2% now married, 5.1% widowed, 10.1% divorced (2005-2009 5-year est.); Foreign born: 1.3% (2005-2009 5-year est.); Ancestry (includes multiple ancestries): 47.0% German, 18.5% Irish, 12.4% American, 10.3% English, 3.9% French (2005-2009 5-year est.).
Economy: Employment by occupation: 11.2% management, 14.6% professional, 12.8% services, 34.1% sales, 0.4% farming, 12.0% construction, 14.8% production (2005-2009 5-year est.).
Income: Per capita income: $22,364 (2010); Median household income: $48,214 (2010); Average household income: $66,696 (2010); Percent of households with income of $100,000 or more: 13.5% (2010); Poverty rate: 1.7% (2005-2009 5-year est.).
Taxes: Total city taxes per capita: $15 (2007); City property taxes per capita: $0 (2007).
Education: Percent of population age 25 and over with: High school diploma (including GED) or higher: 82.5% (2010); Bachelor's degree or higher: 12.4% (2010); Master's degree or higher: 4.7% (2010).
Housing: Homeownership rate: 79.1% (2010); Median home value: $119,853 (2010); Median contract rent: $833 per month (2005-2009 5-year est.); Median year structure built: 1989 (2005-2009 5-year est.).
Transportation: Commute to work: 91.5% car, 0.0% public transportation, 0.0% walk, 8.5% work from home (2005-2009 5-year est.); Travel time to work: 17.4% less than 15 minutes, 45.6% 15 to 30 minutes, 21.8% 30 to 45 minutes, 7.9% 45 to 60 minutes, 7.3% 60 minutes or more (2005-2009 5-year est.)

SCHERTZ (city). Covers a land area of 24.731 square miles and a water area of 0 square miles. Located at 29.56° N. Lat; 98.26° W. Long. Elevation is 712 feet.
Population: 10,628 (1990); 18,694 (2000); 28,066 (2010); 32,947 (2015 projected); Race: 76.5% White, 9.5% Black, 2.3% Asian, 11.7% Other, 23.7% Hispanic of any race (2010); Density: 1,134.9 persons per square mile (2010); Average household size: 2.91 (2010); Median age: 35.2 (2010); Males per 100 females: 95.6 (2010); Marriage status: 24.1% never married, 58.1% now married, 7.0% widowed, 10.8% divorced (2005-2009 5-year est.); Foreign born: 4.9% (2005-2009 5-year est.); Ancestry (includes multiple ancestries): 21.7% German, 12.8% Irish, 9.9% English, 5.3% American, 3.9% French (2005-2009 5-year est.).
Economy: Unemployment rate: 6.4% (June 2011); Total civilian labor force: 16,643 (June 2011); Single-family building permits issued: 446 (2010); Multi-family building permits issued: 0 (2010); Employment by occupation: 22.3% management, 20.4% professional, 15.1% services, 27.7% sales, 0.0% farming, 6.8% construction, 7.6% production (2005-2009 5-year est.).
Income: Per capita income: $28,935 (2010); Median household income: $71,133 (2010); Average household income: $84,399 (2010); Percent of households with income of $100,000 or more: 27.8% (2010); Poverty rate: 4.9% (2005-2009 5-year est.).
Taxes: Total city taxes per capita: $329 (2007); City property taxes per capita: $153 (2007).
Education: Percent of population age 25 and over with: High school diploma (including GED) or higher: 92.2% (2010); Bachelor's degree or higher: 30.4% (2010); Master's degree or higher: 10.8% (2010).

School District(s)

Schertz-Cibolo-Universal City ISD (PK-12)
 2009-10 Enrollment: 11,718 . . . . (210) 945-6200
Shekinah Radiance Academy (PK-12)
 2009-10 Enrollment: 1,125 . . . . (210) 658-6848
Housing: Homeownership rate: 80.1% (2010); Median home value: $159,017 (2010); Median contract rent: $734 per month (2005-2009 5-year est.); Median year structure built: 1993 (2005-2009 5-year est.).
Safety: Violent crime rate: 26.9 per 10,000 population; Property crime rate: 197.0 per 10,000 population (2009).
Transportation: Commute to work: 94.8% car, 0.1% public transportation, 1.0% walk, 2.9% work from home (2005-2009 5-year est.); Travel time to work: 25.6% less than 15 minutes, 38.2% 15 to 30 minutes, 24.3% 30 to 45 minutes, 8.1% 45 to 60 minutes, 3.8% 60 minutes or more (2005-2009 5-year est.)
Additional Information Contacts
City of Schertz . . . . (210) 619-1000
 http://www.schertz.com

SEGUIN (city). County seat. Covers a land area of 19.021 square miles and a water area of 0.170 square miles. Located at 29.57° N. Lat; 97.96° W. Long. Elevation is 522 feet.
History: Named for Juan Seguin (1807-1890), a colonel in the Texas Cavalry at the Battle of San Jacinto. Seguin was founded in 1838 by planters from other southern states, who called it Walnut Springs. The name was changed to honor resident Colonel Juan N. Seguin, commander of a detachment of Texas-born Mexicans in the Battle of San Jacinto.
Population: 20,666 (1990); 22,011 (2000); 25,020 (2010); 27,797 (2015 projected); Race: 66.9% White, 7.3% Black, 1.1% Asian, 24.8% Other, 59.0% Hispanic of any race (2010); Density: 1,315.4 persons per square mile (2010); Average household size: 2.73 (2010); Median age: 32.3 (2010); Males per 100 females: 92.5 (2010); Marriage status: 33.6% never married, 45.6% now married, 8.0% widowed, 12.8% divorced (2005-2009 5-year est.); Foreign born: 7.2% (2005-2009 5-year est.); Ancestry (includes multiple ancestries): 16.3% German, 5.2% Irish, 4.7% English, 4.1% American, 1.7% Scotch-Irish (2005-2009 5-year est.).
Economy: Unemployment rate: 8.2% (June 2011); Total civilian labor force: 12,373 (June 2011); Single-family building permits issued: 62 (2010); Multi-family building permits issued: 187 (2010); Employment by occupation: 10.2% management, 13.5% professional, 17.5% services, 25.3% sales, 0.1% farming, 11.7% construction, 21.7% production (2005-2009 5-year est.).
Income: Per capita income: $16,522 (2010); Median household income: $38,940 (2010); Average household income: $46,694 (2010); Percent of households with income of $100,000 or more: 6.4% (2010); Poverty rate: 17.9% (2005-2009 5-year est.).

Taxes: Total city taxes per capita: $359 (2007); City property taxes per capita: $162 (2007).
Education: Percent of population age 25 and over with: High school diploma (including GED) or higher: 66.2% (2010); Bachelor's degree or higher: 16.0% (2010); Master's degree or higher: 6.0% (2010).
School District(s)
Navarro ISD (PK-12)
   2009-10 Enrollment: 1,560 . . . . (830) 372-1930
Seguin ISD (PK-12)
   2009-10 Enrollment: 7,562 . . . . (830) 372-5771
Four-year College(s)
Texas Lutheran University (Private, Not-for-profit, American Evangelical Lutheran Church)
   Fall 2009 Enrollment: 1,387. . . . . (830) 372-8000
   2010-11 Tuition: In-state $22,890; Out-of-state $22,890
Vocational/Technical School(s)
Seguin Beauty School (Private, For-profit)
   Fall 2009 Enrollment: 44 . . . . (830) 372-0935
   2010-11 Tuition: $13,500
Housing: Homeownership rate: 54.9% (2010); Median home value: $92,362 (2010); Median contract rent: $520 per month (2005-2009 5-year est.); Median year structure built: 1971 (2005-2009 5-year est.).
Hospitals: Guadalupe Valley Hospital (117 beds)
Safety: Violent crime rate: 46.1 per 10,000 population; Property crime rate: 496.2 per 10,000 population (2009).
Newspapers: Seguin Gazette-Enterprise (Local news)
Transportation: Commute to work: 90.8% car, 0.0% public transportation, 5.2% walk, 1.1% work from home (2005-2009 5-year est.); Travel time to work: 56.1% less than 15 minutes, 23.1% 15 to 30 minutes, 10.9% 30 to 45 minutes, 5.3% 45 to 60 minutes, 4.6% 60 minutes or more (2005-2009 5-year est.)
Additional Information Contacts
City of Seguin. . . . . (830) 401-2468
   http://www.seguintexas.gov
Seguin Area Chamber of Commerce. . . . . (830) 379-6382
   http://www.seguinchamber.com

ZUEHL (CDP). Covers a land area of 7.113 square miles and a water area of 0 square miles. Located at 29.49° N. Lat; 98.15° W. Long. Elevation is 584 feet.
Population: 288 (1990); 346 (2000); 315 (2010); 318 (2015 projected); Race: 91.4% White, 1.3% Black, 1.6% Asian, 5.7% Other, 12.4% Hispanic of any race (2010); Density: 44.3 persons per square mile (2010); Average household size: 2.76 (2010); Median age: 40.4 (2010); Males per 100 females: 98.1 (2010); Marriage status: 47.7% never married, 41.3% now married, 5.5% widowed, 5.5% divorced (2005-2009 5-year est.); Foreign born: 1.9% (2005-2009 5-year est.); Ancestry (includes multiple ancestries): 46.2% German, 30.6% English, 21.4% Irish, 12.6% Scottish, 8.7% Portuguese (2005-2009 5-year est.).
Economy: Employment by occupation: 3.1% management, 6.8% professional, 13.3% services, 52.2% sales, 0.0% farming, 6.1% construction, 18.4% production (2005-2009 5-year est.).
Income: Per capita income: $26,296 (2010); Median household income: $54,861 (2010); Average household income: $72,281 (2010); Percent of households with income of $100,000 or more: 17.5% (2010); Poverty rate: 27.8% (2005-2009 5-year est.).
Education: Percent of population age 25 and over with: High school diploma (including GED) or higher: 82.4% (2010); Bachelor's degree or higher: 21.7% (2010); Master's degree or higher: 9.5% (2010).
Housing: Homeownership rate: 84.2% (2010); Median home value: $104,762 (2010); Median contract rent: $616 per month (2005-2009 5-year est.); Median year structure built: 1987 (2005-2009 5-year est.).
Transportation: Commute to work: 100.0% car, 0.0% public transportation, 0.0% walk, 0.0% work from home (2005-2009 5-year est.); Travel time to work: 11.3% less than 15 minutes, 30.4% 15 to 30 minutes, 55.1% 30 to 45 minutes, 0.0% 45 to 60 minutes, 3.2% 60 minutes or more (2005-2009 5-year est.)

Hale County

Located in northwestern Texas; drained by the White River. Covers a land area of 1,004.65 square miles, a water area of 0.12 square miles, and is located in the Central Time Zone at 34.09° N. Lat., 101.79° W. Long. The county was founded in 1876. County seat is Plainview.

Hale County is part of the Plainview, TX Micropolitan Statistical Area. The entire metro area includes: Hale County, TX

Weather Station: Plainview   Elevation: 3,370 feet

	Jan	Feb	Mar	Apr	May	Jun	Jul	Aug	Sep	Oct	Nov	Dec
High	52	56	63	72	81	88	92	90	83	73	61	52
Low	26	29	36	44	55	63	67	66	58	47	36	27
Precip	0.7	0.6	1.1	1.5	2.9	3.2	2.2	2.2	2.3	1.7	0.9	0.8
Snow	3.2	1.9	0.8	0.2	0.0	0.0	0.0	0.0	0.0	0.1	1.7	3.0

High and Low temperatures in degrees Fahrenheit; Precipitation and Snow in inches

Population: 34,671 (1990); 36,602 (2000); 35,227 (2010); 34,497 (2015 projected); Race: 63.0% White, 5.7% Black, 0.6% Asian, 30.8% Other, 54.0% Hispanic of any race (2010); Density: 35.1 persons per square mile (2010); Average household size: 2.83 (2010); Median age: 32.5 (2010); Males per 100 females: 103.8 (2010).
Religion: Five largest groups: 42.6% Southern Baptist Convention, 25.3% Catholic Church, 6.8% The United Methodist Church, 5.1% Churches of Christ, 1.7% Assemblies of God (2000).
Economy: Unemployment rate: 8.4% (June 2011); Total civilian labor force: 17,534 (June 2011); Leading industries: 22.2% manufacturing; 13.8% retail trade; 10.2% accommodation & food services (2009); Farms: 957 totaling 588,724 acres (2007); Companies that employ 500 or more persons: 3 (2009); Companies that employ 100 to 499 persons: 11 (2009); Companies that employ less than 100 persons: 724 (2009); Black-owned businesses: n/a (2007); Hispanic-owned businesses: 662 (2007); Asian-owned businesses: n/a (2007); Women-owned businesses: 358 (2007); Retail sales per capita: $7,450 (2010). Single-family building permits issued: 13 (2010); Multi-family building permits issued: 0 (2010).
Income: Per capita income: $16,131 (2010); Median household income: $36,122 (2010); Average household income: $47,547 (2010); Percent of households with income of $100,000 or more: 8.1% (2010); Poverty rate: 19.2% (2009); Bankruptcy rate: 1.17% (2010).
Taxes: Total county taxes per capita: $247 (2007); County property taxes per capita: $191 (2007).
Education: Percent of population age 25 and over with: High school diploma (including GED) or higher: 69.8% (2010); Bachelor's degree or higher: 15.3% (2010); Master's degree or higher: 5.2% (2010).
Housing: Homeownership rate: 65.5% (2010); Median home value: $68,816 (2010); Median contract rent: $381 per month (2005-2009 5-year est.); Median year structure built: 1960 (2005-2009 5-year est.).
Health: Birth rate: 174.3 per 10,000 population (2009); Death rate: 78.5 per 10,000 population (2009); Age-adjusted cancer mortality rate: 153.3 deaths per 100,000 population (2007); Number of physicians: 8.8 per 10,000 population (2008); Hospital beds: 15.1 per 10,000 population (2007); Hospital admissions: 643.0 per 10,000 population (2007).
Elections: 2008 Presidential election results: 27.2% Obama, 72.1% McCain, 0.0% Nader
Additional Information Contacts
Hale County Government . . . . (806) 291-5214

City of Plainview. . . . . (806) 296-1100
   http://www.ci.plainview.tx.us
Plainview Chamber of Commerce . . . . (806) 296-7431
   http://www.plainviewtexaschamber.com

Hale County Communities

ABERNATHY (city). Covers a land area of 1.182 square miles and a water area of 0 square miles. Located at 33.83° N. Lat; 101.84° W. Long. Elevation is 3,356 feet.
Population: 2,731 (1990); 2,839 (2000); 2,707 (2010); 2,659 (2015 projected); Race: 79.2% White, 1.5% Black, 0.3% Asian, 19.0% Other, 43.4% Hispanic of any race (2010); Density: 2,290.3 persons per square mile (2010); Average household size: 2.80 (2010); Median age: 34.8 (2010); Males per 100 females: 97.9 (2010); Marriage status: 17.4% never married, 64.0% now married, 8.7% widowed, 10.0% divorced (2005-2009 5-year est.); Foreign born: 4.9% (2005-2009 5-year est.); Ancestry (includes multiple ancestries): 9.8% American, 6.2% Irish, 6.0% German, 4.9% English, 3.1% Italian (2005-2009 5-year est.).
Economy: Single-family building permits issued: 8 (2010); Multi-family building permits issued: 0 (2010); Employment by occupation: 5.9% management, 16.5% professional, 23.4% services, 30.8% sales, 3.2% farming, 7.7% construction, 12.5% production (2005-2009 5-year est.).
Income: Per capita income: $18,036 (2010); Median household income: $36,915 (2010); Average household income: $50,525 (2010); Percent of

households with income of $100,000 or more: 8.9% (2010); Poverty rate: 24.5% (2005-2009 5-year est.).
Taxes: Total city taxes per capita: $208 (2007); City property taxes per capita: $166 (2007).
Education: Percent of population age 25 and over with: High school diploma (including GED) or higher: 72.2% (2010); Bachelor's degree or higher: 13.1% (2010); Master's degree or higher: 4.3% (2010).

School District(s)

Abernathy ISD (PK-12)
   2009-10 Enrollment: 809 . . . . (806) 298-2563
Housing: Homeownership rate: 74.4% (2010); Median home value: $61,193 (2010); Median contract rent: $467 per month (2005-2009 5-year est.); Median year structure built: 1958 (2005-2009 5-year est.).
Safety: Violent crime rate: 25.7 per 10,000 population; Property crime rate: 80.9 per 10,000 population (2009).
Newspapers: Abernathy Weekly Review (Community news; Circulation 850)
Transportation: Commute to work: 94.8% car, 0.0% public transportation, 2.9% walk, 1.3% work from home (2005-2009 5-year est.); Travel time to work: 34.7% less than 15 minutes, 29.7% 15 to 30 minutes, 32.7% 30 to 45 minutes, 1.7% 45 to 60 minutes, 1.2% 60 minutes or more (2005-2009 5-year est.)

EDMONSON (town). Covers a land area of 0.434 square miles and a water area of 0 square miles. Located at 34.28° N. Lat; 101.90° W. Long. Elevation is 3,504 feet.
Population: 107 (1990); 123 (2000); 112 (2010); 106 (2015 projected); Race: 74.1% White, 0.9% Black, 0.9% Asian, 24.1% Other, 36.6% Hispanic of any race (2010); Density: 258.0 persons per square mile (2010); Average household size: 2.87 (2010); Median age: 26.3 (2010); Males per 100 females: 115.4 (2010); Marriage status: 16.2% never married, 45.9% now married, 0.0% widowed, 37.8% divorced (2005-2009 5-year est.); Foreign born: 9.7% (2005-2009 5-year est.); Ancestry (includes multiple ancestries): 41.9% German, 3.2% Irish (2005-2009 5-year est.).
Economy: Employment by occupation: 0.0% management, 7.4% professional, 25.9% services, 25.9% sales, 18.5% farming, 14.8% construction, 7.4% production (2005-2009 5-year est.).
Income: Per capita income: $25,325 (2010); Median household income: $48,929 (2010); Average household income: $70,000 (2010); Percent of households with income of $100,000 or more: 23.1% (2010); Poverty rate: 38.7% (2005-2009 5-year est.).
Taxes: Total city taxes per capita: $24 (2007); City property taxes per capita: $0 (2007).
Education: Percent of population age 25 and over with: High school diploma (including GED) or higher: 80.7% (2010); Bachelor's degree or higher: 26.3% (2010); Master's degree or higher: 15.8% (2010).
Housing: Homeownership rate: 66.7% (2010); Median home value: $100,000 (2010); Median contract rent: $275 per month (2005-2009 5-year est.); Median year structure built: 1958 (2005-2009 5-year est.).
Transportation: Commute to work: 100.0% car, 0.0% public transportation, 0.0% walk, 0.0% work from home (2005-2009 5-year est.); Travel time to work: 7.4% less than 15 minutes, 92.6% 15 to 30 minutes, 0.0% 30 to 45 minutes, 0.0% 45 to 60 minutes, 0.0% 60 minutes or more (2005-2009 5-year est.)

HALE CENTER (city). Covers a land area of 1.087 square miles and a water area of 0 square miles. Located at 34.06° N. Lat; 101.84° W. Long. Elevation is 3,422 feet.
History: Hale Center, business center for an area of irrigated farms, claimed the Texas record for snowfall in 1956 with 33 inches in a single snowstorm.
Population: 2,076 (1990); 2,263 (2000); 2,087 (2010); 1,999 (2015 projected); Race: 77.6% White, 3.2% Black, 0.1% Asian, 19.1% Other, 63.2% Hispanic of any race (2010); Density: 1,920.5 persons per square mile (2010); Average household size: 2.72 (2010); Median age: 32.9 (2010); Males per 100 females: 94.7 (2010); Marriage status: 22.6% never married, 59.1% now married, 9.4% widowed, 8.9% divorced (2005-2009 5-year est.); Foreign born: 10.3% (2005-2009 5-year est.); Ancestry (includes multiple ancestries): 10.1% German, 6.2% English, 5.0% Irish, 1.9% French, 1.5% African (2005-2009 5-year est.).
Economy: Single-family building permits issued: 2 (2010); Multi-family building permits issued: 0 (2010); Employment by occupation: 11.0% management, 13.1% professional, 23.5% services, 15.1% sales, 4.9% farming, 8.5% construction, 23.9% production (2005-2009 5-year est.).

Income: Per capita income: $16,204 (2010); Median household income: $34,813 (2010); Average household income: $43,949 (2010); Percent of households with income of $100,000 or more: 5.9% (2010); Poverty rate: 23.2% (2005-2009 5-year est.).
Taxes: Total city taxes per capita: $398 (2007); City property taxes per capita: $163 (2007).
Education: Percent of population age 25 and over with: High school diploma (including GED) or higher: 61.4% (2010); Bachelor's degree or higher: 13.5% (2010); Master's degree or higher: 3.2% (2010).

School District(s)

Hale Center ISD (PK-12)
   2009-10 Enrollment: 628 . . . . (806) 839-2451
Housing: Homeownership rate: 70.5% (2010); Median home value: $41,684 (2010); Median contract rent: $354 per month (2005-2009 5-year est.); Median year structure built: 1956 (2005-2009 5-year est.).
Safety: Violent crime rate: 19.0 per 10,000 population; Property crime rate: 114.2 per 10,000 population (2009).
Newspapers: Hale Center American (Community news; Circulation 1,184)
Transportation: Commute to work: 92.6% car, 0.0% public transportation, 3.1% walk, 4.4% work from home (2005-2009 5-year est.); Travel time to work: 32.7% less than 15 minutes, 48.3% 15 to 30 minutes, 9.1% 30 to 45 minutes, 8.8% 45 to 60 minutes, 1.1% 60 minutes or more (2005-2009 5-year est.)

PETERSBURG (city). Covers a land area of 0.801 square miles and a water area of 0 square miles. Located at 33.87° N. Lat; 101.59° W. Long. Elevation is 3,255 feet.
Population: 1,303 (1990); 1,262 (2000); 1,170 (2010); 1,124 (2015 projected); Race: 49.6% White, 1.2% Black, 0.0% Asian, 49.2% Other, 61.8% Hispanic of any race (2010); Density: 1,460.0 persons per square mile (2010); Average household size: 2.79 (2010); Median age: 33.9 (2010); Males per 100 females: 97.6 (2010); Marriage status: 25.4% never married, 61.7% now married, 5.8% widowed, 7.0% divorced (2005-2009 5-year est.); Foreign born: 15.8% (2005-2009 5-year est.); Ancestry (includes multiple ancestries): 9.4% German, 8.5% English, 4.0% Irish, 1.9% American, 1.9% Dutch (2005-2009 5-year est.).
Economy: Employment by occupation: 7.0% management, 11.2% professional, 21.5% services, 16.2% sales, 16.0% farming, 6.6% construction, 21.5% production (2005-2009 5-year est.).
Income: Per capita income: $17,631 (2010); Median household income: $34,527 (2010); Average household income: $49,678 (2010); Percent of households with income of $100,000 or more: 9.3% (2010); Poverty rate: 23.5% (2005-2009 5-year est.).
Taxes: Total city taxes per capita: $189 (2007); City property taxes per capita: $132 (2007).
Education: Percent of population age 25 and over with: High school diploma (including GED) or higher: 66.6% (2010); Bachelor's degree or higher: 15.4% (2010); Master's degree or higher: 2.7% (2010).

School District(s)

Petersburg ISD (PK-12)
   2009-10 Enrollment: 279 . . . . (806) 667-3585
Housing: Homeownership rate: 77.1% (2010); Median home value: $44,756 (2010); Median contract rent: $355 per month (2005-2009 5-year est.); Median year structure built: 1956 (2005-2009 5-year est.).
Newspapers: Petersburg Post (Community news; Circulation 650)
Transportation: Commute to work: 91.3% car, 0.0% public transportation, 3.0% walk, 5.7% work from home (2005-2009 5-year est.); Travel time to work: 47.6% less than 15 minutes, 3.6% 15 to 30 minutes, 35.0% 30 to 45 minutes, 13.8% 45 to 60 minutes, 0.0% 60 minutes or more (2005-2009 5-year est.)

PLAINVIEW (city). County seat. Covers a land area of 13.779 square miles and a water area of 0 square miles. Located at 34.19° N. Lat; 101.71° W. Long. Elevation is 3,366 feet.
History: Plainview grew as the center of a grain producing region, with cotton as the second crop. Petroleum and natural gas later added to the economic base.
Population: 21,934 (1990); 22,336 (2000); 21,392 (2010); 20,950 (2015 projected); Race: 59.5% White, 4.9% Black, 0.8% Asian, 34.8% Other, 56.8% Hispanic of any race (2010); Density: 1,552.5 persons per square mile (2010); Average household size: 2.82 (2010); Median age: 32.4 (2010); Males per 100 females: 92.8 (2010); Marriage status: 23.6% never married, 58.1% now married, 7.3% widowed, 11.0% divorced (2005-2009 5-year est.); Foreign born: 10.9% (2005-2009 5-year est.); Ancestry

(includes multiple ancestries): 8.9% German, 6.8% Irish, 5.4% English, 5.2% American, 1.4% Scotch-Irish (2005-2009 5-year est.).
Economy: Single-family building permits issued: 3 (2010); Multi-family building permits issued: 0 (2010); Employment by occupation: 9.8% management, 15.8% professional, 19.0% services, 22.1% sales, 1.7% farming, 10.1% construction, 21.5% production (2005-2009 5-year est.).
Income: Per capita income: $15,865 (2010); Median household income: $35,468 (2010); Average household income: $45,574 (2010); Percent of households with income of $100,000 or more: 6.9% (2010); Poverty rate: 19.3% (2005-2009 5-year est.).
Taxes: Total city taxes per capita: $358 (2007); City property taxes per capita: $160 (2007).
Education: Percent of population age 25 and over with: High school diploma (including GED) or higher: 70.4% (2010); Bachelor's degree or higher: 17.7% (2010); Master's degree or higher: 6.3% (2010).

School District(s)
Abernathy ISD (PK-12)
    2009-10 Enrollment: 809 . . . . (806) 298-2563
Petersburg ISD (PK-12)
    2009-10 Enrollment: 279 . . . . (806) 667-3585
Plainview ISD (PK-12)
    2009-10 Enrollment: 5,859 . . . . (806) 296-6392
Shallowater ISD (PK-12)
    2009-10 Enrollment: 1,457 . . . . (806) 832-4531
Slaton ISD (PK-12)
    2009-10 Enrollment: 1,290 . . . . (806) 828-6591

Four-year College(s)
Wayland Baptist University (Private, Not-for-profit, Southern Baptist)
    Fall 2009 Enrollment: 5,886. . . . . (806) 291-1000
    2010-11 Tuition: In-state $10,796; Out-of-state $10,796
Housing: Homeownership rate: 63.1% (2010); Median home value: $73,208 (2010); Median contract rent: $383 per month (2005-2009 5-year est.); Median year structure built: 1961 (2005-2009 5-year est.).
Hospitals: Covenant Hospital Plainview (100 beds)
Safety: Violent crime rate: 39.1 per 10,000 population; Property crime rate: 511.1 per 10,000 population (2009).
Newspapers: Plainview Daily Herald (Local news)
Transportation: Commute to work: 93.4% car, 0.0% public transportation, 2.7% walk, 3.7% work from home (2005-2009 5-year est.); Travel time to work: 72.5% less than 15 minutes, 19.2% 15 to 30 minutes, 3.9% 30 to 45 minutes, 2.6% 45 to 60 minutes, 1.8% 60 minutes or more (2005-2009 5-year est.)
Airports: Hale County (general aviation)
Additional Information Contacts
City of Plainview. . . . . (806) 296-1100
    http://www.ci.plainview.tx.us
Plainview Chamber of Commerce . . . . (806) 296-7431
    http://www.plainviewtexaschamber.com

SETH WARD (CDP).
Covers a land area of 1.607 square miles and a water area of 0 square miles. Located at 34.21° N. Lat; 101.69° W. Long. Elevation is 3,373 feet.
Population: 1,818 (1990); 1,926 (2000); 1,848 (2010); 1,798 (2015 projected); Race: 63.8% White, 3.4% Black, 0.1% Asian, 32.8% Other, 68.5% Hispanic of any race (2010); Density: 1,150.2 persons per square mile (2010); Average household size: 3.24 (2010); Median age: 28.4 (2010); Males per 100 females: 94.5 (2010); Marriage status: 34.3% never married, 53.7% now married, 2.8% widowed, 9.1% divorced (2005-2009 5-year est.); Foreign born: 12.3% (2005-2009 5-year est.); Ancestry (includes multiple ancestries): 3.0% American, 2.7% English, 1.3% Irish, 0.7% French, 0.4% German (2005-2009 5-year est.).
Economy: Employment by occupation: 6.8% management, 1.6% professional, 24.8% services, 7.8% sales, 3.3% farming, 5.6% construction, 50.2% production (2005-2009 5-year est.).
Income: Per capita income: $10,619 (2010); Median household income: $27,500 (2010); Average household income: $34,654 (2010); Percent of households with income of $100,000 or more: 2.6% (2010); Poverty rate: 29.9% (2005-2009 5-year est.).
Education: Percent of population age 25 and over with: High school diploma (including GED) or higher: 49.1% (2010); Bachelor's degree or higher: 1.3% (2010); Master's degree or higher: 0.0% (2010).
Housing: Homeownership rate: 64.6% (2010); Median home value: $40,429 (2010); Median contract rent: $265 per month (2005-2009 5-year est.); Median year structure built: 1959 (2005-2009 5-year est.).

Transportation: Commute to work: 92.6% car, 0.0% public transportation, 4.7% walk, 2.7% work from home (2005-2009 5-year est.); Travel time to work: 81.1% less than 15 minutes, 10.6% 15 to 30 minutes, 1.7% 30 to 45 minutes, 3.4% 45 to 60 minutes, 3.2% 60 minutes or more (2005-2009 5-year est.)

Hall County

Located in northwestern Texas; plains area, crossed by the Prairie Dog Town Fork of the Red River. Covers a land area of 903.09 square miles, a water area of 0.99 square miles, and is located in the Central Time Zone at 34.53° N. Lat., 100.65° W. Long. The county was founded in 1876. County seat is Memphis.

Weather Station: Memphis   Elevation: 2,089 feet

	Jan	Feb	Mar	Apr	May	Jun	Jul	Aug	Sep	Oct	Nov	Dec
High	53	57	66	75	83	91	96	95	87	76	64	53
Low	27	30	37	46	56	65	69	68	60	48	36	27
Precip	0.7	0.9	1.5	1.8	3.5	3.3	1.9	2.6	2.5	2.0	1.1	0.9
Snow	1.2	0.8	0.1	0.1	0.0	0.0	0.0	0.0	0.0	tr	0.3	1.2

High and Low temperatures in degrees Fahrenheit; Precipitation and Snow in inches

Weather Station: Turkey   Elevation: 2,330 feet

	Jan	Feb	Mar	Apr	May	Jun	Jul	Aug	Sep	Oct	Nov	Dec
High	55	60	68	77	84	91	95	94	87	77	65	55
Low	28	31	38	46	56	65	69	68	60	49	37	28
Precip	0.8	1.1	1.6	1.8	3.1	4.0	2.2	2.6	2.5	1.9	1.2	1.0
Snow	2.5	1.5	0.6	0.1	0.0	0.0	0.0	0.0	0.0	tr	0.8	1.7

High and Low temperatures in degrees Fahrenheit; Precipitation and Snow in inches

Population: 3,905 (1990); 3,782 (2000); 3,421 (2010); 3,239 (2015 projected); Race: 66.6% White, 9.1% Black, 0.2% Asian, 24.1% Other, 33.8% Hispanic of any race (2010); Density: 3.8 persons per square mile (2010); Average household size: 2.47 (2010); Median age: 41.1 (2010); Males per 100 females: 92.1 (2010).
Religion: Five largest groups: 50.4% Southern Baptist Convention, 14.5% The United Methodist Church, 9.3% Catholic Church, 8.4% Churches of Christ, 1.0% Christian Churches and Churches of Christ (2000).
Economy: Unemployment rate: 9.8% (June 2011); Total civilian labor force: 1,358 (June 2011); Leading industries: 16.9% health care and social assistance; 9.8% manufacturing; 8.4% finance & insurance (2009); Farms: 382 totaling 533,874 acres (2007); Companies that employ 500 or more persons: 0 (2009); Companies that employ 100 to 499 persons: 0 (2009); Companies that employ less than 100 persons: 90 (2009); Black-owned businesses: n/a (2007); Hispanic-owned businesses: n/a (2007); Asian-owned businesses: n/a (2007); Women-owned businesses: n/a (2007); Retail sales per capita: $19,962 (2010). Single-family building permits issued: 0 (2010); Multi-family building permits issued: 0 (2010).
Income: Per capita income: $15,780 (2010); Median household income: $27,522 (2010); Average household income: $36,081 (2010); Percent of households with income of $100,000 or more: 4.1% (2010); Poverty rate: 25.3% (2009); Bankruptcy rate: 1.79% (2010).
Taxes: Total county taxes per capita: $425 (2007); County property taxes per capita: $314 (2007).
Education: Percent of population age 25 and over with: High school diploma (including GED) or higher: 67.5% (2010); Bachelor's degree or higher: 11.7% (2010); Master's degree or higher: 2.9% (2010).
Housing: Homeownership rate: 72.2% (2010); Median home value: $31,358 (2010); Median contract rent: $313 per month (2005-2009 5-year est.); Median year structure built: 1953 (2005-2009 5-year est.).
Health: Birth rate: 129.2 per 10,000 population (2009); Death rate: 93.2 per 10,000 population (2009); Age-adjusted cancer mortality rate: 185.2 (Unreliable) deaths per 100,000 population (2007); Number of physicians: 3.0 per 10,000 population (2008); Hospital beds: 0.0 per 10,000 population (2007); Hospital admissions: 0.0 per 10,000 population (2007).
Elections: 2008 Presidential election results: 25.6% Obama, 73.6% McCain, 0.1% Nader
Additional Information Contacts
Hall County Government . . . . (806) 259-2511

Memphis Chamber of Commerce . . . . (806) 259-3144

Hall County Communities

ESTELLINE (town). Covers a land area of 0.734 square miles and a water area of 0 square miles. Located at 34.54° N. Lat; 100.43° W. Long. Elevation is 1,834 feet.
History: Estelline was an early cattle shipping point for livestock from the surrounding ranches, including the 62 Wells, the Mill Iron, the Diamond Tail, and the Shoe Nail.
Population: 194 (1990); 168 (2000); 145 (2010); 137 (2015 projected); Race: 84.1% White, 4.1% Black, 0.7% Asian, 11.0% Other, 47.6% Hispanic of any race (2010); Density: 197.6 persons per square mile (2010); Average household size: 2.46 (2010); Median age: 48.1 (2010); Males per 100 females: 95.9 (2010); Marriage status: 24.8% never married, 41.6% now married, 15.9% widowed, 17.7% divorced (2005-2009 5-year est.); Foreign born: 9.0% (2005-2009 5-year est.); Ancestry (includes multiple ancestries): 15.0% American, 12.0% German, 10.5% Irish, 1.5% Dutch West Indian, 1.5% Dutch (2005-2009 5-year est.).
Economy: Employment by occupation: 5.7% management, 28.6% professional, 25.7% services, 0.0% sales, 22.9% farming, 0.0% construction, 17.1% production (2005-2009 5-year est.).
Income: Per capita income: $17,390 (2010); Median household income: $35,682 (2010); Average household income: $41,864 (2010); Percent of households with income of $100,000 or more: 1.7% (2010); Poverty rate: 23.8% (2005-2009 5-year est.).
Taxes: Total city taxes per capita: $198 (2007); City property taxes per capita: $108 (2007).
Education: Percent of population age 25 and over with: High school diploma (including GED) or higher: 74.5% (2010); Bachelor's degree or higher: 20.8% (2010); Master's degree or higher: 0.0% (2010).
Housing: Homeownership rate: 74.6% (2010); Median home value: $29,000 (2010); Median contract rent: $308 per month (2005-2009 5-year est.); Median year structure built: 1949 (2005-2009 5-year est.).
Transportation: Commute to work: 100.0% car, 0.0% public transportation, 0.0% walk, 0.0% work from home (2005-2009 5-year est.); Travel time to work: 34.4% less than 15 minutes, 53.1% 15 to 30 minutes, 12.5% 30 to 45 minutes, 0.0% 45 to 60 minutes, 0.0% 60 minutes or more (2005-2009 5-year est.)

LAKEVIEW (town). Covers a land area of 0.208 square miles and a water area of 0 square miles. Located at 34.67° N. Lat; 100.69° W. Long. Elevation is 2,129 feet.
Population: 202 (1990); 152 (2000); 132 (2010); 125 (2015 projected); Race: 59.1% White, 7.6% Black, 0.0% Asian, 33.3% Other, 45.5% Hispanic of any race (2010); Density: 634.0 persons per square mile (2010); Average household size: 2.69 (2010); Median age: 42.7 (2010); Males per 100 females: 97.0 (2010); Marriage status: 22.2% never married, 61.1% now married, 9.3% widowed, 7.4% divorced (2005-2009 5-year est.); Foreign born: 20.0% (2005-2009 5-year est.); Ancestry (includes multiple ancestries): 9.2% American, 6.2% English, 3.1% German, 1.5% Irish (2005-2009 5-year est.).
Economy: Employment by occupation: 12.5% management, 12.5% professional, 12.5% services, 25.0% sales, 18.8% farming, 18.8% construction, 0.0% production (2005-2009 5-year est.).
Income: Per capita income: $13,483 (2010); Median household income: $31,250 (2010); Average household income: $37,041 (2010); Percent of households with income of $100,000 or more: 4.1% (2010); Poverty rate: 32.3% (2005-2009 5-year est.).
Taxes: Total city taxes per capita: $46 (2007); City property taxes per capita: $33 (2007).
Education: Percent of population age 25 and over with: High school diploma (including GED) or higher: 61.9% (2010); Bachelor's degree or higher: 15.5% (2010); Master's degree or higher: 3.6% (2010).
Housing: Homeownership rate: 77.6% (2010); Median home value: $32,000 (2010); Median contract rent: $400 per month (2005-2009 5-year est.); Median year structure built: 1955 (2005-2009 5-year est.).
Safety: Violent crime rate: 1.5 per 10,000 population; Property crime rate: 140.5 per 10,000 population (2009).
Transportation: Commute to work: 100.0% car, 0.0% public transportation, 0.0% walk, 0.0% work from home (2005-2009 5-year est.); Travel time to work: 37.5% less than 15 minutes, 43.8% 15 to 30 minutes, 18.8% 30 to 45 minutes, 0.0% 45 to 60 minutes, 0.0% 60 minutes or more (2005-2009 5-year est.)

MEMPHIS (city). County seat. Covers a land area of 2.243 square miles and a water area of 0 square miles. Located at 34.72° N. Lat; 100.54° W. Long. Elevation is 2,057 feet.
History: Memphis developed as the center of a productive and diversified agricultural area, where scientific farming methods produced cotton, vegetables, and fruits.
Population: 2,465 (1990); 2,479 (2000); 2,223 (2010); 2,101 (2015 projected); Race: 64.2% White, 10.3% Black, 0.1% Asian, 25.5% Other, 32.4% Hispanic of any race (2010); Density: 991.1 persons per square mile (2010); Average household size: 2.45 (2010); Median age: 41.3 (2010); Males per 100 females: 89.8 (2010); Marriage status: 16.6% never married, 57.0% now married, 11.0% widowed, 15.3% divorced (2005-2009 5-year est.); Foreign born: 9.7% (2005-2009 5-year est.); Ancestry (includes multiple ancestries): 12.5% German, 8.2% English, 8.2% Irish, 5.8% American, 2.6% Dutch (2005-2009 5-year est.).
Economy: Single-family building permits issued: 0 (2010); Multi-family building permits issued: 0 (2010); Employment by occupation: 10.6% management, 21.0% professional, 20.8% services, 20.9% sales, 2.5% farming, 7.4% construction, 17.0% production (2005-2009 5-year est.).
Income: Per capita income: $16,251 (2010); Median household income: $27,143 (2010); Average household income: $35,568 (2010); Percent of households with income of $100,000 or more: 4.4% (2010); Poverty rate: 25.1% (2005-2009 5-year est.).
Taxes: Total city taxes per capita: $247 (2007); City property taxes per capita: $100 (2007).
Education: Percent of population age 25 and over with: High school diploma (including GED) or higher: 68.0% (2010); Bachelor's degree or higher: 10.7% (2010); Master's degree or higher: 3.1% (2010).

School District(s)
Memphis ISD (PK-12)
   2009-10 Enrollment: 556 . . . . (806) 259-2443
Housing: Homeownership rate: 69.7% (2010); Median home value: $35,470 (2010); Median contract rent: $304 per month (2005-2009 5-year est.); Median year structure built: 1953 (2005-2009 5-year est.).
Hospitals: Hall County Hospital (42 beds)
Safety: Violent crime rate: 18.4 per 10,000 population; Property crime rate: 87.6 per 10,000 population (2009).
Newspapers: Memphis Democrat (Community news; Circulation 1,700)
Transportation: Commute to work: 90.0% car, 0.0% public transportation, 2.1% walk, 4.4% work from home (2005-2009 5-year est.); Travel time to work: 69.5% less than 15 minutes, 12.8% 15 to 30 minutes, 15.5% 30 to 45 minutes, 1.8% 45 to 60 minutes, 0.5% 60 minutes or more (2005-2009 5-year est.)
Additional Information Contacts
Memphis Chamber of Commerce . . . . (806) 259-3144

TURKEY (city). Covers a land area of 0.825 square miles and a water area of 0 square miles. Located at 34.39° N. Lat; 100.89° W. Long. Elevation is 2,333 feet.
Population: 507 (1990); 494 (2000); 447 (2010); 427 (2015 projected); Race: 71.4% White, 6.0% Black, 0.4% Asian, 22.1% Other, 32.0% Hispanic of any race (2010); Density: 541.9 persons per square mile (2010); Average household size: 2.46 (2010); Median age: 42.1 (2010); Males per 100 females: 96.1 (2010); Marriage status: 21.2% never married, 61.5% now married, 11.1% widowed, 6.2% divorced (2005-2009 5-year est.); Foreign born: 34.0% (2005-2009 5-year est.); Ancestry (includes multiple ancestries): 12.9% German, 9.2% Irish, 8.1% American, 7.4% English, 5.1% Scottish (2005-2009 5-year est.).
Economy: Employment by occupation: 17.7% management, 15.5% professional, 12.7% services, 20.4% sales, 29.8% farming, 3.9% construction, 0.0% production (2005-2009 5-year est.).
Income: Per capita income: $14,246 (2010); Median household income: $24,487 (2010); Average household income: $35,096 (2010); Percent of households with income of $100,000 or more: 3.3% (2010); Poverty rate: 46.1% (2005-2009 5-year est.).
Taxes: Total city taxes per capita: $153 (2007); City property taxes per capita: $82 (2007).
Education: Percent of population age 25 and over with: High school diploma (including GED) or higher: 62.9% (2010); Bachelor's degree or higher: 9.2% (2010); Master's degree or higher: 2.4% (2010).

School District(s)
Turkey-Quitaque ISD (PK-12)
   2009-10 Enrollment: 207 . . . . (806) 455-1411

Housing: Homeownership rate: 79.7% (2010); Median home value: $19,999 (2010); Median contract rent: n/a per month (2005-2009 5-year est.); Median year structure built: 1955 (2005-2009 5-year est.).
Transportation: Commute to work: 95.8% car, 0.0% public transportation, 3.0% walk, 1.2% work from home (2005-2009 5-year est.); Travel time to work: 42.7% less than 15 minutes, 26.2% 15 to 30 minutes, 14.6% 30 to 45 minutes, 0.0% 45 to 60 minutes, 16.5% 60 minutes or more (2005-2009 5-year est.)

Hamilton County

Located in central Texas; prairie area, drained by the Leon, Bosque, and Lampasas Rivers. Covers a land area of 835.71 square miles, a water area of 0.67 square miles, and is located in the Central Time Zone at 31.75° N. Lat., 98.10° W. Long. The county was founded in 1858. County seat is Hamilton.

Weather Station: Hico   Elevation: 1,024 feet

	Jan	Feb	Mar	Apr	May	Jun	Jul	Aug	Sep	Oct	Nov	Dec
High	59	62	70	78	84	91	95	95	88	79	68	59
Low	33	36	44	51	61	68	71	70	63	53	43	33
Precip	1.9	2.5	3.2	2.6	5.0	4.5	2.0	2.7	3.4	3.3	2.4	2.0
Snow	0.4	0.1	tr	0.0	0.6	0.0	0.0	0.0	0.0	0.0	tr	0.3

High and Low temperatures in degrees Fahrenheit; Precipitation and Snow in inches

Population: 7,733 (1990); 8,229 (2000); 8,395 (2010); 8,460 (2015 projected); Race: 91.4% White, 0.7% Black, 0.2% Asian, 7.8% Other, 10.0% Hispanic of any race (2010); Density: 10.0 persons per square mile (2010); Average household size: 2.41 (2010); Median age: 42.7 (2010); Males per 100 females: 95.6 (2010).
Religion: Five largest groups: 35.0% Southern Baptist Convention, 12.6% The United Methodist Church, 7.3% Lutheran Church—Missouri Synod, 6.3% Churches of Christ, 2.7% Evangelical Lutheran Church in America (2000).
Economy: Unemployment rate: 6.4% (June 2011); Total civilian labor force: 4,426 (June 2011); Leading industries: 23.0% health care and social assistance; 17.1% retail trade; 9.1% accommodation & food services (2009); Farms: 1,045 totaling 470,850 acres (2007); Companies that employ 500 or more persons: 0 (2009); Companies that employ 100 to 499 persons: 2 (2009); Companies that employ less than 100 persons: 227 (2009); Black-owned businesses: n/a (2007); Hispanic-owned businesses: n/a (2007); Asian-owned businesses: n/a (2007); Women-owned businesses: n/a (2007); Retail sales per capita: $8,359 (2010). Single-family building permits issued: 0 (2010); Multi-family building permits issued: 0 (2010).
Income: Per capita income: $21,628 (2010); Median household income: $40,688 (2010); Average household income: $52,872 (2010); Percent of households with income of $100,000 or more: 11.1% (2010); Poverty rate: 15.9% (2009); Bankruptcy rate: 1.86% (2010).
Taxes: Total county taxes per capita: $374 (2007); County property taxes per capita: $265 (2007).
Education: Percent of population age 25 and over with: High school diploma (including GED) or higher: 79.0% (2010); Bachelor's degree or higher: 18.7% (2010); Master's degree or higher: 6.6% (2010).
Housing: Homeownership rate: 76.4% (2010); Median home value: $79,471 (2010); Median contract rent: $358 per month (2005-2009 5-year est.); Median year structure built: 1963 (2005-2009 5-year est.)
Health: Birth rate: 120.6 per 10,000 population (2009); Death rate: 156.7 per 10,000 population (2009); Age-adjusted cancer mortality rate: 166.1 deaths per 100,000 population (2007); Number of physicians: 14.8 per 10,000 population (2008); Hospital beds: 42.1 per 10,000 population (2007); Hospital admissions: 2,452.6 per 10,000 population (2007).
Elections: 2008 Presidential election results: 22.8% Obama, 76.1% McCain, 0.1% Nader

Additional Information Contacts
Hamilton County Government . . . . (254) 386-3815
   http://www.co.hamilton.tx.us/ips/cms
City of Hamilton . . . . (254) 386-8116
   http://www.hamiltontexas.com
Hamilton Chamber of Commerce . . . . (254) 386-3216
   http://hamiltontexas.com/chamber.php

Hamilton County Communities

CARLTON (unincorporated postal area, zip code 76436). Covers a land area of 6.403 square miles and a water area of 0 square miles. Located at 31.91° N. Lat; 98.17° W. Long. Elevation is 1,332 feet.
Population: 126 (2000); Race: 81.1% White, 0.0% Black, 0.0% Asian, 18.9% Other, 25.4% Hispanic of any race (2000); Density: 19.7 persons per square mile (2000); Age: 22.1% under 18, 18.0% over 64 (2000); Marriage status: 18.1% never married, 66.7% now married, 12.4% widowed, 2.9% divorced (2000); Foreign born: 23.0% (2000); Ancestry (includes multiple ancestries): 12.3% German, 12.3% English, 8.2% Irish, 8.2% American (2000).
Economy: Employment by occupation: 3.6% management, 8.9% professional, 10.7% services, 12.5% sales, 37.5% farming, 19.6% construction, 7.1% production (2000).
Income: Per capita income: $11,702 (2000); Median household income: $18,125 (2000); Poverty rate: 179.1% (2000).
Education: Percent of population age 25 and over with: High school diploma (including GED) or higher: 55.7% (2000); Bachelor's degree or higher: 9.1% (2000).
Housing: Homeownership rate: 83.3% (2000); Median home value: $34,300 (2000); Median contract rent: $225 per month (2000); Median year structure built: 1949 (2000).
Transportation: Commute to work: 91.1% car, 0.0% public transportation, 0.0% walk, 8.9% work from home (2000); Travel time to work: 19.6% less than 15 minutes, 33.3% 15 to 30 minutes, 13.7% 30 to 45 minutes, 7.8% 45 to 60 minutes, 25.5% 60 minutes or more (2000)

HAMILTON (city). County seat. Covers a land area of 2.832 square miles and a water area of 0.054 square miles. Located at 31.70° N. Lat; 98.12° W. Long. Elevation is 1,168 feet.
Population: 2,945 (1990); 2,977 (2000); 2,962 (2010); 2,917 (2015 projected); Race: 94.5% White, 0.2% Black, 0.3% Asian, 5.0% Other, 8.0% Hispanic of any race (2010); Density: 1,045.7 persons per square mile (2010); Average household size: 2.40 (2010); Median age: 40.6 (2010); Males per 100 females: 87.8 (2010); Marriage status: 18.1% never married, 62.6% now married, 8.3% widowed, 10.9% divorced (2005-2009 5-year est.); Foreign born: 2.4% (2005-2009 5-year est.); Ancestry (includes multiple ancestries): 19.7% American, 19.3% German, 18.9% English, 11.2% Irish, 9.4% French (2005-2009 5-year est.).
Economy: Single-family building permits issued: 0 (2010); Multi-family building permits issued: 0 (2010); Employment by occupation: 11.9% management, 14.6% professional, 19.4% services, 20.2% sales, 0.6% farming, 15.3% construction, 18.1% production (2005-2009 5-year est.).
Income: Per capita income: $20,009 (2010); Median household income: $36,285 (2010); Average household income: $48,988 (2010); Percent of households with income of $100,000 or more: 8.6% (2010); Poverty rate: 8.4% (2005-2009 5-year est.).
Taxes: Total city taxes per capita: $371 (2007); City property taxes per capita: $170 (2007).
Education: Percent of population age 25 and over with: High school diploma (including GED) or higher: 76.8% (2010); Bachelor's degree or higher: 14.5% (2010); Master's degree or higher: 5.2% (2010).
School District(s)
Hamilton ISD (PK-12)
   2009-10 Enrollment: 847 . . . . (254) 386-3149
Housing: Homeownership rate: 73.9% (2010); Median home value: $60,959 (2010); Median contract rent: $381 per month (2005-2009 5-year est.); Median year structure built: 1962 (2005-2009 5-year est.).
Hospitals: Hamilton General Hospital
Newspapers: The Hamilton Herald-News (Local news; Circulation 3,750)
Transportation: Commute to work: 94.7% car, 0.0% public transportation, 1.5% walk, 3.8% work from home (2005-2009 5-year est.); Travel time to work: 74.1% less than 15 minutes, 10.1% 15 to 30 minutes, 7.2% 30 to 45 minutes, 5.1% 45 to 60 minutes, 3.5% 60 minutes or more (2005-2009 5-year est.)
Additional Information Contacts
City of Hamilton . . . . (254) 386-8116
   http://www.hamiltontexas.com
Hamilton Chamber of Commerce . . . . (254) 386-3216
   http://hamiltontexas.com/chamber.php

HICO (city). Covers a land area of 1.471 square miles and a water area of 0 square miles. Located at 31.98° N. Lat; 98.03° W. Long. Elevation is 1,027 feet.

Population: 1,342 (1990); 1,341 (2000); 1,402 (2010); 1,432 (2015 projected); Race: 87.2% White, 0.1% Black, 0.0% Asian, 12.7% Other, 14.8% Hispanic of any race (2010); Density: 952.8 persons per square mile (2010); Average household size: 2.42 (2010); Median age: 37.8 (2010); Males per 100 females: 89.7 (2010); Marriage status: 19.0% never married, 43.3% now married, 16.2% widowed, 21.5% divorced (2005-2009 5-year est.); Foreign born: 9.4% (2005-2009 5-year est.); Ancestry (includes multiple ancestries): 16.4% German, 13.9% American, 9.0% Irish, 6.8% English, 3.2% Scottish (2005-2009 5-year est.).
Economy: Employment by occupation: 10.3% management, 14.4% professional, 24.5% services, 8.7% sales, 5.1% farming, 25.3% construction, 11.7% production (2005-2009 5-year est.).
Income: Per capita income: $17,783 (2010); Median household income: $34,267 (2010); Average household income: $43,298 (2010); Percent of households with income of $100,000 or more: 6.5% (2010); Poverty rate: 22.5% (2005-2009 5-year est.).
Taxes: Total city taxes per capita: $434 (2007); City property taxes per capita: $245 (2007).
Education: Percent of population age 25 and over with: High school diploma (including GED) or higher: 76.5% (2010); Bachelor's degree or higher: 13.6% (2010); Master's degree or higher: 3.4% (2010).

School District(s)

Hico ISD (PK-12)
  2009-10 Enrollment: 667 . . . . (254) 796-2181
Housing: Homeownership rate: 72.8% (2010); Median home value: $71,176 (2010); Median contract rent: $243 per month (2005-2009 5-year est.); Median year structure built: 1961 (2005-2009 5-year est.).
Newspapers: Hico News Review (Community news; Circulation 1,500)
Transportation: Commute to work: 86.1% car, 0.0% public transportation, 8.4% walk, 3.2% work from home (2005-2009 5-year est.); Travel time to work: 48.0% less than 15 minutes, 23.2% 15 to 30 minutes, 17.2% 30 to 45 minutes, 6.4% 45 to 60 minutes, 5.2% 60 minutes or more (2005-2009 5-year est.)

POTTSVILLE (unincorporated postal area, zip code 76565). Covers a land area of 37.390 square miles and a water area of 0 square miles. Located at 31.65° N. Lat; 98.36° W. Long. Elevation is 1,322 feet.
Population: 142 (2000); Race: 100.0% White, 0.0% Black, 0.0% Asian, 0.0% Other, 0.0% Hispanic of any race (2000); Density: 3.8 persons per square mile (2000); Age: 16.8% under 18, 32.0% over 64 (2000); Marriage status: 7.1% never married, 68.8% now married, 17.9% widowed, 6.3% divorced (2000); Foreign born: 0.0% (2000); Ancestry (includes multiple ancestries): 60.8% German, 22.4% English, 8.8% Irish, 5.6% Hungarian (2000).
Economy: Employment by occupation: 21.8% management, 25.5% professional, 0.0% services, 27.3% sales, 0.0% farming, 0.0% construction, 25.5% production (2000).
Income: Per capita income: $18,237 (2000); Median household income: $33,750 (2000); Poverty rate: 179.1% (2000).
Education: Percent of population age 25 and over with: High school diploma (including GED) or higher: 78.6% (2000); Bachelor's degree or higher: 21.4% (2000).
Housing: Homeownership rate: 91.2% (2000); Median home value: $95,000 (2000); Median contract rent: n/a per month (2000); Median year structure built: 1965 (2000).
Transportation: Commute to work: 67.3% car, 0.0% public transportation, 0.0% walk, 32.7% work from home (2000); Travel time to work: 0.0% less than 15 minutes, 59.5% 15 to 30 minutes, 21.6% 30 to 45 minutes, 0.0% 45 to 60 minutes, 18.9% 60 minutes or more (2000)

Hansford County

Located in north Texas, in the high plains area of the Panhandle; bounded on the north by Oklahoma. Covers a land area of 919.80 square miles, a water area of 0.60 square miles, and is located in the Central Time Zone at 36.27° N. Lat., 101.30° W. Long. The county was founded in 1876. County seat is Spearman.

Weather Station: Gruver   Elevation: 3,169 feet

	Jan	Feb	Mar	Apr	May	Jun	Jul	Aug	Sep	Oct	Nov	Dec
High	49	53	61	71	79	88	93	91	83	72	60	48
Low	21	24	31	40	51	60	65	64	55	42	30	22
Precip	0.5	0.6	1.5	1.6	2.7	3.3	2.8	2.2	1.8	1.7	0.9	0.9
Snow	2.9	1.7	2.8	0.5	0.0	0.0	0.0	0.0	0.0	0.1	1.2	3.5

High and Low temperatures in degrees Fahrenheit; Precipitation and Snow in inches

Weather Station: Spearman   Elevation: 3,094 feet

	Jan	Feb	Mar	Apr	May	Jun	Jul	Aug	Sep	Oct	Nov	Dec
High	52	56	65	74	82	90	95	93	86	76	63	51
Low	24	27	34	43	53	62	67	66	58	46	33	25
Precip	0.6	0.6	1.6	1.7	2.9	3.6	2.7	2.4	2.1	1.4	0.8	0.8
Snow	4.4	3.6	4.5	0.9	0.0	0.0	0.0	0.0	tr	0.3	1.5	5.0

High and Low temperatures in degrees Fahrenheit; Precipitation and Snow in inches

Population: 5,848 (1990); 5,369 (2000); 5,241 (2010); 5,171 (2015 projected); Race: 71.5% White, 0.0% Black, 0.4% Asian, 28.1% Other, 45.1% Hispanic of any race (2010); Density: 5.7 persons per square mile (2010); Average household size: 2.58 (2010); Median age: 35.4 (2010); Males per 100 females: 99.7 (2010).
Religion: Five largest groups: 34.8% Southern Baptist Convention, 26.4% The United Methodist Church, 11.6% Catholic Church, 7.7% Churches of Christ, 6.9% Christian Church (Disciples of Christ) (2000).
Economy: Unemployment rate: 5.4% (June 2011); Total civilian labor force: 2,834 (June 2011); Leading industries: 11.7% wholesale trade; 9.1% construction; 8.7% mining (2009); Farms: 242 totaling 585,286 acres (2007); Companies that employ 500 or more persons: 0 (2009); Companies that employ 100 to 499 persons: 1 (2009); Companies that employ less than 100 persons: 147 (2009); Black-owned businesses: n/a (2007); Hispanic-owned businesses: n/a (2007); Asian-owned businesses: n/a (2007); Women-owned businesses: n/a (2007); Retail sales per capita: $8,896 (2010). Single-family building permits issued: 0 (2010); Multi-family building permits issued: 0 (2010).
Income: Per capita income: $21,727 (2010); Median household income: $43,880 (2010); Average household income: $56,942 (2010); Percent of households with income of $100,000 or more: 11.0% (2010); Poverty rate: 12.3% (2009); Bankruptcy rate: 0.18% (2010).
Taxes: Total county taxes per capita: $407 (2007); County property taxes per capita: $337 (2007).
Education: Percent of population age 25 and over with: High school diploma (including GED) or higher: 74.6% (2010); Bachelor's degree or higher: 20.8% (2010); Master's degree or higher: 4.4% (2010).
Housing: Homeownership rate: 72.8% (2010); Median home value: $56,625 (2010); Median contract rent: $399 per month (2005-2009 5-year est.); Median year structure built: 1959 (2005-2009 5-year est.)
Health: Birth rate: 253.4 per 10,000 population (2009); Death rate: 96.2 per 10,000 population (2009); Age-adjusted cancer mortality rate: 201.1 (Unreliable) deaths per 100,000 population (2007); Number of physicians: 3.7 per 10,000 population (2008); Hospital beds: 38.4 per 10,000 population (2007); Hospital admissions: 378.7 per 10,000 population (2007).
Elections: 2008 Presidential election results: 11.4% Obama, 87.9% McCain, 0.0% Nader
Additional Information Contacts
Hansford County Government . . . . (806) 659-4100
  http://www.co.hansford.tx.us/ips/cms
Gruver Chamber of Commerce . . . . (806) 733-5114
  http://www.gruvertexas.com/chamber.html
Spearman Chamber of Commerce . . . . (806) 659-5555
  http://www.spearman.org

Hansford County Communities

GRUVER (city). Covers a land area of 1.067 square miles and a water area of 0 square miles. Located at 36.26° N. Lat; 101.40° W. Long. Elevation is 3,176 feet.
Population: 1,172 (1990); 1,162 (2000); 1,122 (2010); 1,099 (2015 projected); Race: 72.1% White, 0.0% Black, 0.0% Asian, 27.9% Other, 40.9% Hispanic of any race (2010); Density: 1,051.5 persons per square mile (2010); Average household size: 2.59 (2010); Median age: 34.9 (2010); Males per 100 females: 104.7 (2010); Marriage status: 16.3% never married, 72.4% now married, 9.6% widowed, 1.6% divorced (2005-2009 5-year est.); Foreign born: 11.4% (2005-2009 5-year est.); Ancestry (includes multiple ancestries): 19.8% English, 19.0% Irish, 17.7% German, 6.7% Dutch, 6.3% French (2005-2009 5-year est.).
Economy: Single-family building permits issued: 0 (2010); Multi-family building permits issued: 0 (2010); Employment by occupation: 18.9% management, 19.9% professional, 10.8% services, 19.1% sales, 6.0% farming, 9.1% construction, 16.2% production (2005-2009 5-year est.).
Income: Per capita income: $20,478 (2010); Median household income: $41,370 (2010); Average household income: $53,450 (2010); Percent of households with income of $100,000 or more: 10.4% (2010); Poverty rate: 2.3% (2005-2009 5-year est.).

Taxes: Total city taxes per capita: $260 (2007); City property taxes per capita: $88 (2007).
Education: Percent of population age 25 and over with: High school diploma (including GED) or higher: 75.1% (2010); Bachelor's degree or higher: 25.0% (2010); Master's degree or higher: 5.3% (2010).

School District(s)

Gruver ISD (PK-12)
   2009-10 Enrollment: 420 . . . . (806) 733-2001
Housing: Homeownership rate: 72.8% (2010); Median home value: $66,857 (2010); Median contract rent: $429 per month (2005-2009 5-year est.); Median year structure built: 1957 (2005-2009 5-year est.).
Transportation: Commute to work: 84.8% car, 1.4% public transportation, 6.4% walk, 3.3% work from home (2005-2009 5-year est.); Travel time to work: 52.2% less than 15 minutes, 26.4% 15 to 30 minutes, 12.5% 30 to 45 minutes, 1.8% 45 to 60 minutes, 7.1% 60 minutes or more (2005-2009 5-year est.)
Additional Information Contacts
Gruver Chamber of Commerce . . . . (806) 733-5114
   http://www.gruvertexas.com/chamber.html

MORSE (CDP). Covers a land area of 0.545 square miles and a water area of 0 square miles. Located at 36.06° N. Lat; 101.47° W. Long. Elevation is 3,205 feet.
Population: 231 (1990); 172 (2000); 167 (2010); 167 (2015 projected); Race: 87.4% White, 0.6% Black, 2.4% Asian, 9.6% Other, 34.1% Hispanic of any race (2010); Density: 306.4 persons per square mile (2010); Average household size: 2.49 (2010); Median age: 41.8 (2010); Males per 100 females: 101.2 (2010); Marriage status: 18.3% never married, 74.6% now married, 0.0% widowed, 7.0% divorced (2005-2009 5-year est.); Foreign born: 17.4% (2005-2009 5-year est.); Ancestry (includes multiple ancestries): 46.5% German, 20.9% Czech, 8.1% Scotch-Irish, 5.8% Welsh, 5.8% Irish (2005-2009 5-year est.).
Economy: Employment by occupation: 0.0% management, 18.6% professional, 4.7% services, 20.9% sales, 18.6% farming, 4.7% construction, 32.6% production (2005-2009 5-year est.).
Income: Per capita income: $20,862 (2010); Median household income: $43,382 (2010); Average household income: $53,246 (2010); Percent of households with income of $100,000 or more: 14.9% (2010); Poverty rate: 0.0% (2005-2009 5-year est.).
Education: Percent of population age 25 and over with: High school diploma (including GED) or higher: 79.1% (2010); Bachelor's degree or higher: 28.2% (2010); Master's degree or higher: 5.5% (2010).

School District(s)

Pringle-Morse CISD (PK-08)
   2009-10 Enrollment: 111 . . . . (806) 733-2507
Housing: Homeownership rate: 68.7% (2010); Median home value: $63,333 (2010); Median contract rent: n/a per month (2005-2009 5-year est.); Median year structure built: 1961 (2005-2009 5-year est.).
Transportation: Commute to work: 90.0% car, 0.0% public transportation, 5.0% walk, 0.0% work from home (2005-2009 5-year est.); Travel time to work: 17.5% less than 15 minutes, 55.0% 15 to 30 minutes, 7.5% 30 to 45 minutes, 7.5% 45 to 60 minutes, 12.5% 60 minutes or more (2005-2009 5-year est.)

SPEARMAN (city). County seat. Covers a land area of 2.091 square miles and a water area of 0 square miles. Located at 36.19° N. Lat; 101.19° W. Long. Elevation is 3,104 feet.
History: Incorporated 1921.
Population: 3,198 (1990); 3,021 (2000); 2,919 (2010); 2,869 (2015 projected); Race: 70.3% White, 0.0% Black, 0.2% Asian, 29.5% Other, 46.9% Hispanic of any race (2010); Density: 1,396.3 persons per square mile (2010); Average household size: 2.53 (2010); Median age: 35.3 (2010); Males per 100 females: 95.5 (2010); Marriage status: 23.4% never married, 64.1% now married, 5.6% widowed, 6.9% divorced (2005-2009 5-year est.); Foreign born: 18.8% (2005-2009 5-year est.); Ancestry (includes multiple ancestries): 8.4% German, 6.2% American, 6.0% English, 5.9% Irish, 2.8% Dutch (2005-2009 5-year est.).
Economy: Single-family building permits issued: 0 (2010); Multi-family building permits issued: 0 (2010); Employment by occupation: 10.5% management, 10.9% professional, 13.1% services, 24.8% sales, 3.2% farming, 18.9% construction, 18.8% production (2005-2009 5-year est.).
Income: Per capita income: $21,751 (2010); Median household income: $44,669 (2010); Average household income: $56,446 (2010); Percent of households with income of $100,000 or more: 10.1% (2010); Poverty rate: 14.9% (2005-2009 5-year est.).

Taxes: Total city taxes per capita: $263 (2007); City property taxes per capita: $108 (2007).
Education: Percent of population age 25 and over with: High school diploma (including GED) or higher: 73.9% (2010); Bachelor's degree or higher: 18.5% (2010); Master's degree or higher: 4.1% (2010).

School District(s)

Spearman ISD (PK-12)
   2009-10 Enrollment: 810 . . . . (806) 659-3233
Housing: Homeownership rate: 75.3% (2010); Median home value: $49,013 (2010); Median contract rent: $394 per month (2005-2009 5-year est.); Median year structure built: 1959 (2005-2009 5-year est.).
Hospitals: Hansford County Hospital District (25 beds)
Safety: Violent crime rate: 30.6 per 10,000 population; Property crime rate: 204.3 per 10,000 population (2009).
Newspapers: Hansford County Reporter-Statesman (Community news; Circulation 1,700)
Transportation: Commute to work: 95.9% car, 0.0% public transportation, 0.9% walk, 2.0% work from home (2005-2009 5-year est.); Travel time to work: 55.9% less than 15 minutes, 13.3% 15 to 30 minutes, 16.3% 30 to 45 minutes, 2.2% 45 to 60 minutes, 12.3% 60 minutes or more (2005-2009 5-year est.)
Airports: Spearman Municipal (general aviation)
Additional Information Contacts
Spearman Chamber of Commerce . . . . (806) 659-5555
   http://www.spearman.org

Hardeman County

Located in north Texas; bounded on the north by Prairie Dog Town Fork of the Red River and the Oklahoma border, and on the south by the Pease River; includes Lake Pauline. Covers a land area of 695.38 square miles, a water area of 1.62 square miles, and is located in the Central Time Zone at 34.28° N. Lat., 99.72° W. Long. The county was founded in 1858. County seat is Quanah.

Weather Station: Quanah 5 SE   Elevation: 1,495 feet

	Jan	Feb	Mar	Apr	May	Jun	Jul	Aug	Sep	Oct	Nov	Dec
High	53	57	66	75	83	91	96	95	87	77	64	54
Low	26	30	39	47	58	67	71	70	61	49	37	28
Precip	1.1	1.2	1.9	1.9	3.6	4.0	2.1	2.8	2.9	2.3	1.8	1.2
Snow	1.7	1.3	0.1	0.0	0.0	0.0	0.0	0.0	0.0	tr	0.8	0.8

High and Low temperatures in degrees Fahrenheit; Precipitation and Snow in inches

Population: 5,283 (1990); 4,724 (2000); 4,080 (2010); 3,760 (2015 projected); Race: 81.5% White, 5.9% Black, 0.3% Asian, 12.3% Other, 18.2% Hispanic of any race (2010); Density: 5.9 persons per square mile (2010); Average household size: 2.37 (2010); Median age: 42.8 (2010); Males per 100 females: 91.5 (2010).
Religion: Five largest groups: 84.3% Southern Baptist Convention, 13.7% The United Methodist Church, 10.1% Churches of Christ, 7.2% Catholic Church, 2.7% Christian Church (Disciples of Christ) (2000).
Economy: Unemployment rate: 6.4% (June 2011); Total civilian labor force: 2,242 (June 2011); Leading industries: 26.4% health care and social assistance; 17.8% retail trade; 12.5% accommodation & food services (2009); Farms: 332 totaling 370,113 acres (2007); Companies that employ 500 or more persons: 0 (2009); Companies that employ 100 to 499 persons: 2 (2009); Companies that employ less than 100 persons: 85 (2009); Black-owned businesses: n/a (2007); Hispanic-owned businesses: n/a (2007); Asian-owned businesses: n/a (2007); Women-owned businesses: n/a (2007); Retail sales per capita: $6,234 (2010). Single-family building permits issued: 0 (2010); Multi-family building permits issued: 0 (2010).
Income: Per capita income: $20,808 (2010); Median household income: $35,260 (2010); Average household income: $49,495 (2010); Percent of households with income of $100,000 or more: 9.5% (2010); Poverty rate: 18.8% (2009); Bankruptcy rate: 3.36% (2010).
Taxes: Total county taxes per capita: $760 (2007); County property taxes per capita: $665 (2007).
Education: Percent of population age 25 and over with: High school diploma (including GED) or higher: 75.8% (2010); Bachelor's degree or higher: 13.9% (2010); Master's degree or higher: 4.7% (2010).
Housing: Homeownership rate: 71.3% (2010); Median home value: $37,775 (2010); Median contract rent: $296 per month (2005-2009 5-year est.); Median year structure built: 1956 (2005-2009 5-year est.)
Health: Birth rate: 134.2 per 10,000 population (2009); Death rate: 90.3 per 10,000 population (2009); Age-adjusted cancer mortality rate: 142.5

(Unreliable) deaths per 100,000 population (2007); Number of physicians: 17.5 per 10,000 population (2008); Hospital beds: 109.1 per 10,000 population (2007); Hospital admissions: 858.0 per 10,000 population (2007).

Elections: 2008 Presidential election results: 23.4% Obama, 75.2% McCain, 0.0% Nader

Additional Information Contacts

Hardeman County Government . . . . (940) 663-2911

Quanah Chamber of Commerce . . . . (940) 663-2222
http://www.quanahnet.com

Hardeman County Communities

CHILLICOTHE (city). Covers a land area of 1.014 square miles and a water area of 0 square miles. Located at 34.25° N. Lat; 99.51° W. Long. Elevation is 1,401 feet.

History: Chillicothe developed around grain elevators, flour and cottonseed oil mills.

Population: 816 (1990); 798 (2000); 695 (2010); 642 (2015 projected); Race: 82.4% White, 4.9% Black, 0.0% Asian, 12.7% Other, 16.5% Hispanic of any race (2010); Density: 685.6 persons per square mile (2010); Average household size: 2.51 (2010); Median age: 40.3 (2010); Males per 100 females: 87.8 (2010); Marriage status: 18.9% never married, 61.1% now married, 7.2% widowed, 12.8% divorced (2005-2009 5-year est.); Foreign born: 4.0% (2005-2009 5-year est.); Ancestry (includes multiple ancestries): 18.0% American, 15.3% Irish, 14.1% English, 8.3% German, 1.7% Dutch (2005-2009 5-year est.).

Economy: Employment by occupation: 14.0% management, 14.2% professional, 30.2% services, 18.0% sales, 4.4% farming, 8.4% construction, 10.8% production (2005-2009 5-year est.).

Income: Per capita income: $18,601 (2010); Median household income: $36,653 (2010); Average household income: $47,356 (2010); Percent of households with income of $100,000 or more: 9.7% (2010); Poverty rate: 16.9% (2005-2009 5-year est.).

Taxes: Total city taxes per capita: $82 (2007); City property taxes per capita: $81 (2007).

Education: Percent of population age 25 and over with: High school diploma (including GED) or higher: 74.3% (2010); Bachelor's degree or higher: 11.4% (2010); Master's degree or higher: 5.8% (2010).

School District(s)

Chillicothe ISD (PK-12)
    2009-10 Enrollment: 185 . . . . (940) 852-5391

Housing: Homeownership rate: 74.0% (2010); Median home value: $31,096 (2010); Median contract rent: $340 per month (2005-2009 5-year est.); Median year structure built: 1946 (2005-2009 5-year est.).

Hospitals: Chillicothe Hospital (21 beds)

Safety: Violent crime rate: 29.6 per 10,000 population; Property crime rate: 74.0 per 10,000 population (2009).

Newspapers: Chillicothe Valley News (Community news; Circulation 684)

Transportation: Commute to work: 98.8% car, 0.0% public transportation, 0.0% walk, 0.0% work from home (2005-2009 5-year est.); Travel time to work: 36.0% less than 15 minutes, 48.8% 15 to 30 minutes, 11.9% 30 to 45 minutes, 3.2% 45 to 60 minutes, 0.0% 60 minutes or more (2005-2009 5-year est.)

QUANAH (city). County seat. Covers a land area of 3.486 square miles and a water area of 0 square miles. Located at 34.29° N. Lat; 99.74° W. Long. Elevation is 1,572 feet.

History: Quanah was founded in the 1880's and named for Quanah Parker, celebrated chief of the Comanches and son of Cynthia Ann Parker. When Quanah, then living as a farmer and tribal leader, was told that the town had been named for him, he gave it a blessing: "May the Great Spirit smile on you, town. May the rains fall in due season; and in the warmth of the sunshine after the rain, may the earth yield bountifully. May peace and contentment dwell with you and your children forever."

Population: 3,413 (1990); 3,022 (2000); 2,607 (2010); 2,407 (2015 projected); Race: 80.3% White, 6.2% Black, 0.3% Asian, 13.3% Other, 20.4% Hispanic of any race (2010); Density: 747.8 persons per square mile (2010); Average household size: 2.34 (2010); Median age: 42.8 (2010); Males per 100 females: 90.6 (2010); Marriage status: 16.1% never married, 65.4% now married, 8.8% widowed, 9.7% divorced (2005-2009 5-year est.); Foreign born: 5.4% (2005-2009 5-year est.); Ancestry (includes multiple ancestries): 21.2% German, 13.8% English, 13.0% American, 8.4% Irish, 2.9% Polish (2005-2009 5-year est.).

Economy: Single-family building permits issued: 0 (2010); Multi-family building permits issued: 0 (2010); Employment by occupation: 10.9% management, 21.5% professional, 25.3% services, 14.0% sales, 2.1% farming, 12.2% construction, 13.9% production (2005-2009 5-year est.).

Income: Per capita income: $19,773 (2010); Median household income: $32,821 (2010); Average household income: $46,427 (2010); Percent of households with income of $100,000 or more: 7.7% (2010); Poverty rate: 8.0% (2005-2009 5-year est.).

Taxes: Total city taxes per capita: $411 (2007); City property taxes per capita: $197 (2007).

Education: Percent of population age 25 and over with: High school diploma (including GED) or higher: 73.8% (2010); Bachelor's degree or higher: 12.3% (2010); Master's degree or higher: 3.5% (2010).

School District(s)

Quanah ISD (PK-12)
    2009-10 Enrollment: 556 . . . . (940) 663-2281

Housing: Homeownership rate: 70.3% (2010); Median home value: $35,489 (2010); Median contract rent: $265 per month (2005-2009 5-year est.); Median year structure built: 1959 (2005-2009 5-year est.).

Newspapers: Quanah Tribune-Chief (Local news; Circulation 1,500)

Transportation: Commute to work: 85.6% car, 0.0% public transportation, 0.0% walk, 3.3% work from home (2005-2009 5-year est.); Travel time to work: 58.9% less than 15 minutes, 14.5% 15 to 30 minutes, 13.4% 30 to 45 minutes, 9.7% 45 to 60 minutes, 3.6% 60 minutes or more (2005-2009 5-year est.)

Additional Information Contacts

Quanah Chamber of Commerce . . . . (940) 663-2222
http://www.quanahnet.com

Hardin County

Located in east Texas; bounded on the east by the Neches River; drained by tributaries of the Neches River. Covers a land area of 894.33 square miles, a water area of 3.04 square miles, and is located in the Central Time Zone at 30.32° N. Lat., 94.33° W. Long. The county was founded in 1858. County seat is Kountze.

Hardin County is part of the Beaumont-Port Arthur, TX Metropolitan Statistical Area. The entire metro area includes: Hardin County, TX; Jefferson County, TX; Orange County, TX

Population: 41,320 (1990); 48,073 (2000); 52,904 (2010); 55,155 (2015 projected); Race: 89.6% White, 7.0% Black, 0.6% Asian, 2.9% Other, 4.2% Hispanic of any race (2010); Density: 59.2 persons per square mile (2010); Average household size: 2.61 (2010); Median age: 36.5 (2010); Males per 100 females: 97.2 (2010).

Religion: Five largest groups: 40.3% Southern Baptist Convention, 5.8% Catholic Church, 5.3% The United Methodist Church, 2.4% Assemblies of God, 1.4% Churches of Christ (2000).

Economy: Unemployment rate: 10.2% (June 2011); Total civilian labor force: 28,059 (June 2011); Leading industries: 24.3% retail trade; 17.7% health care and social assistance; 15.9% construction (2009); Farms: 699 totaling 91,189 acres (2007); Companies that employ 500 or more persons: 1 (2009); Companies that employ 100 to 499 persons: 9 (2009); Companies that employ less than 100 persons: 767 (2009); Black-owned businesses: n/a (2007); Hispanic-owned businesses: n/a (2007); Asian-owned businesses: n/a (2007); Women-owned businesses: n/a (2007); Retail sales per capita: $12,459 (2010). Single-family building permits issued: 87 (2010); Multi-family building permits issued: 0 (2010).

Income: Per capita income: $24,855 (2010); Median household income: $51,536 (2010); Average household income: $65,164 (2010); Percent of households with income of $100,000 or more: 18.5% (2010); Poverty rate: 11.3% (2009); Bankruptcy rate: 1.80% (2010).

Taxes: Total county taxes per capita: $230 (2007); County property taxes per capita: $205 (2007).

Education: Percent of population age 25 and over with: High school diploma (including GED) or higher: 84.4% (2010); Bachelor's degree or higher: 15.6% (2010); Master's degree or higher: 3.3% (2010).

Housing: Homeownership rate: 77.6% (2010); Median home value: $88,908 (2010); Median contract rent: $465 per month (2005-2009 5-year est.); Median year structure built: 1982 (2005-2009 5-year est.)

Health: Birth rate: 131.8 per 10,000 population (2009); Death rate: 95.3 per 10,000 population (2009); Age-adjusted cancer mortality rate: 202.2 deaths per 100,000 population (2007); Number of physicians: 4.4 per 10,000 population (2008); Hospital beds: 0.0 per 10,000 population (2007); Hospital admissions: 0.0 per 10,000 population (2007).

Elections: 2008 Presidential election results: 19.0% Obama, 80.2% McCain, 0.0% Nader
National and State Parks: Big Thicket National Preserve
Additional Information Contacts
Hardin County Government . . . . (409) 246-5120
  http://www.co.hardin.tx.us/ips/cms
City of Lumberton . . . . (409) 755-3700
  http://www.cityoflumberton.com
City of Silsbee . . . . (409) 385-2863
  http://www.cityofsilsbee.com
Kountze Chamber of Commerce . . . . (409) 246-3413
  http://www.kountzechamber.org
Lumberton Chamber of Commerce . . . . (409) 755-0554
  http://www.lumbertoncoc.com
Silsbee Chamber of Commerce . . . . (409) 385-5562
  http://www.bigthicketdirectory.com/pages/silsbeechamber.html
Sour Lake Chamber of Commerce . . . . (409) 287-3828

Hardin County Communities

BATSON (unincorporated postal area, zip code 77519). Covers a land area of 64.890 square miles and a water area of 0.109 square miles. Located at 30.25° N. Lat; 94.60° W. Long. Elevation is 82 feet.
Population: 1,298 (2000); Race: 97.3% White, 0.0% Black, 0.0% Asian, 2.7% Other, 1.9% Hispanic of any race (2000); Density: 20.0 persons per square mile (2000); Age: 24.8% under 18, 13.6% over 64 (2000); Marriage status: 16.6% never married, 69.0% now married, 3.8% widowed, 10.6% divorced (2000); Foreign born: 0.0% (2000); Ancestry (includes multiple ancestries): 37.4% American, 9.8% Irish, 7.3% German, 6.9% French (2000).
Economy: Employment by occupation: 10.6% management, 18.2% professional, 10.1% services, 21.4% sales, 0.0% farming, 15.1% construction, 24.7% production (2000).
Income: Per capita income: $17,323 (2000); Median household income: $31,538 (2000); Poverty rate: 179.1% (2000).
Education: Percent of population age 25 and over with: High school diploma (including GED) or higher: 73.1% (2000); Bachelor's degree or higher: 12.0% (2000).
Housing: Homeownership rate: 89.2% (2000); Median home value: $50,200 (2000); Median contract rent: $725 per month (2000); Median year structure built: 1980 (2000).
Transportation: Commute to work: 96.4% car, 0.0% public transportation, 1.8% walk, 0.0% work from home (2000); Travel time to work: 24.7% less than 15 minutes, 21.8% 15 to 30 minutes, 20.6% 30 to 45 minutes, 6.7% 45 to 60 minutes, 26.2% 60 minutes or more (2000)

KOUNTZE (city). County seat. Covers a land area of 3.970 square miles and a water area of 0 square miles. Located at 30.37° N. Lat; 94.31° W. Long. Elevation is 85 feet.
History: Kountze developed around a sawmill. The village was located near the area known as the Big Thicket, a thickly forested section of hardwood and pine trees with undergrowth forming an almost impenetrable jungle. The once abundant wildlife of the Big Thicket began to disappear when lumber and oil companies set up operations.
Population: 2,137 (1990); 2,115 (2000); 2,163 (2010); 2,198 (2015 projected); Race: 71.7% White, 24.0% Black, 1.1% Asian, 3.2% Other, 4.4% Hispanic of any race (2010); Density: 544.8 persons per square mile (2010); Average household size: 2.59 (2010); Median age: 35.3 (2010); Males per 100 females: 97.0 (2010); Marriage status: 24.7% never married, 51.2% now married, 11.1% widowed, 13.0% divorced (2005-2009 5-year est.); Foreign born: 3.0% (2005-2009 5-year est.); Ancestry (includes multiple ancestries): 15.9% Irish, 10.9% German, 9.4% French, 8.0% American, 5.7% English (2005-2009 5-year est.).
Economy: Single-family building permits issued: 2 (2010); Multi-family building permits issued: 0 (2010); Employment by occupation: 11.2% management, 14.1% professional, 24.9% services, 20.3% sales, 2.0% farming, 10.3% construction, 17.1% production (2005-2009 5-year est.).
Income: Per capita income: $20,997 (2010); Median household income: $41,838 (2010); Average household income: $55,806 (2010); Percent of households with income of $100,000 or more: 11.8% (2010); Poverty rate: 22.1% (2005-2009 5-year est.).
Taxes: Total city taxes per capita: $31 (2007); City property taxes per capita: $0 (2007).

Education: Percent of population age 25 and over with: High school diploma (including GED) or higher: 78.6% (2010); Bachelor's degree or higher: 13.8% (2010); Master's degree or higher: 3.5% (2010).
School District(s)
Hardin-Jefferson ISD (PK-12)
  2009-10 Enrollment: 2,014 . . . . (409) 981-6400
Kountze ISD (PK-12)
  2009-10 Enrollment: 1,373 . . . . (409) 246-3352
West Hardin County CISD (PK-12)
  2009-10 Enrollment: 597 . . . . (936) 274-5061
Housing: Homeownership rate: 66.4% (2010); Median home value: $58,785 (2010); Median contract rent: $452 per month (2005-2009 5-year est.); Median year structure built: 1973 (2005-2009 5-year est.).
Safety: Violent crime rate: 73.5 per 10,000 population; Property crime rate: 271.0 per 10,000 population (2009).
Newspapers: Kountze Journal (Local news; Circulation 2,000)
Transportation: Commute to work: 94.0% car, 0.0% public transportation, 2.3% walk, 0.4% work from home (2005-2009 5-year est.); Travel time to work: 35.6% less than 15 minutes, 23.5% 15 to 30 minutes, 14.9% 30 to 45 minutes, 9.8% 45 to 60 minutes, 16.3% 60 minutes or more (2005-2009 5-year est.)
Additional Information Contacts
Kountze Chamber of Commerce . . . . (409) 246-3413
  http://www.kountzechamber.org

LUMBERTON (city). Aka Ariola. Covers a land area of 9.403 square miles and a water area of 0 square miles. Located at 30.26° N. Lat; 94.20° W. Long. Elevation is 59 feet.
Population: 6,943 (1990); 8,731 (2000); 10,234 (2010); 10,967 (2015 projected); Race: 96.4% White, 0.2% Black, 0.6% Asian, 2.8% Other, 4.9% Hispanic of any race (2010); Density: 1,088.4 persons per square mile (2010); Average household size: 2.63 (2010); Median age: 35.4 (2010); Males per 100 females: 94.7 (2010); Marriage status: 26.0% never married, 57.3% now married, 4.2% widowed, 12.5% divorced (2005-2009 5-year est.); Foreign born: 0.8% (2005-2009 5-year est.); Ancestry (includes multiple ancestries): 18.8% Irish, 14.8% German, 11.5% American, 9.7% French, 8.4% English (2005-2009 5-year est.).
Economy: Single-family building permits issued: 55 (2010); Multi-family building permits issued: 0 (2010); Employment by occupation: 7.4% management, 24.1% professional, 14.3% services, 31.0% sales, 0.7% farming, 9.5% construction, 12.9% production (2005-2009 5-year est.).
Income: Per capita income: $25,168 (2010); Median household income: $54,817 (2010); Average household income: $66,253 (2010); Percent of households with income of $100,000 or more: 19.4% (2010); Poverty rate: 9.5% (2005-2009 5-year est.).
Taxes: Total city taxes per capita: $284 (2007); City property taxes per capita: $0 (2007).
Education: Percent of population age 25 and over with: High school diploma (including GED) or higher: 91.5% (2010); Bachelor's degree or higher: 19.3% (2010); Master's degree or higher: 3.3% (2010).
School District(s)
Lumberton ISD (PK-12)
  2009-10 Enrollment: 3,900 . . . . (409) 923-7580
Housing: Homeownership rate: 72.9% (2010); Median home value: $119,559 (2010); Median contract rent: $568 per month (2005-2009 5-year est.); Median year structure built: 1987 (2005-2009 5-year est.).
Safety: Violent crime rate: 11.4 per 10,000 population; Property crime rate: 248.8 per 10,000 population (2009).
Newspapers: Hardin County News (Community news; Circulation 26,000)
Transportation: Commute to work: 94.6% car, 0.0% public transportation, 0.9% walk, 2.2% work from home (2005-2009 5-year est.); Travel time to work: 23.2% less than 15 minutes, 40.0% 15 to 30 minutes, 24.8% 30 to 45 minutes, 7.3% 45 to 60 minutes, 4.7% 60 minutes or more (2005-2009 5-year est.)
Additional Information Contacts
City of Lumberton . . . . (409) 755-3700
  http://www.cityoflumberton.com
Lumberton Chamber of Commerce . . . . (409) 755-0554
  http://www.lumbertoncoc.com

PINEWOOD ESTATES (CDP). Covers a land area of 13.225 square miles and a water area of 0 square miles. Located at 30.15° N. Lat; 94.32° W. Long. Elevation is 26 feet.
Population: 1,168 (1990); 1,633 (2000); 1,861 (2010); 1,983 (2015 projected); Race: 96.0% White, 0.4% Black, 0.8% Asian, 2.8% Other, 5.6%

Hispanic of any race (2010); Density: 140.7 persons per square mile (2010); Average household size: 2.96 (2010); Median age: 40.3 (2010); Males per 100 females: 101.4 (2010); Marriage status: 22.7% never married, 70.6% now married, 2.5% widowed, 4.3% divorced (2005-2009 5-year est.); Foreign born: 0.7% (2005-2009 5-year est.); Ancestry (includes multiple ancestries): 18.7% Irish, 18.5% English, 14.2% German, 11.4% French, 5.2% Scottish (2005-2009 5-year est.).
Economy: Employment by occupation: 12.4% management, 35.3% professional, 12.3% services, 20.8% sales, 0.0% farming, 8.2% construction, 10.9% production (2005-2009 5-year est.).
Income: Per capita income: $35,024 (2010); Median household income: $87,500 (2010); Average household income: $102,923 (2010); Percent of households with income of $100,000 or more: 43.2% (2010); Poverty rate: 0.4% (2005-2009 5-year est.).
Education: Percent of population age 25 and over with: High school diploma (including GED) or higher: 95.9% (2010); Bachelor's degree or higher: 39.6% (2010); Master's degree or higher: 8.6% (2010).
Housing: Homeownership rate: 92.7% (2010); Median home value: $153,320 (2010); Median contract rent: $1,302 per month (2005-2009 5-year est.); Median year structure built: 1982 (2005-2009 5-year est.).
Transportation: Commute to work: 95.4% car, 0.0% public transportation, 0.0% walk, 1.3% work from home (2005-2009 5-year est.); Travel time to work: 10.5% less than 15 minutes, 58.3% 15 to 30 minutes, 16.8% 30 to 45 minutes, 7.1% 45 to 60 minutes, 7.4% 60 minutes or more (2005-2009 5-year est.)

ROSE HILL ACRES (city).
Covers a land area of 0.405 square miles and a water area of 0 square miles. Located at 30.19° N. Lat; 94.19° W. Long. Elevation is 23 feet.
Population: 468 (1990); 480 (2000); 462 (2010); 474 (2015 projected); Race: 97.0% White, 0.0% Black, 0.6% Asian, 2.4% Other, 7.6% Hispanic of any race (2010); Density: 1,141.4 persons per square mile (2010); Average household size: 2.75 (2010); Median age: 37.5 (2010); Males per 100 females: 100.0 (2010); Marriage status: 19.5% never married, 59.0% now married, 7.2% widowed, 14.2% divorced (2005-2009 5-year est.); Foreign born: 2.4% (2005-2009 5-year est.); Ancestry (includes multiple ancestries): 20.0% American, 16.7% Irish, 16.5% French, 15.7% German, 7.9% English (2005-2009 5-year est.).
Economy: Single-family building permits issued: 1 (2010); Multi-family building permits issued: 0 (2010); Employment by occupation: 5.8% management, 19.1% professional, 14.7% services, 24.4% sales, 0.0% farming, 18.2% construction, 17.8% production (2005-2009 5-year est.).
Income: Per capita income: $28,018 (2010); Median household income: $68,333 (2010); Average household income: $78,110 (2010); Percent of households with income of $100,000 or more: 25.6% (2010); Poverty rate: 7.8% (2005-2009 5-year est.).
Taxes: Total city taxes per capita: $66 (2007); City property taxes per capita: $20 (2007).
Education: Percent of population age 25 and over with: High school diploma (including GED) or higher: 90.3% (2010); Bachelor's degree or higher: 21.3% (2010); Master's degree or higher: 1.9% (2010).
Housing: Homeownership rate: 89.3% (2010); Median home value: $111,000 (2010); Median contract rent: $1,025 per month (2005-2009 5-year est.); Median year structure built: 1973 (2005-2009 5-year est.).
Transportation: Commute to work: 92.2% car, 0.0% public transportation, 3.7% walk, 4.1% work from home (2005-2009 5-year est.); Travel time to work: 17.1% less than 15 minutes, 44.8% 15 to 30 minutes, 25.7% 30 to 45 minutes, 4.3% 45 to 60 minutes, 8.1% 60 minutes or more (2005-2009 5-year est.)

SARATOGA (unincorporated postal area, zip code 77585).
Covers a land area of 100.808 square miles and a water area of 0.029 square miles. Located at 30.30° N. Lat; 94.52° W. Long. Elevation is 89 feet.
History: Big Thicket Museum is here. Settled 1850s; oil discovered 1901.
Population: 946 (2000); Race: 93.2% White, 0.0% Black, 5.5% Asian, 1.3% Other, 0.0% Hispanic of any race (2000); Density: 9.4 persons per square mile (2000); Age: 21.4% under 18, 16.8% over 64 (2000); Marriage status: 19.7% never married, 61.9% now married, 7.3% widowed, 11.1% divorced (2000); Foreign born: 5.5% (2000); Ancestry (includes multiple ancestries): 36.9% American, 5.5% Irish, 5.4% German, 3.8% English (2000).
Economy: Employment by occupation: 6.6% management, 10.9% professional, 16.5% services, 17.3% sales, 0.0% farming, 23.9% construction, 24.9% production (2000).

Income: Per capita income: $14,558 (2000); Median household income: $31,856 (2000); Poverty rate: 179.1% (2000).
Education: Percent of population age 25 and over with: High school diploma (including GED) or higher: 63.4% (2000); Bachelor's degree or higher: 6.9% (2000).
School District(s)
West Hardin County CISD (PK-12)
    2009-10 Enrollment: 597 . . . . (936) 274-5061
Housing: Homeownership rate: 94.5% (2000); Median home value: $40,000 (2000); Median contract rent: $375 per month (2000); Median year structure built: 1978 (2000).
Transportation: Commute to work: 96.1% car, 0.0% public transportation, 3.9% walk, 0.0% work from home (2000); Travel time to work: 17.9% less than 15 minutes, 24.4% 15 to 30 minutes, 19.4% 30 to 45 minutes, 14.2% 45 to 60 minutes, 24.1% 60 minutes or more (2000)

SILSBEE (city).
Covers a land area of 7.530 square miles and a water area of 0 square miles. Located at 30.34° N. Lat; 94.18° W. Long. Elevation is 82 feet.
History: Silsbee was founded in 1892 around the logging camp of John H. Kirby. The town was named for a railway official.
Population: 6,654 (1990); 6,393 (2000); 6,771 (2010); 6,919 (2015 projected); Race: 62.6% White, 33.7% Black, 0.9% Asian, 2.7% Other, 3.8% Hispanic of any race (2010); Density: 899.2 persons per square mile (2010); Average household size: 2.50 (2010); Median age: 37.1 (2010); Males per 100 females: 90.3 (2010); Marriage status: 26.0% never married, 50.3% now married, 12.0% widowed, 11.7% divorced (2005-2009 5-year est.); Foreign born: 0.9% (2005-2009 5-year est.); Ancestry (includes multiple ancestries): 10.8% Irish, 10.8% German, 7.8% French, 7.5% American, 6.5% English (2005-2009 5-year est.).
Economy: Single-family building permits issued: 29 (2010); Multi-family building permits issued: 0 (2010); Employment by occupation: 10.1% management, 14.5% professional, 22.3% services, 17.1% sales, 1.8% farming, 14.1% construction, 20.1% production (2005-2009 5-year est.).
Income: Per capita income: $24,727 (2010); Median household income: $46,800 (2010); Average household income: $62,794 (2010); Percent of households with income of $100,000 or more: 16.7% (2010); Poverty rate: 16.7% (2005-2009 5-year est.).
Taxes: Total city taxes per capita: $535 (2007); City property taxes per capita: $96 (2007).
Education: Percent of population age 25 and over with: High school diploma (including GED) or higher: 81.6% (2010); Bachelor's degree or higher: 18.5% (2010); Master's degree or higher: 4.3% (2010).
School District(s)
Silsbee ISD (PK-12)
    2009-10 Enrollment: 3,000 . . . . (409) 980-7800
Vocational/Technical School(s)
Southeast Texas Career Institute (Private, For-profit)
    Fall 2009 Enrollment: 114 . . . . (409) 386-2020
    2010-11 Tuition: $8,000
Housing: Homeownership rate: 62.7% (2010); Median home value: $82,996 (2010); Median contract rent: $415 per month (2005-2009 5-year est.); Median year structure built: 1970 (2005-2009 5-year est.).
Safety: Violent crime rate: 40.4 per 10,000 population; Property crime rate: 231.1 per 10,000 population (2009).
Newspapers: Silsbee Bee (Local news; Circulation 6,460)
Transportation: Commute to work: 95.5% car, 0.0% public transportation, 2.0% walk, 0.2% work from home (2005-2009 5-year est.); Travel time to work: 44.2% less than 15 minutes, 20.9% 15 to 30 minutes, 19.6% 30 to 45 minutes, 11.6% 45 to 60 minutes, 3.6% 60 minutes or more (2005-2009 5-year est.)
Additional Information Contacts
City of Silsbee . . . . (409) 385-2863
    http://www.cityofsilsbee.com
Silsbee Chamber of Commerce . . . . (409) 385-5562
    http://www.bigthicketdirectory.com/pages/silsbeechamber.html

SOUR LAKE (city).
Aka Sourlake. Covers a land area of 1.729 square miles and a water area of 0.011 square miles. Located at 30.13° N. Lat; 94.40° W. Long. Elevation is 49 feet.
History: Settled 1836, incorporated 1939.
Population: 1,561 (1990); 1,667 (2000); 1,799 (2010); 1,875 (2015 projected); Race: 92.6% White, 2.9% Black, 1.3% Asian, 3.2% Other, 3.1% Hispanic of any race (2010); Density: 1,040.3 persons per square mile (2010); Average household size: 2.52 (2010); Median age: 37.0 (2010);

Males per 100 females: 95.3 (2010); Marriage status: 20.6% never married, 49.3% now married, 13.1% widowed, 17.0% divorced (2005-2009 5-year est.); Foreign born: 0.6% (2005-2009 5-year est.); Ancestry (includes multiple ancestries): 14.3% American, 14.0% Irish, 11.4% German, 9.9% English, 5.4% French (2005-2009 5-year est.).

Economy: Employment by occupation: 3.6% management, 10.4% professional, 9.6% services, 31.3% sales, 0.0% farming, 25.6% construction, 19.5% production (2005-2009 5-year est.).

Income: Per capita income: $23,134 (2010); Median household income: $42,992 (2010); Average household income: $58,186 (2010); Percent of households with income of $100,000 or more: 14.1% (2010); Poverty rate: 11.4% (2005-2009 5-year est.).

Taxes: Total city taxes per capita: $285 (2007); City property taxes per capita: $112 (2007).

Education: Percent of population age 25 and over with: High school diploma (including GED) or higher: 83.9% (2010); Bachelor's degree or higher: 13.6% (2010); Master's degree or higher: 4.0% (2010).

School District(s)

Hardin-Jefferson ISD (PK-12)
    2009-10 Enrollment: 2,014 . . . . (409) 981-6400

Housing: Homeownership rate: 73.0% (2010); Median home value: $65,000 (2010); Median contract rent: $386 per month (2005-2009 5-year est.); Median year structure built: 1966 (2005-2009 5-year est.).

Safety: Violent crime rate: 11.5 per 10,000 population; Property crime rate: 275.2 per 10,000 population (2009).

Transportation: Commute to work: 93.7% car, 0.0% public transportation, 3.2% walk, 2.6% work from home (2005-2009 5-year est.); Travel time to work: 35.8% less than 15 minutes, 12.9% 15 to 30 minutes, 37.5% 30 to 45 minutes, 5.0% 45 to 60 minutes, 8.7% 60 minutes or more (2005-2009 5-year est.)

Additional Information Contacts

Sour Lake Chamber of Commerce . . . . (409) 287-3828

Harris County

Located in south Texas, on the Gulf Coast plains; bounded on the southeast by Galveston Bay; drained by the San Jacinto River; includes part of Sam Houston National Forest. Covers a land area of 1,728.83 square miles, a water area of 48.87 square miles, and is located in the Central Time Zone at 29.78° N. Lat., 95.36° W. Long. The county was founded in 1836. County seat is Houston.

Harris County is part of the Houston-Sugar Land-Baytown, TX Metropolitan Statistical Area. The entire metro area includes: Austin County, TX; Brazoria County, TX; Chambers County, TX; Fort Bend County, TX; Galveston County, TX; Harris County, TX; Liberty County, TX; Montgomery County, TX; San Jacinto County, TX; Waller County, TX

Weather Station: Baytown   Elevation: 34 feet

	Jan	Feb	Mar	Apr	May	Jun	Jul	Aug	Sep	Oct	Nov	Dec
High	63	66	72	78	84	89	92	93	88	81	72	64
Low	43	47	53	60	68	74	76	75	70	61	52	44
Precip	4.7	3.9	3.7	3.7	5.5	7.1	4.8	4.9	5.7	6.1	5.2	4.7
Snow	0.0	0.0	0.0	0.0	0.0	0.0	0.0	0.0	0.0	0.0	0.0	0.0

High and Low temperatures in degrees Fahrenheit; Precipitation and Snow in inches

Weather Station: Houston Bush Intercontinental   Elevation: 95 feet

	Jan	Feb	Mar	Apr	May	Jun	Jul	Aug	Sep	Oct	Nov	Dec
High	63	66	73	79	86	91	94	94	90	82	72	64
Low	43	46	52	59	67	73	74	74	69	60	51	44
Precip	3.5	3.2	3.5	3.3	5.2	5.8	3.4	3.8	4.2	5.8	4.3	3.7
Snow	0.1	0.1	tr	tr	tr	tr	0.0	0.0	0.0	0.0	0.0	0.1

High and Low temperatures in degrees Fahrenheit; Precipitation and Snow in inches

Weather Station: Houston William P Hobby Arpt   Elevation: 49 feet

	Jan	Feb	Mar	Apr	May	Jun	Jul	Aug	Sep	Oct	Nov	Dec
High	63	66	72	79	85	90	92	93	88	81	72	64
Low	45	48	54	61	69	74	75	76	72	63	54	47
Precip	4.0	3.2	3.3	3.3	4.9	7.0	4.3	4.8	4.9	5.8	4.2	3.8
Snow	na	na	na	na	na	na	na	na	na	na	na	na

High and Low temperatures in degrees Fahrenheit; Precipitation and Snow in inches

Weather Station: Marshall   Elevation: 352 feet

	Jan	Feb	Mar	Apr	May	Jun	Jul	Aug	Sep	Oct	Nov	Dec
High	56	60	67	75	82	89	93	93	87	77	67	57
Low	35	39	46	53	62	69	72	72	65	53	45	37
Precip	3.8	4.3	4.5	3.8	5.0	5.1	3.2	2.6	3.4	4.9	4.6	5.0
Snow	0.3	0.1	0.1	0.0	0.0	0.0	0.0	0.0	0.0	0.0	0.0	tr

High and Low temperatures in degrees Fahrenheit; Precipitation and Snow in inches

Population: 2,818,199 (1990); 3,400,578 (2000); 4,078,460 (2010); 4,400,897 (2015 projected); Race: 55.1% White, 18.1% Black, 5.3% Asian, 21.5% Other, 40.0% Hispanic of any race (2010); Density: 2,359.1 persons per square mile (2010); Average household size: 2.85 (2010); Median age: 33.3 (2010); Males per 100 females: 100.7 (2010).

Religion: Five largest groups: 18.2% Catholic Church, 14.3% Southern Baptist Convention, 5.0% The United Methodist Church, 1.4% Muslim Estimate, 1.3% Independent, Charismatic Churches (2000).

Economy: Unemployment rate: 9.0% (June 2011); Total civilian labor force: 2,048,651 (June 2011); Leading industries: 11.4% health care and social assistance; 10.1% retail trade; 9.1% professional, scientific & technical services (2009); Farms: 2,210 totaling 259,039 acres (2007); Companies that employ 500 or more persons: 346 (2009); Companies that employ 100 to 499 persons: 2,703 (2009); Companies that employ less than 100 persons: 88,033 (2009); Black-owned businesses: 47,278 (2007); Hispanic-owned businesses: 85,170 (2007); Asian-owned businesses: 36,718 (2007); Women-owned businesses: 108,132 (2007); Retail sales per capita: $14,307 (2010). Single-family building permits issued: 11,057 (2010); Multi-family building permits issued: 3,982 (2010).

Income: Per capita income: $25,831 (2010); Median household income: $53,157 (2010); Average household income: $73,906 (2010); Percent of households with income of $100,000 or more: 21.9% (2010); Poverty rate: 17.1% (2009); Bankruptcy rate: 2.05% (2010).

Taxes: Total county taxes per capita: $383 (2007); County property taxes per capita: $357 (2007).

Education: Percent of population age 25 and over with: High school diploma (including GED) or higher: 77.3% (2010); Bachelor's degree or higher: 27.4% (2010); Master's degree or higher: 9.3% (2010).

Housing: Homeownership rate: 58.3% (2010); Median home value: $130,827 (2010); Median contract rent: $639 per month (2005-2009 5-year est.); Median year structure built: 1979 (2005-2009 5-year est.)

Health: Birth rate: 171.2 per 10,000 population (2009); Death rate: 54.2 per 10,000 population (2009); Age-adjusted cancer mortality rate: 174.9 deaths per 100,000 population (2007); Number of physicians: 29.3 per 10,000 population (2008); Hospital beds: 36.1 per 10,000 population (2007); Hospital admissions: 1,351.0 per 10,000 population (2007).

Environment: Air Quality Index: 41.8% good, 51.3% moderate, 6.2% unhealthy for sensitive individuals, 0.7% unhealthy (percent of days in 2008)

Elections: 2008 Presidential election results: 50.4% Obama, 48.8% McCain, 0.1% Nader

National and State Parks: San Jacinto State Park

Additional Information Contacts

Harris County Government . . . . (281) 755-4000
    http://www.co.harris.tx.us
Baytown Chamber of Commerce. (281) 422-8359
    http://www.baytownchamber.com
Caribbean Chamber of Commerce . . . . (281) 652-8404
    http://www.caribbeanchamber.org
City of Baytown . . . . (281) 422-8281
    http://www.baytown.org
City of Bellaire . . . . (713) 662-8222
    http://www.ci.bellaire.tx.us
City of Bunker Hill Village. . . . . (713) 467-9762
    http://www.bunkerhill.net
City of Deer Park . . . . (281) 478-7248
    http://www.deerparktx.gov
City of Galena Park . . . . (713) 672-2556
    http://www.cityofgalenapark-tx.gov
City of Hilshire Village . . . . (713) 973-1779
    http://hilshirevillagetexas.com
City of Houston . . . . (713) 837-0311
    http://www.houstontx.gov
City of Humble . . . . (281) 446-3061
    http://www.cityofhumble.org
City of Hunters Creek Village. . . . . (713) 465-2150
    http://cityofhunterscreek.com

City of Jacinto City	(713) 674-8424
http://www.jacintocity-tx.gov	
City of Jersey Village	(713) 466-2102
http://www.jerseyvillage.info	
City of Katy	(281) 391-4800
http://ci.katy.tx.us	
City of La Porte	(281) 471-5020
http://www.ci.la-porte.tx.us	
City of Nassau Bay	(281) 333-4211
http://www.nassaubay.com	
City of Pasadena	(713) 477-1511
http://www.ci.pasadena.tx.us	
City of Seabrook	(281) 291-5600
http://www.ci.seabrook.tx.us	
City of South Houston	(713) 947-7700
http://www.southhoustontx.org	
City of Southside Place	(713) 668-2341
http://www.ci.southside-place.tx.us	
City of Spring Valley	(713) 465-8308
http://www.springvalleytx.com	
City of Tomball	(281) 351-5484
http://www.ci.tomball.tx.us	
City of Webster	(281) 332-1826
http://www.cityofwebster.com	
City of West University Place	(713) 668-4441
http://www.westu.org	
Clear Lake Area Chamber of Commerce	(281) 488-7676
http://www.clearlakearea.com	
Community Chamber of Commerce	(281) 348-1531
http://www.communitychamber.com	
Crosby Huffman Chamber of Commerce	(281) 328-6984
http://www.crosbyhuffmancc.org	
Deer Park Chamber of Commerce	(281) 479-1559
http://www.deerpark.org	
French American Chamber of Commerce	(713) 960-0575
http://www.facchouston.com	
Greater Highlands Chamber of Commerce	(281) 426-7227
http://allabouthighlands.com	
Greater Houston Partnership	(713) 844-3600
http://www.houston.org	
Greater Tomball Area Chamber of Commerce	(281) 351-7222
http://www.tomballchamber.org	
Houston Citizens Chamber of Commerce	(713) 522-9745
http://www.hccoc.org	
Houston East End Chamber of Commerce	(713) 926-3305
http://www.eecoc.org	
Houston Hispanic Chamber of Commerce	(713) 644-7070
http://www.houstonhispanicchamber.com	
Houston Intercontinenal Chamber of Commerce	(281) 260-3163
http://www.nhgcc.org	
Houston Metropolitan Chamber of Commerce	(713) 666-1521
http://www.gswhcc.org	
Houston NW Chamber of Commerce	(281) 440-4160
http://www.hnwcc.com	
Interamerican Chamber of Commerce	(713) 975-6171
Italy-America Chamber of Commerce	(713) 626-9303
http://www.iacctexas.com	
Katy Area Chamber of Commerce	(281) 391-5289
http://www.katychamber.com	
La Porte-Bayshore Chamber of Commerce	(281) 471-1123
http://www.laportechamber.org	
Lake Houston Area Chamber of Commerce	(281) 446-2128
http://www.humbleareachamber.org	
National Acres Home Chamber of Commerce	(281) 820-2620
http://www.nahc-of-c.org/home.htm	
North Channel Chamber of Commerce	(713) 450-3600
http://www.northchannelarea.com	
Pasadena Chamber of Commerce	(281) 487-7871
http://www.pasadenachamber.org	
South Asian Chamber of Commerce	(713) 570-0199
South Houston Chamber of Commerce	(713) 943-0244
http://www.southhoustonchamber.org	
Swedish American Chamber of Commerce	(713) 914-0015
http://www.sacctx.com	
Texas-Israel Chamber of Commerce	(214) 576-9639
http://www.texasisrael.org	

Harris County Communities

ALDINE (CDP). Covers a land area of 8.095 square miles and a water area of 0 square miles. Located at 29.91° N. Lat; 95.38° W. Long. Elevation is 79 feet.
Population: 11,133 (1990); 13,979 (2000); 13,799 (2010); 14,111 (2015 projected); Race: 50.7% White, 6.5% Black, 2.7% Asian, 40.0% Other, 71.7% Hispanic of any race (2010); Density: 1,704.7 persons per square mile (2010); Average household size: 3.58 (2010); Median age: 30.2 (2010); Males per 100 females: 107.3 (2010); Marriage status: 31.7% never married, 57.0% now married, 3.0% widowed, 8.3% divorced (2005-2009 5-year est.); Foreign born: 35.5% (2005-2009 5-year est.); Ancestry (includes multiple ancestries): 3.9% American, 3.6% German, 3.0% Irish, 1.9% English, 0.9% Italian (2005-2009 5-year est.).
Economy: Employment by occupation: 5.1% management, 2.8% professional, 16.1% services, 24.6% sales, 0.0% farming, 24.8% construction, 26.6% production (2005-2009 5-year est.).
Income: Per capita income: $13,536 (2010); Median household income: $39,557 (2010); Average household income: $48,384 (2010); Percent of households with income of $100,000 or more: 7.3% (2010); Poverty rate: 23.8% (2005-2009 5-year est.).
Education: Percent of population age 25 and over with: High school diploma (including GED) or higher: 52.2% (2010); Bachelor's degree or higher: 5.3% (2010); Master's degree or higher: 1.9% (2010).
Housing: Homeownership rate: 73.2% (2010); Median home value: $81,353 (2010); Median contract rent: $515 per month (2005-2009 5-year est.); Median year structure built: 1976 (2005-2009 5-year est.).
Transportation: Commute to work: 92.3% car, 0.0% public transportation, 2.2% walk, 3.4% work from home (2005-2009 5-year est.); Travel time to work: 22.5% less than 15 minutes, 32.5% 15 to 30 minutes, 31.7% 30 to 45 minutes, 7.8% 45 to 60 minutes, 5.5% 60 minutes or more (2005-2009 5-year est.)

ATASCOCITA (CDP). Covers a land area of 27.584 square miles and a water area of 0.007 square miles. Located at 29.99° N. Lat; 95.18° W. Long. Elevation is 72 feet.
Population: 20,455 (1990); 35,757 (2000); 57,800 (2010); 64,367 (2015 projected); Race: 72.2% White, 14.7% Black, 2.5% Asian, 10.6% Other, 17.6% Hispanic of any race (2010); Density: 2,095.4 persons per square mile (2010); Average household size: 3.02 (2010); Median age: 34.5 (2010); Males per 100 females: 106.7 (2010); Marriage status: 25.3% never married, 64.5% now married, 2.4% widowed, 7.8% divorced (2005-2009 5-year est.); Foreign born: 9.6% (2005-2009 5-year est.); Ancestry (includes multiple ancestries): 12.3% German, 10.2% Irish, 9.9% American, 7.5% English, 4.3% French (2005-2009 5-year est.).
Economy: Employment by occupation: 19.7% management, 23.4% professional, 13.9% services, 25.9% sales, 0.2% farming, 6.8% construction, 10.1% production (2005-2009 5-year est.).
Income: Per capita income: $32,456 (2010); Median household income: $88,474 (2010); Average household income: $100,672 (2010); Percent of households with income of $100,000 or more: 40.0% (2010); Poverty rate: 4.1% (2005-2009 5-year est.).
Education: Percent of population age 25 and over with: High school diploma (including GED) or higher: 92.4% (2010); Bachelor's degree or higher: 32.2% (2010); Master's degree or higher: 9.8% (2010).
Housing: Homeownership rate: 87.3% (2010); Median home value: $165,795 (2010); Median contract rent: $931 per month (2005-2009 5-year est.); Median year structure built: 1996 (2005-2009 5-year est.).
Transportation: Commute to work: 93.9% car, 1.0% public transportation, 0.2% walk, 3.4% work from home (2005-2009 5-year est.); Travel time to work: 13.5% less than 15 minutes, 29.2% 15 to 30 minutes, 27.5% 30 to 45 minutes, 16.9% 45 to 60 minutes, 12.8% 60 minutes or more (2005-2009 5-year est.)

BARRETT (CDP). Covers a land area of 6.486 square miles and a water area of 0.058 square miles. Located at 29.87° N. Lat; 95.06° W. Long. Elevation is 43 feet.
Population: 3,139 (1990); 2,872 (2000); 3,274 (2010); 3,516 (2015 projected); Race: 27.9% White, 62.1% Black, 0.0% Asian, 9.9% Other, 14.0% Hispanic of any race (2010); Density: 504.8 persons per square mile (2010); Average household size: 2.96 (2010); Median age: 35.6 (2010); Males per 100 females: 97.8 (2010); Marriage status: 34.2% never married, 33.2% now married, 16.0% widowed, 16.6% divorced (2005-2009 5-year est.); Foreign born: 3.2% (2005-2009 5-year est.); Ancestry (includes

multiple ancestries): 17.8% African, 6.4% German, 2.7% Ukrainian, 2.1% French, 2.1% Trinidadian and Tobagonian (2005-2009 5-year est.).
Economy: Employment by occupation: 10.9% management, 8.5% professional, 23.0% services, 26.0% sales, 0.0% farming, 10.4% construction, 21.3% production (2005-2009 5-year est.).
Income: Per capita income: $17,894 (2010); Median household income: $41,414 (2010); Average household income: $52,584 (2010); Percent of households with income of $100,000 or more: 15.2% (2010); Poverty rate: 18.6% (2005-2009 5-year est.).
Education: Percent of population age 25 and over with: High school diploma (including GED) or higher: 76.5% (2010); Bachelor's degree or higher: 8.1% (2010); Master's degree or higher: 1.4% (2010).
Housing: Homeownership rate: 81.3% (2010); Median home value: $77,123 (2010); Median contract rent: $612 per month (2005-2009 5-year est.); Median year structure built: 1973 (2005-2009 5-year est.).
Transportation: Commute to work: 98.9% car, 0.0% public transportation, 1.1% walk, 0.0% work from home (2005-2009 5-year est.); Travel time to work: 9.2% less than 15 minutes, 40.1% 15 to 30 minutes, 34.3% 30 to 45 minutes, 12.8% 45 to 60 minutes, 3.7% 60 minutes or more (2005-2009 5-year est.)

BAYTOWN (city). Covers a land area of 32.654 square miles and a water area of 0.496 square miles. Located at 29.74° N. Lat; 94.96° W. Long. Elevation is 26 feet.

Population: 64,638 (1990); 66,430 (2000); 71,729 (2010); 75,507 (2015 projected); Race: 62.1% White, 14.5% Black, 1.1% Asian, 22.3% Other, 45.5% Hispanic of any race (2010); Density: 2,196.6 persons per square mile (2010); Average household size: 2.86 (2010); Median age: 32.3 (2010); Males per 100 females: 96.9 (2010); Marriage status: 26.6% never married, 56.5% now married, 6.6% widowed, 10.3% divorced (2005-2009 5-year est.); Foreign born: 16.4% (2005-2009 5-year est.); Ancestry (includes multiple ancestries): 8.0% German, 7.8% American, 6.7% Irish, 6.6% English, 2.6% French (2005-2009 5-year est.).
Economy: Unemployment rate: 13.0% (June 2011); Total civilian labor force: 33,889 (June 2011); Single-family building permits issued: 57 (2010); Multi-family building permits issued: 66 (2010); Employment by occupation: 7.1% management, 16.5% professional, 17.6% services, 22.8% sales, 0.3% farming, 18.5% construction, 17.2% production (2005-2009 5-year est.).
Income: Per capita income: $21,353 (2010); Median household income: $48,679 (2010); Average household income: $61,421 (2010); Percent of households with income of $100,000 or more: 15.9% (2010); Poverty rate: 15.0% (2005-2009 5-year est.).
Taxes: Total city taxes per capita: $513 (2007); City property taxes per capita: $232 (2007).
Education: Percent of population age 25 and over with: High school diploma (including GED) or higher: 75.2% (2010); Bachelor's degree or higher: 13.8% (2010); Master's degree or higher: 5.0% (2010).
School District(s)
Goose Creek CISD (PK-12)
    2009-10 Enrollment: 20,954 . . . . (281) 420-4842
Two-year College(s)
Lee College (Public)
    Fall 2009 Enrollment: 6,658. . . . . (281) 427-5611
    2010-11 Tuition: In-state $1,710; Out-of-state $2,502
Housing: Homeownership rate: 62.5% (2010); Median home value: $89,955 (2010); Median contract rent: $541 per month (2005-2009 5-year est.); Median year structure built: 1974 (2005-2009 5-year est.).
Hospitals: San Jacinto Methodist Hospital (262 beds); San Jacinto Methodist Hospital (335 beds)
Safety: Violent crime rate: 46.6 per 10,000 population; Property crime rate: 565.4 per 10,000 population (2009).
Newspapers: The Baytown Sun (Local news; Circulation 10,000)
Transportation: Commute to work: 93.9% car, 0.2% public transportation, 1.3% walk, 1.4% work from home (2005-2009 5-year est.); Travel time to work: 32.0% less than 15 minutes, 36.0% 15 to 30 minutes, 17.5% 30 to 45 minutes, 6.8% 45 to 60 minutes, 7.8% 60 minutes or more (2005-2009 5-year est.)
Additional Information Contacts
Baytown Chamber of Commerce. (281) 422-8359
    http://www.baytownchamber.com
City of Baytown . . . . (281) 422-8281
    http://www.baytown.org

BELLAIRE (city). Covers a land area of 3.622 square miles and a water area of 0 square miles. Located at 29.70° N. Lat; 95.46° W. Long. Elevation is 56 feet.

History: Named for Bellaire, Ohio, which is the French translation of "beautiful air". Bellaire developed as an independent city almost surrounded by Houston. Incorporated in 1918, it called itself the "Biggest City in Houston."
Population: 13,844 (1990); 15,642 (2000); 18,731 (2010); 20,773 (2015 projected); Race: 84.4% White, 1.4% Black, 9.4% Asian, 4.8% Other, 9.2% Hispanic of any race (2010); Density: 5,172.0 persons per square mile (2010); Average household size: 2.67 (2010); Median age: 40.6 (2010); Males per 100 females: 95.2 (2010); Marriage status: 20.6% never married, 66.6% now married, 4.5% widowed, 8.2% divorced (2005-2009 5-year est.); Foreign born: 13.1% (2005-2009 5-year est.); Ancestry (includes multiple ancestries): 18.0% German, 15.2% English, 11.9% Irish, 7.9% American, 5.1% French (2005-2009 5-year est.).
Economy: Single-family building permits issued: 57 (2010); Multi-family building permits issued: 0 (2010); Employment by occupation: 29.4% management, 41.2% professional, 6.3% services, 18.5% sales, 0.0% farming, 2.1% construction, 2.4% production (2005-2009 5-year est.).
Income: Per capita income: $61,560 (2010); Median household income: $119,482 (2010); Average household income: $165,806 (2010); Percent of households with income of $100,000 or more: 58.6% (2010); Poverty rate: 2.7% (2005-2009 5-year est.).
Taxes: Total city taxes per capita: $868 (2007); City property taxes per capita: $630 (2007).
Education: Percent of population age 25 and over with: High school diploma (including GED) or higher: 96.3% (2010); Bachelor's degree or higher: 66.9% (2010); Master's degree or higher: 32.5% (2010).
School District(s)
Houston ISD (PK-12)
    2009-10 Enrollment: 202,773 . . . . (713) 556-6000
Housing: Homeownership rate: 84.6% (2010); Median home value: $413,919 (2010); Median contract rent: $1,048 per month (2005-2009 5-year est.); Median year structure built: 1983 (2005-2009 5-year est.).
Hospitals: Foundation Surgical Hospital (64 beds)
Safety: Violent crime rate: 17.8 per 10,000 population; Property crime rate: 197.4 per 10,000 population (2009).
Newspapers: El Rincón (Community news; Circulation 15,000); Southwest News (Community news; Circulation 40,000); Village News (Community news; Circulation 40,000)
Transportation: Commute to work: 91.6% car, 0.9% public transportation, 1.6% walk, 4.7% work from home (2005-2009 5-year est.); Travel time to work: 31.0% less than 15 minutes, 50.0% 15 to 30 minutes, 14.4% 30 to 45 minutes, 3.0% 45 to 60 minutes, 1.7% 60 minutes or more (2005-2009 5-year est.)
Additional Information Contacts
City of Bellaire . . . . (713) 662-8222
    http://www.ci.bellaire.tx.us
Houston Metropolitan Chamber of Commerce . . . . (713) 666-1521
    http://www.gswhcc.org

BUNKER HILL VILLAGE (city). Aka Bunker Hill. Covers a land area of 1.459 square miles and a water area of 0 square miles. Located at 29.76° N. Lat; 95.53° W. Long. Elevation is 82 feet.

History: Prior to the city's incorporation, German farmers settled the area and built sawmills to process local lumber. The city incorporated in December 1954 with a mayor-council government.
Population: 3,391 (1990); 3,654 (2000); 3,966 (2010); 4,210 (2015 projected); Race: 89.7% White, 0.2% Black, 7.4% Asian, 2.7% Other, 4.5% Hispanic of any race (2010); Density: 2,719.0 persons per square mile (2010); Average household size: 3.09 (2010); Median age: 46.1 (2010); Males per 100 females: 93.2 (2010); Marriage status: 20.9% never married, 68.9% now married, 4.5% widowed, 5.6% divorced (2005-2009 5-year est.); Foreign born: 12.0% (2005-2009 5-year est.); Ancestry (includes multiple ancestries): 20.1% German, 19.0% English, 18.3% Irish, 8.1% American, 5.2% Italian (2005-2009 5-year est.).
Economy: Single-family building permits issued: 13 (2010); Multi-family building permits issued: 0 (2010); Employment by occupation: 35.9% management, 37.5% professional, 9.8% services, 14.8% sales, 0.7% farming, 1.4% construction, 0.0% production (2005-2009 5-year est.).
Income: Per capita income: $84,735 (2010); Median household income: $231,132 (2010); Average household income: $262,435 (2010); Percent of

households with income of $100,000 or more: 71.6% (2010); Poverty rate: 5.3% (2005-2009 5-year est.).

Taxes: Total city taxes per capita: $1,024 (2007); City property taxes per capita: $861 (2007).

Education: Percent of population age 25 and over with: High school diploma (including GED) or higher: 97.9% (2010); Bachelor's degree or higher: 81.0% (2010); Master's degree or higher: 31.4% (2010).

Housing: Homeownership rate: 98.4% (2010); Median home value: $865,767 (2010); Median contract rent: $955 per month (2005-2009 5-year est.); Median year structure built: 1966 (2005-2009 5-year est.).

Transportation: Commute to work: 90.4% car, 0.0% public transportation, 1.5% walk, 6.0% work from home (2005-2009 5-year est.); Travel time to work: 28.3% less than 15 minutes, 39.9% 15 to 30 minutes, 30.9% 30 to 45 minutes, 0.8% 45 to 60 minutes, 0.0% 60 minutes or more (2005-2009 5-year est.)

Additional Information Contacts
City of Bunker Hill Village. . . . . (713) 467-9762
  http://www.bunkerhill.net

CHANNELVIEW (CDP). Covers a land area of 16.211 square miles and a water area of 1.758 square miles. Located at 29.78° N. Lat; 95.12° W. Long. Elevation is 30 feet.

History: Named for its location on the Houston Ship Channel. Major chemical plant explosion 1990.

Population: 25,568 (1990); 29,685 (2000); 32,871 (2010); 35,101 (2015 projected); Race: 52.3% White, 16.3% Black, 1.7% Asian, 29.7% Other, 52.2% Hispanic of any race (2010); Density: 2,027.7 persons per square mile (2010); Average household size: 3.36 (2010); Median age: 30.6 (2010); Males per 100 females: 101.0 (2010); Marriage status: 31.3% never married, 53.9% now married, 3.9% widowed, 11.0% divorced (2005-2009 5-year est.); Foreign born: 22.1% (2005-2009 5-year est.); Ancestry (includes multiple ancestries): 5.5% American, 4.5% German, 3.7% English, 3.3% Irish, 1.7% French (2005-2009 5-year est.).

Economy: Employment by occupation: 8.5% management, 10.5% professional, 13.2% services, 25.0% sales, 0.1% farming, 19.7% construction, 22.9% production (2005-2009 5-year est.).

Income: Per capita income: $18,087 (2010); Median household income: $53,195 (2010); Average household income: $60,656 (2010); Percent of households with income of $100,000 or more: 13.6% (2010); Poverty rate: 17.0% (2005-2009 5-year est.).

Education: Percent of population age 25 and over with: High school diploma (including GED) or higher: 72.4% (2010); Bachelor's degree or higher: 8.2% (2010); Master's degree or higher: 2.4% (2010).

School District(s)
Channelview ISD (PK-12)
  2009-10 Enrollment: 8,644 . . . . (281) 452-8002

Housing: Homeownership rate: 74.9% (2010); Median home value: $95,866 (2010); Median contract rent: $597 per month (2005-2009 5-year est.); Median year structure built: 1982 (2005-2009 5-year est.).

Transportation: Commute to work: 94.7% car, 0.5% public transportation, 1.4% walk, 0.4% work from home (2005-2009 5-year est.); Travel time to work: 23.3% less than 15 minutes, 34.6% 15 to 30 minutes, 28.5% 30 to 45 minutes, 8.5% 45 to 60 minutes, 5.1% 60 minutes or more (2005-2009 5-year est.)

CLOVERLEAF (CDP). Covers a land area of 3.568 square miles and a water area of 0 square miles. Located at 29.78° N. Lat; 95.17° W. Long. Elevation is 26 feet.

Population: 18,230 (1990); 23,508 (2000); 23,976 (2010); 24,791 (2015 projected); Race: 48.0% White, 20.1% Black, 1.3% Asian, 30.5% Other, 56.7% Hispanic of any race (2010); Density: 6,720.4 persons per square mile (2010); Average household size: 3.35 (2010); Median age: 30.3 (2010); Males per 100 females: 102.5 (2010); Marriage status: 32.2% never married, 55.6% now married, 4.9% widowed, 7.3% divorced (2005-2009 5-year est.); Foreign born: 30.5% (2005-2009 5-year est.); Ancestry (includes multiple ancestries): 5.4% American, 3.1% English, 3.0% German, 2.9% Irish, 1.7% African (2005-2009 5-year est.).

Economy: Employment by occupation: 4.2% management, 7.9% professional, 13.5% services, 23.5% sales, 0.0% farming, 21.8% construction, 29.0% production (2005-2009 5-year est.).

Income: Per capita income: $17,502 (2010); Median household income: $45,034 (2010); Average household income: $58,584 (2010); Percent of households with income of $100,000 or more: 14.0% (2010); Poverty rate: 22.2% (2005-2009 5-year est.).

Education: Percent of population age 25 and over with: High school diploma (including GED) or higher: 63.6% (2010); Bachelor's degree or higher: 9.9% (2010); Master's degree or higher: 2.0% (2010).

Housing: Homeownership rate: 63.6% (2010); Median home value: $103,904 (2010); Median contract rent: $513 per month (2005-2009 5-year est.); Median year structure built: 1976 (2005-2009 5-year est.).

Transportation: Commute to work: 95.9% car, 1.0% public transportation, 0.7% walk, 0.3% work from home (2005-2009 5-year est.); Travel time to work: 19.9% less than 15 minutes, 38.2% 15 to 30 minutes, 29.4% 30 to 45 minutes, 6.7% 45 to 60 minutes, 5.8% 60 minutes or more (2005-2009 5-year est.)

CROSBY (CDP). Covers a land area of 2.261 square miles and a water area of 0 square miles. Located at 29.91° N. Lat; 95.06° W. Long. Elevation is 46 feet.

Population: 1,811 (1990); 1,714 (2000); 1,763 (2010); 1,816 (2015 projected); Race: 67.8% White, 13.7% Black, 0.6% Asian, 17.9% Other, 20.3% Hispanic of any race (2010); Density: 779.9 persons per square mile (2010); Average household size: 2.62 (2010); Median age: 32.4 (2010); Males per 100 females: 100.6 (2010); Marriage status: 13.0% never married, 63.0% now married, 4.1% widowed, 19.9% divorced (2005-2009 5-year est.); Foreign born: 15.0% (2005-2009 5-year est.); Ancestry (includes multiple ancestries): 10.6% American, 7.5% Irish, 5.7% African, 4.9% German, 4.7% Czech (2005-2009 5-year est.).

Economy: Employment by occupation: 15.4% management, 7.9% professional, 10.1% services, 19.9% sales, 0.0% farming, 6.3% construction, 40.3% production (2005-2009 5-year est.).

Income: Per capita income: $23,833 (2010); Median household income: $49,564 (2010); Average household income: $62,418 (2010); Percent of households with income of $100,000 or more: 18.3% (2010); Poverty rate: 18.5% (2005-2009 5-year est.).

Education: Percent of population age 25 and over with: High school diploma (including GED) or higher: 75.1% (2010); Bachelor's degree or higher: 8.3% (2010); Master's degree or higher: 3.2% (2010).

School District(s)
Crosby ISD (PK-12)
  2009-10 Enrollment: 5,034 . . . . (281) 328-9200

Housing: Homeownership rate: 68.9% (2010); Median home value: $107,547 (2010); Median contract rent: $536 per month (2005-2009 5-year est.); Median year structure built: 1974 (2005-2009 5-year est.).

Transportation: Commute to work: 99.2% car, 0.0% public transportation, 0.0% walk, 0.8% work from home (2005-2009 5-year est.); Travel time to work: 29.1% less than 15 minutes, 34.3% 15 to 30 minutes, 14.7% 30 to 45 minutes, 6.5% 45 to 60 minutes, 15.3% 60 minutes or more (2005-2009 5-year est.)

Additional Information Contacts
Crosby Huffman Chamber of Commerce. . . . . (281) 328-6984
  http://www.crosbyhuffmancc.org

DEER PARK (city). Covers a land area of 10.361 square miles and a water area of 0.001 square miles. Located at 29.69° N. Lat; 95.11° W. Long. Elevation is 30 feet.

Population: 27,653 (1990); 28,520 (2000); 29,866 (2010); 31,335 (2015 projected); Race: 88.6% White, 1.4% Black, 1.0% Asian, 8.9% Other, 19.9% Hispanic of any race (2010); Density: 2,882.6 persons per square mile (2010); Average household size: 2.96 (2010); Median age: 36.1 (2010); Males per 100 females: 99.5 (2010); Marriage status: 24.8% never married, 58.9% now married, 4.9% widowed, 11.4% divorced (2005-2009 5-year est.); Foreign born: 5.8% (2005-2009 5-year est.); Ancestry (includes multiple ancestries): 13.1% German, 11.6% Irish, 11.5% American, 9.4% English, 4.1% French (2005-2009 5-year est.).

Economy: Unemployment rate: 9.0% (June 2011); Total civilian labor force: 17,159 (June 2011); Single-family building permits issued: 84 (2010); Multi-family building permits issued: 0 (2010); Employment by occupation: 15.1% management, 21.0% professional, 9.5% services, 28.0% sales, 0.0% farming, 12.1% construction, 14.2% production (2005-2009 5-year est.).

Income: Per capita income: $30,014 (2010); Median household income: $77,428 (2010); Average household income: $89,243 (2010); Percent of households with income of $100,000 or more: 34.4% (2010); Poverty rate: 7.2% (2005-2009 5-year est.).

Taxes: Total city taxes per capita: $499 (2007); City property taxes per capita: $303 (2007).

Education: Percent of population age 25 and over with: High school diploma (including GED) or higher: 91.2% (2010); Bachelor's degree or higher: 17.2% (2010); Master's degree or higher: 5.3% (2010).

School District(s)

Deer Park ISD (PK-12)
 2009-10 Enrollment: 12,502 . . . . (832) 668-7000
La Porte ISD (PK-12)
 2009-10 Enrollment: 7,847 . . . . (281) 604-7015

Housing: Homeownership rate: 82.9% (2010); Median home value: $138,022 (2010); Median contract rent: $720 per month (2005-2009 5-year est.); Median year structure built: 1977 (2005-2009 5-year est.).

Safety: Violent crime rate: 25.4 per 10,000 population; Property crime rate: 268.6 per 10,000 population (2009).

Newspapers: Deer Park Progress (Community news; Circulation 15,000)

Transportation: Commute to work: 96.0% car, 0.4% public transportation, 1.0% walk, 1.8% work from home (2005-2009 5-year est.); Travel time to work: 29.2% less than 15 minutes, 36.0% 15 to 30 minutes, 19.3% 30 to 45 minutes, 8.9% 45 to 60 minutes, 6.6% 60 minutes or more (2005-2009 5-year est.)

Additional Information Contacts

City of Deer Park . . . . (281) 478-7248
 http://www.deerparktx.gov
Deer Park Chamber of Commerce . . . . (281) 479-1559
 http://www.deerpark.org

EL LAGO (city). Covers a land area of 0.653 square miles and a water area of 0.057 square miles. Located at 29.57° N. Lat; 95.04° W. Long. Elevation is 10 feet.

History: El Lago is on Taylor Lake, Clear Lake, and NASA Parkway (also called NASA Road 1 and Farm Road 528) in southeastern Harris County. The community was started in the 1950s, incorporated in 1961, and grew from a population of 750 in 1967 to 3,550 by 1975, as workers were drawn to the nearby Lyndon B. Johnson Space Center.

Population: 3,269 (1990); 3,075 (2000); 3,015 (2010); 3,100 (2015 projected); Race: 88.0% White, 1.8% Black, 2.1% Asian, 8.1% Other, 14.8% Hispanic of any race (2010); Density: 4,617.4 persons per square mile (2010); Average household size: 2.08 (2010); Median age: 40.4 (2010); Males per 100 females: 108.7 (2010); Marriage status: 25.3% never married, 59.1% now married, 1.6% widowed, 14.0% divorced (2005-2009 5-year est.); Foreign born: 8.4% (2005-2009 5-year est.); Ancestry (includes multiple ancestries): 24.8% English, 21.1% German, 16.0% Irish, 8.7% Scotch-Irish, 6.7% Scottish (2005-2009 5-year est.).

Economy: Single-family building permits issued: 1 (2010); Multi-family building permits issued: 0 (2010); Employment by occupation: 27.5% management, 33.5% professional, 4.2% services, 22.0% sales, 0.0% farming, 9.8% construction, 3.1% production (2005-2009 5-year est.).

Income: Per capita income: $38,817 (2010); Median household income: $64,784 (2010); Average household income: $80,269 (2010); Percent of households with income of $100,000 or more: 26.0% (2010); Poverty rate: 15.7% (2005-2009 5-year est.).

Taxes: Total city taxes per capita: $314 (2007); City property taxes per capita: $216 (2007).

Education: Percent of population age 25 and over with: High school diploma (including GED) or higher: 95.2% (2010); Bachelor's degree or higher: 49.7% (2010); Master's degree or higher: 17.9% (2010).

School District(s)

Bay Area Charter Inc (PK-12)
 2009-10 Enrollment: 369 . . . . (281) 316-0001

Housing: Homeownership rate: 46.2% (2010); Median home value: $183,040 (2010); Median contract rent: $858 per month (2005-2009 5-year est.); Median year structure built: 1969 (2005-2009 5-year est.).

Transportation: Commute to work: 78.2% car, 3.7% public transportation, 2.4% walk, 12.6% work from home (2005-2009 5-year est.); Travel time to work: 19.1% less than 15 minutes, 39.3% 15 to 30 minutes, 17.9% 30 to 45 minutes, 8.9% 45 to 60 minutes, 14.8% 60 minutes or more (2005-2009 5-year est.)

GALENA PARK (city). Covers a land area of 4.987 square miles and a water area of 0 square miles. Located at 29.73° N. Lat; 95.23° W. Long. Elevation is 10 feet.

History: Named for the Galena-Signal Oil Company, the leading industry in the town. Absorbed 1948 by Houston.

Population: 10,033 (1990); 10,592 (2000); 10,310 (2010); 10,399 (2015 projected); Race: 65.0% White, 5.2% Black, 0.4% Asian, 29.4% Other, 80.4% Hispanic of any race (2010); Density: 2,067.5 persons per square mile (2010); Average household size: 3.61 (2010); Median age: 29.3 (2010); Males per 100 females: 101.4 (2010); Marriage status: 27.7% never married, 58.8% now married, 4.9% widowed, 8.6% divorced (2005-2009 5-year est.); Foreign born: 33.5% (2005-2009 5-year est.); Ancestry (includes multiple ancestries): 2.7% American, 2.6% Irish, 2.3% English, 2.3% German, 1.2% Scotch-Irish (2005-2009 5-year est.).

Economy: Single-family building permits issued: 2 (2010); Multi-family building permits issued: 2 (2010); Employment by occupation: 2.4% management, 6.4% professional, 15.0% services, 22.4% sales, 0.3% farming, 18.0% construction, 35.4% production (2005-2009 5-year est.).

Income: Per capita income: $13,931 (2010); Median household income: $38,807 (2010); Average household income: $49,550 (2010); Percent of households with income of $100,000 or more: 7.7% (2010); Poverty rate: 24.9% (2005-2009 5-year est.).

Taxes: Total city taxes per capita: $472 (2007); City property taxes per capita: $295 (2007).

Education: Percent of population age 25 and over with: High school diploma (including GED) or higher: 50.2% (2010); Bachelor's degree or higher: 7.1% (2010); Master's degree or higher: 2.6% (2010).

School District(s)

Galena Park ISD (PK-12)
 2009-10 Enrollment: 21,536 . . . . (832) 386-1000

Housing: Homeownership rate: 74.7% (2010); Median home value: $69,923 (2010); Median contract rent: $530 per month (2005-2009 5-year est.); Median year structure built: 1957 (2005-2009 5-year est.).

Safety: Violent crime rate: 30.5 per 10,000 population; Property crime rate: 280.3 per 10,000 population (2009).

Transportation: Commute to work: 72.5% car, 8.4% public transportation, 3.2% walk, 2.5% work from home (2005-2009 5-year est.); Travel time to work: 20.0% less than 15 minutes, 51.0% 15 to 30 minutes, 22.1% 30 to 45 minutes, 4.1% 45 to 60 minutes, 2.9% 60 minutes or more (2005-2009 5-year est.)

Additional Information Contacts

City of Galena Park . . . . (713) 672-2556
 http://www.cityofgalenapark-tx.gov
North Channel Chamber of Commerce . . . . (713) 450-3600
 http://www.northchannelarea.com

HEDWIG VILLAGE (city). Covers a land area of 0.862 square miles and a water area of 0 square miles. Located at 29.78° N. Lat; 95.51° W. Long. Elevation is 75 feet.

Population: 2,616 (1990); 2,334 (2000); 2,290 (2010); 2,309 (2015 projected); Race: 78.3% White, 1.2% Black, 15.0% Asian, 5.5% Other, 5.0% Hispanic of any race (2010); Density: 2,655.5 persons per square mile (2010); Average household size: 2.43 (2010); Median age: 43.1 (2010); Males per 100 females: 91.6 (2010); Marriage status: 24.8% never married, 58.7% now married, 2.2% widowed, 14.3% divorced (2005-2009 5-year est.); Foreign born: 19.5% (2005-2009 5-year est.); Ancestry (includes multiple ancestries): 17.3% English, 14.6% Irish, 13.8% German, 7.6% American, 4.5% Italian (2005-2009 5-year est.).

Economy: Single-family building permits issued: 3 (2010); Multi-family building permits issued: 0 (2010); Employment by occupation: 22.8% management, 31.4% professional, 2.6% services, 29.7% sales, 0.0% farming, 8.2% construction, 5.4% production (2005-2009 5-year est.).

Income: Per capita income: $57,357 (2010); Median household income: $79,598 (2010); Average household income: $139,657 (2010); Percent of households with income of $100,000 or more: 42.4% (2010); Poverty rate: 2.7% (2005-2009 5-year est.).

Taxes: Total city taxes per capita: $1,288 (2007); City property taxes per capita: $389 (2007).

Education: Percent of population age 25 and over with: High school diploma (including GED) or higher: 97.3% (2010); Bachelor's degree or higher: 66.3% (2010); Master's degree or higher: 27.7% (2010).

Housing: Homeownership rate: 68.9% (2010); Median home value: $591,176 (2010); Median contract rent: $822 per month (2005-2009 5-year est.); Median year structure built: 1966 (2005-2009 5-year est.).

Safety: Violent crime rate: 29.9 per 10,000 population; Property crime rate: 648.2 per 10,000 population (2009).

Transportation: Commute to work: 99.1% car, 0.0% public transportation, 0.0% walk, 0.3% work from home (2005-2009 5-year est.); Travel time to work: 16.0% less than 15 minutes, 54.6% 15 to 30 minutes, 20.2% 30 to 45 minutes, 3.1% 45 to 60 minutes, 6.1% 60 minutes or more (2005-2009 5-year est.)

HIGHLANDS (CDP). Covers a land area of 6.175 square miles and a water area of 0.399 square miles. Located at 29.81° N. Lat; 95.05° W. Long. Elevation is 36 feet.
Population: 6,632 (1990); 7,089 (2000); 7,306 (2010); 7,426 (2015 projected); Race: 83.1% White, 3.7% Black, 0.5% Asian, 12.8% Other, 22.1% Hispanic of any race (2010); Density: 1,183.2 persons per square mile (2010); Average household size: 2.77 (2010); Median age: 35.6 (2010); Males per 100 females: 100.7 (2010); Marriage status: 25.2% never married, 51.3% now married, 10.8% widowed, 12.7% divorced (2005-2009 5-year est.); Foreign born: 6.8% (2005-2009 5-year est.); Ancestry (includes multiple ancestries): 14.7% German, 13.9% Irish, 11.7% American, 5.1% English, 4.1% French (2005-2009 5-year est.).
Economy: Employment by occupation: 10.6% management, 19.6% professional, 10.4% services, 24.7% sales, 0.0% farming, 20.3% construction, 14.4% production (2005-2009 5-year est.).
Income: Per capita income: $22,372 (2010); Median household income: $49,777 (2010); Average household income: $62,030 (2010); Percent of households with income of $100,000 or more: 17.5% (2010); Poverty rate: 12.3% (2005-2009 5-year est.).
Education: Percent of population age 25 and over with: High school diploma (including GED) or higher: 80.9% (2010); Bachelor's degree or higher: 7.2% (2010); Master's degree or higher: 3.0% (2010).
School District(s)
Goose Creek CISD (PK-12)
    2009-10 Enrollment: 20,954 . . . . (281) 420-4842
Housing: Homeownership rate: 82.3% (2010); Median home value: $77,311 (2010); Median contract rent: $449 per month (2005-2009 5-year est.); Median year structure built: 1975 (2005-2009 5-year est.).
Transportation: Commute to work: 90.7% car, 0.0% public transportation, 0.4% walk, 6.3% work from home (2005-2009 5-year est.); Travel time to work: 20.3% less than 15 minutes, 39.0% 15 to 30 minutes, 17.1% 30 to 45 minutes, 10.9% 45 to 60 minutes, 12.8% 60 minutes or more (2005-2009 5-year est.)
Additional Information Contacts
Greater Highlands Chamber of Commerce . . . . (281) 426-7227
    http://allabouthighlands.com

HILSHIRE VILLAGE (city). Covers a land area of 0.271 square miles and a water area of 0 square miles. Located at 29.79° N. Lat; 95.48° W. Long. Elevation is 69 feet.
Population: 665 (1990); 720 (2000); 745 (2010); 771 (2015 projected); Race: 91.9% White, 0.4% Black, 4.0% Asian, 3.6% Other, 7.4% Hispanic of any race (2010); Density: 2,753.4 persons per square mile (2010); Average household size: 2.60 (2010); Median age: 48.3 (2010); Males per 100 females: 90.1 (2010); Marriage status: 16.3% never married, 70.8% now married, 6.5% widowed, 6.3% divorced (2005-2009 5-year est.); Foreign born: 9.4% (2005-2009 5-year est.); Ancestry (includes multiple ancestries): 23.5% German, 22.1% English, 17.1% Irish, 7.0% American, 4.6% European (2005-2009 5-year est.).
Economy: Single-family building permits issued: 1 (2010); Multi-family building permits issued: 0 (2010); Employment by occupation: 33.5% management, 39.4% professional, 8.5% services, 16.1% sales, 0.0% farming, 0.0% construction, 2.5% production (2005-2009 5-year est.).
Income: Per capita income: $71,785 (2010); Median household income: $143,478 (2010); Average household income: $186,993 (2010); Percent of households with income of $100,000 or more: 65.4% (2010); Poverty rate: 1.1% (2005-2009 5-year est.).
Taxes: Total city taxes per capita: $729 (2007); City property taxes per capita: $502 (2007).
Education: Percent of population age 25 and over with: High school diploma (including GED) or higher: 97.6% (2010); Bachelor's degree or higher: 61.1% (2010); Master's degree or higher: 28.4% (2010).
Housing: Homeownership rate: 98.3% (2010); Median home value: $481,897 (2010); Median contract rent: $2,000+ per month (2005-2009 5-year est.); Median year structure built: 1969 (2005-2009 5-year est.).
Transportation: Commute to work: 93.6% car, 0.9% public transportation, 0.0% walk, 4.6% work from home (2005-2009 5-year est.); Travel time to work: 27.6% less than 15 minutes, 51.5% 15 to 30 minutes, 18.5% 30 to 45 minutes, 1.5% 45 to 60 minutes, 0.9% 60 minutes or more (2005-2009 5-year est.)
Additional Information Contacts
City of Hilshire Village . . . . (713) 973-1779
    http://hilshirevillagetexas.com

HOCKLEY (unincorporated postal area, zip code 77447). Covers a land area of 102.844 square miles and a water area of 1.019 square miles. Located at 30.06° N. Lat; 95.81° W. Long. Elevation is 220 feet.
Population: 8,242 (2000); Race: 80.7% White, 8.6% Black, 0.8% Asian, 9.9% Other, 16.3% Hispanic of any race (2000); Density: 80.1 persons per square mile (2000); Age: 32.2% under 18, 7.0% over 64 (2000); Marriage status: 21.4% never married, 68.7% now married, 3.0% widowed, 7.0% divorced (2000); Foreign born: 6.2% (2000); Ancestry (includes multiple ancestries): 16.9% German, 11.4% Irish, 9.3% English, 9.2% American (2000).
Economy: Employment by occupation: 13.1% management, 16.0% professional, 10.0% services, 32.1% sales, 0.6% farming, 15.7% construction, 12.4% production (2000).
Income: Per capita income: $20,103 (2000); Median household income: $51,628 (2000); Poverty rate: 179.1% (2000).
Education: Percent of population age 25 and over with: High school diploma (including GED) or higher: 81.1% (2000); Bachelor's degree or higher: 13.7% (2000).
School District(s)
Waller ISD (PK-12)
    2009-10 Enrollment: 5,407 . . . . (936) 931-3685
Housing: Homeownership rate: 84.6% (2000); Median home value: $96,300 (2000); Median contract rent: $515 per month (2000); Median year structure built: 1986 (2000).
Transportation: Commute to work: 92.9% car, 1.1% public transportation, 1.8% walk, 2.0% work from home (2000); Travel time to work: 9.4% less than 15 minutes, 24.0% 15 to 30 minutes, 25.0% 30 to 45 minutes, 19.8% 45 to 60 minutes, 21.8% 60 minutes or more (2000)

HOUSTON (city). County seat. Covers a land area of 579.416 square miles and a water area of 22.277 square miles. Located at 29.76° N. Lat; 95.38° W. Long. Elevation is 39 feet.
History: Houston owes its existence to John K. and Augustus C. Allen who came from New York in 1832. In 1836, they bought land that had been granted to John Austin, platted a town, and named it for Sam Houston, who had defeated the Mexicans in an encounter near here, earlier that year. The Allens mounted a promotional campaign that brought a string of settlers from other states. In 1837, when it was incoporated, Houston was the capital of the Republic and an inland port, with boats navigating the bayous from Galveston Bay. When the capital was moved to Austin in 1839, Houston began to concentrate on commercial development. Harrisonburg, established to the southeast 13 years before Houston, was Houston's rival for the railroad, as well as for the improvement of the ship channel to the Gulf of Mexico. Houston was connected by rail in 1856. By 1915 the ship channel was made adequate for large cargo vessels and Houston became a busy port, leading to its later role as a financial and business center for major oil companies.
Population: 1,697,610 (1990); 1,953,631 (2000); 2,269,768 (2010); 2,451,441 (2015 projected); Race: 47.2% White, 23.6% Black, 5.4% Asian, 23.7% Other, 44.6% Hispanic of any race (2010); Density: 3,917.3 persons per square mile (2010); Average household size: 2.73 (2010); Median age: 33.3 (2010); Males per 100 females: 101.6 (2010); Marriage status: 36.4% never married, 48.3% now married, 5.1% widowed, 10.2% divorced (2005-2009 5-year est.); Foreign born: 27.9% (2005-2009 5-year est.); Ancestry (includes multiple ancestries): 6.5% German, 4.7% English, 4.5% Irish, 3.1% American, 1.8% French (2005-2009 5-year est.).
Economy: Unemployment rate: 8.8% (June 2011); Total civilian labor force: 1,094,492 (June 2011); Single-family building permits issued: 2,452 (2010); Multi-family building permits issued: 2,139 (2010); Employment by occupation: 12.4% management, 19.5% professional, 18.3% services, 23.7% sales, 0.2% farming, 13.0% construction, 12.8% production (2005-2009 5-year est.).
Income: Per capita income: $23,910 (2010); Median household income: $44,923 (2010); Average household income: $65,640 (2010); Percent of households with income of $100,000 or more: 17.2% (2010); Poverty rate: 20.8% (2005-2009 5-year est.).
Taxes: Total city taxes per capita: $749 (2007); City property taxes per capita: $392 (2007).
Education: Percent of population age 25 and over with: High school diploma (including GED) or higher: 72.8% (2010); Bachelor's degree or higher: 27.4% (2010); Master's degree or higher: 10.0% (2010).
School District(s)
Academy of Accelerated Learning Inc (PK-05)
    2009-10 Enrollment: 574 . . . . (713) 773-4766

Accelerated Intermediate Academy (PK-08)
2009-10 Enrollment: 454 . . . . (713) 283-6298
Aldine ISD (PK-12)
2009-10 Enrollment: 62,792 . . . . (281) 449-1011
Alief ISD (PK-12)
2009-10 Enrollment: 45,553 . . . . (281) 498-8110
Alief Montessori Community School (PK-05)
2009-10 Enrollment: 238 . . . . (281) 530-9406
Alphonso Crutch's-Life Support Center
2009-10 Enrollment: n/a . . . . (713) 779-9990
Amigos Por Vida-Friends for Life Pub Chtr Sch (PK-08)
2009-10 Enrollment: 482 . . . . (713) 349-9945
Beatrice Mayes Institute Charter School (KG-08)
2009-10 Enrollment: 415 . . . . (713) 747-5629
Benji's Special Educational Academy Charter School (PK-12)
2009-10 Enrollment: 496 . . . . (713) 229-0560
Brazos School for Inquiry & Creativity (PK-12)
2009-10 Enrollment: 490 . . . . (979) 268-8884
Calvin Nelms Charter Schools (04-12)
2009-10 Enrollment: 297 . . . . (281) 398-8031
Channelview ISD (PK-12)
2009-10 Enrollment: 8,644 . . . . (281) 452-8002
Children First Academy of Houston (PK-07)
2009-10 Enrollment: 432 . . . . (713) 491-9030
Clear Creek ISD (PK-12)
2009-10 Enrollment: 37,611 . . . . (281) 284-0079
Crosby ISD (PK-12)
2009-10 Enrollment: 5,034 . . . . (281) 328-9200
Cypress-Fairbanks ISD (PK-12)
2009-10 Enrollment: 104,231 . . . . (281) 897-4000
Draw Academy (PK-08)
2009-10 Enrollment: 280 . . . . (713) 706-3729
Excel Academy (04-12)
2009-10 Enrollment: 529 . . . . (713) 222-4340
Fort Bend ISD (PK-12)
2009-10 Enrollment: 69,374 . . . . (281) 634-1000
Galena Park ISD (PK-12)
2009-10 Enrollment: 21,536 . . . . (832) 386-1000
George I Sanchez Charter (PK-12)
2009-10 Enrollment: 691 . . . . (713) 926-1112
Girls & Boys Preparatory Academy (PK-12)
2009-10 Enrollment: 746 . . . . (713) 270-5994
Goose Creek CISD (PK-12)
2009-10 Enrollment: 20,954 . . . . (281) 420-4842
Harmony School of Excellence (KG-11)
2009-10 Enrollment: 1,125 . . . . (713) 343-3333
Harmony School of Innovation (KG-09)
2009-10 Enrollment: 1,005 . . . . (713) 541-3030
Harmony Science Academy (KG-12)
2009-10 Enrollment: 1,804 . . . . (713) 343-3333
Harris County Dept of Ed
2009-10 Enrollment: n/a . . . . (713) 694-6300
Houston Alternative Preparatory Charter School (PK-12)
2009-10 Enrollment: 170 . . . . (713) 721-6905
Houston Can Academy Charter School (09-12)
2009-10 Enrollment: 809 . . . . (214) 943-2244
Houston Gateway Academy Inc (PK-10)
2009-10 Enrollment: 864 . . . . (713) 644-8292
Houston Heights High School (09-12)
2009-10 Enrollment: 201 . . . . (713) 868-9797
Houston Heights Learning Academy Inc (PK-05)
2009-10 Enrollment: 124 . . . . (713) 869-9453
Houston ISD (PK-12)
2009-10 Enrollment: 202,773 . . . . (713) 556-6000
Huffman ISD (PK-12)
2009-10 Enrollment: 3,152 . . . . (281) 324-1871
Humble ISD (PK-12)
2009-10 Enrollment: 34,923 . . . . (281) 641-1000
Jamie's House Charter School (05-12)
2009-10 Enrollment: 96 . . . . (281) 866-9777
Jesse Jackson Academy
2009-10 Enrollment: n/a . . . . (713) 845-2451
Juan B Galaviz Charter School (06-12)
2009-10 Enrollment: 77 . . . . (832) 300-6010
Katy ISD (PK-12)
2009-10 Enrollment: 59,078 . . . . (281) 396-6000

Kipp Inc Charter (PK-12)
2009-10 Enrollment: 3,864 . . . . (832) 328-1051
Kipp Southeast Houston (KG-08)
2009-10 Enrollment: 794 . . . . (832) 328-1051
Klein ISD (PK-12)
2009-10 Enrollment: 44,824 . . . . (832) 249-4000
Koinonia Community Learning Academy
2009-10 Enrollment: n/a . . . . (713) 659-7753
La Amistad Love & Learning Academy (PK-05)
2009-10 Enrollment: 347 . . . . (281) 988-9231
Medical Center Charter School (PK-06)
2009-10 Enrollment: 222 . . . . (713) 791-9980
Meyerpark Elementary (PK-05)
2009-10 Enrollment: 174 . . . . (713) 729-9712
North Forest ISD (PK-12)
2009-10 Enrollment: 7,665 . . . . (713) 633-1600
North Houston HS for Business (01-05)
2009-10 Enrollment: 24 . . . . (832) 390-8337
Northwest Preparatory (PK-08)
2009-10 Enrollment: 283 . . . . (713) 688-3649
Pasadena ISD (PK-12)
2009-10 Enrollment: 52,303 . . . .
Raul Yzaguirre School for Success (PK-12)
2009-10 Enrollment: 1,145 . . . . (713) 649-6201
Richard Milburn Academy (Suburban Houston) (09-12)
2009-10 Enrollment: 275 . . . . (830) 557-6181
Ripley House Charter School (PK-05)
2009-10 Enrollment: 1,530 . . . . (713) 315-6429
Ser-Ninos Charter School (PK-08)
2009-10 Enrollment: 622 . . . . (713) 667-6145
Shekinah Radiance Academy (PK-12)
2009-10 Enrollment: 1,125 . . . . (210) 658-6848
Sheldon ISD (PK-12)
2009-10 Enrollment: 6,570 . . . . (281) 727-2000
Southwest School (PK-12)
2009-10 Enrollment: 3,598 . . . . (713) 784-6345
Spring Branch ISD (PK-12)
2009-10 Enrollment: 32,502 . . . . (713) 464-1511
Spring ISD (PK-12)
2009-10 Enrollment: 35,350 . . . . (281) 891-6000
Stepping Stones Charter Elementary (KG-06)
2009-10 Enrollment: 203 . . . . (281) 988-7797
Texas Serenity Academy (KG-08)
2009-10 Enrollment: 390 . . . . (281) 931-8887
The Rhodes School (PK-05)
2009-10 Enrollment: 298 . . . . (281) 458-4334
The Varnett Public School (PK-05)
2009-10 Enrollment: 1,552 . . . . (713) 723-4699
Tomball ISD (PK-12)
2009-10 Enrollment: 10,266 . . . . (281) 357-3100
Two Dimensions Preparatory Academy (PK-05)
2009-10 Enrollment: 428 . . . . (281) 893-9349
University of Houston Charter School (KG-05)
2009-10 Enrollment: 133 . . . . (713) 743-9107
University of Texas University Charter School (KG-12)
2009-10 Enrollment: 907 . . . . (512) 471-5652
Yes Preparatory Public Schools (06-12)
2009-10 Enrollment: 3,374 . . . . (713) 574-7600
Zoe Learning Academy (PK-06)
2009-10 Enrollment: 553 . . . . (713) 748-4228

Four-year College(s)
American College of Acupuncture and Oriental Med (Private, For-profit)
Fall 2009 Enrollment: 130 . . . . (713) 780-9777
American InterContinental University (Private, For-profit)
Fall 2009 Enrollment: 514 . . . . (832) 201-3600
2010-11 Tuition: In-state $15,015; Out-of-state $15,015
Baylor College of Medicine (Private, Not-for-profit)
Fall 2009 Enrollment: 1,428. . . . . (713) 798-4951
Center for Advanced Legal Studies (Private, For-profit)
Fall 2009 Enrollment: 208 . . . . (713) 529-2778
College of Biblical Studies-Houston (Private, Not-for-profit, Undenominational)
Fall 2009 Enrollment: 617 . . . . (713) 785-5995
2010-11 Tuition: In-state $8,784; Out-of-state $8,784

Houston Baptist University (Private, Not-for-profit, Southern Baptist)
Fall 2009 Enrollment: 2,710 . . . . (281) 649-3000
2010-11 Tuition: In-state $23,180; Out-of-state $23,180
Houston Graduate School of Theology (Private, Not-for-profit, Multiple
Protestant Denomination)
Fall 2009 Enrollment: 213 . . . . (713) 942-9505
ITT Technical Institute-Houston North (Private, For-profit)
Fall 2009 Enrollment: 905 . . . . (281) 873-0512
2010-11 Tuition: In-state $18,048; Out-of-state $18,048
ITT Technical Institute-Houston West (Private, For-profit)
Fall 2009 Enrollment: 622 . . . . (713) 952-2294
2010-11 Tuition: In-state $18,048; Out-of-state $18,048
Institute of Ocean Technology (Private, For-profit)
Fall 2009 Enrollment: n/a . . . . (713) 464-0771
Rice University (Private, Not-for-profit)
Fall 2009 Enrollment: 5,576 . . . . (713) 348-0000
2010-11 Tuition: In-state $33,771; Out-of-state $33,771
South Texas College of Law (Private, Not-for-profit)
Fall 2009 Enrollment: 1,278 . . . . (713) 659-8040
Texas Southern University (Public, Historically black)
Fall 2009 Enrollment: 9,394 . . . . (713) 313-7011
2010-11 Tuition: In-state $7,360; Out-of-state $15,772
The Art Institute of Houston (Private, For-profit)
Fall 2009 Enrollment: 2,223 . . . . (713) 623-2040
2010-11 Tuition: In-state $17,618; Out-of-state $17,618
The University of Texas Health Science Center at Houston (Public)
Fall 2009 Enrollment: 3,969 . . . . (713) 500-4472
The University of Texas M.D. Anderson Cancer Center (Public)
Fall 2009 Enrollment: 208 . . . . (800) 392-1611
University of Houston (Public)
Fall 2009 Enrollment: 37,000 . . . . (713) 743-1000
2010-11 Tuition: In-state $7,342; Out-of-state $14,782
University of Houston-Clear Lake (Public)
Fall 2009 Enrollment: 7,643 . . . . (281) 283-7600
University of Houston-Downtown (Public)
Fall 2009 Enrollment: 12,742 . . . . (713) 221-8000
2010-11 Tuition: In-state $4,604; Out-of-state $12,044
University of Phoenix-Houston Westside Campus (Private, For-profit)
Fall 2009 Enrollment: 2,987 . . . . (713) 465-9966
2010-11 Tuition: In-state $11,640; Out-of-state $11,640
University of St Thomas (Private, Not-for-profit, Roman Catholic)
Fall 2009 Enrollment: 3,132 . . . . (713) 522-7911
2010-11 Tuition: In-state $23,500; Out-of-state $23,500
Westwood College-Houston South (Private, For-profit)
Fall 2009 Enrollment: 478 . . . . (713) 777-4433
2010-11 Tuition: In-state $13,825; Out-of-state $13,825

Two-year College(s)

Commonwealth Institute of Funeral Service (Private, Not-for-profit)
Fall 2009 Enrollment: 154 . . . . (281) 873-0262
2010-11 Tuition: In-state $10,320; Out-of-state $10,320
Culinary Institute Inc (Private, For-profit)
Fall 2009 Enrollment: 199 . . . . (713) 692-0077
Houston Community College (Public)
Fall 2009 Enrollment: 54,942 . . . . (877) 422-6111
2010-11 Tuition: In-state $2,858; Out-of-state $3,410
Medvance Institute-Houston (Private, For-profit)
Fall 2009 Enrollment: 516 . . . . (713) 266-6594
Remington College-Houston Campus (Private, For-profit)
Fall 2009 Enrollment: 651 . . . . (281) 899-1240
2010-11 Tuition: In-state $14,745; Out-of-state $14,745
Remington College-North Houston Campus (Private, For-profit)
Fall 2009 Enrollment: 796 . . . . (281) 885-4450
2010-11 Tuition: In-state $14,745; Out-of-state $14,745
Sanford-Brown College (Private, For-profit)
Fall 2009 Enrollment: 1,513 . . . . (800) 445-6108
2010-11 Tuition: In-state $25,782; Out-of-state $25,782
Texas School of Business Inc (Private, For-profit)
Fall 2009 Enrollment: 1,206 . . . . (281) 443-7300
Texas School of Business-Southwest Inc (Private, For-profit)
Fall 2009 Enrollment: 388 . . . . (713) 975-7527
The Academy of Health Care Professions (Private, For-profit)
Fall 2009 Enrollment: 392 . . . . (713) 425-3100
Universal Technical Institute of Texas Inc (Private, For-profit)
Fall 2009 Enrollment: 3,479 . . . . (281) 443-6262

Vet Tech Institute of Houston (Private, For-profit)
Fall 2009 Enrollment: 134 . . . . (713) 629-1500
2010-11 Tuition: In-state $13,530; Out-of-state $13,530

Vocational/Technical School(s)

360 Degrees Beauty Academy (Private, For-profit)
Fall 2009 Enrollment: 23 . . . . (281) 656-2626
2010-11 Tuition: $15,000
ATI Career Training Center (Private, For-profit)
Fall 2009 Enrollment: 106 . . . . (713) 581-8001
2010-11 Tuition: $16,700
Astrodome Career Centers (Private, For-profit)
Fall 2009 Enrollment: n/a . . . . (713) 664-5300
2010-11 Tuition: $3,560
Aviation Institute of Maintenance-Houston (Private, For-profit)
Fall 2009 Enrollment: 105 . . . . (713) 644-7777
2010-11 Tuition: In-state $13,020; Out-of-state $13,020
Champion Beauty College (Private, For-profit)
Fall 2009 Enrollment: 34 . . . . (281) 583-9117
2010-11 Tuition: $12,850
Everest Institute-Bissonnet (Private, For-profit)
Fall 2009 Enrollment: 1,331 . . . . (713) 772-4200
2010-11 Tuition: $15,600
Everest Institute-Greenspoint (Private, For-profit)
Fall 2009 Enrollment: 1,226 . . . . (281) 447-7037
2010-11 Tuition: $15,475
Everest Institute-Hobby (Private, For-profit)
Fall 2009 Enrollment: 1,137 . . . . (713) 645-7404
2010-11 Tuition: $15,180
Franklin Beauty School (Private, For-profit)
Fall 2009 Enrollment: 132 . . . . (713) 645-9060
2010-11 Tuition: $10,125
HTEC-Houston's Training and Education Center Inc (Private, For-profit)
Fall 2009 Enrollment: 75 . . . . (281) 219-3305
2010-11 Tuition: $7,575
Houston Training School (Private, For-profit)
Fall 2009 Enrollment: 33 . . . . (281) 535-0290
2010-11 Tuition: $11,000
Houston Training School-South (Private, For-profit)
Fall 2009 Enrollment: 259 . . . . (281) 535-0290
2010-11 Tuition: $11,000
ICC Technical Institute (Private, Not-for-profit)
Fall 2009 Enrollment: 73 . . . . (713) 522-7799
2010-11 Tuition: $6,600
Interactive Learning Systems (Private, For-profit)
Fall 2009 Enrollment: 33 . . . . (281) 931-7717
2010-11 Tuition: $11,375
Interactive Learning Systems (Private, For-profit)
Fall 2009 Enrollment: 21 . . . . (713) 771-5336
2010-11 Tuition: $11,375
Jay's Technical Institute (Private, For-profit)
Fall 2009 Enrollment: 150 . . . . (713) 772-2410
2010-11 Tuition: $10,850
Mai-trix Beauty College (Private, For-profit)
Fall 2009 Enrollment: 66 . . . . (713) 957-0050
2010-11 Tuition: $10,033
MediaTech Institute-Houston (Private, For-profit)
Fall 2009 Enrollment: 116 . . . . (832) 242-3426
North West Beauty School (Private, For-profit)
Fall 2009 Enrollment: 148 . . . . (713) 263-8333
2010-11 Tuition: $11,520
Northwest Educational Center (Private, For-profit)
Fall 2009 Enrollment: 297 . . . . (713) 680-2929
2010-11 Tuition: $8,500
Ocean Corporation (Private, For-profit)
Fall 2009 Enrollment: 344 . . . . (281) 776-3322
2010-11 Tuition: $16,500
Paul Mitchell The School- Houston (Private, For-profit)
Fall 2009 Enrollment: 249 . . . . (713) 465-6300
2010-11 Tuition: $15,900
Professional Careers Institute (Private, For-profit)
Fall 2009 Enrollment: 98 . . . . (713) 783-3999
2010-11 Tuition: $8,800
Royal Beauty Careers (Private, For-profit)
Fall 2009 Enrollment: 124 . . . . (770) 446-1333
2010-11 Tuition: $14,500

Sanford-Brown Institute (Private, For-profit)
Fall 2009 Enrollment: 505 . . . . (832) 325-4500
2010-11 Tuition: $13,772
School of Automotive Machinists (Private, For-profit)
Fall 2009 Enrollment: 96 . . . . (713) 683-3817
2010-11 Tuition: $31,750
Sebring Career Schools (Private, For-profit)
Fall 2009 Enrollment: 107 . . . . (281) 561-0592
2010-11 Tuition: $9,050
Texas Barber Colleges and Hairstyling Schools (Private, For-profit)
Fall 2009 Enrollment: 1,375. . . . . (713) 953-0262
2010-11 Tuition: $12,050
Texas Health School (Private, For-profit)
Fall 2009 Enrollment: 163 . . . . (713) 932-9333
2010-11 Tuition: $817
Texas School of Business East Inc (Private, For-profit)
Fall 2009 Enrollment: 360 . . . . (713) 455-8555
2010-11 Tuition: $15,506
The Academy of Health Care Professions (Private, For-profit)
Fall 2009 Enrollment: 34 . . . . (713) 470-2427
2010-11 Tuition: $20,600
Trend Barber College (Private, For-profit)
Fall 2009 Enrollment: 150 . . . . (713) 721-0000
2010-11 Tuition: $10,995
Housing: Homeownership rate: 47.7% (2010); Median home value: $121,005 (2010); Median contract rent: $629 per month (2005-2009 5-year est.); Median year structure built: 1975 (2005-2009 5-year est.).
Hospitals: Ben Taub General Hospital (650 beds); CHRISTUS St. John Hospital (178 beds); Columbia Spring Branch Medical Center (350 beds); Cypress Fairbanks Medical Center Hospital (160 beds); Doctor's Hospital Parkway + Tidwell (263 beds); Doctors Hospital Parkway & Tidwell (285 beds); East Houston Regional Medical Center; Harris County Psychiatric Center (250 beds); Healthsouth Hospital For Specialized Surgery; Herman Memorial Prevention & Recovery Center (176 beds); Houston Northwest Medical Center (494 beds); Institute for Rehabilitation & Research (70 beds); Intracare Hospital (142 beds); Intracare North Hospital (90 beds); Lyndon B. Johnson General Hospital (332 beds); Memorial Hermann - Texas Medical Center (908 beds); Memorial Hermann Healthcare System; Memorial Hermann Hospital Southeast (267 beds); Memorial Hermann Hospital Southwest (600 beds); Memorial Hermann Memorial City; Memorial Hermann Northwest Hospital; Menninger Clinic (130 beds); Methodist Hospital, The; Methodist Willowbrook Hospital; Michael E. Debakey VA Medical Center (343 beds); Park Plaza Hospital (446 beds); Renaissance Hospital Houston (39 beds); Riverside General Hospital (98 beds); Select Specialty Hospital - Houston Heights (300 beds); Shriners Hospitals for Children (40 beds); St. Joseph Medical Center (792 beds); St. Luke's Episcopal Hospital (946 beds); TOPS Surgical Specialty Hospital; Texas Children's Hospital (456 beds); Texas Orthopedic Hospital; The Methodist Hospital (300 beds); Twelve Oaks Hospital (190 beds); Twelve Oaks Medical Center (526 beds); University General Hospital; University of Houston Health Center (4 beds); University of Texas M.D. Anderson Cancer Center, The (517 beds); West Houston Medical Center (221 beds); West Oaks Hospital (144 beds); Womans Hospital of Texas (275 beds)
Safety: Violent crime rate: 112.6 per 10,000 population; Property crime rate: 531.9 per 10,000 population (2009).
Newspapers: African News Digest (Local news; Circulation 85,000); African-American News & Issues (National news; Circulation 350,000); Al Madar; Barbers Hill Press (Local news; Circulation 2,500); Bellaire Examiner (Community news); Children's Software Press; Daily Court Review (Local news; Circulation 500,000); El Dia (Local news; Circulation 60,000); Exchange News (Community news; Circulation 15,002); Financial Times - Houston Bureau (Regional news); Greater Greenspoint Reporter (Local news; Circulation 20,000); Greater Houston Weekly (Community news); Highlands Star/Crosby Courier (Community news; Circulation 7,000); Houston Chronicle (Regional news; Circulation 503,114); Houston Forward Times (Local news; Circulation 64,580); Houston Press (Local news; Circulation 75,000); Houston Tribune (Local news; Indo-American News (Local news; Circulation 4,000); The Informer and Texas Freeman (Community news; Circulation 40,000); Jewish Herald-Voice (Local news; Circulation 7,000); Korea Times Houston Edition (Local news; Circulation 8,500); La Informacion (Local news; Circulation 100,000); La Voz De Houston (Local news; Circulation 90,000); The Leader (Community news; Circulation 77,160); Los Angeles Times - Houston Bureau (Local news); Memorial Examiner (Community news; Circulation 21,000); Metro Weekender (National news); Neighbourhood News (Community news); The New York Times - Houston Bureau (International news); North Forest News (Community news; Circulation 13,000); Northeast News (Community news; Circulation 32,000); River Oaks Examiner (Community news); Rumbo de Houston (Local news; Circulation 25,000); Semana News (Local news; Circulation 146,500); South Belt-Ellington Leader (Community news; Circulation 10,000); Southern Chinese Daily News (Local news; Circulation 25,000); Texas Catholic Herald (Regional news; Circulation 72,000); The Wall Street Journal - Houston Bureau (Regional news); Weekly Petroleum Argus - Houston Bureau (International news); West University Examiner (Community news)
Transportation: Commute to work: 87.9% car, 4.8% public transportation, 2.1% walk, 3.1% work from home (2005-2009 5-year est.); Travel time to work: 21.1% less than 15 minutes, 38.8% 15 to 30 minutes, 24.7% 30 to 45 minutes, 7.8% 45 to 60 minutes, 7.5% 60 minutes or more (2005-2009 5-year est.); Amtrak: train service available.
Airports: David Wayne Hooks Memorial (general aviation); Ellington Field (general aviation); George Bush Intercontinental/Houston (primary service/large hub); Houston-Southwest (general aviation); Pearland Regional (general aviation); Sugar Land Regional (general aviation); Weiser Air Park (general aviation); William P Hobby (primary service/medium hub)
Additional Information Contacts
Caribbean Chamber of Commerce . . . . (281) 652-8404
  http://www.caribbeanchamber.org
City of Houston . . . . (713) 837-0311
  http://www.houstontx.gov
Clear Lake Area Chamber of Commerce. . . . . (281) 488-7676
  http://www.clearlakearea.com
French American Chamber of Commerce . . . . (713) 960-0575
  http://www.facchouston.com
Greater Houston Partnership . . . . (713) 844-3600
  http://www.houston.org
Houston Citizens Chamber of Commerce . . . . (713) 522-9745
  http://www.hccoc.org
Houston East End Chamber of Commerce . . . . (713) 926-3305
  http://www.eecoc.org
Houston Hispanic Chamber of Commerce . . . . (713) 644-7070
  http://www.houstonhispanicchamber.com
Houston Intercontinenal Chamber of Commerce. . . . . (281) 260-3163
  http://www.nhgcc.org
Houston NW Chamber of Commerce . . . . (281) 440-4160
  http://www.hnwcc.com
Interamerican Chamber of Commerce. . . . . (713) 975-6171
Italy-America Chamber of Commerce . . . . (713) 626-9303
  http://www.iacctexas.com
National Acres Home Chamber of Commerce. . . . . (281) 820-2620
  http://www.nahc-of-c.org/home.htm
South Asian Chamber of Commerce . . . . (713) 570-0199
Swedish American Chamber of Commerce. . . . . (713) 914-0015
  http://www.sacctx.com
Texas-Israel Chamber of Commerce. . . . . (214) 576-9639
  http://www.texasisrael.org

HUFFMAN (unincorporated postal area, zip code 77336). Covers a land area of 42.108 square miles and a water area of 0.175 square miles. Located at 30.04° N. Lat; 95.10° W. Long. Elevation is 69 feet.
Population: 8,678 (2000); Race: 94.5% White, 0.4% Black, 0.9% Asian, 4.2% Other, 6.0% Hispanic of any race (2000); Density: 206.1 persons per square mile (2000); Age: 29.2% under 18, 8.3% over 64 (2000); Marriage status: 20.5% never married, 65.6% now married, 5.2% widowed, 8.6% divorced (2000); Foreign born: 2.8% (2000); Ancestry (includes multiple ancestries): 13.7% German, 11.7% American, 11.2% Irish, 11.1% English (2000).
Economy: Employment by occupation: 11.6% management, 12.5% professional, 11.2% services, 33.5% sales, 0.0% farming, 17.6% construction, 13.6% production (2000).
Income: Per capita income: $21,151 (2000); Median household income: $51,989 (2000); Poverty rate: 179.1% (2000).
Education: Percent of population age 25 and over with: High school diploma (including GED) or higher: 81.9% (2000); Bachelor's degree or higher: 11.6% (2000).

School District(s)

Huffman ISD (PK-12)
2009-10 Enrollment: 3,152 . . . . (281) 324-1871

Housing: Homeownership rate: 86.0% (2000); Median home value: $78,600 (2000); Median contract rent: $498 per month (2000); Median year structure built: 1978 (2000).

Transportation: Commute to work: 97.0% car, 0.7% public transportation, 0.6% walk, 1.3% work from home (2000); Travel time to work: 12.7% less than 15 minutes, 20.1% 15 to 30 minutes, 25.9% 30 to 45 minutes, 21.6% 45 to 60 minutes, 19.8% 60 minutes or more (2000)

HUMBLE (city). Covers a land area of 9.867 square miles and a water area of 0.013 square miles. Located at 29.99° N. Lat; 95.26° W. Long. Elevation is 95 feet.

History: Named for Pleasant Humble, first postmaster and judge. The discovery of oil in 1904 changed Humble from a prairie town into an oil center. After the oil diminished, Humble returned to small truck farming and ranching.

Population: 12,060 (1990); 14,579 (2000); 15,293 (2010); 16,048 (2015 projected); Race: 55.7% White, 23.6% Black, 3.5% Asian, 17.3% Other, 32.5% Hispanic of any race (2010); Density: 1,549.8 persons per square mile (2010); Average household size: 2.75 (2010); Median age: 33.3 (2010); Males per 100 females: 98.8 (2010); Marriage status: 31.7% never married, 45.6% now married, 7.7% widowed, 15.1% divorced (2005-2009 5-year est.); Foreign born: 16.3% (2005-2009 5-year est.); Ancestry (includes multiple ancestries): 10.8% German, 10.2% Irish, 6.7% American, 4.5% English, 2.4% French (2005-2009 5-year est.).

Economy: Single-family building permits issued: 4 (2010); Multi-family building permits issued: 0 (2010); Employment by occupation: 8.7% management, 13.6% professional, 22.2% services, 29.3% sales, 0.0% farming, 13.4% construction, 12.8% production (2005-2009 5-year est.).

Income: Per capita income: $20,292 (2010); Median household income: $46,839 (2010); Average household income: $56,174 (2010); Percent of households with income of $100,000 or more: 13.5% (2010); Poverty rate: 19.4% (2005-2009 5-year est.).

Taxes: Total city taxes per capita: $1,023 (2007); City property taxes per capita: $143 (2007).

Education: Percent of population age 25 and over with: High school diploma (including GED) or higher: 81.8% (2010); Bachelor's degree or higher: 15.3% (2010); Master's degree or higher: 5.1% (2010).

School District(s)
Aldine ISD (PK-12)
    2009-10 Enrollment: 62,792 . . . . (281) 449-1011
Humble ISD (PK-12)
    2009-10 Enrollment: 34,923 . . . . (281) 641-1000

Housing: Homeownership rate: 52.6% (2010); Median home value: $123,948 (2010); Median contract rent: $637 per month (2005-2009 5-year est.); Median year structure built: 1980 (2005-2009 5-year est.).

Hospitals: Healthsouth Humble Rehabilitation Hospital; Northeast Medical Center Hospital (237 beds)

Safety: Violent crime rate: 114.5 per 10,000 population; Property crime rate: 1,364.7 per 10,000 population (2009).

Newspapers: Atascocita Observer (Community news; Circulation 11,000); East Montgomery County Observer (Community news; Circulation 10,700); Humble Observer (Community news; Circulation 19,500); Kingwood Observer (Community news; Circulation 21,975); Kingwood Sun (Community news; Circulation 15,975); Spring Observer East (Community news; Circulation 11,000); Spring Observer West (Community news; Circulation 10,700)

Transportation: Commute to work: 91.9% car, 0.6% public transportation, 3.8% walk, 1.4% work from home (2005-2009 5-year est.); Travel time to work: 27.8% less than 15 minutes, 36.7% 15 to 30 minutes, 24.1% 30 to 45 minutes, 6.2% 45 to 60 minutes, 5.2% 60 minutes or more (2005-2009 5-year est.)

Additional Information Contacts
City of Humble . . . . (281) 446-3061
    http://www.cityofhumble.org
Community Chamber of Commerce . . . . (281) 348-1531
    http://www.communitychamber.org
Lake Houston Area Chamber of Commerce . . . . (281) 446-2128
    http://www.humbleareachamber.org

HUNTERS CREEK VILLAGE (city). Covers a land area of 1.941 square miles and a water area of 0 square miles. Located at 29.77° N. Lat; 95.50° W. Long. Elevation is 66 feet.

History: By 1936 the community had a sawmill and several residences. In the mid-1950s, effort to form a Spring Branch municipality failed. The city incorporated in 1954 with a mayor-alderman government.

Population: 3,954 (1990); 4,374 (2000); 4,693 (2010); 4,958 (2015 projected); Race: 91.6% White, 0.5% Black, 6.0% Asian, 1.9% Other, 4.7% Hispanic of any race (2010); Density: 2,417.3 persons per square mile (2010); Average household size: 3.09 (2010); Median age: 45.4 (2010); Males per 100 females: 94.1 (2010); Marriage status: 18.5% never married, 74.6% now married, 3.9% widowed, 3.0% divorced (2005-2009 5-year est.); Foreign born: 9.8% (2005-2009 5-year est.); Ancestry (includes multiple ancestries): 18.7% English, 17.8% German, 10.8% Irish, 8.5% American, 7.2% Scotch-Irish (2005-2009 5-year est.).

Economy: Single-family building permits issued: 16 (2010); Multi-family building permits issued: 0 (2010); Employment by occupation: 29.7% management, 40.6% professional, 2.1% services, 23.0% sales, 0.0% farming, 3.4% construction, 1.1% production (2005-2009 5-year est.).

Income: Per capita income: $79,714 (2010); Median household income: $218,000 (2010); Average household income: $246,603 (2010); Percent of households with income of $100,000 or more: 76.1% (2010); Poverty rate: 1.1% (2005-2009 5-year est.).

Taxes: Total city taxes per capita: $995 (2007); City property taxes per capita: $751 (2007).

Education: Percent of population age 25 and over with: High school diploma (including GED) or higher: 96.8% (2010); Bachelor's degree or higher: 76.2% (2010); Master's degree or higher: 33.6% (2010).

Housing: Homeownership rate: 97.8% (2010); Median home value: $876,712 (2010); Median contract rent: $2,000+ per month (2005-2009 5-year est.); Median year structure built: 1975 (2005-2009 5-year est.).

Transportation: Commute to work: 95.7% car, 0.0% public transportation, 0.0% walk, 4.3% work from home (2005-2009 5-year est.); Travel time to work: 28.5% less than 15 minutes, 41.8% 15 to 30 minutes, 29.0% 30 to 45 minutes, 0.0% 45 to 60 minutes, 0.8% 60 minutes or more (2005-2009 5-year est.)

Additional Information Contacts
City of Hunters Creek Village. . . . . (713) 465-2150
    http://cityofhunterscreek.com

JACINTO CITY (city). Covers a land area of 1.859 square miles and a water area of 0 square miles. Located at 29.76° N. Lat; 95.24° W. Long. Elevation is 30 feet.

History: Incorporated since 1940.

Population: 9,343 (1990); 10,302 (2000); 10,012 (2010); 10,118 (2015 projected); Race: 69.2% White, 1.3% Black, 0.2% Asian, 29.3% Other, 84.2% Hispanic of any race (2010); Density: 5,384.9 persons per square mile (2010); Average household size: 3.58 (2010); Median age: 29.7 (2010); Males per 100 females: 101.3 (2010); Marriage status: 32.5% never married, 53.9% now married, 4.9% widowed, 8.7% divorced (2005-2009 5-year est.); Foreign born: 39.2% (2005-2009 5-year est.); Ancestry (includes multiple ancestries): 3.8% Irish, 2.6% American, 2.3% German, 1.2% English, 0.7% Greek (2005-2009 5-year est.).

Economy: Single-family building permits issued: 3 (2010); Multi-family building permits issued: 0 (2010); Employment by occupation: 2.9% management, 7.6% professional, 18.2% services, 21.2% sales, 2.0% farming, 14.3% construction, 33.8% production (2005-2009 5-year est.).

Income: Per capita income: $14,099 (2010); Median household income: $43,882 (2010); Average household income: $50,742 (2010); Percent of households with income of $100,000 or more: 7.7% (2010); Poverty rate: 18.7% (2005-2009 5-year est.).

Taxes: Total city taxes per capita: $398 (2007); City property taxes per capita: $252 (2007).

Education: Percent of population age 25 and over with: High school diploma (including GED) or higher: 48.7% (2010); Bachelor's degree or higher: 4.8% (2010); Master's degree or higher: 1.7% (2010).

Housing: Homeownership rate: 70.4% (2010); Median home value: $63,027 (2010); Median contract rent: $488 per month (2005-2009 5-year est.); Median year structure built: 1957 (2005-2009 5-year est.).

Safety: Violent crime rate: 35.4 per 10,000 population; Property crime rate: 331.9 per 10,000 population (2009).

Transportation: Commute to work: 90.3% car, 2.0% public transportation, 1.4% walk, 0.3% work from home (2005-2009 5-year est.); Travel time to work: 26.4% less than 15 minutes, 40.8% 15 to 30 minutes, 20.4% 30 to 45 minutes, 6.2% 45 to 60 minutes, 6.2% 60 minutes or more (2005-2009 5-year est.)

Additional Information Contacts
City of Jacinto City . . . . (713) 674-8424
    http://www.jacintocity-tx.gov
North Channel Chamber of Commerce . . . . (713) 450-3600
    http://www.northchannelarea.com

JERSEY VILLAGE (city). Covers a land area of 3.416 square miles and a water area of 0.031 square miles. Located at 29.89° N. Lat; 95.56° W. Long. Elevation is 105 feet.

History: The first family moved to the subdivision in late October 1954. The community developed a school, a park, and an 18-hole golf course. Jersey Village incorporated on April 16, 1956 with all 58 votes in favor of incorporation and a volunteer police force.

Population: 5,292 (1990); 6,880 (2000); 7,345 (2010); 7,610 (2015 projected); Race: 80.4% White, 5.2% Black, 6.6% Asian, 7.8% Other, 12.4% Hispanic of any race (2010); Density: 2,150.5 persons per square mile (2010); Average household size: 2.38 (2010); Median age: 36.9 (2010); Males per 100 females: 100.2 (2010); Marriage status: 30.9% never married, 53.5% now married, 4.2% widowed, 11.4% divorced (2005-2009 5-year est.); Foreign born: 11.4% (2005-2009 5-year est.); Ancestry (includes multiple ancestries): 18.1% German, 11.4% English, 10.2% Irish, 5.6% American, 5.3% Italian (2005-2009 5-year est.).

Economy: Single-family building permits issued: 9 (2010); Multi-family building permits issued: 0 (2010); Employment by occupation: 22.6% management, 28.5% professional, 6.6% services, 30.6% sales, 0.0% farming, 4.3% construction, 7.3% production (2005-2009 5-year est.).

Income: Per capita income: $39,432 (2010); Median household income: $73,378 (2010); Average household income: $93,905 (2010); Percent of households with income of $100,000 or more: 34.8% (2010); Poverty rate: 3.2% (2005-2009 5-year est.).

Taxes: Total city taxes per capita: $350 (2007); City property taxes per capita: $138 (2007).

Education: Percent of population age 25 and over with: High school diploma (including GED) or higher: 92.7% (2010); Bachelor's degree or higher: 42.3% (2010); Master's degree or higher: 13.7% (2010).

Housing: Homeownership rate: 50.0% (2010); Median home value: $204,552 (2010); Median contract rent: $839 per month (2005-2009 5-year est.); Median year structure built: 1991 (2005-2009 5-year est.).

Safety: Violent crime rate: 27.3 per 10,000 population; Property crime rate: 434.2 per 10,000 population (2009).

Transportation: Commute to work: 95.4% car, 1.5% public transportation, 0.4% walk, 2.4% work from home (2005-2009 5-year est.); Travel time to work: 19.1% less than 15 minutes, 35.3% 15 to 30 minutes, 25.7% 30 to 45 minutes, 10.0% 45 to 60 minutes, 10.0% 60 minutes or more (2005-2009 5-year est.)

Additional Information Contacts

City of Jersey Village . . . . (713) 466-2102
   http://www.jerseyvillage.info

KATY (city). Covers a land area of 10.668 square miles and a water area of 0 square miles. Located at 29.79° N. Lat; 95.82° W. Long. Elevation is 141 feet.

Population: 8,059 (1990); 11,775 (2000); 13,983 (2010); 15,615 (2015 projected); Race: 77.7% White, 5.0% Black, 0.7% Asian, 16.5% Other, 33.6% Hispanic of any race (2010); Density: 1,310.7 persons per square mile (2010); Average household size: 3.05 (2010); Median age: 33.4 (2010); Males per 100 females: 99.9 (2010); Marriage status: 28.4% never married, 59.3% now married, 2.9% widowed, 9.3% divorced (2005-2009 5-year est.); Foreign born: 15.7% (2005-2009 5-year est.); Ancestry (includes multiple ancestries): 13.1% American, 13.0% German, 10.0% Irish, 8.8% English, 2.8% Italian (2005-2009 5-year est.).

Economy: Single-family building permits issued: 48 (2010); Multi-family building permits issued: 0 (2010); Employment by occupation: 15.3% management, 16.7% professional, 17.1% services, 24.8% sales, 0.2% farming, 13.1% construction, 12.8% production (2005-2009 5-year est.).

Income: Per capita income: $25,944 (2010); Median household income: $62,001 (2010); Average household income: $79,615 (2010); Percent of households with income of $100,000 or more: 28.1% (2010); Poverty rate: 11.4% (2005-2009 5-year est.).

Taxes: Total city taxes per capita: $1,000 (2007); City property taxes per capita: $413 (2007).

Education: Percent of population age 25 and over with: High school diploma (including GED) or higher: 84.4% (2010); Bachelor's degree or higher: 24.4% (2010); Master's degree or higher: 6.6% (2010).

School District(s)

Calvin Nelms Charter Schools (04-12)
   2009-10 Enrollment: 297 . . . . (281) 398-8031
Cypress-Fairbanks ISD (PK-12)
   2009-10 Enrollment: 104,231 . . . . (281) 897-4000

Excel Academy (04-12)
   2009-10 Enrollment: 529 . . . . (713) 222-4340
Katy ISD (PK-12)
   2009-10 Enrollment: 59,078 . . . . (281) 396-6000
Southwest School (PK-12)
   2009-10 Enrollment: 3,598 . . . . (713) 784-6345
Trinity Charter School (KG-12)
   2009-10 Enrollment: 277 . . . . (512) 706-7564
West Houston Charter School (KG-08)
   2009-10 Enrollment: 307 . . . . (281) 391-5003

Housing: Homeownership rate: 74.5% (2010); Median home value: $136,056 (2010); Median contract rent: $819 per month (2005-2009 5-year est.); Median year structure built: 1987 (2005-2009 5-year est.).

Hospitals: Christus Saint Catherine Hospital; Memorial Herman Katy Hospital (118 beds)

Safety: Violent crime rate: 34.6 per 10,000 population; Property crime rate: 457.4 per 10,000 population (2009).

Newspapers: Katy Courier (Local news); Katy Sun (Community news; Circulation 22,000); The Katy Times (Local news; Circulation 8,000)

Transportation: Commute to work: 93.7% car, 1.6% public transportation, 0.7% walk, 2.1% work from home (2005-2009 5-year est.); Travel time to work: 29.9% less than 15 minutes, 26.2% 15 to 30 minutes, 18.5% 30 to 45 minutes, 13.4% 45 to 60 minutes, 11.9% 60 minutes or more (2005-2009 5-year est.)

Airports: Houston Executive (general aviation)

Additional Information Contacts

City of Katy . . . . (281) 391-4800
   http://ci.katy.tx.us
Katy Area Chamber of Commerce . . . . (281) 391-5289
   http://www.katychamber.com

LA PORTE (city). Covers a land area of 18.939 square miles and a water area of 1.028 square miles. Located at 29.66° N. Lat; 95.04° W. Long. Elevation is 20 feet.

History: Named for the French translation of "entrance," for its location as a "gateway to the sea". San Jacinto Battleground and Battleship Texas State Historic Site to North. Settled 1889. Incorporated 1892.

Population: 27,923 (1990); 31,880 (2000); 33,876 (2010); 35,605 (2015 projected); Race: 75.8% White, 6.3% Black, 1.3% Asian, 16.6% Other, 28.8% Hispanic of any race (2010); Density: 1,788.7 persons per square mile (2010); Average household size: 2.91 (2010); Median age: 34.5 (2010); Males per 100 females: 99.5 (2010); Marriage status: 25.5% never married, 56.4% now married, 5.4% widowed, 12.7% divorced (2005-2009 5-year est.); Foreign born: 8.7% (2005-2009 5-year est.); Ancestry (includes multiple ancestries): 13.7% German, 9.6% American, 9.6% English, 8.3% Irish, 3.5% European (2005-2009 5-year est.).

Economy: Unemployment rate: 9.2% (June 2011); Total civilian labor force: 18,673 (June 2011); Single-family building permits issued: 21 (2010); Multi-family building permits issued: 0 (2010); Employment by occupation: 11.1% management, 18.3% professional, 14.6% services, 24.6% sales, 0.3% farming, 14.3% construction, 16.9% production (2005-2009 5-year est.).

Income: Per capita income: $26,817 (2010); Median household income: $69,117 (2010); Average household income: $77,651 (2010); Percent of households with income of $100,000 or more: 25.4% (2010); Poverty rate: 10.0% (2005-2009 5-year est.).

Taxes: Total city taxes per capita: $556 (2007); City property taxes per capita: $359 (2007).

Education: Percent of population age 25 and over with: High school diploma (including GED) or higher: 85.9% (2010); Bachelor's degree or higher: 13.2% (2010); Master's degree or higher: 3.8% (2010).

School District(s)

La Porte ISD (PK-12)
   2009-10 Enrollment: 7,847 . . . . (281) 604-7015
Trinity Charter School (KG-12)
   2009-10 Enrollment: 277 . . . . (512) 706-7564

Housing: Homeownership rate: 79.5% (2010); Median home value: $122,312 (2010); Median contract rent: $693 per month (2005-2009 5-year est.); Median year structure built: 1981 (2005-2009 5-year est.).

Safety: Violent crime rate: 19.7 per 10,000 population; Property crime rate: 196.3 per 10,000 population (2009).

Newspapers: Bayshore Sun (Community news; Circulation 11,000)

Transportation: Commute to work: 96.0% car, 0.2% public transportation, 0.1% walk, 1.2% work from home (2005-2009 5-year est.); Travel time to work: 32.2% less than 15 minutes, 34.3% 15 to 30 minutes, 21.1% 30 to 45

minutes, 7.0% 45 to 60 minutes, 5.5% 60 minutes or more (2005-2009 5-year est.)

Additional Information Contacts
City of La Porte .... (281) 471-5020
http://www.ci.la-porte.tx.us
La Porte-Bayshore Chamber of Commerce............. (281) 471-1123
http://www.laportechamber.org

MORGAN'S POINT (city). Covers a land area of 1.614 square miles and a water area of 0.151 square miles. Located at 29.67° N. Lat; 95.00° W. Long.

Population: 341 (1990); 336 (2000); 315 (2010); 310 (2015 projected); Race: 80.6% White, 9.8% Black, 0.0% Asian, 9.5% Other, 13.3% Hispanic of any race (2010); Density: 195.1 persons per square mile (2010); Average household size: 2.45 (2010); Median age: 40.4 (2010); Males per 100 females: 111.4 (2010); Marriage status: 30.3% never married, 55.5% now married, 6.6% widowed, 7.6% divorced (2005-2009 5-year est.); Foreign born: 4.8% (2005-2009 5-year est.); Ancestry (includes multiple ancestries): 23.8% English, 23.4% Irish, 14.3% German, 9.5% Italian, 6.5% French (2005-2009 5-year est.).

Economy: Single-family building permits issued: 2 (2010); Multi-family building permits issued: 0 (2010); Employment by occupation: 13.5% management, 16.9% professional, 9.0% services, 29.2% sales, 0.0% farming, 21.3% construction, 10.1% production (2005-2009 5-year est.).

Income: Per capita income: $32,026 (2010); Median household income: $59,524 (2010); Average household income: $93,822 (2010); Percent of households with income of $100,000 or more: 22.1% (2010); Poverty rate: 25.5% (2005-2009 5-year est.).

Taxes: Total city taxes per capita: $2,466 (2007); City property taxes per capita: $930 (2007).

Education: Percent of population age 25 and over with: High school diploma (including GED) or higher: 77.3% (2010); Bachelor's degree or higher: 20.8% (2010); Master's degree or higher: 9.2% (2010).

Housing: Homeownership rate: 86.5% (2010); Median home value: $134,375 (2010); Median contract rent: $295 per month (2005-2009 5-year est.); Median year structure built: 1951 (2005-2009 5-year est.).

Transportation: Commute to work: 88.2% car, 0.0% public transportation, 0.0% walk, 4.7% work from home (2005-2009 5-year est.); Travel time to work: 11.1% less than 15 minutes, 44.4% 15 to 30 minutes, 32.1% 30 to 45 minutes, 7.4% 45 to 60 minutes, 4.9% 60 minutes or more (2005-2009 5-year est.)

NASSAU BAY (city). Covers a land area of 1.326 square miles and a water area of 0.386 square miles. Located at 29.54° N. Lat; 95.09° W. Long. Elevation is 16 feet.

History: The name was chosen by the original developers of raw land known as Colonel Pearson's 1776 Ranch. The name was chosen because of the tropical feeling it generates. The developers sought to create an atmosphere that would be familiar and comfortable to people moving from warmer areas of the country. When Nassau Bay was incorporated in 1970, the name of the development was retained as the City's name.

Population: 4,320 (1990); 4,170 (2000); 3,958 (2010); 3,947 (2015 projected); Race: 85.3% White, 3.1% Black, 4.1% Asian, 7.4% Other, 9.9% Hispanic of any race (2010); Density: 2,986.0 persons per square mile (2010); Average household size: 2.05 (2010); Median age: 49.2 (2010); Males per 100 females: 96.6 (2010); Marriage status: 26.8% never married, 53.4% now married, 5.3% widowed, 14.4% divorced (2005-2009 5-year est.); Foreign born: 12.3% (2005-2009 5-year est.); Ancestry (includes multiple ancestries): 25.5% German, 20.2% English, 16.0% Irish, 7.3% French, 7.3% Scotch-Irish (2005-2009 5-year est.).

Economy: Single-family building permits issued: 0 (2010); Multi-family building permits issued: 0 (2010); Employment by occupation: 24.5% management, 34.0% professional, 11.8% services, 20.7% sales, 0.0% farming, 3.4% construction, 5.5% production (2005-2009 5-year est.).

Income: Per capita income: $45,983 (2010); Median household income: $69,527 (2010); Average household income: $94,400 (2010); Percent of households with income of $100,000 or more: 34.6% (2010); Poverty rate: 5.4% (2005-2009 5-year est.).

Taxes: Total city taxes per capita: $1,070 (2007); City property taxes per capita: $640 (2007).

Education: Percent of population age 25 and over with: High school diploma (including GED) or higher: 96.7% (2010); Bachelor's degree or higher: 52.9% (2010); Master's degree or higher: 26.0% (2010).

Housing: Homeownership rate: 62.5% (2010); Median home value: $232,809 (2010); Median contract rent: $612 per month (2005-2009 5-year est.); Median year structure built: 1969 (2005-2009 5-year est.).

Safety: Violent crime rate: 12.4 per 10,000 population; Property crime rate: 313.0 per 10,000 population (2009).

Transportation: Commute to work: 83.6% car, 0.6% public transportation, 3.2% walk, 10.9% work from home (2005-2009 5-year est.); Travel time to work: 31.9% less than 15 minutes, 21.2% 15 to 30 minutes, 21.5% 30 to 45 minutes, 16.6% 45 to 60 minutes, 8.8% 60 minutes or more (2005-2009 5-year est.)

Additional Information Contacts
City of Nassau Bay .... (281) 333-4211
http://www.nassaubay.com

PASADENA (city). Covers a land area of 44.162 square miles and a water area of 0.359 square miles. Located at 29.67° N. Lat; 95.17° W. Long. Elevation is 30 feet.

History: Named for Pasadena, California, which was named for the Ojibway Indian translation of "crown of the valley". Pasadena developed as a residential community for people working in Houston and in nearby oil refineries. It was at this site that Mexican General Santa Anna was captured after the Battle of San Jacinto in 1836.

Population: 119,344 (1990); 141,674 (2000); 149,217 (2010); 155,189 (2015 projected); Race: 63.5% White, 2.1% Black, 2.7% Asian, 31.8% Other, 59.1% Hispanic of any race (2010); Density: 3,378.9 persons per square mile (2010); Average household size: 3.08 (2010); Median age: 31.3 (2010); Males per 100 females: 101.0 (2010); Marriage status: 29.7% never married, 54.5% now married, 5.0% widowed, 10.8% divorced (2005-2009 5-year est.); Foreign born: 25.2% (2005-2009 5-year est.); Ancestry (includes multiple ancestries): 7.3% German, 6.3% Irish, 5.2% English, 5.0% American, 2.0% French (2005-2009 5-year est.).

Economy: Unemployment rate: 11.1% (June 2011); Total civilian labor force: 68,133 (June 2011); Single-family building permits issued: 47 (2010); Multi-family building permits issued: 159 (2010); Employment by occupation: 9.5% management, 13.3% professional, 16.8% services, 23.0% sales, 0.1% farming, 20.8% construction, 16.5% production (2005-2009 5-year est.).

Income: Per capita income: $19,986 (2010); Median household income: $47,061 (2010); Average household income: $61,754 (2010); Percent of households with income of $100,000 or more: 16.1% (2010); Poverty rate: 18.8% (2005-2009 5-year est.).

Taxes: Total city taxes per capita: $451 (2007); City property taxes per capita: $188 (2007).

Education: Percent of population age 25 and over with: High school diploma (including GED) or higher: 70.4% (2010); Bachelor's degree or higher: 14.1% (2010); Master's degree or higher: 5.2% (2010).

School District(s)
Deer Park ISD (PK-12)
2009-10 Enrollment: 12,502 .... (832) 668-7000
Pasadena ISD (PK-12)
2009-10 Enrollment: 52,303 ....

Four-year College(s)
Texas Chiropractic College Foundation Inc (Private, Not-for-profit)
Fall 2009 Enrollment: 343 .... (281) 487-1170

Two-year College(s)
San Jacinto Community College (Public)
Fall 2009 Enrollment: 27,011...................... (281) 998-6150
2010-11 Tuition: In-state $2,160; Out-of-state $3,660

Vocational/Technical School(s)
Interactive Learning Systems (Private, For-profit)
Fall 2009 Enrollment: 35 .... (713) 920-1120
2010-11 Tuition: $11,375
Regency Beauty Institute-Pasadena (Private, For-profit)
Fall 2009 Enrollment: 85 .... (800) 787-6456
2010-11 Tuition: $16,075

Housing: Homeownership rate: 60.7% (2010); Median home value: $107,939 (2010); Median contract rent: $579 per month (2005-2009 5-year est.); Median year structure built: 1973 (2005-2009 5-year est.).

Hospitals: Bayshore Medical Center (373 beds); Vista Medical Center Hospital

Safety: Violent crime rate: 48.0 per 10,000 population; Property crime rate: 381.7 per 10,000 population (2009).

Newspapers: Deer Park Broadcaster (Community news; Circulation 15,000); The Lake Houston Sentinel (Local news; Circulation 14,105); The North Channel Sentinel (Community news; Circulation 33,714)

Transportation: Commute to work: 93.0% car, 0.6% public transportation, 1.5% walk, 2.1% work from home (2005-2009 5-year est.); Travel time to work: 26.4% less than 15 minutes, 36.9% 15 to 30 minutes, 21.1% 30 to 45 minutes, 8.0% 45 to 60 minutes, 7.6% 60 minutes or more (2005-2009 5-year est.)

Additional Information Contacts

City of Pasadena . . . . (713) 477-1511
    http://www.ci.pasadena.tx.us
Pasadena Chamber of Commerce . . . . (281) 487-7871
    http://www.pasadenachamber.org

PINEY POINT VILLAGE (city). Aka Piney Point. Covers a land
area of 2.139 square miles and a water area of 0 square miles. Located at 29.76° N. Lat; 95.51° W. Long. Elevation is 72 feet.

History: In 1885 Piney Point Village began as a station on the Texas Western Railroad. German farmers settled in the area. According to 1936 state highway maps, the community was near a sawmill. In the mid 1950s, effort to form a Spring Branch municipality failed. Piney Point Village incorporated in 1955 with an alderman form of government.

Population: 3,214 (1990); 3,380 (2000); 3,482 (2010); 3,596 (2015 projected); Race: 85.7% White, 0.7% Black, 11.0% Asian, 2.6% Other, 4.8% Hispanic of any race (2010); Density: 1,627.9 persons per square mile (2010); Average household size: 2.76 (2010); Median age: 47.4 (2010); Males per 100 females: 96.7 (2010); Marriage status: 20.4% never married, 71.4% now married, 4.3% widowed, 3.9% divorced (2005-2009 5-year est.); Foreign born: 17.2% (2005-2009 5-year est.); Ancestry (includes multiple ancestries): 20.3% English, 11.1% Irish, 10.7% German, 8.1% American, 7.3% Scotch-Irish (2005-2009 5-year est.).

Economy: Single-family building permits issued: 4 (2010); Multi-family building permits issued: 0 (2010); Employment by occupation: 36.3% management, 40.9% professional, 3.8% services, 14.6% sales, 0.0% farming, 1.8% construction, 2.5% production (2005-2009 5-year est.).

Income: Per capita income: $93,828 (2010); Median household income: $258,315 (2010); Average household income: $258,676 (2010); Percent of households with income of $100,000 or more: 77.0% (2010); Poverty rate: 2.0% (2005-2009 5-year est.).

Taxes: Total city taxes per capita: $156 (2007); City property taxes per capita: $66 (2007).

Education: Percent of population age 25 and over with: High school diploma (including GED) or higher: 99.3% (2010); Bachelor's degree or higher: 74.0% (2010); Master's degree or higher: 33.6% (2010).

Housing: Homeownership rate: 95.3% (2010); Median home value: $1 million+ (2010); Median contract rent: $1,039 per month (2005-2009 5-year est.); Median year structure built: 1976 (2005-2009 5-year est.).

Transportation: Commute to work: 93.8% car, 0.0% public transportation, 0.0% walk, 5.6% work from home (2005-2009 5-year est.); Travel time to work: 26.5% less than 15 minutes, 51.4% 15 to 30 minutes, 18.8% 30 to 45 minutes, 1.7% 45 to 60 minutes, 1.7% 60 minutes or more (2005-2009 5-year est.)

SEABROOK (city). Covers a land area of 5.732 square miles and a
water area of 15.780 square miles. Located at 29.56° N. Lat; 95.02° W. Long. Elevation is 13 feet.

Population: 6,685 (1990); 9,443 (2000); 11,926 (2010); 13,225 (2015 projected); Race: 86.9% White, 2.4% Black, 3.2% Asian, 7.6% Other, 14.1% Hispanic of any race (2010); Density: 2,080.7 persons per square mile (2010); Average household size: 2.53 (2010); Median age: 38.4 (2010); Males per 100 females: 105.8 (2010); Marriage status: 28.4% never married, 55.5% now married, 3.7% widowed, 12.3% divorced (2005-2009 5-year est.); Foreign born: 7.3% (2005-2009 5-year est.); Ancestry (includes multiple ancestries): 22.0% German, 14.8% Irish, 14.5% English, 5.7% French, 4.5% American (2005-2009 5-year est.).

Economy: Single-family building permits issued: 45 (2010); Multi-family building permits issued: 0 (2010); Employment by occupation: 19.0% management, 26.2% professional, 11.9% services, 22.1% sales, 1.4% farming, 7.5% construction, 11.9% production (2005-2009 5-year est.).

Income: Per capita income: $37,681 (2010); Median household income: $78,189 (2010); Average household income: $95,136 (2010); Percent of households with income of $100,000 or more: 36.4% (2010); Poverty rate: 7.5% (2005-2009 5-year est.).

Taxes: Total city taxes per capita: $758 (2007); City property taxes per capita: $364 (2007).

Education: Percent of population age 25 and over with: High school diploma (including GED) or higher: 94.2% (2010); Bachelor's degree or higher: 45.3% (2010); Master's degree or higher: 15.2% (2010).

School District(s)

Clear Creek ISD (PK-12)
    2009-10 Enrollment: 37,611 . . . . (281) 284-0079
Excel Academy (04-12)
    2009-10 Enrollment: 529 . . . . (713) 222-4340

Housing: Homeownership rate: 68.7% (2010); Median home value: $181,913 (2010); Median contract rent: $666 per month (2005-2009 5-year est.); Median year structure built: 1988 (2005-2009 5-year est.).

Safety: Violent crime rate: 11.9 per 10,000 population; Property crime rate: 205.5 per 10,000 population (2009).

Transportation: Commute to work: 92.3% car, 0.5% public transportation, 0.5% walk, 3.9% work from home (2005-2009 5-year est.); Travel time to work: 28.9% less than 15 minutes, 37.1% 15 to 30 minutes, 17.8% 30 to 45 minutes, 8.2% 45 to 60 minutes, 8.0% 60 minutes or more (2005-2009 5-year est.)

Additional Information Contacts

City of Seabrook . . . . (281) 291-5600
    http://www.ci.seabrook.tx.us

SHELDON (CDP). Covers a land area of 2.582 square miles and a
water area of 0 square miles. Located at 29.86° N. Lat; 95.13° W. Long. Elevation is 46 feet.

Population: 1,653 (1990); 1,831 (2000); 1,638 (2010); 1,619 (2015 projected); Race: 68.3% White, 3.2% Black, 0.4% Asian, 28.1% Other, 61.7% Hispanic of any race (2010); Density: 634.3 persons per square mile (2010); Average household size: 3.60 (2010); Median age: 29.1 (2010); Males per 100 females: 106.6 (2010); Marriage status: 34.7% never married, 48.4% now married, 6.6% widowed, 10.3% divorced (2005-2009 5-year est.); Foreign born: 18.7% (2005-2009 5-year est.); Ancestry (includes multiple ancestries): 6.7% American, 2.9% Irish, 2.4% English, 1.1% Scottish, 0.8% Greek (2005-2009 5-year est.).

Economy: Employment by occupation: 1.4% management, 3.7% professional, 23.3% services, 14.5% sales, 0.0% farming, 26.5% construction, 30.5% production (2005-2009 5-year est.).

Income: Per capita income: $17,028 (2010); Median household income: $48,700 (2010); Average household income: $61,401 (2010); Percent of households with income of $100,000 or more: 17.6% (2010); Poverty rate: 22.8% (2005-2009 5-year est.).

Education: Percent of population age 25 and over with: High school diploma (including GED) or higher: 69.4% (2010); Bachelor's degree or higher: 8.2% (2010); Master's degree or higher: 3.3% (2010).

Housing: Homeownership rate: 75.6% (2010); Median home value: $70,469 (2010); Median contract rent: $665 per month (2005-2009 5-year est.); Median year structure built: 1969 (2005-2009 5-year est.).

Transportation: Commute to work: 95.7% car, 0.0% public transportation, 4.3% walk, 0.0% work from home (2005-2009 5-year est.); Travel time to work: 17.7% less than 15 minutes, 39.8% 15 to 30 minutes, 27.5% 30 to 45 minutes, 9.2% 45 to 60 minutes, 5.8% 60 minutes or more (2005-2009 5-year est.)

SHOREACRES (city). Covers a land area of 0.898 square miles and
a water area of 1.027 square miles. Located at 29.62° N. Lat; 95.01° W. Long. Elevation is 10 feet.

Population: 1,316 (1990); 1,488 (2000); 1,653 (2010); 1,649 (2015 projected); Race: 84.5% White, 3.7% Black, 0.8% Asian, 11.1% Other, 16.0% Hispanic of any race (2010); Density: 1,839.8 persons per square mile (2010); Average household size: 2.58 (2010); Median age: 41.0 (2010); Males per 100 females: 104.1 (2010); Marriage status: 24.2% never married, 57.8% now married, 4.0% widowed, 14.1% divorced (2005-2009 5-year est.); Foreign born: 3.6% (2005-2009 5-year est.); Ancestry (includes multiple ancestries): 21.6% German, 16.7% English, 15.1% Irish, 9.0% American, 8.5% Scottish (2005-2009 5-year est.).

Economy: Single-family building permits issued: 7 (2010); Multi-family building permits issued: 0 (2010); Employment by occupation: 17.4% management, 24.8% professional, 16.3% services, 19.8% sales, 0.0% farming, 11.1% construction, 10.5% production (2005-2009 5-year est.).

Income: Per capita income: $33,768 (2010); Median household income: $73,646 (2010); Average household income: $86,634 (2010); Percent of households with income of $100,000 or more: 31.4% (2010); Poverty rate: 4.1% (2005-2009 5-year est.).

Taxes: Total city taxes per capita: $1,019 (2007); City property taxes per capita: $0 (2007).

Education: Percent of population age 25 and over with: High school diploma (including GED) or higher: 92.5% (2010); Bachelor's degree or higher: 27.5% (2010); Master's degree or higher: 8.3% (2010).

Housing: Homeownership rate: 81.3% (2010); Median home value: $147,488 (2010); Median contract rent: $897 per month (2005-2009 5-year est.); Median year structure built: 1969 (2005-2009 5-year est.).
Transportation: Commute to work: 97.5% car, 0.0% public transportation, 0.0% walk, 2.5% work from home (2005-2009 5-year est.); Travel time to work: 20.9% less than 15 minutes, 42.4% 15 to 30 minutes, 20.5% 30 to 45 minutes, 7.7% 45 to 60 minutes, 8.6% 60 minutes or more (2005-2009 5-year est.)

SOUTH HOUSTON (city). Aka Dumont. Covers a land area of 3.027 square miles and a water area of 0 square miles. Located at 29.66° N. Lat; 95.23° W. Long. Elevation is 30 feet.

History: Named for its location south of Houston, which was named for Samuel Houston, Texas patriot. Incorporated 1911.
Population: 14,207 (1990); 15,833 (2000); 16,557 (2010); 17,263 (2015 projected); Race: 65.1% White, 0.8% Black, 0.6% Asian, 33.4% Other, 86.1% Hispanic of any race (2010); Density: 5,470.4 persons per square mile (2010); Average household size: 3.56 (2010); Median age: 29.4 (2010); Males per 100 females: 104.6 (2010); Marriage status: 31.9% never married, 53.9% now married, 5.3% widowed, 8.9% divorced (2005-2009 5-year est.); Foreign born: 35.7% (2005-2009 5-year est.); Ancestry (includes multiple ancestries): 2.3% German, 1.9% American, 1.8% Irish, 1.5% English, 0.8% French (2005-2009 5-year est.).
Economy: Single-family building permits issued: 9 (2010); Multi-family building permits issued: 2 (2010); Employment by occupation: 7.7% management, 10.3% professional, 20.3% services, 20.9% sales, 0.0% farming, 22.0% construction, 18.8% production (2005-2009 5-year est.).
Income: Per capita income: $13,972 (2010); Median household income: $40,067 (2010); Average household income: $49,684 (2010); Percent of households with income of $100,000 or more: 9.7% (2010); Poverty rate: 25.5% (2005-2009 5-year est.).
Taxes: Total city taxes per capita: $387 (2007); City property taxes per capita: $182 (2007).
Education: Percent of population age 25 and over with: High school diploma (including GED) or higher: 47.1% (2010); Bachelor's degree or higher: 3.4% (2010); Master's degree or higher: 1.3% (2010).

School District(s)

Pasadena ISD (PK-12)
   2009-10 Enrollment: 52,303 . . . .

Vocational/Technical School(s)

Royal Beauty Careers (Private, For-profit)
   Fall 2009 Enrollment: 96 . . . . (770) 446-1333
   2010-11 Tuition: $14,500
Housing: Homeownership rate: 61.1% (2010); Median home value: $73,852 (2010); Median contract rent: $485 per month (2005-2009 5-year est.); Median year structure built: 1970 (2005-2009 5-year est.).
Safety: Violent crime rate: 64.0 per 10,000 population; Property crime rate: 465.0 per 10,000 population (2009).
Transportation: Commute to work: 90.3% car, 0.7% public transportation, 5.0% walk, 1.9% work from home (2005-2009 5-year est.); Travel time to work: 24.3% less than 15 minutes, 32.0% 15 to 30 minutes, 20.6% 30 to 45 minutes, 10.6% 45 to 60 minutes, 12.6% 60 minutes or more (2005-2009 5-year est.)
Additional Information Contacts
City of South Houston . . . . (713) 947-7700
   http://www.southhoustontx.org
South Houston Chamber of Commerce. . . . . (713) 943-0244
   http://www.southhoustonchamber.org

SOUTHSIDE PLACE (city). Covers a land area of 0.247 square miles and a water area of 0 square miles. Located at 29.71° N. Lat; 95.43° W. Long. Elevation is 49 feet.

Population: 1,392 (1990); 1,546 (2000); 1,706 (2010); 1,826 (2015 projected); Race: 90.0% White, 1.3% Black, 4.8% Asian, 3.8% Other, 8.1% Hispanic of any race (2010); Density: 6,919.9 persons per square mile (2010); Average household size: 2.58 (2010); Median age: 37.8 (2010); Males per 100 females: 96.8 (2010); Marriage status: 28.6% never married, 63.2% now married, 2.2% widowed, 5.9% divorced (2005-2009 5-year est.); Foreign born: 19.7% (2005-2009 5-year est.); Ancestry (includes multiple ancestries): 20.0% English, 15.9% German, 12.7% Irish, 7.3% American, 5.4% Scottish (2005-2009 5-year est.).
Economy: Single-family building permits issued: 3 (2010); Multi-family building permits issued: 0 (2010); Employment by occupation: 23.0% management, 46.9% professional, 5.3% services, 19.5% sales, 0.0% farming, 2.5% construction, 2.7% production (2005-2009 5-year est.).

Income: Per capita income: $68,277 (2010); Median household income: $115,152 (2010); Average household income: $176,485 (2010); Percent of households with income of $100,000 or more: 53.0% (2010); Poverty rate: 4.2% (2005-2009 5-year est.).
Taxes: Total city taxes per capita: $127 (2007); City property taxes per capita: $113 (2007).
Education: Percent of population age 25 and over with: High school diploma (including GED) or higher: 95.8% (2010); Bachelor's degree or higher: 70.1% (2010); Master's degree or higher: 43.0% (2010).
Housing: Homeownership rate: 61.8% (2010); Median home value: $720,982 (2010); Median contract rent: $642 per month (2005-2009 5-year est.); Median year structure built: 1978 (2005-2009 5-year est.).
Safety: Violent crime rate: 11.9 per 10,000 population; Property crime rate: 41.7 per 10,000 population (2009).
Transportation: Commute to work: 82.4% car, 2.2% public transportation, 3.6% walk, 9.3% work from home (2005-2009 5-year est.); Travel time to work: 32.3% less than 15 minutes, 48.3% 15 to 30 minutes, 17.1% 30 to 45 minutes, 1.5% 45 to 60 minutes, 0.7% 60 minutes or more (2005-2009 5-year est.)
Additional Information Contacts
City of Southside Place . . . . (713) 668-2341
   http://www.ci.southside-place.tx.us

SPRING (CDP). Covers a land area of 23.937 square miles and a water area of 0.028 square miles. Located at 30.05° N. Lat; 95.38° W. Long. Elevation is 121 feet.

Population: 33,122 (1990); 36,385 (2000); 44,425 (2010); 47,659 (2015 projected); Race: 77.7% White, 8.3% Black, 1.7% Asian, 12.2% Other, 23.2% Hispanic of any race (2010); Density: 1,855.9 persons per square mile (2010); Average household size: 2.91 (2010); Median age: 35.3 (2010); Males per 100 females: 96.6 (2010); Marriage status: 28.4% never married, 57.4% now married, 3.5% widowed, 10.7% divorced (2005-2009 5-year est.); Foreign born: 10.8% (2005-2009 5-year est.); Ancestry (includes multiple ancestries): 14.0% German, 8.3% Irish, 7.5% English, 6.2% American, 3.5% French (2005-2009 5-year est.).
Economy: Employment by occupation: 12.6% management, 18.8% professional, 14.0% services, 30.4% sales, 0.0% farming, 10.6% construction, 13.6% production (2005-2009 5-year est.).
Income: Per capita income: $27,110 (2010); Median household income: $68,079 (2010); Average household income: $78,773 (2010); Percent of households with income of $100,000 or more: 23.8% (2010); Poverty rate: 8.3% (2005-2009 5-year est.).
Education: Percent of population age 25 and over with: High school diploma (including GED) or higher: 90.7% (2010); Bachelor's degree or higher: 19.7% (2010); Master's degree or higher: 5.5% (2010).

School District(s)

Conroe ISD (PK-12)
   2009-10 Enrollment: 49,629 . . . . (936) 709-7702
Klein ISD (PK-12)
   2009-10 Enrollment: 44,824 . . . . (832) 249-4000
Spring ISD (PK-12)
   2009-10 Enrollment: 35,350 . . . . (281) 891-6000

Vocational/Technical School(s)

Regency Beauty Institute-Cypresswood (Private, For-profit)
   Fall 2009 Enrollment: 92 . . . . (800) 787-6456
   2010-11 Tuition: $16,075
Housing: Homeownership rate: 78.3% (2010); Median home value: $119,496 (2010); Median contract rent: $813 per month (2005-2009 5-year est.); Median year structure built: 1985 (2005-2009 5-year est.).
Transportation: Commute to work: 93.2% car, 2.1% public transportation, 0.3% walk, 3.1% work from home (2005-2009 5-year est.); Travel time to work: 14.8% less than 15 minutes, 36.7% 15 to 30 minutes, 22.2% 30 to 45 minutes, 14.6% 45 to 60 minutes, 11.7% 60 minutes or more (2005-2009 5-year est.)

SPRING VALLEY (city). Covers a land area of 1.311 square miles and a water area of 0 square miles. Located at 29.79° N. Lat; 95.50° W. Long. Elevation is 75 feet.

History: In the mid-1950s, effort to form a Spring Branch municipality failed. The city incorporated in 1955. In 1960 the city had 3,004 residents and two businesses. The city had 3,800 residents in 1976 and 3,392 residents in 1990. In 2007, the name of the city was officially changed from Spring Valley to Spring Valley Village.
Population: 3,392 (1990); 3,611 (2000); 4,025 (2010); 4,321 (2015 projected); Race: 93.7% White, 0.5% Black, 3.2% Asian, 2.6% Other, 5.1%

Hispanic of any race (2010); Density: 3,070.8 persons per square mile (2010); Average household size: 2.75 (2010); Median age: 41.7 (2010); Males per 100 females: 96.6 (2010); Marriage status: n/a never married, n/a now married, n/a widowed, n/a divorced (2005-2009 5-year est.); Foreign born: n/a (2005-2009 5-year est.); Ancestry (includes multiple ancestries): n/a (2005-2009 5-year est.).
Economy: Employment by occupation: n/a management, n/a professional, n/a services, n/a sales, n/a farming, n/a construction, n/a production (2005-2009 5-year est.).
Income: Per capita income: $54,624 (2010); Median household income: $117,434 (2010); Average household income: $150,075 (2010); Percent of households with income of $100,000 or more: 59.0% (2010); Poverty rate: n/a (2005-2009 5-year est.).
Taxes: Total city taxes per capita: $977 (2007); City property taxes per capita: $582 (2007).
Education: Percent of population age 25 and over with: High school diploma (including GED) or higher: 97.5% (2010); Bachelor's degree or higher: 64.3% (2010); Master's degree or higher: 21.2% (2010).
Housing: Homeownership rate: 95.0% (2010); Median home value: $374,580 (2010); Median contract rent: n/a per month (2005-2009 5-year est.); Median year structure built: n/a (2005-2009 5-year est.).
Safety: Violent crime rate: 15.3 per 10,000 population; Property crime rate: 248.1 per 10,000 population (2009).
Transportation: Commute to work: n/a car, n/a public transportation, n/a walk, n/a work from home (2005-2009 5-year est.); Travel time to work: n/a less than 15 minutes, n/a 15 to 30 minutes, n/a 30 to 45 minutes, n/a 45 to 60 minutes, n/a 60 minutes or more (2005-2009 5-year est.)
Additional Information Contacts
City of Spring Valley. . . . . (713) 465-8308
  http://www.springvalleytx.com

TAYLOR LAKE VILLAGE (city). Covers a land area of 1.242 square miles and a water area of 0.146 square miles. Located at 29.57° N. Lat; 95.05° W. Long. Elevation is 3 feet.
History: The community was incorporated in December 1961 with a mayor-alderman form of city government. The town permits no business establishments within its corporate limits.
Population: 3,414 (1990); 3,694 (2000); 3,621 (2010); 3,773 (2015 projected); Race: 85.7% White, 3.9% Black, 3.3% Asian, 7.1% Other, 10.3% Hispanic of any race (2010); Density: 2,915.4 persons per square mile (2010); Average household size: 2.65 (2010); Median age: 42.7 (2010); Males per 100 females: 102.3 (2010); Marriage status: 17.5% never married, 76.5% now married, 2.0% widowed, 3.9% divorced (2005-2009 5-year est.); Foreign born: 7.8% (2005-2009 5-year est.); Ancestry (includes multiple ancestries): 34.2% German, 15.4% English, 8.6% Irish, 7.7% American, 6.9% Polish (2005-2009 5-year est.).
Economy: Single-family building permits issued: 5 (2010); Multi-family building permits issued: 0 (2010); Employment by occupation: 26.2% management, 39.1% professional, 4.0% services, 21.8% sales, 0.0% farming, 2.1% construction, 6.9% production (2005-2009 5-year est.).
Income: Per capita income: $47,771 (2010); Median household income: $102,140 (2010); Average household income: $128,127 (2010); Percent of households with income of $100,000 or more: 51.4% (2010); Poverty rate: 1.6% (2005-2009 5-year est.).
Taxes: Total city taxes per capita: $409 (2007); City property taxes per capita: $320 (2007).
Education: Percent of population age 25 and over with: High school diploma (including GED) or higher: 97.7% (2010); Bachelor's degree or higher: 58.0% (2010); Master's degree or higher: 24.0% (2010).
Housing: Homeownership rate: 85.6% (2010); Median home value: $225,630 (2010); Median contract rent: n/a per month (2005-2009 5-year est.); Median year structure built: 1974 (2005-2009 5-year est.).
Transportation: Commute to work: 88.1% car, 1.0% public transportation, 0.0% walk, 10.2% work from home (2005-2009 5-year est.); Travel time to work: 33.6% less than 15 minutes, 35.4% 15 to 30 minutes, 15.7% 30 to 45 minutes, 7.3% 45 to 60 minutes, 8.0% 60 minutes or more (2005-2009 5-year est.)

TOMBALL (city). Covers a land area of 10.151 square miles and a water area of 0.005 square miles. Located at 30.09° N. Lat; 95.61° W. Long. Elevation is 187 feet.
History: Incorporated 1935.
Population: 6,431 (1990); 9,089 (2000); 10,138 (2010); 10,742 (2015 projected); Race: 83.9% White, 4.0% Black, 0.6% Asian, 11.5% Other, 17.7% Hispanic of any race (2010); Density: 998.8 persons per square mile

(2010); Average household size: 2.48 (2010); Median age: 36.8 (2010); Males per 100 females: 91.8 (2010); Marriage status: 21.6% never married, 55.1% now married, 12.5% widowed, 10.7% divorced (2005-2009 5-year est.); Foreign born: 13.8% (2005-2009 5-year est.); Ancestry (includes multiple ancestries): 19.7% German, 12.4% English, 10.9% American, 10.5% Irish, 4.1% Polish (2005-2009 5-year est.).
Economy: Single-family building permits issued: 12 (2010); Multi-family building permits issued: 0 (2010); Employment by occupation: 15.4% management, 17.7% professional, 19.6% services, 26.1% sales, 0.6% farming, 9.5% construction, 11.1% production (2005-2009 5-year est.).
Income: Per capita income: $26,638 (2010); Median household income: $51,329 (2010); Average household income: $67,987 (2010); Percent of households with income of $100,000 or more: 18.7% (2010); Poverty rate: 10.0% (2005-2009 5-year est.).
Taxes: Total city taxes per capita: $409 (2007); City property taxes per capita: $208 (2007).
Education: Percent of population age 25 and over with: High school diploma (including GED) or higher: 79.4% (2010); Bachelor's degree or higher: 22.8% (2010); Master's degree or higher: 6.2% (2010).
School District(s)
Comquest Academy (09-12)
  2009-10 Enrollment: 75 . . . . (281) 516-0611
Klein ISD (PK-12)
  2009-10 Enrollment: 44,824 . . . . (832) 249-4000
Tomball ISD (PK-12)
  2009-10 Enrollment: 10,266 . . . . (281) 357-3100
Housing: Homeownership rate: 49.5% (2010); Median home value: $149,713 (2010); Median contract rent: $706 per month (2005-2009 5-year est.); Median year structure built: 1990 (2005-2009 5-year est.).
Hospitals: Tomball Regional Hospital (205 beds)
Safety: Violent crime rate: 31.9 per 10,000 population; Property crime rate: 433.1 per 10,000 population (2009).
Newspapers: The Potpourri (Community news; Circulation 42,000)
Transportation: Commute to work: 91.6% car, 0.8% public transportation, 0.9% walk, 3.8% work from home (2005-2009 5-year est.); Travel time to work: 27.0% less than 15 minutes, 23.2% 15 to 30 minutes, 28.6% 30 to 45 minutes, 11.8% 45 to 60 minutes, 9.4% 60 minutes or more (2005-2009 5-year est.)
Additional Information Contacts
City of Tomball . . . . (281) 351-5484
  http://www.ci.tomball.tx.us
Greater Tomball Area Chamber of Commerce . . . . (281) 351-7222
  http://www.tomballchamber.org

WEBSTER (city). Covers a land area of 6.616 square miles and a water area of 0.037 square miles. Located at 29.53° N. Lat; 95.11° W. Long. Elevation is 26 feet.
Population: 5,662 (1990); 9,083 (2000); 12,424 (2010); 13,926 (2015 projected); Race: 54.8% White, 11.6% Black, 4.2% Asian, 29.4% Other, 35.0% Hispanic of any race (2010); Density: 1,877.9 persons per square mile (2010); Average household size: 2.14 (2010); Median age: 33.5 (2010); Males per 100 females: 108.0 (2010); Marriage status: 45.5% never married, 35.8% now married, 8.0% widowed, 10.7% divorced (2005-2009 5-year est.); Foreign born: 23.9% (2005-2009 5-year est.); Ancestry (includes multiple ancestries): 9.9% German, 9.2% Irish, 4.7% American, 4.1% Italian, 3.8% English (2005-2009 5-year est.).
Economy: Single-family building permits issued: 16 (2010); Multi-family building permits issued: 0 (2010); Employment by occupation: 11.6% management, 20.6% professional, 25.0% services, 21.2% sales, 0.9% farming, 10.2% construction, 10.4% production (2005-2009 5-year est.).
Income: Per capita income: $24,379 (2010); Median household income: $45,369 (2010); Average household income: $53,103 (2010); Percent of households with income of $100,000 or more: 10.0% (2010); Poverty rate: 16.1% (2005-2009 5-year est.).
Taxes: Total city taxes per capita: $1,748 (2007); City property taxes per capita: $225 (2007).
Education: Percent of population age 25 and over with: High school diploma (including GED) or higher: 81.5% (2010); Bachelor's degree or higher: 30.5% (2010); Master's degree or higher: 10.8% (2010).
School District(s)
Clear Creek ISD (PK-12)
  2009-10 Enrollment: 37,611 . . . . (281) 284-0079

Four-year College(s)
ITT Technical Institute-Webster (Private, For-profit)
  Fall 2009 Enrollment: 439 . . . . (281) 316-4700
  2010-11 Tuition: In-state $18,048; Out-of-state $18,048
Two-year College(s)
Remington College-Houston Southeast (Private, For-profit)
  Fall 2009 Enrollment: 423 . . . . (281) 554-1700
  2010-11 Tuition: In-state $14,745; Out-of-state $14,745
Housing: Homeownership rate: 18.3% (2010); Median home value: $104,395 (2010); Median contract rent: $761 per month (2005-2009 5-year est.); Median year structure built: 1987 (2005-2009 5-year est.).
Hospitals: Clear Lake Regional Medical Center (595 beds); Houston Physicians' Hospital
Safety: Violent crime rate: 42.3 per 10,000 population; Property crime rate: 733.3 per 10,000 population (2009).
Newspapers: The Citizen Bay Area (Local news; Circulation 26,700)
Transportation: Commute to work: 91.8% car, 1.8% public transportation, 2.4% walk, 0.5% work from home (2005-2009 5-year est.); Travel time to work: 40.0% less than 15 minutes, 27.3% 15 to 30 minutes, 15.4% 30 to 45 minutes, 12.0% 45 to 60 minutes, 5.4% 60 minutes or more (2005-2009 5-year est.)
Additional Information Contacts
City of Webster . . . . (281) 332-1826
  http://www.cityofwebster.com

WEST UNIVERSITY PLACE (city). Covers a land area of 2.010 square miles and a water area of 0 square miles. Located at 29.71° N. Lat; 95.43° W. Long. Elevation is 49 feet.
History: Named for its location near Rice University. West University Place grew up near Rice University. It was incorporated as a city, almost surrounded by the bigger city of Houston.
Population: 12,920 (1990); 14,211 (2000); 16,072 (2010); 17,352 (2015 projected); Race: 89.2% White, 0.7% Black, 6.5% Asian, 3.6% Other, 6.5% Hispanic of any race (2010); Density: 7,994.2 persons per square mile (2010); Average household size: 2.79 (2010); Median age: 38.9 (2010); Males per 100 females: 97.4 (2010); Marriage status: 18.9% never married, 72.1% now married, 2.1% widowed, 6.9% divorced (2005-2009 5-year est.); Foreign born: 13.2% (2005-2009 5-year est.); Ancestry (includes multiple ancestries): 18.7% German, 16.1% English, 12.7% Irish, 6.7% Italian, 6.0% French (2005-2009 5-year est.).
Economy: Single-family building permits issued: 36 (2010); Multi-family building permits issued: 0 (2010); Employment by occupation: 29.8% management, 47.4% professional, 3.0% services, 17.8% sales, 0.0% farming, 0.7% construction, 1.3% production (2005-2009 5-year est.).
Income: Per capita income: $76,901 (2010); Median household income: $168,305 (2010); Average household income: $214,726 (2010); Percent of households with income of $100,000 or more: 71.7% (2010); Poverty rate: 1.9% (2005-2009 5-year est.).
Taxes: Total city taxes per capita: $1,007 (2007); City property taxes per capita: $834 (2007).
Education: Percent of population age 25 and over with: High school diploma (including GED) or higher: 98.3% (2010); Bachelor's degree or higher: 79.6% (2010); Master's degree or higher: 44.9% (2010).
Housing: Homeownership rate: 91.5% (2010); Median home value: $611,387 (2010); Median contract rent: $1,295 per month (2005-2009 5-year est.); Median year structure built: 1982 (2005-2009 5-year est.).
Safety: Violent crime rate: 2.5 per 10,000 population; Property crime rate: 123.9 per 10,000 population (2009).
Transportation: Commute to work: 88.0% car, 0.5% public transportation, 0.5% walk, 8.9% work from home (2005-2009 5-year est.); Travel time to work: 32.3% less than 15 minutes, 52.1% 15 to 30 minutes, 12.0% 30 to 45 minutes, 3.0% 45 to 60 minutes, 0.7% 60 minutes or more (2005-2009 5-year est.)
Additional Information Contacts
City of West University Place . . . . (713) 668-4441
  http://www.westu.org

Harrison County

Located in east Texas; bounded on the east by Louisiana, on the northeast by Caddo Lake, and on the southwest by the Sabine River; drained by Little Cypress Bayou. Covers a land area of 898.71 square miles, a water area of 16.38 square miles, and is located in the Central Time Zone at 32.54° N. Lat., 94.35° W. Long. The county was founded in 1839. County seat is Marshall.

Harrison County is part of the Marshall, TX Micropolitan Statistical Area. The entire metro area includes: Harrison County, TX

Weather Station: Marshall										Elevation: 352 feet		
	Jan	Feb	Mar	Apr	May	Jun	Jul	Aug	Sep	Oct	Nov	Dec
High	56	60	67	75	82	89	93	93	87	77	67	57
Low	35	39	46	53	62	69	72	72	65	53	45	37
Precip	3.8	4.3	4.5	3.8	5.0	5.1	3.2	2.6	3.4	4.9	4.6	5.0
Snow	0.3	0.1	0.1	0.0	0.0	0.0	0.0	0.0	0.0	0.0	0.0	tr

High and Low temperatures in degrees Fahrenheit; Precipitation and Snow in inches

Population: 57,483 (1990); 62,110 (2000); 64,727 (2010); 65,880 (2015 projected); Race: 70.3% White, 22.1% Black, 0.5% Asian, 7.1% Other, 9.2% Hispanic of any race (2010); Density: 72.0 persons per square mile (2010); Average household size: 2.57 (2010); Median age: 36.6 (2010); Males per 100 females: 95.8 (2010).
Religion: Five largest groups: 36.8% Southern Baptist Convention, 6.6% The United Methodist Church, 5.1% Catholic Church, 2.0% Churches of Christ, 1.2% Independent, Non-Charismatic Churches (2000).
Economy: Unemployment rate: 8.9% (June 2011); Total civilian labor force: 33,574 (June 2011); Leading industries: 20.8% manufacturing; 12.6% retail trade; 9.9% mining (2009); Farms: 1,205 totaling 200,875 acres (2007); Companies that employ 500 or more persons: 2 (2009); Companies that employ 100 to 499 persons: 28 (2009); Companies that employ less than 100 persons: 1,265 (2009); Black-owned businesses: 537 (2007); Hispanic-owned businesses: n/a (2007); Asian-owned businesses: 75 (2007); Women-owned businesses: 1,676 (2007); Retail sales per capita: $10,528 (2010). Single-family building permits issued: 36 (2010); Multi-family building permits issued: 51 (2010).
Income: Per capita income: $22,003 (2010); Median household income: $44,574 (2010); Average household income: $57,285 (2010); Percent of households with income of $100,000 or more: 13.0% (2010); Poverty rate: 15.4% (2009); Bankruptcy rate: 2.09% (2010).
Taxes: Total county taxes per capita: $249 (2007); County property taxes per capita: $228 (2007).
Education: Percent of population age 25 and over with: High school diploma (including GED) or higher: 83.3% (2010); Bachelor's degree or higher: 15.6% (2010); Master's degree or higher: 4.9% (2010).
Housing: Homeownership rate: 74.4% (2010); Median home value: $85,927 (2010); Median contract rent: $447 per month (2005-2009 5-year est.); Median year structure built: 1975 (2005-2009 5-year est.)
Health: Birth rate: 140.0 per 10,000 population (2009); Death rate: 88.9 per 10,000 population (2009); Age-adjusted cancer mortality rate: 237.8 deaths per 100,000 population (2007); Number of physicians: 7.7 per 10,000 population (2008); Hospital beds: 20.9 per 10,000 population (2007); Hospital admissions: 600.2 per 10,000 population (2007).
Environment: Air Quality Index: 82.0% good, 18.0% moderate, 0.0% unhealthy for sensitive individuals, 0.0% unhealthy (percent of days in 2008)
Elections: 2008 Presidential election results: 34.0% Obama, 65.4% McCain, 0.0% Nader
National and State Parks: Caddo Lake State Park
Additional Information Contacts
Harrison County Government . . . . (903) 935-4845
  http://www.co.harrison.tx.us
City of Marshall . . . . (903) 935-4419
  http://www.marshalltexas.net
Hallsville Chamber of Commerce . . . . (903) 668-2592
Marshall Chamber of Commerce . . . . (903) 935-7868
  http://www.marshall-chamber.com
Waskom Chamber of Commerce . . . . (903) 687-3000

Harrison County Communities

HALLSVILLE (city). Covers a land area of 2.277 square miles and a water area of 0 square miles. Located at 32.50° N. Lat; 94.57° W. Long. Elevation is 364 feet.
Population: 2,295 (1990); 2,772 (2000); 3,107 (2010); 3,225 (2015 projected); Race: 90.5% White, 6.1% Black, 0.6% Asian, 2.8% Other, 3.2% Hispanic of any race (2010); Density: 1,364.5 persons per square mile (2010); Average household size: 2.68 (2010); Median age: 34.2 (2010); Males per 100 females: 91.9 (2010); Marriage status: 18.3% never married, 62.6% now married, 4.9% widowed, 14.1% divorced (2005-2009 5-year est.); Foreign born: 3.7% (2005-2009 5-year est.); Ancestry (includes multiple ancestries): 14.9% American, 14.6% Irish, 12.5% English, 12.0% German, 2.6% Scottish (2005-2009 5-year est.).

Economy: Single-family building permits issued: 9 (2010); Multi-family building permits issued: 51 (2010); Employment by occupation: 11.1% management, 21.0% professional, 11.8% services, 29.6% sales, 0.0% farming, 11.7% construction, 14.8% production (2005-2009 5-year est.).
Income: Per capita income: $24,920 (2010); Median household income: $58,666 (2010); Average household income: $67,076 (2010); Percent of households with income of $100,000 or more: 16.9% (2010); Poverty rate: 9.6% (2005-2009 5-year est.).
Taxes: Total city taxes per capita: $121 (2007); City property taxes per capita: $42 (2007).
Education: Percent of population age 25 and over with: High school diploma (including GED) or higher: 92.1% (2010); Bachelor's degree or higher: 18.0% (2010); Master's degree or higher: 6.5% (2010).

School District(s)
Hallsville ISD (PK-12)
   2009-10 Enrollment: 4,265 . . . . (903) 668-5990
Housing: Homeownership rate: 69.5% (2010); Median home value: $104,867 (2010); Median contract rent: $545 per month (2005-2009 5-year est.); Median year structure built: 1983 (2005-2009 5-year est.).
Safety: Violent crime rate: 0.0 per 10,000 population; Property crime rate: 174.5 per 10,000 population (2009).
Transportation: Commute to work: 96.5% car, 0.0% public transportation, 0.4% walk, 1.6% work from home (2005-2009 5-year est.); Travel time to work: 20.4% less than 15 minutes, 52.1% 15 to 30 minutes, 20.8% 30 to 45 minutes, 3.7% 45 to 60 minutes, 3.0% 60 minutes or more (2005-2009 5-year est.)
Additional Information Contacts
Hallsville Chamber of Commerce . . . . (903) 668-2592

HARLETON (unincorporated postal area, zip code 75651). Covers a land area of 56.627 square miles and a water area of 0.212 square miles. Located at 32.69° N. Lat; 94.54° W. Long. Elevation is 318 feet.
Population: 1,832 (2000); Race: 88.3% White, 8.3% Black, 0.2% Asian, 3.2% Other, 2.5% Hispanic of any race (2000); Density: 32.4 persons per square mile (2000); Age: 28.2% under 18, 11.9% over 64 (2000); Marriage status: 17.8% never married, 61.6% now married, 9.8% widowed, 10.8% divorced (2000); Foreign born: 1.0% (2000); Ancestry (includes multiple ancestries): 36.5% American, 8.8% Irish, 5.6% German, 4.4% English (2000).
Economy: Employment by occupation: 7.2% management, 11.8% professional, 14.6% services, 23.7% sales, 0.5% farming, 13.7% construction, 28.5% production (2000).
Income: Per capita income: $14,976 (2000); Median household income: $30,179 (2000); Poverty rate: 179.1% (2000).
Education: Percent of population age 25 and over with: High school diploma (including GED) or higher: 70.1% (2000); Bachelor's degree or higher: 11.3% (2000).

School District(s)
Harleton ISD (PK-12)
   2009-10 Enrollment: 737 . . . . (903) 777-2372
Housing: Homeownership rate: 88.1% (2000); Median home value: $63,800 (2000); Median contract rent: $277 per month (2000); Median year structure built: 1978 (2000).
Transportation: Commute to work: 92.7% car, 0.0% public transportation, 2.4% walk, 3.5% work from home (2000); Travel time to work: 16.5% less than 15 minutes, 30.9% 15 to 30 minutes, 33.4% 30 to 45 minutes, 10.0% 45 to 60 minutes, 9.2% 60 minutes or more (2000)

KARNACK (unincorporated postal area, zip code 75661). Covers a land area of 117.083 square miles and a water area of 0.653 square miles. Located at 32.65° N. Lat; 94.15° W. Long. Elevation is 240 feet.
Population: 2,558 (2000); Race: 61.6% White, 36.8% Black, 0.8% Asian, 0.8% Other, 2.0% Hispanic of any race (2000); Density: 21.8 persons per square mile (2000); Age: 21.4% under 18, 18.9% over 64 (2000); Marriage status: 19.0% never married, 63.1% now married, 8.0% widowed, 9.8% divorced (2000); Foreign born: 2.1% (2000); Ancestry (includes multiple ancestries): 20.8% American, 6.8% Irish, 6.6% German, 6.3% English (2000).
Economy: Employment by occupation: 13.9% management, 10.5% professional, 15.2% services, 22.7% sales, 1.0% farming, 14.4% construction, 22.4% production (2000).
Income: Per capita income: $18,670 (2000); Median household income: $27,981 (2000); Poverty rate: 179.1% (2000).

Education: Percent of population age 25 and over with: High school diploma (including GED) or higher: 71.7% (2000); Bachelor's degree or higher: 10.9% (2000).

School District(s)
Karnack ISD (PK-12)
   2009-10 Enrollment: 183 . . . . (903) 679-3117
Housing: Homeownership rate: 84.8% (2000); Median home value: $58,800 (2000); Median contract rent: $323 per month (2000); Median year structure built: 1979 (2000).
Transportation: Commute to work: 92.3% car, 0.0% public transportation, 1.2% walk, 4.7% work from home (2000); Travel time to work: 22.1% less than 15 minutes, 30.7% 15 to 30 minutes, 32.0% 30 to 45 minutes, 7.7% 45 to 60 minutes, 7.5% 60 minutes or more (2000)

MARSHALL (city). County seat. Covers a land area of 29.566 square miles and a water area of 0.078 square miles. Located at 32.54° N. Lat; 94.36° W. Long. Elevation is 413 feet.
History: Marshall, established in 1841, was named for U.S. Chief Justice John Marshall. During the Civil War, Marshall was the administrative capital of Confederate Missouri, while Missouri itself was held by the Union.
Population: 25,073 (1990); 23,935 (2000); 23,928 (2010); 23,830 (2015 projected); Race: 51.8% White, 36.8% Black, 0.9% Asian, 10.5% Other, 15.4% Hispanic of any race (2010); Density: 809.3 persons per square mile (2010); Average household size: 2.50 (2010); Median age: 34.0 (2010); Males per 100 females: 91.8 (2010); Marriage status: 33.8% never married, 46.2% now married, 8.1% widowed, 11.9% divorced (2005-2009 5-year est.); Foreign born: 8.8% (2005-2009 5-year est.); Ancestry (includes multiple ancestries): 13.4% American, 7.4% English, 7.0% German, 6.4% Irish, 2.2% African (2005-2009 5-year est.).
Economy: Single-family building permits issued: 27 (2010); Multi-family building permits issued: 0 (2010); Employment by occupation: 6.7% management, 17.9% professional, 20.4% services, 24.1% sales, 0.3% farming, 10.5% construction, 20.0% production (2005-2009 5-year est.).
Income: Per capita income: $20,395 (2010); Median household income: $38,857 (2010); Average household income: $52,607 (2010); Percent of households with income of $100,000 or more: 10.9% (2010); Poverty rate: 23.6% (2005-2009 5-year est.).
Taxes: Total city taxes per capita: $564 (2007); City property taxes per capita: $158 (2007).
Education: Percent of population age 25 and over with: High school diploma (including GED) or higher: 81.8% (2010); Bachelor's degree or higher: 18.8% (2010); Master's degree or higher: 6.1% (2010).

School District(s)
Marshall ISD (PK-12)
   2009-10 Enrollment: 5,789 . . . . (903) 927-8701
Panola Charter School (08-12)
   2009-10 Enrollment: 140 . . . . (903) 693-6355

Four-year College(s)
East Texas Baptist University (Private, Not-for-profit, Baptist)
   Fall 2009 Enrollment: 1,179 . . . . (903) 935-7963
   2010-11 Tuition: In-state $19,550; Out-of-state $19,550
Wiley College (Private, Not-for-profit, Historically black, United Methodist)
   Fall 2009 Enrollment: 1,237 . . . . (903) 927-3300
   2010-11 Tuition: In-state $11,050; Out-of-state $11,050

Two-year College(s)
Texas State Technical College-Marshall (Public)
   Fall 2009 Enrollment: 963 . . . . (903) 935-1010
   2010-11 Tuition: In-state $4,248; Out-of-state $9,756
Housing: Homeownership rate: 62.8% (2010); Median home value: $75,768 (2010); Median contract rent: $446 per month (2005-2009 5-year est.); Median year structure built: 1962 (2005-2009 5-year est.).
Hospitals: Marshall Regional Medical Center (139 beds)
Safety: Violent crime rate: 73.1 per 10,000 population; Property crime rate: 485.5 per 10,000 population (2009).
Newspapers: Marshall News Messenger (Local news; Circulation 70,000)
Transportation: Commute to work: 92.6% car, 0.0% public transportation, 5.3% walk, 1.4% work from home (2005-2009 5-year est.); Travel time to work: 50.2% less than 15 minutes, 25.2% 15 to 30 minutes, 16.0% 30 to 45 minutes, 4.7% 45 to 60 minutes, 3.8% 60 minutes or more (2005-2009 5-year est.); Amtrak: train service available.
Airports: Harrison County (general aviation)
Additional Information Contacts
City of Marshall . . . . (903) 935-4419
   http://www.marshalltexas.net

Marshall Chamber of Commerce . . . . (903) 935-7868
http://www.marshall-chamber.com

NESBITT (town). Covers a land area of 1.747 square miles and a water area of 0 square miles. Located at 32.59° N. Lat; 94.44° W. Long. Elevation is 358 feet.
Population: 327 (1990); 302 (2000); 328 (2010); 343 (2015 projected); Race: 79.6% White, 17.7% Black, 0.0% Asian, 2.7% Other, 2.7% Hispanic of any race (2010); Density: 187.7 persons per square mile (2010); Average household size: 2.76 (2010); Median age: 36.0 (2010); Males per 100 females: 106.3 (2010); Marriage status: 17.6% never married, 62.6% now married, 12.2% widowed, 7.7% divorced (2005-2009 5-year est.); Foreign born: 0.0% (2005-2009 5-year est.); Ancestry (includes multiple ancestries): 16.8% American, 8.4% Scotch-Irish, 7.1% French, 6.2% Scottish, 3.5% German (2005-2009 5-year est.).
Economy: Employment by occupation: 3.1% management, 13.5% professional, 9.2% services, 43.6% sales, 0.0% farming, 7.4% construction, 23.3% production (2005-2009 5-year est.).
Income: Per capita income: $18,883 (2010); Median household income: $40,921 (2010); Average household income: $53,592 (2010); Percent of households with income of $100,000 or more: 10.1% (2010); Poverty rate: 1.3% (2005-2009 5-year est.).
Education: Percent of population age 25 and over with: High school diploma (including GED) or higher: 73.6% (2010); Bachelor's degree or higher: 6.1% (2010); Master's degree or higher: 2.8% (2010).
Housing: Homeownership rate: 85.7% (2010); Median home value: $78,462 (2010); Median contract rent: n/a per month (2005-2009 5-year est.); Median year structure built: 1981 (2005-2009 5-year est.).
Transportation: Commute to work: 96.9% car, 0.0% public transportation, 0.0% walk, 3.1% work from home (2005-2009 5-year est.); Travel time to work: 20.3% less than 15 minutes, 65.2% 15 to 30 minutes, 7.6% 30 to 45 minutes, 4.4% 45 to 60 minutes, 2.5% 60 minutes or more (2005-2009 5-year est.)

SCOTTSVILLE (city). Covers a land area of 1.312 square miles and a water area of 0 square miles. Located at 32.53° N. Lat; 94.24° W. Long. Elevation is 410 feet.
History: Scottsville was founded in 1834 as a non-denominational camp meeting site.
Population: 283 (1990); 263 (2000); 272 (2010); 276 (2015 projected); Race: 63.2% White, 34.9% Black, 0.0% Asian, 1.8% Other, 1.8% Hispanic of any race (2010); Density: 207.4 persons per square mile (2010); Average household size: 2.62 (2010); Median age: 38.9 (2010); Males per 100 females: 100.0 (2010); Marriage status: 32.4% never married, 30.8% now married, 18.5% widowed, 18.2% divorced (2005-2009 5-year est.); Foreign born: 12.1% (2005-2009 5-year est.); Ancestry (includes multiple ancestries): 11.7% Nigerian, 8.9% American, 3.5% European, 2.8% German, 2.6% Irish (2005-2009 5-year est.).
Economy: Employment by occupation: 3.9% management, 7.2% professional, 36.6% services, 25.5% sales, 0.0% farming, 15.7% construction, 11.1% production (2005-2009 5-year est.).
Income: Per capita income: $27,568 (2010); Median household income: $43,077 (2010); Average household income: $70,625 (2010); Percent of households with income of $100,000 or more: 16.3% (2010); Poverty rate: 10.7% (2005-2009 5-year est.).
Taxes: Total city taxes per capita: $201 (2007); City property taxes per capita: $128 (2007).
Education: Percent of population age 25 and over with: High school diploma (including GED) or higher: 78.1% (2010); Bachelor's degree or higher: 8.7% (2010); Master's degree or higher: 3.3% (2010).
Housing: Homeownership rate: 84.6% (2010); Median home value: $82,000 (2010); Median contract rent: $775 per month (2005-2009 5-year est.); Median year structure built: 1974 (2005-2009 5-year est.).
Transportation: Commute to work: 97.4% car, 0.0% public transportation, 0.0% walk, 0.0% work from home (2005-2009 5-year est.); Travel time to work: 26.1% less than 15 minutes, 22.2% 15 to 30 minutes, 21.6% 30 to 45 minutes, 28.8% 45 to 60 minutes, 1.3% 60 minutes or more (2005-2009 5-year est.)

UNCERTAIN (city). Covers a land area of 0.510 square miles and a water area of 0.001 square miles. Located at 32.71° N. Lat; 94.12° W. Long. Elevation is 180 feet.
History: Named by steamboat captains who had difficulty mooring here. Home of Uncertain Club Society, early 1900s. Incorporated 1961.

Population: 194 (1990); 150 (2000); 152 (2010); 154 (2015 projected); Race: 83.6% White, 14.5% Black, 0.0% Asian, 2.0% Other, 0.7% Hispanic of any race (2010); Density: 298.1 persons per square mile (2010); Average household size: 2.05 (2010); Median age: 54.6 (2010); Males per 100 females: 120.3 (2010); Marriage status: 7.6% never married, 52.2% now married, 10.9% widowed, 29.3% divorced (2005-2009 5-year est.); Foreign born: 0.0% (2005-2009 5-year est.); Ancestry (includes multiple ancestries): 46.5% American, 20.8% German, 8.9% English, 6.9% Irish, 5.9% French (2005-2009 5-year est.).
Economy: Employment by occupation: 4.9% management, 7.3% professional, 22.0% services, 24.4% sales, 0.0% farming, 24.4% construction, 17.1% production (2005-2009 5-year est.).
Income: Per capita income: $26,582 (2010); Median household income: $41,818 (2010); Average household income: $58,547 (2010); Percent of households with income of $100,000 or more: 9.5% (2010); Poverty rate: 26.7% (2005-2009 5-year est.).
Taxes: Total city taxes per capita: $147 (2007); City property taxes per capita: $64 (2007).
Education: Percent of population age 25 and over with: High school diploma (including GED) or higher: 79.5% (2010); Bachelor's degree or higher: 12.0% (2010); Master's degree or higher: 4.3% (2010).
Housing: Homeownership rate: 85.1% (2010); Median home value: $85,833 (2010); Median contract rent: n/a per month (2005-2009 5-year est.); Median year structure built: 1973 (2005-2009 5-year est.).
Transportation: Commute to work: 80.5% car, 0.0% public transportation, 9.8% walk, 9.8% work from home (2005-2009 5-year est.); Travel time to work: 10.8% less than 15 minutes, 0.0% 15 to 30 minutes, 21.6% 30 to 45 minutes, 43.2% 45 to 60 minutes, 24.3% 60 minutes or more (2005-2009 5-year est.)

WASKOM (city). Covers a land area of 2.757 square miles and a water area of 0 square miles. Located at 32.47° N. Lat; 94.06° W. Long. Elevation is 285 feet.
History: Established 1850 as Powellton, changed to Waskom Station 1872.
Population: 1,914 (1990); 2,068 (2000); 2,104 (2010); 2,116 (2015 projected); Race: 69.2% White, 20.7% Black, 0.1% Asian, 10.1% Other, 10.0% Hispanic of any race (2010); Density: 763.0 persons per square mile (2010); Average household size: 2.63 (2010); Median age: 36.5 (2010); Males per 100 females: 99.6 (2010); Marriage status: 26.3% never married, 45.3% now married, 9.3% widowed, 19.1% divorced (2005-2009 5-year est.); Foreign born: 9.0% (2005-2009 5-year est.); Ancestry (includes multiple ancestries): 28.0% American, 9.1% Irish, 5.8% English, 5.1% French, 3.2% German (2005-2009 5-year est.).
Economy: Employment by occupation: 6.0% management, 18.8% professional, 12.5% services, 14.9% sales, 0.9% farming, 22.6% construction, 24.2% production (2005-2009 5-year est.).
Income: Per capita income: $16,858 (2010); Median household income: $37,078 (2010); Average household income: $43,967 (2010); Percent of households with income of $100,000 or more: 7.4% (2010); Poverty rate: 24.0% (2005-2009 5-year est.).
Taxes: Total city taxes per capita: $202 (2007); City property taxes per capita: $126 (2007).
Education: Percent of population age 25 and over with: High school diploma (including GED) or higher: 78.9% (2010); Bachelor's degree or higher: 7.5% (2010); Master's degree or higher: 1.7% (2010).

School District(s)
Waskom ISD (PK-12)
    2009-10 Enrollment: 790 . . . . (903) 687-3361
Housing: Homeownership rate: 72.9% (2010); Median home value: $65,435 (2010); Median contract rent: $429 per month (2005-2009 5-year est.); Median year structure built: 1971 (2005-2009 5-year est.).
Newspapers: Waskom Review (Community news; Circulation 500)
Transportation: Commute to work: 96.4% car, 0.0% public transportation, 2.6% walk, 0.0% work from home (2005-2009 5-year est.); Travel time to work: 28.8% less than 15 minutes, 28.1% 15 to 30 minutes, 26.2% 30 to 45 minutes, 12.9% 45 to 60 minutes, 4.0% 60 minutes or more (2005-2009 5-year est.)
Additional Information Contacts
Waskom Chamber of Commerce . . . . (903) 687-3000

Hartley County

Located in north Texas, in the high plains of the Panhandle; bounded on the west by New Mexico; includes Rita Blanca Lake. Covers a land area of

1,462.25 square miles, a water area of 0.95 square miles, and is located in the Central Time Zone at 35.87° N. Lat., 102.55° W. Long. The county was founded in 1876. County seat is Channing.

Weather Station: Bravo — Elevation: 4,160 feet

	Jan	Feb	Mar	Apr	May	Jun	Jul	Aug	Sep	Oct	Nov	Dec
High	52	56	63	72	80	88	92	90	83	73	61	51
Low	21	24	30	38	48	57	62	61	53	41	29	21
Precip	0.4	0.4	0.9	1.0	2.5	2.6	2.3	3.3	1.8	1.4	0.6	0.5
Snow	0.7	0.1	0.2	0.1	0.0	0.0	0.0	0.0	0.0	tr	tr	0.3

High and Low temperatures in degrees Fahrenheit; Precipitation and Snow in inches

Population: 3,634 (1990); 5,537 (2000); 5,445 (2010); 5,389 (2015 projected); Race: 75.8% White, 8.9% Black, 0.3% Asian, 14.9% Other, 19.7% Hispanic of any race (2010); Density: 3.7 persons per square mile (2010); Average household size: 2.53 (2010); Median age: 39.3 (2010); Males per 100 females: 166.7 (2010).
Religion: Five largest groups: 48.8% Southern Baptist Convention, 4.6% The United Methodist Church, 2.7% Church of the Nazarene, 2.2% Lutheran Church—Missouri Synod, 0.7% Churches of Christ (2000).
Economy: Unemployment rate: 5.8% (June 2011); Total civilian labor force: 2,548 (June 2011); Leading industries: 17.4% retail trade; 10.8% other services (except public administration); 5.2% wholesale trade (2009); Farms: 282 totaling 910,965 acres (2007); Companies that employ 500 or more persons: 0 (2009); Companies that employ 100 to 499 persons: 2 (2009); Companies that employ less than 100 persons: 87 (2009); Black-owned businesses: n/a (2007); Hispanic-owned businesses: n/a (2007); Asian-owned businesses: n/a (2007); Women-owned businesses: n/a (2007); Retail sales per capita: $3,678 (2010); Single-family building permits issued: n/a (2010); Multi-family building permits issued: n/a (2010).
Income: Per capita income: $23,072 (2010); Median household income: $56,250 (2010); Average household income: $72,446 (2010); Percent of households with income of $100,000 or more: 18.6% (2010); Poverty rate: 11.4% (2009); Bankruptcy rate: 1.47% (2010).
Taxes: Total county taxes per capita: $286 (2007); County property taxes per capita: $230 (2007).
Education: Percent of population age 25 and over with: High school diploma (including GED) or higher: 81.1% (2010); Bachelor's degree or higher: 19.0% (2010); Master's degree or higher: 4.4% (2010).
Housing: Homeownership rate: 74.5% (2010); Median home value: $124,460 (2010); Median contract rent: $427 per month (2005-2009 5-year est.); Median year structure built: 1971 (2005-2009 5-year est.)
Health: Birth rate: 161.0 per 10,000 population (2009); Death rate: 82.5 per 10,000 population (2009); Age-adjusted cancer mortality rate: 140.2 (Unreliable) deaths per 100,000 population (2007); Number of physicians: 0.0 per 10,000 population (2008); Hospital beds: 0.0 per 10,000 population (2007); Hospital admissions: 0.0 per 10,000 population (2007).
Elections: 2008 Presidential election results: 12.6% Obama, 86.2% McCain, 0.1% Nader
Additional Information Contacts
Hartley County Government . . . . (806) 235-3442
http://www.co.hartley.tx.us/ips/cms

Hartley County Communities

CHANNING (city). County seat. Covers a land area of 0.995 square miles and a water area of 0 square miles. Located at 35.68° N. Lat; 102.33° W. Long. Elevation is 3,806 feet.
Population: 277 (1990); 356 (2000); 371 (2010); 371 (2015 projected); Race: 91.9% White, 0.5% Black, 0.3% Asian, 7.3% Other, 9.2% Hispanic of any race (2010); Density: 373.0 persons per square mile (2010); Average household size: 2.79 (2010); Median age: 30.9 (2010); Males per 100 females: 107.3 (2010); Marriage status: 16.7% never married, 80.3% now married, 1.9% widowed, 1.1% divorced (2005-2009 5-year est.); Foreign born: 1.2% (2005-2009 5-year est.); Ancestry (includes multiple ancestries): 35.9% German, 18.4% French, 11.4% Scotch-Irish, 10.7% Irish, 8.5% American (2005-2009 5-year est.).
Economy: Employment by occupation: 13.6% management, 13.0% professional, 34.5% services, 10.7% sales, 0.6% farming, 11.9% construction, 15.8% production (2005-2009 5-year est.).
Income: Per capita income: $19,998 (2010); Median household income: $47,813 (2010); Average household income: $56,053 (2010); Percent of households with income of $100,000 or more: 12.8% (2010); Poverty rate: 7.3% (2005-2009 5-year est.).
Taxes: Total city taxes per capita: $81 (2007); City property taxes per capita: $64 (2007).

Education: Percent of population age 25 and over with: High school diploma (including GED) or higher: 87.9% (2010); Bachelor's degree or higher: 20.6% (2010); Master's degree or higher: 3.7% (2010).
School District(s)
Channing ISD (KG-12)
    2009-10 Enrollment: 147 . . . . (806) 235-3432
Housing: Homeownership rate: 61.7% (2010); Median home value: $72,727 (2010); Median contract rent: $450 per month (2005-2009 5-year est.); Median year structure built: 1955 (2005-2009 5-year est.).
Transportation: Commute to work: 87.5% car, 0.0% public transportation, 8.9% walk, 1.8% work from home (2005-2009 5-year est.); Travel time to work: 52.7% less than 15 minutes, 10.9% 15 to 30 minutes, 14.5% 30 to 45 minutes, 17.6% 45 to 60 minutes, 4.2% 60 minutes or more (2005-2009 5-year est.)

HARTLEY (CDP). Covers a land area of 6.976 square miles and a water area of 0 square miles. Located at 35.88° N. Lat; 102.39° W. Long. Elevation is 3,907 feet.
Population: 323 (1990); 441 (2000); 441 (2010); 441 (2015 projected); Race: 91.8% White, 0.7% Black, 0.2% Asian, 7.3% Other, 9.1% Hispanic of any race (2010); Density: 63.2 persons per square mile (2010); Average household size: 2.79 (2010); Median age: 30.8 (2010); Males per 100 females: 100.5 (2010); Marriage status: 13.3% never married, 72.6% now married, 3.0% widowed, 11.1% divorced (2005-2009 5-year est.); Foreign born: 6.1% (2005-2009 5-year est.); Ancestry (includes multiple ancestries): 30.3% German, 20.7% Irish, 13.2% American, 9.4% Scotch-Irish, 3.0% Swedish (2005-2009 5-year est.).
Economy: Employment by occupation: 9.8% management, 17.0% professional, 11.3% services, 23.2% sales, 6.7% farming, 17.0% construction, 14.9% production (2005-2009 5-year est.).
Income: Per capita income: $19,998 (2010); Median household income: $47,931 (2010); Average household income: $57,911 (2010); Percent of households with income of $100,000 or more: 12.7% (2010); Poverty rate: 1.9% (2005-2009 5-year est.).
Education: Percent of population age 25 and over with: High school diploma (including GED) or higher: 88.1% (2010); Bachelor's degree or higher: 20.6% (2010); Master's degree or higher: 4.0% (2010).
School District(s)
Hartley ISD (PK-12)
    2009-10 Enrollment: 199 . . . . (806) 365-4458
Housing: Homeownership rate: 61.4% (2010); Median home value: $69,286 (2010); Median contract rent: $413 per month (2005-2009 5-year est.); Median year structure built: 1962 (2005-2009 5-year est.).
Transportation: Commute to work: 93.3% car, 0.0% public transportation, 2.2% walk, 0.0% work from home (2005-2009 5-year est.); Travel time to work: 53.9% less than 15 minutes, 33.3% 15 to 30 minutes, 9.4% 30 to 45 minutes, 3.3% 45 to 60 minutes, 0.0% 60 minutes or more (2005-2009 5-year est.)

Haskell County

Located in northwest central Texas; drained by the Double Mountain Fork of the Brazos River. Covers a land area of 902.97 square miles, a water area of 7.29 square miles, and is located in the Central Time Zone at 33.20° N. Lat., 99.78° W. Long. The county was founded in 1858. County seat is Haskell.

Weather Station: Haskell — Elevation: 1,600 feet

	Jan	Feb	Mar	Apr	May	Jun	Jul	Aug	Sep	Oct	Nov	Dec
High	56	60	68	78	85	92	96	95	88	78	65	56
Low	30	34	41	50	60	68	72	71	63	52	41	31
Precip	1.0	1.6	1.8	1.9	3.5	3.8	1.8	2.4	2.6	2.4	1.4	1.4
Snow	1.1	1.2	0.1	0.0	0.0	0.0	0.0	0.0	0.0	tr	0.9	0.7

High and Low temperatures in degrees Fahrenheit; Precipitation and Snow in inches

Population: 6,820 (1990); 6,093 (2000); 5,325 (2010); 4,944 (2015 projected); Race: 78.1% White, 3.6% Black, 0.2% Asian, 18.0% Other, 24.9% Hispanic of any race (2010); Density: 5.9 persons per square mile (2010); Average household size: 2.28 (2010); Median age: 48.5 (2010); Males per 100 females: 87.8 (2010).
Religion: Five largest groups: 70.1% Southern Baptist Convention, 10.3% Catholic Church, 9.5% The United Methodist Church, 7.0% Churches of Christ, 4.6% Evangelical Lutheran Church in America (2000).
Economy: Unemployment rate: 5.9% (June 2011); Total civilian labor force: 3,053 (June 2011); Leading industries: 32.8% retail trade; 15.7% health care and social assistance; 12.5% accommodation & food services

(2009); Farms: 553 totaling 494,932 acres (2007); Companies that employ 500 or more persons: 0 (2009); Companies that employ 100 to 499 persons: 0 (2009); Companies that employ less than 100 persons: 130 (2009); Black-owned businesses: n/a (2007); Hispanic-owned businesses: n/a (2007); Asian-owned businesses: n/a (2007); Women-owned businesses: n/a (2007); Retail sales per capita: $12,804 (2010). Single-family building permits issued: 2 (2010); Multi-family building permits issued: 0 (2010).

Income: Per capita income: $19,031 (2010); Median household income: $30,016 (2010); Average household income: $43,751 (2010); Percent of households with income of $100,000 or more: 9.2% (2010); Poverty rate: 22.6% (2009); Bankruptcy rate: 1.19% (2010).

Taxes: Total county taxes per capita: $406 (2007); County property taxes per capita: $346 (2007).

Education: Percent of population age 25 and over with: High school diploma (including GED) or higher: 76.3% (2010); Bachelor's degree or higher: 16.3% (2010); Master's degree or higher: 5.5% (2010).

Housing: Homeownership rate: 77.2% (2010); Median home value: $39,044 (2010); Median contract rent: $244 per month (2005-2009 5-year est.); Median year structure built: 1958 (2005-2009 5-year est.)

Health: Birth rate: 116.0 per 10,000 population (2009); Death rate: 147.9 per 10,000 population (2009); Age-adjusted cancer mortality rate: 237.6 deaths per 100,000 population (2007); Number of physicians: 3.9 per 10,000 population (2008); Hospital beds: 48.6 per 10,000 population (2007); Hospital admissions: 382.7 per 10,000 population (2007).

Elections: 2008 Presidential election results: 33.0% Obama, 65.6% McCain, 0.1% Nader

Additional Information Contacts
Haskell County Government . . . . (940) 864-2451
   http://www.co.haskell.tx.us/ips/cms
Haskell Chamber of Commerce . . . . (940) 864-2477
   http://www.haskelltxchamber.com

Haskell County Communities

HASKELL (city). County seat. Covers a land area of 3.403 square miles and a water area of 0 square miles. Located at 33.16° N. Lat; 99.73° W. Long. Elevation is 1,581 feet.

History: Haskell was settled in 1882, with the post office in the home of Mrs. R.A. Standefer, who kept the mail in her bureau drawers. Many of the early residents of Haskell were of Swedish and German descent.

Population: 3,362 (1990); 3,106 (2000); 2,684 (2010); 2,488 (2015 projected); Race: 75.5% White, 5.0% Black, 0.1% Asian, 19.4% Other, 27.3% Hispanic of any race (2010); Density: 788.8 persons per square mile (2010); Average household size: 2.26 (2010); Median age: 47.5 (2010); Males per 100 females: 82.6 (2010); Marriage status: 14.5% never married, 68.6% now married, 10.0% widowed, 6.9% divorced (2005-2009 5-year est.); Foreign born: 1.3% (2005-2009 5-year est.); Ancestry (includes multiple ancestries): 13.4% Irish, 9.6% English, 8.0% German, 7.6% American, 2.3% Scotch-Irish (2005-2009 5-year est.).

Economy: Single-family building permits issued: 2 (2010); Multi-family building permits issued: 0 (2010); Employment by occupation: 5.5% management, 13.4% professional, 27.8% services, 25.6% sales, 1.4% farming, 16.8% construction, 9.4% production (2005-2009 5-year est.).

Income: Per capita income: $16,456 (2010); Median household income: $26,044 (2010); Average household income: $37,540 (2010); Percent of households with income of $100,000 or more: 6.0% (2010); Poverty rate: 20.7% (2005-2009 5-year est.).

Taxes: Total city taxes per capita: $222 (2007); City property taxes per capita: $92 (2007).

Education: Percent of population age 25 and over with: High school diploma (including GED) or higher: 73.3% (2010); Bachelor's degree or higher: 14.1% (2010); Master's degree or higher: 5.3% (2010).

School District(s)
Haskell CISD (PK-12)
   2009-10 Enrollment: 632 . . . . (940) 864-2602
Paint Creek ISD (PK-12)
   2009-10 Enrollment: 162 . . . . (940) 864-2471

Housing: Homeownership rate: 71.9% (2010); Median home value: $41,346 (2010); Median contract rent: $213 per month (2005-2009 5-year est.); Median year structure built: 1956 (2005-2009 5-year est.).

Hospitals: Haskell Memorial Hospital

Safety: Violent crime rate: 23.3 per 10,000 population; Property crime rate: 333.7 per 10,000 population (2009).

Newspapers: Haskell Free Press (Local news; Circulation 2,100)

Transportation: Commute to work: 91.8% car, 0.0% public transportation, 3.1% walk, 2.5% work from home (2005-2009 5-year est.); Travel time to work: 58.7% less than 15 minutes, 16.7% 15 to 30 minutes, 9.0% 30 to 45 minutes, 3.4% 45 to 60 minutes, 12.2% 60 minutes or more (2005-2009 5-year est.)

Additional Information Contacts
Haskell Chamber of Commerce . . . . (940) 864-2477
   http://www.haskelltxchamber.com

O'BRIEN (city). Covers a land area of 0.504 square miles and a water area of 0 square miles. Located at 33.38° N. Lat; 99.84° W. Long. Elevation is 1,575 feet.

Population: 152 (1990); 132 (2000); 117 (2010); 109 (2015 projected); Race: 69.2% White, 2.6% Black, 0.9% Asian, 27.4% Other, 32.5% Hispanic of any race (2010); Density: 232.3 persons per square mile (2010); Average household size: 2.32 (2010); Median age: 48.2 (2010); Males per 100 females: 95.0 (2010); Marriage status: 27.3% never married, 54.5% now married, 12.1% widowed, 6.1% divorced (2005-2009 5-year est.); Foreign born: 7.1% (2005-2009 5-year est.); Ancestry (includes multiple ancestries): 11.1% Dutch, 11.1% Irish, 6.3% German, 4.8% English, 4.8% Swedish (2005-2009 5-year est.).

Economy: Employment by occupation: 3.7% management, 13.0% professional, 14.8% services, 1.9% sales, 24.1% farming, 37.0% construction, 5.6% production (2005-2009 5-year est.).

Income: Per capita income: $18,423 (2010); Median household income: $29,000 (2010); Average household income: $44,550 (2010); Percent of households with income of $100,000 or more: 10.0% (2010); Poverty rate: 53.2% (2005-2009 5-year est.).

Taxes: Total city taxes per capita: $150 (2007); City property taxes per capita: $100 (2007).

Education: Percent of population age 25 and over with: High school diploma (including GED) or higher: 75.3% (2010); Bachelor's degree or higher: 16.9% (2010); Master's degree or higher: 4.5% (2010).

School District(s)
Knox City-O'brien CISD (PK-12)
   2009-10 Enrollment: 298 . . . . (940) 657-3521

Housing: Homeownership rate: 80.0% (2010); Median home value: $31,111 (2010); Median contract rent: n/a per month (2005-2009 5-year est.); Median year structure built: 1962 (2005-2009 5-year est.).

Transportation: Commute to work: 87.0% car, 0.0% public transportation, 13.0% walk, 0.0% work from home (2005-2009 5-year est.); Travel time to work: 77.8% less than 15 minutes, 5.6% 15 to 30 minutes, 16.7% 30 to 45 minutes, 0.0% 45 to 60 minutes, 0.0% 60 minutes or more (2005-2009 5-year est.)

ROCHESTER (town). Covers a land area of 0.351 square miles and a water area of 0 square miles. Located at 33.31° N. Lat; 99.85° W. Long. Elevation is 1,594 feet.

Population: 458 (1990); 378 (2000); 326 (2010); 303 (2015 projected); Race: 69.6% White, 3.1% Black, 1.2% Asian, 26.1% Other, 31.9% Hispanic of any race (2010); Density: 928.0 persons per square mile (2010); Average household size: 2.33 (2010); Median age: 47.7 (2010); Males per 100 females: 94.0 (2010); Marriage status: 17.6% never married, 68.3% now married, 7.7% widowed, 6.3% divorced (2005-2009 5-year est.); Foreign born: 3.5% (2005-2009 5-year est.); Ancestry (includes multiple ancestries): 13.2% Irish, 11.2% German, 10.9% American, 6.2% English, 2.7% Scottish (2005-2009 5-year est.).

Economy: Employment by occupation: 5.4% management, 6.2% professional, 14.6% services, 20.0% sales, 1.5% farming, 42.3% construction, 10.0% production (2005-2009 5-year est.).

Income: Per capita income: $18,423 (2010); Median household income: $27,813 (2010); Average household income: $43,741 (2010); Percent of households with income of $100,000 or more: 8.6% (2010); Poverty rate: 19.0% (2005-2009 5-year est.).

Taxes: Total city taxes per capita: $255 (2007); City property taxes per capita: $100 (2007).

Education: Percent of population age 25 and over with: High school diploma (including GED) or higher: 74.5% (2010); Bachelor's degree or higher: 15.2% (2010); Master's degree or higher: 2.9% (2010).

School District(s)
Haskell CISD (PK-12)
   2009-10 Enrollment: 632 . . . . (940) 864-2602

Housing: Homeownership rate: 79.9% (2010); Median home value: $35,217 (2010); Median contract rent: $275 per month (2005-2009 5-year est.); Median year structure built: 1956 (2005-2009 5-year est.).

Transportation: Commute to work: 96.6% car, 1.7% public transportation, 1.7% walk, 0.0% work from home (2005-2009 5-year est.); Travel time to work: 44.5% less than 15 minutes, 22.7% 15 to 30 minutes, 16.8% 30 to 45 minutes, 0.0% 45 to 60 minutes, 16.0% 60 minutes or more (2005-2009 5-year est.)

RULE (town). Covers a land area of 0.696 square miles and a water area of 0 square miles. Located at 33.18° N. Lat; 99.89° W. Long. Elevation is 1,680 feet.
History: Incorporated 1909.
Population: 783 (1990); 698 (2000); 621 (2010); 579 (2015 projected); Race: 85.2% White, 2.3% Black, 0.0% Asian, 12.6% Other, 23.2% Hispanic of any race (2010); Density: 892.7 persons per square mile (2010); Average household size: 2.29 (2010); Median age: 48.5 (2010); Males per 100 females: 95.9 (2010); Marriage status: 26.6% never married, 50.7% now married, 11.3% widowed, 11.3% divorced (2005-2009 5-year est.); Foreign born: 9.3% (2005-2009 5-year est.); Ancestry (includes multiple ancestries): 15.2% Irish, 13.7% American, 10.0% German, 6.8% English, 3.6% Czech (2005-2009 5-year est.).
Economy: Employment by occupation: 5.2% management, 20.4% professional, 27.0% services, 14.2% sales, 6.6% farming, 8.5% construction, 18.0% production (2005-2009 5-year est.).
Income: Per capita income: $19,194 (2010); Median household income: $33,295 (2010); Average household income: $43,875 (2010); Percent of households with income of $100,000 or more: 6.6% (2010); Poverty rate: 32.7% (2005-2009 5-year est.).
Taxes: Total city taxes per capita: $191 (2007); City property taxes per capita: $121 (2007).
Education: Percent of population age 25 and over with: High school diploma (including GED) or higher: 79.1% (2010); Bachelor's degree or higher: 12.6% (2010); Master's degree or higher: 5.2% (2010).
School District(s)
Rule ISD (PK-12)
    2009-10 Enrollment: 154 . . . . (940) 997-2521
Housing: Homeownership rate: 81.5% (2010); Median home value: $26,812 (2010); Median contract rent: $235 per month (2005-2009 5-year est.); Median year structure built: 1955 (2005-2009 5-year est.).
Transportation: Commute to work: 98.0% car, 0.0% public transportation, 2.0% walk, 0.0% work from home (2005-2009 5-year est.); Travel time to work: 37.2% less than 15 minutes, 32.7% 15 to 30 minutes, 16.1% 30 to 45 minutes, 7.5% 45 to 60 minutes, 6.5% 60 minutes or more (2005-2009 5-year est.)

WEINERT (city). Covers a land area of 0.483 square miles and a water area of 0 square miles. Located at 33.32° N. Lat; 99.67° W. Long. Elevation is 1,526 feet.
Population: 235 (1990); 177 (2000); 153 (2010); 142 (2015 projected); Race: 69.9% White, 2.6% Black, 0.7% Asian, 26.8% Other, 32.7% Hispanic of any race (2010); Density: 316.9 persons per square mile (2010); Average household size: 2.34 (2010); Median age: 46.5 (2010); Males per 100 females: 96.2 (2010); Marriage status: 20.5% never married, 59.8% now married, 13.2% widowed, 6.4% divorced (2005-2009 5-year est.); Foreign born: 1.1% (2005-2009 5-year est.); Ancestry (includes multiple ancestries): 17.9% American, 15.7% Irish, 15.7% German, 6.0% English, 5.2% French (2005-2009 5-year est.).
Economy: Employment by occupation: 24.3% management, 6.1% professional, 17.4% services, 14.8% sales, 14.8% farming, 14.8% construction, 7.8% production (2005-2009 5-year est.).
Income: Per capita income: $18,423 (2010); Median household income: $25,714 (2010); Average household income: $49,269 (2010); Percent of households with income of $100,000 or more: 9.2% (2010); Poverty rate: 20.9% (2005-2009 5-year est.).
Taxes: Total city taxes per capita: $106 (2007); City property taxes per capita: $81 (2007).
Education: Percent of population age 25 and over with: High school diploma (including GED) or higher: 75.0% (2010); Bachelor's degree or higher: 14.3% (2010); Master's degree or higher: 2.7% (2010).
Housing: Homeownership rate: 80.0% (2010); Median home value: $32,727 (2010); Median contract rent: n/a per month (2005-2009 5-year est.); Median year structure built: 1963 (2005-2009 5-year est.).
Transportation: Commute to work: 100.0% car, 0.0% public transportation, 0.0% walk, 0.0% work from home (2005-2009 5-year est.); Travel time to work: 65.5% less than 15 minutes, 27.4% 15 to 30 minutes, 7.1% 30 to 45 minutes, 0.0% 45 to 60 minutes, 0.0% 60 minutes or more (2005-2009 5-year est.)

Hays County

Located in south central Texas, partly on the Edwards Plateau; drained by the San Marcos and Blanco Rivers. Covers a land area of 677.87 square miles, a water area of 1.92 square miles, and is located in the Central Time Zone at 29.99° N. Lat., 97.97° W. Long. The county was founded in 1848. County seat is San Marcos.

Hays County is part of the Austin-Round Rock-San Marcos, TX Metropolitan Statistical Area. The entire metro area includes: Bastrop County, TX; Caldwell County, TX; Hays County, TX; Travis County, TX; Williamson County, TX

Weather Station: Dripping Springs 6 E — Elevation: 1,120 feet

	Jan	Feb	Mar	Apr	May	Jun	Jul	Aug	Sep	Oct	Nov	Dec
High	61	65	72	80	86	91	94	96	90	80	70	62
Low	39	43	48	56	64	69	71	71	65	57	48	40
Precip	2.4	2.3	2.9	2.4	4.0	4.7	2.2	1.8	2.8	4.0	3.4	2.8
Snow	0.5	0.2	tr	tr	0.0	0.0	0.0	0.0	0.0	0.0	tr	0.1

High and Low temperatures in degrees Fahrenheit; Precipitation and Snow in inches

Weather Station: San Marcos — Elevation: 611 feet

	Jan	Feb	Mar	Apr	May	Jun	Jul	Aug	Sep	Oct	Nov	Dec
High	63	66	73	80	86	92	95	96	91	82	72	63
Low	40	42	49	56	65	71	73	73	68	58	49	40
Precip	2.1	1.9	2.4	2.4	4.6	4.9	2.3	2.2	3.4	4.2	3.1	2.3
Snow	tr	0.1	0.0	0.0	0.0	0.0	0.0	0.0	0.0	0.0	tr	tr

High and Low temperatures in degrees Fahrenheit; Precipitation and Snow in inches

Population: 65,614 (1990); 97,589 (2000); 156,281 (2010); 184,560 (2015 projected); Race: 76.1% White, 4.3% Black, 1.1% Asian, 18.5% Other, 32.8% Hispanic of any race (2010); Density: 230.5 persons per square mile (2010); Average household size: 2.78 (2010); Median age: 29.4 (2010); Males per 100 females: 100.9 (2010).
Religion: Five largest groups: 19.8% Catholic Church, 11.7% Southern Baptist Convention, 4.4% The United Methodist Church, 1.4% Episcopal Church, 1.0% The Church of Jesus Christ of Latter-day Saints (2000).
Economy: Unemployment rate: 7.6% (June 2011); Total civilian labor force: 81,892 (June 2011); Leading industries: 24.9% retail trade; 17.1% accommodation & food services; 12.7% health care and social assistance (2009); Farms: 1,136 totaling 235,568 acres (2007); Companies that employ 500 or more persons: 2 (2009); Companies that employ 100 to 499 persons: 50 (2009); Companies that employ less than 100 persons: 3,054 (2009); Black-owned businesses: 260 (2007); Hispanic-owned businesses: 2,574 (2007); Asian-owned businesses: 130 (2007); Women-owned businesses: 3,725 (2007); Retail sales per capita: $11,829 (2010). Single-family building permits issued: 1,130 (2010); Multi-family building permits issued: 1,250 (2010).
Income: Per capita income: $24,846 (2010); Median household income: $57,196 (2010); Average household income: $73,035 (2010); Percent of households with income of $100,000 or more: 22.6% (2010); Poverty rate: 19.2% (2009); Bankruptcy rate: 2.14% (2010).
Taxes: Total county taxes per capita: $346 (2007); County property taxes per capita: $259 (2007).
Education: Percent of population age 25 and over with: High school diploma (including GED) or higher: 87.6% (2010); Bachelor's degree or higher: 32.3% (2010); Master's degree or higher: 9.8% (2010).
Housing: Homeownership rate: 65.8% (2010); Median home value: $168,169 (2010); Median contract rent: $651 per month (2005-2009 5-year est.); Median year structure built: 1993 (2005-2009 5-year est.)
Health: Birth rate: 147.0 per 10,000 population (2009); Death rate: 48.9 per 10,000 population (2009); Age-adjusted cancer mortality rate: 172.4 deaths per 100,000 population (2007); Number of physicians: 11.7 per 10,000 population (2008); Hospital beds: 8.0 per 10,000 population (2007); Hospital admissions: 348.8 per 10,000 population (2007).
Environment: Air Quality Index: 93.0% good, 7.0% moderate, 0.0% unhealthy for sensitive individuals, 0.0% unhealthy (percent of days in 2008)
Elections: 2008 Presidential election results: 48.1% Obama, 50.2% McCain, 0.2% Nader
Additional Information Contacts
Hays County Government . . . . (512) 393-2205
    http://www.co.hays.tx.us
City of Kyle . . . . (512) 262-1010
    http://www.cityofkyle.com
City of San Marcos . . . . (512) 393-8000
    http://www.ci.san-marcos.tx.us

Dripping Springs Chamber of Commerce . . . . (512) 858-4740
  http://www.drippingspringstx.org
San Marcos Area Chamber of Commerce . . . . (512) 393-5900
  http://www.sanmarcostexas.com
Town of Buda . . . . (512) 312-0084
  http://www.ci.buda.tx.us
Town of Niederwald . . . . (512) 398-6338
Wimberley Chamber of Commerce . . . . (512) 847-2201
  http://www.wimberley.org

Hays County Communities

BEAR CREEK (village). Covers a land area of 1.152 square miles and a water area of 0 square miles. Located at 30.18° N. Lat; 97.93° W. Long. Elevation is 991 feet.
Population: 232 (1990); 360 (2000); 338 (2010); 383 (2015 projected); Race: 94.4% White, 0.9% Black, 2.1% Asian, 2.7% Other, 10.1% Hispanic of any race (2010); Density: 293.5 persons per square mile (2010); Average household size: 2.89 (2010); Median age: 38.3 (2010); Males per 100 females: 97.7 (2010); Marriage status: 23.2% never married, 69.3% now married, 3.1% widowed, 4.4% divorced (2005-2009 5-year est.); Foreign born: 2.6% (2005-2009 5-year est.); Ancestry (includes multiple ancestries): 19.4% German, 18.5% English, 13.8% Scottish, 8.4% Italian, 4.3% Irish (2005-2009 5-year est.).
Economy: Employment by occupation: 33.0% management, 18.6% professional, 14.9% services, 22.6% sales, 0.0% farming, 9.0% construction, 1.8% production (2005-2009 5-year est.).
Income: Per capita income: $42,284 (2010); Median household income: $98,214 (2010); Average household income: $121,368 (2010); Percent of households with income of $100,000 or more: 48.7% (2010); Poverty rate: 4.5% (2005-2009 5-year est.).
Taxes: Total city taxes per capita: $101 (2007); City property taxes per capita: $88 (2007).
Education: Percent of population age 25 and over with: High school diploma (including GED) or higher: 95.0% (2010); Bachelor's degree or higher: 47.3% (2010); Master's degree or higher: 15.5% (2010).
Housing: Homeownership rate: 93.2% (2010); Median home value: $339,706 (2010); Median contract rent: $1,679 per month (2005-2009 5-year est.); Median year structure built: 1995 (2005-2009 5-year est.).
Transportation: Commute to work: 88.6% car, 0.0% public transportation, 0.0% walk, 10.5% work from home (2005-2009 5-year est.); Travel time to work: 4.1% less than 15 minutes, 36.2% 15 to 30 minutes, 36.7% 30 to 45 minutes, 18.9% 45 to 60 minutes, 4.1% 60 minutes or more (2005-2009 5-year est.)

BUDA (city). Covers a land area of 2.408 square miles and a water area of 0.006 square miles. Located at 30.08° N. Lat; 97.83° W. Long. Elevation is 702 feet.
Population: 1,948 (1990); 2,404 (2000); 4,650 (2010); 5,582 (2015 projected); Race: 76.3% White, 1.6% Black, 1.2% Asian, 20.9% Other, 39.9% Hispanic of any race (2010); Density: 1,931.3 persons per square mile (2010); Average household size: 2.82 (2010); Median age: 31.6 (2010); Males per 100 females: 97.8 (2010); Marriage status: 24.3% never married, 58.8% now married, 6.0% widowed, 10.9% divorced (2005-2009 5-year est.); Foreign born: 2.7% (2005-2009 5-year est.); Ancestry (includes multiple ancestries): 26.0% German, 13.6% English, 10.4% Irish, 7.5% Scotch-Irish, 5.2% French (2005-2009 5-year est.).
Economy: Single-family building permits issued: 272 (2010); Multi-family building permits issued: 144 (2010); Employment by occupation: 19.2% management, 20.4% professional, 13.6% services, 30.4% sales, 0.0% farming, 9.9% construction, 6.4% production (2005-2009 5-year est.).
Income: Per capita income: $28,713 (2010); Median household income: $66,979 (2010); Average household income: $80,778 (2010); Percent of households with income of $100,000 or more: 22.8% (2010); Poverty rate: 1.4% (2005-2009 5-year est.).
Taxes: Total city taxes per capita: $818 (2007); City property taxes per capita: $93 (2007).
Education: Percent of population age 25 and over with: High school diploma (including GED) or higher: 90.4% (2010); Bachelor's degree or higher: 29.5% (2010); Master's degree or higher: 3.7% (2010).
School District(s)
Hays CISD (PK-12)
  2009-10 Enrollment: 14,649 . . . . (512) 268-2141
San Marcos CISD (PK-12)
  2009-10 Enrollment: 7,434 . . . . (512) 393-6700

University of Texas University Charter School (KG-12)
  2009-10 Enrollment: 907 . . . . (512) 471-5652
Housing: Homeownership rate: 84.3% (2010); Median home value: $167,431 (2010); Median contract rent: $833 per month (2005-2009 5-year est.); Median year structure built: 1994 (2005-2009 5-year est.).
Newspapers: Free Press (Local news; Circulation 4,300)
Transportation: Commute to work: 95.3% car, 0.0% public transportation, 1.2% walk, 3.1% work from home (2005-2009 5-year est.); Travel time to work: 19.0% less than 15 minutes, 21.7% 15 to 30 minutes, 24.9% 30 to 45 minutes, 17.5% 45 to 60 minutes, 16.9% 60 minutes or more (2005-2009 5-year est.)
Additional Information Contacts
Town of Buda . . . . (512) 312-0084
  http://www.ci.buda.tx.us

DRIFTWOOD (unincorporated postal area, zip code 78619). Covers a land area of 34.192 square miles and a water area of 0 square miles. Located at 30.10° N. Lat; 98.03° W. Long. Elevation is 1,043 feet.
Population: 1,585 (2000); Race: 96.7% White, 0.0% Black, 1.2% Asian, 2.1% Other, 3.1% Hispanic of any race (2000); Density: 46.4 persons per square mile (2000); Age: 25.1% under 18, 10.0% over 64 (2000); Marriage status: 14.4% never married, 72.2% now married, 4.6% widowed, 8.9% divorced (2000); Foreign born: 4.6% (2000); Ancestry (includes multiple ancestries): 26.1% German, 17.3% English, 11.4% Irish, 9.1% American (2000).
Economy: Employment by occupation: 13.0% management, 28.7% professional, 8.7% services, 26.0% sales, 0.0% farming, 16.5% construction, 7.2% production (2000).
Income: Per capita income: $31,190 (2000); Median household income: $61,875 (2000); Poverty rate: 179.1% (2000).
Education: Percent of population age 25 and over with: High school diploma (including GED) or higher: 96.9% (2000); Bachelor's degree or higher: 42.0% (2000).
School District(s)
University of Texas University Charter School (KG-12)
  2009-10 Enrollment: 907 . . . . (512) 471-5652
Housing: Homeownership rate: 85.0% (2000); Median home value: $109,900 (2000); Median contract rent: $345 per month (2000); Median year structure built: 1987 (2000).
Newspapers: News-Dispatch (Community news; Circulation 2,500)
Transportation: Commute to work: 90.2% car, 2.5% public transportation, 0.0% walk, 7.3% work from home (2000); Travel time to work: 15.8% less than 15 minutes, 25.8% 15 to 30 minutes, 24.8% 30 to 45 minutes, 19.4% 45 to 60 minutes, 14.3% 60 minutes or more (2000)

DRIPPING SPRINGS (city). Covers a land area of 3.303 square miles and a water area of 0 square miles. Located at 30.19° N. Lat; 98.08° W. Long. Elevation is 1,148 feet.
Population: 1,069 (1990); 1,548 (2000); 1,519 (2010); 1,776 (2015 projected); Race: 92.1% White, 0.6% Black, 0.5% Asian, 6.8% Other, 9.8% Hispanic of any race (2010); Density: 459.9 persons per square mile (2010); Average household size: 2.93 (2010); Median age: 35.6 (2010); Males per 100 females: 100.9 (2010); Marriage status: 28.0% never married, 52.7% now married, 3.5% widowed, 15.8% divorced (2005-2009 5-year est.); Foreign born: 15.0% (2005-2009 5-year est.); Ancestry (includes multiple ancestries): 28.0% German, 18.0% Irish, 10.3% English, 4.2% French, 3.6% Scotch-Irish (2005-2009 5-year est.).
Economy: Single-family building permits issued: 5 (2010); Multi-family building permits issued: 0 (2010); Employment by occupation: 14.0% management, 21.7% professional, 21.3% services, 21.8% sales, 0.3% farming, 13.4% construction, 7.4% production (2005-2009 5-year est.).
Income: Per capita income: $35,832 (2010); Median household income: $87,649 (2010); Average household income: $105,475 (2010); Percent of households with income of $100,000 or more: 41.9% (2010); Poverty rate: 11.5% (2005-2009 5-year est.).
Taxes: Total city taxes per capita: $424 (2007); City property taxes per capita: $76 (2007).
Education: Percent of population age 25 and over with: High school diploma (including GED) or higher: 94.5% (2010); Bachelor's degree or higher: 40.4% (2010); Master's degree or higher: 12.1% (2010).
School District(s)
Dripping Springs ISD (PK-12)
  2009-10 Enrollment: 4,331 . . . . (512) 858-3000

Housing: Homeownership rate: 84.5% (2010); Median home value: $275,540 (2010); Median contract rent: $850 per month (2005-2009 5-year est.); Median year structure built: 1986 (2005-2009 5-year est.).
Transportation: Commute to work: 89.4% car, 0.0% public transportation, 1.2% walk, 8.2% work from home (2005-2009 5-year est.); Travel time to work: 24.7% less than 15 minutes, 13.2% 15 to 30 minutes, 40.0% 30 to 45 minutes, 12.4% 45 to 60 minutes, 9.6% 60 minutes or more (2005-2009 5-year est.)
Additional Information Contacts
Dripping Springs Chamber of Commerce . . . . (512) 858-4740
  http://www.drippingspringstx.org

HAYS (city). Covers a land area of 0.173 square miles and a water area of 0 square miles. Located at 30.11° N. Lat; 97.87° W. Long. Elevation is 728 feet.
Population: 251 (1990); 233 (2000); 197 (2010); 227 (2015 projected); Race: 91.4% White, 1.0% Black, 1.0% Asian, 6.6% Other, 17.3% Hispanic of any race (2010); Density: 1,138.2 persons per square mile (2010); Average household size: 3.03 (2010); Median age: 38.1 (2010); Males per 100 females: 99.0 (2010); Marriage status: 24.5% never married, 50.0% now married, 7.7% widowed, 17.9% divorced (2005-2009 5-year est.); Foreign born: 2.6% (2005-2009 5-year est.); Ancestry (includes multiple ancestries): 23.5% English, 23.5% German, 14.8% American, 10.9% Irish, 7.8% Scottish (2005-2009 5-year est.).
Economy: Employment by occupation: 18.2% management, 17.2% professional, 10.1% services, 22.2% sales, 0.0% farming, 23.2% construction, 9.1% production (2005-2009 5-year est.).
Income: Per capita income: $36,202 (2010); Median household income: $99,038 (2010); Average household income: $107,385 (2010); Percent of households with income of $100,000 or more: 49.2% (2010); Poverty rate: 0.9% (2005-2009 5-year est.).
Taxes: Total city taxes per capita: $133 (2007); City property taxes per capita: $41 (2007).
Education: Percent of population age 25 and over with: High school diploma (including GED) or higher: 93.9% (2010); Bachelor's degree or higher: 30.5% (2010); Master's degree or higher: 7.6% (2010).
Housing: Homeownership rate: 96.9% (2010); Median home value: $248,214 (2010); Median contract rent: $646 per month (2005-2009 5-year est.); Median year structure built: 1971 (2005-2009 5-year est.).
Transportation: Commute to work: 87.8% car, 0.0% public transportation, 2.0% walk, 8.2% work from home (2005-2009 5-year est.); Travel time to work: 31.1% less than 15 minutes, 28.9% 15 to 30 minutes, 20.0% 30 to 45 minutes, 17.8% 45 to 60 minutes, 2.2% 60 minutes or more (2005-2009 5-year est.)

KYLE (city). Covers a land area of 5.911 square miles and a water area of 0.081 square miles. Located at 29.98° N. Lat; 97.87° W. Long. Elevation is 728 feet.
Population: 2,892 (1990); 5,314 (2000); 20,867 (2010); 24,862 (2015 projected); Race: 73.3% White, 4.8% Black, 0.3% Asian, 21.5% Other, 44.5% Hispanic of any race (2010); Density: 3,530.2 persons per square mile (2010); Average household size: 3.31 (2010); Median age: 29.0 (2010); Males per 100 females: 101.4 (2010); Marriage status: 26.1% never married, 58.8% now married, 3.2% widowed, 12.0% divorced (2005-2009 5-year est.); Foreign born: 4.3% (2005-2009 5-year est.); Ancestry (includes multiple ancestries): 15.6% German, 8.6% Irish, 6.8% English, 3.1% American, 2.9% Scottish (2005-2009 5-year est.).
Economy: Unemployment rate: 6.1% (June 2011); Total civilian labor force: 13,331 (June 2011); Single-family building permits issued: 299 (2010); Multi-family building permits issued: 0 (2010); Employment by occupation: 16.5% management, 20.7% professional, 12.5% services, 31.6% sales, 0.0% farming, 8.1% construction, 10.6% production (2005-2009 5-year est.).
Income: Per capita income: $22,749 (2010); Median household income: $64,426 (2010); Average household income: $75,745 (2010); Percent of households with income of $100,000 or more: 22.8% (2010); Poverty rate: 7.3% (2005-2009 5-year est.).
Taxes: Total city taxes per capita: $381 (2007); City property taxes per capita: $109 (2007).
Education: Percent of population age 25 and over with: High school diploma (including GED) or higher: 79.0% (2010); Bachelor's degree or higher: 18.2% (2010); Master's degree or higher: 3.7% (2010).
School District(s)
Hays CISD (PK-12)
  2009-10 Enrollment: 14,649 . . . . (512) 268-2141

Housing: Homeownership rate: 76.0% (2010); Median home value: $135,840 (2010); Median contract rent: $1,041 per month (2005-2009 5-year est.); Median year structure built: 2002 (2005-2009 5-year est.).
Safety: Violent crime rate: 5.5 per 10,000 population; Property crime rate: 110.9 per 10,000 population (2009).
Transportation: Commute to work: 95.0% car, 0.5% public transportation, 0.7% walk, 3.2% work from home (2005-2009 5-year est.); Travel time to work: 13.2% less than 15 minutes, 27.0% 15 to 30 minutes, 30.8% 30 to 45 minutes, 14.2% 45 to 60 minutes, 14.7% 60 minutes or more (2005-2009 5-year est.)
Additional Information Contacts
City of Kyle. . . . . (512) 262-1010
  http://www.cityofkyle.com

MOUNTAIN CITY (city). Covers a land area of 0.461 square miles and a water area of 0 square miles. Located at 30.04° N. Lat; 97.89° W. Long. Elevation is 823 feet.
Population: 374 (1990); 671 (2000); 1,119 (2010); 1,371 (2015 projected); Race: 89.5% White, 1.4% Black, 0.8% Asian, 8.2% Other, 17.2% Hispanic of any race (2010); Density: 2,426.6 persons per square mile (2010); Average household size: 2.99 (2010); Median age: 34.6 (2010); Males per 100 females: 96.7 (2010); Marriage status: 21.0% never married, 71.7% now married, 1.2% widowed, 6.1% divorced (2005-2009 5-year est.); Foreign born: 0.9% (2005-2009 5-year est.); Ancestry (includes multiple ancestries): 30.1% German, 16.0% English, 14.1% Irish, 9.8% American, 4.7% Scottish (2005-2009 5-year est.).
Economy: Employment by occupation: 15.9% management, 24.9% professional, 12.5% services, 28.7% sales, 0.0% farming, 9.7% construction, 8.3% production (2005-2009 5-year est.).
Income: Per capita income: $38,102 (2010); Median household income: $105,714 (2010); Average household income: $112,868 (2010); Percent of households with income of $100,000 or more: 54.3% (2010); Poverty rate: 2.6% (2005-2009 5-year est.).
Taxes: Total city taxes per capita: $73 (2007); City property taxes per capita: $59 (2007).
Education: Percent of population age 25 and over with: High school diploma (including GED) or higher: 95.4% (2010); Bachelor's degree or higher: 41.5% (2010); Master's degree or higher: 12.6% (2010).
Housing: Homeownership rate: 93.3% (2010); Median home value: $248,106 (2010); Median contract rent: $725 per month (2005-2009 5-year est.); Median year structure built: 1986 (2005-2009 5-year est.).
Transportation: Commute to work: 93.3% car, 0.0% public transportation, 1.4% walk, 3.5% work from home (2005-2009 5-year est.); Travel time to work: 20.6% less than 15 minutes, 20.6% 15 to 30 minutes, 32.0% 30 to 45 minutes, 10.7% 45 to 60 minutes, 16.2% 60 minutes or more (2005-2009 5-year est.)

NIEDERWALD (town). Covers a land area of 2.968 square miles and a water area of 0 square miles. Located at 30.00° N. Lat; 97.75° W. Long.
Population: 378 (1990); 584 (2000); 749 (2010); 862 (2015 projected); Race: 64.5% White, 2.8% Black, 0.8% Asian, 31.9% Other, 55.3% Hispanic of any race (2010); Density: 252.4 persons per square mile (2010); Average household size: 3.40 (2010); Median age: 31.1 (2010); Males per 100 females: 106.3 (2010); Marriage status: 30.8% never married, 54.3% now married, 3.6% widowed, 11.2% divorced (2005-2009 5-year est.); Foreign born: 7.5% (2005-2009 5-year est.); Ancestry (includes multiple ancestries): 15.9% English, 15.5% German, 11.2% Irish, 6.3% Italian, 4.7% American (2005-2009 5-year est.).
Economy: Employment by occupation: 8.8% management, 5.4% professional, 22.6% services, 38.1% sales, 1.7% farming, 11.7% construction, 11.7% production (2005-2009 5-year est.).
Income: Per capita income: $18,753 (2010); Median household income: $55,085 (2010); Average household income: $62,659 (2010); Percent of households with income of $100,000 or more: 12.7% (2010); Poverty rate: 6.1% (2005-2009 5-year est.).
Taxes: Total city taxes per capita: $167 (2007); City property taxes per capita: $89 (2007).
Education: Percent of population age 25 and over with: High school diploma (including GED) or higher: 75.3% (2010); Bachelor's degree or higher: 11.2% (2010); Master's degree or higher: 3.1% (2010).
School District(s)
Hays CISD (PK-12)
  2009-10 Enrollment: 14,649 . . . . (512) 268-2141

Housing: Homeownership rate: 83.2% (2010); Median home value: $94,800 (2010); Median contract rent: $650 per month (2005-2009 5-year est.); Median year structure built: 1990 (2005-2009 5-year est.).
Transportation: Commute to work: 87.0% car, 0.0% public transportation, 0.8% walk, 12.1% work from home (2005-2009 5-year est.); Travel time to work: 8.6% less than 15 minutes, 26.7% 15 to 30 minutes, 32.9% 30 to 45 minutes, 19.0% 45 to 60 minutes, 12.9% 60 minutes or more (2005-2009 5-year est.)
Additional Information Contacts
Town of Niederwald. . . . . (512) 398-6338

SAN MARCOS (city). County seat. Covers a land area of 18.209 square miles and a water area of 0.113 square miles. Located at 29.87° N. Lat; 97.93° W. Long. Elevation is 617 feet.
History: San Marcos was settled about 1846 on land purchased by William Lindsey and General Edward Burleson. The town was named for an earlier settlement of San Marcos de Neve, that had existed at the Camino Real Crossing of the San Marcos from 1808 to 1812.
Population: 28,859 (1990); 34,733 (2000); 48,926 (2010); 57,237 (2015 projected); Race: 70.6% White, 6.9% Black, 2.0% Asian, 20.5% Other, 34.1% Hispanic of any race (2010); Density: 2,686.9 persons per square mile (2010); Average household size: 2.30 (2010); Median age: 24.8 (2010); Males per 100 females: 98.8 (2010); Marriage status: 65.3% never married, 23.4% now married, 3.7% widowed, 7.7% divorced (2005-2009 5-year est.); Foreign born: 5.6% (2005-2009 5-year est.); Ancestry (includes multiple ancestries): 16.7% German, 7.9% English, 7.7% Irish, 3.5% American, 3.1% Italian (2005-2009 5-year est.).
Economy: Unemployment rate: 6.6% (June 2011); Total civilian labor force: 28,637 (June 2011); Single-family building permits issued: 190 (2010); Multi-family building permits issued: 1,104 (2010); Employment by occupation: 7.2% management, 20.9% professional, 25.7% services, 30.0% sales, 0.2% farming, 8.0% construction, 7.9% production (2005-2009 5-year est.).
Income: Per capita income: $17,572 (2010); Median household income: $33,339 (2010); Average household income: $46,871 (2010); Percent of households with income of $100,000 or more: 9.3% (2010); Poverty rate: 36.8% (2005-2009 5-year est.).
Taxes: Total city taxes per capita: $753 (2007); City property taxes per capita: $189 (2007).
Education: Percent of population age 25 and over with: High school diploma (including GED) or higher: 86.7% (2010); Bachelor's degree or higher: 34.2% (2010); Master's degree or higher: 11.6% (2010).

School District(s)
Hays CISD (PK-12)
    2009-10 Enrollment: 14,649 . . . . (512) 268-2141
John H Wood Jr Public Charter District (05-12)
    2009-10 Enrollment: 348 . . . . (210) 638-5003
San Marcos CISD (PK-12)
    2009-10 Enrollment: 7,434 . . . . (512) 393-6700
Texas Preparatory School (KG-06)
    2009-10 Enrollment: 105 . . . . (512) 805-7737
University of Texas University Charter School (KG-12)
    2009-10 Enrollment: 907 . . . . (512) 471-5652

Four-year College(s)
Texas State University-San Marcos (Public)
    Fall 2009 Enrollment: 30,803 . . . . (512) 245-2111
    2010-11 Tuition: In-state $6,458; Out-of-state $13,898
Housing: Homeownership rate: 33.4% (2010); Median home value: $119,092 (2010); Median contract rent: $616 per month (2005-2009 5-year est.); Median year structure built: 1984 (2005-2009 5-year est.).
Hospitals: Central Texas Medical Center (113 beds); San Marcos Treatment Center (209 beds)
Safety: Violent crime rate: 33.0 per 10,000 population; Property crime rate: 308.4 per 10,000 population (2009).
Newspapers: San Marcos Daily Record (Local news; Circulation 5,600)
Transportation: Commute to work: 85.9% car, 2.9% public transportation, 5.9% walk, 4.3% work from home (2005-2009 5-year est.); Travel time to work: 50.8% less than 15 minutes, 23.1% 15 to 30 minutes, 12.3% 30 to 45 minutes, 6.0% 45 to 60 minutes, 7.8% 60 minutes or more (2005-2009 5-year est.); Amtrak: train service available.
Airports: San Marcos Municipal (general aviation)
Additional Information Contacts
City of San Marcos. . . . . (512) 393-8000
    http://www.ci.san-marcos.tx.us

San Marcos Area Chamber of Commerce. . . . . (512) 393-5900
    http://www.sanmarcostexas.com

UHLAND (city). Covers a land area of 1.827 square miles and a water area of 0 square miles. Located at 29.96° N. Lat; 97.79° W. Long. Elevation is 545 feet.
Population: 381 (1990); 386 (2000); 1,242 (2010); 1,479 (2015 projected); Race: 70.5% White, 4.4% Black, 0.6% Asian, 24.4% Other, 50.1% Hispanic of any race (2010); Density: 679.8 persons per square mile (2010); Average household size: 3.27 (2010); Median age: 29.0 (2010); Males per 100 females: 97.1 (2010); Marriage status: 35.6% never married, 60.7% now married, 1.0% widowed, 2.7% divorced (2005-2009 5-year est.); Foreign born: 4.5% (2005-2009 5-year est.); Ancestry (includes multiple ancestries): 13.8% German, 10.7% English, 2.6% American, 2.3% Irish, 1.5% Scotch-Irish (2005-2009 5-year est.).
Economy: Employment by occupation: 22.3% management, 9.4% professional, 20.8% services, 21.8% sales, 0.0% farming, 12.5% construction, 13.2% production (2005-2009 5-year est.).
Income: Per capita income: $23,520 (2010); Median household income: $68,814 (2010); Average household income: $77,829 (2010); Percent of households with income of $100,000 or more: 22.6% (2010); Poverty rate: 20.5% (2005-2009 5-year est.).
Taxes: Total city taxes per capita: $104 (2007); City property taxes per capita: $0 (2007).
Education: Percent of population age 25 and over with: High school diploma (including GED) or higher: 84.3% (2010); Bachelor's degree or higher: 19.8% (2010); Master's degree or higher: 3.0% (2010).
Housing: Homeownership rate: 88.4% (2010); Median home value: $148,131 (2010); Median contract rent: $304 per month (2005-2009 5-year est.); Median year structure built: 1969 (2005-2009 5-year est.).
Transportation: Commute to work: 98.2% car, 0.0% public transportation, 0.0% walk, 1.8% work from home (2005-2009 5-year est.); Travel time to work: 13.0% less than 15 minutes, 40.5% 15 to 30 minutes, 25.1% 30 to 45 minutes, 11.9% 45 to 60 minutes, 9.5% 60 minutes or more (2005-2009 5-year est.)

WIMBERLEY (CDP). Covers a land area of 16.138 square miles and a water area of 0 square miles. Located at 29.99° N. Lat; 98.10° W. Long. Elevation is 860 feet.
History: On March 5, 1874, Pleasant Wimberley (son of Zachariah and Quinnie Vaughn Wimberley) from Blanco County bought the mill from the Cudes for $8,000 in gold, and the settlement then came to be known as Wimberley's Mill.
Population: 2,519 (1990); 3,797 (2000); 4,293 (2010); 4,919 (2015 projected); Race: 92.7% White, 0.1% Black, 0.2% Asian, 6.9% Other, 9.4% Hispanic of any race (2010); Density: 266.0 persons per square mile (2010); Average household size: 2.47 (2010); Median age: 44.7 (2010); Males per 100 females: 97.7 (2010); Marriage status: 11.3% never married, 57.7% now married, 14.3% widowed, 16.7% divorced (2005-2009 5-year est.); Foreign born: 1.5% (2005-2009 5-year est.); Ancestry (includes multiple ancestries): 23.4% Irish, 22.0% English, 17.7% French, 15.9% German, 4.9% Scottish (2005-2009 5-year est.).
Economy: Employment by occupation: 19.0% management, 33.3% professional, 8.0% services, 32.0% sales, 0.6% farming, 3.8% construction, 3.5% production (2005-2009 5-year est.).
Income: Per capita income: $33,308 (2010); Median household income: $65,509 (2010); Average household income: $82,123 (2010); Percent of households with income of $100,000 or more: 27.9% (2010); Poverty rate: 5.3% (2005-2009 5-year est.).
Taxes: Total city taxes per capita: $248 (2007); City property taxes per capita: $0 (2007).
Education: Percent of population age 25 and over with: High school diploma (including GED) or higher: 94.9% (2010); Bachelor's degree or higher: 44.3% (2010); Master's degree or higher: 15.9% (2010).

School District(s)
Katherine Anne Porter School (09-12)
    2009-10 Enrollment: 130 . . . . (512) 847-6867
Wimberley ISD (PK-12)
    2009-10 Enrollment: 2,003 . . . . (512) 847-2414
Housing: Homeownership rate: 79.2% (2010); Median home value: $226,673 (2010); Median contract rent: $896 per month (2005-2009 5-year est.); Median year structure built: 1984 (2005-2009 5-year est.).
Newspapers: Dripping Springs Century (Local news; Circulation 1,110); Kyle Eagle (Community news; Circulation 5,131); Wimberley View (Local news; Circulation 2,000)

Transportation: Commute to work: 88.4% car, 0.0% public transportation, 1.4% walk, 10.3% work from home (2005-2009 5-year est.); Travel time to work: 26.5% less than 15 minutes, 17.2% 15 to 30 minutes, 15.8% 30 to 45 minutes, 26.5% 45 to 60 minutes, 14.0% 60 minutes or more (2005-2009 5-year est.)

Additional Information Contacts

Wimberley Chamber of Commerce . . . . (512) 847-2201
    http://www.wimberley.org

WOODCREEK (city). Covers a land area of 1.058 square miles and a water area of 0 square miles. Located at 30.02° N. Lat; 98.11° W. Long. Elevation is 961 feet.

Population: 833 (1990); 1,274 (2000); 1,594 (2010); 1,892 (2015 projected); Race: 94.5% White, 0.1% Black, 0.1% Asian, 5.3% Other, 5.5% Hispanic of any race (2010); Density: 1,507.2 persons per square mile (2010); Average household size: 2.34 (2010); Median age: 49.2 (2010); Males per 100 females: 89.5 (2010); Marriage status: 14.3% never married, 68.0% now married, 10.3% widowed, 7.5% divorced (2005-2009 5-year est.); Foreign born: 4.1% (2005-2009 5-year est.); Ancestry (includes multiple ancestries): 22.0% English, 20.1% German, 10.2% Irish, 10.2% American, 7.5% French (2005-2009 5-year est.).

Economy: Single-family building permits issued: 7 (2010); Multi-family building permits issued: 0 (2010); Employment by occupation: 16.5% management, 27.9% professional, 14.5% services, 23.1% sales, 0.0% farming, 12.4% construction, 5.6% production (2005-2009 5-year est.).

Income: Per capita income: $35,203 (2010); Median household income: $66,512 (2010); Average household income: $81,983 (2010); Percent of households with income of $100,000 or more: 26.0% (2010); Poverty rate: 3.2% (2005-2009 5-year est.).

Taxes: Total city taxes per capita: $174 (2007); City property taxes per capita: $82 (2007).

Education: Percent of population age 25 and over with: High school diploma (including GED) or higher: 97.1% (2010); Bachelor's degree or higher: 44.4% (2010); Master's degree or higher: 13.4% (2010).

Housing: Homeownership rate: 83.1% (2010); Median home value: $210,538 (2010); Median contract rent: $806 per month (2005-2009 5-year est.); Median year structure built: 1988 (2005-2009 5-year est.).

Transportation: Commute to work: 89.7% car, 0.0% public transportation, 0.6% walk, 9.7% work from home (2005-2009 5-year est.); Travel time to work: 36.7% less than 15 minutes, 14.0% 15 to 30 minutes, 18.6% 30 to 45 minutes, 15.8% 45 to 60 minutes, 14.9% 60 minutes or more (2005-2009 5-year est.)

Hemphill County

Located in north Texas, on the high plains of the Panhandle; bounded on the east by Oklahoma; drained by the Canadian and Washita Rivers. Covers a land area of 909.68 square miles, a water area of 2.38 square miles, and is located in the Central Time Zone at 35.81° N. Lat., 100.27° W. Long. The county was founded in 1876. County seat is Canadian.

Population: 3,720 (1990); 3,351 (2000); 3,603 (2010); 3,720 (2015 projected); Race: 83.9% White, 1.5% Black, 0.2% Asian, 14.3% Other, 21.9% Hispanic of any race (2010); Density: 4.0 persons per square mile (2010); Average household size: 2.39 (2010); Median age: 38.7 (2010); Males per 100 females: 101.7 (2010).

Religion: Five largest groups: 33.4% Southern Baptist Convention, 15.1% The United Methodist Church, 9.2% Christian Churches and Churches of Christ, 7.5% Catholic Church, 7.3% The Church of Jesus Christ of Latter-day Saints (2000).

Economy: Unemployment rate: 3.6% (June 2011); Total civilian labor force: 2,588 (June 2011); Leading industries: 22.4% mining; 12.7% health care and social assistance; 11.3% retail trade (2009); Farms: 233 totaling 548,746 acres (2007); Companies that employ 500 or more persons: 0 (2009); Companies that employ 100 to 499 persons: 0 (2009); Companies that employ less than 100 persons: 160 (2009); Black-owned businesses: n/a (2007); Hispanic-owned businesses: n/a (2007); Asian-owned businesses: n/a (2007); Women-owned businesses: n/a (2007); Retail sales per capita: $7,782 (2010). Single-family building permits issued: 0 (2010); Multi-family building permits issued: 0 (2010).

Income: Per capita income: $23,834 (2010); Median household income: $46,899 (2010); Average household income: $58,923 (2010); Percent of households with income of $100,000 or more: 14.8% (2010); Poverty rate: 7.6% (2009); Bankruptcy rate: 1.57% (2010).

Taxes: Total county taxes per capita: $437 (2007); County property taxes per capita: $353 (2007).

Education: Percent of population age 25 and over with: High school diploma (including GED) or higher: 83.7% (2010); Bachelor's degree or higher: 19.7% (2010); Master's degree or higher: 4.0% (2010).

Housing: Homeownership rate: 75.2% (2010); Median home value: $69,492 (2010); Median contract rent: $430 per month (2005-2009 5-year est.); Median year structure built: 1967 (2005-2009 5-year est.)

Health: Birth rate: 167.5 per 10,000 population (2009); Death rate: 40.4 per 10,000 population (2009); Age-adjusted cancer mortality rate: 233.0 (Unreliable) deaths per 100,000 population (2007); Number of physicians: 11.7 per 10,000 population (2008); Hospital beds: 57.5 per 10,000 population (2007); Hospital admissions: 635.0 per 10,000 population (2007).

Elections: 2008 Presidential election results: 13.8% Obama, 85.7% McCain, 0.1% Nader

Additional Information Contacts

Hemphill County Government . . . . (806) 323-6521
    http://www.co.hemphill.tx.us/ips/cms
Canadian Chamber of Commerce . . . . (806) 323-6234
    http://www.canadiantx.org

Hemphill County Communities

CANADIAN (city). County seat. Covers a land area of 1.290 square miles and a water area of 0 square miles. Located at 35.91° N. Lat; 100.38° W. Long. Elevation is 2,425 feet.

History: Canadian, established on the Canadian River, was first called Hogtown, and then Desperado City. It was settled by railroad construction men, buffalo hunters, and soldiers.

Population: 2,499 (1990); 2,233 (2000); 2,439 (2010); 2,534 (2015 projected); Race: 81.8% White, 1.7% Black, 0.3% Asian, 16.2% Other, 26.2% Hispanic of any race (2010); Density: 1,890.7 persons per square mile (2010); Average household size: 2.42 (2010); Median age: 35.3 (2010); Males per 100 females: 100.9 (2010); Marriage status: 9.9% never married, 72.5% now married, 7.9% widowed, 9.7% divorced (2005-2009 5-year est.); Foreign born: 4.6% (2005-2009 5-year est.); Ancestry (includes multiple ancestries): 17.7% German, 12.4% English, 9.5% Irish, 9.0% American, 3.9% Scotch-Irish (2005-2009 5-year est.).

Economy: Single-family building permits issued: 0 (2010); Multi-family building permits issued: 0 (2010); Employment by occupation: 14.8% management, 18.9% professional, 10.9% services, 15.2% sales, 2.1% farming, 14.6% construction, 23.5% production (2005-2009 5-year est.).

Income: Per capita income: $21,388 (2010); Median household income: $42,774 (2010); Average household income: $54,012 (2010); Percent of households with income of $100,000 or more: 12.4% (2010); Poverty rate: 14.8% (2005-2009 5-year est.).

Taxes: Total city taxes per capita: $551 (2007); City property taxes per capita: $180 (2007).

Education: Percent of population age 25 and over with: High school diploma (including GED) or higher: 80.4% (2010); Bachelor's degree or higher: 20.0% (2010); Master's degree or higher: 4.6% (2010).

School District(s)

Canadian ISD (PK-12)
    2009-10 Enrollment: 792 . . . . (806) 323-5393

Housing: Homeownership rate: 75.6% (2010); Median home value: $61,641 (2010); Median contract rent: $438 per month (2005-2009 5-year est.); Median year structure built: 1964 (2005-2009 5-year est.).

Hospitals: Hemphill County Hospital (26 beds)

Newspapers: The Canadian Record (Community news; Circulation 2,000)

Transportation: Commute to work: 93.9% car, 0.0% public transportation, 0.0% walk, 5.7% work from home (2005-2009 5-year est.); Travel time to work: 73.9% less than 15 minutes, 12.0% 15 to 30 minutes, 6.6% 30 to 45 minutes, 2.3% 45 to 60 minutes, 5.2% 60 minutes or more (2005-2009 5-year est.)

Airports: En Gedi Ranch (general aviation); Hemphill County (general aviation)

Additional Information Contacts

Canadian Chamber of Commerce . . . . (806) 323-6234
    http://www.canadiantx.org

Henderson County

Located in east Texas; bounded on the west by the Trinity River, and on the east by the Neches River. Covers a land area of 874.24 square miles, a water area of 74.76 square miles, and is located in the Central Time Zone at 32.22° N. Lat., 95.91° W. Long. The county was founded in 1846. County seat is Athens.

Henderson County is part of the Athens, TX Micropolitan Statistical Area. The entire metro area includes: Henderson County, TX

Weather Station: Athens   Elevation: 448 feet

	Jan	Feb	Mar	Apr	May	Jun	Jul	Aug	Sep	Oct	Nov	Dec
High	58	62	70	77	83	89	93	95	89	79	68	59
Low	36	39	46	53	62	69	71	71	65	55	45	37
Precip	3.1	3.9	4.0	3.2	4.9	4.3	2.0	2.4	2.5	5.0	3.8	3.8
Snow	0.3	0.3	tr	0.0	0.0	0.0	0.0	0.0	0.0	0.0	0.0	0.2

High and Low temperatures in degrees Fahrenheit; Precipitation and Snow in inches

Population: 58,543 (1990); 73,277 (2000); 80,182 (2010); 83,391 (2015 projected); Race: 86.7% White, 6.4% Black, 0.3% Asian, 6.6% Other, 10.3% Hispanic of any race (2010); Density: 91.7 persons per square mile (2010); Average household size: 2.52 (2010); Median age: 39.3 (2010); Males per 100 females: 96.7 (2010).
Religion: Five largest groups: 24.6% Southern Baptist Convention, 6.6% Catholic Church, 5.5% Baptist Missionary Association of America, 4.9% The United Methodist Church, 2.2% Assemblies of God (2000).
Economy: Unemployment rate: 9.3% (June 2011); Total civilian labor force: 36,503 (June 2011); Leading industries: 20.5% retail trade; 18.6% health care and social assistance; 14.5% manufacturing (2009); Farms: 2,109 totaling 318,452 acres (2007); Companies that employ 500 or more persons: 0 (2009); Companies that employ 100 to 499 persons: 16 (2009); Companies that employ less than 100 persons: 1,228 (2009); Black-owned businesses: n/a (2007); Hispanic-owned businesses: n/a (2007); Asian-owned businesses: n/a (2007); Women-owned businesses: n/a (2007); Retail sales per capita: $9,154 (2010). Single-family building permits issued: 60 (2010); Multi-family building permits issued: 0 (2010).
Income: Per capita income: $21,348 (2010); Median household income: $40,783 (2010); Average household income: $54,342 (2010); Percent of households with income of $100,000 or more: 11.6% (2010); Poverty rate: 18.2% (2009); Bankruptcy rate: 2.39% (2010).
Taxes: Total county taxes per capita: $274 (2007); County property taxes per capita: $254 (2007).
Education: Percent of population age 25 and over with: High school diploma (including GED) or higher: 79.2% (2010); Bachelor's degree or higher: 14.1% (2010); Master's degree or higher: 4.6% (2010).
Housing: Homeownership rate: 76.8% (2010); Median home value: $82,614 (2010); Median contract rent: $438 per month (2005-2009 5-year est.); Median year structure built: 1983 (2005-2009 5-year est.)
Health: Birth rate: 121.3 per 10,000 population (2009); Death rate: 117.5 per 10,000 population (2009); Age-adjusted cancer mortality rate: 210.1 deaths per 100,000 population (2007); Number of physicians: 9.0 per 10,000 population (2008); Hospital beds: 14.8 per 10,000 population (2007); Hospital admissions: 1,014.3 per 10,000 population (2007).
Elections: 2008 Presidential election results: 27.3% Obama, 71.9% McCain, 0.0% Nader
Additional Information Contacts
Henderson County Government . . . . (903) 675-6120
    http://www.co.henderson.tx.us/ips/cms
Athens Chamber of Commerce . . . . (903) 675-5181
    http://www.athenscc.org
Cedar Creek Lake Area Chamber of Commerce . . . . (903) 887-3152
    http://www.cclake.net
Chandler-Brownsboro Area Chamber of Commerce . . . . . . (903) 849-5930
    http://www.cbacc.net
City of Athens . . . . (903) 675-5131
    http://athenstexas.us
City of Gun Barrel City . . . . (903) 887-1087
    http://www.gunbarrelcity.net
Malakoff Chamber of Commerce . . . . (903) 489-1518

Henderson County Communities

ATHENS (city). County seat. Covers a land area of 14.618 square miles and a water area of 2.350 square miles. Located at 32.20° N. Lat; 95.84° W. Long. Elevation is 489 feet.
History: Athens was the home of Cynthia Ann Parker, mother of the Comanche war chief Quanah Parker, during the last years before her death.
Population: 10,686 (1990); 11,297 (2000); 12,272 (2010); 12,767 (2015 projected); Race: 70.8% White, 18.8% Black, 0.6% Asian, 9.8% Other,

26.4% Hispanic of any race (2010); Density: 839.5 persons per square mile (2010); Average household size: 2.63 (2010); Median age: 34.2 (2010); Males per 100 females: 93.8 (2010); Marriage status: 31.6% never married, 46.3% now married, 13.1% widowed, 9.1% divorced (2005-2009 5-year est.); Foreign born: 13.8% (2005-2009 5-year est.); Ancestry (includes multiple ancestries): 14.0% American, 7.9% English, 7.7% German, 7.4% Irish, 2.0% Scottish (2005-2009 5-year est.).
Economy: Single-family building permits issued: 6 (2010); Multi-family building permits issued: 0 (2010); Employment by occupation: 7.7% management, 17.4% professional, 26.5% services, 21.2% sales, 1.1% farming, 9.3% construction, 16.7% production (2005-2009 5-year est.).
Income: Per capita income: $19,478 (2010); Median household income: $37,279 (2010); Average household income: $53,251 (2010); Percent of households with income of $100,000 or more: 12.1% (2010); Poverty rate: 23.6% (2005-2009 5-year est.).
Taxes: Total city taxes per capita: $609 (2007); City property taxes per capita: $180 (2007).
Education: Percent of population age 25 and over with: High school diploma (including GED) or higher: 74.1% (2010); Bachelor's degree or higher: 20.8% (2010); Master's degree or higher: 7.2% (2010).
School District(s)
Athens ISD (PK-12)
    2009-10 Enrollment: 3,460 . . . . (903) 677-6991
Two-year College(s)
Trinity Valley Community College (Public)
    Fall 2009 Enrollment: 7,012 . . . . (903) 675-6200
    2010-11 Tuition: In-state $2,400; Out-of-state $3,200
Housing: Homeownership rate: 57.2% (2010); Median home value: $91,143 (2010); Median contract rent: $449 per month (2005-2009 5-year est.); Median year structure built: 1976 (2005-2009 5-year est.).
Hospitals: East Texas Medical Center - Athens (117 beds)
Safety: Violent crime rate: 59.7 per 10,000 population; Property crime rate: 426.5 per 10,000 population (2009).
Newspapers: Athens Daily Review (Local news; Circulation 65,000)
Transportation: Commute to work: 93.9% car, 1.0% public transportation, 0.4% walk, 3.5% work from home (2005-2009 5-year est.); Travel time to work: 62.0% less than 15 minutes, 20.4% 15 to 30 minutes, 6.2% 30 to 45 minutes, 7.2% 45 to 60 minutes, 4.2% 60 minutes or more (2005-2009 5-year est.)
Additional Information Contacts
Athens Chamber of Commerce . . . . (903) 675-5181
    http://www.athenscc.org
City of Athens . . . . (903) 675-5131
    http://athenstexas.us

BERRYVILLE (town). Covers a land area of 1.314 square miles and a water area of 0 square miles. Located at 32.09° N. Lat; 95.46° W. Long. Elevation is 364 feet.
Population: 738 (1990); 891 (2000); 880 (2010); 870 (2015 projected); Race: 88.2% White, 6.9% Black, 0.2% Asian, 4.7% Other, 7.3% Hispanic of any race (2010); Density: 669.7 persons per square mile (2010); Average household size: 2.44 (2010); Median age: 41.3 (2010); Males per 100 females: 98.2 (2010); Marriage status: 16.6% never married, 62.1% now married, 7.2% widowed, 14.1% divorced (2005-2009 5-year est.); Foreign born: 0.0% (2005-2009 5-year est.); Ancestry (includes multiple ancestries): 32.7% American, 13.0% Irish, 11.6% German, 8.0% English, 2.8% French (2005-2009 5-year est.).
Economy: Single-family building permits issued: 4 (2010); Multi-family building permits issued: 0 (2010); Employment by occupation: 8.8% management, 14.3% professional, 16.4% services, 24.5% sales, 2.4% farming, 15.4% construction, 18.3% production (2005-2009 5-year est.).
Income: Per capita income: $20,687 (2010); Median household income: $39,792 (2010); Average household income: $49,986 (2010); Percent of households with income of $100,000 or more: 8.3% (2010); Poverty rate: 14.4% (2005-2009 5-year est.).
Taxes: Total city taxes per capita: $11 (2007); City property taxes per capita: $0 (2007).
Education: Percent of population age 25 and over with: High school diploma (including GED) or higher: 85.3% (2010); Bachelor's degree or higher: 12.3% (2010); Master's degree or higher: 4.4% (2010).
Housing: Homeownership rate: 80.8% (2010); Median home value: $66,944 (2010); Median contract rent: $400 per month (2005-2009 5-year est.); Median year structure built: 1984 (2005-2009 5-year est.).
Transportation: Commute to work: 96.9% car, 0.0% public transportation, 1.0% walk, 1.4% work from home (2005-2009 5-year est.); Travel time to

work: 21.8% less than 15 minutes, 26.7% 15 to 30 minutes, 30.6% 30 to 45 minutes, 11.5% 45 to 60 minutes, 9.5% 60 minutes or more (2005-2009 5-year est.)

BROWNSBORO (city).
Covers a land area of 1.956 square miles and a water area of 0 square miles. Located at 32.30° N. Lat; 95.61° W. Long. Elevation is 381 feet.
Population: 577 (1990); 796 (2000); 926 (2010); 987 (2015 projected); Race: 83.9% White, 6.9% Black, 0.0% Asian, 9.2% Other, 16.4% Hispanic of any race (2010); Density: 473.5 persons per square mile (2010); Average household size: 2.85 (2010); Median age: 33.7 (2010); Males per 100 females: 95.8 (2010); Marriage status: 15.8% never married, 58.3% now married, 13.6% widowed, 12.3% divorced (2005-2009 5-year est.); Foreign born: 14.1% (2005-2009 5-year est.); Ancestry (includes multiple ancestries): 39.6% American, 7.1% German, 5.8% Irish, 5.6% English, 2.5% French (2005-2009 5-year est.).
Economy: Employment by occupation: 10.9% management, 16.3% professional, 26.6% services, 21.1% sales, 2.7% farming, 8.8% construction, 13.6% production (2005-2009 5-year est.).
Income: Per capita income: $19,676 (2010); Median household income: $42,227 (2010); Average household income: $55,954 (2010); Percent of households with income of $100,000 or more: 13.2% (2010); Poverty rate: 12.9% (2005-2009 5-year est.).
Taxes: Total city taxes per capita: $334 (2007); City property taxes per capita: $143 (2007).
Education: Percent of population age 25 and over with: High school diploma (including GED) or higher: 79.1% (2010); Bachelor's degree or higher: 17.8% (2010); Master's degree or higher: 4.7% (2010).
School District(s)
Brownsboro ISD (PK-12)
   2009-10 Enrollment: 2,842 . . . . (903) 852-3701
Housing: Homeownership rate: 81.5% (2010); Median home value: $75,870 (2010); Median contract rent: $467 per month (2005-2009 5-year est.); Median year structure built: 1980 (2005-2009 5-year est.).
Newspapers: Brownsboro & Chandler Statesman (Community news; Circulation 1,575)
Transportation: Commute to work: 91.6% car, 0.0% public transportation, 5.0% walk, 3.4% work from home (2005-2009 5-year est.); Travel time to work: 14.7% less than 15 minutes, 38.8% 15 to 30 minutes, 27.2% 30 to 45 minutes, 14.1% 45 to 60 minutes, 5.1% 60 minutes or more (2005-2009 5-year est.)
Additional Information Contacts
Chandler-Brownsboro Area Chamber of Commerce . . . . . . (903) 849-5930
   http://www.cbacc.net

CANEY CITY (town).
Covers a land area of 1.163 square miles and a water area of 0 square miles. Located at 32.21° N. Lat; 96.03° W. Long. Elevation is 354 feet.
Population: 129 (1990); 236 (2000); 271 (2010); 291 (2015 projected); Race: 90.0% White, 5.5% Black, 0.4% Asian, 4.1% Other, 4.4% Hispanic of any race (2010); Density: 232.9 persons per square mile (2010); Average household size: 2.40 (2010); Median age: 48.6 (2010); Males per 100 females: 102.2 (2010); Marriage status: 7.6% never married, 57.6% now married, 15.1% widowed, 19.8% divorced (2005-2009 5-year est.); Foreign born: 0.0% (2005-2009 5-year est.); Ancestry (includes multiple ancestries): 27.7% American, 10.7% Irish, 9.6% English, 5.6% European, 4.5% German (2005-2009 5-year est.).
Economy: Single-family building permits issued: 0 (2010); Multi-family building permits issued: 0 (2010); Employment by occupation: 9.3% management, 8.1% professional, 22.1% services, 12.8% sales, 0.0% farming, 12.8% construction, 34.9% production (2005-2009 5-year est.).
Income: Per capita income: $28,079 (2010); Median household income: $43,750 (2010); Average household income: $68,053 (2010); Percent of households with income of $100,000 or more: 19.5% (2010); Poverty rate: 17.5% (2005-2009 5-year est.).
Taxes: Total city taxes per capita: $12 (2007); City property taxes per capita: $0 (2007).
Education: Percent of population age 25 and over with: High school diploma (including GED) or higher: 81.5% (2010); Bachelor's degree or higher: 18.5% (2010); Master's degree or higher: 3.4% (2010).
Housing: Homeownership rate: 82.3% (2010); Median home value: $110,294 (2010); Median contract rent: n/a per month (2005-2009 5-year est.); Median year structure built: 1986 (2005-2009 5-year est.).
Transportation: Commute to work: 71.4% car, 0.0% public transportation, 0.0% walk, 23.8% work from home (2005-2009 5-year est.); Travel time to

work: 31.3% less than 15 minutes, 12.5% 15 to 30 minutes, 18.8% 30 to 45 minutes, 15.6% 45 to 60 minutes, 21.9% 60 minutes or more (2005-2009 5-year est.)

CHANDLER (city).
Covers a land area of 3.505 square miles and a water area of 0.046 square miles. Located at 32.30° N. Lat; 95.47° W. Long. Elevation is 404 feet.
Population: 1,630 (1990); 2,099 (2000); 2,670 (2010); 2,910 (2015 projected); Race: 87.1% White, 8.2% Black, 1.0% Asian, 3.7% Other, 2.8% Hispanic of any race (2010); Density: 761.8 persons per square mile (2010); Average household size: 2.52 (2010); Median age: 38.2 (2010); Males per 100 females: 90.9 (2010); Marriage status: 16.5% never married, 63.1% now married, 13.8% widowed, 6.5% divorced (2005-2009 5-year est.); Foreign born: 1.4% (2005-2009 5-year est.); Ancestry (includes multiple ancestries): 29.5% American, 20.7% English, 12.9% Irish, 4.8% German, 2.8% Scottish (2005-2009 5-year est.).
Economy: Single-family building permits issued: 7 (2010); Multi-family building permits issued: 0 (2010); Employment by occupation: 14.9% management, 25.1% professional, 9.4% services, 25.4% sales, 1.3% farming, 12.7% construction, 11.3% production (2005-2009 5-year est.).
Income: Per capita income: $25,361 (2010); Median household income: $54,965 (2010); Average household income: $64,683 (2010); Percent of households with income of $100,000 or more: 17.1% (2010); Poverty rate: 6.8% (2005-2009 5-year est.).
Taxes: Total city taxes per capita: $298 (2007); City property taxes per capita: $127 (2007).
Education: Percent of population age 25 and over with: High school diploma (including GED) or higher: 87.6% (2010); Bachelor's degree or higher: 22.5% (2010); Master's degree or higher: 6.5% (2010).
School District(s)
Brownsboro ISD (PK-12)
   2009-10 Enrollment: 2,842 . . . . (903) 852-3701
Housing: Homeownership rate: 71.4% (2010); Median home value: $126,087 (2010); Median contract rent: $478 per month (2005-2009 5-year est.); Median year structure built: 1987 (2005-2009 5-year est.).
Transportation: Commute to work: 96.2% car, 0.0% public transportation, 0.0% walk, 3.3% work from home (2005-2009 5-year est.); Travel time to work: 26.5% less than 15 minutes, 45.2% 15 to 30 minutes, 25.0% 30 to 45 minutes, 1.1% 45 to 60 minutes, 2.2% 60 minutes or more (2005-2009 5-year est.)
Additional Information Contacts
Chandler-Brownsboro Area Chamber of Commerce . . . . . . (903) 849-5930
   http://www.cbacc.net

COFFEE CITY (town).
Covers a land area of 1.831 square miles and a water area of 4.697 square miles. Located at 32.14° N. Lat; 95.49° W. Long. Elevation is 381 feet.
Population: 216 (1990); 193 (2000); 192 (2010); 190 (2015 projected); Race: 88.0% White, 7.3% Black, 0.0% Asian, 4.7% Other, 7.3% Hispanic of any race (2010); Density: 104.9 persons per square mile (2010); Average household size: 2.43 (2010); Median age: 40.0 (2010); Males per 100 females: 100.0 (2010); Marriage status: 17.0% never married, 72.2% now married, 7.2% widowed, 3.6% divorced (2005-2009 5-year est.); Foreign born: 6.5% (2005-2009 5-year est.); Ancestry (includes multiple ancestries): 29.3% American, 17.7% German, 14.4% Irish, 13.0% Belgian, 7.0% English (2005-2009 5-year est.).
Economy: Employment by occupation: 8.6% management, 10.5% professional, 28.6% services, 39.0% sales, 0.0% farming, 5.7% construction, 7.6% production (2005-2009 5-year est.).
Income: Per capita income: $20,695 (2010); Median household income: $39,219 (2010); Average household income: $53,070 (2010); Percent of households with income of $100,000 or more: 8.9% (2010); Poverty rate: 7.4% (2005-2009 5-year est.).
Taxes: Total city taxes per capita: $233 (2007); City property taxes per capita: $34 (2007).
Education: Percent of population age 25 and over with: High school diploma (including GED) or higher: 85.1% (2010); Bachelor's degree or higher: 11.9% (2010); Master's degree or higher: 3.7% (2010).
Housing: Homeownership rate: 81.0% (2010); Median home value: $65,714 (2010); Median contract rent: $433 per month (2005-2009 5-year est.); Median year structure built: 1984 (2005-2009 5-year est.).
Safety: Violent crime rate: 0.0 per 10,000 population; Property crime rate: 334.9 per 10,000 population (2009).
Transportation: Commute to work: 89.5% car, 0.0% public transportation, 6.7% walk, 3.8% work from home (2005-2009 5-year est.); Travel time to

work: 15.8% less than 15 minutes, 22.8% 15 to 30 minutes, 32.7% 30 to 45 minutes, 16.8% 45 to 60 minutes, 11.9% 60 minutes or more (2005-2009 5-year est.)

ENCHANTED OAKS (town). Covers a land area of 0.389 square miles and a water area of 0 square miles. Located at 32.26° N. Lat; 96.10° W. Long. Elevation is 344 feet.

Population: 290 (1990); 357 (2000); 427 (2010); 459 (2015 projected); Race: 92.5% White, 1.4% Black, 0.2% Asian, 5.9% Other, 5.6% Hispanic of any race (2010); Density: 1,097.7 persons per square mile (2010); Average household size: 2.54 (2010); Median age: 41.8 (2010); Males per 100 females: 97.7 (2010); Marriage status: 10.4% never married, 69.2% now married, 12.5% widowed, 8.0% divorced (2005-2009 5-year est.); Foreign born: 0.3% (2005-2009 5-year est.); Ancestry (includes multiple ancestries): 25.2% American, 19.6% English, 15.2% Irish, 11.8% German, 5.3% French (2005-2009 5-year est.).
Economy: Single-family building permits issued: 2 (2010); Multi-family building permits issued: 0 (2010); Employment by occupation: 9.1% management, 27.3% professional, 9.1% services, 33.0% sales, 0.0% farming, 11.4% construction, 10.2% production (2005-2009 5-year est.).
Income: Per capita income: $20,413 (2010); Median household income: $42,500 (2010); Average household income: $55,268 (2010); Percent of households with income of $100,000 or more: 10.7% (2010); Poverty rate: 3.4% (2005-2009 5-year est.).
Taxes: Total city taxes per capita: $392 (2007); City property taxes per capita: $331 (2007).
Education: Percent of population age 25 and over with: High school diploma (including GED) or higher: 81.0% (2010); Bachelor's degree or higher: 11.3% (2010); Master's degree or higher: 2.7% (2010).
Housing: Homeownership rate: 85.1% (2010); Median home value: $73,158 (2010); Median contract rent: n/a per month (2005-2009 5-year est.); Median year structure built: 1982 (2005-2009 5-year est.).
Transportation: Commute to work: 89.8% car, 0.0% public transportation, 0.0% walk, 1.1% work from home (2005-2009 5-year est.); Travel time to work: 20.7% less than 15 minutes, 20.7% 15 to 30 minutes, 12.6% 30 to 45 minutes, 6.9% 45 to 60 minutes, 39.1% 60 minutes or more (2005-2009 5-year est.)

EUSTACE (city). Covers a land area of 1.720 square miles and a water area of 0 square miles. Located at 32.30° N. Lat; 96.00° W. Long. Elevation is 423 feet.

Population: 623 (1990); 798 (2000); 855 (2010); 879 (2015 projected); Race: 94.7% White, 0.1% Black, 0.5% Asian, 4.7% Other, 5.6% Hispanic of any race (2010); Density: 497.1 persons per square mile (2010); Average household size: 2.72 (2010); Median age: 36.2 (2010); Males per 100 females: 96.1 (2010); Marriage status: 33.2% never married, 52.1% now married, 4.3% widowed, 10.4% divorced (2005-2009 5-year est.); Foreign born: 2.7% (2005-2009 5-year est.); Ancestry (includes multiple ancestries): 50.4% American, 8.4% Irish, 5.4% German, 4.0% English, 3.5% Dutch (2005-2009 5-year est.).
Economy: Single-family building permits issued: 0 (2010); Multi-family building permits issued: 0 (2010); Employment by occupation: 9.5% management, 10.6% professional, 17.2% services, 35.0% sales, 0.0% farming, 6.9% construction, 20.9% production (2005-2009 5-year est.).
Income: Per capita income: $23,858 (2010); Median household income: $57,566 (2010); Average household income: $65,422 (2010); Percent of households with income of $100,000 or more: 15.9% (2010); Poverty rate: 16.8% (2005-2009 5-year est.).
Taxes: Total city taxes per capita: $170 (2007); City property taxes per capita: $77 (2007).
Education: Percent of population age 25 and over with: High school diploma (including GED) or higher: 84.9% (2010); Bachelor's degree or higher: 11.4% (2010); Master's degree or higher: 3.5% (2010).
School District(s)
Eustace ISD (PK-12)
    2009-10 Enrollment: 1,462 . . . . (903) 425-5151
Housing: Homeownership rate: 72.0% (2010); Median home value: $86,923 (2010); Median contract rent: $473 per month (2005-2009 5-year est.); Median year structure built: 1974 (2005-2009 5-year est.).
Transportation: Commute to work: 95.4% car, 0.0% public transportation, 0.9% walk, 3.8% work from home (2005-2009 5-year est.); Travel time to work: 29.1% less than 15 minutes, 34.2% 15 to 30 minutes, 13.8% 30 to 45 minutes, 8.4% 45 to 60 minutes, 14.4% 60 minutes or more (2005-2009 5-year est.)

GUN BARREL CITY (town). Covers a land area of 5.143 square miles and a water area of 0.054 square miles. Located at 32.32° N. Lat; 96.13° W. Long. Elevation is 351 feet.

Population: 4,075 (1990); 5,145 (2000); 5,868 (2010); 6,192 (2015 projected); Race: 90.4% White, 3.3% Black, 0.8% Asian, 5.6% Other, 5.5% Hispanic of any race (2010); Density: 1,141.1 persons per square mile (2010); Average household size: 2.39 (2010); Median age: 41.5 (2010); Males per 100 females: 97.0 (2010); Marriage status: 14.7% never married, 63.9% now married, 8.8% widowed, 12.5% divorced (2005-2009 5-year est.); Foreign born: 1.9% (2005-2009 5-year est.); Ancestry (includes multiple ancestries): 33.2% American, 9.4% German, 9.0% Irish, 8.4% English, 3.2% French (2005-2009 5-year est.).
Economy: Single-family building permits issued: 29 (2010); Multi-family building permits issued: 0 (2010); Employment by occupation: 6.5% management, 11.0% professional, 18.7% services, 29.7% sales, 0.0% farming, 15.5% construction, 18.5% production (2005-2009 5-year est.).
Income: Per capita income: $20,823 (2010); Median household income: $33,852 (2010); Average household income: $49,602 (2010); Percent of households with income of $100,000 or more: 9.1% (2010); Poverty rate: 23.3% (2005-2009 5-year est.).
Taxes: Total city taxes per capita: $459 (2007); City property taxes per capita: $0 (2007).
Education: Percent of population age 25 and over with: High school diploma (including GED) or higher: 76.9% (2010); Bachelor's degree or higher: 9.3% (2010); Master's degree or higher: 2.8% (2010).
School District(s)
Mabank ISD (PK-12)
    2009-10 Enrollment: 3,325 . . . . (903) 880-1300
Housing: Homeownership rate: 77.3% (2010); Median home value: $78,022 (2010); Median contract rent: $467 per month (2005-2009 5-year est.); Median year structure built: 1984 (2005-2009 5-year est.).
Safety: Violent crime rate: 42.9 per 10,000 population; Property crime rate: 432.6 per 10,000 population (2009).
Newspapers: Cedar Creek Pilot (Local news)
Transportation: Commute to work: 96.2% car, 0.0% public transportation, 0.0% walk, 2.4% work from home (2005-2009 5-year est.); Travel time to work: 30.3% less than 15 minutes, 16.8% 15 to 30 minutes, 20.6% 30 to 45 minutes, 6.8% 45 to 60 minutes, 25.5% 60 minutes or more (2005-2009 5-year est.)
Additional Information Contacts
Cedar Creek Lake Area Chamber of Commerce. . . . . (903) 887-3152
    http://www.cclake.net
City of Gun Barrel City . . . . (903) 887-1087
    http://www.gunbarrelcity.net

LARUE (unincorporated postal area, zip code 75770). Aka La Rue. Covers a land area of 115.513 square miles and a water area of 1.772 square miles. Located at 32.13° N. Lat; 95.64° W. Long.

Population: 2,327 (2000); Race: 75.7% White, 21.2% Black, 0.1% Asian, 3.0% Other, 2.9% Hispanic of any race (2000); Density: 20.1 persons per square mile (2000); Age: 22.6% under 18, 15.6% over 64 (2000); Marriage status: 21.2% never married, 64.8% now married, 5.5% widowed, 8.4% divorced (2000); Foreign born: 1.1% (2000); Ancestry (includes multiple ancestries): 16.0% American, 8.4% Irish, 6.5% German, 6.2% English (2000).
Economy: Employment by occupation: 7.4% management, 14.7% professional, 19.6% services, 19.5% sales, 1.8% farming, 12.2% construction, 24.8% production (2000).
Income: Per capita income: $18,613 (2000); Median household income: $35,625 (2000); Poverty rate: 179.1% (2000).
Education: Percent of population age 25 and over with: High school diploma (including GED) or higher: 74.7% (2000); Bachelor's degree or higher: 12.6% (2000).
School District(s)
Lapoynor ISD (PK-12)
    2009-10 Enrollment: 469 . . . . (903) 876-4057
Housing: Homeownership rate: 86.0% (2000); Median home value: $53,500 (2000); Median contract rent: $296 per month (2000); Median year structure built: 1980 (2000).
Transportation: Commute to work: 92.2% car, 0.1% public transportation, 1.4% walk, 3.5% work from home (2000); Travel time to work: 15.3% less than 15 minutes, 38.5% 15 to 30 minutes, 20.1% 30 to 45 minutes, 11.5% 45 to 60 minutes, 14.6% 60 minutes or more (2000)

LOG CABIN (city).
Covers a land area of 1.060 square miles and a water area of 0 square miles. Located at 32.22° N. Lat; 96.02° W. Long. Elevation is 371 feet.
Population: 552 (1990); 733 (2000); 866 (2010); 928 (2015 projected); Race: 94.6% White, 0.6% Black, 0.3% Asian, 4.5% Other, 4.5% Hispanic of any race (2010); Density: 816.7 persons per square mile (2010); Average household size: 2.54 (2010); Median age: 42.9 (2010); Males per 100 females: 101.4 (2010); Marriage status: 24.5% never married, 43.2% now married, 6.8% widowed, 25.6% divorced (2005-2009 5-year est.); Foreign born: 0.2% (2005-2009 5-year est.); Ancestry (includes multiple ancestries): 40.1% American, 13.1% German, 12.5% Irish, 6.6% French, 4.1% Italian (2005-2009 5-year est.).
Economy: Single-family building permits issued: 0 (2010); Multi-family building permits issued: 0 (2010); Employment by occupation: 1.2% management, 6.9% professional, 20.1% services, 18.5% sales, 0.0% farming, 18.9% construction, 34.4% production (2005-2009 5-year est.).
Income: Per capita income: $18,899 (2010); Median household income: $36,250 (2010); Average household income: $48,482 (2010); Percent of households with income of $100,000 or more: 9.4% (2010); Poverty rate: 26.9% (2005-2009 5-year est.).
Taxes: Total city taxes per capita: $183 (2007); City property taxes per capita: $168 (2007).
Education: Percent of population age 25 and over with: High school diploma (including GED) or higher: 79.1% (2010); Bachelor's degree or higher: 7.0% (2010); Master's degree or higher: 1.3% (2010).
Housing: Homeownership rate: 83.6% (2010); Median home value: $54,444 (2010); Median contract rent: $367 per month (2005-2009 5-year est.); Median year structure built: 1984 (2005-2009 5-year est.).
Transportation: Commute to work: 98.8% car, 0.0% public transportation, 0.0% walk, 1.2% work from home (2005-2009 5-year est.); Travel time to work: 19.9% less than 15 minutes, 44.6% 15 to 30 minutes, 10.8% 30 to 45 minutes, 12.4% 45 to 60 minutes, 12.4% 60 minutes or more (2005-2009 5-year est.)

MALAKOFF (city).
Covers a land area of 2.806 square miles and a water area of 0.017 square miles. Located at 32.17° N. Lat; 96.01° W. Long. Elevation is 374 feet.
History: Incorporated after 1940.
Population: 2,059 (1990); 2,257 (2000); 2,353 (2010); 2,405 (2015 projected); Race: 74.6% White, 20.2% Black, 0.0% Asian, 5.1% Other, 13.3% Hispanic of any race (2010); Density: 838.6 persons per square mile (2010); Average household size: 2.55 (2010); Median age: 36.3 (2010); Males per 100 females: 88.4 (2010); Marriage status: 26.6% never married, 52.0% now married, 8.0% widowed, 13.3% divorced (2005-2009 5-year est.); Foreign born: 11.6% (2005-2009 5-year est.); Ancestry (includes multiple ancestries): 24.0% American, 9.2% Irish, 7.3% English, 5.6% German, 5.2% South African (2005-2009 5-year est.).
Economy: Single-family building permits issued: 1 (2010); Multi-family building permits issued: 0 (2010); Employment by occupation: 6.6% management, 17.4% professional, 33.2% services, 14.9% sales, 4.4% farming, 5.9% construction, 17.6% production (2005-2009 5-year est.).
Income: Per capita income: $14,882 (2010); Median household income: $27,791 (2010); Average household income: $38,567 (2010); Percent of households with income of $100,000 or more: 6.0% (2010); Poverty rate: 29.5% (2005-2009 5-year est.).
Taxes: Total city taxes per capita: $411 (2007); City property taxes per capita: $103 (2007).
Education: Percent of population age 25 and over with: High school diploma (including GED) or higher: 79.0% (2010); Bachelor's degree or higher: 13.2% (2010); Master's degree or higher: 4.3% (2010).
School District(s)
Cross Roads ISD (PK-12)
   2009-10 Enrollment: 590 . . . . (903) 489-2001
Malakoff ISD (PK-12)
   2009-10 Enrollment: 1,217 . . . . (903) 489-1152
Housing: Homeownership rate: 61.6% (2010); Median home value: $57,308 (2010); Median contract rent: $355 per month (2005-2009 5-year est.); Median year structure built: 1977 (2005-2009 5-year est.).
Safety: Violent crime rate: 30.0 per 10,000 population; Property crime rate: 222.9 per 10,000 population (2009).
Newspapers: Lake Country Weekender (Local news; Circulation 5,500); Malakoff News (Community news; Circulation 2,000)
Transportation: Commute to work: 93.0% car, 0.8% public transportation, 3.4% walk, 2.0% work from home (2005-2009 5-year est.); Travel time to work: 34.7% less than 15 minutes, 42.1% 15 to 30 minutes, 11.9% 30 to 45 minutes, 3.4% 45 to 60 minutes, 7.9% 60 minutes or more (2005-2009 5-year est.)
Additional Information Contacts
Malakoff Chamber of Commerce . . . . (903) 489-1518

MOORE STATION (city).
Covers a land area of 1.295 square miles and a water area of 0 square miles. Located at 32.18° N. Lat; 95.56° W. Long. Elevation is 420 feet.
Population: 256 (1990); 184 (2000); 175 (2010); 171 (2015 projected); Race: 46.3% White, 49.1% Black, 0.6% Asian, 4.0% Other, 4.6% Hispanic of any race (2010); Density: 135.2 persons per square mile (2010); Average household size: 2.65 (2010); Median age: 40.0 (2010); Males per 100 females: 101.1 (2010); Marriage status: 32.8% never married, 43.1% now married, 10.9% widowed, 13.2% divorced (2005-2009 5-year est.); Foreign born: 0.0% (2005-2009 5-year est.); Ancestry (includes multiple ancestries): 9.7% American (2005-2009 5-year est.).
Economy: Employment by occupation: 0.0% management, 7.1% professional, 50.6% services, 17.6% sales, 0.0% farming, 0.0% construction, 24.7% production (2005-2009 5-year est.).
Income: Per capita income: $16,359 (2010); Median household income: $32,778 (2010); Average household income: $41,667 (2010); Percent of households with income of $100,000 or more: 6.1% (2010); Poverty rate: 9.2% (2005-2009 5-year est.).
Taxes: Total city taxes per capita: $10 (2007); City property taxes per capita: $0 (2007).
Education: Percent of population age 25 and over with: High school diploma (including GED) or higher: 76.2% (2010); Bachelor's degree or higher: 13.9% (2010); Master's degree or higher: 3.3% (2010).
Housing: Homeownership rate: 86.4% (2010); Median home value: $56,429 (2010); Median contract rent: n/a per month (2005-2009 5-year est.); Median year structure built: 1983 (2005-2009 5-year est.).
Transportation: Commute to work: 100.0% car, 0.0% public transportation, 0.0% walk, 0.0% work from home (2005-2009 5-year est.); Travel time to work: 17.6% less than 15 minutes, 38.8% 15 to 30 minutes, 8.2% 30 to 45 minutes, 20.0% 45 to 60 minutes, 15.3% 60 minutes or more (2005-2009 5-year est.)

MURCHISON (city).
Covers a land area of 1.583 square miles and a water area of 0 square miles. Located at 32.27° N. Lat; 95.75° W. Long. Elevation is 456 feet.
Population: 510 (1990); 592 (2000); 585 (2010); 583 (2015 projected); Race: 85.8% White, 1.4% Black, 0.2% Asian, 12.6% Other, 10.1% Hispanic of any race (2010); Density: 369.4 persons per square mile (2010); Average household size: 2.65 (2010); Median age: 34.9 (2010); Males per 100 females: 95.7 (2010); Marriage status: 21.9% never married, 57.8% now married, 6.5% widowed, 13.9% divorced (2005-2009 5-year est.); Foreign born: 2.9% (2005-2009 5-year est.); Ancestry (includes multiple ancestries): 50.8% American, 14.3% Irish, 6.1% German, 2.4% Greek, 1.9% English (2005-2009 5-year est.).
Economy: Employment by occupation: 12.5% management, 11.7% professional, 11.4% services, 38.5% sales, 0.0% farming, 7.7% construction, 18.3% production (2005-2009 5-year est.).
Income: Per capita income: $24,887 (2010); Median household income: $55,769 (2010); Average household income: $67,602 (2010); Percent of households with income of $100,000 or more: 19.5% (2010); Poverty rate: 10.4% (2005-2009 5-year est.).
Taxes: Total city taxes per capita: $85 (2007); City property taxes per capita: $0 (2007).
Education: Percent of population age 25 and over with: High school diploma (including GED) or higher: 79.7% (2010); Bachelor's degree or higher: 16.8% (2010); Master's degree or higher: 5.3% (2010).
School District(s)
Murchison ISD (PK-08)
   2009-10 Enrollment: 169 . . . . (903) 469-3636
Housing: Homeownership rate: 80.5% (2010); Median home value: $87,813 (2010); Median contract rent: $420 per month (2005-2009 5-year est.); Median year structure built: 1979 (2005-2009 5-year est.).
Transportation: Commute to work: 98.1% car, 0.0% public transportation, 0.0% walk, 1.9% work from home (2005-2009 5-year est.); Travel time to work: 43.8% less than 15 minutes, 36.9% 15 to 30 minutes, 5.8% 30 to 45 minutes, 3.8% 45 to 60 minutes, 9.6% 60 minutes or more (2005-2009 5-year est.)

PAYNE SPRINGS (town). Covers a land area of 1.889 square miles and a water area of <.001 square miles. Located at 32.28° N. Lat; 96.09° W. Long. Elevation is 367 feet.
Population: 606 (1990); 683 (2000); 806 (2010); 865 (2015 projected); Race: 92.8% White, 1.2% Black, 0.2% Asian, 5.7% Other, 5.5% Hispanic of any race (2010); Density: 426.8 persons per square mile (2010); Average household size: 2.55 (2010); Median age: 41.6 (2010); Males per 100 females: 99.0 (2010); Marriage status: 17.2% never married, 65.9% now married, 7.1% widowed, 9.8% divorced (2005-2009 5-year est.); Foreign born: 3.2% (2005-2009 5-year est.); Ancestry (includes multiple ancestries): 38.6% American, 10.6% Irish, 8.5% German, 6.6% English, 4.0% French (2005-2009 5-year est.).
Economy: Employment by occupation: 7.0% management, 10.7% professional, 17.0% services, 17.3% sales, 5.0% farming, 26.0% construction, 17.0% production (2005-2009 5-year est.).
Income: Per capita income: $20,472 (2010); Median household income: $41,500 (2010); Average household income: $53,117 (2010); Percent of households with income of $100,000 or more: 9.8% (2010); Poverty rate: 18.0% (2005-2009 5-year est.).
Taxes: Total city taxes per capita: $252 (2007); City property taxes per capita: $111 (2007).
Education: Percent of population age 25 and over with: High school diploma (including GED) or higher: 81.2% (2010); Bachelor's degree or higher: 11.2% (2010); Master's degree or higher: 2.8% (2010).
Housing: Homeownership rate: 84.8% (2010); Median home value: $73,143 (2010); Median contract rent: $339 per month (2005-2009 5-year est.); Median year structure built: 1981 (2005-2009 5-year est.).
Transportation: Commute to work: 94.1% car, 0.0% public transportation, 1.4% walk, 2.8% work from home (2005-2009 5-year est.); Travel time to work: 17.9% less than 15 minutes, 37.5% 15 to 30 minutes, 21.4% 30 to 45 minutes, 1.1% 45 to 60 minutes, 22.1% 60 minutes or more (2005-2009 5-year est.)

POYNOR (town). Covers a land area of 2.366 square miles and a water area of 0 square miles. Located at 32.07° N. Lat; 95.59° W. Long. Elevation is 440 feet.
Population: 237 (1990); 314 (2000); 276 (2010); 261 (2015 projected); Race: 88.8% White, 5.4% Black, 0.4% Asian, 5.4% Other, 8.0% Hispanic of any race (2010); Density: 116.7 persons per square mile (2010); Average household size: 2.68 (2010); Median age: 38.0 (2010); Males per 100 females: 100.0 (2010); Marriage status: 20.0% never married, 68.0% now married, 6.0% widowed, 6.0% divorced (2005-2009 5-year est.); Foreign born: 0.0% (2005-2009 5-year est.); Ancestry (includes multiple ancestries): 42.8% American, 16.4% Irish, 13.0% English, 10.8% German, 6.7% Scottish (2005-2009 5-year est.).
Economy: Employment by occupation: 17.2% management, 14.9% professional, 18.7% services, 15.7% sales, 0.0% farming, 13.4% construction, 20.1% production (2005-2009 5-year est.).
Income: Per capita income: $20,176 (2010); Median household income: $43,382 (2010); Average household income: $51,845 (2010); Percent of households with income of $100,000 or more: 10.7% (2010); Poverty rate: 16.7% (2005-2009 5-year est.).
Taxes: Total city taxes per capita: $175 (2007); City property taxes per capita: $0 (2007).
Education: Percent of population age 25 and over with: High school diploma (including GED) or higher: 86.6% (2010); Bachelor's degree or higher: 16.0% (2010); Master's degree or higher: 6.2% (2010).
Housing: Homeownership rate: 84.5% (2010); Median home value: $87,000 (2010); Median contract rent: $438 per month (2005-2009 5-year est.); Median year structure built: 1971 (2005-2009 5-year est.).
Transportation: Commute to work: 91.7% car, 0.0% public transportation, 8.3% walk, 0.0% work from home (2005-2009 5-year est.); Travel time to work: 17.4% less than 15 minutes, 14.4% 15 to 30 minutes, 34.8% 30 to 45 minutes, 17.4% 45 to 60 minutes, 15.9% 60 minutes or more (2005-2009 5-year est.)

SEVEN POINTS (city). Covers a land area of 2.489 square miles and a water area of 0.006 square miles. Located at 32.33° N. Lat; 96.21° W. Long. Elevation is 384 feet.
Population: 750 (1990); 1,145 (2000); 1,191 (2010); 1,210 (2015 projected); Race: 89.1% White, 0.7% Black, 0.0% Asian, 10.2% Other, 9.7% Hispanic of any race (2010); Density: 478.4 persons per square mile (2010); Average household size: 2.50 (2010); Median age: 37.6 (2010); Males per 100 females: 100.5 (2010); Marriage status: 15.0% never

married, 61.0% now married, 9.1% widowed, 14.9% divorced (2005-2009 5-year est.); Foreign born: 0.8% (2005-2009 5-year est.); Ancestry (includes multiple ancestries): 52.3% American, 15.7% German, 11.1% Irish, 9.0% English, 2.6% Polish (2005-2009 5-year est.).
Economy: Single-family building permits issued: 0 (2010); Multi-family building permits issued: 0 (2010); Employment by occupation: 10.9% management, 5.0% professional, 15.4% services, 29.7% sales, 0.0% farming, 27.8% construction, 11.3% production (2005-2009 5-year est.).
Income: Per capita income: $18,882 (2010); Median household income: $35,789 (2010); Average household income: $47,311 (2010); Percent of households with income of $100,000 or more: 8.6% (2010); Poverty rate: 12.6% (2005-2009 5-year est.).
Taxes: Total city taxes per capita: $344 (2007); City property taxes per capita: $0 (2007).
Education: Percent of population age 25 and over with: High school diploma (including GED) or higher: 67.4% (2010); Bachelor's degree or higher: 4.9% (2010); Master's degree or higher: 1.3% (2010).
Housing: Homeownership rate: 77.7% (2010); Median home value: $57,556 (2010); Median contract rent: $463 per month (2005-2009 5-year est.); Median year structure built: 1987 (2005-2009 5-year est.).
Safety: Violent crime rate: 52.7 per 10,000 population; Property crime rate: 459.3 per 10,000 population (2009).
Transportation: Commute to work: 94.0% car, 0.0% public transportation, 3.0% walk, 2.4% work from home (2005-2009 5-year est.); Travel time to work: 25.0% less than 15 minutes, 10.2% 15 to 30 minutes, 20.3% 30 to 45 minutes, 11.8% 45 to 60 minutes, 32.7% 60 minutes or more (2005-2009 5-year est.)
Additional Information Contacts
Cedar Creek Lake Area Chamber of Commerce . . . . (903) 887-3152
   http://www.cclake.net

STAR HARBOR (city). Covers a land area of 0.493 square miles and a water area of 0.059 square miles. Located at 32.19° N. Lat; 96.05° W. Long. Elevation is 341 feet.
Population: 368 (1990); 416 (2000); 497 (2010); 533 (2015 projected); Race: 87.9% White, 7.8% Black, 0.4% Asian, 3.8% Other, 4.2% Hispanic of any race (2010); Density: 1,007.2 persons per square mile (2010); Average household size: 2.33 (2010); Median age: 52.3 (2010); Males per 100 females: 94.1 (2010); Marriage status: 7.2% never married, 80.6% now married, 6.7% widowed, 5.6% divorced (2005-2009 5-year est.); Foreign born: 6.7% (2005-2009 5-year est.); Ancestry (includes multiple ancestries): 33.1% English, 17.2% German, 14.7% Irish, 12.8% American, 5.0% French (2005-2009 5-year est.).
Economy: Single-family building permits issued: 3 (2010); Multi-family building permits issued: 0 (2010); Employment by occupation: 32.1% management, 7.3% professional, 11.0% services, 36.7% sales, 0.0% farming, 8.3% construction, 4.6% production (2005-2009 5-year est.).
Income: Per capita income: $32,508 (2010); Median household income: $47,250 (2010); Average household income: $75,869 (2010); Percent of households with income of $100,000 or more: 23.0% (2010); Poverty rate: 6.4% (2005-2009 5-year est.).
Taxes: Total city taxes per capita: $287 (2007); City property taxes per capita: $287 (2007).
Education: Percent of population age 25 and over with: High school diploma (including GED) or higher: 82.6% (2010); Bachelor's degree or higher: 24.4% (2010); Master's degree or higher: 4.7% (2010).
Housing: Homeownership rate: 81.2% (2010); Median home value: $132,576 (2010); Median contract rent: $825 per month (2005-2009 5-year est.); Median year structure built: 1983 (2005-2009 5-year est.).
Transportation: Commute to work: 92.7% car, 0.0% public transportation, 0.0% walk, 7.3% work from home (2005-2009 5-year est.); Travel time to work: 37.6% less than 15 minutes, 24.8% 15 to 30 minutes, 17.8% 30 to 45 minutes, 6.9% 45 to 60 minutes, 12.9% 60 minutes or more (2005-2009 5-year est.)

TOOL (city). Covers a land area of 3.608 square miles and a water area of 0.016 square miles. Located at 32.28° N. Lat; 96.17° W. Long. Elevation is 341 feet.
Population: 1,703 (1990); 2,275 (2000); 2,504 (2010); 2,608 (2015 projected); Race: 93.5% White, 0.4% Black, 0.0% Asian, 6.0% Other, 4.2% Hispanic of any race (2010); Density: 694.1 persons per square mile (2010); Average household size: 2.27 (2010); Median age: 47.7 (2010); Males per 100 females: 98.3 (2010); Marriage status: 21.0% never married, 56.8% now married, 9.5% widowed, 12.8% divorced (2005-2009 5-year est.); Foreign born: 6.6% (2005-2009 5-year est.); Ancestry (includes

multiple ancestries): 30.8% American, 11.9% English, 9.8% Irish, 9.7% German, 5.0% Scottish (2005-2009 5-year est.).
Economy: Single-family building permits issued: 8 (2010); Multi-family building permits issued: 0 (2010); Employment by occupation: 8.4% management, 11.6% professional, 12.9% services, 27.6% sales, 2.0% farming, 19.5% construction, 18.0% production (2005-2009 5-year est.).
Income: Per capita income: $22,478 (2010); Median household income: $38,143 (2010); Average household income: $50,695 (2010); Percent of households with income of $100,000 or more: 10.8% (2010); Poverty rate: 14.2% (2005-2009 5-year est.).
Taxes: Total city taxes per capita: $285 (2007); City property taxes per capita: $204 (2007).
Education: Percent of population age 25 and over with: High school diploma (including GED) or higher: 75.5% (2010); Bachelor's degree or higher: 11.8% (2010); Master's degree or higher: 4.6% (2010).

School District(s)
Malakoff ISD (PK-12)
    2009-10 Enrollment: 1,217 . . . . (903) 489-1152
Housing: Homeownership rate: 85.1% (2010); Median home value: $80,663 (2010); Median contract rent: $436 per month (2005-2009 5-year est.); Median year structure built: 1979 (2005-2009 5-year est.).
Safety: Violent crime rate: 61.1 per 10,000 population; Property crime rate: 394.8 per 10,000 population (2009).
Transportation: Commute to work: 96.4% car, 0.0% public transportation, 2.1% walk, 0.7% work from home (2005-2009 5-year est.); Travel time to work: 16.6% less than 15 minutes, 24.2% 15 to 30 minutes, 18.7% 30 to 45 minutes, 9.4% 45 to 60 minutes, 31.1% 60 minutes or more (2005-2009 5-year est.)

TRINIDAD (city). Covers a land area of 14.856 square miles and a water area of 0.232 square miles. Located at 32.14° N. Lat; 96.09° W. Long. Elevation is 302 feet.
Population: 1,056 (1990); 1,091 (2000); 1,098 (2010); 1,094 (2015 projected); Race: 87.5% White, 7.7% Black, 0.0% Asian, 4.8% Other, 8.8% Hispanic of any race (2010); Density: 73.9 persons per square mile (2010); Average household size: 2.55 (2010); Median age: 35.2 (2010); Males per 100 females: 94.3 (2010); Marriage status: 20.1% never married, 56.5% now married, 5.4% widowed, 18.0% divorced (2005-2009 5-year est.); Foreign born: 0.0% (2005-2009 5-year est.); Ancestry (includes multiple ancestries): 27.0% American, 7.8% Irish, 4.9% German, 4.8% English, 2.9% Czechoslovakian (2005-2009 5-year est.).
Economy: Single-family building permits issued: 0 (2010); Multi-family building permits issued: 0 (2010); Employment by occupation: 6.8% management, 10.4% professional, 22.2% services, 21.6% sales, 0.0% farming, 17.3% construction, 21.6% production (2005-2009 5-year est.).
Income: Per capita income: $16,774 (2010); Median household income: $33,725 (2010); Average household income: $42,697 (2010); Percent of households with income of $100,000 or more: 5.6% (2010); Poverty rate: 28.9% (2005-2009 5-year est.).
Taxes: Total city taxes per capita: $282 (2007); City property taxes per capita: $164 (2007).
Education: Percent of population age 25 and over with: High school diploma (including GED) or higher: 76.2% (2010); Bachelor's degree or higher: 8.6% (2010); Master's degree or higher: 3.5% (2010).

School District(s)
Trinidad ISD (PK-12)
    2009-10 Enrollment: 189 . . . . (903) 778-2673
Housing: Homeownership rate: 66.6% (2010); Median home value: $46,364 (2010); Median contract rent: $306 per month (2005-2009 5-year est.); Median year structure built: 1962 (2005-2009 5-year est.).
Transportation: Commute to work: 97.1% car, 0.0% public transportation, 0.0% walk, 2.9% work from home (2005-2009 5-year est.); Travel time to work: 32.9% less than 15 minutes, 17.6% 15 to 30 minutes, 18.8% 30 to 45 minutes, 11.5% 45 to 60 minutes, 19.1% 60 minutes or more (2005-2009 5-year est.)

Hidalgo County

Located in south Texas, in the valley of the Rio Grande; bounded on the south by the Mexican border. Covers a land area of 1,569.75 square miles, a water area of 12.92 square miles, and is located in the Central Time Zone at 26.24° N. Lat., 98.16° W. Long. The county was founded in 1852. County seat is Edinburg.

Hidalgo County is part of the McAllen-Edinburg-Mission, TX Metropolitan Statistical Area. The entire metro area includes: Hidalgo County, TX

Weather Station: McAllen   Elevation: 100 feet

	Jan	Feb	Mar	Apr	May	Jun	Jul	Aug	Sep	Oct	Nov	Dec
High	70	74	80	86	90	95	96	97	93	87	79	71
Low	49	53	58	65	71	75	76	76	73	66	58	50
Precip	1.0	1.2	0.9	1.3	2.2	2.1	1.9	2.0	3.7	2.2	1.0	1.0
Snow	tr	0.0	0.0	0.0	0.0	0.0	0.0	0.0	0.0	0.0	0.0	0.1

High and Low temperatures in degrees Fahrenheit; Precipitation and Snow in inches

Weather Station: McAllen Miller Intl Arpt   Elevation: 100 feet

	Jan	Feb	Mar	Apr	May	Jun	Jul	Aug	Sep	Oct	Nov	Dec
High	71	75	82	88	92	96	97	98	93	88	80	72
Low	51	54	60	66	72	76	76	77	73	67	59	52
Precip	1.1	1.1	0.8	1.1	2.4	2.3	2.1	2.5	4.2	2.0	1.0	1.3
Snow	na	na	na	na	na	na	na	na	na	na	na	na

High and Low temperatures in degrees Fahrenheit; Precipitation and Snow in inches

Weather Station: McCook   Elevation: 220 feet

	Jan	Feb	Mar	Apr	May	Jun	Jul	Aug	Sep	Oct	Nov	Dec
High	70	74	81	87	91	96	98	99	93	87	79	70
Low	48	52	57	63	70	74	75	74	71	64	57	49
Precip	0.9	1.1	0.8	1.1	2.5	2.4	2.1	1.5	3.6	2.7	1.0	1.1
Snow	0.0	0.0	tr	0.0	0.0	0.0	0.0	0.0	0.0	0.0	0.0	0.1

High and Low temperatures in degrees Fahrenheit; Precipitation and Snow in inches

Weather Station: Weslaco 2 E   Elevation: 75 feet

	Jan	Feb	Mar	Apr	May	Jun	Jul	Aug	Sep	Oct	Nov	Dec
High	71	75	81	86	90	94	96	97	92	87	79	72
Low	50	53	59	64	71	75	75	75	72	65	58	51
Precip	1.1	1.3	1.1	1.4	2.7	2.5	2.2	2.3	5.0	2.4	1.4	1.3
Snow	0.0	0.0	0.0	0.0	0.0	0.0	0.0	0.0	0.0	0.0	0.0	0.0

High and Low temperatures in degrees Fahrenheit; Precipitation and Snow in inches

Population: 383,545 (1990); 569,463 (2000); 760,181 (2010); 851,581 (2015 projected); Race: 76.8% White, 0.7% Black, 0.8% Asian, 21.7% Other, 89.7% Hispanic of any race (2010); Density: 484.3 persons per square mile (2010); Average household size: 3.51 (2010); Median age: 27.7 (2010); Males per 100 females: 95.0 (2010).
Religion: Five largest groups: 39.0% Catholic Church, 4.1% Southern Baptist Convention, 1.8% The United Methodist Church, 1.0% Assemblies of God, 1.0% The Church of Jesus Christ of Latter-day Saints (2000).
Economy: Unemployment rate: 13.0% (June 2011); Total civilian labor force: 311,386 (June 2011); Leading industries: 30.2% health care and social assistance; 20.5% retail trade; 11.2% accommodation & food services (2009); Farms: 2,151 totaling 722,582 acres (2007); Companies that employ 500 or more persons: 27 (2009); Companies that employ 100 to 499 persons: 216 (2009); Companies that employ less than 100 persons: 10,417 (2009); Black-owned businesses: n/a (2007); Hispanic-owned businesses: 45,054 (2007); Asian-owned businesses: 1,192 (2007); Women-owned businesses: 20,078 (2007); Retail sales per capita: $9,298 (2010). Single-family building permits issued: 3,096 (2010); Multi-family building permits issued: 456 (2010).
Income: Per capita income: $12,816 (2010); Median household income: $31,552 (2010); Average household income: $45,150 (2010); Percent of households with income of $100,000 or more: 8.5% (2010); Poverty rate: 35.2% (2009); Bankruptcy rate: 1.27% (2010).
Taxes: Total county taxes per capita: $186 (2007); County property taxes per capita: $180 (2007).
Education: Percent of population age 25 and over with: High school diploma (including GED) or higher: 58.7% (2010); Bachelor's degree or higher: 14.9% (2010); Master's degree or higher: 4.6% (2010).
Housing: Homeownership rate: 69.7% (2010); Median home value: $66,341 (2010); Median contract rent: $417 per month (2005-2009 5-year est.); Median year structure built: 1990 (2005-2009 5-year est.).
Health: Birth rate: 240.6 per 10,000 population (2009); Death rate: 48.0 per 10,000 population (2009); Age-adjusted cancer mortality rate: 119.7 deaths per 100,000 population (2007); Number of physicians: 11.4 per 10,000 population (2008); Hospital beds: 40.7 per 10,000 population (2007); Hospital admissions: 1,354.6 per 10,000 population (2007).
Environment: Air Quality Index: 72.3% good, 27.4% moderate, 0.3% unhealthy for sensitive individuals, 0.0% unhealthy (percent of days in 2008)
Elections: 2008 Presidential election results: 68.9% Obama, 30.3% McCain, 0.1% Nader

National and State Parks: Bentsen Rio Grande Valley State Park; Santa Ana National Wildlife Refuge

Additional Information Contacts

Hidalgo County Government . . . . (956) 318-2600
  http://www.co.hidalgo.tx.us
Alamo Chamber of Commerce . . . . (956) 787-2117
  http://www.alamochamber.com
City of Alamo . . . . (956) 787-0006
  http://www.alamotexas.org
City of Donna . . . . (956) 464-3314
  http://www.ci.donna.lib.tx.us
City of Edinburg . . . . (956) 388-8204
  http://www.cityofedinburg.com
City of Elsa . . . . (956) 262-2127
City of Hidalgo . . . . (956) 843-2286
  http://www.hidalgotexas.com
City of McAllen . . . . (956) 681-1000
  http://www.mcallen.net
City of Mercedes . . . . (956) 565-3114
  http://www.cityofmercedes.net
City of Mission . . . . (956) 580-8650
  http://www.missiontexas.us
City of Pharr . . . . (956) 702-5335
  http://www.pharr-tx.gov
City of San Juan . . . . (956) 223-2200
  http://www.cityofsanjuantexas.com
City of Weslaco . . . . (956) 968-3181
  http://www.weslacotx.gov
Donna Chamber of Commerce . . . . (956) 464-3314
Edinburg Chamber of Commerce . . . . (956) 383-4974
  http://www.edinburg.com
Edinburg Hispanic Chamber of Commerce . . . . (956) 383-5163
Greater Mission Chamber of Commerce . . . . (956) 585-2727
  http://www.missionchamber.com
Hidalgo Chamber of Commerce . . . . (956) 843-2734
  http://www.hidalgotexas.com/Chamber
Mc Allen Chamber of Commerce . . . . (956) 682-2871
  http://www.mcallen.org
Mercedes Area Chamber of Commerce . . . . (956) 565-2221
  http://www.hiline.net/macoc
Pharr Chamber of Commerce . . . . (956) 787-1481
  http://www.pharrchamberofcommerce.com
Rio Grande Valley Hispanic Chamber of Commerce . . . . . . (956) 928-0060
  http://www.rgvhcc.com
Weslaco Chamber of Commerce . . . . (956) 968-2102
  http://www.weslaco.com

Hidalgo County Communities

ABRAM-PEREZVILLE (CDP). Covers a land area of 5.069 square miles and a water area of 0.193 square miles. Located at 26.23° N. Lat; 98.40° W. Long. Elevation is 151 feet.
Population: 2,326 (1990); 5,444 (2000); 7,515 (2010); 8,574 (2015 projected); Race: 53.0% White, 0.1% Black, 0.1% Asian, 46.8% Other, 83.7% Hispanic of any race (2010); Density: 1,482.5 persons per square mile (2010); Average household size: 3.37 (2010); Median age: 27.6 (2010); Males per 100 females: 95.5 (2010); Marriage status: 22.9% never married, 62.3% now married, 7.5% widowed, 7.3% divorced (2005-2009 5-year est.); Foreign born: 32.2% (2005-2009 5-year est.); Ancestry (includes multiple ancestries): 5.4% German, 4.2% English, 3.8% Irish, 2.4% American, 2.1% Czech (2005-2009 5-year est.).
Economy: Employment by occupation: 9.9% management, 9.1% professional, 40.9% services, 22.2% sales, 0.9% farming, 11.2% construction, 5.7% production (2005-2009 5-year est.).
Income: Per capita income: $10,494 (2010); Median household income: $27,939 (2010); Average household income: $35,496 (2010); Percent of households with income of $100,000 or more: 3.0% (2010); Poverty rate: 35.1% (2005-2009 5-year est.).
Education: Percent of population age 25 and over with: High school diploma (including GED) or higher: 54.2% (2010); Bachelor's degree or higher: 7.6% (2010); Master's degree or higher: 3.2% (2010).
Housing: Homeownership rate: 87.0% (2010); Median home value: $53,953 (2010); Median contract rent: $387 per month (2005-2009 5-year est.); Median year structure built: 1990 (2005-2009 5-year est.).

Transportation: Commute to work: 83.4% car, 0.0% public transportation, 0.0% walk, 1.8% work from home (2005-2009 5-year est.); Travel time to work: 35.7% less than 15 minutes, 41.4% 15 to 30 minutes, 9.8% 30 to 45 minutes, 3.8% 45 to 60 minutes, 9.2% 60 minutes or more (2005-2009 5-year est.)

ALAMO (city). Covers a land area of 5.719 square miles and a water area of 0 square miles. Located at 26.18° N. Lat; 98.11° W. Long. Elevation is 98 feet.
History: Incorporated 1924.
Population: 10,047 (1990); 14,760 (2000); 18,333 (2010); 20,337 (2015 projected); Race: 84.8% White, 0.2% Black, 0.1% Asian, 14.8% Other, 85.8% Hispanic of any race (2010); Density: 3,205.5 persons per square mile (2010); Average household size: 3.36 (2010); Median age: 29.1 (2010); Males per 100 females: 94.8 (2010); Marriage status: 25.8% never married, 60.5% now married, 7.5% widowed, 6.1% divorced (2005-2009 5-year est.); Foreign born: 25.7% (2005-2009 5-year est.); Ancestry (includes multiple ancestries): 6.7% German, 2.4% English, 1.2% Norwegian, 1.1% Irish, 0.9% Dutch (2005-2009 5-year est.).
Economy: Single-family building permits issued: 39 (2010); Multi-family building permits issued: 0 (2010); Employment by occupation: 9.0% management, 13.8% professional, 27.3% services, 26.8% sales, 2.9% farming, 10.3% construction, 9.9% production (2005-2009 5-year est.).
Income: Per capita income: $11,810 (2010); Median household income: $29,166 (2010); Average household income: $39,634 (2010); Percent of households with income of $100,000 or more: 5.2% (2010); Poverty rate: 30.9% (2005-2009 5-year est.).
Taxes: Total city taxes per capita: $319 (2007); City property taxes per capita: $120 (2007).
Education: Percent of population age 25 and over with: High school diploma (including GED) or higher: 58.2% (2010); Bachelor's degree or higher: 10.4% (2010); Master's degree or higher: 1.8% (2010).

School District(s)
Donna ISD (PK-12)
  2009-10 Enrollment: 14,873 . . . . (956) 464-1600
Idea Public Schools (PK-12)
  2009-10 Enrollment: 5,515 . . . . (956) 377-8000
Pharr-San Juan-Alamo ISD (PK-12)
  2009-10 Enrollment: 31,329 . . . . (956) 354-2000
Housing: Homeownership rate: 74.1% (2010); Median home value: $50,601 (2010); Median contract rent: $374 per month (2005-2009 5-year est.); Median year structure built: 1986 (2005-2009 5-year est.).
Safety: Violent crime rate: 79.1 per 10,000 population; Property crime rate: 859.0 per 10,000 population (2009).
Transportation: Commute to work: 92.4% car, 0.0% public transportation, 2.4% walk, 4.8% work from home (2005-2009 5-year est.); Travel time to work: 33.3% less than 15 minutes, 46.7% 15 to 30 minutes, 16.2% 30 to 45 minutes, 1.4% 45 to 60 minutes, 2.4% 60 minutes or more (2005-2009 5-year est.)
Additional Information Contacts
Alamo Chamber of Commerce . . . . (956) 787-2117
  http://www.alamochamber.com
City of Alamo . . . . (956) 787-0006
  http://www.alamotexas.org

ALTON (city). Covers a land area of 2.112 square miles and a water area of 0 square miles. Located at 26.28° N. Lat; 98.30° W. Long. Elevation is 161 feet.
Population: 3,298 (1990); 4,384 (2000); 5,366 (2010); 6,001 (2015 projected); Race: 88.3% White, 0.1% Black, 0.7% Asian, 10.9% Other, 95.7% Hispanic of any race (2010); Density: 2,540.4 persons per square mile (2010); Average household size: 4.05 (2010); Median age: 25.4 (2010); Males per 100 females: 96.0 (2010); Marriage status: 25.1% never married, 66.1% now married, 5.7% widowed, 3.1% divorced (2005-2009 5-year est.); Foreign born: 34.2% (2005-2009 5-year est.); Ancestry (includes multiple ancestries): 1.5% Irish, 1.2% English, 0.6% American, 0.2% Swedish, 0.2% French (2005-2009 5-year est.).
Economy: Single-family building permits issued: 67 (2010); Multi-family building permits issued: 0 (2010); Employment by occupation: 9.4% management, 5.2% professional, 24.1% services, 35.1% sales, 3.0% farming, 15.6% construction, 7.7% production (2005-2009 5-year est.).
Income: Per capita income: $9,740 (2010); Median household income: $28,079 (2010); Average household income: $39,475 (2010); Percent of households with income of $100,000 or more: 5.7% (2010); Poverty rate: 38.6% (2005-2009 5-year est.).

Taxes: Total city taxes per capita: $198 (2007); City property taxes per capita: $117 (2007).
Education: Percent of population age 25 and over with: High school diploma (including GED) or higher: 44.4% (2010); Bachelor's degree or higher: 7.0% (2010); Master's degree or higher: 2.3% (2010).

School District(s)
Mission CISD (PK-12)
    2009-10 Enrollment: 15,412 . . . . (956) 323-5500
Housing: Homeownership rate: 76.7% (2010); Median home value: $58,976 (2010); Median contract rent: $324 per month (2005-2009 5-year est.); Median year structure built: 1992 (2005-2009 5-year est.).
Safety: Violent crime rate: 28.5 per 10,000 population; Property crime rate: 348.3 per 10,000 population (2009).
Transportation: Commute to work: 85.6% car, 0.0% public transportation, 1.1% walk, 4.1% work from home (2005-2009 5-year est.); Travel time to work: 26.3% less than 15 minutes, 46.1% 15 to 30 minutes, 22.6% 30 to 45 minutes, 2.9% 45 to 60 minutes, 2.1% 60 minutes or more (2005-2009 5-year est.)

ALTON NORTH (CDP).
Covers a land area of 4.191 square miles and a water area of 0 square miles. Located at 26.29° N. Lat; 98.31° W. Long. Elevation is 154 feet.
Population: 2,304 (1990); 5,051 (2000); 6,542 (2010); 7,434 (2015 projected); Race: 91.6% White, 0.0% Black, 0.0% Asian, 8.4% Other, 98.5% Hispanic of any race (2010); Density: 1,561.0 persons per square mile (2010); Average household size: 4.39 (2010); Median age: 24.3 (2010); Males per 100 females: 98.2 (2010); Marriage status: n/a never married, n/a now married, n/a widowed, n/a divorced (2005-2009 5-year est.); Foreign born: n/a (2005-2009 5-year est.); Ancestry (includes multiple ancestries): n/a (2005-2009 5-year est.).
Economy: Employment by occupation: n/a management, n/a professional, n/a services, n/a sales, n/a farming, n/a construction, n/a production (2005-2009 5-year est.).
Income: Per capita income: $6,979 (2010); Median household income: $22,768 (2010); Average household income: $30,839 (2010); Percent of households with income of $100,000 or more: 2.0% (2010); Poverty rate: n/a (2005-2009 5-year est.).
Education: Percent of population age 25 and over with: High school diploma (including GED) or higher: 35.5% (2010); Bachelor's degree or higher: 2.9% (2010); Master's degree or higher: 1.5% (2010).
Housing: Homeownership rate: 81.6% (2010); Median home value: $48,088 (2010); Median contract rent: n/a per month (2005-2009 5-year est.); Median year structure built: n/a (2005-2009 5-year est.).
Transportation: Commute to work: n/a car, n/a public transportation, n/a walk, n/a work from home (2005-2009 5-year est.); Travel time to work: n/a less than 15 minutes, n/a 15 to 30 minutes, n/a 30 to 45 minutes, n/a 45 to 60 minutes, n/a 60 minutes or more (2005-2009 5-year est.)

CESAR CHAVEZ (CDP).
Covers a land area of 3.210 square miles and a water area of 0 square miles. Located at 26.30° N. Lat; 98.10° W. Long. Elevation is 85 feet.
Population: 724 (1990); 1,469 (2000); 2,314 (2010); 2,671 (2015 projected); Race: 81.6% White, 0.6% Black, 0.0% Asian, 17.8% Other, 92.3% Hispanic of any race (2010); Density: 720.8 persons per square mile (2010); Average household size: 3.67 (2010); Median age: 25.7 (2010); Males per 100 females: 96.8 (2010); Marriage status: 21.4% never married, 67.0% now married, 7.2% widowed, 4.4% divorced (2005-2009 5-year est.); Foreign born: 17.1% (2005-2009 5-year est.); Ancestry (includes multiple ancestries): 4.4% German, 2.5% Dutch, 2.1% Irish, 1.0% French, 0.9% English (2005-2009 5-year est.).
Economy: Employment by occupation: 12.2% management, 17.9% professional, 17.9% services, 18.5% sales, 0.0% farming, 21.7% construction, 11.8% production (2005-2009 5-year est.).
Income: Per capita income: $10,566 (2010); Median household income: $28,800 (2010); Average household income: $38,918 (2010); Percent of households with income of $100,000 or more: 6.2% (2010); Poverty rate: 40.3% (2005-2009 5-year est.).
Education: Percent of population age 25 and over with: High school diploma (including GED) or higher: 52.8% (2010); Bachelor's degree or higher: 11.3% (2010); Master's degree or higher: 5.1% (2010).
Housing: Homeownership rate: 78.1% (2010); Median home value: $58,440 (2010); Median contract rent: $300 per month (2005-2009 5-year est.); Median year structure built: 1989 (2005-2009 5-year est.).
Transportation: Commute to work: 92.7% car, 0.0% public transportation, 0.0% walk, 7.3% work from home (2005-2009 5-year est.); Travel time to

work: 23.3% less than 15 minutes, 54.7% 15 to 30 minutes, 22.0% 30 to 45 minutes, 0.0% 45 to 60 minutes, 0.0% 60 minutes or more (2005-2009 5-year est.)

CITRUS CITY (CDP).
Covers a land area of 2.033 square miles and a water area of 0 square miles. Located at 26.32° N. Lat; 98.39° W. Long. Elevation is 217 feet.
Population: 287 (1990); 941 (2000); 1,344 (2010); 1,553 (2015 projected); Race: 73.1% White, 0.5% Black, 0.0% Asian, 26.3% Other, 97.6% Hispanic of any race (2010); Density: 661.3 persons per square mile (2010); Average household size: 4.48 (2010); Median age: 21.7 (2010); Males per 100 females: 98.2 (2010); Marriage status: 27.5% never married, 71.1% now married, 1.3% widowed, 0.0% divorced (2005-2009 5-year est.); Foreign born: 36.6% (2005-2009 5-year est.); Ancestry (includes multiple ancestries): 2.6% French Canadian, 2.1% American (2005-2009 5-year est.).
Economy: Employment by occupation: 0.0% management, 10.9% professional, 19.3% services, 18.4% sales, 2.7% farming, 48.6% construction, 0.0% production (2005-2009 5-year est.).
Income: Per capita income: $4,915 (2010); Median household income: $14,999 (2010); Average household income: $22,133 (2010); Percent of households with income of $100,000 or more: 2.3% (2010); Poverty rate: 78.6% (2005-2009 5-year est.).
Education: Percent of population age 25 and over with: High school diploma (including GED) or higher: 30.3% (2010); Bachelor's degree or higher: 5.9% (2010); Master's degree or higher: 0.8% (2010).
Housing: Homeownership rate: 84.7% (2010); Median home value: $40,299 (2010); Median contract rent: $553 per month (2005-2009 5-year est.); Median year structure built: 2000 (2005-2009 5-year est.).
Transportation: Commute to work: 95.7% car, 0.0% public transportation, 0.0% walk, 0.0% work from home (2005-2009 5-year est.); Travel time to work: 2.6% less than 15 minutes, 46.9% 15 to 30 minutes, 13.1% 30 to 45 minutes, 24.8% 45 to 60 minutes, 12.6% 60 minutes or more (2005-2009 5-year est.)

CUEVITAS (CDP).
Aka Curvitas. Covers a land area of 0.271 square miles and a water area of 0.027 square miles. Located at 26.26° N. Lat; 98.57° W. Long. Elevation is 141 feet.
Population: 24 (1990); 37 (2000); 42 (2010); 46 (2015 projected); Race: 64.3% White, 0.0% Black, 0.0% Asian, 35.7% Other, 97.6% Hispanic of any race (2010); Density: 154.7 persons per square mile (2010); Average household size: 3.82 (2010); Median age: 29.5 (2010); Males per 100 females: 100.0 (2010); Marriage status: n/a never married, n/a now married, n/a widowed, n/a divorced (2005-2009 5-year est.); Foreign born: n/a (2005-2009 5-year est.); Ancestry (includes multiple ancestries): n/a (2005-2009 5-year est.).
Economy: Employment by occupation: n/a management, n/a professional, n/a services, n/a sales, n/a farming, n/a construction, n/a production (2005-2009 5-year est.).
Income: Per capita income: $6,962 (2010); Median household income: $22,500 (2010); Average household income: $25,909 (2010); Percent of households with income of $100,000 or more: 0.0% (2010); Poverty rate: n/a (2005-2009 5-year est.).
Education: Percent of population age 25 and over with: High school diploma (including GED) or higher: 38.5% (2010); Bachelor's degree or higher: 11.5% (2010); Master's degree or higher: 7.7% (2010).
Housing: Homeownership rate: 81.8% (2010); Median home value: $70,000 (2010); Median contract rent: n/a per month (2005-2009 5-year est.); Median year structure built: n/a (2005-2009 5-year est.).
Transportation: Commute to work: n/a car, n/a public transportation, n/a walk, n/a work from home (2005-2009 5-year est.); Travel time to work: n/a less than 15 minutes, n/a 15 to 30 minutes, n/a 30 to 45 minutes, n/a 45 to 60 minutes, n/a 60 minutes or more (2005-2009 5-year est.)

DOFFING (CDP).
Covers a land area of 4.334 square miles and a water area of 0 square miles. Located at 26.27° N. Lat; 98.38° W. Long. Elevation is 194 feet.
Population: 1,252 (1990); 4,256 (2000); 6,013 (2010); 6,898 (2015 projected); Race: 32.5% White, 0.0% Black, 0.0% Asian, 67.5% Other, 99.2% Hispanic of any race (2010); Density: 1,387.4 persons per square mile (2010); Average household size: 4.46 (2010); Median age: 22.8 (2010); Males per 100 females: 98.3 (2010); Marriage status: 27.8% never married, 61.8% now married, 4.0% widowed, 6.4% divorced (2005-2009 5-year est.); Foreign born: 43.8% (2005-2009 5-year est.); Ancestry (includes multiple ancestries): n/a (2005-2009 5-year est.).

Economy: Employment by occupation: 4.5% management, 8.5% professional, 21.5% services, 28.9% sales, 6.1% farming, 17.3% construction, 13.1% production (2005-2009 5-year est.).
Income: Per capita income: $7,054 (2010); Median household income: $24,729 (2010); Average household income: $31,383 (2010); Percent of households with income of $100,000 or more: 4.1% (2010); Poverty rate: 35.3% (2005-2009 5-year est.).
Education: Percent of population age 25 and over with: High school diploma (including GED) or higher: 35.9% (2010); Bachelor's degree or higher: 3.2% (2010); Master's degree or higher: 2.0% (2010).
Housing: Homeownership rate: 82.0% (2010); Median home value: $56,239 (2010); Median contract rent: $317 per month (2005-2009 5-year est.); Median year structure built: 1995 (2005-2009 5-year est.).
Transportation: Commute to work: 82.2% car, 0.0% public transportation, 0.0% walk, 6.3% work from home (2005-2009 5-year est.); Travel time to work: 21.2% less than 15 minutes, 35.7% 15 to 30 minutes, 36.6% 30 to 45 minutes, 0.9% 45 to 60 minutes, 5.6% 60 minutes or more (2005-2009 5-year est.)

DONNA (city). Covers a land area of 5.041 square miles and a water area of 0.011 square miles. Located at 26.17° N. Lat; 98.04° W. Long. Elevation is 92 feet.
History: Founded c.1902.
Population: 12,523 (1990); 14,768 (2000); 17,518 (2010); 19,240 (2015 projected); Race: 72.6% White, 0.3% Black, 0.2% Asian, 26.9% Other, 85.5% Hispanic of any race (2010); Density: 3,475.0 persons per square mile (2010); Average household size: 3.34 (2010); Median age: 28.8 (2010); Males per 100 females: 93.3 (2010); Marriage status: 26.4% never married, 60.2% now married, 6.9% widowed, 6.4% divorced (2005-2009 5-year est.); Foreign born: 25.7% (2005-2009 5-year est.); Ancestry (includes multiple ancestries): 4.3% German, 3.6% Irish, 2.3% English, 1.8% American, 0.8% Norwegian (2005-2009 5-year est.).
Economy: Single-family building permits issued: 30 (2010); Multi-family building permits issued: 8 (2010); Employment by occupation: 6.8% management, 13.3% professional, 24.1% services, 27.6% sales, 9.6% farming, 11.7% construction, 6.9% production (2005-2009 5-year est.).
Income: Per capita income: $10,781 (2010); Median household income: $26,387 (2010); Average household income: $36,037 (2010); Percent of households with income of $100,000 or more: 4.6% (2010); Poverty rate: 40.4% (2005-2009 5-year est.).
Taxes: Total city taxes per capita: $310 (2007); City property taxes per capita: $177 (2007).
Education: Percent of population age 25 and over with: High school diploma (including GED) or higher: 57.7% (2010); Bachelor's degree or higher: 10.3% (2010); Master's degree or higher: 2.8% (2010).

School District(s)
Donna ISD (PK-12)
    2009-10 Enrollment: 14,873 . . . . (956) 464-1600
Idea Public Schools (PK-12)
    2009-10 Enrollment: 5,515 . . . . (956) 377-8000
Housing: Homeownership rate: 67.6% (2010); Median home value: $52,101 (2010); Median contract rent: $266 per month (2005-2009 5-year est.); Median year structure built: 1984 (2005-2009 5-year est.).
Safety: Violent crime rate: 77.4 per 10,000 population; Property crime rate: 685.8 per 10,000 population (2009).
Transportation: Commute to work: 95.1% car, 0.0% public transportation, 1.1% walk, 2.3% work from home (2005-2009 5-year est.); Travel time to work: 33.1% less than 15 minutes, 38.0% 15 to 30 minutes, 19.4% 30 to 45 minutes, 2.6% 45 to 60 minutes, 6.9% 60 minutes or more (2005-2009 5-year est.)
Additional Information Contacts
City of Donna . . . . (956) 464-3314
    http://www.ci.donna.lib.tx.us
Donna Chamber of Commerce . . . . (956) 464-3314

DOOLITTLE (CDP). Covers a land area of 4.255 square miles and a water area of 0 square miles. Located at 26.36° N. Lat; 98.12° W. Long. Elevation is 85 feet.
Population: 874 (1990); 2,358 (2000); 3,460 (2010); 3,970 (2015 projected); Race: 41.2% White, 1.2% Black, 0.2% Asian, 57.4% Other, 93.7% Hispanic of any race (2010); Density: 813.1 persons per square mile (2010); Average household size: 4.07 (2010); Median age: 23.0 (2010); Males per 100 females: 103.1 (2010); Marriage status: 23.0% never married, 72.2% now married, 4.5% widowed, 0.3% divorced (2005-2009 5-year est.); Foreign born: 34.2% (2005-2009 5-year est.); Ancestry

(includes multiple ancestries): 0.9% English, 0.9% Polish, 0.6% Irish, 0.6% Scotch-Irish, 0.2% Scottish (2005-2009 5-year est.).
Economy: Employment by occupation: 5.3% management, 12.2% professional, 20.3% services, 27.0% sales, 2.9% farming, 13.3% construction, 19.1% production (2005-2009 5-year est.).
Income: Per capita income: $8,925 (2010); Median household income: $27,409 (2010); Average household income: $36,318 (2010); Percent of households with income of $100,000 or more: 4.1% (2010); Poverty rate: 59.5% (2005-2009 5-year est.).
Education: Percent of population age 25 and over with: High school diploma (including GED) or higher: 39.6% (2010); Bachelor's degree or higher: 6.2% (2010); Master's degree or higher: 1.4% (2010).
Housing: Homeownership rate: 84.4% (2010); Median home value: $53,333 (2010); Median contract rent: $467 per month (2005-2009 5-year est.); Median year structure built: 1995 (2005-2009 5-year est.).
Transportation: Commute to work: 78.1% car, 0.0% public transportation, 0.0% walk, 10.6% work from home (2005-2009 5-year est.); Travel time to work: 24.9% less than 15 minutes, 50.6% 15 to 30 minutes, 21.6% 30 to 45 minutes, 2.2% 45 to 60 minutes, 0.8% 60 minutes or more (2005-2009 5-year est.)

EDCOUCH (city). Covers a land area of 0.935 square miles and a water area of 0 square miles. Located at 26.29° N. Lat; 97.96° W. Long. Elevation is 59 feet.
History: Incorporated 1928.
Population: 3,005 (1990); 3,342 (2000); 4,316 (2010); 4,843 (2015 projected); Race: 74.3% White, 0.9% Black, 0.0% Asian, 24.8% Other, 97.1% Hispanic of any race (2010); Density: 4,615.4 persons per square mile (2010); Average household size: 3.67 (2010); Median age: 25.9 (2010); Males per 100 females: 94.9 (2010); Marriage status: 23.1% never married, 59.8% now married, 9.8% widowed, 7.3% divorced (2005-2009 5-year est.); Foreign born: 17.6% (2005-2009 5-year est.); Ancestry (includes multiple ancestries): 2.3% American, 2.0% Welsh, 0.6% Scottish, 0.5% German, 0.5% English (2005-2009 5-year est.).
Economy: Single-family building permits issued: 0 (2010); Multi-family building permits issued: 0 (2010); Employment by occupation: 6.7% management, 28.0% professional, 22.3% services, 19.3% sales, 3.0% farming, 7.4% construction, 13.4% production (2005-2009 5-year est.).
Income: Per capita income: $9,600 (2010); Median household income: $24,488 (2010); Average household income: $35,393 (2010); Percent of households with income of $100,000 or more: 3.5% (2010); Poverty rate: 40.9% (2005-2009 5-year est.).
Taxes: Total city taxes per capita: $305 (2007); City property taxes per capita: $121 (2007).
Education: Percent of population age 25 and over with: High school diploma (including GED) or higher: 47.5% (2010); Bachelor's degree or higher: 6.4% (2010); Master's degree or higher: 1.3% (2010).

School District(s)
Edcouch-Elsa ISD (PK-12)
    2009-10 Enrollment: 5,404 . . . . (956) 262-6000
Housing: Homeownership rate: 70.8% (2010); Median home value: $50,172 (2010); Median contract rent: $303 per month (2005-2009 5-year est.); Median year structure built: 1977 (2005-2009 5-year est.).
Safety: Violent crime rate: 31.4 per 10,000 population; Property crime rate: 270.4 per 10,000 population (2009).
Transportation: Commute to work: 92.2% car, 0.0% public transportation, 0.0% walk, 1.2% work from home (2005-2009 5-year est.); Travel time to work: 27.9% less than 15 minutes, 42.9% 15 to 30 minutes, 15.5% 30 to 45 minutes, 11.3% 45 to 60 minutes, 2.3% 60 minutes or more (2005-2009 5-year est.)

EDINBURG (city). County seat. Covers a land area of 37.369 square miles and a water area of 0.045 square miles. Located at 26.30° N. Lat; 98.16° W. Long. Elevation is 95 feet.
History: Edinburg was first called Chapin when it was located along the Rio Grande. It was moved north in 1908 and renamed in 1911.
Population: 35,988 (1990); 48,465 (2000); 71,278 (2010); 80,649 (2015 projected); Race: 73.6% White, 0.6% Black, 0.7% Asian, 25.1% Other, 90.9% Hispanic of any race (2010); Density: 1,907.4 persons per square mile (2010); Average household size: 3.19 (2010); Median age: 27.9 (2010); Males per 100 females: 93.9 (2010); Marriage status: 31.1% never married, 56.8% now married, 4.6% widowed, 7.5% divorced (2005-2009 5-year est.); Foreign born: 18.8% (2005-2009 5-year est.); Ancestry (includes multiple ancestries): 2.3% German, 1.9% Irish, 1.7% English, 1.1% American, 0.7% French (2005-2009 5-year est.).

Economy: Unemployment rate: 10.0% (June 2011); Total civilian labor force: 33,650 (June 2011); Single-family building permits issued: 535 (2010); Multi-family building permits issued: 46 (2010); Employment by occupation: 8.4% management, 25.0% professional, 22.3% services, 26.0% sales, 0.9% farming, 9.0% construction, 8.3% production (2005-2009 5-year est.).

Income: Per capita income: $15,050 (2010); Median household income: $35,838 (2010); Average household income: $48,428 (2010); Percent of households with income of $100,000 or more: 9.9% (2010); Poverty rate: 29.2% (2005-2009 5-year est.).

Taxes: Total city taxes per capita: $407 (2007); City property taxes per capita: $218 (2007).

Education: Percent of population age 25 and over with: High school diploma (including GED) or higher: 68.8% (2010); Bachelor's degree or higher: 22.1% (2010); Master's degree or higher: 7.7% (2010).

School District(s)

Edinburg CISD (PK-12)
    2009-10 Enrollment: 32,011 . . . . (956) 289-2300
Evins Regional Juvenile Center (08-12)
    2009-10 Enrollment: 135 . . . . (956) 289-5500
Mercedes ISD (PK-12)
    2009-10 Enrollment: 5,545 . . . . (956) 514-2000
Monte Alto ISD (PK-09)
    2009-10 Enrollment: 820 . . . . (956) 262-1381
One Stop Multiservice Charter School (PK-12)
    2009-10 Enrollment: 746 . . . . (956) 393-2227
South Texas ISD (07-12)
    2009-10 Enrollment: 3,023 . . . . (956) 514-4216

Four-year College(s)

The University of Texas-Pan American (Public)
    Fall 2009 Enrollment: 18,337 . . . . (956) 665-2011
    2010-11 Tuition: In-state $4,795; Out-of-state $12,235

Housing: Homeownership rate: 57.4% (2010); Median home value: $79,164 (2010); Median contract rent: $476 per month (2005-2009 5-year est.); Median year structure built: 1994 (2005-2009 5-year est.).

Hospitals: Cornerstone Regional Hospital; Doctors Hospital at Renaissance (142 beds); Edinburg Regional Medical Center (250 beds)

Safety: Violent crime rate: 35.8 per 10,000 population; Property crime rate: 625.8 per 10,000 population (2009).

Newspapers: Edinburg Daily Review (Local news; Circulation 5,600)

Transportation: Commute to work: 90.2% car, 0.4% public transportation, 1.8% walk, 2.9% work from home (2005-2009 5-year est.); Travel time to work: 37.7% less than 15 minutes, 41.6% 15 to 30 minutes, 13.7% 30 to 45 minutes, 3.5% 45 to 60 minutes, 3.4% 60 minutes or more (2005-2009 5-year est.)

Additional Information Contacts

City of Edinburg . . . . (956) 388-8204
    http://www.cityofedinburg.com
Edinburg Chamber of Commerce . . . . (956) 383-4974
    http://www.edinburg.com
Edinburg Hispanic Chamber of Commerce . . . . (956) 383-5163

ELSA (city). Covers a land area of 1.477 square miles and a water area of 0 square miles. Located at 26.29° N. Lat; 97.99° W. Long. Elevation is 66 feet.

History: Settled 1927, incorporated 1933.

Population: 5,320 (1990); 5,549 (2000); 6,409 (2010); 7,002 (2015 projected); Race: 77.5% White, 0.4% Black, 0.0% Asian, 22.0% Other, 98.1% Hispanic of any race (2010); Density: 4,339.1 persons per square mile (2010); Average household size: 3.46 (2010); Median age: 27.4 (2010); Males per 100 females: 92.3 (2010); Marriage status: 23.1% never married, 54.8% now married, 11.6% widowed, 10.4% divorced (2005-2009 5-year est.); Foreign born: 18.0% (2005-2009 5-year est.); Ancestry (includes multiple ancestries): 1.0% American, 0.8% French, 0.5% German, 0.4% Dutch (2005-2009 5-year est.).

Economy: Single-family building permits issued: 116 (2010); Multi-family building permits issued: 0 (2010); Employment by occupation: 12.8% management, 28.9% professional, 25.6% services, 13.9% sales, 0.0% farming, 15.4% construction, 3.4% production (2005-2009 5-year est.).

Income: Per capita income: $10,737 (2010); Median household income: $26,952 (2010); Average household income: $37,046 (2010); Percent of households with income of $100,000 or more: 5.6% (2010); Poverty rate: 46.7% (2005-2009 5-year est.).

Taxes: Total city taxes per capita: $179 (2007); City property taxes per capita: $92 (2007).

Education: Percent of population age 25 and over with: High school diploma (including GED) or higher: 53.7% (2010); Bachelor's degree or higher: 7.5% (2010); Master's degree or higher: 1.2% (2010).

School District(s)

Edcouch-Elsa ISD (PK-12)
    2009-10 Enrollment: 5,404 . . . . (956) 262-6000

Housing: Homeownership rate: 67.2% (2010); Median home value: $51,170 (2010); Median contract rent: $215 per month (2005-2009 5-year est.); Median year structure built: 1980 (2005-2009 5-year est.).

Safety: Violent crime rate: 50.4 per 10,000 population; Property crime rate: 659.8 per 10,000 population (2009).

Transportation: Commute to work: 92.3% car, 0.0% public transportation, 0.0% walk, 1.2% work from home (2005-2009 5-year est.); Travel time to work: 32.7% less than 15 minutes, 42.2% 15 to 30 minutes, 22.8% 30 to 45 minutes, 2.3% 45 to 60 minutes, 0.0% 60 minutes or more (2005-2009 5-year est.)

Additional Information Contacts

City of Elsa . . . . (956) 262-2127

FAYSVILLE (CDP). Covers a land area of 0.932 square miles and a water area of 0 square miles. Located at 26.40° N. Lat; 98.13° W. Long. Elevation is 85 feet.

Population: 111 (1990); 348 (2000); 407 (2010); 437 (2015 projected); Race: 33.7% White, 47.9% Black, 0.2% Asian, 18.2% Other, 38.6% Hispanic of any race (2010); Density: 436.5 persons per square mile (2010); Average household size: 3.82 (2010); Median age: 32.9 (2010); Males per 100 females: 402.5 (2010); Marriage status: 55.6% never married, 0.0% now married, 44.4% widowed, 0.0% divorced (2005-2009 5-year est.); Foreign born: 100.0% (2005-2009 5-year est.); Ancestry (includes multiple ancestries): n/a (2005-2009 5-year est.).

Economy: Employment by occupation: 0.0% management, 0.0% professional, 0.0% services, 100.0% sales, 0.0% farming, 0.0% construction, 0.0% production (2005-2009 5-year est.).

Income: Per capita income: $7,529 (2010); Median household income: $32,500 (2010); Average household income: $36,023 (2010); Percent of households with income of $100,000 or more: 6.8% (2010); Poverty rate: 100.0% (2005-2009 5-year est.).

Education: Percent of population age 25 and over with: High school diploma (including GED) or higher: 64.6% (2010); Bachelor's degree or higher: 3.6% (2010); Master's degree or higher: 0.4% (2010).

Housing: Homeownership rate: 72.7% (2010); Median home value: $60,000 (2010); Median contract rent: n/a per month (2005-2009 5-year est.); Median year structure built: n/a (2005-2009 5-year est.).

Transportation: Commute to work: 100.0% car, 0.0% public transportation, 0.0% walk, 0.0% work from home (2005-2009 5-year est.); Travel time to work: 0.0% less than 15 minutes, 100.0% 15 to 30 minutes, 0.0% 30 to 45 minutes, 0.0% 45 to 60 minutes, 0.0% 60 minutes or more (2005-2009 5-year est.)

GRANJENO (city). Covers a land area of 0.349 square miles and a water area of 0 square miles. Located at 26.13° N. Lat; 98.30° W. Long. Elevation is 108 feet.

Population: 93 (1990); 313 (2000); 620 (2010); 704 (2015 projected); Race: 86.0% White, 0.0% Black, 0.0% Asian, 14.0% Other, 99.0% Hispanic of any race (2010); Density: 1,775.3 persons per square mile (2010); Average household size: 4.28 (2010); Median age: 25.7 (2010); Males per 100 females: 92.0 (2010); Marriage status: 23.4% never married, 65.9% now married, 10.7% widowed, 0.0% divorced (2005-2009 5-year est.); Foreign born: 13.9% (2005-2009 5-year est.); Ancestry (includes multiple ancestries): 2.9% French, 1.4% American, 1.1% English, 0.4% Irish (2005-2009 5-year est.).

Economy: Single-family building permits issued: 0 (2010); Multi-family building permits issued: 0 (2010); Employment by occupation: 3.1% management, 28.1% professional, 29.2% services, 13.5% sales, 0.0% farming, 3.1% construction, 22.9% production (2005-2009 5-year est.).

Income: Per capita income: $7,943 (2010); Median household income: $28,036 (2010); Average household income: $33,103 (2010); Percent of households with income of $100,000 or more: 2.1% (2010); Poverty rate: 35.4% (2005-2009 5-year est.).

Taxes: Total city taxes per capita: $399 (2007); City property taxes per capita: $100 (2007).

Education: Percent of population age 25 and over with: High school diploma (including GED) or higher: 50.0% (2010); Bachelor's degree or higher: 5.4% (2010); Master's degree or higher: 1.6% (2010).

Housing: Homeownership rate: 88.3% (2010); Median home value: $91,351 (2010); Median contract rent: n/a per month (2005-2009 5-year est.); Median year structure built: 1980 (2005-2009 5-year est.).
Transportation: Commute to work: 92.7% car, 0.0% public transportation, 7.3% walk, 0.0% work from home (2005-2009 5-year est.); Travel time to work: 25.0% less than 15 minutes, 52.1% 15 to 30 minutes, 17.7% 30 to 45 minutes, 2.1% 45 to 60 minutes, 3.1% 60 minutes or more (2005-2009 5-year est.)

HARGILL (unincorporated postal area, zip code 78549). Covers a land area of 14.105 square miles and a water area of 0.105 square miles. Located at 26.44° N. Lat; 98.01° W. Long. Elevation is 66 feet.
Population: 1,009 (2000); Race: 81.9% White, 0.0% Black, 0.0% Asian, 18.1% Other, 95.7% Hispanic of any race (2000); Density: 71.5 persons per square mile (2000); Age: 34.9% under 18, 10.3% over 64 (2000); Marriage status: 32.9% never married, 51.4% now married, 9.2% widowed, 6.5% divorced (2000); Foreign born: 19.1% (2000); Ancestry (includes multiple ancestries): 0.8% English, 0.5% American (2000).
Economy: Employment by occupation: 7.1% management, 14.7% professional, 14.7% services, 24.1% sales, 16.1% farming, 7.1% construction, 16.1% production (2000).
Income: Per capita income: $5,797 (2000); Median household income: $17,679 (2000); Poverty rate: 179.1% (2000).
Education: Percent of population age 25 and over with: High school diploma (including GED) or higher: 34.7% (2000); Bachelor's degree or higher: 11.1% (2000).

School District(s)
Edinburg CISD (PK-12)
   2009-10 Enrollment: 32,011 . . . . (956) 289-2300
Housing: Homeownership rate: 84.3% (2000); Median home value: $26,300 (2000); Median contract rent: n/a per month (2000); Median year structure built: 1976 (2000).
Transportation: Commute to work: 78.3% car, 0.0% public transportation, 8.7% walk, 5.8% work from home (2000); Travel time to work: 23.1% less than 15 minutes, 28.2% 15 to 30 minutes, 14.9% 30 to 45 minutes, 28.2% 45 to 60 minutes, 5.6% 60 minutes or more (2000)

HAVANA (CDP). Covers a land area of 0.820 square miles and a water area of 0.003 square miles. Located at 26.25° N. Lat; 98.50° W. Long. Elevation is 157 feet.
Population: 203 (1990); 452 (2000); 530 (2010); 582 (2015 projected); Race: 55.7% White, 0.0% Black, 0.0% Asian, 44.3% Other, 99.1% Hispanic of any race (2010); Density: 646.4 persons per square mile (2010); Average household size: 3.90 (2010); Median age: 25.9 (2010); Males per 100 females: 93.4 (2010); Marriage status: 19.7% never married, 42.3% now married, 27.5% widowed, 10.6% divorced (2005-2009 5-year est.); Foreign born: 73.4% (2005-2009 5-year est.); Ancestry (includes multiple ancestries): n/a (2005-2009 5-year est.).
Economy: Employment by occupation: 0.0% management, 0.0% professional, 52.7% services, 5.5% sales, 0.0% farming, 10.9% construction, 30.9% production (2005-2009 5-year est.).
Income: Per capita income: $7,473 (2010); Median household income: $23,889 (2010); Average household income: $28,676 (2010); Percent of households with income of $100,000 or more: 0.7% (2010); Poverty rate: 39.2% (2005-2009 5-year est.).
Education: Percent of population age 25 and over with: High school diploma (including GED) or higher: 35.7% (2010); Bachelor's degree or higher: 2.9% (2010); Master's degree or higher: 1.1% (2010).
Housing: Homeownership rate: 75.0% (2010); Median home value: $55,385 (2010); Median contract rent: n/a per month (2005-2009 5-year est.); Median year structure built: 1974 (2005-2009 5-year est.).
Transportation: Commute to work: 100.0% car, 0.0% public transportation, 0.0% walk, 0.0% work from home (2005-2009 5-year est.); Travel time to work: 89.1% less than 15 minutes, 10.9% 15 to 30 minutes, 0.0% 30 to 45 minutes, 0.0% 45 to 60 minutes, 0.0% 60 minutes or more (2005-2009 5-year est.)

HEIDELBERG (CDP). Covers a land area of 2.841 square miles and a water area of 0 square miles. Located at 26.18° N. Lat; 97.88° W. Long. Elevation is 59 feet.
Population: 926 (1990); 1,586 (2000); 1,839 (2010); 2,031 (2015 projected); Race: 70.5% White, 0.5% Black, 0.0% Asian, 29.0% Other, 96.6% Hispanic of any race (2010); Density: 647.2 persons per square mile (2010); Average household size: 4.37 (2010); Median age: 23.1 (2010); Males per 100 females: 97.3 (2010); Marriage status: 28.8% never married,

63.5% now married, 4.7% widowed, 3.0% divorced (2005-2009 5-year est.); Foreign born: 17.2% (2005-2009 5-year est.); Ancestry (includes multiple ancestries): 7.1% German, 2.6% Irish (2005-2009 5-year est.).
Economy: Employment by occupation: 2.0% management, 23.8% professional, 33.9% services, 12.7% sales, 0.0% farming, 17.0% construction, 10.6% production (2005-2009 5-year est.).
Income: Per capita income: $7,082 (2010); Median household income: $23,820 (2010); Average household income: $30,849 (2010); Percent of households with income of $100,000 or more: 2.6% (2010); Poverty rate: 47.5% (2005-2009 5-year est.).
Education: Percent of population age 25 and over with: High school diploma (including GED) or higher: 37.6% (2010); Bachelor's degree or higher: 4.6% (2010); Master's degree or higher: 0.0% (2010).
Housing: Homeownership rate: 86.9% (2010); Median home value: $39,863 (2010); Median contract rent: n/a per month (2005-2009 5-year est.); Median year structure built: 1983 (2005-2009 5-year est.).
Transportation: Commute to work: 77.5% car, 0.0% public transportation, 3.4% walk, 19.1% work from home (2005-2009 5-year est.); Travel time to work: 46.9% less than 15 minutes, 38.4% 15 to 30 minutes, 11.1% 30 to 45 minutes, 0.0% 45 to 60 minutes, 3.6% 60 minutes or more (2005-2009 5-year est.)

HIDALGO (city). Covers a land area of 4.353 square miles and a water area of 0.088 square miles. Located at 26.10° N. Lat; 98.24° W. Long. Elevation is 102 feet.
History: Hidalgo, on the Rio Grande, has a history of floods, droughts, and bandit raids. Texas Ranger camps and U.S. customs offices were located here.
Population: 3,735 (1990); 7,322 (2000); 12,004 (2010); 13,610 (2015 projected); Race: 86.9% White, 0.1% Black, 0.1% Asian, 12.9% Other, 97.8% Hispanic of any race (2010); Density: 2,757.9 persons per square mile (2010); Average household size: 4.07 (2010); Median age: 25.9 (2010); Males per 100 females: 90.7 (2010); Marriage status: 25.1% never married, 63.9% now married, 6.4% widowed, 4.6% divorced (2005-2009 5-year est.); Foreign born: 41.6% (2005-2009 5-year est.); Ancestry (includes multiple ancestries): 1.4% Irish, 0.6% American, 0.4% Armenian, 0.3% Russian, 0.1% German (2005-2009 5-year est.).
Economy: Single-family building permits issued: 44 (2010); Multi-family building permits issued: 0 (2010); Employment by occupation: 8.8% management, 10.1% professional, 22.2% services, 28.0% sales, 2.7% farming, 14.3% construction, 13.9% production (2005-2009 5-year est.).
Income: Per capita income: $8,334 (2010); Median household income: $26,973 (2010); Average household income: $33,654 (2010); Percent of households with income of $100,000 or more: 2.9% (2010); Poverty rate: 25.8% (2005-2009 5-year est.).
Taxes: Total city taxes per capita: $288 (2007); City property taxes per capita: $89 (2007).
Education: Percent of population age 25 and over with: High school diploma (including GED) or higher: 50.1% (2010); Bachelor's degree or higher: 6.7% (2010); Master's degree or higher: 2.0% (2010).

School District(s)
Hidalgo ISD (PK-12)
   2009-10 Enrollment: 3,516 . . . . (956) 843-4405
Valley View ISD (PK-12)
   2009-10 Enrollment: 4,650 . . . . (956) 843-3025
Housing: Homeownership rate: 71.2% (2010); Median home value: $87,824 (2010); Median contract rent: $340 per month (2005-2009 5-year est.); Median year structure built: 1999 (2005-2009 5-year est.).
Safety: Violent crime rate: 8.7 per 10,000 population; Property crime rate: 119.9 per 10,000 population (2009).
Transportation: Commute to work: 89.7% car, 2.2% public transportation, 3.8% walk, 3.0% work from home (2005-2009 5-year est.); Travel time to work: 32.8% less than 15 minutes, 34.4% 15 to 30 minutes, 25.5% 30 to 45 minutes, 2.4% 45 to 60 minutes, 4.9% 60 minutes or more (2005-2009 5-year est.)
Additional Information Contacts
City of Hidalgo . . . . (956) 843-2286
   http://www.hidalgotexas.com
Hidalgo Chamber of Commerce . . . . (956) 843-2734
   http://www.hidalgotexas.com/Chamber

INDIAN HILLS (CDP). Covers a land area of 2.393 square miles and a water area of 0.103 square miles. Located at 26.21° N. Lat; 97.91° W. Long. Elevation is 66 feet.

Population: 785 (1990); 2,036 (2000); 2,421 (2010); 2,681 (2015 projected); Race: 70.8% White, 0.2% Black, 0.2% Asian, 28.9% Other, 96.4% Hispanic of any race (2010); Density: 1,011.6 persons per square mile (2010); Average household size: 4.31 (2010); Median age: 22.3 (2010); Males per 100 females: 95.7 (2010); Marriage status: 23.7% never married, 66.9% now married, 5.3% widowed, 4.1% divorced (2005-2009 5-year est.); Foreign born: 36.8% (2005-2009 5-year est.); Ancestry (includes multiple ancestries): 3.5% Irish, 1.5% Ukrainian, 1.4% English (2005-2009 5-year est.).
Economy: Employment by occupation: 0.0% management, 9.7% professional, 19.6% services, 19.2% sales, 12.5% farming, 29.6% construction, 9.5% production (2005-2009 5-year est.).
Income: Per capita income: $7,193 (2010); Median household income: $22,846 (2010); Average household income: $30,449 (2010); Percent of households with income of $100,000 or more: 2.7% (2010); Poverty rate: 70.2% (2005-2009 5-year est.).
Education: Percent of population age 25 and over with: High school diploma (including GED) or higher: 43.3% (2010); Bachelor's degree or higher: 5.0% (2010); Master's degree or higher: 0.1% (2010).
Housing: Homeownership rate: 79.5% (2010); Median home value: $41,228 (2010); Median contract rent: $818 per month (2005-2009 5-year est.); Median year structure built: 1993 (2005-2009 5-year est.).
Transportation: Commute to work: 100.0% car, 0.0% public transportation, 0.0% walk, 0.0% work from home (2005-2009 5-year est.); Travel time to work: 19.1% less than 15 minutes, 41.9% 15 to 30 minutes, 29.0% 30 to 45 minutes, 5.8% 45 to 60 minutes, 4.2% 60 minutes or more (2005-2009 5-year est.)

LA BLANCA (CDP). Covers a land area of 4.150 square miles and a water area of 0 square miles. Located at 26.30° N. Lat; 98.03° W. Long. Elevation is 69 feet.
Population: 1,231 (1990); 2,351 (2000); 3,028 (2010); 3,407 (2015 projected); Race: 85.9% White, 0.2% Black, 0.1% Asian, 13.8% Other, 97.6% Hispanic of any race (2010); Density: 729.6 persons per square mile (2010); Average household size: 4.09 (2010); Median age: 24.3 (2010); Males per 100 females: 98.0 (2010); Marriage status: 33.4% never married, 55.3% now married, 9.8% widowed, 1.5% divorced (2005-2009 5-year est.); Foreign born: 17.2% (2005-2009 5-year est.); Ancestry (includes multiple ancestries): n/a (2005-2009 5-year est.).
Economy: Employment by occupation: 7.1% management, 25.1% professional, 36.4% services, 28.2% sales, 0.0% farming, 0.0% construction, 3.1% production (2005-2009 5-year est.).
Income: Per capita income: $8,093 (2010); Median household income: $27,000 (2010); Average household income: $32,976 (2010); Percent of households with income of $100,000 or more: 2.0% (2010); Poverty rate: 39.5% (2005-2009 5-year est.).
Education: Percent of population age 25 and over with: High school diploma (including GED) or higher: 50.4% (2010); Bachelor's degree or higher: 5.9% (2010); Master's degree or higher: 1.6% (2010).
Housing: Homeownership rate: 81.2% (2010); Median home value: $54,529 (2010); Median contract rent: n/a per month (2005-2009 5-year est.); Median year structure built: 1986 (2005-2009 5-year est.).
Transportation: Commute to work: 96.2% car, 0.0% public transportation, 0.0% walk, 3.8% work from home (2005-2009 5-year est.); Travel time to work: 21.7% less than 15 minutes, 46.5% 15 to 30 minutes, 24.1% 30 to 45 minutes, 3.3% 45 to 60 minutes, 4.3% 60 minutes or more (2005-2009 5-year est.)

LA HOMA (CDP). Covers a land area of 6.857 square miles and a water area of 0 square miles. Located at 26.27° N. Lat; 98.35° W. Long. Elevation is 164 feet.
Population: 3,714 (1990); 10,433 (2000); 15,417 (2010); 17,641 (2015 projected); Race: 77.8% White, 0.1% Black, 0.1% Asian, 22.1% Other, 98.3% Hispanic of any race (2010); Density: 2,248.5 persons per square mile (2010); Average household size: 4.20 (2010); Median age: 23.5 (2010); Males per 100 females: 97.8 (2010); Marriage status: 34.3% never married, 57.0% now married, 5.3% widowed, 3.5% divorced (2005-2009 5-year est.); Foreign born: 43.6% (2005-2009 5-year est.); Ancestry (includes multiple ancestries): 1.0% German, 0.8% English, 0.5% Irish, 0.4% American, 0.1% Canadian (2005-2009 5-year est.).
Economy: Employment by occupation: 7.1% management, 4.7% professional, 28.5% services, 20.7% sales, 5.5% farming, 16.0% construction, 17.5% production (2005-2009 5-year est.).
Income: Per capita income: $7,153 (2010); Median household income: $22,518 (2010); Average household income: $29,949 (2010); Percent of

households with income of $100,000 or more: 2.9% (2010); Poverty rate: 43.0% (2005-2009 5-year est.).
Education: Percent of population age 25 and over with: High school diploma (including GED) or higher: 36.3% (2010); Bachelor's degree or higher: 3.6% (2010); Master's degree or higher: 1.1% (2010).
Housing: Homeownership rate: 78.4% (2010); Median home value: $53,772 (2010); Median contract rent: $373 per month (2005-2009 5-year est.); Median year structure built: 1994 (2005-2009 5-year est.).
Transportation: Commute to work: 79.6% car, 0.0% public transportation, 1.0% walk, 8.1% work from home (2005-2009 5-year est.); Travel time to work: 15.3% less than 15 minutes, 48.5% 15 to 30 minutes, 20.4% 30 to 45 minutes, 7.5% 45 to 60 minutes, 8.2% 60 minutes or more (2005-2009 5-year est.)

LA JOYA (city). Covers a land area of 2.781 square miles and a water area of 0.097 square miles. Located at 26.24° N. Lat; 98.48° W. Long. Elevation is 174 feet.
Population: 2,721 (1990); 3,303 (2000); 4,205 (2010); 4,714 (2015 projected); Race: 54.0% White, 0.2% Black, 0.7% Asian, 45.1% Other, 94.1% Hispanic of any race (2010); Density: 1,511.9 persons per square mile (2010); Average household size: 3.56 (2010); Median age: 29.2 (2010); Males per 100 females: 90.8 (2010); Marriage status: 21.0% never married, 69.8% now married, 5.4% widowed, 3.8% divorced (2005-2009 5-year est.); Foreign born: 33.3% (2005-2009 5-year est.); Ancestry (includes multiple ancestries): 0.4% English, 0.2% Irish, 0.1% Austrian (2005-2009 5-year est.).
Economy: Single-family building permits issued: 16 (2010); Multi-family building permits issued: 0 (2010); Employment by occupation: 4.6% management, 9.9% professional, 16.4% services, 27.2% sales, 1.9% farming, 20.4% construction, 19.7% production (2005-2009 5-year est.).
Income: Per capita income: $10,633 (2010); Median household income: $29,106 (2010); Average household income: $37,761 (2010); Percent of households with income of $100,000 or more: 5.1% (2010); Poverty rate: 52.8% (2005-2009 5-year est.).
Taxes: Total city taxes per capita: $104 (2007); City property taxes per capita: $66 (2007).
Education: Percent of population age 25 and over with: High school diploma (including GED) or higher: 51.7% (2010); Bachelor's degree or higher: 7.5% (2010); Master's degree or higher: 2.3% (2010).
School District(s)
La Joya ISD (PK-12)
    2009-10 Enrollment: 28,004 . . . . (956) 580-5441
Housing: Homeownership rate: 69.2% (2010); Median home value: $60,462 (2010); Median contract rent: $274 per month (2005-2009 5-year est.); Median year structure built: 1987 (2005-2009 5-year est.).
Safety: Violent crime rate: 10.0 per 10,000 population; Property crime rate: 76.3 per 10,000 population (2009).
Transportation: Commute to work: 91.9% car, 0.0% public transportation, 2.3% walk, 1.1% work from home (2005-2009 5-year est.); Travel time to work: 39.5% less than 15 minutes, 36.0% 15 to 30 minutes, 11.2% 30 to 45 minutes, 8.7% 45 to 60 minutes, 4.6% 60 minutes or more (2005-2009 5-year est.)

LA VILLA (city). Covers a land area of 0.268 square miles and a water area of 0 square miles. Located at 26.29° N. Lat; 97.92° W. Long. Elevation is 52 feet.
Population: 1,388 (1990); 1,305 (2000); 1,412 (2010); 1,509 (2015 projected); Race: 61.8% White, 0.6% Black, 0.0% Asian, 37.6% Other, 97.6% Hispanic of any race (2010); Density: 5,269.8 persons per square mile (2010); Average household size: 3.97 (2010); Median age: 25.9 (2010); Males per 100 females: 95.0 (2010); Marriage status: 35.3% never married, 45.0% now married, 9.8% widowed, 9.9% divorced (2005-2009 5-year est.); Foreign born: 14.5% (2005-2009 5-year est.); Ancestry (includes multiple ancestries): 4.4% American, 1.6% German (2005-2009 5-year est.).
Economy: Single-family building permits issued: 1 (2010); Multi-family building permits issued: 0 (2010); Employment by occupation: 4.1% management, 16.6% professional, 32.1% services, 21.0% sales, 6.7% farming, 7.9% construction, 11.7% production (2005-2009 5-year est.).
Income: Per capita income: $7,779 (2010); Median household income: $24,333 (2010); Average household income: $30,758 (2010); Percent of households with income of $100,000 or more: 2.2% (2010); Poverty rate: 55.5% (2005-2009 5-year est.).
Taxes: Total city taxes per capita: $167 (2007); City property taxes per capita: $139 (2007).

Education: Percent of population age 25 and over with: High school diploma (including GED) or higher: 48.5% (2010); Bachelor's degree or higher: 4.8% (2010); Master's degree or higher: 1.2% (2010).

School District(s)

La Villa ISD (PK-12)
   2009-10 Enrollment: 603 . . . . (956) 262-4755
Housing: Homeownership rate: 80.1% (2010); Median home value: $40,319 (2010); Median contract rent: $198 per month (2005-2009 5-year est.); Median year structure built: 1973 (2005-2009 5-year est.).
Safety: Violent crime rate: 89.8 per 10,000 population; Property crime rate: 559.8 per 10,000 population (2009).
Transportation: Commute to work: 91.7% car, 0.0% public transportation, 0.9% walk, 0.0% work from home (2005-2009 5-year est.); Travel time to work: 28.1% less than 15 minutes, 37.3% 15 to 30 minutes, 27.8% 30 to 45 minutes, 5.6% 45 to 60 minutes, 1.2% 60 minutes or more (2005-2009 5-year est.)

LAGUNA SECA (CDP). Covers a land area of 2.254 square miles and a water area of 0 square miles. Located at 26.27° N. Lat; 97.92° W. Long. Elevation is 105 feet.
Population: 149 (1990); 251 (2000); 288 (2010); 315 (2015 projected); Race: 76.7% White, 0.0% Black, 0.0% Asian, 23.3% Other, 95.5% Hispanic of any race (2010); Density: 127.8 persons per square mile (2010); Average household size: 4.04 (2010); Median age: 24.3 (2010); Males per 100 females: 101.4 (2010); Marriage status: 41.8% never married, 49.0% now married, 9.2% widowed, 0.0% divorced (2005-2009 5-year est.); Foreign born: 0.0% (2005-2009 5-year est.); Ancestry (includes multiple ancestries): n/a (2005-2009 5-year est.).
Economy: Employment by occupation: 8.2% management, 44.9% professional, 0.0% services, 24.5% sales, 0.0% farming, 22.4% construction, 0.0% production (2005-2009 5-year est.).
Income: Per capita income: $9,249 (2010); Median household income: $24,688 (2010); Average household income: $36,549 (2010); Percent of households with income of $100,000 or more: 4.2% (2010); Poverty rate: 25.4% (2005-2009 5-year est.).
Education: Percent of population age 25 and over with: High school diploma (including GED) or higher: 46.8% (2010); Bachelor's degree or higher: 12.1% (2010); Master's degree or higher: 1.4% (2010).
Housing: Homeownership rate: 78.9% (2010); Median home value: $66,667 (2010); Median contract rent: n/a per month (2005-2009 5-year est.); Median year structure built: 1971 (2005-2009 5-year est.).
Transportation: Commute to work: 100.0% car, 0.0% public transportation, 0.0% walk, 0.0% work from home (2005-2009 5-year est.); Travel time to work: 24.5% less than 15 minutes, 30.6% 15 to 30 minutes, 22.4% 30 to 45 minutes, 0.0% 45 to 60 minutes, 22.4% 60 minutes or more (2005-2009 5-year est.)

LINN (unincorporated postal area, zip code 78563). Aka San Manuel. Covers a land area of 209.384 square miles and a water area of 0.114 square miles. Located at 26.63° N. Lat; 98.21° W. Long. Elevation is 75 feet.
Population: 565 (2000); Race: 51.4% White, 0.0% Black, 0.0% Asian, 48.6% Other, 97.2% Hispanic of any race (2000); Density: 2.7 persons per square mile (2000); Age: 43.9% under 18, 8.5% over 64 (2000); Marriage status: 19.8% never married, 58.2% now married, 11.2% widowed, 10.8% divorced (2000); Foreign born: 35.4% (2000); **Economy:** Employment by occupation: 0.0% management, 18.9% professional, 12.3% services, 12.3% sales, 13.2% farming, 0.0% construction, 43.4% production (2000).
Income: Per capita income: $6,088 (2000); Median household income: $12,500 (2000); Poverty rate: 179.1% (2000).
Education: Percent of population age 25 and over with: High school diploma (including GED) or higher: 47.6% (2000); Bachelor's degree or higher: 0.0% (2000).
Housing: Homeownership rate: 83.2% (2000); Median home value: $60,000 (2000); Median contract rent: n/a per month (2000); Median year structure built: 1978 (2000).
Transportation: Commute to work: 86.8% car, 0.0% public transportation, 0.0% walk, 0.0% work from home (2000); Travel time to work: 26.4% less than 15 minutes, 35.8% 15 to 30 minutes, 17.9% 30 to 45 minutes, 19.8% 45 to 60 minutes, 0.0% 60 minutes or more (2000)

LLANO GRANDE (CDP). Covers a land area of 1.726 square miles and a water area of 0 square miles. Located at 26.13° N. Lat; 97.96° W. Long. Elevation is 72 feet.

Population: 2,769 (1990); 3,333 (2000); 3,496 (2010); 3,686 (2015 projected); Race: 74.4% White, 0.3% Black, 0.2% Asian, 25.1% Other, 82.0% Hispanic of any race (2010); Density: 2,025.4 persons per square mile (2010); Average household size: 3.24 (2010); Median age: 30.1 (2010); Males per 100 females: 94.8 (2010); Marriage status: 28.0% never married, 62.6% now married, 4.0% widowed, 5.4% divorced (2005-2009 5-year est.); Foreign born: 25.9% (2005-2009 5-year est.); Ancestry (includes multiple ancestries): 5.0% German, 2.7% English, 2.0% American, 1.6% Irish, 0.6% Welsh (2005-2009 5-year est.).
Economy: Employment by occupation: 5.7% management, 9.0% professional, 26.6% services, 20.6% sales, 0.0% farming, 11.9% construction, 26.2% production (2005-2009 5-year est.).
Income: Per capita income: $10,682 (2010); Median household income: $27,158 (2010); Average household income: $34,738 (2010); Percent of households with income of $100,000 or more: 3.3% (2010); Poverty rate: 35.4% (2005-2009 5-year est.).
Education: Percent of population age 25 and over with: High school diploma (including GED) or higher: 54.3% (2010); Bachelor's degree or higher: 8.5% (2010); Master's degree or higher: 2.6% (2010).
Housing: Homeownership rate: 79.8% (2010); Median home value: $46,770 (2010); Median contract rent: $284 per month (2005-2009 5-year est.); Median year structure built: 1984 (2005-2009 5-year est.).
Transportation: Commute to work: 87.3% car, 0.0% public transportation, 2.7% walk, 3.4% work from home (2005-2009 5-year est.); Travel time to work: 42.6% less than 15 minutes, 35.1% 15 to 30 minutes, 13.3% 30 to 45 minutes, 1.7% 45 to 60 minutes, 7.3% 60 minutes or more (2005-2009 5-year est.)

LOPEZVILLE (CDP). Covers a land area of 1.776 square miles and a water area of 0 square miles. Located at 26.24° N. Lat; 98.15° W. Long. Elevation is 105 feet.
Population: 2,958 (1990); 4,476 (2000); 5,959 (2010); 6,600 (2015 projected); Race: 91.9% White, 1.1% Black, 0.1% Asian, 6.9% Other, 95.8% Hispanic of any race (2010); Density: 3,355.6 persons per square mile (2010); Average household size: 3.93 (2010); Median age: 26.4 (2010); Males per 100 females: 121.4 (2010); Marriage status: 32.4% never married, 60.9% now married, 3.3% widowed, 3.4% divorced (2005-2009 5-year est.); Foreign born: 26.1% (2005-2009 5-year est.); Ancestry (includes multiple ancestries): 0.8% Irish, 0.8% German, 0.3% American (2005-2009 5-year est.).
Economy: Employment by occupation: 0.0% management, 9.7% professional, 35.9% services, 26.2% sales, 0.0% farming, 20.2% construction, 8.0% production (2005-2009 5-year est.).
Income: Per capita income: $9,653 (2010); Median household income: $25,565 (2010); Average household income: $38,555 (2010); Percent of households with income of $100,000 or more: 4.2% (2010); Poverty rate: 39.9% (2005-2009 5-year est.).
Education: Percent of population age 25 and over with: High school diploma (including GED) or higher: 46.5% (2010); Bachelor's degree or higher: 6.4% (2010); Master's degree or higher: 1.6% (2010).
Housing: Homeownership rate: 67.6% (2010); Median home value: $63,765 (2010); Median contract rent: $370 per month (2005-2009 5-year est.); Median year structure built: 1988 (2005-2009 5-year est.).
Transportation: Commute to work: 86.1% car, 0.0% public transportation, 2.5% walk, 2.4% work from home (2005-2009 5-year est.); Travel time to work: 27.8% less than 15 minutes, 60.7% 15 to 30 minutes, 10.2% 30 to 45 minutes, 0.4% 45 to 60 minutes, 1.0% 60 minutes or more (2005-2009 5-year est.)

LOS EBANOS (CDP). Covers a land area of 0.566 square miles and a water area of 0 square miles. Located at 26.24° N. Lat; 98.56° W. Long. Elevation is 141 feet.
Population: 478 (1990); 403 (2000); 413 (2010); 428 (2015 projected); Race: 90.8% White, 0.2% Black, 0.0% Asian, 9.0% Other, 96.4% Hispanic of any race (2010); Density: 729.5 persons per square mile (2010); Average household size: 2.97 (2010); Median age: 32.1 (2010); Males per 100 females: 82.7 (2010); Marriage status: 21.2% never married, 68.4% now married, 4.1% widowed, 6.3% divorced (2005-2009 5-year est.); Foreign born: 30.1% (2005-2009 5-year est.); Ancestry (includes multiple ancestries): 4.3% Italian, 4.3% German (2005-2009 5-year est.).
Economy: Employment by occupation: 0.0% management, 46.4% professional, 21.6% services, 11.1% sales, 0.0% farming, 0.0% construction, 20.9% production (2005-2009 5-year est.).
Income: Per capita income: $6,359 (2010); Median household income: $14,999 (2010); Average household income: $18,849 (2010); Percent of

households with income of $100,000 or more: 2.2% (2010); Poverty rate: 46.1% (2005-2009 5-year est.).

Education: Percent of population age 25 and over with: High school diploma (including GED) or higher: 44.8% (2010); Bachelor's degree or higher: 18.4% (2010); Master's degree or higher: 9.6% (2010).

Housing: Homeownership rate: 78.4% (2010); Median home value: $49,444 (2010); Median contract rent: n/a per month (2005-2009 5-year est.); Median year structure built: 1963 (2005-2009 5-year est.).

Transportation: Commute to work: 90.2% car, 0.0% public transportation, 0.0% walk, 9.8% work from home (2005-2009 5-year est.); Travel time to work: 33.3% less than 15 minutes, 58.0% 15 to 30 minutes, 0.0% 30 to 45 minutes, 8.7% 45 to 60 minutes, 0.0% 60 minutes or more (2005-2009 5-year est.)

MCALLEN (city).
Covers a land area of 45.974 square miles and a water area of 0.286 square miles. Located at 26.21° N. Lat; 98.23° W. Long. Elevation is 121 feet.

History: McAllen, the City of Palms, developed as a center for citrus fruits, cotton, and petroleum products, as well as recreation in the Lower Rio Grande Valley.

Population: 86,145 (1990); 106,414 (2000); 133,373 (2010); 146,936 (2015 projected); Race: 79.7% White, 0.8% Black, 2.6% Asian, 16.9% Other, 83.4% Hispanic of any race (2010); Density: 2,901.1 persons per square mile (2010); Average household size: 3.11 (2010); Median age: 31.1 (2010); Males per 100 females: 91.4 (2010); Marriage status: 28.3% never married, 58.4% now married, 5.5% widowed, 7.8% divorced (2005-2009 5-year est.); Foreign born: 26.9% (2005-2009 5-year est.); Ancestry (includes multiple ancestries): 4.9% German, 2.4% Irish, 2.1% English, 1.8% American, 1.3% Italian (2005-2009 5-year est.).

Economy: Unemployment rate: 8.7% (June 2011); Total civilian labor force: 63,641 (June 2011); Single-family building permits issued: 472 (2010); Multi-family building permits issued: 178 (2010); Employment by occupation: 13.3% management, 23.8% professional, 18.0% services, 28.6% sales, 0.5% farming, 7.7% construction, 7.9% production (2005-2009 5-year est.).

Income: Per capita income: $19,060 (2010); Median household income: $42,446 (2010); Average household income: $59,544 (2010); Percent of households with income of $100,000 or more: 15.2% (2010); Poverty rate: 27.2% (2005-2009 5-year est.).

Taxes: Total city taxes per capita: $705 (2007); City property taxes per capita: $194 (2007).

Education: Percent of population age 25 and over with: High school diploma (including GED) or higher: 73.8% (2010); Bachelor's degree or higher: 26.7% (2010); Master's degree or higher: 8.7% (2010).

School District(s)
Donna ISD (PK-12)
　　2009-10 Enrollment: 14,873 . . . . (956) 464-1600
Edcouch-Elsa ISD (PK-12)
　　2009-10 Enrollment: 5,404 . . . . (956) 262-6000
Edinburg CISD (PK-12)
　　2009-10 Enrollment: 32,011 . . . . (956) 289-2300
Idea Public Schools (PK-12)
　　2009-10 Enrollment: 5,515 . . . . (956) 377-8000
McAllen ISD (PK-12)
　　2009-10 Enrollment: 25,172 . . . . (956) 618-6000
Mid-Valley Academy (09-12)
　　2009-10 Enrollment: 380 . . . . (210) 227-0295
Sharyland ISD (PK-12)
　　2009-10 Enrollment: 9,566 . . . . (956) 580-5200
South Texas Educational Technologies Inc (PK-06)
　　2009-10 Enrollment: 620 . . . . (956) 969-3092
Weslaco ISD (PK-12)
　　2009-10 Enrollment: 17,279 . . . . (956) 969-6500

Four-year College(s)
South Texas College (Public)
　　Fall 2009 Enrollment: 26,338. . . . . (956) 872-8311
　　2010-11 Tuition: In-state $2,678; Out-of-state $5,700

Two-year College(s)
Kaplan Career Institute - McAllen (Private, For-profit)
　　Fall 2009 Enrollment: 1,015. . . . . (956) 630-1499

Vocational/Technical School(s)
South Texas Vocational Technical Institute-McAllen (Private, For-profit)
　　Fall 2009 Enrollment: 474 . . . . (956) 631-1107
　　2010-11 Tuition: $16,700

University of Cosmetology Arts and Sciences (Private, For-profit)
　　Fall 2009 Enrollment: 487 . . . . (956) 687-9444
　　2010-11 Tuition: $14,905

Housing: Homeownership rate: 60.4% (2010); Median home value: $97,292 (2010); Median contract rent: $495 per month (2005-2009 5-year est.); Median year structure built: 1986 (2005-2009 5-year est.).

Hospitals: McAllen Medical Center (589 beds); Rio Grande Regional Hospital (319 beds)

Safety: Violent crime rate: 26.2 per 10,000 population; Property crime rate: 604.8 per 10,000 population (2009).

Newspapers: El Periodico USA (Local news; Circulation 24,115); La Frontera (Local news; Circulation 15,000); Mid-Valley Town Crier (Community news; Circulation 93,000); The Monitor (Community news; Circulation 47,648); Rumbo del Valle (Regional news; Circulation 6,600)

Transportation: Commute to work: 92.3% car, 0.7% public transportation, 1.7% walk, 3.6% work from home (2005-2009 5-year est.); Travel time to work: 35.1% less than 15 minutes, 48.0% 15 to 30 minutes, 11.6% 30 to 45 minutes, 2.2% 45 to 60 minutes, 3.0% 60 minutes or more (2005-2009 5-year est.)

Airports: McAllen Miller International (primary service/small hub)

Additional Information Contacts
City of McAllen . . . . (956) 681-1000
　　http://www.mcallen.net
Mc Allen Chamber of Commerce. . . . . (956) 682-2871
　　http://www.mcallen.org
Rio Grande Valley Hispanic Chamber of Commerce. . . . . . (956) 928-0060
　　http://www.rgvhcc.com

MERCEDES (city).
Covers a land area of 8.578 square miles and a water area of 0.062 square miles. Located at 26.14° N. Lat; 97.91° W. Long. Elevation is 69 feet.

History: Mercedes was established in 1906 by St. Louis capitalists, and named for the wife of Mexican President Diaz.

Population: 13,226 (1990); 13,649 (2000); 15,354 (2010); 16,587 (2015 projected); Race: 79.1% White, 0.5% Black, 0.0% Asian, 20.4% Other, 90.8% Hispanic of any race (2010); Density: 1,790.0 persons per square mile (2010); Average household size: 3.25 (2010); Median age: 28.9 (2010); Males per 100 females: 92.1 (2010); Marriage status: 27.2% never married, 56.7% now married, 8.1% widowed, 8.1% divorced (2005-2009 5-year est.); Foreign born: 18.1% (2005-2009 5-year est.); Ancestry (includes multiple ancestries): 3.0% German, 1.6% American, 1.0% Irish, 0.9% French, 0.8% English (2005-2009 5-year est.).

Economy: Single-family building permits issued: 64 (2010); Multi-family building permits issued: 10 (2010); Employment by occupation: 6.8% management, 12.7% professional, 33.3% services, 23.4% sales, 1.0% farming, 11.8% construction, 11.0% production (2005-2009 5-year est.).

Income: Per capita income: $11,603 (2010); Median household income: $29,222 (2010); Average household income: $37,712 (2010); Percent of households with income of $100,000 or more: 4.8% (2010); Poverty rate: 44.5% (2005-2009 5-year est.).

Taxes: Total city taxes per capita: $411 (2007); City property taxes per capita: $132 (2007).

Education: Percent of population age 25 and over with: High school diploma (including GED) or higher: 60.5% (2010); Bachelor's degree or higher: 12.4% (2010); Master's degree or higher: 3.0% (2010).

School District(s)
Mercedes ISD (PK-12)
　　2009-10 Enrollment: 5,545 . . . . (956) 514-2000
Mid-Valley Academy (09-12)
　　2009-10 Enrollment: 380 . . . . (210) 227-0295
Santa Maria ISD (PK-12)
　　2009-10 Enrollment: 666 . . . . (956) 565-6308
South Texas ISD (07-12)
　　2009-10 Enrollment: 3,023 . . . . (956) 514-4216
Weslaco ISD (PK-12)
　　2009-10 Enrollment: 17,279 . . . . (956) 969-6500

Housing: Homeownership rate: 61.5% (2010); Median home value: $49,783 (2010); Median contract rent: $279 per month (2005-2009 5-year est.); Median year structure built: 1978 (2005-2009 5-year est.).

Safety: Violent crime rate: 55.0 per 10,000 population; Property crime rate: 540.6 per 10,000 population (2009).

Newspapers: Mercedes Enterprise (Local news; Circulation 2,200)

Transportation: Commute to work: 91.9% car, 0.0% public transportation, 2.0% walk, 2.9% work from home (2005-2009 5-year est.); Travel time to work: 41.2% less than 15 minutes, 38.5% 15 to 30 minutes, 14.3% 30 to 45

minutes, 4.4% 45 to 60 minutes, 1.6% 60 minutes or more (2005-2009 5-year est.)

Additional Information Contacts

City of Mercedes . . . . (956) 565-3114
  http://www.cityofmercedes.net
Mercedes Area Chamber of Commerce . . . . (956) 565-2221
  http://www.hiline.net/macoc

MIDWAY NORTH (CDP). Covers a land area of 2.067 square miles and a water area of 0 square miles. Located at 26.18° N. Lat; 98.01° W. Long. Elevation is 79 feet.

Population: 1,992 (1990); 3,946 (2000); 4,991 (2010); 5,650 (2015 projected); Race: 89.6% White, 0.2% Black, 0.1% Asian, 10.1% Other, 97.6% Hispanic of any race (2010); Density: 2,414.2 persons per square mile (2010); Average household size: 4.39 (2010); Median age: 23.6 (2010); Males per 100 females: 100.8 (2010); Marriage status: 24.8% never married, 63.6% now married, 3.8% widowed, 7.8% divorced (2005-2009 5-year est.); Foreign born: 39.7% (2005-2009 5-year est.); Ancestry (includes multiple ancestries): 0.7% English, 0.2% Italian, 0.2% Dutch, 0.1% American (2005-2009 5-year est.).

Economy: Employment by occupation: 2.5% management, 4.0% professional, 40.3% services, 21.2% sales, 5.6% farming, 14.2% construction, 12.1% production (2005-2009 5-year est.).

Income: Per capita income: $9,275 (2010); Median household income: $32,861 (2010); Average household income: $40,664 (2010); Percent of households with income of $100,000 or more: 5.4% (2010); Poverty rate: 53.6% (2005-2009 5-year est.).

Education: Percent of population age 25 and over with: High school diploma (including GED) or higher: 52.6% (2010); Bachelor's degree or higher: 11.7% (2010); Master's degree or higher: 2.9% (2010).

Housing: Homeownership rate: 81.9% (2010); Median home value: $65,514 (2010); Median contract rent: $331 per month (2005-2009 5-year est.); Median year structure built: 1992 (2005-2009 5-year est.).

Transportation: Commute to work: 95.0% car, 0.0% public transportation, 1.1% walk, 3.9% work from home (2005-2009 5-year est.); Travel time to work: 39.7% less than 15 minutes, 40.3% 15 to 30 minutes, 10.3% 30 to 45 minutes, 5.5% 45 to 60 minutes, 4.2% 60 minutes or more (2005-2009 5-year est.)

MIDWAY SOUTH (CDP). Covers a land area of 1.243 square miles and a water area of 0 square miles. Located at 26.16° N. Lat; 98.01° W. Long. Elevation is 79 feet.

Population: 1,046 (1990); 1,711 (2000); 2,000 (2010); 2,192 (2015 projected); Race: 83.3% White, 0.0% Black, 0.3% Asian, 16.4% Other, 90.7% Hispanic of any race (2010); Density: 1,608.8 persons per square mile (2010); Average household size: 3.38 (2010); Median age: 26.4 (2010); Males per 100 females: 93.4 (2010); Marriage status: 41.1% never married, 45.3% now married, 9.1% widowed, 4.6% divorced (2005-2009 5-year est.); Foreign born: 44.1% (2005-2009 5-year est.); Ancestry (includes multiple ancestries): 5.5% German, 0.5% Danish (2005-2009 5-year est.).

Economy: Employment by occupation: 3.6% management, 1.8% professional, 34.2% services, 14.4% sales, 3.1% farming, 29.8% construction, 13.1% production (2005-2009 5-year est.).

Income: Per capita income: $9,130 (2010); Median household income: $19,832 (2010); Average household income: $29,434 (2010); Percent of households with income of $100,000 or more: 3.6% (2010); Poverty rate: 52.6% (2005-2009 5-year est.).

Education: Percent of population age 25 and over with: High school diploma (including GED) or higher: 46.1% (2010); Bachelor's degree or higher: 8.7% (2010); Master's degree or higher: 3.7% (2010).

Housing: Homeownership rate: 61.7% (2010); Median home value: $47,907 (2010); Median contract rent: $293 per month (2005-2009 5-year est.); Median year structure built: 1992 (2005-2009 5-year est.).

Transportation: Commute to work: 92.9% car, 0.0% public transportation, 0.0% walk, 1.6% work from home (2005-2009 5-year est.); Travel time to work: 33.1% less than 15 minutes, 42.0% 15 to 30 minutes, 18.6% 30 to 45 minutes, 6.3% 45 to 60 minutes, 0.0% 60 minutes or more (2005-2009 5-year est.)

MILA DOCE (CDP). Covers a land area of 3.288 square miles and a water area of 0 square miles. Located at 26.22° N. Lat; 97.96° W. Long. Elevation is 59 feet.

Population: 2,845 (1990); 4,907 (2000); 5,922 (2010); 6,599 (2015 projected); Race: 91.4% White, 0.1% Black, 0.1% Asian, 8.5% Other,

97.8% Hispanic of any race (2010); Density: 1,800.9 persons per square mile (2010); Average household size: 4.41 (2010); Median age: 22.9 (2010); Males per 100 females: 95.3 (2010); Marriage status: 35.3% never married, 60.2% now married, 0.9% widowed, 3.6% divorced (2005-2009 5-year est.); Foreign born: 41.0% (2005-2009 5-year est.); Ancestry (includes multiple ancestries): 0.3% French (2005-2009 5-year est.).

Economy: Employment by occupation: 0.9% management, 9.0% professional, 20.4% services, 15.4% sales, 7.0% farming, 30.6% construction, 16.6% production (2005-2009 5-year est.).

Income: Per capita income: $7,070 (2010); Median household income: $25,417 (2010); Average household income: $31,290 (2010); Percent of households with income of $100,000 or more: 2.2% (2010); Poverty rate: 64.3% (2005-2009 5-year est.).

Education: Percent of population age 25 and over with: High school diploma (including GED) or higher: 40.9% (2010); Bachelor's degree or higher: 6.0% (2010); Master's degree or higher: 1.2% (2010).

Housing: Homeownership rate: 78.7% (2010); Median home value: $48,723 (2010); Median contract rent: $309 per month (2005-2009 5-year est.); Median year structure built: 1991 (2005-2009 5-year est.).

Transportation: Commute to work: 93.7% car, 0.0% public transportation, 3.4% walk, 0.0% work from home (2005-2009 5-year est.); Travel time to work: 25.8% less than 15 minutes, 43.0% 15 to 30 minutes, 20.0% 30 to 45 minutes, 9.0% 45 to 60 minutes, 2.3% 60 minutes or more (2005-2009 5-year est.)

MISSION (city). Covers a land area of 24.129 square miles and a water area of 0.007 square miles. Located at 26.21° N. Lat; 98.32° W. Long. Elevation is 141 feet.

History: The town of Mission was established on La Lomita Rancho, owned by the Oblate Fathers who continued a work started by the Franciscan Order in 1824.

Population: 31,523 (1990); 45,408 (2000); 69,180 (2010); 79,173 (2015 projected); Race: 77.2% White, 0.5% Black, 0.9% Asian, 21.5% Other, 81.4% Hispanic of any race (2010); Density: 2,867.1 persons per square mile (2010); Average household size: 3.22 (2010); Median age: 30.5 (2010); Males per 100 females: 92.9 (2010); Marriage status: 24.6% never married, 63.4% now married, 5.6% widowed, 6.4% divorced (2005-2009 5-year est.); Foreign born: 28.0% (2005-2009 5-year est.); Ancestry (includes multiple ancestries): 4.8% German, 3.2% Irish, 2.2% English, 2.0% American, 0.8% Italian (2005-2009 5-year est.).

Economy: Unemployment rate: 10.9% (June 2011); Total civilian labor force: 29,164 (June 2011); Single-family building permits issued: 346 (2010); Multi-family building permits issued: 40 (2010); Employment by occupation: 11.2% management, 19.4% professional, 18.4% services, 31.3% sales, 1.1% farming, 9.5% construction, 9.1% production (2005-2009 5-year est.).

Income: Per capita income: $17,658 (2010); Median household income: $39,241 (2010); Average household income: $56,912 (2010); Percent of households with income of $100,000 or more: 12.8% (2010); Poverty rate: 25.6% (2005-2009 5-year est.).

Taxes: Total city taxes per capita: $380 (2007); City property taxes per capita: $199 (2007).

Education: Percent of population age 25 and over with: High school diploma (including GED) or higher: 67.6% (2010); Bachelor's degree or higher: 20.4% (2010); Master's degree or higher: 6.0% (2010).

School District(s)

Idea Public Schools (PK-12)
  2009-10 Enrollment: 5,515 . . . . (956) 377-8000
La Joya ISD (PK-12)
  2009-10 Enrollment: 28,004 . . . . (956) 580-5441
Mission CISD (PK-12)
  2009-10 Enrollment: 15,412 . . . . (956) 323-5500
One Stop Multiservice Charter School (PK-12)
  2009-10 Enrollment: 746 . . . . (956) 393-2227
Responsive Education Solutions (KG-12)
  2009-10 Enrollment: 5,022 . . . . (972) 316-3663
Sharyland ISD (PK-12)
  2009-10 Enrollment: 9,566 . . . . (956) 580-5200

Housing: Homeownership rate: 72.8% (2010); Median home value: $79,282 (2010); Median contract rent: $442 per month (2005-2009 5-year est.); Median year structure built: 1993 (2005-2009 5-year est.).

Hospitals: Mission Hospital (138 beds)

Safety: Violent crime rate: 17.7 per 10,000 population; Property crime rate: 489.3 per 10,000 population (2009).

Newspapers: Mission Progress-Times; Progress-Times (Community news); Winter Texan Times (Regional news; Circulation 19,000)
Transportation: Commute to work: 89.9% car, 0.2% public transportation, 1.0% walk, 3.7% work from home (2005-2009 5-year est.); Travel time to work: 30.5% less than 15 minutes, 44.1% 15 to 30 minutes, 16.3% 30 to 45 minutes, 2.6% 45 to 60 minutes, 6.5% 60 minutes or more (2005-2009 5-year est.)
Additional Information Contacts
City of Mission . . . . (956) 580-8650
    http://www.missiontexas.us
Greater Mission Chamber of Commerce . . . . (956) 585-2727
    http://www.missionchamber.com

MONTE ALTO (CDP). Covers a land area of 2.243 square miles and a water area of 0 square miles. Located at 26.37° N. Lat; 97.97° W. Long. Elevation is 52 feet.
Population: 1,371 (1990); 1,611 (2000); 1,722 (2010); 1,832 (2015 projected); Race: 57.1% White, 0.0% Black, 0.1% Asian, 42.8% Other, 94.0% Hispanic of any race (2010); Density: 767.8 persons per square mile (2010); Average household size: 3.66 (2010); Median age: 26.9 (2010); Males per 100 females: 93.9 (2010); Marriage status: 24.5% never married, 64.0% now married, 4.6% widowed, 6.8% divorced (2005-2009 5-year est.); Foreign born: 23.2% (2005-2009 5-year est.); Ancestry (includes multiple ancestries): 0.8% American, 0.6% German, 0.3% French (2005-2009 5-year est.).
Economy: Employment by occupation: 4.0% management, 23.1% professional, 21.0% services, 17.0% sales, 3.4% farming, 17.9% construction, 13.6% production (2005-2009 5-year est.).
Income: Per capita income: $8,482 (2010); Median household income: $24,400 (2010); Average household income: $31,096 (2010); Percent of households with income of $100,000 or more: 2.6% (2010); Poverty rate: 39.1% (2005-2009 5-year est.).
Education: Percent of population age 25 and over with: High school diploma (including GED) or higher: 52.9% (2010); Bachelor's degree or higher: 9.9% (2010); Master's degree or higher: 2.3% (2010).
                                  School District(s)
Monte Alto ISD (PK-09)
    2009-10 Enrollment: 820 . . . . (956) 262-1381
Housing: Homeownership rate: 72.6% (2010); Median home value: $44,588 (2010); Median contract rent: $248 per month (2005-2009 5-year est.); Median year structure built: 1987 (2005-2009 5-year est.).
Transportation: Commute to work: 88.9% car, 1.8% public transportation, 0.8% walk, 5.8% work from home (2005-2009 5-year est.); Travel time to work: 39.2% less than 15 minutes, 32.3% 15 to 30 minutes, 24.6% 30 to 45 minutes, 1.9% 45 to 60 minutes, 1.9% 60 minutes or more (2005-2009 5-year est.)

MUNIZ (CDP). Covers a land area of 1.066 square miles and a water area of 0 square miles. Located at 26.25° N. Lat; 98.09° W. Long. Elevation is 89 feet.
Population: 476 (1990); 1,106 (2000); 1,451 (2010); 1,659 (2015 projected); Race: 86.4% White, 0.4% Black, 0.0% Asian, 13.2% Other, 98.3% Hispanic of any race (2010); Density: 1,361.0 persons per square mile (2010); Average household size: 4.40 (2010); Median age: 22.9 (2010); Males per 100 females: 100.7 (2010); Marriage status: 26.4% never married, 71.2% now married, 2.4% widowed, 0.0% divorced (2005-2009 5-year est.); Foreign born: 48.9% (2005-2009 5-year est.); Ancestry (includes multiple ancestries): n/a (2005-2009 5-year est.).
Economy: Employment by occupation: 5.1% management, 8.0% professional, 31.6% services, 21.4% sales, 0.0% farming, 9.2% construction, 24.6% production (2005-2009 5-year est.).
Income: Per capita income: $5,764 (2010); Median household income: $20,977 (2010); Average household income: $25,379 (2010); Percent of households with income of $100,000 or more: 1.5% (2010); Poverty rate: 55.5% (2005-2009 5-year est.).
Education: Percent of population age 25 and over with: High school diploma (including GED) or higher: 43.6% (2010); Bachelor's degree or higher: 6.6% (2010); Master's degree or higher: 1.3% (2010).
Housing: Homeownership rate: 76.4% (2010); Median home value: $47,013 (2010); Median contract rent: n/a per month (2005-2009 5-year est.); Median year structure built: 1995 (2005-2009 5-year est.).
Transportation: Commute to work: 87.2% car, 0.0% public transportation, 0.0% walk, 12.8% work from home (2005-2009 5-year est.); Travel time to work: 14.4% less than 15 minutes, 22.9% 15 to 30 minutes, 52.9% 30 to 45

minutes, 3.5% 45 to 60 minutes, 6.2% 60 minutes or more (2005-2009 5-year est.)

NORTH ALAMO (CDP). Covers a land area of 1.794 square miles and a water area of 0 square miles. Located at 26.21° N. Lat; 98.12° W. Long. Elevation is 98 feet.
Population: 880 (1990); 2,061 (2000); 2,312 (2010); 2,499 (2015 projected); Race: 96.7% White, 0.1% Black, 0.0% Asian, 3.2% Other, 79.0% Hispanic of any race (2010); Density: 1,288.8 persons per square mile (2010); Average household size: 3.07 (2010); Median age: 29.6 (2010); Males per 100 females: 98.3 (2010); Marriage status: 13.1% never married, 71.9% now married, 7.4% widowed, 7.6% divorced (2005-2009 5-year est.); Foreign born: 25.7% (2005-2009 5-year est.); Ancestry (includes multiple ancestries): 6.5% German, 4.2% English, 2.5% Irish, 2.0% American, 1.9% Swedish (2005-2009 5-year est.).
Economy: Employment by occupation: 8.0% management, 10.7% professional, 32.7% services, 26.2% sales, 0.0% farming, 17.6% construction, 4.7% production (2005-2009 5-year est.).
Income: Per capita income: $10,888 (2010); Median household income: $27,171 (2010); Average household income: $33,296 (2010); Percent of households with income of $100,000 or more: 3.2% (2010); Poverty rate: 35.6% (2005-2009 5-year est.).
Education: Percent of population age 25 and over with: High school diploma (including GED) or higher: 61.8% (2010); Bachelor's degree or higher: 9.1% (2010); Master's degree or higher: 4.2% (2010).
Housing: Homeownership rate: 79.0% (2010); Median home value: $44,088 (2010); Median contract rent: $360 per month (2005-2009 5-year est.); Median year structure built: 1986 (2005-2009 5-year est.).
Transportation: Commute to work: 99.2% car, 0.0% public transportation, 0.0% walk, 0.8% work from home (2005-2009 5-year est.); Travel time to work: 41.4% less than 15 minutes, 36.3% 15 to 30 minutes, 7.7% 30 to 45 minutes, 5.1% 45 to 60 minutes, 9.6% 60 minutes or more (2005-2009 5-year est.)

NURILLO (CDP). Covers a land area of 6.965 square miles and a water area of 0 square miles. Located at 26.26° N. Lat; 98.13° W. Long. Elevation is 95 feet.
Population: 2,486 (1990); 5,056 (2000); 9,119 (2010); 10,426 (2015 projected); Race: 81.1% White, 0.6% Black, 0.4% Asian, 18.0% Other, 95.2% Hispanic of any race (2010); Density: 1,309.4 persons per square mile (2010); Average household size: 3.85 (2010); Median age: 24.8 (2010); Males per 100 females: 95.1 (2010); Marriage status: 32.8% never married, 57.6% now married, 5.8% widowed, 3.7% divorced (2005-2009 5-year est.); Foreign born: 27.8% (2005-2009 5-year est.); Ancestry (includes multiple ancestries): 3.6% Italian, 1.3% American, 1.0% Portuguese, 0.4% Polish (2005-2009 5-year est.).
Economy: Employment by occupation: 10.7% management, 10.3% professional, 29.8% services, 20.6% sales, 0.5% farming, 15.4% construction, 12.6% production (2005-2009 5-year est.).
Income: Per capita income: $10,355 (2010); Median household income: $29,076 (2010); Average household income: $39,864 (2010); Percent of households with income of $100,000 or more: 4.8% (2010); Poverty rate: 34.0% (2005-2009 5-year est.).
Education: Percent of population age 25 and over with: High school diploma (including GED) or higher: 57.6% (2010); Bachelor's degree or higher: 10.2% (2010); Master's degree or higher: 2.8% (2010).
Housing: Homeownership rate: 66.9% (2010); Median home value: $64,009 (2010); Median contract rent: $501 per month (2005-2009 5-year est.); Median year structure built: 1994 (2005-2009 5-year est.).
Transportation: Commute to work: 90.3% car, 0.0% public transportation, 0.0% walk, 1.8% work from home (2005-2009 5-year est.); Travel time to work: 23.2% less than 15 minutes, 53.6% 15 to 30 minutes, 21.2% 30 to 45 minutes, 1.9% 45 to 60 minutes, 0.0% 60 minutes or more (2005-2009 5-year est.)

OLIVAREZ (CDP). Covers a land area of 3.687 square miles and a water area of 0 square miles. Located at 26.23° N. Lat; 97.99° W. Long. Elevation is 66 feet.
Population: 1,442 (1990); 2,445 (2000); 3,044 (2010); 3,424 (2015 projected); Race: 91.7% White, 0.2% Black, 0.4% Asian, 7.7% Other, 98.6% Hispanic of any race (2010); Density: 825.6 persons per square mile (2010); Average household size: 4.61 (2010); Median age: 23.3 (2010); Males per 100 females: 100.0 (2010); Marriage status: 39.6% never married, 54.8% now married, 2.2% widowed, 3.4% divorced (2005-2009 5-year est.); Foreign born: 35.5% (2005-2009 5-year est.); Ancestry

(includes multiple ancestries): 2.1% German, 1.0% English, 0.8% American, 0.5% Scottish, 0.3% Dutch (2005-2009 5-year est.).
Economy: Employment by occupation: 7.2% management, 5.5% professional, 46.5% services, 14.2% sales, 1.7% farming, 13.0% construction, 11.9% production (2005-2009 5-year est.).
Income: Per capita income: $6,932 (2010); Median household income: $26,579 (2010); Average household income: $31,864 (2010); Percent of households with income of $100,000 or more: 2.7% (2010); Poverty rate: 47.9% (2005-2009 5-year est.).
Education: Percent of population age 25 and over with: High school diploma (including GED) or higher: 40.0% (2010); Bachelor's degree or higher: 5.7% (2010); Master's degree or higher: 1.5% (2010).
Housing: Homeownership rate: 85.2% (2010); Median home value: $51,304 (2010); Median contract rent: $320 per month (2005-2009 5-year est.); Median year structure built: 1992 (2005-2009 5-year est.).
Transportation: Commute to work: 87.1% car, 1.8% public transportation, 0.0% walk, 5.1% work from home (2005-2009 5-year est.); Travel time to work: 25.1% less than 15 minutes, 41.6% 15 to 30 minutes, 15.6% 30 to 45 minutes, 12.2% 45 to 60 minutes, 5.5% 60 minutes or more (2005-2009 5-year est.)

PALMHURST (city). Covers a land area of 6.060 square miles and a water area of 0 square miles. Located at 26.25° N. Lat; 98.30° W. Long. Elevation is 161 feet.
Population: 1,957 (1990); 4,872 (2000); 6,036 (2010); 6,725 (2015 projected); Race: 88.0% White, 0.3% Black, 1.6% Asian, 10.1% Other, 88.5% Hispanic of any race (2010); Density: 996.0 persons per square mile (2010); Average household size: 3.76 (2010); Median age: 26.7 (2010); Males per 100 females: 94.5 (2010); Marriage status: 25.9% never married, 68.8% now married, 3.6% widowed, 1.7% divorced (2005-2009 5-year est.); Foreign born: 17.3% (2005-2009 5-year est.); Ancestry (includes multiple ancestries): 3.6% German, 2.3% Irish, 0.9% Scotch-Irish, 0.8% American, 0.6% English (2005-2009 5-year est.).
Economy: Single-family building permits issued: 5 (2010); Multi-family building permits issued: 0 (2010); Employment by occupation: 24.3% management, 21.9% professional, 14.8% services, 21.2% sales, 1.7% farming, 14.4% construction, 1.8% production (2005-2009 5-year est.).
Income: Per capita income: $15,153 (2010); Median household income: $32,461 (2010); Average household income: $56,921 (2010); Percent of households with income of $100,000 or more: 16.4% (2010); Poverty rate: 16.7% (2005-2009 5-year est.).
Taxes: Total city taxes per capita: $100 (2007); City property taxes per capita: $67 (2007).
Education: Percent of population age 25 and over with: High school diploma (including GED) or higher: 58.7% (2010); Bachelor's degree or higher: 16.3% (2010); Master's degree or higher: 4.9% (2010).
School District(s)
Mission CISD (PK-12)
    2009-10 Enrollment: 15,412 . . . . (956) 323-5500
Housing: Homeownership rate: 74.8% (2010); Median home value: $95,043 (2010); Median contract rent: n/a per month (2005-2009 5-year est.); Median year structure built: 1995 (2005-2009 5-year est.).
Safety: Violent crime rate: 18.0 per 10,000 population; Property crime rate: 431.8 per 10,000 population (2009).
Transportation: Commute to work: 82.9% car, 0.0% public transportation, 0.0% walk, 4.8% work from home (2005-2009 5-year est.); Travel time to work: 27.9% less than 15 minutes, 41.7% 15 to 30 minutes, 22.0% 30 to 45 minutes, 1.5% 45 to 60 minutes, 6.8% 60 minutes or more (2005-2009 5-year est.)

PALMVIEW (city). Covers a land area of 2.398 square miles and a water area of 0 square miles. Located at 26.22° N. Lat; 98.37° W. Long. Elevation is 148 feet.
Population: 2,244 (1990); 4,107 (2000); 6,183 (2010); 7,131 (2015 projected); Race: 48.9% White, 0.3% Black, 0.0% Asian, 50.8% Other, 98.4% Hispanic of any race (2010); Density: 2,578.1 persons per square mile (2010); Average household size: 4.11 (2010); Median age: 25.2 (2010); Males per 100 females: 97.7 (2010); Marriage status: 20.0% never married, 72.8% now married, 3.7% widowed, 3.6% divorced (2005-2009 5-year est.); Foreign born: 31.1% (2005-2009 5-year est.); Ancestry (includes multiple ancestries): 1.0% German, 0.9% English, 0.8% Dutch, 0.5% American, 0.5% French (2005-2009 5-year est.).
Economy: Single-family building permits issued: 5 (2010); Multi-family building permits issued: 0 (2010); Employment by occupation: 8.9%

management, 14.2% professional, 22.7% services, 31.3% sales, 0.7% farming, 12.0% construction, 10.2% production (2005-2009 5-year est.).
Income: Per capita income: $10,536 (2010); Median household income: $29,381 (2010); Average household income: $43,376 (2010); Percent of households with income of $100,000 or more: 9.4% (2010); Poverty rate: 31.3% (2005-2009 5-year est.).
Taxes: Total city taxes per capita: $245 (2007); City property taxes per capita: $110 (2007).
Education: Percent of population age 25 and over with: High school diploma (including GED) or higher: 39.0% (2010); Bachelor's degree or higher: 11.5% (2010); Master's degree or higher: 3.2% (2010).
School District(s)
Responsive Education Solutions (KG-12)
    2009-10 Enrollment: 5,022 . . . . (972) 316-3663
Housing: Homeownership rate: 75.5% (2010); Median home value: $68,782 (2010); Median contract rent: $387 per month (2005-2009 5-year est.); Median year structure built: 1993 (2005-2009 5-year est.).
Safety: Violent crime rate: 21.7 per 10,000 population; Property crime rate: 675.5 per 10,000 population (2009).
Transportation: Commute to work: 91.0% car, 1.4% public transportation, 0.0% walk, 3.0% work from home (2005-2009 5-year est.); Travel time to work: 24.5% less than 15 minutes, 51.1% 15 to 30 minutes, 18.8% 30 to 45 minutes, 1.6% 45 to 60 minutes, 4.0% 60 minutes or more (2005-2009 5-year est.)

PALMVIEW SOUTH (CDP). Covers a land area of 3.009 square miles and a water area of 0.028 square miles. Located at 26.22° N. Lat; 98.37° W. Long. Elevation is 135 feet.
Population: 3,008 (1990); 6,219 (2000); 8,578 (2010); 9,781 (2015 projected); Race: 56.8% White, 0.3% Black, 0.1% Asian, 42.8% Other, 91.5% Hispanic of any race (2010); Density: 2,850.7 persons per square mile (2010); Average household size: 3.83 (2010); Median age: 26.4 (2010); Males per 100 females: 96.1 (2010); Marriage status: 20.0% never married, 68.9% now married, 5.6% widowed, 5.6% divorced (2005-2009 5-year est.); Foreign born: 28.1% (2005-2009 5-year est.); Ancestry (includes multiple ancestries): 4.2% German, 3.1% English, 1.4% Irish, 0.9% Norwegian, 0.8% American (2005-2009 5-year est.).
Economy: Employment by occupation: 3.9% management, 17.7% professional, 37.4% services, 17.3% sales, 0.0% farming, 9.5% construction, 14.1% production (2005-2009 5-year est.).
Income: Per capita income: $9,829 (2010); Median household income: $27,699 (2010); Average household income: $37,536 (2010); Percent of households with income of $100,000 or more: 5.5% (2010); Poverty rate: 46.3% (2005-2009 5-year est.).
Education: Percent of population age 25 and over with: High school diploma (including GED) or higher: 43.8% (2010); Bachelor's degree or higher: 10.5% (2010); Master's degree or higher: 3.7% (2010).
Housing: Homeownership rate: 79.8% (2010); Median home value: $58,728 (2010); Median contract rent: $419 per month (2005-2009 5-year est.); Median year structure built: 1989 (2005-2009 5-year est.).
Transportation: Commute to work: 86.4% car, 0.0% public transportation, 3.0% walk, 2.5% work from home (2005-2009 5-year est.); Travel time to work: 33.7% less than 15 minutes, 46.7% 15 to 30 minutes, 17.0% 30 to 45 minutes, 1.1% 45 to 60 minutes, 1.5% 60 minutes or more (2005-2009 5-year est.)

PENITAS (city). Covers a land area of 2.005 square miles and a water area of 0.006 square miles. Located at 26.24° N. Lat; 98.44° W. Long. Elevation is 144 feet.
Population: 897 (1990); 1,167 (2000); 1,485 (2010); 1,665 (2015 projected); Race: 54.1% White, 0.1% Black, 0.1% Asian, 45.7% Other, 89.9% Hispanic of any race (2010); Density: 740.7 persons per square mile (2010); Average household size: 3.60 (2010); Median age: 27.7 (2010); Males per 100 females: 93.1 (2010); Marriage status: 23.2% never married, 67.1% now married, 2.9% widowed, 6.7% divorced (2005-2009 5-year est.); Foreign born: 33.4% (2005-2009 5-year est.); Ancestry (includes multiple ancestries): 4.0% American, 2.0% German, 0.3% Czech, 0.3% Irish, 0.2% Scotch-Irish (2005-2009 5-year est.).
Economy: Employment by occupation: 10.4% management, 6.1% professional, 15.6% services, 23.6% sales, 3.5% farming, 20.6% construction, 20.1% production (2005-2009 5-year est.).
Income: Per capita income: $9,851 (2010); Median household income: $27,581 (2010); Average household income: $34,879 (2010); Percent of households with income of $100,000 or more: 3.4% (2010); Poverty rate: 36.3% (2005-2009 5-year est.).

Taxes: Total city taxes per capita: $280 (2007); City property taxes per capita: $131 (2007).

Education: Percent of population age 25 and over with: High school diploma (including GED) or higher: 50.8% (2010); Bachelor's degree or higher: 7.7% (2010); Master's degree or higher: 3.6% (2010).

School District(s)

La Joya ISD (PK-12)

  2009-10 Enrollment: 28,004 . . . . (956) 580-5441

Housing: Homeownership rate: 79.6% (2010); Median home value: $58,082 (2010); Median contract rent: $353 per month (2005-2009 5-year est.); Median year structure built: 1988 (2005-2009 5-year est.).

Safety: Violent crime rate: 25.4 per 10,000 population; Property crime rate: 355.0 per 10,000 population (2009).

Transportation: Commute to work: 84.6% car, 0.0% public transportation, 1.4% walk, 9.9% work from home (2005-2009 5-year est.); Travel time to work: 28.6% less than 15 minutes, 34.4% 15 to 30 minutes, 24.4% 30 to 45 minutes, 1.3% 45 to 60 minutes, 11.3% 60 minutes or more (2005-2009 5-year est.)

PHARR (city). Covers a land area of 20.828 square miles and a water area of 0.006 square miles. Located at 26.20° N. Lat; 98.18° W. Long. Elevation is 112 feet.

History: Pharr developed as a shipping center for produce from the surrounding farms and citrus groves.

Population: 34,775 (1990); 46,660 (2000); 67,984 (2010); 76,316 (2015 projected); Race: 82.0% White, 0.2% Black, 0.3% Asian, 17.5% Other, 92.8% Hispanic of any race (2010); Density: 3,264.1 persons per square mile (2010); Average household size: 3.60 (2010); Median age: 27.4 (2010); Males per 100 females: 92.9 (2010); Marriage status: 25.3% never married, 63.8% now married, 6.1% widowed, 4.7% divorced (2005-2009 5-year est.); Foreign born: 31.2% (2005-2009 5-year est.); Ancestry (includes multiple ancestries): 1.8% German, 1.3% English, 1.0% Irish, 0.8% American, 0.5% Italian (2005-2009 5-year est.).

Economy: Unemployment rate: 11.6% (June 2011); Total civilian labor force: 26,824 (June 2011); Single-family building permits issued: 282 (2010); Multi-family building permits issued: 0 (2010); Employment by occupation: 6.9% management, 12.8% professional, 25.0% services, 30.9% sales, 0.5% farming, 12.3% construction, 11.6% production (2005-2009 5-year est.).

Income: Per capita income: $11,841 (2010); Median household income: $31,708 (2010); Average household income: $42,600 (2010); Percent of households with income of $100,000 or more: 6.5% (2010); Poverty rate: 38.2% (2005-2009 5-year est.).

Taxes: Total city taxes per capita: $416 (2007); City property taxes per capita: $170 (2007).

Education: Percent of population age 25 and over with: High school diploma (including GED) or higher: 53.9% (2010); Bachelor's degree or higher: 12.2% (2010); Master's degree or higher: 3.4% (2010).

School District(s)

Hidalgo ISD (PK-12)

  2009-10 Enrollment: 3,516 . . . . (956) 843-4405

Idea Public Schools (PK-12)

  2009-10 Enrollment: 5,515 . . . . (956) 377-8000

Pharr-San Juan-Alamo ISD (PK-12)

  2009-10 Enrollment: 31,329 . . . . (956) 354-2000

Responsive Education Solutions (KG-12)

  2009-10 Enrollment: 5,022 . . . . (972) 316-3663

Valley View ISD (PK-12)

  2009-10 Enrollment: 4,650 . . . . (956) 843-3025

Vanguard Academy (PK-09)

  2009-10 Enrollment: 860 . . . . (956) 283-1700

Vocational/Technical School(s)

Southern Careers Institute Inc-South Texas (Private, For-profit)

  Fall 2009 Enrollment: 245 . . . . (512) 437-7507

  2010-11 Tuition: $13,600

Housing: Homeownership rate: 71.0% (2010); Median home value: $56,655 (2010); Median contract rent: $432 per month (2005-2009 5-year est.); Median year structure built: 1992 (2005-2009 5-year est.).

Safety: Violent crime rate: 44.7 per 10,000 population; Property crime rate: 585.3 per 10,000 population (2009).

Newspapers: Advance News Journal (Local news; Circulation 11,000)

Transportation: Commute to work: 94.3% car, 0.2% public transportation, 1.1% walk, 2.6% work from home (2005-2009 5-year est.); Travel time to work: 35.5% less than 15 minutes, 47.3% 15 to 30 minutes, 11.5% 30 to 45

minutes, 2.9% 45 to 60 minutes, 2.8% 60 minutes or more (2005-2009 5-year est.)

Additional Information Contacts

City of Pharr . . . . (956) 702-5335

  http://www.pharr-tx.gov

Pharr Chamber of Commerce . . . . (956) 787-1481

  http://www.pharrchamberofcommerce.com

PROGRESO (city). Covers a land area of 2.983 square miles and a water area of 0 square miles. Located at 26.09° N. Lat; 97.95° W. Long. Elevation is 69 feet.

Population: 3,281 (1990); 4,851 (2000); 5,527 (2010); 6,001 (2015 projected); Race: 89.7% White, 0.1% Black, 0.1% Asian, 10.2% Other, 98.6% Hispanic of any race (2010); Density: 1,852.6 persons per square mile (2010); Average household size: 4.34 (2010); Median age: 23.3 (2010); Males per 100 females: 101.9 (2010); Marriage status: 29.4% never married, 64.9% now married, 3.4% widowed, 2.3% divorced (2005-2009 5-year est.); Foreign born: 30.5% (2005-2009 5-year est.); Ancestry (includes multiple ancestries): 1.0% American, 0.7% Italian, 0.4% French, 0.3% German, 0.2% Portuguese (2005-2009 5-year est.).

Economy: Single-family building permits issued: 16 (2010); Multi-family building permits issued: 0 (2010); Employment by occupation: 2.1% management, 8.8% professional, 29.2% services, 19.3% sales, 3.9% farming, 14.4% construction, 22.4% production (2005-2009 5-year est.).

Income: Per capita income: $7,212 (2010); Median household income: $22,934 (2010); Average household income: $31,207 (2010); Percent of households with income of $100,000 or more: 3.8% (2010); Poverty rate: 43.7% (2005-2009 5-year est.).

Taxes: Total city taxes per capita: $77 (2007); City property taxes per capita: $32 (2007).

Education: Percent of population age 25 and over with: High school diploma (including GED) or higher: 36.2% (2010); Bachelor's degree or higher: 6.0% (2010); Master's degree or higher: 1.8% (2010).

School District(s)

Progreso ISD (PK-12)

  2009-10 Enrollment: 2,224 . . . . (956) 565-3002

Housing: Homeownership rate: 82.1% (2010); Median home value: $50,922 (2010); Median contract rent: $313 per month (2005-2009 5-year est.); Median year structure built: 1990 (2005-2009 5-year est.).

Safety: Violent crime rate: 30.4 per 10,000 population; Property crime rate: 220.1 per 10,000 population (2009).

Transportation: Commute to work: 93.5% car, 0.0% public transportation, 1.3% walk, 3.5% work from home (2005-2009 5-year est.); Travel time to work: 42.4% less than 15 minutes, 38.1% 15 to 30 minutes, 12.5% 30 to 45 minutes, 2.8% 45 to 60 minutes, 4.2% 60 minutes or more (2005-2009 5-year est.)

PROGRESO LAKES (city). Covers a land area of 2.101 square miles and a water area of 0.090 square miles. Located at 26.07° N. Lat; 97.96° W. Long. Elevation is 75 feet.

Population: 154 (1990); 234 (2000); 270 (2010); 297 (2015 projected); Race: 94.4% White, 0.4% Black, 0.4% Asian, 4.8% Other, 87.4% Hispanic of any race (2010); Density: 128.5 persons per square mile (2010); Average household size: 3.86 (2010); Median age: 26.3 (2010); Males per 100 females: 98.5 (2010); Marriage status: 11.6% never married, 77.6% now married, 3.0% widowed, 7.8% divorced (2005-2009 5-year est.); Foreign born: 11.1% (2005-2009 5-year est.); Ancestry (includes multiple ancestries): 18.8% German, 8.3% Irish, 5.9% English, 3.8% Italian, 3.5% Norwegian (2005-2009 5-year est.).

Economy: Single-family building permits issued: 0 (2010); Multi-family building permits issued: 0 (2010); Employment by occupation: 25.0% management, 32.3% professional, 5.2% services, 34.4% sales, 0.0% farming, 1.0% construction, 2.1% production (2005-2009 5-year est.).

Income: Per capita income: $13,675 (2010); Median household income: $31,923 (2010); Average household income: $48,286 (2010); Percent of households with income of $100,000 or more: 10.0% (2010); Poverty rate: 13.5% (2005-2009 5-year est.).

Taxes: Total city taxes per capita: $74 (2007); City property taxes per capita: $74 (2007).

Education: Percent of population age 25 and over with: High school diploma (including GED) or higher: 57.9% (2010); Bachelor's degree or higher: 10.7% (2010); Master's degree or higher: 2.9% (2010).

Housing: Homeownership rate: 85.7% (2010); Median home value: $68,000 (2010); Median contract rent: n/a per month (2005-2009 5-year est.); Median year structure built: 1977 (2005-2009 5-year est.).

Transportation: Commute to work: 92.7% car, 0.0% public transportation, 0.0% walk, 1.0% work from home (2005-2009 5-year est.); Travel time to work: 26.3% less than 15 minutes, 38.9% 15 to 30 minutes, 18.9% 30 to 45 minutes, 1.1% 45 to 60 minutes, 14.7% 60 minutes or more (2005-2009 5-year est.)

RELAMPAGO (CDP). Covers a land area of 1.296 square miles and a water area of 0 square miles. Located at 26.08° N. Lat; 97.90° W. Long. Elevation is 69 feet.
Population: 65 (1990); 104 (2000); 120 (2010); 132 (2015 projected); Race: 86.7% White, 0.0% Black, 0.0% Asian, 13.3% Other, 98.3% Hispanic of any race (2010); Density: 92.6 persons per square mile (2010); Average household size: 4.62 (2010); Median age: 23.4 (2010); Males per 100 females: 100.0 (2010); Marriage status: 0.0% never married, 100.0% now married, 0.0% widowed, 0.0% divorced (2005-2009 5-year est.); Foreign born: 0.0% (2005-2009 5-year est.); Ancestry (includes multiple ancestries): n/a (2005-2009 5-year est.).
Economy: Employment by occupation: 0.0% management, 0.0% professional, 0.0% services, 0.0% sales, 0.0% farming, 100.0% construction, 0.0% production (2005-2009 5-year est.).
Income: Per capita income: $7,634 (2010); Median household income: $27,500 (2010); Average household income: $36,442 (2010); Percent of households with income of $100,000 or more: 7.7% (2010); Poverty rate: 0.0% (2005-2009 5-year est.).
Education: Percent of population age 25 and over with: High school diploma (including GED) or higher: 32.8% (2010); Bachelor's degree or higher: 3.4% (2010); Master's degree or higher: 1.7% (2010).
Housing: Homeownership rate: 88.5% (2010); Median home value: $54,000 (2010); Median contract rent: n/a per month (2005-2009 5-year est.); Median year structure built: n/a (2005-2009 5-year est.).
Transportation: Commute to work: n/a car, n/a public transportation, n/a walk, n/a work from home (2005-2009 5-year est.); Travel time to work: n/a less than 15 minutes, n/a 15 to 30 minutes, n/a 30 to 45 minutes, n/a 45 to 60 minutes, n/a 60 minutes or more (2005-2009 5-year est.)

SAN CARLOS (CDP). Covers a land area of 1.795 square miles and a water area of 0 square miles. Located at 26.29° N. Lat; 98.06° W. Long. Elevation is 75 feet.
Population: 1,211 (1990); 2,650 (2000); 3,707 (2010); 4,285 (2015 projected); Race: 74.5% White, 0.5% Black, 0.1% Asian, 24.9% Other, 96.4% Hispanic of any race (2010); Density: 2,065.4 persons per square mile (2010); Average household size: 4.02 (2010); Median age: 25.3 (2010); Males per 100 females: 98.2 (2010); Marriage status: 28.6% never married, 65.4% now married, 4.4% widowed, 1.7% divorced (2005-2009 5-year est.); Foreign born: 37.7% (2005-2009 5-year est.); Ancestry (includes multiple ancestries): n/a (2005-2009 5-year est.).
Economy: Employment by occupation: 6.5% management, 9.2% professional, 26.7% services, 28.6% sales, 2.3% farming, 14.9% construction, 11.8% production (2005-2009 5-year est.).
Income: Per capita income: $8,312 (2010); Median household income: $25,036 (2010); Average household income: $33,434 (2010); Percent of households with income of $100,000 or more: 3.6% (2010); Poverty rate: 34.3% (2005-2009 5-year est.).
Education: Percent of population age 25 and over with: High school diploma (including GED) or higher: 53.2% (2010); Bachelor's degree or higher: 7.7% (2010); Master's degree or higher: 1.8% (2010).
Housing: Homeownership rate: 79.4% (2010); Median home value: $57,235 (2010); Median contract rent: $256 per month (2005-2009 5-year est.); Median year structure built: 1992 (2005-2009 5-year est.).
Transportation: Commute to work: 92.2% car, 0.0% public transportation, 0.0% walk, 2.9% work from home (2005-2009 5-year est.); Travel time to work: 11.6% less than 15 minutes, 48.6% 15 to 30 minutes, 27.6% 30 to 45 minutes, 3.0% 45 to 60 minutes, 9.1% 60 minutes or more (2005-2009 5-year est.)

SAN JUAN (city). Covers a land area of 11.007 square miles and a water area of 0 square miles. Located at 26.19° N. Lat; 98.15° W. Long. Elevation is 105 feet.
History: San Juan was laid out in 1909.
Population: 16,628 (1990); 26,229 (2000); 35,348 (2010); 40,165 (2015 projected); Race: 79.8% White, 0.3% Black, 0.1% Asian, 19.9% Other, 96.6% Hispanic of any race (2010); Density: 3,211.5 persons per square mile (2010); Average household size: 3.91 (2010); Median age: 26.3 (2010); Males per 100 females: 94.4 (2010); Marriage status: 26.9% never married, 63.4% now married, 4.9% widowed, 4.8% divorced (2005-2009

5-year est.); Foreign born: 32.3% (2005-2009 5-year est.); Ancestry (includes multiple ancestries): 1.5% German, 1.1% American, 0.6% Irish, 0.4% English, 0.2% Italian (2005-2009 5-year est.).
Economy: Unemployment rate: 12.4% (June 2011); Total civilian labor force: 13,906 (June 2011); Single-family building permits issued: 123 (2010); Multi-family building permits issued: 0 (2010); Employment by occupation: 8.5% management, 14.9% professional, 24.3% services, 24.6% sales, 0.2% farming, 15.3% construction, 12.2% production (2005-2009 5-year est.).
Income: Per capita income: $10,367 (2010); Median household income: $29,566 (2010); Average household income: $40,698 (2010); Percent of households with income of $100,000 or more: 6.7% (2010); Poverty rate: 35.4% (2005-2009 5-year est.).
Taxes: Total city taxes per capita: $205 (2007); City property taxes per capita: $117 (2007).
Education: Percent of population age 25 and over with: High school diploma (including GED) or higher: 53.9% (2010); Bachelor's degree or higher: 9.2% (2010); Master's degree or higher: 2.7% (2010).
School District(s)
Idea Public Schools (PK-12)
   2009-10 Enrollment: 5,515 . . . . (956) 377-8000
Pharr-San Juan-Alamo ISD (PK-12)
   2009-10 Enrollment: 31,329 . . . . (956) 354-2000
Responsive Education Solutions (KG-12)
   2009-10 Enrollment: 5,022 . . . . (972) 316-3663
Housing: Homeownership rate: 73.4% (2010); Median home value: $59,233 (2010); Median contract rent: $333 per month (2005-2009 5-year est.); Median year structure built: 1989 (2005-2009 5-year est.).
Safety: Violent crime rate: 51.9 per 10,000 population; Property crime rate: 509.8 per 10,000 population (2009).
Transportation: Commute to work: 94.6% car, 0.2% public transportation, 2.0% walk, 2.8% work from home (2005-2009 5-year est.); Travel time to work: 37.9% less than 15 minutes, 44.9% 15 to 30 minutes, 12.5% 30 to 45 minutes, 2.7% 45 to 60 minutes, 1.9% 60 minutes or more (2005-2009 5-year est.)
Additional Information Contacts
City of San Juan. . . . . (956) 223-2200
   http://www.cityofsanjuantexas.com

SAN MANUEL-LINN (CDP). Covers a land area of 48.606 square miles and a water area of 0.080 square miles. Located at 26.56° N. Lat; 98.12° W. Long.
Population: 700 (1990); 958 (2000); 1,107 (2010); 1,210 (2015 projected); Race: 69.0% White, 0.3% Black, 0.2% Asian, 30.5% Other, 73.1% Hispanic of any race (2010); Density: 22.8 persons per square mile (2010); Average household size: 2.77 (2010); Median age: 35.5 (2010); Males per 100 females: 96.3 (2010); Marriage status: 14.5% never married, 78.2% now married, 4.0% widowed, 3.4% divorced (2005-2009 5-year est.); Foreign born: 21.0% (2005-2009 5-year est.); Ancestry (includes multiple ancestries): 7.1% German, 2.7% French Canadian, 2.3% Dutch (2005-2009 5-year est.).
Economy: Employment by occupation: 0.0% management, 21.9% professional, 13.0% services, 0.0% sales, 0.0% farming, 33.6% construction, 31.5% production (2005-2009 5-year est.).
Income: Per capita income: $12,696 (2010); Median household income: $26,000 (2010); Average household income: $35,242 (2010); Percent of households with income of $100,000 or more: 5.6% (2010); Poverty rate: 0.0% (2005-2009 5-year est.).
Education: Percent of population age 25 and over with: High school diploma (including GED) or higher: 60.1% (2010); Bachelor's degree or higher: 13.3% (2010); Master's degree or higher: 3.8% (2010).
Housing: Homeownership rate: 82.9% (2010); Median home value: $50,179 (2010); Median contract rent: n/a per month (2005-2009 5-year est.); Median year structure built: 1983 (2005-2009 5-year est.).
Transportation: Commute to work: 92.5% car, 0.0% public transportation, 0.0% walk, 0.0% work from home (2005-2009 5-year est.); Travel time to work: 33.6% less than 15 minutes, 41.1% 15 to 30 minutes, 25.3% 30 to 45 minutes, 0.0% 45 to 60 minutes, 0.0% 60 minutes or more (2005-2009 5-year est.)

SCISSORS (CDP). Aka La Tijera. Covers a land area of 1.707 square miles and a water area of 0 square miles. Located at 26.13° N. Lat; 98.04° W. Long. Elevation is 79 feet.
Population: 1,892 (1990); 2,805 (2000); 2,778 (2010); 2,854 (2015 projected); Race: 88.4% White, 0.0% Black, 0.1% Asian, 11.5% Other,

97.4% Hispanic of any race (2010); Density: 1,627.1 persons per square mile (2010); Average household size: 4.28 (2010); Median age: 24.2 (2010); Males per 100 females: 97.3 (2010); Marriage status: 29.0% never married, 54.0% now married, 8.5% widowed, 8.5% divorced (2005-2009 5-year est.); Foreign born: 27.6% (2005-2009 5-year est.); Ancestry (includes multiple ancestries): 0.1% American (2005-2009 5-year est.).
Economy: Employment by occupation: 3.5% management, 11.0% professional, 35.1% services, 10.1% sales, 8.0% farming, 10.6% construction, 21.6% production (2005-2009 5-year est.).
Income: Per capita income: $7,516 (2010); Median household income: $24,684 (2010); Average household income: $32,265 (2010); Percent of households with income of $100,000 or more: 2.9% (2010); Poverty rate: 32.1% (2005-2009 5-year est.).
Education: Percent of population age 25 and over with: High school diploma (including GED) or higher: 31.5% (2010); Bachelor's degree or higher: 6.0% (2010); Master's degree or higher: 1.4% (2010).
Housing: Homeownership rate: 75.0% (2010); Median home value: $45,179 (2010); Median contract rent: $375 per month (2005-2009 5-year est.); Median year structure built: 1987 (2005-2009 5-year est.).
Transportation: Commute to work: 93.3% car, 0.0% public transportation, 2.1% walk, 3.0% work from home (2005-2009 5-year est.); Travel time to work: 45.6% less than 15 minutes, 24.8% 15 to 30 minutes, 28.4% 30 to 45 minutes, 0.0% 45 to 60 minutes, 1.2% 60 minutes or more (2005-2009 5-year est.)

SOUTH ALAMO (CDP).
Covers a land area of 2.019 square miles and a water area of 0 square miles. Located at 26.15° N. Lat; 98.11° W. Long. Elevation is 95 feet.
Population: 1,295 (1990); 3,101 (2000); 3,599 (2010); 4,005 (2015 projected); Race: 92.7% White, 0.2% Black, 0.1% Asian, 7.0% Other, 93.7% Hispanic of any race (2010); Density: 1,783.0 persons per square mile (2010); Average household size: 4.08 (2010); Median age: 24.3 (2010); Males per 100 females: 99.2 (2010); Marriage status: 28.7% never married, 63.5% now married, 3.2% widowed, 4.6% divorced (2005-2009 5-year est.); Foreign born: 38.0% (2005-2009 5-year est.); Ancestry (includes multiple ancestries): n/a (2005-2009 5-year est.).
Economy: Employment by occupation: 1.9% management, 7.3% professional, 36.2% services, 21.7% sales, 0.0% farming, 10.8% construction, 22.2% production (2005-2009 5-year est.).
Income: Per capita income: $5,642 (2010); Median household income: $19,618 (2010); Average household income: $23,056 (2010); Percent of households with income of $100,000 or more: 0.3% (2010); Poverty rate: 48.8% (2005-2009 5-year est.).
Education: Percent of population age 25 and over with: High school diploma (including GED) or higher: 40.4% (2010); Bachelor's degree or higher: 4.4% (2010); Master's degree or higher: 1.1% (2010).
Housing: Homeownership rate: 76.6% (2010); Median home value: $38,157 (2010); Median contract rent: n/a per month (2005-2009 5-year est.); Median year structure built: 1991 (2005-2009 5-year est.).
Transportation: Commute to work: 85.1% car, 0.0% public transportation, 2.8% walk, 12.1% work from home (2005-2009 5-year est.); Travel time to work: 18.4% less than 15 minutes, 51.8% 15 to 30 minutes, 20.3% 30 to 45 minutes, 4.5% 45 to 60 minutes, 5.0% 60 minutes or more (2005-2009 5-year est.)

SULLIVAN CITY (city).
Covers a land area of 3.579 square miles and a water area of 0 square miles. Located at 26.27° N. Lat; 98.56° W. Long. Elevation is 200 feet.
Population: 2,605 (1990); 3,998 (2000); 4,634 (2010); 5,071 (2015 projected); Race: 55.8% White, 0.0% Black, 0.0% Asian, 44.1% Other, 99.0% Hispanic of any race (2010); Density: 1,294.8 persons per square mile (2010); Average household size: 3.90 (2010); Median age: 26.2 (2010); Males per 100 females: 95.1 (2010); Marriage status: 26.0% never married, 61.1% now married, 6.0% widowed, 6.9% divorced (2005-2009 5-year est.); Foreign born: 37.9% (2005-2009 5-year est.); Ancestry (includes multiple ancestries): 0.8% Arab, 0.3% American (2005-2009 5-year est.).
Economy: Single-family building permits issued: 0 (2010); Multi-family building permits issued: 0 (2010); Employment by occupation: 9.9% management, 10.3% professional, 25.9% services, 23.0% sales, 0.9% farming, 9.0% construction, 21.0% production (2005-2009 5-year est.).
Income: Per capita income: $7,554 (2010); Median household income: $23,700 (2010); Average household income: $29,640 (2010); Percent of households with income of $100,000 or more: 1.3% (2010); Poverty rate: 60.3% (2005-2009 5-year est.).

Taxes: Total city taxes per capita: $182 (2007); City property taxes per capita: $69 (2007).
Education: Percent of population age 25 and over with: High school diploma (including GED) or higher: 36.1% (2010); Bachelor's degree or higher: 3.0% (2010); Master's degree or higher: 1.0% (2010).
School District(s)
La Joya ISD (PK-12)
    2009-10 Enrollment: 28,004 . . . . (956) 580-5441
Housing: Homeownership rate: 74.1% (2010); Median home value: $54,969 (2010); Median contract rent: $259 per month (2005-2009 5-year est.); Median year structure built: 1984 (2005-2009 5-year est.).
Safety: Violent crime rate: 6.7 per 10,000 population; Property crime rate: 111.5 per 10,000 population (2009).
Transportation: Commute to work: 91.9% car, 0.0% public transportation, 3.7% walk, 1.6% work from home (2005-2009 5-year est.); Travel time to work: 34.6% less than 15 minutes, 28.5% 15 to 30 minutes, 24.3% 30 to 45 minutes, 7.3% 45 to 60 minutes, 5.2% 60 minutes or more (2005-2009 5-year est.)

VILLA VERDE (CDP).
Covers a land area of 0.376 square miles and a water area of 0 square miles. Located at 26.13° N. Lat; 97.99° W. Long. Elevation is 75 feet.
Population: 613 (1990); 891 (2000); 1,339 (2010); 1,531 (2015 projected); Race: 43.6% White, 0.1% Black, 3.0% Asian, 53.2% Other, 86.9% Hispanic of any race (2010); Density: 3,558.4 persons per square mile (2010); Average household size: 3.59 (2010); Median age: 27.7 (2010); Males per 100 females: 93.8 (2010); Marriage status: 36.9% never married, 55.5% now married, 7.6% widowed, 0.0% divorced (2005-2009 5-year est.); Foreign born: 31.9% (2005-2009 5-year est.); Ancestry (includes multiple ancestries): 4.3% American (2005-2009 5-year est.).
Economy: Employment by occupation: 0.0% management, 0.0% professional, 40.4% services, 6.0% sales, 14.7% farming, 6.4% construction, 32.6% production (2005-2009 5-year est.).
Income: Per capita income: $13,220 (2010); Median household income: $30,267 (2010); Average household income: $48,693 (2010); Percent of households with income of $100,000 or more: 10.2% (2010); Poverty rate: 55.6% (2005-2009 5-year est.).
Education: Percent of population age 25 and over with: High school diploma (including GED) or higher: 69.4% (2010); Bachelor's degree or higher: 14.0% (2010); Master's degree or higher: 0.7% (2010).
Housing: Homeownership rate: 85.3% (2010); Median home value: $75,484 (2010); Median contract rent: n/a per month (2005-2009 5-year est.); Median year structure built: 1977 (2005-2009 5-year est.).
Transportation: Commute to work: 96.8% car, 0.0% public transportation, 3.2% walk, 0.0% work from home (2005-2009 5-year est.); Travel time to work: 15.1% less than 15 minutes, 33.9% 15 to 30 minutes, 43.6% 30 to 45 minutes, 0.0% 45 to 60 minutes, 7.3% 60 minutes or more (2005-2009 5-year est.)

WESLACO (city).
Covers a land area of 12.687 square miles and a water area of 0.070 square miles. Located at 26.15° N. Lat; 97.98° W. Long. Elevation is 79 feet.
History: Weslaco was established in 1919.
Population: 24,801 (1990); 26,935 (2000); 33,350 (2010); 36,694 (2015 projected); Race: 71.8% White, 0.3% Black, 1.3% Asian, 26.6% Other, 86.1% Hispanic of any race (2010); Density: 2,628.7 persons per square mile (2010); Average household size: 3.16 (2010); Median age: 29.8 (2010); Males per 100 females: 89.9 (2010); Marriage status: 25.3% never married, 59.9% now married, 7.7% widowed, 7.1% divorced (2005-2009 5-year est.); Foreign born: 19.6% (2005-2009 5-year est.); Ancestry (includes multiple ancestries): 5.9% German, 3.5% English, 2.2% Irish, 2.0% American, 0.8% French (2005-2009 5-year est.).
Economy: Unemployment rate: 13.1% (June 2011); Total civilian labor force: 14,786 (June 2011); Single-family building permits issued: 119 (2010); Multi-family building permits issued: 147 (2010); Employment by occupation: 9.3% management, 26.6% professional, 22.5% services, 23.6% sales, 0.5% farming, 7.4% construction, 10.1% production (2005-2009 5-year est.).
Income: Per capita income: $13,886 (2010); Median household income: $33,127 (2010); Average household income: $43,941 (2010); Percent of households with income of $100,000 or more: 7.8% (2010); Poverty rate: 31.8% (2005-2009 5-year est.).
Taxes: Total city taxes per capita: $545 (2007); City property taxes per capita: $217 (2007).

Education: Percent of population age 25 and over with: High school diploma (including GED) or higher: 62.0% (2010); Bachelor's degree or higher: 14.4% (2010); Master's degree or higher: 3.7% (2010).

School District(s)

Edinburg CISD (PK-12)
  2009-10 Enrollment: 32,011 . . . . (956) 289-2300
Idea Public Schools (PK-12)
  2009-10 Enrollment: 5,515 . . . . (956) 377-8000
One Stop Multiservice Charter School (PK-12)
  2009-10 Enrollment: 746 . . . . (956) 393-2227
Santa Maria ISD (PK-12)
  2009-10 Enrollment: 666 . . . . (956) 565-6308
South Texas Educational Technologies Inc (PK-06)
  2009-10 Enrollment: 620 . . . . (956) 969-3092
Weslaco ISD (PK-12)
  2009-10 Enrollment: 17,279 . . . . (956) 969-6500

Vocational/Technical School(s)

Advanced Barber College and Hair Design (Private, For-profit)
  Fall 2009 Enrollment: 117 . . . . (956) 969-0341
  2010-11 Tuition: $6,810
South Texas Vo-Tech Institute (Private, For-profit)
  Fall 2009 Enrollment: 818 . . . . (956) 969-1564
  2010-11 Tuition: $16,700
Valley Grande Institute for Academic Studies (Private, Not-for-profit)
  Fall 2009 Enrollment: 454 . . . . (956) 973-1945
  2010-11 Tuition: $22,185

Housing: Homeownership rate: 62.1% (2010); Median home value: $58,243 (2010); Median contract rent: $356 per month (2005-2009 5-year est.); Median year structure built: 1984 (2005-2009 5-year est.).

Hospitals: Knapp Medical Center (200 beds)

Safety: Violent crime rate: 65.3 per 10,000 population; Property crime rate: 730.9 per 10,000 population (2009).

Transportation: Commute to work: 94.6% car, 0.1% public transportation, 1.5% walk, 0.9% work from home (2005-2009 5-year est.); Travel time to work: 45.5% less than 15 minutes, 35.3% 15 to 30 minutes, 13.6% 30 to 45 minutes, 3.5% 45 to 60 minutes, 2.1% 60 minutes or more (2005-2009 5-year est.)

Additional Information Contacts

City of Weslaco . . . . (956) 968-3181
  http://www.weslacotx.gov
Weslaco Chamber of Commerce. (956) 968-2102
  http://www.weslaco.com

WEST SHARYLAND (CDP).

Covers a land area of 2.310 square miles and a water area of 0 square miles. Located at 26.27° N. Lat; 98.33° W. Long. Elevation is 171 feet.

Population: 948 (1990); 2,947 (2000); 3,775 (2010); 4,218 (2015 projected); Race: 87.9% White, 0.0% Black, 0.1% Asian, 11.9% Other, 98.3% Hispanic of any race (2010); Density: 1,633.9 persons per square mile (2010); Average household size: 4.14 (2010); Median age: 24.1 (2010); Males per 100 females: 95.8 (2010); Marriage status: 21.7% never married, 73.1% now married, 1.8% widowed, 3.4% divorced (2005-2009 5-year est.); Foreign born: 42.7% (2005-2009 5-year est.); Ancestry (includes multiple ancestries): 3.6% German (2005-2009 5-year est.).

Economy: Employment by occupation: 6.1% management, 14.8% professional, 36.9% services, 7.9% sales, 1.0% farming, 13.1% construction, 20.3% production (2005-2009 5-year est.).

Income: Per capita income: $7,454 (2010); Median household income: $23,781 (2010); Average household income: $30,752 (2010); Percent of households with income of $100,000 or more: 3.1% (2010); Poverty rate: 43.9% (2005-2009 5-year est.).

Education: Percent of population age 25 and over with: High school diploma (including GED) or higher: 35.7% (2010); Bachelor's degree or higher: 5.1% (2010); Master's degree or higher: 1.8% (2010).

Housing: Homeownership rate: 76.0% (2010); Median home value: $63,548 (2010); Median contract rent: $451 per month (2005-2009 5-year est.); Median year structure built: 1992 (2005-2009 5-year est.).

Transportation: Commute to work: 83.0% car, 0.0% public transportation, 0.0% walk, 2.1% work from home (2005-2009 5-year est.); Travel time to work: 30.7% less than 15 minutes, 30.6% 15 to 30 minutes, 33.2% 30 to 45 minutes, 0.0% 45 to 60 minutes, 5.5% 60 minutes or more (2005-2009 5-year est.)

Hill County

Located in north central Texas; bounded on the west by the Brazos River. Covers a land area of 962.36 square miles, a water area of 23.29 square miles, and is located in the Central Time Zone at 31.99° N. Lat., 97.15° W. Long. The county was founded in 1853. County seat is Hillsboro.

Weather Station: Hillsboro   Elevation: 549 feet

	Jan	Feb	Mar	Apr	May	Jun	Jul	Aug	Sep	Oct	Nov	Dec
High	59	63	70	77	84	90	95	96	89	79	68	59
Low	36	40	47	54	63	70	73	73	66	56	46	38
Precip	2.4	2.9	3.7	3.0	4.5	4.1	1.4	2.1	2.9	4.3	2.9	3.1
Snow	0.3	0.2	0.1	0.0	0.0	0.0	0.0	0.0	0.0	0.0	0.0	0.1

High and Low temperatures in degrees Fahrenheit; Precipitation and Snow in inches

Population: 27,146 (1990); 32,321 (2000); 36,247 (2010); 38,091 (2015 projected); Race: 81.6% White, 6.9% Black, 0.4% Asian, 11.1% Other, 18.7% Hispanic of any race (2010); Density: 37.7 persons per square mile (2010); Average household size: 2.60 (2010); Median age: 37.1 (2010); Males per 100 females: 98.6 (2010).

Religion: Five largest groups: 22.5% Southern Baptist Convention, 7.0% The United Methodist Church, 4.8% Catholic Church, 3.0% Baptist Missionary Association of America, 3.0% Churches of Christ (2000).

Economy: Unemployment rate: 9.3% (June 2011); Total civilian labor force: 16,269 (June 2011); Leading industries: 23.3% retail trade; 16.3% health care and social assistance; 14.3% accommodation & food services (2009); Farms: 2,113 totaling 524,907 acres (2007); Companies that employ 500 or more persons: 0 (2009); Companies that employ 100 to 499 persons: 8 (2009); Companies that employ less than 100 persons: 671 (2009); Black-owned businesses: n/a (2007); Hispanic-owned businesses: 204 (2007); Asian-owned businesses: n/a (2007); Women-owned businesses: 751 (2007); Retail sales per capita: $18,125 (2010). Single-family building permits issued: 9 (2010); Multi-family building permits issued: 0 (2010).

Income: Per capita income: $19,563 (2010); Median household income: $40,300 (2010); Average household income: $51,658 (2010); Percent of households with income of $100,000 or more: 10.5% (2010); Poverty rate: 16.0% (2009); Bankruptcy rate: 2.18% (2010).

Taxes: Total county taxes per capita: $236 (2007); County property taxes per capita: $145 (2007).

Education: Percent of population age 25 and over with: High school diploma (including GED) or higher: 77.3% (2010); Bachelor's degree or higher: 14.1% (2010); Master's degree or higher: 3.5% (2010).

Housing: Homeownership rate: 76.5% (2010); Median home value: $82,357 (2010); Median contract rent: $402 per month (2005-2009 5-year est.); Median year structure built: 1976 (2005-2009 5-year est.)

Health: Birth rate: 137.6 per 10,000 population (2009); Death rate: 111.3 per 10,000 population (2009); Age-adjusted cancer mortality rate: 215.9 deaths per 100,000 population (2007); Number of physicians: 4.8 per 10,000 population (2008); Hospital beds: 31.8 per 10,000 population (2007); Hospital admissions: 1,052.4 per 10,000 population (2007).

Elections: 2008 Presidential election results: 28.9% Obama, 70.2% McCain, 0.0% Nader

National and State Parks: Lake Whitney State Park

Additional Information Contacts

Hill County Government. . . . . (254) 582-4020
  http://www.co.hill.tx.us/ips/cms
City of Hillsboro . . . . (254) 582-3271
  http://www.hillsborotx.org
Hillsboro Chamber of Commerce. . . . . (254) 582-2481
  http://www.hillsborochamber.org
Hubbard Chamber of Commerce. . . . . (254) 576-2521
  http://hubbardchamber.com
Whitney Chamber of Commerce . . . . (254) 694-2540
  http://www.lakewhitneychamber.com

Hill County Communities

ABBOTT (city).

Covers a land area of 0.579 square miles and a water area of 0 square miles. Located at 31.88° N. Lat; 97.07° W. Long. Elevation is 712 feet.

Population: 348 (1990); 300 (2000); 316 (2010); 324 (2015 projected); Race: 94.3% White, 0.6% Black, 0.3% Asian, 4.7% Other, 9.8% Hispanic of any race (2010); Density: 545.6 persons per square mile (2010); Average household size: 2.59 (2010); Median age: 38.6 (2010); Males per 100 females: 107.9 (2010); Marriage status: 30.5% never married, 54.5%

now married, 7.6% widowed, 7.3% divorced (2005-2009 5-year est.); Foreign born: 0.0% (2005-2009 5-year est.); Ancestry (includes multiple ancestries): 37.4% Czech, 20.6% Irish, 14.6% German, 5.4% English, 5.4% French (2005-2009 5-year est.).
Economy: Employment by occupation: 11.8% management, 23.0% professional, 21.4% services, 20.3% sales, 2.1% farming, 11.2% construction, 10.2% production (2005-2009 5-year est.).
Income: Per capita income: $19,951 (2010); Median household income: $42,500 (2010); Average household income: $50,430 (2010); Percent of households with income of $100,000 or more: 10.7% (2010); Poverty rate: 2.0% (2005-2009 5-year est.).
Taxes: Total city taxes per capita: $6 (2007); City property taxes per capita: $0 (2007).
Education: Percent of population age 25 and over with: High school diploma (including GED) or higher: 82.6% (2010); Bachelor's degree or higher: 23.7% (2010); Master's degree or higher: 6.8% (2010).

School District(s)

Abbott ISD (PK-12)
    2009-10 Enrollment: 297 . . . . (254) 582-3011
Housing: Homeownership rate: 82.8% (2010); Median home value: $103,409 (2010); Median contract rent: $363 per month (2005-2009 5-year est.); Median year structure built: 1952 (2005-2009 5-year est.).
Transportation: Commute to work: 93.0% car, 0.0% public transportation, 0.0% walk, 5.4% work from home (2005-2009 5-year est.); Travel time to work: 45.1% less than 15 minutes, 15.4% 15 to 30 minutes, 20.6% 30 to 45 minutes, 12.0% 45 to 60 minutes, 6.9% 60 minutes or more (2005-2009 5-year est.)

AQUILLA (city). Covers a land area of 0.278 square miles and a water area of 0 square miles. Located at 31.85° N. Lat; 97.21° W. Long. Elevation is 522 feet.
Population: 136 (1990); 136 (2000); 151 (2010); 158 (2015 projected); Race: 92.1% White, 0.7% Black, 0.0% Asian, 7.3% Other, 7.3% Hispanic of any race (2010); Density: 542.2 persons per square mile (2010); Average household size: 2.60 (2010); Median age: 38.4 (2010); Males per 100 females: 96.1 (2010); Marriage status: 26.0% never married, 69.0% now married, 2.0% widowed, 3.0% divorced (2005-2009 5-year est.); Foreign born: 0.0% (2005-2009 5-year est.); Ancestry (includes multiple ancestries): 39.5% Irish, 28.6% German, 19.3% English, 6.7% Polish, 5.0% American (2005-2009 5-year est.).
Economy: Employment by occupation: 23.3% management, 6.8% professional, 12.3% services, 20.5% sales, 0.0% farming, 16.4% construction, 20.5% production (2005-2009 5-year est.).
Income: Per capita income: $21,484 (2010); Median household income: $50,000 (2010); Average household income: $60,129 (2010); Percent of households with income of $100,000 or more: 15.5% (2010); Poverty rate: 0.0% (2005-2009 5-year est.).
Taxes: Total city taxes per capita: $66 (2007); City property taxes per capita: $66 (2007).
Education: Percent of population age 25 and over with: High school diploma (including GED) or higher: 81.4% (2010); Bachelor's degree or higher: 12.7% (2010); Master's degree or higher: 2.9% (2010).

School District(s)

Aquilla ISD (PK-12)
    2009-10 Enrollment: 237 . . . . (254) 694-3770
Housing: Homeownership rate: 81.0% (2010); Median home value: $98,333 (2010); Median contract rent: $467 per month (2005-2009 5-year est.); Median year structure built: 1954 (2005-2009 5-year est.).
Transportation: Commute to work: 97.3% car, 0.0% public transportation, 2.7% walk, 0.0% work from home (2005-2009 5-year est.); Travel time to work: 6.8% less than 15 minutes, 24.7% 15 to 30 minutes, 28.8% 30 to 45 minutes, 27.4% 45 to 60 minutes, 12.3% 60 minutes or more (2005-2009 5-year est.)

BLUM (town). Covers a land area of 1.008 square miles and a water area of 0 square miles. Located at 32.14° N. Lat; 97.39° W. Long. Elevation is 591 feet.
Population: 358 (1990); 399 (2000); 418 (2010); 423 (2015 projected); Race: 94.7% White, 0.7% Black, 0.0% Asian, 4.5% Other, 5.0% Hispanic of any race (2010); Density: 414.7 persons per square mile (2010); Average household size: 2.56 (2010); Median age: 36.0 (2010); Males per 100 females: 100.0 (2010); Marriage status: 26.4% never married, 58.7% now married, 6.3% widowed, 8.6% divorced (2005-2009 5-year est.); Foreign born: 0.7% (2005-2009 5-year est.); Ancestry (includes multiple

ancestries): 43.3% English, 10.4% Irish, 8.9% German, 8.4% Scottish, 8.2% American (2005-2009 5-year est.).
Economy: Employment by occupation: 7.5% management, 7.5% professional, 9.4% services, 22.6% sales, 0.0% farming, 38.2% construction, 14.6% production (2005-2009 5-year est.).
Income: Per capita income: $20,497 (2010); Median household income: $44,300 (2010); Average household income: $51,518 (2010); Percent of households with income of $100,000 or more: 9.8% (2010); Poverty rate: 20.0% (2005-2009 5-year est.).
Taxes: Total city taxes per capita: $112 (2007); City property taxes per capita: $63 (2007).
Education: Percent of population age 25 and over with: High school diploma (including GED) or higher: 77.0% (2010); Bachelor's degree or higher: 12.3% (2010); Master's degree or higher: 2.2% (2010).

School District(s)

Blum ISD (PK-12)
    2009-10 Enrollment: 375 . . . . (254) 874-5231
Housing: Homeownership rate: 82.2% (2010); Median home value: $69,000 (2010); Median contract rent: $389 per month (2005-2009 5-year est.); Median year structure built: 1975 (2005-2009 5-year est.).
Transportation: Commute to work: 93.6% car, 0.0% public transportation, 4.0% walk, 0.0% work from home (2005-2009 5-year est.); Travel time to work: 25.7% less than 15 minutes, 14.9% 15 to 30 minutes, 36.1% 30 to 45 minutes, 3.0% 45 to 60 minutes, 20.3% 60 minutes or more (2005-2009 5-year est.)

BYNUM (town). Covers a land area of 0.146 square miles and a water area of 0 square miles. Located at 31.97° N. Lat; 97.00° W. Long. Elevation is 653 feet.
Population: 205 (1990); 225 (2000); 252 (2010); 266 (2015 projected); Race: 87.3% White, 1.2% Black, 0.4% Asian, 11.1% Other, 13.5% Hispanic of any race (2010); Density: 1,725.4 persons per square mile (2010); Average household size: 2.61 (2010); Median age: 39.3 (2010); Males per 100 females: 106.6 (2010); Marriage status: 40.0% never married, 47.6% now married, 1.6% widowed, 10.8% divorced (2005-2009 5-year est.); Foreign born: 0.0% (2005-2009 5-year est.); Ancestry (includes multiple ancestries): 36.8% Irish, 20.5% German, 15.5% French, 14.5% Norwegian, 10.0% English (2005-2009 5-year est.).
Economy: Employment by occupation: 15.7% management, 3.5% professional, 31.3% services, 16.5% sales, 0.0% farming, 4.3% construction, 28.7% production (2005-2009 5-year est.).
Income: Per capita income: $20,885 (2010); Median household income: $45,714 (2010); Average household income: $54,167 (2010); Percent of households with income of $100,000 or more: 12.5% (2010); Poverty rate: 21.4% (2005-2009 5-year est.).
Taxes: Total city taxes per capita: $270 (2007); City property taxes per capita: $238 (2007).
Education: Percent of population age 25 and over with: High school diploma (including GED) or higher: 80.9% (2010); Bachelor's degree or higher: 18.5% (2010); Master's degree or higher: 4.0% (2010).

School District(s)

Bynum ISD (PK-12)
    2009-10 Enrollment: 233 . . . . (254) 623-4251
Housing: Homeownership rate: 84.4% (2010); Median home value: $89,000 (2010); Median contract rent: $413 per month (2005-2009 5-year est.); Median year structure built: before 1940 (2005-2009 5-year est.).
Transportation: Commute to work: 88.3% car, 0.0% public transportation, 5.4% walk, 0.0% work from home (2005-2009 5-year est.); Travel time to work: 40.5% less than 15 minutes, 39.6% 15 to 30 minutes, 1.8% 30 to 45 minutes, 6.3% 45 to 60 minutes, 11.7% 60 minutes or more (2005-2009 5-year est.)

CARL'S CORNER (town). Covers a land area of 1.905 square miles and a water area of 0.004 square miles. Located at 32.08° N. Lat; 97.04° W. Long.
Population: 94 (1990); 134 (2000); 150 (2010); 158 (2015 projected); Race: 82.0% White, 6.0% Black, 2.0% Asian, 10.0% Other, 16.0% Hispanic of any race (2010); Density: 78.8 persons per square mile (2010); Average household size: 2.58 (2010); Median age: 35.0 (2010); Males per 100 females: 94.8 (2010); Marriage status: 13.0% never married, 77.4% now married, 1.1% widowed, 8.5% divorced (2005-2009 5-year est.); Foreign born: 0.0% (2005-2009 5-year est.); Ancestry (includes multiple ancestries): 53.4% German, 33.5% Irish, 8.1% Italian, 7.7% French, 7.2% Scotch-Irish (2005-2009 5-year est.).

Economy: Employment by occupation: 23.9% management, 19.7% professional, 29.6% services, 0.0% sales, 0.0% farming, 5.6% construction, 21.1% production (2005-2009 5-year est.).
Income: Per capita income: $19,103 (2010); Median household income: $45,714 (2010); Average household income: $57,552 (2010); Percent of households with income of $100,000 or more: 14.6% (2010); Poverty rate: 4.5% (2005-2009 5-year est.).
Taxes: Total city taxes per capita: $119 (2007); City property taxes per capita: $0 (2007).
Education: Percent of population age 25 and over with: High school diploma (including GED) or higher: 80.0% (2010); Bachelor's degree or higher: 8.4% (2010); Master's degree or higher: 3.2% (2010).
Housing: Homeownership rate: 72.9% (2010); Median home value: $125,000 (2010); Median contract rent: $238 per month (2005-2009 5-year est.); Median year structure built: 1984 (2005-2009 5-year est.).
Transportation: Commute to work: 100.0% car, 0.0% public transportation, 0.0% walk, 0.0% work from home (2005-2009 5-year est.); Travel time to work: 26.7% less than 15 minutes, 48.3% 15 to 30 minutes, 0.0% 30 to 45 minutes, 1.7% 45 to 60 minutes, 23.3% 60 minutes or more (2005-2009 5-year est.)

COVINGTON (city). Covers a land area of 0.830 square miles and a water area of 0 square miles. Located at 32.17° N. Lat; 97.25° W. Long. Elevation is 758 feet.
Population: 238 (1990); 282 (2000); 345 (2010); 371 (2015 projected); Race: 85.2% White, 2.9% Black, 0.0% Asian, 11.9% Other, 18.6% Hispanic of any race (2010); Density: 415.7 persons per square mile (2010); Average household size: 2.75 (2010); Median age: 33.9 (2010); Males per 100 females: 106.6 (2010); Marriage status: 37.2% never married, 39.9% now married, 2.2% widowed, 20.6% divorced (2005-2009 5-year est.); Foreign born: 3.4% (2005-2009 5-year est.); Ancestry (includes multiple ancestries): 24.3% English, 23.2% Irish, 13.5% American, 7.1% German, 2.6% Swiss (2005-2009 5-year est.).
Economy: Single-family building permits issued: 0 (2010); Multi-family building permits issued: 0 (2010); Employment by occupation: 7.5% management, 9.8% professional, 12.0% services, 19.5% sales, 15.8% farming, 21.1% construction, 14.3% production (2005-2009 5-year est.).
Income: Per capita income: $22,929 (2010); Median household income: $54,464 (2010); Average household income: $67,036 (2010); Percent of households with income of $100,000 or more: 16.1% (2010); Poverty rate: 14.6% (2005-2009 5-year est.).
Taxes: Total city taxes per capita: $316 (2007); City property taxes per capita: $199 (2007).
Education: Percent of population age 25 and over with: High school diploma (including GED) or higher: 81.9% (2010); Bachelor's degree or higher: 13.0% (2010); Master's degree or higher: 3.2% (2010).
School District(s)
Covington ISD (PK-12)
   2009-10 Enrollment: 299 . . . . (254) 854-2215
Housing: Homeownership rate: 80.6% (2010); Median home value: $98,462 (2010); Median contract rent: $475 per month (2005-2009 5-year est.); Median year structure built: 1955 (2005-2009 5-year est.).
Transportation: Commute to work: 93.9% car, 0.0% public transportation, 1.5% walk, 2.3% work from home (2005-2009 5-year est.); Travel time to work: 17.2% less than 15 minutes, 26.6% 15 to 30 minutes, 16.4% 30 to 45 minutes, 25.8% 45 to 60 minutes, 14.1% 60 minutes or more (2005-2009 5-year est.)

HILLSBORO (city). County seat. Covers a land area of 9.065 square miles and a water area of 0.095 square miles. Located at 32.01° N. Lat; 97.12° W. Long. Elevation is 633 feet.
History: Hillsboro developed as the center of a wide cotton growing area. Early industries here were a textile mill, cotton gins, and a furniture factory.
Population: 7,085 (1990); 8,232 (2000); 8,845 (2010); 9,178 (2015 projected); Race: 66.4% White, 15.0% Black, 0.6% Asian, 18.0% Other, 39.2% Hispanic of any race (2010); Density: 975.7 persons per square mile (2010); Average household size: 2.77 (2010); Median age: 33.1 (2010); Males per 100 females: 100.1 (2010); Marriage status: 27.1% never married, 49.5% now married, 9.7% widowed, 13.6% divorced (2005-2009 5-year est.); Foreign born: 19.7% (2005-2009 5-year est.); Ancestry (includes multiple ancestries): 10.9% German, 8.9% Irish, 6.1% English, 5.3% American, 1.5% Scotch-Irish (2005-2009 5-year est.).
Economy: Single-family building permits issued: 4 (2010); Multi-family building permits issued: 0 (2010); Employment by occupation: 6.7%

management, 11.8% professional, 24.0% services, 14.3% sales, 2.9% farming, 21.0% construction, 19.2% production (2005-2009 5-year est.).
Income: Per capita income: $15,771 (2010); Median household income: $33,929 (2010); Average household income: $44,865 (2010); Percent of households with income of $100,000 or more: 7.4% (2010); Poverty rate: 30.4% (2005-2009 5-year est.).
Taxes: Total city taxes per capita: $653 (2007); City property taxes per capita: $270 (2007).
Education: Percent of population age 25 and over with: High school diploma (including GED) or higher: 69.2% (2010); Bachelor's degree or higher: 14.7% (2010); Master's degree or higher: 3.4% (2010).
School District(s)
Bynum ISD (PK-12)
   2009-10 Enrollment: 233 . . . . (254) 623-4251
Covington ISD (PK-12)
   2009-10 Enrollment: 299 . . . . (254) 854-2215
Ft Hancock ISD (PK-12)
   2009-10 Enrollment: 516 . . . . (915) 769-3811
Hillsboro ISD (PK-12)
   2009-10 Enrollment: 1,902 . . . . (254) 582-8585
Hubbard ISD (PK-12)
   2009-10 Enrollment: 399 . . . . (254) 576-2564
Malone ISD (PK-08)
   2009-10 Enrollment: 91 . . . . (254) 533-2321
Penelope ISD (PK-12)
   2009-10 Enrollment: 196 . . . . (254) 533-2215
Whitney ISD (PK-12)
   2009-10 Enrollment: 1,575 . . . . (254) 694-2254
Two-year College(s)
Hill College (Public)
   Fall 2009 Enrollment: 4,294 . . . . (254) 659-7500
   2010-11 Tuition: In-state $2,520; Out-of-state $2,920
Housing: Homeownership rate: 61.0% (2010); Median home value: $73,310 (2010); Median contract rent: $411 per month (2005-2009 5-year est.); Median year structure built: 1969 (2005-2009 5-year est.).
Hospitals: Hill Regional Hospital (92 beds)
Safety: Violent crime rate: 31.1 per 10,000 population; Property crime rate: 307.7 per 10,000 population (2009).
Newspapers: Reporter (Community news; Circulation 5,000)
Transportation: Commute to work: 96.5% car, 0.0% public transportation, 1.7% walk, 0.2% work from home (2005-2009 5-year est.); Travel time to work: 54.2% less than 15 minutes, 15.1% 15 to 30 minutes, 14.5% 30 to 45 minutes, 10.4% 45 to 60 minutes, 5.8% 60 minutes or more (2005-2009 5-year est.)
Additional Information Contacts
City of Hillsboro . . . . (254) 582-3271
   http://www.hillsborotx.org
Hillsboro Chamber of Commerce . . . . (254) 582-2481
   http://www.hillsborochamber.org

HUBBARD (city). Covers a land area of 1.980 square miles and a water area of 0.012 square miles. Located at 31.84° N. Lat; 96.79° W. Long. Elevation is 650 feet.
Population: 1,589 (1990); 1,586 (2000); 1,865 (2010); 2,002 (2015 projected); Race: 75.6% White, 16.1% Black, 0.8% Asian, 7.5% Other, 7.8% Hispanic of any race (2010); Density: 941.7 persons per square mile (2010); Average household size: 2.51 (2010); Median age: 36.2 (2010); Males per 100 females: 87.1 (2010); Marriage status: 26.5% never married, 47.3% now married, 11.8% widowed, 14.4% divorced (2005-2009 5-year est.); Foreign born: 0.3% (2005-2009 5-year est.); Ancestry (includes multiple ancestries): 21.4% Irish, 10.3% German, 9.4% American, 8.5% English, 4.3% French (2005-2009 5-year est.).
Economy: Single-family building permits issued: 0 (2010); Multi-family building permits issued: 0 (2010); Employment by occupation: 12.5% management, 15.9% professional, 28.8% services, 17.8% sales, 0.0% farming, 8.0% construction, 17.1% production (2005-2009 5-year est.).
Income: Per capita income: $19,305 (2010); Median household income: $36,316 (2010); Average household income: $49,685 (2010); Percent of households with income of $100,000 or more: 10.2% (2010); Poverty rate: 28.7% (2005-2009 5-year est.).
Taxes: Total city taxes per capita: $260 (2007); City property taxes per capita: $150 (2007).
Education: Percent of population age 25 and over with: High school diploma (including GED) or higher: 81.5% (2010); Bachelor's degree or higher: 14.8% (2010); Master's degree or higher: 3.9% (2010).

School District(s)

Hubbard ISD (PK-12)

   2009-10 Enrollment: 399 . . . . (254) 576-2564

Housing: Homeownership rate: 76.5% (2010); Median home value: $63,881 (2010); Median contract rent: $342 per month (2005-2009 5-year est.); Median year structure built: 1963 (2005-2009 5-year est.).

Safety: Violent crime rate: 11.3 per 10,000 population; Property crime rate: 22.6 per 10,000 population (2009).

Transportation: Commute to work: 94.6% car, 0.0% public transportation, 2.7% walk, 2.0% work from home (2005-2009 5-year est.); Travel time to work: 32.9% less than 15 minutes, 7.9% 15 to 30 minutes, 26.2% 30 to 45 minutes, 16.1% 45 to 60 minutes, 16.8% 60 minutes or more (2005-2009 5-year est.)

Additional Information Contacts

Hubbard Chamber of Commerce . . . . (254) 576-2521
   http://hubbardchamber.com

ITASCA (city). Covers a land area of 1.209 square miles and a water area of 0 square miles. Located at 32.15° N. Lat; 97.14° W. Long. Elevation is 702 feet.

History: Itasca developed around a textile mill.

Population: 1,523 (1990); 1,503 (2000); 1,744 (2010); 1,857 (2015 projected); Race: 60.4% White, 13.0% Black, 0.1% Asian, 26.5% Other, 30.4% Hispanic of any race (2010); Density: 1,442.2 persons per square mile (2010); Average household size: 2.67 (2010); Median age: 35.3 (2010); Males per 100 females: 101.2 (2010); Marriage status: 22.8% never married, 55.9% now married, 11.3% widowed, 10.0% divorced (2005-2009 5-year est.); Foreign born: 19.6% (2005-2009 5-year est.); Ancestry (includes multiple ancestries): 15.0% German, 11.0% Irish, 7.2% English, 5.6% American, 4.0% Italian (2005-2009 5-year est.).

Economy: Single-family building permits issued: 0 (2010); Multi-family building permits issued: 0 (2010); Employment by occupation: 4.6% management, 6.2% professional, 27.9% services, 14.0% sales, 1.6% farming, 20.2% construction, 25.5% production (2005-2009 5-year est.).

Income: Per capita income: $18,773 (2010); Median household income: $41,260 (2010); Average household income: $51,638 (2010); Percent of households with income of $100,000 or more: 8.2% (2010); Poverty rate: 28.7% (2005-2009 5-year est.).

Taxes: Total city taxes per capita: $165 (2007); City property taxes per capita: $0 (2007).

Education: Percent of population age 25 and over with: High school diploma (including GED) or higher: 69.3% (2010); Bachelor's degree or higher: 11.2% (2010); Master's degree or higher: 2.0% (2010).

School District(s)

Itasca ISD (PK-12)

   2009-10 Enrollment: 742 . . . . (254) 687-2922

Housing: Homeownership rate: 76.3% (2010); Median home value: $63,947 (2010); Median contract rent: $364 per month (2005-2009 5-year est.); Median year structure built: 1964 (2005-2009 5-year est.).

Safety: Violent crime rate: 5.8 per 10,000 population; Property crime rate: 75.7 per 10,000 population (2009).

Transportation: Commute to work: 93.5% car, 0.0% public transportation, 0.4% walk, 1.2% work from home (2005-2009 5-year est.); Travel time to work: 27.1% less than 15 minutes, 33.9% 15 to 30 minutes, 21.6% 30 to 45 minutes, 9.0% 45 to 60 minutes, 8.4% 60 minutes or more (2005-2009 5-year est.)

MALONE (town). Covers a land area of 0.458 square miles and a water area of 0 square miles. Located at 31.91° N. Lat; 96.89° W. Long. Elevation is 479 feet.

Population: 306 (1990); 278 (2000); 282 (2010); 279 (2015 projected); Race: 83.3% White, 5.7% Black, 0.0% Asian, 11.0% Other, 20.2% Hispanic of any race (2010); Density: 615.3 persons per square mile (2010); Average household size: 2.56 (2010); Median age: 36.4 (2010); Males per 100 females: 102.9 (2010); Marriage status: 19.1% never married, 51.6% now married, 3.2% widowed, 26.1% divorced (2005-2009 5-year est.); Foreign born: 1.3% (2005-2009 5-year est.); Ancestry (includes multiple ancestries): 52.0% German, 24.9% Irish, 17.0% English, 5.7% Czech, 4.8% Welsh (2005-2009 5-year est.).

Economy: Employment by occupation: 11.6% management, 15.8% professional, 15.8% services, 15.8% sales, 0.0% farming, 31.6% construction, 9.5% production (2005-2009 5-year est.).

Income: Per capita income: $19,480 (2010); Median household income: $40,833 (2010); Average household income: $52,341 (2010); Percent of

households with income of $100,000 or more: 11.8% (2010); Poverty rate: 11.8% (2005-2009 5-year est.).

Taxes: Total city taxes per capita: $164 (2007); City property taxes per capita: $98 (2007).

Education: Percent of population age 25 and over with: High school diploma (including GED) or higher: 77.0% (2010); Bachelor's degree or higher: 12.3% (2010); Master's degree or higher: 2.7% (2010).

School District(s)

Malone ISD (PK-08)

   2009-10 Enrollment: 91 . . . . (254) 533-2321

Housing: Homeownership rate: 81.8% (2010); Median home value: $60,000 (2010); Median contract rent: n/a per month (2005-2009 5-year est.); Median year structure built: 1956 (2005-2009 5-year est.).

Transportation: Commute to work: 87.9% car, 0.0% public transportation, 0.0% walk, 5.5% work from home (2005-2009 5-year est.); Travel time to work: 7.0% less than 15 minutes, 46.5% 15 to 30 minutes, 15.1% 30 to 45 minutes, 18.6% 45 to 60 minutes, 12.8% 60 minutes or more (2005-2009 5-year est.)

MERTENS (town). Covers a land area of 0.439 square miles and a water area of 0 square miles. Located at 32.05° N. Lat; 96.89° W. Long. Elevation is 538 feet.

Population: 104 (1990); 146 (2000); 163 (2010); 172 (2015 projected); Race: 87.1% White, 1.2% Black, 0.0% Asian, 11.7% Other, 14.1% Hispanic of any race (2010); Density: 371.0 persons per square mile (2010); Average household size: 2.61 (2010); Median age: 41.4 (2010); Males per 100 females: 111.7 (2010); Marriage status: 16.7% never married, 58.3% now married, 22.9% widowed, 2.1% divorced (2005-2009 5-year est.); Foreign born: 23.5% (2005-2009 5-year est.); Ancestry (includes multiple ancestries): 16.2% Irish, 5.9% English, 4.4% American, 4.4% German, 4.4% French (2005-2009 5-year est.).

Economy: Employment by occupation: 15.2% management, 23.9% professional, 6.5% services, 10.9% sales, 4.3% farming, 28.3% construction, 10.9% production (2005-2009 5-year est.).

Income: Per capita income: $20,885 (2010); Median household income: $45,500 (2010); Average household income: $52,218 (2010); Percent of households with income of $100,000 or more: 12.9% (2010); Poverty rate: 8.1% (2005-2009 5-year est.).

Taxes: Total city taxes per capita: $62 (2007); City property taxes per capita: $62 (2007).

Education: Percent of population age 25 and over with: High school diploma (including GED) or higher: 81.0% (2010); Bachelor's degree or higher: 19.0% (2010); Master's degree or higher: 5.2% (2010).

Housing: Homeownership rate: 83.9% (2010); Median home value: $90,000 (2010); Median contract rent: n/a per month (2005-2009 5-year est.); Median year structure built: 1959 (2005-2009 5-year est.).

Transportation: Commute to work: 100.0% car, 0.0% public transportation, 0.0% walk, 0.0% work from home (2005-2009 5-year est.); Travel time to work: 18.6% less than 15 minutes, 20.9% 15 to 30 minutes, 4.7% 30 to 45 minutes, 44.2% 45 to 60 minutes, 11.6% 60 minutes or more (2005-2009 5-year est.)

MOUNT CALM (city). Covers a land area of 0.834 square miles and a water area of 0.003 square miles. Located at 31.75° N. Lat; 96.88° W. Long. Elevation is 604 feet.

Population: 303 (1990); 310 (2000); 382 (2010); 415 (2015 projected); Race: 84.0% White, 11.5% Black, 0.8% Asian, 3.7% Other, 3.7% Hispanic of any race (2010); Density: 458.2 persons per square mile (2010); Average household size: 2.59 (2010); Median age: 37.3 (2010); Males per 100 females: 87.3 (2010); Marriage status: 9.0% never married, 74.4% now married, 9.4% widowed, 7.3% divorced (2005-2009 5-year est.); Foreign born: 0.0% (2005-2009 5-year est.); Ancestry (includes multiple ancestries): 22.3% German, 18.9% Irish, 16.2% English, 4.8% Czech, 4.5% Scotch-Irish (2005-2009 5-year est.).

Economy: Employment by occupation: 6.9% management, 28.4% professional, 14.7% services, 16.7% sales, 2.9% farming, 13.7% construction, 16.7% production (2005-2009 5-year est.).

Income: Per capita income: $20,126 (2010); Median household income: $42,143 (2010); Average household income: $50,993 (2010); Percent of households with income of $100,000 or more: 11.6% (2010); Poverty rate: 26.5% (2005-2009 5-year est.).

Taxes: Total city taxes per capita: $96 (2007); City property taxes per capita: $81 (2007).

Education: Percent of population age 25 and over with: High school diploma (including GED) or higher: 85.5% (2010); Bachelor's degree or higher: 11.4% (2010); Master's degree or higher: 2.7% (2010).

School District(s)

Mount Calm ISD (PK-08)

   2009-10 Enrollment: 154 . . . . (254) 993-2611

Housing: Homeownership rate: 81.5% (2010); Median home value: $81,000 (2010); Median contract rent: $325 per month (2005-2009 5-year est.); Median year structure built: 1961 (2005-2009 5-year est.).

Transportation: Commute to work: 91.9% car, 0.0% public transportation, 3.0% walk, 5.1% work from home (2005-2009 5-year est.); Travel time to work: 18.1% less than 15 minutes, 27.7% 15 to 30 minutes, 31.9% 30 to 45 minutes, 14.9% 45 to 60 minutes, 7.4% 60 minutes or more (2005-2009 5-year est.)

PENELOPE (town). Covers a land area of 1.021 square miles and a water area of 0 square miles. Located at 31.85° N. Lat; 96.92° W. Long. Elevation is 568 feet.

Population: 210 (1990); 211 (2000); 204 (2010); 202 (2015 projected); Race: 83.3% White, 5.9% Black, 0.0% Asian, 10.8% Other, 20.1% Hispanic of any race (2010); Density: 199.8 persons per square mile (2010); Average household size: 2.58 (2010); Median age: 37.1 (2010); Males per 100 females: 104.0 (2010); Marriage status: 19.8% never married, 57.7% now married, 15.0% widowed, 7.5% divorced (2005-2009 5-year est.); Foreign born: 2.2% (2005-2009 5-year est.); Ancestry (includes multiple ancestries): 32.6% Czech, 12.6% German, 11.7% Irish, 7.4% Dutch, 4.3% French (2005-2009 5-year est.).

Economy: Employment by occupation: 12.1% management, 15.0% professional, 23.7% services, 20.2% sales, 1.2% farming, 17.3% construction, 10.4% production (2005-2009 5-year est.).

Income: Per capita income: $19,481 (2010); Median household income: $40,893 (2010); Average household income: $49,177 (2010); Percent of households with income of $100,000 or more: 11.4% (2010); Poverty rate: 5.8% (2005-2009 5-year est.).

Taxes: Total city taxes per capita: $325 (2007); City property taxes per capita: $128 (2007).

Education: Percent of population age 25 and over with: High school diploma (including GED) or higher: 77.0% (2010); Bachelor's degree or higher: 13.3% (2010); Master's degree or higher: 3.0% (2010).

School District(s)

Penelope ISD (PK-12)

   2009-10 Enrollment: 196 . . . . (254) 533-2215

Housing: Homeownership rate: 82.3% (2010); Median home value: $63,750 (2010); Median contract rent: $438 per month (2005-2009 5-year est.); Median year structure built: 1954 (2005-2009 5-year est.).

Transportation: Commute to work: 91.6% car, 6.6% public transportation, 0.0% walk, 0.0% work from home (2005-2009 5-year est.); Travel time to work: 18.6% less than 15 minutes, 28.1% 15 to 30 minutes, 43.1% 30 to 45 minutes, 0.0% 45 to 60 minutes, 10.2% 60 minutes or more (2005-2009 5-year est.)

WHITNEY (town). Covers a land area of 1.619 square miles and a water area of 0 square miles. Located at 31.95° N. Lat; 97.32° W. Long. Elevation is 594 feet.

History: Established 1879.

Population: 1,654 (1990); 1,833 (2000); 2,087 (2010); 2,207 (2015 projected); Race: 88.1% White, 5.3% Black, 0.2% Asian, 6.5% Other, 16.1% Hispanic of any race (2010); Density: 1,289.2 persons per square mile (2010); Average household size: 2.54 (2010); Median age: 40.4 (2010); Males per 100 females: 83.1 (2010); Marriage status: 18.5% never married, 52.1% now married, 20.7% widowed, 8.7% divorced (2005-2009 5-year est.); Foreign born: 10.0% (2005-2009 5-year est.); Ancestry (includes multiple ancestries): 18.7% English, 13.8% Irish, 12.0% German, 11.2% American, 3.8% French (2005-2009 5-year est.).

Economy: Single-family building permits issued: 5 (2010); Multi-family building permits issued: 0 (2010); Employment by occupation: 6.2% management, 13.2% professional, 20.6% services, 27.6% sales, 0.8% farming, 17.1% construction, 14.5% production (2005-2009 5-year est.).

Income: Per capita income: $17,041 (2010); Median household income: $33,956 (2010); Average household income: $45,673 (2010); Percent of households with income of $100,000 or more: 7.6% (2010); Poverty rate: 17.2% (2005-2009 5-year est.).

Taxes: Total city taxes per capita: $428 (2007); City property taxes per capita: $162 (2007).

Education: Percent of population age 25 and over with: High school diploma (including GED) or higher: 71.8% (2010); Bachelor's degree or higher: 10.0% (2010); Master's degree or higher: 3.0% (2010).

School District(s)

Whitney ISD (PK-12)

   2009-10 Enrollment: 1,575 . . . . (254) 694-2254

Housing: Homeownership rate: 68.5% (2010); Median home value: $78,721 (2010); Median contract rent: $375 per month (2005-2009 5-year est.); Median year structure built: 1971 (2005-2009 5-year est.).

Hospitals: Lake Whitney Medical Center (49 beds)

Safety: Violent crime rate: 14.5 per 10,000 population; Property crime rate: 327.6 per 10,000 population (2009).

Transportation: Commute to work: 91.5% car, 0.0% public transportation, 2.2% walk, 5.1% work from home (2005-2009 5-year est.); Travel time to work: 46.9% less than 15 minutes, 25.3% 15 to 30 minutes, 12.8% 30 to 45 minutes, 6.3% 45 to 60 minutes, 8.8% 60 minutes or more (2005-2009 5-year est.)

Additional Information Contacts

Whitney Chamber of Commerce . . . . (254) 694-2540
   http://www.lakewhitneychamber.com

Hockley County

Located in northwestern Texas; bounded on the west by New Mexico; crossed by the Punta de Agua and Rita Blanca Rivers. Covers a land area of 908.28 square miles, a water area of 0.27 square miles, and is located in the Central Time Zone at 33.62° N. Lat., 102.36° W. Long. The county was founded in 1921. County seat is Levelland.

Hockley County is part of the Levelland, TX Micropolitan Statistical Area. The entire metro area includes: Hockley County, TX

Weather Station: Levelland									Elevation: 3,549 feet			
	Jan	Feb	Mar	Apr	May	Jun	Jul	Aug	Sep	Oct	Nov	Dec
High	54	59	67	75	84	91	93	91	84	75	64	54
Low	25	28	34	42	53	62	65	64	56	45	34	26
Precip	0.7	0.6	1.0	1.0	2.6	2.7	2.0	2.6	2.9	1.6	1.0	0.9
Snow	2.4	1.5	0.5	0.2	0.0	0.0	0.0	0.0	0.0	tr	1.0	2.6

High and Low temperatures in degrees Fahrenheit; Precipitation and Snow in inches

Population: 24,199 (1990); 22,716 (2000); 22,241 (2010); 21,972 (2015 projected); Race: 70.6% White, 3.6% Black, 0.2% Asian, 25.5% Other, 43.5% Hispanic of any race (2010); Density: 24.5 persons per square mile (2010); Average household size: 2.66 (2010); Median age: 33.6 (2010); Males per 100 females: 96.1 (2010).

Religion: Five largest groups: 40.1% Southern Baptist Convention, 20.4% Catholic Church, 6.8% The United Methodist Church, 6.6% Churches of Christ, 6.1% Baptist Missionary Association of America (2000).

Economy: Unemployment rate: 6.7% (June 2011); Total civilian labor force: 12,145 (June 2011); Leading industries: 18.4% health care and social assistance; 16.4% retail trade; 15.7% mining (2009); Farms: 842 totaling 484,286 acres (2007); Companies that employ 500 or more persons: 0 (2009); Companies that employ 100 to 499 persons: 8 (2009); Companies that employ less than 100 persons: 497 (2009); Black-owned businesses: n/a (2007); Hispanic-owned businesses: n/a (2007); Asian-owned businesses: n/a (2007); Women-owned businesses: 425 (2007); Retail sales per capita: $9,881 (2010). Single-family building permits issued: 8 (2010); Multi-family building permits issued: 0 (2010).

Income: Per capita income: $20,820 (2010); Median household income: $42,710 (2010); Average household income: $56,082 (2010); Percent of households with income of $100,000 or more: 12.2% (2010); Poverty rate: 16.7% (2009); Bankruptcy rate: 1.12% (2010).

Taxes: Total county taxes per capita: $370 (2007); County property taxes per capita: $351 (2007).

Education: Percent of population age 25 and over with: High school diploma (including GED) or higher: 72.8% (2010); Bachelor's degree or higher: 14.7% (2010); Master's degree or higher: 4.0% (2010).

Housing: Homeownership rate: 74.2% (2010); Median home value: $63,150 (2010); Median contract rent: $413 per month (2005-2009 5-year est.); Median year structure built: 1969 (2005-2009 5-year est.)

Health: Birth rate: 162.1 per 10,000 population (2009); Death rate: 86.2 per 10,000 population (2009); Age-adjusted cancer mortality rate: 171.1 deaths per 100,000 population (2007); Number of physicians: 6.7 per 10,000 population (2008); Hospital beds: 9.9 per 10,000 population (2007); Hospital admissions: 838.3 per 10,000 population (2007).

Elections: 2008 Presidential election results: 23.5% Obama, 75.8% McCain, 0.1% Nader

Additional Information Contacts

Hockley County Government . . . . (806) 894-6856
  http://www.co.hockley.tx.us/ips/cms
City of Levelland . . . . (806) 894-0113
  http://www.ci.levelland.tx.us
Levelland Chamber of Commerce . . . . (806) 894-3157
  http://www.levellandtexas.org

Hockley County Communities

ANTON (city). Covers a land area of 0.793 square miles and a water area of 0 square miles. Located at 33.81° N. Lat; 102.16° W. Long. Elevation is 3,389 feet.

Population: 1,212 (1990); 1,200 (2000); 1,111 (2010); 1,072 (2015 projected); Race: 71.9% White, 5.1% Black, 0.0% Asian, 23.0% Other, 48.2% Hispanic of any race (2010); Density: 1,400.2 persons per square mile (2010); Average household size: 2.73 (2010); Median age: 33.2 (2010); Males per 100 females: 94.9 (2010); Marriage status: 25.9% never married, 55.2% now married, 7.0% widowed, 12.0% divorced (2005-2009 5-year est.); Foreign born: 6.2% (2005-2009 5-year est.); Ancestry (includes multiple ancestries): 7.9% Irish, 4.4% English, 3.0% German, 2.9% Greek, 2.6% Polish (2005-2009 5-year est.).

Economy: Single-family building permits issued: 0 (2010); Multi-family building permits issued: 0 (2010); Employment by occupation: 8.8% management, 20.1% professional, 16.6% services, 23.1% sales, 1.7% farming, 10.7% construction, 18.9% production (2005-2009 5-year est.).

Income: Per capita income: $22,351 (2010); Median household income: $47,794 (2010); Average household income: $60,565 (2010); Percent of households with income of $100,000 or more: 12.0% (2010); Poverty rate: 23.1% (2005-2009 5-year est.).

Taxes: Total city taxes per capita: $142 (2007); City property taxes per capita: $86 (2007).

Education: Percent of population age 25 and over with: High school diploma (including GED) or higher: 67.5% (2010); Bachelor's degree or higher: 11.2% (2010); Master's degree or higher: 2.0% (2010).

School District(s)

Anton ISD (PK-12)
  2009-10 Enrollment: 271 . . . . (806) 997-2301

Housing: Homeownership rate: 73.7% (2010); Median home value: $48,732 (2010); Median contract rent: $268 per month (2005-2009 5-year est.); Median year structure built: 1960 (2005-2009 5-year est.).

Transportation: Commute to work: 97.3% car, 0.0% public transportation, 0.0% walk, 2.7% work from home (2005-2009 5-year est.); Travel time to work: 33.8% less than 15 minutes, 20.1% 15 to 30 minutes, 34.6% 30 to 45 minutes, 5.6% 45 to 60 minutes, 5.8% 60 minutes or more (2005-2009 5-year est.)

LEVELLAND (city). County seat. Covers a land area of 9.923 square miles and a water area of 0.017 square miles. Located at 33.58° N. Lat; 102.37° W. Long. Elevation is 3,520 feet.

History: Levelland was settled in 1921 as a station on the Panhandle & Santa Fe Railroad. Its name reflects the flat land on which it is located.

Population: 14,001 (1990); 12,866 (2000); 12,405 (2010); 12,177 (2015 projected); Race: 66.9% White, 4.9% Black, 0.3% Asian, 27.9% Other, 44.7% Hispanic of any race (2010); Density: 1,250.1 persons per square mile (2010); Average household size: 2.57 (2010); Median age: 33.1 (2010); Males per 100 females: 94.3 (2010); Marriage status: 27.1% never married, 57.9% now married, 6.8% widowed, 8.1% divorced (2005-2009 5-year est.); Foreign born: 6.1% (2005-2009 5-year est.); Ancestry (includes multiple ancestries): 10.5% German, 8.0% English, 7.0% Irish, 5.2% American, 2.9% Scotch-Irish (2005-2009 5-year est.).

Economy: Single-family building permits issued: 7 (2010); Multi-family building permits issued: 0 (2010); Employment by occupation: 9.6% management, 17.3% professional, 20.3% services, 24.7% sales, 1.5% farming, 16.5% construction, 10.1% production (2005-2009 5-year est.).

Income: Per capita income: $18,715 (2010); Median household income: $38,182 (2010); Average household income: $49,276 (2010); Percent of households with income of $100,000 or more: 9.5% (2010); Poverty rate: 19.3% (2005-2009 5-year est.).

Taxes: Total city taxes per capita: $371 (2007); City property taxes per capita: $189 (2007).

Education: Percent of population age 25 and over with: High school diploma (including GED) or higher: 72.2% (2010); Bachelor's degree or higher: 14.8% (2010); Master's degree or higher: 4.2% (2010).

School District(s)

Levelland ISD (PK-12)
  2009-10 Enrollment: 2,957 . . . . (806) 894-9628

Two-year College(s)

South Plains College (Public)
  Fall 2009 Enrollment: 10,011 . . . . (806) 894-9611
  2010-11 Tuition: In-state $1,946; Out-of-state $2,330

Housing: Homeownership rate: 71.3% (2010); Median home value: $63,021 (2010); Median contract rent: $446 per month (2005-2009 5-year est.); Median year structure built: 1967 (2005-2009 5-year est.).

Hospitals: Covenant Hospital Levelland (48 beds)

Safety: Violent crime rate: 56.4 per 10,000 population; Property crime rate: 397.3 per 10,000 population (2009).

Newspapers: Hockley County News-Press (Community news; Circulation 5,150)

Transportation: Commute to work: 93.9% car, 0.1% public transportation, 0.9% walk, 3.2% work from home (2005-2009 5-year est.); Travel time to work: 58.7% less than 15 minutes, 13.8% 15 to 30 minutes, 18.1% 30 to 45 minutes, 4.1% 45 to 60 minutes, 5.2% 60 minutes or more (2005-2009 5-year est.)

Additional Information Contacts

City of Levelland . . . . (806) 894-0113
  http://www.ci.levelland.tx.us
Levelland Chamber of Commerce . . . . (806) 894-3157
  http://www.levellandtexas.org

OPDYKE WEST (town). Covers a land area of 0.237 square miles and a water area of 0 square miles. Located at 33.59° N. Lat; 102.29° W. Long. Elevation is 3,471 feet.

Population: 100 (1990); 188 (2000); 224 (2010); 239 (2015 projected); Race: 77.2% White, 0.0% Black, 0.0% Asian, 22.8% Other, 30.8% Hispanic of any race (2010); Density: 943.6 persons per square mile (2010); Average household size: 2.64 (2010); Median age: 35.0 (2010); Males per 100 females: 101.8 (2010); Marriage status: 21.2% never married, 70.2% now married, 4.8% widowed, 3.8% divorced (2005-2009 5-year est.); Foreign born: 31.6% (2005-2009 5-year est.); Ancestry (includes multiple ancestries): 2.4% Irish, 2.4% German, 1.2% English, 1.2% American, 0.9% French Canadian (2005-2009 5-year est.).

Economy: Employment by occupation: 8.8% management, 0.0% professional, 9.6% services, 20.2% sales, 1.8% farming, 54.4% construction, 5.3% production (2005-2009 5-year est.).

Income: Per capita income: $23,967 (2010); Median household income: $53,804 (2010); Average household income: $62,912 (2010); Percent of households with income of $100,000 or more: 14.1% (2010); Poverty rate: 17.7% (2005-2009 5-year est.).

Education: Percent of population age 25 and over with: High school diploma (including GED) or higher: 79.1% (2010); Bachelor's degree or higher: 14.2% (2010); Master's degree or higher: 2.7% (2010).

Housing: Homeownership rate: 82.4% (2010); Median home value: $60,000 (2010); Median contract rent: $285 per month (2005-2009 5-year est.); Median year structure built: 1996 (2005-2009 5-year est.).

Transportation: Commute to work: 100.0% car, 0.0% public transportation, 0.0% walk, 0.0% work from home (2005-2009 5-year est.); Travel time to work: 18.8% less than 15 minutes, 26.7% 15 to 30 minutes, 3.0% 30 to 45 minutes, 9.9% 45 to 60 minutes, 41.6% 60 minutes or more (2005-2009 5-year est.)

PEP (unincorporated postal area, zip code 79353). Covers a land area of 13.959 square miles and a water area of 0.223 square miles. Located at 33.78° N. Lat; 102.59° W. Long. Elevation is 3,697 feet.

Population: 24 (2000); Race: 100.0% White, 0.0% Black, 0.0% Asian, 0.0% Other, 59.5% Hispanic of any race (2000); Density: 1.7 persons per square mile (2000); Age: 35.1% under 18, 21.6% over 64 (2000); Marriage status: 12.5% never married, 58.3% now married, 20.8% widowed, 8.3% divorced (2000); Foreign born: 8.1% (2000); Ancestry (includes multiple ancestries): 21.6% German, 5.4% Czech (2000).

Economy: Employment by occupation: 33.3% management, 0.0% professional, 0.0% services, 0.0% sales, 0.0% farming, 33.3% construction, 33.3% production (2000).

Income: Per capita income: $16,222 (2000); Median household income: $33,750 (2000); Poverty rate: 179.1% (2000).

Education: Percent of population age 25 and over with: High school diploma (including GED) or higher: 66.7% (2000); Bachelor's degree or higher: 12.5% (2000).

School District(s)

Amherst ISD (PK-12)
  2009-10 Enrollment: 180 . . . . (806) 246-3501
Morton ISD (PK-12)
  2009-10 Enrollment: 470 . . . . (806) 266-5505
Muleshoe ISD (PK-12)
  2009-10 Enrollment: 1,446 . . . . (806) 272-7404
Whiteface CISD (PK-12)
  2009-10 Enrollment: 310 . . . . (806) 287-1154

Housing: Homeownership rate: 25.0% (2000); Median home value: $107,500 (2000); Median contract rent: $150 per month (2000); Median year structure built: 1947 (2000).
Transportation: Commute to work: 66.7% car, 0.0% public transportation, 33.3% walk, 0.0% work from home (2000); Travel time to work: 33.3% less than 15 minutes, 33.3% 15 to 30 minutes, 33.3% 30 to 45 minutes, 0.0% 45 to 60 minutes, 0.0% 60 minutes or more (2000)

ROPESVILLE (city). Aka Ropes. Covers a land area of 0.359 square miles and a water area of 0 square miles. Located at 33.41° N. Lat; 102.15° W. Long. Elevation is 3,363 feet.
Population: 508 (1990); 517 (2000); 520 (2010); 519 (2015 projected); Race: 87.5% White, 1.0% Black, 0.2% Asian, 11.3% Other, 46.3% Hispanic of any race (2010); Density: 1,449.9 persons per square mile (2010); Average household size: 2.78 (2010); Median age: 33.8 (2010); Males per 100 females: 103.1 (2010); Marriage status: 22.3% never married, 62.4% now married, 7.0% widowed, 8.3% divorced (2005-2009 5-year est.); Foreign born: 4.8% (2005-2009 5-year est.); Ancestry (includes multiple ancestries): 8.2% German, 8.0% American, 7.2% English, 3.4% Irish, 2.1% Dutch (2005-2009 5-year est.).
Economy: Single-family building permits issued: 0 (2010); Multi-family building permits issued: 0 (2010); Employment by occupation: 4.8% management, 20.0% professional, 20.9% services, 18.3% sales, 5.2% farming, 8.3% construction, 22.6% production (2005-2009 5-year est.).
Income: Per capita income: $23,594 (2010); Median household income: $47,214 (2010); Average household income: $65,936 (2010); Percent of households with income of $100,000 or more: 16.0% (2010); Poverty rate: 18.3% (2005-2009 5-year est.).
Taxes: Total city taxes per capita: $340 (2007); City property taxes per capita: $98 (2007).
Education: Percent of population age 25 and over with: High school diploma (including GED) or higher: 76.8% (2010); Bachelor's degree or higher: 20.9% (2010); Master's degree or higher: 4.2% (2010).

School District(s)

Ropes ISD (PK-12)
  2009-10 Enrollment: 324 . . . . (806) 562-4031

Housing: Homeownership rate: 74.9% (2010); Median home value: $63,571 (2010); Median contract rent: $325 per month (2005-2009 5-year est.); Median year structure built: 1959 (2005-2009 5-year est.).
Transportation: Commute to work: 95.2% car, 0.0% public transportation, 2.2% walk, 0.0% work from home (2005-2009 5-year est.); Travel time to work: 28.5% less than 15 minutes, 24.6% 15 to 30 minutes, 39.5% 30 to 45 minutes, 7.5% 45 to 60 minutes, 0.0% 60 minutes or more (2005-2009 5-year est.)

SMYER (town). Covers a land area of 0.778 square miles and a water area of 0 square miles. Located at 33.58° N. Lat; 102.16° W. Long. Elevation is 3,389 feet.
Population: 442 (1990); 480 (2000); 471 (2010); 468 (2015 projected); Race: 77.3% White, 2.1% Black, 0.4% Asian, 20.2% Other, 33.5% Hispanic of any race (2010); Density: 605.7 persons per square mile (2010); Average household size: 2.79 (2010); Median age: 33.8 (2010); Males per 100 females: 101.3 (2010); Marriage status: 19.8% never married, 63.1% now married, 3.4% widowed, 13.7% divorced (2005-2009 5-year est.); Foreign born: 4.5% (2005-2009 5-year est.); Ancestry (includes multiple ancestries): 16.2% German, 8.1% French, 7.8% Irish, 7.2% English, 5.3% American (2005-2009 5-year est.).
Economy: Employment by occupation: 10.3% management, 6.3% professional, 16.7% services, 21.4% sales, 5.6% farming, 24.6% construction, 15.1% production (2005-2009 5-year est.).
Income: Per capita income: $22,392 (2010); Median household income: $48,864 (2010); Average household income: $61,509 (2010); Percent of

households with income of $100,000 or more: 13.6% (2010); Poverty rate: 28.4% (2005-2009 5-year est.).
Taxes: Total city taxes per capita: $115 (2007); City property taxes per capita: $115 (2007).
Education: Percent of population age 25 and over with: High school diploma (including GED) or higher: 75.6% (2010); Bachelor's degree or higher: 14.1% (2010); Master's degree or higher: 3.5% (2010).

School District(s)

Smyer ISD (PK-12)
  2009-10 Enrollment: 369 . . . . (806) 234-2935

Housing: Homeownership rate: 81.1% (2010); Median home value: $77,407 (2010); Median contract rent: $364 per month (2005-2009 5-year est.); Median year structure built: 1973 (2005-2009 5-year est.).
Transportation: Commute to work: 100.0% car, 0.0% public transportation, 0.0% walk, 0.0% work from home (2005-2009 5-year est.); Travel time to work: 16.7% less than 15 minutes, 43.7% 15 to 30 minutes, 34.1% 30 to 45 minutes, 0.0% 45 to 60 minutes, 5.6% 60 minutes or more (2005-2009 5-year est.)

SUNDOWN (city). Covers a land area of 1.513 square miles and a water area of 0 square miles. Located at 33.45° N. Lat; 102.48° W. Long. Elevation is 3,540 feet.
History: Incorporated after 1940.
Population: 1,759 (1990); 1,505 (2000); 1,490 (2010); 1,483 (2015 projected); Race: 74.9% White, 0.9% Black, 0.1% Asian, 24.2% Other, 49.7% Hispanic of any race (2010); Density: 985.0 persons per square mile (2010); Average household size: 2.93 (2010); Median age: 31.7 (2010); Males per 100 females: 93.5 (2010); Marriage status: 18.4% never married, 73.6% now married, 5.2% widowed, 2.8% divorced (2005-2009 5-year est.); Foreign born: 12.5% (2005-2009 5-year est.); Ancestry (includes multiple ancestries): 9.9% German, 9.3% Irish, 8.3% English, 3.5% Arab, 3.5% French (2005-2009 5-year est.).
Economy: Single-family building permits issued: 1 (2010); Multi-family building permits issued: 0 (2010); Employment by occupation: 11.4% management, 16.1% professional, 12.4% services, 22.8% sales, 0.0% farming, 29.7% construction, 7.5% production (2005-2009 5-year est.).
Income: Per capita income: $20,273 (2010); Median household income: $48,309 (2010); Average household income: $59,226 (2010); Percent of households with income of $100,000 or more: 13.8% (2010); Poverty rate: 13.8% (2005-2009 5-year est.).
Taxes: Total city taxes per capita: $513 (2007); City property taxes per capita: $229 (2007).
Education: Percent of population age 25 and over with: High school diploma (including GED) or higher: 68.4% (2010); Bachelor's degree or higher: 11.7% (2010); Master's degree or higher: 2.8% (2010).

School District(s)

Sundown ISD (PK-12)
  2009-10 Enrollment: 688 . . . . (806) 229-3021

Housing: Homeownership rate: 79.1% (2010); Median home value: $46,628 (2010); Median contract rent: $408 per month (2005-2009 5-year est.); Median year structure built: 1975 (2005-2009 5-year est.).
Transportation: Commute to work: 88.2% car, 0.0% public transportation, 0.0% walk, 7.9% work from home (2005-2009 5-year est.); Travel time to work: 59.4% less than 15 minutes, 22.2% 15 to 30 minutes, 6.0% 30 to 45 minutes, 6.9% 45 to 60 minutes, 5.3% 60 minutes or more (2005-2009 5-year est.)

Hood County

Located in north central Texas; drained by the Brazos River. Covers a land area of 421.61 square miles, a water area of 15.19 square miles, and is located in the Central Time Zone at 32.43° N. Lat., 97.79° W. Long. The county was founded in 1865. County seat is Granbury.

Hood County is part of the Granbury, TX Micropolitan Statistical Area. The entire metro area includes: Hood County, TX; Somervell County, TX

Population: 28,981 (1990); 41,100 (2000); 52,847 (2010); 58,462 (2015 projected); Race: 92.2% White, 1.4% Black, 0.6% Asian, 5.8% Other, 10.3% Hispanic of any race (2010); Density: 125.3 persons per square mile (2010); Average household size: 2.46 (2010); Median age: 40.2 (2010); Males per 100 females: 97.1 (2010).
Religion: Five largest groups: 26.3% Southern Baptist Convention, 9.9% The United Methodist Church, 6.1% Catholic Church, 3.4% Churches of Christ, 1.2% Christian Church (Disciples of Christ) (2000).

Economy: Unemployment rate: 8.1% (June 2011); Total civilian labor force: 26,661 (June 2011); Leading industries: 21.1% retail trade; 16.1% health care and social assistance; 13.8% accommodation & food services (2009); Farms: 1,076 totaling 205,672 acres (2007); Companies that employ 500 or more persons: 1 (2009); Companies that employ 100 to 499 persons: 14 (2009); Companies that employ less than 100 persons: 1,205 (2009); Black-owned businesses: n/a (2007); Hispanic-owned businesses: n/a (2007); Asian-owned businesses: n/a (2007); Women-owned businesses: 1,678 (2007); Retail sales per capita: $13,305 (2010). Single-family building permits issued: 76 (2010); Multi-family building permits issued: 0 (2010).

Income: Per capita income: $29,618 (2010); Median household income: $56,521 (2010); Average household income: $73,648 (2010); Percent of households with income of $100,000 or more: 20.2% (2010); Poverty rate: 11.6% (2009); Bankruptcy rate: 2.63% (2010).

Taxes: Total county taxes per capita: $316 (2007); County property taxes per capita: $229 (2007).

Education: Percent of population age 25 and over with: High school diploma (including GED) or higher: 85.9% (2010); Bachelor's degree or higher: 23.6% (2010); Master's degree or higher: 5.5% (2010).

Housing: Homeownership rate: 76.1% (2010); Median home value: $137,138 (2010); Median contract rent: $598 per month (2005-2009 5-year est.); Median year structure built: 1987 (2005-2009 5-year est.)

Health: Birth rate: 123.0 per 10,000 population (2009); Death rate: 109.0 per 10,000 population (2009); Age-adjusted cancer mortality rate: 176.7 deaths per 100,000 population (2007); Number of physicians: 12.4 per 10,000 population (2008); Hospital beds: 11.9 per 10,000 population (2007); Hospital admissions: 529.0 per 10,000 population (2007).

Environment: Air Quality Index: 95.1% good, 4.6% moderate, 0.3% unhealthy for sensitive individuals, 0.0% unhealthy (percent of days in 2008)

Elections: 2008 Presidential election results: 22.5% Obama, 76.6% McCain, 0.1% Nader

National and State Parks: Acton State Park

Additional Information Contacts
Hood County Government . . . . (817) 579-3200
   http://www.co.hood.tx.us
City of Granbury . . . . (817) 573-1114
   http://www.granbury.org
Granbury Chamber of Commerce . . . . (817) 573-1622
   http://www.granburychamber.com

Hood County Communities

CRESSON (unincorporated postal area, zip code 76035). Aka City of Cresson (incorporated in 2001). Covers a land area of 31.035 square miles and a water area of 0 square miles. Located at 32.54° N. Lat; 97.64° W. Long. Elevation is 1,053 feet.

Population: 414 (2000); Race: 98.1% White, 0.0% Black, 0.0% Asian, 1.9% Other, 10.7% Hispanic of any race (2000); Density: 13.3 persons per square mile (2000); Age: 26.0% under 18, 9.3% over 64 (2000); Marriage status: 14.8% never married, 76.5% now married, 2.0% widowed, 6.7% divorced (2000); Foreign born: 0.0% (2000); Ancestry (includes multiple ancestries): 28.6% German, 17.7% American, 15.3% English, 7.2% Irish (2000).

Economy: Employment by occupation: 3.5% management, 16.2% professional, 12.6% services, 20.7% sales, 0.0% farming, 16.7% construction, 30.3% production (2000).

Income: Per capita income: $16,153 (2000); Median household income: $54,038 (2000); Poverty rate: 179.1% (2000).

Education: Percent of population age 25 and over with: High school diploma (including GED) or higher: 76.8% (2000); Bachelor's degree or higher: 2.8% (2000).

Housing: Homeownership rate: 100.0% (2000); Median home value: $58,000 (2000); Median contract rent: n/a per month (2000); Median year structure built: 1980 (2000).

Transportation: Commute to work: 92.9% car, 0.0% public transportation, 0.0% walk, 7.1% work from home (2000); Travel time to work: 32.5% less than 15 minutes, 14.2% 15 to 30 minutes, 33.1% 30 to 45 minutes, 4.1% 45 to 60 minutes, 16.0% 60 minutes or more (2000)

GRANBURY (city). County seat. Covers a land area of 5.536 square miles and a water area of 0.589 square miles. Located at 32.44° N. Lat; 97.78° W. Long. Elevation is 735 feet.

History: Granbury was the home of Ashley W. Crockett, grandson of Davy Crockett and publisher of the county newspaper.

Population: 4,552 (1990); 5,718 (2000); 7,784 (2010); 8,683 (2015 projected); Race: 91.8% White, 1.2% Black, 0.7% Asian, 6.2% Other, 10.0% Hispanic of any race (2010); Density: 1,406.2 persons per square mile (2010); Average household size: 2.25 (2010); Median age: 38.5 (2010); Males per 100 females: 92.6 (2010); Marriage status: 20.6% never married, 50.2% now married, 12.5% widowed, 16.7% divorced (2005-2009 5-year est.); Foreign born: 3.4% (2005-2009 5-year est.); Ancestry (includes multiple ancestries): 14.5% English, 13.5% German, 12.9% Irish, 7.6% American, 3.6% Scotch-Irish (2005-2009 5-year est.).

Economy: Single-family building permits issued: 71 (2010); Multi-family building permits issued: 0 (2010); Employment by occupation: 13.2% management, 17.7% professional, 10.0% services, 28.9% sales, 0.4% farming, 15.1% construction, 14.7% production (2005-2009 5-year est.).

Income: Per capita income: $26,476 (2010); Median household income: $47,094 (2010); Average household income: $61,460 (2010); Percent of households with income of $100,000 or more: 14.7% (2010); Poverty rate: 15.6% (2005-2009 5-year est.).

Taxes: Total city taxes per capita: $1,256 (2007); City property taxes per capita: $300 (2007).

Education: Percent of population age 25 and over with: High school diploma (including GED) or higher: 86.3% (2010); Bachelor's degree or higher: 21.8% (2010); Master's degree or higher: 4.6% (2010).

School District(s)
Granbury ISD (PK-12)
   2009-10 Enrollment: 6,791 . . . . (817) 408-4000
John H Wood Jr Public Charter District (05-12)
   2009-10 Enrollment: 348 . . . . (210) 638-5003

Housing: Homeownership rate: 53.6% (2010); Median home value: $127,929 (2010); Median contract rent: $592 per month (2005-2009 5-year est.); Median year structure built: 1983 (2005-2009 5-year est.).

Hospitals: Lake Granbury Medical Center (56 beds)

Safety: Violent crime rate: 25.8 per 10,000 population; Property crime rate: 459.1 per 10,000 population (2009).

Newspapers: Hood County News (Local news; Circulation 10,683)

Transportation: Commute to work: 92.1% car, 0.3% public transportation, 2.1% walk, 3.1% work from home (2005-2009 5-year est.); Travel time to work: 56.0% less than 15 minutes, 20.2% 15 to 30 minutes, 8.1% 30 to 45 minutes, 7.4% 45 to 60 minutes, 8.3% 60 minutes or more (2005-2009 5-year est.)

Airports: Granbury Regional (general aviation)

Additional Information Contacts
City of Granbury . . . . (817) 573-1114
   http://www.granbury.org
Granbury Chamber of Commerce . . . . (817) 573-1622
   http://www.granburychamber.com

LIPAN (city). Covers a land area of 1.060 square miles and a water area of 0 square miles. Located at 32.51° N. Lat; 98.04° W. Long. Elevation is 919 feet.

Population: 354 (1990); 425 (2000); 499 (2010); 540 (2015 projected); Race: 93.2% White, 1.2% Black, 1.0% Asian, 4.6% Other, 6.8% Hispanic of any race (2010); Density: 470.7 persons per square mile (2010); Average household size: 2.59 (2010); Median age: 34.7 (2010); Males per 100 females: 98.8 (2010); Marriage status: 13.2% never married, 62.5% now married, 12.5% widowed, 11.8% divorced (2005-2009 5-year est.); Foreign born: 4.9% (2005-2009 5-year est.); Ancestry (includes multiple ancestries): 20.7% German, 11.7% English, 11.1% Irish, 8.5% American, 6.5% French (2005-2009 5-year est.).

Economy: Employment by occupation: 10.1% management, 11.5% professional, 27.7% services, 16.2% sales, 5.4% farming, 12.8% construction, 16.2% production (2005-2009 5-year est.).

Income: Per capita income: $23,473 (2010); Median household income: $46,250 (2010); Average household income: $59,845 (2010); Percent of households with income of $100,000 or more: 11.4% (2010); Poverty rate: 9.8% (2005-2009 5-year est.).

Taxes: Total city taxes per capita: $207 (2007); City property taxes per capita: $0 (2007).

Education: Percent of population age 25 and over with: High school diploma (including GED) or higher: 75.5% (2010); Bachelor's degree or higher: 15.8% (2010); Master's degree or higher: 3.7% (2010).

School District(s)
Lipan ISD (PK-12)
   2009-10 Enrollment: 287 . . . . (254) 646-2266

Housing: Homeownership rate: 81.9% (2010); Median home value: $75,556 (2010); Median contract rent: $330 per month (2005-2009 5-year est.); Median year structure built: 1959 (2005-2009 5-year est.).
Transportation: Commute to work: 95.7% car, 4.3% public transportation, 0.0% walk, 0.0% work from home (2005-2009 5-year est.); Travel time to work: 35.7% less than 15 minutes, 18.6% 15 to 30 minutes, 23.6% 30 to 45 minutes, 15.0% 45 to 60 minutes, 7.1% 60 minutes or more (2005-2009 5-year est.)

OAK TRAIL SHORES (CDP). Covers a land area of 2.513 square miles and a water area of 0 square miles. Located at 32.48° N. Lat; 97.83° W. Long. Elevation is 810 feet.

Population: 1,750 (1990); 2,475 (2000); 2,878 (2010); 3,122 (2015 projected); Race: 83.1% White, 4.3% Black, 0.0% Asian, 12.5% Other, 28.8% Hispanic of any race (2010); Density: 1,145.2 persons per square mile (2010); Average household size: 2.67 (2010); Median age: 36.0 (2010); Males per 100 females: 101.8 (2010); Marriage status: 31.8% never married, 51.1% now married, 7.8% widowed, 9.2% divorced (2005-2009 5-year est.); Foreign born: 28.7% (2005-2009 5-year est.); Ancestry (includes multiple ancestries): 10.7% German, 10.1% Irish, 8.2% American, 4.9% English, 1.5% Welsh (2005-2009 5-year est.).
Economy: Employment by occupation: 5.3% management, 4.2% professional, 22.4% services, 9.1% sales, 0.0% farming, 44.7% construction, 14.2% production (2005-2009 5-year est.).
Income: Per capita income: $15,370 (2010); Median household income: $34,319 (2010); Average household income: $41,041 (2010); Percent of households with income of $100,000 or more: 3.8% (2010); Poverty rate: 32.6% (2005-2009 5-year est.).
Education: Percent of population age 25 and over with: High school diploma (including GED) or higher: 74.4% (2010); Bachelor's degree or higher: 11.3% (2010); Master's degree or higher: 0.2% (2010).
Housing: Homeownership rate: 74.9% (2010); Median home value: $49,082 (2010); Median contract rent: $483 per month (2005-2009 5-year est.); Median year structure built: 1979 (2005-2009 5-year est.).
Transportation: Commute to work: 93.3% car, 0.0% public transportation, 3.4% walk, 3.3% work from home (2005-2009 5-year est.); Travel time to work: 20.7% less than 15 minutes, 24.4% 15 to 30 minutes, 25.9% 30 to 45 minutes, 7.9% 45 to 60 minutes, 21.1% 60 minutes or more (2005-2009 5-year est.)

PECAN PLANTATION (CDP). Covers a land area of 6.993 square miles and a water area of 0.157 square miles. Located at 32.36° N. Lat; 97.66° W. Long. Elevation is 719 feet.

History: By 1971 work on infrastructure and amenities such as a country club, golf course, airport, and recreational areas had begun, and in 1972 the Pecan Plantation Owners Association was formed.
Population: 1,526 (1990); 3,544 (2000); 4,969 (2010); 5,605 (2015 projected); Race: 96.8% White, 0.2% Black, 1.4% Asian, 1.5% Other, 3.3% Hispanic of any race (2010); Density: 710.5 persons per square mile (2010); Average household size: 2.36 (2010); Median age: 53.5 (2010); Males per 100 females: 95.7 (2010); Marriage status: 11.2% never married, 76.7% now married, 4.7% widowed, 7.4% divorced (2005-2009 5-year est.); Foreign born: 2.1% (2005-2009 5-year est.); Ancestry (includes multiple ancestries): 17.1% English, 15.0% American, 14.9% German, 13.8% Irish, 4.9% Scottish (2005-2009 5-year est.).
Economy: Employment by occupation: 20.8% management, 31.2% professional, 9.9% services, 28.0% sales, 0.0% farming, 2.3% construction, 7.7% production (2005-2009 5-year est.).
Income: Per capita income: $52,311 (2010); Median household income: $96,875 (2010); Average household income: $123,483 (2010); Percent of households with income of $100,000 or more: 47.6% (2010); Poverty rate: 4.8% (2005-2009 5-year est.).
Education: Percent of population age 25 and over with: High school diploma (including GED) or higher: 97.5% (2010); Bachelor's degree or higher: 51.2% (2010); Master's degree or higher: 13.9% (2010).
Housing: Homeownership rate: 94.0% (2010); Median home value: $249,874 (2010); Median contract rent: n/a per month (2005-2009 5-year est.); Median year structure built: 1995 (2005-2009 5-year est.).
Transportation: Commute to work: 91.4% car, 1.0% public transportation, 1.4% walk, 5.8% work from home (2005-2009 5-year est.); Travel time to work: 14.2% less than 15 minutes, 21.5% 15 to 30 minutes, 13.8% 30 to 45 minutes, 19.1% 45 to 60 minutes, 31.3% 60 minutes or more (2005-2009 5-year est.)

TOLAR (city). Covers a land area of 0.911 square miles and a water area of 0 square miles. Located at 32.39° N. Lat; 97.92° W. Long. Elevation is 1,020 feet.

History: Many of the homes in Tolar were constructed of petrified wood, which was also an export of the town.
Population: 491 (1990); 504 (2000); 600 (2010); 652 (2015 projected); Race: 87.2% White, 4.8% Black, 1.5% Asian, 6.5% Other, 7.8% Hispanic of any race (2010); Density: 658.6 persons per square mile (2010); Average household size: 2.68 (2010); Median age: 34.4 (2010); Males per 100 females: 97.4 (2010); Marriage status: 19.5% never married, 61.8% now married, 6.1% widowed, 12.5% divorced (2005-2009 5-year est.); Foreign born: 2.5% (2005-2009 5-year est.); Ancestry (includes multiple ancestries): 10.2% English, 9.8% Irish, 9.4% Scottish, 7.9% German, 3.2% European (2005-2009 5-year est.).
Economy: Single-family building permits issued: 5 (2010); Multi-family building permits issued: 0 (2010); Employment by occupation: 17.6% management, 21.3% professional, 17.6% services, 20.4% sales, 0.0% farming, 12.0% construction, 11.1% production (2005-2009 5-year est.).
Income: Per capita income: $27,072 (2010); Median household income: $58,190 (2010); Average household income: $73,626 (2010); Percent of households with income of $100,000 or more: 20.3% (2010); Poverty rate: 16.7% (2005-2009 5-year est.).
Taxes: Total city taxes per capita: $281 (2007); City property taxes per capita: $117 (2007).
Education: Percent of population age 25 and over with: High school diploma (including GED) or higher: 85.5% (2010); Bachelor's degree or higher: 21.6% (2010); Master's degree or higher: 5.3% (2010).

School District(s)

Tolar ISD (PK-12)
    2009-10 Enrollment: 610 . . . . (254) 835-4718
Housing: Homeownership rate: 72.1% (2010); Median home value: $104,412 (2010); Median contract rent: $475 per month (2005-2009 5-year est.); Median year structure built: 1975 (2005-2009 5-year est.).
Safety: Violent crime rate: 0.0 per 10,000 population; Property crime rate: 71.0 per 10,000 population (2009).
Transportation: Commute to work: 94.0% car, 0.0% public transportation, 0.0% walk, 4.3% work from home (2005-2009 5-year est.); Travel time to work: 25.2% less than 15 minutes, 39.3% 15 to 30 minutes, 11.5% 30 to 45 minutes, 3.0% 45 to 60 minutes, 21.1% 60 minutes or more (2005-2009 5-year est.)

Hopkins County

Located in northeastern Texas; bounded on the north by the South Fork of the Sulphur River; drained by White Oak Bayou. Covers a land area of 782.40 square miles, a water area of 10.35 square miles, and is located in the Central Time Zone at 33.12° N. Lat., 95.58° W. Long. The county was founded in 1846. County seat is Sulphur Springs.

Hopkins County is part of the Sulphur Springs, TX Micropolitan Statistical Area. The entire metro area includes: Hopkins County, TX

Weather Station: Sulphur Springs									Elevation: 501 feet		
	Jan	Feb	Mar	Apr	May	Jun	Jul	Aug	Sep	Oct	Nov	Dec
High	55	59	67	75	82	89	94	95	88	78	66	56
Low	32	36	43	51	61	68	72	71	63	52	43	34
Precip	3.1	3.6	4.4	3.9	4.9	4.5	3.3	2.3	3.1	5.3	4.5	4.3
Snow	tr	0.1	tr	0.0	0.0	0.0	0.0	0.0	0.0	0.0	0.0	0.2

High and Low temperatures in degrees Fahrenheit; Precipitation and Snow in inches

Population: 28,833 (1990); 31,960 (2000); 34,520 (2010); 35,703 (2015 projected); Race: 82.0% White, 7.5% Black, 0.7% Asian, 9.8% Other, 14.1% Hispanic of any race (2010); Density: 44.1 persons per square mile (2010); Average household size: 2.55 (2010); Median age: 36.4 (2010); Males per 100 females: 98.2 (2010).
Religion: Five largest groups: 34.4% Southern Baptist Convention, 9.9% Baptist Missionary Association of America, 9.3% The United Methodist Church, 5.2% Churches of Christ, 4.9% Catholic Church (2000).
Economy: Unemployment rate: 7.8% (June 2011); Total civilian labor force: 17,695 (June 2011); Leading industries: 16.8% retail trade; 11.8% health care and social assistance; 11.2% wholesale trade (2009); Farms: 1,955 totaling 390,466 acres (2007); Companies that employ 500 or more persons: 1 (2009); Companies that employ 100 to 499 persons: 14 (2009); Companies that employ less than 100 persons: 726 (2009); Black-owned businesses: n/a (2007); Hispanic-owned businesses: n/a (2007);

Asian-owned businesses: n/a (2007); Women-owned businesses: 665 (2007); Retail sales per capita: $16,490 (2010). Single-family building permits issued: 8 (2010); Multi-family building permits issued: 6 (2010).
Income: Per capita income: $21,069 (2010); Median household income: $40,487 (2010); Average household income: $54,151 (2010); Percent of households with income of $100,000 or more: 10.9% (2010); Poverty rate: 18.0% (2009); Bankruptcy rate: 1.71% (2010).
Taxes: Total county taxes per capita: $278 (2007); County property taxes per capita: $204 (2007).
Education: Percent of population age 25 and over with: High school diploma (including GED) or higher: 79.7% (2010); Bachelor's degree or higher: 16.0% (2010); Master's degree or higher: 4.4% (2010).
Housing: Homeownership rate: 70.1% (2010); Median home value: $86,732 (2010); Median contract rent: $429 per month (2005-2009 5-year est.); Median year structure built: 1977 (2005-2009 5-year est.).
Health: Birth rate: 137.6 per 10,000 population (2009); Death rate: 97.2 per 10,000 population (2009); Age-adjusted cancer mortality rate: 224.1 deaths per 100,000 population (2007); Number of physicians: 9.4 per 10,000 population (2008); Hospital beds: 15.9 per 10,000 population (2007); Hospital admissions: 1,260.3 per 10,000 population (2007).
Elections: 2008 Presidential election results: 27.3% Obama, 72.0% McCain, 0.0% Nader
Additional Information Contacts
Hopkins County Government . . . . (903) 438-4009
   http://www.hopkinscountytx.org
City of Sulphur Springs . . . . (903) 885-7541
   http://www.sulphurspringstx.org

Hopkins County Communities

BRASHEAR (unincorporated postal area, zip code 75420). Covers a land area of 38.376 square miles and a water area of 0.420 square miles. Located at 33.05° N. Lat; 95.72° W. Long. Elevation is 554 feet.
Population: 1,020 (2000); Race: 91.9% White, 0.4% Black, 0.0% Asian, 7.7% Other, 8.6% Hispanic of any race (2000); Density: 26.6 persons per square mile (2000); Age: 23.7% under 18, 14.7% over 64 (2000); Marriage status: 15.1% never married, 66.3% now married, 7.7% widowed, 10.9% divorced (2000); Foreign born: 3.6% (2000); Ancestry (includes multiple ancestries): 32.9% American, 10.1% Irish, 6.2% English, 6.0% German (2000).
Economy: Employment by occupation: 10.3% management, 15.6% professional, 11.3% services, 24.7% sales, 2.4% farming, 10.5% construction, 25.1% production (2000).
Income: Per capita income: $17,988 (2000); Median household income: $35,156 (2000); Poverty rate: 179.1% (2000).
Education: Percent of population age 25 and over with: High school diploma (including GED) or higher: 69.0% (2000); Bachelor's degree or higher: 7.3% (2000).
Housing: Homeownership rate: 86.9% (2000); Median home value: $49,000 (2000); Median contract rent: $417 per month (2000); Median year structure built: 1975 (2000).
Transportation: Commute to work: 87.3% car, 0.0% public transportation, 2.5% walk, 8.5% work from home (2000); Travel time to work: 19.1% less than 15 minutes, 45.3% 15 to 30 minutes, 14.8% 30 to 45 minutes, 4.8% 45 to 60 minutes, 15.9% 60 minutes or more (2000)

COMO (town). Covers a land area of 1.106 square miles and a water area of 0 square miles. Located at 33.06° N. Lat; 95.47° W. Long. Elevation is 535 feet.
Population: 563 (1990); 621 (2000); 657 (2010); 678 (2015 projected); Race: 88.7% White, 2.3% Black, 0.0% Asian, 9.0% Other, 25.9% Hispanic of any race (2010); Density: 593.9 persons per square mile (2010); Average household size: 2.91 (2010); Median age: 33.5 (2010); Males per 100 females: 104.0 (2010); Marriage status: 22.8% never married, 59.7% now married, 2.1% widowed, 15.4% divorced (2005-2009 5-year est.); Foreign born: 11.7% (2005-2009 5-year est.); Ancestry (includes multiple ancestries): 28.1% American, 15.0% German, 9.0% Irish, 8.8% English, 4.1% Italian (2005-2009 5-year est.).
Economy: Employment by occupation: 0.7% management, 17.1% professional, 22.5% services, 21.6% sales, 3.8% farming, 11.6% construction, 22.7% production (2005-2009 5-year est.).
Income: Per capita income: $16,930 (2010); Median household income: $35,000 (2010); Average household income: $50,033 (2010); Percent of households with income of $100,000 or more: 9.7% (2010); Poverty rate: 26.7% (2005-2009 5-year est.).

Taxes: Total city taxes per capita: $110 (2007); City property taxes per capita: $54 (2007).
Education: Percent of population age 25 and over with: High school diploma (including GED) or higher: 71.6% (2010); Bachelor's degree or higher: 7.5% (2010); Master's degree or higher: 2.0% (2010).
School District(s)
Como-Pickton CISD (PK-12)
   2009-10 Enrollment: 825 . . . . (903) 488-3671
Housing: Homeownership rate: 70.4% (2010); Median home value: $59,677 (2010); Median contract rent: $380 per month (2005-2009 5-year est.); Median year structure built: 1971 (2005-2009 5-year est.).
Transportation: Commute to work: 92.7% car, 0.0% public transportation, 3.7% walk, 3.7% work from home (2005-2009 5-year est.); Travel time to work: 31.0% less than 15 minutes, 44.9% 15 to 30 minutes, 9.4% 30 to 45 minutes, 5.6% 45 to 60 minutes, 9.1% 60 minutes or more (2005-2009 5-year est.)

CUMBY (city). Covers a land area of 0.870 square miles and a water area of 0 square miles. Located at 33.13° N. Lat; 95.84° W. Long. Elevation is 646 feet.
Population: 576 (1990); 616 (2000); 653 (2010); 671 (2015 projected); Race: 95.1% White, 0.2% Black, 0.0% Asian, 4.7% Other, 5.2% Hispanic of any race (2010); Density: 750.6 persons per square mile (2010); Average household size: 2.31 (2010); Median age: 42.1 (2010); Males per 100 females: 98.5 (2010); Marriage status: 23.2% never married, 57.1% now married, 6.7% widowed, 12.9% divorced (2005-2009 5-year est.); Foreign born: 0.0% (2005-2009 5-year est.); Ancestry (includes multiple ancestries): 21.7% American, 17.5% Irish, 13.0% English, 7.1% Scotch-Irish, 6.9% German (2005-2009 5-year est.).
Economy: Single-family building permits issued: 2 (2010); Multi-family building permits issued: 0 (2010); Employment by occupation: 14.2% management, 11.2% professional, 23.6% services, 20.4% sales, 0.5% farming, 17.2% construction, 12.9% production (2005-2009 5-year est.).
Income: Per capita income: $21,215 (2010); Median household income: $40,119 (2010); Average household income: $48,719 (2010); Percent of households with income of $100,000 or more: 8.8% (2010); Poverty rate: 10.0% (2005-2009 5-year est.).
Taxes: Total city taxes per capita: $215 (2007); City property taxes per capita: $90 (2007).
Education: Percent of population age 25 and over with: High school diploma (including GED) or higher: 80.5% (2010); Bachelor's degree or higher: 15.5% (2010); Master's degree or higher: 5.0% (2010).
School District(s)
Cumby ISD (PK-12)
   2009-10 Enrollment: 450 . . . . (903) 994-2775
Miller Grove ISD (PK-12)
   2009-10 Enrollment: 260 . . . . (903) 459-3288
Housing: Homeownership rate: 69.3% (2010); Median home value: $46,400 (2010); Median contract rent: $425 per month (2005-2009 5-year est.); Median year structure built: 1972 (2005-2009 5-year est.).
Transportation: Commute to work: 93.9% car, 0.0% public transportation, 2.5% walk, 3.5% work from home (2005-2009 5-year est.); Travel time to work: 23.1% less than 15 minutes, 50.7% 15 to 30 minutes, 14.7% 30 to 45 minutes, 8.9% 45 to 60 minutes, 2.6% 60 minutes or more (2005-2009 5-year est.)

DIKE (unincorporated postal area, zip code 75437). Covers a land area of 63.312 square miles and a water area of 0.513 square miles. Located at 33.25° N. Lat; 95.47° W. Long. Elevation is 472 feet.
Population: 986 (2000); Race: 98.0% White, 0.0% Black, 0.0% Asian, 2.0% Other, 5.7% Hispanic of any race (2000); Density: 15.6 persons per square mile (2000); Age: 28.3% under 18, 11.0% over 64 (2000); Marriage status: 13.9% never married, 69.6% now married, 6.0% widowed, 10.5% divorced (2000); Foreign born: 2.8% (2000); Ancestry (includes multiple ancestries): 16.5% American, 10.4% Irish, 9.6% German, 5.7% English (2000).
Economy: Employment by occupation: 11.4% management, 10.4% professional, 11.8% services, 27.7% sales, 5.1% farming, 13.5% construction, 20.1% production (2000).
Income: Per capita income: $15,830 (2000); Median household income: $35,071 (2000); Poverty rate: 179.1% (2000).
Education: Percent of population age 25 and over with: High school diploma (including GED) or higher: 72.9% (2000); Bachelor's degree or higher: 8.3% (2000).

Housing: Homeownership rate: 81.6% (2000); Median home value: $44,400 (2000); Median contract rent: $354 per month (2000); Median year structure built: 1979 (2000).
Transportation: Commute to work: 91.1% car, 0.0% public transportation, 1.5% walk, 5.8% work from home (2000); Travel time to work: 20.2% less than 15 minutes, 48.4% 15 to 30 minutes, 11.7% 30 to 45 minutes, 7.3% 45 to 60 minutes, 12.4% 60 minutes or more (2000)

PICKTON (unincorporated postal area, zip code 75471). Covers a land area of 44.099 square miles and a water area of 0.079 square miles. Located at 33.04° N. Lat; 95.39° W. Long. Elevation is 518 feet.
Population: 1,103 (2000); Race: 88.2% White, 0.8% Black, 0.0% Asian, 11.0% Other, 15.2% Hispanic of any race (2000); Density: 25.0 persons per square mile (2000); Age: 28.4% under 18, 13.1% over 64 (2000); Marriage status: 15.0% never married, 66.5% now married, 9.3% widowed, 9.2% divorced (2000); Foreign born: 12.5% (2000); Ancestry (includes multiple ancestries): 14.1% American, 12.8% Irish, 8.2% English, 6.4% German (2000).
Economy: Employment by occupation: 20.7% management, 9.3% professional, 14.9% services, 18.5% sales, 9.3% farming, 10.7% construction, 16.7% production (2000).
Income: Per capita income: $15,317 (2000); Median household income: $34,886 (2000); Poverty rate: 179.1% (2000).
Education: Percent of population age 25 and over with: High school diploma (including GED) or higher: 71.7% (2000); Bachelor's degree or higher: 10.4% (2000).

School District(s)
Como-Pickton CISD (PK-12)
    2009-10 Enrollment: 825 . . . . (903) 488-3671
Housing: Homeownership rate: 74.1% (2000); Median home value: $56,700 (2000); Median contract rent: $320 per month (2000); Median year structure built: 1975 (2000).
Transportation: Commute to work: 88.8% car, 0.0% public transportation, 4.1% walk, 6.3% work from home (2000); Travel time to work: 37.4% less than 15 minutes, 37.4% 15 to 30 minutes, 17.3% 30 to 45 minutes, 3.2% 45 to 60 minutes, 4.5% 60 minutes or more (2000)

SALTILLO (unincorporated postal area, zip code 75478). Covers a land area of 52.855 square miles and a water area of 0.156 square miles. Located at 33.17° N. Lat; 95.36° W. Long. Elevation is 453 feet.
Population: 805 (2000); Race: 94.1% White, 0.6% Black, 0.0% Asian, 5.3% Other, 4.4% Hispanic of any race (2000); Density: 15.2 persons per square mile (2000); Age: 27.3% under 18, 17.1% over 64 (2000); Marriage status: 19.5% never married, 60.9% now married, 8.4% widowed, 11.1% divorced (2000); Foreign born: 3.5% (2000); Ancestry (includes multiple ancestries): 21.0% American, 13.7% English, 12.0% Irish, 5.5% German (2000).
Economy: Employment by occupation: 14.0% management, 14.3% professional, 12.0% services, 26.4% sales, 3.4% farming, 8.0% construction, 21.8% production (2000).
Income: Per capita income: $14,195 (2000); Median household income: $29,609 (2000); Poverty rate: 179.1% (2000).
Education: Percent of population age 25 and over with: High school diploma (including GED) or higher: 82.1% (2000); Bachelor's degree or higher: 11.4% (2000).

School District(s)
Saltillo ISD (PK-12)
    2009-10 Enrollment: 257 . . . . (903) 537-2386
Housing: Homeownership rate: 90.8% (2000); Median home value: $43,700 (2000); Median contract rent: $388 per month (2000); Median year structure built: 1976 (2000).
Transportation: Commute to work: 85.3% car, 1.5% public transportation, 3.8% walk, 7.1% work from home (2000); Travel time to work: 32.1% less than 15 minutes, 34.9% 15 to 30 minutes, 16.8% 30 to 45 minutes, 5.1% 45 to 60 minutes, 11.1% 60 minutes or more (2000)

SULPHUR BLUFF (unincorporated postal area, zip code 75481). Covers a land area of 57.747 square miles and a water area of 0.651 square miles. Located at 33.32° N. Lat; 95.39° W. Long. Elevation is 459 feet.
Population: 306 (2000); Race: 97.7% White, 2.3% Black, 0.0% Asian, 0.0% Other, 6.1% Hispanic of any race (2000); Density: 5.3 persons per square mile (2000); Age: 17.2% under 18, 23.3% over 64 (2000); Marriage status: 20.4% never married, 61.9% now married, 8.8% widowed, 8.8% divorced (2000); Foreign born: 6.1% (2000); Ancestry (includes multiple

ancestries): 13.0% American, 9.9% German, 5.7% Irish, 3.1% English (2000).
Economy: Employment by occupation: 15.6% management, 11.1% professional, 12.6% services, 17.8% sales, 8.1% farming, 20.0% construction, 14.8% production (2000).
Income: Per capita income: $15,958 (2000); Median household income: $33,929 (2000); Poverty rate: 179.1% (2000).
Education: Percent of population age 25 and over with: High school diploma (including GED) or higher: 72.4% (2000); Bachelor's degree or higher: 8.7% (2000).

School District(s)
Sulphur Bluff ISD (PK-12)
    2009-10 Enrollment: 233 . . . . (903) 945-2460
Housing: Homeownership rate: 84.3% (2000); Median home value: $65,000 (2000); Median contract rent: $238 per month (2000); Median year structure built: 1969 (2000).
Transportation: Commute to work: 84.7% car, 2.3% public transportation, 6.1% walk, 6.9% work from home (2000); Travel time to work: 25.4% less than 15 minutes, 23.0% 15 to 30 minutes, 29.5% 30 to 45 minutes, 7.4% 45 to 60 minutes, 14.8% 60 minutes or more (2000)

SULPHUR SPRINGS (city). County seat. Covers a land area of 17.859 square miles and a water area of 3.181 square miles. Located at 33.13° N. Lat; 95.60° W. Long. Elevation is 502 feet.
History: Many farmers of Dutch origin. The city became the county seat in 1871.
Population: 14,178 (1990); 14,551 (2000); 15,482 (2010); 15,907 (2015 projected); Race: 76.0% White, 13.8% Black, 1.1% Asian, 9.1% Other, 13.1% Hispanic of any race (2010); Density: 866.9 persons per square mile (2010); Average household size: 2.41 (2010); Median age: 35.6 (2010); Males per 100 females: 92.5 (2010); Marriage status: 20.8% never married, 54.7% now married, 11.4% widowed, 13.0% divorced (2005-2009 5-year est.); Foreign born: 7.3% (2005-2009 5-year est.); Ancestry (includes multiple ancestries): 18.3% American, 12.1% German, 12.0% Irish, 10.8% English, 2.0% Dutch (2005-2009 5-year est.).
Economy: Single-family building permits issued: 8 (2010); Multi-family building permits issued: 6 (2010); Employment by occupation: 7.6% management, 18.0% professional, 19.3% services, 25.1% sales, 0.0% farming, 9.3% construction, 20.8% production (2005-2009 5-year est.).
Income: Per capita income: $19,911 (2010); Median household income: $36,004 (2010); Average household income: $48,817 (2010); Percent of households with income of $100,000 or more: 8.1% (2010); Poverty rate: 16.9% (2005-2009 5-year est.).
Taxes: Total city taxes per capita: $558 (2007); City property taxes per capita: $204 (2007).
Education: Percent of population age 25 and over with: High school diploma (including GED) or higher: 78.7% (2010); Bachelor's degree or higher: 18.5% (2010); Master's degree or higher: 4.9% (2010).

School District(s)
North Hopkins ISD (PK-12)
    2009-10 Enrollment: 457 . . . . (903) 945-2192
Sulphur Springs ISD (PK-12)
    2009-10 Enrollment: 4,121 . . . . (903) 885-2153
Housing: Homeownership rate: 58.7% (2010); Median home value: $87,708 (2010); Median contract rent: $433 per month (2005-2009 5-year est.); Median year structure built: 1975 (2005-2009 5-year est.).
Hospitals: Hopkins County Memorial Hospital
Safety: Violent crime rate: 25.1 per 10,000 population; Property crime rate: 190.2 per 10,000 population (2009).
Newspapers: Country World (National news; Circulation 20,000); Hopkins County Echo (Community news; Circulation 891); Sulphur Springs News-Telegram (Regional news; Circulation 6,000)
Transportation: Commute to work: 90.8% car, 0.3% public transportation, 2.8% walk, 5.4% work from home (2005-2009 5-year est.); Travel time to work: 62.8% less than 15 minutes, 17.7% 15 to 30 minutes, 10.9% 30 to 45 minutes, 3.3% 45 to 60 minutes, 5.3% 60 minutes or more (2005-2009 5-year est.)
Airports: Sulphur Springs Municipal (general aviation)
Additional Information Contacts
City of Sulphur Springs . . . . (903) 885-7541
    http://www.sulphurspringstx.org

TIRA (town). Covers a land area of 1.438 square miles and a water area of 0 square miles. Located at 33.32° N. Lat; 95.57° W. Long. Elevation is 469 feet.

Population: 253 (1990); 248 (2000); 257 (2010); 262 (2015 projected); Race: 94.9% White, 0.8% Black, 0.0% Asian, 4.3% Other, 5.4% Hispanic of any race (2010); Density: 178.7 persons per square mile (2010); Average household size: 2.71 (2010); Median age: 34.4 (2010); Males per 100 females: 100.8 (2010); Marriage status: 20.8% never married, 61.8% now married, 12.1% widowed, 5.3% divorced (2005-2009 5-year est.); Foreign born: 3.4% (2005-2009 5-year est.); Ancestry (includes multiple ancestries): 56.5% American, 12.3% Irish, 8.6% English, 4.1% Dutch, 4.1% German (2005-2009 5-year est.).

Economy: Employment by occupation: 24.6% management, 6.2% professional, 10.8% services, 20.0% sales, 0.0% farming, 15.4% construction, 23.1% production (2005-2009 5-year est.).

Income: Per capita income: $22,301 (2010); Median household income: $50,568 (2010); Average household income: $59,237 (2010); Percent of households with income of $100,000 or more: 14.7% (2010); Poverty rate: 7.2% (2005-2009 5-year est.).

Taxes: Total city taxes per capita: $918 (2007); City property taxes per capita: $367 (2007).

Education: Percent of population age 25 and over with: High school diploma (including GED) or higher: 80.0% (2010); Bachelor's degree or higher: 14.1% (2010); Master's degree or higher: 4.7% (2010).

Housing: Homeownership rate: 84.2% (2010); Median home value: $67,500 (2010); Median contract rent: $275 per month (2005-2009 5-year est.); Median year structure built: 1977 (2005-2009 5-year est.).

Transportation: Commute to work: 87.3% car, 0.0% public transportation, 0.0% walk, 12.7% work from home (2005-2009 5-year est.); Travel time to work: 21.8% less than 15 minutes, 41.8% 15 to 30 minutes, 32.7% 30 to 45 minutes, 0.0% 45 to 60 minutes, 3.6% 60 minutes or more (2005-2009 5-year est.)

Houston County

Located in east Texas; bounded on the west by the Trinity River, and on the east by the Neches River; includes part of Davy Crockett National Forest. Covers a land area of 1,230.89 square miles, a water area of 5.94 square miles, and is located in the Central Time Zone at 31.32° N. Lat., 95.43° W. Long. The county was founded in 1837. County seat is Crockett.

Weather Station: Crockett										Elevation: 347 feet		
	Jan	Feb	Mar	Apr	May	Jun	Jul	Aug	Sep	Oct	Nov	Dec
High	59	63	70	77	84	90	94	95	89	80	69	60
Low	37	40	47	54	63	70	72	72	66	56	46	38
Precip	3.9	3.5	3.7	3.2	4.7	4.6	3.0	3.0	3.3	4.7	3.9	3.9
Snow	0.2	tr	0.0	0.0	0.0	0.0	0.0	0.0	0.0	0.0	tr	tr

High and Low temperatures in degrees Fahrenheit; Precipitation and Snow in inches

Population: 21,375 (1990); 23,185 (2000); 23,270 (2010); 23,274 (2015 projected); Race: 69.5% White, 25.8% Black, 0.4% Asian, 4.3% Other, 10.1% Hispanic of any race (2010); Density: 18.9 persons per square mile (2010); Average household size: 2.41 (2010); Median age: 41.2 (2010); Males per 100 females: 116.4 (2010).

Religion: Five largest groups: 29.0% Southern Baptist Convention, 5.5% The United Methodist Church, 4.7% Baptist Missionary Association of America, 3.5% Churches of Christ, 3.1% Catholic Church (2000).

Economy: Unemployment rate: 11.2% (June 2011); Total civilian labor force: 8,700 (June 2011); Leading industries: 20.2% retail trade; 19.4% health care and social assistance; 18.7% manufacturing (2009); Farms: 1,562 totaling 440,462 acres (2007); Companies that employ 500 or more persons: 0 (2009); Companies that employ 100 to 499 persons: 3 (2009); Companies that employ less than 100 persons: 364 (2009); Black-owned businesses: n/a (2007); Hispanic-owned businesses: n/a (2007); Asian-owned businesses: n/a (2007); Women-owned businesses: 376 (2007); Retail sales per capita: $9,455 (2010). Single-family building permits issued: 2 (2010); Multi-family building permits issued: 0 (2010).

Income: Per capita income: $16,918 (2010); Median household income: $32,570 (2010); Average household income: $43,500 (2010); Percent of households with income of $100,000 or more: 6.8% (2010); Poverty rate: 23.9% (2009); Bankruptcy rate: 1.37% (2010).

Taxes: Total county taxes per capita: $186 (2007); County property taxes per capita: $120 (2007).

Education: Percent of population age 25 and over with: High school diploma (including GED) or higher: 75.7% (2010); Bachelor's degree or higher: 10.5% (2010); Master's degree or higher: 2.0% (2010).

Housing: Homeownership rate: 70.5% (2010); Median home value: $66,152 (2010); Median contract rent: $336 per month (2005-2009 5-year est.); Median year structure built: 1975 (2005-2009 5-year est.)

Health: Birth rate: 116.3 per 10,000 population (2009); Death rate: 134.6 per 10,000 population (2009); Age-adjusted cancer mortality rate: 248.8 deaths per 100,000 population (2007); Number of physicians: 5.8 per 10,000 population (2008); Hospital beds: 21.6 per 10,000 population (2007); Hospital admissions: 1,019.5 per 10,000 population (2007).

Elections: 2008 Presidential election results: 30.8% Obama, 68.1% McCain, 0.2% Nader

National and State Parks: Davy Crockett National Forest; Mission Tejas State Park; Mission Tejas State Park

Additional Information Contacts

Houston County Government	(936) 544-3256
http://www.co.houston.tx.us/ips/cms	
City of Crockett	(936) 544-5156
http://www.crocketttexas.org	
Crockett Area Chamber of Commerce.	(936) 544-2359
http://crockettareachamber.org	

Houston County Communities

CROCKETT (city). County seat. Covers a land area of 8.865 square miles and a water area of <.001 square miles. Located at 31.31° N. Lat; 95.45° W. Long. Elevation is 364 feet.

History: Crockett was founded in the 1830's on the Old San Antonio Road. The town was named for Davy Crockett, who may have camped here on his way to the Alamo.

Population: 7,024 (1990); 7,141 (2000); 7,361 (2010); 7,521 (2015 projected); Race: 48.3% White, 42.0% Black, 0.8% Asian, 8.9% Other, 13.9% Hispanic of any race (2010); Density: 830.4 persons per square mile (2010); Average household size: 2.47 (2010); Median age: 37.9 (2010); Males per 100 females: 84.6 (2010); Marriage status: 40.9% never married, 42.5% now married, 8.4% widowed, 8.2% divorced (2005-2009 5-year est.); Foreign born: 11.4% (2005-2009 5-year est.); Ancestry (includes multiple ancestries): 6.3% Irish, 6.3% English, 4.7% German, 2.7% American, 2.1% French (2005-2009 5-year est.).

Economy: Single-family building permits issued: 2 (2010); Multi-family building permits issued: 0 (2010); Employment by occupation: 8.4% management, 11.4% professional, 31.8% services, 20.0% sales, 1.9% farming, 6.7% construction, 19.8% production (2005-2009 5-year est.).

Income: Per capita income: $15,399 (2010); Median household income: $27,335 (2010); Average household income: $39,111 (2010); Percent of households with income of $100,000 or more: 6.1% (2010); Poverty rate: 38.2% (2005-2009 5-year est.).

Taxes: Total city taxes per capita: $386 (2007); City property taxes per capita: $148 (2007).

Education: Percent of population age 25 and over with: High school diploma (including GED) or higher: 72.7% (2010); Bachelor's degree or higher: 9.0% (2010); Master's degree or higher: 1.6% (2010).

School District(s)

Crockett ISD (PK-12)
    2009-10 Enrollment: 1,455 . . . . (936) 544-2125
Crockett State School (09-12)
    2009-10 Enrollment: 136 . . . . (936) 852-5000

Housing: Homeownership rate: 55.9% (2010); Median home value: $58,143 (2010); Median contract rent: $325 per month (2005-2009 5-year est.); Median year structure built: 1966 (2005-2009 5-year est.).

Hospitals: East Texas Medical Center - Crockett (93 beds)

Safety: Violent crime rate: 22.1 per 10,000 population; Property crime rate: 407.0 per 10,000 population (2009).

Newspapers: Houston County Courier (Local news; Circulation 6,000)

Transportation: Commute to work: 83.5% car, 0.0% public transportation, 8.5% walk, 1.6% work from home (2005-2009 5-year est.); Travel time to work: 46.8% less than 15 minutes, 33.2% 15 to 30 minutes, 6.9% 30 to 45 minutes, 7.8% 45 to 60 minutes, 5.3% 60 minutes or more (2005-2009 5-year est.)

Additional Information Contacts

City of Crockett	(936) 544-5156
http://www.crocketttexas.org	
Crockett Area Chamber of Commerce.	(936) 544-2359
http://crockettareachamber.org	

GRAPELAND (city). Covers a land area of 1.978 square miles and a water area of 0.008 square miles. Located at 31.49° N. Lat; 95.48° W. Long. Elevation is 472 feet.

History: Mission Tejas State Historical Park and Davy Crockett National Forest are to the East. Incorporated 1924.

Population: 1,725 (1990); 1,451 (2000); 1,362 (2010); 1,309 (2015 projected); Race: 75.3% White, 22.1% Black, 0.1% Asian, 2.5% Other, 2.1% Hispanic of any race (2010); Density: 688.5 persons per square mile (2010); Average household size: 2.29 (2010); Median age: 45.4 (2010); Males per 100 females: 88.6 (2010); Marriage status: 31.5% never married, 41.3% now married, 17.4% widowed, 9.8% divorced (2005-2009 5-year est.); Foreign born: 1.5% (2005-2009 5-year est.); Ancestry (includes multiple ancestries): 12.8% Irish, 10.4% American, 9.2% English, 6.5% German, 3.9% French (2005-2009 5-year est.).
Economy: Single-family building permits issued: 0 (2010); Multi-family building permits issued: 0 (2010); Employment by occupation: 5.0% management, 7.5% professional, 44.2% services, 12.1% sales, 0.7% farming, 8.7% construction, 21.8% production (2005-2009 5-year est.).
Income: Per capita income: $16,126 (2010); Median household income: $27,831 (2010); Average household income: $37,430 (2010); Percent of households with income of $100,000 or more: 3.7% (2010); Poverty rate: 20.1% (2005-2009 5-year est.).
Taxes: Total city taxes per capita: $528 (2007); City property taxes per capita: $160 (2007).
Education: Percent of population age 25 and over with: High school diploma (including GED) or higher: 74.9% (2010); Bachelor's degree or higher: 8.6% (2010); Master's degree or higher: 1.4% (2010).
School District(s)
Grapeland ISD (PK-12)
    2009-10 Enrollment: 526 . . . . (936) 687-4619
Housing: Homeownership rate: 66.4% (2010); Median home value: $70,270 (2010); Median contract rent: $228 per month (2005-2009 5-year est.); Median year structure built: 1973 (2005-2009 5-year est.).
Safety: Violent crime rate: 72.8 per 10,000 population; Property crime rate: 211.2 per 10,000 population (2009).
Newspapers: Grapeland Messenger (Community news; Circulation 2,500)
Transportation: Commute to work: 94.2% car, 0.0% public transportation, 1.7% walk, 0.9% work from home (2005-2009 5-year est.); Travel time to work: 27.6% less than 15 minutes, 25.9% 15 to 30 minutes, 21.1% 30 to 45 minutes, 5.0% 45 to 60 minutes, 20.5% 60 minutes or more (2005-2009 5-year est.)

KENNARD (city). Covers a land area of 1.265 square miles and a water area of 0 square miles. Located at 31.35° N. Lat; 95.18° W. Long. Elevation is 361 feet.
Population: 341 (1990); 317 (2000); 320 (2010); 320 (2015 projected); Race: 87.2% White, 11.3% Black, 0.3% Asian, 1.3% Other, 1.3% Hispanic of any race (2010); Density: 252.9 persons per square mile (2010); Average household size: 2.60 (2010); Median age: 38.6 (2010); Males per 100 females: 100.0 (2010); Marriage status: 29.5% never married, 45.9% now married, 5.3% widowed, 19.3% divorced (2005-2009 5-year est.); Foreign born: 13.7% (2005-2009 5-year est.); Ancestry (includes multiple ancestries): 20.8% Irish, 17.9% English, 6.5% German, 2.3% Dutch, 2.0% American (2005-2009 5-year est.).
Economy: Employment by occupation: 2.8% management, 20.4% professional, 25.4% services, 10.6% sales, 0.0% farming, 21.1% construction, 19.7% production (2005-2009 5-year est.).
Income: Per capita income: $20,976 (2010); Median household income: $44,063 (2010); Average household income: $53,679 (2010); Percent of households with income of $100,000 or more: 11.4% (2010); Poverty rate: 16.4% (2005-2009 5-year est.).
Taxes: Total city taxes per capita: $120 (2007); City property taxes per capita: $69 (2007).
Education: Percent of population age 25 and over with: High school diploma (including GED) or higher: 79.6% (2010); Bachelor's degree or higher: 8.8% (2010); Master's degree or higher: 2.3% (2010).
School District(s)
Kennard ISD (PK-12)
    2009-10 Enrollment: 353 . . . . (936) 655-2008
Housing: Homeownership rate: 78.9% (2010); Median home value: $75,625 (2010); Median contract rent: $573 per month (2005-2009 5-year est.); Median year structure built: 1970 (2005-2009 5-year est.).
Transportation: Commute to work: 71.8% car, 0.0% public transportation, 23.2% walk, 4.9% work from home (2005-2009 5-year est.); Travel time to work: 53.3% less than 15 minutes, 5.9% 15 to 30 minutes, 20.0% 30 to 45 minutes, 11.9% 45 to 60 minutes, 8.9% 60 minutes or more (2005-2009 5-year est.)

LATEXO (city). Covers a land area of 0.986 square miles and a water area of 0 square miles. Located at 31.38° N. Lat; 95.47° W. Long. Elevation is 397 feet.
Population: 289 (1990); 272 (2000); 273 (2010); 272 (2015 projected); Race: 90.5% White, 5.1% Black, 0.0% Asian, 4.4% Other, 6.6% Hispanic of any race (2010); Density: 277.0 persons per square mile (2010); Average household size: 2.39 (2010); Median age: 46.0 (2010); Males per 100 females: 92.3 (2010); Marriage status: 30.4% never married, 55.2% now married, 7.3% widowed, 7.1% divorced (2005-2009 5-year est.); Foreign born: 4.0% (2005-2009 5-year est.); Ancestry (includes multiple ancestries): 14.9% English, 14.4% German, 11.6% Scotch-Irish, 9.8% Irish, 8.4% French (2005-2009 5-year est.).
Economy: Employment by occupation: 3.7% management, 7.0% professional, 27.6% services, 37.9% sales, 1.2% farming, 11.9% construction, 10.7% production (2005-2009 5-year est.).
Income: Per capita income: $20,818 (2010); Median household income: $37,727 (2010); Average household income: $52,456 (2010); Percent of households with income of $100,000 or more: 8.8% (2010); Poverty rate: 35.9% (2005-2009 5-year est.).
Taxes: Total city taxes per capita: $121 (2007); City property taxes per capita: $0 (2007).
Education: Percent of population age 25 and over with: High school diploma (including GED) or higher: 81.3% (2010); Bachelor's degree or higher: 12.6% (2010); Master's degree or higher: 1.5% (2010).
School District(s)
Latexo ISD (PK-12)
    2009-10 Enrollment: 450 . . . . (936) 544-5664
Housing: Homeownership rate: 82.5% (2010); Median home value: $76,667 (2010); Median contract rent: $360 per month (2005-2009 5-year est.); Median year structure built: 1967 (2005-2009 5-year est.).
Transportation: Commute to work: 85.6% car, 0.0% public transportation, 9.5% walk, 2.9% work from home (2005-2009 5-year est.); Travel time to work: 47.0% less than 15 minutes, 22.5% 15 to 30 minutes, 17.4% 30 to 45 minutes, 6.8% 45 to 60 minutes, 6.4% 60 minutes or more (2005-2009 5-year est.)

LOVELADY (city). Covers a land area of 1.118 square miles and a water area of 0.009 square miles. Located at 31.12° N. Lat; 95.44° W. Long. Elevation is 299 feet.
Population: 587 (1990); 608 (2000); 619 (2010); 616 (2015 projected); Race: 90.3% White, 8.2% Black, 0.0% Asian, 1.5% Other, 3.2% Hispanic of any race (2010); Density: 553.7 persons per square mile (2010); Average household size: 2.58 (2010); Median age: 32.7 (2010); Males per 100 females: 95.9 (2010); Marriage status: 17.4% never married, 45.8% now married, 15.0% widowed, 21.8% divorced (2005-2009 5-year est.); Foreign born: 0.0% (2005-2009 5-year est.); Ancestry (includes multiple ancestries): 21.8% Irish, 14.8% German, 14.0% English, 4.4% French, 4.2% American (2005-2009 5-year est.).
Economy: Employment by occupation: 8.7% management, 18.1% professional, 29.6% services, 27.8% sales, 0.0% farming, 3.2% construction, 12.6% production (2005-2009 5-year est.).
Income: Per capita income: $16,198 (2010); Median household income: $35,000 (2010); Average household income: $41,607 (2010); Percent of households with income of $100,000 or more: 5.0% (2010); Poverty rate: 13.5% (2005-2009 5-year est.).
Taxes: Total city taxes per capita: $198 (2007); City property taxes per capita: $74 (2007).
Education: Percent of population age 25 and over with: High school diploma (including GED) or higher: 86.6% (2010); Bachelor's degree or higher: 18.4% (2010); Master's degree or higher: 3.0% (2010).
School District(s)
Lovelady ISD (PK-12)
    2009-10 Enrollment: 557 . . . . (936) 636-7616
Housing: Homeownership rate: 74.4% (2010); Median home value: $58,200 (2010); Median contract rent: $379 per month (2005-2009 5-year est.); Median year structure built: 1979 (2005-2009 5-year est.).
Transportation: Commute to work: 91.0% car, 0.0% public transportation, 2.5% walk, 6.5% work from home (2005-2009 5-year est.); Travel time to work: 24.3% less than 15 minutes, 41.3% 15 to 30 minutes, 12.7% 30 to 45 minutes, 2.7% 45 to 60 minutes, 18.9% 60 minutes or more (2005-2009 5-year est.)

Howard County

Located in northwestern Texas; rolling plains area, drained by tributaries of the Colorado River. Covers a land area of 902.84 square miles, a water area of 1.36 square miles, and is located in the Central Time Zone at 32.23° N. Lat., 101.43° W. Long. The county was founded in 1876. County seat is Big Spring.

Howard County is part of the Big Spring, TX Micropolitan Statistical Area. The entire metro area includes: Howard County, TX

Weather Station: Big Spring   Elevation: 2,571 feet

	Jan	Feb	Mar	Apr	May	Jun	Jul	Aug	Sep	Oct	Nov	Dec
High	57	61	69	78	87	92	95	93	87	78	67	57
Low	32	35	42	50	60	68	71	71	64	53	41	32
Precip	0.7	0.9	1.0	1.2	2.5	2.7	1.4	2.7	3.0	1.9	0.9	0.7
Snow	0.4	0.3	0.1	tr	0.0	0.0	0.0	0.0	0.0	0.0	0.6	0.7

High and Low temperatures in degrees Fahrenheit; Precipitation and Snow in inches

Population: 32,343 (1990); 33,627 (2000); 32,725 (2010); 32,224 (2015 projected); Race: 77.4% White, 4.5% Black, 0.7% Asian, 17.3% Other, 42.5% Hispanic of any race (2010); Density: 36.2 persons per square mile (2010); Average household size: 2.48 (2010); Median age: 35.9 (2010); Males per 100 females: 121.4 (2010).
Religion: Five largest groups: 34.9% Southern Baptist Convention, 14.6% Catholic Church, 5.1% The United Methodist Church, 4.0% Churches of Christ, 1.5% Church of the Nazarene (2000).
Economy: Unemployment rate: 7.9% (June 2011); Total civilian labor force: 14,154 (June 2011); Leading industries: 23.5% health care and social assistance; 14.7% retail trade; 11.7% accommodation & food services (2009); Farms: 519 totaling 522,791 acres (2007); Companies that employ 500 or more persons: 1 (2009); Companies that employ 100 to 499 persons: 14 (2009); Companies that employ less than 100 persons: 675 (2009); Black-owned businesses: n/a (2007); Hispanic-owned businesses: 193 (2007); Asian-owned businesses: n/a (2007); Women-owned businesses: 541 (2007); Retail sales per capita: $10,919 (2010). Single-family building permits issued: 2 (2010); Multi-family building permits issued: 0 (2010).
Income: Per capita income: $18,726 (2010); Median household income: $38,705 (2010); Average household income: $50,872 (2010); Percent of households with income of $100,000 or more: 9.7% (2010); Poverty rate: 18.7% (2009); Bankruptcy rate: 1.02% (2010).
Taxes: Total county taxes per capita: $233 (2007); County property taxes per capita: $211 (2007).
Education: Percent of population age 25 and over with: High school diploma (including GED) or higher: 70.8% (2010); Bachelor's degree or higher: 10.4% (2010); Master's degree or higher: 4.1% (2010).
Housing: Homeownership rate: 65.8% (2010); Median home value: $51,946 (2010); Median contract rent: $408 per month (2005-2009 5-year est.); Median year structure built: 1963 (2005-2009 5-year est.)
Health: Birth rate: 148.5 per 10,000 population (2009); Death rate: 103.5 per 10,000 population (2009); Age-adjusted cancer mortality rate: 161.6 deaths per 100,000 population (2007); Number of physicians: 12.3 per 10,000 population (2008); Hospital beds: 158.9 per 10,000 population (2007); Hospital admissions: 2,964.2 per 10,000 population (2007).
Elections: 2008 Presidential election results: 26.3% Obama, 72.5% McCain, 0.0% Nader
National and State Parks: Big Spring State Park
Additional Information Contacts
Howard County Government . . . . (432) 264-2202
http://www.co.howard.tx.us/ips/cms
Big Spring Area Chamber of Commerce . . . . (915) 263-7641
http://www.crcom.net/~bscc
City of Big Spring . . . . (432) 264-2401
http://www.mybigspring.com

Howard County Communities

BIG SPRING (city). County seat. Covers a land area of 19.110 square miles and a water area of 0.078 square miles. Located at 32.24° N. Lat; 101.47° W. Long. Elevation is 2,441 feet.
History: The buffalo spring for which Big Spring was named ran dry, but for a time it was a watering place for buffalo hunters and bone gatherers. The town became the trading center for many ranches in the area, followed by farmlands and then oil fields.

Population: 23,252 (1990); 25,233 (2000); 24,399 (2010); 23,987 (2015 projected); Race: 73.6% White, 5.6% Black, 0.7% Asian, 20.1% Other, 50.9% Hispanic of any race (2010); Density: 1,276.8 persons per square mile (2010); Average household size: 2.46 (2010); Median age: 34.5 (2010); Males per 100 females: 129.6 (2010); Marriage status: 24.7% never married, 55.2% now married, 7.1% widowed, 12.9% divorced (2005-2009 5-year est.); Foreign born: 20.4% (2005-2009 5-year est.); Ancestry (includes multiple ancestries): 8.9% Irish, 8.2% German, 6.8% English, 4.4% American, 2.7% Scottish (2005-2009 5-year est.).
Economy: Unemployment rate: 8.7% (June 2011); Total civilian labor force: 9,735 (June 2011); Single-family building permits issued: 2 (2010); Multi-family building permits issued: 0 (2010); Employment by occupation: 9.4% management, 19.0% professional, 23.1% services, 21.8% sales, 0.7% farming, 14.4% construction, 11.7% production (2005-2009 5-year est.).
Income: Per capita income: $16,889 (2010); Median household income: $34,547 (2010); Average household income: $46,563 (2010); Percent of households with income of $100,000 or more: 8.4% (2010); Poverty rate: 24.1% (2005-2009 5-year est.).
Taxes: Total city taxes per capita: $484 (2007); City property taxes per capita: $128 (2007).
Education: Percent of population age 25 and over with: High school diploma (including GED) or higher: 67.8% (2010); Bachelor's degree or higher: 9.8% (2010); Master's degree or higher: 4.0% (2010).

School District(s)
Big Spring ISD (PK-12)
   2009-10 Enrollment: 3,882 . . . . (432) 264-3600
Forsan ISD (PK-12)
   2009-10 Enrollment: 699 . . . . (432) 457-2223

Two-year College(s)
Howard College (Public)
   Fall 2009 Enrollment: 3,984 . . . . (432) 264-5000
   2010-11 Tuition: In-state $2,132; Out-of-state $2,832
Southwest Collegiate Institute for the Deaf (Public)
   Fall 2009 Enrollment: 119 . . . . (432) 264-3700
   2010-11 Tuition: In-state $2,132; Out-of-state $10,142
Housing: Homeownership rate: 59.7% (2010); Median home value: $46,467 (2010); Median contract rent: $423 per month (2005-2009 5-year est.); Median year structure built: 1960 (2005-2009 5-year est.).
Hospitals: Big Spring State Hospital (195 beds); Scenic Mountain Medical Center (150 beds); West Texas VA Health Care System
Safety: Violent crime rate: 75.3 per 10,000 population; Property crime rate: 713.4 per 10,000 population (2009).
Newspapers: Big Spring Herald (Local news; Circulation 48,000)
Transportation: Commute to work: 92.2% car, 0.0% public transportation, 2.3% walk, 2.2% work from home (2005-2009 5-year est.); Travel time to work: 69.2% less than 15 minutes, 20.8% 15 to 30 minutes, 5.1% 30 to 45 minutes, 1.4% 45 to 60 minutes, 3.6% 60 minutes or more (2005-2009 5-year est.)
Airports: Big Spring McMahon-Wrinkle (general aviation)
Additional Information Contacts
Big Spring Area Chamber of Commerce . . . . (915) 263-7641
http://www.crcom.net/~bscc
City of Big Spring . . . . (432) 264-2401
http://www.mybigspring.com

COAHOMA (town). Covers a land area of 1.203 square miles and a water area of 0 square miles. Located at 32.29° N. Lat; 101.30° W. Long. Elevation is 2,411 feet.
Population: 1,133 (1990); 932 (2000); 892 (2010); 868 (2015 projected); Race: 90.2% White, 0.8% Black, 0.0% Asian, 9.0% Other, 21.5% Hispanic of any race (2010); Density: 741.7 persons per square mile (2010); Average household size: 2.54 (2010); Median age: 39.2 (2010); Males per 100 females: 95.6 (2010); Marriage status: 10.7% never married, 64.0% now married, 16.5% widowed, 8.9% divorced (2005-2009 5-year est.); Foreign born: 4.9% (2005-2009 5-year est.); Ancestry (includes multiple ancestries): 12.2% Irish, 12.2% English, 6.8% German, 5.9% American, 2.8% French (2005-2009 5-year est.).
Economy: Employment by occupation: 8.9% management, 20.2% professional, 19.2% services, 17.5% sales, 0.0% farming, 15.6% construction, 18.5% production (2005-2009 5-year est.).
Income: Per capita income: $22,489 (2010); Median household income: $48,625 (2010); Average household income: $56,282 (2010); Percent of households with income of $100,000 or more: 10.0% (2010); Poverty rate: 10.7% (2005-2009 5-year est.).

Taxes: Total city taxes per capita: $192 (2007); City property taxes per capita: $166 (2007).
Education: Percent of population age 25 and over with: High school diploma (including GED) or higher: 74.6% (2010); Bachelor's degree or higher: 8.7% (2010); Master's degree or higher: 3.8% (2010).

School District(s)
Coahoma ISD (PK-12)
    2009-10 Enrollment: 772 . . . . (432) 394-5000
Housing: Homeownership rate: 78.3% (2010); Median home value: $53,509 (2010); Median contract rent: $322 per month (2005-2009 5-year est.); Median year structure built: 1957 (2005-2009 5-year est.).
Transportation: Commute to work: 98.7% car, 0.0% public transportation, 0.0% walk, 0.0% work from home (2005-2009 5-year est.); Travel time to work: 30.2% less than 15 minutes, 46.6% 15 to 30 minutes, 13.1% 30 to 45 minutes, 2.7% 45 to 60 minutes, 7.4% 60 minutes or more (2005-2009 5-year est.)

FORSAN (city). Covers a land area of 0.290 square miles and a water area of 0 square miles. Located at 32.10° N. Lat; 101.36° W. Long. Elevation is 2,789 feet.
Population: 256 (1990); 226 (2000); 197 (2010); 186 (2015 projected); Race: 94.4% White, 0.5% Black, 1.5% Asian, 3.6% Other, 8.6% Hispanic of any race (2010); Density: 678.9 persons per square mile (2010); Average household size: 2.70 (2010); Median age: 40.8 (2010); Males per 100 females: 91.3 (2010); Marriage status: 25.9% never married, 63.8% now married, 6.3% widowed, 4.0% divorced (2005-2009 5-year est.); Foreign born: 0.0% (2005-2009 5-year est.); Ancestry (includes multiple ancestries): 43.8% German, 27.4% Irish, 13.9% English, 7.0% Dutch, 2.5% American (2005-2009 5-year est.).
Economy: Employment by occupation: 11.7% management, 10.8% professional, 32.4% services, 27.0% sales, 0.0% farming, 5.4% construction, 12.6% production (2005-2009 5-year est.).
Income: Per capita income: $25,454 (2010); Median household income: $55,208 (2010); Average household income: $69,966 (2010); Percent of households with income of $100,000 or more: 15.1% (2010); Poverty rate: 7.5% (2005-2009 5-year est.).
Taxes: Total city taxes per capita: $462 (2007); City property taxes per capita: $81 (2007).
Education: Percent of population age 25 and over with: High school diploma (including GED) or higher: 85.2% (2010); Bachelor's degree or higher: 12.5% (2010); Master's degree or higher: 6.3% (2010).

School District(s)
Forsan ISD (PK-12)
    2009-10 Enrollment: 699 . . . . (432) 457-2223
Housing: Homeownership rate: 83.6% (2010); Median home value: $71,250 (2010); Median contract rent: $158 per month (2005-2009 5-year est.); Median year structure built: 1963 (2005-2009 5-year est.).
Transportation: Commute to work: 77.5% car, 1.8% public transportation, 5.4% walk, 15.3% work from home (2005-2009 5-year est.); Travel time to work: 42.6% less than 15 minutes, 46.8% 15 to 30 minutes, 0.0% 30 to 45 minutes, 6.4% 45 to 60 minutes, 4.3% 60 minutes or more (2005-2009 5-year est.)

KNOTT (unincorporated postal area, zip code 79748). Covers a land area of 41.403 square miles and a water area of 0 square miles. Located at 32.38° N. Lat; 101.66° W. Long. Elevation is 2,612 feet.
Population: 247 (2000); Race: 77.7% White, 0.0% Black, 0.0% Asian, 22.3% Other, 33.5% Hispanic of any race (2000); Density: 6.0 persons per square mile (2000); Age: 29.9% under 18, 14.7% over 64 (2000); Marriage status: 21.7% never married, 75.0% now married, 2.2% widowed, 1.1% divorced (2000); Foreign born: 25.9% (2000); Ancestry (includes multiple ancestries): 10.3% American, 5.8% Pennsylvania German, 5.8% Irish, 3.6% Hungarian (2000).
Economy: Employment by occupation: 18.4% management, 5.7% professional, 17.2% services, 21.8% sales, 26.4% farming, 3.4% construction, 6.9% production (2000).
Income: Per capita income: $11,527 (2000); Median household income: $24,659 (2000); Poverty rate: 179.1% (2000).
Education: Percent of population age 25 and over with: High school diploma (including GED) or higher: 59.3% (2000); Bachelor's degree or higher: 6.7% (2000).
Housing: Homeownership rate: 48.6% (2000); Median home value: $80,000 (2000); Median contract rent: $225 per month (2000); Median year structure built: 1951 (2000).

Transportation: Commute to work: 84.5% car, 0.0% public transportation, 2.4% walk, 13.1% work from home (2000); Travel time to work: 47.9% less than 15 minutes, 16.4% 15 to 30 minutes, 26.0% 30 to 45 minutes, 9.6% 45 to 60 minutes, 0.0% 60 minutes or more (2000)

Hudspeth County

Located in west Texas; bounded on the north by New Mexico, and on the south by the Rio Grande and the Mexican border; high plateau area with many mountains. Covers a land area of 4,571.00 square miles, a water area of 0.93 square miles, and is located in the Mountain Time Zone at 31.49° N. Lat., 105.40° W. Long. The county was founded in 1917. County seat is Sierra Blanca.

Weather Station: Dell City 5 SSW   Elevation: 3,770 feet

	Jan	Feb	Mar	Apr	May	Jun	Jul	Aug	Sep	Oct	Nov	Dec
High	60	65	72	80	89	97	97	94	89	80	68	59
Low	26	31	36	43	53	61	65	63	56	45	32	26
Precip	0.4	0.5	0.3	0.2	1.0	1.0	1.5	1.9	1.8	1.1	0.5	0.5
Snow	0.3	0.1	0.0	0.0	0.0	0.0	0.0	0.0	0.0	0.0	0.1	0.1

High and Low temperatures in degrees Fahrenheit; Precipitation and Snow in inches

Weather Station: Fort Hancock 5 SSE   Elevation: 3,904 feet

	Jan	Feb	Mar	Apr	May	Jun	Jul	Aug	Sep	Oct	Nov	Dec
High	61	67	74	82	91	98	96	93	89	81	70	60
Low	26	30	37	43	53	63	66	65	58	46	33	26
Precip	0.5	0.3	0.2	0.3	0.5	0.9	1.6	1.5	1.6	1.0	0.4	0.6
Snow	0.1	tr	0.0	0.0	0.0	0.0	0.0	0.0	0.0	0.0	tr	0.3

High and Low temperatures in degrees Fahrenheit; Precipitation and Snow in inches

Population: 2,915 (1990); 3,344 (2000); 3,292 (2010); 3,262 (2015 projected); Race: 86.3% White, 1.1% Black, 0.2% Asian, 12.5% Other, 75.4% Hispanic of any race (2010); Density: 0.7 persons per square mile (2010); Average household size: 3.06 (2010); Median age: 37.9 (2010); Males per 100 females: 96.1 (2010).
Religion: Five largest groups: 49.2% Catholic Church, 3.0% Southern Baptist Convention, 2.1% The United Methodist Church, 1.3% Assemblies of God, 0.7% Churches of Christ (2000).
Economy: Unemployment rate: 6.6% (June 2011); Total civilian labor force: 1,816 (June 2011); Leading industries: Farms: 169 totaling 2,257,579 acres (2007); Companies that employ 500 or more persons: 0 (2009); Companies that employ 100 to 499 persons: 0 (2009); Companies that employ less than 100 persons: 32 (2009); Black-owned businesses: n/a (2007); Hispanic-owned businesses: n/a (2007); Asian-owned businesses: n/a (2007); Women-owned businesses: n/a (2007); Retail sales per capita: $2,274 (2010). Single-family building permits issued: n/a (2010); Multi-family building permits issued: n/a (2010).
Income: Per capita income: $12,041 (2010); Median household income: $26,548 (2010); Average household income: $37,180 (2010); Percent of households with income of $100,000 or more: 4.3% (2010); Poverty rate: 29.8% (2009); Bankruptcy rate: 1.42% (2010).
Taxes: Total county taxes per capita: $607 (2007); County property taxes per capita: $551 (2007).
Education: Percent of population age 25 and over with: High school diploma (including GED) or higher: 52.6% (2010); Bachelor's degree or higher: 11.3% (2010); Master's degree or higher: 3.5% (2010).
Housing: Homeownership rate: 79.4% (2010); Median home value: $36,105 (2010); Median contract rent: $240 per month (2005-2009 5-year est.); Median year structure built: 1974 (2005-2009 5-year est.).
Health: Birth rate: 144.5 per 10,000 population (2009); Death rate: 9.6 per 10,000 population (2009); Age-adjusted cancer mortality rate: 171.4 (Unreliable) deaths per 100,000 population (2007); Number of physicians: 3.2 per 10,000 population (2008); Hospital beds: 0.0 per 10,000 population (2007); Hospital admissions: 0.0 per 10,000 population (2007).
Elections: 2008 Presidential election results: 47.9% Obama, 51.0% McCain, 0.0% Nader
Additional Information Contacts
Hudspeth County Government . . . . (915) 369-2301
    http://www.co.hudspeth.tx.us/ips/cms

Hudspeth County Communities

DELL CITY (city). Covers a land area of 1.651 square miles and a water area of 0 square miles. Located at 31.93° N. Lat; 105.20° W. Long. Elevation is 3,701 feet.

History: Dell City was settled about 1950 at the place where a rancher struck an abundant supply of well water.
Population: 569 (1990); 413 (2000); 351 (2010); 326 (2015 projected); Race: 57.0% White, 3.4% Black, 0.3% Asian, 39.3% Other, 54.4% Hispanic of any race (2010); Density: 212.6 persons per square mile (2010); Average household size: 2.58 (2010); Median age: 49.8 (2010); Males per 100 females: 91.8 (2010); Marriage status: 17.9% never married, 75.3% now married, 5.7% widowed, 1.2% divorced (2005-2009 5-year est.); Foreign born: 27.2% (2005-2009 5-year est.); Ancestry (includes multiple ancestries): 16.2% German, 12.5% American, 5.0% Irish, 2.9% French, 2.6% Swiss (2005-2009 5-year est.).
Economy: Employment by occupation: 27.3% management, 13.9% professional, 1.0% services, 22.7% sales, 15.5% farming, 13.4% construction, 6.2% production (2005-2009 5-year est.).
Income: Per capita income: $14,240 (2010); Median household income: $27,500 (2010); Average household income: $37,077 (2010); Percent of households with income of $100,000 or more: 4.4% (2010); Poverty rate: 15.4% (2005-2009 5-year est.).
Taxes: Total city taxes per capita: $190 (2007); City property taxes per capita: $97 (2007).
Education: Percent of population age 25 and over with: High school diploma (including GED) or higher: 66.3% (2010); Bachelor's degree or higher: 7.0% (2010); Master's degree or higher: 3.1% (2010).

School District(s)
Dell City ISD (PK-12)
   2009-10 Enrollment: 100 . . . . (915) 964-2663
Housing: Homeownership rate: 74.3% (2010); Median home value: $38,889 (2010); Median contract rent: n/a per month (2005-2009 5-year est.); Median year structure built: 1967 (2005-2009 5-year est.).
Newspapers: Hudspeth County Herald-Dell Valley Review (Community news; Circulation 800)
Transportation: Commute to work: 67.2% car, 0.0% public transportation, 0.0% walk, 10.4% work from home (2005-2009 5-year est.); Travel time to work: 77.3% less than 15 minutes, 9.3% 15 to 30 minutes, 0.0% 30 to 45 minutes, 3.5% 45 to 60 minutes, 9.9% 60 minutes or more (2005-2009 5-year est.)

FORT HANCOCK (CDP). Covers a land area of 37.653 square miles and a water area of 0.157 square miles. Located at 31.29° N. Lat; 105.86° W. Long. Elevation is 3,579 feet.
History: Ruins of old Fort Hancock are nearby.
Population: 979 (1990); 1,713 (2000); 1,834 (2010); 1,885 (2015 projected); Race: 93.3% White, 0.9% Black, 0.2% Asian, 5.7% Other, 85.2% Hispanic of any race (2010); Density: 48.7 persons per square mile (2010); Average household size: 3.37 (2010); Median age: 34.8 (2010); Males per 100 females: 96.4 (2010); Marriage status: 30.6% never married, 57.2% now married, 8.4% widowed, 3.8% divorced (2005-2009 5-year est.); Foreign born: 42.4% (2005-2009 5-year est.); Ancestry (includes multiple ancestries): 7.1% American, 2.1% Norwegian, 1.2% British, 0.8% German (2005-2009 5-year est.).
Economy: Employment by occupation: 12.9% management, 6.4% professional, 18.7% services, 14.1% sales, 7.2% farming, 17.1% construction, 23.7% production (2005-2009 5-year est.).
Income: Per capita income: $9,042 (2010); Median household income: $22,074 (2010); Average household income: $30,450 (2010); Percent of households with income of $100,000 or more: 2.8% (2010); Poverty rate: 59.3% (2005-2009 5-year est.).
Education: Percent of population age 25 and over with: High school diploma (including GED) or higher: 40.8% (2010); Bachelor's degree or higher: 10.8% (2010); Master's degree or higher: 3.5% (2010).

School District(s)
Ft Hancock ISD (PK-12)
   2009-10 Enrollment: 516 . . . . (915) 769-3811
Housing: Homeownership rate: 85.7% (2010); Median home value: $33,022 (2010); Median contract rent: $203 per month (2005-2009 5-year est.); Median year structure built: 1983 (2005-2009 5-year est.).
Transportation: Commute to work: 86.8% car, 2.0% public transportation, 3.6% walk, 1.8% work from home (2005-2009 5-year est.); Travel time to work: 43.5% less than 15 minutes, 3.6% 15 to 30 minutes, 25.6% 30 to 45 minutes, 14.5% 45 to 60 minutes, 12.9% 60 minutes or more (2005-2009 5-year est.)

SALT FLAT (unincorporated postal area, zip code 79847). Covers a land area of 464.663 square miles and a water area of 0 square miles. Located at 31.82° N. Lat; 105.30° W. Long. Elevation is 3,730 feet.

Population: 44 (2000); Race: 93.5% White, 0.0% Black, 6.5% Asian, 0.0% Other, 6.5% Hispanic of any race (2000); Density: 0.1 persons per square mile (2000); Age: 9.7% under 18, 9.7% over 64 (2000); Marriage status: 10.7% never married, 67.9% now married, 10.7% widowed, 10.7% divorced (2000); Foreign born: 0.0% (2000); Ancestry (includes multiple ancestries): 9.7% Russian, 9.7% English (2000).
Economy: Employment by occupation: 20.0% management, 20.0% professional, 0.0% services, 0.0% sales, 45.0% farming, 0.0% construction, 15.0% production (2000).
Income: Per capita income: $13,303 (2000); Median household income: $25,833 (2000); Poverty rate: 179.1% (2000).
Education: Percent of population age 25 and over with: High school diploma (including GED) or higher: 63.6% (2000); Bachelor's degree or higher: 18.2% (2000).
Housing: Homeownership rate: 73.3% (2000); Median home value: n/a (2000); Median contract rent: n/a per month (2000); Median year structure built: 1981 (2000).
Transportation: Commute to work: 100.0% car, 0.0% public transportation, 0.0% walk, 0.0% work from home (2000); Travel time to work: 55.0% less than 15 minutes, 30.0% 15 to 30 minutes, 15.0% 30 to 45 minutes, 0.0% 45 to 60 minutes, 0.0% 60 minutes or more (2000)

SIERRA BLANCA (CDP). County seat. Covers a land area of 4.069 square miles and a water area of 0.028 square miles. Located at 31.18° N. Lat; 105.34° W. Long. Elevation is 4,528 feet.
History: Established 1881 at railroad junction.
Population: 664 (1990); 533 (2000); 454 (2010); 418 (2015 projected); Race: 87.4% White, 0.0% Black, 0.2% Asian, 12.3% Other, 61.5% Hispanic of any race (2010); Density: 111.6 persons per square mile (2010); Average household size: 2.68 (2010); Median age: 40.8 (2010); Males per 100 females: 94.0 (2010); Marriage status: 26.4% never married, 42.8% now married, 19.1% widowed, 11.7% divorced (2005-2009 5-year est.); Foreign born: 16.2% (2005-2009 5-year est.); Ancestry (includes multiple ancestries): 19.1% American, 5.6% Scotch-Irish, 5.2% Welsh, 2.3% Irish, 2.3% German (2005-2009 5-year est.).
Economy: Employment by occupation: 9.6% management, 8.2% professional, 53.4% services, 15.8% sales, 0.0% farming, 13.0% construction, 0.0% production (2005-2009 5-year est.).
Income: Per capita income: $19,909 (2010); Median household income: $42,708 (2010); Average household income: $56,196 (2010); Percent of households with income of $100,000 or more: 8.1% (2010); Poverty rate: 18.1% (2005-2009 5-year est.).
Education: Percent of population age 25 and over with: High school diploma (including GED) or higher: 75.3% (2010); Bachelor's degree or higher: 17.0% (2010); Master's degree or higher: 3.8% (2010).

School District(s)
Sierra Blanca ISD (KG-12)
   2009-10 Enrollment: 166 . . . . (915) 369-3741
Housing: Homeownership rate: 67.1% (2010); Median home value: $56,250 (2010); Median contract rent: $298 per month (2005-2009 5-year est.); Median year structure built: 1955 (2005-2009 5-year est.).
Transportation: Commute to work: 76.1% car, 0.0% public transportation, 2.1% walk, 2.8% work from home (2005-2009 5-year est.); Travel time to work: 85.5% less than 15 minutes, 2.9% 15 to 30 minutes, 6.5% 30 to 45 minutes, 5.1% 45 to 60 minutes, 0.0% 60 minutes or more (2005-2009 5-year est.)

Hunt County

Located in northeastern Texas; drained by the Sabine River and South Fork of the Sulphur River. Covers a land area of 841.16 square miles, a water area of 40.87 square miles, and is located in the Central Time Zone at 33.11° N. Lat., 96.08° W. Long. The county was founded in 1846. County seat is Greenville.

Hunt County is part of the Dallas-Fort Worth-Arlington, TX Metropolitan Statistical Area. The entire metro area includes: Dallas-Plano-Irving, TX Metropolitan Division (Collin County, TX; Dallas County, TX; Delta County, TX; Denton County, TX; Ellis County, TX; Hunt County, TX; Kaufman County, TX; Rockwall County, TX); Fort Worth-Arlington, TX Metropolitan Division (Johnson County, TX; Parker County, TX; Tarrant County, TX; Wise County, TX)

Weather Station: Greenville Kgvl Radio   Elevation: 544 feet

	Jan	Feb	Mar	Apr	May	Jun	Jul	Aug	Sep	Oct	Nov	Dec
High	54	58	66	74	82	89	94	95	88	77	66	56
Low	32	35	43	51	61	68	72	72	64	53	43	34
Precip	2.7	3.4	4.1	3.7	5.4	4.3	2.9	2.0	3.3	5.2	4.0	3.4
Snow	0.3	0.7	0.1	0.0	0.0	0.0	0.0	0.0	0.0	0.0	tr	0.2

High and Low temperatures in degrees Fahrenheit; Precipitation and Snow in inches

Population: 64,343 (1990); 76,596 (2000); 84,923 (2010); 88,821 (2015 projected); Race: 81.4% White, 8.8% Black, 0.7% Asian, 9.1% Other, 12.4% Hispanic of any race (2010); Density: 101.0 persons per square mile (2010); Average household size: 2.66 (2010); Median age: 35.6 (2010); Males per 100 females: 99.4 (2010).
Religion: Five largest groups: 35.4% Southern Baptist Convention, 5.7% The United Methodist Church, 3.3% Churches of Christ, 2.3% Catholic Church, 1.4% Independent, Non-Charismatic Churches (2000).
Economy: Unemployment rate: 9.9% (June 2011); Total civilian labor force: 38,044 (June 2011); Leading industries: 34.9% manufacturing; 16.6% retail trade; 13.6% health care and social assistance (2009); Farms: 3,139 totaling 388,422 acres (2007); Companies that employ 500 or more persons: 3 (2009); Companies that employ 100 to 499 persons: 22 (2009); Companies that employ less than 100 persons: 1,370 (2009); Black-owned businesses: 176 (2007); Hispanic-owned businesses: n/a (2007); Asian-owned businesses: n/a (2007); Women-owned businesses: 1,912 (2007); Retail sales per capita: $10,920 (2010). Single-family building permits issued: 37 (2010); Multi-family building permits issued: 10 (2010).
Income: Per capita income: $20,911 (2010); Median household income: $44,694 (2010); Average household income: $56,617 (2010); Percent of households with income of $100,000 or more: 12.6% (2010); Poverty rate: 19.9% (2009); Bankruptcy rate: 2.13% (2010).
Taxes: Total county taxes per capita: $256 (2007); County property taxes per capita: $203 (2007).
Education: Percent of population age 25 and over with: High school diploma (including GED) or higher: 79.5% (2010); Bachelor's degree or higher: 18.2% (2010); Master's degree or higher: 6.0% (2010).
Housing: Homeownership rate: 71.8% (2010); Median home value: $87,174 (2010); Median contract rent: $517 per month (2005-2009 5-year est.); Median year structure built: 1981 (2005-2009 5-year est.)
Health: Birth rate: 135.1 per 10,000 population (2009); Death rate: 96.1 per 10,000 population (2009); Age-adjusted cancer mortality rate: 230.3 deaths per 100,000 population (2007); Number of physicians: 7.4 per 10,000 population (2008); Hospital beds: 31.1 per 10,000 population (2007); Hospital admissions: 1,368.0 per 10,000 population (2007).
Environment: Air Quality Index: 94.8% good, 5.2% moderate, 0.0% unhealthy for sensitive individuals, 0.0% unhealthy (percent of days in 2008)
Elections: 2008 Presidential election results: 29.1% Obama, 69.7% McCain, 0.1% Nader
Additional Information Contacts

Hunt County Government	(903) 408-4100
http://www.huntcounty.net	
City of Commerce	(903) 886-1100
http://commercetx.org	
City of Greenville	(903) 457-3121
http://www.ci.greenville.tx.us	
Commerce Chamber of Commerce	(903) 886-3950
http://www.commerce-chamber.com	
Greenville Chamber of Commerce	(903) 455-1510
http://www.greenville-chamber.org	
Lake Tawakoni Regional Chamber of Commerce	(903) 447-3020
http://laketawakonichamber.org	
Wolfe City Chamber of Commerce	(903) 496-2323

Hunt County Communities

CADDO MILLS (city). Covers a land area of 2.616 square miles and a water area of 0.011 square miles. Located at 33.06° N. Lat; 96.22° W. Long. Elevation is 531 feet.
Population: 1,093 (1990); 1,149 (2000); 1,255 (2010); 1,309 (2015 projected); Race: 92.3% White, 3.3% Black, 0.0% Asian, 4.4% Other, 4.1% Hispanic of any race (2010); Density: 479.8 persons per square mile (2010); Average household size: 2.68 (2010); Median age: 35.0 (2010); Males per 100 females: 88.4 (2010); Marriage status: 20.1% never married, 59.3% now married, 6.0% widowed, 14.6% divorced (2005-2009 5-year est.); Foreign born: 3.1% (2005-2009 5-year est.); Ancestry (includes

multiple ancestries): 25.8% Irish, 16.6% English, 9.4% American, 8.7% German, 5.2% Scotch-Irish (2005-2009 5-year est.).
Economy: Single-family building permits issued: 3 (2010); Multi-family building permits issued: 0 (2010); Employment by occupation: 12.6% management, 9.7% professional, 18.7% services, 24.5% sales, 0.0% farming, 19.2% construction, 15.4% production (2005-2009 5-year est.).
Income: Per capita income: $19,543 (2010); Median household income: $42,411 (2010); Average household income: $52,308 (2010); Percent of households with income of $100,000 or more: 11.5% (2010); Poverty rate: 9.8% (2005-2009 5-year est.).
Taxes: Total city taxes per capita: $579 (2007); City property taxes per capita: $551 (2007).
Education: Percent of population age 25 and over with: High school diploma (including GED) or higher: 75.6% (2010); Bachelor's degree or higher: 10.8% (2010); Master's degree or higher: 4.4% (2010).

School District(s)

Caddo Mills ISD (PK-12)
   2009-10 Enrollment: 1,460 .... (903) 527-6056
Celeste ISD (PK-12)
   2009-10 Enrollment: 513 .... (903) 568-4825
Housing: Homeownership rate: 70.8% (2010); Median home value: $77,647 (2010); Median contract rent: $540 per month (2005-2009 5-year est.); Median year structure built: 1976 (2005-2009 5-year est.).
Safety: Violent crime rate: 99.2 per 10,000 population; Property crime rate: 405.0 per 10,000 population (2009).
Transportation: Commute to work: 99.5% car, 0.0% public transportation, 0.5% walk, 0.0% work from home (2005-2009 5-year est.); Travel time to work: 27.7% less than 15 minutes, 18.8% 15 to 30 minutes, 20.4% 30 to 45 minutes, 11.5% 45 to 60 minutes, 21.7% 60 minutes or more (2005-2009 5-year est.)

CAMPBELL (city). Covers a land area of 2.291 square miles and a water area of 0 square miles. Located at 33.15° N. Lat; 95.95° W. Long. Elevation is 591 feet.
Population: 683 (1990); 734 (2000); 764 (2010); 772 (2015 projected); Race: 92.0% White, 1.7% Black, 0.4% Asian, 5.9% Other, 4.7% Hispanic of any race (2010); Density: 333.5 persons per square mile (2010); Average household size: 2.72 (2010); Median age: 39.6 (2010); Males per 100 females: 100.0 (2010); Marriage status: 24.6% never married, 55.1% now married, 12.0% widowed, 8.3% divorced (2005-2009 5-year est.); Foreign born: 2.1% (2005-2009 5-year est.); Ancestry (includes multiple ancestries): 18.0% Irish, 14.4% German, 9.2% American, 8.2% Scotch-Irish, 8.2% English (2005-2009 5-year est.).
Economy: Employment by occupation: 4.5% management, 8.8% professional, 13.0% services, 29.6% sales, 0.9% farming, 21.1% construction, 22.1% production (2005-2009 5-year est.).
Income: Per capita income: $23,576 (2010); Median household income: $49,306 (2010); Average household income: $64,297 (2010); Percent of households with income of $100,000 or more: 13.5% (2010); Poverty rate: 7.6% (2005-2009 5-year est.).
Taxes: Total city taxes per capita: $143 (2007); City property taxes per capita: $140 (2007).
Education: Percent of population age 25 and over with: High school diploma (including GED) or higher: 82.9% (2010); Bachelor's degree or higher: 21.9% (2010); Master's degree or higher: 8.2% (2010).

School District(s)

Campbell ISD (PK-12)
   2009-10 Enrollment: 392 .... (903) 862-3259
Housing: Homeownership rate: 85.8% (2010); Median home value: $98,780 (2010); Median contract rent: $501 per month (2005-2009 5-year est.); Median year structure built: 1979 (2005-2009 5-year est.).
Transportation: Commute to work: 90.3% car, 0.0% public transportation, 9.7% walk, 0.0% work from home (2005-2009 5-year est.); Travel time to work: 28.4% less than 15 minutes, 40.3% 15 to 30 minutes, 4.7% 30 to 45 minutes, 1.9% 45 to 60 minutes, 24.7% 60 minutes or more (2005-2009 5-year est.)

CELESTE (city). Covers a land area of 0.813 square miles and a water area of 0 square miles. Located at 33.29° N. Lat; 96.19° W. Long. Elevation is 669 feet.
Population: 725 (1990); 817 (2000); 894 (2010); 932 (2015 projected); Race: 94.2% White, 2.2% Black, 0.1% Asian, 3.5% Other, 2.5% Hispanic of any race (2010); Density: 1,099.9 persons per square mile (2010); Average household size: 2.85 (2010); Median age: 33.2 (2010); Males per 100 females: 93.5 (2010); Marriage status: 31.4% never married, 45.5%

now married, 5.7% widowed, 17.4% divorced (2005-2009 5-year est.); Foreign born: 0.3% (2005-2009 5-year est.); Ancestry (includes multiple ancestries): 29.3% Irish, 15.2% German, 11.6% English, 7.8% American, 6.1% French (2005-2009 5-year est.).

Economy: Single-family building permits issued: 1 (2010); Multi-family building permits issued: 0 (2010); Employment by occupation: 8.7% management, 15.6% professional, 18.9% services, 30.0% sales, 1.1% farming, 6.4% construction, 19.3% production (2005-2009 5-year est.).

Income: Per capita income: $18,258 (2010); Median household income: $47,500 (2010); Average household income: $51,768 (2010); Percent of households with income of $100,000 or more: 8.0% (2010); Poverty rate: 21.2% (2005-2009 5-year est.).

Taxes: Total city taxes per capita: $206 (2007); City property taxes per capita: $111 (2007).

Education: Percent of population age 25 and over with: High school diploma (including GED) or higher: 83.9% (2010); Bachelor's degree or higher: 12.1% (2010); Master's degree or higher: 4.1% (2010).

School District(s)

Celeste ISD (PK-12)
    2009-10 Enrollment: 513 . . . . (903) 568-4825

Housing: Homeownership rate: 78.0% (2010); Median home value: $61,373 (2010); Median contract rent: $487 per month (2005-2009 5-year est.); Median year structure built: 1975 (2005-2009 5-year est.).

Transportation: Commute to work: 90.1% car, 0.0% public transportation, 6.6% walk, 2.1% work from home (2005-2009 5-year est.); Travel time to work: 20.6% less than 15 minutes, 39.8% 15 to 30 minutes, 20.1% 30 to 45 minutes, 1.9% 45 to 60 minutes, 17.5% 60 minutes or more (2005-2009 5-year est.)

COMMERCE (city).

Covers a land area of 6.481 square miles and a water area of 0.056 square miles. Located at 33.24° N. Lat; 95.90° W. Long. Elevation is 554 feet.

History: East Texas State University was established in Commerce in 1889 as Teachers College.

Population: 6,828 (1990); 7,669 (2000); 9,428 (2010); 10,242 (2015 projected); Race: 70.8% White, 19.8% Black, 2.5% Asian, 7.0% Other, 11.2% Hispanic of any race (2010); Density: 1,454.7 persons per square mile (2010); Average household size: 2.38 (2010); Median age: 29.4 (2010); Males per 100 females: 97.8 (2010); Marriage status: 47.9% never married, 34.9% now married, 5.0% widowed, 12.3% divorced (2005-2009 5-year est.); Foreign born: 9.0% (2005-2009 5-year est.); Ancestry (includes multiple ancestries): 19.6% Irish, 11.6% German, 7.1% English, 3.6% American, 2.9% Scotch-Irish (2005-2009 5-year est.).

Economy: Single-family building permits issued: 2 (2010); Multi-family building permits issued: 10 (2010); Employment by occupation: 6.7% management, 27.7% professional, 17.2% services, 26.1% sales, 1.1% farming, 4.8% construction, 16.5% production (2005-2009 5-year est.).

Income: Per capita income: $17,437 (2010); Median household income: $29,113 (2010); Average household income: $45,587 (2010); Percent of households with income of $100,000 or more: 9.5% (2010); Poverty rate: 32.7% (2005-2009 5-year est.).

Taxes: Total city taxes per capita: $374 (2007); City property taxes per capita: $151 (2007).

Education: Percent of population age 25 and over with: High school diploma (including GED) or higher: 82.3% (2010); Bachelor's degree or higher: 32.8% (2010); Master's degree or higher: 14.3% (2010).

School District(s)

Commerce ISD (PK-12)
    2009-10 Enrollment: 1,629 . . . . (903) 886-3755

Four-year College(s)

Texas A & M University-Commerce (Public)
    Fall 2009 Enrollment: 9,021. . . . . (903) 886-5081
    2010-11 Tuition: In-state $5,998; Out-of-state $15,298

Housing: Homeownership rate: 45.8% (2010); Median home value: $80,435 (2010); Median contract rent: $456 per month (2005-2009 5-year est.); Median year structure built: 1967 (2005-2009 5-year est.).

Safety: Violent crime rate: 33.9 per 10,000 population; Property crime rate: 342.6 per 10,000 population (2009).

Transportation: Commute to work: 86.9% car, 0.4% public transportation, 10.0% walk, 0.1% work from home (2005-2009 5-year est.); Travel time to work: 52.6% less than 15 minutes, 24.5% 15 to 30 minutes, 11.6% 30 to 45 minutes, 3.4% 45 to 60 minutes, 7.9% 60 minutes or more (2005-2009 5-year est.)

Additional Information Contacts

City of Commerce . . . . (903) 886-1100
    http://commercetx.org
Commerce Chamber of Commerce. . . . . (903) 886-3950
    http://www.commerce-chamber.com

GREENVILLE (city).

County seat. Covers a land area of 33.913 square miles and a water area of 0.796 square miles. Located at 33.12° N. Lat; 96.11° W. Long. Elevation is 541 feet.

History: Named for General Thomas J. Green, soldier in the Texas Revolution. Greenville developed as a major cotton center, later turning to diversified industry manufacturing aircraft and oil well equipment.

Population: 23,364 (1990); 23,960 (2000); 26,163 (2010); 27,230 (2015 projected); Race: 67.5% White, 16.2% Black, 0.7% Asian, 15.6% Other, 22.0% Hispanic of any race (2010); Density: 771.5 persons per square mile (2010); Average household size: 2.62 (2010); Median age: 35.3 (2010); Males per 100 females: 97.1 (2010); Marriage status: 26.2% never married, 48.7% now married, 12.0% widowed, 13.0% divorced (2005-2009 5-year est.); Foreign born: 8.5% (2005-2009 5-year est.); Ancestry (includes multiple ancestries): 14.5% Irish, 12.6% German, 8.4% English, 5.7% American, 2.6% Scotch-Irish (2005-2009 5-year est.).

Economy: Unemployment rate: 9.6% (June 2011); Total civilian labor force: 11,368 (June 2011); Single-family building permits issued: 29 (2010); Multi-family building permits issued: 0 (2010); Employment by occupation: 9.6% management, 16.8% professional, 14.8% services, 28.1% sales, 0.2% farming, 13.0% construction, 17.5% production (2005-2009 5-year est.).

Income: Per capita income: $19,558 (2010); Median household income: $40,476 (2010); Average household income: $51,841 (2010); Percent of households with income of $100,000 or more: 10.2% (2010); Poverty rate: 22.3% (2005-2009 5-year est.).

Taxes: Total city taxes per capita: $621 (2007); City property taxes per capita: $299 (2007).

Education: Percent of population age 25 and over with: High school diploma (including GED) or higher: 77.9% (2010); Bachelor's degree or higher: 20.6% (2010); Master's degree or higher: 6.8% (2010).

School District(s)

Bland ISD (PK-12)
    2009-10 Enrollment: 591 . . . . (903) 776-2239
Greenville ISD (PK-12)
    2009-10 Enrollment: 4,956 . . . . (903) 457-2500
Lone Oak ISD (PK-12)
    2009-10 Enrollment: 925 . . . . (903) 662-5427
Phoenix Charter School (PK-12)
    2009-10 Enrollment: 452 . . . . (903) 454-7153

Vocational/Technical School(s)

Touch of Class School of Cosmetology (Private, For-profit)
    Fall 2009 Enrollment: 47 . . . . (903) 455-1144
    2010-11 Tuition: $18,000

Housing: Homeownership rate: 58.4% (2010); Median home value: $80,283 (2010); Median contract rent: $571 per month (2005-2009 5-year est.); Median year structure built: 1971 (2005-2009 5-year est.).

Hospitals: Glen Oaks Hospital (54 beds); Presbyterian Hospital of Greenville (109 beds)

Safety: Violent crime rate: 75.0 per 10,000 population; Property crime rate: 469.0 per 10,000 population (2009).

Newspapers: Commerce Journal (Local news; Circulation 1,300); Herald-Banner (Local news; Circulation 11,800)

Transportation: Commute to work: 95.1% car, 0.6% public transportation, 0.8% walk, 2.1% work from home (2005-2009 5-year est.); Travel time to work: 54.8% less than 15 minutes, 30.0% 15 to 30 minutes, 4.8% 30 to 45 minutes, 3.5% 45 to 60 minutes, 6.9% 60 minutes or more (2005-2009 5-year est.)

Additional Information Contacts

City of Greenville . . . . (903) 457-3121
    http://www.ci.greenville.tx.us
Greenville Chamber of Commerce . . . . (903) 455-1510
    http://www.greenville-chamber.org

HAWK COVE (city).

Covers a land area of 0.312 square miles and a water area of 0 square miles. Located at 32.88° N. Lat; 96.08° W. Long. Elevation is 472 feet.

Population: 359 (1990); 457 (2000); 478 (2010); 488 (2015 projected); Race: 93.7% White, 0.4% Black, 0.0% Asian, 5.9% Other, 7.3% Hispanic of any race (2010); Density: 1,533.0 persons per square mile (2010); Average household size: 2.70 (2010); Median age: 36.1 (2010); Males per

100 females: 94.3 (2010); Marriage status: 21.3% never married, 64.7% now married, 4.6% widowed, 9.4% divorced (2005-2009 5-year est.); Foreign born: 0.0% (2005-2009 5-year est.); Ancestry (includes multiple ancestries): 27.2% Irish, 22.3% English, 8.8% German, 6.0% American, 3.2% French (2005-2009 5-year est.).

Economy: Single-family building permits issued: 0 (2010); Multi-family building permits issued: 0 (2010); Employment by occupation: 12.0% management, 11.5% professional, 24.0% services, 19.7% sales, 3.3% farming, 12.6% construction, 16.9% production (2005-2009 5-year est.).

Income: Per capita income: $16,557 (2010); Median household income: $34,000 (2010); Average household income: $47,726 (2010); Percent of households with income of $100,000 or more: 7.9% (2010); Poverty rate: 50.0% (2005-2009 5-year est.).

Taxes: Total city taxes per capita: $159 (2007); City property taxes per capita: $126 (2007).

Education: Percent of population age 25 and over with: High school diploma (including GED) or higher: 71.9% (2010); Bachelor's degree or higher: 7.8% (2010); Master's degree or higher: 1.0% (2010).

Housing: Homeownership rate: 87.0% (2010); Median home value: $57,143 (2010); Median contract rent: $295 per month (2005-2009 5-year est.); Median year structure built: 1985 (2005-2009 5-year est.).

Safety: Violent crime rate: 48.5 per 10,000 population; Property crime rate: 80.9 per 10,000 population (2009).

Transportation: Commute to work: 95.5% car, 0.0% public transportation, 2.8% walk, 0.0% work from home (2005-2009 5-year est.); Travel time to work: 39.7% less than 15 minutes, 25.7% 15 to 30 minutes, 3.4% 30 to 45 minutes, 0.0% 45 to 60 minutes, 31.3% 60 minutes or more (2005-2009 5-year est.)

Additional Information Contacts

Lake Tawakoni Regional Chamber of Commerce . . . . (903) 447-3020
http://laketawakonichamber.org

LONE OAK (town). Covers a land area of 0.797 square miles and a water area of 0 square miles. Located at 32.99° N. Lat; 95.94° W. Long. Elevation is 564 feet.

Population: 549 (1990); 521 (2000); 567 (2010); 584 (2015 projected); Race: 91.9% White, 2.6% Black, 0.2% Asian, 5.3% Other, 8.1% Hispanic of any race (2010); Density: 711.2 persons per square mile (2010); Average household size: 2.88 (2010); Median age: 35.6 (2010); Males per 100 females: 105.4 (2010); Marriage status: 25.1% never married, 52.9% now married, 8.5% widowed, 13.5% divorced (2005-2009 5-year est.); Foreign born: 0.0% (2005-2009 5-year est.); Ancestry (includes multiple ancestries): 15.9% German, 12.3% Irish, 12.1% English, 5.6% Polish, 4.3% American (2005-2009 5-year est.).

Economy: Employment by occupation: 1.1% management, 11.2% professional, 24.2% services, 18.8% sales, 1.1% farming, 17.7% construction, 26.0% production (2005-2009 5-year est.).

Income: Per capita income: $18,310 (2010); Median household income: $42,045 (2010); Average household income: $54,201 (2010); Percent of households with income of $100,000 or more: 7.1% (2010); Poverty rate: 20.8% (2005-2009 5-year est.).

Taxes: Total city taxes per capita: $223 (2007); City property taxes per capita: $89 (2007).

Education: Percent of population age 25 and over with: High school diploma (including GED) or higher: 78.1% (2010); Bachelor's degree or higher: 11.6% (2010); Master's degree or higher: 2.7% (2010).

School District(s)

Lone Oak ISD (PK-12)
2009-10 Enrollment: 925 . . . . (903) 662-5427

Housing: Homeownership rate: 78.2% (2010); Median home value: $71,667 (2010); Median contract rent: $608 per month (2005-2009 5-year est.); Median year structure built: 1964 (2005-2009 5-year est.).

Transportation: Commute to work: 98.0% car, 0.0% public transportation, 0.0% walk, 2.0% work from home (2005-2009 5-year est.); Travel time to work: 40.2% less than 15 minutes, 43.0% 15 to 30 minutes, 9.6% 30 to 45 minutes, 0.0% 45 to 60 minutes, 7.2% 60 minutes or more (2005-2009 5-year est.)

NEYLANDVILLE (town). Covers a land area of 0.316 square miles and a water area of 0 square miles. Located at 33.20° N. Lat; 96.00° W. Long. Elevation is 535 feet.

History: Neylandville was founded by a former slave, Jim Brigham, who purchased his own freedom and that of his wife and one of his ten children. He named the town for the son of his former owner.

Population: 94 (1990); 56 (2000); 56 (2010); 56 (2015 projected); Race: 76.8% White, 8.9% Black, 0.0% Asian, 14.3% Other, 19.6% Hispanic of any race (2010); Density: 177.2 persons per square mile (2010); Average household size: 2.67 (2010); Median age: 38.7 (2010); Males per 100 females: 80.6 (2010); Marriage status: 17.0% never married, 50.0% now married, 25.0% widowed, 8.0% divorced (2005-2009 5-year est.); Foreign born: 0.0% (2005-2009 5-year est.); Ancestry (includes multiple ancestries): 11.1% American (2005-2009 5-year est.).

Economy: Employment by occupation: 0.0% management, 18.8% professional, 27.1% services, 54.2% sales, 0.0% farming, 0.0% construction, 0.0% production (2005-2009 5-year est.).

Income: Per capita income: $19,208 (2010); Median household income: $48,125 (2010); Average household income: $61,667 (2010); Percent of households with income of $100,000 or more: 14.3% (2010); Poverty rate: 25.2% (2005-2009 5-year est.).

Taxes: Total city taxes per capita: $220 (2007); City property taxes per capita: $136 (2007).

Education: Percent of population age 25 and over with: High school diploma (including GED) or higher: 83.3% (2010); Bachelor's degree or higher: 13.9% (2010); Master's degree or higher: 5.6% (2010).

Housing: Homeownership rate: 81.0% (2010); Median home value: $95,000 (2010); Median contract rent: $500 per month (2005-2009 5-year est.); Median year structure built: 1978 (2005-2009 5-year est.).

Transportation: Commute to work: 100.0% car, 0.0% public transportation, 0.0% walk, 0.0% work from home (2005-2009 5-year est.); Travel time to work: 16.7% less than 15 minutes, 47.9% 15 to 30 minutes, 35.4% 30 to 45 minutes, 0.0% 45 to 60 minutes, 0.0% 60 minutes or more (2005-2009 5-year est.)

QUINLAN (city). Covers a land area of 1.248 square miles and a water area of 0 square miles. Located at 32.90° N. Lat; 96.13° W. Long. Elevation is 512 feet.

Population: 1,360 (1990); 1,370 (2000); 1,394 (2010); 1,407 (2015 projected); Race: 93.0% White, 1.1% Black, 0.2% Asian, 5.7% Other, 6.2% Hispanic of any race (2010); Density: 1,117.2 persons per square mile (2010); Average household size: 2.52 (2010); Median age: 35.6 (2010); Males per 100 females: 94.7 (2010); Marriage status: 29.4% never married, 48.0% now married, 7.3% widowed, 15.4% divorced (2005-2009 5-year est.); Foreign born: 0.3% (2005-2009 5-year est.); Ancestry (includes multiple ancestries): 24.7% Irish, 19.0% German, 14.6% American, 11.8% English, 6.5% French (2005-2009 5-year est.).

Economy: Single-family building permits issued: 0 (2010); Multi-family building permits issued: 0 (2010); Employment by occupation: 5.1% management, 15.2% professional, 13.8% services, 30.1% sales, 0.0% farming, 15.0% construction, 20.7% production (2005-2009 5-year est.).

Income: Per capita income: $20,639 (2010); Median household income: $41,722 (2010); Average household income: $52,862 (2010); Percent of households with income of $100,000 or more: 9.4% (2010); Poverty rate: 18.0% (2005-2009 5-year est.).

Taxes: Total city taxes per capita: $428 (2007); City property taxes per capita: $153 (2007).

Education: Percent of population age 25 and over with: High school diploma (including GED) or higher: 72.6% (2010); Bachelor's degree or higher: 7.6% (2010); Master's degree or higher: 1.8% (2010).

School District(s)

Boles ISD (PK-12)
2009-10 Enrollment: 529 . . . . (903) 883-4464
Quinlan ISD (PK-12)
2009-10 Enrollment: 2,543 . . . . (903) 356-1200

Housing: Homeownership rate: 72.2% (2010); Median home value: $71,905 (2010); Median contract rent: $469 per month (2005-2009 5-year est.); Median year structure built: 1977 (2005-2009 5-year est.).

Safety: Violent crime rate: 20.9 per 10,000 population; Property crime rate: 340.8 per 10,000 population (2009).

Newspapers: Tawakoni News (Community news; Circulation 4,000)

Transportation: Commute to work: 89.7% car, 1.7% public transportation, 5.5% walk, 0.7% work from home (2005-2009 5-year est.); Travel time to work: 17.3% less than 15 minutes, 25.7% 15 to 30 minutes, 16.9% 30 to 45 minutes, 12.6% 45 to 60 minutes, 27.5% 60 minutes or more (2005-2009 5-year est.)

Additional Information Contacts

Lake Tawakoni Regional Chamber of Commerce . . . . (903) 447-3020
http://laketawakonichamber.org

WEST TAWAKONI (town).
Covers a land area of 2.098 square miles and a water area of 0.013 square miles. Located at 32.90° N. Lat; 96.02° W. Long. Elevation is 456 feet.
Population: 932 (1990); 1,462 (2000); 1,679 (2010); 1,782 (2015 projected); Race: 92.1% White, 0.6% Black, 0.7% Asian, 6.6% Other, 5.4% Hispanic of any race (2010); Density: 800.4 persons per square mile (2010); Average household size: 2.59 (2010); Median age: 38.1 (2010); Males per 100 females: 104.8 (2010); Marriage status: 28.2% never married, 51.5% now married, 6.4% widowed, 13.8% divorced (2005-2009 5-year est.); Foreign born: 0.7% (2005-2009 5-year est.); Ancestry (includes multiple ancestries): 14.1% Irish, 9.5% American, 8.8% German, 6.1% English, 3.2% French (2005-2009 5-year est.).
Economy: Single-family building permits issued: 2 (2010); Multi-family building permits issued: 0 (2010); Employment by occupation: 8.2% management, 7.7% professional, 13.4% services, 47.2% sales, 0.0% farming, 11.3% construction, 12.3% production (2005-2009 5-year est.).
Income: Per capita income: $19,269 (2010); Median household income: $40,283 (2010); Average household income: $49,857 (2010); Percent of households with income of $100,000 or more: 9.7% (2010); Poverty rate: 46.5% (2005-2009 5-year est.).
Taxes: Total city taxes per capita: $274 (2007); City property taxes per capita: $113 (2007).
Education: Percent of population age 25 and over with: High school diploma (including GED) or higher: 70.4% (2010); Bachelor's degree or higher: 7.8% (2010); Master's degree or higher: 0.9% (2010).
Housing: Homeownership rate: 78.6% (2010); Median home value: $55,573 (2010); Median contract rent: $378 per month (2005-2009 5-year est.); Median year structure built: 1976 (2005-2009 5-year est.).
Safety: Violent crime rate: 28.4 per 10,000 population; Property crime rate: 284.1 per 10,000 population (2009).
Transportation: Commute to work: 95.2% car, 0.0% public transportation, 0.0% walk, 4.1% work from home (2005-2009 5-year est.); Travel time to work: 12.1% less than 15 minutes, 15.4% 15 to 30 minutes, 24.2% 30 to 45 minutes, 5.1% 45 to 60 minutes, 43.2% 60 minutes or more (2005-2009 5-year est.)

WOLFE CITY (city).
Covers a land area of 1.443 square miles and a water area of 0.095 square miles. Located at 33.36° N. Lat; 96.07° W. Long. Elevation is 692 feet.
History: Incorporated 1873.
Population: 1,505 (1990); 1,566 (2000); 1,622 (2010); 1,651 (2015 projected); Race: 86.4% White, 8.9% Black, 0.2% Asian, 4.5% Other, 4.3% Hispanic of any race (2010); Density: 1,124.1 persons per square mile (2010); Average household size: 2.50 (2010); Median age: 36.3 (2010); Males per 100 females: 89.5 (2010); Marriage status: 21.9% never married, 50.6% now married, 9.4% widowed, 18.2% divorced (2005-2009 5-year est.); Foreign born: 1.0% (2005-2009 5-year est.); Ancestry (includes multiple ancestries): 17.2% German, 13.7% Irish, 12.4% English, 8.2% American, 4.6% Scotch-Irish (2005-2009 5-year est.).
Economy: Employment by occupation: 4.0% management, 15.3% professional, 21.4% services, 25.3% sales, 0.0% farming, 14.4% construction, 19.6% production (2005-2009 5-year est.).
Income: Per capita income: $19,998 (2010); Median household income: $40,678 (2010); Average household income: $51,068 (2010); Percent of households with income of $100,000 or more: 10.7% (2010); Poverty rate: 24.1% (2005-2009 5-year est.).
Taxes: Total city taxes per capita: $199 (2007); City property taxes per capita: $155 (2007).
Education: Percent of population age 25 and over with: High school diploma (including GED) or higher: 77.1% (2010); Bachelor's degree or higher: 12.5% (2010); Master's degree or higher: 4.3% (2010).

School District(s)
Wolfe City ISD (PK-12)
    2009-10 Enrollment: 640 . . . . (903) 496-7333
Housing: Homeownership rate: 70.1% (2010); Median home value: $55,238 (2010); Median contract rent: $318 per month (2005-2009 5-year est.); Median year structure built: 1969 (2005-2009 5-year est.).
Safety: Violent crime rate: 24.4 per 10,000 population; Property crime rate: 122.0 per 10,000 population (2009).
Newspapers: Wolfe City Mirror (Community news; Circulation 1,050)
Transportation: Commute to work: 87.3% car, 0.0% public transportation, 3.1% walk, 3.2% work from home (2005-2009 5-year est.); Travel time to work: 35.3% less than 15 minutes, 31.6% 15 to 30 minutes, 18.9% 30 to 45

minutes, 3.6% 45 to 60 minutes, 10.7% 60 minutes or more (2005-2009 5-year est.)
Additional Information Contacts
Wolfe City Chamber of Commerce . . . . (903) 496-2323

Hutchinson County

Located in north Texas, on the high plains of the Panhandle; crossed by the gorge of the Canadian River. Covers a land area of 887.37 square miles, a water area of 7.58 square miles, and is located in the Central Time Zone at 35.73° N. Lat., 101.42° W. Long. The county was founded in 1876. County seat is Stinnett.

Hutchinson County is part of the Borger, TX Micropolitan Statistical Area. The entire metro area includes: Hutchinson County, TX

Weather Station: Borger   Elevation: 3,140 feet

	Jan	Feb	Mar	Apr	May	Jun	Jul	Aug	Sep	Oct	Nov	Dec
High	51	56	64	72	81	89	93	91	84	73	61	50
Low	25	28	35	43	53	62	67	66	58	46	34	26
Precip	0.8	0.7	1.7	1.8	2.8	3.3	2.7	3.6	2.1	1.9	1.0	0.8
Snow	5.3	4.0	3.5	0.9	tr	tr	0.0	tr	tr	0.2	2.4	5.3

High and Low temperatures in degrees Fahrenheit; Precipitation and Snow in inches

Population: 25,689 (1990); 23,857 (2000); 21,965 (2010); 21,006 (2015 projected); Race: 82.9% White, 3.0% Black, 0.5% Asian, 13.6% Other, 19.7% Hispanic of any race (2010); Density: 24.8 persons per square mile (2010); Average household size: 2.49 (2010); Median age: 38.3 (2010); Males per 100 females: 96.4 (2010).
Religion: Five largest groups: 52.6% Southern Baptist Convention, 7.4% The United Methodist Church, 7.1% Catholic Church, 6.0% Churches of Christ, 2.3% Christian Church (Disciples of Christ) (2000).
Economy: Unemployment rate: 7.7% (June 2011); Total civilian labor force: 11,344 (June 2011); Leading industries: 27.1% manufacturing; 14.3% retail trade; 11.9% construction (2009); Farms: 259 totaling 557,262 acres (2007); Companies that employ 500 or more persons: 1 (2009); Companies that employ 100 to 499 persons: 7 (2009); Companies that employ less than 100 persons: 485 (2009); Black-owned businesses: n/a (2007); Hispanic-owned businesses: n/a (2007); Asian-owned businesses: n/a (2007); Women-owned businesses: n/a (2007); Retail sales per capita: $8,992 (2010). Single-family building permits issued: 0 (2010); Multi-family building permits issued: 0 (2010).
Income: Per capita income: $22,227 (2010); Median household income: $45,204 (2010); Average household income: $55,867 (2010); Percent of households with income of $100,000 or more: 12.3% (2010); Poverty rate: 12.3% (2009); Bankruptcy rate: 1.75% (2010).
Taxes: Total county taxes per capita: $354 (2007); County property taxes per capita: $331 (2007).
Education: Percent of population age 25 and over with: High school diploma (including GED) or higher: 81.8% (2010); Bachelor's degree or higher: 12.5% (2010); Master's degree or higher: 3.8% (2010).
Housing: Homeownership rate: 82.0% (2010); Median home value: $50,389 (2010); Median contract rent: $402 per month (2005-2009 5-year est.); Median year structure built: 1961 (2005-2009 5-year est.).
Health: Birth rate: 136.0 per 10,000 population (2009); Death rate: 103.5 per 10,000 population (2009); Age-adjusted cancer mortality rate: 202.4 deaths per 100,000 population (2007); Number of physicians: 7.9 per 10,000 population (2008); Hospital beds: 11.5 per 10,000 population (2007); Hospital admissions: 590.8 per 10,000 population (2007).
Elections: 2008 Presidential election results: 15.1% Obama, 84.0% McCain, 0.0% Nader
Additional Information Contacts
Hutchinson County Government . . . . (806) 878-4002
   http://www.co.hutchinson.tx.us/ips/cms
Borger Chamber of Commerce . . . . (806) 274-2211
   http://www.borgerchamber.org
City of Borger . . . . (806) 273-0900
   http://www.ci.borger.tx.us

Hutchinson County Communities

BORGER (city).
Covers a land area of 8.732 square miles and a water area of 0.006 square miles. Located at 35.66° N. Lat; 101.40° W. Long. Elevation is 3,077 feet.
History: Borger developed with the natural gas industry, and as a base for Phillips Petroleum Company and other petrochemical industries.

Population: 15,728 (1990); 14,302 (2000); 13,050 (2010); 12,448 (2015 projected); Race: 76.8% White, 4.5% Black, 0.6% Asian, 18.1% Other, 27.6% Hispanic of any race (2010); Density: 1,494.5 persons per square mile (2010); Average household size: 2.49 (2010); Median age: 35.6 (2010); Males per 100 females: 94.9 (2010); Marriage status: 23.3% never married, 57.2% now married, 10.3% widowed, 9.2% divorced (2005-2009 5-year est.); Foreign born: 8.1% (2005-2009 5-year est.); Ancestry (includes multiple ancestries): 14.6% Irish, 13.3% German, 10.1% English, 6.6% American, 2.2% French (2005-2009 5-year est.).
Economy: Single-family building permits issued: 0 (2010); Multi-family building permits issued: 0 (2010); Employment by occupation: 8.3% management, 14.5% professional, 18.2% services, 24.5% sales, 1.1% farming, 18.5% construction, 14.9% production (2005-2009 5-year est.).
Income: Per capita income: $21,008 (2010); Median household income: $42,549 (2010); Average household income: $53,123 (2010); Percent of households with income of $100,000 or more: 10.6% (2010); Poverty rate: 18.5% (2005-2009 5-year est.).
Taxes: Total city taxes per capita: $433 (2007); City property taxes per capita: $117 (2007).
Education: Percent of population age 25 and over with: High school diploma (including GED) or higher: 79.3% (2010); Bachelor's degree or higher: 12.1% (2010); Master's degree or higher: 4.1% (2010).

School District(s)
Borger ISD (PK-12)
    2009-10 Enrollment: 2,815 . . . . (806) 273-6481

Two-year College(s)
Frank Phillips College (Public)
    Fall 2009 Enrollment: 1,239. . . . . (806) 457-4200
    2010-11 Tuition: In-state $3,250; Out-of-state $3,460

Housing: Homeownership rate: 77.9% (2010); Median home value: $46,985 (2010); Median contract rent: $402 per month (2005-2009 5-year est.); Median year structure built: 1957 (2005-2009 5-year est.).
Hospitals: Golden Plains Community Hospital (25 beds)
Safety: Violent crime rate: 164.6 per 10,000 population; Property crime rate: 545.7 per 10,000 population (2009).
Newspapers: Borger News-Herald (Local news; Circulation 4,600)
Transportation: Commute to work: 95.1% car, 0.6% public transportation, 1.7% walk, 2.2% work from home (2005-2009 5-year est.); Travel time to work: 72.1% less than 15 minutes, 13.8% 15 to 30 minutes, 6.6% 30 to 45 minutes, 2.6% 45 to 60 minutes, 4.9% 60 minutes or more (2005-2009 5-year est.)
Airports: Hutchinson County (general aviation)
Additional Information Contacts
Borger Chamber of Commerce . . . . (806) 274-2211
    http://www.borgerchamber.org
City of Borger. . . . . (806) 273-0900
    http://www.ci.borger.tx.us

FRITCH (city). Covers a land area of 1.214 square miles and a water area of 0 square miles. Located at 35.64° N. Lat; 101.60° W. Long. Elevation is 3,196 feet.
History: Alibates Flint Quarries National Monument to Southwest.
Population: 2,335 (1990); 2,235 (2000); 2,094 (2010); 2,009 (2015 projected); Race: 93.8% White, 0.5% Black, 0.2% Asian, 5.4% Other, 7.2% Hispanic of any race (2010); Density: 1,724.7 persons per square mile (2010); Average household size: 2.48 (2010); Median age: 40.7 (2010); Males per 100 females: 95.2 (2010); Marriage status: 13.5% never married, 71.4% now married, 8.4% widowed, 6.7% divorced (2005-2009 5-year est.); Foreign born: 2.8% (2005-2009 5-year est.); Ancestry (includes multiple ancestries): 16.4% German, 15.1% Irish, 11.5% English, 9.0% Scottish, 6.9% Dutch (2005-2009 5-year est.).
Economy: Employment by occupation: 5.5% management, 17.9% professional, 10.3% services, 31.2% sales, 0.0% farming, 12.8% construction, 22.3% production (2005-2009 5-year est.).
Income: Per capita income: $23,143 (2010); Median household income: $50,648 (2010); Average household income: $57,654 (2010); Percent of households with income of $100,000 or more: 12.8% (2010); Poverty rate: 14.5% (2005-2009 5-year est.).
Taxes: Total city taxes per capita: $238 (2007); City property taxes per capita: $152 (2007).
Education: Percent of population age 25 and over with: High school diploma (including GED) or higher: 87.8% (2010); Bachelor's degree or higher: 12.6% (2010); Master's degree or higher: 2.7% (2010).

School District(s)
Borger ISD (PK-12)
    2009-10 Enrollment: 2,815 . . . . (806) 273-6481
Dumas ISD (PK-12)
    2009-10 Enrollment: 4,476 . . . . (806) 935-6461
Plemons-Stinnett-Phillips CISD (PK-12)
    2009-10 Enrollment: 612 . . . . (806) 878-2858
Sanford-Fritch ISD (PK-12)
    2009-10 Enrollment: 865 . . . . (806) 857-3122
Housing: Homeownership rate: 87.6% (2010); Median home value: $52,156 (2010); Median contract rent: $290 per month (2005-2009 5-year est.); Median year structure built: 1965 (2005-2009 5-year est.).
Newspapers: The Eagle Press (Community news; Circulation 1,300)
Transportation: Commute to work: 95.1% car, 0.0% public transportation, 0.0% walk, 0.0% work from home (2005-2009 5-year est.); Travel time to work: 29.4% less than 15 minutes, 40.3% 15 to 30 minutes, 11.5% 30 to 45 minutes, 14.8% 45 to 60 minutes, 3.9% 60 minutes or more (2005-2009 5-year est.)

SANFORD (town). Covers a land area of 0.134 square miles and a water area of 0 square miles. Located at 35.70° N. Lat; 101.53° W. Long. Elevation is 3,035 feet.
Population: 218 (1990); 203 (2000); 185 (2010); 176 (2015 projected); Race: 93.0% White, 2.2% Black, 0.0% Asian, 4.9% Other, 5.4% Hispanic of any race (2010); Density: 1,382.6 persons per square mile (2010); Average household size: 2.50 (2010); Median age: 42.5 (2010); Males per 100 females: 110.2 (2010); Marriage status: 14.6% never married, 77.2% now married, 1.9% widowed, 6.3% divorced (2005-2009 5-year est.); Foreign born: 1.1% (2005-2009 5-year est.); Ancestry (includes multiple ancestries): 21.2% Irish, 12.7% German, 12.7% American, 9.5% Italian, 6.3% English (2005-2009 5-year est.).
Economy: Employment by occupation: 4.5% management, 19.3% professional, 14.8% services, 19.3% sales, 11.4% farming, 20.5% construction, 10.2% production (2005-2009 5-year est.).
Income: Per capita income: $19,528 (2010); Median household income: $48,750 (2010); Average household income: $52,279 (2010); Percent of households with income of $100,000 or more: 11.8% (2010); Poverty rate: 7.9% (2005-2009 5-year est.).
Taxes: Total city taxes per capita: $117 (2007); City property taxes per capita: $30 (2007).
Education: Percent of population age 25 and over with: High school diploma (including GED) or higher: 81.0% (2010); Bachelor's degree or higher: 9.9% (2010); Master's degree or higher: 1.7% (2010).
Housing: Homeownership rate: 83.8% (2010); Median home value: $67,778 (2010); Median contract rent: $1,071 per month (2005-2009 5-year est.); Median year structure built: 1966 (2005-2009 5-year est.).
Transportation: Commute to work: 100.0% car, 0.0% public transportation, 0.0% walk, 0.0% work from home (2005-2009 5-year est.); Travel time to work: 25.0% less than 15 minutes, 39.8% 15 to 30 minutes, 13.6% 30 to 45 minutes, 13.6% 45 to 60 minutes, 8.0% 60 minutes or more (2005-2009 5-year est.)

STINNETT (city). County seat. Covers a land area of 1.990 square miles and a water area of 0 square miles. Located at 35.82° N. Lat; 101.44° W. Long. Elevation is 3,186 feet.
History: Established 1901.
Population: 2,182 (1990); 1,936 (2000); 1,826 (2010); 1,762 (2015 projected); Race: 90.5% White, 0.3% Black, 0.2% Asian, 9.0% Other, 7.2% Hispanic of any race (2010); Density: 917.6 persons per square mile (2010); Average household size: 2.44 (2010); Median age: 39.7 (2010); Males per 100 females: 99.8 (2010); Marriage status: 21.4% never married, 62.7% now married, 5.7% widowed, 10.2% divorced (2005-2009 5-year est.); Foreign born: 1.4% (2005-2009 5-year est.); Ancestry (includes multiple ancestries): 23.5% Irish, 20.3% German, 10.5% English, 5.1% Dutch, 4.6% Scotch-Irish (2005-2009 5-year est.).
Economy: Employment by occupation: 15.4% management, 18.8% professional, 12.3% services, 21.8% sales, 0.0% farming, 17.3% construction, 14.5% production (2005-2009 5-year est.).
Income: Per capita income: $21,537 (2010); Median household income: $42,965 (2010); Average household income: $53,034 (2010); Percent of households with income of $100,000 or more: 9.9% (2010); Poverty rate: 14.6% (2005-2009 5-year est.).
Taxes: Total city taxes per capita: $140 (2007); City property taxes per capita: $63 (2007).

Education: Percent of population age 25 and over with: High school diploma (including GED) or higher: 78.6% (2010); Bachelor's degree or higher: 8.2% (2010); Master's degree or higher: 2.3% (2010).

School District(s)
Plemons-Stinnett-Phillips CISD (PK-12)
2009-10 Enrollment: 612 . . . . (806) 878-2858

Housing: Homeownership rate: 85.6% (2010); Median home value: $39,953 (2010); Median contract rent: $370 per month (2005-2009 5-year est.); Median year structure built: 1961 (2005-2009 5-year est.).

Transportation: Commute to work: 91.8% car, 0.0% public transportation, 0.4% walk, 3.0% work from home (2005-2009 5-year est.); Travel time to work: 38.2% less than 15 minutes, 41.4% 15 to 30 minutes, 12.6% 30 to 45 minutes, 0.8% 45 to 60 minutes, 6.9% 60 minutes or more (2005-2009 5-year est.)

Irion County

Located in west Texas; drained by the Middle Concho River. Covers a land area of 1,051.48 square miles, a water area of 0.11 square miles, and is located in the Central Time Zone at 31.28° N. Lat., 100.97° W. Long. The county was founded in 1889. County seat is Mertzon.

Irion County is part of the San Angelo, TX Metropolitan Statistical Area. The entire metro area includes: Irion County, TX; Tom Green County, TX

Population: 1,629 (1990); 1,771 (2000); 1,701 (2010); 1,663 (2015 projected); Race: 86.8% White, 3.4% Black, 0.0% Asian, 9.8% Other, 26.0% Hispanic of any race (2010); Density: 1.6 persons per square mile (2010); Average household size: 2.47 (2010); Median age: 41.6 (2010); Males per 100 females: 100.6 (2010).

Religion: Five largest groups: 38.3% Southern Baptist Convention, 15.9% The United Methodist Church, 15.7% Catholic Church, 2.1% Churches of Christ, 1.2% Christian Church (Disciples of Christ) (2000).

Economy: Unemployment rate: 6.7% (June 2011); Total civilian labor force: 928 (June 2011); Leading industries: 15.6% construction; 15.6% mining (2009); Farms: 156 totaling 624,626 acres (2007); Companies that employ 500 or more persons: 0 (2009); Companies that employ 100 to 499 persons: 0 (2009); Companies that employ less than 100 persons: 45 (2009); Black-owned businesses: n/a (2007); Hispanic-owned businesses: n/a (2007); Asian-owned businesses: n/a (2007); Women-owned businesses: n/a (2007); Retail sales per capita: $2,836 (2010). Single-family building permits issued: n/a (2010); Multi-family building permits issued: n/a (2010).

Income: Per capita income: $28,480 (2010); Median household income: $50,195 (2010); Average household income: $70,210 (2010); Percent of households with income of $100,000 or more: 17.1% (2010); Poverty rate: 10.9% (2009); Bankruptcy rate: 1.24% (2010).

Taxes: Total county taxes per capita: $960 (2007); County property taxes per capita: $862 (2007).

Education: Percent of population age 25 and over with: High school diploma (including GED) or higher: 83.0% (2010); Bachelor's degree or higher: 23.6% (2010); Master's degree or higher: 4.3% (2010).

Housing: Homeownership rate: 75.9% (2010); Median home value: $96,061 (2010); Median contract rent: $451 per month (2005-2009 5-year est.); Median year structure built: 1969 (2005-2009 5-year est.)

Health: Birth rate: 63.2 per 10,000 population (2009); Death rate: 17.2 per 10,000 population (2009); Age-adjusted cancer mortality rate: Suppressed deaths per 100,000 population (2007); Number of physicians: 0.0 per 10,000 population (2008); Hospital beds: 0.0 per 10,000 population (2007); Hospital admissions: 0.0 per 10,000 population (2007).

Elections: 2008 Presidential election results: 20.1% Obama, 78.8% McCain, 0.0% Nader

Additional Information Contacts

Irion County Government . . . . (325) 835-2421
http://www.co.irion.tx.us/ips/cms

Irion County Communities

BARNHART (unincorporated postal area, zip code 76930). Covers a land area of 74.652 square miles and a water area of 0 square miles. Located at 31.14° N. Lat; 101.18° W. Long. Elevation is 2,559 feet.
Population: 145 (2000); Race: 98.4% White, 0.0% Black, 0.0% Asian, 1.6% Other, 9.7% Hispanic of any race (2000); Density: 1.9 persons per square mile (2000); Age: 25.0% under 18, 16.1% over 64 (2000); Marriage status: 5.2% never married, 70.1% now married, 16.5% widowed, 8.2%

divorced (2000); Foreign born: 3.2% (2000); Ancestry (includes multiple ancestries): 24.2% German, 18.5% Irish, 10.5% American, 4.8% English (2000).

Economy: Employment by occupation: 11.3% management, 8.1% professional, 12.9% services, 24.2% sales, 8.1% farming, 9.7% construction, 25.8% production (2000).

Income: Per capita income: $15,143 (2000); Median household income: $26,250 (2000); Poverty rate: 179.1% (2000).

Education: Percent of population age 25 and over with: High school diploma (including GED) or higher: 89.2% (2000); Bachelor's degree or higher: 10.8% (2000).

Housing: Homeownership rate: 85.7% (2000); Median home value: $38,800 (2000); Median contract rent: $475 per month (2000); Median year structure built: 1963 (2000).

Transportation: Commute to work: 91.8% car, 0.0% public transportation, 6.6% walk, 0.0% work from home (2000); Travel time to work: 36.1% less than 15 minutes, 32.8% 15 to 30 minutes, 19.7% 30 to 45 minutes, 0.0% 45 to 60 minutes, 11.5% 60 minutes or more (2000)

MERTZON (city). County seat. Covers a land area of 1.522 square miles and a water area of 0 square miles. Located at 31.26° N. Lat; 100.82° W. Long. Elevation is 2,201 feet.
Population: 778 (1990); 839 (2000); 802 (2010); 781 (2015 projected); Race: 80.9% White, 3.7% Black, 0.0% Asian, 15.3% Other, 34.4% Hispanic of any race (2010); Density: 527.1 persons per square mile (2010); Average household size: 2.55 (2010); Median age: 39.1 (2010); Males per 100 females: 96.1 (2010); Marriage status: 21.7% never married, 65.0% now married, 7.1% widowed, 6.2% divorced (2005-2009 5-year est.); Foreign born: 4.0% (2005-2009 5-year est.); Ancestry (includes multiple ancestries): 7.7% Irish, 5.4% English, 5.4% American, 4.0% German, 3.3% French (2005-2009 5-year est.).

Economy: Employment by occupation: 4.0% management, 11.6% professional, 20.7% services, 18.1% sales, 11.4% farming, 15.1% construction, 19.1% production (2005-2009 5-year est.).

Income: Per capita income: $21,184 (2010); Median household income: $44,545 (2010); Average household income: $53,869 (2010); Percent of households with income of $100,000 or more: 8.9% (2010); Poverty rate: 4.3% (2005-2009 5-year est.).

Taxes: Total city taxes per capita: $174 (2007); City property taxes per capita: $94 (2007).

Education: Percent of population age 25 and over with: High school diploma (including GED) or higher: 77.9% (2010); Bachelor's degree or higher: 17.9% (2010); Master's degree or higher: 3.1% (2010).

School District(s)
Irion County ISD (KG-12)
2009-10 Enrollment: 335 . . . . (325) 835-6111

Housing: Homeownership rate: 77.4% (2010); Median home value: $87,674 (2010); Median contract rent: $447 per month (2005-2009 5-year est.); Median year structure built: 1958 (2005-2009 5-year est.).

Transportation: Commute to work: 93.3% car, 0.0% public transportation, 0.7% walk, 2.3% work from home (2005-2009 5-year est.); Travel time to work: 46.4% less than 15 minutes, 12.9% 15 to 30 minutes, 28.3% 30 to 45 minutes, 3.6% 45 to 60 minutes, 8.8% 60 minutes or more (2005-2009 5-year est.)

Jack County

Located in north Texas; drained by the West Fork of the Trinity River; includes part of Lake Bridgeport. Covers a land area of 916.61 square miles, a water area of 3.50 square miles, and is located in the Central Time Zone at 33.20° N. Lat., 98.17° W. Long. The county was founded in 1857. County seat is Jacksboro.

Weather Station: Jacksboro   Elevation: 1,100 feet

	Jan	Feb	Mar	Apr	May	Jun	Jul	Aug	Sep	Oct	Nov	Dec
High	56	59	67	76	83	90	95	95	88	77	66	56
Low	32	35	43	51	61	68	72	72	64	54	43	33
Precip	1.2	2.2	2.7	2.5	4.9	4.0	1.7	1.8	3.3	3.9	2.1	2.0
Snow	0.4	0.1	tr	tr	0.0	0.0	0.0	0.0	0.0	0.0	0.1	0.2

High and Low temperatures in degrees Fahrenheit; Precipitation and Snow in inches

Population: 6,981 (1990); 8,763 (2000); 8,861 (2010); 8,893 (2015 projected); Race: 85.3% White, 6.4% Black, 0.4% Asian, 7.9% Other, 11.8% Hispanic of any race (2010); Density: 9.7 persons per square mile (2010); Average household size: 2.53 (2010); Median age: 38.2 (2010); Males per 100 females: 120.6 (2010).

Religion: Five largest groups: 34.6% Southern Baptist Convention, 5.7% The United Methodist Church, 3.4% Churches of Christ, 2.4% Christian Church (Disciples of Christ), 2.3% Catholic Church (2000).

Economy: Unemployment rate: 6.5% (June 2011); Total civilian labor force: 4,879 (June 2011); Leading industries: 39.4% mining; 14.2% construction; 8.3% accommodation & food services (2009); Farms: 902 totaling 576,091 acres (2007); Companies that employ 500 or more persons: 0 (2009); Companies that employ 100 to 499 persons: 4 (2009); Companies that employ less than 100 persons: 229 (2009); Black-owned businesses: n/a (2007); Hispanic-owned businesses: n/a (2007); Asian-owned businesses: n/a (2007); Women-owned businesses: n/a (2007); Retail sales per capita: $4,157 (2010). Single-family building permits issued: 4 (2010); Multi-family building permits issued: 0 (2010).

Income: Per capita income: $21,402 (2010); Median household income: $46,444 (2010); Average household income: $58,997 (2010); Percent of households with income of $100,000 or more: 12.3% (2010); Poverty rate: 14.9% (2009); Bankruptcy rate: 1.42% (2010).

Taxes: Total county taxes per capita: $254 (2007); County property taxes per capita: $216 (2007).

Education: Percent of population age 25 and over with: High school diploma (including GED) or higher: 80.6% (2010); Bachelor's degree or higher: 14.5% (2010); Master's degree or higher: 4.1% (2010).

Housing: Homeownership rate: 74.9% (2010); Median home value: $62,186 (2010); Median contract rent: $346 per month (2005-2009 5-year est.); Median year structure built: 1970 (2005-2009 5-year est.)

Health: Birth rate: 100.0 per 10,000 population (2009); Death rate: 102.4 per 10,000 population (2009); Age-adjusted cancer mortality rate: 198.7 deaths per 100,000 population (2007); Number of physicians: 5.8 per 10,000 population (2008); Hospital beds: 19.6 per 10,000 population (2007); Hospital admissions: 597.2 per 10,000 population (2007).

Elections: 2008 Presidential election results: 15.5% Obama, 83.6% McCain, 0.1% Nader

Additional Information Contacts

Jack County Government . . . . (940) 567-2241
  http://jackcounty.org
Jacksboro Chamber of Commerce . . . . (940) 567-2602
  http://www.jacksborochamber.com

Jack County Communities

BRYSON (city). Covers a land area of 1.240 square miles and a water area of 0.094 square miles. Located at 33.16° N. Lat; 98.38° W. Long. Elevation is 1,250 feet.

Population: 520 (1990); 528 (2000); 552 (2010); 558 (2015 projected); Race: 94.6% White, 0.4% Black, 0.2% Asian, 4.9% Other, 4.3% Hispanic of any race (2010); Density: 445.3 persons per square mile (2010); Average household size: 2.37 (2010); Median age: 44.5 (2010); Males per 100 females: 95.7 (2010); Marriage status: 28.8% never married, 59.3% now married, 3.1% widowed, 8.8% divorced (2005-2009 5-year est.); Foreign born: 0.0% (2005-2009 5-year est.); Ancestry (includes multiple ancestries): 15.1% American, 9.2% Irish, 6.5% German, 6.3% English, 3.9% Dutch (2005-2009 5-year est.).

Economy: Single-family building permits issued: 0 (2010); Multi-family building permits issued: 0 (2010); Employment by occupation: 9.1% management, 7.1% professional, 21.6% services, 19.9% sales, 0.0% farming, 20.9% construction, 21.3% production (2005-2009 5-year est.).

Income: Per capita income: $25,428 (2010); Median household income: $45,338 (2010); Average household income: $59,893 (2010); Percent of households with income of $100,000 or more: 12.9% (2010); Poverty rate: 23.5% (2005-2009 5-year est.).

Taxes: Total city taxes per capita: $173 (2007); City property taxes per capita: $71 (2007).

Education: Percent of population age 25 and over with: High school diploma (including GED) or higher: 77.1% (2010); Bachelor's degree or higher: 9.4% (2010); Master's degree or higher: 2.2% (2010).

School District(s)

Bryson ISD (PK-12)
  2009-10 Enrollment: 206 . . . . (940) 392-3281

Housing: Homeownership rate: 73.8% (2010); Median home value: $51,429 (2010); Median contract rent: $354 per month (2005-2009 5-year est.); Median year structure built: 1971 (2005-2009 5-year est.).

Transportation: Commute to work: 85.1% car, 0.0% public transportation, 10.5% walk, 4.4% work from home (2005-2009 5-year est.); Travel time to work: 36.4% less than 15 minutes, 44.5% 15 to 30 minutes, 12.0% 30 to 45

minutes, 2.8% 45 to 60 minutes, 4.2% 60 minutes or more (2005-2009 5-year est.)

JACKSBORO (city). County seat. Covers a land area of 5.821 square miles and a water area of 0.986 square miles. Located at 33.22° N. Lat; 98.16° W. Long. Elevation is 1,083 feet.

History: Fort Richardson State Historic Site (founded 1867; extant). Settled 1855; incorporated 1899.

Population: 3,680 (1990); 4,533 (2000); 4,164 (2010); 4,003 (2015 projected); Race: 84.8% White, 6.1% Black, 0.5% Asian, 8.6% Other, 14.6% Hispanic of any race (2010); Density: 715.3 persons per square mile (2010); Average household size: 2.51 (2010); Median age: 37.5 (2010); Males per 100 females: 111.9 (2010); Marriage status: 29.0% never married, 48.2% now married, 7.0% widowed, 15.8% divorced (2005-2009 5-year est.); Foreign born: 7.9% (2005-2009 5-year est.); Ancestry (includes multiple ancestries): 9.9% Irish, 9.8% American, 6.5% German, 5.5% English, 3.3% Scotch-Irish (2005-2009 5-year est.).

Economy: Single-family building permits issued: 4 (2010); Multi-family building permits issued: 0 (2010); Employment by occupation: 10.7% management, 13.3% professional, 19.0% services, 29.2% sales, 0.2% farming, 15.2% construction, 12.4% production (2005-2009 5-year est.).

Income: Per capita income: $21,169 (2010); Median household income: $45,966 (2010); Average household income: $57,799 (2010); Percent of households with income of $100,000 or more: 12.2% (2010); Poverty rate: 17.9% (2005-2009 5-year est.).

Taxes: Total city taxes per capita: $524 (2007); City property taxes per capita: $193 (2007).

Education: Percent of population age 25 and over with: High school diploma (including GED) or higher: 79.8% (2010); Bachelor's degree or higher: 16.3% (2010); Master's degree or higher: 5.2% (2010).

School District(s)

Jacksboro ISD (PK-12)
  2009-10 Enrollment: 956 . . . . (940) 567-7203

Housing: Homeownership rate: 72.6% (2010); Median home value: $59,116 (2010); Median contract rent: $387 per month (2005-2009 5-year est.); Median year structure built: 1960 (2005-2009 5-year est.).

Hospitals: Faith Community Hospital (41 beds)

Safety: Violent crime rate: 2.2 per 10,000 population; Property crime rate: 169.3 per 10,000 population (2009).

Newspapers: Jack County Herald (Community news; Circulation 2,700); Jacksboro Gazette News (Community news; Circulation 2,956)

Transportation: Commute to work: 97.2% car, 0.0% public transportation, 0.0% walk, 1.7% work from home (2005-2009 5-year est.); Travel time to work: 72.9% less than 15 minutes, 8.9% 15 to 30 minutes, 5.7% 30 to 45 minutes, 4.0% 45 to 60 minutes, 8.5% 60 minutes or more (2005-2009 5-year est.)

Additional Information Contacts

Jacksboro Chamber of Commerce . . . . (940) 567-2602
  http://www.jacksborochamber.com

JERMYN (unincorporated postal area, zip code 76459). Covers a land area of 24.424 square miles and a water area of 0.004 square miles. Located at 33.27° N. Lat; 98.39° W. Long. Elevation is 1,168 feet.

Population: 163 (2000); Race: 95.9% White, 0.0% Black, 0.0% Asian, 4.1% Other, 10.3% Hispanic of any race (2000); Density: 6.7 persons per square mile (2000); Age: 27.7% under 18, 15.4% over 64 (2000); Marriage status: 17.2% never married, 66.2% now married, 9.3% widowed, 7.3% divorced (2000); Foreign born: 3.1% (2000); Ancestry (includes multiple ancestries): 29.2% American, 13.8% English, 8.2% German, 4.1% Irish (2000).

Economy: Employment by occupation: 9.6% management, 25.3% professional, 16.9% services, 7.2% sales, 3.6% farming, 19.3% construction, 18.1% production (2000).

Income: Per capita income: $13,831 (2000); Median household income: $37,250 (2000); Poverty rate: 179.1% (2000).

Education: Percent of population age 25 and over with: High school diploma (including GED) or higher: 77.0% (2000); Bachelor's degree or higher: 14.1% (2000).

Housing: Homeownership rate: 80.0% (2000); Median home value: $32,500 (2000); Median contract rent: $288 per month (2000); Median year structure built: 1957 (2000).

Transportation: Commute to work: 86.7% car, 0.0% public transportation, 0.0% walk, 8.4% work from home (2000); Travel time to work: 40.8% less than 15 minutes, 28.9% 15 to 30 minutes, 15.8% 30 to 45 minutes, 2.6% 45 to 60 minutes, 11.8% 60 minutes or more (2000)

PERRIN (unincorporated postal area, zip code 76486). Covers a land area of 75.280 square miles and a water area of 0.536 square miles. Located at 33.02° N. Lat; 98.05° W. Long. Elevation is 1,047 feet.
Population: 1,092 (2000); Race: 96.7% White, 0.0% Black, 0.0% Asian, 3.3% Other, 6.0% Hispanic of any race (2000); Density: 14.5 persons per square mile (2000); Age: 28.7% under 18, 13.2% over 64 (2000); Marriage status: 15.0% never married, 69.2% now married, 5.8% widowed, 10.0% divorced (2000); Foreign born: 1.2% (2000); Ancestry (includes multiple ancestries): 20.0% American, 9.9% Irish, 7.2% English, 5.5% German (2000).
Economy: Employment by occupation: 12.4% management, 11.1% professional, 16.2% services, 26.2% sales, 1.9% farming, 18.3% construction, 13.9% production (2000).
Income: Per capita income: $13,984 (2000); Median household income: $32,188 (2000); Poverty rate: 179.1% (2000).
Education: Percent of population age 25 and over with: High school diploma (including GED) or higher: 77.3% (2000); Bachelor's degree or higher: 10.5% (2000).

School District(s)
Perrin-Whitt CISD (PK-12)
    2009-10 Enrollment: 397 . . . . (940) 798-3718
Housing: Homeownership rate: 80.8% (2000); Median home value: $40,000 (2000); Median contract rent: $263 per month (2000); Median year structure built: 1969 (2000).
Transportation: Commute to work: 93.2% car, 0.0% public transportation, 1.8% walk, 4.0% work from home (2000); Travel time to work: 14.9% less than 15 minutes, 28.6% 15 to 30 minutes, 22.2% 30 to 45 minutes, 11.0% 45 to 60 minutes, 23.3% 60 minutes or more (2000)

Jackson County

Located in south Texas, on the Gulf coastal plain; touches Lavaca and Matagorda Bays in the south; drained by the Lavaca and Navidad Rivers. Covers a land area of 829.49 square miles, a water area of 27.54 square miles, and is located in the Central Time Zone at 28.92° N. Lat., 96.57° W. Long. The county was founded in 1836. County seat is Edna.
Population: 13,039 (1990); 14,391 (2000); 14,628 (2010); 14,718 (2015 projected); Race: 74.1% White, 7.5% Black, 0.5% Asian, 18.0% Other, 28.6% Hispanic of any race (2010); Density: 17.6 persons per square mile (2010); Average household size: 2.64 (2010); Median age: 38.6 (2010); Males per 100 females: 97.4 (2010).
Religion: Five largest groups: 31.0% Catholic Church, 23.1% Southern Baptist Convention, 7.0% The United Methodist Church, 3.9% Churches of Christ, 1.9% Lutheran Church—Missouri Synod (2000).
Economy: Unemployment rate: 8.2% (June 2011); Total civilian labor force: 7,022 (June 2011); Leading industries: 13.6% retail trade; 8.5% construction; 7.7% accommodation & food services (2009); Farms: 847 totaling 492,580 acres (2007); Companies that employ 500 or more persons: 1 (2009); Companies that employ 100 to 499 persons: 3 (2009); Companies that employ less than 100 persons: 275 (2009); Black-owned businesses: n/a (2007); Hispanic-owned businesses: n/a (2007); Asian-owned businesses: n/a (2007); Women-owned businesses: n/a (2007); Retail sales per capita: $9,564 (2010). Single-family building permits issued: 12 (2010); Multi-family building permits issued: 0 (2010).
Income: Per capita income: $20,898 (2010); Median household income: $44,543 (2010); Average household income: $55,392 (2010); Percent of households with income of $100,000 or more: 11.1% (2010); Poverty rate: 13.8% (2009); Bankruptcy rate: 1.12% (2010).
Taxes: Total county taxes per capita: $431 (2007); County property taxes per capita: $350 (2007).
Education: Percent of population age 25 and over with: High school diploma (including GED) or higher: 77.7% (2010); Bachelor's degree or higher: 14.3% (2010); Master's degree or higher: 3.4% (2010).
Housing: Homeownership rate: 71.8% (2010); Median home value: $67,481 (2010); Median contract rent: $385 per month (2005-2009 5-year est.); Median year structure built: 1972 (2005-2009 5-year est.).
Health: Birth rate: 151.3 per 10,000 population (2009); Death rate: 102.3 per 10,000 population (2009); Age-adjusted cancer mortality rate: 181.1 deaths per 100,000 population (2007); Number of physicians: 4.3 per 10,000 population (2008); Hospital beds: 44.3 per 10,000 population (2007); Hospital admissions: 281.4 per 10,000 population (2007).
Elections: 2008 Presidential election results: 25.7% Obama, 73.6% McCain, 0.0% Nader
Additional Information Contacts

Jackson County Government. . . . . (361) 782-2352
    http://www.co.jackson.tx.us/ips/cms
City of Edna . . . . (361) 782-3122
    http://www.cityofedna.com
Jackson County Chamber of Commerce . . . . (361) 782-7146
    http://www.ykc.com/jccc

Jackson County Communities

EDNA (city). County seat. Covers a land area of 3.901 square miles and a water area of <.001 square miles. Located at 28.97° N. Lat; 96.64° W. Long. Elevation is 66 feet.
History: Incorporated 1926.
Population: 5,610 (1990); 5,899 (2000); 5,969 (2010); 5,980 (2015 projected); Race: 64.3% White, 12.0% Black, 0.8% Asian, 22.8% Other, 31.5% Hispanic of any race (2010); Density: 1,530.0 persons per square mile (2010); Average household size: 2.56 (2010); Median age: 37.2 (2010); Males per 100 females: 93.2 (2010); Marriage status: 25.4% never married, 57.0% now married, 5.8% widowed, 11.7% divorced (2005-2009 5-year est.); Foreign born: 3.1% (2005-2009 5-year est.); Ancestry (includes multiple ancestries): 19.8% German, 8.6% Irish, 8.1% English, 4.5% American, 3.7% French (2005-2009 5-year est.).
Economy: Single-family building permits issued: 6 (2010); Multi-family building permits issued: 0 (2010); Employment by occupation: 9.9% management, 15.8% professional, 25.8% services, 18.4% sales, 0.0% farming, 9.7% construction, 20.3% production (2005-2009 5-year est.).
Income: Per capita income: $19,501 (2010); Median household income: $40,208 (2010); Average household income: $50,398 (2010); Percent of households with income of $100,000 or more: 9.3% (2010); Poverty rate: 11.3% (2005-2009 5-year est.).
Taxes: Total city taxes per capita: $310 (2007); City property taxes per capita: $93 (2007).
Education: Percent of population age 25 and over with: High school diploma (including GED) or higher: 74.3% (2010); Bachelor's degree or higher: 14.6% (2010); Master's degree or higher: 3.7% (2010).

School District(s)
Edna ISD (PK-12)
    2009-10 Enrollment: 1,470 . . . . (361) 782-3573
Housing: Homeownership rate: 64.0% (2010); Median home value: $65,263 (2010); Median contract rent: $385 per month (2005-2009 5-year est.); Median year structure built: 1970 (2005-2009 5-year est.).
Hospitals: Jackson Healthcare Center (54 beds)
Safety: Violent crime rate: 29.4 per 10,000 population; Property crime rate: 227.9 per 10,000 population (2009).
Newspapers: Jackson County Herald-Tribune (Community news; Circulation 3,751)
Transportation: Commute to work: 91.2% car, 0.0% public transportation, 3.2% walk, 4.7% work from home (2005-2009 5-year est.); Travel time to work: 50.5% less than 15 minutes, 13.4% 15 to 30 minutes, 22.5% 30 to 45 minutes, 7.4% 45 to 60 minutes, 6.3% 60 minutes or more (2005-2009 5-year est.)
Additional Information Contacts
City of Edna . . . . (361) 782-3122
    http://www.cityofedna.com
Jackson County Chamber of Commerce . . . . (361) 782-7146
    http://www.ykc.com/jccc

GANADO (city). Covers a land area of 1.164 square miles and a water area of 0.004 square miles. Located at 29.04° N. Lat; 96.51° W. Long. Elevation is 66 feet.
History: The name of Ganado means cattle, reflecting the numbers of longhorns that roamed the prairies when the settlement was founded in 1883.
Population: 1,800 (1990); 1,915 (2000); 1,908 (2010); 1,903 (2015 projected); Race: 79.1% White, 3.2% Black, 0.2% Asian, 17.5% Other, 36.4% Hispanic of any race (2010); Density: 1,639.3 persons per square mile (2010); Average household size: 2.79 (2010); Median age: 37.6 (2010); Males per 100 females: 103.2 (2010); Marriage status: 22.4% never married, 60.5% now married, 10.9% widowed, 6.1% divorced (2005-2009 5-year est.); Foreign born: 7.7% (2005-2009 5-year est.); Ancestry (includes multiple ancestries): 19.6% Czech, 18.0% German, 13.3% Irish, 6.5% English, 2.5% French (2005-2009 5-year est.).
Economy: Single-family building permits issued: 2 (2010); Multi-family building permits issued: 0 (2010); Employment by occupation: 5.9%

management, 16.9% professional, 18.8% services, 22.3% sales, 1.5% farming, 20.8% construction, 13.9% production (2005-2009 5-year est.).
Income: Per capita income: $20,093 (2010); Median household income: $44,167 (2010); Average household income: $55,785 (2010); Percent of households with income of $100,000 or more: 11.7% (2010); Poverty rate: 7.6% (2005-2009 5-year est.).
Taxes: Total city taxes per capita: $300 (2007); City property taxes per capita: $166 (2007).
Education: Percent of population age 25 and over with: High school diploma (including GED) or higher: 75.2% (2010); Bachelor's degree or higher: 13.6% (2010); Master's degree or higher: 3.6% (2010).

School District(s)
Ganado ISD (PK-12)
    2009-10 Enrollment: 651 . . . . (361) 771-4200
Housing: Homeownership rate: 73.9% (2010); Median home value: $63,298 (2010); Median contract rent: $387 per month (2005-2009 5-year est.); Median year structure built: 1969 (2005-2009 5-year est.).
Safety: Violent crime rate: 5.5 per 10,000 population; Property crime rate: 21.8 per 10,000 population (2009).
Transportation: Commute to work: 93.8% car, 0.0% public transportation, 2.5% walk, 3.3% work from home (2005-2009 5-year est.); Travel time to work: 41.0% less than 15 minutes, 19.0% 15 to 30 minutes, 18.7% 30 to 45 minutes, 14.2% 45 to 60 minutes, 7.1% 60 minutes or more (2005-2009 5-year est.)

LA WARD (city). Aka Laward. Covers a land area of 0.814 square miles and a water area of 0 square miles. Located at 28.84° N. Lat; 96.46° W. Long. Elevation is 39 feet.
Population: 162 (1990); 200 (2000); 218 (2010); 229 (2015 projected); Race: 86.7% White, 0.5% Black, 0.0% Asian, 12.8% Other, 22.0% Hispanic of any race (2010); Density: 267.9 persons per square mile (2010); Average household size: 2.73 (2010); Median age: 40.4 (2010); Males per 100 females: 109.6 (2010); Marriage status: 34.8% never married, 44.3% now married, 13.0% widowed, 7.8% divorced (2005-2009 5-year est.); Foreign born: 0.0% (2005-2009 5-year est.); Ancestry (includes multiple ancestries): 31.6% German, 22.8% Czech, 21.5% Irish, 20.3% English, 8.9% Welsh (2005-2009 5-year est.).
Economy: Single-family building permits issued: 0 (2010); Multi-family building permits issued: 0 (2010); Employment by occupation: 0.0% management, 15.1% professional, 17.8% services, 30.1% sales, 0.0% farming, 19.2% construction, 17.8% production (2005-2009 5-year est.).
Income: Per capita income: $20,125 (2010); Median household income: $45,714 (2010); Average household income: $51,688 (2010); Percent of households with income of $100,000 or more: 8.8% (2010); Poverty rate: 20.9% (2005-2009 5-year est.).
Taxes: Total city taxes per capita: $66 (2007); City property taxes per capita: $0 (2007).
Education: Percent of population age 25 and over with: High school diploma (including GED) or higher: 81.8% (2010); Bachelor's degree or higher: 12.2% (2010); Master's degree or higher: 2.7% (2010).
Housing: Homeownership rate: 83.8% (2010); Median home value: $61,250 (2010); Median contract rent: n/a per month (2005-2009 5-year est.); Median year structure built: 1945 (2005-2009 5-year est.).
Transportation: Commute to work: 86.8% car, 0.0% public transportation, 0.0% walk, 13.2% work from home (2005-2009 5-year est.); Travel time to work: 10.2% less than 15 minutes, 28.8% 15 to 30 minutes, 32.2% 30 to 45 minutes, 28.8% 45 to 60 minutes, 0.0% 60 minutes or more (2005-2009 5-year est.)

LOLITA (CDP). Covers a land area of 2.599 square miles and a water area of 0 square miles. Located at 28.83° N. Lat; 96.54° W. Long. Elevation is 39 feet.
Population: 488 (1990); 548 (2000); 600 (2010); 624 (2015 projected); Race: 87.5% White, 0.2% Black, 0.0% Asian, 12.3% Other, 22.7% Hispanic of any race (2010); Density: 230.9 persons per square mile (2010); Average household size: 2.86 (2010); Median age: 37.7 (2010); Males per 100 females: 98.7 (2010); Marriage status: 36.8% never married, 47.4% now married, 15.9% widowed, 0.0% divorced (2005-2009 5-year est.); Foreign born: 0.0% (2005-2009 5-year est.); Ancestry (includes multiple ancestries): 53.9% German, 40.8% Czech, 20.2% French, 13.6% Irish, 10.1% English (2005-2009 5-year est.).
Economy: Employment by occupation: 20.5% management, 35.1% professional, 0.0% services, 29.3% sales, 0.0% farming, 0.0% construction, 15.1% production (2005-2009 5-year est.).

Income: Per capita income: $19,339 (2010); Median household income: $48,256 (2010); Average household income: $55,131 (2010); Percent of households with income of $100,000 or more: 11.4% (2010); Poverty rate: 0.0% (2005-2009 5-year est.).
Education: Percent of population age 25 and over with: High school diploma (including GED) or higher: 83.8% (2010); Bachelor's degree or higher: 9.6% (2010); Master's degree or higher: 0.3% (2010).
Housing: Homeownership rate: 83.3% (2010); Median home value: $56,875 (2010); Median contract rent: n/a per month (2005-2009 5-year est.); Median year structure built: 1977 (2005-2009 5-year est.).
Transportation: Commute to work: 100.0% car, 0.0% public transportation, 0.0% walk, 0.0% work from home (2005-2009 5-year est.); Travel time to work: 16.3% less than 15 minutes, 42.7% 15 to 30 minutes, 18.8% 30 to 45 minutes, 22.2% 45 to 60 minutes, 0.0% 60 minutes or more (2005-2009 5-year est.)

VANDERBILT (CDP). Covers a land area of 1.892 square miles and a water area of 0 square miles. Located at 28.82° N. Lat; 96.61° W. Long. Elevation is 39 feet.
Population: 421 (1990); 411 (2000); 358 (2010); 335 (2015 projected); Race: 80.4% White, 5.9% Black, 0.0% Asian, 13.7% Other, 19.0% Hispanic of any race (2010); Density: 189.2 persons per square mile (2010); Average household size: 2.67 (2010); Median age: 40.5 (2010); Males per 100 females: 87.4 (2010); Marriage status: 48.8% never married, 51.2% now married, 0.0% widowed, 0.0% divorced (2005-2009 5-year est.); Foreign born: 0.0% (2005-2009 5-year est.); Ancestry (includes multiple ancestries): 44.2% German, 22.5% Irish, 20.4% Czech (2005-2009 5-year est.).
Economy: Employment by occupation: 13.3% management, 20.4% professional, 0.0% services, 4.4% sales, 22.2% farming, 0.0% construction, 39.6% production (2005-2009 5-year est.).
Income: Per capita income: $24,719 (2010); Median household income: $54,000 (2010); Average household income: $65,448 (2010); Percent of households with income of $100,000 or more: 12.7% (2010); Poverty rate: 0.0% (2005-2009 5-year est.).
Education: Percent of population age 25 and over with: High school diploma (including GED) or higher: 79.3% (2010); Bachelor's degree or higher: 20.7% (2010); Master's degree or higher: 6.2% (2010).

School District(s)
Industrial ISD (PK-12)
    2009-10 Enrollment: 1,107 . . . . (361) 284-3226
Housing: Homeownership rate: 80.6% (2010); Median home value: $79,286 (2010); Median contract rent: n/a per month (2005-2009 5-year est.); Median year structure built: 1976 (2005-2009 5-year est.).
Transportation: Commute to work: 95.6% car, 0.0% public transportation, 0.0% walk, 4.4% work from home (2005-2009 5-year est.); Travel time to work: 77.7% less than 15 minutes, 16.7% 15 to 30 minutes, 0.0% 30 to 45 minutes, 5.6% 45 to 60 minutes, 0.0% 60 minutes or more (2005-2009 5-year est.)

Jasper County

Located in east Texas; bounded on the west by the Neches River; includes part of Angelina National Forest. Covers a land area of 937.40 square miles, a water area of 32.22 square miles, and is located in the Central Time Zone at 30.77° N. Lat., 94.00° W. Long. The county was founded in 1836. County seat is Jasper.

Weather Station: Sam Rayburn Dam   Elevation: 188 feet

	Jan	Feb	Mar	Apr	May	Jun	Jul	Aug	Sep	Oct	Nov	Dec
High	58	62	70	77	84	90	93	94	89	79	69	60
Low	37	40	47	53	62	69	71	70	65	55	46	39
Precip	5.3	4.7	5.2	4.1	4.9	6.2	4.0	4.0	4.3	5.6	6.2	6.1
Snow	tr	0.0	0.0	0.0	0.0	0.0	0.0	0.0	0.0	0.0	0.0	tr

High and Low temperatures in degrees Fahrenheit; Precipitation and Snow in inches

Population: 31,102 (1990); 35,604 (2000); 34,987 (2010); 34,627 (2015 projected); Race: 77.5% White, 17.2% Black, 0.5% Asian, 4.8% Other, 5.3% Hispanic of any race (2010); Density: 37.3 persons per square mile (2010); Average household size: 2.52 (2010); Median age: 39.0 (2010); Males per 100 females: 94.8 (2010).
Religion: Five largest groups: 36.0% Southern Baptist Convention, 7.1% The United Methodist Church, 4.1% Catholic Church, 3.8% Baptist Missionary Association of America, 3.5% Churches of Christ (2000).
Economy: Unemployment rate: 12.5% (June 2011); Total civilian labor force: 15,969 (June 2011); Leading industries: 26.5% health care and

social assistance; 17.9% retail trade; 8.6% accommodation & food services (2009); Farms: 920 totaling 95,928 acres (2007); Companies that employ 500 or more persons: 2 (2009); Companies that employ 100 to 499 persons: 9 (2009); Companies that employ less than 100 persons: 639 (2009); Black-owned businesses: 386 (2007); Hispanic-owned businesses: 110 (2007); Asian-owned businesses: n/a (2007); Women-owned businesses: 997 (2007); Retail sales per capita: $12,668 (2010). Single-family building permits issued: 40 (2010); Multi-family building permits issued: 0 (2010).

Income: Per capita income: $19,275 (2010); Median household income: $39,188 (2010); Average household income: $49,310 (2010); Percent of households with income of $100,000 or more: 8.9% (2010); Poverty rate: 16.5% (2009); Bankruptcy rate: 1.41% (2010).

Taxes: Total county taxes per capita: $305 (2007); County property taxes per capita: $260 (2007).

Education: Percent of population age 25 and over with: High school diploma (including GED) or higher: 80.5% (2010); Bachelor's degree or higher: 14.3% (2010); Master's degree or higher: 3.1% (2010).

Housing: Homeownership rate: 79.1% (2010); Median home value: $72,859 (2010); Median contract rent: $349 per month (2005-2009 5-year est.); Median year structure built: 1980 (2005-2009 5-year est.)

Health: Birth rate: 132.4 per 10,000 population (2009); Death rate: 117.3 per 10,000 population (2009); Age-adjusted cancer mortality rate: 183.4 deaths per 100,000 population (2007); Number of physicians: 8.5 per 10,000 population (2008); Hospital beds: 14.6 per 10,000 population (2007); Hospital admissions: 665.0 per 10,000 population (2007).

Elections: 2008 Presidential election results: 28.6% Obama, 70.6% McCain, 0.0% Nader

National and State Parks: Big Thicket National Preserve

Additional Information Contacts

Jasper County Government . . . . (409) 384-2612
  http://www.co.jasper.tx.us/ips/cms
Buna Chamber of Commerce . . . . (409) 994-5586
  http://www.bunatexas.net/chamber.htm
City of Jasper . . . . (409) 384-4651
  http://www.jaspertx.org
Jasper-Lake Sam Rayburn Area Chamber of Commerce . . (409) 384-2762
  http://www.jaspercoc.org
Kirbyville Chamber of Commerce . . . . (409) 423-5827

Jasper County Communities

BROWNDELL (city). Covers a land area of 2.421 square miles and a water area of 0 square miles. Located at 31.12° N. Lat; 93.98° W. Long. Elevation is 253 feet.

Population: 192 (1990); 219 (2000); 216 (2010); 215 (2015 projected); Race: 77.3% White, 15.7% Black, 0.5% Asian, 6.5% Other, 6.5% Hispanic of any race (2010); Density: 89.2 persons per square mile (2010); Average household size: 2.54 (2010); Median age: 41.1 (2010); Males per 100 females: 92.9 (2010); Marriage status: 34.3% never married, 40.6% now married, 14.7% widowed, 10.4% divorced (2005-2009 5-year est.); Foreign born: 0.0% (2005-2009 5-year est.); Ancestry (includes multiple ancestries): 16.6% German, 14.2% Irish, 12.5% French, 3.7% English, 3.4% American (2005-2009 5-year est.).

Economy: Employment by occupation: 3.3% management, 8.3% professional, 49.6% services, 14.9% sales, 1.7% farming, 6.6% construction, 15.7% production (2005-2009 5-year est.).

Income: Per capita income: $22,000 (2010); Median household income: $39,583 (2010); Average household income: $55,824 (2010); Percent of households with income of $100,000 or more: 9.4% (2010); Poverty rate: 15.2% (2005-2009 5-year est.).

Taxes: Total city taxes per capita: $90 (2007); City property taxes per capita: $81 (2007).

Education: Percent of population age 25 and over with: High school diploma (including GED) or higher: 74.5% (2010); Bachelor's degree or higher: 4.0% (2010); Master's degree or higher: 2.0% (2010).

Housing: Homeownership rate: 84.7% (2010); Median home value: $60,000 (2010); Median contract rent: n/a per month (2005-2009 5-year est.); Median year structure built: 1981 (2005-2009 5-year est.).

Transportation: Commute to work: 97.4% car, 0.0% public transportation, 0.0% walk, 0.0% work from home (2005-2009 5-year est.); Travel time to work: 32.8% less than 15 minutes, 38.8% 15 to 30 minutes, 19.0% 30 to 45 minutes, 0.0% 45 to 60 minutes, 9.5% 60 minutes or more (2005-2009 5-year est.)

BUNA (CDP). Covers a land area of 5.949 square miles and a water area of 0.009 square miles. Located at 30.43° N. Lat; 93.96° W. Long. Elevation is 75 feet.

History: Buna began as a sawmill community. Later tung orchards were planted, producing nuts whose oil was used in paints.

Population: 2,127 (1990); 2,269 (2000); 2,216 (2010); 2,184 (2015 projected); Race: 86.4% White, 10.3% Black, 0.3% Asian, 3.1% Other, 1.4% Hispanic of any race (2010); Density: 372.5 persons per square mile (2010); Average household size: 2.53 (2010); Median age: 38.7 (2010); Males per 100 females: 87.6 (2010); Marriage status: 25.2% never married, 52.3% now married, 7.1% widowed, 15.4% divorced (2005-2009 5-year est.); Foreign born: 0.0% (2005-2009 5-year est.); Ancestry (includes multiple ancestries): 18.0% Irish, 17.7% English, 11.9% German, 10.1% French, 5.9% Dutch (2005-2009 5-year est.).

Economy: Employment by occupation: 3.7% management, 15.9% professional, 20.0% services, 25.7% sales, 0.0% farming, 18.9% construction, 15.9% production (2005-2009 5-year est.).

Income: Per capita income: $15,898 (2010); Median household income: $33,577 (2010); Average household income: $40,893 (2010); Percent of households with income of $100,000 or more: 5.8% (2010); Poverty rate: 11.5% (2005-2009 5-year est.).

Education: Percent of population age 25 and over with: High school diploma (including GED) or higher: 85.8% (2010); Bachelor's degree or higher: 13.3% (2010); Master's degree or higher: 3.8% (2010).

School District(s)

Buna ISD (PK-12)
  2009-10 Enrollment: 1,494 . . . . (409) 994-5101

Housing: Homeownership rate: 75.6% (2010); Median home value: $67,416 (2010); Median contract rent: $429 per month (2005-2009 5-year est.); Median year structure built: 1976 (2005-2009 5-year est.).

Newspapers: The Buna Beacon Shopper (Community news); The Buna Beacon (Community news; Circulation 1,400)

Transportation: Commute to work: 95.9% car, 0.0% public transportation, 1.6% walk, 0.0% work from home (2005-2009 5-year est.); Travel time to work: 30.8% less than 15 minutes, 15.0% 15 to 30 minutes, 37.6% 30 to 45 minutes, 9.4% 45 to 60 minutes, 7.2% 60 minutes or more (2005-2009 5-year est.)

Additional Information Contacts

Buna Chamber of Commerce . . . . (409) 994-5586
  http://www.bunatexas.net/chamber.htm

EVADALE (CDP). Covers a land area of 17.051 square miles and a water area of 0.663 square miles. Located at 30.35° N. Lat; 94.06° W. Long. Elevation is 46 feet.

Population: 1,422 (1990); 1,430 (2000); 1,389 (2010); 1,365 (2015 projected); Race: 98.6% White, 0.0% Black, 0.0% Asian, 1.4% Other, 2.6% Hispanic of any race (2010); Density: 81.5 persons per square mile (2010); Average household size: 2.60 (2010); Median age: 36.3 (2010); Males per 100 females: 96.7 (2010); Marriage status: 17.7% never married, 64.9% now married, 8.1% widowed, 9.4% divorced (2005-2009 5-year est.); Foreign born: 1.1% (2005-2009 5-year est.); Ancestry (includes multiple ancestries): 27.2% Irish, 22.9% English, 14.4% German, 10.7% French, 7.6% American (2005-2009 5-year est.).

Economy: Employment by occupation: 7.1% management, 24.7% professional, 9.2% services, 22.4% sales, 1.6% farming, 9.4% construction, 25.6% production (2005-2009 5-year est.).

Income: Per capita income: $18,174 (2010); Median household income: $38,989 (2010); Average household income: $47,392 (2010); Percent of households with income of $100,000 or more: 9.2% (2010); Poverty rate: 17.5% (2005-2009 5-year est.).

Education: Percent of population age 25 and over with: High school diploma (including GED) or higher: 79.2% (2010); Bachelor's degree or higher: 8.9% (2010); Master's degree or higher: 1.6% (2010).

School District(s)

Evadale ISD (PK-12)
  2009-10 Enrollment: 451 . . . . (409) 276-1337

Housing: Homeownership rate: 84.6% (2010); Median home value: $58,333 (2010); Median contract rent: $375 per month (2005-2009 5-year est.); Median year structure built: 1980 (2005-2009 5-year est.).

Transportation: Commute to work: 92.8% car, 0.0% public transportation, 2.9% walk, 1.4% work from home (2005-2009 5-year est.); Travel time to work: 35.6% less than 15 minutes, 26.8% 15 to 30 minutes, 18.5% 30 to 45 minutes, 11.5% 45 to 60 minutes, 7.6% 60 minutes or more (2005-2009 5-year est.)

JASPER

JASPER (city). County seat. Covers a land area of 10.342 square miles and a water area of 0.061 square miles. Located at 30.92° N. Lat; 93.99° W. Long. Elevation is 203 feet.

History: Jasper was settled in 1824 by John Bevil, and was named for Sergeant William Jasper of South Carolina, a hero of the Revolutionary War. Jasper developed as a lumber town, and as a trading center for an area that produced livestock and agricultural products.

Population: 7,880 (1990); 8,247 (2000); 7,765 (2010); 7,529 (2015 projected); Race: 46.8% White, 42.5% Black, 1.3% Asian, 9.3% Other, 11.6% Hispanic of any race (2010); Density: 750.8 persons per square mile (2010); Average household size: 2.52 (2010); Median age: 36.3 (2010); Males per 100 females: 94.1 (2010); Marriage status: 27.0% never married, 43.4% now married, 11.7% widowed, 17.8% divorced (2005-2009 5-year est.); Foreign born: 5.8% (2005-2009 5-year est.); Ancestry (includes multiple ancestries): 11.2% German, 8.5% Irish, 8.1% American, 4.8% English, 2.9% Scotch-Irish (2005-2009 5-year est.).

Economy: Single-family building permits issued: 36 (2010); Multi-family building permits issued: 0 (2010); Employment by occupation: 9.8% management, 23.3% professional, 25.2% services, 21.3% sales, 1.0% farming, 6.5% construction, 12.8% production (2005-2009 5-year est.).

Income: Per capita income: $16,325 (2010); Median household income: $31,818 (2010); Average household income: $42,446 (2010); Percent of households with income of $100,000 or more: 6.7% (2010); Poverty rate: 27.5% (2005-2009 5-year est.).

Taxes: Total city taxes per capita: $562 (2007); City property taxes per capita: $94 (2007).

Education: Percent of population age 25 and over with: High school diploma (including GED) or higher: 76.3% (2010); Bachelor's degree or higher: 16.4% (2010); Master's degree or higher: 3.6% (2010).

School District(s)

Jasper ISD (PK-12)
    2009-10 Enrollment: 2,814 . . . . (409) 384-2401
Responsive Education Solutions (KG-12)
    2009-10 Enrollment: 5,022 . . . . (972) 316-3663

Vocational/Technical School(s)

Academy of Hair Design (Private, For-profit)
    Fall 2009 Enrollment: 50 . . . . (409) 384-8200
    2010-11 Tuition: $8,500

Housing: Homeownership rate: 64.1% (2010); Median home value: $71,090 (2010); Median contract rent: $338 per month (2005-2009 5-year est.); Median year structure built: 1973 (2005-2009 5-year est.).

Hospitals: Christus Jasper Memorial Hospital (81 beds); Dickerson Memorial Hospital

Safety: Violent crime rate: 39.6 per 10,000 population; Property crime rate: 465.9 per 10,000 population (2009).

Newspapers: Jasper News-Boy (Community news; Circulation 8,620)

Transportation: Commute to work: 87.5% car, 0.0% public transportation, 3.5% walk, 5.3% work from home (2005-2009 5-year est.); Travel time to work: 69.9% less than 15 minutes, 16.5% 15 to 30 minutes, 6.2% 30 to 45 minutes, 1.3% 45 to 60 minutes, 6.2% 60 minutes or more (2005-2009 5-year est.)

Additional Information Contacts
City of Jasper. . . . . (409) 384-4651
    http://www.jaspertx.org
Jasper-Lake Sam Rayburn Area Chamber of Commerce . . (409) 384-2762
    http://www.jaspercoc.org

KIRBYVILLE

KIRBYVILLE (city). Covers a land area of 2.436 square miles and a water area of 0.009 square miles. Located at 30.65° N. Lat; 93.89° W. Long. Elevation is 112 feet.

History: Kirbyville grew up around a lumber mill, and was named for John Kirby, a sawmill operator.

Population: 1,930 (1990); 2,085 (2000); 2,006 (2010); 1,961 (2015 projected); Race: 77.6% White, 18.2% Black, 0.5% Asian, 3.7% Other, 3.9% Hispanic of any race (2010); Density: 823.6 persons per square mile (2010); Average household size: 2.38 (2010); Median age: 37.6 (2010); Males per 100 females: 84.5 (2010); Marriage status: 23.6% never married, 49.5% now married, 8.0% widowed, 18.8% divorced (2005-2009 5-year est.); Foreign born: 3.4% (2005-2009 5-year est.); Ancestry (includes multiple ancestries): 14.4% Irish, 12.6% English, 11.2% German, 7.6% American, 5.1% French (2005-2009 5-year est.).

Economy: Single-family building permits issued: 4 (2010); Multi-family building permits issued: 0 (2010); Employment by occupation: 8.3% management, 20.4% professional, 14.2% services, 14.1% sales, 2.0% farming, 19.9% construction, 21.0% production (2005-2009 5-year est.).

Income: Per capita income: $16,265 (2010); Median household income: $30,709 (2010); Average household income: $38,547 (2010); Percent of households with income of $100,000 or more: 5.3% (2010); Poverty rate: 41.9% (2005-2009 5-year est.).

Taxes: Total city taxes per capita: $213 (2007); City property taxes per capita: $78 (2007).

Education: Percent of population age 25 and over with: High school diploma (including GED) or higher: 75.5% (2010); Bachelor's degree or higher: 16.2% (2010); Master's degree or higher: 3.8% (2010).

School District(s)

Kirbyville CISD (PK-12)
    2009-10 Enrollment: 1,477 . . . . (409) 423-2284

Housing: Homeownership rate: 66.1% (2010); Median home value: $51,615 (2010); Median contract rent: $243 per month (2005-2009 5-year est.); Median year structure built: 1964 (2005-2009 5-year est.).

Safety: Violent crime rate: 41.4 per 10,000 population; Property crime rate: 181.3 per 10,000 population (2009).

Newspapers: East Texas Banner (Community news; Circulation 3,300)

Transportation: Commute to work: 92.4% car, 0.0% public transportation, 3.2% walk, 2.5% work from home (2005-2009 5-year est.); Travel time to work: 45.6% less than 15 minutes, 15.6% 15 to 30 minutes, 14.1% 30 to 45 minutes, 7.8% 45 to 60 minutes, 16.8% 60 minutes or more (2005-2009 5-year est.)

Additional Information Contacts
Kirbyville Chamber of Commerce . . . . (409) 423-5827

Jeff Davis County

Located in west Texas, in a high plateau area; touches the Rio Grande at the southwestern tip, rising to the Davis Mountains; includes Mt. Livermore and Mt. Locke. Covers a land area of 2,264.43 square miles, a water area of 0.18 square miles, and is located in the Central Time Zone at 30.68° N. Lat., 104.13° W. Long. The county was founded in 1887. County seat is Fort Davis.

Weather Station: Fort Davis   Elevation: 4,879 feet

	Jan	Feb	Mar	Apr	May	Jun	Jul	Aug	Sep	Oct	Nov	Dec
High	61	65	71	79	86	90	89	87	83	78	68	61
Low	29	32	37	44	53	60	62	61	55	46	36	30
Precip	0.5	0.5	0.4	0.6	1.5	2.3	3.2	3.1	2.3	1.5	0.5	0.7
Snow	0.4	0.3	0.0	tr	0.0	0.0	0.0	0.0	0.0	0.1	0.4	0.9

High and Low temperatures in degrees Fahrenheit; Precipitation and Snow in inches

Weather Station: Mount Locke   Elevation: 6,790 feet

	Jan	Feb	Mar	Apr	May	Jun	Jul	Aug	Sep	Oct	Nov	Dec
High	55	58	65	72	80	85	84	82	78	72	62	55
Low	33	35	38	45	53	59	59	59	55	48	39	33
Precip	0.5	0.6	0.4	0.7	1.7	2.7	3.6	3.7	2.9	1.7	0.6	0.7
Snow	0.8	0.7	0.1	0.0	0.0	0.0	0.0	0.0	0.0	0.1	0.4	2.0

High and Low temperatures in degrees Fahrenheit; Precipitation and Snow in inches

Weather Station: Valentine   Elevation: 4,430 feet

	Jan	Feb	Mar	Apr	May	Jun	Jul	Aug	Sep	Oct	Nov	Dec
High	60	65	72	80	88	94	92	90	86	79	68	60
Low	27	31	36	43	53	61	63	62	56	47	35	28
Precip	0.4	0.5	0.3	0.4	0.8	2.1	2.3	2.2	2.1	1.4	0.5	0.5
Snow	0.8	tr	tr	0.1	0.0	0.0	0.0	0.0	0.0	tr	0.1	0.8

High and Low temperatures in degrees Fahrenheit; Precipitation and Snow in inches

Population: 1,946 (1990); 2,207 (2000); 2,579 (2010); 2,756 (2015 projected); Race: 90.3% White, 1.0% Black, 0.1% Asian, 8.5% Other, 36.3% Hispanic of any race (2010); Density: 1.1 persons per square mile (2010); Average household size: 2.36 (2010); Median age: 45.4 (2010); Males per 100 females: 104.4 (2010).

Religion: Five largest groups: 23.3% Catholic Church, 12.1% Southern Baptist Convention, 7.3% Christian Churches and Churches of Christ, 6.0% The United Methodist Church, 3.9% Presbyterian Church (U.S.A.) (2000).

Economy: Unemployment rate: 5.4% (June 2011); Total civilian labor force: 1,233 (June 2011); Leading industries: 12.1% retail trade; 10.9% other services (except public administration); 6.7% professional, scientific & technical services (2009); Farms: 105 totaling 1,390,903 acres (2007); Companies that employ 500 or more persons: 0 (2009); Companies that employ 100 to 499 persons: 0 (2009); Companies that employ less than 100 persons: 59 (2009); Black-owned businesses: n/a (2007); Hispanic-owned businesses: n/a (2007); Asian-owned businesses: n/a

(2007); Women-owned businesses: n/a (2007); Retail sales per capita: $3,465 (2010). Single-family building permits issued: n/a (2010); Multi-family building permits issued: n/a (2010).

Income: Per capita income: $24,606 (2010); Median household income: $42,751 (2010); Average household income: $59,412 (2010); Percent of households with income of $100,000 or more: 13.2% (2010); Poverty rate: 13.6% (2009); Bankruptcy rate: 0.83% (2010).

Taxes: Total county taxes per capita: $300 (2007); County property taxes per capita: $163 (2007).

Education: Percent of population age 25 and over with: High school diploma (including GED) or higher: 79.7% (2010); Bachelor's degree or higher: 38.0% (2010); Master's degree or higher: 14.4% (2010).

Housing: Homeownership rate: 68.0% (2010); Median home value: $104,801 (2010); Median contract rent: $238 per month (2005-2009 5-year est.); Median year structure built: 1972 (2005-2009 5-year est.)

Health: Birth rate: 79.7 per 10,000 population (2009); Death rate: 22.1 per 10,000 population (2009); Age-adjusted cancer mortality rate: Suppressed deaths per 100,000 population (2007); Number of physicians: 4.5 per 10,000 population (2008); Hospital beds: 0.0 per 10,000 population (2007); Hospital admissions: 0.0 per 10,000 population (2007).

Environment: Air Quality Index: 99.7% good, 0.3% moderate, 0.0% unhealthy for sensitive individuals, 0.0% unhealthy (percent of days in 2008)

Elections: 2008 Presidential election results: 37.9% Obama, 60.6% McCain, 0.0% Nader

National and State Parks: Davis Mountains State Park; Fort Davis National Historic Site

Additional Information Contacts
Jeff Davis County Government . . . . (432) 426-3968
   http://www.co.jeff-davis.tx.us/ips/cms
Fort Davis Chamber of Commerce . . . . (432) 426-3015
   http://www.fortdavis.com

Jeff Davis County Communities

FORT DAVIS (CDP). County seat. Covers a land area of 5.580 square miles and a water area of 0 square miles. Located at 30.59° N. Lat; 103.89° W. Long. Elevation is 4,892 feet.

History: The original Fort Davis was built in 1854 and abandoned in 1891.

Population: 896 (1990); 1,050 (2000); 1,214 (2010); 1,294 (2015 projected); Race: 88.0% White, 0.2% Black, 0.2% Asian, 11.7% Other, 50.7% Hispanic of any race (2010); Density: 217.6 persons per square mile (2010); Average household size: 2.49 (2010); Median age: 40.7 (2010); Males per 100 females: 103.0 (2010); Marriage status: 8.8% never married, 69.8% now married, 7.9% widowed, 13.5% divorced (2005-2009 5-year est.); Foreign born: 9.4% (2005-2009 5-year est.); Ancestry (includes multiple ancestries): 14.5% German, 14.4% English, 10.6% American, 7.9% Irish, 4.6% Scotch-Irish (2005-2009 5-year est.).

Economy: Employment by occupation: 19.8% management, 12.9% professional, 24.9% services, 20.4% sales, 3.5% farming, 9.8% construction, 8.6% production (2005-2009 5-year est.).

Income: Per capita income: $18,875 (2010); Median household income: $32,500 (2010); Average household income: $47,002 (2010); Percent of households with income of $100,000 or more: 8.8% (2010); Poverty rate: 9.2% (2005-2009 5-year est.).

Education: Percent of population age 25 and over with: High school diploma (including GED) or higher: 71.9% (2010); Bachelor's degree or higher: 27.2% (2010); Master's degree or higher: 8.9% (2010).

School District(s)
Ft Davis ISD (PK-12)
   2009-10 Enrollment: 330 . . . . (432) 426-4440

Housing: Homeownership rate: 72.1% (2010); Median home value: $85,000 (2010); Median contract rent: $237 per month (2005-2009 5-year est.); Median year structure built: 1959 (2005-2009 5-year est.).

Newspapers: Jeff Davis County Mountain Dispatch (Community news; Circulation 1,600)

Transportation: Commute to work: 83.8% car, 0.0% public transportation, 3.2% walk, 11.3% work from home (2005-2009 5-year est.); Travel time to work: 77.2% less than 15 minutes, 8.9% 15 to 30 minutes, 12.0% 30 to 45 minutes, 1.9% 45 to 60 minutes, 0.0% 60 minutes or more (2005-2009 5-year est.)

Additional Information Contacts
Fort Davis Chamber of Commerce . . . . (432) 426-3015
   http://www.fortdavis.com

VALENTINE (town). Covers a land area of 0.481 square miles and a water area of 0 square miles. Located at 30.58° N. Lat; 104.49° W. Long. Elevation is 4,432 feet.

Population: 217 (1990); 187 (2000); 183 (2010); 185 (2015 projected); Race: 91.8% White, 0.0% Black, 0.0% Asian, 8.2% Other, 53.0% Hispanic of any race (2010); Density: 380.5 persons per square mile (2010); Average household size: 2.47 (2010); Median age: 52.2 (2010); Males per 100 females: 101.1 (2010); Marriage status: 15.9% never married, 77.0% now married, 3.5% widowed, 3.5% divorced (2005-2009 5-year est.); Foreign born: 12.5% (2005-2009 5-year est.); Ancestry (includes multiple ancestries): 18.8% German, 12.5% English, 9.7% Irish (2005-2009 5-year est.).

Economy: Employment by occupation: 21.0% management, 25.8% professional, 12.9% services, 16.1% sales, 0.0% farming, 0.0% construction, 24.2% production (2005-2009 5-year est.).

Income: Per capita income: $25,266 (2010); Median household income: $50,000 (2010); Average household income: $60,980 (2010); Percent of households with income of $100,000 or more: 14.9% (2010); Poverty rate: 42.0% (2005-2009 5-year est.).

Taxes: Total city taxes per capita: $521 (2007); City property taxes per capita: $103 (2007).

Education: Percent of population age 25 and over with: High school diploma (including GED) or higher: 62.8% (2010); Bachelor's degree or higher: 28.5% (2010); Master's degree or higher: 12.4% (2010).

School District(s)
Valentine ISD (PK-12)
   2009-10 Enrollment: 48 . . . . (432) 467-2671

Housing: Homeownership rate: 55.4% (2010); Median home value: $33,636 (2010); Median contract rent: n/a per month (2005-2009 5-year est.); Median year structure built: before 1940 (2005-2009 5-year est.).

Transportation: Commute to work: 56.5% car, 6.5% public transportation, 27.4% walk, 4.8% work from home (2005-2009 5-year est.); Travel time to work: 62.7% less than 15 minutes, 6.8% 15 to 30 minutes, 22.0% 30 to 45 minutes, 6.8% 45 to 60 minutes, 1.7% 60 minutes or more (2005-2009 5-year est.)

Jefferson County

Located in southeastern Texas, on the Gulf coastal plain; bounded on the east by Sabine Lake, the Louisiana border, and the Neches River, and on the south by the Gulf of Mexico. Covers a land area of 903.55 square miles, a water area of 207.71 square miles, and is located in the Central Time Zone at 29.98° N. Lat., 94.06° W. Long. The county was founded in 1836. County seat is Beaumont.

Jefferson County is part of the Beaumont-Port Arthur, TX Metropolitan Statistical Area. The entire metro area includes: Hardin County, TX; Jefferson County, TX; Orange County, TX

Weather Station: Beaumont Research Ctr										Elevation: 26 feet		
	Jan	Feb	Mar	Apr	May	Jun	Jul	Aug	Sep	Oct	Nov	Dec
High	62	65	72	78	85	90	92	93	89	81	72	64
Low	42	45	51	58	66	72	73	73	68	59	50	43
Precip	4.6	3.9	3.6	3.0	5.5	8.1	4.8	4.9	5.6	5.9	4.6	4.8
Snow	tr	0.0	0.0	0.0	0.0	0.0	0.0	0.0	0.0	0.0	0.0	0.0

High and Low temperatures in degrees Fahrenheit; Precipitation and Snow in inches

Weather Station: Port Arthur Jefferson County										Elevation: 16 feet		
	Jan	Feb	Mar	Apr	May	Jun	Jul	Aug	Sep	Oct	Nov	Dec
High	62	66	72	78	85	90	92	92	88	81	72	64
Low	44	47	53	59	67	73	74	74	70	61	52	45
Precip	5.3	3.5	3.7	3.2	5.5	7.0	5.6	5.3	6.5	5.8	4.4	5.2
Snow	na	na	na	na	na	na	na	na	na	na	na	na

High and Low temperatures in degrees Fahrenheit; Precipitation and Snow in inches

Population: 239,397 (1990); 252,051 (2000); 245,147 (2010); 241,351 (2015 projected); Race: 54.5% White, 34.4% Black, 2.7% Asian, 8.5% Other, 14.9% Hispanic of any race (2010); Density: 271.3 persons per square mile (2010); Average household size: 2.52 (2010); Median age: 36.3 (2010); Males per 100 females: 104.6 (2010).

Religion: Five largest groups: 25.4% Catholic Church, 22.6% Southern Baptist Convention, 5.9% The United Methodist Church, 1.7% Churches of Christ, 1.4% The Salvation Army (2000).

Economy: Unemployment rate: 12.1% (June 2011); Total civilian labor force: 120,199 (June 2011); Leading industries: 16.2% health care and

social assistance; 13.7% retail trade; 12.9% manufacturing (2009); Farms: 793 totaling 333,255 acres (2007); Companies that employ 500 or more persons: 24 (2009); Companies that employ 100 to 499 persons: 134 (2009); Companies that employ less than 100 persons: 5,563 (2009); Black-owned businesses: 3,503 (2007); Hispanic-owned businesses: 1,156 (2007); Asian-owned businesses: 1,179 (2007); Women-owned businesses: 5,091 (2007); Retail sales per capita: $16,684 (2010). Single-family building permits issued: 959 (2010); Multi-family building permits issued: 152 (2010).

Income: Per capita income: $21,675 (2010); Median household income: $42,908 (2010); Average household income: $57,715 (2010); Percent of households with income of $100,000 or more: 14.3% (2010); Poverty rate: 19.1% (2009); Bankruptcy rate: 1.64% (2010).

Taxes: Total county taxes per capita: $349 (2007); County property taxes per capita: $251 (2007).

Education: Percent of population age 25 and over with: High school diploma (including GED) or higher: 80.9% (2010); Bachelor's degree or higher: 18.0% (2010); Master's degree or higher: 5.7% (2010).

Housing: Homeownership rate: 65.5% (2010); Median home value: $87,104 (2010); Median contract rent: $491 per month (2005-2009 5-year est.); Median year structure built: 1969 (2005-2009 5-year est.)

Health: Birth rate: 137.4 per 10,000 population (2009); Death rate: 102.0 per 10,000 population (2009); Age-adjusted cancer mortality rate: 187.6 deaths per 100,000 population (2007); Number of physicians: 23.0 per 10,000 population (2008); Hospital beds: 69.3 per 10,000 population (2007); Hospital admissions: 2,532.9 per 10,000 population (2007).

Environment: Air Quality Index: 72.0% good, 26.7% moderate, 1.3% unhealthy for sensitive individuals, 0.0% unhealthy (percent of days in 2008)

Elections: 2008 Presidential election results: 50.8% Obama, 48.6% McCain, 0.0% Nader

National and State Parks: Texas Point National Wildlife Refuge

Additional Information Contacts

Jefferson County Government . . . . (409) 835-8466
  http://www.co.jefferson.tx.us
Beaumont Chamber of Commerce . . . . (409) 838-6581
  http://www.bmtcoc.org
City of Beaumont . . . . (409) 980-8311
  http://www.cityofbeaumont.com
City of Groves . . . . (409) 962-4471
  http://www.cigrovestx.com
City of Nederland . . . . (409) 723-1503
  http://www.ci.nederland.tx.us
City of Port Arthur . . . . (409) 983-8101
  http://www.portarthur.net
City of Port Neches . . . . (409) 719-4208
  http://www.ci.port-neches.tx.us
Golden Triangle Hispanic Chamber of Commerce . . . . (409) 983-1169
  http://www.gthcc.org/contactus2.html
Groves Chamber of Commerce . . . . (409) 962-3631
  http://www.grovescofc.com
Nederland Chamber of Commerce . . . . (409) 722-0279
  http://www.nederlandtx.com
Port Arthur Chamber of Commerce . . . . (409) 963-1107
  http://www.portarthurtexas.com
Port Neches Chamber of Commerce . . . . (409) 722-9155
  http://www.portnecheschamber.com

Jefferson County Communities

BEAUMONT (city). County seat. Covers a land area of 85.015 square miles and a water area of 0.921 square miles. Located at 30.08° N. Lat; 94.12° W. Long. Elevation is 16 feet.

History: Beaumont's geology created its wealth, first with the low prairies making good rice paddies, and by the early 1900's with the oil gushers. The first settlers here were Noah and Nancy Tevis, who came about 1825. The settlement that grew up around their home was called Tevis Bluff and River Neches Settlement. In 1835 Henry Millard, of Thomas B. Huling and Company, purchased land from Tevis and laid out a town that he named Beaumont. Lumbering was the first industry, but soon the settlers began to plant rice. In 1892 a commercial rice mill was opened. Life changed for Beaumonters on January 10, 1901, when the Spindletop well spouted a geyser of oil 200 feet into the air. The town boomed, with all the problems inherent in fast growth and people hoping for instant riches. An Englishman, James Roche, helped to bring order from chaos by

encouraging the organization of the Producers' Oil Company, which became the Texas Company.

Population: 114,387 (1990); 113,866 (2000); 110,755 (2010); 108,917 (2015 projected); Race: 44.6% White, 45.6% Black, 2.4% Asian, 7.4% Other, 11.2% Hispanic of any race (2010); Density: 1,302.8 persons per square mile (2010); Average household size: 2.48 (2010); Median age: 36.1 (2010); Males per 100 females: 92.2 (2010); Marriage status: 34.0% never married, 47.6% now married, 7.2% widowed, 11.2% divorced (2005-2009 5-year est.); Foreign born: 8.2% (2005-2009 5-year est.); Ancestry (includes multiple ancestries): 6.8% German, 5.9% Irish, 5.4% English, 5.2% French, 4.1% American (2005-2009 5-year est.).

Economy: Unemployment rate: 10.5% (June 2011); Total civilian labor force: 56,682 (June 2011); Single-family building permits issued: 351 (2010); Multi-family building permits issued: 128 (2010); Employment by occupation: 10.0% management, 22.7% professional, 20.4% services, 24.4% sales, 0.2% farming, 9.8% construction, 12.6% production (2005-2009 5-year est.).

Income: Per capita income: $22,847 (2010); Median household income: $40,180 (2010); Average household income: $57,154 (2010); Percent of households with income of $100,000 or more: 13.8% (2010); Poverty rate: 21.3% (2005-2009 5-year est.).

Taxes: Total city taxes per capita: $720 (2007); City property taxes per capita: $298 (2007).

Education: Percent of population age 25 and over with: High school diploma (including GED) or higher: 83.4% (2010); Bachelor's degree or higher: 23.8% (2010); Master's degree or higher: 8.0% (2010).

School District(s)
Al Price State Juvenile Correctional Facility (09-12)
  2009-10 Enrollment: 168 . . . . (409) 724-6388
Beaumont ISD (PK-12)
  2009-10 Enrollment: 19,551 . . . . (409) 617-5000
Cypress-Fairbanks ISD (PK-12)
  2009-10 Enrollment: 104,231 . . . . (281) 897-4000
Ehrhart School (PK-08)
  2009-10 Enrollment: 214 . . . . (409) 839-8200
Hamshire-Fannett ISD (PK-12)
  2009-10 Enrollment: 1,757 . . . . (409) 243-2514
Harmony Science Academy (Beaumont) (KG-10)
  2009-10 Enrollment: 502 . . . . (409) 838-4000
Nederland ISD (PK-12)
  2009-10 Enrollment: 5,041 . . . . (409) 724-2391
Port Arthur ISD (PK-12)
  2009-10 Enrollment: 9,238 . . . . (409) 989-6244
Port Neches-Groves ISD (PK-12)
  2009-10 Enrollment: 4,593 . . . . (409) 722-4244
Responsive Education Solutions (KG-12)
  2009-10 Enrollment: 5,022 . . . . (972) 316-3663
Richard Milburn Academy (Beaumont) (09-12)
  2009-10 Enrollment: 154 . . . . (830) 557-6181

Four-year College(s)
Lamar University (Public)
  Fall 2009 Enrollment: 13,992. . . . . (409) 880-7011
  2010-11 Tuition: In-state $6,924; Out-of-state $16,224

Two-year College(s)
Lamar Institute of Technology (Public)
  Fall 2009 Enrollment: 3,154. . . . . (409) 880-8321
  2010-11 Tuition: In-state $3,422; Out-of-state $10,862
Texas Careers-Beaumont (Private, For-profit)
  Fall 2009 Enrollment: 532 . . . . (409) 833-2722

Vocational/Technical School(s)
Academy of Hair Design (Private, For-profit)
  Fall 2009 Enrollment: 67 . . . . (409) 813-3100
  2010-11 Tuition: $8,500

Housing: Homeownership rate: 59.9% (2010); Median home value: $94,181 (2010); Median contract rent: $506 per month (2005-2009 5-year est.); Median year structure built: 1971 (2005-2009 5-year est.).

Hospitals: Beaumont Bone & Joint Institute; Christus St. Elizabeth Hospital (461 beds); Memorial Hermann Baptist Beaumont (352 beds); Memorial Hermann Baptist Beaumont Hospital (355 beds)

Safety: Violent crime rate: 90.9 per 10,000 population; Property crime rate: 574.3 per 10,000 population (2009).

Newspapers: Beaumont Enterprise (Local news; Circulation 80,000); East Texas Catholic (Regional news); The Examiner (Local news)

Transportation: Commute to work: 93.4% car, 1.3% public transportation, 2.0% walk, 1.7% work from home (2005-2009 5-year est.); Travel time to

work: 43.1% less than 15 minutes, 39.3% 15 to 30 minutes, 11.4% 30 to 45 minutes, 2.2% 45 to 60 minutes, 4.0% 60 minutes or more (2005-2009 5-year est.); Amtrak: train service available.
Airports: Southeast Texas Regional (primary service)
Additional Information Contacts
Beaumont Chamber of Commerce . . . . (409) 838-6581
  http://www.bmtcoc.org
City of Beaumont . . . . (409) 980-8311
  http://www.cityofbeaumont.com

BEVIL OAKS (city). Aka Bevel Acres. Covers a land area of 2.102 square miles and a water area of 0 square miles. Located at 30.15° N. Lat; 94.26° W. Long. Elevation is 26 feet.
Population: 1,348 (1990); 1,346 (2000); 1,270 (2010); 1,226 (2015 projected); Race: 93.1% White, 3.1% Black, 0.1% Asian, 3.8% Other, 3.9% Hispanic of any race (2010); Density: 604.1 persons per square mile (2010); Average household size: 2.49 (2010); Median age: 46.6 (2010); Males per 100 females: 102.9 (2010); Marriage status: 17.5% never married, 67.4% now married, 5.7% widowed, 9.4% divorced (2005-2009 5-year est.); Foreign born: 1.4% (2005-2009 5-year est.); Ancestry (includes multiple ancestries): 14.7% German, 11.3% Irish, 10.9% French, 10.4% American, 8.5% English (2005-2009 5-year est.).
Economy: Single-family building permits issued: 0 (2010); Multi-family building permits issued: 0 (2010); Employment by occupation: 15.4% management, 26.7% professional, 14.4% services, 24.3% sales, 0.0% farming, 7.0% construction, 12.3% production (2005-2009 5-year est.).
Income: Per capita income: $31,817 (2010); Median household income: $65,726 (2010); Average household income: $78,666 (2010); Percent of households with income of $100,000 or more: 23.8% (2010); Poverty rate: 5.1% (2005-2009 5-year est.).
Taxes: Total city taxes per capita: $136 (2007); City property taxes per capita: $88 (2007).
Education: Percent of population age 25 and over with: High school diploma (including GED) or higher: 90.7% (2010); Bachelor's degree or higher: 23.9% (2010); Master's degree or higher: 6.9% (2010).
Housing: Homeownership rate: 89.6% (2010); Median home value: $130,605 (2010); Median contract rent: $750 per month (2005-2009 5-year est.); Median year structure built: 1977 (2005-2009 5-year est.).
Transportation: Commute to work: 97.1% car, 0.0% public transportation, 2.4% walk, 0.5% work from home (2005-2009 5-year est.); Travel time to work: 12.4% less than 15 minutes, 59.7% 15 to 30 minutes, 23.3% 30 to 45 minutes, 2.0% 45 to 60 minutes, 2.6% 60 minutes or more (2005-2009 5-year est.)

CENTRAL GARDENS (CDP). Covers a land area of 2.549 square miles and a water area of 0 square miles. Located at 29.98° N. Lat; 94.01° W. Long. Elevation is 16 feet.
Population: 3,755 (1990); 4,106 (2000); 4,083 (2010); 4,043 (2015 projected); Race: 81.5% White, 13.7% Black, 0.8% Asian, 4.0% Other, 5.8% Hispanic of any race (2010); Density: 1,601.9 persons per square mile (2010); Average household size: 2.58 (2010); Median age: 37.7 (2010); Males per 100 females: 120.8 (2010); Marriage status: 24.1% never married, 64.0% now married, 4.9% widowed, 6.9% divorced (2005-2009 5-year est.); Foreign born: 2.8% (2005-2009 5-year est.); Ancestry (includes multiple ancestries): 22.1% French, 13.4% German, 12.8% Irish, 9.7% American, 8.5% English (2005-2009 5-year est.).
Economy: Employment by occupation: 5.1% management, 17.0% professional, 12.0% services, 31.4% sales, 0.0% farming, 12.2% construction, 22.3% production (2005-2009 5-year est.).
Income: Per capita income: $27,460 (2010); Median household income: $60,987 (2010); Average household income: $77,480 (2010); Percent of households with income of $100,000 or more: 25.9% (2010); Poverty rate: 3.3% (2005-2009 5-year est.).
Education: Percent of population age 25 and over with: High school diploma (including GED) or higher: 89.5% (2010); Bachelor's degree or higher: 23.0% (2010); Master's degree or higher: 9.0% (2010).
Housing: Homeownership rate: 82.3% (2010); Median home value: $119,527 (2010); Median contract rent: $510 per month (2005-2009 5-year est.); Median year structure built: 1979 (2005-2009 5-year est.).
Transportation: Commute to work: 99.1% car, 0.0% public transportation, 0.3% walk, 0.0% work from home (2005-2009 5-year est.); Travel time to work: 34.7% less than 15 minutes, 46.4% 15 to 30 minutes, 14.0% 30 to 45 minutes, 0.6% 45 to 60 minutes, 4.4% 60 minutes or more (2005-2009 5-year est.)

CHINA (city). Covers a land area of 1.289 square miles and a water area of 0.008 square miles. Located at 30.05° N. Lat; 94.33° W. Long. Elevation is 39 feet.
Population: 1,059 (1990); 1,112 (2000); 1,018 (2010); 969 (2015 projected); Race: 75.4% White, 19.3% Black, 0.6% Asian, 4.7% Other, 3.5% Hispanic of any race (2010); Density: 789.9 persons per square mile (2010); Average household size: 2.60 (2010); Median age: 42.4 (2010); Males per 100 females: 95.8 (2010); Marriage status: 27.2% never married, 62.1% now married, 3.1% widowed, 7.6% divorced (2005-2009 5-year est.); Foreign born: 1.9% (2005-2009 5-year est.); Ancestry (includes multiple ancestries): 34.1% American, 15.2% Irish, 11.2% German, 10.5% French, 5.3% English (2005-2009 5-year est.).
Economy: Employment by occupation: 7.5% management, 25.9% professional, 26.0% services, 28.2% sales, 0.4% farming, 6.9% construction, 5.2% production (2005-2009 5-year est.).
Income: Per capita income: $24,084 (2010); Median household income: $53,052 (2010); Average household income: $62,986 (2010); Percent of households with income of $100,000 or more: 16.6% (2010); Poverty rate: 2.4% (2005-2009 5-year est.).
Taxes: Total city taxes per capita: $267 (2007); City property taxes per capita: $94 (2007).
Education: Percent of population age 25 and over with: High school diploma (including GED) or higher: 79.7% (2010); Bachelor's degree or higher: 17.1% (2010); Master's degree or higher: 5.2% (2010).
School District(s)
Hardin-Jefferson ISD (PK-12)
  2009-10 Enrollment: 2,014 . . . . (409) 981-6400
Housing: Homeownership rate: 85.9% (2010); Median home value: $100,538 (2010); Median contract rent: $485 per month (2005-2009 5-year est.); Median year structure built: 1987 (2005-2009 5-year est.).
Transportation: Commute to work: 96.1% car, 0.0% public transportation, 1.0% walk, 1.4% work from home (2005-2009 5-year est.); Travel time to work: 41.4% less than 15 minutes, 40.3% 15 to 30 minutes, 17.1% 30 to 45 minutes, 1.3% 45 to 60 minutes, 0.0% 60 minutes or more (2005-2009 5-year est.)

GROVES (city). Covers a land area of 5.181 square miles and a water area of 0.007 square miles. Located at 29.94° N. Lat; 93.91° W. Long. Elevation is 10 feet.
Population: 15,869 (1990); 15,733 (2000); 14,126 (2010); 13,443 (2015 projected); Race: 90.3% White, 2.9% Black, 2.0% Asian, 4.7% Other, 9.0% Hispanic of any race (2010); Density: 2,726.5 persons per square mile (2010); Average household size: 2.48 (2010); Median age: 40.1 (2010); Males per 100 females: 93.1 (2010); Marriage status: 21.2% never married, 55.0% now married, 12.3% widowed, 11.6% divorced (2005-2009 5-year est.); Foreign born: 4.8% (2005-2009 5-year est.); Ancestry (includes multiple ancestries): 22.3% French, 12.9% Irish, 9.8% English, 8.3% German, 7.2% American (2005-2009 5-year est.).
Economy: Single-family building permits issued: 22 (2010); Multi-family building permits issued: 0 (2010); Employment by occupation: 6.4% management, 18.1% professional, 14.2% services, 29.6% sales, 0.0% farming, 15.4% construction, 16.3% production (2005-2009 5-year est.).
Income: Per capita income: $26,002 (2010); Median household income: $51,999 (2010); Average household income: $64,809 (2010); Percent of households with income of $100,000 or more: 17.5% (2010); Poverty rate: 8.2% (2005-2009 5-year est.).
Taxes: Total city taxes per capita: $415 (2007); City property taxes per capita: $266 (2007).
Education: Percent of population age 25 and over with: High school diploma (including GED) or higher: 87.0% (2010); Bachelor's degree or higher: 16.0% (2010); Master's degree or higher: 3.8% (2010).
School District(s)
Port Arthur ISD (PK-12)
  2009-10 Enrollment: 9,238 . . . . (409) 989-6244
Port Neches-Groves ISD (PK-12)
  2009-10 Enrollment: 4,593 . . . . (409) 722-4244
Housing: Homeownership rate: 77.7% (2010); Median home value: $89,415 (2010); Median contract rent: $605 per month (2005-2009 5-year est.); Median year structure built: 1958 (2005-2009 5-year est.).
Hospitals: Renaissance Hospital - East Texas (87 beds)
Safety: Violent crime rate: 37.2 per 10,000 population; Property crime rate: 333.2 per 10,000 population (2009).
Transportation: Commute to work: 97.0% car, 0.4% public transportation, 1.2% walk, 0.8% work from home (2005-2009 5-year est.); Travel time to

work: 44.5% less than 15 minutes, 38.5% 15 to 30 minutes, 11.9% 30 to 45 minutes, 1.5% 45 to 60 minutes, 3.5% 60 minutes or more (2005-2009 5-year est.)

Additional Information Contacts
City of Groves . . . . (409) 962-4471
    http://www.cigrovestx.com
Groves Chamber of Commerce. . . . . (409) 962-3631
    http://www.grovescofc.com

HAMSHIRE (unincorporated postal area, zip code 77622). Covers a land area of 40.234 square miles and a water area of 0 square miles. Located at 29.87° N. Lat; 94.29° W. Long. Elevation is 16 feet.
Population: 1,326 (2000); Race: 99.1% White, 0.0% Black, 0.4% Asian, 0.5% Other, 6.2% Hispanic of any race (2000); Density: 33.0 persons per square mile (2000); Age: 27.0% under 18, 12.5% over 64 (2000); Marriage status: 21.9% never married, 64.1% now married, 7.3% widowed, 6.8% divorced (2000); Foreign born: 0.5% (2000); Ancestry (includes multiple ancestries): 35.0% American, 8.8% French, 8.2% Irish, 6.1% German (2000).
Economy: Employment by occupation: 12.7% management, 12.9% professional, 13.9% services, 32.7% sales, 0.0% farming, 12.3% construction, 15.4% production (2000).
Income: Per capita income: $24,567 (2000); Median household income: $51,300 (2000); Poverty rate: 179.1% (2000).
Education: Percent of population age 25 and over with: High school diploma (including GED) or higher: 85.3% (2000); Bachelor's degree or higher: 18.0% (2000).

School District(s)
Hamshire-Fannett ISD (PK-12)
    2009-10 Enrollment: 1,757 . . . . (409) 243-2514
Housing: Homeownership rate: 81.8% (2000); Median home value: $65,700 (2000); Median contract rent: $459 per month (2000); Median year structure built: 1973 (2000).
Transportation: Commute to work: 99.4% car, 0.0% public transportation, 0.0% walk, 0.0% work from home (2000); Travel time to work: 29.6% less than 15 minutes, 33.3% 15 to 30 minutes, 28.0% 30 to 45 minutes, 6.7% 45 to 60 minutes, 2.3% 60 minutes or more (2000)

NEDERLAND (city). Covers a land area of 5.688 square miles and a water area of 0.009 square miles. Located at 29.97° N. Lat; 93.99° W. Long. Elevation is 16 feet.
History: Nederland was founded in 1896 by a group of settlers from Holland.
Population: 17,002 (1990); 17,422 (2000); 15,707 (2010); 14,956 (2015 projected); Race: 92.1% White, 0.8% Black, 2.1% Asian, 5.0% Other, 7.8% Hispanic of any race (2010); Density: 2,761.6 persons per square mile (2010); Average household size: 2.51 (2010); Median age: 38.7 (2010); Males per 100 females: 96.3 (2010); Marriage status: 20.7% never married, 58.7% now married, 7.7% widowed, 12.9% divorced (2005-2009 5-year est.); Foreign born: 3.5% (2005-2009 5-year est.); Ancestry (includes multiple ancestries): 16.5% German, 15.6% French, 14.6% Irish, 9.4% American, 8.5% English (2005-2009 5-year est.).
Economy: Single-family building permits issued: 57 (2010); Multi-family building permits issued: 24 (2010); Employment by occupation: 12.4% management, 24.1% professional, 12.7% services, 26.9% sales, 0.0% farming, 11.9% construction, 12.1% production (2005-2009 5-year est.).
Income: Per capita income: $26,078 (2010); Median household income: $55,225 (2010); Average household income: $65,246 (2010); Percent of households with income of $100,000 or more: 15.8% (2010); Poverty rate: 6.0% (2005-2009 5-year est.).
Taxes: Total city taxes per capita: $548 (2007); City property taxes per capita: $267 (2007).
Education: Percent of population age 25 and over with: High school diploma (including GED) or higher: 88.9% (2010); Bachelor's degree or higher: 18.2% (2010); Master's degree or higher: 5.0% (2010).

School District(s)
Nederland ISD (PK-12)
    2009-10 Enrollment: 5,041 . . . . (409) 724-2391

Vocational/Technical School(s)
Faris Computer School Inc (Private, For-profit)
    Fall 2009 Enrollment: 34 . . . . (409) 722-4072
    2010-11 Tuition: $10,550
Housing: Homeownership rate: 75.1% (2010); Median home value: $97,638 (2010); Median contract rent: $578 per month (2005-2009 5-year est.); Median year structure built: 1969 (2005-2009 5-year est.).

Hospitals: Mid-Jefferson Hospital (138 beds)
Safety: Violent crime rate: 32.0 per 10,000 population; Property crime rate: 400.4 per 10,000 population (2009).
Newspapers: Mid County Chronicle (Community news; Circulation 25,000)
Transportation: Commute to work: 94.7% car, 0.2% public transportation, 2.2% walk, 1.3% work from home (2005-2009 5-year est.); Travel time to work: 43.6% less than 15 minutes, 43.4% 15 to 30 minutes, 10.4% 30 to 45 minutes, 0.5% 45 to 60 minutes, 2.2% 60 minutes or more (2005-2009 5-year est.)

Additional Information Contacts
City of Nederland . . . . (409) 723-1503
    http://www.ci.nederland.tx.us
Nederland Chamber of Commerce . . . . (409) 722-0279
    http://www.nederlandtx.com

NOME (city). Covers a land area of 1.245 square miles and a water area of 0 square miles. Located at 30.03° N. Lat; 94.41° W. Long. Elevation is 46 feet.
Population: 485 (1990); 515 (2000); 480 (2010); 463 (2015 projected); Race: 86.7% White, 10.4% Black, 0.4% Asian, 2.5% Other, 2.9% Hispanic of any race (2010); Density: 385.6 persons per square mile (2010); Average household size: 2.62 (2010); Median age: 37.6 (2010); Males per 100 females: 97.5 (2010); Marriage status: 29.4% never married, 47.6% now married, 10.7% widowed, 12.3% divorced (2005-2009 5-year est.); Foreign born: 0.9% (2005-2009 5-year est.); Ancestry (includes multiple ancestries): 31.9% English, 20.4% French, 15.6% German, 12.7% Irish, 7.7% Italian (2005-2009 5-year est.).
Economy: Employment by occupation: 1.3% management, 17.2% professional, 19.2% services, 25.8% sales, 5.3% farming, 26.5% construction, 4.6% production (2005-2009 5-year est.).
Income: Per capita income: $25,344 (2010); Median household income: $56,419 (2010); Average household income: $64,877 (2010); Percent of households with income of $100,000 or more: 16.4% (2010); Poverty rate: 18.9% (2005-2009 5-year est.).
Taxes: Total city taxes per capita: $422 (2007); City property taxes per capita: $210 (2007).
Education: Percent of population age 25 and over with: High school diploma (including GED) or higher: 86.4% (2010); Bachelor's degree or higher: 13.9% (2010); Master's degree or higher: 4.7% (2010).
Housing: Homeownership rate: 86.3% (2010); Median home value: $102,500 (2010); Median contract rent: $446 per month (2005-2009 5-year est.); Median year structure built: 1980 (2005-2009 5-year est.).
Transportation: Commute to work: 94.0% car, 0.0% public transportation, 0.0% walk, 0.7% work from home (2005-2009 5-year est.); Travel time to work: 29.3% less than 15 minutes, 34.0% 15 to 30 minutes, 24.0% 30 to 45 minutes, 6.0% 45 to 60 minutes, 6.7% 60 minutes or more (2005-2009 5-year est.)

PORT ARTHUR (city). Covers a land area of 82.919 square miles and a water area of 60.839 square miles. Located at 29.88° N. Lat; 93.94° W. Long. Elevation is 7 feet.
History: Port Arthur was established on Lake Sabine, connected by a seven-mile canal with the Gulf of Mexico. Its founder was Arthur Edward Stilwell, a wealthy New Yorker who believed in hunches and little creatures that he called Brownies. His Brownies, he said, told him to choose the site of Port Arthur as a Gulf terminus for his railroad. He had the town site surveyed in 1895, and named the town for himself. Stilwell promoted his town and it grew, acquiring incorporation in 1897. About 1900, John Warne Gates bought stock in Stilwell's companies, and was in control of Port Arthur's development when the nearby oil gushers brought the boom to the area. Port Arthur became the refining and shipping center for the oil industry.
Population: 58,531 (1990); 57,755 (2000); 56,204 (2010); 55,282 (2015 projected); Race: 35.7% White, 43.3% Black, 5.0% Asian, 16.1% Other, 23.7% Hispanic of any race (2010); Density: 677.8 persons per square mile (2010); Average household size: 2.59 (2010); Median age: 35.2 (2010); Males per 100 females: 92.4 (2010); Marriage status: 29.8% never married, 49.0% now married, 9.6% widowed, 11.6% divorced (2005-2009 5-year est.); Foreign born: 15.6% (2005-2009 5-year est.); Ancestry (includes multiple ancestries): 6.5% French, 4.4% German, 3.4% Irish, 3.0% English, 2.7% American (2005-2009 5-year est.).
Economy: Unemployment rate: 16.3% (June 2011); Total civilian labor force: 25,483 (June 2011); Single-family building permits issued: 414 (2010); Multi-family building permits issued: 0 (2010); Employment by occupation: 6.7% management, 14.3% professional, 20.9% services,

22.5% sales, 0.6% farming, 15.8% construction, 19.2% production (2005-2009 5-year est.).
Income: Per capita income: $17,891 (2010); Median household income: $33,341 (2010); Average household income: $46,381 (2010); Percent of households with income of $100,000 or more: 9.3% (2010); Poverty rate: 23.4% (2005-2009 5-year est.).
Taxes: Total city taxes per capita: $486 (2007); City property taxes per capita: $219 (2007).
Education: Percent of population age 25 and over with: High school diploma (including GED) or higher: 73.4% (2010); Bachelor's degree or higher: 11.1% (2010); Master's degree or higher: 3.2% (2010).

School District(s)
Bob Hope School
  2009-10 Enrollment: n/a . . . . (409) 983-6659
Port Arthur ISD (PK-12)
  2009-10 Enrollment: 9,238 . . . . (409) 989-6244
Port Neches-Groves ISD (PK-12)
  2009-10 Enrollment: 4,593 . . . . (409) 722-4244
Tekoa Academy of Accelerated Studies (PK-12)
  2009-10 Enrollment: 421 . . . . (409) 982-5400

Two-year College(s)
Lamar State College-Port Arthur (Public)
  Fall 2009 Enrollment: 2,208. . . . . (409) 984-6342
  2010-11 Tuition: In-state $4,232; Out-of-state $12,542
Housing: Homeownership rate: 60.2% (2010); Median home value: $52,916 (2010); Median contract rent: $411 per month (2005-2009 5-year est.); Median year structure built: 1961 (2005-2009 5-year est.).
Hospitals: Christus St. Mary Hospital (246 beds); Medical Center of Southeast Texas (224 beds)
Safety: Violent crime rate: 77.7 per 10,000 population; Property crime rate: 474.5 per 10,000 population (2009).
Newspapers: Port Arthur News (Local news; Circulation 20,000)
Transportation: Commute to work: 94.9% car, 0.6% public transportation, 1.5% walk, 1.8% work from home (2005-2009 5-year est.); Travel time to work: 36.0% less than 15 minutes, 44.7% 15 to 30 minutes, 14.0% 30 to 45 minutes, 1.8% 45 to 60 minutes, 3.5% 60 minutes or more (2005-2009 5-year est.)
Airports: Southeast Texas Regional (primary service)
Additional Information Contacts
City of Port Arthur . . . . (409) 983-8101
  http://www.portarthur.net
Golden Triangle Hispanic Chamber of Commerce . . . . (409) 983-1169
  http://www.gthcc.org/contactus2.html
Port Arthur Chamber of Commerce . . . . (409) 963-1107
  http://www.portarthurtexas.com

PORT NECHES (city). Covers a land area of 9.126 square miles and a water area of 0.072 square miles. Located at 29.98° N. Lat; 93.96° W. Long. Elevation is 16 feet.
History: Incorporated 1927.
Population: 13,150 (1990); 13,601 (2000); 12,498 (2010); 11,985 (2015 projected); Race: 93.5% White, 1.4% Black, 1.5% Asian, 3.5% Other, 6.7% Hispanic of any race (2010); Density: 1,369.5 persons per square mile (2010); Average household size: 2.56 (2010); Median age: 39.9 (2010); Males per 100 females: 97.2 (2010); Marriage status: 19.1% never married, 65.9% now married, 5.4% widowed, 9.5% divorced (2005-2009 5-year est.); Foreign born: 3.6% (2005-2009 5-year est.); Ancestry (includes multiple ancestries): 20.5% French, 17.0% German, 12.6% English, 12.0% Irish, 5.9% American (2005-2009 5-year est.).
Economy: Single-family building permits issued: 29 (2010); Multi-family building permits issued: 0 (2010); Employment by occupation: 11.0% management, 23.5% professional, 12.8% services, 26.4% sales, 0.0% farming, 13.1% construction, 13.1% production (2005-2009 5-year est.).
Income: Per capita income: $28,172 (2010); Median household income: $60,886 (2010); Average household income: $72,098 (2010); Percent of households with income of $100,000 or more: 24.2% (2010); Poverty rate: 11.9% (2005-2009 5-year est.).
Taxes: Total city taxes per capita: $484 (2007); City property taxes per capita: $399 (2007).
Education: Percent of population age 25 and over with: High school diploma (including GED) or higher: 90.9% (2010); Bachelor's degree or higher: 22.4% (2010); Master's degree or higher: 5.7% (2010).

School District(s)
Port Neches-Groves ISD (PK-12)
  2009-10 Enrollment: 4,593 . . . . (409) 722-4244

Housing: Homeownership rate: 77.7% (2010); Median home value: $115,797 (2010); Median contract rent: $522 per month (2005-2009 5-year est.); Median year structure built: 1971 (2005-2009 5-year est.).
Safety: Violent crime rate: 12.8 per 10,000 population; Property crime rate: 272.0 per 10,000 population (2009).
Transportation: Commute to work: 98.5% car, 0.0% public transportation, 0.0% walk, 1.5% work from home (2005-2009 5-year est.); Travel time to work: 43.5% less than 15 minutes, 48.2% 15 to 30 minutes, 7.5% 30 to 45 minutes, 0.3% 45 to 60 minutes, 0.5% 60 minutes or more (2005-2009 5-year est.)
Additional Information Contacts
City of Port Neches . . . . (409) 719-4208
  http://www.ci.port-neches.tx.us
Port Neches Chamber of Commerce. . . . . (409) 722-9155
  http://www.portnecheschamber.com

SABINE PASS (unincorporated postal area, zip code 77655). Covers a land area of 54.477 square miles and a water area of 4.254 square miles. Located at 29.78° N. Lat; 94.09° W. Long. Elevation is 3 feet.
Population: 661 (2000); Race: 95.3% White, 2.9% Black, 0.7% Asian, 1.1% Other, 2.1% Hispanic of any race (2000); Density: 12.1 persons per square mile (2000); Age: 27.1% under 18, 11.8% over 64 (2000); Marriage status: 21.4% never married, 60.0% now married, 7.1% widowed, 11.5% divorced (2000); Foreign born: 2.9% (2000); Ancestry (includes multiple ancestries): 20.1% French, 16.8% American, 8.5% German, 7.9% English (2000).
Economy: Employment by occupation: 12.3% management, 20.7% professional, 9.1% services, 22.5% sales, 0.0% farming, 21.0% construction, 14.5% production (2000).
Income: Per capita income: $16,598 (2000); Median household income: $39,167 (2000); Poverty rate: 179.1% (2000).
Education: Percent of population age 25 and over with: High school diploma (including GED) or higher: 71.9% (2000); Bachelor's degree or higher: 5.7% (2000).

School District(s)
Sabine Pass ISD (PK-12)
  2009-10 Enrollment: 304 . . . . (409) 971-2321
Housing: Homeownership rate: 82.5% (2000); Median home value: $46,000 (2000); Median contract rent: $327 per month (2000); Median year structure built: 1967 (2000).
Transportation: Commute to work: 88.4% car, 0.0% public transportation, 3.3% walk, 6.9% work from home (2000); Travel time to work: 53.3% less than 15 minutes, 13.2% 15 to 30 minutes, 27.2% 30 to 45 minutes, 5.1% 45 to 60 minutes, 1.2% 60 minutes or more (2000)

Jim Hogg County

Located in south Texas. Covers a land area of 1,136.11 square miles, a water area of 0.05 square miles, and is located in the Central Time Zone at 27.12° N. Lat., 98.70° W. Long. The county was founded in 1913. County seat is Hebbronville.

Weather Station: Hebbronville								Elevation: 580 feet			
	Jan	Feb	Mar	Apr	May	Jun	Jul	Aug	Sep	Oct	Nov	Dec
High	68	72	79	85	91	96	97	98	92	86	77	68
Low	44	48	55	61	69	73	74	73	70	62	53	45
Precip	1.2	1.3	1.2	1.3	3.1	2.5	2.3	2.0	3.1	2.3	1.4	1.2
Snow	tr	tr	0.0	0.0	0.0	0.0	0.0	0.0	0.0	0.0	0.0	0.2

High and Low temperatures in degrees Fahrenheit; Precipitation and Snow in inches

Population: 5,109 (1990); 5,281 (2000); 5,060 (2010); 4,945 (2015 projected); Race: 80.5% White, 0.5% Black, 0.2% Asian, 18.8% Other, 89.4% Hispanic of any race (2010); Density: 4.5 persons per square mile (2010); Average household size: 2.80 (2010); Median age: 36.4 (2010); Males per 100 females: 95.9 (2010).
Religion: Five largest groups: 91.1% Catholic Church, 5.6% Southern Baptist Convention, 2.5% The United Methodist Church, 0.7% Assemblies of God, 0.7% Churches of Christ (2000).
Economy: Unemployment rate: 7.6% (June 2011); Total civilian labor force: 2,928 (June 2011); Leading industries: 17.4% retail trade; 7.0% finance & insurance; 2.6% construction (2009); Farms: 240 totaling 640,270 acres (2007); Companies that employ 500 or more persons: 0 (2009); Companies that employ 100 to 499 persons: 1 (2009); Companies that employ less than 100 persons: 100 (2009); Black-owned businesses: n/a (2007); Hispanic-owned businesses: n/a (2007); Asian-owned businesses: n/a (2007); Women-owned businesses: 137 (2007); Retail

sales per capita: $9,864 (2010). Single-family building permits issued: n/a (2010); Multi-family building permits issued: n/a (2010).

Income: Per capita income: $17,977 (2010); Median household income: $37,132 (2010); Average household income: $50,077 (2010); Percent of households with income of $100,000 or more: 10.6% (2010); Poverty rate: 22.6% (2009); Bankruptcy rate: 1.50% (2010).

Taxes: Total county taxes per capita: $955 (2007); County property taxes per capita: $824 (2007).

Education: Percent of population age 25 and over with: High school diploma (including GED) or higher: 64.5% (2010); Bachelor's degree or higher: 11.4% (2010); Master's degree or higher: 4.3% (2010).

Housing: Homeownership rate: 75.9% (2010); Median home value: $39,471 (2010); Median contract rent: $325 per month (2005-2009 5-year est.); Median year structure built: 1973 (2005-2009 5-year est.)

Health: Birth rate: 202.1 per 10,000 population (2009); Death rate: 92.1 per 10,000 population (2009); Age-adjusted cancer mortality rate: 91.6 (Unreliable) deaths per 100,000 population (2007); Number of physicians: 2.0 per 10,000 population (2008); Hospital beds: 0.0 per 10,000 population (2007); Hospital admissions: 0.0 per 10,000 population (2007).

Elections: 2008 Presidential election results: 73.6% Obama, 26.0% McCain, 0.0% Nader

Additional Information Contacts
Jim Hogg County Government . . . . (361) 527-3015
   http://www.co.jim-hogg.tx.us/ips/cms

Jim Hogg County Communities

GUERRA (CDP). Covers a land area of 5.913 square miles and a water area of 0 square miles. Located at 26.88° N. Lat; 98.89° W. Long. Elevation is 564 feet.

Population: 9 (1990); 8 (2000); 9 (2010); 9 (2015 projected); Race: 77.8% White, 11.1% Black, 0.0% Asian, 11.1% Other, 77.8% Hispanic of any race (2010); Density: 1.5 persons per square mile (2010); Average household size: 3.00 (2010); Median age: 40.0 (2010); Males per 100 females: 200.0 (2010); Marriage status: n/a never married, n/a now married, n/a widowed, n/a divorced (2005-2009 5-year est.); Foreign born: n/a (2005-2009 5-year est.); Ancestry (includes multiple ancestries): n/a (2005-2009 5-year est.).

Economy: Employment by occupation: n/a management, n/a professional, n/a services, n/a sales, n/a farming, n/a construction, n/a production (2005-2009 5-year est.).

Income: Per capita income: $14,326 (2010); Median household income: $14,999 (2010); Average household income: $24,167 (2010); Percent of households with income of $100,000 or more: 0.0% (2010); Poverty rate: n/a (2005-2009 5-year est.).

Education: Percent of population age 25 and over with: High school diploma (including GED) or higher: 66.7% (2010); Bachelor's degree or higher: 16.7% (2010); Master's degree or higher: 0.0% (2010).

Housing: Homeownership rate: 66.7% (2010); Median home value: $40,000 (2010); Median contract rent: n/a per month (2005-2009 5-year est.); Median year structure built: n/a (2005-2009 5-year est.).

Transportation: Commute to work: n/a car, n/a public transportation, n/a walk, n/a work from home (2005-2009 5-year est.); Travel time to work: n/a less than 15 minutes, n/a 15 to 30 minutes, n/a 30 to 45 minutes, n/a 45 to 60 minutes, n/a 60 minutes or more (2005-2009 5-year est.).

HEBBRONVILLE (CDP). County seat. Covers a land area of 5.892 square miles and a water area of 0 square miles. Located at 27.31° N. Lat; 98.68° W. Long. Elevation is 548 feet.

Population: 4,433 (1990); 4,498 (2000); 4,311 (2010); 4,217 (2015 projected); Race: 80.6% White, 0.4% Black, 0.2% Asian, 18.8% Other, 89.3% Hispanic of any race (2010); Density: 731.7 persons per square mile (2010); Average household size: 2.79 (2010); Median age: 36.5 (2010); Males per 100 females: 95.7 (2010); Marriage status: 32.0% never married, 54.3% now married, 8.6% widowed, 5.1% divorced (2005-2009 5-year est.); Foreign born: 11.7% (2005-2009 5-year est.); Ancestry (includes multiple ancestries): 3.4% Italian, 2.0% American, 1.0% Irish, 0.7% English, 0.6% French (2005-2009 5-year est.).

Economy: Employment by occupation: 7.2% management, 9.0% professional, 35.1% services, 11.5% sales, 3.2% farming, 13.7% construction, 20.3% production (2005-2009 5-year est.).

Income: Per capita income: $18,212 (2010); Median household income: $37,430 (2010); Average household income: $50,703 (2010); Percent of households with income of $100,000 or more: 11.0% (2010); Poverty rate: 14.5% (2005-2009 5-year est.).

Education: Percent of population age 25 and over with: High school diploma (including GED) or higher: 65.0% (2010); Bachelor's degree or higher: 11.7% (2010); Master's degree or higher: 4.6% (2010).

School District(s)
Jim Hogg County ISD (PK-12)
   2009-10 Enrollment: 1,138 . . . . (361) 527-3203
Housing: Homeownership rate: 75.9% (2010); Median home value: $39,887 (2010); Median contract rent: $325 per month (2005-2009 5-year est.); Median year structure built: 1971 (2005-2009 5-year est.).

Newspapers: Enterprise (Community news; Circulation 1,500); Hebbronville View (Community news; Circulation 1,200)

Transportation: Commute to work: 91.4% car, 0.0% public transportation, 1.3% walk, 5.7% work from home (2005-2009 5-year est.); Travel time to work: 66.9% less than 15 minutes, 11.4% 15 to 30 minutes, 5.4% 30 to 45 minutes, 6.1% 45 to 60 minutes, 10.2% 60 minutes or more (2005-2009 5-year est.)

Airports: Jim Hogg County (general aviation)

LAS LOMITAS (CDP). Covers a land area of 3.956 square miles and a water area of 0 square miles. Located at 27.34° N. Lat; 98.66° W. Long. Elevation is 571 feet.

Population: 207 (1990); 267 (2000); 258 (2010); 252 (2015 projected); Race: 82.2% White, 0.4% Black, 0.8% Asian, 16.7% Other, 95.0% Hispanic of any race (2010); Density: 65.2 persons per square mile (2010); Average household size: 3.07 (2010); Median age: 31.1 (2010); Males per 100 females: 95.5 (2010); Marriage status: 13.5% never married, 66.5% now married, 0.0% widowed, 20.0% divorced (2005-2009 5-year est.); Foreign born: 57.2% (2005-2009 5-year est.); Ancestry (includes multiple ancestries): 13.5% African (2005-2009 5-year est.).

Economy: Employment by occupation: 0.0% management, 0.0% professional, 55.3% services, 0.0% sales, 0.0% farming, 44.7% construction, 0.0% production (2005-2009 5-year est.).

Income: Per capita income: $15,990 (2010); Median household income: $39,737 (2010); Average household income: $50,565 (2010); Percent of households with income of $100,000 or more: 7.1% (2010); Poverty rate: 0.0% (2005-2009 5-year est.).

Education: Percent of population age 25 and over with: High school diploma (including GED) or higher: 63.7% (2010); Bachelor's degree or higher: 9.6% (2010); Master's degree or higher: 1.4% (2010).

Housing: Homeownership rate: 82.1% (2010); Median home value: $33,500 (2010); Median contract rent: n/a per month (2005-2009 5-year est.); Median year structure built: 1994 (2005-2009 5-year est.).

Transportation: Commute to work: 100.0% car, 0.0% public transportation, 0.0% walk, 0.0% work from home (2005-2009 5-year est.); Travel time to work: 55.3% less than 15 minutes, 0.0% 15 to 30 minutes, 31.9% 30 to 45 minutes, 0.0% 45 to 60 minutes, 12.8% 60 minutes or more (2005-2009 5-year est.)

SOUTH FORK ESTATES (CDP). Covers a land area of 3.367 square miles and a water area of 0 square miles. Located at 27.26° N. Lat; 98.72° W. Long. Elevation is 607 feet.

Population: 33 (1990); 47 (2000); 46 (2010); 44 (2015 projected); Race: 73.9% White, 0.0% Black, 0.0% Asian, 26.1% Other, 87.0% Hispanic of any race (2010); Density: 13.7 persons per square mile (2010); Average household size: 2.71 (2010); Median age: 35.0 (2010); Males per 100 females: 91.7 (2010); Marriage status: 0.0% never married, 100.0% now married, 0.0% widowed, 0.0% divorced (2005-2009 5-year est.); Foreign born: 0.0% (2005-2009 5-year est.); Ancestry (includes multiple ancestries): n/a (2005-2009 5-year est.).

Economy: Employment by occupation: n/a management, n/a professional, n/a services, n/a sales, n/a farming, n/a construction, n/a production (2005-2009 5-year est.).

Income: Per capita income: $16,530 (2010); Median household income: $33,333 (2010); Average household income: $41,471 (2010); Percent of households with income of $100,000 or more: 5.9% (2010); Poverty rate: 0.0% (2005-2009 5-year est.).

Education: Percent of population age 25 and over with: High school diploma (including GED) or higher: 53.8% (2010); Bachelor's degree or higher: 0.0% (2010); Master's degree or higher: 0.0% (2010).

Housing: Homeownership rate: 76.5% (2010); Median home value: $31,667 (2010); Median contract rent: n/a per month (2005-2009 5-year est.); Median year structure built: 1982 (2005-2009 5-year est.).

Transportation: Commute to work: n/a car, n/a public transportation, n/a walk, n/a work from home (2005-2009 5-year est.); Travel time to work: n/a

less than 15 minutes, n/a 15 to 30 minutes, n/a 30 to 45 minutes, n/a 45 to 60 minutes, n/a 60 minutes or more (2005-2009 5-year est.)

Jim Wells County

Located in south Texas; bounded on the northeast by the Nueces River and Agua Dulce and San Diego Creeks. Covers a land area of 864.52 square miles, a water area of 3.71 square miles, and is located in the Central Time Zone at 27.70° N. Lat., 98.08° W. Long. The county was founded in 1911. County seat is Alice.

Jim Wells County is part of the Alice, TX Micropolitan Statistical Area. The entire metro area includes: Jim Wells County, TX

Weather Station: Alice   Elevation: 201 feet

	Jan	Feb	Mar	Apr	May	Jun	Jul	Aug	Sep	Oct	Nov	Dec
High	68	72	78	85	89	94	96	97	92	86	77	69
Low	46	49	55	62	69	73	74	75	71	63	55	47
Precip	1.2	1.5	1.5	1.3	3.1	2.7	2.9	2.7	4.1	3.0	1.7	1.1
Snow	0.0	0.0	0.0	0.0	0.0	0.0	0.0	0.0	0.0	0.0	0.0	0.3

High and Low temperatures in degrees Fahrenheit; Precipitation and Snow in inches

Weather Station: Mathis 4 SSW   Elevation: 138 feet

	Jan	Feb	Mar	Apr	May	Jun	Jul	Aug	Sep	Oct	Nov	Dec
High	66	70	76	82	88	93	95	96	91	84	75	67
Low	45	48	54	60	68	72	73	74	71	63	54	46
Precip	1.7	1.6	2.0	1.7	3.2	3.2	2.4	2.4	3.2	3.4	2.1	1.5
Snow	0.0	tr	0.0	0.0	0.0	0.0	0.0	0.0	0.0	0.0	0.0	tr

High and Low temperatures in degrees Fahrenheit; Precipitation and Snow in inches

Population: 37,679 (1990); 39,326 (2000); 41,734 (2010); 42,830 (2015 projected); Race: 77.2% White, 0.8% Black, 0.5% Asian, 21.4% Other, 76.9% Hispanic of any race (2010); Density: 48.3 persons per square mile (2010); Average household size: 2.93 (2010); Median age: 33.9 (2010); Males per 100 females: 94.9 (2010).
Religion: Five largest groups: 37.8% Catholic Church, 14.1% Southern Baptist Convention, 2.1% Evangelical Lutheran Church in America, 1.7% The United Methodist Church, 1.0% The Church of Jesus Christ of Latter-day Saints (2000).
Economy: Unemployment rate: 8.3% (June 2011); Total civilian labor force: 21,644 (June 2011); Leading industries: 32.6% health care and social assistance; 16.4% mining; 12.2% retail trade (2009); Farms: 1,109 totaling 462,721 acres (2007); Companies that employ 500 or more persons: 3 (2009); Companies that employ 100 to 499 persons: 16 (2009); Companies that employ less than 100 persons: 827 (2009); Black-owned businesses: n/a (2007); Hispanic-owned businesses: n/a (2007); Asian-owned businesses: n/a (2007); Women-owned businesses: 811 (2007); Retail sales per capita: $12,159 (2010). Single-family building permits issued: 18 (2010); Multi-family building permits issued: 0 (2010).
Income: Per capita income: $17,526 (2010); Median household income: $39,526 (2010); Average household income: $51,602 (2010); Percent of households with income of $100,000 or more: 10.7% (2010); Poverty rate: 23.2% (2009); Bankruptcy rate: 1.35% (2010).
Taxes: Total county taxes per capita: $839 (2007); County property taxes per capita: $776 (2007).
Education: Percent of population age 25 and over with: High school diploma (including GED) or higher: 70.4% (2010); Bachelor's degree or higher: 9.6% (2010); Master's degree or higher: 3.2% (2010).
Housing: Homeownership rate: 70.6% (2010); Median home value: $59,789 (2010); Median contract rent: $402 per month (2005-2009 5-year est.); Median year structure built: 1972 (2005-2009 5-year est.)
Health: Birth rate: 163.4 per 10,000 population (2009); Death rate: 90.0 per 10,000 population (2009); Age-adjusted cancer mortality rate: 163.7 deaths per 100,000 population (2007); Number of physicians: 8.1 per 10,000 population (2008); Hospital beds: 37.0 per 10,000 population (2007); Hospital admissions: 1,442.2 per 10,000 population (2007).
Elections: 2008 Presidential election results: 57.8% Obama, 41.7% McCain, 0.0% Nader
Additional Information Contacts
Jim Wells County Government . . . . (361) 668-5706
   http://www.co.jim-wells.tx.us/ips/cms
Alice Chamber of Commerce . . . . (361) 664-3454
   http://www.alicetxchamber.org
City of Alice . . . . (361) 668-7210
   http://www.ci.alice.tx.us

Jim Wells County Communities

ALFRED-SOUTH LA PALOMA (CDP). Covers a land area of 4.460 square miles and a water area of 0.011 square miles. Located at 27.89° N. Lat; 97.97° W. Long. Elevation is 167 feet.
Population: 366 (1990); 451 (2000); 467 (2010); 475 (2015 projected); Race: 84.6% White, 0.9% Black, 0.9% Asian, 13.7% Other, 55.7% Hispanic of any race (2010); Density: 104.7 persons per square mile (2010); Average household size: 2.99 (2010); Median age: 34.5 (2010); Males per 100 females: 96.2 (2010); Marriage status: 66.3% never married, 15.1% now married, 0.0% widowed, 18.6% divorced (2005-2009 5-year est.); Foreign born: 0.0% (2005-2009 5-year est.); Ancestry (includes multiple ancestries): 73.4% American (2005-2009 5-year est.).
Economy: Employment by occupation: 0.0% management, 14.0% professional, 52.9% services, 9.9% sales, 0.0% farming, 23.3% construction, 0.0% production (2005-2009 5-year est.).
Income: Per capita income: $17,854 (2010); Median household income: $44,500 (2010); Average household income: $51,362 (2010); Percent of households with income of $100,000 or more: 7.7% (2010); Poverty rate: 73.4% (2005-2009 5-year est.).
Education: Percent of population age 25 and over with: High school diploma (including GED) or higher: 75.0% (2010); Bachelor's degree or higher: 5.6% (2010); Master's degree or higher: 1.4% (2010).
Housing: Homeownership rate: 83.3% (2010); Median home value: $73,636 (2010); Median contract rent: n/a per month (2005-2009 5-year est.); Median year structure built: 1987 (2005-2009 5-year est.).
Transportation: Commute to work: 100.0% car, 0.0% public transportation, 0.0% walk, 0.0% work from home (2005-2009 5-year est.); Travel time to work: 16.7% less than 15 minutes, 65.9% 15 to 30 minutes, 17.4% 30 to 45 minutes, 0.0% 45 to 60 minutes, 0.0% 60 minutes or more (2005-2009 5-year est.)

ALICE (city). County seat. Covers a land area of 11.900 square miles and a water area of 0.400 square miles. Located at 27.75° N. Lat; 98.07° W. Long. Elevation is 200 feet.
History: Alice had been a cattle shipping point since 1888 when it was incorporated in 1910. The town was named for a daughter of the founder of the King Ranch.
Population: 19,785 (1990); 19,010 (2000); 20,085 (2010); 20,562 (2015 projected); Race: 73.9% White, 1.1% Black, 0.9% Asian, 24.1% Other, 80.4% Hispanic of any race (2010); Density: 1,687.7 persons per square mile (2010); Average household size: 2.87 (2010); Median age: 34.3 (2010); Males per 100 females: 92.2 (2010); Marriage status: 27.8% never married, 51.9% now married, 8.5% widowed, 11.9% divorced (2005-2009 5-year est.); Foreign born: 4.5% (2005-2009 5-year est.); Ancestry (includes multiple ancestries): 4.4% German, 3.4% Irish, 3.2% American, 2.0% English, 0.8% French (2005-2009 5-year est.).
Economy: Single-family building permits issued: 18 (2010); Multi-family building permits issued: 0 (2010); Employment by occupation: 10.0% management, 13.6% professional, 22.0% services, 28.6% sales, 0.2% farming, 12.6% construction, 12.9% production (2005-2009 5-year est.).
Income: Per capita income: $18,147 (2010); Median household income: $40,135 (2010); Average household income: $52,450 (2010); Percent of households with income of $100,000 or more: 11.0% (2010); Poverty rate: 23.0% (2005-2009 5-year est.).
Taxes: Total city taxes per capita: $602 (2007); City property taxes per capita: $141 (2007).
Education: Percent of population age 25 and over with: High school diploma (including GED) or higher: 70.6% (2010); Bachelor's degree or higher: 11.0% (2010); Master's degree or higher: 3.5% (2010).
School District(s)
Alice ISD (PK-12)
   2009-10 Enrollment: 5,389 . . . . (361) 664-0981
Housing: Homeownership rate: 63.3% (2010); Median home value: $60,399 (2010); Median contract rent: $425 per month (2005-2009 5-year est.); Median year structure built: 1965 (2005-2009 5-year est.).
Hospitals: Christus Spohn Hospital Alice (148 beds)
Safety: Violent crime rate: 93.5 per 10,000 population; Property crime rate: 707.0 per 10,000 population (2009).
Newspapers: Alice Echo-News Journal (Local news; Circulation 4,000)
Transportation: Commute to work: 93.6% car, 0.4% public transportation, 0.6% walk, 2.9% work from home (2005-2009 5-year est.); Travel time to work: 62.6% less than 15 minutes, 17.7% 15 to 30 minutes, 6.1% 30 to 45 minutes, 5.4% 45 to 60 minutes, 8.2% 60 minutes or more (2005-2009 5-year est.)

Airports: Alice International (general aviation)
Additional Information Contacts
Alice Chamber of Commerce . . . . (361) 664-3454
    http://www.alicetxchamber.org
City of Alice . . . . (361) 668-7210
    http://www.ci.alice.tx.us

ALICE ACRES (CDP). Covers a land area of 5.899 square miles and a water area of 0 square miles. Located at 27.72° N. Lat; 98.11° W. Long. Elevation is 233 feet.
Population: 290 (1990); 491 (2000); 548 (2010); 574 (2015 projected); Race: 79.9% White, 0.4% Black, 0.0% Asian, 19.7% Other, 89.4% Hispanic of any race (2010); Density: 92.9 persons per square mile (2010); Average household size: 3.43 (2010); Median age: 29.5 (2010); Males per 100 females: 96.4 (2010); Marriage status: 0.0% never married, 40.7% now married, 0.0% widowed, 59.3% divorced (2005-2009 5-year est.); Foreign born: 0.0% (2005-2009 5-year est.); Ancestry (includes multiple ancestries): n/a (2005-2009 5-year est.).
Economy: Employment by occupation: 0.0% management, 68.4% professional, 0.0% services, 19.0% sales, 0.0% farming, 12.7% construction, 0.0% production (2005-2009 5-year est.).
Income: Per capita income: $17,219 (2010); Median household income: $48,295 (2010); Average household income: $57,610 (2010); Percent of households with income of $100,000 or more: 13.8% (2010); Poverty rate: 6.1% (2005-2009 5-year est.).
Education: Percent of population age 25 and over with: High school diploma (including GED) or higher: 73.2% (2010); Bachelor's degree or higher: 10.6% (2010); Master's degree or higher: 5.3% (2010).
Housing: Homeownership rate: 83.6% (2010); Median home value: $56,452 (2010); Median contract rent: n/a per month (2005-2009 5-year est.); Median year structure built: 1996 (2005-2009 5-year est.).
Transportation: Commute to work: 100.0% car, 0.0% public transportation, 0.0% walk, 0.0% work from home (2005-2009 5-year est.); Travel time to work: 21.7% less than 15 minutes, 0.0% 15 to 30 minutes, 0.0% 30 to 45 minutes, 0.0% 45 to 60 minutes, 78.3% 60 minutes or more (2005-2009 5-year est.)

COYOTE ACRES (CDP). Covers a land area of 5.108 square miles and a water area of 0 square miles. Located at 27.72° N. Lat; 98.13° W. Long. Elevation is 230 feet.
Population: 211 (1990); 389 (2000); 442 (2010); 469 (2015 projected); Race: 79.2% White, 0.5% Black, 0.0% Asian, 20.4% Other, 86.4% Hispanic of any race (2010); Density: 86.5 persons per square mile (2010); Average household size: 3.27 (2010); Median age: 31.9 (2010); Males per 100 females: 92.2 (2010); Marriage status: 55.3% never married, 39.8% now married, 4.9% widowed, 0.0% divorced (2005-2009 5-year est.); Foreign born: 8.7% (2005-2009 5-year est.); Ancestry (includes multiple ancestries): 32.1% French, 4.3% Dutch (2005-2009 5-year est.).
Economy: Employment by occupation: 0.0% management, 0.0% professional, 31.4% services, 44.2% sales, 0.0% farming, 19.0% construction, 5.4% production (2005-2009 5-year est.).
Income: Per capita income: $17,709 (2010); Median household income: $46,591 (2010); Average household income: $59,130 (2010); Percent of households with income of $100,000 or more: 20.0% (2010); Poverty rate: 3.2% (2005-2009 5-year est.).
Education: Percent of population age 25 and over with: High school diploma (including GED) or higher: 71.1% (2010); Bachelor's degree or higher: 7.6% (2010); Master's degree or higher: 1.9% (2010).
Housing: Homeownership rate: 83.0% (2010); Median home value: $69,167 (2010); Median contract rent: n/a per month (2005-2009 5-year est.); Median year structure built: 1999 (2005-2009 5-year est.).
Transportation: Commute to work: 100.0% car, 0.0% public transportation, 0.0% walk, 0.0% work from home (2005-2009 5-year est.); Travel time to work: 15.3% less than 15 minutes, 84.7% 15 to 30 minutes, 0.0% 30 to 45 minutes, 0.0% 45 to 60 minutes, 0.0% 60 minutes or more (2005-2009 5-year est.)

K-BAR RANCH (CDP). Covers a land area of 3.411 square miles and a water area of 0 square miles. Located at 27.99° N. Lat; 97.92° W. Long. Elevation is 194 feet.
Population: 284 (1990); 350 (2000); 361 (2010); 367 (2015 projected); Race: 84.5% White, 0.8% Black, 0.8% Asian, 13.9% Other, 55.4% Hispanic of any race (2010); Density: 105.8 persons per square mile (2010); Average household size: 2.98 (2010); Median age: 34.6 (2010); Males per 100 females: 93.0 (2010); Marriage status: 22.6% never married,

54.9% now married, 7.5% widowed, 15.0% divorced (2005-2009 5-year est.); Foreign born: 0.0% (2005-2009 5-year est.); Ancestry (includes multiple ancestries): 27.7% American, 7.6% French, 7.6% Irish, 2.9% Polish (2005-2009 5-year est.).
Economy: Employment by occupation: 0.0% management, 0.0% professional, 0.0% services, 62.2% sales, 0.0% farming, 37.8% construction, 0.0% production (2005-2009 5-year est.).
Income: Per capita income: $17,854 (2010); Median household income: $44,886 (2010); Average household income: $53,202 (2010); Percent of households with income of $100,000 or more: 9.1% (2010); Poverty rate: 40.8% (2005-2009 5-year est.).
Education: Percent of population age 25 and over with: High school diploma (including GED) or higher: 75.5% (2010); Bachelor's degree or higher: 6.0% (2010); Master's degree or higher: 1.9% (2010).
Housing: Homeownership rate: 83.5% (2010); Median home value: $73,529 (2010); Median contract rent: n/a per month (2005-2009 5-year est.); Median year structure built: 1977 (2005-2009 5-year est.).
Transportation: Commute to work: 100.0% car, 0.0% public transportation, 0.0% walk, 0.0% work from home (2005-2009 5-year est.); Travel time to work: 8.7% less than 15 minutes, 0.0% 15 to 30 minutes, 53.6% 30 to 45 minutes, 30.6% 45 to 60 minutes, 7.1% 60 minutes or more (2005-2009 5-year est.)

LOMA LINDA EAST (CDP). Covers a land area of 5.191 square miles and a water area of 0 square miles. Located at 27.76° N. Lat; 98.19° W. Long.
Population: 211 (1990); 214 (2000); 253 (2010); 272 (2015 projected); Race: 71.1% White, 0.0% Black, 0.0% Asian, 28.9% Other, 74.3% Hispanic of any race (2010); Density: 48.7 persons per square mile (2010); Average household size: 2.83 (2010); Median age: 32.1 (2010); Males per 100 females: 97.7 (2010); Marriage status: 20.0% never married, 80.0% now married, 0.0% widowed, 0.0% divorced (2005-2009 5-year est.); Foreign born: 0.0% (2005-2009 5-year est.); Ancestry (includes multiple ancestries): n/a (2005-2009 5-year est.).
Economy: Employment by occupation: 25.6% management, 0.0% professional, 0.0% services, 53.8% sales, 0.0% farming, 0.0% construction, 20.5% production (2005-2009 5-year est.).
Income: Per capita income: $21,021 (2010); Median household income: $46,500 (2010); Average household income: $58,764 (2010); Percent of households with income of $100,000 or more: 13.5% (2010); Poverty rate: 0.0% (2005-2009 5-year est.).
Education: Percent of population age 25 and over with: High school diploma (including GED) or higher: 79.3% (2010); Bachelor's degree or higher: 13.3% (2010); Master's degree or higher: 3.3% (2010).
Housing: Homeownership rate: 84.3% (2010); Median home value: $79,231 (2010); Median contract rent: n/a per month (2005-2009 5-year est.); Median year structure built: 1987 (2005-2009 5-year est.).
Transportation: Commute to work: 100.0% car, 0.0% public transportation, 0.0% walk, 0.0% work from home (2005-2009 5-year est.); Travel time to work: 20.5% less than 15 minutes, 79.5% 15 to 30 minutes, 0.0% 30 to 45 minutes, 0.0% 45 to 60 minutes, 0.0% 60 minutes or more (2005-2009 5-year est.)

ORANGE GROVE (city). Covers a land area of 1.080 square miles and a water area of 0 square miles. Located at 27.95° N. Lat; 97.93° W. Long. Elevation is 194 feet.
Population: 1,202 (1990); 1,288 (2000); 1,445 (2010); 1,516 (2015 projected); Race: 91.9% White, 0.3% Black, 0.5% Asian, 7.3% Other, 52.6% Hispanic of any race (2010); Density: 1,338.0 persons per square mile (2010); Average household size: 2.75 (2010); Median age: 34.3 (2010); Males per 100 females: 86.9 (2010); Marriage status: 29.8% never married, 48.5% now married, 8.7% widowed, 13.0% divorced (2005-2009 5-year est.); Foreign born: 5.6% (2005-2009 5-year est.); Ancestry (includes multiple ancestries): 19.0% German, 6.0% Irish, 4.1% English, 3.3% American, 2.0% French (2005-2009 5-year est.).
Economy: Single-family building permits issued: 0 (2010); Multi-family building permits issued: 0 (2010); Employment by occupation: 9.5% management, 18.0% professional, 16.1% services, 24.7% sales, 1.1% farming, 4.9% construction, 25.6% production (2005-2009 5-year est.).
Income: Per capita income: $21,892 (2010); Median household income: $48,306 (2010); Average household income: $59,905 (2010); Percent of households with income of $100,000 or more: 15.6% (2010); Poverty rate: 14.2% (2005-2009 5-year est.).
Taxes: Total city taxes per capita: $327 (2007); City property taxes per capita: $119 (2007).

Education: Percent of population age 25 and over with: High school diploma (including GED) or higher: 77.1% (2010); Bachelor's degree or higher: 13.4% (2010); Master's degree or higher: 6.4% (2010).

School District(s)

Orange Grove ISD (PK-12)
    2009-10 Enrollment: 1,761 . . . . (361) 384-2495

Housing: Homeownership rate: 64.3% (2010); Median home value: $83,500 (2010); Median contract rent: $304 per month (2005-2009 5-year est.); Median year structure built: 1968 (2005-2009 5-year est.).

Safety: Violent crime rate: 0.0 per 10,000 population; Property crime rate: 84.7 per 10,000 population (2009).

Transportation: Commute to work: 95.9% car, 0.0% public transportation, 0.9% walk, 0.5% work from home (2005-2009 5-year est.); Travel time to work: 37.1% less than 15 minutes, 24.2% 15 to 30 minutes, 19.3% 30 to 45 minutes, 10.8% 45 to 60 minutes, 8.5% 60 minutes or more (2005-2009 5-year est.)

Additional Information Contacts

Greater Orange Area Chamber of Commerce. . . . . (409) 883-3536
    http://www.orangetexaschamber.org

OWL RANCH-AMARGOSA (CDP). Covers a land area of 2.259 square miles and a water area of 0.006 square miles. Located at 27.88° N. Lat; 98.10° W. Long. Elevation is 292 feet.

Population: 443 (1990); 527 (2000); 506 (2010); 498 (2015 projected); Race: 82.8% White, 0.6% Black, 0.2% Asian, 16.4% Other, 87.5% Hispanic of any race (2010); Density: 224.0 persons per square mile (2010); Average household size: 3.10 (2010); Median age: 31.5 (2010); Males per 100 females: 97.7 (2010); Marriage status: 29.4% never married, 23.5% now married, 28.9% widowed, 18.2% divorced (2005-2009 5-year est.); Foreign born: 0.0% (2005-2009 5-year est.); Ancestry (includes multiple ancestries): n/a (2005-2009 5-year est.).

Economy: Employment by occupation: 9.1% management, 0.0% professional, 53.0% services, 29.8% sales, 0.0% farming, 0.0% construction, 8.1% production (2005-2009 5-year est.).

Income: Per capita income: $12,049 (2010); Median household income: $32,051 (2010); Average household income: $36,396 (2010); Percent of households with income of $100,000 or more: 4.3% (2010); Poverty rate: 17.5% (2005-2009 5-year est.).

Education: Percent of population age 25 and over with: High school diploma (including GED) or higher: 57.0% (2010); Bachelor's degree or higher: 3.1% (2010); Master's degree or higher: 3.1% (2010).

Housing: Homeownership rate: 82.8% (2010); Median home value: $34,490 (2010); Median contract rent: n/a per month (2005-2009 5-year est.); Median year structure built: 1965 (2005-2009 5-year est.).

Transportation: Commute to work: 83.3% car, 0.0% public transportation, 16.7% walk, 0.0% work from home (2005-2009 5-year est.); Travel time to work: 16.7% less than 15 minutes, 44.9% 15 to 30 minutes, 0.0% 30 to 45 minutes, 30.3% 45 to 60 minutes, 8.1% 60 minutes or more (2005-2009 5-year est.)

PREMONT (city). Covers a land area of 1.708 square miles and a water area of 0 square miles. Located at 27.35° N. Lat; 98.12° W. Long. Elevation is 161 feet.

History: Incorporated 1938.

Population: 2,914 (1990); 2,772 (2000); 2,804 (2010); 2,817 (2015 projected); Race: 78.2% White, 0.7% Black, 0.0% Asian, 21.1% Other, 86.3% Hispanic of any race (2010); Density: 1,641.3 persons per square mile (2010); Average household size: 2.89 (2010); Median age: 35.1 (2010); Males per 100 females: 97.6 (2010); Marriage status: 31.2% never married, 51.1% now married, 6.3% widowed, 11.4% divorced (2005-2009 5-year est.); Foreign born: 4.9% (2005-2009 5-year est.); Ancestry (includes multiple ancestries): 11.6% German, 3.8% Scotch-Irish, 2.2% Italian, 2.0% American, 1.9% Irish (2005-2009 5-year est.).

Economy: Single-family building permits issued: 0 (2010); Multi-family building permits issued: 0 (2010); Employment by occupation: 7.7% management, 25.1% professional, 20.2% services, 20.6% sales, 1.9% farming, 12.7% construction, 11.7% production (2005-2009 5-year est.).

Income: Per capita income: $11,408 (2010); Median household income: $25,388 (2010); Average household income: $33,240 (2010); Percent of households with income of $100,000 or more: 2.9% (2010); Poverty rate: 35.2% (2005-2009 5-year est.).

Taxes: Total city taxes per capita: $188 (2007); City property taxes per capita: $168 (2007).

Education: Percent of population age 25 and over with: High school diploma (including GED) or higher: 63.2% (2010); Bachelor's degree or higher: 9.5% (2010); Master's degree or higher: 3.4% (2010).

School District(s)

Premont ISD (PK-12)
    2009-10 Enrollment: 614 . . . . (361) 348-3915

Housing: Homeownership rate: 72.3% (2010); Median home value: $37,852 (2010); Median contract rent: $335 per month (2005-2009 5-year est.); Median year structure built: 1961 (2005-2009 5-year est.).

Safety: Violent crime rate: 39.4 per 10,000 population; Property crime rate: 215.0 per 10,000 population (2009).

Transportation: Commute to work: 89.2% car, 0.0% public transportation, 8.2% walk, 0.0% work from home (2005-2009 5-year est.); Travel time to work: 63.2% less than 15 minutes, 17.1% 15 to 30 minutes, 13.6% 30 to 45 minutes, 2.4% 45 to 60 minutes, 3.7% 60 minutes or more (2005-2009 5-year est.)

RANCHO ALEGRE (CDP). Covers a land area of 1.257 square miles and a water area of 0 square miles. Located at 27.74° N. Lat; 98.09° W. Long. Elevation is 213 feet.

Population: 1,811 (1990); 1,775 (2000); 1,697 (2010); 1,656 (2015 projected); Race: 82.3% White, 0.8% Black, 0.1% Asian, 16.7% Other, 86.2% Hispanic of any race (2010); Density: 1,350.5 persons per square mile (2010); Average household size: 2.99 (2010); Median age: 31.7 (2010); Males per 100 females: 97.1 (2010); Marriage status: 34.0% never married, 48.8% now married, 6.6% widowed, 10.6% divorced (2005-2009 5-year est.); Foreign born: 6.8% (2005-2009 5-year est.); Ancestry (includes multiple ancestries): 3.1% German, 1.6% American, 0.8% English (2005-2009 5-year est.).

Economy: Employment by occupation: 0.0% management, 5.1% professional, 22.7% services, 15.7% sales, 0.0% farming, 33.9% construction, 22.5% production (2005-2009 5-year est.).

Income: Per capita income: $14,054 (2010); Median household income: $34,000 (2010); Average household income: $42,179 (2010); Percent of households with income of $100,000 or more: 5.0% (2010); Poverty rate: 39.0% (2005-2009 5-year est.).

Education: Percent of population age 25 and over with: High school diploma (including GED) or higher: 59.4% (2010); Bachelor's degree or higher: 2.5% (2010); Master's degree or higher: 1.0% (2010).

Housing: Homeownership rate: 67.1% (2010); Median home value: $46,076 (2010); Median contract rent: $389 per month (2005-2009 5-year est.); Median year structure built: 1973 (2005-2009 5-year est.).

Transportation: Commute to work: 93.9% car, 3.6% public transportation, 2.5% walk, 0.0% work from home (2005-2009 5-year est.); Travel time to work: 58.9% less than 15 minutes, 23.7% 15 to 30 minutes, 6.4% 30 to 45 minutes, 0.0% 45 to 60 minutes, 11.0% 60 minutes or more (2005-2009 5-year est.)

SANDIA (CDP). Covers a land area of 0.968 square miles and a water area of 0.004 square miles. Located at 28.02° N. Lat; 97.87° W. Long. Elevation is 125 feet.

Population: 308 (1990); 431 (2000); 452 (2010); 460 (2015 projected); Race: 84.7% White, 0.9% Black, 0.7% Asian, 13.7% Other, 55.5% Hispanic of any race (2010); Density: 467.0 persons per square mile (2010); Average household size: 2.99 (2010); Median age: 34.4 (2010); Males per 100 females: 97.4 (2010); Marriage status: 45.1% never married, 39.1% now married, 7.5% widowed, 8.3% divorced (2005-2009 5-year est.); Foreign born: 0.0% (2005-2009 5-year est.); Ancestry (includes multiple ancestries): 19.6% German, 16.7% English, 10.0% Polish, 2.6% Irish (2005-2009 5-year est.).

Economy: Employment by occupation: 7.5% management, 12.1% professional, 0.0% services, 20.2% sales, 9.2% farming, 8.1% construction, 42.8% production (2005-2009 5-year est.).

Income: Per capita income: $17,854 (2010); Median household income: $44,375 (2010); Average household income: $54,305 (2010); Percent of households with income of $100,000 or more: 7.9% (2010); Poverty rate: 13.8% (2005-2009 5-year est.).

Education: Percent of population age 25 and over with: High school diploma (including GED) or higher: 75.0% (2010); Bachelor's degree or higher: 6.6% (2010); Master's degree or higher: 2.2% (2010).

Housing: Homeownership rate: 82.8% (2010); Median home value: $74,762 (2010); Median contract rent: n/a per month (2005-2009 5-year est.); Median year structure built: 1956 (2005-2009 5-year est.).

Transportation: Commute to work: 100.0% car, 0.0% public transportation, 0.0% walk, 0.0% work from home (2005-2009 5-year est.);

Travel time to work: 17.3% less than 15 minutes, 35.3% 15 to 30 minutes, 8.1% 30 to 45 minutes, 34.1% 45 to 60 minutes, 5.2% 60 minutes or more (2005-2009 5-year est.)

WESTDALE (CDP). Covers a land area of 3.783 square miles and a water area of 0 square miles. Located at 27.96° N. Lat; 97.97° W. Long. Elevation is 213 feet.
Population: 190 (1990); 295 (2000); 336 (2010); 355 (2015 projected); Race: 88.1% White, 0.6% Black, 0.0% Asian, 11.3% Other, 45.5% Hispanic of any race (2010); Density: 88.8 persons per square mile (2010); Average household size: 2.90 (2010); Median age: 36.6 (2010); Males per 100 females: 94.2 (2010); Marriage status: 33.0% never married, 63.8% now married, 0.0% widowed, 3.3% divorced (2005-2009 5-year est.); Foreign born: 7.6% (2005-2009 5-year est.); Ancestry (includes multiple ancestries): 27.5% German, 21.2% Irish, 2.5% French (2005-2009 5-year est.).
Economy: Employment by occupation: 13.0% management, 12.3% professional, 0.0% services, 59.4% sales, 0.0% farming, 3.9% construction, 11.4% production (2005-2009 5-year est.).
Income: Per capita income: $18,958 (2010); Median household income: $41,136 (2010); Average household income: $53,728 (2010); Percent of households with income of $100,000 or more: 12.1% (2010); Poverty rate: 44.8% (2005-2009 5-year est.).
Education: Percent of population age 25 and over with: High school diploma (including GED) or higher: 80.8% (2010); Bachelor's degree or higher: 11.7% (2010); Master's degree or higher: 4.2% (2010).
Housing: Homeownership rate: 80.2% (2010); Median home value: $90,833 (2010); Median contract rent: n/a per month (2005-2009 5-year est.); Median year structure built: 1976 (2005-2009 5-year est.).
Transportation: Commute to work: 100.0% car, 0.0% public transportation, 0.0% walk, 0.0% work from home (2005-2009 5-year est.); Travel time to work: 55.4% less than 15 minutes, 15.9% 15 to 30 minutes, 0.0% 30 to 45 minutes, 16.9% 45 to 60 minutes, 11.8% 60 minutes or more (2005-2009 5-year est.)

Johnson County

Located in north central Texas; bounded on the southwest by the Brazos River; drained by tributaries of the Brazos and Trinity Rivers. Covers a land area of 729.42 square miles, a water area of 5.03 square miles, and is located in the Central Time Zone at 32.40° N. Lat., 97.33° W. Long. The county was founded in 1854. County seat is Cleburne.

Johnson County is part of the Dallas-Fort Worth-Arlington, TX Metropolitan Statistical Area. The entire metro area includes: Dallas-Plano-Irving, TX Metropolitan Division (Collin County, TX; Dallas County, TX; Delta County, TX; Denton County, TX; Ellis County, TX; Hunt County, TX; Kaufman County, TX; Rockwall County, TX); Fort Worth-Arlington, TX Metropolitan Division (Johnson County, TX; Parker County, TX; Tarrant County, TX; Wise County, TX)

Weather Station: Cleburne   Elevation: 783 feet

	Jan	Feb	Mar	Apr	May	Jun	Jul	Aug	Sep	Oct	Nov	Dec
High	59	63	71	79	85	92	97	97	90	80	69	59
Low	35	39	46	53	63	69	72	72	65	55	45	36
Precip	2.2	2.6	3.5	3.0	5.0	4.2	2.0	2.5	2.9	3.9	2.8	2.6
Snow	0.3	0.3	0.1	tr	0.0	0.0	0.0	0.0	0.0	tr	tr	0.3

High and Low temperatures in degrees Fahrenheit; Precipitation and Snow in inches

Population: 97,165 (1990); 126,811 (2000); 161,137 (2010); 177,549 (2015 projected); Race: 85.9% White, 3.7% Black, 0.8% Asian, 9.6% Other, 17.1% Hispanic of any race (2010); Density: 220.9 persons per square mile (2010); Average household size: 2.90 (2010); Median age: 34.7 (2010); Males per 100 females: 100.0 (2010).
Religion: Five largest groups: 25.3% Southern Baptist Convention, 5.8% The United Methodist Church, 4.6% Seventh-day Adventist Church, 4.1% Catholic Church, 2.6% Churches of Christ (2000).
Economy: Unemployment rate: 8.5% (June 2011); Total civilian labor force: 76,761 (June 2011); Leading industries: 14.9% mining; 13.6% retail trade; 13.3% manufacturing (2009); Farms: 2,746 totaling 331,347 acres (2007); Companies that employ 500 or more persons: 6 (2009); Companies that employ 100 to 499 persons: 45 (2009); Companies that employ less than 100 persons: 2,508 (2009); Black-owned businesses: 399 (2007); Hispanic-owned businesses: 912 (2007); Asian-owned businesses: n/a (2007); Women-owned businesses: 3,095 (2007); Retail sales per capita:

$10,137 (2010). Single-family building permits issued: 436 (2010); Multi-family building permits issued: 397 (2010).
Income: Per capita income: $22,394 (2010); Median household income: $54,643 (2010); Average household income: $65,700 (2010); Percent of households with income of $100,000 or more: 17.1% (2010); Poverty rate: 11.4% (2009); Bankruptcy rate: 3.23% (2010).
Taxes: Total county taxes per capita: $190 (2007); County property taxes per capita: $175 (2007).
Education: Percent of population age 25 and over with: High school diploma (including GED) or higher: 80.4% (2010); Bachelor's degree or higher: 14.7% (2010); Master's degree or higher: 4.3% (2010).
Housing: Homeownership rate: 74.5% (2010); Median home value: $106,903 (2010); Median contract rent: $564 per month (2005-2009 5-year est.); Median year structure built: 1987 (2005-2009 5-year est.)
Health: Birth rate: 141.5 per 10,000 population (2009); Death rate: 74.3 per 10,000 population (2009); Age-adjusted cancer mortality rate: 189.3 deaths per 100,000 population (2007); Number of physicians: 9.2 per 10,000 population (2008); Hospital beds: 3.2 per 10,000 population (2007); Hospital admissions: 243.6 per 10,000 population (2007).
Environment: Air Quality Index: 83.9% good, 12.8% moderate, 3.3% unhealthy for sensitive individuals, 0.0% unhealthy (percent of days in 2008)
Elections: 2008 Presidential election results: 25.8% Obama, 73.3% McCain, 0.1% Nader
National and State Parks: Cleburne State Park
Additional Information Contacts
Johnson County Government . . . . (817) 556-6300
   http://www.johnsoncountytx.org
Burleson Area Chamber of Commerce . . . . (817) 295-6121
   http://www.burleson.org
City of Alvarado . . . . (817) 790-3351
   http://www.cityofalvarado.org
City of Burleson . . . . (817) 426-9600
   http://www.burlesontx.com
City of Cleburne . . . . (817) 645-0908
   http://www.ci.cleburne.tx.us
City of Keene . . . . (817) 641-3336
   http://www.keenetx.com
Cleburne Chamber of Commerce . . . . (817) 645-2455
   http://www.cleburnechamber.com
Grandview Chamber of Commerce . . . . (817) 866-4881
   http://www.grandviewchamber.net
Johnson County Hispanic Chamber of Commerce . . . . (817) 641-8644
Joshua Area Chamber of Commerce . . . . (817) 558-2821
   http://www.joshuachamber.org
Keene Chamber of Commerce . . . . (817) 556-2995
   http://www.keenechamber.org

Johnson County Communities

ALVARADO (city). Covers a land area of 3.903 square miles and a water area of 0.011 square miles. Located at 32.40° N. Lat; 97.21° W. Long. Elevation is 764 feet.
History: Alvarado was on the trail for cattle being herded both north and west. The first school here had an eight-foot log barricade around it to protect the students from the cattle herds trampling through the town.
Population: 2,792 (1990); 3,288 (2000); 4,236 (2010); 4,762 (2015 projected); Race: 75.6% White, 5.7% Black, 0.4% Asian, 18.3% Other, 26.6% Hispanic of any race (2010); Density: 1,085.5 persons per square mile (2010); Average household size: 2.91 (2010); Median age: 33.9 (2010); Males per 100 females: 103.0 (2010); Marriage status: 25.4% never married, 57.4% now married, 5.3% widowed, 11.9% divorced (2005-2009 5-year est.); Foreign born: 7.4% (2005-2009 5-year est.); Ancestry (includes multiple ancestries): 13.9% English, 11.8% Irish, 6.5% German, 4.8% American, 3.6% Dutch (2005-2009 5-year est.).
Economy: Single-family building permits issued: 6 (2010); Multi-family building permits issued: 2 (2010); Employment by occupation: 7.5% management, 14.6% professional, 19.6% services, 12.2% sales, 0.5% farming, 21.5% construction, 24.1% production (2005-2009 5-year est.).
Income: Per capita income: $18,165 (2010); Median household income: $43,797 (2010); Average household income: $53,509 (2010); Percent of households with income of $100,000 or more: 11.3% (2010); Poverty rate: 14.8% (2005-2009 5-year est.).
Taxes: Total city taxes per capita: $564 (2007); City property taxes per capita: $235 (2007).

Education: Percent of population age 25 and over with: High school diploma (including GED) or higher: 66.3% (2010); Bachelor's degree or higher: 6.8% (2010); Master's degree or higher: 1.6% (2010).

School District(s)

Alvarado ISD (PK-12)

    2009-10 Enrollment: 3,402 . . . . (817) 783-6800

Housing: Homeownership rate: 64.3% (2010); Median home value: $66,387 (2010); Median contract rent: $378 per month (2005-2009 5-year est.); Median year structure built: 1985 (2005-2009 5-year est.).

Safety: Violent crime rate: 14.0 per 10,000 population; Property crime rate: 359.0 per 10,000 population (2009).

Newspapers: Post (Community news; Circulation 3,000)

Transportation: Commute to work: 98.3% car, 0.0% public transportation, 0.0% walk, 1.7% work from home (2005-2009 5-year est.); Travel time to work: 37.5% less than 15 minutes, 27.9% 15 to 30 minutes, 16.3% 30 to 45 minutes, 7.6% 45 to 60 minutes, 10.7% 60 minutes or more (2005-2009 5-year est.)

Additional Information Contacts

City of Alvarado . . . . (817) 790-3351
    http://www.cityofalvarado.org

BRIAROAKS (city). Covers a land area of 1.032 square miles and a water area of 0 square miles. Located at 32.49° N. Lat; 97.30° W. Long. Elevation is 738 feet.

Population: 535 (1990); 493 (2000); 543 (2010); 576 (2015 projected); Race: 94.7% White, 0.2% Black, 0.2% Asian, 5.0% Other, 5.0% Hispanic of any race (2010); Density: 525.9 persons per square mile (2010); Average household size: 2.69 (2010); Median age: 41.0 (2010); Males per 100 females: 97.5 (2010); Marriage status: 22.1% never married, 64.4% now married, 5.1% widowed, 8.4% divorced (2005-2009 5-year est.); Foreign born: 2.6% (2005-2009 5-year est.); Ancestry (includes multiple ancestries): 21.8% American, 18.8% German, 16.2% Irish, 14.2% English, 4.9% Scottish (2005-2009 5-year est.).

Economy: Employment by occupation: 14.0% management, 21.0% professional, 9.1% services, 24.5% sales, 0.3% farming, 12.9% construction, 18.2% production (2005-2009 5-year est.).

Income: Per capita income: $24,724 (2010); Median household income: $54,514 (2010); Average household income: $67,960 (2010); Percent of households with income of $100,000 or more: 21.4% (2010); Poverty rate: 0.7% (2005-2009 5-year est.).

Education: Percent of population age 25 and over with: High school diploma (including GED) or higher: 87.1% (2010); Bachelor's degree or higher: 30.7% (2010); Master's degree or higher: 10.6% (2010).

Housing: Homeownership rate: 76.1% (2010); Median home value: $147,159 (2010); Median contract rent: n/a per month (2005-2009 5-year est.); Median year structure built: 1976 (2005-2009 5-year est.).

Transportation: Commute to work: 86.9% car, 0.7% public transportation, 2.5% walk, 7.4% work from home (2005-2009 5-year est.); Travel time to work: 21.1% less than 15 minutes, 24.5% 15 to 30 minutes, 30.7% 30 to 45 minutes, 13.8% 45 to 60 minutes, 10.0% 60 minutes or more (2005-2009 5-year est.)

BURLESON (city). Covers a land area of 19.645 square miles and a water area of 0.061 square miles. Located at 32.53° N. Lat; 97.32° W. Long. Elevation is 712 feet.

Population: 16,275 (1990); 20,976 (2000); 35,135 (2010); 40,108 (2015 projected); Race: 93.7% White, 0.9% Black, 0.7% Asian, 4.7% Other, 8.3% Hispanic of any race (2010); Density: 1,788.5 persons per square mile (2010); Average household size: 2.77 (2010); Median age: 35.1 (2010); Males per 100 females: 96.4 (2010); Marriage status: 21.7% never married, 59.7% now married, 5.7% widowed, 12.9% divorced (2005-2009 5-year est.); Foreign born: 3.0% (2005-2009 5-year est.); Ancestry (includes multiple ancestries): 18.8% English, 17.5% German, 14.1% Irish, 9.7% American, 3.0% French (2005-2009 5-year est.).

Economy: Unemployment rate: 7.8% (June 2011); Total civilian labor force: 19,053 (June 2011); Single-family building permits issued: 197 (2010); Multi-family building permits issued: 393 (2010); Employment by occupation: 14.1% management, 21.6% professional, 14.2% services, 28.6% sales, 0.3% farming, 8.4% construction, 12.8% production (2005-2009 5-year est.).

Income: Per capita income: $24,553 (2010); Median household income: $60,147 (2010); Average household income: $68,268 (2010); Percent of households with income of $100,000 or more: 19.0% (2010); Poverty rate: 5.3% (2005-2009 5-year est.).

Taxes: Total city taxes per capita: $679 (2007); City property taxes per capita: $275 (2007).

Education: Percent of population age 25 and over with: High school diploma (including GED) or higher: 88.5% (2010); Bachelor's degree or higher: 16.5% (2010); Master's degree or higher: 4.5% (2010).

School District(s)

Burleson ISD (PK-12)

    2009-10 Enrollment: 9,896 . . . . (817) 245-1000

Joshua ISD (PK-12)

    2009-10 Enrollment: 4,731 . . . . (817) 202-2500

Mansfield ISD (PK-12)

    2009-10 Enrollment: 31,662 . . . . (817) 299-6300

Housing: Homeownership rate: 74.1% (2010); Median home value: $119,611 (2010); Median contract rent: $686 per month (2005-2009 5-year est.); Median year structure built: 1991 (2005-2009 5-year est.).

Hospitals: Huguley Memorial Medical Center (213 beds)

Safety: Violent crime rate: 18.7 per 10,000 population; Property crime rate: 306.2 per 10,000 population (2009).

Newspapers: Burleson Star (Local news; Circulation 7,214); Crowley Star (Local news; Circulation 3,000); Joshua Star (Local news; Circulation 2,000); Keene Star (Local news; Circulation 1,000)

Transportation: Commute to work: 95.2% car, 0.4% public transportation, 0.7% walk, 2.0% work from home (2005-2009 5-year est.); Travel time to work: 26.1% less than 15 minutes, 31.0% 15 to 30 minutes, 25.0% 30 to 45 minutes, 9.6% 45 to 60 minutes, 8.2% 60 minutes or more (2005-2009 5-year est.)

Additional Information Contacts

Burleson Area Chamber of Commerce . . . . (817) 295-6121
    http://www.burleson.org

City of Burleson . . . . (817) 426-9600
    http://www.burlesontx.com

CLEBURNE (city). County seat. Covers a land area of 27.786 square miles and a water area of 2.674 square miles. Located at 32.35° N. Lat; 97.39° W. Long. Elevation is 764 feet.

History: Named for Patrick R. Cleburne, Confederate general killed in battle. Cleburne grew up on both sides of West Buffalo Creek, as a shipping and trading center for a large agricultural area, with cotton as the principal crop.

Population: 22,749 (1990); 26,005 (2000); 30,835 (2010); 33,501 (2015 projected); Race: 81.9% White, 5.8% Black, 0.5% Asian, 11.8% Other, 28.6% Hispanic of any race (2010); Density: 1,109.7 persons per square mile (2010); Average household size: 2.78 (2010); Median age: 33.9 (2010); Males per 100 females: 97.7 (2010); Marriage status: 23.2% never married, 54.4% now married, 6.8% widowed, 15.6% divorced (2005-2009 5-year est.); Foreign born: 10.6% (2005-2009 5-year est.); Ancestry (includes multiple ancestries): 18.4% English, 13.9% German, 13.6% Irish, 7.5% American, 2.7% Scottish (2005-2009 5-year est.).

Economy: Unemployment rate: 8.9% (June 2011); Total civilian labor force: 13,671 (June 2011); Single-family building permits issued: 25 (2010); Multi-family building permits issued: 2 (2010); Employment by occupation: 9.0% management, 14.8% professional, 19.0% services, 22.4% sales, 0.3% farming, 14.7% construction, 19.8% production (2005-2009 5-year est.).

Income: Per capita income: $19,299 (2010); Median household income: $41,892 (2010); Average household income: $54,466 (2010); Percent of households with income of $100,000 or more: 11.2% (2010); Poverty rate: 19.3% (2005-2009 5-year est.).

Taxes: Total city taxes per capita: $642 (2007); City property taxes per capita: $326 (2007).

Education: Percent of population age 25 and over with: High school diploma (including GED) or higher: 74.5% (2010); Bachelor's degree or higher: 15.4% (2010); Master's degree or higher: 4.0% (2010).

School District(s)

Alvarado ISD (PK-12)

    2009-10 Enrollment: 3,402 . . . . (817) 783-6800

Cleburne ISD (PK-12)

    2009-10 Enrollment: 6,907 . . . . (817) 202-1100

Godley ISD (PK-12)

    2009-10 Enrollment: 1,555 . . . . (817) 389-2536

Rio Vista ISD (PK-12)

    2009-10 Enrollment: 882 . . . . (817) 373-2241

Venus ISD (PK-12)

    2009-10 Enrollment: 1,858 . . . . (972) 366-3448

Housing: Homeownership rate: 61.6% (2010); Median home value: $93,269 (2010); Median contract rent: $561 per month (2005-2009 5-year est.); Median year structure built: 1977 (2005-2009 5-year est.).
Hospitals: Walls Regional Hospital (137 beds)
Safety: Violent crime rate: 64.7 per 10,000 population; Property crime rate: 430.2 per 10,000 population (2009).
Newspapers: Cleburne Times-Review (Local news; Circulation 78,500)
Transportation: Commute to work: 93.4% car, 0.3% public transportation, 1.7% walk, 2.6% work from home (2005-2009 5-year est.); Travel time to work: 44.0% less than 15 minutes, 21.4% 15 to 30 minutes, 14.5% 30 to 45 minutes, 8.9% 45 to 60 minutes, 11.2% 60 minutes or more (2005-2009 5-year est.); Amtrak: train service available.
Airports: Cleburne Municipal (general aviation)
Additional Information Contacts
City of Cleburne . . . . (817) 645-0908
   http://www.ci.cleburne.tx.us
Cleburne Chamber of Commerce . . . . (817) 645-2455
   http://www.cleburnechamber.com
Johnson County Hispanic Chamber of Commerce . . . . (817) 641-8644

CROSS TIMBER (town). Covers a land area of 1.381 square miles and a water area of 0 square miles. Located at 32.48° N. Lat; 97.32° W. Long. Elevation is 709 feet.
Population: 251 (1990); 277 (2000); 339 (2010); 372 (2015 projected); Race: 92.3% White, 1.2% Black, 0.3% Asian, 6.2% Other, 10.0% Hispanic of any race (2010); Density: 245.4 persons per square mile (2010); Average household size: 2.65 (2010); Median age: 42.0 (2010); Males per 100 females: 97.1 (2010); Marriage status: 18.4% never married, 48.8% now married, 7.4% widowed, 25.3% divorced (2005-2009 5-year est.); Foreign born: 1.9% (2005-2009 5-year est.); Ancestry (includes multiple ancestries): 33.8% German, 28.5% English, 17.5% Irish, 8.7% Scotch-Irish, 7.2% American (2005-2009 5-year est.).
Economy: Single-family building permits issued: 1 (2010); Multi-family building permits issued: 0 (2010); Employment by occupation: 11.9% management, 21.0% professional, 18.2% services, 21.7% sales, 3.5% farming, 7.0% construction, 16.8% production (2005-2009 5-year est.).
Income: Per capita income: $26,205 (2010); Median household income: $55,208 (2010); Average household income: $69,023 (2010); Percent of households with income of $100,000 or more: 18.0% (2010); Poverty rate: 3.6% (2005-2009 5-year est.).
Taxes: Total city taxes per capita: $188 (2007); City property taxes per capita: $115 (2007).
Education: Percent of population age 25 and over with: High school diploma (including GED) or higher: 82.3% (2010); Bachelor's degree or higher: 12.0% (2010); Master's degree or higher: 6.0% (2010).
Housing: Homeownership rate: 87.5% (2010); Median home value: $134,211 (2010); Median contract rent: $713 per month (2005-2009 5-year est.); Median year structure built: 1977 (2005-2009 5-year est.).
Transportation: Commute to work: 93.7% car, 0.0% public transportation, 0.0% walk, 4.2% work from home (2005-2009 5-year est.); Travel time to work: 19.0% less than 15 minutes, 24.1% 15 to 30 minutes, 21.2% 30 to 45 minutes, 21.9% 45 to 60 minutes, 13.9% 60 minutes or more (2005-2009 5-year est.)

GODLEY (city). Covers a land area of 1.678 square miles and a water area of 0 square miles. Located at 32.44° N. Lat; 97.53° W. Long. Elevation is 928 feet.
Population: 643 (1990); 879 (2000); 961 (2010); 1,014 (2015 projected); Race: 91.8% White, 0.7% Black, 0.0% Asian, 7.5% Other, 16.9% Hispanic of any race (2010); Density: 572.6 persons per square mile (2010); Average household size: 2.93 (2010); Median age: 32.3 (2010); Males per 100 females: 89.2 (2010); Marriage status: 29.1% never married, 49.0% now married, 3.2% widowed, 18.7% divorced (2005-2009 5-year est.); Foreign born: 0.7% (2005-2009 5-year est.); Ancestry (includes multiple ancestries): 28.6% Irish, 22.4% English, 20.2% German, 6.6% Polish, 6.5% Italian (2005-2009 5-year est.).
Economy: Single-family building permits issued: 4 (2010); Multi-family building permits issued: 0 (2010); Employment by occupation: 9.2% management, 17.7% professional, 18.1% services, 17.7% sales, 0.6% farming, 22.5% construction, 14.1% production (2005-2009 5-year est.).
Income: Per capita income: $23,922 (2010); Median household income: $61,699 (2010); Average household income: $70,535 (2010); Percent of households with income of $100,000 or more: 22.3% (2010); Poverty rate: 16.5% (2005-2009 5-year est.).

Taxes: Total city taxes per capita: $810 (2007); City property taxes per capita: $202 (2007).
Education: Percent of population age 25 and over with: High school diploma (including GED) or higher: 80.2% (2010); Bachelor's degree or higher: 11.1% (2010); Master's degree or higher: 2.1% (2010).
School District(s)
Godley ISD (PK-12)
   2009-10 Enrollment: 1,555 . . . . (817) 389-2536
Housing: Homeownership rate: 64.5% (2010); Median home value: $91,951 (2010); Median contract rent: $483 per month (2005-2009 5-year est.); Median year structure built: 1981 (2005-2009 5-year est.).
Safety: Violent crime rate: 29.4 per 10,000 population; Property crime rate: 244.9 per 10,000 population (2009).
Transportation: Commute to work: 98.4% car, 0.0% public transportation, 0.0% walk, 0.0% work from home (2005-2009 5-year est.); Travel time to work: 26.6% less than 15 minutes, 30.7% 15 to 30 minutes, 17.2% 30 to 45 minutes, 17.8% 45 to 60 minutes, 7.8% 60 minutes or more (2005-2009 5-year est.)

GRANDVIEW (city). Covers a land area of 1.696 square miles and a water area of 0 square miles. Located at 32.26° N. Lat; 97.17° W. Long. Elevation is 692 feet.
Population: 1,279 (1990); 1,358 (2000); 1,642 (2010); 1,811 (2015 projected); Race: 86.2% White, 8.9% Black, 0.0% Asian, 4.9% Other, 13.5% Hispanic of any race (2010); Density: 968.2 persons per square mile (2010); Average household size: 2.71 (2010); Median age: 35.1 (2010); Males per 100 females: 89.0 (2010); Marriage status: 25.6% never married, 47.4% now married, 13.7% widowed, 13.4% divorced (2005-2009 5-year est.); Foreign born: 5.2% (2005-2009 5-year est.); Ancestry (includes multiple ancestries): 18.2% German, 17.6% English, 17.2% Irish, 6.9% American, 6.1% Dutch (2005-2009 5-year est.).
Economy: Single-family building permits issued: 3 (2010); Multi-family building permits issued: 0 (2010); Employment by occupation: 11.6% management, 8.9% professional, 12.5% services, 29.5% sales, 0.0% farming, 13.5% construction, 24.0% production (2005-2009 5-year est.).
Income: Per capita income: $22,612 (2010); Median household income: $46,897 (2010); Average household income: $62,749 (2010); Percent of households with income of $100,000 or more: 17.0% (2010); Poverty rate: 11.4% (2005-2009 5-year est.).
Taxes: Total city taxes per capita: $915 (2007); City property taxes per capita: $190 (2007).
Education: Percent of population age 25 and over with: High school diploma (including GED) or higher: 70.7% (2010); Bachelor's degree or higher: 17.1% (2010); Master's degree or higher: 3.6% (2010).
School District(s)
Grandview ISD (PK-12)
   2009-10 Enrollment: 1,118 . . . . (817) 866-2450
Housing: Homeownership rate: 62.5% (2010); Median home value: $89,123 (2010); Median contract rent: $433 per month (2005-2009 5-year est.); Median year structure built: 1974 (2005-2009 5-year est.).
Newspapers: Grandview Tribune (Community news; Circulation 1,500)
Transportation: Commute to work: 95.0% car, 0.0% public transportation, 3.9% walk, 0.5% work from home (2005-2009 5-year est.); Travel time to work: 27.9% less than 15 minutes, 29.3% 15 to 30 minutes, 28.2% 30 to 45 minutes, 11.5% 45 to 60 minutes, 3.1% 60 minutes or more (2005-2009 5-year est.)
Additional Information Contacts
Grandview Chamber of Commerce . . . . (817) 866-4881
   http://www.grandviewchamber.net

JOSHUA (city). Covers a land area of 6.512 square miles and a water area of 0.010 square miles. Located at 32.45° N. Lat; 97.39° W. Long. Elevation is 928 feet.
Population: 3,873 (1990); 4,528 (2000); 6,384 (2010); 7,097 (2015 projected); Race: 92.2% White, 1.0% Black, 0.5% Asian, 6.3% Other, 11.6% Hispanic of any race (2010); Density: 980.3 persons per square mile (2010); Average household size: 2.89 (2010); Median age: 34.4 (2010); Males per 100 females: 99.4 (2010); Marriage status: 25.6% never married, 54.6% now married, 5.5% widowed, 14.3% divorced (2005-2009 5-year est.); Foreign born: 2.9% (2005-2009 5-year est.); Ancestry (includes multiple ancestries): 28.4% English, 15.0% American, 12.5% German, 11.4% Irish, 4.4% French (2005-2009 5-year est.).
Economy: Single-family building permits issued: 12 (2010); Multi-family building permits issued: 0 (2010); Employment by occupation: 8.8%

management, 21.4% professional, 11.7% services, 27.5% sales, 1.5% farming, 15.0% construction, 14.2% production (2005-2009 5-year est.).
Income: Per capita income: $23,948 (2010); Median household income: $59,009 (2010); Average household income: $69,156 (2010); Percent of households with income of $100,000 or more: 16.8% (2010); Poverty rate: 4.5% (2005-2009 5-year est.).
Taxes: Total city taxes per capita: $448 (2007); City property taxes per capita: $239 (2007).
Education: Percent of population age 25 and over with: High school diploma (including GED) or higher: 84.5% (2010); Bachelor's degree or higher: 20.4% (2010); Master's degree or higher: 6.8% (2010).

School District(s)
Joshua ISD (PK-12)
    2009-10 Enrollment: 4,731 . . . . (817) 202-2500
Housing: Homeownership rate: 77.8% (2010); Median home value: $125,357 (2010); Median contract rent: $521 per month (2005-2009 5-year est.); Median year structure built: 1982 (2005-2009 5-year est.).
Safety: Violent crime rate: 21.8 per 10,000 population; Property crime rate: 93.9 per 10,000 population (2009).
Transportation: Commute to work: 97.0% car, 0.0% public transportation, 1.3% walk, 0.9% work from home (2005-2009 5-year est.); Travel time to work: 29.6% less than 15 minutes, 24.3% 15 to 30 minutes, 23.4% 30 to 45 minutes, 14.6% 45 to 60 minutes, 8.1% 60 minutes or more (2005-2009 5-year est.)
Additional Information Contacts
Joshua Area Chamber of Commerce . . . . (817) 558-2821
    http://www.joshuachamber.org

KEENE (city). Covers a land area of 2.806 square miles and a water area of 0.012 square miles. Located at 32.39° N. Lat; 97.32° W. Long. Elevation is 892 feet.
History: Keene was settled by a group of Seventh Day Adventists and named for a leader of the church.
Population: 4,358 (1990); 5,003 (2000); 5,855 (2010); 6,359 (2015 projected); Race: 68.5% White, 9.9% Black, 3.6% Asian, 17.9% Other, 27.3% Hispanic of any race (2010); Density: 2,086.8 persons per square mile (2010); Average household size: 2.79 (2010); Median age: 31.4 (2010); Males per 100 females: 94.6 (2010); Marriage status: 27.6% never married, 47.9% now married, 11.3% widowed, 13.3% divorced (2005-2009 5-year est.); Foreign born: 19.9% (2005-2009 5-year est.); Ancestry (includes multiple ancestries): 11.7% English, 10.3% German, 8.6% Irish, 5.2% American, 2.8% French (2005-2009 5-year est.).
Economy: Single-family building permits issued: 2 (2010); Multi-family building permits issued: 0 (2010); Employment by occupation: 6.2% management, 30.3% professional, 16.8% services, 16.1% sales, 0.0% farming, 9.5% construction, 21.0% production (2005-2009 5-year est.).
Income: Per capita income: $17,566 (2010); Median household income: $42,908 (2010); Average household income: $51,319 (2010); Percent of households with income of $100,000 or more: 9.7% (2010); Poverty rate: 19.8% (2005-2009 5-year est.).
Taxes: Total city taxes per capita: $186 (2007); City property taxes per capita: $148 (2007).
Education: Percent of population age 25 and over with: High school diploma (including GED) or higher: 83.1% (2010); Bachelor's degree or higher: 25.3% (2010); Master's degree or higher: 10.2% (2010).

School District(s)
Alvarado ISD (PK-12)
    2009-10 Enrollment: 3,402 . . . . (817) 783-6800
Godley ISD (PK-12)
    2009-10 Enrollment: 1,555 . . . . (817) 389-2536
Grandview ISD (PK-12)
    2009-10 Enrollment: 1,118 . . . . (817) 866-2450
Keene ISD (PK-12)
    2009-10 Enrollment: 834 . . . . (817) 774-5200
Four-year College(s)
Southwestern Adventist University (Private, Not-for-profit, Seventh Day Adventists)
    Fall 2009 Enrollment: 809 . . . . (817) 645-3921
    2010-11 Tuition: In-state $16,456; Out-of-state $16,456
Housing: Homeownership rate: 47.8% (2010); Median home value: $90,679 (2010); Median contract rent: $464 per month (2005-2009 5-year est.); Median year structure built: 1977 (2005-2009 5-year est.).
Safety: Violent crime rate: 3.1 per 10,000 population; Property crime rate: 173.6 per 10,000 population (2009).

Transportation: Commute to work: 95.9% car, 0.0% public transportation, 0.6% walk, 3.6% work from home (2005-2009 5-year est.); Travel time to work: 37.0% less than 15 minutes, 17.6% 15 to 30 minutes, 31.5% 30 to 45 minutes, 7.6% 45 to 60 minutes, 6.3% 60 minutes or more (2005-2009 5-year est.)
Additional Information Contacts
City of Keene . . . . (817) 641-3336
    http://www.keenetx.com
Keene Chamber of Commerce . . . . (817) 556-2995
    http://www.keenechamber.org

RIO VISTA (city). Covers a land area of 0.792 square miles and a water area of 0 square miles. Located at 32.23° N. Lat; 97.37° W. Long. Elevation is 732 feet.
Population: 501 (1990); 656 (2000); 761 (2010); 823 (2015 projected); Race: 96.3% White, 0.0% Black, 0.1% Asian, 3.5% Other, 4.1% Hispanic of any race (2010); Density: 960.9 persons per square mile (2010); Average household size: 2.81 (2010); Median age: 34.5 (2010); Males per 100 females: 107.9 (2010); Marriage status: 13.0% never married, 63.9% now married, 4.0% widowed, 19.2% divorced (2005-2009 5-year est.); Foreign born: 0.6% (2005-2009 5-year est.); Ancestry (includes multiple ancestries): 37.1% English, 22.2% Irish, 15.9% American, 8.6% French, 7.0% German (2005-2009 5-year est.).
Economy: Single-family building permits issued: 4 (2010); Multi-family building permits issued: 0 (2010); Employment by occupation: 10.1% management, 8.8% professional, 9.8% services, 32.2% sales, 0.0% farming, 14.7% construction, 24.5% production (2005-2009 5-year est.).
Income: Per capita income: $18,446 (2010); Median household income: $43,816 (2010); Average household income: $53,441 (2010); Percent of households with income of $100,000 or more: 8.9% (2010); Poverty rate: 6.1% (2005-2009 5-year est.).
Taxes: Total city taxes per capita: $338 (2007); City property taxes per capita: $190 (2007).
Education: Percent of population age 25 and over with: High school diploma (including GED) or higher: 78.3% (2010); Bachelor's degree or higher: 7.7% (2010); Master's degree or higher: 0.8% (2010).

School District(s)
Rio Vista ISD (PK-12)
    2009-10 Enrollment: 882 . . . . (817) 373-2241
Housing: Homeownership rate: 77.5% (2010); Median home value: $87,273 (2010); Median contract rent: $629 per month (2005-2009 5-year est.); Median year structure built: 1991 (2005-2009 5-year est.).
Transportation: Commute to work: 96.6% car, 0.0% public transportation, 0.0% walk, 2.6% work from home (2005-2009 5-year est.); Travel time to work: 17.6% less than 15 minutes, 37.6% 15 to 30 minutes, 16.8% 30 to 45 minutes, 5.7% 45 to 60 minutes, 22.4% 60 minutes or more (2005-2009 5-year est.)

VENUS (town). Covers a land area of 2.283 square miles and a water area of 0 square miles. Located at 32.42° N. Lat; 97.10° W. Long. Elevation is 666 feet.
Population: 987 (1990); 910 (2000); 1,013 (2010); 1,076 (2015 projected); Race: 60.3% White, 23.2% Black, 8.5% Asian, 8.0% Other, 23.0% Hispanic of any race (2010); Density: 443.8 persons per square mile (2010); Average household size: 2.94 (2010); Median age: 36.1 (2010); Males per 100 females: 179.1 (2010); Marriage status: 36.8% never married, 42.9% now married, 2.3% widowed, 18.0% divorced (2005-2009 5-year est.); Foreign born: 7.3% (2005-2009 5-year est.); Ancestry (includes multiple ancestries): 22.0% English, 9.2% German, 5.8% Irish, 3.3% American, 3.1% French (2005-2009 5-year est.).
Economy: Single-family building permits issued: 20 (2010); Multi-family building permits issued: 0 (2010); Employment by occupation: 10.5% management, 11.8% professional, 13.8% services, 34.8% sales, 1.5% farming, 6.1% construction, 21.5% production (2005-2009 5-year est.).
Income: Per capita income: $15,485 (2010); Median household income: $50,410 (2010); Average household income: $60,784 (2010); Percent of households with income of $100,000 or more: 15.5% (2010); Poverty rate: 8.8% (2005-2009 5-year est.).
Taxes: Total city taxes per capita: $117 (2007); City property taxes per capita: $86 (2007).
Education: Percent of population age 25 and over with: High school diploma (including GED) or higher: 66.1% (2010); Bachelor's degree or higher: 6.0% (2010); Master's degree or higher: 1.5% (2010).

School District(s)
Venus ISD (PK-12)
  2009-10 Enrollment: 1,858 . . . . (972) 366-3448
Housing: Homeownership rate: 80.2% (2010); Median home value: $80,465 (2010); Median contract rent: $479 per month (2005-2009 5-year est.); Median year structure built: 1995 (2005-2009 5-year est.).
Transportation: Commute to work: 88.2% car, 0.0% public transportation, 0.6% walk, 3.1% work from home (2005-2009 5-year est.); Travel time to work: 28.6% less than 15 minutes, 27.4% 15 to 30 minutes, 14.7% 30 to 45 minutes, 22.5% 45 to 60 minutes, 6.9% 60 minutes or more (2005-2009 5-year est.)

Jones County

Located in west central Texas; rolling plains area, drained by the Clear Fork of the Brazos River. Covers a land area of 930.99 square miles, a water area of 6.14 square miles, and is located in the Central Time Zone at 32.78° N. Lat., 99.91° W. Long. The county was founded in 1881. County seat is Anson.

Jones County is part of the Abilene, TX Metropolitan Statistical Area. The entire metro area includes: Callahan County, TX; Jones County, TX; Taylor County, TX

Weather Station: Anson   Elevation: 1,709 feet

	Jan	Feb	Mar	Apr	May	Jun	Jul	Aug	Sep	Oct	Nov	Dec
High	58	61	69	79	86	92	96	95	88	78	66	57
Low	33	36	43	51	61	69	72	71	64	54	42	33
Precip	1.0	1.7	1.6	1.9	3.3	3.8	2.0	2.7	2.8	2.5	1.7	1.5
Snow	1.1	0.5	0.3	0.5	0.0	0.0	0.0	0.0	0.0	0.0	1.0	1.2

High and Low temperatures in degrees Fahrenheit; Precipitation and Snow in inches

Weather Station: Stamford 1   Elevation: 1,640 feet

	Jan	Feb	Mar	Apr	May	Jun	Jul	Aug	Sep	Oct	Nov	Dec
High	56	61	69	78	86	93	97	96	89	78	66	57
Low	30	34	41	49	59	67	71	70	63	52	41	31
Precip	1.0	1.7	1.7	2.0	3.5	3.9	1.7	2.3	2.9	2.8	1.5	1.4
Snow	1.3	0.7	0.1	0.3	0.0	0.0	0.0	0.0	0.0	tr	0.9	0.8

High and Low temperatures in degrees Fahrenheit; Precipitation and Snow in inches

Population: 16,490 (1990); 20,785 (2000); 19,722 (2010); 19,168 (2015 projected); Race: 76.1% White, 12.8% Black, 0.5% Asian, 10.6% Other, 23.7% Hispanic of any race (2010); Density: 21.2 persons per square mile (2010); Average household size: 2.56 (2010); Median age: 36.7 (2010); Males per 100 females: 164.1 (2010).
Religion: Five largest groups: 36.5% Southern Baptist Convention, 8.3% Catholic Church, 6.7% Churches of Christ, 4.7% The United Methodist Church, 1.8% Evangelical Lutheran Church in America (2000).
Economy: Unemployment rate: 9.1% (June 2011); Total civilian labor force: 7,484 (June 2011); Leading industries: 32.5% health care and social assistance; 10.9% retail trade; 9.1% mining (2009); Farms: 1,053 totaling 573,323 acres (2007); Companies that employ 500 or more persons: 0 (2009); Companies that employ 100 to 499 persons: 2 (2009); Companies that employ less than 100 persons: 299 (2009); Black-owned businesses: n/a (2007); Hispanic-owned businesses: n/a (2007); Asian-owned businesses: n/a (2007); Women-owned businesses: 283 (2007); Retail sales per capita: $12,696 (2010). Single-family building permits issued: 0 (2010); Multi-family building permits issued: 0 (2010).
Income: Per capita income: $16,963 (2010); Median household income: $39,201 (2010); Average household income: $51,911 (2010); Percent of households with income of $100,000 or more: 9.5% (2010); Poverty rate: 23.9% (2009); Bankruptcy rate: 1.57% (2010).
Taxes: Total county taxes per capita: $220 (2007); County property taxes per capita: $176 (2007).
Education: Percent of population age 25 and over with: High school diploma (including GED) or higher: 69.6% (2010); Bachelor's degree or higher: 9.1% (2010); Master's degree or higher: 2.4% (2010).
Housing: Homeownership rate: 77.6% (2010); Median home value: $56,808 (2010); Median contract rent: $287 per month (2005-2009 5-year est.); Median year structure built: 1964 (2005-2009 5-year est.)
Health: Birth rate: 98.1 per 10,000 population (2009); Death rate: 92.3 per 10,000 population (2009); Age-adjusted cancer mortality rate: 182.4 deaths per 100,000 population (2007); Number of physicians: 4.2 per 10,000 population (2008); Hospital beds: 41.2 per 10,000 population (2007); Hospital admissions: 733.0 per 10,000 population (2007).
Elections: 2008 Presidential election results: 26.3% Obama, 72.4% McCain, 0.1% Nader

Additional Information Contacts
Jones County Government . . . . (325) 823-3741
  http://www.co.jones.tx.us/ips/cms
Anson Chamber of Commerce . . . . (325) 823-3259
Stamford Chamber of Commerce . . . . (325) 773-2411
  http://www.stamfordcoc.org

Jones County Communities

ANSON (city). County seat. Covers a land area of 2.096 square miles and a water area of 0 square miles. Located at 32.75° N. Lat; 99.89° W. Long. Elevation is 1,729 feet.
History: Anson developed as a cotton shipping center, named for Anson Jones, the last president of the Republic of Texas, for whom Jones County is also named. The Cowboys' Christmas Ball, made known by local poet Larry Chittenden, took place in Anson.
Population: 2,644 (1990); 2,556 (2000); 2,242 (2010); 2,094 (2015 projected); Race: 76.4% White, 1.9% Black, 1.0% Asian, 20.7% Other, 32.3% Hispanic of any race (2010); Density: 1,069.4 persons per square mile (2010); Average household size: 2.60 (2010); Median age: 38.0 (2010); Males per 100 females: 92.3 (2010); Marriage status: 14.8% never married, 68.7% now married, 5.9% widowed, 10.6% divorced (2005-2009 5-year est.); Foreign born: 4.7% (2005-2009 5-year est.); Ancestry (includes multiple ancestries): 12.0% German, 8.4% American, 8.1% Irish, 8.1% English, 3.3% Swedish (2005-2009 5-year est.).
Economy: Single-family building permits issued: 0 (2010); Multi-family building permits issued: 0 (2010); Employment by occupation: 10.2% management, 19.5% professional, 32.0% services, 12.0% sales, 0.0% farming, 13.0% construction, 13.3% production (2005-2009 5-year est.).
Income: Per capita income: $15,020 (2010); Median household income: $30,130 (2010); Average household income: $39,793 (2010); Percent of households with income of $100,000 or more: 5.0% (2010); Poverty rate: 9.8% (2005-2009 5-year est.).
Taxes: Total city taxes per capita: $149 (2007); City property taxes per capita: $59 (2007).
Education: Percent of population age 25 and over with: High school diploma (including GED) or higher: 68.4% (2010); Bachelor's degree or higher: 11.1% (2010); Master's degree or higher: 2.8% (2010).
School District(s)
Anson ISD (PK-12)
  2009-10 Enrollment: 736 . . . . (325) 823-3671
Housing: Homeownership rate: 71.2% (2010); Median home value: $42,348 (2010); Median contract rent: $278 per month (2005-2009 5-year est.); Median year structure built: 1961 (2005-2009 5-year est.).
Hospitals: Anson General Hospital (45 beds)
Safety: Violent crime rate: 13.3 per 10,000 population; Property crime rate: 142.1 per 10,000 population (2009).
Newspapers: Western Observer (Community news; Circulation 1,250)
Transportation: Commute to work: 94.7% car, 0.0% public transportation, 3.6% walk, 1.7% work from home (2005-2009 5-year est.); Travel time to work: 48.4% less than 15 minutes, 25.1% 15 to 30 minutes, 25.9% 30 to 45 minutes, 0.5% 45 to 60 minutes, 0.1% 60 minutes or more (2005-2009 5-year est.)
Additional Information Contacts
Anson Chamber of Commerce . . . . (325) 823-3259

AVOCA (unincorporated postal area, zip code 79503). Covers a land area of 88.251 square miles and a water area of 0.031 square miles. Located at 32.75° N. Lat; 99.78° W. Long. Elevation is 1,542 feet.
Population: 284 (2000); Race: 89.5% White, 0.0% Black, 0.7% Asian, 9.8% Other, 8.4% Hispanic of any race (2000); Density: 3.2 persons per square mile (2000); Age: 36.7% under 18, 13.1% over 64 (2000); Marriage status: 20.1% never married, 66.0% now married, 7.2% widowed, 6.7% divorced (2000); Foreign born: 0.7% (2000); Ancestry (includes multiple ancestries): 24.0% American, 14.2% German, 10.9% English, 10.9% Italian (2000).
Economy: Employment by occupation: 27.4% management, 15.4% professional, 12.8% services, 24.8% sales, 1.7% farming, 4.3% construction, 13.7% production (2000).
Income: Per capita income: $13,450 (2000); Median household income: $36,458 (2000); Poverty rate: 179.1% (2000).
Education: Percent of population age 25 and over with: High school diploma (including GED) or higher: 84.2% (2000); Bachelor's degree or higher: 7.0% (2000).

Lueders-Avoca ISD (PK-12)
   2009-10 Enrollment: 114 . . . . (325) 228-4211
Housing: Homeownership rate: 81.8% (2000); Median home value: $35,800 (2000); Median contract rent: $185 per month (2000); Median year structure built: 1947 (2000).
Transportation: Commute to work: 98.3% car, 0.0% public transportation, 0.0% walk, 1.7% work from home (2000); Travel time to work: 29.6% less than 15 minutes, 27.8% 15 to 30 minutes, 19.1% 30 to 45 minutes, 18.3% 45 to 60 minutes, 5.2% 60 minutes or more (2000)

HAMLIN (city).
Covers a land area of 5.322 square miles and a water area of 0.004 square miles. Located at 32.88° N. Lat; 100.12° W. Long.
History: Hamlin grew up around a railroad division point. Gypsum, sand, and gravel deposits formed the base for the early economy.
Population: 2,791 (1990); 2,248 (2000); 1,884 (2010); 1,721 (2015 projected); Race: 83.2% White, 3.0% Black, 0.5% Asian, 13.3% Other, 20.0% Hispanic of any race (2010); Density: 354.0 persons per square mile (2010); Average household size: 2.36 (2010); Median age: 43.2 (2010); Males per 100 females: 92.4 (2010); Marriage status: 23.1% never married, 41.4% now married, 22.0% widowed, 13.5% divorced (2005-2009 5-year est.); Foreign born: 2.4% (2005-2009 5-year est.); Ancestry (includes multiple ancestries): 16.7% Irish, 11.5% German, 9.6% American, 7.8% English, 3.5% Dutch (2005-2009 5-year est.).
Economy: Single-family building permits issued: 0 (2010); Multi-family building permits issued: 0 (2010); Employment by occupation: 10.3% management, 19.5% professional, 20.6% services, 19.3% sales, 4.3% farming, 13.9% construction, 12.1% production (2005-2009 5-year est.).
Income: Per capita income: $19,194 (2010); Median household income: $35,475 (2010); Average household income: $45,955 (2010); Percent of households with income of $100,000 or more: 7.8% (2010); Poverty rate: 14.5% (2005-2009 5-year est.).
Taxes: Total city taxes per capita: $381 (2007); City property taxes per capita: $148 (2007).
Education: Percent of population age 25 and over with: High school diploma (including GED) or higher: 75.6% (2010); Bachelor's degree or higher: 10.4% (2010); Master's degree or higher: 2.0% (2010).
Hamlin ISD (PK-12)
   2009-10 Enrollment: 496 . . . . (325) 576-2722
Housing: Homeownership rate: 78.2% (2010); Median home value: $53,111 (2010); Median contract rent: $310 per month (2005-2009 5-year est.); Median year structure built: 1959 (2005-2009 5-year est.).
Hospitals: Hamlin Memorial Hospital (25 beds)
Safety: Violent crime rate: 10.7 per 10,000 population; Property crime rate: 53.5 per 10,000 population (2009).
Newspapers: Herald (Local news; Circulation 1,250)
Transportation: Commute to work: 96.1% car, 0.0% public transportation, 3.4% walk, 0.4% work from home (2005-2009 5-year est.); Travel time to work: 50.4% less than 15 minutes, 21.7% 15 to 30 minutes, 11.1% 30 to 45 minutes, 8.2% 45 to 60 minutes, 8.6% 60 minutes or more (2005-2009 5-year est.)

HAWLEY (city).
Covers a land area of 2.940 square miles and a water area of 0 square miles. Located at 32.61° N. Lat; 99.81° W. Long. Elevation is 1,640 feet.
Population: 606 (1990); 646 (2000); 625 (2010); 606 (2015 projected); Race: 93.4% White, 0.3% Black, 0.5% Asian, 5.8% Other, 7.0% Hispanic of any race (2010); Density: 212.6 persons per square mile (2010); Average household size: 2.78 (2010); Median age: 37.9 (2010); Males per 100 females: 103.6 (2010); Marriage status: 18.0% never married, 66.3% now married, 4.7% widowed, 11.0% divorced (2005-2009 5-year est.); Foreign born: 0.0% (2005-2009 5-year est.); Ancestry (includes multiple ancestries): 17.0% Irish, 8.4% German, 7.2% Dutch, 6.3% American, 4.7% English (2005-2009 5-year est.).
Economy: Employment by occupation: 7.9% management, 22.3% professional, 14.9% services, 16.5% sales, 0.0% farming, 20.2% construction, 18.2% production (2005-2009 5-year est.).
Income: Per capita income: $18,308 (2010); Median household income: $44,167 (2010); Average household income: $50,778 (2010); Percent of households with income of $100,000 or more: 7.6% (2010); Poverty rate: 6.3% (2005-2009 5-year est.).
Taxes: Total city taxes per capita: $211 (2007); City property taxes per capita: $87 (2007).

Education: Percent of population age 25 and over with: High school diploma (including GED) or higher: 84.4% (2010); Bachelor's degree or higher: 10.1% (2010); Master's degree or higher: 2.5% (2010).
Hawley ISD (PK-12)
   2009-10 Enrollment: 749 . . . . (325) 537-2214
Housing: Homeownership rate: 84.0% (2010); Median home value: $63,793 (2010); Median contract rent: $425 per month (2005-2009 5-year est.); Median year structure built: 1966 (2005-2009 5-year est.).
Safety: Violent crime rate: 0.0 per 10,000 population; Property crime rate: 193.3 per 10,000 population (2009).
Transportation: Commute to work: 95.8% car, 0.0% public transportation, 0.0% walk, 0.4% work from home (2005-2009 5-year est.); Travel time to work: 8.0% less than 15 minutes, 64.1% 15 to 30 minutes, 3.4% 30 to 45 minutes, 0.0% 45 to 60 minutes, 24.5% 60 minutes or more (2005-2009 5-year est.)

LUEDERS (city).
Covers a land area of 0.618 square miles and a water area of 0 square miles. Located at 32.80° N. Lat; 99.62° W. Long. Elevation is 1,562 feet.
Population: 368 (1990); 300 (2000); 243 (2010); 219 (2015 projected); Race: 93.0% White, 0.8% Black, 0.0% Asian, 6.2% Other, 4.9% Hispanic of any race (2010); Density: 393.1 persons per square mile (2010); Average household size: 2.48 (2010); Median age: 39.6 (2010); Males per 100 females: 117.0 (2010); Marriage status: 4.4% never married, 62.9% now married, 7.3% widowed, 25.4% divorced (2005-2009 5-year est.); Foreign born: 0.0% (2005-2009 5-year est.); Ancestry (includes multiple ancestries): 21.1% German, 20.1% Irish, 7.2% English, 4.3% Dutch, 3.0% Swedish (2005-2009 5-year est.).
Economy: Employment by occupation: 0.0% management, 9.9% professional, 11.6% services, 13.2% sales, 0.0% farming, 52.9% construction, 12.4% production (2005-2009 5-year est.).
Income: Per capita income: $20,770 (2010); Median household income: $43,125 (2010); Average household income: $51,454 (2010); Percent of households with income of $100,000 or more: 9.2% (2010); Poverty rate: 14.8% (2005-2009 5-year est.).
Taxes: Total city taxes per capita: $128 (2007); City property taxes per capita: $66 (2007).
Education: Percent of population age 25 and over with: High school diploma (including GED) or higher: 77.8% (2010); Bachelor's degree or higher: 9.3% (2010); Master's degree or higher: 5.6% (2010).
Lueders-Avoca ISD (PK-12)
   2009-10 Enrollment: 114 . . . . (325) 228-4211
Housing: Homeownership rate: 83.7% (2010); Median home value: $45,714 (2010); Median contract rent: n/a per month (2005-2009 5-year est.); Median year structure built: 1948 (2005-2009 5-year est.).
Transportation: Commute to work: 98.3% car, 0.0% public transportation, 0.0% walk, 1.7% work from home (2005-2009 5-year est.); Travel time to work: 57.1% less than 15 minutes, 22.7% 15 to 30 minutes, 14.3% 30 to 45 minutes, 0.0% 45 to 60 minutes, 5.9% 60 minutes or more (2005-2009 5-year est.)

STAMFORD (city).
Covers a land area of 5.959 square miles and a water area of 6.886 square miles. Located at 32.94° N. Lat; 99.79° W. Long. Elevation is 1,614 feet.
History: Stamford developed as an agricultural center, settled by many immigrants from Germany and Sweden. The annual Texas Cowboy Reunion was begun here.
Population: 3,817 (1990); 3,636 (2000); 3,218 (2010); 3,019 (2015 projected); Race: 70.0% White, 5.3% Black, 0.1% Asian, 24.5% Other, 29.0% Hispanic of any race (2010); Density: 540.0 persons per square mile (2010); Average household size: 2.55 (2010); Median age: 41.9 (2010); Males per 100 females: 93.7 (2010); Marriage status: 23.4% never married, 53.3% now married, 12.1% widowed, 11.2% divorced (2005-2009 5-year est.); Foreign born: 1.7% (2005-2009 5-year est.); Ancestry (includes multiple ancestries): 7.9% German, 7.3% English, 7.2% Irish, 6.3% American, 2.7% Scottish (2005-2009 5-year est.).
Economy: Single-family building permits issued: 0 (2010); Multi-family building permits issued: 0 (2010); Employment by occupation: 7.1% management, 14.2% professional, 15.8% services, 31.6% sales, 2.9% farming, 12.9% construction, 15.5% production (2005-2009 5-year est.).
Income: Per capita income: $18,308 (2010); Median household income: $32,397 (2010); Average household income: $47,386 (2010); Percent of

households with income of $100,000 or more: 9.7% (2010); Poverty rate: 31.5% (2005-2009 5-year est.).

Taxes: Total city taxes per capita: $281 (2007); City property taxes per capita: $80 (2007).

Education: Percent of population age 25 and over with: High school diploma (including GED) or higher: 73.5% (2010); Bachelor's degree or higher: 9.2% (2010); Master's degree or higher: 3.1% (2010).

School District(s)

Stamford ISD (PK-12)

    2009-10 Enrollment: 642 . . . . (325) 773-2705

Housing: Homeownership rate: 73.4% (2010); Median home value: $50,791 (2010); Median contract rent: $254 per month (2005-2009 5-year est.); Median year structure built: 1958 (2005-2009 5-year est.).

Hospitals: Stamford Memorial Hospital (34 beds)

Safety: Violent crime rate: 39.2 per 10,000 population; Property crime rate: 437.9 per 10,000 population (2009).

Newspapers: Stamford American (Community news; Circulation 2,450)

Transportation: Commute to work: 95.4% car, 0.0% public transportation, 0.8% walk, 0.8% work from home (2005-2009 5-year est.); Travel time to work: 46.4% less than 15 minutes, 21.0% 15 to 30 minutes, 4.1% 30 to 45 minutes, 20.6% 45 to 60 minutes, 7.8% 60 minutes or more (2005-2009 5-year est.)

Additional Information Contacts

Stamford Chamber of Commerce . . . . (325) 773-2411
    http://www.stamfordcoc.org

Karnes County

Located in south Texas; drained by the San Antonio River. Covers a land area of 750.32 square miles, a water area of 3.27 square miles, and is located in the Central Time Zone at 28.88° N. Lat., 97.86° W. Long. The county was founded in 1854. County seat is Karnes City.

Weather Station: Karnes City 2 N										Elevation: 450 feet	
	Jan	Feb	Mar	Apr	May	Jun	Jul	Aug	Sep	Oct	Nov	Dec
High	65	68	74	81	87	93	95	96	91	83	74	65
Low	43	45	52	59	67	72	73	73	68	61	51	43
Precip	1.5	1.8	1.9	2.2	3.2	3.5	2.4	1.9	2.9	3.2	2.1	1.8
Snow	0.0	0.0	0.0	0.0	0.0	0.0	0.0	0.0	0.0	0.0	0.0	0.2

High and Low temperatures in degrees Fahrenheit; Precipitation and Snow in inches

Population: 12,455 (1990); 15,446 (2000); 15,334 (2010); 15,248 (2015 projected); Race: 67.4% White, 11.2% Black, 0.4% Asian, 21.0% Other, 49.1% Hispanic of any race (2010); Density: 20.4 persons per square mile (2010); Average household size: 2.56 (2010); Median age: 34.1 (2010); Males per 100 females: 145.9 (2010).

Religion: Five largest groups: 39.8% Catholic Church, 13.5% Southern Baptist Convention, 4.6% Evangelical Lutheran Church in America, 2.4% The United Methodist Church, 1.3% Churches of Christ (2000).

Economy: Unemployment rate: 10.0% (June 2011); Total civilian labor force: 5,505 (June 2011); Leading industries: 20.7% retail trade; 10.9% manufacturing; 9.5% accommodation & food services (2009); Farms: 1,208 totaling 417,484 acres (2007); Companies that employ 500 or more persons: 0 (2009); Companies that employ 100 to 499 persons: 3 (2009); Companies that employ less than 100 persons: 238 (2009); Black-owned businesses: n/a (2007); Hispanic-owned businesses: n/a (2007); Asian-owned businesses: n/a (2007); Women-owned businesses: n/a (2007); Retail sales per capita: $6,197 (2010). Single-family building permits issued: 25 (2010); Multi-family building permits issued: 0 (2010).

Income: Per capita income: $17,190 (2010); Median household income: $34,777 (2010); Average household income: $48,726 (2010); Percent of households with income of $100,000 or more: 9.8% (2010); Poverty rate: 25.8% (2009); Bankruptcy rate: 0.53% (2010).

Taxes: Total county taxes per capita: $256 (2007); County property taxes per capita: $201 (2007).

Education: Percent of population age 25 and over with: High school diploma (including GED) or higher: 65.0% (2010); Bachelor's degree or higher: 11.0% (2010); Master's degree or higher: 3.5% (2010).

Housing: Homeownership rate: 72.2% (2010); Median home value: $55,222 (2010); Median contract rent: $305 per month (2005-2009 5-year est.); Median year structure built: 1970 (2005-2009 5-year est.)

Health: Birth rate: 122.4 per 10,000 population (2009); Death rate: 97.8 per 10,000 population (2009); Age-adjusted cancer mortality rate: 156.6 deaths per 100,000 population (2007); Number of physicians: 4.6 per 10,000 population (2008); Hospital beds: 14.0 per 10,000 population (2007); Hospital admissions: 221.3 per 10,000 population (2007).

Elections: 2008 Presidential election results: 38.9% Obama, 60.4% McCain, 0.1% Nader

Additional Information Contacts

Karnes County Government . . . . (830) 780-3732
    http://www.co.karnes.tx.us/ips/cms
Karnes City Community Chamber of Commerce. . . . . (830) 780-3112
    http://karnescitychamberofcommerce.com
Kenedy Chamber of Commerce . . . . (830) 583-3223
    http://www.kenedychamber.com

Karnes County Communities

FALLS CITY (city). Covers a land area of 0.905 square miles and a water area of 0 square miles. Located at 28.98° N. Lat; 98.02° W. Long. Elevation is 308 feet.

Population: 478 (1990); 591 (2000); 647 (2010); 675 (2015 projected); Race: 92.9% White, 0.0% Black, 0.0% Asian, 7.1% Other, 17.5% Hispanic of any race (2010); Density: 715.3 persons per square mile (2010); Average household size: 2.57 (2010); Median age: 40.5 (2010); Males per 100 females: 99.7 (2010); Marriage status: 13.1% never married, 75.7% now married, 3.9% widowed, 7.3% divorced (2005-2009 5-year est.); Foreign born: 1.2% (2005-2009 5-year est.); Ancestry (includes multiple ancestries): 73.2% Polish, 18.1% German, 4.0% English, 2.2% Irish, 1.0% British (2005-2009 5-year est.).

Economy: Single-family building permits issued: 2 (2010); Multi-family building permits issued: 0 (2010); Employment by occupation: 6.5% management, 12.5% professional, 9.9% services, 26.6% sales, 0.0% farming, 4.0% construction, 40.5% production (2005-2009 5-year est.).

Income: Per capita income: $21,806 (2010); Median household income: $44,695 (2010); Average household income: $55,986 (2010); Percent of households with income of $100,000 or more: 12.4% (2010); Poverty rate: 24.1% (2005-2009 5-year est.).

Taxes: Total city taxes per capita: $182 (2007); City property taxes per capita: $142 (2007).

Education: Percent of population age 25 and over with: High school diploma (including GED) or higher: 79.5% (2010); Bachelor's degree or higher: 14.4% (2010); Master's degree or higher: 3.7% (2010).

School District(s)

Falls City ISD (KG-12)

    2009-10 Enrollment: 329 . . . . (830) 254-3551

Housing: Homeownership rate: 81.7% (2010); Median home value: $78,421 (2010); Median contract rent: $291 per month (2005-2009 5-year est.); Median year structure built: 1976 (2005-2009 5-year est.).

Transportation: Commute to work: 96.9% car, 0.0% public transportation, 1.4% walk, 1.7% work from home (2005-2009 5-year est.); Travel time to work: 49.7% less than 15 minutes, 36.2% 15 to 30 minutes, 0.0% 30 to 45 minutes, 5.5% 45 to 60 minutes, 8.6% 60 minutes or more (2005-2009 5-year est.)

GILLETT (unincorporated postal area, zip code 78116). Covers a land area of 96.302 square miles and a water area of 0.239 square miles. Located at 29.11° N. Lat; 97.78° W. Long. Elevation is 351 feet.

Population: 240 (2000); Race: 100.0% White, 0.0% Black, 0.0% Asian, 0.0% Other, 7.2% Hispanic of any race (2000); Density: 2.5 persons per square mile (2000); Age: 11.0% under 18, 22.5% over 64 (2000); Marriage status: 15.7% never married, 63.9% now married, 10.5% widowed, 9.9% divorced (2000); Foreign born: 5.3% (2000); Ancestry (includes multiple ancestries): 59.3% Polish, 36.8% German, 7.7% Irish, 6.7% Czech (2000).

Economy: Employment by occupation: 22.1% management, 12.5% professional, 5.8% services, 23.1% sales, 11.5% farming, 13.5% construction, 11.5% production (2000).

Income: Per capita income: $16,767 (2000); Median household income: $25,714 (2000); Poverty rate: 179.1% (2000).

Education: Percent of population age 25 and over with: High school diploma (including GED) or higher: 73.4% (2000); Bachelor's degree or higher: 3.5% (2000).

Housing: Homeownership rate: 84.9% (2000); Median home value: $61,300 (2000); Median contract rent: n/a per month (2000); Median year structure built: 1967 (2000).

Transportation: Commute to work: 85.6% car, 0.0% public transportation, 4.8% walk, 9.6% work from home (2000); Travel time to work: 11.7% less than 15 minutes, 27.7% 15 to 30 minutes, 28.7% 30 to 45 minutes, 5.3% 45 to 60 minutes, 26.6% 60 minutes or more (2000)

HOBSON (unincorporated postal area, zip code 78117). Covers a land area of 65.460 square miles and a water area of 0.345 square miles. Located at 28.95° N. Lat; 97.95° W. Long. Elevation is 312 feet.

Population: 577 (2000); Race: 90.3% White, 0.0% Black, 0.0% Asian, 9.7% Other, 13.9% Hispanic of any race (2000); Density: 8.8 persons per square mile (2000); Age: 27.0% under 18, 13.8% over 64 (2000); Marriage status: 19.9% never married, 73.1% now married, 3.3% widowed, 3.7% divorced (2000); Foreign born: 0.7% (2000); Ancestry (includes multiple ancestries): 35.5% Polish, 26.5% German, 10.4% Czech, 4.3% Irish (2000).

Economy: Employment by occupation: 10.0% management, 15.0% professional, 7.9% services, 29.6% sales, 1.1% farming, 12.9% construction, 23.6% production (2000).

Income: Per capita income: $18,179 (2000); Median household income: $40,500 (2000); Poverty rate: 179.1% (2000).

Education: Percent of population age 25 and over with: High school diploma (including GED) or higher: 82.8% (2000); Bachelor's degree or higher: 15.6% (2000).

Housing: Homeownership rate: 84.3% (2000); Median home value: $54,200 (2000); Median contract rent: $308 per month (2000); Median year structure built: 1967 (2000).

Transportation: Commute to work: 97.4% car, 0.0% public transportation, 0.0% walk, 2.6% work from home (2000); Travel time to work: 31.8% less than 15 minutes, 26.4% 15 to 30 minutes, 6.9% 30 to 45 minutes, 9.2% 45 to 60 minutes, 25.7% 60 minutes or more (2000)

KARNES CITY (city). County seat. Covers a land area of 2.124 square miles and a water area of 0 square miles. Located at 28.88° N. Lat; 97.90° W. Long. Elevation is 430 feet.

History: Flax was a part of the early economy of Karnes City, a marketing and shipping center for beef and dairy cattle as well as farm products.

Population: 2,916 (1990); 3,457 (2000); 3,251 (2010); 3,131 (2015 projected); Race: 74.7% White, 2.4% Black, 0.4% Asian, 22.5% Other, 63.1% Hispanic of any race (2010); Density: 1,530.6 persons per square mile (2010); Average household size: 2.68 (2010); Median age: 34.2 (2010); Males per 100 females: 111.5 (2010); Marriage status: 31.7% never married, 54.6% now married, 6.3% widowed, 7.5% divorced (2005-2009 5-year est.); Foreign born: 41.8% (2005-2009 5-year est.); Ancestry (includes multiple ancestries): 6.0% German, 3.6% Italian, 3.3% Irish, 3.2% Polish, 2.7% American (2005-2009 5-year est.).

Economy: Single-family building permits issued: 8 (2010); Multi-family building permits issued: 0 (2010); Employment by occupation: 11.4% management, 10.3% professional, 36.3% services, 16.3% sales, 0.6% farming, 18.9% construction, 6.2% production (2005-2009 5-year est.).

Income: Per capita income: $16,592 (2010); Median household income: $34,429 (2010); Average household income: $45,360 (2010); Percent of households with income of $100,000 or more: 8.5% (2010); Poverty rate: 18.5% (2005-2009 5-year est.).

Taxes: Total city taxes per capita: $51 (2007); City property taxes per capita: $0 (2007).

Education: Percent of population age 25 and over with: High school diploma (including GED) or higher: 61.6% (2010); Bachelor's degree or higher: 14.6% (2010); Master's degree or higher: 5.2% (2010).

School District(s)
Karnes City ISD (PK-12)
    2009-10 Enrollment: 960 . . . . (830) 780-2321
Kenedy ISD (PK-12)
    2009-10 Enrollment: 694 . . . . (830) 583-4100

Housing: Homeownership rate: 70.2% (2010); Median home value: $46,667 (2010); Median contract rent: $294 per month (2005-2009 5-year est.); Median year structure built: 1967 (2005-2009 5-year est.).

Safety: Violent crime rate: 30.1 per 10,000 population; Property crime rate: 243.5 per 10,000 population (2009).

Newspapers: County Wide (Local news; Circulation 4,000)

Transportation: Commute to work: 95.9% car, 0.0% public transportation, 2.6% walk, 0.5% work from home (2005-2009 5-year est.); Travel time to work: 57.6% less than 15 minutes, 12.4% 15 to 30 minutes, 11.5% 30 to 45 minutes, 3.7% 45 to 60 minutes, 14.8% 60 minutes or more (2005-2009 5-year est.)

Additional Information Contacts
Karnes City Community Chamber of Commerce . . . . (830) 780-3112
    http://karnescitychamberofcommerce.com

KENEDY (city). Covers a land area of 3.324 square miles and a water area of 0 square miles. Located at 28.81° N. Lat; 97.85° W. Long. Elevation is 266 feet.

History: Kenedy was founded in 1882 around hot mineral wells. It grew as a health resort, and as a cotton and food processing center.

Population: 3,832 (1990); 3,487 (2000); 3,492 (2010); 3,488 (2015 projected); Race: 72.9% White, 4.8% Black, 0.7% Asian, 21.6% Other, 60.3% Hispanic of any race (2010); Density: 1,050.7 persons per square mile (2010); Average household size: 2.55 (2010); Median age: 34.8 (2010); Males per 100 females: 94.1 (2010); Marriage status: 20.7% never married, 61.0% now married, 11.7% widowed, 6.6% divorced (2005-2009 5-year est.); Foreign born: 7.9% (2005-2009 5-year est.); Ancestry (includes multiple ancestries): 10.7% German, 3.9% American, 3.8% English, 2.8% Irish, 1.3% Dutch (2005-2009 5-year est.).

Economy: Single-family building permits issued: 1 (2010); Multi-family building permits issued: 0 (2010); Employment by occupation: 14.4% management, 17.6% professional, 22.9% services, 11.6% sales, 6.0% farming, 11.4% construction, 16.2% production (2005-2009 5-year est.).

Income: Per capita income: $18,601 (2010); Median household income: $33,357 (2010); Average household income: $48,864 (2010); Percent of households with income of $100,000 or more: 8.8% (2010); Poverty rate: 35.3% (2005-2009 5-year est.).

Taxes: Total city taxes per capita: $280 (2007); City property taxes per capita: $60 (2007).

Education: Percent of population age 25 and over with: High school diploma (including GED) or higher: 63.9% (2010); Bachelor's degree or higher: 11.3% (2010); Master's degree or higher: 2.9% (2010).

School District(s)
Kenedy ISD (PK-12)
    2009-10 Enrollment: 694 . . . . (830) 583-4100

Housing: Homeownership rate: 66.2% (2010); Median home value: $55,097 (2010); Median contract rent: $413 per month (2005-2009 5-year est.); Median year structure built: 1966 (2005-2009 5-year est.).

Hospitals: Otto Kaiser Memorial Hospital (25 beds)

Safety: Violent crime rate: 33.5 per 10,000 population; Property crime rate: 328.5 per 10,000 population (2009).

Transportation: Commute to work: 95.5% car, 0.0% public transportation, 0.0% walk, 4.0% work from home (2005-2009 5-year est.); Travel time to work: 64.9% less than 15 minutes, 11.4% 15 to 30 minutes, 5.0% 30 to 45 minutes, 7.7% 45 to 60 minutes, 11.1% 60 minutes or more (2005-2009 5-year est.)

Additional Information Contacts
Kenedy Chamber of Commerce . . . . (830) 583-3223
    http://www.kenedychamber.com

RUNGE (town). Covers a land area of 1.176 square miles and a water area of 0 square miles. Located at 28.88° N. Lat; 97.71° W. Long. Elevation is 312 feet.

History: Settled 1884, incorporated 1913.

Population: 1,139 (1990); 1,080 (2000); 1,056 (2010); 1,041 (2015 projected); Race: 79.0% White, 0.6% Black, 0.0% Asian, 20.5% Other, 66.0% Hispanic of any race (2010); Density: 898.3 persons per square mile (2010); Average household size: 2.54 (2010); Median age: 37.9 (2010); Males per 100 females: 92.3 (2010); Marriage status: 15.4% never married, 71.9% now married, 6.5% widowed, 6.2% divorced (2005-2009 5-year est.); Foreign born: 4.6% (2005-2009 5-year est.); Ancestry (includes multiple ancestries): 12.4% German, 7.1% Irish, 2.2% English, 1.3% Czech, 1.0% French (2005-2009 5-year est.).

Economy: Employment by occupation: 8.6% management, 8.2% professional, 25.1% services, 31.4% sales, 3.6% farming, 9.0% construction, 14.2% production (2005-2009 5-year est.).

Income: Per capita income: $16,242 (2010); Median household income: $30,385 (2010); Average household income: $41,701 (2010); Percent of households with income of $100,000 or more: 7.2% (2010); Poverty rate: 26.9% (2005-2009 5-year est.).

Taxes: Total city taxes per capita: $191 (2007); City property taxes per capita: $95 (2007).

Education: Percent of population age 25 and over with: High school diploma (including GED) or higher: 66.2% (2010); Bachelor's degree or higher: 12.6% (2010); Master's degree or higher: 4.5% (2010).

School District(s)
Runge ISD (PK-12)
    2009-10 Enrollment: 300 . . . . (830) 239-4315

Housing: Homeownership rate: 70.0% (2010); Median home value: $36,377 (2010); Median contract rent: $271 per month (2005-2009 5-year est.); Median year structure built: 1963 (2005-2009 5-year est.).
Transportation: Commute to work: 84.2% car, 0.0% public transportation, 10.5% walk, 4.7% work from home (2005-2009 5-year est.); Travel time to work: 31.7% less than 15 minutes, 47.4% 15 to 30 minutes, 10.1% 30 to 45 minutes, 4.7% 45 to 60 minutes, 6.1% 60 minutes or more (2005-2009 5-year est.)

Kaufman County

Located in northeastern Texas; prairie area, bounded on the west by the Trinity River; drained by its East Fork and other tributaries. Covers a land area of 786.04 square miles, a water area of 20.76 square miles, and is located in the Central Time Zone at 32.61° N. Lat., 96.30° W. Long. The county was founded in 1848. County seat is Kaufman.

Kaufman County is part of the Dallas-Fort Worth-Arlington, TX Metropolitan Statistical Area. The entire metro area includes: Dallas-Plano-Irving, TX Metropolitan Division (Collin County, TX; Dallas County, TX; Delta County, TX; Denton County, TX; Ellis County, TX; Hunt County, TX; Kaufman County, TX; Rockwall County, TX); Fort Worth-Arlington, TX Metropolitan Division (Johnson County, TX; Parker County, TX; Tarrant County, TX; Wise County, TX)

Weather Station: Kaufman 3 SE										Elevation: 419 feet		
	Jan	Feb	Mar	Apr	May	Jun	Jul	Aug	Sep	Oct	Nov	Dec
High	56	60	67	75	82	90	94	96	89	78	67	58
Low	34	37	45	52	62	69	72	72	65	54	44	35
Precip	2.8	3.0	3.8	2.7	4.4	3.5	2.2	2.5	2.8	4.9	3.6	3.3
Snow	0.2	0.3	tr	0.0	0.0	0.0	0.0	0.0	0.0	0.0	tr	0.3

High and Low temperatures in degrees Fahrenheit; Precipitation and Snow in inches

Population: 52,220 (1990); 71,313 (2000); 105,215 (2010); 121,528 (2015 projected); Race: 76.5% White, 10.5% Black, 0.9% Asian, 12.1% Other, 18.0% Hispanic of any race (2010); Density: 133.9 persons per square mile (2010); Average household size: 2.87 (2010); Median age: 32.9 (2010); Males per 100 females: 98.3 (2010).
Religion: Five largest groups: 24.9% Southern Baptist Convention, 6.9% Baptist Missionary Association of America, 6.6% Catholic Church, 4.6% The United Methodist Church, 3.7% Churches of Christ (2000).
Economy: Unemployment rate: 9.6% (June 2011); Total civilian labor force: 48,796 (June 2011); Leading industries: 17.4% manufacturing; 17.3% retail trade; 14.9% health care and social assistance (2009); Farms: 2,563 totaling 421,803 acres (2007); Companies that employ 500 or more persons: 3 (2009); Companies that employ 100 to 499 persons: 28 (2009); Companies that employ less than 100 persons: 1,661 (2009); Black-owned businesses: n/a (2007); Hispanic-owned businesses: n/a (2007); Asian-owned businesses: n/a (2007); Women-owned businesses: 2,786 (2007); Retail sales per capita: $12,652 (2010). Single-family building permits issued: 187 (2010); Multi-family building permits issued: 2 (2010).
Income: Per capita income: $24,107 (2010); Median household income: $57,352 (2010); Average household income: $69,736 (2010); Percent of households with income of $100,000 or more: 19.9% (2010); Poverty rate: 12.2% (2009); Bankruptcy rate: 3.76% (2010).
Taxes: Total county taxes per capita: $291 (2007); County property taxes per capita: $265 (2007).
Education: Percent of population age 25 and over with: High school diploma (including GED) or higher: 80.4% (2010); Bachelor's degree or higher: 15.5% (2010); Master's degree or higher: 4.4% (2010).
Housing: Homeownership rate: 77.0% (2010); Median home value: $122,940 (2010); Median contract rent: $615 per month (2005-2009 5-year est.); Median year structure built: 1990 (2005-2009 5-year est.)
Health: Birth rate: 164.5 per 10,000 population (2009); Death rate: 77.5 per 10,000 population (2009); Age-adjusted cancer mortality rate: 210.9 deaths per 100,000 population (2007); Number of physicians: 6.4 per 10,000 population (2008); Hospital beds: 50.7 per 10,000 population (2007); Hospital admissions: 741.1 per 10,000 population (2007).
Environment: Air Quality Index: 80.7% good, 18.4% moderate, 1.0% unhealthy for sensitive individuals, 0.0% unhealthy (percent of days in 2008)
Elections: 2008 Presidential election results: 31.8% Obama, 67.5% McCain, 0.0% Nader
Additional Information Contacts
Kaufman County Government . . . . (972) 932-4331
  http://www.kaufmancounty.net

City of Forney. . . . . (972) 564-7300
  http://www.cityofforney.org
City of Kaufman . . . . (972) 932-2216
  http://www.kaufmantx.org
City of Terrell . . . . (972) 551-6600
  http://www.cityofterrell.org
Forney Chamber of Commerce . . . . (972) 564-2233
  http://www.forneychamber.com
Kaufman Chamber of Commerce . . . . (972) 932-3118
  http://www.kaufmantx.com
Terrell Chamber of Commerce . . . . (972) 563-5703
  http://www.terrelltexas.com

Kaufman County Communities

COMBINE (city). Covers a land area of 7.207 square miles and a water area of 0 square miles. Located at 32.58° N. Lat; 96.51° W. Long. Elevation is 413 feet.
Population: 1,329 (1990); 1,788 (2000); 2,045 (2010); 2,256 (2015 projected); Race: 93.1% White, 1.0% Black, 0.2% Asian, 5.7% Other, 7.7% Hispanic of any race (2010); Density: 283.7 persons per square mile (2010); Average household size: 2.96 (2010); Median age: 35.7 (2010); Males per 100 females: 102.3 (2010); Marriage status: 17.2% never married, 65.3% now married, 4.6% widowed, 12.9% divorced (2005-2009 5-year est.); Foreign born: 2.6% (2005-2009 5-year est.); Ancestry (includes multiple ancestries): 14.0% German, 13.1% Irish, 12.0% English, 10.9% American, 2.6% French (2005-2009 5-year est.).
Economy: Single-family building permits issued: 2 (2010); Multi-family building permits issued: 0 (2010); Employment by occupation: 17.3% management, 20.1% professional, 7.4% services, 29.4% sales, 0.3% farming, 11.8% construction, 13.6% production (2005-2009 5-year est.).
Income: Per capita income: $27,981 (2010); Median household income: $68,627 (2010); Average household income: $83,262 (2010); Percent of households with income of $100,000 or more: 26.9% (2010); Poverty rate: 9.1% (2005-2009 5-year est.).
Taxes: Total city taxes per capita: $57 (2007); City property taxes per capita: $0 (2007).
Education: Percent of population age 25 and over with: High school diploma (including GED) or higher: 82.0% (2010); Bachelor's degree or higher: 15.6% (2010); Master's degree or higher: 3.1% (2010).
Housing: Homeownership rate: 89.3% (2010); Median home value: $158,929 (2010); Median contract rent: $492 per month (2005-2009 5-year est.); Median year structure built: 1988 (2005-2009 5-year est.).
Transportation: Commute to work: 96.8% car, 0.0% public transportation, 0.8% walk, 2.0% work from home (2005-2009 5-year est.); Travel time to work: 8.7% less than 15 minutes, 16.2% 15 to 30 minutes, 29.1% 30 to 45 minutes, 28.8% 45 to 60 minutes, 17.1% 60 minutes or more (2005-2009 5-year est.)

COTTONWOOD (city). Covers a land area of 1.546 square miles and a water area of 0 square miles. Located at 32.46° N. Lat; 96.39° W. Long. Elevation is 417 feet.
Population: 134 (1990); 181 (2000); 187 (2010); 204 (2015 projected); Race: 94.7% White, 1.1% Black, 0.0% Asian, 4.3% Other, 4.3% Hispanic of any race (2010); Density: 121.0 persons per square mile (2010); Average household size: 2.88 (2010); Median age: 34.5 (2010); Males per 100 females: 105.5 (2010); Marriage status: 33.5% never married, 55.7% now married, 1.1% widowed, 9.7% divorced (2005-2009 5-year est.); Foreign born: 0.5% (2005-2009 5-year est.); Ancestry (includes multiple ancestries): 27.5% English, 26.1% German, 16.6% Irish, 16.1% American, 4.3% Czech (2005-2009 5-year est.).
Economy: Single-family building permits issued: 1 (2010); Multi-family building permits issued: 0 (2010); Employment by occupation: 9.8% management, 17.4% professional, 15.2% services, 35.9% sales, 0.0% farming, 0.0% construction, 21.7% production (2005-2009 5-year est.).
Income: Per capita income: $24,984 (2010); Median household income: $61,029 (2010); Average household income: $71,538 (2010); Percent of households with income of $100,000 or more: 18.5% (2010); Poverty rate: 7.6% (2005-2009 5-year est.).
Education: Percent of population age 25 and over with: High school diploma (including GED) or higher: 79.7% (2010); Bachelor's degree or higher: 12.2% (2010); Master's degree or higher: 7.5% (2010).
Housing: Homeownership rate: 89.2% (2010); Median home value: $96,000 (2010); Median contract rent: n/a per month (2005-2009 5-year est.); Median year structure built: 1980 (2005-2009 5-year est.); Median year structure built: 1980 (2005-2009 5-year est.).

Transportation: Commute to work: 100.0% car, 0.0% public transportation, 0.0% walk, 0.0% work from home (2005-2009 5-year est.); Travel time to work: 20.9% less than 15 minutes, 7.7% 15 to 30 minutes, 25.3% 30 to 45 minutes, 20.9% 45 to 60 minutes, 25.3% 60 minutes or more (2005-2009 5-year est.)

CRANDALL (city). Covers a land area of 2.841 square miles and a water area of 0 square miles. Located at 32.62° N. Lat; 96.45° W. Long. Elevation is 423 feet.

Population: 1,849 (1990); 2,774 (2000); 3,530 (2010); 4,087 (2015 projected); Race: 83.5% White, 4.9% Black, 0.2% Asian, 11.4% Other, 13.0% Hispanic of any race (2010); Density: 1,242.5 persons per square mile (2010); Average household size: 3.01 (2010); Median age: 31.4 (2010); Males per 100 females: 97.3 (2010); Marriage status: 28.5% never married, 58.5% now married, 2.4% widowed, 10.6% divorced (2005-2009 5-year est.); Foreign born: 3.4% (2005-2009 5-year est.); Ancestry (includes multiple ancestries): 22.3% Irish, 9.7% English, 9.7% German, 5.6% American, 3.1% French (2005-2009 5-year est.).

Economy: Single-family building permits issued: 15 (2010); Multi-family building permits issued: 0 (2010); Employment by occupation: 14.9% management, 21.1% professional, 9.5% services, 30.0% sales, 0.0% farming, 13.7% construction, 10.9% production (2005-2009 5-year est.).

Income: Per capita income: $22,342 (2010); Median household income: $59,566 (2010); Average household income: $67,308 (2010); Percent of households with income of $100,000 or more: 16.4% (2010); Poverty rate: 5.9% (2005-2009 5-year est.).

Taxes: Total city taxes per capita: $387 (2007); City property taxes per capita: $235 (2007).

Education: Percent of population age 25 and over with: High school diploma (including GED) or higher: 84.4% (2010); Bachelor's degree or higher: 13.3% (2010); Master's degree or higher: 3.9% (2010).

School District(s)

Crandall ISD (PK-12)

    2009-10 Enrollment: 2,774 . . . . (972) 427-6000

Housing: Homeownership rate: 79.6% (2010); Median home value: $119,936 (2010); Median contract rent: $689 per month (2005-2009 5-year est.); Median year structure built: 1990 (2005-2009 5-year est.).

Safety: Violent crime rate: 30.1 per 10,000 population; Property crime rate: 168.2 per 10,000 population (2009).

Transportation: Commute to work: 99.3% car, 0.0% public transportation, 0.0% walk, 0.7% work from home (2005-2009 5-year est.); Travel time to work: 24.4% less than 15 minutes, 27.6% 15 to 30 minutes, 25.7% 30 to 45 minutes, 12.9% 45 to 60 minutes, 9.4% 60 minutes or more (2005-2009 5-year est.)

FORNEY (city). Covers a land area of 7.843 square miles and a water area of 0 square miles. Located at 32.75° N. Lat; 96.46° W. Long. Elevation is 472 feet.

History: Settled 1872, incorporated 1910.

Population: 4,099 (1990); 5,588 (2000); 11,443 (2010); 13,553 (2015 projected); Race: 77.1% White, 7.6% Black, 0.6% Asian, 14.8% Other, 16.9% Hispanic of any race (2010); Density: 1,459.0 persons per square mile (2010); Average household size: 2.94 (2010); Median age: 32.1 (2010); Males per 100 females: 97.6 (2010); Marriage status: 23.1% never married, 62.8% now married, 2.5% widowed, 11.6% divorced (2005-2009 5-year est.); Foreign born: 2.6% (2005-2009 5-year est.); Ancestry (includes multiple ancestries): 16.1% German, 13.4% Irish, 13.2% English, 9.1% American, 5.1% Italian (2005-2009 5-year est.).

Economy: Single-family building permits issued: 155 (2010); Multi-family building permits issued: 0 (2010); Employment by occupation: 12.7% management, 20.1% professional, 11.6% services, 33.9% sales, 0.1% farming, 9.4% construction, 12.1% production (2005-2009 5-year est.).

Income: Per capita income: $26,491 (2010); Median household income: $67,907 (2010); Average household income: $77,978 (2010); Percent of households with income of $100,000 or more: 25.9% (2010); Poverty rate: 5.1% (2005-2009 5-year est.).

Taxes: Total city taxes per capita: $666 (2007); City property taxes per capita: $212 (2007).

Education: Percent of population age 25 and over with: High school diploma (including GED) or higher: 84.1% (2010); Bachelor's degree or higher: 18.7% (2010); Master's degree or higher: 4.8% (2010).

School District(s)

Forney ISD (PK-12)

    2009-10 Enrollment: 7,813 . . . . (972) 564-4055

Housing: Homeownership rate: 78.2% (2010); Median home value: $141,473 (2010); Median contract rent: $1,014 per month (2005-2009 5-year est.); Median year structure built: 2000 (2005-2009 5-year est.).

Safety: Violent crime rate: 14.1 per 10,000 population; Property crime rate: 205.6 per 10,000 population (2009).

Newspapers: Forney Messenger (Community news; Circulation 2,300)

Transportation: Commute to work: 95.7% car, 1.1% public transportation, 0.7% walk, 2.3% work from home (2005-2009 5-year est.); Travel time to work: 16.3% less than 15 minutes, 28.3% 15 to 30 minutes, 26.0% 30 to 45 minutes, 18.8% 45 to 60 minutes, 10.6% 60 minutes or more (2005-2009 5-year est.)

Additional Information Contacts

City of Forney. . . . . (972) 564-7300

    http://www.cityofforney.org

Forney Chamber of Commerce . . . . (972) 564-2233

    http://www.forneychamber.com

GRAYS PRAIRIE (village). Aka Peede's Mill. Covers a land area of 1.257 square miles and a water area of 0 square miles. Located at 32.47° N. Lat; 96.35° W. Long. Elevation is 449 feet.

Population: 286 (1990); 296 (2000); 338 (2010); 375 (2015 projected); Race: 89.9% White, 3.3% Black, 0.9% Asian, 5.9% Other, 7.4% Hispanic of any race (2010); Density: 268.9 persons per square mile (2010); Average household size: 2.81 (2010); Median age: 34.1 (2010); Males per 100 females: 98.8 (2010); Marriage status: 22.1% never married, 60.2% now married, 7.2% widowed, 10.5% divorced (2005-2009 5-year est.); Foreign born: 0.4% (2005-2009 5-year est.); Ancestry (includes multiple ancestries): 26.0% German, 11.5% American, 8.9% Czech, 7.2% Irish, 3.0% French Canadian (2005-2009 5-year est.).

Economy: Single-family building permits issued: 0 (2010); Multi-family building permits issued: 0 (2010); Employment by occupation: 7.1% management, 24.5% professional, 19.4% services, 18.4% sales, 0.0% farming, 18.4% construction, 12.2% production (2005-2009 5-year est.).

Income: Per capita income: $25,598 (2010); Median household income: $58,621 (2010); Average household income: $69,958 (2010); Percent of households with income of $100,000 or more: 18.6% (2010); Poverty rate: 1.7% (2005-2009 5-year est.).

Taxes: Total city taxes per capita: $35 (2007); City property taxes per capita: $0 (2007).

Education: Percent of population age 25 and over with: High school diploma (including GED) or higher: 82.8% (2010); Bachelor's degree or higher: 13.6% (2010); Master's degree or higher: 4.1% (2010).

Housing: Homeownership rate: 83.1% (2010); Median home value: $103,846 (2010); Median contract rent: $725 per month (2005-2009 5-year est.); Median year structure built: 1982 (2005-2009 5-year est.).

Transportation: Commute to work: 94.8% car, 0.0% public transportation, 0.0% walk, 2.1% work from home (2005-2009 5-year est.); Travel time to work: 9.6% less than 15 minutes, 30.9% 15 to 30 minutes, 17.0% 30 to 45 minutes, 30.9% 45 to 60 minutes, 11.7% 60 minutes or more (2005-2009 5-year est.)

KAUFMAN (city). County seat. Covers a land area of 6.636 square miles and a water area of 0.179 square miles. Located at 32.58° N. Lat; 96.30° W. Long. Elevation is 459 feet.

History: Founded 1848, incorporated 1873.

Population: 5,490 (1990); 6,490 (2000); 8,096 (2010); 9,369 (2015 projected); Race: 64.8% White, 10.0% Black, 0.7% Asian, 24.4% Other, 42.1% Hispanic of any race (2010); Density: 1,219.9 persons per square mile (2010); Average household size: 2.90 (2010); Median age: 31.2 (2010); Males per 100 females: 96.5 (2010); Marriage status: 27.8% never married, 50.2% now married, 6.0% widowed, 16.0% divorced (2005-2009 5-year est.); Foreign born: 14.9% (2005-2009 5-year est.); Ancestry (includes multiple ancestries): 14.1% Irish, 6.3% American, 6.2% English, 5.8% German, 3.0% French (2005-2009 5-year est.).

Economy: Single-family building permits issued: 0 (2010); Multi-family building permits issued: 0 (2010); Employment by occupation: 12.4% management, 12.0% professional, 15.1% services, 25.8% sales, 0.0% farming, 16.4% construction, 18.3% production (2005-2009 5-year est.).

Income: Per capita income: $19,232 (2010); Median household income: $43,043 (2010); Average household income: $55,819 (2010); Percent of households with income of $100,000 or more: 11.6% (2010); Poverty rate: 21.3% (2005-2009 5-year est.).

Taxes: Total city taxes per capita: $367 (2007); City property taxes per capita: $175 (2007).

Education: Percent of population age 25 and over with: High school diploma (including GED) or higher: 73.6% (2010); Bachelor's degree or higher: 16.0% (2010); Master's degree or higher: 2.8% (2010).

School District(s)

Honors Academy (KG-12)
2009-10 Enrollment: 1,068 . . . . (214) 521-6365
Kaufman ISD (PK-12)
2009-10 Enrollment: 3,738 . . . . (972) 932-2622

Housing: Homeownership rate: 62.4% (2010); Median home value: $88,020 (2010); Median contract rent: $537 per month (2005-2009 5-year est.); Median year structure built: 1979 (2005-2009 5-year est.).
Hospitals: Presbyterian Hospital of Kaufman (91 beds)
Safety: Violent crime rate: 16.5 per 10,000 population; Property crime rate: 187.4 per 10,000 population (2009).
Newspapers: Kaufman Herald (Local news; Circulation 4,500)
Transportation: Commute to work: 94.4% car, 0.3% public transportation, 2.9% walk, 1.4% work from home (2005-2009 5-year est.); Travel time to work: 32.0% less than 15 minutes, 17.0% 15 to 30 minutes, 17.7% 30 to 45 minutes, 19.9% 45 to 60 minutes, 13.3% 60 minutes or more (2005-2009 5-year est.)

Additional Information Contacts

City of Kaufman . . . . (972) 932-2216
http://www.kaufmantx.org
Kaufman Chamber of Commerce . . . . (972) 932-3118
http://www.kaufmantx.com

KEMP (town). Covers a land area of 1.769 square miles and a water area of 0.052 square miles. Located at 32.43° N. Lat; 96.22° W. Long. Elevation is 381 feet.
Population: 1,184 (1990); 1,133 (2000); 1,247 (2010); 1,377 (2015 projected); Race: 90.5% White, 6.2% Black, 0.3% Asian, 3.0% Other, 8.2% Hispanic of any race (2010); Density: 704.9 persons per square mile (2010); Average household size: 2.53 (2010); Median age: 34.7 (2010); Males per 100 females: 93.6 (2010); Marriage status: 19.7% never married, 48.2% now married, 20.5% widowed, 11.6% divorced (2005-2009 5-year est.); Foreign born: 0.9% (2005-2009 5-year est.); Ancestry (includes multiple ancestries): 18.8% Irish, 11.4% English, 10.3% German, 10.2% American, 6.8% French (2005-2009 5-year est.).
Economy: Single-family building permits issued: 0 (2010); Multi-family building permits issued: 0 (2010); Employment by occupation: 3.8% management, 18.3% professional, 14.0% services, 34.5% sales, 3.2% farming, 10.6% construction, 15.5% production (2005-2009 5-year est.).
Income: Per capita income: $22,753 (2010); Median household income: $45,776 (2010); Average household income: $59,041 (2010); Percent of households with income of $100,000 or more: 11.5% (2010); Poverty rate: 11.2% (2005-2009 5-year est.).
Taxes: Total city taxes per capita: $357 (2007); City property taxes per capita: $194 (2007).
Education: Percent of population age 25 and over with: High school diploma (including GED) or higher: 76.0% (2010); Bachelor's degree or higher: 11.0% (2010); Master's degree or higher: 5.6% (2010).

School District(s)

Kemp ISD (PK-12)
2009-10 Enrollment: 1,566 . . . . (903) 498-1314

Housing: Homeownership rate: 70.3% (2010); Median home value: $78,636 (2010); Median contract rent: $375 per month (2005-2009 5-year est.); Median year structure built: 1969 (2005-2009 5-year est.).
Safety: Violent crime rate: 0.0 per 10,000 population; Property crime rate: 147.6 per 10,000 population (2009).
Transportation: Commute to work: 96.4% car, 0.0% public transportation, 0.7% walk, 2.9% work from home (2005-2009 5-year est.); Travel time to work: 28.0% less than 15 minutes, 36.2% 15 to 30 minutes, 12.8% 30 to 45 minutes, 11.9% 45 to 60 minutes, 11.0% 60 minutes or more (2005-2009 5-year est.)

Additional Information Contacts

Cedar Creek Lake Area Chamber of Commerce. . . . . (903) 887-3152
http://www.cclake.net

MABANK (town). Covers a land area of 2.970 square miles and a water area of 0.033 square miles. Located at 32.36° N. Lat; 96.10° W. Long. Elevation is 394 feet.
Population: 1,838 (1990); 2,151 (2000); 2,989 (2010); 3,408 (2015 projected); Race: 86.4% White, 5.2% Black, 0.3% Asian, 8.1% Other, 8.8% Hispanic of any race (2010); Density: 1,006.3 persons per square mile (2010); Average household size: 2.44 (2010); Median age: 33.0 (2010);

Males per 100 females: 86.9 (2010); Marriage status: 23.3% never married, 54.5% now married, 6.2% widowed, 16.0% divorced (2005-2009 5-year est.); Foreign born: 2.7% (2005-2009 5-year est.); Ancestry (includes multiple ancestries): 21.2% American, 17.1% German, 12.0% Irish, 8.4% English, 2.1% Scotch-Irish (2005-2009 5-year est.).
Economy: Single-family building permits issued: 6 (2010); Multi-family building permits issued: 0 (2010); Employment by occupation: 11.0% management, 15.4% professional, 19.1% services, 26.5% sales, 0.0% farming, 11.3% construction, 16.7% production (2005-2009 5-year est.).
Income: Per capita income: $21,150 (2010); Median household income: $43,260 (2010); Average household income: $51,823 (2010); Percent of households with income of $100,000 or more: 10.8% (2010); Poverty rate: 23.7% (2005-2009 5-year est.).
Taxes: Total city taxes per capita: $473 (2007); City property taxes per capita: $127 (2007).
Education: Percent of population age 25 and over with: High school diploma (including GED) or higher: 76.3% (2010); Bachelor's degree or higher: 13.4% (2010); Master's degree or higher: 2.8% (2010).

School District(s)

Mabank ISD (PK-12)
2009-10 Enrollment: 3,325 . . . . (903) 880-1300

Housing: Homeownership rate: 60.5% (2010); Median home value: $78,257 (2010); Median contract rent: $488 per month (2005-2009 5-year est.); Median year structure built: 1987 (2005-2009 5-year est.).
Newspapers: Monitor (Local news; Circulation 4,300)
Transportation: Commute to work: 93.6% car, 0.0% public transportation, 0.4% walk, 4.5% work from home (2005-2009 5-year est.); Travel time to work: 46.4% less than 15 minutes, 12.4% 15 to 30 minutes, 7.7% 30 to 45 minutes, 9.9% 45 to 60 minutes, 23.5% 60 minutes or more (2005-2009 5-year est.)

Additional Information Contacts

Cedar Creek Lake Area Chamber of Commerce. . . . . (903) 887-3152
http://www.cclake.net

OAK GROVE (town). Covers a land area of 2.110 square miles and a water area of 0 square miles. Located at 32.54° N. Lat; 96.31° W. Long. Elevation is 420 feet.
Population: 557 (1990); 710 (2000); 911 (2010); 1,044 (2015 projected); Race: 82.2% White, 6.5% Black, 1.6% Asian, 9.7% Other, 14.7% Hispanic of any race (2010); Density: 431.7 persons per square mile (2010); Average household size: 2.70 (2010); Median age: 33.2 (2010); Males per 100 females: 98.9 (2010); Marriage status: 18.0% never married, 62.6% now married, 7.1% widowed, 12.3% divorced (2005-2009 5-year est.); Foreign born: 0.3% (2005-2009 5-year est.); Ancestry (includes multiple ancestries): 20.3% German, 15.6% Irish, 9.6% English, 7.0% French, 6.4% American (2005-2009 5-year est.).
Economy: Single-family building permits issued: 1 (2010); Multi-family building permits issued: 0 (2010); Employment by occupation: 17.7% management, 22.4% professional, 7.6% services, 30.7% sales, 0.0% farming, 13.4% construction, 8.3% production (2005-2009 5-year est.).
Income: Per capita income: $26,620 (2010); Median household income: $58,824 (2010); Average household income: $72,842 (2010); Percent of households with income of $100,000 or more: 22.4% (2010); Poverty rate: 3.1% (2005-2009 5-year est.).
Education: Percent of population age 25 and over with: High school diploma (including GED) or higher: 86.9% (2010); Bachelor's degree or higher: 19.3% (2010); Master's degree or higher: 3.5% (2010).
Housing: Homeownership rate: 73.6% (2010); Median home value: $116,558 (2010); Median contract rent: $675 per month (2005-2009 5-year est.); Median year structure built: 1984 (2005-2009 5-year est.).
Transportation: Commute to work: 97.0% car, 0.0% public transportation, 0.0% walk, 3.0% work from home (2005-2009 5-year est.); Travel time to work: 30.2% less than 15 minutes, 17.6% 15 to 30 minutes, 11.4% 30 to 45 minutes, 17.3% 45 to 60 minutes, 23.5% 60 minutes or more (2005-2009 5-year est.)

OAK RIDGE (town). Covers a land area of 2.237 square miles and a water area of 0 square miles. Located at 32.65° N. Lat; 96.26° W. Long. Elevation is 420 feet.
Population: 248 (1990); 400 (2000); 524 (2010); 609 (2015 projected); Race: 73.5% White, 15.1% Black, 2.7% Asian, 8.8% Other, 10.5% Hispanic of any race (2010); Density: 234.2 persons per square mile (2010); Average household size: 2.91 (2010); Median age: 34.5 (2010); Males per 100 females: 97.7 (2010); Marriage status: 22.2% never married, 62.0% now married, 3.9% widowed, 11.9% divorced (2005-2009 5-year

est.); Foreign born: 13.2% (2005-2009 5-year est.); Ancestry (includes multiple ancestries): 17.2% German, 12.8% Irish, 9.6% Welsh, 7.4% American, 6.4% English (2005-2009 5-year est.).

Economy: Single-family building permits issued: 2 (2010); Multi-family building permits issued: 0 (2010); Employment by occupation: 15.4% management, 9.0% professional, 16.5% services, 33.7% sales, 4.7% farming, 4.7% construction, 16.1% production (2005-2009 5-year est.).

Income: Per capita income: $21,594 (2010); Median household income: $51,786 (2010); Average household income: $63,958 (2010); Percent of households with income of $100,000 or more: 13.9% (2010); Poverty rate: 5.3% (2005-2009 5-year est.).

Taxes: Total city taxes per capita: $389 (2007); City property taxes per capita: $137 (2007).

Education: Percent of population age 25 and over with: High school diploma (including GED) or higher: 86.8% (2010); Bachelor's degree or higher: 16.2% (2010); Master's degree or higher: 7.8% (2010).

Housing: Homeownership rate: 90.6% (2010); Median home value: $119,737 (2010); Median contract rent: n/a per month (2005-2009 5-year est.); Median year structure built: 1987 (2005-2009 5-year est.).

Transportation: Commute to work: 88.5% car, 0.0% public transportation, 1.8% walk, 8.6% work from home (2005-2009 5-year est.); Travel time to work: 22.4% less than 15 minutes, 25.1% 15 to 30 minutes, 25.5% 30 to 45 minutes, 9.8% 45 to 60 minutes, 17.3% 60 minutes or more (2005-2009 5-year est.)

POST OAK BEND CITY (town). Covers a land area of 2.054 square miles and a water area of 0 square miles. Located at 32.63° N. Lat; 96.31° W. Long. Elevation is 440 feet.

Population: 264 (1990); 404 (2000); 449 (2010); 502 (2015 projected); Race: 81.5% White, 4.5% Black, 2.7% Asian, 11.4% Other, 16.0% Hispanic of any race (2010); Density: 218.5 persons per square mile (2010); Average household size: 2.89 (2010); Median age: 37.4 (2010); Males per 100 females: 93.5 (2010); Marriage status: 15.1% never married, 70.8% now married, 12.3% divorced (2005-2009 5-year est.); Foreign born: 1.6% (2005-2009 5-year est.); Ancestry (includes multiple ancestries): 23.9% English, 23.2% German, 10.1% American, 8.1% Irish, 5.9% Scottish (2005-2009 5-year est.).

Economy: Employment by occupation: 15.3% management, 29.3% professional, 23.5% services, 22.8% sales, 0.7% farming, 5.8% construction, 2.7% production (2005-2009 5-year est.).

Income: Per capita income: $27,242 (2010); Median household income: $62,805 (2010); Average household income: $78,569 (2010); Percent of households with income of $100,000 or more: 23.0% (2010); Poverty rate: 3.1% (2005-2009 5-year est.).

Taxes: Total city taxes per capita: $67 (2007); City property taxes per capita: $0 (2007).

Education: Percent of population age 25 and over with: High school diploma (including GED) or higher: 80.3% (2010); Bachelor's degree or higher: 14.8% (2010); Master's degree or higher: 3.0% (2010).

Housing: Homeownership rate: 89.5% (2010); Median home value: $132,895 (2010); Median contract rent: $575 per month (2005-2009 5-year est.); Median year structure built: 1995 (2005-2009 5-year est.).

Transportation: Commute to work: 91.8% car, 0.0% public transportation, 0.0% walk, 8.2% work from home (2005-2009 5-year est.); Travel time to work: 18.4% less than 15 minutes, 15.4% 15 to 30 minutes, 15.7% 30 to 45 minutes, 24.0% 45 to 60 minutes, 26.6% 60 minutes or more (2005-2009 5-year est.)

ROSSER (village). Covers a land area of 2.010 square miles and a water area of 0.019 square miles. Located at 32.46° N. Lat; 96.45° W. Long. Elevation is 361 feet.

Population: 349 (1990); 379 (2000); 489 (2010); 567 (2015 projected); Race: 89.6% White, 4.1% Black, 0.2% Asian, 6.1% Other, 8.0% Hispanic of any race (2010); Density: 243.3 persons per square mile (2010); Average household size: 3.00 (2010); Median age: 32.9 (2010); Males per 100 females: 99.6 (2010); Marriage status: 36.6% never married, 47.2% now married, 7.9% widowed, 8.3% divorced (2005-2009 5-year est.); Foreign born: 1.8% (2005-2009 5-year est.); Ancestry (includes multiple ancestries): 11.9% Irish, 8.5% English, 7.9% German, 4.0% Scottish, 2.4% Czech (2005-2009 5-year est.).

Economy: Employment by occupation: 12.4% management, 7.9% professional, 19.8% services, 20.3% sales, 4.5% farming, 1.7% construction, 33.3% production (2005-2009 5-year est.).

Income: Per capita income: $25,244 (2010); Median household income: $65,705 (2010); Average household income: $75,230 (2010); Percent of

households with income of $100,000 or more: 22.7% (2010); Poverty rate: 11.9% (2005-2009 5-year est.).

Taxes: Total city taxes per capita: $7 (2007); City property taxes per capita: $0 (2007).

Education: Percent of population age 25 and over with: High school diploma (including GED) or higher: 86.0% (2010); Bachelor's degree or higher: 16.6% (2010); Master's degree or higher: 3.9% (2010).

Housing: Homeownership rate: 89.0% (2010); Median home value: $152,083 (2010); Median contract rent: $460 per month (2005-2009 5-year est.); Median year structure built: 1975 (2005-2009 5-year est.).

Transportation: Commute to work: 98.3% car, 0.0% public transportation, 1.2% walk, 0.6% work from home (2005-2009 5-year est.); Travel time to work: 15.1% less than 15 minutes, 29.1% 15 to 30 minutes, 36.6% 30 to 45 minutes, 9.9% 45 to 60 minutes, 9.3% 60 minutes or more (2005-2009 5-year est.)

SCURRY (unincorporated postal area, zip code 75158). Covers a land area of 75.129 square miles and a water area of 0.245 square miles. Located at 32.46° N. Lat; 96.38° W. Long. Elevation is 440 feet.

Population: 3,861 (2000); Race: 96.8% White, 0.7% Black, 0.1% Asian, 2.4% Other, 3.3% Hispanic of any race (2000); Density: 51.4 persons per square mile (2000); Age: 28.7% under 18, 8.6% over 64 (2000); Marriage status: 15.3% never married, 72.6% now married, 4.5% widowed, 7.7% divorced (2000); Foreign born: 0.4% (2000); Ancestry (includes multiple ancestries): 24.6% American, 14.6% Irish, 10.9% English, 8.9% German (2000).

Economy: Employment by occupation: 14.2% management, 14.4% professional, 11.1% services, 25.1% sales, 1.1% farming, 19.2% construction, 14.8% production (2000).

Income: Per capita income: $20,446 (2000); Median household income: $50,851 (2000); Poverty rate: 179.1% (2000).

Education: Percent of population age 25 and over with: High school diploma (including GED) or higher: 77.2% (2000); Bachelor's degree or higher: 11.1% (2000).

School District(s)
Scurry-Rosser ISD (PK-12)
    2009-10 Enrollment: 899 . . . . (972) 452-8823

Housing: Homeownership rate: 89.0% (2000); Median home value: $79,900 (2000); Median contract rent: $402 per month (2000); Median year structure built: 1984 (2000).

Transportation: Commute to work: 96.2% car, 0.0% public transportation, 0.5% walk, 2.7% work from home (2000); Travel time to work: 12.0% less than 15 minutes, 16.7% 15 to 30 minutes, 15.6% 30 to 45 minutes, 24.6% 45 to 60 minutes, 31.2% 60 minutes or more (2000)

TALTY (city). Covers a land area of 2.986 square miles and a water area of 0 square miles. Located at 32.69° N. Lat; 96.39° W. Long. Elevation is 440 feet.

Population: 333 (1990); 1,028 (2000); 2,553 (2010); 3,054 (2015 projected); Race: 87.3% White, 5.8% Black, 1.2% Asian, 5.6% Other, 8.8% Hispanic of any race (2010); Density: 855.0 persons per square mile (2010); Average household size: 3.15 (2010); Median age: 33.6 (2010); Males per 100 females: 103.3 (2010); Marriage status: 23.4% never married, 67.2% now married, 2.4% widowed, 6.9% divorced (2005-2009 5-year est.); Foreign born: 1.7% (2005-2009 5-year est.); Ancestry (includes multiple ancestries): 15.1% Irish, 14.5% German, 9.3% English, 9.2% American, 3.6% Welsh (2005-2009 5-year est.).

Economy: Employment by occupation: 21.4% management, 14.6% professional, 9.2% services, 36.4% sales, 0.0% farming, 10.4% construction, 8.1% production (2005-2009 5-year est.).

Income: Per capita income: $31,367 (2010); Median household income: $86,139 (2010); Average household income: $98,967 (2010); Percent of households with income of $100,000 or more: 40.0% (2010); Poverty rate: 5.6% (2005-2009 5-year est.).

Taxes: Total city taxes per capita: $95 (2007); City property taxes per capita: $0 (2007).

Education: Percent of population age 25 and over with: High school diploma (including GED) or higher: 91.1% (2010); Bachelor's degree or higher: 20.8% (2010); Master's degree or higher: 4.4% (2010).

Housing: Homeownership rate: 94.8% (2010); Median home value: $200,171 (2010); Median contract rent: n/a per month (2005-2009 5-year est.); Median year structure built: 2002 (2005-2009 5-year est.).

Transportation: Commute to work: 96.8% car, 0.0% public transportation, 0.0% walk, 2.4% work from home (2005-2009 5-year est.); Travel time to work: 15.7% less than 15 minutes, 23.0% 15 to 30 minutes, 25.1% 30 to 45

minutes, 24.5% 45 to 60 minutes, 11.6% 60 minutes or more (2005-2009 5-year est.)

TERRELL (city). Covers a land area of 18.315 square miles and a water area of 0.336 square miles. Located at 32.73° N. Lat; 96.28° W. Long. Elevation is 509 feet.
History: Named for Alexander Watkins Terrell (1827-1912), Texas statesman and soldier. Southwest Christian College in Terrell. Incorporated 1883.
Population: 12,565 (1990); 13,606 (2000); 19,470 (2010); 22,879 (2015 projected); Race: 47.3% White, 32.0% Black, 0.8% Asian, 19.8% Other, 30.6% Hispanic of any race (2010); Density: 1,063.1 persons per square mile (2010); Average household size: 2.75 (2010); Median age: 31.4 (2010); Males per 100 females: 96.8 (2010); Marriage status: 31.7% never married, 47.5% now married, 8.9% widowed, 12.0% divorced (2005-2009 5-year est.); Foreign born: 15.1% (2005-2009 5-year est.); Ancestry (includes multiple ancestries): 10.8% Irish, 7.0% English, 6.3% German, 5.4% American, 1.7% Dutch (2005-2009 5-year est.).
Economy: Single-family building permits issued: 5 (2010); Multi-family building permits issued: 2 (2010); Employment by occupation: 9.0% management, 14.5% professional, 25.1% services, 23.6% sales, 0.0% farming, 9.7% construction, 18.1% production (2005-2009 5-year est.).
Income: Per capita income: $18,415 (2010); Median household income: $40,239 (2010); Average household income: $51,635 (2010); Percent of households with income of $100,000 or more: 10.6% (2010); Poverty rate: 22.6% (2005-2009 5-year est.).
Taxes: Total city taxes per capita: $730 (2007); City property taxes per capita: $211 (2007).
Education: Percent of population age 25 and over with: High school diploma (including GED) or higher: 71.0% (2010); Bachelor's degree or higher: 14.5% (2010); Master's degree or higher: 6.3% (2010).

School District(s)

Terrell ISD (PK-12)
 2009-10 Enrollment: 4,178 . . . . (972) 563-7504

Four-year College(s)

Southwestern Christian College (Private, Not-for-profit, Historically black, Churches of Christ)
 Fall 2009 Enrollment: 201 . . . . (972) 524-3341
 2010-11 Tuition: In-state $6,185; Out-of-state $6,185
Housing: Homeownership rate: 53.7% (2010); Median home value: $92,330 (2010); Median contract rent: $635 per month (2005-2009 5-year est.); Median year structure built: 1981 (2005-2009 5-year est.).
Hospitals: Medical Center at Terrell (130 beds); Terrell State Hospital (316 beds)
Safety: Violent crime rate: 63.1 per 10,000 population; Property crime rate: 493.1 per 10,000 population (2009).
Newspapers: Rockwall County News (Regional news; Circulation 4,300); Terrell Tribune (Local news; Circulation 6,700)
Transportation: Commute to work: 87.0% car, 1.3% public transportation, 2.8% walk, 6.6% work from home (2005-2009 5-year est.); Travel time to work: 40.4% less than 15 minutes, 28.5% 15 to 30 minutes, 13.0% 30 to 45 minutes, 10.0% 45 to 60 minutes, 8.2% 60 minutes or more (2005-2009 5-year est.)
Airports: Terrell Municipal (general aviation)
Additional Information Contacts
City of Terrell . . . . (972) 551-6600
 http://www.cityofterrell.org
Terrell Chamber of Commerce . . . . (972) 563-5703
 http://www.terrelltexas.com

Kendall County

Located in south central Texas, on the south edge of Edwards Plateau; drained by the Guadalupe and Blanco Rivers. Covers a land area of 662.44 square miles, a water area of 0.60 square miles, and is located in the Central Time Zone at 29.89° N. Lat., 98.73° W. Long. The county was founded in 1862. County seat is Boerne.

Kendall County is part of the San Antonio-New Braunfels, TX Metropolitan Statistical Area. The entire metro area includes: Atascosa County, TX; Bandera County, TX; Bexar County, TX; Comal County, TX; Guadalupe County, TX; Kendall County, TX; Medina County, TX; Wilson County, TX

Weather Station: Boerne										Elevation: 1,443 feet		
	Jan	Feb	Mar	Apr	May	Jun	Jul	Aug	Sep	Oct	Nov	Dec
High	61	65	71	79	84	90	93	94	89	80	70	62
Low	36	39	45	53	62	68	70	69	64	55	45	37
Precip	2.0	2.2	3.0	2.2	4.6	4.6	3.0	2.8	3.3	4.3	3.2	2.2
Snow	0.3	tr	0.0	0.0	0.0	0.0	0.0	0.0	0.0	0.0	tr	tr

High and Low temperatures in degrees Fahrenheit; Precipitation and Snow in inches

Population: 14,589 (1990); 23,743 (2000); 34,762 (2010); 40,059 (2015 projected); Race: 90.4% White, 1.3% Black, 0.7% Asian, 7.6% Other, 20.4% Hispanic of any race (2010); Density: 52.5 persons per square mile (2010); Average household size: 2.73 (2010); Median age: 37.5 (2010); Males per 100 females: 97.6 (2010).
Religion: Five largest groups: 24.0% Catholic Church, 16.0% Southern Baptist Convention, 9.6% The United Methodist Church, 6.3% Evangelical Lutheran Church in America, 3.0% Episcopal Church (2000).
Economy: Unemployment rate: 6.7% (June 2011); Total civilian labor force: 17,390 (June 2011); Leading industries: 21.0% retail trade; 13.2% health care and social assistance; 11.8% accommodation & food services (2009); Farms: 1,164 totaling 342,515 acres (2007); Companies that employ 500 or more persons: 0 (2009); Companies that employ 100 to 499 persons: 12 (2009); Companies that employ less than 100 persons: 1,071 (2009); Black-owned businesses: 57 (2007); Hispanic-owned businesses: 406 (2007); Asian-owned businesses: n/a (2007); Women-owned businesses: 1,465 (2007); Retail sales per capita: $28,097 (2010). Single-family building permits issued: 202 (2010); Multi-family building permits issued: 0 (2010).
Income: Per capita income: $33,404 (2010); Median household income: $68,012 (2010); Average household income: $91,707 (2010); Percent of households with income of $100,000 or more: 30.2% (2010); Poverty rate: 8.6% (2009); Bankruptcy rate: 2.30% (2010).
Taxes: Total county taxes per capita: $406 (2007); County property taxes per capita: $302 (2007).
Education: Percent of population age 25 and over with: High school diploma (including GED) or higher: 91.7% (2010); Bachelor's degree or higher: 36.7% (2010); Master's degree or higher: 12.4% (2010).
Housing: Homeownership rate: 72.0% (2010); Median home value: $212,395 (2010); Median contract rent: $724 per month (2005-2009 5-year est.); Median year structure built: 1992 (2005-2009 5-year est.)
Health: Birth rate: 142.4 per 10,000 population (2009); Death rate: 91.0 per 10,000 population (2009); Age-adjusted cancer mortality rate: 175.4 deaths per 100,000 population (2007); Number of physicians: 29.8 per 10,000 population (2008); Hospital beds: 0.0 per 10,000 population (2007); Hospital admissions: 0.0 per 10,000 population (2007).
Elections: 2008 Presidential election results: 21.5% Obama, 77.5% McCain, 0.1% Nader
Additional Information Contacts
Kendall County Government . . . . (830) 249-9343
 http://www.co.kendall.tx.us
City of Boerne . . . . (830) 249-9511
 http://www.ci.boerne.tx.us
Comfort Chamber of Commerce . . . . (830) 995-3131
 http://www.comfort-texas.com
Greater Boerne Chamber of Commerce . . . . (830) 249-8000
 http://www.boerne.org

Kendall County Communities

BERGHEIM (unincorporated postal area, zip code 78004). Covers a land area of 38.843 square miles and a water area of 0 square miles. Located at 29.90° N. Lat; 98.55° W. Long. Elevation is 1,437 feet.
Population: 676 (2000); Race: 98.3% White, 0.0% Black, 0.0% Asian, 1.7% Other, 3.4% Hispanic of any race (2000); Density: 17.4 persons per square mile (2000); Age: 29.9% under 18, 8.5% over 64 (2000); Marriage status: 15.7% never married, 74.3% now married, 4.3% widowed, 5.8% divorced (2000); Foreign born: 1.6% (2000); Ancestry (includes multiple ancestries): 36.6% German, 17.0% American, 15.4% Irish, 15.0% English (2000).
Economy: Employment by occupation: 19.9% management, 22.5% professional, 17.7% services, 19.1% sales, 1.7% farming, 16.4% construction, 2.8% production (2000).
Income: Per capita income: $17,943 (2000); Median household income: $52,321 (2000); Poverty rate: 179.1% (2000).
Education: Percent of population age 25 and over with: High school diploma (including GED) or higher: 94.8% (2000); Bachelor's degree or higher: 30.0% (2000).

Housing: Homeownership rate: 89.8% (2000); Median home value: $149,000 (2000); Median contract rent: $818 per month (2000); Median year structure built: 1988 (2000).
Transportation: Commute to work: 90.5% car, 0.0% public transportation, 1.7% walk, 5.6% work from home (2000); Travel time to work: 11.0% less than 15 minutes, 25.0% 15 to 30 minutes, 38.4% 30 to 45 minutes, 21.7% 45 to 60 minutes, 3.9% 60 minutes or more (2000)

BOERNE (city). County seat. Covers a land area of 5.822 square miles and a water area of 0.294 square miles. Located at 29.79° N. Lat; 98.73° W. Long. Elevation is 1,411 feet.
History: Boerne was founded in 1849 by members of the German colony of Bettina, and named for Ludwig Boerne, one of the founders. The aim of the settlement was to promote the study of the Latin classics. Boerne was the home of George Wilkins Kendall, an early war correspondent, for whom the county was named.
Population: 4,812 (1990); 6,178 (2000); 9,556 (2010); 10,976 (2015 projected); Race: 93.7% White, 1.5% Black, 0.4% Asian, 4.5% Other, 18.9% Hispanic of any race (2010); Density: 1,641.2 persons per square mile (2010); Average household size: 2.54 (2010); Median age: 38.0 (2010); Males per 100 females: 90.0 (2010); Marriage status: 23.6% never married, 54.6% now married, 10.3% widowed, 11.5% divorced (2005-2009 5-year est.); Foreign born: 6.0% (2005-2009 5-year est.); Ancestry (includes multiple ancestries): 29.1% German, 15.6% English, 13.1% Irish, 5.1% Scottish, 4.5% French (2005-2009 5-year est.).
Economy: Single-family building permits issued: 113 (2010); Multi-family building permits issued: 0 (2010); Employment by occupation: 19.0% management, 21.1% professional, 17.8% services, 25.2% sales, 0.9% farming, 8.4% construction, 7.6% production (2005-2009 5-year est.).
Income: Per capita income: $29,493 (2010); Median household income: $56,547 (2010); Average household income: $75,464 (2010); Percent of households with income of $100,000 or more: 21.7% (2010); Poverty rate: 7.2% (2005-2009 5-year est.).
Taxes: Total city taxes per capita: $927 (2007); City property taxes per capita: $300 (2007).
Education: Percent of population age 25 and over with: High school diploma (including GED) or higher: 90.0% (2010); Bachelor's degree or higher: 34.8% (2010); Master's degree or higher: 10.8% (2010).
School District(s)
Boerne ISD (PK-12)
    2009-10 Enrollment: 6,392 . . . . (830) 357-2000
Meadowland Charter School (07-12)
    2009-10 Enrollment: 60 . . . . (830) 331-4094
Housing: Homeownership rate: 57.0% (2010); Median home value: $191,141 (2010); Median contract rent: $837 per month (2005-2009 5-year est.); Median year structure built: 1994 (2005-2009 5-year est.).
Safety: Violent crime rate: 12.0 per 10,000 population; Property crime rate: 277.8 per 10,000 population (2009).
Newspapers: Boerne Star (Community news; Circulation 6,000); Hill Country Recorder (Community news; Circulation 7,100)
Transportation: Commute to work: 88.0% car, 0.7% public transportation, 1.9% walk, 7.2% work from home (2005-2009 5-year est.); Travel time to work: 40.7% less than 15 minutes, 20.8% 15 to 30 minutes, 23.0% 30 to 45 minutes, 10.2% 45 to 60 minutes, 5.3% 60 minutes or more (2005-2009 5-year est.)
Additional Information Contacts
City of Boerne . . . . (830) 249-9511
    http://www.ci.boerne.tx.us
Greater Boerne Chamber of Commerce . . . . (830) 249-8000
    http://www.boerne.org

COMFORT (CDP). Covers a land area of 3.206 square miles and a water area of 0.015 square miles. Located at 29.97° N. Lat; 98.90° W. Long. Elevation is 1,427 feet.
History: Comfort developed as a retail and recreational center on the edge of the Guadalupe River Valley.
Population: 1,477 (1990); 2,358 (2000); 2,509 (2010); 2,693 (2015 projected); Race: 61.8% White, 1.4% Black, 0.4% Asian, 36.5% Other, 60.0% Hispanic of any race (2010); Density: 782.7 persons per square mile (2010); Average household size: 2.87 (2010); Median age: 31.2 (2010); Males per 100 females: 99.1 (2010); Marriage status: 16.2% never married, 57.7% now married, 20.9% widowed, 5.1% divorced (2005-2009 5-year est.); Foreign born: 15.0% (2005-2009 5-year est.); Ancestry (includes multiple ancestries): 27.5% German, 10.1% Irish, 9.4% English, 8.0% Dutch, 4.5% Italian (2005-2009 5-year est.).

Economy: Employment by occupation: 25.3% management, 8.3% professional, 29.8% services, 9.7% sales, 1.3% farming, 16.9% construction, 8.7% production (2005-2009 5-year est.).
Income: Per capita income: $17,149 (2010); Median household income: $39,552 (2010); Average household income: $49,741 (2010); Percent of households with income of $100,000 or more: 10.1% (2010); Poverty rate: 19.6% (2005-2009 5-year est.).
Education: Percent of population age 25 and over with: High school diploma (including GED) or higher: 71.9% (2010); Bachelor's degree or higher: 20.0% (2010); Master's degree or higher: 6.1% (2010).
School District(s)
Comfort ISD (PK-12)
    2009-10 Enrollment: 1,159 . . . . (830) 995-6400
Housing: Homeownership rate: 69.0% (2010); Median home value: $68,780 (2010); Median contract rent: $230 per month (2005-2009 5-year est.); Median year structure built: 1978 (2005-2009 5-year est.).
Newspapers: Comfort News (Community news)
Transportation: Commute to work: 100.0% car, 0.0% public transportation, 0.0% walk, 0.0% work from home (2005-2009 5-year est.); Travel time to work: 50.9% less than 15 minutes, 33.0% 15 to 30 minutes, 8.3% 30 to 45 minutes, 6.9% 45 to 60 minutes, 0.9% 60 minutes or more (2005-2009 5-year est.)
Additional Information Contacts
Comfort Chamber of Commerce . . . . (830) 995-3131
    http://www.comfort-texas.com

KENDALIA (unincorporated postal area, zip code 78027). Covers a land area of 101.636 square miles and a water area of 0.028 square miles. Located at 30.00° N. Lat; 98.57° W. Long. Elevation is 1,385 feet.
Population: 374 (2000); Race: 98.1% White, 0.0% Black, 0.0% Asian, 1.9% Other, 0.0% Hispanic of any race (2000); Density: 3.7 persons per square mile (2000); Age: 15.9% under 18, 15.6% over 64 (2000); Marriage status: 10.0% never married, 73.6% now married, 10.4% widowed, 5.9% divorced (2000); Foreign born: 0.0% (2000); Ancestry (includes multiple ancestries): 57.2% German, 17.2% Irish, 14.7% English, 6.6% Scotch-Irish, 6.6% Polish (2000).
Economy: Employment by occupation: 13.3% management, 13.3% professional, 9.7% services, 33.3% sales, 3.6% farming, 22.4% construction, 4.2% production (2000).
Income: Per capita income: $21,375 (2000); Median household income: $37,500 (2000); Poverty rate: 179.1% (2000).
Education: Percent of population age 25 and over with: High school diploma (including GED) or higher: 84.1% (2000); Bachelor's degree or higher: 14.7% (2000).
Housing: Homeownership rate: 97.2% (2000); Median home value: $106,300 (2000); Median contract rent: $775 per month (2000); Median year structure built: 1980 (2000).
Transportation: Commute to work: 87.3% car, 0.0% public transportation, 0.0% walk, 6.7% work from home (2000); Travel time to work: 16.2% less than 15 minutes, 17.5% 15 to 30 minutes, 31.2% 30 to 45 minutes, 19.5% 45 to 60 minutes, 15.6% 60 minutes or more (2000)

WARING (unincorporated postal area, zip code 78074). Covers a land area of 2.864 square miles and a water area of 0 square miles. Located at 29.95° N. Lat; 98.79° W. Long. Elevation is 1,345 feet.
Population: 59 (2000); Race: 100.0% White, 0.0% Black, 0.0% Asian, 0.0% Other, 0.0% Hispanic of any race (2000); Density: 20.6 persons per square mile (2000); Age: 0.0% under 18, 64.0% over 64 (2000); Marriage status: 0.0% never married, 64.0% now married, 0.0% widowed, 36.0% divorced (2000); Foreign born: 0.0% (2000); Ancestry (includes multiple ancestries): 64.0% German, 32.0% Irish (2000).
Economy: Employment by occupation: 0.0% management, 0.0% professional, 0.0% services, 100.0% sales, 0.0% farming, 0.0% construction, 0.0% production (2000).
Income: Per capita income: $16,380 (2000); Median household income: $17,361 (2000); Poverty rate: 179.1% (2000).
Education: Percent of population age 25 and over with: High school diploma (including GED) or higher: 100.0% (2000); Bachelor's degree or higher: 0.0% (2000).
Housing: Homeownership rate: 42.1% (2000); Median home value: n/a (2000); Median contract rent: n/a per month (2000); Median year structure built: 1977 (2000).
Transportation: Commute to work: 100.0% car, 0.0% public transportation, 0.0% walk, 0.0% work from home (2000); Travel time to

work: 0.0% less than 15 minutes, 100.0% 15 to 30 minutes, 0.0% 30 to 45 minutes, 0.0% 45 to 60 minutes, 0.0% 60 minutes or more (2000)

Kenedy County

Located in south Texas; coastal plains area, bounded on the east by Laguna Madre, with Padre Island separating the mainland from the Gulf of Mexico. Covers a land area of 1,456.77 square miles, a water area of 488.83 square miles, and is located in the Central Time Zone at 26.86° N. Lat., 97.73° W. Long. The county was founded in 1911. County seat is Sarita.

Kenedy County is part of the Kingsville, TX Micropolitan Statistical Area. The entire metro area includes: Kenedy County, TX; Kleberg County, TX

Population: 460 (1990); 414 (2000); 360 (2010); 334 (2015 projected); Race: 65.8% White, 0.6% Black, 0.6% Asian, 33.1% Other, 75.8% Hispanic of any race (2010); Density: 0.2 persons per square mile (2010); Average household size: 2.89 (2010); Median age: 39.7 (2010); Males per 100 females: 105.7 (2010).
Religion: Two largest groups: 29.0% Catholic Church, 12.1% International Pentecostal Holiness Church (2000).
Economy: Unemployment rate: 3.9% (June 2011); Total civilian labor force: 229 (June 2011); Leading industries: Farms: 25 totaling 909,048 acres (2007); Companies that employ 500 or more persons: 0 (2009); Companies that employ 100 to 499 persons: 0 (2009); Companies that employ less than 100 persons: 12 (2009); Black-owned businesses: n/a (2007); Hispanic-owned businesses: n/a (2007); Asian-owned businesses: n/a (2007); Women-owned businesses: n/a (2007); Retail sales per capita: $1,269 (2010). Single-family building permits issued: n/a (2010); Multi-family building permits issued: n/a (2010).
Income: Per capita income: $19,368 (2010); Median household income: $33,958 (2010); Average household income: $49,614 (2010); Percent of households with income of $100,000 or more: 5.7% (2010); Poverty rate: 15.9% (2009); Bankruptcy rate: n/a (2010).
Taxes: Total county taxes per capita: $1,475 (2007); County property taxes per capita: $1,391 (2007).
Education: Percent of population age 25 and over with: High school diploma (including GED) or higher: 64.4% (2010); Bachelor's degree or higher: 24.0% (2010); Master's degree or higher: 10.0% (2010).
Housing: Homeownership rate: 32.5% (2010); Median home value: $53,333 (2010); Median contract rent: $500 per month (2005-2009 5-year est.); Median year structure built: 1970 (2005-2009 5-year est.)
Health: Birth rate: 108.4 per 10,000 population (2009); Death rate: 0.0 per 10,000 population (2009); Age-adjusted cancer mortality rate: n/a deaths per 100,000 population (2007); Number of physicians: 0.0 per 10,000 population (2008); Hospital beds: 0.0 per 10,000 population (2007); Hospital admissions: 0.0 per 10,000 population (2007).
Elections: 2008 Presidential election results: 53.5% Obama, 46.5% McCain, 0.0% Nader
National and State Parks: Padre Island National Seashore
Additional Information Contacts
Kenedy County Government . . . . (361) 294-5220
    http://www.co.kenedy.tx.us/ips/cms

Kenedy County Communities

ARMSTRONG (unincorporated postal area, zip code 78338). Covers a land area of 67.323 square miles and a water area of 0.172 square miles. Located at 26.87° N. Lat; 97.77° W. Long. Elevation is 23 feet.
Population: 86 (2000); Race: 88.7% White, 0.0% Black, 0.0% Asian, 11.3% Other, 88.7% Hispanic of any race (2000); Density: 1.3 persons per square mile (2000); Age: 39.2% under 18, 7.2% over 64 (2000); Marriage status: 28.8% never married, 52.5% now married, 13.6% widowed, 5.1% divorced (2000); Foreign born: 8.2% (2000); Ancestry (includes multiple ancestries): 4.1% French, 3.1% Scotch-Irish, 3.1% German, 2.1% Irish (2000).
Economy: Employment by occupation: 49.0% management, 0.0% professional, 8.2% services, 16.3% sales, 26.5% farming, 0.0% construction, 0.0% production (2000).
Income: Per capita income: $34,546 (2000); Median household income: $33,438 (2000); Poverty rate: 179.1% (2000).
Education: Percent of population age 25 and over with: High school diploma (including GED) or higher: 83.3% (2000); Bachelor's degree or higher: 29.6% (2000).

Housing: Homeownership rate: 19.0% (2000); Median home value: n/a (2000); Median contract rent: n/a per month (2000); Median year structure built: 1977 (2000).
Transportation: Commute to work: 44.9% car, 0.0% public transportation, 42.9% walk, 12.2% work from home (2000); Travel time to work: 72.1% less than 15 minutes, 7.0% 15 to 30 minutes, 14.0% 30 to 45 minutes, 7.0% 45 to 60 minutes, 0.0% 60 minutes or more (2000)

SARITA (unincorporated postal area, zip code 78385). County seat. Covers a land area of 202.165 square miles and a water area of 2.288 square miles. Located at 27.17° N. Lat; 97.82° W. Long. Elevation is 36 feet.
History: Sarita was named for the granddaughter of Captain Mifflin Kenedy, developer of a large ranch, for whom Kenedy County was named.
Population: 278 (2000); Race: 56.9% White, 0.7% Black, 0.0% Asian, 42.4% Other, 86.1% Hispanic of any race (2000); Density: 1.4 persons per square mile (2000); Age: 27.8% under 18, 14.6% over 64 (2000); Marriage status: 28.9% never married, 55.3% now married, 7.9% widowed, 7.9% divorced (2000); Foreign born: 13.5% (2000); Ancestry (includes multiple ancestries): 5.3% Irish, 4.3% German, 2.8% English, 2.1% French (2000).
Economy: Employment by occupation: 10.9% management, 16.8% professional, 25.2% services, 16.8% sales, 19.3% farming, 7.6% construction, 3.4% production (2000).
Income: Per capita income: $10,148 (2000); Median household income: $22,109 (2000); Poverty rate: 179.1% (2000).
Education: Percent of population age 25 and over with: High school diploma (including GED) or higher: 47.5% (2000); Bachelor's degree or higher: 12.0% (2000).

School District(s)
Kenedy County Wide CSD (PK-06)
    2009-10 Enrollment: 83 . . . . (361) 294-5381
Housing: Homeownership rate: 44.1% (2000); Median home value: $22,500 (2000); Median contract rent: $242 per month (2000); Median year structure built: 1958 (2000).
Transportation: Commute to work: 88.2% car, 0.0% public transportation, 7.6% walk, 0.0% work from home (2000); Travel time to work: 47.9% less than 15 minutes, 29.4% 15 to 30 minutes, 13.4% 30 to 45 minutes, 0.0% 45 to 60 minutes, 9.2% 60 minutes or more (2000)

Kent County

Located in northwestern Texas; rolling plains area, drained by the Salt and Double Mountain Forks of the Brazos River. Covers a land area of 902.33 square miles, a water area of 0.58 square miles, and is located in the Central Time Zone at 33.23° N. Lat., 100.71° W. Long. The county was founded in 1876. County seat is Jayton.

Weather Station: Jayton   Elevation: 2,009 feet

	Jan	Feb	Mar	Apr	May	Jun	Jul	Aug	Sep	Oct	Nov	Dec
High	55	59	67	77	84	91	96	94	87	77	65	55
Low	27	31	38	46	57	65	70	69	61	50	38	28
Precip	0.9	1.1	1.4	1.6	3.0	3.8	1.9	2.4	2.4	2.4	1.2	1.0
Snow	1.0	0.7	0.1	tr	0.0	0.0	0.0	0.0	0.0	0.0	0.7	0.4

High and Low temperatures in degrees Fahrenheit; Precipitation and Snow in inches

Population: 1,010 (1990); 859 (2000); 753 (2010); 700 (2015 projected); Race: 92.7% White, 0.3% Black, 0.0% Asian, 7.0% Other, 14.9% Hispanic of any race (2010); Density: 0.8 persons per square mile (2010); Average household size: 2.25 (2010); Median age: 49.4 (2010); Males per 100 females: 92.1 (2010).
Religion: Five largest groups: 57.3% Southern Baptist Convention, 9.4% The United Methodist Church, 7.3% Catholic Church, 7.1% Churches of Christ, 5.0% Assemblies of God (2000).
Economy: Unemployment rate: 6.3% (June 2011); Total civilian labor force: 429 (June 2011); Leading industries: Farms: 212 totaling 567,607 acres (2007); Companies that employ 500 or more persons: 0 (2009); Companies that employ 100 to 499 persons: 0 (2009); Companies that employ less than 100 persons: 10 (2009); Black-owned businesses: n/a (2007); Hispanic-owned businesses: n/a (2007); Asian-owned businesses: n/a (2007); Women-owned businesses: n/a (2007); Retail sales per capita: $8,765 (2010). Single-family building permits issued: n/a (2010); Multi-family building permits issued: n/a (2010).
Income: Per capita income: $22,363 (2010); Median household income: $38,811 (2010); Average household income: $52,390 (2010); Percent of households with income of $100,000 or more: 11.4% (2010); Poverty rate: 12.2% (2009); Bankruptcy rate: 1.28% (2010).

Taxes: Total county taxes per capita: $252 (2007); County property taxes per capita: $192 (2007).
Education: Percent of population age 25 and over with: High school diploma (including GED) or higher: 81.4% (2010); Bachelor's degree or higher: 16.5% (2010); Master's degree or higher: 5.4% (2010).
Housing: Homeownership rate: 77.6% (2010); Median home value: $31,803 (2010); Median contract rent: $310 per month (2005-2009 5-year est.); Median year structure built: 1958 (2005-2009 5-year est.)
Health: Birth rate: 113.8 per 10,000 population (2009); Death rate: 71.1 per 10,000 population (2009); Age-adjusted cancer mortality rate: Suppressed deaths per 100,000 population (2007); Number of physicians: 14.1 per 10,000 population (2008); Hospital beds: 0.0 per 10,000 population (2007); Hospital admissions: 0.0 per 10,000 population (2007).
Elections: 2008 Presidential election results: 22.1% Obama, 76.3% McCain, 0.0% Nader
Additional Information Contacts
Kent County Government . . . . (806) 237-3373
http://www.co.kent.tx.us/ips/cms

Kent County Communities

GIRARD (CDP). Covers a land area of 1.462 square miles and a water area of 0 square miles. Located at 33.36° N. Lat; 100.66° W. Long. Elevation is 2,116 feet.
Population: 82 (1990); 62 (2000); 57 (2010); 52 (2015 projected); Race: 89.5% White, 0.0% Black, 0.0% Asian, 10.5% Other, 15.8% Hispanic of any race (2010); Density: 39.0 persons per square mile (2010); Average household size: 2.38 (2010); Median age: 47.3 (2010); Males per 100 females: 111.1 (2010); Marriage status: 0.0% never married, 88.0% now married, 0.0% widowed, 12.0% divorced (2005-2009 5-year est.); Foreign born: 28.0% (2005-2009 5-year est.); Ancestry (includes multiple ancestries): 36.0% German, 12.0% English (2005-2009 5-year est.).
Economy: Employment by occupation: 30.0% management, 0.0% professional, 0.0% services, 0.0% sales, 0.0% farming, 0.0% construction, 70.0% production (2005-2009 5-year est.).
Income: Per capita income: $20,421 (2010); Median household income: $31,667 (2010); Average household income: $40,729 (2010); Percent of households with income of $100,000 or more: 8.3% (2010); Poverty rate: 0.0% (2005-2009 5-year est.).
Education: Percent of population age 25 and over with: High school diploma (including GED) or higher: 87.8% (2010); Bachelor's degree or higher: 14.6% (2010); Master's degree or higher: 4.9% (2010).
Housing: Homeownership rate: 75.0% (2010); Median home value: $45,000 (2010); Median contract rent: n/a per month (2005-2009 5-year est.); Median year structure built: 1973 (2005-2009 5-year est.).
Transportation: Commute to work: 70.0% car, 0.0% public transportation, 0.0% walk, 30.0% work from home (2005-2009 5-year est.); Travel time to work: 0.0% less than 15 minutes, 0.0% 15 to 30 minutes, 100.0% 30 to 45 minutes, 0.0% 45 to 60 minutes, 0.0% 60 minutes or more (2005-2009 5-year est.)

JAYTON (city). County seat. Covers a land area of 1.701 square miles and a water area of 0 square miles. Located at 33.24° N. Lat; 100.57° W. Long. Elevation is 2,005 feet.
Population: 608 (1990); 513 (2000); 451 (2010); 422 (2015 projected); Race: 94.9% White, 0.2% Black, 0.0% Asian, 4.9% Other, 14.9% Hispanic of any race (2010); Density: 265.2 persons per square mile (2010); Average household size: 2.16 (2010); Median age: 52.9 (2010); Males per 100 females: 85.6 (2010); Marriage status: 24.1% never married, 55.0% now married, 14.1% widowed, 6.8% divorced (2005-2009 5-year est.); Foreign born: 4.8% (2005-2009 5-year est.); Ancestry (includes multiple ancestries): 19.8% German, 15.4% English, 11.5% American, 11.0% Irish, 3.8% Scottish (2005-2009 5-year est.).
Economy: Employment by occupation: 26.5% management, 21.1% professional, 10.8% services, 14.0% sales, 3.6% farming, 7.9% construction, 16.1% production (2005-2009 5-year est.).
Income: Per capita income: $23,664 (2010); Median household income: $44,000 (2010); Average household income: $53,961 (2010); Percent of households with income of $100,000 or more: 11.6% (2010); Poverty rate: 8.7% (2005-2009 5-year est.).
Taxes: Total city taxes per capita: $174 (2007); City property taxes per capita: $120 (2007).
Education: Percent of population age 25 and over with: High school diploma (including GED) or higher: 77.8% (2010); Bachelor's degree or higher: 16.6% (2010); Master's degree or higher: 5.5% (2010).

Jayton-Girard ISD (PK-12)
2009-10 Enrollment: 144 . . . . (806) 237-2991
Housing: Homeownership rate: 78.9% (2010); Median home value: $27,391 (2010); Median contract rent: $310 per month (2005-2009 5-year est.); Median year structure built: 1959 (2005-2009 5-year est.).
Transportation: Commute to work: 98.9% car, 0.0% public transportation, 1.1% walk, 0.0% work from home (2005-2009 5-year est.); Travel time to work: 63.1% less than 15 minutes, 17.9% 15 to 30 minutes, 17.2% 30 to 45 minutes, 1.1% 45 to 60 minutes, 0.7% 60 minutes or more (2005-2009 5-year est.)

Kerr County

Located in southwestern Texas, on the Edwards Plateau; drained by the Guadalupe River. Covers a land area of 1,106.12 square miles, a water area of 1.54 square miles, and is located in the Central Time Zone at 30.04° N. Lat., 99.19° W. Long. The county was founded in 1856. County seat is Kerrville.

Kerr County is part of the Kerrville, TX Micropolitan Statistical Area. The entire metro area includes: Kerr County, TX

Weather Station: Kerrville 3 NNE — Elevation: 1,782 feet

	Jan	Feb	Mar	Apr	May	Jun	Jul	Aug	Sep	Oct	Nov	Dec
High	60	64	70	78	84	90	92	93	88	79	69	61
Low	34	38	45	52	62	68	70	69	63	54	44	35
Precip	1.5	1.8	2.5	2.0	4.1	3.8	2.7	1.7	3.8	3.7	2.5	1.8
Snow	0.7	0.2	tr	tr	0.0	0.0	0.0	0.0	0.0	0.0	0.2	0.1

High and Low temperatures in degrees Fahrenheit; Precipitation and Snow in inches

Population: 36,304 (1990); 43,653 (2000); 49,055 (2010); 51,597 (2015 projected); Race: 87.0% White, 1.9% Black, 0.6% Asian, 10.4% Other, 23.0% Hispanic of any race (2010); Density: 44.3 persons per square mile (2010); Average household size: 2.33 (2010); Median age: 43.5 (2010); Males per 100 females: 92.8 (2010).
Religion: Five largest groups: 16.9% Southern Baptist Convention, 14.4% Catholic Church, 7.8% The United Methodist Church, 2.8% Presbyterian Church (U.S.A.), 2.4% Episcopal Church (2000).
Economy: Unemployment rate: 7.1% (June 2011); Total civilian labor force: 23,617 (June 2011); Leading industries: 23.0% health care and social assistance; 19.0% retail trade; 12.7% accommodation & food services (2009); Farms: 1,226 totaling 613,555 acres (2007); Companies that employ 500 or more persons: 3 (2009); Companies that employ 100 to 499 persons: 15 (2009); Companies that employ less than 100 persons: 1,403 (2009); Black-owned businesses: n/a (2007); Hispanic-owned businesses: 564 (2007); Asian-owned businesses: n/a (2007); Women-owned businesses: 1,462 (2007); Retail sales per capita: $18,347 (2010). Single-family building permits issued: 41 (2010); Multi-family building permits issued: 0 (2010).
Income: Per capita income: $25,318 (2010); Median household income: $43,783 (2010); Average household income: $60,413 (2010); Percent of households with income of $100,000 or more: 13.9% (2010); Poverty rate: 14.5% (2009); Bankruptcy rate: 1.58% (2010).
Taxes: Total county taxes per capita: $313 (2007); County property taxes per capita: $230 (2007).
Education: Percent of population age 25 and over with: High school diploma (including GED) or higher: 85.1% (2010); Bachelor's degree or higher: 24.8% (2010); Master's degree or higher: 8.9% (2010).
Housing: Homeownership rate: 74.4% (2010); Median home value: $120,360 (2010); Median contract rent: $573 per month (2005-2009 5-year est.); Median year structure built: 1982 (2005-2009 5-year est.)
Health: Birth rate: 126.3 per 10,000 population (2009); Death rate: 139.5 per 10,000 population (2009); Age-adjusted cancer mortality rate: 200.2 deaths per 100,000 population (2007); Number of physicians: 25.5 per 10,000 population (2008); Hospital beds: 68.0 per 10,000 population (2007); Hospital admissions: 1,376.1 per 10,000 population (2007).
Elections: 2008 Presidential election results: 24.7% Obama, 74.3% McCain, 0.2% Nader
National and State Parks: Kerrville State Park
Additional Information Contacts
Kerr County Government . . . . (830) 792-2200
http://www.co.kerr.tx.us
City of Kerrville . . . . (830) 257-8000
http://www.kerrville.org

Kerrville Area Chamber of Commerce . . . . (830) 896-1155
    http://www.kerrvilletx.com
West Kerr County Chamber of Commerce . . . . (830) 367-4322
    http://www.wkcc.com

Kerr County Communities

CENTER POINT (unincorporated postal area, zip code 78010).
Covers a land area of 71.717 square miles and a water area of 0.242
square miles. Located at 29.94° N. Lat; 99.05° W. Long. Elevation is 1,532
feet.
Population: 2,383 (2000); Race: 92.8% White, 0.3% Black, 0.6% Asian,
6.3% Other, 15.1% Hispanic of any race (2000); Density: 33.2 persons per
square mile (2000); Age: 24.8% under 18, 17.3% over 64 (2000); Marriage
status: 17.7% never married, 61.0% now married, 10.3% widowed, 10.9%
divorced (2000); Foreign born: 5.8% (2000); Ancestry (includes multiple
ancestries): 16.5% German, 11.8% American, 11.0% English, 8.4% Irish
(2000).
Economy: Employment by occupation: 9.5% management, 15.1%
professional, 20.4% services, 23.2% sales, 1.1% farming, 16.5%
construction, 14.2% production (2000).
Income: Per capita income: $18,405 (2000); Median household income:
$35,121 (2000); Poverty rate: 179.1% (2000).
Education: Percent of population age 25 and over with: High school
diploma (including GED) or higher: 79.3% (2000); Bachelor's degree or
higher: 18.5% (2000).

School District(s)
Center Point ISD (PK-12)
    2009-10 Enrollment: 624 . . . . (830) 634-2171
Housing: Homeownership rate: 80.5% (2000); Median home value:
$76,000 (2000); Median contract rent: $369 per month (2000); Median year
structure built: 1980 (2000).
Hospitals: Starlite Recovery Center (65 beds)
Transportation: Commute to work: 91.8% car, 0.0% public transportation,
3.7% walk, 2.7% work from home (2000); Travel time to work: 20.0% less
than 15 minutes, 40.9% 15 to 30 minutes, 23.4% 30 to 45 minutes, 5.3%
45 to 60 minutes, 10.4% 60 minutes or more (2000)

HUNT (unincorporated postal area, zip code 78024). Covers a land area
of 264.585 square miles and a water area of 0.398 square miles. Located
at 30.05° N. Lat; 99.42° W. Long. Elevation is 1,808 feet.
Population: 1,107 (2000); Race: 97.4% White, 0.0% Black, 0.0% Asian,
2.6% Other, 12.7% Hispanic of any race (2000); Density: 4.2 persons per
square mile (2000); Age: 23.0% under 18, 14.3% over 64 (2000); Marriage
status: 13.9% never married, 73.8% now married, 2.7% widowed, 9.7%
divorced (2000); Foreign born: 10.4% (2000); Ancestry (includes multiple
ancestries): 17.1% German, 16.5% English, 10.9% American, 10.8% Irish
(2000).
Economy: Employment by occupation: 24.5% management, 19.2%
professional, 17.4% services, 20.8% sales, 1.6% farming, 10.9%
construction, 5.6% production (2000).
Income: Per capita income: $26,506 (2000); Median household income:
$43,500 (2000); Poverty rate: 179.1% (2000).
Education: Percent of population age 25 and over with: High school
diploma (including GED) or higher: 87.8% (2000); Bachelor's degree or
higher: 41.3% (2000).

School District(s)
Hunt ISD (PK-08)
    2009-10 Enrollment: 187 . . . . (830) 238-4893
Housing: Homeownership rate: 68.7% (2000); Median home value:
$187,500 (2000); Median contract rent: $325 per month (2000); Median
year structure built: 1976 (2000).
Hospitals: La Hacienda Treatment Center
Transportation: Commute to work: 75.0% car, 0.0% public transportation,
6.6% walk, 16.1% work from home (2000); Travel time to work: 39.5% less
than 15 minutes, 28.3% 15 to 30 minutes, 16.3% 30 to 45 minutes, 9.3%
45 to 60 minutes, 6.6% 60 minutes or more (2000)

INGRAM (city). Covers a land area of 1.276 square miles and a water
area of 0 square miles. Located at 30.07° N. Lat; 99.23° W. Long.
Elevation is 1,732 feet.
History: Established 1883; new section built after flood of 1936.
Population: 1,451 (1990); 1,740 (2000); 1,887 (2010); 1,961 (2015
projected); Race: 93.1% White, 0.2% Black, 1.1% Asian, 5.7% Other,
20.7% Hispanic of any race (2010); Density: 1,479.4 persons per square

mile (2010); Average household size: 2.60 (2010); Median age: 37.9
(2010); Males per 100 females: 93.9 (2010); Marriage status: 19.9% never
married, 61.9% now married, 8.3% widowed, 10.0% divorced (2005-2009
5-year est.); Foreign born: 4.3% (2005-2009 5-year est.); Ancestry
(includes multiple ancestries): 23.1% German, 22.8% Irish, 22.5% English,
5.1% French, 4.0% Dutch (2005-2009 5-year est.).
Economy: Employment by occupation: 6.7% management, 12.7%
professional, 28.4% services, 28.2% sales, 0.5% farming, 13.6%
construction, 9.8% production (2005-2009 5-year est.).
Income: Per capita income: $20,502 (2010); Median household income:
$45,170 (2010); Average household income: $53,086 (2010); Percent of
households with income of $100,000 or more: 11.3% (2010); Poverty rate:
23.9% (2005-2009 5-year est.).
Taxes: Total city taxes per capita: $251 (2007); City property taxes per
capita: $102 (2007).
Education: Percent of population age 25 and over with: High school
diploma (including GED) or higher: 80.1% (2010); Bachelor's degree or
higher: 14.1% (2010); Master's degree or higher: 5.1% (2010).

School District(s)
Big Springs Charter School (01-12)
    2009-10 Enrollment: 125 . . . . (830) 232-7101
Ingram ISD (PK-12)
    2009-10 Enrollment: 1,139 . . . . (830) 367-5517
Housing: Homeownership rate: 82.3% (2010); Median home value:
$85,658 (2010); Median contract rent: $528 per month (2005-2009 5-year
est.); Median year structure built: 1980 (2005-2009 5-year est.).
Safety: Violent crime rate: 57.1 per 10,000 population; Property crime rate:
321.6 per 10,000 population (2009).
Transportation: Commute to work: 95.5% car, 0.0% public transportation,
2.5% walk, 2.1% work from home (2005-2009 5-year est.); Travel time to
work: 39.2% less than 15 minutes, 37.5% 15 to 30 minutes, 10.5% 30 to 45
minutes, 9.0% 45 to 60 minutes, 3.9% 60 minutes or more (2005-2009
5-year est.)
Additional Information Contacts
West Kerr County Chamber of Commerce . . . . (830) 367-4322
    http://www.wkcc.com

KERRVILLE (city). County seat. Covers a land area of 16.708 square
miles and a water area of 0.232 square miles. Located at 30.04° N. Lat;
99.14° W. Long. Elevation is 1,637 feet.
History: Kerrville developed as a recreation and health resort, founded on
the Guadalupe River and noted for its clear air.
Population: 17,146 (1990); 20,425 (2000); 23,047 (2010); 24,267 (2015
projected); Race: 85.6% White, 2.4% Black, 0.6% Asian, 11.4% Other,
24.8% Hispanic of any race (2010); Density: 1,379.4 persons per square
mile (2010); Average household size: 2.23 (2010); Median age: 44.4
(2010); Males per 100 females: 88.8 (2010); Marriage status: 25.0% never
married, 50.1% now married, 10.8% widowed, 14.2% divorced (2005-2009
5-year est.); Foreign born: 6.2% (2005-2009 5-year est.); Ancestry
(includes multiple ancestries): 24.0% German, 12.5% English, 10.8% Irish,
5.4% American, 4.6% French (2005-2009 5-year est.).
Economy: Single-family building permits issued: 41 (2010); Multi-family
building permits issued: 0 (2010); Employment by occupation: 11.4%
management, 19.3% professional, 23.4% services, 25.6% sales, 0.1%
farming, 8.0% construction, 12.3% production (2005-2009 5-year est.).
Income: Per capita income: $24,966 (2010); Median household income:
$39,291 (2010); Average household income: $57,185 (2010); Percent of
households with income of $100,000 or more: 13.0% (2010); Poverty rate:
13.8% (2005-2009 5-year est.).
Taxes: Total city taxes per capita: $786 (2007); City property taxes per
capita: $332 (2007).
Education: Percent of population age 25 and over with: High school
diploma (including GED) or higher: 85.1% (2010); Bachelor's degree or
higher: 25.0% (2010); Master's degree or higher: 9.5% (2010).

School District(s)
Kerrville ISD (PK-12)
    2009-10 Enrollment: 4,884 . . . . (830) 257-2200

Four-year College(s)
Schreiner University (Private, Not-for-profit, Presbyterian Church (USA))
    Fall 2009 Enrollment: 1,049 . . . . (830) 896-5411
    2010-11 Tuition: In-state $19,548; Out-of-state $19,548

Vocational/Technical School(s)
Conlee's College of Cosmetology (Private, For-profit)
    Fall 2009 Enrollment: 83 . . . . (830) 896-2380
    2010-11 Tuition: $8,725

Housing: Homeownership rate: 67.0% (2010); Median home value: $122,148 (2010); Median contract rent: $589 per month (2005-2009 5-year est.); Median year structure built: 1977 (2005-2009 5-year est.).
Hospitals: Kerrville State Hospital; Kerrville Veterans Affairs Medical Center (226 beds); Sid Peterson Memorial Hospital (148 beds)
Safety: Violent crime rate: 22.5 per 10,000 population; Property crime rate: 378.1 per 10,000 population (2009).
Newspapers: Kerrville Daily Times (Local news; Circulation 10,000)
Transportation: Commute to work: 91.5% car, 0.3% public transportation, 2.9% walk, 4.8% work from home (2005-2009 5-year est.); Travel time to work: 57.8% less than 15 minutes, 31.4% 15 to 30 minutes, 6.1% 30 to 45 minutes, 1.7% 45 to 60 minutes, 3.0% 60 minutes or more (2005-2009 5-year est.)
Airports: Kerrville Municipal/Louis Schreiner Field (general aviation)
Additional Information Contacts
City of Kerrville. . . . . (830) 257-8000
   http://www.kerrville.org
Kerrville Area Chamber of Commerce . . . . (830) 896-1155
   http://www.kerrvilletx.com

MOUNTAIN HOME (unincorporated postal area, zip code 78058).
Covers a land area of 457.038 square miles and a water area of 0.026 square miles. Located at 30.07° N. Lat; 99.69° W. Long. Elevation is 1,909 feet.
Population: 608 (2000); Race: 91.2% White, 0.0% Black, 0.0% Asian, 8.8% Other, 18.5% Hispanic of any race (2000); Density: 1.3 persons per square mile (2000); Age: 25.9% under 18, 9.2% over 64 (2000); Marriage status: 16.6% never married, 69.4% now married, 4.7% widowed, 9.4% divorced (2000); Foreign born: 9.6% (2000); Ancestry (includes multiple ancestries): 20.3% German, 15.9% English, 15.5% Irish, 8.6% American (2000).
Economy: Employment by occupation: 19.1% management, 29.8% professional, 8.8% services, 7.9% sales, 12.1% farming, 12.6% construction, 9.8% production (2000).
Income: Per capita income: $18,923 (2000); Median household income: $35,385 (2000); Poverty rate: 179.1% (2000).
Education: Percent of population age 25 and over with: High school diploma (including GED) or higher: 81.1% (2000); Bachelor's degree or higher: 27.8% (2000).

School District(s)
Divide ISD (PK-06)
   2009-10 Enrollment: 28 . . . . (830) 640-3322
University of Texas University Charter School (KG-12)
   2009-10 Enrollment: 907 . . . . (512) 471-5652
Housing: Homeownership rate: 72.6% (2000); Median home value: $128,300 (2000); Median contract rent: $208 per month (2000); Median year structure built: 1983 (2000).
Transportation: Commute to work: 71.6% car, 0.0% public transportation, 8.8% walk, 19.5% work from home (2000); Travel time to work: 50.3% less than 15 minutes, 2.3% 15 to 30 minutes, 35.3% 30 to 45 minutes, 9.2% 45 to 60 minutes, 2.9% 60 minutes or more (2000)

Kimble County

Located in west central Texas, on the Edwards Plateau; drained by the North Llano and South Llano Rivers. Covers a land area of 1,250.70 square miles, a water area of 0.23 square miles, and is located in the Central Time Zone at 30.51° N. Lat., 99.74° W. Long. The county was founded in 1858. County seat is Junction.

Weather Station: Junction 4 SSW								Elevation: 1,747 feet			
	Jan	Feb	Mar	Apr	May	Jun	Jul	Aug	Sep	Oct	Nov	Dec
High	63	66	73	81	87	92	95	95	89	81	70	62
Low	31	35	43	50	60	67	68	67	61	51	40	31
Precip	0.8	1.4	2.0	1.8	2.7	3.3	1.5	1.7	2.7	2.4	1.6	1.3
Snow	0.6	tr	0.0	tr	0.0	0.0	0.0	0.0	0.0	0.0	0.2	tr

High and Low temperatures in degrees Fahrenheit; Precipitation and Snow in inches

Population: 4,122 (1990); 4,468 (2000); 4,584 (2010); 4,631 (2015 projected); Race: 88.1% White, 0.3% Black, 0.4% Asian, 11.2% Other, 25.2% Hispanic of any race (2010); Density: 3.7 persons per square mile (2010); Average household size: 2.30 (2010); Median age: 43.7 (2010); Males per 100 females: 95.6 (2010).
Religion: Five largest groups: 31.0% Southern Baptist Convention, 7.8% Catholic Church, 6.2% Churches of Christ, 5.8% The United Methodist Church, 3.0% Presbyterian Church (U.S.A.) (2000).

Economy: Unemployment rate: 8.3% (June 2011); Total civilian labor force: 1,997 (June 2011); Leading industries: 25.9% retail trade; 18.2% manufacturing; 17.3% accommodation & food services (2009); Farms: 639 totaling 619,961 acres (2007); Companies that employ 500 or more persons: 0 (2009); Companies that employ 100 to 499 persons: 0 (2009); Companies that employ less than 100 persons: 150 (2009); Black-owned businesses: n/a (2007); Hispanic-owned businesses: n/a (2007); Asian-owned businesses: n/a (2007); Women-owned businesses: 145 (2007); Retail sales per capita: $11,864 (2010). Single-family building permits issued: 1 (2010); Multi-family building permits issued: 0 (2010).
Income: Per capita income: $22,868 (2010); Median household income: $39,111 (2010); Average household income: $52,685 (2010); Percent of households with income of $100,000 or more: 9.4% (2010); Poverty rate: 18.5% (2009); Bankruptcy rate: 0.43% (2010).
Taxes: Total county taxes per capita: $309 (2007); County property taxes per capita: $202 (2007).
Education: Percent of population age 25 and over with: High school diploma (including GED) or higher: 77.4% (2010); Bachelor's degree or higher: 18.9% (2010); Master's degree or higher: 5.9% (2010).
Housing: Homeownership rate: 71.6% (2010); Median home value: $79,752 (2010); Median contract rent: $364 per month (2005-2009 5-year est.); Median year structure built: 1967 (2005-2009 5-year est.)
Health: Birth rate: 101.3 per 10,000 population (2009); Death rate: 119.0 per 10,000 population (2009); Age-adjusted cancer mortality rate: 206.2 (Unreliable) deaths per 100,000 population (2007); Number of physicians: 6.8 per 10,000 population (2008); Hospital beds: 33.9 per 10,000 population (2007); Hospital admissions: 350.3 per 10,000 population (2007).
Elections: 2008 Presidential election results: 18.6% Obama, 80.7% McCain, 0.1% Nader
Additional Information Contacts
Kimble County Government. . . . . (915) 446-2724
   http://www.co.kimble.tx.us/ips/cms
Junction-Kimble County Chamber of Commerce. . . . . (325) 446-3190
   http://www.junctiontexas.net

Kimble County Communities

JUNCTION (city). County seat. Covers a land area of 2.286 square miles and a water area of 0.007 square miles. Located at 30.49° N. Lat; 99.77° W. Long. Elevation is 1,703 feet.
History: Junction was the site, in 1877, of a major round-up of men by the Texas Rangers. After bringing in everyone they could find in the arroyos and hills, the Rangers sorted out the "bad guys" from the good, and escorted the chosen ones to justice.
Population: 2,654 (1990); 2,618 (2000); 2,582 (2010); 2,571 (2015 projected); Race: 83.5% White, 0.0% Black, 0.7% Asian, 15.8% Other, 33.6% Hispanic of any race (2010); Density: 1,129.3 persons per square mile (2010); Average household size: 2.42 (2010); Median age: 37.7 (2010); Males per 100 females: 91.3 (2010); Marriage status: 20.9% never married, 59.7% now married, 8.2% widowed, 11.2% divorced (2005-2009 5-year est.); Foreign born: 12.2% (2005-2009 5-year est.); Ancestry (includes multiple ancestries): 21.0% American, 11.2% German, 9.8% Irish, 9.8% English, 2.5% French (2005-2009 5-year est.).
Economy: Single-family building permits issued: 1 (2010); Multi-family building permits issued: 0 (2010); Employment by occupation: 6.5% management, 11.5% professional, 27.1% services, 16.1% sales, 7.3% farming, 22.8% construction, 8.6% production (2005-2009 5-year est.).
Income: Per capita income: $19,529 (2010); Median household income: $34,704 (2010); Average household income: $47,125 (2010); Percent of households with income of $100,000 or more: 7.0% (2010); Poverty rate: 18.1% (2005-2009 5-year est.).
Taxes: Total city taxes per capita: $330 (2007); City property taxes per capita: $0 (2007).
Education: Percent of population age 25 and over with: High school diploma (including GED) or higher: 72.7% (2010); Bachelor's degree or higher: 13.2% (2010); Master's degree or higher: 5.1% (2010).
School District(s)
Junction ISD (PK-12)
   2009-10 Enrollment: 662 . . . . (325) 446-3510
Housing: Homeownership rate: 67.2% (2010); Median home value: $60,631 (2010); Median contract rent: $362 per month (2005-2009 5-year est.); Median year structure built: 1962 (2005-2009 5-year est.).
Hospitals: Kimble Hospital (15 beds)

Safety: Violent crime rate: 43.2 per 10,000 population; Property crime rate: 282.8 per 10,000 population (2009).
Newspapers: Eagle (Community news; Circulation 2,700)
Transportation: Commute to work: 94.0% car, 0.0% public transportation, 3.0% walk, 2.4% work from home (2005-2009 5-year est.); Travel time to work: 75.4% less than 15 minutes, 10.5% 15 to 30 minutes, 11.3% 30 to 45 minutes, 2.2% 45 to 60 minutes, 0.6% 60 minutes or more (2005-2009 5-year est.)
Additional Information Contacts
Junction-Kimble County Chamber of Commerce . . . . (325) 446-3190
    http://www.junctiontexas.net

LONDON (unincorporated postal area, zip code 76854). Covers a land area of 106.980 square miles and a water area of 0 square miles. Located at 30.64° N. Lat; 99.54° W. Long. Elevation is 1,699 feet.
Population: 322 (2000); Race: 89.7% White, 7.1% Black, 0.0% Asian, 3.2% Other, 18.4% Hispanic of any race (2000); Density: 3.0 persons per square mile (2000); Age: 19.0% under 18, 28.1% over 64 (2000); Marriage status: 15.3% never married, 65.7% now married, 8.8% widowed, 10.2% divorced (2000); Foreign born: 0.0% (2000); Ancestry (includes multiple ancestries): 17.1% German, 16.1% Irish, 10.6% English, 7.1% American (2000).
Economy: Employment by occupation: 17.6% management, 5.6% professional, 27.2% services, 28.0% sales, 5.6% farming, 4.0% construction, 12.0% production (2000).
Income: Per capita income: $12,226 (2000); Median household income: $21,591 (2000); Poverty rate: 179.1% (2000).
Education: Percent of population age 25 and over with: High school diploma (including GED) or higher: 69.4% (2000); Bachelor's degree or higher: 5.2% (2000).
Housing: Homeownership rate: 83.2% (2000); Median home value: $23,400 (2000); Median contract rent: $206 per month (2000); Median year structure built: 1962 (2000).
Transportation: Commute to work: 91.7% car, 0.0% public transportation, 0.0% walk, 0.0% work from home (2000); Travel time to work: 2.5% less than 15 minutes, 23.3% 15 to 30 minutes, 31.7% 30 to 45 minutes, 10.8% 45 to 60 minutes, 31.7% 60 minutes or more (2000)

ROOSEVELT (unincorporated postal area, zip code 76874). Covers a land area of 65.796 square miles and a water area of 0 square miles. Located at 30.48° N. Lat; 100.11° W. Long. Elevation is 1,909 feet.
Population: 98 (2000); Race: 100.0% White, 0.0% Black, 0.0% Asian, 0.0% Other, 0.0% Hispanic of any race (2000); Density: 1.5 persons per square mile (2000); Age: 17.0% under 18, 10.0% over 64 (2000); Marriage status: 8.4% never married, 66.3% now married, 12.0% widowed, 13.3% divorced (2000); Foreign born: 0.0% (2000); Ancestry (includes multiple ancestries): 59.0% German, 33.0% English, 20.0% Irish, 17.0% Welsh, 5.0% French (2000).
Economy: Employment by occupation: 9.1% management, 10.9% professional, 0.0% services, 61.8% sales, 7.3% farming, 10.9% construction, 0.0% production (2000).
Income: Per capita income: $14,671 (2000); Median household income: $30,577 (2000); Poverty rate: 179.1% (2000).
Education: Percent of population age 25 and over with: High school diploma (including GED) or higher: 100.0% (2000); Bachelor's degree or higher: 51.8% (2000).
Housing: Homeownership rate: 86.0% (2000); Median home value: n/a (2000); Median contract rent: n/a per month (2000); Median year structure built: 1973 (2000).
Transportation: Commute to work: 90.9% car, 0.0% public transportation, 0.0% walk, 9.1% work from home (2000); Travel time to work: 76.0% less than 15 minutes, 0.0% 15 to 30 minutes, 24.0% 30 to 45 minutes, 0.0% 45 to 60 minutes, 0.0% 60 minutes or more (2000)

King County

Located in northwestern Texas; rolling plains area, drained by tributaries of the Wichita and Brazos Rivers. Covers a land area of 912.29 square miles, a water area of 1.04 square miles, and is located in the Central Time Zone at 33.60° N. Lat., 100.25° W. Long. The county was founded in 1850. County seat is Guthrie.

Weather Station: Guthrie										Elevation: 1,740 feet		
	Jan	Feb	Mar	Apr	May	Jun	Jul	Aug	Sep	Oct	Nov	Dec
High	56	60	68	78	86	92	97	96	88	78	66	56
Low	26	30	37	45	56	65	69	68	60	48	36	27
Precip	1.1	1.4	1.5	1.8	3.4	3.7	2.1	2.7	2.6	2.5	1.3	1.2
Snow	1.2	0.6	0.1	tr	0.0	0.0	0.0	0.0	0.0	tr	0.8	0.6

High and Low temperatures in degrees Fahrenheit; Precipitation and Snow in inches

Population: 354 (1990); 356 (2000); 315 (2010); 294 (2015 projected); Race: 92.4% White, 0.0% Black, 0.0% Asian, 7.6% Other, 14.9% Hispanic of any race (2010); Density: 0.3 persons per square mile (2010); Average household size: 2.73 (2010); Median age: 39.2 (2010); Males per 100 females: 120.3 (2010).
Religion: Largest group: 50.6% Southern Baptist Convention (2000).
Economy: Unemployment rate: 7.1% (June 2011); Total civilian labor force: 196 (June 2011); Leading industries: Farms: 64 totaling 542,166 acres (2007); Companies that employ 500 or more persons: n/a (2009); Companies that employ 100 to 499 persons: n/a (2009); Companies that employ less than 100 persons: n/a (2009); Black-owned businesses: n/a (2007); Hispanic-owned businesses: n/a (2007); Asian-owned businesses: n/a (2007); Women-owned businesses: n/a (2007); Retail sales per capita: $580 (2010). Single-family building permits issued: n/a (2010); Multi-family building permits issued: n/a (2010).
Income: Per capita income: $14,564 (2010); Median household income: $39,167 (2010); Average household income: $40,479 (2010); Percent of households with income of $100,000 or more: 1.1% (2010); Poverty rate: 15.4% (2009); Bankruptcy rate: n/a (2010).
Taxes: Total county taxes per capita: $8,610 (2007); County property taxes per capita: $8,606 (2007).
Education: Percent of population age 25 and over with: High school diploma (including GED) or higher: 81.1% (2010); Bachelor's degree or higher: 25.2% (2010); Master's degree or higher: 3.4% (2010).
Housing: Homeownership rate: 33.0% (2010); Median home value: $23,333 (2010); Median contract rent: $441 per month (2005-2009 5-year est.); Median year structure built: 1967 (2005-2009 5-year est.)
Health: Birth rate: 69.9 per 10,000 population (2009); Death rate: 0.0 per 10,000 population (2009); Age-adjusted cancer mortality rate: n/a deaths per 100,000 population (2007); Number of physicians: 0.0 per 10,000 population (2008); Hospital beds: 0.0 per 10,000 population (2007); Hospital admissions: 0.0 per 10,000 population (2007).
Elections: 2008 Presidential election results: 4.9% Obama, 92.6% McCain, 0.0% Nader
Additional Information Contacts
King County Government . . . . (806) 596-4411
    http://www.kingcountytx.com

King County Communities

DUMONT (unincorporated postal area, zip code 79232). Covers a land area of 71.545 square miles and a water area of 0.003 square miles. Located at 33.77° N. Lat; 100.61° W. Long. Elevation is 2,051 feet.
Population: 42 (2000); Race: 93.6% White, 0.0% Black, 0.0% Asian, 6.4% Other, 6.4% Hispanic of any race (2000); Density: 0.6 persons per square mile (2000); Age: 14.9% under 18, 23.4% over 64 (2000); Marriage status: 4.9% never married, 90.2% now married, 4.9% widowed, 0.0% divorced (2000); Foreign born: 0.0% (2000); Ancestry (includes multiple ancestries): 12.8% American (2000).
Economy: Employment by occupation: 38.5% management, 0.0% professional, 23.1% services, 0.0% sales, 15.4% farming, 7.7% construction, 15.4% production (2000).
Income: Per capita income: $9,432 (2000); Median household income: $16,000 (2000); Poverty rate: 179.1% (2000).
Education: Percent of population age 25 and over with: High school diploma (including GED) or higher: 86.1% (2000); Bachelor's degree or higher: 0.0% (2000).
Housing: Homeownership rate: 90.5% (2000); Median home value: n/a (2000); Median contract rent: n/a per month (2000); Median year structure built: 1963 (2000).
Transportation: Commute to work: 69.2% car, 15.4% public transportation, 0.0% walk, 15.4% work from home (2000); Travel time to work: 36.4% less than 15 minutes, 9.1% 15 to 30 minutes, 9.1% 30 to 45 minutes, 27.3% 45 to 60 minutes, 18.2% 60 minutes or more (2000)

Kinney County

Located in southwestern Texas, on the south edge of the Edwards Plateau; bounded on the southwest by the Rio Grande and the Mexican border; drained by tributaries of the Nueces River and the Rio Grande. Covers a land area of 1,363.44 square miles, a water area of 1.87 square miles, and is located in the Central Time Zone at 29.30° N. Lat., 100.43° W. Long. The county was founded in 1876. County seat is Brackettville.

Weather Station: Brackettville   Elevation: 1,118 feet

	Jan	Feb	Mar	Apr	May	Jun	Jul	Aug	Sep	Oct	Nov	Dec
High	na	70	76	83	88	93	95	96	91	83	na	65
Low	38	43	50	56	65	71	73	73	67	58	48	40
Precip	0.8	0.9	1.4	1.7	3.2	3.1	2.1	1.9	3.1	2.2	1.5	0.9
Snow	0.5	tr	0.0	0.0	0.0	0.0	0.0	0.0	0.0	0.0	0.0	0.0

High and Low temperatures in degrees Fahrenheit; Precipitation and Snow in inches

Population: 3,119 (1990); 3,379 (2000); 3,247 (2010); 3,177 (2015 projected); Race: 74.2% White, 2.7% Black, 0.5% Asian, 22.5% Other, 50.9% Hispanic of any race (2010); Density: 2.4 persons per square mile (2010); Average household size: 2.53 (2010); Median age: 44.7 (2010); Males per 100 females: 100.3 (2010).

Religion: Five largest groups: 52.1% Catholic Church, 13.0% Southern Baptist Convention, 3.3% The United Methodist Church, 3.0% Churches of Christ, 2.0% Evangelical Lutheran Church in America (2000).

Economy: Unemployment rate: 8.9% (June 2011); Total civilian labor force: 1,474 (June 2011); Leading industries: Farms: 220 totaling 601,224 acres (2007); Companies that employ 500 or more persons: 0 (2009); Companies that employ 100 to 499 persons: 0 (2009); Companies that employ less than 100 persons: 36 (2009); Black-owned businesses: n/a (2007); Hispanic-owned businesses: n/a (2007); Asian-owned businesses: n/a (2007); Women-owned businesses: 41 (2007); Retail sales per capita: $1,797 (2010). Single-family building permits issued: 0 (2010); Multi-family building permits issued: 0 (2010).

Income: Per capita income: $21,085 (2010); Median household income: $40,012 (2010); Average household income: $53,769 (2010); Percent of households with income of $100,000 or more: 11.9% (2010); Poverty rate: 20.7% (2009); Bankruptcy rate: 0.28% (2010).

Taxes: Total county taxes per capita: $394 (2007); County property taxes per capita: $322 (2007).

Education: Percent of population age 25 and over with: High school diploma (including GED) or higher: 72.5% (2010); Bachelor's degree or higher: 20.0% (2010); Master's degree or higher: 5.3% (2010).

Housing: Homeownership rate: 75.7% (2010); Median home value: $59,597 (2010); Median contract rent: $203 per month (2005-2009 5-year est.); Median year structure built: 1978 (2005-2009 5-year est.)

Health: Birth rate: 106.9 per 10,000 population (2009); Death rate: 61.1 per 10,000 population (2009); Age-adjusted cancer mortality rate: Suppressed deaths per 100,000 population (2007); Number of physicians: 0.0 per 10,000 population (2008); Hospital beds: 0.0 per 10,000 population (2007); Hospital admissions: 0.0 per 10,000 population (2007).

Elections: 2008 Presidential election results: 40.8% Obama, 58.5% McCain, 0.0% Nader

Additional Information Contacts

Kinney County Government . . . . (830) 563-2401
    http://www.co.kinney.tx.us/ips/cms
Brackettville Chamber of Commerce . . . . (830) 563-2466

Kinney County Communities

BRACKETTVILLE (city). County seat. Covers a land area of 3.170 square miles and a water area of 0 square miles. Located at 29.31° N. Lat; 100.41° W. Long. Elevation is 1,106 feet.

History: Brackettville grew up around a U.S. Army post founded in 1852 as Fort Riley, and later called Fort Clark. Officers once stationed here included Robert E. Lee, George S. Patton, Jr., and J.M. Wainwright.

Population: 1,740 (1990); 1,876 (2000); 1,758 (2010); 1,700 (2015 projected); Race: 62.9% White, 3.6% Black, 0.4% Asian, 33.1% Other, 75.8% Hispanic of any race (2010); Density: 554.6 persons per square mile (2010); Average household size: 2.97 (2010); Median age: 33.8 (2010); Males per 100 females: 101.1 (2010); Marriage status: 28.2% never married, 55.7% now married, 7.3% widowed, 8.8% divorced (2005-2009 5-year est.); Foreign born: 17.3% (2005-2009 5-year est.); Ancestry (includes multiple ancestries): 14.6% American, 4.2% English, 4.2% Scotch-Irish, 3.4% German, 1.9% Dutch (2005-2009 5-year est.).

Economy: Single-family building permits issued: 0 (2010); Multi-family building permits issued: 0 (2010); Employment by occupation: 15.2% management, 4.7% professional, 28.9% services, 15.1% sales, 9.9% farming, 17.1% construction, 9.2% production (2005-2009 5-year est.).

Income: Per capita income: $11,456 (2010); Median household income: $25,854 (2010); Average household income: $34,658 (2010); Percent of households with income of $100,000 or more: 3.4% (2010); Poverty rate: 39.3% (2005-2009 5-year est.).

Taxes: Total city taxes per capita: $208 (2007); City property taxes per capita: $166 (2007).

Education: Percent of population age 25 and over with: High school diploma (including GED) or higher: 53.9% (2010); Bachelor's degree or higher: 8.1% (2010); Master's degree or higher: 1.9% (2010).

School District(s)

Brackett ISD (PK-12)
    2009-10 Enrollment: 597 . . . . (830) 563-2491

Housing: Homeownership rate: 71.7% (2010); Median home value: $38,411 (2010); Median contract rent: $203 per month (2005-2009 5-year est.); Median year structure built: 1965 (2005-2009 5-year est.).

Transportation: Commute to work: 92.9% car, 0.0% public transportation, 2.3% walk, 0.0% work from home (2005-2009 5-year est.); Travel time to work: 66.6% less than 15 minutes, 14.1% 15 to 30 minutes, 12.5% 30 to 45 minutes, 2.3% 45 to 60 minutes, 4.5% 60 minutes or more (2005-2009 5-year est.)

Additional Information Contacts

Brackettville Chamber of Commerce . . . . (830) 563-2466

SPOFFORD (city). Covers a land area of 0.251 square miles and a water area of 0 square miles. Located at 29.17° N. Lat; 100.41° W. Long. Elevation is 1,010 feet.

Population: 68 (1990); 75 (2000); 71 (2010); 71 (2015 projected); Race: 88.7% White, 1.4% Black, 0.0% Asian, 9.9% Other, 19.7% Hispanic of any race (2010); Density: 282.9 persons per square mile (2010); Average household size: 2.15 (2010); Median age: 56.0 (2010); Males per 100 females: 108.8 (2010); Marriage status: 27.6% never married, 68.1% now married, 4.3% widowed, 0.0% divorced (2005-2009 5-year est.); Foreign born: 10.0% (2005-2009 5-year est.); Ancestry (includes multiple ancestries): 17.9% American, 15.7% French, 10.0% German, 5.0% Irish, 2.9% Welsh (2005-2009 5-year est.).

Economy: Employment by occupation: 8.0% management, 0.0% professional, 64.0% services, 16.0% sales, 6.0% farming, 6.0% construction, 0.0% production (2005-2009 5-year est.).

Income: Per capita income: $33,232 (2010); Median household income: $54,688 (2010); Average household income: $67,652 (2010); Percent of households with income of $100,000 or more: 18.2% (2010); Poverty rate: 23.6% (2005-2009 5-year est.).

Taxes: Total city taxes per capita: $560 (2007); City property taxes per capita: $293 (2007).

Education: Percent of population age 25 and over with: High school diploma (including GED) or higher: 91.1% (2010); Bachelor's degree or higher: 32.1% (2010); Master's degree or higher: 8.9% (2010).

Housing: Homeownership rate: 78.8% (2010); Median home value: $70,000 (2010); Median contract rent: n/a per month (2005-2009 5-year est.); Median year structure built: 1957 (2005-2009 5-year est.).

Transportation: Commute to work: 95.7% car, 0.0% public transportation, 0.0% walk, 0.0% work from home (2005-2009 5-year est.); Travel time to work: 39.1% less than 15 minutes, 50.0% 15 to 30 minutes, 0.0% 30 to 45 minutes, 0.0% 45 to 60 minutes, 10.9% 60 minutes or more (2005-2009 5-year est.)

Kleberg County

Located in south Texas, on the Gulf Coast, protected by Padre Island and indented by Baffin Bay. Covers a land area of 870.97 square miles, a water area of 219.32 square miles, and is located in the Central Time Zone at 27.46° N. Lat., 97.85° W. Long. The county was founded in 1913. County seat is Kingsville.

Kleberg County is part of the Kingsville, TX Micropolitan Statistical Area. The entire metro area includes: Kenedy County, TX; Kleberg County, TX

Weather Station: Kingsville   Elevation: 59 feet

	Jan	Feb	Mar	Apr	May	Jun	Jul	Aug	Sep	Oct	Nov	Dec
High	69	73	79	85	90	94	96	97	92	86	78	70
Low	46	50	55	62	69	73	74	75	71	63	55	46
Precip	1.5	1.8	1.2	1.5	3.5	3.2	2.5	3.2	5.0	3.2	1.9	1.2
Snow	tr	tr	0.0	0.0	0.0	0.0	0.0	0.0	0.0	0.0	0.0	0.0

High and Low temperatures in degrees Fahrenheit; Precipitation and Snow in inches

Population: 30,274 (1990); 31,549 (2000); 30,613 (2010); 30,103 (2015 projected); Race: 70.0% White, 3.5% Black, 2.1% Asian, 24.4% Other, 68.7% Hispanic of any race (2010); Density: 35.1 persons per square mile (2010); Average household size: 2.71 (2010); Median age: 30.3 (2010); Males per 100 females: 101.3 (2010).
Religion: Five largest groups: 13.8% Catholic Church, 12.4% Southern Baptist Convention, 3.1% The United Methodist Church, 2.2% Assemblies of God, 0.9% Presbyterian Church (U.S.A.) (2000).
Economy: Unemployment rate: 8.0% (June 2011); Total civilian labor force: 17,210 (June 2011); Leading industries: 25.3% retail trade; 19.5% health care and social assistance; 17.8% accommodation & food services (2009); Farms: 349 totaling 498,417 acres (2007); Companies that employ 500 or more persons: 0 (2009); Companies that employ 100 to 499 persons: 10 (2009); Companies that employ less than 100 persons: 548 (2009); Black-owned businesses: n/a (2007); Hispanic-owned businesses: 923 (2007); Asian-owned businesses: n/a (2007); Women-owned businesses: n/a (2007); Retail sales per capita: $14,358 (2010). Single-family building permits issued: 19 (2010); Multi-family building permits issued: 0 (2010).
Income: Per capita income: $16,998 (2010); Median household income: $35,466 (2010); Average household income: $47,550 (2010); Percent of households with income of $100,000 or more: 10.0% (2010); Poverty rate: 22.3% (2009); Bankruptcy rate: 1.11% (2010).
Taxes: Total county taxes per capita: $261 (2007); County property taxes per capita: $177 (2007).
Education: Percent of population age 25 and over with: High school diploma (including GED) or higher: 74.8% (2010); Bachelor's degree or higher: 17.9% (2010); Master's degree or higher: 5.9% (2010).
Housing: Homeownership rate: 55.8% (2010); Median home value: $67,516 (2010); Median contract rent: $461 per month (2005-2009 5-year est.); Median year structure built: 1968 (2005-2009 5-year est.)
Health: Birth rate: 172.0 per 10,000 population (2009); Death rate: 61.7 per 10,000 population (2009); Age-adjusted cancer mortality rate: 153.5 deaths per 100,000 population (2007); Number of physicians: 8.1 per 10,000 population (2008); Hospital beds: 32.6 per 10,000 population (2007); Hospital admissions: 1,434.5 per 10,000 population (2007).
Environment: Air Quality Index: 81.7% good, 18.3% moderate, 0.0% unhealthy for sensitive individuals, 0.0% unhealthy (percent of days in 2008)
Elections: 2008 Presidential election results: 53.2% Obama, 46.0% McCain, 0.1% Nader
Additional Information Contacts
Kleberg County Government . . . . (361) 595-8585
   http://www.co.kleberg.tx.us/ips/cms
City of Kingsville. . . . . (361) 595-8002
   http://www.cityofkingsville.com
Kingsville Chamber of Commerce . . . . (361) 592-6438
   http://www.kingsville.org

Kleberg County Communities

KINGSVILLE (city). County seat. Covers a land area of 13.833 square miles and a water area of 0.034 square miles. Located at 27.51° N. Lat; 97.86° W. Long. Elevation is 59 feet.
History: Kingsville was named for Captain Richard King, who developed the large King Ranch in Kleberg County. The town grew as the center for several large ranches raising Herefords, Shorthorns, and Brahmas. The Texas College of Arts and Industries was established here.
Population: 25,446 (1990); 25,575 (2000); 24,583 (2010); 24,094 (2015 projected); Race: 69.3% White, 4.1% Black, 2.5% Asian, 24.1% Other, 70.5% Hispanic of any race (2010); Density: 1,777.1 persons per square mile (2010); Average household size: 2.67 (2010); Median age: 29.4 (2010); Males per 100 females: 100.5 (2010); Marriage status: 42.0% never married, 43.6% now married, 4.7% widowed, 9.7% divorced (2005-2009 5-year est.); Foreign born: 7.0% (2005-2009 5-year est.); Ancestry (includes multiple ancestries): 6.4% German, 4.5% Irish, 3.7% American, 2.8% English, 0.9% Scottish (2005-2009 5-year est.).

Economy: Unemployment rate: 7.8% (June 2011); Total civilian labor force: 13,712 (June 2011); Single-family building permits issued: 19 (2010); Multi-family building permits issued: 0 (2010); Employment by occupation: 8.6% management, 24.0% professional, 23.2% services, 21.2% sales, 1.0% farming, 12.0% construction, 10.0% production (2005-2009 5-year est.).
Income: Per capita income: $15,637 (2010); Median household income: $32,734 (2010); Average household income: $43,307 (2010); Percent of households with income of $100,000 or more: 7.6% (2010); Poverty rate: 28.8% (2005-2009 5-year est.).
Taxes: Total city taxes per capita: $385 (2007); City property taxes per capita: $169 (2007).
Education: Percent of population age 25 and over with: High school diploma (including GED) or higher: 74.4% (2010); Bachelor's degree or higher: 18.1% (2010); Master's degree or higher: 6.3% (2010).

School District(s)
Kingsville ISD (PK-12)
   2009-10 Enrollment: 3,981 . . . . (361) 592-3387
Ricardo ISD (PK-08)
   2009-10 Enrollment: 617 . . . . (361) 592-6465
Santa Gertrudis ISD (PK-12)
   2009-10 Enrollment: 397 . . . . (361) 592-3937

Four-year College(s)
Texas A & M University-Kingsville (Public)
   Fall 2009 Enrollment: 8,194. . . . . (361) 593-2111
   2010-11 Tuition: In-state $6,346; Out-of-state $13,426
Housing: Homeownership rate: 50.9% (2010); Median home value: $64,636 (2010); Median contract rent: $458 per month (2005-2009 5-year est.); Median year structure built: 1965 (2005-2009 5-year est.).
Hospitals: Christus Spohn Hospital Kleberg (100 beds)
Safety: Violent crime rate: 86.9 per 10,000 population; Property crime rate: 529.4 per 10,000 population (2009).
Newspapers: Kingsville Record & Bishop News (Local news; Circulation 7,000)
Transportation: Commute to work: 90.7% car, 0.0% public transportation, 3.9% walk, 1.2% work from home (2005-2009 5-year est.); Travel time to work: 62.5% less than 15 minutes, 14.9% 15 to 30 minutes, 12.2% 30 to 45 minutes, 4.5% 45 to 60 minutes, 5.9% 60 minutes or more (2005-2009 5-year est.)
Additional Information Contacts
City of Kingsville. . . . . (361) 595-8002
   http://www.cityofkingsville.com
Kingsville Chamber of Commerce . . . . (361) 592-6438
   http://www.kingsville.org

RIVIERA (unincorporated postal area, zip code 78379). Covers a land area of 49.515 square miles and a water area of 0.094 square miles. Located at 27.29° N. Lat; 97.78° W. Long. Elevation is 43 feet.
Population: 1,384 (2000); Race: 75.1% White, 0.1% Black, 0.4% Asian, 24.4% Other, 54.9% Hispanic of any race (2000); Density: 28.0 persons per square mile (2000); Age: 28.6% under 18, 15.2% over 64 (2000); Marriage status: 22.8% never married, 58.9% now married, 8.3% widowed, 9.9% divorced (2000); Foreign born: 7.0% (2000); Ancestry (includes multiple ancestries): 13.2% German, 8.1% Irish, 5.8% English, 4.5% American (2000).
Economy: Employment by occupation: 10.6% management, 14.8% professional, 20.3% services, 18.8% sales, 11.8% farming, 13.1% construction, 10.6% production (2000).
Income: Per capita income: $15,425 (2000); Median household income: $30,750 (2000); Poverty rate: 179.1% (2000).
Education: Percent of population age 25 and over with: High school diploma (including GED) or higher: 63.9% (2000); Bachelor's degree or higher: 14.6% (2000).

School District(s)
Riviera ISD (PK-12)
   2009-10 Enrollment: 475 . . . . (361) 296-3101
Housing: Homeownership rate: 81.6% (2000); Median home value: $40,000 (2000); Median contract rent: $306 per month (2000); Median year structure built: 1975 (2000).
Transportation: Commute to work: 92.4% car, 0.0% public transportation, 2.3% walk, 4.2% work from home (2000); Travel time to work: 32.3% less than 15 minutes, 41.3% 15 to 30 minutes, 13.2% 30 to 45 minutes, 4.6% 45 to 60 minutes, 8.6% 60 minutes or more (2000)

Knox County

Located in north Texas; plains area, drained by the Brazos River, and North and South Forks of the Wichita River. Covers a land area of 849.00 square miles, a water area of 6.43 square miles, and is located in the Central Time Zone at 33.53° N. Lat., 99.71° W. Long. The county was founded in 1858. County seat is Benjamin.

Weather Station: Munday   Elevation: 1,479 feet

	Jan	Feb	Mar	Apr	May	Jun	Jul	Aug	Sep	Oct	Nov	Dec
High	58	62	70	80	87	93	98	97	89	80	68	58
Low	30	34	41	50	60	68	72	71	63	52	41	32
Precip	1.1	1.7	1.9	1.9	3.9	4.0	1.5	2.1	2.9	2.5	1.5	1.4
Snow	0.8	0.9	0.2	0.0	0.0	0.0	0.0	0.0	0.0	0.0	1.4	0.4

High and Low temperatures in degrees Fahrenheit; Precipitation and Snow in inches

Weather Station: Truscott 3 W   Elevation: 1,570 feet

	Jan	Feb	Mar	Apr	May	Jun	Jul	Aug	Sep	Oct	Nov	Dec
High	55	59	67	77	85	92	97	96	88	78	66	55
Low	29	32	39	48	59	67	71	70	62	50	39	30
Precip	1.1	1.4	1.8	2.0	3.9	3.5	1.9	2.3	3.0	2.9	1.5	1.1
Snow	0.7	0.2	0.1	0.0	0.0	0.0	0.0	0.0	0.0	0.0	0.2	0.4

High and Low temperatures in degrees Fahrenheit; Precipitation and Snow in inches

Population: 4,837 (1990); 4,253 (2000); 3,501 (2010); 3,316 (2015 projected); Race: 70.6% White, 9.0% Black, 0.5% Asian, 20.0% Other, 26.3% Hispanic of any race (2010); Density: 4.1 persons per square mile (2010); Average household size: 2.40 (2010); Median age: 45.3 (2010); Males per 100 females: 89.7 (2010).
Religion: Five largest groups: 57.3% Southern Baptist Convention, 28.1% Catholic Church, 14.6% The United Methodist Church, 10.2% Churches of Christ, 4.5% International Church of the Foursquare Gospel (2000).
Economy: Unemployment rate: 6.7% (June 2011); Total civilian labor force: 1,788 (June 2011); Leading industries: 25.1% health care and social assistance; 16.9% retail trade; 13.9% wholesale trade (2009); Farms: 219 totaling 493,464 acres (2007); Companies that employ 500 or more persons: 0 (2009); Companies that employ 100 to 499 persons: 0 (2009); Companies that employ less than 100 persons: 113 (2009); Black-owned businesses: n/a (2007); Hispanic-owned businesses: n/a (2007); Asian-owned businesses: n/a (2007); Women-owned businesses: n/a (2007); Retail sales per capita: $6,797 (2010). Single-family building permits issued: n/a (2010); Multi-family building permits issued: n/a (2010).
Income: Per capita income: $18,324 (2010); Median household income: $33,159 (2010); Average household income: $44,431 (2010); Percent of households with income of $100,000 or more: 7.8% (2010); Poverty rate: 23.1% (2009); Bankruptcy rate: n/a (2010).
Taxes: Total county taxes per capita: $359 (2007); County property taxes per capita: $285 (2007).
Education: Percent of population age 25 and over with: High school diploma (including GED) or higher: 72.7% (2010); Bachelor's degree or higher: 13.7% (2010); Master's degree or higher: 2.8% (2010).
Housing: Homeownership rate: 73.5% (2010); Median home value: $33,523 (2010); Median contract rent: $245 per month (2005-2009 5-year est.); Median year structure built: 1958 (2005-2009 5-year est.)
Health: Birth rate: 126.4 per 10,000 population (2009); Death rate: 144.5 per 10,000 population (2009); Age-adjusted cancer mortality rate: 223.7 (Unreliable) deaths per 100,000 population (2007); Number of physicians: 8.9 per 10,000 population (2008); Hospital beds: 40.4 per 10,000 population (2007); Hospital admissions: 943.2 per 10,000 population (2007).
Elections: 2008 Presidential election results: 26.8% Obama, 72.1% McCain, 0.0% Nader
Additional Information Contacts
Knox County Government . . . . (940) 454-2191
   http://www.knoxcountytexas.org
Knox City Chamber of Commerce . . . . (940) 658-3442
   http://www.knoxcitychamberofcommerce.com
Munday Chamber of Commerce . . . . (940) 422-4540
   http://mundaychamber.googlepages.com

Knox County Communities

BENJAMIN (city). County seat. Covers a land area of 1.037 square miles and a water area of 0 square miles. Located at 33.58° N. Lat; 99.79° W. Long. Elevation is 1,476 feet.

Population: 225 (1990); 264 (2000); 225 (2010); 214 (2015 projected); Race: 85.3% White, 3.6% Black, 2.2% Asian, 8.9% Other, 16.0% Hispanic of any race (2010); Density: 216.9 persons per square mile (2010); Average household size: 2.37 (2010); Median age: 47.7 (2010); Males per 100 females: 97.4 (2010); Marriage status: 16.7% never married, 66.7% now married, 15.6% widowed, 1.0% divorced (2005-2009 5-year est.); Foreign born: 9.7% (2005-2009 5-year est.); Ancestry (includes multiple ancestries): 37.8% German, 16.2% American, 13.9% English, 10.0% Irish, 6.2% Scotch-Irish (2005-2009 5-year est.).
Economy: Employment by occupation: 15.8% management, 36.7% professional, 14.2% services, 13.3% sales, 1.7% farming, 9.2% construction, 9.2% production (2005-2009 5-year est.).
Income: Per capita income: $17,848 (2010); Median household income: $34,118 (2010); Average household income: $42,688 (2010); Percent of households with income of $100,000 or more: 5.4% (2010); Poverty rate: 0.0% (2005-2009 5-year est.).
Taxes: Total city taxes per capita: $269 (2007); City property taxes per capita: $179 (2007).
Education: Percent of population age 25 and over with: High school diploma (including GED) or higher: 79.4% (2010); Bachelor's degree or higher: 13.8% (2010); Master's degree or higher: 2.5% (2010).
School District(s)
Benjamin ISD (PK-12)
   2009-10 Enrollment: 86 . . . . (940) 459-2231
Housing: Homeownership rate: 76.3% (2010); Median home value: $30,625 (2010); Median contract rent: $221 per month (2005-2009 5-year est.); Median year structure built: 1960 (2005-2009 5-year est.).
Transportation: Commute to work: 99.1% car, 0.0% public transportation, 0.9% walk, 0.0% work from home (2005-2009 5-year est.); Travel time to work: 38.5% less than 15 minutes, 55.6% 15 to 30 minutes, 0.9% 30 to 45 minutes, 2.6% 45 to 60 minutes, 2.6% 60 minutes or more (2005-2009 5-year est.)

GOREE (city). Covers a land area of 1.455 square miles and a water area of 0 square miles. Located at 33.46° N. Lat; 99.52° W. Long. Elevation is 1,453 feet.
Population: 412 (1990); 321 (2000); 261 (2010); 246 (2015 projected); Race: 76.2% White, 3.8% Black, 0.0% Asian, 19.9% Other, 28.0% Hispanic of any race (2010); Density: 179.4 persons per square mile (2010); Average household size: 2.44 (2010); Median age: 46.5 (2010); Males per 100 females: 85.1 (2010); Marriage status: 5.9% never married, 80.5% now married, 9.2% widowed, 4.3% divorced (2005-2009 5-year est.); Foreign born: 7.0% (2005-2009 5-year est.); Ancestry (includes multiple ancestries): 10.4% German, 7.8% American, 7.4% Irish, 3.0% English, 3.0% French (2005-2009 5-year est.).
Economy: Employment by occupation: 14.2% management, 2.7% professional, 21.2% services, 9.7% sales, 15.9% farming, 25.7% construction, 10.6% production (2005-2009 5-year est.).
Income: Per capita income: $23,986 (2010); Median household income: $42,083 (2010); Average household income: $55,958 (2010); Percent of households with income of $100,000 or more: 14.0% (2010); Poverty rate: 11.1% (2005-2009 5-year est.).
Taxes: Total city taxes per capita: $234 (2007); City property taxes per capita: $57 (2007).
Education: Percent of population age 25 and over with: High school diploma (including GED) or higher: 74.3% (2010); Bachelor's degree or higher: 13.4% (2010); Master's degree or higher: 3.4% (2010).
Housing: Homeownership rate: 78.5% (2010); Median home value: $33,684 (2010); Median contract rent: $177 per month (2005-2009 5-year est.); Median year structure built: 1948 (2005-2009 5-year est.).
Transportation: Commute to work: 87.6% car, 0.0% public transportation, 0.9% walk, 2.7% work from home (2005-2009 5-year est.); Travel time to work: 80.0% less than 15 minutes, 15.5% 15 to 30 minutes, 0.9% 30 to 45 minutes, 0.0% 45 to 60 minutes, 3.6% 60 minutes or more (2005-2009 5-year est.)

KNOX CITY (town). Covers a land area of 0.837 square miles and a water area of 0 square miles. Located at 33.41° N. Lat; 99.81° W. Long. Elevation is 1,529 feet.
History: Incorporated 1916.
Population: 1,450 (1990); 1,219 (2000); 1,003 (2010); 950 (2015 projected); Race: 64.7% White, 10.2% Black, 0.7% Asian, 24.4% Other, 24.6% Hispanic of any race (2010); Density: 1,199.0 persons per square mile (2010); Average household size: 2.35 (2010); Median age: 47.3 (2010); Males per 100 females: 87.8 (2010); Marriage status: 11.9% never

married, 60.3% now married, 22.9% widowed, 4.9% divorced (2005-2009 5-year est.); Foreign born: 4.8% (2005-2009 5-year est.); Ancestry (includes multiple ancestries): 9.8% Irish, 9.6% English, 9.3% German, 8.9% American, 2.5% French (2005-2009 5-year est.).
Economy: Employment by occupation: 10.1% management, 19.9% professional, 18.1% services, 26.4% sales, 4.2% farming, 14.2% construction, 7.1% production (2005-2009 5-year est.).
Income: Per capita income: $17,281 (2010); Median household income: $29,697 (2010); Average household income: $41,622 (2010); Percent of households with income of $100,000 or more: 6.1% (2010); Poverty rate: 22.4% (2005-2009 5-year est.).
Taxes: Total city taxes per capita: $398 (2007); City property taxes per capita: $163 (2007).
Education: Percent of population age 25 and over with: High school diploma (including GED) or higher: 73.6% (2010); Bachelor's degree or higher: 17.4% (2010); Master's degree or higher: 4.4% (2010).

School District(s)
Knox City-O'brien CISD (PK-12)
   2009-10 Enrollment: 298 . . . . (940) 657-3521
Housing: Homeownership rate: 75.1% (2010); Median home value: $35,699 (2010); Median contract rent: $229 per month (2005-2009 5-year est.); Median year structure built: 1958 (2005-2009 5-year est.).
Hospitals: Knox County Hospital (14 beds)
Transportation: Commute to work: 96.4% car, 0.6% public transportation, 3.0% walk, 0.0% work from home (2005-2009 5-year est.); Travel time to work: 75.8% less than 15 minutes, 13.0% 15 to 30 minutes, 3.6% 30 to 45 minutes, 0.0% 45 to 60 minutes, 7.6% 60 minutes or more (2005-2009 5-year est.)
Additional Information Contacts
Knox City Chamber of Commerce . . . . (940) 658-3442
   http://www.knoxcitychamberofcommerce.com

MUNDAY (city). Covers a land area of 1.416 square miles and a water area of 0 square miles. Located at 33.44° N. Lat; 99.62° W. Long. Elevation is 1,480 feet.
History: Incorporated 1906.
Population: 1,600 (1990); 1,527 (2000); 1,258 (2010); 1,192 (2015 projected); Race: 68.6% White, 11.9% Black, 0.0% Asian, 19.5% Other, 30.5% Hispanic of any race (2010); Density: 888.5 persons per square mile (2010); Average household size: 2.44 (2010); Median age: 40.4 (2010); Males per 100 females: 86.6 (2010); Marriage status: 23.5% never married, 58.8% now married, 11.0% widowed, 6.7% divorced (2005-2009 5-year est.); Foreign born: 15.3% (2005-2009 5-year est.); Ancestry (includes multiple ancestries): 18.3% German, 11.5% Irish, 6.2% English, 4.6% Scotch-Irish, 2.9% American (2005-2009 5-year est.).
Economy: Employment by occupation: 14.0% management, 18.0% professional, 19.5% services, 17.5% sales, 9.8% farming, 9.8% construction, 11.5% production (2005-2009 5-year est.).
Income: Per capita income: $17,018 (2010); Median household income: $33,220 (2010); Average household income: $41,558 (2010); Percent of households with income of $100,000 or more: 7.0% (2010); Poverty rate: 20.1% (2005-2009 5-year est.).
Taxes: Total city taxes per capita: $196 (2007); City property taxes per capita: $108 (2007).
Education: Percent of population age 25 and over with: High school diploma (including GED) or higher: 68.9% (2010); Bachelor's degree or higher: 10.1% (2010); Master's degree or higher: 1.4% (2010).

School District(s)
Munday CISD (PK-12)
   2009-10 Enrollment: 378 . . . . (940) 422-4321
Housing: Homeownership rate: 68.5% (2010); Median home value: $32,281 (2010); Median contract rent: $229 per month (2005-2009 5-year est.); Median year structure built: 1960 (2005-2009 5-year est.).
Safety: Violent crime rate: 34.0 per 10,000 population; Property crime rate: 144.3 per 10,000 population (2009).
Newspapers: Munday Courier (Community news; Circulation 1,300)
Transportation: Commute to work: 92.4% car, 0.0% public transportation, 3.2% walk, 1.1% work from home (2005-2009 5-year est.); Travel time to work: 50.3% less than 15 minutes, 29.3% 15 to 30 minutes, 13.8% 30 to 45 minutes, 0.2% 45 to 60 minutes, 6.5% 60 minutes or more (2005-2009 5-year est.)
Additional Information Contacts
Munday Chamber of Commerce . . . . (940) 422-4540
   http://mundaychamber.googlepages.com

La Salle County

Located in south Texas; drained by the Nueces and Frio Rivers. Covers a land area of 1,488.85 square miles, a water area of 5.38 square miles, and is located in the Central Time Zone at 28.35° N. Lat., 99.16° W. Long. The county was founded in 1858. County seat is Cotulla.

Weather Station: Fowlerton   Elevation: 319 feet

	Jan	Feb	Mar	Apr	May	Jun	Jul	Aug	Sep	Oct	Nov	Dec
High	67	71	78	85	91	96	98	98	93	85	76	67
Low	41	44	51	57	67	72	73	73	68	60	49	41
Precip	0.9	1.1	1.8	1.6	2.8	2.7	2.6	2.0	3.1	3.2	1.5	1.3
Snow	0.0	0.0	0.0	0.0	0.0	0.0	0.0	0.0	0.0	0.0	0.0	0.2

High and Low temperatures in degrees Fahrenheit; Precipitation and Snow in inches

Population: 5,254 (1990); 5,866 (2000); 5,905 (2010); 5,914 (2015 projected); Race: 81.1% White, 3.9% Black, 0.3% Asian, 14.6% Other, 76.7% Hispanic of any race (2010); Density: 4.0 persons per square mile (2010); Average household size: 2.80 (2010); Median age: 33.7 (2010); Males per 100 females: 115.6 (2010).
Religion: Five largest groups: 85.7% Catholic Church, 10.7% Southern Baptist Convention, 3.5% The United Methodist Church, 2.0% Churches of Christ, 1.0% International Church of the Foursquare Gospel (2000).
Economy: Unemployment rate: 7.4% (June 2011); Total civilian labor force: 3,300 (June 2011); Leading industries: 13.8% retail trade; 9.8% accommodation & food services; 7.3% health care and social assistance (2009); Farms: 399 totaling 649,126 acres (2007); Companies that employ 500 or more persons: 1 (2009); Companies that employ 100 to 499 persons: 0 (2009); Companies that employ less than 100 persons: 82 (2009); Black-owned businesses: n/a (2007); Hispanic-owned businesses: 147 (2007); Asian-owned businesses: n/a (2007); Women-owned businesses: 128 (2007); Retail sales per capita: $4,689 (2010). Single-family building permits issued: 6 (2010); Multi-family building permits issued: 0 (2010).
Income: Per capita income: $12,410 (2010); Median household income: $28,528 (2010); Average household income: $38,141 (2010); Percent of households with income of $100,000 or more: 6.8% (2010); Poverty rate: 31.6% (2009); Bankruptcy rate: 1.14% (2010).
Taxes: Total county taxes per capita: $202 (2007); County property taxes per capita: $142 (2007).
Education: Percent of population age 25 and over with: High school diploma (including GED) or higher: 56.0% (2010); Bachelor's degree or higher: 7.7% (2010); Master's degree or higher: 1.2% (2010).
Housing: Homeownership rate: 72.8% (2010); Median home value: $36,277 (2010); Median contract rent: $323 per month (2005-2009 5-year est.); Median year structure built: 1969 (2005-2009 5-year est.)
Health: Birth rate: 161.8 per 10,000 population (2009); Death rate: 60.2 per 10,000 population (2009); Age-adjusted cancer mortality rate: Suppressed deaths per 100,000 population (2007); Number of physicians: 0.0 per 10,000 population (2008); Hospital beds: 0.0 per 10,000 population (2007); Hospital admissions: 0.0 per 10,000 population (2007).
Elections: 2008 Presidential election results: 59.2% Obama, 40.2% McCain, 0.0% Nader
Additional Information Contacts
La Salle County Government . . . . (830) 879-3033

Cottula-La Salle Chamber of Commerce . . . . (830) 879-2326
   http://www.cotulla-chamber.com

La Salle County Communities

COTULLA (city). County seat. Covers a land area of 1.973 square miles and a water area of 0 square miles. Located at 28.43° N. Lat; 99.23° W. Long. Elevation is 427 feet.
History: Cotulla had an early reputation as a tough western town where gunplay was frequent and killings rather commonplace. The author O.Henry (W.S. Porter) lived on a ranch near Cotulla for a time during his boyhood.
Population: 3,694 (1990); 3,614 (2000); 3,535 (2010); 3,487 (2015 projected); Race: 83.0% White, 0.5% Black, 0.6% Asian, 15.9% Other, 83.1% Hispanic of any race (2010); Density: 1,791.8 persons per square mile (2010); Average household size: 2.84 (2010); Median age: 31.9 (2010); Males per 100 females: 91.1 (2010); Marriage status: 34.9% never married, 51.1% now married, 7.2% widowed, 6.7% divorced (2005-2009 5-year est.); Foreign born: 7.3% (2005-2009 5-year est.); Ancestry

(includes multiple ancestries): 5.0% German, 3.4% English, 3.1% Irish, 2.8% American, 1.0% Cajun (2005-2009 5-year est.).
Economy: Single-family building permits issued: 6 (2010); Multi-family building permits issued: 0 (2010); Employment by occupation: 12.5% management, 7.9% professional, 28.5% services, 14.9% sales, 3.1% farming, 26.6% construction, 6.5% production (2005-2009 5-year est.).
Income: Per capita income: $13,540 (2010); Median household income: $29,403 (2010); Average household income: $38,914 (2010); Percent of households with income of $100,000 or more: 6.8% (2010); Poverty rate: 25.7% (2005-2009 5-year est.).
Taxes: Total city taxes per capita: $254 (2007); City property taxes per capita: $101 (2007).
Education: Percent of population age 25 and over with: High school diploma (including GED) or higher: 58.5% (2010); Bachelor's degree or higher: 7.9% (2010); Master's degree or higher: 0.5% (2010).

School District(s)
Cotulla ISD (PK-12)
    2009-10 Enrollment: 1,178 . . . . (830) 879-3073
Housing: Homeownership rate: 69.1% (2010); Median home value: $34,504 (2010); Median contract rent: $303 per month (2005-2009 5-year est.); Median year structure built: 1965 (2005-2009 5-year est.).
Transportation: Commute to work: 90.9% car, 0.0% public transportation, 2.8% walk, 4.9% work from home (2005-2009 5-year est.); Travel time to work: 46.6% less than 15 minutes, 24.9% 15 to 30 minutes, 15.0% 30 to 45 minutes, 6.0% 45 to 60 minutes, 7.5% 60 minutes or more (2005-2009 5-year est.)
Airports: Cotulla-La Salle County (general aviation)
Additional Information Contacts
Cottula-La Salle Chamber of Commerce . . . . (830) 879-2326
    http://www.cotulla-chamber.com

ENCINAL (city). Covers a land area of 0.389 square miles and a water area of 0 square miles. Located at 28.04° N. Lat; 99.35° W. Long. Elevation is 558 feet.
Population: 620 (1990); 629 (2000); 701 (2010); 734 (2015 projected); Race: 77.0% White, 0.1% Black, 0.0% Asian, 22.8% Other, 84.3% Hispanic of any race (2010); Density: 1,801.4 persons per square mile (2010); Average household size: 2.87 (2010); Median age: 33.8 (2010); Males per 100 females: 100.3 (2010); Marriage status: 20.3% never married, 54.7% now married, 10.0% widowed, 15.0% divorced (2005-2009 5-year est.); Foreign born: 14.1% (2005-2009 5-year est.); Ancestry (includes multiple ancestries): 2.2% Scottish (2005-2009 5-year est.).
Economy: Single-family building permits issued: 0 (2010); Multi-family building permits issued: 0 (2010); Employment by occupation: 21.8% management, 0.0% professional, 24.1% services, 10.3% sales, 4.0% farming, 21.8% construction, 17.8% production (2005-2009 5-year est.).
Income: Per capita income: $11,713 (2010); Median household income: $25,000 (2010); Average household income: $33,432 (2010); Percent of households with income of $100,000 or more: 2.9% (2010); Poverty rate: 22.2% (2005-2009 5-year est.).
Taxes: Total city taxes per capita: $231 (2007); City property taxes per capita: $32 (2007).
Education: Percent of population age 25 and over with: High school diploma (including GED) or higher: 41.9% (2010); Bachelor's degree or higher: 2.1% (2010); Master's degree or higher: 0.2% (2010).

School District(s)
Cotulla ISD (PK-12)
    2009-10 Enrollment: 1,178 . . . . (830) 879-3073
Housing: Homeownership rate: 79.9% (2010); Median home value: $31,667 (2010); Median contract rent: $280 per month (2005-2009 5-year est.); Median year structure built: 1972 (2005-2009 5-year est.).
Transportation: Commute to work: 85.6% car, 4.6% public transportation, 4.0% walk, 5.7% work from home (2005-2009 5-year est.); Travel time to work: 55.5% less than 15 minutes, 12.8% 15 to 30 minutes, 1.8% 30 to 45 minutes, 17.1% 45 to 60 minutes, 12.8% 60 minutes or more (2005-2009 5-year est.)

FOWLERTON (CDP). Covers a land area of 2.178 square miles and a water area of 0 square miles. Located at 28.46° N. Lat; 98.81° W. Long. Elevation is 322 feet.
Population: 47 (1990); 62 (2000); 61 (2010); 62 (2015 projected); Race: 78.7% White, 16.4% Black, 0.0% Asian, 4.9% Other, 52.5% Hispanic of any race (2010); Density: 28.0 persons per square mile (2010); Average household size: 2.43 (2010); Median age: 36.3 (2010); Males per 100 females: 281.3 (2010); Marriage status: 33.8% never married, 53.7% now

married, 12.5% widowed, 0.0% divorced (2005-2009 5-year est.); Foreign born: 0.0% (2005-2009 5-year est.); Ancestry (includes multiple ancestries): 58.1% German, 36.8% French, 27.7% English, 16.1% Dutch West Indian, 11.6% Irish (2005-2009 5-year est.).
Economy: Employment by occupation: 0.0% management, 0.0% professional, 0.0% services, 0.0% sales, 0.0% farming, 0.0% construction, 100.0% production (2005-2009 5-year est.).
Income: Per capita income: $10,100 (2010); Median household income: $30,000 (2010); Average household income: $40,893 (2010); Percent of households with income of $100,000 or more: 14.3% (2010); Poverty rate: 0.0% (2005-2009 5-year est.).
Education: Percent of population age 25 and over with: High school diploma (including GED) or higher: 63.6% (2010); Bachelor's degree or higher: 13.6% (2010); Master's degree or higher: 4.5% (2010).
Housing: Homeownership rate: 78.6% (2010); Median home value: $137,500 (2010); Median contract rent: n/a per month (2005-2009 5-year est.); Median year structure built: before 1940 (2005-2009 5-year est.).
Transportation: Commute to work: 100.0% car, 0.0% public transportation, 0.0% walk, 0.0% work from home (2005-2009 5-year est.); Travel time to work: 0.0% less than 15 minutes, 0.0% 15 to 30 minutes, 0.0% 30 to 45 minutes, 0.0% 45 to 60 minutes, 100.0% 60 minutes or more (2005-2009 5-year est.)

Lamar County

Located in northeastern Texas; bounded on the north by the Red River and the Oklahoma border, and on the south by the North Fork of the Sulphur River. Covers a land area of 916.81 square miles, a water area of 15.66 square miles, and is located in the Central Time Zone at 33.65° N. Lat., 95.56° W. Long. The county was founded in 1840. County seat is Paris.

Lamar County is part of the Paris, TX Micropolitan Statistical Area. The entire metro area includes: Lamar County, TX

Weather Station: Paris									Elevation: 541 feet			
	Jan	Feb	Mar	Apr	May	Jun	Jul	Aug	Sep	Oct	Nov	Dec
High	53	58	66	75	82	90	95	96	88	77	64	54
Low	32	36	44	52	62	69	73	73	65	53	43	34
Precip	2.8	3.4	4.4	3.5	5.5	4.1	3.6	2.2	4.0	5.1	4.3	4.0
Snow	0.5	0.4	tr	0.0	0.0	0.0	0.0	0.0	0.0	0.0	tr	0.5

High and Low temperatures in degrees Fahrenheit; Precipitation and Snow in inches

Population: 43,949 (1990); 48,499 (2000); 50,062 (2010); 50,737 (2015 projected); Race: 81.1% White, 13.1% Black, 0.6% Asian, 5.3% Other, 5.7% Hispanic of any race (2010); Density: 54.6 persons per square mile (2010); Average household size: 2.44 (2010); Median age: 38.2 (2010); Males per 100 females: 91.8 (2010).
Religion: Five largest groups: 36.3% Southern Baptist Convention, 7.1% The United Methodist Church, 5.6% Catholic Church, 4.9% Churches of Christ, 4.5% Church of God (Cleveland, Tennessee) (2000).
Economy: Unemployment rate: 10.6% (June 2011); Total civilian labor force: 23,790 (June 2011); Leading industries: 24.5% manufacturing; 19.3% health care and social assistance; 14.7% retail trade (2009); Farms: 1,817 totaling 521,001 acres (2007); Companies that employ 500 or more persons: 7 (2009); Companies that employ 100 to 499 persons: 12 (2009); Companies that employ less than 100 persons: 1,151 (2009); Black-owned businesses: n/a (2007); Hispanic-owned businesses: n/a (2007); Asian-owned businesses: n/a (2007); Women-owned businesses: 1,721 (2007); Retail sales per capita: $14,694 (2010). Single-family building permits issued: 46 (2010); Multi-family building permits issued: 0 (2010).
Income: Per capita income: $19,942 (2010); Median household income: $36,895 (2010); Average household income: $49,326 (2010); Percent of households with income of $100,000 or more: 8.8% (2010); Poverty rate: 18.6% (2009); Bankruptcy rate: 1.28% (2010).
Taxes: Total county taxes per capita: $226 (2007); County property taxes per capita: $159 (2007).
Education: Percent of population age 25 and over with: High school diploma (including GED) or higher: 81.8% (2010); Bachelor's degree or higher: 16.6% (2010); Master's degree or higher: 5.3% (2010).
Housing: Homeownership rate: 69.5% (2010); Median home value: $74,597 (2010); Median contract rent: $396 per month (2005-2009 5-year est.); Median year structure built: 1978 (2005-2009 5-year est.)
Health: Birth rate: 131.7 per 10,000 population (2009); Death rate: 117.2 per 10,000 population (2009); Age-adjusted cancer mortality rate: 223.4 deaths per 100,000 population (2007); Number of physicians: 19.4 per

10,000 population (2008); Hospital beds: 65.5 per 10,000 population (2007); Hospital admissions: 1,826.7 per 10,000 population (2007).
Elections: 2008 Presidential election results: 28.6% Obama, 70.5% McCain, 0.1% Nader
National and State Parks: Pat Mayse State Park 1; Pat Mayse State Park 2
Additional Information Contacts
Lamar County Government . . . . (903) 737-2410
   http://www.co.lamar.tx.us
City of Paris . . . . (903) 784-9202
   http://www.paristexas.gov
Paris-Lamar County Chamber of Commerce . . . . (903) 784-2501
   http://www.paristexas.com

Lamar County Communities

ARTHUR CITY (unincorporated postal area, zip code 75411). Covers a land area of 78.636 square miles and a water area of 0.309 square miles. Located at 33.86° N. Lat; 95.60° W. Long. Elevation is 430 feet.
History: Arthur City was established near the site of a French trading post on the Red River.
Population: 1,046 (2000); Race: 82.7% White, 6.5% Black, 0.7% Asian, 10.1% Other, 7.4% Hispanic of any race (2000); Density: 13.3 persons per square mile (2000); Age: 27.1% under 18, 16.5% over 64 (2000); Marriage status: 20.2% never married, 62.5% now married, 3.8% widowed, 13.6% divorced (2000); Foreign born: 4.5% (2000); Ancestry (includes multiple ancestries): 13.8% American, 9.6% Irish, 9.4% German, 3.9% Scottish (2000).
Economy: Employment by occupation: 15.0% management, 11.9% professional, 10.2% services, 18.6% sales, 2.8% farming, 11.6% construction, 29.9% production (2000).
Income: Per capita income: $13,156 (2000); Median household income: $25,526 (2000); Poverty rate: 179.1% (2000).
Education: Percent of population age 25 and over with: High school diploma (including GED) or higher: 64.4% (2000); Bachelor's degree or higher: 10.4% (2000).
Housing: Homeownership rate: 77.4% (2000); Median home value: $44,400 (2000); Median contract rent: $175 per month (2000); Median year structure built: 1980 (2000).
Transportation: Commute to work: 88.8% car, 0.0% public transportation, 4.7% walk, 4.2% work from home (2000); Travel time to work: 25.1% less than 15 minutes, 52.2% 15 to 30 minutes, 16.9% 30 to 45 minutes, 3.8% 45 to 60 minutes, 2.0% 60 minutes or more (2000)

BLOSSOM (city). Covers a land area of 2.510 square miles and a water area of 0.042 square miles. Located at 33.66° N. Lat; 95.38° W. Long. Elevation is 528 feet.
Population: 1,515 (1990); 1,439 (2000); 1,460 (2010); 1,472 (2015 projected); Race: 94.8% White, 0.9% Black, 0.1% Asian, 4.2% Other, 8.4% Hispanic of any race (2010); Density: 581.6 persons per square mile (2010); Average household size: 2.54 (2010); Median age: 38.8 (2010); Males per 100 females: 101.7 (2010); Marriage status: 17.5% never married, 62.6% now married, 6.8% widowed, 13.1% divorced (2005-2009 5-year est.); Foreign born: 2.6% (2005-2009 5-year est.); Ancestry (includes multiple ancestries): 14.8% American, 12.8% Irish, 9.0% German, 8.0% English, 4.3% Dutch (2005-2009 5-year est.).
Economy: Single-family building permits issued: 16 (2010); Multi-family building permits issued: 0 (2010); Employment by occupation: 4.7% management, 14.9% professional, 14.3% services, 26.4% sales, 0.7% farming, 11.0% construction, 28.0% production (2005-2009 5-year est.).
Income: Per capita income: $16,334 (2010); Median household income: $32,500 (2010); Average household income: $41,109 (2010); Percent of households with income of $100,000 or more: 4.9% (2010); Poverty rate: 9.8% (2005-2009 5-year est.).
Taxes: Total city taxes per capita: $83 (2007); City property taxes per capita: $81 (2007).
Education: Percent of population age 25 and over with: High school diploma (including GED) or higher: 81.9% (2010); Bachelor's degree or higher: 15.0% (2010); Master's degree or higher: 4.4% (2010).
School District(s)
Prairiland ISD (PK-12)
   2009-10 Enrollment: 1,127 . . . . (903) 652-6476
Housing: Homeownership rate: 81.9% (2010); Median home value: $72,319 (2010); Median contract rent: $376 per month (2005-2009 5-year est.); Median year structure built: 1979 (2005-2009 5-year est.).

Transportation: Commute to work: 94.2% car, 0.0% public transportation, 0.7% walk, 2.7% work from home (2005-2009 5-year est.); Travel time to work: 26.5% less than 15 minutes, 57.4% 15 to 30 minutes, 6.1% 30 to 45 minutes, 4.2% 45 to 60 minutes, 5.7% 60 minutes or more (2005-2009 5-year est.)

BROOKSTON (unincorporated postal area, zip code 75421). Covers a land area of 69.938 square miles and a water area of 0.048 square miles. Located at 33.64° N. Lat; 95.69° W. Long. Elevation is 591 feet.
Population: 1,225 (2000); Race: 89.2% White, 8.5% Black, 0.2% Asian, 2.1% Other, 1.7% Hispanic of any race (2000); Density: 17.5 persons per square mile (2000); Age: 24.2% under 18, 12.9% over 64 (2000); Marriage status: 18.7% never married, 65.3% now married, 4.9% widowed, 11.1% divorced (2000); Foreign born: 2.3% (2000); Ancestry (includes multiple ancestries): 16.9% American, 10.1% German, 7.4% Irish, 5.9% English (2000).
Economy: Employment by occupation: 9.7% management, 13.0% professional, 15.3% services, 29.8% sales, 0.5% farming, 11.7% construction, 20.0% production (2000).
Income: Per capita income: $16,774 (2000); Median household income: $33,571 (2000); Poverty rate: 179.1% (2000).
Education: Percent of population age 25 and over with: High school diploma (including GED) or higher: 80.1% (2000); Bachelor's degree or higher: 7.7% (2000).
Housing: Homeownership rate: 89.8% (2000); Median home value: $50,000 (2000); Median contract rent: $275 per month (2000); Median year structure built: 1979 (2000).
Transportation: Commute to work: 94.8% car, 0.0% public transportation, 1.2% walk, 4.1% work from home (2000); Travel time to work: 26.8% less than 15 minutes, 56.2% 15 to 30 minutes, 10.6% 30 to 45 minutes, 3.7% 45 to 60 minutes, 2.8% 60 minutes or more (2000)

DEPORT (city). Covers a land area of 1.115 square miles and a water area of 0 square miles. Located at 33.52° N. Lat; 95.31° W. Long. Elevation is 413 feet.
Population: 746 (1990); 718 (2000); 662 (2010); 635 (2015 projected); Race: 91.5% White, 2.4% Black, 0.0% Asian, 6.0% Other, 2.1% Hispanic of any race (2010); Density: 593.9 persons per square mile (2010); Average household size: 2.29 (2010); Median age: 47.1 (2010); Males per 100 females: 89.1 (2010); Marriage status: 14.6% never married, 56.4% now married, 9.0% widowed, 20.0% divorced (2005-2009 5-year est.); Foreign born: 0.4% (2005-2009 5-year est.); Ancestry (includes multiple ancestries): 25.4% Irish, 21.8% American, 11.0% German, 9.4% English, 8.3% Scotch-Irish (2005-2009 5-year est.).
Economy: Single-family building permits issued: 0 (2010); Multi-family building permits issued: 0 (2010); Employment by occupation: 13.1% management, 17.4% professional, 13.1% services, 20.0% sales, 4.6% farming, 14.8% construction, 17.0% production (2005-2009 5-year est.).
Income: Per capita income: $15,768 (2010); Median household income: $29,583 (2010); Average household income: $39,303 (2010); Percent of households with income of $100,000 or more: 5.9% (2010); Poverty rate: 12.6% (2005-2009 5-year est.).
Taxes: Total city taxes per capita: $32 (2007); City property taxes per capita: $0 (2007).
Education: Percent of population age 25 and over with: High school diploma (including GED) or higher: 72.9% (2010); Bachelor's degree or higher: 13.5% (2010); Master's degree or higher: 3.8% (2010).
School District(s)
Prairiland ISD (PK-12)
   2009-10 Enrollment: 1,127 . . . . (903) 652-6476
Housing: Homeownership rate: 72.5% (2010); Median home value: $55,161 (2010); Median contract rent: $271 per month (2005-2009 5-year est.); Median year structure built: 1971 (2005-2009 5-year est.).
Newspapers: Blossom Times (Community news; Circulation 450); Bogata News (Community news; Circulation 1,700); Deport Times (Community news; Circulation 2,000); Detroit Weekly (Community news; Circulation 450); Talco Times (Community news; Circulation 475)
Transportation: Commute to work: 97.6% car, 0.0% public transportation, 1.0% walk, 0.0% work from home (2005-2009 5-year est.); Travel time to work: 34.5% less than 15 minutes, 40.8% 15 to 30 minutes, 16.4% 30 to 45 minutes, 8.4% 45 to 60 minutes, 0.0% 60 minutes or more (2005-2009 5-year est.)

PARIS (city). County seat. Covers a land area of 42.754 square miles and a water area of 1.663 square miles. Located at 33.66° N. Lat; 95.54° W. Long. Elevation is 600 feet.

History: Paris has twice been the victim of disastrous fires that destroyed the town. This was the home of Claiborne Chisum's son, John, whom Parisians claim was the blazer of the Old Chisholm Trail. The Central National Road of the Republic of Texas, surveyed in 1844, ran from San Antonio northward through Paris.

Population: 25,676 (1990); 25,898 (2000); 26,530 (2010); 26,875 (2015 projected); Race: 71.4% White, 21.7% Black, 0.9% Asian, 6.0% Other, 7.1% Hispanic of any race (2010); Density: 620.5 persons per square mile (2010); Average household size: 2.32 (2010); Median age: 37.6 (2010); Males per 100 females: 88.1 (2010); Marriage status: 25.0% never married, 51.8% now married, 10.0% widowed, 13.2% divorced (2005-2009 5-year est.); Foreign born: 4.2% (2005-2009 5-year est.); Ancestry (includes multiple ancestries): 13.1% Irish, 11.7% American, 10.7% German, 6.8% English, 2.6% African (2005-2009 5-year est.).

Economy: Unemployment rate: 11.9% (June 2011); Total civilian labor force: 11,946 (June 2011); Single-family building permits issued: 16 (2010); Multi-family building permits issued: 0 (2010); Employment by occupation: 7.3% management, 21.0% professional, 20.3% services, 25.5% sales, 0.1% farming, 9.7% construction, 16.1% production (2005-2009 5-year est.).

Income: Per capita income: $19,401 (2010); Median household income: $32,131 (2010); Average household income: $46,056 (2010); Percent of households with income of $100,000 or more: 8.1% (2010); Poverty rate: 24.2% (2005-2009 5-year est.).

Taxes: Total city taxes per capita: $665 (2007); City property taxes per capita: $286 (2007).

Education: Percent of population age 25 and over with: High school diploma (including GED) or higher: 80.0% (2010); Bachelor's degree or higher: 17.5% (2010); Master's degree or higher: 5.8% (2010).

School District(s)
Chisum ISD (PK-12)
    2009-10 Enrollment: 854 . . . . (903) 737-2830
North Lamar ISD (PK-12)
    2009-10 Enrollment: 2,963 . . . . (903) 737-2000
Paris ISD (PK-12)
    2009-10 Enrollment: 3,716 . . . . (903) 737-7473
Two-year College(s)
Paris Junior College (Public)
    Fall 2009 Enrollment: 5,580 . . . . (903) 785-7661
    2010-11 Tuition: In-state $1,908; Out-of-state $2,892

Housing: Homeownership rate: 58.0% (2010); Median home value: $68,468 (2010); Median contract rent: $395 per month (2005-2009 5-year est.); Median year structure built: 1973 (2005-2009 5-year est.).

Hospitals: Paris Regional Medical Center (365 beds); Paris Regional Medical Center - South Campus (228 beds)

Safety: Violent crime rate: 64.8 per 10,000 population; Property crime rate: 661.0 per 10,000 population (2009).

Newspapers: The Paris News (Local news; Circulation 13,000)

Transportation: Commute to work: 91.7% car, 0.1% public transportation, 1.7% walk, 2.1% work from home (2005-2009 5-year est.); Travel time to work: 62.7% less than 15 minutes, 22.0% 15 to 30 minutes, 6.8% 30 to 45 minutes, 2.8% 45 to 60 minutes, 5.6% 60 minutes or more (2005-2009 5-year est.)

Airports: Cox Field (general aviation)
Additional Information Contacts
City of Paris . . . . (903) 784-9202
    http://www.paristexas.gov
Paris-Lamar County Chamber of Commerce . . . . (903) 784-2501
    http://www.paristexas.com

PATTONVILLE (unincorporated postal area, zip code 75468). Covers a land area of 42.536 square miles and a water area of 0.034 square miles. Located at 33.53° N. Lat; 95.39° W. Long. Elevation is 499 feet.

Population: 839 (2000); Race: 94.7% White, 4.0% Black, 1.0% Asian, 0.3% Other, 0.0% Hispanic of any race (2000); Density: 19.7 persons per square mile (2000); Age: 29.0% under 18, 9.7% over 64 (2000); Marriage status: 13.3% never married, 77.5% now married, 3.9% widowed, 5.4% divorced (2000); Foreign born: 1.0% (2000); Ancestry (includes multiple ancestries): 21.8% American, 15.0% Irish, 2.3% German, 2.3% Dutch (2000).

Economy: Employment by occupation: 4.6% management, 5.8% professional, 28.3% services, 22.2% sales, 2.4% farming, 17.3% construction, 19.5% production (2000).

Income: Per capita income: $11,299 (2000); Median household income: $27,417 (2000); Poverty rate: 179.1% (2000).

Education: Percent of population age 25 and over with: High school diploma (including GED) or higher: 82.6% (2000); Bachelor's degree or higher: 11.8% (2000).

School District(s)
Prairiland ISD (PK-12)
    2009-10 Enrollment: 1,127 . . . . (903) 652-6476

Housing: Homeownership rate: 86.3% (2000); Median home value: $39,300 (2000); Median contract rent: $292 per month (2000); Median year structure built: 1977 (2000).

Transportation: Commute to work: 91.8% car, 0.0% public transportation, 2.1% walk, 6.1% work from home (2000); Travel time to work: 12.3% less than 15 minutes, 49.8% 15 to 30 minutes, 24.3% 30 to 45 minutes, 3.9% 45 to 60 minutes, 9.7% 60 minutes or more (2000)

PETTY (unincorporated postal area, zip code 75470). Covers a land area of 38.202 square miles and a water area of 0.095 square miles. Located at 33.60° N. Lat; 95.81° W. Long. Elevation is 617 feet.

Population: 371 (2000); Race: 94.1% White, 5.2% Black, 0.0% Asian, 0.7% Other, 0.0% Hispanic of any race (2000); Density: 9.7 persons per square mile (2000); Age: 26.5% under 18, 15.5% over 64 (2000); Marriage status: 16.1% never married, 74.0% now married, 6.0% widowed, 3.9% divorced (2000); Foreign born: 5.6% (2000); Ancestry (includes multiple ancestries): 23.0% American, 9.4% German, 5.9% Irish, 3.5% Dutch (2000).

Economy: Employment by occupation: 13.9% management, 8.6% professional, 3.7% services, 34.8% sales, 0.0% farming, 12.3% construction, 26.7% production (2000).

Income: Per capita income: $15,142 (2000); Median household income: $34,250 (2000); Poverty rate: 179.1% (2000).

Education: Percent of population age 25 and over with: High school diploma (including GED) or higher: 81.8% (2000); Bachelor's degree or higher: 11.0% (2000).

Housing: Homeownership rate: 89.3% (2000); Median home value: $44,400 (2000); Median contract rent: $225 per month (2000); Median year structure built: 1971 (2000).

Transportation: Commute to work: 90.7% car, 0.0% public transportation, 0.0% walk, 7.7% work from home (2000); Travel time to work: 21.9% less than 15 minutes, 29.0% 15 to 30 minutes, 29.0% 30 to 45 minutes, 10.7% 45 to 60 minutes, 9.5% 60 minutes or more (2000)

POWDERLY (unincorporated postal area, zip code 75473). Covers a land area of 78.550 square miles and a water area of 1.150 square miles. Located at 33.80° N. Lat; 95.50° W. Long. Elevation is 528 feet.

Population: 3,919 (2000); Race: 95.7% White, 1.4% Black, 0.2% Asian, 2.7% Other, 0.9% Hispanic of any race (2000); Density: 49.9 persons per square mile (2000); Age: 27.4% under 18, 12.0% over 64 (2000); Marriage status: 11.7% never married, 73.8% now married, 5.5% widowed, 8.9% divorced (2000); Foreign born: 0.6% (2000); Ancestry (includes multiple ancestries): 17.6% Irish, 13.9% American, 12.1% German, 8.2% English (2000).

Economy: Employment by occupation: 8.0% management, 17.2% professional, 14.8% services, 25.0% sales, 0.0% farming, 12.4% construction, 22.7% production (2000).

Income: Per capita income: $18,994 (2000); Median household income: $44,625 (2000); Poverty rate: 179.1% (2000).

Education: Percent of population age 25 and over with: High school diploma (including GED) or higher: 79.1% (2000); Bachelor's degree or higher: 14.5% (2000).

School District(s)
North Lamar ISD (PK-12)
    2009-10 Enrollment: 2,963 . . . . (903) 737-2000

Housing: Homeownership rate: 87.2% (2000); Median home value: $76,000 (2000); Median contract rent: $307 per month (2000); Median year structure built: 1981 (2000).

Transportation: Commute to work: 95.5% car, 0.0% public transportation, 0.0% walk, 4.5% work from home (2000); Travel time to work: 19.7% less than 15 minutes, 49.5% 15 to 30 minutes, 19.1% 30 to 45 minutes, 2.4% 45 to 60 minutes, 9.3% 60 minutes or more (2000)

RENO (city). Covers a land area of 3.784 square miles and a water area of 0.006 square miles. Located at 33.67° N. Lat; 95.47° W. Long. Elevation is 561 feet.
Population: 2,021 (1990); 2,767 (2000); 3,216 (2010); 3,390 (2015 projected); Race: 89.5% White, 3.5% Black, 0.7% Asian, 6.3% Other, 4.6% Hispanic of any race (2010); Density: 849.8 persons per square mile (2010); Average household size: 2.58 (2010); Median age: 36.2 (2010); Males per 100 females: 92.8 (2010); Marriage status: 20.1% never married, 64.6% now married, 6.3% widowed, 9.1% divorced (2005-2009 5-year est.); Foreign born: 2.2% (2005-2009 5-year est.); Ancestry (includes multiple ancestries): 17.8% American, 17.2% English, 12.1% German, 7.6% Irish, 3.7% Italian (2005-2009 5-year est.).
Economy: Single-family building permits issued: 14 (2010); Multi-family building permits issued: 0 (2010); Employment by occupation: 10.5% management, 25.5% professional, 16.4% services, 19.7% sales, 0.0% farming, 10.8% construction, 17.1% production (2005-2009 5-year est.).
Income: Per capita income: $25,921 (2010); Median household income: $51,964 (2010); Average household income: $66,784 (2010); Percent of households with income of $100,000 or more: 15.8% (2010); Poverty rate: 4.2% (2005-2009 5-year est.).
Taxes: Total city taxes per capita: $156 (2007); City property taxes per capita: $66 (2007).
Education: Percent of population age 25 and over with: High school diploma (including GED) or higher: 90.1% (2010); Bachelor's degree or higher: 21.7% (2010); Master's degree or higher: 6.9% (2010).
Housing: Homeownership rate: 82.6% (2010); Median home value: $95,867 (2010); Median contract rent: $498 per month (2005-2009 5-year est.); Median year structure built: 1990 (2005-2009 5-year est.).
Safety: Violent crime rate: 12.8 per 10,000 population; Property crime rate: 128.2 per 10,000 population (2009).
Transportation: Commute to work: 97.7% car, 0.0% public transportation, 0.0% walk, 1.5% work from home (2005-2009 5-year est.); Travel time to work: 59.5% less than 15 minutes, 26.8% 15 to 30 minutes, 6.1% 30 to 45 minutes, 2.2% 45 to 60 minutes, 5.5% 60 minutes or more (2005-2009 5-year est.)

ROXTON (city). Covers a land area of 0.870 square miles and a water area of 0.006 square miles. Located at 33.54° N. Lat; 95.72° W. Long. Elevation is 512 feet.
Population: 638 (1990); 694 (2000); 722 (2010); 740 (2015 projected); Race: 81.7% White, 13.2% Black, 0.0% Asian, 5.1% Other, 5.4% Hispanic of any race (2010); Density: 829.5 persons per square mile (2010); Average household size: 2.51 (2010); Median age: 36.4 (2010); Males per 100 females: 84.7 (2010); Marriage status: 29.4% never married, 41.4% now married, 10.9% widowed, 18.3% divorced (2005-2009 5-year est.); Foreign born: 0.5% (2005-2009 5-year est.); Ancestry (includes multiple ancestries): 16.6% Irish, 11.6% German, 10.6% English, 7.7% American, 7.0% Scotch-Irish (2005-2009 5-year est.).
Economy: Employment by occupation: 1.8% management, 13.7% professional, 21.5% services, 17.8% sales, 0.0% farming, 19.2% construction, 26.0% production (2005-2009 5-year est.).
Income: Per capita income: $17,236 (2010); Median household income: $33,293 (2010); Average household income: $43,576 (2010); Percent of households with income of $100,000 or more: 6.9% (2010); Poverty rate: 40.2% (2005-2009 5-year est.).
Taxes: Total city taxes per capita: $320 (2007); City property taxes per capita: $148 (2007).
Education: Percent of population age 25 and over with: High school diploma (including GED) or higher: 80.7% (2010); Bachelor's degree or higher: 9.3% (2010); Master's degree or higher: 4.8% (2010).

School District(s)
Roxton ISD (PK-12)
    2009-10 Enrollment: 217 . . . . (903) 346-3213
Housing: Homeownership rate: 74.0% (2010); Median home value: $50,889 (2010); Median contract rent: $245 per month (2005-2009 5-year est.); Median year structure built: 1971 (2005-2009 5-year est.).
Transportation: Commute to work: 99.1% car, 0.0% public transportation, 0.9% walk, 0.0% work from home (2005-2009 5-year est.); Travel time to work: 20.1% less than 15 minutes, 61.6% 15 to 30 minutes, 12.3% 30 to 45 minutes, 0.9% 45 to 60 minutes, 5.0% 60 minutes or more (2005-2009 5-year est.)

SUMNER (unincorporated postal area, zip code 75486). Covers a land area of 102.712 square miles and a water area of 0.807 square miles. Located at 33.73° N. Lat; 95.76° W. Long. Elevation is 568 feet.
Population: 1,946 (2000); Race: 97.2% White, 0.6% Black, 0.0% Asian, 2.2% Other, 1.6% Hispanic of any race (2000); Density: 18.9 persons per square mile (2000); Age: 26.1% under 18, 12.8% over 64 (2000); Marriage status: 9.0% never married, 75.4% now married, 4.5% widowed, 11.0% divorced (2000); Foreign born: 7.5% (2000); Ancestry (includes multiple ancestries): 17.7% American, 15.0% Irish, 13.9% German, 6.2% English (2000).
Economy: Employment by occupation: 18.0% management, 16.8% professional, 7.7% services, 26.2% sales, 1.6% farming, 10.2% construction, 19.5% production (2000).
Income: Per capita income: $15,255 (2000); Median household income: $37,596 (2000); Poverty rate: 179.1% (2000).
Education: Percent of population age 25 and over with: High school diploma (including GED) or higher: 81.1% (2000); Bachelor's degree or higher: 12.5% (2000).
Housing: Homeownership rate: 86.5% (2000); Median home value: $61,000 (2000); Median contract rent: $276 per month (2000); Median year structure built: 1983 (2000).
Transportation: Commute to work: 97.1% car, 0.0% public transportation, 0.0% walk, 2.5% work from home (2000); Travel time to work: 23.7% less than 15 minutes, 44.7% 15 to 30 minutes, 18.1% 30 to 45 minutes, 3.4% 45 to 60 minutes, 10.0% 60 minutes or more (2000)

SUN VALLEY (city). Covers a land area of 0.154 square miles and a water area of 0 square miles. Located at 33.66° N. Lat; 95.42° W. Long. Elevation is 535 feet.
Population: 60 (1990); 51 (2000); 56 (2010); 58 (2015 projected); Race: 89.3% White, 3.6% Black, 0.0% Asian, 7.1% Other, 5.4% Hispanic of any race (2010); Density: 364.6 persons per square mile (2010); Average household size: 2.67 (2010); Median age: 35.0 (2010); Males per 100 females: 86.7 (2010); Marriage status: 35.1% never married, 22.8% now married, 0.0% widowed, 42.1% divorced (2005-2009 5-year est.); Foreign born: 6.3% (2005-2009 5-year est.); Ancestry (includes multiple ancestries): 34.9% Irish, 17.5% German, 9.5% American, 4.8% English, 4.8% Italian (2005-2009 5-year est.).
Economy: Employment by occupation: 0.0% management, 0.0% professional, 39.0% services, 26.8% sales, 7.3% farming, 26.8% construction, 0.0% production (2005-2009 5-year est.).
Income: Per capita income: $22,424 (2010); Median household income: $44,375 (2010); Average household income: $49,048 (2010); Percent of households with income of $100,000 or more: 4.8% (2010); Poverty rate: 30.2% (2005-2009 5-year est.).
Taxes: Total city taxes per capita: $1,019 (2007); City property taxes per capita: $0 (2007).
Education: Percent of population age 25 and over with: High school diploma (including GED) or higher: 89.2% (2010); Bachelor's degree or higher: 18.9% (2010); Master's degree or higher: 5.4% (2010).
Housing: Homeownership rate: 81.0% (2010); Median home value: $72,500 (2010); Median contract rent: n/a per month (2005-2009 5-year est.); Median year structure built: 1989 (2005-2009 5-year est.).
Transportation: Commute to work: 100.0% car, 0.0% public transportation, 0.0% walk, 0.0% work from home (2005-2009 5-year est.); Travel time to work: 51.2% less than 15 minutes, 31.7% 15 to 30 minutes, 12.2% 30 to 45 minutes, 0.0% 45 to 60 minutes, 4.9% 60 minutes or more (2005-2009 5-year est.)

TOCO (city). Covers a land area of 0.170 square miles and a water area of 0 square miles. Located at 33.65° N. Lat; 95.64° W. Long. Elevation is 568 feet.
Population: 127 (1990); 89 (2000); 85 (2010); 83 (2015 projected); Race: 94.1% White, 4.7% Black, 0.0% Asian, 1.2% Other, 2.4% Hispanic of any race (2010); Density: 500.2 persons per square mile (2010); Average household size: 2.58 (2010); Median age: 43.1 (2010); Males per 100 females: 112.5 (2010); Marriage status: 10.3% never married, 65.4% now married, 21.8% widowed, 2.6% divorced (2005-2009 5-year est.); Foreign born: 14.4% (2005-2009 5-year est.); Ancestry (includes multiple ancestries): 8.9% American (2005-2009 5-year est.).
Economy: Employment by occupation: 0.0% management, 0.0% professional, 24.1% services, 24.1% sales, 0.0% farming, 0.0% construction, 51.9% production (2005-2009 5-year est.).

Income: Per capita income: $21,920 (2010); Median household income: $53,750 (2010); Average household income: $54,848 (2010); Percent of households with income of $100,000 or more: 9.1% (2010); Poverty rate: 2.2% (2005-2009 5-year est.).
Taxes: Total city taxes per capita: $689 (2007); City property taxes per capita: $0 (2007).
Education: Percent of population age 25 and over with: High school diploma (including GED) or higher: 90.0% (2010); Bachelor's degree or higher: 16.7% (2010); Master's degree or higher: 3.3% (2010).
Housing: Homeownership rate: 90.9% (2010); Median home value: $86,667 (2010); Median contract rent: n/a per month (2005-2009 5-year est.); Median year structure built: 1975 (2005-2009 5-year est.).
Transportation: Commute to work: 100.0% car, 0.0% public transportation, 0.0% walk, 0.0% work from home (2005-2009 5-year est.); Travel time to work: 27.8% less than 15 minutes, 53.7% 15 to 30 minutes, 0.0% 30 to 45 minutes, 11.1% 45 to 60 minutes, 7.4% 60 minutes or more (2005-2009 5-year est.)

Lamb County

Located in northwestern Texas; drained by intermittent Double Mountain Fork of the Brazos River. Covers a land area of 1,016.21 square miles, a water area of 1.52 square miles, and is located in the Central Time Zone at 34.05° N. Lat., 102.35° W. Long. The county was founded in 1876. County seat is Littlefield.

Weather Station: Littlefield 2 NW   Elevation: 3,504 feet

	Jan	Feb	Mar	Apr	May	Jun	Jul	Aug	Sep	Oct	Nov	Dec
High	53	58	66	74	83	90	92	90	84	75	63	53
Low	24	27	33	41	52	61	65	64	56	44	33	25
Precip	0.6	0.6	1.0	1.1	2.0	3.1	2.2	2.5	2.2	1.6	0.9	0.8
Snow	1.3	0.9	0.4	0.4	0.0	0.0	0.0	0.0	0.0	tr	1.2	2.1

High and Low temperatures in degrees Fahrenheit; Precipitation and Snow in inches

Weather Station: Olton   Elevation: 3,609 feet

	Jan	Feb	Mar	Apr	May	Jun	Jul	Aug	Sep	Oct	Nov	Dec
High	51	57	64	72	81	88	90	88	82	73	61	52
Low	23	26	32	41	52	60	64	62	55	43	32	24
Precip	0.6	0.5	1.0	1.0	2.5	3.0	1.6	2.6	2.0	1.7	0.9	0.8
Snow	2.2	0.8	0.9	0.2	0.0	0.0	0.0	0.0	0.0	0.1	1.2	3.0

High and Low temperatures in degrees Fahrenheit; Precipitation and Snow in inches

Population: 15,072 (1990); 14,709 (2000); 13,829 (2010); 13,374 (2015 projected); Race: 72.2% White, 4.6% Black, 0.2% Asian, 23.0% Other, 50.8% Hispanic of any race (2010); Density: 13.6 persons per square mile (2010); Average household size: 2.68 (2010); Median age: 37.0 (2010); Males per 100 females: 94.4 (2010).
Religion: Five largest groups: 44.6% Southern Baptist Convention, 22.4% Catholic Church, 12.2% The United Methodist Church, 7.7% Churches of Christ, 1.2% Baptist Missionary Association of America (2000).
Economy: Unemployment rate: 7.8% (June 2011); Total civilian labor force: 6,932 (June 2011); Leading industries: 18.1% health care and social assistance; 13.4% retail trade; 8.8% utilities (2009); Farms: 987 totaling 634,703 acres (2007); Companies that employ 500 or more persons: 1 (2009); Companies that employ 100 to 499 persons: 3 (2009); Companies that employ less than 100 persons: 270 (2009); Black-owned businesses: n/a (2007); Hispanic-owned businesses: n/a (2007); Asian-owned businesses: n/a (2007); Women-owned businesses: 165 (2007); Retail sales per capita: $8,771 (2010). Single-family building permits issued: 0 (2010); Multi-family building permits issued: 0 (2010).
Income: Per capita income: $17,272 (2010); Median household income: $33,656 (2010); Average household income: $46,412 (2010); Percent of households with income of $100,000 or more: 8.3% (2010); Poverty rate: 20.5% (2009); Bankruptcy rate: 1.69% (2010).
Taxes: Total county taxes per capita: $531 (2007); County property taxes per capita: $494 (2007).
Education: Percent of population age 25 and over with: High school diploma (including GED) or higher: 69.7% (2010); Bachelor's degree or higher: 12.7% (2010); Master's degree or higher: 3.4% (2010).
Housing: Homeownership rate: 73.8% (2010); Median home value: $43,744 (2010); Median contract rent: $358 per month (2005-2009 5-year est.); Median year structure built: 1961 (2005-2009 5-year est.)
Health: Birth rate: 170.9 per 10,000 population (2009); Death rate: 120.0 per 10,000 population (2009); Age-adjusted cancer mortality rate: 153.4 deaths per 100,000 population (2007); Number of physicians: 3.7 per

10,000 population (2008); Hospital beds: 29.7 per 10,000 population (2007); Hospital admissions: 642.8 per 10,000 population (2007).
Elections: 2008 Presidential election results: 25.5% Obama, 73.9% McCain, 0.1% Nader
Additional Information Contacts
Lamb County Government . . . . (806) 385-4222
  http://www.co.lamb.tx.us/ips/cms
City of Littlefield . . . . (806) 385-5161
  http://www.littlefieldtexas.org
Littlefield Chamber of Commerce . . . . (806) 385-5331
  http://www.littlefieldtexas.org
Olton Chamber of Commerce . . . . (806) 285-2292
  http://www.oltonchamber.org

Lamb County Communities

AMHERST (city). Covers a land area of 0.831 square miles and a water area of 0 square miles. Located at 34.01° N. Lat; 102.41° W. Long. Elevation is 3,652 feet.
History: Amherst was established in 1923 when the railroad arrived. It was located on land that once belonged to the Mashed O Ranch.
Population: 742 (1990); 791 (2000); 708 (2010); 676 (2015 projected); Race: 66.4% White, 8.2% Black, 0.0% Asian, 25.4% Other, 39.0% Hispanic of any race (2010); Density: 851.6 persons per square mile (2010); Average household size: 2.70 (2010); Median age: 39.1 (2010); Males per 100 females: 91.9 (2010); Marriage status: 20.0% never married, 65.3% now married, 7.8% widowed, 6.9% divorced (2005-2009 5-year est.); Foreign born: 18.6% (2005-2009 5-year est.); Ancestry (includes multiple ancestries): 14.3% Irish, 8.5% English, 6.7% German, 3.2% American, 1.8% French (2005-2009 5-year est.).
Economy: Single-family building permits issued: 0 (2010); Multi-family building permits issued: 0 (2010); Employment by occupation: 0.0% management, 11.5% professional, 4.1% services, 35.7% sales, 17.8% farming, 7.8% construction, 23.0% production (2005-2009 5-year est.).
Income: Per capita income: $20,339 (2010); Median household income: $39,865 (2010); Average household income: $55,266 (2010); Percent of households with income of $100,000 or more: 11.4% (2010); Poverty rate: 24.1% (2005-2009 5-year est.).
Taxes: Total city taxes per capita: $127 (2007); City property taxes per capita: $113 (2007).
Education: Percent of population age 25 and over with: High school diploma (including GED) or higher: 67.5% (2010); Bachelor's degree or higher: 12.9% (2010); Master's degree or higher: 2.0% (2010).
School District(s)
Amherst ISD (PK-12)
  2009-10 Enrollment: 180 . . . . (806) 246-3501
Housing: Homeownership rate: 76.0% (2010); Median home value: $41,200 (2010); Median contract rent: $173 per month (2005-2009 5-year est.); Median year structure built: 1956 (2005-2009 5-year est.).
Transportation: Commute to work: 91.4% car, 0.0% public transportation, 7.1% walk, 1.5% work from home (2005-2009 5-year est.); Travel time to work: 44.2% less than 15 minutes, 45.7% 15 to 30 minutes, 4.5% 30 to 45 minutes, 0.0% 45 to 60 minutes, 5.7% 60 minutes or more (2005-2009 5-year est.)

EARTH (city). Covers a land area of 1.197 square miles and a water area of 0 square miles. Located at 34.23° N. Lat; 102.40° W. Long. Elevation is 3,694 feet.
History: The town of Earth was named during a sandstorm. Earth developed in an area of irrigated farms.
Population: 1,228 (1990); 1,109 (2000); 993 (2010); 932 (2015 projected); Race: 66.5% White, 2.5% Black, 0.0% Asian, 31.0% Other, 53.0% Hispanic of any race (2010); Density: 829.3 persons per square mile (2010); Average household size: 2.73 (2010); Median age: 34.4 (2010); Males per 100 females: 91.0 (2010); Marriage status: 25.8% never married, 54.1% now married, 9.6% widowed, 10.4% divorced (2005-2009 5-year est.); Foreign born: 3.1% (2005-2009 5-year est.); Ancestry (includes multiple ancestries): 7.1% German, 5.8% Irish, 3.9% African, 3.8% American, 2.9% English (2005-2009 5-year est.).
Economy: Single-family building permits issued: 0 (2010); Multi-family building permits issued: 0 (2010); Employment by occupation: 8.4% management, 23.4% professional, 22.7% services, 17.4% sales, 9.0% farming, 3.9% construction, 15.1% production (2005-2009 5-year est.).
Income: Per capita income: $15,756 (2010); Median household income: $31,349 (2010); Average household income: $43,276 (2010); Percent of

households with income of $100,000 or more: 5.5% (2010); Poverty rate: 23.5% (2005-2009 5-year est.).

Taxes: Total city taxes per capita: $201 (2007); City property taxes per capita: $127 (2007).

Education: Percent of population age 25 and over with: High school diploma (including GED) or higher: 63.1% (2010); Bachelor's degree or higher: 13.2% (2010); Master's degree or higher: 1.7% (2010).

School District(s)

Springlake-Earth ISD (PK-12)

    2009-10 Enrollment: 425 . . . . (806) 257-3310

Housing: Homeownership rate: 81.3% (2010); Median home value: $32,632 (2010); Median contract rent: $228 per month (2005-2009 5-year est.); Median year structure built: 1956 (2005-2009 5-year est.).

Newspapers: Earth Weekly News (Community news; Circulation 950)

Transportation: Commute to work: 83.4% car, 0.0% public transportation, 8.9% walk, 7.7% work from home (2005-2009 5-year est.); Travel time to work: 33.9% less than 15 minutes, 37.5% 15 to 30 minutes, 17.2% 30 to 45 minutes, 6.0% 45 to 60 minutes, 5.5% 60 minutes or more (2005-2009 5-year est.)

FIELDTON (unincorporated postal area, zip code 79326). Covers a land area of 7.334 square miles and a water area of 0 square miles. Located at 34.04° N. Lat; 102.21° W. Long. Elevation is 3,579 feet.

Population: 42 (2000); Race: 100.0% White, 0.0% Black, 0.0% Asian, 0.0% Other, 17.9% Hispanic of any race (2000); Density: 5.7 persons per square mile (2000); Age: 7.7% under 18, 92.3% over 64 (2000); Marriage status: 0.0% never married, 88.9% now married, 11.1% widowed, 0.0% divorced (2000); Foreign born: 10.3% (2000); Ancestry (includes multiple ancestries): 46.2% American, 43.6% English, 20.5% French (2000).

Income: Per capita income: $9,613 (2000); Median household income: $9,375 (2000); Poverty rate: 179.1% (2000).

Education: Percent of population age 25 and over with: High school diploma (including GED) or higher: 22.2% (2000); Bachelor's degree or higher: 0.0% (2000).

Housing: Homeownership rate: 77.8% (2000); Median home value: $12,500 (2000); Median contract rent: n/a per month (2000); Median year structure built: 1957 (2000).

LITTLEFIELD (city). County seat. Covers a land area of 5.995 square miles and a water area of 0 square miles. Located at 33.92° N. Lat; 102.33° W. Long. Elevation is 3,556 feet.

History: Littlefield came into existence about 1912, on land that had been grazing grounds until then. The town developed as a shipping center for cattle and a processing center for cotton, with gins, compresses, and cottonseed oil mills.

Population: 6,489 (1990); 6,507 (2000); 6,098 (2010); 5,916 (2015 projected); Race: 77.1% White, 5.4% Black, 0.3% Asian, 17.2% Other, 56.0% Hispanic of any race (2010); Density: 1,017.2 persons per square mile (2010); Average household size: 2.65 (2010); Median age: 36.1 (2010); Males per 100 females: 94.6 (2010); Marriage status: 27.0% never married, 54.4% now married, 9.7% widowed, 9.0% divorced (2005-2009 5-year est.); Foreign born: 10.7% (2005-2009 5-year est.); Ancestry (includes multiple ancestries): 6.6% American, 6.4% English, 5.6% Irish, 4.0% German, 1.6% Scottish (2005-2009 5-year est.).

Economy: Single-family building permits issued: 0 (2010); Multi-family building permits issued: 0 (2010); Employment by occupation: 10.5% management, 10.3% professional, 21.3% services, 22.6% sales, 1.9% farming, 9.7% construction, 23.8% production (2005-2009 5-year est.).

Income: Per capita income: $14,868 (2010); Median household income: $29,725 (2010); Average household income: $39,558 (2010); Percent of households with income of $100,000 or more: 5.6% (2010); Poverty rate: 19.3% (2005-2009 5-year est.).

Taxes: Total city taxes per capita: $283 (2007); City property taxes per capita: $163 (2007).

Education: Percent of population age 25 and over with: High school diploma (including GED) or higher: 70.5% (2010); Bachelor's degree or higher: 10.4% (2010); Master's degree or higher: 3.3% (2010).

School District(s)

Littlefield ISD (PK-12)

    2009-10 Enrollment: 1,479 . . . . (806) 385-3844

Housing: Homeownership rate: 71.8% (2010); Median home value: $37,831 (2010); Median contract rent: $394 per month (2005-2009 5-year est.); Median year structure built: 1966 (2005-2009 5-year est.).

Hospitals: Lamb Healthcare Center (75 beds)

Safety: Violent crime rate: 42.6 per 10,000 population; Property crime rate: 350.9 per 10,000 population (2009).

Newspapers: Lamb County Leader-News (Local news; Circulation 2,850)

Transportation: Commute to work: 93.7% car, 0.0% public transportation, 3.0% walk, 2.0% work from home (2005-2009 5-year est.); Travel time to work: 74.2% less than 15 minutes, 6.6% 15 to 30 minutes, 9.5% 30 to 45 minutes, 3.8% 45 to 60 minutes, 5.9% 60 minutes or more (2005-2009 5-year est.)

Additional Information Contacts

City of Littlefield . . . . (806) 385-5161

    http://www.littlefieldtexas.org

Littlefield Chamber of Commerce . . . . (806) 385-5331

    http://www.littlefieldtexas.org

OLTON (city). Covers a land area of 1.359 square miles and a water area of 0 square miles. Located at 34.18° N. Lat; 102.13° W. Long. Elevation is 3,612 feet.

History: Olton was known for its prevailing winds, which made everything in the town lean toward the north.

Population: 2,116 (1990); 2,288 (2000); 2,163 (2010); 2,087 (2015 projected); Race: 57.7% White, 1.8% Black, 0.2% Asian, 40.3% Other, 70.2% Hispanic of any race (2010); Density: 1,591.8 persons per square mile (2010); Average household size: 2.92 (2010); Median age: 33.6 (2010); Males per 100 females: 96.8 (2010); Marriage status: 21.3% never married, 59.7% now married, 8.3% widowed, 10.8% divorced (2005-2009 5-year est.); Foreign born: 14.3% (2005-2009 5-year est.); Ancestry (includes multiple ancestries): 6.8% German, 3.7% Irish, 2.2% English, 1.1% American, 0.7% Italian (2005-2009 5-year est.).

Economy: Single-family building permits issued: 0 (2010); Multi-family building permits issued: 0 (2010); Employment by occupation: 8.1% management, 8.5% professional, 20.7% services, 19.1% sales, 12.6% farming, 12.0% construction, 18.9% production (2005-2009 5-year est.).

Income: Per capita income: $13,598 (2010); Median household income: $32,132 (2010); Average household income: $39,899 (2010); Percent of households with income of $100,000 or more: 5.7% (2010); Poverty rate: 21.5% (2005-2009 5-year est.).

Taxes: Total city taxes per capita: $260 (2007); City property taxes per capita: $169 (2007).

Education: Percent of population age 25 and over with: High school diploma (including GED) or higher: 59.4% (2010); Bachelor's degree or higher: 12.2% (2010); Master's degree or higher: 3.9% (2010).

School District(s)

Olton ISD (PK-12)

    2009-10 Enrollment: 711 . . . . (806) 285-2641

Housing: Homeownership rate: 73.6% (2010); Median home value: $41,971 (2010); Median contract rent: $317 per month (2005-2009 5-year est.); Median year structure built: 1961 (2005-2009 5-year est.).

Safety: Violent crime rate: 28.1 per 10,000 population; Property crime rate: 102.9 per 10,000 population (2009).

Newspapers: Olton Enterprise (Community news; Circulation 1,000)

Transportation: Commute to work: 91.8% car, 0.0% public transportation, 2.7% walk, 4.1% work from home (2005-2009 5-year est.); Travel time to work: 56.0% less than 15 minutes, 13.9% 15 to 30 minutes, 24.8% 30 to 45 minutes, 1.8% 45 to 60 minutes, 3.5% 60 minutes or more (2005-2009 5-year est.)

Additional Information Contacts

Olton Chamber of Commerce . . . . (806) 285-2292

    http://www.oltonchamber.org

SPADE (CDP). Covers a land area of 1.959 square miles and a water area of 0 square miles. Located at 33.91° N. Lat; 102.15° W. Long. Elevation is 3,517 feet.

Population: 129 (1990); 100 (2000); 89 (2010); 85 (2015 projected); Race: 86.5% White, 5.6% Black, 0.0% Asian, 7.9% Other, 16.9% Hispanic of any race (2010); Density: 45.4 persons per square mile (2010); Average household size: 2.54 (2010); Median age: 48.7 (2010); Males per 100 females: 111.9 (2010); Marriage status: 11.8% never married, 79.4% now married, 8.8% widowed, 0.0% divorced (2005-2009 5-year est.); Foreign born: 0.0% (2005-2009 5-year est.); Ancestry (includes multiple ancestries): 10.3% English, 5.2% German, 5.2% Irish (2005-2009 5-year est.).

Economy: Employment by occupation: 36.0% management, 28.0% professional, 0.0% services, 20.0% sales, 0.0% farming, 16.0% construction, 0.0% production (2005-2009 5-year est.).

Income: Per capita income: $24,066 (2010); Median household income: $51,786 (2010); Average household income: $77,929 (2010); Percent of households with income of $100,000 or more: 22.9% (2010); Poverty rate: 29.3% (2005-2009 5-year est.).

Education: Percent of population age 25 and over with: High school diploma (including GED) or higher: 82.1% (2010); Bachelor's degree or higher: 13.4% (2010); Master's degree or higher: 4.5% (2010).

Housing: Homeownership rate: 77.1% (2010); Median home value: $87,500 (2010); Median contract rent: $206 per month (2005-2009 5-year est.); Median year structure built: 1970 (2005-2009 5-year est.).

Transportation: Commute to work: 56.3% car, 0.0% public transportation, 43.8% walk, 0.0% work from home (2005-2009 5-year est.); Travel time to work: 100.0% less than 15 minutes, 0.0% 15 to 30 minutes, 0.0% 30 to 45 minutes, 0.0% 45 to 60 minutes, 0.0% 60 minutes or more (2005-2009 5-year est.)

SPRINGLAKE (town). Covers a land area of 1.018 square miles and a water area of 0 square miles. Located at 34.23° N. Lat; 102.30° W. Long. Elevation is 3,681 feet.

Population: 132 (1990); 135 (2000); 127 (2010); 122 (2015 projected); Race: 85.8% White, 0.8% Black, 0.0% Asian, 13.4% Other, 34.6% Hispanic of any race (2010); Density: 124.7 persons per square mile (2010); Average household size: 2.49 (2010); Median age: 42.5 (2010); Males per 100 females: 89.6 (2010); Marriage status: 45.9% never married, 37.6% now married, 9.4% widowed, 7.1% divorced (2005-2009 5-year est.); Foreign born: 6.8% (2005-2009 5-year est.); Ancestry (includes multiple ancestries): 19.3% Irish, 18.2% German, 13.6% French, 8.0% Scottish, 3.4% English (2005-2009 5-year est.).

Economy: Employment by occupation: 5.8% management, 3.8% professional, 28.8% services, 0.0% sales, 34.6% farming, 21.2% construction, 5.8% production (2005-2009 5-year est.).

Income: Per capita income: $25,729 (2010); Median household income: $38,750 (2010); Average household income: $70,000 (2010); Percent of households with income of $100,000 or more: 15.7% (2010); Poverty rate: 1.1% (2005-2009 5-year est.).

Taxes: Total city taxes per capita: $346 (2007); City property taxes per capita: $346 (2007).

Education: Percent of population age 25 and over with: High school diploma (including GED) or higher: 81.3% (2010); Bachelor's degree or higher: 19.8% (2010); Master's degree or higher: 6.6% (2010).

Housing: Homeownership rate: 72.5% (2010); Median home value: $58,333 (2010); Median contract rent: n/a per month (2005-2009 5-year est.); Median year structure built: 1962 (2005-2009 5-year est.).

Transportation: Commute to work: 100.0% car, 0.0% public transportation, 0.0% walk, 0.0% work from home (2005-2009 5-year est.); Travel time to work: 57.1% less than 15 minutes, 22.4% 15 to 30 minutes, 20.4% 30 to 45 minutes, 0.0% 45 to 60 minutes, 0.0% 60 minutes or more (2005-2009 5-year est.)

SUDAN (city). Covers a land area of 0.907 square miles and a water area of 0 square miles. Located at 34.06° N. Lat; 102.52° W. Long. Elevation is 3,753 feet.

History: Sudan, settled as a service center for the surrounding ranches, was named for the sudan grass that was a principal crop.

Population: 983 (1990); 1,039 (2000); 1,023 (2010); 1,002 (2015 projected); Race: 66.4% White, 4.4% Black, 0.0% Asian, 29.2% Other, 38.0% Hispanic of any race (2010); Density: 1,127.6 persons per square mile (2010); Average household size: 2.56 (2010); Median age: 38.4 (2010); Males per 100 females: 88.1 (2010); Marriage status: 17.1% never married, 57.1% now married, 18.1% widowed, 7.7% divorced (2005-2009 5-year est.); Foreign born: 4.6% (2005-2009 5-year est.); Ancestry (includes multiple ancestries): 13.4% German, 13.2% English, 12.9% American, 7.1% Irish, 4.7% Scotch-Irish (2005-2009 5-year est.).

Economy: Employment by occupation: 11.7% management, 13.2% professional, 19.9% services, 14.0% sales, 7.6% farming, 14.9% construction, 18.7% production (2005-2009 5-year est.).

Income: Per capita income: $25,449 (2010); Median household income: $47,976 (2010); Average household income: $65,633 (2010); Percent of households with income of $100,000 or more: 18.8% (2010); Poverty rate: 18.8% (2005-2009 5-year est.).

Taxes: Total city taxes per capita: $311 (2007); City property taxes per capita: $147 (2007).

Education: Percent of population age 25 and over with: High school diploma (including GED) or higher: 71.5% (2010); Bachelor's degree or higher: 17.1% (2010); Master's degree or higher: 4.7% (2010).

School District(s)
Sudan ISD (PK-12)
  2009-10 Enrollment: 405 . . . . (806) 227-2431

Housing: Homeownership rate: 77.9% (2010); Median home value: $50,282 (2010); Median contract rent: $403 per month (2005-2009 5-year est.); Median year structure built: 1959 (2005-2009 5-year est.).

Safety: Violent crime rate: 10.3 per 10,000 population; Property crime rate: 82.2 per 10,000 population (2009).

Newspapers: Sudan Beacon News (Community news; Circulation 700)

Transportation: Commute to work: 94.5% car, 0.0% public transportation, 1.5% walk, 3.4% work from home (2005-2009 5-year est.); Travel time to work: 41.1% less than 15 minutes, 50.9% 15 to 30 minutes, 4.1% 30 to 45 minutes, 3.2% 45 to 60 minutes, 0.6% 60 minutes or more (2005-2009 5-year est.)

Lampasas County

Located in central Texas; bounded on the west by the Colorado River; drained by the Lampasas River. Covers a land area of 712.04 square miles, a water area of 1.92 square miles, and is located in the Central Time Zone at 31.14° N. Lat., 98.21° W. Long. The county was founded in 1856. County seat is Lampasas.

Lampasas County is part of the Killeen-Temple-Fort Hood, TX Metropolitan Statistical Area. The entire metro area includes: Bell County, TX; Coryell County, TX; Lampasas County, TX

Weather Station: Lampasas										Elevation: 1,023 feet		
	Jan	Feb	Mar	Apr	May	Jun	Jul	Aug	Sep	Oct	Nov	Dec
High	59	63	69	78	84	90	94	95	89	79	69	59
Low	32	36	43	51	61	68	71	70	63	53	42	33
Precip	1.8	2.2	2.7	2.3	4.4	3.8	2.0	2.1	2.7	3.5	2.4	2.2
Snow	0.2	0.1	0.0	0.0	0.0	0.0	0.0	0.0	0.0	0.0	0.1	tr

High and Low temperatures in degrees Fahrenheit; Precipitation and Snow in inches

Population: 13,521 (1990); 17,762 (2000); 21,861 (2010); 23,816 (2015 projected); Race: 84.9% White, 3.6% Black, 1.0% Asian, 10.4% Other, 16.5% Hispanic of any race (2010); Density: 30.7 persons per square mile (2010); Average household size: 2.66 (2010); Median age: 37.9 (2010); Males per 100 females: 95.7 (2010).

Religion: Five largest groups: 22.6% Southern Baptist Convention, 11.7% Catholic Church, 4.4% The United Methodist Church, 3.4% Churches of Christ, 1.7% Episcopal Church (2000).

Economy: Unemployment rate: 7.5% (June 2011); Total civilian labor force: 10,877 (June 2011); Leading industries: 20.7% construction; 17.8% retail trade; 16.0% manufacturing (2009); Farms: 966 totaling 416,018 acres (2007); Companies that employ 500 or more persons: 0 (2009); Companies that employ 100 to 499 persons: 4 (2009); Companies that employ less than 100 persons: 392 (2009); Black-owned businesses: n/a (2007); Hispanic-owned businesses: n/a (2007); Asian-owned businesses: n/a (2007); Women-owned businesses: 476 (2007); Retail sales per capita: $10,232 (2010). Single-family building permits issued: 14 (2010); Multi-family building permits issued: 0 (2010).

Income: Per capita income: $23,524 (2010); Median household income: $49,526 (2010); Average household income: $63,417 (2010); Percent of households with income of $100,000 or more: 14.5% (2010); Poverty rate: 17.9% (2009); Bankruptcy rate: 0.86% (2010).

Taxes: Total county taxes per capita: $186 (2007); County property taxes per capita: $140 (2007).

Education: Percent of population age 25 and over with: High school diploma (including GED) or higher: 79.2% (2010); Bachelor's degree or higher: 16.9% (2010); Master's degree or higher: 3.8% (2010).

Housing: Homeownership rate: 77.3% (2010); Median home value: $108,760 (2010); Median contract rent: $439 per month (2005-2009 5-year est.); Median year structure built: 1982 (2005-2009 5-year est.).

Health: Birth rate: 119.1 per 10,000 population (2009); Death rate: 93.7 per 10,000 population (2009); Age-adjusted cancer mortality rate: 250.9 deaths per 100,000 population (2007); Number of physicians: 6.7 per 10,000 population (2008); Hospital beds: 12.1 per 10,000 population (2007); Hospital admissions: 428.1 per 10,000 population (2007).

Elections: 2008 Presidential election results: 24.9% Obama, 74.0% McCain, 0.1% Nader

Additional Information Contacts
Lampasas County Government . . . . (512) 556-8271
  http://www.co.lampasas.tx.us/ips/cms

City of Lampasas . . . . (512) 556-6831
　　http://www.cityoflampasas.com
Lampasas County Chamber of Commerce . . . . (512) 556-5172
　　http://www.lampaschamber.org

Lampasas County Communities

KEMPNER (city). Covers a land area of 2.230 square miles and a water area of 0 square miles. Located at 31.07° N. Lat; 97.98° W. Long. Elevation is 866 feet.
Population: 714 (1990); 1,004 (2000); 1,208 (2010); 1,308 (2015 projected); Race: 80.0% White, 8.1% Black, 2.4% Asian, 9.4% Other, 10.4% Hispanic of any race (2010); Density: 541.8 persons per square mile (2010); Average household size: 2.82 (2010); Median age: 39.0 (2010); Males per 100 females: 95.5 (2010); Marriage status: 25.1% never married, 43.7% now married, 4.5% widowed, 26.7% divorced (2005-2009 5-year est.); Foreign born: 6.6% (2005-2009 5-year est.); Ancestry (includes multiple ancestries): 23.8% German, 21.7% Irish, 15.3% English, 4.3% French, 4.3% Portuguese (2005-2009 5-year est.).
Economy: Employment by occupation: 2.9% management, 19.1% professional, 20.3% services, 31.4% sales, 0.0% farming, 12.2% construction, 14.1% production (2005-2009 5-year est.).
Income: Per capita income: $23,005 (2010); Median household income: $53,784 (2010); Average household income: $65,076 (2010); Percent of households with income of $100,000 or more: 15.9% (2010); Poverty rate: 17.2% (2005-2009 5-year est.).
Taxes: Total city taxes per capita: $121 (2007); City property taxes per capita: $62 (2007).
Education: Percent of population age 25 and over with: High school diploma (including GED) or higher: 91.7% (2010); Bachelor's degree or higher: 13.2% (2010); Master's degree or higher: 4.0% (2010).
Housing: Homeownership rate: 84.1% (2010); Median home value: $115,323 (2010); Median contract rent: $426 per month (2005-2009 5-year est.); Median year structure built: 1984 (2005-2009 5-year est.).
Safety: Violent crime rate: 0.0 per 10,000 population; Property crime rate: 0.0 per 10,000 population (2009).
Transportation: Commute to work: 99.2% car, 0.0% public transportation, 0.0% walk, 0.0% work from home (2005-2009 5-year est.); Travel time to work: 11.2% less than 15 minutes, 44.5% 15 to 30 minutes, 31.8% 30 to 45 minutes, 0.5% 45 to 60 minutes, 12.1% 60 minutes or more (2005-2009 5-year est.)

LAMPASAS (city). County seat. Covers a land area of 6.184 square miles and a water area of 0.036 square miles. Located at 31.06° N. Lat; 98.18° W. Long. Elevation is 1,027 feet.
History: Lampasas was a cattle town in the 1870's, and became a shipping center for livestock, pecans, wool, and furs.
Population: 6,234 (1990); 6,786 (2000); 8,108 (2010); 8,774 (2015 projected); Race: 86.7% White, 1.4% Black, 0.7% Asian, 11.1% Other, 22.0% Hispanic of any race (2010); Density: 1,311.1 persons per square mile (2010); Average household size: 2.57 (2010); Median age: 36.5 (2010); Males per 100 females: 90.9 (2010); Marriage status: 26.2% never married, 50.6% now married, 11.8% widowed, 11.4% divorced (2005-2009 5-year est.); Foreign born: 8.2% (2005-2009 5-year est.); Ancestry (includes multiple ancestries): 18.2% German, 14.8% Irish, 10.9% English, 8.2% American, 3.4% French (2005-2009 5-year est.).
Economy: Single-family building permits issued: 14 (2010); Multi-family building permits issued: 0 (2010); Employment by occupation: 5.9% management, 11.1% professional, 21.9% services, 30.3% sales, 2.1% farming, 15.6% construction, 13.1% production (2005-2009 5-year est.).
Income: Per capita income: $20,078 (2010); Median household income: $42,829 (2010); Average household income: $52,778 (2010); Percent of households with income of $100,000 or more: 10.5% (2010); Poverty rate: 23.8% (2005-2009 5-year est.).
Taxes: Total city taxes per capita: $304 (2007); City property taxes per capita: $117 (2007).
Education: Percent of population age 25 and over with: High school diploma (including GED) or higher: 71.2% (2010); Bachelor's degree or higher: 15.7% (2010); Master's degree or higher: 3.1% (2010).
School District(s)
Lampasas ISD (PK-12)
　　2009-10 Enrollment: 3,372 . . . . (512) 556-6224
Housing: Homeownership rate: 68.2% (2010); Median home value: $88,100 (2010); Median contract rent: $457 per month (2005-2009 5-year est.); Median year structure built: 1969 (2005-2009 5-year est.).

Hospitals: Rollins Brook Community Hospital
Safety: Violent crime rate: 24.7 per 10,000 population; Property crime rate: 235.6 per 10,000 population (2009).
Newspapers: Lampasas Dispatch Record (Local news; Circulation 4,238)
Transportation: Commute to work: 84.1% car, 0.0% public transportation, 8.4% walk, 3.6% work from home (2005-2009 5-year est.); Travel time to work: 56.2% less than 15 minutes, 14.3% 15 to 30 minutes, 16.2% 30 to 45 minutes, 3.9% 45 to 60 minutes, 9.3% 60 minutes or more (2005-2009 5-year est.)
Additional Information Contacts
City of Lampasas . . . . (512) 556-6831
　　http://www.cityoflampasas.com
Lampasas County Chamber of Commerce . . . . (512) 556-5172
　　http://www.lampaschamber.org

LOMETA (city). Covers a land area of 0.902 square miles and a water area of 0 square miles. Located at 31.21° N. Lat; 98.39° W. Long. Elevation is 1,493 feet.
Population: 625 (1990); 782 (2000); 901 (2010); 962 (2015 projected); Race: 84.2% White, 3.6% Black, 0.4% Asian, 11.8% Other, 29.3% Hispanic of any race (2010); Density: 998.5 persons per square mile (2010); Average household size: 2.50 (2010); Median age: 33.2 (2010); Males per 100 females: 102.5 (2010); Marriage status: 33.3% never married, 40.6% now married, 13.1% widowed, 13.0% divorced (2005-2009 5-year est.); Foreign born: 5.1% (2005-2009 5-year est.); Ancestry (includes multiple ancestries): 9.8% Irish, 8.4% German, 6.5% English, 5.0% American, 3.7% Scotch-Irish (2005-2009 5-year est.).
Economy: Employment by occupation: 0.0% management, 16.3% professional, 44.0% services, 5.1% sales, 2.3% farming, 12.5% construction, 19.8% production (2005-2009 5-year est.).
Income: Per capita income: $19,920 (2010); Median household income: $39,950 (2010); Average household income: $51,924 (2010); Percent of households with income of $100,000 or more: 13.7% (2010); Poverty rate: 32.0% (2005-2009 5-year est.).
Taxes: Total city taxes per capita: $191 (2007); City property taxes per capita: $60 (2007).
Education: Percent of population age 25 and over with: High school diploma (including GED) or higher: 56.8% (2010); Bachelor's degree or higher: 11.6% (2010); Master's degree or higher: 2.5% (2010).
School District(s)
Lometa ISD (PK-12)
　　2009-10 Enrollment: 314 . . . . (512) 752-3384
Orenda Charter School (01-12)
　　2009-10 Enrollment: 185 . . . . (512) 869-3020
Housing: Homeownership rate: 72.9% (2010); Median home value: $57,260 (2010); Median contract rent: $292 per month (2005-2009 5-year est.); Median year structure built: 1969 (2005-2009 5-year est.).
Transportation: Commute to work: 82.0% car, 0.0% public transportation, 15.6% walk, 1.2% work from home (2005-2009 5-year est.); Travel time to work: 54.8% less than 15 minutes, 25.7% 15 to 30 minutes, 10.8% 30 to 45 minutes, 0.0% 45 to 60 minutes, 8.7% 60 minutes or more (2005-2009 5-year est.)

Lavaca County

Located in south Texas; coastal plains area, drained by the Lavaca and Navidad Rivers. Covers a land area of 969.90 square miles, a water area of 0.45 square miles, and is located in the Central Time Zone at 29.39° N. Lat; 97.00° W. Long. The county was founded in 1846. County seat is Hallettsville.

Weather Station: Hallettsville 2 N　　　　　　　　　Elevation: 274 feet

	Jan	Feb	Mar	Apr	May	Jun	Jul	Aug	Sep	Oct	Nov	Dec
High	64	67	73	80	86	91	94	95	90	83	73	65
Low	43	46	52	59	67	72	73	73	68	60	51	44
Precip	2.9	2.4	2.6	3.1	4.8	4.6	2.6	2.9	3.8	4.6	3.8	2.6
Snow	0.1	tr	tr	0.0	0.0	0.0	0.0	0.0	0.0	0.0	0.0	tr

High and Low temperatures in degrees Fahrenheit; Precipitation and Snow in inches

Weather Station: Yoakum　　　　　　　　　　　　　Elevation: 325 feet

	Jan	Feb	Mar	Apr	May	Jun	Jul	Aug	Sep	Oct	Nov	Dec
High	62	67	73	80	86	92	95	96	91	82	73	64
Low	40	44	51	58	66	71	72	72	67	59	50	42
Precip	2.7	2.2	2.8	3.0	4.4	4.2	2.7	3.5	3.1	5.1	3.4	2.7
Snow	tr	tr	0.0	0.0	0.0	0.0	0.0	0.0	0.0	0.0	0.0	tr

High and Low temperatures in degrees Fahrenheit; Precipitation and Snow in inches

Population: 18,690 (1990); 19,210 (2000); 19,184 (2010); 19,135 (2015 projected); Race: 84.6% White, 6.7% Black, 0.2% Asian, 8.4% Other, 15.5% Hispanic of any race (2010); Density: 19.8 persons per square mile (2010); Average household size: 2.42 (2010); Median age: 42.7 (2010); Males per 100 females: 93.4 (2010).

Religion: Five largest groups: 70.0% Catholic Church, 10.6% Evangelical Lutheran Church in America, 10.1% Southern Baptist Convention, 4.6% The United Methodist Church, 1.4% Churches of Christ (2000).

Economy: Unemployment rate: 6.6% (June 2011); Total civilian labor force: 9,874 (June 2011); Leading industries: 26.6% manufacturing; 18.2% health care and social assistance; 14.1% retail trade (2009); Farms: 2,747 totaling 566,648 acres (2007); Companies that employ 500 or more persons: 0 (2009); Companies that employ 100 to 499 persons: 10 (2009); Companies that employ less than 100 persons: 443 (2009); Black-owned businesses: n/a (2007); Hispanic-owned businesses: n/a (2007); Asian-owned businesses: n/a (2007); Women-owned businesses: 488 (2007); Retail sales per capita: $9,555 (2010). Single-family building permits issued: 9 (2010); Multi-family building permits issued: 0 (2010).

Income: Per capita income: $21,608 (2010); Median household income: $39,220 (2010); Average household income: $52,888 (2010); Percent of households with income of $100,000 or more: 10.6% (2010); Poverty rate: 12.6% (2009); Bankruptcy rate: 0.77% (2010).

Taxes: Total county taxes per capita: $170 (2007); County property taxes per capita: $147 (2007).

Education: Percent of population age 25 and over with: High school diploma (including GED) or higher: 74.3% (2010); Bachelor's degree or higher: 12.8% (2010); Master's degree or higher: 3.6% (2010).

Housing: Homeownership rate: 76.8% (2010); Median home value: $83,364 (2010); Median contract rent: $340 per month (2005-2009 5-year est.); Median year structure built: 1968 (2005-2009 5-year est.)

Health: Birth rate: 137.0 per 10,000 population (2009); Death rate: 130.0 per 10,000 population (2009); Age-adjusted cancer mortality rate: 156.4 deaths per 100,000 population (2007); Number of physicians: 10.8 per 10,000 population (2008); Hospital beds: 26.8 per 10,000 population (2007); Hospital admissions: 1,042.5 per 10,000 population (2007).

Elections: 2008 Presidential election results: 22.7% Obama, 76.5% McCain, 0.0% Nader

Additional Information Contacts

Lavaca County Government . . . . (361) 798-2301
   http://www.co.lavaca.tx.us/ips/cms
City of Yoakum . . . . (361) 293-6321
   http://www.cityofyoakum.org
Hallettsville Chamber of Commerce . . . . (361) 798-2662
   http://www.hallettsville.com
Moulton Chamber of Commerce . . . . (361) 596-7205
   http://www.moultontexas.com
Shiner Chamber of Commerce . . . . (361) 594-4180
   http://www.shinertx.com
Yoakum Area Chamber of Commerce. . . . . (361) 293-2309
   http://www.yoakumareachamber.com

Lavaca County Communities

HALLETTSVILLE (city). County seat. Covers a land area of 2.231 square miles and a water area of 0 square miles. Located at 29.44° N. Lat; 96.94° W. Long. Elevation is 233 feet.

History: Many of the early residents of Hallettsville were German and Polish immigrants. A local legend hints of a Lost Dutchman's Lead Mine in the vicinity.

Population: 2,776 (1990); 2,345 (2000); 2,409 (2010); 2,436 (2015 projected); Race: 82.0% White, 10.8% Black, 0.1% Asian, 7.1% Other, 12.0% Hispanic of any race (2010); Density: 1,079.7 persons per square mile (2010); Average household size: 2.29 (2010); Median age: 42.0 (2010); Males per 100 females: 88.9 (2010); Marriage status: 28.1% never married, 53.2% now married, 7.0% widowed, 11.7% divorced (2005-2009 5-year est.); Foreign born: 0.9% (2005-2009 5-year est.); Ancestry (includes multiple ancestries): 48.1% German, 28.2% Czech, 15.9% Irish, 4.3% American, 3.8% English (2005-2009 5-year est.).

Economy: Single-family building permits issued: 0 (2010); Multi-family building permits issued: 0 (2010); Employment by occupation: 9.5% management, 21.1% professional, 21.0% services, 20.9% sales, 0.0% farming, 10.5% construction, 17.1% production (2005-2009 5-year est.).

Income: Per capita income: $19,883 (2010); Median household income: $33,186 (2010); Average household income: $46,488 (2010); Percent of

households with income of $100,000 or more: 8.5% (2010); Poverty rate: 16.6% (2005-2009 5-year est.).

Taxes: Total city taxes per capita: $305 (2007); City property taxes per capita: $121 (2007).

Education: Percent of population age 25 and over with: High school diploma (including GED) or higher: 75.3% (2010); Bachelor's degree or higher: 12.6% (2010); Master's degree or higher: 3.4% (2010).

School District(s)

Ezzell ISD (KG-08)
   2009-10 Enrollment: 59 . . . . (361) 798-4448
Hallettsville ISD (PK-12)
   2009-10 Enrollment: 867 . . . . (361) 798-2242
Vysehrad ISD (KG-08)
   2009-10 Enrollment: 95 . . . . (361) 798-4118

Housing: Homeownership rate: 70.0% (2010); Median home value: $77,813 (2010); Median contract rent: $341 per month (2005-2009 5-year est.); Median year structure built: 1968 (2005-2009 5-year est.).

Hospitals: Lavaca Medical Center (43 beds)

Safety: Violent crime rate: 24.2 per 10,000 population; Property crime rate: 262.1 per 10,000 population (2009).

Newspapers: Tribune Herald (Local news; Circulation 4,000)

Transportation: Commute to work: 93.2% car, 0.0% public transportation, 4.6% walk, 0.5% work from home (2005-2009 5-year est.); Travel time to work: 58.5% less than 15 minutes, 19.1% 15 to 30 minutes, 11.9% 30 to 45 minutes, 6.1% 45 to 60 minutes, 4.4% 60 minutes or more (2005-2009 5-year est.)

Additional Information Contacts

Hallettsville Chamber of Commerce . . . . (361) 798-2662
   http://www.hallettsville.com

MOULTON (town). Covers a land area of 0.823 square miles and a water area of 0 square miles. Located at 29.57° N. Lat; 97.14° W. Long. Elevation is 361 feet.

Population: 923 (1990); 944 (2000); 955 (2010); 958 (2015 projected); Race: 96.1% White, 0.7% Black, 0.0% Asian, 3.1% Other, 17.4% Hispanic of any race (2010); Density: 1,160.6 persons per square mile (2010); Average household size: 2.38 (2010); Median age: 46.3 (2010); Males per 100 females: 91.0 (2010); Marriage status: 21.2% never married, 51.3% now married, 16.1% widowed, 11.4% divorced (2005-2009 5-year est.); Foreign born: 4.1% (2005-2009 5-year est.); Ancestry (includes multiple ancestries): 42.2% Czech, 28.4% German, 5.2% Ukrainian, 5.0% Irish, 4.5% American (2005-2009 5-year est.).

Economy: Employment by occupation: 5.0% management, 16.5% professional, 19.2% services, 16.0% sales, 2.5% farming, 15.8% construction, 24.9% production (2005-2009 5-year est.).

Income: Per capita income: $21,439 (2010); Median household income: $40,077 (2010); Average household income: $53,618 (2010); Percent of households with income of $100,000 or more: 10.8% (2010); Poverty rate: 6.9% (2005-2009 5-year est.).

Taxes: Total city taxes per capita: $201 (2007); City property taxes per capita: $108 (2007).

Education: Percent of population age 25 and over with: High school diploma (including GED) or higher: 64.3% (2010); Bachelor's degree or higher: 9.1% (2010); Master's degree or higher: 2.2% (2010).

School District(s)

Moulton ISD (PK-12)
   2009-10 Enrollment: 311 . . . . (361) 596-4609

Housing: Homeownership rate: 77.8% (2010); Median home value: $64,000 (2010); Median contract rent: $354 per month (2005-2009 5-year est.); Median year structure built: 1956 (2005-2009 5-year est.).

Newspapers: Moulton Eagle (Community news; Circulation 1,400)

Transportation: Commute to work: 92.5% car, 0.0% public transportation, 6.1% walk, 1.4% work from home (2005-2009 5-year est.); Travel time to work: 38.3% less than 15 minutes, 24.4% 15 to 30 minutes, 23.4% 30 to 45 minutes, 5.5% 45 to 60 minutes, 8.4% 60 minutes or more (2005-2009 5-year est.)

Additional Information Contacts

Moulton Chamber of Commerce . . . . (361) 596-7205
   http://www.moultontexas.com

SHINER (city). Covers a land area of 2.436 square miles and a water area of 0.007 square miles. Located at 29.43° N. Lat; 97.17° W. Long. Elevation is 358 feet.

History: Settled 1887, incorporated 1890.

Population: 2,075 (1990); 2,070 (2000); 1,968 (2010); 1,923 (2015 projected); Race: 84.5% White, 10.2% Black, 0.5% Asian, 4.9% Other, 8.6% Hispanic of any race (2010); Density: 808.0 persons per square mile (2010); Average household size: 2.19 (2010); Median age: 46.8 (2010); Males per 100 females: 82.2 (2010); Marriage status: 19.4% never married, 59.7% now married, 13.7% widowed, 7.3% divorced (2005-2009 5-year est.); Foreign born: 1.8% (2005-2009 5-year est.); Ancestry (includes multiple ancestries): 44.6% German, 31.6% Czech, 13.5% Irish, 6.4% English, 5.1% French (2005-2009 5-year est.).

Economy: Single-family building permits issued: 3 (2010); Multi-family building permits issued: 0 (2010); Employment by occupation: 8.7% management, 15.9% professional, 13.5% services, 17.6% sales, 1.7% farming, 14.8% construction, 27.8% production (2005-2009 5-year est.).

Income: Per capita income: $21,248 (2010); Median household income: $37,641 (2010); Average household income: $47,686 (2010); Percent of households with income of $100,000 or more: 5.9% (2010); Poverty rate: 6.8% (2005-2009 5-year est.).

Taxes: Total city taxes per capita: $168 (2007); City property taxes per capita: $140 (2007).

Education: Percent of population age 25 and over with: High school diploma (including GED) or higher: 79.4% (2010); Bachelor's degree or higher: 17.0% (2010); Master's degree or higher: 4.2% (2010).

School District(s)

Shiner ISD (PK-12)

    2009-10 Enrollment: 559 . . . . (361) 594-3121

Housing: Homeownership rate: 78.0% (2010); Median home value: $63,846 (2010); Median contract rent: $387 per month (2005-2009 5-year est.); Median year structure built: 1959 (2005-2009 5-year est.).

Newspapers: Shiner Gazette (Local news; Circulation 2,800)

Transportation: Commute to work: 91.7% car, 0.0% public transportation, 2.4% walk, 4.2% work from home (2005-2009 5-year est.); Travel time to work: 62.4% less than 15 minutes, 20.8% 15 to 30 minutes, 6.3% 30 to 45 minutes, 3.9% 45 to 60 minutes, 6.6% 60 minutes or more (2005-2009 5-year est.)

Additional Information Contacts

Shiner Chamber of Commerce . . . . (361) 594-4180

    http://www.shinertx.com

YOAKUM (city). Covers a land area of 4.562 square miles and a water area of 0.009 square miles. Located at 29.29° N. Lat; 97.14° W. Long. Elevation is 322 feet.

History: Yoakum was founded on 1887 on land granted to Irishman John May in 1835. The site became a gathering point for cattle herds heading north. Later, a leather tannery and railroad shops formed the economic base.

Population: 5,618 (1990); 5,731 (2000); 5,602 (2010); 5,544 (2015 projected); Race: 74.9% White, 8.2% Black, 0.2% Asian, 16.8% Other, 34.0% Hispanic of any race (2010); Density: 1,227.9 persons per square mile (2010); Average household size: 2.59 (2010); Median age: 36.7 (2010); Males per 100 females: 93.5 (2010); Marriage status: 24.0% never married, 57.8% now married, 10.5% widowed, 7.7% divorced (2005-2009 5-year est.); Foreign born: 12.6% (2005-2009 5-year est.); Ancestry (includes multiple ancestries): 16.9% German, 9.3% Irish, 9.1% Czech, 5.9% English, 2.6% American (2005-2009 5-year est.).

Economy: Single-family building permits issued: 6 (2010); Multi-family building permits issued: 0 (2010); Employment by occupation: 6.0% management, 13.5% professional, 15.3% services, 18.9% sales, 0.8% farming, 14.0% construction, 31.5% production (2005-2009 5-year est.).

Income: Per capita income: $20,000 (2010); Median household income: $37,273 (2010); Average household income: $52,525 (2010); Percent of households with income of $100,000 or more: 11.0% (2010); Poverty rate: 23.6% (2005-2009 5-year est.).

Taxes: Total city taxes per capita: $183 (2007); City property taxes per capita: $29 (2007).

Education: Percent of population age 25 and over with: High school diploma (including GED) or higher: 72.0% (2010); Bachelor's degree or higher: 14.9% (2010); Master's degree or higher: 4.8% (2010).

School District(s)

Yoakum ISD (PK-12)

    2009-10 Enrollment: 1,544 . . . . (361) 293-3162

Housing: Homeownership rate: 69.9% (2010); Median home value: $68,722 (2010); Median contract rent: $292 per month (2005-2009 5-year est.); Median year structure built: 1960 (2005-2009 5-year est.).

Hospitals: Yoakum Community Hospital (25 beds)

Safety: Violent crime rate: 23.9 per 10,000 population; Property crime rate: 415.2 per 10,000 population (2009).

Newspapers: Yoakum Herald-Times (Local news; Circulation 3,100)

Transportation: Commute to work: 93.7% car, 0.0% public transportation, 1.8% walk, 2.9% work from home (2005-2009 5-year est.); Travel time to work: 64.5% less than 15 minutes, 20.4% 15 to 30 minutes, 6.1% 30 to 45 minutes, 3.3% 45 to 60 minutes, 5.8% 60 minutes or more (2005-2009 5-year est.)

Additional Information Contacts

City of Yoakum. . . . . (361) 293-6321

    http://www.cityofyoakum.org

Yoakum Area Chamber of Commerce. . . . . (361) 293-2309

    http://www.yoakumareachamber.com

Lee County

Located in south central Texas; drained by Yegua Creek. Covers a land area of 628.50 square miles, a water area of 5.53 square miles, and is located in the Central Time Zone at 30.27° N. Lat., 96.94° W. Long. The county was founded in 1874. County seat is Giddings.

Weather Station: Lexington										Elevation: 464 feet		
	Jan	Feb	Mar	Apr	May	Jun	Jul	Aug	Sep	Oct	Nov	Dec
High	60	64	71	78	85	91	94	95	90	81	70	62
Low	38	42	49	56	65	71	73	73	67	58	48	39
Precip	2.6	2.4	2.9	2.1	4.3	3.6	2.0	2.0	2.9	5.4	3.5	2.9
Snow	0.0	tr	0.0	0.0	0.0	0.0	0.0	0.0	0.0	0.0	0.0	0.0

High and Low temperatures in degrees Fahrenheit; Precipitation and Snow in inches

Population: 12,854 (1990); 15,657 (2000); 17,216 (2010); 17,944 (2015 projected); Race: 75.9% White, 11.0% Black, 0.2% Asian, 12.8% Other, 21.1% Hispanic of any race (2010); Density: 27.4 persons per square mile (2010); Average household size: 2.67 (2010); Median age: 38.1 (2010); Males per 100 females: 100.2 (2010).

Religion: Five largest groups: 24.0% Lutheran Church—Missouri Synod, 10.9% Southern Baptist Convention, 7.5% Evangelical Lutheran Church in America, 7.3% Catholic Church, 5.2% The United Methodist Church (2000).

Economy: Unemployment rate: 6.9% (June 2011); Total civilian labor force: 9,604 (June 2011); Leading industries: 17.6% retail trade; 12.4% mining; 11.5% construction (2009); Farms: 1,844 totaling 325,643 acres (2007); Companies that employ 500 or more persons: 0 (2009); Companies that employ 100 to 499 persons: 3 (2009); Companies that employ less than 100 persons: 405 (2009); Black-owned businesses: n/a (2007); Hispanic-owned businesses: n/a (2007); Asian-owned businesses: n/a (2007); Women-owned businesses: 255 (2007); Retail sales per capita: $9,624 (2010). Single-family building permits issued: 4 (2010); Multi-family building permits issued: 16 (2010).

Income: Per capita income: $22,467 (2010); Median household income: $48,619 (2010); Average household income: $61,805 (2010); Percent of households with income of $100,000 or more: 15.0% (2010); Poverty rate: 10.7% (2009); Bankruptcy rate: 1.01% (2010).

Taxes: Total county taxes per capita: $314 (2007); County property taxes per capita: $231 (2007).

Education: Percent of population age 25 and over with: High school diploma (including GED) or higher: 77.1% (2010); Bachelor's degree or higher: 14.6% (2010); Master's degree or higher: 3.8% (2010).

Housing: Homeownership rate: 77.7% (2010); Median home value: $104,102 (2010); Median contract rent: $421 per month (2005-2009 5-year est.); Median year structure built: 1979 (2005-2009 5-year est.)

Health: Birth rate: 123.8 per 10,000 population (2009); Death rate: 91.2 per 10,000 population (2009); Age-adjusted cancer mortality rate: 189.2 deaths per 100,000 population (2007); Number of physicians: 3.1 per 10,000 population (2008); Hospital beds: 0.0 per 10,000 population (2007); Hospital admissions: 0.0 per 10,000 population (2007).

Elections: 2008 Presidential election results: 31.4% Obama, 67.6% McCain, 0.0% Nader

National and State Parks: Nails Creek State Park

Additional Information Contacts

Lee County Government . . . . (979) 542-3178

    http://www.co.lee.tx.us/ips/cms

City of Giddings . . . . (979) 540-2714

    http://www.giddings.net

Giddings Area Chamber of Commerce . . . . (979) 542-3455

    http://www.giddingstx.com

Lexington Chamber of Commerce . . . . (979) 773-4337
http://lexingtontexas.com

Lee County Communities

DIME BOX (unincorporated postal area, zip code 77853). Covers a land area of 55.042 square miles and a water area of 0.075 square miles. Located at 30.35° N. Lat; 96.85° W. Long. Elevation is 371 feet.
Population: 1,050 (2000); Race: 57.9% White, 32.8% Black, 0.0% Asian, 9.3% Other, 17.4% Hispanic of any race (2000); Density: 19.1 persons per square mile (2000); Age: 27.0% under 18, 18.3% over 64 (2000); Marriage status: 16.1% never married, 63.0% now married, 11.7% widowed, 9.2% divorced (2000); Foreign born: 4.4% (2000); Ancestry (includes multiple ancestries): 16.1% German, 8.2% Czech, 6.5% American, 3.2% Irish (2000).
Economy: Employment by occupation: 8.5% management, 15.8% professional, 23.9% services, 19.4% sales, 2.8% farming, 15.6% construction, 13.9% production (2000).
Income: Per capita income: $14,502 (2000); Median household income: $27,639 (2000); Poverty rate: 179.1% (2000).
Education: Percent of population age 25 and over with: High school diploma (including GED) or higher: 63.2% (2000); Bachelor's degree or higher: 10.1% (2000).
School District(s)
Dime Box ISD (PK-12)
    2009-10 Enrollment: 178 . . . . (979) 884-2324
Housing: Homeownership rate: 82.7% (2000); Median home value: $51,300 (2000); Median contract rent: $317 per month (2000); Median year structure built: 1974 (2000).
Transportation: Commute to work: 93.8% car, 0.0% public transportation, 2.1% walk, 4.0% work from home (2000); Travel time to work: 23.6% less than 15 minutes, 31.5% 15 to 30 minutes, 20.6% 30 to 45 minutes, 11.2% 45 to 60 minutes, 13.2% 60 minutes or more (2000)

GIDDINGS (city). County seat. Covers a land area of 5.147 square miles and a water area of 0.031 square miles. Located at 30.18° N. Lat; 96.93° W. Long. Elevation is 505 feet.
History: Giddings was established in 1872 by a West Slavic group known as the Wends, who had immigrated to Texas in 1854 seeking civil and religious freedom.
Population: 4,093 (1990); 5,105 (2000); 5,688 (2010); 5,912 (2015 projected); Race: 65.9% White, 11.5% Black, 0.6% Asian, 22.0% Other, 37.7% Hispanic of any race (2010); Density: 1,105.2 persons per square mile (2010); Average household size: 2.81 (2010); Median age: 33.0 (2010); Males per 100 females: 107.0 (2010); Marriage status: 30.9% never married, 48.7% now married, 8.0% widowed, 12.4% divorced (2005-2009 5-year est.); Foreign born: 14.0% (2005-2009 5-year est.); Ancestry (includes multiple ancestries): 18.2% German, 6.8% English, 5.0% Irish, 4.7% American, 4.1% French (2005-2009 5-year est.).
Economy: Single-family building permits issued: 1 (2010); Multi-family building permits issued: 16 (2010); Employment by occupation: 8.8% management, 13.2% professional, 10.7% services, 33.1% sales, 2.3% farming, 17.5% construction, 14.4% production (2005-2009 5-year est.).
Income: Per capita income: $17,683 (2010); Median household income: $40,150 (2010); Average household income: $53,542 (2010); Percent of households with income of $100,000 or more: 10.6% (2010); Poverty rate: 19.6% (2005-2009 5-year est.).
Taxes: Total city taxes per capita: $426 (2007); City property taxes per capita: $163 (2007).
Education: Percent of population age 25 and over with: High school diploma (including GED) or higher: 69.9% (2010); Bachelor's degree or higher: 12.8% (2010); Master's degree or higher: 3.2% (2010).
School District(s)
Giddings ISD (PK-12)
    2009-10 Enrollment: 1,919 . . . . (979) 542-2854
Giddings State School (08-12)
    2009-10 Enrollment: 297 . . . . (979) 542-3686
Housing: Homeownership rate: 65.4% (2010); Median home value: $87,174 (2010); Median contract rent: $417 per month (2005-2009 5-year est.); Median year structure built: 1973 (2005-2009 5-year est.).
Safety: Violent crime rate: 78.8 per 10,000 population; Property crime rate: 346.5 per 10,000 population (2009).
Newspapers: Times & News (Local news; Circulation 6,400)
Transportation: Commute to work: 91.6% car, 0.0% public transportation, 5.3% walk, 1.4% work from home (2005-2009 5-year est.); Travel time to

work: 67.9% less than 15 minutes, 13.2% 15 to 30 minutes, 8.2% 30 to 45 minutes, 6.0% 45 to 60 minutes, 4.7% 60 minutes or more (2005-2009 5-year est.)
Additional Information Contacts
City of Giddings . . . . (979) 540-2714
http://www.giddings.net
Giddings Area Chamber of Commerce . . . . (979) 542-3455
http://www.giddingstx.com

LEXINGTON (town). Covers a land area of 1.187 square miles and a water area of 0 square miles. Located at 30.41° N. Lat; 97.00° W. Long. Elevation is 456 feet.
History: Established 1850s.
Population: 955 (1990); 1,178 (2000); 1,279 (2010); 1,318 (2015 projected); Race: 87.0% White, 6.2% Black, 0.0% Asian, 6.8% Other, 7.7% Hispanic of any race (2010); Density: 1,077.5 persons per square mile (2010); Average household size: 2.51 (2010); Median age: 40.4 (2010); Males per 100 females: 95.0 (2010); Marriage status: 21.1% never married, 57.9% now married, 9.7% widowed, 11.3% divorced (2005-2009 5-year est.); Foreign born: 1.5% (2005-2009 5-year est.); Ancestry (includes multiple ancestries): 34.7% German, 12.4% English, 12.2% Irish, 5.9% Scotch-Irish, 3.0% Scottish (2005-2009 5-year est.).
Economy: Single-family building permits issued: 3 (2010); Multi-family building permits issued: 0 (2010); Employment by occupation: 7.1% management, 22.2% professional, 18.2% services, 22.7% sales, 0.0% farming, 11.6% construction, 18.2% production (2005-2009 5-year est.).
Income: Per capita income: $28,923 (2010); Median household income: $58,960 (2010); Average household income: $73,168 (2010); Percent of households with income of $100,000 or more: 19.4% (2010); Poverty rate: 11.6% (2005-2009 5-year est.).
Taxes: Total city taxes per capita: $280 (2007); City property taxes per capita: $131 (2007).
Education: Percent of population age 25 and over with: High school diploma (including GED) or higher: 86.5% (2010); Bachelor's degree or higher: 17.6% (2010); Master's degree or higher: 4.2% (2010).
School District(s)
Lexington ISD (PK-12)
    2009-10 Enrollment: 929 . . . . (979) 773-2254
Housing: Homeownership rate: 80.6% (2010); Median home value: $107,075 (2010); Median contract rent: $409 per month (2005-2009 5-year est.); Median year structure built: 1976 (2005-2009 5-year est.).
Safety: Violent crime rate: 8.1 per 10,000 population; Property crime rate: 265.9 per 10,000 population (2009).
Transportation: Commute to work: 91.1% car, 0.0% public transportation, 1.8% walk, 2.4% work from home (2005-2009 5-year est.); Travel time to work: 45.8% less than 15 minutes, 18.0% 15 to 30 minutes, 12.0% 30 to 45 minutes, 4.6% 45 to 60 minutes, 19.7% 60 minutes or more (2005-2009 5-year est.)
Additional Information Contacts
Lexington Chamber of Commerce . . . . (979) 773-4337
http://lexingtontexas.com

LINCOLN (unincorporated postal area, zip code 78948). Covers a land area of 75.390 square miles and a water area of 0.244 square miles. Located at 30.29° N. Lat; 96.95° W. Long. Elevation is 371 feet.
Population: 969 (2000); Race: 73.7% White, 24.7% Black, 0.0% Asian, 1.6% Other, 6.3% Hispanic of any race (2000); Density: 12.9 persons per square mile (2000); Age: 29.0% under 18, 15.8% over 64 (2000); Marriage status: 16.7% never married, 69.8% now married, 9.0% widowed, 4.5% divorced (2000); Foreign born: 0.8% (2000); Ancestry (includes multiple ancestries): 39.5% German, 7.6% Irish, 5.1% Czech, 3.5% American (2000).
Economy: Employment by occupation: 16.8% management, 14.1% professional, 20.4% services, 19.3% sales, 1.1% farming, 16.8% construction, 11.6% production (2000).
Income: Per capita income: $18,234 (2000); Median household income: $30,284 (2000); Poverty rate: 179.1% (2000).
Education: Percent of population age 25 and over with: High school diploma (including GED) or higher: 72.3% (2000); Bachelor's degree or higher: 10.5% (2000).
Housing: Homeownership rate: 86.4% (2000); Median home value: $82,100 (2000); Median contract rent: $417 per month (2000); Median year structure built: 1980 (2000).
Transportation: Commute to work: 94.4% car, 0.0% public transportation, 1.3% walk, 4.3% work from home (2000); Travel time to work: 18.2% less

than 15 minutes, 32.2% 15 to 30 minutes, 23.0% 30 to 45 minutes, 8.6% 45 to 60 minutes, 18.0% 60 minutes or more (2000)

Leon County

Located in east central Texas; bounded on the west by the Navasota River, and on the east by the Trinity River. Covers a land area of 1,072.04 square miles, a water area of 8.34 square miles, and is located in the Central Time Zone at 31.27° N. Lat., 96.06° W. Long. The county was founded in 1846. County seat is Centerville.

Weather Station: Centerville   Elevation: 319 feet

	Jan	Feb	Mar	Apr	May	Jun	Jul	Aug	Sep	Oct	Nov	Dec
High	59	63	70	77	84	90	94	95	89	79	69	60
Low	36	39	46	53	62	69	71	71	64	54	45	37
Precip	3.3	3.4	3.8	2.8	4.8	4.1	2.5	2.7	2.8	5.0	3.9	3.7
Snow	0.2	0.2	tr	0.1	0.0	0.0	0.0	0.0	0.0	0.0	0.0	0.0

High and Low temperatures in degrees Fahrenheit; Precipitation and Snow in inches

Population: 12,665 (1990); 15,335 (2000); 16,802 (2010); 17,483 (2015 projected); Race: 81.3% White, 9.8% Black, 0.3% Asian, 8.6% Other, 11.8% Hispanic of any race (2010); Density: 15.7 persons per square mile (2010); Average household size: 2.43 (2010); Median age: 40.3 (2010); Males per 100 females: 97.4 (2010).
Religion: Five largest groups: 27.7% Southern Baptist Convention, 11.4% Baptist Missionary Association of America, 9.7% The United Methodist Church, 5.0% Catholic Church, 3.6% Churches of Christ (2000).
Economy: Unemployment rate: 8.4% (June 2011); Total civilian labor force: 8,209 (June 2011); Leading industries: 19.6% construction; 13.2% manufacturing; 12.7% retail trade (2009); Farms: 2,066 totaling 569,101 acres (2007); Companies that employ 500 or more persons: 0 (2009); Companies that employ 100 to 499 persons: 6 (2009); Companies that employ less than 100 persons: 355 (2009); Black-owned businesses: n/a (2007); Hispanic-owned businesses: n/a (2007); Asian-owned businesses: n/a (2007); Women-owned businesses: n/a (2007); Retail sales per capita: $9,332 (2010). Single-family building permits issued: n/a (2010); Multi-family building permits issued: n/a (2010).
Income: Per capita income: $22,254 (2010); Median household income: $39,917 (2010); Average household income: $54,255 (2010); Percent of households with income of $100,000 or more: 12.7% (2010); Poverty rate: 16.9% (2009); Bankruptcy rate: 0.94% (2010).
Taxes: Total county taxes per capita: $344 (2007); County property taxes per capita: $257 (2007).
Education: Percent of population age 25 and over with: High school diploma (including GED) or higher: 79.0% (2010); Bachelor's degree or higher: 13.7% (2010); Master's degree or higher: 3.9% (2010).
Housing: Homeownership rate: 81.4% (2010); Median home value: $85,879 (2010); Median contract rent: $371 per month (2005-2009 5-year est.); Median year structure built: 1980 (2005-2009 5-year est.)
Health: Birth rate: 138.3 per 10,000 population (2009); Death rate: 115.8 per 10,000 population (2009); Age-adjusted cancer mortality rate: 220.7 deaths per 100,000 population (2007); Number of physicians: 4.7 per 10,000 population (2008); Hospital beds: 0.0 per 10,000 population (2007); Hospital admissions: 0.0 per 10,000 population (2007).
Elections: 2008 Presidential election results: 20.1% Obama, 79.1% McCain, 0.0% Nader
Additional Information Contacts
Leon County Government . . . . (903) 536-2331
  http://www.co.leon.tx.us/ips/cms
Buffalo Chamber of Commerce . . . . (903) 322-5810
  http://www.buffalotxchamberofcommerce.org
Centerville Chamber of Commerce . . . . (903) 536-7261
  http://www.centervilletexas.com
Jewett Area Chamber of Commerce . . . . (903) 626-4202
  http://jewetttexas.org

Leon County Communities

BUFFALO (city). Covers a land area of 4.020 square miles and a water area of 0.018 square miles. Located at 31.46° N. Lat; 96.06° W. Long. Elevation is 384 feet.
Population: 1,640 (1990); 1,804 (2000); 1,947 (2010); 2,009 (2015 projected); Race: 75.4% White, 8.9% Black, 0.7% Asian, 15.0% Other, 20.9% Hispanic of any race (2010); Density: 484.3 persons per square mile (2010); Average household size: 2.58 (2010); Median age: 33.6 (2010); Males per 100 females: 96.5 (2010); Marriage status: 26.6% never married,

49.7% now married, 8.0% widowed, 15.8% divorced (2005-2009 5-year est.); Foreign born: 11.9% (2005-2009 5-year est.); Ancestry (includes multiple ancestries): 17.7% Irish, 12.1% German, 12.1% English, 3.2% American, 2.8% Scotch-Irish (2005-2009 5-year est.).
Economy: Employment by occupation: 14.8% management, 9.2% professional, 34.1% services, 11.4% sales, 0.7% farming, 14.6% construction, 15.2% production (2005-2009 5-year est.).
Income: Per capita income: $18,139 (2010); Median household income: $37,295 (2010); Average household income: $46,644 (2010); Percent of households with income of $100,000 or more: 8.9% (2010); Poverty rate: 26.9% (2005-2009 5-year est.).
Taxes: Total city taxes per capita: $175 (2007); City property taxes per capita: $128 (2007).
Education: Percent of population age 25 and over with: High school diploma (including GED) or higher: 78.6% (2010); Bachelor's degree or higher: 10.9% (2010); Master's degree or higher: 4.0% (2010).
School District(s)
Buffalo ISD (PK-12)
  2009-10 Enrollment: 889 . . . . (903) 322-3765
Housing: Homeownership rate: 76.6% (2010); Median home value: $69,506 (2010); Median contract rent: $344 per month (2005-2009 5-year est.); Median year structure built: 1976 (2005-2009 5-year est.).
Newspapers: Buffalo Press (Local news; Circulation 3,500)
Transportation: Commute to work: 85.6% car, 0.0% public transportation, 5.3% walk, 4.9% work from home (2005-2009 5-year est.); Travel time to work: 50.1% less than 15 minutes, 29.9% 15 to 30 minutes, 11.4% 30 to 45 minutes, 1.4% 45 to 60 minutes, 7.1% 60 minutes or more (2005-2009 5-year est.)
Additional Information Contacts
Buffalo Chamber of Commerce . . . . (903) 322-5810
  http://www.buffalotxchamberofcommerce.org

CENTERVILLE (city). County seat. Covers a land area of 1.454 square miles and a water area of 0 square miles. Located at 31.25° N. Lat; 95.97° W. Long. Elevation is 354 feet.
Population: 848 (1990); 903 (2000); 939 (2010); 960 (2015 projected); Race: 82.0% White, 10.3% Black, 0.6% Asian, 7.0% Other, 7.6% Hispanic of any race (2010); Density: 645.7 persons per square mile (2010); Average household size: 2.25 (2010); Median age: 45.4 (2010); Males per 100 females: 91.2 (2010); Marriage status: 18.2% never married, 48.1% now married, 18.5% widowed, 15.2% divorced (2005-2009 5-year est.); Foreign born: 0.8% (2005-2009 5-year est.); Ancestry (includes multiple ancestries): 24.6% Irish, 22.3% German, 16.3% English, 5.1% French, 3.7% Italian (2005-2009 5-year est.).
Economy: Employment by occupation: 18.3% management, 7.8% professional, 15.3% services, 33.3% sales, 1.6% farming, 15.5% construction, 8.2% production (2005-2009 5-year est.).
Income: Per capita income: $26,971 (2010); Median household income: $41,085 (2010); Average household income: $61,679 (2010); Percent of households with income of $100,000 or more: 15.3% (2010); Poverty rate: 10.3% (2005-2009 5-year est.).
Taxes: Total city taxes per capita: $484 (2007); City property taxes per capita: $69 (2007).
Education: Percent of population age 25 and over with: High school diploma (including GED) or higher: 72.7% (2010); Bachelor's degree or higher: 16.7% (2010); Master's degree or higher: 3.2% (2010).
School District(s)
Centerville ISD (PK-12)
  2009-10 Enrollment: 730 . . . . (903) 536-7812
Housing: Homeownership rate: 76.3% (2010); Median home value: $82,800 (2010); Median contract rent: $289 per month (2005-2009 5-year est.); Median year structure built: 1961 (2005-2009 5-year est.).
Newspapers: Centerville News (Community news; Circulation 2,300)
Transportation: Commute to work: 90.6% car, 0.0% public transportation, 4.2% walk, 0.6% work from home (2005-2009 5-year est.); Travel time to work: 51.5% less than 15 minutes, 23.3% 15 to 30 minutes, 19.5% 30 to 45 minutes, 1.1% 45 to 60 minutes, 4.6% 60 minutes or more (2005-2009 5-year est.)
Additional Information Contacts
Centerville Chamber of Commerce . . . . (903) 536-7261
  http://www.centervilletexas.com

JEWETT (city). Covers a land area of 2.058 square miles and a water area of 0.015 square miles. Located at 31.36° N. Lat; 96.14° W. Long. Elevation is 492 feet.

Population: 816 (1990); 861 (2000); 931 (2010); 961 (2015 projected); Race: 71.2% White, 7.4% Black, 0.0% Asian, 21.4% Other, 30.0% Hispanic of any race (2010); Density: 452.4 persons per square mile (2010); Average household size: 2.54 (2010); Median age: 31.7 (2010); Males per 100 females: 102.4 (2010); Marriage status: 33.0% never married, 49.1% now married, 9.9% widowed, 8.1% divorced (2005-2009 5-year est.); Foreign born: 23.9% (2005-2009 5-year est.); Ancestry (includes multiple ancestries): 12.6% Irish, 7.8% English, 6.2% German, 2.7% Dutch, 1.7% American (2005-2009 5-year est.).
Economy: Employment by occupation: 8.4% management, 9.2% professional, 28.1% services, 9.2% sales, 2.6% farming, 21.7% construction, 20.9% production (2005-2009 5-year est.).
Income: Per capita income: $19,720 (2010); Median household income: $36,967 (2010); Average household income: $49,857 (2010); Percent of households with income of $100,000 or more: 10.9% (2010); Poverty rate: 23.9% (2005-2009 5-year est.).
Taxes: Total city taxes per capita: $401 (2007); City property taxes per capita: $99 (2007).
Education: Percent of population age 25 and over with: High school diploma (including GED) or higher: 72.4% (2010); Bachelor's degree or higher: 9.4% (2010); Master's degree or higher: 3.6% (2010).

School District(s)

Leon ISD (PK-12)
   2009-10 Enrollment: 732 . . . . (903) 626-1400
Housing: Homeownership rate: 69.7% (2010); Median home value: $53,529 (2010); Median contract rent: $376 per month (2005-2009 5-year est.); Median year structure built: 1975 (2005-2009 5-year est.).
Newspapers: Jewett Messenger (Community news; Circulation 1,800)
Transportation: Commute to work: 88.9% car, 1.0% public transportation, 4.4% walk, 3.1% work from home (2005-2009 5-year est.); Travel time to work: 61.5% less than 15 minutes, 24.9% 15 to 30 minutes, 8.8% 30 to 45 minutes, 4.8% 45 to 60 minutes, 0.0% 60 minutes or more (2005-2009 5-year est.)
Additional Information Contacts
Jewett Area Chamber of Commerce . . . . (903) 626-4202
   http://jewetttexas.org

LEONA (city). Covers a land area of 2.175 square miles and a water area of 0 square miles. Located at 31.15° N. Lat; 95.97° W. Long. Elevation is 341 feet.
Population: 178 (1990); 181 (2000); 209 (2010); 224 (2015 projected); Race: 87.6% White, 9.6% Black, 0.0% Asian, 2.9% Other, 5.7% Hispanic of any race (2010); Density: 96.1 persons per square mile (2010); Average household size: 2.49 (2010); Median age: 43.8 (2010); Males per 100 females: 101.0 (2010); Marriage status: 26.6% never married, 51.4% now married, 18.5% widowed, 3.5% divorced (2005-2009 5-year est.); Foreign born: 0.0% (2005-2009 5-year est.); Ancestry (includes multiple ancestries): 12.8% English, 8.4% Irish, 6.6% German, 4.0% French, 3.1% Lithuanian (2005-2009 5-year est.).
Economy: Employment by occupation: 16.3% management, 12.8% professional, 17.4% services, 11.6% sales, 0.0% farming, 19.8% construction, 22.1% production (2005-2009 5-year est.).
Income: Per capita income: $23,964 (2010); Median household income: $42,500 (2010); Average household income: $58,780 (2010); Percent of households with income of $100,000 or more: 14.3% (2010); Poverty rate: 20.4% (2005-2009 5-year est.).
Education: Percent of population age 25 and over with: High school diploma (including GED) or higher: 80.3% (2010); Bachelor's degree or higher: 7.5% (2010); Master's degree or higher: 2.7% (2010).
Housing: Homeownership rate: 89.3% (2010); Median home value: $92,500 (2010); Median contract rent: $625 per month (2005-2009 5-year est.); Median year structure built: 1949 (2005-2009 5-year est.).
Transportation: Commute to work: 81.1% car, 0.0% public transportation, 0.0% walk, 12.2% work from home (2005-2009 5-year est.); Travel time to work: 44.3% less than 15 minutes, 24.1% 15 to 30 minutes, 6.3% 30 to 45 minutes, 16.5% 45 to 60 minutes, 8.9% 60 minutes or more (2005-2009 5-year est.)

MARQUEZ (city). Covers a land area of 1.200 square miles and a water area of 0 square miles. Located at 31.24° N. Lat; 96.25° W. Long. Elevation is 407 feet.
Population: 270 (1990); 220 (2000); 236 (2010); 242 (2015 projected); Race: 88.1% White, 3.8% Black, 0.4% Asian, 7.6% Other, 8.5% Hispanic of any race (2010); Density: 196.6 persons per square mile (2010); Average household size: 2.48 (2010); Median age: 39.3 (2010); Males per

100 females: 108.8 (2010); Marriage status: 14.0% never married, 57.3% now married, 16.0% widowed, 12.7% divorced (2005-2009 5-year est.); Foreign born: 0.0% (2005-2009 5-year est.); Ancestry (includes multiple ancestries): 46.2% Irish, 20.6% American, 11.1% German, 9.0% English, 4.5% Norwegian (2005-2009 5-year est.).
Economy: Employment by occupation: 15.6% management, 6.7% professional, 14.4% services, 18.9% sales, 0.0% farming, 2.2% construction, 42.2% production (2005-2009 5-year est.).
Income: Per capita income: $22,140 (2010); Median household income: $44,375 (2010); Average household income: $55,000 (2010); Percent of households with income of $100,000 or more: 13.7% (2010); Poverty rate: 5.0% (2005-2009 5-year est.).
Taxes: Total city taxes per capita: $167 (2007); City property taxes per capita: $90 (2007).
Education: Percent of population age 25 and over with: High school diploma (including GED) or higher: 80.5% (2010); Bachelor's degree or higher: 15.9% (2010); Master's degree or higher: 4.9% (2010).
Housing: Homeownership rate: 84.2% (2010); Median home value: $86,667 (2010); Median contract rent: $240 per month (2005-2009 5-year est.); Median year structure built: 1977 (2005-2009 5-year est.).
Transportation: Commute to work: 87.8% car, 12.2% public transportation, 0.0% walk, 0.0% work from home (2005-2009 5-year est.); Travel time to work: 44.4% less than 15 minutes, 36.7% 15 to 30 minutes, 2.2% 30 to 45 minutes, 12.2% 45 to 60 minutes, 4.4% 60 minutes or more (2005-2009 5-year est.)

NORMANGEE (town). Covers a land area of 1.110 square miles and a water area of 0 square miles. Located at 31.02° N. Lat; 96.11° W. Long. Elevation is 377 feet.
Population: 689 (1990); 719 (2000); 765 (2010); 783 (2015 projected); Race: 81.0% White, 10.6% Black, 0.3% Asian, 8.1% Other, 10.1% Hispanic of any race (2010); Density: 689.4 persons per square mile (2010); Average household size: 2.51 (2010); Median age: 35.8 (2010); Males per 100 females: 91.7 (2010); Marriage status: 26.7% never married, 52.1% now married, 13.0% widowed, 8.3% divorced (2005-2009 5-year est.); Foreign born: 0.0% (2005-2009 5-year est.); Ancestry (includes multiple ancestries): 15.4% Irish, 13.8% German, 12.6% English, 2.1% French, 0.8% Scotch-Irish (2005-2009 5-year est.).
Economy: Employment by occupation: 6.6% management, 5.5% professional, 31.4% services, 24.5% sales, 1.8% farming, 17.9% construction, 12.4% production (2005-2009 5-year est.).
Income: Per capita income: $21,358 (2010); Median household income: $41,167 (2010); Average household income: $53,861 (2010); Percent of households with income of $100,000 or more: 12.5% (2010); Poverty rate: 33.1% (2005-2009 5-year est.).
Taxes: Total city taxes per capita: $286 (2007); City property taxes per capita: $205 (2007).
Education: Percent of population age 25 and over with: High school diploma (including GED) or higher: 76.0% (2010); Bachelor's degree or higher: 15.4% (2010); Master's degree or higher: 3.5% (2010).

School District(s)

Normangee ISD (PK-12)
   2009-10 Enrollment: 545 . . . . (936) 396-3111
Housing: Homeownership rate: 77.0% (2010); Median home value: $87,391 (2010); Median contract rent: $190 per month (2005-2009 5-year est.); Median year structure built: 1970 (2005-2009 5-year est.).
Newspapers: Normangee Star (Community news; Circulation 1,450)
Transportation: Commute to work: 90.1% car, 0.0% public transportation, 5.1% walk, 2.9% work from home (2005-2009 5-year est.); Travel time to work: 54.1% less than 15 minutes, 5.6% 15 to 30 minutes, 17.3% 30 to 45 minutes, 5.6% 45 to 60 minutes, 17.3% 60 minutes or more (2005-2009 5-year est.)

OAKWOOD (town). Covers a land area of 1.096 square miles and a water area of 0 square miles. Located at 31.58° N. Lat; 95.85° W. Long. Elevation is 279 feet.
Population: 536 (1990); 471 (2000); 517 (2010); 536 (2015 projected); Race: 70.4% White, 25.9% Black, 0.2% Asian, 3.5% Other, 6.4% Hispanic of any race (2010); Density: 471.9 persons per square mile (2010); Average household size: 2.31 (2010); Median age: 41.8 (2010); Males per 100 females: 95.8 (2010); Marriage status: 35.2% never married, 36.7% now married, 9.0% widowed, 19.1% divorced (2005-2009 5-year est.); Foreign born: 1.5% (2005-2009 5-year est.); Ancestry (includes multiple ancestries): 17.1% Irish, 13.4% English, 4.5% Scotch-Irish, 4.1% Dutch, 3.5% German (2005-2009 5-year est.).

Economy: Employment by occupation: 1.3% management, 11.0% professional, 24.2% services, 17.4% sales, 8.1% farming, 23.7% construction, 14.4% production (2005-2009 5-year est.).
Income: Per capita income: $20,660 (2010); Median household income: $31,667 (2010); Average household income: $46,741 (2010); Percent of households with income of $100,000 or more: 11.6% (2010); Poverty rate: 33.4% (2005-2009 5-year est.).
Taxes: Total city taxes per capita: $86 (2007); City property taxes per capita: $46 (2007).
Education: Percent of population age 25 and over with: High school diploma (including GED) or higher: 78.0% (2010); Bachelor's degree or higher: 16.0% (2010); Master's degree or higher: 3.8% (2010).

School District(s)

Oakwood ISD (PK-12)
　　2009-10 Enrollment: 228 . . . . (903) 545-2666
Housing: Homeownership rate: 83.0% (2010); Median home value: $71,579 (2010); Median contract rent: $275 per month (2005-2009 5-year est.); Median year structure built: 1955 (2005-2009 5-year est.).
Transportation: Commute to work: 68.5% car, 3.9% public transportation, 3.9% walk, 18.1% work from home (2005-2009 5-year est.); Travel time to work: 20.0% less than 15 minutes, 37.9% 15 to 30 minutes, 33.7% 30 to 45 minutes, 4.2% 45 to 60 minutes, 4.2% 60 minutes or more (2005-2009 5-year est.)

Liberty County

Located in east Texas; drained by the Trinity River. Covers a land area of 1,159.68 square miles, a water area of 16.54 square miles, and is located in the Central Time Zone at 30.16° N. Lat., 94.84° W. Long. The county was founded in 1836. County seat is Liberty.

Liberty County is part of the Houston-Sugar Land-Baytown, TX Metropolitan Statistical Area. The entire metro area includes: Austin County, TX; Brazoria County, TX; Chambers County, TX; Fort Bend County, TX; Galveston County, TX; Harris County, TX; Liberty County, TX; Montgomery County, TX; San Jacinto County, TX; Waller County, TX

Weather Station: Cleveland　　　　　　　　　　　　　　Elevation: 195 feet

	Jan	Feb	Mar	Apr	May	Jun	Jul	Aug	Sep	Oct	Nov	Dec
High	61	65	72	78	84	89	92	93	88	80	70	62
Low	39	42	48	55	64	70	72	71	66	57	48	40
Precip	4.1	4.1	3.9	3.4	5.5	5.6	3.3	3.5	4.5	6.3	5.6	4.6
Snow	0.2	0.2	0.0	0.0	0.0	0.0	0.0	0.0	0.0	0.0	0.0	tr

High and Low temperatures in degrees Fahrenheit; Precipitation and Snow in inches

Weather Station: Liberty　　　　　　　　　　　　　　　　Elevation: 35 feet

	Jan	Feb	Mar	Apr	May	Jun	Jul	Aug	Sep	Oct	Nov	Dec
High	63	66	73	78	85	90	93	93	89	81	72	64
Low	42	45	51	58	66	72	74	74	69	59	50	43
Precip	4.5	4.1	4.0	3.8	5.5	7.1	4.8	4.6	6.0	7.2	5.3	5.0
Snow	0.1	tr	0.0	0.0	0.0	0.0	0.0	0.0	0.0	0.0	0.0	0.1

High and Low temperatures in degrees Fahrenheit; Precipitation and Snow in inches

Population: 52,726 (1990); 70,154 (2000); 77,835 (2010); 81,429 (2015 projected); Race: 76.5% White, 11.8% Black, 0.4% Asian, 11.3% Other, 15.9% Hispanic of any race (2010); Density: 67.1 persons per square mile (2010); Average household size: 2.82 (2010); Median age: 34.8 (2010); Males per 100 females: 96.3 (2010).
Religion: Five largest groups: 33.0% Southern Baptist Convention, 11.1% Catholic Church, 3.8% The United Methodist Church, 2.5% Assemblies of God, 1.9% Muslim Estimate (2000).
Economy: Unemployment rate: 11.8% (June 2011); Total civilian labor force: 32,778 (June 2011); Leading industries: 22.5% retail trade; 15.4% health care and social assistance; 10.8% accommodation & food services (2009); Farms: 1,589 totaling 297,855 acres (2007); Companies that employ 500 or more persons: 1 (2009); Companies that employ 100 to 499 persons: 12 (2009); Companies that employ less than 100 persons: 1,014 (2009); Black-owned businesses: n/a (2007); Hispanic-owned businesses: 477 (2007); Asian-owned businesses: n/a (2007); Women-owned businesses: n/a (2007); Retail sales per capita: $10,633 (2010). Single-family building permits issued: 193 (2010); Multi-family building permits issued: 76 (2010).
Income: Per capita income: $20,017 (2010); Median household income: $48,974 (2010); Average household income: $58,950 (2010); Percent of households with income of $100,000 or more: 13.4% (2010); Poverty rate: 17.9% (2009); Bankruptcy rate: 1.31% (2010).

Taxes: Total county taxes per capita: $343 (2007); County property taxes per capita: $282 (2007).
Education: Percent of population age 25 and over with: High school diploma (including GED) or higher: 74.1% (2010); Bachelor's degree or higher: 9.3% (2010); Master's degree or higher: 2.2% (2010).
Housing: Homeownership rate: 76.2% (2010); Median home value: $77,370 (2010); Median contract rent: $484 per month (2005-2009 5-year est.); Median year structure built: 1983 (2005-2009 5-year est.)
Health: Birth rate: 140.7 per 10,000 population (2009); Death rate: 92.5 per 10,000 population (2009); Age-adjusted cancer mortality rate: 271.1 deaths per 100,000 population (2008); Number of physicians: 4.0 per 10,000 population (2008); Hospital beds: 17.2 per 10,000 population (2007); Hospital admissions: 640.0 per 10,000 population (2007).
Elections: 2008 Presidential election results: 27.7% Obama, 71.4% McCain, 0.1% Nader
Additional Information Contacts
Liberty County Government . . . . (936) 336-4600
　　http://www.co.liberty.tx.us
City of Cleveland . . . . (281) 592-2667
　　http://www.clevelandtexas.com
City of Dayton . . . . (936) 258-2642
　　http://daytontx.com
City of Liberty . . . . (512) 778-5449
　　http://www.ci.liberty-hill.tx.us
Greater Cleveland Chamber of Commerce . . . . (281) 592-8786
　　http://clevelandtxchamber.com
Liberty-Dayton Area Chamber of Commerce. . . . . (936) 336-5736
　　http://www.libertydaytonchamber.com

Liberty County Communities

AMES (city). Covers a land area of 3.169 square miles and a water area of 0 square miles. Located at 30.05° N. Lat; 94.74° W. Long. Elevation is 72 feet.
Population: 1,156 (1990); 1,079 (2000); 1,220 (2010); 1,288 (2015 projected); Race: 52.0% White, 38.6% Black, 0.2% Asian, 9.2% Other, 12.4% Hispanic of any race (2010); Density: 385.0 persons per square mile (2010); Average household size: 2.74 (2010); Median age: 36.7 (2010); Males per 100 females: 92.1 (2010); Marriage status: 33.9% never married, 42.0% now married, 15.3% widowed, 8.7% divorced (2005-2009 5-year est.); Foreign born: 10.3% (2005-2009 5-year est.); Ancestry (includes multiple ancestries): 10.3% German, 6.7% Irish, 4.2% French, 1.1% Italian, 1.0% Trinidadian and Tobagonian (2005-2009 5-year est.).
Economy: Employment by occupation: 1.2% management, 12.2% professional, 35.6% services, 19.8% sales, 0.0% farming, 17.5% construction, 13.6% production (2005-2009 5-year est.).
Income: Per capita income: $23,148 (2010); Median household income: $48,350 (2010); Average household income: $63,511 (2010); Percent of households with income of $100,000 or more: 16.4% (2010); Poverty rate: 36.1% (2005-2009 5-year est.).
Taxes: Total city taxes per capita: $100 (2007); City property taxes per capita: $67 (2007).
Education: Percent of population age 25 and over with: High school diploma (including GED) or higher: 78.7% (2010); Bachelor's degree or higher: 14.5% (2010); Master's degree or higher: 3.0% (2010).
Housing: Homeownership rate: 81.6% (2010); Median home value: $71,094 (2010); Median contract rent: $279 per month (2005-2009 5-year est.); Median year structure built: 1975 (2005-2009 5-year est.).
Transportation: Commute to work: 99.1% car, 0.9% public transportation, 0.0% walk, 0.0% work from home (2005-2009 5-year est.); Travel time to work: 31.3% less than 15 minutes, 43.8% 15 to 30 minutes, 19.0% 30 to 45 minutes, 2.6% 45 to 60 minutes, 3.2% 60 minutes or more (2005-2009 5-year est.)

CLEVELAND (city). Covers a land area of 4.812 square miles and a water area of 0 square miles. Located at 30.34° N. Lat; 95.08° W. Long. Elevation is 157 feet.
History: Incorporated 1929.
Population: 7,132 (1990); 7,605 (2000); 7,981 (2010); 8,153 (2015 projected); Race: 56.1% White, 24.3% Black, 0.9% Asian, 18.7% Other, 28.5% Hispanic of any race (2010); Density: 1,658.7 persons per square mile (2010); Average household size: 2.65 (2010); Median age: 33.8 (2010); Males per 100 females: 103.0 (2010); Marriage status: 30.4% never married, 49.5% now married, 6.6% widowed, 13.5% divorced (2005-2009 5-year est.); Foreign born: 11.8% (2005-2009 5-year est.);

Ancestry (includes multiple ancestries): 8.8% Irish, 8.7% German, 8.5% American, 4.4% English, 3.2% French (2005-2009 5-year est.).
Economy: Single-family building permits issued: 5 (2010); Multi-family building permits issued: 0 (2010); Employment by occupation: 6.8% management, 17.5% professional, 15.2% services, 17.6% sales, 1.0% farming, 25.9% construction, 16.0% production (2005-2009 5-year est.).
Income: Per capita income: $16,930 (2010); Median household income: $31,801 (2010); Average household income: $47,065 (2010); Percent of households with income of $100,000 or more: 8.0% (2010); Poverty rate: 26.5% (2005-2009 5-year est.).
Taxes: Total city taxes per capita: $554 (2007); City property taxes per capita: $228 (2007).
Education: Percent of population age 25 and over with: High school diploma (including GED) or higher: 66.7% (2010); Bachelor's degree or higher: 8.5% (2010); Master's degree or higher: 1.5% (2010).

School District(s)
Cleveland ISD (PK-12)
    2009-10 Enrollment: 3,779 . . . . (281) 592-8717
Tarkington ISD (PK-12)
    2009-10 Enrollment: 1,986 . . . . (281) 592-8781
Housing: Homeownership rate: 49.9% (2010); Median home value: $65,819 (2010); Median contract rent: $480 per month (2005-2009 5-year est.); Median year structure built: 1977 (2005-2009 5-year est.).
Hospitals: Cleveland Regional Medical Center (107 beds)
Safety: Violent crime rate: 90.2 per 10,000 population; Property crime rate: 872.3 per 10,000 population (2009).
Newspapers: Cleveland Advocate (Community news); Dayton News (Community news; Circulation 7,000); Eastex Advocate (Local news); Eastex Shopper (Community news; Circulation 13,400)
Transportation: Commute to work: 96.3% car, 0.0% public transportation, 0.3% walk, 1.3% work from home (2005-2009 5-year est.); Travel time to work: 33.5% less than 15 minutes, 21.1% 15 to 30 minutes, 28.8% 30 to 45 minutes, 6.1% 45 to 60 minutes, 10.7% 60 minutes or more (2005-2009 5-year est.)
Airports: Cleveland Municipal (general aviation)
Additional Information Contacts
City of Cleveland . . . . (281) 592-2667
    http://www.clevelandtexas.com
Greater Cleveland Chamber of Commerce . . . . (281) 592-8786
    http://clevelandtxchamber.com

DAISETTA (city). Covers a land area of 1.475 square miles and a water area of <.001 square miles. Located at 30.11° N. Lat; 94.64° W. Long. Elevation is 82 feet.
History: Incorporated since 1940.
Population: 969 (1990); 1,034 (2000); 1,062 (2010); 1,078 (2015 projected); Race: 96.0% White, 1.6% Black, 0.0% Asian, 2.4% Other, 2.7% Hispanic of any race (2010); Density: 720.0 persons per square mile (2010); Average household size: 2.70 (2010); Median age: 34.3 (2010); Males per 100 females: 96.3 (2010); Marriage status: 23.4% never married, 49.2% now married, 12.9% widowed, 14.4% divorced (2005-2009 5-year est.); Foreign born: 2.2% (2005-2009 5-year est.); Ancestry (includes multiple ancestries): 15.3% French, 14.8% American, 12.5% Irish, 10.1% German, 8.1% English (2005-2009 5-year est.).
Economy: Employment by occupation: 4.1% management, 6.1% professional, 24.0% services, 14.6% sales, 0.0% farming, 32.9% construction, 18.3% production (2005-2009 5-year est.).
Income: Per capita income: $21,209 (2010); Median household income: $45,236 (2010); Average household income: $57,125 (2010); Percent of households with income of $100,000 or more: 13.5% (2010); Poverty rate: 27.7% (2005-2009 5-year est.).
Taxes: Total city taxes per capita: $60 (2007); City property taxes per capita: $0 (2007).
Education: Percent of population age 25 and over with: High school diploma (including GED) or higher: 75.1% (2010); Bachelor's degree or higher: 12.3% (2010); Master's degree or higher: 4.2% (2010).

School District(s)
Hull-Daisetta ISD (PK-12)
    2009-10 Enrollment: 500 . . . . (936) 536-6321
Housing: Homeownership rate: 73.8% (2010); Median home value: $50,313 (2010); Median contract rent: $394 per month (2005-2009 5-year est.); Median year structure built: 1970 (2005-2009 5-year est.).
Transportation: Commute to work: 93.5% car, 0.0% public transportation, 0.0% walk, 4.1% work from home (2005-2009 5-year est.); Travel time to work: 24.2% less than 15 minutes, 36.4% 15 to 30 minutes, 16.5% 30 to 45

minutes, 14.8% 45 to 60 minutes, 8.1% 60 minutes or more (2005-2009 5-year est.)

DAYTON (city). Covers a land area of 11.040 square miles and a water area of 0 square miles. Located at 30.05° N. Lat; 94.89° W. Long. Elevation is 82 feet.
History: Incorporated 1925.
Population: 4,988 (1990); 5,709 (2000); 6,389 (2010); 6,681 (2015 projected); Race: 72.2% White, 15.5% Black, 0.5% Asian, 11.8% Other, 15.1% Hispanic of any race (2010); Density: 578.7 persons per square mile (2010); Average household size: 2.70 (2010); Median age: 33.0 (2010); Males per 100 females: 91.9 (2010); Marriage status: 35.7% never married, 44.9% now married, 7.6% widowed, 11.8% divorced (2005-2009 5-year est.); Foreign born: 4.6% (2005-2009 5-year est.); Ancestry (includes multiple ancestries): 13.0% German, 9.7% Irish, 6.8% English, 6.7% French, 6.2% American (2005-2009 5-year est.).
Economy: Single-family building permits issued: 33 (2010); Multi-family building permits issued: 0 (2010); Employment by occupation: 10.5% management, 12.7% professional, 20.3% services, 19.0% sales, 0.0% farming, 16.3% construction, 21.2% production (2005-2009 5-year est.).
Income: Per capita income: $19,615 (2010); Median household income: $47,658 (2010); Average household income: $53,530 (2010); Percent of households with income of $100,000 or more: 10.9% (2010); Poverty rate: 17.9% (2005-2009 5-year est.).
Taxes: Total city taxes per capita: $635 (2007); City property taxes per capita: $470 (2007).
Education: Percent of population age 25 and over with: High school diploma (including GED) or higher: 79.5% (2010); Bachelor's degree or higher: 13.3% (2010); Master's degree or higher: 2.4% (2010).

School District(s)
Dayton ISD (PK-12)
    2009-10 Enrollment: 4,912 . . . . (936) 258-2667
Housing: Homeownership rate: 57.9% (2010); Median home value: $89,797 (2010); Median contract rent: $459 per month (2005-2009 5-year est.); Median year structure built: 1984 (2005-2009 5-year est.).
Safety: Violent crime rate: 25.5 per 10,000 population; Property crime rate: 288.2 per 10,000 population (2009).
Transportation: Commute to work: 97.9% car, 0.0% public transportation, 1.0% walk, 0.0% work from home (2005-2009 5-year est.); Travel time to work: 28.6% less than 15 minutes, 27.5% 15 to 30 minutes, 22.5% 30 to 45 minutes, 10.3% 45 to 60 minutes, 11.1% 60 minutes or more (2005-2009 5-year est.)
Additional Information Contacts
City of Dayton . . . . (936) 258-2642
    http://daytontx.com

DAYTON LAKES (city). Covers a land area of 0.839 square miles and a water area of 0.122 square miles. Located at 30.14° N. Lat; 94.82° W. Long. Elevation is 30 feet.
Population: 191 (1990); 101 (2000); 144 (2010); 161 (2015 projected); Race: 98.6% White, 1.4% Black, 0.0% Asian, 0.0% Other, 0.7% Hispanic of any race (2010); Density: 171.7 persons per square mile (2010); Average household size: 2.72 (2010); Median age: 40.0 (2010); Males per 100 females: 100.0 (2010); Marriage status: 21.0% never married, 79.0% now married, 0.0% widowed, 0.0% divorced (2005-2009 5-year est.); Foreign born: 0.0% (2005-2009 5-year est.); Ancestry (includes multiple ancestries): 51.5% German, 29.4% English, 23.5% Irish, 10.3% Czech (2005-2009 5-year est.).
Economy: Employment by occupation: 0.0% management, 24.1% professional, 75.9% services, 0.0% sales, 0.0% farming, 0.0% construction, 0.0% production (2005-2009 5-year est.).
Income: Per capita income: $20,589 (2010); Median household income: $53,906 (2010); Average household income: $56,038 (2010); Percent of households with income of $100,000 or more: 5.7% (2010); Poverty rate: 39.7% (2005-2009 5-year est.).
Taxes: Total city taxes per capita: $104 (2007); City property taxes per capita: $66 (2007).
Education: Percent of population age 25 and over with: High school diploma (including GED) or higher: 74.0% (2010); Bachelor's degree or higher: 4.8% (2010); Master's degree or higher: 2.9% (2010).
Housing: Homeownership rate: 77.4% (2010); Median home value: $78,000 (2010); Median contract rent: n/a per month (2005-2009 5-year est.); Median year structure built: 1986 (2005-2009 5-year est.).
Transportation: Commute to work: 100.0% car, 0.0% public transportation, 0.0% walk, 0.0% work from home (2005-2009 5-year est.);

Travel time to work: 10.5% less than 15 minutes, 36.8% 15 to 30 minutes, 0.0% 30 to 45 minutes, 0.0% 45 to 60 minutes, 52.6% 60 minutes or more (2005-2009 5-year est.)

DEVERS (city). Covers a land area of 1.871 square miles and a water area of 0 square miles. Located at 30.02° N. Lat; 94.59° W. Long. Elevation is 59 feet.
Population: 318 (1990); 416 (2000); 430 (2010); 438 (2015 projected); Race: 75.6% White, 7.4% Black, 0.0% Asian, 17.0% Other, 17.7% Hispanic of any race (2010); Density: 229.8 persons per square mile (2010); Average household size: 2.77 (2010); Median age: 36.4 (2010); Males per 100 females: 97.2 (2010); Marriage status: 33.7% never married, 59.3% now married, 2.6% widowed, 4.4% divorced (2005-2009 5-year est.); Foreign born: 13.0% (2005-2009 5-year est.); Ancestry (includes multiple ancestries): 21.5% American, 12.3% French, 8.8% Irish, 6.2% English, 4.4% German (2005-2009 5-year est.).
Economy: Employment by occupation: 4.5% management, 10.3% professional, 10.7% services, 27.7% sales, 0.0% farming, 14.0% construction, 32.6% production (2005-2009 5-year est.).
Income: Per capita income: $27,721 (2010); Median household income: $59,926 (2010); Average household income: $75,306 (2010); Percent of households with income of $100,000 or more: 20.6% (2010); Poverty rate: 6.2% (2005-2009 5-year est.).
Taxes: Total city taxes per capita: $105 (2007); City property taxes per capita: $0 (2007).
Education: Percent of population age 25 and over with: High school diploma (including GED) or higher: 72.6% (2010); Bachelor's degree or higher: 10.6% (2010); Master's degree or higher: 2.2% (2010).

Housing: Homeownership rate: 83.9% (2010); Median home value: $80,000 (2010); Median contract rent: $531 per month (2005-2009 5-year est.); Median year structure built: 1961 (2005-2009 5-year est.).
Transportation: Commute to work: 97.1% car, 0.8% public transportation, 0.0% walk, 2.1% work from home (2005-2009 5-year est.); Travel time to work: 19.8% less than 15 minutes, 35.4% 15 to 30 minutes, 19.8% 30 to 45 minutes, 16.0% 45 to 60 minutes, 8.9% 60 minutes or more (2005-2009 5-year est.)

HARDIN (city). Covers a land area of 2.292 square miles and a water area of 0 square miles. Located at 30.15° N. Lat; 94.73° W. Long. Elevation is 82 feet.
Population: 656 (1990); 755 (2000); 813 (2010); 844 (2015 projected); Race: 91.3% White, 2.8% Black, 0.2% Asian, 5.7% Other, 7.1% Hispanic of any race (2010); Density: 354.7 persons per square mile (2010); Average household size: 2.73 (2010); Median age: 35.4 (2010); Males per 100 females: 96.4 (2010); Marriage status: 19.2% never married, 56.0% now married, 10.4% widowed, 14.5% divorced (2005-2009 5-year est.); Foreign born: 1.6% (2005-2009 5-year est.); Ancestry (includes multiple ancestries): 14.2% American, 14.1% French, 10.8% Irish, 9.8% English, 8.5% German (2005-2009 5-year est.).
Economy: Employment by occupation: 8.0% management, 8.7% professional, 5.9% services, 29.1% sales, 0.0% farming, 28.2% construction, 20.1% production (2005-2009 5-year est.).
Income: Per capita income: $25,082 (2010); Median household income: $61,161 (2010); Average household income: $67,878 (2010); Percent of households with income of $100,000 or more: 21.5% (2010); Poverty rate: 3.9% (2005-2009 5-year est.).
Taxes: Total city taxes per capita: $88 (2007); City property taxes per capita: $28 (2007).
Education: Percent of population age 25 and over with: High school diploma (including GED) or higher: 78.5% (2010); Bachelor's degree or higher: 12.8% (2010); Master's degree or higher: 3.3% (2010).

Housing: Homeownership rate: 82.9% (2010); Median home value: $76,452 (2010); Median contract rent: $442 per month (2005-2009 5-year est.); Median year structure built: 1963 (2005-2009 5-year est.).
Transportation: Commute to work: 92.5% car, 0.0% public transportation, 3.7% walk, 0.0% work from home (2005-2009 5-year est.); Travel time to work: 51.7% less than 15 minutes, 26.2% 15 to 30 minutes, 1.0% 30 to 45 minutes, 6.5% 45 to 60 minutes, 14.6% 60 minutes or more (2005-2009 5-year est.)

HULL (unincorporated postal area, zip code 77564). Covers a land area of 61.560 square miles and a water area of 0.126 square miles. Located at 30.16° N. Lat; 94.65° W. Long. Elevation is 69 feet.
Population: 2,313 (2000); Race: 95.9% White, 0.2% Black, 0.4% Asian, 3.5% Other, 3.8% Hispanic of any race (2000); Density: 37.6 persons per square mile (2000); Age: 29.9% under 18, 11.5% over 64 (2000); Marriage status: 16.2% never married, 68.9% now married, 5.8% widowed, 9.1% divorced (2000); Foreign born: 1.8% (2000); Ancestry (includes multiple ancestries): 17.8% American, 8.6% French, 6.8% English, 6.1% Irish (2000).
Economy: Employment by occupation: 5.8% management, 16.1% professional, 12.0% services, 26.0% sales, 0.7% farming, 16.3% construction, 23.0% production (2000).
Income: Per capita income: $15,263 (2000); Median household income: $36,689 (2000); Poverty rate: 179.1% (2000).
Education: Percent of population age 25 and over with: High school diploma (including GED) or higher: 72.1% (2000); Bachelor's degree or higher: 9.3% (2000).

Housing: Homeownership rate: 88.9% (2000); Median home value: $43,400 (2000); Median contract rent: $336 per month (2000); Median year structure built: 1976 (2000).
Transportation: Commute to work: 96.1% car, 0.0% public transportation, 1.3% walk, 1.3% work from home (2000); Travel time to work: 15.6% less than 15 minutes, 26.6% 15 to 30 minutes, 14.8% 30 to 45 minutes, 11.1% 45 to 60 minutes, 31.9% 60 minutes or more (2000)

KENEFICK (town). Covers a land area of 1.524 square miles and a water area of 0.006 square miles. Located at 30.10° N. Lat; 94.85° W. Long. Elevation is 66 feet.
Population: 555 (1990); 667 (2000); 663 (2010); 662 (2015 projected); Race: 91.0% White, 1.2% Black, 0.6% Asian, 7.2% Other, 6.5% Hispanic of any race (2010); Density: 435.0 persons per square mile (2010); Average household size: 3.06 (2010); Median age: 35.5 (2010); Males per 100 females: 99.7 (2010); Marriage status: 12.9% never married, 73.5% now married, 8.9% widowed, 4.7% divorced (2005-2009 5-year est.); Foreign born: 0.0% (2005-2009 5-year est.); Ancestry (includes multiple ancestries): 22.1% Irish, 20.6% English, 15.6% German, 11.3% American, 6.7% French (2005-2009 5-year est.).
Economy: Employment by occupation: 5.3% management, 10.5% professional, 16.5% services, 24.8% sales, 1.1% farming, 27.8% construction, 13.9% production (2005-2009 5-year est.).
Income: Per capita income: $22,237 (2010); Median household income: $61,750 (2010); Average household income: $67,108 (2010); Percent of households with income of $100,000 or more: 17.5% (2010); Poverty rate: 3.0% (2005-2009 5-year est.).
Taxes: Total city taxes per capita: $32 (2007); City property taxes per capita: $0 (2007).
Education: Percent of population age 25 and over with: High school diploma (including GED) or higher: 81.4% (2010); Bachelor's degree or higher: 9.4% (2010); Master's degree or higher: 2.6% (2010).
Housing: Homeownership rate: 90.8% (2010); Median home value: $107,328 (2010); Median contract rent: $696 per month (2005-2009 5-year est.); Median year structure built: 1978 (2005-2009 5-year est.).
Transportation: Commute to work: 94.3% car, 0.0% public transportation, 0.0% walk, 5.7% work from home (2005-2009 5-year est.); Travel time to work: 10.5% less than 15 minutes, 11.3% 15 to 30 minutes, 27.0% 30 to 45 minutes, 4.8% 45 to 60 minutes, 46.4% 60 minutes or more (2005-2009 5-year est.)

LIBERTY (city). County seat. Covers a land area of 35.052 square miles and a water area of 0.355 square miles. Located at 30.05° N. Lat; 94.79° W. Long. Elevation is 30 feet.
History: A Mexican settlement named Trinita de la Libertad occupied this site before the town of Liberty was established in 1837.
Population: 7,592 (1990); 8,033 (2000); 8,313 (2010); 8,479 (2015 projected); Race: 70.5% White, 14.4% Black, 0.9% Asian, 14.2% Other, 20.1% Hispanic of any race (2010); Density: 237.2 persons per square mile (2010); Average household size: 2.62 (2010); Median age: 35.6 (2010); Males per 100 females: 98.8 (2010); Marriage status: 29.2% never married, 49.8% now married, 7.5% widowed, 13.5% divorced (2005-2009 5-year est.); Foreign born: 9.3% (2005-2009 5-year est.); Ancestry (includes

multiple ancestries): 13.8% Irish, 11.2% English, 11.2% German, 7.1% French, 6.7% American (2005-2009 5-year est.).

Economy: Single-family building permits issued: 7 (2010); Multi-family building permits issued: 76 (2010); Employment by occupation: 12.8% management, 20.5% professional, 14.1% services, 21.0% sales, 0.8% farming, 16.3% construction, 14.5% production (2005-2009 5-year est.).

Income: Per capita income: $22,241 (2010); Median household income: $45,084 (2010); Average household income: $61,036 (2010); Percent of households with income of $100,000 or more: 16.1% (2010); Poverty rate: 12.0% (2005-2009 5-year est.).

Taxes: Total city taxes per capita: $453 (2007); City property taxes per capita: $240 (2007).

Education: Percent of population age 25 and over with: High school diploma (including GED) or higher: 77.0% (2010); Bachelor's degree or higher: 19.8% (2010); Master's degree or higher: 4.3% (2010).

School District(s)

Anahuac ISD (PK-12)
  2009-10 Enrollment: 1,289 . . . . (409) 267-3600
Barbers Hill ISD (PK-12)
  2009-10 Enrollment: 4,121 . . . . (281) 576-2221
Cleveland ISD (PK-12)
  2009-10 Enrollment: 3,779 . . . . (281) 592-8717
Dayton ISD (PK-12)
  2009-10 Enrollment: 4,912 . . . . (936) 258-2667
East Chambers ISD (PK-12)
  2009-10 Enrollment: 1,297 . . . . (409) 296-6100
Hardin ISD (PK-12)
  2009-10 Enrollment: 1,243 . . . . (936) 298-2112
Hull-Daisetta ISD (PK-12)
  2009-10 Enrollment: 500 . . . . (936) 536-6321
Liberty ISD (PK-12)
  2009-10 Enrollment: 2,238 . . . . (936) 336-7213

Housing: Homeownership rate: 64.2% (2010); Median home value: $78,977 (2010); Median contract rent: $563 per month (2005-2009 5-year est.); Median year structure built: 1971 (2005-2009 5-year est.).

Hospitals: Liberty-Dayton Hospital (35 beds)

Safety: Violent crime rate: 61.0 per 10,000 population; Property crime rate: 502.3 per 10,000 population (2009).

Newspapers: Liberty Gazette (Community news; Circulation 8,800); Pony Express Mail (Community news; Circulation 9,682); Vindicator (Local news; Circulation 4,500)

Transportation: Commute to work: 95.5% car, 0.0% public transportation, 1.3% walk, 2.8% work from home (2005-2009 5-year est.); Travel time to work: 44.9% less than 15 minutes, 12.2% 15 to 30 minutes, 11.0% 30 to 45 minutes, 10.4% 45 to 60 minutes, 21.6% 60 minutes or more (2005-2009 5-year est.)

Airports: Liberty Municipal (general aviation)

Additional Information Contacts
City of Liberty . . . . (512) 778-5449
  http://www.ci.liberty-hill.tx.us
Liberty-Dayton Area Chamber of Commerce . . . . (936) 336-5736
  http://www.libertydaytonchamber.com

NORTH CLEVELAND (city). Covers a land area of 1.922 square miles and a water area of 0.031 square miles. Located at 30.35° N. Lat; 95.09° W. Long. Elevation is 161 feet.

Population: 177 (1990); 263 (2000); 252 (2010); 247 (2015 projected); Race: 65.5% White, 5.6% Black, 1.2% Asian, 27.8% Other, 49.2% Hispanic of any race (2010); Density: 131.1 persons per square mile (2010); Average household size: 2.77 (2010); Median age: 34.2 (2010); Males per 100 females: 98.4 (2010); Marriage status: 30.0% never married, 60.1% now married, 3.3% widowed, 6.6% divorced (2005-2009 5-year est.); Foreign born: 11.9% (2005-2009 5-year est.); Ancestry (includes multiple ancestries): 18.1% Cajun, 9.4% German, 8.4% Irish, 8.1% English, 7.7% Scandinavian (2005-2009 5-year est.).

Economy: Employment by occupation: 2.2% management, 26.1% professional, 37.0% services, 7.2% sales, 0.0% farming, 14.5% construction, 13.0% production (2005-2009 5-year est.).

Income: Per capita income: $20,330 (2010); Median household income: $46,250 (2010); Average household income: $53,214 (2010); Percent of households with income of $100,000 or more: 11.0% (2010); Poverty rate: 18.4% (2005-2009 5-year est.).

Taxes: Total city taxes per capita: $1,153 (2007); City property taxes per capita: $611 (2007).

Education: Percent of population age 25 and over with: High school diploma (including GED) or higher: 79.9% (2010); Bachelor's degree or higher: 5.0% (2010); Master's degree or higher: 1.3% (2010).

Housing: Homeownership rate: 69.2% (2010); Median home value: $59,091 (2010); Median contract rent: $442 per month (2005-2009 5-year est.); Median year structure built: 1990 (2005-2009 5-year est.).

Transportation: Commute to work: 100.0% car, 0.0% public transportation, 0.0% walk, 0.0% work from home (2005-2009 5-year est.); Travel time to work: 41.1% less than 15 minutes, 14.5% 15 to 30 minutes, 5.6% 30 to 45 minutes, 10.5% 45 to 60 minutes, 28.2% 60 minutes or more (2005-2009 5-year est.)

PLUM GROVE (city). Covers a land area of 7.313 square miles and a water area of 0 square miles. Located at 30.20° N. Lat; 95.09° W. Long. Elevation is 95 feet.

Population: 480 (1990); 930 (2000); 1,075 (2010); 1,155 (2015 projected); Race: 74.7% White, 1.6% Black, 0.0% Asian, 23.7% Other, 30.1% Hispanic of any race (2010); Density: 147.0 persons per square mile (2010); Average household size: 3.22 (2010); Median age: 32.7 (2010); Males per 100 females: 105.9 (2010); Marriage status: 11.8% never married, 74.5% now married, 4.6% widowed, 9.1% divorced (2005-2009 5-year est.); Foreign born: 3.0% (2005-2009 5-year est.); Ancestry (includes multiple ancestries): 12.7% English, 11.4% German, 10.8% American, 7.8% Irish, 3.4% Scottish (2005-2009 5-year est.).

Economy: Employment by occupation: 14.1% management, 12.2% professional, 9.9% services, 24.0% sales, 1.9% farming, 15.2% construction, 22.8% production (2005-2009 5-year est.).

Income: Per capita income: $19,280 (2010); Median household income: $55,163 (2010); Average household income: $63,249 (2010); Percent of households with income of $100,000 or more: 13.5% (2010); Poverty rate: 16.8% (2005-2009 5-year est.).

Taxes: Total city taxes per capita: $19 (2007); City property taxes per capita: $0 (2007).

Education: Percent of population age 25 and over with: High school diploma (including GED) or higher: 68.1% (2010); Bachelor's degree or higher: 3.9% (2010); Master's degree or higher: 0.3% (2010).

Housing: Homeownership rate: 86.5% (2010); Median home value: $80,980 (2010); Median contract rent: $344 per month (2005-2009 5-year est.); Median year structure built: 1989 (2005-2009 5-year est.).

Transportation: Commute to work: 92.2% car, 0.0% public transportation, 3.5% walk, 4.3% work from home (2005-2009 5-year est.); Travel time to work: 19.9% less than 15 minutes, 18.3% 15 to 30 minutes, 18.3% 30 to 45 minutes, 11.4% 45 to 60 minutes, 32.1% 60 minutes or more (2005-2009 5-year est.)

RAYWOOD (unincorporated postal area, zip code 77582). Covers a land area of 26.656 square miles and a water area of 0.278 square miles. Located at 30.05° N. Lat; 94.67° W. Long. Elevation is 62 feet.

Population: 771 (2000); Race: 58.9% White, 34.7% Black, 0.6% Asian, 5.8% Other, 0.4% Hispanic of any race (2000); Density: 28.9 persons per square mile (2000); Age: 31.1% under 18, 14.7% over 64 (2000); Marriage status: 18.4% never married, 61.5% now married, 12.0% widowed, 8.1% divorced (2000); Foreign born: 0.6% (2000); Ancestry (includes multiple ancestries): 7.8% American, 7.4% French, 6.0% Irish, 5.4% German (2000).

Economy: Employment by occupation: 2.1% management, 12.6% professional, 15.1% services, 21.0% sales, 1.7% farming, 23.9% construction, 23.5% production (2000).

Income: Per capita income: $23,470 (2000); Median household income: $40,000 (2000); Poverty rate: 179.1% (2000).

Education: Percent of population age 25 and over with: High school diploma (including GED) or higher: 58.8% (2000); Bachelor's degree or higher: 6.0% (2000).

Housing: Homeownership rate: 91.4% (2000); Median home value: $53,000 (2000); Median contract rent: $250 per month (2000); Median year structure built: 1967 (2000).

Transportation: Commute to work: 98.3% car, 0.0% public transportation, 0.0% walk, 0.0% work from home (2000); Travel time to work: 15.0% less than 15 minutes, 40.6% 15 to 30 minutes, 13.7% 30 to 45 minutes, 6.4% 45 to 60 minutes, 24.4% 60 minutes or more (2000)

Limestone County

Located in east central Texas; drained by the Navasota River. Covers a land area of 908.88 square miles, a water area of 24.27 square miles, and

is located in the Central Time Zone at 31.57° N. Lat., 96.55° W. Long. The county was founded in 1846. County seat is Groesbeck.
Population: 20,946 (1990); 22,051 (2000); 22,234 (2010); 22,279 (2015 projected); Race: 67.3% White, 18.5% Black, 0.3% Asian, 13.9% Other, 18.0% Hispanic of any race (2010); Density: 24.5 persons per square mile (2010); Average household size: 2.56 (2010); Median age: 36.9 (2010); Males per 100 females: 104.7 (2010).
Religion: Five largest groups: 29.0% Southern Baptist Convention, 8.7% The United Methodist Church, 5.0% Churches of Christ, 3.6% Catholic Church, 2.9% National Primitive Baptist Convention, USA (2000).
Economy: Unemployment rate: 7.4% (June 2011); Total civilian labor force: 12,318 (June 2011); Leading industries: 23.0% retail trade; 19.1% health care and social assistance; 17.7% manufacturing (2009); Farms: 1,494 totaling 505,846 acres (2007); Companies that employ 500 or more persons: 0 (2009); Companies that employ 100 to 499 persons: 9 (2009); Companies that employ less than 100 persons: 393 (2009); Black-owned businesses: n/a (2007); Hispanic-owned businesses: n/a (2007); Asian-owned businesses: n/a (2007); Women-owned businesses: 651 (2007); Retail sales per capita: $9,412 (2010). Single-family building permits issued: 4 (2010); Multi-family building permits issued: 0 (2010).
Income: Per capita income: $19,126 (2010); Median household income: $39,740 (2010); Average household income: $51,766 (2010); Percent of households with income of $100,000 or more: 10.4% (2010); Poverty rate: 19.9% (2009); Bankruptcy rate: 1.14% (2010).
Taxes: Total county taxes per capita: $212 (2007); County property taxes per capita: $159 (2007).
Education: Percent of population age 25 and over with: High school diploma (including GED) or higher: 70.4% (2010); Bachelor's degree or higher: 12.7% (2010); Master's degree or higher: 5.7% (2010).
Housing: Homeownership rate: 74.8% (2010); Median home value: $67,455 (2010); Median contract rent: $375 per month (2005-2009 5-year est.); Median year structure built: 1975 (2005-2009 5-year est.)
Health: Birth rate: 130.6 per 10,000 population (2009); Death rate: 118.5 per 10,000 population (2009); Age-adjusted cancer mortality rate: 200.3 deaths per 100,000 population (2007); Number of physicians: 6.7 per 10,000 population (2008); Hospital beds: 29.5 per 10,000 population (2007); Hospital admissions: 1,242.5 per 10,000 population (2007).
Elections: 2008 Presidential election results: 32.9% Obama, 66.4% McCain, 0.0% Nader
National and State Parks: Fort Parker State Park
Additional Information Contacts
Limestone County Government . . . . (254) 729-5504
   http://www.co.limestone.tx.us/ips/cms
City of Mexia . . . . (254) 562-4110
   http://www.cityofmexia.com
Groesbeck Chamber of Commerce . . . . (254) 729-3894
Mexia Area Chamber of Commerce . . . . (254) 562-5569
   http://www.mexiachamber.com

Limestone County Communities

COOLIDGE (town). Covers a land area of 0.965 square miles and a water area of 0.034 square miles. Located at 31.75° N. Lat; 96.65° W. Long. Elevation is 535 feet.
History: Settled 1903, incorporated 1905.
Population: 748 (1990); 848 (2000); 876 (2010); 889 (2015 projected); Race: 58.1% White, 16.2% Black, 0.5% Asian, 25.2% Other, 41.0% Hispanic of any race (2010); Density: 907.7 persons per square mile (2010); Average household size: 2.82 (2010); Median age: 31.0 (2010); Males per 100 females: 95.1 (2010); Marriage status: 26.0% never married, 57.5% now married, 5.8% widowed, 10.7% divorced (2005-2009 5-year est.); Foreign born: 7.6% (2005-2009 5-year est.); Ancestry (includes multiple ancestries): 11.4% German, 8.9% Irish, 5.8% African, 5.7% English, 4.4% Italian (2005-2009 5-year est.).
Economy: Employment by occupation: 18.2% management, 14.3% professional, 21.4% services, 20.1% sales, 0.3% farming, 1.0% construction, 24.7% production (2005-2009 5-year est.).
Income: Per capita income: $16,555 (2010); Median household income: $34,135 (2010); Average household income: $45,941 (2010); Percent of households with income of $100,000 or more: 6.4% (2010); Poverty rate: 30.7% (2005-2009 5-year est.).
Taxes: Total city taxes per capita: $5 (2007); City property taxes per capita: $0 (2007).

Education: Percent of population age 25 and over with: High school diploma (including GED) or higher: 54.4% (2010); Bachelor's degree or higher: 9.7% (2010); Master's degree or higher: 6.9% (2010).
School District(s)
Coolidge ISD (PK-12)
   2009-10 Enrollment: 288 . . . . (254) 786-2206
Housing: Homeownership rate: 66.6% (2010); Median home value: $36,622 (2010); Median contract rent: $296 per month (2005-2009 5-year est.); Median year structure built: 1976 (2005-2009 5-year est.).
Transportation: Commute to work: 97.3% car, 0.0% public transportation, 2.7% walk, 0.0% work from home (2005-2009 5-year est.); Travel time to work: 28.5% less than 15 minutes, 52.8% 15 to 30 minutes, 6.1% 30 to 45 minutes, 11.7% 45 to 60 minutes, 0.8% 60 minutes or more (2005-2009 5-year est.)

GROESBECK (city). County seat. Covers a land area of 3.760 square miles and a water area of 0.010 square miles. Located at 31.52° N. Lat; 96.53° W. Long. Elevation is 479 feet.
History: Old Fort Parker State Historic Site to North.
Population: 3,289 (1990); 4,291 (2000); 4,361 (2010); 4,376 (2015 projected); Race: 50.1% White, 25.7% Black, 0.0% Asian, 24.1% Other, 24.7% Hispanic of any race (2010); Density: 1,159.9 persons per square mile (2010); Average household size: 2.59 (2010); Median age: 32.0 (2010); Males per 100 females: 144.3 (2010); Marriage status: 36.1% never married, 42.2% now married, 6.9% widowed, 14.9% divorced (2005-2009 5-year est.); Foreign born: 24.1% (2005-2009 5-year est.); Ancestry (includes multiple ancestries): 13.7% Irish, 10.1% German, 4.2% English, 2.2% Scotch-Irish, 2.1% American (2005-2009 5-year est.).
Economy: Single-family building permits issued: 2 (2010); Multi-family building permits issued: 0 (2010); Employment by occupation: 8.2% management, 11.7% professional, 13.2% services, 14.9% sales, 0.7% farming, 32.0% construction, 19.3% production (2005-2009 5-year est.).
Income: Per capita income: $15,180 (2010); Median household income: $34,103 (2010); Average household income: $44,709 (2010); Percent of households with income of $100,000 or more: 7.2% (2010); Poverty rate: 23.5% (2005-2009 5-year est.).
Taxes: Total city taxes per capita: $306 (2007); City property taxes per capita: $126 (2007).
Education: Percent of population age 25 and over with: High school diploma (including GED) or higher: 61.3% (2010); Bachelor's degree or higher: 9.6% (2010); Master's degree or higher: 2.9% (2010).
School District(s)
Groesbeck ISD (PK-12)
   2009-10 Enrollment: 1,583 . . . . (254) 729-4100
Housing: Homeownership rate: 65.9% (2010); Median home value: $59,837 (2010); Median contract rent: $364 per month (2005-2009 5-year est.); Median year structure built: 1967 (2005-2009 5-year est.).
Hospitals: Limestone Medical Center (20 beds)
Safety: Violent crime rate: 21.0 per 10,000 population; Property crime rate: 212.7 per 10,000 population (2009).
Newspapers: Groesbeck Journal (Local news; Circulation 3,600); Journal (Local news; Circulation 4,300)
Transportation: Commute to work: 95.4% car, 0.0% public transportation, 1.2% walk, 3.1% work from home (2005-2009 5-year est.); Travel time to work: 37.6% less than 15 minutes, 17.9% 15 to 30 minutes, 12.4% 30 to 45 minutes, 15.7% 45 to 60 minutes, 16.4% 60 minutes or more (2005-2009 5-year est.)
Additional Information Contacts
Groesbeck Chamber of Commerce . . . . (254) 729-3894

KOSSE (town). Covers a land area of 1.302 square miles and a water area of 0 square miles. Located at 31.30° N. Lat; 96.63° W. Long. Elevation is 499 feet.
Population: 505 (1990); 497 (2000); 515 (2010); 519 (2015 projected); Race: 74.6% White, 13.4% Black, 0.8% Asian, 11.3% Other, 15.7% Hispanic of any race (2010); Density: 395.5 persons per square mile (2010); Average household size: 2.43 (2010); Median age: 37.7 (2010); Males per 100 females: 106.8 (2010); Marriage status: 16.1% never married, 52.8% now married, 15.1% widowed, 16.1% divorced (2005-2009 5-year est.); Foreign born: 2.6% (2005-2009 5-year est.); Ancestry (includes multiple ancestries): 32.6% English, 20.8% Irish, 18.3% German, 4.6% American, 2.3% Scotch-Irish (2005-2009 5-year est.).
Economy: Employment by occupation: 12.7% management, 27.5% professional, 28.6% services, 16.4% sales, 3.2% farming, 6.3% construction, 5.3% production (2005-2009 5-year est.).

Income: Per capita income: $19,688 (2010); Median household income: $38,409 (2010); Average household income: $48,134 (2010); Percent of households with income of $100,000 or more: 8.8% (2010); Poverty rate: 16.5% (2005-2009 5-year est.).

Taxes: Total city taxes per capita: $52 (2007); City property taxes per capita: $47 (2007).

Education: Percent of population age 25 and over with: High school diploma (including GED) or higher: 73.5% (2010); Bachelor's degree or higher: 7.1% (2010); Master's degree or higher: 1.8% (2010).

Housing: Homeownership rate: 74.1% (2010); Median home value: $50,000 (2010); Median contract rent: $231 per month (2005-2009 5-year est.); Median year structure built: 1970 (2005-2009 5-year est.).

Transportation: Commute to work: 94.9% car, 0.0% public transportation, 0.0% walk, 5.1% work from home (2005-2009 5-year est.); Travel time to work: 38.6% less than 15 minutes, 39.2% 15 to 30 minutes, 17.5% 30 to 45 minutes, 0.0% 45 to 60 minutes, 4.8% 60 minutes or more (2005-2009 5-year est.)

MEXIA (city). Covers a land area of 5.152 square miles and a water area of 0 square miles. Located at 31.68° N. Lat; 96.48° W. Long. Elevation is 522 feet.

History: Mexia was named for Colonel Jose Antonio Mejia, who owned land here through a Spanish grant. His son, H.A. Mexia, changed the spelling of the name.

Population: 6,933 (1990); 6,563 (2000); 6,460 (2010); 6,407 (2015 projected); Race: 53.8% White, 28.9% Black, 0.4% Asian, 16.9% Other, 25.0% Hispanic of any race (2010); Density: 1,253.9 persons per square mile (2010); Average household size: 2.65 (2010); Median age: 33.7 (2010); Males per 100 females: 88.0 (2010); Marriage status: 25.8% never married, 50.5% now married, 11.1% widowed, 12.6% divorced (2005-2009 5-year est.); Foreign born: 10.2% (2005-2009 5-year est.); Ancestry (includes multiple ancestries): 9.3% English, 9.3% Irish, 8.7% American, 6.7% German, 1.7% Scottish (2005-2009 5-year est.).

Economy: Single-family building permits issued: 2 (2010); Multi-family building permits issued: 0 (2010); Employment by occupation: 7.5% management, 24.6% professional, 24.2% services, 18.6% sales, 0.8% farming, 10.1% construction, 14.2% production (2005-2009 5-year est.).

Income: Per capita income: $16,453 (2010); Median household income: $32,130 (2010); Average household income: $44,535 (2010); Percent of households with income of $100,000 or more: 7.7% (2010); Poverty rate: 25.7% (2005-2009 5-year est.).

Taxes: Total city taxes per capita: $592 (2007); City property taxes per capita: $232 (2007).

Education: Percent of population age 25 and over with: High school diploma (including GED) or higher: 68.3% (2010); Bachelor's degree or higher: 12.7% (2010); Master's degree or higher: 5.4% (2010).

School District(s)

Mexia ISD (PK-12)
    2009-10 Enrollment: 2,215 . . . . (254) 562-4000

Housing: Homeownership rate: 66.4% (2010); Median home value: $52,722 (2010); Median contract rent: $406 per month (2005-2009 5-year est.); Median year structure built: 1971 (2005-2009 5-year est.).

Hospitals: Parkview Regional Hospital (59 beds)

Safety: Violent crime rate: 81.0 per 10,000 population; Property crime rate: 704.4 per 10,000 population (2009).

Newspapers: Hubbard City News (Community news; Circulation 1,350); The Mexia Daily News (Local news; Circulation 4,000)

Transportation: Commute to work: 94.8% car, 0.0% public transportation, 1.6% walk, 1.4% work from home (2005-2009 5-year est.); Travel time to work: 59.4% less than 15 minutes, 25.9% 15 to 30 minutes, 6.6% 30 to 45 minutes, 2.9% 45 to 60 minutes, 5.2% 60 minutes or more (2005-2009 5-year est.)

Additional Information Contacts

City of Mexia . . . . (254) 562-4110
  http://www.cityofmexia.com
Mexia Area Chamber of Commerce . . . . (254) 562-5569
  http://www.mexiachamber.com

PRAIRIE HILL (unincorporated postal area, zip code 76678). Covers a land area of 21.286 square miles and a water area of 0.020 square miles. Located at 31.65° N. Lat; 96.78° W. Long. Elevation is 594 feet.

Population: 168 (2000); Race: 95.0% White, 0.0% Black, 0.0% Asian, 5.0% Other, 2.9% Hispanic of any race (2000); Density: 7.9 persons per square mile (2000); Age: 17.3% under 18, 24.5% over 64 (2000); Marriage status: 8.5% never married, 66.9% now married, 15.3% widowed, 9.3%

divorced (2000); Foreign born: 0.0% (2000); Ancestry (includes multiple ancestries): 13.7% German, 9.4% Irish, 7.9% American, 7.2% Czech (2000).

Economy: Employment by occupation: 10.7% management, 1.8% professional, 23.2% services, 23.2% sales, 0.0% farming, 14.3% construction, 26.8% production (2000).

Income: Per capita income: $15,989 (2000); Median household income: $25,417 (2000); Poverty rate: 179.1% (2000).

Education: Percent of population age 25 and over with: High school diploma (including GED) or higher: 80.6% (2000); Bachelor's degree or higher: 11.1% (2000).

Housing: Homeownership rate: 84.1% (2000); Median home value: $42,000 (2000); Median contract rent: $292 per month (2000); Median year structure built: 1963 (2000).

Transportation: Commute to work: 94.6% car, 0.0% public transportation, 0.0% walk, 5.4% work from home (2000); Travel time to work: 9.4% less than 15 minutes, 15.1% 15 to 30 minutes, 41.5% 30 to 45 minutes, 24.5% 45 to 60 minutes, 9.4% 60 minutes or more (2000)

TEHUACANA (town). Covers a land area of 1.613 square miles and a water area of 0 square miles. Located at 31.74° N. Lat; 96.54° W. Long. Elevation is 640 feet.

History: Tehuacana was founded about 1844 and named for an Indian tribe that had lived nearby.

Population: 366 (1990); 307 (2000); 287 (2010); 275 (2015 projected); Race: 80.1% White, 13.9% Black, 0.3% Asian, 5.6% Other, 6.3% Hispanic of any race (2010); Density: 177.9 persons per square mile (2010); Average household size: 2.41 (2010); Median age: 41.0 (2010); Males per 100 females: 106.5 (2010); Marriage status: 23.0% never married, 51.3% now married, 0.4% widowed, 25.2% divorced (2005-2009 5-year est.); Foreign born: 0.0% (2005-2009 5-year est.); Ancestry (includes multiple ancestries): 41.4% Irish, 17.2% English, 13.4% German, 9.0% Dutch, 5.9% Scottish (2005-2009 5-year est.).

Economy: Employment by occupation: 8.0% management, 12.3% professional, 34.0% services, 21.6% sales, 0.6% farming, 13.6% construction, 9.9% production (2005-2009 5-year est.).

Income: Per capita income: $21,889 (2010); Median household income: $42,857 (2010); Average household income: $52,325 (2010); Percent of households with income of $100,000 or more: 11.4% (2010); Poverty rate: 20.7% (2005-2009 5-year est.).

Taxes: Total city taxes per capita: $66 (2007); City property taxes per capita: $66 (2007).

Education: Percent of population age 25 and over with: High school diploma (including GED) or higher: 77.2% (2010); Bachelor's degree or higher: 23.8% (2010); Master's degree or higher: 12.4% (2010).

Housing: Homeownership rate: 86.0% (2010); Median home value: $85,000 (2010); Median contract rent: $383 per month (2005-2009 5-year est.); Median year structure built: 1963 (2005-2009 5-year est.).

Transportation: Commute to work: 100.0% car, 0.0% public transportation, 0.0% walk, 0.0% work from home (2005-2009 5-year est.); Travel time to work: 38.4% less than 15 minutes, 28.9% 15 to 30 minutes, 6.3% 30 to 45 minutes, 11.9% 45 to 60 minutes, 14.5% 60 minutes or more (2005-2009 5-year est.)

THORNTON (town). Covers a land area of 0.992 square miles and a water area of 0.006 square miles. Located at 31.41° N. Lat; 96.57° W. Long. Elevation is 492 feet.

Population: 540 (1990); 525 (2000); 537 (2010); 541 (2015 projected); Race: 90.7% White, 3.9% Black, 0.6% Asian, 4.8% Other, 10.1% Hispanic of any race (2010); Density: 541.6 persons per square mile (2010); Average household size: 2.57 (2010); Median age: 39.4 (2010); Males per 100 females: 100.4 (2010); Marriage status: 6.2% never married, 68.6% now married, 7.1% widowed, 18.2% divorced (2005-2009 5-year est.); Foreign born: 0.0% (2005-2009 5-year est.); Ancestry (includes multiple ancestries): 22.4% German, 14.1% English, 13.9% American, 13.5% Irish, 6.3% French (2005-2009 5-year est.).

Economy: Employment by occupation: 14.3% management, 8.9% professional, 19.4% services, 17.8% sales, 0.0% farming, 17.8% construction, 21.7% production (2005-2009 5-year est.).

Income: Per capita income: $18,244 (2010); Median household income: $34,571 (2010); Average household income: $47,189 (2010); Percent of households with income of $100,000 or more: 7.2% (2010); Poverty rate: 15.8% (2005-2009 5-year est.).

Taxes: Total city taxes per capita: $92 (2007); City property taxes per capita: $42 (2007).

Education: Percent of population age 25 and over with: High school diploma (including GED) or higher: 71.2% (2010); Bachelor's degree or higher: 5.5% (2010); Master's degree or higher: 2.2% (2010).
Housing: Homeownership rate: 75.1% (2010); Median home value: $52,895 (2010); Median contract rent: $328 per month (2005-2009 5-year est.); Median year structure built: 1964 (2005-2009 5-year est.).
Transportation: Commute to work: 94.0% car, 0.0% public transportation, 4.8% walk, 1.2% work from home (2005-2009 5-year est.); Travel time to work: 30.9% less than 15 minutes, 29.3% 15 to 30 minutes, 28.9% 30 to 45 minutes, 0.0% 45 to 60 minutes, 10.8% 60 minutes or more (2005-2009 5-year est.)

Lipscomb County

Located in north Texas, in the Panhandle; bounded on the north and east by Oklahoma. Covers a land area of 932.11 square miles, a water area of 0.11 square miles, and is located in the Central Time Zone at 36.29° N. Lat., 100.28° W. Long. The county was founded in 1876. County seat is Lipscomb.

Weather Station: Follett   Elevation: 2,769 feet

	Jan	Feb	Mar	Apr	May	Jun	Jul	Aug	Sep	Oct	Nov	Dec
High	47	52	59	69	77	86	91	91	82	71	59	46
Low	22	25	32	41	52	61	66	65	56	44	32	23
Precip	0.5	0.9	2.3	2.0	3.2	3.1	2.7	2.7	2.0	1.8	1.0	0.9
Snow	3.1	2.4	4.8	0.6	0.0	0.0	0.0	0.0	tr	tr	2.0	3.0

High and Low temperatures in degrees Fahrenheit; Precipitation and Snow in inches

Weather Station: Lipscomb   Elevation: 2,450 feet

	Jan	Feb	Mar	Apr	May	Jun	Jul	Aug	Sep	Oct	Nov	Dec
High	49	53	62	71	79	88	94	93	85	73	61	49
Low	19	22	31	40	51	61	66	65	55	42	29	19
Precip	0.7	0.8	1.8	1.9	3.1	3.6	2.3	2.8	1.9	1.8	0.9	0.9
Snow	2.4	2.0	2.8	0.4	0.0	0.0	0.0	0.0	0.0	0.1	1.1	4.2

High and Low temperatures in degrees Fahrenheit; Precipitation and Snow in inches

Population: 3,143 (1990); 3,057 (2000); 3,118 (2010); 3,143 (2015 projected); Race: 75.5% White, 0.6% Black, 0.0% Asian, 23.9% Other, 30.6% Hispanic of any race (2010); Density: 3.3 persons per square mile (2010); Average household size: 2.46 (2010); Median age: 38.1 (2010); Males per 100 females: 100.0 (2010).
Religion: Five largest groups: 33.9% Southern Baptist Convention, 23.9% The United Methodist Church, 9.1% Catholic Church, 4.9% Christian Churches and Churches of Christ, 4.1% Friends (Quakers) (2000).
Economy: Unemployment rate: 5.0% (June 2011); Total civilian labor force: 1,681 (June 2011); Leading industries: Farms: 294 totaling 571,057 acres (2007); Companies that employ 500 or more persons: 0 (2009); Companies that employ 100 to 499 persons: 2 (2009); Companies that employ less than 100 persons: 97 (2009); Black-owned businesses: n/a (2007); Hispanic-owned businesses: n/a (2007); Asian-owned businesses: n/a (2007); Women-owned businesses: n/a (2007); Retail sales per capita: $5,018 (2010). Single-family building permits issued: 2 (2010); Multi-family building permits issued: 0 (2010).
Income: Per capita income: $22,057 (2010); Median household income: $42,079 (2010); Average household income: $54,308 (2010); Percent of households with income of $100,000 or more: 10.9% (2010); Poverty rate: 12.2% (2009); Bankruptcy rate: 1.21% (2010).
Taxes: Total county taxes per capita: $915 (2007); County property taxes per capita: $828 (2007).
Education: Percent of population age 25 and over with: High school diploma (including GED) or higher: 79.2% (2010); Bachelor's degree or higher: 21.2% (2010); Master's degree or higher: 5.6% (2010).
Housing: Homeownership rate: 76.1% (2010); Median home value: $47,024 (2010); Median contract rent: $406 per month (2005-2009 5-year est.); Median year structure built: 1959 (2005-2009 5-year est.)
Health: Birth rate: 158.4 per 10,000 population (2009); Death rate: 74.3 per 10,000 population (2009); Age-adjusted cancer mortality rate: 270.1 (Unreliable) deaths per 100,000 population (2007); Number of physicians: 0.0 per 10,000 population (2008); Hospital beds: 0.0 per 10,000 population (2007); Hospital admissions: 0.0 per 10,000 population (2007).
Elections: 2008 Presidential election results: 12.3% Obama, 87.0% McCain, 0.0% Nader
Additional Information Contacts
Lipscomb County Government . . . . (806) 862-4131
  http://www.co.lipscomb.tx.us/ips/cms

Booker Chamber of Commerce . . . . (806) 658-2416
  http://bookerchamber.com

Lipscomb County Communities

BOOKER (town). Covers a land area of 1.043 square miles and a water area of 0 square miles. Located at 36.45° N. Lat; 100.53° W. Long. Elevation is 2,831 feet.
Population: 1,236 (1990); 1,315 (2000); 1,338 (2010); 1,350 (2015 projected); Race: 60.2% White, 0.6% Black, 0.1% Asian, 39.1% Other, 54.3% Hispanic of any race (2010); Density: 1,282.4 persons per square mile (2010); Average household size: 2.76 (2010); Median age: 32.4 (2010); Males per 100 females: 99.4 (2010); Marriage status: 13.4% never married, 71.6% now married, 6.8% widowed, 8.2% divorced (2005-2009 5-year est.); Foreign born: 26.8% (2005-2009 5-year est.); Ancestry (includes multiple ancestries): 10.2% German, 8.4% Irish, 7.9% American, 7.8% English, 1.9% Czech (2005-2009 5-year est.).
Economy: Single-family building permits issued: 0 (2010); Multi-family building permits issued: 0 (2010); Employment by occupation: 14.5% management, 11.6% professional, 17.4% services, 14.5% sales, 6.5% farming, 19.5% construction, 15.9% production (2005-2009 5-year est.).
Income: Per capita income: $17,618 (2010); Median household income: $39,701 (2010); Average household income: $48,451 (2010); Percent of households with income of $100,000 or more: 7.9% (2010); Poverty rate: 21.5% (2005-2009 5-year est.).
Taxes: Total city taxes per capita: $210 (2007); City property taxes per capita: $124 (2007).
Education: Percent of population age 25 and over with: High school diploma (including GED) or higher: 71.1% (2010); Bachelor's degree or higher: 18.5% (2010); Master's degree or higher: 5.7% (2010).
School District(s)
Booker ISD (PK-12)
  2009-10 Enrollment: 390 . . . . (806) 658-4501
Housing: Homeownership rate: 75.6% (2010); Median home value: $49,870 (2010); Median contract rent: $409 per month (2005-2009 5-year est.); Median year structure built: 1973 (2005-2009 5-year est.).
Newspapers: Booker News (Community news; Circulation 1,100)
Transportation: Commute to work: 92.5% car, 0.0% public transportation, 3.7% walk, 0.0% work from home (2005-2009 5-year est.); Travel time to work: 59.4% less than 15 minutes, 19.8% 15 to 30 minutes, 8.1% 30 to 45 minutes, 5.0% 45 to 60 minutes, 7.7% 60 minutes or more (2005-2009 5-year est.)
Additional Information Contacts
Booker Chamber of Commerce . . . . (806) 658-2416
  http://bookerchamber.com

DARROUZETT (town). Covers a land area of 0.374 square miles and a water area of 0 square miles. Located at 36.44° N. Lat; 100.32° W. Long. Elevation is 2,556 feet.
Population: 343 (1990); 303 (2000); 300 (2010); 296 (2015 projected); Race: 82.7% White, 0.7% Black, 0.0% Asian, 16.7% Other, 25.7% Hispanic of any race (2010); Density: 801.6 persons per square mile (2010); Average household size: 2.40 (2010); Median age: 40.3 (2010); Males per 100 females: 106.9 (2010); Marriage status: 27.9% never married, 55.0% now married, 3.8% widowed, 13.3% divorced (2005-2009 5-year est.); Foreign born: 1.6% (2005-2009 5-year est.); Ancestry (includes multiple ancestries): 29.3% German, 10.2% Irish, 9.5% English, 6.3% American, 6.3% French (2005-2009 5-year est.).
Economy: Single-family building permits issued: 2 (2010); Multi-family building permits issued: 0 (2010); Employment by occupation: 18.0% management, 18.6% professional, 17.4% services, 8.7% sales, 11.2% farming, 10.6% construction, 15.5% production (2005-2009 5-year est.).
Income: Per capita income: $24,632 (2010); Median household income: $49,674 (2010); Average household income: $58,760 (2010); Percent of households with income of $100,000 or more: 10.4% (2010); Poverty rate: 20.7% (2005-2009 5-year est.).
Taxes: Total city taxes per capita: $272 (2007); City property taxes per capita: $238 (2007).
Education: Percent of population age 25 and over with: High school diploma (including GED) or higher: 85.9% (2010); Bachelor's degree or higher: 23.7% (2010); Master's degree or higher: 6.6% (2010).
School District(s)
Darrouzett ISD (PK-12)
  2009-10 Enrollment: 132 . . . . (806) 624-2221

Housing: Homeownership rate: 72.0% (2010); Median home value: $43,750 (2010); Median contract rent: $393 per month (2005-2009 5-year est.); Median year structure built: 1960 (2005-2009 5-year est.).
Transportation: Commute to work: 92.5% car, 0.0% public transportation, 1.4% walk, 4.8% work from home (2005-2009 5-year est.); Travel time to work: 43.2% less than 15 minutes, 10.8% 15 to 30 minutes, 37.4% 30 to 45 minutes, 3.6% 45 to 60 minutes, 5.0% 60 minutes or more (2005-2009 5-year est.)

FOLLETT (city). Covers a land area of 0.969 square miles and a water area of 0 square miles. Located at 36.43° N. Lat; 100.14° W. Long. Elevation is 2,598 feet.
Population: 441 (1990); 412 (2000); 428 (2010); 433 (2015 projected); Race: 87.9% White, 0.7% Black, 0.0% Asian, 11.4% Other, 11.0% Hispanic of any race (2010); Density: 441.6 persons per square mile (2010); Average household size: 2.31 (2010); Median age: 44.3 (2010); Males per 100 females: 104.8 (2010); Marriage status: 22.8% never married, 64.6% now married, 2.9% widowed, 9.7% divorced (2005-2009 5-year est.); Foreign born: 2.1% (2005-2009 5-year est.); Ancestry (includes multiple ancestries): 35.5% German, 18.0% English, 14.8% French, 12.1% Irish, 5.2% Scottish (2005-2009 5-year est.).
Economy: Single-family building permits issued: 0 (2010); Multi-family building permits issued: 0 (2010); Employment by occupation: 21.3% management, 17.5% professional, 7.2% services, 16.8% sales, 2.7% farming, 17.5% construction, 16.8% production (2005-2009 5-year est.).
Income: Per capita income: $25,611 (2010); Median household income: $42,905 (2010); Average household income: $59,162 (2010); Percent of households with income of $100,000 or more: 16.2% (2010); Poverty rate: 3.1% (2005-2009 5-year est.).
Taxes: Total city taxes per capita: $276 (2007); City property taxes per capita: $137 (2007).
Education: Percent of population age 25 and over with: High school diploma (including GED) or higher: 85.2% (2010); Bachelor's degree or higher: 22.5% (2010); Master's degree or higher: 4.9% (2010).

School District(s)
Follett ISD (PK-12)
   2009-10 Enrollment: 173 . . . . (806) 653-2301
Housing: Homeownership rate: 80.5% (2010); Median home value: $51,923 (2010); Median contract rent: $410 per month (2005-2009 5-year est.); Median year structure built: 1952 (2005-2009 5-year est.).
Newspapers: Golden Spread (Local news; Circulation 800)
Transportation: Commute to work: 91.3% car, 0.0% public transportation, 2.1% walk, 6.6% work from home (2005-2009 5-year est.); Travel time to work: 63.8% less than 15 minutes, 19.0% 15 to 30 minutes, 12.3% 30 to 45 minutes, 4.1% 45 to 60 minutes, 0.7% 60 minutes or more (2005-2009 5-year est.)

HIGGINS (city). Covers a land area of 1.094 square miles and a water area of 0 square miles. Located at 36.12° N. Lat; 100.02° W. Long. Elevation is 2,569 feet.
History: Near Higgins, it is believed, Father Juan de Padilla was buried. Padilla accompanied Coronado to Gran Quivira, and returned later to work among the people of the area. He died in 1544.
Population: 464 (1990); 425 (2000); 447 (2010); 455 (2015 projected); Race: 89.3% White, 0.7% Black, 0.0% Asian, 10.1% Other, 4.9% Hispanic of any race (2010); Density: 408.8 persons per square mile (2010); Average household size: 2.19 (2010); Median age: 47.9 (2010); Males per 100 females: 103.2 (2010); Marriage status: 15.0% never married, 62.6% now married, 12.5% widowed, 9.9% divorced (2005-2009 5-year est.); Foreign born: 4.2% (2005-2009 5-year est.); Ancestry (includes multiple ancestries): 32.5% German, 17.9% Irish, 11.2% English, 3.9% American, 3.4% Welsh (2005-2009 5-year est.).
Economy: Employment by occupation: 5.7% management, 13.0% professional, 21.4% services, 14.1% sales, 1.0% farming, 18.8% construction, 26.0% production (2005-2009 5-year est.).
Income: Per capita income: $25,842 (2010); Median household income: $39,342 (2010); Average household income: $56,973 (2010); Percent of households with income of $100,000 or more: 10.8% (2010); Poverty rate: 7.4% (2005-2009 5-year est.).
Taxes: Total city taxes per capita: $317 (2007); City property taxes per capita: $198 (2007).
Education: Percent of population age 25 and over with: High school diploma (including GED) or higher: 82.7% (2010); Bachelor's degree or higher: 22.7% (2010); Master's degree or higher: 5.4% (2010).

School District(s)
Higgins ISD (PK-12)
   2009-10 Enrollment: 94 . . . . (806) 852-2171
Housing: Homeownership rate: 76.0% (2010); Median home value: $37,000 (2010); Median contract rent: $340 per month (2005-2009 5-year est.); Median year structure built: 1951 (2005-2009 5-year est.).
Transportation: Commute to work: 96.3% car, 0.0% public transportation, 0.0% walk, 3.7% work from home (2005-2009 5-year est.); Travel time to work: 31.1% less than 15 minutes, 44.3% 15 to 30 minutes, 7.1% 30 to 45 minutes, 11.5% 45 to 60 minutes, 6.0% 60 minutes or more (2005-2009 5-year est.)

LIPSCOMB (CDP). County seat. Covers a land area of 5.105 square miles and a water area of 0 square miles. Located at 36.23° N. Lat; 100.27° W. Long. Elevation is 2,392 feet.
Population: 51 (1990); 44 (2000); 55 (2010); 56 (2015 projected); Race: 90.9% White, 0.0% Black, 0.0% Asian, 9.1% Other, 5.5% Hispanic of any race (2010); Density: 10.8 persons per square mile (2010); Average household size: 2.20 (2010); Median age: 48.2 (2010); Males per 100 females: 111.5 (2010); Marriage status: 0.0% never married, 65.5% now married, 10.3% widowed, 24.1% divorced (2005-2009 5-year est.); Foreign born: 0.0% (2005-2009 5-year est.); Ancestry (includes multiple ancestries): 65.5% German, 34.5% Irish, 20.7% English, 13.8% American, 13.8% Russian (2005-2009 5-year est.).
Economy: Employment by occupation: 61.1% management, 0.0% professional, 0.0% services, 38.9% sales, 0.0% farming, 0.0% construction, 0.0% production (2005-2009 5-year est.).
Income: Per capita income: $25,842 (2010); Median household income: $45,500 (2010); Average household income: $64,500 (2010); Percent of households with income of $100,000 or more: 16.0% (2010); Poverty rate: 24.1% (2005-2009 5-year est.).
Education: Percent of population age 25 and over with: High school diploma (including GED) or higher: 85.4% (2010); Bachelor's degree or higher: 24.4% (2010); Master's degree or higher: 7.3% (2010).
Housing: Homeownership rate: 76.0% (2010); Median home value: $32,500 (2010); Median contract rent: n/a per month (2005-2009 5-year est.); Median year structure built: before 1940 (2005-2009 5-year est.).
Transportation: Commute to work: 100.0% car, 0.0% public transportation, 0.0% walk, 0.0% work from home (2005-2009 5-year est.); Travel time to work: 83.3% less than 15 minutes, 16.7% 15 to 30 minutes, 0.0% 30 to 45 minutes, 0.0% 45 to 60 minutes, 0.0% 60 minutes or more (2005-2009 5-year est.)

Live Oak County

Located in south Texas; drained by the Frio, Atascosa, and Nueces Rivers. Covers a land area of 1,036.30 square miles, a water area of 42.53 square miles, and is located in the Central Time Zone at 28.31° N. Lat., 98.10° W. Long. The county was founded in 1856. County seat is George West.

Weather Station: Choke Canyon Dam   Elevation: 229 feet

	Jan	Feb	Mar	Apr	May	Jun	Jul	Aug	Sep	Oct	Nov	Dec
High	66	70	77	84	90	95	97	98	93	86	75	67
Low	44	47	53	60	68	73	74	74	70	62	53	45
Precip	1.4	1.3	1.9	2.0	2.5	3.1	3.2	1.6	3.0	2.1	1.7	1.6
Snow	0.0	tr	0.0	0.0	0.0	0.0	0.0	0.0	0.0	0.0	0.0	0.2

High and Low temperatures in degrees Fahrenheit; Precipitation and Snow in inches

Population: 9,556 (1990); 12,309 (2000); 11,665 (2010); 11,330 (2015 projected); Race: 85.7% White, 2.9% Black, 0.2% Asian, 11.2% Other, 42.2% Hispanic of any race (2010); Density: 11.3 persons per square mile (2010); Average household size: 2.46 (2010); Median age: 42.1 (2010); Males per 100 females: 125.2 (2010).
Religion: Five largest groups: 20.9% Southern Baptist Convention, 17.9% Catholic Church, 5.1% The United Methodist Church, 2.9% Churches of Christ, 2.7% Evangelical Lutheran Church in America (2000).
Economy: Unemployment rate: 7.2% (June 2011); Total civilian labor force: 5,392 (June 2011); Leading industries: 20.6% retail trade; 12.8% accommodation & food services; 12.5% construction (2009); Farms: 896 totaling 501,191 acres (2007); Companies that employ 500 or more persons: 0 (2009); Companies that employ 100 to 499 persons: 1 (2009); Companies that employ less than 100 persons: 228 (2009); Black-owned businesses: n/a (2007); Hispanic-owned businesses: n/a (2007); Asian-owned businesses: n/a (2007); Women-owned businesses: n/a (2007); Retail sales per capita: $11,901 (2010). Single-family building permits issued: 8 (2010); Multi-family building permits issued: 0 (2010).

Income: Per capita income: $21,023 (2010); Median household income: $45,252 (2010); Average household income: $59,785 (2010); Percent of households with income of $100,000 or more: 14.4% (2010); Poverty rate: 21.2% (2009); Bankruptcy rate: 1.21% (2010).

Taxes: Total county taxes per capita: $393 (2007); County property taxes per capita: $352 (2007).

Education: Percent of population age 25 and over with: High school diploma (including GED) or higher: 73.0% (2010); Bachelor's degree or higher: 13.6% (2010); Master's degree or higher: 4.8% (2010).

Housing: Homeownership rate: 79.9% (2010); Median home value: $70,561 (2010); Median contract rent: $386 per month (2005-2009 5-year est.); Median year structure built: 1976 (2005-2009 5-year est.)

Health: Birth rate: 108.6 per 10,000 population (2009); Death rate: 82.4 per 10,000 population (2009); Age-adjusted cancer mortality rate: 155.5 deaths per 100,000 population (2007); Number of physicians: 0.9 per 10,000 population (2008); Hospital beds: 0.0 per 10,000 population (2007); Hospital admissions: 0.0 per 10,000 population (2007).

Elections: 2008 Presidential election results: 25.1% Obama, 74.1% McCain, 0.1% Nader

Additional Information Contacts

Live Oak County Government . . . . (361) 449-2733
   http://www.co.live-oak.tx.us/ips/cms
George West Chamber of Cmmrc . . . . (361) 449-2033
   http://www.georgewest.org
Three Rivers Chamber of Commerce . . . . (361) 786-4330
   http://www.threeriverstx.org

Live Oak County Communities

GEORGE WEST (city). County seat. Covers a land area of 1.902 square miles and a water area of 0 square miles. Located at 28.33° N. Lat; 98.11° W. Long. Elevation is 157 feet.

History: The town of George West was named for the ranch owner who gave the town its public buildings and bridges.

Population: 2,586 (1990); 2,524 (2000); 2,255 (2010); 2,127 (2015 projected); Race: 84.2% White, 0.2% Black, 0.1% Asian, 15.5% Other, 61.4% Hispanic of any race (2010); Density: 1,185.8 persons per square mile (2010); Average household size: 2.68 (2010); Median age: 36.3 (2010); Males per 100 females: 94.4 (2010); Marriage status: 31.0% never married, 48.5% now married, 12.8% widowed, 7.7% divorced (2005-2009 5-year est.); Foreign born: 4.8% (2005-2009 5-year est.); Ancestry (includes multiple ancestries): 18.7% German, 11.2% English, 10.7% Irish, 4.7% Scotch-Irish, 2.7% Czech (2005-2009 5-year est.).

Economy: Single-family building permits issued: 7 (2010); Multi-family building permits issued: 0 (2010); Employment by occupation: 14.4% management, 15.3% professional, 16.9% services, 16.5% sales, 0.0% farming, 25.0% construction, 12.0% production (2005-2009 5-year est.).

Income: Per capita income: $19,674 (2010); Median household income: $43,196 (2010); Average household income: $53,555 (2010); Percent of households with income of $100,000 or more: 12.1% (2010); Poverty rate: 21.2% (2005-2009 5-year est.).

Taxes: Total city taxes per capita: $364 (2007); City property taxes per capita: $114 (2007).

Education: Percent of population age 25 and over with: High school diploma (including GED) or higher: 63.3% (2010); Bachelor's degree or higher: 12.7% (2010); Master's degree or higher: 4.3% (2010).

School District(s)

George West ISD (PK-12)
   2009-10 Enrollment: 1,132 . . . . (361) 449-1914

Housing: Homeownership rate: 74.1% (2010); Median home value: $59,922 (2010); Median contract rent: $488 per month (2005-2009 5-year est.); Median year structure built: 1972 (2005-2009 5-year est.).

Transportation: Commute to work: 82.4% car, 0.0% public transportation, 6.5% walk, 2.7% work from home (2005-2009 5-year est.); Travel time to work: 48.4% less than 15 minutes, 19.3% 15 to 30 minutes, 14.2% 30 to 45 minutes, 0.9% 45 to 60 minutes, 17.2% 60 minutes or more (2005-2009 5-year est.)

Additional Information Contacts

George West Chamber of Cmmrc . . . . (361) 449-2033
   http://www.georgewest.org

PERNITAS POINT (village). Covers a land area of 0.554 square miles and a water area of 0 square miles. Located at 28.05° N. Lat; 97.90° W. Long. Elevation is 171 feet.

Population: 174 (1990); 269 (2000); 267 (2010); 264 (2015 projected); Race: 90.6% White, 0.4% Black, 0.4% Asian, 8.6% Other, 29.6% Hispanic of any race (2010); Density: 482.0 persons per square mile (2010); Average household size: 2.39 (2010); Median age: 50.2 (2010); Males per 100 females: 100.8 (2010); Marriage status: n/a never married, n/a now married, n/a widowed, n/a divorced (2005-2009 5-year est.); Foreign born: n/a (2005-2009 5-year est.); Ancestry (includes multiple ancestries): n/a (2005-2009 5-year est.).

Economy: Employment by occupation: n/a management, n/a professional, n/a services, n/a sales, n/a farming, n/a construction, n/a production (2005-2009 5-year est.).

Income: Per capita income: $23,279 (2010); Median household income: $44,545 (2010); Average household income: $59,364 (2010); Percent of households with income of $100,000 or more: 11.8% (2010); Poverty rate: n/a (2005-2009 5-year est.).

Education: Percent of population age 25 and over with: High school diploma (including GED) or higher: 81.7% (2010); Bachelor's degree or higher: 11.9% (2010); Master's degree or higher: 4.5% (2010).

Housing: Homeownership rate: 85.5% (2010); Median home value: $68,235 (2010); Median contract rent: n/a per month (2005-2009 5-year est.); Median year structure built: n/a (2005-2009 5-year est.).

Transportation: Commute to work: n/a car, n/a public transportation, n/a walk, n/a work from home (2005-2009 5-year est.); Travel time to work: n/a less than 15 minutes, n/a 15 to 30 minutes, n/a 30 to 45 minutes, n/a 45 to 60 minutes, n/a 60 minutes or more (2005-2009 5-year est.)

THREE RIVERS (city). Covers a land area of 1.445 square miles and a water area of 0.004 square miles. Located at 28.46° N. Lat; 98.17° W. Long. Elevation is 144 feet.

History: Established 1913, incorporated 1927.

Population: 2,038 (1990); 1,878 (2000); 1,811 (2010); 1,786 (2015 projected); Race: 80.2% White, 3.0% Black, 0.3% Asian, 16.5% Other, 49.4% Hispanic of any race (2010); Density: 1,253.3 persons per square mile (2010); Average household size: 2.53 (2010); Median age: 36.7 (2010); Males per 100 females: 121.7 (2010); Marriage status: 26.0% never married, 59.8% now married, 11.1% widowed, 3.1% divorced (2005-2009 5-year est.); Foreign born: 4.1% (2005-2009 5-year est.); Ancestry (includes multiple ancestries): 11.5% German, 9.4% English, 8.3% Irish, 3.9% American, 3.4% Norwegian (2005-2009 5-year est.).

Economy: Single-family building permits issued: 1 (2010); Multi-family building permits issued: 0 (2010); Employment by occupation: 12.1% management, 12.1% professional, 25.2% services, 22.8% sales, 1.2% farming, 16.7% construction, 9.9% production (2005-2009 5-year est.).

Income: Per capita income: $19,099 (2010); Median household income: $44,032 (2010); Average household income: $55,371 (2010); Percent of households with income of $100,000 or more: 13.2% (2010); Poverty rate: 22.3% (2005-2009 5-year est.).

Taxes: Total city taxes per capita: $921 (2007); City property taxes per capita: $369 (2007).

Education: Percent of population age 25 and over with: High school diploma (including GED) or higher: 70.5% (2010); Bachelor's degree or higher: 10.6% (2010); Master's degree or higher: 2.9% (2010).

School District(s)

Three Rivers ISD (PK-12)
   2009-10 Enrollment: 635 . . . . (361) 786-3626

Housing: Homeownership rate: 68.7% (2010); Median home value: $62,029 (2010); Median contract rent: $366 per month (2005-2009 5-year est.); Median year structure built: 1969 (2005-2009 5-year est.).

Safety: Violent crime rate: 42.3 per 10,000 population; Property crime rate: 259.8 per 10,000 population (2009).

Newspapers: The Progress (Local news; Circulation 3,300)

Transportation: Commute to work: 90.7% car, 0.0% public transportation, 0.0% walk, 0.0% work from home (2005-2009 5-year est.); Travel time to work: 59.2% less than 15 minutes, 20.6% 15 to 30 minutes, 5.3% 30 to 45 minutes, 3.2% 45 to 60 minutes, 11.7% 60 minutes or more (2005-2009 5-year est.)

Additional Information Contacts

Three Rivers Chamber of Commerce . . . . (361) 786-4330
   http://www.threeriverstx.org

WHITSETT (unincorporated postal area, zip code 78075). Covers a land area of 39.240 square miles and a water area of 0.074 square miles. Located at 28.63° N. Lat; 98.27° W. Long. Elevation is 200 feet.

Population: 123 (2000); Race: 88.8% White, 0.0% Black, 0.0% Asian, 11.2% Other, 13.6% Hispanic of any race (2000); Density: 3.1 persons per

square mile (2000); Age: 18.4% under 18, 19.2% over 64 (2000); Marriage status: 6.9% never married, 87.3% now married, 0.0% widowed, 5.9% divorced (2000); Foreign born: 0.0% (2000); Ancestry (includes multiple ancestries): 25.6% German, 20.0% American, 11.2% Irish (2000).
Economy: Employment by occupation: 9.5% management, 14.3% professional, 0.0% services, 38.1% sales, 19.0% farming, 7.9% construction, 11.1% production (2000).
Income: Per capita income: $16,801 (2000); Median household income: $41,250 (2000); Poverty rate: 179.1% (2000).
Education: Percent of population age 25 and over with: High school diploma (including GED) or higher: 78.4% (2000); Bachelor's degree or higher: 22.5% (2000).
Housing: Homeownership rate: 85.7% (2000); Median home value: $31,700 (2000); Median contract rent: n/a per month (2000); Median year structure built: 1973 (2000).
Transportation: Commute to work: 77.8% car, 0.0% public transportation, 7.9% walk, 0.0% work from home (2000); Travel time to work: 31.7% less than 15 minutes, 19.0% 15 to 30 minutes, 30.2% 30 to 45 minutes, 9.5% 45 to 60 minutes, 9.5% 60 minutes or more (2000)

Llano County

Located in central Texas, on the Edwards Plateau; bounded on the east by the Colorado River and Lake Buchanan; drained by the Llano River and tributaries. Covers a land area of 934.76 square miles, a water area of 31.41 square miles, and is located in the Central Time Zone at 30.70° N. Lat., 98.55° W. Long. The county was founded in 1856. County seat is Llano.

Weather Station: Llano											Elevation: 1,020 feet	
	Jan	Feb	Mar	Apr	May	Jun	Jul	Aug	Sep	Oct	Nov	Dec
High	61	65	72	79	86	92	96	96	90	81	71	62
Low	33	37	45	53	63	70	72	71	65	54	43	34
Precip	1.3	1.7	2.4	1.8	3.8	3.7	1.8	1.6	2.4	3.0	2.3	1.9
Snow	0.3	0.1	tr	0.0	0.0	0.0	0.0	0.0	0.0	0.0	0.0	0.0

High and Low temperatures in degrees Fahrenheit; Precipitation and Snow in inches

Population: 11,631 (1990); 17,044 (2000); 19,224 (2010); 20,253 (2015 projected); Race: 93.9% White, 1.1% Black, 0.4% Asian, 4.7% Other, 8.6% Hispanic of any race (2010); Density: 20.6 persons per square mile (2010); Average household size: 2.12 (2010); Median age: 49.6 (2010); Males per 100 females: 94.9 (2010).
Religion: Five largest groups: 24.7% Southern Baptist Convention, 6.9% The United Methodist Church, 3.7% Catholic Church, 3.5% Churches of Christ, 1.9% The Church of Jesus Christ of Latter-day Saints (2000).
Economy: Unemployment rate: 8.1% (June 2011); Total civilian labor force: 8,442 (June 2011); Leading industries: 27.8% accommodation & food services; 21.5% health care and social assistance; 12.8% retail trade (2009); Farms: 791 totaling 538,890 acres (2007); Companies that employ 500 or more persons: 1 (2009); Companies that employ 100 to 499 persons: 3 (2009); Companies that employ less than 100 persons: 430 (2009); Black-owned businesses: n/a (2007); Hispanic-owned businesses: n/a (2007); Asian-owned businesses: n/a (2007); Women-owned businesses: n/a (2007); Retail sales per capita: $7,342 (2010). Single-family building permits issued: 195 (2010); Multi-family building permits issued: 2 (2010).
Income: Per capita income: $31,363 (2010); Median household income: $47,614 (2010); Average household income: $67,057 (2010); Percent of households with income of $100,000 or more: 16.3% (2010); Poverty rate: 13.2% (2009); Bankruptcy rate: 2.25% (2010).
Taxes: Total county taxes per capita: $460 (2007); County property taxes per capita: $423 (2007).
Education: Percent of population age 25 and over with: High school diploma (including GED) or higher: 87.2% (2010); Bachelor's degree or higher: 22.5% (2010); Master's degree or higher: 7.1% (2010).
Housing: Homeownership rate: 79.3% (2010); Median home value: $128,667 (2010); Median contract rent: $491 per month (2005-2009 5-year est.); Median year structure built: 1979 (2005-2009 5-year est.)
Health: Birth rate: 91.9 per 10,000 population (2009); Death rate: 149.4 per 10,000 population (2009); Age-adjusted cancer mortality rate: 211.8 deaths per 100,000 population (2007); Number of physicians: 13.7 per 10,000 population (2008); Hospital beds: 16.4 per 10,000 population (2007); Hospital admissions: 896.7 per 10,000 population (2007).
Elections: 2008 Presidential election results: 23.4% Obama, 75.6% McCain, 0.1% Nader
Additional Information Contacts

Llano County Government . . . . (325) 247-5054
  http://www.co.llano.tx.us/ips/cms
Kingsland/Lake LBJ Chamber of Commerce . . . . (325) 388-6211
  http://www.kingslandchamber.org
Lake Buchanan/Inks Lake Chamber of Commerce . . . . (512) 793-2803
  http://www.buchanan-inks.com
Llano County Chamber of Commerce . . . . (325) 247-5354
  http://www.llanochamber.org

Llano County Communities

BLUFFTON (unincorporated postal area, zip code 78607). Covers a land area of 18.778 square miles and a water area of 0.022 square miles. Located at 30.83° N. Lat; 98.47° W. Long. Elevation is 1,063 feet.
Population: 198 (2000); Race: 100.0% White, 0.0% Black, 0.0% Asian, 0.0% Other, 6.3% Hispanic of any race (2000); Density: 10.5 persons per square mile (2000); Age: 10.2% under 18, 62.4% over 64 (2000); Marriage status: 5.2% never married, 57.7% now married, 21.6% widowed, 15.5% divorced (2000); Foreign born: 3.4% (2000); Ancestry (includes multiple ancestries): 22.9% German, 12.2% American, 6.8% Scotch-Irish, 6.3% English (2000).
Economy: Employment by occupation: 29.5% management, 0.0% professional, 0.0% services, 34.1% sales, 0.0% farming, 0.0% construction, 36.4% production (2000).
Income: Per capita income: $16,888 (2000); Median household income: $23,977 (2000); Poverty rate: 179.1% (2000).
Education: Percent of population age 25 and over with: High school diploma (including GED) or higher: 65.8% (2000); Bachelor's degree or higher: 7.6% (2000).
Housing: Homeownership rate: 95.3% (2000); Median home value: $92,100 (2000); Median contract rent: n/a per month (2000); Median year structure built: 1976 (2000).
Transportation: Commute to work: 70.5% car, 0.0% public transportation, 0.0% walk, 29.5% work from home (2000); Travel time to work: 48.4% less than 15 minutes, 0.0% 15 to 30 minutes, 0.0% 30 to 45 minutes, 22.6% 45 to 60 minutes, 29.0% 60 minutes or more (2000)

BUCHANAN DAM (CDP). Covers a land area of 7.614 square miles and a water area of 12.531 square miles. Located at 30.76° N. Lat; 98.45° W. Long. Elevation is 1,043 feet.
Population: 1,099 (1990); 1,688 (2000); 1,882 (2010); 1,974 (2015 projected); Race: 93.7% White, 1.4% Black, 0.1% Asian, 4.9% Other, 11.1% Hispanic of any race (2010); Density: 247.2 persons per square mile (2010); Average household size: 1.99 (2010); Median age: 54.0 (2010); Males per 100 females: 96.2 (2010); Marriage status: 17.5% never married, 57.8% now married, 13.6% widowed, 11.1% divorced (2005-2009 5-year est.); Foreign born: 11.5% (2005-2009 5-year est.); Ancestry (includes multiple ancestries): 26.3% German, 21.1% English, 16.7% Irish, 7.0% Scotch-Irish, 3.8% French (2005-2009 5-year est.).
Economy: Employment by occupation: 5.5% management, 11.8% professional, 15.4% services, 32.3% sales, 0.0% farming, 8.5% construction, 26.6% production (2005-2009 5-year est.).
Income: Per capita income: $32,221 (2010); Median household income: $45,071 (2010); Average household income: $64,600 (2010); Percent of households with income of $100,000 or more: 11.5% (2010); Poverty rate: 3.6% (2005-2009 5-year est.).
Education: Percent of population age 25 and over with: High school diploma (including GED) or higher: 87.1% (2010); Bachelor's degree or higher: 15.3% (2010); Master's degree or higher: 2.8% (2010).
Housing: Homeownership rate: 76.1% (2010); Median home value: $131,132 (2010); Median contract rent: $563 per month (2005-2009 5-year est.); Median year structure built: 1976 (2005-2009 5-year est.).
Transportation: Commute to work: 91.2% car, 0.0% public transportation, 2.7% walk, 1.6% work from home (2005-2009 5-year est.); Travel time to work: 29.8% less than 15 minutes, 20.4% 15 to 30 minutes, 29.2% 30 to 45 minutes, 13.7% 45 to 60 minutes, 7.0% 60 minutes or more (2005-2009 5-year est.)
Additional Information Contacts
Lake Buchanan/Inks Lake Chamber of Commerce . . . . (512) 793-2803
  http://www.buchanan-inks.com

CASTELL (unincorporated postal area, zip code 76831). Covers a land area of 11.864 square miles and a water area of 0 square miles. Located at 30.77° N. Lat; 98.95° W. Long. Elevation is 1,201 feet.

Population: 12 (2000); Race: 100.0% White, 0.0% Black, 0.0% Asian, 0.0% Other, 0.0% Hispanic of any race (2000); Density: 1.0 persons per square mile (2000); Age: 0.0% under 18, 0.0% over 64 (2000); Marriage status: 45.5% never married, 0.0% now married, 0.0% widowed, 54.5% divorced (2000); Foreign born: 0.0% (2000); Ancestry (includes multiple ancestries): 100.0% German (2000).
Economy: Employment by occupation: 0.0% management, 0.0% professional, 45.5% services, 54.5% sales, 0.0% farming, 0.0% construction, 0.0% production (2000).
Income: Per capita income: $10,309 (2000); Median household income: $18,750 (2000); Poverty rate: 179.1% (2000).
Education: Percent of population age 25 and over with: High school diploma (including GED) or higher: 100.0% (2000); Bachelor's degree or higher: 0.0% (2000).
Housing: Homeownership rate: 100.0% (2000); Median home value: $112,500 (2000); Median contract rent: n/a per month (2000); Median year structure built: 1993 (2000).
Transportation: Commute to work: 100.0% car, 0.0% public transportation, 0.0% walk, 0.0% work from home (2000); Travel time to work: 0.0% less than 15 minutes, 0.0% 15 to 30 minutes, 100.0% 30 to 45 minutes, 0.0% 45 to 60 minutes, 0.0% 60 minutes or more (2000)

HORSESHOE BAY (CDP).

Covers a land area of 23.365 square miles and a water area of 3.329 square miles. Located at 30.54° N. Lat; 98.36° W. Long. Elevation is 846 feet.
Population: 1,509 (1990); 3,337 (2000); 4,173 (2010); 4,553 (2015 projected); Race: 94.0% White, 1.2% Black, 0.7% Asian, 4.1% Other, 8.1% Hispanic of any race (2010); Density: 178.6 persons per square mile (2010); Average household size: 2.06 (2010); Median age: 57.3 (2010); Males per 100 females: 95.7 (2010); Marriage status: 6.5% never married, 76.1% now married, 8.4% widowed, 9.0% divorced (2005-2009 5-year est.); Foreign born: 4.0% (2005-2009 5-year est.); Ancestry (includes multiple ancestries): 19.2% German, 16.8% English, 12.5% Irish, 10.7% Scotch-Irish, 8.0% Scottish (2005-2009 5-year est.).
Economy: Single-family building permits issued: 14 (2010); Multi-family building permits issued: 2 (2010); Employment by occupation: 21.2% management, 20.5% professional, 12.2% services, 33.5% sales, 0.0% farming, 4.2% construction, 8.3% production (2005-2009 5-year est.).
Income: Per capita income: $47,944 (2010); Median household income: $70,135 (2010); Average household income: $98,452 (2010); Percent of households with income of $100,000 or more: 35.0% (2010); Poverty rate: 9.2% (2005-2009 5-year est.).
Education: Percent of population age 25 and over with: High school diploma (including GED) or higher: 94.7% (2010); Bachelor's degree or higher: 40.4% (2010); Master's degree or higher: 11.2% (2010).
Housing: Homeownership rate: 82.7% (2010); Median home value: $240,073 (2010); Median contract rent: $954 per month (2005-2009 5-year est.); Median year structure built: 1986 (2005-2009 5-year est.).
Safety: Violent crime rate: 12.1 per 10,000 population; Property crime rate: 185.0 per 10,000 population (2009).
Transportation: Commute to work: 77.1% car, 0.0% public transportation, 0.0% walk, 17.5% work from home (2005-2009 5-year est.); Travel time to work: 39.9% less than 15 minutes, 49.3% 15 to 30 minutes, 5.9% 30 to 45 minutes, 0.0% 45 to 60 minutes, 4.9% 60 minutes or more (2005-2009 5-year est.)

KINGSLAND (CDP).

Covers a land area of 8.998 square miles and a water area of 0.771 square miles. Located at 30.66° N. Lat; 98.44° W. Long. Elevation is 837 feet.
Population: 2,725 (1990); 4,584 (2000); 5,421 (2010); 5,830 (2015 projected); Race: 93.3% White, 0.4% Black, 0.4% Asian, 5.9% Other, 10.0% Hispanic of any race (2010); Density: 602.4 persons per square mile (2010); Average household size: 2.15 (2010); Median age: 45.1 (2010); Males per 100 females: 93.9 (2010); Marriage status: 6.9% never married, 65.3% now married, 13.4% widowed, 14.3% divorced (2005-2009 5-year est.); Foreign born: 2.2% (2005-2009 5-year est.); Ancestry (includes multiple ancestries): 22.8% German, 19.6% Irish, 16.8% English, 10.3% American, 6.4% Scottish (2005-2009 5-year est.).
Economy: Employment by occupation: 15.0% management, 17.8% professional, 16.5% services, 24.5% sales, 0.0% farming, 14.6% construction, 11.6% production (2005-2009 5-year est.).
Income: Per capita income: $23,453 (2010); Median household income: $39,182 (2010); Average household income: $50,975 (2010); Percent of households with income of $100,000 or more: 8.8% (2010); Poverty rate: 12.7% (2005-2009 5-year est.).

Education: Percent of population age 25 and over with: High school diploma (including GED) or higher: 82.2% (2010); Bachelor's degree or higher: 14.2% (2010); Master's degree or higher: 5.9% (2010).

School District(s)

Llano ISD (PK-12)
    2009-10 Enrollment: 1,951 . . . . (325) 247-4747
Housing: Homeownership rate: 75.7% (2010); Median home value: $102,344 (2010); Median contract rent: $587 per month (2005-2009 5-year est.); Median year structure built: 1983 (2005-2009 5-year est.).
Transportation: Commute to work: 87.2% car, 0.7% public transportation, 1.6% walk, 10.5% work from home (2005-2009 5-year est.); Travel time to work: 39.7% less than 15 minutes, 30.0% 15 to 30 minutes, 12.7% 30 to 45 minutes, 1.6% 45 to 60 minutes, 16.0% 60 minutes or more (2005-2009 5-year est.)

Additional Information Contacts

Kingsland/Lake LBJ Chamber of Commerce . . . . (325) 388-6211
    http://www.kingslandchamber.org

LLANO (city).

County seat. Covers a land area of 4.445 square miles and a water area of 0.255 square miles. Located at 30.75° N. Lat; 98.68° W. Long. Elevation is 1,030 feet.
History: Founded 1855; incorporated 1901.
Population: 3,059 (1990); 3,325 (2000); 3,297 (2010); 3,289 (2015 projected); Race: 89.9% White, 1.6% Black, 0.2% Asian, 8.2% Other, 14.1% Hispanic of any race (2010); Density: 741.8 persons per square mile (2010); Average household size: 2.37 (2010); Median age: 34.2 (2010); Males per 100 females: 94.7 (2010); Marriage status: 18.9% never married, 55.3% now married, 9.3% widowed, 16.6% divorced (2005-2009 5-year est.); Foreign born: 4.6% (2005-2009 5-year est.); Ancestry (includes multiple ancestries): 18.0% English, 15.3% German, 12.2% Irish, 10.1% American, 7.1% French (2005-2009 5-year est.).
Economy: Single-family building permits issued: 69 (2010); Multi-family building permits issued: 0 (2010); Employment by occupation: 12.0% management, 16.3% professional, 20.2% services, 27.2% sales, 0.0% farming, 6.8% construction, 17.4% production (2005-2009 5-year est.).
Income: Per capita income: $23,423 (2010); Median household income: $46,328 (2010); Average household income: $56,732 (2010); Percent of households with income of $100,000 or more: 8.7% (2010); Poverty rate: 17.8% (2005-2009 5-year est.).
Taxes: Total city taxes per capita: $377 (2007); City property taxes per capita: $136 (2007).
Education: Percent of population age 25 and over with: High school diploma (including GED) or higher: 83.5% (2010); Bachelor's degree or higher: 19.7% (2010); Master's degree or higher: 6.0% (2010).

School District(s)

Llano ISD (PK-12)
    2009-10 Enrollment: 1,951 . . . . (325) 247-4747
Housing: Homeownership rate: 69.2% (2010); Median home value: $73,448 (2010); Median contract rent: $393 per month (2005-2009 5-year est.); Median year structure built: 1964 (2005-2009 5-year est.).
Hospitals: Llano Memorial Hospital (30 beds)
Safety: Violent crime rate: 9.3 per 10,000 population; Property crime rate: 347.2 per 10,000 population (2009).
Newspapers: Llano News (Community news; Circulation 3,300)
Transportation: Commute to work: 84.8% car, 2.5% public transportation, 4.2% walk, 3.8% work from home (2005-2009 5-year est.); Travel time to work: 69.3% less than 15 minutes, 11.8% 15 to 30 minutes, 7.3% 30 to 45 minutes, 8.4% 45 to 60 minutes, 3.3% 60 minutes or more (2005-2009 5-year est.)

Additional Information Contacts

Llano County Chamber of Commerce . . . . (325) 247-5354
    http://www.llanochamber.org

SUNRISE BEACH VILLAGE (city).

Covers a land area of 1.655 square miles and a water area of 0.636 square miles. Located at 30.59° N. Lat; 98.41° W. Long. Elevation is 843 feet.
Population: 497 (1990); 704 (2000); 867 (2010); 940 (2015 projected); Race: 97.1% White, 1.4% Black, 0.0% Asian, 1.5% Other, 2.0% Hispanic of any race (2010); Density: 524.0 persons per square mile (2010); Average household size: 1.99 (2010); Median age: 59.6 (2010); Males per 100 females: 92.2 (2010); Marriage status: 10.4% never married, 70.3% now married, 8.9% widowed, 10.3% divorced (2005-2009 5-year est.); Foreign born: 0.7% (2005-2009 5-year est.); Ancestry (includes multiple ancestries): 26.1% German, 20.9% English, 19.9% Irish, 10.4% American, 5.1% French (2005-2009 5-year est.).

Economy: Single-family building permits issued: 0 (2010); Multi-family building permits issued: 0 (2010); Employment by occupation: 17.8% management, 16.2% professional, 21.1% services, 32.4% sales, 0.0% farming, 7.3% construction, 5.3% production (2005-2009 5-year est.).
Income: Per capita income: $35,337 (2010); Median household income: $56,490 (2010); Average household income: $70,269 (2010); Percent of households with income of $100,000 or more: 17.4% (2010); Poverty rate: 8.0% (2005-2009 5-year est.).
Taxes: Total city taxes per capita: $92 (2007); City property taxes per capita: $92 (2007).
Education: Percent of population age 25 and over with: High school diploma (including GED) or higher: 93.7% (2010); Bachelor's degree or higher: 29.8% (2010); Master's degree or higher: 11.4% (2010).
Housing: Homeownership rate: 91.5% (2010); Median home value: $184,659 (2010); Median contract rent: $480 per month (2005-2009 5-year est.); Median year structure built: 1976 (2005-2009 5-year est.).
Safety: Violent crime rate: 0.0 per 10,000 population; Property crime rate: 699.2 per 10,000 population (2009).
Transportation: Commute to work: 90.9% car, 0.0% public transportation, 0.0% walk, 9.1% work from home (2005-2009 5-year est.); Travel time to work: 24.2% less than 15 minutes, 20.1% 15 to 30 minutes, 39.3% 30 to 45 minutes, 1.4% 45 to 60 minutes, 15.1% 60 minutes or more (2005-2009 5-year est.)

TOW (unincorporated postal area, zip code 78672). Covers a land area of 28.275 square miles and a water area of 0 square miles. Located at 30.86° N. Lat; 98.45° W. Long. Elevation is 1,037 feet.
Population: 1,060 (2000); Race: 95.0% White, 0.0% Black, 0.9% Asian, 4.1% Other, 3.8% Hispanic of any race (2000); Density: 37.5 persons per square mile (2000); Age: 8.9% under 18, 36.5% over 64 (2000); Marriage status: 10.9% never married, 63.1% now married, 12.7% widowed, 13.3% divorced (2000); Foreign born: 1.3% (2000); Ancestry (includes multiple ancestries): 19.0% American, 11.1% German, 11.0% Irish, 9.1% English (2000).
Economy: Employment by occupation: 11.6% management, 6.1% professional, 20.3% services, 24.2% sales, 1.6% farming, 21.6% construction, 14.7% production (2000).
Income: Per capita income: $15,536 (2000); Median household income: $24,500 (2000); Poverty rate: 179.1% (2000).
Education: Percent of population age 25 and over with: High school diploma (including GED) or higher: 77.3% (2000); Bachelor's degree or higher: 5.1% (2000).
Housing: Homeownership rate: 87.2% (2000); Median home value: $76,000 (2000); Median contract rent: $183 per month (2000); Median year structure built: 1974 (2000).
Transportation: Commute to work: 86.3% car, 0.0% public transportation, 2.5% walk, 8.5% work from home (2000); Travel time to work: 31.8% less than 15 minutes, 25.8% 15 to 30 minutes, 15.9% 30 to 45 minutes, 11.4% 45 to 60 minutes, 15.0% 60 minutes or more (2000)

VALLEY SPRING (unincorporated postal area, zip code 76885). Covers a land area of 35.040 square miles and a water area of 0.008 square miles. Located at 30.90° N. Lat; 98.79° W. Long. Elevation is 1,306 feet.
Population: 41 (2000); Race: 100.0% White, 0.0% Black, 0.0% Asian, 0.0% Other, 0.0% Hispanic of any race (2000); Density: 1.2 persons per square mile (2000); Age: 0.0% under 18, 0.0% over 64 (2000); Marriage status: 0.0% never married, 100.0% now married, 0.0% widowed, 0.0% divorced (2000); Foreign born: 0.0% (2000); Ancestry (includes multiple ancestries): 28.6% English, 28.6% Scottish, 23.8% German (2000).
Economy: Employment by occupation: 23.8% management, 0.0% professional, 0.0% services, 23.8% sales, 0.0% farming, 28.6% construction, 23.8% production (2000).
Income: Per capita income: $30,724 (2000); Median household income: $80,067 (2000); Poverty rate: 179.1% (2000).
Education: Percent of population age 25 and over with: High school diploma (including GED) or higher: 100.0% (2000); Bachelor's degree or higher: 76.2% (2000).
Housing: Homeownership rate: 100.0% (2000); Median home value: $100,000 (2000); Median contract rent: n/a per month (2000); Median year structure built: 1975 (2000).
Transportation: Commute to work: 76.2% car, 0.0% public transportation, 0.0% walk, 23.8% work from home (2000); Travel time to work: 0.0% less than 15 minutes, 100.0% 15 to 30 minutes, 0.0% 30 to 45 minutes, 0.0% 45 to 60 minutes, 0.0% 60 minutes or more (2000)

Loving County

Located in west Texas; high prairie area, bounded on the north by New Mexico, and on the west by the Pecos River; includes part of Red Bluff Lake. Covers a land area of 673.08 square miles, a water area of 3.77 square miles, and is located in the Central Time Zone at 31.81° N. Lat., 103.60° W. Long. The county was founded in 1887. County seat is Mentone.
Population: 107 (1990); 67 (2000); 48 (2010); 44 (2015 projected); Race: 85.4% White, 0.0% Black, 0.0% Asian, 14.6% Other, 14.6% Hispanic of any race (2010); Density: 0.1 persons per square mile (2010); Average household size: 1.92 (2010); Median age: 52.1 (2010); Males per 100 females: 71.4 (2010).
Religion: Largest group: 0.0% Data not available. (2000).
Economy: Unemployment rate: 8.0% (June 2011); Total civilian labor force: 50 (June 2011); Leading industries: Farms: 9 totaling 426,792 acres (2007); Companies that employ 500 or more persons: 0 (2009); Companies that employ 100 to 499 persons: 0 (2009); Companies that employ less than 100 persons: 1 (2009); Black-owned businesses: n/a (2007); Hispanic-owned businesses: n/a (2007); Asian-owned businesses: n/a (2007); Women-owned businesses: n/a (2007); Retail sales per capita: $8,549 (2010). Single-family building permits issued: n/a (2010); Multi-family building permits issued: n/a (2010).
Income: Per capita income: $43,698 (2010); Median household income: $56,250 (2010); Average household income: $83,900 (2010); Percent of households with income of $100,000 or more: 28.0% (2010); Poverty rate: 11.1% (2009); Bankruptcy rate: n/a (2010).
Taxes: Total county taxes per capita: $40,100 (2007); County property taxes per capita: $39,867 (2007).
Education: Percent of population age 25 and over with: High school diploma (including GED) or higher: 83.7% (2010); Bachelor's degree or higher: 7.0% (2010); Master's degree or higher: 7.0% (2010).
Housing: Homeownership rate: 80.0% (2010); Median home value: $19,999 (2010); Median contract rent: n/a per month (2005-2009 5-year est.); Median year structure built: 1974 (2005-2009 5-year est.)
Health: Birth rate: 0.0 per 10,000 population (2009); Death rate: 0.0 per 10,000 population (2009); Age-adjusted cancer mortality rate: Suppressed deaths per 100,000 population (2007); Number of physicians: 0.0 per 10,000 population (2008); Hospital beds: 0.0 per 10,000 population (2007); Hospital admissions: 0.0 per 10,000 population (2007).
Elections: 2008 Presidential election results: 15.2% Obama, 84.8% McCain, 0.0% Nader
Additional Information Contacts
Loving County Government . . . . (432) 377-2362
    http://www.lovingcountytexas.us

Loving County Communities

MENTONE (unincorporated postal area, zip code 79754). County seat. Covers a land area of 158.735 square miles and a water area of 0 square miles. Located at 31.72° N. Lat; 103.57° W. Long. Elevation is 2,687 feet.
History: One of the smallest county seats in U.S., only locality within county.
Population: 58 (2000); Race: 82.1% White, 0.0% Black, 0.0% Asian, 17.9% Other, 17.9% Hispanic of any race (2000); Density: 0.4 persons per square mile (2000); Age: 20.9% under 18, 14.9% over 64 (2000); Marriage status: 12.1% never married, 65.5% now married, 10.3% widowed, 12.1% divorced (2000); Foreign born: 0.0% (2000); Ancestry (includes multiple ancestries): 20.9% Irish, 16.4% English, 9.0% American, 4.5% Scotch-Irish (2000).
Economy: Employment by occupation: 19.0% management, 7.1% professional, 14.3% services, 23.8% sales, 0.0% farming, 21.4% construction, 14.3% production (2000).
Income: Per capita income: $24,084 (2000); Median household income: $40,000 (2000); Poverty rate: 179.1% (2000).
Education: Percent of population age 25 and over with: High school diploma (including GED) or higher: 86.3% (2000); Bachelor's degree or higher: 5.9% (2000).
Housing: Homeownership rate: 80.6% (2000); Median home value: n/a (2000); Median contract rent: $425 per month (2000); Median year structure built: 1960 (2000).
Transportation: Commute to work: 78.9% car, 0.0% public transportation, 21.1% walk, 0.0% work from home (2000); Travel time to work: 52.6% less than 15 minutes, 31.6% 15 to 30 minutes, 7.9% 30 to 45 minutes, 0.0% 45 to 60 minutes, 7.9% 60 minutes or more (2000)

Lubbock County

Located in northwest Texas; drained by the intermittent Double Mountain Fork of the Brazos River. Covers a land area of 899.49 square miles, a water area of 1.20 square miles, and is located in the Central Time Zone at 33.57° N. Lat., 101.85° W. Long. The county was founded in 1891. County seat is Lubbock.

Lubbock County is part of the Lubbock, TX Metropolitan Statistical Area. The entire metro area includes: Crosby County, TX; Lubbock County, TX

Weather Station: Lubbock Regional Arpt   Elevation: 3,253 feet

	Jan	Feb	Mar	Apr	May	Jun	Jul	Aug	Sep	Oct	Nov	Dec
High	54	59	67	76	84	91	93	91	84	75	63	54
Low	27	31	37	46	56	65	68	67	59	48	36	28
Precip	0.6	0.7	1.0	1.3	2.4	3.0	1.7	1.9	2.6	1.9	0.9	0.8
Snow	2.6	1.5	0.5	0.3	tr	tr	tr	0.0	tr	tr	1.6	2.2

High and Low temperatures in degrees Fahrenheit; Precipitation and Snow in inches

Population: 222,636 (1990); 242,628 (2000); 269,474 (2010); 282,041 (2015 projected); Race: 72.5% White, 7.1% Black, 1.4% Asian, 19.0% Other, 31.0% Hispanic of any race (2010); Density: 299.6 persons per square mile (2010); Average household size: 2.48 (2010); Median age: 31.6 (2010); Males per 100 females: 97.1 (2010).
Religion: Five largest groups: 21.9% Southern Baptist Convention, 16.2% Catholic Church, 6.6% The United Methodist Church, 4.8% Churches of Christ, 1.6% Independent, Non-Charismatic Churches (2000).
Economy: Unemployment rate: 7.2% (June 2011); Total civilian labor force: 145,125 (June 2011); Leading industries: 20.9% health care and social assistance; 16.1% retail trade; 12.9% accommodation & food services (2009); Farms: 1,205 totaling 515,741 acres (2007); Companies that employ 500 or more persons: 9 (2009); Companies that employ 100 to 499 persons: 145 (2009); Companies that employ less than 100 persons: 6,659 (2009); Black-owned businesses: 500 (2007); Hispanic-owned businesses: 3,027 (2007); Asian-owned businesses: 479 (2007); Women-owned businesses: 5,461 (2007); Retail sales per capita: $15,329 (2010). Single-family building permits issued: 896 (2010); Multi-family building permits issued: 555 (2010).
Income: Per capita income: $22,727 (2010); Median household income: $42,081 (2010); Average household income: $57,888 (2010); Percent of households with income of $100,000 or more: 13.4% (2010); Poverty rate: 20.1% (2009); Bankruptcy rate: 1.48% (2010).
Taxes: Total county taxes per capita: $231 (2007); County property taxes per capita: $165 (2007).
Education: Percent of population age 25 and over with: High school diploma (including GED) or higher: 83.5% (2010); Bachelor's degree or higher: 27.7% (2010); Master's degree or higher: 9.6% (2010).
Housing: Homeownership rate: 61.0% (2010); Median home value: $94,230 (2010); Median contract rent: $563 per month (2005-2009 5-year est.); Median year structure built: 1976 (2005-2009 5-year est.)
Health: Birth rate: 157.2 per 10,000 population (2009); Death rate: 79.9 per 10,000 population (2009); Age-adjusted cancer mortality rate: 196.9 deaths per 100,000 population (2007); Number of physicians: 38.7 per 10,000 population (2008); Hospital beds: 53.9 per 10,000 population (2007); Hospital admissions: 2,354.6 per 10,000 population (2007).
Elections: 2008 Presidential election results: 31.3% Obama, 68.0% McCain, 0.1% Nader
National and State Parks: Mac Kenzie State Park
Additional Information Contacts

Lubbock County Government . . . . (806) 775-1086
  http://www.co.lubbock.tx.us
City of Lubbock . . . . (806) 775-3000
  http://www.ci.lubbock.tx.us
City of Slaton . . . . (806) 828-2000
  http://www.slaton.tx.us
Idalou Chamber of Commerce . . . . (806) 892-2531
Lubbock Chamber of Commerce . . . . (806) 761-7000
  http://www.lubbockbiz.org
Slaton Chamber of Commerce . . . . (806) 828-6238
  http://www.slatonchamberofcommerce.org

Lubbock County Communities

BUFFALO SPRINGS (village). Covers a land area of 1.575 square miles and a water area of 0.354 square miles. Located at 33.53° N. Lat; 101.70° W. Long. Elevation is 3,018 feet.

Population: 468 (1990); 493 (2000); 495 (2010); 502 (2015 projected); Race: 87.1% White, 1.2% Black, 0.0% Asian, 11.7% Other, 17.2% Hispanic of any race (2010); Density: 314.2 persons per square mile (2010); Average household size: 2.46 (2010); Median age: 44.2 (2010); Males per 100 females: 98.0 (2010); Marriage status: 11.4% never married, 64.3% now married, 5.5% widowed, 18.8% divorced (2005-2009 5-year est.); Foreign born: 0.0% (2005-2009 5-year est.); Ancestry (includes multiple ancestries): 22.4% German, 14.7% Irish, 10.3% American, 7.8% English, 6.3% French (2005-2009 5-year est.).
Economy: Employment by occupation: 10.5% management, 10.5% professional, 8.1% services, 33.5% sales, 3.8% farming, 21.1% construction, 12.4% production (2005-2009 5-year est.).
Income: Per capita income: $34,117 (2010); Median household income: $63,438 (2010); Average household income: $84,851 (2010); Percent of households with income of $100,000 or more: 26.9% (2010); Poverty rate: 4.6% (2005-2009 5-year est.).
Taxes: Total city taxes per capita: $61 (2007); City property taxes per capita: $40 (2007).
Education: Percent of population age 25 and over with: High school diploma (including GED) or higher: 84.5% (2010); Bachelor's degree or higher: 30.7% (2010); Master's degree or higher: 12.6% (2010).
Housing: Homeownership rate: 84.6% (2010); Median home value: $114,706 (2010); Median contract rent: $344 per month (2005-2009 5-year est.); Median year structure built: 1961 (2005-2009 5-year est.).
Transportation: Commute to work: 100.0% car, 0.0% public transportation, 0.0% walk, 0.0% work from home (2005-2009 5-year est.); Travel time to work: 8.3% less than 15 minutes, 70.6% 15 to 30 minutes, 19.1% 30 to 45 minutes, 0.0% 45 to 60 minutes, 2.0% 60 minutes or more (2005-2009 5-year est.)

IDALOU (city). Covers a land area of 0.980 square miles and a water area of 0 square miles. Located at 33.66° N. Lat; 101.68° W. Long. Elevation is 3,192 feet.
Population: 2,084 (1990); 2,157 (2000); 2,063 (2010); 2,050 (2015 projected); Race: 59.6% White, 0.7% Black, 0.2% Asian, 39.5% Other, 47.6% Hispanic of any race (2010); Density: 2,105.6 persons per square mile (2010); Average household size: 2.62 (2010); Median age: 34.4 (2010); Males per 100 females: 90.3 (2010); Marriage status: 20.3% never married, 59.6% now married, 7.9% widowed, 12.1% divorced (2005-2009 5-year est.); Foreign born: 1.7% (2005-2009 5-year est.); Ancestry (includes multiple ancestries): 14.1% Irish, 11.4% German, 9.2% English, 6.7% American, 1.5% French (2005-2009 5-year est.).
Economy: Single-family building permits issued: 4 (2010); Multi-family building permits issued: 0 (2010); Employment by occupation: 9.6% management, 15.9% professional, 25.6% services, 26.0% sales, 3.7% farming, 3.8% construction, 15.4% production (2005-2009 5-year est.).
Income: Per capita income: $21,550 (2010); Median household income: $44,968 (2010); Average household income: $56,801 (2010); Percent of households with income of $100,000 or more: 11.9% (2010); Poverty rate: 14.6% (2005-2009 5-year est.).
Taxes: Total city taxes per capita: $228 (2007); City property taxes per capita: $150 (2007).
Education: Percent of population age 25 and over with: High school diploma (including GED) or higher: 76.0% (2010); Bachelor's degree or higher: 19.0% (2010); Master's degree or higher: 6.1% (2010).
School District(s)
Idalou ISD (PK-12)
  2009-10 Enrollment: 964 . . . . (806) 892-1900
Housing: Homeownership rate: 75.5% (2010); Median home value: $83,182 (2010); Median contract rent: $431 per month (2005-2009 5-year est.); Median year structure built: 1964 (2005-2009 5-year est.).
Safety: Violent crime rate: 14.2 per 10,000 population; Property crime rate: 108.8 per 10,000 population (2009).
Transportation: Commute to work: 95.7% car, 0.0% public transportation, 1.7% walk, 2.6% work from home (2005-2009 5-year est.); Travel time to work: 32.2% less than 15 minutes, 48.8% 15 to 30 minutes, 17.0% 30 to 45 minutes, 1.4% 45 to 60 minutes, 0.6% 60 minutes or more (2005-2009 5-year est.)
Additional Information Contacts
Idalou Chamber of Commerce . . . . (806) 892-2531

LUBBOCK (city). County seat. Covers a land area of 114.808 square miles and a water area of 0.101 square miles. Located at 33.56° N. Lat; 101.87° W. Long. Elevation is 3,202 feet.

History: Lubbock was formed by the union of two small towns in 1891, and was incorporated in 1909. Cotton was first planted here in 1900 and became a major crop, along with grain sorghum. Texas Technological College was established in Lubbock in 1925, specializing in textile, agricultural, and petroleum engineering.
Population: 187,170 (1990); 199,564 (2000); 222,184 (2010); 232,190 (2015 projected); Race: 71.4% White, 7.9% Black, 1.6% Asian, 19.1% Other, 31.4% Hispanic of any race (2010); Density: 1,935.3 persons per square mile (2010); Average household size: 2.44 (2010); Median age: 31.2 (2010); Males per 100 females: 96.4 (2010); Marriage status: 37.5% never married, 46.9% now married, 5.6% widowed, 10.0% divorced (2005-2009 5-year est.); Foreign born: 5.0% (2005-2009 5-year est.); Ancestry (includes multiple ancestries): 12.0% German, 9.6% Irish, 9.3% English, 6.5% American, 2.6% French (2005-2009 5-year est.).
Economy: Unemployment rate: 7.1% (June 2011); Total civilian labor force: 121,847 (June 2011); Single-family building permits issued: 844 (2010); Multi-family building permits issued: 555 (2010); Employment by occupation: 11.4% management, 20.6% professional, 19.3% services, 29.1% sales, 0.7% farming, 8.1% construction, 10.7% production (2005-2009 5-year est.).
Income: Per capita income: $22,883 (2010); Median household income: $41,425 (2010); Average household income: $57,418 (2010); Percent of households with income of $100,000 or more: 13.2% (2010); Poverty rate: 20.4% (2005-2009 5-year est.).
Taxes: Total city taxes per capita: $511 (2007); City property taxes per capita: $202 (2007).
Education: Percent of population age 25 and over with: High school diploma (including GED) or higher: 84.3% (2010); Bachelor's degree or higher: 29.8% (2010); Master's degree or higher: 10.5% (2010).

School District(s)

Frenship ISD (PK-12)
   2009-10 Enrollment: 7,342 . . . . (806) 866-9541
Harmony Science Academy (Lubbock) (KG-10)
   2009-10 Enrollment: 379 . . . . (806) 747-1000
Idalou ISD (PK-12)
   2009-10 Enrollment: 964 . . . . (806) 892-1900
Lubbock ISD (PK-12)
   2009-10 Enrollment: 28,680 . . . . (806) 766-1000
Lubbock-Cooper ISD (PK-12)
   2009-10 Enrollment: 3,746 . . . . (806) 863-7100
New Deal ISD (PK-12)
   2009-10 Enrollment: 731 . . . . (806) 746-5833
Orenda Charter School (01-12)
   2009-10 Enrollment: 185 . . . . (512) 869-3020
Responsive Education Solutions (KG-12)
   2009-10 Enrollment: 5,022 . . . . (972) 316-3663
Richard Milburn Academy (Ector County) (09-12)
   2009-10 Enrollment: 481 . . . . (830) 557-6181
Rise Academy (PK-08)
   2009-10 Enrollment: 222 . . . . (806) 744-0430
Roosevelt ISD (PK-12)
   2009-10 Enrollment: 1,124 . . . . (806) 842-3282
Slaton ISD (PK-12)
   2009-10 Enrollment: 1,290 . . . . (806) 828-6591
South Plains (09-12)
   2009-10 Enrollment: 186 . . . . (210) 227-0295

Four-year College(s)

Lubbock Christian University (Private, Not-for-profit, Churches of Christ)
   Fall 2009 Enrollment: 1,906 . . . . (806) 796-8800
   2010-11 Tuition: In-state $16,180; Out-of-state $16,180
Texas Tech University (Public)
   Fall 2009 Enrollment: 30,049 . . . . (806) 742-2011
   2010-11 Tuition: In-state $6,970; Out-of-state $14,410
Texas Tech University Health Sciences Center (Public)
   Fall 2009 Enrollment: 3,250 . . . . (806) 743-2484

Two-year College(s)

Covenant School of Nursing and Allied Health (Private, Not-for-profit, Roman Catholic)
   Fall 2009 Enrollment: 376 . . . . (806) 797-0955
Texas Careers-Lubbock (Private, For-profit)
   Fall 2009 Enrollment: 490 . . . . (806) 765-7051

Vocational/Technical School(s)

American Commercial College (Private, For-profit)
   Fall 2009 Enrollment: 185 . . . . (806) 747-4339
   2010-11 Tuition: $12,700

Lubbock Hair Academy (Private, For-profit)
   Fall 2009 Enrollment: 15 . . . . (806) 795-0806
   2010-11 Tuition: $8,273
Housing: Homeownership rate: 57.9% (2010); Median home value: $96,540 (2010); Median contract rent: $573 per month (2005-2009 5-year est.); Median year structure built: 1976 (2005-2009 5-year est.).
Hospitals: Covenant Medical Center (920 beds); Covenant Medical Center: Lakeside Campus (422 beds); Highland Community Hospital (123 beds); Lubbock Heart Hospital (74 beds); University Medical Center (388 beds)
Safety: Violent crime rate: 93.3 per 10,000 population; Property crime rate: 583.7 per 10,000 population (2009).
Newspapers: El Editor (Local news; Circulation 15,000); Lubbock Avalanche-Journal (Local news; Circulation 66,921); South Plains Catholic (Regional news; Circulation 10,000)
Transportation: Commute to work: 92.5% car, 1.0% public transportation, 2.4% walk, 3.0% work from home (2005-2009 5-year est.); Travel time to work: 49.4% less than 15 minutes, 42.4% 15 to 30 minutes, 4.7% 30 to 45 minutes, 1.4% 45 to 60 minutes, 2.1% 60 minutes or more (2005-2009 5-year est.)
Airports: Lubbock Preston Smith International (primary service/small hub)
Additional Information Contacts
City of Lubbock . . . . (806) 775-3000
   http://www.ci.lubbock.tx.us
Lubbock Chamber of Commerce . . . . (806) 761-7000
   http://www.lubbockbiz.org

NEW DEAL (town). Aka Monroe. Covers a land area of 1.035 square miles and a water area of 0 square miles. Located at 33.73° N. Lat; 101.83° W. Long. Elevation is 3,301 feet.
Population: 562 (1990); 708 (2000); 517 (2010); 525 (2015 projected); Race: 75.8% White, 1.9% Black, 0.2% Asian, 22.1% Other, 33.5% Hispanic of any race (2010); Density: 499.6 persons per square mile (2010); Average household size: 2.77 (2010); Median age: 33.3 (2010); Males per 100 females: 100.4 (2010); Marriage status: 14.1% never married, 76.5% now married, 2.4% widowed, 7.1% divorced (2005-2009 5-year est.); Foreign born: 3.3% (2005-2009 5-year est.); Ancestry (includes multiple ancestries): 16.5% German, 12.6% Irish, 8.5% American, 5.0% English, 2.2% Scotch-Irish (2005-2009 5-year est.).
Economy: Single-family building permits issued: 2 (2010); Multi-family building permits issued: 0 (2010); Employment by occupation: 8.4% management, 10.1% professional, 15.4% services, 25.2% sales, 2.1% farming, 18.5% construction, 20.3% production (2005-2009 5-year est.).
Income: Per capita income: $22,983 (2010); Median household income: $50,000 (2010); Average household income: $64,462 (2010); Percent of households with income of $100,000 or more: 15.1% (2010); Poverty rate: 10.4% (2005-2009 5-year est.).
Taxes: Total city taxes per capita: $199 (2007); City property taxes per capita: $155 (2007).
Education: Percent of population age 25 and over with: High school diploma (including GED) or higher: 81.7% (2010); Bachelor's degree or higher: 21.9% (2010); Master's degree or higher: 5.8% (2010).

School District(s)

New Deal ISD (PK-12)
   2009-10 Enrollment: 731 . . . . (806) 746-5833
Housing: Homeownership rate: 76.9% (2010); Median home value: $74,348 (2010); Median contract rent: $500 per month (2005-2009 5-year est.); Median year structure built: 1969 (2005-2009 5-year est.).
Safety: Violent crime rate: 0.0 per 10,000 population; Property crime rate: 106.2 per 10,000 population (2009).
Transportation: Commute to work: 92.9% car, 0.0% public transportation, 0.0% walk, 6.4% work from home (2005-2009 5-year est.); Travel time to work: 8.7% less than 15 minutes, 74.6% 15 to 30 minutes, 13.3% 30 to 45 minutes, 0.0% 45 to 60 minutes, 3.4% 60 minutes or more (2005-2009 5-year est.)

RANSOM CANYON (town). Aka Lake Ransom Canyon. Covers a land area of 0.833 square miles and a water area of 0.109 square miles. Located at 33.53° N. Lat; 101.68° W. Long. Elevation is 3,104 feet.
Population: 750 (1990); 1,011 (2000); 1,000 (2010); 1,013 (2015 projected); Race: 87.0% White, 1.1% Black, 0.1% Asian, 11.8% Other, 16.9% Hispanic of any race (2010); Density: 1,199.9 persons per square mile (2010); Average household size: 2.46 (2010); Median age: 43.7 (2010); Males per 100 females: 99.2 (2010); Marriage status: 10.5% never married, 79.5% now married, 2.8% widowed, 7.2% divorced (2005-2009

5-year est.); Foreign born: 2.4% (2005-2009 5-year est.); Ancestry (includes multiple ancestries): 17.1% English, 15.1% German, 12.1% Irish, 9.4% American, 3.9% French (2005-2009 5-year est.).
Economy: Single-family building permits issued: 3 (2010); Multi-family building permits issued: 0 (2010); Employment by occupation: 23.4% management, 30.9% professional, 6.0% services, 29.1% sales, 0.7% farming, 3.7% construction, 6.2% production (2005-2009 5-year est.).
Income: Per capita income: $34,117 (2010); Median household income: $63,554 (2010); Average household income: $84,347 (2010); Percent of households with income of $100,000 or more: 26.8% (2010); Poverty rate: 0.6% (2005-2009 5-year est.).
Taxes: Total city taxes per capita: $579 (2007); City property taxes per capita: $551 (2007).
Education: Percent of population age 25 and over with: High school diploma (including GED) or higher: 84.0% (2010); Bachelor's degree or higher: 31.2% (2010); Master's degree or higher: 13.0% (2010).
Housing: Homeownership rate: 84.5% (2010); Median home value: $114,855 (2010); Median contract rent: n/a per month (2005-2009 5-year est.); Median year structure built: 1987 (2005-2009 5-year est.).
Safety: Violent crime rate: 0.0 per 10,000 population; Property crime rate: 62.2 per 10,000 population (2009).
Transportation: Commute to work: 98.1% car, 0.0% public transportation, 0.0% walk, 1.9% work from home (2005-2009 5-year est.); Travel time to work: 13.4% less than 15 minutes, 68.5% 15 to 30 minutes, 13.8% 30 to 45 minutes, 1.5% 45 to 60 minutes, 2.7% 60 minutes or more (2005-2009 5-year est.)

REESE CENTER (CDP).
Covers a land area of 6.522 square miles and a water area of 0 square miles. Located at 33.59° N. Lat; 102.03° W. Long.
Population: 1,278 (1990); 42 (2000); 39 (2010); 42 (2015 projected); Race: 79.5% White, 0.0% Black, 0.0% Asian, 20.5% Other, 56.4% Hispanic of any race (2010); Density: 6.0 persons per square mile (2010); Average household size: 2.85 (2010); Median age: 42.0 (2010); Males per 100 females: 105.3 (2010); Marriage status: n/a never married, n/a now married, n/a widowed, n/a divorced (2005-2009 5-year est.); Foreign born: n/a (2005-2009 5-year est.); Ancestry (includes multiple ancestries): n/a (2005-2009 5-year est.).
Economy: Employment by occupation: n/a management, n/a professional, n/a services, n/a sales, n/a farming, n/a construction, n/a production (2005-2009 5-year est.).
Income: Per capita income: $14,911 (2010); Median household income: $42,500 (2010); Average household income: $43,654 (2010); Percent of households with income of $100,000 or more: 0.0% (2010); Poverty rate: n/a (2005-2009 5-year est.).
Education: Percent of population age 25 and over with: High school diploma (including GED) or higher: 85.2% (2010); Bachelor's degree or higher: 7.4% (2010); Master's degree or higher: 7.4% (2010).
Housing: Homeownership rate: 69.2% (2010); Median home value: $50,000 (2010); Median contract rent: n/a per month (2005-2009 5-year est.); Median year structure built: n/a (2005-2009 5-year est.).
Transportation: Commute to work: n/a car, n/a public transportation, n/a walk, n/a work from home (2005-2009 5-year est.); Travel time to work: n/a less than 15 minutes, n/a 15 to 30 minutes, n/a 30 to 45 minutes, n/a 45 to 60 minutes, n/a 60 minutes or more (2005-2009 5-year est.)

SHALLOWATER (city).
Covers a land area of 0.918 square miles and a water area of 0 square miles. Located at 33.68° N. Lat; 101.99° W. Long. Elevation is 3,294 feet.
Population: 1,706 (1990); 2,086 (2000); 2,304 (2010); 2,437 (2015 projected); Race: 87.5% White, 0.6% Black, 0.3% Asian, 11.7% Other, 17.9% Hispanic of any race (2010); Density: 2,510.3 persons per square mile (2010); Average household size: 2.76 (2010); Median age: 34.0 (2010); Males per 100 females: 93.8 (2010); Marriage status: 21.1% never married, 66.1% now married, 6.2% widowed, 6.5% divorced (2005-2009 5-year est.); Foreign born: 1.2% (2005-2009 5-year est.); Ancestry (includes multiple ancestries): 15.2% English, 14.6% Irish, 13.0% German, 12.3% American, 6.6% Scotch-Irish (2005-2009 5-year est.).
Economy: Single-family building permits issued: 5 (2010); Multi-family building permits issued: 0 (2010); Employment by occupation: 14.5% management, 21.9% professional, 14.0% services, 23.7% sales, 0.0% farming, 7.8% construction, 18.1% production (2005-2009 5-year est.).
Income: Per capita income: $24,038 (2010); Median household income: $52,621 (2010); Average household income: $66,536 (2010); Percent of

households with income of $100,000 or more: 18.3% (2010); Poverty rate: 15.1% (2005-2009 5-year est.).
Taxes: Total city taxes per capita: $192 (2007); City property taxes per capita: $166 (2007).
Education: Percent of population age 25 and over with: High school diploma (including GED) or higher: 82.2% (2010); Bachelor's degree or higher: 20.0% (2010); Master's degree or higher: 4.8% (2010).

School District(s)
Shallowater ISD (PK-12)
    2009-10 Enrollment: 1,457 . . . . (806) 832-4531
Housing: Homeownership rate: 79.6% (2010); Median home value: $92,338 (2010); Median contract rent: $552 per month (2005-2009 5-year est.); Median year structure built: 1978 (2005-2009 5-year est.).
Safety: Violent crime rate: 0.0 per 10,000 population; Property crime rate: 99.5 per 10,000 population (2009).
Transportation: Commute to work: 93.0% car, 0.0% public transportation, 0.9% walk, 4.1% work from home (2005-2009 5-year est.); Travel time to work: 29.6% less than 15 minutes, 51.5% 15 to 30 minutes, 15.1% 30 to 45 minutes, 0.7% 45 to 60 minutes, 3.1% 60 minutes or more (2005-2009 5-year est.)

SLATON (city).
Covers a land area of 5.422 square miles and a water area of 0 square miles. Located at 33.43° N. Lat; 101.64° W. Long. Elevation is 3,084 feet.
History: Slaton's early economy was based on cotton, with gins, compresses, and warehouses encircling the town.
Population: 6,070 (1990); 6,109 (2000); 5,738 (2010); 5,663 (2015 projected); Race: 72.1% White, 5.5% Black, 0.2% Asian, 22.2% Other, 48.3% Hispanic of any race (2010); Density: 1,058.2 persons per square mile (2010); Average household size: 2.61 (2010); Median age: 31.7 (2010); Males per 100 females: 90.2 (2010); Marriage status: 25.1% never married, 52.6% now married, 10.2% widowed, 12.2% divorced (2005-2009 5-year est.); Foreign born: 5.7% (2005-2009 5-year est.); Ancestry (includes multiple ancestries): 10.9% German, 8.0% American, 7.3% Irish, 6.1% English, 1.6% French (2005-2009 5-year est.).
Economy: Single-family building permits issued: 0 (2010); Multi-family building permits issued: 0 (2010); Employment by occupation: 7.7% management, 7.8% professional, 22.5% services, 26.7% sales, 1.9% farming, 15.4% construction, 18.0% production (2005-2009 5-year est.).
Income: Per capita income: $17,289 (2010); Median household income: $33,746 (2010); Average household income: $43,923 (2010); Percent of households with income of $100,000 or more: 8.2% (2010); Poverty rate: 19.8% (2005-2009 5-year est.).
Taxes: Total city taxes per capita: $271 (2007); City property taxes per capita: $172 (2007).
Education: Percent of population age 25 and over with: High school diploma (including GED) or higher: 66.1% (2010); Bachelor's degree or higher: 7.8% (2010); Master's degree or higher: 3.4% (2010).

School District(s)
Slaton ISD (PK-12)
    2009-10 Enrollment: 1,290 . . . . (806) 828-6591
Housing: Homeownership rate: 69.4% (2010); Median home value: $51,306 (2010); Median contract rent: $387 per month (2005-2009 5-year est.); Median year structure built: 1959 (2005-2009 5-year est.).
Safety: Violent crime rate: 67.6 per 10,000 population; Property crime rate: 265.2 per 10,000 population (2009).
Newspapers: Slatonite (Community news; Circulation 2,450)
Transportation: Commute to work: 97.1% car, 0.0% public transportation, 1.8% walk, 0.4% work from home (2005-2009 5-year est.); Travel time to work: 21.4% less than 15 minutes, 39.9% 15 to 30 minutes, 33.8% 30 to 45 minutes, 2.1% 45 to 60 minutes, 2.8% 60 minutes or more (2005-2009 5-year est.)
Additional Information Contacts
City of Slaton . . . . (806) 828-2000
    http://www.slaton.tx.us
Slaton Chamber of Commerce . . . . (806) 828-6238
    http://www.slatonchamberofcommerce.org

WOLFFORTH (city).
Covers a land area of 1.502 square miles and a water area of 0 square miles. Located at 33.50° N. Lat; 102.01° W. Long. Elevation is 3,317 feet.
Population: 2,309 (1990); 2,554 (2000); 3,085 (2010); 3,380 (2015 projected); Race: 81.8% White, 1.1% Black, 0.3% Asian, 16.7% Other, 24.6% Hispanic of any race (2010); Density: 2,054.2 persons per square mile (2010); Average household size: 2.72 (2010); Median age: 34.7

(2010); Males per 100 females: 91.7 (2010); Marriage status: 16.8% never married, 70.8% now married, 3.9% widowed, 8.5% divorced (2005-2009 5-year est.); Foreign born: 0.4% (2005-2009 5-year est.); Ancestry (includes multiple ancestries): 16.7% German, 12.0% English, 9.1% American, 9.0% Irish, 4.9% French (2005-2009 5-year est.).
Economy: Single-family building permits issued: 38 (2010); Multi-family building permits issued: 0 (2010); Employment by occupation: 16.2% management, 22.8% professional, 12.9% services, 26.4% sales, 0.3% farming, 8.4% construction, 13.0% production (2005-2009 5-year est.).
Income: Per capita income: $20,767 (2010); Median household income: $46,632 (2010); Average household income: $57,172 (2010); Percent of households with income of $100,000 or more: 11.4% (2010); Poverty rate: 6.5% (2005-2009 5-year est.).
Taxes: Total city taxes per capita: $340 (2007); City property taxes per capita: $212 (2007).
Education: Percent of population age 25 and over with: High school diploma (including GED) or higher: 80.9% (2010); Bachelor's degree or higher: 21.7% (2010); Master's degree or higher: 7.2% (2010).

School District(s)
Frenship ISD (PK-12)
   2009-10 Enrollment: 7,342 . . . . (806) 866-9541
Housing: Homeownership rate: 79.2% (2010); Median home value: $76,789 (2010); Median contract rent: $709 per month (2005-2009 5-year est.); Median year structure built: 1984 (2005-2009 5-year est.).
Safety: Violent crime rate: 19.3 per 10,000 population; Property crime rate: 146.4 per 10,000 population (2009).
Transportation: Commute to work: 95.0% car, 0.0% public transportation, 0.0% walk, 4.8% work from home (2005-2009 5-year est.); Travel time to work: 24.8% less than 15 minutes, 64.4% 15 to 30 minutes, 8.1% 30 to 45 minutes, 1.6% 45 to 60 minutes, 1.2% 60 minutes or more (2005-2009 5-year est.)

Lynn County

Located in northwestern Texas; includes Tahoka Lake. Covers a land area of 891.88 square miles, a water area of 1.58 square miles, and is located in the Central Time Zone at 33.15° N. Lat., 101.80° W. Long. The county was founded in 1876. County seat is Tahoka.

Weather Station: Tahoka   Elevation: 3,120 feet

	Jan	Feb	Mar	Apr	May	Jun	Jul	Aug	Sep	Oct	Nov	Dec
High	55	60	67	76	84	90	93	91	84	76	64	55
Low	27	30	36	45	56	64	67	66	59	48	37	28
Precip	0.7	0.8	1.0	1.3	2.9	3.1	2.3	2.3	2.3	2.1	1.0	1.0
Snow	2.5	1.5	0.2	0.4	0.0	0.0	0.0	0.0	0.0	tr	1.2	1.8

High and Low temperatures in degrees Fahrenheit; Precipitation and Snow in inches

Population: 6,758 (1990); 6,550 (2000); 5,773 (2010); 5,386 (2015 projected); Race: 73.5% White, 3.8% Black, 0.2% Asian, 22.6% Other, 46.2% Hispanic of any race (2010); Density: 6.5 persons per square mile (2010); Average household size: 2.74 (2010); Median age: 39.0 (2010); Males per 100 females: 99.7 (2010).
Religion: Five largest groups: 42.4% Southern Baptist Convention, 21.4% Catholic Church, 10.5% The United Methodist Church, 3.5% Churches of Christ, 2.7% Church of the Nazarene (2000).
Economy: Unemployment rate: 8.5% (June 2011); Total civilian labor force: 2,835 (June 2011); Leading industries: 12.4% retail trade; 9.5% finance & insurance; 5.1% accommodation & food services (2009); Farms: 506 totaling 493,691 acres (2007); Companies that employ 500 or more persons: 0 (2009); Companies that employ 100 to 499 persons: 1 (2009); Companies that employ less than 100 persons: 94 (2009); Black-owned businesses: n/a (2007); Hispanic-owned businesses: n/a (2007); Asian-owned businesses: n/a (2007); Women-owned businesses: 75 (2007); Retail sales per capita: $9,946 (2010). Single-family building permits issued: 1 (2010); Multi-family building permits issued: 0 (2010).
Income: Per capita income: $18,452 (2010); Median household income: $34,220 (2010); Average household income: $50,663 (2010); Percent of households with income of $100,000 or more: 11.8% (2010); Poverty rate: 19.3% (2009); Bankruptcy rate: 0.68% (2010).
Taxes: Total county taxes per capita: $865 (2007); County property taxes per capita: $835 (2007).
Education: Percent of population age 25 and over with: High school diploma (including GED) or higher: 68.6% (2010); Bachelor's degree or higher: 15.6% (2010); Master's degree or higher: 4.8% (2010).

Housing: Homeownership rate: 72.4% (2010); Median home value: $48,866 (2010); Median contract rent: $274 per month (2005-2009 5-year est.); Median year structure built: 1965 (2005-2009 5-year est.)
Health: Birth rate: 156.9 per 10,000 population (2009); Death rate: 72.3 per 10,000 population (2009); Age-adjusted cancer mortality rate: 239.3 (Unreliable) deaths per 100,000 population (2007); Number of physicians: 5.3 per 10,000 population (2008); Hospital beds: 32.9 per 10,000 population (2007); Hospital admissions: 275.0 per 10,000 population (2007).
Elections: 2008 Presidential election results: 29.6% Obama, 69.6% McCain, 0.0% Nader
Additional Information Contacts
Lynn County Government . . . . (806) 998-4222
   http://www.co.lynn.tx.us/ips/cms
City of Tahoka . . . . (806) 561-4211
   http://www.tahoka-texas.com

Lynn County Communities

NEW HOME (city). Covers a land area of 1.002 square miles and a water area of 0 square miles. Located at 33.32° N. Lat; 101.91° W. Long. Elevation is 3,238 feet.
Population: 175 (1990); 320 (2000); 292 (2010); 278 (2015 projected); Race: 86.0% White, 0.3% Black, 0.3% Asian, 13.4% Other, 32.9% Hispanic of any race (2010); Density: 291.3 persons per square mile (2010); Average household size: 2.97 (2010); Median age: 38.1 (2010); Males per 100 females: 104.2 (2010); Marriage status: 21.4% never married, 71.1% now married, 2.4% widowed, 5.1% divorced (2005-2009 5-year est.); Foreign born: 6.3% (2005-2009 5-year est.); Ancestry (includes multiple ancestries): 11.0% German, 9.1% Irish, 7.2% English, 6.1% American, 3.0% Dutch (2005-2009 5-year est.).
Economy: Single-family building permits issued: 0 (2010); Multi-family building permits issued: 0 (2010); Employment by occupation: 7.5% management, 16.2% professional, 31.2% services, 8.7% sales, 5.8% farming, 14.5% construction, 16.2% production (2005-2009 5-year est.).
Income: Per capita income: $17,064 (2010); Median household income: $34,375 (2010); Average household income: $54,592 (2010); Percent of households with income of $100,000 or more: 10.2% (2010); Poverty rate: 0.0% (2005-2009 5-year est.).
Taxes: Total city taxes per capita: $92 (2007); City property taxes per capita: $82 (2007).
Education: Percent of population age 25 and over with: High school diploma (including GED) or higher: 76.2% (2010); Bachelor's degree or higher: 20.0% (2010); Master's degree or higher: 4.9% (2010).

School District(s)
New Home ISD (PK-12)
   2009-10 Enrollment: 184 . . . . (806) 924-7542
Housing: Homeownership rate: 70.4% (2010); Median home value: $85,000 (2010); Median contract rent: $250 per month (2005-2009 5-year est.); Median year structure built: 1979 (2005-2009 5-year est.).
Transportation: Commute to work: 95.2% car, 0.0% public transportation, 3.0% walk, 1.8% work from home (2005-2009 5-year est.); Travel time to work: 27.3% less than 15 minutes, 44.2% 15 to 30 minutes, 24.2% 30 to 45 minutes, 4.2% 45 to 60 minutes, 0.0% 60 minutes or more (2005-2009 5-year est.)

O'DONNELL (city). Covers a land area of 0.859 square miles and a water area of 0 square miles. Located at 32.96° N. Lat; 101.82° W. Long. Elevation is 3,048 feet.
Population: 1,102 (1990); 1,011 (2000); 876 (2010); 814 (2015 projected); Race: 52.2% White, 1.8% Black, 0.5% Asian, 45.5% Other, 63.6% Hispanic of any race (2010); Density: 1,020.3 persons per square mile (2010); Average household size: 2.69 (2010); Median age: 38.1 (2010); Males per 100 females: 100.9 (2010); Marriage status: 14.3% never married, 75.8% now married, 4.2% widowed, 5.8% divorced (2005-2009 5-year est.); Foreign born: 3.5% (2005-2009 5-year est.); Ancestry (includes multiple ancestries): 9.8% English, 6.0% Irish, 3.6% German, 2.1% French, 2.0% Scottish (2005-2009 5-year est.).
Economy: Employment by occupation: 9.1% management, 15.3% professional, 24.1% services, 17.5% sales, 13.1% farming, 6.4% construction, 14.6% production (2005-2009 5-year est.).
Income: Per capita income: $21,576 (2010); Median household income: $39,186 (2010); Average household income: $57,784 (2010); Percent of households with income of $100,000 or more: 15.3% (2010); Poverty rate: 24.5% (2005-2009 5-year est.).

Taxes: Total city taxes per capita: $137 (2007); City property taxes per capita: $39 (2007).
Education: Percent of population age 25 and over with: High school diploma (including GED) or higher: 61.0% (2010); Bachelor's degree or higher: 11.9% (2010); Master's degree or higher: 3.2% (2010).
School District(s)
O'Donnell ISD (PK-12)
    2009-10 Enrollment: 338 . . . . (806) 428-3241
Housing: Homeownership rate: 74.2% (2010); Median home value: $26,557 (2010); Median contract rent: $237 per month (2005-2009 5-year est.); Median year structure built: 1962 (2005-2009 5-year est.).
Transportation: Commute to work: 94.8% car, 0.0% public transportation, 2.7% walk, 2.5% work from home (2005-2009 5-year est.); Travel time to work: 49.4% less than 15 minutes, 36.0% 15 to 30 minutes, 2.1% 30 to 45 minutes, 5.1% 45 to 60 minutes, 7.4% 60 minutes or more (2005-2009 5-year est.)

ODONNELL (unincorporated postal area, zip code 79351). Covers a land area of 352.582 square miles and a water area of 0.115 square miles. Located at 32.97° N. Lat; 101.93° W. Long.
Population: 1,595 (2000); Race: 69.2% White, 1.1% Black, 1.0% Asian, 28.7% Other, 51.2% Hispanic of any race (2000); Density: 4.5 persons per square mile (2000); Age: 29.5% under 18, 17.0% over 64 (2000); Marriage status: 19.0% never married, 68.4% now married, 6.2% widowed, 6.3% divorced (2000); Foreign born: 7.1% (2000); Ancestry (includes multiple ancestries): 11.8% American, 4.4% German, 4.2% English, 3.5% Irish (2000).
Economy: Employment by occupation: 24.1% management, 12.4% professional, 17.0% services, 16.4% sales, 13.9% farming, 7.7% construction, 8.6% production (2000).
Income: Per capita income: $16,342 (2000); Median household income: $27,667 (2000); Poverty rate: 179.1% (2000).
Education: Percent of population age 25 and over with: High school diploma (including GED) or higher: 59.6% (2000); Bachelor's degree or higher: 13.1% (2000).
Housing: Homeownership rate: 76.0% (2000); Median home value: $26,200 (2000); Median contract rent: $174 per month (2000); Median year structure built: 1959 (2000).
Newspapers: O'Donnell Index Press (Community news; Circulation 650)
Transportation: Commute to work: 92.1% car, 0.0% public transportation, 2.4% walk, 4.9% work from home (2000); Travel time to work: 54.3% less than 15 minutes, 26.2% 15 to 30 minutes, 11.0% 30 to 45 minutes, 4.8% 45 to 60 minutes, 3.7% 60 minutes or more (2000)

TAHOKA (city). County seat. Covers a land area of 2.397 square miles and a water area of 0.007 square miles. Located at 33.16° N. Lat; 101.79° W. Long. Elevation is 3,081 feet.
History: Tahoka developed as a shipping center for cotton, cattle, and grain.
Population: 2,868 (1990); 2,910 (2000); 2,502 (2010); 2,312 (2015 projected); Race: 74.7% White, 6.8% Black, 0.2% Asian, 18.3% Other, 49.3% Hispanic of any race (2010); Density: 1,043.7 persons per square mile (2010); Average household size: 2.67 (2010); Median age: 38.5 (2010); Males per 100 females: 94.4 (2010); Marriage status: 23.1% never married, 57.2% now married, 8.3% widowed, 11.4% divorced (2005-2009 5-year est.); Foreign born: 7.0% (2005-2009 5-year est.); Ancestry (includes multiple ancestries): 13.4% German, 9.0% English, 4.4% Irish, 3.6% French, 2.9% Scottish (2005-2009 5-year est.).
Economy: Single-family building permits issued: 1 (2010); Multi-family building permits issued: 0 (2010); Employment by occupation: 8.1% management, 10.2% professional, 26.6% services, 28.6% sales, 4.5% farming, 13.3% construction, 8.9% production (2005-2009 5-year est.).
Income: Per capita income: $16,779 (2010); Median household income: $31,096 (2010); Average household income: $45,135 (2010); Percent of households with income of $100,000 or more: 9.7% (2010); Poverty rate: 17.5% (2005-2009 5-year est.).
Taxes: Total city taxes per capita: $220 (2007); City property taxes per capita: $137 (2007).
Education: Percent of population age 25 and over with: High school diploma (including GED) or higher: 66.1% (2010); Bachelor's degree or higher: 14.1% (2010); Master's degree or higher: 4.8% (2010).
School District(s)
Tahoka ISD (PK-12)
    2009-10 Enrollment: 641 . . . . (806) 561-4105

Housing: Homeownership rate: 72.9% (2010); Median home value: $48,429 (2010); Median contract rent: $287 per month (2005-2009 5-year est.); Median year structure built: 1965 (2005-2009 5-year est.).
Hospitals: Lynn County Hospital (24 beds)
Safety: Violent crime rate: 4.0 per 10,000 population; Property crime rate: 165.4 per 10,000 population (2009).
Transportation: Commute to work: 94.1% car, 0.0% public transportation, 1.7% walk, 3.1% work from home (2005-2009 5-year est.); Travel time to work: 66.9% less than 15 minutes, 12.6% 15 to 30 minutes, 17.4% 30 to 45 minutes, 1.5% 45 to 60 minutes, 1.5% 60 minutes or more (2005-2009 5-year est.)
Additional Information Contacts
City of Tahoka . . . . (806) 561-4211
    http://www.tahoka-texas.com

WILSON (city). Covers a land area of 0.651 square miles and a water area of 0 square miles. Located at 33.31° N. Lat; 101.72° W. Long. Elevation is 3,120 feet.
Population: 568 (1990); 532 (2000); 467 (2010); 436 (2015 projected); Race: 66.6% White, 1.9% Black, 0.0% Asian, 31.5% Other, 54.4% Hispanic of any race (2010); Density: 717.0 persons per square mile (2010); Average household size: 2.94 (2010); Median age: 34.6 (2010); Males per 100 females: 104.8 (2010); Marriage status: 20.6% never married, 68.6% now married, 4.1% widowed, 6.6% divorced (2005-2009 5-year est.); Foreign born: 9.7% (2005-2009 5-year est.); Ancestry (includes multiple ancestries): 16.3% German, 7.5% Irish, 1.7% Italian, 1.2% English, 0.5% French (2005-2009 5-year est.).
Economy: Single-family building permits issued: 0 (2010); Multi-family building permits issued: 0 (2010); Employment by occupation: 6.7% management, 11.9% professional, 19.8% services, 22.8% sales, 16.0% farming, 10.4% construction, 12.3% production (2005-2009 5-year est.).
Income: Per capita income: $17,829 (2010); Median household income: $37,100 (2010); Average household income: $53,208 (2010); Percent of households with income of $100,000 or more: 8.8% (2010); Poverty rate: 9.5% (2005-2009 5-year est.).
Taxes: Total city taxes per capita: $143 (2007); City property taxes per capita: $141 (2007).
Education: Percent of population age 25 and over with: High school diploma (including GED) or higher: 69.7% (2010); Bachelor's degree or higher: 13.9% (2010); Master's degree or higher: 4.5% (2010).
School District(s)
Wilson ISD (PK-12)
    2009-10 Enrollment: 151 . . . . (806) 628-6271
Housing: Homeownership rate: 76.7% (2010); Median home value: $41,600 (2010); Median contract rent: $294 per month (2005-2009 5-year est.); Median year structure built: 1964 (2005-2009 5-year est.).
Transportation: Commute to work: 83.0% car, 1.9% public transportation, 7.5% walk, 7.5% work from home (2005-2009 5-year est.); Travel time to work: 38.0% less than 15 minutes, 28.6% 15 to 30 minutes, 24.1% 30 to 45 minutes, 8.6% 45 to 60 minutes, 0.8% 60 minutes or more (2005-2009 5-year est.)

Madison County

Located in east central Texas; bounded on the west by the Navassota River, and on the east by the Trinity River. Covers a land area of 469.65 square miles, a water area of 2.80 square miles, and is located in the Central Time Zone at 30.95° N. Lat., 95.96° W. Long. The county was founded in 1854. County seat is Madisonville.

Weather Station: Madisonville   Elevation: 251 feet

	Jan	Feb	Mar	Apr	May	Jun	Jul	Aug	Sep	Oct	Nov	Dec
High	62	66	73	79	86	92	95	96	91	82	72	63
Low	39	43	49	56	64	70	73	72	67	57	48	40
Precip	3.9	3.3	3.4	2.9	4.8	4.3	2.8	3.1	3.5	5.0	4.3	4.0
Snow	0.1	tr	0.0	0.0	0.0	0.0	0.0	0.0	0.0	0.0	tr	0.1

High and Low temperatures in degrees Fahrenheit; Precipitation and Snow in inches

Population: 10,931 (1990); 12,940 (2000); 13,828 (2010); 14,233 (2015 projected); Race: 65.3% White, 21.3% Black, 0.7% Asian, 12.7% Other, 20.1% Hispanic of any race (2010); Density: 29.4 persons per square mile (2010); Average household size: 2.59 (2010); Median age: 34.1 (2010); Males per 100 females: 137.8 (2010).
Religion: Five largest groups: 25.6% Southern Baptist Convention, 6.9% Churches of Christ, 6.4% The United Methodist Church, 3.0% Catholic Church, 2.3% Baptist Missionary Association of America (2000).

Economy: Unemployment rate: 9.0% (June 2011); Total civilian labor force: 5,756 (June 2011); Leading industries: 26.3% retail trade; 11.2% mining; 5.4% finance & insurance (2009); Farms: 1,057 totaling 273,109 acres (2007); Companies that employ 500 or more persons: 0 (2009); Companies that employ 100 to 499 persons: 4 (2009); Companies that employ less than 100 persons: 201 (2009); Black-owned businesses: 82 (2007); Hispanic-owned businesses: n/a (2007); Asian-owned businesses: n/a (2007); Women-owned businesses: 205 (2007); Retail sales per capita: $18,178 (2010). Single-family building permits issued: 19 (2010); Multi-family building permits issued: 0 (2010).
Income: Per capita income: $17,599 (2010); Median household income: $37,556 (2010); Average household income: $51,770 (2010); Percent of households with income of $100,000 or more: 9.6% (2010); Poverty rate: 25.9% (2009); Bankruptcy rate: 0.60% (2010).
Taxes: Total county taxes per capita: $293 (2007); County property taxes per capita: $198 (2007).
Education: Percent of population age 25 and over with: High school diploma (including GED) or higher: 77.6% (2010); Bachelor's degree or higher: 13.0% (2010); Master's degree or higher: 3.3% (2010).
Housing: Homeownership rate: 75.2% (2010); Median home value: $74,541 (2010); Median contract rent: $361 per month (2005-2009 5-year est.); Median year structure built: 1979 (2005-2009 5-year est.)
Health: Birth rate: 120.8 per 10,000 population (2009); Death rate: 82.5 per 10,000 population (2009); Age-adjusted cancer mortality rate: 212.9 deaths per 100,000 population (2007); Number of physicians: 1.5 per 10,000 population (2008); Hospital beds: 18.9 per 10,000 population (2007); Hospital admissions: 363.2 per 10,000 population (2007).
Elections: 2008 Presidential election results: 28.1% Obama, 71.0% McCain, 0.1% Nader
Additional Information Contacts
Madison County Government . . . . (936) 348-2670
    http://www.co.madison.tx.us/ips/cms
Madison County Chamber of Commerce. . . . . (936) 348-3591
    http://www.madisoncountytxchamber.com

Madison County Communities

MADISONVILLE (city). County seat. Covers a land area of 4.145 square miles and a water area of 0.155 square miles. Located at 30.95° N. Lat; 95.91° W. Long. Elevation is 249 feet.
Population: 3,720 (1990); 4,159 (2000); 4,536 (2010); 4,742 (2015 projected); Race: 57.6% White, 26.3% Black, 0.6% Asian, 15.5% Other, 29.2% Hispanic of any race (2010); Density: 1,094.2 persons per square mile (2010); Average household size: 2.74 (2010); Median age: 34.7 (2010); Males per 100 females: 90.7 (2010); Marriage status: 35.5% never married, 42.1% now married, 11.8% widowed, 10.6% divorced (2005-2009 5-year est.); Foreign born: 19.8% (2005-2009 5-year est.); Ancestry (includes multiple ancestries): 6.0% English, 5.7% German, 4.7% Irish, 4.0% American, 1.3% French (2005-2009 5-year est.).
Economy: Single-family building permits issued: 19 (2010); Multi-family building permits issued: 0 (2010); Employment by occupation: 3.7% management, 8.8% professional, 20.1% services, 25.2% sales, 13.8% farming, 11.8% construction, 16.6% production (2005-2009 5-year est.).
Income: Per capita income: $15,357 (2010); Median household income: $30,948 (2010); Average household income: $42,670 (2010); Percent of households with income of $100,000 or more: 5.7% (2010); Poverty rate: 22.9% (2005-2009 5-year est.).
Taxes: Total city taxes per capita: $387 (2007); City property taxes per capita: $137 (2007).
Education: Percent of population age 25 and over with: High school diploma (including GED) or higher: 72.8% (2010); Bachelor's degree or higher: 13.8% (2010); Master's degree or higher: 3.6% (2010).
School District(s)
Madisonville CISD (PK-12)
    2009-10 Enrollment: 2,322 . . . . (936) 348-2797
Housing: Homeownership rate: 64.5% (2010); Median home value: $59,882 (2010); Median contract rent: $341 per month (2005-2009 5-year est.); Median year structure built: 1973 (2005-2009 5-year est.).
Hospitals: Madison Saint Joseph Health Center
Safety: Violent crime rate: 109.2 per 10,000 population; Property crime rate: 509.6 per 10,000 population (2009).
Newspapers: Madisonville Meteor (Community news; Circulation 3,400)
Transportation: Commute to work: 91.8% car, 0.0% public transportation, 4.1% walk, 2.9% work from home (2005-2009 5-year est.); Travel time to work: 54.1% less than 15 minutes, 16.1% 15 to 30 minutes, 17.9% 30 to 45

minutes, 5.8% 45 to 60 minutes, 6.2% 60 minutes or more (2005-2009 5-year est.)
Additional Information Contacts
Madison County Chamber of Commerce. . . . . (936) 348-3591
    http://www.madisoncountytxchamber.com

MIDWAY (city). Covers a land area of 1.603 square miles and a water area of 0 square miles. Located at 31.02° N. Lat; 95.75° W. Long. Elevation is 249 feet.
Population: 274 (1990); 288 (2000); 285 (2010); 287 (2015 projected); Race: 60.7% White, 27.0% Black, 0.7% Asian, 11.6% Other, 15.1% Hispanic of any race (2010); Density: 177.8 persons per square mile (2010); Average household size: 2.49 (2010); Median age: 32.4 (2010); Males per 100 females: 161.5 (2010); Marriage status: 30.5% never married, 53.5% now married, 8.9% widowed, 7.0% divorced (2005-2009 5-year est.); Foreign born: 3.0% (2005-2009 5-year est.); Ancestry (includes multiple ancestries): 26.2% Irish, 17.0% English, 10.3% Italian, 9.6% German, 9.6% American (2005-2009 5-year est.).
Economy: Employment by occupation: 4.8% management, 8.4% professional, 49.4% services, 8.4% sales, 0.0% farming, 20.5% construction, 8.4% production (2005-2009 5-year est.).
Income: Per capita income: $19,095 (2010); Median household income: $44,107 (2010); Average household income: $56,883 (2010); Percent of households with income of $100,000 or more: 12.3% (2010); Poverty rate: 37.3% (2005-2009 5-year est.).
Taxes: Total city taxes per capita: $330 (2007); City property taxes per capita: $0 (2007).
Education: Percent of population age 25 and over with: High school diploma (including GED) or higher: 76.3% (2010); Bachelor's degree or higher: 9.1% (2010); Master's degree or higher: 2.2% (2010).
Housing: Homeownership rate: 79.0% (2010); Median home value: $90,000 (2010); Median contract rent: $405 per month (2005-2009 5-year est.); Median year structure built: 1976 (2005-2009 5-year est.).
Transportation: Commute to work: 85.7% car, 0.0% public transportation, 2.6% walk, 0.0% work from home (2005-2009 5-year est.); Travel time to work: 22.1% less than 15 minutes, 27.3% 15 to 30 minutes, 3.9% 30 to 45 minutes, 31.2% 45 to 60 minutes, 15.6% 60 minutes or more (2005-2009 5-year est.)

NORTH ZULCH (unincorporated postal area, zip code 77872). Covers a land area of 85.520 square miles and a water area of 0.322 square miles. Located at 30.89° N. Lat; 96.10° W. Long. Elevation is 351 feet.
Population: 1,682 (2000); Race: 96.5% White, 0.0% Black, 0.0% Asian, 3.5% Other, 6.1% Hispanic of any race (2000); Density: 19.7 persons per square mile (2000); Age: 21.6% under 18, 19.4% over 64 (2000); Marriage status: 17.6% never married, 65.8% now married, 8.9% widowed, 7.6% divorced (2000); Foreign born: 2.7% (2000); Ancestry (includes multiple ancestries): 19.7% German, 14.2% Irish, 11.9% English, 9.2% American (2000).
Economy: Employment by occupation: 12.1% management, 12.5% professional, 19.5% services, 20.9% sales, 3.9% farming, 16.8% construction, 14.3% production (2000).
Income: Per capita income: $17,796 (2000); Median household income: $34,635 (2000); Poverty rate: 179.1% (2000).
Education: Percent of population age 25 and over with: High school diploma (including GED) or higher: 76.8% (2000); Bachelor's degree or higher: 11.4% (2000).
School District(s)
North Zulch ISD (PK-12)
    2009-10 Enrollment: 355 . . . . (936) 399-1000
Housing: Homeownership rate: 86.8% (2000); Median home value: $56,100 (2000); Median contract rent: $400 per month (2000); Median year structure built: 1981 (2000).
Transportation: Commute to work: 91.6% car, 0.3% public transportation, 0.3% walk, 6.9% work from home (2000); Travel time to work: 12.7% less than 15 minutes, 30.4% 15 to 30 minutes, 31.4% 30 to 45 minutes, 13.6% 45 to 60 minutes, 11.9% 60 minutes or more (2000)

Marion County

Located in east Texas; bounded on the east by Louisiana; drained by Cypress Bayou; includes part of Caddo Lake. Covers a land area of 381.21 square miles, a water area of 39.15 square miles, and is located in the

Central Time Zone at 32.78° N. Lat., 94.41° W. Long. The county was founded in 1860. County seat is Jefferson.
Population: 9,984 (1990); 10,941 (2000); 10,547 (2010); 10,338 (2015 projected); Race: 74.7% White, 20.9% Black, 0.4% Asian, 3.9% Other, 3.3% Hispanic of any race (2010); Density: 27.7 persons per square mile (2010); Average household size: 2.30 (2010); Median age: 45.4 (2010); Males per 100 females: 93.0 (2010).
Religion: Five largest groups: 25.2% Southern Baptist Convention, 6.8% The United Methodist Church, 3.9% Seventh-day Adventist Church, 2.9% Catholic Church, 1.7% Churches of Christ (2000).
Economy: Unemployment rate: 10.0% (June 2011); Total civilian labor force: 5,141 (June 2011); Leading industries: 24.3% health care and social assistance; 24.2% manufacturing; 16.1% accommodation & food services (2009); Farms: 258 totaling 42,270 acres (2007); Companies that employ 500 or more persons: 0 (2009); Companies that employ 100 to 499 persons: 2 (2009); Companies that employ less than 100 persons: 156 (2009); Black-owned businesses: n/a (2007); Hispanic-owned businesses: n/a (2007); Asian-owned businesses: n/a (2007); Women-owned businesses: n/a (2007); Retail sales per capita: $6,564 (2010). Single-family building permits issued: 5 (2010); Multi-family building permits issued: 0 (2010).
Income: Per capita income: $20,131 (2010); Median household income: $33,837 (2010); Average household income: $46,682 (2010); Percent of households with income of $100,000 or more: 8.8% (2010); Poverty rate: 24.6% (2009); Bankruptcy rate: 2.06% (2010).
Taxes: Total county taxes per capita: $321 (2007); County property taxes per capita: $255 (2007).
Education: Percent of population age 25 and over with: High school diploma (including GED) or higher: 73.8% (2010); Bachelor's degree or higher: 9.7% (2010); Master's degree or higher: 3.2% (2010).
Housing: Homeownership rate: 80.6% (2010); Median home value: $57,252 (2010); Median contract rent: $315 per month (2005-2009 5-year est.); Median year structure built: 1976 (2005-2009 5-year est.).
Health: Birth rate: 95.1 per 10,000 population (2009); Death rate: 132.0 per 10,000 population (2009); Age-adjusted cancer mortality rate: 200.9 deaths per 100,000 population (2007); Number of physicians: 2.9 per 10,000 population (2008); Hospital beds: 0.0 per 10,000 population (2007); Hospital admissions: 0.0 per 10,000 population (2007).
Elections: 2008 Presidential election results: 38.7% Obama, 60.4% McCain, 0.1% Nader
Additional Information Contacts
Marion County Government . . . . (903) 665-3971
http://www.co.marion.tx.us/ips/cms
Marion County Chamber of Commerce . . . . (903) 665-2672
http://www.jefferson-texas.com

Marion County Communities

JEFFERSON (city). County seat. Covers a land area of 4.347 square miles and a water area of 0.070 square miles. Located at 32.76° N. Lat; 94.34° W. Long. Elevation is 194 feet.
History: Jefferson was established in 1836 on land donated by Allen Urquart. Sawmills were built, and the town became a river port, connected by bayous to the Red River and on to the Mississippi River. Jefferson was located on Trammel's Trace, over which Sam Houston and, later, Davey Crockett entered Texas.
Population: 2,237 (1990); 2,024 (2000); 1,955 (2010); 1,906 (2015 projected); Race: 65.0% White, 31.5% Black, 1.5% Asian, 2.0% Other, 1.8% Hispanic of any race (2010); Density: 449.8 persons per square mile (2010); Average household size: 2.20 (2010); Median age: 45.1 (2010); Males per 100 females: 81.4 (2010); Marriage status: 21.4% never married, 46.0% now married, 14.7% widowed, 17.9% divorced (2005-2009 5-year est.); Foreign born: 0.7% (2005-2009 5-year est.); Ancestry (includes multiple ancestries): 17.1% Irish, 10.2% German, 9.7% English, 8.7% American, 2.4% Scottish (2005-2009 5-year est.).
Economy: Single-family building permits issued: 5 (2010); Multi-family building permits issued: 0 (2010); Employment by occupation: 6.1% management, 18.7% professional, 30.0% services, 31.9% sales, 0.9% farming, 5.2% construction, 7.1% production (2005-2009 5-year est.).
Income: Per capita income: $16,811 (2010); Median household income: $22,355 (2010); Average household income: $38,138 (2010); Percent of households with income of $100,000 or more: 7.0% (2010); Poverty rate: 24.5% (2005-2009 5-year est.).
Taxes: Total city taxes per capita: $627 (2007); City property taxes per capita: $299 (2007).

Education: Percent of population age 25 and over with: High school diploma (including GED) or higher: 79.1% (2010); Bachelor's degree or higher: 13.5% (2010); Master's degree or higher: 5.7% (2010).
School District(s)
Jefferson ISD (PK-12)
    2009-10 Enrollment: 1,244 . . . . (903) 665-2461
Housing: Homeownership rate: 62.7% (2010); Median home value: $75,373 (2010); Median contract rent: $323 per month (2005-2009 5-year est.); Median year structure built: 1957 (2005-2009 5-year est.).
Safety: Violent crime rate: 21.0 per 10,000 population; Property crime rate: 398.3 per 10,000 population (2009).
Newspapers: Jimplecute (Local news; Circulation 2,250)
Transportation: Commute to work: 92.2% car, 0.0% public transportation, 7.0% walk, 0.0% work from home (2005-2009 5-year est.); Travel time to work: 44.0% less than 15 minutes, 29.5% 15 to 30 minutes, 14.5% 30 to 45 minutes, 11.1% 45 to 60 minutes, 1.0% 60 minutes or more (2005-2009 5-year est.)
Additional Information Contacts
Marion County Chamber of Commerce . . . . (903) 665-2672
http://www.jefferson-texas.com

Martin County

Located in west Texas; crossed by Mustang Draw. Covers a land area of 914.78 square miles, a water area of 0.84 square miles, and is located in the Central Time Zone at 32.25° N. Lat., 101.88° W. Long. The county was founded in 1876. County seat is Stanton.
Population: 4,956 (1990); 4,746 (2000); 4,756 (2010); 4,754 (2015 projected); Race: 77.2% White, 1.9% Black, 0.4% Asian, 20.5% Other, 43.0% Hispanic of any race (2010); Density: 5.2 persons per square mile (2010); Average household size: 2.79 (2010); Median age: 34.5 (2010); Males per 100 females: 96.5 (2010).
Religion: Five largest groups: 31.0% Southern Baptist Convention, 18.0% Catholic Church, 10.4% The United Methodist Church, 6.6% Churches of Christ, 0.7% Community of Christ (2000).
Economy: Unemployment rate: 6.4% (June 2011); Total civilian labor force: 2,270 (June 2011); Leading industries: 18.0% health care and social assistance; 7.0% construction; 5.0% other services (except public administration) (2009); Farms: 464 totaling 457,990 acres (2007); Companies that employ 500 or more persons: 0 (2009); Companies that employ 100 to 499 persons: 0 (2009); Companies that employ less than 100 persons: 93 (2009); Black-owned businesses: n/a (2007); Hispanic-owned businesses: n/a (2007); Asian-owned businesses: n/a (2007); Women-owned businesses: n/a (2007); Retail sales per capita: $11,263 (2010). Single-family building permits issued: 9 (2010); Multi-family building permits issued: 0 (2010).
Income: Per capita income: $22,151 (2010); Median household income: $45,050 (2010); Average household income: $61,027 (2010); Percent of households with income of $100,000 or more: 15.0% (2010); Poverty rate: 15.1% (2009); Bankruptcy rate: 1.40% (2010).
Taxes: Total county taxes per capita: $583 (2007); County property taxes per capita: $494 (2007).
Education: Percent of population age 25 and over with: High school diploma (including GED) or higher: 71.3% (2010); Bachelor's degree or higher: 13.5% (2010); Master's degree or higher: 3.0% (2010).
Housing: Homeownership rate: 72.1% (2010); Median home value: $67,234 (2010); Median contract rent: $143 per month (2005-2009 5-year est.); Median year structure built: 1967 (2005-2009 5-year est.)
Health: Birth rate: 187.7 per 10,000 population (2009); Death rate: 67.7 per 10,000 population (2009); Age-adjusted cancer mortality rate: Suppressed deaths per 100,000 population (2007); Number of physicians: 6.7 per 10,000 population (2008); Hospital beds: 45.3 per 10,000 population (2007); Hospital admissions: 760.9 per 10,000 population (2007).
Elections: 2008 Presidential election results: 18.3% Obama, 81.0% McCain, 0.0% Nader
Additional Information Contacts
Martin County Government . . . . (432) 756-2231

Martin County Chamber of Commerce . . . . (432) 756-3386
http://stantontex.com/Local/Chamber

Martin County Communities

LENORAH (unincorporated postal area, zip code 79749). Covers a land area of 79.963 square miles and a water area of 0 square miles. Located at 32.25° N. Lat; 101.81° W. Long. Elevation is 2,844 feet.
Population: 249 (2000); Race: 69.9% White, 0.0% Black, 0.0% Asian, 30.1% Other, 41.5% Hispanic of any race (2000); Density: 3.1 persons per square mile (2000); Age: 42.4% under 18, 10.5% over 64 (2000); Marriage status: 22.4% never married, 67.1% now married, 2.6% widowed, 7.9% divorced (2000); Foreign born: 11.4% (2000); Ancestry (includes multiple ancestries): 11.8% American, 9.2% Irish, 6.1% German, 4.4% French (2000).
Economy: Employment by occupation: 18.3% management, 12.7% professional, 16.9% services, 5.6% sales, 16.9% farming, 5.6% construction, 23.9% production (2000).
Income: Per capita income: $15,712 (2000); Median household income: $38,438 (2000); Poverty rate: 179.1% (2000).
Education: Percent of population age 25 and over with: High school diploma (including GED) or higher: 69.0% (2000); Bachelor's degree or higher: 14.7% (2000).

School District(s)
Grady ISD (KG-12)
    2009-10 Enrollment: 206 . . . . (432) 459-2444
Housing: Homeownership rate: 62.1% (2000); Median home value: $53,800 (2000); Median contract rent: $267 per month (2000); Median year structure built: 1968 (2000).
Transportation: Commute to work: 93.9% car, 0.0% public transportation, 3.0% walk, 3.0% work from home (2000); Travel time to work: 45.3% less than 15 minutes, 21.9% 15 to 30 minutes, 25.0% 30 to 45 minutes, 4.7% 45 to 60 minutes, 3.1% 60 minutes or more (2000)

STANTON (city). County seat. Covers a land area of 1.753 square miles and a water area of 0.013 square miles. Located at 32.13° N. Lat; 101.79° W. Long. Elevation is 2,664 feet.
History: Stanton was called Mariensfeld when it was first established by monks as a colony for German immigrants.
Population: 2,603 (1990); 2,556 (2000); 2,307 (2010); 2,197 (2015 projected); Race: 71.5% White, 3.7% Black, 0.9% Asian, 23.9% Other, 53.8% Hispanic of any race (2010); Density: 1,316.0 persons per square mile (2010); Average household size: 2.79 (2010); Median age: 32.7 (2010); Males per 100 females: 90.0 (2010); Marriage status: 23.7% never married, 59.4% now married, 9.8% widowed, 7.2% divorced (2005-2009 5-year est.); Foreign born: 3.7% (2005-2009 5-year est.); Ancestry (includes multiple ancestries): 16.3% Irish, 6.3% German, 5.1% English, 1.8% Dutch West Indian, 1.2% American (2005-2009 5-year est.).
Economy: Single-family building permits issued: 9 (2010); Multi-family building permits issued: 0 (2010); Employment by occupation: 12.6% management, 18.7% professional, 17.0% services, 27.4% sales, 0.0% farming, 12.3% construction, 12.0% production (2005-2009 5-year est.).
Income: Per capita income: $21,439 (2010); Median household income: $43,740 (2010); Average household income: $58,705 (2010); Percent of households with income of $100,000 or more: 14.7% (2010); Poverty rate: 6.0% (2005-2009 5-year est.).
Taxes: Total city taxes per capita: $271 (2007); City property taxes per capita: $181 (2007).
Education: Percent of population age 25 and over with: High school diploma (including GED) or higher: 68.2% (2010); Bachelor's degree or higher: 13.6% (2010); Master's degree or higher: 3.1% (2010).

School District(s)
Stanton ISD (PK-12)
    2009-10 Enrollment: 784 . . . . (432) 756-2244
Housing: Homeownership rate: 73.0% (2010); Median home value: $54,151 (2010); Median contract rent: $131 per month (2005-2009 5-year est.); Median year structure built: 1967 (2005-2009 5-year est.).
Hospitals: Martin County Hospital District
Safety: Violent crime rate: 4.6 per 10,000 population; Property crime rate: 150.5 per 10,000 population (2009).
Transportation: Commute to work: 95.5% car, 0.0% public transportation, 1.5% walk, 3.0% work from home (2005-2009 5-year est.); Travel time to work: 60.7% less than 15 minutes, 19.4% 15 to 30 minutes, 12.2% 30 to 45 minutes, 6.7% 45 to 60 minutes, 1.0% 60 minutes or more (2005-2009 5-year est.)
Additional Information Contacts
Martin County Chamber of Commerce . . . . (432) 756-3386
    http://stantontex.com/Local/Chamber

TARZAN (unincorporated postal area, zip code 79783). Covers a land area of 193.207 square miles and a water area of 0 square miles. Located at 32.37° N. Lat; 102.03° W. Long. Elevation is 2,822 feet.
Population: 179 (2000); Race: 91.4% White, 0.0% Black, 0.0% Asian, 8.6% Other, 10.1% Hispanic of any race (2000); Density: 0.9 persons per square mile (2000); Age: 37.9% under 18, 3.5% over 64 (2000); Marriage status: 18.6% never married, 69.3% now married, 2.1% widowed, 10.0% divorced (2000); Foreign born: 15.2% (2000); Ancestry (includes multiple ancestries): 26.3% German, 9.6% American, 5.6% Irish, 4.0% Pennsylvania German (2000).
Economy: Employment by occupation: 42.3% management, 7.7% professional, 9.0% services, 12.8% sales, 10.3% farming, 0.0% construction, 17.9% production (2000).
Income: Per capita income: $15,753 (2000); Median household income: $35,000 (2000); Poverty rate: 179.1% (2000).
Education: Percent of population age 25 and over with: High school diploma (including GED) or higher: 71.3% (2000); Bachelor's degree or higher: 8.9% (2000).
Housing: Homeownership rate: 57.1% (2000); Median home value: $82,000 (2000); Median contract rent: $175 per month (2000); Median year structure built: 1965 (2000).
Transportation: Commute to work: 80.8% car, 0.0% public transportation, 6.4% walk, 12.8% work from home (2000); Travel time to work: 58.8% less than 15 minutes, 20.6% 15 to 30 minutes, 14.7% 30 to 45 minutes, 2.9% 45 to 60 minutes, 2.9% 60 minutes or more (2000)

Mason County

Located in central Texas, on the Edwards Plateau; drained by the San Saba and Llano Rivers. Covers a land area of 932.07 square miles, a water area of 0.11 square miles, and is located in the Central Time Zone at 30.75° N. Lat., 99.21° W. Long. The county was founded in 1858. County seat is Mason.
Population: 3,423 (1990); 3,738 (2000); 3,805 (2010); 3,829 (2015 projected); Race: 91.0% White, 0.1% Black, 0.1% Asian, 8.9% Other, 23.0% Hispanic of any race (2010); Density: 4.1 persons per square mile (2010); Average household size: 2.28 (2010); Median age: 45.8 (2010); Males per 100 females: 94.7 (2010).
Religion: Five largest groups: 21.5% Catholic Church, 21.1% The United Methodist Church, 16.5% Southern Baptist Convention, 12.8% Evangelical Lutheran Church in America, 3.8% Churches of Christ (2000).
Economy: Unemployment rate: 5.6% (June 2011); Total civilian labor force: 2,369 (June 2011); Leading industries: 25.0% health care and social assistance; 18.7% retail trade; 14.2% accommodation & food services (2009); Farms: 647 totaling 536,402 acres (2007); Companies that employ 500 or more persons: 0 (2009); Companies that employ 100 to 499 persons: 0 (2009); Companies that employ less than 100 persons: 141 (2009); Black-owned businesses: n/a (2007); Hispanic-owned businesses: n/a (2007); Asian-owned businesses: n/a (2007); Women-owned businesses: n/a (2007); Retail sales per capita: $4,821 (2010).
Single-family building permits issued: 9 (2010); Multi-family building permits issued: 0 (2010).
Income: Per capita income: $27,754 (2010); Median household income: $45,966 (2010); Average household income: $63,754 (2010); Percent of households with income of $100,000 or more: 15.8% (2010); Poverty rate: 16.5% (2009); Bankruptcy rate: 0.72% (2010).
Taxes: Total county taxes per capita: $370 (2007); County property taxes per capita: $295 (2007).
Education: Percent of population age 25 and over with: High school diploma (including GED) or higher: 82.1% (2010); Bachelor's degree or higher: 20.3% (2010); Master's degree or higher: 4.9% (2010).
Housing: Homeownership rate: 78.5% (2010); Median home value: $99,840 (2010); Median contract rent: $318 per month (2005-2009 5-year est.); Median year structure built: 1951 (2005-2009 5-year est.)
Health: Birth rate: 95.8 per 10,000 population (2009); Death rate: 111.0 per 10,000 population (2009); Age-adjusted cancer mortality rate: 197.0 (Unreliable) deaths per 100,000 population (2007); Number of physicians: 0.0 per 10,000 population (2008); Hospital beds: 0.0 per 10,000 population (2007); Hospital admissions: 0.0 per 10,000 population (2007).
Elections: 2008 Presidential election results: 25.7% Obama, 72.8% McCain, 0.0% Nader
Additional Information Contacts
Mason County Government . . . . (325) 347-5556
    http://www.co.mason.tx.us/ips/cms

Mason County Chamber of Commerce . . . . (325) 347-5758
http://www.masontxcoc.com

Mason County Communities

FREDONIA (unincorporated postal area, zip code 76842). Covers a land area of 82.974 square miles and a water area of 0 square miles. Located at 30.92° N. Lat; 99.09° W. Long. Elevation is 1,654 feet.
Population: 165 (2000); Race: 87.0% White, 0.0% Black, 0.0% Asian, 13.0% Other, 39.8% Hispanic of any race (2000); Density: 2.0 persons per square mile (2000); Age: 16.1% under 18, 46.0% over 64 (2000); Marriage status: 10.6% never married, 69.7% now married, 10.6% widowed, 9.2% divorced (2000); Foreign born: 44.1% (2000); Ancestry (includes multiple ancestries): 20.5% English, 18.0% German, 5.6% Irish, 5.6% American (2000).
Economy: Employment by occupation: 57.4% management, 0.0% professional, 14.9% services, 0.0% sales, 12.8% farming, 14.9% construction, 0.0% production (2000).
Income: Per capita income: $35,822 (2000); Median household income: $17,115 (2000); Poverty rate: 179.1% (2000).
Education: Percent of population age 25 and over with: High school diploma (including GED) or higher: 46.7% (2000); Bachelor's degree or higher: 16.3% (2000).
Housing: Homeownership rate: 91.8% (2000); Median home value: $37,100 (2000); Median contract rent: n/a per month (2000); Median year structure built: before 1940 (2000).
Transportation: Commute to work: 47.4% car, 0.0% public transportation, 0.0% walk, 31.6% work from home (2000); Travel time to work: 23.1% less than 15 minutes, 0.0% 15 to 30 minutes, 50.0% 30 to 45 minutes, 0.0% 45 to 60 minutes, 26.9% 60 minutes or more (2000)

MASON (city). County seat. Covers a land area of 3.681 square miles and a water area of 0 square miles. Located at 30.74° N. Lat; 99.23° W. Long. Elevation is 1,539 feet.
History: Site of historic Fort Mason, foundations of 23 buildings. Settled by Germans before Civil War. Incorporated after 1940.
Population: 2,053 (1990); 2,134 (2000); 2,165 (2010); 2,175 (2015 projected); Race: 87.6% White, 0.1% Black, 0.0% Asian, 12.2% Other, 32.4% Hispanic of any race (2010); Density: 588.1 persons per square mile (2010); Average household size: 2.27 (2010); Median age: 42.5 (2010); Males per 100 females: 90.6 (2010); Marriage status: 29.1% never married, 48.2% now married, 8.0% widowed, 14.7% divorced (2005-2009 5-year est.); Foreign born: 3.0% (2005-2009 5-year est.); Ancestry (includes multiple ancestries): 47.9% German, 15.9% Irish, 11.7% English, 9.8% American, 4.6% French (2005-2009 5-year est.).
Economy: Single-family building permits issued: 9 (2010); Multi-family building permits issued: 0 (2010); Employment by occupation: 11.4% management, 15.2% professional, 14.4% services, 38.5% sales, 8.8% farming, 10.9% construction, 0.8% production (2005-2009 5-year est.).
Income: Per capita income: $26,010 (2010); Median household income: $43,396 (2010); Average household income: $59,764 (2010); Percent of households with income of $100,000 or more: 14.1% (2010); Poverty rate: 19.5% (2005-2009 5-year est.).
Taxes: Total city taxes per capita: $152 (2007); City property taxes per capita: $56 (2007).
Education: Percent of population age 25 and over with: High school diploma (including GED) or higher: 77.8% (2010); Bachelor's degree or higher: 16.3% (2010); Master's degree or higher: 4.6% (2010).
School District(s)
Mason ISD (PK-12)
    2009-10 Enrollment: 681 . . . . (325) 347-1144
Housing: Homeownership rate: 76.4% (2010); Median home value: $78,073 (2010); Median contract rent: $345 per month (2005-2009 5-year est.); Median year structure built: 1950 (2005-2009 5-year est.).
Newspapers: Mason County News (Community news; Circulation 2,850)
Transportation: Commute to work: 81.3% car, 0.0% public transportation, 7.7% walk, 4.5% work from home (2005-2009 5-year est.); Travel time to work: 73.5% less than 15 minutes, 7.2% 15 to 30 minutes, 10.5% 30 to 45 minutes, 5.6% 45 to 60 minutes, 3.2% 60 minutes or more (2005-2009 5-year est.)
Additional Information Contacts
Mason County Chamber of Commerce . . . . (325) 347-5758
    http://www.masontxcoc.com

PONTOTOC (unincorporated postal area, zip code 76869). Covers a land area of 94.422 square miles and a water area of 0 square miles. Located at 30.91° N. Lat; 98.98° W. Long. Elevation is 1,562 feet.
Population: 207 (2000); Race: 92.3% White, 0.0% Black, 3.6% Asian, 4.1% Other, 10.7% Hispanic of any race (2000); Density: 2.2 persons per square mile (2000); Age: 19.0% under 18, 34.5% over 64 (2000); Marriage status: 2.9% never married, 77.9% now married, 8.6% widowed, 10.7% divorced (2000); Foreign born: 14.3% (2000); Ancestry (includes multiple ancestries): 46.4% German, 13.1% English, 3.6% Welsh, 3.6% Scotch-Irish (2000).
Economy: Employment by occupation: 29.5% management, 0.0% professional, 8.2% services, 8.2% sales, 31.1% farming, 8.2% construction, 14.8% production (2000).
Income: Per capita income: $16,674 (2000); Median household income: $24,821 (2000); Poverty rate: 179.1% (2000).
Education: Percent of population age 25 and over with: High school diploma (including GED) or higher: 77.9% (2000); Bachelor's degree or higher: 22.8% (2000).
Housing: Homeownership rate: 97.3% (2000); Median home value: $38,300 (2000); Median contract rent: n/a per month (2000); Median year structure built: 1954 (2000).
Transportation: Commute to work: 80.3% car, 0.0% public transportation, 0.0% walk, 16.4% work from home (2000); Travel time to work: 43.1% less than 15 minutes, 41.2% 15 to 30 minutes, 11.8% 30 to 45 minutes, 3.9% 45 to 60 minutes, 0.0% 60 minutes or more (2000)

Matagorda County

Located in south Texas, on Matagorda Bay of the Gulf of Mexico; drained by the Colorado River. Covers a land area of 1,114.46 square miles, a water area of 497.73 square miles, and is located in the Central Time Zone at 28.86° N. Lat., 96.00° W. Long. The county was founded in 1836. County seat is Bay City.

Matagorda County is part of the Bay City, TX Micropolitan Statistical Area. The entire metro area includes: Matagorda County, TX

Weather Station: Bay City Waterworks   Elevation: 51 feet

	Jan	Feb	Mar	Apr	May	Jun	Jul	Aug	Sep	Oct	Nov	Dec
High	64	67	73	79	84	90	92	92	89	82	74	66
Low	45	48	54	61	68	73	75	75	70	63	54	46
Precip	4.0	2.9	3.2	3.1	4.9	4.7	4.5	3.8	4.8	6.7	4.1	3.5
Snow	0.0	0.0	0.0	0.0	0.0	0.0	0.0	0.0	0.0	0.0	0.0	0.0

High and Low temperatures in degrees Fahrenheit; Precipitation and Snow in inches

Weather Station: Matagorda 2   Elevation: 9 feet

	Jan	Feb	Mar	Apr	May	Jun	Jul	Aug	Sep	Oct	Nov	Dec
High	64	66	72	77	83	88	90	91	89	82	74	66
Low	46	49	55	62	70	76	77	77	72	64	56	47
Precip	3.8	2.6	2.7	2.5	4.1	4.9	4.0	2.8	4.8	4.4	3.9	2.6
Snow	tr	tr	tr	0.0	0.0	0.0	0.0	0.0	0.0	0.0	tr	0.2

High and Low temperatures in degrees Fahrenheit; Precipitation and Snow in inches

Weather Station: Palacios Municipal Arpt   Elevation: 16 feet

	Jan	Feb	Mar	Apr	May	Jun	Jul	Aug	Sep	Oct	Nov	Dec
High	64	67	72	78	84	89	90	91	89	82	73	65
Low	45	49	54	62	70	75	77	77	71	63	54	47
Precip	3.3	2.2	3.1	2.6	4.2	4.4	4.5	3.0	5.0	5.0	3.6	2.8
Snow	na	na	na	na	na	na	na	na	na	na	na	na

High and Low temperatures in degrees Fahrenheit; Precipitation and Snow in inches

Population: 36,928 (1990); 37,957 (2000); 37,214 (2010); 36,786 (2015 projected); Race: 65.8% White, 11.8% Black, 2.0% Asian, 20.4% Other, 37.6% Hispanic of any race (2010); Density: 33.4 persons per square mile (2010); Average household size: 2.65 (2010); Median age: 36.3 (2010); Males per 100 females: 99.8 (2010).
Religion: Five largest groups: 23.9% Southern Baptist Convention, 23.4% Catholic Church, 5.3% The United Methodist Church, 1.9% Presbyterian Church (U.S.A.), 1.7% Churches of Christ (2000).
Economy: Unemployment rate: 12.6% (June 2011); Total civilian labor force: 18,178 (June 2011); Leading industries: 18.1% retail trade; 14.9% health care and social assistance; 13.4% accommodation & food services (2009); Farms: 903 totaling 577,594 acres (2007); Companies that employ 500 or more persons: 1 (2009); Companies that employ 100 to 499 persons: 7 (2009); Companies that employ less than 100 persons: 721 (2009); Black-owned businesses: n/a (2007); Hispanic-owned businesses:

n/a (2007); Asian-owned businesses: n/a (2007); Women-owned businesses: 681 (2007); Retail sales per capita: $7,628 (2010). Single-family building permits issued: 68 (2010); Multi-family building permits issued: 0 (2010).
Income: Per capita income: $19,613 (2010); Median household income: $39,420 (2010); Average household income: $52,350 (2010); Percent of households with income of $100,000 or more: 12.6% (2010); Poverty rate: 21.2% (2009); Bankruptcy rate: 1.69% (2010).
Taxes: Total county taxes per capita: $242 (2007); County property taxes per capita: $221 (2007).
Education: Percent of population age 25 and over with: High school diploma (including GED) or higher: 74.3% (2010); Bachelor's degree or higher: 14.9% (2010); Master's degree or higher: 3.8% (2010).
Housing: Homeownership rate: 70.7% (2010); Median home value: $72,910 (2010); Median contract rent: $342 per month (2005-2009 5-year est.); Median year structure built: 1973 (2005-2009 5-year est.)
Health: Birth rate: 150.6 per 10,000 population (2009); Death rate: 91.9 per 10,000 population (2009); Age-adjusted cancer mortality rate: 214.5 deaths per 100,000 population (2007); Number of physicians: 10.8 per 10,000 population (2008); Hospital beds: 19.1 per 10,000 population (2007); Hospital admissions: 640.0 per 10,000 population (2007).
Elections: 2008 Presidential election results: 35.9% Obama, 63.3% McCain, 0.0% Nader
Additional Information Contacts
Matagorda County Government . . . . (979) 244-7680
   http://www.co.matagorda.tx.us/ips/cms
Bay City Chamber of Commerce . . . . (979) 245-8333
   http://baycitychamber.org
City of Bay City . . . . (979) 245-5311
   http://www.cityofbaycity.org
City of Palacios . . . . (361) 972-3605
   http://www.cityofpalacios.org
Palacios Chamber of Commerce . . . . (361) 972-2615
   http://www.palacioschamber.com

Matagorda County Communities

BAY CITY (city). County seat. Covers a land area of 8.500 square miles and a water area of 0.011 square miles. Located at 28.98° N. Lat; 95.96° W. Long. Elevation is 52 feet.
History: Bay City's economy developed around the oil and natural gas found here. When the Port of Bay City was opened, it was connected by a barge channel up the Colorado River from the Gulf of Mexico.
Population: 18,682 (1990); 18,667 (2000); 17,815 (2010); 17,436 (2015 projected); Race: 59.6% White, 17.0% Black, 0.6% Asian, 22.8% Other, 40.6% Hispanic of any race (2010); Density: 2,095.8 persons per square mile (2010); Average household size: 2.60 (2010); Median age: 34.6 (2010); Males per 100 females: 96.6 (2010); Marriage status: 28.7% never married, 54.9% now married, 5.9% widowed, 10.5% divorced (2005-2009 5-year est.); Foreign born: 12.0% (2005-2009 5-year est.); Ancestry (includes multiple ancestries): 11.5% German, 6.0% Irish, 5.5% English, 4.8% Czech, 4.7% American (2005-2009 5-year est.).
Economy: Single-family building permits issued: 16 (2010); Multi-family building permits issued: 0 (2010); Employment by occupation: 8.7% management, 15.9% professional, 20.7% services, 20.5% sales, 3.0% farming, 15.9% construction, 15.2% production (2005-2009 5-year est.).
Income: Per capita income: $19,071 (2010); Median household income: $37,349 (2010); Average household income: $50,311 (2010); Percent of households with income of $100,000 or more: 11.6% (2010); Poverty rate: 31.1% (2005-2009 5-year est.).
Taxes: Total city taxes per capita: $388 (2007); City property taxes per capita: $133 (2007).
Education: Percent of population age 25 and over with: High school diploma (including GED) or higher: 74.0% (2010); Bachelor's degree or higher: 14.9% (2010); Master's degree or higher: 3.9% (2010).
School District(s)
Bay City ISD (PK-12)
   2009-10 Enrollment: 3,793 . . . . (979) 245-5766
Palacios ISD (PK-12)
   2009-10 Enrollment: 1,509 . . . . (361) 972-5491
Van Vleck ISD (PK-12)
   2009-10 Enrollment: 973 . . . . (979) 245-8518
Housing: Homeownership rate: 57.4% (2010); Median home value: $77,607 (2010); Median contract rent: $349 per month (2005-2009 5-year est.); Median year structure built: 1972 (2005-2009 5-year est.).

Hospitals: Matagorda General Hospital (66 beds)
Safety: Violent crime rate: 36.5 per 10,000 population; Property crime rate: 506.4 per 10,000 population (2009).
Newspapers: The Bay City Tribune (Local news; Circulation 6,000); Victoria Advocate - Bay City Bureau (Local news)
Transportation: Commute to work: 91.3% car, 0.0% public transportation, 4.9% walk, 2.9% work from home (2005-2009 5-year est.); Travel time to work: 50.5% less than 15 minutes, 25.3% 15 to 30 minutes, 12.1% 30 to 45 minutes, 5.3% 45 to 60 minutes, 6.7% 60 minutes or more (2005-2009 5-year est.)
Additional Information Contacts
Bay City Chamber of Commerce . . . . (979) 245-8333
   http://baycitychamber.org
City of Bay City . . . . (979) 245-5311
   http://www.cityofbaycity.org

BLESSING (CDP). Covers a land area of 2.032 square miles and a water area of 0 square miles. Located at 28.87° N. Lat; 96.22° W. Long. Elevation is 39 feet.
Population: 761 (1990); 861 (2000); 931 (2010); 965 (2015 projected); Race: 81.2% White, 2.5% Black, 0.0% Asian, 16.3% Other, 43.8% Hispanic of any race (2010); Density: 458.2 persons per square mile (2010); Average household size: 2.81 (2010); Median age: 34.9 (2010); Males per 100 females: 106.4 (2010); Marriage status: 25.8% never married, 61.5% now married, 3.2% widowed, 9.5% divorced (2005-2009 5-year est.); Foreign born: 19.4% (2005-2009 5-year est.); Ancestry (includes multiple ancestries): 10.9% Irish, 10.9% German, 3.6% English, 2.1% Swedish, 2.0% Welsh (2005-2009 5-year est.).
Economy: Employment by occupation: 12.8% management, 11.2% professional, 12.0% services, 36.4% sales, 5.9% farming, 0.0% construction, 21.7% production (2005-2009 5-year est.).
Income: Per capita income: $18,213 (2010); Median household income: $35,174 (2010); Average household income: $51,835 (2010); Percent of households with income of $100,000 or more: 8.8% (2010); Poverty rate: 40.2% (2005-2009 5-year est.).
Education: Percent of population age 25 and over with: High school diploma (including GED) or higher: 76.1% (2010); Bachelor's degree or higher: 14.8% (2010); Master's degree or higher: 5.4% (2010).
School District(s)
Tidehaven ISD (PK-12)
   2009-10 Enrollment: 808 . . . . (361) 588-6321
Housing: Homeownership rate: 82.2% (2010); Median home value: $66,462 (2010); Median contract rent: n/a per month (2005-2009 5-year est.); Median year structure built: 1975 (2005-2009 5-year est.).
Transportation: Commute to work: 87.2% car, 0.0% public transportation, 5.9% walk, 7.0% work from home (2005-2009 5-year est.); Travel time to work: 66.1% less than 15 minutes, 3.4% 15 to 30 minutes, 18.1% 30 to 45 minutes, 0.0% 45 to 60 minutes, 12.4% 60 minutes or more (2005-2009 5-year est.)

CEDAR LANE (unincorporated postal area, zip code 77415). Covers a land area of 13.233 square miles and a water area of 0.050 square miles. Located at 28.81° N. Lat; 95.84° W. Long. Elevation is 26 feet.
Population: 209 (2000); Race: 69.9% White, 20.5% Black, 0.0% Asian, 9.6% Other, 9.7% Hispanic of any race (2000); Density: 15.8 persons per square mile (2000); Age: 16.5% under 18, 30.7% over 64 (2000); Marriage status: 4.1% never married, 76.2% now married, 15.0% widowed, 4.8% divorced (2000); Foreign born: 0.0% (2000); Ancestry (includes multiple ancestries): 4.5% Irish, 4.5% German, 4.0% American (2000).
Economy: Employment by occupation: 0.0% management, 9.8% professional, 13.7% services, 15.7% sales, 9.8% farming, 41.2% construction, 9.8% production (2000).
Income: Per capita income: $12,105 (2000); Median household income: $37,917 (2000); Poverty rate: 179.1% (2000).
Education: Percent of population age 25 and over with: High school diploma (including GED) or higher: 78.2% (2000); Bachelor's degree or higher: 3.4% (2000).
Housing: Homeownership rate: 86.8% (2000); Median home value: $85,000 (2000); Median contract rent: $325 per month (2000); Median year structure built: 1970 (2000).
Transportation: Commute to work: 100.0% car, 0.0% public transportation, 0.0% walk, 0.0% work from home (2000); Travel time to work: 0.0% less than 15 minutes, 10.9% 15 to 30 minutes, 41.3% 30 to 45 minutes, 0.0% 45 to 60 minutes, 47.8% 60 minutes or more (2000)

COLLEGEPORT (unincorporated postal area, zip code 77428). Covers a land area of 14.311 square miles and a water area of 0 square miles. Located at 28.75° N. Lat; 95.94° W. Long. Elevation is 13 feet.
Population: 77 (2000); Race: 100.0% White, 0.0% Black, 0.0% Asian, 0.0% Other, 0.0% Hispanic of any race (2000); Density: 5.4 persons per square mile (2000); Age: 0.0% under 18, 46.5% over 64 (2000); Marriage status: 0.0% never married, 67.4% now married, 32.6% widowed, 0.0% divorced (2000); Foreign born: 0.0% (2000); Ancestry (includes multiple ancestries): 18.6% Swedish, 14.0% English, 14.0% Scotch-Irish, 14.0% Irish (2000).
Economy: Employment by occupation: 25.0% management, 25.0% professional, 50.0% services, 0.0% sales, 0.0% farming, 0.0% construction, 0.0% production (2000).
Income: Per capita income: $45,193 (2000); Median household income: $63,750 (2000); Poverty rate: 179.1% (2000).
Education: Percent of population age 25 and over with: High school diploma (including GED) or higher: 100.0% (2000); Bachelor's degree or higher: 58.1% (2000).
Housing: Homeownership rate: 100.0% (2000); Median home value: $65,000 (2000); Median contract rent: n/a per month (2000); Median year structure built: 1971 (2000).
Transportation: Commute to work: 100.0% car, 0.0% public transportation, 0.0% walk, 0.0% work from home (2000); Travel time to work: 50.0% less than 15 minutes, 50.0% 15 to 30 minutes, 0.0% 30 to 45 minutes, 0.0% 45 to 60 minutes, 0.0% 60 minutes or more (2000)

ELMATON (unincorporated postal area, zip code 77440). Covers a land area of 15.795 square miles and a water area of 0 square miles. Located at 28.88° N. Lat; 96.14° W. Long. Elevation is 36 feet.
Population: 194 (2000); Race: 97.3% White, 2.7% Black, 0.0% Asian, 0.0% Other, 10.0% Hispanic of any race (2000); Density: 12.3 persons per square mile (2000); Age: 19.9% under 18, 20.4% over 64 (2000); Marriage status: 18.9% never married, 69.7% now married, 11.4% widowed, 0.0% divorced (2000); Foreign born: 7.7% (2000); Ancestry (includes multiple ancestries): 33.0% Czech, 8.6% Irish, 8.6% German, 7.7% French (2000).
Economy: Employment by occupation: 19.6% management, 15.2% professional, 9.8% services, 10.9% sales, 22.8% farming, 15.2% construction, 6.5% production (2000).
Income: Per capita income: $20,043 (2000); Median household income: $38,472 (2000); Poverty rate: 179.1% (2000).
Education: Percent of population age 25 and over with: High school diploma (including GED) or higher: 72.5% (2000); Bachelor's degree or higher: 6.0% (2000).
Housing: Homeownership rate: 92.8% (2000); Median home value: $68,100 (2000); Median contract rent: n/a per month (2000); Median year structure built: 1969 (2000).
Transportation: Commute to work: 80.4% car, 0.0% public transportation, 0.0% walk, 19.6% work from home (2000); Travel time to work: 35.1% less than 15 minutes, 37.8% 15 to 30 minutes, 27.0% 30 to 45 minutes, 0.0% 45 to 60 minutes, 0.0% 60 minutes or more (2000)

MARKHAM (CDP). Covers a land area of 2.288 square miles and a water area of 0 square miles. Located at 28.96° N. Lat; 96.06° W. Long. Elevation is 52 feet.
Population: 1,221 (1990); 1,138 (2000); 1,167 (2010); 1,179 (2015 projected); Race: 85.8% White, 6.5% Black, 0.1% Asian, 7.6% Other, 43.6% Hispanic of any race (2010); Density: 510.1 persons per square mile (2010); Average household size: 2.88 (2010); Median age: 35.5 (2010); Males per 100 females: 95.5 (2010); Marriage status: 13.1% never married, 75.4% now married, 5.3% widowed, 6.2% divorced (2005-2009 5-year est.); Foreign born: 5.5% (2005-2009 5-year est.); Ancestry (includes multiple ancestries): 15.1% Scottish, 10.7% German, 5.2% English, 5.0% Irish, 4.3% Italian (2005-2009 5-year est.).
Economy: Employment by occupation: 7.0% management, 21.0% professional, 19.6% services, 41.0% sales, 0.0% farming, 7.7% construction, 3.7% production (2005-2009 5-year est.).
Income: Per capita income: $25,415 (2010); Median household income: $63,949 (2010); Average household income: $73,025 (2010); Percent of households with income of $100,000 or more: 24.0% (2010); Poverty rate: 16.9% (2005-2009 5-year est.).
Education: Percent of population age 25 and over with: High school diploma (including GED) or higher: 77.7% (2010); Bachelor's degree or higher: 5.2% (2010); Master's degree or higher: 0.1% (2010).

School District(s)
Tidehaven ISD (PK-12)
   2009-10 Enrollment: 808 . . . . (361) 588-6321
Housing: Homeownership rate: 80.5% (2010); Median home value: $61,798 (2010); Median contract rent: $285 per month (2005-2009 5-year est.); Median year structure built: 1968 (2005-2009 5-year est.).
Transportation: Commute to work: 100.0% car, 0.0% public transportation, 0.0% walk, 0.0% work from home (2005-2009 5-year est.); Travel time to work: 26.9% less than 15 minutes, 51.7% 15 to 30 minutes, 0.0% 30 to 45 minutes, 0.0% 45 to 60 minutes, 21.4% 60 minutes or more (2005-2009 5-year est.)

MATAGORDA (unincorporated postal area, zip code 77457). Covers a land area of 23.639 square miles and a water area of 1.002 square miles. Located at 28.67° N. Lat; 95.96° W. Long. Elevation is 3 feet.
History: Matagorda was designated as a port of entry by the Mexican government in 1831, after the town was settled in 1825. Near Matagorda lived Samuel A. Maverick, a pioneer whose name, through little fault of his, came to be synonymous with unbranded cattle.
Population: 665 (2000); Race: 92.5% White, 0.3% Black, 0.3% Asian, 6.9% Other, 13.4% Hispanic of any race (2000); Density: 28.1 persons per square mile (2000); Age: 12.7% under 18, 22.8% over 64 (2000); Marriage status: 14.4% never married, 57.8% now married, 15.1% widowed, 12.7% divorced (2000); Foreign born: 7.8% (2000); Ancestry (includes multiple ancestries): 20.5% German, 11.8% English, 10.4% Irish, 9.3% American (2000).
Economy: Employment by occupation: 11.6% management, 13.3% professional, 18.1% services, 20.5% sales, 8.0% farming, 17.7% construction, 10.8% production (2000).
Income: Per capita income: $17,550 (2000); Median household income: $24,671 (2000); Poverty rate: 179.1% (2000).
Education: Percent of population age 25 and over with: High school diploma (including GED) or higher: 80.3% (2000); Bachelor's degree or higher: 16.1% (2000).

School District(s)
Matagorda ISD (PK-06)
   2009-10 Enrollment: 99 . . . . (979) 863-7693
Housing: Homeownership rate: 83.2% (2000); Median home value: $61,600 (2000); Median contract rent: $318 per month (2000); Median year structure built: 1976 (2000).
Transportation: Commute to work: 89.3% car, 0.0% public transportation, 4.5% walk, 0.8% work from home (2000); Travel time to work: 36.5% less than 15 minutes, 25.3% 15 to 30 minutes, 22.4% 30 to 45 minutes, 2.9% 45 to 60 minutes, 12.9% 60 minutes or more (2000)

MIDFIELD (unincorporated postal area, zip code 77458). Covers a land area of 12.163 square miles and a water area of 0.155 square miles. Located at 28.93° N. Lat; 96.21° W. Long. Elevation is 46 feet.
Population: 210 (2000); Race: 69.3% White, 0.0% Black, 0.0% Asian, 30.7% Other, 34.1% Hispanic of any race (2000); Density: 17.3 persons per square mile (2000); Age: 31.2% under 18, 17.6% over 64 (2000); Marriage status: 4.7% never married, 79.1% now married, 4.1% widowed, 12.2% divorced (2000); Foreign born: 6.8% (2000); Ancestry (includes multiple ancestries): 17.6% German, 16.1% Czech, 10.2% American, 7.8% Scotch-Irish (2000).
Economy: Employment by occupation: 21.3% management, 0.0% professional, 17.5% services, 30.0% sales, 8.8% farming, 22.5% construction, 0.0% production (2000).
Income: Per capita income: $32,557 (2000); Median household income: $33,750 (2000); Poverty rate: 179.1% (2000).
Education: Percent of population age 25 and over with: High school diploma (including GED) or higher: 50.4% (2000); Bachelor's degree or higher: 5.0% (2000).
Housing: Homeownership rate: 85.0% (2000); Median home value: $44,400 (2000); Median contract rent: $275 per month (2000); Median year structure built: 1969 (2000).
Transportation: Commute to work: 100.0% car, 0.0% public transportation, 0.0% walk, 0.0% work from home (2000); Travel time to work: 0.0% less than 15 minutes, 22.5% 15 to 30 minutes, 61.3% 30 to 45 minutes, 10.0% 45 to 60 minutes, 6.3% 60 minutes or more (2000)

PALACIOS (city). Covers a land area of 5.045 square miles and a water area of 0.230 square miles. Located at 28.70° N. Lat; 96.21° W. Long. Elevation is 13 feet.

History: Palacios was founded in the 1820's, and became the center of a large fishing industry.
Population: 4,551 (1990); 5,153 (2000); 5,341 (2010); 5,402 (2015 projected); Race: 54.6% White, 4.4% Black, 7.1% Asian, 33.9% Other, 59.6% Hispanic of any race (2010); Density: 1,058.7 persons per square mile (2010); Average household size: 2.99 (2010); Median age: 31.7 (2010); Males per 100 females: 101.7 (2010); Marriage status: 20.4% never married, 63.6% now married, 5.6% widowed, 10.5% divorced (2005-2009 5-year est.); Foreign born: 30.6% (2005-2009 5-year est.); Ancestry (includes multiple ancestries): 5.8% English, 4.7% Irish, 3.4% German, 2.1% Scotch-Irish, 2.1% Czech (2005-2009 5-year est.).
Economy: Single-family building permits issued: 2 (2010); Multi-family building permits issued: 0 (2010); Employment by occupation: 5.4% management, 9.1% professional, 30.2% services, 13.6% sales, 6.5% farming, 11.4% construction, 23.8% production (2005-2009 5-year est.).
Income: Per capita income: $16,537 (2010); Median household income: $34,615 (2010); Average household income: $49,439 (2010); Percent of households with income of $100,000 or more: 12.3% (2010); Poverty rate: 18.9% (2005-2009 5-year est.).
Taxes: Total city taxes per capita: $292 (2007); City property taxes per capita: $179 (2007).
Education: Percent of population age 25 and over with: High school diploma (including GED) or higher: 63.3% (2010); Bachelor's degree or higher: 16.7% (2010); Master's degree or higher: 4.2% (2010).

School District(s)
Palacios ISD (PK-12)
    2009-10 Enrollment: 1,509 . . . . (361) 972-5491
Housing: Homeownership rate: 74.1% (2010); Median home value: $64,795 (2010); Median contract rent: $266 per month (2005-2009 5-year est.); Median year structure built: 1971 (2005-2009 5-year est.).
Safety: Violent crime rate: 13.8 per 10,000 population; Property crime rate: 371.7 per 10,000 population (2009).
Newspapers: Palacios Beacon (Community news; Circulation 2,200)
Transportation: Commute to work: 92.0% car, 0.0% public transportation, 5.1% walk, 2.1% work from home (2005-2009 5-year est.); Travel time to work: 54.9% less than 15 minutes, 18.8% 15 to 30 minutes, 17.4% 30 to 45 minutes, 5.4% 45 to 60 minutes, 3.5% 60 minutes or more (2005-2009 5-year est.)
Airports: Palacios Municipal (general aviation)
Additional Information Contacts
City of Palacios . . . . (361) 972-3605
    http://www.cityofpalacios.org
Palacios Chamber of Commerce . . . . (361) 972-2615
    http://www.palacioschamber.com

PLEDGER (unincorporated postal area, zip code 77468). Covers a land area of 23.665 square miles and a water area of 0.030 square miles. Located at 29.17° N. Lat; 95.89° W. Long. Elevation is 66 feet.
Population: 300 (2000); Race: 65.7% White, 34.3% Black, 0.0% Asian, 0.0% Other, 3.3% Hispanic of any race (2000); Density: 12.7 persons per square mile (2000); Age: 24.3% under 18, 6.7% over 64 (2000); Marriage status: 27.0% never married, 34.0% now married, 21.4% widowed, 17.6% divorced (2000); Foreign born: 0.0% (2000); Ancestry (includes multiple ancestries): 21.4% American, 16.2% Dutch, 3.3% English, 3.3% Czech (2000).
Economy: Employment by occupation: 0.0% management, 25.0% professional, 25.0% services, 8.0% sales, 0.0% farming, 14.3% construction, 27.7% production (2000).
Income: Per capita income: $18,019 (2000); Median household income: $25,375 (2000); Poverty rate: 179.1% (2000).
Education: Percent of population age 25 and over with: High school diploma (including GED) or higher: 81.2% (2000); Bachelor's degree or higher: 6.5% (2000).
Housing: Homeownership rate: 79.2% (2000); Median home value: $57,400 (2000); Median contract rent: $675 per month (2000); Median year structure built: 1965 (2000).
Transportation: Commute to work: 91.1% car, 0.0% public transportation, 0.0% walk, 0.0% work from home (2000); Travel time to work: 15.2% less than 15 minutes, 30.4% 15 to 30 minutes, 42.9% 30 to 45 minutes, 11.6% 45 to 60 minutes, 0.0% 60 minutes or more (2000)

VAN VLECK (CDP). Covers a land area of 3.175 square miles and a water area of 0 square miles. Located at 29.02° N. Lat; 95.89° W. Long. Elevation is 46 feet.

Population: 1,533 (1990); 1,411 (2000); 1,301 (2010); 1,248 (2015 projected); Race: 70.3% White, 17.2% Black, 0.0% Asian, 12.5% Other, 26.9% Hispanic of any race (2010); Density: 409.8 persons per square mile (2010); Average household size: 2.61 (2010); Median age: 39.9 (2010); Males per 100 females: 99.5 (2010); Marriage status: 19.2% never married, 68.8% now married, 5.5% widowed, 6.5% divorced (2005-2009 5-year est.); Foreign born: 0.0% (2005-2009 5-year est.); Ancestry (includes multiple ancestries): 19.2% Irish, 14.8% Italian, 8.8% German, 4.5% French, 1.1% English (2005-2009 5-year est.).
Economy: Employment by occupation: 6.4% management, 4.7% professional, 19.1% services, 14.4% sales, 0.0% farming, 28.7% construction, 26.6% production (2005-2009 5-year est.).
Income: Per capita income: $20,246 (2010); Median household income: $37,614 (2010); Average household income: $52,756 (2010); Percent of households with income of $100,000 or more: 12.0% (2010); Poverty rate: 8.0% (2005-2009 5-year est.).
Education: Percent of population age 25 and over with: High school diploma (including GED) or higher: 75.6% (2010); Bachelor's degree or higher: 6.2% (2010); Master's degree or higher: 0.6% (2010).

School District(s)
Van Vleck ISD (PK-12)
    2009-10 Enrollment: 973 . . . . (979) 245-8518
Housing: Homeownership rate: 85.2% (2010); Median home value: $62,024 (2010); Median contract rent: $717 per month (2005-2009 5-year est.); Median year structure built: 1978 (2005-2009 5-year est.).
Transportation: Commute to work: 97.0% car, 0.0% public transportation, 3.0% walk, 0.0% work from home (2005-2009 5-year est.); Travel time to work: 48.2% less than 15 minutes, 20.8% 15 to 30 minutes, 3.4% 30 to 45 minutes, 0.0% 45 to 60 minutes, 27.6% 60 minutes or more (2005-2009 5-year est.)

WADSWORTH (unincorporated postal area, zip code 77483). Covers a land area of 11.992 square miles and a water area of 0 square miles. Located at 28.83° N. Lat; 95.93° W. Long. Elevation is 36 feet.
Population: 365 (2000); Race: 93.2% White, 0.0% Black, 0.0% Asian, 6.8% Other, 5.3% Hispanic of any race (2000); Density: 30.4 persons per square mile (2000); Age: 36.9% under 18, 9.9% over 64 (2000); Marriage status: 14.5% never married, 73.5% now married, 9.0% widowed, 2.9% divorced (2000); Foreign born: 7.0% (2000); Ancestry (includes multiple ancestries): 35.6% American, 10.5% Irish, 9.7% English, 9.5% German (2000).
Economy: Employment by occupation: 23.7% management, 13.0% professional, 0.0% services, 29.6% sales, 13.6% farming, 3.6% construction, 16.6% production (2000).
Income: Per capita income: $14,561 (2000); Median household income: $23,889 (2000); Poverty rate: 179.1% (2000).
Education: Percent of population age 25 and over with: High school diploma (including GED) or higher: 65.9% (2000); Bachelor's degree or higher: 9.6% (2000).
Housing: Homeownership rate: 92.0% (2000); Median home value: $51,800 (2000); Median contract rent: $175 per month (2000); Median year structure built: 1978 (2000).
Transportation: Commute to work: 100.0% car, 0.0% public transportation, 0.0% walk, 0.0% work from home (2000); Travel time to work: 16.6% less than 15 minutes, 72.2% 15 to 30 minutes, 4.1% 30 to 45 minutes, 4.1% 45 to 60 minutes, 3.0% 60 minutes or more (2000)

Maverick County

Located in southwestern Texas; bounded on the southwest by the Rio Grande and the Mexican border. Covers a land area of 1,280.08 square miles, a water area of 11.66 square miles, and is located in the Central Time Zone at 28.74° N. Lat., 100.38° W. Long. The county was founded in 1856. County seat is Eagle Pass.

Maverick County is part of the Eagle Pass, TX Micropolitan Statistical Area. The entire metro area includes: Maverick County, TX

Weather Station: Eagle Pass										Elevation: 808 feet		
	Jan	Feb	Mar	Apr	May	Jun	Jul	Aug	Sep	Oct	Nov	Dec
High	65	69	77	85	91	96	99	99	93	84	74	65
Low	41	45	52	60	68	74	75	75	70	61	51	42
Precip	0.9	0.9	0.9	1.8	2.6	2.7	1.9	1.5	2.8	2.2	1.1	0.8
Snow	0.7	tr	0.0	0.0	0.0	0.0	0.0	0.0	0.0	tr	0.0	0.0

High and Low temperatures in degrees Fahrenheit; Precipitation and Snow in inches

Population: 36,378 (1990); 47,297 (2000); 53,820 (2010); 56,898 (2015 projected); Race: 70.5% White, 0.6% Black, 0.5% Asian, 28.4% Other, 94.5% Hispanic of any race (2010); Density: 42.0 persons per square mile (2010); Average household size: 3.56 (2010); Median age: 29.7 (2010); Males per 100 females: 91.6 (2010).
Religion: Five largest groups: 27.7% Catholic Church, 2.2% Southern Baptist Convention, 1.2% The Church of Jesus Christ of Latter-day Saints, 0.7% The United Methodist Church, 0.6% Assemblies of God (2000).
Economy: Unemployment rate: 14.8% (June 2011); Total civilian labor force: 23,471 (June 2011); Leading industries: 34.8% health care and social assistance; 23.0% retail trade; 10.5% accommodation & food services (2009); Farms: 312 totaling 473,683 acres (2007); Companies that employ 500 or more persons: 2 (2009); Companies that employ 100 to 499 persons: 14 (2009); Companies that employ less than 100 persons: 754 (2009); Black-owned businesses: n/a (2007); Hispanic-owned businesses: 3,447 (2007); Asian-owned businesses: n/a (2007); Women-owned businesses: n/a (2007); Retail sales per capita: $9,287 (2010). Single-family building permits issued: 156 (2010); Multi-family building permits issued: 49 (2010).
Income: Per capita income: $12,051 (2010); Median household income: $30,280 (2010); Average household income: $42,949 (2010); Percent of households with income of $100,000 or more: 7.3% (2010); Poverty rate: 29.8% (2009); Bankruptcy rate: 0.62% (2010).
Taxes: Total county taxes per capita: $151 (2007); County property taxes per capita: $84 (2007).
Education: Percent of population age 25 and over with: High school diploma (including GED) or higher: 52.5% (2010); Bachelor's degree or higher: 12.7% (2010); Master's degree or higher: 3.3% (2010).
Housing: Homeownership rate: 70.4% (2010); Median home value: $68,459 (2010); Median contract rent: $340 per month (2005-2009 5-year est.); Median year structure built: 1984 (2005-2009 5-year est.)
Health: Birth rate: 208.4 per 10,000 population (2009); Death rate: 59.0 per 10,000 population (2009); Age-adjusted cancer mortality rate: 126.0 deaths per 100,000 population (2007); Number of physicians: 6.8 per 10,000 population (2008); Hospital beds: 19.8 per 10,000 population (2007); Hospital admissions: 997.7 per 10,000 population (2007).
Environment: Air Quality Index: 87.9% good, 12.1% moderate, 0.0% unhealthy for sensitive individuals, 0.0% unhealthy (percent of days in 2008)
Elections: 2008 Presidential election results: 78.2% Obama, 21.2% McCain, 0.0% Nader
Additional Information Contacts
Maverick County Government . . . . (830) 773-3824
  http://www.co.maverick.tx.us/ips/cms
City of Eagle Pass . . . . (830) 773-1111
  http://www.eaglepasstx.us
Eagle Pass Chamber of Commerce . . . . (830) 773-3224
  http://www.eaglepasstexas.com

Maverick County Communities

EAGLE PASS (city). County seat. Covers a land area of 7.396 square miles and a water area of 0.033 square miles. Located at 28.71° N. Lat; 100.48° W. Long. Elevation is 732 feet.
History: The town of El Paso del Aguila (Eagle Pass) was laid out in 1850 near Fort Duncan, which had been established halfway between Old Camp Eagle Pass (from the Mexican War days) and Camp California (a tent city to supply prospectors on their way to California). The name first came from the observation of an eagle that flew back and forth across the Rio Grande daily to its nest on the Mexican side. Eagle Pass was an important cotton port during the Civil War, later becoming a commercial and recreational center and a U.S. Immigration and Customs Station.
Population: 21,650 (1990); 22,413 (2000); 26,193 (2010); 27,776 (2015 projected); Race: 78.8% White, 0.6% Black, 0.9% Asian, 19.7% Other, 94.3% Hispanic of any race (2010); Density: 3,541.4 persons per square mile (2010); Average household size: 3.20 (2010); Median age: 32.8 (2010); Males per 100 females: 89.6 (2010); Marriage status: 27.5% never married, 58.8% now married, 6.9% widowed, 6.8% divorced (2005-2009 5-year est.); Foreign born: 33.0% (2005-2009 5-year est.); Ancestry (includes multiple ancestries): 1.1% German, 1.0% Scotch-Irish, 0.8% American, 0.3% Celtic, 0.3% English (2005-2009 5-year est.).
Economy: Unemployment rate: 15.1% (June 2011); Total civilian labor force: 13,526 (June 2011); Single-family building permits issued: 156 (2010); Multi-family building permits issued: 49 (2010); Employment by occupation: 10.8% management, 19.1% professional, 23.0% services,

26.6% sales, 0.7% farming, 6.6% construction, 13.1% production (2005-2009 5-year est.).
Income: Per capita income: $14,231 (2010); Median household income: $30,179 (2010); Average household income: $45,550 (2010); Percent of households with income of $100,000 or more: 9.4% (2010); Poverty rate: 27.7% (2005-2009 5-year est.).
Taxes: Total city taxes per capita: $298 (2007); City property taxes per capita: $99 (2007).
Education: Percent of population age 25 and over with: High school diploma (including GED) or higher: 60.4% (2010); Bachelor's degree or higher: 18.3% (2010); Master's degree or higher: 5.1% (2010).
School District(s)
Eagle Pass ISD (PK-12)
  2009-10 Enrollment: 14,463 . . . . (830) 773-5181
Vocational/Technical School(s)
SW School of Business and Technical Careers (Private, For-profit)
  Fall 2009 Enrollment: 48 . . . . (830) 626-7007
  2010-11 Tuition: $10,500
Housing: Homeownership rate: 60.6% (2010); Median home value: $86,865 (2010); Median contract rent: $344 per month (2005-2009 5-year est.); Median year structure built: 1979 (2005-2009 5-year est.).
Hospitals: Fort Duncan Regional Medical Center (92 beds)
Safety: Violent crime rate: 15.1 per 10,000 population; Property crime rate: 397.1 per 10,000 population (2009).
Newspapers: Eagle Pass Business Journal (Local news; Circulation 5,000); Eagle Pass Sunday News (Community news; Circulation 5,000); The News Gram (Regional news; Circulation 2,500); News Guide (Community news; Circulation 4,300)
Transportation: Commute to work: 90.6% car, 0.4% public transportation, 2.9% walk, 2.6% work from home (2005-2009 5-year est.); Travel time to work: 66.8% less than 15 minutes, 22.8% 15 to 30 minutes, 3.4% 30 to 45 minutes, 1.2% 45 to 60 minutes, 5.7% 60 minutes or more (2005-2009 5-year est.)
Airports: Comanche Ranch (general aviation)
Additional Information Contacts
City of Eagle Pass . . . . (830) 773-1111
  http://www.eaglepasstx.us
Eagle Pass Chamber of Commerce . . . . (830) 773-3224
  http://www.eaglepasstexas.com

EIDSON ROAD (CDP). Covers a land area of 7.108 square miles and a water area of 0.372 square miles. Located at 28.67° N. Lat; 100.48° W. Long. Elevation is 751 feet.
Population: 5,625 (1990); 9,348 (2000); 10,027 (2010); 10,454 (2015 projected); Race: 64.9% White, 0.8% Black, 0.0% Asian, 34.3% Other, 98.2% Hispanic of any race (2010); Density: 1,410.7 persons per square mile (2010); Average household size: 4.26 (2010); Median age: 26.6 (2010); Males per 100 females: 93.0 (2010); Marriage status: 33.5% never married, 54.4% now married, 3.9% widowed, 8.2% divorced (2005-2009 5-year est.); Foreign born: 37.6% (2005-2009 5-year est.); Ancestry (includes multiple ancestries): 0.2% Irish (2005-2009 5-year est.).
Economy: Employment by occupation: 4.7% management, 4.0% professional, 31.5% services, 23.2% sales, 0.4% farming, 14.2% construction, 21.9% production (2005-2009 5-year est.).
Income: Per capita income: $9,341 (2010); Median household income: $29,143 (2010); Average household income: $39,816 (2010); Percent of households with income of $100,000 or more: 5.1% (2010); Poverty rate: 34.8% (2005-2009 5-year est.).
Education: Percent of population age 25 and over with: High school diploma (including GED) or higher: 34.1% (2010); Bachelor's degree or higher: 5.5% (2010); Master's degree or higher: 1.1% (2010).
Housing: Homeownership rate: 81.1% (2010); Median home value: $51,774 (2010); Median contract rent: $269 per month (2005-2009 5-year est.); Median year structure built: 1987 (2005-2009 5-year est.).
Transportation: Commute to work: 84.2% car, 0.0% public transportation, 3.8% walk, 4.6% work from home (2005-2009 5-year est.); Travel time to work: 46.4% less than 15 minutes, 43.1% 15 to 30 minutes, 3.1% 30 to 45 minutes, 1.0% 45 to 60 minutes, 6.3% 60 minutes or more (2005-2009 5-year est.)

EL INDIO (CDP). Covers a land area of 1.761 square miles and a water area of 0 square miles. Located at 28.51° N. Lat; 100.31° W. Long. Elevation is 735 feet.
Population: 162 (1990); 263 (2000); 263 (2010); 270 (2015 projected); Race: 42.2% White, 0.8% Black, 0.0% Asian, 57.0% Other, 80.6%

Hispanic of any race (2010); Density: 149.3 persons per square mile (2010); Average household size: 3.91 (2010); Median age: 26.1 (2010); Males per 100 females: 93.4 (2010); Marriage status: 37.6% never married, 62.4% now married, 0.0% widowed, 0.0% divorced (2005-2009 5-year est.); Foreign born: 36.2% (2005-2009 5-year est.); Ancestry (includes multiple ancestries): 13.2% Scotch-Irish, 7.5% German (2005-2009 5-year est.).
Economy: Employment by occupation: 26.5% management, 0.0% professional, 24.5% services, 0.0% sales, 0.0% farming, 28.6% construction, 20.4% production (2005-2009 5-year est.).
Income: Per capita income: $9,523 (2010); Median household income: $30,357 (2010); Average household income: $38,918 (2010); Percent of households with income of $100,000 or more: 4.5% (2010); Poverty rate: 70.1% (2005-2009 5-year est.).
Education: Percent of population age 25 and over with: High school diploma (including GED) or higher: 40.0% (2010); Bachelor's degree or higher: 2.2% (2010); Master's degree or higher: 1.5% (2010).
Housing: Homeownership rate: 83.6% (2010); Median home value: $38,889 (2010); Median contract rent: n/a per month (2005-2009 5-year est.); Median year structure built: 1970 (2005-2009 5-year est.).
Transportation: Commute to work: 75.5% car, 0.0% public transportation, 24.5% walk, 0.0% work from home (2005-2009 5-year est.); Travel time to work: 71.4% less than 15 minutes, 28.6% 15 to 30 minutes, 0.0% 30 to 45 minutes, 0.0% 45 to 60 minutes, 0.0% 60 minutes or more (2005-2009 5-year est.)

ELM CREEK (CDP). Covers a land area of 2.824 square miles and a water area of 0 square miles. Located at 28.77° N. Lat; 100.49° W. Long. Elevation is 751 feet.
Population: 1,318 (1990); 1,928 (2000); 2,109 (2010); 2,208 (2015 projected); Race: 56.2% White, 0.1% Black, 0.1% Asian, 43.5% Other, 94.5% Hispanic of any race (2010); Density: 746.9 persons per square mile (2010); Average household size: 3.88 (2010); Median age: 26.3 (2010); Males per 100 females: 89.3 (2010); Marriage status: 25.6% never married, 68.6% now married, 2.5% widowed, 3.3% divorced (2005-2009 5-year est.); Foreign born: 30.1% (2005-2009 5-year est.); Ancestry (includes multiple ancestries): 0.5% Dutch, 0.5% English (2005-2009 5-year est.).
Economy: Employment by occupation: 5.3% management, 5.7% professional, 25.9% services, 39.5% sales, 2.8% farming, 9.8% construction, 11.0% production (2005-2009 5-year est.).
Income: Per capita income: $11,242 (2010); Median household income: $40,086 (2010); Average household income: $43,757 (2010); Percent of households with income of $100,000 or more: 4.2% (2010); Poverty rate: 29.6% (2005-2009 5-year est.).
Education: Percent of population age 25 and over with: High school diploma (including GED) or higher: 57.0% (2010); Bachelor's degree or higher: 6.8% (2010); Master's degree or higher: 2.1% (2010).
Housing: Homeownership rate: 89.0% (2010); Median home value: $45,949 (2010); Median contract rent: $347 per month (2005-2009 5-year est.); Median year structure built: 1988 (2005-2009 5-year est.).
Transportation: Commute to work: 90.0% car, 3.0% public transportation, 3.0% walk, 1.3% work from home (2005-2009 5-year est.); Travel time to work: 29.6% less than 15 minutes, 40.8% 15 to 30 minutes, 13.8% 30 to 45 minutes, 4.9% 45 to 60 minutes, 10.9% 60 minutes or more (2005-2009 5-year est.)

LAS QUINTAS FRONTERIZAS (CDP). Covers a land area of 0.666 square miles and a water area of 0 square miles. Located at 28.69° N. Lat; 100.47° W. Long. Elevation is 745 feet.
Population: 841 (1990); 2,030 (2000); 2,642 (2010); 2,937 (2015 projected); Race: 74.1% White, 0.5% Black, 0.4% Asian, 25.0% Other, 97.0% Hispanic of any race (2010); Density: 3,966.1 persons per square mile (2010); Average household size: 4.02 (2010); Median age: 28.1 (2010); Males per 100 females: 91.9 (2010); Marriage status: 23.9% never married, 60.4% now married, 10.9% widowed, 4.8% divorced (2005-2009 5-year est.); Foreign born: 35.8% (2005-2009 5-year est.); Ancestry (includes multiple ancestries): n/a (2005-2009 5-year est.).
Economy: Employment by occupation: 0.0% management, 18.0% professional, 28.3% services, 22.1% sales, 0.0% farming, 8.6% construction, 23.0% production (2005-2009 5-year est.).
Income: Per capita income: $13,001 (2010); Median household income: $40,566 (2010); Average household income: $52,679 (2010); Percent of households with income of $100,000 or more: 7.9% (2010); Poverty rate: 19.8% (2005-2009 5-year est.).

Education: Percent of population age 25 and over with: High school diploma (including GED) or higher: 61.5% (2010); Bachelor's degree or higher: 13.9% (2010); Master's degree or higher: 2.3% (2010).
Housing: Homeownership rate: 83.1% (2010); Median home value: $59,588 (2010); Median contract rent: $483 per month (2005-2009 5-year est.); Median year structure built: 1982 (2005-2009 5-year est.).
Transportation: Commute to work: 97.2% car, 0.0% public transportation, 0.0% walk, 0.0% work from home (2005-2009 5-year est.); Travel time to work: 59.3% less than 15 minutes, 23.6% 15 to 30 minutes, 3.1% 30 to 45 minutes, 0.0% 45 to 60 minutes, 14.0% 60 minutes or more (2005-2009 5-year est.)

QUEMADO (CDP). Covers a land area of 0.118 square miles and a water area of 0 square miles. Located at 28.94° N. Lat; 100.62° W. Long. Elevation is 784 feet.
Population: 252 (1990); 243 (2000); 194 (2010); 177 (2015 projected); Race: 46.4% White, 3.1% Black, 0.0% Asian, 50.5% Other, 77.3% Hispanic of any race (2010); Density: 1,639.2 persons per square mile (2010); Average household size: 2.85 (2010); Median age: 40.0 (2010); Males per 100 females: 108.6 (2010); Marriage status: 37.7% never married, 62.3% now married, 0.0% widowed, 0.0% divorced (2005-2009 5-year est.); Foreign born: 16.0% (2005-2009 5-year est.); Ancestry (includes multiple ancestries): 32.8% American (2005-2009 5-year est.).
Economy: Employment by occupation: 12.2% management, 0.0% professional, 0.0% services, 24.3% sales, 21.6% farming, 0.0% construction, 41.9% production (2005-2009 5-year est.).
Income: Per capita income: $10,351 (2010); Median household income: $19,118 (2010); Average household income: $28,934 (2010); Percent of households with income of $100,000 or more: 2.9% (2010); Poverty rate: 5.0% (2005-2009 5-year est.).
Education: Percent of population age 25 and over with: High school diploma (including GED) or higher: 59.7% (2010); Bachelor's degree or higher: 17.7% (2010); Master's degree or higher: 4.0% (2010).
School District(s)
Eagle Pass ISD (PK-12)
    2009-10 Enrollment: 14,463 . . . . (830) 773-5181
Housing: Homeownership rate: 79.4% (2010); Median home value: $62,000 (2010); Median contract rent: n/a per month (2005-2009 5-year est.); Median year structure built: 1968 (2005-2009 5-year est.).
Transportation: Commute to work: 100.0% car, 0.0% public transportation, 0.0% walk, 0.0% work from home (2005-2009 5-year est.); Travel time to work: 0.0% less than 15 minutes, 33.8% 15 to 30 minutes, 48.6% 30 to 45 minutes, 0.0% 45 to 60 minutes, 17.6% 60 minutes or more (2005-2009 5-year est.)

RADAR BASE (CDP). Covers a land area of 4.216 square miles and a water area of 0 square miles. Located at 28.85° N. Lat; 100.52° W. Long. Elevation is 869 feet.
Population: 167 (1990); 162 (2000); 125 (2010); 117 (2015 projected); Race: 75.2% White, 0.0% Black, 0.0% Asian, 24.8% Other, 72.0% Hispanic of any race (2010); Density: 29.6 persons per square mile (2010); Average household size: 3.21 (2010); Median age: 29.6 (2010); Males per 100 females: 108.3 (2010); Marriage status: 55.2% never married, 35.1% now married, 0.0% widowed, 9.7% divorced (2005-2009 5-year est.); Foreign born: 11.4% (2005-2009 5-year est.); Ancestry (includes multiple ancestries): 18.3% American (2005-2009 5-year est.).
Economy: Employment by occupation: 42.5% management, 0.0% professional, 0.0% services, 57.5% sales, 0.0% farming, 0.0% construction, 0.0% production (2005-2009 5-year est.).
Income: Per capita income: $10,566 (2010); Median household income: $22,917 (2010); Average household income: $33,718 (2010); Percent of households with income of $100,000 or more: 7.7% (2010); Poverty rate: 81.7% (2005-2009 5-year est.).
Education: Percent of population age 25 and over with: High school diploma (including GED) or higher: 52.9% (2010); Bachelor's degree or higher: 8.8% (2010); Master's degree or higher: 4.4% (2010).
Housing: Homeownership rate: 76.9% (2010); Median home value: $44,000 (2010); Median contract rent: n/a per month (2005-2009 5-year est.); Median year structure built: 1955 (2005-2009 5-year est.).
Transportation: Commute to work: 100.0% car, 0.0% public transportation, 0.0% walk, 0.0% work from home (2005-2009 5-year est.); Travel time to work: 0.0% less than 15 minutes, 85.1% 15 to 30 minutes, 14.9% 30 to 45 minutes, 0.0% 45 to 60 minutes, 0.0% 60 minutes or more (2005-2009 5-year est.)

ROSITA NORTH (CDP). Covers a land area of 3.058 square miles and a water area of 0.010 square miles. Located at 28.65° N. Lat; 100.42° W. Long. Elevation is 810 feet.
Population: 1,483 (1990); 3,400 (2000); 3,988 (2010); 4,265 (2015 projected); Race: 64.3% White, 0.3% Black, 0.0% Asian, 35.4% Other, 97.2% Hispanic of any race (2010); Density: 1,304.0 persons per square mile (2010); Average household size: 4.08 (2010); Median age: 25.4 (2010); Males per 100 females: 96.5 (2010); Marriage status: 28.1% never married, 60.1% now married, 3.0% widowed, 8.9% divorced (2005-2009 5-year est.); Foreign born: 26.0% (2005-2009 5-year est.); Ancestry (includes multiple ancestries): 0.3% Scottish, 0.3% English, 0.2% African (2005-2009 5-year est.).
Economy: Employment by occupation: 5.8% management, 3.9% professional, 23.8% services, 24.6% sales, 1.1% farming, 13.1% construction, 27.6% production (2005-2009 5-year est.).
Income: Per capita income: $7,366 (2010); Median household income: $24,785 (2010); Average household income: $30,077 (2010); Percent of households with income of $100,000 or more: 1.1% (2010); Poverty rate: 28.0% (2005-2009 5-year est.).
Education: Percent of population age 25 and over with: High school diploma (including GED) or higher: 39.1% (2010); Bachelor's degree or higher: 4.7% (2010); Master's degree or higher: 1.7% (2010).
Housing: Homeownership rate: 90.3% (2010); Median home value: $45,343 (2010); Median contract rent: $343 per month (2005-2009 5-year est.); Median year structure built: 1995 (2005-2009 5-year est.).
Transportation: Commute to work: 92.0% car, 0.0% public transportation, 4.2% walk, 1.5% work from home (2005-2009 5-year est.); Travel time to work: 24.0% less than 15 minutes, 61.5% 15 to 30 minutes, 7.1% 30 to 45 minutes, 0.0% 45 to 60 minutes, 7.4% 60 minutes or more (2005-2009 5-year est.)

ROSITA SOUTH (CDP). Covers a land area of 7.759 square miles and a water area of 0.205 square miles. Located at 28.62° N. Lat; 100.43° W. Long. Elevation is 771 feet.
Population: 1,557 (1990); 2,574 (2000); 2,700 (2010); 2,769 (2015 projected); Race: 39.1% White, 0.9% Black, 0.0% Asian, 60.0% Other, 81.3% Hispanic of any race (2010); Density: 348.0 persons per square mile (2010); Average household size: 4.00 (2010); Median age: 24.5 (2010); Males per 100 females: 95.5 (2010); Marriage status: 30.1% never married, 66.0% now married, 2.6% widowed, 1.3% divorced (2005-2009 5-year est.); Foreign born: 33.7% (2005-2009 5-year est.); Ancestry (includes multiple ancestries): n/a (2005-2009 5-year est.).
Economy: Employment by occupation: 5.0% management, 6.8% professional, 27.0% services, 19.6% sales, 4.1% farming, 20.5% construction, 16.8% production (2005-2009 5-year est.).
Income: Per capita income: $8,933 (2010); Median household income: $28,250 (2010); Average household income: $35,873 (2010); Percent of households with income of $100,000 or more: 4.5% (2010); Poverty rate: 46.9% (2005-2009 5-year est.).
Education: Percent of population age 25 and over with: High school diploma (including GED) or higher: 35.1% (2010); Bachelor's degree or higher: 1.4% (2010); Master's degree or higher: 0.5% (2010).
Housing: Homeownership rate: 85.7% (2010); Median home value: $36,083 (2010); Median contract rent: $414 per month (2005-2009 5-year est.); Median year structure built: 1993 (2005-2009 5-year est.).
Transportation: Commute to work: 92.8% car, 0.0% public transportation, 6.3% walk, 0.9% work from home (2005-2009 5-year est.); Travel time to work: 39.6% less than 15 minutes, 50.6% 15 to 30 minutes, 3.7% 30 to 45 minutes, 0.0% 45 to 60 minutes, 6.1% 60 minutes or more (2005-2009 5-year est.)

McCulloch County

Located in central Texas, on the North Edwards Plateau; bounded on the north by the Colorado River; crossed by the Brady Mountains. Covers a land area of 1,069.31 square miles, a water area of 4.05 square miles, and is located in the Central Time Zone at 31.15° N. Lat., 99.34° W. Long. The county was founded in 1856. County seat is Brady.

Weather Station: Brady									Elevation: 1,720 feet			
	Jan	Feb	Mar	Apr	May	Jun	Jul	Aug	Sep	Oct	Nov	Dec
High	59	63	70	79	85	91	95	95	89	80	69	60
Low	34	38	44	51	61	68	70	70	63	54	44	35
Precip	1.1	1.7	2.2	1.9	3.7	3.3	2.1	2.1	3.0	2.7	1.9	1.6
Snow	0.0	0.0	0.0	0.0	0.0	0.0	0.0	0.0	0.0	0.0	tr	0.1

High and Low temperatures in degrees Fahrenheit; Precipitation and Snow in inches

Population: 8,778 (1990); 8,205 (2000); 8,115 (2010); 8,058 (2015 projected); Race: 82.0% White, 2.4% Black, 0.2% Asian, 15.4% Other, 30.5% Hispanic of any race (2010); Density: 7.6 persons per square mile (2010); Average household size: 2.44 (2010); Median age: 40.5 (2010); Males per 100 females: 90.7 (2010).
Religion: Five largest groups: 18.7% Catholic Church, 18.7% Southern Baptist Convention, 9.0% The United Methodist Church, 6.6% Churches of Christ, 4.8% Christian Church (Disciples of Christ) (2000).
Economy: Unemployment rate: 7.2% (June 2011); Total civilian labor force: 4,163 (June 2011); Leading industries: 23.1% retail trade; 13.7% health care and social assistance; 7.0% accommodation & food services (2009); Farms: 694 totaling 612,627 acres (2007); Companies that employ 500 or more persons: 0 (2009); Companies that employ 100 to 499 persons: 3 (2009); Companies that employ less than 100 persons: 215 (2009); Black-owned businesses: n/a (2007); Hispanic-owned businesses: n/a (2007); Asian-owned businesses: n/a (2007); Women-owned businesses: n/a (2007); Retail sales per capita: $25,029 (2010). Single-family building permits issued: 0 (2010); Multi-family building permits issued: 0 (2010).
Income: Per capita income: $17,437 (2010); Median household income: $32,139 (2010); Average household income: $42,802 (2010); Percent of households with income of $100,000 or more: 6.1% (2010); Poverty rate: 18.6% (2009); Bankruptcy rate: 0.25% (2010).
Taxes: Total county taxes per capita: $271 (2007); County property taxes per capita: $156 (2007).
Education: Percent of population age 25 and over with: High school diploma (including GED) or higher: 76.0% (2010); Bachelor's degree or higher: 15.7% (2010); Master's degree or higher: 4.5% (2010).
Housing: Homeownership rate: 70.8% (2010); Median home value: $42,047 (2010); Median contract rent: $292 per month (2005-2009 5-year est.); Median year structure built: 1962 (2005-2009 5-year est.)
Health: Birth rate: 134.1 per 10,000 population (2009); Death rate: 117.8 per 10,000 population (2009); Age-adjusted cancer mortality rate: 187.7 deaths per 100,000 population (2007); Number of physicians: 6.4 per 10,000 population (2008); Hospital beds: 32.0 per 10,000 population (2007); Hospital admissions: 553.4 per 10,000 population (2007).
Elections: 2008 Presidential election results: 24.2% Obama, 75.2% McCain, 0.0% Nader
Additional Information Contacts
McCulloch County Government . . . . (325) 597-0733
   http://www.co.mcculloch.tx.us/ips/cms
Brady/McCulloch County Chamber of Commerce . . . . (325) 597-3491
   http://www.bradytx.com
City of Brady . . . . (325) 597-2152
   http://www.bradytx.us

McCulloch County Communities

BRADY (city). County seat. Covers a land area of 9.188 square miles and a water area of 2.324 square miles. Located at 31.13° N. Lat; 99.34° W. Long. Elevation is 1,677 feet.
History: Brady, settled along Brady Creek, became the seat of McCulloch County. The county was named for Confederate General Ben McCulloch who fought at San Jacinto.
Population: 5,946 (1990); 5,523 (2000); 5,429 (2010); 5,371 (2015 projected); Race: 78.1% White, 3.1% Black, 0.2% Asian, 18.6% Other, 36.2% Hispanic of any race (2010); Density: 590.9 persons per square mile (2010); Average household size: 2.43 (2010); Median age: 37.5 (2010); Males per 100 females: 88.2 (2010); Marriage status: 22.1% never married, 52.3% now married, 13.2% widowed, 12.4% divorced (2005-2009 5-year est.); Foreign born: 7.1% (2005-2009 5-year est.); Ancestry (includes multiple ancestries): 17.9% American, 9.9% German, 7.2% English, 7.0% Irish, 3.7% French (2005-2009 5-year est.).
Economy: Single-family building permits issued: 0 (2010); Multi-family building permits issued: 0 (2010); Employment by occupation: 12.5% management, 11.6% professional, 31.1% services, 16.3% sales, 0.0% farming, 9.1% construction, 19.4% production (2005-2009 5-year est.).

Income: Per capita income: $15,751 (2010); Median household income: $28,838 (2010); Average household income: $38,703 (2010); Percent of households with income of $100,000 or more: 4.3% (2010); Poverty rate: 27.7% (2005-2009 5-year est.).

Taxes: Total city taxes per capita: $245 (2007); City property taxes per capita: $72 (2007).

Education: Percent of population age 25 and over with: High school diploma (including GED) or higher: 73.1% (2010); Bachelor's degree or higher: 13.5% (2010); Master's degree or higher: 3.4% (2010).

School District(s)
Brady ISD (PK-12)
   2009-10 Enrollment: 1,272 . . . . (325) 597-2301

Housing: Homeownership rate: 66.3% (2010); Median home value: $33,621 (2010); Median contract rent: $283 per month (2005-2009 5-year est.); Median year structure built: 1961 (2005-2009 5-year est.).

Hospitals: Heart of Texas Memorial Hospital (49 beds)

Safety: Violent crime rate: 20.7 per 10,000 population; Property crime rate: 275.2 per 10,000 population (2009).

Newspapers: Brady Standard (Community news; Circulation 3,333)

Transportation: Commute to work: 94.5% car, 0.0% public transportation, 0.2% walk, 3.3% work from home (2005-2009 5-year est.); Travel time to work: 79.1% less than 15 minutes, 11.7% 15 to 30 minutes, 3.5% 30 to 45 minutes, 2.8% 45 to 60 minutes, 2.9% 60 minutes or more (2005-2009 5-year est.)

Airports: Curtis Field (general aviation)

Additional Information Contacts
Brady/McCulloch County Chamber of Commerce . . . . (325) 597-3491
   http://www.bradytx.com
City of Brady . . . . (325) 597-2152
   http://www.bradytx.us

LOHN (unincorporated postal area, zip code 76852). Covers a land area of 138.528 square miles and a water area of 0.047 square miles. Located at 31.40° N. Lat; 99.49° W. Long. Elevation is 1,565 feet.

Population: 163 (2000); Race: 97.7% White, 0.0% Black, 0.0% Asian, 2.3% Other, 2.3% Hispanic of any race (2000); Density: 1.2 persons per square mile (2000); Age: 21.7% under 18, 23.4% over 64 (2000); Marriage status: 15.4% never married, 75.5% now married, 9.1% widowed, 0.0% divorced (2000); Foreign born: 0.6% (2000); Ancestry (includes multiple ancestries): 35.4% American, 19.4% German, 10.3% Irish, 3.4% English (2000).

Economy: Employment by occupation: 50.6% management, 21.5% professional, 2.5% services, 5.1% sales, 10.1% farming, 2.5% construction, 7.6% production (2000).

Income: Per capita income: $28,084 (2000); Median household income: $35,750 (2000); Poverty rate: 179.1% (2000).

Education: Percent of population age 25 and over with: High school diploma (including GED) or higher: 89.2% (2000); Bachelor's degree or higher: 23.8% (2000).

School District(s)
Lohn ISD (PK-12)
   2009-10 Enrollment: 98 . . . . (325) 344-5749

Housing: Homeownership rate: 95.5% (2000); Median home value: $87,500 (2000); Median contract rent: n/a per month (2000); Median year structure built: 1942 (2000).

Transportation: Commute to work: 88.3% car, 0.0% public transportation, 0.0% walk, 11.7% work from home (2000); Travel time to work: 45.6% less than 15 minutes, 10.3% 15 to 30 minutes, 35.3% 30 to 45 minutes, 5.9% 45 to 60 minutes, 2.9% 60 minutes or more (2000)

MELVIN (town). Covers a land area of 0.471 square miles and a water area of 0 square miles. Located at 31.19° N. Lat; 99.58° W. Long. Elevation is 1,857 feet.

Population: 184 (1990); 155 (2000); 153 (2010); 148 (2015 projected); Race: 88.9% White, 0.0% Black, 0.0% Asian, 11.1% Other, 21.6% Hispanic of any race (2010); Density: 324.9 persons per square mile (2010); Average household size: 2.47 (2010); Median age: 49.0 (2010); Males per 100 females: 121.7 (2010); Marriage status: 20.0% never married, 45.0% now married, 14.0% widowed, 21.0% divorced (2005-2009 5-year est.); Foreign born: 4.4% (2005-2009 5-year est.); Ancestry (includes multiple ancestries): 41.2% American, 7.0% Scotch-Irish, 4.4% Irish, 2.6% German, 1.8% Dutch (2005-2009 5-year est.).

Economy: Employment by occupation: 17.9% management, 0.0% professional, 39.3% services, 0.0% sales, 0.0% farming, 35.7% construction, 7.1% production (2005-2009 5-year est.).

Income: Per capita income: $19,185 (2010); Median household income: $30,714 (2010); Average household income: $43,911 (2010); Percent of households with income of $100,000 or more: 9.7% (2010); Poverty rate: 15.8% (2005-2009 5-year est.).

Taxes: Total city taxes per capita: $101 (2007); City property taxes per capita: $74 (2007).

Education: Percent of population age 25 and over with: High school diploma (including GED) or higher: 84.1% (2010); Bachelor's degree or higher: 17.7% (2010); Master's degree or higher: 3.5% (2010).

Housing: Homeownership rate: 82.3% (2010); Median home value: $77,500 (2010); Median contract rent: n/a per month (2005-2009 5-year est.); Median year structure built: 1948 (2005-2009 5-year est.).

Transportation: Commute to work: 100.0% car, 0.0% public transportation, 0.0% walk, 0.0% work from home (2005-2009 5-year est.); Travel time to work: 26.8% less than 15 minutes, 41.1% 15 to 30 minutes, 19.6% 30 to 45 minutes, 3.6% 45 to 60 minutes, 8.9% 60 minutes or more (2005-2009 5-year est.)

ROCHELLE (unincorporated postal area, zip code 76872). Covers a land area of 139.723 square miles and a water area of 0.436 square miles. Located at 31.31° N. Lat; 99.17° W. Long. Elevation is 1,781 feet.

Population: 565 (2000); Race: 95.3% White, 0.0% Black, 0.0% Asian, 4.7% Other, 5.6% Hispanic of any race (2000); Density: 4.0 persons per square mile (2000); Age: 21.4% under 18, 23.0% over 64 (2000); Marriage status: 17.3% never married, 63.3% now married, 11.5% widowed, 7.9% divorced (2000); Foreign born: 1.4% (2000); Ancestry (includes multiple ancestries): 19.3% German, 15.7% English, 12.3% Irish, 9.7% American (2000).

Economy: Employment by occupation: 20.1% management, 29.5% professional, 3.6% services, 21.0% sales, 0.0% farming, 12.1% construction, 13.8% production (2000).

Income: Per capita income: $16,110 (2000); Median household income: $31,172 (2000); Poverty rate: 179.1% (2000).

Education: Percent of population age 25 and over with: High school diploma (including GED) or higher: 78.6% (2000); Bachelor's degree or higher: 26.7% (2000).

School District(s)
Rochelle ISD (PK-12)
   2009-10 Enrollment: 213 . . . . (325) 243-5224

Housing: Homeownership rate: 82.9% (2000); Median home value: $52,500 (2000); Median contract rent: $304 per month (2000); Median year structure built: 1959 (2000).

Transportation: Commute to work: 94.2% car, 0.0% public transportation, 0.9% walk, 3.1% work from home (2000); Travel time to work: 26.7% less than 15 minutes, 41.5% 15 to 30 minutes, 17.1% 30 to 45 minutes, 8.3% 45 to 60 minutes, 6.5% 60 minutes or more (2000)

VOCA (unincorporated postal area, zip code 76887). Covers a land area of 40.900 square miles and a water area of 0.170 square miles. Located at 30.97° N. Lat; 99.17° W. Long. Elevation is 1,555 feet.

Population: 143 (2000); Race: 79.4% White, 5.6% Black, 0.0% Asian, 15.0% Other, 15.1% Hispanic of any race (2000); Density: 3.5 persons per square mile (2000); Age: 7.1% under 18, 19.0% over 64 (2000); Marriage status: 20.5% never married, 75.2% now married, 4.3% widowed, 0.0% divorced (2000); Foreign born: 4.0% (2000); Ancestry (includes multiple ancestries): 18.3% German, 15.9% Irish, 8.7% Scotch-Irish, 8.7% English (2000).

Economy: Employment by occupation: 61.7% management, 6.7% professional, 16.7% services, 5.0% sales, 0.0% farming, 10.0% construction, 0.0% production (2000).

Income: Per capita income: $18,841 (2000); Median household income: $38,438 (2000); Poverty rate: 179.1% (2000).

Education: Percent of population age 25 and over with: High school diploma (including GED) or higher: 87.4% (2000); Bachelor's degree or higher: 6.8% (2000).

Housing: Homeownership rate: 100.0% (2000); Median home value: $57,500 (2000); Median contract rent: n/a per month (2000); Median year structure built: 1974 (2000).

Transportation: Commute to work: 70.4% car, 0.0% public transportation, 29.6% walk, 0.0% work from home (2000); Travel time to work: 55.6% less than 15 minutes, 9.3% 15 to 30 minutes, 27.8% 30 to 45 minutes, 0.0% 45 to 60 minutes, 7.4% 60 minutes or more (2000)

McLennan County

Located in east central Texas; drained by the Brazos River; includes Lake Waco. Covers a land area of 1,041.88 square miles, a water area of 18.34 square miles, and is located in the Central Time Zone at 31.54° N. Lat., 97.16° W. Long. The county was founded in 1850. County seat is Waco.

McLennan County is part of the Waco, TX Metropolitan Statistical Area. The entire metro area includes: McLennan County, TX

Weather Station: McGregor   Elevation: 723 feet

	Jan	Feb	Mar	Apr	May	Jun	Jul	Aug	Sep	Oct	Nov	Dec
High	57	61	68	76	83	90	95	95	89	79	67	58
Low	35	39	46	53	62	69	72	72	66	56	46	37
Precip	2.2	2.6	3.3	2.8	4.6	3.7	1.7	2.3	2.6	4.3	3.0	2.9
Snow	0.2	tr	0.0	0.0	0.0	0.0	0.0	0.0	0.0	0.0	tr	0.0

High and Low temperatures in degrees Fahrenheit; Precipitation and Snow in inches

Weather Station: Waco Dam   Elevation: 495 feet

	Jan	Feb	Mar	Apr	May	Jun	Jul	Aug	Sep	Oct	Nov	Dec
High	58	62	69	77	84	91	96	96	90	79	69	59
Low	35	38	46	54	64	71	74	74	66	55	46	36
Precip	2.1	2.8	3.5	2.7	4.6	3.5	1.8	1.8	3.0	3.8	3.1	3.2
Snow	tr	tr	tr	0.0	0.0	0.0	0.0	0.0	0.0	0.0	tr	0.0

High and Low temperatures in degrees Fahrenheit; Precipitation and Snow in inches

Weather Station: Waco Madison Cooper Arpt   Elevation: 500 feet

	Jan	Feb	Mar	Apr	May	Jun	Jul	Aug	Sep	Oct	Nov	Dec
High	59	62	70	78	85	92	97	97	90	80	69	60
Low	37	40	47	55	64	71	74	74	67	57	47	38
Precip	2.0	2.6	3.1	2.7	4.4	3.3	1.7	1.9	2.8	3.9	2.9	2.8
Snow	0.4	na	0.1	0.2	tr	0.0	0.0	tr	0.0	tr	0.1	tr

High and Low temperatures in degrees Fahrenheit; Precipitation and Snow in inches

Population: 189,123 (1990); 213,517 (2000); 232,469 (2010); 241,263 (2015 projected); Race: 69.6% White, 14.5% Black, 1.5% Asian, 14.4% Other, 22.2% Hispanic of any race (2010); Density: 223.1 persons per square mile (2010); Average household size: 2.61 (2010); Median age: 32.4 (2010); Males per 100 females: 95.8 (2010).
Religion: Five largest groups: 30.0% Southern Baptist Convention, 10.7% Catholic Church, 8.2% The United Methodist Church, 2.0% Churches of Christ, 1.5% Assemblies of God (2000).
Economy: Unemployment rate: 8.4% (June 2011); Total civilian labor force: 118,722 (June 2011); Leading industries: 16.1% health care and social assistance; 15.5% manufacturing; 12.4% retail trade (2009); Farms: 2,798 totaling 529,621 acres (2007); Companies that employ 500 or more persons: 15 (2009); Companies that employ 100 to 499 persons: 136 (2009); Companies that employ less than 100 persons: 4,804 (2009); Black-owned businesses: 864 (2007); Hispanic-owned businesses: 1,508 (2007); Asian-owned businesses: 263 (2007); Women-owned businesses: 4,792 (2007); Retail sales per capita: $12,673 (2010). Single-family building permits issued: 442 (2010); Multi-family building permits issued: 160 (2010).
Income: Per capita income: $20,672 (2010); Median household income: $41,022 (2010); Average household income: $55,525 (2010); Percent of households with income of $100,000 or more: 12.6% (2010); Poverty rate: 22.8% (2009); Bankruptcy rate: 0.67% (2010).
Taxes: Total county taxes per capita: $225 (2007); County property taxes per capita: $166 (2007).
Education: Percent of population age 25 and over with: High school diploma (including GED) or higher: 80.4% (2010); Bachelor's degree or higher: 20.3% (2010); Master's degree or higher: 6.8% (2010).
Housing: Homeownership rate: 59.2% (2010); Median home value: $97,675 (2010); Median contract rent: $528 per month (2005-2009 5-year est.); Median year structure built: 1975 (2005-2009 5-year est.)
Health: Birth rate: 151.6 per 10,000 population (2009); Death rate: 86.0 per 10,000 population (2009); Age-adjusted cancer mortality rate: 199.0 deaths per 100,000 population (2007); Number of physicians: 20.7 per 10,000 population (2008); Hospital beds: 37.9 per 10,000 population (2007); Hospital admissions: 1,258.5 per 10,000 population (2007).
Environment: Air Quality Index: 83.8% good, 15.8% moderate, 0.3% unhealthy for sensitive individuals, 0.0% unhealthy (percent of days in 2008)
Elections: 2008 Presidential election results: 37.7% Obama, 61.6% McCain, 0.1% Nader
Additional Information Contacts

McLennan County Government . . . . (254) 757-5049
  http://www.co.mclennan.tx.us
Cen-Tex African American Chamber of Commerce . . . . . . (254) 235-3204
  http://centexchamber.com
Cen-Tex Hispanic Chamber of Commerce . . . . (254) 754-7111
  http://www.wacohispanicchamber.com
City of Bellmead . . . . (254) 799-2436
  http://www.bellmead.com
City of Hewitt . . . . (254) 666-6171
  http://www.cityofhewitt.com
City of Lacy Lakeview . . . . (254) 799-2458
  http://www.lacylakeview.org
City of Robinson . . . . (254) 662-1415
  http://www.robinsontexas.org
City of Waco . . . . (254) 750-5600
  http://www.waco-texas.com
City of Woodway . . . . (254) 772-4480
  http://www.woodway-texas.com
Greater Hewitt Chamber of Commerce . . . . (254) 666-1200
  http://www.hewitt-texas.com
Greater Robinson Chamber of Commerce . . . . (254) 662-6434
  http://www.robinsontexaschamber.org
Greater Waco Chamber of Commerce . . . . (254) 752-6551
  http://www.waco-chamber.com
Lacy Lakeview Chamber of Commerce . . . . (254) 799-2458
  http://www.lacylakeview.org/chamber.html
Mart Chamber of Commerce . . . . (254) 876-2462
Mc Gregor Chamber of Commerce . . . . (254) 840-2292
  http://www.mcgregor-texas.com
West Chamber of Commerce . . . . (254) 826-3188
  http://westtxchamber.com

McLennan County Communities

AXTELL (unincorporated postal area, zip code 76624). Covers a land area of 73.944 square miles and a water area of 0.974 square miles. Located at 31.66° N. Lat; 96.95° W. Long. Elevation is 525 feet.
Population: 2,284 (2000); Race: 94.0% White, 2.3% Black, 0.1% Asian, 3.6% Other, 3.9% Hispanic of any race (2000); Density: 30.9 persons per square mile (2000); Age: 26.0% under 18, 13.1% over 64 (2000); Marriage status: 18.0% never married, 67.2% now married, 5.2% widowed, 9.7% divorced (2000); Foreign born: 1.8% (2000); Ancestry (includes multiple ancestries): 18.0% German, 12.4% Irish, 8.7% English, 8.1% American (2000).
Economy: Employment by occupation: 12.8% management, 16.3% professional, 11.7% services, 29.9% sales, 0.4% farming, 12.3% construction, 16.7% production (2000).
Income: Per capita income: $18,200 (2000); Median household income: $40,884 (2000); Poverty rate: 179.1% (2000).
Education: Percent of population age 25 and over with: High school diploma (including GED) or higher: 82.4% (2000); Bachelor's degree or higher: 10.2% (2000).

School District(s)
Axtell ISD (PK-12)
    2009-10 Enrollment: 767 . . . . (254) 863-5301
Housing: Homeownership rate: 83.3% (2000); Median home value: $72,200 (2000); Median contract rent: $316 per month (2000); Median year structure built: 1980 (2000).
Transportation: Commute to work: 94.5% car, 0.0% public transportation, 2.1% walk, 3.4% work from home (2000); Travel time to work: 18.0% less than 15 minutes, 44.3% 15 to 30 minutes, 27.1% 30 to 45 minutes, 6.7% 45 to 60 minutes, 3.9% 60 minutes or more (2000)

BELLMEAD (city). Covers a land area of 6.233 square miles and a water area of 0 square miles. Located at 31.59° N. Lat; 97.09° W. Long. Elevation is 436 feet.
Population: 8,328 (1990); 9,214 (2000); 9,619 (2010); 9,822 (2015 projected); Race: 61.5% White, 18.1% Black, 0.8% Asian, 19.6% Other, 30.4% Hispanic of any race (2010); Density: 1,543.1 persons per square mile (2010); Average household size: 2.75 (2010); Median age: 32.3 (2010); Males per 100 females: 97.5 (2010); Marriage status: 29.1% never married, 46.2% now married, 7.1% widowed, 17.7% divorced (2005-2009 5-year est.); Foreign born: 14.5% (2005-2009 5-year est.); Ancestry (includes multiple ancestries): 13.7% American, 11.1% German, 8.3% Irish, 2.8% English, 2.5% Italian (2005-2009 5-year est.).

Economy: Single-family building permits issued: 1 (2010); Multi-family building permits issued: 0 (2010); Employment by occupation: 5.2% management, 9.3% professional, 19.4% services, 29.4% sales, 0.5% farming, 18.6% construction, 17.5% production (2005-2009 5-year est.).
Income: Per capita income: $16,174 (2010); Median household income: $35,063 (2010); Average household income: $44,692 (2010); Percent of households with income of $100,000 or more: 5.8% (2010); Poverty rate: 19.6% (2005-2009 5-year est.).
Taxes: Total city taxes per capita: $460 (2007); City property taxes per capita: $77 (2007).
Education: Percent of population age 25 and over with: High school diploma (including GED) or higher: 70.7% (2010); Bachelor's degree or higher: 8.9% (2010); Master's degree or higher: 3.2% (2010).
Housing: Homeownership rate: 62.8% (2010); Median home value: $52,809 (2010); Median contract rent: $513 per month (2005-2009 5-year est.); Median year structure built: 1968 (2005-2009 5-year est.).
Safety: Violent crime rate: 146.7 per 10,000 population; Property crime rate: 1,149.8 per 10,000 population (2009).
Transportation: Commute to work: 95.8% car, 0.0% public transportation, 2.0% walk, 1.8% work from home (2005-2009 5-year est.); Travel time to work: 33.7% less than 15 minutes, 46.2% 15 to 30 minutes, 14.4% 30 to 45 minutes, 4.3% 45 to 60 minutes, 1.4% 60 minutes or more (2005-2009 5-year est.).
Additional Information Contacts
City of Bellmead.................................. (254) 799-2436
    http://www.bellmead.com

BEVERLY HILLS (city). Aka Beverly. Covers a land area of 0.650 square miles and a water area of 0 square miles. Located at 31.52° N. Lat; 97.15° W. Long. Elevation is 528 feet.
Population: 2,048 (1990); 2,113 (2000); 2,237 (2010); 2,300 (2015 projected); Race: 55.4% White, 13.4% Black, 0.5% Asian, 30.6% Other, 52.3% Hispanic of any race (2010); Density: 3,443.7 persons per square mile (2010); Average household size: 2.96 (2010); Median age: 31.8 (2010); Males per 100 females: 104.3 (2010); Marriage status: 30.0% never married, 49.6% now married, 5.8% widowed, 14.6% divorced (2005-2009 5-year est.); Foreign born: 16.1% (2005-2009 5-year est.); Ancestry (includes multiple ancestries): 9.1% German, 6.8% Irish, 6.3% English, 2.7% French, 2.2% American (2005-2009 5-year est.).
Economy: Single-family building permits issued: 0 (2010); Multi-family building permits issued: 0 (2010); Employment by occupation: 7.3% management, 3.4% professional, 25.6% services, 25.7% sales, 0.6% farming, 14.4% construction, 23.1% production (2005-2009 5-year est.).
Income: Per capita income: $14,232 (2010); Median household income: $34,963 (2010); Average household income: $40,990 (2010); Percent of households with income of $100,000 or more: 4.8% (2010); Poverty rate: 22.0% (2005-2009 5-year est.).
Taxes: Total city taxes per capita: $500 (2007); City property taxes per capita: $103 (2007).
Education: Percent of population age 25 and over with: High school diploma (including GED) or higher: 64.3% (2010); Bachelor's degree or higher: 5.0% (2010); Master's degree or higher: 1.2% (2010).
Housing: Homeownership rate: 66.1% (2010); Median home value: $58,652 (2010); Median contract rent: $523 per month (2005-2009 5-year est.); Median year structure built: 1961 (2005-2009 5-year est.).
Safety: Violent crime rate: 29.4 per 10,000 population; Property crime rate: 225.5 per 10,000 population (2009).
Transportation: Commute to work: 95.4% car, 1.0% public transportation, 1.3% walk, 1.4% work from home (2005-2009 5-year est.); Travel time to work: 51.9% less than 15 minutes, 40.5% 15 to 30 minutes, 4.8% 30 to 45 minutes, 0.7% 45 to 60 minutes, 2.0% 60 minutes or more (2005-2009 5-year est.)

BRUCEVILLE-EDDY (city). Covers a land area of 3.233 square miles and a water area of 0.003 square miles. Located at 31.30° N. Lat; 97.24° W. Long. Elevation is 692 feet.
Population: 1,242 (1990); 1,490 (2000); 1,562 (2010); 1,603 (2015 projected); Race: 83.2% White, 0.4% Black, 0.1% Asian, 16.3% Other, 20.8% Hispanic of any race (2010); Density: 483.1 persons per square mile (2010); Average household size: 2.90 (2010); Median age: 34.3 (2010); Males per 100 females: 101.8 (2010); Marriage status: 21.8% never married, 53.2% now married, 9.0% widowed, 16.0% divorced (2005-2009 5-year est.); Foreign born: 5.0% (2005-2009 5-year est.); Ancestry (includes multiple ancestries): 31.8% German, 15.8% Irish, 12.0% American, 9.5% English, 6.7% Czech (2005-2009 5-year est.).

Economy: Employment by occupation: 9.7% management, 13.3% professional, 13.5% services, 31.5% sales, 0.0% farming, 13.0% construction, 19.0% production (2005-2009 5-year est.).
Income: Per capita income: $19,199 (2010); Median household income: $45,304 (2010); Average household income: $55,776 (2010); Percent of households with income of $100,000 or more: 11.2% (2010); Poverty rate: 11.7% (2005-2009 5-year est.).
Taxes: Total city taxes per capita: $163 (2007); City property taxes per capita: $80 (2007).
Education: Percent of population age 25 and over with: High school diploma (including GED) or higher: 82.0% (2010); Bachelor's degree or higher: 8.6% (2010); Master's degree or higher: 2.0% (2010).
Housing: Homeownership rate: 84.8% (2010); Median home value: $76,308 (2010); Median contract rent: $441 per month (2005-2009 5-year est.); Median year structure built: 1980 (2005-2009 5-year est.).
Safety: Violent crime rate: 25.9 per 10,000 population; Property crime rate: 440.4 per 10,000 population (2009).
Transportation: Commute to work: 97.2% car, 0.0% public transportation, 0.8% walk, 0.4% work from home (2005-2009 5-year est.); Travel time to work: 18.4% less than 15 minutes, 43.9% 15 to 30 minutes, 30.4% 30 to 45 minutes, 3.2% 45 to 60 minutes, 4.2% 60 minutes or more (2005-2009 5-year est.)

CHINA SPRING (unincorporated postal area, zip code 76633). Covers a land area of 47.664 square miles and a water area of 0.025 square miles. Located at 31.66° N. Lat; 97.32° W. Long.
Population: 3,579 (2000); Race: 95.0% White, 0.4% Black, 0.0% Asian, 4.6% Other, 7.0% Hispanic of any race (2000); Density: 75.1 persons per square mile (2000); Age: 30.0% under 18, 8.4% over 64 (2000); Marriage status: 15.9% never married, 72.8% now married, 4.2% widowed, 7.1% divorced (2000); Foreign born: 1.7% (2000); Ancestry (includes multiple ancestries): 15.5% German, 14.0% American, 12.5% Irish, 7.8% English (2000).
Economy: Employment by occupation: 14.2% management, 19.2% professional, 14.6% services, 25.4% sales, 0.6% farming, 12.8% construction, 13.3% production (2000).
Income: Per capita income: $20,708 (2000); Median household income: $49,375 (2000); Poverty rate: 179.1% (2000).
Education: Percent of population age 25 and over with: High school diploma (including GED) or higher: 89.8% (2000); Bachelor's degree or higher: 17.2% (2000).

School District(s)
China Spring ISD (PK-12)
    2009-10 Enrollment: 2,288 .... (254) 836-1115
Housing: Homeownership rate: 88.4% (2000); Median home value: $89,300 (2000); Median contract rent: $419 per month (2000); Median year structure built: 1985 (2000).
Transportation: Commute to work: 95.9% car, 0.0% public transportation, 0.5% walk, 2.7% work from home (2000); Travel time to work: 11.4% less than 15 minutes, 54.2% 15 to 30 minutes, 30.0% 30 to 45 minutes, 2.4% 45 to 60 minutes, 2.0% 60 minutes or more (2000)

CRAWFORD (town). Covers a land area of 0.924 square miles and a water area of 0 square miles. Located at 31.53° N. Lat; 97.44° W. Long. Elevation is 689 feet.
Population: 665 (1990); 705 (2000); 710 (2010); 717 (2015 projected); Race: 92.3% White, 1.1% Black, 0.0% Asian, 6.6% Other, 7.6% Hispanic of any race (2010); Density: 768.5 persons per square mile (2010); Average household size: 2.77 (2010); Median age: 35.0 (2010); Males per 100 females: 97.8 (2010); Marriage status: 21.2% never married, 55.5% now married, 11.8% widowed, 11.6% divorced (2005-2009 5-year est.); Foreign born: 0.2% (2005-2009 5-year est.); Ancestry (includes multiple ancestries): 29.6% German, 23.9% American, 16.7% Irish, 12.3% English, 4.4% Dutch (2005-2009 5-year est.).
Economy: Single-family building permits issued: 2 (2010); Multi-family building permits issued: 0 (2010); Employment by occupation: 11.8% management, 26.7% professional, 12.8% services, 23.6% sales, 0.0% farming, 10.8% construction, 14.4% production (2005-2009 5-year est.).
Income: Per capita income: $24,570 (2010); Median household income: $58,673 (2010); Average household income: $69,336 (2010); Percent of households with income of $100,000 or more: 20.3% (2010); Poverty rate: 2.3% (2005-2009 5-year est.).
Taxes: Total city taxes per capita: $53 (2007); City property taxes per capita: $50 (2007).

Education: Percent of population age 25 and over with: High school diploma (including GED) or higher: 86.9% (2010); Bachelor's degree or higher: 24.9% (2010); Master's degree or higher: 8.4% (2010).

School District(s)

Crawford ISD (PK-12)

2009-10 Enrollment: 603 . . . . (254) 486-2381

Housing: Homeownership rate: 80.1% (2010); Median home value: $115,625 (2010); Median contract rent: $508 per month (2005-2009 5-year est.); Median year structure built: 1972 (2005-2009 5-year est.).

Transportation: Commute to work: 95.6% car, 0.0% public transportation, 2.1% walk, 2.3% work from home (2005-2009 5-year est.); Travel time to work: 21.2% less than 15 minutes, 45.0% 15 to 30 minutes, 22.5% 30 to 45 minutes, 5.6% 45 to 60 minutes, 5.8% 60 minutes or more (2005-2009 5-year est.)

EDDY (unincorporated postal area, zip code 76524). Covers a land area of 50.629 square miles and a water area of 0.081 square miles. Located at 31.30° N. Lat; 97.27° W. Long. Elevation is 679 feet.

Population: 2,434 (2000); Race: 88.1% White, 0.5% Black, 0.4% Asian, 11.0% Other, 15.6% Hispanic of any race (2000); Density: 48.1 persons per square mile (2000); Age: 32.1% under 18, 9.1% over 64 (2000); Marriage status: 18.2% never married, 69.0% now married, 5.0% widowed, 7.8% divorced (2000); Foreign born: 5.0% (2000); Ancestry (includes multiple ancestries): 16.7% German, 12.3% American, 12.0% Irish, 8.1% English (2000).

Economy: Employment by occupation: 10.2% management, 14.2% professional, 12.5% services, 27.1% sales, 0.2% farming, 11.3% construction, 24.6% production (2000).

Income: Per capita income: $16,297 (2000); Median household income: $40,125 (2000); Poverty rate: 179.1% (2000).

Education: Percent of population age 25 and over with: High school diploma (including GED) or higher: 80.1% (2000); Bachelor's degree or higher: 11.1% (2000).

School District(s)

Bruceville-Eddy ISD (PK-12)

2009-10 Enrollment: 854 . . . . (254) 859-5832

Housing: Homeownership rate: 85.1% (2000); Median home value: $69,400 (2000); Median contract rent: $323 per month (2000); Median year structure built: 1982 (2000).

Transportation: Commute to work: 96.0% car, 0.0% public transportation, 2.1% walk, 0.7% work from home (2000); Travel time to work: 18.0% less than 15 minutes, 42.9% 15 to 30 minutes, 30.0% 30 to 45 minutes, 4.8% 45 to 60 minutes, 4.3% 60 minutes or more (2000)

ELM MOTT (unincorporated postal area, zip code 76640). Covers a land area of 28.636 square miles and a water area of 0.071 square miles. Located at 31.68° N. Lat; 97.08° W. Long. Elevation is 525 feet.

Population: 3,113 (2000); Race: 89.7% White, 5.0% Black, 0.0% Asian, 5.3% Other, 7.8% Hispanic of any race (2000); Density: 108.7 persons per square mile (2000); Age: 30.0% under 18, 10.6% over 64 (2000); Marriage status: 18.4% never married, 64.0% now married, 7.7% widowed, 9.8% divorced (2000); Foreign born: 1.3% (2000); Ancestry (includes multiple ancestries): 17.7% German, 14.1% American, 11.6% Irish, 9.6% Czech (2000).

Economy: Employment by occupation: 10.0% management, 13.1% professional, 12.8% services, 25.4% sales, 0.4% farming, 14.8% construction, 23.5% production (2000).

Income: Per capita income: $20,118 (2000); Median household income: $38,702 (2000); Poverty rate: 179.1% (2000).

Education: Percent of population age 25 and over with: High school diploma (including GED) or higher: 72.3% (2000); Bachelor's degree or higher: 10.1% (2000).

School District(s)

Connally ISD (PK-12)

2009-10 Enrollment: 2,464 . . . . (254) 296-6460

Housing: Homeownership rate: 81.0% (2000); Median home value: $58,200 (2000); Median contract rent: $297 per month (2000); Median year structure built: 1979 (2000).

Transportation: Commute to work: 94.3% car, 0.5% public transportation, 0.4% walk, 3.9% work from home (2000); Travel time to work: 26.5% less than 15 minutes, 46.3% 15 to 30 minutes, 16.3% 30 to 45 minutes, 5.1% 45 to 60 minutes, 5.9% 60 minutes or more (2000)

GHOLSON (city). Covers a land area of 11.728 square miles and a water area of 0 square miles. Located at 31.73° N. Lat; 97.22° W. Long. Elevation is 430 feet.

Population: 692 (1990); 922 (2000); 959 (2010); 977 (2015 projected); Race: 83.0% White, 7.3% Black, 0.0% Asian, 9.7% Other, 9.1% Hispanic of any race (2010); Density: 81.8 persons per square mile (2010); Average household size: 2.63 (2010); Median age: 34.5 (2010); Males per 100 females: 110.8 (2010); Marriage status: 13.8% never married, 63.0% now married, 6.1% widowed, 17.1% divorced (2005-2009 5-year est.); Foreign born: 5.4% (2005-2009 5-year est.); Ancestry (includes multiple ancestries): 15.7% American, 15.2% Irish, 11.1% German, 6.8% French, 4.5% Scotch-Irish (2005-2009 5-year est.).

Economy: Employment by occupation: 10.5% management, 24.7% professional, 14.7% services, 16.1% sales, 0.0% farming, 10.8% construction, 23.2% production (2005-2009 5-year est.).

Income: Per capita income: $20,101 (2010); Median household income: $46,140 (2010); Average household income: $54,419 (2010); Percent of households with income of $100,000 or more: 11.9% (2010); Poverty rate: 9.8% (2005-2009 5-year est.).

Taxes: Total city taxes per capita: $59 (2007); City property taxes per capita: $59 (2007).

Education: Percent of population age 25 and over with: High school diploma (including GED) or higher: 74.8% (2010); Bachelor's degree or higher: 9.2% (2010); Master's degree or higher: 3.0% (2010).

Housing: Homeownership rate: 76.2% (2010); Median home value: $96,053 (2010); Median contract rent: $437 per month (2005-2009 5-year est.); Median year structure built: 1987 (2005-2009 5-year est.).

Transportation: Commute to work: 95.1% car, 0.0% public transportation, 3.2% walk, 1.6% work from home (2005-2009 5-year est.); Travel time to work: 8.0% less than 15 minutes, 26.6% 15 to 30 minutes, 45.9% 30 to 45 minutes, 15.1% 45 to 60 minutes, 4.4% 60 minutes or more (2005-2009 5-year est.)

HALLSBURG (city). Covers a land area of 8.400 square miles and a water area of 0.181 square miles. Located at 31.55° N. Lat; 96.95° W. Long. Elevation is 499 feet.

Population: 450 (1990); 518 (2000); 527 (2010); 532 (2015 projected); Race: 87.5% White, 5.7% Black, 0.6% Asian, 6.3% Other, 5.7% Hispanic of any race (2010); Density: 62.7 persons per square mile (2010); Average household size: 2.80 (2010); Median age: 35.9 (2010); Males per 100 females: 103.5 (2010); Marriage status: 23.1% never married, 63.2% now married, 4.6% widowed, 9.1% divorced (2005-2009 5-year est.); Foreign born: 2.6% (2005-2009 5-year est.); Ancestry (includes multiple ancestries): 26.7% German, 18.8% Irish, 13.6% American, 9.2% Czech, 5.0% Scottish (2005-2009 5-year est.).

Economy: Employment by occupation: 10.6% management, 10.6% professional, 16.3% services, 28.4% sales, 1.0% farming, 10.6% construction, 22.6% production (2005-2009 5-year est.).

Income: Per capita income: $23,685 (2010); Median household income: $52,035 (2010); Average household income: $64,398 (2010); Percent of households with income of $100,000 or more: 15.5% (2010); Poverty rate: 5.0% (2005-2009 5-year est.).

Taxes: Total city taxes per capita: $102 (2007); City property taxes per capita: $82 (2007).

Education: Percent of population age 25 and over with: High school diploma (including GED) or higher: 82.6% (2010); Bachelor's degree or higher: 11.2% (2010); Master's degree or higher: 2.9% (2010).

Housing: Homeownership rate: 81.8% (2010); Median home value: $92,353 (2010); Median contract rent: $527 per month (2005-2009 5-year est.); Median year structure built: 1986 (2005-2009 5-year est.).

Transportation: Commute to work: 98.1% car, 1.0% public transportation, 0.0% walk, 1.0% work from home (2005-2009 5-year est.); Travel time to work: 12.1% less than 15 minutes, 66.5% 15 to 30 minutes, 15.0% 30 to 45 minutes, 1.0% 45 to 60 minutes, 5.3% 60 minutes or more (2005-2009 5-year est.)

HEWITT (city). Covers a land area of 6.894 square miles and a water area of 0 square miles. Located at 31.45° N. Lat; 97.19° W. Long. Elevation is 646 feet.

Population: 9,042 (1990); 11,085 (2000); 13,347 (2010); 14,498 (2015 projected); Race: 81.8% White, 7.6% Black, 3.3% Asian, 7.2% Other, 11.4% Hispanic of any race (2010); Density: 1,936.1 persons per square mile (2010); Average household size: 2.80 (2010); Median age: 35.1 (2010); Males per 100 females: 96.5 (2010); Marriage status: 25.0% never

married, 61.9% now married, 2.9% widowed, 10.3% divorced (2005-2009 5-year est.); Foreign born: 6.0% (2005-2009 5-year est.); Ancestry (includes multiple ancestries): 18.9% German, 13.9% English, 12.8% Irish, 7.4% American, 4.8% Italian (2005-2009 5-year est.).
Economy: Single-family building permits issued: 18 (2010); Multi-family building permits issued: 24 (2010); Employment by occupation: 12.1% management, 29.5% professional, 14.0% services, 26.2% sales, 0.7% farming, 7.5% construction, 10.0% production (2005-2009 5-year est.).
Income: Per capita income: $27,171 (2010); Median household income: $67,903 (2010); Average household income: $75,857 (2010); Percent of households with income of $100,000 or more: 22.8% (2010); Poverty rate: 6.9% (2005-2009 5-year est.).
Taxes: Total city taxes per capita: $311 (2007); City property taxes per capita: $172 (2007).
Education: Percent of population age 25 and over with: High school diploma (including GED) or higher: 96.0% (2010); Bachelor's degree or higher: 35.1% (2010); Master's degree or higher: 11.5% (2010).

School District(s)

Midway ISD (PK-12)
    2009-10 Enrollment: 6,883 . . . . (254) 761-5610
Housing: Homeownership rate: 74.0% (2010); Median home value: $136,751 (2010); Median contract rent: $769 per month (2005-2009 5-year est.); Median year structure built: 1987 (2005-2009 5-year est.).
Safety: Violent crime rate: 10.1 per 10,000 population; Property crime rate: 145.1 per 10,000 population (2009).
Transportation: Commute to work: 93.2% car, 0.0% public transportation, 1.3% walk, 4.4% work from home (2005-2009 5-year est.); Travel time to work: 37.2% less than 15 minutes, 47.5% 15 to 30 minutes, 9.9% 30 to 45 minutes, 2.7% 45 to 60 minutes, 2.8% 60 minutes or more (2005-2009 5-year est.)

Additional Information Contacts

City of Hewitt . . . . (254) 666-6171
    http://www.cityofhewitt.com
Greater Hewitt Chamber of Commerce . . . . (254) 666-1200
    http://www.hewitt-texas.com

LACY-LAKEVIEW (city). Covers a land area of 3.810 square miles and a water area of 0 square miles. Located at 31.62° N. Lat; 97.10° W. Long. Elevation is 486 feet.

Population: 5,499 (1990); 5,764 (2000); 5,841 (2010); 5,895 (2015 projected); Race: 66.5% White, 20.0% Black, 0.8% Asian, 12.7% Other, 21.0% Hispanic of any race (2010); Density: 1,533.0 persons per square mile (2010); Average household size: 2.42 (2010); Median age: 32.0 (2010); Males per 100 females: 101.1 (2010); Marriage status: 33.7% never married, 45.2% now married, 6.9% widowed, 14.2% divorced (2005-2009 5-year est.); Foreign born: 8.1% (2005-2009 5-year est.); Ancestry (includes multiple ancestries): 16.3% German, 12.7% Irish, 9.3% American, 5.2% English, 3.6% Czech (2005-2009 5-year est.).
Economy: Single-family building permits issued: 1 (2010); Multi-family building permits issued: 4 (2010); Employment by occupation: 4.4% management, 17.4% professional, 13.9% services, 32.7% sales, 0.2% farming, 12.4% construction, 19.1% production (2005-2009 5-year est.).
Income: Per capita income: $18,761 (2010); Median household income: $37,448 (2010); Average household income: $45,461 (2010); Percent of households with income of $100,000 or more: 6.2% (2010); Poverty rate: 17.5% (2005-2009 5-year est.).
Taxes: Total city taxes per capita: $267 (2007); City property taxes per capita: $94 (2007).
Education: Percent of population age 25 and over with: High school diploma (including GED) or higher: 86.0% (2010); Bachelor's degree or higher: 11.6% (2010); Master's degree or higher: 4.1% (2010).
Housing: Homeownership rate: 49.9% (2010); Median home value: $80,237 (2010); Median contract rent: $426 per month (2005-2009 5-year est.); Median year structure built: 1974 (2005-2009 5-year est.).
Safety: Violent crime rate: 69.5 per 10,000 population; Property crime rate: 405.4 per 10,000 population (2009).
Transportation: Commute to work: 98.0% car, 0.0% public transportation, 0.0% walk, 0.6% work from home (2005-2009 5-year est.); Travel time to work: 40.8% less than 15 minutes, 48.0% 15 to 30 minutes, 8.9% 30 to 45 minutes, 1.1% 45 to 60 minutes, 1.2% 60 minutes or more (2005-2009 5-year est.)

Additional Information Contacts

City of Lacy Lakeview . . . . (254) 799-2458
    http://www.lacylakeview.org

LEROY (city). Covers a land area of 1.907 square miles and a water area of 0 square miles. Located at 31.73° N. Lat; 97.02° W. Long. Elevation is 495 feet.

Population: 292 (1990); 335 (2000); 309 (2010); 298 (2015 projected); Race: 92.9% White, 1.6% Black, 0.0% Asian, 5.5% Other, 9.1% Hispanic of any race (2010); Density: 162.0 persons per square mile (2010); Average household size: 2.66 (2010); Median age: 37.4 (2010); Males per 100 females: 96.8 (2010); Marriage status: 26.5% never married, 62.2% now married, 2.4% widowed, 8.8% divorced (2005-2009 5-year est.); Foreign born: 1.8% (2005-2009 5-year est.); Ancestry (includes multiple ancestries): 40.4% Czech, 38.6% German, 15.7% American, 10.5% English, 5.1% Irish (2005-2009 5-year est.).
Economy: Employment by occupation: 16.9% management, 5.5% professional, 13.2% services, 27.4% sales, 0.0% farming, 10.5% construction, 26.5% production (2005-2009 5-year est.).
Income: Per capita income: $25,876 (2010); Median household income: $58,750 (2010); Average household income: $72,609 (2010); Percent of households with income of $100,000 or more: 19.1% (2010); Poverty rate: 5.4% (2005-2009 5-year est.).
Taxes: Total city taxes per capita: $51 (2007); City property taxes per capita: $0 (2007).
Education: Percent of population age 25 and over with: High school diploma (including GED) or higher: 78.8% (2010); Bachelor's degree or higher: 8.9% (2010); Master's degree or higher: 1.0% (2010).
Housing: Homeownership rate: 85.2% (2010); Median home value: $98,182 (2010); Median contract rent: $608 per month (2005-2009 5-year est.); Median year structure built: 1986 (2005-2009 5-year est.).
Transportation: Commute to work: 95.0% car, 0.0% public transportation, 2.7% walk, 0.9% work from home (2005-2009 5-year est.); Travel time to work: 21.2% less than 15 minutes, 51.6% 15 to 30 minutes, 21.2% 30 to 45 minutes, 0.9% 45 to 60 minutes, 5.1% 60 minutes or more (2005-2009 5-year est.)

LORENA (city). Covers a land area of 3.222 square miles and a water area of 0 square miles. Located at 31.38° N. Lat; 97.21° W. Long. Elevation is 604 feet.

Population: 1,280 (1990); 1,433 (2000); 1,655 (2010); 1,761 (2015 projected); Race: 91.4% White, 0.9% Black, 0.7% Asian, 7.1% Other, 7.6% Hispanic of any race (2010); Density: 513.7 persons per square mile (2010); Average household size: 2.85 (2010); Median age: 35.1 (2010); Males per 100 females: 95.9 (2010); Marriage status: 28.4% never married, 60.3% now married, 3.6% widowed, 7.7% divorced (2005-2009 5-year est.); Foreign born: 2.8% (2005-2009 5-year est.); Ancestry (includes multiple ancestries): 25.3% German, 22.6% English, 13.7% Irish, 7.9% American, 3.8% Italian (2005-2009 5-year est.).
Economy: Single-family building permits issued: 2 (2010); Multi-family building permits issued: 0 (2010); Employment by occupation: 14.4% management, 26.3% professional, 6.4% services, 27.7% sales, 0.0% farming, 8.8% construction, 16.4% production (2005-2009 5-year est.).
Income: Per capita income: $25,369 (2010); Median household income: $61,774 (2010); Average household income: $72,043 (2010); Percent of households with income of $100,000 or more: 21.2% (2010); Poverty rate: 3.5% (2005-2009 5-year est.).
Taxes: Total city taxes per capita: $400 (2007); City property taxes per capita: $220 (2007).
Education: Percent of population age 25 and over with: High school diploma (including GED) or higher: 91.0% (2010); Bachelor's degree or higher: 19.0% (2010); Master's degree or higher: 4.6% (2010).

School District(s)

Lorena ISD (PK-12)
    2009-10 Enrollment: 1,611 . . . . (254) 857-3239
Housing: Homeownership rate: 80.2% (2010); Median home value: $124,133 (2010); Median contract rent: $559 per month (2005-2009 5-year est.); Median year structure built: 1983 (2005-2009 5-year est.).
Safety: Violent crime rate: 5.9 per 10,000 population; Property crime rate: 253.2 per 10,000 population (2009).
Transportation: Commute to work: 93.9% car, 0.0% public transportation, 0.4% walk, 4.9% work from home (2005-2009 5-year est.); Travel time to work: 17.7% less than 15 minutes, 65.9% 15 to 30 minutes, 13.5% 30 to 45 minutes, 0.8% 45 to 60 minutes, 2.1% 60 minutes or more (2005-2009 5-year est.)

MART (city). Covers a land area of 1.343 square miles and a water area of 0 square miles. Located at 31.54° N. Lat; 96.83° W. Long. Elevation is 525 feet.
History: Settled 1875, incorporated 1903.
Population: 2,135 (1990); 2,273 (2000); 2,432 (2010); 2,521 (2015 projected); Race: 69.2% White, 24.6% Black, 0.0% Asian, 6.2% Other, 9.6% Hispanic of any race (2010); Density: 1,810.3 persons per square mile (2010); Average household size: 2.63 (2010); Median age: 34.2 (2010); Males per 100 females: 87.4 (2010); Marriage status: 46.7% never married, 36.3% now married, 6.6% widowed, 10.5% divorced (2005-2009 5-year est.); Foreign born: 5.2% (2005-2009 5-year est.); Ancestry (includes multiple ancestries): 11.1% German, 9.3% American, 7.8% English, 6.2% Irish, 2.9% French (2005-2009 5-year est.).
Economy: Single-family building permits issued: 0 (2010); Multi-family building permits issued: 0 (2010); Employment by occupation: 7.0% management, 14.9% professional, 25.2% services, 21.5% sales, 0.8% farming, 2.4% construction, 28.2% production (2005-2009 5-year est.).
Income: Per capita income: $17,653 (2010); Median household income: $37,889 (2010); Average household income: $49,317 (2010); Percent of households with income of $100,000 or more: 9.8% (2010); Poverty rate: 23.9% (2005-2009 5-year est.).
Taxes: Total city taxes per capita: $117 (2007); City property taxes per capita: $86 (2007).
Education: Percent of population age 25 and over with: High school diploma (including GED) or higher: 71.9% (2010); Bachelor's degree or higher: 12.3% (2010); Master's degree or higher: 4.2% (2010).
School District(s)
Mart ISD (PK-12)
   2009-10 Enrollment: 575 . . . . (254) 876-2523
McLennan Co St Juvenile Correction Facility I (07-12)
   2009-10 Enrollment: 133 . . . . (254) 297-8243
McLennan Co St Juvenile Correction Facility II (06-12)
   2009-10 Enrollment: 204 . . . . (254) 297-8200
Housing: Homeownership rate: 68.0% (2010); Median home value: $56,903 (2010); Median contract rent: $444 per month (2005-2009 5-year est.); Median year structure built: 1958 (2005-2009 5-year est.).
Safety: Violent crime rate: 24.7 per 10,000 population; Property crime rate: 139.7 per 10,000 population (2009).
Transportation: Commute to work: 96.6% car, 0.0% public transportation, 1.8% walk, 0.0% work from home (2005-2009 5-year est.); Travel time to work: 28.9% less than 15 minutes, 22.0% 15 to 30 minutes, 41.8% 30 to 45 minutes, 6.0% 45 to 60 minutes, 1.3% 60 minutes or more (2005-2009 5-year est.)
Additional Information Contacts
Mart Chamber of Commerce . . . . (254) 876-2462

MCGREGOR (city). Covers a land area of 21.816 square miles and a water area of 0 square miles. Located at 31.43° N. Lat; 97.41° W. Long. Elevation is 692 feet.
History: An ordnance plant was nearby in World War II. Established 1882.
Population: 4,706 (1990); 4,727 (2000); 4,958 (2010); 5,111 (2015 projected); Race: 78.3% White, 5.1% Black, 0.6% Asian, 16.0% Other, 25.9% Hispanic of any race (2010); Density: 227.3 persons per square mile (2010); Average household size: 2.70 (2010); Median age: 35.0 (2010); Males per 100 females: 91.1 (2010); Marriage status: 34.3% never married, 49.6% now married, 5.9% widowed, 10.2% divorced (2005-2009 5-year est.); Foreign born: 11.1% (2005-2009 5-year est.); Ancestry (includes multiple ancestries): 16.7% German, 16.4% Irish, 12.1% English, 7.4% American, 2.4% Italian (2005-2009 5-year est.).
Economy: Single-family building permits issued: 4 (2010); Multi-family building permits issued: 2 (2010); Employment by occupation: 7.5% management, 18.0% professional, 18.1% services, 21.4% sales, 3.0% farming, 10.4% construction, 21.7% production (2005-2009 5-year est.).
Income: Per capita income: $28,516 (2010); Median household income: $53,528 (2010); Average household income: $79,135 (2010); Percent of households with income of $100,000 or more: 20.6% (2010); Poverty rate: 21.0% (2005-2009 5-year est.).
Taxes: Total city taxes per capita: $420 (2007); City property taxes per capita: $210 (2007).
Education: Percent of population age 25 and over with: High school diploma (including GED) or higher: 73.2% (2010); Bachelor's degree or higher: 16.2% (2010); Master's degree or higher: 6.1% (2010).

School District(s)
McGregor ISD (PK-12)
   2009-10 Enrollment: 1,318 . . . . (254) 840-2828
Housing: Homeownership rate: 72.3% (2010); Median home value: $77,456 (2010); Median contract rent: $396 per month (2005-2009 5-year est.); Median year structure built: 1965 (2005-2009 5-year est.).
Safety: Violent crime rate: 28.5 per 10,000 population; Property crime rate: 238.3 per 10,000 population (2009).
Newspapers: McGregor Mirror (Community news; Circulation 2,450)
Transportation: Commute to work: 93.8% car, 0.0% public transportation, 2.8% walk, 0.5% work from home (2005-2009 5-year est.); Travel time to work: 33.5% less than 15 minutes, 46.7% 15 to 30 minutes, 15.1% 30 to 45 minutes, 3.5% 45 to 60 minutes, 1.1% 60 minutes or more (2005-2009 5-year est.); Amtrak: train service available.
Additional Information Contacts
Mc Gregor Chamber of Commerce . . . . (254) 840-2292
   http://www.mcgregor-texas.com

MOODY (city). Covers a land area of 0.851 square miles and a water area of 0 square miles. Located at 31.30° N. Lat; 97.36° W. Long. Elevation is 781 feet.
History: Incorporated 1901.
Population: 1,377 (1990); 1,400 (2000); 1,381 (2010); 1,381 (2015 projected); Race: 86.1% White, 4.6% Black, 0.0% Asian, 9.3% Other, 14.6% Hispanic of any race (2010); Density: 1,623.4 persons per square mile (2010); Average household size: 2.63 (2010); Median age: 36.0 (2010); Males per 100 females: 94.0 (2010); Marriage status: 24.5% never married, 46.0% now married, 15.7% widowed, 13.9% divorced (2005-2009 5-year est.); Foreign born: 2.1% (2005-2009 5-year est.); Ancestry (includes multiple ancestries): 20.7% Irish, 17.5% German, 15.5% English, 10.1% American, 4.5% Welsh (2005-2009 5-year est.).
Economy: Single-family building permits issued: 0 (2010); Multi-family building permits issued: 0 (2010); Employment by occupation: 4.5% management, 7.4% professional, 18.3% services, 39.1% sales, 0.0% farming, 18.7% construction, 12.0% production (2005-2009 5-year est.).
Income: Per capita income: $18,903 (2010); Median household income: $41,553 (2010); Average household income: $50,121 (2010); Percent of households with income of $100,000 or more: 8.7% (2010); Poverty rate: 22.8% (2005-2009 5-year est.).
Taxes: Total city taxes per capita: $186 (2007); City property taxes per capita: $114 (2007).
Education: Percent of population age 25 and over with: High school diploma (including GED) or higher: 73.5% (2010); Bachelor's degree or higher: 10.3% (2010); Master's degree or higher: 2.2% (2010).
School District(s)
Moody ISD (PK-12)
   2009-10 Enrollment: 712 . . . . (254) 853-2172
Housing: Homeownership rate: 74.3% (2010); Median home value: $75,758 (2010); Median contract rent: $308 per month (2005-2009 5-year est.); Median year structure built: 1960 (2005-2009 5-year est.).
Transportation: Commute to work: 98.9% car, 0.0% public transportation, 0.0% walk, 0.5% work from home (2005-2009 5-year est.); Travel time to work: 28.5% less than 15 minutes, 27.3% 15 to 30 minutes, 37.2% 30 to 45 minutes, 1.7% 45 to 60 minutes, 5.3% 60 minutes or more (2005-2009 5-year est.)

RIESEL (city). Covers a land area of 3.974 square miles and a water area of <.001 square miles. Located at 31.47° N. Lat; 96.93° W. Long. Elevation is 505 feet.
Population: 943 (1990); 973 (2000); 934 (2010); 921 (2015 projected); Race: 89.0% White, 3.2% Black, 0.6% Asian, 7.2% Other, 8.4% Hispanic of any race (2010); Density: 235.0 persons per square mile (2010); Average household size: 2.75 (2010); Median age: 37.1 (2010); Males per 100 females: 96.2 (2010); Marriage status: 22.9% never married, 51.5% now married, 4.9% widowed, 20.8% divorced (2005-2009 5-year est.); Foreign born: 0.0% (2005-2009 5-year est.); Ancestry (includes multiple ancestries): 41.9% German, 16.0% Irish, 8.1% American, 7.7% English, 6.2% Welsh (2005-2009 5-year est.).
Economy: Employment by occupation: 11.1% management, 12.4% professional, 17.1% services, 30.4% sales, 0.9% farming, 16.7% construction, 11.3% production (2005-2009 5-year est.).
Income: Per capita income: $19,982 (2010); Median household income: $46,036 (2010); Average household income: $55,074 (2010); Percent of households with income of $100,000 or more: 9.4% (2010); Poverty rate: 7.0% (2005-2009 5-year est.).

Taxes: Total city taxes per capita: $31 (2007); City property taxes per capita: $0 (2007).
Education: Percent of population age 25 and over with: High school diploma (including GED) or higher: 81.7% (2010); Bachelor's degree or higher: 11.7% (2010); Master's degree or higher: 3.3% (2010).

School District(s)

Riesel ISD (PK-12)
    2009-10 Enrollment: 581 . . . . (254) 896-6411
Housing: Homeownership rate: 80.8% (2010); Median home value: $79,111 (2010); Median contract rent: $465 per month (2005-2009 5-year est.); Median year structure built: 1970 (2005-2009 5-year est.).
Safety: Violent crime rate: 19.7 per 10,000 population; Property crime rate: 196.9 per 10,000 population (2009).
Transportation: Commute to work: 98.4% car, 0.0% public transportation, 0.0% walk, 0.9% work from home (2005-2009 5-year est.); Travel time to work: 23.3% less than 15 minutes, 27.2% 15 to 30 minutes, 42.5% 30 to 45 minutes, 3.2% 45 to 60 minutes, 3.9% 60 minutes or more (2005-2009 5-year est.)

ROBINSON (city). Covers a land area of 31.555 square miles and a water area of 0 square miles. Located at 31.47° N. Lat; 97.11° W. Long. Elevation is 495 feet.
Population: 7,005 (1990); 7,845 (2000); 10,700 (2010); 11,619 (2015 projected); Race: 86.5% White, 3.4% Black, 0.6% Asian, 9.6% Other, 13.1% Hispanic of any race (2010); Density: 339.1 persons per square mile (2010); Average household size: 2.82 (2010); Median age: 38.2 (2010); Males per 100 females: 94.7 (2010); Marriage status: 20.9% never married, 63.0% now married, 7.4% widowed, 8.7% divorced (2005-2009 5-year est.); Foreign born: 0.9% (2005-2009 5-year est.); Ancestry (includes multiple ancestries): 21.5% German, 15.0% Irish, 10.7% English, 9.8% American, 2.4% Scotch-Irish (2005-2009 5-year est.).
Economy: Single-family building permits issued: 88 (2010); Multi-family building permits issued: 0 (2010); Employment by occupation: 15.4% management, 16.0% professional, 13.5% services, 30.1% sales, 0.0% farming, 9.0% construction, 15.9% production (2005-2009 5-year est.).
Income: Per capita income: $24,938 (2010); Median household income: $56,675 (2010); Average household income: $70,416 (2010); Percent of households with income of $100,000 or more: 15.7% (2010); Poverty rate: 8.7% (2005-2009 5-year est.).
Taxes: Total city taxes per capita: $280 (2007); City property taxes per capita: $146 (2007).
Education: Percent of population age 25 and over with: High school diploma (including GED) or higher: 87.4% (2010); Bachelor's degree or higher: 17.5% (2010); Master's degree or higher: 4.4% (2010).

School District(s)

Robinson ISD (PK-12)
    2009-10 Enrollment: 2,160 . . . . (254) 662-0194
Housing: Homeownership rate: 81.3% (2010); Median home value: $120,638 (2010); Median contract rent: $651 per month (2005-2009 5-year est.); Median year structure built: 1982 (2005-2009 5-year est.).
Safety: Violent crime rate: 14.1 per 10,000 population; Property crime rate: 193.6 per 10,000 population (2009).
Transportation: Commute to work: 95.9% car, 0.0% public transportation, 0.8% walk, 2.5% work from home (2005-2009 5-year est.); Travel time to work: 30.7% less than 15 minutes, 58.9% 15 to 30 minutes, 7.6% 30 to 45 minutes, 1.3% 45 to 60 minutes, 1.5% 60 minutes or more (2005-2009 5-year est.)
Additional Information Contacts
City of Robinson. . . . . (254) 662-1415
   http://www.robinsontexas.org

ROSS (city). Covers a land area of 1.744 square miles and a water area of 0 square miles. Located at 31.72° N. Lat; 97.10° W. Long. Elevation is 571 feet.
Population: 182 (1990); 228 (2000); 233 (2010); 235 (2015 projected); Race: 93.6% White, 0.9% Black, 0.4% Asian, 5.2% Other, 6.9% Hispanic of any race (2010); Density: 133.6 persons per square mile (2010); Average household size: 2.77 (2010); Median age: 35.2 (2010); Males per 100 females: 100.9 (2010); Marriage status: 30.4% never married, 59.5% now married, 1.4% widowed, 8.8% divorced (2005-2009 5-year est.); Foreign born: 2.8% (2005-2009 5-year est.); Ancestry (includes multiple ancestries): 33.5% Czech, 31.0% German, 11.8% Scotch-Irish, 10.8% Irish, 8.3% American (2005-2009 5-year est.).

Economy: Employment by occupation: 5.0% management, 13.4% professional, 11.4% services, 31.7% sales, 0.0% farming, 10.4% construction, 28.2% production (2005-2009 5-year est.).
Income: Per capita income: $23,693 (2010); Median household income: $54,762 (2010); Average household income: $64,583 (2010); Percent of households with income of $100,000 or more: 15.5% (2010); Poverty rate: 7.8% (2005-2009 5-year est.).
Taxes: Total city taxes per capita: $52 (2007); City property taxes per capita: $0 (2007).
Education: Percent of population age 25 and over with: High school diploma (including GED) or higher: 84.6% (2010); Bachelor's degree or higher: 14.1% (2010); Master's degree or higher: 4.7% (2010).
Housing: Homeownership rate: 84.5% (2010); Median home value: $98,571 (2010); Median contract rent: $371 per month (2005-2009 5-year est.); Median year structure built: 1982 (2005-2009 5-year est.).
Transportation: Commute to work: 96.0% car, 0.0% public transportation, 3.0% walk, 1.0% work from home (2005-2009 5-year est.); Travel time to work: 20.5% less than 15 minutes, 52.0% 15 to 30 minutes, 10.5% 30 to 45 minutes, 13.5% 45 to 60 minutes, 3.5% 60 minutes or more (2005-2009 5-year est.)

WACO (city). County seat. Covers a land area of 84.201 square miles and a water area of 11.322 square miles. Located at 31.55° N. Lat; 97.15° W. Long. Elevation is 469 feet.
History: Waco was laid out as a village on the Brazos River in 1849 by land agent Jacob de Cordova, following sporadic settlement in the area during the 1840's. The town grew up around the ferry established by Shapley P. Ross, who later built a hotel. Education achieved early importance with the founding in 1861 of Waco University, absorbed by Baylor University in 1885.
Population: 104,455 (1990); 113,726 (2000); 124,070 (2010); 128,953 (2015 projected); Race: 58.0% White, 21.1% Black, 1.9% Asian, 19.0% Other, 29.4% Hispanic of any race (2010); Density: 1,473.5 persons per square mile (2010); Average household size: 2.51 (2010); Median age: 29.7 (2010); Males per 100 females: 94.2 (2010); Marriage status: 41.8% never married, 39.9% now married, 7.1% widowed, 11.2% divorced (2005-2009 5-year est.); Foreign born: 10.6% (2005-2009 5-year est.); Ancestry (includes multiple ancestries): 12.4% German, 8.9% Irish, 7.7% English, 5.5% American, 1.9% Scotch-Irish (2005-2009 5-year est.).
Economy: Unemployment rate: 9.2% (June 2011); Total civilian labor force: 59,101 (June 2011); Single-family building permits issued: 308 (2010); Multi-family building permits issued: 130 (2010); Employment by occupation: 8.4% management, 19.4% professional, 21.2% services, 26.5% sales, 0.3% farming, 9.6% construction, 14.6% production (2005-2009 5-year est.).
Income: Per capita income: $16,890 (2010); Median household income: $30,942 (2010); Average household income: $44,294 (2010); Percent of households with income of $100,000 or more: 8.1% (2010); Poverty rate: 28.8% (2005-2009 5-year est.).
Taxes: Total city taxes per capita: $653 (2007); City property taxes per capita: $300 (2007).
Education: Percent of population age 25 and over with: High school diploma (including GED) or higher: 76.0% (2010); Bachelor's degree or higher: 19.6% (2010); Master's degree or higher: 7.0% (2010).

School District(s)

Axtell ISD (PK-12)
    2009-10 Enrollment: 767 . . . . (254) 863-5301
Bosqueville ISD (PK-12)
    2009-10 Enrollment: 565 . . . . (254) 757-3113
Bruceville-Eddy ISD (PK-12)
    2009-10 Enrollment: 854 . . . . (254) 859-5832
China Spring ISD (PK-12)
    2009-10 Enrollment: 2,288 . . . . (254) 836-1115
Connally ISD (PK-12)
    2009-10 Enrollment: 2,464 . . . . (254) 296-6460
Crawford ISD (PK-12)
    2009-10 Enrollment: 603 . . . . (254) 486-2381
Gholson ISD (PK-08)
    2009-10 Enrollment: 154 . . . . (254) 829-1528
Hallsburg ISD (KG-09)
    2009-10 Enrollment: 99 . . . . (254) 875-2331
Harmony Science Academy (Waco) (KG-10)
    2009-10 Enrollment: 433 . . . . (254) 751-7878
La Vega ISD (PK-12)
    2009-10 Enrollment: 2,932 . . . . (254) 799-4963

Profiles of Texas

392 McLennan County

Lorena ISD (PK-12)
2009-10 Enrollment: 1,611 .... (254) 857-3239
Mart ISD (PK-12)
2009-10 Enrollment: 575 .... (254) 876-2523
McGregor ISD (PK-12)
2009-10 Enrollment: 1,318 .... (254) 840-2828
Midway ISD (PK-12)
2009-10 Enrollment: 6,883 .... (254) 761-5610
Rapoport Academy Public School (PK-12)
2009-10 Enrollment: 369 .... (254) 754-8000
Responsive Education Solutions (KG-12)
2009-10 Enrollment: 5,022 .... (972) 316-3663
Riesel ISD (PK-12)
2009-10 Enrollment: 581 .... (254) 896-6411
Robinson ISD (PK-12)
2009-10 Enrollment: 2,160 .... (254) 662-0194
University of Texas University Charter School (KG-12)
2009-10 Enrollment: 907 .... (512) 471-5652
Waco Charter School (KG-05)
2009-10 Enrollment: 182 .... (254) 754-8169
Waco ISD (PK-12)
2009-10 Enrollment: 15,337 .... (254) 755-9420
West ISD (PK-12)
2009-10 Enrollment: 1,552 .... (254) 826-7500

Four-year College(s)
Baylor University (Private, Not-for-profit, Baptist)
Fall 2009 Enrollment: 14,614 .... (254) 710-1011
2010-11 Tuition: In-state $29,884; Out-of-state $29,884

Two-year College(s)
McLennan Community College (Public)
Fall 2009 Enrollment: 9,128 .... (254) 299-8000
2010-11 Tuition: In-state $2,448; Out-of-state $3,600
Texas State Technical College Waco (Public)
Fall 2009 Enrollment: 6,816 .... (800) 792-8784
2010-11 Tuition: In-state $3,636; Out-of-state $7,992

Vocational/Technical School(s)
ATI Career Training Center (Private, For-profit)
Fall 2009 Enrollment: 483 .... (254) 230-4950
2010-11 Tuition: $16,700

Housing: Homeownership rate: 45.2% (2010); Median home value: $77,247 (2010); Median contract rent: $531 per month (2005-2009 5-year est.); Median year structure built: 1970 (2005-2009 5-year est.).
Hospitals: Hillcrest Baptist Medical Center (393 beds); Providence DePaul Center; Providence Health Center (214 beds); Waco Center for Youth (90 beds); Waco VA Medical Center (1063 beds)
Safety: Violent crime rate: 70.6 per 10,000 population; Property crime rate: 568.4 per 10,000 population (2009).
Newspapers: Hometown News (Community news); Moody Courier (Community news; Circulation 1,000); Rustler (Community news); Waco Citizen (Community news; Circulation 1,000); Waco Tribune-Herald (Local news; Circulation 48,500)
Transportation: Commute to work: 91.4% car, 0.7% public transportation, 4.7% walk, 2.1% work from home (2005-2009 5-year est.); Travel time to work: 46.4% less than 15 minutes, 42.9% 15 to 30 minutes, 6.2% 30 to 45 minutes, 1.4% 45 to 60 minutes, 3.1% 60 minutes or more (2005-2009 5-year est.)
Airports: McGregor Executive (general aviation); TSTC Waco (general aviation); Waco Regional (primary service)
Additional Information Contacts
Cen-Tex African American Chamber of Commerce ...... (254) 235-3204
http://centexchamber.com
Cen-Tex Hispanic Chamber of Commerce .... (254) 754-7111
http://www.wacohispanicchamber.com
City of Waco.................................... (254) 750-5600
http://www.waco-texas.com
Greater Robinson Chamber of Commerce .... (254) 662-6434
http://www.robinsontexaschamber.org
Greater Waco Chamber of Commerce .... (254) 752-6551
http://www.waco-chamber.com
Lacy Lakeview Chamber of Commerce................ (254) 799-2458
http://www.lacylakeview.org/chamber.html

WEST (city). Covers a land area of 1.555 square miles and a water area of 0 square miles. Located at 31.80° N. Lat; 97.09° W. Long. Elevation is 650 feet.

History: Settled 1878, incorporated 1894.
Population: 2,498 (1990); 2,692 (2000); 2,678 (2010); 2,676 (2015 projected); Race: 93.6% White, 2.9% Black, 0.1% Asian, 3.3% Other, 9.7% Hispanic of any race (2010); Density: 1,722.1 persons per square mile (2010); Average household size: 2.50 (2010); Median age: 38.8 (2010); Males per 100 females: 89.4 (2010); Marriage status: 24.1% never married, 46.0% now married, 20.1% widowed, 9.7% divorced (2005-2009 5-year est.); Foreign born: 7.8% (2005-2009 5-year est.); Ancestry (includes multiple ancestries): 34.6% Czech, 16.5% German, 12.7% American, 7.6% Irish, 3.2% Polish (2005-2009 5-year est.).
Economy: Single-family building permits issued: 4 (2010); Multi-family building permits issued: 0 (2010); Employment by occupation: 11.2% management, 18.2% professional, 8.3% services, 27.6% sales, 0.4% farming, 16.1% construction, 18.2% production (2005-2009 5-year est.).
Income: Per capita income: $20,009 (2010); Median household income: $44,214 (2010); Average household income: $51,725 (2010); Percent of households with income of $100,000 or more: 9.7% (2010); Poverty rate: 16.2% (2005-2009 5-year est.).
Taxes: Total city taxes per capita: $342 (2007); City property taxes per capita: $146 (2007).
Education: Percent of population age 25 and over with: High school diploma (including GED) or higher: 71.1% (2010); Bachelor's degree or higher: 14.5% (2010); Master's degree or higher: 5.2% (2010).

School District(s)
West ISD (PK-12)
2009-10 Enrollment: 1,552 .... (254) 826-7500
Housing: Homeownership rate: 71.5% (2010); Median home value: $78,831 (2010); Median contract rent: $379 per month (2005-2009 5-year est.); Median year structure built: 1957 (2005-2009 5-year est.).
Hospitals: Hillcrest Medical Center at West (49 beds)
Safety: Violent crime rate: 0.0 per 10,000 population; Property crime rate: 141.4 per 10,000 population (2009).
Newspapers: West News (Local news; Circulation 3,100)
Transportation: Commute to work: 96.9% car, 0.0% public transportation, 0.9% walk, 1.8% work from home (2005-2009 5-year est.); Travel time to work: 40.6% less than 15 minutes, 38.7% 15 to 30 minutes, 16.9% 30 to 45 minutes, 2.0% 45 to 60 minutes, 1.8% 60 minutes or more (2005-2009 5-year est.)
Additional Information Contacts
West Chamber of Commerce .... (254) 826-3188
http://westtxchamber.com

WOODWAY (city). Covers a land area of 6.596 square miles and a water area of 0 square miles. Located at 31.50° N. Lat; 97.22° W. Long. Elevation is 633 feet.
History: The unofficial slogan of Woodway is "Keep Woodway Woody", referring to the picturesque and magnificent trees found in the area.
Population: 8,693 (1990); 8,733 (2000); 8,826 (2010); 8,966 (2015 projected); Race: 91.5% White, 3.6% Black, 2.2% Asian, 2.8% Other, 5.3% Hispanic of any race (2010); Density: 1,338.2 persons per square mile (2010); Average household size: 2.52 (2010); Median age: 46.2 (2010); Males per 100 females: 94.2 (2010); Marriage status: 17.6% never married, 69.5% now married, 7.1% widowed, 5.9% divorced (2005-2009 5-year est.); Foreign born: 4.6% (2005-2009 5-year est.); Ancestry (includes multiple ancestries): 20.3% German, 14.5% English, 11.0% American, 10.5% Irish, 4.8% Scotch-Irish (2005-2009 5-year est.).
Economy: Single-family building permits issued: 14 (2010); Multi-family building permits issued: 0 (2010); Employment by occupation: 15.2% management, 26.3% professional, 8.1% services, 32.0% sales, 0.3% farming, 7.1% construction, 11.0% production (2005-2009 5-year est.).
Income: Per capita income: $39,912 (2010); Median household income: $77,221 (2010); Average household income: $102,024 (2010); Percent of households with income of $100,000 or more: 35.5% (2010); Poverty rate: 3.5% (2005-2009 5-year est.).
Taxes: Total city taxes per capita: $645 (2007); City property taxes per capita: $337 (2007).
Education: Percent of population age 25 and over with: High school diploma (including GED) or higher: 95.3% (2010); Bachelor's degree or higher: 51.1% (2010); Master's degree or higher: 18.3% (2010).
Housing: Homeownership rate: 79.9% (2010); Median home value: $183,099 (2010); Median contract rent: $753 per month (2005-2009 5-year est.); Median year structure built: 1977 (2005-2009 5-year est.).
Safety: Violent crime rate: 23.8 per 10,000 population; Property crime rate: 167.7 per 10,000 population (2009).

Transportation: Commute to work: 94.8% car, 0.3% public transportation, 1.2% walk, 2.2% work from home (2005-2009 5-year est.); Travel time to work: 56.2% less than 15 minutes, 38.5% 15 to 30 minutes, 2.4% 30 to 45 minutes, 2.2% 45 to 60 minutes, 0.7% 60 minutes or more (2005-2009 5-year est.)

Additional Information Contacts
City of Woodway . . . . (254) 772-4480
   http://www.woodway-texas.com

McMullen County

Located in south Texas; drained by the Frio and Nueces Rivers. Covers a land area of 1,113.00 square miles, a water area of 29.60 square miles, and is located in the Central Time Zone at 28.35° N. Lat., 98.53° W. Long. The county was founded in 1858. County seat is Tilden.

Weather Station: Tilden 4 SSE — Elevation: 345 feet

	Jan	Feb	Mar	Apr	May	Jun	Jul	Aug	Sep	Oct	Nov	Dec
High	67	71	78	84	91	96	98	99	93	86	76	68
Low	42	46	53	59	67	72	73	73	69	60	51	44
Precip	1.2	1.3	1.6	1.8	3.1	3.0	2.3	2.3	3.0	2.1	1.4	1.4
Snow	0.0	0.0	0.0	0.0	0.0	0.0	0.0	0.0	0.0	tr	0.0	0.2

High and Low temperatures in degrees Fahrenheit; Precipitation and Snow in inches

Population: 817 (1990); 851 (2000); 848 (2010); 845 (2015 projected); Race: 87.1% White, 1.2% Black, 0.0% Asian, 11.7% Other, 37.1% Hispanic of any race (2010); Density: 0.8 persons per square mile (2010); Average household size: 2.32 (2010); Median age: 46.9 (2010); Males per 100 females: 97.7 (2010).
Religion: Two largest groups: 41.4% Catholic Church, 15.5% Southern Baptist Convention (2000).
Economy: Unemployment rate: 6.8% (June 2011); Total civilian labor force: 426 (June 2011); Leading industries: Farms: 225 totaling 506,492 acres (2007); Companies that employ 500 or more persons: 0 (2009); Companies that employ 100 to 499 persons: 0 (2009); Companies that employ less than 100 persons: 14 (2009); Black-owned businesses: n/a (2007); Hispanic-owned businesses: n/a (2007); Asian-owned businesses: n/a (2007); Women-owned businesses: n/a (2007); Retail sales per capita: $5,423 (2010). Single-family building permits issued: n/a (2010); Multi-family building permits issued: n/a (2010).
Income: Per capita income: $24,116 (2010); Median household income: $39,100 (2010); Average household income: $56,027 (2010); Percent of households with income of $100,000 or more: 12.1% (2010); Poverty rate: 13.2% (2009); Bankruptcy rate: 0.45% (2010).
Taxes: Total county taxes per capita: $2,461 (2007); County property taxes per capita: $2,285 (2007).
Education: Percent of population age 25 and over with: High school diploma (including GED) or higher: 79.2% (2010); Bachelor's degree or higher: 18.2% (2010); Master's degree or higher: 3.0% (2010).
Housing: Homeownership rate: 78.9% (2010); Median home value: $57,931 (2010); Median contract rent: $290 per month (2005-2009 5-year est.); Median year structure built: 1979 (2005-2009 5-year est.)
Health: Birth rate: 74.1 per 10,000 population (2009); Death rate: 24.7 per 10,000 population (2009); Age-adjusted cancer mortality rate: Suppressed deaths per 100,000 population (2007); Number of physicians: 11.9 per 10,000 population (2008); Hospital beds: 0.0 per 10,000 population (2007); Hospital admissions: 0.0 per 10,000 population (2007).
Elections: 2008 Presidential election results: 24.6% Obama, 74.5% McCain, 0.0% Nader
Additional Information Contacts
McMullen County Government . . . . (361) 274-3341

McMullen County Communities

CALLIHAM (unincorporated postal area, zip code 78007). Covers a land area of 32.612 square miles and a water area of 0.069 square miles. Located at 28.45° N. Lat; 98.37° W. Long. Elevation is 226 feet.
Population: 182 (2000); Race: 86.9% White, 0.0% Black, 0.0% Asian, 13.1% Other, 31.3% Hispanic of any race (2000); Density: 5.6 persons per square mile (2000); Age: 21.3% under 18, 15.6% over 64 (2000); Marriage status: 13.3% never married, 66.7% now married, 9.6% widowed, 10.4% divorced (2000); Foreign born: 4.4% (2000); Ancestry (includes multiple ancestries): 13.1% German, 10.6% American, 8.1% English, 7.5% Irish (2000).

Economy: Employment by occupation: 18.5% management, 12.3% professional, 18.5% services, 23.1% sales, 3.1% farming, 16.9% construction, 7.7% production (2000).
Income: Per capita income: $17,669 (2000); Median household income: $27,344 (2000); Poverty rate: 179.1% (2000).
Education: Percent of population age 25 and over with: High school diploma (including GED) or higher: 79.0% (2000); Bachelor's degree or higher: 3.4% (2000).
Housing: Homeownership rate: 91.4% (2000); Median home value: $52,000 (2000); Median contract rent: $325 per month (2000); Median year structure built: 1987 (2000).
Transportation: Commute to work: 100.0% car, 0.0% public transportation, 0.0% walk, 0.0% work from home (2000); Travel time to work: 53.1% less than 15 minutes, 25.0% 15 to 30 minutes, 9.4% 30 to 45 minutes, 3.1% 45 to 60 minutes, 9.4% 60 minutes or more (2000)

TILDEN (unincorporated postal area, zip code 78072). County seat. Covers a land area of 678.857 square miles and a water area of 2.805 square miles. Located at 28.31° N. Lat; 98.49° W. Long. Elevation is 249 feet.
Population: 588 (2000); Race: 84.9% White, 0.7% Black, 0.0% Asian, 14.4% Other, 37.7% Hispanic of any race (2000); Density: 0.9 persons per square mile (2000); Age: 22.9% under 18, 21.6% over 64 (2000); Marriage status: 16.9% never married, 65.5% now married, 10.9% widowed, 6.7% divorced (2000); Foreign born: 3.6% (2000); Ancestry (includes multiple ancestries): 9.8% German, 9.4% English, 7.0% American, 6.8% Irish (2000).
Economy: Employment by occupation: 20.5% management, 12.6% professional, 7.9% services, 15.0% sales, 5.9% farming, 17.7% construction, 20.5% production (2000).
Income: Per capita income: $23,931 (2000); Median household income: $33,295 (2000); Poverty rate: 179.1% (2000).
Education: Percent of population age 25 and over with: High school diploma (including GED) or higher: 71.6% (2000); Bachelor's degree or higher: 17.6% (2000).

School District(s)
McMullen County ISD (PK-12)
   2009-10 Enrollment: 170 . . . . (361) 274-3315
Housing: Homeownership rate: 78.8% (2000); Median home value: $45,900 (2000); Median contract rent: $295 per month (2000); Median year structure built: 1973 (2000).
Transportation: Commute to work: 89.9% car, 2.0% public transportation, 2.8% walk, 5.2% work from home (2000); Travel time to work: 50.6% less than 15 minutes, 31.1% 15 to 30 minutes, 11.9% 30 to 45 minutes, 1.3% 45 to 60 minutes, 5.1% 60 minutes or more (2000)

Medina County

Located in southwestern Texas; drained by the Medina River; includes part of Medina Lake. Covers a land area of 1,327.76 square miles, a water area of 6.77 square miles, and is located in the Central Time Zone at 29.29° N. Lat., 99.03° W. Long. The county was founded in 1848. County seat is Hondo.

Medina County is part of the San Antonio-New Braunfels, TX Metropolitan Statistical Area. The entire metro area includes: Atascosa County, TX; Bandera County, TX; Bexar County, TX; Comal County, TX; Guadalupe County, TX; Kendall County, TX; Medina County, TX; Wilson County, TX

Weather Station: Hondo Municipal Arpt — Elevation: 919 feet

	Jan	Feb	Mar	Apr	May	Jun	Jul	Aug	Sep	Oct	Nov	Dec
High	63	67	74	81	87	92	95	96	90	82	72	64
Low	39	43	50	57	66	71	72	72	67	59	48	40
Precip	1.4	1.4	2.0	1.9	3.5	3.2	2.2	1.6	2.5	2.9	1.7	1.2
Snow	na	na	na	na	na	na	na	na	na	na	na	na

High and Low temperatures in degrees Fahrenheit; Precipitation and Snow in inches

Weather Station: Lytle 3 W — Elevation: 722 feet

	Jan	Feb	Mar	Apr	May	Jun	Jul	Aug	Sep	Oct	Nov	Dec
High	65	69	76	83	88	93	95	96	91	83	73	66
Low	41	45	51	58	66	71	73	72	68	60	51	43
Precip	1.6	1.8	2.0	2.1	3.3	3.8	2.3	1.6	2.8	3.7	2.1	1.6
Snow	0.5	tr	0.0	0.0	0.0	0.0	0.0	0.0	0.0	tr	0.0	0.0

High and Low temperatures in degrees Fahrenheit; Precipitation and Snow in inches

Population: 27,312 (1990); 39,304 (2000); 45,338 (2010); 48,189 (2015 projected); Race: 78.2% White, 2.6% Black, 0.4% Asian, 18.9% Other, 47.5% Hispanic of any race (2010); Density: 34.1 persons per square mile (2010); Average household size: 2.90 (2010); Median age: 34.9 (2010); Males per 100 females: 102.9 (2010).
Religion: Five largest groups: 38.0% Catholic Church, 11.4% Southern Baptist Convention, 4.3% The United Methodist Church, 2.6% Evangelical Lutheran Church in America, 0.8% Churches of Christ (2000).
Economy: Unemployment rate: 7.9% (June 2011); Total civilian labor force: 20,736 (June 2011); Leading industries: 23.3% retail trade; 15.6% health care and social assistance; 15.0% accommodation & food services (2009); Farms: 2,139 totaling 748,144 acres (2007); Companies that employ 500 or more persons: 0 (2009); Companies that employ 100 to 499 persons: 5 (2009); Companies that employ less than 100 persons: 632 (2009); Black-owned businesses: n/a (2007); Hispanic-owned businesses: 1,109 (2007); Asian-owned businesses: n/a (2007); Women-owned businesses: n/a (2007); Retail sales per capita: $7,778 (2010). Single-family building permits issued: 12 (2010); Multi-family building permits issued: 0 (2010).
Income: Per capita income: $20,041 (2010); Median household income: $46,693 (2010); Average household income: $58,909 (2010); Percent of households with income of $100,000 or more: 13.1% (2010); Poverty rate: 17.6% (2009); Bankruptcy rate: 1.77% (2010).
Taxes: Total county taxes per capita: $258 (2007); County property taxes per capita: $219 (2007).
Education: Percent of population age 25 and over with: High school diploma (including GED) or higher: 78.4% (2010); Bachelor's degree or higher: 18.5% (2010); Master's degree or higher: 6.5% (2010).
Housing: Homeownership rate: 80.2% (2010); Median home value: $94,940 (2010); Median contract rent: $462 per month (2005-2009 5-year est.); Median year structure built: 1984 (2005-2009 5-year est.)
Health: Birth rate: 141.5 per 10,000 population (2009); Death rate: 86.5 per 10,000 population (2009); Age-adjusted cancer mortality rate: 202.5 deaths per 100,000 population (2007); Number of physicians: 4.3 per 10,000 population (2008); Hospital beds: 5.7 per 10,000 population (2007); Hospital admissions: 257.6 per 10,000 population (2007).
Elections: 2008 Presidential election results: 32.7% Obama, 66.6% McCain, 0.0% Nader
Additional Information Contacts
Medina County Government . . . . (830) 741-6020
    http://www.medinacountytexas.org
Castroville Area Chamber of Commerce . . . . (830) 538-3142
    http://www.castroville.com
City of Hondo . . . . (830) 426-3378
    http://cityofhondo.com
Hondo Area Chamber of Commerce . . . . (830) 426-3037
    http://www.hondochamber.com

Medina County Communities

CASTROVILLE (city). Covers a land area of 2.548 square miles and a water area of 0.006 square miles. Located at 29.35° N. Lat; 98.88° W. Long. Elevation is 758 feet.
History: Castroville was founded in 1844 by a group of colonists under Count Henri de Castro. Many of Castro's first colonists came from Alsace. They established their town on the Medina River, where they suffered many hardships before being joined by other settlers. Castroville was for 44 years the seat of Medina County, but lost it to Hondo in 1892.
Population: 2,248 (1990); 2,664 (2000); 3,102 (2010); 3,307 (2015 projected); Race: 78.7% White, 0.2% Black, 0.8% Asian, 20.3% Other, 34.5% Hispanic of any race (2010); Density: 1,217.2 persons per square mile (2010); Average household size: 2.75 (2010); Median age: 39.8 (2010); Males per 100 females: 96.0 (2010); Marriage status: 28.6% never married, 52.0% now married, 9.2% widowed, 10.2% divorced (2005-2009 5-year est.); Foreign born: 0.8% (2005-2009 5-year est.); Ancestry (includes multiple ancestries): 26.1% German, 10.9% Irish, 7.5% English, 7.2% American, 4.3% Alsatian (2005-2009 5-year est.).
Economy: Single-family building permits issued: 4 (2010); Multi-family building permits issued: 0 (2010); Employment by occupation: 11.0% management, 31.6% professional, 12.1% services, 30.5% sales, 0.0% farming, 7.9% construction, 6.8% production (2005-2009 5-year est.).
Income: Per capita income: $24,502 (2010); Median household income: $54,333 (2010); Average household income: $68,078 (2010); Percent of households with income of $100,000 or more: 18.2% (2010); Poverty rate: 13.1% (2005-2009 5-year est.).

Taxes: Total city taxes per capita: $319 (2007); City property taxes per capita: $148 (2007).
Education: Percent of population age 25 and over with: High school diploma (including GED) or higher: 89.7% (2010); Bachelor's degree or higher: 34.0% (2010); Master's degree or higher: 15.6% (2010).
School District(s)
Medina Valley ISD (PK-12)
    2009-10 Enrollment: 3,382 . . . . (830) 931-2243
Housing: Homeownership rate: 80.0% (2010); Median home value: $117,016 (2010); Median contract rent: $613 per month (2005-2009 5-year est.); Median year structure built: 1974 (2005-2009 5-year est.).
Safety: Violent crime rate: 41.9 per 10,000 population; Property crime rate: 225.5 per 10,000 population (2009).
Newspapers: Medina Valley Times (Community news; Circulation 3,900); News Bulletin (Community news; Circulation 2,400)
Transportation: Commute to work: 85.8% car, 0.5% public transportation, 9.3% walk, 3.3% work from home (2005-2009 5-year est.); Travel time to work: 37.5% less than 15 minutes, 31.3% 15 to 30 minutes, 11.0% 30 to 45 minutes, 11.2% 45 to 60 minutes, 9.0% 60 minutes or more (2005-2009 5-year est.)
Additional Information Contacts
Castroville Area Chamber of Commerce . . . . (830) 538-3142
    http://www.castroville.com

D'HANIS (unincorporated postal area, zip code 78850). Covers a land area of 250.695 square miles and a water area of 0.685 square miles. Located at 29.33° N. Lat; 99.33° W. Long.
Population: 1,095 (2000); Race: 84.0% White, 0.2% Black, 0.0% Asian, 15.8% Other, 46.4% Hispanic of any race (2000); Density: 4.4 persons per square mile (2000); Age: 28.4% under 18, 18.1% over 64 (2000); Marriage status: 21.8% never married, 63.0% now married, 7.7% widowed, 7.5% divorced (2000); Foreign born: 3.0% (2000); Ancestry (includes multiple ancestries): 26.2% German, 4.4% French, 4.2% Alsatian, 4.2% American (2000).
Economy: Employment by occupation: 14.7% management, 13.4% professional, 14.7% services, 22.1% sales, 5.7% farming, 9.9% construction, 19.5% production (2000).
Income: Per capita income: $14,459 (2000); Median household income: $31,359 (2000); Poverty rate: 179.1% (2000).
Education: Percent of population age 25 and over with: High school diploma (including GED) or higher: 75.6% (2000); Bachelor's degree or higher: 14.4% (2000).
School District(s)
D'hanis ISD (PK-12)
    2009-10 Enrollment: 317 . . . . (830) 363-7215
Housing: Homeownership rate: 79.9% (2000); Median home value: $50,000 (2000); Median contract rent: $179 per month (2000); Median year structure built: 1971 (2000).
Transportation: Commute to work: 85.0% car, 0.0% public transportation, 4.3% walk, 6.4% work from home (2000); Travel time to work: 37.6% less than 15 minutes, 37.0% 15 to 30 minutes, 12.5% 30 to 45 minutes, 4.2% 45 to 60 minutes, 8.8% 60 minutes or more (2000)

DEVINE (city). Covers a land area of 3.109 square miles and a water area of 0 square miles. Located at 29.14° N. Lat; 98.90° W. Long. Elevation is 646 feet.
History: Incorporated 1904.
Population: 4,000 (1990); 4,140 (2000); 4,623 (2010); 4,798 (2015 projected); Race: 77.3% White, 0.6% Black, 0.3% Asian, 21.9% Other, 51.8% Hispanic of any race (2010); Density: 1,486.8 persons per square mile (2010); Average household size: 2.79 (2010); Median age: 34.9 (2010); Males per 100 females: 96.6 (2010); Marriage status: 35.0% never married, 47.5% now married, 5.1% widowed, 12.4% divorced (2005-2009 5-year est.); Foreign born: 8.8% (2005-2009 5-year est.); Ancestry (includes multiple ancestries): 19.1% German, 6.2% Irish, 5.5% English, 3.4% French, 2.4% American (2005-2009 5-year est.).
Economy: Single-family building permits issued: 6 (2010); Multi-family building permits issued: 0 (2010); Employment by occupation: 8.2% management, 11.0% professional, 23.2% services, 15.0% sales, 1.9% farming, 17.8% construction, 22.9% production (2005-2009 5-year est.).
Income: Per capita income: $19,147 (2010); Median household income: $38,498 (2010); Average household income: $54,067 (2010); Percent of households with income of $100,000 or more: 10.5% (2010); Poverty rate: 33.1% (2005-2009 5-year est.).

Taxes: Total city taxes per capita: $311 (2007); City property taxes per capita: $147 (2007).
Education: Percent of population age 25 and over with: High school diploma (including GED) or higher: 73.3% (2010); Bachelor's degree or higher: 16.1% (2010); Master's degree or higher: 7.6% (2010).

School District(s)

Devine ISD (PK-12)
    2009-10 Enrollment: 1,913 . . . . (830) 851-0795
Housing: Homeownership rate: 72.6% (2010); Median home value: $69,874 (2010); Median contract rent: $305 per month (2005-2009 5-year est.); Median year structure built: 1965 (2005-2009 5-year est.).
Safety: Violent crime rate: 28.3 per 10,000 population; Property crime rate: 172.2 per 10,000 population (2009).
Newspapers: Devine News (Community news; Circulation 4,100)
Transportation: Commute to work: 94.0% car, 0.0% public transportation, 2.5% walk, 2.2% work from home (2005-2009 5-year est.); Travel time to work: 40.8% less than 15 minutes, 18.0% 15 to 30 minutes, 15.4% 30 to 45 minutes, 11.5% 45 to 60 minutes, 14.4% 60 minutes or more (2005-2009 5-year est.)

HONDO (city). County seat. Covers a land area of 9.586 square miles and a water area of 0.019 square miles. Located at 29.34° N. Lat; 99.14° W. Long. Elevation is 892 feet.
History: Hondo was first incorporated in 1890 as Hondo City, though the incorporation was allowed to dissolve for a time because of the expense to the taxpayers. Many of Hondo's early residents were of German ancestry. The town was named for the Hondo River, which means "deep river."
Population: 6,098 (1990); 7,897 (2000); 8,839 (2010); 9,284 (2015 projected); Race: 74.8% White, 10.1% Black, 0.3% Asian, 14.8% Other, 55.7% Hispanic of any race (2010); Density: 922.1 persons per square mile (2010); Average household size: 2.81 (2010); Median age: 32.2 (2010); Males per 100 females: 129.3 (2010); Marriage status: 35.1% never married, 40.3% now married, 9.7% widowed, 14.9% divorced (2005-2009 5-year est.); Foreign born: 5.8% (2005-2009 5-year est.); Ancestry (includes multiple ancestries): 19.2% German, 5.9% American, 4.6% Irish, 3.6% Italian, 3.5% English (2005-2009 5-year est.).
Economy: Single-family building permits issued: 1 (2010); Multi-family building permits issued: 0 (2010); Employment by occupation: 11.4% management, 22.0% professional, 17.2% services, 24.3% sales, 2.5% farming, 9.5% construction, 13.2% production (2005-2009 5-year est.).
Income: Per capita income: $16,989 (2010); Median household income: $38,230 (2010); Average household income: $49,452 (2010); Percent of households with income of $100,000 or more: 8.8% (2010); Poverty rate: 13.3% (2005-2009 5-year est.).
Taxes: Total city taxes per capita: $162 (2007); City property taxes per capita: $86 (2007).
Education: Percent of population age 25 and over with: High school diploma (including GED) or higher: 69.3% (2010); Bachelor's degree or higher: 11.8% (2010); Master's degree or higher: 3.2% (2010).

School District(s)

Hondo ISD (PK-12)
    2009-10 Enrollment: 2,276 . . . . (830) 426-3027
Housing: Homeownership rate: 70.9% (2010); Median home value: $84,146 (2010); Median contract rent: $467 per month (2005-2009 5-year est.); Median year structure built: 1975 (2005-2009 5-year est.).
Hospitals: Medina Community Hospital
Safety: Violent crime rate: 55.9 per 10,000 population; Property crime rate: 341.0 per 10,000 population (2009).
Newspapers: Hondo Anvil Herald (Community news; Circulation 4,430); Sabinal Sampler (Community news; Circulation 800)
Transportation: Commute to work: 94.1% car, 0.0% public transportation, 2.9% walk, 1.1% work from home (2005-2009 5-year est.); Travel time to work: 56.5% less than 15 minutes, 7.8% 15 to 30 minutes, 14.5% 30 to 45 minutes, 11.7% 45 to 60 minutes, 9.5% 60 minutes or more (2005-2009 5-year est.)
Airports: Hondo Municipal (general aviation)
Additional Information Contacts
City of Hondo . . . . (830) 426-3378
    http://cityofhondo.com
Hondo Area Chamber of Commerce . . . . (830) 426-3037
    http://www.hondochamber.com

LA COSTE (city). Aka Lacoste. Covers a land area of 0.642 square miles and a water area of 0 square miles. Located at 29.31° N. Lat; 98.81° W. Long. Elevation is 712 feet.

Population: 1,021 (1990); 1,255 (2000); 1,390 (2010); 1,462 (2015 projected); Race: 82.4% White, 1.3% Black, 0.3% Asian, 16.0% Other, 40.6% Hispanic of any race (2010); Density: 2,164.2 persons per square mile (2010); Average household size: 2.96 (2010); Median age: 34.4 (2010); Males per 100 females: 93.3 (2010); Marriage status: 32.7% never married, 51.7% now married, 4.3% widowed, 11.3% divorced (2005-2009 5-year est.); Foreign born: 5.3% (2005-2009 5-year est.); Ancestry (includes multiple ancestries): 19.5% German, 10.6% Irish, 6.6% Scotch-Irish, 5.5% English, 3.9% Alsatian (2005-2009 5-year est.).
Economy: Employment by occupation: 3.8% management, 14.6% professional, 22.9% services, 28.9% sales, 1.6% farming, 9.0% construction, 19.1% production (2005-2009 5-year est.).
Income: Per capita income: $19,788 (2010); Median household income: $49,242 (2010); Average household income: $58,422 (2010); Percent of households with income of $100,000 or more: 12.4% (2010); Poverty rate: 18.9% (2005-2009 5-year est.).
Taxes: Total city taxes per capita: $112 (2007); City property taxes per capita: $47 (2007).
Education: Percent of population age 25 and over with: High school diploma (including GED) or higher: 82.3% (2010); Bachelor's degree or higher: 21.4% (2010); Master's degree or higher: 7.4% (2010).

School District(s)

Medina Valley ISD (PK-12)
    2009-10 Enrollment: 3,382 . . . . (830) 931-2243
Housing: Homeownership rate: 86.6% (2010); Median home value: $76,053 (2010); Median contract rent: $462 per month (2005-2009 5-year est.); Median year structure built: 1977 (2005-2009 5-year est.).
Transportation: Commute to work: 95.0% car, 0.0% public transportation, 2.8% walk, 2.2% work from home (2005-2009 5-year est.); Travel time to work: 28.9% less than 15 minutes, 12.7% 15 to 30 minutes, 33.8% 30 to 45 minutes, 19.6% 45 to 60 minutes, 4.9% 60 minutes or more (2005-2009 5-year est.)

MICO (unincorporated postal area, zip code 78056). Covers a land area of 87.224 square miles and a water area of 0.042 square miles. Located at 29.54° N. Lat; 98.90° W. Long. Elevation is 1,135 feet.
Population: 852 (2000); Race: 84.7% White, 0.0% Black, 0.0% Asian, 15.3% Other, 17.2% Hispanic of any race (2000); Density: 9.8 persons per square mile (2000); Age: 25.3% under 18, 16.6% over 64 (2000); Marriage status: 12.5% never married, 74.0% now married, 6.6% widowed, 6.9% divorced (2000); Foreign born: 2.6% (2000); Ancestry (includes multiple ancestries): 32.9% German, 13.1% English, 5.5% Irish, 4.9% American (2000).
Economy: Employment by occupation: 20.3% management, 22.5% professional, 18.0% services, 17.6% sales, 3.9% farming, 10.7% construction, 7.1% production (2000).
Income: Per capita income: $21,956 (2000); Median household income: $40,982 (2000); Poverty rate: 179.1% (2000).
Education: Percent of population age 25 and over with: High school diploma (including GED) or higher: 92.2% (2000); Bachelor's degree or higher: 32.5% (2000).
Housing: Homeownership rate: 86.9% (2000); Median home value: $121,800 (2000); Median contract rent: $379 per month (2000); Median year structure built: 1974 (2000).
Transportation: Commute to work: 85.0% car, 0.0% public transportation, 5.1% walk, 9.9% work from home (2000); Travel time to work: 18.8% less than 15 minutes, 15.7% 15 to 30 minutes, 24.9% 30 to 45 minutes, 25.9% 45 to 60 minutes, 14.7% 60 minutes or more (2000)

NATALIA (city). Covers a land area of 1.020 square miles and a water area of 0 square miles. Located at 29.18° N. Lat; 98.85° W. Long. Elevation is 686 feet.
History: Natalia developed as a center of an agricultural area that produced vegetables on land irrigated by the Medina Dam project. Canning was a leading early industry.
Population: 1,216 (1990); 1,663 (2000); 1,898 (2010); 2,018 (2015 projected); Race: 67.2% White, 0.6% Black, 0.3% Asian, 31.8% Other, 70.3% Hispanic of any race (2010); Density: 1,860.8 persons per square mile (2010); Average household size: 3.29 (2010); Median age: 31.2 (2010); Males per 100 females: 95.5 (2010); Marriage status: 33.8% never married, 55.8% now married, 1.7% widowed, 8.7% divorced (2005-2009 5-year est.); Foreign born: 8.8% (2005-2009 5-year est.); Ancestry (includes multiple ancestries): 2.9% German, 2.5% Irish, 1.6% African, 1.1% Scottish, 0.8% English (2005-2009 5-year est.).

Economy: Single-family building permits issued: 1 (2010); Multi-family building permits issued: 0 (2010); Employment by occupation: 10.4% management, 12.1% professional, 16.5% services, 29.4% sales, 0.0% farming, 20.3% construction, 11.3% production (2005-2009 5-year est.).
Income: Per capita income: $15,984 (2010); Median household income: $42,580 (2010); Average household income: $52,075 (2010); Percent of households with income of $100,000 or more: 9.0% (2010); Poverty rate: 29.2% (2005-2009 5-year est.).
Taxes: Total city taxes per capita: $175 (2007); City property taxes per capita: $128 (2007).
Education: Percent of population age 25 and over with: High school diploma (including GED) or higher: 67.1% (2010); Bachelor's degree or higher: 10.0% (2010); Master's degree or higher: 4.2% (2010).

School District(s)

Natalia ISD (PK-12)
   2009-10 Enrollment: 1,102 . . . . (830) 663-4416
Housing: Homeownership rate: 84.6% (2010); Median home value: $69,067 (2010); Median contract rent: $351 per month (2005-2009 5-year est.); Median year structure built: 1976 (2005-2009 5-year est.).
Transportation: Commute to work: 96.4% car, 0.0% public transportation, 0.9% walk, 0.4% work from home (2005-2009 5-year est.); Travel time to work: 29.9% less than 15 minutes, 16.1% 15 to 30 minutes, 23.0% 30 to 45 minutes, 16.7% 45 to 60 minutes, 14.3% 60 minutes or more (2005-2009 5-year est.)

RIO MEDINA (unincorporated postal area, zip code 78066). Covers a land area of 26.793 square miles and a water area of 0.025 square miles. Located at 29.46° N. Lat; 98.89° W. Long.
Population: 432 (2000); Race: 96.5% White, 0.0% Black, 0.0% Asian, 3.5% Other, 8.0% Hispanic of any race (2000); Density: 16.1 persons per square mile (2000); Age: 38.6% under 18, 10.2% over 64 (2000); Marriage status: 27.9% never married, 72.1% now married, 0.0% widowed, 0.0% divorced (2000); Foreign born: 0.0% (2000); Ancestry (includes multiple ancestries): 26.6% German, 18.2% English, 15.2% Irish, 13.7% Alsatian (2000).
Economy: Employment by occupation: 24.3% management, 26.2% professional, 13.1% services, 22.4% sales, 2.8% farming, 3.4% construction, 7.8% production (2000).
Income: Per capita income: $16,740 (2000); Median household income: $64,500 (2000); Poverty rate: 179.1% (2000).
Education: Percent of population age 25 and over with: High school diploma (including GED) or higher: 97.5% (2000); Bachelor's degree or higher: 19.7% (2000).
Housing: Homeownership rate: 83.6% (2000); Median home value: $86,200 (2000); Median contract rent: n/a per month (2000); Median year structure built: 1988 (2000).
Transportation: Commute to work: 100.0% car, 0.0% public transportation, 0.0% walk, 0.0% work from home (2000); Travel time to work: 26.2% less than 15 minutes, 4.5% 15 to 30 minutes, 43.8% 30 to 45 minutes, 12.5% 45 to 60 minutes, 13.1% 60 minutes or more (2000)

YANCEY (unincorporated postal area, zip code 78886). Covers a land area of 100.461 square miles and a water area of 0.176 square miles. Located at 29.14° N. Lat; 99.19° W. Long. Elevation is 673 feet.
Population: 526 (2000); Race: 81.9% White, 0.5% Black, 0.0% Asian, 17.6% Other, 33.4% Hispanic of any race (2000); Density: 5.2 persons per square mile (2000); Age: 25.6% under 18, 20.9% over 64 (2000); Marriage status: 15.5% never married, 70.3% now married, 10.3% widowed, 3.9% divorced (2000); Foreign born: 2.3% (2000); Ancestry (includes multiple ancestries): 16.0% German, 10.5% American, 5.9% Irish, 5.7% English (2000).
Economy: Employment by occupation: 13.5% management, 13.1% professional, 20.7% services, 16.3% sales, 5.2% farming, 24.7% construction, 6.4% production (2000).
Income: Per capita income: $17,818 (2000); Median household income: $37,955 (2000); Poverty rate: 179.1% (2000).
Education: Percent of population age 25 and over with: High school diploma (including GED) or higher: 75.9% (2000); Bachelor's degree or higher: 22.8% (2000).
Housing: Homeownership rate: 76.0% (2000); Median home value: $47,200 (2000); Median contract rent: $292 per month (2000); Median year structure built: 1974 (2000).
Transportation: Commute to work: 96.5% car, 0.0% public transportation, 0.9% walk, 2.6% work from home (2000); Travel time to work: 19.7% less

than 15 minutes, 29.6% 15 to 30 minutes, 23.8% 30 to 45 minutes, 7.6% 45 to 60 minutes, 19.3% 60 minutes or more (2000)

Menard County

Located in west central Texas, on the Edwards Plateau; drained by the San Saba River. Covers a land area of 901.91 square miles, a water area of 0.34 square miles, and is located in the Central Time Zone at 30.89° N. Lat., 99.81° W. Long. The county was founded in 1858. County seat is Menard.

Weather Station: Menard   Elevation: 1,951 feet

	Jan	Feb	Mar	Apr	May	Jun	Jul	Aug	Sep	Oct	Nov	Dec
High	61	65	72	81	86	91	95	94	88	79	69	61
Low	32	36	43	50	60	66	68	68	61	52	41	32
Precip	1.0	1.5	1.9	1.5	3.3	3.3	1.9	2.0	2.3	2.5	1.7	1.2
Snow	0.8	0.2	tr	0.0	0.0	0.0	0.0	0.0	0.0	0.0	tr	0.3

High and Low temperatures in degrees Fahrenheit; Precipitation and Snow in inches

Population: 2,252 (1990); 2,360 (2000); 2,248 (2010); 2,191 (2015 projected); Race: 86.9% White, 0.7% Black, 0.3% Asian, 12.1% Other, 32.4% Hispanic of any race (2010); Density: 2.5 persons per square mile (2010); Average household size: 2.32 (2010); Median age: 48.5 (2010); Males per 100 females: 99.6 (2010).
Religion: Five largest groups: 23.9% Southern Baptist Convention, 16.5% Catholic Church, 9.2% The United Methodist Church, 3.1% Churches of Christ, 2.8% Episcopal Church (2000).
Economy: Unemployment rate: 7.6% (June 2011); Total civilian labor force: 1,015 (June 2011); Leading industries: 30.0% retail trade; 12.7% accommodation & food services; 3.2% other services (except public administration) (2009); Farms: 356 totaling 491,293 acres (2007); Companies that employ 500 or more persons: 0 (2009); Companies that employ 100 to 499 persons: 0 (2009); Companies that employ less than 100 persons: 53 (2009); Black-owned businesses: n/a (2007); Hispanic-owned businesses: n/a (2007); Asian-owned businesses: n/a (2007); Women-owned businesses: n/a (2007); Retail sales per capita: $7,381 (2010). Single-family building permits issued: n/a (2010); Multi-family building permits issued: n/a (2010).
Income: Per capita income: $21,121 (2010); Median household income: $35,000 (2010); Average household income: $49,918 (2010); Percent of households with income of $100,000 or more: 12.2% (2010); Poverty rate: 25.6% (2009); Bankruptcy rate: n/a (2010).
Taxes: Total county taxes per capita: $483 (2007); County property taxes per capita: $333 (2007).
Education: Percent of population age 25 and over with: High school diploma (including GED) or higher: 74.6% (2010); Bachelor's degree or higher: 19.4% (2010); Master's degree or higher: 6.2% (2010).
Housing: Homeownership rate: 72.7% (2010); Median home value: $40,841 (2010); Median contract rent: $290 per month (2005-2009 5-year est.); Median year structure built: 1955 (2005-2009 5-year est.).
Health: Birth rate: 108.1 per 10,000 population (2009); Death rate: 131.6 per 10,000 population (2009); Age-adjusted cancer mortality rate: 146.5 (Unreliable) deaths per 100,000 population (2007); Number of physicians: 9.4 per 10,000 population (2008); Hospital beds: 0.0 per 10,000 population (2007); Hospital admissions: 0.0 per 10,000 population (2007).
Elections: 2008 Presidential election results: 29.0% Obama, 69.9% McCain, 0.1% Nader

Additional Information Contacts
Menard County Government . . . . (325) 396-4682
  http://www.menardtexas.com
Menard County Chamber of Commerce . . . . (325) 396-2365
  http://site.menardchamber.com

Menard County Communities

FORT MC KAVETT (unincorporated postal area, zip code 76841). Covers a land area of 40.714 square miles and a water area of 0.030 square miles. Located at 30.83° N. Lat; 100.09° W. Long.
Population: 31 (2000); Race: 77.8% White, 0.0% Black, 0.0% Asian, 22.2% Other, 22.2% Hispanic of any race (2000); Density: 0.8 persons per square mile (2000); Age: 19.4% under 18, 0.0% over 64 (2000); Marriage status: 24.2% never married, 51.5% now married, 0.0% widowed, 24.2% divorced (2000); Foreign born: 0.0% (2000); Ancestry (includes multiple ancestries): 41.7% American, 11.1% English (2000).

Economy: Employment by occupation: 38.9% management, 22.2% professional, 22.2% services, 16.7% sales, 0.0% farming, 0.0% construction, 0.0% production (2000).
Income: Per capita income: $22,147 (2000); Median household income: $50,417 (2000); Poverty rate: 179.1% (2000).
Education: Percent of population age 25 and over with: High school diploma (including GED) or higher: 86.2% (2000); Bachelor's degree or higher: 24.1% (2000).
Housing: Homeownership rate: 61.1% (2000); Median home value: $12,500 (2000); Median contract rent: n/a per month (2000); Median year structure built: 1952 (2000).
Transportation: Commute to work: 77.8% car, 0.0% public transportation, 0.0% walk, 22.2% work from home (2000); Travel time to work: 21.4% less than 15 minutes, 28.6% 15 to 30 minutes, 0.0% 30 to 45 minutes, 28.6% 45 to 60 minutes, 21.4% 60 minutes or more (2000)

HEXT (unincorporated postal area, zip code 76848). Covers a land area of 77.633 square miles and a water area of 0.006 square miles. Located at 30.84° N. Lat; 99.52° W. Long. Elevation is 1,847 feet.
Population: 64 (2000); Race: 100.0% White, 0.0% Black, 0.0% Asian, 0.0% Other, 13.7% Hispanic of any race (2000); Density: 0.8 persons per square mile (2000); Age: 15.7% under 18, 9.8% over 64 (2000); Marriage status: 0.0% never married, 83.7% now married, 7.0% widowed, 9.3% divorced (2000); Foreign born: 0.0% (2000); Ancestry (includes multiple ancestries): 21.6% English, 9.8% Scottish, 7.8% Irish, 5.9% Scotch-Irish (2000).
Economy: Employment by occupation: 10.7% management, 14.3% professional, 25.0% services, 10.7% sales, 0.0% farming, 14.3% construction, 25.0% production (2000).
Income: Per capita income: $20,704 (2000); Median household income: $30,625 (2000); Poverty rate: 179.1% (2000).
Education: Percent of population age 25 and over with: High school diploma (including GED) or higher: 90.7% (2000); Bachelor's degree or higher: 30.2% (2000).
Housing: Homeownership rate: 88.0% (2000); Median home value: $17,500 (2000); Median contract rent: n/a per month (2000); Median year structure built: before 1940 (2000).
Transportation: Commute to work: 100.0% car, 0.0% public transportation, 0.0% walk, 0.0% work from home (2000); Travel time to work: 14.3% less than 15 minutes, 60.7% 15 to 30 minutes, 10.7% 30 to 45 minutes, 14.3% 45 to 60 minutes, 0.0% 60 minutes or more (2000)

MENARD (city). County seat. Covers a land area of 2.057 square miles and a water area of 0 square miles. Located at 30.92° N. Lat; 99.78° W. Long. Elevation is 1,883 feet.
History: Menard, established in a valley along the San Saba River, became a shipping center for wool and mohair.
Population: 1,655 (1990); 1,653 (2000); 1,541 (2010); 1,490 (2015 projected); Race: 83.7% White, 0.9% Black, 0.3% Asian, 15.1% Other, 38.7% Hispanic of any race (2010); Density: 749.0 persons per square mile (2010); Average household size: 2.37 (2010); Median age: 45.3 (2010); Males per 100 females: 96.8 (2010); Marriage status: 23.1% never married, 55.4% now married, 10.5% widowed, 11.1% divorced (2005-2009 5-year est.); Foreign born: 6.3% (2005-2009 5-year est.); Ancestry (includes multiple ancestries): 30.5% American, 6.7% German, 4.7% Irish, 4.0% English, 1.0% French Canadian (2005-2009 5-year est.).
Economy: Employment by occupation: 13.0% management, 8.2% professional, 35.0% services, 13.3% sales, 1.3% farming, 19.5% construction, 9.7% production (2005-2009 5-year est.).
Income: Per capita income: $15,647 (2010); Median household income: $27,816 (2010); Average household income: $38,016 (2010); Percent of households with income of $100,000 or more: 5.8% (2010); Poverty rate: 26.5% (2005-2009 5-year est.).
Taxes: Total city taxes per capita: $173 (2007); City property taxes per capita: $92 (2007).
Education: Percent of population age 25 and over with: High school diploma (including GED) or higher: 69.4% (2010); Bachelor's degree or higher: 15.6% (2010); Master's degree or higher: 4.8% (2010).
School District(s)
Menard ISD (PK-12)
    2009-10 Enrollment: 333 . . . . (325) 396-2404
Housing: Homeownership rate: 72.4% (2010); Median home value: $33,833 (2010); Median contract rent: $287 per month (2005-2009 5-year est.); Median year structure built: 1955 (2005-2009 5-year est.).
Newspapers: News And Messenger (Community news; Circulation 1,198)

Transportation: Commute to work: 89.8% car, 0.0% public transportation, 8.7% walk, 0.0% work from home (2005-2009 5-year est.); Travel time to work: 60.5% less than 15 minutes, 15.8% 15 to 30 minutes, 9.4% 30 to 45 minutes, 4.0% 45 to 60 minutes, 10.3% 60 minutes or more (2005-2009 5-year est.)
Additional Information Contacts
Menard County Chamber of Commerce . . . . (325) 396-2365
    http://site.menardchamber.com

Midland County

Located in west Texas; drained by tributaries of the Colorado River. Covers a land area of 900.25 square miles, a water area of 1.72 square miles, and is located in the Central Time Zone at 31.96° N. Lat., 102.07° W. Long. The county was founded in 1885. County seat is Midland.

Midland County is part of the Midland, TX Metropolitan Statistical Area. The entire metro area includes: Midland County, TX

Weather Station: Midland 4 ENE									Elevation: 2,740 feet			
	Jan	Feb	Mar	Apr	May	Jun	Jul	Aug	Sep	Oct	Nov	Dec
High	60	65	73	82	89	95	96	95	89	80	69	61
Low	31	35	42	50	60	67	70	69	62	52	40	32
Precip	0.6	0.6	0.6	0.6	2.0	1.4	1.4	2.0	2.4	1.5	0.9	0.6
Snow	0.8	0.1	0.1	0.0	0.0	0.0	0.0	0.0	0.0	tr	0.7	0.5

High and Low temperatures in degrees Fahrenheit; Precipitation and Snow in inches

Weather Station: Midland Regional Air Terminal									Elevation: 2,861 feet			
	Jan	Feb	Mar	Apr	May	Jun	Jul	Aug	Sep	Oct	Nov	Dec
High	57	63	70	79	87	93	95	93	87	78	66	58
Low	30	35	41	49	59	67	70	69	62	52	39	31
Precip	0.5	0.7	0.6	0.6	1.8	1.7	1.8	1.9	2.1	1.7	0.7	0.6
Snow	2.0	0.5	0.2	0.2	tr	tr	tr	tr	tr	tr	0.9	1.6

High and Low temperatures in degrees Fahrenheit; Precipitation and Snow in inches

Population: 106,611 (1990); 116,009 (2000); 131,542 (2010); 138,861 (2015 projected); Race: 73.3% White, 6.6% Black, 0.9% Asian, 19.2% Other, 37.8% Hispanic of any race (2010); Density: 146.1 persons per square mile (2010); Average household size: 2.66 (2010); Median age: 33.7 (2010); Males per 100 females: 94.9 (2010).
Religion: Five largest groups: 24.5% Southern Baptist Convention, 13.7% Catholic Church, 5.7% The United Methodist Church, 4.1% Churches of Christ, 2.5% Presbyterian Church (U.S.A.) (2000).
Economy: Unemployment rate: 5.2% (June 2011); Total civilian labor force: 78,089 (June 2011); Leading industries: 17.6% mining; 12.8% retail trade; 10.6% health care and social assistance (2009); Farms: 601 totaling 456,633 acres (2007); Companies that employ 500 or more persons: 6 (2009); Companies that employ 100 to 499 persons: 80 (2009); Companies that employ less than 100 persons: 4,410 (2009); Black-owned businesses: 410 (2007); Hispanic-owned businesses: 2,582 (2007); Asian-owned businesses: 507 (2007); Women-owned businesses: 3,873 (2007); Retail sales per capita: $14,585 (2010). Single-family building permits issued: 394 (2010); Multi-family building permits issued: 0 (2010).
Income: Per capita income: $28,476 (2010); Median household income: $54,791 (2010); Average household income: $75,955 (2010); Percent of households with income of $100,000 or more: 22.4% (2010); Poverty rate: 12.5% (2009); Bankruptcy rate: 1.16% (2010).
Taxes: Total county taxes per capita: $281 (2007); County property taxes per capita: $155 (2007).
Education: Percent of population age 25 and over with: High school diploma (including GED) or higher: 81.4% (2010); Bachelor's degree or higher: 22.5% (2010); Master's degree or higher: 5.8% (2010).
Housing: Homeownership rate: 69.8% (2010); Median home value: $122,253 (2010); Median contract rent: $546 per month (2005-2009 5-year est.); Median year structure built: 1977 (2005-2009 5-year est.)
Health: Birth rate: 170.5 per 10,000 population (2009); Death rate: 75.7 per 10,000 population (2009); Age-adjusted cancer mortality rate: 165.0 deaths per 100,000 population (2007); Number of physicians: 19.1 per 10,000 population (2008); Hospital beds: 39.2 per 10,000 population (2007); Hospital admissions: 1,299.9 per 10,000 population (2007).
Elections: 2008 Presidential election results: 21.0% Obama, 78.2% McCain, 0.1% Nader
Additional Information Contacts
Midland County Government . . . . (432) 688-1147
    http://www.co.midland.tx.us

City of Midland . . . . (432) 685-7100
   http://www.ci.midland.tx.us
Midland Chamber of Commerce . . . . (432) 683-3381
   http://www.midlandtxchamber.com
Midland Hispanic Chamber of Commerce . . . . (432) 682-2960
   http://www.midlandhcc.com

Midland County Communities

MIDLAND (city). County seat. Covers a land area of 66.608 square miles and a water area of 0.185 square miles. Located at 32.00° N. Lat; 102.09° W. Long. Elevation is 2,782 feet.

History: Midland became the headquarters for hundreds of oil corporations working in the Permian Basin.

Population: 89,358 (1990); 94,996 (2000); 107,175 (2010); 112,843 (2015 projected); Race: 71.8% White, 7.7% Black, 0.9% Asian, 19.5% Other, 37.5% Hispanic of any race (2010); Density: 1,609.0 persons per square mile (2010); Average household size: 2.60 (2010); Median age: 33.8 (2010); Males per 100 females: 94.1 (2010); Marriage status: 25.6% never married, 58.4% now married, 6.3% widowed, 9.8% divorced (2005-2009 5-year est.); Foreign born: 8.5% (2005-2009 5-year est.); Ancestry (includes multiple ancestries): 9.8% German, 9.4% English, 9.1% American, 8.3% Irish, 2.1% Scotch-Irish (2005-2009 5-year est.).

Economy: Unemployment rate: 5.2% (June 2011); Total civilian labor force: 64,307 (June 2011); Single-family building permits issued: 394 (2010); Multi-family building permits issued: 0 (2010); Employment by occupation: 13.3% management, 19.6% professional, 16.5% services, 27.7% sales, 0.2% farming, 12.8% construction, 9.8% production (2005-2009 5-year est.).

Income: Per capita income: $29,148 (2010); Median household income: $54,441 (2010); Average household income: $76,152 (2010); Percent of households with income of $100,000 or more: 22.8% (2010); Poverty rate: 12.6% (2005-2009 5-year est.).

Taxes: Total city taxes per capita: $634 (2007); City property taxes per capita: $253 (2007).

Education: Percent of population age 25 and over with: High school diploma (including GED) or higher: 82.6% (2010); Bachelor's degree or higher: 24.6% (2010); Master's degree or higher: 6.4% (2010).

School District(s)
Greenwood ISD (PK-12)
   2009-10 Enrollment: 1,641 . . . . (432) 685-7800
Midland Academy Charter School (PK-12)
   2009-10 Enrollment: 538 . . . . (432) 686-0003
Midland ISD (PK-12)
   2009-10 Enrollment: 21,374 . . . . (432) 689-1000
Responsive Education Solutions (KG-12)
   2009-10 Enrollment: 5,022 . . . . (972) 316-3663
Richard Milburn Academy (Ector County) (09-12)
   2009-10 Enrollment: 481 . . . . (830) 557-6181

Four-year College(s)
Midland College (Public)
   Fall 2009 Enrollment: 6,227 . . . . (432) 685-4500
   2010-11 Tuition: In-state $2,940; Out-of-state $3,930

Two-year College(s)
Kaplan College-Midland (Private, For-profit)
   Fall 2009 Enrollment: 494 . . . . (432) 681-3390

Housing: Homeownership rate: 66.4% (2010); Median home value: $128,067 (2010); Median contract rent: $568 per month (2005-2009 5-year est.); Median year structure built: 1975 (2005-2009 5-year est.).

Hospitals: Desert Springs Medical Center (64 beds); Midland Memorial Hospital (321 beds); Midland Memorial Hospital - West Campus (107 beds); Rehabcare Rehabilitation Hospital Permian Basin (38 beds); West Texas Medical Center

Safety: Violent crime rate: 39.5 per 10,000 population; Property crime rate: 363.7 per 10,000 population (2009).

Newspapers: Midland Reporter-Telegram (Local news; Circulation 26,500)

Transportation: Commute to work: 95.0% car, 0.4% public transportation, 0.8% walk, 2.9% work from home (2005-2009 5-year est.); Travel time to work: 48.9% less than 15 minutes, 38.9% 15 to 30 minutes, 7.5% 30 to 45 minutes, 1.4% 45 to 60 minutes, 3.4% 60 minutes or more (2005-2009 5-year est.)

Airports: Midland Airpark (general aviation); Midland International (primary service/small hub)

Additional Information Contacts

City of Midland . . . . (432) 685-7100
   http://www.ci.midland.tx.us
Midland Chamber of Commerce . . . . (432) 683-3381
   http://www.midlandtxchamber.com
Midland Hispanic Chamber of Commerce . . . . (432) 682-2960
   http://www.midlandhcc.com

Milam County

Located in central Texas; bounded on the east by the Brazos River; drained by the Little River. Covers a land area of 1,016.71 square miles, a water area of 4.95 square miles, and is located in the Central Time Zone at 30.78° N. Lat., 97.00° W. Long. The county was founded in 1836. County seat is Cameron.

Weather Station: Cameron								Elevation: 363 feet			
	Jan	Feb	Mar	Apr	May	Jun	Jul	Aug	Sep	Oct	Nov	Dec
High	61	65	72	79	85	90	94	95	89	81	71	62
Low	39	43	49	57	65	71	73	73	67	58	49	40
Precip	2.3	2.6	2.7	2.4	5.3	3.7	2.0	2.1	2.9	4.0	3.3	2.9
Snow	tr	tr	tr	0.0	0.0	0.0	0.0	0.0	0.0	0.0	0.0	0.0

High and Low temperatures in degrees Fahrenheit; Precipitation and Snow in inches

Population: 22,946 (1990); 24,238 (2000); 25,481 (2010); 26,036 (2015 projected); Race: 77.7% White, 10.1% Black, 0.4% Asian, 11.8% Other, 22.5% Hispanic of any race (2010); Density: 25.1 persons per square mile (2010); Average household size: 2.58 (2010); Median age: 37.6 (2010); Males per 100 females: 97.9 (2010).

Religion: Five largest groups: 22.5% Southern Baptist Convention, 22.0% Catholic Church, 5.7% The United Methodist Church, 3.5% Evangelical Lutheran Church in America, 3.3% Lutheran Church—Missouri Synod (2000).

Economy: Unemployment rate: 10.8% (June 2011); Total civilian labor force: 10,885 (June 2011); Leading industries: 17.4% health care and social assistance; 16.9% retail trade; 12.2% construction (2009); Farms: 2,045 totaling 538,678 acres (2007); Companies that employ 500 or more persons: 0 (2009); Companies that employ 100 to 499 persons: 8 (2009); Companies that employ less than 100 persons: 408 (2009); Black-owned businesses: n/a (2007); Hispanic-owned businesses: n/a (2007); Asian-owned businesses: n/a (2007); Women-owned businesses: 494 (2007); Retail sales per capita: $6,655 (2010). Single-family building permits issued: 3 (2010); Multi-family building permits issued: 0 (2010).

Income: Per capita income: $20,492 (2010); Median household income: $41,760 (2010); Average household income: $53,406 (2010); Percent of households with income of $100,000 or more: 10.5% (2010); Poverty rate: 18.0% (2009); Bankruptcy rate: 1.27% (2010).

Taxes: Total county taxes per capita: $318 (2007); County property taxes per capita: $253 (2007).

Education: Percent of population age 25 and over with: High school diploma (including GED) or higher: 80.1% (2010); Bachelor's degree or higher: 14.4% (2010); Master's degree or higher: 4.6% (2010).

Housing: Homeownership rate: 72.2% (2010); Median home value: $77,709 (2010); Median contract rent: $360 per month (2005-2009 5-year est.); Median year structure built: 1973 (2005-2009 5-year est.)

Health: Birth rate: 149.0 per 10,000 population (2009); Death rate: 100.7 per 10,000 population (2009); Age-adjusted cancer mortality rate: 219.5 deaths per 100,000 population (2007); Number of physicians: 6.0 per 10,000 population (2008); Hospital beds: 23.9 per 10,000 population (2007); Hospital admissions: 1,200.2 per 10,000 population (2007).

Elections: 2008 Presidential election results: 36.4% Obama, 62.4% McCain, 0.1% Nader

Additional Information Contacts
Milam County Government . . . . (254) 697-7000
   http://milamcounty.net/
Cameron Chamber of Commerce . . . . (254) 697-4979
   http://www.cameron-tx.com
City of Cameron . . . . (254) 697-6646
   http://camerontexas.net
City of Rockdale . . . . (512) 446-2511
Rockdale Chamber of Commerce . . . . (512) 446-2030
   http://www.rockdalechamber.com
Thorndale Area Chamber of Commerce . . . . (512) 658-5378
   http://thorndaletx.com
Thorndale Chamber of Commerce . . . . (512) 898-0053

Milam County Communities

BUCKHOLTS (town). Covers a land area of 1.326 square miles and a water area of 0 square miles. Located at 30.87° N. Lat; 97.12° W. Long. Elevation is 522 feet.
Population: 335 (1990); 387 (2000); 400 (2010); 408 (2015 projected); Race: 83.8% White, 1.3% Black, 0.0% Asian, 15.0% Other, 30.5% Hispanic of any race (2010); Density: 301.5 persons per square mile (2010); Average household size: 2.67 (2010); Median age: 38.2 (2010); Males per 100 females: 100.0 (2010); Marriage status: 29.5% never married, 59.4% now married, 5.7% widowed, 5.3% divorced (2005-2009 5-year est.); Foreign born: 20.1% (2005-2009 5-year est.); Ancestry (includes multiple ancestries): 11.1% German, 5.3% Irish, 3.9% American, 3.6% English, 2.5% Czech (2005-2009 5-year est.).
Economy: Employment by occupation: 1.7% management, 16.8% professional, 5.9% services, 6.7% sales, 19.3% farming, 33.6% construction, 16.0% production (2005-2009 5-year est.).
Income: Per capita income: $22,925 (2010); Median household income: $43,333 (2010); Average household income: $61,317 (2010); Percent of households with income of $100,000 or more: 12.0% (2010); Poverty rate: 46.0% (2005-2009 5-year est.).
Taxes: Total city taxes per capita: $165 (2007); City property taxes per capita: $49 (2007).
Education: Percent of population age 25 and over with: High school diploma (including GED) or higher: 81.2% (2010); Bachelor's degree or higher: 17.7% (2010); Master's degree or higher: 4.9% (2010).
School District(s)
Buckholts ISD (PK-12)
    2009-10 Enrollment: 172 . . . . (254) 593-3011
Housing: Homeownership rate: 78.7% (2010); Median home value: $82,500 (2010); Median contract rent: $323 per month (2005-2009 5-year est.); Median year structure built: 1952 (2005-2009 5-year est.).
Transportation: Commute to work: 82.4% car, 0.0% public transportation, 13.9% walk, 3.7% work from home (2005-2009 5-year est.); Travel time to work: 37.5% less than 15 minutes, 28.8% 15 to 30 minutes, 8.7% 30 to 45 minutes, 15.4% 45 to 60 minutes, 9.6% 60 minutes or more (2005-2009 5-year est.)

BURLINGTON (unincorporated postal area, zip code 76519). Covers a land area of 61.306 square miles and a water area of 0.076 square miles. Located at 31.00° N. Lat; 97.03° W. Long. Elevation is 430 feet.
Population: 530 (2000); Race: 92.0% White, 2.9% Black, 0.0% Asian, 5.1% Other, 5.1% Hispanic of any race (2000); Density: 8.6 persons per square mile (2000); Age: 19.2% under 18, 17.1% over 64 (2000); Marriage status: 22.1% never married, 65.0% now married, 3.5% widowed, 9.3% divorced (2000); Foreign born: 1.8% (2000); Ancestry (includes multiple ancestries): 37.1% German, 18.8% Czech, 12.0% Irish, 8.2% English, 5.5% American (2000).
Economy: Employment by occupation: 21.0% management, 24.8% professional, 6.5% services, 22.4% sales, 2.3% farming, 5.6% construction, 17.3% production (2000).
Income: Per capita income: $17,198 (2000); Median household income: $31,058 (2000); Poverty rate: 179.1% (2000).
Education: Percent of population age 25 and over with: High school diploma (including GED) or higher: 64.9% (2000); Bachelor's degree or higher: 23.0% (2000).
Housing: Homeownership rate: 82.2% (2000); Median home value: $42,300 (2000); Median contract rent: $182 per month (2000); Median year structure built: 1965 (2000).
Transportation: Commute to work: 76.1% car, 0.0% public transportation, 0.0% walk, 23.9% work from home (2000); Travel time to work: 13.2% less than 15 minutes, 41.5% 15 to 30 minutes, 21.4% 30 to 45 minutes, 19.5% 45 to 60 minutes, 4.4% 60 minutes or more (2000)

CAMERON (city). County seat. Covers a land area of 4.243 square miles and a water area of 0 square miles. Located at 30.85° N. Lat; 96.97° W. Long. Elevation is 400 feet.
History: Cameron was named for Captain Ewen Cameron, a pioneer cattleman. The town grew as a center for farm products, cattle, and peanuts.
Population: 5,580 (1990); 5,634 (2000); 5,783 (2010); 5,844 (2015 projected); Race: 71.1% White, 16.4% Black, 0.1% Asian, 12.4% Other, 30.2% Hispanic of any race (2010); Density: 1,363.0 persons per square mile (2010); Average household size: 2.56 (2010); Median age: 36.0 (2010); Males per 100 females: 92.1 (2010); Marriage status: 21.4% never married, 57.5% now married, 14.6% widowed, 6.5% divorced (2005-2009 5-year est.); Foreign born: 9.6% (2005-2009 5-year est.); Ancestry (includes multiple ancestries): 16.2% German, 6.9% English, 5.0% Irish, 4.5% Czech, 1.6% Scottish (2005-2009 5-year est.).
Economy: Single-family building permits issued: 2 (2010); Multi-family building permits issued: 0 (2010); Employment by occupation: 9.4% management, 14.8% professional, 18.0% services, 15.9% sales, 2.8% farming, 16.1% construction, 23.0% production (2005-2009 5-year est.).
Income: Per capita income: $18,087 (2010); Median household income: $33,193 (2010); Average household income: $46,970 (2010); Percent of households with income of $100,000 or more: 8.5% (2010); Poverty rate: 25.3% (2005-2009 5-year est.).
Taxes: Total city taxes per capita: $392 (2007); City property taxes per capita: $183 (2007).
Education: Percent of population age 25 and over with: High school diploma (including GED) or higher: 77.4% (2010); Bachelor's degree or higher: 16.5% (2010); Master's degree or higher: 3.8% (2010).
School District(s)
Cameron ISD (PK-12)
    2009-10 Enrollment: 1,606 . . . . (254) 697-3512
Housing: Homeownership rate: 65.4% (2010); Median home value: $66,840 (2010); Median contract rent: $347 per month (2005-2009 5-year est.); Median year structure built: 1969 (2005-2009 5-year est.).
Hospitals: Central Texas Hospital
Safety: Violent crime rate: 20.9 per 10,000 population; Property crime rate: 328.7 per 10,000 population (2009).
Newspapers: Cameron Herald (Local news; Circulation 4,000)
Transportation: Commute to work: 90.7% car, 0.0% public transportation, 2.9% walk, 2.4% work from home (2005-2009 5-year est.); Travel time to work: 44.7% less than 15 minutes, 19.7% 15 to 30 minutes, 20.4% 30 to 45 minutes, 11.6% 45 to 60 minutes, 3.6% 60 minutes or more (2005-2009 5-year est.)
Additional Information Contacts
Cameron Chamber of Commerce . . . . (254) 697-4979
    http://www.cameron-tx.com
City of Cameron . . . . (254) 697-6646
    http://camerontexas.net

DAVILLA (unincorporated postal area, zip code 76523). Covers a land area of 11.446 square miles and a water area of 0.215 square miles. Located at 30.78° N. Lat; 97.28° W. Long. Elevation is 545 feet.
Population: 248 (2000); Race: 85.7% White, 12.9% Black, 0.0% Asian, 1.4% Other, 0.9% Hispanic of any race (2000); Density: 21.7 persons per square mile (2000); Age: 21.7% under 18, 18.0% over 64 (2000); Marriage status: 20.2% never married, 68.3% now married, 7.7% widowed, 3.8% divorced (2000); Foreign born: 0.0% (2000); Ancestry (includes multiple ancestries): 15.2% German, 15.2% Irish, 12.4% English, 3.7% American (2000).
Economy: Employment by occupation: 6.7% management, 9.6% professional, 12.5% services, 23.1% sales, 2.9% farming, 25.0% construction, 20.2% production (2000).
Income: Per capita income: $18,018 (2000); Median household income: $36,250 (2000); Poverty rate: 179.1% (2000).
Education: Percent of population age 25 and over with: High school diploma (including GED) or higher: 78.5% (2000); Bachelor's degree or higher: 11.4% (2000).
Housing: Homeownership rate: 86.2% (2000); Median home value: $51,700 (2000); Median contract rent: $508 per month (2000); Median year structure built: 1978 (2000).
Transportation: Commute to work: 98.0% car, 0.0% public transportation, 0.0% walk, 2.0% work from home (2000); Travel time to work: 1.0% less than 15 minutes, 24.0% 15 to 30 minutes, 21.9% 30 to 45 minutes, 22.9% 45 to 60 minutes, 30.2% 60 minutes or more (2000)

MILANO (city). Covers a land area of 1.948 square miles and a water area of 0.009 square miles. Located at 30.70° N. Lat; 96.86° W. Long. Elevation is 522 feet.
Population: 408 (1990); 400 (2000); 421 (2010); 427 (2015 projected); Race: 87.2% White, 10.0% Black, 0.7% Asian, 2.1% Other, 11.2% Hispanic of any race (2010); Density: 216.1 persons per square mile (2010); Average household size: 2.68 (2010); Median age: 35.7 (2010); Males per 100 females: 91.4 (2010); Marriage status: 21.0% never married, 65.7% now married, 1.3% widowed, 12.0% divorced (2005-2009 5-year est.); Foreign born: 7.2% (2005-2009 5-year est.); Ancestry (includes

multiple ancestries): 12.5% Irish, 11.7% English, 5.6% German, 3.5% Czech, 3.2% Welsh (2005-2009 5-year est.).
Economy: Employment by occupation: 3.6% management, 12.4% professional, 28.5% services, 7.3% sales, 2.6% farming, 21.2% construction, 24.4% production (2005-2009 5-year est.).
Income: Per capita income: $19,674 (2010); Median household income: $44,900 (2010); Average household income: $55,573 (2010); Percent of households with income of $100,000 or more: 10.2% (2010); Poverty rate: 16.9% (2005-2009 5-year est.).
Taxes: Total city taxes per capita: $60 (2007); City property taxes per capita: $0 (2007).
Education: Percent of population age 25 and over with: High school diploma (including GED) or higher: 85.2% (2010); Bachelor's degree or higher: 15.2% (2010); Master's degree or higher: 3.6% (2010).

School District(s)
Milano ISD (PK-12)
    2009-10 Enrollment: 418 . . . . (512) 455-2533
Housing: Homeownership rate: 77.1% (2010); Median home value: $72,273 (2010); Median contract rent: $193 per month (2005-2009 5-year est.); Median year structure built: 1969 (2005-2009 5-year est.).
Transportation: Commute to work: 93.5% car, 0.0% public transportation, 4.9% walk, 0.0% work from home (2005-2009 5-year est.); Travel time to work: 46.5% less than 15 minutes, 18.9% 15 to 30 minutes, 17.8% 30 to 45 minutes, 5.4% 45 to 60 minutes, 11.4% 60 minutes or more (2005-2009 5-year est.)

ROCKDALE (city).
Covers a land area of 3.133 square miles and a water area of 0 square miles. Located at 30.65° N. Lat; 97.00° W. Long. Elevation is 466 feet.
History: Rockdale developed as a lignite mining area, with an oil refinery and an aluminum plant.
Population: 5,235 (1990); 5,439 (2000); 5,833 (2010); 5,984 (2015 projected); Race: 65.7% White, 14.3% Black, 0.9% Asian, 19.1% Other, 25.3% Hispanic of any race (2010); Density: 1,861.5 persons per square mile (2010); Average household size: 2.58 (2010); Median age: 34.8 (2010); Males per 100 females: 93.7 (2010); Marriage status: 23.7% never married, 59.5% now married, 7.8% widowed, 8.9% divorced (2005-2009 5-year est.); Foreign born: 7.0% (2005-2009 5-year est.); Ancestry (includes multiple ancestries): 13.6% German, 7.4% English, 6.1% Irish, 5.9% American, 2.1% Czech (2005-2009 5-year est.).
Economy: Single-family building permits issued: 0 (2010); Multi-family building permits issued: 0 (2010); Employment by occupation: 8.0% management, 16.3% professional, 21.2% services, 23.9% sales, 0.0% farming, 14.0% construction, 16.6% production (2005-2009 5-year est.).
Income: Per capita income: $21,565 (2010); Median household income: $45,782 (2010); Average household income: $57,091 (2010); Percent of households with income of $100,000 or more: 12.3% (2010); Poverty rate: 26.5% (2005-2009 5-year est.).
Taxes: Total city taxes per capita: $243 (2007); City property taxes per capita: $144 (2007).
Education: Percent of population age 25 and over with: High school diploma (including GED) or higher: 80.0% (2010); Bachelor's degree or higher: 13.5% (2010); Master's degree or higher: 4.7% (2010).

School District(s)
John H Wood Jr Public Charter District (05-12)
    2009-10 Enrollment: 348 . . . . (210) 638-5003
Rockdale ISD (PK-12)
    2009-10 Enrollment: 1,753 . . . . (512) 430-6000
Housing: Homeownership rate: 63.5% (2010); Median home value: $69,440 (2010); Median contract rent: $396 per month (2005-2009 5-year est.); Median year structure built: 1970 (2005-2009 5-year est.).
Hospitals: Richards Memorial Hospital (25 beds)
Safety: Violent crime rate: 20.1 per 10,000 population; Property crime rate: 272.4 per 10,000 population (2009).
Newspapers: The Rockdale Reporter (Community news; Circulation 4,888)
Transportation: Commute to work: 93.7% car, 0.0% public transportation, 2.9% walk, 2.2% work from home (2005-2009 5-year est.); Travel time to work: 60.5% less than 15 minutes, 18.3% 15 to 30 minutes, 6.6% 30 to 45 minutes, 5.4% 45 to 60 minutes, 9.2% 60 minutes or more (2005-2009 5-year est.)
Additional Information Contacts
City of Rockdale. . . . . (512) 446-2511
Rockdale Chamber of Commerce . . . . (512) 446-2030
    http://www.rockdalechamber.com

THORNDALE (city).
Covers a land area of 0.978 square miles and a water area of 0.004 square miles. Located at 30.61° N. Lat; 97.20° W. Long. Elevation is 453 feet.
History: Thorndale was established in an area that had seen three Spanish missions, all abandoned by 1755. The town developed around plants processing cotton and mineral water crystals.
Population: 1,119 (1990); 1,278 (2000); 1,345 (2010); 1,374 (2015 projected); Race: 88.1% White, 3.6% Black, 0.4% Asian, 7.9% Other, 16.5% Hispanic of any race (2010); Density: 1,375.7 persons per square mile (2010); Average household size: 2.62 (2010); Median age: 37.4 (2010); Males per 100 females: 103.2 (2010); Marriage status: 18.0% never married, 62.9% now married, 12.3% widowed, 6.8% divorced (2005-2009 5-year est.); Foreign born: 4.3% (2005-2009 5-year est.); Ancestry (includes multiple ancestries): 42.1% German, 8.3% English, 6.6% Czech, 6.5% Irish, 3.3% Scottish (2005-2009 5-year est.).
Economy: Single-family building permits issued: 1 (2010); Multi-family building permits issued: 0 (2010); Employment by occupation: 7.5% management, 15.4% professional, 9.0% services, 31.0% sales, 0.8% farming, 21.8% construction, 14.6% production (2005-2009 5-year est.).
Income: Per capita income: $21,087 (2010); Median household income: $41,848 (2010); Average household income: $55,224 (2010); Percent of households with income of $100,000 or more: 10.1% (2010); Poverty rate: 6.7% (2005-2009 5-year est.).
Taxes: Total city taxes per capita: $287 (2007); City property taxes per capita: $205 (2007).
Education: Percent of population age 25 and over with: High school diploma (including GED) or higher: 82.0% (2010); Bachelor's degree or higher: 13.7% (2010); Master's degree or higher: 3.6% (2010).

School District(s)
Thorndale ISD (PK-12)
    2009-10 Enrollment: 548 . . . . (512) 898-2538
Housing: Homeownership rate: 73.0% (2010); Median home value: $94,474 (2010); Median contract rent: $298 per month (2005-2009 5-year est.); Median year structure built: 1965 (2005-2009 5-year est.).
Safety: Violent crime rate: 45.7 per 10,000 population; Property crime rate: 53.3 per 10,000 population (2009).
Newspapers: Thorndale Champion (Community news; Circulation 1,270)
Transportation: Commute to work: 97.6% car, 0.0% public transportation, 1.2% walk, 1.2% work from home (2005-2009 5-year est.); Travel time to work: 26.4% less than 15 minutes, 39.6% 15 to 30 minutes, 12.8% 30 to 45 minutes, 12.2% 45 to 60 minutes, 9.0% 60 minutes or more (2005-2009 5-year est.)
Additional Information Contacts
Thorndale Area Chamber of Commerce . . . . (512) 658-5378
    http://thorndaletx.com
Thorndale Chamber of Commerce . . . . (512) 898-0053

Mills County

Located in central Texas; bounded on the southwest by the Colorado River; drained by Pecan Bayou. Covers a land area of 748.11 square miles, a water area of 1.78 square miles, and is located in the Central Time Zone at 31.49° N. Lat., 98.59° W. Long. The county was founded in 1887. County seat is Goldthwaite.

Weather Station: Goldthwaite 1 WSW   Elevation: 1,500 feet

	Jan	Feb	Mar	Apr	May	Jun	Jul	Aug	Sep	Oct	Nov	Dec
High	60	63	70	78	84	89	93	93	87	79	69	60
Low	36	40	46	54	62	69	71	71	66	56	46	37
Precip	1.3	2.2	2.5	2.1	4.0	4.9	1.7	2.2	2.7	3.1	2.1	1.7
Snow	0.0	0.0	0.0	0.0	0.0	0.0	0.0	0.0	0.0	0.0	0.0	tr

High and Low temperatures in degrees Fahrenheit; Precipitation and Snow in inches

Population: 4,531 (1990); 5,151 (2000); 5,135 (2010); 5,118 (2015 projected); Race: 86.8% White, 1.9% Black, 0.1% Asian, 11.3% Other, 15.7% Hispanic of any race (2010); Density: 6.9 persons per square mile (2010); Average household size: 2.45 (2010); Median age: 44.6 (2010); Males per 100 females: 103.8 (2010).
Religion: Five largest groups: 42.8% Southern Baptist Convention, 11.3% The United Methodist Church, 9.9% Catholic Church, 8.5% Churches of Christ, 6.7% Evangelical Lutheran Church in America (2000).
Economy: Unemployment rate: 6.8% (June 2011); Total civilian labor force: 2,369 (June 2011); Leading industries: 24.8% retail trade; 24.4% health care and social assistance; 7.4% accommodation & food services (2009); Farms: 921 totaling 474,226 acres (2007); Companies that employ

500 or more persons: 0 (2009); Companies that employ 100 to 499 persons: 0 (2009); Companies that employ less than 100 persons: 126 (2009); Black-owned businesses: n/a (2007); Hispanic-owned businesses: n/a (2007); Asian-owned businesses: n/a (2007); Women-owned businesses: n/a (2007); Retail sales per capita: $9,497 (2010). Single-family building permits issued: n/a (2010); Multi-family building permits issued: n/a (2010).

Income: Per capita income: $20,829 (2010); Median household income: $39,636 (2010); Average household income: $53,280 (2010); Percent of households with income of $100,000 or more: 10.9% (2010); Poverty rate: 19.4% (2009); Bankruptcy rate: n/a (2010).

Taxes: Total county taxes per capita: $365 (2007); County property taxes per capita: $280 (2007).

Education: Percent of population age 25 and over with: High school diploma (including GED) or higher: 81.2% (2010); Bachelor's degree or higher: 22.0% (2010); Master's degree or higher: 7.4% (2010).

Housing: Homeownership rate: 79.0% (2010); Median home value: $87,561 (2010); Median contract rent: $196 per month (2005-2009 5-year est.); Median year structure built: 1970 (2005-2009 5-year est.)

Health: Birth rate: 112.1 per 10,000 population (2009); Death rate: 128.2 per 10,000 population (2009); Age-adjusted cancer mortality rate: 178.1 (Unreliable) deaths per 100,000 population (2007); Number of physicians: 6.0 per 10,000 population (2008); Hospital beds: 0.0 per 10,000 population (2007); Hospital admissions: 0.0 per 10,000 population (2007).

Elections: 2008 Presidential election results: 18.3% Obama, 80.5% McCain, 0.0% Nader

Additional Information Contacts
Mills County Government. . . . . (325) 648-2222
  http://www.co.mills.tx.us/ips/cms
Mills County Chamber of Commerce . . . . (325) 648-3619
  http://www.goldthwaite.biz

Mills County Communities

GOLDTHWAITE (city). County seat. Covers a land area of 1.720 square miles and a water area of <.001 square miles. Located at 31.45° N. Lat; 98.57° W. Long. Elevation is 1,572 feet.

History: The early economy in Goldthwaite depended on wool, mohair, turkeys, and peanuts.

Population: 1,689 (1990); 1,802 (2000); 1,734 (2010); 1,696 (2015 projected); Race: 85.2% White, 0.5% Black, 0.2% Asian, 14.1% Other, 22.3% Hispanic of any race (2010); Density: 1,007.9 persons per square mile (2010); Average household size: 2.24 (2010); Median age: 42.6 (2010); Males per 100 females: 89.7 (2010); Marriage status: 21.3% never married, 54.9% now married, 11.1% widowed, 12.7% divorced (2005-2009 5-year est.); Foreign born: 11.3% (2005-2009 5-year est.); Ancestry (includes multiple ancestries): 13.9% Irish, 12.6% English, 11.6% German, 4.5% Scotch-Irish, 2.7% American (2005-2009 5-year est.).

Economy: Employment by occupation: 4.9% management, 18.2% professional, 28.6% services, 18.9% sales, 2.7% farming, 14.3% construction, 12.5% production (2005-2009 5-year est.).

Income: Per capita income: $18,603 (2010); Median household income: $34,115 (2010); Average household income: $43,781 (2010); Percent of households with income of $100,000 or more: 6.8% (2010); Poverty rate: 26.9% (2005-2009 5-year est.).

Taxes: Total city taxes per capita: $144 (2007); City property taxes per capita: $0 (2007).

Education: Percent of population age 25 and over with: High school diploma (including GED) or higher: 76.2% (2010); Bachelor's degree or higher: 20.1% (2010); Master's degree or higher: 5.6% (2010).

School District(s)
Goldthwaite ISD (PK-12)
  2009-10 Enrollment: 576 . . . . (325) 648-3531
Orenda Charter School (01-12)
  2009-10 Enrollment: 185 . . . . (512) 869-3020

Housing: Homeownership rate: 72.9% (2010); Median home value: $68,750 (2010); Median contract rent: $193 per month (2005-2009 5-year est.); Median year structure built: 1963 (2005-2009 5-year est.).

Newspapers: Goldthwaite Eagle (Local news; Circulation 2,700)

Transportation: Commute to work: 93.3% car, 0.0% public transportation, 4.9% walk, 1.8% work from home (2005-2009 5-year est.); Travel time to work: 63.1% less than 15 minutes, 18.8% 15 to 30 minutes, 11.1% 30 to 45 minutes, 1.4% 45 to 60 minutes, 5.6% 60 minutes or more (2005-2009 5-year est.)

Additional Information Contacts

Mills County Chamber of Commerce . . . . (325) 648-3619
  http://www.goldthwaite.biz

MULLIN (town). Covers a land area of 0.465 square miles and a water area of 0 square miles. Located at 31.55° N. Lat; 98.66° W. Long. Elevation is 1,437 feet.

Population: 194 (1990); 175 (2000); 196 (2010); 205 (2015 projected); Race: 84.2% White, 5.6% Black, 0.0% Asian, 10.2% Other, 10.7% Hispanic of any race (2010); Density: 421.6 persons per square mile (2010); Average household size: 2.71 (2010); Median age: 43.5 (2010); Males per 100 females: 133.3 (2010); Marriage status: 22.8% never married, 56.4% now married, 8.1% widowed, 12.8% divorced (2005-2009 5-year est.); Foreign born: 0.0% (2005-2009 5-year est.); Ancestry (includes multiple ancestries): 39.1% German, 27.9% Irish, 23.4% English, 11.2% French, 2.0% Scotch-Irish (2005-2009 5-year est.).

Economy: Employment by occupation: 13.8% management, 5.7% professional, 62.1% services, 12.6% sales, 0.0% farming, 0.0% construction, 5.7% production (2005-2009 5-year est.).

Income: Per capita income: $19,309 (2010); Median household income: $40,250 (2010); Average household income: $60,538 (2010); Percent of households with income of $100,000 or more: 13.8% (2010); Poverty rate: 24.4% (2005-2009 5-year est.).

Education: Percent of population age 25 and over with: High school diploma (including GED) or higher: 85.5% (2010); Bachelor's degree or higher: 22.1% (2010); Master's degree or higher: 9.9% (2010).

School District(s)
Mullin ISD (PK-12)
  2009-10 Enrollment: 109 . . . . (325) 985-3374

Housing: Homeownership rate: 83.1% (2010); Median home value: $100,000 (2010); Median contract rent: $263 per month (2005-2009 5-year est.); Median year structure built: before 1940 (2005-2009 5-year est.).

Transportation: Commute to work: 85.1% car, 0.0% public transportation, 14.9% walk, 0.0% work from home (2005-2009 5-year est.); Travel time to work: 34.5% less than 15 minutes, 37.9% 15 to 30 minutes, 16.1% 30 to 45 minutes, 11.5% 45 to 60 minutes, 0.0% 60 minutes or more (2005-2009 5-year est.)

Additional Information Contacts
Mills County Chamber of Commerce . . . . (325) 648-3619
  http://www.goldthwaite.biz

PRIDDY (unincorporated postal area, zip code 76870). Covers a land area of 18.604 square miles and a water area of 0.006 square miles. Located at 31.65° N. Lat; 98.50° W. Long. Elevation is 1,539 feet.

Population: 230 (2000); Race: 99.0% White, 0.0% Black, 0.0% Asian, 1.0% Other, 1.0% Hispanic of any race (2000); Density: 12.4 persons per square mile (2000); Age: 29.4% under 18, 13.9% over 64 (2000); Marriage status: 12.5% never married, 62.5% now married, 15.8% widowed, 9.2% divorced (2000); Foreign born: 0.0% (2000); Ancestry (includes multiple ancestries): 33.8% German, 10.4% Irish, 9.0% Italian, 7.5% American (2000).

Economy: Employment by occupation: 9.5% management, 20.2% professional, 8.3% services, 22.6% sales, 0.0% farming, 26.2% construction, 13.1% production (2000).

Income: Per capita income: $16,696 (2000); Median household income: $36,250 (2000); Poverty rate: 179.1% (2000).

Education: Percent of population age 25 and over with: High school diploma (including GED) or higher: 81.3% (2000); Bachelor's degree or higher: 12.5% (2000).

School District(s)
Priddy ISD (PK-12)
  2009-10 Enrollment: 107 . . . . (325) 966-3323

Housing: Homeownership rate: 93.8% (2000); Median home value: $36,700 (2000); Median contract rent: $475 per month (2000); Median year structure built: 1962 (2000).

Transportation: Commute to work: 96.3% car, 0.0% public transportation, 0.0% walk, 3.7% work from home (2000); Travel time to work: 26.6% less than 15 minutes, 43.0% 15 to 30 minutes, 7.6% 30 to 45 minutes, 11.4% 45 to 60 minutes, 11.4% 60 minutes or more (2000)

Mitchell County

Located in west Texas; prairie area, crossed by the Colorado River. Covers a land area of 910.04 square miles, a water area of 5.86 square miles, and is located in the Central Time Zone at 32.34° N. Lat., 100.89° W. Long. The county was founded in 1876. County seat is Colorado City.

Population: 8,016 (1990); 9,698 (2000); 9,371 (2010); 9,192 (2015 projected); Race: 71.8% White, 14.3% Black, 0.4% Asian, 13.5% Other, 33.5% Hispanic of any race (2010); Density: 10.3 persons per square mile (2010); Average household size: 2.43 (2010); Median age: 36.9 (2010); Males per 100 females: 171.2 (2010).
Religion: Five largest groups: 32.7% Southern Baptist Convention, 11.8% Catholic Church, 5.6% The United Methodist Church, 4.4% Churches of Christ, 0.7% Assemblies of God (2000).
Economy: Unemployment rate: 9.0% (June 2011); Total civilian labor force: 3,643 (June 2011); Leading industries: 23.2% retail trade; 11.6% accommodation & food services; 7.0% mining (2009); Farms: 519 totaling 574,995 acres (2007); Companies that employ 500 or more persons: 0 (2009); Companies that employ 100 to 499 persons: 1 (2009); Companies that employ less than 100 persons: 125 (2009); Black-owned businesses: n/a (2007); Hispanic-owned businesses: n/a (2007); Asian-owned businesses: n/a (2007); Women-owned businesses: 161 (2007); Retail sales per capita: $4,968 (2010). Single-family building permits issued: 1 (2010); Multi-family building permits issued: 0 (2010).
Income: Per capita income: $15,588 (2010); Median household income: $33,300 (2010); Average household income: $46,657 (2010); Percent of households with income of $100,000 or more: 7.8% (2010); Poverty rate: 22.6% (2009); Bankruptcy rate: 1.16% (2010).
Taxes: Total county taxes per capita: $394 (2007); County property taxes per capita: $323 (2007).
Education: Percent of population age 25 and over with: High school diploma (including GED) or higher: 76.9% (2010); Bachelor's degree or higher: 11.7% (2010); Master's degree or higher: 2.6% (2010).
Housing: Homeownership rate: 74.0% (2010); Median home value: $40,223 (2010); Median contract rent: $335 per month (2005-2009 5-year est.); Median year structure built: 1966 (2005-2009 5-year est.).
Health: Birth rate: 107.0 per 10,000 population (2009); Death rate: 98.4 per 10,000 population (2009); Age-adjusted cancer mortality rate: 221.8 deaths per 100,000 population (2007); Number of physicians: 3.2 per 10,000 population (2008); Hospital beds: 26.9 per 10,000 population (2007); Hospital admissions: 664.4 per 10,000 population (2007).
Elections: 2008 Presidential election results: 24.1% Obama, 74.7% McCain, 0.2% Nader
Additional Information Contacts
Mitchell County Government . . . . (325) 728-3457

Colorado City Area Chamber of Commerce . . . . (325) 728-3403
   http://coloradocitychamberofcommerce.com

Mitchell County Communities

COLORADO CITY (city). County seat. Covers a land area of 5.290 square miles and a water area of 0 square miles. Located at 32.39° N. Lat; 100.86° W. Long. Elevation is 2,067 feet.
History: Colorado City developed as an industrial and agricultural center, with plants processing petroleum and cotton products. It was also a major livestock shipping point.
Population: 4,749 (1990); 4,281 (2000); 4,005 (2010); 3,850 (2015 projected); Race: 75.2% White, 3.9% Black, 0.5% Asian, 20.4% Other, 35.4% Hispanic of any race (2010); Density: 757.1 persons per square mile (2010); Average household size: 2.48 (2010); Median age: 35.2 (2010); Males per 100 females: 96.9 (2010); Marriage status: 16.3% never married, 66.3% now married, 10.7% widowed, 6.7% divorced (2005-2009 5-year est.); Foreign born: 2.2% (2005-2009 5-year est.); Ancestry (includes multiple ancestries): 17.9% German, 9.0% American, 8.4% English, 6.1% Irish, 1.6% French (2005-2009 5-year est.).
Economy: Single-family building permits issued: 1 (2010); Multi-family building permits issued: 0 (2010); Employment by occupation: 10.1% management, 17.5% professional, 23.3% services, 22.3% sales, 0.0% farming, 13.3% construction, 13.5% production (2005-2009 5-year est.).
Income: Per capita income: $16,404 (2010); Median household income: $29,387 (2010); Average household income: $41,609 (2010); Percent of households with income of $100,000 or more: 5.0% (2010); Poverty rate: 21.3% (2005-2009 5-year est.).
Taxes: Total city taxes per capita: $351 (2007); City property taxes per capita: $129 (2007).
Education: Percent of population age 25 and over with: High school diploma (including GED) or higher: 75.3% (2010); Bachelor's degree or higher: 11.9% (2010); Master's degree or higher: 3.7% (2010).

Colorado ISD (PK-12)
   2009-10 Enrollment: 1,052 . . . . (325) 728-3721
Housing: Homeownership rate: 68.2% (2010); Median home value: $35,643 (2010); Median contract rent: $337 per month (2005-2009 5-year est.); Median year structure built: 1959 (2005-2009 5-year est.).
Hospitals: Mitchell County Hospital (39 beds)
Safety: Violent crime rate: 36.4 per 10,000 population; Property crime rate: 410.3 per 10,000 population (2009).
Newspapers: Record (Community news; Circulation 4,000)
Transportation: Commute to work: 97.3% car, 0.0% public transportation, 0.0% walk, 0.5% work from home (2005-2009 5-year est.); Travel time to work: 65.8% less than 15 minutes, 12.3% 15 to 30 minutes, 11.4% 30 to 45 minutes, 6.3% 45 to 60 minutes, 4.2% 60 minutes or more (2005-2009 5-year est.)
Airports: Colorado City (general aviation)
Additional Information Contacts
Colorado City Area Chamber of Commerce . . . . (325) 728-3403
   http://coloradocitychamberofcommerce.com

LORAINE (town). Covers a land area of 1.053 square miles and a water area of 0 square miles. Located at 32.40° N. Lat; 100.71° W. Long. Elevation is 2,267 feet.
History: Incorporated 1907.
Population: 734 (1990); 656 (2000); 595 (2010); 561 (2015 projected); Race: 66.6% White, 2.9% Black, 0.2% Asian, 30.4% Other, 44.7% Hispanic of any race (2010); Density: 565.3 persons per square mile (2010); Average household size: 2.43 (2010); Median age: 42.1 (2010); Males per 100 females: 93.2 (2010); Marriage status: 7.7% never married, 76.0% now married, 12.3% widowed, 3.9% divorced (2005-2009 5-year est.); Foreign born: 2.1% (2005-2009 5-year est.); Ancestry (includes multiple ancestries): 13.3% Irish, 12.6% English, 8.7% German, 7.7% European, 6.6% American (2005-2009 5-year est.).
Economy: Single-family building permits issued: 0 (2010); Multi-family building permits issued: 0 (2010); Employment by occupation: 8.6% management, 19.8% professional, 14.2% services, 21.3% sales, 4.1% farming, 14.9% construction, 17.2% production (2005-2009 5-year est.).
Income: Per capita income: $21,266 (2010); Median household income: $32,375 (2010); Average household income: $51,076 (2010); Percent of households with income of $100,000 or more: 11.0% (2010); Poverty rate: 10.1% (2005-2009 5-year est.).
Taxes: Total city taxes per capita: $123 (2007); City property taxes per capita: $107 (2007).
Education: Percent of population age 25 and over with: High school diploma (including GED) or higher: 78.7% (2010); Bachelor's degree or higher: 15.5% (2010); Master's degree or higher: 5.8% (2010).
Loraine ISD (PK-12)
   2009-10 Enrollment: 180 . . . . (325) 737-2235
Housing: Homeownership rate: 80.2% (2010); Median home value: $31,500 (2010); Median contract rent: $145 per month (2005-2009 5-year est.); Median year structure built: 1957 (2005-2009 5-year est.).
Transportation: Commute to work: 93.7% car, 0.0% public transportation, 6.3% walk, 0.0% work from home (2005-2009 5-year est.); Travel time to work: 34.0% less than 15 minutes, 35.4% 15 to 30 minutes, 7.5% 30 to 45 minutes, 1.5% 45 to 60 minutes, 21.6% 60 minutes or more (2005-2009 5-year est.)

WESTBROOK (city). Covers a land area of 0.403 square miles and a water area of 0 square miles. Located at 32.35° N. Lat; 101.01° W. Long. Elevation is 2,162 feet.
Population: 237 (1990); 203 (2000); 196 (2010); 191 (2015 projected); Race: 94.4% White, 0.0% Black, 0.0% Asian, 5.6% Other, 10.7% Hispanic of any race (2010); Density: 486.9 persons per square mile (2010); Average household size: 2.28 (2010); Median age: 45.9 (2010); Males per 100 females: 100.0 (2010); Marriage status: 31.7% never married, 50.0% now married, 12.7% widowed, 5.6% divorced (2005-2009 5-year est.); Foreign born: 0.0% (2005-2009 5-year est.); Ancestry (includes multiple ancestries): 7.3% American, 7.3% Irish, 5.3% Scottish, 4.7% German, 3.3% English (2005-2009 5-year est.).
Economy: Employment by occupation: 0.0% management, 36.7% professional, 20.4% services, 0.0% sales, 0.0% farming, 20.4% construction, 22.4% production (2005-2009 5-year est.).
Income: Per capita income: $24,187 (2010); Median household income: $45,313 (2010); Average household income: $59,651 (2010); Percent of

households with income of $100,000 or more: 11.6% (2010); Poverty rate: 17.3% (2005-2009 5-year est.).
Taxes: Total city taxes per capita: $51 (2007); City property taxes per capita: $46 (2007).
Education: Percent of population age 25 and over with: High school diploma (including GED) or higher: 82.4% (2010); Bachelor's degree or higher: 14.8% (2010); Master's degree or higher: 2.8% (2010).

School District(s)

Westbrook ISD (PK-12)
    2009-10 Enrollment: 237 . . . . (325) 644-2311
Housing: Homeownership rate: 81.4% (2010); Median home value: $54,545 (2010); Median contract rent: $505 per month (2005-2009 5-year est.); Median year structure built: 1972 (2005-2009 5-year est.).
Transportation: Commute to work: 83.0% car, 0.0% public transportation, 0.0% walk, 17.0% work from home (2005-2009 5-year est.); Travel time to work: 51.3% less than 15 minutes, 0.0% 15 to 30 minutes, 33.3% 30 to 45 minutes, 15.4% 45 to 60 minutes, 0.0% 60 minutes or more (2005-2009 5-year est.)

Montague County

Located in north Texas; bounded on the north by the Red River and the Oklahoma border; drained by tributaries of the Red and Trinity Rivers. Covers a land area of 930.66 square miles, a water area of 7.78 square miles, and is located in the Central Time Zone at 33.66° N. Lat., 97.74° W. Long. The county was founded in 1857. County seat is Montague.

Weather Station: Bowie										Elevation: 1,080 feet	
	Jan	Feb	Mar	Apr	May	Jun	Jul	Aug	Sep	Oct	Nov	Dec
High	54	58	67	75	82	89	94	94	87	76	65	54
Low	31	35	42	50	60	68	72	72	64	53	42	32
Precip	1.4	2.4	2.9	2.9	5.0	4.2	1.8	2.1	3.4	4.0	2.0	2.0
Snow	0.5	0.4	tr	0.0	0.0	0.0	0.0	0.0	0.0	0.0	0.1	0.5

High and Low temperatures in degrees Fahrenheit; Precipitation and Snow in inches

Population: 17,274 (1990); 19,117 (2000); 20,001 (2010); 20,396 (2015 projected); Race: 93.4% White, 1.2% Black, 0.3% Asian, 5.0% Other, 8.0% Hispanic of any race (2010); Density: 21.5 persons per square mile (2010); Average household size: 2.38 (2010); Median age: 40.1 (2010); Males per 100 females: 93.4 (2010).
Religion: Five largest groups: 38.2% Southern Baptist Convention, 5.5% The United Methodist Church, 3.8% Churches of Christ, 3.3% Catholic Church, 2.6% Independent, Non-Charismatic Churches (2000).
Economy: Unemployment rate: 6.8% (June 2011); Total civilian labor force: 10,327 (June 2011); Leading industries: 20.6% retail trade; 18.2% health care and social assistance; 14.3% mining (2009); Farms: 1,545 totaling 507,690 acres (2007); Companies that employ 500 or more persons: 0 (2009); Companies that employ 100 to 499 persons: 6 (2009); Companies that employ less than 100 persons: 451 (2009); Black-owned businesses: n/a (2007); Hispanic-owned businesses: n/a (2007); Asian-owned businesses: n/a (2007); Women-owned businesses: 695 (2007); Retail sales per capita: $7,441 (2010). Single-family building permits issued: 0 (2010); Multi-family building permits issued: 0 (2010).
Income: Per capita income: $24,463 (2010); Median household income: $45,009 (2010); Average household income: $59,081 (2010); Percent of households with income of $100,000 or more: 14.2% (2010); Poverty rate: 15.4% (2009); Bankruptcy rate: 1.65% (2010).
Taxes: Total county taxes per capita: $233 (2007); County property taxes per capita: $188 (2007).
Education: Percent of population age 25 and over with: High school diploma (including GED) or higher: 77.9% (2010); Bachelor's degree or higher: 12.6% (2010); Master's degree or higher: 3.1% (2010).
Housing: Homeownership rate: 77.2% (2010); Median home value: $80,895 (2010); Median contract rent: $377 per month (2005-2009 5-year est.); Median year structure built: 1971 (2005-2009 5-year est.)
Health: Birth rate: 140.0 per 10,000 population (2009); Death rate: 151.3 per 10,000 population (2009); Age-adjusted cancer mortality rate: 207.1 deaths per 100,000 population (2007); Number of physicians: 6.1 per 10,000 population (2008); Hospital beds: 37.7 per 10,000 population (2007); Hospital admissions: 1,155.3 per 10,000 population (2007).
Elections: 2008 Presidential election results: 20.1% Obama, 78.6% McCain, 0.0% Nader
Additional Information Contacts
Montague County Government . . . . (940) 894-2401
    http://www.co.montague.tx.us/ips/cms

Bowie Chamber of Commerce. . . . . (940) 872-1173
    http://www.bowietxchamber.org
City of Bowie . . . . (940) 872-1114
    http://www.cityofbowietx.com
Nacona Chamber of Commerce . . . . (940) 825-3526
    http://nocona.org/chamber.php
Saint Jo Chamber of Commerce . . . . (940) 995-2188
    http://www.saintjochamber.com

Montague County Communities

BOWIE (city). Covers a land area of 3.786 square miles and a water area of 0.017 square miles. Located at 33.56° N. Lat; 97.84° W. Long. Elevation is 1,129 feet.
History: Bowie was once known as the "chicken and bread town," for the chicken sandwiches which residents peddled to the passengers when the train stopped at the Bowie station.
Population: 4,999 (1990); 5,219 (2000); 5,505 (2010); 5,622 (2015 projected); Race: 93.8% White, 0.7% Black, 0.6% Asian, 4.9% Other, 6.8% Hispanic of any race (2010); Density: 1,454.1 persons per square mile (2010); Average household size: 2.39 (2010); Median age: 36.7 (2010); Males per 100 females: 85.2 (2010); Marriage status: 16.8% never married, 57.3% now married, 12.2% widowed, 13.7% divorced (2005-2009 5-year est.); Foreign born: 4.0% (2005-2009 5-year est.); Ancestry (includes multiple ancestries): 17.2% American, 11.2% Irish, 10.4% German, 7.4% English, 4.2% French (2005-2009 5-year est.).
Economy: Employment by occupation: 9.9% management, 12.4% professional, 21.3% services, 32.1% sales, 0.0% farming, 10.9% construction, 13.4% production (2005-2009 5-year est.).
Income: Per capita income: $20,962 (2010); Median household income: $41,918 (2010); Average household income: $51,273 (2010); Percent of households with income of $100,000 or more: 10.1% (2010); Poverty rate: 12.6% (2005-2009 5-year est.).
Taxes: Total city taxes per capita: $371 (2007); City property taxes per capita: $174 (2007).
Education: Percent of population age 25 and over with: High school diploma (including GED) or higher: 74.6% (2010); Bachelor's degree or higher: 13.3% (2010); Master's degree or higher: 3.4% (2010).

School District(s)

Bowie ISD (PK-12)
    2009-10 Enrollment: 1,613 . . . . (940) 872-1151
Housing: Homeownership rate: 69.0% (2010); Median home value: $81,159 (2010); Median contract rent: $424 per month (2005-2009 5-year est.); Median year structure built: 1964 (2005-2009 5-year est.).
Hospitals: Bowie Memorial Hospital (49 beds)
Safety: Violent crime rate: 19.6 per 10,000 population; Property crime rate: 546.3 per 10,000 population (2009).
Newspapers: Bowie News (Community news; Circulation 4,500)
Transportation: Commute to work: 97.9% car, 0.0% public transportation, 0.0% walk, 2.1% work from home (2005-2009 5-year est.); Travel time to work: 40.5% less than 15 minutes, 22.2% 15 to 30 minutes, 20.3% 30 to 45 minutes, 5.4% 45 to 60 minutes, 11.6% 60 minutes or more (2005-2009 5-year est.)
Additional Information Contacts
Bowie Chamber of Commerce. . . . . (940) 872-1173
    http://www.bowietxchamber.org
City of Bowie . . . . (940) 872-1114
    http://www.cityofbowietx.com

FORESTBURG (unincorporated postal area, zip code 76239). Covers a land area of 130.216 square miles and a water area of 0.568 square miles. Located at 33.53° N. Lat; 97.54° W. Long. Elevation is 1,165 feet.
Population: 1,108 (2000); Race: 91.7% White, 0.0% Black, 0.3% Asian, 8.0% Other, 6.9% Hispanic of any race (2000); Density: 8.5 persons per square mile (2000); Age: 24.6% under 18, 17.0% over 64 (2000); Marriage status: 15.2% never married, 68.3% now married, 6.5% widowed, 10.0% divorced (2000); Foreign born: 4.5% (2000); Ancestry (includes multiple ancestries): 17.1% American, 13.0% German, 10.6% English, 10.1% Irish (2000).
Economy: Employment by occupation: 13.9% management, 16.6% professional, 15.3% services, 16.2% sales, 6.2% farming, 12.7% construction, 19.1% production (2000).
Income: Per capita income: $20,240 (2000); Median household income: $34,044 (2000); Poverty rate: 179.1% (2000).

Education: Percent of population age 25 and over with: High school diploma (including GED) or higher: 83.1% (2000); Bachelor's degree or higher: 18.1% (2000).

School District(s)

Forestburg ISD (PK-12)

2009-10 Enrollment: 204 . . . . (940) 964-2323

Housing: Homeownership rate: 79.7% (2000); Median home value: $62,000 (2000); Median contract rent: $280 per month (2000); Median year structure built: 1975 (2000).

Transportation: Commute to work: 88.3% car, 0.4% public transportation, 5.8% walk, 5.6% work from home (2000); Travel time to work: 19.1% less than 15 minutes, 14.5% 15 to 30 minutes, 20.2% 30 to 45 minutes, 20.6% 45 to 60 minutes, 25.6% 60 minutes or more (2000)

MONTAGUE (unincorporated postal area, zip code 76251). County seat. Covers a land area of 55.449 square miles and a water area of 0.262 square miles. Located at 33.66° N. Lat; 97.71° W. Long. Elevation is 1,073 feet.

Population: 678 (2000); Race: 94.5% White, 0.0% Black, 0.0% Asian, 5.5% Other, 5.0% Hispanic of any race (2000); Density: 12.2 persons per square mile (2000); Age: 17.3% under 18, 15.9% over 64 (2000); Marriage status: 11.7% never married, 71.5% now married, 7.8% widowed, 9.0% divorced (2000); Foreign born: 1.2% (2000); Ancestry (includes multiple ancestries): 12.2% Irish, 12.2% German, 10.6% American, 10.2% Italian (2000).

Economy: Employment by occupation: 13.7% management, 13.7% professional, 16.2% services, 20.3% sales, 1.9% farming, 13.3% construction, 21.0% production (2000).

Income: Per capita income: $22,938 (2000); Median household income: $32,014 (2000); Poverty rate: 179.1% (2000).

Education: Percent of population age 25 and over with: High school diploma (including GED) or higher: 78.4% (2000); Bachelor's degree or higher: 12.7% (2000).

School District(s)

Montague ISD (PK-08)

2009-10 Enrollment: 103 . . . . (940) 894-2811

Housing: Homeownership rate: 89.6% (2000); Median home value: $42,000 (2000); Median contract rent: $225 per month (2000); Median year structure built: 1977 (2000).

Transportation: Commute to work: 87.9% car, 0.0% public transportation, 2.9% walk, 7.9% work from home (2000); Travel time to work: 29.7% less than 15 minutes, 40.3% 15 to 30 minutes, 4.8% 30 to 45 minutes, 4.1% 45 to 60 minutes, 21.0% 60 minutes or more (2000)

NOCONA (city). Covers a land area of 2.819 square miles and a water area of 0 square miles. Located at 33.78° N. Lat; 97.72° W. Long. Elevation is 981 feet.

History: Nocona developed as a producer of leather goods, known for the cowboy boots and footballs made in the plants here, which are the outgrowth of a pioneer saddle shop.

Population: 2,993 (1990); 3,198 (2000); 3,279 (2010); 3,321 (2015 projected); Race: 91.7% White, 1.2% Black, 0.2% Asian, 6.9% Other, 18.6% Hispanic of any race (2010); Density: 1,163.3 persons per square mile (2010); Average household size: 2.41 (2010); Median age: 36.2 (2010); Males per 100 females: 88.0 (2010); Marriage status: 18.7% never married, 53.7% now married, 14.7% widowed, 12.9% divorced (2005-2009 5-year est.); Foreign born: 7.8% (2005-2009 5-year est.); Ancestry (includes multiple ancestries): 13.7% American, 11.2% Irish, 8.2% English, 6.9% German, 3.0% Scottish (2005-2009 5-year est.).

Economy: Employment by occupation: 4.9% management, 13.2% professional, 20.3% services, 18.2% sales, 1.5% farming, 22.2% construction, 19.8% production (2005-2009 5-year est.).

Income: Per capita income: $20,856 (2010); Median household income: $36,897 (2010); Average household income: $50,932 (2010); Percent of households with income of $100,000 or more: 11.3% (2010); Poverty rate: 21.2% (2005-2009 5-year est.).

Taxes: Total city taxes per capita: $276 (2007); City property taxes per capita: $136 (2007).

Education: Percent of population age 25 and over with: High school diploma (including GED) or higher: 73.3% (2010); Bachelor's degree or higher: 11.2% (2010); Master's degree or higher: 2.4% (2010).

School District(s)

Nocona ISD (PK-12)

2009-10 Enrollment: 832 . . . . (940) 825-3267

Prairie Valley ISD (PK-12)

2009-10 Enrollment: 156 . . . . (940) 825-4425

Housing: Homeownership rate: 67.0% (2010); Median home value: $59,281 (2010); Median contract rent: $303 per month (2005-2009 5-year est.); Median year structure built: 1958 (2005-2009 5-year est.).

Hospitals: Nocona General Hospital (38 beds)

Safety: Violent crime rate: 9.3 per 10,000 population; Property crime rate: 74.1 per 10,000 population (2009).

Newspapers: Nocona News (Community news; Circulation 2,200)

Transportation: Commute to work: 83.8% car, 1.5% public transportation, 6.6% walk, 5.1% work from home (2005-2009 5-year est.); Travel time to work: 56.0% less than 15 minutes, 12.3% 15 to 30 minutes, 6.4% 30 to 45 minutes, 6.0% 45 to 60 minutes, 19.4% 60 minutes or more (2005-2009 5-year est.)

Additional Information Contacts

Nacona Chamber of Commerce . . . . (940) 825-3526

http://nocona.org/chamber.php

RINGGOLD (unincorporated postal area, zip code 76261). Covers a land area of 59.978 square miles and a water area of 0.006 square miles. Located at 33.81° N. Lat; 97.94° W. Long. Elevation is 902 feet.

Population: 233 (2000); Race: 89.3% White, 0.0% Black, 0.0% Asian, 10.7% Other, 9.4% Hispanic of any race (2000); Density: 3.9 persons per square mile (2000); Age: 29.1% under 18, 16.2% over 64 (2000); Marriage status: 17.4% never married, 65.7% now married, 9.0% widowed, 7.9% divorced (2000); Foreign born: 9.4% (2000); Ancestry (includes multiple ancestries): 9.4% Irish, 8.5% American, 8.5% English, 7.7% German (2000).

Economy: Employment by occupation: 11.8% management, 15.1% professional, 9.7% services, 15.1% sales, 4.3% farming, 16.1% construction, 28.0% production (2000).

Income: Per capita income: $11,562 (2000); Median household income: $28,056 (2000); Poverty rate: 179.1% (2000).

Education: Percent of population age 25 and over with: High school diploma (including GED) or higher: 68.5% (2000); Bachelor's degree or higher: 14.8% (2000).

School District(s)

Gold Burg ISD (KG-12)

2009-10 Enrollment: 115 . . . . (940) 872-3562

Housing: Homeownership rate: 89.4% (2000); Median home value: $28,000 (2000); Median contract rent: $213 per month (2000); Median year structure built: 1959 (2000).

Transportation: Commute to work: 86.7% car, 0.0% public transportation, 2.2% walk, 8.9% work from home (2000); Travel time to work: 14.6% less than 15 minutes, 37.8% 15 to 30 minutes, 25.6% 30 to 45 minutes, 13.4% 45 to 60 minutes, 8.5% 60 minutes or more (2000)

SAINT JO (city). Covers a land area of 1.072 square miles and a water area of 0 square miles. Located at 33.69° N. Lat; 97.52° W. Long. Elevation is 1,142 feet.

History: St. Jo was established on the Old California Trail of 1849, which passed through this valley. Several cattle trails used in the 1870's also came along this route.

Population: 1,048 (1990); 977 (2000); 955 (2010); 942 (2015 projected); Race: 92.3% White, 2.0% Black, 0.2% Asian, 5.5% Other, 5.9% Hispanic of any race (2010); Density: 891.0 persons per square mile (2010); Average household size: 2.31 (2010); Median age: 37.4 (2010); Males per 100 females: 90.6 (2010); Marriage status: 14.0% never married, 63.4% now married, 11.0% widowed, 11.5% divorced (2005-2009 5-year est.); Foreign born: 0.8% (2005-2009 5-year est.); Ancestry (includes multiple ancestries): 24.6% German, 15.6% English, 15.0% Irish, 12.2% American, 6.0% Scotch-Irish (2005-2009 5-year est.).

Economy: Single-family building permits issued: 0 (2010); Multi-family building permits issued: 0 (2010); Employment by occupation: 7.2% management, 19.3% professional, 17.6% services, 13.2% sales, 0.0% farming, 17.9% construction, 24.8% production (2005-2009 5-year est.).

Income: Per capita income: $24,031 (2010); Median household income: $42,500 (2010); Average household income: $56,183 (2010); Percent of households with income of $100,000 or more: 14.4% (2010); Poverty rate: 15.4% (2005-2009 5-year est.).

Taxes: Total city taxes per capita: $328 (2007); City property taxes per capita: $152 (2007).

Education: Percent of population age 25 and over with: High school diploma (including GED) or higher: 81.5% (2010); Bachelor's degree or higher: 13.4% (2010); Master's degree or higher: 3.2% (2010).

School District(s)

Saint Jo ISD (PK-12)

2009-10 Enrollment: 314 . . . . (940) 995-2668

Housing: Homeownership rate: 74.4% (2010); Median home value: $69,219 (2010); Median contract rent: $442 per month (2005-2009 5-year est.); Median year structure built: 1959 (2005-2009 5-year est.).

Newspapers: Saint Jo Tribune (Local news; Circulation 1,050)

Transportation: Commute to work: 89.5% car, 0.8% public transportation, 3.3% walk, 4.7% work from home (2005-2009 5-year est.); Travel time to work: 34.1% less than 15 minutes, 26.3% 15 to 30 minutes, 19.7% 30 to 45 minutes, 9.0% 45 to 60 minutes, 11.0% 60 minutes or more (2005-2009 5-year est.)

Additional Information Contacts

Saint Jo Chamber of Commerce . . . . (940) 995-2188
   http://www.saintjochamber.com

SUNSET (city). Covers a land area of 1.063 square miles and a water area of 0 square miles. Located at 33.45° N. Lat; 97.76° W. Long. Elevation is 991 feet.

Population: 335 (1990); 339 (2000); 329 (2010); 324 (2015 projected); Race: 94.8% White, 0.6% Black, 0.9% Asian, 3.6% Other, 3.6% Hispanic of any race (2010); Density: 309.4 persons per square mile (2010); Average household size: 2.41 (2010); Median age: 40.5 (2010); Males per 100 females: 110.9 (2010); Marriage status: n/a never married, n/a now married, n/a widowed, n/a divorced (2005-2009 5-year est.); Foreign born: n/a (2005-2009 5-year est.); Ancestry (includes multiple ancestries): n/a (2005-2009 5-year est.).

Economy: Employment by occupation: n/a management, n/a professional, n/a services, n/a sales, n/a farming, n/a construction, n/a production (2005-2009 5-year est.).

Income: Per capita income: $22,928 (2010); Median household income: $46,000 (2010); Average household income: $54,848 (2010); Percent of households with income of $100,000 or more: 15.2% (2010); Poverty rate: n/a (2005-2009 5-year est.).

Taxes: Total city taxes per capita: $92 (2007); City property taxes per capita: $92 (2007).

Education: Percent of population age 25 and over with: High school diploma (including GED) or higher: 77.2% (2010); Bachelor's degree or higher: 3.1% (2010); Master's degree or higher: 1.3% (2010).

Housing: Homeownership rate: 83.3% (2010); Median home value: $84,615 (2010); Median contract rent: n/a per month (2005-2009 5-year est.); Median year structure built: n/a (2005-2009 5-year est.).

Transportation: Commute to work: n/a car, n/a public transportation, n/a walk, n/a work from home (2005-2009 5-year est.); Travel time to work: n/a less than 15 minutes, n/a 15 to 30 minutes, n/a 30 to 45 minutes, n/a 45 to 60 minutes, n/a 60 minutes or more (2005-2009 5-year est.)

Montgomery County

Located in east Texas; drained by tributaries of the San Jacinto River; includes part of Sam Houston National Forest. Covers a land area of 1,044.03 square miles, a water area of 32.78 square miles, and is located in the Central Time Zone at 30.26° N. Lat., 95.46° W. Long. The county was founded in 1837. County seat is Conroe.

Montgomery County is part of the Houston-Sugar Land-Baytown, TX Metropolitan Statistical Area. The entire metro area includes: Austin County, TX; Brazoria County, TX; Chambers County, TX; Fort Bend County, TX; Galveston County, TX; Harris County, TX; Liberty County, TX; Montgomery County, TX; San Jacinto County, TX; Waller County, TX

Weather Station: Conroe   Elevation: 245 feet

	Jan	Feb	Mar	Apr	May	Jun	Jul	Aug	Sep	Oct	Nov	Dec
High	62	65	72	79	85	91	94	94	89	81	71	62
Low	40	43	50	57	65	71	73	73	68	58	50	41
Precip	3.9	3.4	3.2	2.9	5.2	5.2	2.9	3.7	3.6	5.8	5.0	3.8
Snow	tr	tr	0.0	0.0	0.0	0.0	0.0	0.0	0.0	0.0	0.0	tr

High and Low temperatures in degrees Fahrenheit; Precipitation and Snow in inches

Population: 182,201 (1990); 293,768 (2000); 456,283 (2010); 534,528 (2015 projected); Race: 82.9% White, 4.8% Black, 1.8% Asian, 10.5% Other, 19.0% Hispanic of any race (2010); Density: 437.0 persons per square mile (2010); Average household size: 2.87 (2010); Median age: 33.8 (2010); Males per 100 females: 99.0 (2010).

Religion: Five largest groups: 22.1% Southern Baptist Convention, 13.4% Catholic Church, 4.8% The United Methodist Church, 1.3% Churches of Christ, 1.1% Assemblies of God (2000).

Economy: Unemployment rate: 8.0% (June 2011); Total civilian labor force: 227,951 (June 2011); Leading industries: 16.9% retail trade; 13.3% accommodation & food services; 11.4% health care and social assistance (2009); Farms: 1,886 totaling 169,914 acres (2007); Companies that employ 500 or more persons: 16 (2009); Companies that employ 100 to 499 persons: 161 (2009); Companies that employ less than 100 persons: 8,566 (2009); Black-owned businesses: n/a (2007); Hispanic-owned businesses: 3,908 (2007); Asian-owned businesses: 854 (2007); Women-owned businesses: 10,432 (2007); Retail sales per capita: $13,115 (2010). Single-family building permits issued: 2,723 (2010); Multi-family building permits issued: 209 (2010).

Income: Per capita income: $31,370 (2010); Median household income: $66,881 (2010); Average household income: $90,376 (2010); Percent of households with income of $100,000 or more: 30.0% (2010); Poverty rate: 11.2% (2009); Bankruptcy rate: 1.99% (2010).

Taxes: Total county taxes per capita: $285 (2007); County property taxes per capita: $265 (2007).

Education: Percent of population age 25 and over with: High school diploma (including GED) or higher: 85.4% (2010); Bachelor's degree or higher: 28.0% (2010); Master's degree or higher: 8.1% (2010).

Housing: Homeownership rate: 75.3% (2010); Median home value: $149,131 (2010); Median contract rent: $712 per month (2005-2009 5-year est.); Median year structure built: 1993 (2005-2009 5-year est.)

Health: Birth rate: 151.2 per 10,000 population (2009); Death rate: 63.6 per 10,000 population (2009); Age-adjusted cancer mortality rate: 168.5 deaths per 100,000 population (2007); Number of physicians: 17.8 per 10,000 population (2008); Hospital beds: 14.6 per 10,000 population (2007); Hospital admissions: 580.0 per 10,000 population (2007).

Environment: Air Quality Index: 75.7% good, 23.3% moderate, 1.0% unhealthy for sensitive individuals, 0.0% unhealthy (percent of days in 2008)

Elections: 2008 Presidential election results: 23.2% Obama, 75.8% McCain, 0.1% Nader

National and State Parks: W G Jones State Forest

Additional Information Contacts

Montgomery County Government . . . . (936) 539-7812
   http://www.co.montgomery.tx.us
City of Conroe . . . . (936) 522-3000
   http://www.cityofconroe.org
City of Oak Ridge North . . . . (281) 292-4648
   http://www.oakridgenorth.com
City of Shenandoah . . . . (281) 298-5522
   http://www.shenandoahtx.com
Community Chamber of Commerce of East Montgomery County . . . . (281) 354-0051
   http://www.communitychamberemc.com
Greater Conroe/Lake Conroe Area Chamber of Commerce (936) 756-6644
   http://www.conroe.org
Magnolia Area Chamber of Commerce . . . . (281) 356-1488
   http://www.magnoliatexas.org

Montgomery County Communities

CONROE (city). County seat. Covers a land area of 37.791 square miles and a water area of 0.076 square miles. Located at 30.31° N. Lat; 95.45° W. Long. Elevation is 220 feet.

History: Named for Captain Isaac Conroe, local sawmill owner. Long a pine-lumbering town, it prospered after oil was discovered in 1932. County Heritage Museum to northeast. Incorporated 1885.

Population: 28,738 (1990); 36,811 (2000); 54,775 (2010); 64,877 (2015 projected); Race: 66.8% White, 12.0% Black, 1.1% Asian, 20.1% Other, 43.9% Hispanic of any race (2010); Density: 1,449.4 persons per square mile (2010); Average household size: 2.83 (2010); Median age: 31.4 (2010); Males per 100 females: 104.0 (2010); Marriage status: 34.1% never married, 48.9% now married, 5.5% widowed, 11.5% divorced (2005-2009 5-year est.); Foreign born: 22.7% (2005-2009 5-year est.); Ancestry (includes multiple ancestries): 11.4% German, 9.6% English, 7.8% Irish, 5.6% American, 3.3% French (2005-2009 5-year est.).

Economy: Unemployment rate: 7.5% (June 2011); Total civilian labor force: 28,799 (June 2011); Single-family building permits issued: 237 (2010); Multi-family building permits issued: 194 (2010); Employment by occupation: 9.6% management, 14.9% professional, 24.3% services,

22.2% sales, 0.2% farming, 13.7% construction, 15.0% production (2005-2009 5-year est.).
Income: Per capita income: $19,704 (2010); Median household income: $42,482 (2010); Average household income: $56,005 (2010); Percent of households with income of $100,000 or more: 12.3% (2010); Poverty rate: 19.1% (2005-2009 5-year est.).
Taxes: Total city taxes per capita: $866 (2007); City property taxes per capita: $197 (2007).
Education: Percent of population age 25 and over with: High school diploma (including GED) or higher: 71.4% (2010); Bachelor's degree or higher: 21.3% (2010); Master's degree or higher: 6.0% (2010).

School District(s)
Conroe ISD (PK-12)
   2009-10 Enrollment: 49,629 . . . . (936) 709-7702
Montgomery ISD (PK-12)
   2009-10 Enrollment: 6,714 . . . . (936) 582-1333
Splendora ISD (PK-12)
   2009-10 Enrollment: 3,382 . . . . (281) 689-3128
Tomball ISD (PK-12)
   2009-10 Enrollment: 10,266 . . . . (281) 357-3100
Housing: Homeownership rate: 44.6% (2010); Median home value: $106,600 (2010); Median contract rent: $626 per month (2005-2009 5-year est.); Median year structure built: 1984 (2005-2009 5-year est.).
Hospitals: Conroe Regional Medical Center (260 beds)
Safety: Violent crime rate: 43.9 per 10,000 population; Property crime rate: 453.5 per 10,000 population (2009).
Newspapers: Arab Times; The Bulletin (Community news; Circulation 20,000); Conroe Bulletin (Local news; Circulation 16,000); The Courier Plus (Community news); The Courier (Local news); Lake Conroe Plus (Community news)
Transportation: Commute to work: 93.6% car, 0.7% public transportation, 1.3% walk, 2.5% work from home (2005-2009 5-year est.); Travel time to work: 31.3% less than 15 minutes, 35.3% 15 to 30 minutes, 18.6% 30 to 45 minutes, 7.2% 45 to 60 minutes, 7.5% 60 minutes or more (2005-2009 5-year est.)
Airports: Lone Star Executive (general aviation)
Additional Information Contacts
City of Conroe . . . . (936) 522-3000
   http://www.cityofconroe.org
Greater Conroe/Lake Conroe Area Chamber of Commerce (936) 756-6644
   http://www.conroe.org

CUT AND SHOOT (town).
Covers a land area of 2.718 square miles and a water area of 0 square miles. Located at 30.33° N. Lat; 95.36° W. Long. Elevation is 190 feet.
Population: 874 (1990); 1,158 (2000); 1,186 (2010); 1,384 (2015 projected); Race: 86.7% White, 0.8% Black, 0.1% Asian, 12.4% Other, 15.0% Hispanic of any race (2010); Density: 436.3 persons per square mile (2010); Average household size: 2.94 (2010); Median age: 33.4 (2010); Males per 100 females: 101.0 (2010); Marriage status: 25.1% never married, 55.9% now married, 9.8% widowed, 9.2% divorced (2005-2009 5-year est.); Foreign born: 6.5% (2005-2009 5-year est.); Ancestry (includes multiple ancestries): 17.6% American, 16.2% English, 10.1% German, 9.5% Irish, 4.6% French (2005-2009 5-year est.).
Economy: Employment by occupation: 10.7% management, 10.0% professional, 9.5% services, 26.1% sales, 3.7% farming, 26.6% construction, 13.4% production (2005-2009 5-year est.).
Income: Per capita income: $22,521 (2010); Median household income: $54,342 (2010); Average household income: $66,197 (2010); Percent of households with income of $100,000 or more: 15.6% (2010); Poverty rate: 19.5% (2005-2009 5-year est.).
Taxes: Total city taxes per capita: $136 (2007); City property taxes per capita: $0 (2007).
Education: Percent of population age 25 and over with: High school diploma (including GED) or higher: 82.1% (2010); Bachelor's degree or higher: 11.1% (2010); Master's degree or higher: 2.9% (2010).
Housing: Homeownership rate: 83.4% (2010); Median home value: $95,667 (2010); Median contract rent: $569 per month (2005-2009 5-year est.); Median year structure built: 1984 (2005-2009 5-year est.).
Transportation: Commute to work: 77.6% car, 0.0% public transportation, 1.1% walk, 20.2% work from home (2005-2009 5-year est.); Travel time to work: 17.9% less than 15 minutes, 27.4% 15 to 30 minutes, 22.7% 30 to 45 minutes, 9.5% 45 to 60 minutes, 22.5% 60 minutes or more (2005-2009 5-year est.)

MAGNOLIA (city).
Covers a land area of 2.103 square miles and a water area of 0 square miles. Located at 30.21° N. Lat; 95.75° W. Long. Elevation is 269 feet.
Population: 940 (1990); 1,111 (2000); 1,603 (2010); 1,808 (2015 projected); Race: 86.1% White, 6.1% Black, 0.2% Asian, 7.7% Other, 9.3% Hispanic of any race (2010); Density: 762.2 persons per square mile (2010); Average household size: 2.83 (2010); Median age: 34.0 (2010); Males per 100 females: 96.2 (2010); Marriage status: 30.1% never married, 51.3% now married, 5.7% widowed, 12.9% divorced (2005-2009 5-year est.); Foreign born: 2.7% (2005-2009 5-year est.); Ancestry (includes multiple ancestries): 23.1% German, 9.5% Irish, 9.2% American, 7.5% English, 4.6% Czech (2005-2009 5-year est.).
Economy: Single-family building permits issued: 9 (2010); Multi-family building permits issued: 0 (2010); Employment by occupation: 12.1% management, 15.0% professional, 20.4% services, 30.3% sales, 1.2% farming, 15.4% construction, 5.6% production (2005-2009 5-year est.).
Income: Per capita income: $24,211 (2010); Median household income: $54,237 (2010); Average household income: $67,836 (2010); Percent of households with income of $100,000 or more: 21.0% (2010); Poverty rate: 6.1% (2005-2009 5-year est.).
Taxes: Total city taxes per capita: $1,811 (2007); City property taxes per capita: $239 (2007).
Education: Percent of population age 25 and over with: High school diploma (including GED) or higher: 85.0% (2010); Bachelor's degree or higher: 19.0% (2010); Master's degree or higher: 3.7% (2010).

School District(s)
Magnolia ISD (PK-12)
   2009-10 Enrollment: 11,691 . . . . (281) 356-3571
Tomball ISD (PK-12)
   2009-10 Enrollment: 10,266 . . . . (281) 357-3100
Housing: Homeownership rate: 75.6% (2010); Median home value: $134,906 (2010); Median contract rent: $617 per month (2005-2009 5-year est.); Median year structure built: 1981 (2005-2009 5-year est.).
Safety: Violent crime rate: 31.6 per 10,000 population; Property crime rate: 307.8 per 10,000 population (2009).
Transportation: Commute to work: 90.6% car, 0.0% public transportation, 0.0% walk, 7.4% work from home (2005-2009 5-year est.); Travel time to work: 25.5% less than 15 minutes, 7.9% 15 to 30 minutes, 29.7% 30 to 45 minutes, 10.4% 45 to 60 minutes, 26.5% 60 minutes or more (2005-2009 5-year est.)
Additional Information Contacts
Magnolia Area Chamber of Commerce . . . . (281) 356-1488
   http://www.magnoliatexas.org

MONTGOMERY (city).
Covers a land area of 4.514 square miles and a water area of 0.056 square miles. Located at 30.38° N. Lat; 95.69° W. Long. Elevation is 295 feet.
Population: 419 (1990); 489 (2000); 659 (2010); 769 (2015 projected); Race: 77.2% White, 19.0% Black, 0.3% Asian, 3.5% Other, 5.2% Hispanic of any race (2010); Density: 146.0 persons per square mile (2010); Average household size: 2.78 (2010); Median age: 36.0 (2010); Males per 100 females: 98.5 (2010); Marriage status: 38.2% never married, 40.8% now married, 7.8% widowed, 13.2% divorced (2005-2009 5-year est.); Foreign born: 16.0% (2005-2009 5-year est.); Ancestry (includes multiple ancestries): 11.4% American, 7.6% English, 7.3% German, 6.4% Irish, 5.9% French (2005-2009 5-year est.).
Economy: Single-family building permits issued: 7 (2010); Multi-family building permits issued: 0 (2010); Employment by occupation: 14.3% management, 8.2% professional, 34.4% services, 29.3% sales, 0.0% farming, 4.8% construction, 9.2% production (2005-2009 5-year est.).
Income: Per capita income: $22,776 (2010); Median household income: $45,057 (2010); Average household income: $62,500 (2010); Percent of households with income of $100,000 or more: 16.0% (2010); Poverty rate: 20.6% (2005-2009 5-year est.).
Taxes: Total city taxes per capita: $329 (2007); City property taxes per capita: $188 (2007).
Education: Percent of population age 25 and over with: High school diploma (including GED) or higher: 83.2% (2010); Bachelor's degree or higher: 18.1% (2010); Master's degree or higher: 6.0% (2010).

School District(s)
Montgomery ISD (PK-12)
   2009-10 Enrollment: 6,714 . . . . (936) 582-1333

Housing: Homeownership rate: 83.5% (2010); Median home value: $114,103 (2010); Median contract rent: $328 per month (2005-2009 5-year est.); Median year structure built: 1978 (2005-2009 5-year est.).
Safety: Violent crime rate: 65.7 per 10,000 population; Property crime rate: 197.0 per 10,000 population (2009).
Newspapers: Montgomery County News (Local news)
Transportation: Commute to work: 89.5% car, 0.0% public transportation, 2.0% walk, 8.5% work from home (2005-2009 5-year est.); Travel time to work: 34.9% less than 15 minutes, 29.0% 15 to 30 minutes, 11.2% 30 to 45 minutes, 6.7% 45 to 60 minutes, 18.2% 60 minutes or more (2005-2009 5-year est.)

NEW CANEY (unincorporated postal area, zip code 77357). Covers a
land area of 54.942 square miles and a water area of 0.029 square miles. Located at 30.17° N. Lat; 95.17° W. Long. Elevation is 95 feet.
Population: 17,189 (2000); Race: 89.8% White, 1.7% Black, 0.4% Asian, 8.1% Other, 11.2% Hispanic of any race (2000); Density: 312.9 persons per square mile (2000); Age: 30.6% under 18, 8.1% over 64 (2000); Marriage status: 19.6% never married, 64.3% now married, 5.8% widowed, 10.3% divorced (2000); Foreign born: 5.1% (2000); Ancestry (includes multiple ancestries): 17.8% American, 11.8% Irish, 11.2% German, 6.7% English (2000).
Economy: Employment by occupation: 9.1% management, 11.8% professional, 12.3% services, 26.3% sales, 0.3% farming, 21.8% construction, 18.5% production (2000).
Income: Per capita income: $15,792 (2000); Median household income: $39,342 (2000); Poverty rate: 179.1% (2000).
Education: Percent of population age 25 and over with: High school diploma (including GED) or higher: 67.5% (2000); Bachelor's degree or higher: 6.9% (2000).

School District(s)
New Caney ISD (PK-12)
   2009-10 Enrollment: 9,609 . . . . (281) 577-8600
Housing: Homeownership rate: 80.7% (2000); Median home value: $74,900 (2000); Median contract rent: $381 per month (2000); Median year structure built: 1983 (2000).
Transportation: Commute to work: 94.3% car, 0.5% public transportation, 1.1% walk, 2.6% work from home (2000); Travel time to work: 18.1% less than 15 minutes, 21.5% 15 to 30 minutes, 23.5% 30 to 45 minutes, 18.4% 45 to 60 minutes, 18.5% 60 minutes or more (2000)
Additional Information Contacts
Community Chamber of Commerce of East Montgomery County . . . . (281) 354-0051
   http://www.communitychamberemc.com

OAK RIDGE NORTH (city). Covers a land area of 1.147 square
miles and a water area of 0 square miles. Located at 30.15° N. Lat; 95.44° W. Long. Elevation is 138 feet.
Population: 2,897 (1990); 2,991 (2000); 3,241 (2010); 3,716 (2015 projected); Race: 90.0% White, 4.5% Black, 1.1% Asian, 4.4% Other, 8.9% Hispanic of any race (2010); Density: 2,825.6 persons per square mile (2010); Average household size: 2.89 (2010); Median age: 41.0 (2010); Males per 100 females: 97.3 (2010); Marriage status: 24.8% never married, 61.0% now married, 6.0% widowed, 8.2% divorced (2005-2009 5-year est.); Foreign born: 7.9% (2005-2009 5-year est.); Ancestry (includes multiple ancestries): 19.1% German, 15.0% English, 14.8% Irish, 7.9% American, 7.2% French (2005-2009 5-year est.).
Economy: Single-family building permits issued: 0 (2010); Multi-family building permits issued: 0 (2010); Employment by occupation: 22.2% management, 22.7% professional, 11.1% services, 28.5% sales, 0.0% farming, 6.9% construction, 8.6% production (2005-2009 5-year est.).
Income: Per capita income: $35,076 (2010); Median household income: $83,314 (2010); Average household income: $101,293 (2010); Percent of households with income of $100,000 or more: 37.4% (2010); Poverty rate: 4.8% (2005-2009 5-year est.).
Taxes: Total city taxes per capita: $860 (2007); City property taxes per capita: $354 (2007).
Education: Percent of population age 25 and over with: High school diploma (including GED) or higher: 95.5% (2010); Bachelor's degree or higher: 35.7% (2010); Master's degree or higher: 11.6% (2010).
Housing: Homeownership rate: 92.1% (2010); Median home value: $171,303 (2010); Median contract rent: $518 per month (2005-2009 5-year est.); Median year structure built: 1978 (2005-2009 5-year est.).
Safety: Violent crime rate: 17.4 per 10,000 population; Property crime rate: 296.0 per 10,000 population (2009).

Transportation: Commute to work: 89.5% car, 1.1% public transportation, 0.9% walk, 6.9% work from home (2005-2009 5-year est.); Travel time to work: 30.3% less than 15 minutes, 29.5% 15 to 30 minutes, 14.8% 30 to 45 minutes, 13.3% 45 to 60 minutes, 12.1% 60 minutes or more (2005-2009 5-year est.)
Additional Information Contacts
City of Oak Ridge North . . . . (281) 292-4648
   http://www.oakridgenorth.com

PANORAMA VILLAGE (city). Covers a land area of 1.098 square
miles and a water area of 0.015 square miles. Located at 30.37° N. Lat; 95.49° W. Long. Elevation is 305 feet.
Population: 1,556 (1990); 1,965 (2000); 2,455 (2010); 2,843 (2015 projected); Race: 94.7% White, 2.1% Black, 0.5% Asian, 2.7% Other, 4.0% Hispanic of any race (2010); Density: 2,236.1 persons per square mile (2010); Average household size: 2.29 (2010); Median age: 50.0 (2010); Males per 100 females: 88.4 (2010); Marriage status: 16.0% never married, 64.4% now married, 8.2% widowed, 11.4% divorced (2005-2009 5-year est.); Foreign born: 1.7% (2005-2009 5-year est.); Ancestry (includes multiple ancestries): 27.7% German, 19.7% Irish, 18.1% English, 13.7% American, 6.1% Scotch-Irish (2005-2009 5-year est.).
Economy: Single-family building permits issued: 1 (2010); Multi-family building permits issued: 0 (2010); Employment by occupation: 19.1% management, 20.6% professional, 10.6% services, 28.4% sales, 0.0% farming, 9.1% construction, 12.2% production (2005-2009 5-year est.).
Income: Per capita income: $34,582 (2010); Median household income: $64,019 (2010); Average household income: $78,995 (2010); Percent of households with income of $100,000 or more: 26.0% (2010); Poverty rate: 3.0% (2005-2009 5-year est.).
Taxes: Total city taxes per capita: $179 (2007); City property taxes per capita: $158 (2007).
Education: Percent of population age 25 and over with: High school diploma (including GED) or higher: 97.1% (2010); Bachelor's degree or higher: 44.6% (2010); Master's degree or higher: 12.9% (2010).
Housing: Homeownership rate: 87.9% (2010); Median home value: $159,412 (2010); Median contract rent: $831 per month (2005-2009 5-year est.); Median year structure built: 1978 (2005-2009 5-year est.).
Transportation: Commute to work: 96.2% car, 0.0% public transportation, 0.6% walk, 3.2% work from home (2005-2009 5-year est.); Travel time to work: 38.4% less than 15 minutes, 24.1% 15 to 30 minutes, 18.1% 30 to 45 minutes, 9.0% 45 to 60 minutes, 10.3% 60 minutes or more (2005-2009 5-year est.)

PATTON VILLAGE (city). Covers a land area of 1.916 square miles
and a water area of 0.138 square miles. Located at 30.19° N. Lat; 95.17° W. Long. Elevation is 89 feet.
Population: 1,299 (1990); 1,391 (2000); 1,668 (2010); 1,915 (2015 projected); Race: 88.1% White, 0.4% Black, 0.5% Asian, 11.0% Other, 15.2% Hispanic of any race (2010); Density: 870.4 persons per square mile (2010); Average household size: 2.98 (2010); Median age: 31.5 (2010); Males per 100 females: 97.2 (2010); Marriage status: 33.9% never married, 46.7% now married, 8.2% widowed, 11.2% divorced (2005-2009 5-year est.); Foreign born: 6.4% (2005-2009 5-year est.); Ancestry (includes multiple ancestries): 20.5% Irish, 15.7% German, 7.2% American, 4.3% English, 2.8% Cajun (2005-2009 5-year est.).
Economy: Employment by occupation: 7.5% management, 7.5% professional, 23.6% services, 25.6% sales, 0.0% farming, 22.2% construction, 13.6% production (2005-2009 5-year est.).
Income: Per capita income: $18,853 (2010); Median household income: $46,929 (2010); Average household income: $56,270 (2010); Percent of households with income of $100,000 or more: 12.3% (2010); Poverty rate: 14.1% (2005-2009 5-year est.).
Taxes: Total city taxes per capita: $62 (2007); City property taxes per capita: $40 (2007).
Education: Percent of population age 25 and over with: High school diploma (including GED) or higher: 75.1% (2010); Bachelor's degree or higher: 8.4% (2010); Master's degree or higher: 2.7% (2010).
Housing: Homeownership rate: 77.1% (2010); Median home value: $68,714 (2010); Median contract rent: $506 per month (2005-2009 5-year est.); Median year structure built: 1976 (2005-2009 5-year est.).
Transportation: Commute to work: 96.1% car, 1.7% public transportation, 0.6% walk, 1.7% work from home (2005-2009 5-year est.); Travel time to work: 24.1% less than 15 minutes, 24.2% 15 to 30 minutes, 18.6% 30 to 45 minutes, 18.9% 45 to 60 minutes, 14.2% 60 minutes or more (2005-2009 5-year est.)

PINEHURST (CDP). Covers a land area of 9.028 square miles and a water area of 0 square miles. Located at 30.17° N. Lat; 95.69° W. Long. Elevation is 223 feet.
Population: 3,277 (1990); 4,266 (2000); 4,984 (2010); 5,716 (2015 projected); Race: 89.3% White, 3.5% Black, 0.3% Asian, 6.9% Other, 14.5% Hispanic of any race (2010); Density: 552.1 persons per square mile (2010); Average household size: 2.93 (2010); Median age: 34.4 (2010); Males per 100 females: 99.8 (2010); Marriage status: 25.5% never married, 60.2% now married, 7.0% widowed, 7.3% divorced (2005-2009 5-year est.); Foreign born: 7.3% (2005-2009 5-year est.); Ancestry (includes multiple ancestries): 22.8% German, 18.8% English, 7.3% Irish, 5.5% French, 5.5% American (2005-2009 5-year est.).
Economy: Employment by occupation: 8.4% management, 8.9% professional, 15.0% services, 25.1% sales, 2.3% farming, 23.3% construction, 17.0% production (2005-2009 5-year est.).
Income: Per capita income: $29,440 (2010); Median household income: $66,172 (2010); Average household income: $85,928 (2010); Percent of households with income of $100,000 or more: 28.4% (2010); Poverty rate: 36.1% (2005-2009 5-year est.).
Education: Percent of population age 25 and over with: High school diploma (including GED) or higher: 83.4% (2010); Bachelor's degree or higher: 21.0% (2010); Master's degree or higher: 5.9% (2010).
Housing: Homeownership rate: 83.9% (2010); Median home value: $115,319 (2010); Median contract rent: $608 per month (2005-2009 5-year est.); Median year structure built: 1985 (2005-2009 5-year est.).
Transportation: Commute to work: 97.1% car, 0.0% public transportation, 0.0% walk, 1.7% work from home (2005-2009 5-year est.); Travel time to work: 14.5% less than 15 minutes, 22.6% 15 to 30 minutes, 23.4% 30 to 45 minutes, 11.2% 45 to 60 minutes, 28.3% 60 minutes or more (2005-2009 5-year est.)

PORTER (unincorporated postal area, zip code 77365). Covers a land area of 37.811 square miles and a water area of 0.015 square miles. Located at 30.10° N. Lat; 95.25° W. Long. Elevation is 102 feet.
Population: 15,982 (2000); Race: 88.0% White, 1.7% Black, 1.0% Asian, 9.3% Other, 15.8% Hispanic of any race (2000); Density: 422.7 persons per square mile (2000); Age: 30.1% under 18, 8.4% over 64 (2000); Marriage status: 21.0% never married, 61.2% now married, 6.6% widowed, 11.2% divorced (2000); Foreign born: 8.9% (2000); Ancestry (includes multiple ancestries): 13.5% American, 13.1% Irish, 13.1% German, 7.1% English (2000).
Economy: Employment by occupation: 6.4% management, 9.2% professional, 16.9% services, 30.7% sales, 0.0% farming, 15.9% construction, 20.8% production (2000).
Income: Per capita income: $16,557 (2000); Median household income: $38,996 (2000); Poverty rate: 179.1% (2000).
Education: Percent of population age 25 and over with: High school diploma (including GED) or higher: 71.6% (2000); Bachelor's degree or higher: 6.7% (2000).

School District(s)
New Caney ISD (PK-12)
    2009-10 Enrollment: 9,609 . . . . (281) 577-8600
Housing: Homeownership rate: 76.1% (2000); Median home value: $75,400 (2000); Median contract rent: $460 per month (2000); Median year structure built: 1984 (2000).
Transportation: Commute to work: 93.6% car, 0.1% public transportation, 1.3% walk, 3.2% work from home (2000); Travel time to work: 16.7% less than 15 minutes, 24.3% 15 to 30 minutes, 25.7% 30 to 45 minutes, 19.9% 45 to 60 minutes, 13.4% 60 minutes or more (2000)

PORTER HEIGHTS (CDP). Covers a land area of 3.159 square miles and a water area of 0.014 square miles. Located at 30.15° N. Lat; 95.31° W. Long. Elevation is 125 feet.
Population: 1,448 (1990); 1,490 (2000); 1,753 (2010); 1,984 (2015 projected); Race: 91.2% White, 1.2% Black, 0.2% Asian, 7.4% Other, 12.8% Hispanic of any race (2010); Density: 554.9 persons per square mile (2010); Average household size: 2.79 (2010); Median age: 34.0 (2010); Males per 100 females: 101.7 (2010); Marriage status: 18.9% never married, 61.1% now married, 8.3% widowed, 11.7% divorced (2005-2009 5-year est.); Foreign born: 9.5% (2005-2009 5-year est.); Ancestry (includes multiple ancestries): 17.4% Irish, 16.6% American, 14.4% German, 8.3% English, 3.7% Italian (2005-2009 5-year est.).

Economy: Employment by occupation: 6.2% management, 16.0% professional, 16.0% services, 25.4% sales, 0.0% farming, 16.0% construction, 20.5% production (2005-2009 5-year est.).
Income: Per capita income: $19,311 (2010); Median household income: $45,813 (2010); Average household income: $53,820 (2010); Percent of households with income of $100,000 or more: 9.5% (2010); Poverty rate: 15.1% (2005-2009 5-year est.).
Education: Percent of population age 25 and over with: High school diploma (including GED) or higher: 85.8% (2010); Bachelor's degree or higher: 13.1% (2010); Master's degree or higher: 3.5% (2010).
Housing: Homeownership rate: 86.8% (2010); Median home value: $95,172 (2010); Median contract rent: $619 per month (2005-2009 5-year est.); Median year structure built: 1983 (2005-2009 5-year est.).
Transportation: Commute to work: 93.6% car, 0.0% public transportation, 0.0% walk, 4.3% work from home (2005-2009 5-year est.); Travel time to work: 11.7% less than 15 minutes, 29.1% 15 to 30 minutes, 33.0% 30 to 45 minutes, 12.2% 45 to 60 minutes, 13.9% 60 minutes or more (2005-2009 5-year est.)

ROMAN FOREST (town). Covers a land area of 1.479 square miles and a water area of 0 square miles. Located at 30.17° N. Lat; 95.15° W. Long. Elevation is 105 feet.
Population: 1,033 (1990); 1,279 (2000); 2,055 (2010); 2,455 (2015 projected); Race: 91.3% White, 1.8% Black, 0.7% Asian, 6.2% Other, 5.9% Hispanic of any race (2010); Density: 1,389.2 persons per square mile (2010); Average household size: 2.93 (2010); Median age: 36.6 (2010); Males per 100 females: 98.6 (2010); Marriage status: 20.2% never married, 72.4% now married, 2.6% widowed, 4.8% divorced (2005-2009 5-year est.); Foreign born: 1.6% (2005-2009 5-year est.); Ancestry (includes multiple ancestries): 24.6% German, 19.2% American, 11.9% English, 10.8% Irish, 5.1% Scotch-Irish (2005-2009 5-year est.).
Economy: Single-family building permits issued: 31 (2010); Multi-family building permits issued: 0 (2010); Employment by occupation: 20.6% management, 19.9% professional, 11.4% services, 25.3% sales, 0.0% farming, 13.1% construction, 9.8% production (2005-2009 5-year est.).
Income: Per capita income: $28,197 (2010); Median household income: $67,446 (2010); Average household income: $82,336 (2010); Percent of households with income of $100,000 or more: 29.1% (2010); Poverty rate: 1.0% (2005-2009 5-year est.).
Taxes: Total city taxes per capita: $103 (2007); City property taxes per capita: $82 (2007).
Education: Percent of population age 25 and over with: High school diploma (including GED) or higher: 89.4% (2010); Bachelor's degree or higher: 18.9% (2010); Master's degree or higher: 5.6% (2010).
Housing: Homeownership rate: 87.6% (2010); Median home value: $125,754 (2010); Median contract rent: $940 per month (2005-2009 5-year est.); Median year structure built: 1984 (2005-2009 5-year est.).
Safety: Violent crime rate: 2.4 per 10,000 population; Property crime rate: 30.8 per 10,000 population (2009).
Transportation: Commute to work: 94.9% car, 0.4% public transportation, 0.0% walk, 3.8% work from home (2005-2009 5-year est.); Travel time to work: 17.0% less than 15 minutes, 25.0% 15 to 30 minutes, 22.9% 30 to 45 minutes, 23.2% 45 to 60 minutes, 11.9% 60 minutes or more (2005-2009 5-year est.)

SHENANDOAH (city). Covers a land area of 1.262 square miles and a water area of 0 square miles. Located at 30.18° N. Lat; 95.45° W. Long. Elevation is 148 feet.
Population: 1,783 (1990); 1,503 (2000); 1,948 (2010); 2,322 (2015 projected); Race: 84.6% White, 8.0% Black, 1.4% Asian, 6.0% Other, 15.4% Hispanic of any race (2010); Density: 1,543.7 persons per square mile (2010); Average household size: 3.05 (2010); Median age: 36.2 (2010); Males per 100 females: 96.4 (2010); Marriage status: 29.7% never married, 48.8% now married, 8.5% widowed, 13.1% divorced (2005-2009 5-year est.); Foreign born: 7.6% (2005-2009 5-year est.); Ancestry (includes multiple ancestries): 24.9% German, 13.2% English, 12.5% Irish, 8.7% American, 7.8% French (2005-2009 5-year est.).
Economy: Single-family building permits issued: 34 (2010); Multi-family building permits issued: 0 (2010); Employment by occupation: 22.5% management, 24.7% professional, 8.6% services, 29.4% sales, 0.0% farming, 5.8% construction, 9.0% production (2005-2009 5-year est.).
Income: Per capita income: $28,510 (2010); Median household income: $76,914 (2010); Average household income: $87,229 (2010); Percent of households with income of $100,000 or more: 33.9% (2010); Poverty rate: 4.6% (2005-2009 5-year est.).

Taxes: Total city taxes per capita: $3,516 (2007); City property taxes per capita: $740 (2007).
Education: Percent of population age 25 and over with: High school diploma (including GED) or higher: 92.0% (2010); Bachelor's degree or higher: 29.0% (2010); Master's degree or higher: 8.0% (2010).
Housing: Homeownership rate: 87.9% (2010); Median home value: $166,406 (2010); Median contract rent: $894 per month (2005-2009 5-year est.); Median year structure built: 1991 (2005-2009 5-year est.).
Safety: Violent crime rate: 19.4 per 10,000 population; Property crime rate: 1,098.7 per 10,000 population (2009).
Transportation: Commute to work: 87.6% car, 2.6% public transportation, 0.7% walk, 7.7% work from home (2005-2009 5-year est.); Travel time to work: 32.1% less than 15 minutes, 24.3% 15 to 30 minutes, 13.1% 30 to 45 minutes, 20.3% 45 to 60 minutes, 10.2% 60 minutes or more (2005-2009 5-year est.)
Additional Information Contacts
City of Shenandoah . . . . (281) 298-5522
　http://www.shenandoahtx.com

SPLENDORA (city).
Covers a land area of 2.112 square miles and a water area of 0 square miles. Located at 30.22° N. Lat; 95.16° W. Long. Elevation is 125 feet.
Population: 959 (1990); 1,275 (2000); 1,686 (2010); 1,960 (2015 projected); Race: 89.5% White, 0.2% Black, 0.8% Asian, 9.5% Other, 13.9% Hispanic of any race (2010); Density: 798.4 persons per square mile (2010); Average household size: 2.99 (2010); Median age: 31.1 (2010); Males per 100 females: 100.2 (2010); Marriage status: 18.3% never married, 63.2% now married, 5.9% widowed, 12.6% divorced (2005-2009 5-year est.); Foreign born: 5.6% (2005-2009 5-year est.); Ancestry (includes multiple ancestries): 20.1% German, 19.3% American, 19.2% Irish, 6.8% English, 4.5% French (2005-2009 5-year est.).
Economy: Employment by occupation: 9.0% management, 14.7% professional, 9.9% services, 27.0% sales, 1.5% farming, 19.4% construction, 18.6% production (2005-2009 5-year est.).
Income: Per capita income: $18,479 (2010); Median household income: $48,087 (2010); Average household income: $54,933 (2010); Percent of households with income of $100,000 or more: 9.8% (2010); Poverty rate: 15.4% (2005-2009 5-year est.).
Taxes: Total city taxes per capita: $137 (2007); City property taxes per capita: $40 (2007).
Education: Percent of population age 25 and over with: High school diploma (including GED) or higher: 73.9% (2010); Bachelor's degree or higher: 4.8% (2010); Master's degree or higher: 0.5% (2010).
School District(s)
Splendora ISD (PK-12)
　2009-10 Enrollment: 3,382 . . . . (281) 689-3128
Housing: Homeownership rate: 82.1% (2010); Median home value: $64,615 (2010); Median contract rent: $459 per month (2005-2009 5-year est.); Median year structure built: 1992 (2005-2009 5-year est.).
Transportation: Commute to work: 93.6% car, 0.0% public transportation, 6.1% walk, 0.3% work from home (2005-2009 5-year est.); Travel time to work: 16.8% less than 15 minutes, 18.4% 15 to 30 minutes, 32.9% 30 to 45 minutes, 16.0% 45 to 60 minutes, 16.0% 60 minutes or more (2005-2009 5-year est.)

STAGECOACH (town).
Covers a land area of 1.138 square miles and a water area of 0.053 square miles. Located at 30.14° N. Lat; 95.71° W. Long. Elevation is 194 feet.
Population: 356 (1990); 455 (2000); 521 (2010); 608 (2015 projected); Race: 92.5% White, 0.8% Black, 0.6% Asian, 6.1% Other, 11.7% Hispanic of any race (2010); Density: 458.0 persons per square mile (2010); Average household size: 2.91 (2010); Median age: 34.9 (2010); Males per 100 females: 97.3 (2010); Marriage status: 12.9% never married, 67.8% now married, 9.6% widowed, 9.6% divorced (2005-2009 5-year est.); Foreign born: 6.7% (2005-2009 5-year est.); Ancestry (includes multiple ancestries): 19.4% German, 16.0% Irish, 14.5% English, 10.8% French, 10.4% American (2005-2009 5-year est.).
Economy: Single-family building permits issued: 1 (2010); Multi-family building permits issued: 0 (2010); Employment by occupation: 25.2% management, 19.4% professional, 10.5% services, 17.8% sales, 0.8% farming, 20.5% construction, 5.8% production (2005-2009 5-year est.).
Income: Per capita income: $33,001 (2010); Median household income: $73,214 (2010); Average household income: $95,587 (2010); Percent of households with income of $100,000 or more: 34.6% (2010); Poverty rate: 1.4% (2005-2009 5-year est.).

Taxes: Total city taxes per capita: $124 (2007); City property taxes per capita: $79 (2007).
Education: Percent of population age 25 and over with: High school diploma (including GED) or higher: 89.0% (2010); Bachelor's degree or higher: 26.5% (2010); Master's degree or higher: 6.9% (2010).
Housing: Homeownership rate: 82.1% (2010); Median home value: $174,107 (2010); Median contract rent: $875 per month (2005-2009 5-year est.); Median year structure built: 1982 (2005-2009 5-year est.).
Transportation: Commute to work: 89.8% car, 0.0% public transportation, 0.8% walk, 8.7% work from home (2005-2009 5-year est.); Travel time to work: 5.2% less than 15 minutes, 19.8% 15 to 30 minutes, 22.0% 30 to 45 minutes, 23.7% 45 to 60 minutes, 29.3% 60 minutes or more (2005-2009 5-year est.)

THE WOODLANDS (CDP).
Covers a land area of 23.409 square miles and a water area of 0.472 square miles. Located at 30.17° N. Lat; 95.50° W. Long. Elevation is 141 feet.
Population: 29,532 (1990); 55,649 (2000); 69,563 (2010); 79,737 (2015 projected); Race: 86.8% White, 2.8% Black, 5.6% Asian, 4.7% Other, 9.4% Hispanic of any race (2010); Density: 2,971.7 persons per square mile (2010); Average household size: 2.88 (2010); Median age: 34.6 (2010); Males per 100 females: 94.9 (2010); Marriage status: 23.3% never married, 62.6% now married, 6.1% widowed, 8.0% divorced (2005-2009 5-year est.); Foreign born: 11.2% (2005-2009 5-year est.); Ancestry (includes multiple ancestries): 20.1% German, 15.1% English, 13.8% Irish, 6.7% American, 5.7% Italian (2005-2009 5-year est.).
Economy: Employment by occupation: 26.7% management, 28.5% professional, 9.1% services, 27.3% sales, 0.0% farming, 3.2% construction, 5.1% production (2005-2009 5-year est.).
Income: Per capita income: $47,184 (2010); Median household income: $108,303 (2010); Average household income: $136,484 (2010); Percent of households with income of $100,000 or more: 53.8% (2010); Poverty rate: 6.0% (2005-2009 5-year est.).
Education: Percent of population age 25 and over with: High school diploma (including GED) or higher: 97.1% (2010); Bachelor's degree or higher: 60.3% (2010); Master's degree or higher: 20.5% (2010).
School District(s)
Conroe ISD (PK-12)
　2009-10 Enrollment: 49,629 . . . . (936) 709-7702
Tomball ISD (PK-12)
　2009-10 Enrollment: 10,266 . . . . (281) 357-3100
Two-year College(s)
Lone Star College System (Public)
　Fall 2009 Enrollment: 46,504. (832) 813-6764
　2010-11 Tuition: In-state $2,880; Out-of-state $3,240
Housing: Homeownership rate: 77.7% (2010); Median home value: $275,734 (2010); Median contract rent: $865 per month (2005-2009 5-year est.); Median year structure built: 1992 (2005-2009 5-year est.).
Hospitals: Memorial Hermann-The Woodland Hospital; St. Luke's Community Medical Center - The Woodlands (86 beds)
Newspapers: The Villager (Community news; Circulation 26,190)
Transportation: Commute to work: 87.2% car, 3.3% public transportation, 0.5% walk, 7.3% work from home (2005-2009 5-year est.); Travel time to work: 27.7% less than 15 minutes, 25.6% 15 to 30 minutes, 17.8% 30 to 45 minutes, 14.5% 45 to 60 minutes, 14.3% 60 minutes or more (2005-2009 5-year est.)

WILLIS (city).
Covers a land area of 3.291 square miles and a water area of 0 square miles. Located at 30.42° N. Lat; 95.47° W. Long. Elevation is 381 feet.
History: Incorporated 1937.
Population: 2,902 (1990); 3,985 (2000); 4,599 (2010); 5,196 (2015 projected); Race: 60.6% White, 19.5% Black, 0.5% Asian, 19.4% Other, 38.0% Hispanic of any race (2010); Density: 1,397.5 persons per square mile (2010); Average household size: 3.15 (2010); Median age: 30.7 (2010); Males per 100 females: 100.7 (2010); Marriage status: 32.0% never married, 50.2% now married, 7.9% widowed, 9.9% divorced (2005-2009 5-year est.); Foreign born: 19.9% (2005-2009 5-year est.); Ancestry (includes multiple ancestries): 5.7% Irish, 5.0% German, 3.8% English, 3.7% French, 3.6% Scotch-Irish (2005-2009 5-year est.).
Economy: Single-family building permits issued: 0 (2010); Multi-family building permits issued: 0 (2010); Employment by occupation: 5.1% management, 10.8% professional, 24.4% services, 23.6% sales, 2.9% farming, 8.5% construction, 24.9% production (2005-2009 5-year est.).

Income: Per capita income: $15,375 (2010); Median household income: $39,505 (2010); Average household income: $48,457 (2010); Percent of households with income of $100,000 or more: 8.2% (2010); Poverty rate: 35.4% (2005-2009 5-year est.).
Taxes: Total city taxes per capita: $471 (2007); City property taxes per capita: $138 (2007).
Education: Percent of population age 25 and over with: High school diploma (including GED) or higher: 71.8% (2010); Bachelor's degree or higher: 10.2% (2010); Master's degree or higher: 3.3% (2010).

School District(s)
Responsive Education Solutions (KG-12)
 2009-10 Enrollment: 5,022 . . . . (972) 316-3663
Texas Serenity Academy (KG-08)
 2009-10 Enrollment: 390 . . . . (281) 931-8887
Willis ISD (PK-12)
 2009-10 Enrollment: 6,264 . . . . (936) 856-1200
Housing: Homeownership rate: 63.9% (2010); Median home value: $77,622 (2010); Median contract rent: $480 per month (2005-2009 5-year est.); Median year structure built: 1989 (2005-2009 5-year est.).
Safety: Violent crime rate: 111.0 per 10,000 population; Property crime rate: 360.7 per 10,000 population (2009).
Transportation: Commute to work: 95.7% car, 0.0% public transportation, 2.4% walk, 1.9% work from home (2005-2009 5-year est.); Travel time to work: 38.8% less than 15 minutes, 33.5% 15 to 30 minutes, 10.5% 30 to 45 minutes, 9.2% 45 to 60 minutes, 8.0% 60 minutes or more (2005-2009 5-year est.)
Additional Information Contacts
Greater Conroe/Lake Conroe Area Chamber of Commerce (936) 756-6644
 http://www.conroe.org

WOODBRANCH (city). Covers a land area of 1.948 square miles and a water area of 0 square miles. Located at 30.18° N. Lat; 95.19° W. Long. Elevation is 95 feet.
Population: 1,316 (1990); 1,305 (2000); 1,979 (2010); 2,363 (2015 projected); Race: 91.7% White, 0.7% Black, 1.3% Asian, 6.4% Other, 6.4% Hispanic of any race (2010); Density: 1,016.0 persons per square mile (2010); Average household size: 2.92 (2010); Median age: 35.1 (2010); Males per 100 females: 95.2 (2010); Marriage status: 16.4% never married, 70.5% now married, 5.4% widowed, 7.8% divorced (2005-2009 5-year est.); Foreign born: 1.0% (2005-2009 5-year est.); Ancestry (includes multiple ancestries): 19.5% German, 18.6% American, 14.1% Irish, 12.2% English, 5.2% French (2005-2009 5-year est.).
Economy: Single-family building permits issued: 4 (2010); Multi-family building permits issued: 0 (2010); Employment by occupation: 15.6% management, 11.4% professional, 15.9% services, 27.5% sales, 0.0% farming, 17.8% construction, 11.9% production (2005-2009 5-year est.).
Income: Per capita income: $24,945 (2010); Median household income: $62,865 (2010); Average household income: $71,831 (2010); Percent of households with income of $100,000 or more: 23.2% (2010); Poverty rate: 3.5% (2005-2009 5-year est.).
Taxes: Total city taxes per capita: $53 (2007); City property taxes per capita: $49 (2007).
Education: Percent of population age 25 and over with: High school diploma (including GED) or higher: 88.9% (2010); Bachelor's degree or higher: 14.6% (2010); Master's degree or higher: 3.4% (2010).
Housing: Homeownership rate: 88.0% (2010); Median home value: $116,118 (2010); Median contract rent: $613 per month (2005-2009 5-year est.); Median year structure built: 1977 (2005-2009 5-year est.).
Transportation: Commute to work: 97.8% car, 0.3% public transportation, 0.0% walk, 1.5% work from home (2005-2009 5-year est.); Travel time to work: 6.3% less than 15 minutes, 27.7% 15 to 30 minutes, 30.5% 30 to 45 minutes, 18.2% 45 to 60 minutes, 17.3% 60 minutes or more (2005-2009 5-year est.)

WOODLOCH (town). Covers a land area of 0.087 square miles and a water area of 0 square miles. Located at 30.21° N. Lat; 95.41° W. Long. Elevation is 108 feet.
Population: 334 (1990); 247 (2000); 232 (2010); 280 (2015 projected); Race: 63.8% White, 3.0% Black, 2.2% Asian, 31.0% Other, 54.7% Hispanic of any race (2010); Density: 2,657.8 persons per square mile (2010); Average household size: 3.46 (2010); Median age: 29.4 (2010); Males per 100 females: 98.3 (2010); Marriage status: 8.8% never married, 84.2% now married, 0.0% widowed, 7.0% divorced (2005-2009 5-year est.); Foreign born: 0.0% (2005-2009 5-year est.); Ancestry (includes

multiple ancestries): 37.8% American, 16.9% German, 4.7% Israeli, 4.1% Dutch, 4.1% Polish (2005-2009 5-year est.).
Economy: Single-family building permits issued: 0 (2010); Multi-family building permits issued: 0 (2010); Employment by occupation: 9.1% management, 24.2% professional, 7.6% services, 28.8% sales, 0.0% farming, 16.7% construction, 13.6% production (2005-2009 5-year est.).
Income: Per capita income: $19,604 (2010); Median household income: $57,031 (2010); Average household income: $65,784 (2010); Percent of households with income of $100,000 or more: 16.4% (2010); Poverty rate: 24.3% (2005-2009 5-year est.).
Taxes: Total city taxes per capita: $240 (2007); City property taxes per capita: $197 (2007).
Education: Percent of population age 25 and over with: High school diploma (including GED) or higher: 79.7% (2010); Bachelor's degree or higher: 18.0% (2010); Master's degree or higher: 3.8% (2010).
Housing: Homeownership rate: 77.6% (2010); Median home value: $111,667 (2010); Median contract rent: n/a per month (2005-2009 5-year est.); Median year structure built: 1975 (2005-2009 5-year est.).
Transportation: Commute to work: 100.0% car, 0.0% public transportation, 0.0% walk, 0.0% work from home (2005-2009 5-year est.); Travel time to work: 14.3% less than 15 minutes, 25.4% 15 to 30 minutes, 31.7% 30 to 45 minutes, 14.3% 45 to 60 minutes, 14.3% 60 minutes or more (2005-2009 5-year est.)

Moore County

Located in north Texas, in the high plains of the Panhandle; drained by the Canadian River. Covers a land area of 899.66 square miles, a water area of 9.95 square miles, and is located in the Central Time Zone at 35.85° N. Lat., 101.89° W. Long. The county was founded in 1876. County seat is Dumas.

Moore County is part of the Dumas, TX Micropolitan Statistical Area. The entire metro area includes: Moore County, TX

Weather Station: Dumas   Elevation: 3,654 feet

	Jan	Feb	Mar	Apr	May	Jun	Jul	Aug	Sep	Oct	Nov	Dec
High	49	52	60	69	78	87	92	90	82	71	59	48
Low	22	25	31	39	50	60	65	64	56	43	31	23
Precip	0.4	0.5	1.2	1.3	2.3	2.4	2.2	2.6	1.9	1.4	0.7	0.6
Snow	3.4	1.9	2.3	0.6	0.0	0.0	0.0	0.0	tr	0.1	1.2	2.9

High and Low temperatures in degrees Fahrenheit; Precipitation and Snow in inches

Population: 17,865 (1990); 20,121 (2000); 20,250 (2010); 20,278 (2015 projected); Race: 57.5% White, 1.6% Black, 1.0% Asian, 40.0% Other, 55.0% Hispanic of any race (2010); Density: 22.5 persons per square mile (2010); Average household size: 2.95 (2010); Median age: 31.2 (2010); Males per 100 females: 101.9 (2010).
Religion: Five largest groups: 23.4% Southern Baptist Convention, 9.9% Catholic Church, 5.5% The United Methodist Church, 5.3% Churches of Christ, 3.4% Assemblies of God (2000).
Economy: Unemployment rate: 5.3% (June 2011); Total civilian labor force: 11,838 (June 2011); Leading industries: 51.2% manufacturing; 12.0% retail trade; 7.5% health care and social assistance (2009); Farms: 283 totaling 553,348 acres (2007); Companies that employ 500 or more persons: 1 (2009); Companies that employ 100 to 499 persons: 4 (2009); Companies that employ less than 100 persons: 442 (2009); Black-owned businesses: n/a (2007); Hispanic-owned businesses: 374 (2007); Asian-owned businesses: n/a (2007); Women-owned businesses: n/a (2007); Retail sales per capita: $11,583 (2010). Single-family building permits issued: 12 (2010); Multi-family building permits issued: 0 (2010).
Income: Per capita income: $18,251 (2010); Median household income: $42,830 (2010); Average household income: $54,195 (2010); Percent of households with income of $100,000 or more: 10.1% (2010); Poverty rate: 11.6% (2009); Bankruptcy rate: 1.49% (2010).
Taxes: Total county taxes per capita: $349 (2007); County property taxes per capita: $321 (2007).
Education: Percent of population age 25 and over with: High school diploma (including GED) or higher: 64.3% (2010); Bachelor's degree or higher: 10.8% (2010); Master's degree or higher: 3.3% (2010).
Housing: Homeownership rate: 62.5% (2010); Median home value: $72,435 (2010); Median contract rent: $446 per month (2005-2009 5-year est.); Median year structure built: 1970 (2005-2009 5-year est.)
Health: Birth rate: 212.7 per 10,000 population (2009); Death rate: 54.5 per 10,000 population (2009); Age-adjusted cancer mortality rate: 173.2 deaths per 100,000 population (2007); Number of physicians: 7.9 per 10,000

population (2008); Hospital beds: 54.0 per 10,000 population (2007); Hospital admissions: 773.1 per 10,000 population (2007).
Elections: 2008 Presidential election results: 20.7% Obama, 78.8% McCain, 0.0% Nader
National and State Parks: Lake Meredith National Recreation Area
Additional Information Contacts
Moore County Government . . . . (806) 935-5588
   http://www.co.moore.tx.us/ips/cms
City of Dumas . . . . (806) 935-4101
   http://www.ci.dumas.tx.us
Dumas-Moore County Chamber of Commerce . . . . (806) 935-2123
   http://www.dumaschamber.com

Moore County Communities

CACTUS (city). Covers a land area of 2.040 square miles and a water area of 0 square miles. Located at 36.04° N. Lat; 102.00° W. Long. Elevation is 3,619 feet.
Population: 1,529 (1990); 2,538 (2000); 2,573 (2010); 2,585 (2015 projected); Race: 28.8% White, 0.6% Black, 0.3% Asian, 70.3% Other, 96.7% Hispanic of any race (2010); Density: 1,261.0 persons per square mile (2010); Average household size: 3.82 (2010); Median age: 24.1 (2010); Males per 100 females: 113.9 (2010); Marriage status: 37.8% never married, 53.0% now married, 6.3% widowed, 2.9% divorced (2005-2009 5-year est.); Foreign born: 45.9% (2005-2009 5-year est.); Ancestry (includes multiple ancestries): 1.6% Scotch-Irish, 1.2% German, 0.7% African, 0.5% Welsh, 0.5% French (2005-2009 5-year est.).
Economy: Employment by occupation: 3.1% management, 4.0% professional, 14.8% services, 7.8% sales, 5.1% farming, 14.7% construction, 50.5% production (2005-2009 5-year est.).
Income: Per capita income: $11,661 (2010); Median household income: $35,000 (2010); Average household income: $44,852 (2010); Percent of households with income of $100,000 or more: 4.5% (2010); Poverty rate: 34.1% (2005-2009 5-year est.).
Taxes: Total city taxes per capita: $186 (2007); City property taxes per capita: $122 (2007).
Education: Percent of population age 25 and over with: High school diploma (including GED) or higher: 22.5% (2010); Bachelor's degree or higher: 1.7% (2010); Master's degree or higher: 0.9% (2010).
School District(s)
Dumas ISD (PK-12)
   2009-10 Enrollment: 4,476 . . . . (806) 935-6461
Housing: Homeownership rate: 54.0% (2010); Median home value: $32,715 (2010); Median contract rent: $476 per month (2005-2009 5-year est.); Median year structure built: 1970 (2005-2009 5-year est.).
Safety: Violent crime rate: 80.4 per 10,000 population; Property crime rate: 153.1 per 10,000 population (2009).
Transportation: Commute to work: 91.7% car, 0.4% public transportation, 5.1% walk, 1.0% work from home (2005-2009 5-year est.); Travel time to work: 73.6% less than 15 minutes, 15.8% 15 to 30 minutes, 4.4% 30 to 45 minutes, 0.0% 45 to 60 minutes, 6.2% 60 minutes or more (2005-2009 5-year est.)

DUMAS (city). County seat. Covers a land area of 5.128 square miles and a water area of 0.019 square miles. Located at 35.86° N. Lat; 101.96° W. Long. Elevation is 3,661 feet.
History: Dumas, once a farming community, prospered with the oil, natural gas, and petrochemicals found here.
Population: 12,900 (1990); 13,747 (2000); 13,831 (2010); 13,857 (2015 projected); Race: 59.5% White, 1.6% Black, 1.3% Asian, 37.6% Other, 51.6% Hispanic of any race (2010); Density: 2,697.4 persons per square mile (2010); Average household size: 2.87 (2010); Median age: 32.1 (2010); Males per 100 females: 99.0 (2010); Marriage status: 24.6% never married, 61.9% now married, 6.0% widowed, 7.6% divorced (2005-2009 5-year est.); Foreign born: 14.5% (2005-2009 5-year est.); Ancestry (includes multiple ancestries): 12.3% German, 9.5% Irish, 6.9% English, 6.2% American, 2.7% Scotch-Irish (2005-2009 5-year est.).
Economy: Single-family building permits issued: 12 (2010); Multi-family building permits issued: 0 (2010); Employment by occupation: 9.2% management, 16.3% professional, 13.3% services, 22.6% sales, 2.2% farming, 11.0% construction, 25.4% production (2005-2009 5-year est.).
Income: Per capita income: $18,273 (2010); Median household income: $42,451 (2010); Average household income: $52,901 (2010); Percent of households with income of $100,000 or more: 9.4% (2010); Poverty rate: 9.6% (2005-2009 5-year est.).

Taxes: Total city taxes per capita: $181 (2007); City property taxes per capita: $36 (2007).
Education: Percent of population age 25 and over with: High school diploma (including GED) or higher: 68.0% (2010); Bachelor's degree or higher: 11.5% (2010); Master's degree or higher: 4.0% (2010).
School District(s)
Dumas ISD (PK-12)
   2009-10 Enrollment: 4,476 . . . . (806) 935-6461
Housing: Homeownership rate: 62.5% (2010); Median home value: $76,224 (2010); Median contract rent: $443 per month (2005-2009 5-year est.); Median year structure built: 1969 (2005-2009 5-year est.).
Hospitals: Memorial Hospital (60 beds)
Safety: Violent crime rate: 36.6 per 10,000 population; Property crime rate: 295.0 per 10,000 population (2009).
Newspapers: Moore County News-Press (Local news; Circulation 4,500)
Transportation: Commute to work: 93.4% car, 0.3% public transportation, 1.4% walk, 0.6% work from home (2005-2009 5-year est.); Travel time to work: 56.9% less than 15 minutes, 32.0% 15 to 30 minutes, 2.4% 30 to 45 minutes, 2.5% 45 to 60 minutes, 6.3% 60 minutes or more (2005-2009 5-year est.)
Airports: Moore County (general aviation)
Additional Information Contacts
City of Dumas . . . . (806) 935-4101
   http://www.ci.dumas.tx.us
Dumas-Moore County Chamber of Commerce . . . . (806) 935-2123
   http://www.dumaschamber.com

SUNRAY (city). Covers a land area of 1.690 square miles and a water area of 0 square miles. Located at 36.01° N. Lat; 101.82° W. Long. Elevation is 3,507 feet.
History: Incorporated after 1940.
Population: 1,729 (1990); 1,950 (2000); 1,875 (2010); 1,838 (2015 projected); Race: 68.9% White, 1.9% Black, 0.1% Asian, 29.2% Other, 40.0% Hispanic of any race (2010); Density: 1,109.7 persons per square mile (2010); Average household size: 2.85 (2010); Median age: 33.1 (2010); Males per 100 females: 102.7 (2010); Marriage status: 17.5% never married, 68.1% now married, 8.2% widowed, 6.2% divorced (2005-2009 5-year est.); Foreign born: 21.0% (2005-2009 5-year est.); Ancestry (includes multiple ancestries): 14.4% German, 12.2% Irish, 5.3% English, 3.8% French, 3.2% Scotch-Irish (2005-2009 5-year est.).
Economy: Single-family building permits issued: 0 (2010); Multi-family building permits issued: 0 (2010); Employment by occupation: 10.1% management, 10.5% professional, 19.4% services, 16.6% sales, 4.9% farming, 17.2% construction, 21.3% production (2005-2009 5-year est.).
Income: Per capita income: $20,894 (2010); Median household income: $45,417 (2010); Average household income: $58,697 (2010); Percent of households with income of $100,000 or more: 12.2% (2010); Poverty rate: 5.9% (2005-2009 5-year est.).
Taxes: Total city taxes per capita: $112 (2007); City property taxes per capita: $47 (2007).
Education: Percent of population age 25 and over with: High school diploma (including GED) or higher: 72.3% (2010); Bachelor's degree or higher: 10.9% (2010); Master's degree or higher: 2.2% (2010).
School District(s)
Sunray ISD (PK-12)
   2009-10 Enrollment: 530 . . . . (806) 948-4411
Housing: Homeownership rate: 67.2% (2010); Median home value: $60,923 (2010); Median contract rent: $350 per month (2005-2009 5-year est.); Median year structure built: 1960 (2005-2009 5-year est.).
Transportation: Commute to work: 95.5% car, 0.0% public transportation, 0.5% walk, 2.3% work from home (2005-2009 5-year est.); Travel time to work: 50.6% less than 15 minutes, 37.8% 15 to 30 minutes, 7.8% 30 to 45 minutes, 1.9% 45 to 60 minutes, 1.9% 60 minutes or more (2005-2009 5-year est.)

Morris County

Located in northeastern Texas; bounded on the north by the Sulphur River, and on the south by Cypress Bayou. Covers a land area of 254.51 square miles, a water area of 4.13 square miles, and is located in the Central Time Zone at 33.05° N. Lat., 94.71° W. Long. The county was founded in 1875. County seat is Daingerfield.

Weather Station: Daingerfield 9 S   Elevation: 299 feet

	Jan	Feb	Mar	Apr	May	Jun	Jul	Aug	Sep	Oct	Nov	Dec
High	57	62	69	77	84	91	94	96	89	78	68	59
Low	36	40	47	54	64	71	74	74	67	56	46	38
Precip	3.2	3.8	4.6	3.6	4.8	4.1	3.1	2.7	3.4	4.6	4.3	4.4
Snow	0.3	0.1	tr	0.0	tr	0.0	0.0	0.0	0.0	0.0	tr	0.2

High and Low temperatures in degrees Fahrenheit; Precipitation and Snow in inches

Population: 13,200 (1990); 13,048 (2000); 13,096 (2010); 13,097 (2015 projected); Race: 71.3% White, 22.5% Black, 0.2% Asian, 6.0% Other, 5.9% Hispanic of any race (2010); Density: 51.5 persons per square mile (2010); Average household size: 2.40 (2010); Median age: 40.5 (2010); Males per 100 females: 91.9 (2010).
Religion: Five largest groups: 38.0% Southern Baptist Convention, 14.1% The American Baptist Association, 8.5% The United Methodist Church, 7.4% Churches of Christ, 6.0% Catholic Church (2000).
Economy: Unemployment rate: 12.1% (June 2011); Total civilian labor force: 6,199 (June 2011); Leading industries: Farms: 457 totaling 85,666 acres (2007); Companies that employ 500 or more persons: 1 (2009); Companies that employ 100 to 499 persons: 3 (2009); Companies that employ less than 100 persons: 222 (2009); Black-owned businesses: 81 (2007); Hispanic-owned businesses: n/a (2007); Asian-owned businesses: n/a (2007); Women-owned businesses: 407 (2007); Retail sales per capita: $4,572 (2010). Single-family building permits issued: 0 (2010); Multi-family building permits issued: 0 (2010).
Income: Per capita income: $20,299 (2010); Median household income: $36,416 (2010); Average household income: $49,172 (2010); Percent of households with income of $100,000 or more: 9.0% (2010); Poverty rate: 18.8% (2009); Bankruptcy rate: 1.68% (2010).
Taxes: Total county taxes per capita: $249 (2007); County property taxes per capita: $161 (2007).
Education: Percent of population age 25 and over with: High school diploma (including GED) or higher: 79.3% (2010); Bachelor's degree or higher: 12.7% (2010); Master's degree or higher: 4.0% (2010).
Housing: Homeownership rate: 76.2% (2010); Median home value: $58,048 (2010); Median contract rent: $293 per month (2005-2009 5-year est.); Median year structure built: 1971 (2005-2009 5-year est.)
Health: Birth rate: 132.2 per 10,000 population (2009); Death rate: 137.7 per 10,000 population (2009); Age-adjusted cancer mortality rate: 238.5 deaths per 100,000 population (2007); Number of physicians: 3.9 per 10,000 population (2008); Hospital beds: 0.0 per 10,000 population (2007); Hospital admissions: 0.0 per 10,000 population (2007).
Elections: 2008 Presidential election results: 39.2% Obama, 60.2% McCain, 0.1% Nader
National and State Parks: Daingerfield State Park
Additional Information Contacts
Morris County Government . . . . (903) 645-3691
   http://www.co.morris.tx.us/ips/cms
Daingerfield Chamber of Commerce . . . . (903) 645-2646
   http://daingerfieldtx.net
Naples Chamber of Commerce . . . . (903) 897-2041

Morris County Communities

DAINGERFIELD (town). County seat. Covers a land area of 2.413 square miles and a water area of <.001 square miles. Located at 33.03° N. Lat; 94.72° W. Long. Elevation is 397 feet.
Population: 2,674 (1990); 2,517 (2000); 2,495 (2010); 2,480 (2015 projected); Race: 63.9% White, 26.2% Black, 0.4% Asian, 9.5% Other, 8.2% Hispanic of any race (2010); Density: 1,033.8 persons per square mile (2010); Average household size: 2.47 (2010); Median age: 36.1 (2010); Males per 100 females: 85.4 (2010); Marriage status: 26.5% never married, 50.5% now married, 10.5% widowed, 12.5% divorced (2005-2009 5-year est.); Foreign born: 7.2% (2005-2009 5-year est.); Ancestry (includes multiple ancestries): 14.2% Irish, 13.8% German, 11.1% African, 9.5% American, 4.6% English (2005-2009 5-year est.).
Economy: Single-family building permits issued: 0 (2010); Multi-family building permits issued: 0 (2010); Employment by occupation: 7.5% management, 17.3% professional, 21.5% services, 22.4% sales, 0.0% farming, 5.8% construction, 25.4% production (2005-2009 5-year est.).
Income: Per capita income: $17,877 (2010); Median household income: $35,409 (2010); Average household income: $45,150 (2010); Percent of households with income of $100,000 or more: 8.3% (2010); Poverty rate: 19.3% (2005-2009 5-year est.).
Taxes: Total city taxes per capita: $329 (2007); City property taxes per capita: $188 (2007).

Education: Percent of population age 25 and over with: High school diploma (including GED) or higher: 82.9% (2010); Bachelor's degree or higher: 14.8% (2010); Master's degree or higher: 3.9% (2010).
School District(s)
Daingerfield-Lone Star ISD (PK-12)
   2009-10 Enrollment: 1,337 . . . . (903) 645-2239
Housing: Homeownership rate: 68.0% (2010); Median home value: $47,500 (2010); Median contract rent: $271 per month (2005-2009 5-year est.); Median year structure built: 1957 (2005-2009 5-year est.).
Safety: Violent crime rate: 45.0 per 10,000 population; Property crime rate: 408.8 per 10,000 population (2009).
Newspapers: Bee (Community news; Circulation 3,200)
Transportation: Commute to work: 94.1% car, 0.0% public transportation, 0.6% walk, 0.0% work from home (2005-2009 5-year est.); Travel time to work: 54.1% less than 15 minutes, 30.2% 15 to 30 minutes, 7.2% 30 to 45 minutes, 6.8% 45 to 60 minutes, 1.7% 60 minutes or more (2005-2009 5-year est.)
Additional Information Contacts
Daingerfield Chamber of Commerce . . . . (903) 645-2646
   http://daingerfieldtx.net

LONE STAR (city). Covers a land area of 1.988 square miles and a water area of 0.011 square miles. Located at 32.94° N. Lat; 94.70° W. Long. Elevation is 348 feet.
Population: 1,615 (1990); 1,631 (2000); 1,614 (2010); 1,601 (2015 projected); Race: 64.1% White, 27.6% Black, 0.4% Asian, 7.9% Other, 10.0% Hispanic of any race (2010); Density: 812.0 persons per square mile (2010); Average household size: 2.38 (2010); Median age: 36.6 (2010); Males per 100 females: 88.1 (2010); Marriage status: 31.7% never married, 43.9% now married, 8.8% widowed, 15.6% divorced (2005-2009 5-year est.); Foreign born: 2.7% (2005-2009 5-year est.); Ancestry (includes multiple ancestries): 16.9% Irish, 14.1% African, 10.9% English, 7.3% German, 4.0% French (2005-2009 5-year est.).
Economy: Single-family building permits issued: 0 (2010); Multi-family building permits issued: 0 (2010); Employment by occupation: 4.9% management, 16.0% professional, 18.5% services, 25.4% sales, 1.7% farming, 7.2% construction, 26.3% production (2005-2009 5-year est.).
Income: Per capita income: $17,991 (2010); Median household income: $31,934 (2010); Average household income: $42,633 (2010); Percent of households with income of $100,000 or more: 5.8% (2010); Poverty rate: 25.4% (2005-2009 5-year est.).
Taxes: Total city taxes per capita: $205 (2007); City property taxes per capita: $84 (2007).
Education: Percent of population age 25 and over with: High school diploma (including GED) or higher: 77.2% (2010); Bachelor's degree or higher: 12.0% (2010); Master's degree or higher: 3.8% (2010).
School District(s)
Daingerfield-Lone Star ISD (PK-12)
   2009-10 Enrollment: 1,337 . . . . (903) 645-2239
Housing: Homeownership rate: 57.2% (2010); Median home value: $68,478 (2010); Median contract rent: $360 per month (2005-2009 5-year est.); Median year structure built: 1970 (2005-2009 5-year est.).
Safety: Violent crime rate: 25.3 per 10,000 population; Property crime rate: 385.1 per 10,000 population (2009).
Transportation: Commute to work: 94.2% car, 0.0% public transportation, 0.0% walk, 3.5% work from home (2005-2009 5-year est.); Travel time to work: 44.9% less than 15 minutes, 19.3% 15 to 30 minutes, 20.0% 30 to 45 minutes, 11.1% 45 to 60 minutes, 4.7% 60 minutes or more (2005-2009 5-year est.)

NAPLES (city). Covers a land area of 2.368 square miles and a water area of 0.018 square miles. Located at 33.20° N. Lat; 94.67° W. Long. Elevation is 407 feet.
History: Incorporated 1909.
Population: 1,510 (1990); 1,410 (2000); 1,416 (2010); 1,420 (2015 projected); Race: 68.3% White, 28.5% Black, 0.1% Asian, 3.1% Other, 1.8% Hispanic of any race (2010); Density: 597.9 persons per square mile (2010); Average household size: 2.19 (2010); Median age: 39.9 (2010); Males per 100 females: 82.7 (2010); Marriage status: 28.3% never married, 47.5% now married, 7.3% widowed, 16.8% divorced (2005-2009 5-year est.); Foreign born: 0.7% (2005-2009 5-year est.); Ancestry (includes multiple ancestries): 19.4% German, 14.7% African, 12.5% English, 11.9% Irish, 4.7% French (2005-2009 5-year est.).

Economy: Employment by occupation: 5.3% management, 21.9% professional, 25.5% services, 22.3% sales, 3.6% farming, 11.9% construction, 9.4% production (2005-2009 5-year est.).
Income: Per capita income: $17,011 (2010); Median household income: $25,575 (2010); Average household income: $37,233 (2010); Percent of households with income of $100,000 or more: 5.6% (2010); Poverty rate: 28.1% (2005-2009 5-year est.).
Taxes: Total city taxes per capita: $201 (2007); City property taxes per capita: $158 (2007).
Education: Percent of population age 25 and over with: High school diploma (including GED) or higher: 76.2% (2010); Bachelor's degree or higher: 13.8% (2010); Master's degree or higher: 3.1% (2010).
Housing: Homeownership rate: 70.3% (2010); Median home value: $52,562 (2010); Median contract rent: $242 per month (2005-2009 5-year est.); Median year structure built: 1966 (2005-2009 5-year est.).
Newspapers: Monitor (Community news; Circulation 4,500)
Transportation: Commute to work: 96.8% car, 0.0% public transportation, 0.0% walk, 2.3% work from home (2005-2009 5-year est.); Travel time to work: 31.2% less than 15 minutes, 44.1% 15 to 30 minutes, 17.6% 30 to 45 minutes, 4.7% 45 to 60 minutes, 2.3% 60 minutes or more (2005-2009 5-year est.)
Additional Information Contacts
Naples Chamber of Commerce . . . . (903) 897-2041

OMAHA (city). Covers a land area of 1.173 square miles and a water area of 0 square miles. Located at 33.18° N. Lat; 94.74° W. Long. Elevation is 400 feet.
Population: 919 (1990); 999 (2000); 979 (2010); 967 (2015 projected); Race: 80.2% White, 14.6% Black, 0.2% Asian, 5.0% Other, 6.4% Hispanic of any race (2010); Density: 834.5 persons per square mile (2010); Average household size: 2.38 (2010); Median age: 38.3 (2010); Males per 100 females: 85.8 (2010); Marriage status: 26.4% never married, 57.0% now married, 11.5% widowed, 5.0% divorced (2005-2009 5-year est.); Foreign born: 3.4% (2005-2009 5-year est.); Ancestry (includes multiple ancestries): 15.9% Irish, 11.4% German, 11.1% English, 6.0% African, 3.3% American (2005-2009 5-year est.).
Economy: Single-family building permits issued: 0 (2010); Multi-family building permits issued: 0 (2010); Employment by occupation: 1.6% management, 12.8% professional, 24.5% services, 21.2% sales, 0.0% farming, 13.2% construction, 26.7% production (2005-2009 5-year est.).
Income: Per capita income: $17,256 (2010); Median household income: $30,082 (2010); Average household income: $41,974 (2010); Percent of households with income of $100,000 or more: 6.2% (2010); Poverty rate: 13.6% (2005-2009 5-year est.).
Taxes: Total city taxes per capita: $124 (2007); City property taxes per capita: $79 (2007).
Education: Percent of population age 25 and over with: High school diploma (including GED) or higher: 77.8% (2010); Bachelor's degree or higher: 10.6% (2010); Master's degree or higher: 4.1% (2010).
School District(s)
Pewitt CISD (PK-12)
    2009-10 Enrollment: 1,000 . . . . (903) 884-2804
Housing: Homeownership rate: 74.5% (2010); Median home value: $55,867 (2010); Median contract rent: $225 per month (2005-2009 5-year est.); Median year structure built: 1968 (2005-2009 5-year est.).
Transportation: Commute to work: 93.8% car, 0.0% public transportation, 2.1% walk, 1.0% work from home (2005-2009 5-year est.); Travel time to work: 38.8% less than 15 minutes, 42.6% 15 to 30 minutes, 16.4% 30 to 45 minutes, 2.3% 45 to 60 minutes, 0.0% 60 minutes or more (2005-2009 5-year est.)

Motley County

Located in northwestern Texas; in plains area, drained by the North, South, and Middle Pease Rivers. Covers a land area of 989.38 square miles, a water area of 0.43 square miles, and is located in the Central Time Zone at 34.08° N. Lat., 100.79° W. Long. The county was founded in 1876. County seat is Matador.

Weather Station: Matador										Elevation: 2,290 feet		
	Jan	Feb	Mar	Apr	May	Jun	Jul	Aug	Sep	Oct	Nov	Dec
High	54	58	66	75	83	90	95	93	85	76	64	54
Low	29	32	39	47	57	65	70	69	61	50	39	30
Precip	0.8	0.9	1.5	1.8	2.9	3.6	2.0	2.4	2.9	2.0	1.2	1.0
Snow	2.3	1.5	0.3	0.1	0.0	0.0	0.0	0.0	0.0	tr	1.4	1.8

High and Low temperatures in degrees Fahrenheit; Precipitation and Snow in inches

Population: 1,532 (1990); 1,426 (2000); 1,362 (2010); 1,329 (2015 projected); Race: 84.9% White, 3.7% Black, 0.1% Asian, 11.2% Other, 15.7% Hispanic of any race (2010); Density: 1.4 persons per square mile (2010); Average household size: 2.35 (2010); Median age: 47.5 (2010); Males per 100 females: 100.6 (2010).
Religion: Five largest groups: 53.2% Southern Baptist Convention, 14.2% The United Methodist Church, 7.7% Churches of Christ, 5.3% Catholic Church, 1.5% Assemblies of God (2000).
Economy: Unemployment rate: 6.3% (June 2011); Total civilian labor force: 703 (June 2011); Leading industries: Farms: 229 totaling 574,812 acres (2007); Companies that employ 500 or more persons: 0 (2009); Companies that employ 100 to 499 persons: 0 (2009); Companies that employ less than 100 persons: 36 (2009); Black-owned businesses: n/a (2007); Hispanic-owned businesses: n/a (2007); Asian-owned businesses: n/a (2007); Women-owned businesses: n/a (2007); Retail sales per capita: $8,266 (2010). Single-family building permits issued: n/a (2010); Multi-family building permits issued: n/a (2010).
Income: Per capita income: $20,530 (2010); Median household income: $35,721 (2010); Average household income: $48,211 (2010); Percent of households with income of $100,000 or more: 8.6% (2010); Poverty rate: 20.7% (2009); Bankruptcy rate: n/a (2010).
Taxes: Total county taxes per capita: $480 (2007); County property taxes per capita: $411 (2007).
Education: Percent of population age 25 and over with: High school diploma (including GED) or higher: 78.5% (2010); Bachelor's degree or higher: 16.6% (2010); Master's degree or higher: 4.4% (2010).
Housing: Homeownership rate: 75.0% (2010); Median home value: $41,705 (2010); Median contract rent: $181 per month (2005-2009 5-year est.); Median year structure built: 1949 (2005-2009 5-year est.)
Health: Birth rate: 124.8 per 10,000 population (2009); Death rate: 70.2 per 10,000 population (2009); Age-adjusted cancer mortality rate: Suppressed deaths per 100,000 population (2007); Number of physicians: 7.9 per 10,000 population (2008); Hospital beds: 0.0 per 10,000 population (2007); Hospital admissions: 0.0 per 10,000 population (2007).
Elections: 2008 Presidential election results: 11.3% Obama, 87.9% McCain, 0.0% Nader
Additional Information Contacts
Motley County Government . . . . (806) 347-2334
    http://www.co.motley.tx.us/ips/cms
Motley County Chamber of Commerce . . . . (806) 347-2968
    http://www.motleycountychamber.org

Motley County Communities

FLOMOT (unincorporated postal area, zip code 79234). Covers a land area of 140.418 square miles and a water area of 0.037 square miles. Located at 34.24° N. Lat; 100.93° W. Long. Elevation is 2,461 feet.
Population: 178 (2000); Race: 78.8% White, 0.0% Black, 0.0% Asian, 21.2% Other, 37.6% Hispanic of any race (2000); Density: 1.3 persons per square mile (2000); Age: 21.2% under 18, 32.4% over 64 (2000); Marriage status: 11.3% never married, 74.5% now married, 9.2% widowed, 5.0% divorced (2000); Foreign born: 22.4% (2000); Ancestry (includes multiple ancestries): 25.9% American, 8.2% English, 5.3% Irish, 1.2% German (2000).
Economy: Employment by occupation: 36.4% management, 5.5% professional, 16.4% services, 9.1% sales, 14.5% farming, 9.1% construction, 9.1% production (2000).
Income: Per capita income: $13,947 (2000); Median household income: $27,500 (2000); Poverty rate: 179.1% (2000).
Education: Percent of population age 25 and over with: High school diploma (including GED) or higher: 67.3% (2000); Bachelor's degree or higher: 11.5% (2000).
Housing: Homeownership rate: 82.9% (2000); Median home value: $29,400 (2000); Median contract rent: n/a per month (2000); Median year structure built: 1955 (2000).
Transportation: Commute to work: 80.0% car, 0.0% public transportation, 7.3% walk, 12.7% work from home (2000); Travel time to work: 35.4% less than 15 minutes, 22.9% 15 to 30 minutes, 33.3% 30 to 45 minutes, 4.2% 45 to 60 minutes, 4.2% 60 minutes or more (2000)

MATADOR (town). County seat. Covers a land area of 1.299 square miles and a water area of 0 square miles. Located at 34.01° N. Lat; 100.82° W. Long. Elevation is 2,382 feet.

History: Matador developed as a service center for ranch hands, with boot and saddle shops as early enterprises. The town took its name from the large Matador Ranch, established in 1879 but later broken into smaller ranches.
Population: 793 (1990); 740 (2000); 699 (2010); 680 (2015 projected); Race: 84.8% White, 5.4% Black, 0.3% Asian, 9.4% Other, 15.0% Hispanic of any race (2010); Density: 537.9 persons per square mile (2010); Average household size: 2.38 (2010); Median age: 45.9 (2010); Males per 100 females: 98.6 (2010); Marriage status: 20.3% never married, 49.7% now married, 15.9% widowed, 14.1% divorced (2005-2009 5-year est.); Foreign born: 0.0% (2005-2009 5-year est.); Ancestry (includes multiple ancestries): 23.7% Irish, 18.4% English, 11.9% German, 7.1% Scottish, 3.9% Italian (2005-2009 5-year est.).
Economy: Employment by occupation: 17.7% management, 15.3% professional, 12.1% services, 20.0% sales, 0.0% farming, 15.8% construction, 19.1% production (2005-2009 5-year est.).
Income: Per capita income: $20,686 (2010); Median household income: $36,731 (2010); Average household income: $49,269 (2010); Percent of households with income of $100,000 or more: 6.5% (2010); Poverty rate: 21.7% (2005-2009 5-year est.).
Taxes: Total city taxes per capita: $158 (2007); City property taxes per capita: $47 (2007).
Education: Percent of population age 25 and over with: High school diploma (including GED) or higher: 78.9% (2010); Bachelor's degree or higher: 18.0% (2010); Master's degree or higher: 6.3% (2010).

School District(s)

Motley County ISD (PK-12)
    2009-10 Enrollment: 187 . . . . (806) 347-2676
Housing: Homeownership rate: 75.5% (2010); Median home value: $36,842 (2010); Median contract rent: $142 per month (2005-2009 5-year est.); Median year structure built: 1949 (2005-2009 5-year est.).
Newspapers: Motley County Tribune (Community news; Circulation 1,100)
Transportation: Commute to work: 86.4% car, 0.0% public transportation, 1.0% walk, 12.6% work from home (2005-2009 5-year est.); Travel time to work: 76.1% less than 15 minutes, 7.2% 15 to 30 minutes, 8.9% 30 to 45 minutes, 0.0% 45 to 60 minutes, 7.8% 60 minutes or more (2005-2009 5-year est.)

Additional Information Contacts

Motley County Chamber of Commerce . . . . (806) 347-2968
    http://www.motleycountychamber.org

ROARING SPRINGS (town). Covers a land area of 1.067 square miles and a water area of 0 square miles. Located at 33.90° N. Lat; 100.85° W. Long. Elevation is 2,507 feet.
Population: 264 (1990); 265 (2000); 251 (2010); 246 (2015 projected); Race: 85.7% White, 1.6% Black, 0.0% Asian, 12.7% Other, 16.7% Hispanic of any race (2010); Density: 235.3 persons per square mile (2010); Average household size: 2.32 (2010); Median age: 48.9 (2010); Males per 100 females: 102.4 (2010); Marriage status: 19.5% never married, 46.5% now married, 21.1% widowed, 13.0% divorced (2005-2009 5-year est.); Foreign born: 0.0% (2005-2009 5-year est.); Ancestry (includes multiple ancestries): 34.8% Irish, 15.4% German, 10.0% English, 5.5% Scottish, 4.5% French (2005-2009 5-year est.).
Economy: Employment by occupation: 2.4% management, 18.3% professional, 17.1% services, 18.3% sales, 8.5% farming, 26.8% construction, 8.5% production (2005-2009 5-year est.).
Income: Per capita income: $20,359 (2010); Median household income: $35,750 (2010); Average household income: $48,194 (2010); Percent of households with income of $100,000 or more: 11.1% (2010); Poverty rate: 20.1% (2005-2009 5-year est.).
Taxes: Total city taxes per capita: $186 (2007); City property taxes per capita: $122 (2007).
Education: Percent of population age 25 and over with: High school diploma (including GED) or higher: 79.1% (2010); Bachelor's degree or higher: 15.5% (2010); Master's degree or higher: 2.7% (2010).
Housing: Homeownership rate: 74.1% (2010); Median home value: $54,545 (2010); Median contract rent: $317 per month (2005-2009 5-year est.); Median year structure built: 1953 (2005-2009 5-year est.).
Transportation: Commute to work: 90.8% car, 0.0% public transportation, 9.2% walk, 0.0% work from home (2005-2009 5-year est.); Travel time to work: 55.3% less than 15 minutes, 18.4% 15 to 30 minutes, 10.5% 30 to 45 minutes, 10.5% 45 to 60 minutes, 5.3% 60 minutes or more (2005-2009 5-year est.)

Nacogdoches County

Located in east Texas; bounded on the west and south by the Angelina River, and partly on the east by Attoyac Bayou; includes part of Angelina National Forest. Covers a land area of 946.77 square miles, a water area of 34.56 square miles, and is located in the Central Time Zone at 31.63° N. Lat., 94.62° W. Long. The county was founded in 1836. County seat is Nacogdoches.

Nacogdoches County is part of the Nacogdoches, TX Micropolitan Statistical Area. The entire metro area includes: Nacogdoches County, TX

Weather Station: Nacogdoches   Elevation: 435 feet

	Jan	Feb	Mar	Apr	May	Jun	Jul	Aug	Sep	Oct	Nov	Dec
High	59	63	70	77	84	90	94	95	89	79	69	60
Low	37	40	47	54	63	70	73	72	66	55	45	37
Precip	4.2	4.4	4.2	3.8	4.5	4.4	3.0	3.3	3.7	4.7	4.8	4.7
Snow	0.2	0.1	0.0	tr	0.0	0.0	0.0	0.0	0.0	0.0	tr	tr

High and Low temperatures in degrees Fahrenheit; Precipitation and Snow in inches

Population: 54,753 (1990); 59,203 (2000); 63,802 (2010); 65,919 (2015 projected); Race: 72.0% White, 16.4% Black, 0.8% Asian, 10.8% Other, 16.4% Hispanic of any race (2010); Density: 67.4 persons per square mile (2010); Average household size: 2.48 (2010); Median age: 30.3 (2010); Males per 100 females: 94.1 (2010).
Religion: Five largest groups: 21.3% Southern Baptist Convention, 16.0% Catholic Church, 5.0% The United Methodist Church, 4.3% Baptist Missionary Association of America, 2.4% Churches of Christ (2000).
Economy: Unemployment rate: 8.0% (June 2011); Total civilian labor force: 32,194 (June 2011); Leading industries: 19.0% manufacturing; 18.5% health care and social assistance; 15.7% retail trade (2009); Farms: 1,277 totaling 265,131 acres (2007); Companies that employ 500 or more persons: 4 (2009); Companies that employ 100 to 499 persons: 18 (2009); Companies that employ less than 100 persons: 1,241 (2009); Black-owned businesses: 391 (2007); Hispanic-owned businesses: 165 (2007); Asian-owned businesses: n/a (2007); Women-owned businesses: 922 (2007); Retail sales per capita: $11,404 (2010). Single-family building permits issued: 38 (2010); Multi-family building permits issued: 212 (2010).
Income: Per capita income: $18,677 (2010); Median household income: $33,632 (2010); Average household income: $48,767 (2010); Percent of households with income of $100,000 or more: 10.5% (2010); Poverty rate: 25.8% (2009); Bankruptcy rate: 1.53% (2010).
Taxes: Total county taxes per capita: $174 (2007); County property taxes per capita: $156 (2007).
Education: Percent of population age 25 and over with: High school diploma (including GED) or higher: 80.8% (2010); Bachelor's degree or higher: 25.6% (2010); Master's degree or higher: 9.2% (2010).
Housing: Homeownership rate: 59.5% (2010); Median home value: $85,670 (2010); Median contract rent: $482 per month (2005-2009 5-year est.); Median year structure built: 1979 (2005-2009 5-year est.)
Health: Birth rate: 161.0 per 10,000 population (2009); Death rate: 86.4 per 10,000 population (2009); Age-adjusted cancer mortality rate: 189.9 deaths per 100,000 population (2007); Number of physicians: 19.1 per 10,000 population (2008); Hospital beds: 39.2 per 10,000 population (2007); Hospital admissions: 1,986.9 per 10,000 population (2007).
Elections: 2008 Presidential election results: 35.9% Obama, 63.4% McCain, 0.1% Nader
National and State Parks: Angelina National Forest
Additional Information Contacts

Nacogdoches County Government . . . . (936) 560-7755
    http://www.co.nacogdoches.tx.us/ips/cms
City of Nacogdoches . . . . (936) 559-2502
    http://www.ci.nacogdoches.tx.us
Nacogdoches County Chamber of Commerce . . . . (936) 560-5533
    http://www.nacogdoches.org

Nacogdoches County Communities

APPLEBY (city). Covers a land area of 2.144 square miles and a water area of 0 square miles. Located at 31.71° N. Lat; 94.60° W. Long. Elevation is 410 feet.
Population: 449 (1990); 444 (2000); 439 (2010); 433 (2015 projected); Race: 87.7% White, 8.2% Black, 0.9% Asian, 3.2% Other, 2.3% Hispanic of any race (2010); Density: 204.8 persons per square mile (2010); Average household size: 2.51 (2010); Median age: 37.8 (2010); Males per 100 females: 95.1 (2010); Marriage status: 34.5% never married, 52.4%

now married, 6.6% widowed, 6.6% divorced (2005-2009 5-year est.); Foreign born: 3.5% (2005-2009 5-year est.); Ancestry (includes multiple ancestries): 31.2% Irish, 13.3% American, 6.6% German, 5.3% Scottish, 5.1% English (2005-2009 5-year est.).

Economy: Employment by occupation: 18.0% management, 20.2% professional, 1.9% services, 25.6% sales, 1.6% farming, 22.1% construction, 10.7% production (2005-2009 5-year est.).

Income: Per capita income: $25,287 (2010); Median household income: $54,545 (2010); Average household income: $64,799 (2010); Percent of households with income of $100,000 or more: 16.7% (2010); Poverty rate: 5.7% (2005-2009 5-year est.).

Taxes: Total city taxes per capita: $417 (2007); City property taxes per capita: $315 (2007).

Education: Percent of population age 25 and over with: High school diploma (including GED) or higher: 91.8% (2010); Bachelor's degree or higher: 30.7% (2010); Master's degree or higher: 9.9% (2010).

Housing: Homeownership rate: 83.9% (2010); Median home value: $117,391 (2010); Median contract rent: $814 per month (2005-2009 5-year est.); Median year structure built: 1985 (2005-2009 5-year est.).

Transportation: Commute to work: 83.7% car, 0.0% public transportation, 3.7% walk, 8.1% work from home (2005-2009 5-year est.); Travel time to work: 35.8% less than 15 minutes, 43.5% 15 to 30 minutes, 10.3% 30 to 45 minutes, 8.5% 45 to 60 minutes, 1.8% 60 minutes or more (2005-2009 5-year est.)

CHIRENO (city).
Covers a land area of 1.874 square miles and a water area of 0 square miles. Located at 31.49° N. Lat; 94.34° W. Long. Elevation is 322 feet.

Population: 415 (1990); 405 (2000); 427 (2010); 434 (2015 projected); Race: 93.7% White, 4.2% Black, 0.0% Asian, 2.1% Other, 3.5% Hispanic of any race (2010); Density: 227.9 persons per square mile (2010); Average household size: 2.53 (2010); Median age: 38.1 (2010); Males per 100 females: 101.4 (2010); Marriage status: 20.7% never married, 62.7% now married, 6.2% widowed, 10.4% divorced (2005-2009 5-year est.); Foreign born: 0.8% (2005-2009 5-year est.); Ancestry (includes multiple ancestries): 20.6% American, 17.7% German, 7.9% English, 5.2% European, 4.2% Norwegian (2005-2009 5-year est.).

Economy: Employment by occupation: 10.4% management, 14.5% professional, 23.5% services, 19.5% sales, 0.0% farming, 30.3% construction, 1.8% production (2005-2009 5-year est.).

Income: Per capita income: $19,278 (2010); Median household income: $36,172 (2010); Average household income: $48,314 (2010); Percent of households with income of $100,000 or more: 8.9% (2010); Poverty rate: 10.1% (2005-2009 5-year est.).

Taxes: Total city taxes per capita: $184 (2007); City property taxes per capita: $100 (2007).

Education: Percent of population age 25 and over with: High school diploma (including GED) or higher: 82.3% (2010); Bachelor's degree or higher: 11.1% (2010); Master's degree or higher: 3.0% (2010).

School District(s)

Chireno ISD (PK-12)
　2009-10 Enrollment: 349 . . . . (936) 362-2132

Housing: Homeownership rate: 83.4% (2010); Median home value: $61,667 (2010); Median contract rent: $338 per month (2005-2009 5-year est.); Median year structure built: 1970 (2005-2009 5-year est.).

Transportation: Commute to work: 86.3% car, 0.0% public transportation, 0.0% walk, 12.3% work from home (2005-2009 5-year est.); Travel time to work: 18.8% less than 15 minutes, 30.1% 15 to 30 minutes, 25.3% 30 to 45 minutes, 8.1% 45 to 60 minutes, 17.7% 60 minutes or more (2005-2009 5-year est.)

CUSHING (city).
Covers a land area of 1.265 square miles and a water area of 0.004 square miles. Located at 31.81° N. Lat; 94.84° W. Long. Elevation is 410 feet.

Population: 565 (1990); 637 (2000); 654 (2010); 670 (2015 projected); Race: 93.1% White, 4.6% Black, 0.8% Asian, 1.5% Other, 2.0% Hispanic of any race (2010); Density: 516.9 persons per square mile (2010); Average household size: 2.47 (2010); Median age: 41.0 (2010); Males per 100 females: 90.7 (2010); Marriage status: 25.4% never married, 41.9% now married, 11.9% widowed, 20.8% divorced (2005-2009 5-year est.); Foreign born: 2.4% (2005-2009 5-year est.); Ancestry (includes multiple ancestries): 22.1% American, 14.3% German, 13.8% English, 11.9% Scottish, 8.5% Irish (2005-2009 5-year est.).

Economy: Employment by occupation: 11.1% management, 24.3% professional, 11.5% services, 22.6% sales, 1.3% farming, 13.7% construction, 15.5% production (2005-2009 5-year est.).

Income: Per capita income: $15,575 (2010); Median household income: $29,024 (2010); Average household income: $37,882 (2010); Percent of households with income of $100,000 or more: 6.3% (2010); Poverty rate: 3.2% (2005-2009 5-year est.).

Taxes: Total city taxes per capita: $155 (2007); City property taxes per capita: $70 (2007).

Education: Percent of population age 25 and over with: High school diploma (including GED) or higher: 82.0% (2010); Bachelor's degree or higher: 14.4% (2010); Master's degree or higher: 6.2% (2010).

School District(s)

Cushing ISD (PK-12)
　2009-10 Enrollment: 496 . . . . (936) 326-4890

Housing: Homeownership rate: 78.0% (2010); Median home value: $59,762 (2010); Median contract rent: $245 per month (2005-2009 5-year est.); Median year structure built: 1957 (2005-2009 5-year est.).

Transportation: Commute to work: 90.0% car, 0.0% public transportation, 10.0% walk, 0.0% work from home (2005-2009 5-year est.); Travel time to work: 32.3% less than 15 minutes, 29.1% 15 to 30 minutes, 19.5% 30 to 45 minutes, 10.0% 45 to 60 minutes, 9.1% 60 minutes or more (2005-2009 5-year est.)

DOUGLASS (unincorporated postal area, zip code 75943).
Covers a land area of 61.755 square miles and a water area of 0.206 square miles. Located at 31.65° N. Lat; 94.91° W. Long. Elevation is 348 feet.

Population: 965 (2000); Race: 92.0% White, 3.6% Black, 0.2% Asian, 4.2% Other, 4.6% Hispanic of any race (2000); Density: 15.6 persons per square mile (2000); Age: 29.0% under 18, 15.2% over 64 (2000); Marriage status: 14.7% never married, 72.5% now married, 6.0% widowed, 6.8% divorced (2000); Foreign born: 1.1% (2000); Ancestry (includes multiple ancestries): 16.9% American, 10.1% Irish, 7.6% German, 7.1% English (2000).

Economy: Employment by occupation: 16.6% management, 14.1% professional, 14.6% services, 23.9% sales, 6.3% farming, 10.8% construction, 13.8% production (2000).

Income: Per capita income: $16,402 (2000); Median household income: $40,096 (2000); Poverty rate: 179.1% (2000).

Education: Percent of population age 25 and over with: High school diploma (including GED) or higher: 76.9% (2000); Bachelor's degree or higher: 18.0% (2000).

School District(s)

Douglass ISD (PK-12)
　2009-10 Enrollment: 363 . . . . (936) 569-9804

Housing: Homeownership rate: 85.4% (2000); Median home value: $63,300 (2000); Median contract rent: $345 per month (2000); Median year structure built: 1980 (2000).

Transportation: Commute to work: 89.1% car, 0.0% public transportation, 1.8% walk, 9.1% work from home (2000); Travel time to work: 22.1% less than 15 minutes, 41.6% 15 to 30 minutes, 24.9% 30 to 45 minutes, 4.7% 45 to 60 minutes, 6.7% 60 minutes or more (2000)

GARRISON (city).
Covers a land area of 1.160 square miles and a water area of <.001 square miles. Located at 31.82° N. Lat; 94.49° W. Long. Elevation is 390 feet.

Population: 883 (1990); 844 (2000); 823 (2010); 815 (2015 projected); Race: 70.6% White, 24.9% Black, 0.4% Asian, 4.1% Other, 6.7% Hispanic of any race (2010); Density: 709.3 persons per square mile (2010); Average household size: 2.52 (2010); Median age: 33.7 (2010); Males per 100 females: 88.8 (2010); Marriage status: 17.1% never married, 50.6% now married, 22.7% widowed, 9.7% divorced (2005-2009 5-year est.); Foreign born: 1.8% (2005-2009 5-year est.); Ancestry (includes multiple ancestries): 23.7% American, 16.5% Irish, 16.0% English, 5.4% German, 4.0% Scotch-Irish (2005-2009 5-year est.).

Economy: Single-family building permits issued: 0 (2010); Multi-family building permits issued: 0 (2010); Employment by occupation: 8.2% management, 6.5% professional, 13.9% services, 17.3% sales, 0.0% farming, 18.7% construction, 35.4% production (2005-2009 5-year est.).

Income: Per capita income: $18,913 (2010); Median household income: $30,167 (2010); Average household income: $47,659 (2010); Percent of households with income of $100,000 or more: 8.6% (2010); Poverty rate: 14.5% (2005-2009 5-year est.).

Taxes: Total city taxes per capita: $158 (2007); City property taxes per capita: $47 (2007).

Education: Percent of population age 25 and over with: High school diploma (including GED) or higher: 77.5% (2010); Bachelor's degree or higher: 13.4% (2010); Master's degree or higher: 5.1% (2010).

School District(s)

Garrison ISD (PK-12)
    2009-10 Enrollment: 686 . . . . (936) 347-7000
Housing: Homeownership rate: 69.2% (2010); Median home value: $55,000 (2010); Median contract rent: $330 per month (2005-2009 5-year est.); Median year structure built: 1969 (2005-2009 5-year est.).
Newspapers: The Garrison News (Community news; Circulation 1,200)
Transportation: Commute to work: 79.3% car, 0.0% public transportation, 6.1% walk, 14.6% work from home (2005-2009 5-year est.); Travel time to work: 46.2% less than 15 minutes, 35.5% 15 to 30 minutes, 13.5% 30 to 45 minutes, 2.0% 45 to 60 minutes, 2.8% 60 minutes or more (2005-2009 5-year est.)

NACOGDOCHES (city). County seat. Covers a land area of 25.226 square miles and a water area of 0.063 square miles. Located at 31.60° N. Lat; 94.65° W. Long. Elevation is 302 feet.
History: Nacogdoches grew up on the site of the old Mission Nuestra Senora de Guadalupe, established in 1716. The town was founded in 1779 when the settlers who had been removed from Los Adaes in 1773 were brought back to their home area by Captain Antonio Gil Ybarbo. Nacogdoches played a role in the Texas Revolution, feeding and arming Sam Houston and many of the volunteers who came to join his army.
Population: 31,093 (1990); 29,914 (2000); 32,546 (2010); 33,723 (2015 projected); Race: 61.0% White, 24.9% Black, 1.2% Asian, 13.0% Other, 18.6% Hispanic of any race (2010); Density: 1,290.2 persons per square mile (2010); Average household size: 2.32 (2010); Median age: 26.1 (2010); Males per 100 females: 90.4 (2010); Marriage status: 52.8% never married, 35.7% now married, 4.6% widowed, 6.9% divorced (2005-2009 5-year est.); Foreign born: 8.5% (2005-2009 5-year est.); Ancestry (includes multiple ancestries): 9.9% German, 9.7% English, 9.7% Irish, 6.1% American, 3.3% French (2005-2009 5-year est.).
Economy: Unemployment rate: 8.4% (June 2011); Total civilian labor force: 17,005 (June 2011); Single-family building permits issued: 38 (2010); Multi-family building permits issued: 212 (2010); Employment by occupation: 10.5% management, 20.9% professional, 24.1% services, 22.8% sales, 1.5% farming, 6.3% construction, 14.0% production (2005-2009 5-year est.).
Income: Per capita income: $17,095 (2010); Median household income: $25,935 (2010); Average household income: $43,762 (2010); Percent of households with income of $100,000 or more: 9.4% (2010); Poverty rate: 32.0% (2005-2009 5-year est.).
Taxes: Total city taxes per capita: $460 (2007); City property taxes per capita: $212 (2007).
Education: Percent of population age 25 and over with: High school diploma (including GED) or higher: 81.0% (2010); Bachelor's degree or higher: 32.1% (2010); Master's degree or higher: 12.7% (2010).

School District(s)

Central Heights ISD (PK-12)
    2009-10 Enrollment: 863 . . . . (936) 564-2681
Douglass ISD (PK-12)
    2009-10 Enrollment: 363 . . . . (936) 569-9804
Etoile ISD (PK-08)
    2009-10 Enrollment: 124 . . . . (936) 465-9404
Nacogdoches ISD (PK-12)
    2009-10 Enrollment: 6,330 . . . . (936) 569-5000
Stephen F Austin State University Charter School (KG-05)
    2009-10 Enrollment: 221 . . . . (936) 468-2336
Woden ISD (PK-12)
    2009-10 Enrollment: 815 . . . . (936) 564-2073

Four-year College(s)

Stephen F Austin State University (Public)
    Fall 2009 Enrollment: 12,845. . . . . (936) 468-2011
    2010-11 Tuition: In-state $6,998; Out-of-state $16,298
Housing: Homeownership rate: 41.3% (2010); Median home value: $92,216 (2010); Median contract rent: $494 per month (2005-2009 5-year est.); Median year structure built: 1978 (2005-2009 5-year est.).
Hospitals: Nacogdoches Medical Center Hospital (150 beds); Nacogdoches Memorial Hospital (202 beds)
Safety: Violent crime rate: 57.0 per 10,000 population; Property crime rate: 431.6 per 10,000 population (2009).
Newspapers: The Daily Sentinel (Local news)

Transportation: Commute to work: 87.0% car, 0.5% public transportation, 8.7% walk, 2.4% work from home (2005-2009 5-year est.); Travel time to work: 69.9% less than 15 minutes, 17.4% 15 to 30 minutes, 8.7% 30 to 45 minutes, 1.1% 45 to 60 minutes, 2.9% 60 minutes or more (2005-2009 5-year est.); Amtrak: bus service available.
Airports: A L Mangham Jr. Regional (general aviation)
Additional Information Contacts
City of Nacogdoches . . . . (936) 559-2502
    http://www.ci.nacogdoches.tx.us
Nacogdoches County Chamber of Commerce . . . . (936) 560-5533
    http://www.nacogdoches.org

Navarro County

Located in east central Texas; prairie area, bounded on the northeast by the Trinity River. Covers a land area of 1,007.66 square miles, a water area of 78.51 square miles, and is located in the Central Time Zone at 32.06° N. Lat., 96.46° W. Long. The county was founded in 1846. County seat is Corsicana.

Navarro County is part of the Corsicana, TX Micropolitan Statistical Area. The entire metro area includes: Navarro County, TX

Weather Station: Corsicana   Elevation: 413 feet

	Jan	Feb	Mar	Apr	May	Jun	Jul	Aug	Sep	Oct	Nov	Dec
High	57	61	68	76	83	90	94	95	89	79	68	59
Low	35	38	45	53	62	70	73	73	66	55	45	36
Precip	2.6	3.4	3.9	3.1	4.9	3.5	2.2	2.1	2.9	4.4	3.3	3.6
Snow	tr	0.1	tr	0.0	0.0	0.0	0.0	0.0	0.0	0.0	tr	0.1

High and Low temperatures in degrees Fahrenheit; Precipitation and Snow in inches

Weather Station: Navarro Mills Dam   Elevation: 454 feet

	Jan	Feb	Mar	Apr	May	Jun	Jul	Aug	Sep	Oct	Nov	Dec
High	57	62	69	77	84	91	96	97	90	80	68	59
Low	33	37	45	52	62	69	72	72	64	54	44	35
Precip	2.3	3.0	3.5	3.1	5.0	4.1	1.7	2.2	2.9	4.4	3.2	3.2
Snow	0.4	tr	0.0	0.0	0.0	0.0	0.0	0.0	0.0	0.0	tr	0.0

High and Low temperatures in degrees Fahrenheit; Precipitation and Snow in inches

Population: 39,926 (1990); 45,124 (2000); 50,315 (2010); 52,749 (2015 projected); Race: 66.8% White, 15.1% Black, 1.0% Asian, 17.2% Other, 23.0% Hispanic of any race (2010); Density: 49.9 persons per square mile (2010); Average household size: 2.67 (2010); Median age: 34.9 (2010); Males per 100 females: 98.8 (2010).
Religion: Five largest groups: 29.9% Southern Baptist Convention, 9.6% The United Methodist Church, 6.3% Catholic Church, 4.3% Churches of Christ, 3.3% Baptist Missionary Association of America (2000).
Economy: Unemployment rate: 10.5% (June 2011); Total civilian labor force: 21,865 (June 2011); Leading industries: 23.2% manufacturing; 16.8% retail trade; 14.7% health care and social assistance (2009); Farms: 2,078 totaling 586,936 acres (2007); Companies that employ 500 or more persons: 1 (2009); Companies that employ 100 to 499 persons: 20 (2009); Companies that employ less than 100 persons: 904 (2009); Black-owned businesses: 104 (2007); Hispanic-owned businesses: n/a (2007); Asian-owned businesses: 26 (2007); Women-owned businesses: 1,066 (2007); Retail sales per capita: $8,639 (2010). Single-family building permits issued: 10 (2010); Multi-family building permits issued: 99 (2010).
Income: Per capita income: $18,567 (2010); Median household income: $38,274 (2010); Average household income: $50,967 (2010); Percent of households with income of $100,000 or more: 10.0% (2010); Poverty rate: 18.3% (2009); Bankruptcy rate: 1.58% (2010).
Taxes: Total county taxes per capita: $275 (2007); County property taxes per capita: $220 (2007).
Education: Percent of population age 25 and over with: High school diploma (including GED) or higher: 74.8% (2010); Bachelor's degree or higher: 13.4% (2010); Master's degree or higher: 5.0% (2010).
Housing: Homeownership rate: 70.8% (2010); Median home value: $77,887 (2010); Median contract rent: $458 per month (2005-2009 5-year est.); Median year structure built: 1975 (2005-2009 5-year est.)
Health: Birth rate: 141.4 per 10,000 population (2009); Death rate: 99.9 per 10,000 population (2009); Age-adjusted cancer mortality rate: 196.5 deaths per 100,000 population (2007); Number of physicians: 9.6 per 10,000 population (2008); Hospital beds: 30.3 per 10,000 population (2007); Hospital admissions: 620.7 per 10,000 population (2007).
Elections: 2008 Presidential election results: 33.1% Obama, 66.2% McCain, 0.0% Nader

Additional Information Contacts
Navarro County Government . . . . (903) 654-3024
    http://www.co.navarro.tx.us/ips/cms
City of Corsicana . . . . (903) 654-4800
    http://www.ci.corsicana.tx.us
Corsicana & Navarro County Chamber of Commerce . . . . . (903) 874-4731
    http://www.corsicana.org
Kerens Area Chamber of Commerce . . . . (903) 396-2391
    http://ci.kerens.tx.us

Navarro County Communities

ANGUS (city). Covers a land area of 3.289 square miles and a water area of 0.022 square miles. Located at 31.98° N. Lat; 96.42° W. Long. Elevation is 436 feet.
Population: 363 (1990); 334 (2000); 440 (2010); 481 (2015 projected); Race: 93.2% White, 0.9% Black, 0.5% Asian, 5.5% Other, 3.6% Hispanic of any race (2010); Density: 133.8 persons per square mile (2010); Average household size: 2.65 (2010); Median age: 40.0 (2010); Males per 100 females: 103.7 (2010); Marriage status: 18.9% never married, 67.0% now married, 3.2% widowed, 10.9% divorced (2005-2009 5-year est.); Foreign born: 10.3% (2005-2009 5-year est.); Ancestry (includes multiple ancestries): 14.7% Irish, 12.6% American, 9.9% German, 8.8% English, 4.6% French (2005-2009 5-year est.).
Economy: Single-family building permits issued: 0 (2010); Multi-family building permits issued: 0 (2010); Employment by occupation: 18.3% management, 7.4% professional, 17.8% services, 31.7% sales, 0.0% farming, 3.5% construction, 21.3% production (2005-2009 5-year est.).
Income: Per capita income: $28,633 (2010); Median household income: $58,333 (2010); Average household income: $76,646 (2010); Percent of households with income of $100,000 or more: 23.2% (2010); Poverty rate: 8.6% (2005-2009 5-year est.).
Taxes: Total city taxes per capita: $190 (2007); City property taxes per capita: $0 (2007).
Education: Percent of population age 25 and over with: High school diploma (including GED) or higher: 82.9% (2010); Bachelor's degree or higher: 19.5% (2010); Master's degree or higher: 8.9% (2010).
Housing: Homeownership rate: 87.2% (2010); Median home value: $102,778 (2010); Median contract rent: $763 per month (2005-2009 5-year est.); Median year structure built: 1984 (2005-2009 5-year est.).
Transportation: Commute to work: 97.0% car, 0.0% public transportation, 0.0% walk, 2.0% work from home (2005-2009 5-year est.); Travel time to work: 41.5% less than 15 minutes, 24.6% 15 to 30 minutes, 5.1% 30 to 45 minutes, 0.0% 45 to 60 minutes, 28.7% 60 minutes or more (2005-2009 5-year est.)

BARRY (city). Covers a land area of 0.447 square miles and a water area of 0 square miles. Located at 32.09° N. Lat; 96.63° W. Long. Elevation is 499 feet.
Population: 175 (1990); 209 (2000); 281 (2010); 312 (2015 projected); Race: 81.5% White, 5.7% Black, 1.8% Asian, 11.0% Other, 13.2% Hispanic of any race (2010); Density: 628.1 persons per square mile (2010); Average household size: 2.93 (2010); Median age: 36.1 (2010); Males per 100 females: 106.6 (2010); Marriage status: 15.0% never married, 78.5% now married, 6.5% widowed, 0.0% divorced (2005-2009 5-year est.); Foreign born: 0.0% (2005-2009 5-year est.); Ancestry (includes multiple ancestries): 38.8% German, 16.9% English, 11.9% Irish, 2.5% French, 2.5% British (2005-2009 5-year est.).
Economy: Employment by occupation: 26.2% management, 34.4% professional, 16.4% services, 8.2% sales, 0.0% farming, 6.6% construction, 8.2% production (2005-2009 5-year est.).
Income: Per capita income: $17,814 (2010); Median household income: $48,235 (2010); Average household income: $51,771 (2010); Percent of households with income of $100,000 or more: 7.3% (2010); Poverty rate: 22.5% (2005-2009 5-year est.).
Taxes: Total city taxes per capita: $189 (2007); City property taxes per capita: $0 (2007).
Education: Percent of population age 25 and over with: High school diploma (including GED) or higher: 88.8% (2010); Bachelor's degree or higher: 10.1% (2010); Master's degree or higher: 1.7% (2010).
Housing: Homeownership rate: 84.4% (2010); Median home value: $59,474 (2010); Median contract rent: n/a per month (2005-2009 5-year est.); Median year structure built: 1981 (2005-2009 5-year est.).
Transportation: Commute to work: 91.0% car, 0.0% public transportation, 0.0% walk, 9.0% work from home (2005-2009 5-year est.); Travel time to

work: 47.5% less than 15 minutes, 18.0% 15 to 30 minutes, 6.6% 30 to 45 minutes, 4.9% 45 to 60 minutes, 23.0% 60 minutes or more (2005-2009 5-year est.)

BLOOMING GROVE (town). Covers a land area of 0.854 square miles and a water area of 0 square miles. Located at 32.09° N. Lat; 96.71° W. Long. Elevation is 597 feet.
Population: 847 (1990); 833 (2000); 919 (2010); 959 (2015 projected); Race: 92.8% White, 3.0% Black, 0.0% Asian, 4.1% Other, 4.8% Hispanic of any race (2010); Density: 1,075.8 persons per square mile (2010); Average household size: 2.42 (2010); Median age: 39.7 (2010); Males per 100 females: 91.1 (2010); Marriage status: 18.0% never married, 53.2% now married, 22.2% widowed, 6.5% divorced (2005-2009 5-year est.); Foreign born: 0.3% (2005-2009 5-year est.); Ancestry (includes multiple ancestries): 21.6% German, 21.3% Irish, 11.8% American, 9.9% English, 6.2% French (2005-2009 5-year est.).
Economy: Single-family building permits issued: 0 (2010); Multi-family building permits issued: 2 (2010); Employment by occupation: 12.0% management, 20.4% professional, 22.4% services, 16.2% sales, 0.0% farming, 17.8% construction, 11.1% production (2005-2009 5-year est.).
Income: Per capita income: $22,915 (2010); Median household income: $43,777 (2010); Average household income: $57,420 (2010); Percent of households with income of $100,000 or more: 13.1% (2010); Poverty rate: 6.5% (2005-2009 5-year est.).
Taxes: Total city taxes per capita: $37 (2007); City property taxes per capita: $37 (2007).
Education: Percent of population age 25 and over with: High school diploma (including GED) or higher: 82.6% (2010); Bachelor's degree or higher: 18.5% (2010); Master's degree or higher: 9.1% (2010).
School District(s)
Blooming Grove ISD (PK-12)
    2009-10 Enrollment: 832 . . . . (903) 695-2541
Housing: Homeownership rate: 77.9% (2010); Median home value: $86,000 (2010); Median contract rent: $472 per month (2005-2009 5-year est.); Median year structure built: 1962 (2005-2009 5-year est.).
Transportation: Commute to work: 96.4% car, 0.0% public transportation, 0.7% walk, 2.9% work from home (2005-2009 5-year est.); Travel time to work: 13.4% less than 15 minutes, 12.7% 15 to 30 minutes, 39.2% 30 to 45 minutes, 11.5% 45 to 60 minutes, 23.3% 60 minutes or more (2005-2009 5-year est.)

CHATFIELD (unincorporated postal area, zip code 75105). Covers a land area of 39.097 square miles and a water area of 0.279 square miles. Located at 32.24° N. Lat; 96.37° W. Long. Elevation is 430 feet.
Population: 323 (2000); Race: 92.0% White, 3.8% Black, 0.0% Asian, 4.2% Other, 5.2% Hispanic of any race (2000); Density: 8.3 persons per square mile (2000); Age: 19.4% under 18, 14.6% over 64 (2000); Marriage status: 21.4% never married, 52.9% now married, 15.1% widowed, 10.5% divorced (2000); Foreign born: 2.1% (2000); Ancestry (includes multiple ancestries): 16.7% Irish, 13.9% American, 11.1% English, 10.8% German (2000).
Economy: Employment by occupation: 27.0% management, 7.9% professional, 5.6% services, 20.6% sales, 7.1% farming, 21.4% construction, 10.3% production (2000).
Income: Per capita income: $17,468 (2000); Median household income: $26,579 (2000); Poverty rate: 179.1% (2000).
Education: Percent of population age 25 and over with: High school diploma (including GED) or higher: 85.1% (2000); Bachelor's degree or higher: 12.7% (2000).
Housing: Homeownership rate: 73.8% (2000); Median home value: $55,000 (2000); Median contract rent: $233 per month (2000); Median year structure built: 1981 (2000).
Transportation: Commute to work: 82.5% car, 0.0% public transportation, 0.0% walk, 6.3% work from home (2000); Travel time to work: 16.1% less than 15 minutes, 52.5% 15 to 30 minutes, 16.1% 30 to 45 minutes, 5.9% 45 to 60 minutes, 9.3% 60 minutes or more (2000)

CORSICANA (city). County seat. Covers a land area of 20.743 square miles and a water area of 0.962 square miles. Located at 32.09° N. Lat; 96.46° W. Long. Elevation is 443 feet.
History: Oil was struck in Corsicana in 1894, the first in the southwest, when the city was drilling for water. Standard Oil opened a refinery here in 1900.
Population: 23,107 (1990); 24,485 (2000); 26,884 (2010); 27,957 (2015 projected); Race: 54.6% White, 21.1% Black, 1.3% Asian, 23.0% Other,

32.4% Hispanic of any race (2010); Density: 1,296.1 persons per square mile (2010); Average household size: 2.67 (2010); Median age: 33.2 (2010); Males per 100 females: 97.6 (2010); Marriage status: 34.8% never married, 43.8% now married, 8.2% widowed, 13.2% divorced (2005-2009 5-year est.); Foreign born: 16.1% (2005-2009 5-year est.); Ancestry (includes multiple ancestries): 6.8% Irish, 6.0% American, 5.6% English, 5.4% German, 1.6% Scotch-Irish (2005-2009 5-year est.).
Economy: Unemployment rate: 11.1% (June 2011); Total civilian labor force: 11,035 (June 2011); Single-family building permits issued: 4 (2010); Multi-family building permits issued: 97 (2010); Employment by occupation: 9.6% management, 12.5% professional, 16.9% services, 24.9% sales, 0.7% farming, 10.1% construction, 25.3% production (2005-2009 5-year est.).
Income: Per capita income: $16,694 (2010); Median household income: $32,660 (2010); Average household income: $46,667 (2010); Percent of households with income of $100,000 or more: 8.6% (2010); Poverty rate: 28.1% (2005-2009 5-year est.).
Taxes: Total city taxes per capita: $490 (2007); City property taxes per capita: $207 (2007).
Education: Percent of population age 25 and over with: High school diploma (including GED) or higher: 71.2% (2010); Bachelor's degree or higher: 14.1% (2010); Master's degree or higher: 5.6% (2010).
School District(s)
Blooming Grove ISD (PK-12)
  2009-10 Enrollment: 832 . . . . (903) 695-2541
Corsicana ISD (PK-12)
  2009-10 Enrollment: 5,638 . . . . (903) 874-7441
Corsicana Residential Treatment Center (07-12)
  2009-10 Enrollment: 140 . . . . (903) 872-4821
Dawson ISD (PK-12)
  2009-10 Enrollment: 459 . . . . (254) 578-1031
Frost ISD (PK-12)
  2009-10 Enrollment: 371 . . . . (903) 682-2711
Mildred ISD (PK-12)
  2009-10 Enrollment: 769 . . . . (903) 872-6505
Two Dimensions Preparatory Academy (PK-05)
  2009-10 Enrollment: 428 . . . . (281) 893-9349
Two-year College(s)
Navarro College (Public)
  Fall 2009 Enrollment: 9,200 . . . . (903) 874-6501
  2010-11 Tuition: In-state $2,472; Out-of-state $3,672
Housing: Homeownership rate: 61.2% (2010); Median home value: $74,961 (2010); Median contract rent: $482 per month (2005-2009 5-year est.); Median year structure built: 1969 (2005-2009 5-year est.).
Hospitals: Navarro Regional Hospital (139 beds)
Safety: Violent crime rate: 37.9 per 10,000 population; Property crime rate: 462.2 per 10,000 population (2009).
Newspapers: Corsicana Daily Sun (Local news; Circulation 7,100); Navarro County Times (Local news)
Transportation: Commute to work: 92.3% car, 0.0% public transportation, 3.4% walk, 2.5% work from home (2005-2009 5-year est.); Travel time to work: 55.7% less than 15 minutes, 25.9% 15 to 30 minutes, 8.7% 30 to 45 minutes, 3.6% 45 to 60 minutes, 6.1% 60 minutes or more (2005-2009 5-year est.)
Airports: C David Campbell Field-Corsicana Municipal (general aviation)
Additional Information Contacts
City of Corsicana . . . . (903) 654-4800
  http://www.ci.corsicana.tx.us
Corsicana & Navarro County Chamber of Commerce . . . . . (903) 874-4731
  http://www.corsicana.org

DAWSON (town). Covers a land area of 1.772 square miles and a water area of 0.012 square miles. Located at 31.89° N. Lat; 96.71° W. Long. Elevation is 482 feet.
History: Settled c.1882, incorporated 1908.
Population: 766 (1990); 852 (2000); 959 (2010); 1,007 (2015 projected); Race: 86.2% White, 8.4% Black, 0.1% Asian, 5.2% Other, 7.7% Hispanic of any race (2010); Density: 541.1 persons per square mile (2010); Average household size: 2.51 (2010); Median age: 40.8 (2010); Males per 100 females: 99.0 (2010); Marriage status: 15.8% never married, 56.0% now married, 7.6% widowed, 20.5% divorced (2005-2009 5-year est.); Foreign born: 2.6% (2005-2009 5-year est.); Ancestry (includes multiple ancestries): 17.3% Irish, 16.5% German, 11.2% English, 4.4% American, 4.0% Dutch (2005-2009 5-year est.).

Economy: Single-family building permits issued: 0 (2010); Multi-family building permits issued: 0 (2010); Employment by occupation: 11.6% management, 24.3% professional, 29.7% services, 14.9% sales, 2.2% farming, 5.9% construction, 11.4% production (2005-2009 5-year est.).
Income: Per capita income: $17,332 (2010); Median household income: $35,000 (2010); Average household income: $43,606 (2010); Percent of households with income of $100,000 or more: 4.5% (2010); Poverty rate: 13.7% (2005-2009 5-year est.).
Taxes: Total city taxes per capita: $155 (2007); City property taxes per capita: $70 (2007).
Education: Percent of population age 25 and over with: High school diploma (including GED) or higher: 72.9% (2010); Bachelor's degree or higher: 11.3% (2010); Master's degree or higher: 3.8% (2010).
School District(s)
Dawson ISD (PK-12)
  2009-10 Enrollment: 459 . . . . (254) 578-1031
Housing: Homeownership rate: 80.1% (2010); Median home value: $54,000 (2010); Median contract rent: $323 per month (2005-2009 5-year est.); Median year structure built: 1961 (2005-2009 5-year est.).
Transportation: Commute to work: 86.5% car, 0.0% public transportation, 2.5% walk, 3.9% work from home (2005-2009 5-year est.); Travel time to work: 26.0% less than 15 minutes, 39.5% 15 to 30 minutes, 17.8% 30 to 45 minutes, 6.1% 45 to 60 minutes, 10.5% 60 minutes or more (2005-2009 5-year est.)

EMHOUSE (town). Covers a land area of 0.269 square miles and a water area of 0 square miles. Located at 32.16° N. Lat; 96.57° W. Long. Elevation is 472 feet.
Population: 221 (1990); 159 (2000); 201 (2010); 220 (2015 projected); Race: 79.6% White, 6.5% Black, 1.5% Asian, 12.4% Other, 14.9% Hispanic of any race (2010); Density: 748.0 persons per square mile (2010); Average household size: 2.91 (2010); Median age: 36.2 (2010); Males per 100 females: 105.1 (2010); Marriage status: 12.1% never married, 60.0% now married, 2.1% widowed, 25.7% divorced (2005-2009 5-year est.); Foreign born: 0.0% (2005-2009 5-year est.); Ancestry (includes multiple ancestries): 9.8% Irish, 7.7% American, 4.6% German, 3.6% Czech, 3.6% English (2005-2009 5-year est.).
Economy: Employment by occupation: 27.0% management, 0.0% professional, 9.5% services, 44.6% sales, 0.0% farming, 13.5% construction, 5.4% production (2005-2009 5-year est.).
Income: Per capita income: $18,219 (2010); Median household income: $47,115 (2010); Average household income: $56,558 (2010); Percent of households with income of $100,000 or more: 8.7% (2010); Poverty rate: 7.7% (2005-2009 5-year est.).
Taxes: Total city taxes per capita: $57 (2007); City property taxes per capita: $23 (2007).
Education: Percent of population age 25 and over with: High school diploma (including GED) or higher: 88.4% (2010); Bachelor's degree or higher: 12.4% (2010); Master's degree or higher: 3.9% (2010).
Housing: Homeownership rate: 84.1% (2010); Median home value: $60,000 (2010); Median contract rent: $559 per month (2005-2009 5-year est.); Median year structure built: 1990 (2005-2009 5-year est.).
Transportation: Commute to work: 86.4% car, 0.0% public transportation, 0.0% walk, 7.6% work from home (2005-2009 5-year est.); Travel time to work: 21.3% less than 15 minutes, 32.8% 15 to 30 minutes, 13.1% 30 to 45 minutes, 11.5% 45 to 60 minutes, 21.3% 60 minutes or more (2005-2009 5-year est.)

EUREKA (city). Covers a land area of 2.318 square miles and a water area of 0.083 square miles. Located at 32.01° N. Lat; 96.29° W. Long. Elevation is 397 feet.
Population: 242 (1990); 340 (2000); 442 (2010); 482 (2015 projected); Race: 93.0% White, 1.6% Black, 0.5% Asian, 5.0% Other, 4.3% Hispanic of any race (2010); Density: 190.7 persons per square mile (2010); Average household size: 2.73 (2010); Median age: 37.5 (2010); Males per 100 females: 101.8 (2010); Marriage status: 14.8% never married, 63.9% now married, 11.4% widowed, 9.9% divorced (2005-2009 5-year est.); Foreign born: 0.0% (2005-2009 5-year est.); Ancestry (includes multiple ancestries): 30.0% German, 19.2% English, 17.5% Irish, 5.3% Russian, 5.3% British (2005-2009 5-year est.).
Economy: Employment by occupation: 13.8% management, 25.6% professional, 10.3% services, 30.8% sales, 0.0% farming, 8.7% construction, 10.8% production (2005-2009 5-year est.).
Income: Per capita income: $28,718 (2010); Median household income: $62,121 (2010); Average household income: $79,094 (2010); Percent of

households with income of $100,000 or more: 24.4% (2010); Poverty rate: 3.9% (2005-2009 5-year est.).
Taxes: Total city taxes per capita: $1,886 (2007); City property taxes per capita: $775 (2007).
Education: Percent of population age 25 and over with: High school diploma (including GED) or higher: 83.3% (2010); Bachelor's degree or higher: 18.4% (2010); Master's degree or higher: 6.9% (2010).
Housing: Homeownership rate: 88.1% (2010); Median home value: $104,464 (2010); Median contract rent: $546 per month (2005-2009 5-year est.); Median year structure built: 1987 (2005-2009 5-year est.).
Transportation: Commute to work: 99.5% car, 0.0% public transportation, 0.0% walk, 0.0% work from home (2005-2009 5-year est.); Travel time to work: 8.7% less than 15 minutes, 60.0% 15 to 30 minutes, 13.3% 30 to 45 minutes, 4.1% 45 to 60 minutes, 13.8% 60 minutes or more (2005-2009 5-year est.)

FROST (city). Covers a land area of 1.131 square miles and a water area of 0.005 square miles. Located at 32.07° N. Lat; 96.80° W. Long. Elevation is 525 feet.
Population: 579 (1990); 648 (2000); 685 (2010); 701 (2015 projected); Race: 78.0% White, 6.3% Black, 2.8% Asian, 13.0% Other, 19.7% Hispanic of any race (2010); Density: 605.5 persons per square mile (2010); Average household size: 2.72 (2010); Median age: 34.8 (2010); Males per 100 females: 106.3 (2010); Marriage status: 21.8% never married, 65.8% now married, 3.1% widowed, 9.2% divorced (2005-2009 5-year est.); Foreign born: 5.8% (2005-2009 5-year est.); Ancestry (includes multiple ancestries): 33.3% Irish, 13.4% German, 6.5% Scotch-Irish, 6.5% English, 6.3% Scottish (2005-2009 5-year est.).
Economy: Single-family building permits issued: 0 (2010); Multi-family building permits issued: 0 (2010); Employment by occupation: 20.5% management, 6.4% professional, 24.2% services, 11.0% sales, 0.0% farming, 22.3% construction, 15.6% production (2005-2009 5-year est.).
Income: Per capita income: $20,339 (2010); Median household income: $46,389 (2010); Average household income: $56,697 (2010); Percent of households with income of $100,000 or more: 9.6% (2010); Poverty rate: 14.4% (2005-2009 5-year est.).
Taxes: Total city taxes per capita: $131 (2007); City property taxes per capita: $72 (2007).
Education: Percent of population age 25 and over with: High school diploma (including GED) or higher: 71.9% (2010); Bachelor's degree or higher: 10.2% (2010); Master's degree or higher: 4.1% (2010).

School District(s)

Frost ISD (PK-12)
    2009-10 Enrollment: 371 . . . . (903) 682-2711
Housing: Homeownership rate: 76.7% (2010); Median home value: $62,308 (2010); Median contract rent: $385 per month (2005-2009 5-year est.); Median year structure built: 1973 (2005-2009 5-year est.).
Transportation: Commute to work: 94.5% car, 0.0% public transportation, 4.5% walk, 1.0% work from home (2005-2009 5-year est.); Travel time to work: 13.1% less than 15 minutes, 19.6% 15 to 30 minutes, 37.6% 30 to 45 minutes, 15.0% 45 to 60 minutes, 14.7% 60 minutes or more (2005-2009 5-year est.)

GOODLOW (city). Covers a land area of 1.033 square miles and a water area of 0 square miles. Located at 32.11° N. Lat; 96.22° W. Long. Elevation is 341 feet.
Population: 319 (1990); 264 (2000); 277 (2010); 283 (2015 projected); Race: 58.8% White, 33.2% Black, 0.0% Asian, 7.9% Other, 9.7% Hispanic of any race (2010); Density: 268.0 persons per square mile (2010); Average household size: 2.54 (2010); Median age: 38.9 (2010); Males per 100 females: 99.3 (2010); Marriage status: 10.3% never married, 49.4% now married, 11.9% widowed, 28.4% divorced (2005-2009 5-year est.); Foreign born: 8.8% (2005-2009 5-year est.); Ancestry (includes multiple ancestries): 9.9% English, 3.6% German, 3.3% Irish, 1.5% African, 0.7% American (2005-2009 5-year est.).
Economy: Single-family building permits issued: 0 (2010); Multi-family building permits issued: 0 (2010); Employment by occupation: 21.2% management, 1.3% professional, 16.7% services, 22.4% sales, 0.0% farming, 18.6% construction, 19.9% production (2005-2009 5-year est.).
Income: Per capita income: $19,502 (2010); Median household income: $37,917 (2010); Average household income: $51,078 (2010); Percent of households with income of $100,000 or more: 7.3% (2010); Poverty rate: 14.6% (2005-2009 5-year est.).
Taxes: Total city taxes per capita: $184 (2007); City property taxes per capita: $80 (2007).

Education: Percent of population age 25 and over with: High school diploma (including GED) or higher: 70.5% (2010); Bachelor's degree or higher: 12.0% (2010); Master's degree or higher: 7.1% (2010).
Housing: Homeownership rate: 78.9% (2010); Median home value: $69,333 (2010); Median contract rent: $146 per month (2005-2009 5-year est.); Median year structure built: 1986 (2005-2009 5-year est.).
Transportation: Commute to work: 91.7% car, 0.0% public transportation, 0.0% walk, 8.3% work from home (2005-2009 5-year est.); Travel time to work: 14.0% less than 15 minutes, 23.8% 15 to 30 minutes, 16.8% 30 to 45 minutes, 0.0% 45 to 60 minutes, 45.5% 60 minutes or more (2005-2009 5-year est.)

KERENS (city). Covers a land area of 2.333 square miles and a water area of 0 square miles. Located at 32.13° N. Lat; 96.22° W. Long. Elevation is 371 feet.
History: Settled 1881.
Population: 1,704 (1990); 1,681 (2000); 1,833 (2010); 1,901 (2015 projected); Race: 61.5% White, 27.7% Black, 0.1% Asian, 10.7% Other, 10.7% Hispanic of any race (2010); Density: 785.6 persons per square mile (2010); Average household size: 2.44 (2010); Median age: 35.5 (2010); Males per 100 females: 86.7 (2010); Marriage status: 27.8% never married, 52.9% now married, 9.0% widowed, 10.3% divorced (2005-2009 5-year est.); Foreign born: 3.4% (2005-2009 5-year est.); Ancestry (includes multiple ancestries): 11.4% English, 9.4% American, 7.7% German, 5.8% Irish, 3.1% Scotch-Irish (2005-2009 5-year est.).
Economy: Single-family building permits issued: 0 (2010); Multi-family building permits issued: 0 (2010); Employment by occupation: 8.9% management, 14.2% professional, 25.9% services, 20.7% sales, 1.7% farming, 9.0% construction, 19.7% production (2005-2009 5-year est.).
Income: Per capita income: $16,942 (2010); Median household income: $34,272 (2010); Average household income: $41,215 (2010); Percent of households with income of $100,000 or more: 4.9% (2010); Poverty rate: 19.5% (2005-2009 5-year est.).
Taxes: Total city taxes per capita: $183 (2007); City property taxes per capita: $99 (2007).
Education: Percent of population age 25 and over with: High school diploma (including GED) or higher: 74.7% (2010); Bachelor's degree or higher: 11.2% (2010); Master's degree or higher: 4.5% (2010).

School District(s)

Kerens ISD (PK-12)
    2009-10 Enrollment: 658 . . . . (903) 396-2924
Housing: Homeownership rate: 65.1% (2010); Median home value: $64,268 (2010); Median contract rent: $278 per month (2005-2009 5-year est.); Median year structure built: 1961 (2005-2009 5-year est.).
Safety: Violent crime rate: 11.0 per 10,000 population; Property crime rate: 191.9 per 10,000 population (2009).
Newspapers: Kerens Tribune (Local news; Circulation 2,000)
Transportation: Commute to work: 97.3% car, 0.0% public transportation, 1.9% walk, 0.3% work from home (2005-2009 5-year est.); Travel time to work: 33.8% less than 15 minutes, 25.9% 15 to 30 minutes, 28.4% 30 to 45 minutes, 3.6% 45 to 60 minutes, 8.3% 60 minutes or more (2005-2009 5-year est.)
Additional Information Contacts
Kerens Area Chamber of Commerce. . . . . (903) 396-2391
    http://ci.kerens.tx.us

MILDRED (town). Covers a land area of 2.215 square miles and a water area of 0.067 square miles. Located at 32.03° N. Lat; 96.34° W. Long. Elevation is 430 feet.
Population: 173 (1990); 405 (2000); 500 (2010); 541 (2015 projected); Race: 91.6% White, 2.6% Black, 0.2% Asian, 5.6% Other, 5.8% Hispanic of any race (2010); Density: 225.7 persons per square mile (2010); Average household size: 2.85 (2010); Median age: 36.0 (2010); Males per 100 females: 107.5 (2010); Marriage status: 13.6% never married, 72.2% now married, 9.5% widowed, 4.2% divorced (2005-2009 5-year est.); Foreign born: 3.6% (2005-2009 5-year est.); Ancestry (includes multiple ancestries): 21.1% American, 11.0% German, 10.3% Irish, 4.9% English, 1.6% Cajun (2005-2009 5-year est.).
Economy: Employment by occupation: 8.0% management, 16.9% professional, 6.8% services, 33.1% sales, 0.0% farming, 17.8% construction, 17.5% production (2005-2009 5-year est.).
Income: Per capita income: $27,992 (2010); Median household income: $67,188 (2010); Average household income: $80,057 (2010); Percent of households with income of $100,000 or more: 25.9% (2010); Poverty rate: 3.5% (2005-2009 5-year est.).

Taxes: Total city taxes per capita: $348 (2007); City property taxes per capita: $270 (2007).

Education: Percent of population age 25 and over with: High school diploma (including GED) or higher: 84.3% (2010); Bachelor's degree or higher: 15.7% (2010); Master's degree or higher: 3.5% (2010).

Housing: Homeownership rate: 88.5% (2010); Median home value: $101,563 (2010); Median contract rent: n/a per month (2005-2009 5-year est.); Median year structure built: 1985 (2005-2009 5-year est.).

Transportation: Commute to work: 98.8% car, 0.0% public transportation, 0.0% walk, 0.0% work from home (2005-2009 5-year est.); Travel time to work: 21.5% less than 15 minutes, 47.9% 15 to 30 minutes, 5.5% 30 to 45 minutes, 3.0% 45 to 60 minutes, 22.1% 60 minutes or more (2005-2009 5-year est.)

MUSTANG (town). Covers a land area of 0.126 square miles and a water area of 0 square miles. Located at 32.01° N. Lat; 96.43° W. Long. Elevation is 390 feet.

Population: 35 (1990); 47 (2000); 62 (2010); 68 (2015 projected); Race: 93.5% White, 0.0% Black, 0.0% Asian, 6.5% Other, 3.2% Hispanic of any race (2010); Density: 491.5 persons per square mile (2010); Average household size: 2.65 (2010); Median age: 47.3 (2010); Males per 100 females: 67.6 (2010); Marriage status: 0.0% never married, 34.2% now married, 43.0% widowed, 22.8% divorced (2005-2009 5-year est.); Foreign born: 0.0% (2005-2009 5-year est.); Ancestry (includes multiple ancestries): 12.2% English, 10.6% German, 8.1% Italian, 4.1% Irish (2005-2009 5-year est.).

Economy: Employment by occupation: 0.0% management, 0.0% professional, 25.8% services, 61.3% sales, 0.0% farming, 6.5% construction, 6.5% production (2005-2009 5-year est.).

Income: Per capita income: $29,318 (2010); Median household income: $62,500 (2010); Average household income: $78,043 (2010); Percent of households with income of $100,000 or more: 26.1% (2010); Poverty rate: 1.6% (2005-2009 5-year est.).

Taxes: Total city taxes per capita: $259 (2007); City property taxes per capita: $148 (2007).

Education: Percent of population age 25 and over with: High school diploma (including GED) or higher: 82.6% (2010); Bachelor's degree or higher: 23.9% (2010); Master's degree or higher: 10.9% (2010).

Housing: Homeownership rate: 87.0% (2010); Median home value: $100,000 (2010); Median contract rent: n/a per month (2005-2009 5-year est.); Median year structure built: 1988 (2005-2009 5-year est.).

Transportation: Commute to work: 100.0% car, 0.0% public transportation, 0.0% walk, 0.0% work from home (2005-2009 5-year est.); Travel time to work: 6.9% less than 15 minutes, 93.1% 15 to 30 minutes, 0.0% 30 to 45 minutes, 0.0% 45 to 60 minutes, 0.0% 60 minutes or more (2005-2009 5-year est.)

NAVARRO (town). Covers a land area of 0.662 square miles and a water area of 0 square miles. Located at 31.99° N. Lat; 96.37° W. Long. Elevation is 417 feet.

Population: 193 (1990); 191 (2000); 250 (2010); 275 (2015 projected); Race: 94.0% White, 0.8% Black, 0.4% Asian, 4.8% Other, 3.2% Hispanic of any race (2010); Density: 377.6 persons per square mile (2010); Average household size: 2.62 (2010); Median age: 42.6 (2010); Males per 100 females: 103.3 (2010); Marriage status: 30.6% never married, 53.0% now married, 6.0% widowed, 10.4% divorced (2005-2009 5-year est.); Foreign born: 0.7% (2005-2009 5-year est.); Ancestry (includes multiple ancestries): 28.8% American, 9.8% English, 7.2% Irish, 5.2% German, 3.9% Czech (2005-2009 5-year est.).

Economy: Single-family building permits issued: 0 (2010); Multi-family building permits issued: 0 (2010); Employment by occupation: 15.2% management, 6.3% professional, 11.4% services, 27.8% sales, 0.0% farming, 29.1% construction, 10.1% production (2005-2009 5-year est.).

Income: Per capita income: $29,318 (2010); Median household income: $60,714 (2010); Average household income: $80,399 (2010); Percent of households with income of $100,000 or more: 24.5% (2010); Poverty rate: 22.2% (2005-2009 5-year est.).

Taxes: Total city taxes per capita: $113 (2007); City property taxes per capita: $47 (2007).

Education: Percent of population age 25 and over with: High school diploma (including GED) or higher: 82.2% (2010); Bachelor's degree or higher: 20.7% (2010); Master's degree or higher: 9.8% (2010).

Housing: Homeownership rate: 87.2% (2010); Median home value: $106,667 (2010); Median contract rent: $384 per month (2005-2009 5-year est.); Median year structure built: 1979 (2005-2009 5-year est.).

Transportation: Commute to work: 97.5% car, 0.0% public transportation, 0.0% walk, 2.5% work from home (2005-2009 5-year est.); Travel time to work: 10.4% less than 15 minutes, 53.2% 15 to 30 minutes, 2.6% 30 to 45 minutes, 2.6% 45 to 60 minutes, 31.2% 60 minutes or more (2005-2009 5-year est.)

OAK VALLEY (town). Covers a land area of 1.969 square miles and a water area of 0 square miles. Located at 32.03° N. Lat; 96.52° W. Long. Elevation is 420 feet.

Population: 387 (1990); 401 (2000); 425 (2010); 439 (2015 projected); Race: 57.2% White, 15.5% Black, 1.4% Asian, 25.9% Other, 27.5% Hispanic of any race (2010); Density: 215.8 persons per square mile (2010); Average household size: 2.78 (2010); Median age: 33.2 (2010); Males per 100 females: 98.6 (2010); Marriage status: 14.2% never married, 65.3% now married, 7.4% widowed, 13.2% divorced (2005-2009 5-year est.); Foreign born: 0.0% (2005-2009 5-year est.); Ancestry (includes multiple ancestries): 15.7% American, 14.8% German, 12.2% Irish, 12.2% English, 10.4% French (2005-2009 5-year est.).

Economy: Single-family building permits issued: 2 (2010); Multi-family building permits issued: 0 (2010); Employment by occupation: 19.3% management, 11.6% professional, 10.3% services, 27.0% sales, 1.3% farming, 9.9% construction, 20.6% production (2005-2009 5-year est.).

Income: Per capita income: $17,872 (2010); Median household income: $38,173 (2010); Average household income: $51,762 (2010); Percent of households with income of $100,000 or more: 8.7% (2010); Poverty rate: 12.3% (2005-2009 5-year est.).

Education: Percent of population age 25 and over with: High school diploma (including GED) or higher: 77.6% (2010); Bachelor's degree or higher: 10.3% (2010); Master's degree or higher: 4.8% (2010).

Housing: Homeownership rate: 58.4% (2010); Median home value: $77,500 (2010); Median contract rent: $413 per month (2005-2009 5-year est.); Median year structure built: 1985 (2005-2009 5-year est.).

Transportation: Commute to work: 94.2% car, 0.0% public transportation, 1.3% walk, 1.3% work from home (2005-2009 5-year est.); Travel time to work: 14.5% less than 15 minutes, 56.6% 15 to 30 minutes, 10.9% 30 to 45 minutes, 2.7% 45 to 60 minutes, 15.4% 60 minutes or more (2005-2009 5-year est.)

POWELL (town). Covers a land area of 1.672 square miles and a water area of 0 square miles. Located at 32.11° N. Lat; 96.32° W. Long. Elevation is 374 feet.

Population: 101 (1990); 105 (2000); 111 (2010); 114 (2015 projected); Race: 76.6% White, 14.4% Black, 0.0% Asian, 9.0% Other, 9.9% Hispanic of any race (2010); Density: 66.4 persons per square mile (2010); Average household size: 2.78 (2010); Median age: 41.3 (2010); Males per 100 females: 101.8 (2010); Marriage status: 5.0% never married, 90.0% now married, 5.0% widowed, 0.0% divorced (2005-2009 5-year est.); Foreign born: 0.0% (2005-2009 5-year est.); Ancestry (includes multiple ancestries): 33.3% English, 21.5% American, 18.3% Irish, 14.0% Czech, 12.9% Scotch-Irish (2005-2009 5-year est.).

Economy: Employment by occupation: 26.9% management, 23.1% professional, 7.7% services, 42.3% sales, 0.0% farming, 0.0% construction, 0.0% production (2005-2009 5-year est.).

Income: Per capita income: $22,127 (2010); Median household income: $47,857 (2010); Average household income: $63,188 (2010); Percent of households with income of $100,000 or more: 17.5% (2010); Poverty rate: 8.6% (2005-2009 5-year est.).

Taxes: Total city taxes per capita: $70 (2007); City property taxes per capita: $0 (2007).

Education: Percent of population age 25 and over with: High school diploma (including GED) or higher: 73.7% (2010); Bachelor's degree or higher: 13.2% (2010); Master's degree or higher: 10.5% (2010).

Housing: Homeownership rate: 85.0% (2010); Median home value: $100,000 (2010); Median contract rent: n/a per month (2005-2009 5-year est.); Median year structure built: 1957 (2005-2009 5-year est.).

Transportation: Commute to work: 78.3% car, 0.0% public transportation, 13.0% walk, 8.7% work from home (2005-2009 5-year est.); Travel time to work: 90.5% less than 15 minutes, 9.5% 15 to 30 minutes, 0.0% 30 to 45 minutes, 0.0% 45 to 60 minutes, 0.0% 60 minutes or more (2005-2009 5-year est.)

PURDON (unincorporated postal area, zip code 76679). Covers a land area of 63.815 square miles and a water area of 0.163 square miles. Located at 31.94° N. Lat; 96.61° W. Long. Elevation is 397 feet.

Population: 1,246 (2000); Race: 95.9% White, 0.9% Black, 0.0% Asian, 3.2% Other, 5.2% Hispanic of any race (2000); Density: 19.5 persons per square mile (2000); Age: 24.1% under 18, 14.4% over 64 (2000); Marriage status: 16.5% never married, 67.6% now married, 7.2% widowed, 8.7% divorced (2000); Foreign born: 1.2% (2000); Ancestry (includes multiple ancestries): 33.9% American, 10.3% Irish, 8.8% English, 4.9% German (2000).
Economy: Employment by occupation: 15.4% management, 16.1% professional, 8.7% services, 24.3% sales, 1.7% farming, 14.3% construction, 19.5% production (2000).
Income: Per capita income: $15,580 (2000); Median household income: $40,526 (2000); Poverty rate: 179.1% (2000).
Education: Percent of population age 25 and over with: High school diploma (including GED) or higher: 79.4% (2000); Bachelor's degree or higher: 9.2% (2000).
Housing: Homeownership rate: 81.2% (2000); Median home value: $58,000 (2000); Median contract rent: $352 per month (2000); Median year structure built: 1977 (2000).
Transportation: Commute to work: 97.3% car, 0.0% public transportation, 0.0% walk, 0.7% work from home (2000); Travel time to work: 5.9% less than 15 minutes, 45.2% 15 to 30 minutes, 24.1% 30 to 45 minutes, 11.1% 45 to 60 minutes, 13.7% 60 minutes or more (2000)

RETREAT (town). Covers a land area of 4.963 square miles and a water area of 0.019 square miles. Located at 32.05° N. Lat; 96.47° W. Long. Elevation is 472 feet.
Population: 334 (1990); 339 (2000); 369 (2010); 384 (2015 projected); Race: 85.1% White, 4.1% Black, 0.5% Asian, 10.3% Other, 8.4% Hispanic of any race (2010); Density: 74.4 persons per square mile (2010); Average household size: 2.80 (2010); Median age: 38.4 (2010); Males per 100 females: 97.3 (2010); Marriage status: 5.0% never married, 67.6% now married, 17.2% widowed, 10.2% divorced (2005-2009 5-year est.); Foreign born: 1.8% (2005-2009 5-year est.); Ancestry (includes multiple ancestries): 27.1% American, 14.2% Irish, 10.1% German, 8.1% English, 3.0% Scottish (2005-2009 5-year est.).
Economy: Single-family building permits issued: 3 (2010); Multi-family building permits issued: 0 (2010); Employment by occupation: 20.3% management, 25.9% professional, 10.3% services, 21.6% sales, 0.0% farming, 7.8% construction, 14.2% production (2005-2009 5-year est.).
Income: Per capita income: $21,171 (2010); Median household income: $49,250 (2010); Average household income: $58,049 (2010); Percent of households with income of $100,000 or more: 12.9% (2010); Poverty rate: 2.3% (2005-2009 5-year est.).
Taxes: Total city taxes per capita: $262 (2007); City property taxes per capita: $145 (2007).
Education: Percent of population age 25 and over with: High school diploma (including GED) or higher: 81.8% (2010); Bachelor's degree or higher: 6.1% (2010); Master's degree or higher: 2.8% (2010).
Housing: Homeownership rate: 87.9% (2010); Median home value: $87,619 (2010); Median contract rent: $367 per month (2005-2009 5-year est.); Median year structure built: 1980 (2005-2009 5-year est.).
Transportation: Commute to work: 98.7% car, 0.0% public transportation, 0.0% walk, 1.3% work from home (2005-2009 5-year est.); Travel time to work: 44.5% less than 15 minutes, 31.9% 15 to 30 minutes, 7.4% 30 to 45 minutes, 3.9% 45 to 60 minutes, 12.2% 60 minutes or more (2005-2009 5-year est.)

RICE (city). Covers a land area of 2.706 square miles and a water area of 0.092 square miles. Located at 32.23° N. Lat; 96.49° W. Long. Elevation is 459 feet.
Population: 619 (1990); 798 (2000); 951 (2010); 1,020 (2015 projected); Race: 75.5% White, 4.6% Black, 0.0% Asian, 19.9% Other, 25.1% Hispanic of any race (2010); Density: 351.5 persons per square mile (2010); Average household size: 2.93 (2010); Median age: 34.5 (2010); Males per 100 females: 101.5 (2010); Marriage status: 21.4% never married, 65.9% now married, 5.4% widowed, 7.2% divorced (2005-2009 5-year est.); Foreign born: 13.9% (2005-2009 5-year est.); Ancestry (includes multiple ancestries): 27.8% Irish, 19.1% German, 10.2% English, 5.8% Scotch-Irish, 4.2% Czech (2005-2009 5-year est.).
Economy: Single-family building permits issued: 1 (2010); Multi-family building permits issued: 0 (2010); Employment by occupation: 6.9% management, 11.5% professional, 17.9% services, 32.9% sales, 0.0% farming, 7.9% construction, 23.0% production (2005-2009 5-year est.).
Income: Per capita income: $16,970 (2010); Median household income: $42,077 (2010); Average household income: $48,631 (2010); Percent of households with income of $100,000 or more: 7.4% (2010); Poverty rate: 15.4% (2005-2009 5-year est.).
Taxes: Total city taxes per capita: $158 (2007); City property taxes per capita: $50 (2007).
Education: Percent of population age 25 and over with: High school diploma (including GED) or higher: 76.1% (2010); Bachelor's degree or higher: 10.1% (2010); Master's degree or higher: 1.8% (2010).

School District(s)
Rice ISD (PK-12)
   2009-10 Enrollment: 777 . . . . (903) 326-4287
Housing: Homeownership rate: 82.8% (2010); Median home value: $75,769 (2010); Median contract rent: $527 per month (2005-2009 5-year est.); Median year structure built: 1986 (2005-2009 5-year est.).
Transportation: Commute to work: 97.0% car, 0.0% public transportation, 0.0% walk, 0.0% work from home (2005-2009 5-year est.); Travel time to work: 39.5% less than 15 minutes, 38.9% 15 to 30 minutes, 14.0% 30 to 45 minutes, 5.3% 45 to 60 minutes, 2.3% 60 minutes or more (2005-2009 5-year est.)

RICHLAND (town). Covers a land area of 1.067 square miles and a water area of 0 square miles. Located at 31.92° N. Lat; 96.42° W. Long. Elevation is 367 feet.
Population: 266 (1990); 291 (2000); 342 (2010); 368 (2015 projected); Race: 88.0% White, 2.0% Black, 0.6% Asian, 9.4% Other, 13.5% Hispanic of any race (2010); Density: 320.6 persons per square mile (2010); Average household size: 2.67 (2010); Median age: 37.2 (2010); Males per 100 females: 97.7 (2010); Marriage status: 13.3% never married, 62.4% now married, 5.0% widowed, 19.4% divorced (2005-2009 5-year est.); Foreign born: 1.1% (2005-2009 5-year est.); Ancestry (includes multiple ancestries): 24.5% Irish, 20.1% German, 10.4% American, 6.3% Polish, 5.2% French (2005-2009 5-year est.).
Economy: Employment by occupation: 12.7% management, 4.7% professional, 17.3% services, 12.0% sales, 10.0% farming, 10.0% construction, 33.3% production (2005-2009 5-year est.).
Income: Per capita income: $19,162 (2010); Median household income: $41,875 (2010); Average household income: $50,059 (2010); Percent of households with income of $100,000 or more: 7.0% (2010); Poverty rate: 25.5% (2005-2009 5-year est.).
Taxes: Total city taxes per capita: $37 (2007); City property taxes per capita: $37 (2007).
Education: Percent of population age 25 and over with: High school diploma (including GED) or higher: 78.7% (2010); Bachelor's degree or higher: 15.7% (2010); Master's degree or higher: 4.3% (2010).
Housing: Homeownership rate: 85.2% (2010); Median home value: $90,000 (2010); Median contract rent: $288 per month (2005-2009 5-year est.); Median year structure built: 1972 (2005-2009 5-year est.).
Transportation: Commute to work: 99.3% car, 0.0% public transportation, 0.7% walk, 0.0% work from home (2005-2009 5-year est.); Travel time to work: 29.9% less than 15 minutes, 30.6% 15 to 30 minutes, 29.9% 30 to 45 minutes, 1.4% 45 to 60 minutes, 8.3% 60 minutes or more (2005-2009 5-year est.)

Newton County

Located in east Texas; bounded on the east by the Sabine River and the Louisiana border; drained by tributaries of the Sabine River. Covers a land area of 932.69 square miles, a water area of 6.82 square miles, and is located in the Central Time Zone at 30.84° N. Lat., 93.73° W. Long. The county was founded in 1846. County seat is Newton.

Weather Station: Toledo Bend Dam   Elevation: 189 feet

	Jan	Feb	Mar	Apr	May	Jun	Jul	Aug	Sep	Oct	Nov	Dec
High	58	61	69	76	84	90	93	93	88	78	68	60
Low	36	40	46	52	61	68	71	70	65	54	45	38
Precip	5.1	4.9	4.9	3.7	5.0	5.6	3.4	3.3	3.4	4.7	5.7	5.8
Snow	tr	tr	0.0	0.0	0.0	0.0	0.0	0.0	0.0	0.0	0.0	tr

High and Low temperatures in degrees Fahrenheit; Precipitation and Snow in inches

Population: 13,569 (1990); 15,072 (2000); 13,857 (2010); 13,242 (2015 projected); Race: 74.7% White, 20.8% Black, 0.7% Asian, 3.8% Other, 4.1% Hispanic of any race (2010); Density: 14.9 persons per square mile (2010); Average household size: 2.51 (2010); Median age: 39.4 (2010); Males per 100 females: 103.6 (2010).
Religion: Five largest groups: 28.1% Southern Baptist Convention, 4.4% The United Methodist Church, 3.4% The American Baptist Association, 2.9% Churches of Christ, 1.4% Church of God (Anderson, Indiana) (2000).

Economy: Unemployment rate: 14.6% (June 2011); Total civilian labor force: 5,975 (June 2011); Leading industries: 26.4% health care and social assistance; 12.7% retail trade; 8.0% forestry, fishing, hunting, and agriculture support (2009); Farms: 403 totaling 59,236 acres (2007); Companies that employ 500 or more persons: 0 (2009); Companies that employ 100 to 499 persons: 2 (2009); Companies that employ less than 100 persons: 136 (2009); Black-owned businesses: n/a (2007); Hispanic-owned businesses: n/a (2007); Asian-owned businesses: n/a (2007); Women-owned businesses: n/a (2007); Retail sales per capita: $2,127 (2010). Single-family building permits issued: 0 (2010); Multi-family building permits issued: 0 (2010).
Income: Per capita income: $18,092 (2010); Median household income: $37,741 (2010); Average household income: $46,754 (2010); Percent of households with income of $100,000 or more: 6.4% (2010); Poverty rate: 20.4% (2009); Bankruptcy rate: 1.03% (2010).
Taxes: Total county taxes per capita: $288 (2007); County property taxes per capita: $248 (2007).
Education: Percent of population age 25 and over with: High school diploma (including GED) or higher: 74.4% (2010); Bachelor's degree or higher: 6.3% (2010); Master's degree or higher: 1.9% (2010).
Housing: Homeownership rate: 83.2% (2010); Median home value: $63,157 (2010); Median contract rent: $278 per month (2005-2009 5-year est.); Median year structure built: 1974 (2005-2009 5-year est.)
Health: Birth rate: 98.8 per 10,000 population (2009); Death rate: 103.9 per 10,000 population (2009); Age-adjusted cancer mortality rate: 274.7 deaths per 100,000 population (2007); Number of physicians: 2.9 per 10,000 population (2008); Hospital beds: 0.0 per 10,000 population (2007); Hospital admissions: 0.0 per 10,000 population (2007).
Elections: 2008 Presidential election results: 33.3% Obama, 65.5% McCain, 0.0% Nader
National and State Parks: E O Siecke State Forest
Additional Information Contacts
Newton County Government . . . . (409) 379-5691
   http://www.co.newton.tx.us/ips/cms
Newton County Chamber of Commerce . . . . (409) 379-5527
   http://newton-texas.com

Newton County Communities

BON WIER (unincorporated postal area, zip code 75928). Covers a land area of 96.179 square miles and a water area of 0.118 square miles. Located at 30.68° N. Lat; 93.68° W. Long. Elevation is 82 feet.
Population: 1,436 (2000); Race: 36.1% White, 59.7% Black, 2.6% Asian, 1.6% Other, 1.5% Hispanic of any race (2000); Density: 14.9 persons per square mile (2000); Age: 32.9% under 18, 15.9% over 64 (2000); Marriage status: 27.0% never married, 60.3% now married, 4.8% widowed, 7.9% divorced (2000); Foreign born: 2.7% (2000); Ancestry (includes multiple ancestries): 10.3% Irish, 9.2% American, 3.2% Dutch, 2.1% German (2000).
Economy: Employment by occupation: 3.1% management, 13.4% professional, 26.7% services, 6.5% sales, 7.1% farming, 21.7% construction, 21.4% production (2000).
Income: Per capita income: $9,194 (2000); Median household income: $23,293 (2000); Poverty rate: 179.1% (2000).
Education: Percent of population age 25 and over with: High school diploma (including GED) or higher: 62.5% (2000); Bachelor's degree or higher: 4.7% (2000).
Housing: Homeownership rate: 86.6% (2000); Median home value: $37,600 (2000); Median contract rent: $256 per month (2000); Median year structure built: 1978 (2000).
Transportation: Commute to work: 95.3% car, 0.0% public transportation, 2.7% walk, 2.0% work from home (2000); Travel time to work: 12.9% less than 15 minutes, 34.0% 15 to 30 minutes, 23.5% 30 to 45 minutes, 13.9% 45 to 60 minutes, 15.6% 60 minutes or more (2000)

BURKEVILLE (unincorporated postal area, zip code 75932). Covers a land area of 139.645 square miles and a water area of 0.703 square miles. Located at 31.06° N. Lat; 93.61° W. Long. Elevation is 210 feet.
History: Burkeville was founded in 1844 by Colonel John R. Burke, who had settled here about 1821. The combined cotton mill and gin was built in 1865.
Population: 1,555 (2000); Race: 91.2% White, 7.7% Black, 0.0% Asian, 1.1% Other, 2.3% Hispanic of any race (2000); Density: 11.1 persons per square mile (2000); Age: 18.1% under 18, 27.5% over 64 (2000); Marriage status: 10.6% never married, 70.1% now married, 9.9% widowed, 9.4%

divorced (2000); Foreign born: 0.7% (2000); Ancestry (includes multiple ancestries): 14.1% American, 11.7% Irish, 6.5% English, 6.0% German (2000).
Economy: Employment by occupation: 5.4% management, 15.0% professional, 15.2% services, 25.7% sales, 2.1% farming, 16.9% construction, 19.6% production (2000).
Income: Per capita income: $16,084 (2000); Median household income: $29,866 (2000); Poverty rate: 179.1% (2000).
Education: Percent of population age 25 and over with: High school diploma (including GED) or higher: 71.9% (2000); Bachelor's degree or higher: 7.9% (2000).
School District(s)
Burkeville ISD (PK-12)
   2009-10 Enrollment: 311 . . . . (409) 565-2201
Housing: Homeownership rate: 87.5% (2000); Median home value: $69,300 (2000); Median contract rent: $275 per month (2000); Median year structure built: 1981 (2000).
Transportation: Commute to work: 90.6% car, 3.3% public transportation, 2.9% walk, 2.1% work from home (2000); Travel time to work: 31.1% less than 15 minutes, 16.2% 15 to 30 minutes, 14.6% 30 to 45 minutes, 7.2% 45 to 60 minutes, 30.9% 60 minutes or more (2000)

CALL (unincorporated postal area, zip code 75933). Covers a land area of 76.158 square miles and a water area of 0.258 square miles. Located at 30.58° N. Lat; 93.81° W. Long. Elevation is 95 feet.
Population: 1,580 (2000); Race: 84.4% White, 15.2% Black, 0.0% Asian, 0.4% Other, 2.3% Hispanic of any race (2000); Density: 20.7 persons per square mile (2000); Age: 27.3% under 18, 13.4% over 64 (2000); Marriage status: 19.9% never married, 61.2% now married, 9.4% widowed, 9.6% divorced (2000); Foreign born: 0.6% (2000); Ancestry (includes multiple ancestries): 30.5% American, 7.4% Irish, 5.7% French, 5.0% English (2000).
Economy: Employment by occupation: 1.6% management, 9.8% professional, 19.4% services, 27.4% sales, 6.1% farming, 24.5% construction, 11.4% production (2000).
Income: Per capita income: $14,008 (2000); Median household income: $28,281 (2000); Poverty rate: 179.1% (2000).
Education: Percent of population age 25 and over with: High school diploma (including GED) or higher: 59.3% (2000); Bachelor's degree or higher: 5.8% (2000).
Housing: Homeownership rate: 91.3% (2000); Median home value: $43,700 (2000); Median contract rent: $252 per month (2000); Median year structure built: 1971 (2000).
Transportation: Commute to work: 91.6% car, 1.8% public transportation, 0.0% walk, 3.8% work from home (2000); Travel time to work: 22.8% less than 15 minutes, 17.3% 15 to 30 minutes, 33.0% 30 to 45 minutes, 4.0% 45 to 60 minutes, 23.0% 60 minutes or more (2000)

DEWEYVILLE (CDP). Covers a land area of 11.239 square miles and a water area of 0.080 square miles. Located at 30.29° N. Lat; 93.74° W. Long. Elevation is 20 feet.
Population: 1,218 (1990); 1,190 (2000); 1,068 (2010); 1,006 (2015 projected); Race: 97.8% White, 0.1% Black, 0.4% Asian, 1.7% Other, 0.5% Hispanic of any race (2010); Density: 95.0 persons per square mile (2010); Average household size: 2.51 (2010); Median age: 39.8 (2010); Males per 100 females: 100.0 (2010); Marriage status: 31.0% never married, 57.8% now married, 1.5% widowed, 9.7% divorced (2005-2009 5-year est.); Foreign born: 0.0% (2005-2009 5-year est.); Ancestry (includes multiple ancestries): 25.9% Irish, 20.8% English, 14.5% French, 13.0% German, 4.2% American (2005-2009 5-year est.).
Economy: Employment by occupation: 11.6% management, 13.6% professional, 15.7% services, 15.3% sales, 0.0% farming, 29.7% construction, 14.0% production (2005-2009 5-year est.).
Income: Per capita income: $20,063 (2010); Median household income: $45,200 (2010); Average household income: $50,299 (2010); Percent of households with income of $100,000 or more: 6.3% (2010); Poverty rate: 14.3% (2005-2009 5-year est.).
Education: Percent of population age 25 and over with: High school diploma (including GED) or higher: 79.9% (2010); Bachelor's degree or higher: 4.8% (2010); Master's degree or higher: 0.7% (2010).
School District(s)
Deweyville ISD (PK-12)
   2009-10 Enrollment: 701 . . . . (409) 746-2731

Housing: Homeownership rate: 83.6% (2010); Median home value: $53,182 (2010); Median contract rent: n/a per month (2005-2009 5-year est.); Median year structure built: 1969 (2005-2009 5-year est.).
Transportation: Commute to work: 90.4% car, 0.0% public transportation, 5.4% walk, 0.0% work from home (2005-2009 5-year est.); Travel time to work: 13.7% less than 15 minutes, 14.3% 15 to 30 minutes, 44.7% 30 to 45 minutes, 14.8% 45 to 60 minutes, 12.5% 60 minutes or more (2005-2009 5-year est.)

NEWTON (city). County seat. Covers a land area of 5.502 square miles and a water area of 0.013 square miles. Located at 30.85° N. Lat; 93.75° W. Long. Elevation is 194 feet.
History: Newton was founded in 1846, and developed as a center for lumber and farming.
Population: 1,952 (1990); 2,459 (2000); 2,252 (2010); 2,156 (2015 projected); Race: 50.3% White, 38.4% Black, 2.8% Asian, 8.5% Other, 14.1% Hispanic of any race (2010); Density: 409.3 persons per square mile (2010); Average household size: 2.48 (2010); Median age: 33.8 (2010); Males per 100 females: 132.2 (2010); Marriage status: 29.4% never married, 50.3% now married, 8.5% widowed, 11.8% divorced (2005-2009 5-year est.); Foreign born: 2.4% (2005-2009 5-year est.); Ancestry (includes multiple ancestries): 15.7% Irish, 13.9% English, 7.0% German, 6.9% Scottish, 3.8% French (2005-2009 5-year est.).
Economy: Single-family building permits issued: 0 (2010); Multi-family building permits issued: 0 (2010); Employment by occupation: 5.5% management, 31.8% professional, 18.4% services, 17.8% sales, 3.4% farming, 14.1% construction, 9.1% production (2005-2009 5-year est.).
Income: Per capita income: $14,597 (2010); Median household income: $35,383 (2010); Average household income: $43,838 (2010); Percent of households with income of $100,000 or more: 5.2% (2010); Poverty rate: 19.5% (2005-2009 5-year est.).
Taxes: Total city taxes per capita: $175 (2007); City property taxes per capita: $0 (2007).
Education: Percent of population age 25 and over with: High school diploma (including GED) or higher: 78.8% (2010); Bachelor's degree or higher: 10.0% (2010); Master's degree or higher: 2.6% (2010).
School District(s)
Newton ISD (PK-12)
    2009-10 Enrollment: 1,156 . . . . (409) 379-8137
Housing: Homeownership rate: 66.4% (2010); Median home value: $64,444 (2010); Median contract rent: $312 per month (2005-2009 5-year est.); Median year structure built: 1968 (2005-2009 5-year est.).
Newspapers: Newton County News (Community news; Circulation 2,400)
Transportation: Commute to work: 93.7% car, 0.0% public transportation, 4.1% walk, 1.8% work from home (2005-2009 5-year est.); Travel time to work: 57.8% less than 15 minutes, 20.3% 15 to 30 minutes, 15.4% 30 to 45 minutes, 3.2% 45 to 60 minutes, 3.2% 60 minutes or more (2005-2009 5-year est.)
Additional Information Contacts
Newton County Chamber of Commerce . . . . (409) 379-5527
    http://newton-texas.com

SOUTH TOLEDO BEND (CDP). Covers a land area of 18.449 square miles and a water area of 2.716 square miles. Located at 31.15° N. Lat; 93.59° W. Long. Elevation is 180 feet.
Population: 456 (1990); 576 (2000); 546 (2010); 527 (2015 projected); Race: 95.6% White, 1.8% Black, 0.4% Asian, 2.2% Other, 0.7% Hispanic of any race (2010); Density: 29.6 persons per square mile (2010); Average household size: 2.14 (2010); Median age: 51.8 (2010); Males per 100 females: 97.1 (2010); Marriage status: 5.4% never married, 58.4% now married, 17.5% widowed, 18.6% divorced (2005-2009 5-year est.); Foreign born: 3.9% (2005-2009 5-year est.); Ancestry (includes multiple ancestries): 16.9% Irish, 13.9% American, 11.6% English, 7.2% French, 6.3% German (2005-2009 5-year est.).
Economy: Employment by occupation: 0.0% management, 4.4% professional, 10.7% services, 24.6% sales, 0.0% farming, 43.3% construction, 17.1% production (2005-2009 5-year est.).
Income: Per capita income: $22,367 (2010); Median household income: $39,943 (2010); Average household income: $47,127 (2010); Percent of households with income of $100,000 or more: 6.7% (2010); Poverty rate: 14.2% (2005-2009 5-year est.).
Education: Percent of population age 25 and over with: High school diploma (including GED) or higher: 76.5% (2010); Bachelor's degree or higher: 9.4% (2010); Master's degree or higher: 3.7% (2010).

Housing: Homeownership rate: 87.8% (2010); Median home value: $80,833 (2010); Median contract rent: n/a per month (2005-2009 5-year est.); Median year structure built: 1982 (2005-2009 5-year est.).
Transportation: Commute to work: 100.0% car, 0.0% public transportation, 0.0% walk, 0.0% work from home (2005-2009 5-year est.); Travel time to work: 16.6% less than 15 minutes, 5.8% 15 to 30 minutes, 36.1% 30 to 45 minutes, 2.1% 45 to 60 minutes, 39.4% 60 minutes or more (2005-2009 5-year est.)

WIERGATE (unincorporated postal area, zip code 75977). Covers a land area of 207.564 square miles and a water area of 0.356 square miles. Located at 31.03° N. Lat; 93.80° W. Long. Elevation is 226 feet.
Population: 793 (2000); Race: 40.8% White, 56.7% Black, 0.0% Asian, 2.5% Other, 2.5% Hispanic of any race (2000); Density: 3.8 persons per square mile (2000); Age: 25.1% under 18, 17.9% over 64 (2000); Marriage status: 24.3% never married, 57.7% now married, 12.8% widowed, 5.3% divorced (2000); Foreign born: 0.0% (2000); Ancestry (includes multiple ancestries): 13.4% American, 6.1% Irish, 4.2% English, 1.9% French (2000).
Economy: Employment by occupation: 11.9% management, 10.8% professional, 21.2% services, 20.4% sales, 2.6% farming, 11.9% construction, 21.2% production (2000).
Income: Per capita income: $12,342 (2000); Median household income: $21,207 (2000); Poverty rate: 179.1% (2000).
Education: Percent of population age 25 and over with: High school diploma (including GED) or higher: 67.6% (2000); Bachelor's degree or higher: 7.1% (2000).
Housing: Homeownership rate: 85.4% (2000); Median home value: $29,000 (2000); Median contract rent: $261 per month (2000); Median year structure built: 1975 (2000).
Transportation: Commute to work: 82.3% car, 4.2% public transportation, 3.5% walk, 6.5% work from home (2000); Travel time to work: 26.7% less than 15 minutes, 31.3% 15 to 30 minutes, 23.5% 30 to 45 minutes, 2.9% 45 to 60 minutes, 15.6% 60 minutes or more (2000)

Nolan County

Located in west Texas; drained by the Colorado River and tributaries of the Colorado and Brazos Rivers; includes Sweetwater and Trammel Lakes. Covers a land area of 911.98 square miles, a water area of 1.94 square miles, and is located in the Central Time Zone at 32.37° N. Lat., 100.40° W. Long. The county was founded in 1876. County seat is Sweetwater.

Nolan County is part of the Sweetwater, TX Micropolitan Statistical Area. The entire metro area includes: Nolan County, TX

Weather Station: Roscoe									Elevation: 2,379 feet		
	Jan	Feb	Mar	Apr	May	Jun	Jul	Aug	Sep	Oct	Nov	Dec
High	56	61	69	78	85	90	94	93	85	77	66	57
Low	31	35	42	50	60	67	70	69	62	53	41	32
Precip	0.9	1.2	1.3	1.5	3.0	3.2	1.7	2.4	2.7	2.3	1.0	1.0
Snow	1.1	0.6	0.2	tr	0.0	0.0	0.0	0.0	0.0	tr	1.0	0.8

High and Low temperatures in degrees Fahrenheit; Precipitation and Snow in inches

Population: 16,594 (1990); 15,802 (2000); 14,702 (2010); 14,141 (2015 projected); Race: 74.5% White, 5.4% Black, 0.5% Asian, 19.6% Other, 32.5% Hispanic of any race (2010); Density: 16.1 persons per square mile (2010); Average household size: 2.42 (2010); Median age: 37.4 (2010); Males per 100 females: 96.1 (2010).
Religion: Five largest groups: 40.8% Southern Baptist Convention, 10.6% Catholic Church, 7.8% The United Methodist Church, 6.8% Churches of Christ, 1.6% Presbyterian Church (U.S.A.) (2000).
Economy: Unemployment rate: 7.5% (June 2011); Total civilian labor force: 7,753 (June 2011); Leading industries: 20.7% manufacturing; 18.2% retail trade; 14.2% health care and social assistance (2009); Farms: 580 totaling 540,221 acres (2007); Companies that employ 500 or more persons: 0 (2009); Companies that employ 100 to 499 persons: 7 (2009); Companies that employ less than 100 persons: 338 (2009); Black-owned businesses: n/a (2007); Hispanic-owned businesses: n/a (2007); Asian-owned businesses: n/a (2007); Women-owned businesses: n/a (2007); Retail sales per capita: $14,395 (2010). Single-family building permits issued: 1 (2010); Multi-family building permits issued: 0 (2010).
Income: Per capita income: $18,239 (2010); Median household income: $32,697 (2010); Average household income: $44,631 (2010); Percent of households with income of $100,000 or more: 7.8% (2010); Poverty rate: 17.6% (2009); Bankruptcy rate: 1.28% (2010).

Taxes: Total county taxes per capita: $331 (2007); County property taxes per capita: $280 (2007).
Education: Percent of population age 25 and over with: High school diploma (including GED) or higher: 75.6% (2010); Bachelor's degree or higher: 14.8% (2010); Master's degree or higher: 3.8% (2010).
Housing: Homeownership rate: 65.3% (2010); Median home value: $44,123 (2010); Median contract rent: $321 per month (2005-2009 5-year est.); Median year structure built: 1961 (2005-2009 5-year est.)
Health: Birth rate: 162.9 per 10,000 population (2009); Death rate: 110.6 per 10,000 population (2009); Age-adjusted cancer mortality rate: 158.4 deaths per 100,000 population (2007); Number of physicians: 8.0 per 10,000 population (2008); Hospital beds: 37.0 per 10,000 population (2007); Hospital admissions: 1,309.3 per 10,000 population (2007).
Elections: 2008 Presidential election results: 30.0% Obama, 68.8% McCain, 0.0% Nader

Additional Information Contacts

Nolan County Government . . . . (325) 235-2263
http://www.co.nolan.tx.us/ips/cms
City of Sweetwater . . . . (325) 236-6313
http://www.sweetwatertexas.org
Sweetwater Chamber of Commerce . . . . (325) 235-5488
http://www.sweetwatertexas.org

Nolan County Communities

BLACKWELL (city). Covers a land area of 0.598 square miles and a water area of 0 square miles. Located at 32.08° N. Lat; 100.32° W. Long. Elevation is 2,126 feet.
Population: 339 (1990); 360 (2000); 343 (2010); 330 (2015 projected); Race: 75.8% White, 3.2% Black, 0.0% Asian, 21.0% Other, 22.7% Hispanic of any race (2010); Density: 574.0 persons per square mile (2010); Average household size: 2.32 (2010); Median age: 38.2 (2010); Males per 100 females: 103.0 (2010); Marriage status: 9.6% never married, 81.5% now married, 3.9% widowed, 5.0% divorced (2005-2009 5-year est.); Foreign born: 3.1% (2005-2009 5-year est.); Ancestry (includes multiple ancestries): 20.0% Irish, 8.6% English, 8.1% American, 7.8% French, 6.7% German (2005-2009 5-year est.).
Economy: Employment by occupation: 21.4% management, 25.0% professional, 3.6% services, 25.7% sales, 6.4% farming, 12.9% construction, 5.0% production (2005-2009 5-year est.).
Income: Per capita income: $20,241 (2010); Median household income: $37,143 (2010); Average household income: $47,230 (2010); Percent of households with income of $100,000 or more: 7.4% (2010); Poverty rate: 6.7% (2005-2009 5-year est.).
Taxes: Total city taxes per capita: $57 (2007); City property taxes per capita: $23 (2007).
Education: Percent of population age 25 and over with: High school diploma (including GED) or higher: 77.9% (2010); Bachelor's degree or higher: 16.1% (2010); Master's degree or higher: 2.8% (2010).
School District(s)
Blackwell CISD (PK-12)
    2009-10 Enrollment: 164 . . . . (325) 282-2311
Housing: Homeownership rate: 75.0% (2010); Median home value: $43,333 (2010); Median contract rent: $138 per month (2005-2009 5-year est.); Median year structure built: 1967 (2005-2009 5-year est.).
Transportation: Commute to work: 90.6% car, 0.0% public transportation, 7.2% walk, 2.2% work from home (2005-2009 5-year est.); Travel time to work: 34.8% less than 15 minutes, 10.4% 15 to 30 minutes, 20.0% 30 to 45 minutes, 8.9% 45 to 60 minutes, 25.9% 60 minutes or more (2005-2009 5-year est.)

MARYNEAL (unincorporated postal area, zip code 79535). Covers a land area of 103.634 square miles and a water area of 0.003 square miles. Located at 32.24° N. Lat; 100.44° W. Long. Elevation is 2,566 feet.
Population: 181 (2000); Race: 98.8% White, 0.0% Black, 0.0% Asian, 1.2% Other, 1.3% Hispanic of any race (2000); Density: 1.7 persons per square mile (2000); Age: 20.0% under 18, 23.1% over 64 (2000); Marriage status: 14.9% never married, 59.0% now married, 11.9% widowed, 14.2% divorced (2000); Foreign born: 1.3% (2000); Ancestry (includes multiple ancestries): 14.4% English, 13.1% Irish, 8.1% German, 6.3% American (2000).
Economy: Employment by occupation: 16.9% management, 13.3% professional, 4.8% services, 22.9% sales, 8.4% farming, 15.7% construction, 18.1% production (2000).

Income: Per capita income: $21,149 (2000); Median household income: $29,583 (2000); Poverty rate: 179.1% (2000).
Education: Percent of population age 25 and over with: High school diploma (including GED) or higher: 78.9% (2000); Bachelor's degree or higher: 17.1% (2000).
Housing: Homeownership rate: 77.5% (2000); Median home value: $25,600 (2000); Median contract rent: $250 per month (2000); Median year structure built: 1955 (2000).
Transportation: Commute to work: 84.8% car, 0.0% public transportation, 6.3% walk, 2.5% work from home (2000); Travel time to work: 24.7% less than 15 minutes, 33.8% 15 to 30 minutes, 22.1% 30 to 45 minutes, 3.9% 45 to 60 minutes, 15.6% 60 minutes or more (2000)

NOLAN (unincorporated postal area, zip code 79537). Covers a land area of 45.903 square miles and a water area of 0.009 square miles. Located at 32.27° N. Lat; 100.23° W. Long. Elevation is 2,493 feet.
Population: 94 (2000); Race: 80.2% White, 0.0% Black, 0.0% Asian, 19.8% Other, 24.4% Hispanic of any race (2000); Density: 2.0 persons per square mile (2000); Age: 22.1% under 18, 25.6% over 64 (2000); Marriage status: 29.7% never married, 52.7% now married, 6.8% widowed, 10.8% divorced (2000); Foreign born: 4.7% (2000); Ancestry (includes multiple ancestries): 29.1% American, 5.8% Irish, 5.8% German, 3.5% English (2000).
Economy: Employment by occupation: 36.4% management, 9.1% professional, 18.2% services, 9.1% sales, 12.1% farming, 9.1% construction, 6.1% production (2000).
Income: Per capita income: $14,608 (2000); Median household income: $23,750 (2000); Poverty rate: 179.1% (2000).
Education: Percent of population age 25 and over with: High school diploma (including GED) or higher: 63.5% (2000); Bachelor's degree or higher: 15.9% (2000).
Housing: Homeownership rate: 65.1% (2000); Median home value: $27,500 (2000); Median contract rent: $175 per month (2000); Median year structure built: 1951 (2000).
Transportation: Commute to work: 72.7% car, 0.0% public transportation, 6.1% walk, 21.2% work from home (2000); Travel time to work: 11.5% less than 15 minutes, 15.4% 15 to 30 minutes, 46.2% 30 to 45 minutes, 26.9% 45 to 60 minutes, 0.0% 60 minutes or more (2000)

ROSCOE (city). Covers a land area of 1.893 square miles and a water area of 0 square miles. Located at 32.44° N. Lat; 100.54° W. Long. Elevation is 2,388 feet.
History: Incorporated 1907.
Population: 1,446 (1990); 1,378 (2000); 1,262 (2010); 1,202 (2015 projected); Race: 63.2% White, 1.6% Black, 0.5% Asian, 34.7% Other, 44.0% Hispanic of any race (2010); Density: 666.8 persons per square mile (2010); Average household size: 2.60 (2010); Median age: 38.7 (2010); Males per 100 females: 92.1 (2010); Marriage status: 18.6% never married, 65.3% now married, 9.2% widowed, 6.8% divorced (2005-2009 5-year est.); Foreign born: 11.0% (2005-2009 5-year est.); Ancestry (includes multiple ancestries): 10.1% German, 8.8% Irish, 7.5% English, 3.3% American, 1.7% Scotch-Irish (2005-2009 5-year est.).
Economy: Single-family building permits issued: 0 (2010); Multi-family building permits issued: 0 (2010); Employment by occupation: 9.1% management, 16.2% professional, 16.1% services, 17.3% sales, 13.0% farming, 5.9% construction, 22.3% production (2005-2009 5-year est.).
Income: Per capita income: $14,977 (2010); Median household income: $30,507 (2010); Average household income: $39,931 (2010); Percent of households with income of $100,000 or more: 5.3% (2010); Poverty rate: 9.8% (2005-2009 5-year est.).
Taxes: Total city taxes per capita: $260 (2007); City property taxes per capita: $144 (2007).
Education: Percent of population age 25 and over with: High school diploma (including GED) or higher: 70.3% (2010); Bachelor's degree or higher: 13.7% (2010); Master's degree or higher: 3.6% (2010).
School District(s)
Highland ISD (PK-12)
    2009-10 Enrollment: 227 . . . . (325) 766-3652
Roscoe ISD (PK-12)
    2009-10 Enrollment: 365 . . . . (325) 766-3629
Housing: Homeownership rate: 73.3% (2010); Median home value: $37,363 (2010); Median contract rent: $239 per month (2005-2009 5-year est.); Median year structure built: 1963 (2005-2009 5-year est.).
Safety: Violent crime rate: 7.9 per 10,000 population; Property crime rate: 7.9 per 10,000 population (2009).

Transportation: Commute to work: 94.8% car, 1.3% public transportation, 0.5% walk, 2.9% work from home (2005-2009 5-year est.); Travel time to work: 51.9% less than 15 minutes, 26.6% 15 to 30 minutes, 12.0% 30 to 45 minutes, 2.6% 45 to 60 minutes, 6.8% 60 minutes or more (2005-2009 5-year est.)

SWEETWATER (city). County seat. Covers a land area of 10.019 square miles and a water area of 0.001 square miles. Located at 32.46° N. Lat; 100.40° W. Long. Elevation is 2,169 feet.

History: Sweetwater was settled in 1877 when Billy Knight opened a store in a dugout on the banks of Sweetwater Creek. The town became a cattle shipping center, and later a producer of gypsum, cement, and cotton-oil.

Population: 12,029 (1990); 11,415 (2000); 10,588 (2010); 10,175 (2015 projected); Race: 72.1% White, 6.8% Black, 0.7% Asian, 20.4% Other, 36.5% Hispanic of any race (2010); Density: 1,056.8 persons per square mile (2010); Average household size: 2.40 (2010); Median age: 35.6 (2010); Males per 100 females: 93.8 (2010); Marriage status: 22.5% never married, 55.0% now married, 7.8% widowed, 14.6% divorced (2005-2009 5-year est.); Foreign born: 4.3% (2005-2009 5-year est.); Ancestry (includes multiple ancestries): 11.4% American, 7.4% German, 6.3% Irish, 5.3% English, 2.7% French (2005-2009 5-year est.).

Economy: Single-family building permits issued: 1 (2010); Multi-family building permits issued: 0 (2010); Employment by occupation: 9.4% management, 15.7% professional, 19.4% services, 25.5% sales, 0.4% farming, 12.5% construction, 17.2% production (2005-2009 5-year est.).

Income: Per capita income: $16,335 (2010); Median household income: $29,431 (2010); Average household income: $39,531 (2010); Percent of households with income of $100,000 or more: 5.9% (2010); Poverty rate: 24.3% (2005-2009 5-year est.).

Taxes: Total city taxes per capita: $445 (2007); City property taxes per capita: $113 (2007).

Education: Percent of population age 25 and over with: High school diploma (including GED) or higher: 73.8% (2010); Bachelor's degree or higher: 13.1% (2010); Master's degree or higher: 3.2% (2010).

School District(s)
Merkel ISD (PK-12)
   2009-10 Enrollment: 1,113 . . . . (325) 928-5813
Sweetwater ISD (PK-12)
   2009-10 Enrollment: 2,320 . . . . (325) 235-8601

Two-year College(s)
Texas State Technical College-West Texas (Public)
   Fall 2009 Enrollment: 1,689 . . . . (325) 235-7300
   2010-11 Tuition: In-state $4,068; Out-of-state $8,424

Housing: Homeownership rate: 60.2% (2010); Median home value: $39,388 (2010); Median contract rent: $321 per month (2005-2009 5-year est.); Median year structure built: 1957 (2005-2009 5-year est.).

Hospitals: Rolling Plains Memorial Hospital

Safety: Violent crime rate: 166.3 per 10,000 population; Property crime rate: 485.8 per 10,000 population (2009).

Newspapers: Nolan County Shopper (Community news; Circulation 5,000); Sweetwater Reporter (Local news; Circulation 5,000)

Transportation: Commute to work: 93.9% car, 0.0% public transportation, 1.7% walk, 2.2% work from home (2005-2009 5-year est.); Travel time to work: 67.7% less than 15 minutes, 12.8% 15 to 30 minutes, 12.9% 30 to 45 minutes, 2.8% 45 to 60 minutes, 3.7% 60 minutes or more (2005-2009 5-year est.)

Airports: Avenger Field (general aviation)

Additional Information Contacts
City of Sweetwater . . . . (325) 236-6313
   http://www.sweetwatertexas.org
Sweetwater Chamber of Commerce . . . . (325) 235-5488
   http://www.sweetwatertexas.org

Nueces County

Located in south Texas, on the Gulf plains; bounded on the north by the Nueces River and Nueces Bay, and on the east and northeast by Corpus Christi Bay and Laguna Madre. Covers a land area of 835.82 square miles, a water area of 330.60 square miles, and is located in the Central Time Zone at 27.74° N. Lat., 97.45° W. Long. The county was founded in 1846. County seat is Corpus Christi.

Nueces County is part of the Corpus Christi, TX Metropolitan Statistical Area. The entire metro area includes: Aransas County, TX; Nueces County, TX; San Patricio County, TX

Weather Station: Corpus Christi Intl Arpt   Elevation: 43 feet

	Jan	Feb	Mar	Apr	May	Jun	Jul	Aug	Sep	Oct	Nov	Dec
High	67	71	76	82	86	91	93	94	90	84	76	68
Low	47	51	56	63	70	74	75	75	72	65	56	49
Precip	1.5	1.8	1.9	1.8	3.2	3.1	2.6	3.4	4.6	3.7	2.0	1.8
Snow	na	na	na	na	na	na	na	na	na	na	na	0.2

High and Low temperatures in degrees Fahrenheit; Precipitation and Snow in inches

Weather Station: Port Aransas   Elevation: 12 feet

	Jan	Feb	Mar	Apr	May	Jun	Jul	Aug	Sep	Oct	Nov	Dec
High	63	66	71	77	83	88	89	90	88	82	74	65
Low	51	54	60	67	74	79	80	80	77	71	61	53
Precip	2.2	2.3	2.5	1.9	3.3	2.9	3.1	2.2	5.6	4.7	3.1	1.7
Snow	0.0	0.0	0.0	0.0	0.0	0.0	0.0	0.0	0.0	0.0	0.0	0.2

High and Low temperatures in degrees Fahrenheit; Precipitation and Snow in inches

Weather Station: Robstown   Elevation: 84 feet

	Jan	Feb	Mar	Apr	May	Jun	Jul	Aug	Sep	Oct	Nov	Dec
High	67	70	76	82	87	92	94	95	91	85	76	68
Low	46	49	56	63	70	74	75	76	72	64	56	48
Precip	1.7	1.9	1.9	1.6	3.1	2.8	3.2	3.3	4.3	3.6	2.3	1.6
Snow	0.0	tr	0.0	0.0	0.0	0.0	0.0	0.0	0.0	0.0	0.0	0.2

High and Low temperatures in degrees Fahrenheit; Precipitation and Snow in inches

Population: 291,204 (1990); 313,645 (2000); 324,919 (2010); 329,820 (2015 projected); Race: 70.5% White, 3.8% Black, 1.3% Asian, 24.4% Other, 60.0% Hispanic of any race (2010); Density: 388.7 persons per square mile (2010); Average household size: 2.73 (2010); Median age: 34.9 (2010); Males per 100 females: 95.5 (2010).

Religion: Five largest groups: 27.5% Catholic Church, 13.8% Southern Baptist Convention, 3.9% The United Methodist Church, 1.6% Assemblies of God, 1.1% Churches of Christ (2000).

Economy: Unemployment rate: 8.4% (June 2011); Total civilian labor force: 173,232 (June 2011); Leading industries: 19.8% health care and social assistance; 13.4% retail trade; 12.6% accommodation & food services (2009); Farms: 712 totaling 509,196 acres (2007); Companies that employ 500 or more persons: 20 (2009); Companies that employ 100 to 499 persons: 154 (2009); Companies that employ less than 100 persons: 7,624 (2009); Black-owned businesses: 696 (2007); Hispanic-owned businesses: 10,275 (2007); Asian-owned businesses: 558 (2007); Women-owned businesses: 7,443 (2007); Retail sales per capita: $12,583 (2010). Single-family building permits issued: 699 (2010); Multi-family building permits issued: 300 (2010).

Income: Per capita income: $21,332 (2010); Median household income: $44,235 (2010); Average household income: $58,583 (2010); Percent of households with income of $100,000 or more: 14.1% (2010); Poverty rate: 19.9% (2009); Bankruptcy rate: 1.83% (2010).

Taxes: Total county taxes per capita: $261 (2007); County property taxes per capita: $249 (2007).

Education: Percent of population age 25 and over with: High school diploma (including GED) or higher: 78.2% (2010); Bachelor's degree or higher: 19.1% (2010); Master's degree or higher: 6.7% (2010).

Housing: Homeownership rate: 61.5% (2010); Median home value: $97,613 (2010); Median contract rent: $577 per month (2005-2009 5-year est.); Median year structure built: 1974 (2005-2009 5-year est.)

Health: Birth rate: 157.6 per 10,000 population (2009); Death rate: 78.2 per 10,000 population (2009); Age-adjusted cancer mortality rate: 166.7 deaths per 100,000 population (2007); Number of physicians: 28.4 per 10,000 population (2008); Hospital beds: 47.8 per 10,000 population (2007); Hospital admissions: 1,874.1 per 10,000 population (2007).

Environment: Air Quality Index: 79.8% good, 19.2% moderate, 1.0% unhealthy for sensitive individuals, 0.0% unhealthy (percent of days in 2008)

Elections: 2008 Presidential election results: 47.3% Obama, 51.8% McCain, 0.1% Nader

Additional Information Contacts
Nueces County Government . . . . (361) 888-0444
   http://www.co.nueces.tx.us
Bishop Chamber of Commerce . . . . (361) 584-2214
   http://www.bishoptx.org
City of Corpus Christi . . . . (361) 826-3220
   http://www.cctexas.com
City of Port Aransas . . . . (361) 749-4111
   http://www.cityofportaransas.org
City of Robstown . . . . (361) 387-4589
Corpus Christi Chamber of Commerce . . . . (361) 881-1800
   http://www.corpuschristichamber.org

Port Aransas Chamber of Commerce . . . . (361) 749-5919
http://www.portaransas.org

Nueces County Communities

AGUA DULCE (city). Covers a land area of 0.315 square miles and a water area of 0 square miles. Located at 27.78° N. Lat; 97.91° W. Long. Elevation is 125 feet.
Population: 794 (1990); 737 (2000); 704 (2010); 688 (2015 projected); Race: 86.1% White, 0.1% Black, 0.0% Asian, 13.8% Other, 69.9% Hispanic of any race (2010); Density: 2,233.4 persons per square mile (2010); Average household size: 3.04 (2010); Median age: 32.9 (2010); Males per 100 females: 93.9 (2010); Marriage status: 21.0% never married, 63.8% now married, 8.6% widowed, 6.6% divorced (2005-2009 5-year est.); Foreign born: 7.0% (2005-2009 5-year est.); Ancestry (includes multiple ancestries): 10.5% German, 5.6% Irish, 3.1% American, 2.1% Czech, 2.0% French (2005-2009 5-year est.).
Economy: Employment by occupation: 8.9% management, 18.6% professional, 16.7% services, 29.7% sales, 3.0% farming, 7.4% construction, 15.6% production (2005-2009 5-year est.).
Income: Per capita income: $14,366 (2010); Median household income: $35,563 (2010); Average household income: $42,781 (2010); Percent of households with income of $100,000 or more: 6.5% (2010); Poverty rate: 10.8% (2005-2009 5-year est.).
Taxes: Total city taxes per capita: $131 (2007); City property taxes per capita: $81 (2007).
Education: Percent of population age 25 and over with: High school diploma (including GED) or higher: 62.4% (2010); Bachelor's degree or higher: 8.0% (2010); Master's degree or higher: 3.5% (2010).
Housing: Homeownership rate: 85.3% (2010); Median home value: $53,051 (2010); Median contract rent: $365 per month (2005-2009 5-year est.); Median year structure built: 1968 (2005-2009 5-year est.).
Transportation: Commute to work: 85.1% car, 0.0% public transportation, 10.8% walk, 0.0% work from home (2005-2009 5-year est.); Travel time to work: 65.1% less than 15 minutes, 17.5% 15 to 30 minutes, 5.9% 30 to 45 minutes, 3.0% 45 to 60 minutes, 8.6% 60 minutes or more (2005-2009 5-year est.)

BISHOP (city). Covers a land area of 2.371 square miles and a water area of 0 square miles. Located at 27.58° N. Lat; 97.79° W. Long. Elevation is 59 feet.
History: Bishop developed around petrochemical plants.
Population: 3,337 (1990); 3,305 (2000); 3,066 (2010); 2,962 (2015 projected); Race: 86.6% White, 1.4% Black, 0.1% Asian, 11.9% Other, 66.7% Hispanic of any race (2010); Density: 1,293.3 persons per square mile (2010); Average household size: 2.83 (2010); Median age: 35.2 (2010); Males per 100 females: 92.6 (2010); Marriage status: 25.7% never married, 52.8% now married, 11.5% widowed, 10.0% divorced (2005-2009 5-year est.); Foreign born: 3.1% (2005-2009 5-year est.); Ancestry (includes multiple ancestries): 10.4% German, 5.3% American, 4.7% English, 4.5% Irish, 3.5% Italian (2005-2009 5-year est.).
Economy: Single-family building permits issued: 2 (2010); Multi-family building permits issued: 0 (2010); Employment by occupation: 6.3% management, 12.4% professional, 20.1% services, 28.5% sales, 2.5% farming, 18.7% construction, 11.5% production (2005-2009 5-year est.).
Income: Per capita income: $18,986 (2010); Median household income: $42,868 (2010); Average household income: $53,758 (2010); Percent of households with income of $100,000 or more: 11.9% (2010); Poverty rate: 30.9% (2005-2009 5-year est.).
Taxes: Total city taxes per capita: $198 (2007); City property taxes per capita: $131 (2007).
Education: Percent of population age 25 and over with: High school diploma (including GED) or higher: 72.7% (2010); Bachelor's degree or higher: 13.9% (2010); Master's degree or higher: 4.8% (2010).
School District(s)
Bishop CISD (PK-12)
    2009-10 Enrollment: 1,227 . . . . (361) 584-3591
Housing: Homeownership rate: 75.6% (2010); Median home value: $59,670 (2010); Median contract rent: $397 per month (2005-2009 5-year est.); Median year structure built: 1959 (2005-2009 5-year est.).
Safety: Violent crime rate: 9.6 per 10,000 population; Property crime rate: 345.9 per 10,000 population (2009).
Transportation: Commute to work: 96.6% car, 0.0% public transportation, 1.3% walk, 0.0% work from home (2005-2009 5-year est.); Travel time to work: 47.6% less than 15 minutes, 25.2% 15 to 30 minutes, 11.1% 30 to 45

minutes, 7.1% 45 to 60 minutes, 9.0% 60 minutes or more (2005-2009 5-year est.)
Additional Information Contacts
Bishop Chamber of Commerce . . . . (361) 584-2214
    http://www.bishoptx.org

CORPUS CHRISTI (city). County seat. Covers a land area of 154.639 square miles and a water area of 305.598 square miles. Located at 27.74° N. Lat; 97.40° W. Long. Elevation is 7 feet.
History: Corpus Christi took its name from that given the bay by Alonso Alvarez de Pineda, who claimed the land for Spain in 1519. One of the many explorers and adventurers who may have come into Corpus Christi Bay was the pirate Jean Lafitte, leaving behind him tales of buried pirate gold. The town of Corpus Christi was founded in 1839 by Colonel Henry L. Kinney from Pennsylvania, who built a trading post. He began promoting his town in 1848, attracting many immigrants. After the Civil War, Corpus Christi became a major port shipping manufactured products, agricultural produce, sea food products, and oil.
Population: 258,425 (1990); 277,454 (2000); 289,001 (2010); 293,937 (2015 projected); Race: 69.4% White, 4.2% Black, 1.4% Asian, 24.9% Other, 59.1% Hispanic of any race (2010); Density: 1,868.9 persons per square mile (2010); Average household size: 2.70 (2010); Median age: 34.9 (2010); Males per 100 females: 95.2 (2010); Marriage status: 30.6% never married, 50.8% now married, 6.4% widowed, 12.2% divorced (2005-2009 5-year est.); Foreign born: 7.7% (2005-2009 5-year est.); Ancestry (includes multiple ancestries): 9.8% German, 6.0% Irish, 5.3% English, 4.0% American, 2.0% French (2005-2009 5-year est.).
Economy: Unemployment rate: 8.1% (June 2011); Total civilian labor force: 155,861 (June 2011); Single-family building permits issued: 628 (2010); Multi-family building permits issued: 284 (2010); Employment by occupation: 11.1% management, 20.2% professional, 19.0% services, 26.0% sales, 0.3% farming, 12.6% construction, 11.0% production (2005-2009 5-year est.).
Income: Per capita income: $21,687 (2010); Median household income: $44,633 (2010); Average household income: $58,929 (2010); Percent of households with income of $100,000 or more: 14.2% (2010); Poverty rate: 19.0% (2005-2009 5-year est.).
Taxes: Total city taxes per capita: $570 (2007); City property taxes per capita: $250 (2007).
Education: Percent of population age 25 and over with: High school diploma (including GED) or higher: 79.5% (2010); Bachelor's degree or higher: 19.9% (2010); Master's degree or higher: 7.0% (2010).
School District(s)
Aransas Pass ISD (PK-12)
    2009-10 Enrollment: 1,881 . . . . (361) 758-3466
Banquete ISD (PK-12)
    2009-10 Enrollment: 835 . . . . (361) 387-2551
Calallen ISD (PK-12)
    2009-10 Enrollment: 3,808 . . . . (361) 242-5600
Corpus Christi ISD (PK-12)
    2009-10 Enrollment: 38,196 . . . . (361) 886-9002
Corpus Christi Montessori School (01-07)
    2009-10 Enrollment: 169 . . . . (361) 852-0707
Dr M L Garza-Gonzalez Charter School (06-12)
    2009-10 Enrollment: 282 . . . . (361) 881-9988
Flour Bluff ISD (PK-12)
    2009-10 Enrollment: 5,474 . . . . (361) 694-9205
London ISD (PK-08)
    2009-10 Enrollment: 353 . . . . (361) 855-0092
Por Vida Academy (09-12)
    2009-10 Enrollment: 305 . . . . (210) 532-8816
Responsive Education Solutions (KG-12)
    2009-10 Enrollment: 5,022 . . . . (972) 316-3663
Richard Milburn Alter High School (Corpus Christi) (09-12)
    2009-10 Enrollment: 279 . . . . (830) 788-0198
School of Science and Technology Corpus Christi (KG-08)
    2009-10 Enrollment: 314 . . . . (361) 851-2420
Seashore Learning Ctr Charter (KG-04)
    2009-10 Enrollment: 204 . . . . (361) 949-1222
Seashore Middle Academy (05-08)
    2009-10 Enrollment: 141 . . . . (361) 654-1134
Trinity Charter School (KG-12)
    2009-10 Enrollment: 277 . . . . (512) 706-7564
Tuloso-Midway ISD (PK-12)
    2009-10 Enrollment: 3,425 . . . . (361) 903-6400

West Oso ISD (PK-12)
    2009-10 Enrollment: 2,090 . . . . (361) 806-5900
Four-year College(s)
Texas A & M University-Corpus Christi (Public)
    Fall 2009 Enrollment: 9,468 . . . . (361) 825-5700
    2010-11 Tuition: In-state $6,294; Out-of-state $13,432
Two-year College(s)
Career Centers of Texas-Corpus Christi (Private, For-profit)
    Fall 2009 Enrollment: 755 . . . . (361) 852-2900
Del Mar College (Public)
    Fall 2009 Enrollment: 12,069 . . . . (361) 698-1255
    2010-11 Tuition: In-state $3,178; Out-of-state $4,066
Vocational/Technical School(s)
South Texas Barber College Inc (Private, For-profit)
    Fall 2009 Enrollment: 44 . . . . (361) 855-0262
    2010-11 Tuition: $7,700
South Texas Vocational Technical Institute (Private, For-profit)
    Fall 2009 Enrollment: 838 . . . . (361) 232-5057
    2010-11 Tuition: $16,700
Southern Careers Institute Inc-Corpus Christi (Private, For-profit)
    Fall 2009 Enrollment: 230 . . . . (512) 437-7507
    2010-11 Tuition: $13,600
Housing: Homeownership rate: 59.9% (2010); Median home value: $101,062 (2010); Median contract rent: $585 per month (2005-2009 5-year est.); Median year structure built: 1974 (2005-2009 5-year est.).
Hospitals: Christus Spohn Hospital Corpus Christi-Shoreline (512 beds); Christus Spohn Memorial Hospital (397 beds); Corpus Christi Medical Center - Doctors Regional (331 beds); Corpus Christi Medical Center - Northwest (89 beds); Driscoll Childrens Hospital (188 beds)
Safety: Violent crime rate: 82.3 per 10,000 population; Property crime rate: 560.4 per 10,000 population (2009).
Newspapers: The Business Journal of Corpus Christi; Corpus Christi Caller-Times (Local news; Circulation 71,300); South Texas Catholic (Regional news; Circulation 42,000)
Transportation: Commute to work: 91.6% car, 1.7% public transportation, 1.7% walk, 2.6% work from home (2005-2009 5-year est.); Travel time to work: 35.4% less than 15 minutes, 47.7% 15 to 30 minutes, 11.0% 30 to 45 minutes, 2.6% 45 to 60 minutes, 3.3% 60 minutes or more (2005-2009 5-year est.)
Airports: Corpus Christi International (primary service/small hub); Corpus Christi NAS/Truax Field (general aviation); Cuddihy Field (general aviation)
Additional Information Contacts
City of Corpus Christi . . . . (361) 826-3220
    http://www.cctexas.com
Corpus Christi Chamber of Commerce . . . . (361) 881-1800
    http://www.corpuschristichamber.org

DRISCOLL (city). Covers a land area of 1.128 square miles and a water area of 0 square miles. Located at 27.67° N. Lat; 97.75° W. Long. Elevation is 62 feet.
History: Driscoll was named for Robert Driscoll.
Population: 688 (1990); 825 (2000); 788 (2010); 765 (2015 projected); Race: 50.8% White, 0.9% Black, 0.8% Asian, 47.6% Other, 85.2% Hispanic of any race (2010); Density: 698.6 persons per square mile (2010); Average household size: 3.13 (2010); Median age: 31.4 (2010); Males per 100 females: 92.2 (2010); Marriage status: 29.0% never married, 53.3% now married, 5.8% widowed, 11.9% divorced (2005-2009 5-year est.); Foreign born: 10.1% (2005-2009 5-year est.); Ancestry (includes multiple ancestries): 6.0% Irish, 3.6% Norwegian, 3.4% American, 1.5% German, 1.5% French (2005-2009 5-year est.).
Economy: Employment by occupation: 12.0% management, 21.2% professional, 18.8% services, 17.8% sales, 2.4% farming, 19.2% construction, 8.7% production (2005-2009 5-year est.).
Income: Per capita income: $19,236 (2010); Median household income: $53,302 (2010); Average household income: $59,851 (2010); Percent of households with income of $100,000 or more: 18.3% (2010); Poverty rate: 23.3% (2005-2009 5-year est.).
Taxes: Total city taxes per capita: $136 (2007); City property taxes per capita: $84 (2007).
Education: Percent of population age 25 and over with: High school diploma (including GED) or higher: 58.9% (2010); Bachelor's degree or higher: 5.3% (2010); Master's degree or higher: 3.1% (2010).
School District(s)
Driscoll ISD (PK-08)
    2009-10 Enrollment: 265 . . . . (361) 387-7349

Housing: Homeownership rate: 77.4% (2010); Median home value: $37,703 (2010); Median contract rent: $405 per month (2005-2009 5-year est.); Median year structure built: 1965 (2005-2009 5-year est.).
Safety: Violent crime rate: 0.0 per 10,000 population; Property crime rate: 212.5 per 10,000 population (2009).
Transportation: Commute to work: 92.4% car, 0.0% public transportation, 7.6% walk, 0.0% work from home (2005-2009 5-year est.); Travel time to work: 36.9% less than 15 minutes, 19.2% 15 to 30 minutes, 38.9% 30 to 45 minutes, 2.5% 45 to 60 minutes, 2.5% 60 minutes or more (2005-2009 5-year est.)

LA PALOMA-LOST CREEK (CDP). Covers a land area of 8.313 square miles and a water area of 0 square miles. Located at 27.71° N. Lat; 97.74° W. Long.
Population: 238 (1990); 323 (2000); 303 (2010); 299 (2015 projected); Race: 76.9% White, 1.0% Black, 0.0% Asian, 22.1% Other, 86.1% Hispanic of any race (2010); Density: 36.4 persons per square mile (2010); Average household size: 3.52 (2010); Median age: 27.6 (2010); Males per 100 females: 113.4 (2010); Marriage status: 31.1% never married, 63.2% now married, 5.7% widowed, 0.0% divorced (2005-2009 5-year est.); Foreign born: 9.4% (2005-2009 5-year est.); Ancestry (includes multiple ancestries): 11.5% Scottish, 11.2% German, 3.5% Dutch (2005-2009 5-year est.).
Economy: Employment by occupation: 0.0% management, 0.0% professional, 35.5% services, 24.3% sales, 0.0% farming, 13.1% construction, 27.1% production (2005-2009 5-year est.).
Income: Per capita income: $10,994 (2010); Median household income: $27,692 (2010); Average household income: $39,235 (2010); Percent of households with income of $100,000 or more: 3.5% (2010); Poverty rate: 11.2% (2005-2009 5-year est.).
Education: Percent of population age 25 and over with: High school diploma (including GED) or higher: 57.1% (2010); Bachelor's degree or higher: 11.2% (2010); Master's degree or higher: 2.5% (2010).
Housing: Homeownership rate: 82.4% (2010); Median home value: $55,294 (2010); Median contract rent: n/a per month (2005-2009 5-year est.); Median year structure built: 1989 (2005-2009 5-year est.).
Transportation: Commute to work: 96.3% car, 0.0% public transportation, 0.0% walk, 3.7% work from home (2005-2009 5-year est.); Travel time to work: 20.4% less than 15 minutes, 28.2% 15 to 30 minutes, 29.1% 30 to 45 minutes, 22.3% 45 to 60 minutes, 0.0% 60 minutes or more (2005-2009 5-year est.)

NORTH SAN PEDRO (CDP). Covers a land area of 0.102 square miles and a water area of 0 square miles. Located at 27.80° N. Lat; 97.68° W. Long. Elevation is 79 feet.
Population: 953 (1990); 920 (2000); 781 (2010); 724 (2015 projected); Race: 67.7% White, 0.1% Black, 0.0% Asian, 32.1% Other, 98.1% Hispanic of any race (2010); Density: 7,662.0 persons per square mile (2010); Average household size: 3.44 (2010); Median age: 27.9 (2010); Males per 100 females: 87.7 (2010); Marriage status: 31.4% never married, 36.0% now married, 13.8% widowed, 18.8% divorced (2005-2009 5-year est.); Foreign born: 3.3% (2005-2009 5-year est.); Ancestry (includes multiple ancestries): n/a (2005-2009 5-year est.).
Economy: Employment by occupation: 0.0% management, 0.0% professional, 20.9% services, 43.3% sales, 17.1% farming, 0.0% construction, 18.7% production (2005-2009 5-year est.).
Income: Per capita income: $9,488 (2010); Median household income: $23,175 (2010); Average household income: $31,795 (2010); Percent of households with income of $100,000 or more: 4.0% (2010); Poverty rate: 62.7% (2005-2009 5-year est.).
Education: Percent of population age 25 and over with: High school diploma (including GED) or higher: 44.4% (2010); Bachelor's degree or higher: 1.2% (2010); Master's degree or higher: 0.5% (2010).
Housing: Homeownership rate: 55.9% (2010); Median home value: $25,932 (2010); Median contract rent: $406 per month (2005-2009 5-year est.); Median year structure built: 1963 (2005-2009 5-year est.).
Transportation: Commute to work: 100.0% car, 0.0% public transportation, 0.0% walk, 0.0% work from home (2005-2009 5-year est.); Travel time to work: 31.9% less than 15 minutes, 58.8% 15 to 30 minutes, 9.3% 30 to 45 minutes, 0.0% 45 to 60 minutes, 0.0% 60 minutes or more (2005-2009 5-year est.)

PETRONILA (city). Covers a land area of 1.792 square miles and a water area of 0 square miles. Located at 27.67° N. Lat; 97.63° W. Long. Elevation is 49 feet.

Population: 157 (1990); 83 (2000); 73 (2010); 69 (2015 projected); Race: 63.0% White, 0.0% Black, 0.0% Asian, 37.0% Other, 78.1% Hispanic of any race (2010); Density: 40.7 persons per square mile (2010); Average household size: 3.17 (2010); Median age: 30.4 (2010); Males per 100 females: 128.1 (2010); Marriage status: 33.8% never married, 35.5% now married, 2.6% widowed, 28.1% divorced (2005-2009 5-year est.); Foreign born: 25.0% (2005-2009 5-year est.); Ancestry (includes multiple ancestries): 2.4% American, 1.0% Scotch-Irish, 0.7% Italian, 0.7% German (2005-2009 5-year est.).
Economy: Employment by occupation: 18.2% management, 11.4% professional, 21.2% services, 22.7% sales, 6.1% farming, 18.9% construction, 1.5% production (2005-2009 5-year est.).
Income: Per capita income: $19,245 (2010); Median household income: $45,500 (2010); Average household income: $62,717 (2010); Percent of households with income of $100,000 or more: 13.0% (2010); Poverty rate: 5.1% (2005-2009 5-year est.).
Taxes: Total city taxes per capita: $175 (2007); City property taxes per capita: $0 (2007).
Education: Percent of population age 25 and over with: High school diploma (including GED) or higher: 65.1% (2010); Bachelor's degree or higher: 9.3% (2010); Master's degree or higher: 0.0% (2010).
Housing: Homeownership rate: 78.3% (2010); Median home value: $73,333 (2010); Median contract rent: $500 per month (2005-2009 5-year est.); Median year structure built: 1983 (2005-2009 5-year est.).
Transportation: Commute to work: 93.2% car, 0.0% public transportation, 3.8% walk, 3.0% work from home (2005-2009 5-year est.); Travel time to work: 18.8% less than 15 minutes, 33.6% 15 to 30 minutes, 47.7% 30 to 45 minutes, 0.0% 45 to 60 minutes, 0.0% 60 minutes or more (2005-2009 5-year est.)

PORT ARANSAS (city). Covers a land area of 8.811 square miles and a water area of 3.263 square miles. Located at 27.82° N. Lat; 97.07° W. Long. Elevation is 7 feet.
History: Port Aransas, on Mustang Island, developed as a fishing resort. A U.S. Coast Guard Station and a Weather Bureau Office were located here, to warn of hurricanes.
Population: 2,258 (1990); 3,370 (2000); 3,904 (2010); 4,123 (2015 projected); Race: 92.8% White, 0.5% Black, 0.5% Asian, 6.2% Other, 6.0% Hispanic of any race (2010); Density: 443.1 persons per square mile (2010); Average household size: 2.12 (2010); Median age: 49.8 (2010); Males per 100 females: 104.8 (2010); Marriage status: 17.5% never married, 63.3% now married, 6.3% widowed, 12.9% divorced (2005-2009 5-year est.); Foreign born: 5.7% (2005-2009 5-year est.); Ancestry (includes multiple ancestries): 20.3% German, 14.1% Irish, 11.2% English, 8.6% American, 6.8% Scotch-Irish (2005-2009 5-year est.).
Economy: Single-family building permits issued: 60 (2010); Multi-family building permits issued: 16 (2010); Employment by occupation: 8.7% management, 16.4% professional, 23.1% services, 27.7% sales, 5.5% farming, 2.6% construction, 16.0% production (2005-2009 5-year est.).
Income: Per capita income: $32,120 (2010); Median household income: $50,732 (2010); Average household income: $68,136 (2010); Percent of households with income of $100,000 or more: 18.2% (2010); Poverty rate: 14.0% (2005-2009 5-year est.).
Taxes: Total city taxes per capita: $1,882 (2007); City property taxes per capita: $774 (2007).
Education: Percent of population age 25 and over with: High school diploma (including GED) or higher: 89.9% (2010); Bachelor's degree or higher: 26.6% (2010); Master's degree or higher: 9.9% (2010).
School District(s)
Port Aransas ISD (PK-12)
    2009-10 Enrollment: 549 . . . . (361) 749-1200
Housing: Homeownership rate: 69.6% (2010); Median home value: $142,784 (2010); Median contract rent: $853 per month (2005-2009 5-year est.); Median year structure built: 1984 (2005-2009 5-year est.).
Safety: Violent crime rate: 64.2 per 10,000 population; Property crime rate: 867.6 per 10,000 population (2009).
Newspapers: South Jetty (Local news; Circulation 4,566)
Transportation: Commute to work: 74.5% car, 0.0% public transportation, 7.2% walk, 5.6% work from home (2005-2009 5-year est.); Travel time to work: 72.6% less than 15 minutes, 8.7% 15 to 30 minutes, 9.7% 30 to 45 minutes, 5.3% 45 to 60 minutes, 3.7% 60 minutes or more (2005-2009 5-year est.)
Additional Information Contacts
City of Port Aransas . . . . (361) 749-4111
    http://www.cityofportaransas.org

Port Aransas Chamber of Commerce . . . . (361) 749-5919
    http://www.portaransas.org

RANCHO BANQUETE (CDP). Covers a land area of 2.850 square miles and a water area of 0 square miles. Located at 27.81° N. Lat; 97.83° W. Long. Elevation is 92 feet.
Population: 377 (1990); 469 (2000); 505 (2010); 524 (2015 projected); Race: 88.3% White, 0.4% Black, 0.2% Asian, 11.1% Other, 52.9% Hispanic of any race (2010); Density: 177.2 persons per square mile (2010); Average household size: 2.99 (2010); Median age: 35.6 (2010); Males per 100 females: 94.2 (2010); Marriage status: 46.9% never married, 47.5% now married, 0.0% widowed, 5.6% divorced (2005-2009 5-year est.); Foreign born: 0.0% (2005-2009 5-year est.); Ancestry (includes multiple ancestries): 6.4% English (2005-2009 5-year est.).
Economy: Employment by occupation: 5.1% management, 16.6% professional, 44.2% services, 0.0% sales, 0.0% farming, 13.8% construction, 20.3% production (2005-2009 5-year est.).
Income: Per capita income: $19,410 (2010); Median household income: $43,534 (2010); Average household income: $57,322 (2010); Percent of households with income of $100,000 or more: 16.0% (2010); Poverty rate: 70.3% (2005-2009 5-year est.).
Education: Percent of population age 25 and over with: High school diploma (including GED) or higher: 76.9% (2010); Bachelor's degree or higher: 16.5% (2010); Master's degree or higher: 3.8% (2010).
Housing: Homeownership rate: 88.2% (2010); Median home value: $76,500 (2010); Median contract rent: n/a per month (2005-2009 5-year est.); Median year structure built: 1987 (2005-2009 5-year est.).
Transportation: Commute to work: 100.0% car, 0.0% public transportation, 0.0% walk, 0.0% work from home (2005-2009 5-year est.); Travel time to work: 0.0% less than 15 minutes, 62.6% 15 to 30 minutes, 31.6% 30 to 45 minutes, 0.0% 45 to 60 minutes, 5.9% 60 minutes or more (2005-2009 5-year est.)

ROBSTOWN (city). Covers a land area of 12.068 square miles and a water area of 0 square miles. Located at 27.79° N. Lat; 97.66° W. Long. Elevation is 72 feet.
History: Robstown was named for Robert Driscoll. The town grew as a center for truck farming and oil supplies.
Population: 12,953 (1990); 12,727 (2000); 11,891 (2010); 11,577 (2015 projected); Race: 73.2% White, 1.0% Black, 0.2% Asian, 25.6% Other, 94.4% Hispanic of any race (2010); Density: 985.3 persons per square mile (2010); Average household size: 3.38 (2010); Median age: 30.3 (2010); Males per 100 females: 94.8 (2010); Marriage status: 34.6% never married, 48.0% now married, 6.7% widowed, 10.7% divorced (2005-2009 5-year est.); Foreign born: 5.7% (2005-2009 5-year est.); Ancestry (includes multiple ancestries): 1.1% American, 1.1% Irish, 1.0% German, 0.5% English, 0.3% Czech (2005-2009 5-year est.).
Economy: Single-family building permits issued: 9 (2010); Multi-family building permits issued: 0 (2010); Employment by occupation: 6.1% management, 13.5% professional, 29.7% services, 19.4% sales, 0.3% farming, 16.0% construction, 15.0% production (2005-2009 5-year est.).
Income: Per capita income: $11,745 (2010); Median household income: $29,602 (2010); Average household income: $39,293 (2010); Percent of households with income of $100,000 or more: 5.8% (2010); Poverty rate: 33.2% (2005-2009 5-year est.).
Taxes: Total city taxes per capita: $275 (2007); City property taxes per capita: $172 (2007).
Education: Percent of population age 25 and over with: High school diploma (including GED) or higher: 54.1% (2010); Bachelor's degree or higher: 5.9% (2010); Master's degree or higher: 2.3% (2010).
School District(s)
Bishop CISD (PK-12)
    2009-10 Enrollment: 1,227 . . . . (361) 584-3591
Robstown ISD (PK-12)
    2009-10 Enrollment: 3,390 . . . . (361) 767-6600
Housing: Homeownership rate: 69.0% (2010); Median home value: $45,053 (2010); Median contract rent: $350 per month (2005-2009 5-year est.); Median year structure built: 1964 (2005-2009 5-year est.).
Safety: Violent crime rate: 18.2 per 10,000 population; Property crime rate: 443.6 per 10,000 population (2009).
Newspapers: Nueces County Record Star (Community news; Circulation 6,000)
Transportation: Commute to work: 94.6% car, 2.1% public transportation, 0.9% walk, 2.3% work from home (2005-2009 5-year est.); Travel time to work: 38.6% less than 15 minutes, 24.9% 15 to 30 minutes, 31.6% 30 to 45

minutes, 2.5% 45 to 60 minutes, 2.3% 60 minutes or more (2005-2009 5-year est.)

Additional Information Contacts

City of Robstown .... (361) 387-4589

SANDY HOLLOW-ESCONDIDAS (CDP). Covers a land area of 7.988 square miles and a water area of 0.205 square miles. Located at 27.94° N. Lat; 97.82° W. Long.

Population: 283 (1990); 433 (2000); 469 (2010); 486 (2015 projected); Race: 88.5% White, 0.4% Black, 0.2% Asian, 10.9% Other, 53.1% Hispanic of any race (2010); Density: 58.7 persons per square mile (2010); Average household size: 2.99 (2010); Median age: 35.6 (2010); Males per 100 females: 93.8 (2010); Marriage status: 21.8% never married, 59.2% now married, 11.9% widowed, 7.2% divorced (2005-2009 5-year est.); Foreign born: 4.8% (2005-2009 5-year est.); Ancestry (includes multiple ancestries): 17.5% German, 1.7% American (2005-2009 5-year est.).
Economy: Employment by occupation: 3.0% management, 10.4% professional, 7.9% services, 30.2% sales, 0.0% farming, 29.7% construction, 18.8% production (2005-2009 5-year est.).
Income: Per capita income: $19,410 (2010); Median household income: $44,167 (2010); Average household income: $58,503 (2010); Percent of households with income of $100,000 or more: 16.6% (2010); Poverty rate: 38.2% (2005-2009 5-year est.).
Education: Percent of population age 25 and over with: High school diploma (including GED) or higher: 75.9% (2010); Bachelor's degree or higher: 16.3% (2010); Master's degree or higher: 3.7% (2010).
Housing: Homeownership rate: 87.9% (2010); Median home value: $74,444 (2010); Median contract rent: n/a per month (2005-2009 5-year est.); Median year structure built: 1979 (2005-2009 5-year est.).
Transportation: Commute to work: 96.8% car, 0.0% public transportation, 0.0% walk, 3.2% work from home (2005-2009 5-year est.); Travel time to work: 19.1% less than 15 minutes, 43.2% 15 to 30 minutes, 15.0% 30 to 45 minutes, 19.4% 45 to 60 minutes, 3.3% 60 minutes or more (2005-2009 5-year est.)

SPRING GARDEN-TERRA VERDE (CDP). Covers a land area of 3.030 square miles and a water area of 0 square miles. Located at 27.76° N. Lat; 97.72° W. Long.

Population: 510 (1990); 693 (2000); 673 (2010); 665 (2015 projected); Race: 76.7% White, 0.7% Black, 0.0% Asian, 22.6% Other, 86.2% Hispanic of any race (2010); Density: 222.1 persons per square mile (2010); Average household size: 3.49 (2010); Median age: 27.3 (2010); Males per 100 females: 106.4 (2010); Marriage status: 33.5% never married, 58.9% now married, 7.5% widowed, 0.0% divorced (2005-2009 5-year est.); Foreign born: 8.0% (2005-2009 5-year est.); Ancestry (includes multiple ancestries): 4.8% American, 4.3% Irish (2005-2009 5-year est.).
Economy: Employment by occupation: 0.0% management, 5.4% professional, 29.2% services, 35.8% sales, 0.0% farming, 20.0% construction, 9.6% production (2005-2009 5-year est.).
Income: Per capita income: $10,994 (2010); Median household income: $27,581 (2010); Average household income: $36,592 (2010); Percent of households with income of $100,000 or more: 2.1% (2010); Poverty rate: 56.5% (2005-2009 5-year est.).
Education: Percent of population age 25 and over with: High school diploma (including GED) or higher: 58.3% (2010); Bachelor's degree or higher: 12.4% (2010); Master's degree or higher: 3.1% (2010).
Housing: Homeownership rate: 82.6% (2010); Median home value: $54,750 (2010); Median contract rent: n/a per month (2005-2009 5-year est.); Median year structure built: 1988 (2005-2009 5-year est.).
Transportation: Commute to work: 100.0% car, 0.0% public transportation, 0.0% walk, 0.0% work from home (2005-2009 5-year est.); Travel time to work: 0.0% less than 15 minutes, 37.2% 15 to 30 minutes, 57.3% 30 to 45 minutes, 5.6% 45 to 60 minutes, 0.0% 60 minutes or more (2005-2009 5-year est.)

TIERRA GRANDE (CDP). Covers a land area of 4.708 square miles and a water area of 0 square miles. Located at 27.69° N. Lat; 97.58° W. Long. Elevation is 56 feet.

Population: 309 (1990); 362 (2000); 402 (2010); 424 (2015 projected); Race: 76.4% White, 3.7% Black, 0.2% Asian, 19.7% Other, 43.8% Hispanic of any race (2010); Density: 85.4 persons per square mile (2010); Average household size: 3.13 (2010); Median age: 32.1 (2010); Males per 100 females: 104.1 (2010); Marriage status: 0.0% never married, 23.1% now married, 44.6% widowed, 32.3% divorced (2005-2009 5-year est.);

Foreign born: 0.0% (2005-2009 5-year est.); Ancestry (includes multiple ancestries): 32.3% Czech (2005-2009 5-year est.).
Economy: Employment by occupation: 0.0% management, 0.0% professional, 0.0% services, 52.4% sales, 0.0% farming, 47.6% construction, 0.0% production (2005-2009 5-year est.).
Income: Per capita income: $15,802 (2010); Median household income: $47,656 (2010); Average household income: $61,869 (2010); Percent of households with income of $100,000 or more: 15.2% (2010); Poverty rate: 35.4% (2005-2009 5-year est.).
Education: Percent of population age 25 and over with: High school diploma (including GED) or higher: 67.6% (2010); Bachelor's degree or higher: 9.5% (2010); Master's degree or higher: 2.5% (2010).
Housing: Homeownership rate: 79.8% (2010); Median home value: $87,857 (2010); Median contract rent: n/a per month (2005-2009 5-year est.); Median year structure built: 1980 (2005-2009 5-year est.).
Transportation: Commute to work: 100.0% car, 0.0% public transportation, 0.0% walk, 0.0% work from home (2005-2009 5-year est.); Travel time to work: 0.0% less than 15 minutes, 100.0% 15 to 30 minutes, 0.0% 30 to 45 minutes, 0.0% 45 to 60 minutes, 0.0% 60 minutes or more (2005-2009 5-year est.)

Ochiltree County

Located in north Texas, on the high plains of the Panhandle; bounded on the north by Oklahoma; drained by tributaries of the Canadian and North Canadian Rivers. Covers a land area of 917.56 square miles, a water area of 0.51 square miles, and is located in the Central Time Zone at 36.32° N. Lat., 100.83° W. Long. The county was founded in 1876. County seat is Perryton.

Weather Station: Perryton									Elevation: 2,941 feet			
	Jan	Feb	Mar	Apr	May	Jun	Jul	Aug	Sep	Oct	Nov	Dec
High	47	51	59	69	78	87	93	91	83	71	59	47
Low	20	22	30	38	49	59	64	63	55	42	30	21
Precip	0.5	0.6	1.8	1.8	3.0	3.2	3.0	2.6	1.9	1.8	0.8	0.9
Snow	3.6	3.1	4.9	0.7	0.0	0.0	0.0	0.0	tr	0.3	1.5	4.0

High and Low temperatures in degrees Fahrenheit; Precipitation and Snow in inches

Population: 9,128 (1990); 9,006 (2000); 9,653 (2010); 9,952 (2015 projected); Race: 80.2% White, 0.4% Black, 0.7% Asian, 18.6% Other, 46.0% Hispanic of any race (2010); Density: 10.5 persons per square mile (2010); Average household size: 2.75 (2010); Median age: 33.1 (2010); Males per 100 females: 101.1 (2010).
Religion: Five largest groups: 29.5% Southern Baptist Convention, 8.2% The United Methodist Church, 7.2% Christian Church (Disciples of Christ), 6.4% Catholic Church, 3.6% Independent, Charismatic Churches (2000).
Economy: Unemployment rate: 4.9% (June 2011); Total civilian labor force: 5,864 (June 2011); Leading industries: 26.1% mining; 12.5% retail trade; 11.6% construction (2009); Farms: 382 totaling 579,476 acres (2007); Companies that employ 500 or more persons: 0 (2009); Companies that employ 100 to 499 persons: 3 (2009); Companies that employ less than 100 persons: 338 (2009); Black-owned businesses: n/a (2007); Hispanic-owned businesses: n/a (2007); Asian-owned businesses: n/a (2007); Women-owned businesses: n/a (2007); Retail sales per capita: $11,652 (2010). Single-family building permits issued: 1 (2010); Multi-family building permits issued: 0 (2010).
Income: Per capita income: $22,383 (2010); Median household income: $50,000 (2010); Average household income: $61,713 (2010); Percent of households with income of $100,000 or more: 14.0% (2010); Poverty rate: 12.1% (2009); Bankruptcy rate: 1.07% (2010).
Taxes: Total county taxes per capita: $468 (2007); County property taxes per capita: $410 (2007).
Education: Percent of population age 25 and over with: High school diploma (including GED) or higher: 74.2% (2010); Bachelor's degree or higher: 18.0% (2010); Master's degree or higher: 3.3% (2010).
Housing: Homeownership rate: 70.5% (2010); Median home value: $54,177 (2010); Median contract rent: $383 per month (2005-2009 5-year est.); Median year structure built: 1968 (2005-2009 5-year est.)
Health: Birth rate: 211.4 per 10,000 population (2009); Death rate: 74.6 per 10,000 population (2009); Age-adjusted cancer mortality rate: 172.4 (Unreliable) deaths per 100,000 population (2007); Number of physicians: 5.2 per 10,000 population (2008); Hospital beds: 26.4 per 10,000 population (2007); Hospital admissions: 922.7 per 10,000 population (2007).
Elections: 2008 Presidential election results: 7.8% Obama, 91.7% McCain, 0.0% Nader

Additional Information Contacts
Ochiltree County Government . . . . (806) 435-8115
    http://www.co.ochiltree.tx.us/ips/cms
City of Perryton . . . . (806) 435-4014
Perryton-Ochiltree Chamber of Commerce . . . . (806) 435-6575
    http://www.perryton.org

Ochiltree County Communities

PERRYTON (city). County seat. Covers a land area of 4.434 square
miles and a water area of 0.025 square miles. Located at 36.39° N. Lat;
100.80° W. Long. Elevation is 2,940 feet.
History: Perryton was founded in 1919 by settlers from Ochiltree, Texas,
and Gray, Oklahoma, who hauled their homes here on platforms pulled by
tractors.
Population: 7,684 (1990); 7,774 (2000); 8,321 (2010); 8,599 (2015
projected); Race: 79.0% White, 0.4% Black, 0.7% Asian, 19.9% Other,
50.3% Hispanic of any race (2010); Density: 1,876.6 persons per square
mile (2010); Average household size: 2.77 (2010); Median age: 32.4
(2010); Males per 100 females: 100.4 (2010); Marriage status: 24.7%
never married, 61.3% now married, 4.8% widowed, 9.2% divorced
(2005-2009 5-year est.); Foreign born: 20.4% (2005-2009 5-year est.);
Ancestry (includes multiple ancestries): 9.8% German, 8.8% Irish, 6.3%
English, 5.4% American, 1.7% Scotch-Irish (2005-2009 5-year est.).
Economy: Single-family building permits issued: 1 (2010); Multi-family
building permits issued: 0 (2010); Employment by occupation: 9.5%
management, 15.0% professional, 15.8% services, 17.4% sales, 2.6%
farming, 21.2% construction, 18.6% production (2005-2009 5-year est.).
Income: Per capita income: $20,790 (2010); Median household income:
$47,089 (2010); Average household income: $57,965 (2010); Percent of
households with income of $100,000 or more: 11.4% (2010); Poverty rate:
18.7% (2005-2009 5-year est.).
Taxes: Total city taxes per capita: $407 (2007); City property taxes per
capita: $112 (2007).
Education: Percent of population age 25 and over with: High school
diploma (including GED) or higher: 71.5% (2010); Bachelor's degree or
higher: 16.0% (2010); Master's degree or higher: 3.0% (2010).
School District(s)
Perryton ISD (PK-12)
    2009-10 Enrollment: 2,256 . . . . (806) 435-5478
Housing: Homeownership rate: 69.5% (2010); Median home value:
$50,105 (2010); Median contract rent: $387 per month (2005-2009 5-year
est.); Median year structure built: 1968 (2005-2009 5-year est.).
Hospitals: Ochiltree General Hospital (49 beds)
Safety: Violent crime rate: 16.7 per 10,000 population; Property crime rate:
132.7 per 10,000 population (2009).
Newspapers: Herald (Local news; Circulation 3,800)
Transportation: Commute to work: 91.1% car, 0.0% public transportation,
1.4% walk, 2.2% work from home (2005-2009 5-year est.); Travel time to
work: 69.4% less than 15 minutes, 12.3% 15 to 30 minutes, 4.7% 30 to 45
minutes, 4.6% 45 to 60 minutes, 8.9% 60 minutes or more (2005-2009
5-year est.)
Airports: Perryton Ochiltree County (general aviation)
Additional Information Contacts
City of Perryton . . . . (806) 435-4014
Perryton-Ochiltree Chamber of Commerce . . . . (806) 435-6575
    http://www.perryton.org

Oldham County

Located in north Texas, in the high plains of the Panhandle; bounded on
the west by New Mexico; drained by the Canadian River. Covers a land
area of 1,500.63 square miles, a water area of 0.79 square miles, and is
located in the Central Time Zone at 35.38° N. Lat., 102.55° W. Long. The
county was founded in 1876. County seat is Vega.

Weather Station: Boys Ranch   Elevation: 3,190 feet

	Jan	Feb	Mar	Apr	May	Jun	Jul	Aug	Sep	Oct	Nov	Dec
High	53	57	64	73	81	89	93	90	84	73	62	52
Low	21	25	32	41	52	61	66	64	56	42	30	21
Precip	0.5	0.4	1.1	1.3	2.1	2.6	2.7	3.5	2.0	1.6	0.7	0.6
Snow	3.3	1.4	1.1	0.3	0.1	0.0	0.0	0.0	0.0	0.0	1.6	2.7

High and Low temperatures in degrees Fahrenheit; Precipitation and Snow in inches

Population: 2,278 (1990); 2,185 (2000); 2,125 (2010); 2,093 (2015
projected); Race: 88.3% White, 2.8% Black, 0.5% Asian, 8.3% Other,

13.2% Hispanic of any race (2010); Density: 1.4 persons per square mile
(2010); Average household size: 2.52 (2010); Median age: 34.6 (2010);
Males per 100 females: 110.6 (2010).
Religion: Four largest groups: 30.1% Southern Baptist Convention, 21.9%
The United Methodist Church, 9.2% Catholic Church, 4.7% Churches of
Christ (2000).
Economy: Unemployment rate: 6.7% (June 2011); Total civilian labor
force: 941 (June 2011); Leading industries: Farms: 150 totaling 880,490
acres (2007); Companies that employ 500 or more persons: 0 (2009);
Companies that employ 100 to 499 persons: 1 (2009); Companies that
employ less than 100 persons: 33 (2009); Black-owned businesses: n/a
(2007); Hispanic-owned businesses: n/a (2007); Asian-owned businesses:
n/a (2007); Women-owned businesses: n/a (2007); Retail sales per capita:
$6,263 (2010); Single-family building permits issued: 4 (2010); Multi-family
building permits issued: 0 (2010).
Income: Per capita income: $17,347 (2010); Median household income:
$38,750 (2010); Average household income: $49,237 (2010); Percent of
households with income of $100,000 or more: 7.7% (2010); Poverty rate:
13.6% (2009); Bankruptcy rate: 0.96% (2010).
Taxes: Total county taxes per capita: $578 (2007); County property taxes
per capita: $452 (2007).
Education: Percent of population age 25 and over with: High school
diploma (including GED) or higher: 85.0% (2010); Bachelor's degree or
higher: 21.9% (2010); Master's degree or higher: 4.4% (2010).
Housing: Homeownership rate: 64.2% (2010); Median home value:
$59,125 (2010); Median contract rent: $628 per month (2005-2009 5-year
est.); Median year structure built: 1966 (2005-2009 5-year est.)
Health: Birth rate: 108.6 per 10,000 population (2009); Death rate: 23.6 per
10,000 population (2009); Age-adjusted cancer mortality rate: Suppressed
deaths per 100,000 population (2007); Number of physicians: 0.0 per
10,000 population (2008); Hospital beds: 0.0 per 10,000 population (2007);
Hospital admissions: 0.0 per 10,000 population (2007).
Elections: 2008 Presidential election results: 11.1% Obama, 88.4%
McCain, 0.1% Nader
Additional Information Contacts
Oldham County Government . . . . (806) 267-2667
    http://www.co.oldham.tx.us/ips/cms
Oldham County Chamber of Commerce . . . . (806) 267-2828
    http://www.oldhamcofc.org

Oldham County Communities

ADRIAN (city). Covers a land area of 0.884 square miles and a water
area of 0 square miles. Located at 35.27° N. Lat; 102.66° W. Long.
Elevation is 4,039 feet.
Population: 220 (1990); 159 (2000); 166 (2010); 166 (2015 projected);
Race: 83.1% White, 2.4% Black, 0.6% Asian, 13.9% Other, 18.1%
Hispanic of any race (2010); Density: 187.8 persons per square mile
(2010); Average household size: 2.58 (2010); Median age: 40.5 (2010);
Males per 100 females: 90.8 (2010); Marriage status: 18.3% never married,
65.5% now married, 4.9% widowed, 11.3% divorced (2005-2009 5-year
est.); Foreign born: 17.0% (2005-2009 5-year est.); Ancestry (includes
multiple ancestries): 26.7% German, 12.5% Irish, 8.0% English, 6.8%
American, 5.7% Norwegian (2005-2009 5-year est.).
Economy: Employment by occupation: 23.9% management, 9.2%
professional, 32.1% services, 9.2% sales, 11.0% farming, 12.8%
construction, 1.8% production (2005-2009 5-year est.).
Income: Per capita income: $21,196 (2010); Median household income:
$40,455 (2010); Average household income: $52,218 (2010); Percent of
households with income of $100,000 or more: 9.7% (2010); Poverty rate:
10.2% (2005-2009 5-year est.).
Taxes: Total city taxes per capita: $135 (2007); City property taxes per
capita: $84 (2007).
Education: Percent of population age 25 and over with: High school
diploma (including GED) or higher: 90.0% (2010); Bachelor's degree or
higher: 25.5% (2010); Master's degree or higher: 4.5% (2010).
School District(s)
Adrian ISD (PK-12)
    2009-10 Enrollment: 131 . . . . (806) 538-6203
Housing: Homeownership rate: 64.5% (2010); Median home value:
$60,000 (2010); Median contract rent: n/a per month (2005-2009 5-year
est.); Median year structure built: 1969 (2005-2009 5-year est.).
Transportation: Commute to work: 100.0% car, 0.0% public
transportation, 0.0% walk, 0.0% work from home (2005-2009 5-year est.);
Travel time to work: 49.5% less than 15 minutes, 16.5% 15 to 30 minutes,

0.0% 30 to 45 minutes, 7.3% 45 to 60 minutes, 26.6% 60 minutes or more (2005-2009 5-year est.)

VEGA (city). County seat. Covers a land area of 1.080 square miles and a water area of 0 square miles. Located at 35.24° N. Lat; 102.42° W. Long. Elevation is 4,029 feet.
Population: 844 (1990); 936 (2000); 901 (2010); 880 (2015 projected); Race: 94.6% White, 1.4% Black, 0.4% Asian, 3.6% Other, 10.2% Hispanic of any race (2010); Density: 834.3 persons per square mile (2010); Average household size: 2.39 (2010); Median age: 41.7 (2010); Males per 100 females: 91.7 (2010); Marriage status: 18.0% never married, 66.2% now married, 10.9% widowed, 4.9% divorced (2005-2009 5-year est.); Foreign born: 4.3% (2005-2009 5-year est.); Ancestry (includes multiple ancestries): 33.3% German, 22.5% Irish, 10.6% American, 8.6% English, 5.6% Swiss (2005-2009 5-year est.).
Economy: Single-family building permits issued: 4 (2010); Multi-family building permits issued: 0 (2010); Employment by occupation: 17.1% management, 30.1% professional, 14.0% services, 18.4% sales, 4.2% farming, 9.2% construction, 7.1% production (2005-2009 5-year est.).
Income: Per capita income: $18,252 (2010); Median household income: $33,482 (2010); Average household income: $43,887 (2010); Percent of households with income of $100,000 or more: 6.4% (2010); Poverty rate: 10.0% (2005-2009 5-year est.).
Taxes: Total city taxes per capita: $458 (2007); City property taxes per capita: $297 (2007).
Education: Percent of population age 25 and over with: High school diploma (including GED) or higher: 80.0% (2010); Bachelor's degree or higher: 19.7% (2010); Master's degree or higher: 3.5% (2010).

School District(s)
Vega ISD (KG-12)
    2009-10 Enrollment: 289 . . . . (806) 267-2123
Housing: Homeownership rate: 76.0% (2010); Median home value: $56,250 (2010); Median contract rent: $653 per month (2005-2009 5-year est.); Median year structure built: 1967 (2005-2009 5-year est.).
Newspapers: Vega Enterprise (Local news; Circulation 900)
Transportation: Commute to work: 86.1% car, 0.9% public transportation, 7.0% walk, 6.1% work from home (2005-2009 5-year est.); Travel time to work: 50.3% less than 15 minutes, 25.3% 15 to 30 minutes, 20.0% 30 to 45 minutes, 0.0% 45 to 60 minutes, 4.4% 60 minutes or more (2005-2009 5-year est.)
Additional Information Contacts
Oldham County Chamber of Commerce . . . . (806) 267-2828
    http://www.oldhamcofc.org

WILDORADO (unincorporated postal area, zip code 79098). Covers a land area of 129.478 square miles and a water area of 0 square miles. Located at 35.15° N. Lat; 102.19° W. Long. Elevation is 3,921 feet.
Population: 472 (2000); Race: 92.3% White, 4.8% Black, 0.0% Asian, 2.9% Other, 4.4% Hispanic of any race (2000); Density: 3.6 persons per square mile (2000); Age: 31.5% under 18, 18.2% over 64 (2000); Marriage status: 14.2% never married, 76.5% now married, 5.2% widowed, 4.1% divorced (2000); Foreign born: 5.1% (2000); Ancestry (includes multiple ancestries): 17.2% German, 13.3% American, 11.7% English, 7.1% Irish (2000).
Economy: Employment by occupation: 22.5% management, 13.7% professional, 11.9% services, 26.4% sales, 6.6% farming, 10.6% construction, 8.4% production (2000).
Income: Per capita income: $16,413 (2000); Median household income: $38,750 (2000); Poverty rate: 179.1% (2000).
Education: Percent of population age 25 and over with: High school diploma (including GED) or higher: 90.4% (2000); Bachelor's degree or higher: 17.9% (2000).

School District(s)
Wildorado ISD (PK-06)
    2009-10 Enrollment: 99 . . . . (806) 426-3317
Housing: Homeownership rate: 60.9% (2000); Median home value: $64,500 (2000); Median contract rent: $338 per month (2000); Median year structure built: 1960 (2000).
Transportation: Commute to work: 88.8% car, 0.0% public transportation, 0.0% walk, 11.2% work from home (2000); Travel time to work: 29.3% less than 15 minutes, 28.3% 15 to 30 minutes, 33.8% 30 to 45 minutes, 6.6% 45 to 60 minutes, 2.0% 60 minutes or more (2000)

Orange County

Located in southeastern Texas; bounded on the east by the Sabine River and the Louisiana border, on the west and southwest by the Neches River, and on the south by Sabine Lake. Covers a land area of 356.40 square miles, a water area of 23.14 square miles, and is located in the Central Time Zone at 30.11° N. Lat., 93.84° W. Long. The county was founded in 1852. County seat is Orange.

Orange County is part of the Beaumont-Port Arthur, TX Metropolitan Statistical Area. The entire metro area includes: Hardin County, TX; Jefferson County, TX; Orange County, TX

Population: 80,509 (1990); 84,966 (2000); 84,130 (2010); 83,559 (2015 projected); Race: 86.0% White, 9.0% Black, 1.0% Asian, 4.0% Other, 5.3% Hispanic of any race (2010); Density: 236.1 persons per square mile (2010); Average household size: 2.58 (2010); Median age: 38.0 (2010); Males per 100 females: 96.1 (2010).
Religion: Five largest groups: 34.4% Southern Baptist Convention, 13.7% Catholic Church, 5.4% The United Methodist Church, 2.8% Assemblies of God, 2.0% The Church of Jesus Christ of Latter-day Saints (2000).
Economy: Unemployment rate: 11.7% (June 2011); Total civilian labor force: 42,773 (June 2011); Leading industries: 29.4% manufacturing; 16.7% retail trade; 10.9% accommodation & food services (2009); Farms: 675 totaling 63,748 acres (2007); Companies that employ 500 or more persons: 2 (2009); Companies that employ 100 to 499 persons: 27 (2009); Companies that employ less than 100 persons: 1,345 (2009); Black-owned businesses: 408 (2007); Hispanic-owned businesses: n/a (2007); Asian-owned businesses: n/a (2007); Women-owned businesses: 1,788 (2007); Retail sales per capita: $11,428 (2010). Single-family building permits issued: 210 (2010); Multi-family building permits issued: 16 (2010).
Income: Per capita income: $23,549 (2010); Median household income: $48,376 (2010); Average household income: $61,129 (2010); Percent of households with income of $100,000 or more: 16.0% (2010); Poverty rate: 15.6% (2009); Bankruptcy rate: 1.92% (2010).
Taxes: Total county taxes per capita: $331 (2007); County property taxes per capita: $259 (2007).
Education: Percent of population age 25 and over with: High school diploma (including GED) or higher: 87.6% (2010); Bachelor's degree or higher: 13.1% (2010); Master's degree or higher: 3.4% (2010).
Housing: Homeownership rate: 78.2% (2010); Median home value: $81,037 (2010); Median contract rent: $447 per month (2005-2009 5-year est.); Median year structure built: 1975 (2005-2009 5-year est.).
Health: Birth rate: 130.0 per 10,000 population (2009); Death rate: 111.5 per 10,000 population (2009); Age-adjusted cancer mortality rate: 194.5 deaths per 100,000 population (2007); Number of physicians: 5.7 per 10,000 population (2008); Hospital beds: 13.7 per 10,000 population (2007); Hospital admissions: 404.3 per 10,000 population (2007).
Environment: Air Quality Index: 83.3% good, 16.4% moderate, 0.3% unhealthy for sensitive individuals, 0.0% unhealthy (percent of days in 2008)
Elections: 2008 Presidential election results: 26.0% Obama, 73.1% McCain, 0.0% Nader
Additional Information Contacts
Orange County Government . . . . (409) 883-7740
    http://www.co.orange.tx.us
Bridge City Chamber of Commerce . . . . (409) 735-5671
    http://www.bridgecitychamber.org
City of Bridge City . . . . (409) 735-6801
    http://www.bridgecitytex.com
City of Orange . . . . (409) 886-3611
    http://www.orangetexas.net
City of Vidor . . . . (409) 769-5473
    http://www.cityofvidor.com
City of West Orange . . . . (409) 883-3468
    http://www.cityofwestorange.com
Greater Orange Area Chamber of Commerce . . . . (409) 883-3536
    http://www.orangetexaschamber.org
Vidor Chamber of Commerce . . . . (409) 769-6339
    http://www.vidorchamber.com

Orange County Communities

BRIDGE CITY (city). Covers a land area of 5.143 square miles and a water area of 0.254 square miles. Located at 30.03° N. Lat; 93.84° W. Long. Elevation is 10 feet.

History: Bridge City grew up near the Port Arthur-Orange Bridge, opened in 1938, 230 feet above the river and one and a half miles long.
Population: 8,385 (1990); 8,651 (2000); 8,672 (2010); 8,685 (2015 projected); Race: 93.4% White, 0.2% Black, 1.9% Asian, 4.4% Other, 5.1% Hispanic of any race (2010); Density: 1,686.1 persons per square mile (2010); Average household size: 2.62 (2010); Median age: 37.7 (2010); Males per 100 females: 96.5 (2010); Marriage status: 19.4% never married, 62.0% now married, 4.8% widowed, 13.8% divorced (2005-2009 5-year est.); Foreign born: 2.9% (2005-2009 5-year est.); Ancestry (includes multiple ancestries): 16.1% Irish, 14.3% French, 9.8% German, 9.6% American, 7.4% English (2005-2009 5-year est.).
Economy: Single-family building permits issued: 20 (2010); Multi-family building permits issued: 8 (2010); Employment by occupation: 12.9% management, 20.3% professional, 12.4% services, 24.9% sales, 0.0% farming, 14.3% construction, 15.2% production (2005-2009 5-year est.).
Income: Per capita income: $24,054 (2010); Median household income: $53,574 (2010); Average household income: $63,212 (2010); Percent of households with income of $100,000 or more: 16.3% (2010); Poverty rate: 8.5% (2005-2009 5-year est.).
Taxes: Total city taxes per capita: $314 (2007); City property taxes per capita: $136 (2007).
Education: Percent of population age 25 and over with: High school diploma (including GED) or higher: 90.0% (2010); Bachelor's degree or higher: 11.3% (2010); Master's degree or higher: 2.8% (2010).

School District(s)

Bridge City ISD (PK-12)
   2009-10 Enrollment: 2,486 . . . . (409) 735-1602
Orangefield ISD (PK-12)
   2009-10 Enrollment: 1,758 . . . . (409) 735-5337
Housing: Homeownership rate: 79.1% (2010); Median home value: $99,286 (2010); Median contract rent: $500 per month (2005-2009 5-year est.); Median year structure built: 1973 (2005-2009 5-year est.).
Safety: Violent crime rate: 10.5 per 10,000 population; Property crime rate: 175.8 per 10,000 population (2009).
Newspapers: Penny Record (Community news; Circulation 22,000)
Transportation: Commute to work: 97.7% car, 0.0% public transportation, 0.3% walk, 0.6% work from home (2005-2009 5-year est.); Travel time to work: 24.7% less than 15 minutes, 50.0% 15 to 30 minutes, 15.8% 30 to 45 minutes, 7.7% 45 to 60 minutes, 1.8% 60 minutes or more (2005-2009 5-year est.)
Additional Information Contacts
Bridge City Chamber of Commerce . . . . (409) 735-5671
   http://www.bridgecitychamber.org
City of Bridge City . . . . (409) 735-6801
   http://www.bridgecitytex.com

MAURICEVILLE (CDP).
Covers a land area of 8.508 square miles and a water area of 0 square miles. Located at 30.21° N. Lat; 93.87° W. Long. Elevation is 26 feet.
Population: 2,065 (1990); 2,743 (2000); 3,069 (2010); 3,222 (2015 projected); Race: 94.2% White, 1.0% Black, 0.1% Asian, 4.7% Other, 6.5% Hispanic of any race (2010); Density: 360.7 persons per square mile (2010); Average household size: 2.79 (2010); Median age: 37.2 (2010); Males per 100 females: 101.5 (2010); Marriage status: 13.2% never married, 74.2% now married, 1.9% widowed, 10.7% divorced (2005-2009 5-year est.); Foreign born: 0.4% (2005-2009 5-year est.); Ancestry (includes multiple ancestries): 11.9% Irish, 11.7% Cajun, 11.2% French, 9.1% American, 8.5% English (2005-2009 5-year est.).
Economy: Employment by occupation: 7.8% management, 17.0% professional, 22.9% services, 18.1% sales, 0.0% farming, 16.7% construction, 17.6% production (2005-2009 5-year est.).
Income: Per capita income: $27,826 (2010); Median household income: $67,018 (2010); Average household income: $78,102 (2010); Percent of households with income of $100,000 or more: 25.2% (2010); Poverty rate: 11.6% (2005-2009 5-year est.).
Education: Percent of population age 25 and over with: High school diploma (including GED) or higher: 90.5% (2010); Bachelor's degree or higher: 11.8% (2010); Master's degree or higher: 2.0% (2010).
Housing: Homeownership rate: 90.6% (2010); Median home value: $94,712 (2010); Median contract rent: $410 per month (2005-2009 5-year est.); Median year structure built: 1991 (2005-2009 5-year est.).
Transportation: Commute to work: 94.8% car, 0.0% public transportation, 1.3% walk, 1.9% work from home (2005-2009 5-year est.); Travel time to work: 11.3% less than 15 minutes, 43.4% 15 to 30 minutes, 39.5% 30 to 45

minutes, 3.8% 45 to 60 minutes, 2.0% 60 minutes or more (2005-2009 5-year est.)

ORANGE (city).
County seat. Covers a land area of 20.078 square miles and a water area of 0.687 square miles. Located at 30.10° N. Lat; 93.75° W. Long. Elevation is 7 feet.
History: Orange was established at the head of navigation on the Sabine River, and on the border with Louisiana. The early economy was based on lumber, cattle, and rice, with a large rice mill established here. Orange became a ship-building port during World War II.
Population: 19,463 (1990); 18,643 (2000); 17,276 (2010); 16,518 (2015 projected); Race: 57.3% White, 37.7% Black, 1.2% Asian, 3.8% Other, 5.2% Hispanic of any race (2010); Density: 860.4 persons per square mile (2010); Average household size: 2.40 (2010); Median age: 37.6 (2010); Males per 100 females: 93.2 (2010); Marriage status: 25.2% never married, 51.8% now married, 8.0% widowed, 15.0% divorced (2005-2009 5-year est.); Foreign born: 4.3% (2005-2009 5-year est.); Ancestry (includes multiple ancestries): 10.1% Irish, 9.1% German, 9.0% French, 7.5% English, 5.4% American (2005-2009 5-year est.).
Economy: Single-family building permits issued: 53 (2010); Multi-family building permits issued: 8 (2010); Employment by occupation: 11.9% management, 19.4% professional, 17.5% services, 18.7% sales, 0.0% farming, 14.8% construction, 17.7% production (2005-2009 5-year est.).
Income: Per capita income: $22,488 (2010); Median household income: $40,605 (2010); Average household income: $54,946 (2010); Percent of households with income of $100,000 or more: 14.7% (2010); Poverty rate: 22.8% (2005-2009 5-year est.).
Taxes: Total city taxes per capita: $446 (2007); City property taxes per capita: $231 (2007).
Education: Percent of population age 25 and over with: High school diploma (including GED) or higher: 87.1% (2010); Bachelor's degree or higher: 19.0% (2010); Master's degree or higher: 5.0% (2010).

School District(s)

Deweyville ISD (PK-12)
   2009-10 Enrollment: 701 . . . . (409) 746-2731
Little Cypress-Mauriceville CISD (PK-12)
   2009-10 Enrollment: 3,638 . . . . (409) 883-2232
Tekoa Academy of Accelerated Studies (PK-12)
   2009-10 Enrollment: 421 . . . . (409) 982-5400
West Orange-Cove CISD (PK-12)
   2009-10 Enrollment: 2,551 . . . . (409) 882-5500

Two-year College(s)

Lamar State College-Orange (Public)
   Fall 2009 Enrollment: 2,262 . . . . (409) 883-7750
   2010-11 Tuition: In-state $3,040; Out-of-state $10,480
Housing: Homeownership rate: 62.7% (2010); Median home value: $77,095 (2010); Median contract rent: $443 per month (2005-2009 5-year est.); Median year structure built: 1966 (2005-2009 5-year est.).
Hospitals: Memorial Herman Baptist Orange Hospital (199 beds)
Safety: Violent crime rate: 83.1 per 10,000 population; Property crime rate: 588.1 per 10,000 population (2009).
Newspapers: Opportunity Valley News (Community news; Circulation 25,000); Orange County News (Local news; Circulation 22,000); Orange Leader (Community news; Circulation 13,000)
Transportation: Commute to work: 90.6% car, 0.6% public transportation, 1.1% walk, 2.1% work from home (2005-2009 5-year est.); Travel time to work: 47.2% less than 15 minutes, 26.6% 15 to 30 minutes, 19.8% 30 to 45 minutes, 4.0% 45 to 60 minutes, 2.4% 60 minutes or more (2005-2009 5-year est.)
Airports: Orange County (general aviation)
Additional Information Contacts
City of Orange . . . . (409) 886-3611
   http://www.orangetexas.net
Greater Orange Area Chamber of Commerce . . . . (409) 883-3536
   http://www.orangetexaschamber.org

PINE FOREST (city).
Covers a land area of 2.769 square miles and a water area of 0 square miles. Located at 30.17° N. Lat; 94.03° W. Long. Elevation is 16 feet.
Population: 797 (1990); 632 (2000); 550 (2010); 541 (2015 projected); Race: 97.3% White, 0.0% Black, 0.4% Asian, 2.4% Other, 2.7% Hispanic of any race (2010); Density: 198.7 persons per square mile (2010); Average household size: 2.71 (2010); Median age: 37.1 (2010); Males per 100 females: 93.0 (2010); Marriage status: 24.7% never married, 60.5% now married, 11.3% widowed, 3.5% divorced (2005-2009 5-year est.);

Foreign born: 2.5% (2005-2009 5-year est.); Ancestry (includes multiple ancestries): 23.3% Irish, 19.8% German, 18.3% French, 10.1% American, 5.4% English (2005-2009 5-year est.).
Economy: Employment by occupation: 7.9% management, 20.8% professional, 13.0% services, 26.4% sales, 0.0% farming, 16.2% construction, 15.7% production (2005-2009 5-year est.).
Income: Per capita income: $26,280 (2010); Median household income: $60,372 (2010); Average household income: $71,207 (2010); Percent of households with income of $100,000 or more: 21.2% (2010); Poverty rate: 12.6% (2005-2009 5-year est.).
Taxes: Total city taxes per capita: $462 (2007); City property taxes per capita: $112 (2007).
Education: Percent of population age 25 and over with: High school diploma (including GED) or higher: 85.2% (2010); Bachelor's degree or higher: 8.1% (2010); Master's degree or higher: 2.2% (2010).
Housing: Homeownership rate: 87.2% (2010); Median home value: $72,778 (2010); Median contract rent: $388 per month (2005-2009 5-year est.); Median year structure built: 1975 (2005-2009 5-year est.).
Transportation: Commute to work: 81.0% car, 0.0% public transportation, 3.3% walk, 0.0% work from home (2005-2009 5-year est.); Travel time to work: 36.7% less than 15 minutes, 21.0% 15 to 30 minutes, 36.2% 30 to 45 minutes, 4.8% 45 to 60 minutes, 1.4% 60 minutes or more (2005-2009 5-year est.)

PINEHURST (city). Covers a land area of 1.775 square miles and a water area of 0 square miles. Located at 30.10° N. Lat; 93.77° W. Long. Elevation is 13 feet.

Population: 2,605 (1990); 2,274 (2000); 2,107 (2010); 2,066 (2015 projected); Race: 74.3% White, 18.9% Black, 0.8% Asian, 6.0% Other, 7.1% Hispanic of any race (2010); Density: 1,186.7 persons per square mile (2010); Average household size: 2.20 (2010); Median age: 42.1 (2010); Males per 100 females: 89.1 (2010); Marriage status: 23.3% never married, 52.3% now married, 9.5% widowed, 14.9% divorced (2005-2009 5-year est.); Foreign born: 4.6% (2005-2009 5-year est.); Ancestry (includes multiple ancestries): 13.9% German, 13.8% French, 9.0% English, 7.3% Irish, 4.3% American (2005-2009 5-year est.).
Economy: Single-family building permits issued: 1 (2010); Multi-family building permits issued: 0 (2010); Employment by occupation: 7.3% management, 10.7% professional, 18.1% services, 25.2% sales, 0.0% farming, 13.7% construction, 25.0% production (2005-2009 5-year est.).
Income: Per capita income: $26,799 (2010); Median household income: $41,549 (2010); Average household income: $60,465 (2010); Percent of households with income of $100,000 or more: 13.8% (2010); Poverty rate: 12.6% (2005-2009 5-year est.).
Taxes: Total city taxes per capita: $458 (2007); City property taxes per capita: $297 (2007).
Education: Percent of population age 25 and over with: High school diploma (including GED) or higher: 86.5% (2010); Bachelor's degree or higher: 17.4% (2010); Master's degree or higher: 6.0% (2010).
Housing: Homeownership rate: 59.2% (2010); Median home value: $103,351 (2010); Median contract rent: $371 per month (2005-2009 5-year est.); Median year structure built: 1975 (2005-2009 5-year est.).
Safety: Violent crime rate: 27.9 per 10,000 population; Property crime rate: 590.4 per 10,000 population (2009).
Transportation: Commute to work: 93.2% car, 0.0% public transportation, 1.1% walk, 5.1% work from home (2005-2009 5-year est.); Travel time to work: 46.0% less than 15 minutes, 27.1% 15 to 30 minutes, 21.5% 30 to 45 minutes, 2.7% 45 to 60 minutes, 2.7% 60 minutes or more (2005-2009 5-year est.)

ROSE CITY (city). Covers a land area of 1.722 square miles and a water area of 0.005 square miles. Located at 30.10° N. Lat; 94.05° W. Long. Elevation is 10 feet.

Population: 572 (1990); 519 (2000); 553 (2010); 535 (2015 projected); Race: 95.5% White, 0.0% Black, 0.7% Asian, 3.8% Other, 4.9% Hispanic of any race (2010); Density: 321.1 persons per square mile (2010); Average household size: 2.62 (2010); Median age: 34.4 (2010); Males per 100 females: 91.3 (2010); Marriage status: 25.6% never married, 41.4% now married, 12.2% widowed, 20.8% divorced (2005-2009 5-year est.); Foreign born: 2.0% (2005-2009 5-year est.); Ancestry (includes multiple ancestries): 20.4% French, 13.3% Irish, 8.3% French Canadian, 7.9% English, 5.5% German (2005-2009 5-year est.).
Economy: Employment by occupation: 6.3% management, 25.4% professional, 10.7% services, 22.0% sales, 0.0% farming, 18.5% construction, 17.1% production (2005-2009 5-year est.).

Income: Per capita income: $19,182 (2010); Median household income: $43,958 (2010); Average household income: $49,941 (2010); Percent of households with income of $100,000 or more: 11.8% (2010); Poverty rate: 11.6% (2005-2009 5-year est.).
Taxes: Total city taxes per capita: $375 (2007); City property taxes per capita: $66 (2007).
Education: Percent of population age 25 and over with: High school diploma (including GED) or higher: 82.9% (2010); Bachelor's degree or higher: 5.9% (2010); Master's degree or higher: 2.0% (2010).
Housing: Homeownership rate: 78.2% (2010); Median home value: $56,122 (2010); Median contract rent: $768 per month (2005-2009 5-year est.); Median year structure built: 1981 (2005-2009 5-year est.).
Safety: Violent crime rate: 59.8 per 10,000 population; Property crime rate: 99.6 per 10,000 population (2009).
Transportation: Commute to work: 98.5% car, 0.0% public transportation, 0.0% walk, 0.0% work from home (2005-2009 5-year est.); Travel time to work: 14.7% less than 15 minutes, 62.3% 15 to 30 minutes, 11.3% 30 to 45 minutes, 10.3% 45 to 60 minutes, 1.5% 60 minutes or more (2005-2009 5-year est.)

VIDOR (city). Covers a land area of 10.557 square miles and a water area of 0.013 square miles. Located at 30.13° N. Lat; 93.99° W. Long. Elevation is 23 feet.

Population: 10,935 (1990); 11,440 (2000); 11,147 (2010); 11,022 (2015 projected); Race: 95.8% White, 0.2% Black, 0.3% Asian, 3.7% Other, 5.4% Hispanic of any race (2010); Density: 1,055.9 persons per square mile (2010); Average household size: 2.60 (2010); Median age: 37.3 (2010); Males per 100 females: 93.7 (2010); Marriage status: 25.1% never married, 52.2% now married, 9.5% widowed, 13.2% divorced (2005-2009 5-year est.); Foreign born: 1.4% (2005-2009 5-year est.); Ancestry (includes multiple ancestries): 15.5% Irish, 11.7% German, 11.3% English, 10.6% American, 7.7% French (2005-2009 5-year est.).
Economy: Single-family building permits issued: 9 (2010); Multi-family building permits issued: 0 (2010); Employment by occupation: 7.7% management, 10.9% professional, 12.6% services, 33.1% sales, 0.2% farming, 16.9% construction, 18.5% production (2005-2009 5-year est.).
Income: Per capita income: $18,834 (2010); Median household income: $40,097 (2010); Average household income: $49,381 (2010); Percent of households with income of $100,000 or more: 9.6% (2010); Poverty rate: 17.7% (2005-2009 5-year est.).
Taxes: Total city taxes per capita: $376 (2007); City property taxes per capita: $127 (2007).
Education: Percent of population age 25 and over with: High school diploma (including GED) or higher: 82.7% (2010); Bachelor's degree or higher: 7.4% (2010); Master's degree or higher: 2.6% (2010).

School District(s)

Vidor ISD (PK-12)
    2009-10 Enrollment: 4,955 . . . . (409) 951-8714
Housing: Homeownership rate: 77.2% (2010); Median home value: $63,717 (2010); Median contract rent: $437 per month (2005-2009 5-year est.); Median year structure built: 1974 (2005-2009 5-year est.).
Safety: Violent crime rate: 35.4 per 10,000 population; Property crime rate: 400.1 per 10,000 population (2009).
Newspapers: Vidorian (Local news; Circulation 1,450); Vidorian Shopper (Community news; Circulation 11,275)
Transportation: Commute to work: 96.6% car, 0.0% public transportation, 0.9% walk, 0.9% work from home (2005-2009 5-year est.); Travel time to work: 27.2% less than 15 minutes, 41.6% 15 to 30 minutes, 22.2% 30 to 45 minutes, 5.2% 45 to 60 minutes, 3.9% 60 minutes or more (2005-2009 5-year est.)
Additional Information Contacts
City of Vidor . . . . (409) 769-5473
    http://www.cityofvidor.com
Vidor Chamber of Commerce . . . . (409) 769-6339
    http://www.vidorchamber.com

WEST ORANGE (city). Covers a land area of 3.168 square miles and a water area of 0.031 square miles. Located at 30.08° N. Lat; 93.75° W. Long. Elevation is 10 feet.

Population: 4,187 (1990); 4,111 (2000); 3,823 (2010); 3,683 (2015 projected); Race: 88.6% White, 3.4% Black, 0.8% Asian, 7.2% Other, 8.6% Hispanic of any race (2010); Density: 1,206.6 persons per square mile (2010); Average household size: 2.39 (2010); Median age: 38.8 (2010); Males per 100 females: 95.0 (2010); Marriage status: 18.6% never married, 61.0% now married, 7.3% widowed, 13.1% divorced (2005-2009 5-year

est.); Foreign born: 3.1% (2005-2009 5-year est.); Ancestry (includes multiple ancestries): 11.9% German, 11.6% Irish, 11.0% French Canadian, 10.5% English, 8.9% French (2005-2009 5-year est.).
Economy: Single-family building permits issued: 5 (2010); Multi-family building permits issued: 0 (2010); Employment by occupation: 4.4% management, 20.2% professional, 13.3% services, 22.7% sales, 0.0% farming, 21.9% construction, 17.5% production (2005-2009 5-year est.).
Income: Per capita income: $20,750 (2010); Median household income: $39,648 (2010); Average household income: $49,458 (2010); Percent of households with income of $100,000 or more: 8.1% (2010); Poverty rate: 17.0% (2005-2009 5-year est.).
Taxes: Total city taxes per capita: $463 (2007); City property taxes per capita: $111 (2007).
Education: Percent of population age 25 and over with: High school diploma (including GED) or higher: 82.7% (2010); Bachelor's degree or higher: 10.9% (2010); Master's degree or higher: 2.8% (2010).
Housing: Homeownership rate: 73.3% (2010); Median home value: $53,500 (2010); Median contract rent: $445 per month (2005-2009 5-year est.); Median year structure built: 1961 (2005-2009 5-year est.).
Safety: Violent crime rate: 31.6 per 10,000 population; Property crime rate: 972.9 per 10,000 population (2009).
Transportation: Commute to work: 97.7% car, 0.0% public transportation, 0.0% walk, 0.0% work from home (2005-2009 5-year est.); Travel time to work: 45.4% less than 15 minutes, 33.8% 15 to 30 minutes, 15.0% 30 to 45 minutes, 1.5% 45 to 60 minutes, 4.4% 60 minutes or more (2005-2009 5-year est.)
Additional Information Contacts
City of West Orange. . . . . (409) 883-3468
  http://www.cityofwestorange.com

Palo Pinto County

Located in north central Texas; crossed by the Brazos River; includes part of Possum Kingdom Lake. Covers a land area of 952.93 square miles, a water area of 32.57 square miles, and is located in the Central Time Zone at 32.75° N. Lat., 98.26° W. Long. The county was founded in 1856. County seat is Palo Pinto.

Palo Pinto County is part of the Mineral Wells, TX Micropolitan Statistical Area. The entire metro area includes: Palo Pinto County, TX

Population: 25,055 (1990); 27,026 (2000); 28,036 (2010); 28,476 (2015 projected); Race: 85.7% White, 2.5% Black, 0.6% Asian, 11.1% Other, 16.9% Hispanic of any race (2010); Density: 29.4 persons per square mile (2010); Average household size: 2.49 (2010); Median age: 37.6 (2010); Males per 100 females: 97.5 (2010).
Religion: Five largest groups: 35.6% Southern Baptist Convention, 5.8% Catholic Church, 5.1% The United Methodist Church, 3.8% Churches of Christ, 2.1% The Church of Jesus Christ of Latter-day Saints (2000).
Economy: Unemployment rate: 8.2% (June 2011); Total civilian labor force: 14,299 (June 2011); Leading industries: 19.2% retail trade; 18.5% manufacturing; 14.8% accommodation & food services (2009); Farms: 1,194 totaling 551,494 acres (2007); Companies that employ 500 or more persons: 0 (2009); Companies that employ 100 to 499 persons: 6 (2009); Companies that employ less than 100 persons: 606 (2009); Black-owned businesses: n/a (2007); Hispanic-owned businesses: n/a (2007); Asian-owned businesses: n/a (2007); Women-owned businesses: n/a (2007); Retail sales per capita: $9,240 (2010). Single-family building permits issued: 16 (2010); Multi-family building permits issued: 80 (2010).
Income: Per capita income: $20,554 (2010); Median household income: $40,994 (2010); Average household income: $51,488 (2010); Percent of households with income of $100,000 or more: 9.8% (2010); Poverty rate: 17.0% (2009); Bankruptcy rate: 2.14% (2010).
Taxes: Total county taxes per capita: $289 (2007); County property taxes per capita: $198 (2007).
Education: Percent of population age 25 and over with: High school diploma (including GED) or higher: 75.7% (2010); Bachelor's degree or higher: 13.2% (2010); Master's degree or higher: 3.4% (2010).
Housing: Homeownership rate: 62.3% (2010); Median home value: $69,400 (2010); Median contract rent: $436 per month (2005-2009 5-year est.); Median year structure built: 1972 (2005-2009 5-year est.).
Health: Birth rate: 142.2 per 10,000 population (2009); Death rate: 111.7 per 10,000 population (2009); Age-adjusted cancer mortality rate: 220.4 deaths per 100,000 population (2007); Number of physicians: 9.8 per 10,000 population (2008); Hospital beds: 15.4 per 10,000 population (2007); Hospital admissions: 944.3 per 10,000 population (2007).

Elections: 2008 Presidential election results: 25.3% Obama, 73.4% McCain, 0.0% Nader
National and State Parks: Possum Kingdom State Park
Additional Information Contacts
Palo Pinto County Government . . . . (940) 659-1253
  http://www.co.palo-pinto.tx.us/ips/cms
City of Mineral Wells . . . . (940) 328-7702
  http://www.mineralwellstx.gov
Mineral Wells Area Chamber of Commerce . . . . (940) 325-2557
  http://www.mineralwellstx.com
Possum Kingdom Chamber of Commerce . . . . (940) 779-2424
  http://www.possumkingdomlake.com

Palo Pinto County Communities

GORDON (city). Covers a land area of 0.965 square miles and a water area of 0 square miles. Located at 32.54° N. Lat; 98.36° W. Long. Elevation is 968 feet.
Population: 465 (1990); 451 (2000); 481 (2010); 497 (2015 projected); Race: 90.9% White, 0.4% Black, 0.4% Asian, 8.3% Other, 8.1% Hispanic of any race (2010); Density: 498.2 persons per square mile (2010); Average household size: 2.35 (2010); Median age: 45.6 (2010); Males per 100 females: 83.6 (2010); Marriage status: 19.5% never married, 61.9% now married, 8.6% widowed, 10.0% divorced (2005-2009 5-year est.); Foreign born: 6.9% (2005-2009 5-year est.); Ancestry (includes multiple ancestries): 18.3% German, 16.5% Irish, 14.7% English, 4.2% American, 3.8% French (2005-2009 5-year est.).
Economy: Employment by occupation: 7.5% management, 17.4% professional, 26.4% services, 13.9% sales, 4.5% farming, 16.4% construction, 13.9% production (2005-2009 5-year est.).
Income: Per capita income: $33,927 (2010); Median household income: $59,797 (2010); Average household income: $80,585 (2010); Percent of households with income of $100,000 or more: 25.9% (2010); Poverty rate: 17.0% (2005-2009 5-year est.).
Taxes: Total city taxes per capita: $410 (2007); City property taxes per capita: $66 (2007).
Education: Percent of population age 25 and over with: High school diploma (including GED) or higher: 85.8% (2010); Bachelor's degree or higher: 23.2% (2010); Master's degree or higher: 9.3% (2010).
School District(s)
Gordon ISD (PK-12)
  2009-10 Enrollment: 204 . . . . (254) 693-5582
Housing: Homeownership rate: 72.7% (2010); Median home value: $79,286 (2010); Median contract rent: $425 per month (2005-2009 5-year est.); Median year structure built: 1963 (2005-2009 5-year est.).
Transportation: Commute to work: 89.4% car, 0.0% public transportation, 0.0% walk, 2.4% work from home (2005-2009 5-year est.); Travel time to work: 31.9% less than 15 minutes, 36.7% 15 to 30 minutes, 13.3% 30 to 45 minutes, 2.4% 45 to 60 minutes, 15.7% 60 minutes or more (2005-2009 5-year est.)

GRAFORD (city). Covers a land area of 0.705 square miles and a water area of 0 square miles. Located at 32.93° N. Lat; 98.24° W. Long. Elevation is 958 feet.
Population: 591 (1990); 578 (2000); 584 (2010); 587 (2015 projected); Race: 92.5% White, 0.0% Black, 0.0% Asian, 7.5% Other, 6.7% Hispanic of any race (2010); Density: 828.4 persons per square mile (2010); Average household size: 2.47 (2010); Median age: 38.4 (2010); Males per 100 females: 106.4 (2010); Marriage status: 16.4% never married, 63.5% now married, 5.8% widowed, 14.3% divorced (2005-2009 5-year est.); Foreign born: 2.6% (2005-2009 5-year est.); Ancestry (includes multiple ancestries): 21.7% American, 13.6% English, 5.3% German, 1.9% Irish, 1.6% French (2005-2009 5-year est.).
Economy: Employment by occupation: 9.1% management, 14.1% professional, 16.4% services, 17.3% sales, 0.0% farming, 23.6% construction, 19.5% production (2005-2009 5-year est.).
Income: Per capita income: $22,382 (2010); Median household income: $48,286 (2010); Average household income: $55,201 (2010); Percent of households with income of $100,000 or more: 9.7% (2010); Poverty rate: 14.1% (2005-2009 5-year est.).
Taxes: Total city taxes per capita: $57 (2007); City property taxes per capita: $41 (2007).
Education: Percent of population age 25 and over with: High school diploma (including GED) or higher: 81.1% (2010); Bachelor's degree or higher: 17.9% (2010); Master's degree or higher: 4.3% (2010).

School District(s)

Graford ISD (PK-12)
  2009-10 Enrollment: 332 . . . . (940) 664-3101
Housing: Homeownership rate: 73.7% (2010); Median home value: $55,000 (2010); Median contract rent: $400 per month (2005-2009 5-year est.); Median year structure built: 1973 (2005-2009 5-year est.).
Transportation: Commute to work: 97.7% car, 0.0% public transportation, 1.4% walk, 0.9% work from home (2005-2009 5-year est.); Travel time to work: 14.4% less than 15 minutes, 35.6% 15 to 30 minutes, 19.4% 30 to 45 minutes, 6.9% 45 to 60 minutes, 23.6% 60 minutes or more (2005-2009 5-year est.)

Additional Information Contacts
Possum Kingdom Chamber of Commerce . . . . (940) 779-2424
  http://www.possumkingdomlake.com

MINERAL WELLS (city). Covers a land area of 20.452 square miles and a water area of 0.730 square miles. Located at 32.80° N. Lat; 98.10° W. Long. Elevation is 883 feet.
History: Water from The Crazy Woman Well, dug in 1878, was thought to have medicinal qualities. More wells were dug, and the town of Mineral Wells became a health resort. Medicinal crystals were produced commercially here.
Population: 14,914 (1990); 16,946 (2000); 17,015 (2010); 17,124 (2015 projected); Race: 73.7% White, 10.5% Black, 0.7% Asian, 15.1% Other, 23.8% Hispanic of any race (2010); Density: 832.0 persons per square mile (2010); Average household size: 2.56 (2010); Median age: 34.5 (2010); Males per 100 females: 109.8 (2010); Marriage status: 29.6% never married, 49.0% now married, 6.4% widowed, 15.0% divorced (2005-2009 5-year est.); Foreign born: 8.5% (2005-2009 5-year est.); Ancestry (includes multiple ancestries): 10.5% Irish, 9.6% German, 8.6% English, 6.1% American, 2.5% French (2005-2009 5-year est.).
Economy: Single-family building permits issued: 16 (2010); Multi-family building permits issued: 80 (2010); Employment by occupation: 9.5% management, 14.2% professional, 25.5% services, 19.9% sales, 0.9% farming, 13.2% construction, 16.8% production (2005-2009 5-year est.).
Income: Per capita income: $16,911 (2010); Median household income: $35,287 (2010); Average household income: $45,097 (2010); Percent of households with income of $100,000 or more: 7.6% (2010); Poverty rate: 16.9% (2005-2009 5-year est.).
Taxes: Total city taxes per capita: $469 (2007); City property taxes per capita: $160 (2007).
Education: Percent of population age 25 and over with: High school diploma (including GED) or higher: 70.7% (2010); Bachelor's degree or higher: 11.7% (2010); Master's degree or higher: 3.5% (2010).

School District(s)

Mineral Wells ISD (PK-12)
  2009-10 Enrollment: 3,568 . . . . (940) 325-6404
Housing: Homeownership rate: 52.5% (2010); Median home value: $60,142 (2010); Median contract rent: $463 per month (2005-2009 5-year est.); Median year structure built: 1964 (2005-2009 5-year est.).
Hospitals: Palo Pinto General Hospital (99 beds)
Safety: Violent crime rate: 49.2 per 10,000 population; Property crime rate: 528.1 per 10,000 population (2009).
Newspapers: Mineral Wells Index (Regional news; Circulation 4,000)
Transportation: Commute to work: 89.3% car, 0.0% public transportation, 1.7% walk, 1.9% work from home (2005-2009 5-year est.); Travel time to work: 56.7% less than 15 minutes, 20.8% 15 to 30 minutes, 8.8% 30 to 45 minutes, 7.2% 45 to 60 minutes, 6.5% 60 minutes or more (2005-2009 5-year est.)
Airports: Mineral Wells (general aviation)

Additional Information Contacts
City of Mineral Wells . . . . (940) 328-7702
  http://www.mineralwellstx.gov
Mineral Wells Area Chamber of Commerce . . . . (940) 325-2557
  http://www.mineralwellstx.com

MINGUS (city). Covers a land area of 1.554 square miles and a water area of 0 square miles. Located at 32.53° N. Lat; 98.42° W. Long. Elevation is 951 feet.
Population: 229 (1990); 246 (2000); 271 (2010); 280 (2015 projected); Race: 90.8% White, 0.4% Black, 0.7% Asian, 8.1% Other, 7.7% Hispanic of any race (2010); Density: 174.4 persons per square mile (2010); Average household size: 2.34 (2010); Median age: 45.1 (2010); Males per 100 females: 88.2 (2010); Marriage status: 11.9% never married, 61.9% now married, 15.5% widowed, 10.7% divorced (2005-2009 5-year est.);

Foreign born: 0.0% (2005-2009 5-year est.); Ancestry (includes multiple ancestries): 20.2% German, 15.4% Irish, 8.5% Dutch, 8.5% English, 5.3% American (2005-2009 5-year est.).
Economy: Employment by occupation: 16.9% management, 15.7% professional, 20.5% services, 10.8% sales, 0.0% farming, 19.3% construction, 16.9% production (2005-2009 5-year est.).
Income: Per capita income: $33,927 (2010); Median household income: $61,364 (2010); Average household income: $81,638 (2010); Percent of households with income of $100,000 or more: 26.7% (2010); Poverty rate: 14.9% (2005-2009 5-year est.).
Taxes: Total city taxes per capita: $143 (2007); City property taxes per capita: $47 (2007).
Education: Percent of population age 25 and over with: High school diploma (including GED) or higher: 85.5% (2010); Bachelor's degree or higher: 22.8% (2010); Master's degree or higher: 9.3% (2010).
Housing: Homeownership rate: 72.4% (2010); Median home value: $80,000 (2010); Median contract rent: $338 per month (2005-2009 5-year est.); Median year structure built: 1948 (2005-2009 5-year est.).
Transportation: Commute to work: 90.7% car, 0.0% public transportation, 0.0% walk, 9.3% work from home (2005-2009 5-year est.); Travel time to work: 39.7% less than 15 minutes, 14.7% 15 to 30 minutes, 13.2% 30 to 45 minutes, 16.2% 45 to 60 minutes, 16.2% 60 minutes or more (2005-2009 5-year est.)

PALO PINTO (unincorporated postal area, zip code 76484). County seat. Covers a land area of 138.671 square miles and a water area of 0.477 square miles. Located at 32.72° N. Lat; 98.33° W. Long. Elevation is 1,043 feet.
History: Palo Pinto got its name from the varicolored petrified wood used as building materials in the town. The name is Spanish for "painted post."
Population: 912 (2000); Race: 91.8% White, 0.6% Black, 0.0% Asian, 7.6% Other, 6.7% Hispanic of any race (2000); Density: 6.6 persons per square mile (2000); Age: 18.8% under 18, 17.4% over 64 (2000); Marriage status: 16.4% never married, 64.6% now married, 6.5% widowed, 12.5% divorced (2000); Foreign born: 1.8% (2000); Ancestry (includes multiple ancestries): 25.9% American, 7.2% English, 5.8% German, 3.8% Irish (2000).
Economy: Employment by occupation: 12.6% management, 20.7% professional, 12.8% services, 21.7% sales, 5.0% farming, 14.4% construction, 12.8% production (2000).
Income: Per capita income: $17,410 (2000); Median household income: $34,861 (2000); Poverty rate: 179.1% (2000).
Education: Percent of population age 25 and over with: High school diploma (including GED) or higher: 80.5% (2000); Bachelor's degree or higher: 20.0% (2000).

School District(s)

Palo Pinto ISD (PK-06)
  2009-10 Enrollment: 91 . . . . (940) 659-2745
Housing: Homeownership rate: 77.2% (2000); Median home value: $79,400 (2000); Median contract rent: $320 per month (2000); Median year structure built: 1976 (2000).
Transportation: Commute to work: 92.4% car, 0.0% public transportation, 1.4% walk, 4.3% work from home (2000); Travel time to work: 29.4% less than 15 minutes, 24.0% 15 to 30 minutes, 16.4% 30 to 45 minutes, 13.6% 45 to 60 minutes, 16.7% 60 minutes or more (2000)

SANTO (unincorporated postal area, zip code 76472). Covers a land area of 91.317 square miles and a water area of 0.375 square miles. Located at 32.61° N. Lat; 98.17° W. Long. Elevation is 830 feet.
Population: 1,262 (2000); Race: 97.0% White, 0.0% Black, 0.0% Asian, 3.0% Other, 5.9% Hispanic of any race (2000); Density: 13.8 persons per square mile (2000); Age: 28.4% under 18, 12.7% over 64 (2000); Marriage status: 11.7% never married, 73.8% now married, 7.2% widowed, 7.2% divorced (2000); Foreign born: 0.9% (2000); Ancestry (includes multiple ancestries): 28.7% American, 8.9% Irish, 8.4% English, 6.5% German (2000).
Economy: Employment by occupation: 13.8% management, 19.0% professional, 19.3% services, 18.6% sales, 3.3% farming, 9.2% construction, 16.8% production (2000).
Income: Per capita income: $15,052 (2000); Median household income: $38,155 (2000); Poverty rate: 179.1% (2000).
Education: Percent of population age 25 and over with: High school diploma (including GED) or higher: 77.4% (2000); Bachelor's degree or higher: 9.5% (2000).

School District(s)
Santo ISD (PK-12)
  2009-10 Enrollment: 510 . . . . (940) 769-2835
Housing: Homeownership rate: 83.7% (2000); Median home value: $42,700 (2000); Median contract rent: $293 per month (2000); Median year structure built: 1970 (2000).
Transportation: Commute to work: 96.9% car, 0.0% public transportation, 1.7% walk, 1.3% work from home (2000); Travel time to work: 23.8% less than 15 minutes, 24.0% 15 to 30 minutes, 27.3% 30 to 45 minutes, 6.4% 45 to 60 minutes, 18.4% 60 minutes or more (2000)

STRAWN (city). Covers a land area of 0.788 square miles and a water area of 0 square miles. Located at 32.55° N. Lat; 98.49° W. Long. Elevation is 1,004 feet.
Population: 733 (1990); 739 (2000); 793 (2010); 821 (2015 projected); Race: 74.0% White, 0.5% Black, 0.1% Asian, 25.3% Other, 28.9% Hispanic of any race (2010); Density: 1,006.6 persons per square mile (2010); Average household size: 2.53 (2010); Median age: 34.1 (2010); Males per 100 females: 100.3 (2010); Marriage status: 27.4% never married, 57.6% now married, 6.7% widowed, 8.3% divorced (2005-2009 5-year est.); Foreign born: 6.1% (2005-2009 5-year est.); Ancestry (includes multiple ancestries): 8.9% German, 7.3% English, 4.9% Scottish, 3.8% Italian, 3.4% Polish (2005-2009 5-year est.).
Economy: Employment by occupation: 9.8% management, 14.7% professional, 18.8% services, 14.7% sales, 2.3% farming, 11.6% construction, 28.0% production (2005-2009 5-year est.).
Income: Per capita income: $22,455 (2010); Median household income: $44,340 (2010); Average household income: $56,369 (2010); Percent of households with income of $100,000 or more: 11.8% (2010); Poverty rate: 5.8% (2005-2009 5-year est.).
Taxes: Total city taxes per capita: $57 (2007); City property taxes per capita: $40 (2007).
Education: Percent of population age 25 and over with: High school diploma (including GED) or higher: 73.5% (2010); Bachelor's degree or higher: 14.3% (2010); Master's degree or higher: 3.3% (2010).
School District(s)
Strawn ISD (PK-12)
  2009-10 Enrollment: 178 . . . . (254) 672-5313
Housing: Homeownership rate: 62.7% (2010); Median home value: $40,682 (2010); Median contract rent: $299 per month (2005-2009 5-year est.); Median year structure built: 1952 (2005-2009 5-year est.).
Transportation: Commute to work: 79.0% car, 0.0% public transportation, 8.0% walk, 4.1% work from home (2005-2009 5-year est.); Travel time to work: 54.9% less than 15 minutes, 3.7% 15 to 30 minutes, 14.2% 30 to 45 minutes, 8.0% 45 to 60 minutes, 19.1% 60 minutes or more (2005-2009 5-year est.)

Panola County

Located in east Texas; bounded on the east by Louisiana; drained by the Sabine River. Covers a land area of 800.92 square miles, a water area of 20.42 square miles, and is located in the Central Time Zone at 32.15° N. Lat., 94.32° W. Long. The county was founded in 1846. County seat is Carthage.

Weather Station: Carthage   Elevation: 339 feet

	Jan	Feb	Mar	Apr	May	Jun	Jul	Aug	Sep	Oct	Nov	Dec
High	57	62	70	76	83	90	94	94	88	78	67	58
Low	35	38	45	52	61	68	71	70	63	53	44	36
Precip	4.3	4.4	4.2	4.0	4.8	4.9	3.1	3.1	3.6	5.1	4.8	5.1
Snow	0.4	0.2	0.1	tr	0.0	0.0	0.0	0.0	0.0	0.0	tr	0.2

High and Low temperatures in degrees Fahrenheit; Precipitation and Snow in inches

Population: 22,035 (1990); 22,756 (2000); 23,470 (2010); 23,775 (2015 projected); Race: 76.5% White, 17.7% Black, 0.5% Asian, 5.4% Other, 6.4% Hispanic of any race (2010); Density: 29.3 persons per square mile (2010); Average household size: 2.47 (2010); Median age: 38.7 (2010); Males per 100 females: 94.4 (2010).
Religion: Five largest groups: 21.7% Southern Baptist Convention, 12.0% Baptist Missionary Association of America, 8.9% The United Methodist Church, 6.4% The American Baptist Association, 2.6% Catholic Church (2000).
Economy: Unemployment rate: 7.5% (June 2011); Total civilian labor force: 14,107 (June 2011); Leading industries: 16.3% construction; 15.6% mining; 12.6% manufacturing (2009); Farms: 1,042 totaling 217,757 acres (2007); Companies that employ 500 or more persons: 1 (2009); Companies

that employ 100 to 499 persons: 13 (2009); Companies that employ less than 100 persons: 478 (2009); Black-owned businesses: n/a (2007); Hispanic-owned businesses: n/a (2007); Asian-owned businesses: n/a (2007); Women-owned businesses: 443 (2007); Retail sales per capita: $7,459 (2010). Single-family building permits issued: 10 (2010); Multi-family building permits issued: 0 (2010).
Income: Per capita income: $21,795 (2010); Median household income: $43,143 (2010); Average household income: $54,784 (2010); Percent of households with income of $100,000 or more: 13.1% (2010); Poverty rate: 13.2% (2009); Bankruptcy rate: 2.16% (2010).
Taxes: Total county taxes per capita: $512 (2007); County property taxes per capita: $493 (2007).
Education: Percent of population age 25 and over with: High school diploma (including GED) or higher: 81.4% (2010); Bachelor's degree or higher: 11.9% (2010); Master's degree or higher: 3.7% (2010).
Housing: Homeownership rate: 80.6% (2010); Median home value: $70,189 (2010); Median contract rent: $374 per month (2005-2009 5-year est.); Median year structure built: 1971 (2005-2009 5-year est.)
Health: Birth rate: 138.6 per 10,000 population (2009); Death rate: 97.8 per 10,000 population (2009); Age-adjusted cancer mortality rate: 216.9 deaths per 100,000 population (2007); Number of physicians: 3.9 per 10,000 population (2008); Hospital beds: 16.1 per 10,000 population (2007); Hospital admissions: 633.1 per 10,000 population (2007).
Elections: 2008 Presidential election results: 25.3% Obama, 74.2% McCain, 0.1% Nader
Additional Information Contacts
Panola County Government. . . . . (903) 693-0391
  http://www.co.panola.tx.us/ips/cms
City of Carthage . . . . (903) 693-3868
  http://www.carthagetexas.com
Panola County Chamber of Commerce . . . . (903) 693-6634
  http://www.carthagetexas.com

Panola County Communities

BECKVILLE (city). Covers a land area of 1.211 square miles and a water area of 0 square miles. Located at 32.24° N. Lat; 94.45° W. Long. Elevation is 341 feet.
Population: 783 (1990); 752 (2000); 748 (2010); 744 (2015 projected); Race: 58.4% White, 28.1% Black, 0.0% Asian, 13.5% Other, 14.2% Hispanic of any race (2010); Density: 617.6 persons per square mile (2010); Average household size: 2.48 (2010); Median age: 35.6 (2010); Males per 100 females: 100.0 (2010); Marriage status: 17.2% never married, 63.3% now married, 8.0% widowed, 11.5% divorced (2005-2009 5-year est.); Foreign born: 2.0% (2005-2009 5-year est.); Ancestry (includes multiple ancestries): 38.4% American, 7.3% Irish, 5.1% German, 4.0% English, 1.7% Italian (2005-2009 5-year est.).
Economy: Employment by occupation: 6.4% management, 20.5% professional, 9.6% services, 25.8% sales, 0.0% farming, 8.0% construction, 29.8% production (2005-2009 5-year est.).
Income: Per capita income: $24,399 (2010); Median household income: $49,625 (2010); Average household income: $60,637 (2010); Percent of households with income of $100,000 or more: 18.5% (2010); Poverty rate: 10.9% (2005-2009 5-year est.).
Taxes: Total city taxes per capita: $92 (2007); City property taxes per capita: $0 (2007).
Education: Percent of population age 25 and over with: High school diploma (including GED) or higher: 86.3% (2010); Bachelor's degree or higher: 8.7% (2010); Master's degree or higher: 3.2% (2010).
School District(s)
Beckville ISD (PK-12)
  2009-10 Enrollment: 656 . . . . (903) 678-3311
Housing: Homeownership rate: 73.2% (2010); Median home value: $54,750 (2010); Median contract rent: $329 per month (2005-2009 5-year est.); Median year structure built: 1962 (2005-2009 5-year est.).
Transportation: Commute to work: 95.5% car, 0.0% public transportation, 4.5% walk, 0.0% work from home (2005-2009 5-year est.); Travel time to work: 20.5% less than 15 minutes, 37.1% 15 to 30 minutes, 30.1% 30 to 45 minutes, 7.5% 45 to 60 minutes, 4.8% 60 minutes or more (2005-2009 5-year est.)

CARTHAGE (city). County seat. Covers a land area of 10.515 square miles and a water area of 0.030 square miles. Located at 32.15° N. Lat; 94.34° W. Long. Elevation is 312 feet.

History: Carthage was founded in 1848. The town developed around the lumber industry and the natural gas deposits.
Population: 6,613 (1990); 6,664 (2000); 6,690 (2010); 6,697 (2015 projected); Race: 69.1% White, 23.7% Black, 1.3% Asian, 6.0% Other, 7.2% Hispanic of any race (2010); Density: 636.2 persons per square mile (2010); Average household size: 2.36 (2010); Median age: 36.9 (2010); Males per 100 females: 84.1 (2010); Marriage status: 23.6% never married, 51.5% now married, 12.9% widowed, 12.0% divorced (2005-2009 5-year est.); Foreign born: 1.6% (2005-2009 5-year est.); Ancestry (includes multiple ancestries): 22.6% American, 10.8% Irish, 9.4% English, 4.1% German, 3.3% French (2005-2009 5-year est.).
Economy: Single-family building permits issued: 10 (2010); Multi-family building permits issued: 0 (2010); Employment by occupation: 5.9% management, 16.3% professional, 20.8% services, 22.6% sales, 0.0% farming, 14.4% construction, 19.9% production (2005-2009 5-year est.).
Income: Per capita income: $22,899 (2010); Median household income: $42,453 (2010); Average household income: $56,676 (2010); Percent of households with income of $100,000 or more: 15.6% (2010); Poverty rate: 12.8% (2005-2009 5-year est.).
Taxes: Total city taxes per capita: $439 (2007); City property taxes per capita: $126 (2007).
Education: Percent of population age 25 and over with: High school diploma (including GED) or higher: 83.9% (2010); Bachelor's degree or higher: 18.8% (2010); Master's degree or higher: 6.0% (2010).

School District(s)
Carthage ISD (PK-12)
    2009-10 Enrollment: 2,779 . . . . (903) 693-3806
Panola Charter School (08-12)
    2009-10 Enrollment: 140 . . . . (903) 693-6355

Two-year College(s)
Panola College (Public)
    Fall 2009 Enrollment: 2,123. . . . . (903) 693-2000
    2010-11 Tuition: In-state $2,328; Out-of-state $2,952
Housing: Homeownership rate: 69.1% (2010); Median home value: $75,827 (2010); Median contract rent: $390 per month (2005-2009 5-year est.); Median year structure built: 1970 (2005-2009 5-year est.).
Hospitals: East Texas Medical Center-Carthage (49 beds)
Safety: Violent crime rate: 34.7 per 10,000 population; Property crime rate: 232.2 per 10,000 population (2009).
Newspapers: Panola County Shopper (Community news; Circulation 5,000); Panola Watchman (Local news; Circulation 5,000)
Transportation: Commute to work: 96.6% car, 0.0% public transportation, 0.8% walk, 2.1% work from home (2005-2009 5-year est.); Travel time to work: 47.2% less than 15 minutes, 21.9% 15 to 30 minutes, 18.1% 30 to 45 minutes, 10.2% 45 to 60 minutes, 2.5% 60 minutes or more (2005-2009 5-year est.)
Additional Information Contacts
City of Carthage. . . . . (903) 693-3868
    http://www.carthagetexas.com
Panola County Chamber of Commerce . . . . (903) 693-6634
    http://www.carthagetexas.com

DE BERRY (unincorporated postal area, zip code 75639). Covers a land area of 164.267 square miles and a water area of 0.637 square miles. Located at 32.28° N. Lat; 94.18° W. Long. Elevation is 361 feet.
Population: 3,305 (2000); Race: 69.0% White, 29.1% Black, 0.0% Asian, 1.9% Other, 0.8% Hispanic of any race (2000); Density: 20.1 persons per square mile (2000); Age: 27.1% under 18, 11.6% over 64 (2000); Marriage status: 23.8% never married, 60.5% now married, 8.4% widowed, 7.3% divorced (2000); Foreign born: 1.6% (2000); Ancestry (includes multiple ancestries): 19.4% American, 7.4% German, 7.1% Irish, 5.3% French (2000).
Economy: Employment by occupation: 9.2% management, 12.2% professional, 13.9% services, 20.0% sales, 1.1% farming, 18.1% construction, 25.5% production (2000).
Income: Per capita income: $15,555 (2000); Median household income: $31,789 (2000); Poverty rate: 179.1% (2000).
Education: Percent of population age 25 and over with: High school diploma (including GED) or higher: 70.8% (2000); Bachelor's degree or higher: 6.7% (2000).
Housing: Homeownership rate: 84.3% (2000); Median home value: $47,100 (2000); Median contract rent: $292 per month (2000); Median year structure built: 1980 (2000).
Transportation: Commute to work: 93.3% car, 0.0% public transportation, 2.4% walk, 3.5% work from home (2000); Travel time to work: 20.6% less

than 15 minutes, 27.7% 15 to 30 minutes, 30.6% 30 to 45 minutes, 12.5% 45 to 60 minutes, 8.6% 60 minutes or more (2000)

GARY CITY (town). Aka Gary. Covers a land area of 1.896 square miles and a water area of 0 square miles. Located at 32.03° N. Lat; 94.36° W. Long. Elevation is 292 feet.
Population: 271 (1990); 303 (2000); 367 (2010); 396 (2015 projected); Race: 85.3% White, 9.3% Black, 0.3% Asian, 5.2% Other, 5.2% Hispanic of any race (2010); Density: 193.6 persons per square mile (2010); Average household size: 2.43 (2010); Median age: 36.8 (2010); Males per 100 females: 96.3 (2010); Marriage status: 29.3% never married, 65.6% now married, 1.1% widowed, 4.0% divorced (2005-2009 5-year est.); Foreign born: 0.9% (2005-2009 5-year est.); Ancestry (includes multiple ancestries): 48.6% American, 11.9% German, 6.3% Irish, 4.4% English, 3.8% Scotch-Irish (2005-2009 5-year est.).
Economy: Employment by occupation: 10.9% management, 7.0% professional, 14.0% services, 18.6% sales, 4.7% farming, 27.1% construction, 17.8% production (2005-2009 5-year est.).
Income: Per capita income: $21,504 (2010); Median household income: $37,500 (2010); Average household income: $49,868 (2010); Percent of households with income of $100,000 or more: 10.6% (2010); Poverty rate: 19.1% (2005-2009 5-year est.).
Taxes: Total city taxes per capita: $23 (2007); City property taxes per capita: $0 (2007).
Education: Percent of population age 25 and over with: High school diploma (including GED) or higher: 72.2% (2010); Bachelor's degree or higher: 10.5% (2010); Master's degree or higher: 3.0% (2010).

School District(s)
Gary ISD (PK-12)
    2009-10 Enrollment: 384 . . . . (903) 685-2291
Housing: Homeownership rate: 84.8% (2010); Median home value: $57,778 (2010); Median contract rent: $344 per month (2005-2009 5-year est.); Median year structure built: 1965 (2005-2009 5-year est.).
Transportation: Commute to work: 86.8% car, 0.0% public transportation, 3.9% walk, 2.3% work from home (2005-2009 5-year est.); Travel time to work: 14.3% less than 15 minutes, 66.7% 15 to 30 minutes, 11.1% 30 to 45 minutes, 5.6% 45 to 60 minutes, 2.4% 60 minutes or more (2005-2009 5-year est.)

LONG BRANCH (unincorporated postal area, zip code 75669). Covers a land area of 65.800 square miles and a water area of 0.040 square miles. Located at 32.03° N. Lat; 94.57° W. Long. Elevation is 371 feet.
Population: 700 (2000); Race: 75.4% White, 24.6% Black, 0.0% Asian, 0.0% Other, 5.6% Hispanic of any race (2000); Density: 10.6 persons per square mile (2000); Age: 29.0% under 18, 14.1% over 64 (2000); Marriage status: 17.6% never married, 63.6% now married, 9.3% widowed, 9.5% divorced (2000); Foreign born: 0.0% (2000); Ancestry (includes multiple ancestries): 29.4% American, 4.5% British, 4.1% English, 2.0% German (2000).
Economy: Employment by occupation: 15.5% management, 11.6% professional, 11.6% services, 31.4% sales, 0.0% farming, 9.3% construction, 20.5% production (2000).
Income: Per capita income: $13,080 (2000); Median household income: $26,875 (2000); Poverty rate: 179.1% (2000).
Education: Percent of population age 25 and over with: High school diploma (including GED) or higher: 70.6% (2000); Bachelor's degree or higher: 0.9% (2000).
Housing: Homeownership rate: 88.7% (2000); Median home value: $42,000 (2000); Median contract rent: $272 per month (2000); Median year structure built: 1972 (2000).
Transportation: Commute to work: 97.3% car, 0.0% public transportation, 0.8% walk, 1.9% work from home (2000); Travel time to work: 18.6% less than 15 minutes, 41.9% 15 to 30 minutes, 23.7% 30 to 45 minutes, 4.7% 45 to 60 minutes, 11.1% 60 minutes or more (2000)

Parker County

Located in north Texas; drained by the Brazos and Clear Fork of the Trinity Rivers. Covers a land area of 903.51 square miles, a water area of 6.58 square miles, and is located in the Central Time Zone at 32.77° N. Lat., 97.76° W. Long. The county was founded in 1855. County seat is Weatherford.

Parker County is part of the Dallas-Fort Worth-Arlington, TX Metropolitan Statistical Area. The entire metro area includes: Dallas-Plano-Irving, TX Metropolitan Division (Collin County, TX; Dallas County, TX; Delta County, TX; Denton County, TX; Ellis County, TX; Hunt County, TX; Kaufman County, TX; Rockwall County, TX); Fort Worth-Arlington, TX Metropolitan Division (Johnson County, TX; Parker County, TX; Tarrant County, TX; Wise County, TX)

Weather Station: Weatherford   Elevation: 955 feet

	Jan	Feb	Mar	Apr	May	Jun	Jul	Aug	Sep	Oct	Nov	Dec
High	56	59	67	76	83	90	95	95	88	78	66	57
Low	30	34	42	50	60	67	71	70	62	51	41	32
Precip	1.6	2.8	3.1	2.5	4.6	4.4	1.9	2.1	3.0	3.9	2.9	2.2
Snow	0.1	0.4	tr	0.0	0.0	0.0	0.0	0.0	0.0	0.0	0.0	0.2

High and Low temperatures in degrees Fahrenheit; Precipitation and Snow in inches

Population: 64,785 (1990); 88,495 (2000); 116,050 (2010); 129,245 (2015 projected); Race: 89.4% White, 2.6% Black, 0.6% Asian, 7.4% Other, 10.4% Hispanic of any race (2010); Density: 128.4 persons per square mile (2010); Average household size: 2.82 (2010); Median age: 36.0 (2010); Males per 100 females: 101.2 (2010).
Religion: Five largest groups: 29.5% Southern Baptist Convention, 7.1% The United Methodist Church, 3.2% Churches of Christ, 2.8% Catholic Church, 1.1% Church of God (Cleveland, Tennessee) (2000).
Economy: Unemployment rate: 8.0% (June 2011); Total civilian labor force: 56,035 (June 2011); Leading industries: 20.7% retail trade; 13.3% accommodation & food services; 11.9% health care and social assistance (2009); Farms: 3,677 totaling 441,575 acres (2007); Companies that employ 500 or more persons: 0 (2009); Companies that employ 100 to 499 persons: 31 (2009); Companies that employ less than 100 persons: 2,145 (2009); Black-owned businesses: n/a (2007); Hispanic-owned businesses: 552 (2007); Asian-owned businesses: n/a (2007); Women-owned businesses: 2,975 (2007); Retail sales per capita: $11,274 (2010). Single-family building permits issued: 144 (2010); Multi-family building permits issued: 3 (2010).
Income: Per capita income: $26,663 (2010); Median household income: $61,033 (2010); Average household income: $76,366 (2010); Percent of households with income of $100,000 or more: 22.9% (2010); Poverty rate: 9.9% (2009); Bankruptcy rate: 3.24% (2010).
Taxes: Total county taxes per capita: $234 (2007); County property taxes per capita: $185 (2007).
Education: Percent of population age 25 and over with: High school diploma (including GED) or higher: 84.0% (2010); Bachelor's degree or higher: 19.5% (2010); Master's degree or higher: 6.6% (2010).
Housing: Homeownership rate: 77.9% (2010); Median home value: $134,006 (2010); Median contract rent: $550 per month (2005-2009 5-year est.); Median year structure built: 1989 (2005-2009 5-year est.)
Health: Birth rate: 126.0 per 10,000 population (2009); Death rate: 76.1 per 10,000 population (2009); Age-adjusted cancer mortality rate: 199.7 deaths per 100,000 population (2007); Number of physicians: 12.3 per 10,000 population (2008); Hospital beds: 6.8 per 10,000 population (2007); Hospital admissions: 456.7 per 10,000 population (2007).
Environment: Air Quality Index: 83.6% good, 14.8% moderate, 1.6% unhealthy for sensitive individuals, 0.0% unhealthy (percent of days in 2008)
Elections: 2008 Presidential election results: 21.9% Obama, 77.1% McCain, 0.1% Nader
National and State Parks: Lake Mineral Wells State Park
Additional Information Contacts
Parker County Government . . . . (817) 599-6591
   http://www.co.parker.tx.us/ips/cms
City of Weatherford . . . . (817) 598-4000
   http://www.ci.weatherford.tx.us
City of Willow Park . . . . (817) 441-7108
   http://www.willowpark.org
East Parker County Chamber of Commerce . . . . (817) 441-7844
   http://www.eastparkchamber.com
Springtown Area Chamber of Commerce . . . . (817) 220-7828
   http://www.springtownchamber.org
Town of Annetta . . . . (817) 441-5770
   http://www.annetta.org
Weatherford Chamber of Commerce . . . . (817) 596-3801
   http://www.weatherford-chamber.com

Parker County Communities

ALEDO (city). Covers a land area of 1.898 square miles and a water area of 0 square miles. Located at 32.69° N. Lat; 97.60° W. Long. Elevation is 883 feet.
Population: 1,172 (1990); 1,726 (2000); 2,558 (2010); 2,948 (2015 projected); Race: 95.4% White, 0.5% Black, 0.3% Asian, 3.9% Other, 3.5% Hispanic of any race (2010); Density: 1,347.5 persons per square mile (2010); Average household size: 3.00 (2010); Median age: 34.3 (2010); Males per 100 females: 88.9 (2010); Marriage status: 21.1% never married, 65.7% now married, 4.0% widowed, 9.2% divorced (2005-2009 5-year est.); Foreign born: 3.4% (2005-2009 5-year est.); Ancestry (includes multiple ancestries): 20.5% German, 20.1% Irish, 14.2% English, 9.2% American, 8.5% Scottish (2005-2009 5-year est.).
Economy: Single-family building permits issued: 11 (2010); Multi-family building permits issued: 0 (2010); Employment by occupation: 15.5% management, 24.2% professional, 13.4% services, 22.5% sales, 0.5% farming, 11.6% construction, 12.3% production (2005-2009 5-year est.).
Income: Per capita income: $29,775 (2010); Median household income: $73,500 (2010); Average household income: $89,368 (2010); Percent of households with income of $100,000 or more: 28.8% (2010); Poverty rate: 11.1% (2005-2009 5-year est.).
Taxes: Total city taxes per capita: $470 (2007); City property taxes per capita: $168 (2007).
Education: Percent of population age 25 and over with: High school diploma (including GED) or higher: 93.6% (2010); Bachelor's degree or higher: 26.7% (2010); Master's degree or higher: 8.4% (2010).

School District(s)
Aledo ISD (PK-12)
   2009-10 Enrollment: 4,589 . . . . (817) 441-8327
Housing: Homeownership rate: 82.8% (2010); Median home value: $144,093 (2010); Median contract rent: $933 per month (2005-2009 5-year est.); Median year structure built: 1994 (2005-2009 5-year est.).
Transportation: Commute to work: 95.7% car, 0.0% public transportation, 1.5% walk, 2.3% work from home (2005-2009 5-year est.); Travel time to work: 20.2% less than 15 minutes, 46.6% 15 to 30 minutes, 23.2% 30 to 45 minutes, 6.4% 45 to 60 minutes, 3.5% 60 minutes or more (2005-2009 5-year est.)
Additional Information Contacts
East Parker County Chamber of Commerce . . . . (817) 441-7844
   http://www.eastparkchamber.com

ANNETTA (town). Covers a land area of 2.170 square miles and a water area of 0.046 square miles. Located at 32.69° N. Lat; 97.65° W. Long. Elevation is 869 feet.
Population: 717 (1990); 1,108 (2000); 1,691 (2010); 1,956 (2015 projected); Race: 95.4% White, 0.1% Black, 0.1% Asian, 4.4% Other, 4.6% Hispanic of any race (2010); Density: 779.1 persons per square mile (2010); Average household size: 3.19 (2010); Median age: 35.3 (2010); Males per 100 females: 98.0 (2010); Marriage status: 21.1% never married, 67.1% now married, 0.7% widowed, 11.1% divorced (2005-2009 5-year est.); Foreign born: 3.0% (2005-2009 5-year est.); Ancestry (includes multiple ancestries): 20.7% German, 16.0% Irish, 14.4% English, 8.3% American, 6.3% Scotch-Irish (2005-2009 5-year est.).
Economy: Single-family building permits issued: 0 (2010); Multi-family building permits issued: 0 (2010); Employment by occupation: 21.1% management, 27.3% professional, 9.1% services, 31.0% sales, 0.0% farming, 6.0% construction, 5.4% production (2005-2009 5-year est.).
Income: Per capita income: $40,358 (2010); Median household income: $102,273 (2010); Average household income: $128,958 (2010); Percent of households with income of $100,000 or more: 51.1% (2010); Poverty rate: 0.9% (2005-2009 5-year est.).
Taxes: Total city taxes per capita: $35 (2007); City property taxes per capita: $0 (2007).
Education: Percent of population age 25 and over with: High school diploma (including GED) or higher: 90.8% (2010); Bachelor's degree or higher: 41.1% (2010); Master's degree or higher: 12.5% (2010).
Housing: Homeownership rate: 89.8% (2010); Median home value: $273,529 (2010); Median contract rent: $1,054 per month (2005-2009 5-year est.); Median year structure built: 1992 (2005-2009 5-year est.).
Transportation: Commute to work: 92.7% car, 0.5% public transportation, 1.4% walk, 4.9% work from home (2005-2009 5-year est.); Travel time to work: 10.7% less than 15 minutes, 36.6% 15 to 30 minutes, 40.4% 30 to 45 minutes, 7.2% 45 to 60 minutes, 5.0% 60 minutes or more (2005-2009 5-year est.)

Additional Information Contacts
Town of Annetta............................... (817) 441-5770
  http://www.annetta.org

ANNETTA NORTH (town). Covers a land area of 3.334 square miles and a water area of 0 square miles. Located at 32.72° N. Lat; 97.68° W. Long. Elevation is 860 feet.

Population: 205 (1990); 467 (2000); 718 (2010); 831 (2015 projected); Race: 95.1% White, 0.0% Black, 0.1% Asian, 4.7% Other, 4.9% Hispanic of any race (2010); Density: 215.4 persons per square mile (2010); Average household size: 3.16 (2010); Median age: 36.4 (2010); Males per 100 females: 97.8 (2010); Marriage status: 22.1% never married, 65.3% now married, 2.9% widowed, 9.7% divorced (2005-2009 5-year est.); Foreign born: 0.4% (2005-2009 5-year est.); Ancestry (includes multiple ancestries): 22.4% English, 16.3% Irish, 13.2% Scotch-Irish, 12.5% German, 8.3% American (2005-2009 5-year est.).

Economy: Employment by occupation: 23.2% management, 33.2% professional, 10.4% services, 17.2% sales, 1.2% farming, 10.8% construction, 4.0% production (2005-2009 5-year est.).

Income: Per capita income: $41,071 (2010); Median household income: $103,879 (2010); Average household income: $131,178 (2010); Percent of households with income of $100,000 or more: 52.0% (2010); Poverty rate: 8.6% (2005-2009 5-year est.).

Taxes: Total city taxes per capita: $87 (2007); City property taxes per capita: $0 (2007).

Education: Percent of population age 25 and over with: High school diploma (including GED) or higher: 91.0% (2010); Bachelor's degree or higher: 41.8% (2010); Master's degree or higher: 13.3% (2010).

Housing: Homeownership rate: 89.9% (2010); Median home value: $277,083 (2010); Median contract rent: $1,025 per month (2005-2009 5-year est.); Median year structure built: 1991 (2005-2009 5-year est.).

Transportation: Commute to work: 83.2% car, 0.8% public transportation, 12.3% walk, 3.7% work from home (2005-2009 5-year est.); Travel time to work: 21.3% less than 15 minutes, 28.1% 15 to 30 minutes, 39.1% 30 to 45 minutes, 6.0% 45 to 60 minutes, 5.5% 60 minutes or more (2005-2009 5-year est.)

ANNETTA SOUTH (town). Covers a land area of 1.902 square miles and a water area of 0.018 square miles. Located at 32.66° N. Lat; 97.65° W. Long. Elevation is 974 feet.

Population: 427 (1990); 555 (2000); 849 (2010); 982 (2015 projected); Race: 95.4% White, 0.1% Black, 0.1% Asian, 4.4% Other, 4.6% Hispanic of any race (2010); Density: 446.3 persons per square mile (2010); Average household size: 3.19 (2010); Median age: 36.0 (2010); Males per 100 females: 98.4 (2010); Marriage status: 27.5% never married, 56.1% now married, 7.3% widowed, 9.1% divorced (2005-2009 5-year est.); Foreign born: 0.0% (2005-2009 5-year est.); Ancestry (includes multiple ancestries): 16.8% German, 11.9% American, 7.0% English, 6.1% Irish, 3.5% French (2005-2009 5-year est.).

Economy: Employment by occupation: 24.4% management, 24.1% professional, 10.7% services, 31.8% sales, 0.0% farming, 4.3% construction, 4.7% production (2005-2009 5-year est.).

Income: Per capita income: $40,358 (2010); Median household income: $102,273 (2010); Average household income: $127,914 (2010); Percent of households with income of $100,000 or more: 51.1% (2010); Poverty rate: 5.8% (2005-2009 5-year est.).

Taxes: Total city taxes per capita: $70 (2007); City property taxes per capita: $0 (2007).

Education: Percent of population age 25 and over with: High school diploma (including GED) or higher: 90.8% (2010); Bachelor's degree or higher: 41.0% (2010); Master's degree or higher: 12.3% (2010).

Housing: Homeownership rate: 89.8% (2010); Median home value: $273,529 (2010); Median contract rent: n/a per month (2005-2009 5-year est.); Median year structure built: 1982 (2005-2009 5-year est.).

Transportation: Commute to work: 94.3% car, 0.0% public transportation, 0.0% walk, 5.7% work from home (2005-2009 5-year est.); Travel time to work: 13.6% less than 15 minutes, 46.4% 15 to 30 minutes, 27.1% 30 to 45 minutes, 7.5% 45 to 60 minutes, 5.4% 60 minutes or more (2005-2009 5-year est.)

COOL (city). Covers a land area of 1.639 square miles and a water area of 0.003 square miles. Located at 32.79° N. Lat; 98.01° W. Long. Elevation is 932 feet.

Population: 214 (1990); 162 (2000); 170 (2010); 175 (2015 projected); Race: 60.6% White, 23.5% Black, 0.0% Asian, 15.9% Other, 17.1% Hispanic of any race (2010); Density: 103.7 persons per square mile (2010); Average household size: 2.80 (2010); Median age: 34.3 (2010); Males per 100 females: 150.0 (2010); Marriage status: 12.8% never married, 70.1% now married, 1.7% widowed, 15.4% divorced (2005-2009 5-year est.); Foreign born: 1.6% (2005-2009 5-year est.); Ancestry (includes multiple ancestries): 18.1% Irish, 14.2% English, 9.4% German, 9.4% Swedish, 8.7% American (2005-2009 5-year est.).

Economy: Employment by occupation: 3.3% management, 11.5% professional, 23.0% services, 31.1% sales, 3.3% farming, 24.6% construction, 3.3% production (2005-2009 5-year est.).

Income: Per capita income: $18,097 (2010); Median household income: $51,923 (2010); Average household income: $56,250 (2010); Percent of households with income of $100,000 or more: 10.9% (2010); Poverty rate: 6.3% (2005-2009 5-year est.).

Education: Percent of population age 25 and over with: High school diploma (including GED) or higher: 78.7% (2010); Bachelor's degree or higher: 9.8% (2010); Master's degree or higher: 2.5% (2010).

Housing: Homeownership rate: 82.6% (2010); Median home value: $100,000 (2010); Median contract rent: $400 per month (2005-2009 5-year est.); Median year structure built: 1969 (2005-2009 5-year est.).

Transportation: Commute to work: 98.3% car, 0.0% public transportation, 0.0% walk, 1.7% work from home (2005-2009 5-year est.); Travel time to work: 27.6% less than 15 minutes, 46.6% 15 to 30 minutes, 5.2% 30 to 45 minutes, 12.1% 45 to 60 minutes, 8.6% 60 minutes or more (2005-2009 5-year est.)

HUDSON OAKS (city). Covers a land area of 2.551 square miles and a water area of 0 square miles. Located at 32.75° N. Lat; 97.69° W. Long. Elevation is 1,043 feet.

Population: 1,388 (1990); 1,637 (2000); 2,189 (2010); 2,449 (2015 projected); Race: 94.1% White, 0.9% Black, 0.3% Asian, 4.7% Other, 6.8% Hispanic of any race (2010); Density: 858.1 persons per square mile (2010); Average household size: 2.80 (2010); Median age: 39.4 (2010); Males per 100 females: 100.3 (2010); Marriage status: 24.4% never married, 67.4% now married, 0.7% widowed, 7.5% divorced (2005-2009 5-year est.); Foreign born: 1.9% (2005-2009 5-year est.); Ancestry (includes multiple ancestries): 17.5% English, 15.1% American, 13.1% German, 10.6% Irish, 5.4% Scotch-Irish (2005-2009 5-year est.).

Economy: Single-family building permits issued: 11 (2010); Multi-family building permits issued: 0 (2010); Employment by occupation: 25.3% management, 19.7% professional, 11.5% services, 32.4% sales, 0.4% farming, 4.8% construction, 6.0% production (2005-2009 5-year est.).

Income: Per capita income: $33,935 (2010); Median household income: $80,777 (2010); Average household income: $94,757 (2010); Percent of households with income of $100,000 or more: 37.0% (2010); Poverty rate: 4.2% (2005-2009 5-year est.).

Taxes: Total city taxes per capita: $711 (2007); City property taxes per capita: $0 (2007).

Education: Percent of population age 25 and over with: High school diploma (including GED) or higher: 92.7% (2010); Bachelor's degree or higher: 28.5% (2010); Master's degree or higher: 9.6% (2010).

Housing: Homeownership rate: 86.1% (2010); Median home value: $199,130 (2010); Median contract rent: $284 per month (2005-2009 5-year est.); Median year structure built: 1990 (2005-2009 5-year est.).

Safety: Violent crime rate: 28.3 per 10,000 population; Property crime rate: 353.3 per 10,000 population (2009).

Transportation: Commute to work: 90.0% car, 0.4% public transportation, 0.2% walk, 8.3% work from home (2005-2009 5-year est.); Travel time to work: 23.4% less than 15 minutes, 35.0% 15 to 30 minutes, 22.2% 30 to 45 minutes, 6.2% 45 to 60 minutes, 13.2% 60 minutes or more (2005-2009 5-year est.)

MILLSAP (town). Covers a land area of 1.315 square miles and a water area of 0.006 square miles. Located at 32.74° N. Lat; 98.01° W. Long. Elevation is 817 feet.

Population: 394 (1990); 353 (2000); 381 (2010); 400 (2015 projected); Race: 91.1% White, 0.3% Black, 0.5% Asian, 8.1% Other, 10.2% Hispanic of any race (2010); Density: 289.8 persons per square mile (2010); Average household size: 2.78 (2010); Median age: 37.2 (2010); Males per 100 females: 100.5 (2010); Marriage status: 30.7% never married, 46.9% now married, 5.7% widowed, 16.7% divorced (2005-2009 5-year est.); Foreign born: 5.8% (2005-2009 5-year est.); Ancestry (includes multiple ancestries): 9.5% American, 7.1% Irish, 6.6% German, 3.2% European, 2.1% Dutch (2005-2009 5-year est.).

Economy: Employment by occupation: 8.6% management, 15.1% professional, 9.7% services, 25.3% sales, 0.0% farming, 25.8% construction, 15.6% production (2005-2009 5-year est.).
Income: Per capita income: $21,418 (2010); Median household income: $52,303 (2010); Average household income: $59,526 (2010); Percent of households with income of $100,000 or more: 12.4% (2010); Poverty rate: 10.1% (2005-2009 5-year est.).
Taxes: Total city taxes per capita: $112 (2007); City property taxes per capita: $0 (2007).
Education: Percent of population age 25 and over with: High school diploma (including GED) or higher: 82.1% (2010); Bachelor's degree or higher: 10.5% (2010); Master's degree or higher: 1.6% (2010).

School District(s)
Millsap ISD (PK-12)
    2009-10 Enrollment: 770 . . . . (940) 682-3101
Housing: Homeownership rate: 81.8% (2010); Median home value: $90,000 (2010); Median contract rent: $503 per month (2005-2009 5-year est.); Median year structure built: 1963 (2005-2009 5-year est.).
Transportation: Commute to work: 97.3% car, 0.0% public transportation, 2.7% walk, 0.0% work from home (2005-2009 5-year est.); Travel time to work: 39.1% less than 15 minutes, 15.2% 15 to 30 minutes, 10.3% 30 to 45 minutes, 16.8% 45 to 60 minutes, 18.5% 60 minutes or more (2005-2009 5-year est.)

POOLVILLE (unincorporated postal area, zip code 76487). Covers a land area of 86.511 square miles and a water area of 0.310 square miles. Located at 33.00° N. Lat; 97.90° W. Long. Elevation is 1,132 feet.
Population: 1,670 (2000); Race: 94.1% White, 0.6% Black, 0.0% Asian, 5.3% Other, 10.7% Hispanic of any race (2000); Density: 19.3 persons per square mile (2000); Age: 30.9% under 18, 10.9% over 64 (2000); Marriage status: 15.2% never married, 70.6% now married, 5.1% widowed, 9.1% divorced (2000); Foreign born: 2.5% (2000); Ancestry (includes multiple ancestries): 17.2% American, 13.7% Irish, 9.5% German, 8.9% English (2000).
Economy: Employment by occupation: 11.5% management, 12.5% professional, 13.7% services, 28.2% sales, 1.0% farming, 16.9% construction, 16.2% production (2000).
Income: Per capita income: $16,495 (2000); Median household income: $36,198 (2000); Poverty rate: 179.1% (2000).
Education: Percent of population age 25 and over with: High school diploma (including GED) or higher: 75.9% (2000); Bachelor's degree or higher: 7.8% (2000).

School District(s)
Poolville ISD (PK-12)
    2009-10 Enrollment: 529 . . . . (817) 594-4452
Housing: Homeownership rate: 86.3% (2000); Median home value: $68,000 (2000); Median contract rent: $329 per month (2000); Median year structure built: 1980 (2000).
Transportation: Commute to work: 89.8% car, 0.0% public transportation, 1.7% walk, 7.8% work from home (2000); Travel time to work: 12.7% less than 15 minutes, 19.8% 15 to 30 minutes, 24.7% 30 to 45 minutes, 16.9% 45 to 60 minutes, 26.0% 60 minutes or more (2000)

RENO (city). Covers a land area of 12.651 square miles and a water area of 0.005 square miles. Located at 32.94° N. Lat; 97.58° W. Long. Elevation is 728 feet.
Population: 2,219 (1990); 2,441 (2000); 2,705 (2010); 2,871 (2015 projected); Race: 92.8% White, 0.5% Black, 0.4% Asian, 6.3% Other, 8.0% Hispanic of any race (2010); Density: 213.8 persons per square mile (2010); Average household size: 2.88 (2010); Median age: 35.3 (2010); Males per 100 females: 98.6 (2010); Marriage status: 22.5% never married, 56.9% now married, 4.1% widowed, 16.5% divorced (2005-2009 5-year est.); Foreign born: 2.0% (2005-2009 5-year est.); Ancestry (includes multiple ancestries): 17.3% Scottish, 15.9% German, 11.1% English, 9.8% Irish, 9.1% American (2005-2009 5-year est.).
Economy: Single-family building permits issued: 4 (2010); Multi-family building permits issued: 0 (2010); Employment by occupation: 9.8% management, 13.2% professional, 15.6% services, 33.8% sales, 0.5% farming, 11.9% construction, 15.2% production (2005-2009 5-year est.).
Income: Per capita income: $21,391 (2010); Median household income: $53,063 (2010); Average household income: $61,297 (2010); Percent of households with income of $100,000 or more: 16.4% (2010); Poverty rate: 18.9% (2005-2009 5-year est.).
Taxes: Total city taxes per capita: $37 (2007); City property taxes per capita: $0 (2007).

Education: Percent of population age 25 and over with: High school diploma (including GED) or higher: 77.8% (2010); Bachelor's degree or higher: 9.6% (2010); Master's degree or higher: 1.8% (2010).
Housing: Homeownership rate: 76.7% (2010); Median home value: $97,674 (2010); Median contract rent: $497 per month (2005-2009 5-year est.); Median year structure built: 1986 (2005-2009 5-year est.).
Transportation: Commute to work: 95.6% car, 0.0% public transportation, 3.1% walk, 1.3% work from home (2005-2009 5-year est.); Travel time to work: 27.5% less than 15 minutes, 18.9% 15 to 30 minutes, 23.1% 30 to 45 minutes, 12.1% 45 to 60 minutes, 18.5% 60 minutes or more (2005-2009 5-year est.)

SANCTUARY (town). Covers a land area of 0.264 square miles and a water area of 0 square miles. Located at 32.90° N. Lat; 97.58° W. Long. Elevation is 768 feet.
Population: 178 (1990); 256 (2000); 396 (2010); 456 (2015 projected); Race: 95.2% White, 0.0% Black, 0.0% Asian, 4.8% Other, 8.1% Hispanic of any race (2010); Density: 1,501.9 persons per square mile (2010); Average household size: 2.69 (2010); Median age: 36.2 (2010); Males per 100 females: 98.0 (2010); Marriage status: 20.3% never married, 68.8% now married, 3.6% widowed, 7.2% divorced (2005-2009 5-year est.); Foreign born: 1.8% (2005-2009 5-year est.); Ancestry (includes multiple ancestries): 28.9% German, 20.5% Irish, 10.0% French, 8.0% English, 6.8% Polish (2005-2009 5-year est.).
Economy: Employment by occupation: 16.4% management, 29.6% professional, 11.7% services, 28.6% sales, 0.0% farming, 11.7% construction, 1.9% production (2005-2009 5-year est.).
Income: Per capita income: $19,788 (2010); Median household income: $42,279 (2010); Average household income: $51,786 (2010); Percent of households with income of $100,000 or more: 8.8% (2010); Poverty rate: 2.0% (2005-2009 5-year est.).
Taxes: Total city taxes per capita: $89 (2007); City property taxes per capita: $0 (2007).
Education: Percent of population age 25 and over with: High school diploma (including GED) or higher: 75.5% (2010); Bachelor's degree or higher: 6.3% (2010); Master's degree or higher: 1.9% (2010).
Housing: Homeownership rate: 73.5% (2010); Median home value: $103,947 (2010); Median contract rent: $475 per month (2005-2009 5-year est.); Median year structure built: 1984 (2005-2009 5-year est.).
Transportation: Commute to work: 95.2% car, 0.0% public transportation, 0.0% walk, 4.8% work from home (2005-2009 5-year est.); Travel time to work: 13.6% less than 15 minutes, 18.2% 15 to 30 minutes, 31.8% 30 to 45 minutes, 31.3% 45 to 60 minutes, 5.1% 60 minutes or more (2005-2009 5-year est.)

SPRINGTOWN (city). Covers a land area of 2.759 square miles and a water area of 0 square miles. Located at 32.96° N. Lat; 97.68° W. Long. Elevation is 860 feet.
Population: 1,756 (1990); 2,062 (2000); 2,662 (2010); 2,963 (2015 projected); Race: 93.8% White, 0.6% Black, 0.1% Asian, 5.5% Other, 5.3% Hispanic of any race (2010); Density: 964.9 persons per square mile (2010); Average household size: 2.80 (2010); Median age: 35.1 (2010); Males per 100 females: 96.6 (2010); Marriage status: 17.8% never married, 59.4% now married, 9.3% widowed, 13.5% divorced (2005-2009 5-year est.); Foreign born: 1.3% (2005-2009 5-year est.); Ancestry (includes multiple ancestries): 20.5% German, 17.6% Irish, 12.1% American, 8.9% English, 4.0% French (2005-2009 5-year est.).
Economy: Single-family building permits issued: 1 (2010); Multi-family building permits issued: 0 (2010); Employment by occupation: 8.4% management, 19.7% professional, 14.0% services, 37.3% sales, 0.0% farming, 10.6% construction, 9.9% production (2005-2009 5-year est.).
Income: Per capita income: $20,938 (2010); Median household income: $50,531 (2010); Average household income: $58,502 (2010); Percent of households with income of $100,000 or more: 15.0% (2010); Poverty rate: 20.6% (2005-2009 5-year est.).
Taxes: Total city taxes per capita: $549 (2007); City property taxes per capita: $238 (2007).
Education: Percent of population age 25 and over with: High school diploma (including GED) or higher: 78.1% (2010); Bachelor's degree or higher: 10.3% (2010); Master's degree or higher: 3.7% (2010).

School District(s)
Springtown ISD (PK-12)
    2009-10 Enrollment: 3,510 . . . . (817) 220-7243

Housing: Homeownership rate: 75.6% (2010); Median home value: $115,969 (2010); Median contract rent: $412 per month (2005-2009 5-year est.); Median year structure built: 1984 (2005-2009 5-year est.).
Safety: Violent crime rate: 45.8 per 10,000 population; Property crime rate: 216.9 per 10,000 population (2009).
Newspapers: Springtown Epigraph (Local news; Circulation 2,100)
Transportation: Commute to work: 94.0% car, 0.0% public transportation, 1.1% walk, 4.5% work from home (2005-2009 5-year est.); Travel time to work: 28.2% less than 15 minutes, 23.8% 15 to 30 minutes, 22.4% 30 to 45 minutes, 15.4% 45 to 60 minutes, 10.2% 60 minutes or more (2005-2009 5-year est.)
Additional Information Contacts
Springtown Area Chamber of Commerce . . . . (817) 220-7828
  http://www.springtownchamber.org

WEATHERFORD (city). County seat. Covers a land area of 20.882 square miles and a water area of 1.781 square miles. Located at 32.75° N. Lat; 97.78° W. Long. Elevation is 1,053 feet.

History: Named for Jefferson Weatherford, one of the creators of Parker County. Weatherford was known as a watermelon town, this being the principal crop of a diversified farming area surrounding the town.
Population: 15,491 (1990); 19,000 (2000); 24,660 (2010); 27,362 (2015 projected); Race: 88.2% White, 1.9% Black, 1.3% Asian, 8.6% Other, 15.2% Hispanic of any race (2010); Density: 1,180.9 persons per square mile (2010); Average household size: 2.54 (2010); Median age: 35.1 (2010); Males per 100 females: 94.4 (2010); Marriage status: 27.2% never married, 50.5% now married, 8.7% widowed, 13.6% divorced (2005-2009 5-year est.); Foreign born: 7.6% (2005-2009 5-year est.); Ancestry (includes multiple ancestries): 15.9% German, 15.3% English, 14.1% Irish, 9.1% American, 3.4% Scotch-Irish (2005-2009 5-year est.).
Economy: Unemployment rate: 8.2% (June 2011); Total civilian labor force: 13,039 (June 2011); Single-family building permits issued: 88 (2010); Multi-family building permits issued: 3 (2010); Employment by occupation: 13.0% management, 18.8% professional, 17.5% services, 27.7% sales, 0.3% farming, 10.8% construction, 12.0% production (2005-2009 5-year est.).
Income: Per capita income: $25,305 (2010); Median household income: $50,662 (2010); Average household income: $65,205 (2010); Percent of households with income of $100,000 or more: 16.6% (2010); Poverty rate: 12.8% (2005-2009 5-year est.).
Taxes: Total city taxes per capita: $663 (2007); City property taxes per capita: $176 (2007).
Education: Percent of population age 25 and over with: High school diploma (including GED) or higher: 84.6% (2010); Bachelor's degree or higher: 23.7% (2010); Master's degree or higher: 9.7% (2010).
School District(s)
Crosstimbers Academy (09-12)
  2009-10 Enrollment: 149 . . . . (817) 648-2047
Garner ISD (PK-08)
  2009-10 Enrollment: 204 . . . . (940) 682-4251
Peaster ISD (PK-12)
  2009-10 Enrollment: 1,074 . . . . (817) 341-5000
Weatherford ISD (PK-12)
  2009-10 Enrollment: 7,530 . . . . (817) 598-2800
Two-year College(s)
Weatherford College (Public)
  Fall 2009 Enrollment: 5,384 . . . . (800) 287-5471
  2010-11 Tuition: In-state $2,980; Out-of-state $4,450
Housing: Homeownership rate: 60.1% (2010); Median home value: $128,584 (2010); Median contract rent: $585 per month (2005-2009 5-year est.); Median year structure built: 1984 (2005-2009 5-year est.).
Hospitals: Campbell Health System (99 beds)
Safety: Violent crime rate: 15.5 per 10,000 population; Property crime rate: 305.1 per 10,000 population (2009).
Newspapers: Weatherford Democrat (Local news; Circulation 5,886)
Transportation: Commute to work: 93.6% car, 0.0% public transportation, 1.3% walk, 3.9% work from home (2005-2009 5-year est.); Travel time to work: 40.8% less than 15 minutes, 24.5% 15 to 30 minutes, 19.4% 30 to 45 minutes, 10.3% 45 to 60 minutes, 4.9% 60 minutes or more (2005-2009 5-year est.)
Additional Information Contacts
City of Weatherford . . . . (817) 598-4000
  http://www.ci.weatherford.tx.us
Weatherford Chamber of Commerce . . . . (817) 596-3801
  http://www.weatherford-chamber.com

WHITT (unincorporated postal area, zip code 76490). Covers a land area of 0.109 square miles and a water area of 0 square miles. Located at 32.95° N. Lat; 98.01° W. Long. Elevation is 1,129 feet.

Population: 60 (2000); Race: 100.0% White, 0.0% Black, 0.0% Asian, 0.0% Other, 0.0% Hispanic of any race (2000); Density: 552.4 persons per square mile (2000); Age: 34.3% under 18, 0.0% over 64 (2000); Marriage status: 25.0% never married, 69.2% now married, 0.0% widowed, 5.8% divorced (2000); Foreign born: 10.0% (2000); Ancestry (includes multiple ancestries): 25.7% English, 15.7% French, 10.0% Irish, 10.0% Dutch (2000).
Economy: Employment by occupation: 0.0% management, 16.1% professional, 29.0% services, 0.0% sales, 0.0% farming, 22.6% construction, 32.3% production (2000).
Income: Per capita income: $8,837 (2000); Median household income: $26,250 (2000); Poverty rate: 179.1% (2000).
Education: Percent of population age 25 and over with: High school diploma (including GED) or higher: 81.6% (2000); Bachelor's degree or higher: 5.3% (2000).
Housing: Homeownership rate: 63.6% (2000); Median home value: $27,500 (2000); Median contract rent: $325 per month (2000); Median year structure built: 1964 (2000).
Transportation: Commute to work: 100.0% car, 0.0% public transportation, 0.0% walk, 0.0% work from home (2000); Travel time to work: 0.0% less than 15 minutes, 40.0% 15 to 30 minutes, 8.0% 30 to 45 minutes, 12.0% 45 to 60 minutes, 40.0% 60 minutes or more (2000)

WILLOW PARK (city). Covers a land area of 6.155 square miles and a water area of 0.105 square miles. Located at 32.75° N. Lat; 97.65° W. Long. Elevation is 932 feet.

Population: 2,469 (1990); 2,849 (2000); 4,122 (2010); 4,677 (2015 projected); Race: 94.8% White, 0.3% Black, 0.4% Asian, 4.5% Other, 4.5% Hispanic of any race (2010); Density: 669.7 persons per square mile (2010); Average household size: 2.88 (2010); Median age: 41.0 (2010); Males per 100 females: 99.4 (2010); Marriage status: 19.0% never married, 67.7% now married, 4.9% widowed, 8.4% divorced (2005-2009 5-year est.); Foreign born: 3.4% (2005-2009 5-year est.); Ancestry (includes multiple ancestries): 24.1% German, 17.2% English, 9.6% Irish, 8.1% American, 5.9% Italian (2005-2009 5-year est.).
Economy: Single-family building permits issued: 29 (2010); Multi-family building permits issued: 0 (2010); Employment by occupation: 20.9% management, 29.4% professional, 9.9% services, 23.1% sales, 0.0% farming, 7.1% construction, 9.6% production (2005-2009 5-year est.).
Income: Per capita income: $38,303 (2010); Median household income: $91,440 (2010); Average household income: $110,356 (2010); Percent of households with income of $100,000 or more: 43.4% (2010); Poverty rate: 5.4% (2005-2009 5-year est.).
Taxes: Total city taxes per capita: $449 (2007); City property taxes per capita: $181 (2007).
Education: Percent of population age 25 and over with: High school diploma (including GED) or higher: 95.4% (2010); Bachelor's degree or higher: 35.9% (2010); Master's degree or higher: 13.0% (2010).
School District(s)
Aledo ISD (PK-12)
  2009-10 Enrollment: 4,589 . . . . (817) 441-8327
Housing: Homeownership rate: 92.9% (2010); Median home value: $202,510 (2010); Median contract rent: $1,133 per month (2005-2009 5-year est.); Median year structure built: 1986 (2005-2009 5-year est.).
Safety: Violent crime rate: 4.2 per 10,000 population; Property crime rate: 117.8 per 10,000 population (2009).
Transportation: Commute to work: 97.0% car, 0.0% public transportation, 1.4% walk, 1.2% work from home (2005-2009 5-year est.); Travel time to work: 15.7% less than 15 minutes, 44.8% 15 to 30 minutes, 27.8% 30 to 45 minutes, 5.4% 45 to 60 minutes, 6.2% 60 minutes or more (2005-2009 5-year est.)
Additional Information Contacts
City of Willow Park . . . . (817) 441-7108
  http://www.willowpark.org
East Parker County Chamber of Commerce . . . . (817) 441-7844
  http://www.eastparkerchamber.com

Parmer County

Located in west Texas; bounded on the west by New Mexico. Covers a land area of 881.66 square miles, a water area of 3.51 square miles, and is located in the Central Time Zone at 34.52° N. Lat., 102.78° W. Long. The county was founded in 1876. County seat is Farwell.

Weather Station: Friona   Elevation: 4,009 feet

	Jan	Feb	Mar	Apr	May	Jun	Jul	Aug	Sep	Oct	Nov	Dec
High	51	56	63	71	80	88	90	88	82	72	60	51
Low	23	25	32	39	50	59	63	62	54	43	31	23
Precip	0.7	0.6	1.2	1.0	2.3	2.6	2.3	3.3	2.3	1.8	0.8	0.9
Snow	3.8	2.7	1.4	0.6	0.0	0.0	0.0	0.0	0.0	0.2	2.2	4.0

High and Low temperatures in degrees Fahrenheit; Precipitation and Snow in inches

Population: 9,863 (1990); 10,016 (2000); 9,387 (2010); 9,066 (2015 projected); Race: 60.1% White, 1.5% Black, 0.5% Asian, 37.9% Other, 57.0% Hispanic of any race (2010); Density: 10.6 persons per square mile (2010); Average household size: 2.94 (2010); Median age: 35.1 (2010); Males per 100 females: 99.2 (2010).
Religion: Five largest groups: 34.0% Southern Baptist Convention, 17.8% Catholic Church, 12.6% The United Methodist Church, 6.3% Churches of Christ, 2.2% The Church of Jesus Christ of Latter-day Saints (2000).
Economy: Unemployment rate: 5.7% (June 2011); Total civilian labor force: 4,700 (June 2011); Leading industries: Farms: 555 totaling 560,788 acres (2007); Companies that employ 500 or more persons: 1 (2009); Companies that employ 100 to 499 persons: 1 (2009); Companies that employ less than 100 persons: 203 (2009); Black-owned businesses: n/a (2007); Hispanic-owned businesses: n/a (2007); Asian-owned businesses: n/a (2007); Women-owned businesses: n/a (2007); Retail sales per capita: $5,926 (2010). Single-family building permits issued: 0 (2010); Multi-family building permits issued: 0 (2010).
Income: Per capita income: $17,092 (2010); Median household income: $37,145 (2010); Average household income: $49,376 (2010); Percent of households with income of $100,000 or more: 8.3% (2010); Poverty rate: 16.9% (2009); Bankruptcy rate: 1.26% (2010).
Taxes: Total county taxes per capita: $338 (2007); County property taxes per capita: $196 (2007).
Education: Percent of population age 25 and over with: High school diploma (including GED) or higher: 66.1% (2010); Bachelor's degree or higher: 15.3% (2010); Master's degree or higher: 3.5% (2010).
Housing: Homeownership rate: 70.3% (2010); Median home value: $63,722 (2010); Median contract rent: $397 per month (2005-2009 5-year est.); Median year structure built: 1962 (2005-2009 5-year est.).
Health: Birth rate: 180.8 per 10,000 population (2009); Death rate: 72.1 per 10,000 population (2009); Age-adjusted cancer mortality rate: 186.7 (Unreliable) deaths per 100,000 population (2007); Number of physicians: 5.4 per 10,000 population (2008); Hospital beds: 25.5 per 10,000 population (2007); Hospital admissions: 299.9 per 10,000 population (2007).
Elections: 2008 Presidential election results: 19.4% Obama, 80.0% McCain, 0.1% Nader
Additional Information Contacts
Parmer County Government . . . . (806) 481-3383
   http://www.co.parmer.tx.us/ips/cms
Friona Chamber of Commerce . . . . (806) 250-3491
   http://www.FrionaChamber.com

Parmer County Communities

BOVINA (city). Covers a land area of 0.867 square miles and a water area of 0 square miles. Located at 34.51° N. Lat; 102.88° W. Long. Elevation is 4,068 feet.
Population: 1,546 (1990); 1,874 (2000); 1,745 (2010); 1,681 (2015 projected); Race: 44.2% White, 2.2% Black, 0.0% Asian, 53.6% Other, 77.0% Hispanic of any race (2010); Density: 2,012.3 persons per square mile (2010); Average household size: 3.29 (2010); Median age: 29.9 (2010); Males per 100 females: 102.0 (2010); Marriage status: 17.8% never married, 69.1% now married, 8.0% widowed, 5.1% divorced (2005-2009 5-year est.); Foreign born: 28.8% (2005-2009 5-year est.); Ancestry (includes multiple ancestries): 3.5% English, 2.1% German, 2.0% American, 1.9% Irish, 1.1% Scotch-Irish (2005-2009 5-year est.).
Economy: Single-family building permits issued: 0 (2010); Multi-family building permits issued: 0 (2010); Employment by occupation: 3.8% management, 3.5% professional, 20.7% services, 14.0% sales, 9.1% farming, 10.8% construction, 38.1% production (2005-2009 5-year est.).
Income: Per capita income: $12,924 (2010); Median household income: $33,143 (2010); Average household income: $42,354 (2010); Percent of households with income of $100,000 or more: 5.6% (2010); Poverty rate: 17.9% (2005-2009 5-year est.).

Taxes: Total city taxes per capita: $77 (2007); City property taxes per capita: $77 (2007).
Education: Percent of population age 25 and over with: High school diploma (including GED) or higher: 48.8% (2010); Bachelor's degree or higher: 10.5% (2010); Master's degree or higher: 2.1% (2010).
School District(s)
Bovina ISD (PK-12)
   2009-10 Enrollment: 515 . . . . (806) 251-1336
Housing: Homeownership rate: 71.0% (2010); Median home value: $39,638 (2010); Median contract rent: $477 per month (2005-2009 5-year est.); Median year structure built: 1965 (2005-2009 5-year est.).
Transportation: Commute to work: 96.8% car, 0.0% public transportation, 0.8% walk, 1.3% work from home (2005-2009 5-year est.); Travel time to work: 55.7% less than 15 minutes, 30.8% 15 to 30 minutes, 9.4% 30 to 45 minutes, 0.8% 45 to 60 minutes, 3.3% 60 minutes or more (2005-2009 5-year est.)

FARWELL (city). County seat. Covers a land area of 0.818 square miles and a water area of 0 square miles. Located at 34.38° N. Lat; 103.03° W. Long. Elevation is 4,144 feet.
History: Farwell was named for two brothers, John V. and Charles B. Farwell, members of a land syndicate. The town was located on the state border with New Mexico.
Population: 1,373 (1990); 1,364 (2000); 1,293 (2010); 1,260 (2015 projected); Race: 66.4% White, 0.5% Black, 2.1% Asian, 31.1% Other, 43.6% Hispanic of any race (2010); Density: 1,580.0 persons per square mile (2010); Average household size: 2.60 (2010); Median age: 43.0 (2010); Males per 100 females: 91.0 (2010); Marriage status: 10.7% never married, 59.6% now married, 17.7% widowed, 12.0% divorced (2005-2009 5-year est.); Foreign born: 13.2% (2005-2009 5-year est.); Ancestry (includes multiple ancestries): 21.0% German, 12.4% Irish, 12.3% English, 3.5% American, 2.0% French (2005-2009 5-year est.).
Economy: Single-family building permits issued: 0 (2010); Multi-family building permits issued: 0 (2010); Employment by occupation: 21.3% management, 23.6% professional, 10.6% services, 18.7% sales, 6.8% farming, 2.8% construction, 16.3% production (2005-2009 5-year est.).
Income: Per capita income: $18,296 (2010); Median household income: $35,147 (2010); Average household income: $41,830 (2010); Percent of households with income of $100,000 or more: 4.7% (2010); Poverty rate: 25.1% (2005-2009 5-year est.).
Taxes: Total city taxes per capita: $201 (2007); City property taxes per capita: $123 (2007).
Education: Percent of population age 25 and over with: High school diploma (including GED) or higher: 73.4% (2010); Bachelor's degree or higher: 12.8% (2010); Master's degree or higher: 4.3% (2010).
School District(s)
Farwell ISD (PK-12)
   2009-10 Enrollment: 543 . . . . (806) 481-3371
Housing: Homeownership rate: 81.5% (2010); Median home value: $63,378 (2010); Median contract rent: $390 per month (2005-2009 5-year est.); Median year structure built: 1966 (2005-2009 5-year est.).
Safety: Violent crime rate: 32.3 per 10,000 population; Property crime rate: 217.7 per 10,000 population (2009).
Newspapers: Farwell State Line Tribune (Community news; Circulation 1,300)
Transportation: Commute to work: 91.6% car, 0.0% public transportation, 0.7% walk, 3.8% work from home (2005-2009 5-year est.); Travel time to work: 54.3% less than 15 minutes, 34.1% 15 to 30 minutes, 10.2% 30 to 45 minutes, 1.5% 45 to 60 minutes, 0.0% 60 minutes or more (2005-2009 5-year est.)

FRIONA (city). Covers a land area of 1.379 square miles and a water area of 0 square miles. Located at 34.63° N. Lat; 102.72° W. Long. Elevation is 4,019 feet.
Population: 3,755 (1990); 3,854 (2000); 3,527 (2010); 3,359 (2015 projected); Race: 56.3% White, 2.0% Black, 0.3% Asian, 41.4% Other, 65.5% Hispanic of any race (2010); Density: 2,557.7 persons per square mile (2010); Average household size: 2.90 (2010); Median age: 34.9 (2010); Males per 100 females: 97.4 (2010); Marriage status: 28.2% never married, 61.5% now married, 4.2% widowed, 6.1% divorced (2005-2009 5-year est.); Foreign born: 24.1% (2005-2009 5-year est.); Ancestry (includes multiple ancestries): 5.6% Irish, 4.7% German, 3.5% English, 3.0% American, 0.9% French Canadian (2005-2009 5-year est.).
Economy: Single-family building permits issued: 0 (2010); Multi-family building permits issued: 0 (2010); Employment by occupation: 11.0%

management, 10.0% professional, 18.1% services, 9.6% sales, 9.3% farming, 10.6% construction, 31.3% production (2005-2009 5-year est.).
Income: Per capita income: $17,888 (2010); Median household income: $38,677 (2010); Average household income: $51,835 (2010); Percent of households with income of $100,000 or more: 8.0% (2010); Poverty rate: 26.4% (2005-2009 5-year est.).
Taxes: Total city taxes per capita: $275 (2007); City property taxes per capita: $174 (2007).
Education: Percent of population age 25 and over with: High school diploma (including GED) or higher: 63.6% (2010); Bachelor's degree or higher: 16.0% (2010); Master's degree or higher: 4.0% (2010).

School District(s)
Friona ISD (PK-12)
    2009-10 Enrollment: 1,249 . . . . (806) 250-2747
Housing: Homeownership rate: 69.9% (2010); Median home value: $61,567 (2010); Median contract rent: $384 per month (2005-2009 5-year est.); Median year structure built: 1965 (2005-2009 5-year est.).
Hospitals: Parmer County Community Hospital (25 beds)
Safety: Violent crime rate: 20.1 per 10,000 population; Property crime rate: 97.4 per 10,000 population (2009).
Newspapers: Star (Community news; Circulation 2,100)
Transportation: Commute to work: 95.6% car, 0.0% public transportation, 0.0% walk, 3.7% work from home (2005-2009 5-year est.); Travel time to work: 77.6% less than 15 minutes, 10.0% 15 to 30 minutes, 8.9% 30 to 45 minutes, 1.3% 45 to 60 minutes, 2.2% 60 minutes or more (2005-2009 5-year est.)
Additional Information Contacts
Friona Chamber of Commerce . . . . (806) 250-3491
    http://www.FrionaChamber.com

Pecos County

Located in west Texas; bounded by the Pecos River on the northeast, extending to the Glass Mountains in the southwest. Covers a land area of 4,763.66 square miles, a water area of 1.07 square miles, and is located in the Central Time Zone at 30.93° N. Lat., 102.74° W. Long. The county was founded in 1871. County seat is Fort Stockton.

Weather Station: Bakersfield | | | | | | | | | Elevation: 2,540 feet

	Jan	Feb	Mar	Apr	May	Jun	Jul	Aug	Sep	Oct	Nov	Dec
High	61	65	73	82	89	94	96	95	89	80	69	61
Low	34	38	45	53	62	69	72	71	65	55	43	34
Precip	0.6	0.7	0.6	1.1	1.6	1.7	1.2	1.6	2.3	2.1	0.7	0.6
Snow	0.7	tr	tr	0.0	0.0	0.0	0.0	0.0	0.0	tr	0.6	0.3

High and Low temperatures in degrees Fahrenheit; Precipitation and Snow in inches

Weather Station: Sheffield | | | | | | | | | Elevation: 2,169 feet

	Jan	Feb	Mar	Apr	May	Jun	Jul	Aug	Sep	Oct	Nov	Dec
High	62	67	75	84	90	94	96	96	90	81	70	62
Low	32	36	44	52	62	70	72	71	64	53	40	32
Precip	0.6	0.8	0.9	1.1	2.1	1.6	1.1	1.8	1.8	2.2	1.0	0.7
Snow	tr	0.0	0.0	0.0	0.0	0.0	0.0	0.0	0.0	0.0	0.1	tr

High and Low temperatures in degrees Fahrenheit; Precipitation and Snow in inches

Population: 14,675 (1990); 16,809 (2000); 16,583 (2010); 16,440 (2015 projected); Race: 73.8% White, 5.1% Black, 0.6% Asian, 20.5% Other, 64.4% Hispanic of any race (2010); Density: 3.5 persons per square mile (2010); Average household size: 2.75 (2010); Median age: 32.8 (2010); Males per 100 females: 126.3 (2010).
Religion: Five largest groups: 17.3% Catholic Church, 15.8% Southern Baptist Convention, 3.3% Churches of Christ, 3.1% The United Methodist Church, 2.7% Presbyterian Church (U.S.A.) (2000).
Economy: Unemployment rate: 6.3% (June 2011); Total civilian labor force: 9,441 (June 2011); Leading industries: 18.2% retail trade; 12.3% accommodation & food services; 10.8% health care and social assistance (2009); Farms: 287 totaling 2,907,965 acres (2007); Companies that employ 500 or more persons: 1 (2009); Companies that employ 100 to 499 persons: 2 (2009); Companies that employ less than 100 persons: 314 (2009); Black-owned businesses: n/a (2007); Hispanic-owned businesses: n/a (2007); Asian-owned businesses: n/a (2007); Women-owned businesses: 182 (2007); Retail sales per capita: $10,394 (2010). Single-family building permits issued: 6 (2010); Multi-family building permits issued: 0 (2010).
Income: Per capita income: $17,152 (2010); Median household income: $40,706 (2010); Average household income: $50,982 (2010); Percent of

households with income of $100,000 or more: 10.3% (2010); Poverty rate: 19.7% (2009); Bankruptcy rate: 0.51% (2010).
Taxes: Total county taxes per capita: $1,075 (2007); County property taxes per capita: $1,041 (2007).
Education: Percent of population age 25 and over with: High school diploma (including GED) or higher: 68.1% (2010); Bachelor's degree or higher: 14.6% (2010); Master's degree or higher: 5.5% (2010).
Housing: Homeownership rate: 72.2% (2010); Median home value: $42,475 (2010); Median contract rent: $342 per month (2005-2009 5-year est.); Median year structure built: 1971 (2005-2009 5-year est.)
Health: Birth rate: 164.9 per 10,000 population (2009); Death rate: 82.5 per 10,000 population (2009); Age-adjusted cancer mortality rate: 165.0 deaths per 100,000 population (2007); Number of physicians: 5.7 per 10,000 population (2008); Hospital beds: 25.3 per 10,000 population (2007); Hospital admissions: 921.9 per 10,000 population (2007).
Elections: 2008 Presidential election results: 36.8% Obama, 61.8% McCain, 0.2% Nader
Additional Information Contacts
Pecos County Government . . . . (432) 336-2792
    http://www.co.pecos.tx.us
City of Fort Stockton . . . . (432) 336-8525
    http://www.cityfs.net
Fort Stockton Chamber of Commerce . . . . (432) 336-2264
    http://www.fortstockton.org
Iraan-Sheffield Chamber of Commerce . . . . (432) 639-2232
    http://www.iraantx.com

Pecos County Communities

COYANOSA (CDP). Covers a land area of 0.120 square miles and a water area of 0 square miles. Located at 31.24° N. Lat; 103.06° W. Long. Elevation is 2,608 feet.
Population: 123 (1990); 138 (2000); 122 (2010); 115 (2015 projected); Race: 86.9% White, 0.0% Black, 0.8% Asian, 12.3% Other, 52.5% Hispanic of any race (2010); Density: 1,019.6 persons per square mile (2010); Average household size: 2.77 (2010); Median age: 37.9 (2010); Males per 100 females: 106.8 (2010); Marriage status: 8.5% never married, 91.5% now married, 0.0% widowed, 0.0% divorced (2005-2009 5-year est.); Foreign born: 60.8% (2005-2009 5-year est.); Ancestry (includes multiple ancestries): n/a (2005-2009 5-year est.).
Economy: Employment by occupation: 0.0% management, 0.0% professional, 50.0% services, 20.0% sales, 0.0% farming, 0.0% construction, 30.0% production (2005-2009 5-year est.).
Income: Per capita income: $17,048 (2010); Median household income: $32,143 (2010); Average household income: $47,443 (2010); Percent of households with income of $100,000 or more: 9.1% (2010); Poverty rate: 76.5% (2005-2009 5-year est.).
Education: Percent of population age 25 and over with: High school diploma (including GED) or higher: 66.2% (2010); Bachelor's degree or higher: 7.8% (2010); Master's degree or higher: 3.9% (2010).
Housing: Homeownership rate: 84.1% (2010); Median home value: $21,000 (2010); Median contract rent: n/a per month (2005-2009 5-year est.); Median year structure built: 1973 (2005-2009 5-year est.).
Transportation: Commute to work: 60.0% car, 0.0% public transportation, 20.0% walk, 0.0% work from home (2005-2009 5-year est.); Travel time to work: 40.0% less than 15 minutes, 0.0% 15 to 30 minutes, 60.0% 30 to 45 minutes, 0.0% 45 to 60 minutes, 0.0% 60 minutes or more (2005-2009 5-year est.)

FORT STOCKTON (city). County seat. Covers a land area of 5.124 square miles and a water area of 0 square miles. Located at 30.89° N. Lat; 102.88° W. Long. Elevation is 2,972 feet.
History: The town of Fort Stockton grew up around a military post built in 1859 near Comanche Springs, on the Camino Real, the California Trail of 1849. This was also the route of the San Antonio to San Diego stage line. Water from Comanche Springs was used to irrigate land around the town.
Population: 8,572 (1990); 7,846 (2000); 7,546 (2010); 7,422 (2015 projected); Race: 67.6% White, 1.6% Black, 0.9% Asian, 29.9% Other, 71.9% Hispanic of any race (2010); Density: 1,472.8 persons per square mile (2010); Average household size: 2.65 (2010); Median age: 33.7 (2010); Males per 100 females: 98.3 (2010); Marriage status: 21.7% never married, 62.6% now married, 9.0% widowed, 6.7% divorced (2005-2009 5-year est.); Foreign born: 16.2% (2005-2009 5-year est.); Ancestry (includes multiple ancestries): 3.6% American, 2.8% German, 2.5% English, 1.7% Irish, 0.7% Scotch-Irish (2005-2009 5-year est.).

Economy: Single-family building permits issued: 6 (2010); Multi-family building permits issued: 0 (2010); Employment by occupation: 7.7% management, 11.5% professional, 30.4% services, 16.1% sales, 2.9% farming, 19.7% construction, 11.7% production (2005-2009 5-year est.).
Income: Per capita income: $17,514 (2010); Median household income: $37,969 (2010); Average household income: $47,172 (2010); Percent of households with income of $100,000 or more: 7.7% (2010); Poverty rate: 19.2% (2005-2009 5-year est.).
Taxes: Total city taxes per capita: $274 (2007); City property taxes per capita: $82 (2007).
Education: Percent of population age 25 and over with: High school diploma (including GED) or higher: 69.9% (2010); Bachelor's degree or higher: 16.6% (2010); Master's degree or higher: 5.7% (2010).

School District(s)
Fort Stockton ISD (PK-12)
    2009-10 Enrollment: 2,378 . . . . (432) 336-4000
Housing: Homeownership rate: 67.0% (2010); Median home value: $46,429 (2010); Median contract rent: $348 per month (2005-2009 5-year est.); Median year structure built: 1969 (2005-2009 5-year est.).
Hospitals: Pecos County Memorial Hosptial (37 beds)
Safety: Violent crime rate: 69.4 per 10,000 population; Property crime rate: 518.8 per 10,000 population (2009).
Newspapers: Fort Stockton Pioneer (Local news; Circulation 4,250)
Transportation: Commute to work: 93.0% car, 0.0% public transportation, 3.4% walk, 3.2% work from home (2005-2009 5-year est.); Travel time to work: 61.9% less than 15 minutes, 20.9% 15 to 30 minutes, 6.7% 30 to 45 minutes, 3.3% 45 to 60 minutes, 7.2% 60 minutes or more (2005-2009 5-year est.)
Airports: Fort Stockton-Pecos County (general aviation)
Additional Information Contacts
City of Fort Stockton . . . . (432) 336-8525
    http://www.cityfs.net
Fort Stockton Chamber of Commerce . . . . (432) 336-2264
    http://www.fortstockton.org

IMPERIAL (CDP). Covers a land area of 4.233 square miles and a water area of 0 square miles. Located at 31.27° N. Lat; 102.69° W. Long. Elevation is 2,392 feet.
Population: 395 (1990); 428 (2000); 380 (2010); 358 (2015 projected); Race: 87.4% White, 0.3% Black, 0.5% Asian, 11.8% Other, 52.9% Hispanic of any race (2010); Density: 89.8 persons per square mile (2010); Average household size: 2.79 (2010); Median age: 35.9 (2010); Males per 100 females: 108.8 (2010); Marriage status: 16.6% never married, 76.4% now married, 5.0% widowed, 1.9% divorced (2005-2009 5-year est.); Foreign born: 10.1% (2005-2009 5-year est.); Ancestry (includes multiple ancestries): 16.6% American, 10.1% Irish, 6.1% Czechoslovakian, 5.2% French, 3.4% Dutch (2005-2009 5-year est.).
Economy: Employment by occupation: 3.9% management, 35.7% professional, 13.6% services, 11.0% sales, 0.0% farming, 4.5% construction, 31.2% production (2005-2009 5-year est.).
Income: Per capita income: $17,048 (2010); Median household income: $32,000 (2010); Average household income: $50,533 (2010); Percent of households with income of $100,000 or more: 10.3% (2010); Poverty rate: 3.1% (2005-2009 5-year est.).
Education: Percent of population age 25 and over with: High school diploma (including GED) or higher: 65.8% (2010); Bachelor's degree or higher: 6.0% (2010); Master's degree or higher: 2.6% (2010).

School District(s)
Buena Vista ISD (PK-12)
    2009-10 Enrollment: 102 . . . . (432) 536-2225
Housing: Homeownership rate: 83.1% (2010); Median home value: $22,333 (2010); Median contract rent: $213 per month (2005-2009 5-year est.); Median year structure built: 1956 (2005-2009 5-year est.).
Transportation: Commute to work: 85.1% car, 0.0% public transportation, 5.2% walk, 9.7% work from home (2005-2009 5-year est.); Travel time to work: 63.3% less than 15 minutes, 2.9% 15 to 30 minutes, 28.8% 30 to 45 minutes, 5.0% 45 to 60 minutes, 0.0% 60 minutes or more (2005-2009 5-year est.)

IRAAN (city). Covers a land area of 0.554 square miles and a water area of 0 square miles. Located at 30.91° N. Lat; 101.89° W. Long. Elevation is 2,221 feet.
History: Iraan was named for Ira and Ann Yates, owners of the land on which the town was founded. Well A No. 1 in Iraan spouted into existence

in 1928 with a force that sent spray four miles away. It was called "the largest producing oil well on the American continent."
Population: 1,322 (1990); 1,238 (2000); 1,174 (2010); 1,143 (2015 projected); Race: 90.2% White, 1.4% Black, 0.0% Asian, 8.4% Other, 43.4% Hispanic of any race (2010); Density: 2,118.8 persons per square mile (2010); Average household size: 2.75 (2010); Median age: 35.6 (2010); Males per 100 females: 113.5 (2010); Marriage status: 17.4% never married, 70.9% now married, 8.2% widowed, 3.5% divorced (2005-2009 5-year est.); Foreign born: 14.9% (2005-2009 5-year est.); Ancestry (includes multiple ancestries): 11.4% American, 7.2% German, 6.8% Irish, 4.3% English, 1.5% Dutch (2005-2009 5-year est.).
Economy: Employment by occupation: 9.1% management, 27.2% professional, 14.6% services, 17.5% sales, 0.0% farming, 18.1% construction, 13.5% production (2005-2009 5-year est.).
Income: Per capita income: $22,556 (2010); Median household income: $53,125 (2010); Average household income: $63,249 (2010); Percent of households with income of $100,000 or more: 14.5% (2010); Poverty rate: 1.4% (2005-2009 5-year est.).
Taxes: Total city taxes per capita: $139 (2007); City property taxes per capita: $0 (2007).
Education: Percent of population age 25 and over with: High school diploma (including GED) or higher: 77.5% (2010); Bachelor's degree or higher: 17.3% (2010); Master's degree or higher: 6.2% (2010).

School District(s)
Iraan-Sheffield ISD (PK-12)
    2009-10 Enrollment: 543 . . . . (432) 639-2512
Housing: Homeownership rate: 66.2% (2010); Median home value: $43,871 (2010); Median contract rent: $278 per month (2005-2009 5-year est.); Median year structure built: 1966 (2005-2009 5-year est.).
Hospitals: Pecos County General Hospital (13 beds)
Newspapers: Iraan News (Community news; Circulation 600)
Transportation: Commute to work: 87.3% car, 0.0% public transportation, 4.5% walk, 6.0% work from home (2005-2009 5-year est.); Travel time to work: 75.3% less than 15 minutes, 16.2% 15 to 30 minutes, 5.7% 30 to 45 minutes, 0.0% 45 to 60 minutes, 2.9% 60 minutes or more (2005-2009 5-year est.)
Additional Information Contacts
Iraan-Sheffield Chamber of Commerce . . . . (432) 639-2232
    http://www.iraantx.com

SHEFFIELD (unincorporated postal area, zip code 79781). Covers a land area of 180.183 square miles and a water area of 0 square miles. Located at 30.70° N. Lat; 101.87° W. Long. Elevation is 2,165 feet.
History: Fort Lancaster State Historic Site to East.
Population: 341 (2000); Race: 93.3% White, 4.8% Black, 0.0% Asian, 1.9% Other, 43.0% Hispanic of any race (2000); Density: 1.9 persons per square mile (2000); Age: 24.2% under 18, 13.4% over 64 (2000); Marriage status: 14.2% never married, 52.7% now married, 27.4% widowed, 5.7% divorced (2000); Foreign born: 5.1% (2000); Ancestry (includes multiple ancestries): 12.1% Irish, 11.3% German, 7.8% English, 7.8% Scottish (2000).
Economy: Employment by occupation: 3.4% management, 14.4% professional, 15.3% services, 26.3% sales, 1.7% farming, 16.1% construction, 22.9% production (2000).
Income: Per capita income: $11,331 (2000); Median household income: $24,028 (2000); Poverty rate: 179.1% (2000).
Education: Percent of population age 25 and over with: High school diploma (including GED) or higher: 66.5% (2000); Bachelor's degree or higher: 4.8% (2000).
Housing: Homeownership rate: 68.4% (2000); Median home value: $47,700 (2000); Median contract rent: $338 per month (2000); Median year structure built: 1973 (2000).
Transportation: Commute to work: 90.4% car, 2.6% public transportation, 1.8% walk, 1.8% work from home (2000); Travel time to work: 43.8% less than 15 minutes, 17.9% 15 to 30 minutes, 27.7% 30 to 45 minutes, 1.8% 45 to 60 minutes, 8.9% 60 minutes or more (2000)

Polk County

Located in east Texas; bounded on the west and southwest by the Trinity River, and on the northeast by the Neches River. Covers a land area of 1,057.26 square miles, a water area of 52.55 square miles, and is located in the Central Time Zone at 30.77° N. Lat., 94.89° W. Long. The county was founded in 1846. County seat is Livingston.

Weather Station: Livingston 2 NNE   Elevation: 178 feet

	Jan	Feb	Mar	Apr	May	Jun	Jul	Aug	Sep	Oct	Nov	Dec
High	60	64	71	78	85	91	94	95	89	80	70	62
Low	37	40	47	53	63	69	72	71	65	55	46	38
Precip	4.2	3.7	4.0	3.3	5.0	5.7	3.3	3.4	4.1	4.8	5.1	4.8
Snow	0.2	0.1	0.0	0.0	0.0	0.0	0.0	0.0	0.0	0.0	0.0	tr

High and Low temperatures in degrees Fahrenheit; Precipitation and Snow in inches

Population: 30,687 (1990); 41,133 (2000); 47,081 (2010); 49,888 (2015 projected); Race: 79.2% White, 12.0% Black, 0.6% Asian, 8.2% Other, 11.7% Hispanic of any race (2010); Density: 44.5 persons per square mile (2010); Average household size: 2.47 (2010); Median age: 38.8 (2010); Males per 100 females: 102.7 (2010).

Religion: Five largest groups: 20.6% Southern Baptist Convention, 11.9% Baptist Missionary Association of America, 5.4% Catholic Church, 4.8% The United Methodist Church, 2.8% Assemblies of God (2000).

Economy: Unemployment rate: 10.7% (June 2011); Total civilian labor force: 18,459 (June 2011); Leading industries: 21.3% retail trade; 14.8% health care and social assistance; 10.9% accommodation & food services (2009); Farms: 812 totaling 131,664 acres (2007); Companies that employ 500 or more persons: 1 (2009); Companies that employ 100 to 499 persons: 13 (2009); Companies that employ less than 100 persons: 684 (2009); Black-owned businesses: n/a (2007); Hispanic-owned businesses: n/a (2007); Asian-owned businesses: n/a (2007); Women-owned businesses: 1,277 (2007); Retail sales per capita: $12,115 (2010). Single-family building permits issued: 346 (2010); Multi-family building permits issued: 0 (2010).

Income: Per capita income: $19,042 (2010); Median household income: $36,909 (2010); Average household income: $49,054 (2010); Percent of households with income of $100,000 or more: 9.5% (2010); Poverty rate: 22.6% (2009); Bankruptcy rate: 1.61% (2010).

Taxes: Total county taxes per capita: $313 (2007); County property taxes per capita: $249 (2007).

Education: Percent of population age 25 and over with: High school diploma (including GED) or higher: 75.7% (2010); Bachelor's degree or higher: 10.9% (2010); Master's degree or higher: 3.7% (2010).

Housing: Homeownership rate: 76.6% (2010); Median home value: $64,480 (2010); Median contract rent: $393 per month (2005-2009 5-year est.); Median year structure built: 1981 (2005-2009 5-year est.)

Health: Birth rate: 109.0 per 10,000 population (2009); Death rate: 131.1 per 10,000 population (2009); Age-adjusted cancer mortality rate: 218.8 deaths per 100,000 population (2007); Number of physicians: 10.1 per 10,000 population (2008); Hospital beds: 14.2 per 10,000 population (2007); Hospital admissions: 713.3 per 10,000 population (2007).

Elections: 2008 Presidential election results: 30.9% Obama, 68.1% McCain, 0.0% Nader

Additional Information Contacts

Polk County Government. . . . . (936) 327-6811
   http://www.co.polk.tx.us/ips/cms
Livingston-Polk County Chamber of Commerce . . . . (936) 327-4929
   http://www.lpcchamber.com
Onalaska Chamber of Commerce . . . . (936) 646-5000
   http://cityofonalaska.us/chamber.htm
Town of Livingston. . . . . (936) 327-4311
   http://www.cityoflivingston-tx.com

Polk County Communities

CORRIGAN (town). Covers a land area of 1.841 square miles and a water area of 0 square miles. Located at 30.99° N. Lat; 94.82° W. Long. Elevation is 236 feet.

History: Incorporated 1938.

Population: 1,808 (1990); 1,721 (2000); 1,742 (2010); 1,756 (2015 projected); Race: 62.5% White, 27.4% Black, 0.1% Asian, 10.0% Other, 18.2% Hispanic of any race (2010); Density: 946.3 persons per square mile (2010); Average household size: 2.62 (2010); Median age: 33.0 (2010); Males per 100 females: 82.2 (2010); Marriage status: 34.8% never married, 38.0% now married, 14.3% widowed, 12.9% divorced (2005-2009 5-year est.); Foreign born: 5.2% (2005-2009 5-year est.); Ancestry (includes multiple ancestries): 3.9% English, 3.8% Irish, 2.3% American, 1.4% German, 0.6% French (2005-2009 5-year est.).

Economy: Employment by occupation: 4.9% management, 8.1% professional, 37.5% services, 18.5% sales, 5.5% farming, 1.5% construction, 24.1% production (2005-2009 5-year est.).

Income: Per capita income: $13,209 (2010); Median household income: $24,714 (2010); Average household income: $35,094 (2010); Percent of

households with income of $100,000 or more: 5.3% (2010); Poverty rate: 45.0% (2005-2009 5-year est.).

Taxes: Total city taxes per capita: $287 (2007); City property taxes per capita: $137 (2007).

Education: Percent of population age 25 and over with: High school diploma (including GED) or higher: 65.3% (2010); Bachelor's degree or higher: 8.3% (2010); Master's degree or higher: 4.1% (2010).

School District(s)

Corrigan-Camden ISD (PK-12)
   2009-10 Enrollment: 1,035 . . . . (936) 398-4040

Housing: Homeownership rate: 55.8% (2010); Median home value: $48,851 (2010); Median contract rent: $147 per month (2005-2009 5-year est.); Median year structure built: 1972 (2005-2009 5-year est.).

Safety: Violent crime rate: 63.6 per 10,000 population; Property crime rate: 159.0 per 10,000 population (2009).

Newspapers: Corrigan Times (Community news; Circulation 1,450)

Transportation: Commute to work: 95.3% car, 0.0% public transportation, 2.9% walk, 1.8% work from home (2005-2009 5-year est.); Travel time to work: 42.5% less than 15 minutes, 30.0% 15 to 30 minutes, 26.8% 30 to 45 minutes, 0.0% 45 to 60 minutes, 0.8% 60 minutes or more (2005-2009 5-year est.)

GOODRICH (city). Covers a land area of 0.707 square miles and a water area of 0 square miles. Located at 30.60° N. Lat; 94.94° W. Long. Elevation is 105 feet.

Population: 239 (1990); 243 (2000); 269 (2010); 286 (2015 projected); Race: 61.7% White, 23.0% Black, 1.5% Asian, 13.8% Other, 17.5% Hispanic of any race (2010); Density: 380.7 persons per square mile (2010); Average household size: 2.69 (2010); Median age: 32.3 (2010); Males per 100 females: 92.1 (2010); Marriage status: 45.5% never married, 30.9% now married, 8.9% widowed, 14.6% divorced (2005-2009 5-year est.); Foreign born: 8.0% (2005-2009 5-year est.); Ancestry (includes multiple ancestries): 35.3% German, 23.1% Portuguese, 3.6% French, 1.9% Irish, 1.7% American (2005-2009 5-year est.).

Economy: Employment by occupation: 1.7% management, 8.6% professional, 29.7% services, 26.9% sales, 0.6% farming, 24.6% construction, 8.0% production (2005-2009 5-year est.).

Income: Per capita income: $12,093 (2010); Median household income: $26,176 (2010); Average household income: $32,525 (2010); Percent of households with income of $100,000 or more: 2.0% (2010); Poverty rate: 22.4% (2005-2009 5-year est.).

Taxes: Total city taxes per capita: $709 (2007); City property taxes per capita: $0 (2007).

Education: Percent of population age 25 and over with: High school diploma (including GED) or higher: 66.9% (2010); Bachelor's degree or higher: 2.5% (2010); Master's degree or higher: 0.0% (2010).

School District(s)

Goodrich ISD (PK-12)
   2009-10 Enrollment: 262 . . . . (936) 365-1100

Housing: Homeownership rate: 77.0% (2010); Median home value: $38,500 (2010); Median contract rent: $558 per month (2005-2009 5-year est.); Median year structure built: 1966 (2005-2009 5-year est.).

Transportation: Commute to work: 93.7% car, 0.0% public transportation, 0.6% walk, 0.0% work from home (2005-2009 5-year est.); Travel time to work: 34.9% less than 15 minutes, 49.1% 15 to 30 minutes, 0.0% 30 to 45 minutes, 2.3% 45 to 60 minutes, 13.7% 60 minutes or more (2005-2009 5-year est.)

Additional Information Contacts

Livingston-Polk County Chamber of Commerce . . . . (936) 327-4929
   http://www.lpcchamber.com

LIVINGSTON (town). County seat. Covers a land area of 8.359 square miles and a water area of 0.013 square miles. Located at 30.71° N. Lat; 94.93° W. Long. Elevation is 167 feet.

History: Livingston was established at one end of the Big Thicket, a densely forested area that once sheltered much wildlife and many lakes and streams. Livingston developed around a sawmill, with livestock and farm products providing revenue.

Population: 4,949 (1990); 5,433 (2000); 6,269 (2010); 6,675 (2015 projected); Race: 69.5% White, 13.0% Black, 1.4% Asian, 16.1% Other, 18.5% Hispanic of any race (2010); Density: 749.9 persons per square mile (2010); Average household size: 2.48 (2010); Median age: 35.7 (2010); Males per 100 females: 83.5 (2010); Marriage status: 27.7% never married, 44.4% now married, 12.6% widowed, 15.2% divorced (2005-2009 5-year est.); Foreign born: 9.2% (2005-2009 5-year est.); Ancestry (includes

multiple ancestries): 10.5% German, 10.3% American, 9.9% English, 8.0% Irish, 4.8% Italian (2005-2009 5-year est.).

Economy: Single-family building permits issued: 4 (2010); Multi-family building permits issued: 0 (2010); Employment by occupation: 4.6% management, 24.0% professional, 21.1% services, 11.4% sales, 0.0% farming, 16.8% construction, 22.1% production (2005-2009 5-year est.).

Income: Per capita income: $19,759 (2010); Median household income: $37,269 (2010); Average household income: $50,843 (2010); Percent of households with income of $100,000 or more: 11.2% (2010); Poverty rate: 28.2% (2005-2009 5-year est.).

Taxes: Total city taxes per capita: $524 (2007); City property taxes per capita: $0 (2007).

Education: Percent of population age 25 and over with: High school diploma (including GED) or higher: 78.5% (2010); Bachelor's degree or higher: 18.2% (2010); Master's degree or higher: 7.1% (2010).

School District(s)
Livingston ISD (PK-12)
    2009-10 Enrollment: 3,999 . . . . (936) 328-2100

Housing: Homeownership rate: 48.6% (2010); Median home value: $80,408 (2010); Median contract rent: $402 per month (2005-2009 5-year est.); Median year structure built: 1977 (2005-2009 5-year est.).

Hospitals: Memorial Medical Center Livingston (50 beds)

Safety: Violent crime rate: 79.6 per 10,000 population; Property crime rate: 552.5 per 10,000 population (2009).

Newspapers: Enterprise (Community news; Circulation 700); Lake Livingston Progress (Local news; Circulation 5,643); Pennysaver (Community news; Circulation 14,043); Polk County Enterprise (Local news; Circulation 8,300)

Transportation: Commute to work: 96.1% car, 0.0% public transportation, 0.7% walk, 2.7% work from home (2005-2009 5-year est.); Travel time to work: 40.0% less than 15 minutes, 26.4% 15 to 30 minutes, 16.0% 30 to 45 minutes, 1.4% 45 to 60 minutes, 16.2% 60 minutes or more (2005-2009 5-year est.)

Additional Information Contacts
Livingston-Polk County Chamber of Commerce . . . . (936) 327-4929
    http://www.lpcchamber.com
Town of Livingston . . . . (936) 327-4311
    http://www.cityoflivingston-tx.com

MOSCOW (unincorporated postal area, zip code 75960). Covers a land area of 51.691 square miles and a water area of 0.055 square miles. Located at 30.90° N. Lat; 94.80° W. Long. Elevation is 344 feet.

Population: 876 (2000); Race: 71.0% White, 13.3% Black, 0.0% Asian, 15.7% Other, 25.6% Hispanic of any race (2000); Density: 16.9 persons per square mile (2000); Age: 28.3% under 18, 10.3% over 64 (2000); Marriage status: 16.8% never married, 67.8% now married, 6.2% widowed, 9.2% divorced (2000); Foreign born: 11.1% (2000); Ancestry (includes multiple ancestries): 10.0% American, 9.1% Irish, 7.7% German, 6.4% English (2000).

Economy: Employment by occupation: 6.2% management, 12.0% professional, 17.9% services, 10.2% sales, 5.9% farming, 10.2% construction, 37.7% production (2000).

Income: Per capita income: $12,877 (2000); Median household income: $33,000 (2000); Poverty rate: 179.1% (2000).

Education: Percent of population age 25 and over with: High school diploma (including GED) or higher: 58.8% (2000); Bachelor's degree or higher: 4.3% (2000).

Housing: Homeownership rate: 84.4% (2000); Median home value: $37,800 (2000); Median contract rent: $316 per month (2000); Median year structure built: 1980 (2000).

Transportation: Commute to work: 95.4% car, 0.0% public transportation, 0.6% walk, 0.9% work from home (2000); Travel time to work: 31.2% less than 15 minutes, 41.7% 15 to 30 minutes, 14.0% 30 to 45 minutes, 2.5% 45 to 60 minutes, 10.6% 60 minutes or more (2000)

ONALASKA (city). Covers a land area of 2.139 square miles and a water area of 0.014 square miles. Located at 30.80° N. Lat; 95.10° W. Long. Elevation is 177 feet.

Population: 919 (1990); 1,174 (2000); 1,317 (2010); 1,388 (2015 projected); Race: 95.1% White, 1.7% Black, 0.8% Asian, 2.4% Other, 2.3% Hispanic of any race (2010); Density: 615.9 persons per square mile (2010); Average household size: 2.13 (2010); Median age: 53.2 (2010); Males per 100 females: 91.4 (2010); Marriage status: 11.0% never married, 52.1% now married, 14.4% widowed, 22.6% divorced (2005-2009 5-year est.); Foreign born: 2.0% (2005-2009 5-year est.); Ancestry (includes

multiple ancestries): 24.4% Irish, 14.4% German, 10.8% English, 9.0% French, 4.9% Scotch-Irish (2005-2009 5-year est.).

Economy: Single-family building permits issued: 10 (2010); Multi-family building permits issued: 0 (2010); Employment by occupation: 10.6% management, 14.6% professional, 28.0% services, 27.1% sales, 3.2% farming, 9.0% construction, 7.5% production (2005-2009 5-year est.).

Income: Per capita income: $23,400 (2010); Median household income: $41,674 (2010); Average household income: $50,340 (2010); Percent of households with income of $100,000 or more: 10.5% (2010); Poverty rate: 36.8% (2005-2009 5-year est.).

Taxes: Total city taxes per capita: $282 (2007); City property taxes per capita: $0 (2007).

Education: Percent of population age 25 and over with: High school diploma (including GED) or higher: 84.0% (2010); Bachelor's degree or higher: 12.4% (2010); Master's degree or higher: 4.7% (2010).

School District(s)
Onalaska ISD (PK-12)
    2009-10 Enrollment: 950 . . . . (936) 646-1000

Housing: Homeownership rate: 82.5% (2010); Median home value: $65,342 (2010); Median contract rent: $393 per month (2005-2009 5-year est.); Median year structure built: 1983 (2005-2009 5-year est.).

Safety: Violent crime rate: 0.0 per 10,000 population; Property crime rate: 6.9 per 10,000 population (2009).

Transportation: Commute to work: 97.5% car, 0.0% public transportation, 1.0% walk, 0.7% work from home (2005-2009 5-year est.); Travel time to work: 29.6% less than 15 minutes, 30.1% 15 to 30 minutes, 19.5% 30 to 45 minutes, 5.4% 45 to 60 minutes, 15.4% 60 minutes or more (2005-2009 5-year est.)

Additional Information Contacts
Livingston-Polk County Chamber of Commerce . . . . (936) 327-4929
    http://www.lpcchamber.com
Onalaska Chamber of Commerce . . . . (936) 646-5000
    http://cityofonalaska.us/chamber.htm

SEVEN OAKS (city). Covers a land area of 1.389 square miles and a water area of 0 square miles. Located at 30.85° N. Lat; 94.85° W. Long. Elevation is 220 feet.

Population: 171 (1990); 131 (2000); 126 (2010); 126 (2015 projected); Race: 80.2% White, 11.1% Black, 0.8% Asian, 7.9% Other, 7.9% Hispanic of any race (2010); Density: 90.7 persons per square mile (2010); Average household size: 2.42 (2010); Median age: 38.3 (2010); Males per 100 females: 96.9 (2010); Marriage status: 17.0% never married, 49.1% now married, 4.5% widowed, 29.5% divorced (2005-2009 5-year est.); Foreign born: 9.2% (2005-2009 5-year est.); Ancestry (includes multiple ancestries): 19.8% Irish, 9.2% Nigerian, 7.6% German, 5.3% Greek, 2.3% English (2005-2009 5-year est.).

Economy: Employment by occupation: 9.1% management, 18.2% professional, 34.5% services, 20.0% sales, 0.0% farming, 3.6% construction, 14.5% production (2005-2009 5-year est.).

Income: Per capita income: $19,039 (2010); Median household income: $36,500 (2010); Average household income: $44,663 (2010); Percent of households with income of $100,000 or more: 7.7% (2010); Poverty rate: 9.9% (2005-2009 5-year est.).

Taxes: Total city taxes per capita: $407 (2007); City property taxes per capita: $100 (2007).

Education: Percent of population age 25 and over with: High school diploma (including GED) or higher: 77.9% (2010); Bachelor's degree or higher: 7.0% (2010); Master's degree or higher: 2.3% (2010).

Housing: Homeownership rate: 82.7% (2010); Median home value: $53,750 (2010); Median contract rent: n/a per month (2005-2009 5-year est.); Median year structure built: 1973 (2005-2009 5-year est.).

Transportation: Commute to work: 85.5% car, 0.0% public transportation, 0.0% walk, 14.5% work from home (2005-2009 5-year est.); Travel time to work: 14.9% less than 15 minutes, 31.9% 15 to 30 minutes, 53.2% 30 to 45 minutes, 0.0% 45 to 60 minutes, 0.0% 60 minutes or more (2005-2009 5-year est.)

WEST LIVINGSTON (CDP). Covers a land area of 23.942 square miles and a water area of 0.036 square miles. Located at 30.70° N. Lat; 95.01° W. Long. Elevation is 141 feet.

Population: 2,419 (1990); 6,612 (2000); 8,055 (2010); 8,688 (2015 projected); Race: 60.2% White, 36.0% Black, 0.6% Asian, 3.2% Other, 19.0% Hispanic of any race (2010); Density: 336.4 persons per square mile (2010); Average household size: 2.50 (2010); Median age: 34.2 (2010); Males per 100 females: 200.2 (2010); Marriage status: 41.5% never married, 35.4% now married, 6.6% widowed, 16.5% divorced (2005-2009 5-year est.); Foreign born: 8.5% (2005-2009 5-year est.); Ancestry (includes multiple ancestries): 12.6% Irish, 11.8% German, 9.7% American, 6.9% English, 5.8% French (2005-2009 5-year est.).

Economy: Employment by occupation: 8.9% management, 8.5% professional, 33.0% services, 17.0% sales, 1.2% farming, 23.6% construction, 7.9% production (2005-2009 5-year est.).

Income: Per capita income: $12,494 (2010); Median household income: $30,460 (2010); Average household income: $36,722 (2010); Percent of households with income of $100,000 or more: 3.2% (2010); Poverty rate: 25.1% (2005-2009 5-year est.).

Education: Percent of population age 25 and over with: High school diploma (including GED) or higher: 71.8% (2010); Bachelor's degree or higher: 8.1% (2010); Master's degree or higher: 3.2% (2010).

Housing: Homeownership rate: 78.6% (2010); Median home value: $60,520 (2010); Median contract rent: $492 per month (2005-2009 5-year est.); Median year structure built: 1985 (2005-2009 5-year est.).

Transportation: Commute to work: 91.6% car, 0.0% public transportation, 0.8% walk, 0.6% work from home (2005-2009 5-year est.); Travel time to work: 23.6% less than 15 minutes, 47.1% 15 to 30 minutes, 10.5% 30 to 45 minutes, 2.6% 45 to 60 minutes, 16.2% 60 minutes or more (2005-2009 5-year est.)

Potter County

Located in north Texas, on the high plains of the Panhandle; drained by the Canadian River. Covers a land area of 909.24 square miles, a water area of 12.74 square miles, and is located in the Central Time Zone at 35.25° N. Lat., 101.84° W. Long. The county was founded in 1876. County seat is Amarillo.

Potter County is part of the Amarillo, TX Metropolitan Statistical Area. The entire metro area includes: Armstrong County, TX; Carson County, TX; Potter County, TX; Randall County, TX

Weather Station: Amarillo Intl Arpt   Elevation: 3,585 feet

	Jan	Feb	Mar	Apr	May	Jun	Jul	Aug	Sep	Oct	Nov	Dec
High	50	54	62	71	79	88	92	89	82	72	60	50
Low	23	26	33	41	52	61	65	64	56	44	32	24
Precip	0.7	0.5	1.4	1.3	2.3	3.2	2.6	2.9	1.9	1.6	0.7	0.7
Snow	4.8	2.6	2.7	0.7	0.2	tr	tr	tr	tr	0.2	2.6	4.0

High and Low temperatures in degrees Fahrenheit; Precipitation and Snow in inches

Population: 97,874 (1990); 113,546 (2000); 123,265 (2010); 127,780 (2015 projected); Race: 65.2% White, 9.7% Black, 2.3% Asian, 22.8% Other, 34.0% Hispanic of any race (2010); Density: 135.6 persons per square mile (2010); Average household size: 2.69 (2010); Median age: 33.1 (2010); Males per 100 females: 103.8 (2010).

Religion: Five largest groups: 41.6% Southern Baptist Convention, 20.2% Catholic Church, 6.0% The United Methodist Church, 4.5% Churches of Christ, 2.4% Presbyterian Church (U.S.A.) (2000).

Economy: Unemployment rate: 7.3% (June 2011); Total civilian labor force: 58,149 (June 2011); Leading industries: 21.4% health care and social assistance; 15.0% retail trade; 12.4% accommodation & food services (2009); Farms: 279 totaling 573,084 acres (2007); Companies that employ 500 or more persons: 6 (2009); Companies that employ 100 to 499 persons: 78 (2009); Companies that employ less than 100 persons: 3,489 (2009); Black-owned businesses: n/a (2007); Hispanic-owned businesses: 1,787 (2007); Asian-owned businesses: n/a (2007); Women-owned businesses: 2,943 (2007); Retail sales per capita: $22,915 (2010). Single-family building permits issued: 510 (2010); Multi-family building permits issued: 345 (2010).

Income: Per capita income: $16,958 (2010); Median household income: $34,934 (2010); Average household income: $47,569 (2010); Percent of households with income of $100,000 or more: 8.4% (2010); Poverty rate: 23.1% (2009); Bankruptcy rate: 2.37% (2010).

Taxes: Total county taxes per capita: $275 (2007); County property taxes per capita: $259 (2007).

Education: Percent of population age 25 and over with: High school diploma (including GED) or higher: 75.2% (2010); Bachelor's degree or higher: 14.1% (2010); Master's degree or higher: 4.3% (2010).

Housing: Homeownership rate: 59.0% (2010); Median home value: $74,705 (2010); Median contract rent: $492 per month (2005-2009 5-year est.); Median year structure built: 1962 (2005-2009 5-year est.)

Health: Birth rate: 184.3 per 10,000 population (2009); Death rate: 101.7 per 10,000 population (2009); Age-adjusted cancer mortality rate: 190.7

deaths per 100,000 population (2007); Number of physicians: 33.6 per 10,000 population (2008); Hospital beds: 98.4 per 10,000 population (2007); Hospital admissions: 4,010.7 per 10,000 population (2007).

Environment: Air Quality Index: 96.7% good, 3.3% moderate, 0.0% unhealthy for sensitive individuals, 0.0% unhealthy (percent of days in 2008)

Elections: 2008 Presidential election results: 29.8% Obama, 69.2% McCain, 0.1% Nader

National and State Parks: Alibates Flint Quarries National Monument

Additional Information Contacts

Potter County Government . . . . (806) 379-2250
  http://www.co.potter.tx.us/home.html
Amarillo Chamber of Commerce . . . . (806) 373-7800
  http://www.amarillo-chamber.org
City of Amarillo. . . . . (806) 378-3000
  http://www.ci.amarillo.tx.us

Potter County Communities

AMARILLO (city). County seat. Covers a land area of 89.863 square miles and a water area of 0.446 square miles. Located at 35.19° N. Lat; 101.84° W. Long. Elevation is 3,668 feet.

History: Amarillo began as a supply and shipping point for buffalo hunters, established around a Fort Worth & Denver City Railway construction camp. The town was laid out in 1887 by Henry B. Sanborn, a land developer, who called it Oneida. When the town won the county seat election, the name was changed to Amarillo. Amarillo, Spanish for "yellow," was the name of a nearby creek with yellow clay banks. One of the early ranchers near Amarillo was J.F. Glidden, who invented barbed wire for fencing.

Population: 158,012 (1990); 173,627 (2000); 191,307 (2010); 199,242 (2015 projected); Race: 74.1% White, 5.9% Black, 2.1% Asian, 17.9% Other, 27.7% Hispanic of any race (2010); Density: 2,128.9 persons per square mile (2010); Average household size: 2.59 (2010); Median age: 34.1 (2010); Males per 100 females: 95.0 (2010); Marriage status: 28.8% never married, 51.8% now married, 6.8% widowed, 12.6% divorced (2005-2009 5-year est.); Foreign born: 9.4% (2005-2009 5-year est.); Ancestry (includes multiple ancestries): 13.6% German, 9.8% Irish, 9.1% English, 8.1% American, 2.3% French (2005-2009 5-year est.).

Economy: Unemployment rate: 6.3% (June 2011); Total civilian labor force: 101,748 (June 2011); Single-family building permits issued: 510 (2010); Multi-family building permits issued: 345 (2010); Employment by occupation: 10.1% management, 18.2% professional, 18.3% services, 27.1% sales, 0.4% farming, 11.1% construction, 14.9% production (2005-2009 5-year est.).

Income: Per capita income: $22,326 (2010); Median household income: $43,383 (2010); Average household income: $58,370 (2010); Percent of households with income of $100,000 or more: 13.5% (2010); Poverty rate: 16.4% (2005-2009 5-year est.).

Taxes: Total city taxes per capita: $516 (2007); City property taxes per capita: $134 (2007).

Education: Percent of population age 25 and over with: High school diploma (including GED) or higher: 82.3% (2010); Bachelor's degree or higher: 20.4% (2010); Master's degree or higher: 6.6% (2010).

School District(s)

Amarillo ISD (PK-12)
  2009-10 Enrollment: 31,890 . . . . (806) 326-1000
Broaddus ISD (PK-12)
  2009-10 Enrollment: 474 . . . . (936) 872-3041
Canyon ISD (PK-12)
  2009-10 Enrollment: 8,745 . . . . (806) 677-2600
Highland Park ISD (PK-12)
  2009-10 Enrollment: 916 . . . . (806) 335-2823
Responsive Education Solutions (KG-12)
  2009-10 Enrollment: 5,022 . . . . (972) 316-3663
Richard Milburn Academy (Amarillo) (09-12)
  2009-10 Enrollment: 236 . . . . (830) 557-6181
River Road ISD (PK-12)
  2009-10 Enrollment: 1,506 . . . . (806) 381-7800

Two-year College(s)

Amarillo College (Public)
  Fall 2009 Enrollment: 11,289 . . . . (806) 371-5000
  2010-11 Tuition: In-state $2,034; Out-of-state $2,994

Vocational/Technical School(s)

Exposito School of Hair Design Ltd (Private, For-profit)
  Fall 2009 Enrollment: 80 . . . . (806) 355-9111
  2010-11 Tuition: $8,308
Milan Institute (Private, For-profit)
  Fall 2009 Enrollment: 231 . . . . (806) 353-3500
  2010-11 Tuition: $10,870
Milan Institute of Cosmetology (Private, For-profit)
  Fall 2009 Enrollment: 212 . . . . (806) 371-7600
  2010-11 Tuition: $15,006

Housing: Homeownership rate: 62.7% (2010); Median home value: $103,742 (2010); Median contract rent: $524 per month (2005-2009 5-year est.); Median year structure built: 1967 (2005-2009 5-year est.).
Hospitals: Baptist-St. Anthony's Health System (451 beds); Northwest Texas Healthcare System (489 beds); Northwest Texas Surgery Center (6 beds); Physicians Surgical Hospital at Quail Creek (32 beds); Thomas E Creek VA Medical Center
Safety: Violent crime rate: 83.7 per 10,000 population; Property crime rate: 584.8 per 10,000 population (2009).
Newspapers: Active Life - Amarillo Globe-News; Amarillo Globe-News (Local news; Circulation 43,572); El Mensajero (Local news; Circulation 15,000); Siglo Veintiuno (Amarillo) (Community news; Circulation 10,000); West Texas Catholic (Regional news; Circulation 9,200)
Transportation: Commute to work: 94.7% car, 0.7% public transportation, 1.2% walk, 2.0% work from home (2005-2009 5-year est.); Travel time to work: 48.1% less than 15 minutes, 41.6% 15 to 30 minutes, 5.9% 30 to 45 minutes, 1.9% 45 to 60 minutes, 2.5% 60 minutes or more (2005-2009 5-year est.)
Airports: Rick Husband Amarillo International (primary service/small hub); Tradewind (general aviation)
Additional Information Contacts
Amarillo Chamber of Commerce . . . . (806) 373-7800
  http://www.amarillo-chamber.org
City of Amarillo. . . . . (806) 378-3000
  http://www.ci.amarillo.tx.us

BISHOP HILLS (town). Covers a land area of 0.311 square miles and a water area of 0 square miles. Located at 35.25° N. Lat; 101.95° W. Long. Elevation is 3,488 feet.
Population: 151 (1990); 210 (2000); 233 (2010); 245 (2015 projected); Race: 94.4% White, 1.3% Black, 0.0% Asian, 4.3% Other, 6.0% Hispanic of any race (2010); Density: 750.1 persons per square mile (2010); Average household size: 2.74 (2010); Median age: 39.2 (2010); Males per 100 females: 83.5 (2010); Marriage status: 23.0% never married, 64.7% now married, 6.3% widowed, 5.9% divorced (2005-2009 5-year est.); Foreign born: 0.7% (2005-2009 5-year est.); Ancestry (includes multiple ancestries): 22.9% English, 22.9% German, 12.0% Irish, 11.3% American, 8.5% Scottish (2005-2009 5-year est.).
Economy: Employment by occupation: 13.2% management, 40.3% professional, 20.1% services, 16.7% sales, 0.0% farming, 2.1% construction, 7.6% production (2005-2009 5-year est.).
Income: Per capita income: $23,349 (2010); Median household income: $50,595 (2010); Average household income: $70,206 (2010); Percent of households with income of $100,000 or more: 15.3% (2010); Poverty rate: 2.5% (2005-2009 5-year est.).
Taxes: Total city taxes per capita: $65 (2007); City property taxes per capita: $65 (2007).
Education: Percent of population age 25 and over with: High school diploma (including GED) or higher: 88.2% (2010); Bachelor's degree or higher: 16.3% (2010); Master's degree or higher: 3.9% (2010).
Housing: Homeownership rate: 88.2% (2010); Median home value: $103,750 (2010); Median contract rent: n/a per month (2005-2009 5-year est.); Median year structure built: 1972 (2005-2009 5-year est.).
Transportation: Commute to work: 100.0% car, 0.0% public transportation, 0.0% walk, 0.0% work from home (2005-2009 5-year est.); Travel time to work: 44.0% less than 15 minutes, 39.0% 15 to 30 minutes, 14.9% 30 to 45 minutes, 2.1% 45 to 60 minutes, 0.0% 60 minutes or more (2005-2009 5-year est.)

Presidio County

Located in west Texas; high plateau area, bounded on the west and south by the Mexican border; includes the Sierra Vieja and Chinati Mountains. Covers a land area of 3,855.51 square miles, a water area of 0.75 square miles, and is located in the Central Time Zone at 29.98° N. Lat., 104.23° W. Long. The county was founded in 1850. County seat is Marfa.

Weather Station: Candelaria   Elevation: 2,875 feet

	Jan	Feb	Mar	Apr	May	Jun	Jul	Aug	Sep	Oct	Nov	Dec
High	67	73	81	89	96	101	100	98	93	86	74	67
Low	32	36	41	48	57	66	69	67	62	51	38	32
Precip	0.5	0.5	0.4	0.5	0.7	2.0	2.1	2.6	2.0	1.5	0.5	0.6
Snow	0.1	0.0	0.0	tr	0.0	0.0	0.0	0.0	0.0	0.0	tr	0.0

High and Low temperatures in degrees Fahrenheit; Precipitation and Snow in inches

Weather Station: Marfa#2   Elevation: 4,759 feet

	Jan	Feb	Mar	Apr	May	Jun	Jul	Aug	Sep	Oct	Nov	Dec
High	60	63	70	78	86	91	90	87	84	77	67	60
Low	26	29	34	41	51	58	61	60	54	45	33	27
Precip	0.5	0.6	0.3	0.7	1.4	1.6	2.9	2.6	2.5	1.5	0.5	0.6
Snow	0.6	0.3	tr	tr	0.0	0.0	0.0	0.0	0.0	tr	0.3	0.4

High and Low temperatures in degrees Fahrenheit; Precipitation and Snow in inches

Weather Station: Presidio   Elevation: 2,582 feet

	Jan	Feb	Mar	Apr	May	Jun	Jul	Aug	Sep	Oct	Nov	Dec
High	69	75	83	91	98	103	101	100	96	88	77	69
Low	35	41	47	55	65	73	75	74	68	57	44	36
Precip	0.5	0.4	0.2	0.3	0.6	1.3	1.6	1.6	1.3	1.0	0.4	0.5
Snow	tr	0.0	0.0	0.0	0.0	0.0	0.0	0.0	0.0	0.0	0.0	tr

High and Low temperatures in degrees Fahrenheit; Precipitation and Snow in inches

Population: 6,637 (1990); 7,304 (2000); 7,903 (2010); 8,178 (2015 projected); Race: 84.3% White, 1.0% Black, 0.1% Asian, 14.6% Other, 83.1% Hispanic of any race (2010); Density: 2.0 persons per square mile (2010); Average household size: 2.81 (2010); Median age: 36.2 (2010); Males per 100 females: 90.3 (2010).
Religion: Five largest groups: 55.4% Catholic Church, 3.1% Southern Baptist Convention, 3.1% The United Methodist Church, 0.8% Churches of Christ, 0.6% Christian Church (Disciples of Christ) (2000).
Economy: Unemployment rate: 16.2% (June 2011); Total civilian labor force: 3,902 (June 2011); Leading industries: 33.8% retail trade; 19.2% accommodation & food services; 8.5% finance & insurance (2009); Farms: 148 totaling 1,559,722 acres (2007); Companies that employ 500 or more persons: 0 (2009); Companies that employ 100 to 499 persons: 0 (2009); Companies that employ less than 100 persons: 129 (2009); Black-owned businesses: n/a (2007); Hispanic-owned businesses: 392 (2007); Asian-owned businesses: n/a (2007); Women-owned businesses: n/a (2007); Retail sales per capita: $4,606 (2010). Single-family building permits issued: 2 (2010); Multi-family building permits issued: 0 (2010).
Income: Per capita income: $13,353 (2010); Median household income: $27,049 (2010); Average household income: $37,352 (2010); Percent of households with income of $100,000 or more: 5.8% (2010); Poverty rate: 23.6% (2009); Bankruptcy rate: 0.38% (2010).
Taxes: Total county taxes per capita: $209 (2007); County property taxes per capita: $166 (2007).
Education: Percent of population age 25 and over with: High school diploma (including GED) or higher: 50.0% (2010); Bachelor's degree or higher: 13.2% (2010); Master's degree or higher: 5.2% (2010).
Housing: Homeownership rate: 68.2% (2010); Median home value: $40,028 (2010); Median contract rent: $209 per month (2005-2009 5-year est.); Median year structure built: 1976 (2005-2009 5-year est.).
Health: Birth rate: 188.8 per 10,000 population (2009); Death rate: 41.5 per 10,000 population (2009); Age-adjusted cancer mortality rate: 120.0 (Unreliable) deaths per 100,000 population (2007); Number of physicians: 4.0 per 10,000 population (2008); Hospital beds: 0.0 per 10,000 population (2007); Hospital admissions: 0.0 per 10,000 population (2007).
Elections: 2008 Presidential election results: 71.3% Obama, 27.8% McCain, 0.1% Nader
National and State Parks: Fort Leaton State Historic Site
Additional Information Contacts
Presidio County Government. . . . . (432) 729-4452
  http://www.co.presidio.tx.us/ips/cms
Marfa Chamber of Commerce . . . . (432) 729-4942
  http://www.marfacc.com

Presidio County Communities

MARFA (city). County seat. Covers a land area of 1.566 square miles and a water area of 0 square miles. Located at 30.31° N. Lat; 104.02° W. Long. Elevation is 4,685 feet.

History: Old Fort D.A. Russell here was founded 1833. Marfa Mystery Lights, unexplained phenomenon first reported in 1883. Founded 1881, incorporated 1887.

Population: 2,424 (1990); 2,121 (2000); 1,904 (2010); 1,813 (2015 projected); Race: 88.5% White, 2.2% Black, 0.1% Asian, 9.2% Other, 67.1% Hispanic of any race (2010); Density: 1,216.0 persons per square mile (2010); Average household size: 2.28 (2010); Median age: 45.4 (2010); Males per 100 females: 97.5 (2010); Marriage status: 20.8% never married, 54.8% now married, 11.4% widowed, 12.9% divorced (2005-2009 5-year est.); Foreign born: 10.7% (2005-2009 5-year est.); Ancestry (includes multiple ancestries): 12.5% English, 11.2% German, 4.3% Swedish, 3.3% Scottish, 3.1% Czech (2005-2009 5-year est.).

Economy: Single-family building permits issued: 0 (2010); Multi-family building permits issued: 0 (2010); Employment by occupation: 10.4% management, 26.2% professional, 17.2% services, 32.0% sales, 4.8% farming, 9.4% construction, 0.0% production (2005-2009 5-year est.).

Income: Per capita income: $18,856 (2010); Median household income: $30,202 (2010); Average household income: $43,670 (2010); Percent of households with income of $100,000 or more: 7.5% (2010); Poverty rate: 21.5% (2005-2009 5-year est.).

Taxes: Total city taxes per capita: $72 (2007); City property taxes per capita: $0 (2007).

Education: Percent of population age 25 and over with: High school diploma (including GED) or higher: 70.0% (2010); Bachelor's degree or higher: 19.6% (2010); Master's degree or higher: 9.0% (2010).

School District(s)
Marfa ISD (PK-12)
    2009-10 Enrollment: 384 . . . . (432) 729-4252

Housing: Homeownership rate: 70.4% (2010); Median home value: $58,058 (2010); Median contract rent: $306 per month (2005-2009 5-year est.); Median year structure built: 1950 (2005-2009 5-year est.).

Transportation: Commute to work: 71.8% car, 0.0% public transportation, 20.4% walk, 7.0% work from home (2005-2009 5-year est.); Travel time to work: 76.9% less than 15 minutes, 11.8% 15 to 30 minutes, 4.8% 30 to 45 minutes, 2.4% 45 to 60 minutes, 4.0% 60 minutes or more (2005-2009 5-year est.)

Airports: Marfa Municipal (general aviation)

Additional Information Contacts
Marfa Chamber of Commerce . . . . (432) 729-4942
    http://www.marfacc.com

PRESIDIO (city). Covers a land area of 2.572 square miles and a water area of 0 square miles. Located at 29.56° N. Lat; 104.36° W. Long. Elevation is 2,582 feet.

History: At the site called by the Spaniards La Junta de los Rios (junction of the rivers), Franciscan priests founded a mission in 1684. The settlement that grew up around the mission was called Presidio del Norte after 1830, and later shortened to Presidio. The Chihuahua Trail, a main freight route to Mexico, crossed the Rio Grande at Presidio.

Population: 3,047 (1990); 4,167 (2000); 4,960 (2010); 5,318 (2015 projected); Race: 83.3% White, 0.4% Black, 0.1% Asian, 16.2% Other, 91.7% Hispanic of any race (2010); Density: 1,928.4 persons per square mile (2010); Average household size: 3.12 (2010); Median age: 32.2 (2010); Males per 100 females: 87.2 (2010); Marriage status: 22.5% never married, 57.1% now married, 11.3% widowed, 9.1% divorced (2005-2009 5-year est.); Foreign born: 40.8% (2005-2009 5-year est.); Ancestry (includes multiple ancestries): 0.6% German, 0.5% Italian, 0.5% Irish (2005-2009 5-year est.).

Economy: Single-family building permits issued: 2 (2010); Multi-family building permits issued: 0 (2010); Employment by occupation: 11.1% management, 12.3% professional, 25.4% services, 24.5% sales, 11.9% farming, 7.9% construction, 7.0% production (2005-2009 5-year est.).

Income: Per capita income: $10,915 (2010); Median household income: $25,731 (2010); Average household income: $33,678 (2010); Percent of households with income of $100,000 or more: 4.6% (2010); Poverty rate: 32.9% (2005-2009 5-year est.).

Taxes: Total city taxes per capita: $159 (2007); City property taxes per capita: $82 (2007).

Education: Percent of population age 25 and over with: High school diploma (including GED) or higher: 38.2% (2010); Bachelor's degree or higher: 8.8% (2010); Master's degree or higher: 2.8% (2010).

School District(s)
Presidio ISD (PK-12)
    2009-10 Enrollment: 1,471 . . . . (432) 229-3275

Housing: Homeownership rate: 66.9% (2010); Median home value: $34,289 (2010); Median contract rent: $200 per month (2005-2009 5-year est.); Median year structure built: 1983 (2005-2009 5-year est.).

Safety: Violent crime rate: 12.6 per 10,000 population; Property crime rate: 82.1 per 10,000 population (2009).

Transportation: Commute to work: 88.7% car, 0.0% public transportation, 6.1% walk, 4.3% work from home (2005-2009 5-year est.); Travel time to work: 67.4% less than 15 minutes, 1.6% 15 to 30 minutes, 0.0% 30 to 45 minutes, 4.2% 45 to 60 minutes, 26.7% 60 minutes or more (2005-2009 5-year est.)

Additional Information Contacts
Marfa Chamber of Commerce . . . . (432) 729-4942
    http://www.marfacc.com

REDFORD (CDP). Covers a land area of 45.045 square miles and a water area of 0.010 square miles. Located at 29.44° N. Lat; 104.18° W. Long. Elevation is 2,520 feet.

Population: 116 (1990); 132 (2000); 156 (2010); 166 (2015 projected); Race: 75.0% White, 0.0% Black, 0.0% Asian, 25.0% Other, 82.1% Hispanic of any race (2010); Density: 3.5 persons per square mile (2010); Average household size: 2.79 (2010); Median age: 35.7 (2010); Males per 100 females: 85.7 (2010); Marriage status: 22.2% never married, 0.0% now married, 77.8% widowed, 0.0% divorced (2005-2009 5-year est.); Foreign born: 58.7% (2005-2009 5-year est.); Ancestry (includes multiple ancestries): n/a (2005-2009 5-year est.).

Economy: Employment by occupation: 0.0% management, 0.0% professional, 33.3% services, 0.0% sales, 0.0% farming, 66.7% construction, 0.0% production (2005-2009 5-year est.).

Income: Per capita income: $13,356 (2010); Median household income: $25,000 (2010); Average household income: $35,759 (2010); Percent of households with income of $100,000 or more: 7.1% (2010); Poverty rate: 0.0% (2005-2009 5-year est.).

Education: Percent of population age 25 and over with: High school diploma (including GED) or higher: 50.5% (2010); Bachelor's degree or higher: 18.6% (2010); Master's degree or higher: 7.2% (2010).

Housing: Homeownership rate: 69.6% (2010); Median home value: $41,000 (2010); Median contract rent: n/a per month (2005-2009 5-year est.); Median year structure built: 1966 (2005-2009 5-year est.).

Transportation: Commute to work: 66.7% car, 0.0% public transportation, 0.0% walk, 33.3% work from home (2005-2009 5-year est.); Travel time to work: 0.0% less than 15 minutes, 0.0% 15 to 30 minutes, 0.0% 30 to 45 minutes, 0.0% 45 to 60 minutes, 100.0% 60 minutes or more (2005-2009 5-year est.)

Rains County

Located in northeastern Texas; bounded on the southwest by the Sabine River; prairie and woodland area, drained by the Sabine River. Covers a land area of 232.05 square miles, a water area of 26.82 square miles, and is located in the Central Time Zone at 32.88° N. Lat., 95.80° W. Long. The county was founded in 1870. County seat is Emory.

Weather Station: Emory										Elevation: 435 feet		
	Jan	Feb	Mar	Apr	May	Jun	Jul	Aug	Sep	Oct	Nov	Dec
High	55	59	67	74	81	88	92	93	87	77	66	57
Low	33	36	44	51	61	69	71	70	63	52	43	34
Precip	3.0	3.5	4.4	3.3	5.2	4.1	2.7	2.2	3.1	5.1	3.8	3.8
Snow	0.2	0.3	tr	0.0	0.0	0.0	0.0	0.0	0.0	0.0	0.0	0.3

High and Low temperatures in degrees Fahrenheit; Precipitation and Snow in inches

Population: 6,715 (1990); 9,139 (2000); 11,276 (2010); 12,295 (2015 projected); Race: 89.8% White, 2.9% Black, 0.6% Asian, 6.7% Other, 8.7% Hispanic of any race (2010); Density: 48.6 persons per square mile (2010); Average household size: 2.49 (2010); Median age: 40.3 (2010); Males per 100 females: 100.2 (2010).

Religion: Five largest groups: 9.3% Southern Baptist Convention, 3.9% Catholic Church, 3.8% Baptist Missionary Association of America, 3.5% The United Methodist Church, 3.4% Church of God (Cleveland, Tennessee) (2000).

Economy: Unemployment rate: 9.6% (June 2011); Total civilian labor force: 5,096 (June 2011); Leading industries: 37.0% retail trade; 14.6% accommodation & food services; 12.5% professional, scientific & technical services (2009); Farms: 657 totaling 97,615 acres (2007); Companies that employ 500 or more persons: 0 (2009); Companies that employ 100 to 499 persons: 0 (2009); Companies that employ less than 100 persons: 143 (2009); Black-owned businesses: n/a (2007); Hispanic-owned businesses:

n/a (2007); Asian-owned businesses: n/a (2007); Women-owned businesses: n/a (2007); Retail sales per capita: $5,347 (2010). Single-family building permits issued: 0 (2010); Multi-family building permits issued: 0 (2010).

Income: Per capita income: $20,849 (2010); Median household income: $42,163 (2010); Average household income: $52,137 (2010); Percent of households with income of $100,000 or more: 10.5% (2010); Poverty rate: 15.8% (2009); Bankruptcy rate: 1.26% (2010).

Taxes: Total county taxes per capita: $284 (2007); County property taxes per capita: $202 (2007).

Education: Percent of population age 25 and over with: High school diploma (including GED) or higher: 77.9% (2010); Bachelor's degree or higher: 12.9% (2010); Master's degree or higher: 4.4% (2010).

Housing: Homeownership rate: 81.3% (2010); Median home value: $80,970 (2010); Median contract rent: $316 per month (2005-2009 5-year est.); Median year structure built: 1981 (2005-2009 5-year est.)

Health: Birth rate: 97.5 per 10,000 population (2009); Death rate: 102.8 per 10,000 population (2009); Age-adjusted cancer mortality rate: 131.3 (Unreliable) deaths per 100,000 population (2007); Number of physicians: 2.7 per 10,000 population (2008); Hospital beds: 0.0 per 10,000 population (2007); Hospital admissions: 0.0 per 10,000 population (2007).

Elections: 2008 Presidential election results: 24.7% Obama, 74.3% McCain, 0.0% Nader

Additional Information Contacts
Rains County Government. . . . . (903) 473-2461
   http://www.co.rains.tx.us/ips/cms
Rains County Chamber of Commerce . . . . (903) 473-3913
   http://www.rainschamber.com

Rains County Communities

EAST TAWAKONI (city). Covers a land area of 1.809 square miles and a water area of 0.043 square miles. Located at 32.90° N. Lat; 95.94° W. Long. Elevation is 469 feet.

Population: 685 (1990); 775 (2000); 983 (2010); 1,082 (2015 projected); Race: 93.5% White, 0.3% Black, 1.4% Asian, 4.8% Other, 5.5% Hispanic of any race (2010); Density: 543.4 persons per square mile (2010); Average household size: 2.45 (2010); Median age: 45.1 (2010); Males per 100 females: 101.0 (2010); Marriage status: 10.8% never married, 68.4% now married, 5.0% widowed, 15.9% divorced (2005-2009 5-year est.); Foreign born: 0.7% (2005-2009 5-year est.); Ancestry (includes multiple ancestries): 31.7% Irish, 20.5% German, 8.1% English, 3.5% American, 2.9% Scotch-Irish (2005-2009 5-year est.).

Economy: Single-family building permits issued: 0 (2010); Multi-family building permits issued: 0 (2010); Employment by occupation: 22.4% management, 23.7% professional, 2.4% services, 25.6% sales, 0.0% farming, 13.6% construction, 12.3% production (2005-2009 5-year est.).

Income: Per capita income: $21,776 (2010); Median household income: $45,697 (2010); Average household income: $53,105 (2010); Percent of households with income of $100,000 or more: 8.7% (2010); Poverty rate: 4.4% (2005-2009 5-year est.).

Taxes: Total city taxes per capita: $196 (2007); City property taxes per capita: $81 (2007).

Education: Percent of population age 25 and over with: High school diploma (including GED) or higher: 81.4% (2010); Bachelor's degree or higher: 7.2% (2010); Master's degree or higher: 1.5% (2010).

Housing: Homeownership rate: 88.3% (2010); Median home value: $76,000 (2010); Median contract rent: $421 per month (2005-2009 5-year est.); Median year structure built: 1975 (2005-2009 5-year est.).

Transportation: Commute to work: 89.6% car, 0.0% public transportation, 0.0% walk, 10.4% work from home (2005-2009 5-year est.); Travel time to work: 12.2% less than 15 minutes, 30.3% 15 to 30 minutes, 20.2% 30 to 45 minutes, 8.0% 45 to 60 minutes, 29.4% 60 minutes or more (2005-2009 5-year est.)

EMORY (city). County seat. Covers a land area of 1.547 square miles and a water area of 0 square miles. Located at 32.87° N. Lat; 95.76° W. Long. Elevation is 479 feet.

Population: 926 (1990); 1,021 (2000); 1,134 (2010); 1,200 (2015 projected); Race: 86.3% White, 3.7% Black, 0.1% Asian, 9.9% Other, 8.8% Hispanic of any race (2010); Density: 733.2 persons per square mile (2010); Average household size: 2.36 (2010); Median age: 37.2 (2010); Males per 100 females: 88.4 (2010); Marriage status: 24.9% never married, 37.9% now married, 16.3% widowed, 20.8% divorced (2005-2009 5-year est.); Foreign born: 1.0% (2005-2009 5-year est.); Ancestry (includes

multiple ancestries): 23.1% Irish, 17.5% German, 9.1% English, 7.5% French, 6.3% Dutch (2005-2009 5-year est.).

Economy: Single-family building permits issued: 0 (2010); Multi-family building permits issued: 0 (2010); Employment by occupation: 9.2% management, 12.9% professional, 17.9% services, 12.2% sales, 0.0% farming, 16.2% construction, 31.5% production (2005-2009 5-year est.).

Income: Per capita income: $19,510 (2010); Median household income: $36,852 (2010); Average household income: $47,188 (2010); Percent of households with income of $100,000 or more: 8.2% (2010); Poverty rate: 17.5% (2005-2009 5-year est.).

Taxes: Total city taxes per capita: $813 (2007); City property taxes per capita: $72 (2007).

Education: Percent of population age 25 and over with: High school diploma (including GED) or higher: 73.0% (2010); Bachelor's degree or higher: 11.5% (2010); Master's degree or higher: 5.4% (2010).

School District(s)
Rains ISD (PK-12)
   2009-10 Enrollment: 1,570 . . . . (903) 473-2222

Housing: Homeownership rate: 62.3% (2010); Median home value: $76,905 (2010); Median contract rent: $192 per month (2005-2009 5-year est.); Median year structure built: 1975 (2005-2009 5-year est.).

Newspapers: Rains County Leader (Local news; Circulation 2,900)

Transportation: Commute to work: 92.5% car, 2.6% public transportation, 0.0% walk, 4.9% work from home (2005-2009 5-year est.); Travel time to work: 32.9% less than 15 minutes, 26.7% 15 to 30 minutes, 23.3% 30 to 45 minutes, 4.0% 45 to 60 minutes, 13.1% 60 minutes or more (2005-2009 5-year est.)

Additional Information Contacts
Rains County Chamber of Commerce . . . . (903) 473-3913
   http://www.rainschamber.com

POINT (city). Covers a land area of 2.773 square miles and a water area of 0 square miles. Located at 32.93° N. Lat; 95.87° W. Long. Elevation is 528 feet.

Population: 645 (1990); 792 (2000); 1,006 (2010); 1,106 (2015 projected); Race: 85.5% White, 5.5% Black, 1.1% Asian, 8.0% Other, 8.4% Hispanic of any race (2010); Density: 362.8 persons per square mile (2010); Average household size: 2.64 (2010); Median age: 35.9 (2010); Males per 100 females: 97.3 (2010); Marriage status: 36.5% never married, 45.7% now married, 4.5% widowed, 13.3% divorced (2005-2009 5-year est.); Foreign born: 5.8% (2005-2009 5-year est.); Ancestry (includes multiple ancestries): 17.7% German, 16.9% Irish, 12.0% English, 5.6% French, 5.1% Dutch (2005-2009 5-year est.).

Economy: Employment by occupation: 27.0% management, 6.1% professional, 21.1% services, 20.2% sales, 0.0% farming, 13.6% construction, 12.0% production (2005-2009 5-year est.).

Income: Per capita income: $17,965 (2010); Median household income: $38,115 (2010); Average household income: $46,804 (2010); Percent of households with income of $100,000 or more: 8.1% (2010); Poverty rate: 17.7% (2005-2009 5-year est.).

Taxes: Total city taxes per capita: $116 (2007); City property taxes per capita: $42 (2007).

Education: Percent of population age 25 and over with: High school diploma (including GED) or higher: 75.7% (2010); Bachelor's degree or higher: 12.6% (2010); Master's degree or higher: 3.8% (2010).

Housing: Homeownership rate: 76.4% (2010); Median home value: $65,345 (2010); Median contract rent: $293 per month (2005-2009 5-year est.); Median year structure built: 1975 (2005-2009 5-year est.).

Transportation: Commute to work: 94.2% car, 0.0% public transportation, 0.0% walk, 3.5% work from home (2005-2009 5-year est.); Travel time to work: 37.6% less than 15 minutes, 14.9% 15 to 30 minutes, 21.9% 30 to 45 minutes, 14.9% 45 to 60 minutes, 10.7% 60 minutes or more (2005-2009 5-year est.)

Randall County

Located in north Texas, on the high plains of the Panhandle; drained by Tierra Blanca and Palo Duro Creeks, which form the Prairie Dog Town Fork of the Red River; includes Palo Duro Canyon. Covers a land area of 914.43 square miles, a water area of 7.99 square miles, and is located in the Central Time Zone at 35.06° N. Lat., 101.89° W. Long. The county was founded in 1876. County seat is Canyon.

Randall County is part of the Amarillo, TX Metropolitan Statistical Area. The entire metro area includes: Armstrong County, TX; Carson County, TX; Potter County, TX; Randall County, TX

Weather Station: Canyon   Elevation: 3,589 feet

	Jan	Feb	Mar	Apr	May	Jun	Jul	Aug	Sep	Oct	Nov	Dec
High	53	57	65	74	82	90	93	91	84	75	62	53
Low	25	27	34	43	53	62	66	65	57	46	34	25
Precip	0.6	0.5	1.1	1.1	2.5	3.3	2.1	3.1	2.2	1.9	0.7	0.7
Snow	2.6	1.9	1.1	0.4	0.1	0.0	0.0	0.0	0.0	tr	1.4	3.0

High and Low temperatures in degrees Fahrenheit; Precipitation and Snow in inches

Population: 89,673 (1990); 104,312 (2000); 119,048 (2010); 125,997 (2015 projected); Race: 85.7% White, 2.5% Black, 1.5% Asian, 10.4% Other, 15.7% Hispanic of any race (2010); Density: 130.2 persons per square mile (2010); Average household size: 2.53 (2010); Median age: 34.5 (2010); Males per 100 females: 96.5 (2010).
Religion: Five largest groups: 20.1% Southern Baptist Convention, 8.3% Christian Churches and Churches of Christ, 6.7% Independent, Charismatic Churches, 4.3% The United Methodist Church, 3.1% Churches of Christ (2000).
Economy: Unemployment rate: 5.6% (June 2011); Total civilian labor force: 69,625 (June 2011); Leading industries: 19.1% retail trade; 12.7% accommodation & food services; 11.4% health care and social assistance (2009); Farms: 887 totaling 575,076 acres (2007); Companies that employ 500 or more persons: 2 (2009); Companies that employ 100 to 499 persons: 28 (2009); Companies that employ less than 100 persons: 2,265 (2009); Black-owned businesses: n/a (2007); Hispanic-owned businesses: 663 (2007); Asian-owned businesses: n/a (2007); Women-owned businesses: 3,172 (2007); Retail sales per capita: $12,000 (2010). Single-family building permits issued: 61 (2010); Multi-family building permits issued: 10 (2010).
Income: Per capita income: $27,500 (2010); Median household income: $55,786 (2010); Average household income: $70,560 (2010); Percent of households with income of $100,000 or more: 19.1% (2010); Poverty rate: 8.9% (2009); Bankruptcy rate: 2.71% (2010).
Taxes: Total county taxes per capita: $192 (2007); County property taxes per capita: $171 (2007).
Education: Percent of population age 25 and over with: High school diploma (including GED) or higher: 91.0% (2010); Bachelor's degree or higher: 28.0% (2010); Master's degree or higher: 9.5% (2010).
Housing: Homeownership rate: 69.3% (2010); Median home value: $129,390 (2010); Median contract rent: $566 per month (2005-2009 5-year est.); Median year structure built: 1975 (2005-2009 5-year est.)
Health: Birth rate: 135.0 per 10,000 population (2009); Death rate: 67.8 per 10,000 population (2009); Age-adjusted cancer mortality rate: 162.4 deaths per 100,000 population (2007); Number of physicians: 20.4 per 10,000 population (2008); Hospital beds: 9.1 per 10,000 population (2007); Hospital admissions: 65.3 per 10,000 population (2007).
Elections: 2008 Presidential election results: 18.3% Obama, 80.9% McCain, 0.1% Nader
National and State Parks: Buffalo Lake National Wildlife Refuge; Palo Duro State Park
Additional Information Contacts
Randall County Government . . . . (806) 655-6270
  http://www.randallcounty.org
Canyon Chamber of Commerce . . . . (806) 655-7815
  http://www.canyonchamber.org
City of Canyon . . . . (806) 655-5000
  http://www.canyon-tx.com

Randall County Communities

CANYON (city). County seat. Covers a land area of 4.952 square miles and a water area of 0 square miles. Located at 34.97° N. Lat; 101.92° W. Long. Elevation is 3,543 feet.
History: Canyon began as a cow town, but became an educational center with the founding of West Texas State University.
Population: 11,365 (1990); 12,875 (2000); 14,972 (2010); 16,139 (2015 projected); Race: 85.0% White, 2.1% Black, 2.3% Asian, 10.6% Other, 14.2% Hispanic of any race (2010); Density: 3,023.4 persons per square mile (2010); Average household size: 2.43 (2010); Median age: 27.6 (2010); Males per 100 females: 96.6 (2010); Marriage status: 46.4% never married, 39.5% now married, 5.4% widowed, 8.6% divorced (2005-2009 5-year est.); Foreign born: 5.3% (2005-2009 5-year est.); Ancestry

(includes multiple ancestries): 20.2% German, 13.4% Irish, 11.3% English, 6.5% American, 4.0% Scotch-Irish (2005-2009 5-year est.).
Economy: Single-family building permits issued: 57 (2010); Multi-family building permits issued: 10 (2010); Employment by occupation: 10.7% management, 22.6% professional, 23.0% services, 29.9% sales, 1.3% farming, 4.7% construction, 7.7% production (2005-2009 5-year est.).
Income: Per capita income: $21,653 (2010); Median household income: $43,621 (2010); Average household income: $57,255 (2010); Percent of households with income of $100,000 or more: 14.2% (2010); Poverty rate: 25.6% (2005-2009 5-year est.).
Taxes: Total city taxes per capita: $291 (2007); City property taxes per capita: $102 (2007).
Education: Percent of population age 25 and over with: High school diploma (including GED) or higher: 89.5% (2010); Bachelor's degree or higher: 40.0% (2010); Master's degree or higher: 15.2% (2010).
School District(s)
Canyon ISD (PK-12)
  2009-10 Enrollment: 8,745 . . . . (806) 677-2600
Four-year College(s)
West Texas A & M University (Public)
  Fall 2009 Enrollment: 7,634. . . . . (806) 651-0000
  2010-11 Tuition: In-state $5,834; Out-of-state $13,274
Housing: Homeownership rate: 50.9% (2010); Median home value: $125,428 (2010); Median contract rent: $498 per month (2005-2009 5-year est.); Median year structure built: 1972 (2005-2009 5-year est.).
Safety: Violent crime rate: 8.8 per 10,000 population; Property crime rate: 92.0 per 10,000 population (2009).
Newspapers: Canyon News (Community news; Circulation 4,335)
Transportation: Commute to work: 87.9% car, 0.9% public transportation, 8.4% walk, 2.6% work from home (2005-2009 5-year est.); Travel time to work: 45.1% less than 15 minutes, 29.0% 15 to 30 minutes, 19.0% 30 to 45 minutes, 3.6% 45 to 60 minutes, 3.4% 60 minutes or more (2005-2009 5-year est.)
Additional Information Contacts
Canyon Chamber of Commerce . . . . (806) 655-7815
  http://www.canyonchamber.org
City of Canyon . . . . (806) 655-5000
  http://www.canyon-tx.com

LAKE TANGLEWOOD (village). Covers a land area of 1.061 square miles and a water area of 0.402 square miles. Located at 35.05° N. Lat; 101.78° W. Long. Elevation is 3,474 feet.
Population: 657 (1990); 825 (2000); 889 (2010); 932 (2015 projected); Race: 91.3% White, 0.3% Black, 0.1% Asian, 8.2% Other, 8.7% Hispanic of any race (2010); Density: 837.7 persons per square mile (2010); Average household size: 2.65 (2010); Median age: 38.7 (2010); Males per 100 females: 104.8 (2010); Marriage status: 11.7% never married, 82.2% now married, 1.8% widowed, 4.3% divorced (2005-2009 5-year est.); Foreign born: 0.6% (2005-2009 5-year est.); Ancestry (includes multiple ancestries): 19.9% German, 17.0% Irish, 10.2% American, 9.8% English, 3.8% European (2005-2009 5-year est.).
Economy: Single-family building permits issued: 3 (2010); Multi-family building permits issued: 0 (2010); Employment by occupation: 42.7% management, 20.6% professional, 3.9% services, 21.0% sales, 0.0% farming, 7.8% construction, 3.9% production (2005-2009 5-year est.).
Income: Per capita income: $35,252 (2010); Median household income: $68,662 (2010); Average household income: $93,631 (2010); Percent of households with income of $100,000 or more: 30.1% (2010); Poverty rate: 0.4% (2005-2009 5-year est.).
Education: Percent of population age 25 and over with: High school diploma (including GED) or higher: 88.3% (2010); Bachelor's degree or higher: 23.5% (2010); Master's degree or higher: 8.3% (2010).
Housing: Homeownership rate: 88.4% (2010); Median home value: $168,243 (2010); Median contract rent: $2,000+ per month (2005-2009 5-year est.); Median year structure built: 1975 (2005-2009 5-year est.).
Transportation: Commute to work: 96.8% car, 0.0% public transportation, 0.0% walk, 2.6% work from home (2005-2009 5-year est.); Travel time to work: 33.1% less than 15 minutes, 43.0% 15 to 30 minutes, 16.9% 30 to 45 minutes, 3.5% 45 to 60 minutes, 3.5% 60 minutes or more (2005-2009 5-year est.)

PALISADES (village). Covers a land area of 0.576 square miles and a water area of 0.004 square miles. Located at 35.06° N. Lat; 101.79° W. Long. Elevation is 3,353 feet.

Population: 275 (1990); 352 (2000); 380 (2010); 400 (2015 projected); Race: 91.6% White, 0.3% Black, 0.0% Asian, 8.2% Other, 8.9% Hispanic of any race (2010); Density: 659.2 persons per square mile (2010); Average household size: 2.64 (2010); Median age: 38.7 (2010); Males per 100 females: 104.3 (2010); Marriage status: 25.3% never married, 51.4% now married, 2.0% widowed, 21.3% divorced (2005-2009 5-year est.); Foreign born: 2.2% (2005-2009 5-year est.); Ancestry (includes multiple ancestries): 39.0% German, 11.2% Irish, 9.2% English, 8.9% American, 4.7% Scotch-Irish (2005-2009 5-year est.).
Economy: Employment by occupation: 10.2% management, 11.9% professional, 19.2% services, 18.6% sales, 0.0% farming, 34.5% construction, 5.6% production (2005-2009 5-year est.).
Income: Per capita income: $35,968 (2010); Median household income: $68,750 (2010); Average household income: $92,795 (2010); Percent of households with income of $100,000 or more: 30.6% (2010); Poverty rate: 13.4% (2005-2009 5-year est.).
Taxes: Total city taxes per capita: $64 (2007); City property taxes per capita: $64 (2007).
Education: Percent of population age 25 and over with: High school diploma (including GED) or higher: 89.5% (2010); Bachelor's degree or higher: 25.4% (2010); Master's degree or higher: 9.0% (2010).
Housing: Homeownership rate: 87.5% (2010); Median home value: $184,375 (2010); Median contract rent: $385 per month (2005-2009 5-year est.); Median year structure built: 1975 (2005-2009 5-year est.).
Transportation: Commute to work: 98.3% car, 0.0% public transportation, 0.0% walk, 1.7% work from home (2005-2009 5-year est.); Travel time to work: 7.5% less than 15 minutes, 64.7% 15 to 30 minutes, 27.7% 30 to 45 minutes, 0.0% 45 to 60 minutes, 0.0% 60 minutes or more (2005-2009 5-year est.)

TIMBERCREEK CANYON (village). Covers a land area of 1.838 square miles and a water area of 0 square miles. Located at 35.05° N. Lat; 101.81° W. Long. Elevation is 3,451 feet.

Population: 289 (1990); 406 (2000); 446 (2010); 468 (2015 projected); Race: 91.7% White, 0.4% Black, 0.2% Asian, 7.6% Other, 9.6% Hispanic of any race (2010); Density: 242.6 persons per square mile (2010); Average household size: 2.67 (2010); Median age: 35.9 (2010); Males per 100 females: 110.4 (2010); Marriage status: 22.6% never married, 70.6% now married, 3.0% widowed, 3.9% divorced (2005-2009 5-year est.); Foreign born: 3.1% (2005-2009 5-year est.); Ancestry (includes multiple ancestries): 22.5% Irish, 18.9% German, 8.4% English, 8.2% American, 7.3% European (2005-2009 5-year est.).
Economy: Single-family building permits issued: 1 (2010); Multi-family building permits issued: 0 (2010); Employment by occupation: 19.0% management, 26.7% professional, 4.7% services, 31.4% sales, 0.0% farming, 7.8% construction, 10.5% production (2005-2009 5-year est.).
Income: Per capita income: $34,835 (2010); Median household income: $71,250 (2010); Average household income: $93,757 (2010); Percent of households with income of $100,000 or more: 29.3% (2010); Poverty rate: 6.3% (2005-2009 5-year est.).
Taxes: Total city taxes per capita: $165 (2007); City property taxes per capita: $135 (2007).
Education: Percent of population age 25 and over with: High school diploma (including GED) or higher: 89.7% (2010); Bachelor's degree or higher: 28.3% (2010); Master's degree or higher: 11.0% (2010).
Housing: Homeownership rate: 86.2% (2010); Median home value: $188,889 (2010); Median contract rent: $1,146 per month (2005-2009 5-year est.); Median year structure built: 1994 (2005-2009 5-year est.).
Transportation: Commute to work: 94.5% car, 0.0% public transportation, 0.8% walk, 4.7% work from home (2005-2009 5-year est.); Travel time to work: 6.1% less than 15 minutes, 52.0% 15 to 30 minutes, 36.5% 30 to 45 minutes, 3.7% 45 to 60 minutes, 1.6% 60 minutes or more (2005-2009 5-year est.)

Reagan County

Located in west Texas, on the north edge of the Edwards Plateau. Covers a land area of 1,175.30 square miles, a water area of 0.68 square miles, and is located in the Central Time Zone at 31.34° N. Lat., 101.51° W. Long. The county was founded in 1903. County seat is Big Lake.

Weather Station: Big Lake 2   Elevation: 2,689 feet

	Jan	Feb	Mar	Apr	May	Jun	Jul	Aug	Sep	Oct	Nov	Dec
High	58	na	70	79	87	91	94	93	87	78	67	58
Low	31	35	42	50	60	66	69	68	61	51	40	31
Precip	0.9	0.9	0.9	1.2	2.2	2.1	1.5	2.0	2.3	1.7	0.8	0.9
Snow	0.7	tr	tr	0.0	0.0	0.0	0.0	0.0	0.0	tr	0.8	0.3

High and Low temperatures in degrees Fahrenheit; Precipitation and Snow in inches

Weather Station: Cope Ranch   Elevation: 2,569 feet

	Jan	Feb	Mar	Apr	May	Jun	Jul	Aug	Sep	Oct	Nov	Dec
High	58	62	70	79	88	93	95	94	87	78	67	58
Low	28	32	39	47	58	66	68	67	59	49	37	29
Precip	0.8	1.0	1.1	1.1	2.3	2.8	1.8	2.3	2.5	2.2	1.0	1.0
Snow	0.3	tr	tr	tr	0.0	0.0	0.0	0.0	0.0	tr	0.3	0.5

High and Low temperatures in degrees Fahrenheit; Precipitation and Snow in inches

Population: 4,514 (1990); 3,326 (2000); 3,292 (2010); 3,268 (2015 projected); Race: 60.3% White, 3.5% Black, 0.3% Asian, 35.9% Other, 55.4% Hispanic of any race (2010); Density: 2.8 persons per square mile (2010); Average household size: 2.79 (2010); Median age: 35.7 (2010); Males per 100 females: 101.0 (2010).
Religion: Five largest groups: 43.6% Southern Baptist Convention, 9.3% The United Methodist Church, 8.2% Catholic Church, 6.8% Assemblies of God, 5.7% Churches of Christ (2000).
Economy: Unemployment rate: 3.9% (June 2011); Total civilian labor force: 2,600 (June 2011); Leading industries: 48.2% mining; 9.6% retail trade; 4.2% transportation & warehousing (2009); Farms: 137 totaling 683,814 acres (2007); Companies that employ 500 or more persons: 0 (2009); Companies that employ 100 to 499 persons: 1 (2009); Companies that employ less than 100 persons: 105 (2009); Black-owned businesses: n/a (2007); Hispanic-owned businesses: n/a (2007); Asian-owned businesses: n/a (2007); Women-owned businesses: n/a (2007); Retail sales per capita: $9,637 (2010). Single-family building permits issued: 0 (2010); Multi-family building permits issued: 0 (2010).
Income: Per capita income: $20,304 (2010); Median household income: $46,807 (2010); Average household income: $57,204 (2010); Percent of households with income of $100,000 or more: 13.3% (2010); Poverty rate: 9.5% (2009); Bankruptcy rate: 0.30% (2010).
Taxes: Total county taxes per capita: $1,645 (2007); County property taxes per capita: $1,451 (2007).
Education: Percent of population age 25 and over with: High school diploma (including GED) or higher: 68.6% (2010); Bachelor's degree or higher: 10.7% (2010); Master's degree or higher: 3.2% (2010).
Housing: Homeownership rate: 76.7% (2010); Median home value: $54,400 (2010); Median contract rent: $354 per month (2005-2009 5-year est.); Median year structure built: 1971 (2005-2009 5-year est.)
Health: Birth rate: 222.3 per 10,000 population (2009); Death rate: 46.4 per 10,000 population (2009); Age-adjusted cancer mortality rate: Suppressed deaths per 100,000 population (2007); Number of physicians: 3.3 per 10,000 population (2008); Hospital beds: 46.8 per 10,000 population (2007); Hospital admissions: 70.3 per 10,000 population (2007).
Elections: 2008 Presidential election results: 19.8% Obama, 80.0% McCain, 0.0% Nader
Additional Information Contacts
Reagan County Government . . . . (325) 884-2665

Reagan County Communities

BIG LAKE (city). County seat. Covers a land area of 1.240 square miles and a water area of 0 square miles. Located at 31.19° N. Lat; 101.45° W. Long. Elevation is 2,690 feet.

Population: 3,672 (1990); 2,885 (2000); 2,850 (2010); 2,829 (2015 projected); Race: 59.6% White, 3.7% Black, 0.3% Asian, 36.4% Other, 57.8% Hispanic of any race (2010); Density: 2,299.1 persons per square mile (2010); Average household size: 2.86 (2010); Median age: 35.0 (2010); Males per 100 females: 98.9 (2010); Marriage status: 12.5% never married, 79.6% now married, 4.5% widowed, 3.5% divorced (2005-2009 5-year est.); Foreign born: 18.4% (2005-2009 5-year est.); Ancestry (includes multiple ancestries): 7.2% American, 6.2% German, 4.3% English, 4.0% Irish, 1.0% French (2005-2009 5-year est.).
Economy: Single-family building permits issued: 0 (2010); Multi-family building permits issued: 0 (2010); Employment by occupation: 9.4% management, 11.1% professional, 10.8% services, 20.2% sales, 1.9% farming, 25.5% construction, 21.3% production (2005-2009 5-year est.).

Income: Per capita income: $19,895 (2010); Median household income: $47,221 (2010); Average household income: $57,783 (2010); Percent of households with income of $100,000 or more: 13.0% (2010); Poverty rate: 4.8% (2005-2009 5-year est.).

Taxes: Total city taxes per capita: $278 (2007); City property taxes per capita: $34 (2007).

Education: Percent of population age 25 and over with: High school diploma (including GED) or higher: 66.3% (2010); Bachelor's degree or higher: 10.5% (2010); Master's degree or higher: 3.2% (2010).

School District(s)

Reagan County ISD (PK-12)
    2009-10 Enrollment: 775 . . . . (325) 884-3705

Housing: Homeownership rate: 79.5% (2010); Median home value: $50,127 (2010); Median contract rent: $365 per month (2005-2009 5-year est.); Median year structure built: 1971 (2005-2009 5-year est.).

Hospitals: Reagan Memorial Hospital (14 beds)

Newspapers: Big Lake Wildcat (Community news; Circulation 1,400)

Transportation: Commute to work: 95.5% car, 0.0% public transportation, 3.0% walk, 1.5% work from home (2005-2009 5-year est.); Travel time to work: 78.9% less than 15 minutes, 2.1% 15 to 30 minutes, 2.0% 30 to 45 minutes, 4.7% 45 to 60 minutes, 12.4% 60 minutes or more (2005-2009 5-year est.)

Airports: Reagan County (general aviation)

Real County

Located in southwestern Texas, on the Edwards Plateau; drained by the Nueces and Frio Rivers. Covers a land area of 699.91 square miles, a water area of 0.13 square miles, and is located in the Central Time Zone at 29.77° N. Lat., 99.87° W. Long. The county was founded in 1913. County seat is Leakey.

Weather Station: Camp Wood   Elevation: 1,470 feet

	Jan	Feb	Mar	Apr	May	Jun	Jul	Aug	Sep	Oct	Nov	Dec
High	62	66	72	80	86	91	94	94	89	80	71	63
Low	34	37	45	53	62	68	70	69	64	55	44	35
Precip	1.2	1.4	2.1	2.0	3.1	3.7	2.3	2.5	3.4	3.4	2.5	1.5
Snow	0.2	0.2	0.0	0.0	0.0	0.0	0.0	0.0	0.0	0.0	0.1	0.0

High and Low temperatures in degrees Fahrenheit; Precipitation and Snow in inches

Population: 2,412 (1990); 3,047 (2000); 3,107 (2010); 3,129 (2015 projected); Race: 90.3% White, 0.3% Black, 0.2% Asian, 9.2% Other, 24.8% Hispanic of any race (2010); Density: 4.4 persons per square mile (2010); Average household size: 2.29 (2010); Median age: 44.4 (2010); Males per 100 females: 94.3 (2010).

Religion: Five largest groups: 31.4% Southern Baptist Convention, 29.8% Catholic Church, 7.9% Churches of Christ, 7.0% The United Methodist Church, 0.8% Assemblies of God (2000).

Economy: Unemployment rate: 6.4% (June 2011); Total civilian labor force: 1,646 (June 2011); Leading industries: 36.0% health care and social assistance; 14.1% accommodation & food services; 11.1% retail trade (2009); Farms: 301 totaling 372,423 acres (2007); Companies that employ 500 or more persons: 0 (2009); Companies that employ 100 to 499 persons: 0 (2009); Companies that employ less than 100 persons: 84 (2009); Black-owned businesses: n/a (2007); Hispanic-owned businesses: n/a (2007); Asian-owned businesses: n/a (2007); Women-owned businesses: n/a (2007); Retail sales per capita: $2,939 (2010). Single-family building permits issued: 0 (2010); Multi-family building permits issued: 0 (2010).

Income: Per capita income: $18,654 (2010); Median household income: $32,904 (2010); Average household income: $42,984 (2010); Percent of households with income of $100,000 or more: 6.1% (2010); Poverty rate: 22.0% (2009); Bankruptcy rate: 1.49% (2010).

Taxes: Total county taxes per capita: $503 (2007); County property taxes per capita: $473 (2007).

Education: Percent of population age 25 and over with: High school diploma (including GED) or higher: 77.8% (2010); Bachelor's degree or higher: 19.2% (2010); Master's degree or higher: 4.5% (2010).

Housing: Homeownership rate: 75.1% (2010); Median home value: $88,191 (2010); Median contract rent: $342 per month (2005-2009 5-year est.); Median year structure built: 1975 (2005-2009 5-year est.).

Health: Birth rate: 106.0 per 10,000 population (2009); Death rate: 102.6 per 10,000 population (2009); Age-adjusted cancer mortality rate: 164.1 (Unreliable) deaths per 100,000 population (2007); Number of physicians: 0.0 per 10,000 population (2008); Hospital beds: 0.0 per 10,000 population (2007); Hospital admissions: 0.0 per 10,000 population (2007).

Elections: 2008 Presidential election results: 23.0% Obama, 76.0% McCain, 0.0% Nader

Additional Information Contacts

Real County Government . . . . (830) 232-5304
    http://www.co.real.tx.us/ips/cms
Frio Canyon Chamber of Commerce . . . . (830) 232-5222
    http://www.friocanyonchamber.com
Nueces Canyon Chamber of Commerce . . . . (830) 597-6241
    http://www.mycampwood.com

Real County Communities

CAMP WOOD (city). Covers a land area of 0.504 square miles and a water area of 0 square miles. Located at 29.66° N. Lat; 100.01° W. Long. Elevation is 1,457 feet.

History: The first settlement on this site was Mission San Lorenzo. A military post with the name of Camp Wood was built here in 1857. When a town was established in 1921, it was given the name of the old camp.

Population: 646 (1990); 822 (2000); 783 (2010); 778 (2015 projected); Race: 89.1% White, 0.4% Black, 0.4% Asian, 10.1% Other, 43.2% Hispanic of any race (2010); Density: 1,552.5 persons per square mile (2010); Average household size: 2.50 (2010); Median age: 37.0 (2010); Males per 100 females: 98.2 (2010); Marriage status: 26.5% never married, 40.6% now married, 18.7% widowed, 14.2% divorced (2005-2009 5-year est.); Foreign born: 4.1% (2005-2009 5-year est.); Ancestry (includes multiple ancestries): 24.9% American, 15.2% German, 10.1% Irish, 6.1% Scotch-Irish, 5.7% English (2005-2009 5-year est.).

Economy: Single-family building permits issued: 0 (2010); Multi-family building permits issued: 0 (2010); Employment by occupation: 3.6% management, 6.1% professional, 23.3% services, 27.8% sales, 5.5% farming, 20.7% construction, 12.9% production (2005-2009 5-year est.).

Income: Per capita income: $14,771 (2010); Median household income: $28,333 (2010); Average household income: $37,179 (2010); Percent of households with income of $100,000 or more: 3.5% (2010); Poverty rate: 32.8% (2005-2009 5-year est.).

Taxes: Total city taxes per capita: $86 (2007); City property taxes per capita: $0 (2007).

Education: Percent of population age 25 and over with: High school diploma (including GED) or higher: 69.4% (2010); Bachelor's degree or higher: 12.9% (2010); Master's degree or higher: 2.5% (2010).

School District(s)

Nueces Canyon CISD (KG-12)
    2009-10 Enrollment: 282 . . . . (830) 234-3514

Housing: Homeownership rate: 73.4% (2010); Median home value: $49,211 (2010); Median contract rent: $355 per month (2005-2009 5-year est.); Median year structure built: 1972 (2005-2009 5-year est.).

Transportation: Commute to work: 58.4% car, 0.0% public transportation, 23.9% walk, 13.0% work from home (2005-2009 5-year est.); Travel time to work: 63.1% less than 15 minutes, 14.5% 15 to 30 minutes, 9.0% 30 to 45 minutes, 0.0% 45 to 60 minutes, 13.3% 60 minutes or more (2005-2009 5-year est.)

Additional Information Contacts

Nueces Canyon Chamber of Commerce . . . . (830) 597-6241
    http://www.mycampwood.com

LEAKEY (city). County seat. Covers a land area of 0.557 square miles and a water area of 0 square miles. Located at 29.72° N. Lat; 99.76° W. Long. Elevation is 1,604 feet.

Population: 430 (1990); 387 (2000); 368 (2010); 359 (2015 projected); Race: 94.3% White, 0.0% Black, 0.0% Asian, 5.7% Other, 22.8% Hispanic of any race (2010); Density: 660.7 persons per square mile (2010); Average household size: 2.23 (2010); Median age: 38.1 (2010); Males per 100 females: 81.3 (2010); Marriage status: 7.1% never married, 69.3% now married, 10.6% widowed, 13.1% divorced (2005-2009 5-year est.); Foreign born: 7.8% (2005-2009 5-year est.); Ancestry (includes multiple ancestries): 37.1% German, 22.9% Irish, 9.9% Scottish, 7.0% English, 6.2% American (2005-2009 5-year est.).

Economy: Employment by occupation: 4.3% management, 15.4% professional, 27.8% services, 19.1% sales, 0.0% farming, 19.8% construction, 13.6% production (2005-2009 5-year est.).

Income: Per capita income: $16,452 (2010); Median household income: $27,857 (2010); Average household income: $36,082 (2010); Percent of households with income of $100,000 or more: 4.9% (2010); Poverty rate: 20.0% (2005-2009 5-year est.).

Taxes: Total city taxes per capita: $88 (2007); City property taxes per capita: $0 (2007).
Education: Percent of population age 25 and over with: High school diploma (including GED) or higher: 75.0% (2010); Bachelor's degree or higher: 19.4% (2010); Master's degree or higher: 6.0% (2010).

School District(s)

Big Springs Charter School (01-12)
   2009-10 Enrollment: 125 . . . . (830) 232-7101
Leakey ISD (PK-12)
   2009-10 Enrollment: 236 . . . . (830) 232-6122
Housing: Homeownership rate: 73.2% (2010); Median home value: $83,529 (2010); Median contract rent: $350 per month (2005-2009 5-year est.); Median year structure built: 1966 (2005-2009 5-year est.).
Transportation: Commute to work: 93.8% car, 0.0% public transportation, 1.9% walk, 4.3% work from home (2005-2009 5-year est.); Travel time to work: 81.3% less than 15 minutes, 7.1% 15 to 30 minutes, 11.6% 30 to 45 minutes, 0.0% 45 to 60 minutes, 0.0% 60 minutes or more (2005-2009 5-year est.)

Additional Information Contacts
Frio Canyon Chamber of Commerce . . . . (830) 232-5222
   http://www.friocanyonchamber.com

RIO FRIO (unincorporated postal area, zip code 78879). Covers a land area of 15.114 square miles and a water area of 0.021 square miles. Located at 29.62° N. Lat; 99.73° W. Long. Elevation is 1,483 feet.
Population: 186 (2000); Race: 79.4% White, 0.0% Black, 0.0% Asian, 20.6% Other, 20.0% Hispanic of any race (2000); Density: 12.3 persons per square mile (2000); Age: 20.0% under 18, 27.8% over 64 (2000); Marriage status: 14.9% never married, 63.0% now married, 11.7% widowed, 10.4% divorced (2000); Foreign born: 6.1% (2000); Ancestry (includes multiple ancestries): 16.1% English, 11.7% German, 7.8% Czech, 7.8% French (2000).
Economy: Employment by occupation: 12.3% management, 20.0% professional, 9.2% services, 18.5% sales, 0.0% farming, 29.2% construction, 10.8% production (2000).
Income: Per capita income: $13,741 (2000); Median household income: $21,500 (2000); Poverty rate: 179.1% (2000).
Education: Percent of population age 25 and over with: High school diploma (including GED) or higher: 85.3% (2000); Bachelor's degree or higher: 29.4% (2000).
Housing: Homeownership rate: 73.3% (2000); Median home value: $104,700 (2000); Median contract rent: $313 per month (2000); Median year structure built: 1984 (2000).
Transportation: Commute to work: 81.5% car, 0.0% public transportation, 7.7% walk, 7.7% work from home (2000); Travel time to work: 71.7% less than 15 minutes, 16.7% 15 to 30 minutes, 0.0% 30 to 45 minutes, 3.3% 45 to 60 minutes, 8.3% 60 minutes or more (2000)

Red River County

Located in northeastern Texas; bounded on the north by the Red River and the Oklahoma border, and on the south by the Sulphur River. Covers a land area of 1,050.18 square miles, a water area of 7.43 square miles, and is located in the Central Time Zone at 33.61° N. Lat., 95.05° W. Long. The county was founded in 1836. County seat is Clarksville.

Weather Station: Clarksville 2 NE										Elevation: 435 feet	
	Jan	Feb	Mar	Apr	May	Jun	Jul	Aug	Sep	Oct	Nov	Dec
High	54	58	66	74	80	88	92	93	86	76	65	55
Low	31	35	42	50	60	68	71	70	63	51	42	33
Precip	2.9	3.3	4.6	3.7	5.8	3.9	3.1	2.3	4.0	5.2	4.8	4.4
Snow	0.6	0.7	0.1	tr	0.0	0.0	0.0	0.0	0.0	0.0	tr	0.1

High and Low temperatures in degrees Fahrenheit; Precipitation and Snow in inches

Population: 14,317 (1990); 14,314 (2000); 13,222 (2010); 12,667 (2015 projected); Race: 77.8% White, 16.8% Black, 0.1% Asian, 5.2% Other, 5.9% Hispanic of any race (2010); Density: 12.6 persons per square mile (2010); Average household size: 2.38 (2010); Median age: 42.6 (2010); Males per 100 females: 92.0 (2010).
Religion: Five largest groups: 24.3% Southern Baptist Convention, 15.8% The American Baptist Association, 10.2% The United Methodist Church, 3.6% Churches of Christ, 1.5% Assemblies of God (2000).
Economy: Unemployment rate: 12.9% (June 2011); Total civilian labor force: 5,838 (June 2011); Leading industries: 27.1% manufacturing; 27.0% health care and social assistance; 14.5% retail trade (2009); Farms: 1,206 totaling 449,525 acres (2007); Companies that employ 500 or more

persons: 0 (2009); Companies that employ 100 to 499 persons: 1 (2009); Companies that employ less than 100 persons: 186 (2009); Black-owned businesses: n/a (2007); Hispanic-owned businesses: n/a (2007); Asian-owned businesses: n/a (2007); Women-owned businesses: n/a (2007); Retail sales per capita: $7,275 (2010). Single-family building permits issued: 11 (2010); Multi-family building permits issued: 0 (2010).
Income: Per capita income: $19,487 (2010); Median household income: $35,374 (2010); Average household income: $47,177 (2010); Percent of households with income of $100,000 or more: 7.8% (2010); Poverty rate: 19.1% (2009); Bankruptcy rate: 1.31% (2010).
Taxes: Total county taxes per capita: $252 (2007); County property taxes per capita: $198 (2007).
Education: Percent of population age 25 and over with: High school diploma (including GED) or higher: 71.5% (2010); Bachelor's degree or higher: 10.2% (2010); Master's degree or higher: 4.0% (2010).
Housing: Homeownership rate: 73.0% (2010); Median home value: $52,686 (2010); Median contract rent: $309 per month (2005-2009 5-year est.); Median year structure built: 1975 (2005-2009 5-year est.)
Health: Birth rate: 115.9 per 10,000 population (2009); Death rate: 142.6 per 10,000 population (2009); Age-adjusted cancer mortality rate: 285.8 deaths per 100,000 population (2007); Number of physicians: 5.4 per 10,000 population (2008); Hospital beds: 27.6 per 10,000 population (2007); Hospital admissions: 1,312.1 per 10,000 population (2007).
Elections: 2008 Presidential election results: 30.5% Obama, 68.5% McCain, 0.1% Nader

Additional Information Contacts
Red River County Government . . . . (903) 427-2680
   http://www.co.red-river.tx.us/ips/cms
Red River County Chamber of Commerce . . . . (903) 427-2645
   http://redrivercoc.com

Red River County Communities

ANNONA (town). Covers a land area of 0.806 square miles and a water area of 0 square miles. Located at 33.58° N. Lat; 94.91° W. Long. Elevation is 374 feet.
Population: 329 (1990); 282 (2000); 281 (2010); 278 (2015 projected); Race: 71.5% White, 14.9% Black, 0.0% Asian, 13.5% Other, 11.4% Hispanic of any race (2010); Density: 348.6 persons per square mile (2010); Average household size: 2.30 (2010); Median age: 44.6 (2010); Males per 100 females: 96.5 (2010); Marriage status: 33.3% never married, 45.8% now married, 8.0% widowed, 12.9% divorced (2005-2009 5-year est.); Foreign born: 11.0% (2005-2009 5-year est.); Ancestry (includes multiple ancestries): 26.2% African, 5.6% American, 4.8% English, 4.2% German, 2.3% Irish (2005-2009 5-year est.).
Economy: Single-family building permits issued: 0 (2010); Multi-family building permits issued: 0 (2010); Employment by occupation: 2.3% management, 3.9% professional, 25.6% services, 12.4% sales, 5.4% farming, 17.1% construction, 33.3% production (2005-2009 5-year est.).
Income: Per capita income: $19,639 (2010); Median household income: $32,647 (2010); Average household income: $43,463 (2010); Percent of households with income of $100,000 or more: 7.4% (2010); Poverty rate: 22.8% (2005-2009 5-year est.).
Taxes: Total city taxes per capita: $336 (2007); City property taxes per capita: $170 (2007).
Education: Percent of population age 25 and over with: High school diploma (including GED) or higher: 70.0% (2010); Bachelor's degree or higher: 12.4% (2010); Master's degree or higher: 5.2% (2010).
Housing: Homeownership rate: 82.0% (2010); Median home value: $57,500 (2010); Median contract rent: $350 per month (2005-2009 5-year est.); Median year structure built: 1970 (2005-2009 5-year est.).
Transportation: Commute to work: 96.6% car, 0.0% public transportation, 3.4% walk, 0.0% work from home (2005-2009 5-year est.); Travel time to work: 40.3% less than 15 minutes, 25.2% 15 to 30 minutes, 14.3% 30 to 45 minutes, 9.2% 45 to 60 minutes, 10.9% 60 minutes or more (2005-2009 5-year est.)

Additional Information Contacts
Red River County Chamber of Commerce . . . . (903) 427-2645
   http://redrivercoc.com

AVERY (town). Covers a land area of 0.947 square miles and a water area of 0.029 square miles. Located at 33.55° N. Lat; 94.78° W. Long. Elevation is 472 feet.
History: Avery developed as the center of a fruit and truck growing area, with tomato packing as an early industry.

Population: 430 (1990); 462 (2000); 467 (2010); 460 (2015 projected); Race: 94.9% White, 2.4% Black, 0.0% Asian, 2.8% Other, 0.4% Hispanic of any race (2010); Density: 493.1 persons per square mile (2010); Average household size: 2.22 (2010); Median age: 42.1 (2010); Males per 100 females: 94.6 (2010); Marriage status: 20.6% never married, 43.3% now married, 12.1% widowed, 23.9% divorced (2005-2009 5-year est.); Foreign born: 1.7% (2005-2009 5-year est.); Ancestry (includes multiple ancestries): 35.1% Irish, 23.9% German, 10.9% American, 9.0% English, 3.8% French (2005-2009 5-year est.).
Economy: Employment by occupation: 2.0% management, 12.9% professional, 17.0% services, 30.6% sales, 3.4% farming, 27.2% construction, 6.8% production (2005-2009 5-year est.).
Income: Per capita income: $17,283 (2010); Median household income: $27,857 (2010); Average household income: $37,821 (2010); Percent of households with income of $100,000 or more: 4.8% (2010); Poverty rate: 30.3% (2005-2009 5-year est.).
Taxes: Total city taxes per capita: $76 (2007); City property taxes per capita: $76 (2007).
Education: Percent of population age 25 and over with: High school diploma (including GED) or higher: 62.5% (2010); Bachelor's degree or higher: 8.1% (2010); Master's degree or higher: 2.7% (2010).
School District(s)
Avery ISD (PK-12)
 2009-10 Enrollment: 414 . . . . (903) 684-3460
Housing: Homeownership rate: 69.5% (2010); Median home value: $49,333 (2010); Median contract rent: $207 per month (2005-2009 5-year est.); Median year structure built: 1973 (2005-2009 5-year est.).
Transportation: Commute to work: 90.5% car, 5.4% public transportation, 2.0% walk, 2.0% work from home (2005-2009 5-year est.); Travel time to work: 15.3% less than 15 minutes, 25.7% 15 to 30 minutes, 15.3% 30 to 45 minutes, 22.2% 45 to 60 minutes, 21.5% 60 minutes or more (2005-2009 5-year est.)
Additional Information Contacts
Red River County Chamber of Commerce . . . . (903) 427-2645
 http://redrivercoc.com

BAGWELL (unincorporated postal area, zip code 75412). Covers a land area of 168.372 square miles and a water area of 0.548 square miles. Located at 33.81° N. Lat; 95.14° W. Long. Elevation is 476 feet.
Population: 935 (2000); Race: 94.1% White, 3.8% Black, 0.0% Asian, 2.1% Other, 1.1% Hispanic of any race (2000); Density: 5.6 persons per square mile (2000); Age: 21.6% under 18, 16.0% over 64 (2000); Marriage status: 20.0% never married, 66.5% now married, 7.4% widowed, 6.1% divorced (2000); Foreign born: 0.2% (2000); Ancestry (includes multiple ancestries): 15.5% American, 8.0% English, 6.7% Irish, 3.8% German (2000).
Economy: Employment by occupation: 10.7% management, 7.7% professional, 17.0% services, 16.5% sales, 5.4% farming, 13.1% construction, 29.6% production (2000).
Income: Per capita income: $15,907 (2000); Median household income: $33,977 (2000); Poverty rate: 179.1% (2000).
Education: Percent of population age 25 and over with: High school diploma (including GED) or higher: 65.2% (2000); Bachelor's degree or higher: 4.7% (2000).
Housing: Homeownership rate: 84.7% (2000); Median home value: $34,900 (2000); Median contract rent: n/a per month (2000); Median year structure built: 1977 (2000).
Transportation: Commute to work: 89.8% car, 0.0% public transportation, 1.1% walk, 6.1% work from home (2000); Travel time to work: 13.1% less than 15 minutes, 36.4% 15 to 30 minutes, 28.6% 30 to 45 minutes, 3.9% 45 to 60 minutes, 18.0% 60 minutes or more (2000)

BOGATA (city). Covers a land area of 1.410 square miles and a water area of 0 square miles. Located at 33.47° N. Lat; 95.21° W. Long. Elevation is 423 feet.
Population: 1,421 (1990); 1,396 (2000); 1,265 (2010); 1,198 (2015 projected); Race: 94.1% White, 2.6% Black, 0.0% Asian, 3.3% Other, 3.8% Hispanic of any race (2010); Density: 897.0 persons per square mile (2010); Average household size: 2.22 (2010); Median age: 45.4 (2010); Males per 100 females: 85.8 (2010); Marriage status: 17.5% never married, 53.8% now married, 12.4% widowed, 16.2% divorced (2005-2009 5-year est.); Foreign born: 0.2% (2005-2009 5-year est.); Ancestry (includes multiple ancestries): 17.8% Irish, 16.1% German, 6.6% American, 4.2% French, 3.9% Dutch (2005-2009 5-year est.).

Economy: Single-family building permits issued: 5 (2010); Multi-family building permits issued: 0 (2010); Employment by occupation: 6.1% management, 10.2% professional, 27.8% services, 17.1% sales, 1.8% farming, 21.8% construction, 15.2% production (2005-2009 5-year est.).
Income: Per capita income: $19,543 (2010); Median household income: $32,162 (2010); Average household income: $44,724 (2010); Percent of households with income of $100,000 or more: 6.4% (2010); Poverty rate: 23.5% (2005-2009 5-year est.).
Taxes: Total city taxes per capita: $152 (2007); City property taxes per capita: $112 (2007).
Education: Percent of population age 25 and over with: High school diploma (including GED) or higher: 68.0% (2010); Bachelor's degree or higher: 8.4% (2010); Master's degree or higher: 3.0% (2010).
School District(s)
Rivercrest ISD (PK-12)
 2009-10 Enrollment: 732 . . . . (903) 632-5203
Housing: Homeownership rate: 68.0% (2010); Median home value: $43,896 (2010); Median contract rent: $322 per month (2005-2009 5-year est.); Median year structure built: 1969 (2005-2009 5-year est.).
Safety: Violent crime rate: 24.6 per 10,000 population; Property crime rate: 196.9 per 10,000 population (2009).
Transportation: Commute to work: 95.0% car, 0.0% public transportation, 1.9% walk, 1.7% work from home (2005-2009 5-year est.); Travel time to work: 25.9% less than 15 minutes, 23.6% 15 to 30 minutes, 31.3% 30 to 45 minutes, 7.7% 45 to 60 minutes, 11.5% 60 minutes or more (2005-2009 5-year est.)

CLARKSVILLE (city). County seat. Covers a land area of 2.989 square miles and a water area of 0 square miles. Located at 33.61° N. Lat; 95.05° W. Long. Elevation is 410 feet.
History: Clarksville was founded in 1835. Its early industries included lumber, cotton, and livestock, with oil contributing to the economy in the 1900's.
Population: 4,311 (1990); 3,883 (2000); 3,563 (2010); 3,391 (2015 projected); Race: 56.0% White, 38.6% Black, 0.3% Asian, 5.1% Other, 9.1% Hispanic of any race (2010); Density: 1,192.1 persons per square mile (2010); Average household size: 2.42 (2010); Median age: 39.6 (2010); Males per 100 females: 86.7 (2010); Marriage status: 27.1% never married, 46.4% now married, 16.1% widowed, 10.4% divorced (2005-2009 5-year est.); Foreign born: 2.5% (2005-2009 5-year est.); Ancestry (includes multiple ancestries): 17.7% African, 7.0% American, 6.1% Irish, 4.8% English, 4.3% German (2005-2009 5-year est.).
Economy: Single-family building permits issued: 6 (2010); Multi-family building permits issued: 0 (2010); Employment by occupation: 15.0% management, 10.1% professional, 11.4% services, 16.4% sales, 0.0% farming, 5.3% construction, 41.8% production (2005-2009 5-year est.).
Income: Per capita income: $16,830 (2010); Median household income: $31,434 (2010); Average household income: $41,895 (2010); Percent of households with income of $100,000 or more: 5.4% (2010); Poverty rate: 24.8% (2005-2009 5-year est.).
Taxes: Total city taxes per capita: $353 (2007); City property taxes per capita: $168 (2007).
Education: Percent of population age 25 and over with: High school diploma (including GED) or higher: 71.7% (2010); Bachelor's degree or higher: 11.8% (2010); Master's degree or higher: 5.2% (2010).
School District(s)
Clarksville ISD (PK-12)
 2009-10 Enrollment: 748 . . . . (903) 427-3891
Housing: Homeownership rate: 62.0% (2010); Median home value: $39,517 (2010); Median contract rent: $278 per month (2005-2009 5-year est.); Median year structure built: 1966 (2005-2009 5-year est.).
Hospitals: East Texas Medical Center-Clarksville (36 beds)
Safety: Violent crime rate: 2.9 per 10,000 population; Property crime rate: 131.0 per 10,000 population (2009).
Newspapers: The Clarksville Times (Regional news; Circulation 3,200)
Transportation: Commute to work: 94.9% car, 0.0% public transportation, 0.0% walk, 2.4% work from home (2005-2009 5-year est.); Travel time to work: 68.0% less than 15 minutes, 7.0% 15 to 30 minutes, 13.4% 30 to 45 minutes, 5.9% 45 to 60 minutes, 5.7% 60 minutes or more (2005-2009 5-year est.)
Additional Information Contacts
Red River County Chamber of Commerce . . . . (903) 427-2645
 http://redrivercoc.com

DETROIT (town). Covers a land area of 1.581 square miles and a water area of 0 square miles. Located at 33.66° N. Lat; 95.26° W. Long. Elevation is 482 feet.

History: Detroit was the boyhood home of John Nance Garner (1868-1967), vice president of the U.S. under Franklin Roosevelt.

Population: 740 (1990); 776 (2000); 725 (2010); 699 (2015 projected); Race: 80.1% White, 14.2% Black, 0.0% Asian, 5.7% Other, 3.6% Hispanic of any race (2010); Density: 458.5 persons per square mile (2010); Average household size: 2.47 (2010); Median age: 36.7 (2010); Males per 100 females: 84.9 (2010); Marriage status: 14.8% never married, 55.4% now married, 9.5% widowed, 20.3% divorced (2005-2009 5-year est.); Foreign born: 0.0% (2005-2009 5-year est.); Ancestry (includes multiple ancestries): 22.6% Irish, 10.2% American, 8.6% English, 8.0% German, 1.6% Scottish (2005-2009 5-year est.).

Economy: Employment by occupation: 5.8% management, 15.0% professional, 16.4% services, 31.7% sales, 0.0% farming, 6.6% construction, 24.5% production (2005-2009 5-year est.).

Income: Per capita income: $18,424 (2010); Median household income: $35,811 (2010); Average household income: $45,825 (2010); Percent of households with income of $100,000 or more: 6.8% (2010); Poverty rate: 12.7% (2005-2009 5-year est.).

Taxes: Total city taxes per capita: $115 (2007); City property taxes per capita: $88 (2007).

Education: Percent of population age 25 and over with: High school diploma (including GED) or higher: 72.7% (2010); Bachelor's degree or higher: 7.4% (2010); Master's degree or higher: 2.1% (2010).

School District(s)

Detroit ISD (PK-12)
    2009-10 Enrollment: 499 . . . . (903) 674-6131

Housing: Homeownership rate: 61.9% (2010); Median home value: $56,538 (2010); Median contract rent: $342 per month (2005-2009 5-year est.); Median year structure built: 1970 (2005-2009 5-year est.).

Transportation: Commute to work: 95.4% car, 0.0% public transportation, 1.9% walk, 2.7% work from home (2005-2009 5-year est.); Travel time to work: 30.6% less than 15 minutes, 57.8% 15 to 30 minutes, 11.7% 30 to 45 minutes, 0.0% 45 to 60 minutes, 0.0% 60 minutes or more (2005-2009 5-year est.)

Additional Information Contacts

Red River County Chamber of Commerce . . . . (903) 427-2645
    http://redrivercoc.com

Reeves County

Located in west Texas; plains area, bounded on the northeast by the Pecos River, and on the southwest by the foothills of the Davis Mountains. Covers a land area of 2,635.88 square miles, a water area of 6.07 square miles, and is located in the Central Time Zone at 31.31° N. Lat., 103.60° W. Long. The county was founded in 1885. County seat is Pecos.

Reeves County is part of the Pecos, TX Micropolitan Statistical Area. The entire metro area includes: Reeves County, TX

Weather Station: Balmorhea   Elevation: 3,219 feet

	Jan	Feb	Mar	Apr	May	Jun	Jul	Aug	Sep	Oct	Nov	Dec
High	61	66	73	81	89	95	95	93	87	80	70	61
Low	31	34	39	47	57	64	67	66	59	49	38	30
Precip	0.6	0.7	0.3	0.7	1.2	1.3	1.6	2.1	2.6	1.3	0.6	0.6
Snow	1.2	0.2	tr	tr	0.0	0.0	0.0	0.0	0.0	0.0	tr	0.3

High and Low temperatures in degrees Fahrenheit; Precipitation and Snow in inches

Population: 15,852 (1990); 13,137 (2000); 11,052 (2010); 10,017 (2015 projected); Race: 79.0% White, 2.6% Black, 0.5% Asian, 17.9% Other, 71.7% Hispanic of any race (2010); Density: 4.2 persons per square mile (2010); Average household size: 2.82 (2010); Median age: 36.4 (2010); Males per 100 females: 117.0 (2010).

Religion: Five largest groups: 48.2% Catholic Church, 18.2% Southern Baptist Convention, 2.6% Churches of Christ, 2.1% The United Methodist Church, 1.1% Christian Church (Disciples of Christ) (2000).

Economy: Unemployment rate: 11.9% (June 2011); Total civilian labor force: 4,893 (June 2011); Leading industries: 27.8% retail trade; 17.3% accommodation & food services; 14.8% mining (2009); Farms: 221 totaling 1,040,344 acres (2007); Companies that employ 500 or more persons: 0 (2009); Companies that employ 100 to 499 persons: 4 (2009); Companies that employ less than 100 persons: 192 (2009); Black-owned businesses: n/a (2007); Hispanic-owned businesses: 237 (2007); Asian-owned

businesses: n/a (2007); Women-owned businesses: 95 (2007); Retail sales per capita: $7,355 (2010). Single-family building permits issued: 1 (2010); Multi-family building permits issued: 0 (2010).

Income: Per capita income: $14,200 (2010); Median household income: $31,670 (2010); Average household income: $42,081 (2010); Percent of households with income of $100,000 or more: 5.6% (2010); Poverty rate: 27.4% (2009); Bankruptcy rate: 1.01% (2010).

Taxes: Total county taxes per capita: $233 (2007); County property taxes per capita: $196 (2007).

Education: Percent of population age 25 and over with: High school diploma (including GED) or higher: 52.3% (2010); Bachelor's degree or higher: 9.3% (2010); Master's degree or higher: 3.4% (2010).

Housing: Homeownership rate: 76.0% (2010); Median home value: $25,880 (2010); Median contract rent: $300 per month (2005-2009 5-year est.); Median year structure built: 1966 (2005-2009 5-year est.)

Health: Birth rate: 148.5 per 10,000 population (2009); Death rate: 95.1 per 10,000 population (2009); Age-adjusted cancer mortality rate: 152.2 deaths per 100,000 population (2007); Number of physicians: 4.5 per 10,000 population (2008); Hospital beds: 22.5 per 10,000 population (2007); Hospital admissions: 616.0 per 10,000 population (2007).

Elections: 2008 Presidential election results: 52.2% Obama, 47.0% McCain, 0.1% Nader

National and State Parks: Balmorhea State Park

Additional Information Contacts

Reeves County Government . . . . (432) 445-5418

City of Pecos . . . . (432) 445-2421
    http://townofpecoscitytx.com
Pecos Area Chamber of Commerce . . . . (432) 445-2406
    http://www.pecostx.com

Reeves County Communities

BALMORHEA (city). Covers a land area of 0.388 square miles and a water area of 0 square miles. Located at 30.98° N. Lat; 103.74° W. Long. Elevation is 3,196 feet.

History: Balmorhea, once a cattle town, became a market center for irrigated farm lands watered by San Solomon Springs.

Population: 765 (1990); 527 (2000); 441 (2010); 395 (2015 projected); Race: 60.5% White, 0.0% Black, 0.0% Asian, 39.5% Other, 87.3% Hispanic of any race (2010); Density: 1,137.7 persons per square mile (2010); Average household size: 2.83 (2010); Median age: 33.7 (2010); Males per 100 females: 102.3 (2010); Marriage status: 15.6% never married, 53.5% now married, 9.2% widowed, 21.7% divorced (2005-2009 5-year est.); Foreign born: 8.8% (2005-2009 5-year est.); Ancestry (includes multiple ancestries): 5.6% English, 4.5% Irish, 3.3% European, 2.1% American, 0.9% German (2005-2009 5-year est.).

Economy: Employment by occupation: 0.0% management, 40.0% professional, 17.9% services, 15.8% sales, 10.0% farming, 1.6% construction, 14.7% production (2005-2009 5-year est.).

Income: Per capita income: $12,113 (2010); Median household income: $23,214 (2010); Average household income: $34,455 (2010); Percent of households with income of $100,000 or more: 3.8% (2010); Poverty rate: 36.7% (2005-2009 5-year est.).

Taxes: Total city taxes per capita: $188 (2007); City property taxes per capita: $43 (2007).

Education: Percent of population age 25 and over with: High school diploma (including GED) or higher: 48.2% (2010); Bachelor's degree or higher: 13.6% (2010); Master's degree or higher: 3.5% (2010).

School District(s)

Balmorhea ISD (PK-12)
    2009-10 Enrollment: 159 . . . . (432) 375-2223

Housing: Homeownership rate: 75.6% (2010); Median home value: $25,000 (2010); Median contract rent: $168 per month (2005-2009 5-year est.); Median year structure built: 1967 (2005-2009 5-year est.).

Transportation: Commute to work: 82.9% car, 0.0% public transportation, 8.8% walk, 3.3% work from home (2005-2009 5-year est.); Travel time to work: 59.4% less than 15 minutes, 17.7% 15 to 30 minutes, 12.6% 30 to 45 minutes, 4.0% 45 to 60 minutes, 6.3% 60 minutes or more (2005-2009 5-year est.)

LINDSAY (CDP). Covers a land area of 1.039 square miles and a water area of 0 square miles. Located at 31.36° N. Lat; 103.53° W. Long. Elevation is 2,628 feet.

Population: 303 (1990); 394 (2000); 316 (2010); 299 (2015 projected); Race: 91.1% White, 2.2% Black, 0.0% Asian, 6.6% Other, 36.7% Hispanic of any race (2010); Density: 304.3 persons per square mile (2010); Average household size: 2.86 (2010); Median age: 31.6 (2010); Males per 100 females: 263.2 (2010); Marriage status: 23.3% never married, 71.2% now married, 0.0% widowed, 5.4% divorced (2005-2009 5-year est.); Foreign born: 47.3% (2005-2009 5-year est.); Ancestry (includes multiple ancestries): n/a (2005-2009 5-year est.).
Economy: Employment by occupation: 0.0% management, 0.0% professional, 63.2% services, 24.6% sales, 0.0% farming, 0.0% construction, 12.3% production (2005-2009 5-year est.).
Income: Per capita income: $10,542 (2010); Median household income: $27,857 (2010); Average household income: $35,388 (2010); Percent of households with income of $100,000 or more: 1.7% (2010); Poverty rate: 59.9% (2005-2009 5-year est.).
Education: Percent of population age 25 and over with: High school diploma (including GED) or higher: 48.1% (2010); Bachelor's degree or higher: 7.7% (2010); Master's degree or higher: 5.5% (2010).
Housing: Homeownership rate: 84.5% (2010); Median home value: $19,999 (2010); Median contract rent: n/a per month (2005-2009 5-year est.); Median year structure built: 1962 (2005-2009 5-year est.).
Transportation: Commute to work: 100.0% car, 0.0% public transportation, 0.0% walk, 0.0% work from home (2005-2009 5-year est.); Travel time to work: 66.7% less than 15 minutes, 33.3% 15 to 30 minutes, 0.0% 30 to 45 minutes, 0.0% 45 to 60 minutes, 0.0% 60 minutes or more (2005-2009 5-year est.)

PECOS (city). County seat. Covers a land area of 7.308 square miles and a water area of 0 square miles. Located at 31.41° N. Lat; 103.50° W. Long. Elevation is 2,582 feet.
History: Pecos was a pioneer cow town with more than its share of violence. The verb "to pecos" meant to kill a man and dispose of his body in the river. The town later settled down to be a marketing center for the surrounding farm lands.
Population: 12,138 (1990); 9,501 (2000); 7,778 (2010); 6,963 (2015 projected); Race: 75.7% White, 3.1% Black, 0.6% Asian, 20.6% Other, 79.5% Hispanic of any race (2010); Density: 1,064.3 persons per square mile (2010); Average household size: 2.84 (2010); Median age: 37.6 (2010); Males per 100 females: 97.0 (2010); Marriage status: 26.3% never married, 56.6% now married, 8.9% widowed, 8.2% divorced (2005-2009 5-year est.); Foreign born: 7.2% (2005-2009 5-year est.); Ancestry (includes multiple ancestries): 5.2% American, 3.0% English, 2.2% German, 1.7% Scotch-Irish, 1.5% Canadian (2005-2009 5-year est.).
Economy: Single-family building permits issued: 1 (2010); Multi-family building permits issued: 0 (2010); Employment by occupation: 11.2% management, 10.1% professional, 32.9% services, 19.6% sales, 0.7% farming, 15.6% construction, 9.8% production (2005-2009 5-year est.).
Income: Per capita income: $15,513 (2010); Median household income: $34,129 (2010); Average household income: $44,493 (2010); Percent of households with income of $100,000 or more: 6.6% (2010); Poverty rate: 27.4% (2005-2009 5-year est.).
Taxes: Total city taxes per capita: $327 (2007); City property taxes per capita: $114 (2007).
Education: Percent of population age 25 and over with: High school diploma (including GED) or higher: 54.9% (2010); Bachelor's degree or higher: 9.9% (2010); Master's degree or higher: 3.0% (2010).

School District(s)
Pecos-Barstow-Toyah ISD (PK-12)
    2009-10 Enrollment: 2,198 . . . . (432) 447-7201
Housing: Homeownership rate: 74.7% (2010); Median home value: $26,805 (2010); Median contract rent: $333 per month (2005-2009 5-year est.); Median year structure built: 1964 (2005-2009 5-year est.).
Hospitals: Reeves County Hospital (49 beds)
Safety: Violent crime rate: 34.0 per 10,000 population; Property crime rate: 260.4 per 10,000 population (2009).
Newspapers: Pecos Enterprise (Local news; Circulation 1,971)
Transportation: Commute to work: 92.4% car, 0.0% public transportation, 2.7% walk, 1.1% work from home (2005-2009 5-year est.); Travel time to work: 69.9% less than 15 minutes, 17.9% 15 to 30 minutes, 6.1% 30 to 45 minutes, 1.0% 45 to 60 minutes, 5.1% 60 minutes or more (2005-2009 5-year est.)
Additional Information Contacts
City of Pecos . . . . (432) 445-2421
    http://townofpecoscitytx.com

Pecos Area Chamber of Commerce . . . . (432) 445-2406
    http://www.pecostx.com

TOYAH (town). Covers a land area of 1.624 square miles and a water area of 0 square miles. Located at 31.31° N. Lat; 103.79° W. Long. Elevation is 2,913 feet.
Population: 115 (1990); 100 (2000); 81 (2010); 77 (2015 projected); Race: 91.4% White, 2.5% Black, 0.0% Asian, 6.2% Other, 37.0% Hispanic of any race (2010); Density: 49.9 persons per square mile (2010); Average household size: 2.80 (2010); Median age: 33.6 (2010); Males per 100 females: 350.0 (2010); Marriage status: 20.5% never married, 59.0% now married, 14.8% widowed, 5.7% divorced (2005-2009 5-year est.); Foreign born: 5.2% (2005-2009 5-year est.); Ancestry (includes multiple ancestries): 30.4% American, 8.1% Italian, 3.0% English, 3.0% French (2005-2009 5-year est.).
Economy: Employment by occupation: 18.2% management, 0.0% professional, 6.8% services, 6.8% sales, 0.0% farming, 59.1% construction, 9.1% production (2005-2009 5-year est.).
Income: Per capita income: $10,543 (2010); Median household income: $26,250 (2010); Average household income: $29,333 (2010); Percent of households with income of $100,000 or more: 0.0% (2010); Poverty rate: 11.1% (2005-2009 5-year est.).
Taxes: Total city taxes per capita: $455 (2007); City property taxes per capita: $284 (2007).
Education: Percent of population age 25 and over with: High school diploma (including GED) or higher: 48.0% (2010); Bachelor's degree or higher: 8.0% (2010); Master's degree or higher: 4.0% (2010).
Housing: Homeownership rate: 86.7% (2010); Median home value: $19,999 (2010); Median contract rent: n/a per month (2005-2009 5-year est.); Median year structure built: 1955 (2005-2009 5-year est.).
Transportation: Commute to work: 100.0% car, 0.0% public transportation, 0.0% walk, 0.0% work from home (2005-2009 5-year est.); Travel time to work: 77.3% less than 15 minutes, 15.9% 15 to 30 minutes, 6.8% 30 to 45 minutes, 0.0% 45 to 60 minutes, 0.0% 60 minutes or more (2005-2009 5-year est.)

Refugio County

Located in south Texas; bounded on the north by the San Antonio River, on the southwest by the Aransas River, on the southeast by Copano Bay, and on the northeast by San Antonio Bay; drained by the Mission River and Copano Creek. Covers a land area of 770.21 square miles, a water area of 48.43 square miles, and is located in the Central Time Zone at 28.28° N. Lat., 97.21° W. Long. The county was founded in 1856. County seat is Refugio.
Population: 7,976 (1990); 7,828 (2000); 7,337 (2010); 7,088 (2015 projected); Race: 79.6% White, 6.7% Black, 0.4% Asian, 13.3% Other, 46.0% Hispanic of any race (2010); Density: 9.5 persons per square mile (2010); Average household size: 2.53 (2010); Median age: 42.8 (2010); Males per 100 females: 94.3 (2010).
Religion: Five largest groups: 26.8% Southern Baptist Convention, 24.8% Catholic Church, 5.7% The United Methodist Church, 2.6% Evangelical Lutheran Church in America, 1.9% Churches of Christ (2000).
Economy: Unemployment rate: 6.8% (June 2011); Total civilian labor force: 4,276 (June 2011); Leading industries: 23.2% mining; 16.5% health care and social assistance; 15.4% retail trade (2009); Farms: 295 totaling 490,565 acres (2007); Companies that employ 500 or more persons: 0 (2009); Companies that employ 100 to 499 persons: 1 (2009); Companies that employ less than 100 persons: 136 (2009); Black-owned businesses: n/a (2007); Hispanic-owned businesses: n/a (2007); Asian-owned businesses: n/a (2007); Women-owned businesses: n/a (2007); Retail sales per capita: $11,525 (2010). Single-family building permits issued: 3 (2010); Multi-family building permits issued: 0 (2010).
Income: Per capita income: $20,100 (2010); Median household income: $38,119 (2010); Average household income: $51,492 (2010); Percent of households with income of $100,000 or more: 9.8% (2010); Poverty rate: 17.2% (2009); Bankruptcy rate: 1.34% (2010).
Taxes: Total county taxes per capita: $612 (2007); County property taxes per capita: $577 (2007).
Education: Percent of population age 25 and over with: High school diploma (including GED) or higher: 73.8% (2010); Bachelor's degree or higher: 13.0% (2010); Master's degree or higher: 4.3% (2010).
Housing: Homeownership rate: 73.0% (2010); Median home value: $46,295 (2010); Median contract rent: $369 per month (2005-2009 5-year est.); Median year structure built: 1965 (2005-2009 5-year est.)

Health: Birth rate: 123.2 per 10,000 population (2009); Death rate: 94.1 per 10,000 population (2009); Age-adjusted cancer mortality rate: 206.4 deaths per 100,000 population (2007); Number of physicians: 1.4 per 10,000 population (2008); Hospital beds: 27.3 per 10,000 population (2007); Hospital admissions: 210.4 per 10,000 population (2007).
Elections: 2008 Presidential election results: 42.4% Obama, 56.9% McCain, 0.1% Nader
Additional Information Contacts
Refugio County Government . . . . (361) 526-4434
    http://www.co.refugio.tx.us/ips/cms
Refugio County Chamber of Commerce . . . . (361) 526-2835
    http://www.refugiocountytx.org

Refugio County Communities

AUSTWELL (city). Covers a land area of 0.364 square miles and a water area of 0 square miles. Located at 28.39° N. Lat; 96.84° W. Long. Elevation is 23 feet.
Population: 189 (1990); 192 (2000); 194 (2010); 191 (2015 projected); Race: 84.0% White, 2.1% Black, 0.5% Asian, 13.4% Other, 68.0% Hispanic of any race (2010); Density: 533.0 persons per square mile (2010); Average household size: 2.49 (2010); Median age: 43.1 (2010); Males per 100 females: 102.1 (2010); Marriage status: 9.5% never married, 50.0% now married, 16.7% widowed, 23.8% divorced (2005-2009 5-year est.); Foreign born: 1.1% (2005-2009 5-year est.); Ancestry (includes multiple ancestries): 25.0% German, 22.8% Irish, 6.5% Italian, 3.3% Swedish, 2.2% English (2005-2009 5-year est.).
Economy: Single-family building permits issued: 0 (2010); Multi-family building permits issued: 0 (2010); Employment by occupation: 11.8% management, 11.8% professional, 32.4% services, 23.5% sales, 11.8% farming, 8.8% construction, 0.0% production (2005-2009 5-year est.).
Income: Per capita income: $19,423 (2010); Median household income: $34,167 (2010); Average household income: $48,045 (2010); Percent of households with income of $100,000 or more: 7.7% (2010); Poverty rate: 21.7% (2005-2009 5-year est.).
Taxes: Total city taxes per capita: $164 (2007); City property taxes per capita: $101 (2007).
Education: Percent of population age 25 and over with: High school diploma (including GED) or higher: 68.4% (2010); Bachelor's degree or higher: 10.3% (2010); Master's degree or higher: 3.7% (2010).
Housing: Homeownership rate: 70.5% (2010); Median home value: $36,154 (2010); Median contract rent: $456 per month (2005-2009 5-year est.); Median year structure built: 1972 (2005-2009 5-year est.).
Transportation: Commute to work: 79.4% car, 0.0% public transportation, 14.7% walk, 5.9% work from home (2005-2009 5-year est.); Travel time to work: 46.9% less than 15 minutes, 40.6% 15 to 30 minutes, 12.5% 30 to 45 minutes, 0.0% 45 to 60 minutes, 0.0% 60 minutes or more (2005-2009 5-year est.)

BAYSIDE (town). Covers a land area of 1.041 square miles and a water area of 0.072 square miles. Located at 28.09° N. Lat; 97.21° W. Long. Elevation is 16 feet.
History: Bayside grew as a resort community on Copano Bay, near the old town of St. Mary's. St. Mary's was founded in 1840 and served as a port for nearly fifty years.
Population: 401 (1990); 360 (2000); 337 (2010); 325 (2015 projected); Race: 90.5% White, 2.1% Black, 0.0% Asian, 7.4% Other, 22.3% Hispanic of any race (2010); Density: 323.9 persons per square mile (2010); Average household size: 2.32 (2010); Median age: 46.8 (2010); Males per 100 females: 101.8 (2010); Marriage status: 11.3% never married, 65.6% now married, 2.4% widowed, 20.7% divorced (2005-2009 5-year est.); Foreign born: 0.0% (2005-2009 5-year est.); Ancestry (includes multiple ancestries): 48.2% German, 23.1% English, 15.3% Irish, 9.2% French, 4.2% Italian (2005-2009 5-year est.).
Economy: Single-family building permits issued: 2 (2010); Multi-family building permits issued: 0 (2010); Employment by occupation: 10.5% management, 22.3% professional, 12.2% services, 17.2% sales, 5.9% farming, 23.5% construction, 8.4% production (2005-2009 5-year est.).
Income: Per capita income: $21,504 (2010); Median household income: $36,974 (2010); Average household income: $50,810 (2010); Percent of households with income of $100,000 or more: 13.8% (2010); Poverty rate: 5.6% (2005-2009 5-year est.).
Taxes: Total city taxes per capita: $201 (2007); City property taxes per capita: $124 (2007).

Education: Percent of population age 25 and over with: High school diploma (including GED) or higher: 80.7% (2010); Bachelor's degree or higher: 21.0% (2010); Master's degree or higher: 1.2% (2010).
Housing: Homeownership rate: 76.6% (2010); Median home value: $51,071 (2010); Median contract rent: n/a per month (2005-2009 5-year est.); Median year structure built: 1970 (2005-2009 5-year est.).
Transportation: Commute to work: 85.0% car, 0.0% public transportation, 12.8% walk, 0.9% work from home (2005-2009 5-year est.); Travel time to work: 34.5% less than 15 minutes, 35.8% 15 to 30 minutes, 13.4% 30 to 45 minutes, 12.5% 45 to 60 minutes, 3.9% 60 minutes or more (2005-2009 5-year est.)

REFUGIO (town). County seat. Covers a land area of 1.564 square miles and a water area of 0 square miles. Located at 28.30° N. Lat; 97.27° W. Long. Elevation is 46 feet.
History: Refugio began in 1790 when Franciscan monks built Mission Nuestra Senora del Refugio (Mission of Our Lady of Refuge). A group of Irish colonists settled in Refugio in 1829 under a grant issued to James Power and James Hewetson, and the Pueblo of Refugio was founded in 1834. For a time in 1836, Refugio was the headquarters for General Sam Houston, and after the fall of the Alamo it was occupied by Mexican forces. The town was chartered in 1842 by the Republic of Texas.
Population: 3,141 (1990); 2,941 (2000); 2,759 (2010); 2,659 (2015 projected); Race: 74.1% White, 14.1% Black, 0.7% Asian, 11.1% Other, 43.2% Hispanic of any race (2010); Density: 1,764.3 persons per square mile (2010); Average household size: 2.50 (2010); Median age: 42.0 (2010); Males per 100 females: 90.0 (2010); Marriage status: 31.8% never married, 40.6% now married, 12.9% widowed, 14.7% divorced (2005-2009 5-year est.); Foreign born: 8.1% (2005-2009 5-year est.); Ancestry (includes multiple ancestries): 10.5% German, 8.7% Irish, 6.0% English, 5.4% American, 2.4% Scottish (2005-2009 5-year est.).
Economy: Single-family building permits issued: 0 (2010); Multi-family building permits issued: 0 (2010); Employment by occupation: 6.8% management, 16.7% professional, 26.1% services, 25.1% sales, 0.8% farming, 12.6% construction, 11.9% production (2005-2009 5-year est.).
Income: Per capita income: $17,635 (2010); Median household income: $34,281 (2010); Average household income: $46,073 (2010); Percent of households with income of $100,000 or more: 6.4% (2010); Poverty rate: 23.4% (2005-2009 5-year est.).
Taxes: Total city taxes per capita: $444 (2007); City property taxes per capita: $128 (2007).
Education: Percent of population age 25 and over with: High school diploma (including GED) or higher: 71.7% (2010); Bachelor's degree or higher: 13.9% (2010); Master's degree or higher: 5.0% (2010).
School District(s)
Refugio ISD (PK-12)
    2009-10 Enrollment: 766 . . . . (361) 526-2325
Housing: Homeownership rate: 69.7% (2010); Median home value: $45,122 (2010); Median contract rent: $308 per month (2005-2009 5-year est.); Median year structure built: 1959 (2005-2009 5-year est.).
Hospitals: Refugio Memorial Hospital
Safety: Violent crime rate: 18.6 per 10,000 population; Property crime rate: 85.4 per 10,000 population (2009).
Transportation: Commute to work: 93.6% car, 0.0% public transportation, 5.8% walk, 0.6% work from home (2005-2009 5-year est.); Travel time to work: 63.4% less than 15 minutes, 5.0% 15 to 30 minutes, 13.2% 30 to 45 minutes, 10.5% 45 to 60 minutes, 7.9% 60 minutes or more (2005-2009 5-year est.)
Additional Information Contacts
Refugio County Chamber of Commerce . . . . (361) 526-2835
    http://www.refugiocountytx.org

TIVOLI (unincorporated postal area, zip code 77990). Covers a land area of 195.843 square miles and a water area of 3.420 square miles. Located at 28.46° N. Lat; 96.88° W. Long. Elevation is 30 feet.
Population: 861 (2000); Race: 82.3% White, 1.7% Black, 0.3% Asian, 15.7% Other, 59.0% Hispanic of any race (2000); Density: 4.4 persons per square mile (2000); Age: 25.7% under 18, 16.7% over 64 (2000); Marriage status: 21.9% never married, 64.8% now married, 7.1% widowed, 6.2% divorced (2000); Foreign born: 5.2% (2000); Ancestry (includes multiple ancestries): 10.0% German, 6.9% Irish, 5.9% English, 3.3% Scotch-Irish (2000).
Economy: Employment by occupation: 7.0% management, 4.6% professional, 20.0% services, 18.8% sales, 6.7% farming, 15.9% construction, 27.0% production (2000).

Income: Per capita income: $16,256 (2000); Median household income: $32,692 (2000); Poverty rate: 179.1% (2000).
Education: Percent of population age 25 and over with: High school diploma (including GED) or higher: 55.5% (2000); Bachelor's degree or higher: 7.4% (2000).

School District(s)
Austwell-Tivoli ISD (PK-12)
   2009-10 Enrollment: 161 . . . . (361) 286-3212
Housing: Homeownership rate: 77.3% (2000); Median home value: $37,700 (2000); Median contract rent: $246 per month (2000); Median year structure built: 1972 (2000).
Transportation: Commute to work: 87.5% car, 0.0% public transportation, 6.4% walk, 2.3% work from home (2000); Travel time to work: 46.6% less than 15 minutes, 26.0% 15 to 30 minutes, 16.4% 30 to 45 minutes, 8.4% 45 to 60 minutes, 2.7% 60 minutes or more (2000)

WOODSBORO (town).
Covers a land area of 0.759 square miles and a water area of 0 square miles. Located at 28.23° N. Lat; 97.32° W. Long. Elevation is 43 feet.
History: Incorporated 1928.
Population: 1,731 (1990); 1,685 (2000); 1,551 (2010); 1,481 (2015 projected); Race: 79.6% White, 2.3% Black, 0.1% Asian, 18.0% Other, 54.5% Hispanic of any race (2010); Density: 2,042.2 persons per square mile (2010); Average household size: 2.64 (2010); Median age: 40.4 (2010); Males per 100 females: 93.9 (2010); Marriage status: 20.0% never married, 65.8% now married, 3.6% widowed, 10.6% divorced (2005-2009 5-year est.); Foreign born: 0.0% (2005-2009 5-year est.); Ancestry (includes multiple ancestries): 23.1% German, 16.7% Irish, 8.5% English, 7.5% Czech, 3.0% American (2005-2009 5-year est.).
Economy: Single-family building permits issued: 0 (2010); Multi-family building permits issued: 0 (2010); Employment by occupation: 10.5% management, 15.3% professional, 22.5% services, 26.1% sales, 1.2% farming, 13.6% construction, 10.8% production (2005-2009 5-year est.).
Income: Per capita income: $19,680 (2010); Median household income: $37,419 (2010); Average household income: $51,648 (2010); Percent of households with income of $100,000 or more: 11.0% (2010); Poverty rate: 9.2% (2005-2009 5-year est.).
Taxes: Total city taxes per capita: $162 (2007); City property taxes per capita: $128 (2007).
Education: Percent of population age 25 and over with: High school diploma (including GED) or higher: 71.0% (2010); Bachelor's degree or higher: 9.6% (2010); Master's degree or higher: 4.1% (2010).

School District(s)
Woodsboro ISD (PK-12)
   2009-10 Enrollment: 535 . . . . (361) 543-4518
Housing: Homeownership rate: 71.6% (2010); Median home value: $39,333 (2010); Median contract rent: $414 per month (2005-2009 5-year est.); Median year structure built: 1963 (2005-2009 5-year est.).
Transportation: Commute to work: 95.1% car, 0.0% public transportation, 1.6% walk, 1.5% work from home (2005-2009 5-year est.); Travel time to work: 49.6% less than 15 minutes, 13.1% 15 to 30 minutes, 7.8% 30 to 45 minutes, 15.1% 45 to 60 minutes, 14.4% 60 minutes or more (2005-2009 5-year est.)

Roberts County

Located in north Texas, on the high plains of the Panhandle; drained by the Canadian River and its tributaries. Covers a land area of 924.09 square miles, a water area of 0.10 square miles, and is located in the Central Time Zone at 35.80° N. Lat., 100.78° W. Long. The county was founded in 1876. County seat is Miami.

Roberts County is part of the Pampa, TX Micropolitan Statistical Area. The entire metro area includes: Gray County, TX; Roberts County, TX

Weather Station: Franklin										Elevation: 469 feet		
	Jan	Feb	Mar	Apr	May	Jun	Jul	Aug	Sep	Oct	Nov	Dec
High	60	64	71	78	84	90	95	96	90	80	70	61
Low	39	42	48	56	64	70	72	72	66	58	48	40
Precip	3.0	3.0	3.2	2.6	4.7	3.2	1.7	2.9	3.1	4.8	3.3	3.6
Snow	0.3	0.4	0.0	0.1	0.0	0.0	0.0	0.0	0.0	0.0	tr	0.1

High and Low temperatures in degrees Fahrenheit; Precipitation and Snow in inches

Weather Station: Miami										Elevation: 2,754 feet		
	Jan	Feb	Mar	Apr	May	Jun	Jul	Aug	Sep	Oct	Nov	Dec
High	49	52	60	70	78	86	92	91	83	72	59	49
Low	22	25	33	41	52	62	66	65	57	44	32	23
Precip	0.8	0.8	2.0	1.9	3.4	3.6	2.2	2.6	2.3	2.1	1.1	1.0
Snow	2.9	2.8	3.7	0.6	0.1	0.0	0.0	0.0	tr	0.1	0.9	4.8

High and Low temperatures in degrees Fahrenheit; Precipitation and Snow in inches

Population: 1,025 (1990); 887 (2000); 839 (2010); 815 (2015 projected); Race: 92.5% White, 0.4% Black, 0.1% Asian, 7.0% Other, 8.2% Hispanic of any race (2010); Density: 0.9 persons per square mile (2010); Average household size: 2.36 (2010); Median age: 44.8 (2010); Males per 100 females: 103.1 (2010).
Religion: Four largest groups: 42.6% Southern Baptist Convention, 24.6% The United Methodist Church, 9.6% Christian Church (Disciples of Christ), 9.4% Churches of Christ (2000).
Economy: Unemployment rate: 4.9% (June 2011); Total civilian labor force: 567 (June 2011); Leading industries: Farms: 108 totaling 485,207 acres (2007); Companies that employ 500 or more persons: 0 (2009); Companies that employ 100 to 499 persons: 0 (2009); Companies that employ less than 100 persons: 12 (2009); Black-owned businesses: n/a (2007); Hispanic-owned businesses: n/a (2007); Asian-owned businesses: n/a (2007); Women-owned businesses: n/a (2007); Retail sales per capita: $3,709 (2010). Single-family building permits issued: n/a (2010); Multi-family building permits issued: n/a (2010).
Income: Per capita income: $28,984 (2010); Median household income: $56,402 (2010); Average household income: $68,308 (2010); Percent of households with income of $100,000 or more: 16.6% (2010); Poverty rate: 6.6% (2009); Bankruptcy rate: 1.08% (2010).
Taxes: Total county taxes per capita: $387 (2007); County property taxes per capita: $299 (2007).
Education: Percent of population age 25 and over with: High school diploma (including GED) or higher: 92.3% (2010); Bachelor's degree or higher: 27.3% (2010); Master's degree or higher: 5.8% (2010).
Housing: Homeownership rate: 77.2% (2010); Median home value: $63,878 (2010); Median contract rent: $431 per month (2005-2009 5-year est.); Median year structure built: 1960 (2005-2009 5-year est.).
Health: Birth rate: 148.1 per 10,000 population (2009); Death rate: 11.4 per 10,000 population (2009); Age-adjusted cancer mortality rate: Suppressed deaths per 100,000 population (2007); Number of physicians: 0.0 per 10,000 population (2008); Hospital beds: 0.0 per 10,000 population (2007); Hospital admissions: 0.0 per 10,000 population (2007).
Elections: 2008 Presidential election results: 7.9% Obama, 92.1% McCain, 0.0% Nader
Additional Information Contacts
Roberts County Government . . . . (806) 868-3721
   http://www.co.roberts.tx.us/ips/cms

Roberts County Communities

MIAMI (city).
County seat. Covers a land area of 1.167 square miles and a water area of 0 square miles. Located at 35.69° N. Lat; 100.63° W. Long. Elevation is 2,756 feet.
History: Miami was established in an area with many prehistoric ruins and fossil beds. Coronado came through this area in the 16th century.
Population: 675 (1990); 588 (2000); 552 (2010); 535 (2015 projected); Race: 90.6% White, 0.0% Black, 0.2% Asian, 9.2% Other, 9.2% Hispanic of any race (2010); Density: 473.1 persons per square mile (2010); Average household size: 2.32 (2010); Median age: 43.1 (2010); Males per 100 females: 100.7 (2010); Marriage status: 9.2% never married, 75.5% now married, 5.0% widowed, 10.3% divorced (2005-2009 5-year est.); Foreign born: 7.3% (2005-2009 5-year est.); Ancestry (includes multiple ancestries): 23.2% English, 15.6% German, 10.4% American, 8.0% Irish, 6.0% French (2005-2009 5-year est.).
Economy: Employment by occupation: 21.0% management, 23.6% professional, 15.9% services, 18.1% sales, 0.0% farming, 12.5% construction, 8.9% production (2005-2009 5-year est.).
Income: Per capita income: $24,281 (2010); Median household income: $48,548 (2010); Average household income: $56,565 (2010); Percent of households with income of $100,000 or more: 12.2% (2010); Poverty rate: 12.4% (2005-2009 5-year est.).
Taxes: Total city taxes per capita: $273 (2007); City property taxes per capita: $174 (2007).
Education: Percent of population age 25 and over with: High school diploma (including GED) or higher: 90.4% (2010); Bachelor's degree or higher: 27.7% (2010); Master's degree or higher: 6.9% (2010).

School District(s)

Miami ISD (PK-12)
  2009-10 Enrollment: 176 . . . . (806) 868-3971
Housing: Homeownership rate: 82.4% (2010); Median home value: $56,471 (2010); Median contract rent: $425 per month (2005-2009 5-year est.); Median year structure built: 1955 (2005-2009 5-year est.).
Newspapers: Miami Chief (Local news; Circulation 630)
Transportation: Commute to work: 79.1% car, 0.0% public transportation, 13.4% walk, 7.5% work from home (2005-2009 5-year est.); Travel time to work: 48.0% less than 15 minutes, 23.8% 15 to 30 minutes, 23.0% 30 to 45 minutes, 4.4% 45 to 60 minutes, 0.8% 60 minutes or more (2005-2009 5-year est.)

Robertson County

Located in east central Texas; bounded on the west by the Brazos River, and on the east by the Navasota River. Covers a land area of 854.56 square miles, a water area of 11.11 square miles, and is located in the Central Time Zone at 30.98° N. Lat., 96.58° W. Long. The county was founded in 1837. County seat is Franklin.

Robertson County is part of the College Station-Bryan, TX Metropolitan Statistical Area. The entire metro area includes: Brazos County, TX; Burleson County, TX; Robertson County, TX

Weather Station: Franklin   Elevation: 469 feet

	Jan	Feb	Mar	Apr	May	Jun	Jul	Aug	Sep	Oct	Nov	Dec
High	60	64	71	78	84	90	95	96	90	80	70	61
Low	39	42	48	56	64	70	72	72	66	58	48	40
Precip	3.0	3.0	3.2	2.6	4.7	3.2	1.7	2.9	3.1	4.8	3.3	3.6
Snow	0.3	0.4	0.0	0.1	0.0	0.0	0.0	0.0	0.0	0.0	tr	0.1

High and Low temperatures in degrees Fahrenheit; Precipitation and Snow in inches

Population: 15,511 (1990); 16,000 (2000); 15,897 (2010); 15,818 (2015 projected); Race: 66.4% White, 21.7% Black, 0.5% Asian, 11.3% Other, 17.6% Hispanic of any race (2010); Density: 18.6 persons per square mile (2010); Average household size: 2.50 (2010); Median age: 37.9 (2010); Males per 100 females: 92.9 (2010).
Religion: Five largest groups: 28.0% Southern Baptist Convention, 13.3% Catholic Church, 5.9% The United Methodist Church, 2.9% Churches of Christ, 0.4% Assemblies of God (2000).
Economy: Unemployment rate: 9.4% (June 2011); Total civilian labor force: 7,343 (June 2011); Leading industries: 16.6% retail trade; 15.4% health care and social assistance; 15.2% accommodation & food services (2009); Farms: 1,562 totaling 455,308 acres (2007); Companies that employ 500 or more persons: 0 (2009); Companies that employ 100 to 499 persons: 3 (2009); Companies that employ less than 100 persons: 250 (2009); Black-owned businesses: n/a (2007); Hispanic-owned businesses: n/a (2007); Asian-owned businesses: n/a (2007); Women-owned businesses: 297 (2007); Retail sales per capita: $5,829 (2010). Single-family building permits issued: 6 (2010); Multi-family building permits issued: 0 (2010).
Income: Per capita income: $20,845 (2010); Median household income: $40,186 (2010); Average household income: $52,540 (2010); Percent of households with income of $100,000 or more: 12.1% (2010); Poverty rate: 20.2% (2009); Bankruptcy rate: 1.01% (2010).
Taxes: Total county taxes per capita: $791 (2007); County property taxes per capita: $701 (2007).
Education: Percent of population age 25 and over with: High school diploma (including GED) or higher: 74.2% (2010); Bachelor's degree or higher: 14.2% (2010); Master's degree or higher: 5.0% (2010).
Housing: Homeownership rate: 69.5% (2010); Median home value: $77,958 (2010); Median contract rent: $327 per month (2005-2009 5-year est.); Median year structure built: 1977 (2005-2009 5-year est.)
Health: Birth rate: 146.4 per 10,000 population (2009); Death rate: 110.1 per 10,000 population (2009); Age-adjusted cancer mortality rate: 177.0 deaths per 100,000 population (2007); Number of physicians: 1.3 per 10,000 population (2008); Hospital beds: 0.0 per 10,000 population (2007); Hospital admissions: 0.0 per 10,000 population (2007).
Elections: 2008 Presidential election results: 39.9% Obama, 59.3% McCain, 0.2% Nader
Additional Information Contacts
Robertson County Government . . . . (979) 828-3542
  http://www.co.robertson.tx.us/ips/cms
Calvert Chamber of Commerce . . . . (979) 364-2559
  http://www.calverttx.com

City of Hearne . . . . (979) 279-3461
  http://www.hearnetexas.info
Franklin Chamber of Commerce . . . . (979) 828-3276
  http://www.franklintexas.com
Hearne Chamber of Commerce . . . . (979) 279-2351
  http://www.hearnetexas.info/index2.htm

Robertson County Communities

BREMOND (city). Covers a land area of 0.906 square miles and a water area of 0 square miles. Located at 31.16° N. Lat; 96.67° W. Long. Elevation is 459 feet.
History: Incorporated 1938.
Population: 1,104 (1990); 876 (2000); 826 (2010); 804 (2015 projected); Race: 82.2% White, 14.2% Black, 0.4% Asian, 3.3% Other, 3.0% Hispanic of any race (2010); Density: 911.5 persons per square mile (2010); Average household size: 2.24 (2010); Median age: 40.3 (2010); Males per 100 females: 88.6 (2010); Marriage status: 23.3% never married, 38.6% now married, 23.4% widowed, 14.7% divorced (2005-2009 5-year est.); Foreign born: 0.3% (2005-2009 5-year est.); Ancestry (includes multiple ancestries): 17.5% Irish, 14.0% Polish, 13.3% German, 6.0% English, 5.1% French (2005-2009 5-year est.).
Economy: Employment by occupation: 4.2% management, 31.3% professional, 28.6% services, 12.7% sales, 0.0% farming, 7.7% construction, 15.4% production (2005-2009 5-year est.).
Income: Per capita income: $26,420 (2010); Median household income: $43,641 (2010); Average household income: $60,566 (2010); Percent of households with income of $100,000 or more: 20.6% (2010); Poverty rate: 27.3% (2005-2009 5-year est.).
Taxes: Total city taxes per capita: $288 (2007); City property taxes per capita: $138 (2007).
Education: Percent of population age 25 and over with: High school diploma (including GED) or higher: 72.9% (2010); Bachelor's degree or higher: 7.9% (2010); Master's degree or higher: 2.6% (2010).
School District(s)
Bremond ISD (PK-12)
  2009-10 Enrollment: 439 . . . . (254) 746-7145
Housing: Homeownership rate: 65.9% (2010); Median home value: $82,000 (2010); Median contract rent: $397 per month (2005-2009 5-year est.); Median year structure built: 1956 (2005-2009 5-year est.).
Safety: Violent crime rate: 46.9 per 10,000 population; Property crime rate: 187.6 per 10,000 population (2009).
Newspapers: Press (Community news; Circulation 1,293)
Transportation: Commute to work: 83.7% car, 0.0% public transportation, 10.2% walk, 2.3% work from home (2005-2009 5-year est.); Travel time to work: 40.0% less than 15 minutes, 45.2% 15 to 30 minutes, 6.7% 30 to 45 minutes, 1.4% 45 to 60 minutes, 6.7% 60 minutes or more (2005-2009 5-year est.)

CALVERT (city). Covers a land area of 3.890 square miles and a water area of 0 square miles. Located at 30.97° N. Lat; 96.67° W. Long. Elevation is 328 feet.
History: Settled nearby as Sterling, c.1840; moved to present site on Railroad and renamed 1869; incorporated 1896.
Population: 1,536 (1990); 1,426 (2000); 1,370 (2010); 1,342 (2015 projected); Race: 41.0% White, 43.0% Black, 0.1% Asian, 15.9% Other, 19.9% Hispanic of any race (2010); Density: 352.2 persons per square mile (2010); Average household size: 2.42 (2010); Median age: 38.7 (2010); Males per 100 females: 91.3 (2010); Marriage status: 26.1% never married, 38.6% now married, 25.0% widowed, 10.3% divorced (2005-2009 5-year est.); Foreign born: 3.7% (2005-2009 5-year est.); Ancestry (includes multiple ancestries): 8.9% German, 8.0% Irish, 6.5% English, 5.9% French, 3.8% Polish (2005-2009 5-year est.).
Economy: Single-family building permits issued: 0 (2010); Multi-family building permits issued: 0 (2010); Employment by occupation: 12.0% management, 22.7% professional, 19.0% services, 9.8% sales, 0.0% farming, 26.1% construction, 10.4% production (2005-2009 5-year est.).
Income: Per capita income: $19,675 (2010); Median household income: $31,210 (2010); Average household income: $48,411 (2010); Percent of households with income of $100,000 or more: 7.7% (2010); Poverty rate: 22.6% (2005-2009 5-year est.).
Taxes: Total city taxes per capita: $234 (2007); City property taxes per capita: $94 (2007).

Education: Percent of population age 25 and over with: High school diploma (including GED) or higher: 68.5% (2010); Bachelor's degree or higher: 13.8% (2010); Master's degree or higher: 3.9% (2010).

School District(s)
Calvert ISD (PK-12)
    2009-10 Enrollment: 159 . . . . (979) 364-2824
Housing: Homeownership rate: 60.5% (2010); Median home value: $61,765 (2010); Median contract rent: $179 per month (2005-2009 5-year est.); Median year structure built: 1955 (2005-2009 5-year est.).
Safety: Violent crime rate: 96.2 per 10,000 population; Property crime rate: 518.1 per 10,000 population (2009).
Transportation: Commute to work: 75.3% car, 2.6% public transportation, 4.2% walk, 7.9% work from home (2005-2009 5-year est.); Travel time to work: 34.6% less than 15 minutes, 27.3% 15 to 30 minutes, 10.9% 30 to 45 minutes, 10.6% 45 to 60 minutes, 16.7% 60 minutes or more (2005-2009 5-year est.)

Additional Information Contacts
Calvert Chamber of Commerce . . . . (979) 364-2559
    http://www.calverttx.com

FRANKLIN (city). County seat. Covers a land area of 0.922 square miles and a water area of 0 square miles. Located at 31.02° N. Lat; 96.48° W. Long. Elevation is 449 feet.
History: Settled 1880, incorporated 1912.
Population: 1,336 (1990); 1,470 (2000); 1,454 (2010); 1,447 (2015 projected); Race: 80.3% White, 14.9% Black, 0.9% Asian, 3.9% Other, 10.7% Hispanic of any race (2010); Density: 1,577.1 persons per square mile (2010); Average household size: 2.51 (2010); Median age: 38.2 (2010); Males per 100 females: 90.1 (2010); Marriage status: 25.2% never married, 50.7% now married, 9.1% widowed, 15.0% divorced (2005-2009 5-year est.); Foreign born: 2.8% (2005-2009 5-year est.); Ancestry (includes multiple ancestries): 21.5% German, 10.0% Irish, 9.4% Scottish, 8.4% English, 4.4% Czech (2005-2009 5-year est.).
Economy: Single-family building permits issued: 1 (2010); Multi-family building permits issued: 0 (2010); Employment by occupation: 15.7% management, 4.3% professional, 19.5% services, 28.1% sales, 0.5% farming, 15.2% construction, 16.7% production (2005-2009 5-year est.).
Income: Per capita income: $21,150 (2010); Median household income: $47,232 (2010); Average household income: $55,198 (2010); Percent of households with income of $100,000 or more: 13.1% (2010); Poverty rate: 14.9% (2005-2009 5-year est.).
Taxes: Total city taxes per capita: $260 (2007); City property taxes per capita: $84 (2007).
Education: Percent of population age 25 and over with: High school diploma (including GED) or higher: 78.0% (2010); Bachelor's degree or higher: 16.0% (2010); Master's degree or higher: 6.8% (2010).

School District(s)
Franklin ISD (PK-12)
    2009-10 Enrollment: 1,049 . . . . (979) 828-7010
Housing: Homeownership rate: 64.5% (2010); Median home value: $73,208 (2010); Median contract rent: $417 per month (2005-2009 5-year est.); Median year structure built: 1977 (2005-2009 5-year est.).
Newspapers: News Weekly (Community news; Circulation 1,050)
Transportation: Commute to work: 84.4% car, 0.0% public transportation, 1.3% walk, 3.8% work from home (2005-2009 5-year est.); Travel time to work: 32.5% less than 15 minutes, 31.9% 15 to 30 minutes, 19.8% 30 to 45 minutes, 7.5% 45 to 60 minutes, 8.3% 60 minutes or more (2005-2009 5-year est.)

Additional Information Contacts
Franklin Chamber of Commerce . . . . (979) 828-3276
    http://www.franklintexas.com

HEARNE (city). Covers a land area of 4.099 square miles and a water area of 0.003 square miles. Located at 30.87° N. Lat; 96.59° W. Long. Elevation is 295 feet.
History: Hearne developed around a railroad junction and railroad shops. Cotton was the basis of the early economy.
Population: 5,132 (1990); 4,690 (2000); 4,509 (2010); 4,416 (2015 projected); Race: 43.3% White, 36.7% Black, 0.4% Asian, 19.5% Other, 31.3% Hispanic of any race (2010); Density: 1,100.0 persons per square mile (2010); Average household size: 2.60 (2010); Median age: 33.5 (2010); Males per 100 females: 89.5 (2010); Marriage status: 35.6% never married, 45.4% now married, 8.0% widowed, 11.0% divorced (2005-2009 5-year est.); Foreign born: 16.9% (2005-2009 5-year est.); Ancestry

(includes multiple ancestries): 5.0% Irish, 4.0% German, 3.6% American, 2.4% Italian, 2.3% English (2005-2009 5-year est.).
Economy: Single-family building permits issued: 5 (2010); Multi-family building permits issued: 0 (2010); Employment by occupation: 6.4% management, 12.4% professional, 26.7% services, 25.4% sales, 5.0% farming, 6.4% construction, 17.6% production (2005-2009 5-year est.).
Income: Per capita income: $14,017 (2010); Median household income: $28,571 (2010); Average household income: $36,685 (2010); Percent of households with income of $100,000 or more: 4.0% (2010); Poverty rate: 34.1% (2005-2009 5-year est.).
Taxes: Total city taxes per capita: $346 (2007); City property taxes per capita: $162 (2007).
Education: Percent of population age 25 and over with: High school diploma (including GED) or higher: 68.5% (2010); Bachelor's degree or higher: 10.6% (2010); Master's degree or higher: 2.7% (2010).

School District(s)
Hearne ISD (PK-12)
    2009-10 Enrollment: 1,091 . . . . (979) 279-3200
Housing: Homeownership rate: 59.9% (2010); Median home value: $65,063 (2010); Median contract rent: $313 per month (2005-2009 5-year est.); Median year structure built: 1967 (2005-2009 5-year est.).
Safety: Violent crime rate: 81.0 per 10,000 population; Property crime rate: 267.2 per 10,000 population (2009).
Newspapers: Calvert Tribune (Community news; Circulation 500); Democrat (Community news; Circulation 3,500); Franklin Advocate (Community news; Circulation 750)
Transportation: Commute to work: 90.4% car, 0.0% public transportation, 5.8% walk, 3.3% work from home (2005-2009 5-year est.); Travel time to work: 41.2% less than 15 minutes, 28.0% 15 to 30 minutes, 26.7% 30 to 45 minutes, 3.6% 45 to 60 minutes, 0.5% 60 minutes or more (2005-2009 5-year est.)

Additional Information Contacts
City of Hearne . . . . (979) 279-3461
    http://www.hearnetexas.info
Hearne Chamber of Commerce . . . . (979) 279-2351
    http://www.hearnetexas.info/index2.htm

Rockwall County

Located in northeastern Texas; drained by the East Fork of the Trinity River. Covers a land area of 128.79 square miles, a water area of 19.91 square miles, and is located in the Central Time Zone at 32.91° N. Lat., 96.43° W. Long. The county was founded in 1873. County seat is Rockwall.

Rockwall County is part of the Dallas-Fort Worth-Arlington, TX Metropolitan Statistical Area. The entire metro area includes: Dallas-Plano-Irving, TX Metropolitan Division (Collin County, TX; Dallas County, TX; Delta County, TX; Denton County, TX; Ellis County, TX; Hunt County, TX; Kaufman County, TX; Rockwall County, TX); Fort Worth-Arlington, TX Metropolitan Division (Johnson County, TX; Parker County, TX; Tarrant County, TX; Wise County, TX)

Population: 25,604 (1990); 43,080 (2000); 82,374 (2010); 101,342 (2015 projected); Race: 81.6% White, 6.5% Black, 2.5% Asian, 9.4% Other, 17.1% Hispanic of any race (2010); Density: 639.6 persons per square mile (2010); Average household size: 2.99 (2010); Median age: 32.9 (2010); Males per 100 females: 100.7 (2010).
Religion: Five largest groups: 39.0% Southern Baptist Convention, 14.3% Catholic Church, 6.0% The United Methodist Church, 2.5% Assemblies of God, 1.9% Churches of Christ (2000).
Economy: Unemployment rate: 7.9% (June 2011); Total civilian labor force: 40,645 (June 2011); Leading industries: 18.8% retail trade; 16.2% accommodation & food services; 15.9% health care and social assistance (2009); Farms: 347 totaling 37,433 acres (2007); Companies that employ 500 or more persons: 2 (2009); Companies that employ 100 to 499 persons: 23 (2009); Companies that employ less than 100 persons: 1,625 (2009); Black-owned businesses: 315 (2007); Hispanic-owned businesses: 481 (2007); Asian-owned businesses: n/a (2007); Women-owned businesses: 2,438 (2007); Retail sales per capita: $10,728 (2010). Single-family building permits issued: 489 (2010); Multi-family building permits issued: 124 (2010).
Income: Per capita income: $32,960 (2010); Median household income: $77,878 (2010); Average household income: $98,906 (2010); Percent of households with income of $100,000 or more: 35.2% (2010); Poverty rate: 6.6% (2009); Bankruptcy rate: 3.67% (2010).

Taxes: Total county taxes per capita: $253 (2007); County property taxes per capita: $250 (2007).
Education: Percent of population age 25 and over with: High school diploma (including GED) or higher: 90.9% (2010); Bachelor's degree or higher: 33.0% (2010); Master's degree or higher: 10.3% (2010).
Housing: Homeownership rate: 82.5% (2010); Median home value: $179,335 (2010); Median contract rent: $927 per month (2005-2009 5-year est.); Median year structure built: 1996 (2005-2009 5-year est.)
Health: Birth rate: 167.3 per 10,000 population (2009); Death rate: 49.1 per 10,000 population (2009); Age-adjusted cancer mortality rate: 157.2 deaths per 100,000 population (2007); Number of physicians: 19.4 per 10,000 population (2008); Hospital beds: 0.0 per 10,000 population (2007); Hospital admissions: 0.0 per 10,000 population (2007).
Environment: Air Quality Index: 90.2% good, 9.4% moderate, 0.3% unhealthy for sensitive individuals, 0.0% unhealthy (percent of days in 2008)
Elections: 2008 Presidential election results: 26.5% Obama, 72.7% McCain, 0.0% Nader
Additional Information Contacts
Rockwall County Government . . . . (972) 882-2882
  http://www.rockwallcountytexas.com
City of Rockwall . . . . (972) 771-7700
  http://www.rockwall.com
City of Royse City . . . . (972) 636-2250
  http://roysecity.com
Rockwall Area Chamber of Commerce . . . . (972) 771-5733
  http://www.rockwallchamber.org
Royse City Chamber of Commerce . . . . (972) 636-5000
  http://www.roysecitychamber.com

Rockwall County Communities

FATE (city). Covers a land area of 4.730 square miles and a water area of 0.017 square miles. Located at 32.93° N. Lat; 96.38° W. Long. Elevation is 587 feet.
Population: 467 (1990); 497 (2000); 1,469 (2010); 1,836 (2015 projected); Race: 79.9% White, 4.8% Black, 2.0% Asian, 13.3% Other, 28.0% Hispanic of any race (2010); Density: 310.6 persons per square mile (2010); Average household size: 3.30 (2010); Median age: 30.3 (2010); Males per 100 females: 101.8 (2010); Marriage status: 12.9% never married, 72.1% now married, 2.2% widowed, 12.9% divorced (2005-2009 5-year est.); Foreign born: 4.7% (2005-2009 5-year est.); Ancestry (includes multiple ancestries): 13.8% German, 10.5% American, 10.4% English, 9.5% Irish, 5.8% French (2005-2009 5-year est.).
Economy: Single-family building permits issued: 190 (2010); Multi-family building permits issued: 0 (2010); Employment by occupation: 23.1% management, 27.1% professional, 11.5% services, 22.5% sales, 0.0% farming, 10.0% construction, 5.8% production (2005-2009 5-year est.).
Income: Per capita income: $22,991 (2010); Median household income: $65,940 (2010); Average household income: $75,545 (2010); Percent of households with income of $100,000 or more: 26.3% (2010); Poverty rate: 2.6% (2005-2009 5-year est.).
Taxes: Total city taxes per capita: $170 (2007); City property taxes per capita: $46 (2007).
Education: Percent of population age 25 and over with: High school diploma (including GED) or higher: 84.2% (2010); Bachelor's degree or higher: 21.8% (2010); Master's degree or higher: 7.3% (2010).
School District(s)
Royse City ISD (PK-12)
  2009-10 Enrollment: 4,450 . . . . (972) 636-2413
Housing: Homeownership rate: 84.3% (2010); Median home value: $133,242 (2010); Median contract rent: $957 per month (2005-2009 5-year est.); Median year structure built: 2004 (2005-2009 5-year est.).
Transportation: Commute to work: 96.4% car, 0.2% public transportation, 0.5% walk, 1.7% work from home (2005-2009 5-year est.); Travel time to work: 11.9% less than 15 minutes, 26.5% 15 to 30 minutes, 29.3% 30 to 45 minutes, 20.0% 45 to 60 minutes, 12.4% 60 minutes or more (2005-2009 5-year est.)

HEATH (city). Covers a land area of 6.864 square miles and a water area of 0.044 square miles. Located at 32.84° N. Lat; 96.47° W. Long. Elevation is 502 feet.
History: In 1840, the Texas Congress ordered a central government road to be built from Austin to the mouth of the Kiamichi Creek at its intersection

with the Red River. This road crossed the east fork of the Trinity River in what is now known as Heath.
Population: 2,230 (1990); 4,149 (2000); 7,558 (2010); 9,318 (2015 projected); Race: 91.0% White, 2.0% Black, 3.1% Asian, 3.9% Other, 5.3% Hispanic of any race (2010); Density: 1,101.1 persons per square mile (2010); Average household size: 2.90 (2010); Median age: 35.6 (2010); Males per 100 females: 99.6 (2010); Marriage status: 21.0% never married, 66.8% now married, 2.9% widowed, 9.3% divorced (2005-2009 5-year est.); Foreign born: 6.5% (2005-2009 5-year est.); Ancestry (includes multiple ancestries): 19.7% English, 14.0% American, 13.0% German, 8.2% Irish, 6.1% Italian (2005-2009 5-year est.).
Economy: Single-family building permits issued: 24 (2010); Multi-family building permits issued: 0 (2010); Employment by occupation: 26.2% management, 24.6% professional, 12.5% services, 26.6% sales, 0.0% farming, 6.9% construction, 3.2% production (2005-2009 5-year est.).
Income: Per capita income: $47,065 (2010); Median household income: $102,712 (2010); Average household income: $136,546 (2010); Percent of households with income of $100,000 or more: 51.3% (2010); Poverty rate: 0.7% (2005-2009 5-year est.).
Taxes: Total city taxes per capita: $613 (2007); City property taxes per capita: $401 (2007).
Education: Percent of population age 25 and over with: High school diploma (including GED) or higher: 96.3% (2010); Bachelor's degree or higher: 41.8% (2010); Master's degree or higher: 15.0% (2010).
School District(s)
Rockwall ISD (PK-12)
  2009-10 Enrollment: 13,843 . . . . (972) 771-0605
Housing: Homeownership rate: 90.9% (2010); Median home value: $243,847 (2010); Median contract rent: $1,452 per month (2005-2009 5-year est.); Median year structure built: 1995 (2005-2009 5-year est.).
Safety: Violent crime rate: 25.4 per 10,000 population; Property crime rate: 101.6 per 10,000 population (2009).
Transportation: Commute to work: 90.0% car, 0.8% public transportation, 0.9% walk, 7.9% work from home (2005-2009 5-year est.); Travel time to work: 20.0% less than 15 minutes, 24.6% 15 to 30 minutes, 25.1% 30 to 45 minutes, 17.8% 45 to 60 minutes, 12.6% 60 minutes or more (2005-2009 5-year est.)

MCLENDON-CHISHOLM (city). Aka McLendon. Covers a land area of 9.866 square miles and a water area of 0.089 square miles. Located at 32.84° N. Lat; 96.39° W. Long. Elevation is 505 feet.
Population: 672 (1990); 914 (2000); 2,443 (2010); 3,023 (2015 projected); Race: 90.8% White, 2.3% Black, 2.7% Asian, 4.2% Other, 6.3% Hispanic of any race (2010); Density: 247.6 persons per square mile (2010); Average household size: 3.06 (2010); Median age: 34.3 (2010); Males per 100 females: 100.6 (2010); Marriage status: 32.2% never married, 50.0% now married, 9.0% widowed, 8.8% divorced (2005-2009 5-year est.); Foreign born: 7.5% (2005-2009 5-year est.); Ancestry (includes multiple ancestries): 31.7% German, 29.9% Irish, 16.1% Italian, 8.6% English, 7.3% American (2005-2009 5-year est.).
Economy: Single-family building permits issued: 15 (2010); Multi-family building permits issued: 0 (2010); Employment by occupation: 13.4% management, 16.7% professional, 14.6% services, 39.0% sales, 0.0% farming, 11.9% construction, 4.4% production (2005-2009 5-year est.).
Income: Per capita income: $46,889 (2010); Median household income: $107,967 (2010); Average household income: $143,571 (2010); Percent of households with income of $100,000 or more: 53.6% (2010); Poverty rate: 8.5% (2005-2009 5-year est.).
Taxes: Total city taxes per capita: $91 (2007); City property taxes per capita: $0 (2007).
Education: Percent of population age 25 and over with: High school diploma (including GED) or higher: 95.1% (2010); Bachelor's degree or higher: 37.0% (2010); Master's degree or higher: 11.0% (2010).
Housing: Homeownership rate: 94.6% (2010); Median home value: $248,378 (2010); Median contract rent: $800 per month (2005-2009 5-year est.); Median year structure built: 1994 (2005-2009 5-year est.).
Transportation: Commute to work: 85.6% car, 0.0% public transportation, 3.4% walk, 10.0% work from home (2005-2009 5-year est.); Travel time to work: 19.5% less than 15 minutes, 22.1% 15 to 30 minutes, 14.4% 30 to 45 minutes, 23.8% 45 to 60 minutes, 20.2% 60 minutes or more (2005-2009 5-year est.)

MOBILE CITY (city). Covers a land area of 0.016 square miles and a water area of 0 square miles. Located at 32.92° N. Lat; 96.41° W. Long. Elevation is 594 feet.

Population: 108 (1990); 196 (2000); 577 (2010); 721 (2015 projected); Race: 79.7% White, 5.0% Black, 1.9% Asian, 13.3% Other, 28.1% Hispanic of any race (2010); Density: 35,065.3 persons per square mile (2010); Average household size: 3.30 (2010); Median age: 30.3 (2010); Males per 100 females: 105.3 (2010); Marriage status: 37.2% never married, 42.6% now married, 4.3% widowed, 16.0% divorced (2005-2009 5-year est.); Foreign born: 29.2% (2005-2009 5-year est.); Ancestry (includes multiple ancestries): 4.4% American, 2.9% Norwegian, 2.9% Italian, 2.2% Irish, 2.2% German (2005-2009 5-year est.).
Economy: Single-family building permits issued: 0 (2010); Multi-family building permits issued: 0 (2010); Employment by occupation: 3.0% management, 0.0% professional, 20.9% services, 19.4% sales, 0.0% farming, 37.3% construction, 19.4% production (2005-2009 5-year est.).
Income: Per capita income: $22,991 (2010); Median household income: $65,988 (2010); Average household income: $75,914 (2010); Percent of households with income of $100,000 or more: 26.3% (2010); Poverty rate: 27.0% (2005-2009 5-year est.).
Taxes: Total city taxes per capita: $930 (2007); City property taxes per capita: $0 (2007).
Education: Percent of population age 25 and over with: High school diploma (including GED) or higher: 83.7% (2010); Bachelor's degree or higher: 21.3% (2010); Master's degree or higher: 7.3% (2010).
Housing: Homeownership rate: 84.0% (2010); Median home value: $132,639 (2010); Median contract rent: $474 per month (2005-2009 5-year est.); Median year structure built: 1989 (2005-2009 5-year est.).
Transportation: Commute to work: 86.6% car, 0.0% public transportation, 6.0% walk, 4.5% work from home (2005-2009 5-year est.); Travel time to work: 62.5% less than 15 minutes, 12.5% 15 to 30 minutes, 17.2% 30 to 45 minutes, 0.0% 45 to 60 minutes, 7.8% 60 minutes or more (2005-2009 5-year est.)

ROCKWALL (city). County seat. Covers a land area of 22.279 square miles and a water area of 0.371 square miles. Located at 32.92° N. Lat; 96.46° W. Long. Elevation is 591 feet.
History: Named for its geological formation that resembles walls. The name of Rockwall, and of Rockwall County, refers to the geological formation underlying the area, which looks like a wall of jointed blocks.
Population: 10,874 (1990); 17,976 (2000); 30,656 (2010); 37,730 (2015 projected); Race: 83.5% White, 6.1% Black, 2.7% Asian, 7.7% Other, 12.6% Hispanic of any race (2010); Density: 1,376.0 persons per square mile (2010); Average household size: 2.79 (2010); Median age: 34.3 (2010); Males per 100 females: 98.5 (2010); Marriage status: 20.3% never married, 66.5% now married, 4.3% widowed, 8.8% divorced (2005-2009 5-year est.); Foreign born: 8.2% (2005-2009 5-year est.); Ancestry (includes multiple ancestries): 15.3% English, 15.3% German, 10.2% Irish, 9.6% American, 5.2% French (2005-2009 5-year est.).
Economy: Unemployment rate: 7.3% (June 2011); Total civilian labor force: 19,190 (June 2011); Single-family building permits issued: 200 (2010); Multi-family building permits issued: 124 (2010); Employment by occupation: 21.4% management, 26.3% professional, 11.3% services, 29.0% sales, 0.1% farming, 6.6% construction, 5.4% production (2005-2009 5-year est.).
Income: Per capita income: $35,108 (2010); Median household income: $78,952 (2010); Average household income: $98,622 (2010); Percent of households with income of $100,000 or more: 36.2% (2010); Poverty rate: 3.8% (2005-2009 5-year est.).
Taxes: Total city taxes per capita: $661 (2007); City property taxes per capita: $279 (2007).
Education: Percent of population age 25 and over with: High school diploma (including GED) or higher: 93.8% (2010); Bachelor's degree or higher: 39.9% (2010); Master's degree or higher: 12.8% (2010).
School District(s)
Rockwall ISD (PK-12)
    2009-10 Enrollment: 13,843 . . . . (972) 771-0605
Housing: Homeownership rate: 77.5% (2010); Median home value: $192,563 (2010); Median contract rent: $967 per month (2005-2009 5-year est.); Median year structure built: 1996 (2005-2009 5-year est.).
Safety: Violent crime rate: 12.2 per 10,000 population; Property crime rate: 276.6 per 10,000 population (2009).
Newspapers: The Dallas Morning News - Rockwall Bureau (Regional news); The Rockwall Express (Local news; Circulation 5,000)
Transportation: Commute to work: 92.3% car, 0.8% public transportation, 0.7% walk, 5.0% work from home (2005-2009 5-year est.); Travel time to work: 20.2% less than 15 minutes, 23.0% 15 to 30 minutes, 28.2% 30 to 45

minutes, 17.3% 45 to 60 minutes, 11.3% 60 minutes or more (2005-2009 5-year est.)
Additional Information Contacts
City of Rockwall . . . . (972) 771-7700
    http://www.rockwall.com
Rockwall Area Chamber of Commerce . . . . (972) 771-5733
    http://www.rockwallchamber.org

ROYSE CITY (city). Covers a land area of 10.203 square miles and a water area of 0 square miles. Located at 32.97° N. Lat; 96.33° W. Long. Elevation is 554 feet.
Population: 2,217 (1990); 2,957 (2000); 8,376 (2010); 10,304 (2015 projected); Race: 69.7% White, 12.2% Black, 0.9% Asian, 17.2% Other, 30.3% Hispanic of any race (2010); Density: 821.0 persons per square mile (2010); Average household size: 2.99 (2010); Median age: 30.9 (2010); Males per 100 females: 101.7 (2010); Marriage status: 26.9% never married, 56.1% now married, 2.9% widowed, 14.1% divorced (2005-2009 5-year est.); Foreign born: 18.2% (2005-2009 5-year est.); Ancestry (includes multiple ancestries): 13.0% American, 9.6% German, 8.6% English, 7.5% Irish, 4.0% French (2005-2009 5-year est.).
Economy: Single-family building permits issued: 60 (2010); Multi-family building permits issued: 0 (2010); Employment by occupation: 11.8% management, 15.8% professional, 13.0% services, 23.2% sales, 0.4% farming, 17.0% construction, 18.9% production (2005-2009 5-year est.).
Income: Per capita income: $21,404 (2010); Median household income: $55,995 (2010); Average household income: $63,955 (2010); Percent of households with income of $100,000 or more: 17.1% (2010); Poverty rate: 8.6% (2005-2009 5-year est.).
Taxes: Total city taxes per capita: $478 (2007); City property taxes per capita: $191 (2007).
Education: Percent of population age 25 and over with: High school diploma (including GED) or higher: 79.3% (2010); Bachelor's degree or higher: 10.2% (2010); Master's degree or higher: 2.7% (2010).
School District(s)
Royse City ISD (PK-12)
    2009-10 Enrollment: 4,450 . . . . (972) 636-2413
Housing: Homeownership rate: 70.0% (2010); Median home value: $101,342 (2010); Median contract rent: $784 per month (2005-2009 5-year est.); Median year structure built: 2001 (2005-2009 5-year est.).
Safety: Violent crime rate: 22.4 per 10,000 population; Property crime rate: 167.4 per 10,000 population (2009).
Transportation: Commute to work: 96.7% car, 1.2% public transportation, 0.0% walk, 1.8% work from home (2005-2009 5-year est.); Travel time to work: 17.9% less than 15 minutes, 30.1% 15 to 30 minutes, 18.7% 30 to 45 minutes, 13.7% 45 to 60 minutes, 19.7% 60 minutes or more (2005-2009 5-year est.)
Additional Information Contacts
City of Royse City . . . . (972) 636-2250
    http://roysecity.com
Royse City Chamber of Commerce . . . . (972) 636-5000
    http://www.roysecitychamber.com

Runnels County

Located in west central Texas; drained by the Colorado River and its tributaries. Covers a land area of 1,050.73 square miles, a water area of 6.40 square miles, and is located in the Central Time Zone at 31.81° N. Lat., 99.97° W. Long. The county was founded in 1858. County seat is Ballinger.

Weather Station: Ballinger 2 NW										Elevation: 1,754 feet	
	Jan	Feb	Mar	Apr	May	Jun	Jul	Aug	Sep	Oct	Nov	Dec
High	60	65	72	81	87	92	95	95	88	80	69	60
Low	32	36	44	52	62	69	71	71	63	53	42	33
Precip	0.9	1.5	1.9	1.4	3.4	3.4	1.5	2.4	2.7	2.5	1.4	1.1
Snow	0.2	0.1	tr	0.0	0.0	0.0	0.0	0.0	0.0	0.0	0.1	0.1

High and Low temperatures in degrees Fahrenheit; Precipitation and Snow in inches

Weather Station: Winters 1 NNE										Elevation: 1,861 feet	
	Jan	Feb	Mar	Apr	May	Jun	Jul	Aug	Sep	Oct	Nov	Dec
High	59	63	71	80	87	92	95	95	88	79	68	59
Low	31	36	43	50	61	68	71	70	63	53	42	33
Precip	0.9	1.4	2.0	1.6	3.1	3.6	1.5	2.0	3.1	3.1	1.3	1.1
Snow	0.5	0.2	0.1	0.1	0.0	0.0	0.0	0.0	0.0	0.0	0.3	0.2

High and Low temperatures in degrees Fahrenheit; Precipitation and Snow in inches

Population: 11,294 (1990); 11,495 (2000); 10,439 (2010); 9,907 (2015 projected); Race: 78.9% White, 1.8% Black, 0.4% Asian, 18.9% Other, 32.7% Hispanic of any race (2010); Density: 9.9 persons per square mile (2010); Average household size: 2.51 (2010); Median age: 42.1 (2010); Males per 100 females: 92.7 (2010).
Religion: Five largest groups: 34.0% Southern Baptist Convention, 28.7% Catholic Church, 10.5% The United Methodist Church, 6.2% Churches of Christ, 4.0% Evangelical Lutheran Church in America (2000).
Economy: Unemployment rate: 9.1% (June 2011); Total civilian labor force: 4,579 (June 2011); Leading industries: 29.2% manufacturing; 20.6% retail trade; 13.9% health care and social assistance (2009); Farms: 953 totaling 656,204 acres (2007); Companies that employ 500 or more persons: 0 (2009); Companies that employ 100 to 499 persons: 3 (2009); Companies that employ less than 100 persons: 248 (2009); Black-owned businesses: n/a (2007); Hispanic-owned businesses: n/a (2007); Asian-owned businesses: n/a (2007); Women-owned businesses: n/a (2007); Retail sales per capita: $9,755 (2007). Single-family building permits issued: 1 (2010); Multi-family building permits issued: 0 (2010).
Income: Per capita income: $17,077 (2010); Median household income: $34,787 (2010); Average household income: $43,844 (2010); Percent of households with income of $100,000 or more: 6.1% (2010); Poverty rate: 16.0% (2009); Bankruptcy rate: 1.60% (2010).
Taxes: Total county taxes per capita: $386 (2007); County property taxes per capita: $296 (2007).
Education: Percent of population age 25 and over with: High school diploma (including GED) or higher: 74.3% (2010); Bachelor's degree or higher: 14.9% (2010); Master's degree or higher: 3.5% (2010).
Housing: Homeownership rate: 75.7% (2010); Median home value: $52,488 (2010); Median contract rent: $309 per month (2005-2009 5-year est.); Median year structure built: 1956 (2005-2009 5-year est.)
Health: Birth rate: 140.6 per 10,000 population (2009); Death rate: 149.5 per 10,000 population (2009); Age-adjusted cancer mortality rate: 199.8 deaths per 100,000 population (2007); Number of physicians: 7.8 per 10,000 population (2008); Hospital beds: 35.8 per 10,000 population (2007); Hospital admissions: 378.8 per 10,000 population (2007).
Elections: 2008 Presidential election results: 18.6% Obama, 80.6% McCain, 0.1% Nader
Additional Information Contacts
Runnels County Government. . . . . (325) 365-2633
   http://www.co.runnels.tx.us/ips/cms
Ballinger Chamber of Commerce. . . . . (325) 365-2633
   http://www.ballingertx.org
Winters Chamber of Commerce . . . . (325) 754-5210
   http://www.winters-texas.us/waccindex.htm

Runnels County Communities

BALLINGER (city). County seat. Covers a land area of 3.350 square miles and a water area of 0.007 square miles. Located at 31.74° N. Lat; 99.95° W. Long. Elevation is 1,627 feet.
History: Laid out 1886, Incorporated 1892.
Population: 3,975 (1990); 4,243 (2000); 3,719 (2010); 3,478 (2015 projected); Race: 77.1% White, 1.9% Black, 0.7% Asian, 20.3% Other, 32.9% Hispanic of any race (2010); Density: 1,110.3 persons per square mile (2010); Average household size: 2.51 (2010); Median age: 41.1 (2010); Males per 100 females: 87.4 (2010); Marriage status: 16.4% never married, 56.0% now married, 18.1% widowed, 9.5% divorced (2005-2009 5-year est.); Foreign born: 3.6% (2005-2009 5-year est.); Ancestry (includes multiple ancestries): 19.8% German, 11.2% Irish, 8.6% English, 6.5% American, 2.2% Czech (2005-2009 5-year est.).
Economy: Single-family building permits issued: 1 (2010); Multi-family building permits issued: 0 (2010); Employment by occupation: 2.9% management, 24.5% professional, 23.2% services, 24.8% sales, 0.0% farming, 6.7% construction, 18.0% production (2005-2009 5-year est.).
Income: Per capita income: $15,692 (2010); Median household income: $33,144 (2010); Average household income: $41,384 (2010); Percent of households with income of $100,000 or more: 5.8% (2010); Poverty rate: 24.5% (2005-2009 5-year est.).
Taxes: Total city taxes per capita: $283 (2007); City property taxes per capita: $0 (2007).
Education: Percent of population age 25 and over with: High school diploma (including GED) or higher: 70.7% (2010); Bachelor's degree or higher: 13.5% (2010); Master's degree or higher: 4.2% (2010).

Ballinger ISD (PK-12)
   2009-10 Enrollment: 1,028 . . . . (325) 365-3588
Housing: Homeownership rate: 74.9% (2010); Median home value: $46,558 (2010); Median contract rent: $335 per month (2005-2009 5-year est.); Median year structure built: 1958 (2005-2009 5-year est.).
Hospitals: Ballinger Memorial Hospital
Safety: Violent crime rate: 13.6 per 10,000 population; Property crime rate: 220.6 per 10,000 population (2009).
Newspapers: The Ballinger Ledger (Local news; Circulation 2,200)
Transportation: Commute to work: 94.3% car, 0.0% public transportation, 1.4% walk, 1.4% work from home (2005-2009 5-year est.); Travel time to work: 69.0% less than 15 minutes, 5.9% 15 to 30 minutes, 20.4% 30 to 45 minutes, 1.9% 45 to 60 minutes, 2.9% 60 minutes or more (2005-2009 5-year est.)
Additional Information Contacts
Ballinger Chamber of Commerce. . . . . (325) 365-2333
   http://www.ballingertx.org

MILES (city). Covers a land area of 1.336 square miles and a water area of 0 square miles. Located at 31.59° N. Lat; 100.18° W. Long. Elevation is 1,801 feet.
History: Old Opera House (1904).
Population: 793 (1990); 850 (2000); 800 (2010); 766 (2015 projected); Race: 79.4% White, 0.3% Black, 0.1% Asian, 20.3% Other, 40.5% Hispanic of any race (2010); Density: 598.8 persons per square mile (2010); Average household size: 2.76 (2010); Median age: 40.8 (2010); Males per 100 females: 97.5 (2010); Marriage status: 18.7% never married, 75.3% now married, 3.1% widowed, 2.9% divorced (2005-2009 5-year est.); Foreign born: 13.5% (2005-2009 5-year est.); Ancestry (includes multiple ancestries): 31.4% German, 12.5% English, 6.7% Irish, 2.7% Czech, 1.1% French (2005-2009 5-year est.).
Economy: Single-family building permits issued: 0 (2010); Multi-family building permits issued: 0 (2010); Employment by occupation: 4.7% management, 19.3% professional, 15.7% services, 17.2% sales, 8.9% farming, 8.1% construction, 26.1% production (2005-2009 5-year est.).
Income: Per capita income: $18,314 (2010); Median household income: $38,529 (2010); Average household income: $51,267 (2010); Percent of households with income of $100,000 or more: 8.6% (2010); Poverty rate: 25.9% (2005-2009 5-year est.).
Taxes: Total city taxes per capita: $148 (2007); City property taxes per capita: $88 (2007).
Education: Percent of population age 25 and over with: High school diploma (including GED) or higher: 74.9% (2010); Bachelor's degree or higher: 14.8% (2010); Master's degree or higher: 4.1% (2010).
Miles ISD (PK-12)
   2009-10 Enrollment: 401 . . . . (325) 468-2861
Wall ISD (PK-12)
   2009-10 Enrollment: 1,040 . . . . (325) 651-7790
Housing: Homeownership rate: 74.1% (2010); Median home value: $63,939 (2010); Median contract rent: $343 per month (2005-2009 5-year est.); Median year structure built: 1955 (2005-2009 5-year est.).
Newspapers: Messenger (Community news; Circulation 600); Paint Rock Concho Herald (Community news; Circulation 400); Rowena Press (Community news; Circulation 275)
Transportation: Commute to work: 96.3% car, 0.0% public transportation, 0.0% walk, 3.7% work from home (2005-2009 5-year est.); Travel time to work: 23.3% less than 15 minutes, 50.9% 15 to 30 minutes, 25.7% 30 to 45 minutes, 0.0% 45 to 60 minutes, 0.0% 60 minutes or more (2005-2009 5-year est.)

NORTON (unincorporated postal area, zip code 76865). Covers a land area of 57.168 square miles and a water area of 0.055 square miles. Located at 31.85° N. Lat; 100.15° W. Long. Elevation is 1,873 feet.
Population: 184 (2000); Race: 85.3% White, 0.0% Black, 0.0% Asian, 14.7% Other, 22.4% Hispanic of any race (2000); Density: 3.2 persons per square mile (2000); Age: 9.6% under 18, 35.3% over 64 (2000); Marriage status: 12.1% never married, 69.5% now married, 14.9% widowed, 3.5% divorced (2000); Foreign born: 6.4% (2000); Ancestry (includes multiple ancestries): 23.1% German, 16.0% English, 12.2% American, 9.0% Czech (2000).
Economy: Employment by occupation: 19.8% management, 21.8% professional, 17.8% services, 19.8% sales, 5.0% farming, 2.0% construction, 13.9% production (2000).

Income: Per capita income: $19,108 (2000); Median household income: $28,750 (2000); Poverty rate: 179.1% (2000).

Education: Percent of population age 25 and over with: High school diploma (including GED) or higher: 78.9% (2000); Bachelor's degree or higher: 17.1% (2000).

Housing: Homeownership rate: 94.3% (2000); Median home value: $26,000 (2000); Median contract rent: $125 per month (2000); Median year structure built: 1960 (2000).

Transportation: Commute to work: 69.1% car, 0.0% public transportation, 5.2% walk, 25.8% work from home (2000); Travel time to work: 15.3% less than 15 minutes, 26.4% 15 to 30 minutes, 27.8% 30 to 45 minutes, 2.8% 45 to 60 minutes, 27.8% 60 minutes or more (2000)

ROWENA (unincorporated postal area, zip code 76875). Covers a land area of 102.280 square miles and a water area of 0.026 square miles. Located at 31.61° N. Lat; 100.03° W. Long. Elevation is 1,762 feet.

Population: 714 (2000); Race: 90.7% White, 0.0% Black, 0.0% Asian, 9.3% Other, 18.3% Hispanic of any race (2000); Density: 7.0 persons per square mile (2000); Age: 19.1% under 18, 30.1% over 64 (2000); Marriage status: 15.9% never married, 70.4% now married, 8.4% widowed, 5.4% divorced (2000); Foreign born: 5.5% (2000); Ancestry (includes multiple ancestries): 52.1% German, 14.8% Czech, 3.2% English, 2.5% Czechoslovakian (2000).

Economy: Employment by occupation: 31.1% management, 11.0% professional, 6.8% services, 30.5% sales, 5.4% farming, 4.8% construction, 10.5% production (2000).

Income: Per capita income: $18,080 (2000); Median household income: $30,652 (2000); Poverty rate: 179.1% (2000).

Education: Percent of population age 25 and over with: High school diploma (including GED) or higher: 73.4% (2000); Bachelor's degree or higher: 14.5% (2000).

School District(s)

Olfen ISD (PK-08)

    2009-10 Enrollment: 75 . . . . (325) 442-4301

Housing: Homeownership rate: 75.6% (2000); Median home value: $46,500 (2000); Median contract rent: $269 per month (2000); Median year structure built: 1945 (2000).

Transportation: Commute to work: 83.6% car, 0.6% public transportation, 0.6% walk, 12.1% work from home (2000); Travel time to work: 24.8% less than 15 minutes, 37.9% 15 to 30 minutes, 22.5% 30 to 45 minutes, 10.6% 45 to 60 minutes, 4.2% 60 minutes or more (2000)

WINGATE (unincorporated postal area, zip code 79566). Covers a land area of 107.501 square miles and a water area of 0.306 square miles. Located at 32.10° N. Lat; 100.10° W. Long. Elevation is 2,001 feet.

Population: 343 (2000); Race: 90.6% White, 0.0% Black, 0.0% Asian, 9.4% Other, 15.8% Hispanic of any race (2000); Density: 3.2 persons per square mile (2000); Age: 14.8% under 18, 17.5% over 64 (2000); Marriage status: 12.3% never married, 71.9% now married, 6.2% widowed, 9.6% divorced (2000); Foreign born: 1.3% (2000); Ancestry (includes multiple ancestries): 18.2% German, 17.5% English, 12.5% American, 7.4% Irish (2000).

Economy: Employment by occupation: 27.9% management, 16.9% professional, 3.7% services, 17.6% sales, 1.5% farming, 22.8% construction, 9.6% production (2000).

Income: Per capita income: $17,101 (2000); Median household income: $27,222 (2000); Poverty rate: 179.1% (2000).

Education: Percent of population age 25 and over with: High school diploma (including GED) or higher: 70.5% (2000); Bachelor's degree or higher: 13.9% (2000).

Housing: Homeownership rate: 79.7% (2000); Median home value: $32,800 (2000); Median contract rent: $188 per month (2000); Median year structure built: 1948 (2000).

Transportation: Commute to work: 88.2% car, 0.0% public transportation, 2.2% walk, 9.6% work from home (2000); Travel time to work: 31.7% less than 15 minutes, 42.3% 15 to 30 minutes, 13.8% 30 to 45 minutes, 8.9% 45 to 60 minutes, 3.3% 60 minutes or more (2000)

WINTERS (city). Covers a land area of 2.249 square miles and a water area of 0.546 square miles. Located at 31.95° N. Lat; 99.95° W. Long. Elevation is 1,841 feet.

History: Settled 1880, incorporated 1909.

Population: 2,975 (1990); 2,880 (2000); 2,598 (2010); 2,457 (2015 projected); Race: 68.6% White, 3.4% Black, 0.4% Asian, 27.6% Other, 45.8% Hispanic of any race (2010); Density: 1,155.3 persons per square

mile (2010); Average household size: 2.60 (2010); Median age: 35.9 (2010); Males per 100 females: 89.4 (2010); Marriage status: 23.7% never married, 58.4% now married, 6.3% widowed, 11.5% divorced (2005-2009 5-year est.); Foreign born: 9.1% (2005-2009 5-year est.); Ancestry (includes multiple ancestries): 14.7% English, 9.7% German, 6.1% Irish, 4.1% American, 2.6% Scotch-Irish (2005-2009 5-year est.).

Economy: Single-family building permits issued: 0 (2010); Multi-family building permits issued: 0 (2010); Employment by occupation: 8.5% management, 10.5% professional, 21.5% services, 19.4% sales, 5.1% farming, 15.9% construction, 19.1% production (2005-2009 5-year est.).

Income: Per capita income: $13,382 (2010); Median household income: $28,392 (2010); Average household income: $35,424 (2010); Percent of households with income of $100,000 or more: 2.6% (2010); Poverty rate: 19.5% (2005-2009 5-year est.).

Taxes: Total city taxes per capita: $324 (2007); City property taxes per capita: $195 (2007).

Education: Percent of population age 25 and over with: High school diploma (including GED) or higher: 66.1% (2010); Bachelor's degree or higher: 9.7% (2010); Master's degree or higher: 2.8% (2010).

School District(s)

Winters ISD (PK-12)

    2009-10 Enrollment: 634 . . . . (325) 754-5574

Housing: Homeownership rate: 73.1% (2010); Median home value: $39,269 (2010); Median contract rent: $289 per month (2005-2009 5-year est.); Median year structure built: 1954 (2005-2009 5-year est.).

Hospitals: North Runnels Hospital (25 beds)

Safety: Violent crime rate: 27.6 per 10,000 population; Property crime rate: 161.7 per 10,000 population (2009).

Newspapers: Winters Enterprise (Local news; Circulation 1,800)

Transportation: Commute to work: 96.1% car, 0.0% public transportation, 2.0% walk, 0.8% work from home (2005-2009 5-year est.); Travel time to work: 60.6% less than 15 minutes, 12.4% 15 to 30 minutes, 8.7% 30 to 45 minutes, 10.7% 45 to 60 minutes, 7.6% 60 minutes or more (2005-2009 5-year est.)

Additional Information Contacts

Winters Chamber of Commerce . . . . (325) 754-5210
    http://www.winters-texas.us/waccindex.htm

Rusk County

Located in east Texas; drained by the Sabine and Angelina Rivers and Attoyac Bayou. Covers a land area of 923.55 square miles, a water area of 15.07 square miles, and is located in the Central Time Zone at 32.15° N. Lat., 94.80° W. Long. The county was founded in 1843. County seat is Henderson.

Rusk County is part of the Longview, TX Metropolitan Statistical Area. The entire metro area includes: Gregg County, TX; Rusk County, TX; Upshur County, TX

Weather Station: Henderson   Elevation: 419 feet

	Jan	Feb	Mar	Apr	May	Jun	Jul	Aug	Sep	Oct	Nov	Dec
High	57	61	68	76	83	89	93	94	88	78	67	59
Low	35	38	45	52	61	68	71	71	64	53	44	36
Precip	3.8	4.2	4.3	3.7	4.8	5.1	3.0	2.8	3.6	4.8	4.7	4.4
Snow	0.4	0.3	tr	tr	0.0	0.0	0.0	0.0	0.0	0.0	tr	0.2

High and Low temperatures in degrees Fahrenheit; Precipitation and Snow in inches

Weather Station: Longview 11 SE   Elevation: 407 feet

	Jan	Feb	Mar	Apr	May	Jun	Jul	Aug	Sep	Oct	Nov	Dec
High	58	62	69	76	83	90	93	94	88	78	67	59
Low	38	41	48	54	63	70	73	72	66	56	47	39
Precip	3.8	4.2	4.4	3.7	5.2	5.2	3.0	2.9	3.4	4.7	4.7	4.8
Snow	0.5	0.4	tr	tr	0.0	0.0	0.0	0.0	0.0	0.0	tr	0.2

High and Low temperatures in degrees Fahrenheit; Precipitation and Snow in inches

Population: 43,735 (1990); 47,372 (2000); 49,257 (2010); 50,086 (2015 projected); Race: 73.6% White, 17.8% Black, 0.5% Asian, 8.2% Other, 12.3% Hispanic of any race (2010); Density: 53.3 persons per square mile (2010); Average household size: 2.53 (2010); Median age: 37.7 (2010); Males per 100 females: 106.3 (2010).

Religion: Five largest groups: 32.6% Southern Baptist Convention, 7.9% The American Baptist Association, 5.9% The United Methodist Church, 2.2% Catholic Church, 1.7% Churches of Christ (2000).

Economy: Unemployment rate: 8.0% (June 2011); Total civilian labor force: 25,619 (June 2011); Leading industries: 14.3% health care and

social assistance; 12.5% retail trade; 12.4% manufacturing (2009); Farms: 1,521 totaling 300,900 acres (2007); Companies that employ 500 or more persons: 0 (2009); Companies that employ 100 to 499 persons: 18 (2009); Companies that employ less than 100 persons: 793 (2009); Black-owned businesses: n/a (2007); Hispanic-owned businesses: n/a (2007); Asian-owned businesses: n/a (2007); Women-owned businesses: n/a (2007); Retail sales per capita: $7,159 (2010). Single-family building permits issued: 0 (2010); Multi-family building permits issued: 0 (2010).
Income: Per capita income: $21,964 (2010); Median household income: $44,644 (2010); Average household income: $58,564 (2010); Percent of households with income of $100,000 or more: 12.9% (2010); Poverty rate: 16.4% (2009); Bankruptcy rate: 1.46% (2010).
Taxes: Total county taxes per capita: $296 (2007); County property taxes per capita: $275 (2007).
Education: Percent of population age 25 and over with: High school diploma (including GED) or higher: 80.0% (2010); Bachelor's degree or higher: 15.7% (2010); Master's degree or higher: 5.1% (2010).
Housing: Homeownership rate: 76.4% (2010); Median home value: $86,124 (2010); Median contract rent: $391 per month (2005-2009 5-year est.); Median year structure built: 1974 (2005-2009 5-year est.)
Health: Birth rate: 138.7 per 10,000 population (2009); Death rate: 103.5 per 10,000 population (2009); Age-adjusted cancer mortality rate: 183.3 deaths per 100,000 population (2007); Number of physicians: 6.3 per 10,000 population (2008); Hospital beds: 15.7 per 10,000 population (2007); Hospital admissions: 550.3 per 10,000 population (2007).
Elections: 2008 Presidential election results: 26.6% Obama, 72.9% McCain, 0.0% Nader
Additional Information Contacts
Rusk County Government . . . . (903) 657-0330
  http://www.co.rusk.tx.us/ips/cms
City of Henderson . . . . (903) 657-6551
  http://www.hendersontx.us
City of Overton . . . . (903) 834-3171
  http://www.ci.overton.tx.us
Henderson Area Chamber of Commerce . . . . (903) 657-5528
  http://www.hendersontx.com

Rusk County Communities

HENDERSON (city). County seat. Covers a land area of 11.897 square miles and a water area of 0.115 square miles. Located at 32.15° N. Lat; 94.80° W. Long. Elevation is 512 feet.
History: Henderson was founded in 1844. Lumber was the earliest industry, followed by farming and, since 1930, oil and gas.
Population: 11,456 (1990); 11,273 (2000); 11,723 (2010); 11,916 (2015 projected); Race: 65.3% White, 21.6% Black, 1.0% Asian, 12.1% Other, 17.7% Hispanic of any race (2010); Density: 985.4 persons per square mile (2010); Average household size: 2.51 (2010); Median age: 36.1 (2010); Males per 100 females: 90.6 (2010); Marriage status: 20.4% never married, 55.9% now married, 10.0% widowed, 13.8% divorced (2005-2009 5-year est.); Foreign born: 5.5% (2005-2009 5-year est.); Ancestry (includes multiple ancestries): 13.0% American, 11.6% Irish, 10.3% English, 8.7% German, 3.5% French (2005-2009 5-year est.).
Economy: Single-family building permits issued: 0 (2010); Multi-family building permits issued: 0 (2010); Employment by occupation: 11.4% management, 17.3% professional, 20.7% services, 22.0% sales, 0.0% farming, 10.7% construction, 17.9% production (2005-2009 5-year est.).
Income: Per capita income: $23,719 (2010); Median household income: $41,216 (2010); Average household income: $60,689 (2010); Percent of households with income of $100,000 or more: 13.5% (2010); Poverty rate: 11.4% (2005-2009 5-year est.).
Taxes: Total city taxes per capita: $652 (2007); City property taxes per capita: $150 (2007).
Education: Percent of population age 25 and over with: High school diploma (including GED) or higher: 80.5% (2010); Bachelor's degree or higher: 21.1% (2010); Master's degree or higher: 6.9% (2010).
School District(s)
Henderson ISD (PK-12)
  2009-10 Enrollment: 3,368 . . . . (903) 657-8511
Housing: Homeownership rate: 65.2% (2010); Median home value: $94,665 (2010); Median contract rent: $406 per month (2005-2009 5-year est.); Median year structure built: 1968 (2005-2009 5-year est.).
Hospitals: Henderson Memorial Hospital (158 beds)
Safety: Violent crime rate: 73.7 per 10,000 population; Property crime rate: 548.2 per 10,000 population (2009).

Newspapers: Henderson Daily News (Local news)
Transportation: Commute to work: 95.9% car, 0.0% public transportation, 0.8% walk, 1.5% work from home (2005-2009 5-year est.); Travel time to work: 57.2% less than 15 minutes, 15.1% 15 to 30 minutes, 18.8% 30 to 45 minutes, 3.9% 45 to 60 minutes, 5.0% 60 minutes or more (2005-2009 5-year est.)
Additional Information Contacts
City of Henderson . . . . (903) 657-6551
  http://www.hendersontx.us
Henderson Area Chamber of Commerce . . . . (903) 657-5528
  http://www.hendersontx.com

LANEVILLE (unincorporated postal area, zip code 75667). Covers a land area of 79.789 square miles and a water area of 0.262 square miles. Located at 31.98° N. Lat; 94.85° W. Long. Elevation is 436 feet.
Population: 1,171 (2000); Race: 73.2% White, 23.5% Black, 0.0% Asian, 3.3% Other, 7.0% Hispanic of any race (2000); Density: 14.7 persons per square mile (2000); Age: 25.0% under 18, 21.2% over 64 (2000); Marriage status: 22.2% never married, 58.2% now married, 12.4% widowed, 7.1% divorced (2000); Foreign born: 3.7% (2000); Ancestry (includes multiple ancestries): 13.4% American, 10.5% Irish, 7.9% English, 7.4% German (2000).
Economy: Employment by occupation: 11.4% management, 12.8% professional, 18.4% services, 21.5% sales, 1.7% farming, 13.3% construction, 20.8% production (2000).
Income: Per capita income: $13,405 (2000); Median household income: $23,050 (2000); Poverty rate: 179.1% (2000).
Education: Percent of population age 25 and over with: High school diploma (including GED) or higher: 75.0% (2000); Bachelor's degree or higher: 10.6% (2000).
School District(s)
Laneville ISD (PK-12)
  2009-10 Enrollment: 182 . . . . (903) 863-5353
Housing: Homeownership rate: 82.9% (2000); Median home value: $52,700 (2000); Median contract rent: $215 per month (2000); Median year structure built: 1968 (2000).
Transportation: Commute to work: 90.6% car, 0.5% public transportation, 3.5% walk, 4.2% work from home (2000); Travel time to work: 19.6% less than 15 minutes, 47.0% 15 to 30 minutes, 15.8% 30 to 45 minutes, 9.0% 45 to 60 minutes, 8.5% 60 minutes or more (2000)

MOUNT ENTERPRISE (city). Covers a land area of 1.475 square miles and a water area of 0 square miles. Located at 31.91° N. Lat; 94.68° W. Long. Elevation is 479 feet.
Population: 501 (1990); 525 (2000); 517 (2010); 512 (2015 projected); Race: 71.0% White, 26.5% Black, 0.0% Asian, 2.5% Other, 4.8% Hispanic of any race (2010); Density: 350.5 persons per square mile (2010); Average household size: 2.45 (2010); Median age: 38.1 (2010); Males per 100 females: 101.2 (2010); Marriage status: 18.9% never married, 61.6% now married, 8.1% widowed, 11.4% divorced (2005-2009 5-year est.); Foreign born: 0.0% (2005-2009 5-year est.); Ancestry (includes multiple ancestries): 22.5% English, 12.4% American, 12.4% German, 12.0% Irish, 4.2% Dutch (2005-2009 5-year est.).
Economy: Employment by occupation: 14.3% management, 15.6% professional, 11.6% services, 32.7% sales, 0.0% farming, 6.8% construction, 19.0% production (2005-2009 5-year est.).
Income: Per capita income: $19,958 (2010); Median household income: $37,961 (2010); Average household income: $50,675 (2010); Percent of households with income of $100,000 or more: 11.4% (2010); Poverty rate: 13.7% (2005-2009 5-year est.).
Taxes: Total city taxes per capita: $203 (2007); City property taxes per capita: $86 (2007).
Education: Percent of population age 25 and over with: High school diploma (including GED) or higher: 77.7% (2010); Bachelor's degree or higher: 16.3% (2010); Master's degree or higher: 8.9% (2010).
School District(s)
Mount Enterprise ISD (PK-12)
  2009-10 Enrollment: 402 . . . . (903) 822-3575
Housing: Homeownership rate: 82.5% (2010); Median home value: $50,189 (2010); Median contract rent: $433 per month (2005-2009 5-year est.); Median year structure built: 1966 (2005-2009 5-year est.).
Transportation: Commute to work: 91.7% car, 0.0% public transportation, 0.0% walk, 3.5% work from home (2005-2009 5-year est.); Travel time to work: 44.6% less than 15 minutes, 17.3% 15 to 30 minutes, 14.4% 30 to 45

minutes, 10.8% 45 to 60 minutes, 12.9% 60 minutes or more (2005-2009 5-year est.)

NEW LONDON (city). Aka Norfolk. Covers a land area of 8.636 square miles and a water area of 0.013 square miles. Located at 32.25° N. Lat; 94.93° W. Long. Elevation is 551 feet.

History: A school explosion here (March 18, 1937) took the lives of hundreds of pupils and teachers.

Population: 997 (1990); 987 (2000); 1,007 (2010); 1,019 (2015 projected); Race: 84.1% White, 12.5% Black, 0.2% Asian, 3.2% Other, 6.8% Hispanic of any race (2010); Density: 116.6 persons per square mile (2010); Average household size: 2.70 (2010); Median age: 35.7 (2010); Males per 100 females: 98.2 (2010); Marriage status: 9.6% never married, 72.1% now married, 5.0% widowed, 13.3% divorced (2005-2009 5-year est.); Foreign born: 2.7% (2005-2009 5-year est.); Ancestry (includes multiple ancestries): 28.5% American, 24.0% Irish, 10.5% German, 8.9% English, 3.4% French (2005-2009 5-year est.).

Economy: Employment by occupation: 8.1% management, 13.5% professional, 22.3% services, 25.5% sales, 0.0% farming, 19.7% construction, 11.0% production (2005-2009 5-year est.).

Income: Per capita income: $20,993 (2010); Median household income: $41,582 (2010); Average household income: $55,510 (2010); Percent of households with income of $100,000 or more: 11.6% (2010); Poverty rate: 23.0% (2005-2009 5-year est.).

Taxes: Total city taxes per capita: $399 (2007); City property taxes per capita: $335 (2007).

Education: Percent of population age 25 and over with: High school diploma (including GED) or higher: 83.2% (2010); Bachelor's degree or higher: 15.0% (2010); Master's degree or higher: 3.0% (2010).

School District(s)
West Rusk ISD (PK-12)
    2009-10 Enrollment: 851 . . . . (903) 895-4503

Housing: Homeownership rate: 84.7% (2010); Median home value: $66,429 (2010); Median contract rent: $414 per month (2005-2009 5-year est.); Median year structure built: 1968 (2005-2009 5-year est.).

Transportation: Commute to work: 90.5% car, 0.0% public transportation, 0.0% walk, 9.5% work from home (2005-2009 5-year est.); Travel time to work: 43.2% less than 15 minutes, 36.1% 15 to 30 minutes, 15.4% 30 to 45 minutes, 3.4% 45 to 60 minutes, 1.9% 60 minutes or more (2005-2009 5-year est.)

OVERTON (city). Covers a land area of 6.711 square miles and a water area of 0.040 square miles. Located at 32.27° N. Lat; 94.97° W. Long. Elevation is 502 feet.

History: Boomed after oil discovery (1930).

Population: 2,105 (1990); 2,350 (2000); 2,431 (2010); 2,486 (2015 projected); Race: 83.4% White, 12.4% Black, 0.0% Asian, 4.2% Other, 3.2% Hispanic of any race (2010); Density: 362.2 persons per square mile (2010); Average household size: 2.47 (2010); Median age: 35.7 (2010); Males per 100 females: 93.2 (2010); Marriage status: 19.0% never married, 62.0% now married, 8.7% widowed, 10.3% divorced (2005-2009 5-year est.); Foreign born: 0.3% (2005-2009 5-year est.); Ancestry (includes multiple ancestries): 12.6% German, 12.4% Irish, 11.7% American, 11.4% English, 2.8% Scottish (2005-2009 5-year est.).

Economy: Single-family building permits issued: 0 (2010); Multi-family building permits issued: 0 (2010); Employment by occupation: 6.2% management, 13.9% professional, 17.2% services, 28.0% sales, 0.7% farming, 12.5% construction, 21.5% production (2005-2009 5-year est.).

Income: Per capita income: $21,721 (2010); Median household income: $39,826 (2010); Average household income: $55,503 (2010); Percent of households with income of $100,000 or more: 11.0% (2010); Poverty rate: 15.0% (2005-2009 5-year est.).

Taxes: Total city taxes per capita: $313 (2007); City property taxes per capita: $174 (2007).

Education: Percent of population age 25 and over with: High school diploma (including GED) or higher: 81.7% (2010); Bachelor's degree or higher: 15.4% (2010); Master's degree or higher: 4.1% (2010).

School District(s)
Leveretts Chapel ISD (PK-12)
    2009-10 Enrollment: 260 . . . . (903) 834-6675
Overton ISD (PK-12)
    2009-10 Enrollment: 531 . . . . (903) 834-6145

Housing: Homeownership rate: 65.3% (2010); Median home value: $73,265 (2010); Median contract rent: $366 per month (2005-2009 5-year est.); Median year structure built: 1968 (2005-2009 5-year est.).

Safety: Violent crime rate: 33.6 per 10,000 population; Property crime rate: 256.2 per 10,000 population (2009).

Newspapers: Overton Press (Community news; Circulation 1,500)

Transportation: Commute to work: 97.4% car, 0.7% public transportation, 0.0% walk, 0.7% work from home (2005-2009 5-year est.); Travel time to work: 32.3% less than 15 minutes, 30.5% 15 to 30 minutes, 15.6% 30 to 45 minutes, 10.8% 45 to 60 minutes, 10.7% 60 minutes or more (2005-2009 5-year est.)

Additional Information Contacts
City of Overton . . . . (903) 834-3171
    http://www.ci.overton.tx.us

TATUM (city). Covers a land area of 3.792 square miles and a water area of 0 square miles. Located at 32.31° N. Lat; 94.51° W. Long. Elevation is 338 feet.

Population: 1,325 (1990); 1,175 (2000); 1,209 (2010); 1,225 (2015 projected); Race: 77.9% White, 7.4% Black, 0.0% Asian, 14.6% Other, 23.6% Hispanic of any race (2010); Density: 318.9 persons per square mile (2010); Average household size: 2.52 (2010); Median age: 34.1 (2010); Males per 100 females: 96.6 (2010); Marriage status: 21.0% never married, 48.3% now married, 13.4% widowed, 17.3% divorced (2005-2009 5-year est.); Foreign born: 11.1% (2005-2009 5-year est.); Ancestry (includes multiple ancestries): 13.3% German, 10.0% American, 9.8% Irish, 4.7% French, 4.2% English (2005-2009 5-year est.).

Economy: Employment by occupation: 7.1% management, 16.1% professional, 18.4% services, 19.9% sales, 3.1% farming, 15.3% construction, 20.2% production (2005-2009 5-year est.).

Income: Per capita income: $18,647 (2010); Median household income: $33,689 (2010); Average household income: $47,656 (2010); Percent of households with income of $100,000 or more: 7.9% (2010); Poverty rate: 31.9% (2005-2009 5-year est.).

Taxes: Total city taxes per capita: $367 (2007); City property taxes per capita: $157 (2007).

Education: Percent of population age 25 and over with: High school diploma (including GED) or higher: 72.0% (2010); Bachelor's degree or higher: 8.8% (2010); Master's degree or higher: 3.7% (2010).

School District(s)
Tatum ISD (PK-12)
    2009-10 Enrollment: 1,507 . . . . (903) 947-6482

Housing: Homeownership rate: 65.4% (2010); Median home value: $66,154 (2010); Median contract rent: $404 per month (2005-2009 5-year est.); Median year structure built: 1973 (2005-2009 5-year est.).

Safety: Violent crime rate: 57.6 per 10,000 population; Property crime rate: 131.7 per 10,000 population (2009).

Newspapers: Tatum Trammel Trace Tribune (Local news; Circulation 750)

Transportation: Commute to work: 90.1% car, 1.1% public transportation, 7.0% walk, 1.9% work from home (2005-2009 5-year est.); Travel time to work: 30.0% less than 15 minutes, 45.5% 15 to 30 minutes, 20.4% 30 to 45 minutes, 3.3% 45 to 60 minutes, 0.8% 60 minutes or more (2005-2009 5-year est.)

Sabine County

Located in east Texas; bounded on the east by the Sabine River and the Louisiana border; includes part of Sabine National Forest. Covers a land area of 490.27 square miles, a water area of 86.34 square miles, and is located in the Central Time Zone at 31.33° N. Lat., 93.85° W. Long. The county was founded in 1836. County seat is Hemphill.

Population: 9,586 (1990); 10,469 (2000); 10,235 (2010); 10,100 (2015 projected); Race: 87.0% White, 9.9% Black, 0.2% Asian, 3.0% Other, 2.9% Hispanic of any race (2010); Density: 20.9 persons per square mile (2010); Average household size: 2.27 (2010); Median age: 45.3 (2010); Males per 100 females: 92.5 (2010).

Religion: Five largest groups: 30.6% Southern Baptist Convention, 8.8% The American Baptist Association, 6.8% Baptist Missionary Association of America, 4.5% The United Methodist Church, 3.7% Landmark Missionary Baptists, Independent Associations a

Economy: Unemployment rate: 16.9% (June 2011); Total civilian labor force: 3,576 (June 2011); Leading industries: 22.1% manufacturing; 19.9% retail trade; 15.8% health care and social assistance (2009); Farms: 223 totaling 31,724 acres (2007); Companies that employ 500 or more persons: 0 (2009); Companies that employ 100 to 499 persons: 3 (2009); Companies that employ less than 100 persons: 148 (2009); Black-owned businesses: n/a (2007); Hispanic-owned businesses: n/a (2007); Asian-owned businesses: n/a (2007); Women-owned businesses: n/a

(2007); Retail sales per capita: $5,273 (2010). Single-family building permits issued: 5 (2010); Multi-family building permits issued: 0 (2010).
Income: Per capita income: $20,665 (2010); Median household income: $34,570 (2010); Average household income: $47,141 (2010); Percent of households with income of $100,000 or more: 8.1% (2010); Poverty rate: 19.2% (2009); Bankruptcy rate: 1.56% (2010).
Taxes: Total county taxes per capita: $214 (2007); County property taxes per capita: $143 (2007).
Education: Percent of population age 25 and over with: High school diploma (including GED) or higher: 77.9% (2010); Bachelor's degree or higher: 11.8% (2010); Master's degree or higher: 4.2% (2010).
Housing: Homeownership rate: 85.0% (2010); Median home value: $70,670 (2010); Median contract rent: $297 per month (2005-2009 5-year est.); Median year structure built: 1980 (2005-2009 5-year est.)
Health: Birth rate: 98.0 per 10,000 population (2009); Death rate: 145.0 per 10,000 population (2009); Age-adjusted cancer mortality rate: 179.9 deaths per 100,000 population (2007); Number of physicians: 6.9 per 10,000 population (2008); Hospital beds: 24.6 per 10,000 population (2007); Hospital admissions: 271.0 per 10,000 population (2007).
Elections: 2008 Presidential election results: 22.1% Obama, 76.9% McCain, 0.0% Nader
National and State Parks: Sabine National Forest
Additional Information Contacts
Sabine County Government. . . . . (409) 787-3543
http://www.sabinecountytexas.com
Sabine County Chamber of Commerce. . . . . (409) 787-2732
http://www.sabinecountytexas.com

Sabine County Communities

BRONSON (unincorporated postal area, zip code 75930). Covers a land area of 150.425 square miles and a water area of 0 square miles. Located at 31.37° N. Lat; 93.82° W. Long. Elevation is 318 feet.
Population: 2,153 (2000); Race: 93.8% White, 2.9% Black, 0.0% Asian, 3.3% Other, 2.5% Hispanic of any race (2000); Density: 14.3 persons per square mile (2000); Age: 29.6% under 18, 13.3% over 64 (2000); Marriage status: 15.3% never married, 62.8% now married, 10.4% widowed, 11.5% divorced (2000); Foreign born: 0.8% (2000); Ancestry (includes multiple ancestries): 19.1% American, 11.9% Irish, 9.1% English, 8.1% German (2000).
Economy: Employment by occupation: 9.1% management, 15.5% professional, 12.1% services, 21.3% sales, 4.9% farming, 15.9% construction, 21.2% production (2000).
Income: Per capita income: $13,346 (2000); Median household income: $28,898 (2000); Poverty rate: 179.1% (2000).
Education: Percent of population age 25 and over with: High school diploma (including GED) or higher: 68.9% (2000); Bachelor's degree or higher: 12.8% (2000).
Housing: Homeownership rate: 83.4% (2000); Median home value: $39,600 (2000); Median contract rent: $231 per month (2000); Median year structure built: 1977 (2000).
Transportation: Commute to work: 95.2% car, 0.0% public transportation, 0.0% walk, 0.0% work from home (2000); Travel time to work: 24.6% less than 15 minutes, 36.8% 15 to 30 minutes, 16.1% 30 to 45 minutes, 4.6% 45 to 60 minutes, 18.0% 60 minutes or more (2000)

BROOKELAND (unincorporated postal area, zip code 75931). Covers a land area of 54.875 square miles and a water area of 0.158 square miles. Located at 31.10° N. Lat; 93.99° W. Long. Elevation is 187 feet.
Population: 1,789 (2000); Race: 88.4% White, 9.5% Black, 0.0% Asian, 2.1% Other, 3.4% Hispanic of any race (2000); Density: 32.6 persons per square mile (2000); Age: 24.8% under 18, 19.9% over 64 (2000); Marriage status: 14.4% never married, 63.5% now married, 11.1% widowed, 11.0% divorced (2000); Foreign born: 1.4% (2000); Ancestry (includes multiple ancestries): 20.0% American, 15.9% Irish, 10.8% English, 6.5% German (2000).
Economy: Employment by occupation: 11.4% management, 20.5% professional, 15.0% services, 18.8% sales, 4.6% farming, 13.9% construction, 15.8% production (2000).
Income: Per capita income: $15,917 (2000); Median household income: $33,257 (2000); Poverty rate: 179.1% (2000).
Education: Percent of population age 25 and over with: High school diploma (including GED) or higher: 72.5% (2000); Bachelor's degree or higher: 14.3% (2000).

Brookeland ISD (PK-12)
   2009-10 Enrollment: 424 . . . . (409) 698-2677
Housing: Homeownership rate: 88.0% (2000); Median home value: $66,000 (2000); Median contract rent: $286 per month (2000); Median year structure built: 1981 (2000).
Transportation: Commute to work: 93.6% car, 0.0% public transportation, 2.1% walk, 2.8% work from home (2000); Travel time to work: 37.4% less than 15 minutes, 34.7% 15 to 30 minutes, 15.9% 30 to 45 minutes, 4.9% 45 to 60 minutes, 7.0% 60 minutes or more (2000)

HEMPHILL (city). County seat. Covers a land area of 2.377 square miles and a water area of 0.038 square miles. Located at 31.34° N. Lat; 93.85° W. Long. Elevation is 279 feet.
History: Incorporated as city 1939.
Population: 1,224 (1990); 1,106 (2000); 1,087 (2010); 1,072 (2015 projected); Race: 77.8% White, 14.7% Black, 0.0% Asian, 7.5% Other, 7.6% Hispanic of any race (2010); Density: 457.3 persons per square mile (2010); Average household size: 2.41 (2010); Median age: 36.3 (2010); Males per 100 females: 83.9 (2010); Marriage status: 27.4% never married, 43.0% now married, 14.5% widowed, 15.1% divorced (2005-2009 5-year est.); Foreign born: 3.4% (2005-2009 5-year est.); Ancestry (includes multiple ancestries): 20.7% English, 17.2% Irish, 8.1% American, 7.2% German, 5.0% Dutch (2005-2009 5-year est.).
Economy: Single-family building permits issued: 2 (2010); Multi-family building permits issued: 0 (2010); Employment by occupation: 7.0% management, 13.8% professional, 30.6% services, 18.2% sales, 1.2% farming, 6.1% construction, 23.1% production (2005-2009 5-year est.).
Income: Per capita income: $19,204 (2010); Median household income: $32,982 (2010); Average household income: $45,351 (2010); Percent of households with income of $100,000 or more: 8.2% (2010); Poverty rate: 32.8% (2005-2009 5-year est.).
Taxes: Total city taxes per capita: $453 (2007); City property taxes per capita: $0 (2007).
Education: Percent of population age 25 and over with: High school diploma (including GED) or higher: 74.6% (2010); Bachelor's degree or higher: 13.9% (2010); Master's degree or higher: 5.5% (2010).
Hemphill ISD (PK-12)
   2009-10 Enrollment: 976 . . . . (409) 787-3371
Housing: Homeownership rate: 71.9% (2010); Median home value: $63,421 (2010); Median contract rent: $285 per month (2005-2009 5-year est.); Median year structure built: 1972 (2005-2009 5-year est.).
Hospitals: Sabine County Hospital (36 beds)
Safety: Violent crime rate: 49.1 per 10,000 population; Property crime rate: 176.8 per 10,000 population (2009).
Newspapers: Sabine County Reporter (Community news; Circulation 52)
Transportation: Commute to work: 87.2% car, 0.0% public transportation, 5.3% walk, 1.2% work from home (2005-2009 5-year est.); Travel time to work: 53.7% less than 15 minutes, 25.4% 15 to 30 minutes, 8.5% 30 to 45 minutes, 5.1% 45 to 60 minutes, 7.3% 60 minutes or more (2005-2009 5-year est.)
Additional Information Contacts
Sabine County Chamber of Commerce . . . . (409) 787-2732
http://www.sabinecountytexas.com

MILAM (CDP). Covers a land area of 32.837 square miles and a water area of 0.565 square miles. Located at 31.45° N. Lat; 93.78° W. Long. Elevation is 312 feet.
Population: 1,181 (1990); 1,329 (2000); 1,331 (2010); 1,323 (2015 projected); Race: 86.6% White, 11.2% Black, 0.6% Asian, 1.7% Other, 1.8% Hispanic of any race (2010); Density: 40.5 persons per square mile (2010); Average household size: 2.16 (2010); Median age: 50.2 (2010); Males per 100 females: 97.5 (2010); Marriage status: 7.8% never married, 63.9% now married, 12.5% widowed, 15.8% divorced (2005-2009 5-year est.); Foreign born: 0.0% (2005-2009 5-year est.); Ancestry (includes multiple ancestries): 17.1% German, 17.0% Irish, 13.6% English, 7.6% Scottish, 6.6% French (2005-2009 5-year est.).
Economy: Employment by occupation: 5.0% management, 19.5% professional, 18.8% services, 13.3% sales, 0.0% farming, 36.4% construction, 7.0% production (2005-2009 5-year est.).
Income: Per capita income: $26,643 (2010); Median household income: $40,022 (2010); Average household income: $57,821 (2010); Percent of households with income of $100,000 or more: 10.9% (2010); Poverty rate: 6.7% (2005-2009 5-year est.).

Education: Percent of population age 25 and over with: High school diploma (including GED) or higher: 79.6% (2010); Bachelor's degree or higher: 18.7% (2010); Master's degree or higher: 9.3% (2010).
Housing: Homeownership rate: 88.8% (2010); Median home value: $76,944 (2010); Median contract rent: n/a per month (2005-2009 5-year est.); Median year structure built: 1982 (2005-2009 5-year est.).
Transportation: Commute to work: 94.3% car, 0.0% public transportation, 0.0% walk, 2.5% work from home (2005-2009 5-year est.); Travel time to work: 25.6% less than 15 minutes, 36.7% 15 to 30 minutes, 5.4% 30 to 45 minutes, 15.8% 45 to 60 minutes, 16.5% 60 minutes or more (2005-2009 5-year est.)

PINELAND (city).

PINELAND (city). Covers a land area of 1.970 square miles and a water area of 0.094 square miles. Located at 31.24° N. Lat; 93.97° W. Long. Elevation is 266 feet.
History: Pineland grew up in an area of piney woods, around a lumber mill.
Population: 1,023 (1990); 980 (2000); 865 (2010); 814 (2015 projected); Race: 77.6% White, 18.2% Black, 0.3% Asian, 3.9% Other, 4.0% Hispanic of any race (2010); Density: 439.1 persons per square mile (2010); Average household size: 2.38 (2010); Median age: 40.6 (2010); Males per 100 females: 89.7 (2010); Marriage status: 28.1% never married, 53.5% now married, 9.9% widowed, 8.4% divorced (2005-2009 5-year est.); Foreign born: 1.5% (2005-2009 5-year est.); Ancestry (includes multiple ancestries): 18.5% Irish, 10.3% English, 9.8% Scottish, 9.7% German, 7.4% French (2005-2009 5-year est.).
Economy: Single-family building permits issued: 3 (2010); Multi-family building permits issued: 0 (2010); Employment by occupation: 1.6% management, 16.1% professional, 18.0% services, 21.5% sales, 0.0% farming, 20.9% construction, 21.9% production (2005-2009 5-year est.).
Income: Per capita income: $19,920 (2010); Median household income: $31,707 (2010); Average household income: $48,824 (2010); Percent of households with income of $100,000 or more: 9.6% (2010); Poverty rate: 32.1% (2005-2009 5-year est.).
Taxes: Total city taxes per capita: $155 (2007); City property taxes per capita: $44 (2007).
Education: Percent of population age 25 and over with: High school diploma (including GED) or higher: 68.2% (2010); Bachelor's degree or higher: 9.7% (2010); Master's degree or higher: 2.5% (2010).

School District(s)
West Sabine ISD (PK-12)
    2009-10 Enrollment: 642 . . . . (409) 584-2655
Housing: Homeownership rate: 74.8% (2010); Median home value: $57,193 (2010); Median contract rent: $251 per month (2005-2009 5-year est.); Median year structure built: 1970 (2005-2009 5-year est.).
Transportation: Commute to work: 74.9% car, 0.0% public transportation, 10.3% walk, 0.0% work from home (2005-2009 5-year est.); Travel time to work: 69.1% less than 15 minutes, 16.4% 15 to 30 minutes, 12.9% 30 to 45 minutes, 0.0% 45 to 60 minutes, 1.6% 60 minutes or more (2005-2009 5-year est.)

San Augustine County

Located in east Texas; bounded on the west by Attoyac Bayou, and on the southwest by the Angelina River; includes part of Angelina National Forest. Covers a land area of 527.87 square miles, a water area of 64.34 square miles, and is located in the Central Time Zone at 31.39° N. Lat., 94.15° W. Long. The county was founded in 1836. County seat is San Augustine.
Population: 7,999 (1990); 8,946 (2000); 8,899 (2010); 8,860 (2015 projected); Race: 69.2% White, 26.5% Black, 0.2% Asian, 4.0% Other, 5.5% Hispanic of any race (2010); Density: 16.9 persons per square mile (2010); Average household size: 2.37 (2010); Median age: 43.8 (2010); Males per 100 females: 91.4 (2010).
Religion: Five largest groups: 22.9% Southern Baptist Convention, 8.8% Baptist Missionary Association of America, 6.9% Catholic Church, 6.5% Landmark Missionary Baptists, Independent Associations and Unaffiliated Churches, 5.4% The American Baptist
Economy: Unemployment rate: 12.5% (June 2011); Total civilian labor force: 3,796 (June 2011); Leading industries: 38.8% health care and social assistance; 18.0% retail trade; 11.1% construction (2009); Farms: 346 totaling 72,640 acres (2007); Companies that employ 500 or more persons: 0 (2009); Companies that employ 100 to 499 persons: 2 (2009); Companies that employ less than 100 persons: 128 (2009); Black-owned businesses: n/a (2007); Hispanic-owned businesses: n/a (2007); Asian-owned businesses: n/a (2007); Women-owned businesses: n/a

(2007); Retail sales per capita: $7,838 (2010). Single-family building permits issued: 0 (2010); Multi-family building permits issued: 0 (2010).
Income: Per capita income: $19,699 (2010); Median household income: $34,874 (2010); Average household income: $48,300 (2010); Percent of households with income of $100,000 or more: 9.3% (2010); Poverty rate: 26.3% (2009); Bankruptcy rate: 1.67% (2010).
Taxes: Total county taxes per capita: $235 (2007); County property taxes per capita: $162 (2007).
Education: Percent of population age 25 and over with: High school diploma (including GED) or higher: 75.7% (2010); Bachelor's degree or higher: 13.5% (2010); Master's degree or higher: 5.9% (2010).
Housing: Homeownership rate: 79.9% (2010); Median home value: $63,390 (2010); Median contract rent: $272 per month (2005-2009 5-year est.); Median year structure built: 1976 (2005-2009 5-year est.).
Health: Birth rate: 114.3 per 10,000 population (2009); Death rate: 142.3 per 10,000 population (2009); Age-adjusted cancer mortality rate: 192.0 deaths per 100,000 population (2007); Number of physicians: 4.6 per 10,000 population (2008); Hospital beds: 20.7 per 10,000 population (2007); Hospital admissions: 773.7 per 10,000 population (2007).
Elections: 2008 Presidential election results: 35.7% Obama, 63.0% McCain, 0.0% Nader
Additional Information Contacts
San Augustine County Government . . . . (936) 275-2762
    http://www.co.san-augustine.tx.us/ips/cms
San Augustine County Chamber of Commerce . . . . (936) 275-3610
    http://www.sanaugustinetx.com

San Augustine County Communities

BROADDUS (town). Covers a land area of 0.377 square miles and a water area of 0 square miles. Located at 31.30° N. Lat; 94.26° W. Long. Elevation is 262 feet.
Population: 212 (1990); 189 (2000); 188 (2010); 186 (2015 projected); Race: 95.2% White, 3.2% Black, 0.0% Asian, 1.6% Other, 2.7% Hispanic of any race (2010); Density: 498.8 persons per square mile (2010); Average household size: 2.29 (2010); Median age: 43.8 (2010); Males per 100 females: 95.8 (2010); Marriage status: 22.5% never married, 50.3% now married, 11.9% widowed, 15.2% divorced (2005-2009 5-year est.); Foreign born: 0.0% (2005-2009 5-year est.); Ancestry (includes multiple ancestries): 47.1% Irish, 41.2% French, 23.5% German, 15.5% Scottish, 10.7% English (2005-2009 5-year est.).
Economy: Employment by occupation: 26.8% management, 14.3% professional, 16.1% services, 0.0% sales, 5.4% farming, 7.1% construction, 30.4% production (2005-2009 5-year est.).
Income: Per capita income: $21,051 (2010); Median household income: $33,571 (2010); Average household income: $46,006 (2010); Percent of households with income of $100,000 or more: 8.5% (2010); Poverty rate: 40.1% (2005-2009 5-year est.).
Taxes: Total city taxes per capita: $813 (2007); City property taxes per capita: $75 (2007).
Education: Percent of population age 25 and over with: High school diploma (including GED) or higher: 73.3% (2010); Bachelor's degree or higher: 14.8% (2010); Master's degree or higher: 5.9% (2010).

School District(s)
Broaddus ISD (PK-12)
    2009-10 Enrollment: 474 . . . . (936) 872-3041
Housing: Homeownership rate: 85.4% (2010); Median home value: $60,000 (2010); Median contract rent: $205 per month (2005-2009 5-year est.); Median year structure built: 1966 (2005-2009 5-year est.).
Transportation: Commute to work: 94.0% car, 0.0% public transportation, 6.0% walk, 0.0% work from home (2005-2009 5-year est.); Travel time to work: 24.0% less than 15 minutes, 56.0% 15 to 30 minutes, 14.0% 30 to 45 minutes, 6.0% 45 to 60 minutes, 0.0% 60 minutes or more (2005-2009 5-year est.)

SAN AUGUSTINE (town). Aka Bland Lake. County seat. Covers a land area of 4.713 square miles and a water area of 0.097 square miles. Located at 31.53° N. Lat; 94.11° W. Long. Elevation is 371 feet.
History: Mission Nuestra Senora de los Dolores de los Ais was established on Ayish Bayou in 1721, followed by the Presidio de San Agustin de Ahumada in 1756. Both were abandoned in the early 1770's, but the presidio's name lived on when settlers came to the area in 1818 and the town of San Augustine was established.
Population: 2,337 (1990); 2,475 (2000); 2,384 (2010); 2,343 (2015 projected); Race: 38.2% White, 54.9% Black, 0.7% Asian, 6.3% Other,

9.9% Hispanic of any race (2010); Density: 505.9 persons per square mile (2010); Average household size: 2.50 (2010); Median age: 40.9 (2010); Males per 100 females: 83.7 (2010); Marriage status: 31.9% never married, 39.6% now married, 17.8% widowed, 10.7% divorced (2005-2009 5-year est.); Foreign born: 10.5% (2005-2009 5-year est.); Ancestry (includes multiple ancestries): 9.9% English, 8.5% American, 3.3% Irish, 2.8% French, 1.9% German (2005-2009 5-year est.).

Economy: Single-family building permits issued: 0 (2010); Multi-family building permits issued: 0 (2010); Employment by occupation: 2.5% management, 11.7% professional, 23.4% services, 16.4% sales, 5.1% farming, 19.8% construction, 21.1% production (2005-2009 5-year est.).

Income: Per capita income: $19,580 (2010); Median household income: $38,750 (2010); Average household income: $53,267 (2010); Percent of households with income of $100,000 or more: 12.0% (2010); Poverty rate: 38.5% (2005-2009 5-year est.).

Taxes: Total city taxes per capita: $160 (2007); City property taxes per capita: $82 (2007).

Education: Percent of population age 25 and over with: High school diploma (including GED) or higher: 73.4% (2010); Bachelor's degree or higher: 16.8% (2010); Master's degree or higher: 6.2% (2010).

School District(s)

San Augustine ISD (PK-12)
    2009-10 Enrollment: 864 . . . . (936) 275-2306

Housing: Homeownership rate: 63.6% (2010); Median home value: $69,286 (2010); Median contract rent: $263 per month (2005-2009 5-year est.); Median year structure built: 1969 (2005-2009 5-year est.).

Hospitals: Memorial Medical Center San Augustine (48 beds)

Safety: Violent crime rate: 42.9 per 10,000 population; Property crime rate: 244.3 per 10,000 population (2009).

Newspapers: San Augustine Tribune (Local news; Circulation 4,750)

Transportation: Commute to work: 95.8% car, 0.0% public transportation, 4.2% walk, 0.0% work from home (2005-2009 5-year est.); Travel time to work: 54.3% less than 15 minutes, 18.4% 15 to 30 minutes, 11.2% 30 to 45 minutes, 10.2% 45 to 60 minutes, 5.9% 60 minutes or more (2005-2009 5-year est.)

Additional Information Contacts

San Augustine County Chamber of Commerce. . . . . (936) 275-3610
    http://www.sanaugustinetx.com

San Jacinto County

Located in east Texas; bounded on the north and east by the Trinity River; drained by headstreams of the San Jacinto River; includes part of the Sam Houston National Forest. Covers a land area of 570.65 square miles, a water area of 57.25 square miles, and is located in the Central Time Zone at 30.59° N. Lat., 95.14° W. Long. The county was founded in 1870. County seat is Coldspring.

San Jacinto County is part of the Houston-Sugar Land-Baytown, TX Metropolitan Statistical Area. The entire metro area includes: Austin County, TX; Brazoria County, TX; Chambers County, TX; Fort Bend County, TX; Galveston County, TX; Harris County, TX; Liberty County, TX; Montgomery County, TX; San Jacinto County, TX; Waller County, TX

Population: 16,372 (1990); 22,246 (2000); 26,087 (2010); 27,910 (2015 projected); Race: 82.7% White, 11.8% Black, 0.6% Asian, 4.9% Other, 8.0% Hispanic of any race (2010); Density: 45.7 persons per square mile (2010); Average household size: 2.52 (2010); Median age: 39.3 (2010); Males per 100 females: 99.0 (2010).

Religion: Five largest groups: 13.9% Southern Baptist Convention, 7.7% Catholic Church, 3.3% The United Methodist Church, 2.9% Baptist Missionary Association of America, 2.6% The American Baptist Association (2000).

Economy: Unemployment rate: 11.0% (June 2011); Total civilian labor force: 10,573 (June 2011); Leading industries: 20.7% retail trade; 12.6% accommodation & food services; 12.3% construction (2009); Farms: 688 totaling 95,492 acres (2007); Companies that employ 500 or more persons: 0 (2009); Companies that employ 100 to 499 persons: 0 (2009); Companies that employ less than 100 persons: 182 (2009); Black-owned businesses: n/a (2007); Hispanic-owned businesses: n/a (2007); Asian-owned businesses: n/a (2007); Women-owned businesses: n/a (2007); Retail sales per capita: $2,289 (2010). Single-family building permits issued: 2 (2010); Multi-family building permits issued: 0 (2010).

Income: Per capita income: $22,310 (2010); Median household income: $43,970 (2010); Average household income: $56,218 (2010); Percent of

households with income of $100,000 or more: 11.7% (2010); Poverty rate: 20.6% (2009); Bankruptcy rate: 1.25% (2010).

Taxes: Total county taxes per capita: $277 (2007); County property taxes per capita: $240 (2007).

Education: Percent of population age 25 and over with: High school diploma (including GED) or higher: 76.6% (2010); Bachelor's degree or higher: 10.6% (2010); Master's degree or higher: 2.4% (2010).

Housing: Homeownership rate: 82.2% (2010); Median home value: $72,066 (2010); Median contract rent: $369 per month (2005-2009 5-year est.); Median year structure built: 1983 (2005-2009 5-year est.)

Health: Birth rate: 105.6 per 10,000 population (2009); Death rate: 95.6 per 10,000 population (2009); Age-adjusted cancer mortality rate: 160.5 deaths per 100,000 population (2007); Number of physicians: 2.0 per 10,000 population (2008); Hospital beds: 0.0 per 10,000 population (2007); Hospital admissions: 0.0 per 10,000 population (2007).

Elections: 2008 Presidential election results: 30.4% Obama, 68.7% McCain, 0.1% Nader

National and State Parks: Sam Houston National Forest

Additional Information Contacts

San Jacinto County Government . . . . (936) 653-2324
    http://www.co.san-jacinto.tx.us/ips/cms
Coldspring-San Jacinto County Chamber of Commerce . . . (936) 653-2184
    http://www.coldspringtexas.org
Greater Shepherd Chamber of Commerce . . . . (936) 628-3890
    http://www.greatershepherdchamberofcommerce.org

San Jacinto County Communities

COLDSPRING (city). County seat. Covers a land area of 1.842 square miles and a water area of 0 square miles. Located at 30.58° N. Lat; 95.13° W. Long. Elevation is 361 feet.

Population: 559 (1990); 691 (2000); 695 (2010); 704 (2015 projected); Race: 72.9% White, 24.6% Black, 0.6% Asian, 1.9% Other, 3.9% Hispanic of any race (2010); Density: 377.3 persons per square mile (2010); Average household size: 2.43 (2010); Median age: 36.4 (2010); Males per 100 females: 98.6 (2010); Marriage status: 40.6% never married, 28.3% now married, 14.3% widowed, 16.9% divorced (2005-2009 5-year est.); Foreign born: 1.1% (2005-2009 5-year est.); Ancestry (includes multiple ancestries): 15.7% English, 11.3% Irish, 8.5% German, 4.0% American, 3.7% Italian (2005-2009 5-year est.).

Economy: Employment by occupation: 9.0% management, 5.0% professional, 30.7% services, 29.6% sales, 0.0% farming, 11.6% construction, 14.1% production (2005-2009 5-year est.).

Income: Per capita income: $22,925 (2010); Median household income: $38,851 (2010); Average household income: $54,391 (2010); Percent of households with income of $100,000 or more: 11.8% (2010); Poverty rate: 32.6% (2005-2009 5-year est.).

Taxes: Total city taxes per capita: $198 (2007); City property taxes per capita: $81 (2007).

Education: Percent of population age 25 and over with: High school diploma (including GED) or higher: 78.5% (2010); Bachelor's degree or higher: 12.4% (2010); Master's degree or higher: 4.8% (2010).

School District(s)

Coldspring-Oakhurst CISD (PK-12)
    2009-10 Enrollment: 1,648 . . . . (936) 653-1115

Housing: Homeownership rate: 72.4% (2010); Median home value: $71,613 (2010); Median contract rent: $355 per month (2005-2009 5-year est.); Median year structure built: 1982 (2005-2009 5-year est.).

Transportation: Commute to work: 95.3% car, 0.0% public transportation, 0.0% walk, 4.7% work from home (2005-2009 5-year est.); Travel time to work: 48.6% less than 15 minutes, 8.3% 15 to 30 minutes, 25.4% 30 to 45 minutes, 6.6% 45 to 60 minutes, 11.0% 60 minutes or more (2005-2009 5-year est.)

Additional Information Contacts

Coldspring-San Jacinto County Chamber of Commerce . . . (936) 653-2184
    http://www.coldspringtexas.org

OAKHURST (city). Covers a land area of 1.570 square miles and a water area of 0 square miles. Located at 30.74° N. Lat; 95.31° W. Long. Elevation is 390 feet.

Population: 218 (1990); 230 (2000); 233 (2010); 237 (2015 projected); Race: 80.3% White, 18.0% Black, 0.0% Asian, 1.7% Other, 3.4% Hispanic of any race (2010); Density: 148.4 persons per square mile (2010); Average household size: 2.43 (2010); Median age: 37.7 (2010); Males per 100 females: 102.6 (2010); Marriage status: n/a never married, n/a now

married, n/a widowed, n/a divorced (2005-2009 5-year est.); Foreign born: n/a (2005-2009 5-year est.); Ancestry (includes multiple ancestries): n/a (2005-2009 5-year est.).
Economy: Employment by occupation: n/a management, n/a professional, n/a services, n/a sales, n/a farming, n/a construction, n/a production (2005-2009 5-year est.).
Income: Per capita income: $22,970 (2010); Median household income: $43,824 (2010); Average household income: $61,927 (2010); Percent of households with income of $100,000 or more: 13.5% (2010); Poverty rate: n/a (2005-2009 5-year est.).
Education: Percent of population age 25 and over with: High school diploma (including GED) or higher: 74.1% (2010); Bachelor's degree or higher: 12.7% (2010); Master's degree or higher: 4.2% (2010).
Housing: Homeownership rate: 75.0% (2010); Median home value: $65,000 (2010); Median contract rent: n/a per month (2005-2009 5-year est.); Median year structure built: n/a (2005-2009 5-year est.).
Transportation: Commute to work: n/a car, n/a public transportation, n/a walk, n/a work from home (2005-2009 5-year est.); Travel time to work: n/a less than 15 minutes, n/a 15 to 30 minutes, n/a 30 to 45 minutes, n/a 45 to 60 minutes, n/a 60 minutes or more (2005-2009 5-year est.)

POINT BLANK (city). Aka Pointblank. Covers a land area of 1.883 square miles and a water area of 0.303 square miles. Located at 30.74° N. Lat; 95.21° W. Long. Elevation is 217 feet.
Population: 443 (1990); 559 (2000); 694 (2010); 753 (2015 projected); Race: 86.6% White, 10.4% Black, 0.1% Asian, 2.9% Other, 4.3% Hispanic of any race (2010); Density: 368.6 persons per square mile (2010); Average household size: 2.18 (2010); Median age: 52.0 (2010); Males per 100 females: 101.7 (2010); Marriage status: 31.0% never married, 41.1% now married, 2.6% widowed, 25.3% divorced (2005-2009 5-year est.); Foreign born: 0.5% (2005-2009 5-year est.); Ancestry (includes multiple ancestries): 28.9% Irish, 17.5% English, 16.6% German, 9.3% Scotch-Irish, 6.7% French (2005-2009 5-year est.).
Economy: Employment by occupation: 21.6% management, 14.7% professional, 16.4% services, 14.7% sales, 0.0% farming, 10.7% construction, 21.9% production (2005-2009 5-year est.).
Income: Per capita income: $20,869 (2010); Median household income: $36,842 (2010); Average household income: $44,866 (2010); Percent of households with income of $100,000 or more: 6.3% (2010); Poverty rate: 19.5% (2005-2009 5-year est.).
Taxes: Total city taxes per capita: $137 (2007); City property taxes per capita: $0 (2007).
Education: Percent of population age 25 and over with: High school diploma (including GED) or higher: 80.0% (2010); Bachelor's degree or higher: 10.4% (2010); Master's degree or higher: 2.7% (2010).
Housing: Homeownership rate: 87.1% (2010); Median home value: $75,208 (2010); Median contract rent: $496 per month (2005-2009 5-year est.); Median year structure built: 1978 (2005-2009 5-year est.).
Transportation: Commute to work: 98.3% car, 1.7% public transportation, 0.0% walk, 0.0% work from home (2005-2009 5-year est.); Travel time to work: 9.8% less than 15 minutes, 13.8% 15 to 30 minutes, 44.7% 30 to 45 minutes, 9.8% 45 to 60 minutes, 21.9% 60 minutes or more (2005-2009 5-year est.)

POINTBLANK (unincorporated postal area, zip code 77364). Aka Point Blank. Covers a land area of 29.014 square miles and a water area of 0.042 square miles. Located at 30.75° N. Lat; 95.21° W. Long. Elevation is 217 feet.
Population: 1,818 (2000); Race: 75.6% White, 21.6% Black, 0.0% Asian, 2.8% Other, 1.3% Hispanic of any race (2000); Density: 62.7 persons per square mile (2000); Age: 19.0% under 18, 25.8% over 64 (2000); Marriage status: 11.2% never married, 67.7% now married, 10.2% widowed, 10.9% divorced (2000); Foreign born: 1.5% (2000); Ancestry (includes multiple ancestries): 16.8% American, 10.3% English, 9.7% German, 9.3% Irish (2000).
Economy: Employment by occupation: 9.0% management, 12.7% professional, 22.5% services, 31.5% sales, 2.9% farming, 14.7% construction, 6.7% production (2000).
Income: Per capita income: $16,776 (2000); Median household income: $27,782 (2000); Poverty rate: 179.1% (2000).
Education: Percent of population age 25 and over with: High school diploma (including GED) or higher: 72.6% (2000); Bachelor's degree or higher: 10.3% (2000).

Housing: Homeownership rate: 89.4% (2000); Median home value: $63,200 (2000); Median contract rent: $290 per month (2000); Median year structure built: 1981 (2000).
Transportation: Commute to work: 98.1% car, 0.0% public transportation, 0.0% walk, 0.3% work from home (2000); Travel time to work: 16.3% less than 15 minutes, 25.0% 15 to 30 minutes, 25.6% 30 to 45 minutes, 12.6% 45 to 60 minutes, 20.5% 60 minutes or more (2000)

SHEPHERD (city). Covers a land area of 6.114 square miles and a water area of 0.009 square miles. Located at 30.49° N. Lat; 95.00° W. Long. Elevation is 144 feet.
Population: 1,853 (1990); 2,029 (2000); 2,336 (2010); 2,499 (2015 projected); Race: 75.8% White, 17.6% Black, 1.3% Asian, 5.3% Other, 8.2% Hispanic of any race (2010); Density: 382.1 persons per square mile (2010); Average household size: 2.63 (2010); Median age: 33.6 (2010); Males per 100 females: 92.3 (2010); Marriage status: 23.3% never married, 46.8% now married, 14.6% widowed, 15.3% divorced (2005-2009 5-year est.); Foreign born: 5.2% (2005-2009 5-year est.); Ancestry (includes multiple ancestries): 16.1% German, 13.1% Irish, 11.0% English, 7.4% French, 6.4% American (2005-2009 5-year est.).
Economy: Single-family building permits issued: 2 (2010); Multi-family building permits issued: 0 (2010); Employment by occupation: 3.5% management, 14.4% professional, 27.9% services, 28.7% sales, 0.0% farming, 10.5% construction, 15.0% production (2005-2009 5-year est.).
Income: Per capita income: $18,530 (2010); Median household income: $39,028 (2010); Average household income: $49,266 (2010); Percent of households with income of $100,000 or more: 9.7% (2010); Poverty rate: 27.8% (2005-2009 5-year est.).
Taxes: Total city taxes per capita: $172 (2007); City property taxes per capita: $53 (2007).
Education: Percent of population age 25 and over with: High school diploma (including GED) or higher: 70.1% (2010); Bachelor's degree or higher: 7.0% (2010); Master's degree or higher: 1.5% (2010).
School District(s)
Shepherd ISD (PK-12)
   2009-10 Enrollment: 1,917 . . . . (936) 628-3396
Housing: Homeownership rate: 66.3% (2010); Median home value: $59,694 (2010); Median contract rent: $270 per month (2005-2009 5-year est.); Median year structure built: 1980 (2005-2009 5-year est.).
Newspapers: San Jacinto News-Times (Community news; Circulation 2,175)
Transportation: Commute to work: 90.6% car, 0.0% public transportation, 3.3% walk, 5.3% work from home (2005-2009 5-year est.); Travel time to work: 24.4% less than 15 minutes, 13.9% 15 to 30 minutes, 20.2% 30 to 45 minutes, 21.7% 45 to 60 minutes, 19.8% 60 minutes or more (2005-2009 5-year est.)
Additional Information Contacts
Greater Shepherd Chamber of Commerce . . . . (936) 628-3890
   http://www.greatershepherdchamberofcommerce.org

San Patricio County

Located in south Texas; bounded on the east by Aransas Bay with St. Joseph and Mustang Islands, on the south by the Nueces River and Nueces and Corpus Christi Bays, and on the north by the Aransas River; includes part of Lake Corpus Christi. Covers a land area of 691.65 square miles, a water area of 15.41 square miles, and is located in the Central Time Zone at 27.97° N. Lat., 97.46° W. Long. The county was founded in 1836. County seat is Sinton.

San Patricio County is part of the Corpus Christi, TX Metropolitan Statistical Area. The entire metro area includes: Aransas County, TX; Nueces County, TX; San Patricio County, TX

Population: 58,690 (1990); 67,138 (2000); 69,464 (2010); 70,472 (2015 projected); Race: 75.5% White, 2.2% Black, 0.8% Asian, 21.6% Other, 53.5% Hispanic of any race (2010); Density: 100.4 persons per square mile (2010); Average household size: 2.84 (2010); Median age: 34.5 (2010); Males per 100 females: 94.7 (2010).
Religion: Five largest groups: 30.8% Catholic Church, 13.6% Southern Baptist Convention, 4.4% The United Methodist Church, 2.0% Churches of Christ, 1.0% Evangelical Lutheran Church in America (2000).
Economy: Unemployment rate: 9.7% (June 2011); Total civilian labor force: 31,881 (June 2011); Leading industries: 18.2% retail trade; 14.1% accommodation & food services; 12.0% health care and social assistance (2009); Farms: 652 totaling 369,737 acres (2007); Companies that employ

500 or more persons: 1 (2009); Companies that employ 100 to 499 persons: 16 (2009); Companies that employ less than 100 persons: 1,026 (2009); Black-owned businesses: n/a (2007); Hispanic-owned businesses: 1,419 (2007); Asian-owned businesses: n/a (2007); Women-owned businesses: 1,444 (2007); Retail sales per capita: $9,809 (2010). Single-family building permits issued: 126 (2010); Multi-family building permits issued: 0 (2010).
Income: Per capita income: $20,135 (2010); Median household income: $44,465 (2010); Average household income: $57,398 (2010); Percent of households with income of $100,000 or more: 13.3% (2010); Poverty rate: 16.3% (2009); Bankruptcy rate: 1.83% (2010).
Taxes: Total county taxes per capita: $251 (2007); County property taxes per capita: $232 (2007).
Education: Percent of population age 25 and over with: High school diploma (including GED) or higher: 75.8% (2010); Bachelor's degree or higher: 15.1% (2010); Master's degree or higher: 2.9% (2010).
Housing: Homeownership rate: 64.2% (2010); Median home value: $85,704 (2010); Median contract rent: $516 per month (2005-2009 5-year est.); Median year structure built: 1975 (2005-2009 5-year est.)
Health: Birth rate: 167.4 per 10,000 population (2009); Death rate: 79.3 per 10,000 population (2009); Age-adjusted cancer mortality rate: 190.9 deaths per 100,000 population (2007); Number of physicians: 5.7 per 10,000 population (2008); Hospital beds: 8.5 per 10,000 population (2007); Hospital admissions: 215.4 per 10,000 population (2007).
Elections: 2008 Presidential election results: 41.4% Obama, 58.0% McCain, 0.1% Nader
National and State Parks: Lake Corpus Christi State Park
Additional Information Contacts
San Patricio County Government . . . . (361) 364-6120
    http://www.co.san-patricio.tx.us/ips/cms
Aransas Pass Chamber of Commerce . . . . (361) 758-2750
    http://www.aransaspass.org
City of Aransas Pass . . . . (361) 758-5301
    http://www.aransaspasstx.gov
City of Ingleside . . . . (361) 776-2517
    http://www.inglesidetx.gov
City of Mathis . . . . (361) 547-3343
    http://www.cityofmathis.com
City of Portland . . . . (361) 777-4500
    http://www.portlandtx.com
City of Sinton . . . . (361) 364-2381
    http://www.sintontexas.org
Ingleside Chamber of Commerce . . . . (361) 776-2906
    http://www.inglesidexchamber.org
Mathis Area Chamber of Commerce . . . . (361) 547-0289
    http://www.mathischamber.org
Portland Chamber of Commerce . . . . (361) 643-2475
    http://www.portlandtx.org
Sinton Chamber of Commerce . . . . (361) 364-2307
    http://www.sintontexas.org
Taft Chamber of Commerce . . . . (361) 528-3230

San Patricio County Communities

ARANSAS PASS (city).
Covers a land area of 10.735 square miles and a water area of 41.111 square miles. Located at 27.90° N. Lat; 97.13° W. Long. Elevation is 16 feet.
History: The town of Aransas Pass was settled by Irish colonists in the 1820's or 1830's. This port town depended on the fish, shrimp, and oyster industry until oil and petrochemical plants were built here.
Population: 7,337 (1990); 8,138 (2000); 8,927 (2010); 9,050 (2015 projected); Race: 79.8% White, 1.7% Black, 0.4% Asian, 18.1% Other, 41.8% Hispanic of any race (2010); Density: 831.6 persons per square mile (2010); Average household size: 2.61 (2010); Median age: 36.8 (2010); Males per 100 females: 94.3 (2010); Marriage status: 23.4% never married, 54.5% now married, 9.1% widowed, 12.9% divorced (2005-2009 5-year est.); Foreign born: 5.9% (2005-2009 5-year est.); Ancestry (includes multiple ancestries): 14.8% German, 14.4% Irish, 11.0% English, 3.9% Dutch, 3.3% American (2005-2009 5-year est.).
Economy: Single-family building permits issued: 13 (2010); Multi-family building permits issued: 0 (2010); Employment by occupation: 12.1% management, 9.6% professional, 27.3% services, 21.4% sales, 1.0% farming, 16.8% construction, 11.8% production (2005-2009 5-year est.).
Income: Per capita income: $19,106 (2010); Median household income: $39,530 (2010); Average household income: $49,890 (2010); Percent of

households with income of $100,000 or more: 9.2% (2010); Poverty rate: 18.3% (2005-2009 5-year est.).
Taxes: Total city taxes per capita: $583 (2007); City property taxes per capita: $281 (2007).
Education: Percent of population age 25 and over with: High school diploma (including GED) or higher: 73.0% (2010); Bachelor's degree or higher: 10.0% (2010); Master's degree or higher: 2.2% (2010).
School District(s)
Aransas Pass ISD (PK-12)
    2009-10 Enrollment: 1,881 . . . . (361) 758-3466
Housing: Homeownership rate: 61.3% (2010); Median home value: $72,431 (2010); Median contract rent: $442 per month (2005-2009 5-year est.); Median year structure built: 1974 (2005-2009 5-year est.).
Hospitals: North Bay Hospital (75 beds)
Safety: Violent crime rate: 33.8 per 10,000 population; Property crime rate: 687.7 per 10,000 population (2009).
Newspapers: The Aransas Pass Progress (Local news; Circulation 2,806); Ingleside Index (Community news; Circulation 869)
Transportation: Commute to work: 83.9% car, 0.0% public transportation, 4.3% walk, 0.9% work from home (2005-2009 5-year est.); Travel time to work: 46.6% less than 15 minutes, 24.4% 15 to 30 minutes, 17.9% 30 to 45 minutes, 4.9% 45 to 60 minutes, 6.3% 60 minutes or more (2005-2009 5-year est.)
Additional Information Contacts
Aransas Pass Chamber of Commerce . . . . (361) 758-2750
    http://www.aransaspass.org
City of Aransas Pass . . . . (361) 758-5301
    http://www.aransaspasstx.gov

DEL SOL-LOMA LINDA (CDP).
Covers a land area of 2.768 square miles and a water area of 0 square miles. Located at 28.01° N. Lat; 97.51° W. Long. Elevation is 49 feet.
Population: 671 (1990); 726 (2000); 716 (2010); 710 (2015 projected); Race: 79.1% White, 1.3% Black, 0.0% Asian, 19.7% Other, 81.3% Hispanic of any race (2010); Density: 258.7 persons per square mile (2010); Average household size: 3.02 (2010); Median age: 32.7 (2010); Males per 100 females: 93.0 (2010); Marriage status: 25.8% never married, 39.0% now married, 13.2% widowed, 21.9% divorced (2005-2009 5-year est.); Foreign born: 1.8% (2005-2009 5-year est.); Ancestry (includes multiple ancestries): 5.6% English, 2.0% Scotch-Irish, 1.2% German, 1.1% Irish (2005-2009 5-year est.).
Economy: Employment by occupation: 0.0% management, 7.4% professional, 11.3% services, 24.8% sales, 0.0% farming, 23.2% construction, 33.4% production (2005-2009 5-year est.).
Income: Per capita income: $17,057 (2010); Median household income: $36,544 (2010); Average household income: $51,055 (2010); Percent of households with income of $100,000 or more: 10.5% (2010); Poverty rate: 14.5% (2005-2009 5-year est.).
Education: Percent of population age 25 and over with: High school diploma (including GED) or higher: 63.8% (2010); Bachelor's degree or higher: 7.8% (2010); Master's degree or higher: 1.9% (2010).
Housing: Homeownership rate: 66.7% (2010); Median home value: $54,902 (2010); Median contract rent: $197 per month (2005-2009 5-year est.); Median year structure built: 1978 (2005-2009 5-year est.).
Transportation: Commute to work: 75.6% car, 0.0% public transportation, 0.0% walk, 0.0% work from home (2005-2009 5-year est.); Travel time to work: 12.5% less than 15 minutes, 40.2% 15 to 30 minutes, 40.8% 30 to 45 minutes, 6.4% 45 to 60 minutes, 0.0% 60 minutes or more (2005-2009 5-year est.)

DOYLE (CDP).
Covers a land area of 0.843 square miles and a water area of 0 square miles. Located at 27.88° N. Lat; 97.34° W. Long. Elevation is 20 feet.
Population: 239 (1990); 285 (2000); 445 (2010); 442 (2015 projected); Race: 72.4% White, 3.6% Black, 0.9% Asian, 23.1% Other, 42.5% Hispanic of any race (2010); Density: 528.1 persons per square mile (2010); Average household size: 2.42 (2010); Median age: 36.1 (2010); Males per 100 females: 98.7 (2010); Marriage status: 28.4% never married, 65.3% now married, 6.3% widowed, 0.0% divorced (2005-2009 5-year est.); Foreign born: 0.0% (2005-2009 5-year est.); Ancestry (includes multiple ancestries): 47.7% German, 37.5% English, 28.4% French, 19.9% Irish, 9.1% Scottish (2005-2009 5-year est.).
Economy: Employment by occupation: 38.7% management, 13.3% professional, 0.0% services, 0.0% sales, 0.0% farming, 48.0% construction, 0.0% production (2005-2009 5-year est.).

Income: Per capita income: $28,914 (2010); Median household income: $54,070 (2010); Average household income: $69,117 (2010); Percent of households with income of $100,000 or more: 20.1% (2010); Poverty rate: 13.6% (2005-2009 5-year est.).
Education: Percent of population age 25 and over with: High school diploma (including GED) or higher: 88.2% (2010); Bachelor's degree or higher: 22.1% (2010); Master's degree or higher: 6.2% (2010).
Housing: Homeownership rate: 43.5% (2010); Median home value: $120,270 (2010); Median contract rent: n/a per month (2005-2009 5-year est.); Median year structure built: 1954 (2005-2009 5-year est.).
Transportation: Commute to work: 100.0% car, 0.0% public transportation, 0.0% walk, 0.0% work from home (2005-2009 5-year est.); Travel time to work: 21.7% less than 15 minutes, 78.3% 15 to 30 minutes, 0.0% 30 to 45 minutes, 0.0% 45 to 60 minutes, 0.0% 60 minutes or more (2005-2009 5-year est.)

EDGEWATER-PAISANO (CDP).
Covers a land area of 0.277 square miles and a water area of 0 square miles. Located at 28.09° N. Lat; 97.86° W. Long. Elevation is 128 feet.
Population: 151 (1990); 182 (2000); 197 (2010); 203 (2015 projected); Race: 78.2% White, 0.5% Black, 0.5% Asian, 20.8% Other, 50.3% Hispanic of any race (2010); Density: 710.4 persons per square mile (2010); Average household size: 2.43 (2010); Median age: 42.8 (2010); Males per 100 females: 97.0 (2010); Marriage status: 40.7% never married, 59.3% now married, 0.0% widowed, 0.0% divorced (2005-2009 5-year est.); Foreign born: 0.0% (2005-2009 5-year est.); Ancestry (includes multiple ancestries): n/a (2005-2009 5-year est.).
Economy: Employment by occupation: 0.0% management, 0.0% professional, 100.0% services, 0.0% sales, 0.0% farming, 0.0% construction, 0.0% production (2005-2009 5-year est.).
Income: Per capita income: $19,821 (2010); Median household income: $34,667 (2010); Average household income: $49,352 (2010); Percent of households with income of $100,000 or more: 9.9% (2010); Poverty rate: 0.0% (2005-2009 5-year est.).
Education: Percent of population age 25 and over with: High school diploma (including GED) or higher: 73.1% (2010); Bachelor's degree or higher: 10.4% (2010); Master's degree or higher: 0.7% (2010).
Housing: Homeownership rate: 72.8% (2010); Median home value: $80,833 (2010); Median contract rent: n/a per month (2005-2009 5-year est.); Median year structure built: n/a (2005-2009 5-year est.).
Transportation: Commute to work: 50.0% car, 0.0% public transportation, 0.0% walk, 50.0% work from home (2005-2009 5-year est.); Travel time to work: 0.0% less than 15 minutes, 100.0% 15 to 30 minutes, 0.0% 30 to 45 minutes, 0.0% 45 to 60 minutes, 0.0% 60 minutes or more (2005-2009 5-year est.)

EDROY (CDP).
Covers a land area of 2.080 square miles and a water area of 0 square miles. Located at 27.97° N. Lat; 97.67° W. Long. Elevation is 95 feet.
Population: 412 (1990); 420 (2000); 405 (2010); 401 (2015 projected); Race: 78.5% White, 0.0% Black, 0.2% Asian, 21.2% Other, 63.7% Hispanic of any race (2010); Density: 194.7 persons per square mile (2010); Average household size: 3.14 (2010); Median age: 33.1 (2010); Males per 100 females: 100.5 (2010); Marriage status: 23.1% never married, 43.7% now married, 0.0% widowed, 33.2% divorced (2005-2009 5-year est.); Foreign born: 8.5% (2005-2009 5-year est.); Ancestry (includes multiple ancestries): 2.7% English, 2.7% Dutch (2005-2009 5-year est.).
Economy: Employment by occupation: 0.0% management, 17.8% professional, 14.2% services, 13.6% sales, 0.0% farming, 26.0% construction, 28.4% production (2005-2009 5-year est.).
Income: Per capita income: $16,733 (2010); Median household income: $40,625 (2010); Average household income: $56,027 (2010); Percent of households with income of $100,000 or more: 13.2% (2010); Poverty rate: 14.6% (2005-2009 5-year est.).
Education: Percent of population age 25 and over with: High school diploma (including GED) or higher: 75.2% (2010); Bachelor's degree or higher: 10.3% (2010); Master's degree or higher: 1.7% (2010).
Housing: Homeownership rate: 81.4% (2010); Median home value: $65,556 (2010); Median contract rent: $325 per month (2005-2009 5-year est.); Median year structure built: 1957 (2005-2009 5-year est.).
Transportation: Commute to work: 100.0% car, 0.0% public transportation, 0.0% walk, 0.0% work from home (2005-2009 5-year est.); Travel time to work: 7.7% less than 15 minutes, 37.3% 15 to 30 minutes,

26.0% 30 to 45 minutes, 29.0% 45 to 60 minutes, 0.0% 60 minutes or more (2005-2009 5-year est.)

FALMAN-COUNTY ACRES (CDP).
Covers a land area of 0.247 square miles and a water area of 0 square miles. Located at 27.92° N. Lat; 97.16° W. Long. Elevation is 10 feet.
Population: 217 (1990); 289 (2000); 261 (2010); 280 (2015 projected); Race: 80.8% White, 1.5% Black, 0.0% Asian, 17.6% Other, 33.0% Hispanic of any race (2010); Density: 1,057.2 persons per square mile (2010); Average household size: 2.66 (2010); Median age: 31.3 (2010); Males per 100 females: 90.5 (2010); Marriage status: 19.9% never married, 26.7% now married, 21.8% widowed, 31.6% divorced (2005-2009 5-year est.); Foreign born: 3.6% (2005-2009 5-year est.); Ancestry (includes multiple ancestries): 48.5% American, 7.9% English, 6.9% Irish, 4.0% Scotch-Irish, 4.0% Russian (2005-2009 5-year est.).
Economy: Employment by occupation: 0.0% management, 0.0% professional, 29.0% services, 12.0% sales, 0.0% farming, 11.0% construction, 48.0% production (2005-2009 5-year est.).
Income: Per capita income: $20,496 (2010); Median household income: $43,000 (2010); Average household income: $54,286 (2010); Percent of households with income of $100,000 or more: 11.2% (2010); Poverty rate: 33.7% (2005-2009 5-year est.).
Education: Percent of population age 25 and over with: High school diploma (including GED) or higher: 78.7% (2010); Bachelor's degree or higher: 14.0% (2010); Master's degree or higher: 4.0% (2010).
Housing: Homeownership rate: 68.4% (2010); Median home value: $53,571 (2010); Median contract rent: n/a per month (2005-2009 5-year est.); Median year structure built: 1986 (2005-2009 5-year est.).
Transportation: Commute to work: 100.0% car, 0.0% public transportation, 0.0% walk, 0.0% work from home (2005-2009 5-year est.); Travel time to work: 24.0% less than 15 minutes, 33.0% 15 to 30 minutes, 31.0% 30 to 45 minutes, 0.0% 45 to 60 minutes, 12.0% 60 minutes or more (2005-2009 5-year est.)

GREGORY (city).
Covers a land area of 1.416 square miles and a water area of 0 square miles. Located at 27.92° N. Lat; 97.29° W. Long. Elevation is 30 feet.
Population: 2,458 (1990); 2,318 (2000); 2,205 (2010); 2,150 (2015 projected); Race: 66.3% White, 0.5% Black, 0.0% Asian, 33.1% Other, 95.8% Hispanic of any race (2010); Density: 1,557.0 persons per square mile (2010); Average household size: 3.35 (2010); Median age: 32.0 (2010); Males per 100 females: 93.4 (2010); Marriage status: 27.1% never married, 56.4% now married, 7.2% widowed, 9.3% divorced (2005-2009 5-year est.); Foreign born: 6.9% (2005-2009 5-year est.); Ancestry (includes multiple ancestries): 1.3% Irish, 1.2% German, 1.0% Norwegian, 0.9% Dutch West Indian, 0.8% Italian (2005-2009 5-year est.).
Economy: Single-family building permits issued: 0 (2010); Multi-family building permits issued: 0 (2010); Employment by occupation: 3.4% management, 8.7% professional, 35.3% services, 17.0% sales, 0.9% farming, 15.0% construction, 19.7% production (2005-2009 5-year est.).
Income: Per capita income: $14,592 (2010); Median household income: $39,879 (2010); Average household income: $48,900 (2010); Percent of households with income of $100,000 or more: 7.9% (2010); Poverty rate: 19.6% (2005-2009 5-year est.).
Taxes: Total city taxes per capita: $120 (2007); City property taxes per capita: $80 (2007).
Education: Percent of population age 25 and over with: High school diploma (including GED) or higher: 55.8% (2010); Bachelor's degree or higher: 5.5% (2010); Master's degree or higher: 0.8% (2010).
School District(s)
Gregory-Portland ISD (PK-12)
    2009-10 Enrollment: 4,197 . . . . (361) 777-1091
Housing: Homeownership rate: 66.8% (2010); Median home value: $48,313 (2010); Median contract rent: $379 per month (2005-2009 5-year est.); Median year structure built: 1965 (2005-2009 5-year est.).
Safety: Violent crime rate: 4.6 per 10,000 population; Property crime rate: 114.3 per 10,000 population (2009).
Transportation: Commute to work: 86.3% car, 1.4% public transportation, 1.1% walk, 4.2% work from home (2005-2009 5-year est.); Travel time to work: 37.4% less than 15 minutes, 39.1% 15 to 30 minutes, 20.1% 30 to 45 minutes, 1.9% 45 to 60 minutes, 1.4% 60 minutes or more (2005-2009 5-year est.)

INGLESIDE (city). Covers a land area of 14.396 square miles and a water area of 0.109 square miles. Located at 27.87° N. Lat; 97.20° W. Long. Elevation is 13 feet.

Population: 6,058 (1990); 9,388 (2000); 9,219 (2010); 9,329 (2015 projected); Race: 78.0% White, 3.9% Black, 2.1% Asian, 16.1% Other, 32.7% Hispanic of any race (2010); Density: 640.4 persons per square mile (2010); Average household size: 2.72 (2010); Median age: 32.6 (2010); Males per 100 females: 99.6 (2010); Marriage status: 34.2% never married, 55.2% now married, 2.5% widowed, 8.0% divorced (2005-2009 5-year est.); Foreign born: 7.8% (2005-2009 5-year est.); Ancestry (includes multiple ancestries): 14.8% German, 14.7% Irish, 7.3% English, 5.6% American, 2.2% Italian (2005-2009 5-year est.).

Economy: Single-family building permits issued: 12 (2010); Multi-family building permits issued: 0 (2010); Employment by occupation: 8.8% management, 17.9% professional, 22.9% services, 19.5% sales, 0.0% farming, 19.6% construction, 11.3% production (2005-2009 5-year est.).

Income: Per capita income: $22,176 (2010); Median household income: $48,580 (2010); Average household income: $60,519 (2010); Percent of households with income of $100,000 or more: 14.0% (2010); Poverty rate: 10.0% (2005-2009 5-year est.).

Taxes: Total city taxes per capita: $328 (2007); City property taxes per capita: $210 (2007).

Education: Percent of population age 25 and over with: High school diploma (including GED) or higher: 86.3% (2010); Bachelor's degree or higher: 16.0% (2010); Master's degree or higher: 2.9% (2010).

School District(s)

Ingleside ISD (PK-12)
    2009-10 Enrollment: 2,150 . . . . (361) 776-7631

Housing: Homeownership rate: 59.4% (2010); Median home value: $97,798 (2010); Median contract rent: $583 per month (2005-2009 5-year est.); Median year structure built: 1983 (2005-2009 5-year est.).

Safety: Violent crime rate: 17.8 per 10,000 population; Property crime rate: 271.0 per 10,000 population (2009).

Transportation: Commute to work: 86.2% car, 0.2% public transportation, 9.8% walk, 2.2% work from home (2005-2009 5-year est.); Travel time to work: 52.2% less than 15 minutes, 25.2% 15 to 30 minutes, 15.3% 30 to 45 minutes, 4.4% 45 to 60 minutes, 2.8% 60 minutes or more (2005-2009 5-year est.)

Additional Information Contacts

City of Ingleside . . . . (361) 776-2517
    http://www.inglesidetx.gov
Ingleside Chamber of Commerce . . . . (361) 776-2906
    http://www.inglesidetxchamber.org

INGLESIDE ON THE BAY (city). Covers a land area of 0.297 square miles and a water area of 0.015 square miles. Located at 27.82° N. Lat; 97.22° W. Long. Elevation is 10 feet.

Population: 231 (1990); 659 (2000); 747 (2010); 766 (2015 projected); Race: 72.6% White, 11.5% Black, 3.9% Asian, 12.0% Other, 21.8% Hispanic of any race (2010); Density: 2,514.8 persons per square mile (2010); Average household size: 2.45 (2010); Median age: 34.2 (2010); Males per 100 females: 145.7 (2010); Marriage status: 17.4% never married, 72.6% now married, 2.2% widowed, 7.7% divorced (2005-2009 5-year est.); Foreign born: 2.3% (2005-2009 5-year est.); Ancestry (includes multiple ancestries): 26.0% German, 23.0% Irish, 18.6% English, 7.6% French, 6.4% Polish (2005-2009 5-year est.).

Economy: Single-family building permits issued: 1 (2010); Multi-family building permits issued: 0 (2010); Employment by occupation: 16.5% management, 17.7% professional, 25.5% services, 18.9% sales, 0.0% farming, 6.6% construction, 14.8% production (2005-2009 5-year est.).

Income: Per capita income: $24,746 (2010); Median household income: $57,212 (2010); Average household income: $66,688 (2010); Percent of households with income of $100,000 or more: 20.5% (2010); Poverty rate: 6.9% (2005-2009 5-year est.).

Taxes: Total city taxes per capita: $189 (2007); City property taxes per capita: $99 (2007).

Education: Percent of population age 25 and over with: High school diploma (including GED) or higher: 93.4% (2010); Bachelor's degree or higher: 22.4% (2010); Master's degree or higher: 3.5% (2010).

Housing: Homeownership rate: 80.8% (2010); Median home value: $106,250 (2010); Median contract rent: $938 per month (2005-2009 5-year est.); Median year structure built: 1975 (2005-2009 5-year est.).

Transportation: Commute to work: 88.5% car, 2.4% public transportation, 0.0% walk, 4.0% work from home (2005-2009 5-year est.); Travel time to

work: 22.6% less than 15 minutes, 37.9% 15 to 30 minutes, 30.9% 30 to 45 minutes, 5.8% 45 to 60 minutes, 2.9% 60 minutes or more (2005-2009 5-year est.)

LAKE CITY (town). Covers a land area of 0.638 square miles and a water area of 0.036 square miles. Located at 28.08° N. Lat; 97.88° W. Long. Elevation is 118 feet.

Population: 465 (1990); 526 (2000); 564 (2010); 580 (2015 projected); Race: 78.4% White, 0.4% Black, 0.2% Asian, 21.1% Other, 50.4% Hispanic of any race (2010); Density: 884.0 persons per square mile (2010); Average household size: 2.43 (2010); Median age: 46.1 (2010); Males per 100 females: 88.6 (2010); Marriage status: 16.1% never married, 59.8% now married, 10.3% widowed, 13.8% divorced (2005-2009 5-year est.); Foreign born: 5.6% (2005-2009 5-year est.); Ancestry (includes multiple ancestries): 13.2% American, 13.0% Irish, 12.7% German, 8.7% English, 4.5% Greek (2005-2009 5-year est.).

Economy: Employment by occupation: 4.9% management, 20.2% professional, 13.5% services, 24.7% sales, 0.0% farming, 19.3% construction, 17.5% production (2005-2009 5-year est.).

Income: Per capita income: $19,821 (2010); Median household income: $35,000 (2010); Average household income: $49,784 (2010); Percent of households with income of $100,000 or more: 9.9% (2010); Poverty rate: 12.3% (2005-2009 5-year est.).

Education: Percent of population age 25 and over with: High school diploma (including GED) or higher: 73.8% (2010); Bachelor's degree or higher: 11.5% (2010); Master's degree or higher: 1.5% (2010).

Housing: Homeownership rate: 73.3% (2010); Median home value: $81,176 (2010); Median contract rent: $145 per month (2005-2009 5-year est.); Median year structure built: 1980 (2005-2009 5-year est.).

Transportation: Commute to work: 88.0% car, 4.6% public transportation, 0.0% walk, 7.4% work from home (2005-2009 5-year est.); Travel time to work: 9.5% less than 15 minutes, 26.4% 15 to 30 minutes, 16.4% 30 to 45 minutes, 41.8% 45 to 60 minutes, 6.0% 60 minutes or more (2005-2009 5-year est.)

LAKESHORE GARDENS-HIDDEN ACRES (CDP). Covers a land area of 1.953 square miles and a water area of 0.008 square miles. Located at 28.12° N. Lat; 97.86° W. Long. Elevation is 95 feet.

Population: 647 (1990); 720 (2000); 668 (2010); 644 (2015 projected); Race: 75.7% White, 0.0% Black, 0.3% Asian, 24.0% Other, 57.2% Hispanic of any race (2010); Density: 342.1 persons per square mile (2010); Average household size: 2.48 (2010); Median age: 46.1 (2010); Males per 100 females: 88.2 (2010); Marriage status: 31.1% never married, 55.1% now married, 10.6% widowed, 3.2% divorced (2005-2009 5-year est.); Foreign born: 0.0% (2005-2009 5-year est.); Ancestry (includes multiple ancestries): 9.6% Irish, 8.7% German, 8.7% English, 7.2% Welsh, 4.1% Scotch-Irish (2005-2009 5-year est.).

Economy: Employment by occupation: 12.0% management, 14.6% professional, 12.7% services, 36.1% sales, 0.0% farming, 10.8% construction, 13.9% production (2005-2009 5-year est.).

Income: Per capita income: $31,989 (2010); Median household income: $44,938 (2010); Average household income: $78,922 (2010); Percent of households with income of $100,000 or more: 20.1% (2010); Poverty rate: 9.8% (2005-2009 5-year est.).

Education: Percent of population age 25 and over with: High school diploma (including GED) or higher: 69.5% (2010); Bachelor's degree or higher: 7.3% (2010); Master's degree or higher: 2.3% (2010).

Housing: Homeownership rate: 86.2% (2010); Median home value: $57,200 (2010); Median contract rent: n/a per month (2005-2009 5-year est.); Median year structure built: 1978 (2005-2009 5-year est.).

Transportation: Commute to work: 100.0% car, 0.0% public transportation, 0.0% walk, 0.0% work from home (2005-2009 5-year est.); Travel time to work: 17.8% less than 15 minutes, 0.0% 15 to 30 minutes, 28.4% 30 to 45 minutes, 53.8% 45 to 60 minutes, 0.0% 60 minutes or more (2005-2009 5-year est.)

LAKESIDE (town). Covers a land area of 0.393 square miles and a water area of 0 square miles. Located at 28.10° N. Lat; 97.86° W. Long. Elevation is 95 feet.

Population: 292 (1990); 333 (2000); 364 (2010); 374 (2015 projected); Race: 78.6% White, 0.0% Black, 0.0% Asian, 21.4% Other, 50.5% Hispanic of any race (2010); Density: 926.8 persons per square mile (2010); Average household size: 2.43 (2010); Median age: 45.5 (2010); Males per 100 females: 91.6 (2010); Marriage status: 15.6% never married, 46.0% now married, 9.5% widowed, 28.9% divorced (2005-2009 5-year

est.); Foreign born: 3.5% (2005-2009 5-year est.); Ancestry (includes multiple ancestries): 26.6% Irish, 8.7% English, 4.0% American, 3.0% German, 2.2% Scotch-Irish (2005-2009 5-year est.).
Economy: Employment by occupation: 8.4% management, 6.3% professional, 18.9% services, 45.5% sales, 4.2% farming, 9.1% construction, 7.7% production (2005-2009 5-year est.).
Income: Per capita income: $19,821 (2010); Median household income: $35,577 (2010); Average household income: $48,883 (2010); Percent of households with income of $100,000 or more: 10.0% (2010); Poverty rate: 33.7% (2005-2009 5-year est.).
Taxes: Total city taxes per capita: $184 (2007); City property taxes per capita: $112 (2007).
Education: Percent of population age 25 and over with: High school diploma (including GED) or higher: 73.8% (2010); Bachelor's degree or higher: 11.7% (2010); Master's degree or higher: 1.2% (2010).
Housing: Homeownership rate: 73.3% (2010); Median home value: $81,739 (2010); Median contract rent: n/a per month (2005-2009 5-year est.); Median year structure built: 1974 (2005-2009 5-year est.).
Transportation: Commute to work: 78.3% car, 0.0% public transportation, 5.6% walk, 8.4% work from home (2005-2009 5-year est.); Travel time to work: 53.4% less than 15 minutes, 6.1% 15 to 30 minutes, 9.9% 30 to 45 minutes, 24.4% 45 to 60 minutes, 6.1% 60 minutes or more (2005-2009 5-year est.)

MATHIS (city). Covers a land area of 1.988 square miles and a water area of 0 square miles. Located at 28.09° N. Lat; 97.82° W. Long. Elevation is 161 feet.
History: Incorporated 1937.
Population: 5,423 (1990); 5,034 (2000); 5,009 (2010); 4,921 (2015 projected); Race: 56.5% White, 0.8% Black, 0.4% Asian, 42.4% Other, 93.8% Hispanic of any race (2010); Density: 2,519.4 persons per square mile (2010); Average household size: 3.14 (2010); Median age: 31.3 (2010); Males per 100 females: 91.3 (2010); Marriage status: 21.4% never married, 51.6% now married, 10.0% widowed, 17.0% divorced (2005-2009 5-year est.); Foreign born: 3.3% (2005-2009 5-year est.); Ancestry (includes multiple ancestries): 5.0% English, 4.1% German, 3.4% Irish, 0.8% Czech, 0.6% Scotch-Irish (2005-2009 5-year est.).
Economy: Single-family building permits issued: 4 (2010); Multi-family building permits issued: 0 (2010); Employment by occupation: 9.8% management, 11.2% professional, 30.1% services, 11.9% sales, 3.1% farming, 20.9% construction, 13.0% production (2005-2009 5-year est.).
Income: Per capita income: $11,782 (2010); Median household income: $24,561 (2010); Average household income: $36,599 (2010); Percent of households with income of $100,000 or more: 5.8% (2010); Poverty rate: 35.4% (2005-2009 5-year est.).
Taxes: Total city taxes per capita: $253 (2007); City property taxes per capita: $131 (2007).
Education: Percent of population age 25 and over with: High school diploma (including GED) or higher: 52.0% (2010); Bachelor's degree or higher: 7.6% (2010); Master's degree or higher: 0.9% (2010).
School District(s)
Mathis ISD (PK-12)
    2009-10 Enrollment: 1,746 . . . . (361) 547-3378
Housing: Homeownership rate: 64.4% (2010); Median home value: $36,972 (2010); Median contract rent: $359 per month (2005-2009 5-year est.); Median year structure built: 1966 (2005-2009 5-year est.).
Safety: Violent crime rate: 66.2 per 10,000 population; Property crime rate: 431.3 per 10,000 population (2009).
Newspapers: Mathis News (Community news; Circulation 2,000)
Transportation: Commute to work: 86.1% car, 0.0% public transportation, 3.8% walk, 7.9% work from home (2005-2009 5-year est.); Travel time to work: 45.1% less than 15 minutes, 10.6% 15 to 30 minutes, 21.6% 30 to 45 minutes, 19.4% 45 to 60 minutes, 3.3% 60 minutes or more (2005-2009 5-year est.)
Additional Information Contacts
City of Mathis . . . . (361) 547-3343
    http://www.cityofmathis.com
Mathis Area Chamber of Commerce . . . . (361) 547-0289
    http://www.mathischamber.org

MORGAN FARM AREA (CDP). Covers a land area of 3.337 square miles and a water area of 0 square miles. Located at 28.01° N. Lat; 97.54° W. Long. Elevation is 52 feet.
Population: 414 (1990); 484 (2000); 519 (2010); 534 (2015 projected); Race: 70.7% White, 1.3% Black, 0.0% Asian, 27.9% Other, 54.1%

Hispanic of any race (2010); Density: 155.5 persons per square mile (2010); Average household size: 2.90 (2010); Median age: 37.1 (2010); Males per 100 females: 95.1 (2010); Marriage status: 18.0% never married, 71.7% now married, 0.0% widowed, 10.2% divorced (2005-2009 5-year est.); Foreign born: 0.0% (2005-2009 5-year est.); Ancestry (includes multiple ancestries): 34.4% German, 11.1% English, 4.7% Scotch-Irish, 3.8% African, 3.0% Czechoslovakian (2005-2009 5-year est.).
Economy: Employment by occupation: 0.0% management, 27.3% professional, 10.0% services, 46.8% sales, 0.0% farming, 16.0% construction, 0.0% production (2005-2009 5-year est.).
Income: Per capita income: $24,748 (2010); Median household income: $48,250 (2010); Average household income: $72,263 (2010); Percent of households with income of $100,000 or more: 17.3% (2010); Poverty rate: 6.3% (2005-2009 5-year est.).
Education: Percent of population age 25 and over with: High school diploma (including GED) or higher: 70.2% (2010); Bachelor's degree or higher: 10.2% (2010); Master's degree or higher: 0.6% (2010).
Housing: Homeownership rate: 76.5% (2010); Median home value: $73,810 (2010); Median contract rent: n/a per month (2005-2009 5-year est.); Median year structure built: 1983 (2005-2009 5-year est.).
Transportation: Commute to work: 79.7% car, 0.0% public transportation, 0.0% walk, 6.5% work from home (2005-2009 5-year est.); Travel time to work: 26.4% less than 15 minutes, 19.9% 15 to 30 minutes, 50.9% 30 to 45 minutes, 2.8% 45 to 60 minutes, 0.0% 60 minutes or more (2005-2009 5-year est.)

ODEM (city). Covers a land area of 1.113 square miles and a water area of 0 square miles. Located at 27.94° N. Lat; 97.58° W. Long. Elevation is 72 feet.
History: Incorporated as city 1929.
Population: 2,366 (1990); 2,499 (2000); 2,554 (2010); 2,575 (2015 projected); Race: 78.9% White, 0.2% Black, 0.0% Asian, 20.9% Other, 76.2% Hispanic of any race (2010); Density: 2,295.4 persons per square mile (2010); Average household size: 3.03 (2010); Median age: 33.1 (2010); Males per 100 females: 88.6 (2010); Marriage status: 27.1% never married, 58.8% now married, 4.4% widowed, 9.6% divorced (2005-2009 5-year est.); Foreign born: 4.3% (2005-2009 5-year est.); Ancestry (includes multiple ancestries): 6.4% Irish, 5.0% German, 3.5% English, 3.1% American, 1.6% Italian (2005-2009 5-year est.).
Economy: Single-family building permits issued: 0 (2010); Multi-family building permits issued: 0 (2010); Employment by occupation: 6.5% management, 15.9% professional, 14.3% services, 32.4% sales, 1.2% farming, 9.0% construction, 20.7% production (2005-2009 5-year est.).
Income: Per capita income: $15,882 (2010); Median household income: $38,392 (2010); Average household income: $47,752 (2010); Percent of households with income of $100,000 or more: 7.9% (2010); Poverty rate: 16.7% (2005-2009 5-year est.).
Taxes: Total city taxes per capita: $289 (2007); City property taxes per capita: $194 (2007).
Education: Percent of population age 25 and over with: High school diploma (including GED) or higher: 68.0% (2010); Bachelor's degree or higher: 9.0% (2010); Master's degree or higher: 2.0% (2010).
School District(s)
Odem-Edroy ISD (PK-12)
    2009-10 Enrollment: 1,134 . . . . (361) 368-2561
Housing: Homeownership rate: 70.0% (2010); Median home value: $65,684 (2010); Median contract rent: $397 per month (2005-2009 5-year est.); Median year structure built: 1970 (2005-2009 5-year est.).
Transportation: Commute to work: 85.8% car, 0.0% public transportation, 0.9% walk, 0.0% work from home (2005-2009 5-year est.); Travel time to work: 32.3% less than 15 minutes, 38.8% 15 to 30 minutes, 22.3% 30 to 45 minutes, 3.7% 45 to 60 minutes, 2.9% 60 minutes or more (2005-2009 5-year est.)

PORTLAND (city). Covers a land area of 6.976 square miles and a water area of 2.639 square miles. Located at 27.88° N. Lat; 97.32° W. Long. Elevation is 43 feet.
History: Incorporated after 1940.
Population: 12,360 (1990); 14,827 (2000); 16,977 (2010); 17,855 (2015 projected); Race: 79.1% White, 3.8% Black, 1.2% Asian, 15.9% Other, 31.6% Hispanic of any race (2010); Density: 2,433.7 persons per square mile (2010); Average household size: 2.86 (2010); Median age: 35.5 (2010); Males per 100 females: 93.6 (2010); Marriage status: 26.0% never married, 59.6% now married, 5.7% widowed, 8.7% divorced (2005-2009 5-year est.); Foreign born: 3.7% (2005-2009 5-year est.); Ancestry

(includes multiple ancestries): 19.6% German, 13.4% Irish, 8.8% English, 6.6% American, 5.8% French (2005-2009 5-year est.).
Economy: Single-family building permits issued: 48 (2010); Multi-family building permits issued: 0 (2010); Employment by occupation: 13.3% management, 25.3% professional, 16.0% services, 27.0% sales, 0.0% farming, 9.0% construction, 9.3% production (2005-2009 5-year est.).
Income: Per capita income: $25,042 (2010); Median household income: $59,778 (2010); Average household income: $71,786 (2010); Percent of households with income of $100,000 or more: 20.1% (2010); Poverty rate: 8.6% (2005-2009 5-year est.).
Taxes: Total city taxes per capita: $459 (2007); City property taxes per capita: $193 (2007).
Education: Percent of population age 25 and over with: High school diploma (including GED) or higher: 92.2% (2010); Bachelor's degree or higher: 27.9% (2010); Master's degree or higher: 5.7% (2010).

School District(s)

Gregory-Portland ISD (PK-12)
    2009-10 Enrollment: 4,197 . . . . (361) 777-1091
Housing: Homeownership rate: 60.4% (2010); Median home value: $134,248 (2010); Median contract rent: $638 per month (2005-2009 5-year est.); Median year structure built: 1977 (2005-2009 5-year est.).
Safety: Violent crime rate: 10.8 per 10,000 population; Property crime rate: 287.3 per 10,000 population (2009).
Newspapers: Portland News (Community news; Circulation 2,500)
Transportation: Commute to work: 92.8% car, 0.3% public transportation, 1.1% walk, 1.8% work from home (2005-2009 5-year est.); Travel time to work: 33.2% less than 15 minutes, 52.3% 15 to 30 minutes, 11.5% 30 to 45 minutes, 1.0% 45 to 60 minutes, 2.0% 60 minutes or more (2005-2009 5-year est.)

Additional Information Contacts
City of Portland . . . . (361) 777-4500
    http://www.portlandtx.com
Portland Chamber of Commerce . . . . (361) 643-2475
    http://www.portlandtx.org

RANCHO CHICO (CDP). Covers a land area of 0.492 square miles and a water area of 0 square miles. Located at 28.02° N. Lat; 97.49° W. Long. Elevation is 49 feet.
Population: 311 (1990); 309 (2000); 298 (2010); 288 (2015 projected); Race: 82.9% White, 1.3% Black, 0.0% Asian, 15.8% Other, 83.9% Hispanic of any race (2010); Density: 605.5 persons per square mile (2010); Average household size: 3.01 (2010); Median age: 33.6 (2010); Males per 100 females: 98.7 (2010); Marriage status: 50.8% never married, 42.7% now married, 6.5% widowed, 0.0% divorced (2005-2009 5-year est.); Foreign born: 0.0% (2005-2009 5-year est.); Ancestry (includes multiple ancestries): n/a (2005-2009 5-year est.).
Economy: Employment by occupation: 0.0% management, 22.3% professional, 56.2% services, 11.2% sales, 0.0% farming, 0.0% construction, 10.4% production (2005-2009 5-year est.).
Income: Per capita income: $19,604 (2010); Median household income: $39,500 (2010); Average household income: $58,030 (2010); Percent of households with income of $100,000 or more: 15.2% (2010); Poverty rate: 8.4% (2005-2009 5-year est.).
Education: Percent of population age 25 and over with: High school diploma (including GED) or higher: 64.8% (2010); Bachelor's degree or higher: 10.1% (2010); Master's degree or higher: 2.8% (2010).
Housing: Homeownership rate: 72.7% (2010); Median home value: $54,783 (2010); Median contract rent: n/a per month (2005-2009 5-year est.); Median year structure built: 1978 (2005-2009 5-year est.).
Transportation: Commute to work: 89.6% car, 0.0% public transportation, 0.0% walk, 0.0% work from home (2005-2009 5-year est.); Travel time to work: 22.3% less than 15 minutes, 0.0% 15 to 30 minutes, 77.7% 30 to 45 minutes, 0.0% 45 to 60 minutes, 0.0% 60 minutes or more (2005-2009 5-year est.)

SAINT PAUL (CDP). Covers a land area of 3.294 square miles and a water area of 0 square miles. Located at 28.09° N. Lat; 97.55° W. Long. Elevation is 82 feet.
Population: 512 (1990); 542 (2000); 613 (2010); 639 (2015 projected); Race: 72.9% White, 0.2% Black, 0.0% Asian, 26.9% Other, 55.1% Hispanic of any race (2010); Density: 186.1 persons per square mile (2010); Average household size: 2.85 (2010); Median age: 36.8 (2010); Males per 100 females: 97.7 (2010); Marriage status: 22.5% never married, 62.2% now married, 11.0% widowed, 4.2% divorced (2005-2009 5-year est.); Foreign born: 5.6% (2005-2009 5-year est.); Ancestry (includes

multiple ancestries): 9.4% Irish, 8.7% German, 4.1% English, 1.6% Austrian, 0.8% Scottish (2005-2009 5-year est.).
Economy: Employment by occupation: 14.2% management, 1.0% professional, 17.2% services, 28.7% sales, 10.5% farming, 28.4% construction, 0.0% production (2005-2009 5-year est.).
Income: Per capita income: $17,411 (2010); Median household income: $35,300 (2010); Average household income: $49,663 (2010); Percent of households with income of $100,000 or more: 8.8% (2010); Poverty rate: 20.7% (2005-2009 5-year est.).
Education: Percent of population age 25 and over with: High school diploma (including GED) or higher: 72.4% (2010); Bachelor's degree or higher: 12.8% (2010); Master's degree or higher: 3.8% (2010).
Housing: Homeownership rate: 78.1% (2010); Median home value: $64,242 (2010); Median contract rent: $233 per month (2005-2009 5-year est.); Median year structure built: 1980 (2005-2009 5-year est.).
Transportation: Commute to work: 89.2% car, 0.0% public transportation, 10.8% walk, 0.0% work from home (2005-2009 5-year est.); Travel time to work: 34.1% less than 15 minutes, 18.9% 15 to 30 minutes, 45.9% 30 to 45 minutes, 0.0% 45 to 60 minutes, 1.0% 60 minutes or more (2005-2009 5-year est.)

SAN PATRICIO (city). Covers a land area of 3.844 square miles and a water area of 0.041 square miles. Located at 27.95° N. Lat; 97.77° W. Long. Elevation is 43 feet.
History: San Patricio was founded in 1828 by Irish immigrant families under a charter from the Mexican government. The town and the county were named for St. Patrick, the patron saint of Ireland.
Population: 369 (1990); 318 (2000); 294 (2010); 286 (2015 projected); Race: 80.6% White, 0.0% Black, 0.0% Asian, 19.4% Other, 49.3% Hispanic of any race (2010); Density: 76.5 persons per square mile (2010); Average household size: 2.85 (2010); Median age: 39.2 (2010); Males per 100 females: 96.0 (2010); Marriage status: 24.5% never married, 59.9% now married, 3.0% widowed, 12.6% divorced (2005-2009 5-year est.); Foreign born: 0.0% (2005-2009 5-year est.); Ancestry (includes multiple ancestries): 15.8% Irish, 13.2% German, 3.4% Scotch-Irish, 2.6% Norwegian, 2.6% Czech (2005-2009 5-year est.).
Economy: Single-family building permits issued: 0 (2010); Multi-family building permits issued: 0 (2010); Employment by occupation: 14.4% management, 23.4% professional, 15.0% services, 6.6% sales, 0.0% farming, 21.6% construction, 19.2% production (2005-2009 5-year est.).
Income: Per capita income: $20,942 (2010); Median household income: $42,969 (2010); Average household income: $57,306 (2010); Percent of households with income of $100,000 or more: 13.6% (2010); Poverty rate: 23.4% (2005-2009 5-year est.).
Taxes: Total city taxes per capita: $81 (2007); City property taxes per capita: $32 (2007).
Education: Percent of population age 25 and over with: High school diploma (including GED) or higher: 70.4% (2010); Bachelor's degree or higher: 13.2% (2010); Master's degree or higher: 1.6% (2010).
Housing: Homeownership rate: 83.5% (2010); Median home value: $83,333 (2010); Median contract rent: $334 per month (2005-2009 5-year est.); Median year structure built: 1980 (2005-2009 5-year est.).
Transportation: Commute to work: 95.2% car, 0.0% public transportation, 0.0% walk, 4.8% work from home (2005-2009 5-year est.); Travel time to work: 12.6% less than 15 minutes, 23.3% 15 to 30 minutes, 8.8% 30 to 45 minutes, 40.3% 45 to 60 minutes, 15.1% 60 minutes or more (2005-2009 5-year est.)

SINTON (city). County seat. Covers a land area of 2.198 square miles and a water area of 0 square miles. Located at 28.03° N. Lat; 97.50° W. Long. Elevation is 49 feet.
History: Sinton was laid out in 1893 and named for David Sinton, a Cincinnati investor and the father-in-law of Charles P. Taft, who owned land here.
Population: 5,549 (1990); 5,676 (2000); 5,390 (2010); 5,310 (2015 projected); Race: 76.6% White, 1.6% Black, 0.0% Asian, 21.8% Other, 78.2% Hispanic of any race (2010); Density: 2,451.9 persons per square mile (2010); Average household size: 2.77 (2010); Median age: 34.2 (2010); Males per 100 females: 93.4 (2010); Marriage status: 34.2% never married, 48.2% now married, 7.4% widowed, 10.2% divorced (2005-2009 5-year est.); Foreign born: 1.8% (2005-2009 5-year est.); Ancestry (includes multiple ancestries): 5.5% Irish, 4.0% German, 2.7% American, 2.3% French, 2.1% English (2005-2009 5-year est.).
Economy: Single-family building permits issued: 6 (2010); Multi-family building permits issued: 0 (2010); Employment by occupation: 5.6%

management, 32.5% professional, 20.9% services, 17.4% sales, 5.1% farming, 3.1% construction, 15.4% production (2005-2009 5-year est.).
Income: Per capita income: $18,151 (2010); Median household income: $33,774 (2010); Average household income: $50,792 (2010); Percent of households with income of $100,000 or more: 10.7% (2010); Poverty rate: 25.6% (2005-2009 5-year est.).
Taxes: Total city taxes per capita: $269 (2007); City property taxes per capita: $138 (2007).
Education: Percent of population age 25 and over with: High school diploma (including GED) or higher: 63.9% (2010); Bachelor's degree or higher: 10.5% (2010); Master's degree or higher: 2.0% (2010).

School District(s)
Sinton ISD (PK-12)
    2009-10 Enrollment: 2,125 . . . . (361) 364-6800
Housing: Homeownership rate: 58.0% (2010); Median home value: $59,500 (2010); Median contract rent: $364 per month (2005-2009 5-year est.); Median year structure built: 1958 (2005-2009 5-year est.).
Safety: Violent crime rate: 47.0 per 10,000 population; Property crime rate: 274.4 per 10,000 population (2009).
Newspapers: Odem Edroy Times (Local news; Circulation 600); San Patricio County News (Community news; Circulation 2,500)
Transportation: Commute to work: 92.9% car, 0.0% public transportation, 2.8% walk, 2.1% work from home (2005-2009 5-year est.); Travel time to work: 47.4% less than 15 minutes, 22.6% 15 to 30 minutes, 18.7% 30 to 45 minutes, 10.9% 45 to 60 minutes, 0.4% 60 minutes or more (2005-2009 5-year est.)
Additional Information Contacts
City of Sinton . . . . (361) 364-2381
   http://www.sintontexas.org
Sinton Chamber of Commerce . . . . (361) 364-2307
   http://www.sintontexas.org

TAFT (city). Covers a land area of 1.499 square miles and a water area of 0 square miles. Located at 27.97° N. Lat; 97.39° W. Long. Elevation is 49 feet.
History: Taft was named for Charles P. Taft, half-brother of U.S. President William Howard Taft.
Population: 3,222 (1990); 3,396 (2000); 3,325 (2010); 3,302 (2015 projected); Race: 68.5% White, 1.2% Black, 0.0% Asian, 30.3% Other, 75.2% Hispanic of any race (2010); Density: 2,218.7 persons per square mile (2010); Average household size: 2.94 (2010); Median age: 32.5 (2010); Males per 100 females: 95.1 (2010); Marriage status: 33.1% never married, 50.3% now married, 4.8% widowed, 11.8% divorced (2005-2009 5-year est.); Foreign born: 1.1% (2005-2009 5-year est.); Ancestry (includes multiple ancestries): 7.2% German, 4.5% Irish, 2.8% American, 2.0% English, 1.3% French (2005-2009 5-year est.).
Economy: Single-family building permits issued: 0 (2010); Multi-family building permits issued: 0 (2010); Employment by occupation: 6.7% management, 13.7% professional, 22.8% services, 23.4% sales, 1.1% farming, 13.7% construction, 18.6% production (2005-2009 5-year est.).
Income: Per capita income: $16,825 (2010); Median household income: $36,582 (2010); Average household income: $50,441 (2010); Percent of households with income of $100,000 or more: 11.0% (2010); Poverty rate: 25.6% (2005-2009 5-year est.).
Taxes: Total city taxes per capita: $64 (2007); City property taxes per capita: $64 (2007).
Education: Percent of population age 25 and over with: High school diploma (including GED) or higher: 66.3% (2010); Bachelor's degree or higher: 9.9% (2010); Master's degree or higher: 2.2% (2010).

School District(s)
Erath Excels Academy Inc (07-12)
    2009-10 Enrollment: 159 . . . . (254) 965-8883
Taft ISD (PK-12)
    2009-10 Enrollment: 1,148 . . . . (361) 528-2636
Housing: Homeownership rate: 63.8% (2010); Median home value: $58,743 (2010); Median contract rent: $330 per month (2005-2009 5-year est.); Median year structure built: 1958 (2005-2009 5-year est.).
Safety: Violent crime rate: 60.0 per 10,000 population; Property crime rate: 285.2 per 10,000 population (2009).
Newspapers: Taft Tribune (Community news; Circulation 1,200)
Transportation: Commute to work: 90.8% car, 0.0% public transportation, 1.6% walk, 0.0% work from home (2005-2009 5-year est.); Travel time to work: 35.6% less than 15 minutes, 32.6% 15 to 30 minutes, 21.0% 30 to 45 minutes, 5.7% 45 to 60 minutes, 5.0% 60 minutes or more (2005-2009 5-year est.)

Additional Information Contacts
Taft Chamber of Commerce . . . . (361) 528-3230

TAFT SOUTHWEST (CDP). Covers a land area of 0.605 square miles and a water area of 0 square miles. Located at 27.97° N. Lat; 97.40° W. Long. Elevation is 52 feet.
Population: 1,958 (1990); 1,721 (2000); 1,649 (2010); 1,609 (2015 projected); Race: 70.7% White, 0.7% Black, 0.0% Asian, 28.6% Other, 93.6% Hispanic of any race (2010); Density: 2,726.2 persons per square mile (2010); Average household size: 3.30 (2010); Median age: 31.3 (2010); Males per 100 females: 91.5 (2010); Marriage status: 26.2% never married, 54.8% now married, 14.6% widowed, 4.3% divorced (2005-2009 5-year est.); Foreign born: 0.7% (2005-2009 5-year est.); Ancestry (includes multiple ancestries): 5.6% American, 0.5% German (2005-2009 5-year est.).
Economy: Employment by occupation: 1.3% management, 0.0% professional, 35.0% services, 20.1% sales, 3.2% farming, 21.2% construction, 19.2% production (2005-2009 5-year est.).
Income: Per capita income: $11,321 (2010); Median household income: $22,786 (2010); Average household income: $37,249 (2010); Percent of households with income of $100,000 or more: 4.4% (2010); Poverty rate: 11.2% (2005-2009 5-year est.).
Education: Percent of population age 25 and over with: High school diploma (including GED) or higher: 47.2% (2010); Bachelor's degree or higher: 2.6% (2010); Master's degree or higher: 0.4% (2010).
Housing: Homeownership rate: 73.1% (2010); Median home value: $40,680 (2010); Median contract rent: $503 per month (2005-2009 5-year est.); Median year structure built: 1967 (2005-2009 5-year est.).
Transportation: Commute to work: 77.9% car, 0.0% public transportation, 0.0% walk, 1.9% work from home (2005-2009 5-year est.); Travel time to work: 23.8% less than 15 minutes, 31.3% 15 to 30 minutes, 30.1% 30 to 45 minutes, 5.4% 45 to 60 minutes, 9.4% 60 minutes or more (2005-2009 5-year est.)

TRADEWINDS (CDP). Covers a land area of 1.079 square miles and a water area of 0 square miles. Located at 27.99° N. Lat; 97.26° W. Long. Elevation is 20 feet.
Population: 112 (1990); 163 (2000); 167 (2010); 168 (2015 projected); Race: 86.8% White, 0.0% Black, 0.6% Asian, 12.6% Other, 58.7% Hispanic of any race (2010); Density: 154.8 persons per square mile (2010); Average household size: 2.98 (2010); Median age: 38.2 (2010); Males per 100 females: 85.6 (2010); Marriage status: 32.3% never married, 67.7% now married, 0.0% widowed, 0.0% divorced (2005-2009 5-year est.); Foreign born: 0.0% (2005-2009 5-year est.); Ancestry (includes multiple ancestries): 50.6% American, 36.4% French, 13.0% Cajun, 11.1% Swedish (2005-2009 5-year est.).
Economy: Employment by occupation: 27.7% management, 0.0% professional, 38.5% services, 0.0% sales, 0.0% farming, 0.0% construction, 33.8% production (2005-2009 5-year est.).
Income: Per capita income: $18,313 (2010); Median household income: $38,750 (2010); Average household income: $49,955 (2010); Percent of households with income of $100,000 or more: 14.3% (2010); Poverty rate: 0.0% (2005-2009 5-year est.).
Education: Percent of population age 25 and over with: High school diploma (including GED) or higher: 70.1% (2010); Bachelor's degree or higher: 13.1% (2010); Master's degree or higher: 2.8% (2010).
Housing: Homeownership rate: 71.4% (2010); Median home value: $86,000 (2010); Median contract rent: n/a per month (2005-2009 5-year est.); Median year structure built: 1944 (2005-2009 5-year est.).
Transportation: Commute to work: 100.0% car, 0.0% public transportation, 0.0% walk, 0.0% work from home (2005-2009 5-year est.); Travel time to work: 33.8% less than 15 minutes, 0.0% 15 to 30 minutes, 66.2% 30 to 45 minutes, 0.0% 45 to 60 minutes, 0.0% 60 minutes or more (2005-2009 5-year est.)

San Saba County

Located in central Texas, on the Edwards Plateau; bounded on the north and east by the Colorado River; drained by the San Saba River; includes part of Lake Buchanan. Covers a land area of 1,134.47 square miles, a water area of 3.78 square miles, and is located in the Central Time Zone at 31.16° N. Lat., 98.80° W. Long. The county was founded in 1856. County seat is San Saba.
Population: 5,401 (1990); 6,186 (2000); 5,969 (2010); 5,852 (2015 projected); Race: 81.7% White, 3.2% Black, 0.1% Asian, 15.0% Other,

25.7% Hispanic of any race (2010); Density: 5.3 persons per square mile (2010); Average household size: 2.46 (2010); Median age: 38.8 (2010); Males per 100 females: 110.4 (2010).
Religion: Five largest groups: 42.5% Southern Baptist Convention, 7.3% Churches of Christ, 4.8% The United Methodist Church, 3.9% Catholic Church, 2.7% Presbyterian Church (U.S.A.) (2000).
Economy: Unemployment rate: 9.3% (June 2011); Total civilian labor force: 2,340 (June 2011); Leading industries: 27.4% retail trade; 17.1% wholesale trade; 8.4% accommodation & food services (2009); Farms: 725 totaling 717,799 acres (2007); Companies that employ 500 or more persons: 0 (2009); Companies that employ 100 to 499 persons: 0 (2009); Companies that employ less than 100 persons: 149 (2009); Black-owned businesses: n/a (2007); Hispanic-owned businesses: n/a (2007); Asian-owned businesses: n/a (2007); Women-owned businesses: n/a (2007); Retail sales per capita: $15,221 (2010). Single-family building permits issued: 0 (2010); Multi-family building permits issued: 0 (2010).
Income: Per capita income: $19,722 (2010); Median household income: $39,346 (2010); Average household income: $52,136 (2010); Percent of households with income of $100,000 or more: 9.7% (2010); Poverty rate: 21.5% (2009); Bankruptcy rate: 0.32% (2010).
Taxes: Total county taxes per capita: $355 (2007); County property taxes per capita: $219 (2007).
Education: Percent of population age 25 and over with: High school diploma (including GED) or higher: 74.9% (2010); Bachelor's degree or higher: 17.5% (2010); Master's degree or higher: 5.4% (2010).
Housing: Homeownership rate: 73.9% (2010); Median home value: $73,318 (2010); Median contract rent: $280 per month (2005-2009 5-year est.); Median year structure built: 1968 (2005-2009 5-year est.)
Health: Birth rate: 122.6 per 10,000 population (2009); Death rate: 117.5 per 10,000 population (2009); Age-adjusted cancer mortality rate: 192.9 (Unreliable) deaths per 100,000 population (2007); Number of physicians: 3.4 per 10,000 population (2008); Hospital beds: 0.0 per 10,000 population (2007); Hospital admissions: 0.0 per 10,000 population (2007).
Elections: 2008 Presidential election results: 19.8% Obama, 79.0% McCain, 0.0% Nader
Additional Information Contacts
San Saba County Government . . . . (325) 372-3635
    http://www.co.san-saba.tx.us/ips/cms
City of San Saba . . . . (325) 372-5144
    http://www.sansabatexas.com/directory.htm
San Saba Chamber of Commerce. . . . . (325) 372-5141
    http://www.sansabachamber.com

San Saba County Communities

BEND (unincorporated postal area, zip code 76824). Covers a land area of 41.783 square miles and a water area of 0.012 square miles. Located at 31.08° N. Lat; 98.51° W. Long. Elevation is 1,119 feet.
Population: 80 (2000); Race: 100.0% White, 0.0% Black, 0.0% Asian, 0.0% Other, 0.0% Hispanic of any race (2000); Density: 1.9 persons per square mile (2000); Age: 16.5% under 18, 13.2% over 64 (2000); Marriage status: 15.8% never married, 76.3% now married, 7.9% widowed, 0.0% divorced (2000); Foreign born: 0.0% (2000); Ancestry (includes multiple ancestries): 25.3% Scottish, 24.2% German, 18.7% Scotch-Irish, 17.6% English (2000).
Economy: Employment by occupation: 17.7% management, 51.6% professional, 3.2% services, 16.1% sales, 0.0% farming, 11.3% construction, 0.0% production (2000).
Income: Per capita income: $31,425 (2000); Median household income: $50,667 (2000); Poverty rate: 179.1% (2000).
Education: Percent of population age 25 and over with: High school diploma (including GED) or higher: 91.4% (2000); Bachelor's degree or higher: 42.9% (2000).
Housing: Homeownership rate: 92.7% (2000); Median home value: n/a (2000); Median contract rent: n/a per month (2000); Median year structure built: 1973 (2000).
Transportation: Commute to work: 100.0% car, 0.0% public transportation, 0.0% walk, 0.0% work from home (2000); Travel time to work: 21.0% less than 15 minutes, 45.2% 15 to 30 minutes, 21.0% 30 to 45 minutes, 0.0% 45 to 60 minutes, 12.9% 60 minutes or more (2000)

CHEROKEE (unincorporated postal area, zip code 76832). Covers a land area of 255.014 square miles and a water area of 0.049 square miles. Located at 30.98° N. Lat; 98.67° W. Long. Elevation is 1,496 feet.

Population: 645 (2000); Race: 83.9% White, 1.3% Black, 0.0% Asian, 14.8% Other, 11.6% Hispanic of any race (2000); Density: 2.5 persons per square mile (2000); Age: 29.7% under 18, 16.2% over 64 (2000); Marriage status: 13.2% never married, 69.8% now married, 7.8% widowed, 9.3% divorced (2000); Foreign born: 7.4% (2000); Ancestry (includes multiple ancestries): 22.2% American, 14.0% German, 8.8% English, 8.5% Irish (2000).
Economy: Employment by occupation: 18.4% management, 20.3% professional, 10.9% services, 26.2% sales, 10.5% farming, 4.7% construction, 9.0% production (2000).
Income: Per capita income: $19,703 (2000); Median household income: $31,875 (2000); Poverty rate: 179.1% (2000).
Education: Percent of population age 25 and over with: High school diploma (including GED) or higher: 75.3% (2000); Bachelor's degree or higher: 17.2% (2000).

School District(s)
Cherokee ISD (KG-12)
    2009-10 Enrollment: 121 . . . . (325) 622-4298
Housing: Homeownership rate: 74.0% (2000); Median home value: $64,700 (2000); Median contract rent: $275 per month (2000); Median year structure built: 1959 (2000).
Transportation: Commute to work: 86.7% car, 0.0% public transportation, 7.0% walk, 6.3% work from home (2000); Travel time to work: 37.9% less than 15 minutes, 31.3% 15 to 30 minutes, 13.8% 30 to 45 minutes, 6.7% 45 to 60 minutes, 10.4% 60 minutes or more (2000)

RICHLAND SPRINGS (town). Covers a land area of 1.004 square miles and a water area of 0 square miles. Located at 31.27° N. Lat; 98.94° W. Long. Elevation is 1,407 feet.
Population: 344 (1990); 350 (2000); 332 (2010); 322 (2015 projected); Race: 93.4% White, 0.0% Black, 0.0% Asian, 6.6% Other, 14.8% Hispanic of any race (2010); Density: 330.7 persons per square mile (2010); Average household size: 2.32 (2010); Median age: 49.3 (2010); Males per 100 females: 108.8 (2010); Marriage status: 32.4% never married, 51.8% now married, 9.7% widowed, 6.2% divorced (2005-2009 5-year est.); Foreign born: 1.4% (2005-2009 5-year est.); Ancestry (includes multiple ancestries): 24.4% English, 20.6% Irish, 13.3% German, 10.7% American, 6.3% Scotch-Irish (2005-2009 5-year est.).
Economy: Employment by occupation: 6.9% management, 6.9% professional, 15.4% services, 21.5% sales, 0.0% farming, 23.8% construction, 25.4% production (2005-2009 5-year est.).
Income: Per capita income: $22,040 (2010); Median household income: $42,500 (2010); Average household income: $52,168 (2010); Percent of households with income of $100,000 or more: 10.5% (2010); Poverty rate: 42.6% (2005-2009 5-year est.).
Taxes: Total city taxes per capita: $176 (2007); City property taxes per capita: $110 (2007).
Education: Percent of population age 25 and over with: High school diploma (including GED) or higher: 82.3% (2010); Bachelor's degree or higher: 24.2% (2010); Master's degree or higher: 6.0% (2010).

School District(s)
Richland Springs ISD (PK-12)
    2009-10 Enrollment: 151 . . . . (325) 452-3524
Housing: Homeownership rate: 78.3% (2010); Median home value: $97,143 (2010); Median contract rent: $225 per month (2005-2009 5-year est.); Median year structure built: 1947 (2005-2009 5-year est.).
Transportation: Commute to work: 96.9% car, 0.0% public transportation, 3.1% walk, 0.0% work from home (2005-2009 5-year est.); Travel time to work: 26.6% less than 15 minutes, 31.3% 15 to 30 minutes, 32.8% 30 to 45 minutes, 3.1% 45 to 60 minutes, 6.3% 60 minutes or more (2005-2009 5-year est.)

SAN SABA (town). County seat. Covers a land area of 1.796 square miles and a water area of 0 square miles. Located at 31.19° N. Lat; 98.72° W. Long. Elevation is 1,204 feet.
History: Settled 1854.
Population: 2,645 (1990); 2,637 (2000); 2,579 (2010); 2,553 (2015 projected); Race: 74.3% White, 1.3% Black, 0.2% Asian, 24.2% Other, 33.3% Hispanic of any race (2010); Density: 1,436.3 persons per square mile (2010); Average household size: 2.55 (2010); Median age: 38.7 (2010); Males per 100 females: 90.3 (2010); Marriage status: 17.6% never married, 49.4% now married, 15.5% widowed, 17.5% divorced (2005-2009 5-year est.); Foreign born: 8.2% (2005-2009 5-year est.); Ancestry (includes multiple ancestries): 15.8% Irish, 13.5% German, 11.4% English, 10.8% American, 2.3% Scottish (2005-2009 5-year est.).

Economy: Single-family building permits issued: 0 (2010); Multi-family building permits issued: 0 (2010); Employment by occupation: 11.1% management, 7.9% professional, 22.7% services, 28.8% sales, 7.3% farming, 3.9% construction, 18.3% production (2005-2009 5-year est.).
Income: Per capita income: $18,301 (2010); Median household income: $36,968 (2010); Average household income: $48,949 (2010); Percent of households with income of $100,000 or more: 8.0% (2010); Poverty rate: 29.3% (2005-2009 5-year est.).
Taxes: Total city taxes per capita: $112 (2007); City property taxes per capita: $91 (2007).
Education: Percent of population age 25 and over with: High school diploma (including GED) or higher: 68.3% (2010); Bachelor's degree or higher: 13.3% (2010); Master's degree or higher: 5.4% (2010).

School District(s)
San Saba ISD (PK-12)
    2009-10 Enrollment: 683 . . . . (325) 372-3771
Housing: Homeownership rate: 72.8% (2010); Median home value: $58,598 (2010); Median contract rent: $213 per month (2005-2009 5-year est.); Median year structure built: 1963 (2005-2009 5-year est.).
Safety: Violent crime rate: 8.1 per 10,000 population; Property crime rate: 108.8 per 10,000 population (2009).
Newspapers: San Saba News & Star (Local news; Circulation 2,800)
Transportation: Commute to work: 91.4% car, 0.0% public transportation, 5.9% walk, 2.0% work from home (2005-2009 5-year est.); Travel time to work: 69.1% less than 15 minutes, 15.2% 15 to 30 minutes, 4.4% 30 to 45 minutes, 10.0% 45 to 60 minutes, 1.4% 60 minutes or more (2005-2009 5-year est.)
Airports: San Saba County Municipal (general aviation)
Additional Information Contacts
City of San Saba . . . . (325) 372-5144
    http://www.sansabatexas.com/directory.htm
San Saba Chamber of Commerce . . . . (325) 372-5141
    http://www.sansabachamber.com

Schleicher County

Located in west Texas, on the Edwards Plateau. Covers a land area of 1,310.61 square miles, a water area of 0.04 square miles, and is located in the Central Time Zone at 30.87° N. Lat., 100.47° W. Long. The county was founded in 1887. County seat is Eldorado.
Population: 2,990 (1990); 2,935 (2000); 2,918 (2010); 2,905 (2015 projected); Race: 73.5% White, 1.9% Black, 0.2% Asian, 24.4% Other, 49.2% Hispanic of any race (2010); Density: 2.2 persons per square mile (2010); Average household size: 2.47 (2010); Median age: 41.3 (2010); Males per 100 females: 97.4 (2010).
Religion: Five largest groups: 26.2% Southern Baptist Convention, 14.7% Catholic Church, 10.2% The United Methodist Church, 4.4% Presbyterian Church (U.S.A.), 3.4% Churches of Christ (2000).
Economy: Unemployment rate: 6.7% (June 2011); Total civilian labor force: 1,497 (June 2011); Leading industries: 22.0% mining; 14.4% retail trade; 6.0% other services (except public administration) (2009); Farms: 332 totaling 800,596 acres (2007); Companies that employ 500 or more persons: 0 (2009); Companies that employ 100 to 499 persons: 0 (2009); Companies that employ less than 100 persons: 58 (2009); Black-owned businesses: n/a (2007); Hispanic-owned businesses: n/a (2007); Asian-owned businesses: n/a (2007); Women-owned businesses: n/a (2007); Retail sales per capita: $2,271 (2010). Single-family building permits issued: 0 (2010); Multi-family building permits issued: 0 (2010).
Income: Per capita income: $22,988 (2010); Median household income: $43,835 (2010); Average household income: $57,031 (2010); Percent of households with income of $100,000 or more: 14.1% (2010); Poverty rate: 15.4% (2009); Bankruptcy rate: 0.87% (2010).
Taxes: Total county taxes per capita: $865 (2007); County property taxes per capita: $702 (2007).
Education: Percent of population age 25 and over with: High school diploma (including GED) or higher: 66.3% (2010); Bachelor's degree or higher: 20.0% (2010); Master's degree or higher: 4.1% (2010).
Housing: Homeownership rate: 73.9% (2010); Median home value: $62,553 (2010); Median contract rent: $384 per month (2005-2009 5-year est.); Median year structure built: 1966 (2005-2009 5-year est.)
Health: Birth rate: 153.8 per 10,000 population (2009); Death rate: 65.9 per 10,000 population (2009); Age-adjusted cancer mortality rate: 166.9 (Unreliable) deaths per 100,000 population (2007); Number of physicians: 7.3 per 10,000 population (2008); Hospital beds: 51.0 per 10,000

population (2007); Hospital admissions: 393.3 per 10,000 population (2007).
Elections: 2008 Presidential election results: 24.8% Obama, 74.4% McCain, 0.0% Nader
Additional Information Contacts
Schleicher County Government . . . . (325) 853-2766
    http://www.co.schleicher.tx.us/ips/cms
Eldorado Chamber of Commerce . . . . (325) 650-9553
    http://www.eldoradotexas.us

Schleicher County Communities

ELDORADO (city). County seat. Covers a land area of 1.386 square miles and a water area of 0 square miles. Located at 30.86° N. Lat; 100.59° W. Long. Elevation is 2,438 feet.
History: Eldorado began as a stage station known as Verand, located in an area called Vermont Pasture. When the town was moved to higher land in 1895, it was renamed El Dorado. The town's slogan was "High - Healthy - Hospitable."
Population: 2,019 (1990); 1,951 (2000); 1,920 (2010); 1,902 (2015 projected); Race: 67.7% White, 2.6% Black, 0.3% Asian, 29.5% Other, 59.5% Hispanic of any race (2010); Density: 1,385.2 persons per square mile (2010); Average household size: 2.56 (2010); Median age: 38.5 (2010); Males per 100 females: 95.5 (2010); Marriage status: 17.5% never married, 62.7% now married, 9.9% widowed, 10.0% divorced (2005-2009 5-year est.); Foreign born: 14.3% (2005-2009 5-year est.); Ancestry (includes multiple ancestries): 13.2% American, 12.9% English, 10.8% German, 7.6% Irish, 1.8% Scotch-Irish (2005-2009 5-year est.).
Economy: Single-family building permits issued: 0 (2010); Multi-family building permits issued: 0 (2010); Employment by occupation: 11.8% management, 23.6% professional, 17.8% services, 11.1% sales, 2.4% farming, 22.4% construction, 11.0% production (2005-2009 5-year est.).
Income: Per capita income: $19,372 (2010); Median household income: $41,069 (2010); Average household income: $49,980 (2010); Percent of households with income of $100,000 or more: 9.5% (2010); Poverty rate: 22.5% (2005-2009 5-year est.).
Taxes: Total city taxes per capita: $205 (2007); City property taxes per capita: $114 (2007).
Education: Percent of population age 25 and over with: High school diploma (including GED) or higher: 63.8% (2010); Bachelor's degree or higher: 13.8% (2010); Master's degree or higher: 3.3% (2010).

School District(s)
Schleicher ISD (PK-12)
    2009-10 Enrollment: 634 . . . . (325) 853-2514
Housing: Homeownership rate: 74.4% (2010); Median home value: $50,417 (2010); Median contract rent: $373 per month (2005-2009 5-year est.); Median year structure built: 1964 (2005-2009 5-year est.).
Hospitals: Schleicher County Medical Center (16 beds)
Newspapers: Eldorado Success (Community news; Circulation 1,300)
Transportation: Commute to work: 92.8% car, 0.0% public transportation, 4.5% walk, 0.8% work from home (2005-2009 5-year est.); Travel time to work: 59.3% less than 15 minutes, 18.4% 15 to 30 minutes, 8.7% 30 to 45 minutes, 4.9% 45 to 60 minutes, 8.6% 60 minutes or more (2005-2009 5-year est.)
Additional Information Contacts
Eldorado Chamber of Commerce . . . . (325) 650-9553
    http://www.eldoradotexas.us

Scurry County

Located in northwest central Texas; plains area, drained by the Colorado River. Covers a land area of 902.50 square miles, a water area of 5.03 square miles, and is located in the Central Time Zone at 32.69° N. Lat., 100.96° W. Long. The county was founded in 1876. County seat is Snyder.

Scurry County is part of the Snyder, TX Micropolitan Statistical Area. The entire metro area includes: Scurry County, TX

Weather Station: Snyder   Elevation: 2,334 feet

	Jan	Feb	Mar	Apr	May	Jun	Jul	Aug	Sep	Oct	Nov	Dec
High	56	59	68	77	85	91	94	93	86	77	66	56
Low	28	32	39	47	58	66	70	69	61	50	38	29
Precip	0.8	1.2	1.4	1.6	3.0	3.4	1.8	2.2	2.5	2.3	1.2	1.0
Snow	tr	0.3	0.0	tr	0.0	0.0	0.0	0.0	0.0	0.0	0.3	0.7

High and Low temperatures in degrees Fahrenheit; Precipitation and Snow in inches

Population: 18,634 (1990); 16,361 (2000); 16,277 (2010); 16,206 (2015 projected); Race: 77.7% White, 6.2% Black, 0.5% Asian, 15.6% Other, 34.7% Hispanic of any race (2010); Density: 18.0 persons per square mile (2010); Average household size: 2.46 (2010); Median age: 35.2 (2010); Males per 100 females: 112.2 (2010).
Religion: Five largest groups: 36.6% Southern Baptist Convention, 16.5% Catholic Church, 8.3% The United Methodist Church, 7.1% Churches of Christ, 2.8% The American Baptist Association (2000).
Economy: Unemployment rate: 6.9% (June 2011); Total civilian labor force: 8,172 (June 2011); Leading industries: 18.6% mining; 14.5% accommodation & food services; 12.6% retail trade (2009); Farms: 681 totaling 519,550 acres (2007); Companies that employ 500 or more persons: 0 (2009); Companies that employ 100 to 499 persons: 9 (2009); Companies that employ less than 100 persons: 413 (2009); Black-owned businesses: n/a (2007); Hispanic-owned businesses: 179 (2007); Asian-owned businesses: n/a (2007); Women-owned businesses: 259 (2007); Retail sales per capita: $12,068 (2010). Single-family building permits issued: 50 (2010); Multi-family building permits issued: 34 (2010).
Income: Per capita income: $22,458 (2010); Median household income: $45,385 (2010); Average household income: $59,997 (2010); Percent of households with income of $100,000 or more: 13.5% (2010); Poverty rate: 17.0% (2009); Bankruptcy rate: 1.00% (2010).
Taxes: Total county taxes per capita: $615 (2007); County property taxes per capita: $376 (2007).
Education: Percent of population age 25 and over with: High school diploma (including GED) or higher: 77.4% (2010); Bachelor's degree or higher: 13.0% (2010); Master's degree or higher: 4.7% (2010).
Housing: Homeownership rate: 71.9% (2010); Median home value: $53,635 (2010); Median contract rent: $364 per month (2005-2009 5-year est.); Median year structure built: 1963 (2005-2009 5-year est.)
Health: Birth rate: 152.3 per 10,000 population (2009); Death rate: 97.4 per 10,000 population (2009); Age-adjusted cancer mortality rate: 126.9 deaths per 100,000 population (2007); Number of physicians: 6.9 per 10,000 population (2008); Hospital beds: 45.5 per 10,000 population (2007); Hospital admissions: 793.1 per 10,000 population (2007).
Elections: 2008 Presidential election results: 19.5% Obama, 79.3% McCain, 0.0% Nader
Additional Information Contacts
Scurry County Government . . . . (325) 573-8576
   http://www.co.scurry.tx.us/ips/cms
City of Snyder . . . . (325) 573-4957
   http://ci.snyder.tx.us
Snyder Chamber of Commerce . . . . (325) 573-3558
   http://snyderchamber.org

Scurry County Communities

FLUVANNA (unincorporated postal area, zip code 79517). Covers a land area of 184.418 square miles and a water area of 0.359 square miles. Located at 32.88° N. Lat; 101.20° W. Long. Elevation is 2,674 feet.
Population: 183 (2000); Race: 86.2% White, 0.0% Black, 0.0% Asian, 13.8% Other, 13.8% Hispanic of any race (2000); Density: 1.0 persons per square mile (2000); Age: 25.0% under 18, 19.9% over 64 (2000); Marriage status: 10.9% never married, 81.6% now married, 5.4% widowed, 2.0% divorced (2000); Foreign born: 4.6% (2000); Ancestry (includes multiple ancestries): 25.0% Irish, 11.7% American, 9.2% English, 2.6% Scotch-Irish (2000).
Economy: Employment by occupation: 50.7% management, 12.3% professional, 16.4% services, 4.1% sales, 0.0% farming, 8.2% construction, 8.2% production (2000).
Income: Per capita income: $14,402 (2000); Median household income: $29,583 (2000); Poverty rate: 179.1% (2000).
Education: Percent of population age 25 and over with: High school diploma (including GED) or higher: 74.0% (2000); Bachelor's degree or higher: 7.6% (2000).
Housing: Homeownership rate: 76.1% (2000); Median home value: $18,800 (2000); Median contract rent: n/a per month (2000); Median year structure built: 1956 (2000).
Transportation: Commute to work: 88.6% car, 0.0% public transportation, 0.0% walk, 11.4% work from home (2000); Travel time to work: 59.7% less than 15 minutes, 32.3% 15 to 30 minutes, 8.1% 30 to 45 minutes, 0.0% 45 to 60 minutes, 0.0% 60 minutes or more (2000)

HERMLEIGH (CDP). Covers a land area of 9.062 square miles and a water area of 0 square miles. Located at 32.63° N. Lat; 100.75° W. Long. Elevation is 2,441 feet.
Population: 470 (1990); 393 (2000); 408 (2010); 415 (2015 projected); Race: 91.2% White, 1.5% Black, 0.0% Asian, 7.4% Other, 21.8% Hispanic of any race (2010); Density: 45.0 persons per square mile (2010); Average household size: 2.43 (2010); Median age: 38.7 (2010); Males per 100 females: 103.0 (2010); Marriage status: 12.9% never married, 72.3% now married, 10.3% widowed, 4.5% divorced (2005-2009 5-year est.); Foreign born: 0.0% (2005-2009 5-year est.); Ancestry (includes multiple ancestries): 14.6% Irish, 9.4% American, 7.8% English, 7.5% German, 2.4% Italian (2005-2009 5-year est.).
Economy: Employment by occupation: 12.7% management, 20.2% professional, 10.4% services, 27.2% sales, 0.0% farming, 17.9% construction, 11.6% production (2005-2009 5-year est.).
Income: Per capita income: $24,235 (2010); Median household income: $45,385 (2010); Average household income: $56,756 (2010); Percent of households with income of $100,000 or more: 14.3% (2010); Poverty rate: 21.3% (2005-2009 5-year est.).
Education: Percent of population age 25 and over with: High school diploma (including GED) or higher: 76.0% (2010); Bachelor's degree or higher: 13.1% (2010); Master's degree or higher: 4.0% (2010).
School District(s)
Hermleigh ISD (PK-12)
   2009-10 Enrollment: 221 . . . . (325) 863-2772
Housing: Homeownership rate: 75.6% (2010); Median home value: $49,545 (2010); Median contract rent: $280 per month (2005-2009 5-year est.); Median year structure built: 1959 (2005-2009 5-year est.).
Transportation: Commute to work: 94.0% car, 0.0% public transportation, 0.0% walk, 2.4% work from home (2005-2009 5-year est.); Travel time to work: 30.7% less than 15 minutes, 55.8% 15 to 30 minutes, 12.9% 30 to 45 minutes, 0.6% 45 to 60 minutes, 0.0% 60 minutes or more (2005-2009 5-year est.)

IRA (unincorporated postal area, zip code 79527). Covers a land area of 44.523 square miles and a water area of 0.006 square miles. Located at 32.58° N. Lat; 101.06° W. Long. Elevation is 2,270 feet.
Population: 271 (2000); Race: 97.2% White, 0.0% Black, 0.0% Asian, 2.8% Other, 15.5% Hispanic of any race (2000); Density: 6.1 persons per square mile (2000); Age: 27.5% under 18, 11.2% over 64 (2000); Marriage status: 14.7% never married, 66.3% now married, 7.4% widowed, 11.6% divorced (2000); Foreign born: 5.2% (2000); Ancestry (includes multiple ancestries): 19.1% American, 17.5% Irish, 15.5% German, 10.4% English (2000).
Economy: Employment by occupation: 20.2% management, 31.5% professional, 4.5% services, 16.9% sales, 0.0% farming, 9.0% construction, 18.0% production (2000).
Income: Per capita income: $13,880 (2000); Median household income: $31,042 (2000); Poverty rate: 179.1% (2000).
Education: Percent of population age 25 and over with: High school diploma (including GED) or higher: 81.0% (2000); Bachelor's degree or higher: 19.7% (2000).
School District(s)
Ira ISD (KG-12)
   2009-10 Enrollment: 258 . . . . (325) 573-2629
Housing: Homeownership rate: 68.4% (2000); Median home value: $52,000 (2000); Median contract rent: $175 per month (2000); Median year structure built: 1962 (2000).
Transportation: Commute to work: 79.8% car, 0.0% public transportation, 19.1% walk, 1.1% work from home (2000); Travel time to work: 39.8% less than 15 minutes, 33.0% 15 to 30 minutes, 11.4% 30 to 45 minutes, 6.8% 45 to 60 minutes, 9.1% 60 minutes or more (2000)

SNYDER (city). County seat. Covers a land area of 8.580 square miles and a water area of 0.020 square miles. Located at 32.71° N. Lat; 100.91° W. Long. Elevation is 2,320 feet.
History: Peter Snyder established a trading post here in 1876, and the town that grew up around it was named Snyder. For a time it was known as Robbers Roost for the many outlaws who built their buffalo-hide huts around the trading post.
Population: 12,272 (1990); 10,783 (2000); 10,385 (2010); 10,178 (2015 projected); Race: 75.3% White, 3.8% Black, 0.5% Asian, 20.4% Other, 38.6% Hispanic of any race (2010); Density: 1,210.4 persons per square mile (2010); Average household size: 2.45 (2010); Median age: 34.5

(2010); Males per 100 females: 89.4 (2010); Marriage status: 24.2% never married, 60.3% now married, 7.5% widowed, 7.9% divorced (2005-2009 5-year est.); Foreign born: 5.6% (2005-2009 5-year est.); Ancestry (includes multiple ancestries): 9.3% Irish, 8.1% German, 8.0% American, 6.7% English, 2.3% French (2005-2009 5-year est.).

Economy: Single-family building permits issued: 50 (2010); Multi-family building permits issued: 34 (2010); Employment by occupation: 12.5% management, 16.2% professional, 15.4% services, 16.7% sales, 0.2% farming, 24.4% construction, 14.5% production (2005-2009 5-year est.).

Income: Per capita income: $23,513 (2010); Median household income: $43,406 (2010); Average household income: $58,471 (2010); Percent of households with income of $100,000 or more: 12.1% (2010); Poverty rate: 17.2% (2005-2009 5-year est.).

Taxes: Total city taxes per capita: $373 (2007); City property taxes per capita: $112 (2007).

Education: Percent of population age 25 and over with: High school diploma (including GED) or higher: 77.3% (2010); Bachelor's degree or higher: 13.5% (2010); Master's degree or higher: 5.2% (2010).

School District(s)

Snyder ISD (PK-12)
    2009-10 Enrollment: 2,715 . . . . (325) 573-5401

Two-year College(s)

Western Texas College (Public)
    Fall 2009 Enrollment: 2,473. . . . . (325) 573-8511
        2010-11 Tuition: In-state $2,112; Out-of-state $2,712

Housing: Homeownership rate: 69.1% (2010); Median home value: $48,496 (2010); Median contract rent: $407 per month (2005-2009 5-year est.); Median year structure built: 1960 (2005-2009 5-year est.).

Hospitals: DM Cogdell Memorial Hospital (99 beds)

Safety: Violent crime rate: 123.4 per 10,000 population; Property crime rate: 404.8 per 10,000 population (2009).

Newspapers: Snyder Daily News (Regional news; Circulation 6,000)

Transportation: Commute to work: 93.9% car, 0.0% public transportation, 2.3% walk, 1.7% work from home (2005-2009 5-year est.); Travel time to work: 73.0% less than 15 minutes, 14.9% 15 to 30 minutes, 6.9% 30 to 45 minutes, 2.3% 45 to 60 minutes, 3.0% 60 minutes or more (2005-2009 5-year est.)

Airports: Winston Field (general aviation)

Additional Information Contacts

City of Snyder . . . . (325) 573-4957
    http://ci.snyder.tx.us
Snyder Chamber of Commerce . . . . (325) 573-3558
    http://snyderchamber.org

Shackelford County

Located in north central Texas; drained by the Clear Fork of the Brazos River; includes part of Lake Fort Phantom Hill. Covers a land area of 913.95 square miles, a water area of 1.59 square miles, and is located in the Central Time Zone at 32.71° N. Lat., 99.33° W. Long. The county was founded in 1858. County seat is Albany.

Weather Station: Albany									Elevation: 1,419 feet		
	Jan	Feb	Mar	Apr	May	Jun	Jul	Aug	Sep	Oct	Nov	Dec
High	58	62	70	78	85	91	95	95	88	79	68	59
Low	33	36	43	50	60	67	71	70	62	52	42	33
Precip	1.0	1.9	2.3	2.4	3.8	4.0	2.0	2.0	2.6	2.9	1.9	1.6
Snow	0.6	0.6	0.3	0.1	0.0	0.0	0.0	0.0	0.0	0.0	0.4	0.8

High and Low temperatures in degrees Fahrenheit; Precipitation and Snow in inches

Population: 3,316 (1990); 3,302 (2000); 3,267 (2010); 3,243 (2015 projected); Race: 92.2% White, 1.0% Black, 0.0% Asian, 6.9% Other, 9.6% Hispanic of any race (2010); Density: 3.6 persons per square mile (2010); Average household size: 2.53 (2010); Median age: 43.5 (2010); Males per 100 females: 91.6 (2010).

Religion: Five largest groups: 53.2% Southern Baptist Convention, 9.4% Christian Church (Disciples of Christ), 8.1% The United Methodist Church, 6.5% Assemblies of God, 6.1% Churches of Christ (2000).

Economy: Unemployment rate: 4.7% (June 2011); Total civilian labor force: 2,302 (June 2011); Leading industries: 29.6% mining; 13.3% manufacturing; 11.9% retail trade (2009); Farms: 254 totaling 552,390 acres (2007); Companies that employ 500 or more persons: 0 (2009); Companies that employ 100 to 499 persons: 0 (2009); Companies that employ less than 100 persons: 129 (2009); Black-owned businesses: n/a (2007); Hispanic-owned businesses: n/a (2007); Asian-owned businesses: n/a (2007); Women-owned businesses: n/a (2007); Retail sales per capita:

$7,710 (2010). Single-family building permits issued: n/a (2010); Multi-family building permits issued: n/a (2010).

Income: Per capita income: $22,298 (2010); Median household income: $43,592 (2010); Average household income: $56,894 (2010); Percent of households with income of $100,000 or more: 13.5% (2010); Poverty rate: 13.1% (2009); Bankruptcy rate: 0.59% (2010).

Taxes: Total county taxes per capita: $505 (2007); County property taxes per capita: $427 (2007).

Education: Percent of population age 25 and over with: High school diploma (including GED) or higher: 83.5% (2010); Bachelor's degree or higher: 22.8% (2010); Master's degree or higher: 5.6% (2010).

Housing: Homeownership rate: 77.3% (2010); Median home value: $56,474 (2010); Median contract rent: $321 per month (2005-2009 5-year est.); Median year structure built: 1958 (2005-2009 5-year est.).

Health: Birth rate: 98.5 per 10,000 population (2009); Death rate: 114.9 per 10,000 population (2009); Age-adjusted cancer mortality rate: 258.7 (Unreliable) deaths per 100,000 population (2007); Number of physicians: 6.6 per 10,000 population (2008); Hospital beds: 0.0 per 10,000 population (2007); Hospital admissions: 0.0 per 10,000 population (2007).

Elections: 2008 Presidential election results: 13.8% Obama, 85.3% McCain, 0.0% Nader

National and State Parks: Fort Griffin State Park

Additional Information Contacts

Shackelford County Government. . . . . (325) 762-2232
    http://www.co.shackelford.tx.us/ips/cms
Albany Chamber of Commerce . . . . (325) 762-2525
    http://www.albanytexas.com

Shackelford County Communities

ALBANY (city). County seat. Covers a land area of 1.471 square miles and a water area of 0 square miles. Located at 32.72° N. Lat; 99.29° W. Long. Elevation is 1,414 feet.

History: Albany, established on the north fork of Hubbard Creek, was the site of the Ledbetter Salt Works, a pioneer industry. The town became a shipping point for Hereford cattle, and for petroleum.

Population: 1,981 (1990); 1,921 (2000); 1,871 (2010); 1,845 (2015 projected); Race: 91.4% White, 1.1% Black, 0.0% Asian, 7.4% Other, 10.6% Hispanic of any race (2010); Density: 1,272.0 persons per square mile (2010); Average household size: 2.54 (2010); Median age: 41.4 (2010); Males per 100 females: 90.1 (2010); Marriage status: 25.7% never married, 56.0% now married, 8.6% widowed, 9.7% divorced (2005-2009 5-year est.); Foreign born: 3.2% (2005-2009 5-year est.); Ancestry (includes multiple ancestries): 12.1% Irish, 10.8% German, 10.7% American, 9.1% English, 3.0% French Canadian (2005-2009 5-year est.).

Economy: Employment by occupation: 11.3% management, 21.3% professional, 18.8% services, 16.9% sales, 2.9% farming, 19.2% construction, 9.6% production (2005-2009 5-year est.).

Income: Per capita income: $22,430 (2010); Median household income: $42,793 (2010); Average household income: $57,784 (2010); Percent of households with income of $100,000 or more: 13.0% (2010); Poverty rate: 10.4% (2005-2009 5-year est.).

Taxes: Total city taxes per capita: $439 (2007); City property taxes per capita: $191 (2007).

Education: Percent of population age 25 and over with: High school diploma (including GED) or higher: 81.4% (2010); Bachelor's degree or higher: 21.7% (2010); Master's degree or higher: 5.1% (2010).

School District(s)

Albany ISD (PK-12)
    2009-10 Enrollment: 517 . . . . (325) 762-2823

Housing: Homeownership rate: 77.0% (2010); Median home value: $53,750 (2010); Median contract rent: $385 per month (2005-2009 5-year est.); Median year structure built: 1952 (2005-2009 5-year est.).

Newspapers: Albany News (Community news; Circulation 1,800)

Transportation: Commute to work: 91.1% car, 0.0% public transportation, 0.8% walk, 3.8% work from home (2005-2009 5-year est.); Travel time to work: 64.7% less than 15 minutes, 14.1% 15 to 30 minutes, 11.4% 30 to 45 minutes, 3.1% 45 to 60 minutes, 6.7% 60 minutes or more (2005-2009 5-year est.)

Additional Information Contacts

Albany Chamber of Commerce . . . . (325) 762-2525
    http://www.albanytexas.com

MORAN (city). Covers a land area of 0.432 square miles and a water area of 0 square miles. Located at 32.54° N. Lat; 99.16° W. Long. Elevation is 1,358 feet.

Population: 285 (1990); 233 (2000); 225 (2010); 218 (2015 projected); Race: 95.6% White, 0.0% Black, 0.0% Asian, 4.4% Other, 6.7% Hispanic of any race (2010); Density: 520.5 persons per square mile (2010); Average household size: 2.32 (2010); Median age: 51.5 (2010); Males per 100 females: 86.0 (2010); Marriage status: 28.3% never married, 48.0% now married, 9.1% widowed, 14.6% divorced (2005-2009 5-year est.); Foreign born: 0.0% (2005-2009 5-year est.); Ancestry (includes multiple ancestries): 31.7% German, 10.4% Irish, 6.3% Portuguese, 5.0% Dutch, 4.2% Italian (2005-2009 5-year est.).

Economy: Employment by occupation: 11.4% management, 14.3% professional, 13.3% services, 22.9% sales, 0.0% farming, 7.6% construction, 30.5% production (2005-2009 5-year est.).

Income: Per capita income: $22,408 (2010); Median household income: $39,500 (2010); Average household income: $52,036 (2010); Percent of households with income of $100,000 or more: 11.3% (2010); Poverty rate: 31.7% (2005-2009 5-year est.).

Taxes: Total city taxes per capita: $152 (2007); City property taxes per capita: $63 (2007).

Education: Percent of population age 25 and over with: High school diploma (including GED) or higher: 86.4% (2010); Bachelor's degree or higher: 23.2% (2010); Master's degree or higher: 6.2% (2010).

School District(s)

Moran ISD (PK-12)
　　2009-10 Enrollment: 181 . . . . (325) 945-3101

Housing: Homeownership rate: 82.5% (2010); Median home value: $43,077 (2010); Median contract rent: $340 per month (2005-2009 5-year est.); Median year structure built: 1969 (2005-2009 5-year est.).

Transportation: Commute to work: 86.7% car, 0.0% public transportation, 4.8% walk, 2.9% work from home (2005-2009 5-year est.); Travel time to work: 33.3% less than 15 minutes, 17.6% 15 to 30 minutes, 35.3% 30 to 45 minutes, 5.9% 45 to 60 minutes, 7.8% 60 minutes or more (2005-2009 5-year est.)

Shelby County

Located in east Texas; bounded on the east by the Sabine River and the Louisiana border, and on the west by Attoyac Bayou; includes part of Sabine National Forest. Covers a land area of 794.11 square miles, a water area of 40.43 square miles, and is located in the Central Time Zone at 31.82° N. Lat., 94.13° W. Long. The county was founded in 1836. County seat is Center.

Weather Station: Center										Elevation: 325 feet		
	Jan	Feb	Mar	Apr	May	Jun	Jul	Aug	Sep	Oct	Nov	Dec
High	58	62	70	77	84	90	94	94	89	79	68	60
Low	35	38	45	52	61	68	71	70	64	53	44	36
Precip	4.5	4.9	4.7	4.4	4.7	5.2	3.2	3.6	3.6	5.3	5.0	5.4
Snow	0.3	0.1	tr	tr	0.0	0.0	0.0	0.0	0.0	0.0	0.1	0.1

High and Low temperatures in degrees Fahrenheit; Precipitation and Snow in inches

Population: 22,034 (1990); 25,224 (2000); 26,454 (2010); 27,005 (2015 projected); Race: 69.6% White, 17.6% Black, 0.2% Asian, 12.5% Other, 16.5% Hispanic of any race (2010); Density: 33.3 persons per square mile (2010); Average household size: 2.61 (2010); Median age: 35.8 (2010); Males per 100 females: 94.5 (2010).

Religion: Five largest groups: 26.4% Southern Baptist Convention, 14.7% The American Baptist Association, 7.0% Baptist Missionary Association of America, 5.5% The United Methodist Church, 2.5% Churches of Christ (2000).

Economy: Unemployment rate: 8.7% (June 2011); Total civilian labor force: 13,249 (June 2011); Leading industries: 33.2% manufacturing; 17.5% retail trade; 9.3% health care and social assistance (2009); Farms: 1,123 totaling 197,791 acres (2007); Companies that employ 500 or more persons: 1 (2009); Companies that employ 100 to 499 persons: 7 (2009); Companies that employ less than 100 persons: 475 (2009); Black-owned businesses: n/a (2007); Hispanic-owned businesses: n/a (2007); Asian-owned businesses: n/a (2007); Women-owned businesses: 503 (2007); Retail sales per capita: $10,498 (2010). Single-family building permits issued: 8 (2010); Multi-family building permits issued: 0 (2010).

Income: Per capita income: $17,264 (2010); Median household income: $33,862 (2010); Average household income: $45,364 (2010); Percent of households with income of $100,000 or more: 8.2% (2010); Poverty rate: 19.9% (2009); Bankruptcy rate: 1.70% (2010).

Taxes: Total county taxes per capita: $211 (2007); County property taxes per capita: $184 (2007).

Education: Percent of population age 25 and over with: High school diploma (including GED) or higher: 73.2% (2010); Bachelor's degree or higher: 14.2% (2010); Master's degree or higher: 5.2% (2010).

Housing: Homeownership rate: 75.6% (2010); Median home value: $58,589 (2010); Median contract rent: $313 per month (2005-2009 5-year est.); Median year structure built: 1974 (2005-2009 5-year est.)

Health: Birth rate: 153.7 per 10,000 population (2009); Death rate: 106.7 per 10,000 population (2009); Age-adjusted cancer mortality rate: 216.9 deaths per 100,000 population (2007); Number of physicians: 3.8 per 10,000 population (2008); Hospital beds: 17.4 per 10,000 population (2007); Hospital admissions: 396.5 per 10,000 population (2007).

Elections: 2008 Presidential election results: 27.6% Obama, 71.9% McCain, 0.0% Nader

Additional Information Contacts
Shelby County Government. . . . . (936) 598-6361
　　http://www.co.shelby.tx.us/ips/cms
City of Center. . . . . (936) 598-2941
　　http://www.centertexas.org
Shelby County Chamber of Commerce . . . . (936) 598-3682
　　http://www.shelbycountychamber.com

Shelby County Communities

CENTER (city). County seat. Covers a land area of 6.232 square miles and a water area of 0.013 square miles. Located at 31.79° N. Lat; 94.17° W. Long. Elevation is 371 feet.

History: Center was established in 1866 when a law was passed requiring that the seat of a county be in the center of the county. Jesse Amason donated the land for a town site for Shelby County, and named it Center. Shelbyville, which had been the county seat, refused to give up the county records to the new town, and placed armed guards around the courthouse. The county clerk spirited them away in the night.

Population: 5,133 (1990); 5,678 (2000); 5,781 (2010); 5,849 (2015 projected); Race: 43.9% White, 32.1% Black, 0.5% Asian, 23.5% Other, 29.3% Hispanic of any race (2010); Density: 927.6 persons per square mile (2010); Average household size: 2.72 (2010); Median age: 34.1 (2010); Males per 100 females: 91.6 (2010); Marriage status: 25.2% never married, 47.3% now married, 14.6% widowed, 12.9% divorced (2005-2009 5-year est.); Foreign born: 18.6% (2005-2009 5-year est.); Ancestry (includes multiple ancestries): 8.1% Irish, 7.4% English, 6.1% American, 4.1% German, 0.9% Dutch (2005-2009 5-year est.).

Economy: Single-family building permits issued: 7 (2010); Multi-family building permits issued: 0 (2010); Employment by occupation: 9.5% management, 10.2% professional, 8.8% services, 21.9% sales, 6.7% farming, 16.0% construction, 26.8% production (2005-2009 5-year est.).

Income: Per capita income: $17,065 (2010); Median household income: $32,760 (2010); Average household income: $47,432 (2010); Percent of households with income of $100,000 or more: 8.0% (2010); Poverty rate: 39.1% (2005-2009 5-year est.).

Taxes: Total city taxes per capita: $689 (2007); City property taxes per capita: $178 (2007).

Education: Percent of population age 25 and over with: High school diploma (including GED) or higher: 66.2% (2010); Bachelor's degree or higher: 15.1% (2010); Master's degree or higher: 6.6% (2010).

School District(s)

Center ISD (PK-12)
　　2009-10 Enrollment: 2,583 . . . . (936) 598-5642
Excelsior ISD (PK-08)
　　2009-10 Enrollment: 116 . . . . (936) 598-5866

Housing: Homeownership rate: 59.0% (2010); Median home value: $53,198 (2010); Median contract rent: $239 per month (2005-2009 5-year est.); Median year structure built: 1967 (2005-2009 5-year est.).

Hospitals: Shelby Regional Medical Center (54 beds)

Safety: Violent crime rate: 104.3 per 10,000 population; Property crime rate: 597.8 per 10,000 population (2009).

Newspapers: Light And Champion (Local news; Circulation 5,300); The Merchandiser (Community news; Circulation 8,083)

Transportation: Commute to work: 86.3% car, 5.0% public transportation, 5.2% walk, 2.3% work from home (2005-2009 5-year est.); Travel time to work: 72.3% less than 15 minutes, 13.8% 15 to 30 minutes, 2.0% 30 to 45

minutes, 1.7% 45 to 60 minutes, 10.3% 60 minutes or more (2005-2009 5-year est.)

Additional Information Contacts
City of Center . . . . (936) 598-2941
   http://www.centertexas.org
Shelby County Chamber of Commerce . . . . (936) 598-3682
   http://www.shelbycountychamber.com

HUXLEY (city). Covers a land area of 2.003 square miles and a water area of 0.039 square miles. Located at 31.76° N. Lat; 93.88° W. Long. Elevation is 279 feet.
Population: 348 (1990); 298 (2000); 306 (2010); 310 (2015 projected); Race: 87.3% White, 9.2% Black, 0.0% Asian, 3.6% Other, 6.5% Hispanic of any race (2010); Density: 152.7 persons per square mile (2010); Average household size: 2.25 (2010); Median age: 46.2 (2010); Males per 100 females: 96.2 (2010); Marriage status: 14.8% never married, 75.2% now married, 6.7% widowed, 3.4% divorced (2005-2009 5-year est.); Foreign born: 0.0% (2005-2009 5-year est.); Ancestry (includes multiple ancestries): 42.2% American, 22.3% Irish, 13.1% German, 5.2% French, 3.5% English (2005-2009 5-year est.).
Economy: Employment by occupation: 16.5% management, 12.6% professional, 6.3% services, 35.4% sales, 0.0% farming, 16.5% construction, 12.6% production (2005-2009 5-year est.).
Income: Per capita income: $21,650 (2010); Median household income: $37,045 (2010); Average household income: $49,559 (2010); Percent of households with income of $100,000 or more: 11.8% (2010); Poverty rate: 7.6% (2005-2009 5-year est.).
Taxes: Total city taxes per capita: $31 (2007); City property taxes per capita: $0 (2007).
Education: Percent of population age 25 and over with: High school diploma (including GED) or higher: 76.5% (2010); Bachelor's degree or higher: 12.8% (2010); Master's degree or higher: 4.7% (2010).
Housing: Homeownership rate: 89.0% (2010); Median home value: $63,500 (2010); Median contract rent: $453 per month (2005-2009 5-year est.); Median year structure built: 1978 (2005-2009 5-year est.).
Transportation: Commute to work: 97.4% car, 0.0% public transportation, 0.0% walk, 1.7% work from home (2005-2009 5-year est.); Travel time to work: 4.3% less than 15 minutes, 52.2% 15 to 30 minutes, 30.4% 30 to 45 minutes, 5.2% 45 to 60 minutes, 7.8% 60 minutes or more (2005-2009 5-year est.)

JOAQUIN (city). Covers a land area of 2.303 square miles and a water area of 0.007 square miles. Located at 31.96° N. Lat; 94.04° W. Long. Elevation is 226 feet.
Population: 873 (1990); 925 (2000); 912 (2010); 901 (2015 projected); Race: 79.4% White, 15.1% Black, 0.1% Asian, 5.4% Other, 6.6% Hispanic of any race (2010); Density: 396.0 persons per square mile (2010); Average household size: 2.58 (2010); Median age: 34.8 (2010); Males per 100 females: 91.6 (2010); Marriage status: 19.5% never married, 63.7% now married, 10.2% widowed, 6.6% divorced (2005-2009 5-year est.); Foreign born: 10.6% (2005-2009 5-year est.); Ancestry (includes multiple ancestries): 25.2% American, 24.6% Irish, 9.6% Dutch, 6.5% French, 6.1% German (2005-2009 5-year est.).
Economy: Single-family building permits issued: 1 (2010); Multi-family building permits issued: 0 (2010); Employment by occupation: 3.9% management, 19.5% professional, 14.4% services, 15.9% sales, 0.0% farming, 32.1% construction, 14.1% production (2005-2009 5-year est.).
Income: Per capita income: $14,074 (2010); Median household income: $26,429 (2010); Average household income: $34,958 (2010); Percent of households with income of $100,000 or more: 5.4% (2010); Poverty rate: 38.5% (2005-2009 5-year est.).
Taxes: Total city taxes per capita: $174 (2007); City property taxes per capita: $35 (2007).
Education: Percent of population age 25 and over with: High school diploma (including GED) or higher: 70.6% (2010); Bachelor's degree or higher: 9.9% (2010); Master's degree or higher: 4.8% (2010).
School District(s)
Joaquin ISD (PK-12)
   2009-10 Enrollment: 735 . . . . (936) 269-3128
Housing: Homeownership rate: 74.6% (2010); Median home value: $45,769 (2010); Median contract rent: $360 per month (2005-2009 5-year est.); Median year structure built: 1970 (2005-2009 5-year est.).
Transportation: Commute to work: 96.0% car, 0.0% public transportation, 1.6% walk, 0.0% work from home (2005-2009 5-year est.); Travel time to work: 44.7% less than 15 minutes, 23.0% 15 to 30 minutes, 12.0% 30 to 45

minutes, 4.5% 45 to 60 minutes, 15.8% 60 minutes or more (2005-2009 5-year est.)

SHELBYVILLE (unincorporated postal area, zip code 75973). Covers a land area of 191.460 square miles and a water area of 0.155 square miles. Located at 31.73° N. Lat; 93.90° W. Long. Elevation is 292 feet.
History: Shelbyville was founded about 1817. It was first known as Tenaha, then Nashville, and finally Shelbyville, in honor of General Isaac Shelby. In the 1840's, Shelbyville was the scene of gang warfare between the Regulators (organized to combat crime but suspected of joining the outlaws) and the Moderators (organized to regulate the Regulators).
Population: 2,763 (2000); Race: 76.4% White, 22.1% Black, 0.0% Asian, 1.5% Other, 1.3% Hispanic of any race (2000); Density: 14.4 persons per square mile (2000); Age: 23.2% under 18, 18.9% over 64 (2000); Marriage status: 14.9% never married, 62.6% now married, 10.3% widowed, 12.2% divorced (2000); Foreign born: 1.2% (2000); Ancestry (includes multiple ancestries): 18.7% American, 8.0% Irish, 7.6% English, 5.6% German (2000).
Economy: Employment by occupation: 11.8% management, 13.0% professional, 13.7% services, 18.5% sales, 6.4% farming, 15.1% construction, 21.5% production (2000).
Income: Per capita income: $16,356 (2000); Median household income: $30,107 (2000); Poverty rate: 179.1% (2000).
Education: Percent of population age 25 and over with: High school diploma (including GED) or higher: 70.1% (2000); Bachelor's degree or higher: 9.3% (2000).
School District(s)
Shelbyville ISD (PK-12)
   2009-10 Enrollment: 751 . . . . (936) 598-2641
Housing: Homeownership rate: 89.4% (2000); Median home value: $60,100 (2000); Median contract rent: $305 per month (2000); Median year structure built: 1977 (2000).
Transportation: Commute to work: 88.6% car, 0.2% public transportation, 4.3% walk, 5.7% work from home (2000); Travel time to work: 20.2% less than 15 minutes, 30.8% 15 to 30 minutes, 23.1% 30 to 45 minutes, 9.1% 45 to 60 minutes, 16.8% 60 minutes or more (2000)

TENAHA (town). Covers a land area of 3.949 square miles and a water area of 0.021 square miles. Located at 31.94° N. Lat; 94.24° W. Long. Elevation is 348 feet.
Population: 1,072 (1990); 1,046 (2000); 1,060 (2010); 1,064 (2015 projected); Race: 67.5% White, 22.8% Black, 0.0% Asian, 9.6% Other, 14.0% Hispanic of any race (2010); Density: 268.4 persons per square mile (2010); Average household size: 2.52 (2010); Median age: 34.2 (2010); Males per 100 females: 92.0 (2010); Marriage status: 29.3% never married, 52.1% now married, 12.0% widowed, 6.5% divorced (2005-2009 5-year est.); Foreign born: 14.3% (2005-2009 5-year est.); Ancestry (includes multiple ancestries): 6.7% American, 5.4% African, 4.8% Irish, 4.2% English, 3.9% French (2005-2009 5-year est.).
Economy: Employment by occupation: 9.1% management, 9.1% professional, 11.7% services, 15.8% sales, 14.2% farming, 6.0% construction, 34.1% production (2005-2009 5-year est.).
Income: Per capita income: $14,398 (2010); Median household income: $27,734 (2010); Average household income: $36,295 (2010); Percent of households with income of $100,000 or more: 4.5% (2010); Poverty rate: 32.1% (2005-2009 5-year est.).
Taxes: Total city taxes per capita: $111 (2007); City property taxes per capita: $48 (2007).
Education: Percent of population age 25 and over with: High school diploma (including GED) or higher: 71.7% (2010); Bachelor's degree or higher: 11.9% (2010); Master's degree or higher: 5.5% (2010).
School District(s)
Tenaha ISD (PK-12)
   2009-10 Enrollment: 470 . . . . (936) 248-5000
Housing: Homeownership rate: 74.3% (2010); Median home value: $55,424 (2010); Median contract rent: $305 per month (2005-2009 5-year est.); Median year structure built: 1974 (2005-2009 5-year est.).
Transportation: Commute to work: 95.7% car, 0.0% public transportation, 1.9% walk, 0.0% work from home (2005-2009 5-year est.); Travel time to work: 54.7% less than 15 minutes, 29.9% 15 to 30 minutes, 13.4% 30 to 45 minutes, 2.1% 45 to 60 minutes, 0.0% 60 minutes or more (2005-2009 5-year est.)

TIMPSON (city). Covers a land area of 2.502 square miles and a water area of 0.007 square miles. Located at 31.90° N. Lat; 94.39° W. Long. Elevation is 390 feet.

Population: 1,029 (1990); 1,094 (2000); 1,182 (2010); 1,225 (2015 projected); Race: 74.2% White, 19.8% Black, 0.1% Asian, 5.9% Other, 8.5% Hispanic of any race (2010); Density: 472.4 persons per square mile (2010); Average household size: 2.57 (2010); Median age: 34.5 (2010); Males per 100 females: 88.5 (2010); Marriage status: 32.5% never married, 46.4% now married, 10.0% widowed, 11.1% divorced (2005-2009 5-year est.); Foreign born: 6.1% (2005-2009 5-year est.); Ancestry (includes multiple ancestries): 16.1% American, 9.6% Irish, 8.7% English, 8.3% African, 4.7% Scotch-Irish (2005-2009 5-year est.).

Economy: Employment by occupation: 6.1% management, 15.1% professional, 26.6% services, 16.4% sales, 4.8% farming, 6.1% construction, 24.9% production (2005-2009 5-year est.).

Income: Per capita income: $18,184 (2010); Median household income: $35,390 (2010); Average household income: $47,076 (2010); Percent of households with income of $100,000 or more: 7.6% (2010); Poverty rate: 35.9% (2005-2009 5-year est.).

Taxes: Total city taxes per capita: $161 (2007); City property taxes per capita: $65 (2007).

Education: Percent of population age 25 and over with: High school diploma (including GED) or higher: 75.8% (2010); Bachelor's degree or higher: 15.4% (2010); Master's degree or higher: 6.3% (2010).

School District(s)

Timpson ISD (PK-12)
    2009-10 Enrollment: 623 . . . . (936) 254-2463

Housing: Homeownership rate: 73.5% (2010); Median home value: $61,579 (2010); Median contract rent: $251 per month (2005-2009 5-year est.); Median year structure built: 1967 (2005-2009 5-year est.).

Newspapers: Timpson & Tenaha News (Local news; Circulation 2,000)

Transportation: Commute to work: 89.3% car, 0.0% public transportation, 8.6% walk, 1.1% work from home (2005-2009 5-year est.); Travel time to work: 46.9% less than 15 minutes, 27.8% 15 to 30 minutes, 20.0% 30 to 45 minutes, 1.3% 45 to 60 minutes, 4.0% 60 minutes or more (2005-2009 5-year est.)

Sherman County

Located in north Texas, on the Panhandle; bounded on the north by Oklahoma; drained by the North Canadian River and its tributaries. Covers a land area of 923.03 square miles, a water area of 0.16 square miles, and is located in the Central Time Zone at 36.27° N. Lat., 101.93° W. Long. The county was founded in 1876. County seat is Stratford.

Weather Station: Stratford									Elevation: 3,690 feet			
	Jan	Feb	Mar	Apr	May	Jun	Jul	Aug	Sep	Oct	Nov	Dec
High	48	52	60	69	78	87	92	89	82	71	59	47
Low	20	22	29	37	48	58	63	62	53	40	29	20
Precip	0.5	0.4	1.3	1.3	2.3	2.2	2.2	2.6	1.7	1.3	0.7	0.7
Snow	5.1	2.5	4.2	1.4	0.1	0.0	0.0	0.0	0.0	0.2	2.1	5.1

High and Low temperatures in degrees Fahrenheit; Precipitation and Snow in inches

Population: 2,858 (1990); 3,186 (2000); 3,027 (2010); 2,944 (2015 projected); Race: 76.8% White, 1.1% Black, 0.0% Asian, 22.1% Other, 36.0% Hispanic of any race (2010); Density: 3.3 persons per square mile (2010); Average household size: 2.80 (2010); Median age: 36.6 (2010); Males per 100 females: 103.2 (2010).

Religion: Five largest groups: 32.3% Southern Baptist Convention, 31.4% Catholic Church, 17.6% The United Methodist Church, 7.6% Christian Church (Disciples of Christ), 4.8% Assemblies of God (2000).

Economy: Unemployment rate: 5.6% (June 2011); Total civilian labor force: 1,470 (June 2011); Leading industries: 24.3% wholesale trade; 5.7% construction (2009); Farms: 362 totaling 584,196 acres (2007); Companies that employ 500 or more persons: 0 (2009); Companies that employ 100 to 499 persons: 0 (2009); Companies that employ less than 100 persons: 56 (2009); Black-owned businesses: n/a (2007); Hispanic-owned businesses: n/a (2007); Asian-owned businesses: n/a (2007); Women-owned businesses: n/a (2007); Retail sales per capita: $4,384 (2010). Single-family building permits issued: 6 (2010); Multi-family building permits issued: 2 (2010).

Income: Per capita income: $19,843 (2010); Median household income: $42,148 (2010); Average household income: $56,094 (2010); Percent of households with income of $100,000 or more: 10.2% (2010); Poverty rate: 13.1% (2009); Bankruptcy rate: 0.99% (2010).

Taxes: Total county taxes per capita: $839 (2007); County property taxes per capita: $791 (2007).

Education: Percent of population age 25 and over with: High school diploma (including GED) or higher: 78.2% (2010); Bachelor's degree or higher: 23.0% (2010); Master's degree or higher: 3.6% (2010).

Housing: Homeownership rate: 71.6% (2010); Median home value: $66,028 (2010); Median contract rent: $351 per month (2005-2009 5-year est.); Median year structure built: 1958 (2005-2009 5-year est.)

Health: Birth rate: 140.7 per 10,000 population (2009); Death rate: 37.8 per 10,000 population (2009); Age-adjusted cancer mortality rate: Suppressed deaths per 100,000 population (2007); Number of physicians: 0.0 per 10,000 population (2008); Hospital beds: 0.0 per 10,000 population (2007); Hospital admissions: 0.0 per 10,000 population (2007).

Elections: 2008 Presidential election results: 12.5% Obama, 86.7% McCain, 0.1% Nader

Additional Information Contacts

Sherman County Government . . . . (806) 396-2021
    http://www.co.sherman.tx.us/ips/cms
Stratford Chamber of Commerce. . . . . (806) 366-2260
    http://stratfordtxchamber.org

Sherman County Communities

STRATFORD (city). County seat. Covers a land area of 2.031 square miles and a water area of 0 square miles. Located at 36.33° N. Lat; 102.07° W. Long. Elevation is 3,691 feet.

History: Until 1901 Coldwater was the seat of Sherman County. Stratford won a county seat election but Coldwater was reluctant to make the change. An armed group from Stratford seized the county records from Coldwater. Coldwater faded out of existence.

Population: 1,781 (1990); 1,991 (2000); 1,954 (2010); 1,929 (2015 projected); Race: 75.6% White, 0.5% Black, 0.1% Asian, 23.8% Other, 42.3% Hispanic of any race (2010); Density: 962.0 persons per square mile (2010); Average household size: 2.73 (2010); Median age: 37.2 (2010); Males per 100 females: 100.8 (2010); Marriage status: 29.7% never married, 55.6% now married, 6.3% widowed, 8.3% divorced (2005-2009 5-year est.); Foreign born: 19.5% (2005-2009 5-year est.); Ancestry (includes multiple ancestries): 13.4% German, 9.3% Irish, 5.9% English, 3.7% American, 3.0% Dutch (2005-2009 5-year est.).

Economy: Single-family building permits issued: 6 (2010); Multi-family building permits issued: 2 (2010); Employment by occupation: 11.7% management, 15.5% professional, 24.0% services, 15.6% sales, 14.4% farming, 5.6% construction, 13.2% production (2005-2009 5-year est.).

Income: Per capita income: $18,225 (2010); Median household income: $40,134 (2010); Average household income: $50,000 (2010); Percent of households with income of $100,000 or more: 8.2% (2010); Poverty rate: 27.0% (2005-2009 5-year est.).

Taxes: Total city taxes per capita: $352 (2007); City property taxes per capita: $168 (2007).

Education: Percent of population age 25 and over with: High school diploma (including GED) or higher: 76.1% (2010); Bachelor's degree or higher: 21.3% (2010); Master's degree or higher: 4.4% (2010).

School District(s)

Stratford ISD (PK-12)
    2009-10 Enrollment: 595 . . . . (806) 366-3300

Housing: Homeownership rate: 74.0% (2010); Median home value: $59,153 (2010); Median contract rent: $336 per month (2005-2009 5-year est.); Median year structure built: 1960 (2005-2009 5-year est.).

Safety: Violent crime rate: 15.7 per 10,000 population; Property crime rate: 78.7 per 10,000 population (2009).

Newspapers: Stratford Star (Community news; Circulation 1,100)

Transportation: Commute to work: 88.5% car, 0.0% public transportation, 3.3% walk, 4.7% work from home (2005-2009 5-year est.); Travel time to work: 59.9% less than 15 minutes, 25.0% 15 to 30 minutes, 9.8% 30 to 45 minutes, 1.4% 45 to 60 minutes, 3.9% 60 minutes or more (2005-2009 5-year est.)

Airports: Stratford Field (general aviation)

Additional Information Contacts

Stratford Chamber of Commerce. . . . . (806) 366-2260
    http://stratfordtxchamber.org

TEXHOMA (city). Covers a land area of 1.890 square miles and a water area of 0 square miles. Located at 36.49° N. Lat; 101.78° W. Long. Elevation is 3,501 feet.

History: Texhoma grew up on the border with Oklahoma, in an area that produced much wheat.
Population: 291 (1990); 371 (2000); 335 (2010); 317 (2015 projected); Race: 77.0% White, 2.7% Black, 0.0% Asian, 20.3% Other, 26.0% Hispanic of any race (2010); Density: 177.2 persons per square mile (2010); Average household size: 3.05 (2010); Median age: 32.4 (2010); Males per 100 females: 109.4 (2010); Marriage status: 19.4% never married, 71.2% now married, 9.4% widowed, 0.0% divorced (2005-2009 5-year est.); Foreign born: 6.2% (2005-2009 5-year est.); Ancestry (includes multiple ancestries): 30.2% German, 11.0% Irish, 10.0% English, 9.5% American, 4.0% Dutch (2005-2009 5-year est.).
Economy: Employment by occupation: 21.7% management, 17.9% professional, 15.2% services, 18.5% sales, 10.3% farming, 3.8% construction, 12.5% production (2005-2009 5-year est.).
Income: Per capita income: $21,297 (2010); Median household income: $45,875 (2010); Average household income: $64,587 (2010); Percent of households with income of $100,000 or more: 11.0% (2010); Poverty rate: 1.8% (2005-2009 5-year est.).
Taxes: Total city taxes per capita: $80 (2007); City property taxes per capita: $80 (2007).
Education: Percent of population age 25 and over with: High school diploma (including GED) or higher: 80.5% (2010); Bachelor's degree or higher: 23.6% (2010); Master's degree or higher: 1.0% (2010).

School District(s)

Texhoma ISD (PK-12)
   2009-10 Enrollment: 373 . . . . (806) 827-7400
Housing: Homeownership rate: 65.1% (2010); Median home value: $75,625 (2010); Median contract rent: $684 per month (2005-2009 5-year est.); Median year structure built: 1956 (2005-2009 5-year est.).
Transportation: Commute to work: 88.2% car, 0.0% public transportation, 8.1% walk, 1.1% work from home (2005-2009 5-year est.); Travel time to work: 53.3% less than 15 minutes, 31.0% 15 to 30 minutes, 10.9% 30 to 45 minutes, 4.9% 45 to 60 minutes, 0.0% 60 minutes or more (2005-2009 5-year est.)

Smith County

Located in east Texas; bounded on the north by the Sabine River, and on the west by the Neches River. Covers a land area of 928.38 square miles, a water area of 21.06 square miles, and is located in the Central Time Zone at 32.33° N. Lat., 95.29° W. Long. The county was founded in 1846. County seat is Tyler.

Smith County is part of the Tyler, TX Metropolitan Statistical Area. The entire metro area includes: Smith County, TX

Weather Station: Tyler											Elevation: 549 feet	
	Jan	Feb	Mar	Apr	May	Jun	Jul	Aug	Sep	Oct	Nov	Dec
High	58	63	71	78	84	90	93	94	88	78	67	59
Low	38	41	48	55	64	70	73	72	66	56	47	39
Precip	3.7	4.2	4.3	3.4	4.5	4.8	2.7	2.8	3.2	5.0	4.5	4.7
Snow	0.2	0.6	0.1	tr	0.0	0.0	0.0	0.0	0.0	0.0	tr	tr

High and Low temperatures in degrees Fahrenheit; Precipitation and Snow in inches

Population: 151,309 (1990); 174,706 (2000); 206,033 (2010); 220,899 (2015 projected); Race: 70.6% White, 17.6% Black, 0.9% Asian, 10.8% Other, 16.1% Hispanic of any race (2010); Density: 221.9 persons per square mile (2010); Average household size: 2.63 (2010); Median age: 35.3 (2010); Males per 100 females: 93.5 (2010).
Religion: Five largest groups: 32.4% Southern Baptist Convention, 9.3% Catholic Church, 7.2% The United Methodist Church, 3.1% Churches of Christ, 1.8% Assemblies of God (2000).
Economy: Unemployment rate: 8.2% (June 2011); Total civilian labor force: 102,765 (June 2011); Leading industries: 22.8% health care and social assistance; 14.0% retail trade; 10.5% accommodation & food services (2009); Farms: 2,514 totaling 302,359 acres (2007); Companies that employ 500 or more persons: 12 (2009); Companies that employ 100 to 499 persons: 109 (2009); Companies that employ less than 100 persons: 5,242 (2009); Black-owned businesses: 1,522 (2007); Hispanic-owned businesses: 1,472 (2007); Asian-owned businesses: n/a (2007); Women-owned businesses: 4,714 (2007); Retail sales per capita: $18,039 (2010). Single-family building permits issued: 201 (2010); Multi-family building permits issued: 65 (2010).
Income: Per capita income: $23,425 (2010); Median household income: $46,592 (2010); Average household income: $62,665 (2010); Percent of

households with income of $100,000 or more: 15.7% (2010); Poverty rate: 16.2% (2009); Bankruptcy rate: 2.18% (2010).
Taxes: Total county taxes per capita: $229 (2007); County property taxes per capita: $137 (2007).
Education: Percent of population age 25 and over with: High school diploma (including GED) or higher: 83.3% (2010); Bachelor's degree or higher: 23.3% (2010); Master's degree or higher: 7.3% (2010).
Housing: Homeownership rate: 71.3% (2010); Median home value: $114,177 (2010); Median contract rent: $561 per month (2005-2009 5-year est.); Median year structure built: 1980 (2005-2009 5-year est.)
Health: Birth rate: 155.8 per 10,000 population (2009); Death rate: 90.1 per 10,000 population (2009); Age-adjusted cancer mortality rate: 167.9 deaths per 100,000 population (2007); Number of physicians: 37.3 per 10,000 population (2008); Hospital beds: 56.8 per 10,000 population (2007); Hospital admissions: 2,461.8 per 10,000 population (2007).
Environment: Air Quality Index: 90.1% good, 9.5% moderate, 0.0% unhealthy for sensitive individuals, 0.3% unhealthy (percent of days in 2008)
Elections: 2008 Presidential election results: 29.8% Obama, 69.4% McCain, 0.1% Nader
National and State Parks: Tyler State Park
Additional Information Contacts
Smith County Government. . . . . (903) 535-0500
   http://www.smith-county.com
Arp Chamber of Commerce . . . . (903) 859-3025
Bullard Area Chamber of Commerce . . . . (903) 894-4238
   http://bullardtexaschamber.com
City of Tyler . . . . (903) 531-1100
   http://www.cityoftyler.org
City of Whitehouse. . . . . (903) 839-4914
   http://www.whitehousetx.org
Lake Palesine Chamber of Commerce . . . . (903) 876-5310
   http://www.lakepalestinechamber.com
Lindale Area Chamber of Commerce . . . . (903) 882-7181
   http://www.lindalechamber.org
Troup Chamber of Commerce . . . . (903) 842-4113
   http://www.trouptexas.org
Tyler Area Chamber of Commerce . . . . (903) 592-1661
   http://www.tylertexas.com

Smith County Communities

ARP (city). Covers a land area of 2.451 square miles and a water area of 0 square miles. Located at 32.22° N. Lat; 95.05° W. Long. Elevation is 495 feet.
Population: 822 (1990); 901 (2000); 945 (2010); 971 (2015 projected); Race: 91.6% White, 5.3% Black, 0.1% Asian, 3.0% Other, 3.2% Hispanic of any race (2010); Density: 385.5 persons per square mile (2010); Average household size: 2.63 (2010); Median age: 35.5 (2010); Males per 100 females: 98.9 (2010); Marriage status: 20.0% never married, 63.5% now married, 3.4% widowed, 13.2% divorced (2005-2009 5-year est.); Foreign born: 5.5% (2005-2009 5-year est.); Ancestry (includes multiple ancestries): 24.7% Irish, 16.3% German, 9.5% English, 6.4% Scottish, 5.4% American (2005-2009 5-year est.).
Economy: Single-family building permits issued: 0 (2010); Multi-family building permits issued: 0 (2010); Employment by occupation: 20.7% management, 22.4% professional, 11.1% services, 23.7% sales, 0.0% farming, 9.1% construction, 13.1% production (2005-2009 5-year est.).
Income: Per capita income: $24,122 (2010); Median household income: $50,313 (2010); Average household income: $62,806 (2010); Percent of households with income of $100,000 or more: 14.2% (2010); Poverty rate: 13.1% (2005-2009 5-year est.).
Taxes: Total city taxes per capita: $103 (2007); City property taxes per capita: $87 (2007).
Education: Percent of population age 25 and over with: High school diploma (including GED) or higher: 82.0% (2010); Bachelor's degree or higher: 13.2% (2010); Master's degree or higher: 3.1% (2010).

School District(s)

Arp ISD (PK-12)
   2009-10 Enrollment: 888 . . . . (903) 859-8482
Housing: Homeownership rate: 83.3% (2010); Median home value: $75,102 (2010); Median contract rent: $322 per month (2005-2009 5-year est.); Median year structure built: 1966 (2005-2009 5-year est.).
Safety: Violent crime rate: 31.0 per 10,000 population; Property crime rate: 92.9 per 10,000 population (2009).

Transportation: Commute to work: 86.7% car, 0.0% public transportation, 2.3% walk, 7.4% work from home (2005-2009 5-year est.); Travel time to work: 21.9% less than 15 minutes, 26.6% 15 to 30 minutes, 36.6% 30 to 45 minutes, 11.1% 45 to 60 minutes, 3.9% 60 minutes or more (2005-2009 5-year est.)

Additional Information Contacts
Arp Chamber of Commerce . . . . (903) 859-3025

BULLARD (town). Covers a land area of 1.417 square miles and a water area of 0 square miles. Located at 32.14° N. Lat; 95.32° W. Long. Elevation is 505 feet.
Population: 748 (1990); 1,150 (2000); 1,565 (2010); 1,750 (2015 projected); Race: 87.8% White, 6.3% Black, 0.8% Asian, 5.2% Other, 5.8% Hispanic of any race (2010); Density: 1,104.7 persons per square mile (2010); Average household size: 2.77 (2010); Median age: 33.5 (2010); Males per 100 females: 89.5 (2010); Marriage status: 24.6% never married, 51.5% now married, 9.3% widowed, 14.6% divorced (2005-2009 5-year est.); Foreign born: 2.5% (2005-2009 5-year est.); Ancestry (includes multiple ancestries): 15.8% Irish, 15.6% English, 12.7% German, 7.2% American, 3.7% Scottish (2005-2009 5-year est.).
Economy: Single-family building permits issued: 15 (2010); Multi-family building permits issued: 0 (2010); Employment by occupation: 19.2% management, 20.5% professional, 13.8% services, 27.0% sales, 0.5% farming, 10.2% construction, 8.9% production (2005-2009 5-year est.).
Income: Per capita income: $20,551 (2010); Median household income: $47,651 (2010); Average household income: $56,970 (2010); Percent of households with income of $100,000 or more: 11.5% (2010); Poverty rate: 4.8% (2005-2009 5-year est.).
Taxes: Total city taxes per capita: $332 (2007); City property taxes per capita: $185 (2007).
Education: Percent of population age 25 and over with: High school diploma (including GED) or higher: 89.0% (2010); Bachelor's degree or higher: 14.4% (2010); Master's degree or higher: 5.4% (2010).
School District(s)
Bullard ISD (PK-12)
   2009-10 Enrollment: 2,004 . . . . (903) 894-6639
Housing: Homeownership rate: 81.4% (2010); Median home value: $98,676 (2010); Median contract rent: $524 per month (2005-2009 5-year est.); Median year structure built: 1990 (2005-2009 5-year est.).
Safety: Violent crime rate: 26.2 per 10,000 population; Property crime rate: 351.0 per 10,000 population (2009).
Newspapers: Bullard Weekly News (Local news; Circulation 1,100)
Transportation: Commute to work: 92.8% car, 0.0% public transportation, 1.3% walk, 3.3% work from home (2005-2009 5-year est.); Travel time to work: 17.0% less than 15 minutes, 38.1% 15 to 30 minutes, 37.5% 30 to 45 minutes, 3.8% 45 to 60 minutes, 3.6% 60 minutes or more (2005-2009 5-year est.)
Additional Information Contacts
Bullard Area Chamber of Commerce . . . . (903) 894-4238
   http://bullardtexaschamber.com

FLINT (unincorporated postal area, zip code 75762). Covers a land area of 42.056 square miles and a water area of 0.076 square miles. Located at 32.20° N. Lat; 95.41° W. Long. Elevation is 522 feet.
Population: 8,056 (2000); Race: 91.9% White, 4.8% Black, 1.8% Asian, 1.5% Other, 3.3% Hispanic of any race (2000); Density: 191.6 persons per square mile (2000); Age: 26.5% under 18, 13.5% over 64 (2000); Marriage status: 13.2% never married, 75.0% now married, 3.3% widowed, 8.4% divorced (2000); Foreign born: 2.5% (2000); Ancestry (includes multiple ancestries): 17.4% American, 14.3% Irish, 13.0% English, 12.1% German (2000).
Economy: Employment by occupation: 15.5% management, 21.5% professional, 11.6% services, 28.2% sales, 0.3% farming, 8.3% construction, 14.6% production (2000).
Income: Per capita income: $24,314 (2000); Median household income: $49,615 (2000); Poverty rate: 179.1% (2000).
Education: Percent of population age 25 and over with: High school diploma (including GED) or higher: 86.0% (2000); Bachelor's degree or higher: 25.6% (2000).
Housing: Homeownership rate: 83.2% (2000); Median home value: $113,200 (2000); Median contract rent: $452 per month (2000); Median year structure built: 1984 (2000).
Transportation: Commute to work: 94.5% car, 0.3% public transportation, 0.8% walk, 2.5% work from home (2000); Travel time to work: 15.2% less

than 15 minutes, 45.8% 15 to 30 minutes, 26.2% 30 to 45 minutes, 5.9% 45 to 60 minutes, 6.9% 60 minutes or more (2000)
Additional Information Contacts
Lake Palesine Chamber of Commerce . . . . (903) 876-5310
   http://www.lakepalestinechamber.com

LINDALE (town). Covers a land area of 4.012 square miles and a water area of 0.018 square miles. Located at 32.50° N. Lat; 95.40° W. Long. Elevation is 551 feet.
Population: 2,676 (1990); 2,954 (2000); 4,230 (2010); 4,764 (2015 projected); Race: 85.4% White, 6.9% Black, 0.7% Asian, 7.0% Other, 7.5% Hispanic of any race (2010); Density: 1,054.2 persons per square mile (2010); Average household size: 2.60 (2010); Median age: 36.8 (2010); Males per 100 females: 89.9 (2010); Marriage status: 28.3% never married, 54.5% now married, 7.8% widowed, 9.4% divorced (2005-2009 5-year est.); Foreign born: 2.5% (2005-2009 5-year est.); Ancestry (includes multiple ancestries): 15.4% Irish, 13.5% German, 12.2% American, 10.2% English, 4.7% French (2005-2009 5-year est.).
Economy: Single-family building permits issued: 56 (2010); Multi-family building permits issued: 0 (2010); Employment by occupation: 13.2% management, 17.9% professional, 17.9% services, 25.2% sales, 0.7% farming, 14.0% construction, 11.2% production (2005-2009 5-year est.).
Income: Per capita income: $18,229 (2010); Median household income: $40,630 (2010); Average household income: $48,362 (2010); Percent of households with income of $100,000 or more: 8.4% (2010); Poverty rate: 14.2% (2005-2009 5-year est.).
Taxes: Total city taxes per capita: $806 (2007); City property taxes per capita: $313 (2007).
Education: Percent of population age 25 and over with: High school diploma (including GED) or higher: 80.0% (2010); Bachelor's degree or higher: 12.0% (2010); Master's degree or higher: 2.6% (2010).
School District(s)
Lindale ISD (PK-12)
   2009-10 Enrollment: 3,595 . . . . (903) 881-4001
Responsive Education Solutions (KG-12)
   2009-10 Enrollment: 5,022 . . . . (972) 316-3663
Housing: Homeownership rate: 72.6% (2010); Median home value: $105,843 (2010); Median contract rent: $557 per month (2005-2009 5-year est.); Median year structure built: 1980 (2005-2009 5-year est.).
Safety: Violent crime rate: 30.6 per 10,000 population; Property crime rate: 391.0 per 10,000 population (2009).
Newspapers: Lindale News & Times (Community news; Circulation 3,000)
Transportation: Commute to work: 91.1% car, 0.5% public transportation, 0.0% walk, 1.7% work from home (2005-2009 5-year est.); Travel time to work: 28.9% less than 15 minutes, 37.1% 15 to 30 minutes, 24.2% 30 to 45 minutes, 6.0% 45 to 60 minutes, 3.8% 60 minutes or more (2005-2009 5-year est.)
Additional Information Contacts
Lindale Area Chamber of Commerce . . . . (903) 882-7181
   http://www.lindalechamber.org

NEW CHAPEL HILL (city). Aka Chapel Hill. Covers a land area of 2.456 square miles and a water area of 0 square miles. Located at 32.30° N. Lat; 95.16° W. Long. Elevation is 430 feet.
Population: 439 (1990); 553 (2000); 703 (2010); 722 (2015 projected); Race: 93.5% White, 1.8% Black, 0.1% Asian, 4.6% Other, 7.5% Hispanic of any race (2010); Density: 286.3 persons per square mile (2010); Average household size: 2.74 (2010); Median age: 37.2 (2010); Males per 100 females: 97.5 (2010); Marriage status: 25.6% never married, 50.8% now married, 10.4% widowed, 13.2% divorced (2005-2009 5-year est.); Foreign born: 1.4% (2005-2009 5-year est.); Ancestry (includes multiple ancestries): 25.9% Irish, 15.4% American, 9.9% English, 7.0% German, 5.4% French (2005-2009 5-year est.).
Economy: Employment by occupation: 11.4% management, 26.2% professional, 15.3% services, 26.6% sales, 0.0% farming, 14.8% construction, 5.7% production (2005-2009 5-year est.).
Income: Per capita income: $25,775 (2010); Median household income: $61,422 (2010); Average household income: $69,553 (2010); Percent of households with income of $100,000 or more: 22.2% (2010); Poverty rate: 10.4% (2005-2009 5-year est.).
Taxes: Total city taxes per capita: $164 (2007); City property taxes per capita: $101 (2007).
Education: Percent of population age 25 and over with: High school diploma (including GED) or higher: 87.6% (2010); Bachelor's degree or higher: 20.0% (2010); Master's degree or higher: 5.8% (2010).

Housing: Homeownership rate: 87.5% (2010); Median home value: $109,810 (2010); Median contract rent: $561 per month (2005-2009 5-year est.); Median year structure built: 1976 (2005-2009 5-year est.).
Transportation: Commute to work: 97.7% car, 0.0% public transportation, 1.4% walk, 0.9% work from home (2005-2009 5-year est.); Travel time to work: 34.9% less than 15 minutes, 45.8% 15 to 30 minutes, 12.7% 30 to 45 minutes, 1.9% 45 to 60 minutes, 4.7% 60 minutes or more (2005-2009 5-year est.)

NOONDAY (city). Covers a land area of 1.992 square miles and a water area of 0 square miles. Located at 32.24° N. Lat; 95.39° W. Long. Elevation is 466 feet.
Population: 466 (1990); 515 (2000); 663 (2010); 737 (2015 projected); Race: 90.2% White, 6.9% Black, 1.1% Asian, 1.8% Other, 4.8% Hispanic of any race (2010); Density: 332.9 persons per square mile (2010); Average household size: 2.60 (2010); Median age: 38.3 (2010); Males per 100 females: 104.6 (2010); Marriage status: 17.3% never married, 68.8% now married, 2.7% widowed, 11.3% divorced (2005-2009 5-year est.); Foreign born: 2.3% (2005-2009 5-year est.); Ancestry (includes multiple ancestries): 21.2% Irish, 20.2% German, 10.0% English, 7.1% American, 2.8% Dutch (2005-2009 5-year est.).
Economy: Employment by occupation: 12.5% management, 13.6% professional, 20.8% services, 20.8% sales, 0.0% farming, 20.1% construction, 12.1% production (2005-2009 5-year est.).
Income: Per capita income: $27,055 (2010); Median household income: $65,351 (2010); Average household income: $72,208 (2010); Percent of households with income of $100,000 or more: 21.0% (2010); Poverty rate: 10.3% (2005-2009 5-year est.).
Taxes: Total city taxes per capita: $443 (2007); City property taxes per capita: $127 (2007).
Education: Percent of population age 25 and over with: High school diploma (including GED) or higher: 88.0% (2010); Bachelor's degree or higher: 27.0% (2010); Master's degree or higher: 8.1% (2010).
Housing: Homeownership rate: 87.9% (2010); Median home value: $170,635 (2010); Median contract rent: $750 per month (2005-2009 5-year est.); Median year structure built: 1985 (2005-2009 5-year est.).
Transportation: Commute to work: 70.3% car, 0.0% public transportation, 1.2% walk, 12.9% work from home (2005-2009 5-year est.); Travel time to work: 28.7% less than 15 minutes, 52.0% 15 to 30 minutes, 13.9% 30 to 45 minutes, 4.0% 45 to 60 minutes, 1.3% 60 minutes or more (2005-2009 5-year est.)

TROUP (city). Covers a land area of 2.348 square miles and a water area of 0 square miles. Located at 32.14° N. Lat; 95.12° W. Long. Elevation is 456 feet.
Population: 1,715 (1990); 1,949 (2000); 2,079 (2010); 2,145 (2015 projected); Race: 74.9% White, 16.3% Black, 0.5% Asian, 8.4% Other, 11.9% Hispanic of any race (2010); Density: 885.3 persons per square mile (2010); Average household size: 2.65 (2010); Median age: 33.3 (2010); Males per 100 females: 87.1 (2010); Marriage status: 24.1% never married, 42.4% now married, 18.0% widowed, 15.6% divorced (2005-2009 5-year est.); Foreign born: 3.1% (2005-2009 5-year est.); Ancestry (includes multiple ancestries): 14.1% Irish, 13.5% German, 13.1% English, 6.0% American, 3.7% French (2005-2009 5-year est.).
Economy: Employment by occupation: 7.1% management, 19.0% professional, 21.4% services, 21.0% sales, 1.0% farming, 11.4% construction, 19.0% production (2005-2009 5-year est.).
Income: Per capita income: $18,371 (2010); Median household income: $39,063 (2010); Average household income: $48,519 (2010); Percent of households with income of $100,000 or more: 7.6% (2010); Poverty rate: 26.9% (2005-2009 5-year est.).
Taxes: Total city taxes per capita: $320 (2007); City property taxes per capita: $179 (2007).
Education: Percent of population age 25 and over with: High school diploma (including GED) or higher: 73.9% (2010); Bachelor's degree or higher: 11.3% (2010); Master's degree or higher: 2.9% (2010).
School District(s)
Troup ISD (PK-12)
    2009-10 Enrollment: 1,077 . . . . (903) 842-3067
Housing: Homeownership rate: 69.3% (2010); Median home value: $73,372 (2010); Median contract rent: $463 per month (2005-2009 5-year est.); Median year structure built: 1971 (2005-2009 5-year est.).
Transportation: Commute to work: 88.5% car, 0.0% public transportation, 3.5% walk, 6.1% work from home (2005-2009 5-year est.); Travel time to work: 25.3% less than 15 minutes, 31.2% 15 to 30 minutes, 34.4% 30 to 45

minutes, 5.8% 45 to 60 minutes, 3.3% 60 minutes or more (2005-2009 5-year est.)
Additional Information Contacts
Troup Chamber of Commerce . . . . (903) 842-4113
    http://www.trouptexas.org

TYLER (city). County seat. Covers a land area of 49.303 square miles and a water area of 0.114 square miles. Located at 32.33° N. Lat; 95.30° W. Long. Elevation is 538 feet.
History: Tyler was incorporated in 1846 and named for John Tyler, tenth president of the United States, who signed the joint resolution under which Texas was admitted to the Union. The East Texas Oil Field made Tyler an oil town. Tyler also earned the reputation as a center of rose cultivation. In addition to hundreds of rose nurseries, the city sported azalea gardens.
Population: 77,653 (1990); 83,650 (2000); 99,059 (2010); 106,150 (2015 projected); Race: 59.5% White, 24.6% Black, 1.3% Asian, 14.6% Other, 22.2% Hispanic of any race (2010); Density: 2,009.2 persons per square mile (2010); Average household size: 2.53 (2010); Median age: 34.4 (2010); Males per 100 females: 90.2 (2010); Marriage status: 32.1% never married, 47.3% now married, 8.5% widowed, 12.1% divorced (2005-2009 5-year est.); Foreign born: 10.8% (2005-2009 5-year est.); Ancestry (includes multiple ancestries): 10.9% English, 9.3% Irish, 8.5% German, 6.8% American, 2.5% Scotch-Irish (2005-2009 5-year est.).
Economy: Unemployment rate: 8.1% (June 2011); Total civilian labor force: 49,797 (June 2011); Single-family building permits issued: 114 (2010); Multi-family building permits issued: 65 (2010); Employment by occupation: 10.0% management, 22.8% professional, 19.9% services, 25.6% sales, 0.7% farming, 7.4% construction, 13.6% production (2005-2009 5-year est.).
Income: Per capita income: $23,657 (2010); Median household income: $41,969 (2010); Average household income: $61,024 (2010); Percent of households with income of $100,000 or more: 15.5% (2010); Poverty rate: 20.5% (2005-2009 5-year est.).
Taxes: Total city taxes per capita: $602 (2007); City property taxes per capita: $130 (2007).
Education: Percent of population age 25 and over with: High school diploma (including GED) or higher: 81.6% (2010); Bachelor's degree or higher: 27.5% (2010); Master's degree or higher: 9.3% (2010).
School District(s)
Accelerated Intermediate Academy (PK-08)
    2009-10 Enrollment: 454 . . . . (713) 283-6298
Azleway Charter School (03-12)
    2009-10 Enrollment: 139 . . . . (903) 566-8444
Chapel Hill ISD (PK-12)
    2009-10 Enrollment: 3,215 . . . . (903) 566-2441
Cumberland Academy (KG-06)
    2009-10 Enrollment: 241 . . . . (903) 581-2890
Ranch Academy (03-12)
    2009-10 Enrollment: 88 . . . . (903) 479-3601
Responsive Education Solutions (KG-12)
    2009-10 Enrollment: 5,022 . . . . (972) 316-3663
Tyler ISD (PK-12)
    2009-10 Enrollment: 18,408 . . . . (903) 262-1000
Four-year College(s)
Texas College (Private, Not-for-profit, Historically black, Christian Methodist Episcopal)
    Fall 2009 Enrollment: 964 . . . . (903) 593-8311
    2010-11 Tuition: In-state $9,482; Out-of-state $9,482
The University of Texas at Tyler (Public)
    Fall 2009 Enrollment: 6,201 . . . . (903) 566-7000
    2010-11 Tuition: In-state $6,322; Out-of-state $15,622
Two-year College(s)
Tyler Junior College (Public)
    Fall 2009 Enrollment: 11,045 . . . . (903) 510-2200
    2010-11 Tuition: In-state $3,230; Out-of-state $3,830
Vocational/Technical School(s)
Star College of Cosmetology 2 (Private, For-profit)
    Fall 2009 Enrollment: 88 . . . . (903) 596-7860
    2010-11 Tuition: $8,700
Housing: Homeownership rate: 58.1% (2010); Median home value: $118,683 (2010); Median contract rent: $578 per month (2005-2009 5-year est.); Median year structure built: 1974 (2005-2009 5-year est.).
Hospitals: ETMC Behavioral Health Center (54 beds); ETMC Quitman (30 beds); East Texas Medical Center - Tyler (454 beds); Mother Frances

Hospital-Tyler (358 beds); Texas Spine and Joint Hospital; University of Texas Health Center at Tyler (204 beds)
Safety: Violent crime rate: 52.9 per 10,000 population; Property crime rate: 587.7 per 10,000 population (2009).
Newspapers: Catholic East Texas (Regional news; Circulation 12,480); Tyler Morning Telegraph (Local news; Circulation 43,668)
Transportation: Commute to work: 89.8% car, 0.8% public transportation, 1.8% walk, 4.7% work from home (2005-2009 5-year est.); Travel time to work: 44.0% less than 15 minutes, 41.1% 15 to 30 minutes, 8.4% 30 to 45 minutes, 3.2% 45 to 60 minutes, 3.3% 60 minutes or more (2005-2009 5-year est.)
Airports: Tyler Pounds Regional (primary service)
Additional Information Contacts
City of Tyler . . . . (903) 531-1100
    http://www.cityoftyler.org
Tyler Area Chamber of Commerce . . . . (903) 592-1661
    http://www.tylertexas.com

WHITEHOUSE (city).
Covers a land area of 3.782 square miles and a water area of 0 square miles. Located at 32.22° N. Lat; 95.21° W. Long. Elevation is 479 feet.
Population: 4,196 (1990); 5,346 (2000); 7,404 (2010); 8,139 (2015 projected); Race: 92.2% White, 2.9% Black, 0.7% Asian, 4.2% Other, 4.8% Hispanic of any race (2010); Density: 1,957.8 persons per square mile (2010); Average household size: 2.92 (2010); Median age: 34.4 (2010); Males per 100 females: 94.8 (2010); Marriage status: 26.1% never married, 55.5% now married, 9.1% widowed, 9.3% divorced (2005-2009 5-year est.); Foreign born: 2.1% (2005-2009 5-year est.); Ancestry (includes multiple ancestries): 16.5% American, 14.1% Irish, 13.4% German, 10.7% English, 4.4% Scotch-Irish (2005-2009 5-year est.).
Economy: Single-family building permits issued: 12 (2010); Multi-family building permits issued: 0 (2010); Employment by occupation: 11.7% management, 26.5% professional, 16.1% services, 25.4% sales, 0.0% farming, 6.5% construction, 13.9% production (2005-2009 5-year est.).
Income: Per capita income: $24,325 (2010); Median household income: $62,175 (2010); Average household income: $71,278 (2010); Percent of households with income of $100,000 or more: 18.9% (2010); Poverty rate: 4.7% (2005-2009 5-year est.).
Taxes: Total city taxes per capita: $332 (2007); City property taxes per capita: $201 (2007).
Education: Percent of population age 25 and over with: High school diploma (including GED) or higher: 91.4% (2010); Bachelor's degree or higher: 24.9% (2010); Master's degree or higher: 6.8% (2010).
School District(s)
Whitehouse ISD (PK-12)
    2009-10 Enrollment: 4,607 . . . . (903) 839-5500
Housing: Homeownership rate: 84.5% (2010); Median home value: $134,471 (2010); Median contract rent: $854 per month (2005-2009 5-year est.); Median year structure built: 1988 (2005-2009 5-year est.).
Safety: Violent crime rate: 12.6 per 10,000 population; Property crime rate: 125.7 per 10,000 population (2009).
Newspapers: Tri-County Leader (Local news; Circulation 2,600)
Transportation: Commute to work: 95.4% car, 0.0% public transportation, 0.2% walk, 3.3% work from home (2005-2009 5-year est.); Travel time to work: 14.6% less than 15 minutes, 60.4% 15 to 30 minutes, 20.6% 30 to 45 minutes, 2.4% 45 to 60 minutes, 2.0% 60 minutes or more (2005-2009 5-year est.)
Additional Information Contacts
City of Whitehouse. . . . . (903) 839-4914
    http://www.whitehousetx.org

WINONA (town).
Covers a land area of 1.561 square miles and a water area of 0.003 square miles. Located at 32.49° N. Lat; 95.17° W. Long. Elevation is 331 feet.
Population: 570 (1990); 582 (2000); 634 (2010); 660 (2015 projected); Race: 87.1% White, 8.7% Black, 0.2% Asian, 4.1% Other, 5.8% Hispanic of any race (2010); Density: 406.1 persons per square mile (2010); Average household size: 2.72 (2010); Median age: 37.2 (2010); Males per 100 females: 94.5 (2010); Marriage status: 25.7% never married, 44.8% now married, 8.2% widowed, 21.3% divorced (2005-2009 5-year est.); Foreign born: 5.2% (2005-2009 5-year est.); Ancestry (includes multiple ancestries): 19.0% Irish, 11.9% English, 7.7% German, 6.3% French, 4.2% American (2005-2009 5-year est.).
Economy: Single-family building permits issued: 0 (2010); Multi-family building permits issued: 0 (2010); Employment by occupation: 4.1%

management, 8.1% professional, 26.2% services, 16.2% sales, 1.1% farming, 7.7% construction, 36.5% production (2005-2009 5-year est.).
Income: Per capita income: $20,284 (2010); Median household income: $47,823 (2010); Average household income: $54,013 (2010); Percent of households with income of $100,000 or more: 8.2% (2010); Poverty rate: 17.2% (2005-2009 5-year est.).
Taxes: Total city taxes per capita: $59 (2007); City property taxes per capita: $59 (2007).
Education: Percent of population age 25 and over with: High school diploma (including GED) or higher: 82.5% (2010); Bachelor's degree or higher: 8.5% (2010); Master's degree or higher: 3.1% (2010).
School District(s)
Winona ISD (PK-12)
    2009-10 Enrollment: 1,041 . . . . (903) 939-4001
Housing: Homeownership rate: 82.0% (2010); Median home value: $88,333 (2010); Median contract rent: $331 per month (2005-2009 5-year est.); Median year structure built: 1974 (2005-2009 5-year est.).
Transportation: Commute to work: 90.9% car, 0.0% public transportation, 0.8% walk, 3.4% work from home (2005-2009 5-year est.); Travel time to work: 18.1% less than 15 minutes, 33.9% 15 to 30 minutes, 37.8% 30 to 45 minutes, 8.3% 45 to 60 minutes, 2.0% 60 minutes or more (2005-2009 5-year est.)

Somervell County

Located in north central Texas; hilly region, drained by the Brazos River and Paluxy Creek. Covers a land area of 187.17 square miles, a water area of 4.73 square miles, and is located in the Central Time Zone at 32.24° N. Lat., 97.75° W. Long. The county was founded in 1875. County seat is Glen Rose.

Somervell County is part of the Granbury, TX Micropolitan Statistical Area. The entire metro area includes: Hood County, TX; Somervell County, TX

Population: 5,360 (1990); 6,809 (2000); 8,329 (2010); 9,055 (2015 projected); Race: 89.6% White, 1.2% Black, 0.3% Asian, 8.9% Other, 17.1% Hispanic of any race (2010); Density: 44.5 persons per square mile (2010); Average household size: 2.72 (2010); Median age: 37.6 (2010); Males per 100 females: 99.6 (2010).
Religion: Five largest groups: 32.8% Southern Baptist Convention, 8.8% The United Methodist Church, 3.0% Catholic Church, 2.8% Churches of Christ, 1.0% Assemblies of God (2000).
Economy: Unemployment rate: 7.9% (June 2011); Total civilian labor force: 4,289 (June 2011); Leading industries: 16.4% health care and social assistance; 15.2% accommodation & food services; 8.7% retail trade (2009); Farms: 366 totaling 82,615 acres (2007); Companies that employ 500 or more persons: 1 (2009); Companies that employ 100 to 499 persons: 4 (2009); Companies that employ less than 100 persons: 194 (2009); Black-owned businesses: n/a (2007); Hispanic-owned businesses: n/a (2007); Asian-owned businesses: n/a (2007); Women-owned businesses: 146 (2007); Retail sales per capita: $10,264 (2010). Single-family building permits issued: 8 (2010); Multi-family building permits issued: 0 (2010).
Income: Per capita income: $22,521 (2010); Median household income: $49,211 (2010); Average household income: $61,666 (2010); Percent of households with income of $100,000 or more: 15.9% (2010); Poverty rate: 10.2% (2009); Bankruptcy rate: 1.14% (2010).
Taxes: Total county taxes per capita: $821 (2007); County property taxes per capita: $821 (2007).
Education: Percent of population age 25 and over with: High school diploma (including GED) or higher: 82.3% (2010); Bachelor's degree or higher: 18.8% (2010); Master's degree or higher: 6.4% (2010).
Housing: Homeownership rate: 73.0% (2010); Median home value: $131,128 (2010); Median contract rent: $404 per month (2005-2009 5-year est.); Median year structure built: 1983 (2005-2009 5-year est.)
Health: Birth rate: 134.5 per 10,000 population (2009); Death rate: 109.6 per 10,000 population (2009); Age-adjusted cancer mortality rate: 177.1 (Unreliable) deaths per 100,000 population (2007); Number of physicians: 11.4 per 10,000 population (2008); Hospital beds: 20.8 per 10,000 population (2007); Hospital admissions: 930.9 per 10,000 population (2007).
Elections: 2008 Presidential election results: 22.6% Obama, 75.8% McCain, 0.7% Nader
National and State Parks: Dinosaur Valley State Park
Additional Information Contacts

Somervell County Government . . . . (254) 897-2206
  http://co.somervell.tx.us/ips/cms
Glen Rose Chamber of Commerce . . . . (254) 897-2286
  http://www.glenrosechamber.com

Somervell County Communities

GLEN ROSE (city). County seat. Covers a land area of 2.729 square miles and a water area of 0.004 square miles. Located at 32.23° N. Lat; 97.75° W. Long. Elevation is 620 feet.

History: Glen Rose developed in an area where many springs and mineral wells were believed to have medicinal value. Petrified wood was found in such quantities here that it was used as an early building material.

Population: 1,953 (1990); 2,122 (2000); 2,822 (2010); 3,126 (2015 projected); Race: 88.0% White, 0.6% Black, 0.6% Asian, 10.8% Other, 19.1% Hispanic of any race (2010); Density: 1,034.2 persons per square mile (2010); Average household size: 2.58 (2010); Median age: 37.6 (2010); Males per 100 females: 95.0 (2010); Marriage status: 21.2% never married, 55.8% now married, 8.9% widowed, 14.1% divorced (2005-2009 5-year est.); Foreign born: 2.2% (2005-2009 5-year est.); Ancestry (includes multiple ancestries): 15.2% German, 14.1% Irish, 11.5% American, 10.4% English, 4.2% Scotch-Irish (2005-2009 5-year est.).

Economy: Single-family building permits issued: 8 (2010); Multi-family building permits issued: 0 (2010); Employment by occupation: 6.4% management, 30.4% professional, 29.5% services, 15.3% sales, 0.0% farming, 5.6% construction, 12.8% production (2005-2009 5-year est.).

Income: Per capita income: $20,285 (2010); Median household income: $42,092 (2010); Average household income: $53,420 (2010); Percent of households with income of $100,000 or more: 12.2% (2010); Poverty rate: 19.8% (2005-2009 5-year est.).

Taxes: Total city taxes per capita: $410 (2007); City property taxes per capita: $191 (2007).

Education: Percent of population age 25 and over with: High school diploma (including GED) or higher: 76.0% (2010); Bachelor's degree or higher: 16.4% (2010); Master's degree or higher: 5.7% (2010).

School District(s)
Glen Rose ISD (PK-12)
  2009-10 Enrollment: 1,656 . . . . (254) 898-3900

Housing: Homeownership rate: 64.1% (2010); Median home value: $100,989 (2010); Median contract rent: $398 per month (2005-2009 5-year est.); Median year structure built: 1968 (2005-2009 5-year est.).

Hospitals: Glen Rose Medical Center (16 beds)

Newspapers: Glen Rose Reporter (Community news; Circulation 3,300)

Transportation: Commute to work: 94.2% car, 0.0% public transportation, 0.9% walk, 2.9% work from home (2005-2009 5-year est.); Travel time to work: 60.9% less than 15 minutes, 20.3% 15 to 30 minutes, 6.9% 30 to 45 minutes, 0.0% 45 to 60 minutes, 11.9% 60 minutes or more (2005-2009 5-year est.)

Additional Information Contacts
Glen Rose Chamber of Commerce . . . . (254) 897-2286
  http://www.glenrosechamber.com

NEMO (unincorporated postal area, zip code 76070). Covers a land area of 23.792 square miles and a water area of 0 square miles. Located at 32.26° N. Lat; 97.65° W. Long. Elevation is 794 feet.

Population: 448 (2000); Race: 94.5% White, 0.0% Black, 1.6% Asian, 3.9% Other, 8.6% Hispanic of any race (2000); Density: 18.8 persons per square mile (2000); Age: 28.1% under 18, 10.1% over 64 (2000); Marriage status: 21.8% never married, 72.8% now married, 3.3% widowed, 2.1% divorced (2000); Foreign born: 1.6% (2000); Ancestry (includes multiple ancestries): 21.4% American, 12.1% English, 9.7% German, 8.8% Irish (2000).

Economy: Employment by occupation: 20.9% management, 22.1% professional, 6.4% services, 12.3% sales, 1.7% farming, 6.0% construction, 30.6% production (2000).

Income: Per capita income: $30,040 (2000); Median household income: $58,333 (2000); Poverty rate: 179.1% (2000).

Education: Percent of population age 25 and over with: High school diploma (including GED) or higher: 88.4% (2000); Bachelor's degree or higher: 22.3% (2000).

School District(s)
Brazos River Charter School (09-12)
  2009-10 Enrollment: 157 . . . . (254) 898-9226

Housing: Homeownership rate: 63.0% (2000); Median home value: $139,600 (2000); Median contract rent: n/a per month (2000); Median year structure built: 1984 (2000).

Transportation: Commute to work: 97.9% car, 0.0% public transportation, 0.0% walk, 2.1% work from home (2000); Travel time to work: 34.8% less than 15 minutes, 32.6% 15 to 30 minutes, 6.5% 30 to 45 minutes, 3.9% 45 to 60 minutes, 22.2% 60 minutes or more (2000)

RAINBOW (unincorporated postal area, zip code 76077). Covers a land area of 8.204 square miles and a water area of 0 square miles. Located at 32.28° N. Lat; 97.70° W. Long. Elevation is 627 feet.

Population: 543 (2000); Race: 94.7% White, 0.0% Black, 0.0% Asian, 5.3% Other, 3.6% Hispanic of any race (2000); Density: 66.2 persons per square mile (2000); Age: 24.6% under 18, 11.9% over 64 (2000); Marriage status: 13.2% never married, 66.8% now married, 6.3% widowed, 13.7% divorced (2000); Foreign born: 0.0% (2000); Ancestry (includes multiple ancestries): 16.1% English, 15.7% Irish, 13.4% American, 7.6% German (2000).

Economy: Employment by occupation: 7.5% management, 14.0% professional, 6.1% services, 38.2% sales, 0.0% farming, 14.0% construction, 20.2% production (2000).

Income: Per capita income: $20,222 (2000); Median household income: $30,000 (2000); Poverty rate: 179.1% (2000).

Education: Percent of population age 25 and over with: High school diploma (including GED) or higher: 85.3% (2000); Bachelor's degree or higher: 14.1% (2000).

Housing: Homeownership rate: 89.6% (2000); Median home value: $119,100 (2000); Median contract rent: $371 per month (2000); Median year structure built: 1983 (2000).

Transportation: Commute to work: 88.5% car, 2.2% public transportation, 3.5% walk, 0.0% work from home (2000); Travel time to work: 49.8% less than 15 minutes, 20.7% 15 to 30 minutes, 3.1% 30 to 45 minutes, 3.5% 45 to 60 minutes, 22.9% 60 minutes or more (2000)

Starr County

Located in south Texas; bounded on the south and southwest by the Rio Grande and the Mexican border. Covers a land area of 1,223.02 square miles, a water area of 6.26 square miles, and is located in the Central Time Zone at 26.45° N. Lat., 98.77° W. Long. The county was founded in 1848. County seat is Rio Grande City.

Starr County is part of the Rio Grande City-Roma, TX Micropolitan Statistical Area. The entire metro area includes: Starr County, TX

Weather Station: Falcon Dam											Elevation: 319 feet	
	Jan	Feb	Mar	Apr	May	Jun	Jul	Aug	Sep	Oct	Nov	Dec
High	69	74	82	89	94	99	100	100	94	88	79	70
Low	47	51	57	63	70	74	75	75	72	64	56	48
Precip	0.9	1.0	0.6	1.4	2.4	2.0	1.8	2.2	3.9	1.8	1.2	0.9
Snow	0.0	0.0	0.0	0.0	0.0	0.0	0.0	0.0	0.0	0.0	0.0	0.0

High and Low temperatures in degrees Fahrenheit; Precipitation and Snow in inches

Weather Station: Rio Grande City 1 SE											Elevation: 171 feet	
	Jan	Feb	Mar	Apr	May	Jun	Jul	Aug	Sep	Oct	Nov	Dec
High	70	75	82	89	93	98	99	100	94	88	79	70
Low	46	50	56	63	70	74	75	75	71	64	55	47
Precip	1.0	1.1	0.8	1.2	2.4	2.9	1.8	1.9	4.1	2.6	1.2	1.0
Snow	tr	0.0	0.0	0.0	0.0	0.0	0.0	0.0	0.0	0.0	0.0	0.1

High and Low temperatures in degrees Fahrenheit; Precipitation and Snow in inches

Population: 40,518 (1990); 53,597 (2000); 64,391 (2010); 69,531 (2015 projected); Race: 87.7% White, 0.3% Black, 0.4% Asian, 11.6% Other, 97.3% Hispanic of any race (2010); Density: 52.6 persons per square mile (2010); Average household size: 3.58 (2010); Median age: 27.1 (2010); Males per 100 females: 92.8 (2010).

Religion: Five largest groups: 74.8% Catholic Church, 1.5% Southern Baptist Convention, 0.7% The United Methodist Church, 0.6% Assemblies of God, 0.4% Mennonite Brethren Churches, U.S. Conference of (2000).

Economy: Unemployment rate: 18.0% (June 2011); Total civilian labor force: 25,251 (June 2011); Leading industries: 52.7% health care and social assistance; 21.7% retail trade; 7.5% accommodation & food services (2009); Farms: 1,104 totaling 652,780 acres (2007); Companies that employ 500 or more persons: 2 (2009); Companies that employ 100 to 499 persons: 8 (2009); Companies that employ less than 100 persons: 490 (2009); Black-owned businesses: n/a (2007); Hispanic-owned businesses:

4,873 (2007); Asian-owned businesses: 128 (2007); Women-owned businesses: 1,736 (2007); Retail sales per capita: $6,265 (2010). Single-family building permits issued: n/a (2010); Multi-family building permits issued: n/a (2010).
Income: Per capita income: $9,974 (2010); Median household income: $23,588 (2010); Average household income: $35,469 (2010); Percent of households with income of $100,000 or more: 5.6% (2010); Poverty rate: 38.5% (2009); Bankruptcy rate: 0.39% (2010).
Taxes: Total county taxes per capita: $176 (2007); County property taxes per capita: $169 (2007).
Education: Percent of population age 25 and over with: High school diploma (including GED) or higher: 49.2% (2010); Bachelor's degree or higher: 10.0% (2010); Master's degree or higher: 3.8% (2010).
Housing: Homeownership rate: 78.5% (2010); Median home value: $52,162 (2010); Median contract rent: $271 per month (2005-2009 5-year est.); Median year structure built: 1985 (2005-2009 5-year est.)
Health: Birth rate: 247.8 per 10,000 population (2009); Death rate: 57.1 per 10,000 population (2009); Age-adjusted cancer mortality rate: 118.5 deaths per 100,000 population (2007); Number of physicians: 3.2 per 10,000 population (2008); Hospital beds: 7.9 per 10,000 population (2007); Hospital admissions: 371.3 per 10,000 population (2007).
Elections: 2008 Presidential election results: 84.5% Obama, 15.2% McCain, 0.0% Nader
National and State Parks: Falcon State Park
Additional Information Contacts
Starr County Government . . . . (956) 487-8015
  http://www.co.starr.tx.us/ips/cms
City of Rio Grande City . . . . (956) 487-0672
  http://www.cityofrgc.com
City of Roma . . . . (956) 849-1411
  http://www.cityofroma.net
Rio Grande Valley Partnership Chamber of Commerce . . . (956) 968-3141
  http://www.valleychamber.com

Starr County Communities

ALTO BONITO (CDP). Covers a land area of 0.121 square miles and a water area of 0 square miles. Located at 26.31° N. Lat; 98.66° W. Long. Elevation is 236 feet.
Population: 346 (1990); 569 (2000); 640 (2010); 682 (2015 projected); Race: 90.8% White, 0.2% Black, 0.0% Asian, 9.1% Other, 98.9% Hispanic of any race (2010); Density: 5,278.4 persons per square mile (2010); Average household size: 3.79 (2010); Median age: 26.2 (2010); Males per 100 females: 96.3 (2010); Marriage status: 22.9% never married, 72.9% now married, 0.0% widowed, 4.2% divorced (2005-2009 5-year est.); Foreign born: 44.2% (2005-2009 5-year est.); Ancestry (includes multiple ancestries): n/a (2005-2009 5-year est.).
Economy: Employment by occupation: 31.6% management, 0.0% professional, 0.0% services, 33.3% sales, 0.0% farming, 0.0% construction, 35.1% production (2005-2009 5-year est.).
Income: Per capita income: $7,703 (2010); Median household income: $23,750 (2010); Average household income: $29,749 (2010); Percent of households with income of $100,000 or more: 3.0% (2010); Poverty rate: 50.7% (2005-2009 5-year est.).
Education: Percent of population age 25 and over with: High school diploma (including GED) or higher: 43.6% (2010); Bachelor's degree or higher: 4.2% (2010); Master's degree or higher: 0.9% (2010).
Housing: Homeownership rate: 84.0% (2010); Median home value: $42,105 (2010); Median contract rent: n/a per month (2005-2009 5-year est.); Median year structure built: 1994 (2005-2009 5-year est.).
Transportation: Commute to work: 100.0% car, 0.0% public transportation, 0.0% walk, 0.0% work from home (2005-2009 5-year est.); Travel time to work: 0.0% less than 15 minutes, 68.4% 15 to 30 minutes, 31.6% 30 to 45 minutes, 0.0% 45 to 60 minutes, 0.0% 60 minutes or more (2005-2009 5-year est.)

EL REFUGIO (CDP). Covers a land area of 0.509 square miles and a water area of 0 square miles. Located at 26.34° N. Lat; 98.75° W. Long. Elevation is 151 feet.
Population: 139 (1990); 221 (2000); 271 (2010); 295 (2015 projected); Race: 90.8% White, 0.0% Black, 0.0% Asian, 9.2% Other, 98.9% Hispanic of any race (2010); Density: 532.8 persons per square mile (2010); Average household size: 3.87 (2010); Median age: 24.6 (2010); Males per 100 females: 95.0 (2010); Marriage status: 21.1% never married, 13.1% now married, 65.7% widowed, 0.0% divorced (2005-2009 5-year est.);

Foreign born: 13.1% (2005-2009 5-year est.); Ancestry (includes multiple ancestries): n/a (2005-2009 5-year est.).
Economy: Employment by occupation: 0.0% management, 0.0% professional, 0.0% services, 100.0% sales, 0.0% farming, 0.0% construction, 0.0% production (2005-2009 5-year est.).
Income: Per capita income: $6,620 (2010); Median household income: $20,294 (2010); Average household income: $26,929 (2010); Percent of households with income of $100,000 or more: 2.9% (2010); Poverty rate: 27.2% (2005-2009 5-year est.).
Education: Percent of population age 25 and over with: High school diploma (including GED) or higher: 34.3% (2010); Bachelor's degree or higher: 1.5% (2010); Master's degree or higher: 0.7% (2010).
Housing: Homeownership rate: 81.4% (2010); Median home value: $38,571 (2010); Median contract rent: n/a per month (2005-2009 5-year est.); Median year structure built: 1964 (2005-2009 5-year est.).
Transportation: Commute to work: 100.0% car, 0.0% public transportation, 0.0% walk, 0.0% work from home (2005-2009 5-year est.); Travel time to work: 0.0% less than 15 minutes, 100.0% 15 to 30 minutes, 0.0% 30 to 45 minutes, 0.0% 45 to 60 minutes, 0.0% 60 minutes or more (2005-2009 5-year est.)

ESCOBARES (CDP). Covers a land area of 0.956 square miles and a water area of 0.065 square miles. Located at 26.40° N. Lat; 98.96° W. Long. Elevation is 180 feet.
Population: 1,583 (1990); 1,954 (2000); 2,084 (2010); 2,168 (2015 projected); Race: 88.5% White, 0.2% Black, 0.0% Asian, 11.3% Other, 99.0% Hispanic of any race (2010); Density: 2,180.8 persons per square mile (2010); Average household size: 3.66 (2010); Median age: 26.3 (2010); Males per 100 females: 94.9 (2010); Marriage status: 36.9% never married, 56.4% now married, 5.5% widowed, 1.2% divorced (2005-2009 5-year est.); Foreign born: 44.6% (2005-2009 5-year est.); Ancestry (includes multiple ancestries): n/a (2005-2009 5-year est.).
Economy: Single-family building permits issued: 2 (2010); Multi-family building permits issued: 0 (2010); Employment by occupation: 0.0% management, 28.6% professional, 29.1% services, 20.2% sales, 0.0% farming, 19.8% construction, 2.2% production (2005-2009 5-year est.).
Income: Per capita income: $10,566 (2010); Median household income: $27,183 (2010); Average household income: $38,888 (2010); Percent of households with income of $100,000 or more: 5.8% (2010); Poverty rate: 92.5% (2005-2009 5-year est.).
Education: Percent of population age 25 and over with: High school diploma (including GED) or higher: 49.0% (2010); Bachelor's degree or higher: 8.5% (2010); Master's degree or higher: 1.3% (2010).
Housing: Homeownership rate: 80.1% (2010); Median home value: $54,833 (2010); Median contract rent: $186 per month (2005-2009 5-year est.); Median year structure built: 1992 (2005-2009 5-year est.).
Transportation: Commute to work: 92.8% car, 0.0% public transportation, 7.0% walk, 0.0% work from home (2005-2009 5-year est.); Travel time to work: 27.0% less than 15 minutes, 68.5% 15 to 30 minutes, 3.3% 30 to 45 minutes, 0.0% 45 to 60 minutes, 1.3% 60 minutes or more (2005-2009 5-year est.)

FALCON HEIGHTS (CDP). Covers a land area of 4.386 square miles and a water area of 0 square miles. Located at 26.55° N. Lat; 99.11° W. Long. Elevation is 272 feet.
Population: 254 (1990); 335 (2000); 349 (2010); 364 (2015 projected); Race: 93.7% White, 0.3% Black, 0.0% Asian, 6.0% Other, 94.8% Hispanic of any race (2010); Density: 79.6 persons per square mile (2010); Average household size: 3.25 (2010); Median age: 29.8 (2010); Males per 100 females: 86.6 (2010); Marriage status: 23.1% never married, 70.2% now married, 6.8% widowed, 0.0% divorced (2005-2009 5-year est.); Foreign born: 46.1% (2005-2009 5-year est.); Ancestry (includes multiple ancestries): n/a (2005-2009 5-year est.).
Economy: Employment by occupation: 0.0% management, 0.0% professional, 100.0% services, 0.0% sales, 0.0% farming, 0.0% construction, 0.0% production (2005-2009 5-year est.).
Income: Per capita income: $9,617 (2010); Median household income: $20,682 (2010); Average household income: $30,841 (2010); Percent of households with income of $100,000 or more: 5.6% (2010); Poverty rate: 90.3% (2005-2009 5-year est.).
Education: Percent of population age 25 and over with: High school diploma (including GED) or higher: 40.7% (2010); Bachelor's degree or higher: 8.8% (2010); Master's degree or higher: 5.2% (2010).

Housing: Homeownership rate: 87.9% (2010); Median home value: $51,818 (2010); Median contract rent: n/a per month (2005-2009 5-year est.); Median year structure built: 1982 (2005-2009 5-year est.).
Transportation: Commute to work: 100.0% car, 0.0% public transportation, 0.0% walk, 0.0% work from home (2005-2009 5-year est.); Travel time to work: 100.0% less than 15 minutes, 0.0% 15 to 30 minutes, 0.0% 30 to 45 minutes, 0.0% 45 to 60 minutes, 0.0% 60 minutes or more (2005-2009 5-year est.)

FALCON VILLAGE (CDP). Covers a land area of 0.865 square miles and a water area of 0 square miles. Located at 26.56° N. Lat; 99.13° W. Long. Elevation is 338 feet.

Population: 59 (1990); 78 (2000); 81 (2010); 85 (2015 projected); Race: 93.8% White, 0.0% Black, 0.0% Asian, 6.2% Other, 95.1% Hispanic of any race (2010); Density: 93.7 persons per square mile (2010); Average household size: 3.24 (2010); Median age: 29.1 (2010); Males per 100 females: 92.9 (2010); Marriage status: 0.0% never married, 76.3% now married, 0.0% widowed, 23.7% divorced (2005-2009 5-year est.); Foreign born: 0.0% (2005-2009 5-year est.); Ancestry (includes multiple ancestries): 23.7% Czech (2005-2009 5-year est.).
Economy: Employment by occupation: 48.3% management, 51.7% professional, 0.0% services, 0.0% sales, 0.0% farming, 0.0% construction, 0.0% production (2005-2009 5-year est.).
Income: Per capita income: $9,617 (2010); Median household income: $22,000 (2010); Average household income: $33,900 (2010); Percent of households with income of $100,000 or more: 8.0% (2010); Poverty rate: 0.0% (2005-2009 5-year est.).
Education: Percent of population age 25 and over with: High school diploma (including GED) or higher: 40.0% (2010); Bachelor's degree or higher: 6.7% (2010); Master's degree or higher: 4.4% (2010).
Housing: Homeownership rate: 88.0% (2010); Median home value: $55,000 (2010); Median contract rent: n/a per month (2005-2009 5-year est.); Median year structure built: 1958 (2005-2009 5-year est.).
Transportation: Commute to work: 100.0% car, 0.0% public transportation, 0.0% walk, 0.0% work from home (2005-2009 5-year est.); Travel time to work: 48.3% less than 15 minutes, 0.0% 15 to 30 minutes, 0.0% 30 to 45 minutes, 51.7% 45 to 60 minutes, 0.0% 60 minutes or more (2005-2009 5-year est.)

FRONTON (CDP). Covers a land area of 4.306 square miles and a water area of 0 square miles. Located at 26.41° N. Lat; 99.08° W. Long. Elevation is 200 feet.

Population: 453 (1990); 599 (2000); 635 (2010); 663 (2015 projected); Race: 93.5% White, 0.0% Black, 0.2% Asian, 6.3% Other, 94.8% Hispanic of any race (2010); Density: 147.5 persons per square mile (2010); Average household size: 3.25 (2010); Median age: 29.1 (2010); Males per 100 females: 92.4 (2010); Marriage status: 38.8% never married, 52.5% now married, 3.9% widowed, 4.8% divorced (2005-2009 5-year est.); Foreign born: 12.3% (2005-2009 5-year est.); Ancestry (includes multiple ancestries): 3.1% American (2005-2009 5-year est.).
Economy: Employment by occupation: 3.6% management, 16.8% professional, 23.0% services, 20.9% sales, 3.6% farming, 23.7% construction, 8.5% production (2005-2009 5-year est.).
Income: Per capita income: $9,617 (2010); Median household income: $20,732 (2010); Average household income: $30,538 (2010); Percent of households with income of $100,000 or more: 5.1% (2010); Poverty rate: 49.0% (2005-2009 5-year est.).
Education: Percent of population age 25 and over with: High school diploma (including GED) or higher: 40.7% (2010); Bachelor's degree or higher: 8.6% (2010); Master's degree or higher: 4.6% (2010).
Housing: Homeownership rate: 87.7% (2010); Median home value: $52,051 (2010); Median contract rent: n/a per month (2005-2009 5-year est.); Median year structure built: 1980 (2005-2009 5-year est.).
Transportation: Commute to work: 89.6% car, 0.0% public transportation, 0.0% walk, 10.4% work from home (2005-2009 5-year est.); Travel time to work: 40.5% less than 15 minutes, 23.0% 15 to 30 minutes, 20.1% 30 to 45 minutes, 2.6% 45 to 60 minutes, 13.8% 60 minutes or more (2005-2009 5-year est.)

GARCENO (CDP). Covers a land area of 3.264 square miles and a water area of 0 square miles. Located at 26.40° N. Lat; 98.94° W. Long. Elevation is 194 feet.

Population: 859 (1990); 1,438 (2000); 1,624 (2010); 1,726 (2015 projected); Race: 83.1% White, 0.1% Black, 0.0% Asian, 16.8% Other, 96.6% Hispanic of any race (2010); Density: 497.6 persons per square mile

(2010); Average household size: 3.82 (2010); Median age: 25.4 (2010); Males per 100 females: 93.1 (2010); Marriage status: 29.6% never married, 48.0% now married, 9.6% widowed, 12.7% divorced (2005-2009 5-year est.); Foreign born: 21.2% (2005-2009 5-year est.); Ancestry (includes multiple ancestries): n/a (2005-2009 5-year est.).
Economy: Employment by occupation: 0.0% management, 0.0% professional, 31.5% services, 0.0% sales, 0.0% farming, 53.0% construction, 15.5% production (2005-2009 5-year est.).
Income: Per capita income: $10,061 (2010); Median household income: $16,404 (2010); Average household income: $38,529 (2010); Percent of households with income of $100,000 or more: 7.5% (2010); Poverty rate: 69.7% (2005-2009 5-year est.).
Education: Percent of population age 25 and over with: High school diploma (including GED) or higher: 45.6% (2010); Bachelor's degree or higher: 5.7% (2010); Master's degree or higher: 2.0% (2010).
Housing: Homeownership rate: 83.5% (2010); Median home value: $49,000 (2010); Median contract rent: $185 per month (2005-2009 5-year est.); Median year structure built: 1970 (2005-2009 5-year est.).
Transportation: Commute to work: 72.5% car, 0.0% public transportation, 4.5% walk, 0.0% work from home (2005-2009 5-year est.); Travel time to work: 66.0% less than 15 minutes, 34.0% 15 to 30 minutes, 0.0% 30 to 45 minutes, 0.0% 45 to 60 minutes, 0.0% 60 minutes or more (2005-2009 5-year est.)

LA CASITA-GARCIASVILLE (CDP). Covers a land area of 4.345 square miles and a water area of 0.034 square miles. Located at 26.32° N. Lat; 98.70° W. Long. Elevation is 207 feet.

Population: 1,683 (1990); 2,177 (2000); 2,464 (2010); 2,626 (2015 projected); Race: 90.8% White, 0.1% Black, 0.0% Asian, 9.1% Other, 99.0% Hispanic of any race (2010); Density: 567.1 persons per square mile (2010); Average household size: 3.79 (2010); Median age: 26.4 (2010); Males per 100 females: 99.8 (2010); Marriage status: 37.8% never married, 55.3% now married, 5.5% widowed, 1.3% divorced (2005-2009 5-year est.); Foreign born: 20.6% (2005-2009 5-year est.); Ancestry (includes multiple ancestries): 2.4% American (2005-2009 5-year est.).
Economy: Employment by occupation: 2.8% management, 19.4% professional, 18.6% services, 39.5% sales, 1.3% farming, 6.9% construction, 11.5% production (2005-2009 5-year est.).
Income: Per capita income: $7,701 (2010); Median household income: $23,705 (2010); Average household income: $28,977 (2010); Percent of households with income of $100,000 or more: 2.6% (2010); Poverty rate: 33.6% (2005-2009 5-year est.).
Education: Percent of population age 25 and over with: High school diploma (including GED) or higher: 43.3% (2010); Bachelor's degree or higher: 4.2% (2010); Master's degree or higher: 0.8% (2010).
School District(s)
Rio Grande City CISD (PK-12)
   2009-10 Enrollment: 10,428 . . . . (956) 716-6750
Housing: Homeownership rate: 84.0% (2010); Median home value: $42,585 (2010); Median contract rent: $231 per month (2005-2009 5-year est.); Median year structure built: 1987 (2005-2009 5-year est.).
Transportation: Commute to work: 82.3% car, 0.0% public transportation, 5.8% walk, 11.9% work from home (2005-2009 5-year est.); Travel time to work: 51.1% less than 15 minutes, 41.3% 15 to 30 minutes, 4.4% 30 to 45 minutes, 0.0% 45 to 60 minutes, 3.2% 60 minutes or more (2005-2009 5-year est.)

LA GRULLA (city). Aka Grulla. Covers a land area of 0.584 square miles and a water area of 0.001 square miles. Located at 26.26° N. Lat; 98.64° W. Long. Elevation is 141 feet.

History: Also called Grulla.
Population: 1,335 (1990); 1,211 (2000); 1,192 (2010); 1,197 (2015 projected); Race: 74.1% White, 3.0% Black, 0.0% Asian, 22.9% Other, 95.1% Hispanic of any race (2010); Density: 2,041.7 persons per square mile (2010); Average household size: 3.31 (2010); Median age: 28.9 (2010); Males per 100 females: 94.1 (2010); Marriage status: 29.1% never married, 58.0% now married, 6.6% widowed, 6.3% divorced (2005-2009 5-year est.); Foreign born: 21.2% (2005-2009 5-year est.); Ancestry (includes multiple ancestries): 2.2% Italian, 2.2% French, 0.9% American, 0.6% German (2005-2009 5-year est.).
Economy: Employment by occupation: 0.8% management, 15.5% professional, 35.1% services, 10.7% sales, 3.5% farming, 14.8% construction, 19.6% production (2005-2009 5-year est.).
Income: Per capita income: $7,899 (2010); Median household income: $20,488 (2010); Average household income: $25,736 (2010); Percent of

households with income of $100,000 or more: 0.3% (2010); Poverty rate: 34.4% (2005-2009 5-year est.).

Taxes: Total city taxes per capita: $7 (2007); City property taxes per capita: $0 (2007).

Education: Percent of population age 25 and over with: High school diploma (including GED) or higher: 43.8% (2010); Bachelor's degree or higher: 6.0% (2010); Master's degree or higher: 2.9% (2010).

Housing: Homeownership rate: 86.4% (2010); Median home value: $33,178 (2010); Median contract rent: $252 per month (2005-2009 5-year est.); Median year structure built: 1974 (2005-2009 5-year est.).

Safety: Violent crime rate: 37.5 per 10,000 population; Property crime rate: 96.4 per 10,000 population (2009).

Transportation: Commute to work: 88.1% car, 0.0% public transportation, 5.4% walk, 6.4% work from home (2005-2009 5-year est.); Travel time to work: 49.8% less than 15 minutes, 23.8% 15 to 30 minutes, 17.8% 30 to 45 minutes, 5.6% 45 to 60 minutes, 3.1% 60 minutes or more (2005-2009 5-year est.)

LA PUERTA (CDP). Covers a land area of 0.856 square miles and a water area of 0 square miles. Located at 26.35° N. Lat; 98.75° W. Long. Elevation is 157 feet.

Population: 1,028 (1990); 1,636 (2000); 1,993 (2010); 2,171 (2015 projected); Race: 90.8% White, 0.2% Black, 0.0% Asian, 9.0% Other, 99.2% Hispanic of any race (2010); Density: 2,329.1 persons per square mile (2010); Average household size: 3.88 (2010); Median age: 24.9 (2010); Males per 100 females: 93.3 (2010); Marriage status: 28.8% never married, 61.4% now married, 5.5% widowed, 4.2% divorced (2005-2009 5-year est.); Foreign born: 49.5% (2005-2009 5-year est.); Ancestry (includes multiple ancestries): n/a (2005-2009 5-year est.).

Economy: Employment by occupation: 0.0% management, 21.2% professional, 29.8% services, 28.5% sales, 5.0% farming, 7.4% construction, 8.1% production (2005-2009 5-year est.).

Income: Per capita income: $6,620 (2010); Median household income: $20,038 (2010); Average household income: $25,734 (2010); Percent of households with income of $100,000 or more: 1.9% (2010); Poverty rate: 44.9% (2005-2009 5-year est.).

Education: Percent of population age 25 and over with: High school diploma (including GED) or higher: 34.4% (2010); Bachelor's degree or higher: 1.8% (2010); Master's degree or higher: 0.7% (2010).

Housing: Homeownership rate: 81.1% (2010); Median home value: $38,526 (2010); Median contract rent: $181 per month (2005-2009 5-year est.); Median year structure built: 1986 (2005-2009 5-year est.).

Transportation: Commute to work: 88.9% car, 0.0% public transportation, 9.7% walk, 0.0% work from home (2005-2009 5-year est.); Travel time to work: 42.4% less than 15 minutes, 37.0% 15 to 30 minutes, 1.4% 30 to 45 minutes, 3.6% 45 to 60 minutes, 15.7% 60 minutes or more (2005-2009 5-year est.)

LA ROSITA (CDP). Covers a land area of 3.212 square miles and a water area of 0.008 square miles. Located at 26.40° N. Lat; 98.92° W. Long. Elevation is 200 feet.

Population: 983 (1990); 1,729 (2000); 2,185 (2010); 2,397 (2015 projected); Race: 85.4% White, 0.0% Black, 0.0% Asian, 14.6% Other, 98.6% Hispanic of any race (2010); Density: 680.3 persons per square mile (2010); Average household size: 3.79 (2010); Median age: 24.8 (2010); Males per 100 females: 97.4 (2010); Marriage status: 24.4% never married, 68.3% now married, 3.8% widowed, 3.5% divorced (2005-2009 5-year est.); Foreign born: 23.5% (2005-2009 5-year est.); Ancestry (includes multiple ancestries): 3.9% Irish (2005-2009 5-year est.).

Economy: Employment by occupation: 5.5% management, 13.1% professional, 14.0% services, 20.2% sales, 7.6% farming, 22.0% construction, 17.6% production (2005-2009 5-year est.).

Income: Per capita income: $9,894 (2010); Median household income: $25,423 (2010); Average household income: $37,179 (2010); Percent of households with income of $100,000 or more: 5.6% (2010); Poverty rate: 42.7% (2005-2009 5-year est.).

Education: Percent of population age 25 and over with: High school diploma (including GED) or higher: 52.8% (2010); Bachelor's degree or higher: 11.2% (2010); Master's degree or higher: 7.6% (2010).

Housing: Homeownership rate: 84.7% (2010); Median home value: $57,143 (2010); Median contract rent: $185 per month (2005-2009 5-year est.); Median year structure built: 1991 (2005-2009 5-year est.).

Transportation: Commute to work: 91.2% car, 1.8% public transportation, 1.2% walk, 5.8% work from home (2005-2009 5-year est.); Travel time to work: 26.1% less than 15 minutes, 38.9% 15 to 30 minutes, 12.3% 30 to 45

minutes, 2.8% 45 to 60 minutes, 19.8% 60 minutes or more (2005-2009 5-year est.)

LA VICTORIA (CDP). Covers a land area of 3.641 square miles and a water area of 0 square miles. Located at 26.33° N. Lat; 98.64° W. Long. Elevation is 253 feet.

Population: 1,022 (1990); 1,683 (2000); 1,916 (2010); 2,042 (2015 projected); Race: 90.8% White, 0.1% Black, 0.1% Asian, 9.1% Other, 99.1% Hispanic of any race (2010); Density: 526.2 persons per square mile (2010); Average household size: 3.79 (2010); Median age: 26.5 (2010); Males per 100 females: 99.6 (2010); Marriage status: 22.6% never married, 73.0% now married, 2.7% widowed, 1.6% divorced (2005-2009 5-year est.); Foreign born: 24.6% (2005-2009 5-year est.); Ancestry (includes multiple ancestries): 0.4% American (2005-2009 5-year est.).

Economy: Employment by occupation: 26.2% management, 26.3% professional, 10.7% services, 15.1% sales, 0.0% farming, 7.5% construction, 14.3% production (2005-2009 5-year est.).

Income: Per capita income: $7,703 (2010); Median household income: $23,578 (2010); Average household income: $29,104 (2010); Percent of households with income of $100,000 or more: 2.8% (2010); Poverty rate: 36.2% (2005-2009 5-year est.).

Education: Percent of population age 25 and over with: High school diploma (including GED) or higher: 43.3% (2010); Bachelor's degree or higher: 4.2% (2010); Master's degree or higher: 0.8% (2010).

Housing: Homeownership rate: 84.0% (2010); Median home value: $42,609 (2010); Median contract rent: $359 per month (2005-2009 5-year est.); Median year structure built: 1992 (2005-2009 5-year est.).

Transportation: Commute to work: 85.2% car, 0.0% public transportation, 6.9% walk, 7.3% work from home (2005-2009 5-year est.); Travel time to work: 46.0% less than 15 minutes, 38.9% 15 to 30 minutes, 3.1% 30 to 45 minutes, 6.8% 45 to 60 minutes, 5.3% 60 minutes or more (2005-2009 5-year est.)

LAS LOMAS (CDP). Covers a land area of 0.557 square miles and a water area of 0 square miles. Located at 26.36° N. Lat; 98.77° W. Long. Elevation is 184 feet.

Population: 1,686 (1990); 2,684 (2000); 3,273 (2010); 3,566 (2015 projected); Race: 90.8% White, 0.2% Black, 0.0% Asian, 9.1% Other, 99.2% Hispanic of any race (2010); Density: 5,874.5 persons per square mile (2010); Average household size: 3.88 (2010); Median age: 24.9 (2010); Males per 100 females: 94.0 (2010); Marriage status: 19.6% never married, 69.4% now married, 6.6% widowed, 4.3% divorced (2005-2009 5-year est.); Foreign born: 44.8% (2005-2009 5-year est.); Ancestry (includes multiple ancestries): 2.7% Italian, 0.7% Arab (2005-2009 5-year est.).

Economy: Employment by occupation: 0.0% management, 10.2% professional, 25.4% services, 20.4% sales, 0.0% farming, 19.6% construction, 24.4% production (2005-2009 5-year est.).

Income: Per capita income: $6,620 (2010); Median household income: $20,000 (2010); Average household income: $25,634 (2010); Percent of households with income of $100,000 or more: 1.8% (2010); Poverty rate: 54.2% (2005-2009 5-year est.).

Education: Percent of population age 25 and over with: High school diploma (including GED) or higher: 34.1% (2010); Bachelor's degree or higher: 1.7% (2010); Master's degree or higher: 0.6% (2010).

Housing: Homeownership rate: 81.0% (2010); Median home value: $38,516 (2010); Median contract rent: $316 per month (2005-2009 5-year est.); Median year structure built: 1992 (2005-2009 5-year est.).

Transportation: Commute to work: 96.5% car, 0.0% public transportation, 0.0% walk, 3.5% work from home (2005-2009 5-year est.); Travel time to work: 60.7% less than 15 minutes, 27.0% 15 to 30 minutes, 6.8% 30 to 45 minutes, 0.0% 45 to 60 minutes, 5.5% 60 minutes or more (2005-2009 5-year est.)

LOS ALVAREZ (CDP). Covers a land area of 3.374 square miles and a water area of 0 square miles. Located at 26.38° N. Lat; 98.89° W. Long. Elevation is 197 feet.

Population: 918 (1990); 1,434 (2000); 1,756 (2010); 1,910 (2015 projected); Race: 79.3% White, 0.1% Black, 0.0% Asian, 20.6% Other, 98.0% Hispanic of any race (2010); Density: 520.4 persons per square mile (2010); Average household size: 3.67 (2010); Median age: 27.0 (2010); Males per 100 females: 90.5 (2010); Marriage status: 28.2% never married, 59.1% now married, 4.2% widowed, 8.5% divorced (2005-2009 5-year est.); Foreign born: 35.7% (2005-2009 5-year est.); Ancestry (includes multiple ancestries): 5.1% Italian, 1.2% American, 0.5% French (2005-2009 5-year est.).

Economy: Employment by occupation: 3.1% management, 17.5% professional, 23.5% services, 28.1% sales, 2.3% farming, 15.0% construction, 10.6% production (2005-2009 5-year est.).

Income: Per capita income: $11,187 (2010); Median household income: $25,347 (2010); Average household income: $41,065 (2010); Percent of households with income of $100,000 or more: 7.5% (2010); Poverty rate: 42.9% (2005-2009 5-year est.).

Education: Percent of population age 25 and over with: High school diploma (including GED) or higher: 51.3% (2010); Bachelor's degree or higher: 16.8% (2010); Master's degree or higher: 11.0% (2010).

Housing: Homeownership rate: 84.6% (2010); Median home value: $56,887 (2010); Median contract rent: $270 per month (2005-2009 5-year est.); Median year structure built: 1984 (2005-2009 5-year est.).

Transportation: Commute to work: 88.8% car, 1.8% public transportation, 0.0% walk, 9.4% work from home (2005-2009 5-year est.); Travel time to work: 34.9% less than 15 minutes, 49.4% 15 to 30 minutes, 9.9% 30 to 45 minutes, 0.0% 45 to 60 minutes, 5.8% 60 minutes or more (2005-2009 5-year est.)

LOS VILLAREALES (CDP).

Covers a land area of 20.469 square miles and a water area of 0.039 square miles. Located at 26.40° N. Lat; 98.87° W. Long. Elevation is 217 feet.

Population: 583 (1990); 930 (2000); 1,174 (2010); 1,291 (2015 projected); Race: 81.3% White, 0.0% Black, 0.0% Asian, 18.7% Other, 98.1% Hispanic of any race (2010); Density: 57.4 persons per square mile (2010); Average household size: 3.76 (2010); Median age: 25.9 (2010); Males per 100 females: 93.1 (2010); Marriage status: 39.0% never married, 54.0% now married, 5.4% widowed, 1.6% divorced (2005-2009 5-year est.); Foreign born: 20.7% (2005-2009 5-year est.); Ancestry (includes multiple ancestries): 4.5% American (2005-2009 5-year est.).

Economy: Employment by occupation: 10.1% management, 15.2% professional, 21.5% services, 21.2% sales, 0.0% farming, 20.2% construction, 11.8% production (2005-2009 5-year est.).

Income: Per capita income: $11,274 (2010); Median household income: $26,515 (2010); Average household income: $42,965 (2010); Percent of households with income of $100,000 or more: 8.3% (2010); Poverty rate: 34.1% (2005-2009 5-year est.).

Education: Percent of population age 25 and over with: High school diploma (including GED) or higher: 52.9% (2010); Bachelor's degree or higher: 12.8% (2010); Master's degree or higher: 9.3% (2010).

Housing: Homeownership rate: 84.9% (2010); Median home value: $58,750 (2010); Median contract rent: n/a per month (2005-2009 5-year est.); Median year structure built: 1998 (2005-2009 5-year est.).

Transportation: Commute to work: 86.3% car, 0.0% public transportation, 11.8% walk, 0.0% work from home (2005-2009 5-year est.); Travel time to work: 35.2% less than 15 minutes, 46.4% 15 to 30 minutes, 1.7% 30 to 45 minutes, 6.0% 45 to 60 minutes, 10.7% 60 minutes or more (2005-2009 5-year est.)

NORTH ESCOBARES (CDP).

Covers a land area of 2.651 square miles and a water area of 0 square miles. Located at 26.41° N. Lat; 98.97° W. Long. Elevation is 184 feet.

Population: 1,010 (1990); 1,692 (2000); 2,083 (2010); 2,277 (2015 projected); Race: 99.4% White, 0.1% Black, 0.0% Asian, 0.5% Other, 95.0% Hispanic of any race (2010); Density: 785.8 persons per square mile (2010); Average household size: 3.98 (2010); Median age: 22.9 (2010); Males per 100 females: 90.2 (2010); Marriage status: 26.9% never married, 64.4% now married, 0.4% widowed, 8.4% divorced (2005-2009 5-year est.); Foreign born: 36.6% (2005-2009 5-year est.); Ancestry (includes multiple ancestries): n/a (2005-2009 5-year est.).

Economy: Employment by occupation: 0.0% management, 13.7% professional, 44.8% services, 11.1% sales, 0.0% farming, 26.8% construction, 3.6% production (2005-2009 5-year est.).

Income: Per capita income: $7,859 (2010); Median household income: $25,058 (2010); Average household income: $31,109 (2010); Percent of households with income of $100,000 or more: 2.9% (2010); Poverty rate: 68.2% (2005-2009 5-year est.).

Education: Percent of population age 25 and over with: High school diploma (including GED) or higher: 34.3% (2010); Bachelor's degree or higher: 2.4% (2010); Master's degree or higher: 2.4% (2010).

Housing: Homeownership rate: 78.0% (2010); Median home value: $52,586 (2010); Median contract rent: $225 per month (2005-2009 5-year est.); Median year structure built: 1993 (2005-2009 5-year est.).

Transportation: Commute to work: 96.4% car, 0.0% public transportation, 0.0% walk, 3.6% work from home (2005-2009 5-year est.); Travel time to work: 36.7% less than 15 minutes, 32.4% 15 to 30 minutes, 15.2% 30 to 45 minutes, 0.7% 45 to 60 minutes, 14.9% 60 minutes or more (2005-2009 5-year est.)

RIO GRANDE CITY (city).

County seat. Covers a land area of 7.587 square miles and a water area of 0 square miles. Located at 26.38° N. Lat; 98.81° W. Long. Elevation is 174 feet.

History: Rio Grande City was occupied by Spanish settlers of Escandon in 1753, and founded as a town in 1847 by Henry Clay Davis, a soldier of fortune. The town was first known as Rancho Davis, and was a stop for steamboats on the Rio Grande.

Population: 10,540 (1990); 11,923 (2000); 14,176 (2010); 15,266 (2015 projected); Race: 83.1% White, 0.8% Black, 1.6% Asian, 14.5% Other, 95.5% Hispanic of any race (2010); Density: 1,868.5 persons per square mile (2010); Average household size: 3.37 (2010); Median age: 29.1 (2010); Males per 100 females: 92.4 (2010); Marriage status: 29.8% never married, 54.7% now married, 7.5% widowed, 8.0% divorced (2005-2009 5-year est.); Foreign born: 25.6% (2005-2009 5-year est.); Ancestry (includes multiple ancestries): 1.3% English, 1.0% French, 0.8% Irish, 0.6% German, 0.5% American (2005-2009 5-year est.).

Economy: Employment by occupation: 6.7% management, 22.1% professional, 28.4% services, 20.7% sales, 2.5% farming, 9.6% construction, 10.0% production (2005-2009 5-year est.).

Income: Per capita income: $12,820 (2010); Median household income: $28,752 (2010); Average household income: $42,701 (2010); Percent of households with income of $100,000 or more: 8.4% (2010); Poverty rate: 34.3% (2005-2009 5-year est.).

Taxes: Total city taxes per capita: $265 (2007); City property taxes per capita: $43 (2007).

Education: Percent of population age 25 and over with: High school diploma (including GED) or higher: 60.3% (2010); Bachelor's degree or higher: 14.4% (2010); Master's degree or higher: 5.3% (2010).

School District(s)

One Stop Multiservice Charter School (PK-12)
   2009-10 Enrollment: 746 . . . . (956) 393-2227
Rio Grande City CISD (PK-12)
   2009-10 Enrollment: 10,428 . . . . (956) 716-6750

Housing: Homeownership rate: 72.7% (2010); Median home value: $58,248 (2010); Median contract rent: $289 per month (2005-2009 5-year est.); Median year structure built: 1983 (2005-2009 5-year est.).

Hospitals: Starr County Memorial Hospital (49 beds)

Safety: Violent crime rate: 31.8 per 10,000 population; Property crime rate: 438.3 per 10,000 population (2009).

Newspapers: Rio Grande City Herald (Community news; Circulation 4,000); Rio Grande Herald (Local news; Circulation 4,000)

Transportation: Commute to work: 93.5% car, 0.5% public transportation, 2.4% walk, 2.7% work from home (2005-2009 5-year est.); Travel time to work: 56.8% less than 15 minutes, 22.4% 15 to 30 minutes, 5.9% 30 to 45 minutes, 4.1% 45 to 60 minutes, 10.7% 60 minutes or more (2005-2009 5-year est.)

Additional Information Contacts

City of Rio Grande City . . . . (956) 487-0672
   http://www.cityofrgc.com
Rio Grande Valley Partnership Chamber of Commerce . . . (956) 968-3141
   http://www.valleychamber.com

ROMA (city).

Aka Roma-Los Saenz. Covers a land area of 2.755 square miles and a water area of 0.133 square miles. Located at 26.40° N. Lat; 99.00° W. Long.

History: Roma, incorporated with Los Saenz, was settled on the banks of the Rio Grande and served as a shipping center for cotton during the Civil War.

Population: 8,495 (1990); 9,617 (2000); 11,501 (2010); 12,463 (2015 projected); Race: 90.4% White, 0.1% Black, 0.0% Asian, 9.4% Other, 97.9% Hispanic of any race (2010); Density: 4,174.0 persons per square mile (2010); Average household size: 3.49 (2010); Median age: 28.1 (2010); Males per 100 females: 87.1 (2010); Marriage status: 29.7% never married, 56.0% now married, 9.6% widowed, 4.6% divorced (2005-2009 5-year est.); Foreign born: 36.0% (2005-2009 5-year est.); Ancestry (includes multiple ancestries): 2.8% American, 0.3% German, 0.2% French, 0.2% Irish, 0.2% Swedish (2005-2009 5-year est.).

Economy: Employment by occupation: 5.3% management, 15.6% professional, 34.2% services, 27.3% sales, 0.7% farming, 11.0% construction, 5.9% production (2005-2009 5-year est.).
Income: Per capita income: $10,262 (2010); Median household income: $23,242 (2010); Average household income: $35,786 (2010); Percent of households with income of $100,000 or more: 5.3% (2010); Poverty rate: 32.4% (2005-2009 5-year est.).
Taxes: Total city taxes per capita: $175 (2007); City property taxes per capita: $46 (2007).
Education: Percent of population age 25 and over with: High school diploma (including GED) or higher: 45.6% (2010); Bachelor's degree or higher: 13.8% (2010); Master's degree or higher: 4.6% (2010).

School District(s)
Roma ISD (PK-12)
  2009-10 Enrollment: 6,320 . . . . (956) 849-1377
Housing: Homeownership rate: 69.8% (2010); Median home value: $60,363 (2010); Median contract rent: $276 per month (2005-2009 5-year est.); Median year structure built: 1981 (2005-2009 5-year est.).
Safety: Violent crime rate: 30.6 per 10,000 population; Property crime rate: 180.9 per 10,000 population (2009).
Newspapers: South Texas Reporter (Local news; Circulation 3,000)
Transportation: Commute to work: 87.2% car, 0.0% public transportation, 5.3% walk, 5.5% work from home (2005-2009 5-year est.); Travel time to work: 55.7% less than 15 minutes, 29.1% 15 to 30 minutes, 9.3% 30 to 45 minutes, 2.4% 45 to 60 minutes, 3.6% 60 minutes or more (2005-2009 5-year est.)

Additional Information Contacts
City of Roma . . . . (956) 849-1411
  http://www.cityofroma.net

ROMA CREEK (CDP). Covers a land area of 5.191 square miles and a water area of 0.014 square miles. Located at 26.42° N. Lat; 99.02° W. Long. Elevation is 249 feet.
Population: 300 (1990); 610 (2000); 724 (2010); 781 (2015 projected); Race: 88.4% White, 0.1% Black, 0.0% Asian, 11.5% Other, 96.8% Hispanic of any race (2010); Density: 139.5 persons per square mile (2010); Average household size: 3.23 (2010); Median age: 31.1 (2010); Males per 100 females: 83.8 (2010); Marriage status: 34.2% never married, 57.4% now married, 6.6% widowed, 1.8% divorced (2005-2009 5-year est.); Foreign born: 39.2% (2005-2009 5-year est.); Ancestry (includes multiple ancestries): 5.6% Irish (2005-2009 5-year est.).
Economy: Employment by occupation: 8.8% management, 3.1% professional, 14.5% services, 50.0% sales, 0.0% farming, 17.9% construction, 5.7% production (2005-2009 5-year est.).
Income: Per capita income: $12,801 (2010); Median household income: $24,898 (2010); Average household income: $41,648 (2010); Percent of households with income of $100,000 or more: 6.7% (2010); Poverty rate: 52.1% (2005-2009 5-year est.).
Education: Percent of population age 25 and over with: High school diploma (including GED) or higher: 50.1% (2010); Bachelor's degree or higher: 14.1% (2010); Master's degree or higher: 5.5% (2010).
Housing: Homeownership rate: 78.0% (2010); Median home value: $70,714 (2010); Median contract rent: $311 per month (2005-2009 5-year est.); Median year structure built: 1994 (2005-2009 5-year est.).
Transportation: Commute to work: 94.0% car, 0.0% public transportation, 6.0% walk, 0.0% work from home (2005-2009 5-year est.); Travel time to work: 29.8% less than 15 minutes, 60.3% 15 to 30 minutes, 9.9% 30 to 45 minutes, 0.0% 45 to 60 minutes, 0.0% 60 minutes or more (2005-2009 5-year est.)

SALINENO (CDP). Covers a land area of 2.792 square miles and a water area of 0 square miles. Located at 26.51° N. Lat; 99.11° W. Long. Elevation is 220 feet.
Population: 230 (1990); 304 (2000); 329 (2010); 343 (2015 projected); Race: 93.6% White, 0.3% Black, 0.0% Asian, 6.1% Other, 94.8% Hispanic of any race (2010); Density: 117.8 persons per square mile (2010); Average household size: 3.25 (2010); Median age: 30.4 (2010); Males per 100 females: 92.4 (2010); Marriage status: 42.4% never married, 38.2% now married, 0.0% widowed, 19.4% divorced (2005-2009 5-year est.); Foreign born: 56.3% (2005-2009 5-year est.); Ancestry (includes multiple ancestries): n/a (2005-2009 5-year est.).
Economy: Employment by occupation: 51.9% management, 0.0% professional, 0.0% services, 0.0% sales, 0.0% farming, 48.1% construction, 0.0% production (2005-2009 5-year est.).

Income: Per capita income: $9,617 (2010); Median household income: $21,250 (2010); Average household income: $31,040 (2010); Percent of households with income of $100,000 or more: 5.0% (2010); Poverty rate: 25.6% (2005-2009 5-year est.).
Education: Percent of population age 25 and over with: High school diploma (including GED) or higher: 40.3% (2010); Bachelor's degree or higher: 8.1% (2010); Master's degree or higher: 4.3% (2010).
Housing: Homeownership rate: 88.1% (2010); Median home value: $54,500 (2010); Median contract rent: n/a per month (2005-2009 5-year est.); Median year structure built: 1966 (2005-2009 5-year est.).
Transportation: Commute to work: 100.0% car, 0.0% public transportation, 0.0% walk, 0.0% work from home (2005-2009 5-year est.); Travel time to work: 51.9% less than 15 minutes, 48.1% 15 to 30 minutes, 0.0% 30 to 45 minutes, 0.0% 45 to 60 minutes, 0.0% 60 minutes or more (2005-2009 5-year est.)

SAN ISIDRO (CDP). Covers a land area of 3.256 square miles and a water area of 0 square miles. Located at 26.71° N. Lat; 98.44° W. Long. Elevation is 282 feet.
Population: 310 (1990); 270 (2000); 259 (2010); 257 (2015 projected); Race: 86.5% White, 0.0% Black, 0.4% Asian, 13.1% Other, 94.2% Hispanic of any race (2010); Density: 79.5 persons per square mile (2010); Average household size: 2.64 (2010); Median age: 42.4 (2010); Males per 100 females: 103.9 (2010); Marriage status: 39.8% never married, 56.2% now married, 4.0% widowed, 0.0% divorced (2005-2009 5-year est.); Foreign born: 22.3% (2005-2009 5-year est.); Ancestry (includes multiple ancestries): 1.5% Italian (2005-2009 5-year est.).
Economy: Employment by occupation: 6.8% management, 28.0% professional, 22.0% services, 7.6% sales, 12.1% farming, 12.9% construction, 10.6% production (2005-2009 5-year est.).
Income: Per capita income: $13,920 (2010); Median household income: $25,000 (2010); Average household income: $39,719 (2010); Percent of households with income of $100,000 or more: 6.1% (2010); Poverty rate: 41.3% (2005-2009 5-year est.).
Education: Percent of population age 25 and over with: High school diploma (including GED) or higher: 73.3% (2010); Bachelor's degree or higher: 14.2% (2010); Master's degree or higher: 2.8% (2010).

School District(s)
San Isidro ISD (PK-12)
  2009-10 Enrollment: 278 . . . . (956) 481-3110
Housing: Homeownership rate: 80.6% (2010); Median home value: $43,846 (2010); Median contract rent: $261 per month (2005-2009 5-year est.); Median year structure built: 1977 (2005-2009 5-year est.).
Transportation: Commute to work: 81.1% car, 0.0% public transportation, 12.9% walk, 6.1% work from home (2005-2009 5-year est.); Travel time to work: 50.0% less than 15 minutes, 16.1% 15 to 30 minutes, 24.2% 30 to 45 minutes, 9.7% 45 to 60 minutes, 0.0% 60 minutes or more (2005-2009 5-year est.)

SANTA CRUZ (CDP). Covers a land area of 0.407 square miles and a water area of 0 square miles. Located at 26.34° N. Lat; 98.76° W. Long. Elevation is 161 feet.
Population: 396 (1990); 630 (2000); 768 (2010); 837 (2015 projected); Race: 90.8% White, 0.3% Black, 0.0% Asian, 9.0% Other, 99.2% Hispanic of any race (2010); Density: 1,886.7 persons per square mile (2010); Average household size: 3.88 (2010); Median age: 25.0 (2010); Males per 100 females: 93.5 (2010); Marriage status: 16.1% never married, 67.0% now married, 8.3% widowed, 8.6% divorced (2005-2009 5-year est.); Foreign born: 42.0% (2005-2009 5-year est.); Ancestry (includes multiple ancestries): n/a (2005-2009 5-year est.).
Economy: Employment by occupation: 0.0% management, 20.6% professional, 0.0% services, 45.0% sales, 0.0% farming, 0.0% construction, 34.4% production (2005-2009 5-year est.).
Income: Per capita income: $6,620 (2010); Median household income: $20,098 (2010); Average household income: $25,871 (2010); Percent of households with income of $100,000 or more: 2.0% (2010); Poverty rate: 54.5% (2005-2009 5-year est.).
Education: Percent of population age 25 and over with: High school diploma (including GED) or higher: 34.1% (2010); Bachelor's degree or higher: 1.6% (2010); Master's degree or higher: 0.5% (2010).
Housing: Homeownership rate: 80.8% (2010); Median home value: $38,333 (2010); Median contract rent: n/a per month (2005-2009 5-year est.); Median year structure built: 1980 (2005-2009 5-year est.).
Transportation: Commute to work: 72.5% car, 0.0% public transportation, 27.5% walk, 0.0% work from home (2005-2009 5-year est.); Travel time to

work: 32.1% less than 15 minutes, 6.9% 15 to 30 minutes, 17.6% 30 to 45 minutes, 16.0% 45 to 60 minutes, 27.5% 60 minutes or more (2005-2009 5-year est.)

Stephens County

Located in north central Texas; drained by the Clear Fork of the Brazos River; includes part of Possum Kingdom Lake. Covers a land area of 894.64 square miles, a water area of 26.84 square miles, and is located in the Central Time Zone at 32.73° N. Lat., 98.85° W. Long. The county was founded in 1858. County seat is Breckenridge.

Weather Station: Breckenridge   Elevation: 1,169 feet

	Jan	Feb	Mar	Apr	May	Jun	Jul	Aug	Sep	Oct	Nov	Dec
High	58	61	69	78	85	92	96	96	89	79	68	58
Low	31	34	43	51	61	69	72	72	64	53	41	31
Precip	1.3	1.8	2.6	2.2	3.8	3.8	2.1	2.3	2.6	3.5	1.6	1.4
Snow	0.3	0.5	0.5	0.3	0.0	0.0	0.0	0.0	0.0	tr	0.4	0.4

High and Low temperatures in degrees Fahrenheit; Precipitation and Snow in inches

Population: 9,010 (1990); 9,674 (2000); 9,776 (2010); 9,808 (2015 projected); Race: 82.3% White, 3.7% Black, 0.6% Asian, 13.3% Other, 19.6% Hispanic of any race (2010); Density: 10.9 persons per square mile (2010); Average household size: 2.45 (2010); Median age: 37.3 (2010); Males per 100 females: 107.9 (2010).
Religion: Five largest groups: 37.4% Southern Baptist Convention, 10.6% Catholic Church, 8.6% The United Methodist Church, 5.9% Churches of Christ, 2.7% Christian Church (Disciples of Christ) (2000).
Economy: Unemployment rate: 8.7% (June 2011); Total civilian labor force: 4,710 (June 2011); Leading industries: 15.9% mining; 15.5% manufacturing; 15.2% health care and social assistance (2009); Farms: 487 totaling 429,279 acres (2007); Companies that employ 500 or more persons: 0 (2009); Companies that employ 100 to 499 persons: 3 (2009); Companies that employ less than 100 persons: 247 (2009); Black-owned businesses: n/a (2007); Hispanic-owned businesses: n/a (2007); Asian-owned businesses: n/a (2007); Women-owned businesses: 255 (2007); Retail sales per capita: $9,681 (2010). Single-family building permits issued: 3 (2010); Multi-family building permits issued: 0 (2010).
Income: Per capita income: $20,840 (2010); Median household income: $40,475 (2010); Average household income: $53,367 (2010); Percent of households with income of $100,000 or more: 10.0% (2010); Poverty rate: 19.7% (2009); Bankruptcy rate: 1.03% (2010).
Taxes: Total county taxes per capita: $368 (2007); County property taxes per capita: $313 (2007).
Education: Percent of population age 25 and over with: High school diploma (including GED) or higher: 77.5% (2010); Bachelor's degree or higher: 14.6% (2010); Master's degree or higher: 5.3% (2010).
Housing: Homeownership rate: 70.4% (2010); Median home value: $57,665 (2010); Median contract rent: $368 per month (2005-2009 5-year est.); Median year structure built: 1965 (2005-2009 5-year est.).
Health: Birth rate: 162.0 per 10,000 population (2009); Death rate: 116.3 per 10,000 population (2009); Age-adjusted cancer mortality rate: 217.2 deaths per 100,000 population (2007); Number of physicians: 5.3 per 10,000 population (2008); Hospital beds: 34.9 per 10,000 population (2007); Hospital admissions: 754.9 per 10,000 population (2007).
Elections: 2008 Presidential election results: 17.8% Obama, 81.4% McCain, 0.0% Nader
Additional Information Contacts
Stephens County Government. . . . . (254) 559-3700
    http://www.co.stephens.tx.us/ips/cms
Breckenridge Chamber of Commerce . . . . (254) 559-2301
    http://www.breckenridgetexas.com
City of Breckenridge. . . . . (254) 559-7322
    http://www.breckenridgetexas.com

Stephens County Communities

BRECKENRIDGE (city). County seat. Covers a land area of 4.153 square miles and a water area of 0.006 square miles. Located at 32.75° N. Lat; 98.90° W. Long. Elevation is 1,204 feet.
History: Breckenridge experienced a boom when oil was struck here in 1916-1917.
Population: 5,674 (1990); 5,868 (2000); 5,791 (2010); 5,711 (2015 projected); Race: 80.7% White, 1.3% Black, 0.9% Asian, 17.1% Other, 26.7% Hispanic of any race (2010); Density: 1,394.3 persons per square mile (2010); Average household size: 2.56 (2010); Median age: 33.3

(2010); Males per 100 females: 92.7 (2010); Marriage status: 20.3% never married, 54.5% now married, 9.8% widowed, 15.5% divorced (2005-2009 5-year est.); Foreign born: 6.5% (2005-2009 5-year est.); Ancestry (includes multiple ancestries): 10.5% English, 9.7% German, 9.1% Irish, 9.0% American, 1.8% Scotch-Irish (2005-2009 5-year est.).
Economy: Single-family building permits issued: 3 (2010); Multi-family building permits issued: 0 (2010); Employment by occupation: 4.3% management, 10.8% professional, 19.9% services, 32.7% sales, 1.0% farming, 14.5% construction, 16.8% production (2005-2009 5-year est.).
Income: Per capita income: $18,966 (2010); Median household income: $39,854 (2010); Average household income: $49,005 (2010); Percent of households with income of $100,000 or more: 7.7% (2010); Poverty rate: 29.4% (2005-2009 5-year est.).
Taxes: Total city taxes per capita: $591 (2007); City property taxes per capita: $276 (2007).
Education: Percent of population age 25 and over with: High school diploma (including GED) or higher: 72.6% (2010); Bachelor's degree or higher: 13.0% (2010); Master's degree or higher: 4.3% (2010).
School District(s)
Breckenridge ISD (PK-12)
    2009-10 Enrollment: 1,581 . . . . (254) 559-2278
Housing: Homeownership rate: 61.8% (2010); Median home value: $46,140 (2010); Median contract rent: $345 per month (2005-2009 5-year est.); Median year structure built: 1956 (2005-2009 5-year est.).
Hospitals: Stephens Memorial Hospital (40 beds)
Safety: Violent crime rate: 12.5 per 10,000 population; Property crime rate: 194.3 per 10,000 population (2009).
Newspapers: Breckenridge American (Local news; Circulation 3,603)
Transportation: Commute to work: 86.9% car, 0.8% public transportation, 2.3% walk, 3.1% work from home (2005-2009 5-year est.); Travel time to work: 75.1% less than 15 minutes, 11.9% 15 to 30 minutes, 6.1% 30 to 45 minutes, 1.2% 45 to 60 minutes, 5.6% 60 minutes or more (2005-2009 5-year est.)
Additional Information Contacts
Breckenridge Chamber of Commerce . . . . (254) 559-2301
    http://www.breckenridgetexas.com
City of Breckenridge. . . . . (254) 559-7322
    http://www.breckenridgetexas.com

CADDO (unincorporated postal area, zip code 76429). Covers a land area of 145.259 square miles and a water area of 0.210 square miles. Located at 32.74° N. Lat; 98.67° W. Long. Elevation is 1,253 feet.
Population: 226 (2000); Race: 100.0% White, 0.0% Black, 0.0% Asian, 0.0% Other, 0.0% Hispanic of any race (2000); Density: 1.6 persons per square mile (2000); Age: 14.8% under 18, 38.8% over 64 (2000); Marriage status: 17.2% never married, 55.2% now married, 17.2% widowed, 10.4% divorced (2000); Foreign born: 1.1% (2000); Ancestry (includes multiple ancestries): 19.7% English, 19.1% American, 12.0% German, 5.5% Scottish (2000).
Economy: Employment by occupation: 12.8% management, 11.5% professional, 11.5% services, 37.2% sales, 7.7% farming, 9.0% construction, 10.3% production (2000).
Income: Per capita income: $21,485 (2000); Median household income: $44,375 (2000); Poverty rate: 179.1% (2000).
Education: Percent of population age 25 and over with: High school diploma (including GED) or higher: 89.9% (2000); Bachelor's degree or higher: 27.5% (2000).
Housing: Homeownership rate: 78.9% (2000); Median home value: $85,600 (2000); Median contract rent: $225 per month (2000); Median year structure built: 1970 (2000).
Transportation: Commute to work: 89.7% car, 0.0% public transportation, 10.3% walk, 0.0% work from home (2000); Travel time to work: 29.5% less than 15 minutes, 38.5% 15 to 30 minutes, 17.9% 30 to 45 minutes, 14.1% 45 to 60 minutes, 0.0% 60 minutes or more (2000)

Sterling County

Located in west Texas; prairie area, drained by the North Concho River. Covers a land area of 923.36 square miles, a water area of 0.13 square miles, and is located in the Central Time Zone at 31.81° N. Lat., 101.04° W. Long. The county was founded in 1891. County seat is Sterling City.

Weather Station: Sterling City   Elevation: 2,265 feet

	Jan	Feb	Mar	Apr	May	Jun	Jul	Aug	Sep	Oct	Nov	Dec
High	59	63	71	80	87	92	95	94	88	79	68	60
Low	30	33	41	49	59	67	69	69	61	50	39	30
Precip	0.9	1.0	1.3	1.4	2.7	2.4	1.5	2.4	2.5	1.8	1.0	1.0
Snow	0.6	0.4	0.2	0.0	0.0	0.0	0.0	0.0	0.0	0.0	0.4	0.4

High and Low temperatures in degrees Fahrenheit; Precipitation and Snow in inches

Population: 1,438 (1990); 1,393 (2000); 1,212 (2010); 1,121 (2015 projected); Race: 83.4% White, 0.1% Black, 0.0% Asian, 16.5% Other, 35.7% Hispanic of any race (2010); Density: 1.3 persons per square mile (2010); Average household size: 2.56 (2010); Median age: 45.0 (2010); Males per 100 females: 94.9 (2010).
Religion: Five largest groups: 39.1% Southern Baptist Convention, 21.1% The United Methodist Church, 14.4% Catholic Church, 7.9% Churches of Christ, 3.6% Presbyterian Church (U.S.A.) (2000).
Economy: Unemployment rate: 5.6% (June 2011); Total civilian labor force: 767 (June 2011); Leading industries: Farms: 74 totaling 578,316 acres (2007); Companies that employ 500 or more persons: 0 (2009); Companies that employ 100 to 499 persons: 0 (2009); Companies that employ less than 100 persons: 28 (2009); Black-owned businesses: n/a (2007); Hispanic-owned businesses: n/a (2007); Asian-owned businesses: n/a (2007); Women-owned businesses: n/a (2007); Retail sales per capita: $20,587 (2010). Single-family building permits issued: n/a (2010); Multi-family building permits issued: n/a (2010).
Income: Per capita income: $24,216 (2010); Median household income: $48,700 (2010); Average household income: $63,272 (2010); Percent of households with income of $100,000 or more: 15.3% (2010); Poverty rate: 13.3% (2009); Bankruptcy rate: n/a (2010).
Taxes: Total county taxes per capita: $1,664 (2007); County property taxes per capita: $1,595 (2007).
Education: Percent of population age 25 and over with: High school diploma (including GED) or higher: 75.3% (2010); Bachelor's degree or higher: 19.0% (2010); Master's degree or higher: 5.1% (2010).
Housing: Homeownership rate: 73.9% (2010); Median home value: $59,452 (2010); Median contract rent: $406 per month (2005-2009 5-year est.); Median year structure built: 1968 (2005-2009 5-year est.)
Health: Birth rate: 111.2 per 10,000 population (2009); Death rate: 79.4 per 10,000 population (2009); Age-adjusted cancer mortality rate: Suppressed deaths per 100,000 population (2007); Number of physicians: 0.0 per 10,000 population (2008); Hospital beds: 0.0 per 10,000 population (2007); Hospital admissions: 0.0 per 10,000 population (2007).
Elections: 2008 Presidential election results: 15.7% Obama, 84.0% McCain, 0.0% Nader
Additional Information Contacts
Sterling County Government . . . . (325) 378-5191
  http://www.co.sterling.tx.us/ips/cms

Sterling County Communities

STERLING CITY (city). County seat. Covers a land area of 0.978 square miles and a water area of 0 square miles. Located at 31.83° N. Lat; 100.98° W. Long. Elevation is 2,287 feet.
Population: 1,108 (1990); 1,081 (2000); 946 (2010); 878 (2015 projected); Race: 79.4% White, 0.1% Black, 0.0% Asian, 20.5% Other, 38.4% Hispanic of any race (2010); Density: 967.8 persons per square mile (2010); Average household size: 2.59 (2010); Median age: 45.2 (2010); Males per 100 females: 92.7 (2010); Marriage status: 18.3% never married, 63.2% now married, 10.9% widowed, 7.6% divorced (2005-2009 5-year est.); Foreign born: 7.2% (2005-2009 5-year est.); Ancestry (includes multiple ancestries): 19.1% German, 18.6% Irish, 8.6% English, 7.8% Italian, 3.3% Egyptian (2005-2009 5-year est.).
Economy: Employment by occupation: 17.3% management, 13.4% professional, 16.5% services, 12.8% sales, 0.0% farming, 20.9% construction, 19.1% production (2005-2009 5-year est.).
Income: Per capita income: $23,033 (2010); Median household income: $50,791 (2010); Average household income: $61,148 (2010); Percent of households with income of $100,000 or more: 16.3% (2010); Poverty rate: 23.6% (2005-2009 5-year est.).
Taxes: Total city taxes per capita: $217 (2007); City property taxes per capita: $110 (2007).
Education: Percent of population age 25 and over with: High school diploma (including GED) or higher: 74.1% (2010); Bachelor's degree or higher: 14.6% (2010); Master's degree or higher: 3.0% (2010).

Eden CISD (PK-12)
  2009-10 Enrollment: 266 . . . . (325) 869-4121
Sterling City ISD (PK-12)
  2009-10 Enrollment: 200 . . . . (325) 378-4781
Housing: Homeownership rate: 79.7% (2010); Median home value: $53,571 (2010); Median contract rent: $421 per month (2005-2009 5-year est.); Median year structure built: 1966 (2005-2009 5-year est.).
Newspapers: News-Record (Local news; Circulation 1,067)
Transportation: Commute to work: 91.2% car, 0.0% public transportation, 1.7% walk, 6.1% work from home (2005-2009 5-year est.); Travel time to work: 57.6% less than 15 minutes, 16.5% 15 to 30 minutes, 5.6% 30 to 45 minutes, 12.1% 45 to 60 minutes, 8.2% 60 minutes or more (2005-2009 5-year est.)

Stonewall County

Located in northwest central Texas; drained by the Salt and Double Mountain Forks of the Brazos River. Covers a land area of 918.67 square miles, a water area of 1.56 square miles, and is located in the Central Time Zone at 33.15° N. Lat., 100.22° W. Long. The county was founded in 1876. County seat is Aspermont.

Weather Station: Aspermont   Elevation: 1,669 feet

	Jan	Feb	Mar	Apr	May	Jun	Jul	Aug	Sep	Oct	Nov	Dec
High	56	60	69	78	86	93	97	96	88	78	65	56
Low	29	32	40	48	58	67	70	69	61	51	39	30
Precip	1.0	1.4	1.6	1.7	3.3	3.4	1.7	2.7	2.2	2.3	1.3	1.2
Snow	1.2	0.5	tr	0.1	0.0	0.0	0.0	0.0	0.0	0.0	0.8	0.5

High and Low temperatures in degrees Fahrenheit; Precipitation and Snow in inches

Population: 2,013 (1990); 1,693 (2000); 1,442 (2010); 1,318 (2015 projected); Race: 83.3% White, 3.6% Black, 0.3% Asian, 12.8% Other, 18.2% Hispanic of any race (2010); Density: 1.6 persons per square mile (2010); Average household size: 2.25 (2010); Median age: 46.3 (2010); Males per 100 females: 96.2 (2010).
Religion: Five largest groups: 52.6% Southern Baptist Convention, 14.9% The United Methodist Church, 14.2% Baptist Missionary Association of America, 10.0% Catholic Church, 5.9% Churches of Christ (2000).
Economy: Unemployment rate: 4.8% (June 2011); Total civilian labor force: 840 (June 2011); Leading industries: 13.8% mining; 11.3% retail trade (2009); Farms: 376 totaling 485,644 acres (2007); Companies that employ 500 or more persons: 0 (2009); Companies that employ 100 to 499 persons: 1 (2009); Companies that employ less than 100 persons: 50 (2009); Black-owned businesses: n/a (2007); Hispanic-owned businesses: n/a (2007); Asian-owned businesses: n/a (2007); Women-owned businesses: n/a (2007); Retail sales per capita: $5,371 (2010). Single-family building permits issued: n/a (2010); Multi-family building permits issued: n/a (2010).
Income: Per capita income: $22,699 (2010); Median household income: $39,853 (2010); Average household income: $52,420 (2010); Percent of households with income of $100,000 or more: 11.2% (2010); Poverty rate: 16.8% (2009); Bankruptcy rate: 0.67% (2010).
Taxes: Total county taxes per capita: $760 (2007); County property taxes per capita: $665 (2007).
Education: Percent of population age 25 and over with: High school diploma (including GED) or higher: 76.2% (2010); Bachelor's degree or higher: 14.7% (2010); Master's degree or higher: 2.9% (2010).
Housing: Homeownership rate: 77.0% (2010); Median home value: $35,099 (2010); Median contract rent: $190 per month (2005-2009 5-year est.); Median year structure built: 1960 (2005-2009 5-year est.)
Health: Birth rate: 251.1 per 10,000 population (2009); Death rate: 118.2 per 10,000 population (2009); Age-adjusted cancer mortality rate: 386.5 (Unreliable) deaths per 100,000 population (2007); Number of physicians: 7.2 per 10,000 population (2008); Hospital beds: 523.3 per 10,000 population (2007); Hospital admissions: 675.9 per 10,000 population (2007).
Elections: 2008 Presidential election results: 28.0% Obama, 71.3% McCain, 0.0% Nader
Additional Information Contacts
Stonewall County Government . . . . (940) 989-2272
  http://stonewallcountytexas.us
Aspermont Chamber of Commerce . . . . (940) 989-3197

Stonewall County Communities

ASPERMONT (town). County seat. Covers a land area of 2.070 square miles and a water area of 0 square miles. Located at 33.13° N. Lat; 100.22° W. Long. Elevation is 1,781 feet.

History: Aspermont developed as a retail and shipping center, situated between the Salt Fork and the Double Mountain Fork of the Brazos River.

Population: 1,214 (1990); 1,021 (2000); 875 (2010); 804 (2015 projected); Race: 80.9% White, 5.1% Black, 0.2% Asian, 13.7% Other, 19.4% Hispanic of any race (2010); Density: 422.7 persons per square mile (2010); Average household size: 2.31 (2010); Median age: 42.0 (2010); Males per 100 females: 91.5 (2010); Marriage status: 20.0% never married, 55.3% now married, 11.2% widowed, 13.5% divorced (2005-2009 5-year est.); Foreign born: 1.6% (2005-2009 5-year est.); Ancestry (includes multiple ancestries): 18.0% English, 13.2% American, 11.6% German, 10.7% Irish, 5.9% French (2005-2009 5-year est.).

Economy: Employment by occupation: 12.7% management, 22.7% professional, 17.1% services, 23.2% sales, 1.7% farming, 10.8% construction, 11.9% production (2005-2009 5-year est.).

Income: Per capita income: $20,323 (2010); Median household income: $37,237 (2010); Average household income: $48,939 (2010); Percent of households with income of $100,000 or more: 9.9% (2010); Poverty rate: 13.4% (2005-2009 5-year est.).

Taxes: Total city taxes per capita: $162 (2007); City property taxes per capita: $128 (2007).

Education: Percent of population age 25 and over with: High school diploma (including GED) or higher: 74.1% (2010); Bachelor's degree or higher: 10.8% (2010); Master's degree or higher: 2.9% (2010).

School District(s)

Aspermont ISD (PK-12)

    2009-10 Enrollment: 238 . . . . (940) 989-3355

Housing: Homeownership rate: 73.8% (2010); Median home value: $31,845 (2010); Median contract rent: $163 per month (2005-2009 5-year est.); Median year structure built: 1959 (2005-2009 5-year est.).

Hospitals: Stonewall Memorial Hospital (25 beds)

Newspapers: Stonewall County Courier (Community news; Circulation 1,000)

Transportation: Commute to work: 86.8% car, 0.0% public transportation, 2.6% walk, 9.1% work from home (2005-2009 5-year est.); Travel time to work: 73.1% less than 15 minutes, 10.0% 15 to 30 minutes, 9.1% 30 to 45 minutes, 0.0% 45 to 60 minutes, 7.8% 60 minutes or more (2005-2009 5-year est.)

Additional Information Contacts

Aspermont Chamber of Commerce . . . . (940) 989-3197

OLD GLORY (unincorporated postal area, zip code 79540). Covers a land area of 47.686 square miles and a water area of 0.084 square miles. Located at 33.15° N. Lat; 100.04° W. Long. Elevation is 1,673 feet.

Population: 116 (2000); Race: 100.0% White, 0.0% Black, 0.0% Asian, 0.0% Other, 5.6% Hispanic of any race (2000); Density: 2.4 persons per square mile (2000); Age: 25.6% under 18, 32.2% over 64 (2000); Marriage status: 17.1% never married, 62.9% now married, 10.0% widowed, 10.0% divorced (2000); Foreign born: 0.0% (2000); Ancestry (includes multiple ancestries): 14.4% German, 7.8% American, 4.4% Irish, 4.4% English (2000).

Economy: Employment by occupation: 20.6% management, 26.5% professional, 0.0% services, 20.6% sales, 8.8% farming, 11.8% construction, 11.8% production (2000).

Income: Per capita income: $33,712 (2000); Median household income: $25,625 (2000); Poverty rate: 179.1% (2000).

Education: Percent of population age 25 and over with: High school diploma (including GED) or higher: 50.8% (2000); Bachelor's degree or higher: 22.2% (2000).

Housing: Homeownership rate: 76.1% (2000); Median home value: $13,800 (2000); Median contract rent: $125 per month (2000); Median year structure built: 1957 (2000).

Transportation: Commute to work: 85.3% car, 0.0% public transportation, 8.8% walk, 5.9% work from home (2000); Travel time to work: 25.0% less than 15 minutes, 68.8% 15 to 30 minutes, 6.3% 30 to 45 minutes, 0.0% 45 to 60 minutes, 0.0% 60 minutes or more (2000)

Sutton County

Located in west Texas, on the Edwards Plateau; drained by the Devils and North Llano Rivers. Covers a land area of 1,453.76 square miles, a water area of 0.63 square miles, and is located in the Central Time Zone at 30.50° N. Lat., 100.60° W. Long. The county was founded in 1887. County seat is Sonora.

Population: 4,135 (1990); 4,077 (2000); 4,335 (2010); 4,453 (2015 projected); Race: 72.6% White, 0.3% Black, 0.2% Asian, 26.9% Other, 57.3% Hispanic of any race (2010); Density: 3.0 persons per square mile (2010); Average household size: 2.61 (2010); Median age: 36.0 (2010); Males per 100 females: 101.2 (2010).

Religion: Five largest groups: 42.9% Catholic Church, 20.1% Southern Baptist Convention, 9.6% The United Methodist Church, 4.5% Churches of Christ, 2.6% Episcopal Church (2000).

Economy: Unemployment rate: 5.3% (June 2011); Total civilian labor force: 2,845 (June 2011); Leading industries: 17.1% mining; 15.9% construction; 14.9% accommodation & food services (2009); Farms: 234 totaling 894,515 acres (2007); Companies that employ 500 or more persons: 0 (2009); Companies that employ 100 to 499 persons: 1 (2009); Companies that employ less than 100 persons: 150 (2009); Black-owned businesses: n/a (2007); Hispanic-owned businesses: n/a (2007); Asian-owned businesses: n/a (2007); Women-owned businesses: 62 (2007); Retail sales per capita: $21,223 (2010). Single-family building permits issued: 0 (2010); Multi-family building permits issued: 0 (2010).

Income: Per capita income: $25,697 (2010); Median household income: $50,575 (2010); Average household income: $67,134 (2010); Percent of households with income of $100,000 or more: 17.0% (2010); Poverty rate: 12.4% (2009); Bankruptcy rate: 0.24% (2010).

Taxes: Total county taxes per capita: $470 (2007); County property taxes per capita: $356 (2007).

Education: Percent of population age 25 and over with: High school diploma (including GED) or higher: 70.4% (2010); Bachelor's degree or higher: 14.8% (2010); Master's degree or higher: 3.2% (2010).

Housing: Homeownership rate: 70.3% (2010); Median home value: $58,312 (2010); Median contract rent: $341 per month (2005-2009 5-year est.); Median year structure built: 1968 (2005-2009 5-year est.)

Health: Birth rate: 159.1 per 10,000 population (2009); Death rate: 28.1 per 10,000 population (2009); Age-adjusted cancer mortality rate: 304.4 (Unreliable) deaths per 100,000 population (2007); Number of physicians: 7.0 per 10,000 population (2008); Hospital beds: 27.9 per 10,000 population (2007); Hospital admissions: 726.6 per 10,000 population (2007).

Elections: 2008 Presidential election results: 24.1% Obama, 75.3% McCain, 0.0% Nader

Additional Information Contacts

Sutton County Government . . . . (325) 387-3815
    http://www.co.sutton.tx.us/ips/cms
City of Sonora . . . . (325) 387-2558
    http://www.sonora-texas.com
Sonora Chamber of Commerce . . . . (325) 387-2880
    http://www.sonoratx-chamber.com

Sutton County Communities

SONORA (city). County seat. Covers a land area of 1.964 square miles and a water area of 0 square miles. Located at 30.56° N. Lat; 100.64° W. Long. Elevation is 2,129 feet.

History: Sonora was settled in 1889 on the Dry Fork of the Devil's River. The town developed as a center for the wool and mohair trade. Nearby, the Caverns of Sonora with their miles of stalactites, coral, and calcite formations were opened to the public in 1960.

Population: 2,777 (1990); 2,924 (2000); 3,090 (2010); 3,168 (2015 projected); Race: 72.1% White, 0.4% Black, 0.2% Asian, 27.4% Other, 59.9% Hispanic of any race (2010); Density: 1,573.3 persons per square mile (2010); Average household size: 2.66 (2010); Median age: 34.8 (2010); Males per 100 females: 99.5 (2010); Marriage status: 27.2% never married, 53.2% now married, 9.0% widowed, 10.6% divorced (2005-2009 5-year est.); Foreign born: 13.5% (2005-2009 5-year est.); Ancestry (includes multiple ancestries): 12.2% American, 11.0% German, 7.1% Irish, 5.1% Italian, 4.8% English (2005-2009 5-year est.).

Economy: Single-family building permits issued: 0 (2010); Multi-family building permits issued: 0 (2010); Employment by occupation: 4.7% management, 21.8% professional, 13.8% services, 21.1% sales, 0.8% farming, 19.8% construction, 17.9% production (2005-2009 5-year est.).

Income: Per capita income: $23,627 (2010); Median household income: $48,831 (2010); Average household income: $62,663 (2010); Percent of households with income of $100,000 or more: 14.7% (2010); Poverty rate: 9.2% (2005-2009 5-year est.).

Taxes: Total city taxes per capita: $437 (2007); City property taxes per capita: $159 (2007).

Education: Percent of population age 25 and over with: High school diploma (including GED) or higher: 70.4% (2010); Bachelor's degree or higher: 13.5% (2010); Master's degree or higher: 3.2% (2010).

School District(s)

Sonora ISD (PK-12)
    2009-10 Enrollment: 935 . . . . (325) 387-6940

Housing: Homeownership rate: 71.6% (2010); Median home value: $56,632 (2010); Median contract rent: $339 per month (2005-2009 5-year est.); Median year structure built: 1968 (2005-2009 5-year est.).

Hospitals: Lillian M. Hudspeth Memorial Hospital (21 beds)

Safety: Violent crime rate: 16.4 per 10,000 population; Property crime rate: 101.5 per 10,000 population (2009).

Newspapers: Devil's River News (Local news; Circulation 1,500)

Transportation: Commute to work: 92.2% car, 0.0% public transportation, 3.0% walk, 2.7% work from home (2005-2009 5-year est.); Travel time to work: 73.1% less than 15 minutes, 17.3% 15 to 30 minutes, 4.4% 30 to 45 minutes, 0.6% 45 to 60 minutes, 4.5% 60 minutes or more (2005-2009 5-year est.)

Additional Information Contacts

City of Sonora . . . . (325) 387-2558
    http://www.sonora-texas.com
Sonora Chamber of Commerce . . . . (325) 387-2880
    http://www.sonoratx-chamber.com

Swisher County

Located in northwestern Texas, on the Llano Estacado. Covers a land area of 900.43 square miles, a water area of 0.25 square miles, and is located in the Central Time Zone at 34.51° N. Lat., 101.75° W. Long. The county was founded in 1876. County seat is Tulia.

Weather Station: Tulia   Elevation: 3,470 feet

	Jan	Feb	Mar	Apr	May	Jun	Jul	Aug	Sep	Oct	Nov	Dec
High	52	56	64	72	81	88	92	90	83	73	61	51
Low	23	26	32	40	51	60	64	63	56	44	32	23
Precip	0.7	0.7	1.3	1.4	2.8	3.4	2.1	2.9	2.2	1.9	1.0	0.9
Snow	3.7	2.8	1.5	0.4	tr	0.0	0.0	0.0	0.0	0.1	2.1	3.9

High and Low temperatures in degrees Fahrenheit; Precipitation and Snow in inches

Population: 8,133 (1990); 8,378 (2000); 7,802 (2010); 7,510 (2015 projected); Race: 68.4% White, 7.2% Black, 0.2% Asian, 24.2% Other, 38.0% Hispanic of any race (2010); Density: 8.7 persons per square mile (2010); Average household size: 2.61 (2010); Median age: 35.8 (2010); Males per 100 females: 114.6 (2010).

Religion: Five largest groups: 48.5% Southern Baptist Convention, 14.6% The United Methodist Church, 11.5% Catholic Church, 7.9% Churches of Christ, 2.9% Assemblies of God (2000).

Economy: Unemployment rate: 7.5% (June 2011); Total civilian labor force: 3,597 (June 2011); Leading industries: 20.0% health care and social assistance; 14.6% retail trade; 12.4% accommodation & food services (2009); Farms: 527 totaling 563,067 acres (2007); Companies that employ 500 or more persons: 0 (2009); Companies that employ 100 to 499 persons: 1 (2009); Companies that employ less than 100 persons: 146 (2009); Black-owned businesses: n/a (2007); Hispanic-owned businesses: 62 (2007); Asian-owned businesses: n/a (2007); Women-owned businesses: 172 (2007); Retail sales per capita: $7,082 (2010). Single-family building permits issued: 0 (2010); Multi-family building permits issued: 0 (2010).

Income: Per capita income: $16,466 (2010); Median household income: $34,691 (2010); Average household income: $45,870 (2010); Percent of households with income of $100,000 or more: 7.7% (2010); Poverty rate: 22.0% (2009); Bankruptcy rate: 1.27% (2010).

Taxes: Total county taxes per capita: $286 (2007); County property taxes per capita: $230 (2007).

Education: Percent of population age 25 and over with: High school diploma (including GED) or higher: 74.6% (2010); Bachelor's degree or higher: 18.4% (2010); Master's degree or higher: 3.4% (2010).

Housing: Homeownership rate: 68.3% (2010); Median home value: $51,339 (2010); Median contract rent: $352 per month (2005-2009 5-year est.); Median year structure built: 1958 (2005-2009 5-year est.)

Health: Birth rate: 179.1 per 10,000 population (2009); Death rate: 83.5 per 10,000 population (2009); Age-adjusted cancer mortality rate: 179.3 (Unreliable) deaths per 100,000 population (2007); Number of physicians: 4.0 per 10,000 population (2008); Hospital beds: 26.2 per 10,000 population (2007); Hospital admissions: 473.1 per 10,000 population (2007).

Elections: 2008 Presidential election results: 32.1% Obama, 66.4% McCain, 0.1% Nader

Additional Information Contacts

Swisher County Government . . . . (806) 995-3294
    http://www.co.swisher.tx.us/ips/cms
City of Tulia . . . . (806) 995-3547
Tulia Chamber of Commerce . . . . (806) 995-2296
    http://www.tuliachamber.com

Swisher County Communities

HAPPY (town). Covers a land area of 1.065 square miles and a water area of 0 square miles. Located at 34.74° N. Lat; 101.85° W. Long. Elevation is 3,615 feet.

Population: 588 (1990); 647 (2000); 676 (2010); 678 (2015 projected); Race: 87.3% White, 0.3% Black, 0.0% Asian, 12.4% Other, 14.2% Hispanic of any race (2010); Density: 634.7 persons per square mile (2010); Average household size: 2.42 (2010); Median age: 42.3 (2010); Males per 100 females: 97.7 (2010); Marriage status: 12.6% never married, 72.2% now married, 6.8% widowed, 8.4% divorced (2005-2009 5-year est.); Foreign born: 7.2% (2005-2009 5-year est.); Ancestry (includes multiple ancestries): 23.1% German, 10.5% English, 8.6% Irish, 4.7% Scottish, 3.0% Swedish (2005-2009 5-year est.).

Economy: Employment by occupation: 6.0% management, 18.5% professional, 10.8% services, 27.6% sales, 2.6% farming, 7.7% construction, 26.8% production (2005-2009 5-year est.).

Income: Per capita income: $18,174 (2010); Median household income: $34,769 (2010); Average household income: $44,633 (2010); Percent of households with income of $100,000 or more: 6.1% (2010); Poverty rate: 21.4% (2005-2009 5-year est.).

Taxes: Total city taxes per capita: $162 (2007); City property taxes per capita: $162 (2007).

Education: Percent of population age 25 and over with: High school diploma (including GED) or higher: 86.9% (2010); Bachelor's degree or higher: 20.6% (2010); Master's degree or higher: 1.7% (2010).

School District(s)

Happy ISD (KG-12)
    2009-10 Enrollment: 244 . . . . (806) 558-5331

Housing: Homeownership rate: 74.6% (2010); Median home value: $40,833 (2010); Median contract rent: $296 per month (2005-2009 5-year est.); Median year structure built: 1963 (2005-2009 5-year est.).

Transportation: Commute to work: 91.8% car, 0.0% public transportation, 3.1% walk, 2.3% work from home (2005-2009 5-year est.); Travel time to work: 24.3% less than 15 minutes, 44.6% 15 to 30 minutes, 19.4% 30 to 45 minutes, 9.9% 45 to 60 minutes, 1.7% 60 minutes or more (2005-2009 5-year est.)

KRESS (city). Covers a land area of 0.568 square miles and a water area of 0 square miles. Located at 34.36° N. Lat; 101.74° W. Long. Elevation is 3,471 feet.

Population: 739 (1990); 826 (2000); 779 (2010); 749 (2015 projected); Race: 62.4% White, 1.8% Black, 0.0% Asian, 35.8% Other, 67.9% Hispanic of any race (2010); Density: 1,371.8 persons per square mile (2010); Average household size: 2.94 (2010); Median age: 34.9 (2010); Males per 100 females: 98.2 (2010); Marriage status: 11.0% never married, 76.3% now married, 4.4% widowed, 8.3% divorced (2005-2009 5-year est.); Foreign born: 11.2% (2005-2009 5-year est.); Ancestry (includes multiple ancestries): 24.4% Irish, 11.2% English, 9.1% German, 4.2% American, 1.5% Czech (2005-2009 5-year est.).

Economy: Employment by occupation: 20.5% management, 12.6% professional, 16.7% services, 23.9% sales, 2.7% farming, 16.4% construction, 7.2% production (2005-2009 5-year est.).

Income: Per capita income: $14,939 (2010); Median household income: $34,528 (2010); Average household income: $43,972 (2010); Percent of households with income of $100,000 or more: 6.4% (2010); Poverty rate: 26.3% (2005-2009 5-year est.).

Taxes: Total city taxes per capita: $87 (2007); City property taxes per capita: $79 (2007).

Education: Percent of population age 25 and over with: High school diploma (including GED) or higher: 68.7% (2010); Bachelor's degree or higher: 10.0% (2010); Master's degree or higher: 2.7% (2010).

School District(s)

Kress ISD (PK-12)

2009-10 Enrollment: 223 . . . . (806) 684-2652

Housing: Homeownership rate: 75.1% (2010); Median home value: $37,013 (2010); Median contract rent: $340 per month (2005-2009 5-year est.); Median year structure built: 1958 (2005-2009 5-year est.).

Safety: Violent crime rate: 0.0 per 10,000 population; Property crime rate: 78.8 per 10,000 population (2009).

Newspapers: Kress Chronicle (Community news; Circulation 450)

Transportation: Commute to work: 98.5% car, 0.0% public transportation, 0.7% walk, 0.7% work from home (2005-2009 5-year est.); Travel time to work: 42.7% less than 15 minutes, 52.1% 15 to 30 minutes, 1.5% 30 to 45 minutes, 2.6% 45 to 60 minutes, 1.1% 60 minutes or more (2005-2009 5-year est.)

TULIA (city). County seat. Covers a land area of 3.535 square miles and a water area of 0 square miles. Located at 34.53° N. Lat; 101.76° W. Long. Elevation is 3,484 feet.

History: Settled 1890, incorporated 1909.

Population: 4,966 (1990); 5,117 (2000); 4,482 (2010); 4,195 (2015 projected); Race: 66.5% White, 8.1% Black, 0.1% Asian, 25.4% Other, 41.7% Hispanic of any race (2010); Density: 1,268.0 persons per square mile (2010); Average household size: 2.61 (2010); Median age: 34.8 (2010); Males per 100 females: 106.7 (2010); Marriage status: 34.1% never married, 46.5% now married, 6.7% widowed, 12.8% divorced (2005-2009 5-year est.); Foreign born: 6.8% (2005-2009 5-year est.); Ancestry (includes multiple ancestries): 8.1% American, 7.2% Irish, 6.9% English, 6.8% German, 1.7% African (2005-2009 5-year est.).

Economy: Single-family building permits issued: 0 (2010); Multi-family building permits issued: 0 (2010); Employment by occupation: 16.1% management, 15.2% professional, 25.4% services, 9.3% sales, 6.9% farming, 11.0% construction, 16.1% production (2005-2009 5-year est.).

Income: Per capita income: $16,055 (2010); Median household income: $33,127 (2010); Average household income: $44,102 (2010); Percent of households with income of $100,000 or more: 7.2% (2010); Poverty rate: 17.4% (2005-2009 5-year est.).

Taxes: Total city taxes per capita: $155 (2007); City property taxes per capita: $55 (2007).

Education: Percent of population age 25 and over with: High school diploma (including GED) or higher: 70.8% (2010); Bachelor's degree or higher: 18.8% (2010); Master's degree or higher: 4.2% (2010).

School District(s)

Tulia ISD (PK-12)

2009-10 Enrollment: 1,028 . . . . (806) 995-4591

Housing: Homeownership rate: 65.7% (2010); Median home value: $50,667 (2010); Median contract rent: $359 per month (2005-2009 5-year est.); Median year structure built: 1960 (2005-2009 5-year est.).

Hospitals: Swisher Memorial Hospital

Safety: Violent crime rate: 37.5 per 10,000 population; Property crime rate: 213.9 per 10,000 population (2009).

Newspapers: Tulia Herald (Community news; Circulation 3,000)

Transportation: Commute to work: 97.1% car, 0.0% public transportation, 0.0% walk, 2.4% work from home (2005-2009 5-year est.); Travel time to work: 65.5% less than 15 minutes, 17.8% 15 to 30 minutes, 12.0% 30 to 45 minutes, 1.3% 45 to 60 minutes, 3.4% 60 minutes or more (2005-2009 5-year est.)

Additional Information Contacts

City of Tulia . . . . (806) 995-3547

Tulia Chamber of Commerce . . . . (806) 995-2296

http://www.tuliachamber.com

Tarrant County

Located in north Texas; drained by the West and Clear Forks of the Trinity River; includes Eagle Mountain Lake. Covers a land area of 863.42 square miles, a water area of 34.06 square miles, and is located in the Central Time Zone at 32.76° N. Lat., 97.26° W. Long. The county was founded in 1849. County seat is Fort Worth.

Tarrant County is part of the Dallas-Fort Worth-Arlington, TX Metropolitan Statistical Area. The entire metro area includes: Dallas-Plano-Irving, TX Metropolitan Division (Collin County, TX; Dallas County, TX; Delta County, TX; Denton County, TX; Ellis County, TX; Hunt County, TX; Kaufman County, TX; Rockwall County, TX); Fort Worth-Arlington, TX Metropolitan Division (Johnson County, TX; Parker County, TX; Tarrant County, TX; Wise County, TX)

Weather Station: Benbrook Dam   Elevation: 790 feet

	Jan	Feb	Mar	Apr	May	Jun	Jul	Aug	Sep	Oct	Nov	Dec
High	57	61	68	76	83	91	96	96	88	79	67	58
Low	33	37	44	52	62	69	72	72	65	54	44	35
Precip	1.9	2.4	3.3	2.8	4.6	3.9	1.8	2.1	3.2	4.0	2.6	2.4
Snow	tr	0.1	tr	0.0	0.0	0.0	0.0	0.0	0.0	0.0	tr	0.1

High and Low temperatures in degrees Fahrenheit; Precipitation and Snow in inches

Weather Station: Dallas-Fort Worth Intl Arpt   Elevation: 560 feet

	Jan	Feb	Mar	Apr	May	Jun	Jul	Aug	Sep	Oct	Nov	Dec
High	56	61	68	76	84	91	96	96	89	78	67	57
Low	36	39	47	55	64	71	75	75	68	57	46	37
Precip	2.1	2.6	3.4	3.0	5.0	3.8	2.1	1.9	2.5	4.2	2.7	2.6
Snow	na	0.6	na	tr	na	na	na	na	na	na	na	0.3

High and Low temperatures in degrees Fahrenheit; Precipitation and Snow in inches

Weather Station: Grapevine Dam   Elevation: 584 feet

	Jan	Feb	Mar	Apr	May	Jun	Jul	Aug	Sep	Oct	Nov	Dec
High	56	60	68	76	83	91	96	96	89	79	67	57
Low	32	36	44	52	61	69	73	72	64	53	43	34
Precip	2.2	2.8	3.5	3.1	4.8	3.9	2.3	1.8	3.1	4.0	2.9	2.7
Snow	0.0	0.2	0.0	0.0	0.0	0.0	0.0	0.0	0.0	0.0	0.0	0.1

High and Low temperatures in degrees Fahrenheit; Precipitation and Snow in inches

Population: 1,170,103 (1990); 1,446,219 (2000); 1,798,962 (2010); 1,967,345 (2015 projected); Race: 65.6% White, 13.8% Black, 4.1% Asian, 16.5% Other, 26.7% Hispanic of any race (2010); Density: 2,083.5 persons per square mile (2010); Average household size: 2.72 (2010); Median age: 33.6 (2010); Males per 100 females: 99.7 (2010).

Religion: Five largest groups: 18.7% Southern Baptist Convention, 11.5% Catholic Church, 6.8% The United Methodist Church, 2.4% Independent, Non-Charismatic Churches, 2.1% Churches of Christ (2000).

Economy: Unemployment rate: 8.6% (June 2011); Total civilian labor force: 924,878 (June 2011); Leading industries: 13.2% retail trade; 11.7% health care and social assistance; 11.2% manufacturing (2009); Farms: 1,248 totaling 154,377 acres (2007); Companies that employ 500 or more persons: 111 (2009); Companies that employ 100 to 499 persons: 929 (2009); Companies that employ less than 100 persons: 35,895 (2009); Black-owned businesses: 16,358 (2007); Hispanic-owned businesses: 18,581 (2007); Asian-owned businesses: 9,719 (2007); Women-owned businesses: 47,419 (2007); Retail sales per capita: $15,211 (2010). Single-family building permits issued: 4,203 (2010); Multi-family building permits issued: 886 (2010).

Income: Per capita income: $26,890 (2010); Median household income: $56,507 (2010); Average household income: $73,622 (2010); Percent of households with income of $100,000 or more: 21.7% (2010); Poverty rate: 14.5% (2009); Bankruptcy rate: 3.69% (2010).

Taxes: Total county taxes per capita: $312 (2007); County property taxes per capita: $291 (2007).

Education: Percent of population age 25 and over with: High school diploma (including GED) or higher: 82.7% (2010); Bachelor's degree or higher: 28.1% (2010); Master's degree or higher: 8.5% (2010).

Housing: Homeownership rate: 63.4% (2010); Median home value: $129,654 (2010); Median contract rent: $637 per month (2005-2009 5-year est.); Median year structure built: 1983 (2005-2009 5-year est.)

Health: Birth rate: 168.2 per 10,000 population (2009); Death rate: 59.7 per 10,000 population (2009); Age-adjusted cancer mortality rate: 179.3 deaths per 100,000 population (2007); Number of physicians: 20.2 per 10,000 population (2008); Hospital beds: 25.9 per 10,000 population (2007); Hospital admissions: 1,179.0 per 10,000 population (2007).

Environment: Air Quality Index: 65.4% good, 27.5% moderate, 6.9% unhealthy for sensitive individuals, 0.3% unhealthy (percent of days in 2008)

Elections: 2008 Presidential election results: 43.7% Obama, 55.4% McCain, 0.1% Nader

Additional Information Contacts

Tarrant County Government . . . . (817) 884-1111

http://www.tarrantcounty.com/eGov/site/default.asp

Arlington Chamber of Commerce . . . . (817) 275-2613

http://www.arlingtontx.com

Azle Area Chamber of Commerce . . . . (817) 444-1112

http://www.azlechamber.com

Benbrook Area Chamber of Commerce.................. (817) 249-4451
  http://www.benbrookchamber.org
City of Arlington .... (817) 459-6777
  http://www.arlingtontx.gov
City of Azle... (817) 444-2541
  http://www.cityofazle.org
City of Bedford .... (817) 952-2100
  http://www.ci.bedford.tx.us
City of Benbrook .... (817) 249-3000
  http://www.ci.benbrook.tx.us
City of Colleyville .... (817) 503-1000
  http://www.colleyville.com
City of Crowley.. (817) 297-2201
  http://www.ci.crowley.tx.us
City of Euless.. (817) 685-1422
  http://www.eulesstx.gov
City of Everman .... (817) 293-0525
  http://www.evermantx.net
City of Forest Hill .... (817) 568-3000
  http://www.foresthilltx.org
City of Fort Worth.. (817) 392-2255
  http://www.fortworthgov.org
City of Grapevine .... (817) 410-3000
  http://www.ci.grapevine.tx.us
City of Haltom City .... (817) 222-7700
  http://www.haltomcitytx.com
City of Hurst... (817) 788-7000
  http://www.ci.hurst.tx.us
City of Keller... (817) 743-4000
  http://www.cityofkeller.com
City of Kennedale.. (817) 985-2100
  http://www.cityofkennedale.com
City of Mansfield .... (817) 276-4200
  http://www.mansfield-tx.gov
City of North Richland Hills .... (817) 427-6000
  http://www.ci.north-richland-hills.tx.us
City of Richland Hills .... (817) 299-1800
  http://www.richlandhills.com
City of River Oaks .... (817) 626-5421
  http://www.riveroakstx.com
City of Saginaw .... (817) 232-4640
  http://www.ci.saginaw.tx.us
City of Southlake .... (817) 748-8400
  http://www.ci.southlake.tx.us
City of Watauga .... (817) 514-5800
  http://www.ci.watauga.tx.us
City of White Settlement .... (817) 246-4971
  http://www.wstx.us
Colleyville Area Chamber of Commerce .... (817) 488-7148
  http://www.colleyvillechamber.org
Crowley Area Chamber of Commerce.................. (817) 297-4211
  http://www.crowleyareachamber.org
Fort Worth Chamber of Commerce .... (817) 336-2491
  http://www.fortworthchamber.com
Fort Worth Hispanic Chamber of Commerce............ (817) 625-5411
  http://www.fwhcc.org
Fort Worth Metropolitan Black Chamber of Commerce.... (817) 871-6538
  http://www.fwmbcc.org
Grapevine Chamber of Commerce .... (817) 481-1522
  http://www.grapevinechamber.org
Greater Keller Chamber of Commerce .... (817) 431-2169
  http://www.KellerChamber.com
HEB Chamber of Commerce............................ (817) 283-1521
  http://www.heb.org
Kennedale Chamber of Commerce .... (817) 985-2109
  http://www.kennedalechamber.com
Mansfield Area Chamber of Commerce................. (817) 473-0507
  http://www.mansfieldchamber.org
Northeast Tarrant County Chamber of Commerce .... (817) 281-9376
  http://www.netarrant.org
Saginaw Area Chamber of Commerce .... (817) 232-0500
  http://www.saginawtxchamber.org
Southlake Chamber of Commerce..................... (817) 481-8200
  http://www.southlakechamber.com
Town of Pantego .... (817) 274-1381
  http://www.townofpantego.com

Town of Westlake .... (817) 430-0941
  http://www.westlake-tx.org
Town of Westover Hills .... (817) 335-5454
White Settlement Area Chamber of Commerce.......... (817) 246-1121
  http://www.whitesettlement-tx.com

Tarrant County Communities

ARLINGTON (city). Covers a land area of 95.818 square miles and a water area of 3.206 square miles. Located at 32.70° N. Lat; 97.12° W. Long. Elevation is 604 feet.

History: Named for the home of George Washington Parke Custis, who named his estate for the 1st Earl of Arlington. North Texas Agricultural College, which became Arlington University and part of the University of Texas sytem, was founded in Arlington in 1895. Early industries in Arlington were medicinal crystals and rose cultivation. The amusement park called Six Flags Over Texas opened in 1961 in Arlington.

Population: 261,643 (1990); 332,969 (2000); 380,432 (2010); 410,218 (2015 projected); Race: 57.9% White, 17.9% Black, 6.4% Asian, 17.8% Other, 26.4% Hispanic of any race (2010); Density: 3,970.3 persons per square mile (2010); Average household size: 2.72 (2010); Median age: 32.5 (2010); Males per 100 females: 101.0 (2010); Marriage status: 32.0% never married, 53.5% now married, 3.9% widowed, 10.6% divorced (2005-2009 5-year est.); Foreign born: 18.9% (2005-2009 5-year est.); Ancestry (includes multiple ancestries): 11.0% German, 8.7% Irish, 7.3% English, 5.4% American, 2.6% Italian (2005-2009 5-year est.).

Economy: Unemployment rate: 8.2% (June 2011); Total civilian labor force: 209,210 (June 2011); Single-family building permits issued: 286 (2010); Multi-family building permits issued: 66 (2010); Employment by occupation: 13.7% management, 18.6% professional, 14.8% services, 28.7% sales, 0.1% farming, 10.6% construction, 13.5% production (2005-2009 5-year est.).

Income: Per capita income: $25,795 (2010); Median household income: $56,739 (2010); Average household income: $70,270 (2010); Percent of households with income of $100,000 or more: 20.0% (2010); Poverty rate: 13.7% (2005-2009 5-year est.).

Taxes: Total city taxes per capita: $610 (2007); City property taxes per capita: $286 (2007).

Education: Percent of population age 25 and over with: High school diploma (including GED) or higher: 85.7% (2010); Bachelor's degree or higher: 31.9% (2010); Master's degree or higher: 9.3% (2010).

School District(s)
Arlington Classics Academy (KG-06)
  2009-10 Enrollment: 502 .... (817) 274-2008
Arlington ISD (PK-12)
  2009-10 Enrollment: 63,487 .... (682) 867-4611
Education Center International Academy (KG-12)
  2009-10 Enrollment: 201 .... (972) 530-6157
Jean Massieu Academy (PK-12)
  2009-10 Enrollment: 104 .... (817) 460-0396
Kennedale ISD (PK-12)
  2009-10 Enrollment: 3,162 .... (817) 563-8000
Mansfield ISD (PK-12)
  2009-10 Enrollment: 31,662 .... (817) 299-6300
Metro Academy of Math and Science (PK-12)
  2009-10 Enrollment: 359 .... (817) 229-5200
Summit International Preparatory (KG-11)
  2009-10 Enrollment: 590 .... (817) 287-5121
Four-year College(s)
Arlington Baptist College (Private, Not-for-profit, Baptist)
  Fall 2009 Enrollment: 158 .... (817) 461-8741
  2010-11 Tuition: In-state $7,340; Out-of-state $7,340
ITT Technical Institute-Arlington (Private, For-profit)
  Fall 2009 Enrollment: 793 .... (817) 794-5100
  2010-11 Tuition: In-state $18,048; Out-of-state $18,048
The University of Texas at Arlington (Public)
  Fall 2009 Enrollment: 28,085.................... (817) 272-2011
  2010-11 Tuition: In-state $8,500; Out-of-state $15,940
Two-year College(s)
Everest College-Arlington (Private, For-profit)
  Fall 2009 Enrollment: 783 .... (817) 652-7790
  2010-11 Tuition: In-state $17,307; Out-of-state $17,307
Iverson Business School and Court Reporting (Private, For-profit)
  Fall 2009 Enrollment: 137 .... (770) 446-1333

Vocational/Technical School(s)

American Broadcasting School (Private, For-profit)
  Fall 2009 Enrollment: 75 . . . . (817) 695-2474
  2010-11 Tuition: $11,625
Arlington Medical Institute (Private, For-profit)
  Fall 2009 Enrollment: 100 . . . . (817) 265-0706
  2010-11 Tuition: $10,065
CCI Training Center (Private, For-profit)
  Fall 2009 Enrollment: 250 . . . . (817) 226-1900
  2010-11 Tuition: $8,740
Concorde Career Institute (Private, For-profit)
  Fall 2009 Enrollment: 798 . . . . (817) 261-1594
  2010-11 Tuition: $23,625
Ogle School Hair Skin Nails (Private, For-profit)
  Fall 2009 Enrollment: 299 . . . . (817) 274-5088
  2010-11 Tuition: $15,600
Regency Beauty Institute-Arlington (Private, For-profit)
  Fall 2009 Enrollment: 78 . . . . (800) 787-6456
  2010-11 Tuition: $16,075

Housing: Homeownership rate: 57.6% (2010); Median home value: $132,719 (2010); Median contract rent: $625 per month (2005-2009 5-year est.); Median year structure built: 1983 (2005-2009 5-year est.).
Hospitals: Arlington Memorial Hospital (417 beds); HealthSouth Rehabilitation Hospital of Arlington (65 beds); Medical Center of Arlington (298 beds); Millwood Hospital (98 beds); USMD Hospital at Arlington (18 beds)
Safety: Violent crime rate: 61.5 per 10,000 population; Property crime rate: 541.2 per 10,000 population (2009).
Newspapers: Amusement Today (Local news; Circulation 400,000)
Transportation: Commute to work: 93.3% car, 0.3% public transportation, 1.6% walk, 3.5% work from home (2005-2009 5-year est.); Travel time to work: 23.3% less than 15 minutes, 38.7% 15 to 30 minutes, 22.5% 30 to 45 minutes, 9.3% 45 to 60 minutes, 6.2% 60 minutes or more (2005-2009 5-year est.)
Airports: Arlington Municipal (general aviation)
Additional Information Contacts
Arlington Chamber of Commerce . . . . (817) 275-2613
  http://www.arlingtontx.com
City of Arlington . . . . (817) 459-6777
  http://www.arlingtontx.gov

AZLE

AZLE (city). Covers a land area of 8.200 square miles and a water area of 0.043 square miles. Located at 32.89° N. Lat; 97.53° W. Long. Elevation is 712 feet.
Population: 9,105 (1990); 9,600 (2000); 10,555 (2010); 11,317 (2015 projected); Race: 93.3% White, 0.2% Black, 0.7% Asian, 5.7% Other, 7.7% Hispanic of any race (2010); Density: 1,287.3 persons per square mile (2010); Average household size: 2.57 (2010); Median age: 37.4 (2010); Males per 100 females: 95.2 (2010); Marriage status: 22.1% never married, 57.8% now married, 7.7% widowed, 12.4% divorced (2005-2009 5-year est.); Foreign born: 2.5% (2005-2009 5-year est.); Ancestry (includes multiple ancestries): 17.1% German, 15.8% English, 15.8% Irish, 13.6% American, 3.0% Dutch (2005-2009 5-year est.).
Economy: Single-family building permits issued: 10 (2010); Multi-family building permits issued: 0 (2010); Employment by occupation: 15.7% management, 14.8% professional, 10.2% services, 33.2% sales, 0.0% farming, 11.7% construction, 14.4% production (2005-2009 5-year est.).
Income: Per capita income: $25,429 (2010); Median household income: $52,313 (2010); Average household income: $65,813 (2010); Percent of households with income of $100,000 or more: 17.5% (2010); Poverty rate: 10.3% (2005-2009 5-year est.).
Taxes: Total city taxes per capita: $560 (2007); City property taxes per capita: $324 (2007).
Education: Percent of population age 25 and over with: High school diploma (including GED) or higher: 83.9% (2010); Bachelor's degree or higher: 17.3% (2010); Master's degree or higher: 5.0% (2010).

School District(s)

Azle ISD (PK-12)
  2009-10 Enrollment: 5,841 . . . . (817) 444-3235
Springtown ISD (PK-12)
  2009-10 Enrollment: 3,510 . . . . (817) 220-7243
Housing: Homeownership rate: 74.4% (2010); Median home value: $114,186 (2010); Median contract rent: $558 per month (2005-2009 5-year est.); Median year structure built: 1978 (2005-2009 5-year est.).
Hospitals: Harris Methodist Northwest (44 beds)

Safety: Violent crime rate: 30.3 per 10,000 population; Property crime rate: 391.2 per 10,000 population (2009).
Newspapers: Azle News (Community news; Circulation 5,000)
Transportation: Commute to work: 92.4% car, 0.0% public transportation, 1.1% walk, 4.5% work from home (2005-2009 5-year est.); Travel time to work: 23.3% less than 15 minutes, 22.9% 15 to 30 minutes, 28.0% 30 to 45 minutes, 11.4% 45 to 60 minutes, 14.5% 60 minutes or more (2005-2009 5-year est.)
Additional Information Contacts
Azle Area Chamber of Commerce . . . . (817) 444-1112
  http://www.azlechamber.com
City of Azle . . . . (817) 444-2541
  http://www.cityofazle.org

BEDFORD

BEDFORD (city). Covers a land area of 10.003 square miles and a water area of 0.007 square miles. Located at 32.84° N. Lat; 97.14° W. Long. Elevation is 597 feet.
History: Named for Bedford County, Tennessee, which was named for army officer Thomas Bedford. The city has grown since the 1970s along with the North Dallas-Fort Worth area. Settled c.1843. Incorporated 1954.
Population: 43,746 (1990); 47,152 (2000); 48,885 (2010); 51,296 (2015 projected); Race: 82.7% White, 4.9% Black, 4.2% Asian, 8.1% Other, 11.8% Hispanic of any race (2010); Density: 4,886.8 persons per square mile (2010); Average household size: 2.27 (2010); Median age: 38.1 (2010); Males per 100 females: 94.9 (2010); Marriage status: 26.4% never married, 54.7% now married, 6.0% widowed, 12.9% divorced (2005-2009 5-year est.); Foreign born: 11.2% (2005-2009 5-year est.); Ancestry (includes multiple ancestries): 17.5% German, 14.3% English, 11.9% Irish, 8.0% American, 3.5% Italian (2005-2009 5-year est.).
Economy: Unemployment rate: 7.4% (June 2011); Total civilian labor force: 30,981 (June 2011); Single-family building permits issued: 23 (2010); Multi-family building permits issued: 0 (2010); Employment by occupation: 18.6% management, 20.9% professional, 13.0% services, 32.0% sales, 0.1% farming, 6.3% construction, 9.0% production (2005-2009 5-year est.).
Income: Per capita income: $33,370 (2010); Median household income: $60,558 (2010); Average household income: $76,289 (2010); Percent of households with income of $100,000 or more: 24.6% (2010); Poverty rate: 5.2% (2005-2009 5-year est.).
Taxes: Total city taxes per capita: $524 (2007); City property taxes per capita: $256 (2007).
Education: Percent of population age 25 and over with: High school diploma (including GED) or higher: 93.8% (2010); Bachelor's degree or higher: 36.6% (2010); Master's degree or higher: 11.0% (2010).

School District(s)

Hurst-Euless-Bedford ISD (PK-12)
  2009-10 Enrollment: 20,762 . . . . (817) 283-4461
Housing: Homeownership rate: 53.4% (2010); Median home value: $149,688 (2010); Median contract rent: $686 per month (2005-2009 5-year est.); Median year structure built: 1983 (2005-2009 5-year est.).
Hospitals: Harris Methodist HEB Hospital (230 beds)
Safety: Violent crime rate: 38.5 per 10,000 population; Property crime rate: 358.3 per 10,000 population (2009).
Transportation: Commute to work: 93.7% car, 0.3% public transportation, 1.5% walk, 2.8% work from home (2005-2009 5-year est.); Travel time to work: 28.0% less than 15 minutes, 40.5% 15 to 30 minutes, 21.1% 30 to 45 minutes, 7.5% 45 to 60 minutes, 3.0% 60 minutes or more (2005-2009 5-year est.)
Additional Information Contacts
City of Bedford . . . . (817) 952-2100
  http://www.ci.bedford.tx.us
HEB Chamber of Commerce . . . . (817) 283-1521
  http://www.heb.org

BENBROOK

BENBROOK (city). Covers a land area of 11.453 square miles and a water area of 0.601 square miles. Located at 32.68° N. Lat; 97.45° W. Long. Elevation is 689 feet.
Population: 19,523 (1990); 20,208 (2000); 22,687 (2010); 24,317 (2015 projected); Race: 84.7% White, 5.4% Black, 1.8% Asian, 8.2% Other, 11.3% Hispanic of any race (2010); Density: 1,980.9 persons per square mile (2010); Average household size: 2.33 (2010); Median age: 41.2 (2010); Males per 100 females: 92.5 (2010); Marriage status: 23.9% never married, 56.9% now married, 7.1% widowed, 12.0% divorced (2005-2009 5-year est.); Foreign born: 6.2% (2005-2009 5-year est.); Ancestry (includes multiple ancestries): 17.8% German, 14.4% American, 12.6% English, 11.8% Irish, 4.3% Scotch-Irish (2005-2009 5-year est.).

Economy: Single-family building permits issued: 56 (2010); Multi-family building permits issued: 0 (2010); Employment by occupation: 16.0% management, 26.6% professional, 15.3% services, 25.5% sales, 0.1% farming, 7.1% construction, 9.5% production (2005-2009 5-year est.).
Income: Per capita income: $31,158 (2010); Median household income: $59,540 (2010); Average household income: $72,784 (2010); Percent of households with income of $100,000 or more: 21.6% (2010); Poverty rate: 6.8% (2005-2009 5-year est.).
Taxes: Total city taxes per capita: $508 (2007); City property taxes per capita: $369 (2007).
Education: Percent of population age 25 and over with: High school diploma (including GED) or higher: 93.3% (2010); Bachelor's degree or higher: 35.3% (2010); Master's degree or higher: 11.4% (2010).
Housing: Homeownership rate: 67.6% (2010); Median home value: $129,833 (2010); Median contract rent: $651 per month (2005-2009 5-year est.); Median year structure built: 1980 (2005-2009 5-year est.).
Safety: Violent crime rate: 14.2 per 10,000 population; Property crime rate: 209.6 per 10,000 population (2009).
Transportation: Commute to work: 93.4% car, 0.3% public transportation, 0.7% walk, 5.5% work from home (2005-2009 5-year est.); Travel time to work: 25.6% less than 15 minutes, 45.8% 15 to 30 minutes, 17.4% 30 to 45 minutes, 5.1% 45 to 60 minutes, 6.1% 60 minutes or more (2005-2009 5-year est.)
Additional Information Contacts
Benbrook Area Chamber of Commerce. . . . . (817) 249-4451
  http://www.benbrookchamber.org
City of Benbrook . . . . (817) 249-3000
  http://www.ci.benbrook.tx.us

BLUE MOUND (city). Aka Saginaw Park. Covers a land area of 0.537 square miles and a water area of 0 square miles. Located at 32.85° N. Lat; 97.33° W. Long. Elevation is 673 feet.
Population: 2,133 (1990); 2,388 (2000); 2,520 (2010); 2,952 (2015 projected); Race: 70.5% White, 4.3% Black, 1.4% Asian, 23.8% Other, 28.6% Hispanic of any race (2010); Density: 4,691.5 persons per square mile (2010); Average household size: 3.10 (2010); Median age: 31.6 (2010); Males per 100 females: 103.1 (2010); Marriage status: 18.6% never married, 65.6% now married, 5.3% widowed, 10.5% divorced (2005-2009 5-year est.); Foreign born: 14.6% (2005-2009 5-year est.); Ancestry (includes multiple ancestries): 11.9% Irish, 10.0% American, 6.7% German, 6.4% English, 2.7% Dutch (2005-2009 5-year est.).
Economy: Single-family building permits issued: 0 (2010); Multi-family building permits issued: 0 (2010); Employment by occupation: 12.0% management, 9.9% professional, 21.2% services, 23.0% sales, 0.5% farming, 14.4% construction, 18.9% production (2005-2009 5-year est.).
Income: Per capita income: $25,864 (2010); Median household income: $72,668 (2010); Average household income: $80,055 (2010); Percent of households with income of $100,000 or more: 24.1% (2010); Poverty rate: 15.8% (2005-2009 5-year est.).
Taxes: Total city taxes per capita: $220 (2007); City property taxes per capita: $176 (2007).
Education: Percent of population age 25 and over with: High school diploma (including GED) or higher: 80.6% (2010); Bachelor's degree or higher: 16.6% (2010); Master's degree or higher: 3.2% (2010).
Housing: Homeownership rate: 86.9% (2010); Median home value: $119,577 (2010); Median contract rent: $817 per month (2005-2009 5-year est.); Median year structure built: 1976 (2005-2009 5-year est.).
Safety: Violent crime rate: 12.7 per 10,000 population; Property crime rate: 241.3 per 10,000 population (2009).
Transportation: Commute to work: 92.8% car, 0.5% public transportation, 3.7% walk, 2.3% work from home (2005-2009 5-year est.); Travel time to work: 20.7% less than 15 minutes, 23.5% 15 to 30 minutes, 24.8% 30 to 45 minutes, 22.5% 45 to 60 minutes, 8.5% 60 minutes or more (2005-2009 5-year est.)

BRIAR (CDP). Covers a land area of 20.573 square miles and a water area of 0 square miles. Located at 32.97° N. Lat; 97.54° W. Long. Elevation is 745 feet.
Population: 4,136 (1990); 5,350 (2000); 5,238 (2010); 5,390 (2015 projected); Race: 94.3% White, 0.5% Black, 0.4% Asian, 4.8% Other, 7.1% Hispanic of any race (2010); Density: 254.6 persons per square mile (2010); Average household size: 2.73 (2010); Median age: 38.8 (2010); Males per 100 females: 99.8 (2010); Marriage status: 28.2% never married, 53.6% now married, 7.7% widowed, 10.5% divorced (2005-2009 5-year est.); Foreign born: 0.0% (2005-2009 5-year est.); Ancestry (includes

multiple ancestries): 15.2% Irish, 14.4% German, 12.6% American, 11.9% English, 3.3% French (2005-2009 5-year est.).
Economy: Employment by occupation: 9.9% management, 14.2% professional, 19.7% services, 28.1% sales, 1.0% farming, 17.0% construction, 10.1% production (2005-2009 5-year est.).
Income: Per capita income: $25,180 (2010); Median household income: $59,763 (2010); Average household income: $68,581 (2010); Percent of households with income of $100,000 or more: 17.5% (2010); Poverty rate: 11.2% (2005-2009 5-year est.).
Education: Percent of population age 25 and over with: High school diploma (including GED) or higher: 80.4% (2010); Bachelor's degree or higher: 12.3% (2010); Master's degree or higher: 2.9% (2010).
Housing: Homeownership rate: 86.1% (2010); Median home value: $120,165 (2010); Median contract rent: $419 per month (2005-2009 5-year est.); Median year structure built: 1987 (2005-2009 5-year est.).
Transportation: Commute to work: 92.8% car, 0.5% public transportation, 1.1% walk, 5.0% work from home (2005-2009 5-year est.); Travel time to work: 12.7% less than 15 minutes, 17.5% 15 to 30 minutes, 27.4% 30 to 45 minutes, 28.3% 45 to 60 minutes, 14.2% 60 minutes or more (2005-2009 5-year est.)

COLLEYVILLE (city). Covers a land area of 13.094 square miles and a water area of 0.006 square miles. Located at 32.88° N. Lat; 97.14° W. Long. Elevation is 614 feet.
History: The first significant settlement of the area began in the 1850s. Samuel C.H. Witten came to Texas from Missouri in 1854 and established a farm along Little Bear Creek. Colleyville was incorporated on January 10, 1956, and its city limits are now contiguous with those of Grapevine and Euless on the east, Bedford and Hurst on the south, Keller and North Richland Hills on the west and Southlake on the north.
Population: 12,726 (1990); 19,636 (2000); 24,831 (2010); 28,190 (2015 projected); Race: 90.2% White, 2.1% Black, 4.0% Asian, 3.7% Other, 5.6% Hispanic of any race (2010); Density: 1,896.4 persons per square mile (2010); Average household size: 3.10 (2010); Median age: 39.5 (2010); Males per 100 females: 97.5 (2010); Marriage status: 18.6% never married, 74.1% now married, 2.0% widowed, 5.4% divorced (2005-2009 5-year est.); Foreign born: 8.6% (2005-2009 5-year est.); Ancestry (includes multiple ancestries): 20.4% German, 17.3% English, 13.9% Irish, 12.7% American, 4.6% Italian (2005-2009 5-year est.).
Economy: Single-family building permits issued: 69 (2010); Multi-family building permits issued: 0 (2010); Employment by occupation: 34.3% management, 24.0% professional, 6.3% services, 25.1% sales, 0.0% farming, 4.7% construction, 5.8% production (2005-2009 5-year est.).
Income: Per capita income: $55,286 (2010); Median household income: $133,647 (2010); Average household income: $171,234 (2010); Percent of households with income of $100,000 or more: 67.5% (2010); Poverty rate: 1.9% (2005-2009 5-year est.).
Taxes: Total city taxes per capita: $889 (2007); City property taxes per capita: $541 (2007).
Education: Percent of population age 25 and over with: High school diploma (including GED) or higher: 97.1% (2010); Bachelor's degree or higher: 56.9% (2010); Master's degree or higher: 19.9% (2010).

School District(s)
Grapevine-Colleyville ISD (PK-12)
  2009-10 Enrollment: 13,671 . . . . (817) 488-9588
Keller ISD (PK-12)
  2009-10 Enrollment: 31,569 . . . . (817) 744-1000
Housing: Homeownership rate: 96.3% (2010); Median home value: $355,613 (2010); Median contract rent: $1,500 per month (2005-2009 5-year est.); Median year structure built: 1990 (2005-2009 5-year est.).
Safety: Violent crime rate: 0.8 per 10,000 population; Property crime rate: 112.4 per 10,000 population (2009).
Transportation: Commute to work: 89.9% car, 0.7% public transportation, 0.2% walk, 7.8% work from home (2005-2009 5-year est.); Travel time to work: 22.0% less than 15 minutes, 39.5% 15 to 30 minutes, 27.6% 30 to 45 minutes, 7.3% 45 to 60 minutes, 3.6% 60 minutes or more (2005-2009 5-year est.)
Additional Information Contacts
City of Colleyville . . . . (817) 503-1000
  http://www.colleyville.com
Colleyville Area Chamber of Commerce . . . . (817) 488-7148
  http://www.colleyvillechamber.org

CROWLEY (city).
Covers a land area of 6.651 square miles and a water area of 0 square miles. Located at 32.57° N. Lat; 97.36° W. Long. Elevation is 778 feet.

Population: 6,976 (1990); 7,467 (2000); 10,375 (2010); 11,875 (2015 projected); Race: 90.8% White, 2.2% Black, 0.5% Asian, 6.4% Other, 11.0% Hispanic of any race (2010); Density: 1,559.9 persons per square mile (2010); Average household size: 2.80 (2010); Median age: 34.1 (2010); Males per 100 females: 92.2 (2010); Marriage status: 24.8% never married, 57.0% now married, 3.4% widowed, 14.9% divorced (2005-2009 5-year est.); Foreign born: 4.6% (2005-2009 5-year est.); Ancestry (includes multiple ancestries): 14.7% German, 13.8% American, 10.8% English, 8.3% Irish, 4.0% Italian (2005-2009 5-year est.).

Economy: Single-family building permits issued: 94 (2010); Multi-family building permits issued: 0 (2010); Employment by occupation: 12.3% management, 18.1% professional, 14.6% services, 29.3% sales, 0.0% farming, 11.8% construction, 14.0% production (2005-2009 5-year est.).

Income: Per capita income: $22,746 (2010); Median household income: $55,647 (2010); Average household income: $63,868 (2010); Percent of households with income of $100,000 or more: 17.1% (2010); Poverty rate: 10.1% (2005-2009 5-year est.).

Taxes: Total city taxes per capita: $471 (2007); City property taxes per capita: $315 (2007).

Education: Percent of population age 25 and over with: High school diploma (including GED) or higher: 87.0% (2010); Bachelor's degree or higher: 18.8% (2010); Master's degree or higher: 5.9% (2010).

School District(s)
Crowley ISD (PK-12)
    2009-10 Enrollment: 15,126 . . . . (817) 297-5800

Housing: Homeownership rate: 80.9% (2010); Median home value: $116,667 (2010); Median contract rent: $623 per month (2005-2009 5-year est.); Median year structure built: 1993 (2005-2009 5-year est.).

Safety: Violent crime rate: 19.9 per 10,000 population; Property crime rate: 243.2 per 10,000 population (2009).

Transportation: Commute to work: 94.3% car, 0.6% public transportation, 1.8% walk, 1.7% work from home (2005-2009 5-year est.); Travel time to work: 15.1% less than 15 minutes, 32.8% 15 to 30 minutes, 29.2% 30 to 45 minutes, 11.2% 45 to 60 minutes, 11.8% 60 minutes or more (2005-2009 5-year est.)

Additional Information Contacts
City of Crowley. . . . . (817) 297-2201
    http://www.ci.crowley.tx.us
Crowley Area Chamber of Commerce . . . . (817) 297-4211
    http://www.crowleyareachamber.org

DALWORTHINGTON GARDENS (city).
Covers a land area of 1.831 square miles and a water area of 0.024 square miles. Located at 32.69° N. Lat; 97.15° W. Long. Elevation is 571 feet.

Population: 1,758 (1990); 2,186 (2000); 2,408 (2010); 2,635 (2015 projected); Race: 80.0% White, 11.7% Black, 2.3% Asian, 6.0% Other, 8.5% Hispanic of any race (2010); Density: 1,315.0 persons per square mile (2010); Average household size: 2.77 (2010); Median age: 39.4 (2010); Males per 100 females: 96.7 (2010); Marriage status: 26.4% never married, 61.9% now married, 4.1% widowed, 7.6% divorced (2005-2009 5-year est.); Foreign born: 4.9% (2005-2009 5-year est.); Ancestry (includes multiple ancestries): 13.4% German, 12.9% English, 9.3% Irish, 6.0% American, 5.4% European (2005-2009 5-year est.).

Economy: Single-family building permits issued: 1 (2010); Multi-family building permits issued: 0 (2010); Employment by occupation: 27.6% management, 32.7% professional, 6.9% services, 17.2% sales, 0.0% farming, 4.4% construction, 11.3% production (2005-2009 5-year est.).

Income: Per capita income: $45,446 (2010); Median household income: $72,826 (2010); Average household income: $126,594 (2010); Percent of households with income of $100,000 or more: 37.3% (2010); Poverty rate: 9.5% (2005-2009 5-year est.).

Taxes: Total city taxes per capita: $91 (2007); City property taxes per capita: $0 (2007).

Education: Percent of population age 25 and over with: High school diploma (including GED) or higher: 94.3% (2010); Bachelor's degree or higher: 47.9% (2010); Master's degree or higher: 16.0% (2010).

Housing: Homeownership rate: 67.8% (2010); Median home value: $311,667 (2010); Median contract rent: $764 per month (2005-2009 5-year est.); Median year structure built: 1982 (2005-2009 5-year est.).

Safety: Violent crime rate: 20.5 per 10,000 population; Property crime rate: 274.9 per 10,000 population (2009).

Transportation: Commute to work: 94.0% car, 0.0% public transportation, 0.0% walk, 1.9% work from home (2005-2009 5-year est.); Travel time to work: 23.2% less than 15 minutes, 28.9% 15 to 30 minutes, 22.6% 30 to 45 minutes, 22.9% 45 to 60 minutes, 2.4% 60 minutes or more (2005-2009 5-year est.)

EAGLE MOUNTAIN (CDP).
Covers a land area of 22.324 square miles and a water area of 0.042 square miles. Located at 32.88° N. Lat; 97.45° W. Long. Elevation is 669 feet.

History: This community takes its name from the numerous American Eagles that made their home on the mountain in the early days of the area's settlement.

Population: 5,032 (1990); 6,599 (2000); 10,509 (2010); 11,719 (2015 projected); Race: 84.0% White, 2.0% Black, 5.2% Asian, 8.8% Other, 10.1% Hispanic of any race (2010); Density: 470.8 persons per square mile (2010); Average household size: 2.66 (2010); Median age: 40.5 (2010); Males per 100 females: 100.6 (2010); Marriage status: n/a never married, n/a now married, n/a widowed, n/a divorced (2005-2009 5-year est.); Foreign born: n/a (2005-2009 5-year est.); Ancestry (includes multiple ancestries): n/a (2005-2009 5-year est.).

Economy: Employment by occupation: n/a management, n/a professional, n/a services, n/a sales, n/a farming, n/a construction, n/a production (2005-2009 5-year est.).

Income: Per capita income: $33,685 (2010); Median household income: $72,064 (2010); Average household income: $89,474 (2010); Percent of households with income of $100,000 or more: 31.9% (2010); Poverty rate: n/a (2005-2009 5-year est.).

Education: Percent of population age 25 and over with: High school diploma (including GED) or higher: 91.1% (2010); Bachelor's degree or higher: 35.9% (2010); Master's degree or higher: 12.6% (2010).

Housing: Homeownership rate: 81.7% (2010); Median home value: $176,485 (2010); Median contract rent: n/a per month (2005-2009 5-year est.); Median year structure built: n/a (2005-2009 5-year est.).

Transportation: Commute to work: n/a car, n/a public transportation, n/a walk, n/a work from home (2005-2009 5-year est.); Travel time to work: n/a less than 15 minutes, n/a 15 to 30 minutes, n/a 30 to 45 minutes, n/a 45 to 60 minutes, n/a 60 minutes or more (2005-2009 5-year est.)

EDGECLIFF VILLAGE (town).
Covers a land area of 1.190 square miles and a water area of 0 square miles. Located at 32.65° N. Lat; 97.34° W. Long. Elevation is 686 feet.

Population: 2,715 (1990); 2,550 (2000); 2,529 (2010); 2,607 (2015 projected); Race: 78.1% White, 10.8% Black, 1.1% Asian, 10.0% Other, 21.0% Hispanic of any race (2010); Density: 2,124.8 persons per square mile (2010); Average household size: 2.53 (2010); Median age: 47.3 (2010); Males per 100 females: 93.1 (2010); Marriage status: 16.9% never married, 59.8% now married, 7.8% widowed, 15.5% divorced (2005-2009 5-year est.); Foreign born: 9.2% (2005-2009 5-year est.); Ancestry (includes multiple ancestries): 17.9% German, 12.9% English, 11.5% Irish, 11.2% American, 3.4% Scottish (2005-2009 5-year est.).

Economy: Single-family building permits issued: 35 (2010); Multi-family building permits issued: 0 (2010); Employment by occupation: 13.6% management, 20.8% professional, 15.3% services, 31.4% sales, 0.0% farming, 8.7% construction, 10.2% production (2005-2009 5-year est.).

Income: Per capita income: $27,617 (2010); Median household income: $61,152 (2010); Average household income: $69,843 (2010); Percent of households with income of $100,000 or more: 17.4% (2010); Poverty rate: 2.2% (2005-2009 5-year est.).

Taxes: Total city taxes per capita: $383 (2007); City property taxes per capita: $157 (2007).

Education: Percent of population age 25 and over with: High school diploma (including GED) or higher: 89.6% (2010); Bachelor's degree or higher: 28.3% (2010); Master's degree or higher: 11.8% (2010).

Housing: Homeownership rate: 95.3% (2010); Median home value: $119,407 (2010); Median contract rent: $919 per month (2005-2009 5-year est.); Median year structure built: 1973 (2005-2009 5-year est.).

Transportation: Commute to work: 96.9% car, 0.0% public transportation, 0.0% walk, 2.0% work from home (2005-2009 5-year est.); Travel time to work: 24.3% less than 15 minutes, 34.1% 15 to 30 minutes, 29.5% 30 to 45 minutes, 5.4% 45 to 60 minutes, 6.6% 60 minutes or more (2005-2009 5-year est.)

EULESS (city).
Covers a land area of 16.266 square miles and a water area of 0 square miles. Located at 32.84° N. Lat; 97.09° W. Long. Elevation is 587 feet.

History: Named for Elisha Adam Euless (1848-1911), owner of a local cotton gin. Euless has grown in 1970s and 1980s along with the surrounding Dallas-Fort Worth area.
Population: 38,149 (1990); 46,005 (2000); 52,526 (2010); 56,884 (2015 projected); Race: 66.8% White, 8.4% Black, 9.0% Asian, 15.8% Other, 20.3% Hispanic of any race (2010); Density: 3,229.2 persons per square mile (2010); Average household size: 2.32 (2010); Median age: 34.6 (2010); Males per 100 females: 100.4 (2010); Marriage status: 30.6% never married, 49.8% now married, 4.3% widowed, 15.3% divorced (2005-2009 5-year est.); Foreign born: 17.3% (2005-2009 5-year est.); Ancestry (includes multiple ancestries): 14.2% German, 10.4% Irish, 9.5% English, 5.6% American, 3.3% Italian (2005-2009 5-year est.).
Economy: Unemployment rate: 7.5% (June 2011); Total civilian labor force: 31,907 (June 2011); Single-family building permits issued: 76 (2010); Multi-family building permits issued: 0 (2010); Employment by occupation: 15.9% management, 16.9% professional, 13.8% services, 30.8% sales, 0.0% farming, 9.2% construction, 13.4% production (2005-2009 5-year est.).
Income: Per capita income: $29,179 (2010); Median household income: $58,275 (2010); Average household income: $67,542 (2010); Percent of households with income of $100,000 or more: 17.6% (2010); Poverty rate: 10.9% (2005-2009 5-year est.).
Taxes: Total city taxes per capita: $788 (2007); City property taxes per capita: $217 (2007).
Education: Percent of population age 25 and over with: High school diploma (including GED) or higher: 90.2% (2010); Bachelor's degree or higher: 32.4% (2010); Master's degree or higher: 7.8% (2010).

School District(s)
Grapevine-Colleyville ISD (PK-12)
    2009-10 Enrollment: 13,671 . . . . (817) 488-9588
Harmony Science Academy (Fort Worth) (KG-11)
    2009-10 Enrollment: 1,948 . . . . (817) 263-0700
Hurst-Euless-Bedford ISD (PK-12)
    2009-10 Enrollment: 20,762 . . . . (817) 283-4461
Housing: Homeownership rate: 41.4% (2010); Median home value: $134,388 (2010); Median contract rent: $708 per month (2005-2009 5-year est.); Median year structure built: 1984 (2005-2009 5-year est.).
Safety: Violent crime rate: 20.2 per 10,000 population; Property crime rate: 353.2 per 10,000 population (2009).
Transportation: Commute to work: 93.0% car, 0.7% public transportation, 1.7% walk, 2.6% work from home (2005-2009 5-year est.); Travel time to work: 27.1% less than 15 minutes, 43.2% 15 to 30 minutes, 22.1% 30 to 45 minutes, 4.7% 45 to 60 minutes, 2.8% 60 minutes or more (2005-2009 5-year est.)
Additional Information Contacts
City of Euless. . . . . (817) 685-1422
    http://www.eulesstx.gov
HEB Chamber of Commerce . . . . (817) 283-1521
    http://www.heb.org

EVERMAN (city). Covers a land area of 1.984 square miles and a water area of 0 square miles. Located at 32.63° N. Lat; 97.28° W. Long. Elevation is 669 feet.
Population: 5,698 (1990); 5,836 (2000); 6,191 (2010); 6,588 (2015 projected); Race: 40.3% White, 34.3% Black, 1.2% Asian, 24.3% Other, 35.4% Hispanic of any race (2010); Density: 3,120.8 persons per square mile (2010); Average household size: 3.07 (2010); Median age: 31.5 (2010); Males per 100 females: 96.1 (2010); Marriage status: 32.6% never married, 47.8% now married, 6.5% widowed, 13.1% divorced (2005-2009 5-year est.); Foreign born: 15.7% (2005-2009 5-year est.); Ancestry (includes multiple ancestries): 8.3% American, 6.5% German, 6.4% Irish, 3.1% English, 1.1% Italian (2005-2009 5-year est.).
Economy: Single-family building permits issued: 0 (2010); Multi-family building permits issued: 0 (2010); Employment by occupation: 5.4% management, 11.5% professional, 19.3% services, 27.5% sales, 0.0% farming, 14.5% construction, 21.9% production (2005-2009 5-year est.).
Income: Per capita income: $15,159 (2010); Median household income: $42,594 (2010); Average household income: $46,387 (2010); Percent of households with income of $100,000 or more: 5.3% (2010); Poverty rate: 23.2% (2005-2009 5-year est.).
Taxes: Total city taxes per capita: $326 (2007); City property taxes per capita: $220 (2007).
Education: Percent of population age 25 and over with: High school diploma (including GED) or higher: 75.0% (2010); Bachelor's degree or higher: 8.9% (2010); Master's degree or higher: 1.2% (2010).

School District(s)
Everman ISD (PK-12)
    2009-10 Enrollment: 5,053 . . . . (817) 568-3500
Housing: Homeownership rate: 77.9% (2010); Median home value: $73,578 (2010); Median contract rent: $638 per month (2005-2009 5-year est.); Median year structure built: 1972 (2005-2009 5-year est.).
Safety: Violent crime rate: 29.5 per 10,000 population; Property crime rate: 326.0 per 10,000 population (2009).
Transportation: Commute to work: 95.0% car, 0.8% public transportation, 0.8% walk, 1.8% work from home (2005-2009 5-year est.); Travel time to work: 22.1% less than 15 minutes, 44.8% 15 to 30 minutes, 19.4% 30 to 45 minutes, 9.4% 45 to 60 minutes, 4.3% 60 minutes or more (2005-2009 5-year est.)
Additional Information Contacts
City of Everman . . . . (817) 293-0525
    http://www.evermantx.net

FOREST HILL (city). Covers a land area of 4.246 square miles and a water area of 0 square miles. Located at 32.66° N. Lat; 97.26° W. Long. Elevation is 682 feet.
History: Named for its location and heavily forested terrain. Incorporated after 1940.
Population: 11,464 (1990); 12,949 (2000); 13,593 (2010); 14,282 (2015 projected); Race: 35.0% White, 50.5% Black, 1.3% Asian, 13.2% Other, 32.1% Hispanic of any race (2010); Density: 3,201.4 persons per square mile (2010); Average household size: 3.00 (2010); Median age: 35.7 (2010); Males per 100 females: 119.6 (2010); Marriage status: 28.1% never married, 54.0% now married, 5.1% widowed, 12.8% divorced (2005-2009 5-year est.); Foreign born: 19.1% (2005-2009 5-year est.); Ancestry (includes multiple ancestries): 2.9% African, 2.4% American, 2.3% German, 2.3% Irish, 1.7% English (2005-2009 5-year est.).
Economy: Single-family building permits issued: 1 (2010); Multi-family building permits issued: 0 (2010); Employment by occupation: 7.1% management, 8.2% professional, 19.0% services, 28.0% sales, 0.4% farming, 17.9% construction, 19.4% production (2005-2009 5-year est.).
Income: Per capita income: $18,490 (2010); Median household income: $41,882 (2010); Average household income: $51,264 (2010); Percent of households with income of $100,000 or more: 9.2% (2010); Poverty rate: 16.1% (2005-2009 5-year est.).
Taxes: Total city taxes per capita: $400 (2007); City property taxes per capita: $253 (2007).
Education: Percent of population age 25 and over with: High school diploma (including GED) or higher: 67.7% (2010); Bachelor's degree or higher: 10.6% (2010); Master's degree or higher: 3.1% (2010).
Housing: Homeownership rate: 83.4% (2010); Median home value: $75,137 (2010); Median contract rent: $638 per month (2005-2009 5-year est.); Median year structure built: 1972 (2005-2009 5-year est.).
Safety: Violent crime rate: 81.7 per 10,000 population; Property crime rate: 404.7 per 10,000 population (2009).
Transportation: Commute to work: 96.0% car, 0.6% public transportation, 0.5% walk, 2.7% work from home (2005-2009 5-year est.); Travel time to work: 20.4% less than 15 minutes, 47.5% 15 to 30 minutes, 21.4% 30 to 45 minutes, 5.1% 45 to 60 minutes, 5.7% 60 minutes or more (2005-2009 5-year est.)
Additional Information Contacts
City of Forest Hill . . . . (817) 568-3000
    http://www.foresthilltx.org

FORT WORTH (city). County seat. Covers a land area of 292.541 square miles and a water area of 6.354 square miles. Located at 32.73° N. Lat; 97.33° W. Long. Elevation is 653 feet.
History: Fort Worth began not as a fort, but as a camp named for General William Jenkins Worth and occupied in 1849 by Brevet Major R.A. Arnold and a troop of dragoons. The community that grew up around the camp became a trading and supply center for the cattle drovers taking their herds north. The town was incorporated in 1873, and then worked desperately for three years to get the first railroad built. Livestock continued to be the basis of the Fort Worth economy; by 1900 meat packing plants were being built by Swift & Company, Armour & Company, and Libby, McNeill & Libby. Fort Worth's nickname as the Panther City began in the slow days of 1873, when a letter to the Dallas newspaper reported that Fort Worth was so dead, a panther had been seen sleeping undisturbed in the main street.
Population: 448,311 (1990); 534,694 (2000); 696,039 (2010); 764,598 (2015 projected); Race: 57.8% White, 18.5% Black, 3.2% Asian, 20.5% Other, 35.9% Hispanic of any race (2010); Density: 2,379.3 persons per square mile (2010); Average household size: 2.73 (2010); Median age:

32.6 (2010); Males per 100 females: 99.6 (2010); Marriage status: 31.4% never married, 51.8% now married, 5.0% widowed, 11.8% divorced (2005-2009 5-year est.); Foreign born: 17.6% (2005-2009 5-year est.); Ancestry (includes multiple ancestries): 9.4% German, 7.4% Irish, 7.4% English, 7.2% American, 2.5% African (2005-2009 5-year est.).

Economy: Unemployment rate: 9.1% (June 2011); Total civilian labor force: 344,363 (June 2011); Single-family building permits issued: 2,759 (2010); Multi-family building permits issued: 818 (2010); Employment by occupation: 12.8% management, 18.6% professional, 16.3% services, 26.2% sales, 0.2% farming, 11.0% construction, 14.9% production (2005-2009 5-year est.).

Income: Per capita income: $22,786 (2010); Median household income: $46,649 (2010); Average household income: $62,573 (2010); Percent of households with income of $100,000 or more: 16.0% (2010); Poverty rate: 17.0% (2005-2009 5-year est.).

Taxes: Total city taxes per capita: $750 (2007); City property taxes per capita: $402 (2007).

Education: Percent of population age 25 and over with: High school diploma (including GED) or higher: 75.3% (2010); Bachelor's degree or higher: 23.5% (2010); Master's degree or higher: 7.8% (2010).

School District(s)

Arlington ISD (PK-12)
    2009-10 Enrollment: 63,487 . . . . (682) 867-4611
Azle ISD (PK-12)
    2009-10 Enrollment: 5,841 . . . . (817) 444-3235
Burleson ISD (PK-12)
    2009-10 Enrollment: 9,896 . . . . (817) 245-1000
Castleberry ISD (PK-12)
    2009-10 Enrollment: 3,641 . . . . (817) 252-2000
Chapel Hill Academy (PK-02)
    2009-10 Enrollment: 268 . . . . (817) 255-2504
Crowley ISD (PK-12)
    2009-10 Enrollment: 15,126 . . . . (817) 297-5800
Eagle Mt-Saginaw ISD (PK-12)
    2009-10 Enrollment: 16,126 . . . . (817) 232-0880
East Fort Worth Montessori Academy (PK-05)
    2009-10 Enrollment: 306 . . . . (817) 496-3003
Everman ISD (PK-12)
    2009-10 Enrollment: 5,053 . . . . (817) 568-3500
Fort Worth Academy of Fine Arts (03-12)
    2009-10 Enrollment: 417 . . . . (817) 924-1482
Fort Worth Can Academy (09-12)
    2009-10 Enrollment: 714 . . . . (214) 943-2244
Fort Worth ISD (PK-12)
    2009-10 Enrollment: 80,209 . . . . (817) 871-2000
Harmony Science Academy (Fort Worth) (KG-11)
    2009-10 Enrollment: 1,948 . . . . (817) 263-0700
Honors Academy (KG-12)
    2009-10 Enrollment: 1,068 . . . . (214) 521-6365
Hurst-Euless-Bedford ISD (PK-12)
    2009-10 Enrollment: 20,762 . . . . (817) 283-4461
Keller ISD (PK-12)
    2009-10 Enrollment: 31,569 . . . . (817) 744-1000
Kennedale ISD (PK-12)
    2009-10 Enrollment: 3,162 . . . . (817) 563-8000
Lake Worth ISD (PK-12)
    2009-10 Enrollment: 2,957 . . . . (817) 306-4205
Metro Academy of Math and Science (PK-12)
    2009-10 Enrollment: 359 . . . . (817) 229-5200
Northwest ISD (PK-12)
    2009-10 Enrollment: 14,164 . . . . (817) 215-0000
Responsive Education Solutions (KG-12)
    2009-10 Enrollment: 5,022 . . . . (972) 316-3663
Richard Milburn Academy (Fort Worth) (09-12)
    2009-10 Enrollment: 201 . . . . (830) 788-0198
Texas Elementary School of the Arts (KG-06)
    2009-10 Enrollment: 155 . . . . (817) 732-8372
Theresa B Lee Academy
    2009-10 Enrollment: n/a . . . . (817) 534-5593
Treetops School International (KG-12)
    2009-10 Enrollment: 367 . . . . (817) 283-1771
White Settlement ISD (PK-12)
    2009-10 Enrollment: 6,051 . . . . (817) 367-5349

Four-year College(s)

Brite Divinity School (Private, Not-for-profit, Christian Church (Disciples of Christ))
    Fall 2009 Enrollment: 242 . . . . (817) 257-7575
Texas Christian University (Private, Not-for-profit, Christian Church (Disciples of Christ))
    Fall 2009 Enrollment: 8,853 . . . . (817) 257-7000
    2010-11 Tuition: In-state $30,090; Out-of-state $30,090
Texas Wesleyan University (Private, Not-for-profit, United Methodist)
    Fall 2009 Enrollment: 3,333 . . . . (817) 531-4444
    2010-11 Tuition: In-state $18,710; Out-of-state $18,710
The College of Saint Thomas More (Private, Not-for-profit, Roman Catholic)
    Fall 2009 Enrollment: 70 . . . . (817) 923-8459
    2010-11 Tuition: In-state $12,800; Out-of-state $12,800
University of North Texas Health Science Center (Public)
    Fall 2009 Enrollment: 1,395 . . . . (817) 735-2000
Westwood College-Ft Worth (Private, For-profit)
    Fall 2009 Enrollment: 367 . . . . (817) 547-9600
    2010-11 Tuition: In-state $13,825; Out-of-state $13,825

Two-year College(s)

Career Centers of Texas-Ft Worth (Private, For-profit)
    Fall 2009 Enrollment: 721 . . . . (817) 413-2000
Everest College-Fort Worth (Private, For-profit)
    Fall 2009 Enrollment: 939 . . . . (817) 838-3000
    2010-11 Tuition: In-state $15,263; Out-of-state $15,263
Remington College-Fort Worth Campus (Private, For-profit)
    Fall 2009 Enrollment: 782 . . . . (817) 451-0017
    2010-11 Tuition: In-state $19,950; Out-of-state $19,950
Tarrant County College District (Public)
    Fall 2009 Enrollment: 44,355 . . . . (817) 515-5100
    2010-11 Tuition: In-state $1,752; Out-of-state $3,960

Vocational/Technical School(s)

Fort Worth Beauty School (Private, For-profit)
    Fall 2009 Enrollment: 129 . . . . (817) 732-2232
    2010-11 Tuition: $11,450
International Renowned Beauty Academy (Private, For-profit)
    Fall 2009 Enrollment: n/a . . . . (817) 531-3716
    2010-11 Tuition: $12,140
Ogle School Hair Skin Nails (Private, For-profit)
    Fall 2009 Enrollment: 297 . . . . (817) 665-1329
    2010-11 Tuition: $15,600

Housing: Homeownership rate: 59.1% (2010); Median home value: $105,338 (2010); Median contract rent: $602 per month (2005-2009 5-year est.); Median year structure built: 1980 (2005-2009 5-year est.).

Hospitals: Baylor All Saints Medical Center at Forth Worth (275 beds); Baylor Medical Center at Southwest Fort Worth (71 beds); Baylor Surgical Hospital at Fort Worth; Cook Children's Medical Center (282 beds); Federal Medical Center Carswell (450 beds); Harris Methodist Continued Care Hospital (628 beds); Harris Methodist Southwest (85 beds); HealthSouth Rehabilitation Hospital of Fort Worth; Healthsouth City View Rehabilitation Hospital (62 beds); John Peter Smith Hospital (459 beds); Kindred Hospital-Fort Worth (67 beds); Plaza Medical Center of Fort Worth (320 beds)

Safety: Violent crime rate: 58.5 per 10,000 population; Property crime rate: 496.0 per 10,000 population (2009).

Newspapers: Benbrook News (Community news; Circulation 7,500); The Dallas Morning News - Fort Worth Bureau (Local news); Diario La Estrella (Regional news; Circulation 32,950); El Informador Hispano (Local news; Circulation 30,000); Fort Worth Star-Telegram (Regional news; Circulation 336,883); Fort Worth Star-Telegram - Arlington Bureau (Local news); Fort Worth Star-Telegram - Dallas Bureau (Community news); Fort Worth Star-Telegram - Northeast Tarrant County Bureau (Local news); Fort Worth Weekly (Local news); La Vida News - The Black Voice (Community news; Circulation 34,929); North Texas Catholic (Regional news; Circulation 26,500); River Oak News (Community news; Circulation 4,500); Star-Telegram.com (Regional news); Tarrant Business - Fort Worth Star-Telegram (Regional news); White Settlement Bomber News (Community news; Circulation 7,000)

Transportation: Commute to work: 92.6% car, 1.4% public transportation, 1.4% walk, 3.0% work from home (2005-2009 5-year est.); Travel time to work: 23.3% less than 15 minutes, 40.7% 15 to 30 minutes, 21.5% 30 to 45 minutes, 7.7% 45 to 60 minutes, 6.8% 60 minutes or more (2005-2009 5-year est.); Amtrak: train service available.

Airports: Bourland Field (general aviation); Dallas/Fort Worth International (primary service/large hub); Fort Worth Alliance (general aviation); Fort

Worth Meacham International (general aviation); Fort Worth NAS Jrb/Carswell Field (general aviation)
Additional Information Contacts
City of Fort Worth . . . . (817) 392-2255
  http://www.fortworthgov.org
Fort Worth Chamber of Commerce . . . . (817) 336-2491
  http://www.fortworthchamber.com
Fort Worth Hispanic Chamber of Commerce . . . . (817) 625-5411
  http://www.fwhcc.org
Fort Worth Metropolitan Black Chamber of Commerce . . . . (817) 871-6538
  http://www.fwmbcc.org
Northeast Tarrant County Chamber of Commerce . . . . (817) 281-9376
  http://www.netarrant.org

GRAPEVINE (city). Covers a land area of 32.280 square miles and a water area of 3.576 square miles. Located at 32.93° N. Lat; 97.08° W. Long. Elevation is 640 feet.
Population: 29,351 (1990); 42,059 (2000); 50,522 (2010); 55,637 (2015 projected); Race: 81.5% White, 3.1% Black, 3.2% Asian, 12.3% Other, 20.1% Hispanic of any race (2010); Density: 1,565.1 persons per square mile (2010); Average household size: 2.69 (2010); Median age: 35.8 (2010); Males per 100 females: 101.8 (2010); Marriage status: 26.4% never married, 56.1% now married, 3.9% widowed, 13.6% divorced (2005-2009 5-year est.); Foreign born: 11.0% (2005-2009 5-year est.); Ancestry (includes multiple ancestries): 19.0% German, 14.3% English, 12.4% Irish, 9.5% American, 3.4% French (2005-2009 5-year est.).
Economy: Unemployment rate: 6.4% (June 2011); Total civilian labor force: 29,450 (June 2011); Single-family building permits issued: 17 (2010); Multi-family building permits issued: 0 (2010); Employment by occupation: 22.4% management, 22.5% professional, 13.9% services, 29.1% sales, 0.0% farming, 4.8% construction, 7.3% production (2005-2009 5-year est.).
Income: Per capita income: $37,130 (2010); Median household income: $80,099 (2010); Average household income: $100,209 (2010); Percent of households with income of $100,000 or more: 38.1% (2010); Poverty rate: 6.8% (2005-2009 5-year est.).
Taxes: Total city taxes per capita: $1,296 (2007); City property taxes per capita: $541 (2007).
Education: Percent of population age 25 and over with: High school diploma (including GED) or higher: 91.4% (2010); Bachelor's degree or higher: 43.5% (2010); Master's degree or higher: 11.8% (2010).

School District(s)

Carroll ISD (PK-12)
  2009-10 Enrollment: 7,745 . . . . (817) 949-8222
Grapevine-Colleyville ISD (PK-12)
  2009-10 Enrollment: 13,671 . . . . (817) 488-9588
Winfree Academy Charter Schools (09-12)
  2009-10 Enrollment: 1,862 . . . . (972) 869-3250
Housing: Homeownership rate: 65.0% (2010); Median home value: $215,138 (2010); Median contract rent: $762 per month (2005-2009 5-year est.); Median year structure built: 1987 (2005-2009 5-year est.).
Hospitals: Baylor Regional Medical Center at Grapevine (190 beds)
Safety: Violent crime rate: 15.9 per 10,000 population; Property crime rate: 332.3 per 10,000 population (2009).
Newspapers: Grapevine Sun (Local news; Circulation 19,000); Hometown Star (Local news; Circulation 15,700)
Transportation: Commute to work: 91.3% car, 0.3% public transportation, 0.9% walk, 6.0% work from home (2005-2009 5-year est.); Travel time to work: 28.0% less than 15 minutes, 38.6% 15 to 30 minutes, 23.8% 30 to 45 minutes, 6.2% 45 to 60 minutes, 3.3% 60 minutes or more (2005-2009 5-year est.)
Additional Information Contacts
City of Grapevine . . . . (817) 410-3000
  http://www.ci.grapevine.tx.us
Grapevine Chamber of Commerce . . . . (817) 481-1522
  http://www.grapevinechamber.org

HALTOM CITY (city). Covers a land area of 12.393 square miles and a water area of 0.017 square miles. Located at 32.81° N. Lat; 97.27° W. Long. Elevation is 535 feet.
History: Incorporated after 1940.
Population: 32,909 (1990); 39,018 (2000); 40,693 (2010); 42,883 (2015 projected); Race: 65.2% White, 4.2% Black, 8.8% Asian, 21.9% Other, 34.0% Hispanic of any race (2010); Density: 3,283.6 persons per square mile (2010); Average household size: 2.68 (2010); Median age: 33.6 (2010); Males per 100 females: 101.4 (2010); Marriage status: 28.2%

never married, 50.8% now married, 6.5% widowed, 14.5% divorced (2005-2009 5-year est.); Foreign born: 22.1% (2005-2009 5-year est.); Ancestry (includes multiple ancestries): 12.1% American, 8.3% German, 7.2% Irish, 7.0% English, 1.6% Scottish (2005-2009 5-year est.).
Economy: Unemployment rate: 8.3% (June 2011); Total civilian labor force: 21,240 (June 2011); Single-family building permits issued: 9 (2010); Multi-family building permits issued: 0 (2010); Employment by occupation: 9.4% management, 11.6% professional, 16.0% services, 26.0% sales, 0.2% farming, 13.7% construction, 23.2% production (2005-2009 5-year est.).
Income: Per capita income: $21,109 (2010); Median household income: $46,372 (2010); Average household income: $56,474 (2010); Percent of households with income of $100,000 or more: 11.9% (2010); Poverty rate: 16.7% (2005-2009 5-year est.).
Taxes: Total city taxes per capita: $346 (2007); City property taxes per capita: $135 (2007).
Education: Percent of population age 25 and over with: High school diploma (including GED) or higher: 75.2% (2010); Bachelor's degree or higher: 14.0% (2010); Master's degree or higher: 3.8% (2010).

School District(s)

Birdville ISD (PK-12)
  2009-10 Enrollment: 22,897 . . . . (817) 547-5700
Housing: Homeownership rate: 62.0% (2010); Median home value: $86,797 (2010); Median contract rent: $594 per month (2005-2009 5-year est.); Median year structure built: 1973 (2005-2009 5-year est.).
Safety: Violent crime rate: 34.5 per 10,000 population; Property crime rate: 475.4 per 10,000 population (2009).
Transportation: Commute to work: 94.1% car, 0.2% public transportation, 1.3% walk, 1.0% work from home (2005-2009 5-year est.); Travel time to work: 26.2% less than 15 minutes, 39.4% 15 to 30 minutes, 22.7% 30 to 45 minutes, 5.7% 45 to 60 minutes, 5.9% 60 minutes or more (2005-2009 5-year est.)
Additional Information Contacts
City of Haltom City . . . . (817) 222-7700
  http://www.haltomcitytx.com

HASLET (city). Covers a land area of 7.499 square miles and a water area of 0 square miles. Located at 32.96° N. Lat; 97.34° W. Long. Elevation is 702 feet.
History: Haslet was first settled in 1880.
Population: 893 (1990); 1,134 (2000); 4,878 (2010); 5,466 (2015 projected); Race: 76.0% White, 7.0% Black, 2.0% Asian, 15.0% Other, 16.7% Hispanic of any race (2010); Density: 650.5 persons per square mile (2010); Average household size: 2.83 (2010); Median age: 37.3 (2010); Males per 100 females: 101.0 (2010); Marriage status: 18.4% never married, 67.7% now married, 6.0% widowed, 7.9% divorced (2005-2009 5-year est.); Foreign born: 4.5% (2005-2009 5-year est.); Ancestry (includes multiple ancestries): 20.5% German, 13.9% English, 12.8% American, 11.3% Irish, 3.5% Scotch-Irish (2005-2009 5-year est.).
Economy: Single-family building permits issued: 1 (2010); Multi-family building permits issued: 0 (2010); Employment by occupation: 23.2% management, 27.3% professional, 9.4% services, 19.2% sales, 0.5% farming, 8.6% construction, 11.8% production (2005-2009 5-year est.).
Income: Per capita income: $34,214 (2010); Median household income: $84,330 (2010); Average household income: $97,141 (2010); Percent of households with income of $100,000 or more: 34.9% (2010); Poverty rate: 0.1% (2005-2009 5-year est.).
Taxes: Total city taxes per capita: $1,301 (2007); City property taxes per capita: $885 (2007).
Education: Percent of population age 25 and over with: High school diploma (including GED) or higher: 94.4% (2010); Bachelor's degree or higher: 29.4% (2010); Master's degree or higher: 6.8% (2010).

School District(s)

Northwest ISD (PK-12)
  2009-10 Enrollment: 14,164 . . . . (817) 215-0000
Housing: Homeownership rate: 94.6% (2010); Median home value: $172,821 (2010); Median contract rent: $706 per month (2005-2009 5-year est.); Median year structure built: 1992 (2005-2009 5-year est.).
Transportation: Commute to work: 90.4% car, 0.0% public transportation, 2.1% walk, 6.6% work from home (2005-2009 5-year est.); Travel time to work: 20.9% less than 15 minutes, 20.0% 15 to 30 minutes, 30.4% 30 to 45 minutes, 20.5% 45 to 60 minutes, 8.2% 60 minutes or more (2005-2009 5-year est.)

HURST

HURST (city). Covers a land area of 9.904 square miles and a water area of 0 square miles. Located at 32.83° N. Lat; 97.18° W. Long. Elevation is 554 feet.

Population: 33,593 (1990); 36,273 (2000); 38,250 (2010); 40,366 (2015 projected); Race: 78.1% White, 6.0% Black, 2.4% Asian, 13.5% Other, 19.0% Hispanic of any race (2010); Density: 3,862.3 persons per square mile (2010); Average household size: 2.58 (2010); Median age: 37.4 (2010); Males per 100 females: 97.0 (2010); Marriage status: 24.3% never married, 55.6% now married, 6.6% widowed, 13.5% divorced (2005-2009 5-year est.); Foreign born: 13.8% (2005-2009 5-year est.); Ancestry (includes multiple ancestries): 16.1% German, 13.4% English, 13.1% American, 10.4% Irish, 2.9% Italian (2005-2009 5-year est.).

Economy: Unemployment rate: 8.0% (June 2011); Total civilian labor force: 21,112 (June 2011); Single-family building permits issued: 11 (2010); Multi-family building permits issued: 2 (2010); Employment by occupation: 15.3% management, 19.5% professional, 14.6% services, 30.9% sales, 0.0% farming, 11.7% construction, 8.0% production (2005-2009 5-year est.).

Income: Per capita income: $28,182 (2010); Median household income: $59,275 (2010); Average household income: $73,018 (2010); Percent of households with income of $100,000 or more: 21.8% (2010); Poverty rate: 10.1% (2005-2009 5-year est.).

Taxes: Total city taxes per capita: $836 (2007); City property taxes per capita: $278 (2007).

Education: Percent of population age 25 and over with: High school diploma (including GED) or higher: 88.3% (2010); Bachelor's degree or higher: 25.8% (2010); Master's degree or higher: 7.1% (2010).

School District(s)

Birdville ISD (PK-12)
 2009-10 Enrollment: 22,897 .... (817) 547-5700
Hurst-Euless-Bedford ISD (PK-12)
 2009-10 Enrollment: 20,762 .... (817) 283-4461

Vocational/Technical School(s)

Ogle School Hair Skin Nails (Private, For-profit)
 Fall 2009 Enrollment: 211 .... (817) 284-8526
 2010-11 Tuition: $15,600

Housing: Homeownership rate: 67.0% (2010); Median home value: $135,716 (2010); Median contract rent: $618 per month (2005-2009 5-year est.); Median year structure built: 1973 (2005-2009 5-year est.).

Hospitals: Southwest Surgical Hospital

Safety: Violent crime rate: 49.2 per 10,000 population; Property crime rate: 602.6 per 10,000 population (2009).

Transportation: Commute to work: 93.1% car, 0.8% public transportation, 0.9% walk, 3.1% work from home (2005-2009 5-year est.); Travel time to work: 27.3% less than 15 minutes, 38.5% 15 to 30 minutes, 21.4% 30 to 45 minutes, 8.3% 45 to 60 minutes, 4.5% 60 minutes or more (2005-2009 5-year est.)

Additional Information Contacts
City of Hurst .... (817) 788-7000
 http://www.ci.hurst.tx.us
HEB Chamber of Commerce .... (817) 283-1521
 http://www.heb.org

KELLER

KELLER (city). Covers a land area of 18.438 square miles and a water area of 0 square miles. Located at 32.92° N. Lat; 97.23° W. Long. Elevation is 709 feet.

Population: 13,683 (1990); 27,345 (2000); 40,551 (2010); 47,390 (2015 projected); Race: 90.4% White, 2.5% Black, 2.5% Asian, 4.6% Other, 7.0% Hispanic of any race (2010); Density: 2,199.3 persons per square mile (2010); Average household size: 3.17 (2010); Median age: 34.6 (2010); Males per 100 females: 99.1 (2010); Marriage status: 20.5% never married, 69.7% now married, 3.1% widowed, 6.7% divorced (2005-2009 5-year est.); Foreign born: 6.3% (2005-2009 5-year est.); Ancestry (includes multiple ancestries): 21.3% German, 17.3% English, 16.0% Irish, 11.0% American, 5.0% Italian (2005-2009 5-year est.).

Economy: Unemployment rate: 7.0% (June 2011); Total civilian labor force: 20,928 (June 2011); Single-family building permits issued: 228 (2010); Multi-family building permits issued: 0 (2010); Employment by occupation: 25.1% management, 22.5% professional, 9.4% services, 30.2% sales, 0.0% farming, 5.0% construction, 7.9% production (2005-2009 5-year est.).

Income: Per capita income: $40,342 (2010); Median household income: $106,949 (2010); Average household income: $127,875 (2010); Percent of households with income of $100,000 or more: 55.2% (2010); Poverty rate: 2.8% (2005-2009 5-year est.).

Taxes: Total city taxes per capita: $763 (2007); City property taxes per capita: $402 (2007).

Education: Percent of population age 25 and over with: High school diploma (including GED) or higher: 95.9% (2010); Bachelor's degree or higher: 45.8% (2010); Master's degree or higher: 11.3% (2010).

School District(s)

Keller ISD (PK-12)
 2009-10 Enrollment: 31,569 .... (817) 744-1000
Northwest ISD (PK-12)
 2009-10 Enrollment: 14,164 .... (817) 215-0000

Housing: Homeownership rate: 92.8% (2010); Median home value: $251,257 (2010); Median contract rent: $832 per month (2005-2009 5-year est.); Median year structure built: 1995 (2005-2009 5-year est.).

Safety: Violent crime rate: 6.7 per 10,000 population; Property crime rate: 124.7 per 10,000 population (2009).

Newspapers: Keller Citizen (Community news; Circulation 36,000)

Transportation: Commute to work: 90.4% car, 0.2% public transportation, 0.5% walk, 7.9% work from home (2005-2009 5-year est.); Travel time to work: 20.5% less than 15 minutes, 31.9% 15 to 30 minutes, 30.4% 30 to 45 minutes, 11.8% 45 to 60 minutes, 5.3% 60 minutes or more (2005-2009 5-year est.)

Additional Information Contacts
City of Keller .... (817) 743-4000
 http://www.cityofkeller.com
Greater Keller Chamber of Commerce .... (817) 431-2169
 http://www.KellerChamber.com

KENNEDALE

KENNEDALE (city). Covers a land area of 6.041 square miles and a water area of 0 square miles. Located at 32.65° N. Lat; 97.21° W. Long. Elevation is 630 feet.

History: Incorporated after 1940.

Population: 5,028 (1990); 5,850 (2000); 6,838 (2010); 7,414 (2015 projected); Race: 79.1% White, 7.7% Black, 1.8% Asian, 11.5% Other, 16.4% Hispanic of any race (2010); Density: 1,132.0 persons per square mile (2010); Average household size: 2.59 (2010); Median age: 34.1 (2010); Males per 100 females: 100.6 (2010); Marriage status: 22.9% never married, 59.8% now married, 4.9% widowed, 12.4% divorced (2005-2009 5-year est.); Foreign born: 6.1% (2005-2009 5-year est.); Ancestry (includes multiple ancestries): 14.9% German, 13.2% English, 12.2% Irish, 6.5% American, 4.0% Scottish (2005-2009 5-year est.).

Economy: Single-family building permits issued: 15 (2010); Multi-family building permits issued: 0 (2010); Employment by occupation: 16.8% management, 14.3% professional, 13.7% services, 26.2% sales, 0.0% farming, 10.0% construction, 19.0% production (2005-2009 5-year est.).

Income: Per capita income: $28,739 (2010); Median household income: $57,215 (2010); Average household income: $74,419 (2010); Percent of households with income of $100,000 or more: 22.6% (2010); Poverty rate: 10.4% (2005-2009 5-year est.).

Taxes: Total city taxes per capita: $607 (2007); City property taxes per capita: $325 (2007).

Education: Percent of population age 25 and over with: High school diploma (including GED) or higher: 85.0% (2010); Bachelor's degree or higher: 20.9% (2010); Master's degree or higher: 5.8% (2010).

School District(s)

Kennedale ISD (PK-12)
 2009-10 Enrollment: 3,162 .... (817) 563-8000

Housing: Homeownership rate: 59.0% (2010); Median home value: $139,559 (2010); Median contract rent: $644 per month (2005-2009 5-year est.); Median year structure built: 1984 (2005-2009 5-year est.).

Safety: Violent crime rate: 40.0 per 10,000 population; Property crime rate: 346.1 per 10,000 population (2009).

Transportation: Commute to work: 93.3% car, 0.6% public transportation, 1.6% walk, 3.3% work from home (2005-2009 5-year est.); Travel time to work: 29.6% less than 15 minutes, 36.6% 15 to 30 minutes, 19.3% 30 to 45 minutes, 6.1% 45 to 60 minutes, 8.3% 60 minutes or more (2005-2009 5-year est.)

Additional Information Contacts
City of Kennedale .... (817) 985-2100
 http://www.cityofkennedale.com
Kennedale Chamber of Commerce .... (817) 985-2109
 http://www.kennedalechamber.com

LAKE WORTH

LAKE WORTH (city). Aka Lake Worth Village. Covers a land area of 2.522 square miles and a water area of 0 square miles. Located at 32.81° N. Lat; 97.43° W. Long. Elevation is 643 feet.

History: Incorporated after 1940.

Population: 4,591 (1990); 4,618 (2000); 4,797 (2010); 5,040 (2015 projected); Race: 80.2% White, 1.4% Black, 0.9% Asian, 17.5% Other, 26.3% Hispanic of any race (2010); Density: 1,902.2 persons per square mile (2010); Average household size: 2.72 (2010); Median age: 38.4 (2010); Males per 100 females: 94.9 (2010); Marriage status: 25.1% never married, 52.0% now married, 7.9% widowed, 15.0% divorced (2005-2009 5-year est.); Foreign born: 8.7% (2005-2009 5-year est.); Ancestry (includes multiple ancestries): 17.6% American, 17.0% German, 13.1% Irish, 8.5% English, 3.6% African (2005-2009 5-year est.).

Economy: Single-family building permits issued: 1 (2010); Multi-family building permits issued: 0 (2010); Employment by occupation: 10.9% management, 11.0% professional, 12.4% services, 30.9% sales, 0.4% farming, 20.0% construction, 14.4% production (2005-2009 5-year est.).

Income: Per capita income: $20,180 (2010); Median household income: $45,864 (2010); Average household income: $56,091 (2010); Percent of households with income of $100,000 or more: 10.1% (2010); Poverty rate: 11.0% (2005-2009 5-year est.).

Taxes: Total city taxes per capita: $1,507 (2007); City property taxes per capita: $191 (2007).

Education: Percent of population age 25 and over with: High school diploma (including GED) or higher: 71.2% (2010); Bachelor's degree or higher: 9.1% (2010); Master's degree or higher: 3.3% (2010).

School District(s)
Lake Worth ISD (PK-12)
   2009-10 Enrollment: 2,957 . . . . (817) 306-4205

Housing: Homeownership rate: 80.3% (2010); Median home value: $85,376 (2010); Median contract rent: $716 per month (2005-2009 5-year est.); Median year structure built: 1957 (2005-2009 5-year est.).

Safety: Violent crime rate: 41.4 per 10,000 population; Property crime rate: 968.5 per 10,000 population (2009).

Transportation: Commute to work: 92.4% car, 1.3% public transportation, 0.5% walk, 5.5% work from home (2005-2009 5-year est.); Travel time to work: 21.0% less than 15 minutes, 44.2% 15 to 30 minutes, 19.3% 30 to 45 minutes, 6.9% 45 to 60 minutes, 8.6% 60 minutes or more (2005-2009 5-year est.)

LAKESIDE

LAKESIDE (town). Covers a land area of 1.513 square miles and a water area of 0 square miles. Located at 32.82° N. Lat; 97.49° W. Long. Elevation is 712 feet.

Population: 816 (1990); 1,040 (2000); 1,192 (2010); 1,328 (2015 projected); Race: 92.5% White, 0.3% Black, 1.4% Asian, 5.7% Other, 9.1% Hispanic of any race (2010); Density: 788.0 persons per square mile (2010); Average household size: 2.42 (2010); Median age: 46.7 (2010); Males per 100 females: 98.0 (2010); Marriage status: 12.2% never married, 70.1% now married, 4.7% widowed, 12.9% divorced (2005-2009 5-year est.); Foreign born: 1.3% (2005-2009 5-year est.); Ancestry (includes multiple ancestries): 19.9% Irish, 18.6% German, 15.0% American, 13.3% English, 3.9% Scottish (2005-2009 5-year est.).

Economy: Single-family building permits issued: 2 (2010); Multi-family building permits issued: 0 (2010); Employment by occupation: 17.5% management, 29.3% professional, 7.6% services, 24.2% sales, 0.0% farming, 10.5% construction, 10.9% production (2005-2009 5-year est.).

Income: Per capita income: $28,780 (2010); Median household income: $58,929 (2010); Average household income: $70,076 (2010); Percent of households with income of $100,000 or more: 20.3% (2010); Poverty rate: 3.5% (2005-2009 5-year est.).

Taxes: Total city taxes per capita: $14 (2007); City property taxes per capita: $8 (2007).

Education: Percent of population age 25 and over with: High school diploma (including GED) or higher: 86.9% (2010); Bachelor's degree or higher: 18.8% (2010); Master's degree or higher: 5.9% (2010).

Housing: Homeownership rate: 90.0% (2010); Median home value: $128,046 (2010); Median contract rent: $860 per month (2005-2009 5-year est.); Median year structure built: 1968 (2005-2009 5-year est.).

Safety: Violent crime rate: 0.0 per 10,000 population; Property crime rate: 125.1 per 10,000 population (2009).

Transportation: Commute to work: 93.4% car, 0.0% public transportation, 1.0% walk, 4.9% work from home (2005-2009 5-year est.); Travel time to work: 10.0% less than 15 minutes, 43.9% 15 to 30 minutes, 19.9% 30 to 45

minutes, 9.7% 45 to 60 minutes, 16.5% 60 minutes or more (2005-2009 5-year est.)

MANSFIELD

MANSFIELD (city). Covers a land area of 36.477 square miles and a water area of 0.036 square miles. Located at 32.57° N. Lat; 97.12° W. Long. Elevation is 604 feet.

Population: 15,390 (1990); 28,031 (2000); 50,896 (2010); 57,988 (2015 projected); Race: 75.5% White, 8.1% Black, 2.6% Asian, 13.8% Other, 20.4% Hispanic of any race (2010); Density: 1,395.3 persons per square mile (2010); Average household size: 3.12 (2010); Median age: 33.2 (2010); Males per 100 females: 102.6 (2010); Marriage status: 24.7% never married, 64.3% now married, 3.0% widowed, 8.0% divorced (2005-2009 5-year est.); Foreign born: 11.3% (2005-2009 5-year est.); Ancestry (includes multiple ancestries): 14.7% German, 11.1% Irish, 9.8% English, 9.0% American, 3.0% French (2005-2009 5-year est.).

Economy: Unemployment rate: 7.3% (June 2011); Total civilian labor force: 25,576 (June 2011); Single-family building permits issued: 236 (2010); Multi-family building permits issued: 0 (2010); Employment by occupation: 19.8% management, 22.8% professional, 12.7% services, 28.5% sales, 0.0% farming, 7.9% construction, 8.2% production (2005-2009 5-year est.).

Income: Per capita income: $33,163 (2010); Median household income: $81,560 (2010); Average household income: $104,055 (2010); Percent of households with income of $100,000 or more: 37.6% (2010); Poverty rate: 6.8% (2005-2009 5-year est.).

Taxes: Total city taxes per capita: $1,011 (2007); City property taxes per capita: $528 (2007).

Education: Percent of population age 25 and over with: High school diploma (including GED) or higher: 87.5% (2010); Bachelor's degree or higher: 34.5% (2010); Master's degree or higher: 9.9% (2010).

School District(s)
Mansfield ISD (PK-12)
   2009-10 Enrollment: 31,662 . . . . (817) 299-6300

Housing: Homeownership rate: 87.3% (2010); Median home value: $175,321 (2010); Median contract rent: $859 per month (2005-2009 5-year est.); Median year structure built: 1999 (2005-2009 5-year est.).

Hospitals: Kindred Hospital - Mansfield (55 beds)

Safety: Violent crime rate: 23.2 per 10,000 population; Property crime rate: 238.6 per 10,000 population (2009).

Newspapers: Mansfield News-Mirror (Community news; Circulation 3,950)

Transportation: Commute to work: 93.3% car, 0.1% public transportation, 0.5% walk, 5.2% work from home (2005-2009 5-year est.); Travel time to work: 19.6% less than 15 minutes, 28.7% 15 to 30 minutes, 30.1% 30 to 45 minutes, 10.8% 45 to 60 minutes, 10.9% 60 minutes or more (2005-2009 5-year est.)

Additional Information Contacts
City of Mansfield . . . . (817) 276-4200
   http://www.mansfield-tx.gov
Mansfield Area Chamber of Commerce. . . . . (817) 473-0507
   http://www.mansfieldchamber.org

NAVAL AIR STATION/JRB

NAVAL AIR STATION/JRB (unincorporated postal area, zip code 76127). Covers a land area of 0.363 square miles and a water area of 0 square miles. Located at 32.76° N. Lat; 97.42° W. Long.

Population: 289 (2000); Race: 49.0% White, 36.3% Black, 0.0% Asian, 14.7% Other, 20.5% Hispanic of any race (2000); Density: 796.1 persons per square mile (2000); Age: 3.8% under 18, 0.0% over 64 (2000); Marriage status: 61.6% never married, 28.1% now married, 0.0% widowed, 10.3% divorced (2000); Foreign born: 3.4% (2000); Ancestry (includes multiple ancestries): 14.7% German, 7.9% Irish, 4.8% Jamaican, 4.5% Finnish (2000).

Economy: Employment by occupation: 0.0% management, 39.4% professional, 39.4% services, 0.0% sales, 0.0% farming, 21.2% construction, 0.0% production (2000).

Income: Per capita income: $17,172 (2000); Median household income: $61,250 (2000); Poverty rate: 179.1% (2000).

Education: Percent of population age 25 and over with: High school diploma (including GED) or higher: 100.0% (2000); Bachelor's degree or higher: 24.4% (2000).

Housing: Homeownership rate: 0.0% (2000); Median home value: n/a (2000); Median contract rent: $525 per month (2000); Median year structure built: 1965 (2000).

Transportation: Commute to work: 76.5% car, 2.5% public transportation, 17.1% walk, 0.0% work from home (2000); Travel time to work: 70.1% less

than 15 minutes, 21.0% 15 to 30 minutes, 5.0% 30 to 45 minutes, 3.9% 45 to 60 minutes, 0.0% 60 minutes or more (2000)

NORTH RICHLAND HILLS (city). Covers a land area of 18.206 square miles and a water area of 0.026 square miles. Located at 32.85° N. Lat; 97.21° W. Long. Elevation is 604 feet.

History: Named for its location north of Richland Hills, which is named for its rich soil. Population more than doubled between 1970 and 1990 as a result of the economic development of the north Texas area. Incorporated 1953.

Population: 45,843 (1990); 55,635 (2000); 64,762 (2010); 70,805 (2015 projected); Race: 83.3% White, 3.9% Black, 3.3% Asian, 9.5% Other, 15.5% Hispanic of any race (2010); Density: 3,557.1 persons per square mile (2010); Average household size: 2.66 (2010); Median age: 35.7 (2010); Males per 100 females: 99.1 (2010); Marriage status: 24.2% never married, 56.8% now married, 7.3% widowed, 11.6% divorced (2005-2009 5-year est.); Foreign born: 7.5% (2005-2009 5-year est.); Ancestry (includes multiple ancestries): 17.6% American, 16.1% German, 12.8% Irish, 12.2% English, 3.1% French (2005-2009 5-year est.).

Economy: Unemployment rate: 7.7% (June 2011); Total civilian labor force: 37,111 (June 2011); Single-family building permits issued: 80 (2010); Multi-family building permits issued: 0 (2010); Employment by occupation: 16.3% management, 20.3% professional, 12.7% services, 33.6% sales, 0.0% farming, 7.7% construction, 9.6% production (2005-2009 5-year est.).

Income: Per capita income: $30,830 (2010); Median household income: $67,573 (2010); Average household income: $82,083 (2010); Percent of households with income of $100,000 or more: 26.4% (2010); Poverty rate: 7.6% (2005-2009 5-year est.).

Taxes: Total city taxes per capita: $685 (2007); City property taxes per capita: $317 (2007).

Education: Percent of population age 25 and over with: High school diploma (including GED) or higher: 90.5% (2010); Bachelor's degree or higher: 27.5% (2010); Master's degree or higher: 6.9% (2010).

School District(s)
Birdville ISD (PK-12)
    2009-10 Enrollment: 22,897 . . . . (817) 547-5700
Winfree Academy Charter Schools (09-12)
    2009-10 Enrollment: 1,862 . . . . (972) 869-3250
Vocational/Technical School(s)
ATI Career Training Center (Private, For-profit)
    Fall 2009 Enrollment: 2,225. . . . . (817) 284-1141
    2010-11 Tuition: $18,100

Housing: Homeownership rate: 67.5% (2010); Median home value: $136,248 (2010); Median contract rent: $702 per month (2005-2009 5-year est.); Median year structure built: 1984 (2005-2009 5-year est.).

Hospitals: North Hills Hospital (144 beds)

Safety: Violent crime rate: 26.9 per 10,000 population; Property crime rate: 308.4 per 10,000 population (2009).

Transportation: Commute to work: 93.4% car, 0.4% public transportation, 0.4% walk, 3.4% work from home (2005-2009 5-year est.); Travel time to work: 22.6% less than 15 minutes, 38.3% 15 to 30 minutes, 24.8% 30 to 45 minutes, 8.2% 45 to 60 minutes, 6.0% 60 minutes or more (2005-2009 5-year est.)

Additional Information Contacts
City of North Richland Hills . . . . (817) 427-6000
    http://www.ci.north-richland-hills.tx.us

PANTEGO (town). Covers a land area of 0.994 square miles and a water area of 0 square miles. Located at 32.71° N. Lat; 97.15° W. Long. Elevation is 571 feet.

Population: 2,371 (1990); 2,318 (2000); 2,444 (2010); 2,512 (2015 projected); Race: 86.0% White, 8.8% Black, 1.5% Asian, 3.8% Other, 4.5% Hispanic of any race (2010); Density: 2,457.7 persons per square mile (2010); Average household size: 2.47 (2010); Median age: 45.0 (2010); Males per 100 females: 90.5 (2010); Marriage status: 18.8% never married, 65.1% now married, 6.8% widowed, 9.3% divorced (2005-2009 5-year est.); Foreign born: 2.3% (2005-2009 5-year est.); Ancestry (includes multiple ancestries): 13.1% Irish, 12.2% German, 11.2% American, 10.7% English, 6.9% Scotch-Irish (2005-2009 5-year est.).

Economy: Single-family building permits issued: 3 (2010); Multi-family building permits issued: 0 (2010); Employment by occupation: 22.1% management, 20.2% professional, 9.5% services, 36.3% sales, 0.0% farming, 4.8% construction, 7.1% production (2005-2009 5-year est.).

Income: Per capita income: $39,981 (2010); Median household income: $79,419 (2010); Average household income: $98,315 (2010); Percent of

households with income of $100,000 or more: 33.5% (2010); Poverty rate: 5.8% (2005-2009 5-year est.).

Taxes: Total city taxes per capita: $1,585 (2007); City property taxes per capita: $381 (2007).

Education: Percent of population age 25 and over with: High school diploma (including GED) or higher: 94.9% (2010); Bachelor's degree or higher: 41.2% (2010); Master's degree or higher: 9.2% (2010).

Housing: Homeownership rate: 86.1% (2010); Median home value: $180,132 (2010); Median contract rent: $633 per month (2005-2009 5-year est.); Median year structure built: 1975 (2005-2009 5-year est.).

Safety: Violent crime rate: 46.1 per 10,000 population; Property crime rate: 565.3 per 10,000 population (2009).

Transportation: Commute to work: 92.3% car, 0.0% public transportation, 0.0% walk, 6.4% work from home (2005-2009 5-year est.); Travel time to work: 34.6% less than 15 minutes, 31.1% 15 to 30 minutes, 23.4% 30 to 45 minutes, 7.4% 45 to 60 minutes, 3.5% 60 minutes or more (2005-2009 5-year est.)

Additional Information Contacts
Town of Pantego . . . . (817) 274-1381
    http://www.townofpantego.com

PELICAN BAY (city). Covers a land area of 0.652 square miles and a water area of 0 square miles. Located at 32.92° N. Lat; 97.51° W. Long. Elevation is 699 feet.

Population: 1,271 (1990); 1,505 (2000); 1,535 (2010); 1,588 (2015 projected); Race: 90.5% White, 0.9% Black, 0.3% Asian, 8.3% Other, 15.2% Hispanic of any race (2010); Density: 2,353.5 persons per square mile (2010); Average household size: 2.82 (2010); Median age: 31.1 (2010); Males per 100 females: 104.1 (2010); Marriage status: 21.6% never married, 55.3% now married, 5.5% widowed, 17.6% divorced (2005-2009 5-year est.); Foreign born: 4.8% (2005-2009 5-year est.); Ancestry (includes multiple ancestries): 17.0% Irish, 14.9% American, 12.8% German, 11.3% English, 3.3% French (2005-2009 5-year est.).

Economy: Employment by occupation: 2.6% management, 9.9% professional, 19.6% services, 24.6% sales, 0.0% farming, 16.7% construction, 26.6% production (2005-2009 5-year est.).

Income: Per capita income: $16,623 (2010); Median household income: $37,857 (2010); Average household income: $47,284 (2010); Percent of households with income of $100,000 or more: 6.1% (2010); Poverty rate: 29.2% (2005-2009 5-year est.).

Taxes: Total city taxes per capita: $291 (2007); City property taxes per capita: $86 (2007).

Education: Percent of population age 25 and over with: High school diploma (including GED) or higher: 69.0% (2010); Bachelor's degree or higher: 5.2% (2010); Master's degree or higher: 1.4% (2010).

Housing: Homeownership rate: 69.3% (2010); Median home value: $45,062 (2010); Median contract rent: $493 per month (2005-2009 5-year est.); Median year structure built: 1987 (2005-2009 5-year est.).

Safety: Violent crime rate: 36.9 per 10,000 population; Property crime rate: 252.2 per 10,000 population (2009).

Transportation: Commute to work: 94.4% car, 0.0% public transportation, 0.0% walk, 2.0% work from home (2005-2009 5-year est.); Travel time to work: 12.4% less than 15 minutes, 18.9% 15 to 30 minutes, 23.3% 30 to 45 minutes, 25.8% 45 to 60 minutes, 19.6% 60 minutes or more (2005-2009 5-year est.)

RENDON (CDP). Covers a land area of 24.761 square miles and a water area of 0 square miles. Located at 32.57° N. Lat; 97.24° W. Long. Elevation is 735 feet.

Population: 7,810 (1990); 9,022 (2000); 8,435 (2010); 9,026 (2015 projected); Race: 84.1% White, 5.0% Black, 0.5% Asian, 10.4% Other, 13.8% Hispanic of any race (2010); Density: 340.7 persons per square mile (2010); Average household size: 2.87 (2010); Median age: 38.9 (2010); Males per 100 females: 99.4 (2010); Marriage status: 22.7% never married, 61.3% now married, 3.8% widowed, 12.1% divorced (2005-2009 5-year est.); Foreign born: 5.8% (2005-2009 5-year est.); Ancestry (includes multiple ancestries): 19.0% English, 16.7% Irish, 15.0% German, 10.8% American, 4.6% French (2005-2009 5-year est.).

Economy: Employment by occupation: 19.9% management, 14.2% professional, 11.2% services, 25.8% sales, 0.4% farming, 13.5% construction, 15.0% production (2005-2009 5-year est.).

Income: Per capita income: $28,511 (2010); Median household income: $68,389 (2010); Average household income: $81,696 (2010); Percent of households with income of $100,000 or more: 29.4% (2010); Poverty rate: 9.8% (2005-2009 5-year est.).

Education: Percent of population age 25 and over with: High school diploma (including GED) or higher: 83.1% (2010); Bachelor's degree or higher: 22.6% (2010); Master's degree or higher: 6.8% (2010).
Housing: Homeownership rate: 87.4% (2010); Median home value: $143,582 (2010); Median contract rent: $567 per month (2005-2009 5-year est.); Median year structure built: 1986 (2005-2009 5-year est.).
Transportation: Commute to work: 90.6% car, 0.0% public transportation, 1.0% walk, 7.3% work from home (2005-2009 5-year est.); Travel time to work: 12.9% less than 15 minutes, 37.7% 15 to 30 minutes, 26.4% 30 to 45 minutes, 10.5% 45 to 60 minutes, 12.6% 60 minutes or more (2005-2009 5-year est.)

RICHLAND HILLS (city). Covers a land area of 3.146 square miles and a water area of 0.003 square miles. Located at 32.81° N. Lat; 97.22° W. Long. Elevation is 568 feet.
Population: 8,013 (1990); 8,132 (2000); 8,114 (2010); 8,368 (2015 projected); Race: 80.4% White, 2.7% Black, 1.4% Asian, 15.5% Other, 22.1% Hispanic of any race (2010); Density: 2,578.9 persons per square mile (2010); Average household size: 2.46 (2010); Median age: 38.4 (2010); Males per 100 females: 89.9 (2010); Marriage status: 25.4% never married, 48.9% now married, 9.7% widowed, 16.0% divorced (2005-2009 5-year est.); Foreign born: 8.4% (2005-2009 5-year est.); Ancestry (includes multiple ancestries): 18.6% American, 16.2% German, 13.0% Irish, 11.1% English, 3.3% Scotch-Irish (2005-2009 5-year est.).
Economy: Single-family building permits issued: 2 (2010); Multi-family building permits issued: 0 (2010); Employment by occupation: 9.5% management, 12.7% professional, 14.4% services, 33.8% sales, 0.3% farming, 14.8% construction, 14.4% production (2005-2009 5-year est.).
Income: Per capita income: $22,399 (2010); Median household income: $48,202 (2010); Average household income: $54,657 (2010); Percent of households with income of $100,000 or more: 10.1% (2010); Poverty rate: 10.3% (2005-2009 5-year est.).
Taxes: Total city taxes per capita: $542 (2007); City property taxes per capita: $230 (2007).
Education: Percent of population age 25 and over with: High school diploma (including GED) or higher: 82.8% (2010); Bachelor's degree or higher: 16.8% (2010); Master's degree or higher: 5.9% (2010).

School District(s)

Birdville ISD (PK-12)
    2009-10 Enrollment: 22,897 . . . . (817) 547-5700
Housing: Homeownership rate: 65.7% (2010); Median home value: $100,893 (2010); Median contract rent: $607 per month (2005-2009 5-year est.); Median year structure built: 1960 (2005-2009 5-year est.).
Safety: Violent crime rate: 13.6 per 10,000 population; Property crime rate: 442.5 per 10,000 population (2009).
Transportation: Commute to work: 92.0% car, 0.7% public transportation, 2.2% walk, 3.5% work from home (2005-2009 5-year est.); Travel time to work: 26.2% less than 15 minutes, 44.7% 15 to 30 minutes, 18.6% 30 to 45 minutes, 6.0% 45 to 60 minutes, 4.5% 60 minutes or more (2005-2009 5-year est.)
Additional Information Contacts
City of Richland Hills . . . . (817) 299-1800
  http://www.richlandhills.com

RIVER OAKS (city). Covers a land area of 1.993 square miles and a water area of 0 square miles. Located at 32.77° N. Lat; 97.39° W. Long. Elevation is 600 feet.
History: Carswell Air Force Base (closed) to West. Formerly called Castleberry. Incorporated after 1940.
Population: 6,580 (1990); 6,985 (2000); 6,931 (2010); 7,143 (2015 projected); Race: 72.1% White, 0.9% Black, 0.8% Asian, 26.3% Other, 48.8% Hispanic of any race (2010); Density: 3,477.7 persons per square mile (2010); Average household size: 2.62 (2010); Median age: 34.7 (2010); Males per 100 females: 97.6 (2010); Marriage status: 25.6% never married, 48.1% now married, 7.8% widowed, 18.5% divorced (2005-2009 5-year est.); Foreign born: 19.5% (2005-2009 5-year est.); Ancestry (includes multiple ancestries): 15.3% American, 12.8% German, 11.3% English, 11.0% Irish, 3.2% French (2005-2009 5-year est.).
Economy: Single-family building permits issued: 3 (2010); Multi-family building permits issued: 0 (2010); Employment by occupation: 8.5% management, 10.3% professional, 19.6% services, 25.0% sales, 0.0% farming, 15.7% construction, 20.8% production (2005-2009 5-year est.).
Income: Per capita income: $17,836 (2010); Median household income: $34,428 (2010); Average household income: $46,671 (2010); Percent of

households with income of $100,000 or more: 6.6% (2010); Poverty rate: 23.4% (2005-2009 5-year est.).
Taxes: Total city taxes per capita: $396 (2007); City property taxes per capita: $248 (2007).
Education: Percent of population age 25 and over with: High school diploma (including GED) or higher: 72.1% (2010); Bachelor's degree or higher: 10.0% (2010); Master's degree or higher: 2.8% (2010).
Housing: Homeownership rate: 72.1% (2010); Median home value: $71,633 (2010); Median contract rent: $571 per month (2005-2009 5-year est.); Median year structure built: 1951 (2005-2009 5-year est.).
Safety: Violent crime rate: 14.4 per 10,000 population; Property crime rate: 212.6 per 10,000 population (2009).
Transportation: Commute to work: 95.9% car, 0.0% public transportation, 0.0% walk, 3.7% work from home (2005-2009 5-year est.); Travel time to work: 17.8% less than 15 minutes, 51.8% 15 to 30 minutes, 14.5% 30 to 45 minutes, 7.5% 45 to 60 minutes, 8.3% 60 minutes or more (2005-2009 5-year est.)
Additional Information Contacts
City of River Oaks . . . . (817) 626-5421
  http://www.riveroaksstx.com

SAGINAW (city). Covers a land area of 7.503 square miles and a water area of 0 square miles. Located at 32.86° N. Lat; 97.36° W. Long. Elevation is 728 feet.
Population: 8,551 (1990); 12,374 (2000); 19,595 (2010); 22,266 (2015 projected); Race: 79.2% White, 2.7% Black, 1.1% Asian, 17.1% Other, 24.6% Hispanic of any race (2010); Density: 2,611.5 persons per square mile (2010); Average household size: 2.92 (2010); Median age: 33.1 (2010); Males per 100 females: 99.0 (2010); Marriage status: 23.1% never married, 61.1% now married, 3.7% widowed, 12.0% divorced (2005-2009 5-year est.); Foreign born: 6.8% (2005-2009 5-year est.); Ancestry (includes multiple ancestries): 16.9% American, 11.9% German, 9.7% English, 9.5% Irish, 2.6% French (2005-2009 5-year est.).
Economy: Single-family building permits issued: 92 (2010); Multi-family building permits issued: 0 (2010); Employment by occupation: 15.6% management, 21.2% professional, 9.2% services, 29.1% sales, 0.0% farming, 11.9% construction, 12.9% production (2005-2009 5-year est.).
Income: Per capita income: $24,482 (2010); Median household income: $65,350 (2010); Average household income: $71,391 (2010); Percent of households with income of $100,000 or more: 19.4% (2010); Poverty rate: 3.5% (2005-2009 5-year est.).
Taxes: Total city taxes per capita: $441 (2007); City property taxes per capita: $193 (2007).
Education: Percent of population age 25 and over with: High school diploma (including GED) or higher: 83.3% (2010); Bachelor's degree or higher: 15.1% (2010); Master's degree or higher: 2.8% (2010).

School District(s)

Eagle Mt-Saginaw ISD (PK-12)
    2009-10 Enrollment: 16,126 . . . . (817) 232-0880
Housing: Homeownership rate: 77.8% (2010); Median home value: $116,170 (2010); Median contract rent: $783 per month (2005-2009 5-year est.); Median year structure built: 1993 (2005-2009 5-year est.).
Safety: Violent crime rate: 23.8 per 10,000 population; Property crime rate: 279.6 per 10,000 population (2009).
Transportation: Commute to work: 96.6% car, 0.2% public transportation, 0.3% walk, 1.6% work from home (2005-2009 5-year est.); Travel time to work: 17.9% less than 15 minutes, 38.8% 15 to 30 minutes, 25.5% 30 to 45 minutes, 10.5% 45 to 60 minutes, 7.3% 60 minutes or more (2005-2009 5-year est.)
Additional Information Contacts
City of Saginaw . . . . (817) 232-4640
  http://www.ci.saginaw.tx.us
Saginaw Area Chamber of Commerce . . . . (817) 232-0500
  http://www.saginawtxchamber.org

SANSOM PARK (city). Covers a land area of 1.238 square miles and a water area of 0 square miles. Located at 32.80° N. Lat; 97.40° W. Long. Elevation is 751 feet.
Population: 3,928 (1990); 4,181 (2000); 4,252 (2010); 4,440 (2015 projected); Race: 70.2% White, 0.7% Black, 0.6% Asian, 28.5% Other, 47.7% Hispanic of any race (2010); Density: 3,434.1 persons per square mile (2010); Average household size: 2.92 (2010); Median age: 33.0 (2010); Males per 100 females: 97.3 (2010); Marriage status: 28.3% never married, 52.8% now married, 8.3% widowed, 10.6% divorced (2005-2009 5-year est.); Foreign born: 18.8% (2005-2009 5-year est.); Ancestry

(includes multiple ancestries): 11.5% American, 8.4% Irish, 5.2% English, 4.7% German, 2.2% Russian (2005-2009 5-year est.).
Economy: Single-family building permits issued: 0 (2010); Multi-family building permits issued: 0 (2010); Employment by occupation: 6.3% management, 6.6% professional, 25.9% services, 24.2% sales, 0.0% farming, 18.5% construction, 18.4% production (2005-2009 5-year est.).
Income: Per capita income: $13,037 (2010); Median household income: $33,127 (2010); Average household income: $38,466 (2010); Percent of households with income of $100,000 or more: 2.6% (2010); Poverty rate: 27.2% (2005-2009 5-year est.).
Taxes: Total city taxes per capita: $194 (2007); City property taxes per capita: $95 (2007).
Education: Percent of population age 25 and over with: High school diploma (including GED) or higher: 57.0% (2010); Bachelor's degree or higher: 4.3% (2010); Master's degree or higher: 1.2% (2010).
Housing: Homeownership rate: 71.6% (2010); Median home value: $54,554 (2010); Median contract rent: $529 per month (2005-2009 5-year est.); Median year structure built: 1955 (2005-2009 5-year est.).
Safety: Violent crime rate: 61.9 per 10,000 population; Property crime rate: 316.8 per 10,000 population (2009).
Transportation: Commute to work: 93.7% car, 0.0% public transportation, 1.0% walk, 2.3% work from home (2005-2009 5-year est.); Travel time to work: 21.4% less than 15 minutes, 43.4% 15 to 30 minutes, 17.4% 30 to 45 minutes, 11.0% 45 to 60 minutes, 6.7% 60 minutes or more (2005-2009 5-year est.)

SOUTHLAKE (city).
Covers a land area of 21.892 square miles and a water area of 0.555 square miles. Located at 32.94° N. Lat; 97.14° W. Long. Elevation is 640 feet.
Population: 7,155 (1990); 21,519 (2000); 28,121 (2010); 32,320 (2015 projected); Race: 90.7% White, 2.9% Black, 2.7% Asian, 3.7% Other, 5.8% Hispanic of any race (2010); Density: 1,284.5 persons per square mile (2010); Average household size: 3.45 (2010); Median age: 32.4 (2010); Males per 100 females: 99.6 (2010); Marriage status: 21.0% never married, 73.5% now married, 1.9% widowed, 3.7% divorced (2005-2009 5-year est.); Foreign born: 7.4% (2005-2009 5-year est.); Ancestry (includes multiple ancestries): 19.7% German, 19.3% Irish, 18.5% English, 8.5% American, 5.9% Italian (2005-2009 5-year est.).
Economy: Unemployment rate: 6.9% (June 2011); Total civilian labor force: 12,701 (June 2011); Single-family building permits issued: 54 (2010); Multi-family building permits issued: 0 (2010); Employment by occupation: 37.0% management, 23.4% professional, 7.8% services, 24.5% sales, 0.0% farming, 3.0% construction, 4.3% production (2005-2009 5-year est.).
Income: Per capita income: $57,548 (2010); Median household income: $160,857 (2010); Average household income: $198,372 (2010); Percent of households with income of $100,000 or more: 75.2% (2010); Poverty rate: 1.9% (2005-2009 5-year est.).
Taxes: Total city taxes per capita: $1,632 (2007); City property taxes per capita: $831 (2007).
Education: Percent of population age 25 and over with: High school diploma (including GED) or higher: 96.4% (2010); Bachelor's degree or higher: 58.8% (2010); Master's degree or higher: 19.4% (2010).
School District(s)
Carroll ISD (PK-12)
    2009-10 Enrollment: 7,745 . . . . (817) 949-8222
Keller ISD (PK-12)
    2009-10 Enrollment: 31,569 . . . . (817) 744-1000
Housing: Homeownership rate: 95.1% (2010); Median home value: $475,115 (2010); Median contract rent: $1,606 per month (2005-2009 5-year est.); Median year structure built: 1994 (2005-2009 5-year est.).
Hospitals: Harris Methodist Southlake Center for Diagnostics
Safety: Violent crime rate: 4.8 per 10,000 population; Property crime rate: 188.3 per 10,000 population (2009).
Newspapers: The Dallas Morning News - Northeast Tarrant County Bureau (Community news); Southlake Journal (Community news)
Transportation: Commute to work: 86.0% car, 0.1% public transportation, 1.1% walk, 11.5% work from home (2005-2009 5-year est.); Travel time to work: 23.9% less than 15 minutes, 29.7% 15 to 30 minutes, 32.9% 30 to 45 minutes, 7.1% 45 to 60 minutes, 6.5% 60 minutes or more (2005-2009 5-year est.)
Additional Information Contacts
City of Southlake . . . . (817) 748-8400
    http://www.ci.southlake.tx.us
Southlake Chamber of Commerce. . . . . (817) 481-8200
    http://www.southlakechamber.com

WATAUGA (city).
Covers a land area of 4.167 square miles and a water area of 0 square miles. Located at 32.87° N. Lat; 97.24° W. Long. Elevation is 607 feet.
Population: 20,009 (1990); 21,908 (2000); 24,413 (2010); 25,868 (2015 projected); Race: 81.3% White, 3.5% Black, 4.3% Asian, 10.9% Other, 16.4% Hispanic of any race (2010); Density: 5,858.0 persons per square mile (2010); Average household size: 3.02 (2010); Median age: 33.1 (2010); Males per 100 females: 99.1 (2010); Marriage status: 27.7% never married, 54.2% now married, 3.5% widowed, 14.7% divorced (2005-2009 5-year est.); Foreign born: 8.9% (2005-2009 5-year est.); Ancestry (includes multiple ancestries): 17.1% American, 14.0% German, 10.6% Irish, 8.0% English, 3.3% French (2005-2009 5-year est.).
Economy: Single-family building permits issued: 0 (2010); Multi-family building permits issued: 0 (2010); Employment by occupation: 12.6% management, 15.1% professional, 18.4% services, 31.4% sales, 0.1% farming, 11.9% construction, 10.5% production (2005-2009 5-year est.).
Income: Per capita income: $23,663 (2010); Median household income: $65,918 (2010); Average household income: $71,429 (2010); Percent of households with income of $100,000 or more: 18.3% (2010); Poverty rate: 9.6% (2005-2009 5-year est.).
Taxes: Total city taxes per capita: $494 (2007); City property taxes per capita: $243 (2007).
Education: Percent of population age 25 and over with: High school diploma (including GED) or higher: 87.5% (2010); Bachelor's degree or higher: 17.9% (2010); Master's degree or higher: 4.2% (2010).
School District(s)
Birdville ISD (PK-12)
    2009-10 Enrollment: 22,897 . . . . (817) 547-5700
Keller ISD (PK-12)
    2009-10 Enrollment: 31,569 . . . . (817) 744-1000
Housing: Homeownership rate: 86.6% (2010); Median home value: $109,255 (2010); Median contract rent: $854 per month (2005-2009 5-year est.); Median year structure built: 1982 (2005-2009 5-year est.).
Safety: Violent crime rate: 42.1 per 10,000 population; Property crime rate: 242.2 per 10,000 population (2009).
Transportation: Commute to work: 95.0% car, 0.1% public transportation, 0.4% walk, 3.1% work from home (2005-2009 5-year est.); Travel time to work: 17.3% less than 15 minutes, 39.9% 15 to 30 minutes, 27.4% 30 to 45 minutes, 7.6% 45 to 60 minutes, 7.8% 60 minutes or more (2005-2009 5-year est.)
Additional Information Contacts
City of Watauga . . . . (817) 514-5800
    http://www.ci.watauga.tx.us

WESTLAKE (town).
Covers a land area of 6.594 square miles and a water area of 0.087 square miles. Located at 32.98° N. Lat; 97.20° W. Long.
Population: 339 (1990); 207 (2000); 737 (2010); 852 (2015 projected); Race: 95.5% White, 1.5% Black, 0.8% Asian, 2.2% Other, 2.6% Hispanic of any race (2010); Density: 111.8 persons per square mile (2010); Average household size: 3.06 (2010); Median age: 38.3 (2010); Males per 100 females: 98.7 (2010); Marriage status: 8.4% never married, 84.7% now married, 0.0% widowed, 6.9% divorced (2005-2009 5-year est.); Foreign born: 5.4% (2005-2009 5-year est.); Ancestry (includes multiple ancestries): 23.9% German, 20.1% English, 13.3% Irish, 12.9% French, 5.4% British (2005-2009 5-year est.).
Economy: Single-family building permits issued: 6 (2010); Multi-family building permits issued: 0 (2010); Employment by occupation: 44.3% management, 17.9% professional, 15.7% services, 11.4% sales, 0.0% farming, 5.0% construction, 5.7% production (2005-2009 5-year est.).
Income: Per capita income: $55,427 (2010); Median household income: $126,563 (2010); Average household income: $170,695 (2010); Percent of households with income of $100,000 or more: 63.9% (2010); Poverty rate: 5.6% (2005-2009 5-year est.).
Education: Percent of population age 25 and over with: High school diploma (including GED) or higher: 95.9% (2010); Bachelor's degree or higher: 45.7% (2010); Master's degree or higher: 9.2% (2010).
School District(s)
Westlake Academy Charter School (KG-12)
    2009-10 Enrollment: 480 . . . . (817) 490-5757
Housing: Homeownership rate: 93.8% (2010); Median home value: $334,783 (2010); Median contract rent: n/a per month (2005-2009 5-year est.); Median year structure built: 2002 (2005-2009 5-year est.).

Transportation: Commute to work: 90.7% car, 0.0% public transportation, 0.0% walk, 4.3% work from home (2005-2009 5-year est.); Travel time to work: 29.9% less than 15 minutes, 14.9% 15 to 30 minutes, 30.6% 30 to 45 minutes, 17.9% 45 to 60 minutes, 6.7% 60 minutes or more (2005-2009 5-year est.)

Additional Information Contacts

Town of Westlake . . . . (817) 430-0941
http://www.westlake-tx.org

WESTOVER HILLS (town). Covers a land area of 0.715 square miles and a water area of 0 square miles. Located at 32.74° N. Lat; 97.41° W. Long. Elevation is 597 feet.

Population: 672 (1990); 658 (2000); 687 (2010); 723 (2015 projected); Race: 98.3% White, 0.0% Black, 0.6% Asian, 1.2% Other, 1.6% Hispanic of any race (2010); Density: 961.5 persons per square mile (2010); Average household size: 2.53 (2010); Median age: 50.8 (2010); Males per 100 females: 96.3 (2010); Marriage status: 13.5% never married, 79.1% now married, 3.7% widowed, 3.7% divorced (2005-2009 5-year est.); Foreign born: 2.6% (2005-2009 5-year est.); Ancestry (includes multiple ancestries): 28.8% English, 19.4% German, 15.9% Irish, 8.5% French, 6.5% American (2005-2009 5-year est.).
Economy: Single-family building permits issued: 1 (2010); Multi-family building permits issued: 0 (2010); Employment by occupation: 38.9% management, 31.1% professional, 1.6% services, 28.5% sales, 0.0% farming, 0.0% construction, 0.0% production (2005-2009 5-year est.).
Income: Per capita income: $112,031 (2010); Median household income: $290,909 (2010); Average household income: $282,960 (2010); Percent of households with income of $100,000 or more: 74.3% (2010); Poverty rate: 3.4% (2005-2009 5-year est.).
Taxes: Total city taxes per capita: $2,206 (2007); City property taxes per capita: $1,990 (2007).
Education: Percent of population age 25 and over with: High school diploma (including GED) or higher: 98.3% (2010); Bachelor's degree or higher: 69.4% (2010); Master's degree or higher: 25.1% (2010).
Housing: Homeownership rate: 99.3% (2010); Median home value: $957,143 (2010); Median contract rent: n/a per month (2005-2009 5-year est.); Median year structure built: 1973 (2005-2009 5-year est.).
Safety: Violent crime rate: 0.0 per 10,000 population; Property crime rate: 315.1 per 10,000 population (2009).
Transportation: Commute to work: 93.7% car, 0.0% public transportation, 0.0% walk, 6.3% work from home (2005-2009 5-year est.); Travel time to work: 45.5% less than 15 minutes, 33.1% 15 to 30 minutes, 11.2% 30 to 45 minutes, 7.3% 45 to 60 minutes, 2.8% 60 minutes or more (2005-2009 5-year est.)

Additional Information Contacts

Town of Westover Hills . . . . (817) 335-5454

WESTWORTH VILLAGE (city). Aka Westworth. Covers a land area of 1.979 square miles and a water area of 0 square miles. Located at 32.75° N. Lat; 97.41° W. Long. Elevation is 573 feet.

Population: 2,350 (1990); 2,124 (2000); 1,704 (2010); 1,715 (2015 projected); Race: 74.1% White, 3.5% Black, 1.0% Asian, 21.4% Other, 32.9% Hispanic of any race (2010); Density: 861.0 persons per square mile (2010); Average household size: 2.67 (2010); Median age: 35.6 (2010); Males per 100 females: 103.3 (2010); Marriage status: n/a never married, n/a now married, n/a widowed, n/a divorced (2005-2009 5-year est.); Foreign born: n/a (2005-2009 5-year est.); Ancestry (includes multiple ancestries): n/a (2005-2009 5-year est.).
Economy: Employment by occupation: n/a management, n/a professional, n/a services, n/a sales, n/a farming, n/a construction, n/a production (2005-2009 5-year est.).
Income: Per capita income: $20,271 (2010); Median household income: $43,833 (2010); Average household income: $54,057 (2010); Percent of households with income of $100,000 or more: 7.7% (2010); Poverty rate: n/a (2005-2009 5-year est.).
Education: Percent of population age 25 and over with: High school diploma (including GED) or higher: 85.5% (2010); Bachelor's degree or higher: 10.3% (2010); Master's degree or higher: 1.9% (2010).
Housing: Homeownership rate: 51.8% (2010); Median home value: $83,506 (2010); Median contract rent: n/a per month (2005-2009 5-year est.); Median year structure built: n/a (2005-2009 5-year est.).
Safety: Violent crime rate: 15.9 per 10,000 population; Property crime rate: 343.8 per 10,000 population (2009).
Transportation: Commute to work: n/a car, n/a public transportation, n/a walk, n/a work from home (2005-2009 5-year est.); Travel time to work: n/a

less than 15 minutes, n/a 15 to 30 minutes, n/a 30 to 45 minutes, n/a 45 to 60 minutes, n/a 60 minutes or more (2005-2009 5-year est.)

WHITE SETTLEMENT (city). Covers a land area of 4.872 square miles and a water area of 0 square miles. Located at 32.75° N. Lat; 97.46° W. Long. Elevation is 666 feet.

History: Named for being the area's only European settlement when it was founded. Formerly called Liberator Village or Liberator. Incorporated after 1940.
Population: 15,472 (1990); 14,831 (2000); 15,787 (2010); 16,713 (2015 projected); Race: 81.2% White, 4.3% Black, 1.3% Asian, 13.3% Other, 23.3% Hispanic of any race (2010); Density: 3,240.1 persons per square mile (2010); Average household size: 2.53 (2010); Median age: 34.4 (2010); Males per 100 females: 94.9 (2010); Marriage status: 28.4% never married, 44.2% now married, 8.8% widowed, 18.6% divorced (2005-2009 5-year est.); Foreign born: 10.4% (2005-2009 5-year est.); Ancestry (includes multiple ancestries): 17.6% American, 15.9% Irish, 12.3% German, 5.9% English, 2.2% Scottish (2005-2009 5-year est.).
Economy: Single-family building permits issued: 31 (2010); Multi-family building permits issued: 0 (2010); Employment by occupation: 8.8% management, 12.3% professional, 21.5% services, 23.6% sales, 0.0% farming, 14.4% construction, 19.3% production (2005-2009 5-year est.).
Income: Per capita income: $16,259 (2010); Median household income: $35,942 (2010); Average household income: $42,012 (2010); Percent of households with income of $100,000 or more: 5.0% (2010); Poverty rate: 21.3% (2005-2009 5-year est.).
Taxes: Total city taxes per capita: $547 (2007); City property taxes per capita: $257 (2007).
Education: Percent of population age 25 and over with: High school diploma (including GED) or higher: 73.6% (2010); Bachelor's degree or higher: 8.3% (2010); Master's degree or higher: 2.2% (2010).

School District(s)

White Settlement ISD (PK-12)
2009-10 Enrollment: 6,051 . . . . (817) 367-5349
Housing: Homeownership rate: 55.2% (2010); Median home value: $67,993 (2010); Median contract rent: $557 per month (2005-2009 5-year est.); Median year structure built: 1966 (2005-2009 5-year est.).
Safety: Violent crime rate: 27.3 per 10,000 population; Property crime rate: 397.7 per 10,000 population (2009).
Transportation: Commute to work: 92.7% car, 1.8% public transportation, 2.8% walk, 2.0% work from home (2005-2009 5-year est.); Travel time to work: 33.4% less than 15 minutes, 42.0% 15 to 30 minutes, 14.6% 30 to 45 minutes, 5.9% 45 to 60 minutes, 4.0% 60 minutes or more (2005-2009 5-year est.)

Additional Information Contacts

City of White Settlement . . . . (817) 246-4971
http://www.wstx.us
White Settlement Area Chamber of Commerce. . . . . (817) 246-1121
http://www.whitesettlement-tx.com

Taylor County

Located in west central Texas; drained by tributaries of the Brazos and Colorado Rivers; includes Lake Abilene. Covers a land area of 915.63 square miles, a water area of 3.63 square miles, and is located in the Central Time Zone at 32.40° N. Lat., 99.81° W. Long. The county was founded in 1858. County seat is Abilene.

Taylor County is part of the Abilene, TX Metropolitan Statistical Area. The entire metro area includes: Callahan County, TX; Jones County, TX; Taylor County, TX

Weather Station: Abilene Municipal Arpt										Elevation: 1,790 feet	
	Jan	Feb	Mar	Apr	May	Jun	Jul	Aug	Sep	Oct	Nov	Dec
High	57	61	69	77	85	91	94	94	87	77	66	57
Low	33	37	44	52	61	69	72	72	64	54	43	34
Precip	0.9	1.3	1.7	1.6	3.2	3.5	1.7	2.6	2.4	3.0	1.5	1.2
Snow	1.8	0.7	0.4	0.4	tr	tr	tr	tr	0.0	tr	0.7	1.3

High and Low temperatures in degrees Fahrenheit; Precipitation and Snow in inches

Population: 119,655 (1990); 126,555 (2000); 128,720 (2010); 129,538 (2015 projected); Race: 78.3% White, 6.3% Black, 1.3% Asian, 14.1% Other, 21.4% Hispanic of any race (2010); Density: 140.6 persons per square mile (2010); Average household size: 2.45 (2010); Median age: 33.4 (2010); Males per 100 females: 93.9 (2010).

Religion: Five largest groups: 33.9% Southern Baptist Convention, 9.5% Churches of Christ, 8.0% The United Methodist Church, 6.6% Catholic Church, 1.2% Presbyterian Church (U.S.A.) (2000).
Economy: Unemployment rate: 7.4% (June 2011); Total civilian labor force: 65,558 (June 2011); Leading industries: 21.0% health care and social assistance; 15.6% retail trade; 12.3% accommodation & food services (2009); Farms: 1,292 totaling 579,484 acres (2007); Companies that employ 500 or more persons: 9 (2009); Companies that employ 100 to 499 persons: 59 (2009); Companies that employ less than 100 persons: 3,289 (2009); Black-owned businesses: n/a (2007); Hispanic-owned businesses: n/a (2007); Asian-owned businesses: n/a (2007); Women-owned businesses: 2,655 (2007); Retail sales per capita: $17,053 (2010). Single-family building permits issued: 270 (2010); Multi-family building permits issued: 118 (2010).
Income: Per capita income: $21,443 (2010); Median household income: $41,842 (2010); Average household income: $54,315 (2010); Percent of households with income of $100,000 or more: 11.2% (2010); Poverty rate: 15.4% (2009); Bankruptcy rate: 2.06% (2010).
Taxes: Total county taxes per capita: $212 (2007); County property taxes per capita: $186 (2007).
Education: Percent of population age 25 and over with: High school diploma (including GED) or higher: 84.7% (2010); Bachelor's degree or higher: 24.3% (2010); Master's degree or higher: 6.5% (2010).
Housing: Homeownership rate: 62.7% (2010); Median home value: $85,783 (2010); Median contract rent: $500 per month (2005-2009 5-year est.); Median year structure built: 1970 (2005-2009 5-year est.)
Health: Birth rate: 161.7 per 10,000 population (2009); Death rate: 94.0 per 10,000 population (2009); Age-adjusted cancer mortality rate: 177.0 deaths per 100,000 population (2007); Number of physicians: 23.8 per 10,000 population (2008); Hospital beds: 51.3 per 10,000 population (2007); Hospital admissions: 1,964.9 per 10,000 population (2007).
Elections: 2008 Presidential election results: 26.8% Obama, 72.3% McCain, 0.1% Nader
National and State Parks: Abilene State Park
Additional Information Contacts
Taylor County Government . . . . (325) 674-1202
  http://www.taylorcountytexas.org
Abilene Chamber of Commerce . . . . (325) 677-7241
  http://www.abilenechamber.com
City of Abilene . . . . (325) 676-6200
  http://www.abilenetx.com
Merkel Chamber of Commerce . . . . (325) 928-5722
  http://merkeltexas.com

Taylor County Communities

ABILENE (city). County seat. Covers a land area of 105.131 square miles and a water area of 5.479 square miles. Located at 32.44° N. Lat; 99.74° W. Long. Elevation is 1,719 feet.
History: Abilene was called the gateway to the Panhandle, and served as a shipping center for cattle, sheep, cotton, and petroleum. Buffalo hunters were followed by cattlemen, who later made room for oil field workers. The city became an education center with the founding of Hardin-Simmons University by the Sweetwater Baptist Association in 1890, and Abilene Christian College by the Texas Church of Christ in 1906.
Population: 106,927 (1990); 115,930 (2000); 117,942 (2010); 118,579 (2015 projected); Race: 75.5% White, 8.5% Black, 1.4% Asian, 14.6% Other, 23.7% Hispanic of any race (2010); Density: 1,121.9 persons per square mile (2010); Average household size: 2.43 (2010); Median age: 32.6 (2010); Males per 100 females: 101.9 (2010); Marriage status: 32.2% never married, 49.2% now married, 7.1% widowed, 11.5% divorced (2005-2009 5-year est.); Foreign born: 4.7% (2005-2009 5-year est.); Ancestry (includes multiple ancestries): 13.3% German, 10.9% Irish, 10.2% English, 6.5% American, 2.7% French (2005-2009 5-year est.).
Economy: Unemployment rate: 7.7% (June 2011); Total civilian labor force: 56,929 (June 2011); Single-family building permits issued: 269 (2010); Multi-family building permits issued: 118 (2010); Employment by occupation: 11.0% management, 20.6% professional, 21.9% services, 25.0% sales, 0.2% farming, 10.3% construction, 11.2% production (2005-2009 5-year est.).
Income: Per capita income: $20,353 (2010); Median household income: $40,256 (2010); Average household income: $52,608 (2010); Percent of households with income of $100,000 or more: 10.3% (2010); Poverty rate: 18.0% (2005-2009 5-year est.).

Taxes: Total city taxes per capita: $569 (2007); City property taxes per capita: $210 (2007).
Education: Percent of population age 25 and over with: High school diploma (including GED) or higher: 82.7% (2010); Bachelor's degree or higher: 23.7% (2010); Master's degree or higher: 6.6% (2010).
School District(s)
Abilene ISD (PK-12)
  2009-10 Enrollment: 17,016 . . . . (325) 677-1444
Jim Ned CISD (PK-12)
  2009-10 Enrollment: 1,031 . . . . (325) 554-7500
Responsive Education Solutions (KG-12)
  2009-10 Enrollment: 5,022 . . . . (972) 316-3663
Wylie ISD (PK-12)
  2009-10 Enrollment: 3,281 . . . . (325) 692-4353
Four-year College(s)
Abilene Christian University (Private, Not-for-profit, Churches of Christ)
  Fall 2009 Enrollment: 4,813 . . . . (325) 674-2000
  2010-11 Tuition: In-state $22,760; Out-of-state $22,760
Hardin-Simmons University (Private, Not-for-profit, Baptist)
  Fall 2009 Enrollment: 2,305 . . . . (325) 670-1000
  2010-11 Tuition: In-state $20,990; Out-of-state $20,990
McMurry University (Private, Not-for-profit, United Methodist)
  Fall 2009 Enrollment: 1,509 . . . . (325) 793-3800
  2010-11 Tuition: In-state $20,830; Out-of-state $20,830
Vocational/Technical School(s)
American Commercial College (Private, For-profit)
  Fall 2009 Enrollment: 138 . . . . (325) 672-8495
  2010-11 Tuition: $12,600
Texas College of Cosmetology (Private, For-profit)
  Fall 2009 Enrollment: 109 . . . . (325) 677-0532
  2010-11 Tuition: $8,915
Housing: Homeownership rate: 59.8% (2010); Median home value: $85,729 (2010); Median contract rent: $503 per month (2005-2009 5-year est.); Median year structure built: 1967 (2005-2009 5-year est.).
Hospitals: Abilene Regional Medical Center (187 beds); Hendrick Medical Center (511 beds)
Safety: Violent crime rate: 56.5 per 10,000 population; Property crime rate: 414.4 per 10,000 population (2009).
Newspapers: Abilene Reporter-News (Local news; Circulation 38,909)
Transportation: Commute to work: 92.2% car, 0.4% public transportation, 2.6% walk, 2.3% work from home (2005-2009 5-year est.); Travel time to work: 57.5% less than 15 minutes, 34.9% 15 to 30 minutes, 4.3% 30 to 45 minutes, 0.9% 45 to 60 minutes, 2.4% 60 minutes or more (2005-2009 5-year est.)
Airports: Abilene Regional (primary service); Dyess AFB (general aviation)
Additional Information Contacts
Abilene Chamber of Commerce . . . . (325) 677-7241
  http://www.abilenechamber.com
City of Abilene . . . . (325) 676-6200
  http://www.abilenetx.com

BUFFALO GAP (town). Covers a land area of 2.295 square miles and a water area of 0 square miles. Located at 32.28° N. Lat; 99.82° W. Long. Elevation is 1,909 feet.
History: The legends of Buffalo Gap tell of gold, buried by prospectors returning from the California gold fields through the narrow pass on the Buffalo Gap Road.
Population: 499 (1990); 463 (2000); 538 (2010); 573 (2015 projected); Race: 94.4% White, 0.7% Black, 0.2% Asian, 4.6% Other, 5.2% Hispanic of any race (2010); Density: 234.4 persons per square mile (2010); Average household size: 2.59 (2010); Median age: 43.2 (2010); Males per 100 females: 90.1 (2010); Marriage status: 14.0% never married, 70.0% now married, 4.4% widowed, 11.7% divorced (2005-2009 5-year est.); Foreign born: 0.0% (2005-2009 5-year est.); Ancestry (includes multiple ancestries): 15.8% German, 14.2% Scotch-Irish, 12.5% Irish, 9.7% American, 9.2% English (2005-2009 5-year est.).
Economy: Single-family building permits issued: 0 (2010); Multi-family building permits issued: 0 (2010); Employment by occupation: 12.3% management, 7.5% professional, 21.7% services, 27.8% sales, 0.0% farming, 19.3% construction, 11.3% production (2005-2009 5-year est.).
Income: Per capita income: $31,710 (2010); Median household income: $69,207 (2010); Average household income: $82,657 (2010); Percent of households with income of $100,000 or more: 26.6% (2010); Poverty rate: 14.2% (2005-2009 5-year est.).

Taxes: Total city taxes per capita: $224 (2007); City property taxes per capita: $76 (2007).
Education: Percent of population age 25 and over with: High school diploma (including GED) or higher: 90.6% (2010); Bachelor's degree or higher: 31.6% (2010); Master's degree or higher: 6.1% (2010).

School District(s)
Jim Ned CISD (PK-12)
   2009-10 Enrollment: 1,031 . . . . (325) 554-7500
Housing: Homeownership rate: 86.5% (2010); Median home value: $123,125 (2010); Median contract rent: $467 per month (2005-2009 5-year est.); Median year structure built: 1954 (2005-2009 5-year est.).
Transportation: Commute to work: 93.3% car, 0.0% public transportation, 3.8% walk, 1.4% work from home (2005-2009 5-year est.); Travel time to work: 23.7% less than 15 minutes, 52.7% 15 to 30 minutes, 19.8% 30 to 45 minutes, 0.0% 45 to 60 minutes, 3.9% 60 minutes or more (2005-2009 5-year est.)

DYESS AFB (unincorporated postal area, zip code 79607). Covers a land area of 8.309 square miles and a water area of 0 square miles. Located at 32.42° N. Lat; 99.74° W. Long.
Population: 4,969 (2000); Race: 71.6% White, 13.0% Black, 3.9% Asian, 11.5% Other, 13.3% Hispanic of any race (2000); Density: 598.0 persons per square mile (2000); Age: 37.0% under 18, 0.2% over 64 (2000); Marriage status: 32.4% never married, 64.6% now married, 0.3% widowed, 2.7% divorced (2000); Foreign born: 5.3% (2000); Ancestry (includes multiple ancestries): 18.2% German, 9.5% Irish, 6.9% English, 6.8% American (2000).
Economy: Employment by occupation: 12.6% management, 19.3% professional, 23.4% services, 31.4% sales, 0.0% farming, 8.3% construction, 5.0% production (2000).
Income: Per capita income: $10,944 (2000); Median household income: $33,846 (2000); Poverty rate: 179.1% (2000).
Education: Percent of population age 25 and over with: High school diploma (including GED) or higher: 94.5% (2000); Bachelor's degree or higher: 13.7% (2000).
Housing: Homeownership rate: 0.6% (2000); Median home value: $37,500 (2000); Median contract rent: $566 per month (2000); Median year structure built: 1958 (2000).
Hospitals: 7th Medical Group
Transportation: Commute to work: 94.3% car, 0.2% public transportation, 3.6% walk, 1.0% work from home (2000); Travel time to work: 72.5% less than 15 minutes, 22.8% 15 to 30 minutes, 3.1% 30 to 45 minutes, 0.6% 45 to 60 minutes, 1.0% 60 minutes or more (2000)

IMPACT (town). Covers a land area of 0.087 square miles and a water area of 0 square miles. Located at 32.50° N. Lat; 99.74° W. Long. Elevation is 1,670 feet.
Population: 41 (1990); 39 (2000); 35 (2010); 33 (2015 projected); Race: 77.1% White, 2.9% Black, 0.0% Asian, 20.0% Other, 54.3% Hispanic of any race (2010); Density: 404.0 persons per square mile (2010); Average household size: 2.69 (2010); Median age: 31.3 (2010); Males per 100 females: 84.2 (2010); Marriage status: 30.4% never married, 39.1% now married, 30.4% widowed, 0.0% divorced (2005-2009 5-year est.); Foreign born: 100.0% (2005-2009 5-year est.); Ancestry (includes multiple ancestries): n/a (2005-2009 5-year est.).
Economy: Employment by occupation: 0.0% management, 0.0% professional, 44.4% services, 0.0% sales, 0.0% farming, 0.0% construction, 55.6% production (2005-2009 5-year est.).
Income: Per capita income: $14,598 (2010); Median household income: $37,500 (2010); Average household income: $39,231 (2010); Percent of households with income of $100,000 or more: 0.0% (2010); Poverty rate: 30.4% (2005-2009 5-year est.).
Education: Percent of population age 25 and over with: High school diploma (including GED) or higher: 40.0% (2010); Bachelor's degree or higher: 5.0% (2010); Master's degree or higher: 0.0% (2010).
Housing: Homeownership rate: 76.9% (2010); Median home value: $30,000 (2010); Median contract rent: n/a per month (2005-2009 5-year est.); Median year structure built: 1958 (2005-2009 5-year est.).
Transportation: Commute to work: 100.0% car, 0.0% public transportation, 0.0% walk, 0.0% work from home (2005-2009 5-year est.); Travel time to work: 77.8% less than 15 minutes, 0.0% 15 to 30 minutes, 22.2% 30 to 45 minutes, 0.0% 45 to 60 minutes, 0.0% 60 minutes or more (2005-2009 5-year est.)

LAWN (town). Covers a land area of 0.564 square miles and a water area of 0 square miles. Located at 32.13° N. Lat; 99.74° W. Long. Elevation is 1,916 feet.
Population: 358 (1990); 353 (2000); 327 (2010); 319 (2015 projected); Race: 95.4% White, 0.0% Black, 0.6% Asian, 4.0% Other, 3.1% Hispanic of any race (2010); Density: 579.4 persons per square mile (2010); Average household size: 2.57 (2010); Median age: 44.9 (2010); Males per 100 females: 105.7 (2010); Marriage status: 17.9% never married, 62.7% now married, 10.9% widowed, 8.4% divorced (2005-2009 5-year est.); Foreign born: 0.5% (2005-2009 5-year est.); Ancestry (includes multiple ancestries): 18.5% German, 18.2% English, 9.2% Irish, 6.7% American, 3.7% Dutch (2005-2009 5-year est.).
Economy: Employment by occupation: 3.9% management, 18.2% professional, 19.5% services, 19.9% sales, 5.2% farming, 9.5% construction, 23.8% production (2005-2009 5-year est.).
Income: Per capita income: $22,412 (2010); Median household income: $47,900 (2010); Average household income: $58,406 (2010); Percent of households with income of $100,000 or more: 11.0% (2010); Poverty rate: 8.3% (2005-2009 5-year est.).
Taxes: Total city taxes per capita: $968 (2007); City property taxes per capita: $428 (2007).
Education: Percent of population age 25 and over with: High school diploma (including GED) or higher: 85.6% (2010); Bachelor's degree or higher: 15.3% (2010); Master's degree or higher: 2.1% (2010).

School District(s)
Jim Ned CISD (PK-12)
   2009-10 Enrollment: 1,031 . . . . (325) 554-7500
Housing: Homeownership rate: 88.2% (2010); Median home value: $70,000 (2010); Median contract rent: $409 per month (2005-2009 5-year est.); Median year structure built: 1959 (2005-2009 5-year est.).
Transportation: Commute to work: 98.2% car, 0.0% public transportation, 0.0% walk, 1.8% work from home (2005-2009 5-year est.); Travel time to work: 24.2% less than 15 minutes, 33.2% 15 to 30 minutes, 36.3% 30 to 45 minutes, 6.3% 45 to 60 minutes, 0.0% 60 minutes or more (2005-2009 5-year est.)

MERKEL (town). Covers a land area of 1.965 square miles and a water area of 0 square miles. Located at 32.46° N. Lat; 100.01° W. Long. Elevation is 1,870 feet.
History: Settled c.1875, incorporated 1906.
Population: 2,541 (1990); 2,637 (2000); 2,583 (2010); 2,592 (2015 projected); Race: 90.2% White, 0.6% Black, 0.3% Asian, 8.9% Other, 13.8% Hispanic of any race (2010); Density: 1,314.6 persons per square mile (2010); Average household size: 2.49 (2010); Median age: 37.2 (2010); Males per 100 females: 90.3 (2010); Marriage status: 22.3% never married, 55.1% now married, 9.5% widowed, 13.1% divorced (2005-2009 5-year est.); Foreign born: 4.9% (2005-2009 5-year est.); Ancestry (includes multiple ancestries): 14.6% Irish, 14.2% German, 11.5% American, 10.9% English, 3.9% French (2005-2009 5-year est.).
Economy: Single-family building permits issued: 1 (2010); Multi-family building permits issued: 0 (2010); Employment by occupation: 7.1% management, 15.3% professional, 28.2% services, 15.9% sales, 2.9% farming, 16.3% construction, 14.3% production (2005-2009 5-year est.).
Income: Per capita income: $18,861 (2010); Median household income: $41,079 (2010); Average household income: $47,243 (2010); Percent of households with income of $100,000 or more: 8.0% (2010); Poverty rate: 19.9% (2005-2009 5-year est.).
Taxes: Total city taxes per capita: $140 (2007); City property taxes per capita: $114 (2007).
Education: Percent of population age 25 and over with: High school diploma (including GED) or higher: 78.8% (2010); Bachelor's degree or higher: 14.8% (2010); Master's degree or higher: 2.2% (2010).

School District(s)
Merkel ISD (PK-12)
   2009-10 Enrollment: 1,113 . . . . (325) 928-5813
Housing: Homeownership rate: 74.9% (2010); Median home value: $48,883 (2010); Median contract rent: $316 per month (2005-2009 5-year est.); Median year structure built: 1962 (2005-2009 5-year est.).
Safety: Violent crime rate: 23.0 per 10,000 population; Property crime rate: 122.5 per 10,000 population (2009).
Newspapers: Mail (Local news; Circulation 1,510)
Transportation: Commute to work: 88.7% car, 2.2% public transportation, 1.5% walk, 3.8% work from home (2005-2009 5-year est.); Travel time to work: 38.3% less than 15 minutes, 30.9% 15 to 30 minutes, 22.8% 30 to 45

minutes, 2.7% 45 to 60 minutes, 5.3% 60 minutes or more (2005-2009 5-year est.)

Additional Information Contacts

Merkel Chamber of Commerce . . . . (325) 928-5722
  http://merkeltexas.com

OVALO (unincorporated postal area, zip code 79541). Covers a land area of 142.275 square miles and a water area of 0.297 square miles. Located at 32.15° N. Lat; 99.84° W. Long. Elevation is 2,021 feet.
Population: 701 (2000); Race: 97.5% White, 0.0% Black, 1.8% Asian, 0.7% Other, 0.8% Hispanic of any race (2000); Density: 4.9 persons per square mile (2000); Age: 32.6% under 18, 11.4% over 64 (2000); Marriage status: 10.4% never married, 72.3% now married, 8.8% widowed, 8.5% divorced (2000); Foreign born: 1.5% (2000); Ancestry (includes multiple ancestries): 21.0% American, 14.6% Irish, 12.8% English, 8.0% German (2000).
Economy: Employment by occupation: 11.9% management, 20.3% professional, 7.5% services, 25.6% sales, 3.4% farming, 15.3% construction, 15.9% production (2000).
Income: Per capita income: $14,923 (2000); Median household income: $39,271 (2000); Poverty rate: 179.1% (2000).
Education: Percent of population age 25 and over with: High school diploma (including GED) or higher: 92.6% (2000); Bachelor's degree or higher: 21.3% (2000).
Housing: Homeownership rate: 82.5% (2000); Median home value: $65,000 (2000); Median contract rent: $144 per month (2000); Median year structure built: 1983 (2000).
Transportation: Commute to work: 87.5% car, 2.2% public transportation, 0.0% walk, 10.3% work from home (2000); Travel time to work: 6.1% less than 15 minutes, 39.6% 15 to 30 minutes, 46.8% 30 to 45 minutes, 0.0% 45 to 60 minutes, 7.5% 60 minutes or more (2000)

POTOSI (CDP). Covers a land area of 18.463 square miles and a water area of 0.003 square miles. Located at 32.33° N. Lat; 99.66° W. Long. Elevation is 1,821 feet.
Population: 1,441 (1990); 1,664 (2000); 1,907 (2010); 1,990 (2015 projected); Race: 92.6% White, 1.0% Black, 1.0% Asian, 5.5% Other, 8.3% Hispanic of any race (2010); Density: 103.3 persons per square mile (2010); Average household size: 2.76 (2010); Median age: 39.4 (2010); Males per 100 females: 95.2 (2010); Marriage status: 13.0% never married, 79.9% now married, 3.8% widowed, 3.3% divorced (2005-2009 5-year est.); Foreign born: 1.0% (2005-2009 5-year est.); Ancestry (includes multiple ancestries): 22.6% English, 19.6% German, 17.1% Irish, 8.4% American, 4.8% Dutch (2005-2009 5-year est.).
Economy: Employment by occupation: 7.8% management, 25.8% professional, 17.9% services, 30.7% sales, 0.0% farming, 14.5% construction, 3.3% production (2005-2009 5-year est.).
Income: Per capita income: $27,884 (2010); Median household income: $66,341 (2010); Average household income: $76,892 (2010); Percent of households with income of $100,000 or more: 22.0% (2010); Poverty rate: 4.1% (2005-2009 5-year est.).
Education: Percent of population age 25 and over with: High school diploma (including GED) or higher: 92.4% (2010); Bachelor's degree or higher: 22.8% (2010); Master's degree or higher: 3.6% (2010).
Housing: Homeownership rate: 90.6% (2010); Median home value: $117,308 (2010); Median contract rent: $330 per month (2005-2009 5-year est.); Median year structure built: 1983 (2005-2009 5-year est.).
Transportation: Commute to work: 98.6% car, 0.0% public transportation, 0.0% walk, 1.4% work from home (2005-2009 5-year est.); Travel time to work: 17.2% less than 15 minutes, 70.6% 15 to 30 minutes, 11.0% 30 to 45 minutes, 0.0% 45 to 60 minutes, 1.2% 60 minutes or more (2005-2009 5-year est.)

TRENT (town). Covers a land area of 0.410 square miles and a water area of 0 square miles. Located at 32.48° N. Lat; 100.12° W. Long. Elevation is 1,913 feet.
Population: 319 (1990); 318 (2000); 248 (2010); 227 (2015 projected); Race: 91.9% White, 1.2% Black, 0.4% Asian, 6.5% Other, 15.7% Hispanic of any race (2010); Density: 605.0 persons per square mile (2010); Average household size: 2.53 (2010); Median age: 40.4 (2010); Males per 100 females: 86.5 (2010); Marriage status: 25.8% never married, 58.3% now married, 7.1% widowed, 8.8% divorced (2005-2009 5-year est.); Foreign born: 0.0% (2005-2009 5-year est.); Ancestry (includes multiple ancestries): 14.5% German, 10.7% Irish, 8.3% American, 6.6% Scotch-Irish, 5.9% Scottish (2005-2009 5-year est.).

Economy: Employment by occupation: 6.9% management, 4.1% professional, 22.1% services, 22.8% sales, 2.8% farming, 13.1% construction, 28.3% production (2005-2009 5-year est.).
Income: Per capita income: $22,648 (2010); Median household income: $50,000 (2010); Average household income: $55,230 (2010); Percent of households with income of $100,000 or more: 10.2% (2010); Poverty rate: 14.5% (2005-2009 5-year est.).
Taxes: Total city taxes per capita: $157 (2007); City property taxes per capita: $45 (2007).
Education: Percent of population age 25 and over with: High school diploma (including GED) or higher: 74.9% (2010); Bachelor's degree or higher: 9.4% (2010); Master's degree or higher: 1.2% (2010).

School District(s)

Trent ISD (PK-12)
    2009-10 Enrollment: 198 . . . . (325) 862-6400
Housing: Homeownership rate: 83.7% (2010); Median home value: $52,500 (2010); Median contract rent: n/a per month (2005-2009 5-year est.); Median year structure built: 1972 (2005-2009 5-year est.).
Transportation: Commute to work: 100.0% car, 0.0% public transportation, 0.0% walk, 0.0% work from home (2005-2009 5-year est.); Travel time to work: 31.5% less than 15 minutes, 35.7% 15 to 30 minutes, 25.2% 30 to 45 minutes, 3.5% 45 to 60 minutes, 4.2% 60 minutes or more (2005-2009 5-year est.)

TUSCOLA (city). Covers a land area of 0.735 square miles and a water area of 0 square miles. Located at 32.20° N. Lat; 99.79° W. Long. Elevation is 1,978 feet.
Population: 620 (1990); 714 (2000); 817 (2010); 866 (2015 projected); Race: 96.8% White, 0.2% Black, 0.0% Asian, 2.9% Other, 5.9% Hispanic of any race (2010); Density: 1,111.3 persons per square mile (2010); Average household size: 2.69 (2010); Median age: 41.6 (2010); Males per 100 females: 98.8 (2010); Marriage status: 12.8% never married, 68.0% now married, 4.6% widowed, 14.6% divorced (2005-2009 5-year est.); Foreign born: 2.5% (2005-2009 5-year est.); Ancestry (includes multiple ancestries): 21.8% Irish, 21.1% German, 13.7% English, 8.7% American, 4.7% Scottish (2005-2009 5-year est.).
Economy: Single-family building permits issued: 0 (2010); Multi-family building permits issued: 0 (2010); Employment by occupation: 7.0% management, 21.3% professional, 15.2% services, 31.7% sales, 0.0% farming, 16.0% construction, 8.7% production (2005-2009 5-year est.).
Income: Per capita income: $24,895 (2010); Median household income: $60,756 (2010); Average household income: $65,938 (2010); Percent of households with income of $100,000 or more: 15.8% (2010); Poverty rate: 8.6% (2005-2009 5-year est.).
Taxes: Total city taxes per capita: $120 (2007); City property taxes per capita: $59 (2007).
Education: Percent of population age 25 and over with: High school diploma (including GED) or higher: 87.7% (2010); Bachelor's degree or higher: 25.7% (2010); Master's degree or higher: 5.7% (2010).

School District(s)

Jim Ned CISD (PK-12)
    2009-10 Enrollment: 1,031 . . . . (325) 554-7500
Housing: Homeownership rate: 87.8% (2010); Median home value: $105,000 (2010); Median contract rent: $483 per month (2005-2009 5-year est.); Median year structure built: 1959 (2005-2009 5-year est.).
Newspapers: Journal (Local news; Circulation 700)
Transportation: Commute to work: 92.9% car, 0.0% public transportation, 2.0% walk, 2.0% work from home (2005-2009 5-year est.); Travel time to work: 23.3% less than 15 minutes, 54.7% 15 to 30 minutes, 17.2% 30 to 45 minutes, 1.2% 45 to 60 minutes, 3.8% 60 minutes or more (2005-2009 5-year est.)

TYE (city). Covers a land area of 4.664 square miles and a water area of 0 square miles. Located at 32.45° N. Lat; 99.86° W. Long. Elevation is 1,795 feet.
Population: 1,073 (1990); 1,158 (2000); 1,119 (2010); 1,101 (2015 projected); Race: 89.5% White, 1.2% Black, 0.4% Asian, 8.8% Other, 13.3% Hispanic of any race (2010); Density: 239.9 persons per square mile (2010); Average household size: 2.58 (2010); Median age: 35.8 (2010); Males per 100 females: 95.3 (2010); Marriage status: 19.4% never married, 51.1% now married, 12.2% widowed, 17.2% divorced (2005-2009 5-year est.); Foreign born: 3.5% (2005-2009 5-year est.); Ancestry (includes multiple ancestries): 12.2% English, 10.5% German, 9.3% Irish, 3.3% American, 3.2% Scotch-Irish (2005-2009 5-year est.).

Economy: Single-family building permits issued: 0 (2010); Multi-family building permits issued: 0 (2010); Employment by occupation: 6.8% management, 7.2% professional, 18.5% services, 30.5% sales, 2.2% farming, 20.7% construction, 14.2% production (2005-2009 5-year est.).
Income: Per capita income: $21,685 (2010); Median household income: $43,051 (2010); Average household income: $56,224 (2010); Percent of households with income of $100,000 or more: 12.2% (2010); Poverty rate: 15.4% (2005-2009 5-year est.).
Taxes: Total city taxes per capita: $602 (2007); City property taxes per capita: $144 (2007).
Education: Percent of population age 25 and over with: High school diploma (including GED) or higher: 83.1% (2010); Bachelor's degree or higher: 11.1% (2010); Master's degree or higher: 2.5% (2010).

School District(s)
Merkel ISD (PK-12)
　　2009-10 Enrollment: 1,113 . . . . (325) 928-5813
Housing: Homeownership rate: 78.3% (2010); Median home value: $52,917 (2010); Median contract rent: $418 per month (2005-2009 5-year est.); Median year structure built: 1979 (2005-2009 5-year est.).
Safety: Violent crime rate: 26.4 per 10,000 population; Property crime rate: 167.0 per 10,000 population (2009).
Transportation: Commute to work: 97.8% car, 0.0% public transportation, 0.0% walk, 1.3% work from home (2005-2009 5-year est.); Travel time to work: 28.6% less than 15 minutes, 51.1% 15 to 30 minutes, 9.0% 30 to 45 minutes, 6.6% 45 to 60 minutes, 4.8% 60 minutes or more (2005-2009 5-year est.)

Terrell County

Located in west Texas; bounded on the south by the Rio Grande and the Mexican border, and on the east by the Pecos River. Covers a land area of 2,357.72 square miles, a water area of 0.03 square miles, and is located in the Central Time Zone at 30.23° N. Lat., 102.12° W. Long. The county was founded in 1905. County seat is Sanderson.

Weather Station: Sanderson　　　　　　　　　　　　Elevation: 2,839 feet

	Jan	Feb	Mar	Apr	May	Jun	Jul	Aug	Sep	Oct	Nov	Dec
High	61	65	72	81	88	92	92	92	87	78	69	61
Low	32	36	43	51	61	68	70	69	63	52	40	33
Precip	0.4	0.6	0.6	0.8	1.6	2.2	1.6	1.6	1.8	1.8	0.8	0.5
Snow	0.4	tr	tr	0.0	0.0	0.0	0.0	0.0	0.0	0.0	tr	0.2

High and Low temperatures in degrees Fahrenheit; Precipitation and Snow in inches

Population: 1,410 (1990); 1,081 (2000); 952 (2010); 889 (2015 projected); Race: 87.3% White, 0.0% Black, 0.9% Asian, 11.8% Other, 51.5% Hispanic of any race (2010); Density: 0.4 persons per square mile (2010); Average household size: 2.30 (2010); Median age: 46.5 (2010); Males per 100 females: 95.9 (2010).
Religion: Five largest groups: 55.5% Catholic Church, 23.4% Southern Baptist Convention, 11.1% The United Methodist Church, 6.2% Presbyterian Church (U.S.A.), 4.4% Churches of Christ (2000).
Economy: Unemployment rate: 10.3% (June 2011); Total civilian labor force: 388 (June 2011); Leading industries: Farms: 107 totaling 1,302,152 acres (2007); Companies that employ 500 or more persons: 0 (2009); Companies that employ 100 to 499 persons: 0 (2009); Companies that employ less than 100 persons: 17 (2009); Black-owned businesses: n/a (2007); Hispanic-owned businesses: n/a (2007); Asian-owned businesses: n/a (2007); Women-owned businesses: n/a (2007); Retail sales per capita: $2,011 (2010). Single-family building permits issued: n/a (2010); Multi-family building permits issued: n/a (2010).
Income: Per capita income: $17,613 (2010); Median household income: $29,118 (2010); Average household income: $40,501 (2010); Percent of households with income of $100,000 or more: 8.2% (2010); Poverty rate: 18.8% (2009); Bankruptcy rate: n/a (2010).
Taxes: Total county taxes per capita: $2,275 (2007); County property taxes per capita: $1,956 (2007).
Education: Percent of population age 25 and over with: High school diploma (including GED) or higher: 76.1% (2010); Bachelor's degree or higher: 20.8% (2010); Master's degree or higher: 3.7% (2010).
Housing: Homeownership rate: 75.1% (2010); Median home value: $29,813 (2010); Median contract rent: $319 per month (2005-2009 5-year est.); Median year structure built: 1959 (2005-2009 5-year est.)
Health: Birth rate: 103.2 per 10,000 population (2009); Death rate: 51.6 per 10,000 population (2009); Age-adjusted cancer mortality rate: Suppressed deaths per 100,000 population (2007); Number of physicians: 0.0 per

10,000 population (2008); Hospital beds: 0.0 per 10,000 population (2007); Hospital admissions: 0.0 per 10,000 population (2007).
Elections: 2008 Presidential election results: 35.8% Obama, 62.2% McCain, 0.2% Nader
Additional Information Contacts
Terrell County Government . . . . (432) 345-2391
　　http://www.co.terrell.tx.us/ips/cms
Sanderson Chamber of Commerce . . . . (432) 345-2509
　　http://www.sandersonchamberofcommerce.info

Terrell County Communities

DRYDEN (unincorporated postal area, zip code 78851). Covers a land area of 807.867 square miles and a water area of 0.033 square miles. Located at 30.07° N. Lat; 101.95° W. Long. Elevation is 2,110 feet.
Population: 85 (2000); Race: 100.0% White, 0.0% Black, 0.0% Asian, 0.0% Other, 45.6% Hispanic of any race (2000); Density: 0.1 persons per square mile (2000); Age: 40.4% under 18, 7.0% over 64 (2000); Marriage status: 12.8% never married, 71.8% now married, 7.7% widowed, 7.7% divorced (2000); Foreign born: 24.6% (2000); Ancestry (includes multiple ancestries): 12.3% Scotch-Irish, 10.5% English, 5.3% Irish, 5.3% German (2000).
Economy: Employment by occupation: 52.0% management, 0.0% professional, 12.0% services, 28.0% sales, 8.0% farming, 0.0% construction, 0.0% production (2000).
Income: Per capita income: $11,868 (2000); Median household income: $27,917 (2000); Poverty rate: 179.1% (2000).
Education: Percent of population age 25 and over with: High school diploma (including GED) or higher: 47.1% (2000); Bachelor's degree or higher: 32.4% (2000).
Housing: Homeownership rate: 52.2% (2000); Median home value: $47,500 (2000); Median contract rent: n/a per month (2000); Median year structure built: 1968 (2000).
Transportation: Commute to work: 60.0% car, 0.0% public transportation, 16.0% walk, 24.0% work from home (2000); Travel time to work: 47.4% less than 15 minutes, 0.0% 15 to 30 minutes, 0.0% 30 to 45 minutes, 15.8% 45 to 60 minutes, 36.8% 60 minutes or more (2000)

SANDERSON (CDP). County seat. Covers a land area of 4.185 square miles and a water area of 0 square miles. Located at 30.14° N. Lat; 102.39° W. Long. Elevation is 2,789 feet.
History: Sanderson began as a wild frontier town, founded by Charlie Wilson in the 1880's. The legendary Judge Roy Bean of Langtry once owned a saloon in Sanderson.
Population: 1,128 (1990); 861 (2000); 749 (2010); 695 (2015 projected); Race: 86.6% White, 0.0% Black, 1.1% Asian, 12.3% Other, 53.4% Hispanic of any race (2010); Density: 179.0 persons per square mile (2010); Average household size: 2.27 (2010); Median age: 46.8 (2010); Males per 100 females: 93.5 (2010); Marriage status: 23.7% never married, 52.3% now married, 11.1% widowed, 13.0% divorced (2005-2009 5-year est.); Foreign born: 11.4% (2005-2009 5-year est.); Ancestry (includes multiple ancestries): 16.0% American, 11.2% Irish, 9.3% German, 4.0% English, 3.0% Scotch-Irish (2005-2009 5-year est.).
Economy: Employment by occupation: 15.7% management, 15.4% professional, 17.7% services, 17.3% sales, 4.7% farming, 16.1% construction, 13.0% production (2005-2009 5-year est.).
Income: Per capita income: $17,729 (2010); Median household income: $27,791 (2010); Average household income: $40,129 (2010); Percent of households with income of $100,000 or more: 8.2% (2005-2009 5-year est.); Poverty rate: 18.5% (2005-2009 5-year est.).
Education: Percent of population age 25 and over with: High school diploma (including GED) or higher: 76.1% (2010); Bachelor's degree or higher: 20.0% (2010); Master's degree or higher: 3.3% (2010).
School District(s)
Terrell County ISD (PK-12)
　　2009-10 Enrollment: 167 . . . . (432) 345-2515
Housing: Homeownership rate: 79.4% (2010); Median home value: $27,917 (2010); Median contract rent: $303 per month (2005-2009 5-year est.); Median year structure built: 1955 (2005-2009 5-year est.).
Newspapers: Terrell County News Leader (Local news)
Transportation: Commute to work: 79.9% car, 0.0% public transportation, 9.4% walk, 10.6% work from home (2005-2009 5-year est.); Travel time to work: 67.0% less than 15 minutes, 6.2% 15 to 30 minutes, 11.9% 30 to 45 minutes, 5.3% 45 to 60 minutes, 9.7% 60 minutes or more (2005-2009 5-year est.); Amtrak: train service available.

Additional Information Contacts

Sanderson Chamber of Commerce . . . . (432) 345-2509
http://www.sandersonchamberofcommerce.info

Terry County

Located in northwestern Texas; crossed by Sulphur Springs Creek. Covers a land area of 889.88 square miles, a water area of 1.06 square miles, and is located in the Central Time Zone at 33.18° N. Lat., 102.31° W. Long. The county was founded in 1876. County seat is Brownfield.

Weather Station: Brownfield 2   Elevation: 3,299 feet

	Jan	Feb	Mar	Apr	May	Jun	Jul	Aug	Sep	Oct	Nov	Dec
High	55	60	67	76	84	91	93	91	85	76	65	55
Low	27	30	36	44	54	63	66	65	58	47	36	28
Precip	0.6	0.7	1.0	1.1	2.8	3.0	2.1	1.9	2.5	1.6	0.9	0.8
Snow	2.1	1.5	0.2	0.2	0.0	0.0	0.0	0.0	0.0	tr	0.6	1.6

High and Low temperatures in degrees Fahrenheit; Precipitation and Snow in inches

Population: 13,218 (1990); 12,761 (2000); 12,118 (2010); 11,782 (2015 projected); Race: 74.0% White, 5.5% Black, 0.3% Asian, 20.2% Other, 48.8% Hispanic of any race (2010); Density: 13.6 persons per square mile (2010); Average household size: 2.67 (2010); Median age: 35.4 (2010); Males per 100 females: 98.0 (2010).
Religion: Five largest groups: 29.7% Southern Baptist Convention, 16.9% Catholic Church, 7.5% Churches of Christ, 4.7% International Church of the Foursquare Gospel, 4.6% The United Methodist Church (2000).
Economy: Unemployment rate: 8.3% (June 2011); Total civilian labor force: 5,749 (June 2011); Leading industries: 21.6% retail trade; 16.7% health care and social assistance; 10.7% accommodation & food services (2009); Farms: 624 totaling 496,692 acres (2007); Companies that employ 500 or more persons: 0 (2009); Companies that employ 100 to 499 persons: 5 (2009); Companies that employ less than 100 persons: 252 (2009); Black-owned businesses: n/a (2007); Hispanic-owned businesses: n/a (2007); Asian-owned businesses: n/a (2007); Women-owned businesses: 146 (2007); Retail sales per capita: $9,133 (2010). Single-family building permits issued: 0 (2010); Multi-family building permits issued: 48 (2010).
Income: Per capita income: $16,457 (2010); Median household income: $33,815 (2010); Average household income: $46,299 (2010); Percent of households with income of $100,000 or more: 9.0% (2010); Poverty rate: 23.1% (2009); Bankruptcy rate: 1.26% (2010).
Taxes: Total county taxes per capita: $437 (2007); County property taxes per capita: $353 (2007).
Education: Percent of population age 25 and over with: High school diploma (including GED) or higher: 67.4% (2010); Bachelor's degree or higher: 10.9% (2010); Master's degree or higher: 2.7% (2010).
Housing: Homeownership rate: 69.1% (2010); Median home value: $51,766 (2010); Median contract rent: $349 per month (2005-2009 5-year est.); Median year structure built: 1964 (2005-2009 5-year est.)
Health: Birth rate: 154.0 per 10,000 population (2009); Death rate: 89.8 per 10,000 population (2009); Age-adjusted cancer mortality rate: 157.5 deaths per 100,000 population (2007); Number of physicians: 5.8 per 10,000 population (2008); Hospital beds: 21.4 per 10,000 population (2007); Hospital admissions: 938.1 per 10,000 population (2007).
Elections: 2008 Presidential election results: 32.2% Obama, 67.3% McCain, 0.0% Nader

Additional Information Contacts

Terry County Government . . . . (806) 637-6421
http://www.co.terry.tx.us/ips/cms
Brownfield Chamber & Visitor Center . . . . (806) 637-2564
http://www.brownfieldchamber.com
City of Brownfield . . . . (806) 637-4547
http://www.ci.brownfield.tx.us

Terry County Communities

BROWNFIELD (city). County seat. Covers a land area of 6.321 square miles and a water area of 0.020 square miles. Located at 33.18° N. Lat; 102.27° W. Long. Elevation is 3,310 feet.
History: The Bibricora feeding pens in Brownfield were the holding area for 10,000 head of cattle, shipped in regularly from Mexico and fattened for market in Brownfield.
Population: 9,609 (1990); 9,488 (2000); 8,948 (2010); 8,649 (2015 projected); Race: 73.4% White, 7.1% Black, 0.3% Asian, 19.2% Other, 50.3% Hispanic of any race (2010); Density: 1,415.6 persons per square

mile (2010); Average household size: 2.59 (2010); Median age: 35.5 (2010); Males per 100 females: 112.2 (2010); Marriage status: 25.7% never married, 50.8% now married, 8.4% widowed, 15.1% divorced (2005-2009 5-year est.); Foreign born: 6.6% (2005-2009 5-year est.); Ancestry (includes multiple ancestries): 4.9% American, 4.8% German, 4.8% English, 3.6% Irish, 2.6% Scotch-Irish (2005-2009 5-year est.).
Economy: Single-family building permits issued: 0 (2010); Multi-family building permits issued: 48 (2010); Employment by occupation: 9.0% management, 17.7% professional, 20.5% services, 27.1% sales, 1.1% farming, 11.4% construction, 13.2% production (2005-2009 5-year est.).
Income: Per capita income: $16,282 (2010); Median household income: $33,148 (2010); Average household income: $45,267 (2010); Percent of households with income of $100,000 or more: 8.9% (2010); Poverty rate: 22.0% (2005-2009 5-year est.).
Taxes: Total city taxes per capita: $224 (2007); City property taxes per capita: $89 (2007).
Education: Percent of population age 25 and over with: High school diploma (including GED) or higher: 65.8% (2010); Bachelor's degree or higher: 9.6% (2010); Master's degree or higher: 2.9% (2010).

School District(s)

Brownfield ISD (PK-12)
    2009-10 Enrollment: 1,762 . . . . (806) 637-2591
Housing: Homeownership rate: 69.0% (2010); Median home value: $51,250 (2010); Median contract rent: $343 per month (2005-2009 5-year est.); Median year structure built: 1962 (2005-2009 5-year est.).
Hospitals: Brownfield Regional Medical Center (71 beds)
Safety: Violent crime rate: 21.4 per 10,000 population; Property crime rate: 192.3 per 10,000 population (2009).
Newspapers: Brownfield News (Local news; Circulation 3,100)
Transportation: Commute to work: 99.4% car, 0.0% public transportation, 0.0% walk, 0.6% work from home (2005-2009 5-year est.); Travel time to work: 68.2% less than 15 minutes, 5.7% 15 to 30 minutes, 10.1% 30 to 45 minutes, 8.3% 45 to 60 minutes, 7.7% 60 minutes or more (2005-2009 5-year est.)

Additional Information Contacts

Brownfield Chamber & Visitor Center . . . . (806) 637-2564
http://www.brownfieldchamber.com
City of Brownfield . . . . (806) 637-4547
http://www.ci.brownfield.tx.us

MEADOW (town). Covers a land area of 1.600 square miles and a water area of 0 square miles. Located at 33.33° N. Lat; 102.20° W. Long. Elevation is 3,333 feet.
Population: 547 (1990); 658 (2000); 658 (2010); 653 (2015 projected); Race: 81.0% White, 0.3% Black, 0.0% Asian, 18.7% Other, 51.5% Hispanic of any race (2010); Density: 411.3 persons per square mile (2010); Average household size: 2.95 (2010); Median age: 36.2 (2010); Males per 100 females: 101.8 (2010); Marriage status: 26.8% never married, 55.1% now married, 7.3% widowed, 10.9% divorced (2005-2009 5-year est.); Foreign born: 12.4% (2005-2009 5-year est.); Ancestry (includes multiple ancestries): 7.7% German, 7.1% American, 3.5% English, 2.5% Irish, 2.4% Dutch (2005-2009 5-year est.).
Economy: Single-family building permits issued: 0 (2010); Multi-family building permits issued: 0 (2010); Employment by occupation: 11.0% management, 9.8% professional, 14.2% services, 24.6% sales, 11.3% farming, 17.5% construction, 11.6% production (2005-2009 5-year est.).
Income: Per capita income: $15,163 (2010); Median household income: $32,889 (2010); Average household income: $45,729 (2010); Percent of households with income of $100,000 or more: 6.7% (2010); Poverty rate: 32.1% (2005-2009 5-year est.).
Taxes: Total city taxes per capita: $122 (2007); City property taxes per capita: $97 (2007).
Education: Percent of population age 25 and over with: High school diploma (including GED) or higher: 70.7% (2010); Bachelor's degree or higher: 10.0% (2010); Master's degree or higher: 1.4% (2010).

School District(s)

Meadow ISD (PK-12)
    2009-10 Enrollment: 280 . . . . (806) 539-2246
Housing: Homeownership rate: 72.6% (2010); Median home value: $43,846 (2010); Median contract rent: $199 per month (2005-2009 5-year est.); Median year structure built: 1969 (2005-2009 5-year est.).
Transportation: Commute to work: 96.3% car, 0.0% public transportation, 3.7% walk, 0.0% work from home (2005-2009 5-year est.); Travel time to work: 45.5% less than 15 minutes, 19.3% 15 to 30 minutes, 29.0% 30 to 45

minutes, 3.7% 45 to 60 minutes, 2.5% 60 minutes or more (2005-2009 5-year est.)

TOKIO (unincorporated postal area, zip code 79376). Covers a land area of 116.713 square miles and a water area of 0 square miles. Located at 33.20° N. Lat; 102.62° W. Long. Elevation is 3,307 feet.
Population: 126 (2000); Race: 85.3% White, 0.0% Black, 0.0% Asian, 14.7% Other, 27.9% Hispanic of any race (2000); Density: 1.1 persons per square mile (2000); Age: 20.6% under 18, 14.7% over 64 (2000); Marriage status: 3.6% never married, 80.4% now married, 3.6% widowed, 12.5% divorced (2000); Foreign born: 8.8% (2000); Ancestry (includes multiple ancestries): 42.6% American, 7.4% German (2000).
Economy: Employment by occupation: 21.1% management, 0.0% professional, 10.5% services, 60.5% sales, 2.6% farming, 0.0% construction, 5.3% production (2000).
Income: Per capita income: $14,219 (2000); Median household income: $21,250 (2000); Poverty rate: 179.1% (2000).
Education: Percent of population age 25 and over with: High school diploma (including GED) or higher: 62.0% (2000); Bachelor's degree or higher: 14.0% (2000).
Housing: Homeownership rate: 71.4% (2000); Median home value: $42,000 (2000); Median contract rent: n/a per month (2000); Median year structure built: 1969 (2000).
Transportation: Commute to work: 100.0% car, 0.0% public transportation, 0.0% walk, 0.0% work from home (2000); Travel time to work: 26.3% less than 15 minutes, 47.4% 15 to 30 minutes, 18.4% 30 to 45 minutes, 7.9% 45 to 60 minutes, 0.0% 60 minutes or more (2000)

WELLMAN (city). Covers a land area of 0.344 square miles and a water area of 0 square miles. Located at 33.04° N. Lat; 102.42° W. Long. Elevation is 3,350 feet.
Population: 235 (1990); 203 (2000); 192 (2010); 185 (2015 projected); Race: 71.9% White, 0.0% Black, 0.0% Asian, 28.1% Other, 39.1% Hispanic of any race (2010); Density: 557.4 persons per square mile (2010); Average household size: 2.91 (2010); Median age: 34.0 (2010); Males per 100 females: 95.9 (2010); Marriage status: 29.2% never married, 64.2% now married, 0.8% widowed, 5.8% divorced (2005-2009 5-year est.); Foreign born: 13.5% (2005-2009 5-year est.); Ancestry (includes multiple ancestries): 8.2% German, 7.9% American, 6.8% English, 6.2% Irish, 3.9% Dutch (2005-2009 5-year est.).
Economy: Employment by occupation: 15.0% management, 12.8% professional, 22.8% services, 18.9% sales, 9.4% farming, 10.0% construction, 11.1% production (2005-2009 5-year est.).
Income: Per capita income: $19,158 (2010); Median household income: $48,125 (2010); Average household income: $54,508 (2010); Percent of households with income of $100,000 or more: 12.1% (2010); Poverty rate: 5.6% (2005-2009 5-year est.).
Taxes: Total city taxes per capita: $189 (2007); City property taxes per capita: $129 (2007).
Education: Percent of population age 25 and over with: High school diploma (including GED) or higher: 77.4% (2010); Bachelor's degree or higher: 19.1% (2010); Master's degree or higher: 2.6% (2010).
School District(s)
Wellman-Union CISD (PK-12)
    2009-10 Enrollment: 214 . . . . (806) 637-4910
Housing: Homeownership rate: 60.6% (2010); Median home value: $70,000 (2010); Median contract rent: $136 per month (2005-2009 5-year est.); Median year structure built: 1965 (2005-2009 5-year est.).
Transportation: Commute to work: 93.2% car, 1.7% public transportation, 2.8% walk, 0.0% work from home (2005-2009 5-year est.); Travel time to work: 40.7% less than 15 minutes, 46.3% 15 to 30 minutes, 2.8% 30 to 45 minutes, 2.3% 45 to 60 minutes, 7.9% 60 minutes or more (2005-2009 5-year est.)

Throckmorton County

Located in northern Texas; drained by the Brazos River and its Clear Fork. Covers a land area of 912.34 square miles, a water area of 3.13 square miles, and is located in the Central Time Zone at 33.15° N. Lat., 99.20° W. Long. The county was founded in 1858. County seat is Throckmorton.
Population: 1,880 (1990); 1,850 (2000); 1,717 (2010); 1,649 (2015 projected); Race: 89.8% White, 0.1% Black, 0.1% Asian, 10.0% Other, 12.5% Hispanic of any race (2010); Density: 1.9 persons per square mile (2010); Average household size: 2.42 (2010); Median age: 48.2 (2010); Males per 100 females: 101.3 (2010).

Religion: Five largest groups: 73.2% Southern Baptist Convention, 11.4% The United Methodist Church, 8.6% Churches of Christ, 5.0% Christian Church (Disciples of Christ), 2.6% Catholic Church (2000).
Economy: Unemployment rate: 6.6% (June 2011); Total civilian labor force: 1,061 (June 2011); Leading industries: 33.2% health care and social assistance; 14.2% mining; 7.3% retail trade (2009); Farms: 264 totaling 573,807 acres (2007); Companies that employ 500 or more persons: 0 (2009); Companies that employ 100 to 499 persons: 0 (2009); Companies that employ less than 100 persons: 50 (2009); Black-owned businesses: n/a (2007); Hispanic-owned businesses: n/a (2007); Asian-owned businesses: n/a (2007); Women-owned businesses: n/a (2007); Retail sales per capita: $3,380 (2010). Single-family building permits issued: n/a (2010); Multi-family building permits issued: n/a (2010).
Income: Per capita income: $20,587 (2010); Median household income: $36,289 (2010); Average household income: $50,039 (2010); Percent of households with income of $100,000 or more: 8.7% (2010); Poverty rate: 15.5% (2009); Bankruptcy rate: 0.61% (2010).
Taxes: Total county taxes per capita: $839 (2007); County property taxes per capita: $776 (2007).
Education: Percent of population age 25 and over with: High school diploma (including GED) or higher: 81.9% (2010); Bachelor's degree or higher: 20.4% (2010); Master's degree or higher: 4.6% (2010).
Housing: Homeownership rate: 75.3% (2010); Median home value: $46,186 (2010); Median contract rent: $155 per month (2005-2009 5-year est.); Median year structure built: 1951 (2005-2009 5-year est.).
Health: Birth rate: 69.1 per 10,000 population (2009); Death rate: 50.2 per 10,000 population (2009); Age-adjusted cancer mortality rate: Suppressed deaths per 100,000 population (2007); Number of physicians: 6.3 per 10,000 population (2008); Hospital beds: 86.2 per 10,000 population (2007); Hospital admissions: 1,557.9 per 10,000 population (2007).
Elections: 2008 Presidential election results: 19.8% Obama, 80.1% McCain, 0.0% Nader
Additional Information Contacts
Throckmorton County Government . . . . (940) 849-3081
    http://www.co.throckmorton.tx.us/ips/cms

Throckmorton County Communities

ELBERT (CDP). Covers a land area of 11.716 square miles and a water area of 0 square miles. Located at 33.27° N. Lat; 98.98° W. Long. Elevation is 1,155 feet.
Population: 70 (1990); 56 (2000); 51 (2010); 49 (2015 projected); Race: 90.2% White, 0.0% Black, 0.0% Asian, 9.8% Other, 9.8% Hispanic of any race (2010); Density: 4.4 persons per square mile (2010); Average household size: 2.50 (2010); Median age: 50.0 (2010); Males per 100 females: 70.0 (2010); Marriage status: 18.2% never married, 67.3% now married, 0.0% widowed, 14.5% divorced (2005-2009 5-year est.); Foreign born: 0.0% (2005-2009 5-year est.); Ancestry (includes multiple ancestries): 28.3% Irish, 16.7% English, 16.7% Scotch-Irish, 13.3% German, 13.3% Czech (2005-2009 5-year est.).
Economy: Employment by occupation: 42.9% management, 28.6% professional, 0.0% services, 0.0% sales, 28.6% farming, 0.0% construction, 0.0% production (2005-2009 5-year est.).
Income: Per capita income: $20,846 (2010); Median household income: $32,500 (2010); Average household income: $38,250 (2010); Percent of households with income of $100,000 or more: 5.0% (2010); Poverty rate: 33.3% (2005-2009 5-year est.).
Education: Percent of population age 25 and over with: High school diploma (including GED) or higher: 84.2% (2010); Bachelor's degree or higher: 15.8% (2010); Master's degree or higher: 0.0% (2010).
Housing: Homeownership rate: 75.0% (2010); Median home value: $52,500 (2010); Median contract rent: n/a per month (2005-2009 5-year est.); Median year structure built: before 1940 (2005-2009 5-year est.).
Transportation: Commute to work: 100.0% car, 0.0% public transportation, 0.0% walk, 0.0% work from home (2005-2009 5-year est.); Travel time to work: 50.0% less than 15 minutes, 50.0% 15 to 30 minutes, 0.0% 30 to 45 minutes, 0.0% 45 to 60 minutes, 0.0% 60 minutes or more (2005-2009 5-year est.)

THROCKMORTON (town). County seat. Covers a land area of 1.678 square miles and a water area of 0 square miles. Located at 33.18° N. Lat; 99.17° W. Long. Elevation is 1,319 feet.
History: Settled before 1880, incorporated 1917.
Population: 1,041 (1990); 905 (2000); 837 (2010); 804 (2015 projected); Race: 88.9% White, 0.2% Black, 0.1% Asian, 10.8% Other, 15.3%

Hispanic of any race (2010); Density: 498.9 persons per square mile (2010); Average household size: 2.38 (2010); Median age: 46.7 (2010); Males per 100 females: 106.2 (2010); Marriage status: 18.2% never married, 60.3% now married, 9.8% widowed, 11.7% divorced (2005-2009 5-year est.); Foreign born: 0.5% (2005-2009 5-year est.); Ancestry (includes multiple ancestries): 14.7% English, 14.7% Irish, 13.3% German, 4.2% Scotch-Irish, 3.9% French (2005-2009 5-year est.).
Economy: Employment by occupation: 12.5% management, 15.0% professional, 23.4% services, 11.5% sales, 9.3% farming, 11.5% construction, 16.8% production (2005-2009 5-year est.).
Income: Per capita income: $20,354 (2010); Median household income: $34,896 (2010); Average household income: $48,632 (2010); Percent of households with income of $100,000 or more: 8.3% (2010); Poverty rate: 9.8% (2005-2009 5-year est.).
Taxes: Total city taxes per capita: $171 (2007); City property taxes per capita: $53 (2007).
Education: Percent of population age 25 and over with: High school diploma (including GED) or higher: 81.0% (2010); Bachelor's degree or higher: 21.1% (2010); Master's degree or higher: 6.9% (2010).
School District(s)
Throckmorton ISD (PK-12)
    2009-10 Enrollment: 205 . . . . (940) 849-2411
Housing: Homeownership rate: 76.4% (2010); Median home value: $40,635 (2010); Median contract rent: $135 per month (2005-2009 5-year est.); Median year structure built: 1954 (2005-2009 5-year est.).
Hospitals: Throckmorton County Memorial Hospital (25 beds)
Newspapers: Throckmorton Tribune (Local news; Circulation 1,300)
Transportation: Commute to work: 96.1% car, 0.0% public transportation, 2.0% walk, 1.3% work from home (2005-2009 5-year est.); Travel time to work: 51.5% less than 15 minutes, 26.1% 15 to 30 minutes, 6.6% 30 to 45 minutes, 10.2% 45 to 60 minutes, 5.6% 60 minutes or more (2005-2009 5-year est.)

WOODSON (town). Covers a land area of 0.640 square miles and a water area of 0 square miles. Located at 33.01° N. Lat; 99.05° W. Long. Elevation is 1,227 feet.
Population: 262 (1990); 296 (2000); 281 (2010); 270 (2015 projected); Race: 90.7% White, 0.0% Black, 0.0% Asian, 9.3% Other, 9.3% Hispanic of any race (2010); Density: 439.3 persons per square mile (2010); Average household size: 2.47 (2010); Median age: 49.5 (2010); Males per 100 females: 92.5 (2010); Marriage status: 12.8% never married, 71.9% now married, 9.1% widowed, 6.2% divorced (2005-2009 5-year est.); Foreign born: 11.2% (2005-2009 5-year est.); Ancestry (includes multiple ancestries): 14.1% Irish, 10.5% American, 7.2% English, 5.9% German, 2.0% Hungarian (2005-2009 5-year est.).
Economy: Employment by occupation: 2.9% management, 12.4% professional, 7.6% services, 26.7% sales, 13.3% farming, 22.9% construction, 14.3% production (2005-2009 5-year est.).
Income: Per capita income: $20,846 (2010); Median household income: $37,100 (2010); Average household income: $49,707 (2010); Percent of households with income of $100,000 or more: 8.1% (2010); Poverty rate: 30.6% (2005-2009 5-year est.).
Taxes: Total city taxes per capita: $134 (2007); City property taxes per capita: $123 (2007).
Education: Percent of population age 25 and over with: High school diploma (including GED) or higher: 82.3% (2010); Bachelor's degree or higher: 19.1% (2010); Master's degree or higher: 1.9% (2010).
School District(s)
Woodson ISD (PK-12)
    2009-10 Enrollment: 117 . . . . (940) 345-6528
Housing: Homeownership rate: 73.9% (2010); Median home value: $54,444 (2010); Median contract rent: n/a per month (2005-2009 5-year est.); Median year structure built: 1943 (2005-2009 5-year est.).
Transportation: Commute to work: 95.2% car, 0.0% public transportation, 0.0% walk, 4.8% work from home (2005-2009 5-year est.); Travel time to work: 21.0% less than 15 minutes, 47.0% 15 to 30 minutes, 22.0% 30 to 45 minutes, 5.0% 45 to 60 minutes, 5.0% 60 minutes or more (2005-2009 5-year est.)

Titus County

Located in northeastern Texas; bounded on the north by the Sulphur River, and on the south by Cypress Bayou; drained by White Oak Bayou. Covers a land area of 410.54 square miles, a water area of 15.15 square miles,

and is located in the Central Time Zone at 33.18° N. Lat., 94.98° W. Long. The county was founded in 1846. County seat is Mount Pleasant.

Titus County is part of the Mount Pleasant, TX Micropolitan Statistical Area. The entire metro area includes: Titus County, TX

Weather Station: Mount Pleasant   Elevation: 424 feet

	Jan	Feb	Mar	Apr	May	Jun	Jul	Aug	Sep	Oct	Nov	Dec
High	56	60	68	76	83	90	94	95	89	78	67	58
Low	31	34	42	49	59	67	70	70	62	50	41	33
Precip	3.3	3.8	4.4	3.6	5.6	4.7	3.5	2.2	3.2	5.3	4.3	4.4
Snow	0.5	0.8	tr	0.0	0.0	0.0	0.0	0.0	0.0	0.0	tr	0.3

High and Low temperatures in degrees Fahrenheit; Precipitation and Snow in inches

Population: 24,009 (1990); 28,118 (2000); 30,870 (2010); 32,154 (2015 projected); Race: 64.0% White, 9.7% Black, 0.7% Asian, 25.7% Other, 39.1% Hispanic of any race (2010); Density: 75.2 persons per square mile (2010); Average household size: 2.94 (2010); Median age: 32.3 (2010); Males per 100 females: 101.2 (2010).
Religion: Five largest groups: 31.8% Southern Baptist Convention, 9.7% Catholic Church, 7.8% The American Baptist Association, 5.4% The United Methodist Church, 5.3% Baptist Missionary Association of America (2000).
Economy: Unemployment rate: 8.2% (June 2011); Total civilian labor force: 14,552 (June 2011); Leading industries: 40.2% manufacturing; 15.1% health care and social assistance; 14.0% retail trade (2009); Farms: 810 totaling 166,405 acres (2007); Companies that employ 500 or more persons: 3 (2009); Companies that employ 100 to 499 persons: 14 (2009); Companies that employ less than 100 persons: 643 (2009); Black-owned businesses: n/a (2007); Hispanic-owned businesses: n/a (2007); Asian-owned businesses: n/a (2007); Women-owned businesses: n/a (2007); Retail sales per capita: $16,530 (2010). Single-family building permits issued: 4 (2010); Multi-family building permits issued: 0 (2010).
Income: Per capita income: $18,540 (2010); Median household income: $41,111 (2010); Average household income: $55,353 (2010); Percent of households with income of $100,000 or more: 12.2% (2010); Poverty rate: 18.4% (2009); Bankruptcy rate: 1.25% (2010).
Taxes: Total county taxes per capita: $381 (2007); County property taxes per capita: $297 (2007).
Education: Percent of population age 25 and over with: High school diploma (including GED) or higher: 72.6% (2010); Bachelor's degree or higher: 13.5% (2010); Master's degree or higher: 3.6% (2010).
Housing: Homeownership rate: 67.7% (2010); Median home value: $87,531 (2010); Median contract rent: $407 per month (2005-2009 5-year est.); Median year structure built: 1980 (2005-2009 5-year est.)
Health: Birth rate: 183.1 per 10,000 population (2009); Death rate: 77.5 per 10,000 population (2009); Age-adjusted cancer mortality rate: 244.3 deaths per 100,000 population (2007); Number of physicians: 15.9 per 10,000 population (2008); Hospital beds: 51.5 per 10,000 population (2007); Hospital admissions: 1,856.6 per 10,000 population (2007).
Elections: 2008 Presidential election results: 34.0% Obama, 65.2% McCain, 0.0% Nader
National and State Parks: Lake Bob Sandlin State Park
Additional Information Contacts
Titus County Government . . . . (903) 577-6791
    http://www.co.titus.tx.us
City of Mount Pleasant . . . . (903) 575-4000
    http://www.mpcity.net
Mt Pleasant/Titus County Chamber of Commerce . . . . . . (903) 572-8567
    http://www.mtpleasanttx.com

Titus County Communities

COOKVILLE (unincorporated postal area, zip code 75558). Covers a land area of 48.316 square miles and a water area of 0.069 square miles. Located at 33.23° N. Lat; 94.84° W. Long. Elevation is 433 feet.
Population: 1,438 (2000); Race: 88.7% White, 0.0% Black, 0.0% Asian, 11.3% Other, 12.9% Hispanic of any race (2000); Density: 29.8 persons per square mile (2000); Age: 23.9% under 18, 16.4% over 64 (2000); Marriage status: 10.9% never married, 68.1% now married, 8.7% widowed, 12.4% divorced (2000); Foreign born: 8.0% (2000); Ancestry (includes multiple ancestries): 19.6% American, 7.6% English, 7.5% Irish, 7.4% German (2000).
Economy: Employment by occupation: 12.7% management, 10.8% professional, 21.4% services, 25.4% sales, 2.3% farming, 15.5% construction, 12.0% production (2000).

Income: Per capita income: $14,144 (2000); Median household income: $30,202 (2000); Poverty rate: 179.1% (2000).

Education: Percent of population age 25 and over with: High school diploma (including GED) or higher: 70.4% (2000); Bachelor's degree or higher: 5.3% (2000).

Housing: Homeownership rate: 78.3% (2000); Median home value: $67,300 (2000); Median contract rent: $243 per month (2000); Median year structure built: 1982 (2000).

Transportation: Commute to work: 94.4% car, 1.8% public transportation, 0.9% walk, 3.0% work from home (2000); Travel time to work: 28.4% less than 15 minutes, 52.1% 15 to 30 minutes, 11.8% 30 to 45 minutes, 1.6% 45 to 60 minutes, 6.1% 60 minutes or more (2000)

MILLER'S COVE (town).
Covers a land area of 0.168 square miles and a water area of 0 square miles. Located at 33.15° N. Lat; 95.11° W. Long.

Population: 75 (1990); 120 (2000); 124 (2010); 127 (2015 projected); Race: 77.4% White, 4.0% Black, 0.0% Asian, 18.5% Other, 28.2% Hispanic of any race (2010); Density: 740.1 persons per square mile (2010); Average household size: 2.70 (2010); Median age: 36.8 (2010); Males per 100 females: 121.4 (2010); Marriage status: 23.0% never married, 77.0% now married, 0.0% widowed, 0.0% divorced (2005-2009 5-year est.); Foreign born: 70.5% (2005-2009 5-year est.); Ancestry (includes multiple ancestries): 8.5% French (2005-2009 5-year est.).

Economy: Employment by occupation: 0.0% management, 2.9% professional, 26.1% services, 8.7% sales, 0.0% farming, 4.3% construction, 58.0% production (2005-2009 5-year est.).

Income: Per capita income: $20,989 (2010); Median household income: $42,500 (2010); Average household income: $54,891 (2010); Percent of households with income of $100,000 or more: 10.9% (2010); Poverty rate: 30.2% (2005-2009 5-year est.).

Taxes: Total city taxes per capita: $182 (2007); City property taxes per capita: $0 (2007).

Education: Percent of population age 25 and over with: High school diploma (including GED) or higher: 80.0% (2010); Bachelor's degree or higher: 23.8% (2010); Master's degree or higher: 3.8% (2010).

Housing: Homeownership rate: 78.3% (2010); Median home value: $143,750 (2010); Median contract rent: $256 per month (2005-2009 5-year est.); Median year structure built: 1977 (2005-2009 5-year est.).

Transportation: Commute to work: 100.0% car, 0.0% public transportation, 0.0% walk, 0.0% work from home (2005-2009 5-year est.); Travel time to work: 47.8% less than 15 minutes, 52.2% 15 to 30 minutes, 0.0% 30 to 45 minutes, 0.0% 45 to 60 minutes, 0.0% 60 minutes or more (2005-2009 5-year est.)

MOUNT PLEASANT (city).
County seat. Covers a land area of 12.532 square miles and a water area of 0.200 square miles. Located at 33.15° N. Lat; 94.97° W. Long. Elevation is 404 feet.

History: Mount Pleasant developed around poultry processing and meat packing plants.

Population: 12,471 (1990); 13,935 (2000); 15,378 (2010); 16,071 (2015 projected); Race: 53.0% White, 13.9% Black, 1.3% Asian, 31.9% Other, 51.3% Hispanic of any race (2010); Density: 1,227.1 persons per square mile (2010); Average household size: 3.03 (2010); Median age: 30.9 (2010); Males per 100 females: 99.5 (2010); Marriage status: 26.0% never married, 55.7% now married, 7.6% widowed, 10.7% divorced (2005-2009 5-year est.); Foreign born: 26.8% (2005-2009 5-year est.); Ancestry (includes multiple ancestries): 6.2% American, 5.5% Irish, 5.3% African, 4.6% English, 4.2% German (2005-2009 5-year est.).

Economy: Single-family building permits issued: 4 (2010); Multi-family building permits issued: 0 (2010); Employment by occupation: 5.2% management, 10.4% professional, 17.0% services, 19.4% sales, 2.1% farming, 11.2% construction, 34.7% production (2005-2009 5-year est.).

Income: Per capita income: $16,163 (2010); Median household income: $35,309 (2010); Average household income: $50,088 (2010); Percent of households with income of $100,000 or more: 9.3% (2010); Poverty rate: 20.6% (2005-2009 5-year est.).

Taxes: Total city taxes per capita: $523 (2007); City property taxes per capita: $138 (2007).

Education: Percent of population age 25 and over with: High school diploma (including GED) or higher: 66.6% (2010); Bachelor's degree or higher: 13.3% (2010); Master's degree or higher: 3.3% (2010).

School District(s)
Chapel Hill ISD (KG-12)
   2009-10 Enrollment: 907 . . . . (903) 572-8096

Harts Bluff ISD (KG-08)
   2009-10 Enrollment: 449 . . . . (903) 572-5427
Lewisville ISD (PK-12)
   2009-10 Enrollment: 50,840 . . . . (469) 713-5200
Mount Pleasant ISD (PK-12)
   2009-10 Enrollment: 5,381 . . . . (903) 575-2000

Two-year College(s)
Northeast Texas Community College (Public)
   Fall 2009 Enrollment: 2,920. (903) 434-8100
   2010-11 Tuition: In-state $2,508; Out-of-state $3,598

Housing: Homeownership rate: 57.1% (2010); Median home value: $79,794 (2010); Median contract rent: $408 per month (2005-2009 5-year est.); Median year structure built: 1974 (2005-2009 5-year est.).

Hospitals: Titus Regional Medical Center (165 beds)

Safety: Violent crime rate: 42.4 per 10,000 population; Property crime rate: 444.7 per 10,000 population (2009).

Newspapers: Mount Pleasant Daily Tribune (Local news; Circulation 5,000)

Transportation: Commute to work: 95.4% car, 0.4% public transportation, 1.1% walk, 0.9% work from home (2005-2009 5-year est.); Travel time to work: 65.9% less than 15 minutes, 23.2% 15 to 30 minutes, 6.1% 30 to 45 minutes, 1.9% 45 to 60 minutes, 3.0% 60 minutes or more (2005-2009 5-year est.)

Airports: Mount Pleasant Regional (general aviation)

Additional Information Contacts
City of Mount Pleasant. . . . . (903) 575-4000
   http://www.mpcity.net
Mt Pleasant/Titus County Chamber of Commerce . . . . (903) 572-8567
   http://www.mtpleasanttx.com

TALCO (city).
Covers a land area of 0.767 square miles and a water area of 0 square miles. Located at 33.36° N. Lat; 95.10° W. Long. Elevation is 364 feet.

History: In 1935 the discovery of oil near Talco changed the population from 140 to more than 5,000 people.

Population: 592 (1990); 570 (2000); 574 (2010); 576 (2015 projected); Race: 79.6% White, 10.6% Black, 0.0% Asian, 9.8% Other, 12.0% Hispanic of any race (2010); Density: 748.2 persons per square mile (2010); Average household size: 2.59 (2010); Median age: 36.6 (2010); Males per 100 females: 104.3 (2010); Marriage status: 13.9% never married, 67.1% now married, 5.0% widowed, 13.9% divorced (2005-2009 5-year est.); Foreign born: 19.5% (2005-2009 5-year est.); Ancestry (includes multiple ancestries): 10.3% Irish, 9.3% German, 4.8% English, 4.7% African, 3.7% Scotch-Irish (2005-2009 5-year est.).

Economy: Single-family building permits issued: 0 (2010); Multi-family building permits issued: 0 (2010); Employment by occupation: 3.9% management, 7.5% professional, 26.4% services, 16.1% sales, 5.1% farming, 22.8% construction, 18.1% production (2005-2009 5-year est.).

Income: Per capita income: $11,769 (2010); Median household income: $24,600 (2010); Average household income: $30,732 (2010); Percent of households with income of $100,000 or more: 1.4% (2010); Poverty rate: 17.9% (2005-2009 5-year est.).

Taxes: Total city taxes per capita: $181 (2007); City property taxes per capita: $119 (2007).

Education: Percent of population age 25 and over with: High school diploma (including GED) or higher: 67.1% (2010); Bachelor's degree or higher: 7.0% (2010); Master's degree or higher: 1.1% (2010).

Housing: Homeownership rate: 76.6% (2010); Median home value: $35,610 (2010); Median contract rent: $303 per month (2005-2009 5-year est.); Median year structure built: 1970 (2005-2009 5-year est.).

Transportation: Commute to work: 95.6% car, 0.0% public transportation, 2.8% walk, 0.0% work from home (2005-2009 5-year est.); Travel time to work: 15.3% less than 15 minutes, 58.9% 15 to 30 minutes, 13.7% 30 to 45 minutes, 4.4% 45 to 60 minutes, 7.7% 60 minutes or more (2005-2009 5-year est.)

WINFIELD (city).
Covers a land area of 0.930 square miles and a water area of 0.014 square miles. Located at 33.16° N. Lat; 95.11° W. Long. Elevation is 456 feet.

Population: 345 (1990); 499 (2000); 532 (2010); 546 (2015 projected); Race: 74.1% White, 1.5% Black, 0.0% Asian, 24.4% Other, 30.8% Hispanic of any race (2010); Density: 572.2 persons per square mile (2010); Average household size: 2.88 (2010); Median age: 33.3 (2010); Males per 100 females: 99.3 (2010); Marriage status: 27.6% never married, 58.0% now married, 11.0% widowed, 3.5% divorced (2005-2009 5-year

est.); Foreign born: 19.9% (2005-2009 5-year est.); Ancestry (includes multiple ancestries): 11.6% American, 9.4% Irish, 9.1% English, 5.1% Dutch, 3.8% German (2005-2009 5-year est.).

Economy: Employment by occupation: 8.1% management, 12.1% professional, 23.5% services, 13.4% sales, 0.0% farming, 20.1% construction, 22.8% production (2005-2009 5-year est.).

Income: Per capita income: $23,308 (2010); Median household income: $51,838 (2010); Average household income: $66,919 (2010); Percent of households with income of $100,000 or more: 18.9% (2010); Poverty rate: 26.1% (2005-2009 5-year est.).

Taxes: Total city taxes per capita: $249 (2007); City property taxes per capita: $136 (2007).

Education: Percent of population age 25 and over with: High school diploma (including GED) or higher: 82.2% (2010); Bachelor's degree or higher: 13.7% (2010); Master's degree or higher: 4.0% (2010).

School District(s)

Winfield ISD (KG-08)

   2009-10 Enrollment: 165 . . . . (903) 524-2221

Housing: Homeownership rate: 76.8% (2010); Median home value: $76,842 (2010); Median contract rent: $413 per month (2005-2009 5-year est.); Median year structure built: 1972 (2005-2009 5-year est.).

Transportation: Commute to work: 98.6% car, 0.0% public transportation, 0.0% walk, 1.4% work from home (2005-2009 5-year est.); Travel time to work: 43.4% less than 15 minutes, 44.1% 15 to 30 minutes, 8.3% 30 to 45 minutes, 0.0% 45 to 60 minutes, 4.1% 60 minutes or more (2005-2009 5-year est.)

Tom Green County

Located in west Texas, on the Edwards Plateau; drained by the North, Middle, and South Concho Rivers. Covers a land area of 1,522.10 square miles, a water area of 18.44 square miles, and is located in the Central Time Zone at 31.44° N. Lat., 100.47° W. Long. The county was founded in 1874. County seat is San Angelo.

Tom Green County is part of the San Angelo, TX Metropolitan Statistical Area. The entire metro area includes: Irion County, TX; Tom Green County, TX

Weather Station: San Angelo Mathis Field   Elevation: 1,916 feet

	Jan	Feb	Mar	Apr	May	Jun	Jul	Aug	Sep	Oct	Nov	Dec
High	60	64	71	80	87	92	95	95	88	79	68	60
Low	33	37	44	51	62	68	71	70	63	53	42	34
Precip	0.9	1.3	1.5	1.4	2.9	2.6	1.2	2.3	2.8	2.6	1.2	0.9
Snow	1.4	0.3	0.1	0.1	tr	tr	tr	0.0	tr	tr	0.3	0.3

High and Low temperatures in degrees Fahrenheit; Precipitation and Snow in inches

Weather Station: Water Valley   Elevation: 2,120 feet

	Jan	Feb	Mar	Apr	May	Jun	Jul	Aug	Sep	Oct	Nov	Dec
High	60	63	71	80	87	92	95	94	88	79	68	59
Low	29	33	41	48	59	67	69	68	61	50	39	30
Precip	0.8	1.2	1.5	1.5	2.9	3.1	1.7	2.8	2.6	2.8	1.1	1.0
Snow	0.7	0.1	0.0	0.2	0.0	0.0	0.0	0.0	0.0	0.0	0.6	0.2

High and Low temperatures in degrees Fahrenheit; Precipitation and Snow in inches

Population: 98,458 (1990); 104,010 (2000); 106,578 (2010); 107,637 (2015 projected); Race: 76.6% White, 4.0% Black, 1.0% Asian, 18.4% Other, 35.0% Hispanic of any race (2010); Density: 70.0 persons per square mile (2010); Average household size: 2.48 (2010); Median age: 34.1 (2010); Males per 100 females: 93.9 (2010).

Religion: Five largest groups: 26.6% Southern Baptist Convention, 15.0% Catholic Church, 4.2% The United Methodist Church, 3.6% Churches of Christ, 2.0% Presbyterian Church (U.S.A.) (2000).

Economy: Unemployment rate: 7.3% (June 2011); Total civilian labor force: 52,950 (June 2011); Leading industries: 19.5% health care and social assistance; 17.1% retail trade; 12.4% accommodation & food services (2009); Farms: 1,180 totaling 923,509 acres (2007); Companies that employ 500 or more persons: 5 (2009); Companies that employ 100 to 499 persons: 41 (2009); Companies that employ less than 100 persons: 2,554 (2009); Black-owned businesses: n/a (2007); Hispanic-owned businesses: n/a (2007); Asian-owned businesses: n/a (2007); Women-owned businesses: 2,521 (2007); Retail sales per capita: $12,026 (2010). Single-family building permits issued: 177 (2010); Multi-family building permits issued: 0 (2010).

Income: Per capita income: $21,792 (2010); Median household income: $41,776 (2010); Average household income: $55,193 (2010); Percent of

households with income of $100,000 or more: 11.0% (2010); Poverty rate: 16.2% (2009); Bankruptcy rate: 1.97% (2010).

Taxes: Total county taxes per capita: $226 (2007); County property taxes per capita: $161 (2007).

Education: Percent of population age 25 and over with: High school diploma (including GED) or higher: 80.7% (2010); Bachelor's degree or higher: 22.1% (2010); Master's degree or higher: 6.8% (2010).

Housing: Homeownership rate: 66.0% (2010); Median home value: $92,021 (2010); Median contract rent: $520 per month (2005-2009 5-year est.); Median year structure built: 1973 (2005-2009 5-year est.)

Health: Birth rate: 157.8 per 10,000 population (2009); Death rate: 95.1 per 10,000 population (2009); Age-adjusted cancer mortality rate: 167.3 deaths per 100,000 population (2007); Number of physicians: 20.8 per 10,000 population (2008); Hospital beds: 50.4 per 10,000 population (2007); Hospital admissions: 2,043.5 per 10,000 population (2007).

Elections: 2008 Presidential election results: 28.7% Obama, 70.4% McCain, 0.1% Nader

Additional Information Contacts

Tom Green County Government . . . . (325) 653-2385
   http://www.co.tom-green.tx.us/ips/cms
Christoval Community Chamber . . . . (325) 896-1065
   http://christoval.org
City of San Angelo . . . . (325) 481-2727
   http://www.sanangelotexas.org
San Angelo Chamber of Commerce . . . . (325) 655-4136
   http://www.sanangelo.org

Tom Green County Communities

CARLSBAD (unincorporated postal area, zip code 76934). Covers a land area of 47.148 square miles and a water area of 0 square miles. Located at 31.60° N. Lat; 100.65° W. Long. Elevation is 2,024 feet.

Population: 1,322 (2000); Race: 86.3% White, 4.6% Black, 0.3% Asian, 8.8% Other, 13.5% Hispanic of any race (2000); Density: 28.0 persons per square mile (2000); Age: 21.0% under 18, 17.2% over 64 (2000); Marriage status: 14.3% never married, 70.9% now married, 5.4% widowed, 9.3% divorced (2000); Foreign born: 2.0% (2000); Ancestry (includes multiple ancestries): 13.0% German, 10.9% Irish, 6.4% English, 6.3% American (2000).

Economy: Employment by occupation: 8.3% management, 11.5% professional, 23.6% services, 23.4% sales, 2.7% farming, 15.2% construction, 15.4% production (2000).

Income: Per capita income: $11,405 (2000); Median household income: $28,214 (2000); Poverty rate: 179.1% (2000).

Education: Percent of population age 25 and over with: High school diploma (including GED) or higher: 59.7% (2000); Bachelor's degree or higher: 7.6% (2000).

Housing: Homeownership rate: 76.0% (2000); Median home value: $45,400 (2000); Median contract rent: $300 per month (2000); Median year structure built: 1980 (2000).

Transportation: Commute to work: 95.0% car, 0.0% public transportation, 1.9% walk, 3.1% work from home (2000); Travel time to work: 23.2% less than 15 minutes, 31.1% 15 to 30 minutes, 36.7% 30 to 45 minutes, 3.4% 45 to 60 minutes, 5.6% 60 minutes or more (2000)

CHRISTOVAL (CDP). Covers a land area of 1.211 square miles and a water area of 0 square miles. Located at 31.19° N. Lat; 100.49° W. Long. Elevation is 2,037 feet.

History: Christoval developed as a health resort with mineral wells known for their medicinal qualities.

Population: 316 (1990); 422 (2000); 471 (2010); 491 (2015 projected); Race: 95.8% White, 0.4% Black, 0.2% Asian, 3.6% Other, 9.8% Hispanic of any race (2010); Density: 388.8 persons per square mile (2010); Average household size: 2.23 (2010); Median age: 48.3 (2010); Males per 100 females: 97.1 (2010); Marriage status: 9.4% never married, 79.8% now married, 1.0% widowed, 9.8% divorced (2005-2009 5-year est.); Foreign born: 3.8% (2005-2009 5-year est.); Ancestry (includes multiple ancestries): 22.0% English, 19.4% German, 14.2% Irish, 12.1% American, 6.2% Scottish (2005-2009 5-year est.).

Economy: Employment by occupation: 5.1% management, 15.8% professional, 2.5% services, 45.6% sales, 0.0% farming, 23.4% construction, 7.6% production (2005-2009 5-year est.).

Income: Per capita income: $27,459 (2010); Median household income: $49,167 (2010); Average household income: $58,235 (2010); Percent of

households with income of $100,000 or more: 12.7% (2010); Poverty rate: 2.4% (2005-2009 5-year est.).

Education: Percent of population age 25 and over with: High school diploma (including GED) or higher: 90.0% (2010); Bachelor's degree or higher: 24.8% (2010); Master's degree or higher: 10.0% (2010).

School District(s)

Christoval ISD (PK-12)
   2009-10 Enrollment: 429 . . . . (325) 896-2520

Housing: Homeownership rate: 79.9% (2010); Median home value: $123,661 (2010); Median contract rent: $675 per month (2005-2009 5-year est.); Median year structure built: 1968 (2005-2009 5-year est.).

Transportation: Commute to work: 89.2% car, 0.0% public transportation, 10.8% walk, 0.0% work from home (2005-2009 5-year est.); Travel time to work: 17.7% less than 15 minutes, 43.0% 15 to 30 minutes, 12.0% 30 to 45 minutes, 25.3% 45 to 60 minutes, 1.9% 60 minutes or more (2005-2009 5-year est.)

Additional Information Contacts

Christoval Community Chamber . . . . (325) 896-1065
   http://christoval.org

GRAPE CREEK (CDP). Covers a land area of 17.215 square miles

and a water area of 0 square miles. Located at 31.57° N. Lat; 100.54° W. Long. Elevation is 2,005 feet.

Population: 2,907 (1990); 3,138 (2000); 2,988 (2010); 2,926 (2015 projected); Race: 88.9% White, 0.5% Black, 0.1% Asian, 10.5% Other, 21.2% Hispanic of any race (2010); Density: 173.6 persons per square mile (2010); Average household size: 2.73 (2010); Median age: 35.8 (2010); Males per 100 females: 94.8 (2010); Marriage status: 25.5% never married, 56.1% now married, 5.7% widowed, 12.7% divorced (2005-2009 5-year est.); Foreign born: 4.1% (2005-2009 5-year est.); Ancestry (includes multiple ancestries): 18.0% German, 16.8% Irish, 9.0% English, 6.8% Scotch-Irish, 6.6% American (2005-2009 5-year est.).

Economy: Employment by occupation: 9.3% management, 17.9% professional, 18.8% services, 26.4% sales, 0.0% farming, 19.0% construction, 8.5% production (2005-2009 5-year est.).

Income: Per capita income: $17,783 (2010); Median household income: $41,235 (2010); Average household income: $48,525 (2010); Percent of households with income of $100,000 or more: 5.2% (2010); Poverty rate: 9.9% (2005-2009 5-year est.).

Education: Percent of population age 25 and over with: High school diploma (including GED) or higher: 77.6% (2010); Bachelor's degree or higher: 9.8% (2010); Master's degree or higher: 1.8% (2010).

Housing: Homeownership rate: 84.4% (2010); Median home value: $73,486 (2010); Median contract rent: $521 per month (2005-2009 5-year est.); Median year structure built: 1978 (2005-2009 5-year est.).

Transportation: Commute to work: 98.4% car, 0.0% public transportation, 0.8% walk, 0.9% work from home (2005-2009 5-year est.); Travel time to work: 21.3% less than 15 minutes, 60.1% 15 to 30 minutes, 10.6% 30 to 45 minutes, 0.9% 45 to 60 minutes, 7.2% 60 minutes or more (2005-2009 5-year est.)

MERETA (unincorporated postal area, zip code 76940). Covers a land

area of 9.931 square miles and a water area of 0 square miles. Located at 31.45° N. Lat; 100.12° W. Long. Elevation is 1,755 feet.

Population: 138 (2000); Race: 76.4% White, 0.0% Black, 0.0% Asian, 23.6% Other, 70.0% Hispanic of any race (2000); Density: 13.9 persons per square mile (2000); Age: 15.7% under 18, 14.3% over 64 (2000); Marriage status: 32.2% never married, 58.5% now married, 4.2% widowed, 5.1% divorced (2000); Foreign born: 27.9% (2000); Ancestry (includes multiple ancestries): 13.6% American, 7.1% German (2000).

Economy: Employment by occupation: 7.9% management, 0.0% professional, 9.5% services, 25.4% sales, 19.0% farming, 28.6% construction, 9.5% production (2000).

Income: Per capita income: $14,744 (2000); Median household income: $43,750 (2000); Poverty rate: 179.1% (2000).

Education: Percent of population age 25 and over with: High school diploma (including GED) or higher: 49.4% (2000); Bachelor's degree or higher: 0.0% (2000).

Housing: Homeownership rate: 95.9% (2000); Median home value: $54,200 (2000); Median contract rent: n/a per month (2000); Median year structure built: 1968 (2000).

Transportation: Commute to work: 87.3% car, 0.0% public transportation, 0.0% walk, 12.7% work from home (2000); Travel time to work: 21.8% less than 15 minutes, 41.8% 15 to 30 minutes, 12.7% 30 to 45 minutes, 23.6% 45 to 60 minutes, 0.0% 60 minutes or more (2000)

SAN ANGELO (city). County seat. Covers a land area of 55.896

square miles and a water area of 2.349 square miles. Located at 31.45° N. Lat; 100.45° W. Long. Elevation is 1,844 feet.

History: The establishment of Camp Concho between the North and Middle Concho Rivers led to the founding of the settlement across the North Concho. First called simply Over-the-River, in 1882 the town was named Santa Angela by Bartholomew De Witt, for his sister-in-law, a nun of the Ursuline Convent at San Antonio. The name was later changed from the feminine Santa Angela to the masculine San Angelo. The Goodnight-Loving Cattle Trail, the Chidester Stage Line, and the California Trail all passed through the present site of San Angelo. The town became a primary wool market, with dozens of wool and mohair warehouses.

Population: 85,280 (1990); 88,439 (2000); 90,878 (2010); 91,930 (2015 projected); Race: 74.7% White, 4.5% Black, 1.1% Asian, 19.7% Other, 37.7% Hispanic of any race (2010); Density: 1,625.8 persons per square mile (2010); Average household size: 2.45 (2010); Median age: 33.3 (2010); Males per 100 females: 93.0 (2010); Marriage status: 29.0% never married, 52.1% now married, 7.1% widowed, 11.8% divorced (2005-2009 5-year est.); Foreign born: 6.5% (2005-2009 5-year est.); Ancestry (includes multiple ancestries): 12.9% German, 8.7% Irish, 8.2% English, 6.9% American, 2.7% Scotch-Irish (2005-2009 5-year est.).

Economy: Unemployment rate: 7.3% (June 2011); Total civilian labor force: 44,605 (June 2011); Single-family building permits issued: 177 (2010); Multi-family building permits issued: 0 (2010); Employment by occupation: 10.0% management, 18.4% professional, 20.7% services, 28.8% sales, 0.7% farming, 10.6% construction, 10.8% production (2005-2009 5-year est.).

Income: Per capita income: $21,683 (2010); Median household income: $40,779 (2010); Average household income: $54,257 (2010); Percent of households with income of $100,000 or more: 10.8% (2010); Poverty rate: 17.4% (2005-2009 5-year est.).

Taxes: Total city taxes per capita: $529 (2007); City property taxes per capita: $258 (2007).

Education: Percent of population age 25 and over with: High school diploma (including GED) or higher: 80.5% (2010); Bachelor's degree or higher: 22.7% (2010); Master's degree or higher: 6.9% (2010).

School District(s)

Ballinger ISD (PK-12)
   2009-10 Enrollment: 1,028 . . . . (325) 365-3588
Bronte ISD (PK-12)
   2009-10 Enrollment: 321 . . . . (325) 473-2511
Christoval ISD (PK-12)
   2009-10 Enrollment: 429 . . . . (325) 896-2520
Eden CISD (PK-12)
   2009-10 Enrollment: 266 . . . . (325) 869-4121
Grape Creek ISD (PK-12)
   2009-10 Enrollment: 1,102 . . . . (325) 658-7823
Miles ISD (PK-12)
   2009-10 Enrollment: 401 . . . . (325) 468-2861
Olfen ISD (PK-08)
   2009-10 Enrollment: 75 . . . . (325) 442-4301
Paint Rock ISD (PK-12)
   2009-10 Enrollment: 139 . . . . (325) 732-4314
Robert Lee ISD (PK-12)
   2009-10 Enrollment: 251 . . . . (325) 453-4555
San Angelo ISD (PK-12)
   2009-10 Enrollment: 14,492 . . . . (325) 947-3700
Sterling City ISD (PK-12)
   2009-10 Enrollment: 200 . . . . (325) 378-4781
Tlc Academy (KG-12)
   2009-10 Enrollment: 633 . . . . (325) 224-2900
Veribest ISD (PK-12)
   2009-10 Enrollment: 258 . . . . (325) 655-4912
Wall ISD (PK-12)
   2009-10 Enrollment: 1,040 . . . . (325) 651-7790
Water Valley ISD (PK-12)
   2009-10 Enrollment: 339 . . . . (325) 484-2478

Four-year College(s)

Angelo State University (Public)
   Fall 2009 Enrollment: 6,387 . . . . (325) 942-2555
   2010-11 Tuition: In-state $5,672; Out-of-state $13,112

Vocational/Technical School(s)

American Commercial College (Private, For-profit)
Fall 2009 Enrollment: 186 . . . . (325) 942-6797
2010-11 Tuition: $12,700
Texas College of Cosmetology (Private, For-profit)
Fall 2009 Enrollment: 57 . . . . (325) 659-2622
2010-11 Tuition: $8,915

Housing: Homeownership rate: 63.1% (2010); Median home value: $89,510 (2010); Median contract rent: $523 per month (2005-2009 5-year est.); Median year structure built: 1971 (2005-2009 5-year est.).

Hospitals: Baptist Memorials (322 beds); River Crest Hospital (80 beds); San Angelo Community Medical Center (168 beds); Shannon Medical Center (400 beds); Shannon Medical Center-St. John's Campus (401 beds)

Safety: Violent crime rate: 39.9 per 10,000 population; Property crime rate: 460.3 per 10,000 population (2009).

Newspapers: San Angelo Standard Times (Local news; Circulation 29,900); West Texas Angelus (Regional news; Circulation 17,500)

Transportation: Commute to work: 89.1% car, 0.5% public transportation, 4.8% walk, 2.9% work from home (2005-2009 5-year est.); Travel time to work: 57.6% less than 15 minutes, 33.4% 15 to 30 minutes, 4.2% 30 to 45 minutes, 1.2% 45 to 60 minutes, 3.6% 60 minutes or more (2005-2009 5-year est.)

Airports: San Angelo Regional/Mathis Field (primary service)

Additional Information Contacts

City of San Angelo . . . . (325) 481-2727
http://www.sanangelotexas.org
San Angelo Chamber of Commerce . . . . (325) 655-4136
http://www.sanangelo.org

VANCOURT (unincorporated postal area, zip code 76955). Covers a land area of 36.343 square miles and a water area of 0 square miles. Located at 31.30° N. Lat; 100.12° W. Long. Elevation is 1,867 feet.

Population: 108 (2000); Race: 68.4% White, 0.0% Black, 0.0% Asian, 31.6% Other, 35.9% Hispanic of any race (2000); Density: 3.0 persons per square mile (2000); Age: 37.6% under 18, 13.7% over 64 (2000); Marriage status: 6.4% never married, 87.2% now married, 6.4% widowed, 0.0% divorced (2000); Foreign born: 16.2% (2000); Ancestry (includes multiple ancestries): 12.0% Irish, 11.1% German, 9.4% American, 2.6% English (2000).

Economy: Employment by occupation: 26.7% management, 11.1% professional, 17.8% services, 13.3% sales, 11.1% farming, 20.0% construction, 0.0% production (2000).

Income: Per capita income: $11,691 (2000); Median household income: $33,750 (2000); Poverty rate: 179.1% (2000).

Education: Percent of population age 25 and over with: High school diploma (including GED) or higher: 75.4% (2000); Bachelor's degree or higher: 22.8% (2000).

Housing: Homeownership rate: 55.6% (2000); Median home value: $76,400 (2000); Median contract rent: n/a per month (2000); Median year structure built: 1982 (2000).

Transportation: Commute to work: 84.4% car, 0.0% public transportation, 11.1% walk, 4.4% work from home (2000); Travel time to work: 37.2% less than 15 minutes, 27.9% 15 to 30 minutes, 23.3% 30 to 45 minutes, 0.0% 45 to 60 minutes, 11.6% 60 minutes or more (2000)

Travis County

Located in south central Texas; drained by the Colorado River. Covers a land area of 989.30 square miles, a water area of 32.77 square miles, and is located in the Central Time Zone at 30.32° N. Lat., 97.77° W. Long. The county was founded in 1840. County seat is Austin.

Travis County is part of the Austin-Round Rock-San Marcos, TX Metropolitan Statistical Area. The entire metro area includes: Bastrop County, TX; Caldwell County, TX; Hays County, TX; Travis County, TX; Williamson County, TX

Weather Station: Austin Municipal Arpt									Elevation: 621 feet		
	Jan	Feb	Mar	Apr	May	Jun	Jul	Aug	Sep	Oct	Nov	Dec
High	62	65	72	80	86	92	96	97	91	82	71	63
Low	42	45	51	58	67	72	74	75	70	61	51	42
Precip	2.1	2.0	2.8	2.1	4.4	4.1	1.8	2.4	2.7	3.9	3.1	2.4
Snow	0.4	0.2	tr	tr	tr	tr	0.0	0.0	0.0	0.0	0.1	tr

High and Low temperatures in degrees Fahrenheit; Precipitation and Snow in inches

Population: 576,407 (1990); 812,280 (2000); 1,017,272 (2010); 1,115,176 (2015 projected); Race: 64.8% White, 8.1% Black, 5.5% Asian, 21.5% Other, 33.4% Hispanic of any race (2010); Density: 1,028.3 persons per square mile (2010); Average household size: 2.51 (2010); Median age: 34.5 (2010); Males per 100 females: 104.5 (2010).

Religion: Five largest groups: 20.4% Catholic Church, 9.5% Southern Baptist Convention, 2.7% The United Methodist Church, 1.7% Jewish Estimate, 1.6% Episcopal Church (2000).

Economy: Unemployment rate: 7.4% (June 2011); Total civilian labor force: 565,717 (June 2011); Leading industries: 12.0% professional, scientific & technical services; 11.7% accommodation & food services; 11.4% retail trade (2009); Farms: 1,214 totaling 262,481 acres (2007); Companies that employ 500 or more persons: 70 (2009); Companies that employ 100 to 499 persons: 639 (2009); Companies that employ less than 100 persons: 27,067 (2009); Black-owned businesses: 4,072 (2007); Hispanic-owned businesses: 13,656 (2007); Asian-owned businesses: 5,121 (2007); Women-owned businesses: 29,153 (2007); Retail sales per capita: $32,023 (2010). Single-family building permits issued: 3,140 (2010); Multi-family building permits issued: 1,257 (2010).

Income: Per capita income: $29,944 (2010); Median household income: $55,338 (2010); Average household income: $76,159 (2010); Percent of households with income of $100,000 or more: 22.4% (2010); Poverty rate: 16.0% (2009); Bankruptcy rate: 1.82% (2010).

Taxes: Total county taxes per capita: $370 (2007); County property taxes per capita: $351 (2007).

Education: Percent of population age 25 and over with: High school diploma (including GED) or higher: 85.6% (2010); Bachelor's degree or higher: 42.7% (2010); Master's degree or higher: 16.1% (2010).

Housing: Homeownership rate: 54.2% (2010); Median home value: $193,722 (2010); Median contract rent: $722 per month (2005-2009 5-year est.); Median year structure built: 1985 (2005-2009 5-year est.)

Health: Birth rate: 158.7 per 10,000 population (2009); Death rate: 44.6 per 10,000 population (2009); Age-adjusted cancer mortality rate: 167.0 deaths per 100,000 population (2007); Number of physicians: 28.9 per 10,000 population (2008); Hospital beds: 26.6 per 10,000 population (2007); Hospital admissions: 1,190.1 per 10,000 population (2007).

Environment: Air Quality Index: 76.8% good, 22.5% moderate, 0.7% unhealthy for sensitive individuals, 0.0% unhealthy (percent of days in 2008)

Elections: 2008 Presidential election results: 63.5% Obama, 34.3% McCain, 0.2% Nader

Additional Information Contacts

Travis County Government . . . . (512) 854-9020
http://www.co.travis.tx.us
Austin Chamber of Commerce. (512) 478-9383
http://www.austinchamber.com
City of Austin . . . . (512) 974-2000
http://www.ci.austin.tx.us
City of Lago Vista. . . . . (512) 267-1155
http://www.lagovistatexas.org
City of Lakeway . . . . (512) 314-7500
http://www.cityoflakeway.com
City of Pflugerville . . . . (512) 990-6101
http://www.cityofpflugerville.com
City of West Lake Hills. . . . . (512) 327-3628
http://www.westlakehills.org
Greater Austin Hispanic Chamber of Commerce. . . . . (512) 476-7502
http://www.gahcc.org
Lago Vista & Jonestown Area Chamber of Commerce . . . . (512) 267-7952
http://www.lagovista.org
Lake Travis Chamber of Commerce . . . . (512) 263-5833
http://www.laketravischamber.com
Swedish American Chamber of Commerce. . . . . (512) 879-4402
http://www.sacctx.com
Village of The Hills. . . . . (512) 261-6281
http://www.villageofthehills.org

Travis County Communities

AUSTIN (city). County seat. Covers a land area of 251.520 square miles and a water area of 6.908 square miles. Located at 30.30° N. Lat; 97.74° W. Long. Elevation is 489 feet.

History: The first settlement at the location of Austin was called Waterloo. In 1839 this site was selected to be the state capital and the name was changed to honor Stephen F. Austin (1793-1836). The capitol building constructed that year was surrounded by an eight-foot-high stockade. When Austin was incorporated in 1840, Sam Houston lived here, as well as Mirabeau B. Lamar, President of the Republic of Texas, who had chosen the site. Transportation was a problem for early Austin, where it took a freight wagon a month to make the round trip to Houston. The Pony Express came through once a week with the mail. The University of Texas, which opened in Austin in 1883, had been part of the plan laid out in 1839. Along with a number of other institutions of higher learning, the University made Austin an educational center.

Population: 499,053 (1990); 656,562 (2000); 764,479 (2010); 824,376 (2015 projected); Race: 62.0% White, 8.0% Black, 5.9% Asian, 24.1% Other, 36.2% Hispanic of any race (2010); Density: 3,039.4 persons per square mile (2010); Average household size: 2.41 (2010); Median age: 33.8 (2010); Males per 100 females: 105.7 (2010); Marriage status: 42.1% never married, 44.0% now married, 3.5% widowed, 10.5% divorced (2005-2009 5-year est.); Foreign born: 19.7% (2005-2009 5-year est.); Ancestry (includes multiple ancestries): 13.1% German, 9.4% English, 8.8% Irish, 3.3% American, 2.9% French (2005-2009 5-year est.).

Economy: Unemployment rate: 7.0% (June 2011); Total civilian labor force: 436,336 (June 2011); Single-family building permits issued: 1,664 (2010); Multi-family building permits issued: 1,110 (2010); Employment by occupation: 15.6% management, 27.4% professional, 16.6% services, 22.7% sales, 0.1% farming, 10.9% construction, 6.6% production (2005-2009 5-year est.).

Income: Per capita income: $28,216 (2010); Median household income: $49,571 (2010); Average household income: $69,121 (2010); Percent of households with income of $100,000 or more: 19.0% (2010); Poverty rate: 17.5% (2005-2009 5-year est.).

Taxes: Total city taxes per capita: $664 (2007); City property taxes per capita: $330 (2007).

Education: Percent of population age 25 and over with: High school diploma (including GED) or higher: 84.1% (2010); Bachelor's degree or higher: 42.7% (2010); Master's degree or higher: 16.6% (2010).

School District(s)

American Youthworks Charter School (09-12)
 2009-10 Enrollment: 310 . . . . (512) 236-6100
Austin Can Academy Charter School (09-12)
 2009-10 Enrollment: 359 . . . . (214) 943-2244
Austin Discovery School (KG-06)
 2009-10 Enrollment: 317 . . . . (512) 674-0700
Austin ISD (PK-12)
 2009-10 Enrollment: 84,676 . . . . (512) 414-1700
Cedars International Academy (PK-07)
 2009-10 Enrollment: 217 . . . . (512) 419-1551
Del Valle ISD (PK-12)
 2009-10 Enrollment: 10,158 . . . . (512) 386-3010
Dripping Springs ISD (PK-12)
 2009-10 Enrollment: 4,331 . . . . (512) 858-3000
Eanes ISD (PK-12)
 2009-10 Enrollment: 7,498 . . . . (512) 732-9001
Eden Park Academy (KG-08)
 2009-10 Enrollment: 188 . . . . (512) 383-0613
Harmony School of Science (Austin) (KG-08)
 2009-10 Enrollment: 526 . . . . (512) 821-1700
Harmony Science Academy (Austin) (KG-12)
 2009-10 Enrollment: 1,104 . . . . (512) 251-5000
Kipp Austin Public Schools Inc (05-10)
 2009-10 Enrollment: 637 . . . . (512) 637-6870
Lago Vista ISD (PK-12)
 2009-10 Enrollment: 1,225 . . . . (512) 267-8300
Lake Travis ISD (PK-12)
 2009-10 Enrollment: 6,577 . . . . (512) 533-6000
Leander ISD (PK-12)
 2009-10 Enrollment: 30,454 . . . . (512) 434-5000
Manor ISD (PK-12)
 2009-10 Enrollment: 6,932 . . . . (512) 278-4000
Nyos Charter School (PK-12)
 2009-10 Enrollment: 678 . . . . (512) 836-7620
Pflugerville ISD (PK-12)
 2009-10 Enrollment: 22,060 . . . . (512) 594-0000
Responsive Education Solutions (KG-12)
 2009-10 Enrollment: 5,022 . . . . (972) 316-3663
Round Rock ISD (PK-12)
 2009-10 Enrollment: 43,008 . . . . (512) 464-5000

Star Charter School (01-12)
 2009-10 Enrollment: 304 . . . . (512) 989-2672
Texas Empowerment Academy (01-09)
 2009-10 Enrollment: 227 . . . . (512) 494-1076
Texas Sch for the Blind & Visually Impaired (02-12)
 2009-10 Enrollment: 129 . . . . (512) 454-8631
Texas Sch for the Deaf (PK-12)
 2009-10 Enrollment: 499 . . . . (512) 462-5353
The East Austin College Prep Academy (06-06)
 2009-10 Enrollment: 88 . . . . (512) 287-5000
University of Texas Elementary Charter School (PK-05)
 2009-10 Enrollment: 256 . . . . (512) 495-9705
University of Texas University Charter School (KG-12)
 2009-10 Enrollment: 907 . . . . (512) 471-5652

Four-year College(s)

Academy of Oriental Medicine at Austin (Private, For-profit)
 Fall 2009 Enrollment: 204 . . . . (512) 454-1188
Austin Graduate School of Theology (Private, Not-for-profit, Churches of Christ)
 Fall 2009 Enrollment: 56 . . . . (512) 476-2772
Austin Presbyterian Theological Seminary (Private, Not-for-profit, Presbyterian Church (USA))
 Fall 2009 Enrollment: 143 . . . . (512) 472-6736
Concordia University Texas (Private, Not-for-profit, Lutheran Church - Missouri Synod)
 Fall 2009 Enrollment: 2,242 . . . . (512) 313-3000
 2010-11 Tuition: In-state $21,700; Out-of-state $21,700
Episcopal Theological Seminary of the Southwest (Private, Not-for-profit, Protestant Episcopal)
 Fall 2009 Enrollment: 108 . . . . (512) 472-4133
Huston-Tillotson University (Private, Not-for-profit, Historically black, Multiple Protestant Denomination)
 Fall 2009 Enrollment: 882 . . . . (512) 505-3000
 2010-11 Tuition: In-state $12,430; Out-of-state $12,430
ITT Technical Institute-Austin (Private, For-profit)
 Fall 2009 Enrollment: 787 . . . . (512) 467-6800
 2010-11 Tuition: In-state $18,048; Out-of-state $18,048
National American University-Austin (Private, For-profit)
 Fall 2009 Enrollment: 129 . . . . (512) 651-4100
 2010-11 Tuition: In-state $11,755; Out-of-state $11,755
Saint Edward's University (Private, Not-for-profit, Roman Catholic)
 Fall 2009 Enrollment: 5,293 . . . . (512) 448-8400
 2010-11 Tuition: In-state $26,484; Out-of-state $26,484
Texas College of Traditional Chinese Medicine (Private, For-profit)
 Fall 2009 Enrollment: 86 . . . . (512) 444-8082
The Art Institute of Austin (Private, For-profit)
 Fall 2009 Enrollment: 873 . . . . (512) 691-1707
 2010-11 Tuition: In-state $17,568; Out-of-state $17,568
The University of Texas at Austin (Public)
 Fall 2009 Enrollment: 50,995 . . . . (512) 471-3434
 2010-11 Tuition: In-state $9,418; Out-of-state $31,218
University of Phoenix-Austin Campus (Private, For-profit)
 Fall 2009 Enrollment: 505 . . . . (512) 344-1450
 2010-11 Tuition: In-state $11,640; Out-of-state $11,640

Two-year College(s)

Academy of Health Care Professions (Private, For-profit)
 Fall 2009 Enrollment: 244 . . . . (512) 892-2835
Allied Health Careers (Private, For-profit)
 Fall 2009 Enrollment: 371 . . . . (512) 892-5210
Austin Community College District (Public)
 Fall 2009 Enrollment: 40,248 . . . . (512) 223-7000
 2010-11 Tuition: In-state $4,980; Out-of-state $9,120
Kussad Institute of Court Reporting (Private, For-profit)
 Fall 2009 Enrollment: 27 . . . . (512) 443-7286
 2010-11 Tuition: In-state $8,500; Out-of-state $8,500
Southwest Institute of Technology (Private, For-profit)
 Fall 2009 Enrollment: 21 . . . . (512) 892-2640
Texas Culinary Academy (Private, For-profit)
 Fall 2009 Enrollment: 1,020 . . . . (888) 553-2433
 2010-11 Tuition: In-state $17,765; Out-of-state $17,765
Virginia College-Austin (Private, For-profit)
 Fall 2009 Enrollment: 865 . . . . (512) 371-3500
 2010-11 Tuition: In-state $11,800; Out-of-state $11,800

Vocational/Technical School(s)

Baldwin Beauty School (Private, For-profit)
Fall 2009 Enrollment: 85 . . . . (512) 441-6898
2010-11 Tuition: $12,100
Baldwin Beauty School (Private, For-profit)
Fall 2009 Enrollment: 124 . . . . (512) 458-4127
2010-11 Tuition: $12,100
Capitol City Careers (Private, For-profit)
Fall 2009 Enrollment: 50 . . . . (512) 892-2640
2010-11 Tuition: $23,674
Capitol City Trade and Technical School (Private, For-profit)
Fall 2009 Enrollment: 215 . . . . (512) 444-3257
2010-11 Tuition: $23,292
Culinary Academy of Austin (Private, For-profit)
Fall 2009 Enrollment: 25 . . . . (512) 451-5743
2010-11 Tuition: $21,000
Everest Institute-Austin (Private, For-profit)
Fall 2009 Enrollment: 1,489. . . . . (512) 928-1933
2010-11 Tuition: $14,810
MediaTech Institute-Austin (Private, For-profit)
Fall 2009 Enrollment: 121 . . . . (512) 447-2002
Regency Beauty Institute-Austin (Private, For-profit)
Fall 2009 Enrollment: 73 . . . . (800) 787-6456
2010-11 Tuition: $16,075
Southern Careers Institute Inc (Private, For-profit)
Fall 2009 Enrollment: 226 . . . . (512) 437-7507
2010-11 Tuition: $13,600
Housing: Homeownership rate: 45.9% (2010); Median home value: $189,950 (2010); Median contract rent: $716 per month (2005-2009 5-year est.); Median year structure built: 1982 (2005-2009 5-year est.).
Hospitals: Austin State Hospital (308 beds); Austin Surgical Hospital; Brackenridge Hospital; Cornerstone Hospital of Austin at North Austin (133 beds); HealthSouth Rehabilitation Hospital of Austin (83 beds); Heart Hospital of Austin (58 beds); Northwest Hills Surgical Hospital; Seton Medical Center (471 beds); Seton Northwest Hospital (103 beds); Seton Southwest Hospital (17 beds); Shoal Creek Hospital (151 beds); South Austin Hospital (252 beds); St. David's Medical Center (518 beds); St. David's Rehabiltation Center (107 beds); Texas NeuroRehab Center (126 beds); The Hospital at Westlake Medical Center
Safety: Violent crime rate: 52.3 per 10,000 population; Property crime rate: 624.6 per 10,000 population (2009).
Newspapers: Austin American-Statesman (Local news; Circulation 173,579); Austin American-Statesman - Williamson County Bureau (Local news); The Austin Chronicle (Community news); The Catholic Spirit (Regional news; Circulation 32,000); The Christian Science Monitor - Southwest Bureau (National news); Club Deportes (Circulation 5,000); The Dallas Morning News - Austin Bureau (Local news); El Mundo (Local news; Circulation 35,000); El Norte de Austin (Regional news; Circulation 2,500); El Paso Times - Austin Bureau (Local news); Fort Worth Star-Telegram - Austin Bureau (Local news); La Prensa-Austin (Local news; Circulation 10,000); Lake Travis View (Community news; Circulation 3,500); Lake and Country Living (Local news; Circulation 15,000); The Lone Star Report (Regional news); Rumbo de Austin (Local news; Circulation 25,000); San Angelo Standard Times - Austin Bureau (Local news); San Antonio Express-News - Austin Bureau (Regional news); Villager News (Regional news; Circulation 6,000); The Villager (Local news; Circulation 6,000); West Austin News (Community news; Circulation 3,200); Westlake Picayune (Community news; Circulation 3,500); ¡Ahora Sí! (Local news)
Transportation: Commute to work: 84.1% car, 5.0% public transportation, 1.9% walk, 5.2% work from home (2005-2009 5-year est.); Travel time to work: 26.6% less than 15 minutes, 44.5% 15 to 30 minutes, 19.9% 30 to 45 minutes, 4.8% 45 to 60 minutes, 4.2% 60 minutes or more (2005-2009 5-year est.); Amtrak: train service available.
Airports: Austin-Bergstrom International (primary service/medium hub); Horseshoe Bay Resort (general aviation)
Additional Information Contacts
Austin Chamber of Commerce. . . . . (512) 478-9383
http://www.austinchamber.com
City of Austin . . . . (512) 974-2000
http://www.ci.austin.tx.us
Greater Austin Hispanic Chamber of Commerce. . . . . (512) 476-7502
http://www.gahcc.org
Lake Travis Chamber of Commerce . . . . (512) 263-5833
http://www.laketravischamber.com
Swedish American Chamber of Commerce. . . . . (512) 879-4402
http://www.sacctx.com

BARTON CREEK (CDP). Covers a land area of 5.361 square miles and a water area of 0 square miles. Located at 30.28° N. Lat; 97.86° W. Long. Elevation is 820 feet.
Population: 208 (1990); 1,589 (2000); 1,714 (2010); 1,945 (2015 projected); Race: 82.3% White, 2.7% Black, 1.7% Asian, 13.3% Other, 24.4% Hispanic of any race (2010); Density: 319.7 persons per square mile (2010); Average household size: 2.42 (2010); Median age: 43.1 (2010); Males per 100 females: 101.9 (2010); Marriage status: 20.2% never married, 70.4% now married, 4.3% widowed, 5.2% divorced (2005-2009 5-year est.); Foreign born: 6.2% (2005-2009 5-year est.); Ancestry (includes multiple ancestries): 23.6% German, 17.8% English, 9.5% Irish, 6.6% American, 5.8% Scottish (2005-2009 5-year est.).
Economy: Employment by occupation: 40.1% management, 23.9% professional, 5.0% services, 28.8% sales, 0.0% farming, 1.3% construction, 1.0% production (2005-2009 5-year est.).
Income: Per capita income: $68,968 (2010); Median household income: $111,919 (2010); Average household income: $166,929 (2010); Percent of households with income of $100,000 or more: 52.9% (2010); Poverty rate: 3.5% (2005-2009 5-year est.).
Education: Percent of population age 25 and over with: High school diploma (including GED) or higher: 90.2% (2010); Bachelor's degree or higher: 62.6% (2010); Master's degree or higher: 28.0% (2010).
Housing: Homeownership rate: 66.4% (2010); Median home value: $823,198 (2010); Median contract rent: $906 per month (2005-2009 5-year est.); Median year structure built: 1998 (2005-2009 5-year est.).
Transportation: Commute to work: 78.9% car, 0.0% public transportation, 1.7% walk, 18.1% work from home (2005-2009 5-year est.); Travel time to work: 20.7% less than 15 minutes, 38.4% 15 to 30 minutes, 39.7% 30 to 45 minutes, 1.1% 45 to 60 minutes, 0.0% 60 minutes or more (2005-2009 5-year est.)

BEE CAVE (village). Covers a land area of 2.603 square miles and a water area of 0 square miles. Located at 30.30° N. Lat; 97.95° W. Long. Elevation is 919 feet.
Population: 273 (1990); 656 (2000); 1,253 (2010); 1,462 (2015 projected); Race: 88.6% White, 0.6% Black, 6.5% Asian, 4.3% Other, 6.1% Hispanic of any race (2010); Density: 481.4 persons per square mile (2010); Average household size: 3.21 (2010); Median age: 37.4 (2010); Males per 100 females: 101.4 (2010); Marriage status: 19.0% never married, 70.3% now married, 2.6% widowed, 8.0% divorced (2005-2009 5-year est.); Foreign born: 9.9% (2005-2009 5-year est.); Ancestry (includes multiple ancestries): 19.3% Irish, 16.2% German, 13.7% English, 7.4% Italian, 5.9% American (2005-2009 5-year est.).
Economy: Single-family building permits issued: 153 (2010); Multi-family building permits issued: 0 (2010); Employment by occupation: 28.0% management, 29.0% professional, 8.7% services, 26.7% sales, 0.4% farming, 2.8% construction, 4.4% production (2005-2009 5-year est.).
Income: Per capita income: $51,876 (2010); Median household income: $131,667 (2010); Average household income: $166,058 (2010); Percent of households with income of $100,000 or more: 65.6% (2010); Poverty rate: 4.4% (2005-2009 5-year est.).
Taxes: Total city taxes per capita: $2,207 (2007); City property taxes per capita: $28 (2007).
Education: Percent of population age 25 and over with: High school diploma (including GED) or higher: 96.7% (2010); Bachelor's degree or higher: 68.4% (2010); Master's degree or higher: 27.9% (2010).
Housing: Homeownership rate: 95.1% (2010); Median home value: $443,333 (2010); Median contract rent: $949 per month (2005-2009 5-year est.); Median year structure built: 2002 (2005-2009 5-year est.).
Safety: Violent crime rate: 50.1 per 10,000 population; Property crime rate: 607.5 per 10,000 population (2009).
Transportation: Commute to work: 77.9% car, 0.0% public transportation, 6.8% walk, 14.2% work from home (2005-2009 5-year est.); Travel time to work: 26.4% less than 15 minutes, 26.3% 15 to 30 minutes, 30.5% 30 to 45 minutes, 14.9% 45 to 60 minutes, 1.8% 60 minutes or more (2005-2009 5-year est.)

BRIARCLIFF (village). Covers a land area of 1.383 square miles and a water area of 0.077 square miles. Located at 30.41° N. Lat; 98.04° W. Long. Elevation is 758 feet.
Population: 335 (1990); 895 (2000); 1,021 (2010); 1,123 (2015 projected); Race: 95.7% White, 0.1% Black, 0.2% Asian, 4.0% Other, 7.5% Hispanic of any race (2010); Density: 738.1 persons per square mile (2010); Average household size: 2.42 (2010); Median age: 46.5 (2010); Males per

100 females: 102.2 (2010); Marriage status: 16.1% never married, 69.0% now married, 3.4% widowed, 11.5% divorced (2005-2009 5-year est.); Foreign born: 5.3% (2005-2009 5-year est.); Ancestry (includes multiple ancestries): 23.8% German, 15.6% Irish, 13.8% American, 9.3% English, 6.3% Scottish (2005-2009 5-year est.).
Economy: Employment by occupation: 22.6% management, 17.6% professional, 9.4% services, 35.7% sales, 0.0% farming, 11.3% construction, 3.4% production (2005-2009 5-year est.).
Income: Per capita income: $44,544 (2010); Median household income: $86,538 (2010); Average household income: $107,536 (2010); Percent of households with income of $100,000 or more: 40.0% (2010); Poverty rate: 3.2% (2005-2009 5-year est.).
Taxes: Total city taxes per capita: $189 (2007); City property taxes per capita: $99 (2007).
Education: Percent of population age 25 and over with: High school diploma (including GED) or higher: 94.6% (2010); Bachelor's degree or higher: 42.4% (2010); Master's degree or higher: 13.3% (2010).
Housing: Homeownership rate: 87.4% (2010); Median home value: $242,083 (2010); Median contract rent: $1,296 per month (2005-2009 5-year est.); Median year structure built: 1996 (2005-2009 5-year est.).
Transportation: Commute to work: 89.8% car, 0.0% public transportation, 1.9% walk, 8.4% work from home (2005-2009 5-year est.); Travel time to work: 17.3% less than 15 minutes, 12.7% 15 to 30 minutes, 33.8% 30 to 45 minutes, 20.5% 45 to 60 minutes, 15.7% 60 minutes or more (2005-2009 5-year est.)

CREEDMOOR (city).
Covers a land area of 2.094 square miles and a water area of 0 square miles. Located at 30.09° N. Lat; 97.74° W. Long. Elevation is 633 feet.
Population: 194 (1990); 211 (2000); 253 (2010); 284 (2015 projected); Race: 74.7% White, 5.9% Black, 0.8% Asian, 18.6% Other, 58.5% Hispanic of any race (2010); Density: 120.8 persons per square mile (2010); Average household size: 3.19 (2010); Median age: 34.6 (2010); Males per 100 females: 88.8 (2010); Marriage status: 21.7% never married, 63.0% now married, 5.1% widowed, 10.1% divorced (2005-2009 5-year est.); Foreign born: 7.4% (2005-2009 5-year est.); Ancestry (includes multiple ancestries): 21.5% Irish, 17.2% German, 6.7% American, 5.5% English, 4.9% Dutch (2005-2009 5-year est.).
Economy: Single-family building permits issued: 2 (2010); Multi-family building permits issued: 0 (2010); Employment by occupation: 10.5% management, 4.7% professional, 24.4% services, 16.3% sales, 0.0% farming, 29.1% construction, 15.1% production (2005-2009 5-year est.).
Income: Per capita income: $21,256 (2010); Median household income: $54,375 (2010); Average household income: $69,589 (2010); Percent of households with income of $100,000 or more: 15.2% (2010); Poverty rate: 8.0% (2005-2009 5-year est.).
Taxes: Total city taxes per capita: $347 (2007); City property taxes per capita: $163 (2007).
Education: Percent of population age 25 and over with: High school diploma (including GED) or higher: 70.4% (2010); Bachelor's degree or higher: 12.6% (2010); Master's degree or higher: 4.4% (2010).
School District(s)
Del Valle ISD (PK-12)
    2009-10 Enrollment: 10,158 . . . . (512) 386-3010
Housing: Homeownership rate: 82.3% (2010); Median home value: $125,000 (2010); Median contract rent: $704 per month (2005-2009 5-year est.); Median year structure built: 1971 (2005-2009 5-year est.).
Transportation: Commute to work: 95.3% car, 0.0% public transportation, 0.0% walk, 0.0% work from home (2005-2009 5-year est.); Travel time to work: 8.1% less than 15 minutes, 32.6% 15 to 30 minutes, 51.2% 30 to 45 minutes, 8.1% 45 to 60 minutes, 0.0% 60 minutes or more (2005-2009 5-year est.)

DEL VALLE (unincorporated postal area, zip code 78617).
Covers a land area of 77.382 square miles and a water area of 0 square miles. Located at 30.16° N. Lat; 97.62° W. Long. Elevation is 486 feet.
Population: 15,227 (2000); Race: 60.1% White, 12.9% Black, 1.8% Asian, 25.2% Other, 48.2% Hispanic of any race (2000); Density: 196.8 persons per square mile (2000); Age: 28.9% under 18, 5.1% over 64 (2000); Marriage status: 31.6% never married, 54.4% now married, 3.1% widowed, 10.9% divorced (2000); Foreign born: 14.3% (2000); Ancestry (includes multiple ancestries): 7.8% German, 5.2% Irish, 4.9% American, 4.7% English (2000).

Economy: Employment by occupation: 9.0% management, 10.8% professional, 15.2% services, 23.9% sales, 0.0% farming, 23.0% construction, 18.1% production (2000).
Income: Per capita income: $15,078 (2000); Median household income: $40,392 (2000); Poverty rate: 179.1% (2000).
Education: Percent of population age 25 and over with: High school diploma (including GED) or higher: 63.2% (2000); Bachelor's degree or higher: 8.0% (2000).
School District(s)
Del Valle ISD (PK-12)
    2009-10 Enrollment: 10,158 . . . . (512) 386-3010
Housing: Homeownership rate: 70.7% (2000); Median home value: $82,900 (2000); Median contract rent: $503 per month (2000); Median year structure built: 1986 (2000).
Transportation: Commute to work: 94.9% car, 1.2% public transportation, 1.2% walk, 1.6% work from home (2000); Travel time to work: 8.1% less than 15 minutes, 28.0% 15 to 30 minutes, 39.6% 30 to 45 minutes, 10.0% 45 to 60 minutes, 14.3% 60 minutes or more (2000)

GARFIELD (CDP).
Covers a land area of 13.684 square miles and a water area of 0.200 square miles. Located at 30.18° N. Lat; 97.55° W. Long. Elevation is 479 feet.
Population: 1,233 (1990); 1,660 (2000); 1,694 (2010); 1,776 (2015 projected); Race: 59.4% White, 3.2% Black, 1.1% Asian, 36.3% Other, 50.5% Hispanic of any race (2010); Density: 123.8 persons per square mile (2010); Average household size: 3.13 (2010); Median age: 34.3 (2010); Males per 100 females: 108.1 (2010); Marriage status: 36.4% never married, 47.3% now married, 6.6% widowed, 9.6% divorced (2005-2009 5-year est.); Foreign born: 11.6% (2005-2009 5-year est.); Ancestry (includes multiple ancestries): 23.4% English, 9.8% German, 8.7% Irish, 3.9% American, 2.0% Scottish (2005-2009 5-year est.).
Economy: Employment by occupation: 11.0% management, 8.9% professional, 17.5% services, 19.7% sales, 0.0% farming, 12.8% construction, 30.1% production (2005-2009 5-year est.).
Income: Per capita income: $19,304 (2010); Median household income: $45,121 (2010); Average household income: $59,616 (2010); Percent of households with income of $100,000 or more: 6.7% (2010); Poverty rate: 23.8% (2005-2009 5-year est.).
Education: Percent of population age 25 and over with: High school diploma (including GED) or higher: 72.1% (2010); Bachelor's degree or higher: 13.8% (2010); Master's degree or higher: 2.6% (2010).
Housing: Homeownership rate: 78.4% (2010); Median home value: $111,066 (2010); Median contract rent: $620 per month (2005-2009 5-year est.); Median year structure built: 1988 (2005-2009 5-year est.).
Transportation: Commute to work: 67.0% car, 0.0% public transportation, 0.0% walk, 7.0% work from home (2005-2009 5-year est.); Travel time to work: 2.1% less than 15 minutes, 20.8% 15 to 30 minutes, 49.5% 30 to 45 minutes, 17.3% 45 to 60 minutes, 10.2% 60 minutes or more (2005-2009 5-year est.)

HUDSON BEND (CDP).
Covers a land area of 3.986 square miles and a water area of 2.694 square miles. Located at 30.41° N. Lat; 97.92° W. Long. Elevation is 755 feet.
Population: 1,365 (1990); 2,369 (2000); 3,047 (2010); 3,478 (2015 projected); Race: 92.4% White, 0.3% Black, 0.9% Asian, 6.4% Other, 8.3% Hispanic of any race (2010); Density: 764.5 persons per square mile (2010); Average household size: 2.23 (2010); Median age: 46.1 (2010); Males per 100 females: 115.6 (2010); Marriage status: 25.7% never married, 53.3% now married, 4.9% widowed, 16.1% divorced (2005-2009 5-year est.); Foreign born: 11.2% (2005-2009 5-year est.); Ancestry (includes multiple ancestries): 28.2% German, 17.2% Irish, 12.0% English, 4.7% Polish, 4.3% Scottish (2005-2009 5-year est.).
Economy: Employment by occupation: 20.3% management, 21.3% professional, 14.3% services, 28.1% sales, 0.7% farming, 6.8% construction, 8.5% production (2005-2009 5-year est.).
Income: Per capita income: $37,473 (2010); Median household income: $61,055 (2010); Average household income: $83,917 (2010); Percent of households with income of $100,000 or more: 25.3% (2010); Poverty rate: 11.0% (2005-2009 5-year est.).
Education: Percent of population age 25 and over with: High school diploma (including GED) or higher: 94.9% (2010); Bachelor's degree or higher: 44.5% (2010); Master's degree or higher: 15.1% (2010).
Housing: Homeownership rate: 79.7% (2010); Median home value: $301,761 (2010); Median contract rent: $765 per month (2005-2009 5-year est.); Median year structure built: 1985 (2005-2009 5-year est.).

Transportation: Commute to work: 80.7% car, 0.0% public transportation, 3.2% walk, 12.9% work from home (2005-2009 5-year est.); Travel time to work: 31.1% less than 15 minutes, 22.4% 15 to 30 minutes, 21.4% 30 to 45 minutes, 13.6% 45 to 60 minutes, 11.5% 60 minutes or more (2005-2009 5-year est.)

JONESTOWN (city). Covers a land area of 4.695 square miles and a water area of 0.596 square miles. Located at 30.48° N. Lat; 97.92° W. Long. Elevation is 814 feet.
Population: 1,182 (1990); 1,681 (2000); 2,355 (2010); 2,721 (2015 projected); Race: 91.6% White, 1.3% Black, 0.7% Asian, 6.4% Other, 9.7% Hispanic of any race (2010); Density: 501.6 persons per square mile (2010); Average household size: 2.48 (2010); Median age: 45.1 (2010); Males per 100 females: 109.0 (2010); Marriage status: 22.1% never married, 61.7% now married, 3.6% widowed, 12.6% divorced (2005-2009 5-year est.); Foreign born: 6.0% (2005-2009 5-year est.); Ancestry (includes multiple ancestries): 28.5% German, 11.3% Irish, 8.6% English, 8.4% Scottish, 5.8% Italian (2005-2009 5-year est.).
Economy: Single-family building permits issued: 19 (2010); Multi-family building permits issued: 0 (2010); Employment by occupation: 10.3% management, 15.7% professional, 13.3% services, 29.5% sales, 0.0% farming, 14.5% construction, 16.9% production (2005-2009 5-year est.).
Income: Per capita income: $35,054 (2010); Median household income: $62,623 (2010); Average household income: $87,429 (2010); Percent of households with income of $100,000 or more: 28.1% (2010); Poverty rate: 6.3% (2005-2009 5-year est.).
Taxes: Total city taxes per capita: $268 (2007); City property taxes per capita: $138 (2007).
Education: Percent of population age 25 and over with: High school diploma (including GED) or higher: 89.9% (2010); Bachelor's degree or higher: 29.8% (2010); Master's degree or higher: 8.5% (2010).
Housing: Homeownership rate: 79.6% (2010); Median home value: $182,407 (2010); Median contract rent: $789 per month (2005-2009 5-year est.); Median year structure built: 1984 (2005-2009 5-year est.).
Safety: Violent crime rate: 63.2 per 10,000 population; Property crime rate: 173.7 per 10,000 population (2009).
Transportation: Commute to work: 95.6% car, 0.0% public transportation, 1.0% walk, 3.3% work from home (2005-2009 5-year est.); Travel time to work: 20.6% less than 15 minutes, 30.6% 15 to 30 minutes, 25.4% 30 to 45 minutes, 10.1% 45 to 60 minutes, 13.3% 60 minutes or more (2005-2009 5-year est.)
Additional Information Contacts
Lago Vista & Jonestown Area Chamber of Commerce . . . . (512) 267-7952
http://www.lagovista.org

LAGO VISTA (city). Covers a land area of 8.712 square miles and a water area of 0.646 square miles. Located at 30.45° N. Lat; 97.99° W. Long. Elevation is 774 feet.
History: Airpower Museum.
Population: 2,205 (1990); 4,507 (2000); 6,268 (2010); 7,230 (2015 projected); Race: 92.8% White, 1.3% Black, 0.8% Asian, 5.2% Other, 10.2% Hispanic of any race (2010); Density: 719.4 persons per square mile (2010); Average household size: 2.32 (2010); Median age: 46.8 (2010); Males per 100 females: 96.2 (2010); Marriage status: 10.2% never married, 73.7% now married, 5.4% widowed, 10.6% divorced (2005-2009 5-year est.); Foreign born: 7.2% (2005-2009 5-year est.); Ancestry (includes multiple ancestries): 19.8% German, 15.9% Irish, 13.2% English, 11.6% American, 5.6% French (2005-2009 5-year est.).
Economy: Single-family building permits issued: 22 (2010); Multi-family building permits issued: 0 (2010); Employment by occupation: 19.4% management, 22.9% professional, 8.1% services, 32.5% sales, 0.0% farming, 9.5% construction, 7.7% production (2005-2009 5-year est.).
Income: Per capita income: $34,330 (2010); Median household income: $66,916 (2010); Average household income: $79,620 (2010); Percent of households with income of $100,000 or more: 26.1% (2010); Poverty rate: 4.5% (2005-2009 5-year est.).
Taxes: Total city taxes per capita: $876 (2007); City property taxes per capita: $567 (2007).
Education: Percent of population age 25 and over with: High school diploma (including GED) or higher: 91.7% (2010); Bachelor's degree or higher: 35.0% (2010); Master's degree or higher: 10.0% (2010).
School District(s)
Lago Vista ISD (PK-12)
  2009-10 Enrollment: 1,225 . . . . (512) 267-8300

Housing: Homeownership rate: 73.8% (2010); Median home value: $200,144 (2010); Median contract rent: $705 per month (2005-2009 5-year est.); Median year structure built: 1990 (2005-2009 5-year est.).
Safety: Violent crime rate: 9.2 per 10,000 population; Property crime rate: 161.4 per 10,000 population (2009).
Newspapers: North Lake Travis Log (Community news; Circulation 6,100)
Transportation: Commute to work: 90.8% car, 0.0% public transportation, 2.6% walk, 6.0% work from home (2005-2009 5-year est.); Travel time to work: 17.1% less than 15 minutes, 10.7% 15 to 30 minutes, 27.2% 30 to 45 minutes, 16.7% 45 to 60 minutes, 28.4% 60 minutes or more (2005-2009 5-year est.)
Additional Information Contacts
City of Lago Vista . . . . (512) 267-1155
http://www.lagovistatexas.org
Lago Vista & Jonestown Area Chamber of Commerce . . . . (512) 267-7952
http://www.lagovista.org

LAKEWAY (city). Covers a land area of 5.801 square miles and a water area of 0.269 square miles. Located at 30.36° N. Lat; 97.97° W. Long. Elevation is 823 feet.
History: The town of Lakeway began with the construction of a 48-room hotel, the Lakeway Inn, now Lakeway Resort and Spa, a 168-room full service resort. Ground was broken October 1962 and the grand opening was July 12, 1963.
Population: 4,342 (1990); 8,002 (2000); 11,531 (2010); 13,511 (2015 projected); Race: 95.6% White, 1.0% Black, 0.9% Asian, 2.5% Other, 5.7% Hispanic of any race (2010); Density: 1,987.7 persons per square mile (2010); Average household size: 2.62 (2010); Median age: 46.6 (2010); Males per 100 females: 97.5 (2010); Marriage status: 16.9% never married, 67.1% now married, 3.9% widowed, 12.0% divorced (2005-2009 5-year est.); Foreign born: 4.1% (2005-2009 5-year est.); Ancestry (includes multiple ancestries): 24.0% German, 18.6% English, 12.4% Irish, 9.6% American, 4.8% Swedish (2005-2009 5-year est.).
Economy: Single-family building permits issued: 69 (2010); Multi-family building permits issued: 0 (2010); Employment by occupation: 27.2% management, 31.1% professional, 3.6% services, 32.5% sales, 0.0% farming, 4.0% construction, 1.5% production (2005-2009 5-year est.).
Income: Per capita income: $45,847 (2010); Median household income: $92,839 (2010); Average household income: $120,090 (2010); Percent of households with income of $100,000 or more: 45.5% (2010); Poverty rate: 4.2% (2005-2009 5-year est.).
Taxes: Total city taxes per capita: $620 (2007); City property taxes per capita: $335 (2007).
Education: Percent of population age 25 and over with: High school diploma (including GED) or higher: 97.2% (2010); Bachelor's degree or higher: 57.7% (2010); Master's degree or higher: 20.3% (2010).
Housing: Homeownership rate: 82.1% (2010); Median home value: $336,803 (2010); Median contract rent: $886 per month (2005-2009 5-year est.); Median year structure built: 1991 (2005-2009 5-year est.).
Safety: Violent crime rate: 12.1 per 10,000 population; Property crime rate: 155.3 per 10,000 population (2009).
Transportation: Commute to work: 83.6% car, 0.0% public transportation, 0.6% walk, 15.6% work from home (2005-2009 5-year est.); Travel time to work: 22.0% less than 15 minutes, 22.9% 15 to 30 minutes, 37.1% 30 to 45 minutes, 12.1% 45 to 60 minutes, 6.0% 60 minutes or more (2005-2009 5-year est.)
Additional Information Contacts
City of Lakeway . . . . (512) 314-7500
http://www.cityoflakeway.com

LOST CREEK (CDP). Covers a land area of 3.133 square miles and a water area of 0 square miles. Located at 30.28° N. Lat; 97.83° W. Long. Elevation is 823 feet.
History: In 1972 developers began to formulate their plane for Lost Creek. The developers started building homes in Lost Creek from the back of their land out towards Loop 360. Lost Creek's area is approximately 775 acres. There are 24 plat sections with 20 residential sections. Lost Creek Boulevard curves 1.8 miles from Loop 360 down to the crystal clear waters of Barton Creek.
Population: 4,134 (1990); 4,729 (2000); 4,999 (2010); 5,375 (2015 projected); Race: 91.3% White, 0.6% Black, 5.4% Asian, 2.7% Other, 4.3% Hispanic of any race (2010); Density: 1,595.8 persons per square mile (2010); Average household size: 3.08 (2010); Median age: 41.3 (2010); Males per 100 females: 99.4 (2010); Marriage status: 16.4% never married, 74.6% now married, 1.1% widowed, 7.9% divorced (2005-2009 5-year

est.); Foreign born: 7.7% (2005-2009 5-year est.); Ancestry (includes multiple ancestries): 29.4% German, 18.8% English, 16.9% Irish, 8.8% American, 4.8% French (2005-2009 5-year est.).
Economy: Employment by occupation: 32.8% management, 40.7% professional, 3.5% services, 19.0% sales, 0.0% farming, 2.2% construction, 1.7% production (2005-2009 5-year est.).
Income: Per capita income: $54,721 (2010); Median household income: $128,915 (2010); Average household income: $168,489 (2010); Percent of households with income of $100,000 or more: 65.9% (2010); Poverty rate: 0.7% (2005-2009 5-year est.).
Education: Percent of population age 25 and over with: High school diploma (including GED) or higher: 98.1% (2010); Bachelor's degree or higher: 77.6% (2010); Master's degree or higher: 39.8% (2010).
Housing: Homeownership rate: 93.8% (2010); Median home value: $412,618 (2010); Median contract rent: $1,442 per month (2005-2009 5-year est.); Median year structure built: 1985 (2005-2009 5-year est.).
Transportation: Commute to work: 89.4% car, 0.0% public transportation, 1.0% walk, 9.0% work from home (2005-2009 5-year est.); Travel time to work: 17.1% less than 15 minutes, 52.0% 15 to 30 minutes, 19.9% 30 to 45 minutes, 10.2% 45 to 60 minutes, 0.8% 60 minutes or more (2005-2009 5-year est.)

MANCHACA (unincorporated postal area, zip code 78652). Covers a land area of 7.913 square miles and a water area of 0 square miles. Located at 30.12° N. Lat; 97.84° W. Long. Elevation is 702 feet.
Population: 3,358 (2000); Race: 81.8% White, 2.9% Black, 1.5% Asian, 13.8% Other, 20.4% Hispanic of any race (2000); Density: 424.4 persons per square mile (2000); Age: 24.4% under 18, 7.3% over 64 (2000); Marriage status: 27.2% never married, 60.7% now married, 3.7% widowed, 8.3% divorced (2000); Foreign born: 6.3% (2000); Ancestry (includes multiple ancestries): 18.9% German, 13.3% Irish, 8.7% English, 6.4% American (2000).
Economy: Employment by occupation: 16.4% management, 28.0% professional, 10.7% services, 21.0% sales, 1.1% farming, 13.3% construction, 9.6% production (2000).
Income: Per capita income: $28,000 (2000); Median household income: $69,831 (2000); Poverty rate: 179.1% (2000).
Education: Percent of population age 25 and over with: High school diploma (including GED) or higher: 88.7% (2000); Bachelor's degree or higher: 29.7% (2000).
School District(s)
Austin ISD (PK-12)
    2009-10 Enrollment: 84,676 . . . . (512) 414-1700
Housing: Homeownership rate: 88.8% (2000); Median home value: $134,800 (2000); Median contract rent: $950 per month (2000); Median year structure built: 1980 (2000).
Transportation: Commute to work: 94.1% car, 0.0% public transportation, 2.3% walk, 2.5% work from home (2000); Travel time to work: 12.6% less than 15 minutes, 41.1% 15 to 30 minutes, 25.6% 30 to 45 minutes, 13.2% 45 to 60 minutes, 7.5% 60 minutes or more (2000)

MANOR (city). Covers a land area of 1.145 square miles and a water area of 0 square miles. Located at 30.34° N. Lat; 97.55° W. Long. Elevation is 531 feet.
Population: 1,041 (1990); 1,204 (2000); 3,289 (2010); 3,857 (2015 projected); Race: 62.1% White, 14.3% Black, 0.0% Asian, 23.6% Other, 43.4% Hispanic of any race (2010); Density: 2,872.9 persons per square mile (2010); Average household size: 2.96 (2010); Median age: 35.9 (2010); Males per 100 females: 96.6 (2010); Marriage status: 28.9% never married, 56.8% now married, 3.4% widowed, 10.9% divorced (2005-2009 5-year est.); Foreign born: 8.3% (2005-2009 5-year est.); Ancestry (includes multiple ancestries): 11.8% German, 8.1% Irish, 4.5% Swedish, 3.5% Polish, 3.2% English (2005-2009 5-year est.).
Economy: Single-family building permits issued: 66 (2010); Multi-family building permits issued: 0 (2010); Employment by occupation: 18.4% management, 12.7% professional, 9.9% services, 35.5% sales, 0.0% farming, 17.2% construction, 6.3% production (2005-2009 5-year est.).
Income: Per capita income: $22,722 (2010); Median household income: $45,583 (2010); Average household income: $67,092 (2010); Percent of households with income of $100,000 or more: 18.1% (2010); Poverty rate: 6.2% (2005-2009 5-year est.).
Taxes: Total city taxes per capita: $435 (2007); City property taxes per capita: $263 (2007).

Education: Percent of population age 25 and over with: High school diploma (including GED) or higher: 65.6% (2010); Bachelor's degree or higher: 8.2% (2010); Master's degree or higher: 2.7% (2010).
School District(s)
Manor ISD (PK-12)
    2009-10 Enrollment: 6,932 . . . . (512) 278-4000
Housing: Homeownership rate: 75.3% (2010); Median home value: $92,987 (2010); Median contract rent: $616 per month (2005-2009 5-year est.); Median year structure built: 2002 (2005-2009 5-year est.).
Safety: Violent crime rate: 25.5 per 10,000 population; Property crime rate: 310.6 per 10,000 population (2009).
Transportation: Commute to work: 95.8% car, 0.0% public transportation, 0.0% walk, 3.2% work from home (2005-2009 5-year est.); Travel time to work: 7.6% less than 15 minutes, 30.7% 15 to 30 minutes, 38.6% 30 to 45 minutes, 4.5% 45 to 60 minutes, 18.7% 60 minutes or more (2005-2009 5-year est.)

ONION CREEK (CDP). Covers a land area of 3.225 square miles and a water area of 0 square miles. Located at 30.14° N. Lat; 97.78° W. Long. Elevation is 574 feet.
History: Home of the Onion Creek Golf Club, the original host for The Legends of Golf, the first senior professional golf tournament. For 11 years, beginning in 1978, golfing greats like Snead, Sarazen and Palmer challenged the Onion Creek course and created what is today's Champions Tour.
Population: 1,632 (1990); 2,116 (2000); 2,270 (2010); 2,581 (2015 projected); Race: 88.2% White, 1.4% Black, 0.7% Asian, 9.7% Other, 18.2% Hispanic of any race (2010); Density: 703.9 persons per square mile (2010); Average household size: 2.03 (2010); Median age: 58.6 (2010); Males per 100 females: 86.5 (2010); Marriage status: n/a never married, n/a now married, n/a widowed, n/a divorced (2005-2009 5-year est.); Foreign born: n/a (2005-2009 5-year est.); Ancestry (includes multiple ancestries): n/a (2005-2009 5-year est.).
Economy: Employment by occupation: n/a management, n/a professional, n/a services, n/a sales, n/a farming, n/a construction, n/a production (2005-2009 5-year est.).
Income: Per capita income: $56,815 (2010); Median household income: $88,264 (2010); Average household income: $115,612 (2010); Percent of households with income of $100,000 or more: 42.4% (2010); Poverty rate: n/a (2005-2009 5-year est.).
Education: Percent of population age 25 and over with: High school diploma (including GED) or higher: 97.1% (2010); Bachelor's degree or higher: 60.1% (2010); Master's degree or higher: 27.2% (2010).
Housing: Homeownership rate: 91.1% (2010); Median home value: $264,491 (2010); Median contract rent: n/a per month (2005-2009 5-year est.); Median year structure built: n/a (2005-2009 5-year est.).
Transportation: Commute to work: n/a car, n/a public transportation, n/a walk, n/a work from home (2005-2009 5-year est.); Travel time to work: n/a less than 15 minutes, n/a 15 to 30 minutes, n/a 30 to 45 minutes, n/a 45 to 60 minutes, n/a 60 minutes or more (2005-2009 5-year est.)

PFLUGERVILLE (city). Covers a land area of 11.339 square miles and a water area of 0 square miles. Located at 30.44° N. Lat; 97.62° W. Long. Elevation is 719 feet.
Population: 5,830 (1990); 16,335 (2000); 33,606 (2010); 39,509 (2015 projected); Race: 67.7% White, 14.0% Black, 5.7% Asian, 12.6% Other, 25.7% Hispanic of any race (2010); Density: 2,963.7 persons per square mile (2010); Average household size: 3.19 (2010); Median age: 34.6 (2010); Males per 100 females: 99.2 (2010); Marriage status: 27.6% never married, 59.7% now married, 3.3% widowed, 9.4% divorced (2005-2009 5-year est.); Foreign born: 12.5% (2005-2009 5-year est.); Ancestry (includes multiple ancestries): 13.5% German, 8.4% Irish, 6.9% English, 4.1% American, 2.8% French (2005-2009 5-year est.).
Economy: Unemployment rate: 6.6% (June 2011); Total civilian labor force: 23,770 (June 2011); Single-family building permits issued: 164 (2010); Multi-family building permits issued: 0 (2010); Employment by occupation: 17.6% management, 28.0% professional, 9.9% services, 27.3% sales, 0.1% farming, 7.5% construction, 9.8% production (2005-2009 5-year est.).
Income: Per capita income: $28,318 (2010); Median household income: $78,420 (2010); Average household income: $90,418 (2010); Percent of households with income of $100,000 or more: 30.8% (2010); Poverty rate: 6.0% (2005-2009 5-year est.).
Taxes: Total city taxes per capita: $552 (2007); City property taxes per capita: $304 (2007).

Education: Percent of population age 25 and over with: High school diploma (including GED) or higher: 94.2% (2010); Bachelor's degree or higher: 38.7% (2010); Master's degree or higher: 11.5% (2010).

School District(s)

Harmony Science Academy (Austin) (KG-12)
2009-10 Enrollment: 1,104 . . . . (512) 251-5000

Pflugerville ISD (PK-12)
2009-10 Enrollment: 22,060 . . . . (512) 594-0000

Vocational/Technical School(s)

Academy at Austin (Private, For-profit)
Fall 2009 Enrollment: 227 . . . . (512) 251-1644
2010-11 Tuition: $14,500

Housing: Homeownership rate: 91.0% (2010); Median home value: $171,335 (2010); Median contract rent: $914 per month (2005-2009 5-year est.); Median year structure built: 2000 (2005-2009 5-year est.).

Safety: Violent crime rate: 16.3 per 10,000 population; Property crime rate: 206.4 per 10,000 population (2009).

Newspapers: Pflugerville Pflag (Community news; Circulation 4,000)

Transportation: Commute to work: 94.0% car, 0.2% public transportation, 0.5% walk, 3.3% work from home (2005-2009 5-year est.); Travel time to work: 19.1% less than 15 minutes, 41.8% 15 to 30 minutes, 24.6% 30 to 45 minutes, 9.4% 45 to 60 minutes, 5.1% 60 minutes or more (2005-2009 5-year est.)

Additional Information Contacts

City of Pflugerville . . . . (512) 990-6101
http://www.cityofpflugerville.com

ROLLINGWOOD (city).

Covers a land area of 0.678 square miles and a water area of 0 square miles. Located at 30.27° N. Lat; 97.78° W. Long. Elevation is 646 feet.

Population: 1,390 (1990); 1,403 (2000); 1,423 (2010); 1,482 (2015 projected); Race: 94.8% White, 0.1% Black, 2.7% Asian, 2.4% Other, 5.4% Hispanic of any race (2010); Density: 2,100.2 persons per square mile (2010); Average household size: 2.88 (2010); Median age: 46.2 (2010); Males per 100 females: 97.1 (2010); Marriage status: 18.5% never married, 73.5% now married, 2.3% widowed, 5.8% divorced (2005-2009 5-year est.); Foreign born: 2.4% (2005-2009 5-year est.); Ancestry (includes multiple ancestries): 24.0% German, 22.4% English, 15.1% Irish, 8.2% American, 7.8% Scottish (2005-2009 5-year est.).

Economy: Single-family building permits issued: 5 (2010); Multi-family building permits issued: 0 (2010); Employment by occupation: 27.8% management, 47.7% professional, 3.2% services, 19.3% sales, 0.0% farming, 0.9% construction, 1.1% production (2005-2009 5-year est.).

Income: Per capita income: $58,688 (2010); Median household income: $123,941 (2010); Average household income: $169,544 (2010); Percent of households with income of $100,000 or more: 61.5% (2010); Poverty rate: 0.7% (2005-2009 5-year est.).

Taxes: Total city taxes per capita: $620 (2007); City property taxes per capita: $276 (2007).

Education: Percent of population age 25 and over with: High school diploma (including GED) or higher: 98.9% (2010); Bachelor's degree or higher: 77.8% (2010); Master's degree or higher: 37.1% (2010).

Housing: Homeownership rate: 93.5% (2010); Median home value: $477,523 (2010); Median contract rent: $2,000 per month (2005-2009 5-year est.); Median year structure built: 1972 (2005-2009 5-year est.).

Safety: Violent crime rate: 0.0 per 10,000 population; Property crime rate: 153.0 per 10,000 population (2009).

Transportation: Commute to work: 89.5% car, 0.0% public transportation, 1.3% walk, 7.5% work from home (2005-2009 5-year est.); Travel time to work: 45.3% less than 15 minutes, 41.5% 15 to 30 minutes, 9.3% 30 to 45 minutes, 1.5% 45 to 60 minutes, 2.5% 60 minutes or more (2005-2009 5-year est.)

SAN LEANNA (village).

Covers a land area of 0.385 square miles and a water area of 0 square miles. Located at 30.14° N. Lat; 97.82° W. Long. Elevation is 669 feet.

Population: 335 (1990); 384 (2000); 324 (2010); 371 (2015 projected); Race: 80.2% White, 0.6% Black, 0.6% Asian, 18.5% Other, 25.9% Hispanic of any race (2010); Density: 842.2 persons per square mile (2010); Average household size: 2.57 (2010); Median age: 47.1 (2010); Males per 100 females: 105.1 (2010); Marriage status: 21.3% never married, 56.8% now married, 4.2% widowed, 17.7% divorced (2005-2009 5-year est.); Foreign born: 7.4% (2005-2009 5-year est.); Ancestry (includes multiple ancestries): 20.4% German, 11.1% English, 10.4% Irish, 6.6% American, 4.7% Scotch-Irish (2005-2009 5-year est.).

Economy: Single-family building permits issued: 0 (2010); Multi-family building permits issued: 0 (2010); Employment by occupation: 23.2% management, 29.2% professional, 9.8% services, 23.2% sales, 0.0% farming, 12.6% construction, 1.9% production (2005-2009 5-year est.).

Income: Per capita income: $30,318 (2010); Median household income: $69,444 (2010); Average household income: $78,770 (2010); Percent of households with income of $100,000 or more: 25.4% (2010); Poverty rate: 3.5% (2005-2009 5-year est.).

Taxes: Total city taxes per capita: $216 (2007); City property taxes per capita: $171 (2007).

Education: Percent of population age 25 and over with: High school diploma (including GED) or higher: 91.1% (2010); Bachelor's degree or higher: 30.8% (2010); Master's degree or higher: 12.1% (2010).

Housing: Homeownership rate: 85.7% (2010); Median home value: $211,765 (2010); Median contract rent: $1,042 per month (2005-2009 5-year est.); Median year structure built: 1976 (2005-2009 5-year est.).

Transportation: Commute to work: 90.2% car, 1.4% public transportation, 0.0% walk, 8.3% work from home (2005-2009 5-year est.); Travel time to work: 26.3% less than 15 minutes, 34.5% 15 to 30 minutes, 32.9% 30 to 45 minutes, 3.4% 45 to 60 minutes, 2.8% 60 minutes or more (2005-2009 5-year est.)

SHADY HOLLOW (CDP).

Covers a land area of 5.369 square miles and a water area of 0 square miles. Located at 30.16° N. Lat; 97.86° W. Long. Elevation is 751 feet.

History: In 1972 Austin Savings and Loan Owners began development on 600 acres of land. In 1978 the homeowners organized the Shady Hollow Homeowners Corporation to counter what they believed was misrepresentation from the developer. The homeowners accused Austin Savings and Loan Owners of installing development more dense than advertised.

Population: 2,623 (1990); 5,140 (2000); 5,334 (2010); 6,172 (2015 projected); Race: 82.9% White, 2.5% Black, 5.2% Asian, 9.4% Other, 17.3% Hispanic of any race (2010); Density: 993.4 persons per square mile (2010); Average household size: 3.05 (2010); Median age: 37.9 (2010); Males per 100 females: 100.4 (2010); Marriage status: 21.9% never married, 69.7% now married, 4.1% widowed, 4.3% divorced (2005-2009 5-year est.); Foreign born: 6.6% (2005-2009 5-year est.); Ancestry (includes multiple ancestries): 18.7% German, 15.2% English, 10.1% Irish, 10.0% French, 9.4% American (2005-2009 5-year est.).

Economy: Employment by occupation: 20.0% management, 37.8% professional, 8.8% services, 27.2% sales, 0.0% farming, 3.6% construction, 2.6% production (2005-2009 5-year est.).

Income: Per capita income: $36,368 (2010); Median household income: $95,295 (2010); Average household income: $112,068 (2010); Percent of households with income of $100,000 or more: 46.2% (2010); Poverty rate: 1.8% (2005-2009 5-year est.).

Education: Percent of population age 25 and over with: High school diploma (including GED) or higher: 97.2% (2010); Bachelor's degree or higher: 55.4% (2010); Master's degree or higher: 19.4% (2010).

Housing: Homeownership rate: 93.2% (2010); Median home value: $253,413 (2010); Median contract rent: n/a per month (2005-2009 5-year est.); Median year structure built: 1986 (2005-2009 5-year est.).

Transportation: Commute to work: 93.2% car, 0.0% public transportation, 0.0% walk, 6.3% work from home (2005-2009 5-year est.); Travel time to work: 12.5% less than 15 minutes, 34.0% 15 to 30 minutes, 39.4% 30 to 45 minutes, 12.3% 45 to 60 minutes, 1.9% 60 minutes or more (2005-2009 5-year est.)

SUNSET VALLEY (city).

Covers a land area of 1.377 square miles and a water area of 0 square miles. Located at 30.22° N. Lat; 97.81° W. Long. Elevation is 666 feet.

Population: 331 (1990); 365 (2000); 442 (2010); 486 (2015 projected); Race: 35.3% White, 2.5% Black, 5.7% Asian, 56.6% Other, 61.1% Hispanic of any race (2010); Density: 321.0 persons per square mile (2010); Average household size: 2.47 (2010); Median age: 30.9 (2010); Males per 100 females: 99.1 (2010); Marriage status: 36.7% never married, 55.7% now married, 2.0% widowed, 5.6% divorced (2005-2009 5-year est.); Foreign born: 9.3% (2005-2009 5-year est.); Ancestry (includes multiple ancestries): 18.9% German, 15.1% Irish, 6.2% English, 4.8% French, 4.5% American (2005-2009 5-year est.).

Economy: Single-family building permits issued: 0 (2010); Multi-family building permits issued: 0 (2010); Employment by occupation: 26.6% management, 38.9% professional, 3.8% services, 26.0% sales, 0.0% farming, 4.7% construction, 0.0% production (2005-2009 5-year est.).

Income: Per capita income: $26,311 (2010); Median household income: $51,351 (2010); Average household income: $65,126 (2010); Percent of households with income of $100,000 or more: 18.0% (2010); Poverty rate: 3.8% (2005-2009 5-year est.).
Taxes: Total city taxes per capita: $6,290 (2007); City property taxes per capita: $0 (2007).
Education: Percent of population age 25 and over with: High school diploma (including GED) or higher: 78.3% (2010); Bachelor's degree or higher: 48.2% (2010); Master's degree or higher: 18.5% (2010).
Housing: Homeownership rate: 22.5% (2010); Median home value: $255,000 (2010); Median contract rent: $762 per month (2005-2009 5-year est.); Median year structure built: 1996 (2005-2009 5-year est.).
Safety: Violent crime rate: 33.2 per 10,000 population; Property crime rate: 1,782.9 per 10,000 population (2009).
Transportation: Commute to work: 91.7% car, 0.0% public transportation, 0.0% walk, 8.3% work from home (2005-2009 5-year est.); Travel time to work: 27.1% less than 15 minutes, 44.8% 15 to 30 minutes, 18.8% 30 to 45 minutes, 6.0% 45 to 60 minutes, 3.3% 60 minutes or more (2005-2009 5-year est.)

THE HILLS (village). Covers a land area of 1.065 square miles and a water area of 0 square miles. Located at 30.34° N. Lat; 97.98° W. Long. Elevation is 817 feet.
Population: 302 (1990); 1,492 (2000); 2,032 (2010); 2,384 (2015 projected); Race: 95.4% White, 1.9% Black, 1.1% Asian, 1.6% Other, 1.9% Hispanic of any race (2010); Density: 1,907.5 persons per square mile (2010); Average household size: 2.50 (2010); Median age: 50.1 (2010); Males per 100 females: 95.0 (2010); Marriage status: 12.9% never married, 80.3% now married, 2.2% widowed, 4.7% divorced (2005-2009 5-year est.); Foreign born: 7.2% (2005-2009 5-year est.); Ancestry (includes multiple ancestries): 20.8% English, 18.3% German, 17.4% American, 14.0% Irish, 7.1% Scottish (2005-2009 5-year est.).
Economy: Single-family building permits issued: 1 (2010); Multi-family building permits issued: 0 (2010); Employment by occupation: 35.1% management, 16.0% professional, 1.6% services, 43.1% sales, 0.0% farming, 1.0% construction, 3.1% production (2005-2009 5-year est.).
Income: Per capita income: $58,408 (2010); Median household income: $108,611 (2010); Average household income: $145,910 (2010); Percent of households with income of $100,000 or more: 53.9% (2010); Poverty rate: 1.4% (2005-2009 5-year est.).
Taxes: Total city taxes per capita: $83 (2007); City property taxes per capita: $58 (2007).
Education: Percent of population age 25 and over with: High school diploma (including GED) or higher: 98.5% (2010); Bachelor's degree or higher: 69.5% (2010); Master's degree or higher: 24.2% (2010).
Housing: Homeownership rate: 87.7% (2010); Median home value: $469,932 (2010); Median contract rent: $2,000+ per month (2005-2009 5-year est.); Median year structure built: 1997 (2005-2009 5-year est.).
Transportation: Commute to work: 75.9% car, 0.0% public transportation, 1.1% walk, 21.8% work from home (2005-2009 5-year est.); Travel time to work: 32.4% less than 15 minutes, 14.7% 15 to 30 minutes, 34.9% 30 to 45 minutes, 14.9% 45 to 60 minutes, 3.1% 60 minutes or more (2005-2009 5-year est.)
Additional Information Contacts
Village of The Hills . . . . (512) 261-6281
    http://www.villageofthehills.org

WELLS BRANCH (CDP). Covers a land area of 2.529 square miles and a water area of 0.006 square miles. Located at 30.44° N. Lat; 97.67° W. Long. Elevation is 820 feet.
Population: 7,242 (1990); 11,271 (2000); 12,782 (2010); 13,676 (2015 projected); Race: 67.0% White, 10.7% Black, 12.7% Asian, 9.6% Other, 19.2% Hispanic of any race (2010); Density: 5,053.8 persons per square mile (2010); Average household size: 2.11 (2010); Median age: 33.2 (2010); Males per 100 females: 101.3 (2010); Marriage status: 45.7% never married, 38.3% now married, 1.8% widowed, 14.2% divorced (2005-2009 5-year est.); Foreign born: 13.3% (2005-2009 5-year est.); Ancestry (includes multiple ancestries): 11.8% German, 9.3% Irish, 8.7% English, 4.6% American, 3.6% Scotch-Irish (2005-2009 5-year est.).
Economy: Employment by occupation: 18.6% management, 26.0% professional, 11.7% services, 31.6% sales, 0.0% farming, 6.7% construction, 5.3% production (2005-2009 5-year est.).
Income: Per capita income: $30,702 (2010); Median household income: $52,973 (2010); Average household income: $64,750 (2010); Percent of

households with income of $100,000 or more: 17.3% (2010); Poverty rate: 10.2% (2005-2009 5-year est.).
Education: Percent of population age 25 and over with: High school diploma (including GED) or higher: 95.4% (2010); Bachelor's degree or higher: 51.5% (2010); Master's degree or higher: 14.6% (2010).
Housing: Homeownership rate: 35.6% (2010); Median home value: $168,718 (2010); Median contract rent: $664 per month (2005-2009 5-year est.); Median year structure built: 1988 (2005-2009 5-year est.).
Transportation: Commute to work: 93.2% car, 1.3% public transportation, 0.8% walk, 2.8% work from home (2005-2009 5-year est.); Travel time to work: 30.9% less than 15 minutes, 42.7% 15 to 30 minutes, 19.4% 30 to 45 minutes, 3.6% 45 to 60 minutes, 3.4% 60 minutes or more (2005-2009 5-year est.)

WEST LAKE HILLS (city). Covers a land area of 3.729 square miles and a water area of 0 square miles. Located at 30.29° N. Lat; 97.80° W. Long. Elevation is 781 feet.
Population: 2,743 (1990); 3,116 (2000); 3,106 (2010); 3,185 (2015 projected); Race: 95.4% White, 0.2% Black, 1.3% Asian, 3.1% Other, 4.4% Hispanic of any race (2010); Density: 833.0 persons per square mile (2010); Average household size: 2.67 (2010); Median age: 46.8 (2010); Males per 100 females: 95.2 (2010); Marriage status: 20.2% never married, 67.5% now married, 2.4% widowed, 10.0% divorced (2005-2009 5-year est.); Foreign born: 5.6% (2005-2009 5-year est.); Ancestry (includes multiple ancestries): 20.4% English, 15.6% German, 13.5% American, 13.3% Irish, 6.8% Scottish (2005-2009 5-year est.).
Economy: Single-family building permits issued: 13 (2010); Multi-family building permits issued: 0 (2010); Employment by occupation: 32.5% management, 38.3% professional, 0.0% services, 26.6% sales, 0.0% farming, 2.6% construction, 0.0% production (2005-2009 5-year est.).
Income: Per capita income: $56,884 (2010); Median household income: $125,606 (2010); Average household income: $151,958 (2010); Percent of households with income of $100,000 or more: 63.3% (2010); Poverty rate: 2.6% (2005-2009 5-year est.).
Taxes: Total city taxes per capita: $882 (2007); City property taxes per capita: $165 (2007).
Education: Percent of population age 25 and over with: High school diploma (including GED) or higher: 98.7% (2010); Bachelor's degree or higher: 81.0% (2010); Master's degree or higher: 41.0% (2010).
Housing: Homeownership rate: 89.4% (2010); Median home value: $510,452 (2010); Median contract rent: $1,194 per month (2005-2009 5-year est.); Median year structure built: 1976 (2005-2009 5-year est.).
Safety: Violent crime rate: 28.5 per 10,000 population; Property crime rate: 275.3 per 10,000 population (2009).
Transportation: Commute to work: 79.2% car, 0.0% public transportation, 1.4% walk, 18.6% work from home (2005-2009 5-year est.); Travel time to work: 31.1% less than 15 minutes, 55.4% 15 to 30 minutes, 9.1% 30 to 45 minutes, 1.1% 45 to 60 minutes, 3.3% 60 minutes or more (2005-2009 5-year est.)
Additional Information Contacts
City of West Lake Hills . . . . (512) 327-3628
    http://www.westlakehills.org

WINDEMERE (CDP). Covers a land area of 2.135 square miles and a water area of 0 square miles. Located at 30.46° N. Lat; 97.64° W. Long. Elevation is 758 feet.
Population: 2,581 (1990); 6,868 (2000); 8,201 (2010); 9,576 (2015 projected); Race: 53.2% White, 22.4% Black, 8.5% Asian, 15.9% Other, 29.2% Hispanic of any race (2010); Density: 3,841.2 persons per square mile (2010); Average household size: 3.16 (2010); Median age: 33.7 (2010); Males per 100 females: 98.2 (2010); Marriage status: 26.6% never married, 55.5% now married, 1.5% widowed, 16.4% divorced (2005-2009 5-year est.); Foreign born: 6.3% (2005-2009 5-year est.); Ancestry (includes multiple ancestries): 14.7% German, 7.5% English, 6.3% Irish, 5.9% Czech, 2.1% Swedish (2005-2009 5-year est.).
Economy: Employment by occupation: 16.7% management, 14.5% professional, 14.1% services, 40.4% sales, 0.0% farming, 6.3% construction, 8.1% production (2005-2009 5-year est.).
Income: Per capita income: $26,819 (2010); Median household income: $74,813 (2010); Average household income: $84,801 (2010); Percent of households with income of $100,000 or more: 27.4% (2010); Poverty rate: 2.4% (2005-2009 5-year est.).
Education: Percent of population age 25 and over with: High school diploma (including GED) or higher: 95.1% (2010); Bachelor's degree or higher: 38.4% (2010); Master's degree or higher: 10.3% (2010).

Housing: Homeownership rate: 87.3% (2010); Median home value: $156,930 (2010); Median contract rent: $1,136 per month (2005-2009 5-year est.); Median year structure built: 1995 (2005-2009 5-year est.).
Transportation: Commute to work: 95.2% car, 1.9% public transportation, 0.0% walk, 0.3% work from home (2005-2009 5-year est.); Travel time to work: 14.3% less than 15 minutes, 45.8% 15 to 30 minutes, 32.8% 30 to 45 minutes, 5.8% 45 to 60 minutes, 1.3% 60 minutes or more (2005-2009 5-year est.)

Trinity County

Located in east Texas; bounded on the southwest by the Trinity River, and on the northeast by the Neches River; includes part of Davy Crockett National Forest. Covers a land area of 692.84 square miles, a water area of 21.16 square miles, and is located in the Central Time Zone at 31.00° N. Lat., 95.20° W. Long. The county was founded in 1850. County seat is Groveton.

Weather Station: Groveton   Elevation: 350 feet

	Jan	Feb	Mar	Apr	May	Jun	Jul	Aug	Sep	Oct	Nov	Dec
High	62	66	73	80	86	91	95	96	91	82	71	63
Low	37	41	46	53	62	69	72	71	65	54	45	38
Precip	3.9	3.5	4.0	na	5.6	5.6	na	na	na	na	na	na
Snow	na	na	na	na	na	na	na	na	na	na	na	na

High and Low temperatures in degrees Fahrenheit; Precipitation and Snow in inches

Population: 11,445 (1990); 13,779 (2000); 14,394 (2010); 14,669 (2015 projected); Race: 82.0% White, 11.4% Black, 0.5% Asian, 6.1% Other, 7.5% Hispanic of any race (2010); Density: 20.8 persons per square mile (2010); Average household size: 2.35 (2010); Median age: 42.0 (2010); Males per 100 females: 91.6 (2010).
Religion: Five largest groups: 32.4% Southern Baptist Convention, 4.6% The United Methodist Church, 3.3% Churches of Christ, 2.6% Church of God (Cleveland, Tennessee), 2.2% Catholic Church (2000).
Economy: Unemployment rate: 9.7% (June 2011); Total civilian labor force: 5,861 (June 2011); Leading industries: 18.2% health care and social assistance; 12.0% accommodation & food services; 11.4% manufacturing (2009); Farms: 576 totaling 108,974 acres (2007); Companies that employ 500 or more persons: 0 (2009); Companies that employ 100 to 499 persons: 2 (2009); Companies that employ less than 100 persons: 188 (2009); Black-owned businesses: n/a (2007); Hispanic-owned businesses: n/a (2007); Asian-owned businesses: n/a (2007); Women-owned businesses: n/a (2007); Retail sales per capita: $5,436 (2010). Single-family building permits issued: 4 (2010); Multi-family building permits issued: 0 (2010).
Income: Per capita income: $19,131 (2010); Median household income: $34,009 (2010); Average household income: $45,043 (2010); Percent of households with income of $100,000 or more: 7.4% (2010); Poverty rate: 19.7% (2009); Bankruptcy rate: 1.49% (2010).
Taxes: Total county taxes per capita: $191 (2007); County property taxes per capita: $169 (2007).
Education: Percent of population age 25 and over with: High school diploma (including GED) or higher: 78.1% (2010); Bachelor's degree or higher: 10.6% (2010); Master's degree or higher: 3.1% (2010).
Housing: Homeownership rate: 79.2% (2010); Median home value: $65,526 (2010); Median contract rent: $333 per month (2005-2009 5-year est.); Median year structure built: 1981 (2005-2009 5-year est.)
Health: Birth rate: 117.3 per 10,000 population (2009); Death rate: 131.7 per 10,000 population (2009); Age-adjusted cancer mortality rate: 170.2 deaths per 100,000 population (2007); Number of physicians: 2.2 per 10,000 population (2008); Hospital beds: 15.7 per 10,000 population (2007); Hospital admissions: 509.2 per 10,000 population (2007).
Elections: 2008 Presidential election results: 31.7% Obama, 67.4% McCain, 0.0% Nader
Additional Information Contacts
Trinity County Government . . . . (936) 642-1746
  http://www.co.trinity.tx.us/ips/cms
Trinity Peninsula Chamber of Commerce . . . . (936) 594-3856
  http://www.trinitychamber.org

Trinity County Communities

APPLE SPRINGS (unincorporated postal area, zip code 75926). Covers a land area of 115.199 square miles and a water area of 0.401 square miles. Located at 31.24° N. Lat; 94.96° W. Long. Elevation is 253 feet.

Population: 1,109 (2000); Race: 74.4% White, 21.6% Black, 0.0% Asian, 4.0% Other, 1.9% Hispanic of any race (2000); Density: 9.6 persons per square mile (2000); Age: 24.7% under 18, 14.4% over 64 (2000); Marriage status: 19.7% never married, 60.8% now married, 8.9% widowed, 10.6% divorced (2000); Foreign born: 1.0% (2000); Ancestry (includes multiple ancestries): 29.3% American, 5.2% Irish, 4.1% English, 3.6% German (2000).
Economy: Employment by occupation: 7.3% management, 10.9% professional, 17.2% services, 22.5% sales, 7.1% farming, 13.9% construction, 21.0% production (2000).
Income: Per capita income: $13,637 (2000); Median household income: $29,519 (2000); Poverty rate: 179.1% (2000).
Education: Percent of population age 25 and over with: High school diploma (including GED) or higher: 73.3% (2000); Bachelor's degree or higher: 6.5% (2000).
School District(s)
Apple Springs ISD (PK-12)
  2009-10 Enrollment: 193 . . . . (936) 831-3344
Housing: Homeownership rate: 88.5% (2000); Median home value: $55,800 (2000); Median contract rent: $319 per month (2000); Median year structure built: 1973 (2000).
Transportation: Commute to work: 95.2% car, 0.4% public transportation, 0.9% walk, 3.5% work from home (2000); Travel time to work: 16.7% less than 15 minutes, 27.7% 15 to 30 minutes, 35.1% 30 to 45 minutes, 9.2% 45 to 60 minutes, 11.3% 60 minutes or more (2000)

GROVETON (city). County seat. Covers a land area of 2.565 square miles and a water area of 0.052 square miles. Located at 31.05° N. Lat; 95.12° W. Long. Elevation is 328 feet.
History: Groveton developed as a market center for farm products and lumber.
Population: 1,081 (1990); 1,107 (2000); 1,127 (2010); 1,137 (2015 projected); Race: 71.3% White, 15.8% Black, 0.4% Asian, 12.6% Other, 18.1% Hispanic of any race (2010); Density: 439.4 persons per square mile (2010); Average household size: 2.33 (2010); Median age: 37.6 (2010); Males per 100 females: 86.6 (2010); Marriage status: 29.1% never married, 45.7% now married, 14.3% widowed, 10.8% divorced (2005-2009 5-year est.); Foreign born: 4.6% (2005-2009 5-year est.); Ancestry (includes multiple ancestries): 22.7% English, 13.9% Irish, 13.5% American, 7.8% German, 3.6% French (2005-2009 5-year est.).
Economy: Employment by occupation: 6.3% management, 11.0% professional, 28.2% services, 32.2% sales, 8.3% farming, 5.2% construction, 8.8% production (2005-2009 5-year est.).
Income: Per capita income: $14,658 (2010); Median household income: $24,390 (2010); Average household income: $35,296 (2010); Percent of households with income of $100,000 or more: 4.2% (2010); Poverty rate: 25.9% (2005-2009 5-year est.).
Taxes: Total city taxes per capita: $363 (2007); City property taxes per capita: $128 (2007).
Education: Percent of population age 25 and over with: High school diploma (including GED) or higher: 71.8% (2010); Bachelor's degree or higher: 10.5% (2010); Master's degree or higher: 2.1% (2010).
School District(s)
Centerville ISD (PK-12)
  2009-10 Enrollment: 152 . . . . (936) 642-1597
Groveton ISD (PK-12)
  2009-10 Enrollment: 712 . . . . (936) 642-1473
Housing: Homeownership rate: 63.6% (2010); Median home value: $46,552 (2010); Median contract rent: $375 per month (2005-2009 5-year est.); Median year structure built: 1965 (2005-2009 5-year est.).
Newspapers: Groveton News (Community news; Circulation 2,000)
Transportation: Commute to work: 97.2% car, 0.0% public transportation, 1.4% walk, 1.4% work from home (2005-2009 5-year est.); Travel time to work: 27.0% less than 15 minutes, 14.4% 15 to 30 minutes, 37.8% 30 to 45 minutes, 11.8% 45 to 60 minutes, 9.0% 60 minutes or more (2005-2009 5-year est.)

PENNINGTON (unincorporated postal area, zip code 75856). Covers a land area of 18.443 square miles and a water area of 0 square miles. Located at 31.21° N. Lat; 95.23° W. Long. Elevation is 344 feet.
Population: 184 (2000); Race: 97.5% White, 0.0% Black, 0.0% Asian, 2.5% Other, 11.8% Hispanic of any race (2000); Density: 10.0 persons per square mile (2000); Age: 25.5% under 18, 19.9% over 64 (2000); Marriage status: 14.2% never married, 63.8% now married, 17.3% widowed, 4.7%

divorced (2000); Foreign born: 0.0% (2000); Ancestry (includes multiple ancestries): 21.7% American, 8.1% German, 7.5% Irish (2000).
Economy: Employment by occupation: 5.3% management, 47.4% professional, 0.0% services, 5.3% sales, 13.2% farming, 10.5% construction, 18.4% production (2000).
Income: Per capita income: $10,710 (2000); Median household income: $22,321 (2000); Poverty rate: 179.1% (2000).
Education: Percent of population age 25 and over with: High school diploma (including GED) or higher: 69.5% (2000); Bachelor's degree or higher: 16.2% (2000).
Housing: Homeownership rate: 80.0% (2000); Median home value: $63,100 (2000); Median contract rent: n/a per month (2000); Median year structure built: 1972 (2000).
Transportation: Commute to work: 81.6% car, 0.0% public transportation, 0.0% walk, 0.0% work from home (2000); Travel time to work: 0.0% less than 15 minutes, 52.6% 15 to 30 minutes, 23.7% 30 to 45 minutes, 0.0% 45 to 60 minutes, 23.7% 60 minutes or more (2000)

TRINITY (city). Covers a land area of 3.778 square miles and a water area of 0 square miles. Located at 30.94° N. Lat; 95.37° W. Long. Elevation is 233 feet.
History: Settled c.1873; incorporated 1903.
Population: 2,648 (1990); 2,721 (2000); 2,764 (2010); 2,782 (2015 projected); Race: 55.2% White, 32.1% Black, 1.0% Asian, 11.7% Other, 15.8% Hispanic of any race (2010); Density: 731.6 persons per square mile (2010); Average household size: 2.47 (2010); Median age: 34.5 (2010); Males per 100 females: 86.5 (2010); Marriage status: 25.9% never married, 52.8% now married, 16.9% widowed, 4.4% divorced (2005-2009 5-year est.); Foreign born: 14.1% (2005-2009 5-year est.); Ancestry (includes multiple ancestries): 12.5% American, 8.7% English, 5.9% Irish, 2.4% French, 2.0% German (2005-2009 5-year est.).
Economy: Single-family building permits issued: 4 (2010); Multi-family building permits issued: 0 (2010); Employment by occupation: 8.3% management, 7.4% professional, 33.5% services, 22.0% sales, 0.9% farming, 7.1% construction, 20.9% production (2005-2009 5-year est.).
Income: Per capita income: $20,718 (2010); Median household income: $39,420 (2010); Average household income: $51,364 (2010); Percent of households with income of $100,000 or more: 8.7% (2010); Poverty rate: 33.3% (2005-2009 5-year est.).
Taxes: Total city taxes per capita: $453 (2007); City property taxes per capita: $129 (2007).
Education: Percent of population age 25 and over with: High school diploma (including GED) or higher: 71.3% (2010); Bachelor's degree or higher: 8.9% (2010); Master's degree or higher: 2.2% (2010).

School District(s)
Trinity ISD (PK-12)
    2009-10 Enrollment: 1,205 . . . . (936) 594-3569
Housing: Homeownership rate: 66.1% (2010); Median home value: $59,380 (2010); Median contract rent: $249 per month (2005-2009 5-year est.); Median year structure built: 1974 (2005-2009 5-year est.).
Hospitals: East Texas Medical Center - Trinity (30 beds)
Safety: Violent crime rate: 99.1 per 10,000 population; Property crime rate: 767.0 per 10,000 population (2009).
Newspapers: Trinity Standard (Community news; Circulation 2,450)
Transportation: Commute to work: 83.7% car, 0.0% public transportation, 0.0% walk, 10.7% work from home (2005-2009 5-year est.); Travel time to work: 36.7% less than 15 minutes, 24.4% 15 to 30 minutes, 23.5% 30 to 45 minutes, 8.8% 45 to 60 minutes, 6.6% 60 minutes or more (2005-2009 5-year est.)
Additional Information Contacts
Trinity Peninsula Chamber of Commerce . . . . (936) 594-3856
    http://www.trinitychamber.org

Tyler County

Located in east Texas; bounded on the north and east by the Neches River. Covers a land area of 922.90 square miles, a water area of 12.81 square miles, and is located in the Central Time Zone at 30.76° N. Lat., 94.37° W. Long. The county was founded in 1846. County seat is Woodville.

Weather Station: Town Bluff Dam   Elevation: 213 feet

	Jan	Feb	Mar	Apr	May	Jun	Jul	Aug	Sep	Oct	Nov	Dec
High	59	64	71	77	84	89	92	93	88	79	70	61
Low	38	42	48	55	64	69	72	71	66	56	48	40
Precip	4.6	4.6	4.2	4.1	4.9	6.1	3.6	3.8	4.4	4.8	5.3	5.6
Snow	tr	0.0	0.0	0.0	0.0	0.0	0.0	0.0	0.0	0.0	0.0	0.1

High and Low temperatures in degrees Fahrenheit; Precipitation and Snow in inches

Population: 16,646 (1990); 20,871 (2000); 21,011 (2010); 21,040 (2015 projected); Race: 82.4% White, 11.7% Black, 0.2% Asian, 5.7% Other, 5.4% Hispanic of any race (2010); Density: 22.8 persons per square mile (2010); Average household size: 2.45 (2010); Median age: 39.0 (2010); Males per 100 females: 106.0 (2010).
Religion: Five largest groups: 46.1% Southern Baptist Convention, 3.7% The United Methodist Church, 2.9% Assemblies of God, 2.7% Catholic Church, 1.8% Churches of Christ (2000).
Economy: Unemployment rate: 12.1% (June 2011); Total civilian labor force: 8,730 (June 2011); Leading industries: 27.2% retail trade; 23.4% health care and social assistance; 12.6% accommodation & food services (2009); Farms: 792 totaling 84,253 acres (2007); Companies that employ 500 or more persons: 0 (2009); Companies that employ 100 to 499 persons: 3 (2009); Companies that employ less than 100 persons: 258 (2009); Black-owned businesses: n/a (2007); Hispanic-owned businesses: n/a (2007); Asian-owned businesses: n/a (2007); Women-owned businesses: n/a (2007); Retail sales per capita: $5,415 (2010). Single-family building permits issued: 4 (2010); Multi-family building permits issued: 0 (2010).
Income: Per capita income: $19,600 (2010); Median household income: $38,108 (2010); Average household income: $50,010 (2010); Percent of households with income of $100,000 or more: 9.0% (2010); Poverty rate: 20.1% (2009); Bankruptcy rate: 1.54% (2010).
Taxes: Total county taxes per capita: $256 (2007); County property taxes per capita: $224 (2007).
Education: Percent of population age 25 and over with: High school diploma (including GED) or higher: 81.8% (2010); Bachelor's degree or higher: 13.8% (2010); Master's degree or higher: 5.3% (2010).
Housing: Homeownership rate: 79.0% (2010); Median home value: $70,540 (2010); Median contract rent: $367 per month (2005-2009 5-year est.); Median year structure built: 1978 (2005-2009 5-year est.)
Health: Birth rate: 117.7 per 10,000 population (2009); Death rate: 108.0 per 10,000 population (2009); Age-adjusted cancer mortality rate: 239.8 deaths per 100,000 population (2007); Number of physicians: 5.4 per 10,000 population (2008); Hospital beds: 12.3 per 10,000 population (2007); Hospital admissions: 470.1 per 10,000 population (2007).
Elections: 2008 Presidential election results: 27.4% Obama, 71.4% McCain, 0.0% Nader
National and State Parks: John H Kirby State Forest
Additional Information Contacts
Tyler County Government . . . . (409) 283-2141
    http://www.co.tyler.tx.us/ips/cms
Tyler County Chamber of Commerce . . . . (409) 283-2632
    http://www.tylercountychamber.com

Tyler County Communities

CHESTER (town). Covers a land area of 1.595 square miles and a water area of 0 square miles. Located at 30.92° N. Lat; 94.59° W. Long. Elevation is 246 feet.
Population: 306 (1990); 265 (2000); 256 (2010); 250 (2015 projected); Race: 95.7% White, 2.3% Black, 0.4% Asian, 1.6% Other, 2.7% Hispanic of any race (2010); Density: 160.5 persons per square mile (2010); Average household size: 2.51 (2010); Median age: 39.6 (2010); Males per 100 females: 93.9 (2010); Marriage status: 16.7% never married, 72.5% now married, 1.3% widowed, 9.6% divorced (2005-2009 5-year est.); Foreign born: 0.0% (2005-2009 5-year est.); Ancestry (includes multiple ancestries): 42.1% Irish, 30.2% German, 30.2% English, 7.0% American, 6.0% French (2005-2009 5-year est.).
Economy: Employment by occupation: 5.4% management, 29.1% professional, 18.2% services, 8.8% sales, 11.5% farming, 20.3% construction, 6.8% production (2005-2009 5-year est.).
Income: Per capita income: $32,860 (2010); Median household income: $62,500 (2010); Average household income: $81,103 (2010); Percent of households with income of $100,000 or more: 20.6% (2010); Poverty rate: 1.1% (2005-2009 5-year est.).
Taxes: Total city taxes per capita: $65 (2007); City property taxes per capita: $0 (2007).

Education: Percent of population age 25 and over with: High school diploma (including GED) or higher: 90.1% (2010); Bachelor's degree or higher: 18.2% (2010); Master's degree or higher: 5.0% (2010).

School District(s)

Chester ISD (KG-12)

    2009-10 Enrollment: 185 . . . . (936) 969-2371

Housing: Homeownership rate: 80.4% (2010); Median home value: $82,000 (2010); Median contract rent: $361 per month (2005-2009 5-year est.); Median year structure built: 1975 (2005-2009 5-year est.).

Transportation: Commute to work: 97.2% car, 0.0% public transportation, 0.0% walk, 0.0% work from home (2005-2009 5-year est.); Travel time to work: 21.7% less than 15 minutes, 32.9% 15 to 30 minutes, 18.2% 30 to 45 minutes, 11.2% 45 to 60 minutes, 16.1% 60 minutes or more (2005-2009 5-year est.)

COLMESNEIL (city). Covers a land area of 2.005 square miles and a water area of 0 square miles. Located at 30.90° N. Lat; 94.42° W. Long. Elevation is 272 feet.

Population: 569 (1990); 638 (2000); 642 (2010); 645 (2015 projected); Race: 91.4% White, 4.2% Black, 0.2% Asian, 4.2% Other, 4.4% Hispanic of any race (2010); Density: 320.1 persons per square mile (2010); Average household size: 2.65 (2010); Median age: 38.6 (2010); Males per 100 females: 88.3 (2010); Marriage status: 22.0% never married, 54.9% now married, 12.6% widowed, 10.6% divorced (2005-2009 5-year est.); Foreign born: 0.0% (2005-2009 5-year est.); Ancestry (includes multiple ancestries): 12.8% German, 12.8% Irish, 11.3% English, 8.3% American, 5.9% Scotch-Irish (2005-2009 5-year est.).

Economy: Employment by occupation: 1.3% management, 25.3% professional, 10.5% services, 24.9% sales, 3.4% farming, 13.1% construction, 21.5% production (2005-2009 5-year est.).

Income: Per capita income: $16,947 (2010); Median household income: $35,000 (2010); Average household income: $45,992 (2010); Percent of households with income of $100,000 or more: 6.6% (2010); Poverty rate: 22.8% (2005-2009 5-year est.).

Taxes: Total city taxes per capita: $113 (2007); City property taxes per capita: $90 (2007).

Education: Percent of population age 25 and over with: High school diploma (including GED) or higher: 81.0% (2010); Bachelor's degree or higher: 12.9% (2010); Master's degree or higher: 3.3% (2010).

School District(s)

Colmesneil ISD (PK-12)

    2009-10 Enrollment: 487 . . . . (409) 837-5757

Housing: Homeownership rate: 80.6% (2010); Median home value: $70,741 (2010); Median contract rent: $268 per month (2005-2009 5-year est.); Median year structure built: 1983 (2005-2009 5-year est.).

Transportation: Commute to work: 93.7% car, 0.0% public transportation, 2.3% walk, 1.4% work from home (2005-2009 5-year est.); Travel time to work: 50.5% less than 15 minutes, 17.4% 15 to 30 minutes, 5.5% 30 to 45 minutes, 10.6% 45 to 60 minutes, 16.1% 60 minutes or more (2005-2009 5-year est.)

FRED (unincorporated postal area, zip code 77616). Covers a land area of 44.216 square miles and a water area of 0.039 square miles. Located at 30.56° N. Lat; 94.20° W. Long. Elevation is 135 feet.

Population: 1,382 (2000); Race: 98.0% White, 1.3% Black, 0.0% Asian, 0.7% Other, 2.3% Hispanic of any race (2000); Density: 31.3 persons per square mile (2000); Age: 29.8% under 18, 10.9% over 64 (2000); Marriage status: 13.6% never married, 68.5% now married, 9.7% widowed, 8.2% divorced (2000); Foreign born: 0.1% (2000); Ancestry (includes multiple ancestries): 31.2% American, 6.1% Irish, 5.8% German, 3.0% French (2000).

Economy: Employment by occupation: 7.1% management, 12.3% professional, 11.9% services, 22.7% sales, 2.1% farming, 12.9% construction, 31.2% production (2000).

Income: Per capita income: $14,757 (2000); Median household income: $28,963 (2000); Poverty rate: 179.1% (2000).

Education: Percent of population age 25 and over with: High school diploma (including GED) or higher: 68.3% (2000); Bachelor's degree or higher: 4.2% (2000).

School District(s)

Warren ISD (PK-12)

    2009-10 Enrollment: 1,223 . . . . (409) 547-2241

Housing: Homeownership rate: 89.3% (2000); Median home value: $37,000 (2000); Median contract rent: $360 per month (2000); Median year structure built: 1977 (2000).

Transportation: Commute to work: 95.2% car, 0.0% public transportation, 0.0% walk, 4.8% work from home (2000); Travel time to work: 8.2% less than 15 minutes, 23.2% 15 to 30 minutes, 22.1% 30 to 45 minutes, 16.2% 45 to 60 minutes, 30.3% 60 minutes or more (2000)

HILLISTER (unincorporated postal area, zip code 77624). Covers a land area of 57.681 square miles and a water area of 0.098 square miles. Located at 30.66° N. Lat; 94.30° W. Long. Elevation is 190 feet.

Population: 786 (2000); Race: 61.4% White, 37.3% Black, 0.4% Asian, 0.9% Other, 0.4% Hispanic of any race (2000); Density: 13.6 persons per square mile (2000); Age: 28.6% under 18, 8.8% over 64 (2000); Marriage status: 21.4% never married, 59.4% now married, 4.9% widowed, 14.3% divorced (2000); Foreign born: 0.6% (2000); Ancestry (includes multiple ancestries): 10.3% English, 6.9% Irish, 6.9% American, 5.3% French (2000).

Economy: Employment by occupation: 4.3% management, 14.0% professional, 20.6% services, 25.3% sales, 3.9% farming, 13.6% construction, 18.3% production (2000).

Income: Per capita income: $11,243 (2000); Median household income: $23,350 (2000); Poverty rate: 179.1% (2000).

Education: Percent of population age 25 and over with: High school diploma (including GED) or higher: 67.2% (2000); Bachelor's degree or higher: 10.3% (2000).

Housing: Homeownership rate: 86.4% (2000); Median home value: $56,800 (2000); Median contract rent: $258 per month (2000); Median year structure built: 1981 (2000).

Transportation: Commute to work: 95.0% car, 0.0% public transportation, 0.4% walk, 0.8% work from home (2000); Travel time to work: 22.4% less than 15 minutes, 32.4% 15 to 30 minutes, 15.4% 30 to 45 minutes, 8.1% 45 to 60 minutes, 21.6% 60 minutes or more (2000)

SPURGER (unincorporated postal area, zip code 77660). Covers a land area of 41.086 square miles and a water area of 0.021 square miles. Located at 30.63° N. Lat; 94.17° W. Long. Elevation is 164 feet.

Population: 1,341 (2000); Race: 97.2% White, 0.0% Black, 0.0% Asian, 2.8% Other, 2.4% Hispanic of any race (2000); Density: 32.6 persons per square mile (2000); Age: 29.4% under 18, 11.2% over 64 (2000); Marriage status: 16.0% never married, 68.4% now married, 5.2% widowed, 10.3% divorced (2000); Foreign born: 1.4% (2000); Ancestry (includes multiple ancestries): 17.2% American, 9.3% German, 8.3% Irish, 6.2% French (2000).

Economy: Employment by occupation: 5.0% management, 7.1% professional, 15.2% services, 30.1% sales, 4.6% farming, 13.9% construction, 24.1% production (2000).

Income: Per capita income: $12,719 (2000); Median household income: $29,750 (2000); Poverty rate: 179.1% (2000).

Education: Percent of population age 25 and over with: High school diploma (including GED) or higher: 71.0% (2000); Bachelor's degree or higher: 4.1% (2000).

School District(s)

Spurger ISD (PK-12)

    2009-10 Enrollment: 362 . . . . (409) 429-3464

Housing: Homeownership rate: 86.4% (2000); Median home value: $38,900 (2000); Median contract rent: $280 per month (2000); Median year structure built: 1978 (2000).

Transportation: Commute to work: 94.3% car, 0.0% public transportation, 2.4% walk, 1.6% work from home (2000); Travel time to work: 22.0% less than 15 minutes, 19.0% 15 to 30 minutes, 25.9% 30 to 45 minutes, 11.0% 45 to 60 minutes, 22.0% 60 minutes or more (2000)

WARREN (unincorporated postal area, zip code 77664). Covers a land area of 148.477 square miles and a water area of 0.125 square miles. Located at 30.60° N. Lat; 94.40° W. Long. Elevation is 167 feet.

Population: 2,627 (2000); Race: 93.6% White, 2.8% Black, 0.0% Asian, 3.6% Other, 1.3% Hispanic of any race (2000); Density: 17.7 persons per square mile (2000); Age: 26.2% under 18, 13.7% over 64 (2000); Marriage status: 16.9% never married, 68.6% now married, 8.1% widowed, 6.4% divorced (2000); Foreign born: 0.6% (2000); Ancestry (includes multiple ancestries): 12.9% Irish, 11.8% English, 11.4% American, 5.2% German (2000).

Economy: Employment by occupation: 9.4% management, 11.0% professional, 14.1% services, 18.6% sales, 4.0% farming, 26.5% construction, 16.3% production (2000).

Income: Per capita income: $16,650 (2000); Median household income: $32,887 (2000); Poverty rate: 179.1% (2000).

Education: Percent of population age 25 and over with: High school diploma (including GED) or higher: 77.5% (2000); Bachelor's degree or higher: 7.2% (2000).

School District(s)

Warren ISD (PK-12)
    2009-10 Enrollment: 1,223 . . . . (409) 547-2241

Housing: Homeownership rate: 87.3% (2000); Median home value: $44,500 (2000); Median contract rent: $275 per month (2000); Median year structure built: 1974 (2000).

Transportation: Commute to work: 88.0% car, 0.4% public transportation, 0.6% walk, 9.1% work from home (2000); Travel time to work: 18.4% less than 15 minutes, 20.5% 15 to 30 minutes, 10.0% 30 to 45 minutes, 24.0% 45 to 60 minutes, 27.0% 60 minutes or more (2000)

WOODVILLE (town). County seat. Covers a land area of 3.152 square miles and a water area of <.001 square miles. Located at 30.77° N. Lat; 94.42° W. Long. Elevation is 269 feet.

History: Settled c.1847, incorporated 1929.

Population: 2,636 (1990); 2,415 (2000); 2,349 (2010); 2,305 (2015 projected); Race: 66.0% White, 30.4% Black, 0.8% Asian, 2.8% Other, 2.0% Hispanic of any race (2010); Density: 745.3 persons per square mile (2010); Average household size: 2.24 (2010); Median age: 41.9 (2010); Males per 100 females: 79.9 (2010); Marriage status: 18.3% never married, 52.8% now married, 13.1% widowed, 15.7% divorced (2005-2009 5-year est.); Foreign born: 0.0% (2005-2009 5-year est.); Ancestry (includes multiple ancestries): 13.5% English, 11.2% Irish, 9.9% German, 7.4% American, 6.4% French (2005-2009 5-year est.).

Economy: Single-family building permits issued: 4 (2010); Multi-family building permits issued: 0 (2010); Employment by occupation: 4.3% management, 36.4% professional, 24.1% services, 10.8% sales, 2.3% farming, 8.7% construction, 13.4% production (2005-2009 5-year est.).

Income: Per capita income: $19,064 (2010); Median household income: $31,739 (2010); Average household income: $44,303 (2010); Percent of households with income of $100,000 or more: 8.7% (2010); Poverty rate: 30.1% (2005-2009 5-year est.).

Taxes: Total city taxes per capita: $587 (2007); City property taxes per capita: $153 (2007).

Education: Percent of population age 25 and over with: High school diploma (including GED) or higher: 83.9% (2010); Bachelor's degree or higher: 23.3% (2010); Master's degree or higher: 8.1% (2010).

School District(s)

Woodville ISD (PK-12)
    2009-10 Enrollment: 1,307 . . . . (409) 283-3752

Housing: Homeownership rate: 57.3% (2010); Median home value: $87,917 (2010); Median contract rent: $466 per month (2005-2009 5-year est.); Median year structure built: 1974 (2005-2009 5-year est.).

Hospitals: Tyler County Hospital District (49 beds)

Safety: Violent crime rate: 35.3 per 10,000 population; Property crime rate: 128.0 per 10,000 population (2009).

Newspapers: Tyler County Advertiser (Community news; Circulation 13,850); Tyler County Booster (Community news; Circulation 4,550)

Transportation: Commute to work: 90.4% car, 0.0% public transportation, 0.6% walk, 2.1% work from home (2005-2009 5-year est.); Travel time to work: 58.1% less than 15 minutes, 11.2% 15 to 30 minutes, 16.1% 30 to 45 minutes, 3.5% 45 to 60 minutes, 11.2% 60 minutes or more (2005-2009 5-year est.)

Additional Information Contacts

Tyler County Chamber of Commerce . . . . (409) 283-2632
    http://www.tylercountychamber.com

Upshur County

Located in northeastern Texas; bounded partly on the south by the Sabine River; drained by Cypress and Little Cypress Bayous. Covers a land area of 587.64 square miles, a water area of 5.02 square miles, and is located in the Central Time Zone at 32.71° N. Lat., 94.94° W. Long. The county was founded in 1846. County seat is Gilmer.

Upshur County is part of the Longview, TX Metropolitan Statistical Area. The entire metro area includes: Gregg County, TX; Rusk County, TX; Upshur County, TX

Weather Station: Gilmer 2 W										Elevation: 390 feet		
	Jan	Feb	Mar	Apr	May	Jun	Jul	Aug	Sep	Oct	Nov	Dec
High	56	61	68	75	82	89	93	94	88	77	67	58
Low	33	36	43	50	60	67	71	70	62	51	43	34
Precip	3.6	4.0	4.4	3.4	4.7	3.8	3.0	2.7	3.5	4.9	4.3	4.4
Snow	0.5	0.7	0.1	0.0	0.0	0.0	0.0	0.0	0.0	0.0	tr	0.3

High and Low temperatures in degrees Fahrenheit; Precipitation and Snow in inches

Population: 31,370 (1990); 35,291 (2000); 38,553 (2010); 40,072 (2015 projected); Race: 84.8% White, 9.7% Black, 0.3% Asian, 5.2% Other, 5.1% Hispanic of any race (2010); Density: 65.6 persons per square mile (2010); Average household size: 2.58 (2010); Median age: 37.7 (2010); Males per 100 females: 96.1 (2010).

Religion: Five largest groups: 27.3% Southern Baptist Convention, 11.4% Baptist Missionary Association of America, 4.3% The United Methodist Church, 4.0% Churches of Christ, 3.8% Catholic Church (2000).

Economy: Unemployment rate: 7.7% (June 2011); Total civilian labor force: 20,728 (June 2011); Leading industries: 18.9% retail trade; 13.6% health care and social assistance; 13.4% accommodation & food services (2009); Farms: 1,507 totaling 198,131 acres (2007); Companies that employ 500 or more persons: 0 (2009); Companies that employ 100 to 499 persons: 4 (2009); Companies that employ less than 100 persons: 470 (2009); Black-owned businesses: n/a (2007); Hispanic-owned businesses: n/a (2007); Asian-owned businesses: n/a (2007); Women-owned businesses: n/a (2007); Retail sales per capita: $5,639 (2010). Single-family building permits issued: 15 (2010); Multi-family building permits issued: 0 (2010).

Income: Per capita income: $21,311 (2010); Median household income: $44,075 (2010); Average household income: $55,362 (2010); Percent of households with income of $100,000 or more: 11.2% (2010); Poverty rate: 15.9% (2009); Bankruptcy rate: 1.78% (2010).

Taxes: Total county taxes per capita: $267 (2007); County property taxes per capita: $223 (2007).

Education: Percent of population age 25 and over with: High school diploma (including GED) or higher: 83.2% (2010); Bachelor's degree or higher: 15.2% (2010); Master's degree or higher: 4.4% (2010).

Housing: Homeownership rate: 77.0% (2010); Median home value: $85,312 (2010); Median contract rent: $413 per month (2005-2009 5-year est.); Median year structure built: 1978 (2005-2009 5-year est.)

Health: Birth rate: 133.0 per 10,000 population (2009); Death rate: 102.5 per 10,000 population (2009); Age-adjusted cancer mortality rate: 226.7 deaths per 100,000 population (2007); Number of physicians: 4.0 per 10,000 population (2008); Hospital beds: 9.9 per 10,000 population (2007); Hospital admissions: 358.3 per 10,000 population (2007).

Elections: 2008 Presidential election results: 25.0% Obama, 74.0% McCain, 0.1% Nader

Additional Information Contacts

Upshur County Government . . . . (903) 843-4015
    http://www.countyofupshur.com
Big Sandy Chamber of Commerce . . . . (903) 636-2238
    http://www.bigsandycdc.com/chamber-of-commerce.html
Gilmer Area Chamber of Commerce . . . . (903) 843-2413
    http://www.gilmerareachamber.com

Upshur County Communities

BIG SANDY (town). Covers a land area of 1.637 square miles and a water area of 0.032 square miles. Located at 32.58° N. Lat; 95.11° W. Long. Elevation is 367 feet.

Population: 1,294 (1990); 1,288 (2000); 1,449 (2010); 1,524 (2015 projected); Race: 78.9% White, 13.7% Black, 2.3% Asian, 5.2% Other, 3.9% Hispanic of any race (2010); Density: 885.1 persons per square mile (2010); Average household size: 2.52 (2010); Median age: 35.3 (2010); Males per 100 females: 94.8 (2010); Marriage status: 28.0% never married, 56.2% now married, 4.6% widowed, 11.2% divorced (2005-2009 5-year est.); Foreign born: 1.3% (2005-2009 5-year est.); Ancestry (includes multiple ancestries): 14.2% German, 14.1% Irish, 13.8% American, 10.8% English, 3.9% French (2005-2009 5-year est.).

Economy: Single-family building permits issued: 1 (2010); Multi-family building permits issued: 0 (2010); Employment by occupation: 9.0% management, 12.6% professional, 12.2% services, 27.9% sales, 0.0% farming, 17.1% construction, 21.2% production (2005-2009 5-year est.).

Income: Per capita income: $19,689 (2010); Median household income: $37,851 (2010); Average household income: $49,874 (2010); Percent of households with income of $100,000 or more: 10.8% (2010); Poverty rate: 19.4% (2005-2009 5-year est.).

Taxes: Total city taxes per capita: $204 (2007); City property taxes per capita: $114 (2007).
Education: Percent of population age 25 and over with: High school diploma (including GED) or higher: 85.8% (2010); Bachelor's degree or higher: 17.4% (2010); Master's degree or higher: 5.3% (2010).
School District(s)
Big Sandy ISD (PK-12)
  2009-10 Enrollment: 704 . . . . (903) 636-5318
Harmony ISD (PK-12)
  2009-10 Enrollment: 1,072 . . . . (903) 725-5492
Housing: Homeownership rate: 60.8% (2010); Median home value: $76,415 (2010); Median contract rent: $489 per month (2005-2009 5-year est.); Median year structure built: 1974 (2005-2009 5-year est.).
Safety: Violent crime rate: 14.6 per 10,000 population; Property crime rate: 124.3 per 10,000 population (2009).
Newspapers: Big Sandy & Hawkins Journal (Community news; Circulation 1,550)
Transportation: Commute to work: 90.2% car, 0.5% public transportation, 1.6% walk, 5.8% work from home (2005-2009 5-year est.); Travel time to work: 33.2% less than 15 minutes, 25.2% 15 to 30 minutes, 21.0% 30 to 45 minutes, 13.9% 45 to 60 minutes, 6.7% 60 minutes or more (2005-2009 5-year est.)
Additional Information Contacts
Big Sandy Chamber of Commerce . . . . (903) 636-2238
  http://www.bigsandycdc.com/chamber-of-commerce.html

DIANA (unincorporated postal area, zip code 75640). Aka James. Covers a land area of 85.154 square miles and a water area of 0.105 square miles. Located at 32.72° N. Lat; 94.69° W. Long. Elevation is 315 feet.
Population: 4,047 (2000); Race: 88.2% White, 10.4% Black, 0.0% Asian, 1.4% Other, 1.7% Hispanic of any race (2000); Density: 47.5 persons per square mile (2000); Age: 26.5% under 18, 13.3% over 64 (2000); Marriage status: 16.3% never married, 70.9% now married, 5.5% widowed, 7.3% divorced; Foreign born: 0.6% (2000); Ancestry (includes multiple ancestries): 18.8% American, 12.3% Irish, 9.5% German, 8.3% English (2000).
Economy: Employment by occupation: 5.2% management, 14.2% professional, 13.4% services, 28.7% sales, 1.3% farming, 16.4% construction, 20.7% production (2000).
Income: Per capita income: $15,501 (2000); Median household income: $35,146 (2000); Poverty rate: 179.1% (2000).
Education: Percent of population age 25 and over with: High school diploma (including GED) or higher: 76.8% (2000); Bachelor's degree or higher: 9.4% (2000).
School District(s)
New Diana ISD (PK-12)
  2009-10 Enrollment: 982 . . . . (903) 663-8000
Housing: Homeownership rate: 87.4% (2000); Median home value: $60,800 (2000); Median contract rent: $352 per month (2000); Median year structure built: 1979 (2000).
Transportation: Commute to work: 96.1% car, 0.3% public transportation, 0.8% walk, 2.2% work from home (2000); Travel time to work: 12.7% less than 15 minutes, 34.9% 15 to 30 minutes, 39.3% 30 to 45 minutes, 7.9% 45 to 60 minutes, 5.2% 60 minutes or more (2000)

EAST MOUNTAIN (city). Covers a land area of 2.031 square miles and a water area of 0 square miles. Located at 32.60° N. Lat; 94.86° W. Long. Elevation is 430 feet.
Population: 779 (1990); 580 (2000); 628 (2010); 650 (2015 projected); Race: 92.5% White, 3.5% Black, 0.2% Asian, 3.8% Other, 3.7% Hispanic of any race (2010); Density: 309.2 persons per square mile (2010); Average household size: 2.52 (2010); Median age: 39.9 (2010); Males per 100 females: 98.1 (2010); Marriage status: 8.7% never married, 75.0% now married, 5.2% widowed, 11.1% divorced (2005-2009 5-year est.); Foreign born: 4.0% (2005-2009 5-year est.); Ancestry (includes multiple ancestries): 36.2% American, 17.8% Irish, 13.3% German, 12.8% English, 8.3% Norwegian (2005-2009 5-year est.).
Economy: Employment by occupation: 6.9% management, 9.4% professional, 17.4% services, 23.9% sales, 0.0% farming, 12.7% construction, 29.7% production (2005-2009 5-year est.).
Income: Per capita income: $22,775 (2010); Median household income: $48,688 (2010); Average household income: $58,614 (2010); Percent of households with income of $100,000 or more: 11.2% (2010); Poverty rate: 16.7% (2005-2009 5-year est.).

Taxes: Total city taxes per capita: $108 (2007); City property taxes per capita: $50 (2007).
Education: Percent of population age 25 and over with: High school diploma (including GED) or higher: 81.1% (2010); Bachelor's degree or higher: 16.6% (2010); Master's degree or higher: 6.0% (2010).
Housing: Homeownership rate: 81.1% (2010); Median home value: $83,571 (2010); Median contract rent: $489 per month (2005-2009 5-year est.); Median year structure built: 1982 (2005-2009 5-year est.).
Safety: Violent crime rate: 47.4 per 10,000 population; Property crime rate: 221.2 per 10,000 population (2009).
Transportation: Commute to work: 88.7% car, 0.0% public transportation, 0.0% walk, 8.0% work from home (2005-2009 5-year est.); Travel time to work: 27.8% less than 15 minutes, 52.4% 15 to 30 minutes, 9.1% 30 to 45 minutes, 1.6% 45 to 60 minutes, 9.1% 60 minutes or more (2005-2009 5-year est.)

GILMER (city). County seat. Covers a land area of 4.621 square miles and a water area of 0 square miles. Located at 32.73° N. Lat; 94.94° W. Long. Elevation is 367 feet.
History: Gilmer was known in its early days for the growing of yams. Later it became an oil center. A story about Sam Houston tells that he gave the name of San Jacinto corn to the corn he was eating in Gilmer, and directed his soldiers to take the corn with them and plant it across the state.
Population: 4,955 (1990); 4,799 (2000); 5,285 (2010); 5,502 (2015 projected); Race: 75.9% White, 19.6% Black, 0.1% Asian, 4.4% Other, 5.6% Hispanic of any race (2010); Density: 1,143.7 persons per square mile (2010); Average household size: 2.37 (2010); Median age: 38.6 (2010); Males per 100 females: 88.1 (2010); Marriage status: 22.3% never married, 44.2% now married, 21.7% widowed, 11.7% divorced (2005-2009 5-year est.); Foreign born: 3.8% (2005-2009 5-year est.); Ancestry (includes multiple ancestries): 12.5% Irish, 12.1% German, 11.5% American, 10.1% English, 3.0% African (2005-2009 5-year est.).
Economy: Single-family building permits issued: 13 (2010); Multi-family building permits issued: 0 (2010); Employment by occupation: 12.1% management, 18.8% professional, 17.8% services, 30.6% sales, 0.0% farming, 8.9% construction, 11.7% production (2005-2009 5-year est.).
Income: Per capita income: $21,965 (2010); Median household income: $39,867 (2010); Average household income: $53,001 (2010); Percent of households with income of $100,000 or more: 12.0% (2010); Poverty rate: 14.6% (2005-2009 5-year est.).
Taxes: Total city taxes per capita: $559 (2007); City property taxes per capita: $275 (2007).
Education: Percent of population age 25 and over with: High school diploma (including GED) or higher: 83.7% (2010); Bachelor's degree or higher: 20.8% (2010); Master's degree or higher: 4.2% (2010).
School District(s)
Big Sandy ISD (PK-12)
  2009-10 Enrollment: 704 . . . . (903) 636-5318
Gilmer ISD (PK-12)
  2009-10 Enrollment: 2,354 . . . . (903) 841-7400
Union Hill ISD (PK-12)
  2009-10 Enrollment: 299 . . . . (903) 762-2140
Housing: Homeownership rate: 64.9% (2010); Median home value: $90,531 (2010); Median contract rent: $335 per month (2005-2009 5-year est.); Median year structure built: 1970 (2005-2009 5-year est.).
Hospitals: East Texas Medical Center-Gilmer
Safety: Violent crime rate: 77.4 per 10,000 population; Property crime rate: 522.6 per 10,000 population (2009).
Newspapers: Gilmer Mirror (Local news; Circulation 5,000)
Transportation: Commute to work: 93.4% car, 0.0% public transportation, 1.8% walk, 4.3% work from home (2005-2009 5-year est.); Travel time to work: 50.1% less than 15 minutes, 17.9% 15 to 30 minutes, 18.1% 30 to 45 minutes, 8.1% 45 to 60 minutes, 5.8% 60 minutes or more (2005-2009 5-year est.)
Additional Information Contacts
Gilmer Area Chamber of Commerce . . . . (903) 843-2413
  http://www.gilmerareachamber.com

ORE CITY (city). Covers a land area of 2.255 square miles and a water area of 0.017 square miles. Located at 32.80° N. Lat; 94.71° W. Long. Elevation is 328 feet.
Population: 898 (1990); 1,106 (2000); 1,178 (2010); 1,214 (2015 projected); Race: 83.6% White, 5.9% Black, 1.3% Asian, 9.2% Other, 10.5% Hispanic of any race (2010); Density: 522.3 persons per square mile (2010); Average household size: 2.67 (2010); Median age: 32.4 (2010);

Males per 100 females: 91.9 (2010); Marriage status: 21.4% never married, 54.8% now married, 5.0% widowed, 18.8% divorced (2005-2009 5-year est.); Foreign born: 8.6% (2005-2009 5-year est.); Ancestry (includes multiple ancestries): 16.4% American, 15.5% German, 11.3% English, 7.2% Irish, 4.5% Scotch-Irish (2005-2009 5-year est.).
Economy: Single-family building permits issued: 1 (2010); Multi-family building permits issued: 0 (2010); Employment by occupation: 6.5% management, 15.5% professional, 8.6% services, 27.6% sales, 1.7% farming, 13.4% construction, 26.6% production (2005-2009 5-year est.).
Income: Per capita income: $20,933 (2010); Median household income: $48,185 (2010); Average household income: $56,122 (2010); Percent of households with income of $100,000 or more: 10.2% (2010); Poverty rate: 13.7% (2005-2009 5-year est.).
Taxes: Total city taxes per capita: $229 (2007); City property taxes per capita: $146 (2007).
Education: Percent of population age 25 and over with: High school diploma (including GED) or higher: 80.9% (2010); Bachelor's degree or higher: 10.4% (2010); Master's degree or higher: 2.2% (2010).

School District(s)
Ore City ISD (PK-12)
    2009-10 Enrollment: 868 . . . . (903) 968-3300
Housing: Homeownership rate: 65.1% (2010); Median home value: $82,500 (2010); Median contract rent: $379 per month (2005-2009 5-year est.); Median year structure built: 1973 (2005-2009 5-year est.).
Transportation: Commute to work: 90.5% car, 0.0% public transportation, 4.2% walk, 5.2% work from home (2005-2009 5-year est.); Travel time to work: 21.6% less than 15 minutes, 38.1% 15 to 30 minutes, 25.1% 30 to 45 minutes, 7.7% 45 to 60 minutes, 7.5% 60 minutes or more (2005-2009 5-year est.)

UNION GROVE (city). Covers a land area of 0.958 square miles and a water area of 0 square miles. Located at 32.58° N. Lat; 94.91° W. Long. Elevation is 410 feet.
Population: 271 (1990); 346 (2000); 349 (2010); 352 (2015 projected); Race: 91.7% White, 2.9% Black, 0.0% Asian, 5.4% Other, 3.2% Hispanic of any race (2010); Density: 364.3 persons per square mile (2010); Average household size: 2.68 (2010); Median age: 39.1 (2010); Males per 100 females: 100.6 (2010); Marriage status: 15.5% never married, 67.1% now married, 8.5% widowed, 8.8% divorced (2005-2009 5-year est.); Foreign born: 0.0% (2005-2009 5-year est.); Ancestry (includes multiple ancestries): 28.8% American, 18.4% Irish, 13.4% German, 4.0% English, 2.1% Norwegian (2005-2009 5-year est.).
Economy: Employment by occupation: 10.3% management, 6.2% professional, 7.5% services, 39.0% sales, 0.0% farming, 19.2% construction, 17.8% production (2005-2009 5-year est.).
Income: Per capita income: $18,878 (2010); Median household income: $43,864 (2010); Average household income: $53,115 (2010); Percent of households with income of $100,000 or more: 8.5% (2010); Poverty rate: 21.5% (2005-2009 5-year est.).
Taxes: Total city taxes per capita: $437 (2007); City property taxes per capita: $190 (2007).
Education: Percent of population age 25 and over with: High school diploma (including GED) or higher: 84.7% (2010); Bachelor's degree or higher: 16.9% (2010); Master's degree or higher: 7.0% (2010).
Housing: Homeownership rate: 82.3% (2010); Median home value: $88,462 (2010); Median contract rent: $650 per month (2005-2009 5-year est.); Median year structure built: 1976 (2005-2009 5-year est.).
Transportation: Commute to work: 97.9% car, 0.0% public transportation, 0.0% walk, 2.1% work from home (2005-2009 5-year est.); Travel time to work: 35.0% less than 15 minutes, 25.2% 15 to 30 minutes, 28.0% 30 to 45 minutes, 4.9% 45 to 60 minutes, 7.0% 60 minutes or more (2005-2009 5-year est.)

Upton County

Located in west Texas; high prairie area, with the Castle and King Mountains in the southwest. Covers a land area of 1,241.68 square miles, a water area of 0.16 square miles, and is located in the Central Time Zone at 31.33° N. Lat., 102.09° W. Long. The county was founded in 1887. County seat is Rankin.

Weather Station: Mccamey   Elevation: 2,450 feet

	Jan	Feb	Mar	Apr	May	Jun	Jul	Aug	Sep	Oct	Nov	Dec
High	60	66	74	82	90	95	96	95	89	80	69	61
Low	33	38	45	52	63	70	73	72	65	55	43	34
Precip	0.6	0.7	0.5	1.0	1.4	1.8	1.1	1.9	2.0	2.2	0.8	0.8
Snow	0.7	0.1	tr	tr	0.0	0.0	0.0	0.0	0.0	tr	0.5	0.2

High and Low temperatures in degrees Fahrenheit; Precipitation and Snow in inches

Population: 4,447 (1990); 3,404 (2000); 3,187 (2010); 3,073 (2015 projected); Race: 74.7% White, 2.0% Black, 0.0% Asian, 23.3% Other, 47.7% Hispanic of any race (2010); Density: 2.6 persons per square mile (2010); Average household size: 2.52 (2010); Median age: 39.8 (2010); Males per 100 females: 97.2 (2010).
Religion: Five largest groups: 30.6% Southern Baptist Convention, 11.3% Catholic Church, 11.0% The United Methodist Church, 5.3% Assemblies of God, 5.0% Churches of Christ (2000).
Economy: Unemployment rate: 5.0% (June 2011); Total civilian labor force: 1,863 (June 2011); Leading industries: 39.2% mining; 9.5% retail trade; 6.6% wholesale trade (2009); Farms: 110 totaling 634,516 acres (2007); Companies that employ 500 or more persons: 0 (2009); Companies that employ 100 to 499 persons: 0 (2009); Companies that employ less than 100 persons: 80 (2009); Black-owned businesses: n/a (2007); Hispanic-owned businesses: n/a (2007); Asian-owned businesses: n/a (2007); Women-owned businesses: n/a (2007); Retail sales per capita: $4,862 (2010). Single-family building permits issued: 1 (2010); Multi-family building permits issued: 0 (2010).
Income: Per capita income: $21,652 (2010); Median household income: $42,064 (2010); Average household income: $55,090 (2010); Percent of households with income of $100,000 or more: 11.8% (2010); Poverty rate: 16.0% (2009); Bankruptcy rate: 0.30% (2010).
Taxes: Total county taxes per capita: $359 (2007); County property taxes per capita: $286 (2007).
Education: Percent of population age 25 and over with: High school diploma (including GED) or higher: 72.9% (2010); Bachelor's degree or higher: 13.5% (2010); Master's degree or higher: 4.0% (2010).
Housing: Homeownership rate: 73.4% (2010); Median home value: $35,153 (2010); Median contract rent: $306 per month (2005-2009 5-year est.); Median year structure built: 1960 (2005-2009 5-year est.)
Health: Birth rate: 185.3 per 10,000 population (2009); Death rate: 19.2 per 10,000 population (2009); Age-adjusted cancer mortality rate: 250.4 (Unreliable) deaths per 100,000 population (2007); Number of physicians: 3.3 per 10,000 population (2008); Hospital beds: 168.0 per 10,000 population (2007); Hospital admissions: 682.1 per 10,000 population (2007).
Elections: 2008 Presidential election results: 24.1% Obama, 75.0% McCain, 0.0% Nader
Additional Information Contacts
Upton County Government . . . . (432) 693-2321
    http://www.co.upton.tx.us/ips/cms
McCamey Chamber of Commerce . . . . (432) 652-8202
    http://www.mccameychamber.com

Upton County Communities

MCCAMEY (city). Covers a land area of 2.005 square miles and a water area of 0 square miles. Located at 31.13° N. Lat; 102.22° W. Long. Elevation is 2,467 feet.
History: McCamey sprang into existence when the No. 1 Baker well began producing in 1925. The well produced on November 16; the first lot was sold on November 18 and carpenters began work within 30 minutes on the building. The world's first recorded Rattlesnake Derby was held in McCamey in 1936.
Population: 2,499 (1990); 1,805 (2000); 1,662 (2010); 1,591 (2015 projected); Race: 73.3% White, 1.6% Black, 0.0% Asian, 25.0% Other, 56.0% Hispanic of any race (2010); Density: 829.1 persons per square mile (2010); Average household size: 2.51 (2010); Median age: 37.6 (2010); Males per 100 females: 98.3 (2010); Marriage status: 18.4% never married, 61.6% now married, 5.6% widowed, 14.4% divorced (2005-2009 5-year est.); Foreign born: 11.0% (2005-2009 5-year est.); Ancestry (includes multiple ancestries): 10.0% Irish, 8.8% German, 3.8% English, 1.7% Dutch, 1.7% Polish (2005-2009 5-year est.).
Economy: Single-family building permits issued: 1 (2010); Multi-family building permits issued: 0 (2010); Employment by occupation: 3.1% management, 17.8% professional, 29.4% services, 17.5% sales, 2.5% farming, 13.2% construction, 16.6% production (2005-2009 5-year est.).

Income: Per capita income: $18,570 (2010); Median household income: $34,615 (2010); Average household income: $46,670 (2010); Percent of households with income of $100,000 or more: 8.7% (2010); Poverty rate: 20.4% (2005-2009 5-year est.).
Taxes: Total city taxes per capita: $217 (2007); City property taxes per capita: $64 (2007).
Education: Percent of population age 25 and over with: High school diploma (including GED) or higher: 67.8% (2010); Bachelor's degree or higher: 10.6% (2010); Master's degree or higher: 5.1% (2010).

School District(s)
McCamey ISD (PK-12)
   2009-10 Enrollment: 478 . . . . (432) 652-3666
Housing: Homeownership rate: 77.2% (2010); Median home value: $32,101 (2010); Median contract rent: $263 per month (2005-2009 5-year est.); Median year structure built: 1958 (2005-2009 5-year est.).
Hospitals: McCamey County Hospital District
Newspapers: McCamey News (Community news; Circulation 1,000)
Transportation: Commute to work: 92.8% car, 0.0% public transportation, 3.3% walk, 3.1% work from home (2005-2009 5-year est.); Travel time to work: 77.5% less than 15 minutes, 5.3% 15 to 30 minutes, 6.5% 30 to 45 minutes, 3.2% 45 to 60 minutes, 7.4% 60 minutes or more (2005-2009 5-year est.)

Additional Information Contacts
McCamey Chamber of Commerce . . . . (432) 652-8202
   http://www.mccameychamber.com

MIDKIFF (unincorporated postal area, zip code 79755). Aka Hadacol Corners. Covers a land area of 199.866 square miles and a water area of 0.127 square miles. Located at 31.60° N. Lat; 101.86° W. Long. Elevation is 2,736 feet.
Population: 245 (2000); Race: 87.3% White, 0.0% Black, 0.0% Asian, 12.7% Other, 50.0% Hispanic of any race (2000); Density: 1.2 persons per square mile (2000); Age: 36.9% under 18, 5.6% over 64 (2000); Marriage status: 19.1% never married, 77.5% now married, 1.1% widowed, 2.2% divorced (2000); Foreign born: 46.4% (2000); Ancestry (includes multiple ancestries): 27.8% German, 9.9% English, 6.3% Dutch, 3.6% Scottish (2000).
Economy: Employment by occupation: 25.5% management, 7.1% professional, 6.1% services, 13.3% sales, 33.7% farming, 10.2% construction, 4.1% production (2000).
Income: Per capita income: $12,752 (2000); Median household income: $26,875 (2000); Poverty rate: 179.1% (2000).
Education: Percent of population age 25 and over with: High school diploma (including GED) or higher: 56.2% (2000); Bachelor's degree or higher: 18.2% (2000).
Housing: Homeownership rate: 48.7% (2000); Median home value: $60,000 (2000); Median contract rent: $242 per month (2000); Median year structure built: 1977 (2000).
Transportation: Commute to work: 78.6% car, 0.0% public transportation, 3.1% walk, 15.3% work from home (2000); Travel time to work: 61.4% less than 15 minutes, 18.1% 15 to 30 minutes, 14.5% 30 to 45 minutes, 6.0% 45 to 60 minutes, 0.0% 60 minutes or more (2000)

RANKIN (city). County seat. Covers a land area of 1.064 square miles and a water area of 0 square miles. Located at 31.22° N. Lat; 101.94° W. Long. Elevation is 2,516 feet.
Population: 1,011 (1990); 800 (2000); 763 (2010); 743 (2015 projected); Race: 76.3% White, 3.1% Black, 0.0% Asian, 20.6% Other, 32.1% Hispanic of any race (2010); Density: 717.1 persons per square mile (2010); Average household size: 2.44 (2010); Median age: 44.0 (2010); Males per 100 females: 96.6 (2010); Marriage status: 21.4% never married, 51.8% now married, 3.8% widowed, 22.9% divorced (2005-2009 5-year est.); Foreign born: 9.7% (2005-2009 5-year est.); Ancestry (includes multiple ancestries): 15.4% Irish, 7.6% English, 6.5% German, 4.3% African, 1.5% Scottish (2005-2009 5-year est.).
Economy: Employment by occupation: 14.9% management, 17.6% professional, 11.2% services, 28.1% sales, 0.0% farming, 8.1% construction, 20.0% production (2005-2009 5-year est.).
Income: Per capita income: $24,983 (2010); Median household income: $52,083 (2010); Average household income: $62,259 (2010); Percent of households with income of $100,000 or more: 15.1% (2010); Poverty rate: 21.0% (2005-2009 5-year est.).
Taxes: Total city taxes per capita: $151 (2007); City property taxes per capita: $63 (2007).

Education: Percent of population age 25 and over with: High school diploma (including GED) or higher: 79.2% (2010); Bachelor's degree or higher: 14.5% (2010); Master's degree or higher: 2.8% (2010).
School District(s)
Rankin ISD (PK-12)
   2009-10 Enrollment: 240 . . . . (432) 693-2461
Housing: Homeownership rate: 70.7% (2010); Median home value: $32,048 (2010); Median contract rent: $309 per month (2005-2009 5-year est.); Median year structure built: 1962 (2005-2009 5-year est.).
Hospitals: Rankin District Hospital (15 beds)
Newspapers: NEWS (Community news; Circulation 710)
Transportation: Commute to work: 98.6% car, 0.0% public transportation, 0.0% walk, 1.4% work from home (2005-2009 5-year est.); Travel time to work: 61.5% less than 15 minutes, 13.5% 15 to 30 minutes, 11.8% 30 to 45 minutes, 3.1% 45 to 60 minutes, 10.1% 60 minutes or more (2005-2009 5-year est.)
Airports: Rankin (general aviation)

Uvalde County

Located in southwestern Texas; drained by the Nueces, Frio, Leona, and Sabinal Rivers. Covers a land area of 1,556.55 square miles, a water area of 2.06 square miles, and is located in the Central Time Zone at 29.28° N. Lat., 99.73° W. Long. The county was founded in 1850. County seat is Uvalde.

Uvalde County is part of the Uvalde, TX Micropolitan Statistical Area. The entire metro area includes: Uvalde County, TX

Population: 23,340 (1990); 25,926 (2000); 26,258 (2010); 26,370 (2015 projected); Race: 74.2% White, 1.0% Black, 0.6% Asian, 24.2% Other, 67.4% Hispanic of any race (2010); Density: 16.9 persons per square mile (2010); Average household size: 2.92 (2010); Median age: 33.2 (2010); Males per 100 females: 94.1 (2010).
Religion: Five largest groups: 58.8% Catholic Church, 15.2% Southern Baptist Convention, 5.7% The United Methodist Church, 2.8% Churches of Christ, 1.4% Assemblies of God (2000).
Economy: Unemployment rate: 10.2% (June 2011); Total civilian labor force: 11,951 (June 2011); Leading industries: 21.2% health care and social assistance; 19.6% retail trade; 14.5% accommodation & food services (2009); Farms: 690 totaling 989,917 acres (2007); Companies that employ 500 or more persons: 0 (2009); Companies that employ 100 to 499 persons: 10 (2009); Companies that employ less than 100 persons: 565 (2009); Black-owned businesses: n/a (2007); Hispanic-owned businesses: 1,287 (2007); Asian-owned businesses: n/a (2007); Women-owned businesses: n/a (2007); Retail sales per capita: $12,834 (2010). Single-family building permits issued: 10 (2010); Multi-family building permits issued: 2 (2010).
Income: Per capita income: $16,497 (2010); Median household income: $35,065 (2010); Average household income: $48,751 (2010); Percent of households with income of $100,000 or more: 9.5% (2010); Poverty rate: 31.5% (2009); Bankruptcy rate: 0.82% (2010).
Taxes: Total county taxes per capita: $261 (2007); County property taxes per capita: $177 (2007).
Education: Percent of population age 25 and over with: High school diploma (including GED) or higher: 70.1% (2010); Bachelor's degree or higher: 14.8% (2010); Master's degree or higher: 5.2% (2010).
Housing: Homeownership rate: 75.1% (2010); Median home value: $59,643 (2010); Median contract rent: $419 per month (2005-2009 5-year est.); Median year structure built: 1974 (2005-2009 5-year est.).
Health: Birth rate: 175.3 per 10,000 population (2009); Death rate: 88.8 per 10,000 population (2009); Age-adjusted cancer mortality rate: 201.2 deaths per 100,000 population (2007); Number of physicians: 10.1 per 10,000 population (2008); Hospital beds: 18.1 per 10,000 population (2007); Hospital admissions: 827.9 per 10,000 population (2007).
Elections: 2008 Presidential election results: 47.1% Obama, 52.4% McCain, 0.0% Nader
National and State Parks: Garner State Park
Additional Information Contacts
Uvalde County Government. . . . . (830) 278-3216
   http://www.uvaldecounty.com
City of Uvalde. . . . . (830) 278-3315
   http://www.uvaldetx.com
Sabinal Chamber of Commerce. (830) 988-2010
   http://www.sabinalchamber.com

Uvalde Area Chamber of Commerce.................(830) 278-3361
http://www.uvalde.org

Uvalde County Communities

CONCAN (unincorporated postal area, zip code 78838). Covers a land area of 24.809 square miles and a water area of 0.025 square miles. Located at 29.54° N. Lat; 99.71° W. Long. Elevation is 1,253 feet.
Population: 224 (2000); Race: 93.7% White, 0.0% Black, 0.0% Asian, 6.3% Other, 29.1% Hispanic of any race (2000); Density: 9.0 persons per square mile (2000); Age: 21.7% under 18, 25.4% over 64 (2000); Marriage status: 13.4% never married, 72.6% now married, 5.1% widowed, 8.9% divorced (2000); Foreign born: 2.6% (2000); Ancestry (includes multiple ancestries): 22.2% German, 10.6% American, 6.9% Irish, 6.9% English (2000).
Economy: Employment by occupation: 17.6% management, 6.8% professional, 31.1% services, 21.6% sales, 9.5% farming, 6.8% construction, 6.8% production (2000).
Income: Per capita income: $20,152 (2000); Median household income: $40,833 (2000); Poverty rate: 179.1% (2000).
Education: Percent of population age 25 and over with: High school diploma (including GED) or higher: 80.3% (2000); Bachelor's degree or higher: 14.4% (2000).
Housing: Homeownership rate: 70.1% (2000); Median home value: $104,500 (2000); Median contract rent: $300 per month (2000); Median year structure built: 1976 (2000).
Transportation: Commute to work: 73.0% car, 0.0% public transportation, 9.5% walk, 17.6% work from home (2000); Travel time to work: 37.7% less than 15 minutes, 39.3% 15 to 30 minutes, 9.8% 30 to 45 minutes, 13.1% 45 to 60 minutes, 0.0% 60 minutes or more (2000)

KNIPPA (CDP). Covers a land area of 10.428 square miles and a water area of 0 square miles. Located at 29.29° N. Lat; 99.63° W. Long. Elevation is 981 feet.
Population: 635 (1990); 739 (2000); 713 (2010); 700 (2015 projected); Race: 75.3% White, 1.0% Black, 0.0% Asian, 23.7% Other, 54.0% Hispanic of any race (2010); Density: 68.4 persons per square mile (2010); Average household size: 2.86 (2010); Median age: 34.8 (2010); Males per 100 females: 101.4 (2010); Marriage status: 17.4% never married, 58.1% now married, 13.5% widowed, 10.9% divorced (2005-2009 5-year est.); Foreign born: 4.0% (2005-2009 5-year est.); Ancestry (includes multiple ancestries): 20.2% German, 7.8% Irish, 7.5% French, 4.3% Scotch-Irish, 2.7% Syrian (2005-2009 5-year est.).
Economy: Employment by occupation: 7.0% management, 22.5% professional, 33.5% services, 13.6% sales, 4.4% farming, 16.5% construction, 2.5% production (2005-2009 5-year est.).
Income: Per capita income: $17,135 (2010); Median household income: $39,953 (2010); Average household income: $49,588 (2010); Percent of households with income of $100,000 or more: 9.2% (2010); Poverty rate: 11.8% (2005-2009 5-year est.).
Education: Percent of population age 25 and over with: High school diploma (including GED) or higher: 76.5% (2010); Bachelor's degree or higher: 16.1% (2010); Master's degree or higher: 7.0% (2010).
School District(s)
Knippa ISD (PK-12)
    2009-10 Enrollment: 239 ....(830) 934-2176
Housing: Homeownership rate: 75.5% (2010); Median home value: $54,839 (2010); Median contract rent: n/a per month (2005-2009 5-year est.); Median year structure built: 1973 (2005-2009 5-year est.).
Transportation: Commute to work: 85.8% car, 0.0% public transportation, 7.0% walk, 0.0% work from home (2005-2009 5-year est.); Travel time to work: 56.6% less than 15 minutes, 32.3% 15 to 30 minutes, 11.1% 30 to 45 minutes, 0.0% 45 to 60 minutes, 0.0% 60 minutes or more (2005-2009 5-year est.)

SABINAL (city). Covers a land area of 1.187 square miles and a water area of 0 square miles. Located at 29.32° N. Lat; 99.46° W. Long. Elevation is 958 feet.
History: Sabinal was founded in the 1850's around Camp Sabinal, a temporary army post. The name means "cypress," referring to the trees along the river. Angora goats were brought here in 1881, and Sabinal became a center for mohair production.
Population: 1,584 (1990); 1,586 (2000); 1,559 (2010); 1,534 (2015 projected); Race: 81.5% White, 0.1% Black, 0.1% Asian, 18.3% Other, 53.2% Hispanic of any race (2010); Density: 1,313.6 persons per square

mile (2010); Average household size: 2.73 (2010); Median age: 36.4 (2010); Males per 100 females: 94.9 (2010); Marriage status: 26.3% never married, 48.2% now married, 18.7% widowed, 6.8% divorced (2005-2009 5-year est.); Foreign born: 9.9% (2005-2009 5-year est.); Ancestry (includes multiple ancestries): 18.3% German, 10.4% English, 8.2% Irish, 2.7% Scotch-Irish, 1.7% Belgian (2005-2009 5-year est.).
Economy: Employment by occupation: 5.3% management, 17.0% professional, 17.0% services, 23.3% sales, 2.7% farming, 10.2% construction, 24.5% production (2005-2009 5-year est.).
Income: Per capita income: $18,746 (2010); Median household income: $38,587 (2010); Average household income: $50,969 (2010); Percent of households with income of $100,000 or more: 11.8% (2010); Poverty rate: 32.8% (2005-2009 5-year est.).
Taxes: Total city taxes per capita: $155 (2007); City property taxes per capita: $92 (2007).
Education: Percent of population age 25 and over with: High school diploma (including GED) or higher: 73.4% (2010); Bachelor's degree or higher: 10.9% (2010); Master's degree or higher: 3.8% (2010).
School District(s)
Sabinal ISD (PK-12)
    2009-10 Enrollment: 508 ....(830) 988-2472
Housing: Homeownership rate: 82.1% (2010); Median home value: $44,565 (2010); Median contract rent: $266 per month (2005-2009 5-year est.); Median year structure built: 1965 (2005-2009 5-year est.).
Safety: Violent crime rate: 24.6 per 10,000 population; Property crime rate: 160.0 per 10,000 population (2009).
Transportation: Commute to work: 87.9% car, 0.0% public transportation, 9.5% walk, 0.0% work from home (2005-2009 5-year est.); Travel time to work: 50.9% less than 15 minutes, 14.4% 15 to 30 minutes, 19.2% 30 to 45 minutes, 6.3% 45 to 60 minutes, 9.2% 60 minutes or more (2005-2009 5-year est.)
Additional Information Contacts
Sabinal Chamber of Commerce.....................(830) 988-2010
    http://www.sabinalchamber.com

UTOPIA (CDP). Covers a land area of 2.952 square miles and a water area of 0 square miles. Located at 29.61° N. Lat; 99.52° W. Long. Elevation is 1,362 feet.
Population: 212 (1990); 241 (2000); 225 (2010); 217 (2015 projected); Race: 91.1% White, 0.0% Black, 0.4% Asian, 8.4% Other, 19.6% Hispanic of any race (2010); Density: 76.2 persons per square mile (2010); Average household size: 2.32 (2010); Median age: 51.6 (2010); Males per 100 females: 108.3 (2010); Marriage status: 16.4% never married, 62.3% now married, 10.1% widowed, 11.3% divorced (2005-2009 5-year est.); Foreign born: 0.0% (2005-2009 5-year est.); Ancestry (includes multiple ancestries): 33.3% German, 25.7% Irish, 10.5% Scotch-Irish, 8.6% French, 7.1% English (2005-2009 5-year est.).
Economy: Employment by occupation: 11.7% management, 33.3% professional, 11.7% services, 16.7% sales, 0.0% farming, 8.3% construction, 18.3% production (2005-2009 5-year est.).
Income: Per capita income: $25,080 (2010); Median household income: $45,147 (2010); Average household income: $58,000 (2010); Percent of households with income of $100,000 or more: 10.5% (2010); Poverty rate: 18.1% (2005-2009 5-year est.).
Education: Percent of population age 25 and over with: High school diploma (including GED) or higher: 86.7% (2010); Bachelor's degree or higher: 21.8% (2010); Master's degree or higher: 7.9% (2010).
School District(s)
Utopia ISD (PK-12)
    2009-10 Enrollment: 217 ....(830) 966-1928
Housing: Homeownership rate: 82.1% (2010); Median home value: $97,500 (2010); Median contract rent: $350 per month (2005-2009 5-year est.); Median year structure built: 1985 (2005-2009 5-year est.).
Transportation: Commute to work: 90.0% car, 0.0% public transportation, 10.0% walk, 0.0% work from home (2005-2009 5-year est.); Travel time to work: 78.3% less than 15 minutes, 0.0% 15 to 30 minutes, 0.0% 30 to 45 minutes, 10.0% 45 to 60 minutes, 11.7% 60 minutes or more (2005-2009 5-year est.)

UVALDE (city). County seat. Covers a land area of 6.724 square miles and a water area of 0 square miles. Located at 29.21° N. Lat; 99.79° W. Long. Elevation is 909 feet.
History: Cattlemen settled the site of Uvalde, near Fort Inge, in 1853. The name came from that of Ugalde, a Spanish military commander in the 1790's. Uvalde was once known as the Honey Capital of the World, and as

the home of John Nance Garner (1868-1967), vice president of the U.S. under Franklin D. Roosevelt.

Population: 14,647 (1990); 14,929 (2000); 14,977 (2010); 14,965 (2015 projected); Race: 71.8% White, 1.0% Black, 0.7% Asian, 26.5% Other, 75.2% Hispanic of any race (2010); Density: 2,227.3 persons per square mile (2010); Average household size: 2.99 (2010); Median age: 32.5 (2010); Males per 100 females: 91.4 (2010); Marriage status: 27.8% never married, 57.2% now married, 6.9% widowed, 8.1% divorced (2005-2009 5-year est.); Foreign born: 9.2% (2005-2009 5-year est.); Ancestry (includes multiple ancestries): 6.0% German, 4.1% English, 3.9% American, 3.0% Irish, 2.3% Scotch-Irish (2005-2009 5-year est.).
Economy: Single-family building permits issued: 10 (2010); Multi-family building permits issued: 2 (2010); Employment by occupation: 9.1% management, 12.7% professional, 17.1% services, 29.0% sales, 3.5% farming, 12.7% construction, 15.9% production (2005-2009 5-year est.).
Income: Per capita income: $15,371 (2010); Median household income: $32,515 (2010); Average household income: $46,578 (2010); Percent of households with income of $100,000 or more: 8.8% (2010); Poverty rate: 25.2% (2005-2009 5-year est.).
Taxes: Total city taxes per capita: $305 (2007); City property taxes per capita: $122 (2007).
Education: Percent of population age 25 and over with: High school diploma (including GED) or higher: 66.6% (2010); Bachelor's degree or higher: 14.4% (2010); Master's degree or higher: 4.5% (2010).

School District(s)
Gabriel Tafolla Academy (PK-12)
    2009-10 Enrollment: 108 . . . . (830) 278-1297
Sabinal ISD (PK-12)
    2009-10 Enrollment: 508 . . . . (830) 988-2472
Uvalde CISD (PK-12)
    2009-10 Enrollment: 5,098 . . . . (830) 278-6655
Two-year College(s)
Southwest Texas Junior College (Public)
    Fall 2009 Enrollment: 5,767 . . . . (830) 278-4401
    2010-11 Tuition: In-state $2,426; Out-of-state $2,726
Housing: Homeownership rate: 71.6% (2010); Median home value: $56,873 (2010); Median contract rent: $426 per month (2005-2009 5-year est.); Median year structure built: 1971 (2005-2009 5-year est.).
Hospitals: Uvalde Memorial Hospital (52 beds)
Safety: Violent crime rate: 42.7 per 10,000 population; Property crime rate: 446.5 per 10,000 population (2009).
Newspapers: Leader-News (Community news; Circulation 6,300)
Transportation: Commute to work: 94.7% car, 0.0% public transportation, 1.7% walk, 2.5% work from home (2005-2009 5-year est.); Travel time to work: 67.8% less than 15 minutes, 18.1% 15 to 30 minutes, 3.2% 30 to 45 minutes, 3.1% 45 to 60 minutes, 7.8% 60 minutes or more (2005-2009 5-year est.)
Airports: Garner Field (general aviation)
Additional Information Contacts
City of Uvalde. . . . . (830) 278-3315
    http://www.uvaldetx.com
Uvalde Area Chamber of Commerce. . . . . (830) 278-3361
    http://www.uvalde.org

UVALDE ESTATES (CDP). Covers a land area of 13.710 square miles and a water area of 0.020 square miles. Located at 29.15° N. Lat; 99.83° W. Long. Elevation is 961 feet.
Population: 1,138 (1990); 1,972 (2000); 2,154 (2010); 2,242 (2015 projected); Race: 67.1% White, 0.2% Black, 0.0% Asian, 32.6% Other, 90.1% Hispanic of any race (2010); Density: 157.1 persons per square mile (2010); Average household size: 3.70 (2010); Median age: 26.5 (2010); Males per 100 females: 96.4 (2010); Marriage status: 39.0% never married, 50.9% now married, 6.4% widowed, 3.7% divorced (2005-2009 5-year est.); Foreign born: 8.9% (2005-2009 5-year est.); Ancestry (includes multiple ancestries): 1.0% Irish, 0.8% English (2005-2009 5-year est.).
Economy: Employment by occupation: 0.0% management, 11.8% professional, 20.0% services, 34.7% sales, 2.7% farming, 13.8% construction, 16.9% production (2005-2009 5-year est.).
Income: Per capita income: $10,325 (2010); Median household income: $31,914 (2010); Average household income: $38,200 (2010); Percent of households with income of $100,000 or more: 3.8% (2010); Poverty rate: 44.4% (2005-2009 5-year est.).
Education: Percent of population age 25 and over with: High school diploma (including GED) or higher: 50.8% (2010); Bachelor's degree or higher: 4.0% (2010); Master's degree or higher: 0.0% (2010).

Housing: Homeownership rate: 85.4% (2010); Median home value: $51,832 (2010); Median contract rent: n/a per month (2005-2009 5-year est.); Median year structure built: 1978 (2005-2009 5-year est.).
Transportation: Commute to work: 82.9% car, 0.0% public transportation, 17.1% walk, 0.0% work from home (2005-2009 5-year est.); Travel time to work: 47.7% less than 15 minutes, 39.0% 15 to 30 minutes, 8.1% 30 to 45 minutes, 5.2% 45 to 60 minutes, 0.0% 60 minutes or more (2005-2009 5-year est.)

Val Verde County

Located in southwestern Texas, partly on the Edwards Plateau; bounded on the south and southwest by the Rio Grande and the Mexican border; drained by the Pecos and Devils River; includes Devils and Walk Lakes. Covers a land area of 3,170.38 square miles, a water area of 62.02 square miles, and is located in the Central Time Zone at 29.57° N. Lat., 100.99° W. Long. The county was founded in 1885. County seat is Del Rio.

Val Verde County is part of the Del Rio, TX Micropolitan Statistical Area. The entire metro area includes: Val Verde County, TX

Weather Station: Amistad Dam — Elevation: 1,157 feet

	Jan	Feb	Mar	Apr	May	Jun	Jul	Aug	Sep	Oct	Nov	Dec
High	64	68	76	84	90	95	98	98	91	82	72	63
Low	40	44	51	58	67	73	74	74	69	60	49	41
Precip	0.7	0.8	1.2	1.1	2.5	1.9	1.8	2.0	2.7	1.9	1.1	0.7
Snow	0.2	0.0	0.0	0.0	0.0	0.0	0.0	0.0	0.0	0.0	0.0	0.0

High and Low temperatures in degrees Fahrenheit; Precipitation and Snow in inches

Weather Station: Del Rio Intl Arpt — Elevation: 999 feet

	Jan	Feb	Mar	Apr	May	Jun	Jul	Aug	Sep	Oct	Nov	Dec
High	64	69	76	84	90	95	97	97	91	82	72	64
Low	41	45	52	60	68	73	75	75	70	61	50	41
Precip	0.7	0.8	1.1	1.5	2.6	2.3	1.6	1.6	2.2	2.2	1.0	0.7
Snow	na	na	na	na	na	na	na	na	na	na	na	na

High and Low temperatures in degrees Fahrenheit; Precipitation and Snow in inches

Weather Station: Langtry — Elevation: 1,290 feet

	Jan	Feb	Mar	Apr	May	Jun	Jul	Aug	Sep	Oct	Nov	Dec
High	64	69	76	85	92	96	98	98	93	83	72	64
Low	36	40	49	57	67	74	76	76	69	59	46	36
Precip	0.6	0.7	0.9	1.0	1.9	1.6	1.1	1.8	1.9	1.9	0.8	0.5
Snow	0.4	0.0	0.0	0.0	0.0	0.0	0.0	0.0	0.0	0.0	0.0	0.0

High and Low temperatures in degrees Fahrenheit; Precipitation and Snow in inches

Weather Station: Pandale 1 N — Elevation: 1,688 feet

	Jan	Feb	Mar	Apr	May	Jun	Jul	Aug	Sep	Oct	Nov	Dec
High	62	67	74	82	90	95	96	96	91	81	70	62
Low	33	37	45	54	65	71	74	73	65	55	42	33
Precip	0.7	0.8	1.3	1.2	2.1	2.2	1.2	2.7	2.3	2.2	1.0	0.6
Snow	0.3	tr	0.0	tr	0.0	0.0	0.0	0.0	0.0	tr	0.1	tr

High and Low temperatures in degrees Fahrenheit; Precipitation and Snow in inches

Population: 38,721 (1990); 44,856 (2000); 48,792 (2010); 50,622 (2015 projected); Race: 75.5% White, 1.3% Black, 0.7% Asian, 22.5% Other, 78.6% Hispanic of any race (2010); Density: 15.4 persons per square mile (2010); Average household size: 3.06 (2010); Median age: 34.2 (2010); Males per 100 females: 93.9 (2010).
Religion: Five largest groups: 30.5% Catholic Church, 9.0% Southern Baptist Convention, 2.1% The United Methodist Church, 1.8% The Church of Jesus Christ of Latter-day Saints, 1.5% Assemblies of God (2000).
Economy: Unemployment rate: 9.4% (June 2011); Total civilian labor force: 21,184 (June 2011); Leading industries: 29.5% health care and social assistance; 21.3% retail trade; 14.5% accommodation & food services (2009); Farms: 402 totaling 1,493,671 acres (2007); Companies that employ 500 or more persons: 0 (2009); Companies that employ 100 to 499 persons: 11 (2009); Companies that employ less than 100 persons: 761 (2009); Black-owned businesses: n/a (2007); Hispanic-owned businesses: 2,269 (2007); Asian-owned businesses: n/a (2007); Women-owned businesses: n/a (2007); Retail sales per capita: $11,765 (2010). Single-family building permits issued: 30 (2010); Multi-family building permits issued: 8 (2010).
Income: Per capita income: $16,588 (2010); Median household income: $37,990 (2010); Average household income: $50,539 (2010); Percent of households with income of $100,000 or more: 9.8% (2010); Poverty rate: 24.5% (2009); Bankruptcy rate: 0.80% (2010).

Taxes: Total county taxes per capita: $202 (2007); County property taxes per capita: $142 (2007).
Education: Percent of population age 25 and over with: High school diploma (including GED) or higher: 61.2% (2010); Bachelor's degree or higher: 14.2% (2010); Master's degree or higher: 4.8% (2010).
Housing: Homeownership rate: 68.3% (2010); Median home value: $73,260 (2010); Median contract rent: $381 per month (2005-2009 5-year est.); Median year structure built: 1977 (2005-2009 5-year est.)
Health: Birth rate: 195.0 per 10,000 population (2009); Death rate: 73.5 per 10,000 population (2009); Age-adjusted cancer mortality rate: 141.0 deaths per 100,000 population (2007); Number of physicians: 8.2 per 10,000 population (2008); Hospital beds: 18.1 per 10,000 population (2007); Hospital admissions: 668.1 per 10,000 population (2007).
Elections: 2008 Presidential election results: 54.5% Obama, 44.9% McCain, 0.1% Nader
National and State Parks: Amistad National Recreation Area; Seminole Canyon State Park
Additional Information Contacts
Val Verde County Government . . . . (830) 774-7501
   http://www.valverdecounty.org
City of Del Rio . . . . (830) 774-8558
   http://www.cityofdelrio.com
Del Rio Chamber of Commerce. (830) 775-3551
   http://www.drchamber.com

Val Verde County Communities

BOX CANYON-AMISTAD (CDP). Covers a land area of 4.019 square miles and a water area of 0 square miles. Located at 29.52° N. Lat; 101.16° W. Long. Elevation is 1,178 feet.
Population: 56 (1990); 76 (2000); 70 (2010); 67 (2015 projected); Race: 74.3% White, 0.0% Black, 0.0% Asian, 25.7% Other, 42.9% Hispanic of any race (2010); Density: 17.4 persons per square mile (2010); Average household size: 2.33 (2010); Median age: 51.0 (2010); Males per 100 females: 100.0 (2010); Marriage status: 0.0% never married, 46.9% now married, 39.1% widowed, 14.1% divorced (2005-2009 5-year est.); Foreign born: 6.3% (2005-2009 5-year est.); Ancestry (includes multiple ancestries): 24.1% English, 20.3% Scotch-Irish, 11.4% German, 11.4% Italian, 10.1% Irish (2005-2009 5-year est.).
Economy: Employment by occupation: 69.2% management, 7.7% professional, 15.4% services, 7.7% sales, 0.0% farming, 0.0% construction, 0.0% production (2005-2009 5-year est.).
Income: Per capita income: $16,969 (2010); Median household income: $29,000 (2010); Average household income: $37,167 (2010); Percent of households with income of $100,000 or more: 3.3% (2010); Poverty rate: 36.7% (2005-2009 5-year est.).
Education: Percent of population age 25 and over with: High school diploma (including GED) or higher: 75.5% (2010); Bachelor's degree or higher: 15.1% (2010); Master's degree or higher: 3.8% (2010).
Housing: Homeownership rate: 83.3% (2010); Median home value: $57,500 (2010); Median contract rent: n/a per month (2005-2009 5-year est.); Median year structure built: 1976 (2005-2009 5-year est.).
Transportation: Commute to work: 100.0% car, 0.0% public transportation, 0.0% walk, 0.0% work from home (2005-2009 5-year est.); Travel time to work: 0.0% less than 15 minutes, 30.8% 15 to 30 minutes, 0.0% 30 to 45 minutes, 69.2% 45 to 60 minutes, 0.0% 60 minutes or more (2005-2009 5-year est.)

CIENEGAS TERRACE (CDP). Covers a land area of 3.204 square miles and a water area of 0.036 square miles. Located at 29.36° N. Lat; 100.94° W. Long. Elevation is 961 feet.
Population: 1,330 (1990); 2,878 (2000); 3,205 (2010); 3,352 (2015 projected); Race: 56.3% White, 0.7% Black, 1.1% Asian, 41.9% Other, 81.2% Hispanic of any race (2010); Density: 1,000.3 persons per square mile (2010); Average household size: 3.14 (2010); Median age: 31.1 (2010); Males per 100 females: 95.2 (2010); Marriage status: 29.1% never married, 58.4% now married, 6.8% widowed, 5.6% divorced (2005-2009 5-year est.); Foreign born: 35.2% (2005-2009 5-year est.); Ancestry (includes multiple ancestries): 1.6% American, 1.1% German, 0.6% Italian, 0.5% Irish (2005-2009 5-year est.).
Economy: Employment by occupation: 2.9% management, 6.9% professional, 33.5% services, 15.6% sales, 0.9% farming, 17.4% construction, 22.8% production (2005-2009 5-year est.).
Income: Per capita income: $15,385 (2010); Median household income: $39,061 (2010); Average household income: $47,807 (2010); Percent of

households with income of $100,000 or more: 8.9% (2010); Poverty rate: 31.4% (2005-2009 5-year est.).
Education: Percent of population age 25 and over with: High school diploma (including GED) or higher: 53.9% (2010); Bachelor's degree or higher: 6.1% (2010); Master's degree or higher: 1.8% (2010).
Housing: Homeownership rate: 76.4% (2010); Median home value: $57,943 (2010); Median contract rent: $286 per month (2005-2009 5-year est.); Median year structure built: 1990 (2005-2009 5-year est.).
Transportation: Commute to work: 97.3% car, 0.0% public transportation, 0.7% walk, 2.0% work from home (2005-2009 5-year est.); Travel time to work: 47.1% less than 15 minutes, 32.9% 15 to 30 minutes, 6.1% 30 to 45 minutes, 6.0% 45 to 60 minutes, 7.9% 60 minutes or more (2005-2009 5-year est.)

COMSTOCK (unincorporated postal area, zip code 78837). Covers a land area of 1,441.197 square miles and a water area of 0.168 square miles. Located at 29.93° N. Lat; 101.40° W. Long. Elevation is 1,549 feet.
History: Comstock was known as Sotol City for many years. It was settled in an area previously inhabited by cave dwellers, whose homes have been excavated by archeologists.
Population: 439 (2000); Race: 74.3% White, 0.0% Black, 0.0% Asian, 25.7% Other, 53.5% Hispanic of any race (2000); Density: 0.3 persons per square mile (2000); Age: 29.8% under 18, 12.4% over 64 (2000); Marriage status: 15.7% never married, 69.5% now married, 7.3% widowed, 7.6% divorced (2000); Foreign born: 14.3% (2000); Ancestry (includes multiple ancestries): 12.0% Irish, 9.8% English, 9.3% German, 6.7% American (2000).
Economy: Employment by occupation: 10.6% management, 19.0% professional, 15.3% services, 18.5% sales, 13.8% farming, 17.5% construction, 5.3% production (2000).
Income: Per capita income: $12,281 (2000); Median household income: $22,330 (2000); Poverty rate: 179.1% (2000).
Education: Percent of population age 25 and over with: High school diploma (including GED) or higher: 71.7% (2000); Bachelor's degree or higher: 16.3% (2000).
School District(s)
Comstock ISD (PK-12)
   2009-10 Enrollment: 204 . . . . (432) 292-4444
Housing: Homeownership rate: 77.2% (2000); Median home value: $42,500 (2000); Median contract rent: $188 per month (2000); Median year structure built: 1970 (2000).
Transportation: Commute to work: 73.8% car, 0.0% public transportation, 15.5% walk, 3.7% work from home (2000); Travel time to work: 58.3% less than 15 minutes, 5.0% 15 to 30 minutes, 17.2% 30 to 45 minutes, 13.3% 45 to 60 minutes, 6.1% 60 minutes or more (2000)

DEL RIO (city). County seat. Covers a land area of 15.436 square miles and a water area of 0.011 square miles. Located at 29.37° N. Lat; 100.89° W. Long. Elevation is 968 feet.
History: Del Rio was founded on the Rio Grande by farmers, who settled in the valley of the San Felipe River. The settlement was first known as San Felipe del Rio. Sheep and goats provided the basis for the early economy, and wool and mohair were exported from Del Rio.
Population: 31,201 (1990); 33,867 (2000); 37,094 (2010); 38,607 (2015 projected); Race: 78.4% White, 1.1% Black, 0.6% Asian, 19.9% Other, 82.9% Hispanic of any race (2010); Density: 2,403.1 persons per square mile (2010); Average household size: 3.07 (2010); Median age: 35.1 (2010); Males per 100 females: 90.9 (2010); Marriage status: 25.9% never married, 56.0% now married, 9.4% widowed, 8.7% divorced (2005-2009 5-year est.); Foreign born: 21.7% (2005-2009 5-year est.); Ancestry (includes multiple ancestries): 4.9% American, 3.4% German, 2.5% English, 2.1% Irish, 1.6% Italian (2005-2009 5-year est.).
Economy: Unemployment rate: 8.9% (June 2011); Total civilian labor force: 16,680 (June 2011); Single-family building permits issued: 30 (2010); Multi-family building permits issued: 8 (2010); Employment by occupation: 8.9% management, 17.5% professional, 23.9% services, 25.8% sales, 0.5% farming, 10.6% construction, 12.8% production (2005-2009 5-year est.).
Income: Per capita income: $16,659 (2010); Median household income: $37,062 (2010); Average household income: $50,874 (2010); Percent of households with income of $100,000 or more: 10.2% (2010); Poverty rate: 23.9% (2005-2009 5-year est.).
Taxes: Total city taxes per capita: $328 (2007); City property taxes per capita: $125 (2007).

Education: Percent of population age 25 and over with: High school diploma (including GED) or higher: 59.4% (2010); Bachelor's degree or higher: 13.3% (2010); Master's degree or higher: 4.7% (2010).

School District(s)

Radiance Academy of Learning (PK-12)
  2009-10 Enrollment: 740 . . . . (210) 658-6848
Responsive Education Solutions (KG-12)
  2009-10 Enrollment: 5,022 . . . . (972) 316-3663
San Felipe-Del Rio CISD (PK-12)
  2009-10 Enrollment: 10,333 . . . . (830) 778-4007

Housing: Homeownership rate: 68.5% (2010); Median home value: $75,484 (2010); Median contract rent: $372 per month (2005-2009 5-year est.); Median year structure built: 1974 (2005-2009 5-year est.).
Hospitals: Val Verde Regional Medical Center (93 beds)
Safety: Violent crime rate: 24.1 per 10,000 population; Property crime rate: 210.8 per 10,000 population (2009).
Newspapers: Border City Shopper (Community news; Circulation 8,000); Border Eagle (Community news; Circulation 3,200); Del Rio News-Herald (Local news; Circulation 5,700)
Transportation: Commute to work: 92.1% car, 0.5% public transportation, 2.8% walk, 2.6% work from home (2005-2009 5-year est.); Travel time to work: 58.7% less than 15 minutes, 29.7% 15 to 30 minutes, 6.5% 30 to 45 minutes, 1.2% 45 to 60 minutes, 3.8% 60 minutes or more (2005-2009 5-year est.); Amtrak: train service available.
Airports: Del Rio International (primary service)
Additional Information Contacts
City of Del Rio . . . . (830) 774-8558
  http://www.cityofdelrio.com
Del Rio Chamber of Commerce. . . . . (830) 775-3551
  http://www.drchamber.com

LAKE VIEW (CDP).

Covers a land area of 0.505 square miles and a water area of 0 square miles. Located at 29.45° N. Lat; 100.94° W. Long. Elevation is 1,171 feet.
Population: 123 (1990); 167 (2000); 211 (2010); 228 (2015 projected); Race: 86.3% White, 1.4% Black, 0.9% Asian, 11.4% Other, 37.9% Hispanic of any race (2010); Density: 418.2 persons per square mile (2010); Average household size: 2.47 (2010); Median age: 47.0 (2010); Males per 100 females: 93.6 (2010); Marriage status: 0.0% never married, 58.8% now married, 27.9% widowed, 13.2% divorced (2005-2009 5-year est.); Foreign born: 0.0% (2005-2009 5-year est.); Ancestry (includes multiple ancestries): 11.6% Irish, 6.8% German, 6.2% English (2005-2009 5-year est.).
Economy: Employment by occupation: 30.7% management, 12.0% professional, 12.0% services, 22.7% sales, 0.0% farming, 22.7% construction, 0.0% production (2005-2009 5-year est.).
Income: Per capita income: $23,521 (2010); Median household income: $46,912 (2010); Average household income: $56,471 (2010); Percent of households with income of $100,000 or more: 14.1% (2010); Poverty rate: 16.4% (2005-2009 5-year est.).
Education: Percent of population age 25 and over with: High school diploma (including GED) or higher: 88.4% (2010); Bachelor's degree or higher: 27.2% (2010); Master's degree or higher: 12.9% (2010).
Housing: Homeownership rate: 87.1% (2010); Median home value: $142,857 (2010); Median contract rent: n/a per month (2005-2009 5-year est.); Median year structure built: 1982 (2005-2009 5-year est.).
Transportation: Commute to work: 86.4% car, 0.0% public transportation, 13.6% walk, 0.0% work from home (2005-2009 5-year est.); Travel time to work: 53.0% less than 15 minutes, 47.0% 15 to 30 minutes, 0.0% 30 to 45 minutes, 0.0% 45 to 60 minutes, 0.0% 60 minutes or more (2005-2009 5-year est.)

LAUGHLIN AFB (CDP).

Covers a land area of 5.893 square miles and a water area of 0 square miles. Located at 29.34° N. Lat; 100.78° W. Long.
Population: 2,556 (1990); 2,225 (2000); 2,122 (2010); 2,091 (2015 projected); Race: 74.8% White, 7.7% Black, 2.5% Asian, 15.0% Other, 20.8% Hispanic of any race (2010); Density: 360.1 persons per square mile (2010); Average household size: 3.03 (2010); Median age: 25.3 (2010); Males per 100 females: 122.9 (2010); Marriage status: 47.0% never married, 50.8% now married, 0.0% widowed, 2.2% divorced (2005-2009 5-year est.); Foreign born: 13.2% (2005-2009 5-year est.); Ancestry (includes multiple ancestries): 15.5% Irish, 14.0% German, 9.5% English, 7.4% Finnish, 5.3% Portuguese (2005-2009 5-year est.).

Economy: Employment by occupation: 0.0% management, 29.2% professional, 10.9% services, 19.0% sales, 0.0% farming, 10.2% construction, 30.6% production (2005-2009 5-year est.).
Income: Per capita income: $18,233 (2010); Median household income: $50,196 (2010); Average household income: $54,907 (2010); Percent of households with income of $100,000 or more: 7.9% (2010); Poverty rate: 0.0% (2005-2009 5-year est.).
Education: Percent of population age 25 and over with: High school diploma (including GED) or higher: 98.9% (2010); Bachelor's degree or higher: 52.7% (2010); Master's degree or higher: 13.0% (2010).
Housing: Homeownership rate: 10.3% (2010); Median home value: $48,750 (2010); Median contract rent: $1,101 per month (2005-2009 5-year est.); Median year structure built: 1971 (2005-2009 5-year est.).
Transportation: Commute to work: 92.0% car, 0.0% public transportation, 1.4% walk, 0.0% work from home (2005-2009 5-year est.); Travel time to work: 89.0% less than 15 minutes, 5.9% 15 to 30 minutes, 5.2% 30 to 45 minutes, 0.0% 45 to 60 minutes, 0.0% 60 minutes or more (2005-2009 5-year est.)

VAL VERDE PARK (CDP).

Covers a land area of 0.815 square miles and a water area of 0 square miles. Located at 29.37° N. Lat; 100.82° W. Long. Elevation is 1,079 feet.
Population: 1,128 (1990); 1,945 (2000); 1,965 (2010); 1,983 (2015 projected); Race: 64.6% White, 0.5% Black, 0.1% Asian, 34.9% Other, 93.6% Hispanic of any race (2010); Density: 2,410.6 persons per square mile (2010); Average household size: 3.55 (2010); Median age: 29.4 (2010); Males per 100 females: 110.4 (2010); Marriage status: 38.0% never married, 49.5% now married, 5.7% widowed, 6.8% divorced (2005-2009 5-year est.); Foreign born: 30.3% (2005-2009 5-year est.); Ancestry (includes multiple ancestries): 0.7% American, 0.6% Dutch, 0.6% Irish (2005-2009 5-year est.).
Economy: Employment by occupation: 2.4% management, 4.8% professional, 39.7% services, 17.1% sales, 5.8% farming, 13.5% construction, 16.7% production (2005-2009 5-year est.).
Income: Per capita income: $9,417 (2010); Median household income: $30,606 (2010); Average household income: $33,371 (2010); Percent of households with income of $100,000 or more: 1.7% (2010); Poverty rate: 16.1% (2005-2009 5-year est.).
Education: Percent of population age 25 and over with: High school diploma (including GED) or higher: 46.5% (2010); Bachelor's degree or higher: 3.8% (2010); Master's degree or higher: 0.8% (2010).
Housing: Homeownership rate: 69.5% (2010); Median home value: $51,687 (2010); Median contract rent: $253 per month (2005-2009 5-year est.); Median year structure built: 1989 (2005-2009 5-year est.).
Transportation: Commute to work: 87.7% car, 0.0% public transportation, 3.5% walk, 4.3% work from home (2005-2009 5-year est.); Travel time to work: 27.0% less than 15 minutes, 35.1% 15 to 30 minutes, 19.5% 30 to 45 minutes, 4.3% 45 to 60 minutes, 14.0% 60 minutes or more (2005-2009 5-year est.)

Van Zandt County

Located in northeastern Texas; bounded on the northeast by the Sabine River, and partly on the east by the Neches River. Covers a land area of 848.64 square miles, a water area of 10.84 square miles, and is located in the Central Time Zone at 32.57° N. Lat., 95.81° W. Long. The county was founded in 1848. County seat is Canton.

Weather Station: Wills Point   Elevation: 521 feet

	Jan	Feb	Mar	Apr	May	Jun	Jul	Aug	Sep	Oct	Nov	Dec
High	55	59	66	74	82	89	93	95	88	77	66	56
Low	34	38	45	52	62	69	72	72	65	55	45	36
Precip	3.1	3.5	4.2	3.0	4.7	4.5	2.1	2.3	3.3	4.9	4.3	3.8
Snow	0.5	0.9	tr	0.0	0.0	0.0	0.0	0.0	0.0	0.0	tr	0.4

High and Low temperatures in degrees Fahrenheit; Precipitation and Snow in inches

Population: 37,944 (1990); 48,140 (2000); 53,269 (2010); 55,668 (2015 projected); Race: 89.3% White, 3.6% Black, 0.4% Asian, 6.7% Other, 9.7% Hispanic of any race (2010); Density: 62.8 persons per square mile (2010); Average household size: 2.59 (2010); Median age: 39.2 (2010); Males per 100 females: 97.6 (2010).
Religion: Five largest groups: 29.6% Southern Baptist Convention, 9.2% Baptist Missionary Association of America, 7.3% The United Methodist Church, 3.6% Churches of Christ, 3.4% Catholic Church (2000).
Economy: Unemployment rate: 8.2% (June 2011); Total civilian labor force: 25,970 (June 2011); Leading industries: 20.1% retail trade; 15.9%

health care and social assistance; 11.9% accommodation & food services (2009); Farms: 3,253 totaling 415,983 acres (2007); Companies that employ 500 or more persons: 0 (2009); Companies that employ 100 to 499 persons: 8 (2009); Companies that employ less than 100 persons: 810 (2009); Black-owned businesses: n/a (2007); Hispanic-owned businesses: n/a (2007); Asian-owned businesses: n/a (2007); Women-owned businesses: 1,098 (2007); Retail sales per capita: $8,266 (2010). Single-family building permits issued: 5 (2010); Multi-family building permits issued: 4 (2010).

Income: Per capita income: $21,908 (2010); Median household income: $45,023 (2010); Average household income: $57,217 (2010); Percent of households with income of $100,000 or more: 12.3% (2010); Poverty rate: 14.5% (2009); Bankruptcy rate: 2.09% (2010).

Taxes: Total county taxes per capita: $170 (2007); County property taxes per capita: $147 (2007).

Education: Percent of population age 25 and over with: High school diploma (including GED) or higher: 77.2% (2010); Bachelor's degree or higher: 11.8% (2010); Master's degree or higher: 4.3% (2010).

Housing: Homeownership rate: 76.6% (2010); Median home value: $93,617 (2010); Median contract rent: $460 per month (2005-2009 5-year est.); Median year structure built: 1981 (2005-2009 5-year est.)

Health: Birth rate: 123.3 per 10,000 population (2009); Death rate: 114.0 per 10,000 population (2009); Age-adjusted cancer mortality rate: 171.1 deaths per 100,000 population (2007); Number of physicians: 2.5 per 10,000 population (2008); Hospital beds: 4.6 per 10,000 population (2007); Hospital admissions: 116.5 per 10,000 population (2007).

Elections: 2008 Presidential election results: 22.1% Obama, 77.1% McCain, 0.0% Nader

Additional Information Contacts
Van Zandt County Government . . . . (903) 567-4071
   http://www.vanzandtcounty.org/ips/cms
Canton Chamber of Commerce . . . . (903) 567-2991
   http://cantontexaschamber.com
Van Area Chamber of Commerce . . . . (903) 963-5051
   http://www.vantexas.com
Wills Point Chamber of Commerce . . . . (903) 873-3111
   http://www.willspoint.org

Van Zandt County Communities

BEN WHEELER (unincorporated postal area, zip code 75754). Covers a land area of 134.493 square miles and a water area of 0.596 square miles. Located at 32.41° N. Lat; 95.66° W. Long. Elevation is 531 feet.

Population: 5,417 (2000); Race: 88.2% White, 4.9% Black, 0.0% Asian, 6.9% Other, 9.4% Hispanic of any race (2000); Density: 40.3 persons per square mile (2000); Age: 25.6% under 18, 16.1% over 64 (2000); Marriage status: 14.1% never married, 70.2% now married, 5.0% widowed, 10.7% divorced (2000); Foreign born: 3.5% (2000); Ancestry (includes multiple ancestries): 18.7% American, 11.0% Irish, 7.1% German, 7.1% English (2000).

Economy: Employment by occupation: 9.7% management, 15.4% professional, 11.4% services, 27.8% sales, 1.9% farming, 17.3% construction, 16.4% production (2000).

Income: Per capita income: $16,441 (2000); Median household income: $33,994 (2000); Poverty rate: 179.1% (2000).

Education: Percent of population age 25 and over with: High school diploma (including GED) or higher: 76.0% (2000); Bachelor's degree or higher: 11.5% (2000).

Housing: Homeownership rate: 86.1% (2000); Median home value: $63,700 (2000); Median contract rent: $367 per month (2000); Median year structure built: 1982 (2000).

Transportation: Commute to work: 92.4% car, 0.4% public transportation, 2.3% walk, 4.1% work from home (2000); Travel time to work: 23.4% less than 15 minutes, 21.8% 15 to 30 minutes, 26.7% 30 to 45 minutes, 12.9% 45 to 60 minutes, 15.3% 60 minutes or more (2000)

CANTON (city). County seat. Covers a land area of 5.194 square miles and a water area of 0.441 square miles. Located at 32.55° N. Lat; 95.86° W. Long. Elevation is 505 feet.

Population: 3,182 (1990); 3,292 (2000); 3,624 (2010); 3,782 (2015 projected); Race: 86.3% White, 7.5% Black, 0.7% Asian, 5.5% Other, 7.4% Hispanic of any race (2010); Density: 697.7 persons per square mile (2010); Average household size: 2.35 (2010); Median age: 40.4 (2010); Males per 100 females: 90.2 (2010); Marriage status: 21.6% never married,

53.1% now married, 10.6% widowed, 14.7% divorced (2005-2009 5-year est.); Foreign born: 2.5% (2005-2009 5-year est.); Ancestry (includes multiple ancestries): 21.5% English, 16.6% German, 12.2% Irish, 7.2% American, 4.7% French (2005-2009 5-year est.).

Economy: Single-family building permits issued: 0 (2010); Multi-family building permits issued: 0 (2010); Employment by occupation: 8.7% management, 18.4% professional, 14.3% services, 26.2% sales, 1.3% farming, 12.5% construction, 18.5% production (2005-2009 5-year est.).

Income: Per capita income: $19,901 (2010); Median household income: $39,942 (2010); Average household income: $47,780 (2010); Percent of households with income of $100,000 or more: 7.2% (2010); Poverty rate: 25.4% (2005-2009 5-year est.).

Taxes: Total city taxes per capita: $1,070 (2007); City property taxes per capita: $233 (2007).

Education: Percent of population age 25 and over with: High school diploma (including GED) or higher: 76.4% (2010); Bachelor's degree or higher: 16.1% (2010); Master's degree or higher: 4.6% (2010).

School District(s)
Canton ISD (PK-12)
   2009-10 Enrollment: 1,985 . . . . (903) 567-4179
Ranch Academy (03-12)
   2009-10 Enrollment: 88 . . . . (903) 479-3601
Housing: Homeownership rate: 64.0% (2010); Median home value: $101,838 (2010); Median contract rent: $538 per month (2005-2009 5-year est.); Median year structure built: 1973 (2005-2009 5-year est.).

Safety: Violent crime rate: 40.5 per 10,000 population; Property crime rate: 405.1 per 10,000 population (2009).

Newspapers: Canton Herald (Community news; Circulation 6,300)

Transportation: Commute to work: 93.4% car, 0.0% public transportation, 0.0% walk, 6.1% work from home (2005-2009 5-year est.); Travel time to work: 45.9% less than 15 minutes, 12.1% 15 to 30 minutes, 17.9% 30 to 45 minutes, 9.1% 45 to 60 minutes, 15.0% 60 minutes or more (2005-2009 5-year est.)

Additional Information Contacts
Canton Chamber of Commerce . . . . (903) 567-2991
   http://cantontexaschamber.com

EDGEWOOD (town). Covers a land area of 1.365 square miles and a water area of 0 square miles. Located at 32.69° N. Lat; 95.88° W. Long. Elevation is 459 feet.

Population: 1,317 (1990); 1,348 (2000); 1,476 (2010); 1,538 (2015 projected); Race: 85.1% White, 7.0% Black, 0.2% Asian, 7.7% Other, 7.8% Hispanic of any race (2010); Density: 1,081.2 persons per square mile (2010); Average household size: 2.47 (2010); Median age: 34.3 (2010); Males per 100 females: 85.4 (2010); Marriage status: 18.5% never married, 58.5% now married, 8.9% widowed, 14.1% divorced (2005-2009 5-year est.); Foreign born: 1.8% (2005-2009 5-year est.); Ancestry (includes multiple ancestries): 18.2% American, 17.9% English, 17.8% Irish, 9.0% German, 3.4% Scotch-Irish (2005-2009 5-year est.).

Economy: Employment by occupation: 6.1% management, 11.1% professional, 20.3% services, 31.2% sales, 0.7% farming, 18.5% construction, 12.2% production (2005-2009 5-year est.).

Income: Per capita income: $20,390 (2010); Median household income: $38,443 (2010); Average household income: $50,431 (2010); Percent of households with income of $100,000 or more: 10.9% (2010); Poverty rate: 19.3% (2005-2009 5-year est.).

Taxes: Total city taxes per capita: $354 (2007); City property taxes per capita: $173 (2007).

Education: Percent of population age 25 and over with: High school diploma (including GED) or higher: 76.1% (2010); Bachelor's degree or higher: 11.5% (2010); Master's degree or higher: 5.6% (2010).

School District(s)
Canton ISD (PK-12)
   2009-10 Enrollment: 1,985 . . . . (903) 567-4179
Edgewood ISD (PK-12)
   2009-10 Enrollment: 939 . . . . (903) 896-4332
Grand Saline ISD (PK-12)
   2009-10 Enrollment: 1,136 . . . . (903) 962-7546
Housing: Homeownership rate: 58.9% (2010); Median home value: $93,077 (2010); Median contract rent: $350 per month (2005-2009 5-year est.); Median year structure built: 1973 (2005-2009 5-year est.).

Safety: Violent crime rate: 55.1 per 10,000 population; Property crime rate: 165.3 per 10,000 population (2009).

Newspapers: Edgewood Enterprise (Community news; Circulation 1,300)

Transportation: Commute to work: 93.1% car, 0.0% public transportation, 1.3% walk, 4.7% work from home (2005-2009 5-year est.); Travel time to work: 21.8% less than 15 minutes, 24.9% 15 to 30 minutes, 18.0% 30 to 45 minutes, 9.4% 45 to 60 minutes, 25.9% 60 minutes or more (2005-2009 5-year est.)

EDOM (city). Covers a land area of 4.149 square miles and a water area of 0.021 square miles. Located at 32.37° N. Lat; 95.61° W. Long. Elevation is 509 feet.
Population: 300 (1990); 322 (2000); 427 (2010); 468 (2015 projected); Race: 89.2% White, 0.7% Black, 0.5% Asian, 9.6% Other, 9.4% Hispanic of any race (2010); Density: 102.9 persons per square mile (2010); Average household size: 2.39 (2010); Median age: 45.4 (2010); Males per 100 females: 94.1 (2010); Marriage status: 9.9% never married, 73.7% now married, 2.9% widowed, 13.5% divorced (2005-2009 5-year est.); Foreign born: 11.0% (2005-2009 5-year est.); Ancestry (includes multiple ancestries): 17.1% English, 16.5% Irish, 11.0% German, 9.5% Scottish, 6.9% Czech (2005-2009 5-year est.).
Economy: Employment by occupation: 11.7% management, 14.0% professional, 16.2% services, 31.8% sales, 5.6% farming, 7.3% construction, 13.4% production (2005-2009 5-year est.).
Income: Per capita income: $23,840 (2010); Median household income: $44,911 (2010); Average household income: $58,883 (2010); Percent of households with income of $100,000 or more: 13.4% (2010); Poverty rate: 21.7% (2005-2009 5-year est.).
Taxes: Total city taxes per capita: $99 (2007); City property taxes per capita: $0 (2007).
Education: Percent of population age 25 and over with: High school diploma (including GED) or higher: 79.5% (2010); Bachelor's degree or higher: 9.3% (2010); Master's degree or higher: 1.6% (2010).
Housing: Homeownership rate: 82.7% (2010); Median home value: $81,176 (2010); Median contract rent: $506 per month (2005-2009 5-year est.); Median year structure built: 1972 (2005-2009 5-year est.).
Transportation: Commute to work: 93.4% car, 0.0% public transportation, 3.3% walk, 2.2% work from home (2005-2009 5-year est.); Travel time to work: 24.3% less than 15 minutes, 46.9% 15 to 30 minutes, 23.2% 30 to 45 minutes, 1.1% 45 to 60 minutes, 4.5% 60 minutes or more (2005-2009 5-year est.)

FRUITVALE (city). Covers a land area of 1.914 square miles and a water area of 0 square miles. Located at 32.68° N. Lat; 95.80° W. Long. Elevation is 466 feet.
Population: 411 (1990); 418 (2000); 438 (2010); 446 (2015 projected); Race: 93.6% White, 0.9% Black, 0.2% Asian, 5.3% Other, 4.8% Hispanic of any race (2010); Density: 228.9 persons per square mile (2010); Average household size: 2.78 (2010); Median age: 36.7 (2010); Males per 100 females: 98.2 (2010); Marriage status: 21.9% never married, 62.3% now married, 1.3% widowed, 14.5% divorced (2005-2009 5-year est.); Foreign born: 0.0% (2005-2009 5-year est.); Ancestry (includes multiple ancestries): 18.7% English, 18.7% American, 15.6% German, 13.3% Irish, 5.1% Czech (2005-2009 5-year est.).
Economy: Employment by occupation: 7.1% management, 25.0% professional, 19.9% services, 8.3% sales, 0.0% farming, 12.2% construction, 27.6% production (2005-2009 5-year est.).
Income: Per capita income: $17,396 (2010); Median household income: $40,081 (2010); Average household income: $48,790 (2010); Percent of households with income of $100,000 or more: 7.0% (2010); Poverty rate: 36.9% (2005-2009 5-year est.).
Taxes: Total city taxes per capita: $112 (2007); City property taxes per capita: $48 (2007).
Education: Percent of population age 25 and over with: High school diploma (including GED) or higher: 73.7% (2010); Bachelor's degree or higher: 9.5% (2010); Master's degree or higher: 4.2% (2010).
School District(s)
Fruitvale ISD (PK-12)
   2009-10 Enrollment: 423 . . . . (903) 896-1191
Housing: Homeownership rate: 74.5% (2010); Median home value: $89,375 (2010); Median contract rent: $289 per month (2005-2009 5-year est.); Median year structure built: 1971 (2005-2009 5-year est.).
Transportation: Commute to work: 98.7% car, 0.0% public transportation, 0.0% walk, 1.3% work from home (2005-2009 5-year est.); Travel time to work: 26.2% less than 15 minutes, 20.8% 15 to 30 minutes, 24.2% 30 to 45 minutes, 7.4% 45 to 60 minutes, 21.5% 60 minutes or more (2005-2009 5-year est.)

GRAND SALINE (city). Covers a land area of 1.989 square miles and a water area of 0.008 square miles. Located at 32.67° N. Lat; 95.71° W. Long. Elevation is 400 feet.
History: Grand Saline developed as the center of the Texas salt industry, situated on salt flats dotted with shafts where hard rock salt was mined. The Morton Salt Company mine was built here.
Population: 2,722 (1990); 3,028 (2000); 3,241 (2010); 3,364 (2015 projected); Race: 88.0% White, 1.4% Black, 0.2% Asian, 10.4% Other, 20.5% Hispanic of any race (2010); Density: 1,629.3 persons per square mile (2010); Average household size: 2.65 (2010); Median age: 36.4 (2010); Males per 100 females: 97.6 (2010); Marriage status: 25.4% never married, 50.9% now married, 11.0% widowed, 12.7% divorced (2005-2009 5-year est.); Foreign born: 14.7% (2005-2009 5-year est.); Ancestry (includes multiple ancestries): 17.0% English, 10.2% German, 8.7% Irish, 8.0% American, 4.2% Scotch-Irish (2005-2009 5-year est.).
Economy: Single-family building permits issued: 0 (2010); Multi-family building permits issued: 0 (2010); Employment by occupation: 7.2% management, 14.4% professional, 23.6% services, 17.9% sales, 0.8% farming, 19.5% construction, 16.6% production (2005-2009 5-year est.).
Income: Per capita income: $15,759 (2010); Median household income: $32,930 (2010); Average household income: $42,927 (2010); Percent of households with income of $100,000 or more: 5.8% (2010); Poverty rate: 25.2% (2005-2009 5-year est.).
Taxes: Total city taxes per capita: $250 (2007); City property taxes per capita: $159 (2007).
Education: Percent of population age 25 and over with: High school diploma (including GED) or higher: 65.6% (2010); Bachelor's degree or higher: 7.5% (2010); Master's degree or higher: 3.0% (2010).
School District(s)
Grand Saline ISD (PK-12)
   2009-10 Enrollment: 1,136 . . . . (903) 962-7546
Martins Mill ISD (PK-12)
   2009-10 Enrollment: 494 . . . . (903) 479-3872
Housing: Homeownership rate: 61.3% (2010); Median home value: $73,333 (2010); Median contract rent: $406 per month (2005-2009 5-year est.); Median year structure built: 1966 (2005-2009 5-year est.).
Hospitals: Cozby-Germany Hospital (52 beds)
Safety: Violent crime rate: 12.6 per 10,000 population; Property crime rate: 160.0 per 10,000 population (2009).
Newspapers: Grand Saline Sun (Community news; Circulation 2,600)
Transportation: Commute to work: 98.8% car, 0.0% public transportation, 0.8% walk, 0.0% work from home (2005-2009 5-year est.); Travel time to work: 41.2% less than 15 minutes, 22.2% 15 to 30 minutes, 9.4% 30 to 45 minutes, 10.3% 45 to 60 minutes, 16.8% 60 minutes or more (2005-2009 5-year est.)

VAN (city). Covers a land area of 2.991 square miles and a water area of 0 square miles. Located at 32.52° N. Lat; 95.63° W. Long. Elevation is 489 feet.
Population: 1,854 (1990); 2,362 (2000); 2,716 (2010); 2,891 (2015 projected); Race: 92.8% White, 0.4% Black, 0.7% Asian, 6.1% Other, 11.4% Hispanic of any race (2010); Density: 908.0 persons per square mile (2010); Average household size: 2.65 (2010); Median age: 36.7 (2010); Males per 100 females: 95.5 (2010); Marriage status: 19.1% never married, 64.6% now married, 7.4% widowed, 9.0% divorced (2005-2009 5-year est.); Foreign born: 6.6% (2005-2009 5-year est.); Ancestry (includes multiple ancestries): 20.0% German, 18.4% English, 15.2% Irish, 9.4% American, 4.2% French (2005-2009 5-year est.).
Economy: Single-family building permits issued: 0 (2010); Multi-family building permits issued: 4 (2010); Employment by occupation: 7.0% management, 20.3% professional, 14.7% services, 27.3% sales, 0.7% farming, 13.4% construction, 16.5% production (2005-2009 5-year est.).
Income: Per capita income: $20,672 (2010); Median household income: $41,774 (2010); Average household income: $55,128 (2010); Percent of households with income of $100,000 or more: 11.6% (2010); Poverty rate: 9.0% (2005-2009 5-year est.).
Taxes: Total city taxes per capita: $174 (2007); City property taxes per capita: $35 (2007).
Education: Percent of population age 25 and over with: High school diploma (including GED) or higher: 83.5% (2010); Bachelor's degree or higher: 19.0% (2010); Master's degree or higher: 8.1% (2010).
School District(s)
Van ISD (PK-12)
   2009-10 Enrollment: 2,299 . . . . (903) 963-8328

Housing: Homeownership rate: 65.9% (2010); Median home value: $88,678 (2010); Median contract rent: $415 per month (2005-2009 5-year est.); Median year structure built: 1971 (2005-2009 5-year est.).

Safety: Violent crime rate: 84.5 per 10,000 population; Property crime rate: 203.6 per 10,000 population (2009).

Transportation: Commute to work: 92.5% car, 0.0% public transportation, 3.0% walk, 2.4% work from home (2005-2009 5-year est.); Travel time to work: 33.8% less than 15 minutes, 15.7% 15 to 30 minutes, 23.3% 30 to 45 minutes, 14.9% 45 to 60 minutes, 12.3% 60 minutes or more (2005-2009 5-year est.)

Additional Information Contacts

Van Area Chamber of Commerce . . . . (903) 963-5051
   http://www.vantexas.com

WILLS POINT (city).

WILLS POINT (city). Covers a land area of 3.581 square miles and a water area of 0 square miles. Located at 32.70° N. Lat; 96.00° W. Long. Elevation is 531 feet.

History: Established 1873.

Population: 3,122 (1990); 3,496 (2000); 3,859 (2010); 4,020 (2015 projected); Race: 78.9% White, 12.5% Black, 0.1% Asian, 8.5% Other, 15.1% Hispanic of any race (2010); Density: 1,077.6 persons per square mile (2010); Average household size: 2.58 (2010); Median age: 36.2 (2010); Males per 100 females: 89.5 (2010); Marriage status: 24.5% never married, 41.3% now married, 22.3% widowed, 11.9% divorced (2005-2009 5-year est.); Foreign born: 5.4% (2005-2009 5-year est.); Ancestry (includes multiple ancestries): 12.0% English, 10.9% Irish, 8.6% German, 7.6% American, 3.3% Scotch-Irish (2005-2009 5-year est.).

Economy: Single-family building permits issued: 5 (2010); Multi-family building permits issued: 0 (2010); Employment by occupation: 4.2% management, 15.1% professional, 25.2% services, 29.7% sales, 1.0% farming, 9.4% construction, 15.5% production (2005-2009 5-year est.).

Income: Per capita income: $20,121 (2010); Median household income: $41,979 (2010); Average household income: $52,803 (2010); Percent of households with income of $100,000 or more: 10.8% (2010); Poverty rate: 19.2% (2005-2009 5-year est.).

Taxes: Total city taxes per capita: $429 (2007); City property taxes per capita: $195 (2007).

Education: Percent of population age 25 and over with: High school diploma (including GED) or higher: 74.6% (2010); Bachelor's degree or higher: 12.8% (2010); Master's degree or higher: 6.5% (2010).

School District(s)

Wills Point ISD (PK-12)
   2009-10 Enrollment: 2,675 . . . . (903) 873-3161

Housing: Homeownership rate: 59.3% (2010); Median home value: $86,959 (2010); Median contract rent: $470 per month (2005-2009 5-year est.); Median year structure built: 1973 (2005-2009 5-year est.).

Safety: Violent crime rate: 15.6 per 10,000 population; Property crime rate: 132.8 per 10,000 population (2009).

Newspapers: Canton Guide (Local news; Circulation 10,000); Van Zandt News (Community news; Circulation 6,000); Wills Point Chronicle (Community news; Circulation 4,600).

Transportation: Commute to work: 94.0% car, 0.0% public transportation, 0.0% walk, 3.1% work from home (2005-2009 5-year est.); Travel time to work: 28.6% less than 15 minutes, 10.6% 15 to 30 minutes, 25.3% 30 to 45 minutes, 19.9% 45 to 60 minutes, 15.6% 60 minutes or more (2005-2009 5-year est.)

Additional Information Contacts

Wills Point Chamber of Commerce . . . . (903) 873-3111
   http://www.willspoint.org

Victoria County

Located in south Texas, touching Lavaca Bay in the southeast; drained by the Guadalupe and San Antonio Rivers. Covers a land area of 882.50 square miles, a water area of 6.23 square miles, and is located in the Central Time Zone at 28.79° N. Lat., 96.97° W. Long. The county was founded in 1836. County seat is Victoria.

Victoria County is part of the Victoria, TX Metropolitan Statistical Area. The entire metro area includes: Calhoun County, TX; Goliad County, TX; Victoria County, TX

Weather Station: Victoria Regional Arpt										Elevation: 115 feet	
	Jan	Feb	Mar	Apr	May	Jun	Jul	Aug	Sep	Oct	Nov	Dec
High	65	68	74	81	86	92	94	95	90	83	74	66
Low	44	47	53	60	68	73	75	74	70	62	52	45
Precip	2.6	2.0	2.8	2.8	5.2	4.4	3.8	3.0	3.9	4.7	3.2	2.3
Snow	na	na	na	na	na	na	na	na	na	na	na	na

High and Low temperatures in degrees Fahrenheit; Precipitation and Snow in inches

Population: 74,361 (1990); 84,088 (2000); 87,878 (2010); 89,555 (2015 projected); Race: 72.8% White, 6.0% Black, 1.0% Asian, 20.2% Other, 42.0% Hispanic of any race (2010); Density: 99.6 persons per square mile (2010); Average household size: 2.70 (2010); Median age: 35.8 (2010); Males per 100 females: 95.0 (2010).

Religion: Five largest groups: 38.0% Catholic Church, 15.9% Southern Baptist Convention, 5.3% Evangelical Lutheran Church in America, 3.7% The United Methodist Church, 1.7% Presbyterian Church (U.S.A.) (2000).

Economy: Unemployment rate: 7.3% (June 2011); Total civilian labor force: 46,768 (June 2011); Leading industries: 20.3% health care and social assistance; 18.2% retail trade; 10.3% accommodation & food services (2009); Farms: 1,351 totaling 493,823 acres (2007); Companies that employ 500 or more persons: 5 (2009); Companies that employ 100 to 499 persons: 39 (2009); Companies that employ less than 100 persons: 2,199 (2009); Black-owned businesses: n/a (2007); Hispanic-owned businesses: 1,806 (2007); Asian-owned businesses: 289 (2007); Women-owned businesses: 1,891 (2007); Retail sales per capita: $20,208 (2010); Single-family building permits issued: 47 (2010); Multi-family building permits issued: 0 (2010).

Income: Per capita income: $22,756 (2010); Median household income: $47,385 (2010); Average household income: $61,699 (2010); Percent of households with income of $100,000 or more: 15.5% (2010); Poverty rate: 14.0% (2009); Bankruptcy rate: 1.07% (2010).

Taxes: Total county taxes per capita: $289 (2007); County property taxes per capita: $185 (2007).

Education: Percent of population age 25 and over with: High school diploma (including GED) or higher: 79.7% (2010); Bachelor's degree or higher: 15.5% (2010); Master's degree or higher: 4.9% (2010).

Housing: Homeownership rate: 66.4% (2010); Median home value: $96,736 (2010); Median contract rent: $489 per month (2005-2009 5-year est.); Median year structure built: 1976 (2005-2009 5-year est.)

Health: Birth rate: 157.2 per 10,000 population (2009); Death rate: 86.0 per 10,000 population (2009); Age-adjusted cancer mortality rate: 198.3 deaths per 100,000 population (2007); Number of physicians: 22.7 per 10,000 population (2008); Hospital beds: 66.5 per 10,000 population (2007); Hospital admissions: 2,387.3 per 10,000 population (2007).

Environment: Air Quality Index: 96.0% good, 4.0% moderate, 0.0% unhealthy for sensitive individuals, 0.0% unhealthy (percent of days in 2008)

Elections: 2008 Presidential election results: 32.8% Obama, 66.4% McCain, 0.1% Nader

Additional Information Contacts

Victoria County Government . . . . (361) 575-4558
   http://www.victoriacountytx.org
City of Victoria . . . . (361) 485-3040
   http://www.victoriatx.org
Victoria Chamber of Commerce . . . . (361) 573-5277
   http://www.victoriachamber.org

Victoria County Communities

BLOOMINGTON (CDP). Covers a land area of 2.665 square miles and a water area of 0 square miles. Located at 28.64° N. Lat; 96.89° W. Long. Elevation is 59 feet.

Population: 1,888 (1990); 2,562 (2000); 2,676 (2010); 2,732 (2015 projected); Race: 39.7% White, 5.0% Black, 0.1% Asian, 55.1% Other, 74.7% Hispanic of any race (2010); Density: 1,004.2 persons per square mile (2010); Average household size: 3.28 (2010); Median age: 27.8 (2010); Males per 100 females: 95.8 (2010); Marriage status: 20.9% never married, 68.4% now married, 2.8% widowed, 7.9% divorced (2005-2009 5-year est.); Foreign born: 12.7% (2005-2009 5-year est.); Ancestry (includes multiple ancestries): 4.0% German, 1.8% Irish, 1.4% African (2005-2009 5-year est.).

Economy: Employment by occupation: 0.0% management, 9.2% professional, 21.6% services, 14.9% sales, 0.0% farming, 26.6% construction, 27.7% production (2005-2009 5-year est.).

Income: Per capita income: $11,757 (2010); Median household income: $32,990 (2010); Average household income: $38,427 (2010); Percent of

households with income of $100,000 or more: 3.4% (2010); Poverty rate: 28.8% (2005-2009 5-year est.).
Education: Percent of population age 25 and over with: High school diploma (including GED) or higher: 58.0% (2010); Bachelor's degree or higher: 2.3% (2010); Master's degree or higher: 0.1% (2010).

School District(s)
Bloomington ISD (PK-12)
   2009-10 Enrollment: 858 . . . . (361) 897-1652
Housing: Homeownership rate: 74.7% (2010); Median home value: $46,444 (2010); Median contract rent: $401 per month (2005-2009 5-year est.); Median year structure built: 1979 (2005-2009 5-year est.).
Transportation: Commute to work: 100.0% car, 0.0% public transportation, 0.0% walk, 0.0% work from home (2005-2009 5-year est.); Travel time to work: 26.6% less than 15 minutes, 39.0% 15 to 30 minutes, 17.7% 30 to 45 minutes, 3.9% 45 to 60 minutes, 12.8% 60 minutes or more (2005-2009 5-year est.)

INEZ (CDP). Covers a land area of 59.544 square miles and a water area of 0.047 square miles. Located at 28.87° N. Lat; 96.79° W. Long. Elevation is 66 feet.
Population: 1,371 (1990); 1,787 (2000); 1,884 (2010); 1,931 (2015 projected); Race: 89.9% White, 1.6% Black, 0.3% Asian, 8.2% Other, 15.9% Hispanic of any race (2010); Density: 31.6 persons per square mile (2010); Average household size: 2.79 (2010); Median age: 37.4 (2010); Males per 100 females: 99.6 (2010); Marriage status: 27.7% never married, 61.1% now married, 3.4% widowed, 7.7% divorced (2005-2009 5-year est.); Foreign born: 0.0% (2005-2009 5-year est.); Ancestry (includes multiple ancestries): 44.4% German, 19.3% Czech, 15.7% Irish, 8.1% American, 6.0% Italian (2005-2009 5-year est.).
Economy: Employment by occupation: 8.0% management, 28.5% professional, 4.4% services, 25.9% sales, 1.5% farming, 16.1% construction, 15.5% production (2005-2009 5-year est.).
Income: Per capita income: $27,184 (2010); Median household income: $67,339 (2010); Average household income: $77,689 (2010); Percent of households with income of $100,000 or more: 23.4% (2010); Poverty rate: 2.9% (2005-2009 5-year est.).
Education: Percent of population age 25 and over with: High school diploma (including GED) or higher: 91.2% (2010); Bachelor's degree or higher: 13.8% (2010); Master's degree or higher: 5.6% (2010).

School District(s)
Industrial ISD (PK-12)
   2009-10 Enrollment: 1,107 . . . . (361) 284-3226
Housing: Homeownership rate: 84.3% (2010); Median home value: $108,717 (2010); Median contract rent: n/a per month (2005-2009 5-year est.); Median year structure built: 1985 (2005-2009 5-year est.).
Transportation: Commute to work: 96.1% car, 0.0% public transportation, 1.5% walk, 2.4% work from home (2005-2009 5-year est.); Travel time to work: 6.4% less than 15 minutes, 68.0% 15 to 30 minutes, 10.9% 30 to 45 minutes, 13.4% 45 to 60 minutes, 1.3% 60 minutes or more (2005-2009 5-year est.)

VICTORIA (city). County seat. Covers a land area of 32.968 square miles and a water area of 0.152 square miles. Located at 28.81° N. Lat; 96.99° W. Long. Elevation is 95 feet.
History: Victoria began as a Spanish colony in 1824, In the 1840's many German immigrants settled here. Cattle, cotton, and then oil provided Victoria's source of revenue.
Population: 55,279 (1990); 60,603 (2000); 63,443 (2010); 64,542 (2015 projected); Race: 69.9% White, 7.1% Black, 1.3% Asian, 21.8% Other, 45.5% Hispanic of any race (2010); Density: 1,924.4 persons per square mile (2010); Average household size: 2.64 (2010); Median age: 35.6 (2010); Males per 100 females: 93.4 (2010); Marriage status: 27.7% never married, 52.5% now married, 7.8% widowed, 12.0% divorced (2005-2009 5-year est.); Foreign born: 6.8% (2005-2009 5-year est.); Ancestry (includes multiple ancestries): 19.1% German, 9.2% Irish, 6.2% English, 4.8% Czech, 3.0% American (2005-2009 5-year est.).
Economy: Unemployment rate: 7.3% (June 2011); Total civilian labor force: 33,705 (June 2011); Single-family building permits issued: 47 (2010); Multi-family building permits issued: 0 (2010); Employment by occupation: 9.8% management, 19.9% professional, 17.0% services, 25.4% sales, 0.4% farming, 12.7% construction, 14.8% production (2005-2009 5-year est.).
Income: Per capita income: $23,175 (2010); Median household income: $45,329 (2010); Average household income: $61,382 (2010); Percent of

households with income of $100,000 or more: 15.5% (2010); Poverty rate: 16.9% (2005-2009 5-year est.).
Taxes: Total city taxes per capita: $475 (2007); City property taxes per capita: $175 (2007).
Education: Percent of population age 25 and over with: High school diploma (including GED) or higher: 79.4% (2010); Bachelor's degree or higher: 17.5% (2010); Master's degree or higher: 5.6% (2010).

School District(s)
Outreach Academy (PK-05)
   2009-10 Enrollment: 218 . . . . (361) 573-4096
Victoria ISD (PK-12)
   2009-10 Enrollment: 13,728 . . . . (361) 576-3131
Four-year College(s)
University of Houston-Victoria (Public)
   Fall 2009 Enrollment: 3,655. . . . . (877) 970-4848
   2010-11 Tuition: In-state $5,604; Out-of-state $14,904
Two-year College(s)
Victoria College (Public)
   Fall 2009 Enrollment: 4,054. . . . . (361) 573-3291
   2010-11 Tuition: In-state $3,480; Out-of-state $4,110
Vocational/Technical School(s)
Texas Vocational Schools Inc (Private, For-profit)
   Fall 2009 Enrollment: 118 . . . . (361) 575-4768
   2010-11 Tuition: $7,300
Victoria Beauty College Inc (Private, For-profit)
   Fall 2009 Enrollment: 110 . . . . (361) 575-4526
   2010-11 Tuition: $11,350
Housing: Homeownership rate: 60.0% (2010); Median home value: $97,185 (2010); Median contract rent: $496 per month (2005-2009 5-year est.); Median year structure built: 1974 (2005-2009 5-year est.).
Hospitals: Citizens Medical Center (344 beds); DeTar Hospital Navarro (266 beds); Devereux - Victoria Center (84 beds)
Safety: Violent crime rate: 68.6 per 10,000 population; Property crime rate: 664.9 per 10,000 population (2009).
Newspapers: The Catholic Lighthouse (Local news; Circulation 21,000); Victoria Advocate (Local news); Victoria Advocate - Port Lavaca Bureau (Local news)
Transportation: Commute to work: 93.7% car, 1.6% public transportation, 1.7% walk, 1.4% work from home (2005-2009 5-year est.); Travel time to work: 48.9% less than 15 minutes, 30.6% 15 to 30 minutes, 9.8% 30 to 45 minutes, 5.7% 45 to 60 minutes, 5.0% 60 minutes or more (2005-2009 5-year est.)
Airports: Victoria Regional (commercial service)
Additional Information Contacts
City of Victoria . . . . (361) 485-3040
   http://www.victoriatx.org
Victoria Chamber of Commerce. (361) 573-5277
   http://www.victoriachamber.org

Walker County

Located in east central Texas; bounded on the northeast by the Trinity River; drained by tributaries of the Trinity and San Jacinto Rivers; includes part of Sam Houston National Forest. Covers a land area of 787.45 square miles, a water area of 13.99 square miles, and is located in the Central Time Zone at 30.74° N. Lat., 95.52° W. Long. The county was founded in 1846. County seat is Huntsville.

Walker County is part of the Huntsville, TX Micropolitan Statistical Area. The entire metro area includes: Walker County, TX

Weather Station: Huntsville										Elevation: 494 feet		
	Jan	Feb	Mar	Apr	May	Jun	Jul	Aug	Sep	Oct	Nov	Dec
High	59	63	71	78	85	91	94	94	89	80	69	61
Low	40	44	50	57	65	71	73	73	68	59	50	42
Precip	4.2	3.3	3.8	3.2	4.6	5.2	2.7	3.7	4.1	4.8	5.2	4.1
Snow	tr	tr	tr	0.0	0.0	0.0	0.0	0.0	0.0	0.0	tr	tr

High and Low temperatures in degrees Fahrenheit; Precipitation and Snow in inches

Population: 50,917 (1990); 61,758 (2000); 65,003 (2010); 66,460 (2015 projected); Race: 69.5% White, 22.5% Black, 0.9% Asian, 7.1% Other, 15.7% Hispanic of any race (2010); Density: 82.5 persons per square mile (2010); Average household size: 2.41 (2010); Median age: 31.5 (2010); Males per 100 females: 153.5 (2010).

Religion: Five largest groups: 19.2% Southern Baptist Convention, 4.3% The United Methodist Church, 2.7% Catholic Church, 1.5% Churches of Christ, 0.9% The Church of Jesus Christ of Latter-day Saints (2000).
Economy: Unemployment rate: 9.2% (June 2011); Total civilian labor force: 28,235 (June 2011); Leading industries: 19.6% retail trade; 18.5% health care and social assistance; 17.7% accommodation & food services (2009); Farms: 1,188 totaling 224,050 acres (2007); Companies that employ 500 or more persons: 2 (2009); Companies that employ 100 to 499 persons: 12 (2009); Companies that employ less than 100 persons: 890 (2009); Black-owned businesses: n/a (2007); Hispanic-owned businesses: 311 (2007); Asian-owned businesses: n/a (2007); Women-owned businesses: 1,197 (2007); Retail sales per capita: $8,812 (2010). Single-family building permits issued: 201 (2010); Multi-family building permits issued: 428 (2010).
Income: Per capita income: $16,443 (2010); Median household income: $36,014 (2010); Average household income: $48,583 (2010); Percent of households with income of $100,000 or more: 9.6% (2010); Poverty rate: 23.2% (2009); Bankruptcy rate: 0.62% (2010).
Taxes: Total county taxes per capita: $212 (2007); County property taxes per capita: $159 (2007).
Education: Percent of population age 25 and over with: High school diploma (including GED) or higher: 78.3% (2010); Bachelor's degree or higher: 16.6% (2010); Master's degree or higher: 5.9% (2010).
Housing: Homeownership rate: 54.5% (2010); Median home value: $91,759 (2010); Median contract rent: $545 per month (2005-2009 5-year est.); Median year structure built: 1985 (2005-2009 5-year est.)
Health: Birth rate: 100.0 per 10,000 population (2009); Death rate: 70.8 per 10,000 population (2009); Age-adjusted cancer mortality rate: 228.2 deaths per 100,000 population (2007); Number of physicians: 9.8 per 10,000 population (2008); Hospital beds: 13.8 per 10,000 population (2007); Hospital admissions: 450.5 per 10,000 population (2007).
Elections: 2008 Presidential election results: 38.3% Obama, 60.7% McCain, 0.1% Nader
National and State Parks: Huntsville State Park
Additional Information Contacts
Walker County Government. . . . . (936) 436-4922
   http://www.co.walker.tx.us
City of Huntsville . . . . (936) 291-5400
   http://ci.huntsville.tx.us
Huntsville-Walker County Chamber of Commerce . . . . . . (936) 295-8113
   http://www.chamber.huntsville.tx.us

Walker County Communities

HUNTSVILLE (city). County seat. Covers a land area of 30.904 square miles and a water area of 0.341 square miles. Located at 30.71° N. Lat; 95.54° W. Long. Elevation is 371 feet.
History: In Huntsville is the place where Sam Houston lived after 1861, and where he died in 1863. A memorial to Houston and a museum were established here.
Population: 30,805 (1990); 35,078 (2000); 38,092 (2010); 39,229 (2015 projected); Race: 65.8% White, 24.4% Black, 1.3% Asian, 8.5% Other, 18.0% Hispanic of any race (2010); Density: 1,232.6 persons per square mile (2010); Average household size: 2.32 (2010); Median age: 30.1 (2010); Males per 100 females: 146.4 (2010); Marriage status: 52.8% never married, 32.1% now married, 4.2% widowed, 10.9% divorced (2005-2009 5-year est.); Foreign born: 10.9% (2005-2009 5-year est.); Ancestry (includes multiple ancestries): 11.8% German, 10.9% American, 8.8% Irish, 8.0% English, 2.2% French (2005-2009 5-year est.).
Economy: Unemployment rate: 9.2% (June 2011); Total civilian labor force: 16,412 (June 2011); Single-family building permits issued: 201 (2010); Multi-family building permits issued: 428 (2010); Employment by occupation: 8.4% management, 20.9% professional, 27.0% services, 26.6% sales, 1.3% farming, 4.4% construction, 11.4% production (2005-2009 5-year est.).
Income: Per capita income: $15,279 (2010); Median household income: $31,051 (2010); Average household income: $44,322 (2010); Percent of households with income of $100,000 or more: 8.7% (2010); Poverty rate: 28.6% (2005-2009 5-year est.).
Taxes: Total city taxes per capita: $328 (2007); City property taxes per capita: $106 (2007).
Education: Percent of population age 25 and over with: High school diploma (including GED) or higher: 78.0% (2010); Bachelor's degree or higher: 19.9% (2010); Master's degree or higher: 7.3% (2010).

School District(s)
Huntsville ISD (PK-12)
   2009-10 Enrollment: 6,291 . . . . (936) 295-3421
Responsive Education Solutions (KG-12)
   2009-10 Enrollment: 5,022 . . . . (972) 316-3663
Four-year College(s)
Sam Houston State University (Public)
   Fall 2009 Enrollment: 16,772. . . . . (936) 294-1111
   2010-11 Tuition: In-state $5,704; Out-of-state $13,144
Vocational/Technical School(s)
Sebring Career Schools (Private, For-profit)
   Fall 2009 Enrollment: 39 . . . . (936) 291-6388
   2010-11 Tuition: $11,612
Housing: Homeownership rate: 41.3% (2010); Median home value: $102,057 (2010); Median contract rent: $552 per month (2005-2009 5-year est.); Median year structure built: 1985 (2005-2009 5-year est.).
Hospitals: Huntsville Memorial Hospital (127 beds)
Safety: Violent crime rate: 48.4 per 10,000 population; Property crime rate: 361.9 per 10,000 population (2009).
Newspapers: Huntsville Item (Local news; Circulation 7,200)
Transportation: Commute to work: 89.7% car, 0.0% public transportation, 6.9% walk, 2.3% work from home (2005-2009 5-year est.); Travel time to work: 49.9% less than 15 minutes, 29.0% 15 to 30 minutes, 11.3% 30 to 45 minutes, 6.3% 45 to 60 minutes, 3.4% 60 minutes or more (2005-2009 5-year est.)
Additional Information Contacts
City of Huntsville . . . . (936) 291-5400
   http://ci.huntsville.tx.us
Huntsville-Walker County Chamber of Commerce . . . . (936) 295-8113
   http://www.chamber.huntsville.tx.us

NEW WAVERLY (city). Covers a land area of 2.244 square miles and a water area of 0.006 square miles. Located at 30.53° N. Lat; 95.48° W. Long. Elevation is 354 feet.
History: New Waverly was settled in 1870 by a group of Polish immigrants. It developed as the center for a plantation area.
Population: 936 (1990); 950 (2000); 935 (2010); 922 (2015 projected); Race: 73.5% White, 22.4% Black, 0.1% Asian, 4.1% Other, 3.3% Hispanic of any race (2010); Density: 416.8 persons per square mile (2010); Average household size: 2.42 (2010); Median age: 35.0 (2010); Males per 100 females: 92.0 (2010); Marriage status: 14.4% never married, 46.4% now married, 12.4% widowed, 26.7% divorced (2005-2009 5-year est.); Foreign born: 11.3% (2005-2009 5-year est.); Ancestry (includes multiple ancestries): 11.4% German, 9.3% Polish, 8.8% Irish, 7.7% English, 5.8% American (2005-2009 5-year est.).
Economy: Employment by occupation: 10.9% management, 14.5% professional, 30.2% services, 18.6% sales, 0.0% farming, 6.8% construction, 19.0% production (2005-2009 5-year est.).
Income: Per capita income: $21,078 (2010); Median household income: $37,647 (2010); Average household income: $50,104 (2010); Percent of households with income of $100,000 or more: 11.9% (2010); Poverty rate: 11.6% (2005-2009 5-year est.).
Taxes: Total city taxes per capita: $230 (2007); City property taxes per capita: $67 (2007).
Education: Percent of population age 25 and over with: High school diploma (including GED) or higher: 72.8% (2010); Bachelor's degree or higher: 8.8% (2010); Master's degree or higher: 4.6% (2010).
School District(s)
New Waverly ISD (PK-12)
   2009-10 Enrollment: 905 . . . . (936) 344-6751
Raven School (09-12)
   2009-10 Enrollment: 136 . . . . (936) 344-6677
Housing: Homeownership rate: 63.5% (2010); Median home value: $90,000 (2010); Median contract rent: $237 per month (2005-2009 5-year est.); Median year structure built: 1973 (2005-2009 5-year est.).
Transportation: Commute to work: 93.2% car, 0.0% public transportation, 3.0% walk, 3.4% work from home (2005-2009 5-year est.); Travel time to work: 18.9% less than 15 minutes, 55.2% 15 to 30 minutes, 10.8% 30 to 45 minutes, 8.4% 45 to 60 minutes, 6.6% 60 minutes or more (2005-2009 5-year est.)

RIVERSIDE (city). Covers a land area of 1.892 square miles and a water area of 0.166 square miles. Located at 30.84° N. Lat; 95.39° W. Long. Elevation is 187 feet.

Population: 476 (1990); 425 (2000); 396 (2010); 381 (2015 projected); Race: 92.2% White, 3.5% Black, 0.3% Asian, 4.0% Other, 4.8% Hispanic of any race (2010); Density: 209.3 persons per square mile (2010); Average household size: 2.34 (2010); Median age: 49.8 (2010); Males per 100 females: 96.0 (2010); Marriage status: 22.1% never married, 65.1% now married, 8.1% widowed, 4.8% divorced (2005-2009 5-year est.); Foreign born: 5.8% (2005-2009 5-year est.); Ancestry (includes multiple ancestries): 18.4% English, 14.6% American, 7.1% Irish, 5.8% German, 4.7% Scotch-Irish (2005-2009 5-year est.).
Economy: Employment by occupation: 13.1% management, 13.8% professional, 32.3% services, 10.0% sales, 0.0% farming, 16.2% construction, 14.6% production (2005-2009 5-year est.).
Income: Per capita income: $25,207 (2010); Median household income: $45,357 (2010); Average household income: $59,349 (2010); Percent of households with income of $100,000 or more: 11.8% (2010); Poverty rate: 17.3% (2005-2009 5-year est.).
Taxes: Total city taxes per capita: $316 (2007); City property taxes per capita: $94 (2007).
Education: Percent of population age 25 and over with: High school diploma (including GED) or higher: 83.5% (2010); Bachelor's degree or higher: 14.8% (2010); Master's degree or higher: 3.8% (2010).
Housing: Homeownership rate: 81.7% (2010); Median home value: $89,565 (2010); Median contract rent: $518 per month (2005-2009 5-year est.); Median year structure built: 1984 (2005-2009 5-year est.).
Transportation: Commute to work: 96.8% car, 0.0% public transportation, 1.6% walk, 0.0% work from home (2005-2009 5-year est.); Travel time to work: 27.0% less than 15 minutes, 45.2% 15 to 30 minutes, 23.0% 30 to 45 minutes, 4.8% 45 to 60 minutes, 0.0% 60 minutes or more (2005-2009 5-year est.)

Waller County

Located in south Texas; bounded on the west by the Brazos River; drained by tributaries of the San Jacinto River. Covers a land area of 513.63 square miles, a water area of 4.87 square miles, and is located in the Central Time Zone at 30.02° N. Lat., 96.00° W. Long. The county was founded in 1873. County seat is Hempstead.

Waller County is part of the Houston-Sugar Land-Baytown, TX Metropolitan Statistical Area. The entire metro area includes: Austin County, TX; Brazoria County, TX; Chambers County, TX; Fort Bend County, TX; Galveston County, TX; Harris County, TX; Liberty County, TX; Montgomery County, TX; San Jacinto County, TX; Waller County, TX

Population: 23,390 (1990); 32,663 (2000); 38,527 (2010); 41,311 (2015 projected); Race: 57.9% White, 25.4% Black, 0.5% Asian, 16.2% Other, 25.4% Hispanic of any race (2010); Density: 75.0 persons per square mile (2010); Average household size: 2.81 (2010); Median age: 31.4 (2010); Males per 100 females: 99.6 (2010).
Religion: Five largest groups: 14.7% Southern Baptist Convention, 8.6% Catholic Church, 4.7% The United Methodist Church, 2.5% Evangelical Lutheran Church in America, 1.0% Churches of Christ (2000).
Economy: Unemployment rate: 9.9% (June 2011); Total civilian labor force: 17,139 (June 2011); Leading industries: 29.2% manufacturing; 13.8% retail trade; 10.8% construction (2009); Farms: 1,640 totaling 271,004 acres (2007); Companies that employ 500 or more persons: 0 (2009); Companies that employ 100 to 499 persons: 16 (2009); Companies that employ less than 100 persons: 664 (2009); Black-owned businesses: 193 (2007); Hispanic-owned businesses: n/a (2007); Asian-owned businesses: n/a (2007); Women-owned businesses: 781 (2007); Retail sales per capita: $32,536 (2010). Single-family building permits issued: 9 (2010); Multi-family building permits issued: 50 (2010).
Income: Per capita income: $22,805 (2010); Median household income: $51,719 (2010); Average household income: $68,135 (2010); Percent of households with income of $100,000 or more: 20.3% (2010); Poverty rate: 19.0% (2009); Bankruptcy rate: 1.59% (2010).
Taxes: Total county taxes per capita: $393 (2007); County property taxes per capita: $352 (2007).
Education: Percent of population age 25 and over with: High school diploma (including GED) or higher: 77.7% (2010); Bachelor's degree or higher: 17.8% (2010); Master's degree or higher: 4.2% (2010).
Housing: Homeownership rate: 69.6% (2010); Median home value: $109,200 (2010); Median contract rent: $520 per month (2005-2009 5-year est.); Median year structure built: 1987 (2005-2009 5-year est.)
Health: Birth rate: 156.6 per 10,000 population (2009); Death rate: 71.2 per 10,000 population (2009); Age-adjusted cancer mortality rate: 180.6 deaths per 100,000 population (2007); Number of physicians: 1.7 per 10,000 population (2008); Hospital beds: 0.0 per 10,000 population (2007); Hospital admissions: 0.0 per 10,000 population (2007).
Elections: 2008 Presidential election results: 46.1% Obama, 53.3% McCain, 0.0% Nader
Additional Information Contacts
Waller County Government . . . . (979) 826-3357
   http://www.co.waller.tx.us/ips/cms
Hempstead Chamber of Commerce . . . . (979) 826-8217
   http://www.hempsteadtxchamber.com
West I-10 Chamber of Commerce . . . . (281) 375-8100
   http://www.westi10chamber.org

Waller County Communities

BROOKSHIRE (city). Covers a land area of 3.509 square miles and a water area of 0 square miles. Located at 29.78° N. Lat; 95.95° W. Long. Elevation is 161 feet.
History: Incorporated after 1940.
Population: 2,922 (1990); 3,450 (2000); 4,155 (2010); 4,488 (2015 projected); Race: 35.7% White, 26.8% Black, 0.5% Asian, 37.0% Other, 45.9% Hispanic of any race (2010); Density: 1,184.1 persons per square mile (2010); Average household size: 3.03 (2010); Median age: 30.5 (2010); Males per 100 females: 98.6 (2010); Marriage status: 34.4% never married, 55.7% now married, 2.4% widowed, 7.5% divorced (2005-2009 5-year est.); Foreign born: 30.4% (2005-2009 5-year est.); Ancestry (includes multiple ancestries): 4.5% German, 2.1% Irish, 1.2% Canadian, 1.0% English, 0.8% Scotch-Irish (2005-2009 5-year est.).
Economy: Single-family building permits issued: 0 (2010); Multi-family building permits issued: 0 (2010); Employment by occupation: 6.8% management, 7.0% professional, 20.0% services, 20.3% sales, 3.8% farming, 25.2% construction, 17.0% production (2005-2009 5-year est.).
Income: Per capita income: $16,911 (2010); Median household income: $39,750 (2010); Average household income: $51,192 (2010); Percent of households with income of $100,000 or more: 10.2% (2010); Poverty rate: 32.2% (2005-2009 5-year est.).
Taxes: Total city taxes per capita: $161 (2007); City property taxes per capita: $65 (2007).
Education: Percent of population age 25 and over with: High school diploma (including GED) or higher: 65.6% (2010); Bachelor's degree or higher: 11.7% (2010); Master's degree or higher: 1.8% (2010).
School District(s)
Royal ISD (PK-12)
   2009-10 Enrollment: 2,057 . . . . (281) 934-2248
Housing: Homeownership rate: 56.3% (2010); Median home value: $59,412 (2010); Median contract rent: $514 per month (2005-2009 5-year est.); Median year structure built: 1990 (2005-2009 5-year est.).
Safety: Violent crime rate: 54.9 per 10,000 population; Property crime rate: 471.4 per 10,000 population (2009).
Transportation: Commute to work: 92.5% car, 1.1% public transportation, 1.6% walk, 3.8% work from home (2005-2009 5-year est.); Travel time to work: 27.3% less than 15 minutes, 40.1% 15 to 30 minutes, 12.3% 30 to 45 minutes, 6.7% 45 to 60 minutes, 13.5% 60 minutes or more (2005-2009 5-year est.)
Additional Information Contacts
West I-10 Chamber of Commerce . . . . (281) 375-8100
   http://www.westi10chamber.org

HEMPSTEAD (city). County seat. Covers a land area of 4.970 square miles and a water area of 0.020 square miles. Located at 30.09° N. Lat; 96.08° W. Long. Elevation is 243 feet.
History: Hempstead served the cotton, truck farming, and ranching area, and later the Raccoon oil field, as a marketing center.
Population: 3,587 (1990); 4,691 (2000); 7,096 (2010); 8,128 (2015 projected); Race: 44.0% White, 34.5% Black, 0.2% Asian, 21.4% Other, 32.4% Hispanic of any race (2010); Density: 1,427.6 persons per square mile (2010); Average household size: 2.81 (2010); Median age: 32.0 (2010); Males per 100 females: 100.6 (2010); Marriage status: 38.6% never married, 42.2% now married, 8.4% widowed, 10.8% divorced (2005-2009 5-year est.); Foreign born: 14.8% (2005-2009 5-year est.); Ancestry (includes multiple ancestries): 11.7% German, 6.6% Irish, 4.2% English, 2.6% Danish, 2.4% Polish (2005-2009 5-year est.).
Economy: Single-family building permits issued: 3 (2010); Multi-family building permits issued: 50 (2010); Employment by occupation: 11.7%

management, 13.9% professional, 25.3% services, 12.3% sales, 2.2% farming, 8.7% construction, 25.8% production (2005-2009 5-year est.).
Income: Per capita income: $16,739 (2010); Median household income: $34,004 (2010); Average household income: $46,706 (2010); Percent of households with income of $100,000 or more: 8.7% (2010); Poverty rate: 17.1% (2005-2009 5-year est.).
Taxes: Total city taxes per capita: $925 (2007); City property taxes per capita: $80 (2007).
Education: Percent of population age 25 and over with: High school diploma (including GED) or higher: 72.2% (2010); Bachelor's degree or higher: 16.8% (2010); Master's degree or higher: 5.1% (2010).

School District(s)
Calvin Nelms Charter Schools (04-12)
    2009-10 Enrollment: 297 . . . . (281) 398-8031
Hempstead ISD (PK-12)
    2009-10 Enrollment: 1,511 . . . . (979) 826-3304
Housing: Homeownership rate: 57.7% (2010); Median home value: $93,478 (2010); Median contract rent: $565 per month (2005-2009 5-year est.); Median year structure built: 1979 (2005-2009 5-year est.).
Safety: Violent crime rate: 38.6 per 10,000 population; Property crime rate: 342.7 per 10,000 population (2009).
Newspapers: Waller County News Citizen (Community news; Circulation 18,500)
Transportation: Commute to work: 93.8% car, 0.0% public transportation, 2.6% walk, 2.7% work from home (2005-2009 5-year est.); Travel time to work: 30.1% less than 15 minutes, 31.6% 15 to 30 minutes, 15.8% 30 to 45 minutes, 8.6% 45 to 60 minutes, 13.9% 60 minutes or more (2005-2009 5-year est.)
Additional Information Contacts
Hempstead Chamber of Commerce . . . . (979) 826-8217
    http://www.hempsteadtxchamber.com
Waller Area Chamber of Commerce . . . . (936) 372-5300
    http://www.wallerchamber.com

PATTISON (city).
Covers a land area of 3.243 square miles and a water area of 0 square miles. Located at 29.81° N. Lat; 95.98° W. Long. Elevation is 171 feet.
Population: 327 (1990); 447 (2000); 454 (2010); 460 (2015 projected); Race: 65.4% White, 8.6% Black, 0.0% Asian, 26.0% Other, 45.8% Hispanic of any race (2010); Density: 140.0 persons per square mile (2010); Average household size: 2.78 (2010); Median age: 35.7 (2010); Males per 100 females: 100.9 (2010); Marriage status: 25.5% never married, 58.9% now married, 4.7% widowed, 10.9% divorced (2005-2009 5-year est.); Foreign born: 16.4% (2005-2009 5-year est.); Ancestry (includes multiple ancestries): 16.7% German, 10.7% English, 10.2% Irish, 7.3% Czech, 3.7% American (2005-2009 5-year est.).
Economy: Single-family building permits issued: 2 (2010); Multi-family building permits issued: 0 (2010); Employment by occupation: 14.9% management, 14.3% professional, 10.9% services, 29.7% sales, 1.1% farming, 11.4% construction, 17.7% production (2005-2009 5-year est.).
Income: Per capita income: $27,379 (2010); Median household income: $63,942 (2010); Average household income: $76,672 (2010); Percent of households with income of $100,000 or more: 27.0% (2010); Poverty rate: 18.1% (2005-2009 5-year est.).
Education: Percent of population age 25 and over with: High school diploma (including GED) or higher: 81.1% (2010); Bachelor's degree or higher: 28.3% (2010); Master's degree or higher: 5.2% (2010).
Housing: Homeownership rate: 85.9% (2010); Median home value: $169,565 (2010); Median contract rent: $563 per month (2005-2009 5-year est.); Median year structure built: 1970 (2005-2009 5-year est.).
Transportation: Commute to work: 86.9% car, 0.0% public transportation, 0.0% walk, 13.1% work from home (2005-2009 5-year est.); Travel time to work: 49.3% less than 15 minutes, 28.3% 15 to 30 minutes, 4.6% 30 to 45 minutes, 7.2% 45 to 60 minutes, 10.5% 60 minutes or more (2005-2009 5-year est.)
Additional Information Contacts
West I-10 Chamber of Commerce . . . . (281) 375-8100
    http://www.westi10chamber.org

PINE ISLAND (town).
Covers a land area of 9.334 square miles and a water area of 0.010 square miles. Located at 30.06° N. Lat; 96.02° W. Long. Elevation is 197 feet.
Population: 571 (1990); 849 (2000); 909 (2010); 946 (2015 projected); Race: 54.7% White, 28.6% Black, 2.4% Asian, 14.3% Other, 25.4% Hispanic of any race (2010); Density: 97.4 persons per square mile (2010);

Average household size: 2.87 (2010); Median age: 31.4 (2010); Males per 100 females: 102.9 (2010); Marriage status: 30.1% never married, 56.5% now married, 8.3% widowed, 5.1% divorced (2005-2009 5-year est.); Foreign born: 14.8% (2005-2009 5-year est.); Ancestry (includes multiple ancestries): 6.3% English, 5.6% American, 5.2% German, 4.8% Italian, 2.9% Irish (2005-2009 5-year est.).
Economy: Employment by occupation: 7.4% management, 21.2% professional, 14.8% services, 19.1% sales, 3.9% farming, 11.8% construction, 21.7% production (2005-2009 5-year est.).
Income: Per capita income: $25,732 (2010); Median household income: $57,570 (2010); Average household income: $74,259 (2010); Percent of households with income of $100,000 or more: 20.5% (2010); Poverty rate: 13.5% (2005-2009 5-year est.).
Taxes: Total city taxes per capita: $81 (2007); City property taxes per capita: $81 (2007).
Education: Percent of population age 25 and over with: High school diploma (including GED) or higher: 80.6% (2010); Bachelor's degree or higher: 15.4% (2010); Master's degree or higher: 2.9% (2010).
Housing: Homeownership rate: 60.6% (2010); Median home value: $100,000 (2010); Median contract rent: $444 per month (2005-2009 5-year est.); Median year structure built: 1991 (2005-2009 5-year est.).
Transportation: Commute to work: 95.6% car, 0.0% public transportation, 1.7% walk, 2.7% work from home (2005-2009 5-year est.); Travel time to work: 24.3% less than 15 minutes, 10.3% 15 to 30 minutes, 16.3% 30 to 45 minutes, 30.4% 45 to 60 minutes, 18.7% 60 minutes or more (2005-2009 5-year est.)

PRAIRIE VIEW (city).
Covers a land area of 7.217 square miles and a water area of 0.001 square miles. Located at 30.08° N. Lat; 95.99° W. Long. Elevation is 269 feet.
History: Seat of Prairie View Agricultural and Mechanical University.
Population: 4,004 (1990); 4,410 (2000); 4,553 (2010); 4,637 (2015 projected); Race: 14.3% White, 81.2% Black, 0.5% Asian, 4.0% Other, 6.4% Hispanic of any race (2010); Density: 630.8 persons per square mile (2010); Average household size: 2.47 (2010); Median age: 21.0 (2010); Males per 100 females: 91.6 (2010); Marriage status: 68.2% never married, 21.8% now married, 3.7% widowed, 6.3% divorced (2005-2009 5-year est.); Foreign born: 11.5% (2005-2009 5-year est.); Ancestry (includes multiple ancestries): 3.5% Slavic, 3.0% Jamaican, 1.7% African, 0.9% German, 0.9% Irish (2005-2009 5-year est.).
Economy: Single-family building permits issued: 3 (2010); Multi-family building permits issued: 0 (2010); Employment by occupation: 5.0% management, 25.3% professional, 21.6% services, 26.5% sales, 0.4% farming, 11.6% construction, 9.7% production (2005-2009 5-year est.).
Income: Per capita income: $14,620 (2010); Median household income: $54,561 (2010); Average household income: $70,924 (2010); Percent of households with income of $100,000 or more: 22.5% (2010); Poverty rate: 33.6% (2005-2009 5-year est.).
Taxes: Total city taxes per capita: $166 (2007); City property taxes per capita: $84 (2007).
Education: Percent of population age 25 and over with: High school diploma (including GED) or higher: 83.7% (2010); Bachelor's degree or higher: 31.7% (2010); Master's degree or higher: 15.8% (2010).

School District(s)
Waller ISD (PK-12)
    2009-10 Enrollment: 5,407 . . . . (936) 931-3685
Four-year College(s)
Prairie View A & M University (Public, Historically black)
    Fall 2009 Enrollment: 8,608. . . . . (936) 261-3311
    2010-11 Tuition: In-state $6,856; Out-of-state $16,156
Housing: Homeownership rate: 56.9% (2010); Median home value: $107,773 (2010); Median contract rent: $475 per month (2005-2009 5-year est.); Median year structure built: 1983 (2005-2009 5-year est.).
Transportation: Commute to work: 87.7% car, 0.0% public transportation, 10.8% walk, 0.6% work from home (2005-2009 5-year est.); Travel time to work: 51.5% less than 15 minutes, 21.4% 15 to 30 minutes, 12.6% 30 to 45 minutes, 3.0% 45 to 60 minutes, 11.4% 60 minutes or more (2005-2009 5-year est.)

WALLER (city).
Covers a land area of 1.493 square miles and a water area of 0 square miles. Located at 30.05° N. Lat; 95.92° W. Long. Elevation is 249 feet.
History: In Waller, an unusual general department store called God's Mercy Store tried a new method of mark-ups. Each item was marked with the cost price paid by the owner, and the purchaser could decide what

amount over that cost was reasonable for the store owner to receive to cover his operating expenses and profit.

Population: 1,554 (1990); 2,092 (2000); 2,133 (2010); 2,173 (2015 projected); Race: 67.7% White, 17.3% Black, 1.0% Asian, 13.9% Other, 29.4% Hispanic of any race (2010); Density: 1,428.5 persons per square mile (2010); Average household size: 2.77 (2010); Median age: 30.8 (2010); Males per 100 females: 99.9 (2010); Marriage status: 33.9% never married, 53.8% now married, 5.1% widowed, 7.3% divorced (2005-2009 5-year est.); Foreign born: 8.0% (2005-2009 5-year est.); Ancestry (includes multiple ancestries): 20.3% German, 8.8% Irish, 8.4% English, 6.1% American, 5.4% French (2005-2009 5-year est.).

Economy: Single-family building permits issued: 1 (2010); Multi-family building permits issued: 0 (2010); Employment by occupation: 12.7% management, 13.9% professional, 24.9% services, 21.6% sales, 2.0% farming, 17.1% construction, 7.9% production (2005-2009 5-year est.).

Income: Per capita income: $24,380 (2010); Median household income: $53,024 (2010); Average household income: $67,783 (2010); Percent of households with income of $100,000 or more: 19.3% (2010); Poverty rate: 21.0% (2005-2009 5-year est.).

Taxes: Total city taxes per capita: $481 (2007); City property taxes per capita: $118 (2007).

Education: Percent of population age 25 and over with: High school diploma (including GED) or higher: 81.4% (2010); Bachelor's degree or higher: 16.0% (2010); Master's degree or higher: 5.7% (2010).

School District(s)

Waller ISD (PK-12)

　2009-10 Enrollment: 5,407 . . . . (936) 931-3685

Housing: Homeownership rate: 53.4% (2010); Median home value: $98,545 (2010); Median contract rent: $572 per month (2005-2009 5-year est.); Median year structure built: 1987 (2005-2009 5-year est.).

Safety: Violent crime rate: 97.5 per 10,000 population; Property crime rate: 385.2 per 10,000 population (2009).

Transportation: Commute to work: 92.5% car, 0.0% public transportation, 1.2% walk, 5.4% work from home (2005-2009 5-year est.); Travel time to work: 53.2% less than 15 minutes, 12.2% 15 to 30 minutes, 16.1% 30 to 45 minutes, 7.7% 45 to 60 minutes, 10.8% 60 minutes or more (2005-2009 5-year est.)

Ward County

Located in west Texas, in the Pecos Valley; bounded on the west and south by the Pecos River. Covers a land area of 835.49 square miles, a water area of 0.25 square miles, and is located in the Central Time Zone at 31.51° N. Lat., 103.01° W. Long. The county was founded in 1892. County seat is Monahans.

Weather Station: Grandfalls 3 SSE　　　　　　　　　　　Elevation: 2,439 feet

	Jan	Feb	Mar	Apr	May	Jun	Jul	Aug	Sep	Oct	Nov	Dec
High	62	67	75	83	91	98	98	97	91	82	71	61
Low	28	32	39	47	58	67	69	68	61	50	37	28
Precip	0.5	0.7	0.5	0.9	1.7	1.5	1.4	1.7	2.5	1.6	0.6	0.8
Snow	1.0	0.1	0.1	0.0	0.0	0.0	0.0	0.0	0.0	0.0	0.4	0.4

High and Low temperatures in degrees Fahrenheit; Precipitation and Snow in inches

Weather Station: Monahans　　　　　　　　　　　　　　　Elevation: 2,660 feet

	Jan	Feb	Mar	Apr	May	Jun	Jul	Aug	Sep	Oct	Nov	Dec
High	62	66	75	83	91	98	99	97	91	82	70	62
Low	29	33	40	48	58	67	69	69	62	50	38	29
Precip	0.5	0.7	0.5	0.7	1.6	1.3	1.6	1.7	2.4	1.6	0.6	0.7
Snow	0.3	0.1	0.1	0.0	0.0	0.0	0.0	0.0	0.0	tr	0.1	0.3

High and Low temperatures in degrees Fahrenheit; Precipitation and Snow in inches

Population: 13,115 (1990); 10,909 (2000); 10,396 (2010); 10,128 (2015 projected); Race: 76.6% White, 5.9% Black, 0.3% Asian, 17.2% Other, 46.7% Hispanic of any race (2010); Density: 12.4 persons per square mile (2010); Average household size: 2.54 (2010); Median age: 35.7 (2010); Males per 100 females: 98.1 (2010).

Religion: Five largest groups: 30.0% Southern Baptist Convention, 27.5% Catholic Church, 6.6% The United Methodist Church, 4.2% Churches of Christ, 2.8% Independent, Non-Charismatic Churches (2000).

Economy: Unemployment rate: 7.6% (June 2011); Total civilian labor force: 4,953 (June 2011); Leading industries: 25.9% mining; 11.6% retail trade; 10.9% accommodation & food services (2009); Farms: 119 totaling 432,920 acres (2007); Companies that employ 500 or more persons: 0 (2009); Companies that employ 100 to 499 persons: 1 (2009); Companies that employ less than 100 persons: 267 (2009); Black-owned businesses:

n/a (2007); Hispanic-owned businesses: n/a (2007); Asian-owned businesses: n/a (2007); Women-owned businesses: n/a (2007); Retail sales per capita: $8,888 (2010). Single-family building permits issued: 7 (2010); Multi-family building permits issued: 0 (2010).

Income: Per capita income: $21,371 (2010); Median household income: $42,391 (2010); Average household income: $55,877 (2010); Percent of households with income of $100,000 or more: 12.8% (2010); Poverty rate: 15.5% (2009); Bankruptcy rate: 0.37% (2010).

Taxes: Total county taxes per capita: $865 (2007); County property taxes per capita: $835 (2007).

Education: Percent of population age 25 and over with: High school diploma (including GED) or higher: 75.2% (2010); Bachelor's degree or higher: 13.8% (2010); Master's degree or higher: 4.6% (2010).

Housing: Homeownership rate: 76.3% (2010); Median home value: $34,891 (2010); Median contract rent: $326 per month (2005-2009 5-year est.); Median year structure built: 1963 (2005-2009 5-year est.)

Health: Birth rate: 193.8 per 10,000 population (2009); Death rate: 95.0 per 10,000 population (2009); Age-adjusted cancer mortality rate: 201.3 deaths per 100,000 population (2007); Number of physicians: 2.9 per 10,000 population (2008); Hospital beds: 24.6 per 10,000 population (2007); Hospital admissions: 359.8 per 10,000 population (2007).

Elections: 2008 Presidential election results: 25.0% Obama, 74.0% McCain, 0.1% Nader

National and State Parks: Monahans Sand Hills State Park

Additional Information Contacts

Ward County Government . . . . (432) 943-3209
　http://www.co.ward.tx.us/ips/cms
City of Monahans . . . . (432) 943-4343
　http://www.cityofmonahans.org
Monahans Chamber of Commerce . . . . (432) 943-2187
　http://www.monahans.org

Ward County Communities

BARSTOW (city). Covers a land area of 0.669 square miles and a water area of 0 square miles. Located at 31.46° N. Lat; 103.39° W. Long. Elevation is 2,566 feet.

History: Water from the Red Bluff Irrigation Project transformed the area around Barstow into fertile agricultural land.

Population: 535 (1990); 406 (2000); 390 (2010); 384 (2015 projected); Race: 73.3% White, 14.1% Black, 0.3% Asian, 12.3% Other, 52.3% Hispanic of any race (2010); Density: 583.3 persons per square mile (2010); Average household size: 2.48 (2010); Median age: 22.6 (2010); Males per 100 females: 156.6 (2010); Marriage status: 19.9% never married, 58.6% now married, 14.5% widowed, 7.1% divorced (2005-2009 5-year est.); Foreign born: 8.6% (2005-2009 5-year est.); Ancestry (includes multiple ancestries): 9.7% English, 5.1% Dutch, 4.3% American, 3.0% Irish, 1.6% German (2005-2009 5-year est.).

Economy: Employment by occupation: 3.9% management, 7.7% professional, 29.0% services, 17.4% sales, 0.0% farming, 14.8% construction, 27.1% production (2005-2009 5-year est.).

Income: Per capita income: $11,039 (2010); Median household income: $29,118 (2010); Average household income: $34,646 (2010); Percent of households with income of $100,000 or more: 2.5% (2010); Poverty rate: 19.6% (2005-2009 5-year est.).

Taxes: Total city taxes per capita: $15 (2007); City property taxes per capita: $0 (2007).

Education: Percent of population age 25 and over with: High school diploma (including GED) or higher: 53.0% (2010); Bachelor's degree or higher: 7.0% (2010); Master's degree or higher: 2.7% (2010).

Housing: Homeownership rate: 75.0% (2010); Median home value: $19,999 (2010); Median contract rent: $144 per month (2005-2009 5-year est.); Median year structure built: 1955 (2005-2009 5-year est.).

Transportation: Commute to work: 91.7% car, 0.0% public transportation, 8.3% walk, 0.0% work from home (2005-2009 5-year est.); Travel time to work: 31.8% less than 15 minutes, 33.3% 15 to 30 minutes, 13.6% 30 to 45 minutes, 14.4% 45 to 60 minutes, 6.8% 60 minutes or more (2005-2009 5-year est.)

GRANDFALLS (town). Covers a land area of 0.536 square miles and a water area of 0 square miles. Located at 31.34° N. Lat; 102.85° W. Long. Elevation is 2,434 feet.

Population: 571 (1990); 391 (2000); 397 (2010); 400 (2015 projected); Race: 74.3% White, 0.3% Black, 0.0% Asian, 25.4% Other, 51.4% Hispanic of any race (2010); Density: 740.3 persons per square mile

(2010); Average household size: 2.56 (2010); Median age: 35.8 (2010); Males per 100 females: 85.5 (2010); Marriage status: 14.3% never married, 60.3% now married, 14.7% widowed, 10.7% divorced (2005-2009 5-year est.); Foreign born: 6.5% (2005-2009 5-year est.); Ancestry (includes multiple ancestries): 13.7% German, 9.8% English, 5.0% Irish, 4.3% French, 4.1% Scottish (2005-2009 5-year est.).

Economy: Employment by occupation: 0.9% management, 29.1% professional, 8.5% services, 6.8% sales, 0.0% farming, 23.1% construction, 31.6% production (2005-2009 5-year est.).

Income: Per capita income: $18,271 (2010); Median household income: $38,068 (2010); Average household income: $47,387 (2010); Percent of households with income of $100,000 or more: 7.7% (2010); Poverty rate: 15.8% (2005-2009 5-year est.).

Taxes: Total city taxes per capita: $332 (2007); City property taxes per capita: $186 (2007).

Education: Percent of population age 25 and over with: High school diploma (including GED) or higher: 70.5% (2010); Bachelor's degree or higher: 11.1% (2010); Master's degree or higher: 2.9% (2010).

School District(s)
Grandfalls-Royalty ISD (PK-12)
    2009-10 Enrollment: 123 . . . . (432) 547-2266

Housing: Homeownership rate: 75.5% (2010); Median home value: $25,429 (2010); Median contract rent: $188 per month (2005-2009 5-year est.); Median year structure built: 1957 (2005-2009 5-year est.).

Transportation: Commute to work: 92.9% car, 0.0% public transportation, 0.0% walk, 0.0% work from home (2005-2009 5-year est.); Travel time to work: 24.8% less than 15 minutes, 21.2% 15 to 30 minutes, 4.4% 30 to 45 minutes, 8.8% 45 to 60 minutes, 40.7% 60 minutes or more (2005-2009 5-year est.)

MONAHANS (city). County seat. Covers a land area of 24.809 square miles and a water area of 0.012 square miles. Located at 31.59° N. Lat; 102.90° W. Long. Elevation is 2,621 feet.

History: Monahans was a supply center for nearby ranches until the Winkler Oil Field, to the north, was developed.

Population: 8,101 (1990); 6,821 (2000); 6,389 (2010); 6,180 (2015 projected); Race: 76.4% White, 5.6% Black, 0.4% Asian, 17.6% Other, 48.4% Hispanic of any race (2010); Density: 257.5 persons per square mile (2010); Average household size: 2.55 (2010); Median age: 35.2 (2010); Males per 100 females: 91.7 (2010); Marriage status: 25.5% never married, 55.1% now married, 8.4% widowed, 10.9% divorced (2005-2009 5-year est.); Foreign born: 7.7% (2005-2009 5-year est.); Ancestry (includes multiple ancestries): 7.9% American, 7.5% Irish, 6.1% English, 3.4% German, 1.5% Swedish (2005-2009 5-year est.).

Economy: Single-family building permits issued: 7 (2010); Multi-family building permits issued: 0 (2010); Employment by occupation: 11.2% management, 13.4% professional, 22.0% services, 21.9% sales, 0.6% farming, 19.4% construction, 11.4% production (2005-2009 5-year est.).

Income: Per capita income: $21,592 (2010); Median household income: $42,703 (2010); Average household income: $55,919 (2010); Percent of households with income of $100,000 or more: 12.9% (2010); Poverty rate: 12.4% (2005-2009 5-year est.).

Taxes: Total city taxes per capita: $255 (2007); City property taxes per capita: $62 (2007).

Education: Percent of population age 25 and over with: High school diploma (including GED) or higher: 77.9% (2010); Bachelor's degree or higher: 16.0% (2010); Master's degree or higher: 5.9% (2010).

School District(s)
Monahans-Wickett-Pyote ISD (PK-12)
    2009-10 Enrollment: 1,983 . . . . (432) 943-6711

Housing: Homeownership rate: 73.1% (2010); Median home value: $38,093 (2010); Median contract rent: $378 per month (2005-2009 5-year est.); Median year structure built: 1964 (2005-2009 5-year est.).

Hospitals: Ward Memorial Hospital (49 beds)

Safety: Violent crime rate: 70.9 per 10,000 population; Property crime rate: 369.9 per 10,000 population (2009).

Newspapers: Monahans News

Transportation: Commute to work: 96.2% car, 0.0% public transportation, 1.2% walk, 2.0% work from home (2005-2009 5-year est.); Travel time to work: 59.6% less than 15 minutes, 11.6% 15 to 30 minutes, 15.0% 30 to 45 minutes, 6.6% 45 to 60 minutes, 7.2% 60 minutes or more (2005-2009 5-year est.)

Additional Information Contacts
City of Monahans . . . . (432) 943-4343
    http://www.cityofmonahans.org

Monahans Chamber of Commerce . . . . (432) 943-2187
    http://www.monahans.org

PYOTE (town). Covers a land area of 1.290 square miles and a water area of 0 square miles. Located at 31.53° N. Lat; 103.12° W. Long. Elevation is 2,625 feet.

Population: 348 (1990); 131 (2000); 131 (2010); 129 (2015 projected); Race: 73.3% White, 14.5% Black, 0.0% Asian, 12.2% Other, 52.7% Hispanic of any race (2010); Density: 101.5 persons per square mile (2010); Average household size: 2.50 (2010); Median age: 22.8 (2010); Males per 100 females: 151.9 (2010); Marriage status: 11.3% never married, 77.4% now married, 0.0% widowed, 11.3% divorced (2005-2009 5-year est.); Foreign born: 1.7% (2005-2009 5-year est.); Ancestry (includes multiple ancestries): 11.6% German, 10.5% Dutch, 10.5% French, 10.5% Irish, 7.7% American (2005-2009 5-year est.).

Economy: Employment by occupation: 4.7% management, 0.0% professional, 3.1% services, 20.3% sales, 0.0% farming, 18.8% construction, 53.1% production (2005-2009 5-year est.).

Income: Per capita income: $11,039 (2010); Median household income: $30,000 (2010); Average household income: $36,813 (2010); Percent of households with income of $100,000 or more: 5.0% (2010); Poverty rate: 3.3% (2005-2009 5-year est.).

Taxes: Total city taxes per capita: $97 (2007); City property taxes per capita: $0 (2007).

Education: Percent of population age 25 and over with: High school diploma (including GED) or higher: 50.8% (2010); Bachelor's degree or higher: 6.6% (2010); Master's degree or higher: 3.3% (2010).

School District(s)
Iraan-Sheffield ISD (PK-12)
    2009-10 Enrollment: 543 . . . . (432) 639-2512

Housing: Homeownership rate: 75.0% (2010); Median home value: $19,999 (2010); Median contract rent: n/a per month (2005-2009 5-year est.); Median year structure built: 1956 (2005-2009 5-year est.).

Transportation: Commute to work: 78.1% car, 0.0% public transportation, 0.0% walk, 21.9% work from home (2005-2009 5-year est.); Travel time to work: 18.0% less than 15 minutes, 36.0% 15 to 30 minutes, 14.0% 30 to 45 minutes, 22.0% 45 to 60 minutes, 10.0% 60 minutes or more (2005-2009 5-year est.)

THORNTONVILLE (town). Covers a land area of 0.783 square miles and a water area of 0 square miles. Located at 31.58° N. Lat; 102.92° W. Long. Elevation is 2,605 feet.

Population: 693 (1990); 442 (2000); 419 (2010); 405 (2015 projected); Race: 77.3% White, 0.0% Black, 0.2% Asian, 22.4% Other, 36.8% Hispanic of any race (2010); Density: 535.3 persons per square mile (2010); Average household size: 2.29 (2010); Median age: 47.2 (2010); Males per 100 females: 91.3 (2010); Marriage status: 14.3% never married, 60.4% now married, 12.2% widowed, 13.1% divorced (2005-2009 5-year est.); Foreign born: 12.6% (2005-2009 5-year est.); Ancestry (includes multiple ancestries): 14.3% German, 13.1% English, 9.7% Irish, 4.2% American, 2.4% Scotch-Irish (2005-2009 5-year est.).

Economy: Employment by occupation: 9.6% management, 4.8% professional, 14.7% services, 15.8% sales, 0.0% farming, 36.3% construction, 18.8% production (2005-2009 5-year est.).

Income: Per capita income: $25,462 (2010); Median household income: $46,691 (2010); Average household income: $58,484 (2010); Percent of households with income of $100,000 or more: 13.7% (2010); Poverty rate: 10.8% (2005-2009 5-year est.).

Taxes: Total city taxes per capita: $40 (2007); City property taxes per capita: $0 (2007).

Education: Percent of population age 25 and over with: High school diploma (including GED) or higher: 68.2% (2010); Bachelor's degree or higher: 6.7% (2010); Master's degree or higher: 0.3% (2010).

Housing: Homeownership rate: 86.3% (2010); Median home value: $31,707 (2010); Median contract rent: $230 per month (2005-2009 5-year est.); Median year structure built: 1967 (2005-2009 5-year est.).

Transportation: Commute to work: 97.9% car, 0.0% public transportation, 2.1% walk, 0.0% work from home (2005-2009 5-year est.); Travel time to work: 43.0% less than 15 minutes, 15.8% 15 to 30 minutes, 11.7% 30 to 45 minutes, 1.4% 45 to 60 minutes, 28.2% 60 minutes or more (2005-2009 5-year est.)

WICKETT (town). Covers a land area of 0.702 square miles and a water area of 0 square miles. Located at 31.56° N. Lat; 103.00° W. Long. Elevation is 2,667 feet.

Population: 560 (1990); 455 (2000); 425 (2010); 408 (2015 projected); Race: 84.5% White, 6.8% Black, 0.0% Asian, 8.7% Other, 34.4% Hispanic of any race (2010); Density: 605.3 persons per square mile (2010); Average household size: 2.53 (2010); Median age: 37.6 (2010); Males per 100 females: 90.6 (2010); Marriage status: 17.3% never married, 61.9% now married, 12.3% widowed, 8.4% divorced (2005-2009 5-year est.); Foreign born: 6.9% (2005-2009 5-year est.); Ancestry (includes multiple ancestries): 18.8% German, 18.2% Irish, 13.9% Italian, 10.1% Dutch West Indian, 9.9% English (2005-2009 5-year est.).

Economy: Single-family building permits issued: 0 (2010); Multi-family building permits issued: 0 (2010); Employment by occupation: 8.9% management, 8.3% professional, 12.5% services, 25.6% sales, 0.0% farming, 22.6% construction, 22.0% production (2005-2009 5-year est.).

Income: Per capita income: $23,522 (2010); Median household income: $44,255 (2010); Average household income: $60,714 (2010); Percent of households with income of $100,000 or more: 14.3% (2010); Poverty rate: 36.2% (2005-2009 5-year est.).

Taxes: Total city taxes per capita: $317 (2007); City property taxes per capita: $59 (2007).

Education: Percent of population age 25 and over with: High school diploma (including GED) or higher: 71.7% (2010); Bachelor's degree or higher: 5.9% (2010); Master's degree or higher: 1.5% (2010).

Housing: Homeownership rate: 90.5% (2010); Median home value: $21,091 (2010); Median contract rent: $267 per month (2005-2009 5-year est.); Median year structure built: 1955 (2005-2009 5-year est.).

Transportation: Commute to work: 85.5% car, 1.9% public transportation, 10.7% walk, 0.0% work from home (2005-2009 5-year est.); Travel time to work: 54.1% less than 15 minutes, 25.2% 15 to 30 minutes, 13.8% 30 to 45 minutes, 1.3% 45 to 60 minutes, 5.7% 60 minutes or more (2005-2009 5-year est.)

Washington County

Located in south central Texas; bounded on the east by the Brazos River, and on the north by Yegua Creek. Covers a land area of 609.22 square miles, a water area of 12.13 square miles, and is located in the Central Time Zone at 30.18° N. Lat., 96.41° W. Long. The county was founded in 1836. County seat is Brenham.

Washington County is part of the Brenham, TX Micropolitan Statistical Area. The entire metro area includes: Washington County, TX

Weather Station: Brenham   Elevation: 312 feet

	Jan	Feb	Mar	Apr	May	Jun	Jul	Aug	Sep	Oct	Nov	Dec
High	62	66	72	80	86	92	95	96	91	82	72	63
Low	41	44	50	57	65	72	74	74	68	59	50	42
Precip	3.5	2.9	3.4	2.9	4.7	4.8	2.5	2.9	4.5	5.2	4.3	3.4
Snow	0.1	tr	tr	0.0	0.0	0.0	0.0	0.0	0.0	0.0	0.0	tr

High and Low temperatures in degrees Fahrenheit; Precipitation and Snow in inches

Weather Station: Navasota   Elevation: 220 feet

	Jan	Feb	Mar	Apr	May	Jun	Jul	Aug	Sep	Oct	Nov	Dec
High	61	65	71	79	85	92	95	96	91	81	71	62
Low	38	42	49	56	64	70	72	72	66	57	48	40
Precip	3.6	2.8	3.5	2.7	4.1	4.6	2.3	2.8	3.5	4.8	3.8	3.4
Snow	0.0	tr	0.0	0.0	0.0	0.0	0.0	0.0	0.0	0.0	0.0	tr

High and Low temperatures in degrees Fahrenheit; Precipitation and Snow in inches

Population: 26,154 (1990); 30,373 (2000); 33,118 (2010); 34,392 (2015 projected); Race: 73.7% White, 17.3% Black, 1.3% Asian, 7.6% Other, 12.5% Hispanic of any race (2010); Density: 54.4 persons per square mile (2010); Average household size: 2.51 (2010); Median age: 37.9 (2010); Males per 100 females: 95.5 (2010).

Religion: Five largest groups: 22.5% Evangelical Lutheran Church in America, 20.2% Catholic Church, 10.0% Southern Baptist Convention, 4.5% The United Methodist Church, 4.2% Lutheran Church—Missouri Synod (2000).

Economy: Unemployment rate: 6.9% (June 2011); Total civilian labor force: 17,170 (June 2011); Leading industries: 21.9% manufacturing; 17.2% retail trade; 13.9% health care and social assistance (2009); Farms: 2,399 totaling 338,384 acres (2007); Companies that employ 500 or more persons: 1 (2009); Companies that employ 100 to 499 persons: 17 (2009); Companies that employ less than 100 persons: 843 (2009); Black-owned businesses: n/a (2007); Hispanic-owned businesses: 141 (2007); Asian-owned businesses: n/a (2007); Women-owned businesses: 1,014

(2007); Retail sales per capita: $12,805 (2010). Single-family building permits issued: 54 (2010); Multi-family building permits issued: 0 (2010).

Income: Per capita income: $22,709 (2010); Median household income: $46,327 (2010); Average household income: $59,417 (2010); Percent of households with income of $100,000 or more: 13.9% (2010); Poverty rate: 14.5% (2009); Bankruptcy rate: 0.64% (2010).

Taxes: Total county taxes per capita: $388 (2007); County property taxes per capita: $300 (2007).

Education: Percent of population age 25 and over with: High school diploma (including GED) or higher: 78.1% (2010); Bachelor's degree or higher: 23.3% (2010); Master's degree or higher: 8.2% (2010).

Housing: Homeownership rate: 68.4% (2010); Median home value: $126,435 (2010); Median contract rent: $526 per month (2005-2009 5-year est.); Median year structure built: 1979 (2005-2009 5-year est.)

Health: Birth rate: 135.6 per 10,000 population (2009); Death rate: 109.4 per 10,000 population (2009); Age-adjusted cancer mortality rate: 155.7 deaths per 100,000 population (2007); Number of physicians: 12.3 per 10,000 population (2008); Hospital beds: 18.7 per 10,000 population (2007); Hospital admissions: 725.6 per 10,000 population (2007).

Elections: 2008 Presidential election results: 28.1% Obama, 70.8% McCain, 0.1% Nader

National and State Parks: Baylor University State Park; Washington State Park

Additional Information Contacts

Washington County Government . . . . (979) 277-6200
   http://www.co.washington.tx.us/ips/cms
City of Brenham . . . . (979) 337-7200
   http://www.ci.brenham.tx.us
Washington Chamber of Commerce . . . . (979) 836-3695
   http://www.brenhamtexas.com

Washington County Communities

BRENHAM (city). County seat. Covers a land area of 8.762 square miles and a water area of 0 square miles. Located at 30.16° N. Lat; 96.39° W. Long. Elevation is 341 feet.

History: Brenham was founded in 1844 and prospered as a shipper of Brazos Valley hogs, beef cattle, and dairy products. Although settled first by people from other states, Brenham's later residents were largely German immigrants who made the town thrifty and efficient.

Population: 12,152 (1990); 13,507 (2000); 14,494 (2010); 15,073 (2015 projected); Race: 67.5% White, 21.0% Black, 1.8% Asian, 9.6% Other, 15.8% Hispanic of any race (2010); Density: 1,654.1 persons per square mile (2010); Average household size: 2.40 (2010); Median age: 34.7 (2010); Males per 100 females: 90.1 (2010); Marriage status: 38.4% never married, 41.7% now married, 10.8% widowed, 9.1% divorced (2005-2009 5-year est.); Foreign born: 6.6% (2005-2009 5-year est.); Ancestry (includes multiple ancestries): 20.7% German, 7.0% English, 4.8% Irish, 2.7% American, 2.1% Polish (2005-2009 5-year est.).

Economy: Single-family building permits issued: 54 (2010); Multi-family building permits issued: 0 (2010); Employment by occupation: 11.9% management, 15.5% professional, 20.2% services, 29.3% sales, 0.3% farming, 6.8% construction, 16.0% production (2005-2009 5-year est.).

Income: Per capita income: $19,984 (2010); Median household income: $40,881 (2010); Average household income: $51,373 (2010); Percent of households with income of $100,000 or more: 10.6% (2010); Poverty rate: 20.7% (2005-2009 5-year est.).

Taxes: Total city taxes per capita: $735 (2007); City property taxes per capita: $236 (2007).

Education: Percent of population age 25 and over with: High school diploma (including GED) or higher: 77.1% (2010); Bachelor's degree or higher: 23.0% (2010); Master's degree or higher: 9.5% (2010).

School District(s)

Brenham ISD (PK-12)
   2009-10 Enrollment: 4,940 . . . . (979) 277-3700

Two-year College(s)

Blinn College (Public)
   Fall 2009 Enrollment: 17,173 . . . . (979) 830-4000
   2010-11 Tuition: In-state $2,352; Out-of-state $4,176

Housing: Homeownership rate: 54.8% (2010); Median home value: $110,876 (2010); Median contract rent: $539 per month (2005-2009 5-year est.); Median year structure built: 1975 (2005-2009 5-year est.).

Hospitals: Trinity Medical Center (60 beds)

Safety: Violent crime rate: 67.5 per 10,000 population; Property crime rate: 400.9 per 10,000 population (2009).

Newspapers: The Brenham Banner-Press (Local news; Circulation 6,500)
Transportation: Commute to work: 92.0% car, 0.3% public transportation, 1.4% walk, 5.3% work from home (2005-2009 5-year est.); Travel time to work: 66.4% less than 15 minutes, 20.5% 15 to 30 minutes, 5.4% 30 to 45 minutes, 3.8% 45 to 60 minutes, 3.9% 60 minutes or more (2005-2009 5-year est.)
Airports: Brenham Municipal (general aviation)
Additional Information Contacts
City of Brenham . . . . (979) 337-7200
   http://www.ci.brenham.tx.us
Washington Chamber of Commerce . . . . (979) 836-3695
   http://www.brenhamtexas.com

BURTON (town). Covers a land area of 1.190 square miles and a water area of 0 square miles. Located at 30.18° N. Lat; 96.59° W. Long. Elevation is 440 feet.
Population: 311 (1990); 359 (2000); 362 (2010); 362 (2015 projected); Race: 74.0% White, 17.4% Black, 1.4% Asian, 7.2% Other, 6.6% Hispanic of any race (2010); Density: 304.3 persons per square mile (2010); Average household size: 2.32 (2010); Median age: 43.6 (2010); Males per 100 females: 94.6 (2010); Marriage status: 23.6% never married, 60.1% now married, 6.3% widowed, 10.1% divorced (2005-2009 5-year est.); Foreign born: 4.3% (2005-2009 5-year est.); Ancestry (includes multiple ancestries): 27.9% German, 13.3% Polish, 6.8% French, 5.1% Irish, 4.6% English (2005-2009 5-year est.).
Economy: Employment by occupation: 5.2% management, 22.7% professional, 19.8% services, 22.7% sales, 0.0% farming, 8.1% construction, 21.5% production (2005-2009 5-year est.).
Income: Per capita income: $20,413 (2010); Median household income: $44,286 (2010); Average household income: $47,500 (2010); Percent of households with income of $100,000 or more: 7.7% (2010); Poverty rate: 14.4% (2005-2009 5-year est.).
Taxes: Total city taxes per capita: $271 (2007); City property taxes per capita: $192 (2007).
Education: Percent of population age 25 and over with: High school diploma (including GED) or higher: 81.1% (2010); Bachelor's degree or higher: 19.3% (2010); Master's degree or higher: 5.3% (2010).
School District(s)
Burton ISD (PK-12)
   2009-10 Enrollment: 340 . . . . (979) 289-3131
Housing: Homeownership rate: 76.9% (2010); Median home value: $127,273 (2010); Median contract rent: $442 per month (2005-2009 5-year est.); Median year structure built: 1968 (2005-2009 5-year est.).
Transportation: Commute to work: 87.6% car, 0.0% public transportation, 5.9% walk, 4.6% work from home (2005-2009 5-year est.); Travel time to work: 28.8% less than 15 minutes, 50.0% 15 to 30 minutes, 6.2% 30 to 45 minutes, 3.4% 45 to 60 minutes, 11.6% 60 minutes or more (2005-2009 5-year est.)

CHAPPELL HILL (unincorporated postal area, zip code 77426). Aka Chapel Hill. Covers a land area of 58.383 square miles and a water area of 0.167 square miles. Located at 30.13° N. Lat; 96.25° W. Long. Elevation is 299 feet.
History: Chappell Hill was founded in 1849 as the home of plantation owners, who lived in nice town houses while overseers handled their vast land holdings.
Population: 1,319 (2000); Race: 74.7% White, 22.5% Black, 1.6% Asian, 1.2% Other, 2.8% Hispanic of any race (2000); Density: 22.6 persons per square mile (2000); Age: 21.0% under 18, 20.6% over 64 (2000); Marriage status: 17.2% never married, 61.4% now married, 12.1% widowed, 9.3% divorced (2000); Foreign born: 8.2% (2000); Ancestry (includes multiple ancestries): 18.4% Polish, 11.9% American, 9.0% English, 7.1% German (2000).
Economy: Employment by occupation: 11.2% management, 18.7% professional, 17.7% services, 27.0% sales, 1.2% farming, 7.3% construction, 16.9% production (2000).
Income: Per capita income: $18,712 (2000); Median household income: $28,333 (2000); Poverty rate: 179.1% (2000).
Education: Percent of population age 25 and over with: High school diploma (including GED) or higher: 71.5% (2000); Bachelor's degree or higher: 20.1% (2000).
Housing: Homeownership rate: 80.8% (2000); Median home value: $63,900 (2000); Median contract rent: $461 per month (2000); Median year structure built: 1969 (2000).

Transportation: Commute to work: 90.6% car, 0.0% public transportation, 1.8% walk, 7.6% work from home (2000); Travel time to work: 27.0% less than 15 minutes, 38.0% 15 to 30 minutes, 7.1% 30 to 45 minutes, 8.2% 45 to 60 minutes, 19.7% 60 minutes or more (2000)

WASHINGTON (unincorporated postal area, zip code 77880). Covers a land area of 86.128 square miles and a water area of 0.341 square miles. Located at 30.28° N. Lat; 96.16° W. Long. Elevation is 226 feet.
History: Washington, on the Brazos River, was the first settlement in Stephen F. Austin's land grant of 1821. The town was founded in 1835, and was first called Washington on the Brazos. The Texas Declaration of Independence was written here in 1836.
Population: 1,413 (2000); Race: 48.9% White, 50.5% Black, 0.0% Asian, 0.6% Other, 2.8% Hispanic of any race (2000); Density: 16.4 persons per square mile (2000); Age: 30.5% under 18, 12.4% over 64 (2000); Marriage status: 27.4% never married, 59.3% now married, 7.1% widowed, 6.2% divorced (2000); Foreign born: 1.5% (2000); Ancestry (includes multiple ancestries): 29.2% German, 4.0% Czechoslovakian, 3.5% Polish, 3.1% Irish (2000).
Economy: Employment by occupation: 10.4% management, 13.3% professional, 18.7% services, 33.2% sales, 0.0% farming, 11.1% construction, 13.4% production (2000).
Income: Per capita income: $15,335 (2000); Median household income: $33,846 (2000); Poverty rate: 179.1% (2000).
Education: Percent of population age 25 and over with: High school diploma (including GED) or higher: 64.8% (2000); Bachelor's degree or higher: 13.4% (2000).
Housing: Homeownership rate: 84.8% (2000); Median home value: $65,400 (2000); Median contract rent: $363 per month (2000); Median year structure built: 1975 (2000).
Transportation: Commute to work: 97.1% car, 0.0% public transportation, 0.0% walk, 2.9% work from home (2000); Travel time to work: 6.8% less than 15 minutes, 50.1% 15 to 30 minutes, 27.5% 30 to 45 minutes, 8.9% 45 to 60 minutes, 6.7% 60 minutes or more (2000)

Webb County

Located in southwestern Texas; bounded on the west and southwest by the Rio Grande and the Mexican border. Covers a land area of 3,356.83 square miles, a water area of 18.69 square miles, and is located in the Central Time Zone at 27.59° N. Lat., 99.39° W. Long. The county was founded in 1848. County seat is Laredo.

Webb County is part of the Laredo, TX Metropolitan Statistical Area. The entire metro area includes: Webb County, TX

Weather Station: Encinal   Elevation: 589 feet

	Jan	Feb	Mar	Apr	May	Jun	Jul	Aug	Sep	Oct	Nov	Dec
High	67	72	80	87	93	98	99	99	94	86	76	68
Low	42	46	52	59	67	72	73	74	69	61	51	43
Precip	0.9	0.7	1.3	1.2	2.9	2.4	2.0	2.1	2.6	2.1	1.1	0.8
Snow	tr	0.0	0.0	0.0	0.0	0.0	0.0	0.0	0.0	0.0	0.0	0.2

High and Low temperatures in degrees Fahrenheit; Precipitation and Snow in inches

Weather Station: Laredo 2   Elevation: 430 feet

	Jan	Feb	Mar	Apr	May	Jun	Jul	Aug	Sep	Oct	Nov	Dec
High	68	73	81	89	94	99	100	101	94	87	77	68
Low	45	50	56	63	71	75	76	76	72	64	54	46
Precip	0.8	0.9	1.1	1.3	2.5	2.2	2.1	2.0	2.8	2.2	1.2	0.9
Snow	tr	tr	0.0	0.0	0.0	0.0	0.0	0.0	0.0	tr	0.0	tr

High and Low temperatures in degrees Fahrenheit; Precipitation and Snow in inches

Population: 133,239 (1990); 193,117 (2000); 248,243 (2010); 274,610 (2015 projected); Race: 82.0% White, 0.4% Black, 0.4% Asian, 17.1% Other, 94.6% Hispanic of any race (2010); Density: 74.0 persons per square mile (2010); Average household size: 3.72 (2010); Median age: 26.5 (2010); Males per 100 females: 93.1 (2010).
Religion: Five largest groups: 68.1% Catholic Church, 1.4% Assemblies of God, 1.3% Southern Baptist Convention, 0.8% The Church of Jesus Christ of Latter-day Saints, 0.4% The United Methodist Church (2000).
Economy: Unemployment rate: 9.0% (June 2011); Total civilian labor force: 97,461 (June 2011); Leading industries: 19.7% health care and social assistance; 19.6% retail trade; 18.9% transportation & warehousing (2009); Farms: 663 totaling 1,855,894 acres (2007); Companies that employ 500 or more persons: 5 (2009); Companies that employ 100 to 499 persons: 85 (2009); Companies that employ less than 100 persons: 4,605

(2009); Black-owned businesses: n/a (2007); Hispanic-owned businesses: 14,717 (2007); Asian-owned businesses: 444 (2007); Women-owned businesses: 5,468 (2007); Retail sales per capita: $12,399 (2010). Single-family building permits issued: 636 (2010); Multi-family building permits issued: 27 (2010).
Income: Per capita income: $13,785 (2010); Median household income: $36,313 (2010); Average household income: $51,474 (2010); Percent of households with income of $100,000 or more: 11.2% (2010); Poverty rate: 30.9% (2009); Bankruptcy rate: 1.26% (2010).
Taxes: Total county taxes per capita: $249 (2007); County property taxes per capita: $184 (2007).
Education: Percent of population age 25 and over with: High school diploma (including GED) or higher: 63.5% (2010); Bachelor's degree or higher: 16.8% (2010); Master's degree or higher: 4.4% (2010).
Housing: Homeownership rate: 64.8% (2010); Median home value: $97,895 (2010); Median contract rent: $487 per month (2005-2009 5-year est.); Median year structure built: 1989 (2005-2009 5-year est.)
Health: Birth rate: 257.0 per 10,000 population (2009); Death rate: 49.7 per 10,000 population (2009); Age-adjusted cancer mortality rate: 119.6 deaths per 100,000 population (2007); Number of physicians: 9.3 per 10,000 population (2008); Hospital beds: 24.8 per 10,000 population (2007); Hospital admissions: 1,126.7 per 10,000 population (2007).
Environment: Air Quality Index: 78.1% good, 21.2% moderate, 0.7% unhealthy for sensitive individuals, 0.0% unhealthy (percent of days in 2008)
Elections: 2008 Presidential election results: 71.4% Obama, 28.0% McCain, 0.1% Nader
Additional Information Contacts
Webb County Government . . . . (956) 721-2500
    http://webbcounty.com
City of Laredo . . . . (956) 791-7300
    http://www.ci.laredo.tx.us
City of Rio Bravo . . . . (956) 725-2807
Laredo Chamber of Commerce . . . . (956) 722-9895
    http://www.laredochamber.com

Webb County Communities

BOTINES (CDP). Covers a land area of 8.591 square miles and a water area of 0 square miles. Located at 27.76° N. Lat; 99.43° W. Long. Elevation is 712 feet.
Population: 37 (1990); 132 (2000); 160 (2010); 174 (2015 projected); Race: 80.0% White, 1.3% Black, 0.6% Asian, 18.1% Other, 89.4% Hispanic of any race (2010); Density: 18.6 persons per square mile (2010); Average household size: 3.72 (2010); Median age: 22.8 (2010); Males per 100 females: 97.5 (2010); Marriage status: 21.1% never married, 66.7% now married, 0.0% widowed, 12.2% divorced (2005-2009 5-year est.); Foreign born: 0.0% (2005-2009 5-year est.); Ancestry (includes multiple ancestries): 25.4% French (2005-2009 5-year est.).
Economy: Employment by occupation: 28.9% management, 28.2% professional, 0.0% services, 25.4% sales, 0.0% farming, 17.6% construction, 0.0% production (2005-2009 5-year est.).
Income: Per capita income: $17,962 (2010); Median household income: $48,750 (2010); Average household income: $75,116 (2010); Percent of households with income of $100,000 or more: 16.3% (2010); Poverty rate: 0.0% (2005-2009 5-year est.).
Education: Percent of population age 25 and over with: High school diploma (including GED) or higher: 77.0% (2010); Bachelor's degree or higher: 24.3% (2010); Master's degree or higher: 5.4% (2010).
Housing: Homeownership rate: 88.4% (2010); Median home value: $93,333 (2010); Median contract rent: n/a per month (2005-2009 5-year est.); Median year structure built: 1993 (2005-2009 5-year est.).
Transportation: Commute to work: 75.4% car, 0.0% public transportation, 0.0% walk, 24.6% work from home (2005-2009 5-year est.); Travel time to work: 0.0% less than 15 minutes, 43.0% 15 to 30 minutes, 57.0% 30 to 45 minutes, 0.0% 45 to 60 minutes, 0.0% 60 minutes or more (2005-2009 5-year est.)

BRUNI (CDP). Covers a land area of 1.309 square miles and a water area of 0 square miles. Located at 27.42° N. Lat; 98.83° W. Long. Elevation is 778 feet.
Population: 412 (1990); 412 (2000); 456 (2010); 491 (2015 projected); Race: 77.6% White, 0.4% Black, 0.0% Asian, 21.9% Other, 92.8% Hispanic of any race (2010); Density: 348.4 persons per square mile (2010); Average household size: 3.21 (2010); Median age: 28.3 (2010);

Males per 100 females: 94.0 (2010); Marriage status: 29.4% never married, 67.8% now married, 1.5% widowed, 1.3% divorced (2005-2009 5-year est.); Foreign born: 2.2% (2005-2009 5-year est.); Ancestry (includes multiple ancestries): 1.3% Italian (2005-2009 5-year est.).
Economy: Employment by occupation: 0.0% management, 6.6% professional, 14.5% services, 63.0% sales, 0.0% farming, 5.7% construction, 10.1% production (2005-2009 5-year est.).
Income: Per capita income: $12,451 (2010); Median household income: $30,952 (2010); Average household income: $39,309 (2010); Percent of households with income of $100,000 or more: 6.4% (2010); Poverty rate: 8.0% (2005-2009 5-year est.).
Education: Percent of population age 25 and over with: High school diploma (including GED) or higher: 65.3% (2010); Bachelor's degree or higher: 13.1% (2010); Master's degree or higher: 4.1% (2010).
School District(s)
Webb CISD (PK-12)
    2009-10 Enrollment: 350 . . . . (361) 747-5415
Housing: Homeownership rate: 75.2% (2010); Median home value: $53,000 (2010); Median contract rent: n/a per month (2005-2009 5-year est.); Median year structure built: 1982 (2005-2009 5-year est.).
Transportation: Commute to work: 97.6% car, 0.0% public transportation, 0.0% walk, 2.4% work from home (2005-2009 5-year est.); Travel time to work: 46.8% less than 15 minutes, 18.2% 15 to 30 minutes, 0.0% 30 to 45 minutes, 0.0% 45 to 60 minutes, 35.0% 60 minutes or more (2005-2009 5-year est.)

EL CENIZO (city). Covers a land area of 0.512 square miles and a water area of 0.014 square miles. Located at 27.32° N. Lat; 99.49° W. Long. Elevation is 390 feet.
Population: 1,399 (1990); 3,545 (2000); 4,338 (2010); 4,812 (2015 projected); Race: 81.0% White, 0.3% Black, 0.0% Asian, 18.7% Other, 99.2% Hispanic of any race (2010); Density: 8,467.5 persons per square mile (2010); Average household size: 4.65 (2010); Median age: 19.7 (2010); Males per 100 females: 99.7 (2010); Marriage status: 34.6% never married, 57.0% now married, 4.0% widowed, 4.4% divorced (2005-2009 5-year est.); Foreign born: 37.0% (2005-2009 5-year est.); Ancestry (includes multiple ancestries): n/a (2005-2009 5-year est.).
Economy: Employment by occupation: 4.8% management, 5.8% professional, 31.8% services, 18.8% sales, 0.6% farming, 18.0% construction, 20.3% production (2005-2009 5-year est.).
Income: Per capita income: $4,868 (2010); Median household income: $18,410 (2010); Average household income: $22,720 (2010); Percent of households with income of $100,000 or more: 0.8% (2010); Poverty rate: 54.5% (2005-2009 5-year est.).
Taxes: Total city taxes per capita: $59 (2007); City property taxes per capita: $59 (2007).
Education: Percent of population age 25 and over with: High school diploma (including GED) or higher: 22.1% (2010); Bachelor's degree or higher: 1.3% (2010); Master's degree or higher: 0.4% (2010).
Housing: Homeownership rate: 78.6% (2010); Median home value: $39,742 (2010); Median contract rent: $301 per month (2005-2009 5-year est.); Median year structure built: 1994 (2005-2009 5-year est.).
Transportation: Commute to work: 86.4% car, 4.2% public transportation, 5.3% walk, 2.4% work from home (2005-2009 5-year est.); Travel time to work: 8.4% less than 15 minutes, 16.4% 15 to 30 minutes, 39.9% 30 to 45 minutes, 16.0% 45 to 60 minutes, 19.3% 60 minutes or more (2005-2009 5-year est.)

LA PRESA (CDP). Covers a land area of 0.479 square miles and a water area of 0.013 square miles. Located at 27.39° N. Lat; 99.44° W. Long. Elevation is 512 feet.
Population: 169 (1990); 508 (2000); 511 (2010); 528 (2015 projected); Race: 87.9% White, 0.4% Black, 0.4% Asian, 11.4% Other, 94.9% Hispanic of any race (2010); Density: 1,065.7 persons per square mile (2010); Average household size: 3.60 (2010); Median age: 27.9 (2010); Males per 100 females: 105.2 (2010); Marriage status: 0.0% never married, 100.0% now married, 0.0% widowed, 0.0% divorced (2005-2009 5-year est.); Foreign born: 41.6% (2005-2009 5-year est.); Ancestry (includes multiple ancestries): n/a (2005-2009 5-year est.).
Economy: Employment by occupation: 16.2% management, 0.0% professional, 64.7% services, 19.1% sales, 0.0% farming, 0.0% construction, 0.0% production (2005-2009 5-year est.).
Income: Per capita income: $14,058 (2010); Median household income: $35,600 (2010); Average household income: $51,761 (2010); Percent of

households with income of $100,000 or more: 12.7% (2010); Poverty rate: 77.7% (2005-2009 5-year est.).

Education: Percent of population age 25 and over with: High school diploma (including GED) or higher: 54.4% (2010); Bachelor's degree or higher: 7.3% (2010); Master's degree or higher: 2.6% (2010).

Housing: Homeownership rate: 81.0% (2010); Median home value: $40,769 (2010); Median contract rent: n/a per month (2005-2009 5-year est.); Median year structure built: 1992 (2005-2009 5-year est.).

Transportation: Commute to work: 50.0% car, 0.0% public transportation, 33.8% walk, 16.2% work from home (2005-2009 5-year est.); Travel time to work: 40.4% less than 15 minutes, 20.2% 15 to 30 minutes, 39.5% 30 to 45 minutes, 0.0% 45 to 60 minutes, 0.0% 60 minutes or more (2005-2009 5-year est.)

LAREDO (city). County seat. Covers a land area of 78.460 square miles and a water area of 1.090 square miles. Located at 27.52° N. Lat; 99.49° W. Long. Elevation is 413 feet.

History: Laredo was founded on the Rio Grande in 1755 by Tomas Sanchez, a Spanish ranchman, on land granted by Don Jose de Escandon, Count of Sierra Gorda and colonizer of the region. Besides being under the six flags that have flown over Texas, Laredo had a seventh flag. In 1837, finding that disagreement over the southern boundary of the Republic of Texas left Laredo in a no-man's land, the town proclaimed the Republic of the Rio Grande and elected Jesus Cardenas as president. Laredo was chartered as a Texas city in 1852. With the arrival of rail lines from Corpus Christi and from Mexico in the 1880's, Laredo became a busy port of entry, an agricultural and oil shipping center, and a tourist destination.

Population: 126,298 (1990); 176,576 (2000); 228,145 (2010); 252,462 (2015 projected); Race: 82.2% White, 0.4% Black, 0.4% Asian, 17.0% Other, 94.4% Hispanic of any race (2010); Density: 2,907.8 persons per square mile (2010); Average household size: 3.69 (2010); Median age: 26.9 (2010); Males per 100 females: 92.7 (2010); Marriage status: 31.0% never married, 54.5% now married, 5.9% widowed, 8.6% divorced (2005-2009 5-year est.); Foreign born: 27.9% (2005-2009 5-year est.); Ancestry (includes multiple ancestries): 1.2% German, 1.1% American, 0.9% Irish, 0.5% English, 0.3% French (2005-2009 5-year est.).

Economy: Unemployment rate: 8.6% (June 2011); Total civilian labor force: 92,448 (June 2011); Single-family building permits issued: 636 (2010); Multi-family building permits issued: 27 (2010); Employment by occupation: 10.4% management, 15.5% professional, 20.5% services, 30.7% sales, 0.3% farming, 9.7% construction, 12.9% production (2005-2009 5-year est.).

Income: Per capita income: $14,248 (2010); Median household income: $37,703 (2010); Average household income: $52,754 (2010); Percent of households with income of $100,000 or more: 11.7% (2010); Poverty rate: 29.3% (2005-2009 5-year est.).

Taxes: Total city taxes per capita: $469 (2007); City property taxes per capita: $229 (2007).

Education: Percent of population age 25 and over with: High school diploma (including GED) or higher: 65.1% (2010); Bachelor's degree or higher: 17.6% (2010); Master's degree or higher: 4.7% (2010).

School District(s)
Gateway (Student Alternative Program Inc) (09-12)
   2009-10 Enrollment: 534 . . . . (956) 727-4700
Harmony Science Academy (Laredo) (KG-09)
   2009-10 Enrollment: 572 . . . . (956) 712-1177
Laredo ISD (PK-12)
   2009-10 Enrollment: 24,707 . . . . (956) 795-3200
Responsive Education Solutions (KG-12)
   2009-10 Enrollment: 5,022 . . . . (972) 316-3663
United ISD (PK-12)
   2009-10 Enrollment: 40,885 . . . . (956) 473-6201

Four-year College(s)
Texas A & M International University (Public)
   Fall 2009 Enrollment: 6,419 . . . . (956) 326-2001
   2010-11 Tuition: In-state $5,105; Out-of-state $12,545

Two-year College(s)
Laredo Community College (Public)
   Fall 2009 Enrollment: 9,361 . . . . (956) 721-5394
   2010-11 Tuition: In-state $3,084; Out-of-state $4,140
Texas Careers-Laredo (Private, For-profit)
   Fall 2009 Enrollment: 380 . . . . (956) 717-5909

Vocational/Technical School(s)
Laredo Beauty College Inc (Private, For-profit)
   Fall 2009 Enrollment: 142 . . . . (956) 723-2059
   2010-11 Tuition: $8,700

Housing: Homeownership rate: 63.6% (2010); Median home value: $102,423 (2010); Median contract rent: $491 per month (2005-2009 5-year est.); Median year structure built: 1989 (2005-2009 5-year est.).

Hospitals: Doctors Hospital of Laredo (180 beds); Mercy Ministries of Laredo (325 beds); Providence Hospital; UHS Doctors Hospital of Laredo (117 beds)

Safety: Violent crime rate: 57.0 per 10,000 population; Property crime rate: 604.8 per 10,000 population (2009).

Newspapers: Laredo Morning Times (Local news; Circulation 23,284); Tiempo de Ambos Laredos (Local news; Circulation 8,500); Tiempo de Laredo (Local news; Circulation 28,300)

Transportation: Commute to work: 91.8% car, 2.0% public transportation, 1.9% walk, 2.8% work from home (2005-2009 5-year est.); Travel time to work: 32.4% less than 15 minutes, 46.0% 15 to 30 minutes, 15.8% 30 to 45 minutes, 2.7% 45 to 60 minutes, 3.1% 60 minutes or more (2005-2009 5-year est.)

Airports: Laredo International (primary service)

Additional Information Contacts
City of Laredo . . . . (956) 791-7300
   http://www.ci.laredo.tx.us
Laredo Chamber of Commerce . . . . (956) 722-9895
   http://www.laredochamber.com

LAREDO RANCHETTES (CDP). Covers a land area of 24.096 square miles and a water area of 0.109 square miles. Located at 27.48° N. Lat; 99.33° W. Long. Elevation is 581 feet.

Population: 531 (1990); 1,845 (2000); 2,604 (2010); 2,987 (2015 projected); Race: 79.5% White, 0.4% Black, 0.0% Asian, 20.0% Other, 97.7% Hispanic of any race (2010); Density: 108.1 persons per square mile (2010); Average household size: 4.08 (2010); Median age: 22.9 (2010); Males per 100 females: 95.6 (2010); Marriage status: 36.6% never married, 52.0% now married, 3.3% widowed, 8.1% divorced (2005-2009 5-year est.); Foreign born: 26.8% (2005-2009 5-year est.); Ancestry (includes multiple ancestries): n/a (2005-2009 5-year est.).

Economy: Employment by occupation: 2.2% management, 6.7% professional, 12.5% services, 35.9% sales, 0.0% farming, 7.6% construction, 35.0% production (2005-2009 5-year est.).

Income: Per capita income: $9,449 (2010); Median household income: $29,245 (2010); Average household income: $38,682 (2010); Percent of households with income of $100,000 or more: 4.4% (2010); Poverty rate: 36.1% (2005-2009 5-year est.).

Education: Percent of population age 25 and over with: High school diploma (including GED) or higher: 55.3% (2010); Bachelor's degree or higher: 4.8% (2010); Master's degree or higher: 0.5% (2010).

Housing: Homeownership rate: 84.7% (2010); Median home value: $74,722 (2010); Median contract rent: n/a per month (2005-2009 5-year est.); Median year structure built: 1992 (2005-2009 5-year est.).

Transportation: Commute to work: 94.2% car, 0.0% public transportation, 0.0% walk, 0.0% work from home (2005-2009 5-year est.); Travel time to work: 5.6% less than 15 minutes, 56.5% 15 to 30 minutes, 35.7% 30 to 45 minutes, 0.0% 45 to 60 minutes, 2.2% 60 minutes or more (2005-2009 5-year est.)

LARGA VISTA (CDP). Covers a land area of 0.774 square miles and a water area of 0 square miles. Located at 27.50° N. Lat; 99.43° W. Long. Elevation is 518 feet.

Population: 342 (1990); 742 (2000); 1,075 (2010); 1,240 (2015 projected); Race: 79.1% White, 0.4% Black, 0.0% Asian, 20.6% Other, 97.8% Hispanic of any race (2010); Density: 1,388.5 persons per square mile (2010); Average household size: 4.10 (2010); Median age: 22.7 (2010); Males per 100 females: 94.4 (2010); Marriage status: n/a never married, n/a now married, n/a widowed, n/a divorced (2005-2009 5-year est.); Foreign born: n/a (2005-2009 5-year est.); Ancestry (includes multiple ancestries): n/a (2005-2009 5-year est.).

Economy: Employment by occupation: n/a management, n/a professional, n/a services, n/a sales, n/a farming, n/a construction, n/a production (2005-2009 5-year est.).

Income: Per capita income: $9,181 (2010); Median household income: $28,913 (2010); Average household income: $37,929 (2010); Percent of households with income of $100,000 or more: 3.8% (2010); Poverty rate: n/a (2005-2009 5-year est.).

Education: Percent of population age 25 and over with: High school diploma (including GED) or higher: 55.2% (2010); Bachelor's degree or higher: 4.6% (2010); Master's degree or higher: 0.4% (2010).
Housing: Homeownership rate: 84.7% (2010); Median home value: $75,111 (2010); Median contract rent: n/a per month (2005-2009 5-year est.); Median year structure built: n/a (2005-2009 5-year est.).
Transportation: Commute to work: n/a car, n/a public transportation, n/a walk, n/a work from home (2005-2009 5-year est.); Travel time to work: n/a less than 15 minutes, n/a 15 to 30 minutes, n/a 30 to 45 minutes, n/a 45 to 60 minutes, n/a 60 minutes or more (2005-2009 5-year est.)

MIRANDO CITY (CDP). Covers a land area of 11.082 square miles and a water area of 0 square miles. Located at 27.44° N. Lat; 98.99° W. Long. Elevation is 758 feet.
Population: 210 (1990); 493 (2000); 487 (2010); 503 (2015 projected); Race: 87.5% White, 0.6% Black, 0.2% Asian, 11.7% Other, 95.1% Hispanic of any race (2010); Density: 43.9 persons per square mile (2010); Average household size: 3.61 (2010); Median age: 27.7 (2010); Males per 100 females: 98.8 (2010); Marriage status: 27.6% never married, 54.1% now married, 8.7% widowed, 9.6% divorced (2005-2009 5-year est.); Foreign born: 12.4% (2005-2009 5-year est.); Ancestry (includes multiple ancestries): 3.3% American, 1.1% French, 1.1% German, 1.1% Greek (2005-2009 5-year est.).
Economy: Employment by occupation: 2.1% management, 16.2% professional, 24.1% services, 9.9% sales, 0.0% farming, 22.0% construction, 25.7% production (2005-2009 5-year est.).
Income: Per capita income: $14,058 (2010); Median household income: $35,938 (2010); Average household income: $49,204 (2010); Percent of households with income of $100,000 or more: 12.6% (2010); Poverty rate: 22.6% (2005-2009 5-year est.).
Education: Percent of population age 25 and over with: High school diploma (including GED) or higher: 54.6% (2010); Bachelor's degree or higher: 8.1% (2010); Master's degree or higher: 2.7% (2010).
Housing: Homeownership rate: 80.7% (2010); Median home value: $39,615 (2010); Median contract rent: $155 per month (2005-2009 5-year est.); Median year structure built: 1966 (2005-2009 5-year est.).
Transportation: Commute to work: 73.2% car, 0.0% public transportation, 12.2% walk, 6.7% work from home (2005-2009 5-year est.); Travel time to work: 55.6% less than 15 minutes, 14.4% 15 to 30 minutes, 12.4% 30 to 45 minutes, 9.2% 45 to 60 minutes, 8.5% 60 minutes or more (2005-2009 5-year est.)

OILTON (CDP). Covers a land area of 0.835 square miles and a water area of 0 square miles. Located at 27.46° N. Lat; 98.97° W. Long. Elevation is 860 feet.
Population: 302 (1990); 310 (2000); 345 (2010); 371 (2015 projected); Race: 78.3% White, 0.6% Black, 0.0% Asian, 21.2% Other, 92.5% Hispanic of any race (2010); Density: 413.0 persons per square mile (2010); Average household size: 3.21 (2010); Median age: 28.7 (2010); Males per 100 females: 91.7 (2010); Marriage status: 43.4% never married, 46.7% now married, 3.3% widowed, 6.6% divorced (2005-2009 5-year est.); Foreign born: 11.8% (2005-2009 5-year est.); Ancestry (includes multiple ancestries): 4.2% Irish (2005-2009 5-year est.).
Economy: Employment by occupation: 0.0% management, 20.0% professional, 27.0% services, 21.0% sales, 6.0% farming, 16.0% construction, 10.0% production (2005-2009 5-year est.).
Income: Per capita income: $12,512 (2010); Median household income: $31,333 (2010); Average household income: $39,112 (2010); Percent of households with income of $100,000 or more: 5.6% (2010); Poverty rate: 19.8% (2005-2009 5-year est.).
Education: Percent of population age 25 and over with: High school diploma (including GED) or higher: 65.2% (2010); Bachelor's degree or higher: 11.8% (2010); Master's degree or higher: 3.2% (2010).

School District(s)
Webb CISD (PK-12)
    2009-10 Enrollment: 350 . . . . (361) 747-5415
Housing: Homeownership rate: 74.8% (2010); Median home value: $53,333 (2010); Median contract rent: $221 per month (2005-2009 5-year est.); Median year structure built: 1984 (2005-2009 5-year est.).
Transportation: Commute to work: 94.0% car, 0.0% public transportation, 6.0% walk, 0.0% work from home (2005-2009 5-year est.); Travel time to work: 42.0% less than 15 minutes, 14.0% 15 to 30 minutes, 38.0% 30 to 45 minutes, 0.0% 45 to 60 minutes, 6.0% 60 minutes or more (2005-2009 5-year est.)

RANCHITOS LAS LOMAS (CDP). Covers a land area of 21.841 square miles and a water area of 0.079 square miles. Located at 27.65° N. Lat; 99.18° W. Long. Elevation is 604 feet.
Population: 120 (1990); 334 (2000); 409 (2010); 453 (2015 projected); Race: 78.2% White, 0.0% Black, 0.0% Asian, 21.8% Other, 95.1% Hispanic of any race (2010); Density: 18.7 persons per square mile (2010); Average household size: 3.58 (2010); Median age: 27.1 (2010); Males per 100 females: 101.5 (2010); Marriage status: 35.6% never married, 32.8% now married, 0.0% widowed, 31.6% divorced (2005-2009 5-year est.); Foreign born: 38.4% (2005-2009 5-year est.); Ancestry (includes multiple ancestries): n/a (2005-2009 5-year est.).
Economy: Employment by occupation: 0.0% management, 0.0% professional, 42.9% services, 57.1% sales, 0.0% farming, 0.0% construction, 0.0% production (2005-2009 5-year est.).
Income: Per capita income: $11,364 (2010); Median household income: $26,364 (2010); Average household income: $35,692 (2010); Percent of households with income of $100,000 or more: 5.4% (2010); Poverty rate: 94.5% (2005-2009 5-year est.).
Education: Percent of population age 25 and over with: High school diploma (including GED) or higher: 52.5% (2010); Bachelor's degree or higher: 9.2% (2010); Master's degree or higher: 0.5% (2010).
Housing: Homeownership rate: 72.3% (2010); Median home value: $70,800 (2010); Median contract rent: n/a per month (2005-2009 5-year est.); Median year structure built: 1987 (2005-2009 5-year est.).
Transportation: Commute to work: 100.0% car, 0.0% public transportation, 0.0% walk, 0.0% work from home (2005-2009 5-year est.); Travel time to work: 0.0% less than 15 minutes, 0.0% 15 to 30 minutes, 42.9% 30 to 45 minutes, 57.1% 45 to 60 minutes, 0.0% 60 minutes or more (2005-2009 5-year est.)

RANCHOS PENITAS WEST (CDP). Covers a land area of 4.655 square miles and a water area of 0 square miles. Located at 27.67° N. Lat; 99.60° W. Long. Elevation is 495 feet.
Population: 123 (1990); 520 (2000); 604 (2010); 658 (2015 projected); Race: 80.3% White, 0.7% Black, 0.3% Asian, 18.7% Other, 89.1% Hispanic of any race (2010); Density: 129.8 persons per square mile (2010); Average household size: 3.71 (2010); Median age: 24.6 (2010); Males per 100 females: 98.7 (2010); Marriage status: 31.5% never married, 58.7% now married, 0.0% widowed, 9.8% divorced (2005-2009 5-year est.); Foreign born: 9.7% (2005-2009 5-year est.); Ancestry (includes multiple ancestries): n/a (2005-2009 5-year est.).
Economy: Employment by occupation: 0.0% management, 7.4% professional, 48.8% services, 11.5% sales, 0.0% farming, 9.2% construction, 23.0% production (2005-2009 5-year est.).
Income: Per capita income: $17,962 (2010); Median household income: $46,250 (2010); Average household income: $65,890 (2010); Percent of households with income of $100,000 or more: 13.5% (2010); Poverty rate: 7.1% (2005-2009 5-year est.).
Education: Percent of population age 25 and over with: High school diploma (including GED) or higher: 75.2% (2010); Bachelor's degree or higher: 22.1% (2010); Master's degree or higher: 5.0% (2010).
Housing: Homeownership rate: 88.3% (2010); Median home value: $87,826 (2010); Median contract rent: n/a per month (2005-2009 5-year est.); Median year structure built: 1994 (2005-2009 5-year est.).
Transportation: Commute to work: 100.0% car, 0.0% public transportation, 0.0% walk, 0.0% work from home (2005-2009 5-year est.); Travel time to work: 0.0% less than 15 minutes, 65.9% 15 to 30 minutes, 0.0% 30 to 45 minutes, 0.0% 45 to 60 minutes, 34.1% 60 minutes or more (2005-2009 5-year est.)

RIO BRAVO (city). Covers a land area of 0.681 square miles and a water area of 0.014 square miles. Located at 27.36° N. Lat; 99.47° W. Long. Elevation is 404 feet.
Population: 2,555 (1990); 5,553 (2000); 6,460 (2010); 7,057 (2015 projected); Race: 78.6% White, 0.4% Black, 0.0% Asian, 21.0% Other, 97.9% Hispanic of any race (2010); Density: 9,485.1 persons per square mile (2010); Average household size: 4.50 (2010); Median age: 20.9 (2010); Males per 100 females: 95.9 (2010); Marriage status: 34.3% never married, 54.5% now married, 6.2% divorced (2005-2009 5-year est.); Foreign born: 29.4% (2005-2009 5-year est.); Ancestry (includes multiple ancestries): 1.8% American, 1.1% Czechoslovakian, 1.1% Scottish, 0.4% Italian (2005-2009 5-year est.).

Economy: Employment by occupation: 5.8% management, 6.6% professional, 36.4% services, 11.8% sales, 0.0% farming, 15.0% construction, 24.4% production (2005-2009 5-year est.).
Income: Per capita income: $5,563 (2010); Median household income: $20,333 (2010); Average household income: $24,991 (2010); Percent of households with income of $100,000 or more: 1.0% (2010); Poverty rate: 41.8% (2005-2009 5-year est.).
Taxes: Total city taxes per capita: $40 (2007); City property taxes per capita: $0 (2007).
Education: Percent of population age 25 and over with: High school diploma (including GED) or higher: 28.5% (2010); Bachelor's degree or higher: 2.6% (2010); Master's degree or higher: 0.3% (2010).
Housing: Homeownership rate: 77.9% (2010); Median home value: $46,988 (2010); Median contract rent: $330 per month (2005-2009 5-year est.); Median year structure built: 1988 (2005-2009 5-year est.).
Transportation: Commute to work: 87.6% car, 3.3% public transportation, 3.9% walk, 4.2% work from home (2005-2009 5-year est.); Travel time to work: 24.2% less than 15 minutes, 9.5% 15 to 30 minutes, 23.1% 30 to 45 minutes, 23.3% 45 to 60 minutes, 19.9% 60 minutes or more (2005-2009 5-year est.)
Additional Information Contacts
City of Rio Bravo . . . . (956) 725-2807

Wharton County

Located in south Texas; drained by the Colorado and San Bernard Rivers. Covers a land area of 1,090.13 square miles, a water area of 4.29 square miles, and is located in the Central Time Zone at 29.25° N. Lat., 96.18° W. Long. The county was founded in 1846. County seat is Wharton.

Wharton County is part of the El Campo, TX Micropolitan Statistical Area. The entire metro area includes: Wharton County, TX

Weather Station: Danevang 1 W   Elevation: 69 feet

	Jan	Feb	Mar	Apr	May	Jun	Jul	Aug	Sep	Oct	Nov	Dec
High	64	67	73	80	85	90	93	94	90	83	74	65
Low	43	46	52	58	66	71	72	72	69	60	52	44
Precip	3.4	2.6	3.0	2.4	5.2	4.7	4.2	3.5	5.1	5.0	4.0	3.0
Snow	tr	tr	tr	0.0	0.0	0.0	0.0	0.0	0.0	0.0	0.0	0.5

High and Low temperatures in degrees Fahrenheit; Precipitation and Snow in inches

Population: 39,955 (1990); 41,188 (2000); 41,856 (2010); 42,110 (2015 projected); Race: 66.8% White, 14.2% Black, 0.5% Asian, 18.4% Other, 36.5% Hispanic of any race (2010); Density: 38.4 persons per square mile (2010); Average household size: 2.71 (2010); Median age: 35.9 (2010); Males per 100 females: 97.4 (2010).
Religion: Five largest groups: 46.3% Catholic Church, 15.7% Southern Baptist Convention, 5.5% The United Methodist Church, 2.7% Evangelical Lutheran Church in America, 1.5% Churches of Christ (2000).
Economy: Unemployment rate: 9.4% (June 2011); Total civilian labor force: 20,846 (June 2011); Leading industries: 18.0% retail trade; 17.1% health care and social assistance; 14.9% manufacturing (2009); Farms: 1,506 totaling 615,851 acres (2007); Companies that employ 500 or more persons: 0 (2009); Companies that employ 100 to 499 persons: 18 (2009); Companies that employ less than 100 persons: 928 (2009); Black-owned businesses: n/a (2007); Hispanic-owned businesses: n/a (2007); Asian-owned businesses: n/a (2007); Women-owned businesses: 1,073 (2007); Retail sales per capita: $13,362 (2010). Single-family building permits issued: 12 (2010); Multi-family building permits issued: 0 (2010).
Income: Per capita income: $19,950 (2010); Median household income: $41,241 (2010); Average household income: $54,510 (2010); Percent of households with income of $100,000 or more: 12.7% (2010); Poverty rate: 18.9% (2009); Bankruptcy rate: 0.79% (2010).
Taxes: Total county taxes per capita: $395 (2007); County property taxes per capita: $324 (2007).
Education: Percent of population age 25 and over with: High school diploma (including GED) or higher: 72.0% (2010); Bachelor's degree or higher: 15.1% (2010); Master's degree or higher: 4.5% (2010).
Housing: Homeownership rate: 68.6% (2010); Median home value: $80,363 (2010); Median contract rent: $399 per month (2005-2009 5-year est.); Median year structure built: 1971 (2005-2009 5-year est.)
Health: Birth rate: 164.1 per 10,000 population (2009); Death rate: 97.8 per 10,000 population (2009); Age-adjusted cancer mortality rate: 215.5 deaths per 100,000 population (2007); Number of physicians: 11.7 per 10,000 population (2008); Hospital beds: 30.9 per 10,000 population (2007); Hospital admissions: 859.0 per 10,000 population (2007).

Elections: 2008 Presidential election results: 34.2% Obama, 65.4% McCain, 0.0% Nader
Additional Information Contacts
Wharton County Government . . . . (979) 532-2381
    http://www.co.wharton.tx.us/ips/cms
City of El Campo . . . . (979) 541-5000
    http://cityofelcampo.org
City of Wharton . . . . (979) 532-2491
    http://www.cityofwharton.com
El Campo Chamber of Commerce . . . . (979) 543-2713
    http://www.elcampochamber.com
Wharton Chamber of Commerce . . . . (979) 532-1862
    http://whartontexas.com

Wharton County Communities

BOLING-IAGO (CDP). Covers a land area of 6.969 square miles and a water area of 0 square miles. Located at 29.26° N. Lat; 95.94° W. Long.
Population: 1,119 (1990); 1,271 (2000); 1,390 (2010); 1,449 (2015 projected); Race: 66.8% White, 7.2% Black, 0.0% Asian, 26.0% Other, 59.1% Hispanic of any race (2010); Density: 199.5 persons per square mile (2010); Average household size: 2.97 (2010); Median age: 34.1 (2010); Males per 100 females: 104.7 (2010); Marriage status: 15.2% never married, 61.8% now married, 10.2% widowed, 12.8% divorced (2005-2009 5-year est.); Foreign born: 3.9% (2005-2009 5-year est.); Ancestry (includes multiple ancestries): 13.6% French, 13.4% Irish, 6.8% German, 3.1% Czech, 2.5% English (2005-2009 5-year est.).
Economy: Employment by occupation: 11.0% management, 22.1% professional, 36.6% services, 3.5% sales, 2.1% farming, 5.4% construction, 19.3% production (2005-2009 5-year est.).
Income: Per capita income: $14,144 (2010); Median household income: $30,402 (2010); Average household income: $42,009 (2010); Percent of households with income of $100,000 or more: 6.4% (2010); Poverty rate: 34.6% (2005-2009 5-year est.).
Education: Percent of population age 25 and over with: High school diploma (including GED) or higher: 53.7% (2010); Bachelor's degree or higher: 4.7% (2010); Master's degree or higher: 1.9% (2010).
School District(s)
Boling ISD (PK-12)
    2009-10 Enrollment: 985 . . . . (979) 657-2770
Housing: Homeownership rate: 75.0% (2010); Median home value: $54,198 (2010); Median contract rent: $352 per month (2005-2009 5-year est.); Median year structure built: 1963 (2005-2009 5-year est.).
Transportation: Commute to work: 94.8% car, 0.0% public transportation, 0.0% walk, 0.0% work from home (2005-2009 5-year est.); Travel time to work: 39.4% less than 15 minutes, 26.2% 15 to 30 minutes, 14.5% 30 to 45 minutes, 19.9% 45 to 60 minutes, 0.0% 60 minutes or more (2005-2009 5-year est.)

DANEVANG (unincorporated postal area, zip code 77432). Covers a land area of 15.647 square miles and a water area of 0 square miles. Located at 29.06° N. Lat; 96.21° W. Long. Elevation is 69 feet.
History: Danevang was founded in 1894 by Danes, who established the Danevang Farmers Cooperative Society to support the cotton farmers.
Population: 517 (2000); Race: 59.1% White, 2.3% Black, 0.0% Asian, 38.6% Other, 79.1% Hispanic of any race (2000); Density: 33.0 persons per square mile (2000); Age: 28.6% under 18, 12.7% over 64 (2000); Marriage status: 23.8% never married, 64.4% now married, 4.7% widowed, 7.2% divorced (2000); Foreign born: 11.3% (2000); Ancestry (includes multiple ancestries): 4.2% Irish, 3.1% French, 2.5% German, 2.1% American (2000).
Economy: Employment by occupation: 3.3% management, 15.6% professional, 6.1% services, 9.0% sales, 2.4% farming, 16.5% construction, 47.2% production (2000).
Income: Per capita income: $13,433 (2000); Median household income: $38,250 (2000); Poverty rate: 179.1% (2000).
Education: Percent of population age 25 and over with: High school diploma (including GED) or higher: 42.7% (2000); Bachelor's degree or higher: 1.5% (2000).
Housing: Homeownership rate: 76.6% (2000); Median home value: $37,200 (2000); Median contract rent: $297 per month (2000); Median year structure built: 1970 (2000).
Transportation: Commute to work: 95.5% car, 0.0% public transportation, 0.0% walk, 0.0% work from home (2000); Travel time to work: 13.1% less

than 15 minutes, 34.3% 15 to 30 minutes, 26.3% 30 to 45 minutes, 11.6% 45 to 60 minutes, 14.6% 60 minutes or more (2000)

EAST BERNARD (CDP). Covers a land area of 1.380 square miles and a water area of 0 square miles. Located at 29.52° N. Lat; 96.06° W. Long. Elevation is 125 feet.

Population: 1,544 (1990); 1,729 (2000); 1,828 (2010); 1,871 (2015 projected); Race: 79.0% White, 2.2% Black, 0.4% Asian, 18.3% Other, 30.5% Hispanic of any race (2010); Density: 1,324.7 persons per square mile (2010); Average household size: 2.69 (2010); Median age: 36.9 (2010); Males per 100 females: 100.0 (2010); Marriage status: 18.4% never married, 66.1% now married, 5.3% widowed, 10.2% divorced (2005-2009 5-year est.); Foreign born: 6.6% (2005-2009 5-year est.); Ancestry (includes multiple ancestries): 30.3% Czech, 20.8% German, 7.2% Irish, 6.3% American, 4.0% English (2005-2009 5-year est.).

Economy: Employment by occupation: 16.5% management, 18.4% professional, 9.0% services, 28.6% sales, 1.7% farming, 17.2% construction, 8.6% production (2005-2009 5-year est.).

Income: Per capita income: $21,235 (2010); Median household income: $46,400 (2010); Average household income: $57,201 (2010); Percent of households with income of $100,000 or more: 12.4% (2010); Poverty rate: 8.3% (2005-2009 5-year est.).

Taxes: Total city taxes per capita: $410 (2007); City property taxes per capita: $192 (2007).

Education: Percent of population age 25 and over with: High school diploma (including GED) or higher: 82.4% (2010); Bachelor's degree or higher: 12.8% (2010); Master's degree or higher: 1.0% (2010).

School District(s)
East Bernard ISD (PK-12)
    2009-10 Enrollment: 956 . . . . (979) 335-7519

Housing: Homeownership rate: 72.0% (2010); Median home value: $89,398 (2010); Median contract rent: $593 per month (2005-2009 5-year est.); Median year structure built: 1976 (2005-2009 5-year est.).

Transportation: Commute to work: 93.7% car, 0.7% public transportation, 1.3% walk, 1.7% work from home (2005-2009 5-year est.); Travel time to work: 43.7% less than 15 minutes, 23.6% 15 to 30 minutes, 8.4% 30 to 45 minutes, 8.2% 45 to 60 minutes, 16.1% 60 minutes or more (2005-2009 5-year est.)

EL CAMPO (city). Covers a land area of 7.467 square miles and a water area of 0 square miles. Located at 29.19° N. Lat; 96.27° W. Long. Elevation is 105 feet.

History: El Campo began as a round-up camp for cowhands from four large ranches. The town developed as a milling, shipping, and trading center for the rice farmers and stockmen of the area.

Population: 10,649 (1990); 10,945 (2000); 10,908 (2010); 10,881 (2015 projected); Race: 68.2% White, 10.1% Black, 0.5% Asian, 21.2% Other, 43.4% Hispanic of any race (2010); Density: 1,460.8 persons per square mile (2010); Average household size: 2.73 (2010); Median age: 34.5 (2010); Males per 100 females: 94.2 (2010); Marriage status: 26.7% never married, 57.5% now married, 7.5% widowed, 8.4% divorced (2005-2009 5-year est.); Foreign born: 12.6% (2005-2009 5-year est.); Ancestry (includes multiple ancestries): 15.0% German, 7.7% Czech, 6.5% Irish, 3.8% Scotch-Irish, 3.3% Polish (2005-2009 5-year est.).

Economy: Single-family building permits issued: 10 (2010); Multi-family building permits issued: 0 (2010); Employment by occupation: 9.2% management, 13.5% professional, 17.2% services, 18.8% sales, 3.2% farming, 17.4% construction, 20.7% production (2005-2009 5-year est.).

Income: Per capita income: $19,741 (2010); Median household income: $41,311 (2010); Average household income: $53,977 (2010); Percent of households with income of $100,000 or more: 13.1% (2010); Poverty rate: 20.5% (2005-2009 5-year est.).

Taxes: Total city taxes per capita: $479 (2007); City property taxes per capita: $204 (2007).

Education: Percent of population age 25 and over with: High school diploma (including GED) or higher: 69.4% (2010); Bachelor's degree or higher: 16.1% (2010); Master's degree or higher: 4.7% (2010).

School District(s)
El Campo ISD (PK-12)
    2009-10 Enrollment: 3,491 . . . . (979) 543-6771

Housing: Homeownership rate: 64.9% (2010); Median home value: $79,474 (2010); Median contract rent: $391 per month (2005-2009 5-year est.); Median year structure built: 1967 (2005-2009 5-year est.).

Hospitals: El Campo Memorial Hospital (49 beds)

Safety: Violent crime rate: 46.6 per 10,000 population; Property crime rate: 296.2 per 10,000 population (2009).

Newspapers: El Campo Leader-News (Local news; Circulation 6,100)

Transportation: Commute to work: 95.2% car, 1.2% public transportation, 1.4% walk, 0.8% work from home (2005-2009 5-year est.); Travel time to work: 56.2% less than 15 minutes, 20.7% 15 to 30 minutes, 8.4% 30 to 45 minutes, 4.4% 45 to 60 minutes, 10.3% 60 minutes or more (2005-2009 5-year est.)

Additional Information Contacts
City of El Campo . . . . (979) 541-5000
    http://cityofelcampo.org
El Campo Chamber of Commerce. . . . . (979) 543-2713
    http://www.elcampochamber.com

GLEN FLORA (unincorporated postal area, zip code 77443). Covers a land area of 5.577 square miles and a water area of 0 square miles. Located at 29.33° N. Lat; 96.17° W. Long. Elevation is 118 feet.

Population: 181 (2000); Race: 52.5% White, 11.5% Black, 0.0% Asian, 36.0% Other, 54.1% Hispanic of any race (2000); Density: 32.5 persons per square mile (2000); Age: 27.9% under 18, 17.2% over 64 (2000); Marriage status: 37.2% never married, 34.0% now married, 22.3% widowed, 6.4% divorced (2000); Foreign born: 13.1% (2000); Ancestry (includes multiple ancestries): 13.1% Irish, 10.7% Dutch, 9.0% German, 4.9% English (2000).

Economy: Employment by occupation: 16.7% management, 0.0% professional, 19.4% services, 47.2% sales, 0.0% farming, 0.0% construction, 16.7% production (2000).

Income: Per capita income: $17,753 (2000); Median household income: $23,750 (2000); Poverty rate: 179.1% (2000).

Education: Percent of population age 25 and over with: High school diploma (including GED) or higher: 69.7% (2000); Bachelor's degree or higher: 5.3% (2000).

Housing: Homeownership rate: 86.4% (2000); Median home value: $53,300 (2000); Median contract rent: $475 per month (2000); Median year structure built: 1966 (2000).

Transportation: Commute to work: 63.9% car, 0.0% public transportation, 0.0% walk, 36.1% work from home (2000); Travel time to work: 47.8% less than 15 minutes, 0.0% 15 to 30 minutes, 26.1% 30 to 45 minutes, 0.0% 45 to 60 minutes, 26.1% 60 minutes or more (2000)

HUNGERFORD (CDP). Covers a land area of 1.832 square miles and a water area of 0 square miles. Located at 29.39° N. Lat; 96.07° W. Long. Elevation is 105 feet.

Population: 633 (1990); 645 (2000); 650 (2010); 652 (2015 projected); Race: 61.5% White, 28.2% Black, 0.0% Asian, 10.3% Other, 17.2% Hispanic of any race (2010); Density: 354.8 persons per square mile (2010); Average household size: 2.67 (2010); Median age: 34.5 (2010); Males per 100 females: 95.8 (2010); Marriage status: 24.3% never married, 75.7% now married, 0.0% widowed, 0.0% divorced (2005-2009 5-year est.); Foreign born: 0.0% (2005-2009 5-year est.); Ancestry (includes multiple ancestries): 27.4% German, 22.8% Czech, 2.4% Lebanese, 1.5% English, 1.4% Swedish (2005-2009 5-year est.).

Economy: Employment by occupation: 0.0% management, 24.6% professional, 29.6% services, 2.9% sales, 0.0% farming, 14.7% construction, 28.2% production (2005-2009 5-year est.).

Income: Per capita income: $24,353 (2010); Median household income: $52,604 (2010); Average household income: $71,776 (2010); Percent of households with income of $100,000 or more: 15.9% (2010); Poverty rate: 5.0% (2005-2009 5-year est.).

Education: Percent of population age 25 and over with: High school diploma (including GED) or higher: 75.4% (2010); Bachelor's degree or higher: 8.6% (2010); Master's degree or higher: 0.8% (2010).

Housing: Homeownership rate: 80.8% (2010); Median home value: $55,938 (2010); Median contract rent: n/a per month (2005-2009 5-year est.); Median year structure built: 1964 (2005-2009 5-year est.).

Transportation: Commute to work: 96.7% car, 0.0% public transportation, 0.0% walk, 3.3% work from home (2005-2009 5-year est.); Travel time to work: 23.6% less than 15 minutes, 30.6% 15 to 30 minutes, 0.0% 30 to 45 minutes, 1.5% 45 to 60 minutes, 44.3% 60 minutes or more (2005-2009 5-year est.)

LISSIE (unincorporated postal area, zip code 77454). Covers a land area of 14.166 square miles and a water area of 0.027 square miles. Located at 29.29° N. Lat; 96.24° W. Long. Elevation is 154 feet.

Population: 190 (2000); Race: 100.0% White, 0.0% Black, 0.0% Asian, 0.0% Other, 25.4% Hispanic of any race (2000); Density: 13.4 persons per square mile (2000); Age: 38.7% under 18, 9.2% over 64 (2000); Marriage status: 25.2% never married, 61.8% now married, 13.0% widowed, 0.0% divorced (2000); Foreign born: 0.0% (2000); Ancestry (includes multiple ancestries): 17.3% American, 13.3% German, 5.8% Czech, 4.6% Slavic (2000).

Economy: Employment by occupation: 24.1% management, 13.9% professional, 0.0% services, 32.9% sales, 0.0% farming, 20.3% construction, 8.9% production (2000).

Income: Per capita income: $15,564 (2000); Median household income: $56,167 (2000); Poverty rate: 179.1% (2000).

Education: Percent of population age 25 and over with: High school diploma (including GED) or higher: 70.6% (2000); Bachelor's degree or higher: 14.1% (2000).

Housing: Homeownership rate: 100.0% (2000); Median home value: $48,800 (2000); Median contract rent: n/a per month (2000); Median year structure built: 1955 (2000).

Transportation: Commute to work: 100.0% car, 0.0% public transportation, 0.0% walk, 0.0% work from home (2000); Travel time to work: 26.6% less than 15 minutes, 21.5% 15 to 30 minutes, 31.6% 30 to 45 minutes, 11.4% 45 to 60 minutes, 8.9% 60 minutes or more (2000)

LOUISE (CDP).
Covers a land area of 6.641 square miles and a water area of 0 square miles. Located at 29.11° N. Lat; 96.41° W. Long. Elevation is 85 feet.

Population: 878 (1990); 977 (2000); 980 (2010); 976 (2015 projected); Race: 81.8% White, 4.0% Black, 0.0% Asian, 14.2% Other, 48.7% Hispanic of any race (2010); Density: 147.6 persons per square mile (2010); Average household size: 2.82 (2010); Median age: 35.0 (2010); Males per 100 females: 100.8 (2010); Marriage status: 27.6% never married, 55.7% now married, 9.1% widowed, 7.5% divorced (2005-2009 5-year est.); Foreign born: 10.7% (2005-2009 5-year est.); Ancestry (includes multiple ancestries): 22.6% Czech, 11.5% German, 5.5% English, 4.7% Irish, 4.5% Swedish (2005-2009 5-year est.).

Economy: Employment by occupation: 9.9% management, 2.9% professional, 22.7% services, 27.7% sales, 1.7% farming, 15.5% construction, 19.5% production (2005-2009 5-year est.).

Income: Per capita income: $21,137 (2010); Median household income: $44,853 (2010); Average household income: $60,994 (2010); Percent of households with income of $100,000 or more: 15.3% (2010); Poverty rate: 16.1% (2005-2009 5-year est.).

Education: Percent of population age 25 and over with: High school diploma (including GED) or higher: 68.3% (2010); Bachelor's degree or higher: 9.1% (2010); Master's degree or higher: 4.2% (2010).

School District(s)
Louise ISD (PK-12)
   2009-10 Enrollment: 508 . . . . (979) 648-2982

Housing: Homeownership rate: 76.1% (2010); Median home value: $77,241 (2010); Median contract rent: $277 per month (2005-2009 5-year est.); Median year structure built: 1969 (2005-2009 5-year est.).

Transportation: Commute to work: 96.6% car, 0.0% public transportation, 0.6% walk, 0.6% work from home (2005-2009 5-year est.); Travel time to work: 48.4% less than 15 minutes, 28.1% 15 to 30 minutes, 14.7% 30 to 45 minutes, 0.9% 45 to 60 minutes, 7.9% 60 minutes or more (2005-2009 5-year est.)

PIERCE (unincorporated postal area, zip code 77467).
Covers a land area of 54.740 square miles and a water area of 0.004 square miles. Located at 29.29° N. Lat; 96.24° W. Long. Elevation is 98 feet.

Population: 117 (2000); Race: 63.3% White, 0.0% Black, 0.0% Asian, 36.7% Other, 58.3% Hispanic of any race (2000); Density: 2.1 persons per square mile (2000); Age: 27.3% under 18, 36.0% over 64 (2000); Marriage status: 9.1% never married, 60.9% now married, 22.7% widowed, 7.3% divorced (2000); Foreign born: 5.8% (2000); Ancestry (includes multiple ancestries): 10.8% Irish, 10.8% Danish, 7.9% German, 6.5% Czech (2000).

Economy: Employment by occupation: 0.0% management, 0.0% professional, 20.0% services, 27.5% sales, 0.0% farming, 17.5% construction, 35.0% production (2000).

Income: Per capita income: $19,399 (2000); Median household income: $36,250 (2000); Poverty rate: 179.1% (2000).

Education: Percent of population age 25 and over with: High school diploma (including GED) or higher: 71.4% (2000); Bachelor's degree or higher: 5.1% (2000).

Housing: Homeownership rate: 45.2% (2000); Median home value: <$10,000 (2000); Median contract rent: $267 per month (2000); Median year structure built: before 1940 (2000).

Transportation: Commute to work: 100.0% car, 0.0% public transportation, 0.0% walk, 0.0% work from home (2000); Travel time to work: 51.9% less than 15 minutes, 48.1% 15 to 30 minutes, 0.0% 30 to 45 minutes, 0.0% 45 to 60 minutes, 0.0% 60 minutes or more (2000)

WHARTON (city).
County seat. Covers a land area of 7.226 square miles and a water area of 0.009 square miles. Located at 29.31° N. Lat; 96.09° W. Long. Elevation is 102 feet.

History: Wharton was named for William and John Wharton, pioneer patriots. John was adjutant general at the Battle of San Jacinto.

Population: 9,536 (1990); 9,237 (2000); 9,248 (2010); 9,343 (2015 projected); Race: 52.9% White, 24.2% Black, 0.9% Asian, 21.9% Other, 37.7% Hispanic of any race (2010); Density: 1,279.9 persons per square mile (2010); Average household size: 2.48 (2010); Median age: 35.7 (2010); Males per 100 females: 92.2 (2010); Marriage status: 36.3% never married, 41.5% now married, 8.2% widowed, 14.0% divorced (2005-2009 5-year est.); Foreign born: 8.1% (2005-2009 5-year est.); Ancestry (includes multiple ancestries): 9.5% Irish, 8.9% German, 7.4% Czech, 5.1% English, 1.5% Polish (2005-2009 5-year est.).

Economy: Single-family building permits issued: 2 (2010); Multi-family building permits issued: 0 (2010); Employment by occupation: 5.7% management, 22.2% professional, 18.9% services, 23.3% sales, 2.0% farming, 14.1% construction, 13.8% production (2005-2009 5-year est.).

Income: Per capita income: $18,669 (2010); Median household income: $33,595 (2010); Average household income: $47,213 (2010); Percent of households with income of $100,000 or more: 9.2% (2010); Poverty rate: 25.9% (2005-2009 5-year est.).

Taxes: Total city taxes per capita: $527 (2007); City property taxes per capita: $202 (2007).

Education: Percent of population age 25 and over with: High school diploma (including GED) or higher: 72.4% (2010); Bachelor's degree or higher: 18.0% (2010); Master's degree or higher: 6.5% (2010).

School District(s)
Wharton ISD (PK-12)
   2009-10 Enrollment: 2,221 . . . . (979) 532-6201

Two-year College(s)
Wharton County Junior College (Public)
   Fall 2009 Enrollment: 6,622. . . . . (979) 532-4560
   2010-11 Tuition: In-state $2,880; Out-of-state $3,648

Housing: Homeownership rate: 57.2% (2010); Median home value: $70,000 (2010); Median contract rent: $402 per month (2005-2009 5-year est.); Median year structure built: 1972 (2005-2009 5-year est.).

Hospitals: Gulf Coast Medical Center (161 beds)

Safety: Violent crime rate: 74.4 per 10,000 population; Property crime rate: 519.9 per 10,000 population (2009).

Newspapers: The Wharton Journal-Spectator (Local news; Circulation 4,595)

Transportation: Commute to work: 97.6% car, 0.0% public transportation, 0.7% walk, 0.8% work from home (2005-2009 5-year est.); Travel time to work: 44.6% less than 15 minutes, 20.2% 15 to 30 minutes, 13.6% 30 to 45 minutes, 9.1% 45 to 60 minutes, 12.5% 60 minutes or more (2005-2009 5-year est.)

Airports: Wharton Regional (general aviation)

Additional Information Contacts
City of Wharton . . . . (979) 532-2491
   http://www.cityofwharton.com
Wharton Chamber of Commerce . . . . (979) 532-1862
   http://whartontexas.com

Wheeler County

Located in north Texas, in the Panhandle; bounded on the east by Oklahoma; drained by the North Fork of the Red River. Covers a land area of 914.26 square miles, a water area of 1.08 square miles, and is located in the Central Time Zone at 35.36° N. Lat., 100.28° W. Long. The county was founded in 1876. County seat is Wheeler.

Weather Station: Shamrock 2   **Elevation: 2,359 feet**

	Jan	Feb	Mar	Apr	May	Jun	Jul	Aug	Sep	Oct	Nov	Dec
High	50	54	62	72	80	88	94	93	84	73	61	50
Low	24	28	35	44	54	63	68	67	59	46	35	25
Precip	0.7	0.8	1.9	2.0	3.5	4.0	2.1	2.5	2.5	2.1	1.3	1.0
Snow	2.4	1.5	1.0	0.0	0.0	0.0	0.0	0.0	0.0	0.0	0.7	2.4

High and Low temperatures in degrees Fahrenheit; Precipitation and Snow in inches

Population: 5,879 (1990); 5,284 (2000); 4,887 (2010); 4,686 (2015 projected); Race: 80.9% White, 4.0% Black, 0.7% Asian, 14.4% Other, 21.1% Hispanic of any race (2010); Density: 5.3 persons per square mile (2010); Average household size: 2.36 (2010); Median age: 40.9 (2010); Males per 100 females: 96.0 (2010).
Religion: Five largest groups: 40.0% Southern Baptist Convention, 19.0% The United Methodist Church, 8.8% Churches of Christ, 2.3% The American Baptist Association, 1.6% Catholic Church (2000).
Economy: Unemployment rate: 4.5% (June 2011); Total civilian labor force: 3,255 (June 2011); Leading industries: 24.5% health care and social assistance; 16.4% accommodation & food services; 15.4% retail trade (2009); Farms: 507 totaling 583,522 acres (2007); Companies that employ 500 or more persons: 0 (2009); Companies that employ 100 to 499 persons: 1 (2009); Companies that employ less than 100 persons: 183 (2009); Black-owned businesses: n/a (2007); Hispanic-owned businesses: n/a (2007); Asian-owned businesses: n/a (2007); Women-owned businesses: n/a (2007); Retail sales per capita: $9,865 (2010). Single-family building permits issued: 0 (2010); Multi-family building permits issued: 0 (2010).
Income: Per capita income: $22,914 (2010); Median household income: $42,520 (2010); Average household income: $54,357 (2010); Percent of households with income of $100,000 or more: 11.4% (2010); Poverty rate: 12.6% (2009); Bankruptcy rate: 0.55% (2010).
Taxes: Total county taxes per capita: $765 (2007); County property taxes per capita: $664 (2007).
Education: Percent of population age 25 and over with: High school diploma (including GED) or higher: 77.3% (2010); Bachelor's degree or higher: 14.5% (2010); Master's degree or higher: 3.3% (2010).
Housing: Homeownership rate: 76.3% (2010); Median home value: $49,593 (2010); Median contract rent: $369 per month (2005-2009 5-year est.); Median year structure built: 1961 (2005-2009 5-year est.)
Health: Birth rate: 153.4 per 10,000 population (2009); Death rate: 122.7 per 10,000 population (2009); Age-adjusted cancer mortality rate: 258.1 (Unreliable) deaths per 100,000 population (2007); Number of physicians: 8.4 per 10,000 population (2008); Hospital beds: 60.9 per 10,000 population (2007); Hospital admissions: 1,367.4 per 10,000 population (2007).
Elections: 2008 Presidential election results: 14.0% Obama, 85.4% McCain, 0.0% Nader
Additional Information Contacts
Wheeler County Government . . . . (806) 826-5544
  http://www.co.wheeler.tx.us/ips/cms
Shamrock Economic Development Corporation . . . . (806) 256-2501
  http://shamrockedc.org
Wheeler Chamber of Commerce . . . . (806) 826-3408
  http://wheelertexas.org/chamberofcommerce.htm

Wheeler County Communities

BRISCOE (unincorporated postal area, zip code 79011). Covers a land area of 145.458 square miles and a water area of 0.653 square miles. Located at 35.66° N. Lat; 100.22° W. Long. Elevation is 2,654 feet.
Population: 300 (2000); Race: 99.0% White, 0.0% Black, 0.0% Asian, 1.0% Other, 1.0% Hispanic of any race (2000); Density: 2.1 persons per square mile (2000); Age: 24.9% under 18, 13.7% over 64 (2000); Marriage status: 18.3% never married, 68.7% now married, 8.3% widowed, 4.8% divorced (2000); Foreign born: 0.0% (2000); Ancestry (includes multiple ancestries): 16.6% American, 12.5% German, 6.4% Scotch-Irish, 5.8% Swiss (2000).
Economy: Employment by occupation: 25.0% management, 20.6% professional, 13.1% services, 16.9% sales, 8.1% farming, 7.5% construction, 8.8% production (2000).
Income: Per capita income: $14,686 (2000); Median household income: $33,750 (2000); Poverty rate: 179.1% (2000).
Education: Percent of population age 25 and over with: High school diploma (including GED) or higher: 88.3% (2000); Bachelor's degree or higher: 22.8% (2000).

School District(s)
Fort Elliott CISD (PK-12)
  2009-10 Enrollment: 147 . . . . (806) 375-2454
Housing: Homeownership rate: 63.5% (2000); Median home value: $50,000 (2000); Median contract rent: n/a per month (2000); Median year structure built: 1967 (2000).
Transportation: Commute to work: 83.6% car, 0.0% public transportation, 8.2% walk, 6.3% work from home (2000); Travel time to work: 38.3% less than 15 minutes, 34.2% 15 to 30 minutes, 9.4% 30 to 45 minutes, 8.1% 45 to 60 minutes, 10.1% 60 minutes or more (2000)

MOBEETIE (city). Aka New Mobeetie. Covers a land area of 0.610 square miles and a water area of 0 square miles. Located at 35.53° N. Lat; 100.43° W. Long. Elevation is 2,641 feet.
History: Nearby is Old Mobeetie, site of old Fort Elliot. Historic jail is now a museum.
Population: 154 (1990); 107 (2000); 107 (2010); 104 (2015 projected); Race: 91.6% White, 0.0% Black, 0.9% Asian, 7.5% Other, 15.9% Hispanic of any race (2010); Density: 175.3 persons per square mile (2010); Average household size: 2.33 (2010); Median age: 48.8 (2010); Males per 100 females: 109.8 (2010); Marriage status: 25.2% never married, 68.5% now married, 2.1% widowed, 4.2% divorced (2005-2009 5-year est.); Foreign born: 0.5% (2005-2009 5-year est.); Ancestry (includes multiple ancestries): 17.4% German, 15.8% Irish, 10.3% English, 4.9% Dutch, 4.3% Norwegian (2005-2009 5-year est.).
Economy: Employment by occupation: 29.5% management, 0.0% professional, 19.3% services, 10.2% sales, 6.8% farming, 20.5% construction, 13.6% production (2005-2009 5-year est.).
Income: Per capita income: $26,158 (2010); Median household income: $47,000 (2010); Average household income: $59,457 (2010); Percent of households with income of $100,000 or more: 10.9% (2010); Poverty rate: 0.0% (2005-2009 5-year est.).
Taxes: Total city taxes per capita: $129 (2007); City property taxes per capita: $119 (2007).
Education: Percent of population age 25 and over with: High school diploma (including GED) or higher: 84.6% (2010); Bachelor's degree or higher: 11.5% (2010); Master's degree or higher: 0.0% (2010).
Housing: Homeownership rate: 78.3% (2010); Median home value: $80,000 (2010); Median contract rent: $940 per month (2005-2009 5-year est.); Median year structure built: 1958 (2005-2009 5-year est.).
Transportation: Commute to work: 100.0% car, 0.0% public transportation, 0.0% walk, 0.0% work from home (2005-2009 5-year est.); Travel time to work: 23.9% less than 15 minutes, 53.4% 15 to 30 minutes, 20.5% 30 to 45 minutes, 2.3% 45 to 60 minutes, 0.0% 60 minutes or more (2005-2009 5-year est.)

SHAMROCK (city). Covers a land area of 2.071 square miles and a water area of 0 square miles. Located at 35.21° N. Lat; 100.24° W. Long. Elevation is 2,343 feet.
History: Shamrock developed around the carbon black plants and gasoline extraction plants, situated in the area of the Panhandle's gas field.
Population: 2,286 (1990); 2,029 (2000); 1,851 (2010); 1,761 (2015 projected); Race: 77.8% White, 7.5% Black, 1.4% Asian, 13.3% Other, 19.9% Hispanic of any race (2010); Density: 893.8 persons per square mile (2010); Average household size: 2.29 (2010); Median age: 40.8 (2010); Males per 100 females: 94.4 (2010); Marriage status: 17.8% never married, 56.9% now married, 13.4% widowed, 11.9% divorced (2005-2009 5-year est.); Foreign born: 2.1% (2005-2009 5-year est.); Ancestry (includes multiple ancestries): 19.2% German, 18.2% American, 12.8% English, 12.6% Irish, 1.8% Scotch-Irish (2005-2009 5-year est.).
Economy: Single-family building permits issued: 0 (2010); Multi-family building permits issued: 0 (2010); Employment by occupation: 10.7% management, 5.5% professional, 27.0% services, 22.6% sales, 0.6% farming, 18.2% construction, 15.3% production (2005-2009 5-year est.).
Income: Per capita income: $21,126 (2010); Median household income: $39,286 (2010); Average household income: $48,819 (2010); Percent of households with income of $100,000 or more: 10.7% (2010); Poverty rate: 16.5% (2005-2009 5-year est.).
Taxes: Total city taxes per capita: $423 (2007); City property taxes per capita: $164 (2007).
Education: Percent of population age 25 and over with: High school diploma (including GED) or higher: 74.3% (2010); Bachelor's degree or higher: 13.4% (2010); Master's degree or higher: 2.7% (2010).

School District(s)

Shamrock ISD (PK-12)
2009-10 Enrollment: 322 . . . . (806) 256-3492
Housing: Homeownership rate: 74.6% (2010); Median home value: $43,191 (2010); Median contract rent: $338 per month (2005-2009 5-year est.); Median year structure built: 1957 (2005-2009 5-year est.).
Hospitals: Shamrock General Hospital (25 beds)
Safety: Violent crime rate: 28.0 per 10,000 population; Property crime rate: 61.6 per 10,000 population (2009).
Transportation: Commute to work: 88.6% car, 0.0% public transportation, 5.7% walk, 2.1% work from home (2005-2009 5-year est.); Travel time to work: 71.3% less than 15 minutes, 9.9% 15 to 30 minutes, 7.5% 30 to 45 minutes, 3.9% 45 to 60 minutes, 7.4% 60 minutes or more (2005-2009 5-year est.)

Additional Information Contacts
Shamrock Economic Development Corporation . . . . (806) 256-2501
http://shamrockedc.org

WHEELER (city). County seat. Covers a land area of 1.530 square miles and a water area of 0 square miles. Located at 35.44° N. Lat; 100.27° W. Long. Elevation is 2,507 feet.
Population: 1,393 (1990); 1,378 (2000); 1,235 (2010); 1,172 (2015 projected); Race: 71.3% White, 3.7% Black, 0.1% Asian, 24.9% Other, 35.9% Hispanic of any race (2010); Density: 807.0 persons per square mile (2010); Average household size: 2.44 (2010); Median age: 38.1 (2010); Males per 100 females: 95.1 (2010); Marriage status: 17.9% never married, 60.7% now married, 12.3% widowed, 9.1% divorced (2005-2009 5-year est.); Foreign born: 16.9% (2005-2009 5-year est.); Ancestry (includes multiple ancestries): 13.8% German, 10.7% English, 8.3% Irish, 3.3% Scottish, 3.0% American (2005-2009 5-year est.).
Economy: Single-family building permits issued: 0 (2010); Multi-family building permits issued: 0 (2010); Employment by occupation: 7.0% management, 12.4% professional, 21.3% services, 10.9% sales, 2.4% farming, 29.9% construction, 16.2% production (2005-2009 5-year est.).
Income: Per capita income: $23,426 (2010); Median household income: $42,577 (2010); Average household income: $57,278 (2010); Percent of households with income of $100,000 or more: 12.6% (2010); Poverty rate: 17.8% (2005-2009 5-year est.).
Taxes: Total city taxes per capita: $274 (2007); City property taxes per capita: $137 (2007).
Education: Percent of population age 25 and over with: High school diploma (including GED) or higher: 71.4% (2010); Bachelor's degree or higher: 11.4% (2010); Master's degree or higher: 2.7% (2010).

School District(s)

Kelton ISD (PK-10)
2009-10 Enrollment: 156 . . . . (806) 826-5795
Wheeler ISD (PK-12)
2009-10 Enrollment: 397 . . . . (806) 826-5241
Housing: Homeownership rate: 80.4% (2010); Median home value: $48,875 (2010); Median contract rent: $385 per month (2005-2009 5-year est.); Median year structure built: 1971 (2005-2009 5-year est.).
Hospitals: Parkview Hospital
Newspapers: Wheeler Times (Local news; Circulation 1,350)
Transportation: Commute to work: 89.7% car, 2.1% public transportation, 0.9% walk, 5.3% work from home (2005-2009 5-year est.); Travel time to work: 44.0% less than 15 minutes, 21.6% 15 to 30 minutes, 17.1% 30 to 45 minutes, 6.4% 45 to 60 minutes, 10.9% 60 minutes or more (2005-2009 5-year est.)

Additional Information Contacts
Wheeler Chamber of Commerce . . . . (806) 826-3408
http://wheelertexas.org/chamberofcommerce.htm

Wichita County

Located in north Texas; bounded on the north by the Red River and the Oklahoma border; drained by the Wichita River; includes Lake Wichita. Covers a land area of 627.66 square miles, a water area of 5.35 square miles, and is located in the Central Time Zone at 33.94° N. Lat., 98.62° W. Long. The county was founded in 1858. County seat is Wichita Falls.

Wichita County is part of the Wichita Falls, TX Metropolitan Statistical Area. The entire metro area includes: Archer County, TX; Clay County, TX; Wichita County, TX

Weather Station: Wichita Falls Municipal Arpt   Elevation: 1,029 feet

	Jan	Feb	Mar	Apr	May	Jun	Jul	Aug	Sep	Oct	Nov	Dec
High	54	59	67	76	84	92	97	97	88	77	65	55
Low	31	34	42	50	60	68	73	72	64	53	41	32
Precip	1.1	1.7	2.2	2.5	3.9	4.0	1.5	2.5	2.9	3.1	1.7	1.7
Snow	1.7	0.8	0.5	tr	tr	tr	tr	0.0	0.0	0.1	0.2	1.0

High and Low temperatures in degrees Fahrenheit; Precipitation and Snow in inches

Population: 122,378 (1990); 131,664 (2000); 128,602 (2010); 126,881 (2015 projected); Race: 75.7% White, 10.3% Black, 2.0% Asian, 12.0% Other, 15.4% Hispanic of any race (2010); Density: 204.9 persons per square mile (2010); Average household size: 2.44 (2010); Median age: 33.7 (2010); Males per 100 females: 103.4 (2010).
Religion: Five largest groups: 32.9% Southern Baptist Convention, 9.6% Catholic Church, 5.5% The United Methodist Church, 3.2% Churches of Christ, 1.9% Assemblies of God (2000).
Economy: Unemployment rate: 8.5% (June 2011); Total civilian labor force: 61,270 (June 2011); Leading industries: 22.0% health care and social assistance; 16.6% retail trade; 13.7% accommodation & food services (2009); Farms: 658 totaling 330,734 acres (2007); Companies that employ 500 or more persons: 7 (2009); Companies that employ 100 to 499 persons: 57 (2009); Companies that employ less than 100 persons: 3,162 (2009); Black-owned businesses: n/a (2007); Hispanic-owned businesses: 727 (2007); Asian-owned businesses: 338 (2007); Women-owned businesses: 2,847 (2007); Retail sales per capita: $15,301 (2010). Single-family building permits issued: 145 (2010); Multi-family building permits issued: 30 (2010).
Income: Per capita income: $21,389 (2010); Median household income: $42,677 (2010); Average household income: $54,866 (2010); Percent of households with income of $100,000 or more: 10.8% (2010); Poverty rate: 15.4% (2009); Bankruptcy rate: 3.18% (2010).
Taxes: Total county taxes per capita: $209 (2007); County property taxes per capita: $191 (2007).
Education: Percent of population age 25 and over with: High school diploma (including GED) or higher: 83.2% (2010); Bachelor's degree or higher: 21.2% (2010); Master's degree or higher: 6.6% (2010).
Housing: Homeownership rate: 64.4% (2010); Median home value: $82,253 (2010); Median contract rent: $511 per month (2005-2009 5-year est.); Median year structure built: 1968 (2005-2009 5-year est.)
Health: Birth rate: 150.5 per 10,000 population (2009); Death rate: 99.4 per 10,000 population (2009); Age-adjusted cancer mortality rate: 211.7 deaths per 100,000 population (2007); Number of physicians: 23.7 per 10,000 population (2008); Hospital beds: 74.2 per 10,000 population (2007); Hospital admissions: 1,767.6 per 10,000 population (2007).
Environment: Air Quality Index: 95.3% good, 4.7% moderate, 0.0% unhealthy for sensitive individuals, 0.0% unhealthy (percent of days in 2008)
Elections: 2008 Presidential election results: 30.2% Obama, 69.0% McCain, 0.1% Nader

Additional Information Contacts
Wichita County Government . . . . (940) 766-8100
http://www.co.wichita.tx.us
Burkburnett Chamber of Commerce . . . . (940) 569-3304
http://www.burkburnett.org/business/chamber_of_commerce
City of Burkburnett . . . . (940) 569-2263
http://www.burkburnett.org
City of Iowa Park . . . . (940) 592-2131
http://www.iowapark.com
City of Wichita Falls . . . . (940) 761-7404
http://www.wichitafallstx.gov
Electra Chamber of Commerce . . . . (940) 495-3577
http://www.electratexas.org
Iowa Park Chamber of Commerce . . . . (940) 592-5441
http://www.iowapark.com

Wichita County Communities

BURKBURNETT (city). Covers a land area of 9.506 square miles and a water area of 0 square miles. Located at 34.08° N. Lat; 98.56° W. Long. Elevation is 1,060 feet.
History: Burkburnett had a boom period between 1911 and 1918, when gusher oil wells were producing, that drew 20,000 people to the town during one six-month period.
Population: 10,145 (1990); 10,927 (2000); 10,414 (2010); 10,156 (2015 projected); Race: 87.9% White, 3.2% Black, 0.6% Asian, 8.2% Other, 8.0% Hispanic of any race (2010); Density: 1,095.6 persons per square mile

(2010); Average household size: 2.57 (2010); Median age: 37.3 (2010); Males per 100 females: 92.5 (2010); Marriage status: 19.7% never married, 62.4% now married, 7.5% widowed, 10.3% divorced (2005-2009 5-year est.); Foreign born: 2.9% (2005-2009 5-year est.); Ancestry (includes multiple ancestries): 22.8% American, 14.8% German, 14.5% Irish, 7.2% English, 2.7% Italian (2005-2009 5-year est.).

Economy: Single-family building permits issued: 21 (2010); Multi-family building permits issued: 0 (2010); Employment by occupation: 8.6% management, 20.9% professional, 17.4% services, 29.9% sales, 0.7% farming, 12.0% construction, 10.5% production (2005-2009 5-year est.).

Income: Per capita income: $22,768 (2010); Median household income: $48,839 (2010); Average household income: $57,956 (2010); Percent of households with income of $100,000 or more: 13.0% (2010); Poverty rate: 11.3% (2005-2009 5-year est.).

Taxes: Total city taxes per capita: $371 (2007); City property taxes per capita: $166 (2007).

Education: Percent of population age 25 and over with: High school diploma (including GED) or higher: 87.2% (2010); Bachelor's degree or higher: 18.7% (2010); Master's degree or higher: 5.9% (2010).

School District(s)

Burkburnett ISD (PK-12)
   2009-10 Enrollment: 3,603 . . . . (940) 569-3326

Housing: Homeownership rate: 78.8% (2010); Median home value: $82,712 (2010); Median contract rent: $469 per month (2005-2009 5-year est.); Median year structure built: 1972 (2005-2009 5-year est.).

Safety: Violent crime rate: 17.4 per 10,000 population; Property crime rate: 146.7 per 10,000 population (2009).

Newspapers: Burkburnett Informer Star (Local news; Circulation 2,850)

Transportation: Commute to work: 92.3% car, 0.0% public transportation, 1.1% walk, 3.3% work from home (2005-2009 5-year est.); Travel time to work: 41.2% less than 15 minutes, 45.8% 15 to 30 minutes, 8.9% 30 to 45 minutes, 1.8% 45 to 60 minutes, 2.2% 60 minutes or more (2005-2009 5-year est.)

Additional Information Contacts

Burkburnett Chamber of Commerce . . . . (940) 569-3304
   http://www.burkburnett.org/business/chamber_of_commerce
City of Burkburnett . . . . (940) 569-2263
   http://www.burkburnett.org

ELECTRA (city). Covers a land area of 2.439 square miles and a water area of 0 square miles. Located at 34.03° N. Lat; 98.91° W. Long. Elevation is 1,220 feet.

History: Electra was named by W.T. Waggoner for his daughter. The town grew from 500 to 5,000 people within five months after a geyser sent a stream of oil 100 feet into the air in 1911. The well was on the W.T. Waggoner ranch.

Population: 3,118 (1990); 3,168 (2000); 2,953 (2010); 2,852 (2015 projected); Race: 85.0% White, 3.4% Black, 0.1% Asian, 11.6% Other, 12.7% Hispanic of any race (2010); Density: 1,210.8 persons per square mile (2010); Average household size: 2.48 (2010); Median age: 36.6 (2010); Males per 100 females: 91.0 (2010); Marriage status: 13.3% never married, 60.2% now married, 11.1% widowed, 15.3% divorced (2005-2009 5-year est.); Foreign born: 0.9% (2005-2009 5-year est.); Ancestry (includes multiple ancestries): 21.9% American, 18.3% German, 12.5% Irish, 6.9% English, 4.3% French (2005-2009 5-year est.).

Economy: Single-family building permits issued: 0 (2010); Multi-family building permits issued: 0 (2010); Employment by occupation: 2.9% management, 13.1% professional, 25.7% services, 15.1% sales, 1.3% farming, 15.1% construction, 26.9% production (2005-2009 5-year est.).

Income: Per capita income: $15,934 (2010); Median household income: $29,848 (2010); Average household income: $39,669 (2010); Percent of households with income of $100,000 or more: 5.7% (2010); Poverty rate: 16.8% (2005-2009 5-year est.).

Taxes: Total city taxes per capita: $292 (2007); City property taxes per capita: $160 (2007).

Education: Percent of population age 25 and over with: High school diploma (including GED) or higher: 73.3% (2010); Bachelor's degree or higher: 8.0% (2010); Master's degree or higher: 2.7% (2010).

School District(s)

Electra ISD (PK-12)
   2009-10 Enrollment: 510 . . . . (940) 495-3683

Housing: Homeownership rate: 74.2% (2010); Median home value: $33,833 (2010); Median contract rent: $293 per month (2005-2009 5-year est.); Median year structure built: 1952 (2005-2009 5-year est.).

Hospitals: Electra Texas Memorial Hospital (25 beds)

Safety: Violent crime rate: 20.9 per 10,000 population; Property crime rate: 251.1 per 10,000 population (2009).

Newspapers: Electra Star News (Community news; Circulation 2,000)

Transportation: Commute to work: 94.7% car, 0.0% public transportation, 1.5% walk, 0.4% work from home (2005-2009 5-year est.); Travel time to work: 59.8% less than 15 minutes, 12.0% 15 to 30 minutes, 21.0% 30 to 45 minutes, 2.8% 45 to 60 minutes, 4.3% 60 minutes or more (2005-2009 5-year est.)

Additional Information Contacts

Electra Chamber of Commerce . . . . (940) 495-3577
   http://www.electratexas.org

IOWA PARK (city). Covers a land area of 3.640 square miles and a water area of 0.390 square miles. Located at 33.95° N. Lat; 98.67° W. Long. Elevation is 1,037 feet.

Population: 6,244 (1990); 6,431 (2000); 6,265 (2010); 6,127 (2015 projected); Race: 94.7% White, 0.5% Black, 0.4% Asian, 4.4% Other, 4.2% Hispanic of any race (2010); Density: 1,721.0 persons per square mile (2010); Average household size: 2.52 (2010); Median age: 37.5 (2010); Males per 100 females: 92.1 (2010); Marriage status: 18.0% never married, 63.6% now married, 5.5% widowed, 13.0% divorced (2005-2009 5-year est.); Foreign born: 1.8% (2005-2009 5-year est.); Ancestry (includes multiple ancestries): 35.4% American, 15.7% Irish, 13.4% German, 11.4% English, 2.0% French (2005-2009 5-year est.).

Economy: Single-family building permits issued: 5 (2010); Multi-family building permits issued: 2 (2010); Employment by occupation: 16.4% management, 17.5% professional, 14.0% services, 28.1% sales, 0.0% farming, 10.3% construction, 13.6% production (2005-2009 5-year est.).

Income: Per capita income: $23,899 (2010); Median household income: $55,145 (2010); Average household income: $60,506 (2010); Percent of households with income of $100,000 or more: 11.5% (2010); Poverty rate: 8.6% (2005-2009 5-year est.).

Taxes: Total city taxes per capita: $414 (2007); City property taxes per capita: $261 (2007).

Education: Percent of population age 25 and over with: High school diploma (including GED) or higher: 84.3% (2010); Bachelor's degree or higher: 13.1% (2010); Master's degree or higher: 2.7% (2010).

School District(s)

Iowa Park CISD (PK-12)
   2009-10 Enrollment: 1,764 . . . . (940) 592-4193

Housing: Homeownership rate: 80.8% (2010); Median home value: $77,490 (2010); Median contract rent: $413 per month (2005-2009 5-year est.); Median year structure built: 1968 (2005-2009 5-year est.).

Safety: Violent crime rate: 12.8 per 10,000 population; Property crime rate: 131.1 per 10,000 population (2009).

Transportation: Commute to work: 94.3% car, 0.0% public transportation, 1.1% walk, 4.6% work from home (2005-2009 5-year est.); Travel time to work: 27.2% less than 15 minutes, 57.4% 15 to 30 minutes, 12.5% 30 to 45 minutes, 0.0% 45 to 60 minutes, 2.9% 60 minutes or more (2005-2009 5-year est.)

Additional Information Contacts

City of Iowa Park . . . . (940) 592-2131
   http://www.iowapark.com
Iowa Park Chamber of Commerce. . . . . (940) 592-5441
   http://www.iowapark.com

PLEASANT VALLEY (town). Covers a land area of 2.593 square miles and a water area of 0 square miles. Located at 33.93° N. Lat; 98.59° W. Long. Elevation is 971 feet.

Population: 378 (1990); 408 (2000); 451 (2010); 460 (2015 projected); Race: 77.2% White, 17.1% Black, 0.4% Asian, 5.3% Other, 24.2% Hispanic of any race (2010); Density: 173.9 persons per square mile (2010); Average household size: 2.60 (2010); Median age: 36.2 (2010); Males per 100 females: 181.9 (2010); Marriage status: 19.6% never married, 64.1% now married, 6.7% widowed, 9.6% divorced (2005-2009 5-year est.); Foreign born: 2.2% (2005-2009 5-year est.); Ancestry (includes multiple ancestries): 29.3% American, 14.0% German, 11.1% Irish, 9.6% English, 8.9% French (2005-2009 5-year est.).

Economy: Single-family building permits issued: 0 (2010); Multi-family building permits issued: 0 (2010); Employment by occupation: 4.6% management, 14.9% professional, 16.7% services, 22.4% sales, 0.0% farming, 18.4% construction, 23.0% production (2005-2009 5-year est.).

Income: Per capita income: $18,209 (2010); Median household income: $47,857 (2010); Average household income: $61,750 (2010); Percent of

households with income of $100,000 or more: 10.9% (2010); Poverty rate: 4.8% (2005-2009 5-year est.).

Taxes: Total city taxes per capita: $38 (2007); City property taxes per capita: $0 (2007).

Education: Percent of population age 25 and over with: High school diploma (including GED) or higher: 73.0% (2010); Bachelor's degree or higher: 10.9% (2010); Master's degree or higher: 3.5% (2010).

Housing: Homeownership rate: 82.7% (2010); Median home value: $90,714 (2010); Median contract rent: $475 per month (2005-2009 5-year est.); Median year structure built: 1972 (2005-2009 5-year est.).

Transportation: Commute to work: 94.4% car, 0.0% public transportation, 0.0% walk, 3.4% work from home (2005-2009 5-year est.); Travel time to work: 47.1% less than 15 minutes, 39.5% 15 to 30 minutes, 4.7% 30 to 45 minutes, 2.9% 45 to 60 minutes, 5.8% 60 minutes or more (2005-2009 5-year est.)

SHEPPARD AFB (unincorporated postal area, zip code 76311).

Covers a land area of 7.009 square miles and a water area of 0 square miles. Located at 33.96° N. Lat; 98.50° W. Long.

Population: 9,395 (2000); Race: 70.6% White, 15.9% Black, 3.0% Asian, 10.5% Other, 10.2% Hispanic of any race (2000); Density: 1,340.4 persons per square mile (2000); Age: 22.3% under 18, 0.2% over 64 (2000); Marriage status: 55.2% never married, 42.3% now married, 0.1% widowed, 2.4% divorced (2000); Foreign born: 4.7% (2000); Ancestry (includes multiple ancestries): 20.0% German, 12.7% Irish, 5.9% American, 5.2% Italian (2000).

Economy: Employment by occupation: 8.1% management, 30.2% professional, 20.4% services, 32.0% sales, 0.0% farming, 4.9% construction, 4.4% production (2000).

Income: Per capita income: $11,245 (2000); Median household income: $35,598 (2000); Poverty rate: 179.1% (2000).

Education: Percent of population age 25 and over with: High school diploma (including GED) or higher: 97.8% (2000); Bachelor's degree or higher: 34.4% (2000).

Housing: Homeownership rate: 0.8% (2000); Median home value: $75,000 (2000); Median contract rent: $566 per month (2000); Median year structure built: 1962 (2000).

Transportation: Commute to work: 36.6% car, 1.4% public transportation, 56.7% walk, 0.8% work from home (2000); Travel time to work: 40.4% less than 15 minutes, 48.1% 15 to 30 minutes, 8.8% 30 to 45 minutes, 1.3% 45 to 60 minutes, 1.3% 60 minutes or more (2000)

WICHITA FALLS (city). County seat. Covers a land area of 70.686 square miles and a water area of 0.024 square miles. Located at 33.89° N. Lat; 98.51° W. Long. Elevation is 948 feet.

History: J.H. Barwise, called the Father of Wichita Falls, came to the site on the Wichita River in 1879. Among those already living here was W.T. Buntin and his family, a large group whose names are remembered in Wichita Falls' pioneer stories for their wild adventures. The railroad arrived in 1882, spurring the cattle industry. An irrigation project involving a dam on Holliday Creek, forming Lake Wichita, made farming more prosperous after 1900. The early 1900's also brought oil to the town. The falls for which Wichita was named was at one time a five-foot waterfall on the river.

Population: 97,153 (1990); 104,197 (2000); 102,024 (2010); 100,812 (2015 projected); Race: 72.3% White, 12.1% Black, 2.3% Asian, 13.3% Other, 17.2% Hispanic of any race (2010); Density: 1,443.3 persons per square mile (2010); Average household size: 2.41 (2010); Median age: 32.8 (2010); Males per 100 females: 105.1 (2010); Marriage status: 31.8% never married, 50.4% now married, 5.9% widowed, 11.9% divorced (2005-2009 5-year est.); Foreign born: 6.6% (2005-2009 5-year est.); Ancestry (includes multiple ancestries): 15.6% American, 13.7% German, 9.7% Irish, 7.9% English, 2.1% French (2005-2009 5-year est.).

Economy: Unemployment rate: 8.7% (June 2011); Total civilian labor force: 46,581 (June 2011); Single-family building permits issued: 119 (2010); Multi-family building permits issued: 28 (2010); Employment by occupation: 10.0% management, 20.1% professional, 21.5% services, 26.1% sales, 0.2% farming, 9.8% construction, 12.3% production (2005-2009 5-year est.).

Income: Per capita income: $21,026 (2010); Median household income: $41,084 (2010); Average household income: $53,841 (2010); Percent of households with income of $100,000 or more: 10.3% (2010); Poverty rate: 16.2% (2005-2009 5-year est.).

Taxes: Total city taxes per capita: $596 (2007); City property taxes per capita: $240 (2007).

Education: Percent of population age 25 and over with: High school diploma (including GED) or higher: 83.1% (2010); Bachelor's degree or higher: 22.8% (2010); Master's degree or higher: 7.2% (2010).

School District(s)

Bright Ideas Charter (KG-12)
    2009-10 Enrollment: 197 . . . . (940) 767-1561
Burkburnett ISD (PK-12)
    2009-10 Enrollment: 3,603 . . . . (940) 569-3326
City View ISD (PK-12)
    2009-10 Enrollment: 937 . . . . (940) 855-4042
Iowa Park CISD (PK-12)
    2009-10 Enrollment: 1,764 . . . . (940) 592-4193
Wichita Falls ISD (PK-12)
    2009-10 Enrollment: 14,584 . . . . (940) 235-1000

Four-year College(s)

Midwestern State University (Public)
    Fall 2009 Enrollment: 6,341. (940) 397-4000
    2010-11 Tuition: In-state $5,470; Out-of-state $6,190

Vocational/Technical School(s)

American Commercial College (Private, For-profit)
    Fall 2009 Enrollment: 234 . . . . (940) 691-0454
    2010-11 Tuition: $10,080

Housing: Homeownership rate: 60.4% (2010); Median home value: $84,083 (2010); Median contract rent: $518 per month (2005-2009 5-year est.); Median year structure built: 1968 (2005-2009 5-year est.).

Hospitals: Kell West Regional Hospital (41 beds); North Texas State Hospital - Wichita Falls Campus; Red River Hospital (66 beds); United Regional Healthcare System (541 beds)

Safety: Violent crime rate: 51.5 per 10,000 population; Property crime rate: 556.9 per 10,000 population (2009).

Newspapers: Times Record News (Local news; Circulation 38,800)

Transportation: Commute to work: 87.1% car, 0.4% public transportation, 7.6% walk, 3.6% work from home (2005-2009 5-year est.); Travel time to work: 55.6% less than 15 minutes, 36.3% 15 to 30 minutes, 5.1% 30 to 45 minutes, 1.3% 45 to 60 minutes, 1.8% 60 minutes or more (2005-2009 5-year est.)

Airports: Sheppard AFB/Wichita Falls Municipal (primary service)

Additional Information Contacts

City of Wichita Falls . . . . (940) 761-7404
    http://www.wichitafallstx.gov

Wilbarger County

Located in north Texas; bounded on the north by the Red River and the Oklahoma border; drained by the Pease River. Covers a land area of 971.06 square miles, a water area of 7.03 square miles, and is located in the Central Time Zone at 34.09° N. Lat., 99.24° W. Long. The county was founded in 1858. County seat is Vernon.

Wilbarger County is part of the Vernon, TX Micropolitan Statistical Area. The entire metro area includes: Wilbarger County, TX

Weather Station: Vernon   Elevation: 1,227 feet

	Jan	Feb	Mar	Apr	May	Jun	Jul	Aug	Sep	Oct	Nov	Dec
High	55	59	67	76	84	92	97	96	88	77	65	55
Low	28	32	40	48	59	68	72	71	63	51	39	29
Precip	1.1	1.4	2.3	2.1	3.4	4.4	1.8	2.8	3.0	2.8	1.7	1.2
Snow	0.8	0.4	tr	0.0	0.0	0.0	0.0	0.0	0.0	tr	0.2	tr

High and Low temperatures in degrees Fahrenheit; Precipitation and Snow in inches

Population: 15,121 (1990); 14,676 (2000); 14,187 (2010); 13,923 (2015 projected); Race: 74.4% White, 9.1% Black, 0.9% Asian, 15.6% Other, 25.5% Hispanic of any race (2010); Density: 14.6 persons per square mile (2010); Average household size: 2.47 (2010); Median age: 35.9 (2010); Males per 100 females: 98.5 (2010).

Religion: Five largest groups: 39.5% Southern Baptist Convention, 7.7% Catholic Church, 6.4% The United Methodist Church, 6.2% Churches of Christ, 5.9% Lutheran Church—Missouri Synod (2000).

Economy: Unemployment rate: 6.7% (June 2011); Total civilian labor force: 7,687 (June 2011); Leading industries: 18.2% retail trade; 14.3% health care and social assistance; 12.5% accommodation & food services (2009); Farms: 461 totaling 613,873 acres (2007); Companies that employ 500 or more persons: 1 (2009); Companies that employ 100 to 499 persons: 2 (2009); Companies that employ less than 100 persons: 302 (2009); Black-owned businesses: n/a (2007); Hispanic-owned businesses: n/a (2007); Asian-owned businesses: 30 (2007); Women-owned

businesses: n/a (2007); Retail sales per capita: $12,992 (2010). Single-family building permits issued: 2 (2010); Multi-family building permits issued: 0 (2010).
Income: Per capita income: $20,139 (2010); Median household income: $36,253 (2010); Average household income: $51,460 (2010); Percent of households with income of $100,000 or more: 10.0% (2010); Poverty rate: 17.2% (2009); Bankruptcy rate: 2.57% (2010).
Taxes: Total county taxes per capita: $359 (2007); County property taxes per capita: $286 (2007).
Education: Percent of population age 25 and over with: High school diploma (including GED) or higher: 77.0% (2010); Bachelor's degree or higher: 18.7% (2010); Master's degree or higher: 4.8% (2010).
Housing: Homeownership rate: 64.1% (2010); Median home value: $60,253 (2010); Median contract rent: $358 per month (2005-2009 5-year est.); Median year structure built: 1962 (2005-2009 5-year est.)
Health: Birth rate: 158.8 per 10,000 population (2009); Death rate: 105.6 per 10,000 population (2009); Age-adjusted cancer mortality rate: 239.4 deaths per 100,000 population (2007); Number of physicians: 12.6 per 10,000 population (2008); Hospital beds: 482.3 per 10,000 population (2007); Hospital admissions: 2,546.0 per 10,000 population (2007).
Elections: 2008 Presidential election results: 26.5% Obama, 72.8% McCain, 0.0% Nader
Additional Information Contacts
Wilbarger County Government . . . . (940) 553-2300
   http://www.co.wilbarger.tx.us
City of Vernon . . . . (940) 552-2581
   http://www.vernontexas.org
Vernon Chamber of Commerce . . . . (940) 552-2564
   http://vernonchamber.chambermaster.com

Wilbarger County Communities

HARROLD (unincorporated postal area, zip code 76364). Covers a land area of 130.902 square miles and a water area of 1.354 square miles. Located at 34.08° N. Lat; 99.06° W. Long. Elevation is 1,240 feet.
Population: 252 (2000); Race: 89.1% White, 1.5% Black, 0.0% Asian, 9.4% Other, 11.6% Hispanic of any race (2000); Density: 1.9 persons per square mile (2000); Age: 20.6% under 18, 32.2% over 64 (2000); Marriage status: 8.3% never married, 66.1% now married, 16.5% widowed, 9.2% divorced (2000); Foreign born: 0.7% (2000); Ancestry (includes multiple ancestries): 22.1% German, 12.7% American, 11.2% Slovene, 4.5% English (2000).
Economy: Employment by occupation: 30.8% management, 6.8% professional, 9.8% services, 17.3% sales, 10.5% farming, 10.5% construction, 14.3% production (2000).
Income: Per capita income: $22,983 (2000); Median household income: $26,563 (2000); Poverty rate: 179.1% (2000).
Education: Percent of population age 25 and over with: High school diploma (including GED) or higher: 60.3% (2000); Bachelor's degree or higher: 8.0% (2000).
School District(s)
Harrold ISD (KG-12)
   2009-10 Enrollment: 96 . . . . (940) 886-2213
Housing: Homeownership rate: 79.2% (2000); Median home value: $39,200 (2000); Median contract rent: $208 per month (2000); Median year structure built: 1942 (2000).
Transportation: Commute to work: 70.7% car, 0.0% public transportation, 23.3% walk, 5.3% work from home (2000); Travel time to work: 58.7% less than 15 minutes, 19.8% 15 to 30 minutes, 13.5% 30 to 45 minutes, 4.8% 45 to 60 minutes, 3.2% 60 minutes or more (2000)

OKLAUNION (unincorporated postal area, zip code 76373). Covers a land area of 32.157 square miles and a water area of 0.036 square miles. Located at 34.14° N. Lat; 99.11° W. Long. Elevation is 1,227 feet.
Population: 194 (2000); Race: 94.4% White, 0.0% Black, 0.0% Asian, 5.6% Other, 0.0% Hispanic of any race (2000); Density: 6.0 persons per square mile (2000); Age: 33.8% under 18, 16.7% over 64 (2000); Marriage status: 8.4% never married, 91.6% now married, 0.0% widowed, 0.0% divorced (2000); Foreign born: 0.0% (2000); Ancestry (includes multiple ancestries): 19.4% English, 18.5% American, 17.6% German, 9.3% Scottish (2000).
Economy: Employment by occupation: 0.0% management, 6.3% professional, 9.5% services, 27.0% sales, 9.5% farming, 7.9% construction, 39.7% production (2000).

Income: Per capita income: $16,113 (2000); Median household income: $33,173 (2000); Poverty rate: 179.1% (2000).
Education: Percent of population age 25 and over with: High school diploma (including GED) or higher: 60.9% (2000); Bachelor's degree or higher: 15.8% (2000).
Housing: Homeownership rate: 68.6% (2000); Median home value: $58,800 (2000); Median contract rent: $175 per month (2000); Median year structure built: before 1940 (2000).
Transportation: Commute to work: 100.0% car, 0.0% public transportation, 0.0% walk, 0.0% work from home (2000); Travel time to work: 18.2% less than 15 minutes, 29.1% 15 to 30 minutes, 41.8% 30 to 45 minutes, 10.9% 45 to 60 minutes, 0.0% 60 minutes or more (2000)

VERNON (city). County seat. Covers a land area of 8.102 square miles and a water area of 0.007 square miles. Located at 34.15° N. Lat; 99.29° W. Long. Elevation is 1,184 feet.
History: In the 1880's Vernon was the supply base for the great herds of cattle that were driven over the Western Trail to the Red River. The W.T. Waggoner Ranch spread over Wilbarger County and five other counties. Vernon was first called Eagle Flats for the number of eagles there. It was renamed Vernon for George Washington's home in Virginia.
Population: 12,001 (1990); 11,660 (2000); 11,250 (2010); 11,026 (2015 projected); Race: 73.3% White, 9.1% Black, 1.0% Asian, 16.6% Other, 27.6% Hispanic of any race (2010); Density: 1,388.6 persons per square mile (2010); Average household size: 2.45 (2010); Median age: 35.8 (2010); Males per 100 females: 94.2 (2010); Marriage status: 26.0% never married, 47.7% now married, 9.7% widowed, 16.5% divorced (2005-2009 5-year est.); Foreign born: 4.0% (2005-2009 5-year est.); Ancestry (includes multiple ancestries): 19.5% American, 10.2% German, 8.4% Irish, 5.5% English, 1.6% Scottish (2005-2009 5-year est.).
Economy: Single-family building permits issued: 2 (2010); Multi-family building permits issued: 0 (2010); Employment by occupation: 7.5% management, 15.5% professional, 27.6% services, 16.3% sales, 0.9% farming, 13.9% construction, 18.2% production (2005-2009 5-year est.).
Income: Per capita income: $19,109 (2010); Median household income: $34,249 (2010); Average household income: $47,719 (2010); Percent of households with income of $100,000 or more: 8.3% (2010); Poverty rate: 27.7% (2005-2009 5-year est.).
Taxes: Total city taxes per capita: $264 (2007); City property taxes per capita: $105 (2007).
Education: Percent of population age 25 and over with: High school diploma (including GED) or higher: 76.4% (2010); Bachelor's degree or higher: 17.0% (2010); Master's degree or higher: 4.5% (2010).
School District(s)
Northside ISD (KG-12)
   2009-10 Enrollment: 193 . . . . (940) 552-2551
Vernon ISD (PK-12)
   2009-10 Enrollment: 2,279 . . . . (940) 553-1900
Victory Field Correctional Academy (09-12)
   2009-10 Enrollment: 81 . . . . (940) 552-9347
Two-year College(s)
Vernon College (Public)
   Fall 2009 Enrollment: 3,163 . . . . (940) 552-6291
   2010-11 Tuition: In-state $3,540; Out-of-state $5,190
Housing: Homeownership rate: 62.4% (2010); Median home value: $56,766 (2010); Median contract rent: $357 per month (2005-2009 5-year est.); Median year structure built: 1962 (2005-2009 5-year est.).
Hospitals: Wilbarger General Hospital (47 beds)
Safety: Violent crime rate: 40.6 per 10,000 population; Property crime rate: 324.5 per 10,000 population (2009).
Newspapers: The Vernon Daily Record (Local news; Circulation 6,000)
Transportation: Commute to work: 96.3% car, 0.0% public transportation, 1.4% walk, 0.6% work from home (2005-2009 5-year est.); Travel time to work: 80.1% less than 15 minutes, 8.9% 15 to 30 minutes, 6.0% 30 to 45 minutes, 3.1% 45 to 60 minutes, 1.8% 60 minutes or more (2005-2009 5-year est.)
Additional Information Contacts
City of Vernon . . . . (940) 552-2581
   http://www.vernontexas.org
Vernon Chamber of Commerce . . . . (940) 552-2564
   http://vernonchamber.chambermaster.com

Willacy County

Located in south Texas, in the Rio Grande Valley; bounded on the east by Laguna Madre, separated from the Gulf of Mexico by Padre Island. Covers a land area of 596.68 square miles, a water area of 187.55 square miles, and is located in the Central Time Zone at 26.47° N. Lat., 97.76° W. Long. The county was founded in 1921. County seat is Raymondville.

Willacy County is part of the Raymondville, TX Micropolitan Statistical Area. The entire metro area includes: Willacy County, TX

Weather Station: Port Mansfield   Elevation: 8 feet

	Jan	Feb	Mar	Apr	May	Jun	Jul	Aug	Sep	Oct	Nov	Dec
High	66	69	74	78	83	88	89	89	87	82	75	68
Low	50	54	60	66	73	77	77	77	73	68	60	52
Precip	1.3	1.7	1.4	1.3	2.6	2.2	1.9	1.6	5.0	3.2	1.8	1.3
Snow	tr	0.0	0.0	0.0	0.0	0.0	0.0	0.0	0.0	0.0	0.0	0.1

High and Low temperatures in degrees Fahrenheit; Precipitation and Snow in inches

Weather Station: Raymondville   Elevation: 30 feet

	Jan	Feb	Mar	Apr	May	Jun	Jul	Aug	Sep	Oct	Nov	Dec
High	71	74	80	86	90	95	97	97	93	87	79	72
Low	48	51	57	63	70	74	74	74	71	64	56	49
Precip	1.2	1.4	1.5	1.3	3.0	2.3	2.2	2.5	5.1	3.4	1.3	1.2
Snow	0.0	0.0	0.0	0.0	0.0	0.0	0.0	0.0	0.0	0.0	0.0	0.1

High and Low temperatures in degrees Fahrenheit; Precipitation and Snow in inches

Population: 17,705 (1990); 20,082 (2000); 21,117 (2010); 21,586 (2015 projected); Race: 69.9% White, 2.3% Black, 0.2% Asian, 27.6% Other, 86.5% Hispanic of any race (2010); Density: 35.4 persons per square mile (2010); Average household size: 3.37 (2010); Median age: 31.5 (2010); Males per 100 females: 104.9 (2010).
Religion: Five largest groups: 59.7% Catholic Church, 8.1% Southern Baptist Convention, 2.9% The United Methodist Church, 1.6% Lutheran Church—Missouri Synod, 1.0% Assemblies of God (2000).
Economy: Unemployment rate: 14.0% (June 2011); Total civilian labor force: 9,476 (June 2011); Leading industries: 44.2% health care and social assistance; 8.6% accommodation & food services; 2.9% finance & insurance (2009); Farms: 352 totaling 338,048 acres (2007); Companies that employ 500 or more persons: 0 (2009); Companies that employ 100 to 499 persons: 4 (2009); Companies that employ less than 100 persons: 198 (2009); Black-owned businesses: n/a (2007); Hispanic-owned businesses: 818 (2007); Asian-owned businesses: n/a (2007); Women-owned businesses: 431 (2007); Retail sales per capita: $5,201 (2010). Single-family building permits issued: 16 (2010); Multi-family building permits issued: 0 (2010).
Income: Per capita income: $10,992 (2010); Median household income: $27,461 (2010); Average household income: $37,098 (2010); Percent of households with income of $100,000 or more: 5.2% (2010); Poverty rate: 41.6% (2009); Bankruptcy rate: 0.94% (2010).
Taxes: Total county taxes per capita: $341 (2007); County property taxes per capita: $254 (2007).
Education: Percent of population age 25 and over with: High school diploma (including GED) or higher: 53.0% (2010); Bachelor's degree or higher: 10.8% (2010); Master's degree or higher: 3.8% (2010).
Housing: Homeownership rate: 68.9% (2010); Median home value: $41,182 (2010); Median contract rent: $339 per month (2005-2009 5-year est.); Median year structure built: 1970 (2005-2009 5-year est.)
Health: Birth rate: 195.6 per 10,000 population (2009); Death rate: 57.4 per 10,000 population (2009); Age-adjusted cancer mortality rate: 153.6 deaths per 100,000 population (2007); Number of physicians: 2.9 per 10,000 population (2008); Hospital beds: 0.0 per 10,000 population (2007); Hospital admissions: 0.0 per 10,000 population (2007).
Elections: 2008 Presidential election results: 69.5% Obama, 29.7% McCain, 0.1% Nader
Additional Information Contacts
Willacy County Government . . . . (956) 689-3393
   http://www.co.willacy.tx.us/ips/cms
City of Raymondville . . . . (956) 689-2443
Port Mansfield Chamber of Commerce . . . . (956) 944-2354
   http://www.port-mansfield.com
Raymondville Chamber of Commerce . . . . (956) 689-1864
   http://www.raymondvillechamber.com

Willacy County Communities

BAUSELL AND ELLIS (CDP). Covers a land area of 0.114 square miles and a water area of 0 square miles. Located at 26.43° N. Lat; 97.78° W. Long. Elevation is 30 feet.
Population: 88 (1990); 112 (2000); 138 (2010); 149 (2015 projected); Race: 65.2% White, 0.0% Black, 0.0% Asian, 34.8% Other, 88.4% Hispanic of any race (2010); Density: 1,212.9 persons per square mile (2010); Average household size: 3.21 (2010); Median age: 35.7 (2010); Males per 100 females: 100.0 (2010); Marriage status: n/a never married, n/a now married, n/a widowed, n/a divorced (2005-2009 5-year est.); Foreign born: n/a (2005-2009 5-year est.); Ancestry (includes multiple ancestries): n/a (2005-2009 5-year est.).
Economy: Employment by occupation: n/a management, n/a professional, n/a services, n/a sales, n/a farming, n/a construction, n/a production (2005-2009 5-year est.).
Income: Per capita income: $15,265 (2010); Median household income: $37,813 (2010); Average household income: $49,593 (2010); Percent of households with income of $100,000 or more: 9.3% (2010); Poverty rate: n/a (2005-2009 5-year est.).
Education: Percent of population age 25 and over with: High school diploma (including GED) or higher: 60.7% (2010); Bachelor's degree or higher: 13.1% (2010); Master's degree or higher: 6.0% (2010).
Housing: Homeownership rate: 69.8% (2010); Median home value: $47,500 (2010); Median contract rent: n/a per month (2005-2009 5-year est.); Median year structure built: n/a (2005-2009 5-year est.).
Transportation: Commute to work: n/a car, n/a public transportation, n/a walk, n/a work from home (2005-2009 5-year est.); Travel time to work: n/a less than 15 minutes, n/a 15 to 30 minutes, n/a 30 to 45 minutes, n/a 45 to 60 minutes, n/a 60 minutes or more (2005-2009 5-year est.)

LASARA (CDP). Aka La Sara. Covers a land area of 1.396 square miles and a water area of 0 square miles. Located at 26.46° N. Lat; 97.91° W. Long. Elevation is 43 feet.
Population: 877 (1990); 1,024 (2000); 1,227 (2010); 1,321 (2015 projected); Race: 67.2% White, 0.6% Black, 0.9% Asian, 31.4% Other, 89.9% Hispanic of any race (2010); Density: 879.1 persons per square mile (2010); Average household size: 3.62 (2010); Median age: 28.4 (2010); Males per 100 females: 92.9 (2010); Marriage status: 33.5% never married, 54.2% now married, 4.4% widowed, 7.9% divorced (2005-2009 5-year est.); Foreign born: 16.6% (2005-2009 5-year est.); Ancestry (includes multiple ancestries): 2.3% Irish, 1.1% Palestinian, 1.1% Greek, 0.3% American (2005-2009 5-year est.).
Economy: Employment by occupation: 8.5% management, 10.9% professional, 35.7% services, 21.1% sales, 7.1% farming, 12.6% construction, 4.1% production (2005-2009 5-year est.).
Income: Per capita income: $10,340 (2010); Median household income: $28,837 (2010); Average household income: $37,153 (2010); Percent of households with income of $100,000 or more: 5.6% (2010); Poverty rate: 47.5% (2005-2009 5-year est.).
Education: Percent of population age 25 and over with: High school diploma (including GED) or higher: 51.6% (2010); Bachelor's degree or higher: 9.7% (2010); Master's degree or higher: 3.2% (2010).
School District(s)
Lasara ISD (PK-11)
   2009-10 Enrollment: 454 . . . . (956) 642-3598
Housing: Homeownership rate: 76.7% (2010); Median home value: $33,913 (2010); Median contract rent: n/a per month (2005-2009 5-year est.); Median year structure built: 1977 (2005-2009 5-year est.).
Transportation: Commute to work: 98.0% car, 0.0% public transportation, 2.0% walk, 0.0% work from home (2005-2009 5-year est.); Travel time to work: 19.7% less than 15 minutes, 36.7% 15 to 30 minutes, 21.1% 30 to 45 minutes, 18.0% 45 to 60 minutes, 4.4% 60 minutes or more (2005-2009 5-year est.)

LOS ANGELES SUBDIVISION (CDP). Covers a land area of 0.165 square miles and a water area of 0 square miles. Located at 26.49° N. Lat; 97.78° W. Long. Elevation is 30 feet.
Population: 105 (1990); 86 (2000); 43 (2010); 40 (2015 projected); Race: 76.7% White, 0.0% Black, 0.0% Asian, 23.3% Other, 97.7% Hispanic of any race (2010); Density: 260.2 persons per square mile (2010); Average household size: 3.91 (2010); Median age: 26.2 (2010); Males per 100 females: 87.0 (2010); Marriage status: n/a never married, n/a now married, n/a widowed, n/a divorced (2005-2009 5-year est.); Foreign born: n/a

(2005-2009 5-year est.); Ancestry (includes multiple ancestries): n/a (2005-2009 5-year est.).

Economy: Employment by occupation: n/a management, n/a professional, n/a services, n/a sales, n/a farming, n/a construction, n/a production (2005-2009 5-year est.).

Income: Per capita income: $6,582 (2010); Median household income: $22,500 (2010); Average household income: $26,136 (2010); Percent of households with income of $100,000 or more: 0.0% (2010); Poverty rate: n/a (2005-2009 5-year est.).

Education: Percent of population age 25 and over with: High school diploma (including GED) or higher: 31.8% (2010); Bachelor's degree or higher: 4.5% (2010); Master's degree or higher: 4.5% (2010).

Housing: Homeownership rate: 72.7% (2010); Median home value: $26,667 (2010); Median contract rent: n/a per month (2005-2009 5-year est.); Median year structure built: n/a (2005-2009 5-year est.).

Transportation: Commute to work: n/a car, n/a public transportation, n/a walk, n/a work from home (2005-2009 5-year est.); Travel time to work: n/a less than 15 minutes, n/a 15 to 30 minutes, n/a 30 to 45 minutes, n/a 45 to 60 minutes, n/a 60 minutes or more (2005-2009 5-year est.)

LYFORD (city).
Covers a land area of 1.070 square miles and a water area of 0.011 square miles. Located at 26.41° N. Lat; 97.79° W. Long. Elevation is 33 feet.

Population: 1,674 (1990); 1,973 (2000); 2,391 (2010); 2,580 (2015 projected); Race: 62.4% White, 0.1% Black, 0.0% Asian, 37.4% Other, 91.4% Hispanic of any race (2010); Density: 2,235.3 persons per square mile (2010); Average household size: 3.42 (2010); Median age: 32.4 (2010); Males per 100 females: 92.0 (2010); Marriage status: 26.3% never married, 60.9% now married, 7.1% widowed, 5.7% divorced (2005-2009 5-year est.); Foreign born: 18.3% (2005-2009 5-year est.); Ancestry (includes multiple ancestries): 1.4% German, 1.1% English, 0.6% Irish, 0.3% Scotch-Irish, 0.3% Polish (2005-2009 5-year est.).

Economy: Employment by occupation: 7.2% management, 11.3% professional, 28.6% services, 21.6% sales, 4.4% farming, 16.5% construction, 10.3% production (2005-2009 5-year est.).

Income: Per capita income: $12,604 (2010); Median household income: $33,480 (2010); Average household income: $42,858 (2010); Percent of households with income of $100,000 or more: 7.2% (2010); Poverty rate: 51.9% (2005-2009 5-year est.).

Taxes: Total city taxes per capita: $157 (2007); City property taxes per capita: $114 (2007).

Education: Percent of population age 25 and over with: High school diploma (including GED) or higher: 56.4% (2010); Bachelor's degree or higher: 12.8% (2010); Master's degree or higher: 4.6% (2010).

School District(s)
Lyford CISD (PK-12)
    2009-10 Enrollment: 1,559 . . . . (956) 347-3900

Housing: Homeownership rate: 74.8% (2010); Median home value: $41,462 (2010); Median contract rent: $345 per month (2005-2009 5-year est.); Median year structure built: 1971 (2005-2009 5-year est.).

Transportation: Commute to work: 95.1% car, 0.0% public transportation, 0.7% walk, 2.1% work from home (2005-2009 5-year est.); Travel time to work: 52.1% less than 15 minutes, 29.9% 15 to 30 minutes, 14.8% 30 to 45 minutes, 2.7% 45 to 60 minutes, 0.5% 60 minutes or more (2005-2009 5-year est.)

LYFORD SOUTH (CDP).
Covers a land area of 0.204 square miles and a water area of 0 square miles. Located at 26.39° N. Lat; 97.79° W. Long. Elevation is 33 feet.

Population: 136 (1990); 172 (2000); 208 (2010); 224 (2015 projected); Race: 61.1% White, 0.0% Black, 0.0% Asian, 38.9% Other, 92.8% Hispanic of any race (2010); Density: 1,019.6 persons per square mile (2010); Average household size: 3.53 (2010); Median age: 32.3 (2010); Males per 100 females: 89.1 (2010); Marriage status: n/a never married, n/a now married, n/a widowed, n/a divorced (2005-2009 5-year est.); Foreign born: n/a (2005-2009 5-year est.); Ancestry (includes multiple ancestries): n/a (2005-2009 5-year est.).

Economy: Employment by occupation: n/a management, n/a professional, n/a services, n/a sales, n/a farming, n/a construction, n/a production (2005-2009 5-year est.).

Income: Per capita income: $10,974 (2010); Median household income: $31,875 (2010); Average household income: $43,432 (2010); Percent of households with income of $100,000 or more: 8.5% (2010); Poverty rate: n/a (2005-2009 5-year est.).

Education: Percent of population age 25 and over with: High school diploma (including GED) or higher: 52.8% (2010); Bachelor's degree or higher: 12.2% (2010); Master's degree or higher: 4.1% (2010).

Housing: Homeownership rate: 78.0% (2010); Median home value: $35,385 (2010); Median contract rent: n/a per month (2005-2009 5-year est.); Median year structure built: n/a (2005-2009 5-year est.).

Transportation: Commute to work: n/a car, n/a public transportation, n/a walk, n/a work from home (2005-2009 5-year est.); Travel time to work: n/a less than 15 minutes, n/a 15 to 30 minutes, n/a 30 to 45 minutes, n/a 45 to 60 minutes, n/a 60 minutes or more (2005-2009 5-year est.)

PORT MANSFIELD (CDP).
Aka Redfish Bay. Covers a land area of 5.212 square miles and a water area of 0.496 square miles. Located at 26.55° N. Lat; 97.43° W. Long. Elevation is 3 feet.

History: Dredged Port Mansfield Channel (1962), across Laguna Madre and through Padre Island, gave direct access to gulf for shipping, fishing and pleasure craft.

Population: 389 (1990); 415 (2000); 425 (2010); 428 (2015 projected); Race: 80.2% White, 0.9% Black, 0.0% Asian, 18.8% Other, 60.5% Hispanic of any race (2010); Density: 81.5 persons per square mile (2010); Average household size: 3.06 (2010); Median age: 38.2 (2010); Males per 100 females: 95.9 (2010); Marriage status: 8.8% never married, 87.6% now married, 2.1% widowed, 1.5% divorced (2005-2009 5-year est.); Foreign born: 2.0% (2005-2009 5-year est.); Ancestry (includes multiple ancestries): 18.1% German, 11.3% Irish, 6.8% English, 5.4% Czech, 5.1% Italian (2005-2009 5-year est.).

Economy: Employment by occupation: 2.0% management, 37.0% professional, 27.0% services, 18.0% sales, 10.0% farming, 6.0% construction, 0.0% production (2005-2009 5-year est.).

Income: Per capita income: $13,552 (2010); Median household income: $31,579 (2010); Average household income: $40,665 (2010); Percent of households with income of $100,000 or more: 4.3% (2010); Poverty rate: 44.2% (2005-2009 5-year est.).

Education: Percent of population age 25 and over with: High school diploma (including GED) or higher: 66.4% (2010); Bachelor's degree or higher: 12.0% (2010); Master's degree or higher: 5.8% (2010).

Housing: Homeownership rate: 73.4% (2010); Median home value: $40,000 (2010); Median contract rent: $504 per month (2005-2009 5-year est.); Median year structure built: 1977 (2005-2009 5-year est.).

Transportation: Commute to work: 100.0% car, 0.0% public transportation, 0.0% walk, 0.0% work from home (2005-2009 5-year est.); Travel time to work: 20.0% less than 15 minutes, 13.3% 15 to 30 minutes, 60.0% 30 to 45 minutes, 6.7% 45 to 60 minutes, 0.0% 60 minutes or more (2005-2009 5-year est.)

Additional Information Contacts
Port Mansfield Chamber of Commerce . . . . (956) 944-2354
   http://www.port-mansfield.com

RANCHETTE ESTATES (CDP).
Covers a land area of 0.614 square miles and a water area of 0 square miles. Located at 26.48° N. Lat; 97.82° W. Long. Elevation is 36 feet.

Population: 87 (1990); 133 (2000); 127 (2010); 124 (2015 projected); Race: 77.2% White, 0.8% Black, 0.0% Asian, 22.0% Other, 87.4% Hispanic of any race (2010); Density: 206.9 persons per square mile (2010); Average household size: 3.43 (2010); Median age: 30.3 (2010); Males per 100 females: 86.8 (2010); Marriage status: n/a never married, n/a now married, n/a widowed, n/a divorced (2005-2009 5-year est.); Foreign born: n/a (2005-2009 5-year est.); Ancestry (includes multiple ancestries): n/a (2005-2009 5-year est.).

Economy: Employment by occupation: n/a management, n/a professional, n/a services, n/a sales, n/a farming, n/a construction, n/a production (2005-2009 5-year est.).

Income: Per capita income: $11,792 (2010); Median household income: $30,000 (2010); Average household income: $39,797 (2010); Percent of households with income of $100,000 or more: 5.4% (2010); Poverty rate: n/a (2005-2009 5-year est.).

Education: Percent of population age 25 and over with: High school diploma (including GED) or higher: 54.1% (2010); Bachelor's degree or higher: 12.2% (2010); Master's degree or higher: 4.1% (2010).

Housing: Homeownership rate: 75.7% (2010); Median home value: $48,571 (2010); Median contract rent: n/a per month (2005-2009 5-year est.); Median year structure built: n/a (2005-2009 5-year est.).

Transportation: Commute to work: n/a car, n/a public transportation, n/a walk, n/a work from home (2005-2009 5-year est.); Travel time to work: n/a

less than 15 minutes, n/a 15 to 30 minutes, n/a 30 to 45 minutes, n/a 45 to 60 minutes, n/a 60 minutes or more (2005-2009 5-year est.)

RAYMONDVILLE (city).
County seat. Covers a land area of 3.795 square miles and a water area of 0.005 square miles. Located at 26.48° N. Lat; 97.78° W. Long. Elevation is 30 feet.
History: Plotted 1904, incorporated as city 1921.
Population: 9,373 (1990); 9,733 (2000); 9,329 (2010); 9,129 (2015 projected); Race: 71.0% White, 2.8% Black, 0.2% Asian, 26.0% Other, 88.5% Hispanic of any race (2010); Density: 2,457.9 persons per square mile (2010); Average household size: 3.40 (2010); Median age: 30.9 (2010); Males per 100 females: 108.6 (2010); Marriage status: 34.6% never married, 47.1% now married, 6.3% widowed, 12.0% divorced (2005-2009 5-year est.); Foreign born: 16.8% (2005-2009 5-year est.); Ancestry (includes multiple ancestries): 3.0% German, 2.4% American, 1.6% English, 1.5% Irish, 0.9% Scotch-Irish (2005-2009 5-year est.).
Economy: Single-family building permits issued: 0 (2010); Multi-family building permits issued: 0 (2010); Employment by occupation: 4.1% management, 19.1% professional, 32.9% services, 25.6% sales, 4.4% farming, 6.3% construction, 7.5% production (2005-2009 5-year est.).
Income: Per capita income: $9,502 (2010); Median household income: $23,265 (2010); Average household income: $31,693 (2010); Percent of households with income of $100,000 or more: 3.6% (2010); Poverty rate: 48.5% (2005-2009 5-year est.).
Taxes: Total city taxes per capita: $258 (2007); City property taxes per capita: $91 (2007).
Education: Percent of population age 25 and over with: High school diploma (including GED) or higher: 50.2% (2010); Bachelor's degree or higher: 11.3% (2010); Master's degree or higher: 3.6% (2010).
School District(s)
One Stop Multiservice Charter School (PK-12)
    2009-10 Enrollment: 746 . . . . (956) 393-2227
Raymondville ISD (PK-12)
    2009-10 Enrollment: 2,209 . . . . (956) 689-8176
Housing: Homeownership rate: 62.5% (2010); Median home value: $39,279 (2010); Median contract rent: $313 per month (2005-2009 5-year est.); Median year structure built: 1964 (2005-2009 5-year est.).
Safety: Violent crime rate: 255.7 per 10,000 population; Property crime rate: 619.9 per 10,000 population (2009).
Transportation: Commute to work: 93.0% car, 0.0% public transportation, 2.2% walk, 3.9% work from home (2005-2009 5-year est.); Travel time to work: 55.6% less than 15 minutes, 24.5% 15 to 30 minutes, 16.0% 30 to 45 minutes, 2.1% 45 to 60 minutes, 1.8% 60 minutes or more (2005-2009 5-year est.)
Additional Information Contacts
City of Raymondville . . . . (956) 689-2443
Raymondville Chamber of Commerce . . . . (956) 689-1864
    http://www.raymondvillechamber.com

SAN PERLITA (city).
Covers a land area of 0.508 square miles and a water area of 0 square miles. Located at 26.50° N. Lat; 97.64° W. Long. Elevation is 20 feet.
Population: 512 (1990); 680 (2000); 688 (2010); 693 (2015 projected); Race: 80.2% White, 1.0% Black, 0.0% Asian, 18.8% Other, 60.6% Hispanic of any race (2010); Density: 1,354.7 persons per square mile (2010); Average household size: 3.06 (2010); Median age: 38.4 (2010); Males per 100 females: 94.9 (2010); Marriage status: 25.4% never married, 60.9% now married, 8.9% widowed, 4.8% divorced (2005-2009 5-year est.); Foreign born: 15.2% (2005-2009 5-year est.); Ancestry (includes multiple ancestries): 5.5% German, 1.0% Scottish, 0.1% American (2005-2009 5-year est.).
Economy: Employment by occupation: 13.7% management, 7.7% professional, 26.9% services, 18.1% sales, 13.2% farming, 13.7% construction, 6.6% production (2005-2009 5-year est.).
Income: Per capita income: $13,552 (2010); Median household income: $32,167 (2010); Average household income: $40,322 (2010); Percent of households with income of $100,000 or more: 4.4% (2010); Poverty rate: 46.9% (2005-2009 5-year est.).
Taxes: Total city taxes per capita: $44 (2007); City property taxes per capita: $44 (2007).
Education: Percent of population age 25 and over with: High school diploma (including GED) or higher: 65.5% (2010); Bachelor's degree or higher: 11.8% (2010); Master's degree or higher: 5.3% (2010).

School District(s)
San Perlita ISD (PK-12)
    2009-10 Enrollment: 281 . . . . (956) 248-5563
Housing: Homeownership rate: 72.9% (2010); Median home value: $39,149 (2010); Median contract rent: $288 per month (2005-2009 5-year est.); Median year structure built: 1972 (2005-2009 5-year est.).
Transportation: Commute to work: 98.4% car, 0.0% public transportation, 1.6% walk, 0.0% work from home (2005-2009 5-year est.); Travel time to work: 30.2% less than 15 minutes, 44.5% 15 to 30 minutes, 20.9% 30 to 45 minutes, 1.6% 45 to 60 minutes, 2.7% 60 minutes or more (2005-2009 5-year est.)

SANTA MONICA (CDP).
Covers a land area of 0.353 square miles and a water area of 0 square miles. Located at 26.36° N. Lat; 97.60° W. Long. Elevation is 16 feet.
Population: 93 (1990); 78 (2000); 97 (2010); 105 (2015 projected); Race: 75.3% White, 1.0% Black, 0.0% Asian, 23.7% Other, 89.7% Hispanic of any race (2010); Density: 274.8 persons per square mile (2010); Average household size: 3.03 (2010); Median age: 35.5 (2010); Males per 100 females: 90.2 (2010); Marriage status: 33.0% never married, 12.2% now married, 54.8% widowed, 0.0% divorced (2005-2009 5-year est.); Foreign born: 0.0% (2005-2009 5-year est.); Ancestry (includes multiple ancestries): n/a (2005-2009 5-year est.).
Economy: Employment by occupation: 0.0% management, 0.0% professional, 0.0% services, 0.0% sales, 0.0% farming, 0.0% construction, 100.0% production (2005-2009 5-year est.).
Income: Per capita income: $11,694 (2010); Median household income: $25,000 (2010); Average household income: $39,375 (2010); Percent of households with income of $100,000 or more: 9.4% (2010); Poverty rate: 7.8% (2005-2009 5-year est.).
Education: Percent of population age 25 and over with: High school diploma (including GED) or higher: 40.7% (2010); Bachelor's degree or higher: 8.5% (2010); Master's degree or higher: 5.1% (2010).
Housing: Homeownership rate: 75.0% (2010); Median home value: $45,714 (2010); Median contract rent: n/a per month (2005-2009 5-year est.); Median year structure built: 1964 (2005-2009 5-year est.).
Transportation: Commute to work: 100.0% car, 0.0% public transportation, 0.0% walk, 0.0% work from home (2005-2009 5-year est.); Travel time to work: 0.0% less than 15 minutes, 100.0% 15 to 30 minutes, 0.0% 30 to 45 minutes, 0.0% 45 to 60 minutes, 0.0% 60 minutes or more (2005-2009 5-year est.)

SEBASTIAN (CDP).
Covers a land area of 1.667 square miles and a water area of 0 square miles. Located at 26.34° N. Lat; 97.79° W. Long. Elevation is 39 feet.
Population: 1,624 (1990); 1,864 (2000); 2,263 (2010); 2,441 (2015 projected); Race: 72.9% White, 0.5% Black, 0.0% Asian, 26.6% Other, 92.1% Hispanic of any race (2010); Density: 1,357.9 persons per square mile (2010); Average household size: 3.36 (2010); Median age: 30.8 (2010); Males per 100 females: 97.5 (2010); Marriage status: 33.8% never married, 56.7% now married, 2.2% widowed, 7.4% divorced (2005-2009 5-year est.); Foreign born: 15.9% (2005-2009 5-year est.); Ancestry (includes multiple ancestries): n/a (2005-2009 5-year est.).
Economy: Employment by occupation: 6.1% management, 13.1% professional, 36.8% services, 15.7% sales, 0.0% farming, 0.0% construction, 28.3% production (2005-2009 5-year est.).
Income: Per capita income: $12,352 (2010); Median household income: $29,045 (2010); Average household income: $41,813 (2010); Percent of households with income of $100,000 or more: 8.0% (2010); Poverty rate: 39.2% (2005-2009 5-year est.).
Education: Percent of population age 25 and over with: High school diploma (including GED) or higher: 48.0% (2010); Bachelor's degree or higher: 4.9% (2010); Master's degree or higher: 2.9% (2010).
Housing: Homeownership rate: 77.9% (2010); Median home value: $45,193 (2010); Median contract rent: $263 per month (2005-2009 5-year est.); Median year structure built: 1981 (2005-2009 5-year est.).
Transportation: Commute to work: 100.0% car, 0.0% public transportation, 0.0% walk, 0.0% work from home (2005-2009 5-year est.); Travel time to work: 20.6% less than 15 minutes, 79.4% 15 to 30 minutes, 0.0% 30 to 45 minutes, 0.0% 45 to 60 minutes, 0.0% 60 minutes or more (2005-2009 5-year est.)

WILLAMAR (CDP).
Covers a land area of 2.428 square miles and a water area of 0 square miles. Located at 26.41° N. Lat; 97.61° W. Long. Elevation is 20 feet.

Population: 7 (1990); 15 (2000); 18 (2010); 19 (2015 projected); Race: 66.7% White, 0.0% Black, 0.0% Asian, 33.3% Other, 88.9% Hispanic of any race (2010); Density: 7.4 persons per square mile (2010); Average household size: 3.00 (2010); Median age: 32.5 (2010); Males per 100 females: 260.0 (2010); Marriage status: n/a never married, n/a now married, n/a widowed, n/a divorced (2005-2009 5-year est.); Foreign born: n/a (2005-2009 5-year est.); Ancestry (includes multiple ancestries): n/a (2005-2009 5-year est.).

Economy: Employment by occupation: n/a management, n/a professional, n/a services, n/a sales, n/a farming, n/a construction, n/a production (2005-2009 5-year est.).

Income: Per capita income: $15,265 (2010); Median household income: $35,000 (2010); Average household income: $44,167 (2010); Percent of households with income of $100,000 or more: 16.7% (2010); Poverty rate: n/a (2005-2009 5-year est.).

Education: Percent of population age 25 and over with: High school diploma (including GED) or higher: 66.7% (2010); Bachelor's degree or higher: 25.0% (2010); Master's degree or higher: 8.3% (2010).

Housing: Homeownership rate: 66.7% (2010); Median home value: $33,333 (2010); Median contract rent: n/a per month (2005-2009 5-year est.); Median year structure built: n/a (2005-2009 5-year est.).

Transportation: Commute to work: n/a car, n/a public transportation, n/a walk, n/a work from home (2005-2009 5-year est.); Travel time to work: n/a less than 15 minutes, n/a 15 to 30 minutes, n/a 30 to 45 minutes, n/a 45 to 60 minutes, n/a 60 minutes or more (2005-2009 5-year est.)

ZAPATA RANCH (CDP). Covers a land area of 1.407 square miles and a water area of 0 square miles. Located at 26.36° N. Lat; 97.82° W. Long. Elevation is 39 feet.

Population: 68 (1990); 88 (2000); 105 (2010); 113 (2015 projected); Race: 71.4% White, 0.0% Black, 0.0% Asian, 28.6% Other, 93.3% Hispanic of any race (2010); Density: 74.6 persons per square mile (2010); Average household size: 3.50 (2010); Median age: 28.9 (2010); Males per 100 females: 98.1 (2010); Marriage status: n/a never married, n/a now married, n/a widowed, n/a divorced (2005-2009 5-year est.); Foreign born: n/a (2005-2009 5-year est.); Ancestry (includes multiple ancestries): n/a (2005-2009 5-year est.).

Economy: Employment by occupation: n/a management, n/a professional, n/a services, n/a sales, n/a farming, n/a construction, n/a production (2005-2009 5-year est.).

Income: Per capita income: $12,644 (2010); Median household income: $35,000 (2010); Average household income: $44,500 (2010); Percent of households with income of $100,000 or more: 10.0% (2010); Poverty rate: n/a (2005-2009 5-year est.).

Education: Percent of population age 25 and over with: High school diploma (including GED) or higher: 48.3% (2010); Bachelor's degree or higher: 0.0% (2010); Master's degree or higher: 0.0% (2010).

Housing: Homeownership rate: 80.0% (2010); Median home value: $46,000 (2010); Median contract rent: n/a per month (2005-2009 5-year est.); Median year structure built: n/a (2005-2009 5-year est.).

Transportation: Commute to work: n/a car, n/a public transportation, n/a walk, n/a work from home (2005-2009 5-year est.); Travel time to work: n/a less than 15 minutes, n/a 15 to 30 minutes, n/a 30 to 45 minutes, n/a 45 to 60 minutes, n/a 60 minutes or more (2005-2009 5-year est.)

Williamson County

Located in central Texas; drained by the San Gabriel River and its forks. Covers a land area of 1,122.77 square miles, a water area of 11.97 square miles, and is located in the Central Time Zone at 30.59° N. Lat., 97.67° W. Long. The county was founded in 1848. County seat is Georgetown.

Williamson County is part of the Austin-Round Rock-San Marcos, TX Metropolitan Statistical Area. The entire metro area includes: Bastrop County, TX; Caldwell County, TX; Hays County, TX; Travis County, TX; Williamson County, TX

Weather Station: Georgetown Lake											Elevation: 839 feet	
	Jan	Feb	Mar	Apr	May	Jun	Jul	Aug	Sep	Oct	Nov	Dec
High	60	64	71	78	85	91	95	96	90	81	70	60
Low	36	40	48	54	64	69	72	72	66	57	47	38
Precip	2.1	2.5	3.1	2.7	4.5	4.3	2.0	2.3	3.3	4.4	3.2	2.6
Snow	0.0	0.0	0.0	0.0	0.0	0.0	0.0	0.0	0.0	0.0	0.0	tr

High and Low temperatures in degrees Fahrenheit; Precipitation and Snow in inches

Weather Station: Granger Dam											Elevation: 564 feet	
	Jan	Feb	Mar	Apr	May	Jun	Jul	Aug	Sep	Oct	Nov	Dec
High	60	64	70	78	85	91	95	96	90	80	70	60
Low	37	41	48	56	64	70	72	72	67	57	48	39
Precip	2.2	2.2	2.7	2.0	5.0	4.2	1.6	2.0	3.0	3.7	2.7	2.9
Snow	0.0	0.0	0.0	0.0	0.0	0.0	0.0	0.0	0.0	0.0	0.0	tr

High and Low temperatures in degrees Fahrenheit; Precipitation and Snow in inches

Population: 139,541 (1990); 249,967 (2000); 417,208 (2010); 497,820 (2015 projected); Race: 76.9% White, 6.3% Black, 4.2% Asian, 12.5% Other, 21.7% Hispanic of any race (2010); Density: 371.6 persons per square mile (2010); Average household size: 2.90 (2010); Median age: 33.3 (2010); Males per 100 females: 99.9 (2010).

Religion: Five largest groups: 12.4% Catholic Church, 10.2% Southern Baptist Convention, 5.7% The United Methodist Church, 2.0% Independent, Charismatic Churches, 1.8% Evangelical Lutheran Church in America (2000).

Economy: Unemployment rate: 7.8% (June 2011); Total civilian labor force: 216,393 (June 2011); Leading industries: 18.3% retail trade; 12.1% wholesale trade; 11.6% accommodation & food services (2009); Farms: 2,728 totaling 541,618 acres (2007); Companies that employ 500 or more persons: 15 (2009); Companies that employ 100 to 499 persons: 131 (2009); Companies that employ less than 100 persons: 7,700 (2009); Black-owned businesses: 1,345 (2007); Hispanic-owned businesses: 3,645 (2007); Asian-owned businesses: 2,013 (2007); Women-owned businesses: 10,316 (2007); Retail sales per capita: $12,120 (2010). Single-family building permits issued: 1,889 (2010); Multi-family building permits issued: 48 (2010).

Income: Per capita income: $28,530 (2010); Median household income: $70,062 (2010); Average household income: $83,310 (2010); Percent of households with income of $100,000 or more: 27.5% (2010); Poverty rate: 5.5% (2009); Bankruptcy rate: 2.42% (2010).

Taxes: Total county taxes per capita: $341 (2007); County property taxes per capita: $325 (2007).

Education: Percent of population age 25 and over with: High school diploma (including GED) or higher: 90.2% (2010); Bachelor's degree or higher: 35.0% (2010); Master's degree or higher: 10.3% (2010).

Housing: Homeownership rate: 71.8% (2010); Median home value: $173,254 (2010); Median contract rent: $774 per month (2005-2009 5-year est.); Median year structure built: 1995 (2005-2009 5-year est.)

Health: Birth rate: 163.4 per 10,000 population (2009); Death rate: 47.0 per 10,000 population (2009); Age-adjusted cancer mortality rate: 137.2 deaths per 100,000 population (2007); Number of physicians: 15.0 per 10,000 population (2008); Hospital beds: 7.0 per 10,000 population (2007); Hospital admissions: 370.7 per 10,000 population (2007).

Elections: 2008 Presidential election results: 42.5% Obama, 55.5% McCain, 0.1% Nader

Additional Information Contacts

Williamson County Government	(512) 930-4300
http://www.williamson-county.org	
Cedar Park Chamber of Commerce	(512) 260-7800
http://www.cedarparkchamber.org	
City of Cedar Park	(512) 401-5000
http://www.cedarparktx.us	
City of Georgetown	(512) 930-3652
http://georgetown.org	
City of Leander	(512) 528-2743
http://www.leandertx.org	
City of Round Rock	(512) 218-5400
http://www.roundrocktexas.gov	
City of Taylor	(512) 352-3675
http://www.ci.taylor.tx.us	
Georgetown Chamber of Commerce	(512) 930-3535
http://www.georgetownchamber.org	
Greater Florence Chamber of Commerce	(512) 635-5170
http://www.florencechamberofcommerce.org	
Leander Chamber of Commerce	(512) 259-1907
http://www.leandercc.org	
Liberty Hill Chamber of Commerce	(512) 548-6343
http://www.libertyhillchamber.org	
Round Rock Chamber of Commerce	(512) 255-5805
http://roundrockchamber.org	
Taylor Chamber of Commerce	(512) 352-6364
http://www.taylorchamber.org	

Williamson County Communities

ANDERSON MILL (CDP). Covers a land area of 1.411 square miles and a water area of 0 square miles. Located at 30.45° N. Lat; 97.80° W. Long. Elevation is 958 feet.
Population: 9,362 (1990); 8,953 (2000); 7,223 (2010); 7,336 (2015 projected); Race: 78.6% White, 4.8% Black, 6.2% Asian, 10.4% Other, 21.4% Hispanic of any race (2010); Density: 5,117.6 persons per square mile (2010); Average household size: 2.72 (2010); Median age: 34.4 (2010); Males per 100 females: 98.4 (2010); Marriage status: n/a never married, n/a now married, n/a widowed, n/a divorced (2005-2009 5-year est.); Foreign born: n/a (2005-2009 5-year est.); Ancestry (includes multiple ancestries): n/a (2005-2009 5-year est.).
Economy: Employment by occupation: n/a management, n/a professional, n/a services, n/a sales, n/a farming, n/a construction, n/a production (2005-2009 5-year est.).
Income: Per capita income: $26,685 (2010); Median household income: $61,531 (2010); Average household income: $72,511 (2010); Percent of households with income of $100,000 or more: 21.7% (2010); Poverty rate: n/a (2005-2009 5-year est.).
Education: Percent of population age 25 and over with: High school diploma (including GED) or higher: 93.8% (2010); Bachelor's degree or higher: 38.7% (2010); Master's degree or higher: 11.4% (2010).
Housing: Homeownership rate: 51.6% (2010); Median home value: $151,136 (2010); Median contract rent: n/a per month (2005-2009 5-year est.); Median year structure built: n/a (2005-2009 5-year est.).
Transportation: Commute to work: n/a car, n/a public transportation, n/a walk, n/a work from home (2005-2009 5-year est.); Travel time to work: n/a less than 15 minutes, n/a 15 to 30 minutes, n/a 30 to 45 minutes, n/a 45 to 60 minutes, n/a 60 minutes or more (2005-2009 5-year est.)

BARTLETT (city). Covers a land area of 1.220 square miles and a water area of 0 square miles. Located at 30.79° N. Lat; 97.43° W. Long. Elevation is 597 feet.
Population: 1,498 (1990); 1,675 (2000); 1,875 (2010); 2,021 (2015 projected); Race: 46.4% White, 25.7% Black, 0.1% Asian, 27.8% Other, 34.0% Hispanic of any race (2010); Density: 1,537.3 persons per square mile (2010); Average household size: 2.80 (2010); Median age: 32.7 (2010); Males per 100 females: 155.4 (2010); Marriage status: 33.1% never married, 50.7% now married, 7.8% widowed, 8.4% divorced (2005-2009 5-year est.); Foreign born: 11.0% (2005-2009 5-year est.); Ancestry (includes multiple ancestries): 8.9% German, 7.8% Irish, 7.5% English, 3.4% Polish, 2.4% American (2005-2009 5-year est.).
Economy: Single-family building permits issued: 2 (2010); Multi-family building permits issued: 0 (2010); Employment by occupation: 6.6% management, 15.2% professional, 24.4% services, 19.6% sales, 1.3% farming, 13.2% construction, 19.7% production (2005-2009 5-year est.).
Income: Per capita income: $12,292 (2010); Median household income: $30,882 (2010); Average household income: $43,676 (2010); Percent of households with income of $100,000 or more: 8.3% (2010); Poverty rate: 6.3% (2005-2009 5-year est.).
Taxes: Total city taxes per capita: $5 (2007); City property taxes per capita: $0 (2007).
Education: Percent of population age 25 and over with: High school diploma (including GED) or higher: 62.7% (2010); Bachelor's degree or higher: 11.2% (2010); Master's degree or higher: 3.4% (2010).
School District(s)
Bartlett ISD (PK-12)
    2009-10 Enrollment: 388 . . . . (254) 527-4247
Housing: Homeownership rate: 64.5% (2010); Median home value: $75,323 (2010); Median contract rent: $275 per month (2005-2009 5-year est.); Median year structure built: 1958 (2005-2009 5-year est.).
Newspapers: Tribune-Progress (Local news; Circulation 1,600)
Transportation: Commute to work: 97.6% car, 0.0% public transportation, 1.0% walk, 0.4% work from home (2005-2009 5-year est.); Travel time to work: 24.2% less than 15 minutes, 21.4% 15 to 30 minutes, 22.9% 30 to 45 minutes, 26.6% 45 to 60 minutes, 5.0% 60 minutes or more (2005-2009 5-year est.)

BRUSHY CREEK (CDP). Covers a land area of 8.710 square miles and a water area of 0 square miles. Located at 30.51° N. Lat; 97.73° W. Long. Elevation is 827 feet.
History: Brushy Creek gets its name from the fact that it is located just west of Round Rock along the shore of Brushy Creek.

Population: 5,726 (1990); 15,371 (2000); 25,963 (2010); 31,633 (2015 projected); Race: 75.2% White, 4.6% Black, 12.7% Asian, 7.5% Other, 12.8% Hispanic of any race (2010); Density: 2,980.9 persons per square mile (2010); Average household size: 3.15 (2010); Median age: 33.1 (2010); Males per 100 females: 97.3 (2010); Marriage status: 24.6% never married, 66.9% now married, 2.8% widowed, 5.8% divorced (2005-2009 5-year est.); Foreign born: 9.2% (2005-2009 5-year est.); Ancestry (includes multiple ancestries): 19.1% German, 11.9% English, 11.0% Irish, 4.8% American, 4.3% Scotch-Irish (2005-2009 5-year est.).
Economy: Employment by occupation: 22.0% management, 33.3% professional, 6.6% services, 28.6% sales, 0.1% farming, 5.4% construction, 4.1% production (2005-2009 5-year est.).
Income: Per capita income: $34,329 (2010); Median household income: $95,197 (2010); Average household income: $108,384 (2010); Percent of households with income of $100,000 or more: 45.9% (2010); Poverty rate: 1.5% (2005-2009 5-year est.).
Education: Percent of population age 25 and over with: High school diploma (including GED) or higher: 96.6% (2010); Bachelor's degree or higher: 56.3% (2010); Master's degree or higher: 18.8% (2010).
Housing: Homeownership rate: 82.8% (2010); Median home value: $230,168 (2010); Median contract rent: $1,196 per month (2005-2009 5-year est.); Median year structure built: 1995 (2005-2009 5-year est.).
Transportation: Commute to work: 92.1% car, 0.6% public transportation, 0.3% walk, 5.5% work from home (2005-2009 5-year est.); Travel time to work: 18.2% less than 15 minutes, 43.3% 15 to 30 minutes, 26.0% 30 to 45 minutes, 6.8% 45 to 60 minutes, 5.7% 60 minutes or more (2005-2009 5-year est.)

CEDAR PARK (city). Covers a land area of 16.970 square miles and a water area of 0.145 square miles. Located at 30.50° N. Lat; 97.83° W. Long. Elevation is 906 feet.
Population: 9,798 (1990); 26,049 (2000); 52,370 (2010); 64,198 (2015 projected); Race: 80.7% White, 5.2% Black, 3.9% Asian, 10.2% Other, 18.8% Hispanic of any race (2010); Density: 3,086.0 persons per square mile (2010); Average household size: 3.06 (2010); Median age: 32.1 (2010); Males per 100 females: 99.0 (2010); Marriage status: 26.5% never married, 56.5% now married, 3.1% widowed, 13.8% divorced (2005-2009 5-year est.); Foreign born: 8.0% (2005-2009 5-year est.); Ancestry (includes multiple ancestries): 20.5% German, 13.3% Irish, 11.2% English, 7.4% American, 4.7% Italian (2005-2009 5-year est.).
Economy: Unemployment rate: 6.6% (June 2011); Total civilian labor force: 33,476 (June 2011); Single-family building permits issued: 595 (2010); Multi-family building permits issued: 48 (2010); Employment by occupation: 22.2% management, 23.5% professional, 11.2% services, 30.2% sales, 0.0% farming, 6.0% construction, 7.0% production (2005-2009 5-year est.).
Income: Per capita income: $29,334 (2010); Median household income: $80,297 (2010); Average household income: $89,903 (2010); Percent of households with income of $100,000 or more: 32.5% (2010); Poverty rate: 5.7% (2005-2009 5-year est.).
Taxes: Total city taxes per capita: $676 (2007); City property taxes per capita: $247 (2007).
Education: Percent of population age 25 and over with: High school diploma (including GED) or higher: 94.5% (2010); Bachelor's degree or higher: 39.5% (2010); Master's degree or higher: 9.9% (2010).
School District(s)
Leander ISD (PK-12)
    2009-10 Enrollment: 30,454 . . . . (512) 434-5000
Housing: Homeownership rate: 82.0% (2010); Median home value: $169,485 (2010); Median contract rent: $798 per month (2005-2009 5-year est.); Median year structure built: 1998 (2005-2009 5-year est.).
Safety: Violent crime rate: 10.2 per 10,000 population; Property crime rate: 143.4 per 10,000 population (2009).
Newspapers: Hill Country News (Community news; Circulation 15,000); Northwest Hill Country News (Community news; Circulation 3,100)
Transportation: Commute to work: 90.7% car, 0.4% public transportation, 0.9% walk, 6.1% work from home (2005-2009 5-year est.); Travel time to work: 18.7% less than 15 minutes, 35.0% 15 to 30 minutes, 28.3% 30 to 45 minutes, 11.7% 45 to 60 minutes, 6.3% 60 minutes or more (2005-2009 5-year est.)
Additional Information Contacts
Cedar Park Chamber of Commerce . . . . (512) 260-7800
    http://www.cedarparkchamber.org
City of Cedar Park . . . . (512) 401-5000
    http://www.cedarparktx.us

COUPLAND (unincorporated postal area, zip code 78615). Covers a land area of 53.069 square miles and a water area of 0.058 square miles. Located at 30.46° N. Lat; 97.39° W. Long. Elevation is 512 feet.
Population: 1,131 (2000); Race: 96.7% White, 0.0% Black, 0.0% Asian, 3.3% Other, 15.8% Hispanic of any race (2000); Density: 21.3 persons per square mile (2000); Age: 35.9% under 18, 11.0% over 64 (2000); Marriage status: 15.6% never married, 66.6% now married, 10.3% widowed, 7.6% divorced (2000); Foreign born: 6.3% (2000); Ancestry (includes multiple ancestries): 34.4% German, 14.9% Irish, 8.0% English, 6.8% Swedish (2000).
Economy: Employment by occupation: 13.6% management, 18.9% professional, 7.4% services, 30.2% sales, 0.9% farming, 17.8% construction, 11.3% production (2000).
Income: Per capita income: $20,242 (2000); Median household income: $41,574 (2000); Poverty rate: 179.1% (2000).
Education: Percent of population age 25 and over with: High school diploma (including GED) or higher: 75.2% (2000); Bachelor's degree or higher: 15.1% (2000).
School District(s)
Coupland ISD (KG-08)
    2009-10 Enrollment: 136 . . . . (512) 856-2422
Housing: Homeownership rate: 87.7% (2000); Median home value: $95,700 (2000); Median contract rent: $397 per month (2000); Median year structure built: 1981 (2000).
Transportation: Commute to work: 94.8% car, 0.0% public transportation, 0.0% walk, 4.7% work from home (2000); Travel time to work: 9.0% less than 15 minutes, 30.5% 15 to 30 minutes, 36.0% 30 to 45 minutes, 18.3% 45 to 60 minutes, 6.2% 60 minutes or more (2000)

FLORENCE (city). Covers a land area of 0.811 square miles and a water area of 0 square miles. Located at 30.84° N. Lat; 97.79° W. Long. Elevation is 994 feet.
Population: 829 (1990); 1,054 (2000); 1,111 (2010); 1,235 (2015 projected); Race: 85.5% White, 1.5% Black, 0.3% Asian, 12.7% Other, 18.3% Hispanic of any race (2010); Density: 1,370.5 persons per square mile (2010); Average household size: 2.96 (2010); Median age: 33.4 (2010); Males per 100 females: 101.6 (2010); Marriage status: 25.5% never married, 54.3% now married, 6.0% widowed, 14.2% divorced (2005-2009 5-year est.); Foreign born: 18.6% (2005-2009 5-year est.); Ancestry (includes multiple ancestries): 15.6% German, 13.4% Irish, 6.9% American, 6.1% English, 3.4% Scotch-Irish (2005-2009 5-year est.).
Economy: Single-family building permits issued: 0 (2010); Multi-family building permits issued: 0 (2010); Employment by occupation: 3.8% management, 13.1% professional, 27.5% services, 14.4% sales, 0.0% farming, 30.6% construction, 10.6% production (2005-2009 5-year est.).
Income: Per capita income: $24,167 (2010); Median household income: $55,093 (2010); Average household income: $70,673 (2010); Percent of households with income of $100,000 or more: 19.2% (2010); Poverty rate: 13.2% (2005-2009 5-year est.).
Taxes: Total city taxes per capita: $218 (2007); City property taxes per capita: $114 (2007).
Education: Percent of population age 25 and over with: High school diploma (including GED) or higher: 79.5% (2010); Bachelor's degree or higher: 12.8% (2010); Master's degree or higher: 2.9% (2010).
School District(s)
Florence ISD (PK-12)
    2009-10 Enrollment: 1,020 . . . . (254) 793-2850
Housing: Homeownership rate: 71.5% (2010); Median home value: $107,143 (2010); Median contract rent: $630 per month (2005-2009 5-year est.); Median year structure built: 1967 (2005-2009 5-year est.).
Safety: Violent crime rate: 8.8 per 10,000 population; Property crime rate: 61.4 per 10,000 population (2009).
Transportation: Commute to work: 90.9% car, 0.0% public transportation, 3.0% walk, 4.0% work from home (2005-2009 5-year est.); Travel time to work: 33.4% less than 15 minutes, 36.3% 15 to 30 minutes, 11.6% 30 to 45 minutes, 8.2% 45 to 60 minutes, 10.5% 60 minutes or more (2005-2009 5-year est.)
Additional Information Contacts
Greater Florence Chamber of Commerce . . . . (512) 635-5170
    http://www.florencechamberofcommerce.org

GEORGETOWN (city). County seat. Covers a land area of 22.830 square miles and a water area of 2.097 square miles. Located at 30.65° N. Lat; 97.68° W. Long. Elevation is 755 feet.

History: Named for George Washington Glasscock (1810-1879), who donated land for the county seat. Southwestern University was established in Georgetown in 1873 by the Methodist Episcopal Church, South. The University was formed from the earlier educational institutions of Rutersville College, McKenzie College, Wesleyan College, and Soule University, founded in the 1840's and 1850's.
Population: 16,988 (1990); 28,339 (2000); 44,984 (2010); 53,811 (2015 projected); Race: 82.2% White, 3.5% Black, 1.1% Asian, 13.2% Other, 20.1% Hispanic of any race (2010); Density: 1,970.4 persons per square mile (2010); Average household size: 2.63 (2010); Median age: 37.8 (2010); Males per 100 females: 97.4 (2010); Marriage status: 21.6% never married, 60.5% now married, 7.5% widowed, 10.3% divorced (2005-2009 5-year est.); Foreign born: 10.2% (2005-2009 5-year est.); Ancestry (includes multiple ancestries): 21.8% German, 15.9% English, 10.7% Irish, 4.9% American, 3.9% Scottish (2005-2009 5-year est.).
Economy: Unemployment rate: 8.1% (June 2011); Total civilian labor force: 22,970 (June 2011); Single-family building permits issued: 542 (2010); Multi-family building permits issued: 0 (2010); Employment by occupation: 16.4% management, 22.5% professional, 15.8% services, 26.0% sales, 0.0% farming, 9.3% construction, 9.8% production (2005-2009 5-year est.).
Income: Per capita income: $29,015 (2010); Median household income: $66,618 (2010); Average household income: $79,534 (2010); Percent of households with income of $100,000 or more: 26.8% (2010); Poverty rate: 6.7% (2005-2009 5-year est.).
Taxes: Total city taxes per capita: $562 (2007); City property taxes per capita: $210 (2007).
Education: Percent of population age 25 and over with: High school diploma (including GED) or higher: 87.9% (2010); Bachelor's degree or higher: 37.7% (2010); Master's degree or higher: 12.6% (2010).
School District(s)
Center Point ISD (PK-12)
    2009-10 Enrollment: 624 . . . . (830) 634-2171
Florence ISD (PK-12)
    2009-10 Enrollment: 1,020 . . . . (254) 793-2850
Georgetown ISD (PK-12)
    2009-10 Enrollment: 10,443 . . . . (512) 943-5015
Hutto ISD (PK-12)
    2009-10 Enrollment: 5,137 . . . . (512) 759-3771
Leander ISD (PK-12)
    2009-10 Enrollment: 30,454 . . . . (512) 434-5000
Liberty Hill ISD (PK-12)
    2009-10 Enrollment: 2,568 . . . . (512) 260-5580
Orenda Charter School (01-12)
    2009-10 Enrollment: 185 . . . . (512) 869-3020
Round Rock ISD (PK-12)
    2009-10 Enrollment: 43,008 . . . . (512) 464-5000
Taylor ISD (PK-12)
    2009-10 Enrollment: 3,168 . . . . (512) 365-1391
Thrall ISD (PK-12)
    2009-10 Enrollment: 644 . . . . (512) 898-0062
University of Texas University Charter School (KG-12)
    2009-10 Enrollment: 907 . . . . (512) 471-5652
Four-year College(s)
Southwestern University (Private, Not-for-profit, United Methodist)
    Fall 2009 Enrollment: 1,301 . . . . (512) 863-6511
    2010-11 Tuition: In-state $31,630; Out-of-state $31,630
Housing: Homeownership rate: 69.3% (2010); Median home value: $205,812 (2010); Median contract rent: $724 per month (2005-2009 5-year est.); Median year structure built: 1994 (2005-2009 5-year est.).
Hospitals: Georgetown Healthcare System (104 beds)
Safety: Violent crime rate: 10.1 per 10,000 population; Property crime rate: 153.2 per 10,000 population (2009).
Newspapers: Williamson County Sun (Local news; Circulation 16,000)
Transportation: Commute to work: 90.3% car, 0.0% public transportation, 2.8% walk, 5.4% work from home (2005-2009 5-year est.); Travel time to work: 36.9% less than 15 minutes, 27.0% 15 to 30 minutes, 18.6% 30 to 45 minutes, 10.9% 45 to 60 minutes, 6.6% 60 minutes or more (2005-2009 5-year est.)
Airports: Georgetown Municipal (general aviation)
Additional Information Contacts
City of Georgetown . . . . (512) 930-3652
    http://georgetown.org
Georgetown Chamber of Commerce . . . . (512) 930-3535
    http://www.georgetownchamber.org

GRANGER (city).
Covers a land area of 0.666 square miles and a water area of 0 square miles. Located at 30.71° N. Lat; 97.44° W. Long. Elevation is 577 feet.
Population: 1,190 (1990); 1,299 (2000); 1,321 (2010); 1,443 (2015 projected); Race: 81.2% White, 6.6% Black, 0.5% Asian, 11.7% Other, 33.2% Hispanic of any race (2010); Density: 1,984.6 persons per square mile (2010); Average household size: 2.57 (2010); Median age: 36.5 (2010); Males per 100 females: 90.6 (2010); Marriage status: 24.6% never married, 51.2% now married, 13.6% widowed, 10.6% divorced (2005-2009 5-year est.); Foreign born: 3.9% (2005-2009 5-year est.); Ancestry (includes multiple ancestries): 19.9% Czech, 18.5% German, 12.5% Irish, 6.5% English, 1.8% American (2005-2009 5-year est.).
Economy: Single-family building permits issued: 1 (2010); Multi-family building permits issued: 0 (2010); Employment by occupation: 13.8% management, 11.2% professional, 34.1% services, 11.2% sales, 0.0% farming, 11.7% construction, 18.0% production (2005-2009 5-year est.).
Income: Per capita income: $16,958 (2010); Median household income: $37,320 (2010); Average household income: $44,541 (2010); Percent of households with income of $100,000 or more: 7.9% (2010); Poverty rate: 21.4% (2005-2009 5-year est.).
Taxes: Total city taxes per capita: $10 (2007); City property taxes per capita: $0 (2007).
Education: Percent of population age 25 and over with: High school diploma (including GED) or higher: 62.0% (2010); Bachelor's degree or higher: 8.3% (2010); Master's degree or higher: 2.7% (2010).

School District(s)
Granger ISD (PK-12)
   2009-10 Enrollment: 427 . . . . (512) 859-2613
Housing: Homeownership rate: 65.9% (2010); Median home value: $69,839 (2010); Median contract rent: $239 per month (2005-2009 5-year est.); Median year structure built: 1951 (2005-2009 5-year est.).
Safety: Violent crime rate: 36.5 per 10,000 population; Property crime rate: 167.8 per 10,000 population (2009).
Transportation: Commute to work: 86.9% car, 0.0% public transportation, 6.3% walk, 6.3% work from home (2005-2009 5-year est.); Travel time to work: 25.4% less than 15 minutes, 27.8% 15 to 30 minutes, 25.4% 30 to 45 minutes, 14.4% 45 to 60 minutes, 6.9% 60 minutes or more (2005-2009 5-year est.)

HUTTO (city).
Covers a land area of 0.963 square miles and a water area of 0 square miles. Located at 30.54° N. Lat; 97.54° W. Long. Elevation is 663 feet.
Population: 689 (1990); 1,250 (2000); 10,434 (2010); 12,305 (2015 projected); Race: 82.2% White, 3.6% Black, 0.1% Asian, 14.1% Other, 26.2% Hispanic of any race (2010); Density: 10,833.3 persons per square mile (2010); Average household size: 3.05 (2010); Median age: 31.4 (2010); Males per 100 females: 102.4 (2010); Marriage status: 26.0% never married, 58.7% now married, 3.4% widowed, 12.0% divorced (2005-2009 5-year est.); Foreign born: 5.7% (2005-2009 5-year est.); Ancestry (includes multiple ancestries): 18.4% German, 9.2% English, 9.1% Irish, 7.5% American, 5.2% Italian (2005-2009 5-year est.).
Economy: Single-family building permits issued: 228 (2010); Multi-family building permits issued: 0 (2010); Employment by occupation: 12.6% management, 18.0% professional, 16.6% services, 36.0% sales, 0.1% farming, 7.7% construction, 9.0% production (2005-2009 5-year est.).
Income: Per capita income: $22,940 (2010); Median household income: $60,241 (2010); Average household income: $69,912 (2010); Percent of households with income of $100,000 or more: 18.7% (2010); Poverty rate: 7.1% (2005-2009 5-year est.).
Taxes: Total city taxes per capita: $338 (2007); City property taxes per capita: $196 (2007).
Education: Percent of population age 25 and over with: High school diploma (including GED) or higher: 83.8% (2010); Bachelor's degree or higher: 15.8% (2010); Master's degree or higher: 2.5% (2010).

School District(s)
Hutto ISD (PK-12)
   2009-10 Enrollment: 5,137 . . . . (512) 759-3771
Housing: Homeownership rate: 77.0% (2010); Median home value: $132,415 (2010); Median contract rent: $1,021 per month (2005-2009 5-year est.); Median year structure built: 2003 (2005-2009 5-year est.).
Safety: Violent crime rate: 16.6 per 10,000 population; Property crime rate: 78.4 per 10,000 population (2009).
Transportation: Commute to work: 93.1% car, 0.9% public transportation, 1.2% walk, 3.6% work from home (2005-2009 5-year est.); Travel time to

work: 11.5% less than 15 minutes, 40.7% 15 to 30 minutes, 32.8% 30 to 45 minutes, 9.9% 45 to 60 minutes, 5.2% 60 minutes or more (2005-2009 5-year est.)

JARRELL (city).
Covers a land area of 48.238 square miles and a water area of <.001 square miles. Located at 30.80° N. Lat; 97.59° W. Long. Elevation is 869 feet.
History: Jarrell incorporated as a city in 2001. Many of the early residents of Jarrell were from Czechoslovakia.
Population: 0 (1990); 2,173 (2000); 0 (2010); 0 (2015 projected); Race: ***.*% White, ***.*% Black, ***.*% Asian, ***.*% Other, ***.*% Hispanic of any race (2010); Density: 0.0 persons per square mile (2010); Average household size: 0.00 (2010); Median age: 0.0 (2010); Males per 100 females: ***.* (2010); Marriage status: 19.0% never married, 69.7% now married, 4.6% widowed, 6.7% divorced (2005-2009 5-year est.); Foreign born: 9.5% (2005-2009 5-year est.); Ancestry (includes multiple ancestries): 14.7% German, 14.3% American, 8.4% Czech, 6.3% English (2005-2009 5-year est.).
Economy: Employment by occupation: 15.2% management, 10.7% professional, 15.0% services, 22.2% sales, 1.1% farming, 21.3% construction, 14.6% production (2005-2009 5-year est.).
Income: Per capita income: $17,305 (2010); Median household income: $39,810 (2010); Average household income: $0 (2010); Percent of households with income of $100,000 or more: 0.0% (2010); Poverty rate: 179.1% (2005-2009 5-year est.).
Education: Percent of population age 25 and over with: High school diploma (including GED) or higher: 0.0% (2010); Bachelor's degree or higher: 0.0% (2010); Master's degree or higher: 0.0% (2010).

School District(s)
Jarrell ISD (PK-12)
   2009-10 Enrollment: 917 . . . . (512) 746-2124
Housing: Homeownership rate: 86.6% (2010); Median home value: $84,100 (2010); Median contract rent: $353 per month (2005-2009 5-year est.); Median year structure built: 1982 (2005-2009 5-year est.).
Safety: Violent crime rate: 6.8 per 10,000 population; Property crime rate: 253.1 per 10,000 population (2009).
Transportation: Commute to work: 92.6% car, 0.0% public transportation, 3.0% walk, 4.4% work from home (2005-2009 5-year est.); Travel time to work: 20.5% less than 15 minutes, 37.0% 15 to 30 minutes, 24.7% 30 to 45 minutes, 10.1% 45 to 60 minutes, 7.7% 60 minutes or more (2005-2009 5-year est.)

JOLLYVILLE (CDP).
Covers a land area of 5.897 square miles and a water area of 0 square miles. Located at 30.45° N. Lat; 97.76° W. Long. Elevation is 938 feet.
History: The area was first settled by Henry Rhodes after obtaining a land grant in 1841 of about 1,000 acres (4 sq. km.) from the Republic of Texas. The name, however, comes from a later settler, John Grey Jolly, who purchased 160 acres (0.65 sq. km.) in 1866.
Population: 9,595 (1990); 15,813 (2000); 15,590 (2010); 17,144 (2015 projected); Race: 72.9% White, 5.1% Black, 13.3% Asian, 8.7% Other, 15.3% Hispanic of any race (2010); Density: 2,643.9 persons per square mile (2010); Average household size: 2.63 (2010); Median age: 33.4 (2010); Males per 100 females: 101.3 (2010); Marriage status: 30.5% never married, 55.1% now married, 2.5% widowed, 11.9% divorced (2005-2009 5-year est.); Foreign born: 13.4% (2005-2009 5-year est.); Ancestry (includes multiple ancestries): 18.8% German, 13.1% English, 11.9% Irish, 5.1% American, 4.1% Scottish (2005-2009 5-year est.).
Economy: Employment by occupation: 20.8% management, 30.5% professional, 11.9% services, 27.3% sales, 0.0% farming, 4.5% construction, 4.9% production (2005-2009 5-year est.).
Income: Per capita income: $32,569 (2010); Median household income: $71,287 (2010); Average household income: $85,900 (2010); Percent of households with income of $100,000 or more: 29.1% (2010); Poverty rate: 7.3% (2005-2009 5-year est.).
Education: Percent of population age 25 and over with: High school diploma (including GED) or higher: 95.6% (2010); Bachelor's degree or higher: 45.7% (2010); Master's degree or higher: 14.8% (2010).
Housing: Homeownership rate: 53.9% (2010); Median home value: $185,182 (2010); Median contract rent: $779 per month (2005-2009 5-year est.); Median year structure built: 1988 (2005-2009 5-year est.).
Transportation: Commute to work: 90.6% car, 0.9% public transportation, 1.0% walk, 5.9% work from home (2005-2009 5-year est.); Travel time to work: 22.5% less than 15 minutes, 48.4% 15 to 30 minutes, 20.9% 30 to 45

minutes, 4.7% 45 to 60 minutes, 3.5% 60 minutes or more (2005-2009 5-year est.)

LEANDER (city). Covers a land area of 7.475 square miles and a water area of 0 square miles. Located at 30.56° N. Lat; 97.86° W. Long. Elevation is 978 feet.

Population: 3,661 (1990); 7,596 (2000); 15,760 (2010); 19,183 (2015 projected); Race: 78.3% White, 5.3% Black, 1.0% Asian, 15.3% Other, 24.5% Hispanic of any race (2010); Density: 2,108.4 persons per square mile (2010); Average household size: 3.10 (2010); Median age: 31.7 (2010); Males per 100 females: 100.7 (2010); Marriage status: 21.2% never married, 62.9% now married, 2.1% widowed, 13.8% divorced (2005-2009 5-year est.); Foreign born: 7.7% (2005-2009 5-year est.); Ancestry (includes multiple ancestries): 20.7% German, 13.0% Irish, 9.2% English, 6.3% American, 6.1% Scotch-Irish (2005-2009 5-year est.).
Economy: Unemployment rate: 6.4% (June 2011); Total civilian labor force: 13,114 (June 2011); Single-family building permits issued: 242 (2010); Multi-family building permits issued: 0 (2010); Employment by occupation: 18.8% management, 21.4% professional, 13.2% services, 27.7% sales, 0.0% farming, 9.4% construction, 9.6% production (2005-2009 5-year est.).
Income: Per capita income: $22,363 (2010); Median household income: $60,558 (2010); Average household income: $69,333 (2010); Percent of households with income of $100,000 or more: 16.5% (2010); Poverty rate: 4.8% (2005-2009 5-year est.).
Taxes: Total city taxes per capita: $393 (2007); City property taxes per capita: $231 (2007).
Education: Percent of population age 25 and over with: High school diploma (including GED) or higher: 88.2% (2010); Bachelor's degree or higher: 22.5% (2010); Master's degree or higher: 5.0% (2010).
School District(s)
Leander ISD (PK-12)
   2009-10 Enrollment: 30,454 . . . . (512) 434-5000
Housing: Homeownership rate: 84.3% (2010); Median home value: $135,311 (2010); Median contract rent: $1,005 per month (2005-2009 5-year est.); Median year structure built: 2001 (2005-2009 5-year est.).
Safety: Violent crime rate: 8.7 per 10,000 population; Property crime rate: 99.1 per 10,000 population (2009).
Transportation: Commute to work: 91.5% car, 2.3% public transportation, 0.4% walk, 5.2% work from home (2005-2009 5-year est.); Travel time to work: 14.3% less than 15 minutes, 25.4% 15 to 30 minutes, 34.1% 30 to 45 minutes, 15.9% 45 to 60 minutes, 10.2% 60 minutes or more (2005-2009 5-year est.)
Additional Information Contacts
City of Leander. . . . . (512) 528-2743
   http://www.leandertx.com
Leander Chamber of Commerce . . . . (512) 259-1907
   http://www.leandercc.org

LIBERTY HILL (city). Covers a land area of 1.907 square miles and a water area of 0.009 square miles. Located at 30.66° N. Lat; 97.91° W. Long. Elevation is 1,024 feet.

Population: 913 (1990); 1,409 (2000); 1,401 (2010); 1,711 (2015 projected); Race: 89.7% White, 0.4% Black, 0.5% Asian, 9.5% Other, 12.3% Hispanic of any race (2010); Density: 734.5 persons per square mile (2010); Average household size: 3.06 (2010); Median age: 34.4 (2010); Males per 100 females: 100.4 (2010); Marriage status: 27.8% never married, 56.0% now married, 4.5% widowed, 11.7% divorced (2005-2009 5-year est.); Foreign born: 18.3% (2005-2009 5-year est.); Ancestry (includes multiple ancestries): 19.4% German, 10.1% English, 8.2% American, 7.1% Irish, 3.9% Scotch-Irish (2005-2009 5-year est.).
Economy: Employment by occupation: 9.9% management, 12.2% professional, 35.4% services, 20.6% sales, 0.6% farming, 15.0% construction, 6.3% production (2005-2009 5-year est.).
Income: Per capita income: $27,749 (2010); Median household income: $68,382 (2010); Average household income: $85,695 (2010); Percent of households with income of $100,000 or more: 26.9% (2010); Poverty rate: 5.7% (2005-2009 5-year est.).
Taxes: Total city taxes per capita: $126 (2007); City property taxes per capita: $0 (2007).
Education: Percent of population age 25 and over with: High school diploma (including GED) or higher: 80.4% (2010); Bachelor's degree or higher: 18.0% (2010); Master's degree or higher: 2.7% (2010).

School District(s)
Liberty Hill ISD (PK-12)
   2009-10 Enrollment: 2,568 . . . . (512) 260-5580
University of Texas University Charter School (KG-12)
   2009-10 Enrollment: 907 . . . . (512) 471-5652
Housing: Homeownership rate: 81.0% (2010); Median home value: $152,273 (2010); Median contract rent: $658 per month (2005-2009 5-year est.); Median year structure built: 1983 (2005-2009 5-year est.).
Hospitals: Meridell Achievement Center (112 beds)
Transportation: Commute to work: 96.3% car, 0.0% public transportation, 0.0% walk, 3.7% work from home (2005-2009 5-year est.); Travel time to work: 19.2% less than 15 minutes, 36.0% 15 to 30 minutes, 10.8% 30 to 45 minutes, 13.4% 45 to 60 minutes, 20.6% 60 minutes or more (2005-2009 5-year est.)
Additional Information Contacts
Liberty Hill Chamber of Commerce . . . . (512) 548-6343
   http://www.libertyhillchamber.org

ROUND ROCK (city). Covers a land area of 26.137 square miles and a water area of 0.127 square miles. Located at 30.51° N. Lat; 97.67° W. Long. Elevation is 735 feet.

History: Named for a round rock by a local creek where travelers stopped to rest. It was at Round Rock that the infamous Texas outlaw, Sam Bass, was betrayed by a member of his gang and mortally wounded by Texas Rangers, thus ending years of bank robberies, train hold-ups and raids on ranches and settlements.
Population: 32,854 (1990); 61,136 (2000); 95,833 (2010); 115,054 (2015 projected); Race: 67.8% White, 10.6% Black, 5.2% Asian, 16.4% Other, 27.9% Hispanic of any race (2010); Density: 3,666.6 persons per square mile (2010); Average household size: 2.94 (2010); Median age: 31.6 (2010); Males per 100 females: 100.2 (2010); Marriage status: 28.0% never married, 57.9% now married, 3.4% widowed, 10.7% divorced (2005-2009 5-year est.); Foreign born: 12.7% (2005-2009 5-year est.); Ancestry (includes multiple ancestries): 17.7% German, 10.6% Irish, 10.5% English, 4.1% American, 3.8% French (2005-2009 5-year est.).
Economy: Unemployment rate: 7.4% (June 2011); Total civilian labor force: 54,775 (June 2011); Single-family building permits issued: 253 (2010); Multi-family building permits issued: 0 (2010); Employment by occupation: 19.0% management, 22.6% professional, 14.0% services, 27.7% sales, 0.1% farming, 7.9% construction, 8.6% production (2005-2009 5-year est.).
Income: Per capita income: $27,783 (2010); Median household income: $68,052 (2010); Average household income: $81,780 (2010); Percent of households with income of $100,000 or more: 24.6% (2010); Poverty rate: 6.5% (2005-2009 5-year est.).
Taxes: Total city taxes per capita: $1,125 (2007); City property taxes per capita: $233 (2007).
Education: Percent of population age 25 and over with: High school diploma (including GED) or higher: 90.4% (2010); Bachelor's degree or higher: 32.6% (2010); Master's degree or higher: 9.6% (2010).
School District(s)
Hutto ISD (PK-12)
   2009-10 Enrollment: 5,137 . . . . (512) 759-3771
Pflugerville ISD (PK-12)
   2009-10 Enrollment: 22,060 . . . . (512) 594-0000
Round Rock ISD (PK-12)
   2009-10 Enrollment: 43,008 . . . . (512) 464-5000
Vocational/Technical School(s)
Central Texas Beauty College (Private, For-profit)
   Fall 2009 Enrollment: 84 . . . . (512) 244-2235
   2010-11 Tuition: $7,995
Housing: Homeownership rate: 64.1% (2010); Median home value: $163,439 (2010); Median contract rent: $757 per month (2005-2009 5-year est.); Median year structure built: 1995 (2005-2009 5-year est.).
Hospitals: Round Rock Medical Center (107 beds)
Safety: Violent crime rate: 11.6 per 10,000 population; Property crime rate: 250.8 per 10,000 population (2009).
Newspapers: Round Rock Leader (Local news; Circulation 7,000); Texas Capital News
Transportation: Commute to work: 93.6% car, 0.2% public transportation, 0.9% walk, 4.3% work from home (2005-2009 5-year est.); Travel time to work: 25.8% less than 15 minutes, 39.3% 15 to 30 minutes, 21.7% 30 to 45 minutes, 7.9% 45 to 60 minutes, 5.3% 60 minutes or more (2005-2009 5-year est.)
Additional Information Contacts

City of Round Rock .... (512) 218-5400
   http://www.roundrocktexas.gov
Round Rock Chamber of Commerce................. (512) 255-5805
   http://roundrockchamber.org

SERENADA (CDP). Covers a land area of 3.546 square miles and a water area of 0 square miles. Located at 30.68° N. Lat; 97.69° W. Long. Elevation is 820 feet.

Population: 1,675 (1990); 1,847 (2000); 2,643 (2010); 3,124 (2015 projected); Race: 96.3% White, 1.0% Black, 0.3% Asian, 2.3% Other, 7.0% Hispanic of any race (2010); Density: 745.3 persons per square mile (2010); Average household size: 2.64 (2010); Median age: 50.9 (2010); Males per 100 females: 98.1 (2010); Marriage status: 15.5% never married, 75.1% now married, 5.9% widowed, 3.5% divorced (2005-2009 5-year est.); Foreign born: 3.6% (2005-2009 5-year est.); Ancestry (includes multiple ancestries): 21.6% English, 21.3% German, 12.8% Irish, 7.8% American, 4.3% Scottish (2005-2009 5-year est.).

Economy: Employment by occupation: 30.4% management, 25.9% professional, 10.2% services, 26.3% sales, 0.0% farming, 7.2% construction, 0.0% production (2005-2009 5-year est.).

Income: Per capita income: $39,690 (2010); Median household income: $82,487 (2010); Average household income: $105,320 (2010); Percent of households with income of $100,000 or more: 36.5% (2010); Poverty rate: 0.0% (2005-2009 5-year est.).

Education: Percent of population age 25 and over with: High school diploma (including GED) or higher: 97.1% (2010); Bachelor's degree or higher: 47.1% (2010); Master's degree or higher: 13.9% (2010).

Housing: Homeownership rate: 94.6% (2010); Median home value: $227,262 (2010); Median contract rent: n/a per month (2005-2009 5-year est.); Median year structure built: 1982 (2005-2009 5-year est.).

Transportation: Commute to work: 84.7% car, 0.0% public transportation, 3.4% walk, 11.8% work from home (2005-2009 5-year est.); Travel time to work: 38.9% less than 15 minutes, 24.3% 15 to 30 minutes, 16.5% 30 to 45 minutes, 13.1% 45 to 60 minutes, 7.3% 60 minutes or more (2005-2009 5-year est.)

TAYLOR (city). Covers a land area of 13.532 square miles and a water area of 0.030 square miles. Located at 30.57° N. Lat; 97.41° W. Long. Elevation is 564 feet.

History: Named, possibly, for three Taylor brothers who died at the Alamo, or for General Zachary Taylor. Taylor was settled by many immigrants from Czechoslovakia. Its early industries included a mattress factory, cheese factory, cotton mills, and poultry raising. Oil refineries added to the economy.

Population: 11,616 (1990); 13,575 (2000); 15,761 (2010); 18,018 (2015 projected); Race: 69.3% White, 11.4% Black, 0.5% Asian, 18.8% Other, 39.4% Hispanic of any race (2010); Density: 1,164.7 persons per square mile (2010); Average household size: 2.77 (2010); Median age: 33.7 (2010); Males per 100 females: 98.9 (2010); Marriage status: 24.4% never married, 57.4% now married, 7.5% widowed, 10.7% divorced (2005-2009 5-year est.); Foreign born: 10.9% (2005-2009 5-year est.); Ancestry (includes multiple ancestries): 17.7% German, 7.1% Czech, 6.4% Irish, 5.9% American, 4.6% English (2005-2009 5-year est.).

Economy: Single-family building permits issued: 23 (2010); Multi-family building permits issued: 0 (2010); Employment by occupation: 12.5% management, 16.2% professional, 15.6% services, 24.2% sales, 0.5% farming, 19.1% construction, 11.9% production (2005-2009 5-year est.).

Income: Per capita income: $20,108 (2010); Median household income: $46,702 (2010); Average household income: $57,400 (2010); Percent of households with income of $100,000 or more: 14.3% (2010); Poverty rate: 19.5% (2005-2009 5-year est.).

Taxes: Total city taxes per capita: $630 (2007); City property taxes per capita: $338 (2007).

Education: Percent of population age 25 and over with: High school diploma (including GED) or higher: 70.8% (2010); Bachelor's degree or higher: 14.3% (2010); Master's degree or higher: 5.3% (2010).

School District(s)
Taylor ISD (PK-12)
   2009-10 Enrollment: 3,168 .... (512) 365-1391

Housing: Homeownership rate: 60.2% (2010); Median home value: $101,853 (2010); Median contract rent: $512 per month (2005-2009 5-year est.); Median year structure built: 1971 (2005-2009 5-year est.).

Hospitals: Johns Community Hospital (53 beds)

Safety: Violent crime rate: 6.1 per 10,000 population; Property crime rate: 249.5 per 10,000 population (2009).

Newspapers: Taylor Daily Press (Local news; Circulation 4,983)

Transportation: Commute to work: 90.5% car, 0.1% public transportation, 1.0% walk, 5.1% work from home (2005-2009 5-year est.); Travel time to work: 30.4% less than 15 minutes, 20.9% 15 to 30 minutes, 22.4% 30 to 45 minutes, 15.5% 45 to 60 minutes, 10.8% 60 minutes or more (2005-2009 5-year est.); Amtrak: train service available.

Additional Information Contacts
City of Taylor .... (512) 352-3675
   http://www.ci.taylor.tx.us
Taylor Chamber of Commerce....................... (512) 352-6364
   http://www.taylorchamber.org

THRALL (city). Covers a land area of 0.406 square miles and a water area of 0 square miles. Located at 30.58° N. Lat; 97.29° W. Long. Elevation is 561 feet.

History: Oil was discovered in Thrall in 1925, bringing overnight prosperity. Another brief boom followed in 1930.

Population: 564 (1990); 710 (2000); 897 (2010); 1,066 (2015 projected); Race: 64.8% White, 6.6% Black, 0.0% Asian, 28.7% Other, 48.0% Hispanic of any race (2010); Density: 2,206.8 persons per square mile (2010); Average household size: 2.82 (2010); Median age: 35.0 (2010); Males per 100 females: 92.9 (2010); Marriage status: 19.8% never married, 58.3% now married, 15.4% widowed, 6.5% divorced (2005-2009 5-year est.); Foreign born: 2.8% (2005-2009 5-year est.); Ancestry (includes multiple ancestries): 37.1% German, 11.5% Irish, 9.0% Czech, 5.8% Swedish, 5.6% Dutch (2005-2009 5-year est.).

Economy: Single-family building permits issued: 2 (2010); Multi-family building permits issued: 0 (2010); Employment by occupation: 6.1% management, 21.5% professional, 17.9% services, 28.5% sales, 1.2% farming, 11.0% construction, 13.8% production (2005-2009 5-year est.).

Income: Per capita income: $15,760 (2010); Median household income: $39,800 (2010); Average household income: $44,355 (2010); Percent of households with income of $100,000 or more: 5.3% (2010); Poverty rate: 18.2% (2005-2009 5-year est.).

Taxes: Total city taxes per capita: $46 (2007); City property taxes per capita: $5 (2007).

Education: Percent of population age 25 and over with: High school diploma (including GED) or higher: 61.9% (2010); Bachelor's degree or higher: 8.0% (2010); Master's degree or higher: 3.2% (2010).

School District(s)
Thrall ISD (PK-12)
   2009-10 Enrollment: 644 .... (512) 898-0062

Housing: Homeownership rate: 75.2% (2010); Median home value: $67,647 (2010); Median contract rent: $550 per month (2005-2009 5-year est.); Median year structure built: 1968 (2005-2009 5-year est.).

Safety: Violent crime rate: 0.0 per 10,000 population; Property crime rate: 63.9 per 10,000 population (2009).

Transportation: Commute to work: 95.9% car, 0.0% public transportation, 4.1% walk, 0.0% work from home (2005-2009 5-year est.); Travel time to work: 30.9% less than 15 minutes, 34.2% 15 to 30 minutes, 7.8% 30 to 45 minutes, 11.9% 45 to 60 minutes, 15.2% 60 minutes or more (2005-2009 5-year est.)

WEIR (city). Covers a land area of 1.593 square miles and a water area of 0 square miles. Located at 30.67° N. Lat; 97.58° W. Long. Elevation is 682 feet.

Population: 221 (1990); 591 (2000); 619 (2010); 685 (2015 projected); Race: 78.7% White, 3.1% Black, 0.2% Asian, 18.1% Other, 32.1% Hispanic of any race (2010); Density: 388.5 persons per square mile (2010); Average household size: 3.13 (2010); Median age: 31.2 (2010); Males per 100 females: 94.0 (2010); Marriage status: 39.1% never married, 30.1% now married, 15.9% widowed, 14.9% divorced (2005-2009 5-year est.); Foreign born: 19.4% (2005-2009 5-year est.); Ancestry (includes multiple ancestries): 32.2% German, 28.4% Irish, 9.9% American, 2.4% French Canadian, 1.2% Scotch-Irish (2005-2009 5-year est.).

Economy: Single-family building permits issued: 1 (2010); Multi-family building permits issued: 0 (2010); Employment by occupation: 3.6% management, 7.8% professional, 28.0% services, 25.9% sales, 2.1% farming, 20.2% construction, 12.4% production (2005-2009 5-year est.).

Income: Per capita income: $20,510 (2010); Median household income: $55,319 (2010); Average household income: $63,434 (2010); Percent of households with income of $100,000 or more: 15.7% (2010); Poverty rate: 10.1% (2005-2009 5-year est.).

Taxes: Total city taxes per capita: $55 (2007); City property taxes per capita: $42 (2007).

Education: Percent of population age 25 and over with: High school diploma (including GED) or higher: 80.5% (2010); Bachelor's degree or higher: 16.5% (2010); Master's degree or higher: 3.3% (2010).
Housing: Homeownership rate: 79.8% (2010); Median home value: $95,714 (2010); Median contract rent: $625 per month (2005-2009 5-year est.); Median year structure built: 1991 (2005-2009 5-year est.).
Transportation: Commute to work: 97.8% car, 0.0% public transportation, 2.2% walk, 0.0% work from home (2005-2009 5-year est.); Travel time to work: 27.6% less than 15 minutes, 34.6% 15 to 30 minutes, 22.7% 30 to 45 minutes, 11.4% 45 to 60 minutes, 3.8% 60 minutes or more (2005-2009 5-year est.)

Wilson County

Located in south Texas; drained by the San Antonio River. Covers a land area of 806.99 square miles, a water area of 1.58 square miles, and is located in the Central Time Zone at 29.19° N. Lat., 98.10° W. Long. The county was founded in 1860. County seat is Floresville.

Wilson County is part of the San Antonio-New Braunfels, TX Metropolitan Statistical Area. The entire metro area includes: Atascosa County, TX; Bandera County, TX; Bexar County, TX; Comal County, TX; Guadalupe County, TX; Kendall County, TX; Medina County, TX; Wilson County, TX

Weather Station: Floresville										Elevation: 399 feet		
	Jan	Feb	Mar	Apr	May	Jun	Jul	Aug	Sep	Oct	Nov	Dec
High	65	69	75	82	88	94	96	97	92	84	75	66
Low	39	42	50	57	66	71	73	73	68	58	49	40
Precip	1.4	1.7	2.1	2.0	3.2	2.9	2.3	2.4	2.9	2.9	2.3	1.5
Snow	0.4	0.0	0.0	0.0	0.0	0.0	0.0	0.0	0.0	tr	0.0	0.0

High and Low temperatures in degrees Fahrenheit; Precipitation and Snow in inches

Population: 22,650 (1990); 32,408 (2000); 42,799 (2010); 47,778 (2015 projected); Race: 79.0% White, 2.4% Black, 0.5% Asian, 18.1% Other, 37.9% Hispanic of any race (2010); Density: 53.0 persons per square mile (2010); Average household size: 2.83 (2010); Median age: 35.6 (2010); Males per 100 females: 99.0 (2010).
Religion: Five largest groups: 37.8% Catholic Church, 10.2% Southern Baptist Convention, 4.6% The United Methodist Church, 3.8% Evangelical Lutheran Church in America, 1.2% Churches of Christ (2000).
Economy: Unemployment rate: 8.2% (June 2011); Total civilian labor force: 19,814 (June 2011); Leading industries: 26.8% health care and social assistance; 19.0% retail trade; 13.0% accommodation & food services (2009); Farms: 2,570 totaling 467,187 acres (2007); Companies that employ 500 or more persons: 0 (2009); Companies that employ 100 to 499 persons: 6 (2009); Companies that employ less than 100 persons: 494 (2009); Black-owned businesses: n/a (2007); Hispanic-owned businesses: n/a (2007); Asian-owned businesses: n/a (2007); Women-owned businesses: n/a (2007); Retail sales per capita: $5,211 (2010).
Single-family building permits issued: 31 (2010); Multi-family building permits issued: 30 (2010).
Income: Per capita income: $24,908 (2010); Median household income: $56,341 (2010); Average household income: $71,130 (2010); Percent of households with income of $100,000 or more: 21.0% (2010); Poverty rate: 12.8% (2009); Bankruptcy rate: 1.62% (2010).
Taxes: Total county taxes per capita: $188 (2007); County property taxes per capita: $159 (2007).
Education: Percent of population age 25 and over with: High school diploma (including GED) or higher: 82.7% (2010); Bachelor's degree or higher: 18.7% (2010); Master's degree or higher: 4.8% (2010).
Housing: Homeownership rate: 83.7% (2010); Median home value: $112,928 (2010); Median contract rent: $465 per month (2005-2009 5-year est.); Median year structure built: 1988 (2005-2009 5-year est.)
Health: Birth rate: 139.6 per 10,000 population (2009); Death rate: 85.2 per 10,000 population (2009); Age-adjusted cancer mortality rate: 206.4 deaths per 100,000 population (2007); Number of physicians: 4.2 per 10,000 population (2008); Hospital beds: 11.2 per 10,000 population (2007); Hospital admissions: 410.4 per 10,000 population (2007).
Elections: 2008 Presidential election results: 32.8% Obama, 66.6% McCain, 0.0% Nader
Additional Information Contacts
Wilson County Government . . . . (830) 393-3126
   http://www.co.wilson.tx.us/ips/cms
City of Floresville . . . . (830) 393-3105
   http://www.cityoffloresville.org

Floresville Chamber of Commerce . . . . (830) 393-0074
   http://floresvillecoc.com
Greater La Vernia Chamber of Commerce . . . . (830) 779-5600
   http://www.vivicom.us/laverniachamber/contactus.html

Wilson County Communities

FLORESVILLE (city). County seat. Covers a land area of 4.753 square miles and a water area of 0 square miles. Located at 29.13° N. Lat; 98.15° W. Long. Elevation is 390 feet.
History: Floresville was established when the railroad was built here, on land donated by Juana Montez Flores, member of an old Spanish family who owned a ranch in the area.
Population: 5,247 (1990); 5,868 (2000); 7,669 (2010); 8,574 (2015 projected); Race: 70.9% White, 2.9% Black, 0.5% Asian, 25.7% Other, 57.7% Hispanic of any race (2010); Density: 1,613.4 persons per square mile (2010); Average household size: 2.78 (2010); Median age: 34.5 (2010); Males per 100 females: 93.5 (2010); Marriage status: 32.1% never married, 49.5% now married, 9.9% widowed, 8.5% divorced (2005-2009 5-year est.); Foreign born: 8.1% (2005-2009 5-year est.); Ancestry (includes multiple ancestries): 9.2% German, 5.1% English, 4.9% Irish, 3.8% Czech, 3.3% Polish (2005-2009 5-year est.).
Economy: Single-family building permits issued: 11 (2010); Multi-family building permits issued: 24 (2010); Employment by occupation: 8.2% management, 14.2% professional, 24.9% services, 19.6% sales, 2.3% farming, 17.6% construction, 13.2% production (2005-2009 5-year est.).
Income: Per capita income: $21,072 (2010); Median household income: $44,650 (2010); Average household income: $59,672 (2010); Percent of households with income of $100,000 or more: 15.0% (2010); Poverty rate: 20.3% (2005-2009 5-year est.).
Taxes: Total city taxes per capita: $255 (2007); City property taxes per capita: $117 (2007).
Education: Percent of population age 25 and over with: High school diploma (including GED) or higher: 73.2% (2010); Bachelor's degree or higher: 18.3% (2010); Master's degree or higher: 5.9% (2010).
School District(s)
East Central ISD (PK-12)
   2009-10 Enrollment: 9,292 . . . . (210) 648-7861
Falls City ISD (KG-12)
   2009-10 Enrollment: 329 . . . . (830) 254-3551
Floresville ISD (PK-12)
   2009-10 Enrollment: 3,801 . . . . (830) 393-5300
La Vernia ISD (PK-12)
   2009-10 Enrollment: 2,983 . . . . (830) 779-6600
Pleasanton ISD (PK-12)
   2009-10 Enrollment: 3,440 . . . . (830) 569-1200
Poth ISD (PK-12)
   2009-10 Enrollment: 816 . . . . (830) 484-3330
Stockdale ISD (PK-12)
   2009-10 Enrollment: 806 . . . . (830) 996-3551
Housing: Homeownership rate: 71.7% (2010); Median home value: $87,808 (2010); Median contract rent: $350 per month (2005-2009 5-year est.); Median year structure built: 1976 (2005-2009 5-year est.).
Hospitals: Connally Memorial Medical Center
Safety: Violent crime rate: 10.2 per 10,000 population; Property crime rate: 272.3 per 10,000 population (2009).
Newspapers: Chronicle-Journal (Community news; Circulation 4,500); Wilson County News (Community news; Circulation 9,500)
Transportation: Commute to work: 96.1% car, 0.0% public transportation, 1.7% walk, 0.8% work from home (2005-2009 5-year est.); Travel time to work: 50.1% less than 15 minutes, 15.6% 15 to 30 minutes, 18.9% 30 to 45 minutes, 11.4% 45 to 60 minutes, 4.0% 60 minutes or more (2005-2009 5-year est.)
Additional Information Contacts
City of Floresville . . . . (830) 393-3105
   http://www.cityoffloresville.org
Floresville Chamber of Commerce . . . . (830) 393-0074
   http://floresvillecoc.com

LA VERNIA (city). Aka Lavernia. Covers a land area of 1.928 square miles and a water area of 0 square miles. Located at 29.35° N. Lat; 98.11° W. Long. Elevation is 489 feet.
Population: 796 (1990); 931 (2000); 1,319 (2010); 1,505 (2015 projected); Race: 93.8% White, 0.4% Black, 0.4% Asian, 5.5% Other, 14.6% Hispanic of any race (2010); Density: 684.0 persons per square mile (2010);

Average household size: 2.79 (2010); Median age: 35.6 (2010); Males per 100 females: 102.0 (2010); Marriage status: 28.3% never married, 58.2% now married, 4.7% widowed, 8.8% divorced (2005-2009 5-year est.); Foreign born: 2.3% (2005-2009 5-year est.); Ancestry (includes multiple ancestries): 61.4% German, 9.2% Irish, 4.4% Polish, 3.2% English, 3.0% American (2005-2009 5-year est.).
Economy: Single-family building permits issued: 16 (2010); Multi-family building permits issued: 6 (2010); Employment by occupation: 9.1% management, 18.5% professional, 7.4% services, 52.6% sales, 0.0% farming, 7.2% construction, 5.3% production (2005-2009 5-year est.).
Income: Per capita income: $26,889 (2010); Median household income: $61,849 (2010); Average household income: $76,354 (2010); Percent of households with income of $100,000 or more: 25.3% (2010); Poverty rate: 4.1% (2005-2009 5-year est.).
Taxes: Total city taxes per capita: $282 (2007); City property taxes per capita: $131 (2007).
Education: Percent of population age 25 and over with: High school diploma (including GED) or higher: 85.9% (2010); Bachelor's degree or higher: 18.0% (2010); Master's degree or higher: 3.5% (2010).
School District(s)
La Vernia ISD (PK-12)
    2009-10 Enrollment: 2,983 . . . . (830) 779-6600
Housing: Homeownership rate: 88.2% (2010); Median home value: $126,020 (2010); Median contract rent: $348 per month (2005-2009 5-year est.); Median year structure built: 1977 (2005-2009 5-year est.).
Safety: Violent crime rate: 0.0 per 10,000 population; Property crime rate: 279.6 per 10,000 population (2009).
Newspapers: La Vernia News (Community news; Circulation 1,500)
Transportation: Commute to work: 93.8% car, 1.0% public transportation, 2.2% walk, 2.4% work from home (2005-2009 5-year est.); Travel time to work: 51.8% less than 15 minutes, 9.7% 15 to 30 minutes, 25.2% 30 to 45 minutes, 4.4% 45 to 60 minutes, 9.0% 60 minutes or more (2005-2009 5-year est.)
Additional Information Contacts
Greater La Vernia Chamber of Commerce . . . . (830) 779-5600
    http://www.vivicom.us/laverniachamber/contactus.html

POTH (town). Covers a land area of 3.191 square miles and a water area of 0 square miles. Located at 29.07° N. Lat; 98.08° W. Long. Elevation is 404 feet.
Population: 1,642 (1990); 1,850 (2000); 2,359 (2010); 2,644 (2015 projected); Race: 72.7% White, 1.6% Black, 0.1% Asian, 25.6% Other, 48.3% Hispanic of any race (2010); Density: 739.2 persons per square mile (2010); Average household size: 2.86 (2010); Median age: 33.6 (2010); Males per 100 females: 99.6 (2010); Marriage status: 27.3% never married, 55.4% now married, 7.0% widowed, 10.3% divorced (2005-2009 5-year est.); Foreign born: 8.2% (2005-2009 5-year est.); Ancestry (includes multiple ancestries): 30.4% Polish, 23.0% German, 2.9% Irish, 2.6% Czech, 1.9% Norwegian (2005-2009 5-year est.).
Economy: Single-family building permits issued: 4 (2010); Multi-family building permits issued: 0 (2010); Employment by occupation: 10.4% management, 14.5% professional, 15.2% services, 26.8% sales, 1.2% farming, 10.0% construction, 22.0% production (2005-2009 5-year est.).
Income: Per capita income: $21,929 (2010); Median household income: $53,707 (2010); Average household income: $62,976 (2010); Percent of households with income of $100,000 or more: 18.9% (2010); Poverty rate: 14.3% (2005-2009 5-year est.).
Taxes: Total city taxes per capita: $105 (2007); City property taxes per capita: $78 (2007).
Education: Percent of population age 25 and over with: High school diploma (including GED) or higher: 79.3% (2010); Bachelor's degree or higher: 15.4% (2010); Master's degree or higher: 4.2% (2010).
School District(s)
Poth ISD (PK-12)
    2009-10 Enrollment: 816 . . . . (830) 484-3330
Housing: Homeownership rate: 76.2% (2010); Median home value: $84,925 (2010); Median contract rent: $455 per month (2005-2009 5-year est.); Median year structure built: 1971 (2005-2009 5-year est.).
Transportation: Commute to work: 96.7% car, 0.0% public transportation, 1.6% walk, 0.5% work from home (2005-2009 5-year est.); Travel time to work: 32.1% less than 15 minutes, 18.2% 15 to 30 minutes, 17.7% 30 to 45 minutes, 18.8% 45 to 60 minutes, 13.1% 60 minutes or more (2005-2009 5-year est.)

STOCKDALE (city). Covers a land area of 1.616 square miles and a water area of 0 square miles. Located at 29.23° N. Lat; 97.96° W. Long. Elevation is 443 feet.
Population: 1,369 (1990); 1,398 (2000); 1,685 (2010); 1,852 (2015 projected); Race: 80.9% White, 2.1% Black, 0.1% Asian, 16.9% Other, 40.0% Hispanic of any race (2010); Density: 1,043.0 persons per square mile (2010); Average household size: 2.62 (2010); Median age: 37.5 (2010); Males per 100 females: 96.4 (2010); Marriage status: 25.4% never married, 52.6% now married, 16.8% widowed, 5.2% divorced (2005-2009 5-year est.); Foreign born: 6.5% (2005-2009 5-year est.); Ancestry (includes multiple ancestries): 21.9% German, 14.1% Irish, 8.1% English, 4.0% American, 4.0% Polish (2005-2009 5-year est.).
Economy: Single-family building permits issued: 0 (2010); Multi-family building permits issued: 0 (2010); Employment by occupation: 10.2% management, 24.2% professional, 16.3% services, 20.1% sales, 0.0% farming, 21.4% construction, 7.7% production (2005-2009 5-year est.).
Income: Per capita income: $25,889 (2010); Median household income: $55,372 (2010); Average household income: $70,467 (2010); Percent of households with income of $100,000 or more: 22.4% (2010); Poverty rate: 14.8% (2005-2009 5-year est.).
Taxes: Total city taxes per capita: $208 (2007); City property taxes per capita: $60 (2007).
Education: Percent of population age 25 and over with: High school diploma (including GED) or higher: 76.6% (2010); Bachelor's degree or higher: 17.3% (2010); Master's degree or higher: 3.9% (2010).
School District(s)
Stockdale ISD (PK-12)
    2009-10 Enrollment: 806 . . . . (830) 996-3551
Housing: Homeownership rate: 70.0% (2010); Median home value: $74,167 (2010); Median contract rent: $371 per month (2005-2009 5-year est.); Median year structure built: 1975 (2005-2009 5-year est.).
Transportation: Commute to work: 88.5% car, 0.0% public transportation, 3.8% walk, 7.1% work from home (2005-2009 5-year est.); Travel time to work: 34.4% less than 15 minutes, 8.1% 15 to 30 minutes, 11.6% 30 to 45 minutes, 23.0% 45 to 60 minutes, 23.0% 60 minutes or more (2005-2009 5-year est.)

SUTHERLAND SPRINGS (unincorporated postal area, zip code 78161). Covers a land area of 3.626 square miles and a water area of 0 square miles. Located at 29.27° N. Lat; 98.05° W. Long. Elevation is 469 feet.
History: Sutherland Springs developed near a health spa that offered 27 varieties of hot and cold mineral waters. The resort declined in the early 1900's, but the town remained.
Population: 335 (2000); Race: 86.2% White, 0.0% Black, 0.0% Asian, 13.8% Other, 22.9% Hispanic of any race (2000); Density: 92.4 persons per square mile (2000); Age: 40.1% under 18, 4.2% over 64 (2000); Marriage status: 28.6% never married, 45.4% now married, 8.6% widowed, 17.5% divorced (2000); Foreign born: 0.0% (2000); Ancestry (includes multiple ancestries): 24.1% English, 17.0% American, 6.9% German, 1.2% Danish (2000).
Economy: Employment by occupation: 0.0% management, 10.0% professional, 5.6% services, 43.8% sales, 0.0% farming, 15.0% construction, 25.6% production (2000).
Income: Per capita income: $17,343 (2000); Median household income: $31,221 (2000); Poverty rate: 179.1% (2000).
Education: Percent of population age 25 and over with: High school diploma (including GED) or higher: 36.6% (2000); Bachelor's degree or higher: 18.5% (2000).
Housing: Homeownership rate: 78.8% (2000); Median home value: $34,800 (2000); Median contract rent: $233 per month (2000); Median year structure built: 1974 (2000).
Transportation: Commute to work: 71.1% car, 0.0% public transportation, 17.4% walk, 5.4% work from home (2000); Travel time to work: 24.8% less than 15 minutes, 24.8% 15 to 30 minutes, 22.0% 30 to 45 minutes, 14.9% 45 to 60 minutes, 13.5% 60 minutes or more (2000)

Winkler County

Located in west Texas; high plains area, bounded on the north by New Mexico. Covers a land area of 841.05 square miles, a water area of 0.19 square miles, and is located in the Central Time Zone at 31.84° N. Lat., 103.09° W. Long. The county was founded in 1887. County seat is Kermit.

Weather Station: Wink Winkler Co Arpt   Elevation: 2,807 feet

	Jan	Feb	Mar	Apr	May	Jun	Jul	Aug	Sep	Oct	Nov	Dec
High	61	66	74	83	91	98	98	96	90	81	70	61
Low	30	34	41	49	60	68	71	70	63	51	38	30
Precip	0.4	0.6	0.7	0.6	1.5	1.6	1.9	1.5	1.7	1.6	0.7	0.6
Snow	na	na	na	na	na	na	na	na	na	na	na	na

High and Low temperatures in degrees Fahrenheit; Precipitation and Snow in inches

Population: 8,626 (1990); 7,173 (2000); 6,807 (2010); 6,619 (2015 projected); Race: 69.9% White, 2.4% Black, 0.2% Asian, 27.5% Other, 52.1% Hispanic of any race (2010); Density: 8.1 persons per square mile (2010); Average household size: 2.62 (2010); Median age: 34.3 (2010); Males per 100 females: 97.2 (2010).

Religion: Five largest groups: 40.7% Southern Baptist Convention, 28.9% Catholic Church, 6.2% The United Methodist Church, 3.3% Churches of Christ, 0.7% Lutheran Church—Missouri Synod (2000).

Economy: Unemployment rate: 7.4% (June 2011); Total civilian labor force: 3,260 (June 2011); Leading industries: 29.0% mining; 14.5% construction; 12.3% retail trade (2009); Farms: 53 totaling 532,883 acres (2007); Companies that employ 500 or more persons: 0 (2009); Companies that employ 100 to 499 persons: 1 (2009); Companies that employ less than 100 persons: 155 (2009); Black-owned businesses: n/a (2007); Hispanic-owned businesses: n/a (2007); Asian-owned businesses: n/a (2007); Women-owned businesses: n/a (2007); Retail sales per capita: $7,672 (2010). Single-family building permits issued: 1 (2010); Multi-family building permits issued: 0 (2010).

Income: Per capita income: $20,432 (2010); Median household income: $44,450 (2010); Average household income: $54,384 (2010); Percent of households with income of $100,000 or more: 11.5% (2010); Poverty rate: 14.6% (2009); Bankruptcy rate: 0.85% (2010).

Taxes: Total county taxes per capita: $934 (2007); County property taxes per capita: $731 (2007).

Education: Percent of population age 25 and over with: High school diploma (including GED) or higher: 66.1% (2010); Bachelor's degree or higher: 12.1% (2010); Master's degree or higher: 3.0% (2010).

Housing: Homeownership rate: 81.7% (2010); Median home value: $29,773 (2010); Median contract rent: $314 per month (2005-2009 5-year est.); Median year structure built: 1962 (2005-2009 5-year est.)

Health: Birth rate: 178.7 per 10,000 population (2009); Death rate: 67.9 per 10,000 population (2009); Age-adjusted cancer mortality rate: 260.3 (Unreliable) deaths per 100,000 population (2007); Number of physicians: 7.4 per 10,000 population (2008); Hospital beds: 22.9 per 10,000 population (2007); Hospital admissions: 495.6 per 10,000 population (2007).

Elections: 2008 Presidential election results: 23.5% Obama, 75.2% McCain, 0.1% Nader

Additional Information Contacts
Winkler County Government . . . . (432) 586-6658
 http://www.co.winkler.tx.us
City of Kermit . . . . (432) 586-3460
 http://www.kermittexas.us
Kermit Chamber of Commerce . . . . (432) 586-2507
Wink Chamber of Commerce. . . . . (915) 527-3441

Winkler County Communities

KERMIT (city). County seat. Covers a land area of 2.497 square miles and a water area of 0 square miles. Located at 31.85° N. Lat; 103.09° W. Long. Elevation is 2,861 feet.

History: Incorporated 1938.

Population: 6,875 (1990); 5,714 (2000); 5,386 (2010); 5,189 (2015 projected); Race: 67.2% White, 2.8% Black, 0.3% Asian, 29.7% Other, 55.7% Hispanic of any race (2010); Density: 2,157.0 persons per square mile (2010); Average household size: 2.62 (2010); Median age: 33.9 (2010); Males per 100 females: 96.4 (2010); Marriage status: 17.7% never married, 59.4% now married, 13.1% widowed, 9.8% divorced (2005-2009 5-year est.); Foreign born: 12.8% (2005-2009 5-year est.); Ancestry (includes multiple ancestries): 15.5% German, 9.3% Irish, 5.5% English, 4.2% American, 2.1% French (2005-2009 5-year est.).

Economy: Single-family building permits issued: 1 (2010); Multi-family building permits issued: 0 (2010); Employment by occupation: 3.3% management, 13.4% professional, 22.0% services, 15.0% sales, 0.0% farming, 30.1% construction, 16.3% production (2005-2009 5-year est.).

Income: Per capita income: $19,062 (2010); Median household income: $42,126 (2010); Average household income: $49,933 (2010); Percent of

households with income of $100,000 or more: 8.8% (2010); Poverty rate: 21.6% (2005-2009 5-year est.).

Taxes: Total city taxes per capita: $238 (2007); City property taxes per capita: $100 (2007).

Education: Percent of population age 25 and over with: High school diploma (including GED) or higher: 62.3% (2010); Bachelor's degree or higher: 10.7% (2010); Master's degree or higher: 2.0% (2010).

School District(s)
Kermit ISD (PK-12)
 2009-10 Enrollment: 1,232 . . . . (432) 586-1000

Housing: Homeownership rate: 81.4% (2010); Median home value: $28,273 (2010); Median contract rent: $331 per month (2005-2009 5-year est.); Median year structure built: 1962 (2005-2009 5-year est.).

Hospitals: Winkler County Memorial Hospital

Safety: Violent crime rate: 27.0 per 10,000 population; Property crime rate: 144.5 per 10,000 population (2009).

Newspapers: Winkler County News (Local news; Circulation 3,700)

Transportation: Commute to work: 90.7% car, 0.0% public transportation, 4.3% walk, 1.1% work from home (2005-2009 5-year est.); Travel time to work: 57.6% less than 15 minutes, 10.8% 15 to 30 minutes, 9.4% 30 to 45 minutes, 9.2% 45 to 60 minutes, 13.0% 60 minutes or more (2005-2009 5-year est.)

Additional Information Contacts
City of Kermit . . . . (432) 586-3460
 http://www.kermittexas.us
Kermit Chamber of Commerce . . . . (432) 586-2507

WINK (city). Covers a land area of 1.136 square miles and a water area of 0 square miles. Located at 31.75° N. Lat; 103.15° W. Long. Elevation is 2,792 feet.

History: Incorporated 1928.

Population: 1,189 (1990); 919 (2000); 954 (2010); 966 (2015 projected); Race: 83.2% White, 0.7% Black, 0.0% Asian, 16.0% Other, 32.3% Hispanic of any race (2010); Density: 839.9 persons per square mile (2010); Average household size: 2.59 (2010); Median age: 37.9 (2010); Males per 100 females: 92.3 (2010); Marriage status: 19.0% never married, 50.9% now married, 12.2% widowed, 17.9% divorced (2005-2009 5-year est.); Foreign born: 2.6% (2005-2009 5-year est.); Ancestry (includes multiple ancestries): 16.7% Irish, 16.0% English, 15.0% American, 11.1% German, 5.5% Scotch-Irish (2005-2009 5-year est.).

Economy: Single-family building permits issued: 0 (2010); Multi-family building permits issued: 0 (2010); Employment by occupation: 11.3% management, 31.6% professional, 11.6% services, 14.2% sales, 2.3% farming, 15.9% construction, 13.0% production (2005-2009 5-year est.).

Income: Per capita income: $25,587 (2010); Median household income: $57,885 (2010); Average household income: $68,600 (2010); Percent of households with income of $100,000 or more: 20.6% (2010); Poverty rate: 18.7% (2005-2009 5-year est.).

Taxes: Total city taxes per capita: $437 (2007); City property taxes per capita: $159 (2007).

Education: Percent of population age 25 and over with: High school diploma (including GED) or higher: 81.5% (2010); Bachelor's degree or higher: 17.7% (2010); Master's degree or higher: 8.2% (2010).

School District(s)
Wink-Loving ISD (PK-12)
 2009-10 Enrollment: 332 . . . . (432) 527-3880

Housing: Homeownership rate: 83.6% (2010); Median home value: $33,548 (2010); Median contract rent: $180 per month (2005-2009 5-year est.); Median year structure built: 1961 (2005-2009 5-year est.).

Safety: Violent crime rate: 0.0 per 10,000 population; Property crime rate: 88.2 per 10,000 population (2009).

Transportation: Commute to work: 89.1% car, 0.0% public transportation, 6.2% walk, 3.6% work from home (2005-2009 5-year est.); Travel time to work: 59.5% less than 15 minutes, 28.8% 15 to 30 minutes, 4.9% 30 to 45 minutes, 1.2% 45 to 60 minutes, 5.5% 60 minutes or more (2005-2009 5-year est.)

Additional Information Contacts
Wink Chamber of Commerce. . . . . (915) 527-3441

Wise County

Located in north Texas; drained by the West Fork of the Trinity River; includes part of Eagle Mountain Lake. Covers a land area of 904.61 square miles, a water area of 18.17 square miles, and is located in the Central

Time Zone at 33.20° N. Lat., 97.67° W. Long. The county was founded in 1856. County seat is Decatur.

Wise County is part of the Dallas-Fort Worth-Arlington, TX Metropolitan Statistical Area. The entire metro area includes: Dallas-Plano-Irving, TX Metropolitan Division (Collin County, TX; Dallas County, TX; Delta County, TX; Denton County, TX; Ellis County, TX; Hunt County, TX; Kaufman County, TX; Rockwall County, TX); Fort Worth-Arlington, TX Metropolitan Division (Johnson County, TX; Parker County, TX; Tarrant County, TX; Wise County, TX)

Weather Station: Bridgeport									Elevation: 745 feet		
	Jan	Feb	Mar	Apr	May	Jun	Jul	Aug	Sep	Oct	Nov	Dec
High	57	61	68	77	84	91	97	97	89	79	67	58
Low	31	35	42	50	60	67	71	69	62	51	42	32
Precip	1.6	2.4	2.9	2.7	5.2	4.1	2.0	1.9	3.1	4.6	2.3	2.1
Snow	0.3	0.8	0.1	0.1	0.0	0.0	0.0	0.0	0.0	0.0	0.2	0.3

High and Low temperatures in degrees Fahrenheit; Precipitation and Snow in inches

Population: 34,679 (1990); 48,793 (2000); 60,350 (2010); 65,860 (2015 projected); Race: 87.7% White, 1.8% Black, 0.4% Asian, 10.1% Other, 15.4% Hispanic of any race (2010); Density: 66.7 persons per square mile (2010); Average household size: 2.77 (2010); Median age: 36.4 (2010); Males per 100 females: 101.2 (2010).
Religion: Five largest groups: 25.0% Southern Baptist Convention, 5.6% The United Methodist Church, 3.8% Catholic Church, 2.6% Churches of Christ, 1.4% Assemblies of God (2000).
Economy: Unemployment rate: 8.5% (June 2011); Total civilian labor force: 28,773 (June 2011); Leading industries: 20.1% mining; 13.8% health care and social assistance; 13.6% retail trade (2009); Farms: 3,164 totaling 442,753 acres (2007); Companies that employ 500 or more persons: 2 (2009); Companies that employ 100 to 499 persons: 18 (2009); Companies that employ less than 100 persons: 1,210 (2009); Black-owned businesses: n/a (2007); Hispanic-owned businesses: 335 (2007); Asian-owned businesses: 160 (2007); Women-owned businesses: 1,531 (2007); Retail sales per capita: $24,723 (2010). Single-family building permits issued: 26 (2010); Multi-family building permits issued: 0 (2010).
Income: Per capita income: $23,923 (2010); Median household income: $56,708 (2010); Average household income: $67,198 (2010); Percent of households with income of $100,000 or more: 18.2% (2010); Poverty rate: 10.6% (2009); Bankruptcy rate: 2.68% (2010).
Taxes: Total county taxes per capita: $417 (2007); County property taxes per capita: $338 (2007).
Education: Percent of population age 25 and over with: High school diploma (including GED) or higher: 79.6% (2010); Bachelor's degree or higher: 14.5% (2010); Master's degree or higher: 4.7% (2010).
Housing: Homeownership rate: 79.8% (2010); Median home value: $114,808 (2010); Median contract rent: $520 per month (2005-2009 5-year est.); Median year structure built: 1987 (2005-2009 5-year est.)
Health: Birth rate: 125.4 per 10,000 population (2009); Death rate: 78.1 per 10,000 population (2009); Age-adjusted cancer mortality rate: 202.0 deaths per 100,000 population (2007); Number of physicians: 7.9 per 10,000 population (2008); Hospital beds: 22.8 per 10,000 population (2007); Hospital admissions: 809.3 per 10,000 population (2007).
Elections: 2008 Presidential election results: 21.7% Obama, 77.4% McCain, 0.1% Nader
National and State Parks: Lyndon B Johnson National Grassland
Additional Information Contacts

Wise County Government . . . . (940) 627-5743
   http://www.co.wise.tx.us
Bridgeport Area Chamber of Commerce . . . . (940) 683-2076
   http://www.bridgeportchamber.org
City of Bridgeport . . . . (940) 683-3400
   http://www.cityofbridgeport.net
City of Decatur . . . . (940) 627-2741
   http://www.decaturtx.org
City of Newark . . . . (817) 489-2201
   http://newarktexas.com
Decatur Chamber of Commerce . . . . (940) 627-3107
   http://www.decaturtx.com
South Wise County Chamber of Commerce . . . . (817) 636-2560
   http://www.southwisechamber.com

Wise County Communities

ALVORD (town). Covers a land area of 1.376 square miles and a water area of 0 square miles. Located at 33.35° N. Lat; 97.69° W. Long. Elevation is 879 feet.
Population: 866 (1990); 1,007 (2000); 1,332 (2010); 1,471 (2015 projected); Race: 92.4% White, 0.8% Black, 0.1% Asian, 6.7% Other, 7.5% Hispanic of any race (2010); Density: 968.3 persons per square mile (2010); Average household size: 2.49 (2010); Median age: 36.5 (2010); Males per 100 females: 96.8 (2010); Marriage status: 20.5% never married, 59.2% now married, 5.9% widowed, 14.3% divorced (2005-2009 5-year est.); Foreign born: 1.4% (2005-2009 5-year est.); Ancestry (includes multiple ancestries): 13.4% German, 11.5% Irish, 9.5% American, 4.6% English, 3.7% French (2005-2009 5-year est.).
Economy: Single-family building permits issued: 0 (2010); Multi-family building permits issued: 0 (2010); Employment by occupation: 9.7% management, 22.0% professional, 19.6% services, 23.5% sales, 0.4% farming, 12.2% construction, 12.5% production (2005-2009 5-year est.).
Income: Per capita income: $26,972 (2010); Median household income: $54,688 (2010); Average household income: $67,331 (2010); Percent of households with income of $100,000 or more: 18.2% (2010); Poverty rate: 7.3% (2005-2009 5-year est.).
Taxes: Total city taxes per capita: $345 (2007); City property taxes per capita: $212 (2007).
Education: Percent of population age 25 and over with: High school diploma (including GED) or higher: 79.2% (2010); Bachelor's degree or higher: 10.9% (2010); Master's degree or higher: 2.3% (2010).
School District(s)
Alvord ISD (PK-12)
   2009-10 Enrollment: 721 . . . . (940) 427-5975
Housing: Homeownership rate: 76.2% (2010); Median home value: $86,721 (2010); Median contract rent: $564 per month (2005-2009 5-year est.); Median year structure built: 1979 (2005-2009 5-year est.).
Newspapers: The Alvord Sunset Gazette (Community news; Circulation 960)
Transportation: Commute to work: 95.3% car, 0.4% public transportation, 0.0% walk, 3.6% work from home (2005-2009 5-year est.); Travel time to work: 31.7% less than 15 minutes, 40.8% 15 to 30 minutes, 10.6% 30 to 45 minutes, 4.4% 45 to 60 minutes, 12.4% 60 minutes or more (2005-2009 5-year est.)

AURORA (town). Covers a land area of 3.228 square miles and a water area of 0 square miles. Located at 33.05° N. Lat; 97.51° W. Long. Elevation is 817 feet.
Population: 623 (1990); 853 (2000); 1,042 (2010); 1,154 (2015 projected); Race: 92.7% White, 0.4% Black, 0.4% Asian, 6.5% Other, 7.8% Hispanic of any race (2010); Density: 322.8 persons per square mile (2010); Average household size: 2.82 (2010); Median age: 37.4 (2010); Males per 100 females: 104.7 (2010); Marriage status: 22.3% never married, 63.2% now married, 8.3% widowed, 6.2% divorced (2005-2009 5-year est.); Foreign born: 9.9% (2005-2009 5-year est.); Ancestry (includes multiple ancestries): 12.9% Irish, 9.1% American, 6.2% German, 5.0% English, 2.5% Dutch (2005-2009 5-year est.).
Economy: Single-family building permits issued: 5 (2010); Multi-family building permits issued: 0 (2010); Employment by occupation: 14.5% management, 15.5% professional, 6.9% services, 25.9% sales, 0.0% farming, 10.2% construction, 27.0% production (2005-2009 5-year est.).
Income: Per capita income: $20,431 (2010); Median household income: $47,712 (2010); Average household income: $56,730 (2010); Percent of households with income of $100,000 or more: 11.6% (2010); Poverty rate: 11.7% (2005-2009 5-year est.).
Taxes: Total city taxes per capita: $148 (2007); City property taxes per capita: $128 (2007).
Education: Percent of population age 25 and over with: High school diploma (including GED) or higher: 80.7% (2010); Bachelor's degree or higher: 15.3% (2010); Master's degree or higher: 1.7% (2010).
Housing: Homeownership rate: 79.7% (2010); Median home value: $133,523 (2010); Median contract rent: $443 per month (2005-2009 5-year est.); Median year structure built: 1988 (2005-2009 5-year est.).
Transportation: Commute to work: 91.2% car, 0.0% public transportation, 0.0% walk, 5.3% work from home (2005-2009 5-year est.); Travel time to work: 20.2% less than 15 minutes, 27.9% 15 to 30 minutes, 18.5% 30 to 45 minutes, 15.6% 45 to 60 minutes, 17.8% 60 minutes or more (2005-2009 5-year est.)

BOYD (town). Covers a land area of 2.876 square miles and a water area of 0 square miles. Located at 33.07° N. Lat; 97.56° W. Long. Elevation is 728 feet.

Population: 1,041 (1990); 1,099 (2000); 1,353 (2010); 1,468 (2015 projected); Race: 85.4% White, 0.3% Black, 0.1% Asian, 14.1% Other, 18.8% Hispanic of any race (2010); Density: 470.4 persons per square mile (2010); Average household size: 2.62 (2010); Median age: 36.2 (2010); Males per 100 females: 98.7 (2010); Marriage status: 27.7% never married, 46.6% now married, 8.5% widowed, 17.2% divorced (2005-2009 5-year est.); Foreign born: 7.4% (2005-2009 5-year est.); Ancestry (includes multiple ancestries): 12.7% Irish, 9.2% American, 7.8% German, 5.5% English, 2.8% Swedish (2005-2009 5-year est.).

Economy: Single-family building permits issued: 0 (2010); Multi-family building permits issued: 0 (2010); Employment by occupation: 13.8% management, 17.2% professional, 18.1% services, 26.3% sales, 0.0% farming, 13.5% construction, 11.1% production (2005-2009 5-year est.).

Income: Per capita income: $21,287 (2010); Median household income: $49,357 (2010); Average household income: $55,649 (2010); Percent of households with income of $100,000 or more: 13.2% (2010); Poverty rate: 23.3% (2005-2009 5-year est.).

Taxes: Total city taxes per capita: $520 (2007); City property taxes per capita: $272 (2007).

Education: Percent of population age 25 and over with: High school diploma (including GED) or higher: 74.7% (2010); Bachelor's degree or higher: 13.1% (2010); Master's degree or higher: 2.6% (2010).

School District(s)

Boyd ISD (PK-12)
    2009-10 Enrollment: 1,032 . . . . (940) 433-2327

Housing: Homeownership rate: 70.3% (2010); Median home value: $90,938 (2010); Median contract rent: $460 per month (2005-2009 5-year est.); Median year structure built: 1983 (2005-2009 5-year est.).

Transportation: Commute to work: 95.6% car, 1.8% public transportation, 1.8% walk, 0.8% work from home (2005-2009 5-year est.); Travel time to work: 26.7% less than 15 minutes, 26.1% 15 to 30 minutes, 13.9% 30 to 45 minutes, 17.2% 45 to 60 minutes, 16.2% 60 minutes or more (2005-2009 5-year est.)

BRIDGEPORT (city). Covers a land area of 3.709 square miles and a water area of 0.021 square miles. Located at 33.21° N. Lat; 97.76° W. Long. Elevation is 801 feet.

History: Bridgeport developed as a coal mining center. The town's later economy was supported by brickyards and a rock-crushing plant.

Population: 3,717 (1990); 4,309 (2000); 4,856 (2010); 5,173 (2015 projected); Race: 73.0% White, 4.7% Black, 0.2% Asian, 22.1% Other, 37.7% Hispanic of any race (2010); Density: 1,309.4 persons per square mile (2010); Average household size: 2.91 (2010); Median age: 33.6 (2010); Males per 100 females: 90.9 (2010); Marriage status: 39.8% never married, 47.2% now married, 6.2% widowed, 6.9% divorced (2005-2009 5-year est.); Foreign born: 12.7% (2005-2009 5-year est.); Ancestry (includes multiple ancestries): 11.7% German, 10.1% English, 8.7% American, 6.2% Irish, 2.4% French (2005-2009 5-year est.).

Economy: Single-family building permits issued: 3 (2010); Multi-family building permits issued: 0 (2010); Employment by occupation: 9.5% management, 10.8% professional, 19.4% services, 18.1% sales, 0.0% farming, 20.6% construction, 21.6% production (2005-2009 5-year est.).

Income: Per capita income: $17,769 (2010); Median household income: $42,898 (2010); Average household income: $53,563 (2010); Percent of households with income of $100,000 or more: 10.6% (2010); Poverty rate: 9.9% (2005-2009 5-year est.).

Taxes: Total city taxes per capita: $578 (2007); City property taxes per capita: $206 (2007).

Education: Percent of population age 25 and over with: High school diploma (including GED) or higher: 68.6% (2010); Bachelor's degree or higher: 12.8% (2010); Master's degree or higher: 4.5% (2010).

School District(s)

Bridgeport ISD (PK-12)
    2009-10 Enrollment: 2,258 . . . . (940) 683-5124

Housing: Homeownership rate: 67.0% (2010); Median home value: $85,168 (2010); Median contract rent: $600 per month (2005-2009 5-year est.); Median year structure built: 1972 (2005-2009 5-year est.).

Safety: Violent crime rate: 14.4 per 10,000 population; Property crime rate: 181.4 per 10,000 population (2009).

Newspapers: The Chico Texan (Community news; Circulation 800); Index (Community news; Circulation 800)

Transportation: Commute to work: 95.6% car, 0.0% public transportation, 2.0% walk, 2.4% work from home (2005-2009 5-year est.); Travel time to work: 54.0% less than 15 minutes, 24.9% 15 to 30 minutes, 14.6% 30 to 45 minutes, 3.2% 45 to 60 minutes, 3.3% 60 minutes or more (2005-2009 5-year est.)

Additional Information Contacts

Bridgeport Area Chamber of Commerce . . . . (940) 683-2076
    http://www.bridgeportchamber.org
City of Bridgeport . . . . (940) 683-3400
    http://www.cityofbridgeport.net

CHICO (city). Covers a land area of 1.256 square miles and a water area of 0 square miles. Located at 33.29° N. Lat; 97.80° W. Long. Elevation is 925 feet.

Population: 800 (1990); 947 (2000); 1,042 (2010); 1,096 (2015 projected); Race: 92.3% White, 1.2% Black, 0.1% Asian, 6.4% Other, 8.3% Hispanic of any race (2010); Density: 829.9 persons per square mile (2010); Average household size: 2.55 (2010); Median age: 36.5 (2010); Males per 100 females: 99.2 (2010); Marriage status: 28.3% never married, 51.3% now married, 6.1% widowed, 14.3% divorced (2005-2009 5-year est.); Foreign born: 2.3% (2005-2009 5-year est.); Ancestry (includes multiple ancestries): 8.8% American, 6.3% Irish, 3.3% English, 2.9% Dutch, 2.7% German (2005-2009 5-year est.).

Economy: Single-family building permits issued: 0 (2010); Multi-family building permits issued: 0 (2010); Employment by occupation: 9.1% management, 12.2% professional, 16.6% services, 31.0% sales, 1.6% farming, 12.6% construction, 16.9% production (2005-2009 5-year est.).

Income: Per capita income: $21,872 (2010); Median household income: $45,750 (2010); Average household income: $55,018 (2010); Percent of households with income of $100,000 or more: 10.3% (2010); Poverty rate: 21.2% (2005-2009 5-year est.).

Taxes: Total city taxes per capita: $485 (2007); City property taxes per capita: $246 (2007).

Education: Percent of population age 25 and over with: High school diploma (including GED) or higher: 68.9% (2010); Bachelor's degree or higher: 7.7% (2010); Master's degree or higher: 1.5% (2010).

School District(s)

Chico ISD (PK-12)
    2009-10 Enrollment: 617 . . . . (940) 644-2228

Housing: Homeownership rate: 74.8% (2010); Median home value: $70,392 (2010); Median contract rent: $483 per month (2005-2009 5-year est.); Median year structure built: 1981 (2005-2009 5-year est.).

Transportation: Commute to work: 91.8% car, 0.0% public transportation, 5.4% walk, 2.8% work from home (2005-2009 5-year est.); Travel time to work: 47.6% less than 15 minutes, 35.3% 15 to 30 minutes, 8.7% 30 to 45 minutes, 2.7% 45 to 60 minutes, 5.8% 60 minutes or more (2005-2009 5-year est.)

DECATUR (city). County seat. Covers a land area of 6.957 square miles and a water area of 0 square miles. Located at 33.23° N. Lat; 97.58° W. Long. Elevation is 1,102 feet.

History: Decatur developed as a shopping and shipping center for the surrounding agricultural and dairy region. Decatur Baptist College was founded here in 1892.

Population: 4,289 (1990); 5,201 (2000); 6,577 (2010); 7,279 (2015 projected); Race: 73.4% White, 1.7% Black, 1.2% Asian, 23.7% Other, 32.3% Hispanic of any race (2010); Density: 945.4 persons per square mile (2010); Average household size: 2.74 (2010); Median age: 34.2 (2010); Males per 100 females: 97.6 (2010); Marriage status: 26.3% never married, 48.4% now married, 11.1% widowed, 14.1% divorced (2005-2009 5-year est.); Foreign born: 19.7% (2005-2009 5-year est.); Ancestry (includes multiple ancestries): 10.2% German, 8.6% American, 7.5% English, 6.7% Irish, 4.1% French (2005-2009 5-year est.).

Economy: Single-family building permits issued: 16 (2010); Multi-family building permits issued: 0 (2010); Employment by occupation: 10.0% management, 16.6% professional, 20.1% services, 14.7% sales, 6.3% farming, 11.1% construction, 21.2% production (2005-2009 5-year est.).

Income: Per capita income: $22,489 (2010); Median household income: $48,698 (2010); Average household income: $63,574 (2010); Percent of households with income of $100,000 or more: 17.5% (2010); Poverty rate: 15.9% (2005-2009 5-year est.).

Taxes: Total city taxes per capita: $1,108 (2007); City property taxes per capita: $586 (2007).

Education: Percent of population age 25 and over with: High school diploma (including GED) or higher: 75.2% (2010); Bachelor's degree or higher: 19.5% (2010); Master's degree or higher: 7.5% (2010).

School District(s)

Decatur ISD (PK-12)
    2009-10 Enrollment: 2,976 . . . . (940) 393-7100
Housing: Homeownership rate: 63.6% (2010); Median home value: $112,852 (2010); Median contract rent: $509 per month (2005-2009 5-year est.); Median year structure built: 1980 (2005-2009 5-year est.).
Hospitals: Wise Regional Health System; Wise Regional Health System - East Campus
Safety: Violent crime rate: 28.9 per 10,000 population; Property crime rate: 389.4 per 10,000 population (2009).
Newspapers: Wise County Messenger (Local news; Circulation 9,981)
Transportation: Commute to work: 97.3% car, 0.0% public transportation, 1.3% walk, 1.1% work from home (2005-2009 5-year est.); Travel time to work: 60.2% less than 15 minutes, 18.7% 15 to 30 minutes, 10.6% 30 to 45 minutes, 6.9% 45 to 60 minutes, 3.6% 60 minutes or more (2005-2009 5-year est.)

Additional Information Contacts

City of Decatur . . . . (940) 627-2741
    http://www.decaturtx.org
Decatur Chamber of Commerce . . . . (940) 627-3107
    http://www.decaturtx.com

LAKE BRIDGEPORT (city). Covers a land area of 0.474 square miles and a water area of 0 square miles. Located at 33.20° N. Lat; 97.83° W. Long. Elevation is 912 feet.

Population: 322 (1990); 372 (2000); 416 (2010); 442 (2015 projected); Race: 95.0% White, 0.5% Black, 0.0% Asian, 4.6% Other, 10.8% Hispanic of any race (2010); Density: 877.9 persons per square mile (2010); Average household size: 2.39 (2010); Median age: 45.8 (2010); Males per 100 females: 104.9 (2010); Marriage status: 21.7% never married, 55.8% now married, 3.1% widowed, 19.4% divorced (2005-2009 5-year est.); Foreign born: 0.0% (2005-2009 5-year est.); Ancestry (includes multiple ancestries): 15.7% American, 13.4% German, 9.6% English, 3.6% Irish, 2.7% French (2005-2009 5-year est.).
Economy: Single-family building permits issued: 0 (2010); Multi-family building permits issued: 0 (2010); Employment by occupation: 14.4% management, 6.5% professional, 14.9% services, 29.3% sales, 0.0% farming, 11.6% construction, 23.3% production (2005-2009 5-year est.).
Income: Per capita income: $28,042 (2010); Median household income: $53,378 (2010); Average household income: $67,069 (2010); Percent of households with income of $100,000 or more: 23.0% (2010); Poverty rate: 6.4% (2005-2009 5-year est.).
Taxes: Total city taxes per capita: $142 (2007); City property taxes per capita: $0 (2007).
Education: Percent of population age 25 and over with: High school diploma (including GED) or higher: 81.3% (2010); Bachelor's degree or higher: 15.8% (2010); Master's degree or higher: 8.6% (2010).
Housing: Homeownership rate: 82.2% (2010); Median home value: $78,125 (2010); Median contract rent: $524 per month (2005-2009 5-year est.); Median year structure built: 1978 (2005-2009 5-year est.).
Transportation: Commute to work: 86.6% car, 0.0% public transportation, 0.0% walk, 10.2% work from home (2005-2009 5-year est.); Travel time to work: 30.5% less than 15 minutes, 42.5% 15 to 30 minutes, 6.0% 30 to 45 minutes, 1.8% 45 to 60 minutes, 19.2% 60 minutes or more (2005-2009 5-year est.)

NEW FAIRVIEW (city). Covers a land area of 15.089 square miles and a water area of 0.014 square miles. Located at 33.11° N. Lat; 97.46° W. Long. Elevation is 938 feet.

Population: 185 (1990); 877 (2000); 1,401 (2010); 1,616 (2015 projected); Race: 86.2% White, 2.9% Black, 0.2% Asian, 10.7% Other, 12.1% Hispanic of any race (2010); Density: 92.9 persons per square mile (2010); Average household size: 2.98 (2010); Median age: 34.9 (2010); Males per 100 females: 101.3 (2010); Marriage status: 31.3% never married, 60.8% now married, 2.9% widowed, 5.0% divorced (2005-2009 5-year est.); Foreign born: 10.1% (2005-2009 5-year est.); Ancestry (includes multiple ancestries): 11.6% English, 11.2% Irish, 7.4% Scottish, 5.0% German, 2.6% American (2005-2009 5-year est.).
Economy: Employment by occupation: 12.5% management, 6.1% professional, 17.5% services, 30.1% sales, 0.0% farming, 13.4% construction, 20.5% production (2005-2009 5-year est.).

Income: Per capita income: $25,145 (2010); Median household income: $65,870 (2010); Average household income: $74,830 (2010); Percent of households with income of $100,000 or more: 21.1% (2010); Poverty rate: 19.0% (2005-2009 5-year est.).
Taxes: Total city taxes per capita: $75 (2007); City property taxes per capita: $0 (2007).
Education: Percent of population age 25 and over with: High school diploma (including GED) or higher: 86.6% (2010); Bachelor's degree or higher: 15.5% (2010); Master's degree or higher: 5.4% (2010).
Housing: Homeownership rate: 86.8% (2010); Median home value: $130,882 (2010); Median contract rent: $472 per month (2005-2009 5-year est.); Median year structure built: 1996 (2005-2009 5-year est.).
Transportation: Commute to work: 98.7% car, 0.0% public transportation, 0.0% walk, 0.7% work from home (2005-2009 5-year est.); Travel time to work: 7.2% less than 15 minutes, 30.4% 15 to 30 minutes, 22.8% 30 to 45 minutes, 27.8% 45 to 60 minutes, 11.8% 60 minutes or more (2005-2009 5-year est.)

NEWARK (city). Covers a land area of 0.689 square miles and a water area of 0 square miles. Located at 33.00° N. Lat; 97.48° W. Long. Elevation is 696 feet.

Population: 658 (1990); 887 (2000); 1,156 (2010); 1,289 (2015 projected); Race: 88.8% White, 0.4% Black, 0.2% Asian, 10.6% Other, 11.7% Hispanic of any race (2010); Density: 1,676.6 persons per square mile (2010); Average household size: 2.95 (2010); Median age: 35.6 (2010); Males per 100 females: 95.3 (2010); Marriage status: 16.9% never married, 62.6% now married, 5.4% widowed, 15.2% divorced (2005-2009 5-year est.); Foreign born: 10.9% (2005-2009 5-year est.); Ancestry (includes multiple ancestries): 10.6% Irish, 9.0% English, 6.5% Dutch, 5.8% German, 3.5% Norwegian (2005-2009 5-year est.).
Economy: Single-family building permits issued: 0 (2010); Multi-family building permits issued: 0 (2010); Employment by occupation: 8.8% management, 16.7% professional, 12.4% services, 26.0% sales, 0.0% farming, 26.0% construction, 10.0% production (2005-2009 5-year est.).
Income: Per capita income: $24,885 (2010); Median household income: $61,859 (2010); Average household income: $74,177 (2010); Percent of households with income of $100,000 or more: 21.9% (2010); Poverty rate: 8.4% (2005-2009 5-year est.).
Taxes: Total city taxes per capita: $161 (2007); City property taxes per capita: $161 (2007).
Education: Percent of population age 25 and over with: High school diploma (including GED) or higher: 82.6% (2010); Bachelor's degree or higher: 10.8% (2010); Master's degree or higher: 1.6% (2010).
Housing: Homeownership rate: 77.0% (2010); Median home value: $103,000 (2010); Median contract rent: $479 per month (2005-2009 5-year est.); Median year structure built: 1983 (2005-2009 5-year est.).
Transportation: Commute to work: 93.3% car, 0.0% public transportation, 1.6% walk, 2.5% work from home (2005-2009 5-year est.); Travel time to work: 19.7% less than 15 minutes, 34.1% 15 to 30 minutes, 27.3% 30 to 45 minutes, 17.5% 45 to 60 minutes, 1.4% 60 minutes or more (2005-2009 5-year est.)

Additional Information Contacts

City of Newark . . . . (817) 489-2201
    http://newarktexas.com

PARADISE (city). Covers a land area of 1.989 square miles and a water area of 0 square miles. Located at 33.15° N. Lat; 97.68° W. Long. Elevation is 758 feet.

Population: 388 (1990); 459 (2000); 483 (2010); 499 (2015 projected); Race: 94.0% White, 0.0% Black, 0.0% Asian, 6.0% Other, 6.8% Hispanic of any race (2010); Density: 242.9 persons per square mile (2010); Average household size: 2.81 (2010); Median age: 37.7 (2010); Males per 100 females: 98.8 (2010); Marriage status: 20.6% never married, 47.9% now married, 14.6% widowed, 16.8% divorced (2005-2009 5-year est.); Foreign born: 2.3% (2005-2009 5-year est.); Ancestry (includes multiple ancestries): 17.2% English, 11.6% Irish, 8.1% German, 7.3% Dutch, 6.7% American (2005-2009 5-year est.).
Economy: Single-family building permits issued: 0 (2010); Multi-family building permits issued: 0 (2010); Employment by occupation: 4.5% management, 14.0% professional, 14.5% services, 25.5% sales, 0.0% farming, 20.0% construction, 21.5% production (2005-2009 5-year est.).
Income: Per capita income: $23,953 (2010); Median household income: $61,111 (2010); Average household income: $66,890 (2010); Percent of households with income of $100,000 or more: 16.9% (2010); Poverty rate: 18.9% (2005-2009 5-year est.).

Taxes: Total city taxes per capita: $178 (2007); City property taxes per capita: $72 (2007).
Education: Percent of population age 25 and over with: High school diploma (including GED) or higher: 80.7% (2010); Bachelor's degree or higher: 14.1% (2010); Master's degree or higher: 4.3% (2010).
School District(s)
Paradise ISD (PK-12)
   2009-10 Enrollment: 1,036 . . . . (940) 969-5000
Housing: Homeownership rate: 81.4% (2010); Median home value: $125,000 (2010); Median contract rent: $491 per month (2005-2009 5-year est.); Median year structure built: 1970 (2005-2009 5-year est.).
Transportation: Commute to work: 96.0% car, 0.0% public transportation, 1.0% walk, 3.0% work from home (2005-2009 5-year est.); Travel time to work: 44.3% less than 15 minutes, 24.7% 15 to 30 minutes, 16.5% 30 to 45 minutes, 6.7% 45 to 60 minutes, 7.7% 60 minutes or more (2005-2009 5-year est.)

PECAN ACRES (CDP). Covers a land area of 19.406 square miles and a water area of 1.851 square miles. Located at 32.98° N. Lat; 97.48° W. Long.
Population: 1,681 (1990); 2,289 (2000); 3,381 (2010); 3,793 (2015 projected); Race: 90.0% White, 1.4% Black, 0.6% Asian, 8.0% Other, 8.8% Hispanic of any race (2010); Density: 174.2 persons per square mile (2010); Average household size: 2.88 (2010); Median age: 36.3 (2010); Males per 100 females: 97.1 (2010); Marriage status: 21.7% never married, 63.7% now married, 3.4% widowed, 11.1% divorced (2005-2009 5-year est.); Foreign born: 6.5% (2005-2009 5-year est.); Ancestry (includes multiple ancestries): 16.5% American, 7.6% German, 7.2% Irish, 5.3% African, 3.4% Scotch-Irish (2005-2009 5-year est.).
Economy: Employment by occupation: 21.8% management, 12.6% professional, 10.7% services, 40.6% sales, 0.0% farming, 4.6% construction, 9.8% production (2005-2009 5-year est.).
Income: Per capita income: $24,899 (2010); Median household income: $61,040 (2010); Average household income: $71,841 (2010); Percent of households with income of $100,000 or more: 20.1% (2010); Poverty rate: 7.3% (2005-2009 5-year est.).
Education: Percent of population age 25 and over with: High school diploma (including GED) or higher: 81.7% (2010); Bachelor's degree or higher: 14.3% (2010); Master's degree or higher: 4.2% (2010).
Housing: Homeownership rate: 81.1% (2010); Median home value: $107,028 (2010); Median contract rent: $461 per month (2005-2009 5-year est.); Median year structure built: 1994 (2005-2009 5-year est.).
Transportation: Commute to work: 78.3% car, 0.0% public transportation, 0.0% walk, 18.4% work from home (2005-2009 5-year est.); Travel time to work: 17.3% less than 15 minutes, 24.7% 15 to 30 minutes, 33.2% 30 to 45 minutes, 21.7% 45 to 60 minutes, 3.1% 60 minutes or more (2005-2009 5-year est.)

RHOME (city). Covers a land area of 1.774 square miles and a water area of 0 square miles. Located at 33.04° N. Lat; 97.46° W. Long. Elevation is 942 feet.
Population: 622 (1990); 551 (2000); 888 (2010); 1,023 (2015 projected); Race: 86.3% White, 2.8% Black, 0.2% Asian, 10.7% Other, 11.9% Hispanic of any race (2010); Density: 500.6 persons per square mile (2010); Average household size: 2.98 (2010); Median age: 34.9 (2010); Males per 100 females: 100.5 (2010); Marriage status: 18.1% never married, 55.6% now married, 4.5% widowed, 21.8% divorced (2005-2009 5-year est.); Foreign born: 5.1% (2005-2009 5-year est.); Ancestry (includes multiple ancestries): 15.9% German, 11.7% American, 7.6% Irish, 4.7% English, 3.8% French (2005-2009 5-year est.).
Economy: Single-family building permits issued: 2 (2010); Multi-family building permits issued: 0 (2010); Employment by occupation: 6.2% management, 8.3% professional, 19.5% services, 33.3% sales, 3.4% farming, 10.1% construction, 19.2% production (2005-2009 5-year est.).
Income: Per capita income: $25,125 (2010); Median household income: $65,625 (2010); Average household income: $74,622 (2010); Percent of households with income of $100,000 or more: 21.1% (2010); Poverty rate: 6.7% (2005-2009 5-year est.).
Taxes: Total city taxes per capita: $86 (2007); City property taxes per capita: $79 (2007).
Education: Percent of population age 25 and over with: High school diploma (including GED) or higher: 86.5% (2010); Bachelor's degree or higher: 15.5% (2010); Master's degree or higher: 5.2% (2010).

School District(s)
Northwest ISD (PK-12)
   2009-10 Enrollment: 14,164 . . . . (817) 215-0000
Housing: Homeownership rate: 86.6% (2010); Median home value: $130,952 (2010); Median contract rent: $492 per month (2005-2009 5-year est.); Median year structure built: 1997 (2005-2009 5-year est.).
Transportation: Commute to work: 94.5% car, 0.0% public transportation, 0.4% walk, 5.0% work from home (2005-2009 5-year est.); Travel time to work: 17.1% less than 15 minutes, 30.7% 15 to 30 minutes, 30.1% 30 to 45 minutes, 13.6% 45 to 60 minutes, 8.6% 60 minutes or more (2005-2009 5-year est.)
Additional Information Contacts
South Wise County Chamber of Commerce . . . . (817) 636-2560
   http://www.southwisechamber.com

RUNAWAY BAY (city). Covers a land area of 2.307 square miles and a water area of 4.194 square miles. Located at 33.17° N. Lat; 97.87° W. Long. Elevation is 912 feet.
Population: 710 (1990); 1,104 (2000); 1,499 (2010); 1,682 (2015 projected); Race: 97.0% White, 1.1% Black, 0.9% Asian, 1.1% Other, 1.3% Hispanic of any race (2010); Density: 649.8 persons per square mile (2010); Average household size: 2.25 (2010); Median age: 49.0 (2010); Males per 100 females: 100.1 (2010); Marriage status: 18.6% never married, 59.4% now married, 3.3% widowed, 18.7% divorced (2005-2009 5-year est.); Foreign born: 2.0% (2005-2009 5-year est.); Ancestry (includes multiple ancestries): 16.3% German, 14.8% Irish, 8.9% American, 8.1% English, 2.6% Scotch-Irish (2005-2009 5-year est.).
Economy: Single-family building permits issued: 5 (2010); Multi-family building permits issued: 0 (2010); Employment by occupation: 17.5% management, 13.6% professional, 8.5% services, 36.2% sales, 0.0% farming, 7.3% construction, 16.8% production (2005-2009 5-year est.).
Income: Per capita income: $32,313 (2010); Median household income: $62,579 (2010); Average household income: $72,741 (2010); Percent of households with income of $100,000 or more: 20.8% (2010); Poverty rate: 3.3% (2005-2009 5-year est.).
Taxes: Total city taxes per capita: $460 (2007); City property taxes per capita: $357 (2007).
Education: Percent of population age 25 and over with: High school diploma (including GED) or higher: 92.8% (2010); Bachelor's degree or higher: 30.4% (2010); Master's degree or higher: 10.7% (2010).
Housing: Homeownership rate: 78.6% (2010); Median home value: $130,710 (2010); Median contract rent: $694 per month (2005-2009 5-year est.); Median year structure built: 1980 (2005-2009 5-year est.).
Safety: Violent crime rate: 0.0 per 10,000 population; Property crime rate: 54.7 per 10,000 population (2009).
Transportation: Commute to work: 95.0% car, 0.0% public transportation, 0.0% walk, 5.0% work from home (2005-2009 5-year est.); Travel time to work: 25.1% less than 15 minutes, 37.3% 15 to 30 minutes, 9.8% 30 to 45 minutes, 9.9% 45 to 60 minutes, 17.9% 60 minutes or more (2005-2009 5-year est.)

Wood County

Located in northeastern Texas; bounded on the south and southwest by the Sabine River; drained by tributaries of the Sabine River. Covers a land area of 650.22 square miles, a water area of 45.58 square miles, and is located in the Central Time Zone at 32.77° N. Lat., 95.37° W. Long. The county was founded in 1850. County seat is Quitman.
Population: 29,380 (1990); 36,752 (2000); 43,511 (2010); 46,720 (2015 projected); Race: 87.7% White, 6.0% Black, 0.3% Asian, 6.0% Other, 8.1% Hispanic of any race (2010); Density: 66.9 persons per square mile (2010); Average household size: 2.38 (2010); Median age: 41.4 (2010); Males per 100 females: 96.5 (2010).
Religion: Five largest groups: 27.5% Southern Baptist Convention, 15.5% Baptist Missionary Association of America, 6.6% The United Methodist Church, 3.3% Catholic Church, 2.6% Churches of Christ (2000).
Economy: Unemployment rate: 9.2% (June 2011); Total civilian labor force: 18,428 (June 2011); Leading industries: 18.3% retail trade; 13.0% health care and social assistance; 12.4% accommodation & food services (2009); Farms: 1,718 totaling 233,796 acres (2007); Companies that employ 500 or more persons: 0 (2009); Companies that employ 100 to 499 persons: 9 (2009); Companies that employ less than 100 persons: 822 (2009); Black-owned businesses: n/a (2007); Hispanic-owned businesses: n/a (2007); Asian-owned businesses: n/a (2007); Women-owned businesses: 1,166 (2007); Retail sales per capita: $8,071 (2010).

Single-family building permits issued: 3 (2010); Multi-family building permits issued: 0 (2010).

Income: Per capita income: $22,308 (2010); Median household income: $41,375 (2010); Average household income: $54,439 (2010); Percent of households with income of $100,000 or more: 10.7% (2010); Poverty rate: 15.0% (2009); Bankruptcy rate: 2.32% (2010).

Taxes: Total county taxes per capita: $282 (2007); County property taxes per capita: $241 (2007).

Education: Percent of population age 25 and over with: High school diploma (including GED) or higher: 80.7% (2010); Bachelor's degree or higher: 14.6% (2010); Master's degree or higher: 4.2% (2010).

Housing: Homeownership rate: 80.2% (2010); Median home value: $90,681 (2010); Median contract rent: $440 per month (2005-2009 5-year est.); Median year structure built: 1982 (2005-2009 5-year est.)

Health: Birth rate: 116.4 per 10,000 population (2009); Death rate: 143.3 per 10,000 population (2009); Age-adjusted cancer mortality rate: 192.7 deaths per 100,000 population (2007); Number of physicians: 6.8 per 10,000 population (2008); Hospital beds: 14.9 per 10,000 population (2007); Hospital admissions: 480.7 per 10,000 population (2007).

Elections: 2008 Presidential election results: 22.5% Obama, 76.8% McCain, 0.1% Nader

Additional Information Contacts

Wood County Government . . . . (903) 763-2716
   http://www.co.wood.tx.us/ips/cms
Greater Quitman Area Chamber of Commerce . . . . (903) 763-4411
   http://www.quitman.com
Hawkins Area Chamber of Commerce . . . . (903) 769-4482
   http://www.hawkinschamberofcommerce.com
Lake Fork Area Chamber of Commerce . . . . (903) 474-3022
   http://www.lakeforkchamber.org
Mineola Area Chamber of Commerce . . . . (903) 569-2087
   http://www.mineolachamber.org
Winnsboro Area Chamber of Commerce . . . . (903) 342-3666
   http://www.winnsboro.com

Wood County Communities

ALBA (town). Covers a land area of 1.109 square miles and a water area of 0 square miles. Located at 32.79° N. Lat; 95.63° W. Long. Elevation is 449 feet.

Population: 489 (1990); 430 (2000); 541 (2010); 596 (2015 projected); Race: 93.0% White, 0.2% Black, 0.0% Asian, 6.8% Other, 7.6% Hispanic of any race (2010); Density: 487.9 persons per square mile (2010); Average household size: 2.46 (2010); Median age: 40.8 (2010); Males per 100 females: 96.0 (2010); Marriage status: 30.6% never married, 46.1% now married, 10.2% widowed, 13.1% divorced (2005-2009 5-year est.); Foreign born: 0.7% (2005-2009 5-year est.); Ancestry (includes multiple ancestries): 31.2% American, 20.0% English, 16.6% Irish, 16.2% German, 5.9% Scottish (2005-2009 5-year est.).

Economy: Employment by occupation: 8.5% management, 20.0% professional, 12.3% services, 16.9% sales, 0.0% farming, 25.4% construction, 16.9% production (2005-2009 5-year est.).

Income: Per capita income: $22,320 (2010); Median household income: $41,667 (2010); Average household income: $54,625 (2010); Percent of households with income of $100,000 or more: 10.9% (2010); Poverty rate: 27.9% (2005-2009 5-year est.).

Taxes: Total city taxes per capita: $396 (2007); City property taxes per capita: $202 (2007).

Education: Percent of population age 25 and over with: High school diploma (including GED) or higher: 82.0% (2010); Bachelor's degree or higher: 12.0% (2010); Master's degree or higher: 1.6% (2010).

School District(s)
Alba-Golden ISD (PK-12)
   2009-10 Enrollment: 870 . . . . (903) 768-2472

Housing: Homeownership rate: 82.7% (2010); Median home value: $101,250 (2010); Median contract rent: $342 per month (2005-2009 5-year est.); Median year structure built: 1974 (2005-2009 5-year est.).

Transportation: Commute to work: 80.0% car, 0.0% public transportation, 0.0% walk, 20.0% work from home (2005-2009 5-year est.); Travel time to work: 23.1% less than 15 minutes, 22.1% 15 to 30 minutes, 3.8% 30 to 45 minutes, 9.6% 45 to 60 minutes, 41.3% 60 minutes or more (2005-2009 5-year est.)

Additional Information Contacts

Lake Fork Area Chamber of Commerce . . . . (903) 474-3022
   http://www.lakeforkchamber.org

HAWKINS (city). Covers a land area of 2.244 square miles and a water area of 0.007 square miles. Located at 32.59° N. Lat; 95.20° W. Long. Elevation is 407 feet.

Population: 1,309 (1990); 1,331 (2000); 1,537 (2010); 1,639 (2015 projected); Race: 80.6% White, 17.7% Black, 0.0% Asian, 1.7% Other, 0.5% Hispanic of any race (2010); Density: 684.9 persons per square mile (2010); Average household size: 2.51 (2010); Median age: 35.0 (2010); Males per 100 females: 81.3 (2010); Marriage status: 17.1% never married, 59.5% now married, 6.1% widowed, 17.2% divorced (2005-2009 5-year est.); Foreign born: 1.4% (2005-2009 5-year est.); Ancestry (includes multiple ancestries): 24.8% American, 18.2% German, 13.8% English, 11.8% Irish, 6.4% Scotch-Irish (2005-2009 5-year est.).

Economy: Single-family building permits issued: 2 (2010); Multi-family building permits issued: 0 (2010); Employment by occupation: 11.4% management, 26.9% professional, 18.1% services, 19.4% sales, 0.0% farming, 11.5% construction, 12.7% production (2005-2009 5-year est.).

Income: Per capita income: $18,488 (2010); Median household income: $38,516 (2010); Average household income: $47,414 (2010); Percent of households with income of $100,000 or more: 9.3% (2010); Poverty rate: 15.3% (2005-2009 5-year est.).

Taxes: Total city taxes per capita: $429 (2007); City property taxes per capita: $310 (2007).

Education: Percent of population age 25 and over with: High school diploma (including GED) or higher: 87.3% (2010); Bachelor's degree or higher: 18.3% (2010); Master's degree or higher: 9.5% (2010).

School District(s)
Hawkins ISD (PK-12)
   2009-10 Enrollment: 737 . . . . (903) 769-2181

Four-year College(s)
Jarvis Christian College (Private, Not-for-profit, Historically black, Christian Church (Disciples of Christ))
   Fall 2009 Enrollment: 628 . . . . (903) 769-5700
   2010-11 Tuition: In-state $11,146; Out-of-state $11,146

Housing: Homeownership rate: 72.8% (2010); Median home value: $60,192 (2010); Median contract rent: $475 per month (2005-2009 5-year est.); Median year structure built: 1966 (2005-2009 5-year est.).

Safety: Violent crime rate: 38.8 per 10,000 population; Property crime rate: 239.2 per 10,000 population (2009).

Transportation: Commute to work: 94.1% car, 0.0% public transportation, 0.0% walk, 4.9% work from home (2005-2009 5-year est.); Travel time to work: 39.4% less than 15 minutes, 20.3% 15 to 30 minutes, 19.3% 30 to 45 minutes, 11.9% 45 to 60 minutes, 9.1% 60 minutes or more (2005-2009 5-year est.)

Additional Information Contacts

Hawkins Area Chamber of Commerce . . . . (903) 769-4482
   http://www.hawkinschamberofcommerce.com

MINEOLA (city). Covers a land area of 5.293 square miles and a water area of 0.042 square miles. Located at 32.66° N. Lat; 95.48° W. Long. Elevation is 417 feet.

History: Settled 1872, incorporated 1873.

Population: 4,306 (1990); 4,550 (2000); 5,347 (2010); 5,735 (2015 projected); Race: 77.0% White, 11.0% Black, 0.5% Asian, 11.5% Other, 17.7% Hispanic of any race (2010); Density: 1,010.2 persons per square mile (2010); Average household size: 2.48 (2010); Median age: 36.5 (2010); Males per 100 females: 89.5 (2010); Marriage status: 32.2% never married, 45.6% now married, 10.5% widowed, 11.6% divorced (2005-2009 5-year est.); Foreign born: 11.9% (2005-2009 5-year est.); Ancestry (includes multiple ancestries): 16.5% American, 15.4% German, 13.1% Irish, 10.2% English, 3.0% British (2005-2009 5-year est.).

Economy: Single-family building permits issued: 1 (2010); Multi-family building permits issued: 0 (2010); Employment by occupation: 6.9% management, 10.8% professional, 26.6% services, 23.0% sales, 3.0% farming, 16.2% construction, 13.6% production (2005-2009 5-year est.).

Income: Per capita income: $19,879 (2010); Median household income: $37,909 (2010); Average household income: $50,236 (2010); Percent of households with income of $100,000 or more: 10.8% (2010); Poverty rate: 24.7% (2005-2009 5-year est.).

Taxes: Total city taxes per capita: $495 (2007); City property taxes per capita: $187 (2007).

Education: Percent of population age 25 and over with: High school diploma (including GED) or higher: 77.1% (2010); Bachelor's degree or higher: 13.3% (2010); Master's degree or higher: 2.5% (2010).

School District(s)

Mineola ISD (PK-12)

   2009-10 Enrollment: 1,581 . . . . (903) 569-2448

Housing: Homeownership rate: 63.8% (2010); Median home value: $83,081 (2010); Median contract rent: $398 per month (2005-2009 5-year est.); Median year structure built: 1960 (2005-2009 5-year est.).

Safety: Violent crime rate: 24.7 per 10,000 population; Property crime rate: 291.3 per 10,000 population (2009).

Newspapers: Mineola Monitor (Community news; Circulation 3,100)

Transportation: Commute to work: 91.4% car, 0.0% public transportation, 4.1% walk, 1.7% work from home (2005-2009 5-year est.); Travel time to work: 32.2% less than 15 minutes, 25.2% 15 to 30 minutes, 13.9% 30 to 45 minutes, 6.6% 45 to 60 minutes, 22.1% 60 minutes or more (2005-2009 5-year est.); Amtrak: train service available.

Additional Information Contacts

Mineola Area Chamber of Commerce . . . . (903) 569-2087
   http://www.mineolachamber.org

QUITMAN (city). County seat. Covers a land area of 1.840 square miles and a water area of 0 square miles. Located at 32.79° N. Lat; 95.44° W. Long. Elevation is 413 feet.

History: Governor Hogg Shrine State Historic Site is here.

Population: 1,694 (1990); 2,030 (2000); 2,318 (2010); 2,482 (2015 projected); Race: 88.3% White, 5.7% Black, 0.4% Asian, 5.6% Other, 6.9% Hispanic of any race (2010); Density: 1,260.1 persons per square mile (2010); Average household size: 2.38 (2010); Median age: 44.2 (2010); Males per 100 females: 87.5 (2010); Marriage status: 18.6% never married, 50.9% now married, 19.7% widowed, 10.8% divorced (2005-2009 5-year est.); Foreign born: 5.2% (2005-2009 5-year est.); Ancestry (includes multiple ancestries): 19.1% American, 12.5% Irish, 12.1% German, 10.2% English, 6.3% French (2005-2009 5-year est.).

Economy: Single-family building permits issued: 0 (2010); Multi-family building permits issued: 0 (2010); Employment by occupation: 2.9% management, 11.5% professional, 22.1% services, 24.7% sales, 7.8% farming, 16.2% construction, 14.8% production (2005-2009 5-year est.).

Income: Per capita income: $24,331 (2010); Median household income: $45,419 (2010); Average household income: $61,051 (2010); Percent of households with income of $100,000 or more: 14.0% (2010); Poverty rate: 15.9% (2005-2009 5-year est.).

Taxes: Total city taxes per capita: $367 (2007); City property taxes per capita: $156 (2007).

Education: Percent of population age 25 and over with: High school diploma (including GED) or higher: 78.0% (2010); Bachelor's degree or higher: 18.1% (2010); Master's degree or higher: 5.3% (2010).

School District(s)

Quitman ISD (PK-12)

   2009-10 Enrollment: 1,115 . . . . (903) 763-5000

Winnsboro ISD (PK-12)

   2009-10 Enrollment: 1,428 . . . . (903) 342-3737

Housing: Homeownership rate: 68.9% (2010); Median home value: $85,698 (2010); Median contract rent: $470 per month (2005-2009 5-year est.); Median year structure built: 1971 (2005-2009 5-year est.).

Safety: Violent crime rate: 93.2 per 10,000 population; Property crime rate: 319.4 per 10,000 population (2009).

Newspapers: Wood County Democrat (Community news; Circulation 3,600)

Transportation: Commute to work: 93.2% car, 0.0% public transportation, 1.9% walk, 2.7% work from home (2005-2009 5-year est.); Travel time to work: 52.7% less than 15 minutes, 28.8% 15 to 30 minutes, 5.0% 30 to 45 minutes, 4.3% 45 to 60 minutes, 9.3% 60 minutes or more (2005-2009 5-year est.)

Additional Information Contacts

Greater Quitman Area Chamber of Commerce . . . . (903) 763-4411
   http://www.quitman.com

WINNSBORO (city). Covers a land area of 3.680 square miles and a water area of <.001 square miles. Located at 32.95° N. Lat; 95.29° W. Long. Elevation is 525 feet.

Population: 2,948 (1990); 3,584 (2000); 4,163 (2010); 4,453 (2015 projected); Race: 77.4% White, 13.1% Black, 1.6% Asian, 7.9% Other, 9.3% Hispanic of any race (2010); Density: 1,131.2 persons per square mile (2010); Average household size: 2.30 (2010); Median age: 37.4 (2010); Males per 100 females: 115.3 (2010); Marriage status: 23.4% never married, 36.6% now married, 22.8% widowed, 17.2% divorced (2005-2009 5-year est.); Foreign born: 0.9% (2005-2009 5-year est.);

Ancestry (includes multiple ancestries): 17.0% American, 13.0% Irish, 11.5% German, 10.9% English, 3.6% Italian (2005-2009 5-year est.).

Economy: Single-family building permits issued: 0 (2010); Multi-family building permits issued: 0 (2010); Employment by occupation: 9.3% management, 17.2% professional, 15.5% services, 25.1% sales, 0.0% farming, 9.2% construction, 23.8% production (2005-2009 5-year est.).

Income: Per capita income: $18,477 (2010); Median household income: $35,267 (2010); Average household income: $45,450 (2010); Percent of households with income of $100,000 or more: 6.0% (2010); Poverty rate: 16.5% (2005-2009 5-year est.).

Taxes: Total city taxes per capita: $322 (2007); City property taxes per capita: $148 (2007).

Education: Percent of population age 25 and over with: High school diploma (including GED) or higher: 77.1% (2010); Bachelor's degree or higher: 12.1% (2010); Master's degree or higher: 5.3% (2010).

School District(s)

Winnsboro ISD (PK-12)

   2009-10 Enrollment: 1,428 . . . . (903) 342-3737

Housing: Homeownership rate: 65.0% (2010); Median home value: $77,629 (2010); Median contract rent: $423 per month (2005-2009 5-year est.); Median year structure built: 1962 (2005-2009 5-year est.).

Hospitals: Presbyterian Hospital of Winnsboro (50 beds)

Safety: Violent crime rate: 50.4 per 10,000 population; Property crime rate: 123.5 per 10,000 population (2009).

Newspapers: Winnsboro News (Local news; Circulation 4,800)

Transportation: Commute to work: 94.1% car, 0.0% public transportation, 3.5% walk, 2.4% work from home (2005-2009 5-year est.); Travel time to work: 53.1% less than 15 minutes, 15.1% 15 to 30 minutes, 16.3% 30 to 45 minutes, 7.3% 45 to 60 minutes, 8.3% 60 minutes or more (2005-2009 5-year est.)

Additional Information Contacts

Winnsboro Area Chamber of Commerce . . . . (903) 342-3666
   http://www.winnsboro.com

YANTIS (town). Covers a land area of 1.868 square miles and a water area of 0 square miles. Located at 32.93° N. Lat; 95.57° W. Long. Elevation is 486 feet.

Population: 210 (1990); 321 (2000); 404 (2010); 441 (2015 projected); Race: 93.1% White, 1.0% Black, 0.2% Asian, 5.7% Other, 10.4% Hispanic of any race (2010); Density: 216.3 persons per square mile (2010); Average household size: 2.26 (2010); Median age: 46.8 (2010); Males per 100 females: 96.1 (2010); Marriage status: 29.5% never married, 49.5% now married, 6.5% widowed, 14.4% divorced (2005-2009 5-year est.); Foreign born: 1.0% (2005-2009 5-year est.); Ancestry (includes multiple ancestries): 18.5% American, 18.2% Irish, 16.8% German, 5.2% English, 4.5% French (2005-2009 5-year est.).

Economy: Employment by occupation: 17.8% management, 19.1% professional, 5.3% services, 27.1% sales, 4.4% farming, 17.3% construction, 8.9% production (2005-2009 5-year est.).

Income: Per capita income: $28,592 (2010); Median household income: $44,044 (2010); Average household income: $63,128 (2010); Percent of households with income of $100,000 or more: 12.3% (2010); Poverty rate: 8.3% (2005-2009 5-year est.).

Taxes: Total city taxes per capita: $120 (2007); City property taxes per capita: $49 (2007).

Education: Percent of population age 25 and over with: High school diploma (including GED) or higher: 80.5% (2010); Bachelor's degree or higher: 12.6% (2010); Master's degree or higher: 2.3% (2010).

School District(s)

Yantis ISD (PK-12)

   2009-10 Enrollment: 384 . . . . (903) 383-2463

Housing: Homeownership rate: 83.8% (2010); Median home value: $99,048 (2010); Median contract rent: $316 per month (2005-2009 5-year est.); Median year structure built: 1989 (2005-2009 5-year est.).

Transportation: Commute to work: 79.1% car, 0.0% public transportation, 2.2% walk, 18.7% work from home (2005-2009 5-year est.); Travel time to work: 25.1% less than 15 minutes, 35.0% 15 to 30 minutes, 5.5% 30 to 45 minutes, 2.7% 45 to 60 minutes, 31.7% 60 minutes or more (2005-2009 5-year est.)

Yoakum County

Located in northwestern Texas; bounded on the west by New Mexico. Covers a land area of 799.75 square miles, a water area of 0.01 square miles, and is located in the Central Time Zone at 33.07° N. Lat., 102.83° W. Long. The county was founded in 1876. County seat is Plains.

Weather Station: Plains   Elevation: 3,680 feet

	Jan	Feb	Mar	Apr	May	Jun	Jul	Aug	Sep	Oct	Nov	Dec
High	54	60	67	75	84	91	93	90	85	76	64	55
Low	25	29	35	42	53	61	64	64	57	45	33	26
Precip	0.6	0.6	1.0	0.9	2.4	2.6	2.1	2.6	2.7	1.4	0.8	0.8
Snow	1.2	1.1	0.3	tr	0.0	0.0	0.0	0.0	0.0	tr	1.1	1.0

High and Low temperatures in degrees Fahrenheit; Precipitation and Snow in inches

Population: 8,786 (1990); 7,322 (2000); 7,567 (2010); 7,674 (2015 projected); Race: 65.4% White, 1.4% Black, 0.1% Asian, 33.1% Other, 54.8% Hispanic of any race (2010); Density: 9.5 persons per square mile (2010); Average household size: 2.88 (2010); Median age: 34.5 (2010); Males per 100 females: 95.4 (2010).
Religion: Five largest groups: 44.2% Catholic Church, 39.5% Southern Baptist Convention, 9.4% The United Methodist Church, 6.1% Churches of Christ, 2.4% Assemblies of God (2000).
Economy: Unemployment rate: 6.2% (June 2011); Total civilian labor force: 3,992 (June 2011); Leading industries: 33.6% mining; 9.6% accommodation & food services; 9.1% wholesale trade (2009); Farms: 348 totaling 443,540 acres (2007); Companies that employ 500 or more persons: 0 (2009); Companies that employ 100 to 499 persons: 4 (2009); Companies that employ less than 100 persons: 173 (2009); Black-owned businesses: n/a (2007); Hispanic-owned businesses: n/a (2007); Asian-owned businesses: n/a (2007); Women-owned businesses: 124 (2007); Retail sales per capita: $7,601 (2010). Single-family building permits issued: 6 (2010); Multi-family building permits issued: 0 (2010).
Income: Per capita income: $21,057 (2010); Median household income: $44,629 (2010); Average household income: $60,757 (2010); Percent of households with income of $100,000 or more: 14.7% (2010); Poverty rate: 12.8% (2009); Bankruptcy rate: 0.63% (2010).
Taxes: Total county taxes per capita: $1,644 (2007); County property taxes per capita: $1,579 (2007).
Education: Percent of population age 25 and over with: High school diploma (including GED) or higher: 65.2% (2010); Bachelor's degree or higher: 11.9% (2010); Master's degree or higher: 3.6% (2010).
Housing: Homeownership rate: 76.4% (2010); Median home value: $37,817 (2010); Median contract rent: $402 per month (2005-2009 5-year est.); Median year structure built: 1972 (2005-2009 5-year est.)
Health: Birth rate: 188.4 per 10,000 population (2009); Death rate: 66.3 per 10,000 population (2009); Age-adjusted cancer mortality rate: 98.7 (Unreliable) deaths per 100,000 population (2007); Number of physicians: 7.9 per 10,000 population (2008); Hospital beds: 29.6 per 10,000 population (2007); Hospital admissions: 867.1 per 10,000 population (2007).
Elections: 2008 Presidential election results: 18.3% Obama, 80.9% McCain, 0.0% Nader
Additional Information Contacts
Yoakum County Government. . . . . (806) 456-2422
    http://www.co.yoakum.tx.us/ips/cms
Denver City Chamber of Commerce . . . . (806) 592-5424
    http://www.denvercitychamber.com

Yoakum County Communities

DENVER CITY (town). Covers a land area of 2.499 square miles and a water area of 0 square miles. Located at 32.96° N. Lat; 102.83° W. Long. Elevation is 3,573 feet.
History: Incorporated after 1940.
Population: 5,227 (1990); 3,985 (2000); 4,077 (2010); 4,113 (2015 projected); Race: 59.1% White, 1.5% Black, 0.2% Asian, 39.1% Other, 58.8% Hispanic of any race (2010); Density: 1,631.3 persons per square mile (2010); Average household size: 2.83 (2010); Median age: 33.2 (2010); Males per 100 females: 94.7 (2010); Marriage status: 15.2% never married, 68.9% now married, 7.9% widowed, 8.0% divorced (2005-2009 5-year est.); Foreign born: 20.6% (2005-2009 5-year est.); Ancestry (includes multiple ancestries): 7.2% German, 4.1% English, 4.1% Irish, 3.4% American, 2.4% Dutch (2005-2009 5-year est.).
Economy: Single-family building permits issued: 3 (2010); Multi-family building permits issued: 0 (2010); Employment by occupation: 5.0% management, 17.5% professional, 15.3% services, 13.8% sales, 6.6% farming, 26.2% construction, 15.7% production (2005-2009 5-year est.).
Income: Per capita income: $19,222 (2010); Median household income: $39,033 (2010); Average household income: $54,540 (2010); Percent of

households with income of $100,000 or more: 11.7% (2010); Poverty rate: 28.1% (2005-2009 5-year est.).
Taxes: Total city taxes per capita: $440 (2007); City property taxes per capita: $285 (2007).
Education: Percent of population age 25 and over with: High school diploma (including GED) or higher: 60.6% (2010); Bachelor's degree or higher: 9.2% (2010); Master's degree or higher: 3.6% (2010).
School District(s)
Denver City ISD (PK-12)
    2009-10 Enrollment: 1,504 . . . . (806) 592-5900
Housing: Homeownership rate: 75.3% (2010); Median home value: $31,782 (2010); Median contract rent: $398 per month (2005-2009 5-year est.); Median year structure built: 1971 (2005-2009 5-year est.).
Hospitals: Yoakum County Hospital (24 beds)
Safety: Violent crime rate: 9.8 per 10,000 population; Property crime rate: 144.4 per 10,000 population (2009).
Newspapers: Denver City Press (Local news; Circulation 2,046)
Transportation: Commute to work: 91.0% car, 0.0% public transportation, 3.1% walk, 2.2% work from home (2005-2009 5-year est.); Travel time to work: 67.3% less than 15 minutes, 16.8% 15 to 30 minutes, 4.9% 30 to 45 minutes, 1.9% 45 to 60 minutes, 9.1% 60 minutes or more (2005-2009 5-year est.)
Additional Information Contacts
Denver City Chamber of Commerce . . . . (806) 592-5424
    http://www.denvercitychamber.com

PLAINS (town). County seat. Covers a land area of 0.989 square miles and a water area of 0 square miles. Located at 33.19° N. Lat; 102.82° W. Long. Elevation is 3,642 feet.
Population: 1,422 (1990); 1,450 (2000); 1,525 (2010); 1,563 (2015 projected); Race: 71.5% White, 0.0% Black, 0.1% Asian, 28.5% Other, 59.3% Hispanic of any race (2010); Density: 1,541.4 persons per square mile (2010); Average household size: 2.97 (2010); Median age: 35.2 (2010); Males per 100 females: 96.3 (2010); Marriage status: 15.3% never married, 72.7% now married, 3.1% widowed, 8.9% divorced (2005-2009 5-year est.); Foreign born: 14.5% (2005-2009 5-year est.); Ancestry (includes multiple ancestries): 12.3% German, 8.2% Irish, 8.1% English, 6.0% American, 2.6% French (2005-2009 5-year est.).
Economy: Single-family building permits issued: 3 (2010); Multi-family building permits issued: 0 (2010); Employment by occupation: 12.1% management, 14.8% professional, 9.9% services, 17.0% sales, 10.5% farming, 20.6% construction, 15.1% production (2005-2009 5-year est.).
Income: Per capita income: $21,229 (2010); Median household income: $47,214 (2010); Average household income: $63,408 (2010); Percent of households with income of $100,000 or more: 16.2% (2010); Poverty rate: 11.3% (2005-2009 5-year est.).
Taxes: Total city taxes per capita: $116 (2007); City property taxes per capita: $71 (2007).
Education: Percent of population age 25 and over with: High school diploma (including GED) or higher: 67.0% (2010); Bachelor's degree or higher: 13.7% (2010); Master's degree or higher: 1.5% (2010).
School District(s)
Plains ISD (PK-12)
    2009-10 Enrollment: 468 . . . . (806) 456-7401
Housing: Homeownership rate: 79.9% (2010); Median home value: $42,911 (2010); Median contract rent: $299 per month (2005-2009 5-year est.); Median year structure built: 1969 (2005-2009 5-year est.).
Transportation: Commute to work: 96.1% car, 0.0% public transportation, 0.4% walk, 3.1% work from home (2005-2009 5-year est.); Travel time to work: 42.2% less than 15 minutes, 42.4% 15 to 30 minutes, 9.0% 30 to 45 minutes, 0.8% 45 to 60 minutes, 5.6% 60 minutes or more (2005-2009 5-year est.)

Young County

Located in north Texas; drained by the Brazos River; includes part of Possum Kingdom Lake. Covers a land area of 922.33 square miles, a water area of 8.51 square miles, and is located in the Central Time Zone at 33.21° N. Lat., 98.65° W. Long. The county was founded in 1856. County seat is Graham.

Weather Station: Graham   Elevation: 1,049 feet

	Jan	Feb	Mar	Apr	May	Jun	Jul	Aug	Sep	Oct	Nov	Dec
High	56	60	69	77	84	91	97	97	89	79	67	57
Low	29	32	41	48	59	68	71	70	62	50	39	30
Precip	1.1	2.0	2.6	2.3	4.5	4.2	2.1	1.9	3.6	3.7	2.0	1.9
Snow	0.4	0.5	0.4	0.1	0.0	0.0	0.0	0.0	0.0	0.0	0.0	0.3

High and Low temperatures in degrees Fahrenheit; Precipitation and Snow in inches

Weather Station: Olney   Elevation: 1,194 feet

	Jan	Feb	Mar	Apr	May	Jun	Jul	Aug	Sep	Oct	Nov	Dec
High	57	61	70	78	85	92	97	97	90	79	67	58
Low	32	35	43	50	60	68	72	71	64	53	42	32
Precip	1.4	1.9	2.5	2.7	5.3	4.2	2.4	1.9	2.7	3.3	2.0	1.6
Snow	0.4	0.2	0.2	0.0	0.0	0.0	0.0	0.0	0.0	0.0	0.1	0.2

High and Low temperatures in degrees Fahrenheit; Precipitation and Snow in inches

Population: 18,126 (1990); 17,943 (2000); 18,068 (2010); 18,097 (2015 projected); Race: 87.3% White, 1.9% Black, 0.4% Asian, 10.4% Other, 14.8% Hispanic of any race (2010); Density: 19.6 persons per square mile (2010); Average household size: 2.41 (2010); Median age: 40.3 (2010); Males per 100 females: 93.2 (2010).
Religion: Five largest groups: 46.1% Southern Baptist Convention, 16.1% The United Methodist Church, 7.5% Catholic Church, 6.2% Churches of Christ, 2.8% Presbyterian Church (U.S.A.) (2000).
Economy: Unemployment rate: 7.2% (June 2011); Total civilian labor force: 9,749 (June 2011); Leading industries: 15.8% health care and social assistance; 15.1% manufacturing; 14.8% retail trade (2009); Farms: 806 totaling 527,356 acres (2007); Companies that employ 500 or more persons: 0 (2009); Companies that employ 100 to 499 persons: 8 (2009); Companies that employ less than 100 persons: 591 (2009); Black-owned businesses: n/a (2007); Hispanic-owned businesses: n/a (2007); Asian-owned businesses: n/a (2007); Women-owned businesses: 402 (2007); Retail sales per capita: $9,453 (2010). Single-family building permits issued: 5 (2010); Multi-family building permits issued: 0 (2010).
Income: Per capita income: $23,473 (2010); Median household income: $42,372 (2010); Average household income: $57,157 (2010); Percent of households with income of $100,000 or more: 12.6% (2010); Poverty rate: 15.1% (2009); Bankruptcy rate: 1.77% (2010).
Taxes: Total county taxes per capita: $332 (2007); County property taxes per capita: $224 (2007).
Education: Percent of population age 25 and over with: High school diploma (including GED) or higher: 77.3% (2010); Bachelor's degree or higher: 16.3% (2010); Master's degree or higher: 4.4% (2010).
Housing: Homeownership rate: 72.0% (2010); Median home value: $54,797 (2010); Median contract rent: $393 per month (2005-2009 5-year est.); Median year structure built: 1969 (2005-2009 5-year est.)
Health: Birth rate: 130.4 per 10,000 population (2009); Death rate: 135.5 per 10,000 population (2009); Age-adjusted cancer mortality rate: 229.0 deaths per 100,000 population (2007); Number of physicians: 8.5 per 10,000 population (2008); Hospital beds: 33.9 per 10,000 population (2007); Hospital admissions: 1,381.2 per 10,000 population (2007).
Elections: 2008 Presidential election results: 17.8% Obama, 81.3% McCain, 0.0% Nader
National and State Parks: Fort Belknap State Park
Additional Information Contacts
Young County Government . . . . (940) 362-4301
    http://www.co.young.tx.us/ips/cms
City of Graham . . . . (940) 549-3322
    http://cityofgrahamtexas.com
Graham Chamber of Commerce . . . . (940) 549-3355
    http://www.grahamtxchamber.com
Olney Chamber of Commerce . . . . (940) 564-5445
    http://www.olneytexas.com

Young County Communities

GRAHAM (city). County seat. Covers a land area of 5.500 square miles and a water area of 0 square miles. Located at 33.10° N. Lat; 98.57° W. Long. Elevation is 1,047 feet.
History: Graham developed as a market town for the surrounding farms and ranches, and later the oil fields, and as the gateway to the recreation area of Graham Lake.
Population: 9,007 (1990); 8,716 (2000); 8,669 (2010); 8,645 (2015 projected); Race: 83.1% White, 1.6% Black, 0.2% Asian, 15.2% Other, 19.6% Hispanic of any race (2010); Density: 1,576.3 persons per square mile (2010); Average household size: 2.45 (2010); Median age: 38.5

(2010); Males per 100 females: 91.3 (2010); Marriage status: 16.1% never married, 65.0% now married, 8.5% widowed, 10.4% divorced (2005-2009 5-year est.); Foreign born: 7.9% (2005-2009 5-year est.); Ancestry (includes multiple ancestries): 13.6% Irish, 13.1% German, 11.8% English, 10.3% American, 2.4% Scottish (2005-2009 5-year est.).
Economy: Single-family building permits issued: 5 (2010); Multi-family building permits issued: 0 (2010); Employment by occupation: 11.6% management, 14.0% professional, 12.8% services, 25.8% sales, 0.7% farming, 14.5% construction, 20.6% production (2005-2009 5-year est.).
Income: Per capita income: $22,978 (2010); Median household income: $43,425 (2010); Average household income: $57,134 (2010); Percent of households with income of $100,000 or more: 13.1% (2010); Poverty rate: 17.8% (2005-2009 5-year est.).
Taxes: Total city taxes per capita: $532 (2007); City property taxes per capita: $192 (2007).
Education: Percent of population age 25 and over with: High school diploma (including GED) or higher: 76.7% (2010); Bachelor's degree or higher: 15.0% (2010); Master's degree or higher: 4.2% (2010).
School District(s)
Graham ISD (PK-12)
    2009-10 Enrollment: 2,550 . . . . (940) 549-0595
Housing: Homeownership rate: 68.3% (2010); Median home value: $50,754 (2010); Median contract rent: $419 per month (2005-2009 5-year est.); Median year structure built: 1965 (2005-2009 5-year est.).
Hospitals: Graham Regional Medical Center (37 beds)
Safety: Violent crime rate: 21.3 per 10,000 population; Property crime rate: 288.6 per 10,000 population (2009).
Newspapers: Graham Leader (Local news; Circulation 5,069)
Transportation: Commute to work: 94.0% car, 0.0% public transportation, 1.1% walk, 2.1% work from home (2005-2009 5-year est.); Travel time to work: 68.4% less than 15 minutes, 11.3% 15 to 30 minutes, 8.3% 30 to 45 minutes, 2.2% 45 to 60 minutes, 9.8% 60 minutes or more (2005-2009 5-year est.)
Airports: Graham Municipal (general aviation)
Additional Information Contacts
City of Graham . . . . (940) 549-3322
    http://cityofgrahamtexas.com
Graham Chamber of Commerce . . . . (940) 549-3355
    http://www.grahamtxchamber.com

LOVING (unincorporated postal area, zip code 76460). Covers a land area of 95.264 square miles and a water area of 0.007 square miles. Located at 33.33° N. Lat; 98.48° W. Long. Elevation is 1,299 feet.
Population: 386 (2000); Race: 95.3% White, 0.0% Black, 0.0% Asian, 4.7% Other, 4.7% Hispanic of any race (2000); Density: 4.1 persons per square mile (2000); Age: 19.8% under 18, 23.2% over 64 (2000); Marriage status: 22.1% never married, 63.5% now married, 7.7% widowed, 6.7% divorced (2000); Foreign born: 2.8% (2000); Ancestry (includes multiple ancestries): 16.8% American, 7.8% English, 7.8% Irish, 7.5% German (2000).
Economy: Employment by occupation: 22.2% management, 17.7% professional, 22.7% services, 9.9% sales, 2.0% farming, 10.8% construction, 14.8% production (2000).
Income: Per capita income: $14,812 (2000); Median household income: $33,625 (2000); Poverty rate: 179.1% (2000).
Education: Percent of population age 25 and over with: High school diploma (including GED) or higher: 80.6% (2000); Bachelor's degree or higher: 11.4% (2000).
Housing: Homeownership rate: 86.2% (2000); Median home value: $47,000 (2000); Median contract rent: $254 per month (2000); Median year structure built: 1957 (2000).
Transportation: Commute to work: 90.8% car, 0.0% public transportation, 0.0% walk, 4.9% work from home (2000); Travel time to work: 21.0% less than 15 minutes, 55.7% 15 to 30 minutes, 15.3% 30 to 45 minutes, 2.8% 45 to 60 minutes, 5.1% 60 minutes or more (2000)

NEWCASTLE (city). Covers a land area of 1.811 square miles and a water area of 0 square miles. Located at 33.19° N. Lat; 98.73° W. Long. Elevation is 1,142 feet.
History: Restored Fort Belknap, established 1851, is just South. Lake Graham reservoir to East, formerly coal-mining center.
Population: 505 (1990); 575 (2000); 559 (2010); 551 (2015 projected); Race: 91.4% White, 1.4% Black, 0.2% Asian, 7.0% Other, 7.0% Hispanic of any race (2010); Density: 308.6 persons per square mile (2010); Average household size: 2.44 (2010); Median age: 40.1 (2010); Males per

100 females: 101.1 (2010); Marriage status: 16.1% never married, 59.9% now married, 12.9% widowed, 11.0% divorced (2005-2009 5-year est.); Foreign born: 3.8% (2005-2009 5-year est.); Ancestry (includes multiple ancestries): 33.4% Irish, 13.3% German, 12.1% English, 7.3% American, 4.3% Dutch West Indian (2005-2009 5-year est.).

Economy: Single-family building permits issued: 0 (2010); Multi-family building permits issued: 0 (2010); Employment by occupation: 12.5% management, 11.0% professional, 17.0% services, 24.0% sales, 0.0% farming, 10.0% construction, 25.5% production (2005-2009 5-year est.).

Income: Per capita income: $22,513 (2010); Median household income: $39,309 (2010); Average household income: $56,288 (2010); Percent of households with income of $100,000 or more: 8.3% (2010); Poverty rate: 20.6% (2005-2009 5-year est.).

Taxes: Total city taxes per capita: $126 (2007); City property taxes per capita: $44 (2007).

Education: Percent of population age 25 and over with: High school diploma (including GED) or higher: 73.4% (2010); Bachelor's degree or higher: 9.4% (2010); Master's degree or higher: 2.1% (2010).

School District(s)
Newcastle ISD (PK-12)
    2009-10 Enrollment: 190 . . . . (940) 846-3551

Housing: Homeownership rate: 74.7% (2010); Median home value: $42,800 (2010); Median contract rent: $284 per month (2005-2009 5-year est.); Median year structure built: 1949 (2005-2009 5-year est.).

Transportation: Commute to work: 98.4% car, 0.0% public transportation, 0.0% walk, 1.6% work from home (2005-2009 5-year est.); Travel time to work: 20.2% less than 15 minutes, 68.1% 15 to 30 minutes, 6.9% 30 to 45 minutes, 4.8% 45 to 60 minutes, 0.0% 60 minutes or more (2005-2009 5-year est.)

OLNEY (city). Covers a land area of 2.052 square miles and a water area of 0 square miles. Located at 33.36° N. Lat; 98.75° W. Long. Elevation is 1,184 feet.

History: Settled 1891, incorporated 1909.

Population: 3,519 (1990); 3,396 (2000); 3,349 (2010); 3,324 (2015 projected); Race: 88.7% White, 4.2% Black, 0.2% Asian, 6.8% Other, 17.9% Hispanic of any race (2010); Density: 1,631.9 persons per square mile (2010); Average household size: 2.32 (2010); Median age: 38.1 (2010); Males per 100 females: 85.5 (2010); Marriage status: 25.4% never married, 51.5% now married, 12.1% widowed, 11.0% divorced (2005-2009 5-year est.); Foreign born: 3.9% (2005-2009 5-year est.); Ancestry (includes multiple ancestries): 15.5% German, 13.9% Irish, 10.1% American, 5.4% French, 4.8% English (2005-2009 5-year est.).

Economy: Single-family building permits issued: 0 (2010); Multi-family building permits issued: 0 (2010); Employment by occupation: 11.6% management, 9.4% professional, 27.1% services, 17.7% sales, 0.6% farming, 15.4% construction, 18.3% production (2005-2009 5-year est.).

Income: Per capita income: $20,386 (2010); Median household income: $32,826 (2010); Average household income: $47,794 (2010); Percent of households with income of $100,000 or more: 9.3% (2010); Poverty rate: 18.9% (2005-2009 5-year est.).

Taxes: Total city taxes per capita: $260 (2007); City property taxes per capita: $142 (2007).

Education: Percent of population age 25 and over with: High school diploma (including GED) or higher: 75.2% (2010); Bachelor's degree or higher: 16.1% (2010); Master's degree or higher: 5.1% (2010).

School District(s)
Olney ISD (PK-12)
    2009-10 Enrollment: 781 . . . . (940) 564-3519

Housing: Homeownership rate: 63.7% (2010); Median home value: $38,872 (2010); Median contract rent: $396 per month (2005-2009 5-year est.); Median year structure built: 1960 (2005-2009 5-year est.).

Hospitals: Hamilton Hospital (49 beds)

Safety: Violent crime rate: 12.4 per 10,000 population; Property crime rate: 288.8 per 10,000 population (2009).

Newspapers: Enterprise (Community news; Circulation 2,188)

Transportation: Commute to work: 93.3% car, 0.0% public transportation, 3.9% walk, 1.8% work from home (2005-2009 5-year est.); Travel time to work: 80.7% less than 15 minutes, 7.6% 15 to 30 minutes, 9.7% 30 to 45 minutes, 0.9% 45 to 60 minutes, 0.9% 60 minutes or more (2005-2009 5-year est.)

Airports: Olney Municipal (general aviation)

Additional Information Contacts
Olney Chamber of Commerce . . . . (940) 564-5445
    http://www.olneytexas.com

SOUTH BEND (unincorporated postal area, zip code 76481). Covers a land area of 51.464 square miles and a water area of 0.153 square miles. Located at 33.00° N. Lat; 98.68° W. Long. Elevation is 1,043 feet.

Population: 304 (2000); Race: 98.0% White, 0.0% Black, 0.0% Asian, 2.0% Other, 0.0% Hispanic of any race (2000); Density: 5.9 persons per square mile (2000); Age: 21.7% under 18, 10.5% over 64 (2000); Marriage status: 15.4% never married, 63.5% now married, 12.9% widowed, 8.3% divorced (2000); Foreign born: 2.0% (2000); Ancestry (includes multiple ancestries): 21.4% American, 15.9% Irish, 11.5% English, 8.8% French (2000).

Economy: Employment by occupation: 18.5% management, 9.6% professional, 22.2% services, 23.7% sales, 3.0% farming, 17.0% construction, 5.9% production (2000).

Income: Per capita income: $12,193 (2000); Median household income: $23,393 (2000); Poverty rate: 179.1% (2000).

Education: Percent of population age 25 and over with: High school diploma (including GED) or higher: 71.6% (2000); Bachelor's degree or higher: 8.8% (2000).

Housing: Homeownership rate: 84.9% (2000); Median home value: $51,300 (2000); Median contract rent: n/a per month (2000); Median year structure built: 1969 (2000).

Transportation: Commute to work: 94.6% car, 5.4% public transportation, 0.0% walk, 0.0% work from home (2000); Travel time to work: 35.4% less than 15 minutes, 34.6% 15 to 30 minutes, 24.6% 30 to 45 minutes, 3.1% 45 to 60 minutes, 2.3% 60 minutes or more (2000)

Zapata County

Located in southern Texas; bounded on the west by the Rio Grande and the Mexican border; drained by tributaries of the Rio Grande. Covers a land area of 996.76 square miles, a water area of 61.34 square miles, and is located in the Central Time Zone at 26.95° N. Lat., 99.20° W. Long. The county was founded in 1858. County seat is Zapata.

Weather Station: Zapata 3 SW									Elevation: 319 feet			
	Jan	Feb	Mar	Apr	May	Jun	Jul	Aug	Sep	Oct	Nov	Dec
High	70	74	82	89	94	98	99	100	94	87	78	69
Low	47	51	57	64	71	75	76	76	72	65	56	48
Precip	0.8	1.0	0.8	1.4	2.6	2.1	2.2	1.6	3.3	1.5	1.3	0.8
Snow	tr	tr	0.0	0.0	0.0	0.0	0.0	0.0	0.0	0.0	0.0	tr

High and Low temperatures in degrees Fahrenheit; Precipitation and Snow in inches

Population: 9,279 (1990); 12,182 (2000); 14,488 (2010); 15,584 (2015 projected); Race: 83.4% White, 0.4% Black, 0.3% Asian, 15.9% Other, 88.3% Hispanic of any race (2010); Density: 14.5 persons per square mile (2010); Average household size: 3.02 (2010); Median age: 30.1 (2010); Males per 100 females: 96.8 (2010).

Religion: Five largest groups: 29.9% Catholic Church, 2.8% Southern Baptist Convention, 0.6% The Church of Jesus Christ of Latter-day Saints, 0.6% Lutheran Church—Missouri Synod, 0.5% Churches of Christ (2000).

Economy: Unemployment rate: 11.0% (June 2011); Total civilian labor force: 5,671 (June 2011); Leading industries: 17.7% mining; 13.8% retail trade; 13.2% health care and social assistance (2009); Farms: 459 totaling 459,440 acres (2007); Companies that employ 500 or more persons: 0 (2009); Companies that employ 100 to 499 persons: 3 (2009); Companies that employ less than 100 persons: 175 (2009); Black-owned businesses: n/a (2007); Hispanic-owned businesses: 773 (2007); Asian-owned businesses: n/a (2007); Women-owned businesses: 317 (2007); Retail sales per capita: $4,933 (2010). Single-family building permits issued: n/a (2010); Multi-family building permits issued: n/a (2010).

Income: Per capita income: $15,922 (2010); Median household income: $34,889 (2010); Average household income: $47,986 (2010); Percent of households with income of $100,000 or more: 8.1% (2010); Poverty rate: 29.3% (2009); Bankruptcy rate: 0.28% (2010).

Taxes: Total county taxes per capita: $282 (2007); County property taxes per capita: $241 (2007).

Education: Percent of population age 25 and over with: High school diploma (including GED) or higher: 59.8% (2010); Bachelor's degree or higher: 10.3% (2010); Master's degree or higher: 3.3% (2010).

Housing: Homeownership rate: 80.4% (2010); Median home value: $49,562 (2010); Median contract rent: $281 per month (2005-2009 5-year est.); Median year structure built: 1983 (2005-2009 5-year est.)

Health: Birth rate: 220.9 per 10,000 population (2009); Death rate: 66.3 per 10,000 population (2009); Age-adjusted cancer mortality rate: 76.7 (Unreliable) deaths per 100,000 population (2007); Number of physicians:

2.2 per 10,000 population (2008); Hospital beds: 0.0 per 10,000 population (2007); Hospital admissions: 0.0 per 10,000 population (2007).
Elections: 2008 Presidential election results: 67.7% Obama, 32.1% McCain, 0.0% Nader
Additional Information Contacts
Zapata County Government.........................(956) 765-9920
   http://www.co.zapata.tx.us/ips/cms
Zapata County Chamber of Commerce...............(956) 765-4871
   http://www.zapatausa.com

Zapata County Communities

FALCON LAKE ESTATES (CDP). Covers a land area of 0.703 square miles and a water area of 0 square miles. Located at 26.87° N. Lat; 99.25° W. Long. Elevation is 354 feet.
Population: 649 (1990); 830 (2000); 1,008 (2010); 1,095 (2015 projected); Race: 83.8% White, 0.8% Black, 1.1% Asian, 14.3% Other, 82.2% Hispanic of any race (2010); Density: 1,433.2 persons per square mile (2010); Average household size: 2.83 (2010); Median age: 31.7 (2010); Males per 100 females: 96.9 (2010); Marriage status: 17.3% never married, 54.5% now married, 13.1% widowed, 15.0% divorced (2005-2009 5-year est.); Foreign born: 5.2% (2005-2009 5-year est.); Ancestry (includes multiple ancestries): 16.3% German, 7.6% American, 5.5% Irish, 2.5% Swiss, 2.5% English (2005-2009 5-year est.).
Economy: Employment by occupation: 11.4% management, 26.5% professional, 24.1% services, 7.9% sales, 0.0% farming, 14.6% construction, 15.5% production (2005-2009 5-year est.).
Income: Per capita income: $19,750 (2010); Median household income: $44,153 (2010); Average household income: $55,976 (2010); Percent of households with income of $100,000 or more: 15.2% (2010); Poverty rate: 20.3% (2005-2009 5-year est.).
Education: Percent of population age 25 and over with: High school diploma (including GED) or higher: 73.9% (2010); Bachelor's degree or higher: 14.7% (2010); Master's degree or higher: 4.2% (2010).
Housing: Homeownership rate: 82.0% (2010); Median home value: $52,963 (2010); Median contract rent: $392 per month (2005-2009 5-year est.); Median year structure built: 1988 (2005-2009 5-year est.).
Transportation: Commute to work: 94.8% car, 0.0% public transportation, 0.0% walk, 5.2% work from home (2005-2009 5-year est.); Travel time to work: 67.7% less than 15 minutes, 8.0% 15 to 30 minutes, 0.0% 30 to 45 minutes, 0.0% 45 to 60 minutes, 24.3% 60 minutes or more (2005-2009 5-year est.)

FALCON MESA (CDP). Covers a land area of 1.528 square miles and a water area of 0 square miles. Located at 26.87° N. Lat; 99.28° W. Long. Elevation is 367 feet.
Population: 274 (1990); 506 (2000); 686 (2010); 760 (2015 projected); Race: 88.0% White, 0.3% Black, 0.1% Asian, 11.5% Other, 64.3% Hispanic of any race (2010); Density: 448.9 persons per square mile (2010); Average household size: 2.30 (2010); Median age: 44.4 (2010); Males per 100 females: 97.7 (2010); Marriage status: 4.7% never married, 60.8% now married, 0.0% widowed, 34.5% divorced (2005-2009 5-year est.); Foreign born: 10.0% (2005-2009 5-year est.); Ancestry (includes multiple ancestries): 13.8% Dutch, 11.6% German, 8.8% American, 6.7% Irish, 2.7% English (2005-2009 5-year est.).
Economy: Employment by occupation: 0.0% management, 9.7% professional, 0.0% services, 53.1% sales, 0.0% farming, 29.2% construction, 8.0% production (2005-2009 5-year est.).
Income: Per capita income: $21,930 (2010); Median household income: $36,596 (2010); Average household income: $50,529 (2010); Percent of households with income of $100,000 or more: 6.4% (2010); Poverty rate: 35.4% (2005-2009 5-year est.).
Education: Percent of population age 25 and over with: High school diploma (including GED) or higher: 73.6% (2010); Bachelor's degree or higher: 10.0% (2010); Master's degree or higher: 2.8% (2010).
Housing: Homeownership rate: 80.9% (2010); Median home value: $46,296 (2010); Median contract rent: $828 per month (2005-2009 5-year est.); Median year structure built: 1993 (2005-2009 5-year est.).
Transportation: Commute to work: 100.0% car, 0.0% public transportation, 0.0% walk, 0.0% work from home (2005-2009 5-year est.); Travel time to work: 58.9% less than 15 minutes, 19.0% 15 to 30 minutes, 0.0% 30 to 45 minutes, 0.0% 45 to 60 minutes, 22.1% 60 minutes or more (2005-2009 5-year est.)

LOPENO (CDP). Covers a land area of 0.764 square miles and a water area of 0 square miles. Located at 26.71° N. Lat; 99.10° W. Long. Elevation is 390 feet.
Population: 126 (1990); 140 (2000); 156 (2010); 166 (2015 projected); Race: 82.7% White, 0.0% Black, 0.6% Asian, 16.7% Other, 85.9% Hispanic of any race (2010); Density: 204.1 persons per square mile (2010); Average household size: 2.84 (2010); Median age: 37.1 (2010); Males per 100 females: 100.0 (2010); Marriage status: n/a never married, n/a now married, n/a widowed, n/a divorced (2005-2009 5-year est.); Foreign born: n/a (2005-2009 5-year est.); Ancestry (includes multiple ancestries): n/a (2005-2009 5-year est.).
Economy: Employment by occupation: n/a management, n/a professional, n/a services, n/a sales, n/a farming, n/a construction, n/a production (2005-2009 5-year est.).
Income: Per capita income: $16,042 (2010); Median household income: $30,000 (2010); Average household income: $44,500 (2010); Percent of households with income of $100,000 or more: 10.9% (2010); Poverty rate: n/a (2005-2009 5-year est.).
Education: Percent of population age 25 and over with: High school diploma (including GED) or higher: 55.3% (2010); Bachelor's degree or higher: 6.8% (2010); Master's degree or higher: 1.9% (2010).
Housing: Homeownership rate: 92.7% (2010); Median home value: $52,500 (2010); Median contract rent: n/a per month (2005-2009 5-year est.); Median year structure built: 1957 (2005-2009 5-year est.).
Transportation: Commute to work: n/a car, n/a public transportation, n/a walk, n/a work from home (2005-2009 5-year est.); Travel time to work: n/a less than 15 minutes, n/a 15 to 30 minutes, n/a 30 to 45 minutes, n/a 45 to 60 minutes, n/a 60 minutes or more (2005-2009 5-year est.)

MEDINA (CDP). Covers a land area of 1.767 square miles and a water area of 0.006 square miles. Located at 26.92° N. Lat; 99.25° W. Long. Elevation is 397 feet.
Population: 1,597 (1990); 2,960 (2000); 3,695 (2010); 4,030 (2015 projected); Race: 81.0% White, 0.4% Black, 0.2% Asian, 18.5% Other, 96.3% Hispanic of any race (2010); Density: 2,091.2 persons per square mile (2010); Average household size: 3.53 (2010); Median age: 24.7 (2010); Males per 100 females: 98.8 (2010); Marriage status: 19.4% never married, 70.2% now married, 4.0% widowed, 6.4% divorced (2005-2009 5-year est.); Foreign born: 51.3% (2005-2009 5-year est.); Ancestry (includes multiple ancestries): 0.6% Czech, 0.4% American, 0.4% German, 0.4% Dutch (2005-2009 5-year est.).
Economy: Employment by occupation: 4.3% management, 1.2% professional, 42.8% services, 22.3% sales, 0.0% farming, 29.5% construction, 0.0% production (2005-2009 5-year est.).
Income: Per capita income: $10,746 (2010); Median household income: $33,571 (2010); Average household income: $37,481 (2010); Percent of households with income of $100,000 or more: 1.3% (2010); Poverty rate: 61.3% (2005-2009 5-year est.).
Education: Percent of population age 25 and over with: High school diploma (including GED) or higher: 47.7% (2010); Bachelor's degree or higher: 7.3% (2010); Master's degree or higher: 1.9% (2010).
School District(s)
Medina ISD (PK-12)
   2009-10 Enrollment: 317........................(830) 589-2855
Housing: Homeownership rate: 80.6% (2010); Median home value: $39,959 (2010); Median contract rent: $276 per month (2005-2009 5-year est.); Median year structure built: 1984 (2005-2009 5-year est.).
Transportation: Commute to work: 83.4% car, 0.0% public transportation, 1.4% walk, 15.2% work from home (2005-2009 5-year est.); Travel time to work: 85.6% less than 15 minutes, 14.4% 15 to 30 minutes, 0.0% 30 to 45 minutes, 0.0% 45 to 60 minutes, 0.0% 60 minutes or more (2005-2009 5-year est.)

MORALES-SANCHEZ (CDP). Covers a land area of 3.615 square miles and a water area of 0 square miles. Located at 26.78° N. Lat; 99.11° W. Long. Elevation is 387 feet.
Population: 77 (1990); 95 (2000); 114 (2010); 124 (2015 projected); Race: 86.0% White, 0.0% Black, 0.0% Asian, 14.0% Other, 88.6% Hispanic of any race (2010); Density: 31.5 persons per square mile (2010); Average household size: 3.00 (2010); Median age: 33.4 (2010); Males per 100 females: 103.6 (2010); Marriage status: 21.3% never married, 78.7% now married, 0.0% widowed, 0.0% divorced (2005-2009 5-year est.); Foreign born: 78.7% (2005-2009 5-year est.); Ancestry (includes multiple ancestries): n/a (2005-2009 5-year est.).

Economy: Employment by occupation: 0.0% management, 0.0% professional, 100.0% services, 0.0% sales, 0.0% farming, 0.0% construction, 0.0% production (2005-2009 5-year est.).
Income: Per capita income: $16,396 (2010); Median household income: $33,000 (2010); Average household income: $49,079 (2010); Percent of households with income of $100,000 or more: 10.5% (2010); Poverty rate: 39.1% (2005-2009 5-year est.).
Education: Percent of population age 25 and over with: High school diploma (including GED) or higher: 54.8% (2010); Bachelor's degree or higher: 6.8% (2010); Master's degree or higher: 1.4% (2010).
Housing: Homeownership rate: 84.2% (2010); Median home value: $53,333 (2010); Median contract rent: n/a per month (2005-2009 5-year est.); Median year structure built: 1967 (2005-2009 5-year est.).
Transportation: Commute to work: 100.0% car, 0.0% public transportation, 0.0% walk, 0.0% work from home (2005-2009 5-year est.); Travel time to work: 0.0% less than 15 minutes, 100.0% 15 to 30 minutes, 0.0% 30 to 45 minutes, 0.0% 45 to 60 minutes, 0.0% 60 minutes or more (2005-2009 5-year est.)

NEW FALCON (CDP).
Covers a land area of 0.202 square miles and a water area of 0 square miles. Located at 26.63° N. Lat; 99.09° W. Long. Elevation is 420 feet.
Population: 166 (1990); 184 (2000); 200 (2010); 213 (2015 projected); Race: 83.5% White, 0.0% Black, 0.5% Asian, 16.0% Other, 86.0% Hispanic of any race (2010); Density: 990.8 persons per square mile (2010); Average household size: 2.86 (2010); Median age: 35.0 (2010); Males per 100 females: 108.3 (2010); Marriage status: 5.9% never married, 87.9% now married, 0.0% widowed, 6.3% divorced (2005-2009 5-year est.); Foreign born: 13.0% (2005-2009 5-year est.); Ancestry (includes multiple ancestries): n/a (2005-2009 5-year est.).
Economy: Employment by occupation: 0.0% management, 25.2% professional, 14.3% services, 9.2% sales, 7.6% farming, 0.0% construction, 43.7% production (2005-2009 5-year est.).
Income: Per capita income: $16,042 (2010); Median household income: $30,000 (2010); Average household income: $45,250 (2010); Percent of households with income of $100,000 or more: 11.4% (2010); Poverty rate: 68.7% (2005-2009 5-year est.).
Education: Percent of population age 25 and over with: High school diploma (including GED) or higher: 55.1% (2010); Bachelor's degree or higher: 6.3% (2010); Master's degree or higher: 1.6% (2010).
Housing: Homeownership rate: 91.4% (2010); Median home value: $52,000 (2010); Median contract rent: n/a per month (2005-2009 5-year est.); Median year structure built: 1967 (2005-2009 5-year est.).
Transportation: Commute to work: 92.4% car, 0.0% public transportation, 7.6% walk, 0.0% work from home (2005-2009 5-year est.); Travel time to work: 31.1% less than 15 minutes, 26.9% 15 to 30 minutes, 42.0% 30 to 45 minutes, 0.0% 45 to 60 minutes, 0.0% 60 minutes or more (2005-2009 5-year est.)

SAN IGNACIO (CDP).
Covers a land area of 1.532 square miles and a water area of 0 square miles. Located at 27.04° N. Lat; 99.44° W. Long. Elevation is 322 feet.
Population: 733 (1990); 853 (2000); 955 (2010); 1,006 (2015 projected); Race: 79.5% White, 1.7% Black, 0.1% Asian, 18.7% Other, 90.4% Hispanic of any race (2010); Density: 623.3 persons per square mile (2010); Average household size: 3.12 (2010); Median age: 30.6 (2010); Males per 100 females: 107.6 (2010); Marriage status: n/a never married, n/a now married, n/a widowed, n/a divorced (2005-2009 5-year est.); Foreign born: n/a (2005-2009 5-year est.); Ancestry (includes multiple ancestries): n/a (2005-2009 5-year est.).
Economy: Employment by occupation: n/a management, n/a professional, n/a services, n/a sales, n/a farming, n/a construction, n/a production (2005-2009 5-year est.).
Income: Per capita income: $13,713 (2010); Median household income: $27,432 (2010); Average household income: $42,565 (2010); Percent of households with income of $100,000 or more: 6.9% (2010); Poverty rate: n/a (2005-2009 5-year est.).
Education: Percent of population age 25 and over with: High school diploma (including GED) or higher: 46.7% (2010); Bachelor's degree or higher: 15.0% (2010); Master's degree or higher: 8.5% (2010).
Housing: Homeownership rate: 74.8% (2010); Median home value: $41,250 (2010); Median contract rent: n/a per month (2005-2009 5-year est.); Median year structure built: n/a (2005-2009 5-year est.).
Transportation: Commute to work: n/a car, n/a public transportation, n/a walk, n/a work from home (2005-2009 5-year est.); Travel time to work: n/a

less than 15 minutes, n/a 15 to 30 minutes, n/a 30 to 45 minutes, n/a 45 to 60 minutes, n/a 60 minutes or more (2005-2009 5-year est.)

SIESTA SHORES (CDP).
Covers a land area of 0.628 square miles and a water area of 0 square miles. Located at 26.85° N. Lat; 99.25° W. Long. Elevation is 374 feet.
Population: 696 (1990); 890 (2000); 1,055 (2010); 1,146 (2015 projected); Race: 83.8% White, 0.7% Black, 1.1% Asian, 14.4% Other, 82.3% Hispanic of any race (2010); Density: 1,681.0 persons per square mile (2010); Average household size: 2.84 (2010); Median age: 31.6 (2010); Males per 100 females: 95.7 (2010); Marriage status: 13.4% never married, 68.3% now married, 8.5% widowed, 9.8% divorced (2005-2009 5-year est.); Foreign born: 32.8% (2005-2009 5-year est.); Ancestry (includes multiple ancestries): 3.3% English (2005-2009 5-year est.).
Economy: Employment by occupation: 0.0% management, 5.5% professional, 9.9% services, 15.7% sales, 0.0% farming, 57.3% construction, 11.6% production (2005-2009 5-year est.).
Income: Per capita income: $19,750 (2010); Median household income: $44,344 (2010); Average household income: $55,638 (2010); Percent of households with income of $100,000 or more: 14.8% (2010); Poverty rate: 15.9% (2005-2009 5-year est.).
Education: Percent of population age 25 and over with: High school diploma (including GED) or higher: 73.9% (2010); Bachelor's degree or higher: 14.6% (2010); Master's degree or higher: 4.1% (2010).
Housing: Homeownership rate: 82.0% (2010); Median home value: $52,679 (2010); Median contract rent: n/a per month (2005-2009 5-year est.); Median year structure built: 1984 (2005-2009 5-year est.).
Transportation: Commute to work: 91.7% car, 0.0% public transportation, 0.0% walk, 8.3% work from home (2005-2009 5-year est.); Travel time to work: 42.9% less than 15 minutes, 24.8% 15 to 30 minutes, 28.7% 30 to 45 minutes, 0.0% 45 to 60 minutes, 3.5% 60 minutes or more (2005-2009 5-year est.)

ZAPATA (CDP).
County seat. Covers a land area of 7.709 square miles and a water area of 0 square miles. Located at 26.90° N. Lat; 99.27° W. Long. Elevation is 394 feet.
History: The original Zapata was founded in 1750 by Spanish ranchmen on land granted by Jose de Escandon. The site later became Camp Drum, built by the U.S. Army in 1852. When the waters of the Falcon Reservoir spread over the area, the town of Zapata developed on the new site.
Population: 4,427 (1990); 4,856 (2000); 5,556 (2010); 5,888 (2015 projected); Race: 84.5% White, 0.2% Black, 0.1% Asian, 15.1% Other, 88.3% Hispanic of any race (2010); Density: 720.7 persons per square mile (2010); Average household size: 2.92 (2010); Median age: 31.4 (2010); Males per 100 females: 92.4 (2010); Marriage status: 35.9% never married, 50.8% now married, 8.5% widowed, 4.8% divorced (2005-2009 5-year est.); Foreign born: 24.5% (2005-2009 5-year est.); Ancestry (includes multiple ancestries): 2.4% German, 1.6% Dutch, 1.3% Irish, 1.3% English, 0.4% American (2005-2009 5-year est.).
Economy: Employment by occupation: 13.8% management, 27.0% professional, 21.3% services, 11.2% sales, 0.5% farming, 14.2% construction, 12.0% production (2005-2009 5-year est.).
Income: Per capita income: $17,385 (2010); Median household income: $33,543 (2010); Average household income: $50,752 (2010); Percent of households with income of $100,000 or more: 8.9% (2010); Poverty rate: 39.7% (2005-2009 5-year est.).
Education: Percent of population age 25 and over with: High school diploma (including GED) or higher: 62.5% (2010); Bachelor's degree or higher: 10.1% (2010); Master's degree or higher: 3.2% (2010).
School District(s)
Zapata County ISD (PK-12)
    2009-10 Enrollment: 3,761 . . . . (956) 765-6546
Housing: Homeownership rate: 79.8% (2010); Median home value: $55,847 (2010); Median contract rent: $246 per month (2005-2009 5-year est.); Median year structure built: 1983 (2005-2009 5-year est.).
Newspapers: Zapata News (Community news; Circulation 3,400)
Transportation: Commute to work: 96.0% car, 0.0% public transportation, 0.0% walk, 3.2% work from home (2005-2009 5-year est.); Travel time to work: 76.7% less than 15 minutes, 10.4% 15 to 30 minutes, 4.7% 30 to 45 minutes, 1.6% 45 to 60 minutes, 6.6% 60 minutes or more (2005-2009 5-year est.)
Additional Information Contacts
Zapata County Chamber of Commerce . . . . (956) 765-4871
    http://www.zapatausa.com

Zavala County

Located in southwestern Texas; drained by the Nueces and Leona Rivers. Covers a land area of 1,298.48 square miles, a water area of 3.24 square miles, and is located in the Central Time Zone at 28.85° N. Lat., 99.76° W. Long. The county was founded in 1858. County seat is Crystal City.

Weather Station: Crystal City — Elevation: 580 feet

	Jan	Feb	Mar	Apr	May	Jun	Jul	Aug	Sep	Oct	Nov	Dec
High	67	72	79	86	91	96	97	98	93	85	75	68
Low	44	48	55	62	70	74	76	76	71	63	53	45
Precip	1.0	1.0	1.4	1.5	2.3	2.6	2.2	1.7	1.9	2.1	1.2	0.8
Snow	0.2	tr	0.0	0.0	0.0	0.0	0.0	0.0	0.0	tr	0.0	0.0

High and Low temperatures in degrees Fahrenheit; Precipitation and Snow in inches

Population: 12,162 (1990); 11,600 (2000); 11,955 (2010); 12,106 (2015 projected); Race: 65.4% White, 0.7% Black, 0.1% Asian, 33.8% Other, 89.7% Hispanic of any race (2010); Density: 9.2 persons per square mile (2010); Average household size: 3.13 (2010); Median age: 30.4 (2010); Males per 100 females: 97.0 (2010).
Religion: Five largest groups: 30.3% Catholic Church, 7.7% Southern Baptist Convention, 5.9% Assemblies of God, 2.7% The United Methodist Church, 0.8% Churches of Christ (2000).
Economy: Unemployment rate: 17.6% (June 2011); Total civilian labor force: 4,094 (June 2011); Leading industries: Farms: 311 totaling 752,017 acres (2007); Companies that employ 500 or more persons: 0 (2009); Companies that employ 100 to 499 persons: 3 (2009); Companies that employ less than 100 persons: 99 (2009); Black-owned businesses: n/a (2007); Hispanic-owned businesses: 827 (2007); Asian-owned businesses: n/a (2007); Women-owned businesses: 382 (2007); Retail sales per capita: $2,987 (2010). Single-family building permits issued: 4 (2010); Multi-family building permits issued: 0 (2010).
Income: Per capita income: $12,360 (2010); Median household income: $21,758 (2010); Average household income: $31,815 (2010); Percent of households with income of $100,000 or more: 4.1% (2010); Poverty rate: 35.8% (2009); Bankruptcy rate: 0.17% (2010).
Taxes: Total county taxes per capita: $190 (2007); County property taxes per capita: $157 (2007).
Education: Percent of population age 25 and over with: High school diploma (including GED) or higher: 50.0% (2010); Bachelor's degree or higher: 8.8% (2010); Master's degree or higher: 3.9% (2010).
Housing: Homeownership rate: 71.2% (2010); Median home value: $30,572 (2010); Median contract rent: $304 per month (2005-2009 5-year est.); Median year structure built: 1972 (2005-2009 5-year est.)
Health: Birth rate: 202.8 per 10,000 population (2009); Death rate: 78.5 per 10,000 population (2009); Age-adjusted cancer mortality rate: 115.2 (Unreliable) deaths per 100,000 population (2007); Number of physicians: 5.1 per 10,000 population (2008); Hospital beds: 0.0 per 10,000 population (2007); Hospital admissions: 0.0 per 10,000 population (2007).
Elections: 2008 Presidential election results: 84.2% Obama, 15.4% McCain, 0.0% Nader
Additional Information Contacts
Zavala County Government . . . . (830) 374-3810
   http://www.co.zavala.tx.us/ips/cms
City of Crystal City . . . . (830) 374-3478

Zavala County Communities

BATESVILLE (CDP). Covers a land area of 11.582 square miles and a water area of 0 square miles. Located at 28.96° N. Lat; 99.61° W. Long. Elevation is 705 feet.
Population: 1,313 (1990); 1,298 (2000); 1,278 (2010); 1,268 (2015 projected); Race: 39.4% White, 1.2% Black, 0.0% Asian, 59.4% Other, 86.7% Hispanic of any race (2010); Density: 110.3 persons per square mile (2010); Average household size: 3.30 (2010); Median age: 31.0 (2010); Males per 100 females: 97.5 (2010); Marriage status: 31.3% never married, 44.6% now married, 11.9% widowed, 12.3% divorced (2005-2009 5-year est.); Foreign born: 11.8% (2005-2009 5-year est.); Ancestry (includes multiple ancestries): 3.1% German, 1.0% Portuguese, 1.0% American (2005-2009 5-year est.).
Economy: Employment by occupation: 0.0% management, 7.6% professional, 44.1% services, 7.6% sales, 12.8% farming, 12.5% construction, 15.5% production (2005-2009 5-year est.).
Income: Per capita income: $10,421 (2010); Median household income: $23,208 (2010); Average household income: $34,457 (2010); Percent of

households with income of $100,000 or more: 6.7% (2010); Poverty rate: 59.0% (2005-2009 5-year est.).
Education: Percent of population age 25 and over with: High school diploma (including GED) or higher: 38.3% (2010); Bachelor's degree or higher: 8.6% (2010); Master's degree or higher: 4.7% (2010).
School District(s)
Uvalde CISD (PK-12)
   2009-10 Enrollment: 5,098 . . . . (830) 278-6655
Housing: Homeownership rate: 78.0% (2010); Median home value: $25,152 (2010); Median contract rent: $272 per month (2005-2009 5-year est.); Median year structure built: 1970 (2005-2009 5-year est.).
Transportation: Commute to work: 84.5% car, 0.0% public transportation, 12.8% walk, 2.7% work from home (2005-2009 5-year est.); Travel time to work: 38.1% less than 15 minutes, 23.4% 15 to 30 minutes, 18.1% 30 to 45 minutes, 0.0% 45 to 60 minutes, 20.3% 60 minutes or more (2005-2009 5-year est.)

CHULA VISTA-RIVER SPUR (CDP). Covers a land area of 0.545 square miles and a water area of 0 square miles. Located at 28.66° N. Lat; 99.80° W. Long. Elevation is 558 feet.
Population: 317 (1990); 400 (2000); 368 (2010); 355 (2015 projected); Race: 71.7% White, 0.0% Black, 0.0% Asian, 28.3% Other, 83.2% Hispanic of any race (2010); Density: 674.7 persons per square mile (2010); Average household size: 3.64 (2010); Median age: 25.6 (2010); Males per 100 females: 86.8 (2010); Marriage status: 47.8% never married, 52.2% now married, 0.0% widowed, 0.0% divorced (2005-2009 5-year est.); Foreign born: 33.0% (2005-2009 5-year est.); Ancestry (includes multiple ancestries): n/a (2005-2009 5-year est.).
Economy: Employment by occupation: 0.0% management, 0.0% professional, 0.0% services, 100.0% sales, 0.0% farming, 0.0% construction, 0.0% production (2005-2009 5-year est.).
Income: Per capita income: $9,125 (2010); Median household income: $21,944 (2010); Average household income: $32,896 (2010); Percent of households with income of $100,000 or more: 4.0% (2010); Poverty rate: 17.6% (2005-2009 5-year est.).
Education: Percent of population age 25 and over with: High school diploma (including GED) or higher: 62.6% (2010); Bachelor's degree or higher: 8.0% (2010); Master's degree or higher: 5.9% (2010).
Housing: Homeownership rate: 76.2% (2010); Median home value: $31,600 (2010); Median contract rent: n/a per month (2005-2009 5-year est.); Median year structure built: 1964 (2005-2009 5-year est.).
Transportation: Commute to work: 100.0% car, 0.0% public transportation, 0.0% walk, 0.0% work from home (2005-2009 5-year est.); Travel time to work: 100.0% less than 15 minutes, 0.0% 15 to 30 minutes, 0.0% 30 to 45 minutes, 0.0% 45 to 60 minutes, 0.0% 60 minutes or more (2005-2009 5-year est.)

CRYSTAL CITY (city). County seat. Covers a land area of 3.642 square miles and a water area of 0 square miles. Located at 28.68° N. Lat; 99.82° W. Long. Elevation is 558 feet.
History: Crystal City celebrated its spinach crops by erecting a statue of Popeye in the town square in 1937.
Population: 8,263 (1990); 7,190 (2000); 7,400 (2010); 7,484 (2015 projected); Race: 74.6% White, 0.8% Black, 0.2% Asian, 24.4% Other, 92.1% Hispanic of any race (2010); Density: 2,031.7 persons per square mile (2010); Average household size: 3.11 (2010); Median age: 30.4 (2010); Males per 100 females: 92.9 (2010); Marriage status: 32.8% never married, 50.1% now married, 9.2% widowed, 7.9% divorced (2005-2009 5-year est.); Foreign born: 11.4% (2005-2009 5-year est.); Ancestry (includes multiple ancestries): 1.5% German, 0.7% Polish, 0.6% Italian, 0.3% American, 0.2% Scotch-Irish (2005-2009 5-year est.).
Economy: Single-family building permits issued: 4 (2010); Multi-family building permits issued: 0 (2010); Employment by occupation: 5.7% management, 12.5% professional, 35.3% services, 23.4% sales, 3.6% farming, 7.6% construction, 12.0% production (2005-2009 5-year est.).
Income: Per capita income: $11,528 (2010); Median household income: $19,762 (2010); Average household income: $29,392 (2010); Percent of households with income of $100,000 or more: 3.5% (2010); Poverty rate: 36.9% (2005-2009 5-year est.).
Taxes: Total city taxes per capita: $135 (2007); City property taxes per capita: $65 (2007).
Education: Percent of population age 25 and over with: High school diploma (including GED) or higher: 50.6% (2010); Bachelor's degree or higher: 8.8% (2010); Master's degree or higher: 3.9% (2010).

School District(s)
Crystal City ISD (PK-12)

2009-10 Enrollment: 1,984 . . . . (830) 374-2367

Housing: Homeownership rate: 66.7% (2010); Median home value: $34,034 (2010); Median contract rent: $326 per month (2005-2009 5-year est.); Median year structure built: 1972 (2005-2009 5-year est.).

Safety: Violent crime rate: 57.3 per 10,000 population; Property crime rate: 115.9 per 10,000 population (2009).

Transportation: Commute to work: 90.2% car, 0.0% public transportation, 1.8% walk, 0.0% work from home (2005-2009 5-year est.); Travel time to work: 66.5% less than 15 minutes, 23.8% 15 to 30 minutes, 4.7% 30 to 45 minutes, 1.3% 45 to 60 minutes, 3.8% 60 minutes or more (2005-2009 5-year est.)

Additional Information Contacts

City of Crystal City . . . . (830) 374-3478

LA PRYOR (CDP). Covers a land area of 2.679 square miles and a water area of 0 square miles. Located at 28.94° N. Lat; 99.84° W. Long. Elevation is 745 feet.

History: La Pryor was established on land that was once part of the large Pryor Ranch. The principal crop here was spinach.

Population: 1,343 (1990); 1,491 (2000); 1,647 (2010); 1,713 (2015 projected); Race: 40.0% White, 0.4% Black, 0.1% Asian, 59.5% Other, 85.5% Hispanic of any race (2010); Density: 614.8 persons per square mile (2010); Average household size: 3.07 (2010); Median age: 30.8 (2010); Males per 100 females: 91.1 (2010); Marriage status: 35.9% never married, 47.6% now married, 8.1% widowed, 8.4% divorced (2005-2009 5-year est.); Foreign born: 13.1% (2005-2009 5-year est.); Ancestry (includes multiple ancestries): 9.4% German, 0.5% Dutch, 0.3% Irish (2005-2009 5-year est.).

Economy: Employment by occupation: 5.6% management, 12.6% professional, 16.6% services, 30.8% sales, 0.0% farming, 25.2% construction, 9.1% production (2005-2009 5-year est.).

Income: Per capita income: $12,052 (2010); Median household income: $26,188 (2010); Average household income: $35,950 (2010); Percent of households with income of $100,000 or more: 3.9% (2010); Poverty rate: 40.4% (2005-2009 5-year est.).

Education: Percent of population age 25 and over with: High school diploma (including GED) or higher: 55.4% (2010); Bachelor's degree or higher: 8.0% (2010); Master's degree or higher: 2.2% (2010).

School District(s)
La Pryor ISD (PK-12)

2009-10 Enrollment: 489 . . . . (830) 365-4000

Housing: Homeownership rate: 84.0% (2010); Median home value: $20,631 (2010); Median contract rent: $280 per month (2005-2009 5-year est.); Median year structure built: 1974 (2005-2009 5-year est.).

Transportation: Commute to work: 94.3% car, 0.0% public transportation, 1.8% walk, 1.3% work from home (2005-2009 5-year est.); Travel time to work: 27.3% less than 15 minutes, 29.5% 15 to 30 minutes, 29.3% 30 to 45 minutes, 0.0% 45 to 60 minutes, 13.9% 60 minutes or more (2005-2009 5-year est.)

LAS COLONIAS (CDP). Covers a land area of 13.548 square miles and a water area of 0.044 square miles. Located at 28.71° N. Lat; 99.82° W. Long. Elevation is 600 feet.

Population: 226 (1990); 283 (2000); 305 (2010); 317 (2015 projected); Race: 77.7% White, 1.3% Black, 0.0% Asian, 21.0% Other, 83.0% Hispanic of any race (2010); Density: 22.5 persons per square mile (2010); Average household size: 3.25 (2010); Median age: 25.9 (2010); Males per 100 females: 102.0 (2010); Marriage status: 33.8% never married, 36.8% now married, 14.7% widowed, 14.7% divorced (2005-2009 5-year est.); Foreign born: 7.9% (2005-2009 5-year est.); Ancestry (includes multiple ancestries): 8.9% Irish, 6.5% English (2005-2009 5-year est.).

Economy: Employment by occupation: 0.0% management, 0.0% professional, 78.9% services, 0.0% sales, 0.0% farming, 21.1% construction, 0.0% production (2005-2009 5-year est.).

Income: Per capita income: $15,464 (2010); Median household income: $26,667 (2010); Average household income: $40,000 (2010); Percent of households with income of $100,000 or more: 5.7% (2010); Poverty rate: 49.6% (2005-2009 5-year est.).

Education: Percent of population age 25 and over with: High school diploma (including GED) or higher: 56.4% (2010); Bachelor's degree or higher: 8.3% (2010); Master's degree or higher: 3.8% (2010).

Housing: Homeownership rate: 51.7% (2010); Median home value: $61,000 (2010); Median contract rent: n/a per month (2005-2009 5-year est.); Median year structure built: 1964 (2005-2009 5-year est.).

Transportation: Commute to work: 78.9% car, 0.0% public transportation, 21.1% walk, 0.0% work from home (2005-2009 5-year est.); Travel time to work: 64.9% less than 15 minutes, 35.1% 15 to 30 minutes, 0.0% 30 to 45 minutes, 0.0% 45 to 60 minutes, 0.0% 60 minutes or more (2005-2009 5-year est.);

A

Abbott city *Hill County*, 286

Abernathy city *Hale County*, 231

Abilene city *Taylor County*, 513

Abram-Perezville CDP *Hidalgo County*, 272

Ackerly city *Dawson County*, 141

Addison town *Dallas County*, 130

Adkins postal area *Bexar County*, 28

Adrian city *Oldham County*, 430

Afton postal area *Dickens County*, 156

Agua Dulce CDP *El Paso County*, 168

Agua Dulce city *Nueces County*, 426

Airport Road Addition CDP *Brooks County*, 58

Alamo Heights city *Bexar County*, 28

Alamo city *Hidalgo County*, 272

Alba town *Wood County*, 580

Albany city *Shackelford County*, 481

Aldine CDP *Harris County*, 242

Aledo city *Parker County*, 438

Alfred-South La Paloma CDP *Jim Wells County*, 319

Alice Acres CDP *Jim Wells County*, 320

Alice city *Jim Wells County*, 319

Allen city *Collin County*, 103

Alleyton postal area *Colorado County*, 112

Alma town *Ellis County*, 173

Alpine city *Brewster County*, 56

Altair postal area *Colorado County*, 112

Alto Bonito CDP *Starr County*, 490

Alto town *Cherokee County*, 93

Alton North CDP *Hidalgo County*, 273

Alton city *Hidalgo County*, 272

Alvarado city *Johnson County*, 322

Alvin city *Brazoria County*, 46

Alvord town *Wise County*, 576

Amarillo city *Potter County*, 447

Ames city *Liberty County*, 358

Amherst city *Lamb County*, 349

Anahuac city *Chambers County*, 90

Anderson County, 1

Anderson Mill CDP *Williamson County*, 568

Anderson city *Grimes County*, 226

Andrews County, 2

Andrews city *Andrews County*, 2

Angelina County, 3 - 4

Angleton city *Brazoria County*, 46

Angus city *Navarro County*, 417

Anna city *Collin County*, 104

Annetta North town *Parker County*, 439

Annetta South town *Parker County*, 439

Annetta town *Parker County*, 438

Annona town *Red River County*, 454

Anson city *Jones County*, 326

Anthony town *El Paso County*, 168

Anton city *Hockley County*, 291

Apple Springs postal area *Trinity County*, 531

Appleby city *Nacogdoches County*, 414

Aquilla city *Hill County*, 287

Aransas County, 5

Aransas Pass city *San Patricio County*, 472

Archer City city *Archer County*, 7

Archer County, 6 - 7

Arcola city *Fort Bend County*, 191

Argyle city *Denton County*, 147

Arlington city *Tarrant County*, 500

Armstrong County, 8

Armstrong postal area *Kenedy County*, 336

Arp city *Smith County*, 485

Arroyo Alto CDP *Cameron County*, 71

Arroyo Colorado Estates CDP *Cameron County*, 72

Arroyo Gardens-La Tina Ranch CDP *Cameron County*, 72

Arthur City postal area *Lamar County*, 346

Asherton city *Dimmit County*, 158

Aspermont town *Stonewall County*, 497

Atascocita CDP *Harris County*, 242

Atascosa County, 9 - 10

Atascosa postal area *Bexar County*, 28

Athens city *Henderson County*, 266

Atlanta city *Cass County*, 86

Aubrey city *Denton County*, 147

Aurora town *Wise County*, 576

Austin County, 11 - 13

Austin city *Travis County*, 523

Austwell city *Refugio County*, 458

Avery town *Red River County*, 454

Avinger town *Cass County*, 86

Avoca postal area *Jones County*, 326

Axtell postal area *McLennan County*, 386

Azle city *Tarrant County*, 501

B

Bacliff CDP *Galveston County*, 205

Bagwell postal area *Red River County*, 455

Bailey County, 14

Bailey city *Fannin County*, 182

Bailey's Prairie village *Brazoria County*, 47

Baird city *Callahan County*, 70

Balch Springs city *Dallas County*, 130

Balcones Heights city *Bexar County*, 28

Ballinger city *Runnels County*, 464

Balmorhea city *Reeves County*, 456

Bandera County, 15

Bandera city *Bandera County*, 15

Bangs city *Brown County*, 60

Bardwell city *Ellis County*, 174

Barksdale postal area *Edwards County*, 166

Barnhart postal area *Irion County*, 307

Barrett CDP *Harris County*, 242

Barry city *Navarro County*, 417

Barstow city *Ward County*, 549

Bartlett city *Williamson County*, 568

Barton Creek CDP *Travis County*, 525

Bartonville town *Denton County*, 147

Bastrop County, 16 - 18

Bastrop city *Bastrop County*, 17

Batesville CDP *Zavala County*, 587

Batson postal area *Hardin County*, 239

Bausell and Ellis CDP *Willacy County*, 564

Bay City city *Matagorda County*, 379

Bayou Vista city *Galveston County*, 205

Bayside town *Refugio County*, 458

Baytown city *Harris County*, 243

Bayview town *Cameron County*, 72

Beach City city *Chambers County*, 91

Bear Creek village *Hays County*, 262

Beasley city *Fort Bend County*, 192

Beaumont city *Jefferson County*, 314

Beckville city *Panola County*, 436

Bedford city *Tarrant County*, 501

Bedias postal area *Grimes County*, 226

Bee Cave village *Travis County*, 525

Bee County, 20 - 22

Beeville city *Bee County*, 21

Bell County, 23 - 26

Bellaire city *Harris County*, 243

Bellevue city *Clay County*, 96

Bellmead city *McLennan County*, 386

Bells town *Grayson County*, 218

Bellville city *Austin County*, 12

Belton city *Bell County*, 23

Ben Franklin postal area *Delta County*, 145

Ben Wheeler postal area *Van Zandt County*, 542

Benavides city *Duval County*, 161

Benbrook city *Tarrant County*, 501

Bend postal area *San Saba County*, 478

Benjamin city *Knox County*, 343

Bergheim postal area *Kendall County*, 334

Berryville town *Henderson County*, 266

Bertram city *Burnet County*, 64

Beverly Hills city *McLennan County*, 387

Bevil Oaks city *Jefferson County*, 315

Bexar County, 27 - 36

Big Lake city *Reagan County*, 452

Big Sandy town *Upshur County*, 534

Big Spring city *Howard County*, 299

Big Wells city *Dimmit County*, 158

Bigfoot CDP *Frio County*, 202

Bishop Hills town *Potter County*, 448

Bishop city *Nueces County*, 426

Bivins postal area *Cass County*, 87

Bixby CDP *Cameron County*, 72

Blackwell city *Nolan County*, 424

Blanco County, 37 - 38

Blanco city *Blanco County*, 38

Blanket town *Brown County*, 60

Blessing CDP *Matagorda County*, 379

Bloomburg town *Cass County*, 87

Blooming Grove town *Navarro County*, 417

Bloomington CDP *Victoria County*, 544

Blossom city *Lamar County*, 346

Blue Berry Hill CDP *Bee County*, 21

Blue Mound city *Tarrant County*, 502

Blue Ridge city *Collin County*, 104

Bluetown-Iglesia Antigua CDP *Cameron County*, 73

Bluff Dale postal area *Erath County*, 178

Bluffton postal area *Llano County*, 367

Blum town *Hill County*, 287

Boerne city *Kendall County*, 335

Bogata city *Red River County*, 455

Boling-Iago CDP *Wharton County*, 556

Bolivar Peninsula CDP *Galveston County*, 205

Bon Wier postal area *Newton County*, 422

Bonham city *Fannin County*, 182

Bonney village *Brazoria County*, 47

Booker town *Lipscomb County*, 364

Borden County, 39

Borger city *Hutchinson County*, 305

Bosque County, 39 - 41

Botines CDP *Webb County*, 553

Bovina city *Parmer County*, 442

Bowie County, 42 - 44

Bowie city *Montague County*, 403

CDP = Census Designated Place

Box Canyon-Amistad CDP *Val Verde County*, 540
Boyd town *Wise County*, 577
Brackettville city *Kinney County*, 341
Brady city *McCulloch County*, 384
Brashear postal area *Hopkins County*, 295
Brazoria County, 45 - 52
Brazoria city *Brazoria County*, 47
Brazos County, 53 - 54
Breckenridge city *Stephens County*, 495
Bremond city *Robertson County*, 460
Brenham city *Washington County*, 551
Brewster County, 55 - 56
Briar CDP *Tarrant County*, 502
Briarcliff village *Travis County*, 525
Briaroaks city *Johnson County*, 323
Bridge City city *Orange County*, 431
Bridgeport city *Wise County*, 577
Briggs postal area *Burnet County*, 64
Briscoe County, 57
Briscoe postal area *Wheeler County*, 559
Broaddus town *San Augustine County*, 469
Bronson postal area *Sabine County*, 468
Bronte town *Coke County*, 99
Brookeland postal area *Sabine County*, 468
Brookesmith postal area *Brown County*, 60
Brooks County, 58
Brookshire city *Waller County*, 547
Brookside Village city *Brazoria County*, 47
Brookston postal area *Lamar County*, 346
Brown County, 59 - 61
Browndell city *Jasper County*, 311
Brownfield city *Terry County*, 517
Brownsboro city *Henderson County*, 267
Brownsville city *Cameron County*, 73
Brownwood city *Brown County*, 60
Bruceville-Eddy city *McLennan County*, 387
Brundage CDP *Dimmit County*, 158
Bruni CDP *Webb County*, 553
Brushy Creek CDP *Williamson County*, 568
Bryan city *Brazos County*, 54
Bryson city *Jack County*, 308
Buchanan Dam CDP *Llano County*, 367
Buckholts town *Milam County*, 399
Buda city *Hays County*, 262
Buffalo Gap town *Taylor County*, 513
Buffalo Springs village *Lubbock County*, 370
Buffalo city *Leon County*, 356
Bula postal area *Bailey County*, 14
Bullard town *Smith County*, 486
Bulverde city *Comal County*, 115
Buna CDP *Jasper County*, 311
Bunker Hill Village city *Harris County*, 243
Burkburnett city *Wichita County*, 560
Burke city *Angelina County*, 3
Burkett postal area *Coleman County*, 100
Burkeville postal area *Newton County*, 422
Burleson County, 62
Burleson city *Johnson County*, 323
Burlington postal area *Milam County*, 399
Burnet County, 63 - 65
Burnet city *Burnet County*, 64
Burton town *Washington County*, 552
Butterfield CDP *El Paso County*, 168
Byers city *Clay County*, 97
Bynum town *Hill County*, 287

C

Cactus city *Moore County*, 411
Caddo Mills city *Hunt County*, 302
Caddo postal area *Stephens County*, 495
Caldwell County, 66 - 67
Caldwell city *Burleson County*, 62
Calhoun County, 68
Call postal area *Newton County*, 422
Callahan County, 69 - 70
Calliham postal area *McMullen County*, 393
Callisburg city *Cooke County*, 120
Calvert city *Robertson County*, 460
Cameron County, 71 - 82
Cameron Park CDP *Cameron County*, 73
Cameron city *Milam County*, 399
Camp County, 83
Camp Swift CDP *Bastrop County*, 17
Camp Wood city *Real County*, 453
Campbell city *Hunt County*, 302
Campbellton postal area *Atascosa County*, 9
Canadian city *Hemphill County*, 265
Caney City town *Henderson County*, 267
Canton city *Van Zandt County*, 542
Cantu Addition CDP *Brooks County*, 58
Canutillo CDP *El Paso County*, 168
Canyon Lake CDP *Comal County*, 115
Canyon city *Randall County*, 451
Carbon town *Eastland County*, 163
Carl's Corner town *Hill County*, 287
Carlsbad postal area *Tom Green County*, 521
Carlton postal area *Hamilton County*, 235
Carmine city *Fayette County*, 185
Carrizo Hill CDP *Dimmit County*, 158
Carrizo Springs city *Dimmit County*, 159
Carrollton city *Denton County*, 147
Carson County, 84 - 85
Carthage city *Panola County*, 436
Cass County, 86 - 88
Castell postal area *Llano County*, 367
Castle Hills city *Bexar County*, 29
Castro County, 89
Castroville city *Medina County*, 394
Cat Spring postal area *Austin County*, 12
Catarina CDP *Dimmit County*, 159
Cedar Creek postal area *Bastrop County*, 18
Cedar Hill city *Dallas County*, 131
Cedar Lane postal area *Matagorda County*, 379
Cedar Park city *Williamson County*, 568
Celeste city *Hunt County*, 302
Celina town *Collin County*, 104
Center Point postal area *Kerr County*, 338
Center city *Shelby County*, 482
Centerville city *Leon County*, 356
Central Gardens CDP *Jefferson County*, 315
Cesar Chavez CDP *Hidalgo County*, 273
Chambers County, 90 - 91
Chandler city *Henderson County*, 267
Channelview CDP *Harris County*, 244
Channing city *Hartley County*, 259
Chappell Hill postal area *Washington County*, 552
Charlotte city *Atascosa County*, 10
Chatfield postal area *Navarro County*, 417
Cherokee County, 92 - 94
Cherokee postal area *San Saba County*, 478

Chester town *Tyler County*, 532
Chico city *Wise County*, 577
Childress County, 95
Childress city *Childress County*, 96
Chillicothe city *Hardeman County*, 238
Chilton postal area *Falls County*, 180
China Grove town *Bexar County*, 29
China Spring postal area *McLennan County*, 387
China city *Jefferson County*, 315
Chireno city *Nacogdoches County*, 415
Christine town *Atascosa County*, 10
Christoval CDP *Tom Green County*, 521
Chula Vista-Orason CDP *Cameron County*, 74
Chula Vista-River Spur CDP *Zavala County*, 587
Cibolo city *Guadalupe County*, 228
Cienegas Terrace CDP *Val Verde County*, 540
Cinco Ranch CDP *Fort Bend County*, 192
Circle D-KC Estates CDP *Bastrop County*, 18
Cisco city *Eastland County*, 163
Citrus City CDP *Hidalgo County*, 273
Clarendon city *Donley County*, 160
Clarksville City city *Gregg County*, 223
Clarksville city *Red River County*, 455
Claude city *Armstrong County*, 9
Clay County, 96 - 97
Clear Lake Shores city *Galveston County*, 206
Cleburne city *Johnson County*, 323
Cleveland city *Liberty County*, 358
Clifton city *Bosque County*, 40
Clint town *El Paso County*, 169
Cloverleaf CDP *Harris County*, 244
Clute city *Brazoria County*, 48
Clyde city *Callahan County*, 70
Coahoma town *Howard County*, 299
Cochran County, 98
Cockrell Hill city *Dallas County*, 131
Coffee City town *Henderson County*, 267
Coke County, 99
Coldspring city *San Jacinto County*, 470
Coleman County, 100 - 102
Coleman city *Coleman County*, 101
College Station city *Brazos County*, 54
Collegeport postal area *Matagorda County*, 380
Colleyville city *Tarrant County*, 502
Collin County, 103 - 109
Collingsworth County, 110 - 111
Collinsville town *Grayson County*, 218
Colmesneil city *Tyler County*, 533
Colorado City city *Mitchell County*, 402
Colorado County, 112 - 113
Columbus city *Colorado County*, 112
Comal County, 114 - 115
Comanche County, 116 - 117
Comanche city *Comanche County*, 117
Combes town *Cameron County*, 74
Combine city *Kaufman County*, 330
Comfort CDP *Kendall County*, 335
Commerce city *Hunt County*, 303
Como town *Hopkins County*, 295
Comstock postal area *Val Verde County*, 540
Concan postal area *Uvalde County*, 538

CDP = Census Designated Place

Estelline town *Hall County*, 234
Euless city *Tarrant County*, 503
Eureka city *Navarro County*, 418
Eustace city *Henderson County*, 268
Evadale CDP *Jasper County*, 311
Evant town *Coryell County*, 123
Everman city *Tarrant County*, 504

F

Fabens CDP *El Paso County*, 170
Fair Oaks Ranch city *Bexar County*, 30
Fairchilds village *Fort Bend County*, 192
Fairfield city *Freestone County*, 200
Fairview town *Collin County*, 104
Falcon Heights CDP *Starr County*, 490
Falcon Lake Estates CDP *Zapata County*, 585
Falcon Mesa CDP *Zapata County*, 585
Falcon Village CDP *Starr County*, 491
Falfurrias city *Brooks County*, 59
Falls City city *Karnes County*, 328
Falls County, 179 - 180
Falman-County Acres CDP *San Patricio County*, 473
Fannin County, 181 - 184
Farmers Branch city *Dallas County*, 134
Farmersville city *Collin County*, 105
Farwell city *Parmer County*, 442
Fate city *Rockwall County*, 462
Fayette County, 185 - 187
Fayetteville city *Fayette County*, 186
Faysville CDP *Hidalgo County*, 275
Ferris city *Ellis County*, 174
Fieldton postal area *Lamb County*, 350
Fifth Street CDP *Fort Bend County*, 193
Fischer postal area *Comal County*, 115
Fisher County, 188
Flatonia town *Fayette County*, 186
Flint postal area *Smith County*, 486
Flomot postal area *Motley County*, 413
Florence city *Williamson County*, 569
Floresville city *Wilson County*, 573
Flowella CDP *Brooks County*, 59
Flower Mound town *Denton County*, 150
Floyd County, 189
Floydada city *Floyd County*, 190
Fluvanna postal area *Scurry County*, 480
Foard County, 190
Follett city *Lipscomb County*, 365
Forest Hill city *Tarrant County*, 504
Forestburg postal area *Montague County*, 403
Forney city *Kaufman County*, 331
Forreston postal area *Ellis County*, 174
Forsan city *Howard County*, 300
Fort Bend County, 191 - 197
Fort Bliss CDP *El Paso County*, 170
Fort Davis CDP *Jeff Davis County*, 313
Fort Hancock CDP *Hudspeth County*, 301
Fort Hood CDP *Bell County*, 24
Fort Mc Kavett postal area *Menard County*, 396
Fort Stockton city *Pecos County*, 443
Fort Worth city *Tarrant County*, 504
Four Corners CDP *Fort Bend County*, 193
Fowlerton CDP *La Salle County*, 345
Franklin County, 198

Franklin city *Robertson County*, 461
Frankston town *Anderson County*, 1
Fred postal area *Tyler County*, 533
Fredericksburg city *Gillespie County*, 212
Fredonia postal area *Mason County*, 378
Freeport city *Brazoria County*, 48
Freer city *Duval County*, 161
Freestone County, 199 - 200
Fresno CDP *Fort Bend County*, 193
Friendswood city *Galveston County*, 206
Frio County, 201 - 202
Friona city *Parmer County*, 442
Frisco city *Collin County*, 105
Fritch city *Hutchinson County*, 306
Fronton CDP *Starr County*, 491
Frost city *Navarro County*, 419
Fruitvale city *Van Zandt County*, 543
Fulshear city *Fort Bend County*, 193
Fulton town *Aransas County*, 6

G

Gail postal area *Borden County*, 39
Gaines County, 203
Gainesville city *Cooke County*, 120
Galena Park city *Harris County*, 245
Gallatin city *Cherokee County*, 93
Galveston County, 204 - 209
Galveston city *Galveston County*, 207
Ganado city *Jackson County*, 309
Garceno CDP *Starr County*, 491
Garden City postal area *Glasscock County*, 213
Garden Ridge city *Comal County*, 115
Gardendale CDP *Ector County*, 165
Garfield CDP *Travis County*, 526
Garland city *Dallas County*, 135
Garrett town *Ellis County*, 175
Garrison city *Nacogdoches County*, 415
Garwood postal area *Colorado County*, 113
Gary City town *Panola County*, 437
Garza County, 210
Gatesville city *Coryell County*, 123
George West city *Live Oak County*, 366
Georgetown city *Williamson County*, 569
Geronimo CDP *Guadalupe County*, 228
Gholson city *McLennan County*, 388
Giddings city *Lee County*, 355
Gilchrist postal area *Galveston County*, 207
Gillespie County, 211 - 212
Gillett postal area *Karnes County*, 328
Gilmer city *Upshur County*, 535
Girard CDP *Kent County*, 337
Gladewater city *Gregg County*, 224
Glasscock County, 213
Glen Flora postal area *Wharton County*, 557
Glen Rose city *Somervell County*, 489
Glenn Heights city *Dallas County*, 135
Glidden postal area *Colorado County*, 113
Godley city *Johnson County*, 324
Goldsboro postal area *Coleman County*, 101
Goldsmith city *Ector County*, 165
Goldthwaite city *Mills County*, 401
Goliad County, 213
Goliad city *Goliad County*, 214
Golinda city *Falls County*, 180
Gonzales County, 214 - 215
Gonzales city *Gonzales County*, 215

Goodlow city *Navarro County*, 419
Goodrich city *Polk County*, 445
Gordon city *Palo Pinto County*, 434
Gordonville postal area *Grayson County*, 219
Goree city *Knox County*, 343
Gorman city *Eastland County*, 164
Gouldbusk postal area *Coleman County*, 101
Graford city *Palo Pinto County*, 434
Graham city *Young County*, 583
Granbury city *Hood County*, 293
Grand Acres CDP *Cameron County*, 75
Grand Prairie city *Dallas County*, 136
Grand Saline city *Van Zandt County*, 543
Grandfalls town *Ward County*, 549
Grandview city *Johnson County*, 324
Granger city *Williamson County*, 570
Granite Shoals city *Burnet County*, 65
Granjeno city *Hidalgo County*, 275
Grape Creek CDP *Tom Green County*, 522
Grapeland city *Houston County*, 297
Grapevine city *Tarrant County*, 506
Gray County, 216
Grays Prairie village *Kaufman County*, 331
Grayson County, 217 - 222
Greatwood CDP *Fort Bend County*, 193
Green Valley Farms CDP *Cameron County*, 75
Greenville city *Hunt County*, 303
Gregg County, 223 - 225
Gregory city *San Patricio County*, 473
Grey Forest city *Bexar County*, 30
Grimes County, 226 - 227
Groesbeck city *Limestone County*, 362
Groom town *Carson County*, 85
Groves city *Jefferson County*, 315
Groveton city *Trinity County*, 531
Gruver city *Hansford County*, 236
Guadalupe County, 228 - 230
Guerra CDP *Jim Hogg County*, 318
Gun Barrel City town *Henderson County*, 268
Gunter city *Grayson County*, 219
Gustine town *Comanche County*, 117
Guy postal area *Fort Bend County*, 194

H

Hackberry town *Denton County*, 150
Hale Center city *Hale County*, 232
Hale County, 231 - 232
Hall County, 233 - 234
Hallettsville city *Lavaca County*, 353
Hallsburg city *McLennan County*, 388
Hallsville city *Harrison County*, 256
Haltom City city *Tarrant County*, 506
Hamilton County, 235
Hamilton city *Hamilton County*, 235
Hamlin city *Jones County*, 327
Hamshire postal area *Jefferson County*, 316
Hankamer postal area *Chambers County*, 91
Hansford County, 236
Happy town *Swisher County*, 498
Hardeman County, 237
Hardin County, 238 - 240
Hardin city *Liberty County*, 360
Hargill postal area *Hidalgo County*, 276
Harker Heights city *Bell County*, 24
Harleton postal area *Harrison County*, 257
Harlingen city *Cameron County*, 75

Harper CDP *Gillespie County*, 212
Harris County, 241 - 255
Harrison County, 256 - 257
Harrold postal area *Wilbarger County*, 563
Hart city *Castro County*, 89
Hartley County, 258
Hartley CDP *Hartley County*, 259
Harwood postal area *Gonzales County*, 215
Haskell County, 259 - 260
Haskell city *Haskell County*, 260
Haslet city *Tarrant County*, 506
Havana CDP *Hidalgo County*, 276
Hawk Cove city *Hunt County*, 303
Hawkins city *Wood County*, 580
Hawley city *Jones County*, 327
Hays County, 261 - 264
Hays city *Hays County*, 263
Hearne city *Robertson County*, 461
Heath city *Rockwall County*, 462
Hebbronville CDP *Jim Hogg County*, 318
Hebron town *Denton County*, 150
Hedley city *Donley County*, 160
Hedwig Village city *Harris County*, 245
Heidelberg CDP *Hidalgo County*, 276
Helotes city *Bexar County*, 30
Hemphill County, 265
Hemphill city *Sabine County*, 468
Hempstead city *Waller County*, 547
Henderson County, 265 - 270
Henderson city *Rusk County*, 466
Henrietta city *Clay County*, 97
Hereford city *Deaf Smith County*, 144
Hermleigh CDP *Scurry County*, 480
Hewitt city *McLennan County*, 388
Hext postal area *Menard County*, 397
Hickory Creek town *Denton County*, 150
Hico city *Hamilton County*, 235
Hidalgo County, 271 - 285
Hidalgo city *Hidalgo County*, 276
Higgins city *Lipscomb County*, 365
High Island postal area *Galveston County*, 207
Highland Haven city *Burnet County*, 65
Highland Park town *Dallas County*, 136
Highland Village city *Denton County*, 151
Highlands CDP *Harris County*, 246
Hill Country Village city *Bexar County*, 31
Hill County, 286 - 289
Hillcrest village *Brazoria County*, 49
Hillister postal area *Tyler County*, 533
Hillsboro city *Hill County*, 288
Hilltop CDP *Frio County*, 202
Hilshire Village city *Harris County*, 246
Hitchcock city *Galveston County*, 207
Hobson postal area *Karnes County*, 329
Hockley County, 290 - 291
Hockley postal area *Harris County*, 246
Holiday Lakes town *Brazoria County*, 49
Holland town *Bell County*, 24
Holliday city *Archer County*, 7
Hollywood Park town *Bexar County*, 31
Homestead Meadows North CDP *El Paso County*, 170
Homestead Meadows South CDP *El Paso County*, 170
Hondo city *Medina County*, 395
Honey Grove city *Fannin County*, 183

Hood County, 292 - 293
Hooks city *Bowie County*, 42
Hopkins County, 294 - 296
Horizon City city *El Paso County*, 171
Horseshoe Bay CDP *Llano County*, 368
Houston County, 297 - 298
Houston city *Harris County*, 246
Howard County, 299
Howardwick city *Donley County*, 160
Howe town *Grayson County*, 220
Hubbard city *Hill County*, 288
Hudson Bend CDP *Travis County*, 526
Hudson Oaks city *Parker County*, 439
Hudson city *Angelina County*, 4
Hudspeth County, 300
Huffman postal area *Harris County*, 249
Hughes Springs city *Cass County*, 88
Hull postal area *Liberty County*, 360
Humble city *Harris County*, 250
Hungerford CDP *Wharton County*, 557
Hunt County, 301 - 304
Hunt postal area *Kerr County*, 338
Hunters Creek Village city *Harris County*, 250
Huntington city *Angelina County*, 4
Huntsville city *Walker County*, 546
Hurst city *Tarrant County*, 507
Hutchins city *Dallas County*, 136
Hutchinson County, 305 - 306
Hutto city *Williamson County*, 570
Huxley city *Shelby County*, 483
Hye postal area *Blanco County*, 38

I

Idalou city *Lubbock County*, 370
Impact town *Taylor County*, 514
Imperial CDP *Pecos County*, 444
Indian Hills CDP *Hidalgo County*, 276
Indian Lake town *Cameron County*, 75
Industry city *Austin County*, 12
Inez CDP *Victoria County*, 545
Ingleside on the Bay city *San Patricio County*, 474
Ingleside city *San Patricio County*, 474
Ingram city *Kerr County*, 338
Iola postal area *Grimes County*, 226
Iowa Colony village *Brazoria County*, 49
Iowa Park city *Wichita County*, 561
Ira postal area *Scurry County*, 480
Iraan city *Pecos County*, 444
Iredell city *Bosque County*, 40
Irion County, 307
Irving city *Dallas County*, 137
Italy town *Ellis County*, 175
Itasca city *Hill County*, 289
Ivanhoe postal area *Fannin County*, 183

J

Jacinto City city *Harris County*, 250
Jack County, 307 - 308
Jacksboro city *Jack County*, 308
Jackson County, 309
Jacksonville city *Cherokee County*, 94
Jamaica Beach city *Galveston County*, 208
Jarrell city *Williamson County*, 570
Jasper County, 310 - 311
Jasper city *Jasper County*, 312
Jayton city *Kent County*, 337

Jeff Davis County, 312
Jefferson County, 313 - 316
Jefferson city *Marion County*, 376
Jermyn postal area *Jack County*, 308
Jersey Village city *Harris County*, 251
Jewett city *Leon County*, 356
Jim Hogg County, 317 - 318
Jim Wells County, 319 - 321
Joaquin city *Shelby County*, 483
Johnson City city *Blanco County*, 38
Johnson County, 322 - 325
Jolly city *Clay County*, 97
Jollyville CDP *Williamson County*, 570
Jones County, 326 - 327
Jones Creek village *Brazoria County*, 49
Jonesboro postal area *Coryell County*, 123
Jonestown city *Travis County*, 527
Josephine city *Collin County*, 105
Joshua city *Johnson County*, 324
Jourdanton city *Atascosa County*, 10
Junction city *Kimble County*, 339
Justin city *Denton County*, 151

K

Karnack postal area *Harrison County*, 257
Karnes City city *Karnes County*, 329
Karnes County, 328 - 329
Katy city *Harris County*, 251
Kaufman County, 330 - 333
Kaufman city *Kaufman County*, 331
K-Bar Ranch CDP *Jim Wells County*, 320
Keene city *Johnson County*, 325
Keller city *Tarrant County*, 507
Kemah city *Galveston County*, 208
Kemp town *Kaufman County*, 332
Kempner city *Lampasas County*, 352
Kendalia postal area *Kendall County*, 335
Kendall County, 334 - 335
Kendleton city *Fort Bend County*, 194
Kenedy County, 336
Kenedy city *Karnes County*, 329
Kenefick town *Liberty County*, 360
Kennard city *Houston County*, 298
Kennedale city *Tarrant County*, 507
Kent County, 336
Kerens city *Navarro County*, 419
Kermit city *Winkler County*, 575
Kerr County, 337 - 338
Kerrville city *Kerr County*, 338
Kilgore city *Gregg County*, 224
Killeen city *Bell County*, 25
Kimble County, 339
King County, 340
Kingsbury CDP *Guadalupe County*, 228
Kingsland CDP *Llano County*, 368
Kingsville city *Kleberg County*, 342
Kinney County, 341
Kirby city *Bexar County*, 31
Kirbyville city *Jasper County*, 312
Kirvin town *Freestone County*, 200
Kleberg County, 341 - 342
Klondike postal area *Delta County*, 145
Knippa CDP *Uvalde County*, 538
Knollwood village *Grayson County*, 220
Knott postal area *Howard County*, 300
Knox City town *Knox County*, 343
Knox County, 343

CDP = Census Designated Place

Kopperl postal area *Bosque County*, 40
Kosse town *Limestone County*, 362
Kountze city *Hardin County*, 239
Kress city *Swisher County*, 498
Krugerville city *Denton County*, 151
Krum city *Denton County*, 152
Kyle city *Hays County*, 263

L

La Blanca CDP *Hidalgo County*, 277
La Casita-Garciasville CDP *Starr County*, 491
La Coste city *Medina County*, 395
La Feria North CDP *Cameron County*, 76
La Feria city *Cameron County*, 76
La Grange city *Fayette County*, 186
La Grulla city *Starr County*, 491
La Homa CDP *Hidalgo County*, 277
La Joya city *Hidalgo County*, 277
La Marque city *Galveston County*, 208
La Paloma CDP *Cameron County*, 76
La Paloma-Lost Creek CDP *Nueces County*, 427
La Porte city *Harris County*, 251
La Presa CDP *Webb County*, 553
La Pryor CDP *Zavala County*, 588
La Puerta CDP *Starr County*, 492
La Rosita CDP *Starr County*, 492
La Salle County, 344
La Vernia city *Wilson County*, 573
La Victoria CDP *Starr County*, 492
La Villa city *Hidalgo County*, 277
La Ward city *Jackson County*, 310
Lackland AFB CDP *Bexar County*, 31
Lacy-Lakeview city *McLennan County*, 389
Ladonia town *Fannin County*, 183
Lago Vista city *Travis County*, 527
Lago CDP *Cameron County*, 76
Laguna Heights CDP *Cameron County*, 77
Laguna Seca CDP *Hidalgo County*, 278
Laguna Vista town *Cameron County*, 77
Lake Bridgeport city *Wise County*, 578
Lake Brownwood CDP *Brown County*, 61
Lake City town *San Patricio County*, 474
Lake Creek postal area *Delta County*, 145
Lake Dallas city *Denton County*, 152
Lake Jackson city *Brazoria County*, 50
Lake Kiowa CDP *Cooke County*, 120
Lake Tanglewood village *Randall County*, 451
Lake View CDP *Val Verde County*, 541
Lake Worth city *Tarrant County*, 508
Lakehills CDP *Bandera County*, 16
Lakeport city *Gregg County*, 224
Lakeshore Gardens-Hidden Acres CDP *San Patricio County*, 474
Lakeside City town *Archer County*, 7
Lakeside town *San Patricio County*, 474
Lakeside town *Tarrant County*, 508
Lakeview town *Hall County*, 234
Lakeway city *Travis County*, 527
Lakewood Village city *Denton County*, 152
Lamar County, 345 - 348
Lamb County, 349 - 350
Lamesa city *Dawson County*, 141
Lampasas County, 351
Lampasas city *Lampasas County*, 352

Lancaster city *Dallas County*, 137
Laneville postal area *Rusk County*, 466
Laredo Ranchettes CDP *Webb County*, 554
Laredo city *Webb County*, 554
Larga Vista CDP *Webb County*, 554
Larue postal area *Henderson County*, 268
Las Colonias CDP *Zavala County*, 588
Las Lomas CDP *Starr County*, 492
Las Lomitas CDP *Jim Hogg County*, 318
Las Palmas-Juarez CDP *Cameron County*, 77
Las Quintas Fronterizas CDP *Maverick County*, 383
Lasana CDP *Cameron County*, 77
Lasara CDP *Willacy County*, 564
Latexo city *Houston County*, 298
Laughlin AFB CDP *Val Verde County*, 541
Laureles CDP *Cameron County*, 77
Lavaca County, 352 - 353
Lavon town *Collin County*, 106
Lawn town *Taylor County*, 514
League City city *Galveston County*, 209
Leakey city *Real County*, 453
Leander city *Williamson County*, 571
Leary city *Bowie County*, 43
Ledbetter postal area *Fayette County*, 187
Lee County, 354 - 355
Leesburg postal area *Camp County*, 83
Leesville postal area *Gonzales County*, 215
Lefors town *Gray County*, 217
Lenorah postal area *Martin County*, 377
Leon County, 356 - 357
Leon Valley city *Bexar County*, 32
Leona city *Leon County*, 357
Leonard city *Fannin County*, 183
Leroy city *McLennan County*, 389
Levelland city *Hockley County*, 291
Lewisville city *Denton County*, 152
Lexington town *Lee County*, 355
Liberty City CDP *Gregg County*, 224
Liberty County, 358 - 360
Liberty Hill city *Williamson County*, 571
Liberty city *Liberty County*, 360
Limestone County, 361 - 363
Lincoln Park town *Denton County*, 153
Lincoln postal area *Lee County*, 355
Lindale town *Smith County*, 486
Linden city *Cass County*, 88
Lindsay CDP *Reeves County*, 456
Lindsay town *Cooke County*, 121
Linn postal area *Hidalgo County*, 278
Lipan city *Hood County*, 293
Lipscomb County, 364
Lipscomb CDP *Lipscomb County*, 365
Lissie postal area *Wharton County*, 557
Little Elm town *Denton County*, 153
Little River-Academy city *Bell County*, 25
Littlefield city *Lamb County*, 350
Live Oak County, 365 - 366
Live Oak city *Bexar County*, 32
Liverpool city *Brazoria County*, 50
Livingston town *Polk County*, 445
Llano County, 367 - 368
Llano Grande CDP *Hidalgo County*, 278
Llano city *Llano County*, 368
Lockhart city *Caldwell County*, 67
Lockney town *Floyd County*, 190

Log Cabin city *Henderson County*, 269
Lohn postal area *McCulloch County*, 385
Lolita CDP *Jackson County*, 310
Loma Linda East CDP *Jim Wells County*, 320
Lometa city *Lampasas County*, 352
London postal area *Kimble County*, 340
Lone Oak town *Hunt County*, 304
Lone Star city *Morris County*, 412
Long Branch postal area *Panola County*, 437
Longview city *Gregg County*, 225
Loop postal area *Gaines County*, 204
Lopeno CDP *Zapata County*, 585
Lopezville CDP *Hidalgo County*, 278
Loraine town *Mitchell County*, 402
Lorena city *McLennan County*, 389
Lorenzo city *Crosby County*, 127
Los Alvarez CDP *Starr County*, 492
Los Angeles Subdivision CDP *Willacy County*, 564
Los Ebanos CDP *Hidalgo County*, 278
Los Fresnos city *Cameron County*, 78
Los Indios town *Cameron County*, 78
Los Villareales CDP *Starr County*, 493
Los Ybanez city *Dawson County*, 141
Lost Creek CDP *Travis County*, 527
Lott city *Falls County*, 180
Louise CDP *Wharton County*, 558
Lovelady city *Houston County*, 298
Loving County, 369
Loving postal area *Young County*, 583
Lowry Crossing city *Collin County*, 106
Lozano CDP *Cameron County*, 78
Lubbock County, 370 - 372
Lubbock city *Lubbock County*, 370
Lucas city *Collin County*, 106
Lueders city *Jones County*, 327
Lufkin city *Angelina County*, 4
Luling city *Caldwell County*, 67
Lumberton city *Hardin County*, 239
Lyford South CDP *Willacy County*, 565
Lyford city *Willacy County*, 565
Lynn County, 373
Lytle city *Atascosa County*, 10

M

Mabank town *Kaufman County*, 332
Madison County, 374
Madisonville city *Madison County*, 375
Magnolia city *Montgomery County*, 406
Malakoff city *Henderson County*, 269
Malone town *Hill County*, 289
Manchaca postal area *Travis County*, 528
Manor city *Travis County*, 528
Mansfield city *Tarrant County*, 508
Manvel city *Brazoria County*, 50
Maple postal area *Bailey County*, 14
Marathon CDP *Brewster County*, 56
Marble Falls city *Burnet County*, 65
Marfa city *Presidio County*, 448
Marietta town *Cass County*, 88
Marion County, 375
Marion city *Guadalupe County*, 229
Markham CDP *Matagorda County*, 380
Marlin city *Falls County*, 180
Marquez city *Leon County*, 357
Marshall Creek town *Denton County*, 153
Marshall city *Harrison County*, 257

CDP = Census Designated Place

Mart city *McLennan County*, 390
Martin County, 376
Martindale city *Caldwell County*, 67
Maryneal postal area *Nolan County*, 424
Mason County, 377
Mason city *Mason County*, 378
Matador town *Motley County*, 413
Matagorda County, 378 - 380
Matagorda postal area *Matagorda County*, 380
Mathis city *San Patricio County*, 475
Maud city *Bowie County*, 43
Mauriceville CDP *Orange County*, 432
Maverick County, 381 - 383
Maxwell postal area *Caldwell County*, 68
May postal area *Brown County*, 61
Maypearl city *Ellis County*, 175
McAdoo postal area *Dickens County*, 157
McAllen city *Hidalgo County*, 279
McCamey city *Upton County*, 536
McCaulley postal area *Fisher County*, 188
McCoy postal area *Atascosa County*, 11
McCulloch County, 384 - 385
McDade postal area *Bastrop County*, 18
McGregor city *McLennan County*, 390
McKinney city *Collin County*, 106
McLean town *Gray County*, 217
McLendon-Chisholm city *Rockwall County*, 462
McLennan County, 386 - 392
McMullen County, 393
McQueeney CDP *Guadalupe County*, 229
Meadow town *Terry County*, 517
Meadowlakes city *Burnet County*, 65
Meadows Place city *Fort Bend County*, 194
Medina County, 393 - 395
Medina CDP *Zapata County*, 585
Megargel town *Archer County*, 7
Melissa city *Collin County*, 107
Melvin town *McCulloch County*, 385
Memphis city *Hall County*, 234
Menard County, 396
Menard city *Menard County*, 397
Mentone postal area *Loving County*, 369
Mercedes city *Hidalgo County*, 279
Mereta postal area *Tom Green County*, 522
Meridian city *Bosque County*, 41
Merkel town *Taylor County*, 514
Mertens town *Hill County*, 289
Mertzon city *Irion County*, 307
Mesquite city *Dallas County*, 138
Mexia city *Limestone County*, 363
Meyersville postal area *DeWitt County*, 143
Miami city *Roberts County*, 459
Mico postal area *Medina County*, 395
Midfield postal area *Matagorda County*, 380
Midkiff postal area *Upton County*, 537
Midland County, 397
Midland city *Midland County*, 398
Midlothian city *Ellis County*, 175
Midway North CDP *Hidalgo County*, 280
Midway South CDP *Hidalgo County*, 280
Midway city *Madison County*, 375
Mila Doce CDP *Hidalgo County*, 280
Milam County, 398 - 399
Milam CDP *Sabine County*, 468
Milano city *Milam County*, 399

Mildred town *Navarro County*, 419
Miles city *Runnels County*, 464
Milford town *Ellis County*, 176
Miller's Cove town *Titus County*, 520
Millersview postal area *Concho County*, 119
Millican town *Brazos County*, 55
Mills County, 400
Millsap town *Parker County*, 439
Mineola city *Wood County*, 580
Mineral Wells city *Palo Pinto County*, 435
Mingus city *Palo Pinto County*, 435
Mirando City CDP *Webb County*, 555
Mission Bend CDP *Fort Bend County*, 194
Mission city *Hidalgo County*, 280
Missouri City city *Fort Bend County*, 195
Mitchell County, 401 - 402
Mobeetie city *Wheeler County*, 559
Mobile City city *Rockwall County*, 462
Monahans city *Ward County*, 550
Mont Belvieu city *Chambers County*, 91
Montague County, 403 - 404
Montague postal area *Montague County*, 404
Montalba postal area *Anderson County*, 1
Monte Alto CDP *Hidalgo County*, 281
Montgomery County, 405 - 409
Montgomery city *Montgomery County*, 406
Moody city *McLennan County*, 390
Moore County, 410
Moore Station city *Henderson County*, 269
Moore CDP *Frio County*, 202
Morales-Sanchez CDP *Zapata County*, 585
Moran city *Shackelford County*, 482
Morgan Farm Area CDP *San Patricio County*, 475
Morgan city *Bosque County*, 41
Morgan's Point Resort city *Bell County*, 25
Morgan's Point city *Harris County*, 252
Morning Glory CDP *El Paso County*, 171
Morris County, 411 - 412
Morse CDP *Hansford County*, 237
Morton city *Cochran County*, 98
Moscow postal area *Polk County*, 446
Motley County, 413
Moulton town *Lavaca County*, 353
Mount Calm city *Hill County*, 289
Mount Enterprise city *Rusk County*, 466
Mount Pleasant city *Titus County*, 520
Mount Vernon town *Franklin County*, 199
Mountain City city *Hays County*, 263
Mountain Home postal area *Kerr County*, 339
Muenster city *Cooke County*, 121
Muldoon postal area *Fayette County*, 187
Muleshoe city *Bailey County*, 15
Mullin town *Mills County*, 401
Munday city *Knox County*, 344
Muniz CDP *Hidalgo County*, 281
Murchison city *Henderson County*, 269
Murphy city *Collin County*, 107
Mustang Ridge city *Caldwell County*, 68
Mustang town *Navarro County*, 420

N

Nacogdoches County, 414 - 415
Nacogdoches city *Nacogdoches County*, 416
Naples city *Morris County*, 412
Nash city *Bowie County*, 43
Nassau Bay city *Harris County*, 252

Natalia city *Medina County*, 395
Naval Air Station/JRB postal area *Tarrant County*, 508
Navarro County, 416 - 420
Navarro town *Navarro County*, 420
Navasota city *Grimes County*, 227
Nazareth city *Castro County*, 90
Nederland city *Jefferson County*, 316
Needville city *Fort Bend County*, 195
Nemo postal area *Somervell County*, 489
Nesbitt town *Harrison County*, 258
Nevada city *Collin County*, 108
New Berlin city *Guadalupe County*, 229
New Boston city *Bowie County*, 44
New Braunfels city *Comal County*, 116
New Caney postal area *Montgomery County*, 407
New Chapel Hill city *Smith County*, 486
New Deal town *Lubbock County*, 371
New Fairview city *Wise County*, 578
New Falcon CDP *Zapata County*, 586
New Home city *Lynn County*, 373
New Hope town *Collin County*, 108
New London city *Rusk County*, 467
New Summerfield city *Cherokee County*, 94
New Territory CDP *Fort Bend County*, 195
New Ulm postal area *Austin County*, 13
New Waverly city *Walker County*, 546
Newark city *Wise County*, 578
Newcastle city *Young County*, 583
Newton County, 421 - 422
Newton city *Newton County*, 423
Neylandville town *Hunt County*, 304
Niederwald town *Hays County*, 263
Nixon city *Gonzales County*, 215
Nocona city *Montague County*, 404
Nolan County, 423 - 424
Nolan postal area *Nolan County*, 424
Nolanville city *Bell County*, 26
Nome city *Jefferson County*, 316
Noonday city *Smith County*, 487
Nordheim city *DeWitt County*, 143
Normangee town *Leon County*, 357
Normanna CDP *Bee County*, 21
North Alamo CDP *Hidalgo County*, 281
North Cleveland city *Liberty County*, 361
North Escobares CDP *Starr County*, 493
North Pearsall CDP *Frio County*, 202
North Richland Hills city *Tarrant County*, 509
North San Pedro CDP *Nueces County*, 427
North Zulch postal area *Madison County*, 375
Northcliff CDP *Guadalupe County*, 229
Northlake town *Denton County*, 154
Norton postal area *Runnels County*, 464
Novice city *Coleman County*, 101
Nueces County, 425 - 428
Nurillo CDP *Hidalgo County*, 281

O

O'Brien city *Haskell County*, 260
O'Donnell city *Lynn County*, 373
Oak Grove town *Kaufman County*, 332
Oak Leaf town *Ellis County*, 176
Oak Point city *Denton County*, 154
Oak Ridge North city *Montgomery County*, 407
Oak Ridge town *Cooke County*, 121

CDP = Census Designated Place

CDP = Census Designated Place

Real County, 453
Realitos CDP *Duval County*, 162
Red Lick city *Bowie County*, 44
Red Oak city *Ellis County*, 177
Red River County, 454 - 455
Red Rock postal area *Bastrop County*, 19
Redford CDP *Presidio County*, 449
Redwater city *Bowie County*, 44
Redwood CDP *Guadalupe County*, 230
Reese Center CDP *Lubbock County*, 372
Reeves County, 456
Refugio County, 457 - 458
Refugio town *Refugio County*, 458
Reid Hope King CDP *Cameron County*, 80
Reklaw city *Cherokee County*, 94
Relampago CDP *Hidalgo County*, 284
Rendon CDP *Tarrant County*, 509
Reno city *Lamar County*, 348
Reno city *Parker County*, 440
Retreat town *Navarro County*, 421
Rhome city *Wise County*, 579
Rice city *Navarro County*, 421
Richards postal area *Grimes County*, 227
Richardson city *Dallas County*, 138
Richland Hills city *Tarrant County*, 510
Richland Springs town *San Saba County*, 478
Richland town *Navarro County*, 421
Richmond city *Fort Bend County*, 196
Richwood city *Brazoria County*, 52
Riesel city *McLennan County*, 390
Ringgold postal area *Montague County*, 404
Rio Bravo city *Webb County*, 555
Rio Frio postal area *Real County*, 454
Rio Grande City city *Starr County*, 493
Rio Hondo city *Cameron County*, 80
Rio Medina postal area *Medina County*, 396
Rio Vista city *Johnson County*, 325
Rising Star town *Eastland County*, 164
River Oaks city *Tarrant County*, 510
Riverside city *Walker County*, 546
Riviera postal area *Kleberg County*, 342
Roanoke city *Denton County*, 155
Roaring Springs town *Motley County*, 414
Robert Lee city *Coke County*, 100
Roberts County, 459
Robertson County, 460
Robinson city *McLennan County*, 391
Robstown city *Nueces County*, 428
Roby city *Fisher County*, 188
Rochelle postal area *McCulloch County*, 385
Rochester town *Haskell County*, 260
Rock Island postal area *Colorado County*, 113
Rockdale city *Milam County*, 400
Rockport city *Aransas County*, 6
Rocksprings town *Edwards County*, 167
Rockwall County, 461 - 462
Rockwall city *Rockwall County*, 463
Rockwood postal area *Coleman County*, 102
Rocky Mound town *Camp County*, 84
Rogers town *Bell County*, 26
Rollingwood city *Travis County*, 529
Roma Creek CDP *Starr County*, 494
Roma city *Starr County*, 493
Roman Forest town *Montgomery County*, 408
Roosevelt postal area *Kimble County*, 340

Ropesville city *Hockley County*, 292
Rosanky postal area *Bastrop County*, 19
Roscoe city *Nolan County*, 424
Rose City city *Orange County*, 433
Rose Hill Acres city *Hardin County*, 240
Rosebud city *Falls County*, 181
Rosenberg city *Fort Bend County*, 197
Rosharon postal area *Brazoria County*, 52
Rosita North CDP *Maverick County*, 384
Rosita South CDP *Maverick County*, 384
Ross city *McLennan County*, 391
Rosser village *Kaufman County*, 333
Rotan city *Fisher County*, 189
Round Mountain town *Blanco County*, 38
Round Rock city *Williamson County*, 571
Round Top town *Fayette County*, 187
Rowena postal area *Runnels County*, 465
Rowlett city *Dallas County*, 139
Roxton city *Lamar County*, 348
Royse City city *Rockwall County*, 463
Rule town *Haskell County*, 261
Runaway Bay city *Wise County*, 579
Runge town *Karnes County*, 329
Runnels County, 463 - 464
Rusk County, 465 - 466
Rusk city *Cherokee County*, 94

S

Sabinal city *Uvalde County*, 538
Sabine County, 467 - 468
Sabine Pass postal area *Jefferson County*, 317
Sachse city *Dallas County*, 139
Sadler city *Grayson County*, 220
Saginaw city *Tarrant County*, 510
Saint Hedwig town *Bexar County*, 33
Saint Jo city *Montague County*, 404
Saint Paul CDP *San Patricio County*, 476
Saint Paul town *Collin County*, 109
Salado village *Bell County*, 26
Salineno CDP *Starr County*, 494
Salt Flat postal area *Hudspeth County*, 301
Saltillo postal area *Hopkins County*, 296
Samnorwood CDP *Collingsworth County*, 111
San Angelo city *Tom Green County*, 522
San Antonio city *Bexar County*, 33
San Augustine County, 469
San Augustine town *San Augustine County*, 469
San Benito city *Cameron County*, 80
San Carlos CDP *Hidalgo County*, 284
San Diego city *Duval County*, 162
San Elizario CDP *El Paso County*, 171
San Felipe town *Austin County*, 13
San Ignacio CDP *Zapata County*, 586
San Isidro CDP *Starr County*, 494
San Jacinto County, 470
San Juan city *Hidalgo County*, 284
San Leanna village *Travis County*, 529
San Leon CDP *Galveston County*, 209
San Manuel-Linn CDP *Hidalgo County*, 284
San Marcos city *Hays County*, 264
San Patricio County, 471 - 476
San Patricio city *San Patricio County*, 476
San Pedro CDP *Cameron County*, 81
San Perlita city *Willacy County*, 566
San Saba County, 477 - 478

San Saba town *San Saba County*, 478
Sanctuary town *Parker County*, 440
Sanderson CDP *Terrell County*, 516
Sandia CDP *Jim Wells County*, 321
Sandy Hollow-Escondidas CDP *Nueces County*, 429
Sanford town *Hutchinson County*, 306
Sanger city *Denton County*, 155
Sansom Park city *Tarrant County*, 510
Santa Anna town *Coleman County*, 102
Santa Clara city *Guadalupe County*, 230
Santa Cruz CDP *Starr County*, 494
Santa Fe city *Galveston County*, 209
Santa Maria CDP *Cameron County*, 81
Santa Monica CDP *Willacy County*, 566
Santa Rosa town *Cameron County*, 81
Santo postal area *Palo Pinto County*, 435
Saratoga postal area *Hardin County*, 240
Sarita postal area *Kenedy County*, 336
Savoy city *Fannin County*, 184
Scenic Oaks CDP *Bexar County*, 35
Schertz city *Guadalupe County*, 230
Schleicher County, 479
Schulenburg city *Fayette County*, 187
Scissors CDP *Hidalgo County*, 284
Scotland city *Archer County*, 8
Scottsville city *Harrison County*, 258
Scroggins postal area *Franklin County*, 199
Scurry County, 479 - 480
Scurry postal area *Kaufman County*, 333
Seabrook city *Harris County*, 253
Seadrift city *Calhoun County*, 69
Seagoville city *Dallas County*, 139
Seagraves city *Gaines County*, 204
Sealy city *Austin County*, 13
Sebastian CDP *Willacy County*, 566
Seguin city *Guadalupe County*, 230
Selma city *Bexar County*, 35
Seminole city *Gaines County*, 204
Serenada CDP *Williamson County*, 572
Seth Ward CDP *Hale County*, 233
Seven Oaks city *Polk County*, 446
Seven Points city *Henderson County*, 270
Seymour city *Baylor County*, 20
Shackelford County, 481
Shady Hollow CDP *Travis County*, 529
Shady Shores town *Denton County*, 155
Shallowater city *Lubbock County*, 372
Shamrock city *Wheeler County*, 559
Shavano Park city *Bexar County*, 35
Sheffield postal area *Pecos County*, 444
Shelby County, 482 - 483
Shelbyville postal area *Shelby County*, 483
Sheldon CDP *Harris County*, 253
Shenandoah city *Montgomery County*, 408
Shepherd city *San Jacinto County*, 471
Sheppard AFB postal area *Wichita County*, 562
Sheridan postal area *Colorado County*, 114
Sherman County, 484
Sherman city *Grayson County*, 221
Shiner city *Lavaca County*, 353
Shoreacres city *Harris County*, 253
Sidney postal area *Comanche County*, 118
Sienna Plantation CDP *Fort Bend County*, 197
Sierra Blanca CDP *Hudspeth County*, 301

CDP = Census Designated Place

Siesta Shores CDP *Zapata County*, 586
Silsbee city *Hardin County*, 240
Silver postal area *Coke County*, 100
Silverton city *Briscoe County*, 57
Simms postal area *Bowie County*, 44
Simonton city *Fort Bend County*, 197
Sinton city *San Patricio County*, 476
Skellytown town *Carson County*, 85
Skidmore CDP *Bee County*, 22
Slaton city *Lubbock County*, 372
Smiley city *Gonzales County*, 216
Smith County, 485 - 487
Smithville city *Bastrop County*, 19
Smyer town *Hockley County*, 292
Snook city *Burleson County*, 63
Snyder city *Scurry County*, 480
Socorro city *El Paso County*, 172
Solis CDP *Cameron County*, 82
Somerset city *Bexar County*, 36
Somervell County, 488
Somerville city *Burleson County*, 63
Sonora city *Sutton County*, 497
Sour Lake city *Hardin County*, 240
South Alamo CDP *Hidalgo County*, 285
South Bend postal area *Young County*, 584
South Fork Estates CDP *Jim Hogg County*, 318
South Houston city *Harris County*, 254
South Mountain town *Coryell County*, 124
South Padre Island town *Cameron County*, 82
South Point CDP *Cameron County*, 82
South Toledo Bend CDP *Newton County*, 423
Southlake city *Tarrant County*, 511
Southmayd city *Grayson County*, 221
Southside Place city *Harris County*, 254
Spade CDP *Lamb County*, 350
Sparks CDP *El Paso County*, 172
Spearman city *Hansford County*, 237
Spicewood postal area *Burnet County*, 66
Splendora city *Montgomery County*, 409
Spofford city *Kinney County*, 341
Spring Branch postal area *Comal County*, 116
Spring Garden-Terra Verde CDP *Nueces County*, 429
Spring Valley city *Harris County*, 254
Spring CDP *Harris County*, 254
Springlake town *Lamb County*, 351
Springtown city *Parker County*, 440
Spur city *Dickens County*, 157
Spurger postal area *Tyler County*, 533
Stafford city *Fort Bend County*, 197
Stagecoach town *Montgomery County*, 409
Stamford city *Jones County*, 327
Stanton city *Martin County*, 377
Star Harbor city *Henderson County*, 270
Starr County, 489 - 494
Stephens County, 495
Stephenville city *Erath County*, 179
Sterling City city *Sterling County*, 496
Sterling County, 495
Stinnett city *Hutchinson County*, 306
Stockdale city *Wilson County*, 574
Stonewall County, 496
Stonewall CDP *Gillespie County*, 212

Stowell CDP *Chambers County*, 92
Stratford city *Sherman County*, 484
Strawn city *Palo Pinto County*, 436
Streetman town *Freestone County*, 200
Study Butte-Terlingua CDP *Brewster County*, 56
Sudan city *Lamb County*, 351
Sugar Land city *Fort Bend County*, 198
Sullivan City city *Hidalgo County*, 285
Sulphur Bluff postal area *Hopkins County*, 296
Sulphur Springs city *Hopkins County*, 296
Sumner postal area *Lamar County*, 348
Sun Valley city *Lamar County*, 348
Sundown city *Hockley County*, 292
Sunnyvale town *Dallas County*, 139
Sunray city *Moore County*, 411
Sunrise Beach Village city *Llano County*, 368
Sunset Valley city *Travis County*, 529
Sunset city *Montague County*, 405
Surfside Beach city *Brazoria County*, 52
Sutherland Springs postal area *Wilson County*, 574
Sutton County, 497
Sweeny city *Brazoria County*, 52
Sweetwater city *Nolan County*, 425
Swisher County, 498
Sylvester postal area *Fisher County*, 189

T

Taft Southwest CDP *San Patricio County*, 477
Taft city *San Patricio County*, 477
Tahoka city *Lynn County*, 374
Talco city *Titus County*, 520
Talpa postal area *Coleman County*, 102
Talty city *Kaufman County*, 333
Tarrant County, 499 - 511
Tarzan postal area *Martin County*, 377
Tatum city *Rusk County*, 467
Taylor County, 512 - 515
Taylor Lake Village city *Harris County*, 255
Taylor city *Williamson County*, 572
Teague city *Freestone County*, 200
Tehuacana town *Limestone County*, 363
Telephone postal area *Fannin County*, 184
Tell postal area *Childress County*, 96
Temple city *Bell County*, 26
Tenaha town *Shelby County*, 483
Terlingua postal area *Brewster County*, 57
Terrell County, 516
Terrell Hills city *Bexar County*, 36
Terrell city *Kaufman County*, 334
Terry County, 517
Texarkana city *Bowie County*, 45
Texas City city *Galveston County*, 210
Texhoma city *Sherman County*, 484
Texline town *Dallam County*, 129
The Colony city *Denton County*, 155
The Hills village *Travis County*, 530
The Woodlands CDP *Montgomery County*, 409
Thompsons town *Fort Bend County*, 198
Thorndale city *Milam County*, 400
Thornton town *Limestone County*, 363
Thorntonville town *Ward County*, 550

Thrall city *Williamson County*, 572
Three Rivers city *Live Oak County*, 366
Throckmorton County, 518
Throckmorton town *Throckmorton County*, 518
Tierra Bonita CDP *Cameron County*, 82
Tierra Grande CDP *Nueces County*, 429
Tiki Island village *Galveston County*, 210
Tilden postal area *McMullen County*, 393
Timbercreek Canyon village *Randall County*, 452
Timberwood Park CDP *Bexar County*, 36
Timpson city *Shelby County*, 484
Tioga town *Grayson County*, 221
Tira town *Hopkins County*, 296
Titus County, 519 - 520
Tivoli postal area *Refugio County*, 458
Toco city *Lamar County*, 348
Todd Mission city *Grimes County*, 227
Tokio postal area *Terry County*, 518
Tolar city *Hood County*, 294
Tom Bean city *Grayson County*, 221
Tom Green County, 521 - 522
Tomball city *Harris County*, 255
Tool city *Henderson County*, 270
Tornillo CDP *El Paso County*, 172
Tow postal area *Llano County*, 369
Toyah town *Reeves County*, 457
Tradewinds CDP *San Patricio County*, 477
Travis County, 523 - 530
Trent town *Taylor County*, 515
Trenton city *Fannin County*, 184
Trinidad city *Henderson County*, 271
Trinity County, 531
Trinity city *Trinity County*, 532
Trophy Club town *Denton County*, 156
Troup city *Smith County*, 487
Troy city *Bell County*, 27
Tuleta CDP *Bee County*, 22
Tulia city *Swisher County*, 499
Tulsita CDP *Bee County*, 22
Turkey city *Hall County*, 234
Tuscola city *Taylor County*, 515
Tye city *Taylor County*, 515
Tyler County, 532 - 533
Tyler city *Smith County*, 487
Tynan CDP *Bee County*, 23

U

Uhland city *Hays County*, 264
Uncertain city *Harrison County*, 258
Union Grove city *Upshur County*, 536
Universal City city *Bexar County*, 36
University Park city *Dallas County*, 140
Upshur County, 534 - 535
Upton County, 536
Utopia CDP *Uvalde County*, 538
Uvalde County, 537 - 538
Uvalde Estates CDP *Uvalde County*, 539
Uvalde city *Uvalde County*, 538

V

Val Verde County, 539 - 540
Val Verde Park CDP *Val Verde County*, 541
Valentine town *Jeff Davis County*, 313
Valera postal area *Coleman County*, 102
Valley Mills city *Bosque County*, 41

CDP = Census Designated Place

Valley Spring postal area *Llano County*, 369
Valley View town *Cooke County*, 121
Van Alstyne city *Grayson County*, 222
Van Horn town *Culberson County*, 128
Van Vleck CDP *Matagorda County*, 381
Van Zandt County, 541 - 543
Van city *Van Zandt County*, 543
Vancourt postal area *Tom Green County*, 523
Vanderbilt CDP *Jackson County*, 310
Vanderpool postal area *Bandera County*, 16
Vega city *Oldham County*, 431
Venus town *Johnson County*, 325
Vernon city *Wilbarger County*, 563
Victoria County, 544
Victoria city *Victoria County*, 545
Vidor city *Orange County*, 433
Villa del Sol CDP *Cameron County*, 82
Villa Pancho CDP *Cameron County*, 83
Villa Verde CDP *Hidalgo County*, 285
Vinton village *El Paso County*, 172
Voca postal area *McCulloch County*, 385
Von Ormy postal area *Bexar County*, 37
Voss postal area *Coleman County*, 102

W

Waco city *McLennan County*, 391
Wadsworth postal area *Matagorda County*, 381
Waelder city *Gonzales County*, 216
Wake Village city *Bowie County*, 45
Walker County, 545 - 546
Waller County, 547 - 548
Waller city *Waller County*, 548
Wallis city *Austin County*, 13
Wallisville postal area *Chambers County*, 92
Walnut Springs city *Bosque County*, 41
Ward County, 549 - 550
Waring postal area *Kendall County*, 335
Warren City city *Gregg County*, 225
Warren postal area *Tyler County*, 533
Washington County, 551
Washington postal area *Washington County*, 552
Waskom city *Harrison County*, 258
Watauga city *Tarrant County*, 511
Waxahachie city *Ellis County*, 177
Weatherford city *Parker County*, 441
Webb County, 552 - 555
Webster city *Harris County*, 255
Weimar city *Colorado County*, 114
Weinert city *Haskell County*, 261
Weir city *Williamson County*, 572

Welch postal area *Dawson County*, 142
Wellington city *Collingsworth County*, 111
Wellman city *Terry County*, 518
Wells Branch CDP *Travis County*, 530
Wells town *Cherokee County*, 95
Weslaco city *Hidalgo County*, 285
West Columbia city *Brazoria County*, 53
West Lake Hills city *Travis County*, 530
West Livingston CDP *Polk County*, 446
West Odessa CDP *Ector County*, 166
West Orange city *Orange County*, 433
West Pearsall CDP *Frio County*, 203
West Point postal area *Fayette County*, 188
West Sharyland CDP *Hidalgo County*, 286
West Tawakoni town *Hunt County*, 305
West University Place city *Harris County*, 256
West city *McLennan County*, 392
Westbrook city *Mitchell County*, 402
Westdale CDP *Jim Wells County*, 322
Westhoff postal area *DeWitt County*, 143
Westlake town *Tarrant County*, 511
Westminster city *Collin County*, 109
Weston city *Collin County*, 110
Westover Hills town *Tarrant County*, 512
Westway CDP *El Paso County*, 173
Westworth Village city *Tarrant County*, 512
Wharton County, 556 - 557
Wharton city *Wharton County*, 558
Wheeler County, 558 - 559
Wheeler city *Wheeler County*, 560
White Deer town *Carson County*, 85
White Oak city *Gregg County*, 225
White Settlement city *Tarrant County*, 512
Whiteface town *Cochran County*, 99
Whitehouse city *Smith County*, 488
Whitesboro city *Grayson County*, 222
Whitewright town *Grayson County*, 222
Whitney town *Hill County*, 290
Whitsett postal area *Live Oak County*, 366
Whitt postal area *Parker County*, 441
Wichita County, 560 - 561
Wichita Falls city *Wichita County*, 562
Wickett town *Ward County*, 550
Wiergate postal area *Newton County*, 423
Wilbarger County, 562 - 563
Wild Peach Village CDP *Brazoria County*, 53
Wildorado postal area *Oldham County*, 431
Willacy County, 564 - 566
Willamar CDP *Willacy County*, 566
Williamson County, 567 - 572
Willis city *Montgomery County*, 409

Willow City postal area *Gillespie County*, 213
Willow Park city *Parker County*, 441
Wills Point city *Van Zandt County*, 544
Wilmer city *Dallas County*, 140
Wilson County, 573
Wilson city *Lynn County*, 374
Wimberley CDP *Hays County*, 264
Windcrest city *Bexar County*, 37
Windemere CDP *Travis County*, 530
Windom town *Fannin County*, 185
Windthorst town *Archer County*, 8
Winfield city *Titus County*, 520
Wingate postal area *Runnels County*, 465
Wink city *Winkler County*, 575
Winkler County, 574
Winnie CDP *Chambers County*, 92
Winnsboro city *Wood County*, 581
Winona town *Smith County*, 488
Winters city *Runnels County*, 465
Wise County, 575 - 578
Wixon Valley city *Brazos County*, 55
Wolfe City city *Hunt County*, 305
Wolfforth city *Lubbock County*, 372
Wood County, 579 - 580
Woodbranch city *Montgomery County*, 410
Woodcreek city *Hays County*, 265
Woodloch town *Montgomery County*, 410
Woodsboro town *Refugio County*, 459
Woodson town *Throckmorton County*, 519
Woodville town *Tyler County*, 534
Woodway city *McLennan County*, 392
Wortham town *Freestone County*, 201
Wyldwood CDP *Bastrop County*, 19
Wylie city *Collin County*, 110

Y

Yancey postal area *Medina County*, 396
Yantis town *Wood County*, 581
Yoakum County, 581
Yoakum city *Lavaca County*, 354
Yorktown city *DeWitt County*, 143
Young County, 582 - 583
Yznaga CDP *Cameron County*, 83

Z

Zapata County, 584 - 586
Zapata Ranch CDP *Willacy County*, 567
Zapata CDP *Zapata County*, 586
Zavala County, 587 - 588
Zavalla city *Angelina County*, 5
Zephyr postal area *Brown County*, 62
Zuehl CDP *Guadalupe County*, 231

Comparative
Statistics

Population

Place	1990	2000	2010 Estimate	2015 Projection
Abilene city *Taylor Co.*	106,927	115,930	117,942	118,579
Allen city *Collin Co.*	19,208	43,554	85,603	104,900
Amarillo city *Potter Co.*	158,012	173,627	191,307	199,242
Arlington city *Tarrant Co.*	261,643	332,969	380,432	410,218
Atascocita CDP *Harris Co.*	20,455	35,757	57,800	64,367
Austin city *Travis Co.*	499,053	656,562	764,479	824,376
Baytown city *Harris Co.*	64,638	66,430	71,729	75,507
Beaumont city *Jefferson Co.*	114,387	113,866	110,755	108,917
Bedford city *Tarrant Co.*	43,746	47,152	48,885	51,296
Brownsville city *Cameron Co.*	114,025	139,722	179,334	195,419
Bryan city *Brazos Co.*	55,759	65,660	71,783	75,758
Burleson city *Johnson Co.*	16,275	20,976	35,135	40,108
Carrollton city *Denton Co.*	82,359	109,576	128,767	140,963
Cedar Hill city *Dallas Co.*	20,267	32,093	45,294	50,263
Cedar Park city *Williamson Co.*	9,798	26,049	52,370	64,198
Channelview CDP *Harris Co.*	25,568	29,685	32,871	35,101
Cleburne city *Johnson Co.*	22,749	26,005	30,835	33,501
College Station city *Brazos Co.*	53,318	67,890	84,952	91,594
Conroe city *Montgomery Co.*	28,738	36,811	54,775	64,877
Coppell city *Dallas Co.*	16,881	35,958	39,175	41,250
Copperas Cove city *Coryell Co.*	24,297	29,592	30,607	31,005
Corpus Christi city *Nueces Co.*	258,425	277,454	289,001	293,937
Dallas city *Dallas Co.*	1,006,971	1,188,580	1,297,289	1,357,127
DeSoto city *Dallas Co.*	30,543	37,646	49,765	54,574
Deer Park city *Harris Co.*	27,653	28,520	29,866	31,335
Del Rio city *Val Verde Co.*	31,201	33,867	37,094	38,607
Denton city *Denton Co.*	65,296	80,537	117,420	137,087
Duncanville city *Dallas Co.*	35,609	36,081	35,634	35,786
Edinburg city *Hidalgo Co.*	35,988	48,465	71,278	80,649
El Paso city *El Paso Co.*	515,541	563,662	614,938	640,686
Euless city *Tarrant Co.*	38,149	46,005	52,526	56,884
Flower Mound town *Denton Co.*	15,788	50,702	72,350	86,064
Fort Hood CDP *Bell Co.*	35,513	33,711	31,532	31,551
Fort Worth city *Tarrant Co.*	448,311	534,694	696,039	764,598
Friendswood city *Galveston Co.*	23,020	29,037	35,622	38,938
Frisco city *Collin Co.*	6,767	33,714	114,030	137,258
Galveston city *Galveston Co.*	59,070	57,247	52,974	49,030
Garland city *Dallas Co.*	180,940	215,768	217,620	220,083
Georgetown city *Williamson Co.*	16,988	28,339	44,984	53,811
Grand Prairie city *Dallas Co.*	99,814	127,427	172,438	189,180
Grapevine city *Tarrant Co.*	29,351	42,059	50,522	55,637
Haltom City city *Tarrant Co.*	32,909	39,018	40,693	42,883
Harlingen city *Cameron Co.*	50,040	57,564	65,547	70,116
Houston city *Harris Co.*	1,697,610	1,953,631	2,269,768	2,451,441
Huntsville city *Walker Co.*	30,805	35,078	38,092	39,229
Hurst city *Tarrant Co.*	33,593	36,273	38,250	40,366
Irving city *Dallas Co.*	155,037	191,615	201,484	206,713
Keller city *Tarrant Co.*	13,683	27,345	40,551	47,390
Killeen city *Bell Co.*	64,711	86,911	116,488	127,959
La Porte city *Harris Co.*	27,923	31,880	33,876	35,605

Place	1990	2000	2010 Estimate	2015 Projection
Lancaster city *Dallas Co.*	22,156	25,894	37,674	41,550
Laredo city *Webb Co.*	126,298	176,576	228,145	252,462
League City city *Galveston Co.*	30,247	45,444	72,973	83,055
Lewisville city *Denton Co.*	46,533	77,737	105,466	123,647
Longview city *Gregg Co.*	70,346	73,344	78,836	81,369
Lubbock city *Lubbock Co.*	187,170	199,564	222,184	232,190
Lufkin city *Angelina Co.*	30,721	32,709	34,425	35,216
Mansfield city *Tarrant Co.*	15,390	28,031	50,896	57,988
McAllen city *Hidalgo Co.*	86,145	106,414	133,373	146,936
McKinney city *Collin Co.*	21,807	54,369	130,459	158,661
Mesquite city *Dallas Co.*	101,507	124,523	134,426	139,286
Midland city *Midland Co.*	89,358	94,996	107,175	112,843
Mission city *Hidalgo Co.*	31,523	45,408	69,180	79,173
Mission Bend CDP *Fort Bend Co.*	24,945	30,831	34,307	38,008
Missouri City city *Fort Bend Co.*	36,681	52,913	78,314	92,673
Nacogdoches city *Nacogdoches Co.*	31,093	29,914	32,546	33,723
New Braunfels city *Comal Co.*	27,952	36,494	52,163	59,607
North Richland Hills city *Tarrant Co.*	45,843	55,635	64,762	70,805
Odessa city *Ector Co.*	90,079	90,943	99,493	103,753
Pasadena city *Harris Co.*	119,344	141,674	149,217	155,189
Pearland city *Brazoria Co.*	23,788	37,640	68,888	79,381
Pflugerville city *Travis Co.*	5,830	16,335	33,606	39,509
Pharr city *Hidalgo Co.*	34,775	46,660	67,984	76,316
Plano city *Collin Co.*	128,507	222,030	280,422	325,345
Port Arthur city *Jefferson Co.*	58,531	57,755	56,204	55,282
Richardson city *Dallas Co.*	74,717	91,802	101,892	108,805
Rockwall city *Rockwall Co.*	10,874	17,976	30,656	37,730
Rosenberg city *Fort Bend Co.*	20,420	24,043	34,922	42,061
Round Rock city *Williamson Co.*	32,854	61,136	95,833	115,054
Rowlett city *Dallas Co.*	23,880	44,503	57,187	62,811
San Angelo city *Tom Green Co.*	85,280	88,439	90,878	91,930
San Antonio city *Bexar Co.*	997,258	1,144,646	1,323,124	1,420,762
San Juan city *Hidalgo Co.*	16,628	26,229	35,348	40,165
San Marcos city *Hays Co.*	28,859	34,733	48,926	57,237
Sherman city *Grayson Co.*	32,235	35,082	38,670	40,318
Socorro city *El Paso Co.*	22,995	27,152	32,215	34,817
Spring CDP *Harris Co.*	33,122	36,385	44,425	47,659
Sugar Land city *Fort Bend Co.*	44,150	63,328	78,697	91,114
Temple city *Bell Co.*	48,442	54,514	59,269	62,887
Texarkana city *Bowie Co.*	34,438	34,782	37,653	38,771
Texas City city *Galveston Co.*	40,735	41,521	46,177	49,864
The Colony city *Denton Co.*	22,178	26,531	38,796	45,698
The Woodlands CDP *Montgomery Co.*	29,532	55,649	69,563	79,737
Tyler city *Smith Co.*	77,653	83,650	99,059	106,150
Victoria city *Victoria Co.*	55,279	60,603	63,443	64,542
Waco city *McLennan Co.*	104,455	113,726	124,070	128,953
Waxahachie city *Ellis Co.*	18,112	21,426	29,971	33,781
Weslaco city *Hidalgo Co.*	24,801	26,935	33,350	36,694
Wichita Falls city *Wichita Co.*	97,153	104,197	102,024	100,812
Wylie city *Collin Co.*	8,930	15,132	37,980	45,891

Physical Characteristics

Place	Density (persons per square mile)	Land Area (square miles)	Water Area (square miles)	Elevation (feet)
Abilene city *Taylor Co.*	1,121.9	105.13	5.48	1,719
Allen city *Collin Co.*	3,250.1	26.34	0.00	659
Amarillo city *Potter Co.*	2,128.9	89.86	0.45	3,668
Arlington city *Tarrant Co.*	3,970.3	95.82	3.21	604
Atascocita CDP *Harris Co.*	2,095.4	27.58	0.01	72
Austin city *Travis Co.*	3,039.4	251.52	6.91	489
Baytown city *Harris Co.*	2,196.6	32.65	0.50	26
Beaumont city *Jefferson Co.*	1,302.8	85.01	0.92	16
Bedford city *Tarrant Co.*	4,886.8	10.00	0.01	597
Brownsville city *Cameron Co.*	2,230.5	80.40	2.62	33
Bryan city *Brazos Co.*	1,656.5	43.34	0.09	374
Burleson city *Johnson Co.*	1,788.5	19.65	0.06	712
Carrollton city *Denton Co.*	3,530.9	36.47	0.18	n/a
Cedar Hill city *Dallas Co.*	1,288.5	35.15	0.09	830
Cedar Park city *Williamson Co.*	3,086.0	16.97	0.15	906
Channelview CDP *Harris Co.*	2,027.7	16.21	1.76	30
Cleburne city *Johnson Co.*	1,109.7	27.79	2.67	764
College Station city *Brazos Co.*	2,110.3	40.26	0.04	338
Conroe city *Montgomery Co.*	1,449.4	37.79	0.08	220
Coppell city *Dallas Co.*	2,634.9	14.87	0.03	518
Copperas Cove city *Coryell Co.*	2,197.8	13.93	0.00	1,093
Corpus Christi city *Nueces Co.*	1,868.9	154.64	305.60	7
Dallas city *Dallas Co.*	3,787.2	342.54	42.46	420
DeSoto city *Dallas Co.*	2,306.1	21.58	0.00	650
Deer Park city *Harris Co.*	2,882.6	10.36	0.00	30
Del Rio city *Val Verde Co.*	2,403.1	15.44	0.01	968
Denton city *Denton Co.*	1,909.4	61.49	0.83	659
Duncanville city *Dallas Co.*	3,157.0	11.29	0.00	725
Edinburg city *Hidalgo Co.*	1,907.4	37.37	0.05	95
El Paso city *El Paso Co.*	2,468.9	249.08	1.46	3,717
Euless city *Tarrant Co.*	3,229.2	16.27	0.00	587
Flower Mound town *Denton Co.*	1,770.0	40.87	2.50	604
Fort Hood CDP *Bell Co.*	2,109.9	14.95	0.05	n/a
Fort Worth city *Tarrant Co.*	2,379.3	292.54	6.35	653
Friendswood city *Galveston Co.*	1,694.5	21.02	0.00	33
Frisco city *Collin Co.*	1,631.8	69.88	0.16	696
Galveston city *Galveston Co.*	1,147.8	46.15	162.19	7
Garland city *Dallas Co.*	3,810.5	57.11	0.00	551
Georgetown city *Williamson Co.*	1,970.4	22.83	2.10	755
Grand Prairie city *Dallas Co.*	2,415.0	71.40	10.14	515
Grapevine city *Tarrant Co.*	1,565.1	32.28	3.58	640
Haltom City city *Tarrant Co.*	3,283.6	12.39	0.02	535
Harlingen city *Cameron Co.*	1,923.9	34.07	0.26	39
Houston city *Harris Co.*	3,917.3	579.42	22.28	39
Huntsville city *Walker Co.*	1,232.6	30.90	0.34	371
Hurst city *Tarrant Co.*	3,862.3	9.90	0.00	554
Irving city *Dallas Co.*	2,997.0	67.23	0.44	482
Keller city *Tarrant Co.*	2,199.3	18.44	0.00	709
Killeen city *Bell Co.*	3,295.7	35.35	0.05	827
La Porte city *Harris Co.*	1,788.7	18.94	1.03	20

Place	Density (persons per square mile)	Land Area (square miles)	Water Area (square miles)	Elevation (feet)
Lancaster city *Dallas Co.*	1,286.1	29.29	0.01	522
Laredo city *Webb Co.*	2,907.8	78.46	1.09	413
League City city *Galveston Co.*	1,424.1	51.24	1.11	20
Lewisville city *Denton Co.*	2,866.4	36.79	5.54	525
Longview city *Gregg Co.*	1,442.3	54.66	0.10	371
Lubbock city *Lubbock Co.*	1,935.3	114.81	0.10	3,202
Lufkin city *Angelina Co.*	1,289.4	26.70	0.13	312
Mansfield city *Tarrant Co.*	1,395.3	36.48	0.04	604
McAllen city *Hidalgo Co.*	2,901.1	45.97	0.29	121
McKinney city *Collin Co.*	2,248.3	58.03	0.48	630
Mesquite city *Dallas Co.*	3,096.2	43.42	0.05	495
Midland city *Midland Co.*	1,609.0	66.61	0.19	2,782
Mission city *Hidalgo Co.*	2,867.1	24.13	0.01	141
Mission Bend CDP *Fort Bend Co.*	6,565.3	5.23	0.03	95
Missouri City city *Fort Bend Co.*	2,637.0	29.70	0.72	79
Nacogdoches city *Nacogdoches Co.*	1,290.2	25.23	0.06	302
New Braunfels city *Comal Co.*	1,783.4	29.25	0.15	630
North Richland Hills city *Tarrant Co.*	3,557.1	18.21	0.03	604
Odessa city *Ector Co.*	2,703.8	36.80	0.07	2,900
Pasadena city *Harris Co.*	3,378.9	44.16	0.36	30
Pearland city *Brazoria Co.*	1,751.5	39.33	0.03	49
Pflugerville city *Travis Co.*	2,963.7	11.34	0.00	719
Pharr city *Hidalgo Co.*	3,264.1	20.83	0.01	112
Plano city *Collin Co.*	3,918.4	71.57	0.06	666
Port Arthur city *Jefferson Co.*	677.8	82.92	60.84	7
Richardson city *Dallas Co.*	3,567.1	28.56	0.00	630
Rockwall city *Rockwall Co.*	1,376.0	22.28	0.37	591
Rosenberg city *Fort Bend Co.*	1,643.8	21.25	0.01	105
Round Rock city *Williamson Co.*	3,666.6	26.14	0.13	735
Rowlett city *Dallas Co.*	2,827.3	20.23	0.02	505
San Angelo city *Tom Green Co.*	1,625.8	55.90	2.35	1,844
San Antonio city *Bexar Co.*	3,246.5	407.56	4.51	650
San Juan city *Hidalgo Co.*	3,211.5	11.01	0.00	105
San Marcos city *Hays Co.*	2,686.9	18.21	0.11	617
Sherman city *Grayson Co.*	1,003.1	38.55	0.07	735
Socorro city *El Paso Co.*	1,840.2	17.51	0.00	3,661
Spring CDP *Harris Co.*	1,855.9	23.94	0.03	121
Sugar Land city *Fort Bend Co.*	3,267.2	24.09	0.83	75
Temple city *Bell Co.*	906.9	65.35	0.09	719
Texarkana city *Bowie Co.*	1,469.3	25.63	0.10	299
Texas City city *Galveston Co.*	740.4	62.37	104.86	10
The Colony city *Denton Co.*	2,839.9	13.66	2.07	591
The Woodlands CDP *Montgomery Co.*	2,971.7	23.41	0.47	141
Tyler city *Smith Co.*	2,009.2	49.30	0.11	538
Victoria city *Victoria Co.*	1,924.4	32.97	0.15	95
Waco city *McLennan Co.*	1,473.5	84.20	11.32	469
Waxahachie city *Ellis Co.*	749.9	39.97	1.20	558
Weslaco city *Hidalgo Co.*	2,628.7	12.69	0.07	79
Wichita Falls city *Wichita Co.*	1,443.3	70.69	0.02	948
Wylie city *Collin Co.*	1,960.8	19.37	13.93	558

NOTE: Population Density figures as of 2010; Land Area and Water Area figures as of 2000.

Population by Race/Hispanic Origin

Place	White (%)	Black (%)	Asian (%)	Other (%)	Hispanic (%)
Abilene city *Taylor Co.*	75.5	8.5	1.4	14.6	23.7
Allen city *Collin Co.*	78.5	7.2	7.2	7.1	10.4
Amarillo city *Potter Co.*	74.1	5.9	2.1	17.9	27.7
Arlington city *Tarrant Co.*	57.9	17.9	6.4	17.8	26.4
Atascocita CDP *Harris Co.*	72.2	14.7	2.5	10.6	17.6
Austin city *Travis Co.*	62.0	8.0	5.9	24.1	36.2
Baytown city *Harris Co.*	62.1	14.5	1.1	22.3	45.5
Beaumont city *Jefferson Co.*	44.6	45.6	2.4	7.4	11.2
Bedford city *Tarrant Co.*	82.7	4.9	4.2	8.1	11.8
Brownsville city *Cameron Co.*	81.3	0.6	0.6	17.5	92.2
Bryan city *Brazos Co.*	61.5	17.7	1.4	19.4	34.6
Burleson city *Johnson Co.*	93.7	0.9	0.7	4.7	8.3
Carrollton city *Denton Co.*	60.3	9.1	15.0	15.6	27.6
Cedar Hill city *Dallas Co.*	44.8	40.9	1.9	12.4	18.2
Cedar Park city *Williamson Co.*	80.7	5.2	3.9	10.2	18.8
Channelview CDP *Harris Co.*	52.3	16.3	1.7	29.7	52.2
Cleburne city *Johnson Co.*	81.9	5.8	0.5	11.8	28.6
College Station city *Brazos Co.*	78.6	5.4	7.8	8.1	11.5
Conroe city *Montgomery Co.*	66.8	12.0	1.1	20.1	43.9
Coppell city *Dallas Co.*	78.3	4.2	11.6	5.9	9.7
Copperas Cove city *Coryell Co.*	65.8	18.1	2.4	13.6	12.5
Corpus Christi city *Nueces Co.*	69.4	4.2	1.4	24.9	59.1
Dallas city *Dallas Co.*	48.1	23.0	3.0	25.9	45.8
DeSoto city *Dallas Co.*	37.5	54.0	1.3	7.2	12.4
Deer Park city *Harris Co.*	88.6	1.4	1.0	8.9	19.9
Del Rio city *Val Verde Co.*	78.4	1.1	0.6	19.9	82.9
Denton city *Denton Co.*	68.5	10.3	4.1	17.1	24.2
Duncanville city *Dallas Co.*	51.0	31.3	1.8	15.9	26.3
Edinburg city *Hidalgo Co.*	73.6	0.6	0.7	25.1	90.9
El Paso city *El Paso Co.*	72.2	2.8	1.2	23.7	80.4
Euless city *Tarrant Co.*	66.8	8.4	9.0	15.8	20.3
Flower Mound town *Denton Co.*	84.9	5.0	5.3	4.8	7.7
Fort Hood CDP *Bell Co.*	54.5	24.6	2.1	18.8	20.0
Fort Worth city *Tarrant Co.*	57.8	18.5	3.2	20.5	35.9
Friendswood city *Galveston Co.*	86.0	3.2	3.7	7.1	12.1
Frisco city *Collin Co.*	79.7	8.1	3.7	8.5	13.7
Galveston city *Galveston Co.*	58.6	21.8	4.4	15.2	30.8
Garland city *Dallas Co.*	56.4	13.2	8.3	22.1	37.1
Georgetown city *Williamson Co.*	82.2	3.5	1.1	13.2	20.1
Grand Prairie city *Dallas Co.*	50.6	16.6	5.1	27.7	44.4
Grapevine city *Tarrant Co.*	81.5	3.1	3.2	12.3	20.1
Haltom City city *Tarrant Co.*	65.2	4.2	8.8	21.9	34.0
Harlingen city *Cameron Co.*	77.6	1.2	1.0	20.2	78.1
Houston city *Harris Co.*	47.2	23.6	5.4	23.7	44.6
Huntsville city *Walker Co.*	65.8	24.4	1.3	8.5	18.0
Hurst city *Tarrant Co.*	78.1	6.0	2.4	13.5	19.0
Irving city *Dallas Co.*	54.7	10.9	10.8	23.6	43.2
Keller city *Tarrant Co.*	90.4	2.5	2.5	4.6	7.0
Killeen city *Bell Co.*	42.0	32.6	4.1	21.3	21.7
La Porte city *Harris Co.*	75.8	6.3	1.3	16.6	28.8

Place	White (%)	Black (%)	Asian (%)	Other (%)	Hispanic (%)
Lancaster city *Dallas Co.*	27.8	55.9	0.3	16.0	19.7
Laredo city *Webb Co.*	82.2	0.4	0.4	17.0	94.4
League City city *Galveston Co.*	80.5	5.7	4.1	9.8	16.3
Lewisville city *Denton Co.*	66.6	11.3	7.0	15.1	23.8
Longview city *Gregg Co.*	66.0	22.8	1.1	10.0	15.4
Lubbock city *Lubbock Co.*	71.4	7.9	1.6	19.1	31.4
Lufkin city *Angelina Co.*	56.9	25.0	1.7	16.4	24.1
Mansfield city *Tarrant Co.*	75.5	8.1	2.6	13.8	20.4
McAllen city *Hidalgo Co.*	79.7	0.8	2.6	16.9	83.4
McKinney city *Collin Co.*	75.9	8.3	2.8	13.0	18.1
Mesquite city *Dallas Co.*	60.8	19.5	4.6	15.1	25.2
Midland city *Midland Co.*	71.8	7.7	0.9	19.5	37.5
Mission city *Hidalgo Co.*	77.2	0.5	0.9	21.5	81.4
Mission Bend CDP *Fort Bend Co.*	35.0	29.2	16.1	19.7	34.5
Missouri City city *Fort Bend Co.*	33.2	41.3	15.5	10.0	15.5
Nacogdoches city *Nacogdoches Co.*	61.0	24.9	1.2	13.0	18.6
New Braunfels city *Comal Co.*	81.4	2.9	1.1	14.6	37.0
North Richland Hills city *Tarrant Co.*	83.3	3.9	3.3	9.5	15.5
Odessa city *Ector Co.*	69.8	5.5	1.0	23.7	50.6
Pasadena city *Harris Co.*	63.5	2.1	2.7	31.8	59.1
Pearland city *Brazoria Co.*	70.5	10.0	7.2	12.3	21.7
Pflugerville city *Travis Co.*	67.7	14.0	5.7	12.6	25.7
Pharr city *Hidalgo Co.*	82.0	0.2	0.3	17.5	92.8
Plano city *Collin Co.*	64.0	8.7	17.4	9.9	14.9
Port Arthur city *Jefferson Co.*	35.7	43.3	5.0	16.1	23.7
Richardson city *Dallas Co.*	64.7	8.2	15.7	11.4	18.3
Rockwall city *Rockwall Co.*	83.5	6.1	2.7	7.7	12.6
Rosenberg city *Fort Bend Co.*	61.9	10.7	0.4	27.0	65.6
Round Rock city *Williamson Co.*	67.8	10.6	5.2	16.4	27.9
Rowlett city *Dallas Co.*	72.9	13.0	4.5	9.7	14.1
San Angelo city *Tom Green Co.*	74.7	4.5	1.1	19.7	37.7
San Antonio city *Bexar Co.*	65.5	6.5	1.9	26.1	62.8
San Juan city *Hidalgo Co.*	79.8	0.3	0.1	19.9	96.6
San Marcos city *Hays Co.*	70.6	6.9	2.0	20.5	34.1
Sherman city *Grayson Co.*	74.8	10.8	1.3	13.1	18.9
Socorro city *El Paso Co.*	72.3	0.5	0.1	27.2	96.6
Spring CDP *Harris Co.*	77.7	8.3	1.7	12.2	23.2
Sugar Land city *Fort Bend Co.*	51.9	7.7	32.3	8.1	11.0
Temple city *Bell Co.*	71.1	13.6	1.7	13.5	21.7
Texarkana city *Bowie Co.*	56.5	38.0	1.2	4.3	4.3
Texas City city *Galveston Co.*	56.2	29.7	1.0	13.1	25.3
The Colony city *Denton Co.*	80.7	7.1	2.3	9.9	17.3
The Woodlands CDP *Montgomery Co.*	86.8	2.8	5.6	4.7	9.4
Tyler city *Smith Co.*	59.5	24.6	1.3	14.6	22.2
Victoria city *Victoria Co.*	69.9	7.1	1.3	21.8	45.5
Waco city *McLennan Co.*	58.0	21.1	1.9	19.0	29.4
Waxahachie city *Ellis Co.*	65.2	18.8	0.7	15.3	24.4
Weslaco city *Hidalgo Co.*	71.8	0.3	1.3	26.6	86.1
Wichita Falls city *Wichita Co.*	72.3	12.1	2.3	13.3	17.2
Wylie city *Collin Co.*	83.7	4.6	1.2	10.5	17.6

NOTE: Data as of 2010; (1) Figures do not include multiple race combinations; (2) Persons of Hispanic Origin may be of any race

Avg. Household Size, Median Age, Male/Female Ratio & Foreign Born

Place	Average Household Size (persons)	Median Age (years)	Male/Female Ratio (males per 100 females)	Foreign Born (%)
Abilene city *Taylor Co.*	2.68	32.6	101.9	4.7
Allen city *Collin Co.*	3.07	33.5	100.3	14.6
Amarillo city *Potter Co.*	2.63	34.1	95.0	9.4
Arlington city *Tarrant Co.*	2.74	32.5	101.0	18.9
Atascocita CDP *Harris Co.*	3.14	34.5	106.7	9.6
Austin city *Travis Co.*	2.48	33.8	105.7	19.7
Baytown city *Harris Co.*	2.89	32.3	96.9	16.4
Beaumont city *Jefferson Co.*	2.55	36.1	92.2	8.2
Bedford city *Tarrant Co.*	2.30	38.1	94.9	11.2
Brownsville city *Cameron Co.*	3.59	28.4	89.8	30.0
Bryan city *Brazos Co.*	2.75	28.7	100.8	12.1
Burleson city *Johnson Co.*	2.79	35.1	96.4	3.0
Carrollton city *Denton Co.*	2.83	35.1	99.8	24.4
Cedar Hill city *Dallas Co.*	3.04	34.1	94.6	7.0
Cedar Park city *Williamson Co.*	3.07	32.1	99.0	8.0
Channelview CDP *Harris Co.*	3.36	30.6	101.0	22.1
Cleburne city *Johnson Co.*	2.85	33.9	97.7	10.6
College Station city *Brazos Co.*	2.72	23.4	106.6	12.4
Conroe city *Montgomery Co.*	2.89	31.4	104.0	22.7
Coppell city *Dallas Co.*	2.99	33.7	99.8	14.9
Copperas Cove city *Coryell Co.*	2.91	30.5	96.5	6.6
Corpus Christi city *Nueces Co.*	2.75	34.9	95.2	7.7
Dallas city *Dallas Co.*	2.69	33.3	105.2	25.4
DeSoto city *Dallas Co.*	2.86	36.9	93.7	4.9
Deer Park city *Harris Co.*	2.99	36.1	99.5	5.8
Del Rio city *Val Verde Co.*	3.10	35.1	90.9	21.7
Denton city *Denton Co.*	2.61	30.3	99.0	12.0
Duncanville city *Dallas Co.*	2.81	37.4	92.9	11.4
Edinburg city *Hidalgo Co.*	3.25	27.9	93.9	18.8
El Paso city *El Paso Co.*	3.03	32.6	90.2	25.7
Euless city *Tarrant Co.*	2.32	34.6	100.4	17.3
Flower Mound town *Denton Co.*	3.15	33.3	98.4	8.2
Fort Hood CDP *Bell Co.*	6.05	22.1	165.0	4.8
Fort Worth city *Tarrant Co.*	2.80	32.6	99.6	17.6
Friendswood city *Galveston Co.*	2.86	36.4	95.1	8.5
Frisco city *Collin Co.*	2.86	32.2	100.3	15.1
Galveston city *Galveston Co.*	2.37	35.7	95.6	12.5
Garland city *Dallas Co.*	3.00	34.6	100.5	27.9
Georgetown city *Williamson Co.*	2.78	37.8	97.4	10.2
Grand Prairie city *Dallas Co.*	3.01	32.6	100.7	20.0
Grapevine city *Tarrant Co.*	2.70	35.8	101.8	11.0
Haltom City city *Tarrant Co.*	2.69	33.6	101.4	22.1
Harlingen city *Cameron Co.*	2.96	31.6	91.1	14.1
Houston city *Harris Co.*	2.77	33.3	101.6	27.9
Huntsville city *Walker Co.*	3.35	30.1	146.4	10.9
Hurst city *Tarrant Co.*	2.60	37.4	97.0	13.8
Irving city *Dallas Co.*	2.55	33.4	107.3	32.1
Keller city *Tarrant Co.*	3.17	34.6	99.1	6.3
Killeen city *Bell Co.*	2.75	30.0	100.7	9.3
La Porte city *Harris Co.*	2.93	34.5	99.5	8.7

Place	Average Household Size (persons)	Median Age (years)	Male/Female Ratio (males per 100 females)	Foreign Born (%)
Lancaster city *Dallas Co.*	2.90	34.2	91.0	7.2
Laredo city *Webb Co.*	3.74	26.9	92.7	27.9
League City city *Galveston Co.*	2.75	35.7	98.4	10.5
Lewisville city *Denton Co.*	2.59	31.9	101.7	20.6
Longview city *Gregg Co.*	2.58	34.6	94.9	8.7
Lubbock city *Lubbock Co.*	2.54	31.2	96.4	5.0
Lufkin city *Angelina Co.*	2.65	35.4	90.8	11.5
Mansfield city *Tarrant Co.*	3.15	33.2	102.6	11.3
McAllen city *Hidalgo Co.*	3.14	31.1	91.4	26.9
McKinney city *Collin Co.*	3.01	31.8	101.2	12.4
Mesquite city *Dallas Co.*	2.94	34.4	96.7	15.2
Midland city *Midland Co.*	2.64	33.8	94.1	8.5
Mission city *Hidalgo Co.*	3.23	30.5	92.9	28.0
Mission Bend CDP *Fort Bend Co.*	3.49	32.8	97.1	35.1
Missouri City city *Fort Bend Co.*	3.16	34.6	95.4	21.0
Nacogdoches city *Nacogdoches Co.*	2.64	26.1	90.4	8.5
New Braunfels city *Comal Co.*	2.64	34.2	95.6	7.0
North Richland Hills city *Tarrant Co.*	2.67	35.7	99.1	7.5
Odessa city *Ector Co.*	2.69	32.2	94.6	10.6
Pasadena city *Harris Co.*	3.11	31.3	101.0	25.2
Pearland city *Brazoria Co.*	2.89	34.2	96.4	12.9
Pflugerville city *Travis Co.*	3.20	34.6	99.2	12.5
Pharr city *Hidalgo Co.*	3.60	27.4	92.9	31.2
Plano city *Collin Co.*	2.66	35.5	100.4	21.8
Port Arthur city *Jefferson Co.*	2.63	35.2	92.4	15.6
Richardson city *Dallas Co.*	2.64	38.1	100.0	20.6
Rockwall city *Rockwall Co.*	2.82	34.3	98.5	8.2
Rosenberg city *Fort Bend Co.*	3.04	31.8	98.7	16.1
Round Rock city *Williamson Co.*	2.96	31.6	100.2	12.7
Rowlett city *Dallas Co.*	3.20	34.2	99.5	10.4
San Angelo city *Tom Green Co.*	2.58	33.3	93.0	6.5
San Antonio city *Bexar Co.*	2.83	32.8	94.7	13.4
San Juan city *Hidalgo Co.*	3.93	26.3	94.4	32.3
San Marcos city *Hays Co.*	2.80	24.8	98.8	5.6
Sherman city *Grayson Co.*	2.58	34.2	94.8	9.9
Socorro city *El Paso Co.*	3.89	28.3	92.4	33.7
Spring CDP *Harris Co.*	2.91	35.3	96.6	10.8
Sugar Land city *Fort Bend Co.*	3.00	36.7	95.5	31.0
Temple city *Bell Co.*	2.54	37.0	93.2	8.1
Texarkana city *Bowie Co.*	2.61	36.3	92.5	3.4
Texas City city *Galveston Co.*	2.62	34.9	90.5	8.6
The Colony city *Denton Co.*	2.96	33.0	99.5	13.1
The Woodlands CDP *Montgomery Co.*	2.89	34.6	94.9	11.2
Tyler city *Smith Co.*	2.62	34.4	90.2	10.8
Victoria city *Victoria Co.*	2.70	35.6	93.4	6.8
Waco city *McLennan Co.*	2.71	29.7	94.2	10.6
Waxahachie city *Ellis Co.*	2.91	32.6	96.4	6.5
Weslaco city *Hidalgo Co.*	3.19	29.8	89.9	19.6
Wichita Falls city *Wichita Co.*	2.70	32.8	105.1	6.6
Wylie city *Collin Co.*	2.96	33.7	99.8	12.7

NOTE: Average Household Size, Median Age, and Male/Female Ratio figures as of 2010. Foreign Born figures are 2005-2009 5-year estimates.

Five Largest Ancestry Groups

Place	Group 1	Group 2	Group 3	Group 4	Group 5
Abilene city *Taylor Co.*	German (13.3%)	Irish (10.9%)	English (10.2%)	American (6.5%)	French (2.7%)
Allen city *Collin Co.*	German (17.5%)	Irish (11.7%)	English (11.1%)	American (5.4%)	Italian (3.9%)
Amarillo city *Potter Co.*	German (13.6%)	Irish (9.8%)	English (9.1%)	American (8.1%)	French (2.3%)
Arlington city *Tarrant Co.*	German (11.0%)	Irish (8.7%)	English (7.3%)	American (5.4%)	Italian (2.6%)
Atascocita CDP *Harris Co.*	German (12.3%)	Irish (10.2%)	American (9.9%)	English (7.5%)	French (4.3%)
Austin city *Travis Co.*	German (13.1%)	English (9.4%)	Irish (8.8%)	American (3.3%)	French (2.9%)
Baytown city *Harris Co.*	German (8.0%)	American (7.8%)	Irish (6.7%)	English (6.6%)	French (2.6%)
Beaumont city *Jefferson Co.*	German (6.8%)	Irish (5.9%)	English (5.4%)	French (5.2%)	American (4.1%)
Bedford city *Tarrant Co.*	German (17.5%)	English (14.3%)	Irish (11.9%)	American (8.0%)	Italian (3.5%)
Brownsville city *Cameron Co.*	German (1.5%)	American (1.3%)	Irish (1.0%)	English (0.9%)	French (0.5%)
Bryan city *Brazos Co.*	German (13.2%)	English (7.8%)	Irish (7.5%)	American (3.9%)	Italian (2.9%)
Burleson city *Johnson Co.*	English (18.8%)	German (17.5%)	Irish (14.1%)	American (9.7%)	French (3.0%)
Carrollton city *Denton Co.*	German (12.7%)	Irish (10.0%)	English (9.7%)	American (5.5%)	French (2.8%)
Cedar Hill city *Dallas Co.*	German (6.3%)	Irish (5.3%)	English (4.9%)	American (4.0%)	French (2.5%)
Cedar Park city *Williamson Co.*	German (20.5%)	Irish (13.3%)	English (11.2%)	American (7.4%)	Italian (4.7%)
Channelview CDP *Harris Co.*	American (5.5%)	German (4.5%)	English (3.7%)	Irish (3.3%)	French (1.7%)
Cleburne city *Johnson Co.*	English (18.4%)	German (13.9%)	Irish (13.6%)	American (7.5%)	Scottish (2.7%)
College Station city *Brazos Co.*	German (18.2%)	English (10.4%)	Irish (8.8%)	American (4.0%)	French (2.9%)
Conroe city *Montgomery Co.*	German (11.4%)	English (9.6%)	Irish (7.8%)	American (5.6%)	French (3.3%)
Coppell city *Dallas Co.*	German (17.2%)	English (15.9%)	Irish (12.1%)	American (6.8%)	Italian (5.9%)
Copperas Cove city *Coryell Co.*	German (18.4%)	Irish (8.8%)	English (8.6%)	American (4.8%)	Italian (3.1%)
Corpus Christi city *Nueces Co.*	German (9.8%)	Irish (6.0%)	English (5.3%)	American (4.0%)	French (2.0%)
Dallas city *Dallas Co.*	German (6.4%)	English (5.7%)	Irish (5.1%)	American (3.0%)	French (1.6%)
DeSoto city *Dallas Co.*	German (5.1%)	English (4.1%)	Irish (3.9%)	American (3.0%)	African (1.4%)
Deer Park city *Harris Co.*	German (13.1%)	Irish (11.6%)	American (11.5%)	English (9.4%)	French (4.1%)
Del Rio city *Val Verde Co.*	American (4.9%)	German (3.4%)	English (2.5%)	Irish (2.1%)	Italian (1.6%)
Denton city *Denton Co.*	German (16.8%)	Irish (11.7%)	English (10.6%)	American (4.9%)	Italian (2.8%)
Duncanville city *Dallas Co.*	German (7.4%)	English (6.8%)	Irish (5.5%)	American (5.2%)	French (2.0%)
Edinburg city *Hidalgo Co.*	German (2.3%)	Irish (1.9%)	English (1.7%)	American (1.1%)	French (0.7%)
El Paso city *El Paso Co.*	German (4.0%)	American (3.5%)	Irish (2.8%)	English (2.4%)	Italian (1.0%)
Euless city *Tarrant Co.*	German (14.2%)	Irish (10.4%)	English (9.5%)	American (5.6%)	Italian (3.3%)
Flower Mound town *Denton Co.*	German (23.8%)	English (15.3%)	Irish (13.5%)	American (5.9%)	Italian (5.2%)
Fort Hood CDP *Bell Co.*	German (15.6%)	Irish (10.6%)	English (4.4%)	Italian (3.9%)	American (3.0%)
Fort Worth city *Tarrant Co.*	German (9.4%)	Irish (7.4%)	English (7.4%)	American (7.2%)	African (2.5%)
Friendswood city *Galveston Co.*	German (22.8%)	English (14.5%)	Irish (14.0%)	American (7.3%)	French (5.0%)
Frisco city *Collin Co.*	German (17.2%)	Irish (12.5%)	English (12.2%)	American (6.1%)	Italian (5.3%)
Galveston city *Galveston Co.*	German (11.8%)	Irish (9.6%)	English (7.9%)	American (4.1%)	Italian (3.8%)
Garland city *Dallas Co.*	German (8.0%)	Irish (7.1%)	English (6.4%)	American (3.9%)	French (2.5%)
Georgetown city *Williamson Co.*	German (21.8%)	English (15.9%)	Irish (10.7%)	American (4.9%)	Scottish (3.9%)
Grand Prairie city *Dallas Co.*	German (7.0%)	Irish (5.9%)	American (5.4%)	English (5.2%)	French (1.7%)
Grapevine city *Tarrant Co.*	German (19.0%)	English (14.3%)	Irish (12.4%)	American (9.5%)	French (3.4%)
Haltom City city *Tarrant Co.*	American (12.1%)	German (8.3%)	Irish (7.2%)	English (7.0%)	Scottish (1.6%)
Harlingen city *Cameron Co.*	German (6.3%)	English (4.1%)	Irish (3.3%)	American (2.4%)	French (1.2%)
Houston city *Harris Co.*	German (6.5%)	English (4.7%)	Irish (4.5%)	American (3.1%)	French (1.8%)
Huntsville city *Walker Co.*	German (11.8%)	American (10.9%)	Irish (8.8%)	English (8.0%)	French (2.2%)
Hurst city *Tarrant Co.*	German (16.1%)	English (13.4%)	American (13.1%)	Irish (10.4%)	Italian (2.9%)
Irving city *Dallas Co.*	German (8.4%)	Irish (6.8%)	English (6.1%)	American (4.8%)	Italian (1.9%)
Keller city *Tarrant Co.*	German (21.3%)	English (17.3%)	Irish (16.0%)	American (11.0%)	Italian (5.0%)
Killeen city *Bell Co.*	German (9.1%)	Irish (4.6%)	English (3.4%)	American (3.1%)	Italian (2.4%)
La Porte city *Harris Co.*	German (13.7%)	American (9.6%)	English (9.6%)	Irish (8.3%)	European (3.5%)

Place	Group 1	Group 2	Group 3	Group 4	Group 5
Lancaster city *Dallas Co.*	Irish (4.3%)	English (2.9%)	German (2.5%)	American (2.3%)	Scotch-Irish (0.9%)
Laredo city *Webb Co.*	German (1.2%)	American (1.1%)	Irish (0.9%)	English (0.5%)	French (0.3%)
League City city *Galveston Co.*	German (17.6%)	Irish (11.8%)	English (10.7%)	Italian (5.3%)	French (5.0%)
Lewisville city *Denton Co.*	German (14.4%)	Irish (10.5%)	English (10.1%)	American (5.7%)	French (2.7%)
Longview city *Gregg Co.*	American (12.9%)	Irish (11.0%)	German (10.1%)	English (9.7%)	French (3.4%)
Lubbock city *Lubbock Co.*	German (12.0%)	Irish (9.6%)	English (9.3%)	American (6.5%)	French (2.6%)
Lufkin city *Angelina Co.*	German (9.8%)	English (9.1%)	American (8.2%)	Irish (7.2%)	African (2.7%)
Mansfield city *Tarrant Co.*	German (14.7%)	Irish (11.1%)	English (9.8%)	American (9.0%)	French (3.0%)
McAllen city *Hidalgo Co.*	German (4.9%)	Irish (2.4%)	English (2.1%)	American (1.8%)	Italian (1.3%)
McKinney city *Collin Co.*	German (16.1%)	Irish (11.2%)	English (11.1%)	American (10.1%)	Italian (3.8%)
Mesquite city *Dallas Co.*	American (14.6%)	German (7.6%)	Irish (6.1%)	English (6.1%)	French (1.7%)
Midland city *Midland Co.*	German (9.8%)	English (9.4%)	American (9.1%)	Irish (8.3%)	Scotch-Irish (2.1%)
Mission city *Hidalgo Co.*	German (4.8%)	Irish (3.2%)	English (2.2%)	American (2.0%)	Italian (0.8%)
Mission Bend CDP *Fort Bend Co.*	German (4.2%)	Nigerian (3.9%)	Irish (3.6%)	English (2.6%)	American (2.5%)
Missouri City city *Fort Bend Co.*	German (8.1%)	English (5.8%)	Irish (4.8%)	American (3.1%)	Nigerian (2.9%)
Nacogdoches city *Nacogdoches Co.*	German (9.9%)	English (9.7%)	Irish (9.7%)	American (6.1%)	French (3.3%)
New Braunfels city *Comal Co.*	German (24.6%)	Irish (11.1%)	English (9.7%)	American (4.7%)	Italian (2.9%)
North Richland Hills city *Tarrant Co.*	American (17.6%)	German (16.1%)	Irish (12.8%)	English (12.2%)	French (3.1%)
Odessa city *Ector Co.*	German (8.5%)	Irish (6.7%)	American (6.2%)	English (6.2%)	French (2.1%)
Pasadena city *Harris Co.*	German (7.3%)	Irish (6.3%)	English (5.2%)	American (5.0%)	French (2.0%)
Pearland city *Brazoria Co.*	German (14.3%)	English (8.9%)	American (8.7%)	Irish (8.6%)	Italian (3.6%)
Pflugerville city *Travis Co.*	German (13.5%)	Irish (8.4%)	English (6.9%)	American (4.1%)	French (2.8%)
Pharr city *Hidalgo Co.*	German (1.8%)	English (1.3%)	Irish (1.0%)	American (0.8%)	Italian (0.5%)
Plano city *Collin Co.*	German (14.9%)	Irish (10.9%)	English (10.2%)	American (7.6%)	Italian (3.7%)
Port Arthur city *Jefferson Co.*	French (6.5%)	German (4.4%)	Irish (3.4%)	English (3.0%)	American (2.7%)
Richardson city *Dallas Co.*	German (12.5%)	American (11.4%)	English (10.8%)	Irish (8.6%)	French (3.0%)
Rockwall city *Rockwall Co.*	English (15.3%)	German (15.3%)	Irish (10.2%)	American (9.6%)	French (5.2%)
Rosenberg city *Fort Bend Co.*	German (9.1%)	American (3.7%)	English (3.4%)	Czech (3.4%)	Irish (3.2%)
Round Rock city *Williamson Co.*	German (17.7%)	Irish (10.6%)	English (10.5%)	American (4.1%)	French (3.8%)
Rowlett city *Dallas Co.*	German (12.1%)	English (9.7%)	Irish (8.0%)	American (6.7%)	French (3.0%)
San Angelo city *Tom Green Co.*	German (12.9%)	Irish (8.7%)	English (8.2%)	American (6.9%)	Scotch-Irish (2.7%)
San Antonio city *Bexar Co.*	German (9.4%)	Irish (5.3%)	English (4.9%)	American (4.0%)	Italian (1.9%)
San Juan city *Hidalgo Co.*	German (1.5%)	American (1.1%)	Irish (0.6%)	English (0.4%)	Italian (0.2%)
San Marcos city *Hays Co.*	German (16.7%)	English (7.9%)	Irish (7.7%)	American (3.5%)	Italian (3.1%)
Sherman city *Grayson Co.*	Irish (13.1%)	German (12.2%)	English (9.8%)	American (7.2%)	French (2.7%)
Socorro city *El Paso Co.*	American (2.8%)	German (0.4%)	French (0.4%)	Irish (0.4%)	Italian (0.2%)
Spring CDP *Harris Co.*	German (14.0%)	Irish (8.3%)	English (7.5%)	American (6.2%)	French (3.5%)
Sugar Land city *Fort Bend Co.*	German (11.5%)	English (9.1%)	Irish (7.6%)	American (5.5%)	French (3.7%)
Temple city *Bell Co.*	German (16.5%)	English (12.3%)	Irish (8.6%)	American (5.5%)	Scotch-Irish (3.2%)
Texarkana city *Bowie Co.*	Irish (11.7%)	American (11.0%)	German (10.6%)	English (7.6%)	African (4.6%)
Texas City city *Galveston Co.*	German (10.3%)	Irish (9.0%)	English (5.9%)	American (3.9%)	French (2.5%)
The Colony city *Denton Co.*	German (17.2%)	Irish (13.6%)	English (10.9%)	American (5.2%)	Italian (3.6%)
The Woodlands CDP *Montgomery Co.*	German (20.1%)	English (15.1%)	Irish (13.8%)	American (6.7%)	Italian (5.7%)
Tyler city *Smith Co.*	English (10.9%)	Irish (9.3%)	German (8.5%)	American (6.8%)	Scotch-Irish (2.5%)
Victoria city *Victoria Co.*	German (19.1%)	Irish (9.2%)	English (6.2%)	Czech (4.8%)	American (3.0%)
Waco city *McLennan Co.*	German (12.4%)	Irish (8.9%)	English (7.7%)	American (5.5%)	Scotch-Irish (1.9%)
Waxahachie city *Ellis Co.*	German (12.3%)	Irish (11.1%)	English (9.5%)	American (6.3%)	French (2.9%)
Weslaco city *Hidalgo Co.*	German (5.9%)	English (3.5%)	Irish (2.2%)	American (2.0%)	French (0.8%)
Wichita Falls city *Wichita Co.*	American (15.6%)	German (13.7%)	Irish (9.7%)	English (7.9%)	French (2.1%)
Wylie city *Collin Co.*	German (12.5%)	Irish (8.3%)	American (7.3%)	English (6.6%)	French (4.0%)

NOTE: Values are 2005-2009 5-year estimates; "French" excludes Basque; Please refer to the Explanation of Data for more information.

Marriage Status

Place	Never Married (%)	Now Married (%)	Widowed (%)	Divorced (%)
Abilene city *Taylor Co.*	32.2	49.2	7.1	11.5
Allen city *Collin Co.*	21.8	64.8	3.4	10.0
Amarillo city *Potter Co.*	28.8	51.8	6.8	12.6
Arlington city *Tarrant Co.*	32.0	53.5	3.9	10.6
Atascocita CDP *Harris Co.*	25.3	64.5	2.4	7.8
Austin city *Travis Co.*	42.1	44.0	3.5	10.5
Baytown city *Harris Co.*	26.6	56.5	6.6	10.3
Beaumont city *Jefferson Co.*	34.0	47.6	7.2	11.2
Bedford city *Tarrant Co.*	26.4	54.7	6.0	12.9
Brownsville city *Cameron Co.*	29.9	57.3	5.8	7.0
Bryan city *Brazos Co.*	40.2	46.1	5.3	8.4
Burleson city *Johnson Co.*	21.7	59.7	5.7	12.9
Carrollton city *Denton Co.*	29.1	57.6	3.5	9.8
Cedar Hill city *Dallas Co.*	31.0	53.6	4.3	11.1
Cedar Park city *Williamson Co.*	26.5	56.5	3.1	13.8
Channelview CDP *Harris Co.*	31.3	53.9	3.9	11.0
Cleburne city *Johnson Co.*	23.2	54.4	6.8	15.6
College Station city *Brazos Co.*	65.3	29.1	1.8	3.8
Conroe city *Montgomery Co.*	34.1	48.9	5.5	11.5
Coppell city *Dallas Co.*	23.5	64.6	2.6	9.3
Copperas Cove city *Coryell Co.*	31.5	53.9	4.3	10.4
Corpus Christi city *Nueces Co.*	30.6	50.8	6.4	12.2
Dallas city *Dallas Co.*	38.5	45.3	5.2	11.0
DeSoto city *Dallas Co.*	27.7	52.4	7.6	12.3
Deer Park city *Harris Co.*	24.8	58.9	4.9	11.4
Del Rio city *Val Verde Co.*	25.9	56.0	9.4	8.7
Denton city *Denton Co.*	45.3	40.6	3.9	10.2
Duncanville city *Dallas Co.*	29.6	55.3	5.5	9.6
Edinburg city *Hidalgo Co.*	31.1	56.8	4.6	7.5
El Paso city *El Paso Co.*	30.3	53.1	6.2	10.4
Euless city *Tarrant Co.*	30.6	49.8	4.3	15.3
Flower Mound town *Denton Co.*	21.0	68.7	3.0	7.2
Fort Hood CDP *Bell Co.*	41.2	53.4	0.7	4.8
Fort Worth city *Tarrant Co.*	31.4	51.8	5.0	11.8
Friendswood city *Galveston Co.*	21.0	64.9	6.5	7.7
Frisco city *Collin Co.*	21.2	66.9	2.5	9.4
Galveston city *Galveston Co.*	35.5	43.6	7.0	13.9
Garland city *Dallas Co.*	30.7	54.2	4.6	10.6
Georgetown city *Williamson Co.*	21.6	60.5	7.5	10.3
Grand Prairie city *Dallas Co.*	30.4	54.5	4.3	10.8
Grapevine city *Tarrant Co.*	26.4	56.1	3.9	13.6
Haltom City city *Tarrant Co.*	28.2	50.8	6.5	14.5
Harlingen city *Cameron Co.*	26.0	58.5	7.2	8.3
Houston city *Harris Co.*	36.4	48.3	5.1	10.2
Huntsville city *Walker Co.*	52.8	32.1	4.2	10.9
Hurst city *Tarrant Co.*	24.3	55.6	6.6	13.5
Irving city *Dallas Co.*	34.9	50.5	4.0	10.7
Keller city *Tarrant Co.*	20.5	69.7	3.1	6.7
Killeen city *Bell Co.*	27.6	55.8	3.7	13.0
La Porte city *Harris Co.*	25.5	56.4	5.4	12.7

Place	Never Married (%)	Now Married (%)	Widowed (%)	Divorced (%)
Lancaster city *Dallas Co.*	32.0	48.9	5.0	14.1
Laredo city *Webb Co.*	31.0	54.5	5.9	8.6
League City city *Galveston Co.*	23.1	64.0	2.9	10.0
Lewisville city *Denton Co.*	34.0	49.9	2.6	13.4
Longview city *Gregg Co.*	26.6	52.6	8.0	12.7
Lubbock city *Lubbock Co.*	37.5	46.9	5.6	10.0
Lufkin city *Angelina Co.*	27.7	50.9	9.8	11.7
Mansfield city *Tarrant Co.*	24.7	64.3	3.0	8.0
McAllen city *Hidalgo Co.*	28.3	58.4	5.5	7.8
McKinney city *Collin Co.*	25.1	61.0	3.7	10.3
Mesquite city *Dallas Co.*	28.8	53.8	5.5	12.0
Midland city *Midland Co.*	25.6	58.4	6.3	9.8
Mission city *Hidalgo Co.*	24.6	63.4	5.6	6.4
Mission Bend CDP *Fort Bend Co.*	32.7	54.3	3.9	9.1
Missouri City city *Fort Bend Co.*	31.4	54.6	4.9	9.1
Nacogdoches city *Nacogdoches Co.*	52.8	35.7	4.6	6.9
New Braunfels city *Comal Co.*	25.1	57.6	7.4	9.9
North Richland Hills city *Tarrant Co.*	24.2	56.8	7.3	11.6
Odessa city *Ector Co.*	27.4	54.5	7.0	11.1
Pasadena city *Harris Co.*	29.7	54.5	5.0	10.8
Pearland city *Brazoria Co.*	21.8	65.1	4.1	9.1
Pflugerville city *Travis Co.*	27.6	59.7	3.3	9.4
Pharr city *Hidalgo Co.*	25.3	63.8	6.1	4.7
Plano city *Collin Co.*	26.2	60.4	3.8	9.6
Port Arthur city *Jefferson Co.*	29.8	49.0	9.6	11.6
Richardson city *Dallas Co.*	29.3	56.2	5.5	8.9
Rockwall city *Rockwall Co.*	20.3	66.5	4.3	8.8
Rosenberg city *Fort Bend Co.*	31.1	50.4	6.3	12.2
Round Rock city *Williamson Co.*	28.0	57.9	3.4	10.7
Rowlett city *Dallas Co.*	24.6	62.8	4.5	8.2
San Angelo city *Tom Green Co.*	29.0	52.1	7.1	11.8
San Antonio city *Bexar Co.*	33.6	48.7	5.7	12.0
San Juan city *Hidalgo Co.*	26.9	63.4	4.9	4.8
San Marcos city *Hays Co.*	65.3	23.4	3.7	7.7
Sherman city *Grayson Co.*	28.3	48.8	8.0	14.9
Socorro city *El Paso Co.*	31.7	55.8	5.4	7.2
Spring CDP *Harris Co.*	28.4	57.4	3.5	10.7
Sugar Land city *Fort Bend Co.*	25.4	61.8	4.6	8.2
Temple city *Bell Co.*	25.7	54.2	8.3	11.8
Texarkana city *Bowie Co.*	33.3	44.7	8.0	14.0
Texas City city *Galveston Co.*	28.0	51.6	7.6	12.9
The Colony city *Denton Co.*	30.4	56.4	2.3	10.9
The Woodlands CDP *Montgomery Co.*	23.3	62.6	6.1	8.0
Tyler city *Smith Co.*	32.1	47.3	8.5	12.1
Victoria city *Victoria Co.*	27.7	52.5	7.8	12.0
Waco city *McLennan Co.*	41.8	39.9	7.1	11.2
Waxahachie city *Ellis Co.*	27.4	54.1	7.0	11.6
Weslaco city *Hidalgo Co.*	25.3	59.9	7.7	7.1
Wichita Falls city *Wichita Co.*	31.8	50.4	5.9	11.9
Wylie city *Collin Co.*	20.9	62.5	3.5	13.1

NOTE: Values are 2005-2009 5-year estimates.

Employment and Building Permits Issued

Place	Unemployment Rate (%)	Total Civilian Labor Force	Single-Family Building Permits	Multi-Family Building Permits
Abilene city *Taylor Co.*	7.7	56,929	269	118
Allen city *Collin Co.*	7.2	44,148	444	0
Amarillo city *Potter Co.*	6.3	101,748	510	345
Arlington city *Tarrant Co.*	8.2	209,210	286	66
Atascocita CDP *Harris Co.*	n/a	n/a	n/a	n/a
Austin city *Travis Co.*	7.0	436,336	1,664	1,110
Baytown city *Harris Co.*	13.0	33,889	57	66
Beaumont city *Jefferson Co.*	10.5	56,682	351	128
Bedford city *Tarrant Co.*	7.4	30,981	23	0
Brownsville city *Cameron Co.*	13.2	68,106	578	22
Bryan city *Brazos Co.*	6.9	40,166	269	4
Burleson city *Johnson Co.*	7.8	19,053	197	393
Carrollton city *Denton Co.*	7.4	72,439	n/a	n/a
Cedar Hill city *Dallas Co.*	9.6	24,117	85	0
Cedar Park city *Williamson Co.*	6.6	33,476	595	48
Channelview CDP *Harris Co.*	n/a	n/a	n/a	n/a
Cleburne city *Johnson Co.*	8.9	13,671	25	2
College Station city *Brazos Co.*	7.3	47,076	491	214
Conroe city *Montgomery Co.*	7.5	28,799	237	194
Coppell city *Dallas Co.*	7.3	20,605	83	0
Copperas Cove city *Coryell Co.*	8.7	13,709	182	111
Corpus Christi city *Nueces Co.*	8.1	155,861	628	284
Dallas city *Dallas Co.*	9.2	608,602	865	1,744
DeSoto city *Dallas Co.*	10.0	25,753	114	0
Deer Park city *Harris Co.*	9.0	17,159	84	0
Del Rio city *Val Verde Co.*	8.9	16,680	30	8
Denton city *Denton Co.*	7.4	65,713	381	477
Duncanville city *Dallas Co.*	9.7	18,541	8	0
Edinburg city *Hidalgo Co.*	10.0	33,650	535	46
El Paso city *El Paso Co.*	10.0	274,948	2,478	1,584
Euless city *Tarrant Co.*	7.5	31,907	76	0
Flower Mound town *Denton Co.*	6.7	36,455	100	0
Fort Hood CDP *Bell Co.*	n/a	n/a	n/a	n/a
Fort Worth city *Tarrant Co.*	9.1	344,363	2,759	818
Friendswood city *Galveston Co.*	7.5	18,141	148	0
Frisco city *Collin Co.*	7.5	55,197	1,284	0
Galveston city *Galveston Co.*	9.5	26,153	105	0
Garland city *Dallas Co.*	9.0	110,544	147	0
Georgetown city *Williamson Co.*	8.1	22,970	542	0
Grand Prairie city *Dallas Co.*	8.9	79,863	387	0
Grapevine city *Tarrant Co.*	6.4	29,450	17	0
Haltom City city *Tarrant Co.*	8.3	21,240	9	0
Harlingen city *Cameron Co.*	11.6	26,962	106	0
Houston city *Harris Co.*	8.8	1,094,492	2,452	2,139
Huntsville city *Walker Co.*	9.2	16,412	201	428
Hurst city *Tarrant Co.*	8.0	21,112	11	2
Irving city *Dallas Co.*	8.2	112,255	338	0
Keller city *Tarrant Co.*	7.0	20,928	228	0
Killeen city *Bell Co.*	9.4	50,596	1,044	66
La Porte city *Harris Co.*	9.2	18,673	21	0

Place	Unemployment Rate (%)	Total Civilian Labor Force	Single-Family Building Permits	Multi-Family Building Permits
Lancaster city *Dallas Co.*	11.3	17,260	54	0
Laredo city *Webb Co.*	8.6	92,448	636	27
League City city *Galveston Co.*	8.3	40,037	770	206
Lewisville city *Denton Co.*	7.4	61,703	79	120
Longview city *Gregg Co.*	7.5	43,828	167	164
Lubbock city *Lubbock Co.*	7.1	121,847	844	555
Lufkin city *Angelina Co.*	8.7	16,411	26	80
Mansfield city *Tarrant Co.*	7.3	25,576	236	0
McAllen city *Hidalgo Co.*	8.7	63,641	472	178
McKinney city *Collin Co.*	9.0	63,515	1,051	0
Mesquite city *Dallas Co.*	8.9	69,666	42	0
Midland city *Midland Co.*	5.2	64,307	394	0
Mission city *Hidalgo Co.*	10.9	29,164	346	40
Mission Bend CDP *Fort Bend Co.*	n/a	n/a	n/a	n/a
Missouri City city *Fort Bend Co.*	8.2	41,813	138	0
Nacogdoches city *Nacogdoches Co.*	8.4	17,005	38	212
New Braunfels city *Comal Co.*	7.0	28,952	356	0
North Richland Hills city *Tarrant Co.*	7.7	37,111	80	0
Odessa city *Ector Co.*	6.9	55,328	268	440
Pasadena city *Harris Co.*	11.1	68,133	47	159
Pearland city *Brazoria Co.*	7.4	47,380	722	126
Pflugerville city *Travis Co.*	6.6	23,770	164	0
Pharr city *Hidalgo Co.*	11.6	26,824	282	0
Plano city *Collin Co.*	7.5	149,182	311	303
Port Arthur city *Jefferson Co.*	16.3	25,483	414	0
Richardson city *Dallas Co.*	7.5	55,591	56	140
Rockwall city *Rockwall Co.*	7.3	19,190	200	124
Rosenberg city *Fort Bend Co.*	8.4	16,344	135	0
Round Rock city *Williamson Co.*	7.4	54,775	253	0
Rowlett city *Dallas Co.*	8.2	29,349	24	0
San Angelo city *Tom Green Co.*	7.3	44,605	177	0
San Antonio city *Bexar Co.*	7.9	660,936	2,337	1,237
San Juan city *Hidalgo Co.*	12.4	13,906	123	0
San Marcos city *Hays Co.*	6.6	28,637	190	1,104
Sherman city *Grayson Co.*	9.3	17,936	35	252
Socorro city *El Paso Co.*	12.9	12,598	76	0
Spring CDP *Harris Co.*	n/a	n/a	n/a	n/a
Sugar Land city *Fort Bend Co.*	6.6	42,993	437	0
Temple city *Bell Co.*	7.5	31,799	408	18
Texarkana city *Bowie Co.*	8.8	17,374	38	111
Texas City city *Galveston Co.*	12.9	20,844	35	31
The Colony city *Denton Co.*	8.0	24,445	37	0
The Woodlands CDP *Montgomery Co.*	n/a	n/a	n/a	n/a
Tyler city *Smith Co.*	8.1	49,797	114	65
Victoria city *Victoria Co.*	7.3	33,705	47	0
Waco city *McLennan Co.*	9.2	59,101	308	130
Waxahachie city *Ellis Co.*	10.4	14,083	150	0
Weslaco city *Hidalgo Co.*	13.1	14,786	119	147
Wichita Falls city *Wichita Co.*	8.7	46,581	119	28
Wylie city *Collin Co.*	7.9	20,658	267	4

NOTE: Unemployment Rate and Civilian Labor Force as of June 2011; Building permit data covers 2010; n/a not available.

Employment by Occupation

Place	Sales (%)	Prof. (%)	Mgmt (%)	Svcs (%)	Prod. (%)	Constr. (%)
Abilene city *Taylor Co.*	25.0	20.6	11.0	21.9	11.2	10.3
Allen city *Collin Co.*	27.5	30.0	22.4	9.9	4.3	5.7
Amarillo city *Potter Co.*	27.1	18.2	10.1	18.3	14.9	11.1
Arlington city *Tarrant Co.*	28.7	18.6	13.7	14.8	13.5	10.6
Atascocita CDP *Harris Co.*	25.9	23.4	19.7	13.9	10.1	6.8
Austin city *Travis Co.*	22.7	27.4	15.6	16.6	6.6	10.9
Baytown city *Harris Co.*	22.8	16.5	7.1	17.6	17.2	18.5
Beaumont city *Jefferson Co.*	24.4	22.7	10.0	20.4	12.6	9.8
Bedford city *Tarrant Co.*	32.0	20.9	18.6	13.0	9.0	6.3
Brownsville city *Cameron Co.*	27.7	17.0	7.7	23.3	13.3	10.4
Bryan city *Brazos Co.*	24.3	19.8	10.6	21.0	11.2	12.7
Burleson city *Johnson Co.*	28.6	21.6	14.1	14.2	12.8	8.4
Carrollton city *Denton Co.*	29.4	19.2	18.5	13.2	11.2	8.5
Cedar Hill city *Dallas Co.*	29.5	22.1	17.6	12.3	11.8	6.5
Cedar Park city *Williamson Co.*	30.2	23.5	22.2	11.2	7.0	6.0
Channelview CDP *Harris Co.*	25.0	10.5	8.5	13.2	22.9	19.7
Cleburne city *Johnson Co.*	22.4	14.8	9.0	19.0	19.8	14.7
College Station city *Brazos Co.*	24.7	34.9	10.6	17.0	6.4	6.1
Conroe city *Montgomery Co.*	22.2	14.9	9.6	24.3	15.0	13.7
Coppell city *Dallas Co.*	25.6	27.8	32.2	7.9	3.6	2.9
Copperas Cove city *Coryell Co.*	26.9	18.2	7.7	21.9	9.9	15.4
Corpus Christi city *Nueces Co.*	26.0	20.2	11.1	19.0	11.0	12.6
Dallas city *Dallas Co.*	24.3	16.8	13.7	18.1	12.9	13.9
DeSoto city *Dallas Co.*	31.2	24.1	16.8	12.0	10.2	5.8
Deer Park city *Harris Co.*	28.0	21.0	15.1	9.5	14.2	12.1
Del Rio city *Val Verde Co.*	25.8	17.5	8.9	23.9	12.8	10.6
Denton city *Denton Co.*	26.2	22.3	12.1	21.4	10.5	7.4
Duncanville city *Dallas Co.*	30.4	18.3	12.1	14.8	13.9	10.4
Edinburg city *Hidalgo Co.*	26.0	25.0	8.4	22.3	8.3	9.0
El Paso city *El Paso Co.*	28.5	19.3	11.3	19.6	12.4	8.7
Euless city *Tarrant Co.*	30.8	16.9	15.9	13.8	13.4	9.2
Flower Mound town *Denton Co.*	30.5	23.4	27.8	7.9	5.8	4.4
Fort Hood CDP *Bell Co.*	39.2	14.4	7.1	21.1	7.9	9.8
Fort Worth city *Tarrant Co.*	26.2	18.6	12.8	16.3	14.9	11.0
Friendswood city *Galveston Co.*	23.8	29.7	21.0	12.0	7.0	6.4
Frisco city *Collin Co.*	28.1	25.7	27.7	10.4	3.8	4.3
Galveston city *Galveston Co.*	22.0	23.5	10.4	24.5	10.1	9.2
Garland city *Dallas Co.*	26.0	16.2	11.3	16.9	14.8	14.4
Georgetown city *Williamson Co.*	26.0	22.5	16.4	15.8	9.8	9.3
Grand Prairie city *Dallas Co.*	27.6	15.7	12.4	15.1	16.7	12.2
Grapevine city *Tarrant Co.*	29.1	22.5	22.4	13.9	7.3	4.8
Haltom City city *Tarrant Co.*	26.0	11.6	9.4	16.0	23.2	13.7
Harlingen city *Cameron Co.*	28.5	22.7	12.4	20.4	9.3	6.2
Houston city *Harris Co.*	23.7	19.5	12.4	18.3	12.8	13.0
Huntsville city *Walker Co.*	26.6	20.9	8.4	27.0	11.4	4.4
Hurst city *Tarrant Co.*	30.9	19.5	15.3	14.6	8.0	11.7
Irving city *Dallas Co.*	26.4	18.7	14.1	14.9	13.1	12.6
Keller city *Tarrant Co.*	30.2	22.5	25.1	9.4	7.9	5.0
Killeen city *Bell Co.*	29.7	16.5	8.7	24.3	9.8	10.8
La Porte city *Harris Co.*	24.6	18.3	11.1	14.6	16.9	14.3

Place	Sales (%)	Prof. (%)	Mgmt (%)	Svcs (%)	Prod. (%)	Constr. (%)
Lancaster city *Dallas Co.*	33.1	14.6	11.2	14.4	18.2	8.5
Laredo city *Webb Co.*	30.7	15.5	10.4	20.5	12.9	9.7
League City city *Galveston Co.*	24.1	33.0	16.8	10.2	8.2	7.7
Lewisville city *Denton Co.*	30.5	19.8	14.6	17.4	9.4	8.4
Longview city *Gregg Co.*	25.2	18.8	10.7	17.6	16.8	10.7
Lubbock city *Lubbock Co.*	29.1	20.6	11.4	19.3	10.7	8.1
Lufkin city *Angelina Co.*	22.1	21.2	10.3	17.4	19.7	8.6
Mansfield city *Tarrant Co.*	28.5	22.8	19.8	12.7	8.2	7.9
McAllen city *Hidalgo Co.*	28.6	23.8	13.3	18.0	7.9	7.7
McKinney city *Collin Co.*	28.7	24.2	21.4	12.6	6.6	6.0
Mesquite city *Dallas Co.*	30.1	16.7	12.4	14.2	13.3	13.0
Midland city *Midland Co.*	27.7	19.6	13.3	16.5	9.8	12.8
Mission city *Hidalgo Co.*	31.3	19.4	11.2	18.4	9.1	9.5
Mission Bend CDP *Fort Bend Co.*	29.2	17.8	11.6	21.3	10.9	9.2
Missouri City city *Fort Bend Co.*	28.2	28.0	17.7	12.2	8.4	5.4
Nacogdoches city *Nacogdoches Co.*	22.8	20.9	10.5	24.1	14.0	6.3
New Braunfels city *Comal Co.*	27.9	19.1	15.4	17.4	10.7	9.3
North Richland Hills city *Tarrant Co.*	33.6	20.3	16.3	12.7	9.6	7.7
Odessa city *Ector Co.*	28.4	15.7	9.5	15.8	15.8	14.7
Pasadena city *Harris Co.*	23.0	13.3	9.5	16.8	16.5	20.8
Pearland city *Brazoria Co.*	24.4	32.4	19.3	9.0	8.6	6.3
Pflugerville city *Travis Co.*	27.3	28.0	17.6	9.9	9.8	7.5
Pharr city *Hidalgo Co.*	30.9	12.8	6.9	25.0	11.6	12.3
Plano city *Collin Co.*	28.2	28.0	22.9	10.8	4.9	5.2
Port Arthur city *Jefferson Co.*	22.5	14.3	6.7	20.9	19.2	15.8
Richardson city *Dallas Co.*	26.2	28.1	19.8	13.5	6.2	6.1
Rockwall city *Rockwall Co.*	29.0	26.3	21.4	11.3	5.4	6.6
Rosenberg city *Fort Bend Co.*	26.4	12.1	10.7	19.2	17.5	13.5
Round Rock city *Williamson Co.*	27.7	22.6	19.0	14.0	8.6	7.9
Rowlett city *Dallas Co.*	30.0	26.7	15.0	12.0	8.0	8.4
San Angelo city *Tom Green Co.*	28.8	18.4	10.0	20.7	10.8	10.6
San Antonio city *Bexar Co.*	28.3	19.2	12.7	18.9	10.1	10.7
San Juan city *Hidalgo Co.*	24.6	14.9	8.5	24.3	12.2	15.3
San Marcos city *Hays Co.*	30.0	20.9	7.2	25.7	7.9	8.0
Sherman city *Grayson Co.*	25.6	18.6	9.4	19.3	16.7	10.1
Socorro city *El Paso Co.*	22.9	12.4	4.7	19.7	22.9	17.0
Spring CDP *Harris Co.*	30.4	18.8	12.6	14.0	13.6	10.6
Sugar Land city *Fort Bend Co.*	27.7	32.9	23.2	7.9	5.5	2.5
Temple city *Bell Co.*	23.6	24.8	11.2	18.7	13.7	7.8
Texarkana city *Bowie Co.*	25.2	25.6	9.1	19.8	12.2	8.1
Texas City city *Galveston Co.*	26.3	16.2	9.2	22.1	13.9	12.3
The Colony city *Denton Co.*	31.8	23.5	16.7	12.3	7.8	8.0
The Woodlands CDP *Montgomery Co.*	27.3	28.5	26.7	9.1	5.1	3.2
Tyler city *Smith Co.*	25.6	22.8	10.0	19.9	13.6	7.4
Victoria city *Victoria Co.*	25.4	19.9	9.8	17.0	14.8	12.7
Waco city *McLennan Co.*	26.5	19.4	8.4	21.2	14.6	9.6
Waxahachie city *Ellis Co.*	26.1	18.5	10.9	18.9	15.9	9.2
Weslaco city *Hidalgo Co.*	23.6	26.6	9.3	22.5	10.1	7.4
Wichita Falls city *Wichita Co.*	26.1	20.1	10.0	21.5	12.3	9.8
Wylie city *Collin Co.*	30.4	23.2	16.3	12.2	8.2	9.7

NOTE: Values are 2005-2009 5-year estimates.

Educational Attainment

Place	Percent of Population 25 Years and Over with:		
	High School Diploma including Equivalency	Bachelor's Degree or Higher	Masters's Degree or Higher
Abilene city *Taylor Co.*	82.7	23.7	6.6
Allen city *Collin Co.*	95.9	50.0	14.4
Amarillo city *Potter Co.*	82.3	20.4	6.6
Arlington city *Tarrant Co.*	85.7	31.9	9.3
Atascocita CDP *Harris Co.*	92.4	32.2	9.8
Austin city *Travis Co.*	84.1	42.7	16.6
Baytown city *Harris Co.*	75.2	13.8	5.0
Beaumont city *Jefferson Co.*	83.4	23.8	8.0
Bedford city *Tarrant Co.*	93.8	36.6	11.0
Brownsville city *Cameron Co.*	60.4	16.2	5.7
Bryan city *Brazos Co.*	75.2	26.7	9.6
Burleson city *Johnson Co.*	88.5	16.5	4.5
Carrollton city *Denton Co.*	86.5	37.6	10.3
Cedar Hill city *Dallas Co.*	90.3	27.6	7.7
Cedar Park city *Williamson Co.*	94.5	39.5	9.9
Channelview CDP *Harris Co.*	72.4	8.2	2.4
Cleburne city *Johnson Co.*	74.5	15.4	4.0
College Station city *Brazos Co.*	94.0	58.7	24.5
Conroe city *Montgomery Co.*	71.4	21.3	6.0
Coppell city *Dallas Co.*	96.6	61.9	19.7
Copperas Cove city *Coryell Co.*	95.5	18.7	5.4
Corpus Christi city *Nueces Co.*	79.5	19.9	7.0
Dallas city *Dallas Co.*	69.4	26.7	9.5
DeSoto city *Dallas Co.*	89.1	30.1	10.3
Deer Park city *Harris Co.*	91.2	17.2	5.3
Del Rio city *Val Verde Co.*	59.4	13.3	4.7
Denton city *Denton Co.*	84.0	36.2	14.3
Duncanville city *Dallas Co.*	85.8	27.2	9.0
Edinburg city *Hidalgo Co.*	68.8	22.1	7.7
El Paso city *El Paso Co.*	74.2	21.6	7.4
Euless city *Tarrant Co.*	90.2	32.4	7.8
Flower Mound town *Denton Co.*	97.6	54.0	14.3
Fort Hood CDP *Bell Co.*	97.3	13.5	3.2
Fort Worth city *Tarrant Co.*	75.3	23.5	7.8
Friendswood city *Galveston Co.*	94.6	41.9	12.1
Frisco city *Collin Co.*	92.6	46.2	12.5
Galveston city *Galveston Co.*	79.1	26.5	11.6
Garland city *Dallas Co.*	78.4	21.4	6.1
Georgetown city *Williamson Co.*	87.9	37.7	12.6
Grand Prairie city *Dallas Co.*	75.8	20.3	5.2
Grapevine city *Tarrant Co.*	91.4	43.5	11.8
Haltom City city *Tarrant Co.*	75.2	14.0	3.8
Harlingen city *Cameron Co.*	72.2	18.0	5.7
Houston city *Harris Co.*	72.8	27.4	10.0
Huntsville city *Walker Co.*	78.0	19.9	7.3
Hurst city *Tarrant Co.*	88.3	25.8	7.1
Irving city *Dallas Co.*	78.3	31.6	11.3
Keller city *Tarrant Co.*	95.9	45.8	11.3
Killeen city *Bell Co.*	92.2	17.6	4.0
La Porte city *Harris Co.*	85.9	13.2	3.8

Place	Percent of Population 25 Years and Over with:		
	High School Diploma including Equivalency	Bachelor's Degree or Higher	Masters's Degree or Higher
Lancaster city *Dallas Co.*	79.8	18.4	6.6
Laredo city *Webb Co.*	65.1	17.6	4.7
League City city *Galveston Co.*	93.4	37.8	11.5
Lewisville city *Denton Co.*	89.3	37.2	8.8
Longview city *Gregg Co.*	84.6	22.7	6.8
Lubbock city *Lubbock Co.*	84.3	29.8	10.5
Lufkin city *Angelina Co.*	77.8	20.2	4.8
Mansfield city *Tarrant Co.*	87.5	34.5	9.9
McAllen city *Hidalgo Co.*	73.8	26.7	8.7
McKinney city *Collin Co.*	89.1	45.9	12.8
Mesquite city *Dallas Co.*	83.4	18.8	5.9
Midland city *Midland Co.*	82.6	24.6	6.4
Mission city *Hidalgo Co.*	67.6	20.4	6.0
Mission Bend CDP *Fort Bend Co.*	87.8	33.0	8.9
Missouri City city *Fort Bend Co.*	91.7	46.1	16.6
Nacogdoches city *Nacogdoches Co.*	81.0	32.1	12.7
New Braunfels city *Comal Co.*	84.3	29.1	9.2
North Richland Hills city *Tarrant Co.*	90.5	27.5	6.9
Odessa city *Ector Co.*	75.7	14.0	4.2
Pasadena city *Harris Co.*	70.4	14.1	5.2
Pearland city *Brazoria Co.*	88.1	31.3	9.2
Pflugerville city *Travis Co.*	94.2	38.7	11.5
Pharr city *Hidalgo Co.*	53.9	12.2	3.4
Plano city *Collin Co.*	94.2	54.1	18.9
Port Arthur city *Jefferson Co.*	73.4	11.1	3.2
Richardson city *Dallas Co.*	90.9	46.8	16.9
Rockwall city *Rockwall Co.*	93.8	39.9	12.8
Rosenberg city *Fort Bend Co.*	67.7	12.4	3.5
Round Rock city *Williamson Co.*	90.4	32.6	9.6
Rowlett city *Dallas Co.*	93.0	31.9	9.5
San Angelo city *Tom Green Co.*	80.5	22.7	6.9
San Antonio city *Bexar Co.*	78.6	23.1	8.1
San Juan city *Hidalgo Co.*	53.9	9.2	2.7
San Marcos city *Hays Co.*	86.7	34.2	11.6
Sherman city *Grayson Co.*	83.3	19.7	6.7
Socorro city *El Paso Co.*	49.9	5.3	2.0
Spring CDP *Harris Co.*	90.7	19.7	5.5
Sugar Land city *Fort Bend Co.*	94.4	55.1	20.6
Temple city *Bell Co.*	83.9	26.2	9.8
Texarkana city *Bowie Co.*	84.2	21.2	6.3
Texas City city *Galveston Co.*	82.1	13.4	3.7
The Colony city *Denton Co.*	93.2	31.5	8.9
The Woodlands CDP *Montgomery Co.*	97.1	60.3	20.5
Tyler city *Smith Co.*	81.6	27.5	9.3
Victoria city *Victoria Co.*	79.4	17.5	5.6
Waco city *McLennan Co.*	76.0	19.6	7.0
Waxahachie city *Ellis Co.*	83.2	22.3	7.4
Weslaco city *Hidalgo Co.*	62.0	14.4	3.7
Wichita Falls city *Wichita Co.*	83.1	22.8	7.2
Wylie city *Collin Co.*	88.0	24.1	5.7

NOTE: Data as of 2010

Income and Poverty

Place	Average Household Income ($)	Median Household Income ($)	Per Capita Income ($)	Households w/$100,000+ Income (%)	Poverty Rate (%)
Abilene city *Taylor Co.*	52,608	40,256	20,353	10.3	18.0
Allen city *Collin Co.*	115,069	94,840	37,472	46.2	3.6
Amarillo city *Potter Co.*	58,370	43,383	22,326	13.5	16.4
Arlington city *Tarrant Co.*	70,270	56,739	25,795	20.0	13.7
Atascocita CDP *Harris Co.*	100,672	88,474	32,456	40.0	4.1
Austin city *Travis Co.*	69,121	49,571	28,216	19.0	17.5
Baytown city *Harris Co.*	61,421	48,679	21,353	15.9	15.0
Beaumont city *Jefferson Co.*	57,154	40,180	22,847	13.8	21.3
Bedford city *Tarrant Co.*	76,289	60,558	33,370	24.6	5.2
Brownsville city *Cameron Co.*	41,815	30,276	11,780	7.3	37.0
Bryan city *Brazos Co.*	52,596	39,949	19,493	10.9	26.9
Burleson city *Johnson Co.*	68,268	60,147	24,553	19.0	5.3
Carrollton city *Denton Co.*	86,457	70,349	30,654	29.6	8.2
Cedar Hill city *Dallas Co.*	77,553	66,655	25,667	22.8	6.0
Cedar Park city *Williamson Co.*	89,903	80,297	29,334	32.5	5.7
Channelview CDP *Harris Co.*	60,656	53,195	18,087	13.6	17.0
Cleburne city *Johnson Co.*	54,466	41,892	19,299	11.2	19.3
College Station city *Brazos Co.*	57,713	31,132	21,810	17.2	39.4
Conroe city *Montgomery Co.*	56,005	42,482	19,704	12.3	19.1
Coppell city *Dallas Co.*	145,039	112,822	48,538	55.9	2.4
Copperas Cove city *Coryell Co.*	61,418	51,032	21,217	12.6	17.2
Corpus Christi city *Nueces Co.*	58,929	44,633	21,687	14.2	19.0
Dallas city *Dallas Co.*	64,560	43,066	24,273	16.0	21.8
DeSoto city *Dallas Co.*	74,318	62,054	26,054	21.7	8.1
Deer Park city *Harris Co.*	89,243	77,428	30,014	34.4	7.2
Del Rio city *Val Verde Co.*	50,874	37,062	16,659	10.2	23.9
Denton city *Denton Co.*	61,693	44,680	24,302	16.2	18.5
Duncanville city *Dallas Co.*	67,550	54,760	24,247	17.8	12.5
Edinburg city *Hidalgo Co.*	48,428	35,838	15,050	9.9	29.2
El Paso city *El Paso Co.*	52,557	38,566	17,492	11.1	25.3
Euless city *Tarrant Co.*	67,542	58,275	29,179	17.6	10.9
Flower Mound town *Denton Co.*	143,913	119,773	45,729	63.2	3.1
Fort Hood CDP *Bell Co.*	46,901	42,456	12,754	3.5	19.9
Fort Worth city *Tarrant Co.*	62,573	46,649	22,786	16.0	17.0
Friendswood city *Galveston Co.*	103,782	84,175	36,324	39.8	5.1
Frisco city *Collin Co.*	114,642	95,132	40,083	46.3	3.7
Galveston city *Galveston Co.*	54,205	36,294	23,414	12.5	21.9
Garland city *Dallas Co.*	66,731	54,066	22,448	17.2	13.4
Georgetown city *Williamson Co.*	79,534	66,618	29,015	26.8	6.7
Grand Prairie city *Dallas Co.*	64,578	53,995	21,545	16.4	14.4
Grapevine city *Tarrant Co.*	100,209	80,099	37,130	38.1	6.8
Haltom City city *Tarrant Co.*	56,474	46,372	21,109	11.9	16.7
Harlingen city *Cameron Co.*	48,348	34,002	16,528	9.7	30.4
Houston city *Harris Co.*	65,640	44,923	23,910	17.2	20.8
Huntsville city *Walker Co.*	44,322	31,051	15,279	8.7	28.6
Hurst city *Tarrant Co.*	73,018	59,275	28,182	21.8	10.1
Irving city *Dallas Co.*	66,820	49,609	26,328	16.2	15.1
Keller city *Tarrant Co.*	127,875	106,949	40,342	55.2	2.8
Killeen city *Bell Co.*	53,881	45,587	19,644	9.3	16.4
La Porte city *Harris Co.*	77,651	69,117	26,817	25.4	10.0

Place	Average Household Income ($)	Median Household Income ($)	Per Capita Income ($)	Households w/$100,000+ Income (%)	Poverty Rate (%)
Lancaster city *Dallas Co.*	55,275	46,805	19,301	11.0	13.4
Laredo city *Webb Co.*	52,754	37,703	14,248	11.7	29.3
League City city *Galveston Co.*	97,181	83,450	35,388	37.2	5.8
Lewisville city *Denton Co.*	78,650	66,500	30,480	25.5	8.5
Longview city *Gregg Co.*	58,508	42,778	23,185	13.4	16.4
Lubbock city *Lubbock Co.*	57,418	41,425	22,883	13.2	20.4
Lufkin city *Angelina Co.*	50,305	36,543	19,570	10.2	19.0
Mansfield city *Tarrant Co.*	104,055	81,560	33,163	37.6	6.8
McAllen city *Hidalgo Co.*	59,544	42,446	19,060	15.2	27.2
McKinney city *Collin Co.*	109,865	86,813	36,765	41.0	9.7
Mesquite city *Dallas Co.*	64,658	55,187	22,105	15.4	9.9
Midland city *Midland Co.*	76,152	54,441	29,148	22.8	12.6
Mission city *Hidalgo Co.*	56,912	39,241	17,658	12.8	25.6
Mission Bend CDP *Fort Bend Co.*	78,056	67,202	22,506	23.1	9.3
Missouri City city *Fort Bend Co.*	102,042	83,792	32,387	39.2	8.6
Nacogdoches city *Nacogdoches Co.*	43,762	25,935	17,095	9.4	32.0
New Braunfels city *Comal Co.*	64,140	51,694	24,785	15.6	11.0
North Richland Hills city *Tarrant Co.*	82,083	67,573	30,830	26.4	7.6
Odessa city *Ector Co.*	61,174	45,426	22,973	14.3	16.1
Pasadena city *Harris Co.*	61,754	47,061	19,986	16.1	18.8
Pearland city *Brazoria Co.*	89,405	75,898	31,033	33.6	4.2
Pflugerville city *Travis Co.*	90,418	78,420	28,318	30.8	6.0
Pharr city *Hidalgo Co.*	42,600	31,708	11,841	6.5	38.2
Plano city *Collin Co.*	113,481	86,954	42,764	42.3	6.0
Port Arthur city *Jefferson Co.*	46,381	33,341	17,891	9.3	23.4
Richardson city *Dallas Co.*	84,067	67,112	32,098	27.9	9.1
Rockwall city *Rockwall Co.*	98,622	78,952	35,108	36.2	3.8
Rosenberg city *Fort Bend Co.*	53,060	43,363	17,621	10.3	19.4
Round Rock city *Williamson Co.*	81,780	68,052	27,783	24.6	6.5
Rowlett city *Dallas Co.*	95,205	82,415	29,896	34.7	5.2
San Angelo city *Tom Green Co.*	54,257	40,779	21,683	10.8	17.4
San Antonio city *Bexar Co.*	58,165	43,723	20,873	13.7	18.6
San Juan city *Hidalgo Co.*	40,698	29,566	10,367	6.7	35.4
San Marcos city *Hays Co.*	46,871	33,339	17,572	9.3	36.8
Sherman city *Grayson Co.*	53,334	40,360	20,921	10.8	17.8
Socorro city *El Paso Co.*	36,303	29,720	9,338	3.3	27.3
Spring CDP *Harris Co.*	78,773	68,079	27,110	23.8	8.3
Sugar Land city *Fort Bend Co.*	118,590	93,025	39,680	45.7	5.8
Temple city *Bell Co.*	62,860	45,840	25,204	14.6	13.0
Texarkana city *Bowie Co.*	53,587	35,812	21,187	12.9	20.4
Texas City city *Galveston Co.*	55,583	42,753	21,430	14.1	15.8
The Colony city *Denton Co.*	104,808	86,623	35,379	39.6	4.7
The Woodlands CDP *Montgomery Co.*	136,484	108,303	47,184	53.8	6.0
Tyler city *Smith Co.*	61,024	41,969	23,657	15.5	20.5
Victoria city *Victoria Co.*	61,382	45,329	23,175	15.5	16.9
Waco city *McLennan Co.*	44,294	30,942	16,890	8.1	28.8
Waxahachie city *Ellis Co.*	64,548	52,176	22,575	16.5	15.6
Weslaco city *Hidalgo Co.*	43,941	33,127	13,886	7.8	31.8
Wichita Falls city *Wichita Co.*	53,841	41,084	21,026	10.3	16.2
Wylie city *Collin Co.*	83,698	70,201	28,346	26.0	6.3

NOTE: Data as of 2010 except for Poverty Rates which are 2005-2009 5-year estimates; (1) Percentage of population with income below the poverty level

Taxes

Place	Total City Taxes Per Capita ($)	City Property Taxes Per Capita ($)
Abilene city *Taylor Co.*	569	210
Allen city *Collin Co.*	767	400
Amarillo city *Potter Co.*	516	134
Arlington city *Tarrant Co.*	610	286
Atascocita CDP *Harris Co.*	n/a	n/a
Austin city *Travis Co.*	664	330
Baytown city *Harris Co.*	513	232
Beaumont city *Jefferson Co.*	720	298
Bedford city *Tarrant Co.*	524	256
Brownsville city *Cameron Co.*	378	164
Bryan city *Brazos Co.*	558	256
Burleson city *Johnson Co.*	679	275
Carrollton city *Denton Co.*	686	421
Cedar Hill city *Dallas Co.*	752	399
Cedar Park city *Williamson Co.*	676	247
Channelview CDP *Harris Co.*	n/a	n/a
Cleburne city *Johnson Co.*	642	326
College Station city *Brazos Co.*	528	225
Conroe city *Montgomery Co.*	866	197
Coppell city *Dallas Co.*	1,085	670
Copperas Cove city *Coryell Co.*	330	202
Corpus Christi city *Nueces Co.*	570	250
Dallas city *Dallas Co.*	761	431
DeSoto city *Dallas Co.*	646	398
Deer Park city *Harris Co.*	499	303
Del Rio city *Val Verde Co.*	328	125
Denton city *Denton Co.*	684	274
Duncanville city *Dallas Co.*	647	343
Edinburg city *Hidalgo Co.*	407	218
El Paso city *El Paso Co.*	488	246
Euless city *Tarrant Co.*	788	217
Flower Mound town *Denton Co.*	566	368
Fort Hood CDP *Bell Co.*	n/a	n/a
Fort Worth city *Tarrant Co.*	750	402
Friendswood city *Galveston Co.*	500	338
Frisco city *Collin Co.*	1,279	498
Galveston city *Galveston Co.*	881	281
Garland city *Dallas Co.*	459	306
Georgetown city *Williamson Co.*	562	210
Grand Prairie city *Dallas Co.*	753	354
Grapevine city *Tarrant Co.*	1,296	541
Haltom City city *Tarrant Co.*	346	135
Harlingen city *Cameron Co.*	558	200
Houston city *Harris Co.*	749	392
Huntsville city *Walker Co.*	328	106
Hurst city *Tarrant Co.*	836	278
Irving city *Dallas Co.*	818	390
Keller city *Tarrant Co.*	763	402
Killeen city *Bell Co.*	463	202
La Porte city *Harris Co.*	556	359

Place	Total City Taxes Per Capita ($)	City Property Taxes Per Capita ($)
Lancaster city *Dallas Co.*	524	273
Laredo city *Webb Co.*	469	229
League City city *Galveston Co.*	540	354
Lewisville city *Denton Co.*	604	270
Longview city *Gregg Co.*	698	261
Lubbock city *Lubbock Co.*	511	202
Lufkin city *Angelina Co.*	684	262
Mansfield city *Tarrant Co.*	1,011	528
McAllen city *Hidalgo Co.*	705	194
McKinney city *Collin Co.*	815	402
Mesquite city *Dallas Co.*	618	269
Midland city *Midland Co.*	634	253
Mission city *Hidalgo Co.*	380	199
Mission Bend CDP *Fort Bend Co.*	n/a	n/a
Missouri City city *Fort Bend Co.*	445	274
Nacogdoches city *Nacogdoches Co.*	460	212
New Braunfels city *Comal Co.*	677	211
North Richland Hills city *Tarrant Co.*	685	317
Odessa city *Ector Co.*	414	173
Pasadena city *Harris Co.*	451	188
Pearland city *Brazoria Co.*	727	403
Pflugerville city *Travis Co.*	552	304
Pharr city *Hidalgo Co.*	416	170
Plano city *Collin Co.*	798	413
Port Arthur city *Jefferson Co.*	486	219
Richardson city *Dallas Co.*	896	466
Rockwall city *Rockwall Co.*	661	279
Rosenberg city *Fort Bend Co.*	478	157
Round Rock city *Williamson Co.*	1,125	233
Rowlett city *Dallas Co.*	622	409
San Angelo city *Tom Green Co.*	529	258
San Antonio city *Bexar Co.*	472	225
San Juan city *Hidalgo Co.*	205	117
San Marcos city *Hays Co.*	753	189
Sherman city *Grayson Co.*	575	190
Socorro city *El Paso Co.*	120	88
Spring CDP *Harris Co.*	n/a	n/a
Sugar Land city *Fort Bend Co.*	808	271
Temple city *Bell Co.*	694	312
Texarkana city *Bowie Co.*	705	274
Texas City city *Galveston Co.*	885	440
The Colony city *Denton Co.*	537	321
The Woodlands CDP *Montgomery Co.*	n/a	n/a
Tyler city *Smith Co.*	602	130
Victoria city *Victoria Co.*	475	175
Waco city *McLennan Co.*	653	300
Waxahachie city *Ellis Co.*	892	404
Weslaco city *Hidalgo Co.*	545	217
Wichita Falls city *Wichita Co.*	596	240
Wylie city *Collin Co.*	542	376

NOTE: Data as of 2007.

Housing

Place	Homeownership Rate (%)	Median Home Value ($)	Median Year Structure Built	Median Rent ($/month)
Abilene city Taylor Co.	59.8	85,729	1967	503
Allen city Collin Co.	85.6	190,876	1998	904
Amarillo city Potter Co.	62.7	103,742	1967	524
Arlington city Tarrant Co.	57.6	132,719	1983	625
Atascocita CDP Harris Co.	87.3	165,795	1996	931
Austin city Travis Co.	45.9	189,950	1982	716
Baytown city Harris Co.	62.5	89,955	1974	541
Beaumont city Jefferson Co.	59.9	94,181	1971	506
Bedford city Tarrant Co.	53.4	149,688	1983	686
Brownsville city Cameron Co.	62.6	73,086	1984	389
Bryan city Brazos Co.	51.5	105,391	1979	543
Burleson city Johnson Co.	74.1	119,611	1991	686
Carrollton city Denton Co.	65.9	164,752	1985	756
Cedar Hill city Dallas Co.	84.2	132,651	1992	843
Cedar Park city Williamson Co.	82.0	169,485	1998	798
Channelview CDP Harris Co.	74.9	95,866	1982	597
Cleburne city Johnson Co.	61.6	93,269	1977	561
College Station city Brazos Co.	36.3	181,040	1988	621
Conroe city Montgomery Co.	44.6	106,600	1984	626
Coppell city Dallas Co.	75.8	276,634	1991	856
Copperas Cove city Coryell Co.	56.2	95,520	1984	560
Corpus Christi city Nueces Co.	59.9	101,062	1974	585
Dallas city Dallas Co.	45.3	125,526	1974	637
DeSoto city Dallas Co.	78.3	142,329	1987	680
Deer Park city Harris Co.	82.9	138,022	1977	720
Del Rio city Val Verde Co.	68.5	75,484	1974	372
Denton city Denton Co.	45.5	126,228	1986	642
Duncanville city Dallas Co.	73.1	119,408	1977	760
Edinburg city Hidalgo Co.	57.4	79,164	1994	476
El Paso city El Paso Co.	62.4	102,897	1976	499
Euless city Tarrant Co.	41.4	134,388	1984	708
Flower Mound town Denton Co.	93.5	232,044	1995	1,154
Fort Hood CDP Bell Co.	2.0	112,281	1980	939
Fort Worth city Tarrant Co.	59.1	105,338	1980	602
Friendswood city Galveston Co.	79.9	196,880	1984	810
Frisco city Collin Co.	83.4	201,643	2001	897
Galveston city Galveston Co.	41.7	115,379	1965	594
Garland city Dallas Co.	68.5	121,794	1977	701
Georgetown city Williamson Co.	69.3	205,812	1994	724
Grand Prairie city Dallas Co.	67.5	121,427	1983	663
Grapevine city Tarrant Co.	65.0	215,138	1987	762
Haltom City city Tarrant Co.	62.0	86,797	1973	594
Harlingen city Cameron Co.	59.8	76,585	1979	455
Houston city Harris Co.	47.7	121,005	1975	629
Huntsville city Walker Co.	41.3	102,057	1985	552
Hurst city Tarrant Co.	67.0	135,716	1973	618
Irving city Dallas Co.	39.1	136,188	1981	683
Keller city Tarrant Co.	92.8	251,257	1995	832
Killeen city Bell Co.	52.6	102,881	1988	596
La Porte city Harris Co.	79.5	122,312	1981	693

Place	Homeownership Rate (%)	Median Home Value ($)	Median Year Structure Built	Median Rent ($/month)
Lancaster city Dallas Co.	69.8	104,077	1986	671
Laredo city Webb Co.	63.6	102,423	1989	491
League City city Galveston Co.	75.8	180,119	1995	801
Lewisville city Denton Co.	52.1	153,630	1991	737
Longview city Gregg Co.	56.4	110,569	1974	526
Lubbock city Lubbock Co.	57.9	96,540	1976	573
Lufkin city Angelina Co.	54.4	86,891	1975	473
Mansfield city Tarrant Co.	87.3	175,321	1999	859
McAllen city Hidalgo Co.	60.4	97,292	1986	495
McKinney city Collin Co.	77.1	197,258	2000	708
Mesquite city Dallas Co.	69.8	118,449	1982	701
Midland city Midland Co.	66.4	128,067	1975	568
Mission city Hidalgo Co.	72.8	79,282	1993	442
Mission Bend CDP Fort Bend Co.	85.2	124,095	1985	903
Missouri City city Fort Bend Co.	89.0	153,948	1989	1,022
Nacogdoches city Nacogdoches Co.	41.3	92,216	1978	494
New Braunfels city Comal Co.	60.6	134,081	1988	677
North Richland Hills city Tarrant Co.	67.5	136,248	1984	702
Odessa city Ector Co.	63.8	79,434	1968	476
Pasadena city Harris Co.	60.7	107,939	1973	579
Pearland city Brazoria Co.	79.5	169,240	1997	813
Pflugerville city Travis Co.	91.0	171,335	2000	914
Pharr city Hidalgo Co.	71.0	56,655	1992	432
Plano city Collin Co.	65.0	205,917	1990	798
Port Arthur city Jefferson Co.	60.2	52,916	1961	411
Richardson city Dallas Co.	65.8	171,531	1976	831
Rockwall city Rockwall Co.	77.5	192,563	1996	967
Rosenberg city Fort Bend Co.	57.5	96,129	1978	569
Round Rock city Williamson Co.	64.1	163,439	1995	757
Rowlett city Dallas Co.	93.4	160,057	1991	933
San Angelo city Tom Green Co.	63.1	89,510	1971	523
San Antonio city Bexar Co.	59.2	102,257	1978	603
San Juan city Hidalgo Co.	73.4	59,233	1989	333
San Marcos city Hays Co.	33.4	119,092	1984	616
Sherman city Grayson Co.	59.1	89,524	1971	536
Socorro city El Paso Co.	80.9	75,246	1987	368
Spring CDP Harris Co.	78.3	119,496	1985	813
Sugar Land city Fort Bend Co.	81.6	206,621	1989	1,028
Temple city Bell Co.	59.5	108,356	1977	536
Texarkana city Bowie Co.	50.7	90,662	1971	463
Texas City city Galveston Co.	61.2	91,350	1972	566
The Colony city Denton Co.	79.2	147,869	1989	948
The Woodlands CDP Montgomery Co.	77.7	275,734	1992	865
Tyler city Smith Co.	58.1	118,683	1974	578
Victoria city Victoria Co.	60.0	97,185	1974	496
Waco city McLennan Co.	45.2	77,247	1970	531
Waxahachie city Ellis Co.	61.2	120,238	1981	622
Weslaco city Hidalgo Co.	62.1	58,243	1984	356
Wichita Falls city Wichita Co.	60.4	84,083	1968	518
Wylie city Collin Co.	84.7	129,066	2000	766

NOTE: Homeownership Rate and Median Home Value as of 2010; Median Rent and Median Age of Housing are 2005-2009 5-year estimates.

Commute to Work

Place	Automobile (%)	Public Transportation (%)	Walk (%)	Work from Home (%)
Abilene city *Taylor Co.*	92.2	0.4	2.6	2.3
Allen city *Collin Co.*	89.9	1.3	0.4	7.1
Amarillo city *Potter Co.*	94.7	0.7	1.2	2.0
Arlington city *Tarrant Co.*	93.3	0.3	1.6	3.5
Atascocita CDP *Harris Co.*	93.9	1.0	0.2	3.4
Austin city *Travis Co.*	84.1	5.0	1.9	5.2
Baytown city *Harris Co.*	93.9	0.2	1.3	1.4
Beaumont city *Jefferson Co.*	93.4	1.3	2.0	1.7
Bedford city *Tarrant Co.*	93.7	0.3	1.5	2.8
Brownsville city *Cameron Co.*	91.2	1.3	2.3	2.3
Bryan city *Brazos Co.*	92.2	1.3	1.4	2.3
Burleson city *Johnson Co.*	95.2	0.4	0.7	2.0
Carrollton city *Denton Co.*	91.9	0.9	1.8	4.0
Cedar Hill city *Dallas Co.*	92.5	1.9	1.7	3.2
Cedar Park city *Williamson Co.*	90.7	0.4	0.9	6.1
Channelview CDP *Harris Co.*	94.7	0.5	1.4	0.4
Cleburne city *Johnson Co.*	93.4	0.3	1.7	2.6
College Station city *Brazos Co.*	86.3	3.6	3.5	2.9
Conroe city *Montgomery Co.*	93.6	0.7	1.3	2.5
Coppell city *Dallas Co.*	90.3	0.4	1.2	7.3
Copperas Cove city *Coryell Co.*	93.9	0.5	2.5	1.1
Corpus Christi city *Nueces Co.*	91.6	1.7	1.7	2.6
Dallas city *Dallas Co.*	89.0	4.3	1.9	3.4
DeSoto city *Dallas Co.*	95.0	1.1	0.5	3.0
Deer Park city *Harris Co.*	96.0	0.4	1.0	1.8
Del Rio city *Val Verde Co.*	92.1	0.5	2.8	2.6
Denton city *Denton Co.*	87.3	1.1	4.7	4.0
Duncanville city *Dallas Co.*	93.1	1.8	0.9	2.9
Edinburg city *Hidalgo Co.*	90.2	0.4	1.8	2.9
El Paso city *El Paso Co.*	90.9	2.2	2.1	2.4
Euless city *Tarrant Co.*	93.0	0.7	1.7	2.6
Flower Mound town *Denton Co.*	89.5	0.3	0.4	8.3
Fort Hood CDP *Bell Co.*	73.2	0.1	18.6	6.9
Fort Worth city *Tarrant Co.*	92.6	1.4	1.4	3.0
Friendswood city *Galveston Co.*	93.5	1.2	1.0	3.6
Frisco city *Collin Co.*	87.4	0.3	0.9	9.0
Galveston city *Galveston Co.*	82.4	2.4	5.9	3.0
Garland city *Dallas Co.*	92.4	2.8	1.4	2.4
Georgetown city *Williamson Co.*	90.3	0.0	2.8	5.4
Grand Prairie city *Dallas Co.*	94.7	0.4	0.8	2.7
Grapevine city *Tarrant Co.*	91.3	0.3	0.9	6.0
Haltom City city *Tarrant Co.*	94.1	0.2	1.3	1.0
Harlingen city *Cameron Co.*	95.1	0.1	1.5	1.6
Houston city *Harris Co.*	87.9	4.8	2.1	3.1
Huntsville city *Walker Co.*	89.7	0.0	6.9	2.3
Hurst city *Tarrant Co.*	93.1	0.8	0.9	3.1
Irving city *Dallas Co.*	92.2	1.8	1.3	2.8
Keller city *Tarrant Co.*	90.4	0.2	0.5	7.9
Killeen city *Bell Co.*	94.7	0.4	1.4	1.6
La Porte city *Harris Co.*	96.0	0.2	0.1	1.2

Place	Automobile (%)	Public Transportation (%)	Walk (%)	Work from Home (%)
Lancaster city *Dallas Co.*	94.2	1.0	1.3	2.5
Laredo city *Webb Co.*	91.8	2.0	1.9	2.8
League City city *Galveston Co.*	93.6	0.6	0.7	2.3
Lewisville city *Denton Co.*	94.4	0.6	0.9	3.0
Longview city *Gregg Co.*	93.0	0.4	0.7	2.6
Lubbock city *Lubbock Co.*	92.5	1.0	2.4	3.0
Lufkin city *Angelina Co.*	95.5	0.5	1.0	1.1
Mansfield city *Tarrant Co.*	93.3	0.1	0.5	5.2
McAllen city *Hidalgo Co.*	92.3	0.7	1.7	3.6
McKinney city *Collin Co.*	88.9	1.0	1.2	6.0
Mesquite city *Dallas Co.*	95.7	0.4	0.8	2.2
Midland city *Midland Co.*	95.0	0.4	0.8	2.9
Mission city *Hidalgo Co.*	89.9	0.2	1.0	3.7
Mission Bend CDP *Fort Bend Co.*	93.7	2.1	0.4	2.5
Missouri City city *Fort Bend Co.*	93.1	1.6	0.3	3.8
Nacogdoches city *Nacogdoches Co.*	87.0	0.5	8.7	2.4
New Braunfels city *Comal Co.*	93.1	0.0	2.0	3.0
North Richland Hills city *Tarrant Co.*	93.4	0.4	0.4	3.4
Odessa city *Ector Co.*	95.4	0.3	1.1	1.9
Pasadena city *Harris Co.*	93.0	0.6	1.5	2.1
Pearland city *Brazoria Co.*	94.9	0.4	0.5	2.7
Pflugerville city *Travis Co.*	94.0	0.2	0.5	3.3
Pharr city *Hidalgo Co.*	94.3	0.2	1.1	2.6
Plano city *Collin Co.*	89.3	1.8	0.9	6.1
Port Arthur city *Jefferson Co.*	94.9	0.6	1.5	1.8
Richardson city *Dallas Co.*	88.7	2.8	2.5	4.9
Rockwall city *Rockwall Co.*	92.3	0.8	0.7	5.0
Rosenberg city *Fort Bend Co.*	94.0	1.2	1.7	1.6
Round Rock city *Williamson Co.*	93.6	0.2	0.9	4.3
Rowlett city *Dallas Co.*	92.7	1.5	0.6	4.7
San Angelo city *Tom Green Co.*	89.1	0.5	4.8	2.9
San Antonio city *Bexar Co.*	90.1	3.3	2.1	2.6
San Juan city *Hidalgo Co.*	94.6	0.2	2.0	2.8
San Marcos city *Hays Co.*	85.9	2.9	5.9	4.3
Sherman city *Grayson Co.*	92.9	0.2	2.0	3.3
Socorro city *El Paso Co.*	90.3	0.0	1.7	2.9
Spring CDP *Harris Co.*	93.2	2.1	0.3	3.1
Sugar Land city *Fort Bend Co.*	91.4	2.1	0.5	5.3
Temple city *Bell Co.*	95.4	0.2	1.7	1.7
Texarkana city *Bowie Co.*	90.2	0.7	2.4	3.1
Texas City city *Galveston Co.*	92.0	0.0	1.6	1.0
The Colony city *Denton Co.*	94.3	0.6	0.4	3.8
The Woodlands CDP *Montgomery Co.*	87.2	3.3	0.5	7.3
Tyler city *Smith Co.*	89.8	0.8	1.8	4.7
Victoria city *Victoria Co.*	93.7	1.6	1.7	1.4
Waco city *McLennan Co.*	91.4	0.7	4.7	2.1
Waxahachie city *Ellis Co.*	93.6	0.4	1.6	3.4
Weslaco city *Hidalgo Co.*	94.6	0.1	1.5	0.9
Wichita Falls city *Wichita Co.*	87.1	0.4	7.6	3.6
Wylie city *Collin Co.*	92.8	0.9	0.7	3.5

NOTE: Values are 2005-2009 5-year estimates.

Travel Time to Work

Place	Less than 15 Minutes (%)	15 to 30 Minutes (%)	30 to 45 Minutes (%)	45 to 60 Minutes (%)	60 Minutes or More (%)
Abilene city *Taylor Co.*	57.5	34.9	4.3	0.9	2.4
Allen city *Collin Co.*	20.3	34.4	25.2	12.0	8.0
Amarillo city *Potter Co.*	48.1	41.6	5.9	1.9	2.5
Arlington city *Tarrant Co.*	23.3	38.7	22.5	9.3	6.2
Atascocita CDP *Harris Co.*	13.5	29.2	27.5	16.9	12.8
Austin city *Travis Co.*	26.6	44.5	19.9	4.8	4.2
Baytown city *Harris Co.*	32.0	36.0	17.5	6.8	7.8
Beaumont city *Jefferson Co.*	43.1	39.3	11.4	2.2	4.0
Bedford city *Tarrant Co.*	28.0	40.5	21.1	7.5	3.0
Brownsville city *Cameron Co.*	33.7	46.8	13.3	3.2	3.0
Bryan city *Brazos Co.*	45.0	44.5	5.2	2.7	2.6
Burleson city *Johnson Co.*	26.1	31.0	25.0	9.6	8.2
Carrollton city *Denton Co.*	21.7	43.6	25.5	5.8	3.4
Cedar Hill city *Dallas Co.*	18.9	27.8	30.0	13.2	10.2
Cedar Park city *Williamson Co.*	18.7	35.0	28.3	11.7	6.3
Channelview CDP *Harris Co.*	23.3	34.6	28.5	8.5	5.1
Cleburne city *Johnson Co.*	44.0	21.4	14.5	8.9	11.2
College Station city *Brazos Co.*	48.6	42.4	5.0	0.9	3.1
Conroe city *Montgomery Co.*	31.3	35.3	18.6	7.2	7.5
Coppell city *Dallas Co.*	25.1	40.0	26.5	5.9	2.6
Copperas Cove city *Coryell Co.*	31.3	45.2	14.4	4.9	4.1
Corpus Christi city *Nueces Co.*	35.4	47.7	11.0	2.6	3.3
Dallas city *Dallas Co.*	22.0	40.6	24.0	6.9	6.5
DeSoto city *Dallas Co.*	16.3	30.7	30.6	14.9	7.6
Deer Park city *Harris Co.*	29.2	36.0	19.3	8.9	6.6
Del Rio city *Val Verde Co.*	58.7	29.7	6.5	1.2	3.8
Denton city *Denton Co.*	37.8	30.3	13.8	9.8	8.2
Duncanville city *Dallas Co.*	20.7	35.8	26.2	10.5	6.8
Edinburg city *Hidalgo Co.*	37.7	41.6	13.7	3.5	3.4
El Paso city *El Paso Co.*	25.9	47.0	20.6	3.8	2.8
Euless city *Tarrant Co.*	27.1	43.2	22.1	4.7	2.8
Flower Mound town *Denton Co.*	19.6	30.8	31.8	12.6	5.2
Fort Hood CDP *Bell Co.*	66.2	29.4	3.1	1.0	0.3
Fort Worth city *Tarrant Co.*	23.3	40.7	21.5	7.7	6.8
Friendswood city *Galveston Co.*	20.4	32.4	25.2	12.4	9.5
Frisco city *Collin Co.*	21.9	30.7	25.6	12.4	9.4
Galveston city *Galveston Co.*	52.2	31.5	7.9	2.9	5.4
Garland city *Dallas Co.*	19.1	36.1	26.0	10.9	7.9
Georgetown city *Williamson Co.*	36.9	27.0	18.6	10.9	6.6
Grand Prairie city *Dallas Co.*	18.4	36.0	28.0	9.7	7.9
Grapevine city *Tarrant Co.*	28.0	38.6	23.8	6.2	3.3
Haltom City city *Tarrant Co.*	26.2	39.4	22.7	5.7	5.9
Harlingen city *Cameron Co.*	49.9	31.6	12.9	4.1	1.4
Houston city *Harris Co.*	21.1	38.8	24.7	7.8	7.5
Huntsville city *Walker Co.*	49.9	29.0	11.3	6.3	3.4
Hurst city *Tarrant Co.*	27.3	38.5	21.4	8.3	4.5
Irving city *Dallas Co.*	27.7	41.7	21.7	5.2	3.7
Keller city *Tarrant Co.*	20.5	31.9	30.4	11.8	5.3
Killeen city *Bell Co.*	35.8	47.8	10.2	3.0	3.2
La Porte city *Harris Co.*	32.2	34.3	21.1	7.0	5.5

Place	Less than 15 Minutes (%)	15 to 30 Minutes (%)	30 to 45 Minutes (%)	45 to 60 Minutes (%)	60 Minutes or More (%)
Lancaster city *Dallas Co.*	12.0	32.8	34.5	14.0	6.6
Laredo city *Webb Co.*	32.4	46.0	15.8	2.7	3.1
League City city *Galveston Co.*	20.4	35.7	23.6	10.4	9.8
Lewisville city *Denton Co.*	25.1	31.7	29.3	9.1	4.7
Longview city *Gregg Co.*	42.9	40.4	8.6	3.7	4.4
Lubbock city *Lubbock Co.*	49.4	42.4	4.7	1.4	2.1
Lufkin city *Angelina Co.*	56.7	27.6	7.9	2.5	5.4
Mansfield city *Tarrant Co.*	19.6	28.7	30.1	10.8	10.9
McAllen city *Hidalgo Co.*	35.1	48.0	11.6	2.2	3.0
McKinney city *Collin Co.*	23.4	26.6	24.4	14.1	11.5
Mesquite city *Dallas Co.*	20.3	29.2	29.7	12.5	8.2
Midland city *Midland Co.*	48.9	38.9	7.5	1.4	3.4
Mission city *Hidalgo Co.*	30.5	44.1	16.3	2.6	6.5
Mission Bend CDP *Fort Bend Co.*	10.9	31.9	31.7	14.2	11.3
Missouri City city *Fort Bend Co.*	13.5	28.7	36.9	13.5	7.4
Nacogdoches city *Nacogdoches Co.*	69.9	17.4	8.7	1.1	2.9
New Braunfels city *Comal Co.*	43.1	29.3	12.5	8.3	6.7
North Richland Hills city *Tarrant Co.*	22.6	38.3	24.8	8.2	6.0
Odessa city *Ector Co.*	46.1	39.9	8.3	1.7	4.1
Pasadena city *Harris Co.*	26.4	36.9	21.1	8.0	7.6
Pearland city *Brazoria Co.*	13.7	28.6	32.8	16.8	8.1
Pflugerville city *Travis Co.*	19.1	41.8	24.6	9.4	5.1
Pharr city *Hidalgo Co.*	35.5	47.3	11.5	2.9	2.8
Plano city *Collin Co.*	20.9	38.9	24.0	9.4	6.8
Port Arthur city *Jefferson Co.*	36.0	44.7	14.0	1.8	3.5
Richardson city *Dallas Co.*	26.8	39.7	23.9	6.4	3.1
Rockwall city *Rockwall Co.*	20.2	23.0	28.2	17.3	11.3
Rosenberg city *Fort Bend Co.*	33.1	29.4	15.2	10.0	12.4
Round Rock city *Williamson Co.*	25.8	39.3	21.7	7.9	5.3
Rowlett city *Dallas Co.*	14.8	28.8	30.7	15.4	10.4
San Angelo city *Tom Green Co.*	57.6	33.4	4.2	1.2	3.6
San Antonio city *Bexar Co.*	23.3	44.4	22.8	5.1	4.4
San Juan city *Hidalgo Co.*	37.9	44.9	12.5	2.7	1.9
San Marcos city *Hays Co.*	50.8	23.1	12.3	6.0	7.8
Sherman city *Grayson Co.*	51.1	30.5	8.9	3.0	6.4
Socorro city *El Paso Co.*	18.1	39.9	32.3	6.6	3.0
Spring CDP *Harris Co.*	14.8	36.7	22.2	14.6	11.7
Sugar Land city *Fort Bend Co.*	19.3	30.2	31.6	12.9	6.0
Temple city *Bell Co.*	50.8	35.0	8.1	4.0	2.0
Texarkana city *Bowie Co.*	57.1	30.8	8.2	1.6	2.3
Texas City city *Galveston Co.*	39.6	32.1	15.5	6.1	6.7
The Colony city *Denton Co.*	13.6	34.2	33.2	12.5	6.5
The Woodlands CDP *Montgomery Co.*	27.7	25.6	17.8	14.5	14.3
Tyler city *Smith Co.*	44.0	41.1	8.4	3.2	3.3
Victoria city *Victoria Co.*	48.9	30.6	9.8	5.7	5.0
Waco city *McLennan Co.*	46.4	42.9	6.2	1.4	3.1
Waxahachie city *Ellis Co.*	46.2	22.5	13.9	8.4	9.0
Weslaco city *Hidalgo Co.*	45.5	35.3	13.6	3.5	2.1
Wichita Falls city *Wichita Co.*	55.6	36.3	5.1	1.3	1.8
Wylie city *Collin Co.*	16.3	25.0	28.5	19.2	10.9

NOTE: Values are 2005-2009 5-year estimates.

Crime

Place	Violent Crime Rate (crimes per 10,000 population)	Property Crime Rate (crimes per 10,000 population)
Abilene city *Taylor Co.*	56.5	414.4
Allen city *Collin Co.*	9.0	176.6
Amarillo city *Potter Co.*	83.7	584.8
Arlington city *Tarrant Co.*	61.5	541.2
Atascocita CDP *Harris Co.*	n/a	n/a
Austin city *Travis Co.*	52.3	624.6
Baytown city *Harris Co.*	46.6	565.4
Beaumont city *Jefferson Co.*	90.9	574.3
Bedford city *Tarrant Co.*	38.5	358.3
Brownsville city *Cameron Co.*	25.3	544.8
Bryan city *Brazos Co.*	77.6	565.4
Burleson city *Johnson Co.*	18.7	306.2
Carrollton city *Denton Co.*	19.6	318.7
Cedar Hill city *Dallas Co.*	26.0	364.2
Cedar Park city *Williamson Co.*	10.2	143.4
Channelview CDP *Harris Co.*	n/a	n/a
Cleburne city *Johnson Co.*	64.7	430.2
College Station city *Brazos Co.*	19.8	379.6
Conroe city *Montgomery Co.*	43.9	453.5
Coppell city *Dallas Co.*	10.9	167.2
Copperas Cove city *Coryell Co.*	35.7	312.4
Corpus Christi city *Nueces Co.*	82.3	560.4
Dallas city *Dallas Co.*	79.2	553.1
DeSoto city *Dallas Co.*	36.5	357.0
Deer Park city *Harris Co.*	25.4	268.6
Del Rio city *Val Verde Co.*	24.1	210.8
Denton city *Denton Co.*	24.6	263.1
Duncanville city *Dallas Co.*	50.7	452.2
Edinburg city *Hidalgo Co.*	35.8	625.8
El Paso city *El Paso Co.*	45.7	299.4
Euless city *Tarrant Co.*	20.2	353.2
Flower Mound town *Denton Co.*	6.6	79.0
Fort Hood CDP *Bell Co.*	n/a	n/a
Fort Worth city *Tarrant Co.*	58.5	496.0
Friendswood city *Galveston Co.*	7.8	129.3
Frisco city *Collin Co.*	10.0	190.1
Galveston city *Galveston Co.*	72.2	573.6
Garland city *Dallas Co.*	27.8	415.7
Georgetown city *Williamson Co.*	10.1	153.2
Grand Prairie city *Dallas Co.*	31.8	482.4
Grapevine city *Tarrant Co.*	15.9	332.3
Haltom City city *Tarrant Co.*	34.5	475.4
Harlingen city *Cameron Co.*	45.8	676.3
Houston city *Harris Co.*	112.6	531.9
Huntsville city *Walker Co.*	48.4	361.9
Hurst city *Tarrant Co.*	49.2	602.6
Irving city *Dallas Co.*	29.8	416.3
Keller city *Tarrant Co.*	6.7	124.7
Killeen city *Bell Co.*	62.2	456.9
La Porte city *Harris Co.*	19.7	196.3

Place	Violent Crime Rate (crimes per 10,000 population)	Property Crime Rate (crimes per 10,000 population)
Lancaster city *Dallas Co.*	n/a	n/a
Laredo city *Webb Co.*	57.0	604.8
League City city *Galveston Co.*	16.3	278.9
Lewisville city *Denton Co.*	18.8	346.0
Longview city *Gregg Co.*	91.2	707.9
Lubbock city *Lubbock Co.*	93.3	583.7
Lufkin city *Angelina Co.*	48.2	739.3
Mansfield city *Tarrant Co.*	23.2	238.6
McAllen city *Hidalgo Co.*	26.2	604.8
McKinney city *Collin Co.*	18.5	252.7
Mesquite city *Dallas Co.*	40.2	506.9
Midland city *Midland Co.*	39.5	363.7
Mission city *Hidalgo Co.*	17.7	489.3
Mission Bend CDP *Fort Bend Co.*	n/a	n/a
Missouri City city *Fort Bend Co.*	15.9	167.6
Nacogdoches city *Nacogdoches Co.*	57.0	431.6
New Braunfels city *Comal Co.*	25.5	386.6
North Richland Hills city *Tarrant Co.*	26.9	308.4
Odessa city *Ector Co.*	78.9	411.8
Pasadena city *Harris Co.*	48.0	381.7
Pearland city *Brazoria Co.*	14.7	226.6
Pflugerville city *Travis Co.*	16.3	206.4
Pharr city *Hidalgo Co.*	44.7	585.3
Plano city *Collin Co.*	17.0	293.1
Port Arthur city *Jefferson Co.*	77.7	474.5
Richardson city *Dallas Co.*	22.4	348.2
Rockwall city *Rockwall Co.*	12.2	276.6
Rosenberg city *Fort Bend Co.*	18.7	193.2
Round Rock city *Williamson Co.*	11.6	250.8
Rowlett city *Dallas Co.*	10.7	189.6
San Angelo city *Tom Green Co.*	39.9	460.3
San Antonio city *Bexar Co.*	57.1	667.1
San Juan city *Hidalgo Co.*	51.9	509.8
San Marcos city *Hays Co.*	33.0	308.4
Sherman city *Grayson Co.*	48.7	415.5
Socorro city *El Paso Co.*	32.0	217.4
Spring CDP *Harris Co.*	n/a	n/a
Sugar Land city *Fort Bend Co.*	13.7	224.2
Temple city *Bell Co.*	n/a	n/a
Texarkana city *Bowie Co.*	150.8	691.1
Texas City city *Galveston Co.*	56.0	424.3
The Colony city *Denton Co.*	11.9	155.9
The Woodlands CDP *Montgomery Co.*	n/a	n/a
Tyler city *Smith Co.*	52.9	587.7
Victoria city *Victoria Co.*	68.6	664.9
Waco city *McLennan Co.*	70.6	568.4
Waxahachie city *Ellis Co.*	35.8	335.4
Weslaco city *Hidalgo Co.*	65.3	730.9
Wichita Falls city *Wichita Co.*	51.5	556.9
Wylie city *Collin Co.*	6.2	166.4

NOTE: Data as of 2009.

Education

Texas Public School Educational Profile

Category	Value	Category	Value
Schools *(2009-2010)*	8,766	**Diploma Recipients** *(2008-2009)*	264,275
Instructional Level		White, Non-Hispanic	112,016
Primary	4,435	Black, Non-Hispanic	35,982
Middle	1,755	Asian/Pacific Islander, Non-Hispanic	10,462
High	1,570	American Indian/Alaskan Native, Non-Hisp.	961
Other/Not Reported	1,006	Hispanic	104,854
Curriculum		**Staff** *(2009-2010)*	
Regular	7,643	Teachers (FTE)	333,170.1
Special Education	25	Salary[1] ($)	48,261
Vocational	0	Librarians/Media Specialists (FTE)	5,141.6
Alternative	1,098	Guidance Counselors (FTE)	11,106.9
Type		**Ratios** *(2009-2010)*	
Magnet	0	Number of Students per Teacher	14.6 to 1
Charter	553	Number of Students per Librarian	943.3 to 1
Title I Eligible	6,594	Number of Students per Guidance Counselor	436.7 to 1
School-wide Title I	6,282	**Finances** *(2007-2008)*	
Students *(2009-2010)*	4,850,210	Current Expenditures ($ per student)	
Gender (%)		Total	8,350
Male	51.4	Instruction	4,993
Female	48.6	Support Services	2,922
Race/Ethnicity (%)		Other	435
White, Non-Hispanic	33.3	General Revenue ($ per student)	
Black, Non-Hispanic	14.0	Total	9,749
Asian/Pacific Islander	3.7	From Federal Sources	978
American Indian/Alaskan Native	0.4	From State Sources	4,364
Hispanic	48.6	From Local Sources	4,407
Special Programs (%)		Long-Term Debt ($ per student)	
Individual Education Program (IEP)	9.2	At beginning of fiscal year	10,382
English Language Learner (ELL)	15.0	At end of fiscal year	11,640
Eligible for Free Lunch Program	42.7	**College Entrance Exam Scores**	
Eligible for Reduced-Price Lunch Program	7.8	SAT Reasoning Test™ *(2010)*	
Average Freshman Grad. Rate (%) *(2008-2009)*	75.4	Participation Rate (%)	53
White, Non-Hispanic	82.7	Mean Critical Reading Score	484
Black, Non-Hispanic	68.0	Mean Math Score	505
Asian/Pacific Islander, Non-Hispanic	100.0	Mean Writing Score	473
American Indian/Alaskan Native, Non-Hisp.	81.9	ACT *(2011)*	
Hispanic	69.6	Participation Rate (%)	36
High School Drop-out Rate (%) *(2008-2009)*	3.2	Mean Composite Score	20.8
White, Non-Hispanic	1.5	Mean English Score	19.6
Black, Non-Hispanic	5.0	Mean Math Score	21.5
Asian/Pacific Islander, Non-Hispanic	1.0	Mean Reading Score	20.7
American Indian/Alaskan Native, Non-Hisp.	2.2	Mean Science Score	20.8
Hispanic	4.2		

Note: For an explanation of data, please refer to the User's Guide in the front of the book; (1) Average salary for classroom teachers in 2010-11

Number of Schools

Rank	Number	District Name	City
1	299	Houston ISD	Houston
2	233	Dallas ISD	Dallas
3	147	Fort Worth ISD	Fort Worth
4	123	Austin ISD	Austin
5	110	Northside ISD	San Antonio
6	101	San Antonio ISD	San Antonio
7	98	El Paso ISD	El Paso
8	82	Aldine ISD	Houston
8	82	Cypress-Fairbanks ISD	Houston
10	77	Arlington ISD	Arlington
10	77	Plano ISD	Plano
12	75	Fort Bend ISD	Sugar Land
12	75	North East ISD	San Antonio
14	74	Garland ISD	Garland
15	70	Lewisville ISD	Flower Mound
16	65	Pasadena ISD	Pasadena
17	62	Ysleta ISD	El Paso
18	61	Corpus Christi ISD	Corpus Christi
18	61	Lubbock ISD	Lubbock
20	59	Brownsville ISD	Brownsville
21	58	Richardson ISD	Richardson
21	58	Round Rock ISD	Round Rock
23	57	Conroe ISD	Conroe
24	56	Katy ISD	Katy
25	55	Amarillo ISD	Amarillo
25	55	Killeen ISD	Killeen
27	49	Spring Branch ISD	Houston
28	47	Mesquite ISD	Mesquite
29	46	Alief ISD	Houston
29	46	Carrollton-Farmers Branch	Carrollton
29	46	Clear Creek ISD	League City
29	46	Edinburg CISD	Edinburg
33	45	Frisco ISD	Frisco
33	45	Klein ISD	Klein
35	43	Socorro ISD	El Paso
36	42	United ISD	Laredo
37	41	Humble ISD	Humble
37	41	Mansfield ISD	Mansfield
37	41	Pharr-San Juan-Alamo ISD	Pharr
40	40	Grand Prairie ISD	Grand Prairie
41	39	Irving ISD	Irving
42	38	Abilene ISD	Abilene
42	38	Ector County ISD	Odessa
42	38	Keller ISD	Keller
42	38	Leander ISD	Leander
42	38	Spring ISD	Houston
47	37	Beaumont ISD	Beaumont
47	37	Midland ISD	Midland
49	36	Eagle Academy of Abilene	Lewisville
49	36	Lamar CISD	Rosenberg
51	35	Denton ISD	Denton
51	35	Mcallen ISD	Mcallen
53	34	La Joya ISD	La Joya
53	34	Mckinney ISD	Mckinney
55	33	Comal ISD	New Braunfels
55	33	Waco ISD	Waco
57	32	Birdville ISD	Haltom City
57	32	Hurst-Euless-Bedford ISD	Bedford
57	32	Wichita Falls ISD	Wichita Falls
60	31	Harlingen CISD	Harlingen
61	30	Harlandale ISD	San Antonio
61	30	Laredo ISD	Laredo
63	28	Bryan ISD	Bryan
63	28	Judson ISD	Live Oak
63	28	Victoria ISD	Victoria
66	27	Goose Creek CISD	Baytown
66	27	Pflugerville ISD	Pflugerville
66	27	San Angelo ISD	San Angelo
66	27	Tyler ISD	Tyler
70	25	Eagle Mt-Saginaw ISD	Fort Worth
71	24	Galena Park ISD	Houston
71	24	Northwest ISD	Justin
71	24	Pearland ISD	Pearland
74	23	Eagle Pass ISD	Eagle Pass
74	23	Hays CISD	Kyle
76	22	Allen ISD	Allen
76	22	Alvin ISD	Alvin
76	22	Donna ISD	Donna
76	22	Edgewood ISD	San Antonio
76	22	Mission CISD	Mission
76	22	San Benito CISD	San Benito
82	21	Brazosport ISD	Clute
82	21	Crowley ISD	Crowley
82	21	Weslaco ISD	Weslaco
82	21	Wylie ISD	Wylie
86	20	South San Antonio ISD	San Antonio
87	19	Duncanville ISD	Duncanville
87	19	Georgetown ISD	Georgetown
87	19	Grapevine-Colleyville ISD	Grapevine
87	19	Lufkin ISD	Lufkin
91	18	Rockwall ISD	Rockwall
92	17	Magnolia ISD	Magnolia
92	17	Port Arthur ISD	Port Arthur
94	16	Burleson ISD	Burleson
94	16	Canyon ISD	Canyon
94	16	Coppell ISD	Coppell
94	16	Idea Academy	Weslaco
94	16	Longview ISD	Longview
94	16	Los Fresnos CISD	Los Fresnos
94	16	New Caney ISD	New Caney
94	16	Temple ISD	Temple
94	16	Tomball ISD	Tomball
103	15	Bastrop ISD	Bastrop
103	15	Cedar Hill ISD	Cedar Hill
103	15	East Central ISD	San Antonio
103	15	Schertz-Cibolo-U City ISD	Schertz
103	15	Sharyland ISD	Mission
108	14	Deer Park ISD	Deer Park
108	14	Forney ISD	Forney
108	14	Galveston ISD	Galveston
108	14	La Porte ISD	La Porte
108	14	Rio Grande City CISD	Rio Grande City
108	14	Seguin ISD	Seguin
108	14	Sherman ISD	Sherman
108	14	Southwest ISD	San Antonio
116	13	Angleton ISD	Angleton
116	13	Belton ISD	Belton
116	13	College Station ISD	College Station
116	13	Del Valle ISD	Del Valle
116	13	Desoto ISD	Desoto
116	13	Dickinson ISD	Dickinson
116	13	Greenville ISD	Greenville
116	13	Manor ISD	Manor
116	13	Plainview ISD	Plainview
116	13	San Felipe-Del Rio CISD	Del Rio
116	13	Waxahachie ISD	Waxahachie
127	12	Channelview ISD	Channelview
127	12	Cleburne ISD	Cleburne
127	12	Clint ISD	El Paso
127	12	Kipp Inc Charter	Houston
127	12	Mercedes ISD	Mercedes
127	12	New Braunfels ISD	New Braunfels
127	12	Port Neches-Groves ISD	Port Neches
134	11	Azle ISD	Azle
134	11	Boerne ISD	Boerne
134	11	Carroll ISD	Grapevine
134	11	Frenship ISD	Wolfforth
134	11	Granbury ISD	Granbury
134	11	Kerrville ISD	Kerrville
134	11	Lancaster ISD	Lancaster
134	11	Little Elm ISD	Little Elm
134	11	Marshall ISD	Marshall
134	11	Midway ISD	Hewitt
134	11	Nacogdoches ISD	Nacogdoches
134	11	North Forest ISD	Houston
134	11	Sheldon ISD	Houston
134	11	Texarkana ISD	Texarkana
134	11	Valley View ISD	Pharr
134	11	Weatherford ISD	Weatherford
150	10	Alice ISD	Alice
150	10	Copperas Cove ISD	Copperas Cove
150	10	Denison ISD	Denison
150	10	Ennis ISD	Ennis
150	10	Huntsville ISD	Huntsville
150	10	Hutto ISD	Hutto
150	10	Joshua ISD	Joshua
150	10	Mount Pleasant ISD	Mount Pleasant
150	10	Roma ISD	Roma
150	10	San Marcos CISD	San Marcos
150	10	White Settlement ISD	White Settlement
150	10	Willis ISD	Willis
162	9	Big Spring ISD	Big Spring
162	9	Brenham ISD	Brenham
162	9	Brownwood ISD	Brownwood
162	9	Calhoun County ISD	Port Lavaca
162	9	Canutillo ISD	El Paso
162	9	Dayton ISD	Dayton
162	9	Dumas ISD	Dumas
162	9	Eanes ISD	Austin
162	9	Floresville ISD	Floresville
162	9	Kingsville ISD	Kingsville
162	9	La Feria Ind SD	La Feria
162	9	La Marque ISD	La Marque
162	9	Lake Travis ISD	Austin
162	9	Lockhart ISD	Lockhart
162	9	Midlothian ISD	Midlothian
162	9	Montgomery ISD	Montgomery
162	9	Nederland ISD	Nederland
162	9	Paris ISD	Paris
162	9	Pleasanton ISD	Pleasanton
162	9	Royse City ISD	Royse City
162	9	Texas City ISD	Texas City
162	9	Uvalde CISD	Uvalde
162	9	Waller ISD	Waller
185	8	Bay City ISD	Bay City
185	8	Connally ISD	Waco
185	8	Corsicana ISD	Corsicana
185	8	Edcouch-Elsa ISD	Edcouch
185	8	Everman ISD	Everman
185	8	Gainesville ISD	Gainesville
185	8	Hereford ISD	Hereford
185	8	Jacksonville ISD	Jacksonville
185	8	La Vernia ISD	La Vernia
185	8	Lake Worth ISD	Lake Worth
185	8	Mabank ISD	Mabank
185	8	Princeton ISD	Princeton
185	8	Red Oak ISD	Red Oak
185	8	Robstown ISD	Robstown
185	8	School of Excellence in Education	San Antonio
185	8	Southside ISD	San Antonio
185	8	Sulphur Springs ISD	Sulphur Springs
185	8	Whitehouse ISD	Whitehouse
203	7	Aledo ISD	Aledo
203	7	Athens ISD	Athens
203	7	Barbers Hill ISD	Mont Belvieu
203	7	Beeville ISD	Beeville
203	7	Borger ISD	Borger
203	7	Brownsboro ISD	Brownsboro
203	7	Burkburnett ISD	Burkburnett
203	7	Burnet CISD	Burnet
203	7	Castleberry ISD	Fort Worth
203	7	China Spring ISD	Waco
203	7	Cleveland ISD	Cleveland
203	7	Cuero ISD	Cuero
203	7	Elgin ISD	Elgin
203	7	Flour Bluff ISD	Corpus Christi
203	7	Friendswood ISD	Friendswood
203	7	Gregory-Portland ISD	Portland
203	7	Hallsville ISD	Hallsville
203	7	Hidalgo ISD	Hidalgo
203	7	Highland Park ISD	Dallas
203	7	Kaufman ISD	Kaufman
203	7	Kennedale ISD	Kennedale
203	7	Levelland ISD	Levelland
203	7	Liberty Hill ISD	Liberty Hill
203	7	Marble Falls ISD	Marble Falls
203	7	Pampa ISD	Pampa
203	7	Pine Tree ISD	Longview
203	7	Robinson ISD	Robinson
203	7	Sanger ISD	Sanger
203	7	Santa Fe ISD	Santa Fe
203	7	Springtown ISD	Springtown
203	7	Sweetwater ISD	Sweetwater
203	7	Terrell ISD	Terrell
203	7	Vidor ISD	Vidor
203	7	West ISD	West
203	7	Yes College Preparatory School	Houston
238	6	Alamo Heights ISD	San Antonio
238	6	Alvarado ISD	Alvarado
238	6	Andrews ISD	Andrews
238	6	Aransas Pass ISD	Aransas Pass
238	6	Bellville ISD	Bellville
238	6	Bonham ISD	Bonham
238	6	Breckenridge ISD	Breckenridge
238	6	Calallen ISD	Corpus Christi
238	6	Carrizo Springs CISD	Carrizo Springs
238	6	Chapel Hill ISD	Tyler
238	6	Crandall ISD	Crandall
238	6	Crosby ISD	Crosby
238	6	Diboll ISD	Diboll
238	6	Fredericksburg ISD	Fredericksburg
238	6	Gladewater ISD	Gladewater
238	6	Gonzales ISD	Gonzales
238	6	Graham ISD	Graham
238	6	Hillsboro ISD	Hillsboro

Note: This section only includes districts with 1,500 or more students; All categories are ranked from high to low

Rank	Number	District Name	City
238	6	Huffman ISD	Huffman
238	6	Jasper ISD	Jasper
238	6	Kilgore ISD	Kilgore
238	6	Krum ISD	Krum
238	6	La Vega ISD	Waco
238	6	Liberty-Eylau ISD	Texarkana
238	6	Lindale ISD	Lindale
238	6	Little Cypress-Mauricevil	Orange
238	6	Lorena ISD	Lorena
238	6	Lubbock-Cooper ISD	Lubbock
238	6	Lumberton ISD	Lumberton
238	6	Lytle ISD	Lytle
238	6	Mexia ISD	Mexia
238	6	Mineral Wells ISD	Mineral Wells
238	6	Monahans-Wickett-Pyote ISD	Monahans
238	6	North Lamar ISD	Paris
238	6	Perryton ISD	Perryton
238	6	Progreso ISD	Progreso
238	6	Quinlan ISD	Quinlan
238	6	San Elizario ISD	San Elizario
238	6	Seminole ISD	Seminole
238	6	Silsbee ISD	Silsbee
238	6	Somerset ISD	Somerset
238	6	Southwest School	Houston
238	6	Spring Hill ISD	Longview
238	6	Stafford MSD	Stafford
238	6	Stephenville	Stephenville
238	6	Taylor ISD	Taylor
238	6	Tuloso-Midway ISD	Corpus Christi
238	6	Vernon ISD	Vernon
238	6	Winfree Academy	Irving
238	6	Zapata County ISD	Zapata
288	5	Aransas County ISD	Rockport
288	5	Atlanta ISD	Atlanta
288	5	Bridge City ISD	Bridge City
288	5	Brownfield ISD	Brownfield
288	5	Bullard ISD	Bullard
288	5	Caldwell ISD	Caldwell
288	5	Canton ISD	Canton
288	5	Carthage ISD	Carthage
288	5	Center ISD	Center
288	5	Columbia-Brazoria ISD	West Columbia
288	5	Commerce ISD	Commerce
288	5	Community ISD	Nevada
288	5	Crystal City ISD	Crystal City
288	5	Dalhart ISD	Dalhart
288	5	Decatur ISD	Decatur
288	5	Devine ISD	Devine
288	5	Dripping Spgs ISD	Dripping Spgs
288	5	El Campo ISD	El Campo
288	5	Ferris ISD	Ferris
288	5	Fort Stockton ISD	Fort Stockton
288	5	Gatesville ISD	Gatesville
288	5	Godley ISD	Godley
288	5	Groesbeck ISD	Groesbeck
288	5	Henderson ISD	Henderson
288	5	Hondo ISD	Hondo
288	5	Hudson ISD	Lufkin
288	5	Huntington ISD	Huntington
288	5	Ingleside ISD	Ingleside
288	5	Iowa Park CISD	Iowa Park
288	5	Kemp ISD	Kemp
288	5	Lake Dallas ISD	Lake Dallas
288	5	Lamesa ISD	Lamesa
288	5	Lampasas ISD	Lampasas
288	5	Liberty ISD	Liberty
288	5	Livingston ISD	Livingston
288	5	Lovejoy ISD	Allen
288	5	Mathis ISD	Mathis
288	5	Medina Valley ISD	Castroville
288	5	Navasota ISD	Navasota
288	5	Needville ISD	Needville
288	5	Palacios ISD	Palacios
288	5	Palestine ISD	Palestine
288	5	Pearsall ISD	Pearsall
288	5	Pecos-Barstow-Toyah ISD	Pecos
288	5	Pittsburg ISD	Pittsburg
288	5	Poteet ISD	Poteet
288	5	Prosper ISD	Prosper
288	5	Rusk ISD	Rusk
288	5	Sinton ISD	Sinton
288	5	Snyder ISD	Snyder
288	5	South Texas ISD	Mercedes
288	5	Splendora ISD	Splendora
288	5	Venus ISD	Venus
288	5	West Orange-Cove CISD	Orange
288	5	Wills Point ISD	Wills Point
288	5	Wylie ISD	Abilene
344	4	Anna ISD	Anna
344	4	Argyle ISD	Argyle
344	4	Aubrey ISD	Aubrey
344	4	Bandera ISD	Bandera
344	4	Bowie ISD	Bowie
344	4	Bridgeport ISD	Bridgeport
344	4	Cameron ISD	Cameron
344	4	Celina ISD	Celina
344	4	Central ISD	Pollok
344	4	Coldspring-Oakhurst CISD	Coldspring
344	4	Dallas Can Academy Charter	Dallas
344	4	Fabens ISD	Fabens
344	4	Fairfield ISD	Fairfield
344	4	Giddings ISD	Giddings
344	4	Gilmer ISD	Gilmer
344	4	Glen Rose ISD	Glen Rose
344	4	Greenwood ISD	Midland
344	4	Hamshire-Fannett ISD	Hamshire
344	4	Hardin-Jefferson ISD	Sour Lake
344	4	Harmony Science Acad (Fort Worth)	Fort Worth
344	4	Hempstead ISD	Hempstead
344	4	La Grange ISD	La Grange
344	4	Life School	Lancaster
344	4	Llano ISD	Llano
344	4	Lyford CISD	Lyford
344	4	Madisonville CISD	Madisonville
344	4	Mineola ISD	Mineola
344	4	Mount Vernon ISD	Mount Vernon
344	4	Navarro ISD	Seguin
344	4	Orange Grove ISD	Orange Grove
344	4	Orangefield ISD	Orangefield
344	4	Pilot Point ISD	Pilot Point
344	4	Pleasant Grove ISD	Texarkana
344	4	Point Isabel ISD	Port Isabel
344	4	Rains ISD	Emory
344	4	Raymondville ISD	Raymondville
344	4	Rio Hondo ISD	Rio Hondo
344	4	Ripley House Charter School	Houston
344	4	River Road ISD	Amarillo
344	4	Rockdale ISD	Rockdale
344	4	Royal ISD	Pattison
344	4	Sealy ISD	Sealy
344	4	Shepherd ISD	Shepherd
344	4	Smithville ISD	Smithville
344	4	Tarkington ISD	Cleveland
344	4	Tatum ISD	Tatum
344	4	Van ISD	Van
344	4	West Oso ISD	Corpus Christi
344	4	Westwood ISD	Palestine
344	4	Whitesboro ISD	Whitesboro
344	4	Whitney ISD	Whitney
344	4	Wimberley ISD	Wimberley
344	4	Yoakum ISD	Yoakum
397	3	Columbus ISD	Columbus
397	3	Denver City ISD	Denver City
397	3	Harmony Science Academy	Houston
397	3	Sweeny ISD	Sweeny
397	3	Varnett Charter School	Houston
397	3	Wharton ISD	Wharton
403	1	Advantage Academy	Dallas

Number of Teachers

Rank	Number	District Name	City
1	12,027.0	Houston ISD	Houston
2	10,704.2	Dallas ISD	Dallas
3	6,725.1	Cypress-Fairbanks ISD	Houston
4	5,975.7	Austin ISD	Austin
5	5,920.8	Northside ISD	San Antonio
6	5,069.2	Fort Worth ISD	Fort Worth
7	4,403.6	El Paso ISD	El Paso
8	4,385.1	Fort Bend ISD	Sugar Land
9	4,373.9	North East ISD	San Antonio
10	4,238.0	Aldine ISD	Houston
11	4,124.0	Arlington ISD	Arlington
12	4,120.3	Katy ISD	Katy
13	3,941.5	Plano ISD	Plano
14	3,744.8	Lewisville ISD	Flower Mound
15	3,720.4	Garland ISD	Garland
16	3,442.2	Pasadena ISD	Pasadena
17	3,401.8	San Antonio ISD	San Antonio
18	3,364.8	Brownsville ISD	Brownsville
19	3,140.9	Conroe ISD	Conroe
20	3,080.8	Alief ISD	Houston
21	3,040.7	Ysleta ISD	El Paso
22	2,937.7	Klein ISD	Klein
23	2,919.5	Round Rock ISD	Round Rock
24	2,729.3	Killeen ISD	Killeen
25	2,629.7	Clear Creek ISD	League City
26	2,538.0	United ISD	Laredo
27	2,503.6	Richardson ISD	Richardson
28	2,493.9	Frisco ISD	Frisco
29	2,493.4	Socorro ISD	El Paso
30	2,428.4	Irving ISD	Irving
31	2,426.3	Humble ISD	Humble
32	2,395.0	Corpus Christi ISD	Corpus Christi
33	2,368.6	Mesquite ISD	Mesquite
34	2,352.7	Spring ISD	Houston
35	2,297.6	Spring Branch ISD	Houston
36	2,190.5	Amarillo ISD	Amarillo
37	2,086.1	Leander ISD	Leander
38	2,057.5	Edinburg CISD	Edinburg
39	2,040.0	Pharr-San Juan-Alamo ISD	Pharr
40	2,023.7	Lubbock ISD	Lubbock
41	1,954.4	Keller ISD	Keller
42	1,928.2	Mansfield ISD	Mansfield
43	1,906.2	La Joya ISD	La Joya
44	1,826.5	Denton ISD	Denton
45	1,727.2	Carrollton-Farmers Branch	Carrollton
46	1,711.6	Ector County ISD	Odessa
47	1,692.0	Mckinney ISD	Mckinney
48	1,681.5	Mcallen ISD	Mcallen
49	1,612.1	Grand Prairie ISD	Grand Prairie
50	1,602.9	Laredo ISD	Laredo
51	1,573.1	Galena Park ISD	Houston
52	1,489.2	Birdville ISD	Haltom City
53	1,474.8	Pflugerville ISD	Pflugerville
54	1,463.4	Goose Creek CISD	Baytown
55	1,456.6	Lamar CISD	Rosenberg
56	1,442.9	Beaumont ISD	Beaumont
57	1,440.0	Midland ISD	Midland
58	1,422.6	Judson ISD	Live Oak
59	1,360.2	Tyler ISD	Tyler
60	1,309.7	Hurst-Euless-Bedford ISD	Bedford
61	1,230.4	Harlingen CISD	Harlingen
62	1,215.7	Allen ISD	Allen
63	1,215.0	Abilene ISD	Abilene
64	1,098.0	Comal ISD	New Braunfels
65	1,097.8	Wichita Falls ISD	Wichita Falls
66	1,087.5	Alvin ISD	Alvin
67	1,086.6	Pearland ISD	Pearland
68	1,077.4	Weslaco ISD	Weslaco
69	1,073.0	Waco ISD	Waco
70	1,059.5	Bryan ISD	Bryan
71	1,026.6	Mission CISD	Mission
72	1,022.1	Eagle Mt-Saginaw ISD	Fort Worth
73	1,016.2	San Angelo ISD	San Angelo
74	994.9	Donna ISD	Donna
75	991.8	Hays CISD	Kyle
76	975.0	Harlandale ISD	San Antonio
77	966.7	Crowley ISD	Crowley
78	957.4	Grapevine-Colleyville ISD	Grapevine
79	945.1	Northwest ISD	Justin
80	926.2	Victoria ISD	Victoria
81	892.0	Eagle Pass ISD	Eagle Pass
82	887.0	Rockwall ISD	Rockwall
83	859.5	Brazosport ISD	Clute
84	839.9	Deer Park ISD	Deer Park
85	821.0	Georgetown ISD	Georgetown
86	808.9	Magnolia ISD	Magnolia
87	806.9	Wylie ISD	Wylie
88	784.8	Schertz-Cibolo-U City ISD	Schertz
89	784.4	Edgewood ISD	San Antonio
90	758.0	Duncanville ISD	Duncanville
91	754.0	Rio Grande City CISD	Rio Grande City
92	732.2	Del Valle ISD	Del Valle
93	721.3	College Station ISD	College Station
94	719.0	San Benito CISD	San Benito
95	709.4	Southwest ISD	San Antonio
96	691.7	Coppell ISD	Coppell
97	684.9	South San Antonio ISD	San Antonio
98	665.2	San Felipe-Del Rio CISD	Del Rio
99	656.4	Clint ISD	El Paso
100	649.0	Tomball ISD	Tomball
101	640.3	New Caney ISD	New Caney
102	634.2	Burleson ISD	Burleson
103	623.8	Lufkin ISD	Lufkin
104	618.9	Temple ISD	Temple
105	614.3	Desoto ISD	Desoto

Note: This section only includes districts with 1,500 or more students; All categories are ranked from high to low

Rank	Value	District	City
106	611.7	Port Arthur ISD	Port Arthur
107	607.3	Bastrop ISD	Bastrop
108	601.8	Los Fresnos CISD	Los Fresnos
109	600.3	Belton ISD	Belton
110	584.6	Sharyland ISD	Mission
111	582.3	Copperas Cove ISD	Copperas Cove
112	574.5	East Central ISD	San Antonio
113	566.1	Channelview ISD	Channelview
114	565.1	Canyon ISD	Canyon
115	558.4	Eanes ISD	Austin
116	558.3	Longview ISD	Longview
117	549.6	Dickinson ISD	Dickinson
118	546.6	San Marcos CISD	San Marcos
119	543.8	Seguin ISD	Seguin
120	543.7	Carroll ISD	Grapevine
121	541.5	Forney ISD	Forney
122	540.5	Frenship ISD	Wolfforth
123	512.2	Cedar Hill ISD	Cedar Hill
124	506.4	La Porte ISD	La Porte
125	503.2	Weatherford ISD	Weatherford
126	502.9	Sherman ISD	Sherman
127	502.4	North Forest ISD	Houston
128	500.7	Granbury ISD	Granbury
129	495.3	Texarkana ISD	Texarkana
130	492.0	New Braunfels ISD	New Braunfels
131	485.7	Cleburne ISD	Cleburne
132	485.1	Midlothian ISD	Midlothian
133	473.0	Waxahachie ISD	Waxahachie
134	471.2	Manor ISD	Manor
135	459.1	Sheldon ISD	Houston
136	457.2	Boerne ISD	Boerne
137	448.1	Midway ISD	Hewitt
138	443.0	Galveston ISD	Galveston
139	442.3	Marshall ISD	Marshall
140	437.3	Roma ISD	Roma
141	435.2	Lake Travis ISD	Austin
142	430.7	Montgomery ISD	Montgomery
143	428.9	Huntsville ISD	Huntsville
144	427.8	Nacogdoches ISD	Nacogdoches
145	417.8	Highland Park ISD	Dallas
146	415.0	Willis ISD	Willis
147	410.8	Mount Pleasant ISD	Mount Pleasant
148	408.2	Little Elm ISD	Little Elm
149	404.1	Canutillo ISD	El Paso
150	403.2	Plainview ISD	Plainview
151	402.9	Angleton ISD	Angleton
152	395.9	Corsicana ISD	Corsicana
153	390.7	Texas City ISD	Texas City
154	387.5	White Settlement ISD	White Settlement
155	381.0	Ennis ISD	Ennis
156	377.0	Brenham ISD	Brenham
157	375.9	Mercedes ISD	Mercedes
158	373.5	Greenville ISD	Greenville
159	373.3	Friendswood ISD	Friendswood
160	368.2	Lancaster ISD	Lancaster
161	368.1	Azle ISD	Azle
162	368.0	Uvalde CISD	Uvalde
163	367.1	Alice ISD	Alice
164	363.7	Vidor ISD	Vidor
165	362.9	Edcouch-Elsa ISD	Edcouch
166	361.2	Southside ISD	San Antonio
167	358.3	Flour Bluff ISD	Corpus Christi
168	356.8	Waller ISD	Waller
169	352.8	Jacksonville ISD	Jacksonville
170	347.4	Joshua ISD	Joshua
171	347.0	Kerrville ISD	Kerrville
172	342.1	Port Neches-Groves ISD	Port Neches
173	340.5	Hutto ISD	Hutto
174	340.1	Royse City ISD	Royse City
175	337.6	Nederland ISD	Nederland
176	337.2	Red Oak ISD	Red Oak
177	335.6	Alamo Heights ISD	San Antonio
178	335.0	Hallsville ISD	Hallsville
179	333.7	Denison ISD	Denison
180	333.5	Everman ISD	Everman
181	332.9	Pine Tree ISD	Longview
182	332.7	Dumas ISD	Dumas
183	326.5	Lockhart ISD	Lockhart
183	326.5	Valley View ISD	Pharr
185	315.4	Hereford ISD	Hereford
186	313.1	Paris ISD	Paris
187	309.7	Marble Falls ISD	Marble Falls
188	309.2	Sulphur Springs ISD	Sulphur Springs
189	306.9	Bay City ISD	Bay City
190	302.7	Aledo ISD	Aledo
191	301.6	Terrell ISD	Terrell
192	300.0	Dayton ISD	Dayton
193	299.1	Santa Fe ISD	Santa Fe
194	299.0	Eagle Academy of Abilene	Lewisville
195	293.1	Whitehouse ISD	Whitehouse
196	292.4	Crosby ISD	Crosby
197	290.6	Calhoun County ISD	Port Lavaca
198	286.9	Lubbock-Cooper ISD	Lubbock
199	283.9	Kilgore ISD	Kilgore
200	282.1	Barbers Hill ISD	Mont Belvieu
201	281.4	Lake Dallas ISD	Lake Dallas
202	281.2	Lumberton ISD	Lumberton
203	279.5	Idea Academy	Weslaco
204	276.8	Livingston ISD	Livingston
205	272.4	Burkburnett ISD	Burkburnett
206	270.0	Henderson ISD	Henderson
207	269.7	Mineral Wells ISD	Mineral Wells
208	269.6	Dripping Spgs ISD	Dripping Spgs
209	268.5	Floresville ISD	Floresville
210	267.4	Hidalgo ISD	Hidalgo
211	266.6	Gregory-Portland ISD	Portland
212	265.7	Cleveland ISD	Cleveland
213	262.4	Big Spring ISD	Big Spring
214	261.8	Pampa ISD	Pampa
214	261.8	Pleasanton ISD	Pleasanton
216	261.5	Little Cypress-Mauricevil	Orange
217	260.6	Kingsville ISD	Kingsville
218	260.3	San Elizario ISD	San Elizario
219	258.4	North Lamar ISD	Paris
220	257.1	Kaufman ISD	Kaufman
221	255.2	El Campo ISD	El Campo
222	252.9	Lovejoy ISD	Allen
223	251.3	Calallen ISD	Corpus Christi
224	250.9	Zapata County ISD	Zapata
225	249.8	Elgin ISD	Elgin
226	249.3	Lindale ISD	Lindale
227	249.1	Prosper ISD	Prosper
228	247.6	La Marque ISD	La Marque
229	247.1	Springtown ISD	Springtown
230	245.1	Brownwood ISD	Brownwood
231	244.4	Levelland ISD	Levelland
232	244.3	Palestine ISD	Palestine
233	243.5	Robstown ISD	Robstown
234	242.3	Aransas County ISD	Rockport
235	240.5	Mabank ISD	Mabank
236	240.0	La Feria Ind SD	La Feria
237	238.7	Somerset ISD	Somerset
238	236.4	Navasota ISD	Navasota
239	235.5	Jasper ISD	Jasper
240	234.0	Athens ISD	Athens
241	232.9	Stephenville	Stephenville
242	232.4	Kipp Inc Charter	Houston
243	231.3	Chapel Hill ISD	Tyler
244	231.0	Liberty-Eylau ISD	Texarkana
245	229.9	Beeville ISD	Beeville
246	229.8	Andrews ISD	Andrews
247	228.5	Splendora ISD	Splendora
248	228.3	Burnet CISD	Burnet
249	223.9	Tuloso-Midway ISD	Corpus Christi
250	222.8	South Texas ISD	Mercedes
251	222.7	Lampasas ISD	Lampasas
252	222.1	Yes College Preparatory School	Houston
253	218.1	Castleberry ISD	Fort Worth
254	216.7	Carthage ISD	Carthage
255	216.4	Silsbee ISD	Silsbee
256	213.8	Medina Valley ISD	Castroville
257	212.8	Decatur ISD	Decatur
258	212.5	Fredericksburg ISD	Fredericksburg
259	211.4	Kennedale ISD	Kennedale
260	211.0	Stafford MSD	Stafford
261	209.0	Pittsburg ISD	Pittsburg
262	208.6	Taylor ISD	Taylor
263	208.0	Borger ISD	Borger
264	205.7	Gatesville ISD	Gatesville
265	205.5	Alvarado ISD	Alvarado
266	205.3	Columbia-Brazoria ISD	West Columbia
267	204.9	Snyder ISD	Snyder
268	204.2	Wylie ISD	Abilene
269	202.7	Lake Worth ISD	Lake Worth
270	202.3	Princeton ISD	Princeton
270	202.3	Sweetwater ISD	Sweetwater
272	202.1	Gainesville ISD	Gainesville
273	198.8	Center ISD	Center
274	198.5	Sealy ISD	Sealy
275	198.0	Life School	Lancaster
276	197.8	Sanger ISD	Sanger
277	194.3	Gilmer ISD	Gilmer
278	193.6	Bandera ISD	Bandera
279	192.8	Gonzales ISD	Gonzales
280	192.2	Brownsboro ISD	Brownsboro
281	191.6	Huffman ISD	Huffman
282	190.2	Seminole ISD	Seminole
283	188.6	Graham ISD	Graham
284	187.3	Fort Stockton ISD	Fort Stockton
285	187.1	Wills Point ISD	Wills Point
286	186.8	West Orange-Cove CISD	Orange
287	186.7	La Vega ISD	Waco
288	186.4	Liberty ISD	Liberty
289	185.0	Liberty Hill ISD	Liberty Hill
290	181.9	Fabens ISD	Fabens
291	179.6	Pearsall ISD	Pearsall
292	179.5	Hondo ISD	Hondo
293	178.8	Pecos-Barstow-Toyah ISD	Pecos
294	178.7	La Vernia ISD	La Vernia
295	178.4	Bridgeport ISD	Bridgeport
296	175.8	Hudson ISD	Lufkin
297	175.0	Perryton ISD	Perryton
298	173.0	Wharton ISD	Wharton
299	172.9	Point Isabel ISD	Port Isabel
300	172.3	Connally ISD	Waco
301	170.9	Needville ISD	Needville
301	170.9	Vernon ISD	Vernon
303	169.2	Anna ISD	Anna
304	167.8	Bellville ISD	Bellville
304	167.8	Quinlan ISD	Quinlan
306	167.6	Crandall ISD	Crandall
307	167.4	Bridge City ISD	Bridge City
308	165.8	Robinson ISD	Robinson
309	164.9	Van ISD	Van
310	164.3	Mexia ISD	Mexia
311	163.7	Royal ISD	Pattison
312	163.4	Gladewater ISD	Gladewater
313	160.4	Hardin-Jefferson ISD	Sour Lake
314	159.4	Carrizo Springs CISD	Carrizo Springs
315	159.0	Bonham ISD	Bonham
316	158.9	Fairfield ISD	Fairfield
316	158.9	Madisonville CISD	Madisonville
318	158.5	Sinton ISD	Sinton
319	158.4	Ferris ISD	Ferris
320	157.5	Cuero ISD	Cuero
321	156.5	Lamesa ISD	Lamesa
322	155.6	Pleasant Grove ISD	Texarkana
323	154.6	Rusk ISD	Rusk
324	152.1	Aransas Pass ISD	Aransas Pass
325	152.0	Raymondville ISD	Raymondville
326	151.4	China Spring ISD	Waco
327	151.1	West Oso ISD	Corpus Christi
328	150.7	Wimberley ISD	Wimberley
329	149.6	Llano ISD	Llano
330	149.1	Shepherd ISD	Shepherd
331	148.9	Glen Rose ISD	Glen Rose
332	148.5	Giddings ISD	Giddings
333	148.4	Monahans-Wickett-Pyote ISD	Monahans
334	145.3	Rio Hondo ISD	Rio Hondo
335	144.9	Brownfield ISD	Brownfield
336	144.0	Tarkington ISD	Cleveland
337	143.4	Hillsboro ISD	Hillsboro
338	143.0	Caldwell ISD	Caldwell
339	142.4	Canton ISD	Canton
339	142.4	La Grange ISD	La Grange
341	142.3	Bullard ISD	Bullard
341	142.3	Diboll ISD	Diboll
343	139.2	Devine ISD	Devine
344	138.7	Dalhart ISD	Dalhart
345	138.6	Ingleside ISD	Ingleside
346	137.1	Sweeny ISD	Sweeny
347	136.9	Breckenridge ISD	Breckenridge
348	135.9	Venus ISD	Venus
349	135.2	Crystal City ISD	Crystal City
350	134.9	Progreso ISD	Progreso
351	134.4	Coldspring-Oakhurst CISD	Coldspring
352	133.9	Atlanta ISD	Atlanta
353	133.5	West ISD	West
354	133.3	Smithville ISD	Smithville
355	132.4	Rains ISD	Emory
356	132.3	Hamshire-Fannett ISD	Hamshire
357	131.2	Spring Hill ISD	Longview
358	129.3	Godley ISD	Godley
359	128.6	Hempstead ISD	Hempstead
360	128.4	Celina ISD	Celina
361	128.3	Westwood ISD	Palestine
362	126.9	Orange Grove ISD	Orange Grove
363	126.7	Mathis ISD	Mathis

Note: This section only includes districts with 1,500 or more students; All categories are ranked from high to low

Rank		District Name	City
364	126.4	Iowa Park CISD	Iowa Park
365	125.9	Huntington ISD	Huntington
366	125.8	Cameron ISD	Cameron
367	125.5	Mount Vernon ISD	Mount Vernon
368	125.1	Lytle ISD	Lytle
369	125.0	Commerce ISD	Commerce
370	124.3	Kemp ISD	Kemp
371	123.6	Poteet ISD	Poteet
372	122.8	Krum ISD	Krum
373	122.6	Whitney ISD	Whitney
374	122.5	Mineola ISD	Mineola
375	122.0	Bowie ISD	Bowie
376	121.4	Whitesboro ISD	Whitesboro
377	120.7	Aubrey ISD	Aubrey
378	120.4	Argyle ISD	Argyle
379	120.1	Groesbeck ISD	Groesbeck
380	120.0	Yoakum ISD	Yoakum
381	119.8	Columbus ISD	Columbus
382	119.1	Orangefield ISD	Orangefield
383	119.0	Rockdale ISD	Rockdale
384	117.6	Palacios ISD	Palacios
385	116.4	Denver City ISD	Denver City
386	114.5	Harmony Science Academy	Houston
387	113.8	Harmony Science Acad (Fort Worth)	Fort Worth
388	113.6	Southwest School	Houston
389	113.3	Lorena ISD	Lorena
390	111.5	Community ISD	Nevada
391	110.8	Lyford CISD	Lyford
392	110.5	Pilot Point ISD	Pilot Point
393	110.3	Advantage Academy	Dallas
394	110.1	Central ISD	Pollok
395	109.8	School of Excellence in Education	San Antonio
396	106.5	Greenwood ISD	Midland
397	103.2	Navarro ISD	Seguin
398	97.7	Dallas Can Academy Charter	Dallas
399	95.0	Tatum ISD	Tatum
400	94.8	River Road ISD	Amarillo
401	80.3	Winfree Academy	Irving
402	70.9	Varnett Charter School	Houston
403	66.0	Ripley House Charter School	Houston

Number of Students

Rank	Number	District Name	City
1	202,773	Houston ISD	Houston
2	157,111	Dallas ISD	Dallas
3	104,231	Cypress-Fairbanks ISD	Houston
4	92,335	Northside ISD	San Antonio
5	84,676	Austin ISD	Austin
6	80,209	Fort Worth ISD	Fort Worth
7	69,374	Fort Bend ISD	Sugar Land
8	65,498	North East ISD	San Antonio
9	63,487	Arlington ISD	Arlington
10	63,378	El Paso ISD	El Paso
11	62,792	Aldine ISD	Houston
12	59,078	Katy ISD	Katy
13	57,861	Garland ISD	Garland
14	55,327	San Antonio ISD	San Antonio
15	54,939	Plano ISD	Plano
16	52,303	Pasadena ISD	Pasadena
17	50,840	Lewisville ISD	Flower Mound
18	49,629	Conroe ISD	Conroe
19	49,121	Brownsville ISD	Brownsville
20	45,553	Alief ISD	Houston
21	44,824	Klein ISD	Klein
22	44,620	Ysleta ISD	El Paso
23	43,008	Round Rock ISD	Round Rock
24	41,357	Socorro ISD	El Paso
25	40,885	United ISD	Laredo
26	39,603	Killeen ISD	Killeen
27	38,196	Corpus Christi ISD	Corpus Christi
28	37,611	Clear Creek ISD	League City
29	37,272	Mesquite ISD	Mesquite
30	35,350	Spring ISD	Houston
31	34,923	Humble ISD	Humble
32	34,843	Richardson ISD	Richardson
33	33,973	Frisco ISD	Frisco
34	33,679	Irving ISD	Irving
35	32,502	Spring Branch ISD	Houston
36	32,011	Edinburg CISD	Edinburg
37	31,890	Amarillo ISD	Amarillo
38	31,662	Mansfield ISD	Mansfield
39	31,569	Keller ISD	Keller
40	31,329	Pharr-San Juan-Alamo ISD	Pharr
41	30,454	Leander ISD	Leander
42	28,680	Lubbock ISD	Lubbock
43	28,004	La Joya ISD	La Joya
44	27,435	Ector County ISD	Odessa
45	26,395	Grand Prairie ISD	Grand Prairie
46	25,920	Carrollton-Farmers Branch	Carrollton
47	25,172	Mcallen ISD	Mcallen
48	24,707	Laredo ISD	Laredo
49	23,933	Mckinney ISD	Mckinney
50	23,864	Lamar CISD	Rosenberg
51	22,897	Birdville ISD	Haltom City
52	22,825	Denton ISD	Denton
53	22,060	Pflugerville ISD	Pflugerville
54	21,750	Judson ISD	Live Oak
55	21,536	Galena Park ISD	Houston
56	21,374	Midland ISD	Midland
57	20,954	Goose Creek CISD	Baytown
58	20,762	Hurst-Euless-Bedford ISD	Bedford
59	19,551	Beaumont ISD	Beaumont
60	18,408	Tyler ISD	Tyler
61	18,308	Pearland ISD	Pearland
62	18,242	Allen ISD	Allen
63	18,205	Harlingen CISD	Harlingen
64	17,279	Weslaco ISD	Weslaco
65	17,016	Abilene ISD	Abilene
66	16,788	Alvin ISD	Alvin
67	16,700	Comal ISD	New Braunfels
68	16,126	Eagle Mt-Saginaw ISD	Fort Worth
69	15,579	Bryan ISD	Bryan
70	15,412	Mission CISD	Mission
71	15,337	Waco ISD	Waco
72	15,126	Crowley ISD	Crowley
73	14,873	Donna ISD	Donna
74	14,649	Hays CISD	Kyle
75	14,584	Wichita Falls ISD	Wichita Falls
76	14,521	Harlandale ISD	San Antonio
77	14,492	San Angelo ISD	San Angelo
78	14,463	Eagle Pass ISD	Eagle Pass
79	14,164	Northwest ISD	Justin
80	13,843	Rockwall ISD	Rockwall
81	13,728	Victoria ISD	Victoria
82	13,671	Grapevine-Colleyville ISD	Grapevine
83	12,903	Duncanville ISD	Duncanville
84	12,861	Brazosport ISD	Clute
85	12,502	Deer Park ISD	Deer Park
86	12,392	Edgewood ISD	San Antonio
87	12,063	Wylie ISD	Wylie
88	11,718	Schertz-Cibolo-U City ISD	Schertz
89	11,691	Magnolia ISD	Magnolia
90	11,531	Southwest ISD	San Antonio
91	11,295	Clint ISD	El Paso
92	11,209	San Benito CISD	San Benito
93	10,443	Georgetown ISD	Georgetown
94	10,428	Rio Grande City CISD	Rio Grande City
95	10,333	San Felipe-Del Rio CISD	Del Rio
96	10,266	Tomball ISD	Tomball
97	10,158	Del Valle ISD	Del Valle
98	10,102	College Station ISD	College Station
99	9,982	Coppell ISD	Coppell
100	9,974	South San Antonio ISD	San Antonio
101	9,896	Burleson ISD	Burleson
102	9,734	Los Fresnos CISD	Los Fresnos
103	9,609	New Caney ISD	New Caney
104	9,566	Sharyland ISD	Mission
105	9,292	East Central ISD	San Antonio
106	9,238	Port Arthur ISD	Port Arthur
107	9,069	Desoto ISD	Desoto
108	8,936	Bastrop ISD	Bastrop
109	8,878	Dickinson ISD	Dickinson
110	8,859	Belton ISD	Belton
111	8,783	Temple ISD	Temple
112	8,745	Canyon ISD	Canyon
113	8,644	Channelview ISD	Channelview
114	8,630	Lufkin ISD	Lufkin
115	8,348	Longview ISD	Longview
116	8,284	Cedar Hill ISD	Cedar Hill
117	8,258	Copperas Cove ISD	Copperas Cove
118	7,856	New Braunfels ISD	New Braunfels
119	7,847	La Porte ISD	La Porte
120	7,813	Forney ISD	Forney
121	7,745	Carroll ISD	Grapevine
122	7,665	North Forest ISD	Houston
123	7,562	Seguin ISD	Seguin
124	7,530	Weatherford ISD	Weatherford
125	7,498	Eanes ISD	Austin
126	7,434	San Marcos CISD	San Marcos
127	7,342	Frenship ISD	Wolfforth
128	7,329	Midlothian ISD	Midlothian
129	6,932	Manor ISD	Manor
130	6,924	Waxahachie ISD	Waxahachie
131	6,907	Cleburne ISD	Cleburne
132	6,883	Midway ISD	Hewitt
133	6,849	Texarkana ISD	Texarkana
134	6,791	Granbury ISD	Granbury
135	6,714	Montgomery ISD	Montgomery
135	6,714	Sherman ISD	Sherman
137	6,577	Lake Travis ISD	Austin
138	6,570	Sheldon ISD	Houston
139	6,448	Highland Park ISD	Dallas
140	6,392	Boerne ISD	Boerne
141	6,358	Galveston ISD	Galveston
142	6,338	Angleton ISD	Angleton
143	6,330	Nacogdoches ISD	Nacogdoches
144	6,320	Roma ISD	Roma
145	6,291	Huntsville ISD	Huntsville
146	6,264	Willis ISD	Willis
147	6,176	Lancaster ISD	Lancaster
148	6,112	Little Elm ISD	Little Elm
149	6,051	White Settlement ISD	White Settlement
150	5,984	Texas City ISD	Texas City
151	5,970	Friendswood ISD	Friendswood
152	5,867	Canutillo ISD	El Paso
153	5,859	Plainview ISD	Plainview
154	5,841	Azle ISD	Azle
155	5,829	Ennis ISD	Ennis
156	5,789	Marshall ISD	Marshall
157	5,638	Corsicana ISD	Corsicana
158	5,545	Mercedes ISD	Mercedes
159	5,515	Idea Academy	Weslaco
160	5,474	Flour Bluff ISD	Corpus Christi
161	5,408	Red Oak ISD	Red Oak
162	5,407	Waller ISD	Waller
163	5,404	Edcouch-Elsa ISD	Edcouch
164	5,389	Alice ISD	Alice
165	5,381	Mount Pleasant ISD	Mount Pleasant
166	5,216	Southside ISD	San Antonio
167	5,137	Hutto ISD	Hutto
168	5,098	Uvalde CISD	Uvalde
169	5,053	Everman ISD	Everman
170	5,041	Nederland ISD	Nederland
171	5,034	Crosby ISD	Crosby
172	5,022	Eagle Academy of Abilene	Lewisville
173	4,956	Greenville ISD	Greenville
174	4,955	Vidor ISD	Vidor
175	4,940	Brenham ISD	Brenham
176	4,912	Dayton ISD	Dayton
177	4,902	Jacksonville ISD	Jacksonville
178	4,884	Kerrville ISD	Kerrville
179	4,762	Alamo Heights ISD	San Antonio
180	4,746	Pine Tree ISD	Longview
181	4,731	Joshua ISD	Joshua
182	4,650	Valley View ISD	Pharr
183	4,636	Lockhart ISD	Lockhart
184	4,607	Whitehouse ISD	Whitehouse
185	4,593	Port Neches-Groves ISD	Port Neches
186	4,589	Aledo ISD	Aledo
187	4,505	Santa Fe ISD	Santa Fe
188	4,492	Denison ISD	Denison
189	4,476	Dumas ISD	Dumas
190	4,450	Royse City ISD	Royse City
191	4,331	Dripping Spgs ISD	Dripping Spgs
192	4,282	Hereford ISD	Hereford
193	4,276	Calhoun County ISD	Port Lavaca
194	4,265	Hallsville ISD	Hallsville
195	4,197	Gregory-Portland ISD	Portland
196	4,178	Terrell ISD	Terrell
197	4,121	Barbers Hill ISD	Mont Belvieu
197	4,121	Sulphur Springs ISD	Sulphur Springs
199	4,090	Lake Dallas ISD	Lake Dallas
200	4,044	San Elizario ISD	San Elizario
201	4,011	Marble Falls ISD	Marble Falls
202	3,999	Livingston ISD	Livingston
203	3,995	Elgin ISD	Elgin
204	3,981	Kingsville ISD	Kingsville
205	3,900	Lumberton ISD	Lumberton
206	3,882	Big Spring ISD	Big Spring
207	3,864	Kipp Inc Charter	Houston
208	3,811	Kilgore ISD	Kilgore
209	3,808	Calallen ISD	Corpus Christi
210	3,801	Floresville ISD	Floresville
211	3,793	Bay City ISD	Bay City
212	3,779	Cleveland ISD	Cleveland
213	3,761	Zapata County ISD	Zapata

Note: This section only includes districts with 1,500 or more students; All categories are ranked from high to low

Rank		District Name	City
214	3,746	Lubbock-Cooper ISD	Lubbock
215	3,738	Kaufman ISD	Kaufman
216	3,726	Somerset ISD	Somerset
217	3,716	Paris ISD	Paris
218	3,641	Castleberry ISD	Fort Worth
219	3,638	Little Cypress-Mauricevil	Orange
220	3,637	Prosper ISD	Prosper
221	3,603	Burkburnett ISD	Burkburnett
222	3,598	Southwest School	Houston
223	3,595	Lindale ISD	Lindale
224	3,568	Mineral Wells ISD	Mineral Wells
225	3,553	Stephenville	Stephenville
226	3,535	Beeville ISD	Beeville
227	3,525	Brownwood ISD	Brownwood
228	3,516	Hidalgo ISD	Hidalgo
229	3,510	Springtown ISD	Springtown
230	3,491	El Campo ISD	El Campo
231	3,474	Pampa ISD	Pampa
232	3,468	La Feria Ind SD	La Feria
233	3,460	Athens ISD	Athens
234	3,440	Pleasanton ISD	Pleasanton
235	3,434	Life School	Lancaster
236	3,425	Tuloso-Midway ISD	Corpus Christi
237	3,402	Alvarado ISD	Alvarado
238	3,398	La Marque ISD	La Marque
239	3,390	Robstown ISD	Robstown
240	3,382	Medina Valley ISD	Castroville
240	3,382	Splendora ISD	Splendora
242	3,374	Yes College Preparatory School	Houston
243	3,372	Lampasas ISD	Lampasas
244	3,368	Henderson ISD	Henderson
245	3,366	Burnet CISD	Burnet
246	3,325	Mabank ISD	Mabank
247	3,281	Wylie ISD	Abilene
248	3,242	Palestine ISD	Palestine
249	3,230	Lovejoy ISD	Allen
250	3,215	Chapel Hill ISD	Tyler
251	3,168	Taylor ISD	Taylor
252	3,162	Kennedale ISD	Kennedale
252	3,162	Stafford MSD	Stafford
254	3,156	Aransas County ISD	Rockport
255	3,152	Huffman ISD	Huffman
256	3,143	Andrews ISD	Andrews
257	3,081	Columbia-Brazoria ISD	West Columbia
258	3,023	South Texas ISD	Mercedes
259	3,000	Silsbee ISD	Silsbee
260	2,996	Princeton ISD	Princeton
261	2,983	La Vernia ISD	La Vernia
262	2,976	Decatur ISD	Decatur
263	2,963	North Lamar ISD	Paris
264	2,957	Lake Worth ISD	Lake Worth
264	2,957	Levelland ISD	Levelland
266	2,941	Fredericksburg ISD	Fredericksburg
267	2,932	La Vega ISD	Waco
268	2,893	Liberty-Eylau ISD	Texarkana
269	2,883	Navasota ISD	Navasota
270	2,842	Brownsboro ISD	Brownsboro
271	2,816	Gatesville ISD	Gatesville
272	2,815	Borger ISD	Borger
273	2,814	Jasper ISD	Jasper
274	2,779	Carthage ISD	Carthage
275	2,774	Crandall ISD	Crandall
276	2,715	Snyder ISD	Snyder
277	2,675	Wills Point ISD	Wills Point
278	2,636	Gainesville ISD	Gainesville
279	2,612	Sealy ISD	Sealy
280	2,602	Needville ISD	Needville
281	2,597	Hudson ISD	Lufkin
282	2,594	Sanger ISD	Sanger
283	2,583	Center ISD	Center
284	2,568	Liberty Hill ISD	Liberty Hill
285	2,551	West Orange-Cove CISD	Orange
286	2,550	Graham ISD	Graham
287	2,543	Quinlan ISD	Quinlan
288	2,539	Bandera ISD	Bandera
289	2,538	Point Isabel ISD	Port Isabel
290	2,532	Gonzales ISD	Gonzales
291	2,491	Fabens ISD	Fabens
292	2,486	Bridge City ISD	Bridge City
293	2,464	Connally ISD	Waco
294	2,437	Pittsburg ISD	Pittsburg
295	2,423	Ferris ISD	Ferris
296	2,395	Carrizo Springs CISD	Carrizo Springs
297	2,380	Seminole ISD	Seminole
298	2,378	Fort Stockton ISD	Fort Stockton
299	2,354	Gilmer ISD	Gilmer

Rank		District Name	City
300	2,322	Madisonville CISD	Madisonville
301	2,320	Sweetwater ISD	Sweetwater
302	2,310	Rio Hondo ISD	Rio Hondo
303	2,299	Van ISD	Van
304	2,288	China Spring ISD	Waco
305	2,279	Vernon ISD	Vernon
306	2,276	Hondo ISD	Hondo
307	2,275	Pearsall ISD	Pearsall
308	2,258	Bridgeport ISD	Bridgeport
309	2,256	Perryton ISD	Perryton
310	2,246	Anna ISD	Anna
311	2,238	Liberty ISD	Liberty
312	2,224	Progreso ISD	Progreso
313	2,221	Wharton ISD	Wharton
314	2,215	Mexia ISD	Mexia
315	2,209	Raymondville ISD	Raymondville
316	2,198	Pecos-Barstow-Toyah ISD	Pecos
317	2,167	Bellville ISD	Bellville
318	2,160	Robinson ISD	Robinson
319	2,150	Ingleside ISD	Ingleside
320	2,141	Rusk ISD	Rusk
321	2,137	Dallas Can Academy Charter	Dallas
322	2,125	Sinton ISD	Sinton
323	2,090	West Oso ISD	Corpus Christi
324	2,087	School of Excellence in Education	San Antonio
325	2,067	Gladewater ISD	Gladewater
326	2,057	Royal ISD	Pattison
327	2,014	Hardin-Jefferson ISD	Sour Lake
328	2,004	Bullard ISD	Bullard
329	2,003	Wimberley ISD	Wimberley
330	1,986	Tarkington ISD	Cleveland
331	1,985	Canton ISD	Canton
332	1,984	Crystal City ISD	Crystal City
333	1,983	Monahans-Wickett-Pyote ISD	Monahans
334	1,971	Pleasant Grove ISD	Texarkana
335	1,962	Diboll ISD	Diboll
336	1,955	Bonham ISD	Bonham
337	1,951	Llano ISD	Llano
338	1,948	Harmony Science Acad (Fort Worth)	Fort Worth
339	1,934	Sweeny ISD	Sweeny
340	1,933	Lamesa ISD	Lamesa
341	1,919	Giddings ISD	Giddings
342	1,917	Shepherd ISD	Shepherd
343	1,913	Devine ISD	Devine
344	1,905	La Grange ISD	La Grange
345	1,904	Celina ISD	Celina
346	1,902	Hillsboro ISD	Hillsboro
347	1,887	Caldwell ISD	Caldwell
348	1,881	Aransas Pass ISD	Aransas Pass
349	1,879	Cuero ISD	Cuero
350	1,862	Winfree Academy	Irving
351	1,858	Venus ISD	Venus
352	1,849	Spring Hill ISD	Longview
353	1,813	Atlanta ISD	Atlanta
354	1,811	Fairfield ISD	Fairfield
355	1,804	Harmony Science Academy	Houston
356	1,790	Argyle ISD	Argyle
357	1,785	Poteet ISD	Poteet
358	1,784	Aubrey ISD	Aubrey
359	1,764	Iowa Park CISD	Iowa Park
360	1,762	Brownfield ISD	Brownfield
361	1,761	Orange Grove ISD	Orange Grove
362	1,758	Orangefield ISD	Orangefield
363	1,757	Hamshire-Fannett ISD	Hamshire
364	1,753	Rockdale ISD	Rockdale
365	1,750	Huntington ISD	Huntington
366	1,746	Mathis ISD	Mathis
367	1,712	Lytle ISD	Lytle
368	1,709	Smithville ISD	Smithville
369	1,698	Westwood ISD	Palestine
370	1,683	Dalhart ISD	Dalhart
371	1,656	Glen Rose ISD	Glen Rose
372	1,648	Coldspring-Oakhurst CISD	Coldspring
373	1,641	Greenwood ISD	Midland
374	1,633	Community ISD	Nevada
375	1,629	Commerce ISD	Commerce
376	1,613	Bowie ISD	Bowie
376	1,613	Krum ISD	Krum
378	1,611	Lorena ISD	Lorena
379	1,606	Cameron ISD	Cameron
380	1,583	Groesbeck ISD	Groesbeck
381	1,581	Breckenridge ISD	Breckenridge
381	1,581	Mineola ISD	Mineola
383	1,575	Whitney ISD	Whitney
384	1,570	Rains ISD	Emory
385	1,566	Kemp ISD	Kemp

Rank		District Name	City
386	1,560	Navarro ISD	Seguin
387	1,559	Lyford CISD	Lyford
388	1,555	Godley ISD	Godley
389	1,554	Whitesboro ISD	Whitesboro
390	1,552	Varnett Charter School	Houston
390	1,552	West ISD	West
392	1,544	Yoakum ISD	Yoakum
393	1,541	Mount Vernon ISD	Mount Vernon
394	1,538	Columbus ISD	Columbus
395	1,530	Central ISD	Pollok
395	1,530	Ripley House Charter School	Houston
397	1,528	Pilot Point ISD	Pilot Point
398	1,511	Hempstead ISD	Hempstead
399	1,509	Palacios ISD	Palacios
400	1,507	Advantage Academy	Dallas
400	1,507	Tatum ISD	Tatum
402	1,506	River Road ISD	Amarillo
403	1,504	Denver City ISD	Denver City

Male Students

Rank	Percent	District Name	City
1	54.8	Kemp ISD	Kemp
1	54.8	West ISD	West
3	54.5	Argyle ISD	Argyle
4	54.4	Hardin-Jefferson ISD	Sour Lake
5	54.2	Whitesboro ISD	Whitesboro
6	54.1	Ripley House Charter School	Houston
6	54.1	West Orange-Cove CISD	Orange
8	54.0	Sweeny ISD	Sweeny
9	53.8	Lorena ISD	Lorena
10	53.7	Navarro ISD	Seguin
10	53.7	Smithville ISD	Smithville
12	53.6	Atlanta ISD	Atlanta
13	53.4	Alvarado ISD	Alvarado
13	53.4	Aransas County ISD	Rockport
13	53.4	Dumas ISD	Dumas
13	53.4	Pleasant Grove ISD	Texarkana
13	53.4	Stafford MSD	Stafford
13	53.4	West Oso ISD	Corpus Christi
19	53.3	Gilmer ISD	Gilmer
19	53.3	Rains ISD	Emory
21	53.2	Mexia ISD	Mexia
22	53.1	Brenham ISD	Brenham
22	53.1	Cameron ISD	Cameron
22	53.1	School of Excellence in Education	San Antonio
25	53.0	East Central ISD	San Antonio
25	53.0	Lubbock-Cooper ISD	Lubbock
25	53.0	Rio Hondo ISD	Rio Hondo
25	53.0	Robstown ISD	Robstown
25	53.0	Royse City ISD	Royse City
30	52.9	Columbus ISD	Columbus
30	52.9	Diboll ISD	Diboll
30	52.9	Godley ISD	Godley
30	52.9	Hallsville ISD	Hallsville
30	52.9	Kerrville ISD	Kerrville
30	52.9	Palestine ISD	Palestine
36	52.8	Gregory-Portland ISD	Portland
36	52.8	Needville ISD	Needville
36	52.8	Wimberley ISD	Wimberley
39	52.7	Bellville ISD	Bellville
39	52.7	Bullard ISD	Bullard
39	52.7	Little Cypress-Mauricevil	Orange
39	52.7	Pecos-Barstow-Toyah ISD	Pecos
39	52.7	Quinlan ISD	Quinlan
39	52.7	Whitehouse ISD	Whitehouse
45	52.6	Aledo ISD	Aledo
45	52.6	Comal ISD	New Braunfels
45	52.6	La Marque ISD	La Marque
45	52.6	Lamesa ISD	Lamesa
45	52.6	Raymondville ISD	Raymondville
45	52.6	Zapata County ISD	Zapata
51	52.5	Boerne ISD	Boerne
51	52.5	Carthage ISD	Carthage
51	52.5	Kaufman ISD	Kaufman
51	52.5	Lake Travis ISD	Austin
51	52.5	Livingston ISD	Livingston
51	52.5	San Benito CISD	San Benito
51	52.5	Santa Fe ISD	Santa Fe
58	52.4	Alice ISD	Alice
58	52.4	Barbers Hill ISD	Mont Belvieu
58	52.4	Caldwell ISD	Caldwell
58	52.4	Crowley ISD	Crowley
58	52.4	El Campo ISD	El Campo
58	52.4	Fredericksburg ISD	Fredericksburg

Note: This section only includes districts with 1,500 or more students; All categories are ranked from high to low

Rank	Score	District	City
58	52.4	Llano ISD	Llano
58	52.4	Mineral Wells ISD	Mineral Wells
58	52.4	Palacios ISD	Palacios
58	52.4	Pittsburg ISD	Pittsburg
58	52.4	White Settlement ISD	White Settlement
69	52.3	Chapel Hill ISD	Tyler
69	52.3	Coldspring-Oakhurst CISD	Coldspring
69	52.3	Cuero ISD	Cuero
69	52.3	Georgetown ISD	Georgetown
69	52.3	Greenville ISD	Greenville
69	52.3	Lyford CISD	Lyford
69	52.3	Montgomery ISD	Montgomery
69	52.3	Waller ISD	Waller
77	52.2	Gainesville ISD	Gainesville
77	52.2	Hondo ISD	Hondo
77	52.2	La Porte ISD	La Porte
77	52.2	Little Elm ISD	Little Elm
77	52.2	Medina Valley ISD	Castroville
77	52.2	Midlothian ISD	Midlothian
77	52.2	Perryton ISD	Perryton
77	52.2	Tatum ISD	Tatum
77	52.2	Vidor ISD	Vidor
86	52.1	Bandera ISD	Bandera
86	52.1	Bastrop ISD	Bastrop
86	52.1	Belton ISD	Belton
86	52.1	Burleson ISD	Burleson
86	52.1	Channelview ISD	Channelview
86	52.1	Coppell ISD	Coppell
86	52.1	Corsicana ISD	Corsicana
86	52.1	Floresville ISD	Floresville
86	52.1	Hempstead ISD	Hempstead
86	52.1	Henderson ISD	Henderson
86	52.1	Ingleside ISD	Ingleside
86	52.1	Pflugerville ISD	Pflugerville
86	52.1	Somerset ISD	Somerset
99	52.0	Alief ISD	Houston
99	52.0	Andrews ISD	Andrews
99	52.0	Athens ISD	Athens
99	52.0	Bridgeport ISD	Bridgeport
99	52.0	Commerce ISD	Commerce
99	52.0	Ennis ISD	Ennis
99	52.0	Madisonville CISD	Madisonville
99	52.0	Pearland ISD	Pearland
99	52.0	Robinson ISD	Robinson
99	52.0	Silsbee ISD	Silsbee
99	52.0	Tarkington ISD	Cleveland
110	51.9	Bonham ISD	Bonham
110	51.9	Canton ISD	Canton
110	51.9	Cedar Hill ISD	Cedar Hill
110	51.9	Dickinson ISD	Dickinson
110	51.9	Greenwood ISD	Midland
110	51.9	Hillsboro ISD	Hillsboro
110	51.9	Jacksonville ISD	Jacksonville
110	51.9	Lake Worth ISD	Lake Worth
110	51.9	Mabank ISD	Mabank
110	51.9	Port Arthur ISD	Port Arthur
110	51.9	Sharyland ISD	Mission
110	51.9	Yoakum ISD	Yoakum
122	51.8	Alvin ISD	Alvin
122	51.8	Bay City ISD	Bay City
122	51.8	Brownsboro ISD	Brownsboro
122	51.8	Forney ISD	Forney
122	51.8	Giddings ISD	Giddings
122	51.8	Granbury ISD	Granbury
122	51.8	Hays CISD	Kyle
122	51.8	Huntington ISD	Huntington
122	51.8	La Feria Ind SD	La Feria
122	51.8	Lytle ISD	Lytle
122	51.8	Mission CISD	Mission
122	51.8	Pilot Point ISD	Pilot Point
122	51.8	Prosper ISD	Prosper
122	51.8	San Marcos CISD	San Marcos
122	51.8	Sanger ISD	Sanger
122	51.8	Sealy ISD	Sealy
122	51.8	Texas City ISD	Texas City
122	51.8	Waxahachie ISD	Waxahachie
140	51.7	Beeville ISD	Beeville
140	51.7	Breckenridge ISD	Breckenridge
140	51.7	Calhoun County ISD	Port Lavaca
140	51.7	Celina ISD	Celina
140	51.7	Eanes ISD	Austin
140	51.7	Goose Creek CISD	Baytown
140	51.7	Groesbeck ISD	Groesbeck
140	51.7	Jasper ISD	Jasper
140	51.7	Lamar CISD	Rosenberg
140	51.7	Leander ISD	Leander
140	51.7	Lewisville ISD	Flower Mound
140	51.7	Lovejoy ISD	Allen
140	51.7	Magnolia ISD	Magnolia
140	51.7	Mckinney ISD	Mckinney
140	51.7	Mineola ISD	Mineola
140	51.7	Richardson ISD	Richardson
140	51.7	San Felipe-Del Rio CISD	Del Rio
140	51.7	Vernon ISD	Vernon
158	51.6	Birdville ISD	Haltom City
158	51.6	Clear Creek ISD	League City
158	51.6	Dayton ISD	Dayton
158	51.6	Harlingen CISD	Harlingen
158	51.6	Huffman ISD	Huffman
158	51.6	Lancaster ISD	Lancaster
158	51.6	North Lamar ISD	Paris
158	51.6	Rockwall ISD	Rockwall
158	51.6	South San Antonio ISD	San Antonio
158	51.6	Southside ISD	San Antonio
158	51.6	Spring Hill ISD	Longview
158	51.6	Wylie ISD	Abilene
170	51.5	Allen ISD	Allen
170	51.5	Aransas Pass ISD	Aransas Pass
170	51.5	Austin ISD	Austin
170	51.5	Burkburnett ISD	Burkburnett
170	51.5	Carroll ISD	Grapevine
170	51.5	Carrollton-Farmers Branch	Carrollton
170	51.5	Castleberry ISD	Fort Worth
170	51.5	Cypress-Fairbanks ISD	Houston
170	51.5	Denison ISD	Denison
170	51.5	Desoto ISD	Desoto
170	51.5	Dripping Spgs ISD	Dripping Spgs
170	51.5	Garland ISD	Garland
170	51.5	Gladewater ISD	Gladewater
170	51.5	Hidalgo ISD	Hidalgo
170	51.5	Hurst-Euless-Bedford ISD	Bedford
170	51.5	Katy ISD	Katy
170	51.5	Klein ISD	Klein
170	51.5	Mansfield ISD	Mansfield
170	51.5	Mount Pleasant ISD	Mount Pleasant
170	51.5	Northside ISD	San Antonio
170	51.5	Northwest ISD	Justin
170	51.5	Orangefield ISD	Orangefield
170	51.5	Pasadena ISD	Pasadena
170	51.5	Port Neches-Groves ISD	Port Neches
170	51.5	Round Rock ISD	Round Rock
170	51.5	Sherman ISD	Sherman
170	51.5	Spring ISD	Houston
170	51.5	Van ISD	Van
170	51.5	Weatherford ISD	Weatherford
170	51.5	Wharton ISD	Wharton
170	51.5	Ysleta ISD	El Paso
201	51.4	Calallen ISD	Corpus Christi
201	51.4	Canyon ISD	Canyon
201	51.4	Cleveland ISD	Cleveland
201	51.4	Eagle Pass ISD	Eagle Pass
201	51.4	Edcouch-Elsa ISD	Edcouch
201	51.4	Flour Bluff ISD	Corpus Christi
201	51.4	Fort Bend ISD	Sugar Land
201	51.4	Fort Stockton ISD	Fort Stockton
201	51.4	La Vega ISD	Waco
201	51.4	Liberty Hill ISD	Liberty Hill
201	51.4	North East ISD	San Antonio
201	51.4	Princeton ISD	Princeton
201	51.4	San Angelo ISD	San Angelo
201	51.4	Spring Branch ISD	Houston
201	51.4	Sulphur Springs ISD	Sulphur Springs
201	51.4	Terrell ISD	Terrell
201	51.4	United ISD	Laredo
201	51.4	Valley View ISD	Pharr
201	51.4	Westwood ISD	Palestine
201	51.4	Wylie ISD	Wylie
221	51.3	Aldine ISD	Houston
221	51.3	Angleton ISD	Angleton
221	51.3	Azle ISD	Azle
221	51.3	Brazosport ISD	Clute
221	51.3	Community ISD	Nevada
221	51.3	Conroe ISD	Conroe
221	51.3	Corpus Christi ISD	Corpus Christi
221	51.3	Everman ISD	Everman
221	51.3	Galena Park ISD	Houston
221	51.3	Highland Park ISD	Dallas
221	51.3	Irving ISD	Irving
221	51.3	Judson ISD	Live Oak
221	51.3	Marshall ISD	Marshall
221	51.3	Plano ISD	Plano
221	51.3	Southwest ISD	San Antonio
221	51.3	Tyler ISD	Tyler
221	51.3	Waco ISD	Waco
238	51.2	College Station ISD	College Station
238	51.2	Columbia-Brazoria ISD	West Columbia
238	51.2	Crandall ISD	Crandall
238	51.2	Devine ISD	Devine
238	51.2	Donna ISD	Donna
238	51.2	El Paso ISD	El Paso
238	51.2	Friendswood ISD	Friendswood
238	51.2	Harlandale ISD	San Antonio
238	51.2	Humble ISD	Humble
238	51.2	Iowa Park CISD	Iowa Park
238	51.2	Keller ISD	Keller
238	51.2	La Joya ISD	La Joya
238	51.2	Mcallen ISD	Mcallen
238	51.2	Navasota ISD	Navasota
238	51.2	New Braunfels ISD	New Braunfels
238	51.2	Sinton ISD	Sinton
238	51.2	Southwest School	Houston
238	51.2	Springtown ISD	Springtown
238	51.2	Uvalde CISD	Uvalde
238	51.2	Weslaco ISD	Weslaco
258	51.1	Anna ISD	Anna
258	51.1	Bridge City ISD	Bridge City
258	51.1	Brownsville ISD	Brownsville
258	51.1	Brownwood ISD	Brownwood
258	51.1	Dalhart ISD	Dalhart
258	51.1	Galveston ISD	Galveston
258	51.1	Grand Prairie ISD	Grand Prairie
258	51.1	Hamshire-Fannett ISD	Hamshire
258	51.1	Houston ISD	Houston
258	51.1	Hutto ISD	Hutto
258	51.1	Kingsville ISD	Kingsville
258	51.1	La Vernia ISD	La Vernia
258	51.1	Mercedes ISD	Mercedes
258	51.1	North Forest ISD	Houston
258	51.1	Pharr-San Juan-Alamo ISD	Pharr
258	51.1	Plainview ISD	Plainview
258	51.1	Progreso ISD	Progreso
258	51.1	Royal ISD	Pattison
258	51.1	Schertz-Cibolo-U City ISD	Schertz
258	51.1	Shepherd ISD	Shepherd
258	51.1	Socorro ISD	El Paso
258	51.1	Sweetwater ISD	Sweetwater
258	51.1	Victoria ISD	Victoria
258	51.1	Willis ISD	Willis
282	51.0	Arlington ISD	Arlington
282	51.0	Burnet CISD	Burnet
282	51.0	Central ISD	Pollok
282	51.0	Connally ISD	Waco
282	51.0	Copperas Cove ISD	Copperas Cove
282	51.0	Crosby ISD	Crosby
282	51.0	Denton ISD	Denton
282	51.0	Ector County ISD	Odessa
282	51.0	Fairfield ISD	Fairfield
282	51.0	Fort Worth ISD	Fort Worth
282	51.0	Lampasas ISD	Lampasas
282	51.0	Lockhart ISD	Lockhart
282	51.0	Longview ISD	Longview
282	51.0	Lumberton ISD	Lumberton
282	51.0	Mesquite ISD	Mesquite
282	51.0	New Caney ISD	New Caney
282	51.0	San Elizario ISD	San Elizario
282	51.0	Seguin ISD	Seguin
282	51.0	Venus ISD	Venus
301	50.9	Amarillo ISD	Amarillo
301	50.9	Big Spring ISD	Big Spring
301	50.9	Bryan ISD	Bryan
301	50.9	Dallas ISD	Dallas
301	50.9	Edinburg CISD	Edinburg
301	50.9	Elgin ISD	Elgin
301	50.9	Gatesville ISD	Gatesville
301	50.9	Hereford ISD	Hereford
301	50.9	Killeen ISD	Killeen
301	50.9	Laredo ISD	Laredo
301	50.9	Los Fresnos CISD	Los Fresnos
301	50.9	Mount Vernon ISD	Mount Vernon
301	50.9	San Antonio ISD	San Antonio
301	50.9	Splendora ISD	Splendora
301	50.9	Wills Point ISD	Wills Point
316	50.8	Abilene ISD	Abilene
316	50.8	Del Valle ISD	Del Valle
316	50.8	Eagle Mt-Saginaw ISD	Fort Worth
316	50.8	Frenship ISD	Wolfforth
316	50.8	Frisco ISD	Frisco
316	50.8	Lake Dallas ISD	Lake Dallas

Note: This section only includes districts with 1,500 or more students; All categories are ranked from high to low

Female Students

Rank	Percent	District Name	City
316	50.8	Liberty ISD	Liberty
316	50.8	Lubbock ISD	Lubbock
316	50.8	Midland ISD	Midland
316	50.8	Paris ISD	Paris
316	50.8	Point Isabel ISD	Port Isabel
316	50.8	Taylor ISD	Taylor
316	50.8	Tomball ISD	Tomball
316	50.8	Wichita Falls ISD	Wichita Falls
330	50.7	Canutillo ISD	El Paso
330	50.7	Carrizo Springs CISD	Carrizo Springs
330	50.7	Cleburne ISD	Cleburne
330	50.7	Clint ISD	El Paso
330	50.7	Decatur ISD	Decatur
330	50.7	Duncanville ISD	Duncanville
330	50.7	Edgewood ISD	San Antonio
330	50.7	Harmony Science Acad (Fort Worth)	Fort Worth
330	50.7	Hudson ISD	Lufkin
330	50.7	Huntsville ISD	Huntsville
330	50.7	Manor ISD	Manor
330	50.7	Orange Grove ISD	Orange Grove
330	50.7	Pearsall ISD	Pearsall
330	50.7	Varnett Charter School	Houston
344	50.6	China Spring ISD	Waco
344	50.6	Grapevine-Colleyville ISD	Grapevine
344	50.6	La Grange ISD	La Grange
344	50.6	Lindale ISD	Lindale
344	50.6	Nacogdoches ISD	Nacogdoches
344	50.6	Red Oak ISD	Red Oak
344	50.6	Sheldon ISD	Houston
344	50.6	Snyder ISD	Snyder
352	50.5	Alamo Heights ISD	San Antonio
352	50.5	Brownfield ISD	Brownfield
352	50.5	Dallas Can Academy Charter	Dallas
352	50.5	Fabens ISD	Fabens
352	50.5	Glen Rose ISD	Glen Rose
352	50.5	Nederland ISD	Nederland
352	50.5	Rio Grande City CISD	Rio Grande City
352	50.5	Rockdale ISD	Rockdale
360	50.4	Advantage Academy	Dallas
360	50.4	Beaumont ISD	Beaumont
360	50.4	Center ISD	Center
360	50.4	Deer Park ISD	Deer Park
360	50.4	Ferris ISD	Ferris
360	50.4	Gonzales ISD	Gonzales
360	50.4	Kipp Inc Charter	Houston
360	50.4	Lufkin ISD	Lufkin
360	50.4	Pleasanton ISD	Pleasanton
369	50.3	Aubrey ISD	Aubrey
369	50.3	Levelland ISD	Levelland
369	50.3	Midway ISD	Hewitt
369	50.3	Seminole ISD	Seminole
369	50.3	Texarkana ISD	Texarkana
374	50.2	Kilgore ISD	Kilgore
374	50.2	Marble Falls ISD	Marble Falls
374	50.2	Pine Tree ISD	Longview
374	50.2	Temple ISD	Temple
378	50.1	Roma ISD	Roma
378	50.1	Tuloso-Midway ISD	Corpus Christi
378	50.1	Winfree Academy	Irving
381	50.0	Graham ISD	Graham
381	50.0	Joshua ISD	Joshua
381	50.0	Kennedale ISD	Kennedale
381	50.0	Mathis ISD	Mathis
385	49.9	Krum ISD	Krum
385	49.9	Pampa ISD	Pampa
387	49.8	Rusk ISD	Rusk
388	49.7	Denver City ISD	Denver City
388	49.7	River Road ISD	Amarillo
390	49.6	Whitney ISD	Whitney
391	49.4	Liberty-Eylau ISD	Texarkana
392	49.3	Bowie ISD	Bowie
392	49.3	Stephenville	Stephenville
394	49.2	Poteet ISD	Poteet
395	49.1	Borger ISD	Borger
396	48.6	Monahans-Wickett-Pyote ISD	Monahans
397	48.3	Eagle Academy of Abilene	Lewisville
397	48.3	Idea Academy	Weslaco
399	47.8	Harmony Science Academy	Houston
400	47.2	Crystal City ISD	Crystal City
400	47.2	South Texas ISD	Mercedes
402	46.5	Yes College Preparatory School	Houston
403	45.8	Life School	Lancaster
1	54.2	Life School	Lancaster
2	53.5	Yes College Preparatory School	Houston
3	52.8	Crystal City ISD	Crystal City
3	52.8	South Texas ISD	Mercedes
5	52.2	Harmony Science Academy	Houston
6	51.7	Eagle Academy of Abilene	Lewisville
6	51.7	Idea Academy	Weslaco
8	51.4	Monahans-Wickett-Pyote ISD	Monahans
9	50.9	Borger ISD	Borger
10	50.8	Poteet ISD	Poteet
11	50.7	Bowie ISD	Bowie
11	50.7	Stephenville	Stephenville
13	50.6	Liberty-Eylau ISD	Texarkana
14	50.4	Whitney ISD	Whitney
15	50.3	Denver City ISD	Denver City
15	50.3	River Road ISD	Amarillo
17	50.2	Rusk ISD	Rusk
18	50.1	Krum ISD	Krum
18	50.1	Pampa ISD	Pampa
20	50.0	Graham ISD	Graham
20	50.0	Joshua ISD	Joshua
20	50.0	Kennedale ISD	Kennedale
20	50.0	Mathis ISD	Mathis
24	49.9	Roma ISD	Roma
24	49.9	Tuloso-Midway ISD	Corpus Christi
24	49.8	Winfree Academy	Irving
27	49.8	Kilgore ISD	Kilgore
27	49.8	Marble Falls ISD	Marble Falls
27	49.8	Pine Tree ISD	Longview
27	49.8	Temple ISD	Temple
31	49.7	Aubrey ISD	Aubrey
31	49.7	Levelland ISD	Levelland
31	49.7	Midway ISD	Hewitt
31	49.7	Seminole ISD	Seminole
31	49.7	Texarkana ISD	Texarkana
36	49.6	Advantage Academy	Dallas
36	49.6	Beaumont ISD	Beaumont
36	49.6	Center ISD	Center
36	49.6	Deer Park ISD	Deer Park
36	49.6	Ferris ISD	Ferris
36	49.6	Gonzales ISD	Gonzales
36	49.6	Kipp Inc Charter	Houston
36	49.6	Lufkin ISD	Lufkin
36	49.6	Pleasanton ISD	Pleasanton
45	49.5	Alamo Heights ISD	San Antonio
45	49.5	Brownfield ISD	Brownfield
45	49.5	Dallas Can Academy Charter	Dallas
45	49.5	Fabens ISD	Fabens
45	49.5	Glen Rose ISD	Glen Rose
45	49.5	Nederland ISD	Nederland
45	49.5	Rio Grande City CISD	Rio Grande City
45	49.5	Rockdale ISD	Rockdale
53	49.4	China Spring ISD	Waco
53	49.4	Grapevine-Colleyville ISD	Grapevine
53	49.4	La Grange ISD	La Grange
53	49.4	Lindale ISD	Lindale
53	49.4	Nacogdoches ISD	Nacogdoches
53	49.4	Red Oak ISD	Red Oak
53	49.4	Sheldon ISD	Houston
53	49.4	Snyder ISD	Snyder
61	49.3	Canutillo ISD	El Paso
61	49.3	Carrizo Springs CISD	Carrizo Springs
61	49.3	Cleburne ISD	Cleburne
61	49.3	Clint ISD	El Paso
61	49.3	Decatur ISD	Decatur
61	49.3	Duncanville ISD	Duncanville
61	49.3	Edgewood ISD	San Antonio
61	49.3	Harmony Science Acad (Fort Worth)	Fort Worth
61	49.3	Hudson ISD	Lufkin
61	49.3	Huntsville ISD	Huntsville
61	49.3	Manor ISD	Manor
61	49.3	Orange Grove ISD	Orange Grove
61	49.3	Pearsall ISD	Pearsall
61	49.3	Varnett Charter School	Houston
75	49.2	Abilene ISD	Abilene
75	49.2	Del Valle ISD	Del Valle
75	49.2	Eagle Mt-Saginaw ISD	Fort Worth
75	49.2	Frenship ISD	Wolfforth
75	49.2	Frisco ISD	Frisco
75	49.2	Lake Dallas ISD	Lake Dallas
75	49.2	Liberty ISD	Liberty
75	49.2	Lubbock ISD	Lubbock
75	49.2	Midland ISD	Midland
75	49.2	Paris ISD	Paris
75	49.2	Point Isabel ISD	Port Isabel
75	49.2	Taylor ISD	Taylor
75	49.2	Tomball ISD	Tomball
75	49.2	Wichita Falls ISD	Wichita Falls
89	49.1	Amarillo ISD	Amarillo
89	49.1	Big Spring ISD	Big Spring
89	49.1	Bryan ISD	Bryan
89	49.1	Dallas ISD	Dallas
89	49.1	Edinburg CISD	Edinburg
89	49.1	Elgin ISD	Elgin
89	49.1	Gatesville ISD	Gatesville
89	49.1	Hereford ISD	Hereford
89	49.1	Killeen ISD	Killeen
89	49.1	Laredo ISD	Laredo
89	49.1	Los Fresnos CISD	Los Fresnos
89	49.1	Mount Vernon ISD	Mount Vernon
89	49.1	San Antonio ISD	San Antonio
89	49.1	Splendora ISD	Splendora
89	49.1	Wills Point ISD	Wills Point
104	49.0	Arlington ISD	Arlington
104	49.0	Burnet CISD	Burnet
104	49.0	Central ISD	Pollok
104	49.0	Connally ISD	Waco
104	49.0	Copperas Cove ISD	Copperas Cove
104	49.0	Crosby ISD	Crosby
104	49.0	Denton ISD	Denton
104	49.0	Ector County ISD	Odessa
104	49.0	Fairfield ISD	Fairfield
104	49.0	Fort Worth ISD	Fort Worth
104	49.0	Lampasas ISD	Lampasas
104	49.0	Lockhart ISD	Lockhart
104	49.0	Longview ISD	Longview
104	49.0	Lumberton ISD	Lumberton
104	49.0	Mesquite ISD	Mesquite
104	49.0	New Caney ISD	New Caney
104	49.0	San Elizario ISD	San Elizario
104	49.0	Seguin ISD	Seguin
104	49.0	Venus ISD	Venus
123	48.9	Anna ISD	Anna
123	48.9	Bridge City ISD	Bridge City
123	48.9	Brownsville ISD	Brownsville
123	48.9	Brownwood ISD	Brownwood
123	48.9	Dalhart ISD	Dalhart
123	48.9	Galveston ISD	Galveston
123	48.9	Grand Prairie ISD	Grand Prairie
123	48.9	Hamshire-Fannett ISD	Hamshire
123	48.9	Houston ISD	Houston
123	48.9	Hutto ISD	Hutto
123	48.9	Kingsville ISD	Kingsville
123	48.9	La Vernia ISD	La Vernia
123	48.9	Mercedes ISD	Mercedes
123	48.9	North Forest ISD	Houston
123	48.9	Pharr-San Juan-Alamo ISD	Pharr
123	48.9	Plainview ISD	Plainview
123	48.9	Progreso ISD	Progreso
123	48.9	Royal ISD	Pattison
123	48.9	Schertz-Cibolo-U City ISD	Schertz
123	48.9	Shepherd ISD	Shepherd
123	48.9	Socorro ISD	El Paso
123	48.9	Sweetwater ISD	Sweetwater
123	48.9	Victoria ISD	Victoria
123	48.9	Willis ISD	Willis
147	48.8	College Station ISD	College Station
147	48.8	Columbia-Brazoria ISD	West Columbia
147	48.8	Crandall ISD	Crandall
147	48.8	Devine ISD	Devine
147	48.8	Donna ISD	Donna
147	48.8	El Paso ISD	El Paso
147	48.8	Friendswood ISD	Friendswood
147	48.8	Harlandale ISD	San Antonio
147	48.8	Humble ISD	Humble
147	48.8	Iowa Park CISD	Iowa Park
147	48.8	Keller ISD	Keller
147	48.8	La Joya ISD	La Joya
147	48.8	Mcallen ISD	Mcallen
147	48.8	Navasota ISD	Navasota
147	48.8	New Braunfels ISD	New Braunfels
147	48.8	Sinton ISD	Sinton
147	48.8	Southwest School	Houston
147	48.8	Springtown ISD	Springtown
147	48.8	Uvalde CISD	Uvalde
147	48.8	Weslaco ISD	Weslaco
167	48.7	Aldine ISD	Houston
167	48.7	Angleton ISD	Angleton
167	48.7	Azle ISD	Azle

Note: This section only includes districts with 1,500 or more students; All categories are ranked from high to low

Rank	Percent	District Name	City
167	48.7	Brazosport ISD	Clute
167	48.7	Community ISD	Nevada
167	48.7	Conroe ISD	Conroe
167	48.7	Corpus Christi ISD	Corpus Christi
167	48.7	Everman ISD	Everman
167	48.7	Galena Park ISD	Houston
167	48.7	Highland Park ISD	Dallas
167	48.7	Irving ISD	Irving
167	48.7	Judson ISD	Live Oak
167	48.7	Marshall ISD	Marshall
167	48.7	Plano ISD	Plano
167	48.7	Southwest ISD	San Antonio
167	48.7	Tyler ISD	Tyler
167	48.7	Waco ISD	Waco
184	48.6	Calallen ISD	Corpus Christi
184	48.6	Canyon ISD	Canyon
184	48.6	Cleveland ISD	Cleveland
184	48.6	Eagle Pass ISD	Eagle Pass
184	48.6	Edcouch-Elsa ISD	Edcouch
184	48.6	Flour Bluff ISD	Corpus Christi
184	48.6	Fort Bend ISD	Sugar Land
184	48.6	Fort Stockton ISD	Fort Stockton
184	48.6	La Vega ISD	Waco
184	48.6	Liberty Hill ISD	Liberty Hill
184	48.6	North East ISD	San Antonio
184	48.6	Princeton ISD	Princeton
184	48.6	San Angelo ISD	San Angelo
184	48.6	Spring Branch ISD	Houston
184	48.6	Sulphur Springs ISD	Sulphur Springs
184	48.6	Terrell ISD	Terrell
184	48.6	United ISD	Laredo
184	48.6	Valley View ISD	Pharr
184	48.6	Westwood ISD	Palestine
184	48.6	Wylie ISD	Wylie
204	48.5	Allen ISD	Allen
204	48.5	Aransas Pass ISD	Aransas Pass
204	48.5	Austin ISD	Austin
204	48.5	Burkburnett ISD	Burkburnett
204	48.5	Carroll ISD	Grapevine
204	48.5	Carrollton-Farmers Branch	Carrollton
204	48.5	Castleberry ISD	Fort Worth
204	48.5	Cypress-Fairbanks ISD	Houston
204	48.5	Denison ISD	Denison
204	48.5	Desoto ISD	Desoto
204	48.5	Dripping Spgs ISD	Dripping Spgs
204	48.5	Garland ISD	Garland
204	48.5	Gladewater ISD	Gladewater
204	48.5	Hidalgo ISD	Hidalgo
204	48.5	Hurst-Euless-Bedford ISD	Bedford
204	48.5	Katy ISD	Katy
204	48.5	Klein ISD	Klein
204	48.5	Mansfield ISD	Mansfield
204	48.5	Mount Pleasant ISD	Mount Pleasant
204	48.5	Northside ISD	San Antonio
204	48.5	Northwest ISD	Justin
204	48.5	Orangefield ISD	Orangefield
204	48.5	Pasadena ISD	Pasadena
204	48.5	Port Neches-Groves ISD	Port Neches
204	48.5	Round Rock ISD	Round Rock
204	48.5	Sherman ISD	Sherman
204	48.5	Spring ISD	Houston
204	48.5	Van ISD	Van
204	48.5	Weatherford ISD	Weatherford
204	48.5	Wharton ISD	Wharton
204	48.5	Ysleta ISD	El Paso
235	48.4	Birdville ISD	Haltom City
235	48.4	Clear Creek ISD	League City
235	48.4	Dayton ISD	Dayton
235	48.4	Harlingen CISD	Harlingen
235	48.4	Huffman ISD	Huffman
235	48.4	Lancaster ISD	Lancaster
235	48.4	North Lamar ISD	Paris
235	48.4	Rockwall ISD	Rockwall
235	48.4	South San Antonio ISD	San Antonio
235	48.4	Southside ISD	San Antonio
235	48.4	Spring Hill ISD	Longview
235	48.4	Wylie ISD	Abilene
247	48.3	Beeville ISD	Beeville
247	48.3	Breckenridge ISD	Breckenridge
247	48.3	Calhoun County ISD	Port Lavaca
247	48.3	Celina ISD	Celina
247	48.3	Eanes ISD	Austin
247	48.3	Goose Creek CISD	Baytown
247	48.3	Groesbeck ISD	Groesbeck
247	48.3	Jasper ISD	Jasper
247	48.3	Lamar CISD	Rosenberg

Rank	Percent	District Name	City
247	48.3	Leander ISD	Leander
247	48.3	Lewisville ISD	Flower Mound
247	48.3	Lovejoy ISD	Allen
247	48.3	Magnolia ISD	Magnolia
247	48.3	Mckinney ISD	Mckinney
247	48.3	Mineola ISD	Mineola
247	48.3	Richardson ISD	Richardson
247	48.3	San Felipe-Del Rio CISD	Del Rio
247	48.3	Vernon ISD	Vernon
265	48.2	Alvin ISD	Alvin
265	48.2	Bay City ISD	Bay City
265	48.2	Brownsboro ISD	Brownsboro
265	48.2	Forney ISD	Forney
265	48.2	Giddings ISD	Giddings
265	48.2	Granbury ISD	Granbury
265	48.2	Hays CISD	Kyle
265	48.2	Huntington ISD	Huntington
265	48.2	La Feria Ind SD	La Feria
265	48.2	Lytle ISD	Lytle
265	48.2	Mission CISD	Mission
265	48.2	Pilot Point ISD	Pilot Point
265	48.2	Prosper ISD	Prosper
265	48.2	San Marcos CISD	San Marcos
265	48.2	Sanger ISD	Sanger
265	48.2	Sealy ISD	Sealy
265	48.2	Texas City ISD	Texas City
265	48.2	Waxahachie ISD	Waxahachie
283	48.1	Bonham ISD	Bonham
283	48.1	Canton ISD	Canton
283	48.1	Cedar Hill ISD	Cedar Hill
283	48.1	Dickinson ISD	Dickinson
283	48.1	Greenwood ISD	Midland
283	48.1	Hillsboro ISD	Hillsboro
283	48.1	Jacksonville ISD	Jacksonville
283	48.1	Lake Worth ISD	Lake Worth
283	48.1	Mabank ISD	Mabank
283	48.1	Port Arthur ISD	Port Arthur
283	48.1	Sharyland ISD	Mission
283	48.1	Yoakum ISD	Yoakum
295	48.0	Alief ISD	Houston
295	48.0	Andrews ISD	Andrews
295	48.0	Athens ISD	Athens
295	48.0	Bridgeport ISD	Bridgeport
295	48.0	Commerce ISD	Commerce
295	48.0	Ennis ISD	Ennis
295	48.0	Madisonville CISD	Madisonville
295	48.0	Pearland ISD	Pearland
295	48.0	Robinson ISD	Robinson
295	48.0	Silsbee ISD	Silsbee
295	48.0	Tarkington ISD	Cleveland
306	47.9	Bandera ISD	Bandera
306	47.9	Bastrop ISD	Bastrop
306	47.9	Belton ISD	Belton
306	47.9	Burleson ISD	Burleson
306	47.9	Channelview ISD	Channelview
306	47.9	Coppell ISD	Coppell
306	47.9	Corsicana ISD	Corsicana
306	47.9	Floresville ISD	Floresville
306	47.9	Hempstead ISD	Hempstead
306	47.9	Henderson ISD	Henderson
306	47.9	Ingleside ISD	Ingleside
306	47.9	Pflugerville ISD	Pflugerville
306	47.9	Somerset ISD	Somerset
319	47.8	Gainesville ISD	Gainesville
319	47.8	Hondo ISD	Hondo
319	47.8	La Porte ISD	La Porte
319	47.8	Little Elm ISD	Little Elm
319	47.8	Medina Valley ISD	Castroville
319	47.8	Midlothian ISD	Midlothian
319	47.8	Perryton ISD	Perryton
319	47.8	Tatum ISD	Tatum
319	47.8	Vidor ISD	Vidor
328	47.7	Chapel Hill ISD	Tyler
328	47.7	Coldspring-Oakhurst CISD	Coldspring
328	47.7	Cuero ISD	Cuero
328	47.7	Georgetown ISD	Georgetown
328	47.7	Greenville ISD	Greenville
328	47.7	Lyford CISD	Lyford
328	47.7	Montgomery ISD	Montgomery
328	47.7	Waller ISD	Waller
336	47.6	Alice ISD	Alice
336	47.6	Barbers Hill ISD	Mont Belvieu
336	47.6	Caldwell ISD	Caldwell
336	47.6	Crowley ISD	Crowley
336	47.6	El Campo ISD	El Campo
336	47.6	Fredericksburg ISD	Fredericksburg

Rank	Percent	District Name	City
336	47.6	Llano ISD	Llano
336	47.6	Mineral Wells ISD	Mineral Wells
336	47.6	Palacios ISD	Palacios
336	47.6	Pittsburg ISD	Pittsburg
336	47.6	White Settlement ISD	White Settlement
347	47.5	Boerne ISD	Boerne
347	47.5	Carthage ISD	Carthage
347	47.5	Kaufman ISD	Kaufman
347	47.5	Lake Travis ISD	Austin
347	47.5	Livingston ISD	Livingston
347	47.5	San Benito CISD	San Benito
347	47.5	Santa Fe ISD	Santa Fe
354	47.4	Aledo ISD	Aledo
354	47.4	Comal ISD	New Braunfels
354	47.4	La Marque ISD	La Marque
354	47.4	Lamesa ISD	Lamesa
354	47.4	Raymondville ISD	Raymondville
354	47.4	Zapata County ISD	Zapata
360	47.3	Bellville ISD	Bellville
360	47.3	Bullard ISD	Bullard
360	47.3	Little Cypress-Mauricevil	Orange
360	47.3	Pecos-Barstow-Toyah ISD	Pecos
360	47.3	Quinlan ISD	Quinlan
360	47.3	Whitehouse ISD	Whitehouse
366	47.2	Gregory-Portland ISD	Portland
366	47.2	Needville ISD	Needville
366	47.2	Wimberley ISD	Wimberley
369	47.1	Columbus ISD	Columbus
369	47.1	Diboll ISD	Diboll
369	47.1	Godley ISD	Godley
369	47.1	Hallsville ISD	Hallsville
369	47.1	Kerrville ISD	Kerrville
369	47.1	Palestine ISD	Palestine
375	47.0	East Central ISD	San Antonio
375	47.0	Lubbock-Cooper ISD	Lubbock
375	47.0	Rio Hondo ISD	Rio Hondo
375	47.0	Robstown ISD	Robstown
375	47.0	Royse City ISD	Royse City
380	46.9	Brenham ISD	Brenham
380	46.9	Cameron ISD	Cameron
380	46.9	School of Excellence in Education	San Antonio
383	46.8	Mexia ISD	Mexia
384	46.7	Gilmer ISD	Gilmer
384	46.7	Rains ISD	Emory
386	46.6	Alvarado ISD	Alvarado
386	46.6	Aransas County ISD	Rockport
386	46.6	Dumas ISD	Dumas
386	46.6	Pleasant Grove ISD	Texarkana
386	46.6	Stafford MSD	Stafford
386	46.6	West Oso ISD	Corpus Christi
392	46.4	Atlanta ISD	Atlanta
393	46.3	Navarro ISD	Seguin
393	46.3	Smithville ISD	Smithville
395	46.2	Lorena ISD	Lorena
396	46.0	Sweeny ISD	Sweeny
397	45.9	Ripley House Charter School	Houston
397	45.9	West Orange-Cove CISD	Orange
399	45.8	Whitesboro ISD	Whitesboro
400	45.6	Hardin-Jefferson ISD	Sour Lake
401	45.5	Argyle ISD	Argyle
402	45.2	Kemp ISD	Kemp
402	45.2	West ISD	West

Individual Education Program Students

Rank	Percent	District Name	City
1	16.6	Denison ISD	Denison
2	15.9	Vidor ISD	Vidor
3	15.0	Gladewater ISD	Gladewater
4	14.6	Wichita Falls ISD	Wichita Falls
5	14.5	Sweetwater ISD	Sweetwater
6	14.4	Abilene ISD	Abilene
7	14.3	Princeton ISD	Princeton
8	14.2	Gatesville ISD	Gatesville
9	13.9	Brenham ISD	Brenham
10	13.8	Pittsburg ISD	Pittsburg
11	13.7	Liberty-Eylau ISD	Texarkana
11	13.7	Mexia ISD	Mexia
13	13.6	Dallas Can Academy Charter	Dallas
14	13.4	Fabens ISD	Fabens
15	13.3	West Orange-Cove CISD	Orange
15	13.3	West Oso ISD	Corpus Christi
17	13.1	Atlanta ISD	Atlanta
18	13.0	Godley ISD	Godley
18	13.0	Wills Point ISD	Wills Point

Note: This section only includes districts with 1,500 or more students; All categories are ranked from high to low

Rank	Value	District	City
20	12.9	Nederland ISD	Nederland
20	12.9	North Lamar ISD	Paris
20	12.9	Winfree Academy	Irving
23	12.8	Bandera ISD	Bandera
23	12.8	Commerce ISD	Commerce
23	12.8	Sherman ISD	Sherman
26	12.7	Jasper ISD	Jasper
26	12.7	Levelland ISD	Levelland
26	12.7	Livingston ISD	Livingston
26	12.7	Lufkin ISD	Lufkin
26	12.7	Plainview ISD	Plainview
31	12.5	Little Cypress-Mauricevil	Orange
31	12.5	Rains ISD	Emory
33	12.4	Calhoun County ISD	Port Lavaca
33	12.4	Central ISD	Pollok
33	12.4	Connally ISD	Waco
33	12.4	Mineral Wells ISD	Mineral Wells
37	12.3	Hempstead ISD	Hempstead
37	12.3	Quinlan ISD	Quinlan
39	12.2	Bonham ISD	Bonham
39	12.2	Floresville ISD	Floresville
39	12.2	Mount Pleasant ISD	Mount Pleasant
39	12.2	Northside ISD	San Antonio
39	12.2	Silsbee ISD	Silsbee
39	12.2	Snyder ISD	Snyder
39	12.2	Whitesboro ISD	Whitesboro
46	12.1	Groesbeck ISD	Groesbeck
47	12.0	Bellville ISD	Bellville
47	12.0	Kemp ISD	Kemp
47	12.0	Mesquite ISD	Mesquite
47	12.0	Red Oak ISD	Red Oak
51	11.9	Lubbock ISD	Lubbock
51	11.9	Texarkana ISD	Texarkana
53	11.8	Bastrop ISD	Bastrop
53	11.8	Marble Falls ISD	Marble Falls
55	11.7	Burnet CISD	Burnet
55	11.7	Coldspring-Oakhurst CISD	Coldspring
55	11.7	Monahans-Wickett-Pyote ISD	Monahans
58	11.6	Big Spring ISD	Big Spring
58	11.6	La Vernia ISD	La Vernia
58	11.6	Lockhart ISD	Lockhart
58	11.6	Magnolia ISD	Magnolia
58	11.6	Tuloso-Midway ISD	Corpus Christi
58	11.6	Whitney ISD	Whitney
64	11.5	Yoakum ISD	Yoakum
65	11.4	Allen ISD	Allen
65	11.4	Ferris ISD	Ferris
65	11.4	Robinson ISD	Robinson
68	11.3	Birdville ISD	Haltom City
68	11.3	Gainesville ISD	Gainesville
68	11.3	Richardson ISD	Richardson
71	11.2	Dalhart ISD	Dalhart
71	11.2	Krum ISD	Krum
71	11.2	Rio Grande City CISD	Rio Grande City
71	11.2	Smithville ISD	Smithville
71	11.2	Waxahachie ISD	Waxahachie
76	11.1	Belton ISD	Belton
76	11.1	Corpus Christi ISD	Corpus Christi
76	11.1	Ennis ISD	Ennis
76	11.1	Granbury ISD	Granbury
76	11.1	Lake Dallas ISD	Lake Dallas
76	11.1	Midlothian ISD	Midlothian
76	11.1	Victoria ISD	Victoria
83	11.0	Brazosport ISD	Clute
83	11.0	Columbus ISD	Columbus
83	11.0	Lubbock-Cooper ISD	Lubbock
83	11.0	Rusk ISD	Rusk
83	11.0	San Angelo ISD	San Angelo
88	10.9	Burkburnett ISD	Burkburnett
88	10.9	Graham ISD	Graham
88	10.9	Lampasas ISD	Lampasas
88	10.9	Paris ISD	Paris
88	10.9	Robstown ISD	Robstown
88	10.9	Southwest ISD	San Antonio
94	10.8	Aransas Pass ISD	Aransas Pass
94	10.8	Fairfield ISD	Fairfield
94	10.8	Gilmer ISD	Gilmer
94	10.8	Killeen ISD	Killeen
94	10.8	Mount Vernon ISD	Mount Vernon
99	10.7	Aubrey ISD	Aubrey
99	10.7	Brownsville ISD	Brownsville
99	10.7	Hillsboro ISD	Hillsboro
99	10.7	Plano ISD	Plano
103	10.6	Angleton ISD	Angleton
103	10.6	Argyle ISD	Argyle
103	10.6	Borger ISD	Borger
103	10.6	Desoto ISD	Desoto
103	10.6	Devine ISD	Devine
103	10.6	East Central ISD	San Antonio
103	10.6	Lorena ISD	Lorena
103	10.6	San Antonio ISD	San Antonio
111	10.5	Azle ISD	Azle
111	10.5	Cameron ISD	Cameron
111	10.5	Orangefield ISD	Orangefield
111	10.5	Rockdale ISD	Rockdale
111	10.5	Seguin ISD	Seguin
111	10.5	Taylor ISD	Taylor
117	10.4	Denton ISD	Denton
117	10.4	Longview ISD	Longview
117	10.4	Needville ISD	Needville
117	10.4	Westwood ISD	Palestine
121	10.3	Anna ISD	Anna
121	10.3	Bowie ISD	Bowie
121	10.3	Edgewood ISD	San Antonio
121	10.3	Jacksonville ISD	Jacksonville
121	10.3	Kaufman ISD	Kaufman
121	10.3	Marshall ISD	Marshall
121	10.3	Sanger ISD	Sanger
121	10.3	Sinton ISD	Sinton
121	10.3	Venus ISD	Venus
121	10.3	White Settlement ISD	White Settlement
131	10.2	Deer Park ISD	Deer Park
131	10.2	Duncanville ISD	Duncanville
131	10.2	Goose Creek CISD	Baytown
131	10.2	Hallsville ISD	Hallsville
131	10.2	Lindale ISD	Lindale
131	10.2	North East ISD	San Antonio
137	10.1	Columbia-Brazoria ISD	West Columbia
137	10.1	Del Valle ISD	Del Valle
137	10.1	Flour Bluff ISD	Corpus Christi
137	10.1	Huntington ISD	Huntington
137	10.1	La Grange ISD	La Grange
137	10.1	Lamesa ISD	Lamesa
137	10.1	New Caney ISD	New Caney
137	10.1	Santa Fe ISD	Santa Fe
137	10.1	Southside ISD	San Antonio
137	10.1	Waco ISD	Waco
137	10.1	West ISD	West
137	10.1	Ysleta ISD	El Paso
149	10.0	Beeville ISD	Beeville
149	10.0	Brownwood ISD	Brownwood
149	10.0	Bullard ISD	Bullard
149	10.0	Celina ISD	Celina
149	10.0	Dripping Spgs ISD	Dripping Spgs
149	10.0	Van ISD	Van
155	9.9	Bridge City ISD	Bridge City
155	9.9	Brownsboro ISD	Brownsboro
155	9.9	Carroll ISD	Grapevine
155	9.9	Kerrville ISD	Kerrville
155	9.9	La Porte ISD	La Porte
155	9.9	Lewisville ISD	Flower Mound
155	9.9	Llano ISD	Llano
155	9.9	Mineola ISD	Mineola
155	9.9	Pecos-Barstow-Toyah ISD	Pecos
164	9.8	Canton ISD	Canton
164	9.8	Decatur ISD	Decatur
164	9.8	Lamar CISD	Rosenberg
164	9.8	Little Elm ISD	Little Elm
164	9.8	River Road ISD	Amarillo
169	9.7	Breckenridge ISD	Breckenridge
169	9.7	Bridgeport ISD	Bridgeport
169	9.7	Canyon ISD	Canyon
169	9.7	Carrollton-Farmers Branch	Carrollton
169	9.7	Elgin ISD	Elgin
169	9.7	Harlandale ISD	San Antonio
169	9.7	Orange Grove ISD	Orange Grove
169	9.7	Springtown ISD	Springtown
169	9.7	Uvalde CISD	Uvalde
178	9.6	Calallen ISD	Corpus Christi
178	9.6	Carthage ISD	Carthage
178	9.6	Gregory-Portland ISD	Portland
178	9.6	Hamshire-Fannett ISD	Hamshire
178	9.6	Huntsville ISD	Huntsville
178	9.6	Judson ISD	Live Oak
178	9.6	La Vega ISD	Waco
178	9.6	Liberty Hill ISD	Liberty Hill
178	9.6	Medina Valley ISD	Castroville
178	9.6	Sealy ISD	Sealy
188	9.5	Alvin ISD	Alvin
188	9.5	Aransas County ISD	Rockport
188	9.5	Athens ISD	Athens
188	9.5	Austin ISD	Austin
188	9.5	Caldwell ISD	Caldwell
188	9.5	Glen Rose ISD	Glen Rose
188	9.5	Lumberton ISD	Lumberton
188	9.5	Pampa ISD	Pampa
188	9.5	Pine Tree ISD	Longview
188	9.5	Schertz-Cibolo-U City ISD	Schertz
188	9.5	Seminole ISD	Seminole
199	9.4	Amarillo ISD	Amarillo
199	9.4	Andrews ISD	Andrews
199	9.4	Center ISD	Center
199	9.4	Clear Creek ISD	League City
199	9.4	Cleburne ISD	Cleburne
199	9.4	Ector County ISD	Odessa
199	9.4	Navarro ISD	Seguin
199	9.4	Pearland ISD	Pearland
199	9.4	Pflugerville ISD	Pflugerville
199	9.4	Port Neches-Groves ISD	Port Neches
199	9.4	San Marcos CISD	San Marcos
199	9.4	Somerset ISD	Somerset
211	9.3	Dickinson ISD	Dickinson
211	9.3	Kilgore ISD	Kilgore
211	9.3	La Marque ISD	La Marque
211	9.3	Mission CISD	Mission
211	9.3	Pleasanton ISD	Pleasanton
211	9.3	Shepherd ISD	Shepherd
211	9.3	Weslaco ISD	Weslaco
218	9.2	Alice ISD	Alice
218	9.2	Carrizo Springs CISD	Carrizo Springs
218	9.2	Comal ISD	New Braunfels
218	9.2	Corsicana ISD	Corsicana
218	9.2	Fredericksburg ISD	Fredericksburg
218	9.2	Garland ISD	Garland
218	9.2	Hardin-Jefferson ISD	Sour Lake
218	9.2	Hurst-Euless-Bedford ISD	Bedford
218	9.2	Leander ISD	Leander
218	9.2	Mabank ISD	Mabank
218	9.2	San Felipe-Del Rio CISD	Del Rio
218	9.2	Temple ISD	Temple
218	9.2	Vernon ISD	Vernon
231	9.1	Bay City ISD	Bay City
231	9.1	Grand Prairie ISD	Grand Prairie
231	9.1	Greenville ISD	Greenville
231	9.1	Henderson ISD	Henderson
231	9.1	Hereford ISD	Hereford
231	9.1	Kingsville ISD	Kingsville
231	9.1	Mathis ISD	Mathis
238	9.0	Burleson ISD	Burleson
238	9.0	El Campo ISD	El Campo
238	9.0	Iowa Park CISD	Iowa Park
238	9.0	Mckinney ISD	Mckinney
238	9.0	Royal ISD	Pattison
243	8.9	Alvarado ISD	Alvarado
243	8.9	Cedar Hill ISD	Cedar Hill
243	8.9	Crosby ISD	Crosby
243	8.9	Lancaster ISD	Lancaster
243	8.9	Northwest ISD	Justin
243	8.9	Tyler ISD	Tyler
249	8.8	Brownfield ISD	Brownfield
249	8.8	Channelview ISD	Channelview
249	8.8	Diboll ISD	Diboll
249	8.8	Frisco ISD	Frisco
249	8.8	Kennedale ISD	Kennedale
249	8.8	Lake Worth ISD	Lake Worth
249	8.8	Pilot Point ISD	Pilot Point
249	8.8	Port Arthur ISD	Port Arthur
249	8.8	School of Excellence in Education	San Antonio
249	8.8	Spring Branch ISD	Houston
249	8.8	Sulphur Springs ISD	Sulphur Springs
260	8.7	Cleveland ISD	Cleveland
260	8.7	Community ISD	Nevada
260	8.7	Copperas Cove ISD	Copperas Cove
260	8.7	Cuero ISD	Cuero
260	8.7	Humble ISD	Humble
260	8.7	Irving ISD	Irving
260	8.7	Manor ISD	Manor
260	8.7	Midway ISD	Hewitt
260	8.7	United ISD	Laredo
260	8.7	Weatherford ISD	Weatherford
270	8.6	Galena Park ISD	Houston
270	8.6	Hays CISD	Kyle
270	8.6	Rockwall ISD	Rockwall
270	8.6	South San Antonio ISD	San Antonio
270	8.6	Spring ISD	Houston
270	8.6	Tatum ISD	Tatum
270	8.6	Texas City ISD	Texas City
270	8.6	Wharton ISD	Wharton

Note: This section only includes districts with 1,500 or more students; All categories are ranked from high to low

278	8.5	Arlington ISD	Arlington
278	8.5	Crowley ISD	Crowley
278	8.5	Friendswood ISD	Friendswood
278	8.5	Point Isabel ISD	Port Isabel
278	8.5	Rio Hondo ISD	Rio Hondo
278	8.5	San Elizario ISD	San Elizario
278	8.5	Terrell ISD	Terrell
285	8.4	China Spring ISD	Waco
285	8.4	Dumas ISD	Dumas
285	8.4	Eagle Mt-Saginaw ISD	Fort Worth
285	8.4	Edinburg CISD	Edinburg
285	8.4	El Paso ISD	El Paso
285	8.4	Frenship ISD	Wolfforth
285	8.4	Ingleside ISD	Ingleside
285	8.4	Sweeny ISD	Sweeny
293	8.3	Canutillo ISD	El Paso
293	8.3	Crandall ISD	Crandall
293	8.3	Huffman ISD	Huffman
293	8.3	Madisonville CISD	Madisonville
297	8.2	Conroe ISD	Conroe
297	8.2	Everman ISD	Everman
297	8.2	Forney ISD	Forney
297	8.2	Mansfield ISD	Mansfield
297	8.2	Montgomery ISD	Montgomery
297	8.2	North Forest ISD	Houston
297	8.2	Raymondville ISD	Raymondville
297	8.2	Stephenville	Stephenville
297	8.2	Wimberley ISD	Wimberley
306	8.1	Houston ISD	Houston
306	8.1	Laredo ISD	Laredo
306	8.1	Lyford CISD	Lyford
306	8.1	Royse City ISD	Royse City
310	8.0	Aledo ISD	Aledo
310	8.0	College Station ISD	College Station
310	8.0	Georgetown ISD	Georgetown
310	8.0	Hutto ISD	Hutto
310	8.0	Pearsall ISD	Pearsall
310	8.0	Splendora ISD	Splendora
316	7.9	Beaumont ISD	Beaumont
316	7.9	Highland Park ISD	Dallas
316	7.9	Joshua ISD	Joshua
316	7.9	New Braunfels ISD	New Braunfels
316	7.9	Southwest School	Houston
316	7.9	Whitehouse ISD	Whitehouse
316	7.9	Wylie ISD	Wylie
316	7.9	Wylie ISD	Abilene
324	7.8	Boerne ISD	Boerne
324	7.8	Eanes ISD	Austin
326	7.7	Alief ISD	Houston
326	7.7	Chapel Hill ISD	Tyler
326	7.7	Crystal City ISD	Crystal City
326	7.7	Dallas ISD	Dallas
326	7.7	Galveston ISD	Galveston
326	7.7	Gonzales ISD	Gonzales
326	7.7	Katy ISD	Katy
326	7.7	Nacogdoches ISD	Nacogdoches
326	7.7	Poteet ISD	Poteet
326	7.7	Round Rock ISD	Round Rock
326	7.7	Socorro ISD	El Paso
337	7.6	Eagle Academy of Abilene	Lewisville
337	7.6	Harlingen CISD	Harlingen
337	7.6	Life School	Lancaster
340	7.5	Keller ISD	Keller
340	7.5	Klein ISD	Klein
340	7.5	Lake Travis ISD	Austin
340	7.5	Lytle ISD	Lytle
340	7.5	Navasota ISD	Navasota
340	7.5	San Benito CISD	San Benito
340	7.5	Stafford MSD	Stafford
340	7.5	Tarkington ISD	Cleveland
348	7.4	Eagle Pass ISD	Eagle Pass
348	7.4	Fort Worth ISD	Fort Worth
348	7.4	Pasadena ISD	Pasadena
351	7.3	Cypress-Fairbanks ISD	Houston
351	7.3	Grapevine-Colleyville ISD	Grapevine
351	7.3	Hondo ISD	Hondo
351	7.3	Palacios ISD	Palacios
355	7.2	Aldine ISD	Houston
355	7.2	Dayton ISD	Dayton
355	7.2	Denver City ISD	Denver City
355	7.2	Hudson ISD	Lufkin
359	7.1	Clint ISD	El Paso
359	7.1	Giddings ISD	Giddings
359	7.1	Liberty ISD	Liberty
359	7.1	Pleasant Grove ISD	Texarkana
363	7.0	Mcallen ISD	Mcallen
363	7.0	Waller ISD	Waller
363	7.0	Willis ISD	Willis
366	6.9	Castleberry ISD	Fort Worth
366	6.9	Tomball ISD	Tomball
368	6.8	Bryan ISD	Bryan
368	6.8	Edcouch-Elsa ISD	Edcouch
368	6.8	Lovejoy ISD	Allen
368	6.8	Midland ISD	Midland
368	6.8	Palestine ISD	Palestine
368	6.8	Pharr-San Juan-Alamo ISD	Pharr
374	6.7	Barbers Hill ISD	Mont Belvieu
374	6.7	Prosper ISD	Prosper
376	6.6	La Joya ISD	La Joya
377	6.5	Donna ISD	Donna
377	6.5	Fort Bend ISD	Sugar Land
379	6.4	Perryton ISD	Perryton
379	6.4	Sharyland ISD	Mission
381	6.3	La Feria Ind SD	La Feria
381	6.3	Zapata County ISD	Zapata
383	6.2	Advantage Academy	Dallas
384	6.1	Coppell ISD	Coppell
384	6.1	Greenwood ISD	Midland
386	6.0	Los Fresnos CISD	Los Fresnos
386	6.0	Sheldon ISD	Houston
388	5.9	Valley View ISD	Pharr
389	5.7	Mercedes ISD	Mercedes
390	5.6	Progreso ISD	Progreso
391	5.5	Alamo Heights ISD	San Antonio
391	5.5	Spring Hill ISD	Longview
393	5.4	Ripley House Charter School	Houston
394	5.3	Fort Stockton ISD	Fort Stockton
394	5.3	Roma ISD	Roma
396	4.6	Yes College Preparatory School	Houston
397	4.4	Hidalgo ISD	Hidalgo
398	3.9	Idea Academy	Weslaco
399	3.8	Kipp Inc Charter	Houston
400	2.7	Harmony Science Academy	Houston
401	2.3	Harmony Science Acad (Fort Worth)	Fort Worth
402	1.8	South Texas ISD	Mercedes
402	1.8	Varnett Charter School	Houston

English Language Learner Students

Rank	Percent	District Name	City
1	63.6	Laredo ISD	Laredo
2	60.4	Roma ISD	Roma
3	57.2	Rio Grande City CISD	Rio Grande City
4	56.0	Valley View ISD	Pharr
5	53.9	Progreso ISD	Progreso
6	53.0	Hidalgo ISD	Hidalgo
7	51.8	Ripley House Charter School	Houston
8	49.9	Donna ISD	Donna
9	44.6	La Joya ISD	La Joya
10	42.6	San Elizario ISD	San Elizario
11	42.2	United ISD	Laredo
12	40.6	Pharr-San Juan-Alamo ISD	Pharr
13	37.6	Edcouch-Elsa ISD	Edcouch
14	35.7	Irving ISD	Irving
15	35.6	Kipp Inc Charter	Houston
16	33.4	Dallas ISD	Dallas
17	32.8	Eagle Pass ISD	Eagle Pass
18	32.5	Clint ISD	El Paso
19	32.1	Brownsville ISD	Brownsville
20	31.7	Mission CISD	Mission
21	30.9	Alief ISD	Houston
22	30.1	Spring Branch ISD	Houston
23	30.0	Edinburg CISD	Edinburg
24	29.5	Fabens ISD	Fabens
24	29.5	Mount Pleasant ISD	Mount Pleasant
26	29.2	Canutillo ISD	El Paso
26	29.2	Castleberry ISD	Fort Worth
28	29.1	Manor ISD	Manor
29	28.6	Del Valle ISD	Del Valle
29	28.6	Dumas ISD	Dumas
29	28.6	Point Isabel ISD	Port Isabel
32	28.5	Houston ISD	Houston
33	27.9	Varnett Charter School	Houston
34	27.6	Sheldon ISD	Houston
35	27.3	Zapata County ISD	Zapata
36	27.0	Fort Worth ISD	Fort Worth
36	27.0	Galena Park ISD	Houston
38	26.4	Sharyland ISD	Mission
39	26.3	Austin ISD	Austin
40	26.1	Mcallen ISD	Mcallen
41	25.9	Mercedes ISD	Mercedes
42	25.2	Channelview ISD	Channelview
42	25.2	Eagle Academy of Abilene	Lewisville
44	24.7	Aldine ISD	Houston
44	24.7	Pasadena ISD	Pasadena
46	23.5	Perryton ISD	Perryton
47	23.3	Weslaco ISD	Weslaco
48	23.2	Center ISD	Center
49	22.7	Jacksonville ISD	Jacksonville
50	22.4	Royal ISD	Pattison
51	22.2	Ysleta ISD	El Paso
52	22.1	El Paso ISD	El Paso
53	21.4	Carrollton-Farmers Branch	Carrollton
54	21.1	Idea Academy	Weslaco
55	20.9	Everman ISD	Everman
56	20.4	Gainesville ISD	Gainesville
57	20.3	Los Fresnos CISD	Los Fresnos
57	20.3	San Benito CISD	San Benito
59	20.0	Socorro ISD	El Paso
60	19.9	Grand Prairie ISD	Grand Prairie
61	19.8	Athens ISD	Athens
62	19.5	Nacogdoches ISD	Nacogdoches
63	19.1	Waller ISD	Waller
64	18.7	Ferris ISD	Ferris
64	18.7	Garland ISD	Garland
64	18.7	Tyler ISD	Tyler
67	18.6	Pilot Point ISD	Pilot Point
68	18.0	Elgin ISD	Elgin
69	17.3	Yes College Preparatory School	Houston
70	16.7	Bryan ISD	Bryan
70	16.7	Edgewood ISD	San Antonio
70	16.7	Little Elm ISD	Little Elm
73	16.6	San Felipe-Del Rio CISD	Del Rio
74	16.5	La Vega ISD	Waco
75	16.4	Arlington ISD	Arlington
75	16.4	Denver City ISD	Denver City
77	16.3	Venus ISD	Venus
78	16.2	Hillsboro ISD	Hillsboro
79	16.0	Corsicana ISD	Corsicana
80	15.9	San Antonio ISD	San Antonio
81	15.8	Cleveland ISD	Cleveland
81	15.8	Southwest School	Houston
81	15.8	Terrell ISD	Terrell
84	15.7	Cleburne ISD	Cleburne
85	15.6	New Caney ISD	New Caney
86	15.3	Spring ISD	Houston
87	15.1	Bridgeport ISD	Bridgeport
87	15.1	Lufkin ISD	Lufkin
89	15.0	Palacios ISD	Palacios
90	14.7	Hereford ISD	Hereford
91	14.5	Diboll ISD	Diboll
91	14.5	South San Antonio ISD	San Antonio
93	14.4	Galveston ISD	Galveston
93	14.4	Richardson ISD	Richardson
95	14.2	Willis ISD	Willis
96	13.8	La Feria Ind SD	La Feria
97	13.7	Bastrop ISD	Bastrop
97	13.7	Denton ISD	Denton
99	13.6	Greenville ISD	Greenville
99	13.6	Longview ISD	Longview
99	13.6	Mesquite ISD	Mesquite
99	13.6	Navasota ISD	Navasota
103	13.5	Stafford MSD	Stafford
103	13.5	Waco ISD	Waco
105	13.4	Cypress-Fairbanks ISD	Houston
105	13.4	Hays CISD	Kyle
107	13.2	Kaufman ISD	Kaufman
107	13.2	Rio Hondo ISD	Rio Hondo
109	13.1	Harlandale ISD	San Antonio
110	12.9	Chapel Hill ISD	Tyler
111	12.8	Gonzales ISD	Gonzales
112	12.7	Madisonville CISD	Madisonville
113	12.6	Alvin ISD	Alvin
113	12.6	Harlingen CISD	Harlingen
113	12.6	Pflugerville ISD	Pflugerville
113	12.6	Pittsburg ISD	Pittsburg
117	12.5	Dallas Can Academy Charter	Dallas
117	12.5	Southwest ISD	San Antonio
119	12.3	Ennis ISD	Ennis
120	12.1	Hempstead ISD	Hempstead
121	11.6	Duncanville ISD	Duncanville
121	11.6	North Forest ISD	Houston
123	11.4	Fort Stockton ISD	Fort Stockton
123	11.4	Giddings ISD	Giddings
123	11.4	Kilgore ISD	Kilgore
123	11.4	Lewisville ISD	Flower Mound
123	11.4	Yoakum ISD	Yoakum

Note: This section only includes districts with 1,500 or more students; All categories are ranked from high to low

Rank	Score	District	City
128	11.3	Fort Bend ISD	Sugar Land
128	11.3	Katy ISD	Katy
128	11.3	Lake Worth ISD	Lake Worth
131	11.1	Advantage Academy	Dallas
132	11.0	Amarillo ISD	Amarillo
133	10.9	Ector County ISD	Odessa
133	10.9	Liberty ISD	Liberty
133	10.9	Southside ISD	San Antonio
136	10.8	Decatur ISD	Decatur
137	10.7	La Grange ISD	La Grange
137	10.7	Taylor ISD	Taylor
139	10.6	Goose Creek CISD	Baytown
139	10.6	Sealy ISD	Sealy
141	10.4	Klein ISD	Klein
141	10.4	Palestine ISD	Palestine
141	10.4	Pampa ISD	Pampa
144	10.0	Plano ISD	Plano
145	9.9	Glen Rose ISD	Glen Rose
145	9.9	Lamar CISD	Rosenberg
147	9.8	Deer Park ISD	Deer Park
147	9.8	Lyford CISD	Lyford
147	9.8	Mexia ISD	Mexia
150	9.7	Harmony Science Academy	Houston
150	9.7	Pine Tree ISD	Longview
152	9.6	Dayton ISD	Dayton
152	9.6	Huntsville ISD	Huntsville
154	9.5	Marble Falls ISD	Marble Falls
155	9.4	Birdville ISD	Haltom City
155	9.4	Calhoun County ISD	Port Lavaca
155	9.4	Conroe ISD	Conroe
158	9.3	Aransas Pass ISD	Aransas Pass
158	9.3	Magnolia ISD	Magnolia
160	9.2	Dickinson ISD	Dickinson
160	9.2	Seminole ISD	Seminole
162	9.1	Tomball ISD	Tomball
163	8.9	Brenham ISD	Brenham
163	8.9	Fredericksburg ISD	Fredericksburg
165	8.8	El Campo ISD	El Campo
165	8.8	Mansfield ISD	Mansfield
165	8.8	Mineral Wells ISD	Mineral Wells
165	8.8	Port Arthur ISD	Port Arthur
165	8.8	Princeton ISD	Princeton
165	8.8	Tatum ISD	Tatum
171	8.7	Marshall ISD	Marshall
172	8.6	Andrews ISD	Andrews
172	8.6	Georgetown ISD	Georgetown
172	8.6	San Marcos CISD	San Marcos
175	8.5	Caldwell ISD	Caldwell
175	8.5	Mckinney ISD	Mckinney
177	8.4	Bellville ISD	Bellville
177	8.4	Winfree Academy	Irving
179	8.3	Breckenridge ISD	Breckenridge
180	8.2	Wharton ISD	Wharton
181	8.1	Needville ISD	Needville
182	8.0	Plainview ISD	Plainview
182	8.0	Seguin ISD	Seguin
184	7.9	Hurst-Euless-Bedford ISD	Bedford
184	7.9	Somerset ISD	Somerset
186	7.8	Midland ISD	Midland
186	7.8	Mineola ISD	Mineola
188	7.7	Borger ISD	Borger
188	7.7	Lockhart ISD	Lockhart
188	7.7	Stephenville	Stephenville
191	7.6	Alvarado ISD	Alvarado
192	7.5	Humble ISD	Humble
193	7.4	Cameron ISD	Cameron
193	7.4	Columbus ISD	Columbus
193	7.4	La Porte ISD	La Porte
193	7.4	Mount Vernon ISD	Mount Vernon
193	7.4	School of Excellence in Education	San Antonio
198	7.3	Grapevine-Colleyville ISD	Grapevine
198	7.3	White Settlement ISD	White Settlement
200	7.2	Crystal City ISD	Crystal City
200	7.2	Sherman ISD	Sherman
202	7.1	Brazosport ISD	Clute
202	7.1	Lytle ISD	Lytle
202	7.1	Raymondville ISD	Raymondville
202	7.1	Texas City ISD	Texas City
206	7.0	Angleton ISD	Angleton
206	7.0	Graham ISD	Graham
208	6.9	Crowley ISD	Crowley
208	6.9	New Braunfels ISD	New Braunfels
210	6.8	Allen ISD	Allen
210	6.8	Beaumont ISD	Beaumont
210	6.8	Temple ISD	Temple
210	6.8	Wylie ISD	Wylie
214	6.7	Carthage ISD	Carthage
214	6.7	Round Rock ISD	Round Rock
214	6.7	Royse City ISD	Royse City
217	6.6	Bay City ISD	Bay City
217	6.6	Brownfield ISD	Brownfield
217	6.6	Commerce ISD	Commerce
217	6.6	Judson ISD	Live Oak
221	6.5	Dalhart ISD	Dalhart
221	6.5	Fairfield ISD	Fairfield
221	6.5	North East ISD	San Antonio
221	6.5	Waxahachie ISD	Waxahachie
225	6.4	Belton ISD	Belton
225	6.4	Killeen ISD	Killeen
225	6.4	Krum ISD	Krum
225	6.4	Shepherd ISD	Shepherd
229	6.3	Eagle Mt-Saginaw ISD	Fort Worth
229	6.3	Pearland ISD	Pearland
229	6.3	Pecos-Barstow-Toyah ISD	Pecos
232	6.2	Northside ISD	San Antonio
233	6.1	Anna ISD	Anna
233	6.1	Coppell ISD	Coppell
233	6.1	Hudson ISD	Lufkin
233	6.1	Rockwall ISD	Rockwall
237	6.0	Carrizo Springs CISD	Carrizo Springs
237	6.0	East Central ISD	San Antonio
237	6.0	Lancaster ISD	Lancaster
240	5.9	Bonham ISD	Bonham
240	5.9	Clear Creek ISD	League City
242	5.8	Connally ISD	Waco
242	5.8	Lake Dallas ISD	Lake Dallas
242	5.8	Life School	Lancaster
242	5.8	Weatherford ISD	Weatherford
246	5.7	Sulphur Springs ISD	Sulphur Springs
246	5.7	Wimberley ISD	Wimberley
248	5.6	Kennedale ISD	Kennedale
248	5.6	Livingston ISD	Livingston
248	5.6	Uvalde CISD	Uvalde
251	5.5	College Station ISD	College Station
251	5.5	Henderson ISD	Henderson
251	5.5	Jasper ISD	Jasper
254	5.4	Hutto ISD	Hutto
254	5.4	Sanger ISD	Sanger
256	5.3	Celina ISD	Celina
256	5.3	Community ISD	Nevada
256	5.3	Ingleside ISD	Ingleside
256	5.3	Rockdale ISD	Rockdale
256	5.3	Snyder ISD	Snyder
261	5.2	Vernon ISD	Vernon
262	5.1	Bowie ISD	Bowie
262	5.1	Prosper ISD	Prosper
262	5.1	Quinlan ISD	Quinlan
262	5.1	Van ISD	Van
266	5.0	Granbury ISD	Granbury
266	5.0	Pearsall ISD	Pearsall
268	4.9	Alamo Heights ISD	San Antonio
268	4.9	Corpus Christi ISD	Corpus Christi
268	4.9	Desoto ISD	Desoto
268	4.9	Greenwood ISD	Midland
268	4.9	Lake Travis ISD	Austin
268	4.9	Northwest ISD	Justin
268	4.9	San Angelo ISD	San Angelo
268	4.9	Wichita Falls ISD	Wichita Falls
276	4.8	Splendora ISD	Splendora
277	4.7	Aubrey ISD	Aubrey
277	4.7	Keller ISD	Keller
277	4.7	Lamesa ISD	Lamesa
277	4.7	Paris ISD	Paris
281	4.6	Tuloso-Midway ISD	Corpus Christi
282	4.5	Joshua ISD	Joshua
282	4.5	Rusk ISD	Rusk
284	4.4	Kemp ISD	Kemp
284	4.4	Leander ISD	Leander
284	4.4	Levelland ISD	Levelland
284	4.4	Medina Valley ISD	Castroville
284	4.4	Nederland ISD	Nederland
284	4.4	Rains ISD	Emory
284	4.4	West Oso ISD	Corpus Christi
291	4.3	Denison ISD	Denison
291	4.3	Forney ISD	Forney
291	4.3	Groesbeck ISD	Groesbeck
291	4.3	Robstown ISD	Robstown
295	4.2	Kerrville ISD	Kerrville
296	4.1	Alice ISD	Alice
296	4.1	Aransas County ISD	Rockport
296	4.1	Bandera ISD	Bandera
296	4.1	Crosby ISD	Crosby
296	4.1	Frisco ISD	Frisco
296	4.1	Godley ISD	Godley
296	4.1	La Marque ISD	La Marque
296	4.1	Poteet ISD	Poteet
296	4.1	Westwood ISD	Palestine
305	4.0	Comal ISD	New Braunfels
305	4.0	Wills Point ISD	Wills Point
307	3.9	Burnet CISD	Burnet
307	3.9	Monahans-Wickett-Pyote ISD	Monahans
309	3.8	Gilmer ISD	Gilmer
309	3.8	Huffman ISD	Huffman
311	3.7	Boerne ISD	Boerne
311	3.7	Bridge City ISD	Bridge City
311	3.7	West ISD	West
311	3.7	Whitney ISD	Whitney
315	3.6	Columbia-Brazoria ISD	West Columbia
315	3.6	Smithville ISD	Smithville
317	3.5	Cedar Hill ISD	Cedar Hill
317	3.5	Crandall ISD	Crandall
317	3.5	Dripping Spgs ISD	Dripping Spgs
317	3.5	Lampasas ISD	Lampasas
321	3.4	Lindale ISD	Lindale
322	3.3	Kingsville ISD	Kingsville
322	3.3	Texarkana ISD	Texarkana
324	3.2	Floresville ISD	Floresville
324	3.2	Llano ISD	Llano
326	3.1	Devine ISD	Devine
326	3.1	Gatesville ISD	Gatesville
326	3.1	Midlothian ISD	Midlothian
326	3.1	Port Neches-Groves ISD	Port Neches
330	3.0	La Vernia ISD	La Vernia
330	3.0	Schertz-Cibolo-U City ISD	Schertz
330	3.0	Spring Hill ISD	Longview
333	2.9	Canton ISD	Canton
333	2.9	Central ISD	Pollok
333	2.9	Lubbock-Cooper ISD	Lubbock
336	2.8	Abilene ISD	Abilene
336	2.8	Hamshire-Fannett ISD	Hamshire
336	2.8	Pleasant Grove ISD	Texarkana
336	2.8	Springtown ISD	Springtown
340	2.7	Frenship ISD	Wolfforth
340	2.7	Liberty Hill ISD	Liberty Hill
340	2.7	West Orange-Cove CISD	Orange
340	2.7	Whitehouse ISD	Whitehouse
344	2.6	Orange Grove ISD	Orange Grove
345	2.5	Argyle ISD	Argyle
345	2.5	Flour Bluff ISD	Corpus Christi
345	2.5	Mabank ISD	Mabank
348	2.4	Barbers Hill ISD	Mont Belvieu
348	2.4	Brownsboro ISD	Brownsboro
348	2.4	Gregory-Portland ISD	Portland
348	2.4	Hardin-Jefferson ISD	Sour Lake
348	2.4	Mathis ISD	Mathis
348	2.4	Midway ISD	Hewitt
354	2.3	Beeville ISD	Beeville
354	2.3	Burleson ISD	Burleson
354	2.3	Hallsville ISD	Hallsville
354	2.3	Pleasanton ISD	Pleasanton
354	2.3	Red Oak ISD	Red Oak
359	2.2	Azle ISD	Azle
359	2.2	Gladewater ISD	Gladewater
359	2.2	Harmony Science Acad (Fort Worth)	Fort Worth
359	2.2	Hondo ISD	Hondo
359	2.2	Montgomery ISD	Montgomery
359	2.2	North Lamar ISD	Paris
365	2.1	Aledo ISD	Aledo
365	2.1	Friendswood ISD	Friendswood
365	2.1	Santa Fe ISD	Santa Fe
365	2.1	Sweetwater ISD	Sweetwater
365	2.1	Whitesboro ISD	Whitesboro
370	2.0	Calallen ISD	Corpus Christi
370	2.0	Cuero ISD	Cuero
370	2.0	Sweeny ISD	Sweeny
373	1.9	Victoria ISD	Victoria
374	1.8	Big Spring ISD	Big Spring
374	1.8	Brownwood ISD	Brownwood
374	1.8	Lubbock ISD	Lubbock
374	1.8	Navarro ISD	Seguin
378	1.7	Eanes ISD	Austin
379	1.6	Atlanta ISD	Atlanta
379	1.6	Little Cypress-Mauricevil	Orange
379	1.6	Orangefield ISD	Orangefield
382	1.5	Bullard ISD	Bullard
383	1.4	China Spring ISD	Waco
383	1.4	Lorena ISD	Lorena
385	1.3	Silsbee ISD	Silsbee

Note: This section only includes districts with 1,500 or more students; All categories are ranked from high to low

386	1.2	Copperas Cove ISD	Copperas Cove
387	1.1	South Texas ISD	Mercedes
388	1.0	Sinton ISD	Sinton
389	0.9	Huntington ISD	Huntington
389	0.9	Liberty-Eylau ISD	Texarkana
391	0.8	Canyon ISD	Canyon
391	0.8	River Road ISD	Amarillo
391	0.8	Robinson ISD	Robinson
391	0.8	Tarkington ISD	Cleveland
395	0.7	Burkburnett ISD	Burkburnett
395	0.7	Coldspring-Oakhurst CISD	Coldspring
395	0.7	Lumberton ISD	Lumberton
395	0.7	Vidor ISD	Vidor
399	0.6	Lovejoy ISD	Allen
399	0.6	Wylie ISD	Abilene
401	0.4	Highland Park ISD	Dallas
402	0.3	Carroll ISD	Grapevine
403	0.2	Iowa Park CISD	Iowa Park

Students Eligible for Free Lunch

Rank	Percent	District Name	City
1	99.6	North Forest ISD	Houston
2	93.7	Ripley House Charter School	Houston
3	87.2	Varnett Charter School	Houston
4	82.0	Kipp Inc Charter	Houston
5	80.4	Dallas Can Academy Charter	Dallas
6	80.3	Dallas ISD	Dallas
7	80.2	Waco ISD	Waco
8	78.1	Mathis ISD	Mathis
9	75.0	Crystal City ISD	Crystal City
10	74.9	Aldine ISD	Houston
11	74.8	La Vega ISD	Waco
12	73.8	Del Valle ISD	Del Valle
12	73.8	Lake Worth ISD	Lake Worth
14	73.2	Hillsboro ISD	Hillsboro
15	73.1	Port Arthur ISD	Port Arthur
16	72.0	Everman ISD	Everman
17	71.7	Jacksonville ISD	Jacksonville
18	71.6	Hereford ISD	Hereford
19	71.5	Southwest ISD	San Antonio
20	71.4	Royal ISD	Pattison
21	70.7	Mount Pleasant ISD	Mount Pleasant
22	70.2	Carrizo Springs CISD	Carrizo Springs
23	70.1	Progreso ISD	Progreso
23	70.1	West Orange-Cove CISD	Orange
25	69.9	Somerset ISD	Somerset
26	69.7	Harlingen CISD	Harlingen
27	69.6	Uvalde CISD	Uvalde
28	69.1	Pearsall ISD	Pearsall
29	68.7	Southside ISD	San Antonio
30	68.5	Alief ISD	Houston
31	68.0	Fort Worth ISD	Fort Worth
32	67.7	San Felipe-Del Rio CISD	Del Rio
32	67.7	School of Excellence in Education	San Antonio
34	67.6	Manor ISD	Manor
34	67.6	Nacogdoches ISD	Nacogdoches
36	67.3	Lancaster ISD	Lancaster
36	67.3	United ISD	Laredo
38	67.2	Alice ISD	Alice
38	67.2	Irving ISD	Irving
40	67.0	Kingsville ISD	Kingsville
41	66.8	Galena Park ISD	Houston
42	66.7	Gainesville ISD	Gainesville
42	66.7	Sheldon ISD	Houston
44	66.5	Lufkin ISD	Lufkin
45	66.4	Ferris ISD	Ferris
46	66.3	Brownfield ISD	Brownfield
47	66.2	Center ISD	Center
47	66.2	La Marque ISD	La Marque
49	65.9	Cleveland ISD	Cleveland
49	65.9	Pasadena ISD	Pasadena
51	65.6	Pittsburg ISD	Pittsburg
51	65.6	Poteet ISD	Poteet
53	65.3	Mexia ISD	Mexia
54	64.9	Paris ISD	Paris
54	64.9	Terrell ISD	Terrell
56	64.6	Navasota ISD	Navasota
56	64.6	Wharton ISD	Wharton
58	64.3	Canutillo ISD	El Paso
59	64.1	Hempstead ISD	Hempstead
60	64.0	Diboll ISD	Diboll
61	63.7	Beaumont ISD	Beaumont
61	63.7	Channelview ISD	Channelview
63	63.5	Bryan ISD	Bryan
64	63.4	Galveston ISD	Galveston
65	63.3	Connally ISD	Waco
66	63.1	Cameron ISD	Cameron
67	63.0	Jasper ISD	Jasper
68	62.9	Idea Academy	Weslaco
68	62.9	Palestine ISD	Palestine
70	62.6	Castleberry ISD	Fort Worth
71	62.3	Madisonville CISD	Madisonville
71	62.3	Plainview ISD	Plainview
73	62.0	Corsicana ISD	Corsicana
74	61.8	Sinton ISD	Sinton
75	61.7	Longview ISD	Longview
76	61.3	Gonzales ISD	Gonzales
77	61.0	Socorro ISD	El Paso
78	60.6	Marshall ISD	Marshall
79	60.5	Liberty-Eylau ISD	Texarkana
80	60.3	Chapel Hill ISD	Tyler
80	60.3	Lytle ISD	Lytle
80	60.3	Venus ISD	Venus
83	60.0	Athens ISD	Athens
84	59.9	Elgin ISD	Elgin
84	59.9	Pecos-Barstow-Toyah ISD	Pecos
86	59.8	Temple ISD	Temple
87	59.6	El Paso ISD	El Paso
88	59.0	Palacios ISD	Palacios
89	58.9	San Marcos CISD	San Marcos
89	58.9	Shepherd ISD	Shepherd
91	58.7	Corpus Christi ISD	Corpus Christi
91	58.7	Yoakum ISD	Yoakum
93	58.6	Grand Prairie ISD	Grand Prairie
94	58.2	Spring ISD	Houston
95	58.1	El Campo ISD	El Campo
96	57.6	Livingston ISD	Livingston
97	57.5	Aransas Pass ISD	Aransas Pass
97	57.5	Tyler ISD	Tyler
99	57.2	Yes College Preparatory School	Houston
100	57.1	Seguin ISD	Seguin
101	56.9	Gladewater ISD	Gladewater
102	56.6	Austin ISD	Austin
102	56.6	Duncanville ISD	Duncanville
104	56.5	Aransas County ISD	Rockport
105	56.3	Big Spring ISD	Big Spring
106	55.9	Taylor ISD	Taylor
107	55.6	Levelland ISD	Levelland
107	55.6	Victoria ISD	Victoria
109	55.5	Sherman ISD	Sherman
109	55.5	Sweetwater ISD	Sweetwater
111	55.4	Fort Stockton ISD	Fort Stockton
112	55.1	Zapata County ISD	Zapata
113	55.0	Amarillo ISD	Amarillo
114	54.9	Bay City ISD	Bay City
114	54.9	Texas City ISD	Texas City
116	54.8	Dumas ISD	Dumas
116	54.8	Texarkana ISD	Texarkana
118	54.6	Bastrop ISD	Bastrop
119	54.5	Liberty ISD	Liberty
119	54.5	Rockdale ISD	Rockdale
121	54.1	Mineral Wells ISD	Mineral Wells
122	53.6	Lockhart ISD	Lockhart
123	53.5	Beeville ISD	Beeville
123	53.5	Calhoun County ISD	Port Lavaca
123	53.5	Pleasanton ISD	Pleasanton
126	53.4	Quinlan ISD	Quinlan
127	53.3	Commerce ISD	Commerce
127	53.3	Goose Creek CISD	Baytown
129	53.0	Lubbock ISD	Lubbock
130	52.9	Mineola ISD	Mineola
131	52.7	Giddings ISD	Giddings
132	52.6	Breckenridge ISD	Breckenridge
132	52.6	Orange Grove ISD	Orange Grove
134	52.5	Harmony Science Academy	Houston
134	52.5	Vernon ISD	Vernon
136	52.3	Abilene ISD	Abilene
137	52.2	Ennis ISD	Ennis
138	52.1	Kaufman ISD	Kaufman
138	52.1	Mesquite ISD	Mesquite
140	51.9	Dickinson ISD	Dickinson
141	51.8	Perryton ISD	Perryton
142	51.7	Atlanta ISD	Atlanta
142	51.7	Coldspring-Oakhurst CISD	Coldspring
144	51.6	Kemp ISD	Kemp
145	51.5	East Central ISD	San Antonio
146	51.3	Mabank ISD	Mabank
147	51.2	Spring Branch ISD	Houston
148	51.1	Brownwood ISD	Brownwood
148	51.1	Waller ISD	Waller
150	51.0	Arlington ISD	Arlington
151	50.9	New Caney ISD	New Caney
152	50.8	Desoto ISD	Desoto
153	50.7	Bonham ISD	Bonham
153	50.7	Houston ISD	Houston
153	50.7	Robstown ISD	Robstown
156	50.5	Cuero ISD	Cuero
157	50.2	Clint ISD	El Paso
157	50.2	Denison ISD	Denison
157	50.2	Rusk ISD	Rusk
157	50.2	Splendora ISD	Splendora
161	50.1	Denver City ISD	Denver City
162	49.9	Devine ISD	Devine
163	49.8	Whitney ISD	Whitney
164	49.7	Cleburne ISD	Cleburne
165	49.5	Willis ISD	Willis
166	49.3	Carrollton-Farmers Branch	Carrollton
167	49.2	Eagle Academy of Abilene	Lewisville
167	49.2	Sulphur Springs ISD	Sulphur Springs
169	49.0	Richardson ISD	Richardson
170	48.9	Wichita Falls ISD	Wichita Falls
171	48.8	Henderson ISD	Henderson
172	48.5	Sharyland ISD	Mission
173	48.4	Ector County ISD	Odessa
173	48.4	Gilmer ISD	Gilmer
175	48.2	Tatum ISD	Tatum
175	48.2	Ysleta ISD	El Paso
177	48.1	Advantage Academy	Dallas
178	48.0	Kilgore ISD	Kilgore
178	48.0	Princeton ISD	Princeton
180	47.9	Southwest School	Houston
181	47.8	Garland ISD	Garland
181	47.8	Judson ISD	Live Oak
183	47.7	Dayton ISD	Dayton
183	47.7	Pampa ISD	Pampa
185	47.2	Marble Falls ISD	Marble Falls
186	47.1	South Texas ISD	Mercedes
187	47.0	San Angelo ISD	San Angelo
188	46.7	Wills Point ISD	Wills Point
189	46.6	Angleton ISD	Angleton
190	46.5	Brazosport ISD	Clute
191	46.2	Groesbeck ISD	Groesbeck
192	46.0	Stafford MSD	Stafford
193	45.8	Westwood ISD	Palestine
194	45.7	Dalhart ISD	Dalhart
194	45.7	Snyder ISD	Snyder
196	45.4	Brownsboro ISD	Brownsboro
197	45.3	Bridgeport ISD	Bridgeport
198	45.2	Brenham ISD	Brenham
198	45.2	Pine Tree ISD	Longview
200	45.1	Hudson ISD	Lufkin
201	44.7	Fairfield ISD	Fairfield
201	44.7	Rio Grande City CISD	Rio Grande City
203	44.6	Central ISD	Pollok
204	44.5	Llano ISD	Llano
205	44.2	Seminole ISD	Seminole
205	44.2	Tuloso-Midway ISD	Corpus Christi
207	44.1	Alvin ISD	Alvin
207	44.1	Floresville ISD	Floresville
209	44.0	Vidor ISD	Vidor
210	43.9	Midland ISD	Midland
211	43.6	Burnet CISD	Burnet
211	43.6	Silsbee ISD	Silsbee
213	43.5	Columbus ISD	Columbus
214	43.3	Smithville ISD	Smithville
215	43.2	Cedar Hill ISD	Cedar Hill
215	43.2	Kerrville ISD	Kerrville
215	43.2	Rains ISD	Emory
215	43.2	Sealy ISD	Sealy
215	43.2	Waxahachie ISD	Waxahachie
220	43.1	Alvarado ISD	Alvarado
220	43.1	Caldwell ISD	Caldwell
222	43.0	La Grange ISD	La Grange
223	42.5	Pilot Point ISD	Pilot Point
224	42.4	Mount Vernon ISD	Mount Vernon
225	42.3	Bandera ISD	Bandera
226	42.1	Birdville ISD	Haltom City
227	42.0	Columbia-Brazoria ISD	West Columbia
227	42.0	Godley ISD	Godley
229	41.7	Monahans-Wickett-Pyote ISD	Monahans
230	41.3	Carthage ISD	Carthage
231	41.1	Springtown ISD	Springtown
232	40.8	Bridge City ISD	Bridge City
233	40.7	Borger ISD	Borger
234	40.2	Fredericksburg ISD	Fredericksburg
234	40.2	Medina Valley ISD	Castroville

Note: This section only includes districts with 1,500 or more students; All categories are ranked from high to low

Rank	Value	District	City		Rank	Value	District	City
236	40.1	Lamar CISD	Rosenberg		322	24.8	Celina ISD	Celina
236	40.1	Van ISD	Van		323	24.7	Comal ISD	New Braunfels
238	40.0	Stephenville	Stephenville		324	24.6	Community ISD	Nevada
239	39.7	Northside ISD	San Antonio		325	24.4	Krum ISD	Krum
239	39.7	River Road ISD	Amarillo		326	23.1	Aubrey ISD	Aubrey
241	39.6	Crosby ISD	Crosby		326	23.1	Burleson ISD	Burleson
241	39.6	San Antonio ISD	San Antonio		328	23.0	Katy ISD	Katy
243	39.4	Whitesboro ISD	Whitesboro		329	22.6	Mckinney ISD	Mckinney
244	39.3	Crowley ISD	Crowley		330	22.5	Spring Hill ISD	Longview
244	39.3	Glen Rose ISD	Glen Rose		331	22.3	Round Rock ISD	Round Rock
244	39.3	Hurst-Euless-Bedford ISD	Bedford		332	21.9	La Vernia ISD	La Vernia
244	39.3	Lampasas ISD	Lampasas		333	21.4	Canyon ISD	Canyon
248	39.1	Hays CISD	Kyle		334	21.2	Wimberley ISD	Wimberley
249	39.0	Joshua ISD	Joshua		335	20.4	Robinson ISD	Robinson
250	38.9	Killeen ISD	Killeen		336	20.3	Wylie ISD	Wylie
251	38.8	Huntington ISD	Huntington		337	20.1	China Spring ISD	Waco
252	38.7	Graham ISD	Graham		338	20.0	Lewisville ISD	Flower Mound
253	38.6	Pflugerville ISD	Pflugerville		338	20.0	Midway ISD	Hewitt
254	38.4	White Settlement ISD	White Settlement		340	19.6	Port Neches-Groves ISD	Port Neches
255	38.1	Lamesa ISD	Lamesa		340	19.6	San Elizario ISD	San Elizario
256	37.0	Sweeny ISD	Sweeny		342	19.3	Montgomery ISD	Montgomery
257	36.8	Huntsville ISD	Huntsville		342	19.3	Schertz-Cibolo-U City ISD	Schertz
258	36.7	Belton ISD	Belton		344	19.2	Forney ISD	Forney
258	36.7	Flour Bluff ISD	Corpus Christi		344	19.2	Liberty Hill ISD	Liberty Hill
260	36.6	Calallen ISD	Corpus Christi		346	18.9	Andrews ISD	Andrews
261	36.5	West ISD	West		346	18.9	Plano ISD	Plano
262	36.4	Fabens ISD	Fabens		348	18.4	Tomball ISD	Tomball
262	36.4	Granbury ISD	Granbury		349	18.2	Pearland ISD	Pearland
264	35.9	Bowie ISD	Bowie		349	18.2	Point Isabel ISD	Port Isabel
265	35.7	Bellville ISD	Bellville		349	18.2	Rockwall ISD	Rockwall
266	35.6	Azle ISD	Azle		352	18.0	Donna ISD	Donna
267	35.0	Harmony Science Acad (Fort Worth)	Fort Worth		353	17.8	Alamo Heights ISD	San Antonio
268	34.7	Tarkington ISD	Cleveland		354	17.6	Midlothian ISD	Midlothian
268	34.7	Weatherford ISD	Weatherford		354	17.6	Pleasant Grove ISD	Texarkana
270	34.6	Cypress-Fairbanks ISD	Houston		356	17.2	Barbers Hill ISD	Mont Belvieu
270	34.6	Little Elm ISD	Little Elm		357	16.9	Clear Creek ISD	League City
272	34.5	La Porte ISD	La Porte		358	16.7	La Joya ISD	La Joya
273	34.4	Gatesville ISD	Gatesville		359	16.5	Leander ISD	Leander
274	34.3	Georgetown ISD	Georgetown		360	16.0	Boerne ISD	Boerne
274	34.3	North East ISD	San Antonio		361	15.8	La Feria Ind SD	La Feria
276	34.1	Magnolia ISD	Magnolia		361	15.8	Northwest ISD	Justin
277	33.9	Deer Park ISD	Deer Park		363	15.7	Raymondville ISD	Raymondville
278	33.8	Denton ISD	Denton		364	14.4	Grapevine-Colleyville ISD	Grapevine
279	33.7	Hallsville ISD	Hallsville		364	14.4	Hondo ISD	Hondo
280	33.4	Ingleside ISD	Ingleside		366	13.5	Rio Hondo ISD	Rio Hondo
281	33.3	Decatur ISD	Decatur		367	13.2	College Station ISD	College Station
281	33.3	Lubbock-Cooper ISD	Lubbock		368	12.7	Keller ISD	Keller
283	33.0	Canton ISD	Canton		369	11.6	Allen ISD	Allen
284	32.5	Life School	Lancaster		369	11.6	Prosper ISD	Prosper
285	32.3	Copperas Cove ISD	Copperas Cove		371	11.0	Lake Travis ISD	Austin
285	32.3	New Braunfels ISD	New Braunfels		372	11.0	South San Antonio ISD	San Antonio
287	32.0	Hutto ISD	Hutto		373	10.4	Dripping Spgs ISD	Dripping Spgs
288	31.9	Sanger ISD	Sanger		374	10.2	West Oso ISD	Corpus Christi
289	31.7	Roma ISD	Roma		375	9.7	Wylie ISD	Abilene
290	31.6	North Lamar ISD	Paris		376	9.5	Aledo ISD	Aledo
291	31.1	Navarro ISD	Seguin		377	9.1	Frisco ISD	Frisco
292	30.8	Lindale ISD	Lindale		378	8.9	Lorena ISD	Lorena
292	30.8	Little Cypress-Mauricevil	Orange		379	8.5	Edgewood ISD	San Antonio
294	30.7	Conroe ISD	Conroe		380	8.4	Argyle ISD	Argyle
295	30.5	Winfree Academy	Irving		381	7.0	Coppell ISD	Coppell
296	30.4	Gregory-Portland ISD	Portland		382	6.8	Weslaco ISD	Weslaco
297	30.3	Red Oak ISD	Red Oak		383	5.9	Los Fresnos CISD	Los Fresnos
298	30.1	Frenship ISD	Wolfforth		384	4.8	Friendswood ISD	Friendswood
299	30.0	Burkburnett ISD	Burkburnett		385	4.3	Edinburg CISD	Edinburg
300	29.9	Anna ISD	Anna		386	2.1	Lovejoy ISD	Allen
301	29.8	Bullard ISD	Bullard		387	2.0	Eanes ISD	Austin
302	29.6	Royse City ISD	Royse City		388	1.4	Carroll ISD	Grapevine
303	29.4	Klein ISD	Klein		389	0.8	Eagle Pass ISD	Eagle Pass
304	29.2	Iowa Park CISD	Iowa Park		389	0.8	Pharr-San Juan-Alamo ISD	Pharr
305	28.6	Eagle Mt-Saginaw ISD	Fort Worth		391	0.6	Greenville ISD	Greenville
306	28.3	Fort Bend ISD	Sugar Land		392	0.2	San Benito CISD	San Benito
307	27.9	Mansfield ISD	Mansfield		393	0.1	Brownsville ISD	Brownsville
308	27.8	Hardin-Jefferson ISD	Sour Lake		393	0.1	Mercedes ISD	Mercedes
309	27.3	Whitehouse ISD	Whitehouse		395	0.0	Edcouch-Elsa ISD	Edcouch
310	27.2	Huffman ISD	Huffman		395	0.0	Harlandale ISD	San Antonio
310	27.2	Nederland ISD	Nederland		395	0.0	Hidalgo ISD	Hidalgo
312	27.1	Needville ISD	Needville		395	0.0	Highland Park ISD	Dallas
313	27.0	Crandall ISD	Crandall		395	0.0	Laredo ISD	Laredo
314	26.8	Orangefield ISD	Orangefield		395	0.0	Lyford CISD	Lyford
315	26.6	Santa Fe ISD	Santa Fe		395	0.0	Mcallen ISD	Mcallen
316	26.4	Kennedale ISD	Kennedale		395	0.0	Mission CISD	Mission
316	26.4	Lake Dallas ISD	Lake Dallas		395	0.0	Valley View ISD	Pharr
316	26.4	Lumberton ISD	Lumberton					
319	26.1	Greenwood ISD	Midland					
320	25.5	Hamshire-Fannett ISD	Hamshire					
320	25.5	Humble ISD	Humble					

Students Eligible for Reduced-Price Lunch

Rank	Percent	District Name	City
1	17.7	River Road ISD	Amarillo
2	17.5	Burkburnett ISD	Burkburnett
3	15.6	Iowa Park CISD	Iowa Park
4	14.8	Idea Academy	Weslaco
5	14.7	Vernon ISD	Vernon
6	14.2	Socorro ISD	El Paso
7	13.9	Life School	Lancaster
8	13.8	Fort Stockton ISD	Fort Stockton
9	13.7	Copperas Cove ISD	Copperas Cove
10	13.4	Killeen ISD	Killeen
11	13.3	Dalhart ISD	Dalhart
11	13.3	Harmony Science Acad (Fort Worth)	Fort Worth
13	13.2	Duncanville ISD	Duncanville
14	13.1	Aransas Pass ISD	Aransas Pass
15	13.0	Channelview ISD	Channelview
15	13.0	Llano ISD	Llano
17	12.9	Poteet ISD	Poteet
18	12.8	Pasadena ISD	Pasadena
19	12.7	Cedar Hill ISD	Cedar Hill
19	12.7	Huntsville ISD	Huntsville
21	12.6	Judson ISD	Live Oak
22	12.5	Anna ISD	Anna
22	12.5	Yes College Preparatory School	Houston
24	12.4	Desoto ISD	Desoto
24	12.4	Ingleside ISD	Ingleside
26	12.3	Crystal City ISD	Crystal City
26	12.3	Huntington ISD	Huntington
28	12.2	Venus ISD	Venus
29	12.1	Beeville ISD	Beeville
29	12.1	Groesbeck ISD	Groesbeck
29	12.1	Southwest ISD	San Antonio
29	12.1	Stafford MSD	Stafford
33	12.0	Harmony Science Academy	Houston
33	12.0	Hutto ISD	Hutto
35	11.9	Clint ISD	El Paso
35	11.9	San Angelo ISD	San Angelo
37	11.8	East Central ISD	San Antonio
37	11.8	Lancaster ISD	Lancaster
37	11.8	Lockhart ISD	Lockhart
37	11.8	Springtown ISD	Springtown
41	11.7	Brownwood ISD	Brownwood
41	11.7	Community ISD	Nevada
41	11.7	Floresville ISD	Floresville
41	11.7	San Antonio ISD	San Antonio
41	11.7	Wills Point ISD	Wills Point
46	11.6	Burnet CISD	Burnet
46	11.6	Denver City ISD	Denver City
46	11.6	Dumas ISD	Dumas
46	11.6	Lytle ISD	Lytle
50	11.3	Ysleta ISD	El Paso
51	11.3	Advantage Academy	Dallas
51	11.3	Pampa ISD	Pampa
53	11.2	Devine ISD	Devine
53	11.2	Kipp Inc Charter	Houston
53	11.2	Liberty-Eylau ISD	Texarkana
53	11.2	Pecos-Barstow-Toyah ISD	Pecos
53	11.2	School of Excellence in Education	San Antonio
53	11.2	Somerset ISD	Somerset
59	11.1	Canutillo ISD	El Paso
60	11.0	Connally ISD	Waco
60	11.0	Grand Prairie ISD	Grand Prairie
60	11.0	Irving ISD	Irving
60	11.0	Manor ISD	Manor
60	11.0	Monahans-Wickett-Pyote ISD	Monahans
60	11.0	Nederland ISD	Nederland
60	11.0	Sheldon ISD	Houston
60	11.0	Splendora ISD	Splendora
68	10.9	White Settlement ISD	White Settlement
68	10.9	Yoakum ISD	Yoakum
70	10.8	Brownsboro ISD	Brownsboro
70	10.8	Hudson ISD	Lufkin
70	10.8	Sulphur Springs ISD	Sulphur Springs
73	10.7	Burleson ISD	Burleson
73	10.7	Del Valle ISD	Del Valle
73	10.7	Gatesville ISD	Gatesville
73	10.7	Marble Falls ISD	Marble Falls
73	10.7	Perryton ISD	Perryton
78	10.6	Fredericksburg ISD	Fredericksburg
79	10.5	Denison ISD	Denison
79	10.5	Orange Grove ISD	Orange Grove
81	10.4	Bandera ISD	Bandera
81	10.4	Breckenridge ISD	Breckenridge

Note: This section only includes districts with 1,500 or more students; All categories are ranked from high to low

Rank	Score	District	City
81	10.4	Graham ISD	Graham
81	10.4	La Vega ISD	Waco
81	10.4	Levelland ISD	Levelland
81	10.4	Medina Valley ISD	Castroville
81	10.4	Rains ISD	Emory
81	10.4	South Texas ISD	Mercedes
81	10.4	Whitney ISD	Whitney
90	10.3	Pflugerville ISD	Pflugerville
90	10.3	Pleasanton ISD	Pleasanton
90	10.3	Winfree Academy	Irving
93	10.2	Abilene ISD	Abilene
93	10.2	Varnett Charter School	Houston
95	10.1	Birdville ISD	Haltom City
95	10.1	Carrollton-Farmers Branch	Carrollton
95	10.1	Everman ISD	Everman
95	10.1	Jasper ISD	Jasper
95	10.1	Mathis ISD	Mathis
95	10.1	Mesquite ISD	Mesquite
95	10.1	New Caney ISD	New Caney
95	10.1	Northside ISD	San Antonio
95	10.1	Westwood ISD	Palestine
104	10.0	Brazosport ISD	Clute
104	10.0	Cameron ISD	Cameron
104	10.0	Cleburne ISD	Cleburne
104	10.0	Diboll ISD	Diboll
104	10.0	Plainview ISD	Plainview
104	10.0	Seminole ISD	Seminole
110	9.9	Godley ISD	Godley
110	9.9	Kilgore ISD	Kilgore
110	9.9	Lampasas ISD	Lampasas
110	9.9	Royal ISD	Pattison
110	9.9	Sealy ISD	Sealy
110	9.9	Spring ISD	Houston
116	9.8	Belton ISD	Belton
116	9.8	Central ISD	Pollok
116	9.8	Giddings ISD	Giddings
116	9.8	Mount Pleasant ISD	Mount Pleasant
116	9.8	Navasota ISD	Navasota
116	9.8	Southside ISD	San Antonio
116	9.8	Sweeny ISD	Sweeny
116	9.8	Van ISD	Van
116	9.8	Vidor ISD	Vidor
125	9.7	Alvarado ISD	Alvarado
125	9.7	Athens ISD	Athens
125	9.7	Hurst-Euless-Bedford ISD	Bedford
125	9.7	Joshua ISD	Joshua
125	9.7	San Marcos CISD	San Marcos
125	9.7	Temple ISD	Temple
131	9.6	Atlanta ISD	Atlanta
131	9.6	Galena Park ISD	Houston
131	9.6	Goose Creek CISD	Baytown
131	9.6	Henderson ISD	Henderson
131	9.6	Kingsville ISD	Kingsville
131	9.6	Pittsburg ISD	Pittsburg
137	9.5	Alief ISD	Houston
137	9.5	Corpus Christi ISD	Corpus Christi
137	9.5	Crowley ISD	Crowley
137	9.5	Hays CISD	Kyle
137	9.5	La Porte ISD	La Porte
137	9.5	Little Elm ISD	Little Elm
137	9.5	Mexia ISD	Mexia
137	9.5	Palacios ISD	Palacios
137	9.5	Quinlan ISD	Quinlan
137	9.5	Rockdale ISD	Rockdale
147	9.4	Aldine ISD	Houston
148	9.3	Amarillo ISD	Amarillo
148	9.3	Bonham ISD	Bonham
148	9.3	Carrizo Springs CISD	Carrizo Springs
148	9.3	Gainesville ISD	Gainesville
148	9.3	Gregory-Portland ISD	Portland
148	9.3	Royse City ISD	Royse City
148	9.3	Tarkington ISD	Cleveland
148	9.3	Victoria ISD	Victoria
156	9.2	Eagle Mt-Saginaw ISD	Fort Worth
156	9.2	Sinton ISD	Sinton
158	9.1	Alice ISD	Alice
158	9.1	Aransas County ISD	Rockport
158	9.1	Crandall ISD	Crandall
158	9.1	Ferris ISD	Ferris
158	9.1	Hondo ISD	Hondo
158	9.1	Kennedale ISD	Kennedale
158	9.1	Lubbock-Cooper ISD	Lubbock
158	9.1	Rusk ISD	Rusk
158	9.1	Seguin ISD	Seguin
158	9.1	Snyder ISD	Snyder
158	9.1	Whitesboro ISD	Whitesboro
169	9.0	Angleton ISD	Angleton
169	9.0	Bowie ISD	Bowie
169	9.0	El Paso ISD	El Paso
169	9.0	Lindale ISD	Lindale
169	9.0	Midland ISD	Midland
169	9.0	Smithville ISD	Smithville
169	9.0	West ISD	West
176	8.9	Beaumont ISD	Beaumont
176	8.9	Chapel Hill ISD	Tyler
176	8.9	Dallas Can Academy Charter	Dallas
176	8.9	Flour Bluff ISD	Corpus Christi
176	8.9	Gladewater ISD	Gladewater
176	8.9	Kemp ISD	Kemp
176	8.9	Kerrville ISD	Kerrville
176	8.9	La Grange ISD	La Grange
176	8.9	Red Oak ISD	Red Oak
176	8.9	Taylor ISD	Taylor
186	8.8	Calallen ISD	Corpus Christi
186	8.8	Castleberry ISD	Fort Worth
186	8.8	El Campo ISD	El Campo
186	8.8	Lubbock ISD	Lubbock
190	8.7	Arlington ISD	Arlington
190	8.7	Dayton ISD	Dayton
190	8.7	Elgin ISD	Elgin
190	8.7	Houston ISD	Houston
190	8.7	Sanger ISD	Sanger
195	8.6	Azle ISD	Azle
195	8.6	Bastrop ISD	Bastrop
195	8.6	Center ISD	Center
195	8.6	Garland ISD	Garland
195	8.6	Gilmer ISD	Gilmer
195	8.6	Krum ISD	Krum
195	8.6	Waxahachie ISD	Waxahachie
195	8.6	Willis ISD	Willis
203	8.5	Andrews ISD	Andrews
203	8.5	Borger ISD	Borger
203	8.5	Bridgeport ISD	Bridgeport
203	8.5	Calhoun County ISD	Port Lavaca
203	8.5	Canton ISD	Canton
203	8.5	Corsicana ISD	Corsicana
203	8.5	Cypress-Fairbanks ISD	Houston
203	8.5	Georgetown ISD	Georgetown
203	8.5	Liberty ISD	Liberty
203	8.5	Sweetwater ISD	Sweetwater
203	8.5	Waller ISD	Waller
214	8.4	Big Spring ISD	Big Spring
214	8.4	Eagle Academy of Abilene	Lewisville
214	8.4	New Braunfels ISD	New Braunfels
214	8.4	North East ISD	San Antonio
214	8.4	Palestine ISD	Palestine
214	8.4	San Felipe-Del Rio CISD	Del Rio
214	8.4	Wharton ISD	Wharton
221	8.3	Brenham ISD	Brenham
221	8.3	Deer Park ISD	Deer Park
221	8.3	Hallsville ISD	Hallsville
221	8.3	Mansfield ISD	Mansfield
221	8.3	Princeton ISD	Princeton
226	8.2	Greenville ISD	Greenville
226	8.2	Lamesa ISD	Lamesa
226	8.2	Marshall ISD	Marshall
226	8.2	Pine Tree ISD	Longview
226	8.2	Sharyland ISD	Mission
226	8.2	Tatum ISD	Tatum
226	8.2	Texarkana ISD	Texarkana
233	8.1	Kaufman ISD	Kaufman
233	8.1	Shepherd ISD	Shepherd
233	8.1	Whitehouse ISD	Whitehouse
233	8.1	Wichita Falls ISD	Wichita Falls
237	8.0	Decatur ISD	Decatur
237	8.0	Frenship ISD	Wolfforth
237	8.0	Granbury ISD	Granbury
237	8.0	Mineral Wells ISD	Mineral Wells
237	8.0	Stephenville ISD	Stephenville
242	7.9	Mount Vernon ISD	Mount Vernon
242	7.9	United ISD	Laredo
244	7.8	Coldspring-Oakhurst CISD	Coldspring
244	7.8	Ennis ISD	Ennis
244	7.8	Mabank ISD	Mabank
244	7.8	Texas City ISD	Texas City
248	7.7	Pearsall ISD	Pearsall
248	7.7	Tyler ISD	Tyler
248	7.7	West Orange-Cove CISD	Orange
251	7.6	Commerce ISD	Commerce
251	7.6	Crosby ISD	Crosby
251	7.6	Cuero ISD	Cuero
251	7.6	Dickinson ISD	Dickinson
251	7.6	La Marque ISD	La Marque
251	7.6	Navarro ISD	Seguin
251	7.6	Waco ISD	Waco
258	7.5	Alvin ISD	Alvin
258	7.5	Ector County ISD	Odessa
258	7.5	Gonzales ISD	Gonzales
258	7.5	Madisonville CISD	Madisonville
258	7.5	Paris ISD	Paris
263	7.4	Brownfield ISD	Brownfield
263	7.4	Lamar CISD	Rosenberg
263	7.4	Midway ISD	Hewitt
263	7.4	Mineola ISD	Mineola
263	7.4	Port Neches-Groves ISD	Port Neches
268	7.3	Canyon ISD	Canyon
268	7.3	Columbia-Brazoria ISD	West Columbia
268	7.3	Fairfield ISD	Fairfield
268	7.3	Forney ISD	Forney
268	7.3	Glen Rose ISD	Glen Rose
268	7.3	Hardin-Jefferson ISD	Sour Lake
268	7.3	Hempstead ISD	Hempstead
268	7.3	Lorena ISD	Lorena
268	7.3	Terrell ISD	Terrell
268	7.3	Uvalde CISD	Uvalde
278	7.2	Columbus ISD	Columbus
278	7.2	Pilot Point ISD	Pilot Point
278	7.2	Zapata County ISD	Zapata
281	7.1	Caldwell ISD	Caldwell
281	7.1	Carthage ISD	Carthage
281	7.1	La Vernia ISD	La Vernia
284	7.0	Bryan ISD	Bryan
284	7.0	Celina ISD	Celina
284	7.0	China Spring ISD	Waco
284	7.0	Cleveland ISD	Cleveland
284	7.0	Longview ISD	Longview
284	7.0	Northwest ISD	Justin
290	6.9	Fabens ISD	Fabens
290	6.9	Livingston ISD	Livingston
290	6.9	Sherman ISD	Sherman
293	6.8	Austin ISD	Austin
293	6.8	Bullard ISD	Bullard
293	6.8	Comal ISD	New Braunfels
293	6.8	Harlingen CISD	Harlingen
293	6.8	Hereford ISD	Hereford
293	6.8	Humble ISD	Humble
293	6.8	Jacksonville ISD	Jacksonville
293	6.8	Lufkin ISD	Lufkin
293	6.8	Schertz-Cibolo-U City ISD	Schertz
293	6.8	Silsbee ISD	Silsbee
303	6.7	Fort Worth ISD	Fort Worth
303	6.7	Klein ISD	Klein
303	6.7	Liberty Hill ISD	Liberty Hill
303	6.7	Needville ISD	Needville
307	6.6	Tuloso-Midway ISD	Corpus Christi
308	6.5	College Station ISD	College Station
308	6.5	Fort Bend ISD	Sugar Land
308	6.5	North Lamar ISD	Paris
308	6.5	Weatherford ISD	Weatherford
312	6.4	Wylie ISD	Wylie
313	6.3	Greenwood ISD	Midland
313	6.3	Hillsboro ISD	Hillsboro
313	6.3	Huffman ISD	Huffman
313	6.3	Lumberton ISD	Lumberton
317	6.2	Dallas ISD	Dallas
317	6.2	Montgomery ISD	Montgomery
317	6.2	Pearland ISD	Pearland
320	6.1	Southwest School	Houston
321	6.0	Leander ISD	Leander
321	6.0	Pleasant Grove ISD	Texarkana
321	6.0	Round Rock ISD	Round Rock
321	6.0	Spring Branch ISD	Houston
325	5.9	Denton ISD	Denton
325	5.9	Richardson ISD	Richardson
325	5.9	Santa Fe ISD	Santa Fe
328	5.8	Clear Creek ISD	League City
328	5.8	Katy ISD	Katy
328	5.8	Lake Dallas ISD	Lake Dallas
328	5.8	Magnolia ISD	Magnolia
332	5.7	Bridge City ISD	Bridge City
332	5.7	Hamshire-Fannett ISD	Hamshire
334	5.6	Galveston ISD	Galveston
334	5.6	Nacogdoches ISD	Nacogdoches
334	5.6	Roma ISD	Roma
334	5.6	Spring Hill ISD	Longview
338	5.5	Keller ISD	Keller
338	5.5	Lewisville ISD	Flower Mound
340	5.4	Bellville ISD	Bellville

Note: This section only includes districts with 1,500 or more students; All categories are ranked from high to low

Rank	Number	District Name	City
341	5.3	Robinson ISD	Robinson
342	5.2	Aubrey ISD	Aubrey
342	5.2	Port Arthur ISD	Port Arthur
342	5.2	Rockwall ISD	Rockwall
342	5.2	Wylie ISD	Abilene
346	5.1	Bay City ISD	Bay City
346	5.1	Midlothian ISD	Midlothian
348	5.0	Tomball ISD	Tomball
349	4.9	Barbers Hill ISD	Mont Belvieu
350	4.8	Little Cypress-Mauricevil	Orange
350	4.8	Wimberley ISD	Wimberley
352	4.6	Orangefield ISD	Orangefield
352	4.6	Plano ISD	Plano
354	4.3	Mckinney ISD	Mckinney
355	4.2	Conroe ISD	Conroe
356	4.1	Boerne ISD	Boerne
356	4.1	Ripley House Charter School	Houston
358	4.0	Allen ISD	Allen
359	3.8	Alamo Heights ISD	San Antonio
360	3.7	Progreso ISD	Progreso
361	3.6	Frisco ISD	Frisco
361	3.6	Grapevine-Colleyville ISD	Grapevine
361	3.6	Prosper ISD	Prosper
364	3.5	La Joya ISD	La Joya
365	2.9	Lake Travis ISD	Austin
366	2.8	Argyle ISD	Argyle
366	2.8	Dripping Spgs ISD	Dripping Spgs
366	2.8	Robstown ISD	Robstown
369	2.7	Coppell ISD	Coppell
370	2.4	Point Isabel ISD	Port Isabel
371	2.3	Aledo ISD	Aledo
371	2.3	South San Antonio ISD	San Antonio
373	2.0	Rio Hondo ISD	Rio Hondo
374	1.9	La Feria Ind SD	La Feria
375	1.7	West Oso ISD	Corpus Christi
376	1.6	Rio Grande City CISD	Rio Grande City
377	1.5	Friendswood ISD	Friendswood
378	1.4	Donna ISD	Donna
379	1.2	Raymondville ISD	Raymondville
380	0.7	Los Fresnos CISD	Los Fresnos
381	0.6	Lovejoy ISD	Allen
382	0.5	Eanes ISD	Austin
382	0.5	Lake Worth ISD	Lake Worth
384	0.4	Edgewood ISD	San Antonio
384	0.4	Edinburg CISD	Edinburg
384	0.4	San Elizario ISD	San Elizario
384	0.4	Weslaco ISD	Weslaco
388	0.3	Carroll ISD	Grapevine
389	0.2	Eagle Pass ISD	Eagle Pass
390	0.1	Pharr-San Juan-Alamo ISD	Pharr
391	0.0	Brownsville ISD	Brownsville
391	0.0	Edcouch-Elsa ISD	Edcouch
391	0.0	Harlandale ISD	San Antonio
391	0.0	Hidalgo ISD	Hidalgo
391	0.0	Highland Park ISD	Dallas
391	0.0	Laredo ISD	Laredo
391	0.0	Lyford CISD	Lyford
391	0.0	Mcallen ISD	Mcallen
391	0.0	Mercedes ISD	Mercedes
391	0.0	Mission CISD	Mission
391	0.0	North Forest ISD	Houston
391	0.0	San Benito CISD	San Benito
391	0.0	Valley View ISD	Pharr

Student/Teacher Ratio

(number of students per teacher)

Rank	Number	District Name	City
1	11.1	Glen Rose ISD	Glen Rose
2	11.4	Fairfield ISD	Fairfield
3	11.5	Breckenridge ISD	Breckenridge
3	11.5	North Lamar ISD	Paris
3	11.5	Sweetwater ISD	Sweetwater
6	11.6	West ISD	West
7	11.7	Hempstead ISD	Hempstead
7	11.7	Pittsburg ISD	Pittsburg
9	11.9	Cuero ISD	Cuero
9	11.9	Jasper ISD	Jasper
9	11.9	Paris ISD	Paris
9	11.9	Rains ISD	Emory
13	12.0	Godley ISD	Godley
13	12.0	Liberty ISD	Liberty
15	12.1	Dalhart ISD	Dalhart
15	12.1	Gilmer ISD	Gilmer
15	12.1	Levelland ISD	Levelland
18	12.2	Brownfield ISD	Brownfield
18	12.2	Navasota ISD	Navasota
20	12.3	Bonham ISD	Bonham
20	12.3	Coldspring-Oakhurst CISD	Coldspring
20	12.3	Mount Vernon ISD	Mount Vernon
20	12.3	Pecos-Barstow-Toyah ISD	Pecos
24	12.4	Aransas Pass ISD	Aransas Pass
24	12.4	Bay City ISD	Bay City
24	12.4	Lamesa ISD	Lamesa
27	12.5	Denton ISD	Denton
27	12.5	Henderson ISD	Henderson
27	12.5	Liberty-Eylau ISD	Texarkana
27	12.5	Seminole ISD	Seminole
31	12.6	Gladewater ISD	Gladewater
31	12.6	Hardin-Jefferson ISD	Sour Lake
31	12.6	Kemp ISD	Kemp
31	12.6	Royal ISD	Pattison
35	12.7	Bridgeport ISD	Bridgeport
35	12.7	Fort Stockton ISD	Fort Stockton
35	12.7	Georgetown ISD	Georgetown
35	12.7	Hallsville ISD	Hallsville
35	12.7	Hondo ISD	Hondo
35	12.7	Pearsall ISD	Pearsall
35	12.7	Pleasant Grove ISD	Texarkana
42	12.8	Cameron ISD	Cameron
42	12.8	Carthage ISD	Carthage
42	12.8	Columbus ISD	Columbus
42	12.8	Lovejoy ISD	Allen
42	12.8	Palacios ISD	Palacios
42	12.8	Smithville ISD	Smithville
42	12.8	Wharton ISD	Wharton
42	12.8	Whitesboro ISD	Whitesboro
42	12.8	Whitney ISD	Whitney
51	12.9	Bellville ISD	Bellville
51	12.9	Denver City ISD	Denver City
51	12.9	Giddings ISD	Giddings
51	12.9	Mineola ISD	Mineola
51	12.9	Perryton ISD	Perryton
51	12.9	Shepherd ISD	Shepherd
51	12.9	Yoakum ISD	Yoakum
58	13.0	Aransas County ISD	Rockport
58	13.0	Center ISD	Center
58	13.0	Commerce ISD	Commerce
58	13.0	Gainesville ISD	Gainesville
58	13.0	Llano ISD	Llano
58	13.0	Marble Falls ISD	Marble Falls
58	13.0	Robinson ISD	Robinson
65	13.1	Bandera ISD	Bandera
65	13.1	Brenham ISD	Brenham
65	13.1	Gonzales ISD	Gonzales
65	13.1	Hidalgo ISD	Hidalgo
65	13.1	Krum ISD	Krum
65	13.1	Lubbock-Cooper ISD	Lubbock
65	13.1	Marshall ISD	Marshall
65	13.1	Mount Pleasant ISD	Mount Pleasant
65	13.1	Pleasanton ISD	Pleasanton
65	13.1	Royse City ISD	Royse City
65	13.1	Sanger ISD	Sanger
76	13.2	Bowie ISD	Bowie
76	13.2	Burkburnett ISD	Burkburnett
76	13.2	Caldwell ISD	Caldwell
76	13.2	Groesbeck ISD	Groesbeck
76	13.2	Mineral Wells ISD	Mineral Wells
76	13.2	Sealy ISD	Sealy
76	13.2	Westwood ISD	Palestine
83	13.3	Anna ISD	Anna
83	13.3	Greenville ISD	Greenville
83	13.3	Hamshire-Fannett ISD	Hamshire
83	13.3	Hillsboro ISD	Hillsboro
83	13.3	Palestine ISD	Palestine
83	13.3	Pampa ISD	Pampa
83	13.3	Snyder ISD	Snyder
83	13.3	Sulphur Springs ISD	Sulphur Springs
83	13.3	Vernon ISD	Vernon
83	13.3	Wichita Falls ISD	Wichita Falls
83	13.3	Wimberley ISD	Wimberley
94	13.4	Eanes ISD	Austin
94	13.4	Kilgore ISD	Kilgore
94	13.4	La Grange ISD	La Grange
94	13.4	Monahans-Wickett-Poyote ISD	Monahans
94	13.4	Port Neches-Groves ISD	Port Neches
94	13.4	Sherman ISD	Sherman
94	13.4	Sinton ISD	Sinton
101	13.5	Atlanta ISD	Atlanta
101	13.5	Beaumont ISD	Beaumont
101	13.5	Borger ISD	Borger
101	13.5	Denison ISD	Denison
101	13.5	Dumas ISD	Dumas
101	13.5	Graham ISD	Graham
101	13.5	Mexia ISD	Mexia
101	13.5	Tyler ISD	Tyler
109	13.6	Frenship ISD	Wolfforth
109	13.6	Frisco ISD	Frisco
109	13.6	Granbury ISD	Granbury
109	13.6	Hereford ISD	Hereford
109	13.6	Joshua ISD	Joshua
109	13.6	Lewisville ISD	Flower Mound
109	13.6	San Marcos CISD	San Marcos
109	13.6	South Texas ISD	Mercedes
109	13.6	Vidor ISD	Vidor
118	13.7	Advantage Academy	Dallas
118	13.7	Andrews ISD	Andrews
118	13.7	Devine ISD	Devine
118	13.7	El Campo ISD	El Campo
118	13.7	Fabens ISD	Fabens
118	13.7	Galena Park ISD	Houston
118	13.7	Gatesville ISD	Gatesville
118	13.7	La Marque ISD	La Marque
118	13.7	Lytle ISD	Lytle
118	13.7	Venus ISD	Venus
118	13.7	West Orange-Cove CISD	Orange
129	13.8	Diboll ISD	Diboll
129	13.8	Fredericksburg ISD	Fredericksburg
129	13.8	Lufkin ISD	Lufkin
129	13.8	Mabank ISD	Mabank
129	13.8	Mathis ISD	Mathis
129	13.8	Pilot Point ISD	Pilot Point
129	13.8	Rio Grande City CISD	Rio Grande City
129	13.8	Rusk ISD	Rusk
129	13.8	Tarkington ISD	Cleveland
129	13.8	Texarkana ISD	Texarkana
129	13.8	West Oso ISD	Corpus Christi
140	13.9	Canton ISD	Canton
140	13.9	Central ISD	Pollok
140	13.9	Chapel Hill ISD	Tyler
140	13.9	Del Valle ISD	Del Valle
140	13.9	Huntington ISD	Huntington
140	13.9	Irving ISD	Irving
140	13.9	Jacksonville ISD	Jacksonville
140	13.9	Liberty Hill ISD	Liberty Hill
140	13.9	Little Cypress-Mauricevil	Orange
140	13.9	Lumberton ISD	Lumberton
140	13.9	Orange Grove ISD	Orange Grove
140	13.9	Plano ISD	Plano
140	13.9	Richardson ISD	Richardson
140	13.9	Robstown ISD	Robstown
140	13.9	Seguin ISD	Seguin
140	13.9	Silsbee ISD	Silsbee
140	13.9	Terrell ISD	Terrell
140	13.9	Uvalde CISD	Uvalde
140	13.9	Van ISD	Van
159	14.0	Abilene ISD	Abilene
159	14.0	Boerne ISD	Boerne
159	14.0	College Station ISD	College Station
159	14.0	Decatur ISD	Decatur
159	14.0	Iowa Park CISD	Iowa Park
164	14.1	Bullard ISD	Bullard
164	14.1	Kerrville ISD	Kerrville
164	14.1	Lyford CISD	Lyford
164	14.1	Mckinney ISD	Mckinney
164	14.1	Spring Branch ISD	Houston
164	14.1	Spring Hill ISD	Longview
164	14.1	Sweeny ISD	Sweeny
171	14.2	Alamo Heights ISD	San Antonio
171	14.2	Austin ISD	Austin
171	14.2	Carroll ISD	Grapevine
171	14.2	Cleburne ISD	Cleburne
171	14.2	Cleveland ISD	Cleveland
171	14.2	Copperas Cove ISD	Copperas Cove
171	14.2	Corsicana ISD	Corsicana
171	14.2	Floresville ISD	Floresville
171	14.2	Lockhart ISD	Lockhart
171	14.2	Lorena ISD	Lorena
171	14.2	Lubbock ISD	Lubbock
171	14.2	Springtown ISD	Springtown
171	14.2	Temple ISD	Temple
171	14.2	Valley View ISD	Pharr
185	14.3	Clear Creek ISD	League City
185	14.3	Connally ISD	Waco
185	14.3	Goose Creek CISD	Baytown
185	14.3	Grapevine-Colleyville ISD	Grapevine
185	14.3	Katy ISD	Katy

Note: This section only includes districts with 1,500 or more students; All categories are ranked from high to low

Rank	Number	District Name	City
185	14.3	Pine Tree ISD	Longview
185	14.3	San Angelo ISD	San Angelo
185	14.3	Sheldon ISD	Houston
185	14.3	Waco ISD	Waco
185	14.3	Wills Point ISD	Wills Point
195	14.4	Brownwood ISD	Brownwood
195	14.4	Coppell ISD	Coppell
195	14.4	El Paso ISD	El Paso
195	14.4	Forney ISD	Forney
195	14.4	Galveston ISD	Galveston
195	14.4	Humble ISD	Humble
195	14.4	Lindale ISD	Lindale
195	14.4	Livingston ISD	Livingston
195	14.4	Poteet ISD	Poteet
195	14.4	Southside ISD	San Antonio
205	14.5	Canutillo ISD	El Paso
205	14.5	Kaufman ISD	Kaufman
205	14.5	Killeen ISD	Killeen
205	14.5	La Feria Ind SD	La Feria
205	14.5	Lake Dallas ISD	Lake Dallas
205	14.5	Magnolia ISD	Magnolia
205	14.5	Plainview ISD	Plainview
205	14.5	Raymondville ISD	Raymondville
205	14.5	Roma ISD	Roma
214	14.6	Amarillo ISD	Amarillo
214	14.6	Barbers Hill ISD	Mont Belvieu
214	14.6	Brownsville ISD	Brownsville
214	14.6	Community ISD	Nevada
214	14.6	Lake Worth ISD	Lake Worth
214	14.6	Leander ISD	Leander
214	14.6	Madisonville CISD	Madisonville
214	14.6	Prosper ISD	Prosper
214	14.6	South San Antonio ISD	San Antonio
214	14.6	Waxahachie ISD	Waxahachie
224	14.7	Alice ISD	Alice
224	14.7	Bastrop ISD	Bastrop
224	14.7	Bryan ISD	Bryan
224	14.7	Burnet CISD	Burnet
224	14.7	Calhoun County ISD	Port Lavaca
224	14.7	Crystal City ISD	Crystal City
224	14.7	Dallas ISD	Dallas
224	14.7	Huntsville ISD	Huntsville
224	14.7	La Joya ISD	La Joya
224	14.7	Manor ISD	Manor
224	14.7	Point Isabel ISD	Port Isabel
224	14.7	Rockdale ISD	Rockdale
224	14.7	Round Rock ISD	Round Rock
224	14.7	Ysleta ISD	El Paso
238	14.8	Aldine ISD	Houston
238	14.8	Alief ISD	Houston
238	14.8	Athens ISD	Athens
238	14.8	Aubrey ISD	Aubrey
238	14.8	Belton ISD	Belton
238	14.8	Big Spring ISD	Big Spring
238	14.8	Brownsboro ISD	Brownsboro
238	14.8	Celina ISD	Celina
238	14.8	Desoto ISD	Desoto
238	14.8	Harlingen CISD	Harlingen
238	14.8	Hays CISD	Kyle
238	14.8	Hudson ISD	Lufkin
238	14.8	Mercedes ISD	Mercedes
238	14.8	Midland ISD	Midland
238	14.8	Nacogdoches ISD	Nacogdoches
238	14.8	Orangefield ISD	Orangefield
238	14.8	Princeton ISD	Princeton
238	14.8	Splendora ISD	Splendora
238	14.8	Victoria ISD	Victoria
257	14.9	Argyle ISD	Argyle
257	14.9	Bridge City ISD	Bridge City
257	14.9	Deer Park ISD	Deer Park
257	14.9	Donna ISD	Donna
257	14.9	Edcouch-Elsa ISD	Edcouch
257	14.9	Harlandale ISD	San Antonio
257	14.9	Nederland ISD	Nederland
257	14.9	Schertz-Cibolo-U City ISD	Schertz
257	14.9	Wylie ISD	Wylie
266	15.0	Allen ISD	Allen
266	15.0	Brazosport ISD	Clute
266	15.0	Carrizo Springs CISD	Carrizo Springs
266	15.0	Carrollton-Farmers Branch	Carrollton
266	15.0	Columbia-Brazoria ISD	West Columbia
266	15.0	Kennedale ISD	Kennedale
266	15.0	Little Elm ISD	Little Elm
266	15.0	Longview ISD	Longview
266	15.0	Mcallen ISD	Mcallen
266	15.0	Mission CISD	Mission

Rank	Number	District Name	City
266	15.0	New Caney ISD	New Caney
266	15.0	North East ISD	San Antonio
266	15.0	Northwest ISD	Justin
266	15.0	Pflugerville ISD	Pflugerville
266	15.0	Spring ISD	Houston
266	15.0	Stafford MSD	Stafford
266	15.0	Weatherford ISD	Weatherford
266	15.0	Zapata County ISD	Zapata
284	15.1	China Spring ISD	Waco
284	15.1	Hutto ISD	Hutto
284	15.1	Lake Travis ISD	Austin
284	15.1	Lampasas ISD	Lampasas
284	15.1	Midlothian ISD	Midlothian
284	15.1	Navarro ISD	Seguin
284	15.1	Port Arthur ISD	Port Arthur
284	15.1	Santa Fe ISD	Santa Fe
284	15.1	Willis ISD	Willis
293	15.2	Aledo ISD	Aledo
293	15.2	Calallen ISD	Corpus Christi
293	15.2	Comal ISD	New Braunfels
293	15.2	Everman ISD	Everman
293	15.2	Needville ISD	Needville
293	15.2	Pasadena ISD	Pasadena
293	15.2	Quinlan ISD	Quinlan
293	15.2	Taylor ISD	Taylor
293	15.2	Waller ISD	Waller
293	15.2	Yes College Preparatory School	Houston
303	15.3	Channelview ISD	Channelview
303	15.3	Ennis ISD	Ennis
303	15.3	Ferris ISD	Ferris
303	15.3	Flour Bluff ISD	Corpus Christi
303	15.3	Judson ISD	Live Oak
303	15.3	Kingsville ISD	Kingsville
303	15.3	Klein ISD	Klein
303	15.3	North Forest ISD	Houston
303	15.3	Stephenville	Stephenville
303	15.3	Texas City	Texas City
303	15.3	Tuloso-Midway ISD	Corpus Christi
314	15.4	Alvin ISD	Alvin
314	15.4	Arlington ISD	Arlington
314	15.4	Beeville ISD	Beeville
314	15.4	Birdville ISD	Haltom City
314	15.4	Greenwood ISD	Midland
314	15.4	Highland Park ISD	Dallas
314	15.4	Laredo ISD	Laredo
314	15.4	Midway ISD	Hewitt
314	15.4	Pharr-San Juan-Alamo ISD	Pharr
323	15.5	Canyon ISD	Canyon
323	15.5	Cypress-Fairbanks ISD	Houston
323	15.5	Ingleside ISD	Ingleside
323	15.5	La Porte ISD	La Porte
323	15.5	San Elizario ISD	San Elizario
323	15.5	San Felipe-Del Rio CISD	Del Rio
329	15.6	Burleson ISD	Burleson
329	15.6	Crowley ISD	Crowley
329	15.6	Edinburg CISD	Edinburg
329	15.6	Garland ISD	Garland
329	15.6	Montgomery ISD	Montgomery
329	15.6	Northside ISD	San Antonio
329	15.6	Rockwall ISD	Rockwall
329	15.6	San Benito CISD	San Benito
329	15.6	Somerset ISD	Somerset
329	15.6	White Settlement ISD	White Settlement
339	15.7	Angleton ISD	Angleton
339	15.7	Gregory-Portland ISD	Portland
339	15.7	La Vega ISD	Waco
339	15.7	Mesquite ISD	Mesquite
339	15.7	Whitehouse ISD	Whitehouse
344	15.8	Conroe ISD	Conroe
344	15.8	Eagle Mt-Saginaw ISD	Fort Worth
344	15.8	Edgewood ISD	San Antonio
344	15.8	Fort Bend ISD	Sugar Land
344	15.8	Fort Worth ISD	Fort Worth
344	15.8	Harmony Science Academy	Houston
344	15.8	Medina Valley ISD	Castroville
344	15.8	Tomball ISD	Tomball
352	15.9	Azle ISD	Azle
352	15.9	Corpus Christi ISD	Corpus Christi
352	15.9	Hurst-Euless-Bedford ISD	Bedford
352	15.9	Rio Hondo ISD	Rio Hondo
352	15.9	River Road ISD	Amarillo
352	15.9	Tatum ISD	Tatum
358	16.0	Ector County ISD	Odessa
358	16.0	Elgin ISD	Elgin
358	16.0	Friendswood ISD	Friendswood
358	16.0	New Braunfels ISD	New Braunfels

Rank	Number	District Name	City
358	16.0	Red Oak ISD	Red Oak
358	16.0	Weslaco ISD	Weslaco
364	16.1	Dripping Spgs ISD	Dripping Spgs
364	16.1	United ISD	Laredo
364	16.1	Wylie ISD	Abilene
367	16.2	Cedar Hill ISD	Cedar Hill
367	16.2	Dickinson ISD	Dickinson
367	16.2	Eagle Pass ISD	Eagle Pass
367	16.2	East Central ISD	San Antonio
367	16.2	Keller ISD	Keller
367	16.2	Los Fresnos CISD	Los Fresnos
373	16.3	San Antonio ISD	San Antonio
373	16.3	Southwest ISD	San Antonio
375	16.4	Dayton ISD	Dayton
375	16.4	Grand Prairie ISD	Grand Prairie
375	16.4	Lamar CISD	Rosenberg
375	16.4	Mansfield ISD	Mansfield
375	16.4	Sharyland ISD	Mission
380	16.5	Huffman ISD	Huffman
380	16.5	Progreso ISD	Progreso
382	16.6	Alvarado ISD	Alvarado
382	16.6	Crandall ISD	Crandall
382	16.6	Kipp Inc Charter	Houston
382	16.6	Socorro ISD	El Paso
386	16.7	Castleberry ISD	Fort Worth
386	16.7	La Vernia ISD	La Vernia
388	16.8	Eagle Academy of Abilene	Lewisville
388	16.8	Lancaster ISD	Lancaster
388	16.8	Pearland ISD	Pearland
391	16.9	Houston ISD	Houston
392	17.0	Duncanville ISD	Duncanville
393	17.1	Harmony Science Acad (Fort Worth)	Fort Worth
394	17.2	Clint ISD	El Paso
394	17.2	Crosby ISD	Crosby
396	17.3	Life School	Lancaster
397	19.0	School of Excellence in Education	San Antonio
398	19.7	Idea Academy	Weslaco
399	21.9	Dallas Can Academy Charter	Dallas
399	21.9	Varnett Charter School	Houston
401	23.2	Ripley House Charter School	Houston
401	23.2	Winfree Academy	Irving
403	31.7	Southwest School	Houston

Student/Librarian Ratio

(number of students per librarian)

Rank	Number	District Name	City
1	376.8	Tatum ISD	Tatum
2	474.7	Smithville ISD	Smithville
3	503.0	Palacios ISD	Palacios
4	503.8	South Texas ISD	Mercedes
5	510.0	Central ISD	Pollok
6	517.3	Varnett Charter School	Houston
6	517.5	West ISD	West
8	527.2	Gainesville ISD	Gainesville
9	527.7	Groesbeck ISD	Groesbeck
10	535.3	Hereford ISD	Hereford
11	537.0	Lorena ISD	Lorena
12	538.9	Alice ISD	Alice
13	541.8	Bellville ISD	Bellville
14	543.0	Commerce ISD	Commerce
15	546.8	Port Neches-Groves ISD	Port Neches
16	563.2	Gatesville ISD	Gatesville
17	566.3	La Marque ISD	La Marque
18	566.8	Hamshire-Fannett ISD	Hamshire
19	576.4	Hidalgo ISD	Hidalgo
20	579.5	Lockhart ISD	Lockhart
21	584.2	Fairfield ISD	Fairfield
22	584.5	Wharton ISD	Wharton
23	586.0	Orangefield ISD	Orangefield
24	587.3	Brownfield ISD	Brownfield
25	588.5	Gilmer ISD	Gilmer
26	599.2	Princeton ISD	Princeton
27	607.3	Decatur ISD	Decatur
28	624.6	Canyon ISD	Canyon
29	626.4	Gladewater ISD	Gladewater
30	626.8	Zapata County ISD	Zapata
31	627.5	Weatherford ISD	Weatherford
32	628.0	Pecos-Barstow-Toyah ISD	Pecos
33	632.2	Carrollton-Farmers Branch	Carrollton
34	634.5	Point Isabel ISD	Port Isabel
35	634.8	Bandera ISD	Bandera
36	639.4	Dumas ISD	Dumas
37	639.7	Monahans-Wickett-Pyote ISD	Monahans
38	642.0	Liberty Hill ISD	Liberty Hill

Note: This section only includes districts with 1,500 or more students; All categories are ranked from high to low

Rank	Value	District	City
39	642.1	Hutto ISD	Hutto
40	644.9	Royse City ISD	Royse City
41	646.0	Lovejoy ISD	Allen
42	649.3	Hudson ISD	Lufkin
43	657.0	Pleasant Grove ISD	Texarkana
44	659.5	El Paso ISD	El Paso
45	661.7	Giddings ISD	Giddings
46	664.3	Valley View ISD	Pharr
47	664.9	South San Antonio ISD	San Antonio
48	667.7	Wimberley ISD	Wimberley
49	674.0	San Elizario ISD	San Elizario
50	674.4	Lampasas ISD	Lampasas
51	679.1	Little Elm ISD	Little Elm
52	680.9	Temple ISD	Temple
53	686.8	Barbers Hill ISD	Mont Belvieu
54	688.3	Midway ISD	Hewitt
55	693.2	Waller ISD	Waller
56	693.5	Crandall ISD	Crandall
57	695.7	Longview ISD	Longview
58	696.3	Terrell ISD	Terrell
59	696.7	West Oso ISD	Corpus Christi
60	696.9	Richardson ISD	Richardson
61	700.5	Mission CISD	Mission
62	701.3	Dalhart ISD	Dalhart
63	701.4	Dallas ISD	Dallas
64	702.2	Roma ISD	Roma
65	703.9	Santa Fe ISD	Santa Fe
66	704.1	Carroll ISD	Grapevine
67	710.6	Stephenville	Stephenville
68	711.3	Victoria ISD	Victoria
69	712.6	Carthage ISD	Carthage
70	713.4	La Porte ISD	La Porte
71	713.6	Mineral Wells ISD	Mineral Wells
72	714.6	Bryan ISD	Bryan
73	720.6	Burkburnett ISD	Burkburnett
74	723.3	Garland ISD	Garland
75	725.9	Fort Worth ISD	Fort Worth
76	733.4	Canutillo ISD	El Paso
77	734.6	Royal ISD	Pattison
78	736.3	Denton ISD	Denton
78	736.3	Raymondville ISD	Raymondville
80	737.4	San Benito CISD	San Benito
81	739.3	Galveston ISD	Galveston
82	739.6	Spring Hill ISD	Longview
83	744.7	Bastrop ISD	Bastrop
84	746.0	Montgomery ISD	Montgomery
85	748.0	Texas City ISD	Texas City
86	748.8	Los Fresnos CISD	Los Fresnos
87	749.2	Lubbock-Cooper ISD	Lubbock
88	749.8	Eanes ISD	Austin
89	752.0	Denver City ISD	Denver City
90	752.7	Bridgeport ISD	Bridgeport
91	753.1	Cedar Hill ISD	Cedar Hill
92	754.6	Diboll ISD	Diboll
93	757.6	Copperas Cove ISD	Copperas Cove
94	758.7	Hondo ISD	Hondo
95	759.0	Duncanville ISD	Duncanville
96	761.0	Brazosport ISD	Clute
97	761.2	Burleson ISD	Burleson
98	764.8	Aledo ISD	Aledo
99	766.6	Andrews ISD	Andrews
100	768.1	Bowie ISD	Bowie
101	768.5	Mesquite ISD	Mesquite
102	769.0	Columbus ISD	Columbus
103	769.3	Ysleta ISD	El Paso
104	770.2	Manor ISD	Manor
105	770.9	Plainview ISD	Plainview
106	771.0	Hays CISD	Kyle
107	772.1	Mcallen ISD	Mcallen
108	773.5	Abilene ISD	Abilene
109	777.5	Godley ISD	Godley
110	779.4	Edgewood ISD	San Antonio
111	781.0	Mercedes ISD	Mercedes
112	783.0	Willis ISD	Willis
113	783.3	Tyler ISD	Tyler
114	783.7	Plano ISD	Plano
115	785.0	Rains ISD	Emory
116	788.0	Huffman ISD	Huffman
117	790.5	Mineola ISD	Mineola
118	790.6	Paris ISD	Paris
119	792.0	Taylor ISD	Taylor
120	793.3	Seminole ISD	Seminole
121	796.2	Kingsville ISD	Kingsville
122	797.2	Sharyland ISD	Mission
123	798.1	Lamar CISD	Rosenberg
124	799.0	Boerne ISD	Boerne
125	802.2	Marble Falls ISD	Marble Falls
126	803.0	Cameron ISD	Cameron
127	803.6	Jacksonville ISD	Jacksonville
128	804.7	Hurst-Euless-Bedford ISD	Bedford
129	806.3	Eagle Mt-Saginaw ISD	Fort Worth
130	812.6	Austin ISD	Austin
131	812.9	Llano ISD	Llano
132	814.3	Midlothian ISD	Midlothian
132	814.3	Rockwall ISD	Rockwall
134	815.9	Georgetown ISD	Georgetown
135	816.5	Community ISD	Nevada
136	816.7	Frisco ISD	Frisco
137	818.0	Lake Dallas ISD	Lake Dallas
138	818.7	Dayton ISD	Dayton
139	820.5	Greenwood ISD	Midland
140	822.1	Lake Travis ISD	Austin
141	823.6	Laredo ISD	Laredo
142	825.8	Vidor ISD	Vidor
143	826.0	Greenville ISD	Greenville
143	826.0	San Marcos CISD	San Marcos
145	826.3	Donna ISD	Donna
146	831.4	Ector County ISD	Odessa
147	833.2	Pharr-San Juan-Alamo ISD	Pharr
148	833.4	Spring Branch ISD	Houston
149	837.0	Schertz-Cibolo-U City ISD	Schertz
150	839.0	Killeen ISD	Killeen
151	840.2	Seguin ISD	Seguin
152	842.8	Harlingen CISD	Harlingen
153	843.1	Northwest ISD	Justin
154	843.3	Grand Prairie ISD	Grand Prairie
155	844.8	Joshua ISD	Joshua
156	847.5	Robstown ISD	Robstown
157	847.7	Comal ISD	New Braunfels
158	848.9	Granbury ISD	Granbury
159	849.0	Westwood ISD	Palestine
160	850.3	West Orange-Cove CISD	Orange
161	851.7	North Forest ISD	Houston
162	854.2	Harlandale ISD	San Antonio
163	855.5	Tomball ISD	Tomball
164	857.2	Bridge City ISD	Bridge City
165	860.0	Pleasanton ISD	Pleasanton
166	860.2	Round Rock ISD	Round Rock
167	861.0	Center ISD	Center
168	861.8	Rio Grande City CISD	Rio Grande City
169	866.2	Dripping Spgs ISD	Dripping Spgs
169	866.2	Little Cypress-Mauricevil	Orange
171	867.3	Needville ISD	Needville
172	869.3	Southside ISD	San Antonio
173	872.2	Mansfield ISD	Mansfield
174	872.8	El Campo ISD	El Campo
175	872.9	New Braunfels ISD	New Braunfels
176	873.1	Goose Creek CISD	Baytown
177	874.4	Alvin ISD	Alvin
178	877.2	Brownsville ISD	Brownsville
179	877.5	Springtown ISD	Springtown
180	878.5	Amarillo ISD	Amarillo
181	880.3	Angleton ISD	Angleton
182	882.3	Lancaster ISD	Lancaster
183	883.8	Beeville ISD	Beeville
184	889.0	La Joya ISD	La Joya
185	889.4	Fort Bend ISD	Sugar Land
186	891.5	Nacogdoches ISD	Nacogdoches
187	891.7	Wills Point ISD	Wills Point
188	895.0	Argyle ISD	Argyle
189	897.9	Birdville ISD	Haltom City
190	902.0	College Station ISD	College Station
191	902.7	Tarkington ISD	Cleveland
192	904.1	Pflugerville ISD	Pflugerville
193	906.4	Spring ISD	Houston
194	906.5	Atlanta ISD	Atlanta
194	906.5	New Caney ISD	New Caney
196	906.9	Desoto ISD	Desoto
197	907.7	Jasper ISD	Jasper
198	908.2	Highland Park ISD	Dallas
199	909.4	Edinburg CISD	Edinburg
200	916.5	Nederland ISD	Nederland
201	917.3	Clear Creek ISD	League City
202	919.3	Deer Park ISD	Deer Park
203	920.0	Glen Rose ISD	Glen Rose
204	921.4	Whitehouse ISD	Whitehouse
205	922.8	Leander ISD	Leander
206	926.3	Palestine ISD	Palestine
207	928.4	Iowa Park CISD	Iowa Park
208	930.0	Grapevine-Colleyville ISD	Grapevine
209	931.5	Somerset ISD	Somerset
210	931.6	Corpus Christi ISD	Corpus Christi
211	933.0	North East ISD	San Antonio
212	934.6	Conroe ISD	Conroe
213	935.6	Henderson ISD	Henderson
214	936.2	Snyder ISD	Snyder
215	938.3	Borger ISD	Borger
216	939.2	Arlington ISD	Arlington
217	940.5	Aransas Pass ISD	Aransas Pass
218	941.3	Clint ISD	El Paso
219	941.4	Aldine ISD	Houston
220	943.7	Pearland ISD	Pearland
221	944.8	Cleveland ISD	Cleveland
222	945.8	Pasadena ISD	Pasadena
223	947.4	San Antonio ISD	San Antonio
224	948.3	Bay City ISD	Bay City
225	949.2	Pine Tree ISD	Longview
226	949.5	Harmony Science Academy	Houston
227	950.0	Midland ISD	Midland
228	951.0	Hillsboro ISD	Hillsboro
229	951.2	Elgin ISD	Elgin
230	953.2	Huntsville ISD	Huntsville
231	958.9	Lufkin ISD	Lufkin
232	963.3	La Feria Ind SD	La Feria
233	973.5	United ISD	Laredo
234	974.3	Magnolia ISD	Magnolia
235	975.0	Lumberton ISD	Lumberton
236	977.5	Bonham ISD	Bonham
237	985.7	Levelland ISD	Levelland
238	986.3	Aransas County ISD	Rockport
239	986.4	Dickinson ISD	Dickinson
240	987.7	North Lamar ISD	Paris
241	989.0	Lubbock ISD	Lubbock
242	991.4	Allen ISD	Allen
243	992.5	Canton ISD	Canton
244	992.8	Northside ISD	San Antonio
245	997.2	Mckinney ISD	Mckinney
246	999.8	Livingston ISD	Livingston
247	1,006.3	Socorro ISD	El Paso
248	1,012.3	Alief ISD	Houston
249	1,015.8	Del Valle ISD	Del Valle
250	1,016.4	Klein ISD	Klein
250	1,016.4	Weslaco ISD	Weslaco
252	1,019.6	Uvalde CISD	Uvalde
253	1,026.4	Port Arthur ISD	Port Arthur
254	1,027.0	Columbia-Brazoria ISD	West Columbia
255	1,027.3	Crosby ISD	Crosby
256	1,028.3	Keller ISD	Keller
257	1,029.1	Coppell ISD	Coppell
258	1,033.3	San Felipe-Del Rio CISD	Del Rio
259	1,035.1	San Angelo ISD	San Angelo
260	1,042.9	Sheldon ISD	Houston
261	1,049.3	Gregory-Portland ISD	Portland
262	1,050.4	Fredericksburg ISD	Fredericksburg
263	1,058.7	Katy ISD	Katy
264	1,060.4	Red Oak ISD	Red Oak
265	1,066.3	Hallsville ISD	Hallsville
266	1,069.0	Calhoun County ISD	Port Lavaca
267	1,071.7	Chapel Hill ISD	Tyler
268	1,081.7	Lewisville ISD	Flower Mound
269	1,087.5	Judson ISD	Live Oak
270	1,094.8	Flour Bluff ISD	Corpus Christi
271	1,110.0	Whitesboro ISD	Whitesboro
272	1,112.0	Progreso ISD	Progreso
273	1,118.4	Sinton ISD	Sinton
274	1,120.6	La Grange ISD	La Grange
275	1,122.6	Irving ISD	Irving
276	1,128.0	Perryton ISD	Perryton
277	1,141.7	Tuloso-Midway ISD	Corpus Christi
278	1,153.1	Southwest ISD	San Antonio
279	1,187.7	Yoakum ISD	Yoakum
280	1,189.0	Fort Stockton ISD	Fort Stockton
281	1,190.5	Alamo Heights ISD	San Antonio
282	1,194.0	Friendswood ISD	Friendswood
283	1,198.3	Lindale ISD	Lindale
284	1,200.1	Humble ISD	Humble
285	1,200.6	Houston ISD	Houston
286	1,204.2	China Spring ISD	Waco
287	1,211.5	Ferris ISD	Ferris
288	1,213.7	Castleberry ISD	Fort Worth
289	1,223.7	Frenship ISD	Wolfforth
290	1,225.5	Wichita Falls ISD	Wichita Falls
291	1,238.9	East Central ISD	San Antonio
292	1,242.9	La Vernia ISD	La Vernia
293	1,245.5	Fabens ISD	Fabens
294	1,255.0	River Road ISD	Amarillo
295	1,266.0	Gonzales ISD	Gonzales
296	1,269.3	Calallen ISD	Corpus Christi

Note: This section only includes districts with 1,500 or more students; All categories are ranked from high to low

Rank	Number	District	City
297	1,296.8	Connally ISD	Waco
298	1,297.0	Sanger ISD	Sanger
299	1,300.0	Navarro ISD	Seguin
300	1,303.4	Beaumont ISD	Beaumont
301	1,306.0	Sealy ISD	Sealy
302	1,346.0	Galena Park ISD	Houston
303	1,346.4	Burnet CISD	Burnet
304	1,381.4	Cleburne ISD	Cleburne
305	1,385.4	Mabank ISD	Mabank
306	1,408.1	Lake Worth ISD	Lake Worth
307	1,423.6	Kemp ISD	Kemp
308	1,428.9	Belton ISD	Belton
309	1,436.9	Van ISD	Van
310	1,440.0	Robinson ISD	Robinson
311	1,446.5	Liberty-Eylau ISD	Texarkana
312	1,447.3	Marshall ISD	Marshall
313	1,460.3	Azle ISD	Azle
314	1,466.0	La Vega ISD	Waco
315	1,500.0	Silsbee ISD	Silsbee
316	1,511.0	Hempstead ISD	Hempstead
317	1,528.0	Pilot Point ISD	Pilot Point
318	1,533.7	Waco ISD	Waco
319	1,541.0	Mount Vernon ISD	Mount Vernon
320	1,559.0	Lyford CISD	Lyford
321	1,581.0	Breckenridge ISD	Breckenridge
321	1,581.0	Kennedale ISD	Kennedale
323	1,613.0	Krum ISD	Krum
324	1,621.8	Aubrey ISD	Aubrey
325	1,624.7	Pittsburg ISD	Pittsburg
326	1,646.6	Cypress-Fairbanks ISD	Houston
327	1,646.7	Brenham ISD	Brenham
328	1,647.6	Athens ISD	Athens
329	1,648.0	Coldspring-Oakhurst CISD	Coldspring
330	1,652.6	Floresville ISD	Floresville
331	1,658.2	Corsicana ISD	Corsicana
332	1,688.8	Waxahachie ISD	Waxahachie
333	1,691.0	Medina Valley ISD	Castroville
334	1,712.0	Lytle ISD	Lytle
335	1,717.0	Life School	Lancaster
336	1,723.3	Wylie ISD	Wylie
337	1,753.1	Vernon ISD	Vernon
338	1,762.5	Brownwood ISD	Brownwood
339	1,858.0	Venus ISD	Venus
340	1,860.2	Forney ISD	Forney
341	1,871.7	Anna ISD	Anna
342	1,879.0	Cuero ISD	Cuero
343	1,887.0	Caldwell ISD	Caldwell
344	1,904.0	Celina ISD	Celina
345	1,913.0	Devine ISD	Devine
346	1,917.0	Shepherd ISD	Shepherd
347	1,933.0	Lamesa ISD	Lamesa
348	1,941.0	Big Spring ISD	Big Spring
349	1,943.0	Ennis ISD	Ennis
350	1,984.0	Crystal City ISD	Crystal City
351	2,014.0	Hardin-Jefferson ISD	Sour Lake
352	2,016.8	Crowley ISD	Crowley
353	2,105.4	Everman ISD	Everman
354	2,141.0	Rusk ISD	Rusk
355	2,150.0	Ingleside ISD	Ingleside
356	2,215.0	Mexia ISD	Mexia
357	2,231.3	Poteet ISD	Poteet
358	2,250.0	Whitney ISD	Whitney
359	2,316.0	Pampa ISD	Pampa
360	2,320.0	Sweetwater ISD	Sweetwater
361	2,322.0	Madisonville CISD	Madisonville
362	2,336.2	Channelview ISD	Channelview
363	2,550.0	Graham ISD	Graham
364	2,620.9	Navasota ISD	Navasota
365	2,690.5	Mount Pleasant ISD	Mount Pleasant
366	2,702.0	Edcouch-Elsa ISD	Edcouch
367	2,757.5	Idea Academy	Weslaco
368	2,842.0	Brownsboro ISD	Brownsboro
369	3,162.0	Stafford MSD	Stafford
370	3,170.0	Sulphur Springs ISD	Sulphur Springs
371	3,281.0	Wylie ISD	Abilene
372	3,357.0	Sherman ISD	Sherman
373	3,402.0	Alvarado ISD	Alvarado
374	3,637.0	Prosper ISD	Prosper
375	3,738.0	Kaufman ISD	Kaufman
376	3,811.0	Kilgore ISD	Kilgore
377	4,083.6	Denison ISD	Denison
378	4,322.1	White Settlement ISD	White Settlement
379	4,566.0	Texarkana ISD	Texarkana
380	4,620.0	Rio Hondo ISD	Rio Hondo
381	4,821.0	Eagle Pass ISD	Eagle Pass
382	5,010.0	Bullard ISD	Bullard
383	5,687.5	Pearsall ISD	Pearsall
384	5,833.3	Huntington ISD	Huntington
385	5,870.0	Orange Grove ISD	Orange Grove
386	6,446.7	Sweeny ISD	Sweeny
387	6,977.1	Kerrville ISD	Kerrville
388	16,910.0	Splendora ISD	Splendora
389	22,380.0	Liberty ISD	Liberty
390	23,950.0	Carrizo Springs CISD	Carrizo Springs
391	25,430.0	Quinlan ISD	Quinlan
n/a	n/a	Advantage Academy	Dallas
n/a	n/a	Dallas Can Academy Charter	Dallas
n/a	n/a	Eagle Academy of Abilene	Lewisville
n/a	n/a	Harmony Science Acad (Fort Worth)	Fort Worth
n/a	n/a	Kipp Inc Charter	Houston
n/a	n/a	Mathis ISD	Mathis
n/a	n/a	Ripley House Charter School	Houston
n/a	n/a	Rockdale ISD	Rockdale
n/a	n/a	School of Excellence in Education	San Antonio
n/a	n/a	Southwest School	Houston
n/a	n/a	Winfree Academy	Irving
n/a	n/a	Yes College Preparatory School	Houston

Student/Counselor Ratio

(number of students per counselor)

Rank	Number	District Name	City
1	213.2	Robstown ISD	Robstown
2	232.5	South Texas ISD	Mercedes
3	232.7	Commerce ISD	Commerce
4	234.9	Cuero ISD	Cuero
5	235.2	Livingston ISD	Livingston
6	265.4	Kingsville ISD	Kingsville
7	266.8	La Feria Ind SD	La Feria
8	271.9	Beeville ISD	Beeville
9	274.7	Coldspring-Oakhurst CISD	Coldspring
10	276.1	Raymondville ISD	Raymondville
11	283.4	Crystal City ISD	Crystal City
12	284.4	Pearsall ISD	Pearsall
13	288.8	Rio Hondo ISD	Rio Hondo
14	289.5	Bay City ISD	Bay City
15	289.9	Levelland ISD	Levelland
16	291.0	Mathis ISD	Mathis
17	293.7	Brownfield ISD	Brownfield
18	295.3	Gladewater ISD	Gladewater
19	295.8	El Campo ISD	El Campo
20	296.3	North Lamar ISD	Paris
21	297.9	La Joya ISD	La Joya
22	299.4	Alice ISD	Alice
22	299.4	Carrizo Springs CISD	Carrizo Springs
24	303.6	Sinton ISD	Sinton
25	305.1	Seminole ISD	Seminole
26	305.9	Rusk ISD	Rusk
27	306.2	Henderson ISD	Henderson
28	307.6	Columbus ISD	Columbus
29	308.9	La Marque ISD	La Marque
30	309.6	Bellville ISD	Bellville
30	309.6	Mcallen ISD	Mcallen
32	311.8	Lyford CISD	Lyford
33	312.2	Central ISD	Pollok
34	312.7	Pleasanton ISD	Pleasanton
35	313.1	Kerrville ISD	Kerrville
36	313.5	Aransas Pass ISD	Aransas Pass
37	317.1	Whitesboro ISD	Whitesboro
38	317.3	Wharton ISD	Wharton
39	319.7	Liberty ISD	Liberty
40	321.2	Cameron ISD	Cameron
41	321.5	Chapel Hill ISD	Tyler
42	321.7	Pampa ISD	Pampa
43	322.9	Richardson ISD	Richardson
44	323.5	Big Spring ISD	Big Spring
45	325.5	Denison ISD	Denison
46	326.2	Alamo Heights ISD	San Antonio
47	326.8	Sweetwater ISD	Sweetwater
48	326.9	Rio Grande City CISD	Rio Grande City
49	329.2	Bowie ISD	Bowie
50	329.4	Hereford ISD	Hereford
51	330.4	Harlingen CISD	Harlingen
52	332.5	Eagle Mt-Saginaw ISD	Fort Worth
53	335.8	Mission CISD	Mission
54	337.5	Robinson ISD	Robinson
55	340.6	Brownsville ISD	Brownsville
56	340.8	Eanes ISD	Austin
57	341.8	Smithville ISD	Smithville
58	342.4	Lytle ISD	Lytle
59	342.9	Ennis ISD	Ennis
60	348.6	Liberty-Eylau ISD	Texarkana
61	350.0	Huntington ISD	Huntington
62	350.5	Sanger ISD	Sanger
63	350.7	Aransas County ISD	Rockport
64	351.0	Springtown ISD	Springtown
65	352.0	Gatesville ISD	Gatesville
66	352.3	Killeen ISD	Killeen
67	352.5	Brownwood ISD	Brownwood
68	352.8	Iowa Park CISD	Iowa Park
69	352.9	Silsbee ISD	Silsbee
70	354.1	Donna ISD	Donna
71	354.2	West Oso ISD	Corpus Christi
72	355.5	Granbury ISD	Granbury
73	355.6	Victoria ISD	Victoria
74	356.4	Del Valle ISD	Del Valle
75	356.7	Lubbock ISD	Lubbock
76	357.5	Mabank ISD	Mabank
77	360.2	Palestine ISD	Palestine
78	360.4	Navasota ISD	Navasota
79	361.7	Cedar Hill ISD	Cedar Hill
79	361.7	Shepherd ISD	Shepherd
81	361.9	Ector County ISD	Odessa
82	364.6	Marble Falls ISD	Marble Falls
83	365.0	North Forest ISD	Houston
84	367.6	Fredericksburg ISD	Fredericksburg
85	367.8	Point Isabel ISD	Port Isabel
86	368.4	Lewisville ISD	Flower Mound
87	368.5	Plainview ISD	Plainview
88	369.0	Center ISD	Center
89	369.2	Weslaco ISD	Weslaco
90	369.4	Corpus Christi ISD	Corpus Christi
91	369.8	Spring Hill ISD	Longview
92	369.9	Abilene ISD	Abilene
92	369.9	Denton ISD	Denton
94	370.1	Hidalgo ISD	Hidalgo
95	370.9	Lockhart ISD	Lockhart
96	371.6	Fort Stockton ISD	Fort Stockton
97	371.8	Roma ISD	Roma
98	372.9	Birdville ISD	Haltom City
99	374.3	Everman ISD	Everman
100	375.0	Sharyland ISD	Mission
101	375.3	Northside ISD	San Antonio
102	376.3	Plano ISD	Plano
103	376.6	Gainesville ISD	Gainesville
104	377.3	Fairfield ISD	Fairfield
104	377.3	Palacios ISD	Palacios
106	377.4	Caldwell ISD	Caldwell
107	379.3	Aledo ISD	Aledo
107	379.3	Hondo ISD	Hondo
109	379.8	Vernon ISD	Vernon
110	380.0	Brenham ISD	Brenham
111	380.8	Celina ISD	Celina
112	381.0	La Grange ISD	La Grange
113	381.1	Desoto ISD	Desoto
114	381.4	San Angelo ISD	San Angelo
115	381.5	Gregory-Portland ISD	Portland
116	381.7	Duncanville ISD	Duncanville
117	382.0	Pilot Point ISD	Pilot Point
118	383.2	Van ISD	Van
119	383.5	Red Oak ISD	Red Oak
120	383.6	Lufkin ISD	Lufkin
121	383.8	Giddings ISD	Giddings
122	383.9	Floresville ISD	Floresville
123	384.1	Vidor ISD	Vidor
124	384.4	Mount Pleasant ISD	Mount Pleasant
125	385.5	Aldine ISD	Houston
126	385.7	Atlanta ISD	Atlanta
127	386.0	Yoakum ISD	Yoakum
128	386.5	Amarillo ISD	Amarillo
129	388.0	West ISD	West
130	389.4	Azle ISD	Azle
131	389.5	Lake Dallas ISD	Lake Dallas
132	390.0	Navarro ISD	Seguin
133	390.2	Llano ISD	Llano
134	390.9	Ingleside ISD	Ingleside
134	390.9	Los Fresnos CISD	Los Fresnos
136	391.0	Bonham ISD	Bonham
137	391.5	Kemp ISD	Kemp
138	391.6	Laredo ISD	Laredo
139	392.3	Gilmer ISD	Gilmer
140	392.5	Rains ISD	Emory
141	393.5	Hudson ISD	Lufkin
142	394.1	Valley View ISD	Pharr
143	394.2	Pleasant Grove ISD	Texarkana
144	394.3	Glen Rose ISD	Glen Rose
145	394.8	Stephenville	Stephenville

Note: This section only includes districts with 1,500 or more students; All categories are ranked from high to low

Rank	Value	District	City
146	394.9	Sherman ISD	Sherman
147	395.3	Mineola ISD	Mineola
147	395.3	Stafford MSD	Stafford
147	395.3	Waco ISD	Waco
150	395.5	Mexia ISD	Mexia
151	396.0	Taylor ISD	Taylor
152	397.0	Canton ISD	Canton
153	398.1	Fort Worth ISD	Fort Worth
154	398.4	Rockdale ISD	Rockdale
155	399.4	Lindale ISD	Lindale
156	400.3	Burkburnett ISD	Burkburnett
157	400.9	Royse City ISD	Royse City
158	401.8	Eagle Pass ISD	Eagle Pass
159	401.9	Brazosport ISD	Clute
160	402.8	Hardin-Jefferson ISD	Sour Lake
161	403.3	Krum ISD	Krum
162	403.8	Ferris ISD	Ferris
163	404.4	Progreso ISD	Progreso
163	404.4	San Elizario ISD	San Elizario
165	404.5	Harlandale ISD	San Antonio
166	404.6	Castleberry ISD	Fort Worth
167	404.8	Copperas Cove ISD	Copperas Cove
168	407.2	Longview ISD	Longview
169	407.3	Beaumont ISD	Beaumont
170	408.3	Spring Branch ISD	Houston
171	409.5	Georgetown ISD	Georgetown
172	410.1	Wylie ISD	Abilene
173	410.2	Midland ISD	Midland
174	410.3	Greenwood ISD	Midland
174	410.3	Socorro ISD	El Paso
176	410.4	Edinburg CISD	Edinburg
177	411.4	Lamar CISD	Rosenberg
178	412.7	Waller ISD	Waller
179	413.3	Santa Fe ISD	Santa Fe
180	413.5	Marshall ISD	Marshall
180	413.5	New Braunfels ISD	New Braunfels
182	414.1	Lovejoy ISD	Allen
183	414.2	Carroll ISD	Grapevine
184	414.3	Bridge City ISD	Bridge City
185	415.0	San Felipe-Del Rio CISD	Del Rio
186	415.6	South San Antonio ISD	San Antonio
187	415.7	Edcouch-Elsa ISD	Edcouch
188	415.9	Coppell ISD	Coppell
189	416.2	Lubbock-Cooper ISD	Lubbock
190	417.1	Dallas ISD	Dallas
191	417.8	Terrell ISD	Terrell
192	418.3	Weatherford ISD	Weatherford
193	418.6	Cleburne ISD	Cleburne
194	418.8	North East ISD	San Antonio
195	418.9	La Vega ISD	Waco
196	419.6	Waxahachie ISD	Waxahachie
197	419.9	Belton ISD	Belton
198	420.0	El Paso ISD	El Paso
199	420.9	Klein ISD	Klein
200	421.1	Flour Bluff ISD	Corpus Christi
201	421.5	Lampasas ISD	Lampasas
202	422.0	Gonzales ISD	Gonzales
203	422.2	Mansfield ISD	Mansfield
204	423.2	Bandera ISD	Bandera
205	423.8	Quinlan ISD	Quinlan
206	423.9	Corsicana ISD	Corsicana
206	423.9	Galveston ISD	Galveston
208	424.5	Westwood ISD	Palestine
209	424.8	Uvalde CISD	Uvalde
210	424.9	Alief ISD	Houston
211	425.2	West Orange-Cove CISD	Orange
212	425.4	Angleton ISD	Angleton
213	425.9	Lancaster ISD	Lancaster
214	426.4	Bullard ISD	Bullard
215	427.6	Calhoun County ISD	Port Lavaca
216	428.0	Liberty Hill ISD	Liberty Hill
217	428.4	Temple ISD	Temple
218	428.5	Royal ISD	Pattison
219	429.5	San Benito CISD	San Benito
220	431.0	Greenville ISD	Greenville
221	431.6	San Antonio ISD	San Antonio
222	431.8	Irving ISD	Irving
223	432.5	Athens ISD	Athens
224	432.9	Jasper ISD	Jasper
225	433.0	Magnolia ISD	Magnolia
226	433.2	Mercedes ISD	Mercedes
227	433.3	Lumberton ISD	Lumberton
228	433.6	Nacogdoches ISD	Nacogdoches
229	435.0	Garland ISD	Garland
230	435.1	Canyon ISD	Canyon
231	435.6	Midway ISD	Hewitt
232	436.5	Conroe ISD	Conroe
233	437.2	Brownsboro ISD	Brownsboro
233	437.2	Paris ISD	Paris
235	437.5	Whitney ISD	Whitney
236	438.0	Sheldon ISD	Houston
237	438.5	Lake Travis ISD	Austin
238	439.5	Orangefield ISD	Orangefield
239	440.3	Orange Grove ISD	Orange Grove
240	440.6	Pharr-San Juan-Alamo ISD	Pharr
241	441.2	Idea Academy	Weslaco
242	443.3	La Porte ISD	La Porte
243	443.5	Southwest ISD	San Antonio
244	444.8	Fabens ISD	Fabens
245	445.3	Comal ISD	New Braunfels
245	445.3	Grapevine-Colleyville ISD	Grapevine
247	445.6	Jacksonville ISD	Jacksonville
248	446.0	Aubrey ISD	Aubrey
249	449.3	United ISD	Laredo
250	450.3	Huffman ISD	Huffman
251	450.5	Hamshire-Fannett ISD	Hamshire
252	450.7	Schertz-Cibolo-U City ISD	Schertz
252	450.7	Tuloso-Midway ISD	Corpus Christi
254	450.9	Highland Park ISD	Dallas
255	451.7	Kennedale ISD	Kennedale
256	452.1	Ysleta ISD	El Paso
257	452.5	Snyder ISD	Snyder
258	453.4	Wills Point ISD	Wills Point
259	453.7	School of Excellence in Education	San Antonio
260	454.3	Grand Prairie ISD	Grand Prairie
261	454.8	Canutillo ISD	El Paso
262	456.8	Tyler ISD	Tyler
263	457.7	Humble ISD	Humble
264	457.9	Pecos-Barstow-Toyah ISD	Pecos
265	458.0	Round Rock ISD	Round Rock
266	458.3	Bastrop ISD	Bastrop
266	458.3	Nederland ISD	Nederland
268	459.1	Manor ISD	Manor
269	459.3	Port Neches-Groves ISD	Port Neches
270	460.1	Mesquite ISD	Mesquite
271	460.3	Lorena ISD	Lorena
272	460.6	Willis ISD	Willis
273	460.7	Whitehouse ISD	Whitehouse
274	461.9	Port Arthur ISD	Port Arthur
275	462.3	Crandall ISD	Crandall
276	463.2	Carthage ISD	Carthage
277	463.9	Texas City ISD	Texas City
278	464.5	Venus ISD	Venus
279	465.7	Judson ISD	Live Oak
280	465.8	Somerset ISD	Somerset
280	465.8	Wimberley ISD	Wimberley
282	466.3	Alvin ISD	Alvin
283	466.7	Frisco ISD	Frisco
284	469.2	Borger ISD	Borger
285	469.9	Southside ISD	San Antonio
286	470.1	Zapata County ISD	Zapata
287	470.2	Little Elm ISD	Little Elm
288	470.5	San Marcos CISD	San Marcos
289	471.0	Hays CISD	Kyle
290	472.1	Monahans-Wickett-Pyote ISD	Monahans
291	472.4	Cleveland ISD	Cleveland
292	473.1	Joshua ISD	Joshua
293	474.6	Pine Tree ISD	Longview
294	475.7	Mineral Wells ISD	Mineral Wells
295	476.0	Calallen ISD	Corpus Christi
296	477.9	Bryan ISD	Bryan
297	478.3	Devine ISD	Devine
298	478.7	Mckinney ISD	Mckinney
299	479.6	Montgomery ISD	Montgomery
300	480.3	Edgewood ISD	San Antonio
301	480.6	Boerne ISD	Boerne
301	480.6	Goose Creek CISD	Baytown
303	480.8	Deer Park ISD	Deer Park
304	482.4	Poteet ISD	Poteet
305	482.9	Spring ISD	Houston
306	483.3	Lamesa ISD	Lamesa
307	483.8	Argyle ISD	Argyle
308	484.0	Galena Park ISD	Houston
309	484.8	Lake Worth ISD	Lake Worth
310	485.2	Austin ISD	Austin
311	486.9	Arlington ISD	Arlington
312	487.4	Pittsburg ISD	Pittsburg
313	488.6	Midlothian ISD	Midlothian
314	489.1	East Central ISD	San Antonio
315	491.0	Clear Creek ISD	League City
316	492.8	Connally ISD	Waco
317	494.4	Rockwall ISD	Rockwall
318	494.8	Burleson ISD	Burleson
319	496.0	Decatur ISD	Decatur
320	496.6	Carrollton-Farmers Branch	Carrollton
321	500.3	Hurst-Euless-Bedford ISD	Bedford
322	501.3	Denver City ISD	Denver City
323	501.8	Hallsville ISD	Hallsville
324	502.0	Northwest ISD	Justin
324	502.3	Tatum ISD	Tatum
326	502.6	Wylie ISD	Wylie
327	503.4	Fort Bend ISD	Sugar Land
328	503.7	Hempstead ISD	Hempstead
329	504.1	Forney ISD	Forney
329	504.1	Seguin ISD	Seguin
331	505.9	Friendswood ISD	Friendswood
332	508.1	Kilgore ISD	Kilgore
333	508.3	Pflugerville ISD	Pflugerville
334	510.0	Graham ISD	Graham
335	512.4	Little Cypress-Mauricevil	Orange
336	513.3	Tomball ISD	Tomball
337	515.1	Barbers Hill ISD	Mont Belvieu
338	515.2	Andrews ISD	Andrews
339	517.0	Frenship ISD	Wolfforth
340	517.1	Dayton ISD	Dayton
341	519.3	River Road ISD	Amarillo
342	519.9	Huntsville ISD	Huntsville
343	520.0	China Spring ISD	Waco
344	520.4	Needville ISD	Needville
345	520.5	Clint ISD	El Paso
346	522.4	Sealy ISD	Sealy
347	522.7	Keller ISD	Keller
348	523.1	Pearland ISD	Pearland
349	527.0	Breckenridge ISD	Breckenridge
350	530.7	Cypress-Fairbanks ISD	Houston
351	531.2	Columbia-Brazoria ISD	West Columbia
352	534.0	Kaufman ISD	Kaufman
353	536.9	Channelview ISD	Channelview
354	540.2	Crowley ISD	Crowley
355	541.4	Dripping Spgs ISD	Dripping Spgs
356	542.8	Prosper ISD	Prosper
357	542.9	Dalhart ISD	Dalhart
358	543.4	Hillsboro ISD	Hillsboro
359	544.3	Community ISD	Nevada
360	545.9	Groesbeck ISD	Groesbeck
361	546.5	Hutto ISD	Hutto
362	550.7	Bridgeport ISD	Bridgeport
363	554.5	Allen ISD	Allen
364	554.9	Dickinson ISD	Dickinson
365	555.1	White Settlement ISD	White Settlement
366	556.6	Wichita Falls ISD	Wichita Falls
367	559.5	Dumas ISD	Dumas
368	560.6	Diboll ISD	Diboll
369	561.0	Burnet CISD	Burnet
370	563.7	Katy ISD	Katy
371	564.0	Leander ISD	Leander
372	565.2	New Caney ISD	New Caney
373	565.6	Crosby ISD	Crosby
374	570.8	Texarkana ISD	Texarkana
375	575.4	Pasadena ISD	Pasadena
376	580.6	Madisonville CISD	Madisonville
377	588.7	Sulphur Springs ISD	Sulphur Springs
378	596.6	La Vernia ISD	La Vernia
379	599.2	Princeton ISD	Princeton
380	614.9	Medina Valley ISD	Castroville
381	620.6	Tarkington ISD	Cleveland
382	634.1	Elgin ISD	Elgin
383	664.6	College Station ISD	College Station
384	676.4	Splendora ISD	Splendora
385	705.0	Perryton ISD	Perryton
386	724.5	Anna ISD	Anna
387	805.8	Sweeny ISD	Sweeny
388	850.5	Alvarado ISD	Alvarado
389	858.5	Life School	Lancaster
390	1,046.3	Houston ISD	Houston
391	1,284.2	Mount Vernon ISD	Mount Vernon
392	2,033.7	Kipp Inc Charter	Houston
393	2,248.8	Southwest School	Houston
n/a	n/a	Advantage Academy	Dallas
n/a	n/a	Dallas Can Academy Charter	Dallas
n/a	n/a	Eagle Academy of Abilene	Lewisville
n/a	n/a	Godley ISD	Godley
n/a	n/a	Harmony Science Acad (Fort Worth)	Fort Worth
n/a	n/a	Harmony Science Academy	Houston
n/a	n/a	Ripley House Charter School	Houston
n/a	n/a	Varnett Charter School	Houston
n/a	n/a	Winfree Academy	Irving
n/a	n/a	Yes College Preparatory School	Houston

Note: This section only includes districts with 1,500 or more students; All categories are ranked from high to low

Current Expenditures per Student

Rank	Dollars	District Name	City
1	11,571	South Texas ISD	Mercedes
2	11,436	Seminole ISD	Seminole
3	11,243	West ISD	West
4	11,218	Glen Rose ISD	Glen Rose
5	10,538	Cuero ISD	Cuero
6	10,526	Fairfield ISD	Fairfield
7	10,465	Mathis ISD	Mathis
8	10,402	Crystal City ISD	Crystal City
9	10,207	Edcouch-Elsa ISD	Edcouch
10	10,169	Palacios ISD	Palacios
11	10,168	Groesbeck ISD	Groesbeck
12	10,133	Kipp Inc Charter	Houston
13	10,036	Rio Grande City CISD	Rio Grande City
14	9,970	Brownfield ISD	Brownfield
15	9,933	Hidalgo ISD	Hidalgo
16	9,846	Raymondville ISD	Raymondville
17	9,845	Pecos-Barstow-Toyah ISD	Pecos
18	9,829	Commerce ISD	Commerce
19	9,820	North Forest ISD	Houston
20	9,805	West Orange-Cove CISD	Orange
21	9,798	Aransas County ISD	Rockport
22	9,623	Andrews ISD	Andrews
23	9,607	Hempstead ISD	Hempstead
24	9,511	Denver City ISD	Denver City
25	9,486	Fort Stockton ISD	Fort Stockton
26	9,436	Sealy ISD	Sealy
27	9,435	Zapata County ISD	Zapata
28	9,430	La Marque ISD	La Marque
29	9,409	Wharton ISD	Wharton
30	9,397	Beaumont ISD	Beaumont
31	9,384	Yes College Preparatory School	Houston
32	9,334	Lyford CISD	Lyford
33	9,322	Carrizo Springs CISD	Carrizo Springs
34	9,288	Galveston ISD	Galveston
35	9,277	Robstown ISD	Robstown
36	9,239	Fabens ISD	Fabens
37	9,236	Dallas ISD	Dallas
38	9,230	Port Arthur ISD	Port Arthur
39	9,228	Coldspring-Oakhurst CISD	Coldspring
40	9,215	Lovejoy ISD	Allen
41	9,211	Caldwell ISD	Caldwell
42	9,209	Uvalde CISD	Uvalde
43	9,201	Liberty ISD	Liberty
44	9,199	Deer Park ISD	Deer Park
45	9,177	Sweetwater ISD	Sweetwater
46	9,149	Donna ISD	Donna
47	9,137	Godley ISD	Godley
48	9,109	Royal ISD	Pattison
49	9,104	Valley View ISD	Pharr
50	9,098	Carthage ISD	Carthage
51	9,092	Mercedes ISD	Mercedes
52	9,043	Sanger ISD	Sanger
53	9,039	Pearsall ISD	Pearsall
54	9,036	Sinton ISD	Sinton
55	9,035	Austin ISD	Austin
56	9,025	Barbers Hill ISD	Mont Belvieu
57	9,013	Mexia ISD	Mexia
58	9,012	Levelland ISD	Levelland
59	8,990	Atlanta ISD	Atlanta
60	8,974	Lake Worth ISD	Lake Worth
61	8,966	Eanes ISD	Austin
62	8,958	Granbury ISD	Granbury
63	8,956	Fredericksburg ISD	Fredericksburg
64	8,949	Edgewood ISD	San Antonio
65	8,946	Jasper ISD	Jasper
66	8,922	Sheldon ISD	Houston
66	8,922	Snyder ISD	Snyder
68	8,910	Spring Branch ISD	Houston
69	8,907	San Elizario ISD	San Elizario
70	8,906	Roma ISD	Roma
71	8,861	Denton ISD	Denton
72	8,850	Aransas Pass ISD	Aransas Pass
72	8,850	Calhoun County ISD	Port Lavaca
74	8,836	El Campo ISD	El Campo
75	8,811	Marble Falls ISD	Marble Falls
76	8,808	Canutillo ISD	El Paso
77	8,803	Texas City ISD	Texas City
78	8,802	Progreso ISD	Progreso
79	8,788	Bay City ISD	Bay City
80	8,773	Navasota ISD	Navasota
81	8,772	Boerne ISD	Boerne
82	8,745	La Joya ISD	La Joya
83	8,739	Silsbee ISD	Silsbee
84	8,733	Pittsburg ISD	Pittsburg
85	8,731	Giddings ISD	Giddings
86	8,720	Lytle ISD	Lytle
87	8,708	West Oso ISD	Corpus Christi
88	8,686	Kingsville ISD	Kingsville
89	8,677	Hardin-Jefferson ISD	Sour Lake
90	8,673	Gainesville ISD	Gainesville
91	8,669	Smithville ISD	Smithville
92	8,659	Brownsville ISD	Brownsville
93	8,657	Weslaco ISD	Weslaco
94	8,656	Manor ISD	Manor
95	8,653	Longview ISD	Longview
96	8,647	Decatur ISD	Decatur
97	8,644	San Antonio ISD	San Antonio
98	8,642	Eagle Pass ISD	Eagle Pass
99	8,637	Gilmer ISD	Gilmer
99	8,637	Rains ISD	Emory
101	8,634	Lamesa ISD	Lamesa
102	8,623	Mount Pleasant ISD	Mount Pleasant
103	8,619	Fort Worth ISD	Fort Worth
104	8,615	El Paso ISD	El Paso
105	8,604	Houston ISD	Houston
106	8,603	Sweeny ISD	Sweeny
107	8,602	Breckenridge ISD	Breckenridge
108	8,595	Paris ISD	Paris
109	8,594	Harlandale ISD	San Antonio
110	8,584	Devine ISD	Devine
111	8,583	San Benito CISD	San Benito
112	8,558	Prosper ISD	Prosper
113	8,549	Mineral Wells ISD	Mineral Wells
113	8,549	Terrell ISD	Terrell
115	8,547	Bridgeport ISD	Bridgeport
115	8,547	La Porte ISD	La Porte
117	8,535	Alamo Heights ISD	San Antonio
118	8,530	Brownsboro ISD	Brownsboro
118	8,530	Edinburg CISD	Edinburg
120	8,519	Shepherd ISD	Shepherd
121	8,512	South San Antonio ISD	San Antonio
122	8,509	Kemp ISD	Kemp
123	8,497	Llano ISD	Llano
123	8,497	Waco ISD	Waco
125	8,494	Point Isabel ISD	Port Isabel
126	8,486	Los Fresnos CISD	Los Fresnos
127	8,477	Hallsville ISD	Hallsville
128	8,468	Hillsboro ISD	Hillsboro
129	8,460	Goose Creek CISD	Baytown
130	8,446	Eagle Academy of Abilene	Lewisville
131	8,435	Carrollton-Farmers Branch	Carrollton
132	8,423	Idea Academy	Weslaco
133	8,413	Monahans-Wickett-Pyote ISD	Monahans
134	8,403	Vidor ISD	Vidor
135	8,392	Mcallen ISD	Mcallen
136	8,381	Cleburne ISD	Cleburne
137	8,370	Pleasanton ISD	Pleasanton
138	8,367	Palestine ISD	Palestine
139	8,366	Stafford MSD	Stafford
140	8,359	Mission CISD	Mission
140	8,359	Wimberley ISD	Wimberley
142	8,357	Laredo ISD	Laredo
143	8,356	Bandera ISD	Bandera
144	8,354	Floresville ISD	Floresville
145	8,347	Diboll ISD	Diboll
146	8,337	Rio Hondo ISD	Rio Hondo
147	8,336	San Marcos CISD	San Marcos
148	8,335	Pharr-San Juan-Alamo ISD	Pharr
149	8,333	Whitney ISD	Whitney
150	8,329	Georgetown ISD	Georgetown
150	8,329	La Feria Ind SD	La Feria
150	8,329	North East ISD	San Antonio
153	8,326	Krum ISD	Krum
154	8,318	Liberty Hill ISD	Liberty Hill
155	8,302	Ysleta ISD	El Paso
156	8,291	Argyle ISD	Argyle
157	8,289	Chapel Hill ISD	Tyler
158	8,275	Aldine ISD	Houston
159	8,274	Carroll ISD	Grapevine
160	8,270	Liberty-Eylau ISD	Texarkana
161	8,258	Vernon ISD	Vernon
162	8,257	Bowie ISD	Bowie
163	8,240	La Grange ISD	La Grange
163	8,240	Sherman ISD	Sherman
165	8,235	Lockhart ISD	Lockhart
166	8,234	Taylor ISD	Taylor
167	8,233	Galena Park ISD	Houston
168	8,232	Hamshire-Fannett ISD	Hamshire
169	8,227	Plano ISD	Plano
169	8,227	Port Neches-Groves ISD	Port Neches
171	8,223	Denison ISD	Denison
172	8,211	Ferris ISD	Ferris
173	8,204	Tyler ISD	Tyler
174	8,202	Montgomery ISD	Montgomery
175	8,197	Brownwood ISD	Brownwood
176	8,194	Bellville ISD	Bellville
177	8,193	Copperas Cove ISD	Copperas Cove
178	8,192	Tuloso-Midway ISD	Corpus Christi
179	8,190	Texarkana ISD	Texarkana
180	8,189	Rockwall ISD	Rockwall
180	8,189	Whitesboro ISD	Whitesboro
182	8,186	Burnet CISD	Burnet
183	8,180	Greenville ISD	Greenville
184	8,174	Cameron ISD	Cameron
185	8,172	Henderson ISD	Henderson
186	8,171	Lubbock-Cooper ISD	Lubbock
187	8,166	Harmony Science Academy	Houston
188	8,155	Livingston ISD	Livingston
189	8,150	Hays CISD	Kyle
189	8,150	Marshall ISD	Marshall
191	8,126	Brazosport ISD	Clute
192	8,125	Dalhart ISD	Dalhart
193	8,123	Somerset ISD	Somerset
194	8,109	Abilene ISD	Abilene
195	8,108	Highland Park ISD	Dallas
196	8,106	Richardson ISD	Richardson
197	8,102	Calallen ISD	Corpus Christi
198	8,085	Lewisville ISD	Flower Mound
199	8,084	New Caney ISD	New Caney
199	8,084	Splendora ISD	Splendora
201	8,078	Bastrop ISD	Bastrop
202	8,077	Kerrville ISD	Kerrville
203	8,069	Alief ISD	Houston
204	8,066	Lubbock ISD	Lubbock
205	8,064	Brenham ISD	Brenham
206	8,055	Perryton ISD	Perryton
207	8,054	Rusk ISD	Rusk
208	8,048	Wichita Falls ISD	Wichita Falls
209	8,045	Channelview ISD	Channelview
210	8,042	Southwest ISD	San Antonio
211	8,038	Bonham ISD	Bonham
212	8,037	Lake Travis ISD	Austin
213	8,036	United ISD	Laredo
214	8,024	Mabank ISD	Mabank
215	8,023	Celina ISD	Celina
216	8,021	Del Valle ISD	Del Valle
217	8,009	Killeen ISD	Killeen
218	8,008	Gladewater ISD	Gladewater
219	8,000	Center ISD	Center
220	7,991	Dallas Can Academy Charter	Dallas
221	7,990	Spring ISD	Houston
222	7,989	Weatherford ISD	Weatherford
223	7,979	Columbus ISD	Columbus
224	7,976	Northwest ISD	Justin
225	7,974	Big Spring ISD	Big Spring
226	7,968	School of Excellence in Education	San Antonio
227	7,964	Poteet ISD	Poteet
228	7,952	Anna ISD	Anna
229	7,949	Gonzales ISD	Gonzales
230	7,947	Alvarado ISD	Alvarado
230	7,947	Seguin ISD	Seguin
232	7,944	Coppell ISD	Coppell
233	7,938	Dripping Spgs ISD	Dripping Spgs
234	7,929	Central ISD	Pollok
235	7,922	Alice ISD	Alice
236	7,912	Leander ISD	Leander
237	7,910	Aledo ISD	Aledo
238	7,899	Waller ISD	Waller
239	7,893	Pasadena ISD	Pasadena
240	7,888	Little Elm ISD	Little Elm
241	7,885	Connally ISD	Waco
242	7,882	Bryan ISD	Bryan
243	7,881	Beeville ISD	Beeville
244	7,880	Corsicana ISD	Corsicana
245	7,875	Kaufman ISD	Kaufman
246	7,874	Clint ISD	El Paso
247	7,871	North Lamar ISD	Paris
247	7,871	Springtown ISD	Springtown
249	7,862	Cleveland ISD	Cleveland
250	7,857	Hereford ISD	Hereford
251	7,856	Southside ISD	San Antonio
252	7,848	Rockdale ISD	Rockdale
253	7,845	Borger ISD	Borger
254	7,842	Lamar CISD	Rosenberg
254	7,842	Orange Grove ISD	Orange Grove

Note: This section only includes districts with 1,500 or more students; All categories are ranked from high to low

Rank	Dollars	District Name	City
256	7,839	Harlingen CISD	Harlingen
257	7,831	Columbia-Brazoria ISD	West Columbia
257	7,831	Pleasant Grove ISD	Texarkana
259	7,822	Mckinney ISD	Mckinney
260	7,821	Jacksonville ISD	Jacksonville
261	7,818	Bridge City ISD	Bridge City
262	7,813	Grapevine-Colleyville ISD	Grapevine
263	7,811	Northside ISD	San Antonio
264	7,802	Princeton ISD	Princeton
265	7,799	Comal ISD	New Braunfels
266	7,794	Lufkin ISD	Lufkin
267	7,792	Amarillo ISD	Amarillo
268	7,784	Magnolia ISD	Magnolia
269	7,763	Joshua ISD	Joshua
270	7,762	Hondo ISD	Hondo
271	7,761	Little Cypress-Mauricevil	Orange
272	7,754	Ennis ISD	Ennis
273	7,742	Kilgore ISD	Kilgore
273	7,742	Waxahachie ISD	Waxahachie
275	7,736	Royse City ISD	Royse City
276	7,735	Dumas ISD	Dumas
277	7,731	Orangefield ISD	Orangefield
278	7,728	Azle ISD	Azle
279	7,726	Medina Valley ISD	Castroville
280	7,725	Sharyland ISD	Mission
281	7,723	Athens ISD	Athens
281	7,723	East Central ISD	San Antonio
283	7,709	Judson ISD	Live Oak
284	7,705	Desoto ISD	Desoto
285	7,702	Corpus Christi ISD	Corpus Christi
286	7,695	Temple ISD	Temple
287	7,689	Alvin ISD	Alvin
288	7,683	Midland ISD	Midland
289	7,682	Arlington ISD	Arlington
290	7,681	Cedar Hill ISD	Cedar Hill
291	7,674	Dickinson ISD	Dickinson
292	7,665	San Felipe-Del Rio CISD	Del Rio
293	7,662	Everman ISD	Everman
294	7,656	Hurst-Euless-Bedford ISD	Bedford
295	7,655	Tomball ISD	Tomball
295	7,655	White Settlement ISD	White Settlement
297	7,654	Pilot Point ISD	Pilot Point
298	7,653	Pflugerville ISD	Pflugerville
299	7,639	Birdville ISD	Haltom City
300	7,636	Fort Bend ISD	Sugar Land
300	7,636	Sulphur Springs ISD	Sulphur Springs
302	7,632	Garland ISD	Garland
303	7,622	La Vega ISD	Waco
304	7,614	Lake Dallas ISD	Lake Dallas
305	7,613	Wills Point ISD	Wills Point
306	7,612	Tatum ISD	Tatum
307	7,610	College Station ISD	College Station
308	7,607	Frenship ISD	Wolfforth
308	7,607	Katy ISD	Katy
310	7,604	Round Rock ISD	Round Rock
311	7,595	Madisonville CISD	Madisonville
312	7,593	Victoria ISD	Victoria
313	7,590	Wylie ISD	Wylie
314	7,587	Plainview ISD	Plainview
315	7,586	Clear Creek ISD	League City
316	7,585	Socorro ISD	El Paso
317	7,584	Pampa ISD	Pampa
318	7,576	Yoakum ISD	Yoakum
319	7,563	Quinlan ISD	Quinlan
320	7,559	Burkburnett ISD	Burkburnett
321	7,553	Lampasas ISD	Lampasas
322	7,548	Ector County ISD	Odessa
323	7,546	Mount Vernon ISD	Mount Vernon
324	7,532	Venus ISD	Venus
325	7,525	Irving ISD	Irving
326	7,521	Mineola ISD	Mineola
327	7,514	Lancaster ISD	Lancaster
328	7,512	Huntsville ISD	Huntsville
329	7,496	Klein ISD	Klein
330	7,486	Nederland ISD	Nederland
331	7,483	Angleton ISD	Angleton
332	7,480	San Angelo ISD	San Angelo
333	7,476	Grand Prairie ISD	Grand Prairie
334	7,471	Harmony Science Acad (Fort Worth)	Fort Worth
334	7,471	Van ISD	Van
336	7,459	Humble ISD	Humble
337	7,457	Elgin ISD	Elgin
338	7,455	Santa Fe ISD	Santa Fe
339	7,452	Red Oak ISD	Red Oak
340	7,451	Needville ISD	Needville
341	7,444	Graham ISD	Graham
342	7,443	Belton ISD	Belton
343	7,434	Frisco ISD	Frisco
344	7,431	Bullard ISD	Bullard
345	7,426	Ingleside ISD	Ingleside
346	7,421	Burleson ISD	Burleson
347	7,417	Midlothian ISD	Midlothian
348	7,411	Robinson ISD	Robinson
349	7,402	Aubrey ISD	Aubrey
350	7,399	Castleberry ISD	Fort Worth
351	7,398	Dayton ISD	Dayton
352	7,397	Lumberton ISD	Lumberton
353	7,392	Huntington ISD	Huntington
354	7,373	Flour Bluff ISD	Corpus Christi
355	7,356	Kennedale ISD	Kennedale
356	7,342	Midway ISD	Hewitt
357	7,335	Nacogdoches ISD	Nacogdoches
358	7,320	Mesquite ISD	Mesquite
359	7,299	Schertz-Cibolo-U City ISD	Schertz
360	7,276	Duncanville ISD	Duncanville
361	7,271	Friendswood ISD	Friendswood
362	7,257	Hudson ISD	Lufkin
362	7,257	Huffman ISD	Huffman
364	7,246	Pine Tree ISD	Longview
365	7,225	Allen ISD	Allen
366	7,224	Crandall ISD	Crandall
367	7,213	Stephenville	Stephenville
368	7,200	Iowa Park CISD	Iowa Park
369	7,199	Hutto ISD	Hutto
370	7,180	Lindale ISD	Lindale
371	7,147	Crosby ISD	Crosby
372	7,144	Willis ISD	Willis
373	7,143	Eagle Mt-Saginaw ISD	Fort Worth
374	7,138	Cypress-Fairbanks ISD	Houston
375	7,123	Canton ISD	Canton
376	7,115	Greenwood ISD	Midland
377	7,113	Crowley ISD	Crowley
378	7,096	Conroe ISD	Conroe
379	7,052	New Braunfels ISD	New Braunfels
380	7,012	La Vernia ISD	La Vernia
381	6,993	Gregory-Portland ISD	Portland
382	6,969	Keller ISD	Keller
383	6,932	Forney ISD	Forney
384	6,917	Pearland ISD	Pearland
385	6,874	Tarkington ISD	Cleveland
386	6,870	Gatesville ISD	Gatesville
387	6,867	Life School	Lancaster
388	6,862	Lorena ISD	Lorena
389	6,807	Spring Hill ISD	Longview
390	6,802	River Road ISD	Amarillo
391	6,798	Advantage Academy	Dallas
392	6,792	Mansfield ISD	Mansfield
393	6,631	Whitehouse ISD	Whitehouse
394	6,606	China Spring ISD	Waco
395	6,602	Navarro ISD	Seguin
396	6,504	Canyon ISD	Canyon
396	6,504	Community ISD	Nevada
398	6,432	Westwood ISD	Palestine
399	6,361	Varnett Charter School	Houston
400	6,005	Winfree Academy	Irving
401	5,572	Southwest School	Houston
402	5,417	Ripley House Charter School	Houston
403	5,409	Wylie ISD	Abilene

Total General Revenue per Student

Rank	Dollars	District Name	City
1	27,239	Seminole ISD	Seminole
2	23,344	Denver City ISD	Denver City
3	19,970	Highland Park ISD	Dallas
4	19,280	Fairfield ISD	Fairfield
5	18,368	Groesbeck ISD	Groesbeck
6	18,268	Glen Rose ISD	Glen Rose
7	18,219	Eanes ISD	Austin
8	18,210	Tatum ISD	Tatum
9	18,064	Llano ISD	Llano
10	17,817	Carthage ISD	Carthage
11	17,807	Andrews ISD	Andrews
12	17,274	Point Isabel ISD	Point Isabel
13	17,045	Palacios ISD	Palacios
14	16,757	Zapata County ISD	Zapata
15	16,472	Barbers Hill ISD	Mont Belvieu
16	16,193	Lake Travis ISD	Austin
17	15,924	South Texas ISD	Mercedes
18	15,843	Snyder ISD	Snyder
19	15,111	Alamo Heights ISD	San Antonio
20	15,002	Sweeny ISD	Sweeny
21	14,988	Fort Stockton ISD	Fort Stockton
22	14,530	Northwest ISD	Justin
23	14,275	Calhoun County ISD	Port Lavaca
24	14,266	Prosper ISD	Prosper
25	13,216	Lovejoy ISD	Allen
26	13,209	Sheldon ISD	Houston
27	13,088	Decatur ISD	Decatur
28	13,032	Hallsville ISD	Hallsville
29	13,013	Carroll ISD	Grapevine
30	12,990	Aransas County ISD	Rockport
31	12,948	Monahans-Wickett-Pyote ISD	Monahans
32	12,808	Coppell ISD	Coppell
33	12,777	Grapevine-Colleyville ISD	Grapevine
34	12,739	Yes College Preparatory School	Houston
35	12,731	La Porte ISD	La Porte
36	12,609	Texas City ISD	Texas City
37	12,419	Manor ISD	Manor
38	12,290	Fredericksburg ISD	Fredericksburg
39	12,220	Port Arthur ISD	Port Arthur
40	12,207	Giddings ISD	Giddings
41	12,158	Deer Park ISD	Deer Park
42	11,998	Pecos-Barstow-Toyah ISD	Pecos
43	11,973	Crystal City ISD	Crystal City
44	11,897	Krum ISD	Krum
45	11,878	Godley ISD	Godley
46	11,850	Mathis ISD	Mathis
47	11,750	Austin ISD	Austin
48	11,732	Galveston ISD	Galveston
49	11,674	Cuero ISD	Cuero
50	11,543	Rio Grande City CISD	Rio Grande City
51	11,397	Plano ISD	Plano
52	11,370	Lake Worth ISD	Lake Worth
53	11,351	Boerne ISD	Boerne
54	11,348	Denton ISD	Denton
55	11,270	Marble Falls ISD	Marble Falls
56	11,253	Carrollton-Farmers Branch	Carrollton
57	11,179	Dripping Spgs ISD	Dripping Spgs
58	11,173	Hidalgo ISD	Hidalgo
59	11,159	Brownfield ISD	Brownfield
60	11,156	Kipp Inc Charter	Houston
61	11,107	Commerce ISD	Commerce
62	11,089	Del Valle ISD	Del Valle
63	11,084	Hempstead ISD	Hempstead
64	11,083	Argyle ISD	Argyle
65	11,040	Port Neches-Groves ISD	Port Neches
66	11,022	Wimberley ISD	Wimberley
67	10,862	West Orange-Cove CISD	Orange
68	10,803	Bridgeport ISD	Bridgeport
69	10,776	Progreso ISD	Progreso
70	10,768	Stafford MSD	Stafford
71	10,732	Edcouch-Elsa ISD	Edcouch
72	10,724	Laredo ISD	Laredo
73	10,714	Lubbock-Cooper ISD	Lubbock
74	10,676	Idea Academy	Weslaco
75	10,669	Comal ISD	New Braunfels
76	10,668	Robstown ISD	Robstown
77	10,646	North East ISD	San Antonio
78	10,639	Valley View ISD	Pharr
79	10,636	Goose Creek CISD	Baytown
80	10,634	Royal ISD	Pattison
81	10,622	Celina ISD	Celina
81	10,622	Edgewood ISD	San Antonio
83	10,598	Kemp ISD	Kemp
84	10,559	Lampasas ISD	Lampasas
85	10,545	Granbury ISD	Granbury
86	10,529	Bullard ISD	Bullard
87	10,523	Spring Branch ISD	Houston
88	10,522	Levelland ISD	Levelland
89	10,501	West Oso ISD	Corpus Christi
90	10,492	Raymondville ISD	Raymondville
91	10,476	Sealy ISD	Sealy
92	10,450	College Station ISD	College Station
93	10,449	Floresville ISD	Floresville
94	10,433	Pearsall ISD	Pearsall
95	10,425	San Marcos CISD	San Marcos
96	10,416	Georgetown ISD	Georgetown
97	10,409	Rockwall ISD	Rockwall
98	10,407	South San Antonio ISD	San Antonio
99	10,404	Aledo ISD	Aledo
100	10,379	Dallas Can Academy Charter	Dallas
101	10,354	Columbus ISD	Columbus
102	10,335	Sinton ISD	Sinton
103	10,330	Lyford CISD	Lyford
104	10,326	Liberty ISD	Liberty
105	10,322	Houston ISD	Houston

Note: This section only includes districts with 1,500 or more students; All categories are ranked from high to low

#	Value	District	City	#	Value	District	City	#	Value	District	City
106	10,320	Mercedes ISD	Mercedes	192	9,700	Tomball ISD	Tomball	278	9,227	Center ISD	Center
107	10,312	Frisco ISD	Frisco	193	9,696	Brownsville ISD	Brownsville	279	9,210	Irving ISD	Irving
108	10,287	Caldwell ISD	Caldwell	194	9,665	Devine ISD	Devine	280	9,197	Fort Worth ISD	Fort Worth
109	10,285	Canutillo ISD	El Paso	195	9,647	Jasper ISD	Jasper	281	9,193	Duncanville ISD	Duncanville
110	10,283	Atlanta ISD	Atlanta	196	9,641	Tyler ISD	Tyler	282	9,189	Cleveland ISD	Cleveland
111	10,258	Carrizo Springs CISD	Carrizo Springs	197	9,640	Judson ISD	Live Oak	283	9,187	Mineola ISD	Mineola
112	10,254	Aubrey ISD	Aubrey	198	9,633	Weslaco ISD	Weslaco	284	9,185	Corsicana ISD	Corsicana
113	10,247	West ISD	West	199	9,620	Copperas Cove ISD	Copperas Cove	285	9,167	Taylor ISD	Taylor
114	10,228	Donna ISD	Donna	200	9,616	Venus ISD	Venus	286	9,157	Pasadena ISD	Pasadena
115	10,222	Dallas ISD	Dallas	201	9,594	Sherman ISD	Sherman	286	9,157	Willis ISD	Willis
116	10,216	Anna ISD	Anna	202	9,588	Mabank ISD	Mabank	288	9,154	Clear Creek ISD	League City
117	10,211	Hays CISD	Kyle	203	9,585	Lancaster ISD	Lancaster	289	9,133	Kaufman ISD	Kaufman
118	10,206	Fabens ISD	Fabens	204	9,584	Brazosport ISD	Clute	290	9,128	New Braunfels ISD	New Braunfels
119	10,190	Montgomery ISD	Montgomery	205	9,579	Paris ISD	Paris	291	9,125	Crandall ISD	Crandall
120	10,179	Mckinney ISD	Mckinney	206	9,575	Harmony Science Acad (Fort Worth)	Fort Worth	292	9,095	Sulphur Springs ISD	Sulphur Springs
121	10,176	El Campo ISD	El Campo	207	9,574	Allen ISD	Allen	293	9,087	Columbia-Brazoria ISD	West Columbia
121	10,176	Midlothian ISD	Midlothian	207	9,574	Sanger ISD	Sanger	294	9,083	Gonzales ISD	Gonzales
123	10,151	Pleasant Grove ISD	Texarkana	209	9,571	Lake Dallas ISD	Lake Dallas	295	9,075	Gregory-Portland ISD	Portland
124	10,146	Henderson ISD	Henderson	209	9,571	Navasota ISD	Navasota	296	9,043	Angleton ISD	Angleton
125	10,132	North Forest ISD	Houston	211	9,566	Whitesboro ISD	Whitesboro	297	9,027	La Vega ISD	Waco
126	10,109	Roma ISD	Roma	212	9,557	Edinburg CISD	Edinburg	298	9,009	Nacogdoches ISD	Nacogdoches
127	10,093	Bastrop ISD	Bastrop	213	9,556	Canton ISD	Canton	299	9,007	Denison ISD	Denison
128	10,092	Round Rock ISD	Round Rock	214	9,553	Hurst-Euless-Bedford ISD	Bedford	300	9,005	Lubbock ISD	Lubbock
129	10,069	La Marque ISD	La Marque	214	9,553	Silsbee ISD	Silsbee	301	9,004	Springtown ISD	Springtown
130	10,062	Leander ISD	Leander	216	9,551	Pharr-San Juan-Alamo ISD	Pharr	302	8,996	Livingston ISD	Livingston
131	10,058	Frenship ISD	Wolfforth	217	9,549	United ISD	Laredo	303	8,980	Quinlan ISD	Quinlan
132	10,033	Medina Valley ISD	Castroville	218	9,543	Joshua ISD	Joshua	304	8,979	Alief ISD	Houston
133	10,020	Breckenridge ISD	Breckenridge	219	9,530	Palestine ISD	Palestine	305	8,974	Wichita Falls ISD	Wichita Falls
134	10,010	Longview ISD	Longview	220	9,523	Liberty Hill ISD	Liberty Hill	306	8,966	Poteet ISD	Poteet
135	10,009	Royse City ISD	Royse City	221	9,522	Ennis ISD	Ennis	307	8,964	China Spring ISD	Waco
136	10,003	Bay City ISD	Bay City	222	9,516	Ferris ISD	Ferris	308	8,952	Socorro ISD	El Paso
137	9,997	Cameron ISD	Cameron	223	9,515	Smithville ISD	Smithville	309	8,948	Pine Tree ISD	Longview
138	9,992	Lewisville ISD	Flower Mound	224	9,514	Cleburne ISD	Cleburne	310	8,932	Mcallen ISD	Mcallen
139	9,975	Richardson ISD	Richardson	225	9,512	Kerrville ISD	Kerrville	310	8,932	North Lamar ISD	Paris
140	9,958	Hillsboro ISD	Hillsboro	226	9,511	Hutto ISD	Hutto	312	8,909	Humble ISD	Humble
140	9,958	Rockdale ISD	Rockdale	227	9,502	Bellville ISD	Bellville	313	8,895	Pleasanton ISD	Pleasanton
142	9,951	Bandera ISD	Bandera	228	9,500	Spring ISD	Houston	314	8,894	Pearland ISD	Pearland
143	9,950	Wharton ISD	Wharton	228	9,500	Tuloso-Midway ISD	Corpus Christi	315	8,891	Northside ISD	San Antonio
144	9,947	Princeton ISD	Princeton	230	9,489	Lockhart ISD	Lockhart	316	8,889	Abilene ISD	Abilene
145	9,940	Alvin ISD	Alvin	231	9,484	Bryan ISD	Bryan	317	8,881	Sharyland ISD	Mission
146	9,936	Eagle Pass ISD	Eagle Pass	232	9,472	Needville ISD	Needville	318	8,876	Orange Grove ISD	Orange Grove
147	9,932	Waxahachie ISD	Waxahachie	233	9,468	White Settlement ISD	White Settlement	319	8,867	Athens ISD	Athens
148	9,924	Hardin-Jefferson ISD	Sour Lake	234	9,467	Brownsboro ISD	Brownsboro	320	8,852	Gladewater ISD	Gladewater
149	9,921	Pittsburg ISD	Pittsburg	234	9,467	Waco ISD	Waco	320	8,852	Victoria ISD	Victoria
150	9,914	Southwest ISD	San Antonio	236	9,463	Van ISD	Van	322	8,829	Castleberry ISD	Fort Worth
150	9,914	Terrell ISD	Terrell	237	9,450	Uvalde CISD	Uvalde	323	8,826	Wylie ISD	Wylie
152	9,912	Brenham ISD	Brenham	238	9,449	Cedar Hill ISD	Cedar Hill	324	8,822	Temple ISD	Temple
153	9,909	Burnet CISD	Burnet	239	9,446	Yoakum ISD	Yoakum	325	8,821	Bridge City ISD	Bridge City
154	9,903	Gainesville ISD	Gainesville	240	9,441	Community ISD	Nevada	326	8,815	Huffman ISD	Huffman
155	9,899	Vernon ISD	Vernon	241	9,439	Desoto ISD	Desoto	327	8,810	Conroe ISD	Conroe
156	9,898	Borger ISD	Borger	242	9,429	Channelview ISD	Channelview	328	8,799	Perryton ISD	Perryton
157	9,896	Beaumont ISD	Beaumont	243	9,424	Brownwood ISD	Brownwood	329	8,779	Lindale ISD	Lindale
158	9,894	La Feria Ind SD	La Feria	244	9,421	Mexia ISD	Mexia	330	8,773	Seguin ISD	Seguin
158	9,894	Lytle ISD	Lytle	245	9,420	Connally ISD	Waco	331	8,746	Bonham ISD	Bonham
158	9,894	Rio Hondo ISD	Rio Hondo	246	9,406	New Caney ISD	New Caney	332	8,743	Belton ISD	Belton
161	9,891	Kingsville ISD	Kingsville	247	9,401	Ysleta ISD	El Paso	333	8,731	Huntsville ISD	Huntsville
162	9,884	La Joya ISD	La Joya	248	9,399	El Paso ISD	El Paso	334	8,729	School of Excellence in Education	San Antonio
163	9,883	San Antonio ISD	San Antonio	249	9,380	Vidor ISD	Vidor	335	8,728	Forney ISD	Forney
164	9,873	La Grange ISD	La Grange	250	9,346	Mansfield ISD	Mansfield	336	8,720	Hereford ISD	Hereford
165	9,862	Weatherford ISD	Weatherford	251	9,345	Katy ISD	Katy	337	8,707	Midland ISD	Midland
166	9,853	Alvarado ISD	Alvarado	252	9,342	Rusk ISD	Rusk	338	8,703	Marshall ISD	Marshall
167	9,851	Dalhart ISD	Dalhart	253	9,337	Aransas Pass ISD	Aransas Pass	339	8,700	Azle ISD	Azle
167	9,851	Harlandale ISD	San Antonio	254	9,333	Shepherd ISD	Shepherd	340	8,697	Dumas ISD	Dumas
169	9,849	Dickinson ISD	Dickinson	255	9,332	Pilot Point ISD	Pilot Point	340	8,697	Kilgore ISD	Kilgore
170	9,829	Clint ISD	El Paso	256	9,325	Rains ISD	Emory	342	8,693	River Road ISD	Amarillo
171	9,820	Mount Pleasant ISD	Mount Pleasant	257	9,319	Aldine ISD	Houston	343	8,683	Splendora ISD	Splendora
172	9,817	Elgin ISD	Elgin	257	9,319	Bowie ISD	Bowie	344	8,681	Greenville ISD	Greenville
173	9,816	Sweetwater ISD	Sweetwater	259	9,308	Burkburnett ISD	Burkburnett	345	8,676	Crosby ISD	Crosby
174	9,813	Midway ISD	Hewitt	260	9,307	Hamshire-Fannett ISD	Hamshire	346	8,670	Jacksonville ISD	Jacksonville
175	9,810	Lamar CISD	Rosenberg	260	9,307	Mount Vernon ISD	Mount Vernon	347	8,666	San Felipe-Del Rio CISD	Del Rio
175	9,810	San Benito CISD	San Benito	262	9,301	Mineral Wells ISD	Mineral Wells	348	8,631	Diboll ISD	Diboll
177	9,801	Coldspring-Oakhurst CISD	Coldspring	263	9,297	Pflugerville ISD	Pflugerville	348	8,631	Hudson ISD	Lufkin
178	9,785	Killeen ISD	Killeen	264	9,293	Alice ISD	Alice	350	8,630	Hondo ISD	Hondo
179	9,766	Birdville ISD	Haltom City	264	9,293	Lamesa ISD	Lamesa	351	8,626	Harlingen CISD	Harlingen
180	9,757	Galena Park ISD	Houston	266	9,292	Mesquite ISD	Mesquite	352	8,621	Dayton ISD	Dayton
181	9,754	Eagle Mt-Saginaw ISD	Fort Worth	267	9,284	Madisonville CISD	Madisonville	353	8,619	Big Spring ISD	Big Spring
181	9,754	Texarkana ISD	Texarkana	268	9,279	Whitney ISD	Whitney	354	8,612	Red Oak ISD	Red Oak
183	9,753	Little Elm ISD	Little Elm	269	9,270	Grand Prairie ISD	Grand Prairie	355	8,599	East Central ISD	San Antonio
183	9,753	Somerset ISD	Somerset	270	9,267	Beeville ISD	Beeville	356	8,598	Crowley ISD	Crowley
185	9,747	Gilmer ISD	Gilmer	271	9,264	Magnolia ISD	Magnolia	357	8,565	Wills Point ISD	Wills Point
186	9,745	Graham ISD	Graham	272	9,256	Southside ISD	San Antonio	358	8,564	Navarro ISD	Seguin
187	9,741	Pampa ISD	Pampa	273	9,254	Liberty-Eylau ISD	Texarkana	359	8,548	Kennedale ISD	Kennedale
188	9,739	Mission CISD	Mission	274	9,251	Schertz-Cibolo-U City ISD	Schertz	360	8,547	Arlington ISD	Arlington
189	9,720	Los Fresnos CISD	Los Fresnos	275	9,244	Everman ISD	Everman	361	8,530	Flour Bluff ISD	Corpus Christi
190	9,718	Waller ISD	Waller	276	9,240	Chapel Hill ISD	Tyler	362	8,524	Gatesville ISD	Gatesville
191	9,707	San Elizario ISD	San Elizario	277	9,238	Burleson ISD	Burleson	363	8,516	Klein ISD	Klein

Note: This section only includes districts with 1,500 or more students; All categories are ranked from high to low

Rank	Dollars	District Name	City
364	8,515	Corpus Christi ISD	Corpus Christi
365	8,503	Amarillo ISD	Amarillo
366	8,463	Keller ISD	Keller
367	8,451	Greenwood ISD	Midland
368	8,443	La Vernia ISD	La Vernia
368	8,443	Robinson ISD	Robinson
370	8,437	Garland ISD	Garland
371	8,415	Central ISD	Pollok
372	8,412	Advantage Academy	Dallas
373	8,405	Fort Bend ISD	Sugar Land
374	8,390	Canyon ISD	Canyon
375	8,363	Stephenville	Stephenville
376	8,330	Little Cypress-Mauricevil	Orange
377	8,312	Lufkin ISD	Lufkin
378	8,287	Eagle Academy of Abilene	Lewisville
378	8,287	Ector County ISD	Odessa
380	8,276	Lorena ISD	Lorena
381	8,225	Huntington ISD	Huntington
382	8,200	Westwood ISD	Palestine
383	8,195	Ingleside ISD	Ingleside
384	8,183	Cypress-Fairbanks ISD	Houston
385	8,177	Santa Fe ISD	Santa Fe
386	8,154	Whitehouse ISD	Whitehouse
387	8,135	San Angelo ISD	San Angelo
388	8,098	Calallen ISD	Corpus Christi
389	8,096	Harmony Science Academy	Houston
390	8,024	Nederland ISD	Nederland
391	8,019	Orangefield ISD	Orangefield
392	8,005	Plainview ISD	Plainview
393	7,968	Lumberton ISD	Lumberton
394	7,934	Varnett Charter School	Houston
395	7,912	Friendswood ISD	Friendswood
396	7,898	Iowa Park CISD	Iowa Park
397	7,658	Wylie ISD	Abilene
398	7,589	Tarkington ISD	Cleveland
399	7,551	Life School	Lancaster
400	7,405	Winfree Academy	Irving
401	7,404	Spring Hill ISD	Longview
402	6,033	Ripley House Charter School	Houston
403	5,695	Southwest School	Houston

Long-Term Debt per Student (end of FY)

Rank	Dollars	District Name	City
1	57,810	Prosper ISD	Prosper
2	45,843	Seminole ISD	Seminole
3	44,805	Lovejoy ISD	Allen
4	39,254	Hutto ISD	Hutto
5	36,354	Northwest ISD	Justin
6	35,687	Frisco ISD	Frisco
7	35,663	Leander ISD	Leander
8	35,390	Celina ISD	Celina
9	34,365	Aledo ISD	Aledo
10	33,344	Aubrey ISD	Aubrey
11	32,853	Lake Travis ISD	Austin
12	32,678	Comal ISD	New Braunfels
13	32,636	Argyle ISD	Argyle
14	32,181	Krum ISD	Krum
15	31,998	White Settlement ISD	White Settlement
16	30,780	Denton ISD	Denton
17	30,576	Forney ISD	Forney
18	30,484	Ennis ISD	Ennis
19	30,050	Manor ISD	Manor
20	29,152	Barbers Hill ISD	Mont Belvieu
21	28,425	Lake Worth ISD	Lake Worth
22	28,296	Royse City ISD	Royse City
23	28,251	Royal ISD	Pattison
24	27,770	Schertz-Cibolo-U City ISD	Schertz
25	27,681	Decatur ISD	Decatur
26	27,583	Rockwall ISD	Rockwall
27	26,786	Sheldon ISD	Houston
28	25,967	Eagle Mt-Saginaw ISD	Fort Worth
29	25,774	Princeton ISD	Princeton
30	25,511	Little Elm ISD	Little Elm
31	24,785	Hays CISD	Kyle
32	24,767	Midlothian ISD	Midlothian
33	24,740	Lake Dallas ISD	Lake Dallas
34	23,746	Frenship ISD	Wolfforth
35	23,719	Anna ISD	Anna
36	23,708	Mansfield ISD	Mansfield
37	23,622	Godley ISD	Godley
38	23,535	La Porte ISD	La Porte
39	23,284	Dickinson ISD	Dickinson
40	22,636	Giddings ISD	Giddings
41	22,578	Bullard ISD	Bullard
42	22,284	Tomball ISD	Tomball
43	22,268	Wylie ISD	Wylie
44	22,200	Lamar CISD	Rosenberg
45	22,106	Elgin ISD	Elgin
46	22,039	Pleasant Grove ISD	Texarkana
47	21,596	Canton ISD	Canton
48	21,276	Grapevine-Colleyville ISD	Grapevine
49	21,170	Crowley ISD	Crowley
50	20,923	North East ISD	San Antonio
51	20,668	Spring Hill ISD	Longview
52	20,596	Friendswood ISD	Friendswood
53	20,580	Port Neches-Groves ISD	Port Neches
54	20,481	Boerne ISD	Boerne
55	20,473	Keller ISD	Keller
56	20,358	Montgomery ISD	Montgomery
57	20,259	Medina Valley ISD	Castroville
58	20,251	Judson ISD	Live Oak
59	20,237	Community ISD	Nevada
60	20,090	Wimberley ISD	Wimberley
61	19,966	Pearland ISD	Pearland
62	19,909	New Caney ISD	New Caney
63	19,666	Alvin ISD	Alvin
64	19,288	Highland Park ISD	Dallas
65	19,276	Red Oak ISD	Red Oak
66	19,223	Crandall ISD	Crandall
67	18,872	Pflugerville ISD	Pflugerville
68	18,870	Springtown ISD	Springtown
69	18,741	Floresville ISD	Floresville
70	18,674	Spring ISD	Houston
71	18,668	Huffman ISD	Huffman
72	18,659	Alvarado ISD	Alvarado
73	18,622	Grand Prairie ISD	Grand Prairie
74	18,589	Carroll ISD	Grapevine
74	18,589	Mckinney ISD	Mckinney
76	18,560	Waller ISD	Waller
77	18,464	Del Valle ISD	Del Valle
78	18,386	Marble Falls ISD	Marble Falls
79	18,322	Port Arthur ISD	Port Arthur
80	18,303	Humble ISD	Humble
81	18,238	Eanes ISD	Austin
82	18,164	West Orange-Cove CISD	Orange
83	18,061	San Marcos CISD	San Marcos
84	18,007	Commerce ISD	Commerce
85	17,824	Bastrop ISD	Bastrop
86	17,758	Van ISD	Van
87	17,596	Katy ISD	Katy
88	17,495	Longview ISD	Longview
89	17,460	Kemp ISD	Kemp
90	17,375	Lancaster ISD	Lancaster
91	17,370	Desoto ISD	Desoto
92	17,251	Clear Creek ISD	League City
93	17,167	Goose Creek CISD	Baytown
94	17,160	Navarro ISD	Seguin
95	17,100	China Spring ISD	Waco
96	16,979	Spring Branch ISD	Houston
97	16,680	Kennedale ISD	Kennedale
98	16,608	Conroe ISD	Conroe
99	16,588	Cypress-Fairbanks ISD	Houston
100	16,499	Rockdale ISD	Rockdale
101	16,412	Joshua ISD	Joshua
102	16,232	Burleson ISD	Burleson
103	16,009	Allen ISD	Allen
104	15,916	Magnolia ISD	Magnolia
105	15,855	Lewisville ISD	Flower Mound
106	15,828	Fairfield ISD	Fairfield
107	15,566	Alamo Heights ISD	San Antonio
108	15,534	Sherman ISD	Sherman
109	15,526	Plano ISD	Plano
110	15,485	Livingston ISD	Livingston
111	15,462	Hempstead ISD	Hempstead
112	15,390	Carrollton-Farmers Branch	Carrollton
113	15,324	Pampa ISD	Pampa
114	15,143	Llano ISD	Llano
115	15,141	La Vernia ISD	La Vernia
116	15,134	Waxahachie ISD	Waxahachie
117	15,070	Graham ISD	Graham
118	14,958	Lampasas ISD	Lampasas
119	14,933	Lubbock-Cooper ISD	Lubbock
120	14,886	South San Antonio ISD	San Antonio
121	14,828	Northside ISD	San Antonio
122	14,726	Weatherford ISD	Weatherford
123	14,530	Georgetown ISD	Georgetown
124	14,509	Deer Park ISD	Deer Park
125	14,424	Harlandale ISD	San Antonio
126	14,384	Midway ISD	Hewitt
127	14,314	Monahans-Wickett-Pyote ISD	Monahans
128	14,287	Dripping Spgs ISD	Dripping Spgs
129	14,275	Tuloso-Midway ISD	Corpus Christi
130	14,230	Cedar Hill ISD	Cedar Hill
131	14,187	Irving ISD	Irving
132	14,176	Willis ISD	Willis
133	14,091	Duncanville ISD	Duncanville
134	14,075	Borger ISD	Borger
135	13,894	Mabank ISD	Mabank
136	13,667	West Oso ISD	Corpus Christi
137	13,632	Hardin-Jefferson ISD	Sour Lake
138	13,599	Gainesville ISD	Gainesville
139	13,581	Southside ISD	San Antonio
140	13,507	Hidalgo ISD	Hidalgo
141	13,469	Victoria ISD	Victoria
142	13,464	Ferris ISD	Ferris
143	13,405	Cameron ISD	Cameron
144	13,381	Coppell ISD	Coppell
145	13,225	New Braunfels ISD	New Braunfels
146	13,162	Liberty Hill ISD	Liberty Hill
147	13,144	Columbia-Brazoria ISD	West Columbia
148	13,114	Everman ISD	Everman
149	13,106	Canutillo ISD	El Paso
150	13,021	Pecos-Barstow-Toyah ISD	Pecos
151	13,020	Pilot Point ISD	Pilot Point
152	12,997	Richardson ISD	Richardson
153	12,864	Navasota ISD	Navasota
154	12,844	Crosby ISD	Crosby
155	12,491	Progreso ISD	Progreso
156	12,488	Burnet ISD	Burnet
157	12,446	River Road ISD	Amarillo
158	12,442	Calallen ISD	Corpus Christi
159	12,403	Round Rock ISD	Round Rock
160	12,396	Pearsall ISD	Pearsall
161	12,388	Huntington ISD	Huntington
162	12,369	Fort Bend ISD	Sugar Land
163	12,338	Birdville ISD	Haltom City
164	12,270	Klein ISD	Klein
165	12,266	Laredo ISD	Laredo
166	12,244	Cleveland ISD	Cleveland
167	12,212	Bowie ISD	Bowie
168	12,209	Sweeny ISD	Sweeny
169	12,030	Sanger ISD	Sanger
170	12,024	Bellville ISD	Bellville
171	12,018	Mesquite ISD	Mesquite
172	11,999	College Station ISD	College Station
173	11,933	Terrell ISD	Terrell
174	11,929	Corsicana ISD	Corsicana
175	11,655	Splendora ISD	Splendora
176	11,651	Crystal City ISD	Crystal City
177	11,647	Galena Park ISD	Houston
178	11,642	Point Isabel ISD	Port Isabel
179	11,572	Pine Tree ISD	Longview
180	11,571	Canyon ISD	Canyon
181	11,532	Waco ISD	Waco
182	11,512	Dalhart ISD	Dalhart
183	11,456	Texas City ISD	Texas City
184	11,243	Sealy ISD	Sealy
185	11,197	Seguin ISD	Seguin
186	11,180	Wharton ISD	Wharton
187	11,171	Clint ISD	El Paso
188	10,899	Paris ISD	Paris
189	10,876	Angleton ISD	Angleton
190	10,857	Rio Hondo ISD	Rio Hondo
191	10,838	Bandera ISD	Bandera
192	10,830	East Central ISD	San Antonio
193	10,810	Brazosport ISD	Clute
194	10,659	Mercedes ISD	Mercedes
195	10,635	Houston ISD	Houston
196	10,551	Rio Grande City CISD	Rio Grande City
197	10,540	Hurst-Euless-Bedford ISD	Bedford
198	10,525	Southwest ISD	San Antonio
199	10,482	Bridge City ISD	Bridge City
200	10,479	Columbus ISD	Columbus
201	10,463	Andrews ISD	Andrews
202	10,416	Hillsboro ISD	Hillsboro
203	10,201	Brownwood ISD	Brownwood
204	10,195	Kingsville ISD	Kingsville
205	9,900	Mineral Wells ISD	Mineral Wells
206	9,781	Valley View ISD	Pharr
207	9,774	Galveston ISD	Galveston
208	9,762	Needville ISD	Needville
209	9,660	Greenwood ISD	Midland
210	9,637	Whitesboro ISD	Whitesboro
211	9,535	Yoakum ISD	Yoakum
212	9,380	Bryan ISD	Bryan
213	9,374	Central ISD	Pollok

Note: This section only includes districts with 1,500 or more students; All categories are ranked from high to low

Rank	Number	District Name	City
214	9,277	Pasadena ISD	Pasadena
215	9,254	Shepherd ISD	Shepherd
216	9,202	La Joya ISD	La Joya
217	9,164	Edcouch-Elsa ISD	Edcouch
218	9,094	Edgewood ISD	San Antonio
219	9,065	Snyder ISD	Snyder
220	9,016	Dallas ISD	Dallas
221	8,906	Smithville ISD	Smithville
222	8,888	Socorro ISD	El Paso
223	8,869	San Antonio ISD	San Antonio
224	8,778	Glen Rose ISD	Glen Rose
225	8,743	Gilmer ISD	Gilmer
226	8,622	North Forest ISD	Houston
227	8,620	Sharyland ISD	Mission
228	8,597	Quinlan ISD	Quinlan
229	8,594	Mount Pleasant ISD	Mount Pleasant
230	8,546	Henderson ISD	Henderson
231	8,540	Cleburne ISD	Cleburne
232	8,519	Whitehouse ISD	Whitehouse
233	8,374	Belton ISD	Belton
234	8,349	Hudson ISD	Lufkin
235	8,291	Lorena ISD	Lorena
236	8,256	Austin ISD	Austin
236	8,256	La Marque ISD	La Marque
238	8,209	La Vega ISD	Waco
239	8,105	Connally ISD	Waco
240	8,074	Chapel Hill ISD	Tyler
241	8,065	Somerset ISD	Somerset
242	7,896	La Feria Ind SD	La Feria
243	7,867	El Campo ISD	El Campo
244	7,850	Kaufman ISD	Kaufman
245	7,842	Granbury ISD	Granbury
246	7,682	Liberty ISD	Liberty
247	7,653	Venus ISD	Venus
248	7,627	Lindale ISD	Lindale
249	7,531	Roma ISD	Roma
250	7,515	Bridgeport ISD	Bridgeport
251	7,431	Channelview ISD	Channelview
252	7,405	Nacogdoches ISD	Nacogdoches
253	7,376	United ISD	Laredo
254	7,336	Texarkana ISD	Texarkana
255	7,326	Robstown ISD	Robstown
256	7,245	Levelland ISD	Levelland
257	7,074	Stafford MSD	Stafford
258	7,070	San Benito CISD	San Benito
259	7,068	Cuero ISD	Cuero
260	7,004	Mission CISD	Mission
261	6,974	Fabens ISD	Fabens
262	6,945	Beaumont ISD	Beaumont
263	6,870	Garland ISD	Garland
264	6,823	Fort Stockton ISD	Fort Stockton
265	6,755	Tarkington ISD	Cleveland
266	6,746	Fort Worth ISD	Fort Worth
267	6,699	Arlington ISD	Arlington
268	6,659	Lyford CISD	Lyford
269	6,640	Pharr-San Juan-Alamo ISD	Pharr
270	6,610	Dumas ISD	Dumas
271	6,547	Orangefield ISD	Orangefield
272	6,491	Raymondville ISD	Raymondville
273	6,463	Huntsville ISD	Huntsville
274	6,435	Kerrville ISD	Kerrville
275	6,384	Hamshire-Fannett ISD	Hamshire
276	6,372	El Paso ISD	El Paso
277	6,338	Midland ISD	Midland
278	6,265	Mathis ISD	Mathis
279	6,196	Tyler ISD	Tyler
280	6,123	Uvalde CISD	Uvalde
281	6,051	Ysleta ISD	El Paso
282	5,993	Lockhart ISD	Lockhart
283	5,961	Orange Grove ISD	Orange Grove
284	5,953	Los Fresnos CISD	Los Fresnos
285	5,901	Bay City ISD	Bay City
286	5,874	Poteet ISD	Poteet
287	5,829	Silsbee ISD	Silsbee
288	5,783	Dayton ISD	Dayton
289	5,702	Robinson ISD	Robinson
290	5,667	Madisonville CISD	Madisonville
291	5,655	Temple ISD	Temple
292	5,484	Taylor ISD	Taylor
293	5,457	San Elizario ISD	San Elizario
294	5,425	Sweetwater ISD	Sweetwater
295	5,384	Center ISD	Center
296	5,320	Castleberry ISD	Fort Worth
297	5,310	Alief ISD	Houston
298	5,271	Copperas Cove ISD	Copperas Cove
299	5,213	Pleasanton ISD	Pleasanton
300	5,160	Gregory-Portland ISD	Portland
301	5,131	Fredericksburg ISD	Fredericksburg
302	5,110	Breckenridge ISD	Breckenridge
303	5,083	Wichita Falls ISD	Wichita Falls
304	5,076	Jasper ISD	Jasper
305	4,924	Donna ISD	Donna
306	4,923	Mcallen ISD	Mcallen
307	4,899	Greenville ISD	Greenville
308	4,877	Beeville ISD	Beeville
309	4,864	Brenham ISD	Brenham
310	4,838	Edinburg CISD	Edinburg
311	4,752	Ingleside ISD	Ingleside
312	4,751	Azle ISD	Azle
313	4,741	Calhoun County ISD	Port Lavaca
314	4,696	Alice ISD	Alice
315	4,689	Lubbock ISD	Lubbock
316	4,681	Aldine ISD	Houston
317	4,607	Brownfield ISD	Brownfield
318	4,547	Athens ISD	Athens
319	4,528	Vidor ISD	Vidor
320	4,294	San Felipe-Del Rio CISD	Del Rio
321	4,223	Brownsville ISD	Brownsville
322	4,132	Pittsburg ISD	Pittsburg
323	4,100	Carthage ISD	Carthage
324	4,063	Lytle ISD	Lytle
325	4,059	Harlingen CISD	Harlingen
326	4,024	Hondo ISD	Hondo
327	3,922	Amarillo ISD	Amarillo
328	3,888	Abilene ISD	Abilene
329	3,842	Little Cypress-Mauricevil	Orange
330	3,819	Weslaco ISD	Weslaco
331	3,751	Lumberton ISD	Lumberton
332	3,708	Whitney ISD	Whitney
333	3,651	Santa Fe ISD	Santa Fe
334	3,619	Lufkin ISD	Lufkin
335	3,555	Caldwell ISD	Caldwell
336	3,533	Killeen ISD	Killeen
337	3,497	Devine ISD	Devine
338	3,434	Sulphur Springs ISD	Sulphur Springs
339	3,431	Ector County ISD	Odessa
340	3,378	West ISD	West
341	3,346	Eagle Pass ISD	Eagle Pass
342	3,292	Stephenville	Stephenville
343	3,252	Rusk ISD	Rusk
344	3,203	Burkburnett ISD	Burkburnett
345	3,019	Aransas County ISD	Rockport
346	2,893	Kilgore ISD	Kilgore
347	2,820	Carrizo Springs CISD	Carrizo Springs
348	2,743	Zapata County ISD	Zapata
349	2,666	Palacios ISD	Palacios
350	2,568	Liberty-Eylau ISD	Texarkana
351	2,566	Sinton ISD	Sinton
352	2,549	Hallsville ISD	Hallsville
353	2,548	Hereford ISD	Hereford
354	2,436	Bonham ISD	Bonham
355	2,416	Wills Point ISD	Wills Point
356	2,402	Coldspring-Oakhurst CISD	Coldspring
357	2,376	Rains ISD	Emory
358	2,308	Iowa Park CISD	Iowa Park
359	2,305	Nederland ISD	Nederland
360	2,243	Big Spring ISD	Big Spring
361	2,191	Perryton ISD	Perryton
362	1,835	Corpus Christi ISD	Corpus Christi
363	1,796	Gonzales ISD	Gonzales
364	1,710	Wylie ISD	Abilene
365	1,654	Denison ISD	Denison
366	1,636	Jacksonville ISD	Jacksonville
367	1,595	Vernon ISD	Vernon
368	1,566	San Angelo ISD	San Angelo
369	1,551	Gatesville ISD	Gatesville
370	1,528	Mount Vernon ISD	Mount Vernon
371	1,482	North Lamar ISD	Paris
372	1,423	Mexia ISD	Mexia
373	1,341	Aransas Pass ISD	Aransas Pass
374	1,267	Palestine ISD	Palestine
375	1,154	Diboll ISD	Diboll
376	1,079	Flour Bluff ISD	Corpus Christi
377	825	La Grange ISD	La Grange
378	647	Marshall ISD	Marshall
379	193	Gladewater ISD	Gladewater
380	180	Atlanta ISD	Atlanta
381	4	Tatum ISD	Tatum
382	0	Advantage Academy	Dallas
382	0	Brownsboro ISD	Brownsboro
382	0	Dallas Can Academy Charter	Dallas
382	0	Denver City ISD	Denver City
382	0	Eagle Academy of Abilene	Lewisville
382	0	Groesbeck ISD	Groesbeck
382	0	Harmony Science Acad (Fort Worth)	Fort Worth
382	0	Harmony Science Academy	Houston
382	0	Idea Academy	Weslaco
382	0	Kipp Inc Charter	Houston
382	0	Lamesa ISD	Lamesa
382	0	Life School	Lancaster
382	0	Mineola ISD	Mineola
382	0	Plainview ISD	Plainview
382	0	Ripley House Charter School	Houston
382	0	School of Excellence in Education	San Antonio
382	0	South Texas ISD	Mercedes
382	0	Southwest School	Houston
382	0	Varnett Charter School	Houston
382	0	Westwood ISD	Palestine
382	0	Winfree Academy	Irving
382	0	Yes College Preparatory School	Houston

Number of Diploma Recipients

Rank	Number	District Name	City
1	8,595	Houston ISD	Houston
2	6,671	Dallas ISD	Dallas
3	5,614	Cypress-Fairbanks ISD	Houston
4	5,000	Northside ISD	San Antonio
5	4,636	Fort Bend ISD	Sugar Land
6	3,961	North East ISD	San Antonio
7	3,914	Austin ISD	Austin
8	3,568	Fort Worth ISD	Fort Worth
9	3,562	Garland ISD	Garland
10	3,539	Katy ISD	Katy
11	3,449	Plano ISD	Plano
12	3,441	Arlington ISD	Arlington
13	3,396	El Paso ISD	El Paso
14	3,158	Lewisville ISD	Flower Mound
15	2,931	Conroe ISD	Conroe
16	2,915	Ysleta ISD	El Paso
17	2,760	Klein ISD	Klein
18	2,652	Aldine ISD	Houston
19	2,545	Round Rock ISD	Round Rock
20	2,524	Brownsville ISD	Brownsville
21	2,428	Pasadena ISD	Pasadena
22	2,412	Clear Creek ISD	League City
23	2,336	Socorro ISD	El Paso
24	2,270	Alief ISD	Houston
24	2,270	San Antonio ISD	San Antonio
26	2,265	Mesquite ISD	Mesquite
27	2,140	Humble ISD	Humble
27	2,140	United ISD	Laredo
29	2,079	Corpus Christi ISD	Corpus Christi
30	1,922	Richardson ISD	Richardson
31	1,818	Spring Branch ISD	Houston
32	1,736	Keller ISD	Keller
33	1,718	Spring ISD	Houston
34	1,706	Amarillo ISD	Amarillo
35	1,666	Mansfield ISD	Mansfield
36	1,660	Killeen ISD	Killeen
37	1,648	Irving ISD	Irving
38	1,603	Lubbock ISD	Lubbock
39	1,594	Pharr-San Juan-Alamo ISD	Pharr
40	1,553	Carrollton-Farmers Branch	Carrollton
41	1,494	Edinburg CISD	Edinburg
42	1,477	Leander ISD	Leander
43	1,323	Hurst-Euless-Bedford ISD	Bedford
44	1,306	Mcallen ISD	Mcallen
45	1,298	Galena Park ISD	Houston
46	1,297	Birdville ISD	Haltom City
47	1,271	Pflugerville ISD	Pflugerville
48	1,270	Ector County ISD	Odessa
48	1,270	Frisco ISD	Frisco
50	1,266	Grand Prairie ISD	Grand Prairie
51	1,234	Mckinney ISD	Mckinney
52	1,230	Allen ISD	Allen
53	1,228	Lamar CISD	Rosenberg
54	1,212	Midland ISD	Midland
55	1,190	La Joya ISD	La Joya
56	1,154	Judson ISD	Live Oak
57	1,113	Grapevine-Colleyville ISD	Grapevine
58	1,103	Goose Creek CISD	Baytown
59	1,091	Beaumont ISD	Beaumont
60	1,081	Denton ISD	Denton
61	1,072	Comal ISD	New Braunfels
62	1,068	Laredo ISD	Laredo
63	991	Pearland ISD	Pearland

Note: This section only includes districts with 1,500 or more students; All categories are ranked from high to low

64	960	Harlingen CISD	Harlingen	150	356	Roma ISD	Roma	236	196	Mabank ISD	Mabank
65	956	San Angelo ISD	San Angelo	151	355	Nederland ISD	Nederland	237	191	Decatur ISD	Decatur
66	908	Wichita Falls ISD	Wichita Falls	152	347	Forney ISD	Forney	238	190	Alvarado ISD	Alvarado
67	901	Tyler ISD	Tyler	152	347	White Settlement ISD	White Settlement	239	188	Brownwood ISD	Brownwood
68	890	Deer Park ISD	Deer Park	154	343	Brenham ISD	Brenham	239	188	Stafford MSD	Stafford
69	879	Abilene ISD	Abilene	155	340	Lancaster ISD	Lancaster	241	187	Pleasanton ISD	Pleasanton
70	848	Schertz-Cibolo-U City ISD	Schertz	156	339	Frenship ISD	Wolfforth	241	187	Zapata County ISD	Zapata
71	839	Rockwall ISD	Rockwall	157	335	Nacogdoches ISD	Nacogdoches	243	186	Brownsboro ISD	Brownsboro
72	826	Eagle Academy of Abilene	Lewisville	158	324	Ennis ISD	Ennis	243	186	Chapel Hill ISD	Tyler
73	821	Eagle Mt-Saginaw ISD	Fort Worth	159	323	Willis ISD	Willis	245	185	Sanger ISD	Sanger
74	808	Alvin ISD	Alvin	160	322	Lockhart ISD	Lockhart	246	183	Gatesville ISD	Gatesville
74	808	Crowley ISD	Crowley	161	311	Kerrville ISD	Kerrville	247	182	La Vernia ISD	La Vernia
76	801	Weslaco ISD	Weslaco	162	310	Crosby ISD	Crosby	247	182	Princeton ISD	Princeton
77	797	Eagle Pass ISD	Eagle Pass	163	309	Calhoun County ISD	Port Lavaca	249	181	Robstown ISD	Robstown
78	782	Brazosport ISD	Clute	164	308	Gregory-Portland ISD	Portland	250	180	Athens ISD	Athens
79	756	Mission CISD	Mission	164	308	Hallsville ISD	Hallsville	250	180	Carthage ISD	Carthage
80	747	Bryan ISD	Bryan	164	308	Plainview ISD	Plainview	250	180	Levelland ISD	Levelland
81	734	Harlandale ISD	San Antonio	167	307	Dayton ISD	Dayton	253	179	Silsbee ISD	Silsbee
82	722	Waco ISD	Waco	168	302	Montgomery ISD	Montgomery	253	179	Wills Point ISD	Wills Point
83	693	Coppell ISD	Coppell	169	300	Canutillo ISD	El Paso	255	178	Hardin-Jefferson ISD	Sour Lake
84	662	Hays CISD	Kyle	169	300	Corsicana ISD	Corsicana	255	178	La Feria Ind SD	La Feria
85	646	Magnolia ISD	Magnolia	171	299	Calallen ISD	Corpus Christi	257	177	Taylor ISD	Taylor
86	645	Victoria ISD	Victoria	172	297	Vidor ISD	Vidor	258	174	Robinson ISD	Robinson
87	622	Wylie ISD	Wylie	173	293	Pine Tree ISD	Longview	259	173	Paris ISD	Paris
88	620	Duncanville ISD	Duncanville	174	291	Little Elm ISD	Little Elm	260	172	Andrews ISD	Andrews
89	605	Georgetown ISD	Georgetown	174	291	Uvalde CISD	Uvalde	260	172	Bellville ISD	Bellville
90	597	Northwest ISD	Justin	174	291	Waller ISD	Waller	262	171	Hidalgo ISD	Hidalgo
91	588	College Station ISD	College Station	177	289	Dripping Spgs ISD	Dripping Spgs	263	169	Gonzales ISD	Gonzales
92	586	Donna ISD	Donna	177	289	Santa Fe ISD	Santa Fe	264	168	Borger ISD	Borger
92	586	Tomball ISD	Tomball	179	286	Mount Pleasant ISD	Mount Pleasant	264	168	Jasper ISD	Jasper
94	561	Eanes ISD	Austin	180	283	Port Neches-Groves ISD	Port Neches	266	164	Cleveland ISD	Cleveland
95	558	Rio Grande City CISD	Rio Grande City	181	280	Whitehouse ISD	Whitehouse	266	164	Seminole ISD	Seminole
96	550	Los Fresnos CISD	Los Fresnos	182	278	Joshua ISD	Joshua	268	163	Somerset ISD	Somerset
97	545	Clint ISD	El Paso	183	274	Denison ISD	Denison	269	161	Palestine ISD	Palestine
98	543	Canyon ISD	Canyon	184	264	Burnet CISD	Burnet	270	160	Bandera ISD	Bandera
99	537	Southwest ISD	San Antonio	185	262	Sheldon ISD	Houston	270	160	Sealy ISD	Sealy
100	535	San Felipe-Del Rio CISD	Del Rio	185	262	Southside ISD	San Antonio	272	159	Gilmer ISD	Gilmer
101	530	San Benito CISD	San Benito	187	261	Edcouch-Elsa ISD	Edcouch	272	159	La Marque ISD	La Marque
102	526	Belton ISD	Belton	188	260	Greenville ISD	Greenville	274	156	Bridgeport ISD	Bridgeport
103	524	Carroll ISD	Grapevine	189	256	Royse City ISD	Royse City	274	156	Perryton ISD	Perryton
103	524	Sharyland ISD	Mission	190	254	Bay City ISD	Bay City	276	154	Castleberry ISD	Fort Worth
105	521	Burleson ISD	Burleson	191	252	Kilgore ISD	Kilgore	277	153	Graham ISD	Graham
106	512	Bastrop ISD	Bastrop	192	250	Marble Falls ISD	Marble Falls	278	152	Bridge City ISD	Bridge City
106	512	Lufkin ISD	Lufkin	192	250	Sulphur Springs ISD	Sulphur Springs	279	151	Navasota ISD	Navasota
108	508	La Porte ISD	La Porte	194	249	Mercedes ISD	Mercedes	279	151	Sinton ISD	Sinton
109	503	Boerne ISD	Boerne	195	247	Hutto ISD	Hutto	279	151	Snyder ISD	Snyder
110	496	Edgewood ISD	San Antonio	195	247	Lampasas ISD	Lampasas	282	150	Prosper ISD	Prosper
111	492	Cedar Hill ISD	Cedar Hill	197	244	Little Cypress-Mauricevil	Orange	283	149	Lubbock-Cooper ISD	Lubbock
112	489	Dallas Can Academy Charter	Dallas	198	242	Everman ISD	Everman	283	149	Needville ISD	Needville
113	486	East Central ISD	San Antonio	198	242	Valley View ISD	Pharr	285	148	Rio Hondo ISD	Rio Hondo
114	484	Highland Park ISD	Dallas	200	241	Floresville ISD	Floresville	286	146	Center ISD	Center
115	482	Midlothian ISD	Midlothian	201	240	Lake Dallas ISD	Lake Dallas	287	145	Ferris ISD	Ferris
116	475	Winfree Academy	Irving	201	240	Lindale ISD	Lindale	287	145	West Orange-Cove CISD	Orange
117	465	Midway ISD	Hewitt	203	239	Alice ISD	Alice	289	144	Crandall ISD	Crandall
118	454	Dickinson ISD	Dickinson	203	239	North Lamar ISD	Paris	289	144	Ingleside ISD	Ingleside
119	453	Galveston ISD	Galveston	205	237	Livingston ISD	Livingston	289	144	Sweetwater ISD	Sweetwater
120	452	Friendswood ISD	Friendswood	206	235	Lumberton ISD	Lumberton	292	140	Bonham ISD	Bonham
120	452	South San Antonio ISD	San Antonio	206	235	Tuloso-Midway ISD	Corpus Christi	292	140	China Spring ISD	Waco
122	448	Waxahachie ISD	Waxahachie	208	234	Dumas ISD	Dumas	292	140	Gainesville ISD	Gainesville
123	438	San Marcos CISD	San Marcos	209	228	Fredericksburg ISD	Fredericksburg	292	140	Pittsburg ISD	Pittsburg
124	434	Granbury ISD	Granbury	210	227	Mineral Wells ISD	Mineral Wells	296	139	Gladewater ISD	Gladewater
125	433	Desoto ISD	Desoto	210	227	Stephenville	Stephenville	296	139	Liberty ISD	Liberty
126	432	Weatherford ISD	Weatherford	212	226	Terrell ISD	Terrell	298	138	Hudson ISD	Lufkin
127	431	South Texas ISD	Mercedes	213	224	El Campo ISD	El Campo	299	137	Hondo ISD	Hondo
128	425	Copperas Cove ISD	Copperas Cove	214	222	North Forest ISD	Houston	300	136	Liberty Hill ISD	Liberty Hill
128	425	Del Valle ISD	Del Valle	215	221	Kingsville ISD	Kingsville	300	136	Quinlan ISD	Quinlan
130	422	Temple ISD	Temple	216	220	Big Spring ISD	Big Spring	302	135	Argyle ISD	Argyle
131	420	Texarkana ISD	Texarkana	217	219	Hereford ISD	Hereford	302	135	Pecos-Barstow-Toyah ISD	Pecos
132	416	New Braunfels ISD	New Braunfels	218	218	Henderson ISD	Henderson	304	134	Connally ISD	Waco
132	416	Seguin ISD	Seguin	219	216	Jacksonville ISD	Jacksonville	304	134	Iowa Park CISD	Iowa Park
134	407	Flour Bluff ISD	Corpus Christi	220	215	Kennedale ISD	Kennedale	306	133	Cuero ISD	Cuero
135	403	Angleton ISD	Angleton	220	215	Medina Valley ISD	Castroville	306	133	Devine ISD	Devine
136	395	New Caney ISD	New Caney	222	214	San Elizario ISD	San Elizario	306	133	Fabens ISD	Fabens
137	391	Cleburne ISD	Cleburne	223	213	Manor ISD	Manor	306	133	Mexia ISD	Mexia
138	390	Channelview ISD	Channelview	224	212	Barbers Hill ISD	Mont Belvieu	306	133	Sweeny ISD	Sweeny
138	390	Longview ISD	Longview	224	212	Beeville ISD	Beeville	306	133	Wimberley ISD	Wimberley
140	388	Port Arthur ISD	Port Arthur	226	210	Burkburnett ISD	Burkburnett	312	132	Fort Stockton ISD	Fort Stockton
141	385	Azle ISD	Azle	227	208	Kaufman ISD	Kaufman	312	132	Huntington ISD	Huntington
142	384	Lake Travis ISD	Austin	228	206	Columbia-Brazoria ISD	West Columbia	312	132	Whitesboro ISD	Whitesboro
143	383	Texas City ISD	Texas City	228	206	Elgin ISD	Elgin	315	128	Mathis ISD	Mathis
144	375	Sherman ISD	Sherman	228	206	Wylie ISD	Abilene	315	128	Point Isabel ISD	Point Isabel
145	373	Alamo Heights ISD	San Antonio	231	205	Aransas County ISD	Rockport	317	127	Van ISD	Van
145	373	Huntsville ISD	Huntsville	232	202	Huffman ISD	Huffman	318	126	Diboll ISD	Diboll
147	371	Marshall ISD	Marshall	233	200	Springtown ISD	Springtown	318	126	Pleasant Grove ISD	Texarkana
148	364	Red Oak ISD	Red Oak	234	198	Splendora ISD	Splendora	318	126	Vernon ISD	Vernon
149	359	Aledo ISD	Aledo	235	197	Pampa ISD	Pampa	318	126	Wharton ISD	Wharton

Note: This section only includes districts with 1,500 or more students; All categories are ranked from high to low

Rank		District Name	City
322	125	Carrizo Springs CISD	Carrizo Springs
323	124	Atlanta ISD	Atlanta
323	124	Canton ISD	Canton
323	124	Giddings ISD	Giddings
326	123	Hamshire-Fannett ISD	Hamshire
327	121	Liberty-Eylau ISD	Texarkana
327	121	Pearsall ISD	Pearsall
329	120	Smithville ISD	Smithville
330	119	Hillsboro ISD	Hillsboro
331	117	Fairfield ISD	Fairfield
332	115	Caldwell ISD	Caldwell
332	115	Monahans-Wickett-Pyote ISD	Monahans
334	114	Mount Vernon ISD	Mount Vernon
335	113	Aransas Pass ISD	Aransas Pass
335	113	Orange Grove ISD	Orange Grove
335	113	Raymondville ISD	Raymondville
335	113	Tarkington ISD	Cleveland
339	112	Central ISD	Pollok
339	112	Tatum ISD	Tatum
339	112	Westwood ISD	Palestine
342	111	Columbus ISD	Columbus
342	111	Crystal City ISD	Crystal City
342	111	Llano ISD	Llano
342	111	West ISD	West
346	110	Brownfield ISD	Brownfield
346	110	Lake Worth ISD	Lake Worth
346	110	Orangefield ISD	Orangefield
349	109	Rains ISD	Emory
349	109	Rusk ISD	Rusk
351	106	Celina ISD	Celina
351	106	La Vega ISD	Waco
351	106	West Oso ISD	Corpus Christi
354	105	Coldspring-Oakhurst CISD	Coldspring
355	103	Community ISD	Nevada
355	103	Madisonville CISD	Madisonville
357	102	Glen Rose ISD	Glen Rose
358	101	Commerce ISD	Commerce
358	101	Dalhart ISD	Dalhart
358	101	Lamesa ISD	Lamesa
358	101	Navarro ISD	Seguin
362	100	Palacios ISD	Palacios
362	100	Rockdale ISD	Rockdale
364	99	Lorena ISD	Lorena
364	99	Poteet ISD	Poteet
366	98	Greenwood ISD	Midland
366	98	Groesbeck ISD	Groesbeck
366	98	Whitney ISD	Whitney
369	97	Mineola ISD	Mineola
369	97	Spring Hill ISD	Longview
369	97	Yoakum ISD	Yoakum
372	96	La Grange ISD	La Grange
373	95	Venus ISD	Venus
374	94	Kemp ISD	Kemp
374	94	Lytle ISD	Lytle
374	94	Shepherd ISD	Shepherd
377	93	Anna ISD	Anna
378	92	Cameron ISD	Cameron
378	92	Progreso ISD	Progreso
380	90	Krum ISD	Krum
381	88	Breckenridge ISD	Breckenridge
381	88	Pilot Point ISD	Pilot Point
383	86	Aubrey ISD	Aubrey
383	86	River Road ISD	Amarillo
383	86	Royal ISD	Pattison
386	84	Denver City ISD	Denver City
387	83	Godley ISD	Godley
387	83	Lyford CISD	Lyford
389	81	Bowie ISD	Bowie
389	81	Bullard ISD	Bullard
389	81	Hempstead ISD	Hempstead
392	78	Yes College Preparatory School	Houston
393	74	Life School	Lancaster
394	73	Kipp Inc Charter	Houston
395	72	Southwest School	Houston
396	66	School of Excellence in Education	San Antonio
397	51	Harmony Science Academy	Houston
398	48	Idea Academy	Weslaco
399	45	Advantage Academy	Dallas
n/a	n/a	Harmony Science Acad (Fort Worth)	Fort Worth
n/a	n/a	Lovejoy ISD	Allen
n/a	n/a	Ripley House Charter School	Houston
n/a	n/a	Varnett Charter School	Houston

High School Drop-out Rate

Rank	Percent	District Name	City
1	37.5	Dallas Can Academy Charter	Dallas
2	22.2	Southwest School	Houston
3	16.0	North Forest ISD	Houston
4	11.9	Winfree Academy	Irving
5	10.4	Robstown ISD	Robstown
6	9.9	Alice ISD	Alice
7	9.5	Galveston ISD	Galveston
8	9.0	San Antonio ISD	San Antonio
9	8.7	Raymondville ISD	Raymondville
10	7.8	Canutillo ISD	El Paso
11	7.5	Waco ISD	Waco
12	7.3	Cleveland ISD	Cleveland
12	7.3	Manor ISD	Manor
12	7.3	South San Antonio ISD	San Antonio
15	7.2	West Orange-Cove CISD	Orange
16	6.7	Dickinson ISD	Dickinson
17	6.6	Edcouch-Elsa ISD	Edcouch
17	6.6	Temple ISD	Temple
19	6.5	Fort Stockton ISD	Fort Stockton
19	6.5	Fort Worth ISD	Fort Worth
19	6.5	Southside ISD	San Antonio
19	6.5	Victoria ISD	Victoria
23	6.4	Pearsall ISD	Pearsall
23	6.4	School of Excellence in Education	San Antonio
25	6.3	Longview ISD	Longview
26	6.2	Lubbock ISD	Lubbock
27	5.9	Dallas ISD	Dallas
27	5.9	Duncanville ISD	Duncanville
27	5.9	Edgewood ISD	San Antonio
27	5.9	La Marque ISD	La Marque
31	5.8	Clint ISD	El Paso
32	5.7	Pleasanton ISD	Pleasanton
33	5.6	Aldine ISD	Houston
33	5.6	Roma ISD	Roma
35	5.5	San Marcos CISD	San Marcos
36	5.4	Donna ISD	Donna
36	5.4	Levelland ISD	Levelland
38	5.3	Crystal City ISD	Crystal City
38	5.3	Plainview ISD	Plainview
40	5.2	Lufkin ISD	Lufkin
41	5.1	Lamesa ISD	Lamesa
41	5.1	San Felipe-Del Rio CISD	Del Rio
43	5.0	Alief ISD	Houston
43	5.0	Pasadena ISD	Pasadena
45	4.9	Austin ISD	Austin
45	4.9	Hereford ISD	Hereford
45	4.9	San Angelo ISD	San Angelo
48	4.8	Bullard ISD	Bullard
48	4.8	El Paso ISD	El Paso
48	4.8	Jacksonville ISD	Jacksonville
48	4.8	Midland ISD	Midland
48	4.8	Palacios ISD	Palacios
48	4.8	Quinlan ISD	Quinlan
54	4.7	Greenville ISD	Greenville
54	4.7	Port Arthur ISD	Port Arthur
54	4.7	Rio Hondo ISD	Rio Hondo
57	4.6	Houston ISD	Houston
57	4.6	Royal ISD	Pattison
59	4.5	Aransas Pass ISD	Aransas Pass
59	4.5	Bridgeport ISD	Bridgeport
59	4.5	Judson ISD	Live Oak
59	4.5	Point Isabel ISD	Port Isabel
63	4.4	Bryan ISD	Bryan
63	4.4	Ector County ISD	Odessa
63	4.4	Grand Prairie ISD	Grand Prairie
63	4.4	Mathis ISD	Mathis
63	4.4	Zapata County ISD	Zapata
68	4.3	Carrizo Springs CISD	Carrizo Springs
68	4.3	Dayton ISD	Dayton
68	4.3	Floresville ISD	Floresville
68	4.3	Harlandale ISD	San Antonio
68	4.3	Hays CISD	Kyle
68	4.3	Ingleside ISD	Ingleside
74	4.2	Beeville ISD	Beeville
74	4.2	Harlingen CISD	Harlingen
74	4.2	Mcallen ISD	Mcallen
74	4.2	Mercedes ISD	Mercedes
78	4.1	Andrews ISD	Andrews
78	4.1	San Benito CISD	San Benito
78	4.1	Sheldon ISD	Houston
78	4.1	Terrell ISD	Terrell
78	4.1	West Oso ISD	Corpus Christi
83	4.0	Alvarado ISD	Alvarado
83	4.0	Galena Park ISD	Houston
83	4.0	La Joya ISD	La Joya
83	4.0	Pflugerville ISD	Pflugerville
83	4.0	Southwest ISD	San Antonio
83	4.0	Ysleta ISD	El Paso
89	3.9	Brownfield ISD	Brownfield
89	3.9	Kaufman ISD	Kaufman
89	3.9	Nacogdoches ISD	Nacogdoches
92	3.8	Somerset ISD	Somerset
93	3.7	Cedar Hill ISD	Cedar Hill
93	3.7	East Central ISD	San Antonio
93	3.7	Edinburg CISD	Edinburg
93	3.7	Tyler ISD	Tyler
97	3.6	Birdville ISD	Haltom City
97	3.6	Gonzales ISD	Gonzales
99	3.5	Eagle Pass ISD	Eagle Pass
99	3.5	Everman ISD	Everman
99	3.5	Spring ISD	Houston
102	3.4	Gainesville ISD	Gainesville
102	3.4	Lockhart ISD	Lockhart
102	3.4	Marshall ISD	Marshall
105	3.3	Bandera ISD	Bandera
105	3.3	Hempstead ISD	Hempstead
105	3.3	West ISD	West
108	3.2	Alvin ISD	Alvin
108	3.2	Castleberry ISD	Fort Worth
108	3.2	Spring Hill ISD	Longview
111	3.1	Amarillo ISD	Amarillo
111	3.1	Beaumont ISD	Beaumont
111	3.1	Crowley ISD	Crowley
111	3.1	Diboll ISD	Diboll
111	3.1	Hondo ISD	Hondo
111	3.1	Pine Tree ISD	Longview
111	3.1	Poteet ISD	Poteet
118	3.0	Fabens ISD	Fabens
118	3.0	Irving ISD	Irving
118	3.0	Livingston ISD	Livingston
118	3.0	Monahans-Wickett-Pyote ISD	Monahans
118	3.0	New Braunfels ISD	New Braunfels
118	3.0	Paris ISD	Paris
118	3.0	Rockdale ISD	Rockdale
125	2.9	Arlington ISD	Arlington
125	2.9	Cleburne ISD	Cleburne
125	2.9	El Campo ISD	El Campo
125	2.9	Georgetown ISD	Georgetown
125	2.9	Laredo ISD	Laredo
130	2.8	Bowie ISD	Bowie
130	2.8	Brazosport ISD	Clute
130	2.8	Chapel Hill ISD	Tyler
130	2.8	Community ISD	Nevada
130	2.8	Corpus Christi ISD	Corpus Christi
130	2.8	Garland ISD	Garland
130	2.8	Goose Creek CISD	Baytown
130	2.8	Huntington ISD	Huntington
130	2.8	Klein ISD	Klein
130	2.8	La Feria Ind SD	La Feria
130	2.8	Lamar CISD	Rosenberg
130	2.8	Mexia ISD	Mexia
130	2.8	Orange Grove ISD	Orange Grove
130	2.8	Rio Grande City CISD	Rio Grande City
130	2.8	Sulphur Springs ISD	Sulphur Springs
145	2.7	Abilene ISD	Abilene
145	2.7	Navasota ISD	Navasota
145	2.7	Santa Fe ISD	Santa Fe
145	2.7	Valley View ISD	Pharr
149	2.6	Desoto ISD	Desoto
149	2.6	Huntsville ISD	Huntsville
149	2.6	Killeen ISD	Killeen
149	2.6	Lyford CISD	Lyford
149	2.6	Texarkana ISD	Texarkana
154	2.5	Burleson ISD	Burleson
154	2.5	Hillsboro ISD	Hillsboro
154	2.5	Huffman ISD	Huffman
154	2.5	La Vega ISD	Waco
154	2.5	Leander ISD	Leander
154	2.5	Royse City ISD	Royse City
154	2.5	San Elizario ISD	San Elizario
154	2.5	Taylor ISD	Taylor
154	2.5	Willis ISD	Willis
163	2.4	Bastrop ISD	Bastrop
163	2.4	Columbia-Brazoria ISD	West Columbia
163	2.4	Lytle ISD	Lytle
163	2.4	Orangefield ISD	Orangefield
163	2.4	Progreso ISD	Progreso
163	2.4	Sharyland ISD	Mission
163	2.4	Wharton ISD	Wharton

Note: This section only includes districts with 1,500 or more students; All categories are ranked from high to low

Rank	Value	District Name	City
170	2.3	Brownsville ISD	Brownsville
170	2.3	Carthage ISD	Carthage
170	2.3	Copperas Cove ISD	Copperas Cove
170	2.3	Denison ISD	Denison
170	2.3	Spring Branch ISD	Houston
170	2.3	Stafford MSD	Stafford
170	2.3	Texas City ISD	Texas City
170	2.3	Uvalde CISD	Uvalde
170	2.3	Weslaco ISD	Weslaco
179	2.2	Hudson ISD	Lufkin
179	2.2	Lancaster ISD	Lancaster
179	2.2	Mineral Wells ISD	Mineral Wells
179	2.2	Springtown ISD	Springtown
183	2.1	Athens ISD	Athens
183	2.1	Aubrey ISD	Aubrey
183	2.1	Breckenridge ISD	Breckenridge
183	2.1	Channelview ISD	Channelview
183	2.1	Eagle Academy of Abilene	Lewisville
183	2.1	Gilmer ISD	Gilmer
183	2.1	Kingsville ISD	Kingsville
183	2.1	Lorena ISD	Lorena
183	2.1	Mansfield ISD	Mansfield
183	2.1	Nederland ISD	Nederland
183	2.1	Pampa ISD	Pampa
183	2.1	Silsbee ISD	Silsbee
183	2.1	Westwood ISD	Palestine
196	2.0	Liberty-Eylau ISD	Texarkana
196	2.0	Northwest ISD	Justin
196	2.0	Pecos-Barstow-Toyah ISD	Pecos
196	2.0	Socorro ISD	El Paso
196	2.0	White Settlement ISD	White Settlement
201	1.9	Bay City ISD	Bay City
201	1.9	Brenham ISD	Brenham
201	1.9	Caldwell ISD	Caldwell
201	1.9	Crosby ISD	Crosby
201	1.9	Richardson ISD	Richardson
201	1.9	Round Rock ISD	Round Rock
201	1.9	Smithville ISD	Smithville
201	1.9	Snyder ISD	Snyder
201	1.9	Whitesboro ISD	Whitesboro
201	1.9	Wills Point ISD	Wills Point
211	1.8	Bridge City ISD	Bridge City
211	1.8	Ferris ISD	Ferris
211	1.8	Lampasas ISD	Lampasas
211	1.8	Mineola ISD	Mineola
211	1.8	Palestine ISD	Palestine
211	1.8	Sweeny ISD	Sweeny
217	1.7	Big Spring ISD	Big Spring
217	1.7	Columbus ISD	Columbus
217	1.7	Devine ISD	Devine
217	1.7	Eagle Mt-Saginaw ISD	Fort Worth
217	1.7	Humble ISD	Humble
217	1.7	Iowa Park CISD	Iowa Park
217	1.7	Kemp ISD	Kemp
217	1.7	La Grange ISD	La Grange
217	1.7	Sealy ISD	Sealy
217	1.7	Waxahachie ISD	Waxahachie
227	1.6	Carrollton-Farmers Branch	Carrollton
227	1.6	Central ISD	Pollok
227	1.6	Dumas ISD	Dumas
227	1.6	Elgin ISD	Elgin
227	1.6	Jasper ISD	Jasper
227	1.6	Life School	Lancaster
227	1.6	Madisonville CISD	Madisonville
227	1.6	New Caney ISD	New Caney
227	1.6	Pearland ISD	Pearland
227	1.6	Pharr-San Juan-Alamo ISD	Pharr
227	1.6	Red Oak ISD	Red Oak
227	1.6	Schertz-Cibolo-U City ISD	Schertz
227	1.6	Venus ISD	Venus
227	1.6	Wylie ISD	Wylie
241	1.5	Bonham ISD	Bonham
241	1.5	Coldspring-Oakhurst CISD	Coldspring
241	1.5	Denver City ISD	Denver City
241	1.5	Fort Bend ISD	Sugar Land
241	1.5	Gladewater ISD	Gladewater
241	1.5	Granbury ISD	Granbury
241	1.5	Gregory-Portland ISD	Portland
241	1.5	Hardin-Jefferson ISD	Sour Lake
241	1.5	Kilgore ISD	Kilgore
241	1.5	La Porte ISD	La Porte
241	1.5	Liberty Hill ISD	Liberty Hill
241	1.5	Liberty ISD	Liberty
241	1.5	Little Cypress-Mauricevil	Orange
241	1.5	Lumberton ISD	Lumberton
241	1.5	Mckinney ISD	Mckinney
241	1.5	Princeton ISD	Princeton
257	1.4	Burkburnett ISD	Burkburnett
257	1.4	Hutto ISD	Hutto
257	1.4	Keller ISD	Keller
257	1.4	Lake Worth ISD	Lake Worth
257	1.4	Little Elm ISD	Little Elm
257	1.4	Magnolia ISD	Magnolia
257	1.4	Mesquite ISD	Mesquite
257	1.4	Mission CISD	Mission
257	1.4	Rusk ISD	Rusk
257	1.4	Tuloso-Midway ISD	Corpus Christi
267	1.3	Barbers Hill ISD	Mont Belvieu
267	1.3	College Station ISD	College Station
267	1.3	Comal ISD	New Braunfels
267	1.3	Fairfield ISD	Fairfield
267	1.3	Forney ISD	Forney
267	1.3	North East ISD	San Antonio
267	1.3	Vernon ISD	Vernon
267	1.3	Waller ISD	Waller
267	1.3	Whitehouse ISD	Whitehouse
267	1.3	Wichita Falls ISD	Wichita Falls
277	1.2	Cypress-Fairbanks ISD	Houston
277	1.2	Deer Park ISD	Deer Park
277	1.2	Glen Rose ISD	Glen Rose
277	1.2	Hallsville ISD	Hallsville
277	1.2	Joshua ISD	Joshua
277	1.2	Lewisville ISD	Flower Mound
277	1.2	Lubbock-Cooper ISD	Lubbock
284	1.1	Angleton ISD	Angleton
284	1.1	Atlanta ISD	Atlanta
284	1.1	Corsicana ISD	Corsicana
284	1.1	Fredericksburg ISD	Fredericksburg
284	1.1	Grapevine-Colleyville ISD	Grapevine
284	1.1	Los Fresnos CISD	Los Fresnos
284	1.1	Midlothian ISD	Midlothian
284	1.1	Northside ISD	San Antonio
284	1.1	Pittsburg ISD	Pittsburg
284	1.1	Sweetwater ISD	Sweetwater
294	1.0	Brownsboro ISD	Brownsboro
294	1.0	Flour Bluff ISD	Corpus Christi
294	1.0	Giddings ISD	Giddings
294	1.0	Katy ISD	Katy
294	1.0	La Vernia ISD	La Vernia
294	1.0	Sanger ISD	Sanger
294	1.0	Van ISD	Van
301	0.9	Clear Creek ISD	League City
301	0.9	Conroe ISD	Conroe
301	0.9	Del Valle ISD	Del Valle
301	0.9	Hurst-Euless-Bedford ISD	Bedford
301	0.9	Navarro ISD	Seguin
301	0.9	North Lamar ISD	Paris
301	0.9	Seminole ISD	Seminole
301	0.9	Tomball ISD	Tomball
309	0.8	Belton ISD	Belton
309	0.8	Burnet CISD	Burnet
309	0.8	Calallen ISD	Corpus Christi
309	0.8	Calhoun County ISD	Port Lavaca
309	0.8	Denton ISD	Denton
309	0.8	Medina Valley ISD	Castroville
309	0.8	Mount Pleasant ISD	Mount Pleasant
309	0.8	Plano ISD	Plano
309	0.8	Rains ISD	Emory
309	0.8	Sherman ISD	Sherman
309	0.8	Stephenville	Stephenville
309	0.8	Wimberley ISD	Wimberley
321	0.7	Azle ISD	Azle
321	0.7	Crandall ISD	Crandall
321	0.7	Cuero ISD	Cuero
321	0.7	Henderson ISD	Henderson
321	0.7	Vidor ISD	Vidor
326	0.6	Alamo Heights ISD	San Antonio
326	0.6	Brownwood ISD	Brownwood
326	0.6	Connally ISD	Waco
326	0.6	Coppell ISD	Coppell
326	0.6	Decatur ISD	Decatur
326	0.6	Gatesville ISD	Gatesville
326	0.6	Lake Travis ISD	Austin
326	0.6	Midway ISD	Hewitt
326	0.6	Montgomery ISD	Montgomery
326	0.6	Rockwall ISD	Rockwall
326	0.6	Sinton ISD	Sinton
337	0.5	Aledo ISD	Aledo
337	0.5	Aransas County ISD	Rockport
337	0.5	Frenship ISD	Wolfforth
337	0.5	Kennedale ISD	Kennedale
337	0.5	Prosper ISD	Prosper
337	0.5	Seguin ISD	Seguin
337	0.5	Weatherford ISD	Weatherford
344	0.4	Ennis ISD	Ennis
344	0.4	Hidalgo ISD	Hidalgo
344	0.4	Marble Falls ISD	Marble Falls
344	0.4	South Texas ISD	Mercedes
344	0.4	United ISD	Laredo
344	0.4	Wylie ISD	Abilene
350	0.3	Allen ISD	Allen
350	0.3	Eanes ISD	Austin
350	0.3	Kerrville ISD	Kerrville
350	0.3	Lake Dallas ISD	Lake Dallas
354	0.2	Frisco ISD	Frisco
355	0.0	Advantage Academy	Dallas
n/a	n/a	Anna ISD	Anna
n/a	n/a	Bellville ISD	Bellville
n/a	n/a	Canton ISD	Canton
n/a	n/a	Graham ISD	Graham
n/a	n/a	Highland Park ISD	Dallas
n/a	n/a	Idea Academy	Weslaco
n/a	n/a	Lindale ISD	Lindale
n/a	n/a	Tarkington ISD	Cleveland
n/a	n/a	Yes College Preparatory School	Houston
n/a	n/a	Harmony Science Acad (Fort Worth)	Fort Worth
n/a	n/a	Lovejoy ISD	Allen
n/a	n/a	Ripley House Charter School	Houston
n/a	n/a	Varnett Charter School	Houston
n/a	n/a	Argyle ISD	Argyle
n/a	n/a	Boerne ISD	Boerne
n/a	n/a	Borger ISD	Borger
n/a	n/a	Cameron ISD	Cameron
n/a	n/a	Canyon ISD	Canyon
n/a	n/a	Carroll ISD	Grapevine
n/a	n/a	Celina ISD	Celina
n/a	n/a	Center ISD	Center
n/a	n/a	China Spring ISD	Waco
n/a	n/a	Commerce ISD	Commerce
n/a	n/a	Dalhart ISD	Dalhart
n/a	n/a	Dripping Spgs ISD	Dripping Spgs
n/a	n/a	Friendswood ISD	Friendswood
n/a	n/a	Godley ISD	Godley
n/a	n/a	Greenwood ISD	Midland
n/a	n/a	Groesbeck ISD	Groesbeck
n/a	n/a	Hamshire-Fannett ISD	Hamshire
n/a	n/a	Harmony Science Academy	Houston
n/a	n/a	Kipp Inc Charter	Houston
n/a	n/a	Krum ISD	Krum
n/a	n/a	Llano ISD	Llano
n/a	n/a	Mabank ISD	Mabank
n/a	n/a	Mount Vernon ISD	Mount Vernon
n/a	n/a	Needville ISD	Needville
n/a	n/a	Perryton ISD	Perryton
n/a	n/a	Pilot Point ISD	Pilot Point
n/a	n/a	Pleasant Grove ISD	Texarkana
n/a	n/a	Port Neches-Groves ISD	Port Neches
n/a	n/a	River Road ISD	Amarillo
n/a	n/a	Robinson ISD	Robinson
n/a	n/a	Shepherd ISD	Shepherd
n/a	n/a	Splendora ISD	Splendora
n/a	n/a	Tatum ISD	Tatum
n/a	n/a	Whitney ISD	Whitney
n/a	n/a	Yoakum ISD	Yoakum

Average Freshman Graduation Rate

Rank	Percent	District Name	City
1	100.0	Aledo ISD	Aledo
1	100.0	Burnet CISD	Burnet
1	100.0	Comal ISD	New Braunfels
1	100.0	Eagle Academy of Abilene	Lewisville
1	100.0	Frisco ISD	Frisco
1	100.0	Hutto ISD	Hutto
1	100.0	Prosper ISD	Prosper
1	100.0	Schertz-Cibolo-U City ISD	Schertz
1	100.0	Tatum ISD	Tatum
10	99.2	Boerne ISD	Boerne
11	98.6	Eanes ISD	Austin
12	98.5	Allen ISD	Allen
13	97.9	China Spring ISD	Waco
14	97.3	Royse City ISD	Royse City
15	97.0	Seminole ISD	Seminole
16	95.9	Forney ISD	Forney
16	95.9	Rockwall ISD	Rockwall
18	95.7	Argyle ISD	Argyle
18	95.7	Huntington ISD	Huntington

Note: This section only includes districts with 1,500 or more students; All categories are ranked from high to low

Rank	Score	District	City
20	95.4	Hallsville ISD	Hallsville
21	94.9	Columbus ISD	Columbus
22	94.5	Highland Park ISD	Dallas
23	94.4	College Station ISD	College Station
24	93.9	Eagle Mt-Saginaw ISD	Fort Worth
25	93.8	Fredericksburg ISD	Fredericksburg
26	93.4	Perryton ISD	Perryton
27	93.3	Katy ISD	Katy
28	92.8	Calhoun County ISD	Port Lavaca
29	92.7	Leander ISD	Leander
30	92.6	Alamo Heights ISD	San Antonio
30	92.6	Robinson ISD	Robinson
32	92.5	Lorena ISD	Lorena
33	92.0	Humble ISD	Humble
34	91.8	Advantage Academy	Dallas
35	91.7	Midway ISD	Hewitt
36	91.5	Friendswood ISD	Friendswood
37	91.2	Anna ISD	Anna
38	91.1	Wylie ISD	Wylie
39	91.0	Bellville ISD	Bellville
40	90.9	Krum ISD	Krum
40	90.9	Midlothian ISD	Midlothian
42	90.6	Celina ISD	Celina
42	90.6	Pearland ISD	Pearland
44	90.5	Devine ISD	Devine
45	90.3	Hurst-Euless-Bedford ISD	Bedford
46	90.2	Hillsboro ISD	Hillsboro
47	90.1	Liberty Hill ISD	Liberty Hill
48	90.0	Crandall ISD	Crandall
49	89.9	Coppell ISD	Coppell
50	89.7	Princeton ISD	Princeton
50	89.7	Whitehouse ISD	Whitehouse
52	89.5	Little Elm ISD	Little Elm
53	89.3	Belton ISD	Belton
53	89.3	Grapevine-Colleyville ISD	Grapevine
55	89.2	Lockhart ISD	Lockhart
56	88.9	Dripping Spgs ISD	Dripping Spgs
57	88.3	Mckinney ISD	Mckinney
57	88.3	South Texas ISD	Mercedes
59	88.2	Round Rock ISD	Round Rock
60	87.8	Keller ISD	Keller
61	87.7	Deer Park ISD	Deer Park
61	87.7	Lake Travis ISD	Austin
61	87.7	Wylie ISD	Abilene
64	87.5	Denver City ISD	Denver City
64	87.5	La Vernia ISD	La Vernia
66	87.4	Calallen ISD	Corpus Christi
66	87.4	White Settlement ISD	White Settlement
68	87.3	Gregory-Portland ISD	Portland
68	87.3	Texarkana ISD	Texarkana
70	87.2	Waxahachie ISD	Waxahachie
71	87.1	Georgetown ISD	Georgetown
72	87.0	Lytle ISD	Lytle
73	86.7	Canton ISD	Canton
73	86.7	Southwest School	Houston
75	86.6	Plano ISD	Plano
76	86.3	Dalhart ISD	Dalhart
76	86.3	Navarro ISD	Seguin
76	86.3	Pleasant Grove ISD	Texarkana
79	86.2	Barbers Hill ISD	Mont Belvieu
80	86.0	Hardin-Jefferson ISD	Sour Lake
80	86.0	North Lamar ISD	Paris
82	85.9	Canyon ISD	Canyon
82	85.9	Cypress-Fairbanks ISD	Houston
82	85.9	Iowa Park CISD	Iowa Park
85	85.8	Tomball ISD	Tomball
86	85.7	Mount Vernon ISD	Mount Vernon
87	85.4	Lindale ISD	Lindale
88	85.3	Orangefield ISD	Orangefield
89	85.2	Carroll ISD	Grapevine
89	85.2	Whitesboro ISD	Whitesboro
91	85.1	Lumberton ISD	Lumberton
92	85.0	Northwest ISD	Justin
93	84.8	Tuloso-Midway ISD	Corpus Christi
94	84.6	Diboll ISD	Diboll
94	84.6	Medina Valley ISD	Castroville
96	84.5	Smithville ISD	Smithville
97	84.3	Pflugerville ISD	Pflugerville
98	84.2	Conroe ISD	Conroe
98	84.2	Lake Dallas ISD	Lake Dallas
98	84.2	Sealy ISD	Sealy
101	84.1	Life School	Lancaster
101	84.1	Sanger ISD	Sanger
103	83.9	Kipp Inc Charter	Houston
104	83.7	Sharyland ISD	Mission
105	83.6	Fairfield ISD	Fairfield
105	83.6	Glen Rose ISD	Glen Rose
107	83.5	Clear Creek ISD	League City
107	83.5	Fort Bend ISD	Sugar Land
109	83.3	Ferris ISD	Ferris
110	83.2	Gatesville ISD	Gatesville
111	83.1	Burleson ISD	Burleson
111	83.1	Floresville ISD	Floresville
111	83.1	Greenwood ISD	Midland
111	83.1	Rio Hondo ISD	Rio Hondo
115	82.9	New Braunfels ISD	New Braunfels
116	82.8	Lewisville ISD	Flower Mound
116	82.8	Magnolia ISD	Magnolia
116	82.8	Marble Falls ISD	Marble Falls
119	82.7	Aubrey ISD	Aubrey
119	82.7	Dumas ISD	Dumas
119	82.7	Kennedale ISD	Kennedale
119	82.7	Lamar CISD	Rosenberg
123	82.6	Hamshire-Fannett ISD	Hamshire
124	82.5	Brenham ISD	Brenham
124	82.5	Tarkington ISD	Cleveland
126	82.4	Community ISD	Nevada
126	82.4	Mabank ISD	Mabank
128	82.3	Decatur ISD	Decatur
128	82.3	Frenship ISD	Wolfforth
130	82.1	Atlanta ISD	Atlanta
130	82.1	Brownfield ISD	Brownfield
130	82.1	Huffman ISD	Huffman
130	82.1	Kilgore ISD	Kilgore
134	82.0	Nederland ISD	Nederland
135	81.7	Bridgeport ISD	Bridgeport
135	81.7	Columbia-Brazoria ISD	West Columbia
135	81.7	La Porte ISD	La Porte
138	81.6	Giddings ISD	Giddings
138	81.6	Granbury ISD	Granbury
138	81.6	West ISD	West
141	81.5	Bastrop ISD	Bastrop
141	81.5	Mineola ISD	Mineola
143	81.4	Burkburnett ISD	Burkburnett
143	81.4	Pine Tree ISD	Longview
145	81.1	Galena Park ISD	Houston
145	81.1	Gilmer ISD	Gilmer
145	81.1	Mansfield ISD	Mansfield
148	81.0	Graham ISD	Graham
148	81.0	North East ISD	San Antonio
150	80.8	Willis ISD	Willis
151	80.7	Carthage ISD	Carthage
151	80.7	Red Oak ISD	Red Oak
153	80.6	Mount Pleasant ISD	Mount Pleasant
153	80.6	Palacios ISD	Palacios
153	80.6	Silsbee ISD	Silsbee
156	80.5	Hays CISD	Kyle
156	80.5	San Angelo ISD	San Angelo
156	80.5	Vidor ISD	Vidor
159	80.4	Andrews ISD	Andrews
159	80.4	Flour Bluff ISD	Corpus Christi
159	80.4	Levelland ISD	Levelland
159	80.4	Northside ISD	San Antonio
159	80.4	United ISD	Laredo
159	80.4	Valley View ISD	Pharr
159	80.4	Van ISD	Van
166	80.3	West Oso ISD	Corpus Christi
166	80.3	Whitney ISD	Whitney
168	80.2	Hempstead ISD	Hempstead
169	80.1	Sulphur Springs ISD	Sulphur Springs
170	80.0	Garland ISD	Garland
171	79.9	Lampasas ISD	Lampasas
171	79.9	Snyder ISD	Snyder
173	79.8	Brownsboro ISD	Brownsboro
173	79.8	Elgin ISD	Elgin
173	79.8	Marshall ISD	Marshall
176	79.7	Kaufman ISD	Kaufman
176	79.7	Klein ISD	Klein
178	79.6	Alvin ISD	Alvin
178	79.6	Orange Grove ISD	Orange Grove
178	79.6	Sweeny ISD	Sweeny
178	79.6	Wimberley ISD	Wimberley
182	79.5	Little Cypress-Mauricevil	Orange
182	79.5	Sinton ISD	Sinton
184	79.1	Bonham ISD	Bonham
185	79.0	Clint ISD	El Paso
186	78.9	El Campo ISD	El Campo
187	78.8	Denton ISD	Denton
187	78.8	Stephenville	Stephenville
189	78.6	Cameron ISD	Cameron
189	78.6	Pharr-San Juan-Alamo ISD	Pharr
191	78.4	Mesquite ISD	Mesquite
192	78.3	Ingleside ISD	Ingleside
192	78.3	Joshua ISD	Joshua
194	78.2	River Road ISD	Amarillo
194	78.2	Spring Hill ISD	Longview
196	78.1	Ennis ISD	Ennis
197	78.0	Hudson ISD	Lufkin
197	78.0	Poteet ISD	Poteet
197	78.0	Spring Branch ISD	Houston
200	77.9	Los Fresnos CISD	Los Fresnos
200	77.9	Lufkin ISD	Lufkin
200	77.9	Ysleta ISD	El Paso
203	77.8	Cuero ISD	Cuero
203	77.8	Jasper ISD	Jasper
205	77.7	Lamesa ISD	Lamesa
205	77.7	San Marcos CISD	San Marcos
205	77.7	Socorro ISD	El Paso
205	77.7	Wichita Falls ISD	Wichita Falls
209	77.6	Dickinson ISD	Dickinson
210	77.4	Hondo ISD	Hondo
210	77.4	Sweetwater ISD	Sweetwater
212	77.2	Gonzales ISD	Gonzales
212	77.2	Wills Point ISD	Wills Point
214	77.1	Mathis ISD	Mathis
215	77.0	Kemp ISD	Kemp
215	77.0	Yoakum ISD	Yoakum
215	77.0	Zapata County ISD	Zapata
218	76.7	Central ISD	Pollok
218	76.7	Fort Stockton ISD	Fort Stockton
218	76.7	Westwood ISD	Palestine
221	76.6	Eagle Pass ISD	Eagle Pass
222	76.5	Montgomery ISD	Montgomery
222	76.5	Pilot Point ISD	Pilot Point
224	76.3	Huntsville ISD	Huntsville
225	76.2	Cleburne ISD	Cleburne
225	76.2	Mineral Wells ISD	Mineral Wells
225	76.2	Monahans-Wickett-Pyote ISD	Monahans
228	76.1	Spring ISD	Houston
228	76.1	Texas City ISD	Texas City
230	76.0	Brazosport ISD	Clute
230	76.0	Hidalgo ISD	Hidalgo
232	75.8	Copperas Cove ISD	Copperas Cove
233	75.7	Denison ISD	Denison
233	75.7	Yes College Preparatory School	Houston
235	75.6	Richardson ISD	Richardson
235	75.6	Rio Grande City CISD	Rio Grande City
237	75.5	Cedar Hill ISD	Cedar Hill
238	75.4	Groesbeck ISD	Groesbeck
239	75.3	Pittsburg ISD	Pittsburg
239	75.3	Taylor ISD	Taylor
241	75.2	Crosby ISD	Crosby
241	75.2	Lubbock ISD	Lubbock
241	75.2	Rains ISD	Emory
244	75.0	Bowie ISD	Bowie
244	75.0	Judson ISD	Live Oak
246	74.9	Edinburg CISD	Edinburg
247	74.8	Azle ISD	Azle
248	74.4	Waller ISD	Waller
249	74.3	Aransas Pass ISD	Aransas Pass
249	74.3	Stafford MSD	Stafford
251	74.1	Crowley ISD	Crowley
251	74.1	Vernon ISD	Vernon
253	74.0	San Elizario ISD	San Elizario
254	73.9	Mexia ISD	Mexia
255	73.8	Amarillo ISD	Amarillo
255	73.8	Angleton ISD	Angleton
255	73.8	Chapel Hill ISD	Tyler
255	73.8	Lubbock-Cooper ISD	Lubbock
255	73.8	Sherman ISD	Sherman
260	73.7	Carrollton-Farmers Branch	Carrollton
260	73.7	Port Neches-Groves ISD	Port Neches
262	73.5	Godley ISD	Godley
263	73.3	Kerrville ISD	Kerrville
264	73.2	Aransas County ISD	Rockport
265	73.1	Midland ISD	Midland
266	73.0	Madisonville CISD	Madisonville
267	72.9	Royal ISD	Pattison
268	72.8	Liberty ISD	Liberty
269	72.7	Bridge City ISD	Bridge City
270	72.6	Center ISD	Center
271	72.5	Corsicana ISD	Corsicana
272	72.3	Santa Fe ISD	Santa Fe
273	72.2	Bay City ISD	Bay City
274	72.1	Bryan ISD	Bryan
275	71.8	Borger ISD	Borger
275	71.8	Pecos-Barstow-Toyah ISD	Pecos
275	71.8	Weatherford ISD	Weatherford

Note: This section only includes districts with 1,500 or more students; All categories are ranked from high to low

Rank	Score	District	City	Rank	Score	District	City	Rank	Score	District	City
278	71.7	Connally ISD	Waco	318	68.9	Mcallen ISD	Mcallen	362	63.4	Pearsall ISD	Pearsall
278	71.7	Splendora ISD	Splendora	318	68.9	Seguin ISD	Seguin	363	63.2	Edcouch-Elsa ISD	Edcouch
280	71.6	Llano ISD	Llano	322	68.7	Brownsville ISD	Brownsville	364	62.9	Channelview ISD	Channelview
280	71.6	Pleasanton ISD	Pleasanton	322	68.7	Manor ISD	Manor	365	62.8	Carrizo Springs CISD	Carrizo Springs
280	71.6	Wharton ISD	Wharton	324	68.6	Austin ISD	Austin	365	62.8	Kingsville ISD	Kingsville
283	71.4	Everman ISD	Everman	324	68.6	Idea Academy	Weslaco	367	62.4	Fort Worth ISD	Fort Worth
284	71.3	Gladewater ISD	Gladewater	326	68.2	Southside ISD	San Antonio	367	62.4	Robstown ISD	Robstown
285	71.1	Athens ISD	Athens	327	68.1	Arlington ISD	Arlington	369	62.3	Laredo ISD	Laredo
285	71.1	Beeville ISD	Beeville	327	68.1	Goose Creek CISD	Baytown	370	62.2	Progreso ISD	Progreso
285	71.1	Hereford ISD	Hereford	327	68.1	Livingston ISD	Livingston	371	61.8	Point Isabel ISD	Port Isabel
285	71.1	Uvalde CISD	Uvalde	327	68.1	Nacogdoches ISD	Nacogdoches	372	61.6	Ector County ISD	Odessa
289	71.0	Big Spring ISD	Big Spring	331	68.0	Del Valle ISD	Del Valle	373	61.5	Longview ISD	Longview
290	70.9	Coldspring-Oakhurst CISD	Coldspring	332	67.8	Roma ISD	Roma	374	61.4	Gainesville ISD	Gainesville
290	70.9	Venus ISD	Venus	333	67.7	Rusk ISD	Rusk	375	61.1	Paris ISD	Paris
292	70.8	Henderson ISD	Henderson	334	67.6	La Grange ISD	La Grange	376	60.9	Mercedes ISD	Mercedes
292	70.8	Southwest ISD	San Antonio	334	67.6	San Felipe-Del Rio CISD	Del Rio	377	60.8	South San Antonio ISD	San Antonio
294	70.7	Birdville ISD	Haltom City	334	67.6	Weslaco ISD	Weslaco	378	60.4	Raymondville ISD	Raymondville
294	70.7	Shepherd ISD	Shepherd	337	67.2	Grand Prairie ISD	Grand Prairie	378	60.4	Victoria ISD	Victoria
294	70.7	Springtown ISD	Springtown	338	66.9	Bullard ISD	Bullard	380	59.2	Houston ISD	Houston
297	70.6	Alvarado ISD	Alvarado	338	66.9	Cleveland ISD	Cleveland	381	59.0	Aldine ISD	Houston
298	70.4	Breckenridge ISD	Breckenridge	338	66.9	Lyford CISD	Lyford	382	58.5	Lake Worth ISD	Lake Worth
298	70.4	Dayton ISD	Dayton	338	66.9	Waco ISD	Waco	383	58.4	Quinlan ISD	Quinlan
298	70.4	Fabens ISD	Fabens	342	66.7	East Central ISD	San Antonio	384	57.7	Desoto ISD	Desoto
301	70.2	Beaumont ISD	Beaumont	343	66.6	Pampa ISD	Pampa	385	57.5	Duncanville ISD	Duncanville
302	70.1	Commerce ISD	Commerce	344	66.5	Needville ISD	Needville	386	57.4	Galveston ISD	Galveston
302	70.1	Mission CISD	Mission	344	66.5	Tyler ISD	Tyler	387	57.1	Dallas ISD	Dallas
304	69.9	Canutillo ISD	El Paso	346	66.4	Harlandale ISD	San Antonio	388	56.8	Liberty-Eylau ISD	Texarkana
305	69.7	Abilene ISD	Abilene	346	66.4	San Benito CISD	San Benito	389	56.1	Alice ISD	Alice
305	69.7	La Joya ISD	La Joya	348	66.3	Somerset ISD	Somerset	390	56.0	Edgewood ISD	San Antonio
307	69.6	Navasota ISD	Navasota	349	66.1	Lancaster ISD	Lancaster	391	55.7	Port Arthur ISD	Port Arthur
308	69.5	Donna ISD	Donna	350	66.0	El Paso ISD	El Paso	391	55.7	San Antonio ISD	San Antonio
308	69.5	La Feria Ind SD	La Feria	350	66.0	Greenville ISD	Greenville	393	55.4	Harmony Science Academy	Houston
308	69.5	New Caney ISD	New Caney	352	65.9	West Orange-Cove CISD	Orange	394	52.7	La Vega ISD	Waco
311	69.4	Corpus Christi ISD	Corpus Christi	353	65.8	Rockdale ISD	Rockdale	395	50.2	La Marque ISD	La Marque
312	69.3	Caldwell ISD	Caldwell	353	65.8	Sheldon ISD	Houston	396	47.8	School of Excellence in Education	San Antonio
313	69.2	Plainview ISD	Plainview	355	65.3	Crystal City ISD	Crystal City	397	31.3	North Forest ISD	Houston
314	69.1	Brownwood ISD	Brownwood	355	65.3	Jacksonville ISD	Jacksonville	n/a	n/a	Dallas Can Academy Charter	Dallas
314	69.1	Killeen ISD	Killeen	357	64.9	Terrell ISD	Terrell	n/a	n/a	Harmony Science Acad (Fort Worth)	Fort Worth
314	69.1	Palestine ISD	Palestine	358	64.6	Alief ISD	Houston	n/a	n/a	Lovejoy ISD	Allen
317	69.0	Bandera ISD	Bandera	359	64.5	Temple ISD	Temple	n/a	n/a	Ripley House Charter School	Houston
318	68.9	Harlingen CISD	Harlingen	360	63.8	Pasadena ISD	Pasadena	n/a	n/a	Varnett Charter School	Houston
318	68.9	Irving ISD	Irving	361	63.6	Castleberry ISD	Fort Worth	n/a	n/a	Winfree Academy	Irving

Note: This section only includes districts with 1,500 or more students; All categories are ranked from high to low

The Nation's Report Card Mathematics 2009
Snapshot State Report

Texas
Grade 4
Public Schools

Overall Results

- In 2009, the average score of fourth-grade students in Texas was 240. This was not significantly different from the average score of 239 for public school students in the nation.
- The average score for students in Texas in 2009 (240) was not significantly different from their average score in 2007 (242) and was higher than their average score in 1992 (218).
- In 2009, the score gap between students in Texas at the 75th percentile and students at the 25th percentile was 34 points. This performance gap was narrower than that of 1992 (40 points).
- The percentage of students in Texas who performed at or above the NAEP *Proficient* level was 38 percent in 2009. This percentage was not significantly different from that in 2007 (40 percent) and was greater than that in 1992 (15 percent).
- The percentage of students in Texas who performed at or above the NAEP *Basic* level was 85 percent in 2009. This percentage was not significantly different from that in 2007 (87 percent) and was greater than that in 1992 (56 percent).

Achievement-Level Percentages and Average Score Results

Texas		Average Score
1992[a]	44* / 41* / 14* / 1*	218*
1996[a]	31* / 44 / 22* / 3*	229*
2000[a]	23* / 50 / 25* / 2*	233*
2000	24* / 50 / 24* / 2*	231*
2003	18* / 49 / 29* / 4	237*
2005	13 / 47 / 35 / 5	242
2007	13 / 47 / 35 / 5	242
2009	15 / 47 / 34 / 4	240
Nation (public)		
2009	19 / 43 / 33 / 6	239

Percent below *Basic* and at *Basic*   Percent at *Proficient* and *Advanced*

■ Below *Basic*   ☐ *Basic*   ☐ *Proficient*   ■ *Advanced*

* Significantly different (*p* < .05) from state's results in 2009.
[a] Accommodations not permitted.
NOTE: Detail may not sum to totals because of rounding.

Compare the Average Score in 2009 to Other States/Jurisdictions

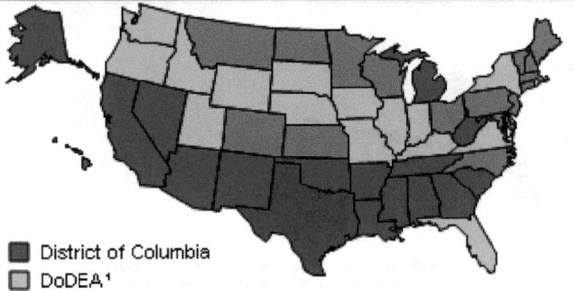

■ District of Columbia
☐ DoDEA.[1]

[1] Department of Defense Education Activity schools (domestic and overseas).

In 2009, the average score in Texas was
- lower than those in 16 states/jurisdictions
- higher than those in 17 states/jurisdictions
- not significantly different from those in 18 states/jurisdictions

Compare the Average Score to Nation (public)

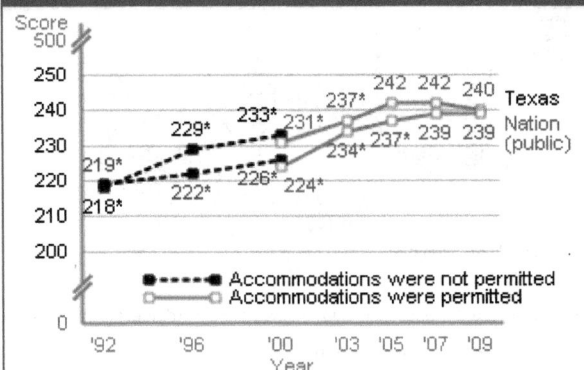

Texas: 218* / 219* / 229* / 233* / 231* / 237* / 242 / 242 / 240
Nation (public): 222* / 226* / 224* / 234* / 237* / 239 / 239

●----● Accommodations were not permitted
☐----☐ Accommodations were permitted

* Significantly different (*p* < .05) from 2009.

Results for Student Groups in 2009

Reporting Groups	Percent of students	Avg. score	Percentages at or above Basic	Proficient	Percent at Advanced
Gender [1]					
Male 51		241	85	39	5
Female	49	240	86	37	3
Race/Ethnicity					
White 31		254	95	61	9
Black 13		231	79	23	1
Hispanic 51		233	80	26	1'
Asian/Pacific Islander	4	259	96	71	17
American Indian/Alaska Native	#	‡	‡	‡	‡
National School Lunch Program					
Eligible 5	9	233	79	26	1'
Not eligible	40	252	94	57	9

Rounds to zero.   ‡ Reporting standards not met.

NOTE: Detail may not sum to totals because of rounding, and because the "Information not available" category for the National School Lunch Program, which provides free/reduced-price lunches, and the "Unclassified" category for race/ethnicity are not displayed.

Score Gaps for Student Groups

- In 2009, male students in Texas had an average score that was not significantly different from that of female students. This performance gap was not significantly different from that in 1992 (2 points). '
- In 2009, Black students had an average score that was 23 points lower than that of White students. This performance gap was narrower than that in 1992 (31 points).
- In 2009, Hispanic students had an average score that was 20 points lower than that of White students. This ' performance gap was not significantly different from that in 1992 (22 points). '
- In 2009, students who were eligible for free/reduced-price school lunch, an indicator of poverty, had an average score that was 20 points lower than that of students who were not eligible for free/reduced-price school lunch. This performance gap was narrower than that in 1996 (25 points).

NOTE: Statistical comparisons are calculated on the basis of unrounded scale scores or percentages.

Mathematics 2009
Snapshot State Report

Texas
Grade 8
Public Schools

Overall Results

- In 2009, the average score of eighth-grade students in Texas was 287. This was higher than the average score of 282 for public school students in the nation.
- The average score for students in Texas in 2009 (287) was not significantly different from their average score in 2007 (286) and was higher than their average score in 1990 (258).
- In 2009, the score gap between students in Texas at the 75th percentile and students at the 25th percentile was 44 points. This performance gap was not significantly different from that of 1990 (49 points).
- The percentage of students in Texas who performed at or above the NAEP *Proficient* level was 36 percent in 2009. This percentage was not significantly different from that in 2007 (35 percent) and was greater than that in 1990 (13 percent). '
- The percentage of students in Texas who performed at or above the NAEP *Basic* level was 78 percent in 2009. This percentage was not significantly different from that in 2007 (78 percent) and ' was greater than that in 1990 (45 percent). '

Achievement-Level Percentages and Average Score Results

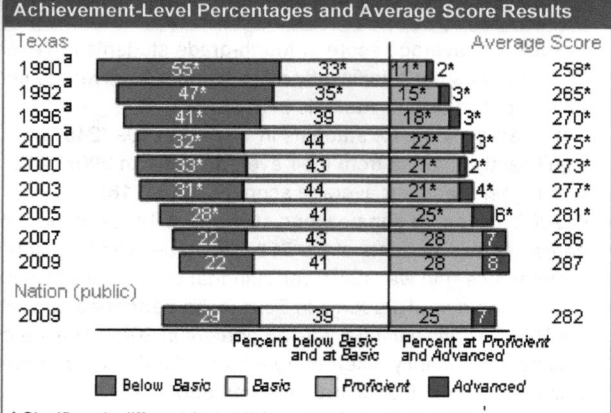

* Significantly different (*p* < .05) from state's results in 2009. '
a Accommodations not permitted. '
NOTE: Detail may not sum to totals because of rounding. '

Compare the Average Score in 2009 to Other States/Jurisdictions

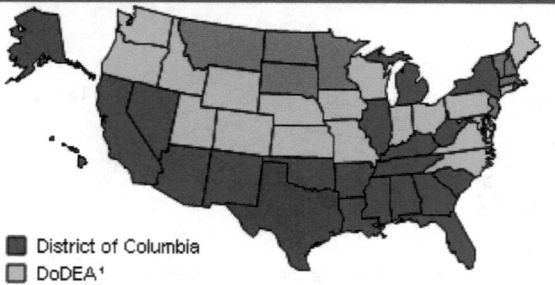

■ District of Columbia
▢ DoDEA '

' Department of Defense Education Activity schools (domestic and overseas).

In 2009, the average score in Texas was
- lower than those in 8 states/jurisdictions
- higher than those in 22 states/jurisdictions
- not significantly different from those in 21 states/jurisdictions

Compare the Average Score to Nation (public)

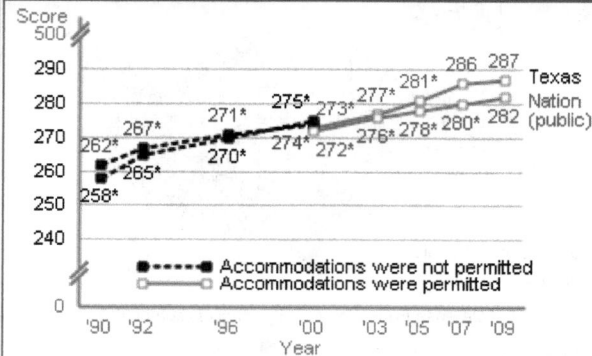

* Significantly different (*p* < .05) from 2009.

Results for Student Groups in 2009

Reporting Groups	Percent of students	Avg. score	Percentages at or above Basic	Percentages at or above Proficient	Percent at Advanced
Gender '					
Male 50		287	78	38	8
Female	50	286	77	35	9
Race/Ethnicity					
White 37		301	89	54	16
Black 14		272	66	17	2
Hispanic 46		277	70	25	2'
Asian/Pacific Islander	4	313	92	67	31
American Indian/Alaska Native	#	‡	‡	‡	‡
National School Lunch Program					
Eligible 5	3	276	69	23	2'
Not eligible	47	299	87	51	15

Rounds to zero.   ‡ Reporting standards not met.

NOTE: Detail may not sum to totals because of rounding, and because the "Information not available" category for the National School Lunch Program, which provides free/reduced-price lunches, and the "Unclassified" category for race/ethnicity are not displayed.

Score Gaps for Student Groups

- In 2009, male students in Texas had an average score that was not significantly different from that of female students. This performance gap was not significantly different from that in 1990 (4 points). '
- In 2009, Black students had an average score that was 28 points lower than that of White students. This performance gap was narrower than that in 1990 (38 points).
- In 2009, Hispanic students had an average score that was 24 points lower than that of White students. This ' performance gap was not significantly different from that in 1990 (28 points). '
- In 2009, students who were eligible for free/reduced-price school lunch, an indicator of poverty, had an average score that was 24 points lower than that of students who were not eligible for free/reduced-price school lunch. This performance gap was narrower than that in 1996 (30 points).

NOTE: Statistical comparisons are calculated on the basis of unrounded scale scores or percentages.
SOURCE: U.S. Department of Education, Institute of Education Sciences, National Center for Education Statistics, National Assessment of Educational Progress (NAEP), various years, 1990–2009 Mathematics Assessments.

The Nation's Report Card   Reading 2009   State Snapshot Report

Texas
Grade 4
Public Schools

Overall Results

- In 2009, the average score of fourth-grade students in Texas was 219. This was not significantly different from the average score of 220 for public school students in the nation.
- The average score for students in Texas in 2009 (219) was not significantly different from their average score in 2007 (220) and was higher than their average score in 1992 (213).
- In 2009, the score gap between students in Texas at the 75th percentile and students at the 25th percentile was 42 points. This performance gap was not significantly different from that of 1992 (46 points).
- The percentage of students in Texas who performed at or above the NAEP *Proficient* level was 28 percent in 2009. This percentage was not significantly different from that in 2007 (30 percent) and was not significantly different from that in 1992 (24 percent).
- The percentage of students in Texas who performed at or above the NAEP *Basic* level was 65 percent in 2009. This percentage was not significantly different from that in 2007 (66 percent) and was greater than that in 1992 (57 percent).

Achievement Level Percentages and Average Score Results

Texas	Below Basic	Basic	Proficient	Advanced	Average Score
1992[a]	43*	33	19	4	213*
1994[a]	42*	32*	20	6	212*
1998[a]	37	34	23	5	217
1998	41*	31*	23	6	214*
2002	38	34	22	6	217
2003	41*	33*	21	6	215*
2005	36	35	23	6	219
2007	34	36	23	6	220
2009	35	37	22	6	219
Nation (public)					
2009	34	34	24	7	220

Percent below *Basic* and at *Basic*   Percent at *Proficient* and *Advanced*

Legend: ■ Below *Basic*   □ *Basic*   ▨ *Proficient*   ■ *Advanced*

* Significantly different (*p* < .05) from state's results in 2009.
a Accommodations not permitted.

NOTE: Detail may not sum to totals because of rounding.

Compare the Average Score in 2009 to Other States/Jurisdictions

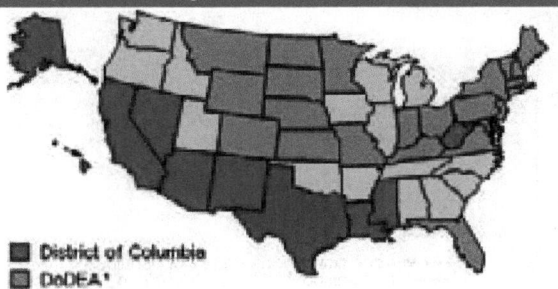

■ District of Columbia
□ DoDEA[1]

[1] Department of Defense Education Activity schools (domestic and overseas).

In 2009, the average score in Texas was
- lower than those in 26 states/jurisdictions
- higher than those in 10 states/jurisdictions
- not significantly different from those in 15 states/jurisdictions

Average Scores for State/Jurisdiction and Nation (public)

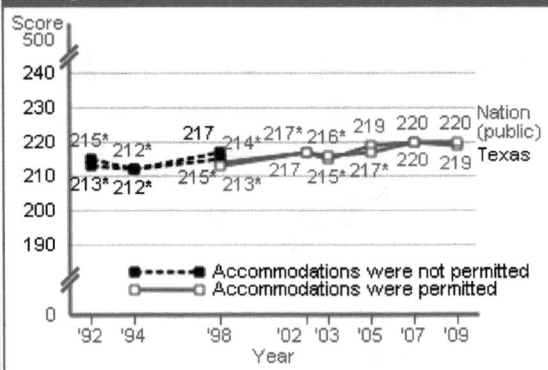

- - - ■ Accommodations were not permitted
———□ Accommodations were permitted

* Significantly different (*p* < .05) from 2009.

Results for Student Groups in 2009

Reporting Groups	Percent of students	Avg. score	Percentages at or above		Percent at Advanced
			Basic	Proficient	
Gender					
Male	51	216	61	25	5
Female	49	222	69	30	7
Race/Ethnicity					
White	32	232	80	43	11
Black	14	213	58	20	2
Hispanic	49	210	54	18	2
Asian/Pacific Islander	4	242	88	52	22
American Indian/Alaska Native	#	‡	‡	‡	‡
National School Lunch Program					
Eligible	58	209	54	17	2
Not eligible	41	232	80	43	11

Rounds to zero.   ‡ Reporting standards not met.

NOTE: Detail may not sum to totals because of rounding, and because the "Information not available" category for the National School Lunch Program, which provides free/reduced-price lunches, and the "Unclassified" category for race/ethnicity are not displayed.

Score Gaps for Student Groups

- In 2009, female students in Texas had an average score that was higher than that of male students.
- In 2009, Black students had an average score that was 19 points lower than that of White students. This performance gap was not significantly different from that in 1992 (24 points).
- In 2009, Hispanic students had an average score that was 22 points lower than that of White students. This performance gap was not significantly different from that in 1992 (23 points).
- In 2009, students who were eligible for free/reduced-price school lunch, an indicator of low income, had an average score that was 23 points lower than that of students who were not eligible for free/reduced-price school lunch. This performance gap was narrower than that in 1998 (31 points).

NOTE: Statistical comparisons are calculated on the basis of unrounded scale scores or percentages.

Reading 2009
State Snapshot Report

Texas
Grade 8
Public Schools

Overall Results

- In 2009, the average score of eighth-grade students in Texas was 260. This was not significantly different from the average score of 262 for public school students in the nation.
- The average score for students in Texas in 2009 (260) was not significantly different from their average score in 2007 (261) and was not significantly different from their average score in 1998 (261).
- In 2009, the score gap between students in Texas at the 75th percentile and students at the 25th percentile was 42 points. This performance gap was not significantly different from that of 1998 (41 points).
- The percentage of students in Texas who performed at or above the NAEP *Proficient* level was 27 percent in 2009. This percentage was not significantly different from that in 2007 (28 percent) and was not significantly different from that in 1998 (27 percent).
- The percentage of students in Texas who performed at or above the NAEP *Basic* level was 73 percent in 2009. This percentage was not significantly different from that in 2007 (73 percent) and was not significantly different from that in 1998 (74 percent).

Achievement-Level Percentages and Average Score Results

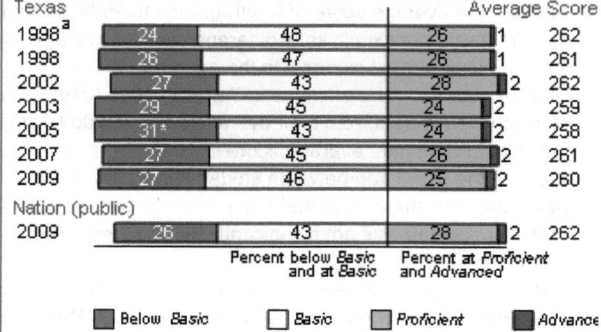

* Significantly different ($p < .05$) from state's results in 2009.
a Accommodations not permitted.

NOTE: Detail may not sum to totals because of rounding.

Compare the Average Score in 2009 to Other States/Jurisdictions

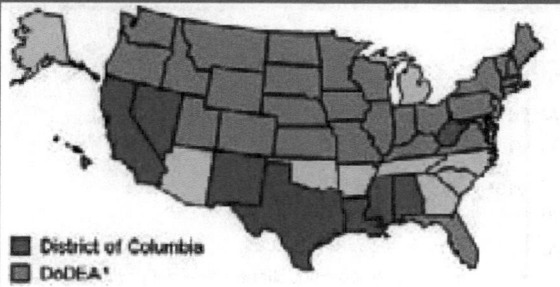

■ District of Columbia
□ DoDEA[1]

[1] Department of Defense Education Activity schools (domestic and overseas).

In 2009, the average score in Texas was
- lower than those in 32 states/jurisdictions
- higher than those in 9 states/jurisdictions
- not significantly different from those in 10 states/jurisdictions

Average Scores for State/Jurisdiction and Nation (public)

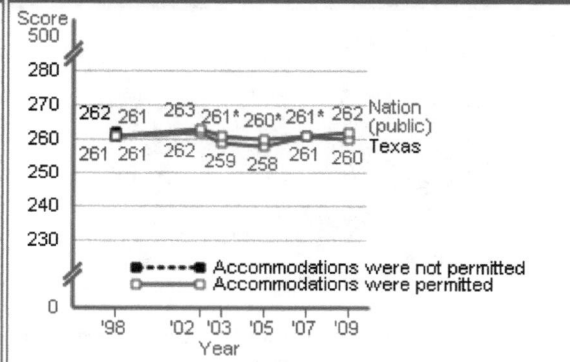

* Significantly different ($p < .05$) from 2009.

Results for Student Groups in 2009

Reporting Groups	Percent of students	Avg. score	Percentages at or above		Percent at Advanced
			Basic	Proficient	
Gender					
Male	50	256	69	23	1
Female	50	264	77	31	2
Race/Ethnicity					
White	37	273	86	42	3
Black	13	249	61	13	#
Hispanic	46	251	64	17	1
Asian/Pacific Islander	4	280	87	53	7
American Indian/Alaska Native	#	‡	‡	‡	‡
National School Lunch Program					
Eligible	53	249	62	15	#
Not eligible	47	273	85	40	3

Rounds to zero.   ‡ Reporting standards not met.

NOTE: Detail may not sum to totals because of rounding, and because the "Information not available" category for the National School Lunch Program, which provides free/reduced-price lunches, and the "Unclassified" category for race/ethnicity are not displayed.

Score Gaps for Student Groups

- In 2009, female students in Texas had an average score that was higher than that of male students.
- In 2009, Black students had an average score that was 25 points lower than that of White students. This performance gap was not significantly different from that in 1998 (25 points).
- In 2009, Hispanic students had an average score that was 22 points lower than that of White students. This performance gap was not significantly different from that in 1998 (22 points).
- In 2009, students who were eligible for free/reduced-price school lunch, an indicator of low income, had an average score that was 23 points lower than that of students who were not eligible for free/reduced-price school lunch. This performance gap was not significantly different from that in 1998 (24 points).

NOTE: Statistical comparisons are calculated on the basis of unrounded scale scores or percentages.

NCES
National Center for Education Statistics

The Nation's Report Card
State **Writing** 2002

Texas
Grade 4
Public School

Snapshot Report

NCES 2003-532TX4

The writing assessment of the National Assessment of Educational Progress (NAEP) measures narrative, informative, and persuasive writing–three purposes identified in the NAEP framework. The NAEP writing scale ranges from 0 to 300.

Overall Writing Results for Texas

- The average scale score for fourth-grade students in Texas was 154.

- Texas' average score (154) was not found to be significantly different[1] from that of the nation's public schools (153).

- Students' average scale scores in Texas were higher than those in 20 jurisdictions[2], not significantly different from those in 21 jurisdictions, and lower than those in 6 jurisdictions.

- The percentage of students who performed at or above the NAEP *Proficient* level was 29 percent. The percentage of students who performed at or above the *Basic* level was 84 percent.

Student Percentage at Each Achievement Level

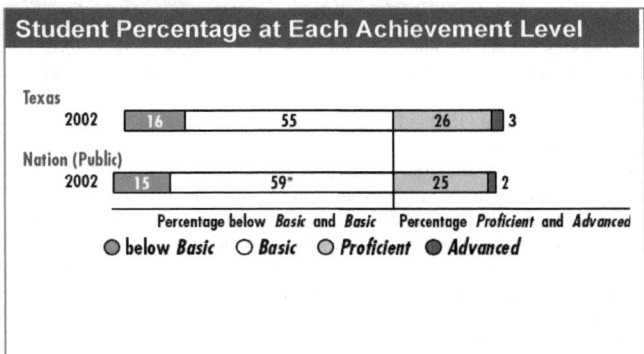

Percentage below *Basic* and *Basic*   Percentage *Proficient* and *Advanced*
● below *Basic*   ○ *Basic*   ○ *Proficient*   ● *Advanced*

Performance of NAEP Reporting Groups in Texas

Reporting groups	Percentage of students	Average Score	Below *Basic*	*Basic*	*Proficient*	*Advanced*
Male	51	145	21	59	19	1
Female	49	163	11	52 ↓	32	5
White	36	168 ↑	8	49 ↓	36 ↑	6 ↑
Black	18	142	22	61	16	1
Hispanic	41	145	22	58	19	1
Asian/Pacific Islander	3	176 ↑	2	49	42	7
American Indian/Alaska Native	1	---	---	---	---	---
Free/reduced-priced school lunch						
Eligible	58	147 ↑	20	58 ↓	20 ↑	2
Not eligible	37	164	11	51	33	5
Information not available	5	160	14	51	29	5

Average Score Gaps Between Selected Groups

- Female students in Texas had an average score that was higher than that of male students (17 points). This performance gap was not significantly different from that of the Nation (18 points).

- White students had an average score that was higher than that of Black students (26 points). This performance gap was not significantly different from that of the Nation (20 points).

- White students had an average score that was higher than that of Hispanic students (23 points). This performance gap was not significantly different from that of the Nation (19 points).

- Students who were not eligible for free/reduced-price school lunch had an average score that was higher than that of students who were eligible (17 points). This performance gap was not significantly different from that of the Nation (22 points).

Writing Scale Scores at Selected Percentiles

Scale Score Distribution

	25th Percentile	50th Percentile	75th Percentile
Texas	127	154	181
Nation (Public)	128	153	178

An examination of scores at different percentiles on the 0-300 NAEP writing scale at each grade indicates how well students at lower, middle, and higher levels of the distribution performed. For example, the data above shows that 75 percent of students in public schools nationally scored below *178,* while 75 percent of students in Texas scored below *181.*

\# Percentage rounds to zero.   --- Reporting standards not met; sample size insufficient to permit a reliable estimate.
* Significantly different from Texas.   ↑ Significantly higher than, ↓ lower than appropriate subgroup in the nation (public).
[1] Comparisons (higher/lower/not different) are based on statistical tests. The .05 level was used for testing statistical significance.
[2] "Jurisdictions" includes participating states and other jurisdictions (such as Guam or the District of Columbia).
NOTE: Detail may not sum to totals because of rounding. Score gaps are calculated based on differences between unrounded average scale scores.
Visit http://nces.ed.gov/nationsreportcard/states/ for additional results and detailed information.
SOURCE: U.S. Department of Education, Institute of Education Sciences, National Center for Education Statistics, National Assessment of Educational Progress (NAEP), 2002 Writing Assessment.

:ies NATIONAL CENTER FOR EDUCATION STATISTICS
Institute of Education Sciences
NCES 2008-470TX8

The Nation's Report Card **Writing 2007**
State Snapshot Report

Texas
Grade 8
Public Schools

The National Assessment of Educational Progress (NAEP) assesses writing for three purposes identified in the NAEP framework: narrative, informative, and persuasive. The NAEP writing scale ranges from 0 to 300.

Overall Writing Results for Texas

- In 2007, the average scale score for eighth-grade students in Texas was 151. This was not significantly different from their average score in 2002 (152) and was not significantly different from their average score in 1998 (154).[1]
- Texas' average score (151) in 2007 was lower than that of the nation's public schools (154).
- Of the 45 states and one other jurisdiction that participated in the 2007 eighth-grade assessment, students' average scale score in Texas was higher than those in 7 jurisdictions, not significantly different from those in 15 jurisdictions, and lower than those in 23 jurisdictions.[2]
- The percentage of students in Texas who performed at or above the NAEP *Proficient* level was 26 percent in 2007. This percentage was not significantly different from that in 2002 (31 percent) and was not significantly different from that in 1998 (31 percent).
- The percentage of students in Texas who performed at or above the NAEP *Basic* level was 86 percent in 2007. This percentage was not significantly different from that in 2002 (83 percent) and was not significantly different from that in 1998 (88 percent).

Percentages at NAEP Achievement Levels and Average Score

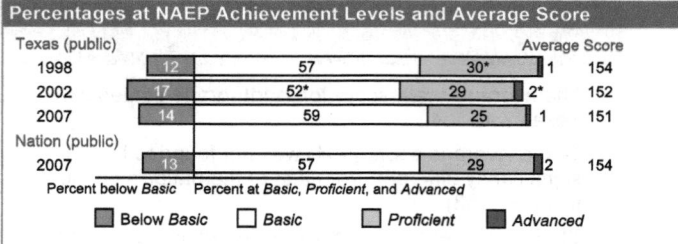

NOTE: The NAEP grade 8 writing achievement levels correspond to the following scale points: Below *Basic*, 113 or lower; *Basic*, 114–172; *Proficient*, 173–223; *Advanced*, 224 or above.

Performance of NAEP Reporting Groups in Texas: 2007

Reporting groups	Percent of students	Average score	Percent below *Basic*	Percent of students at or above *Basic*	Proficient	Percent *Advanced*
Male	51	142	20	80	18	#
Female	49	160	9	91	36	2
White	37↓	165	7	93	41	2
Black	16	142	20	80	17	#
Hispanic	44	142	19↓	81↑	16	#
Asian/Pacific Islander	3	167	6	94	41	3
American Indian/Alaska Native	#	‡	‡	‡	‡	‡
Eligible for National School Lunch Program	50↑	140	21	79	15	#
Not eligible for National School Lunch Program	50	162	8	92	38	2↓

Average Score Gaps Between Selected Groups

- In 2007, male students in Texas had an average score that was lower than that of female students by 18 points. This performance gap was not significantly different from that of 1998 (21 points).
- In 2007, Black students had an average score that was lower than that of White students by 23 points. This performance gap was not significantly different from that of 1998 (17 points).
- In 2007, Hispanic students had an average score that was lower than that of White students by 23 points. This performance gap was not significantly different from that of 1998 (20 points).
- In 2007, students who were eligible for free/reduced-price school lunch, an indicator of poverty, had an average score that was lower than that of students who were not eligible for free/reduced-price school lunch by 22 points. This performance gap was the same as that of 1998 (22 points).
- In 2007, the score gap between students at the 75th percentile and students at the 25th percentile was 46 points. This performance gap was not significantly different from that of 1998 (47 points).

Writing Scores at Selected Percentiles in Texas

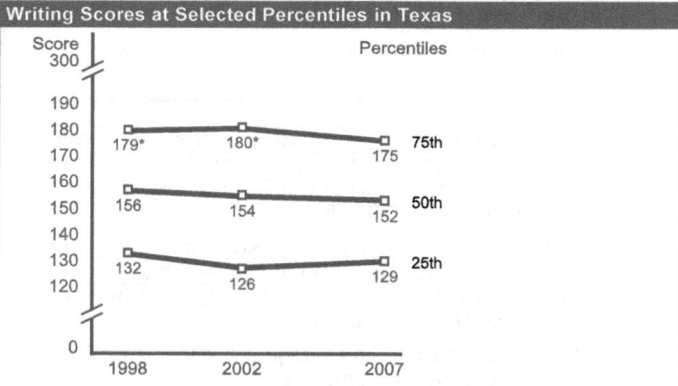

NOTE: Scores at selected percentiles on the NAEP writing scale indicate how well students at lower, middle, and higher levels performed.

Rounds to zero.
* Significantly different from 2007.
‡ Reporting standards not met.
↑ Significantly higher than 2002. ↓ Significantly lower than 2002.
[1] Comparisons (higher/lower/narrower/wider/not different) are based on statistical tests. The .05 level with appropriate adjustments for multiple comparisons was used for testing statistical significance. Statistical comparisons are calculated on the basis of unrounded scale scores or percentages. Comparisons across jurisdictions and comparisons with the nation or within a jurisdiction across years may be affected by differences in exclusion rates for students with disabilities (SD) and English language learners (ELL). The exclusion rates for SD and ELL in Texas were 6 percent and 2 percent in 2007, respectively. For more information on NAEP significance testing, see http://nces.ed.gov/nationsreportcard/writing/interpret-results.asp#statistical.
[2] "Jurisdiction" refers to states, the District of Columbia, and the Department of Defense Education Activity schools.
NOTE: Detail may not sum to totals because of rounding and because the "Information not available" category for the National School Lunch Program, which provides free and reduced-price lunches, and the "Unclassified" category for race/ethnicity are not displayed. Visit http://nces.ed.gov/nationsreportcard/states/ for additional results and detailed information.
SOURCE: U.S. Department of Education, Institute of Education Sciences, National Center for Education Statistics, National Assessment of Educational Progress (NAEP), 1998, 2002, and 2007 Writing Assessments.

NATIONAL CENTER for EDUCATION STATISTICS
Institute of Education Sciences

The Nation's Report Card
Science 2009
State Snapshot Report

Texas
Grade 4
Public Schools

2009 Science Assessment Content

Guided by a new framework, the NAEP science assessment was updated in 2009 to keep the content current with key developments in science, curriculum standards, assessments, and research. The 2009 framework organizes science content into three broad content areas.

Physical science includes concepts related to properties and changes of matter, forms of energy, energy transfer and conservation, position and motion of objects, and forces affecting motion.

Life science includes concepts related to organization and development, matter and energy transformations, interdependence, heredity and reproduction, and evolution and diversity.

Earth and space sciences includes concepts related to objects in the universe, the history of the Earth, properties of Earth materials, tectonics, energy in Earth systems, climate and weather, and biogeochemical cycles.

The 2009 science assessment was composed of 143 questions at grade 4, 162 at grade 8, and 179 at grade 12. Students responded to only a portion of the questions, which included both multiple-choice questions and questions that required a written response.

Compare the Average Score in 2009 to Other States/Jurisdictions

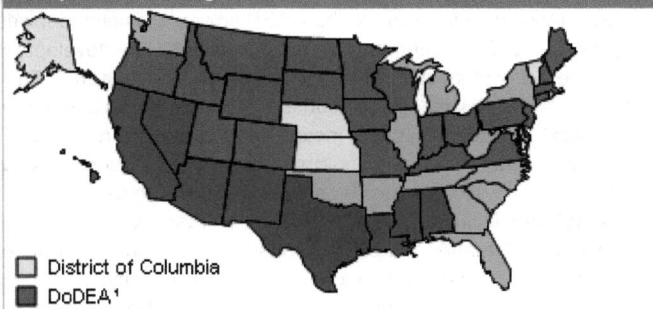

☐ District of Columbia
■ DoDEA[1]

[1] Department of Defense Education Activity (overseas and domestic schools).

In 2009, the average score in **Texas** was
- lower than those in 24 states/jurisdictions
- higher than those in 8 states/jurisdictions
- not significantly different from those in 14 states/jurisdictions
- 5 states/jurisdictions did not participate

Overall Results

- In 2009, the average score of fourth-grade students in Texas was 148. This was not significantly different from the average score of 149 for public school students in the nation.
- The percentage of students in Texas who performed at or above the NAEP *Proficient* level was 29 percent in 2009. This percentage was smaller than the nation (32 percent).
- The percentage of students in Texas who performed at or above the NAEP *Basic* level was 70 percent in 2009. This percentage was not significantly different from the nation (71 percent).

Achievement-Level Percentages and Average Score Results

				Average Score
Texas 2009	30	41	29	1 148
Nation (public) 2009	29	39	32*	1 149

Percent below *Basic* and at *Basic* | Percent at *Proficient* and *Advanced*

■ Below *Basic*   ☐ *Basic*   ▨ *Proficient*   ■ *Advanced*

* Significantly different ($p < .05$) from Texas. Significance tests were performed using unrounded numbers.

NOTE: Detail may not sum to totals because of rounding.

Results for Student Groups in 2009

Reporting Groups	Percent of students	Avg. score	Percentages at or above Basic	Proficient	Percent at Advanced
Gender					
Male	51	148	70	30	1
Female	49	147	69	28	1
Race/Ethnicity					
White	31	168	90	53	2
Black	13	139	62	18	#
Hispanic	51	136	58	16	#
Asian/Pacific Islander	4	163	84	47	2
American Indian/Alaska Native	#	‡	‡	‡	‡
National School Lunch Program					
Eligible	59	135	58	15	#
Not eligible	40	166	88	51	2

\# Rounds to zero.   ‡ Reporting standards not met.

NOTE: Detail may not sum to totals because of rounding, and because the "Information not available" category for the National School Lunch Program, which provides free/reduced-price lunches, and the "Unclassified" category for race/ethnicity are not displayed.

Score Gaps for Student Groups

- In 2009, male students in Texas had an average score that was not significantly different from female students.
- In 2009, Black students had an average score that was 29 points lower than White students. This performance gap was narrower than the nation (35 points).
- In 2009, Hispanic students had an average score that was 31 points lower than White students. This performance gap was not significantly different from the nation (32 points).
- In 2009, students who were eligible for free/reduced-price school lunch, an indicator of low family income, had an average score that was 31 points lower than students who were not eligible for free/reduced-price school lunch. This performance gap was not significantly different from the nation (29 points).

NOTE: Statistical comparisons are calculated on the basis of unrounded scale scores or percentages.
SOURCE: U.S. Department of Education, Institute of Education Sciences, National Center for Education Statistics, National Assessment of Educational Progress (NAEP), 2009 Science Assessment.

NATIONAL CENTER for EDUCATION STATISTICS
Institute of Education Sciences

The Nation's Report Card
Science 2009
State Snapshot Report

Texas
Grade 8
Public Schools

2009 Science Assessment Content

Guided by a new framework, the NAEP science assessment was updated in 2009 to keep the content current with key developments in science, curriculum standards, assessments, and research. The 2009 framework organizes science content into three broad content areas.
Physical science includes concepts related to properties and changes of matter, forms of energy, energy transfer and conservation, position and motion of objects, and forces affecting motion.
Life science includes concepts related to organization and development, matter and energy transformations, interdependence, heredity and reproduction, and evolution and diversity.
Earth and space sciences includes concepts related to objects in the universe, the history of the Earth, properties of Earth materials, tectonics, energy in Earth systems, climate and weather, and biogeochemical cycles.
The 2009 science assessment was composed of 143 questions at grade 4, 162 at grade 8, and 179 at grade 12. Students responded to only a portion of the questions, which included both multiple-choice questions and questions that required a written response.

Compare the Average Score in 2009 to Other States/Jurisdictions

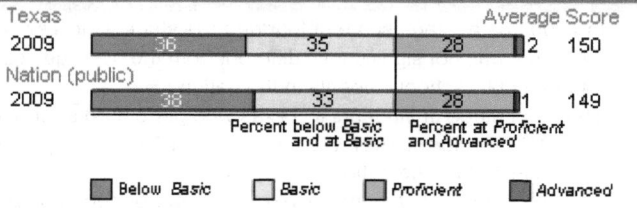

☐ District of Columbia
■ DoDEA[1]

[1] Department of Defense Education Activity (overseas and domestic schools).

In 2009, the average score in **Texas** was
- lower than those in 23 states/jurisdictions
- higher than those in 16 states/jurisdictions
- not significantly different from those in 7 states/jurisdictions
- 5 states/jurisdictions did not participate

Overall Results

- In 2009, the average score of eighth-grade students in Texas was 150. This was not significantly different from the average score of 149 for public school students in the nation.
- The percentage of students in Texas who performed at or above the NAEP *Proficient* level was 29 percent in 2009. This percentage was not significantly different from the nation (29 percent).
- The percentage of students in Texas who performed at or above the NAEP *Basic* level was 64 percent in 2009. This percentage was not significantly different from the nation (62 percent).

Achievement-Level Percentages and Average Score Results

			Average Score
Texas			
2009	36	35	28	2	150
Nation (public)			
2009	38	33	28	1	149

Percent below *Basic* and at *Basic* | Percent at *Proficient* and *Advanced*

■ Below *Basic*   ☐ *Basic*   ▦ *Proficient*   ■ *Advanced*

NOTE: Detail may not sum to totals because of rounding.

Results for Student Groups in 2009

Reporting Groups	Percent of students	Avg. score	Percentages at or above Basic	Proficient	Percent at Advanced
Gender					
Male	50	152	67	32	2
Female	50	148	61	26	1
Race/Ethnicity					
White	37	167	83	47	3
Black	14	133	43	13	#
Hispanic	45	141	53	17	#
Asian/Pacific Islander	4	170	82	55	5
American Indian/Alaska Native	#	‡	‡	‡	‡
National School Lunch Program					
Eligible	52	140	52	17	#
Not eligible	47	162	77	43	3

\# Rounds to zero.   ‡ Reporting standards not met.

NOTE: Detail may not sum to totals because of rounding, and because the "Information not available" category for the National School Lunch Program, which provides free/reduced-price lunches, and the "Unclassified" category for race/ethnicity are not displayed.

Score Gaps for Student Groups

- In 2009, male students in Texas had an average score that was higher than female students.
- In 2009, Black students had an average score that was 33 points lower than White students. This performance gap was not significantly different from the nation (36 points).
- In 2009, Hispanic students had an average score that was 26 points lower than White students. This performance gap was not significantly different from the nation (30 points).
- In 2009, students who were eligible for free/reduced-price school lunch, an indicator of low family income, had an average score that was 22 points lower than students who were not eligible for free/reduced-price school lunch. This performance gap was narrower than the nation (28 points).

NOTE: Statistical comparisons are calculated on the basis of unrounded scale scores or percentages.
SOURCE: U.S. Department of Education, Institute of Education Sciences, National Center for Education Statistics, National Assessment of Educational Progress (NAEP), 2009 Science Assessment.

Texas Assessment of Knowledge and Skills

Summary Report - Group Performance

All Students

Grade 3 English

STATEWIDE
Report Date: MAY 2011
Date of Testing: SPRING 2011
Page 2 of 2

"- - -" = No Data Reported For Fewer Than Five Students

	Reading			Mathematics				All Tests Taken		
	Number of Students Tested	Average Scale Score	Percent Met Standard	Percent Commended	Number of Students Tested	Average Scale Score	Percent Met Standard	Percent Commended	Number of Students Tested	Percent Met Standard	Percent Commended
All Students	321705	E- 608	89	41	336976	E- 593	87	33	338323	83	25
Male	162802	E- 601	88	39	170959	E- 594	87	34	171656	82	24
Female	158824	E- 616	91	44	165930	E- 591	87	33	166578	83	25
No Information Provided	79	E- 556	67	29	87	E- 529	56	21	89	52	15
Hispanic/Latino	149072	E- 592	87	34	163580	E- 581	85	28	164268	80	19
Am. Indian or Alaskan Native	1392	E- 608	90	41	1425	E- 588	86	30	1430	82	22
Asian	12305	E- 660	96	63	12369	E- 658	97	63	12384	95	50
Black or African American	43686	E- 576	82	30	43865	E- 559	77	21	44079	71	14
Native Hawaiian/Pacific Islander	362	E- 610	91	41	369	E- 593	88	34	370	84	23
White	108704	E- 638	94	53	109168	E- 616	92	43	109567	90	34
Two or More Races	5935	E- 629	93	49	5942	E- 607	90	39	5965	87	31
No Information Provided	249	E- 570	78	32	258	E- 552	71	23	260	64	18
Economically Disadvantaged Yes	190970	E- 583	85	31	205389	E- 573	83	25	206313	77	17
No	130555	E- 646	95	56	131399	E- 624	94	47	131820	92	37
No Information Provided	180	E- 564	73	30	188	E- 535	66	15	190	59	12
Title I, Part A Participants	240006	E- 595	87	36	254751	E- 582	85	29	255761	80	20
Nonparticipants	81378	E- 647	96	57	81895	E- 626	94	48	82229	92	38
No Information Provided	321	E- 586	79	36	330	E- 562	72	25	333	66	18
Migrant Yes	2257	E- 561	79	24	2443	E- 564	80	22	2450	72	13
No	319157	E- 609	89	42	334234	E- 593	87	33	335571	83	25
No Information Provided	291	E- 569	76	30	299	E- 548	70	19	302	62	14
LEP Current LEP	58267	E- 579	85	29	72313	E- 578	85	26	72657	79	17
Non-LEP (Monitored 1st Year)	4114	E- 667	99	66	4130	E- 649	98	59	4135	97	46
Non-LEP (Monitored 2nd Year)	2279	E- 670	98	67	2283	E- 656	98	62	2284	97	49
Other Non-LEP	256795	E- 614	90	44	257994	E- 595	87	35	258987	83	26
No Information Provided	250	E- 569	77	29	256	E- 547	68	20	260	61	15
Bilingual Participants	32366	E- 582	85	30	46141	E- 580	86	27	46416	81	19
Nonparticipants	289065	E- 611	90	43	290551	E- 595	87	34	291620	83	26
No Information Provided	274	E- 564	76	29	284	E- 545	69	19	287	61	14
ESL Participants	20638	E- 577	85	28	20846	E- 576	84	26	20941	77	16
Nonparticipants	300795	E- 611	90	42	315849	E- 594	87	34	317097	83	25
No Information Provided	272	E- 566	77	29	281	E- 546	69	19	285	62	14
Special Education Yes	16572	E- 550	74	22	18183	E- 543	71	17	19045	63	11
No	304979	E- 612	90	43	318633	E- 595	88	34	319117	84	25
No Information Provided	154	E- 561	73	28	160	E- 539	66	18	161	59	13
Gifted/Talented Participants	25984	E- 709	100	84	27026	E- 687	100	78	27066	99	71
Nonparticipants	295468	E- 600	88	38	309689	E- 584	86	29	310994	81	21
No Information Provided	253	E- 565	77	27	261	E- 541	66	17	263	60	12
At-Risk Yes	140341	E- 566	82	25	155249	E- 563	80	21	156189	73	13
No	181104	E- 641	95	54	181459	E- 618	93	44	181864	90	35
No Information Provided	260	E- 572	77	31	268	E- 545	69	18	270	62	14

Texas Assessment of Knowledge and Skills
Summary Report - Group Performance

STATEWIDE

Report Date: MAY 2011
Date of Testing: SPRING 2011

Grade 4 English

All Students

"---" = No Data Reported For Fewer Than Five Students

Group	Reading Number of Students Tested	Reading Average Scale Score	Reading Percent Met Standard	Reading Percent Commended	Mathematics Number of Students Tested	Mathematics Average Scale Score	Mathematics Percent Met Standard	Mathematics Percent Commended	Writing Number of Students Tested	Writing Average Scale Score	Writing Percent Met Standard	Writing Percent Commended	All Tests Taken Number of Students Tested	All Tests Taken Percent Met Standard	All Tests Taken Percent Commended
All Students	331009	E- 652	85	36	343178	E- 658	88	37	324816	2340	90	28	348886	77	15
Male	166843	E- 647	84	34	173488	E- 657	88	37	163151	2317	88	23	176357	75	13
Female	163963	E- 658	87	38	169483	E- 658	89	37	161594	2363	93	33	172286	80	17
No Information Provided	203	E- 606	70	22	207	E- 582	62	10	71	2267	80	18	243	58	8
Hispanic/Latino	158294	E- 632	81	27	170171	E- 648	87	32	155213	2315	90	22	172840	74	11
Am. Indian or Alaskan Native	1316	E- 649	86	34	1341	E- 651	89	32	1287	2318	89	24	1385	77	12
Asian	12466	E- 707	95	58	12524	E- 731	97	70	12371	2463	97	54	12640	93	39
Black or African American	43272	E- 623	79	24	43315	E- 621	79	23	42798	2295	86	19	44350	66	7
Native Hawaiian/Pacific Islander	414	E- 647	85	34	411	E- 660	90	37	397	2349	93	30	421	81	15
White	109155	E- 686	93	50	109304	E- 679	93	46	106841	2378	93	37	110976	85	22
Two or More Races	5889	E- 674	90	45	5905	E- 670	91	43	5752	2367	92	34	6008	82	20
No Information Provided	203	E- 630	78	28	207	E- 624	74	29	157	2291	82	22	266	67	14
Economically Disadvantaged Yes	196224	E- 625	80	25	207852	E- 638	85	29	192485	2300	88	19	211785	70	9
Economically Disadvantaged No	134596	E- 692	94	52	135133	E- 688	94	50	132187	2399	95	41	136839	88	25
No Information Provided	189	E- 616	77	24	193	E- 602	70	17	144	2271	74	19	262	63	11
Title I, Part A Participants	247300	E- 638	83	30	259177	E- 647	86	32	242680	2317	89	23	263620	73	11
Nonparticipants	83518	E- 695	94	54	83806	E- 692	94	52	81983	2407	95	43	85004	89	27
No Information Provided	191	E- 620	76	26	195	E- 605	70	19	153	2277	76	21	262	63	12
Migrant Yes	2300	E- 596	71	16	2468	E- 627	81	25	2312	2279	84	16	2567	63	7
No	328512	E- 653	86	36	340509	E- 658	88	37	322355	2340	91	28	346049	77	15
No Information Provided	197	E- 610	75	22	201	E- 601	71	16	149	2266	75	17	270	63	11
LEP Current LEP	52968	E- 600	72	17	64454	E- 638	85	28	51317	2275	86	14	65545	67	9
Non-LEP (Monitored 1st Year)	15025	E- 670	93	40	15063	E- 692	96	51	14941	2387	97	35	15152	90	17
Non-LEP (Monitored 2nd Year)	4232	E- 710	98	59	4243	E- 724	99	67	4208	2453	99	52	4263	96	33
Other Non-LEP	258606	E- 661	88	39	259235	E- 659	88	38	254208	2348	91	30	263675	79	17
No Information Provided	178	E- 609	73	23	183	E- 599	69	17	142	2263	73	18	251	61	12
Bilingual Participants	31195	E- 602	73	17	42409	E- 644	87	30	29728	2284	87	15	43086	70	11
Nonparticipants	299638	E- 657	87	38	300587	E- 660	88	38	294948	2346	91	29	305549	78	16
No Information Provided	176	E- 609	73	25	182	E- 598	68	16	140	2263	74	18	251	61	12
ESL Participants	18080	E- 599	72	16	18361	E- 630	82	25	17916	2266	84	12	18729	62	4
Nonparticipants	312754	E- 655	86	37	324636	E- 659	89	38	306758	2344	91	29	329906	78	16
No Information Provided	175	E- 612	75	23	181	E- 599	69	17	142	2267	74	18	251	62	12
Special Education Participants	17744	E- 590	65	17	18732	E- 599	70	17	16151	2216	68	10	21310	50	5
Nonparticipants	313098	E- 656	87	37	324279	E- 661	89	38	308527	2346	92	29	327343	79	16
No Information Provided	167	E- 622	77	25	167	E- 607	72	19	138	2268	72	19	233	63	13
Gifted/Talented Participants	31661	E- 749	99	79	32766	E- 754	100	81	31343	2515	99	65	32915	98	53
Nonparticipants	299168	E- 642	84	31	310228	E- 647	87	32	293333	2321	90	24	315718	75	11
No Information Provided	180	E- 609	73	23	184	E- 596	67	16	140	2264	72	19	253	60	12
At-Risk Yes	115946	E- 596	71	15	127737	E- 617	78	21	113118	2255	82	12	130942	60	6
No	214877	E- 682	93	47	215250	E- 682	94	47	211552	2386	95	37	217680	88	21
No Information Provided	186	E- 614	76	23	191	E- 601	70	16	146	2275	77	18	264	64	12

|

Texas Assessment of Knowledge and Skills

Summary Report - Group Performance

All Students

Grade 5 English

STATEWIDE
Report Date: JULY 2011
Date of Testing: JUNE 2011

(Page 2 of 2)

"-.-" = No Data Reported For Fewer Than Five Students

Group		Reading				Mathematics				Science			
		Number of Students Tested	Average Scale Score	Percent Met Standard	Percent Commended	Number of Students Tested	Average Scale Score	Percent Met Standard	Percent Commended	Number of Students Tested	Average Scale Score	Percent Met Standard	Percent Commended
All Students		21893	E- 570	23	0	22621	E- 572	32	0				
Male		12237	E- 566	21	0	10999	E- 570	30	0				
Female		9643	E- 576	25	0	11608	E- 574	33	0				
No Information Provided		13	E- 572	23	0	14	E- 569	21	0				
Hispanic/Latino		14709	E- 569	22	0	13483	E- 571	31	0				
Am. Indian or Alaskan Native		70	E- 581	34	1	72	E- 578	35	0				
Asian		180	E- 586	33	1	121	E- 592	44	0				
Black or African American		4059	E- 568	23	0	5406	E- 570	30	0				
Native Hawaiian/Pacific Islander		18	E- 564	28	0	27	E- 581	44	0				
White		2623	E- 580	29	1	3222	E- 580	36	0				
Two or More Races		210	E- 581	31	1	253	E- 579	37	0				
No Information Provided		24	E- 601	29	13	37	E- 569	22	0				
Economically Disadvantaged	Yes	18970	E- 569	22	0	19002	E- 571	30	0				
	No	2874	E- 582	29	1	3556	E- 581	38	0				
	No Information Provided	49	E- 588	31	6	63	E- 574	35	0				
Title I, Part A	Participants	20155	E- 569	22	0	20395	E- 571	31	0				
	Nonparticipants	1695	E- 586	34	1	2173	E- 583	40	0				
	No Information Provided	43	E- 585	26	7	53	E- 571	30	0				
Migrant	Yes	359	E- 561	19	0	287	E- 568	26	1				
	No	21485	E- 570	23	0	22274	E- 572	32	0				
	No Information Provided	49	E- 584	29	6	60	E- 570	30	0				
LEP	Current LEP	8368	E- 563	18	0	6108	E- 567	28	0				
	Non-LEP (Monitored 1st Year)	523	E- 604	43	1	601	E- 591	46	0				
	Non-LEP (Monitored 2nd Year)	239	E- 593	36	0	286	E- 586	42	1				
	Other Non-LEP	12716	E- 573	25	0	15569	E- 573	32	0				
	No Information Provided	47	E- 583	28	6	57	E- 572	32	0				
Bilingual	Participants	5702	E- 562	18	0	4059	E- 566	27	0				
	Nonparticipants	16141	E- 573	25	0	18502	E- 574	33	0				
	No Information Provided	50	E- 584	28	6	60	E- 571	32	0				
ESL	Participants	2167	E- 566	20	0	1689	E- 570	30	0				
	Nonparticipants	19674	E- 571	23	0	20874	E- 572	32	0				
	No Information Provided	52	E- 586	29	6	58	E- 570	29	0				
Special Education	Yes	2684	E- 556	17	0	2680	E- 563	26	1				
	No	19163	E- 572	24	0	19884	E- 573	32	0				
	No Information Provided	46	E- 586	33	7	57	E- 570	30	0				
Gifted/Talented	Participants	78	E- 601	42	0	50	E- 593	48	2				
	Nonparticipants	21767	E- 570	23	0	22515	E- 572	32	0				
	No Information Provided	48	E- 582	29	6	56	E- 569	29	0				
At-Risk	Yes	18517	E- 567	21	0	18601	E- 570	30	0				
	No	3327	E- 589	35	1	3959	E- 583	41	0				
	No Information Provided	49	E- 585	29	6	61	E- 572	31	0				

Science Test was Administered on April 28, 2011

Texas Assessment of Knowledge and Skills

Summary Report - Group Performance

All Students

Grade 6

"- - -" = No Data Reported For Fewer Than Five Students	Reading				Mathematics				All Tests Taken		
	Number of Students Tested	Average Scale Score	Percent Met Standard	Percent Commended	Number of Students Tested	Average Scale Score	Percent Met Standard	Percent Commended	Number of Students Tested	Percent Met Standard	Percent Commended
All Students	339483	E- 733	84	35	339328	E- 723	83	31	342036	75	21
Male	170700	E- 723	81	32	171033	E- 722	82	31	172470	73	20
Female	168667	E- 743	87	39	168180	E- 725	83	32	169448	78	23
No Information Provided	116	E- 689	69	28	115	E- 669	63	15	118	55	9
Hispanic/Latino	167405	E- 712	80	27	167696	E- 709	79	25	168823	70	15
Am. Indian or Alaskan Native	1554	E- 734	86	36	1551	E- 721	84	28	1564	76	19
Asian	11393	E- 796	95	62	11444	E- 810	96	68	11468	93	52
Black or African American	42542	E- 714	80	27	42317	E- 689	72	19	42876	65	12
Native Hawaiian/Pacific Islander	371	E- 734	86	34	372	E- 732	86	34	373	78	21
White	110376	E- 764	91	48	110111	E- 749	90	41	111030	85	31
Two or More Races	5622	E- 758	89	46	5599	E- 741	87	38	5660	82	29
No Information Provided	240	E- 708	80	29	238	E- 687	72	18	242	65	11
Economically Disadvantaged *Yes*	200170	E- 707	78	24	200251	E- 700	77	22	202048	67	13
No	139136	E- 771	93	51	138902	E- 756	91	44	139808	87	34
No Information Provided	177	E- 704	76	28	175	E- 677	67	13	180	60	8
Title I, Part A *Participants*	226355	E- 718	81	29	226420	E- 711	80	26	228153	71	16
Nonparticipants	112839	E- 762	90	47	112621	E- 748	89	41	113590	84	31
No Information Provided	289	E- 698	73	28	287	E- 677	66	17	293	58	11
Migrant *Yes*	2647	E- 681	69	17	2654	E- 688	73	18	2668	58	9
No	336542	E- 733	84	35	336383	E- 724	83	31	339071	75	21
No Information Provided	294	E- 695	74	26	291	E- 672	64	16	297	56	10
LEP *Current LEP*	36095	E- 653	57	8	36508	E- 673	68	13	36796	48	4
Non-LEP (Monitored 1st Year)	9590	E- 715	85	24	9600	E- 718	84	27	9651	76	13
Non-LEP (Monitored 2nd Year)	19505	E- 732	91	30	19498	E- 733	89	33	19555	83	17
Other Non-LEP	274037	E- 744	87	40	273467	E- 729	84	34	275773	78	24
No Information Provided	256	E- 698	75	27	255	E- 677	65	16	261	58	10
Bilingual *Participants*	5864	E- 679	68	15	5928	E- 701	79	21	5950	61	8
Nonparticipants	333329	E- 734	84	36	333112	E- 724	83	31	335792	76	22
No Information Provided	290	E- 690	70	25	288	E- 674	64	16	294	55	11
ESL *Participants*	28291	E- 648	55	8	28618	E- 669	66	12	28857	46	4
Nonparticipants	310919	E- 741	87	38	310439	E- 728	84	33	312902	78	23
No Information Provided	273	E- 695	73	25	271	E- 677	65	17	277	57	11
Special Education *Participants*	17217	E- 646	52	10	16805	E- 645	52	9	19219	39	4
Nonparticipants	322083	E- 738	86	37	322341	E- 727	84	32	322633	77	22
No Information Provided	183	E- 698	72	28	182	E- 681	69	16	184	61	11
Gifted/Talented *Participants*	36394	E- 831	99	78	36398	E- 824	99	75	36420	99	65
Nonparticipants	302823	E- 721	82	30	302668	E- 711	81	26	305347	73	16
No Information Provided	266	E- 692	72	25	262	E- 671	65	14	269	57	9
At-Risk *Yes*	116047	E- 669	65	11	116014	E- 665	64	11	117920	50	4
No	223192	E- 767	94	48	223072	E- 753	92	42	223869	89	30
No Information Provided	244	E- 697	74	27	242	E- 679	68	16	247	60	11

Texas Assessment of Knowledge and Skills

Summary Report - Group Performance

Grade 7

All Students

STATEWIDE

Report Date: MAY 2011
Date of Testing: SPRING 2011

Page 2 of 2

"- - -" = No Data Reported For Fewer Than Five Students

Group	Reading Number of Students Tested	Reading Average Scale Score	Reading Percent Met Standard	Reading Percent Commended	Mathematics Number of Students Tested	Mathematics Average Scale Score	Mathematics Percent Met Standard	Mathematics Percent Commended	Writing Number of Students Tested	Writing Average Scale Score	Writing Percent Met Standard	Writing Percent Commended	All Tests Taken Number of Students Tested	All Tests Taken Percent Met Standard	All Tests Taken Percent Commended
All Students	334640	E- 765	86	30	334319	E- 743	81	23	330783	2380	94	36	340862	74	13
Male	169102	E- 760	84	28	169360	E- 743	81	23	166773	2348	91	29	172808	73	11
Female	165440	E- 770	87	31	164857	E- 744	81	23	163959	2413	97	43	167919	76	15
No Information Provided	98	E- 712	69	14	102	E- 682	54	8	51	2321	88	27	135	54	7
Hispanic/Latino	163384	E- 743	82	21	163566	E- 729	77	17	161892	2342	93	28	166614	69	8
Am. Indian or Alaskan Native	1530	E- 762	86	27	1539	E- 735	81	20	1516	2362	94	33	1575	73	11
Asian	11261	E- 830	96	55	11298	E- 829	96	60	11203	2541	98	66	11402	93	40
Black or African American	42930	E- 736	80	19	42697	E- 708	68	12	42412	2331	92	26	43917	62	6
Native Hawaiian/Pacific Islander	404	E- 765	86	31	404	E- 749	83	25	396	2399	95	40	409	78	14
White	109590	E- 801	93	44	109300	E- 769	89	32	107941	2437	96	47	111269	85	20
Two or More Races	5359	E- 793	91	41	5332	E- 762	86	30	5265	2428	96	46	5439	82	19
No Information Provided	182	E- 727	74	20	183	E- 692	61	9	158	2319	87	24	237	60	8
Economically Disadvantaged Yes	191399	E- 736	80	19	191329	E- 721	74	15	189522	2328	92	25	195842	66	6
Disadvantaged No	143087	E- 804	94	45	142836	E- 774	89	34	141123	2450	97	50	144793	86	22
No Information Provided	154	E- 721	71	19	154	E- 690	58	12	138	2294	87	17	227	60	10
Title I, Part A Participants	208061	E- 749	82	23	208137	E- 730	77	18	205961	2350	93	29	212202	69	9
Nonparticipants	126421	E- 792	91	41	126022	E- 765	87	31	124682	2430	96	46	128432	82	20
No Information Provided	158	E- 720	70	20	160	E- 689	55	13	140	2310	88	20	228	60	11
Migrant Yes	2673	E- 705	68	10	2689	E- 705	67	10	2677	2285	87	15	2795	55	3
No	331800	E- 765	86	30	331462	E- 744	81	23	327960	2381	94	36	337828	74	13
No Information Provided	167	E- 715	68	19	168	E- 684	54	12	146	2298	87	16	239	59	9
LEP Current LEP	28815	E- 676	55	4	29202	E- 690	61	7	28591	2218	79	6	30024	41	1
Non-LEP (Monitored 1st Year)	7283	E- 732	84	12	7318	E- 733	82	16	7220	2326	96	19	7401	73	4
Non-LEP (Monitored 2nd Year)	9698	E- 745	87	18	9720	E- 740	83	19	9662	2350	97	26	9833	76	6
Other Non-LEP	288698	E- 775	89	33	287932	E- 749	83	25	285173	2399	95	39	293386	78	15
No Information Provided	146	E- 714	67	18	147	E- 684	52	12	137	2287	85	15	218	58	9
Bilingual Participants	978	E- 748	80	24	986	E- 751	83	25	969	2352	91	31	994	72	11
Nonparticipants	333512	E- 765	86	30	333180	E- 743	81	23	329674	2380	94	36	339641	74	13
No Information Provided	150	E- 711	65	19	153	E- 680	51	12	140	2283	84	15	227	57	9
ESL Participants	26451	E- 675	55	4	26788	E- 690	60	7	26246	2216	79	6	27518	40	1
Nonparticipants	308044	E- 773	88	32	307385	E- 748	82	25	304397	2394	95	38	313124	77	14
No Information Provided	145	E- 716	66	19	146	E- 686	53	12	140	2288	85	15	220	58	9
Special Education Yes	17659	E- 680	54	7	17025	E- 671	48	5	16503	2191	69	7	20367	35	1
No	316847	E- 770	87	31	317161	E- 747	82	24	314156	2390	95	37	320299	77	14
No Information Provided	134	E- 722	72	20	133	E- 690	56	14	124	2306	89	18	196	62	11
Gifted/Talented Participants	37568	E- 866	99	73	37584	E- 840	99	66	37324	2581	100	74	37713	98	49
Nonparticipants	296926	E- 752	84	24	296588	E- 731	78	18	293330	2354	93	31	302935	71	8
No Information Provided	146	E- 718	68	19	147	E- 690	56	13	129	2225	88	16	214	60	10
At-Risk Yes	124913	E- 701	69	8	124693	E- 688	60	5	123307	2259	87	11	128975	48	1
No	209565	E- 803	96	43	209464	E- 776	93	34	207335	2452	98	50	211656	90	20
No Information Provided	162	E- 723	72	20	162	E- 690	57	12	141	2302	89	17	231	61	10
Career/Technical Participants	51993	E- 761	86	28	51918	E- 742	81	22	51588	2367	94	33	52860	74	11
Education Nonparticipants	282425	E- 766	86	30	282181	E- 744	81	23	279027	2382	94	36	287701	74	13
No Information Provided	222	E- 717	69	18	220	E- 688	57	10	168	2294	86	17	301	59	8

Texas Assessment of Knowledge and Skills

Summary Report - Group Performance

All Students

Grade 8

Report Date: JULY 2011
Date of Testing: JUNE 2011
STATEWIDE
Page 2 of 2

"---" = No Data Reported For Fewer Than Five Students

Group	Reading — Number of Students Tested	Reading — Average Scale Score	Reading — Percent Met Standard	Reading — Percent Commended	Mathematics — Number of Students Tested	Mathematics — Average Scale Score	Mathematics — Percent Met Standard	Mathematics — Percent Commended
All Students	15986	E- 658	29	0	34208	E- 664	22	0
Male	9522	E- 658	31	0	17943	E- 663	22	0
Female	6460	E- 657	27	0	16256	E- 665	22	0
No Information Provided	4	---	---	---	9	E- 640	11	0
Hispanic/Latino	10684	E- 653	27	0	20571	E- 662	21	0
Am. Indian or Alaskan Native	71	E- 668	34	0	201	E- 671	27	0
Asian	159	E- 664	31	1	195	E- 672	27	0
Black or African American	2928	E- 659	28	0	7323	E- 659	19	0
Native Hawaiian/Pacific Islander	26	E- 672	42	0	31	E- 667	26	0
White	1976	E- 678	43	1	5498	E- 676	32	0
Two or More Races	115	E- 676	38	3	329	E- 677	32	0
No Information Provided	27	E- 676	41	7	60	E- 655	13	0
Economically Disadvantaged Yes	13402	E- 655	27	0	26602	E- 662	21	0
No	2551	E- 674	38	1	7541	E- 672	29	0
No Information Provided	33	E- 686	48	9	65	E- 657	15	0
Title I, Part A Participants	12816	E- 654	27	0	26082	E- 662	21	0
Nonparticipants	3133	E- 673	38	1	8055	E- 672	28	0
No Information Provided	37	E- 682	46	8	71	E- 656	14	0
Migrant Yes	305	E- 643	22	0	460	E- 657	16	0
No	15641	E- 658	29	0	33672	E- 664	22	0
No Information Provided	40	E- 681	45	8	76	E- 654	13	0
LEP Current LEP	5270	E- 638	18	0	5701	E- 651	14	0
Non-LEP (Monitored 1st Year)	375	E- 670	34	1	846	E- 667	22	0
Non-LEP (Monitored 2nd Year)	352	E- 673	39	1	766	E- 672	27	0
Other Non-LEP	9954	E- 667	34	1	26826	E- 667	24	0
No Information Provided	35	E- 683	49	9	69	E- 655	16	0
Bilingual Participants	45	E- 645	20	0	64	E- 653	17	0
Nonparticipants	15905	E- 658	29	0	34075	E- 664	22	0
No Information Provided	36	E- 685	47	8	69	E- 655	16	0
ESL Participants	5006	E- 637	17	0	5355	E- 651	14	0
Nonparticipants	10943	E- 667	34	1	28783	E- 667	24	0
No Information Provided	37	E- 680	46	8	70	E- 654	16	0
Special Education Yes	3050	E- 647	24	0	4007	E- 655	17	0
No	12906	E- 660	30	0	30139	E- 665	23	0
No Information Provided	30	E- 687	50	10	62	E- 656	16	0
Gifted/Talented Participants	51	E- 686	39	4	179	E- 675	30	0
Nonparticipants	15900	E- 658	29	0	33962	E- 664	22	0
No Information Provided	35	E- 685	46	9	67	E- 655	15	0
At-Risk Yes	14445	E- 656	28	0	29229	E- 662	20	0
No	1504	E- 678	41	1	4911	E- 676	34	0
No Information Provided	37	E- 679	49	8	68	E- 654	16	0
Career/Technical Education Participants	4471	E- 658	28	0	9776	E- 665	23	0
Nonparticipants	11475	E- 657	29	0	24350	E- 664	22	0
No Information Provided	40	E- 673	43	8	82	E- 649	12	0

Social Studies (Number of Students Tested, Average Scale Score, Percent Met Standard, Percent Commended):

Social Studies Test was Administered on April 29, 2011

Science (Number of Students Tested, Average Scale Score, Percent Met Standard, Percent Commended):

Science Test was Administered on April 28, 2011

Texas Assessment of Knowledge and Skills

Summary Report - Group Performance

Grade 9   STATEWIDE   Report Date: MAY 2011   Date of Testing: SPRING 2011   (Page 2 of 2)

All Students

"– – –" = No Data Reported For Fewer Than Five Students

	Reading				Mathematics				All Tests Taken		
	Number of Students Tested	Average Scale Score	Percent Met Standard	Percent Commended	Number of Students Tested	Average Scale Score	Percent Met Standard	Percent Commended	Number of Students Tested	Percent Met Standard	Percent Commended
All Students	349976	2285	89	31	345503	2229	70	24	360192	68	16
Male	179830	2264	87	27	177204	2226	70	24	185670	67	15
Female	170051	2307	91	35	168214	2232	71	24	174365	70	17
No Information Provided	95	2188	68	16	85	2036	40	8	157	50	10
Hispanic/Latino	169852	2245	85	23	167467	2182	65	17	174997	62	10
Am. Indian or Alaskan Native	1673	2283	90	29	1648	2217	71	21	1737	69	13
Asian	11749	2397	95	54	11850	2488	92	62	11977	90	44
Black or African American	46101	2231	83	20	45090	2131	56	11	47824	54	7
Native Hawaiian/Pacific Islander	415	2308	90	34	417	2242	73	26	432	71	16
White	114478	2352	95	44	113390	2309	82	35	117272	81	25
Two or More Races	5454	2343	94	42	5403	2286	79	32	5598	77	23
No Information Provided	254	2196	77	15	238	2084	45	7	355	52	6
Economically Disadvantaged *Yes*	189442	2233	84	21	185885	2162	62	15	195725	59	8
No	160308	2347	94	43	159390	2307	81	35	164111	80	25
No Information Provided	226	2171	71	15	228	2054	41	6	356	49	7
Title I, Part A *Participants*	162433	2250	85	24	159972	2185	65	18	167440	62	11
Nonparticipants	187282	2315	92	37	185290	2268	75	30	192364	74	20
No Information Provided	261	2177	72	16	241	2061	41	8	388	49	7
Migrant *Yes*	3042	2178	73	14	2904	2126	55	11	3147	50	6
No	346689	2286	89	31	342362	2230	71	24	356659	68	16
No Information Provided	245	2172	73	13	237	2053	40	7	386	49	7
LEP *Current LEP*	20404	2086	52	4	19985	2064	41	6	21461	32	2
Non-LEP (Monitored 1st Year)	5375	2179	78	10	5321	2142	59	11	5532	53	4
Non-LEP (Monitored 2nd Year)	7143	2222	87	16	7044	2176	66	14	7256	63	6
Other Non-LEP	316803	2301	91	33	312923	2243	73	26	325566	71	17
No Information Provided	251	2172	72	13	230	2038	38	6	377	48	6
Bilingual *Participants*	173	2290	94	30	169	2286	80	33	174	79	18
Nonparticipants	349553	2285	89	31	345098	2229	71	24	359634	68	16
No Information Provided	250	2171	72	12	236	2044	39	6	384	48	7
ESL *Participants*	19065	2085	52	4	18699	2064	41	6	20040	32	2
Nonparticipants	330662	2297	91	32	326573	2239	72	25	339775	70	17
No Information Provided	249	2168	71	12	231	2038	38	6	377	47	6
Special Education *Yes*	22795	2101	56	6	20035	2009	27	3	24690	28	2
No	326966	2298	91	33	325267	2243	73	25	335174	71	17
No Information Provided	215	2191	76	14	201	2055	40	7	328	52	8
Gifted/Talented *Participants*	35499	2462	99	68	35467	2522	97	71	35763	97	54
Nonparticipants	314232	2265	87	27	309821	2196	67	19	324067	65	11
No Information Provided	245	2167	71	13	215	2053	40	7	362	49	7
At-Risk *Yes*	148613	2179	77	11	144137	2083	47	5	154873	44	3
No	201119	2364	97	45	201147	2334	88	38	204957	87	26
No Information Provided	244	2173	70	15	219	2058	42	6	362	50	7
Career/Technical *Participants*	193047	2279	89	29	190158	2220	70	22	197475	68	14
Education *Nonparticipants*	156660	2293	88	33	155088	2241	71	26	162305	69	18
No Information Provided	269	2160	70	11	257	2041	39	6	412	46	6

Texas Assessment of Knowledge and Skills

Summary Report - Group Performance

STATEWIDE

Grade 10

All Students

Report Date: MAY 2011
Date of Testing: SPRING 2011

Page 2 of 2

"–––" = No Data Reported For Fewer Than Five Students	English Language Arts				Mathematics				Social Studies				Science				All Tests Taken		
	Number of Students Tested	Average Scale Score	Percent Met Standard	Percent Commended	Number of Students Tested	Average Scale Score	Percent Met Standard	Percent Commended	Number of Students Tested	Average Scale Score	Percent Met Standard	Percent Commended	Number of Students Tested	Average Scale Score	Percent Met Standard	Percent Commended	Number of Students Tested	Percent Met Standard	Percent Commended
All Students	311827	2270	91	15	305827	2204	74	18	305900	2357	93	44	306077	2212	76	18	318753	65	6
Male	156914	2249	87	12	153761	2207	74	19	154196	2370	93	47	154147	2225	77	21	161023	64	5
Female	154788	2292	94	19	151931	2202	75	17	151567	2344	94	40	151795	2200	74	16	157501	65	6
No Information Provided	125	2166	70	3	135	2045	33	4	137	2181	74	12	135	2069	41	2	229	41	1
Hispanic/Latino	143715	2246	88	11	140744	2173	70	12	140277	2321	92	35	140620	2162	69	11	146946	58	3
Am. Indian or Alaskan Native	1681	2269	90	13	1634	2198	73	16	1644	2366	94	46	1647	2216	78	17	1719	66	4
Asian	11188	2347	96	34	11202	2372	92	50	11107	2485	98	72	11165	2350	92	44	11350	87	22
Black or African American	40845	2233	87	8	39626	2130	61	7	39963	2292	88	29	39833	2141	62	8	42127	49	2
Native Hawaiian/Pacific Islander	405	2261	90	15	397	2202	73	16	394	2349	92	43	394	2199	73	15	418	65	4
White	108812	2308	94	22	107102	2255	83	26	107363	2414	97	56	107277	2280	88	28	110804	77	9
Two or More Races	4939	2304	94	22	4892	2240	81	23	4917	2405	96	55	4908	2266	86	26	5047	75	9
No Information Provided	242	2202	80	5	230	2083	46	5	235	2240	82	22	233	2111	56	6	342	48	2
Economically Disadvantaged　Yes	156886	2235	87	9	152651	2158	66	10	152761	2305	90	32	152814	2157	66	10	160927	54	2
No	154754	2306	94	22	152995	2251	82	25	152956	2410	96	56	153082	2268	85	27	157519	76	9
No Information Provided	187	2191	76	5	181	2061	38	4	183	2223	79	17	181	2082	50	6	307	44	3
Title I, Part A　Participants	135734	2249	88	11	132925	2176	70	13	132775	2324	92	36	132870	2176	70	12	138808	58	3
Nonparticipants	175878	2287	92	19	172707	2226	78	22	172925	2383	94	50	173011	2241	80	23	179620	70	8
No Information Provided	215	2189	73	7	195	2066	42	4	200	2225	78	19	196	2091	52	5	325	45	3
Migrant　Yes	2371	2203	82	5	2280	2137	63	8	2251	2257	85	22	2261	2110	54	5	2441	46	1
No	309251	2271	91	15	303377	2205	74	18	303476	2358	93	44	303642	2213	76	18	315994	65	6
No Information Provided	205	2188	74	8	170	2058	39	5	173	2219	77	16	174	2079	48	4	318	47	3
LEP　Current LEP	13341	2115	55	1	12916	2073	44	4	12626	2186	73	10	12922	2032	33	2	14004	23	0
Non-LEP (Monitored 1st Year)	3182	2184	81	2	3128	2145	64	8	3147	2269	88	22	3124	2117	57	5	3267	44	1
Non-LEP (Monitored 2nd Year)	4121	2188	81	3	4023	2136	62	7	4068	2261	87	22	4045	2106	53	4	4218	42	1
Other Non-LEP	290963	2280	92	16	285579	2212	76	19	285874	2367	94	46	285803	2223	78	19	296934	67	6
No Information Provided	220	2185	72	8	181	2053	38	4	185	2219	77	17	183	2078	48	5	330	45	3
Bilingual　Participants	140	2273	93	11	140	2235	81	24	140	2361	95	42	138	2197	78	14	142	73	4
Nonparticipants	311467	2270	91	15	305506	2204	74	18	305576	2358	93	44	305757	2213	76	18	318281	65	6
No Information Provided	220	2180	70	7	181	2045	36	4	184	2202	73	15	182	2067	46	4	330	45	3
ESL　Participants	12501	2113	54	1	12157	2073	44	4	11838	2186	73	10	12140	2031	33	2	13141	22	0
Nonparticipants	299105	2277	92	16	293488	2210	76	18	293878	2364	94	45	293755	2220	77	19	305281	67	6
No Information Provided	221	2181	71	6	182	2047	37	3	184	2213	76	15	182	2072	47	5	331	45	3
Special Education　Yes	19030	2121	54	1	15964	2033	29	2	19186	2169	67	10	17703	2039	33	3	21201	20	0
No	292602	2280	93	16	289703	2214	77	19	286558	2370	95	46	288219	2223	78	19	297265	68	6
No Information Provided	195	2199	78	7	160	2060	39	4	156	2227	80	15	155	2091	50	5	287	50	3
Gifted/Talented　Participants	32443	2392	99	45	32391	2411	98	59	32237	2543	100	85	32304	2408	98	57	32573	96	28
Nonparticipants	279162	2256	90	12	273254	2180	71	13	273479	2336	92	39	273589	2189	73	14	285850	61	3
No Information Provided	222	2184	73	6	182	2049	37	4	184	2208	74	14	184	2072	46	4	330	45	1
At-Risk　Yes	135154	2200	82	4	129958	2099	52	3	130542	2252	86	19	130456	2103	54	4	139678	38	1
No	176460	2324	97	24	175691	2283	90	28	175175	2436	98	62	175439	2294	92	29	178754	86	10
No Information Provided	213	2192	75	8	178	2057	40	4	183	2219	78	15	182	2079	48	4	321	46	3
Career/Technical Education　Participants	207600	2266	91	14	203457	2199	74	16	204038	2351	93	42	203862	2206	75	16	211261	64	5
Nonparticipants	104005	2279	90	18	102147	2216	74	21	101638	2372	93	47	101994	2226	76	22	107129	66	8
No Information Provided	222	2186	75	5	223	2063	40	4	224	2212	76	16	221	2078	48	5	363	45	2

Texas Assessment of Knowledge and Skills

Summary Report – Group Performance

All Students

Grade 11 Exit Level

STATEWIDE
Report Date: MAY 2011
Date of Testing: SPRING 2011
Page 2 of 2

"– – –" = No Data Reported For Fewer Than Five Students

Group	ELA No. Tested	ELA Avg Scale Score	ELA % Met Std	ELA % Comm	Math No. Tested	Math Avg Scale Score	Math % Met Std	Math % Comm	Soc. St. No. Tested	Soc. St. Avg Scale Score	Soc. St. % Met Std	Soc. St. % Comm	Sci. No. Tested	Sci. Avg Scale Score	Sci. % Met Std	Sci. % Comm	All Tests No. Tested	All Tests % Met Std	All Tests % Comm
All Students	278348	2303	95	22	275134	2290	90	25	277224	2415	99	58	276238	2287	91	25	285633	84	10
Male	138893	2285	93	18	137152	2296	90	27	138580	2434	99	63	137966	2302	92	29	142992	84	9
Female	139371	2320	96	26	137912	2285	90	23	138578	2396	99	52	138199	2272	90	22	142497	85	10
No Information Provided	84	2267	90	14	70	2198	70	16	66	2344	95	41	73	2209	74	18	144	76	11
Hispanic/Latino	124347	2272	93	15	122876	2259	88	18	123610	2378	98	47	123197	2249	87	17	127579	80	5
Am. Indian or Alaskan Native	1415	2305	95	22	1394	2286	90	24	1396	2423	99	60	1396	2293	92	26	1454	86	9
Asian	10586	2362	95	41	10574	2429	96	56	10569	2497	99	77	10574	2386	96	51	10716	92	29
Black or African American	35868	2269	93	13	35265	2223	83	12	35757	2372	98	46	35481	2230	86	12	37074	76	3
Native Hawaiian/Pacific Islander	396	2295	94	18	393	2282	91	23	397	2406	99	56	394	2277	90	23	410	85	8
White	101107	2344	98	32	100027	2337	95	34	100841	2465	99	71	100557	2341	97	37	103555	92	15
Two or More Races	4468	2336	98	30	4427	2326	94	32	4474	2457	99	70	4457	2332	95	35	4574	91	14
No Information Provided	161	2266	92	14	178	2197	72	12	180	2350	94	42	182	2204	77	13	271	71	7
Economically Disadvantaged — Yes	131224	2264	92	13	128983	2246	86	16	130274	2368	98	45	129545	2239	86	15	135158	77	4
Economically Disadvantaged — No	146978	2337	97	30	145988	2330	94	33	146788	2457	99	69	146528	2329	95	34	150214	91	15
No Information Provided	146	2264	90	14	163	2186	67	13	162	2328	92	40	165	2198	75	12	261	70	8
Title I, Part A — Participants	121613	2278	93	16	119906	2262	88	19	120676	2381	98	49	120247	2256	88	18	124683	80	6
Nonparticipants	156576	2322	96	26	155056	2313	92	30	156576	2441	99	65	155817	2311	93	31	160678	88	13
No Information Provided	159	2268	91	15	172	2188	69	13	174	2337	94	43	174	2208	78	11	272	71	7
Migrant — Yes	2101	2231	86	7	2064	2226	82	14	2063	2326	95	34	2071	2208	80	10	2178	70	2
Migrant — No	276094	2303	95	22	272907	2291	90	25	274998	2415	99	58	274000	2288	91	25	283185	84	10
No Information Provided	153	2254	90	14	163	2187	69	12	163	2343	93	43	167	2199	77	13	270	70	7
LEP — Current LEP	11220	2109	54	1	10900	2155	65	6	11007	2249	88	16	10932	2121	56	2	11640	37	0
Non-LEP (Monitored 1st Year)	3231	2200	88	3	3178	2232	85	13	3222	2322	97	30	3205	2190	77	7	3329	68	1
Non-LEP (Monitored 2nd Year)	2197	2217	89	5	2163	2241	85	14	2198	2336	97	36	2166	2209	82	10	2267	73	2
Other Non-LEP	261558	2313	97	23	258733	2297	91	26	260636	2424	99	60	259772	2296	93	26	268140	87	10
No Information Provided	142	2264	91	14	160	2183	69	12	161	2343	93	43	163	2197	77	12	257	71	7
Bilingual — Participants	78	2276	92	14	79	2288	87	24	76	2362	97	45	79	2247	86	18	79	82	9
Nonparticipants	278126	2303	95	22	274892	2290	90	25	276983	2415	99	58	275992	2287	91	25	285290	84	10
No Information Provided	144	2254	90	12	163	2177	66	12	165	2335	92	42	167	2190	75	11	264	69	6
ESL — Participants	10655	2107	54	1	10379	2155	65	6	10457	2247	88	15	10395	2120	56	2	11042	36	0
Nonparticipants	267545	2310	96	23	264591	2296	91	26	266602	2421	99	59	265675	2294	92	26	274325	86	10
No Information Provided	148	2247	89	10	164	2178	66	11	165	2337	92	42	168	2193	75	11	266	68	6
Special Education — Yes	15794	2154	69	2	13343	2119	55	3	16327	2268	90	20	14651	2134	60	4	17809	43	1
Special Education — No	262414	2312	96	23	261640	2299	92	26	260753	2424	99	60	261437	2296	93	26	267585	87	10
No Information Provided	140	2256	91	11	151	2197	72	13	144	2362	95	47	150	2212	81	13	239	74	8
Gifted/Talented — Participants	30271	2419	100	55	30277	2467	99	66	30198	2544	100	88	30262	2444	100	65	30497	99	38
Nonparticipants	247929	2288	94	18	244697	2269	89	20	246865	2399	98	54	245812	2268	90	20	254874	83	6
No Information Provided	148	2261	91	11	160	2192	71	13	161	2347	93	44	164	2202	77	12	262	73	6
At-Risk — Yes	123750	2234	89	7	120688	2194	81	6	122647	2334	97	34	121610	2198	82	7	128361	70	1
At-Risk — No	154461	2358	99	34	154295	2366	98	39	154427	2479	100	76	154474	2357	98	40	157026	96	16
No Information Provided	137	2259	90	13	151	2184	69	12	150	2344	94	45	154	2201	77	11	246	72	7
Career/Technical Education — Participants	205358	2297	95	20	202632	2283	91	23	204507	2407	99	56	203567	2279	91	23	209940	84	8
Nonparticipants	72828	2318	94	28	72314	2312	89	31	72528	2436	98	63	72479	2310	91	32	75406	84	15
No Information Provided	162	2257	89	10	188	2179	68	11	189	2335	93	42	192	2201	77	11	287	69	6

Ancestry

Acadian/Cajun

Top 10 Places Sorted by Number
Based on all places, regardless of population

Place	Number	%
Houston (city) Harris County	882	0.05
Austin (city) Travis County	601	0.09
Beaumont (city) Jefferson County	501	0.44
Port Arthur (city) Jefferson County	409	0.71
San Antonio (city) Bexar County	337	0.03
Nederland (city) Jefferson County	286	1.65
Port Neches (city) Jefferson County	244	1.80
Orange (city) Orange County	235	1.27
Dallas (city) Dallas County	221	0.02
Fort Worth (city) Tarrant County	191	0.04

Top 10 Places Sorted by Percent
Based on all places, regardless of population

Place	Number	%
Stowell (cdp) Chambers County	58	3.65
Hardin (city) Liberty County	29	3.62
Zuehl (cdp) Guadalupe County	7	2.75
Pinehurst (city) Orange County	62	2.61
Talty (city) Kaufman County	20	2.45
China (city) Jefferson County	27	2.37
Central Gardens (cdp) Jefferson County	97	2.31
West Orange (city) Orange County	93	2.22
Latexo (city) Houston County	6	2.02
Port Neches (city) Jefferson County	244	1.80

Top 10 Places Sorted by Percent
Based on places with populations of 10,000 or more

Place	Number	%
Port Neches (city) Jefferson County	244	1.80
Nederland (city) Jefferson County	286	1.65
Vidor (city) Orange County	152	1.34
Orange (city) Orange County	235	1.27
Groves (city) Jefferson County	187	1.18
Port Arthur (city) Jefferson County	409	0.71
Beaumont (city) Jefferson County	501	0.44
Rockwall (city) Rockwall County	77	0.42
Clute (city) Brazoria County	42	0.41
Jollyville (cdp) Williamson County	58	0.38

Afghan

Top 10 Places Sorted by Number
Based on all places, regardless of population

Place	Number	%
Richardson (city) Dallas County	146	0.16
Plano (city) Collin County	132	0.06
Irving (city) Dallas County	98	0.05
Dallas (city) Dallas County	83	0.01
Fort Worth (city) Tarrant County	52	0.01
San Antonio (city) Bexar County	49	0.00
Houston (city) Harris County	44	0.00
Arlington (city) Tarrant County	38	0.01
Keller (city) Tarrant County	35	0.13
New Territory (cdp) Fort Bend County	31	0.22

Top 10 Places Sorted by Percent
Based on all places, regardless of population

Place	Number	%
New Territory (cdp) Fort Bend County	31	0.22
Richardson (city) Dallas County	146	0.16
Keller (city) Tarrant County	35	0.13
Frisco (city) Collin County	30	0.09
Highland Park (town) Dallas County	6	0.07
Plano (city) Collin County	132	0.06
Flower Mound (town) Denton County	31	0.06
Allen (city) Collin County	25	0.06
Harker Heights (city) Bell County	10	0.06

Addison (town) Dallas County	8	0.06

Top 10 Places Sorted by Percent
Based on places with populations of 10,000 or more

Place	Number	%
New Territory (cdp) Fort Bend County	31	0.22
Richardson (city) Dallas County	146	0.16
Keller (city) Tarrant County	35	0.13
Frisco (city) Collin County	30	0.09
Plano (city) Collin County	132	0.06
Flower Mound (town) Denton County	31	0.06
Allen (city) Collin County	25	0.06
Harker Heights (city) Bell County	10	0.06
Addison (town) Dallas County	8	0.06
Irving (city) Dallas County	98	0.05

African American/Black

Top 10 Places Sorted by Number
Based on all places, regardless of population

Place	Number	%
Houston (city) Harris County	505,101	25.85
Dallas (city) Dallas County	314,678	26.48
Fort Worth (city) Tarrant County	111,298	20.82
San Antonio (city) Bexar County	84,250	7.36
Austin (city) Travis County	69,943	10.65
Beaumont (city) Jefferson County	52,829	46.40
Arlington (city) Tarrant County	48,196	14.47
Killeen (city) Bell County	31,408	36.14
Garland (city) Dallas County	26,810	12.43
Waco (city) McLennan County	26,461	23.27

Top 10 Places Sorted by Percent
Based on all places, regardless of population

Place	Number	%
Moore Station (city) Henderson County	182	98.91
Neylandville (town) Hunt County	54	96.43
Goodlow (city) Navarro County	251	95.08
Prairie View (city) Waller County	4,160	94.33
Ames (city) Liberty County	974	90.27
Barrett (cdp) Harris County	2,503	87.15
Cuney (town) Cherokee County	126	86.90
Kendleton (city) Fort Bend County	370	79.40
Toco (city) Lamar County	68	76.40
Easton (city) Gregg County	355	67.75

Top 10 Places Sorted by Percent
Based on places with populations of 10,000 or more

Place	Number	%
Forest Hill (city) Tarrant County	7,463	57.63
Lancaster (city) Dallas County	13,920	53.76
Beaumont (city) Jefferson County	52,829	46.40
De Soto (city) Dallas County	17,350	46.09
Port Arthur (city) Jefferson County	25,564	44.26
Missouri City (city) Fort Bend County	20,683	39.09
Marshall (city) Harrison County	9,309	38.89
Texarkana (city) Bowie County	13,063	37.56
Killeen (city) Bell County	31,408	36.14
Orange (city) Orange County	6,700	35.94

African American/Black: Not Hispanic

Top 10 Places Sorted by Number
Based on all places, regardless of population

Place	Number	%
Houston (city) Harris County	495,338	25.35
Dallas (city) Dallas County	310,185	26.10
Fort Worth (city) Tarrant County	109,379	20.46
San Antonio (city) Bexar County	78,542	6.86
Austin (city) Travis County	67,117	10.22
Beaumont (city) Jefferson County	52,461	46.07
Arlington (city) Tarrant County	47,116	14.15

Killeen (city) Bell County	30,013	34.53
Garland (city) Dallas County	26,293	12.19
Waco (city) McLennan County	26,028	22.89

Top 10 Places Sorted by Percent
Based on all places, regardless of population

Place	Number	%
Moore Station (city) Henderson County	182	98.91
Neylandville (town) Hunt County	54	96.43
Goodlow (city) Navarro County	250	94.70
Prairie View (city) Waller County	4,139	93.85
Ames (city) Liberty County	972	90.08
Cuney (town) Cherokee County	126	86.90
Barrett (cdp) Harris County	2,493	86.80
Kendleton (city) Fort Bend County	368	78.97
Toco (city) Lamar County	68	76.40
Easton (city) Gregg County	353	67.37

Top 10 Places Sorted by Percent
Based on places with populations of 10,000 or more

Place	Number	%
Forest Hill (city) Tarrant County	7,414	57.26
Lancaster (city) Dallas County	13,814	53.35
Beaumont (city) Jefferson County	52,461	46.07
De Soto (city) Dallas County	17,242	45.80
Port Arthur (city) Jefferson County	25,360	43.91
Missouri City (city) Fort Bend County	20,486	38.72
Marshall (city) Harrison County	9,263	38.70
Texarkana (city) Bowie County	12,974	37.30
Orange (city) Orange County	6,655	35.70
La Marque (city) Galveston County	4,767	34.84

African American/Black: Hispanic

Top 10 Places Sorted by Number
Based on all places, regardless of population

Place	Number	%
Houston (city) Harris County	9,763	0.50
San Antonio (city) Bexar County	5,708	0.50
Dallas (city) Dallas County	4,493	0.38
El Paso (city) El Paso County	2,928	0.52
Austin (city) Travis County	2,826	0.43
Fort Worth (city) Tarrant County	1,919	0.36
Killeen (city) Bell County	1,395	1.61
Arlington (city) Tarrant County	1,080	0.32
Corpus Christi (city) Nueces County	1,039	0.37
Lubbock (city) Lubbock County	670	0.34

Top 10 Places Sorted by Percent
Based on all places, regardless of population

Place	Number	%
Impact (town) Taylor County	2	5.13
Samnorwood (cdp) Collingsworth County	2	5.13
Rangerville (village) Cameron County	7	3.45
Ranchitos Las Lomas (cdp) Webb County	11	3.29
Del Mar Heights (cdp) Cameron County	7	2.70
Chula Vista-Orason (cdp) Cameron County	9	2.28
Turkey (city) Hall County	11	2.23
Agua Dulce (cdp) El Paso County	13	1.76
Reid Hope King (cdp) Cameron County	14	1.75
Warren City (city) Gregg County	6	1.75

Top 10 Places Sorted by Percent
Based on places with populations of 10,000 or more

Place	Number	%
Killeen (city) Bell County	1,395	1.61
Fort Hood (cdp) Coryell County	466	1.38
Copperas Cove (city) Coryell County	265	0.90
Clute (city) Brazoria County	56	0.54
El Paso (city) El Paso County	2,928	0.52
Temple (city) Bell County	283	0.52
Houston (city) Harris County	9,763	0.50

Notes: (cdp) census designated place; Refer to the User's Guide in the front of the book for more detailed information.

Place	Number	%
San Antonio (city) Bexar County	5,708	0.50
Stafford (city) Fort Bend County	78	0.50
La Marque (city) Galveston County	68	0.50

African, sub-Saharan

Top 10 Places Sorted by Number
Based on all places, regardless of population

Place	Number	%
Houston (city) Harris County	27,841	1.42
Dallas (city) Dallas County	18,242	1.54
Arlington (city) Tarrant County	5,245	1.58
Austin (city) Travis County	4,683	0.71
Fort Worth (city) Tarrant County	4,417	0.82
San Antonio (city) Bexar County	4,192	0.37
Irving (city) Dallas County	2,903	1.52
Garland (city) Dallas County	2,497	1.16
Beaumont (city) Jefferson County	1,483	1.30
Plano (city) Collin County	1,421	0.64

Top 10 Places Sorted by Percent
Based on all places, regardless of population

Place	Number	%
Neylandville (town) Hunt County	7	17.07
Fate (city) Rockwall County	43	9.29
Lyford South (cdp) Willacy County	16	6.13
Coffee City (town) Henderson County	10	5.65
Emhouse (town) Navarro County	9	5.49
Toco (city) Lamar County	5	5.49
Four Corners (cdp) Fort Bend County	134	4.53
Prado Verde (cdp) El Paso County	9	4.25
Lovelady (city) Houston County	24	4.01
Hedley (city) Donley County	14	3.75

Top 10 Places Sorted by Percent
Based on places with populations of 10,000 or more

Place	Number	%
Mission Bend (cdp) Fort Bend County	954	3.09
Addison (town) Dallas County	394	2.86
Missouri City (city) Fort Bend County	1,323	2.52
Cedar Hill (city) Dallas County	794	2.47
Stafford (city) Fort Bend County	386	2.47
New Territory (cdp) Fort Bend County	300	2.16
Texas City (city) Galveston County	861	2.08
Corsicana (city) Navarro County	501	2.05
Lancaster (city) Dallas County	445	1.72
De Soto (city) Dallas County	641	1.70

African, Subsaharan: African

Top 10 Places Sorted by Number
Based on all places, regardless of population

Place	Number	%
Houston (city) Harris County	15,009	0.77
Dallas (city) Dallas County	10,470	0.88
Fort Worth (city) Tarrant County	3,840	0.72
San Antonio (city) Bexar County	3,508	0.31
Austin (city) Travis County	2,935	0.45
Arlington (city) Tarrant County	2,568	0.77
Beaumont (city) Jefferson County	1,353	1.19
Irving (city) Dallas County	1,212	0.63
Garland (city) Dallas County	1,127	0.52
Killeen (city) Bell County	1,061	1.22

Top 10 Places Sorted by Percent
Based on all places, regardless of population

Place	Number	%
Neylandville (town) Hunt County	7	17.07
Fate (city) Rockwall County	43	9.29
Lyford South (cdp) Willacy County	16	6.13
Coffee City (town) Henderson County	10	5.65
Emhouse (town) Navarro County	9	5.49

Place	Number	%
Toco (city) Lamar County	5	5.49
Prado Verde (cdp) El Paso County	9	4.25
Lovelady (city) Houston County	24	4.01
Hedley (city) Donley County	14	3.75
Hearne (city) Robertson County	150	3.40

Top 10 Places Sorted by Percent
Based on places with populations of 10,000 or more

Place	Number	%
Cedar Hill (city) Dallas County	703	2.19
Texas City (city) Galveston County	838	2.02
Corsicana (city) Navarro County	465	1.90
Lancaster (city) Dallas County	426	1.65
El Campo (city) Wharton County	175	1.62
Brenham (city) Washington County	213	1.59
Orange (city) Orange County	286	1.54
De Soto (city) Dallas County	548	1.46
Kilgore (city) Gregg County	163	1.46
Palestine (city) Anderson County	256	1.44

African, Subsaharan: Cape Verdean

Top 10 Places Sorted by Number
Based on all places, regardless of population

Place	Number	%
Dallas (city) Dallas County	71	0.01
San Antonio (city) Bexar County	34	0.00
Flower Mound (town) Denton County	29	0.06
Houston (city) Harris County	26	0.00
Carrollton (city) Denton County	22	0.02
De Soto (city) Dallas County	21	0.06
Austin (city) Travis County	19	0.00
El Paso (city) El Paso County	11	0.00
White Settlement (city) Tarrant County	8	0.05
Grand Prairie (city) Dallas County	8	0.01

Top 10 Places Sorted by Percent
Based on all places, regardless of population

Place	Number	%
Lexington (town) Lee County	2	0.18
Flower Mound (town) Denton County	29	0.06
De Soto (city) Dallas County	21	0.06
White Settlement (city) Tarrant County	8	0.05
Carrollton (city) Denton County	22	0.02
Cedar Hill (city) Dallas County	5	0.02
Dallas (city) Dallas County	71	0.01
Grand Prairie (city) Dallas County	8	0.01
Waco (city) McLennan County	8	0.01
Killeen (city) Bell County	7	0.01

Top 10 Places Sorted by Percent
Based on places with populations of 10,000 or more

Place	Number	%
Flower Mound (town) Denton County	29	0.06
De Soto (city) Dallas County	21	0.06
White Settlement (city) Tarrant County	8	0.05
Carrollton (city) Denton County	22	0.02
Cedar Hill (city) Dallas County	5	0.02
Dallas (city) Dallas County	71	0.01
Grand Prairie (city) Dallas County	8	0.01
Waco (city) McLennan County	8	0.01
Killeen (city) Bell County	7	0.01
McAllen (city) Hidalgo County	6	0.01

African, Subsaharan: Ethiopian

Top 10 Places Sorted by Number
Based on all places, regardless of population

Place	Number	%
Dallas (city) Dallas County	3,006	0.25
Houston (city) Harris County	848	0.04
Plano (city) Collin County	375	0.17

Place	Number	%
Garland (city) Dallas County	316	0.15
Irving (city) Dallas County	286	0.15
Richardson (city) Dallas County	266	0.29
Austin (city) Travis County	254	0.04
Addison (town) Dallas County	115	0.83
Arlington (city) Tarrant County	107	0.03
Mesquite (city) Dallas County	49	0.04

Top 10 Places Sorted by Percent
Based on all places, regardless of population

Place	Number	%
Linden (city) Cass County	19	0.84
Addison (town) Dallas County	115	0.83
Barrett (cdp) Harris County	17	0.62
Rochester (town) Haskell County	2	0.56
Murphy (city) Collin County	15	0.48
Richardson (city) Dallas County	266	0.29
Olmos Park (city) Bexar County	7	0.28
Dallas (city) Dallas County	3,006	0.25
Plano (city) Collin County	375	0.17
Miami (city) Roberts County	1	0.17

Top 10 Places Sorted by Percent
Based on places with populations of 10,000 or more

Place	Number	%
Addison (town) Dallas County	115	0.83
Richardson (city) Dallas County	266	0.29
Dallas (city) Dallas County	3,006	0.25
Plano (city) Collin County	375	0.17
Garland (city) Dallas County	316	0.15
Irving (city) Dallas County	286	0.15
Rowlett (city) Dallas County	35	0.08
Allen (city) Collin County	29	0.07
Balch Springs (city) Dallas County	12	0.06
Round Rock (city) Williamson County	33	0.05

African, Subsaharan: Ghanian

Top 10 Places Sorted by Number
Based on all places, regardless of population

Place	Number	%
Houston (city) Harris County	532	0.03
Arlington (city) Tarrant County	244	0.07
Irving (city) Dallas County	237	0.12
Dallas (city) Dallas County	172	0.01
Grand Prairie (city) Dallas County	152	0.12
Mesquite (city) Dallas County	67	0.05
Missouri City (city) Fort Bend County	62	0.12
Pflugerville (city) Travis County	60	0.37
North Richland Hills (city) Tarrant County	51	0.09
Beaumont (city) Jefferson County	51	0.04

Top 10 Places Sorted by Percent
Based on all places, regardless of population

Place	Number	%
Blessing (cdp) Matagorda County	6	0.70
Pflugerville (city) Travis County	60	0.37
Hickory Creek (town) Denton County	6	0.29
Royse City (city) Rockwall County	6	0.20
University Park (city) Dallas County	32	0.14
The Hills (village) Travis County	2	0.13
Irving (city) Dallas County	237	0.12
Grand Prairie (city) Dallas County	152	0.12
Missouri City (city) Fort Bend County	62	0.12
Keller (city) Tarrant County	27	0.10

Top 10 Places Sorted by Percent
Based on places with populations of 10,000 or more

Place	Number	%
Pflugerville (city) Travis County	60	0.37
University Park (city) Dallas County	32	0.14
Irving (city) Dallas County	237	0.12

Notes: (cdp) census designated place; Refer to the User's Guide in the front of the book for more detailed information.

Grand Prairie (city) Dallas County	152	0.12
Missouri City (city) Fort Bend County	62	0.12
Keller (city) Tarrant County	27	0.10
North Richland Hills (city) Tarrant County	51	0.09
Wells Branch (cdp) Travis County	10	0.09
Arlington (city) Tarrant County	244	0.07
Texas City (city) Galveston County	23	0.06

African, Subsaharan: Kenyan

Top 10 Places Sorted by Number
Based on all places, regardless of population

Place	Number	%
Houston (city) Harris County	457	0.02
Arlington (city) Tarrant County	408	0.12
Dallas (city) Dallas County	361	0.03
Irving (city) Dallas County	102	0.05
Mission Bend (cdp) Fort Bend County	60	0.19
Austin (city) Travis County	58	0.01
Fort Worth (city) Tarrant County	55	0.01
New Territory (cdp) Fort Bend County	47	0.34
Brushy Creek (cdp) Williamson County	41	0.26
Denton (city) Denton County	39	0.05

Top 10 Places Sorted by Percent
Based on all places, regardless of population

Place	Number	%
New Territory (cdp) Fort Bend County	47	0.34
Prairie View (city) Waller County	12	0.27
Brushy Creek (cdp) Williamson County	41	0.26
Mission Bend (cdp) Fort Bend County	60	0.19
Rockwall (city) Rockwall County	27	0.15
Arlington (city) Tarrant County	408	0.12
Canyon (city) Randall County	13	0.10
Haltom City (city) Tarrant County	29	0.07
Frisco (city) Collin County	23	0.07
Bedford (city) Tarrant County	28	0.06

Top 10 Places Sorted by Percent
Based on places with populations of 10,000 or more

Place	Number	%
New Territory (cdp) Fort Bend County	47	0.34
Brushy Creek (cdp) Williamson County	41	0.26
Mission Bend (cdp) Fort Bend County	60	0.19
Rockwall (city) Rockwall County	27	0.15
Arlington (city) Tarrant County	408	0.12
Canyon (city) Randall County	13	0.10
Haltom City (city) Tarrant County	29	0.07
Frisco (city) Collin County	23	0.07
Bedford (city) Tarrant County	28	0.06
Irving (city) Dallas County	102	0.05

African, Subsaharan: Liberian

Top 10 Places Sorted by Number
Based on all places, regardless of population

Place	Number	%
Houston (city) Harris County	251	0.01
Hurst (city) Tarrant County	106	0.29
Euless (city) Tarrant County	100	0.22
Arlington (city) Tarrant County	70	0.02
Richardson (city) Dallas County	38	0.04
Fort Worth (city) Tarrant County	29	0.01
Round Rock (city) Williamson County	23	0.04
Mission Bend (cdp) Fort Bend County	22	0.07
Austin (city) Travis County	17	0.00
Irving (city) Dallas County	15	0.01

Top 10 Places Sorted by Percent
Based on all places, regardless of population

Place	Number	%
New Hope (town) Collin County	2	0.30

Hurst (city) Tarrant County	106	0.29
Euless (city) Tarrant County	100	0.22
Lackland AFB (cdp) Bexar County	6	0.08
Mission Bend (cdp) Fort Bend County	22	0.07
Richardson (city) Dallas County	38	0.04
Round Rock (city) Williamson County	23	0.04
New Territory (cdp) Fort Bend County	6	0.04
Huntsville (city) Walker County	12	0.03
Arlington (city) Tarrant County	70	0.02

Top 10 Places Sorted by Percent
Based on places with populations of 10,000 or more

Place	Number	%
Hurst (city) Tarrant County	106	0.29
Euless (city) Tarrant County	100	0.22
Mission Bend (cdp) Fort Bend County	22	0.07
Richardson (city) Dallas County	38	0.04
Round Rock (city) Williamson County	23	0.04
New Territory (cdp) Fort Bend County	6	0.04
Huntsville (city) Walker County	12	0.03
Arlington (city) Tarrant County	70	0.02
Houston (city) Harris County	251	0.01
Fort Worth (city) Tarrant County	29	0.01

African, Subsaharan: Nigerian

Top 10 Places Sorted by Number
Based on all places, regardless of population

Place	Number	%
Houston (city) Harris County	8,726	0.45
Dallas (city) Dallas County	2,365	0.20
Arlington (city) Tarrant County	1,302	0.39
Garland (city) Dallas County	820	0.38
Austin (city) Travis County	713	0.11
Irving (city) Dallas County	679	0.35
Missouri City (city) Fort Bend County	578	1.10
Mission Bend (cdp) Fort Bend County	496	1.61
Grand Prairie (city) Dallas County	462	0.36
Mesquite (city) Dallas County	383	0.31

Top 10 Places Sorted by Percent
Based on all places, regardless of population

Place	Number	%
Four Corners (cdp) Fort Bend County	105	3.55
Mission Bend (cdp) Fort Bend County	496	1.61
Glenn Heights (city) Dallas County	108	1.49
Windemere (cdp) Travis County	95	1.35
Dalworthington Gardens (city) Tarrant County	28	1.26
Missouri City (city) Fort Bend County	578	1.10
Stafford (city) Fort Bend County	158	1.01
Frost (city) Navarro County	7	0.99
New Territory (cdp) Fort Bend County	110	0.79
Addison (town) Dallas County	86	0.62

Top 10 Places Sorted by Percent
Based on places with populations of 10,000 or more

Place	Number	%
Mission Bend (cdp) Fort Bend County	496	1.61
Missouri City (city) Fort Bend County	578	1.10
Stafford (city) Fort Bend County	158	1.01
New Territory (cdp) Fort Bend County	110	0.79
Addison (town) Dallas County	86	0.62
Sugar Land (city) Fort Bend County	363	0.57
Cinco Ranch (cdp) Fort Bend County	61	0.54
Rowlett (city) Dallas County	221	0.50
Brushy Creek (cdp) Williamson County	76	0.48
Houston (city) Harris County	8,726	0.45

African, Subsaharan: Senegalese

Top 10 Places Sorted by Number
Based on all places, regardless of population

Place	Number	%
San Antonio (city) Bexar County	56	0.00
Irving (city) Dallas County	33	0.02
Houston (city) Harris County	31	0.00
Arlington (city) Tarrant County	28	0.01
Fort Worth (city) Tarrant County	10	0.00
Lubbock (city) Lubbock County	9	0.00

Top 10 Places Sorted by Percent
Based on all places, regardless of population

Place	Number	%
Irving (city) Dallas County	33	0.02
Arlington (city) Tarrant County	28	0.01
San Antonio (city) Bexar County	56	0.00
Houston (city) Harris County	31	0.00
Fort Worth (city) Tarrant County	10	0.00
Lubbock (city) Lubbock County	9	0.00

Top 10 Places Sorted by Percent
Based on places with populations of 10,000 or more

Place	Number	%
Irving (city) Dallas County	33	0.02
Arlington (city) Tarrant County	28	0.01
San Antonio (city) Bexar County	56	0.00
Houston (city) Harris County	31	0.00
Fort Worth (city) Tarrant County	10	0.00
Lubbock (city) Lubbock County	9	0.00

African, Subsaharan: Sierra Leonean

Top 10 Places Sorted by Number
Based on all places, regardless of population

Place	Number	%
Dallas (city) Dallas County	264	0.02
Houston (city) Harris County	84	0.00
Mesquite (city) Dallas County	63	0.05
Euless (city) Tarrant County	28	0.06
Garland (city) Dallas County	25	0.01
Waxahachie (city) Ellis County	20	0.09
Arlington (city) Tarrant County	18	0.01
Lubbock (city) Lubbock County	17	0.01
Colleyville (city) Tarrant County	12	0.06
Hurst (city) Tarrant County	12	0.03

Top 10 Places Sorted by Percent
Based on all places, regardless of population

Place	Number	%
Waxahachie (city) Ellis County	20	0.09
Euless (city) Tarrant County	28	0.06
Colleyville (city) Tarrant County	12	0.06
Mesquite (city) Dallas County	63	0.05
Hurst (city) Tarrant County	12	0.03
Dallas (city) Dallas County	264	0.02
College Station (city) Brazos County	11	0.02
Garland (city) Dallas County	25	0.01
Arlington (city) Tarrant County	18	0.01
Lubbock (city) Lubbock County	17	0.01

Top 10 Places Sorted by Percent
Based on places with populations of 10,000 or more

Place	Number	%
Waxahachie (city) Ellis County	20	0.09
Euless (city) Tarrant County	28	0.06
Colleyville (city) Tarrant County	12	0.06
Mesquite (city) Dallas County	63	0.05
Hurst (city) Tarrant County	12	0.03
Dallas (city) Dallas County	264	0.02

Notes: (cdp) census designated place; Refer to the User's Guide in the front of the book for more detailed information.

Place	Number	%
College Station (city) Brazos County	11	0.02
Garland (city) Dallas County	25	0.01
Arlington (city) Tarrant County	18	0.01
Lubbock (city) Lubbock County	17	0.01

African, Subsaharan: Somalian

Top 10 Places Sorted by Number
Based on all places, regardless of population

Place	Number	%
Houston (city) Harris County	300	0.02
Arlington (city) Tarrant County	211	0.06
Dallas (city) Dallas County	167	0.01
Austin (city) Travis County	94	0.01
Euless (city) Tarrant County	55	0.12
Irving (city) Dallas County	54	0.03
Flower Mound (town) Denton County	37	0.07
Addison (town) Dallas County	30	0.22
Round Rock (city) Williamson County	23	0.04
Lewisville (city) Denton County	12	0.02

Top 10 Places Sorted by Percent
Based on all places, regardless of population

Place	Number	%
Addison (town) Dallas County	30	0.22
Euless (city) Tarrant County	55	0.12
Flower Mound (town) Denton County	37	0.07
Arlington (city) Tarrant County	211	0.06
Round Rock (city) Williamson County	23	0.04
Irving (city) Dallas County	54	0.03
Seguin (city) Guadalupe County	6	0.03
Houston (city) Harris County	300	0.02
Lewisville (city) Denton County	12	0.02
Dallas (city) Dallas County	167	0.01

Top 10 Places Sorted by Percent
Based on places with populations of 10,000 or more

Place	Number	%
Addison (town) Dallas County	30	0.22
Euless (city) Tarrant County	55	0.12
Flower Mound (town) Denton County	37	0.07
Arlington (city) Tarrant County	211	0.06
Round Rock (city) Williamson County	23	0.04
Irving (city) Dallas County	54	0.03
Seguin (city) Guadalupe County	6	0.03
Houston (city) Harris County	300	0.02
Lewisville (city) Denton County	12	0.02
Dallas (city) Dallas County	167	0.01

African, Subsaharan: South African

Top 10 Places Sorted by Number
Based on all places, regardless of population

Place	Number	%
Houston (city) Harris County	764	0.04
Dallas (city) Dallas County	680	0.06
Austin (city) Travis County	320	0.05
Plano (city) Collin County	167	0.08
San Antonio (city) Bexar County	83	0.01
Grapevine (city) Tarrant County	77	0.18
Irving (city) Dallas County	67	0.03
Sugar Land (city) Fort Bend County	54	0.09
University Park (city) Dallas County	52	0.22
Garland (city) Dallas County	48	0.02

Top 10 Places Sorted by Percent
Based on all places, regardless of population

Place	Number	%
Double Oak (town) Denton County	14	0.65
Greatwood (cdp) Fort Bend County	40	0.61
Madisonville (city) Madison County	23	0.55
Oak Ridge North (city) Montgomery County	15	0.50

Place	Number	%
Hickory Creek (town) Denton County	10	0.49
Keene (city) Johnson County	23	0.47
Wheeler (city) Wheeler County	5	0.36
Valley Mills (city) Bosque County	4	0.36
Bee Cave (village) Travis County	2	0.33
Seymour (city) Baylor County	9	0.31

Top 10 Places Sorted by Percent
Based on places with populations of 10,000 or more

Place	Number	%
West University Place (city) Harris County	43	0.30
Cinco Ranch (cdp) Fort Bend County	28	0.25
University Park (city) Dallas County	52	0.22
Grapevine (city) Tarrant County	77	0.18
Canyon Lake (cdp) Comal County	27	0.16
Bellaire (city) Harris County	17	0.11
Sugar Land (city) Fort Bend County	54	0.09
Friendswood (city) Galveston County	25	0.09
Plano (city) Collin County	167	0.08
Atascocita (cdp) Harris County	26	0.07

African, Subsaharan: Sudanese

Top 10 Places Sorted by Number
Based on all places, regardless of population

Place	Number	%
Dallas (city) Dallas County	116	0.01
Houston (city) Harris County	99	0.01
San Antonio (city) Bexar County	83	0.01
Fort Worth (city) Tarrant County	60	0.01
Arlington (city) Tarrant County	51	0.02
Bedford (city) Tarrant County	43	0.09
Irving (city) Dallas County	31	0.02
Hurst (city) Tarrant County	24	0.07
Richardson (city) Dallas County	24	0.03
Plano (city) Collin County	24	0.01

Top 10 Places Sorted by Percent
Based on all places, regardless of population

Place	Number	%
Bedford (city) Tarrant County	43	0.09
Hurst (city) Tarrant County	24	0.07
Burleson (city) Johnson County	10	0.05
Saginaw (city) Tarrant County	6	0.05
Richardson (city) Dallas County	24	0.03
Euless (city) Tarrant County	15	0.03
Arlington (city) Tarrant County	51	0.02
Irving (city) Dallas County	31	0.02
Dallas (city) Dallas County	116	0.01
Houston (city) Harris County	99	0.01

Top 10 Places Sorted by Percent
Based on places with populations of 10,000 or more

Place	Number	%
Bedford (city) Tarrant County	43	0.09
Hurst (city) Tarrant County	24	0.07
Burleson (city) Johnson County	10	0.05
Saginaw (city) Tarrant County	6	0.05
Richardson (city) Dallas County	24	0.03
Euless (city) Tarrant County	15	0.03
Arlington (city) Tarrant County	51	0.02
Irving (city) Dallas County	31	0.02
Dallas (city) Dallas County	116	0.01
Houston (city) Harris County	99	0.01

African, Subsaharan: Ugandan

Top 10 Places Sorted by Number
Based on all places, regardless of population

Place	Number	%
Houston (city) Harris County	46	0.00
Dallas (city) Dallas County	34	0.00

Place	Number	%
Angleton (city) Brazoria County	23	0.13
North Richland Hills (city) Tarrant County	17	0.03
Grand Prairie (city) Dallas County	16	0.01
Euless (city) Tarrant County	15	0.03
Irving (city) Dallas County	15	0.01
Atascocita (cdp) Harris County	13	0.04
Arlington (city) Tarrant County	12	0.00
Bulverde (city) Comal County	11	0.29

Top 10 Places Sorted by Percent
Based on all places, regardless of population

Place	Number	%
Bulverde (city) Comal County	11	0.29
Hughes Springs (city) Cass County	3	0.16
Angleton (city) Brazoria County	23	0.13
Atascocita (cdp) Harris County	13	0.04
Weatherford (city) Parker County	8	0.04
North Richland Hills (city) Tarrant County	17	0.03
Euless (city) Tarrant County	15	0.03
Grand Prairie (city) Dallas County	16	0.01
Irving (city) Dallas County	15	0.01
Killeen (city) Bell County	10	0.01

Top 10 Places Sorted by Percent
Based on places with populations of 10,000 or more

Place	Number	%
Angleton (city) Brazoria County	23	0.13
Atascocita (cdp) Harris County	13	0.04
Weatherford (city) Parker County	8	0.04
North Richland Hills (city) Tarrant County	17	0.03
Euless (city) Tarrant County	15	0.03
Grand Prairie (city) Dallas County	16	0.01
Irving (city) Dallas County	15	0.01
Killeen (city) Bell County	10	0.01
Houston (city) Harris County	46	0.00
Dallas (city) Dallas County	34	0.00

African, Subsaharan: Zairian

Top 10 Places Sorted by Number
Based on all places, regardless of population

Place	Number	%
Bedford (city) Tarrant County	85	0.18
Dallas (city) Dallas County	52	0.00
Irving (city) Dallas County	40	0.02
North Richland Hills (city) Tarrant County	36	0.06
Fort Worth (city) Tarrant County	14	0.00
Richardson (city) Dallas County	13	0.01
Haltom City (city) Tarrant County	11	0.03
San Antonio (city) Bexar County	9	0.00
Grand Prairie (city) Dallas County	7	0.01
McAllen (city) Hidalgo County	6	0.01

Top 10 Places Sorted by Percent
Based on all places, regardless of population

Place	Number	%
Bedford (city) Tarrant County	85	0.18
North Richland Hills (city) Tarrant County	36	0.06
Haltom City (city) Tarrant County	11	0.03
Irving (city) Dallas County	40	0.02
Richardson (city) Dallas County	13	0.01
Grand Prairie (city) Dallas County	7	0.01
McAllen (city) Hidalgo County	6	0.01
Dallas (city) Dallas County	52	0.00
Fort Worth (city) Tarrant County	14	0.00
San Antonio (city) Bexar County	9	0.00

Top 10 Places Sorted by Percent
Based on places with populations of 10,000 or more

Place	Number	%
Bedford (city) Tarrant County	85	0.18
North Richland Hills (city) Tarrant County	36	0.06

Place	Number	%
Haltom City (city) Tarrant County	11	0.03
Irving (city) Dallas County	40	0.02
Richardson (city) Dallas County	13	0.01
Grand Prairie (city) Dallas County	7	0.01
McAllen (city) Hidalgo County	6	0.01
Dallas (city) Dallas County	52	0.00
Fort Worth (city) Tarrant County	14	0.00
San Antonio (city) Bexar County	9	0.00

African, Subsaharan: Zimbabwean

Top 10 Places Sorted by Number
Based on all places, regardless of population

Place	Number	%
Dallas (city) Dallas County	222	0.02
Irving (city) Dallas County	43	0.02
Austin (city) Travis County	31	0.00
Lewisville (city) Denton County	19	0.02
San Antonio (city) Bexar County	18	0.00
Keene (city) Johnson County	13	0.27
Marshall (city) Harrison County	9	0.04
West University Place (city) Harris County	7	0.05
Cedar Park (city) Williamson County	6	0.02
Lake Jackson (city) Brazoria County	6	0.02

Top 10 Places Sorted by Percent
Based on all places, regardless of population

Place	Number	%
Keene (city) Johnson County	13	0.27
West University Place (city) Harris County	7	0.05
Marshall (city) Harrison County	9	0.04
Dallas (city) Dallas County	222	0.02
Irving (city) Dallas County	43	0.02
Lewisville (city) Denton County	19	0.02
Cedar Park (city) Williamson County	6	0.02
Lake Jackson (city) Brazoria County	6	0.02
Austin (city) Travis County	31	0.00
San Antonio (city) Bexar County	18	0.00

Top 10 Places Sorted by Percent
Based on places with populations of 10,000 or more

Place	Number	%
West University Place (city) Harris County	7	0.05
Marshall (city) Harrison County	9	0.04
Dallas (city) Dallas County	222	0.02
Irving (city) Dallas County	43	0.02
Lewisville (city) Denton County	19	0.02
Cedar Park (city) Williamson County	6	0.02
Lake Jackson (city) Brazoria County	6	0.02
Austin (city) Travis County	31	0.00
San Antonio (city) Bexar County	18	0.00
Houston (city) Harris County	3	0.00

African, Subsaharan: Other

Top 10 Places Sorted by Number
Based on all places, regardless of population

Place	Number	%
Houston (city) Harris County	665	0.03
Dallas (city) Dallas County	248	0.02
Arlington (city) Tarrant County	195	0.06
Austin (city) Travis County	172	0.03
Euless (city) Tarrant County	134	0.29
Plano (city) Collin County	126	0.06
Irving (city) Dallas County	89	0.05
Garland (city) Dallas County	72	0.03
El Paso (city) El Paso County	58	0.01
Fort Worth (city) Tarrant County	55	0.01

Top 10 Places Sorted by Percent
Based on all places, regardless of population

Place	Number	%
Spring Garden-Terra Verde (cdp) Nueces County	6	0.83
Seadrift (city) Calhoun County	5	0.37
Shallowater (city) Lubbock County	7	0.34
Euless (city) Tarrant County	134	0.29
Windemere (cdp) Travis County	18	0.26
Walnut Springs (city) Bosque County	2	0.26
Hillsboro (city) Hill County	17	0.21
Wharton (city) Wharton County	18	0.19
White Oak (city) Gregg County	10	0.18
Four Corners (cdp) Fort Bend County	5	0.17

Top 10 Places Sorted by Percent
Based on places with populations of 10,000 or more

Place	Number	%
Euless (city) Tarrant County	134	0.29
Corsicana (city) Navarro County	36	0.15
Cedar Hill (city) Dallas County	42	0.13
Allen (city) Collin County	50	0.12
Farmers Branch (city) Dallas County	33	0.12
Kilgore (city) Gregg County	10	0.09
Stafford (city) Fort Bend County	13	0.08
North Richland Hills (city) Tarrant County	41	0.07
Addison (town) Dallas County	9	0.07
Arlington (city) Tarrant County	195	0.06

Alaska Native tribes, specified

Top 10 Places Sorted by Number
Based on all places, regardless of population

Place	Number	%
San Antonio (city) Bexar County	52	0.00
Dallas (city) Dallas County	48	0.00
Houston (city) Harris County	40	0.00
Austin (city) Travis County	38	0.01
Fort Hood (cdp) Coryell County	25	0.07
Plano (city) Collin County	23	0.01
Fort Worth (city) Tarrant County	21	0.00
Arlington (city) Tarrant County	20	0.01
Corpus Christi (city) Nueces County	15	0.01
Lewisville (city) Denton County	13	0.02

Top 10 Places Sorted by Percent
Based on all places, regardless of population

Place	Number	%
Westbrook (city) Mitchell County	1	0.49
Alvord (town) Wise County	2	0.20
Loraine (town) Mitchell County	1	0.15
Glen Rose (city) Somervell County	3	0.14
Fort Bliss (cdp) El Paso County	10	0.12
Keene (city) Johnson County	6	0.12
Lakeport (city) Gregg County	1	0.12
San Leon (cdp) Galveston County	5	0.11
De Kalb (city) Bowie County	2	0.11
Lake Kiowa (cdp) Cooke County	2	0.11

Top 10 Places Sorted by Percent
Based on places with populations of 10,000 or more

Place	Number	%
Fort Hood (cdp) Coryell County	25	0.07
Pampa (city) Gray County	11	0.06
Gainesville (city) Cooke County	6	0.04
Freeport (city) Brazoria County	5	0.04
Burleson (city) Johnson County	7	0.03
Harker Heights (city) Bell County	5	0.03
Lockhart (city) Caldwell County	4	0.03
Lewisville (city) Denton County	13	0.02
League City (city) Galveston County	10	0.02
Texas City (city) Galveston County	7	0.02

Alaska Native: Alaska Athabascan

Top 10 Places Sorted by Number
Based on all places, regardless of population

Place	Number	%
Fort Hood (cdp) Coryell County	10	0.03
San Antonio (city) Bexar County	10	0.00
Houston (city) Harris County	7	0.00
Pampa (city) Gray County	6	0.03
Denton (city) Denton County	6	0.01
Dallas (city) Dallas County	6	0.00
Plano (city) Collin County	6	0.00
Harker Heights (city) Bell County	5	0.03
Carrollton (city) Denton County	5	0.00
Waco (city) McLennan County	5	0.00

Top 10 Places Sorted by Percent
Based on all places, regardless of population

Place	Number	%
Alvord (town) Wise County	2	0.20
Lakeport (city) Gregg County	1	0.12
De Kalb (city) Bowie County	2	0.11
Lake Kiowa (cdp) Cooke County	2	0.11
San Leon (cdp) Galveston County	4	0.09
Red Oak (city) Ellis County	3	0.07
Shoreacres (city) Harris County	1	0.07
Glen Rose (city) Somervell County	1	0.05
Fort Bliss (cdp) El Paso County	3	0.04
Roanoke (city) Denton County	1	0.04

Top 10 Places Sorted by Percent
Based on places with populations of 10,000 or more

Place	Number	%
Fort Hood (cdp) Coryell County	10	0.03
Pampa (city) Gray County	6	0.03
Harker Heights (city) Bell County	5	0.03
Gainesville (city) Cooke County	3	0.02
Mount Pleasant (city) Titus County	3	0.02
Converse (city) Bexar County	2	0.02
Denton (city) Denton County	6	0.01
Big Spring (city) Howard County	2	0.01
Friendswood (city) Galveston County	2	0.01
Jollyville (cdp) Williamson County	2	0.01

Alaska Native: Aleut

Top 10 Places Sorted by Number
Based on all places, regardless of population

Place	Number	%
San Antonio (city) Bexar County	12	0.00
Mesquite (city) Dallas County	9	0.01
Houston (city) Harris County	8	0.00
Dallas (city) Dallas County	7	0.00
League City (city) Galveston County	5	0.01
Abilene (city) Taylor County	5	0.00
Bay City (city) Matagorda County	4	0.02
Burleson (city) Johnson County	4	0.02
Lewisville (city) Denton County	4	0.01
Texas City (city) Galveston County	4	0.01

Top 10 Places Sorted by Percent
Based on all places, regardless of population

Place	Number	%
Tahoka (city) Lynn County	2	0.07
Quinlan (city) Hunt County	1	0.07
Double Oak (town) Denton County	1	0.05
Dublin (city) Erath County	1	0.03
Fairfield (city) Freestone County	1	0.03
Lucas (city) Collin County	1	0.03
Bay City (city) Matagorda County	4	0.02
Burleson (city) Johnson County	4	0.02
Dickinson (city) Galveston County	3	0.02

Notes: (cdp) census designated place; Refer to the User's Guide in the front of the book for more detailed information.

Place	Number	%
Gainesville (city) Cooke County	3	0.02

Top 10 Places Sorted by Percent
Based on places with populations of 10,000 or more

Place	Number	%
Bay City (city) Matagorda County	4	0.02
Burleson (city) Johnson County	4	0.02
Dickinson (city) Galveston County	3	0.02
Gainesville (city) Cooke County	3	0.02
Pampa (city) Gray County	3	0.02
Mesquite (city) Dallas County	9	0.01
League City (city) Galveston County	5	0.01
Lewisville (city) Denton County	4	0.01
Texas City (city) Galveston County	4	0.01
The Woodlands (cdp) Montgomery County	4	0.01

Alaska Native: Eskimo

Top 10 Places Sorted by Number
Based on all places, regardless of population

Place	Number	%
Austin (city) Travis County	22	0.00
Houston (city) Harris County	18	0.00
San Antonio (city) Bexar County	17	0.00
Dallas (city) Dallas County	16	0.00
Fort Worth (city) Tarrant County	12	0.00
Fort Hood (cdp) Coryell County	10	0.03
Keene (city) Johnson County	6	0.12
Fort Bliss (cdp) El Paso County	6	0.07
Lewisville (city) Denton County	6	0.01
Irving (city) Dallas County	6	0.00

Top 10 Places Sorted by Percent
Based on all places, regardless of population

Place	Number	%
Westbrook (city) Mitchell County	1	0.49
Loraine (town) Mitchell County	1	0.15
Keene (city) Johnson County	6	0.12
Glen Rose (city) Somervell County	2	0.09
Fort Bliss (cdp) El Paso County	6	0.07
Kyle (city) Hays County	3	0.06
Lake Worth (city) Tarrant County	3	0.06
Garfield (cdp) Travis County	1	0.06
Freeport (city) Brazoria County	5	0.04
Pantego (town) Tarrant County	1	0.04

Top 10 Places Sorted by Percent
Based on places with populations of 10,000 or more

Place	Number	%
Freeport (city) Brazoria County	5	0.04
Fort Hood (cdp) Coryell County	10	0.03
Lockhart (city) Caldwell County	4	0.03
Humble (city) Harris County	3	0.02
Lewisville (city) Denton County	6	0.01
League City (city) Galveston County	5	0.01
Burleson (city) Johnson County	3	0.01
Cedar Hill (city) Dallas County	3	0.01
Cedar Park (city) Williamson County	3	0.01
Texas City (city) Galveston County	3	0.01

Alaska Native: Tlingit-Haida

Top 10 Places Sorted by Number
Based on all places, regardless of population

Place	Number	%
Dallas (city) Dallas County	16	0.00
Plano (city) Collin County	13	0.01
San Antonio (city) Bexar County	13	0.00
Amarillo (city) Potter County	10	0.01
Arlington (city) Tarrant County	9	0.00
Corpus Christi (city) Nueces County	8	0.00
Austin (city) Travis County	6	0.00

Place	Number	%
Fort Worth (city) Tarrant County	6	0.00
Houston (city) Harris County	6	0.00
El Paso (city) El Paso County	5	0.00

Top 10 Places Sorted by Percent
Based on all places, regardless of population

Place	Number	%
Saint Jo (city) Montague County	1	0.10
Rockdale (city) Milam County	3	0.06
Kerens (city) Navarro County	1	0.06
Lake Dallas (city) Denton County	2	0.03
Jasper (city) Jasper County	2	0.02
Red Oak (city) Ellis County	1	0.02
Wake Village (city) Bowie County	1	0.02
Plano (city) Collin County	13	0.01
Amarillo (city) Potter County	10	0.01
Grapevine (city) Tarrant County	4	0.01

Top 10 Places Sorted by Percent
Based on places with populations of 10,000 or more

Place	Number	%
Plano (city) Collin County	13	0.01
Amarillo (city) Potter County	10	0.01
Grapevine (city) Tarrant County	4	0.01
Victoria (city) Victoria County	4	0.01
Haltom City (city) Tarrant County	3	0.01
Fort Hood (cdp) Coryell County	2	0.01
Hurst (city) Tarrant County	2	0.01
Kingsville (city) Kleberg County	2	0.01
Pampa (city) Gray County	2	0.01
Spring (cdp) Harris County	2	0.01

Alaska Native: All other tribes

Top 10 Places Sorted by Number
Based on all places, regardless of population

Place	Number	%
Austin (city) Travis County	3	0.00
Dallas (city) Dallas County	3	0.00
Trinity (city) Trinity County	2	0.07
Amarillo (city) Potter County	2	0.00
El Paso (city) El Paso County	2	0.00
Lewisville (city) Denton County	2	0.00
Early (city) Brown County	1	0.04
Ingleside (city) San Patricio County	1	0.01
Bedford (city) Tarrant County	1	0.00
Brownsville (city) Cameron County	1	0.00

Top 10 Places Sorted by Percent
Based on all places, regardless of population

Place	Number	%
Trinity (city) Trinity County	2	0.07
Early (city) Brown County	1	0.04
Ingleside (city) San Patricio County	1	0.01
Austin (city) Travis County	3	0.00
Dallas (city) Dallas County	3	0.00
Amarillo (city) Potter County	2	0.00
El Paso (city) El Paso County	2	0.00
Lewisville (city) Denton County	2	0.00
Bedford (city) Tarrant County	1	0.00
Brownsville (city) Cameron County	1	0.00

Top 10 Places Sorted by Percent
Based on places with populations of 10,000 or more

Place	Number	%
Austin (city) Travis County	3	0.00
Dallas (city) Dallas County	3	0.00
Amarillo (city) Potter County	2	0.00
El Paso (city) El Paso County	2	0.00
Lewisville (city) Denton County	2	0.00
Bedford (city) Tarrant County	1	0.00
Brownsville (city) Cameron County	1	0.00

Place	Number	%
Houston (city) Harris County	1	0.00
Irving (city) Dallas County	1	0.00

Alaska Native tribes, not specified

Top 10 Places Sorted by Number
Based on all places, regardless of population

Place	Number	%
San Antonio (city) Bexar County	23	0.00
Fort Worth (city) Tarrant County	19	0.00
Houston (city) Harris County	15	0.00
Dallas (city) Dallas County	14	0.00
El Paso (city) El Paso County	14	0.00
Austin (city) Travis County	13	0.00
San Marcos (city) Hays County	9	0.03
Amarillo (city) Potter County	7	0.00
Keene (city) Johnson County	6	0.12
Lewisville (city) Denton County	6	0.01

Top 10 Places Sorted by Percent
Based on all places, regardless of population

Place	Number	%
San Felipe (town) Austin County	2	0.23
Van Vleck (cdp) Matagorda County	2	0.14
Hubbard (city) Hill County	2	0.13
Keene (city) Johnson County	6	0.12
De Leon (city) Comanche County	2	0.08
Liberty Hill (city) Williamson County	1	0.07
Jonestown (city) Travis County	1	0.06
Natalia (city) Medina County	1	0.06
Laredo Ranchettes (cdp) Webb County	1	0.05
Sealy (city) Austin County	2	0.04

Top 10 Places Sorted by Percent
Based on places with populations of 10,000 or more

Place	Number	%
San Marcos (city) Hays County	9	0.03
Canyon (city) Randall County	3	0.02
Lewisville (city) Denton County	6	0.01
Sherman (city) Grayson County	4	0.01
Edinburg (city) Hidalgo County	3	0.01
Jacksonville (city) Cherokee County	2	0.01
Wylie (city) Collin County	2	0.01
Hereford (city) Deaf Smith County	1	0.01
Jollyville (cdp) Williamson County	1	0.01
Universal City (city) Bexar County	1	0.01

American Indian or Alaska Native, not specified

Top 10 Places Sorted by Number
Based on all places, regardless of population

Place	Number	%
Houston (city) Harris County	7,193	0.37
San Antonio (city) Bexar County	6,958	0.61
Dallas (city) Dallas County	4,171	0.35
Austin (city) Travis County	2,871	0.44
El Paso (city) El Paso County	2,810	0.50
Fort Worth (city) Tarrant County	2,082	0.39
Corpus Christi (city) Nueces County	1,229	0.44
Arlington (city) Tarrant County	1,116	0.34
Garland (city) Dallas County	745	0.35
Amarillo (city) Potter County	729	0.42

Top 10 Places Sorted by Percent
Based on all places, regardless of population

Place	Number	%
Quintana (town) Brazoria County	2	5.26
Ranchette Estates (cdp) Willacy County	6	4.51
Mertens (town) Hill County	6	4.11
Goree (city) Knox County	12	3.74
Dodson (town) Collingsworth County	4	3.48

Place	Number	%
Opdyke West (town) Hockley County	6	3.19
Pyote (town) Ward County	4	3.05
Chula Vista-River Spur (cdp) Zavala County	12	3.00
Realitos (cdp) Duval County	6	2.87
Walnut Springs (city) Bosque County	20	2.65

Top 10 Places Sorted by Percent
Based on places with populations of 10,000 or more

Place	Number	%
Galena Park (city) Harris County	96	0.91
Plainview (city) Hale County	169	0.76
Mercedes (city) Hidalgo County	103	0.75
Gainesville (city) Cooke County	106	0.68
Denison (city) Grayson County	153	0.67
Jacinto City (city) Harris County	69	0.67
Pampa (city) Gray County	116	0.65
San Antonio (city) Bexar County	6,958	0.61
Balch Springs (city) Dallas County	119	0.61
Levelland (city) Hockley County	78	0.61

Albanian

Top 10 Places Sorted by Number
Based on all places, regardless of population

Place	Number	%
Houston (city) Harris County	301	0.02
Fort Worth (city) Tarrant County	279	0.05
Plano (city) Collin County	240	0.11
Dallas (city) Dallas County	202	0.02
Bedford (city) Tarrant County	165	0.35
Austin (city) Travis County	92	0.01
North Richland Hills (city) Tarrant County	84	0.15
Garland (city) Dallas County	77	0.04
Flower Mound (town) Denton County	63	0.12
Grapevine (city) Tarrant County	52	0.12

Top 10 Places Sorted by Percent
Based on all places, regardless of population

Place	Number	%
Melissa (city) Collin County	11	0.85
West Lake Hills (city) Travis County	24	0.77
Dalworthington Gardens (city) Tarrant County	12	0.54
Bacliff (cdp) Galveston County	29	0.41
Bedford (city) Tarrant County	165	0.35
Murphy (city) Collin County	11	0.35
Hedwig Village (city) Harris County	8	0.34
Lakeside City (town) Archer County	3	0.31
Dickinson (city) Galveston County	36	0.21
Terrell (city) Kaufman County	28	0.21

Top 10 Places Sorted by Percent
Based on places with populations of 10,000 or more

Place	Number	%
Bedford (city) Tarrant County	165	0.35
Dickinson (city) Galveston County	36	0.21
Terrell (city) Kaufman County	28	0.21
Keller (city) Tarrant County	47	0.17
North Richland Hills (city) Tarrant County	84	0.15
Waxahachie (city) Ellis County	32	0.15
Flower Mound (town) Denton County	63	0.12
Grapevine (city) Tarrant County	52	0.12
Plano (city) Collin County	240	0.11
Southlake (city) Tarrant County	24	0.11

Alsatian

Top 10 Places Sorted by Number
Based on all places, regardless of population

Place	Number	%
San Antonio (city) Bexar County	482	0.04
Houston (city) Harris County	193	0.01
Castroville (city) Medina County	168	6.29

Place	Number	%
Dallas (city) Dallas County	125	0.01
La Coste (city) Medina County	92	7.32
Austin (city) Travis County	87	0.01
Devine (city) Medina County	71	1.65
Kingsbury (cdp) Guadalupe County	60	9.65
El Paso (city) El Paso County	56	0.01
Kerrville (city) Kerr County	39	0.19

Top 10 Places Sorted by Percent
Based on all places, regardless of population

Place	Number	%
Kingsbury (cdp) Guadalupe County	60	9.65
La Coste (city) Medina County	92	7.32
Castroville (city) Medina County	168	6.29
Devine (city) Medina County	71	1.65
Moore (cdp) Frio County	7	0.92
Hollywood Park (town) Bexar County	15	0.58
Lakehills (cdp) Bandera County	19	0.43
El Lago (city) Harris County	12	0.36
Castle Hills (city) Bexar County	14	0.33
Lytle (city) Atascosa County	7	0.29

Top 10 Places Sorted by Percent
Based on places with populations of 10,000 or more

Place	Number	%
Kerrville (city) Kerr County	39	0.19
Brushy Creek (cdp) Williamson County	25	0.16
Wells Branch (cdp) Travis County	10	0.09
Bay City (city) Matagorda County	14	0.08
San Marcos (city) Hays County	24	0.07
Cedar Park (city) Williamson County	16	0.06
West University Place (city) Harris County	8	0.06
Benbrook (city) Tarrant County	10	0.05
Universal City (city) Bexar County	8	0.05
San Antonio (city) Bexar County	482	0.04

American Indian tribes, specified

Top 10 Places Sorted by Number
Based on all places, regardless of population

Place	Number	%
Houston (city) Harris County	7,618	0.39
San Antonio (city) Bexar County	6,814	0.60
Dallas (city) Dallas County	6,578	0.55
Austin (city) Travis County	4,148	0.63
Fort Worth (city) Tarrant County	3,553	0.66
El Paso (city) El Paso County	3,279	0.58
Arlington (city) Tarrant County	2,641	0.79
Corpus Christi (city) Nueces County	1,749	0.63
Amarillo (city) Potter County	1,674	0.96
Garland (city) Dallas County	1,653	0.77

Top 10 Places Sorted by Percent
Based on all places, regardless of population

Place	Number	%
Quail (cdp) Collingsworth County	7	21.21
Rosita South (cdp) Maverick County	394	15.31
Lipscomb (cdp) Lipscomb County	4	9.09
Elbert (cdp) Throckmorton County	4	7.14
Aquilla (city) Hill County	9	6.62
Rocky Mound (town) Camp County	6	6.45
Rosser (village) Kaufman County	24	6.33
Southmayd (city) Grayson County	54	5.44
Bausell and Ellis (cdp) Willacy County	6	5.36
Pyote (town) Ward County	6	4.58

Top 10 Places Sorted by Percent
Based on places with populations of 10,000 or more

Place	Number	%
Denison (city) Grayson County	623	2.74
Pampa (city) Gray County	352	1.97
Borger (city) Hutchinson County	273	1.91

Place	Number	%
Sherman (city) Grayson County	625	1.78
Burkburnett (city) Wichita County	179	1.64
Fort Hood (cdp) Coryell County	471	1.40
White Settlement (city) Tarrant County	206	1.39
Paris (city) Lamar County	355	1.37
Gainesville (city) Cooke County	207	1.33
Copperas Cove (city) Coryell County	385	1.30

American Indian: Apache

Top 10 Places Sorted by Number
Based on all places, regardless of population

Place	Number	%
San Antonio (city) Bexar County	590	0.05
Houston (city) Harris County	297	0.02
El Paso (city) El Paso County	285	0.05
Austin (city) Travis County	219	0.03
Dallas (city) Dallas County	192	0.02
Corpus Christi (city) Nueces County	162	0.06
Fort Worth (city) Tarrant County	162	0.03
Arlington (city) Tarrant County	134	0.04
Amarillo (city) Potter County	108	0.06
Lubbock (city) Lubbock County	107	0.05

Top 10 Places Sorted by Percent
Based on all places, regardless of population

Place	Number	%
Quail (cdp) Collingsworth County	1	3.03
Valentine (town) Jeff Davis County	3	1.60
Darrouzett (town) Lipscomb County	3	0.99
Del Sol-Loma Linda (cdp) San Patricio County	7	0.96
Sandia (cdp) Jim Wells County	4	0.93
North Pearsall (cdp) Frio County	5	0.89
Weir (city) Williamson County	5	0.85
Callisburg (city) Cooke County	3	0.82
Mustang Ridge (city) Caldwell County	6	0.76
Pyote (town) Ward County	1	0.76

Top 10 Places Sorted by Percent
Based on places with populations of 10,000 or more

Place	Number	%
San Elizario (cdp) El Paso County	22	0.20
Fort Hood (cdp) Coryell County	40	0.12
Pampa (city) Gray County	21	0.12
Plainview (city) Hale County	24	0.11
Harker Heights (city) Bell County	16	0.09
Port Lavaca (city) Calhoun County	11	0.09
Kerrville (city) Kerr County	16	0.08
Killeen (city) Bell County	62	0.07
Brownwood (city) Brown County	14	0.07
West Odessa (cdp) Ector County	13	0.07

American Indian: Blackfeet

Top 10 Places Sorted by Number
Based on all places, regardless of population

Place	Number	%
Houston (city) Harris County	170	0.01
San Antonio (city) Bexar County	148	0.01
Dallas (city) Dallas County	127	0.01
Austin (city) Travis County	108	0.02
Fort Worth (city) Tarrant County	77	0.01
Arlington (city) Tarrant County	74	0.02
El Paso (city) El Paso County	48	0.01
Killeen (city) Bell County	47	0.05
Corpus Christi (city) Nueces County	40	0.01
Amarillo (city) Potter County	37	0.02

Top 10 Places Sorted by Percent
Based on all places, regardless of population

Place	Number	%
Mount Calm (city) Hill County	3	0.97

Notes: (cdp) census designated place; Refer to the User's Guide in the front of the book for more detailed information.

Stagecoach (town) Montgomery County	4	0.88
Evant (town) Coryell County	3	0.76
Bellevue (city) Clay County	2	0.52
Lometa (city) Lampasas County	4	0.51
Groveton (city) Trinity County	5	0.45
Oak Ridge (town) Cooke County	1	0.45
Southmayd (city) Grayson County	4	0.40
Tira (town) Hopkins County	1	0.40
Splendora (city) Montgomery County	5	0.39

Top 10 Places Sorted by Percent
Based on places with populations of 10,000 or more

Place	Number	%
Pampa (city) Gray County	18	0.10
Harker Heights (city) Bell County	13	0.08
Fort Hood (cdp) Coryell County	24	0.07
Copperas Cove (city) Coryell County	21	0.07
Katy (city) Harris County	8	0.07
Killeen (city) Bell County	47	0.05
Canyon Lake (cdp) Comal County	8	0.05
Pflugerville (city) Travis County	8	0.05
Stafford (city) Fort Bend County	8	0.05
Humble (city) Harris County	7	0.05

American Indian: Cherokee

Top 10 Places Sorted by Number
Based on all places, regardless of population

Place	Number	%
Houston (city) Harris County	2,159	0.11
San Antonio (city) Bexar County	1,963	0.17
Dallas (city) Dallas County	1,889	0.16
Austin (city) Travis County	1,429	0.22
Fort Worth (city) Tarrant County	1,214	0.23
Arlington (city) Tarrant County	1,042	0.31
Corpus Christi (city) Nueces County	578	0.21
Amarillo (city) Potter County	557	0.32
Garland (city) Dallas County	557	0.26
El Paso (city) El Paso County	464	0.08

Top 10 Places Sorted by Percent
Based on all places, regardless of population

Place	Number	%
Lipscomb (cdp) Lipscomb County	3	6.82
Westdale (cdp) Jim Wells County	7	2.37
Bailey (city) Fannin County	5	2.35
Chireno (city) Nacogdoches County	9	2.22
South Fork Estates (cdp) Jim Hogg County	1	2.13
Cranfills Gap (city) Bosque County	7	2.09
Morgan (city) Bosque County	10	2.06
Rose City (city) Orange County	10	1.93
Trent (town) Taylor County	6	1.89
Lavon (town) Collin County	7	1.81

Top 10 Places Sorted by Percent
Based on places with populations of 10,000 or more

Place	Number	%
Pampa (city) Gray County	160	0.89
Borger (city) Hutchinson County	125	0.87
Denison (city) Grayson County	185	0.81
White Settlement (city) Tarrant County	87	0.59
Copperas Cove (city) Coryell County	153	0.52
Burkburnett (city) Wichita County	55	0.50
Sherman (city) Grayson County	172	0.49
Saginaw (city) Tarrant County	58	0.47
Gainesville (city) Cooke County	71	0.46
Wylie (city) Collin County	68	0.45

American Indian: Cheyenne

Top 10 Places Sorted by Number
Based on all places, regardless of population

Place	Number	%
Dallas (city) Dallas County	43	0.00
El Paso (city) El Paso County	35	0.01
San Antonio (city) Bexar County	32	0.00
Houston (city) Harris County	22	0.00
Fort Worth (city) Tarrant County	17	0.00
Austin (city) Travis County	15	0.00
Amarillo (city) Potter County	11	0.01
Irving (city) Dallas County	11	0.01
Lubbock (city) Lubbock County	11	0.01
Garland (city) Dallas County	10	0.00

Top 10 Places Sorted by Percent
Based on all places, regardless of population

Place	Number	%
Dodd City (town) Fannin County	3	0.72
Opdyke West (town) Hockley County	1	0.53
Redwater (city) Bowie County	4	0.46
Mountain City (city) Hays County	2	0.30
Cranfills Gap (city) Bosque County	1	0.30
Dickens (city) Dickens County	1	0.30
Shamrock (city) Wheeler County	4	0.20
Tolar (city) Hood County	1	0.20
Point Blank (city) San Jacinto County	1	0.18
Seven Points (city) Henderson County	2	0.17

Top 10 Places Sorted by Percent
Based on places with populations of 10,000 or more

Place	Number	%
Port Lavaca (city) Calhoun County	4	0.03
Cedar Park (city) Williamson County	6	0.02
Kerrville (city) Kerr County	4	0.02
Pampa (city) Gray County	4	0.02
The Colony (city) Denton County	4	0.02
Dumas (city) Moore County	3	0.02
Mineral Wells (city) Palo Pinto County	3	0.02
Sulphur Springs (city) Hopkins County	3	0.02
Vidor (city) Orange County	2	0.02
El Paso (city) El Paso County	35	0.01

American Indian: Chickasaw

Top 10 Places Sorted by Number
Based on all places, regardless of population

Place	Number	%
Dallas (city) Dallas County	236	0.02
Houston (city) Harris County	134	0.01
Fort Worth (city) Tarrant County	123	0.02
San Antonio (city) Bexar County	102	0.01
Garland (city) Dallas County	85	0.04
Arlington (city) Tarrant County	83	0.02
Wichita Falls (city) Wichita County	81	0.08
Irving (city) Dallas County	79	0.04
Austin (city) Travis County	75	0.01
Denison (city) Grayson County	71	0.31

Top 10 Places Sorted by Percent
Based on all places, regardless of population

Place	Number	%
Rocky Mound (town) Camp County	3	3.23
Rosser (village) Kaufman County	5	1.32
Bellevue (city) Clay County	4	1.04
Texline (town) Dallam County	5	0.98
Byers (city) Clay County	5	0.97
Sunset (city) Montague County	3	0.88
Windthorst (town) Archer County	3	0.68
Bee Cave (village) Travis County	4	0.61
Kempner (city) Lampasas County	6	0.60

Southmayd (city) Grayson County	6	0.60

Top 10 Places Sorted by Percent
Based on places with populations of 10,000 or more

Place	Number	%
Denison (city) Grayson County	71	0.31
Burkburnett (city) Wichita County	32	0.29
Gainesville (city) Cooke County	39	0.25
Sherman (city) Grayson County	57	0.16
Wylie (city) Collin County	16	0.11
Mineral Wells (city) Palo Pinto County	16	0.09
Pampa (city) Gray County	16	0.09
Borger (city) Hutchinson County	13	0.09
Wichita Falls (city) Wichita County	81	0.08
The Colony (city) Denton County	20	0.08

American Indian: Chippewa

Top 10 Places Sorted by Number
Based on all places, regardless of population

Place	Number	%
San Antonio (city) Bexar County	111	0.01
Houston (city) Harris County	88	0.00
Austin (city) Travis County	63	0.01
Fort Worth (city) Tarrant County	61	0.01
Dallas (city) Dallas County	55	0.00
Corpus Christi (city) Nueces County	44	0.02
Arlington (city) Tarrant County	37	0.01
Plano (city) Collin County	31	0.01
Killeen (city) Bell County	30	0.01
Lubbock (city) Lubbock County	28	0.01

Top 10 Places Sorted by Percent
Based on all places, regardless of population

Place	Number	%
Payne Springs (town) Henderson County	4	0.59
Florence (city) Williamson County	3	0.28
Bartlett (city) Williamson County	4	0.24
Thorntonville (town) Ward County	1	0.23
Gholson (city) McLennan County	2	0.22
Bangs (city) Brown County	3	0.19
Earth (city) Lamb County	2	0.18
Edgewood (town) Van Zandt County	2	0.15
Hico (city) Hamilton County	2	0.15
Bee Cave (village) Travis County	1	0.15

Top 10 Places Sorted by Percent
Based on places with populations of 10,000 or more

Place	Number	%
Universal City (city) Bexar County	13	0.09
Harker Heights (city) Bell County	8	0.05
Cedar Hill (city) Dallas County	13	0.04
Waxahachie (city) Ellis County	9	0.04
Converse (city) Bexar County	5	0.04
Henderson (city) Rusk County	4	0.04
Killeen (city) Bell County	30	0.03
Wichita Falls (city) Wichita County	27	0.03
Kingsville (city) Kleberg County	7	0.03
Alvin (city) Brazoria County	6	0.03

American Indian: Choctaw

Top 10 Places Sorted by Number
Based on all places, regardless of population

Place	Number	%
Dallas (city) Dallas County	1,112	0.09
Houston (city) Harris County	662	0.03
Fort Worth (city) Tarrant County	470	0.09
San Antonio (city) Bexar County	411	0.04
Arlington (city) Tarrant County	390	0.12
Austin (city) Travis County	366	0.06
Garland (city) Dallas County	324	0.15

Notes: (cdp) census designated place; Refer to the User's Guide in the front of the book for more detailed information.

Place	Number	%
Amarillo (city) Potter County	283	0.16
Wichita Falls (city) Wichita County	281	0.27
Denison (city) Grayson County	275	1.21

Top 10 Places Sorted by Percent
Based on all places, regardless of population

Place	Number	%
Quail (cdp) Collingsworth County	6	18.18
Rosser (village) Kaufman County	12	3.17
Southmayd (city) Grayson County	24	2.42
Deport (city) Lamar County	17	2.37
Pyote (town) Ward County	3	2.29
Leona (city) Leon County	4	2.21
Mustang (town) Navarro County	1	2.13
Elbert (cdp) Throckmorton County	1	1.79
Byers (city) Clay County	9	1.74
Bryson (city) Jack County	9	1.70

Top 10 Places Sorted by Percent
Based on places with populations of 10,000 or more

Place	Number	%
Denison (city) Grayson County	275	1.21
Paris (city) Lamar County	212	0.82
Sherman (city) Grayson County	255	0.73
Burkburnett (city) Wichita County	49	0.45
Balch Springs (city) Dallas County	68	0.35
Borger (city) Hutchinson County	47	0.33
The Colony (city) Denton County	81	0.31
White Settlement (city) Tarrant County	43	0.29
Wylie (city) Collin County	43	0.28
Wichita Falls (city) Wichita County	281	0.27

American Indian: Colville

Top 10 Places Sorted by Number
Based on all places, regardless of population

Place	Number	%
Lake Jackson (city) Brazoria County	3	0.01
Waco (city) McLennan County	3	0.00
Smithville (city) Bastrop County	2	0.05
Austin (city) Travis County	2	0.00
Dallas (city) Dallas County	2	0.00
El Paso (city) El Paso County	2	0.00
Garland (city) Dallas County	2	0.00
North Richland Hills (city) Tarrant County	2	0.00
Plano (city) Collin County	2	0.00
Stinnett (city) Hutchinson County	1	0.05

Top 10 Places Sorted by Percent
Based on all places, regardless of population

Place	Number	%
Smithville (city) Bastrop County	2	0.05
Stinnett (city) Hutchinson County	1	0.05
Windcrest (city) Bexar County	1	0.02
Lake Jackson (city) Brazoria County	3	0.01
Waco (city) McLennan County	3	0.00
Austin (city) Travis County	2	0.00
Dallas (city) Dallas County	2	0.00
El Paso (city) El Paso County	2	0.00
Garland (city) Dallas County	2	0.00
North Richland Hills (city) Tarrant County	2	0.00

Top 10 Places Sorted by Percent
Based on places with populations of 10,000 or more

Place	Number	%
Lake Jackson (city) Brazoria County	3	0.01
Waco (city) McLennan County	3	0.00
Austin (city) Travis County	2	0.00
Dallas (city) Dallas County	2	0.00
El Paso (city) El Paso County	2	0.00
Garland (city) Dallas County	2	0.00
North Richland Hills (city) Tarrant County	2	0.00

Place	Number	%
Plano (city) Collin County	2	0.00
Arlington (city) Tarrant County	1	0.00
Duncanville (city) Dallas County	1	0.00

American Indian: Comanche

Top 10 Places Sorted by Number
Based on all places, regardless of population

Place	Number	%
Fort Worth (city) Tarrant County	150	0.03
Dallas (city) Dallas County	144	0.01
San Antonio (city) Bexar County	140	0.01
Houston (city) Harris County	120	0.01
Austin (city) Travis County	112	0.02
Arlington (city) Tarrant County	84	0.03
Amarillo (city) Potter County	64	0.04
Wichita Falls (city) Wichita County	61	0.06
Corpus Christi (city) Nueces County	51	0.02
Irving (city) Dallas County	49	0.03

Top 10 Places Sorted by Percent
Based on all places, regardless of population

Place	Number	%
Aquilla (city) Hill County	7	5.15
Toco (city) Lamar County	1	1.12
Uncertain (city) Harrison County	1	0.67
Tolar (city) Hood County	3	0.60
Morgan's Point (city) Harris County	2	0.60
Nazareth (city) Castro County	2	0.56
Westbrook (city) Mitchell County	1	0.49
Fruitvale (city) Van Zandt County	2	0.48
Kosse (town) Limestone County	2	0.40
Pernitas Point (village) Live Oak County	1	0.37

Top 10 Places Sorted by Percent
Based on places with populations of 10,000 or more

Place	Number	%
Denison (city) Grayson County	15	0.07
Converse (city) Bexar County	8	0.07
Wichita Falls (city) Wichita County	61	0.06
Hurst (city) Tarrant County	21	0.06
Mineral Wells (city) Palo Pinto County	11	0.06
Pampa (city) Gray County	11	0.06
White Settlement (city) Tarrant County	9	0.06
Bedford (city) Tarrant County	22	0.05
Big Spring (city) Howard County	13	0.05
Kerrville (city) Kerr County	10	0.05

American Indian: Cree

Top 10 Places Sorted by Number
Based on all places, regardless of population

Place	Number	%
Houston (city) Harris County	20	0.00
Austin (city) Travis County	16	0.00
San Antonio (city) Bexar County	14	0.00
Plano (city) Collin County	8	0.00
Pampa (city) Gray County	5	0.03
McKinney (city) Collin County	5	0.01
Dallas (city) Dallas County	5	0.00
Kerrville (city) Kerr County	4	0.02
Pharr (city) Hidalgo County	4	0.01
Denton (city) Denton County	4	0.00

Top 10 Places Sorted by Percent
Based on all places, regardless of population

Place	Number	%
Blessing (cdp) Matagorda County	2	0.23
Queen City (city) Cass County	3	0.19
Fulshear (city) Fort Bend County	1	0.14
Gholson (city) McLennan County	1	0.11
Blanco (city) Blanco County	1	0.07

Place	Number	%
Circle D-KC Estates (cdp) Bastrop County	1	0.05
McQueeney (cdp) Guadalupe County	1	0.04
Pampa (city) Gray County	5	0.03
Freer (city) Duval County	1	0.03
Jourdanton (city) Atascosa County	1	0.03

Top 10 Places Sorted by Percent
Based on places with populations of 10,000 or more

Place	Number	%
Pampa (city) Gray County	5	0.03
Kerrville (city) Kerr County	4	0.02
McKinney (city) Collin County	5	0.01
Pharr (city) Hidalgo County	4	0.01
Copperas Cove (city) Coryell County	3	0.01
Port Arthur (city) Jefferson County	3	0.01
Burleson (city) Johnson County	2	0.01
Ennis (city) Ellis County	2	0.01
Fort Hood (cdp) Coryell County	2	0.01
Hurst (city) Tarrant County	2	0.01

American Indian: Creek

Top 10 Places Sorted by Number
Based on all places, regardless of population

Place	Number	%
Dallas (city) Dallas County	248	0.02
Houston (city) Harris County	175	0.01
San Antonio (city) Bexar County	116	0.01
Arlington (city) Tarrant County	98	0.03
Austin (city) Travis County	89	0.01
Fort Worth (city) Tarrant County	78	0.01
Garland (city) Dallas County	63	0.03
Corpus Christi (city) Nueces County	63	0.02
Amarillo (city) Potter County	55	0.03
Irving (city) Dallas County	52	0.03

Top 10 Places Sorted by Percent
Based on all places, regardless of population

Place	Number	%
Reese Center (cdp) Lubbock County	1	2.38
Opdyke West (town) Hockley County	4	2.13
Petronila (city) Nueces County	1	1.20
Sundown (city) Hockley County	7	0.47
Meadow (town) Terry County	3	0.46
Point Comfort (city) Calhoun County	3	0.38
Latexo (city) Houston County	1	0.37
Lakeport (city) Gregg County	3	0.35
Doyle (cdp) San Patricio County	1	0.35
Nordheim (city) De Witt County	1	0.31

Top 10 Places Sorted by Percent
Based on places with populations of 10,000 or more

Place	Number	%
Keller (city) Tarrant County	21	0.08
Haltom City (city) Tarrant County	27	0.07
Highland Village (city) Denton County	8	0.07
Euless (city) Tarrant County	26	0.06
Allen (city) Collin County	24	0.06
Gainesville (city) Cooke County	9	0.06
Portland (city) San Patricio County	9	0.06
Corinth (city) Denton County	7	0.06
Vernon (city) Wilbarger County	7	0.06
Grapevine (city) Tarrant County	23	0.05

American Indian: Crow

Top 10 Places Sorted by Number
Based on all places, regardless of population

Place	Number	%
San Antonio (city) Bexar County	22	0.00
Houston (city) Harris County	12	0.00
Austin (city) Travis County	11	0.00

Notes: (cdp) census designated place; Refer to the User's Guide in the front of the book for more detailed information.

Place	Number	%
Dallas (city) Dallas County	11	0.00
Fort Worth (city) Tarrant County	11	0.00
Arlington (city) Tarrant County	6	0.00
Archer City (city) Archer County	4	0.22
Muleshoe (city) Bailey County	4	0.09
Abilene (city) Taylor County	4	0.00
Tyler (city) Smith County	4	0.00

Top 10 Places Sorted by Percent
Based on all places, regardless of population

Place	Number	%
Archer City (city) Archer County	4	0.22
Pineland (city) Sabine County	2	0.20
Lytle (city) Atascosa County	3	0.13
Mart (city) McLennan County	3	0.13
Walnut Springs (city) Bosque County	1	0.13
Willow Park (city) Parker County	3	0.11
Talty (city) Kaufman County	1	0.10
Muleshoe (city) Bailey County	4	0.09
Mabank (town) Kaufman County	2	0.09
Comfort (cdp) Kendall County	2	0.08

Top 10 Places Sorted by Percent
Based on places with populations of 10,000 or more

Place	Number	%
Corinth (city) Denton County	2	0.02
Cedar Hill (city) Dallas County	3	0.01
Pampa (city) Gray County	2	0.01
Texarkana (city) Bowie County	2	0.01
Addison (town) Dallas County	1	0.01
Dickinson (city) Galveston County	1	0.01
Gainesville (city) Cooke County	1	0.01
Gatesville (city) Coryell County	1	0.01
Hereford (city) Deaf Smith County	1	0.01
La Marque (city) Galveston County	1	0.01

American Indian: Delaware

Top 10 Places Sorted by Number
Based on all places, regardless of population

Place	Number	%
Dallas (city) Dallas County	35	0.00
Austin (city) Travis County	30	0.00
San Antonio (city) Bexar County	22	0.00
Houston (city) Harris County	21	0.00
Arlington (city) Tarrant County	17	0.01
Amarillo (city) Potter County	14	0.01
Fort Worth (city) Tarrant County	14	0.00
Corpus Christi (city) Nueces County	12	0.00
Garland (city) Dallas County	11	0.01
Borger (city) Hutchinson County	10	0.07

Top 10 Places Sorted by Percent
Based on all places, regardless of population

Place	Number	%
Bear Creek (village) Hays County	2	0.56
Groom (town) Carson County	2	0.34
Fritch (city) Hutchinson County	6	0.27
Pecan Acres (cdp) Wise County	5	0.22
Argyle (city) Denton County	5	0.21
Bells (town) Grayson County	2	0.17
Kress (city) Swisher County	1	0.12
Crowell (city) Foard County	1	0.09
Gladewater (city) Gregg County	5	0.08
Spring Valley (city) Harris County	3	0.08

Top 10 Places Sorted by Percent
Based on places with populations of 10,000 or more

Place	Number	%
Borger (city) Hutchinson County	10	0.07
Dickinson (city) Galveston County	7	0.04
Highland Village (city) Denton County	5	0.04

Place	Number	%
Belton (city) Bell County	4	0.03
Lake Jackson (city) Brazoria County	6	0.02
Sherman (city) Grayson County	6	0.02
Friendswood (city) Galveston County	5	0.02
Watauga (city) Tarrant County	5	0.02
Balch Springs (city) Dallas County	4	0.02
Cedar Park (city) Williamson County	4	0.02

American Indian: Houma

Top 10 Places Sorted by Number
Based on all places, regardless of population

Place	Number	%
Fort Worth (city) Tarrant County	18	0.00
Houston (city) Harris County	10	0.00
Dallas (city) Dallas County	9	0.00
Bridge City (city) Orange County	6	0.07
Plano (city) Collin County	5	0.00
Garrison (city) Nacogdoches County	4	0.47
Schulenburg (city) Fayette County	4	0.15
Temple (city) Bell County	4	0.01
Corpus Christi (city) Nueces County	4	0.01
Navarro (town) Navarro County	3	1.57

Top 10 Places Sorted by Percent
Based on all places, regardless of population

Place	Number	%
Navarro (town) Navarro County	3	1.57
Garrison (city) Nacogdoches County	4	0.47
Hemphill (city) Sabine County	2	0.18
Schulenburg (city) Fayette County	4	0.15
Brownsboro (city) Henderson County	1	0.13
Murphy (city) Collin County	3	0.10
Bridge City (city) Orange County	6	0.07
Bolivar Peninsula (cdp) Galveston County	2	0.05
Lake Worth (city) Tarrant County	2	0.04
West (city) McLennan County	1	0.04

Top 10 Places Sorted by Percent
Based on places with populations of 10,000 or more

Place	Number	%
Colleyville (city) Tarrant County	3	0.02
Temple (city) Bell County	4	0.01
Alvin (city) Brazoria County	3	0.01
Friendswood (city) Galveston County	3	0.01
Spring (cdp) Harris County	3	0.01
Texas City (city) Galveston County	3	0.01
Cedar Hill (city) Dallas County	2	0.01
Ennis (city) Ellis County	2	0.01
Haltom City (city) Tarrant County	2	0.01
Humble (city) Harris County	2	0.01

American Indian: Iroquois

Top 10 Places Sorted by Number
Based on all places, regardless of population

Place	Number	%
San Antonio (city) Bexar County	102	0.01
Houston (city) Harris County	97	0.00
Austin (city) Travis County	79	0.01
Dallas (city) Dallas County	54	0.00
Arlington (city) Tarrant County	46	0.01
Fort Worth (city) Tarrant County	40	0.01
El Paso (city) El Paso County	33	0.01
Corpus Christi (city) Nueces County	27	0.01
Plano (city) Collin County	25	0.01
Fort Hood (cdp) Coryell County	23	0.07

Top 10 Places Sorted by Percent
Based on all places, regardless of population

Place	Number	%
Falls City (city) Karnes County	3	0.51

Place	Number	%
Roxton (city) Lamar County	3	0.43
Silverton (city) Briscoe County	3	0.39
Savoy (city) Fannin County	3	0.35
Itasca (city) Hill County	5	0.33
Nolanville (city) Bell County	6	0.28
Spur (city) Dickens County	3	0.28
Rankin (city) Upton County	2	0.25
Timbercreek Canyon (village) Randall County	1	0.25
Double Oak (town) Denton County	5	0.23

Top 10 Places Sorted by Percent
Based on places with populations of 10,000 or more

Place	Number	%
Fort Hood (cdp) Coryell County	23	0.07
Portland (city) San Patricio County	8	0.05
Copperas Cove (city) Coryell County	12	0.04
Forest Hill (city) Tarrant County	5	0.04
Bedford (city) Tarrant County	12	0.03
Pearland (city) Brazoria County	10	0.03
Deer Park (city) Harris County	9	0.03
Channelview (cdp) Harris County	8	0.03
The Colony (city) Denton County	7	0.03
Balch Springs (city) Dallas County	5	0.03

American Indian: Kiowa

Top 10 Places Sorted by Number
Based on all places, regardless of population

Place	Number	%
Dallas (city) Dallas County	95	0.01
Fort Worth (city) Tarrant County	42	0.01
Arlington (city) Tarrant County	28	0.01
Grand Prairie (city) Dallas County	27	0.02
Wichita Falls (city) Wichita County	23	0.02
Irving (city) Dallas County	23	0.01
Denton (city) Denton County	17	0.02
Houston (city) Harris County	17	0.00
Lewisville (city) Denton County	15	0.02
Amarillo (city) Potter County	14	0.01

Top 10 Places Sorted by Percent
Based on all places, regardless of population

Place	Number	%
Tolar (city) Hood County	3	0.60
Thrall (city) Williamson County	3	0.42
Knippa (cdp) Uvalde County	3	0.41
Westworth Village (city) Tarrant County	6	0.28
Combine (city) Kaufman County	3	0.17
Niederwald (town) Hays County	1	0.17
Fritch (city) Hutchinson County	3	0.13
Berryville (town) Henderson County	1	0.11
Santa Clara (city) Guadalupe County	1	0.11
Saint Jo (city) Montague County	1	0.10

Top 10 Places Sorted by Percent
Based on places with populations of 10,000 or more

Place	Number	%
Burkburnett (city) Wichita County	10	0.09
Saginaw (city) Tarrant County	9	0.07
Copperas Cove (city) Coryell County	8	0.03
White Settlement (city) Tarrant County	4	0.03
Grand Prairie (city) Dallas County	27	0.02
Wichita Falls (city) Wichita County	23	0.02
Denton (city) Denton County	17	0.02
Lewisville (city) Denton County	15	0.02
De Soto (city) Dallas County	7	0.02
Haltom City (city) Tarrant County	7	0.02

Notes: (cdp) census designated place; Refer to the User's Guide in the front of the book for more detailed information.

American Indian: Latin American Indians

Top 10 Places Sorted by Number
Based on all places, regardless of population

Place	Number	%
Houston (city) Harris County	2,425	0.12
San Antonio (city) Bexar County	1,624	0.14
Dallas (city) Dallas County	1,219	0.10
Austin (city) Travis County	776	0.12
El Paso (city) El Paso County	670	0.12
Fort Worth (city) Tarrant County	545	0.10
Corpus Christi (city) Nueces County	282	0.10
Pasadena (city) Harris County	220	0.16
Brownsville (city) Cameron County	196	0.14
Laredo (city) Webb County	176	0.10

Top 10 Places Sorted by Percent
Based on all places, regardless of population

Place	Number	%
Bausell and Ellis (cdp) Willacy County	6	5.36
El Indio (cdp) Maverick County	5	1.90
Sandy Hollow-Escondidas (cdp) Nueces County	8	1.85
Ratamosa (cdp) Cameron County	4	1.83
Morgan (city) Bosque County	8	1.65
Evant (town) Coryell County	6	1.53
Lasana (cdp) Cameron County	2	1.48
Bixby (cdp) Cameron County	5	1.40
Manor (city) Travis County	14	1.16
Sandia (cdp) Jim Wells County	5	1.16

Top 10 Places Sorted by Percent
Based on places with populations of 10,000 or more

Place	Number	%
Humble (city) Harris County	34	0.23
South Houston (city) Harris County	35	0.22
West Odessa (cdp) Ector County	36	0.20
Richmond (city) Fort Bend County	22	0.20
Jacinto City (city) Harris County	21	0.20
San Juan (city) Hidalgo County	47	0.18
Stephenville (city) Erath County	27	0.18
Edinburg (city) Hidalgo County	82	0.17
Pasadena (city) Harris County	220	0.16
Port Arthur (city) Jefferson County	91	0.16

American Indian: Lumbee

Top 10 Places Sorted by Number
Based on all places, regardless of population

Place	Number	%
San Antonio (city) Bexar County	23	0.00
Houston (city) Harris County	20	0.00
Killeen (city) Bell County	16	0.02
Austin (city) Travis County	16	0.00
Wichita Falls (city) Wichita County	14	0.01
Fort Hood (cdp) Coryell County	13	0.04
El Paso (city) El Paso County	12	0.00
Palestine (city) Anderson County	11	0.06
Copperas Cove (city) Coryell County	10	0.03
Allen (city) Collin County	9	0.02

Top 10 Places Sorted by Percent
Based on all places, regardless of population

Place	Number	%
Thornton (town) Limestone County	2	0.38
Rose City (city) Orange County	1	0.19
Franklin (city) Robertson County	2	0.14
Buda (city) Hays County	3	0.12
Pearsall (city) Frio County	7	0.10
West Orange (city) Orange County	4	0.10
Westworth Village (city) Tarrant County	2	0.09
Florence (city) Williamson County	1	0.09
Moody (city) McLennan County	1	0.07

Place	Number	%
Patton Village (city) Montgomery County	1	0.07

Top 10 Places Sorted by Percent
Based on places with populations of 10,000 or more

Place	Number	%
Palestine (city) Anderson County	11	0.06
Fort Hood (cdp) Coryell County	13	0.04
Copperas Cove (city) Coryell County	10	0.03
Sulphur Springs (city) Hopkins County	4	0.03
Killeen (city) Bell County	16	0.02
Allen (city) Collin County	9	0.02
University Park (city) Dallas County	5	0.02
Schertz (city) Guadalupe County	4	0.02
Converse (city) Bexar County	2	0.02
Wichita Falls (city) Wichita County	14	0.01

American Indian: Menominee

Top 10 Places Sorted by Number
Based on all places, regardless of population

Place	Number	%
Austin (city) Travis County	9	0.00
Copperas Cove (city) Coryell County	5	0.02
Balch Springs (city) Dallas County	4	0.02
Haltom City (city) Tarrant County	4	0.01
San Antonio (city) Bexar County	4	0.00
Wake Village (city) Bowie County	3	0.06
Arlington (city) Tarrant County	3	0.00
Plains (town) Yoakum County	2	0.14
Vidor (city) Orange County	2	0.02
Canyon Lake (cdp) Comal County	2	0.01

Top 10 Places Sorted by Percent
Based on places with populations of 10,000 or more

Place	Number	%
Highland Haven (city) Burnet County	1	0.22
Plains (town) Yoakum County	2	0.14
Wake Village (city) Bowie County	3	0.06
Copperas Cove (city) Coryell County	5	0.02
Balch Springs (city) Dallas County	4	0.02
Vidor (city) Orange County	2	0.02
Keene (city) Johnson County	1	0.02
New Boston (city) Bowie County	1	0.02
Haltom City (city) Tarrant County	4	0.01
Canyon Lake (cdp) Comal County	2	0.01

Top 10 Places Sorted by Percent
Based on places with populations of 10,000 or more

Place	Number	%
Copperas Cove (city) Coryell County	5	0.02
Balch Springs (city) Dallas County	4	0.02
Vidor (city) Orange County	2	0.02
Haltom City (city) Tarrant County	4	0.01
Canyon Lake (cdp) Comal County	2	0.01
Fort Hood (cdp) Coryell County	2	0.01
Harker Heights (city) Bell County	1	0.01
Austin (city) Travis County	9	0.00
San Antonio (city) Bexar County	4	0.00
Arlington (city) Tarrant County	3	0.00

American Indian: Navajo

Top 10 Places Sorted by Number
Based on all places, regardless of population

Place	Number	%
San Antonio (city) Bexar County	191	0.02
Dallas (city) Dallas County	189	0.02
El Paso (city) El Paso County	131	0.02
Houston (city) Harris County	103	0.01
Austin (city) Travis County	88	0.01
Killeen (city) Bell County	72	0.08
Amarillo (city) Potter County	70	0.04

Place	Number	%
Arlington (city) Tarrant County	64	0.02
Fort Worth (city) Tarrant County	64	0.01
Irving (city) Dallas County	55	0.03

Top 10 Places Sorted by Percent
Based on all places, regardless of population

Place	Number	%
Toyah (town) Reeves County	2	2.00
Westdale (cdp) Jim Wells County	4	1.36
Sierra Blanca (cdp) Hudspeth County	7	1.31
Lindsay (cdp) Reeves County	3	0.76
Camp Wood (city) Real County	6	0.73
Sanderson (cdp) Terrell County	5	0.58
Big Wells (city) Dimmit County	4	0.57
Bonney (village) Brazoria County	2	0.52
New Deal (town) Lubbock County	3	0.42
Plains (town) Yoakum County	6	0.41

Top 10 Places Sorted by Percent
Based on places with populations of 10,000 or more

Place	Number	%
Fort Hood (cdp) Coryell County	42	0.12
Schertz (city) Guadalupe County	16	0.09
Killeen (city) Bell County	72	0.08
West Odessa (cdp) Ector County	12	0.07
Big Spring (city) Howard County	15	0.06
Plainview (city) Hale County	13	0.06
Pampa (city) Gray County	10	0.06
Copperas Cove (city) Coryell County	14	0.05
Waxahachie (city) Ellis County	11	0.05
Watauga (city) Tarrant County	10	0.05

American Indian: Osage

Top 10 Places Sorted by Number
Based on all places, regardless of population

Place	Number	%
Dallas (city) Dallas County	53	0.00
Houston (city) Harris County	51	0.00
Austin (city) Travis County	38	0.01
San Antonio (city) Bexar County	28	0.00
Arlington (city) Tarrant County	24	0.01
Plano (city) Collin County	23	0.01
Garland (city) Dallas County	20	0.01
Richardson (city) Dallas County	19	0.02
Irving (city) Dallas County	16	0.01
Fort Worth (city) Tarrant County	16	0.00

Top 10 Places Sorted by Percent
Based on all places, regardless of population

Place	Number	%
Hilshire Village (city) Harris County	3	0.42
Latexo (city) Houston County	1	0.37
Richland Springs (town) San Saba County	1	0.29
Blanket (town) Brown County	1	0.25
Wild Peach Village (cdp) Brazoria County	6	0.24
Howardwick (city) Donley County	1	0.23
Huntington (city) Angelina County	4	0.19
Hill Country Village (city) Bexar County	2	0.19
Pecan Acres (cdp) Wise County	4	0.17
Bullard (town) Smith County	2	0.17

Top 10 Places Sorted by Percent
Based on places with populations of 10,000 or more

Place	Number	%
Borger (city) Hutchinson County	6	0.04
Katy (city) Harris County	5	0.04
Bedford (city) Tarrant County	13	0.03
The Colony (city) Denton County	9	0.03
Canyon Lake (cdp) Comal County	5	0.03
Henderson (city) Rusk County	3	0.03
Wells Branch (cdp) Travis County	3	0.03

Notes: (cdp) census designated place; Refer to the User's Guide in the front of the book for more detailed information.

Place	Number	%
Richardson (city) Dallas County	19	0.02
Euless (city) Tarrant County	10	0.02
Flower Mound (town) Denton County	10	0.02

American Indian: Ottawa

Top 10 Places Sorted by Number
Based on all places, regardless of population

Place	Number	%
Houston (city) Harris County	15	0.00
Austin (city) Travis County	12	0.00
San Antonio (city) Bexar County	10	0.00
Pearland (city) Brazoria County	9	0.02
Dallas (city) Dallas County	8	0.00
El Paso (city) El Paso County	7	0.00
Hereford (city) Deaf Smith County	6	0.04
Angleton (city) Brazoria County	6	0.03
Spring (cdp) Harris County	6	0.02
Texas City (city) Galveston County	6	0.01

Top 10 Places Sorted by Percent
Based on all places, regardless of population

Place	Number	%
Blossom (city) Lamar County	3	0.21
Brookside Village (city) Brazoria County	4	0.20
Byers (city) Clay County	1	0.19
Pinehurst (city) Orange County	3	0.13
Yorktown (city) De Witt County	3	0.13
Buda (city) Hays County	3	0.12
Morgan's Point Resort (city) Bell County	3	0.10
Southmayd (city) Grayson County	1	0.10
Thorndale (city) Milam County	1	0.08
Hereford (city) Deaf Smith County	6	0.04

Top 10 Places Sorted by Percent
Based on places with populations of 10,000 or more

Place	Number	%
Hereford (city) Deaf Smith County	6	0.04
Clute (city) Brazoria County	4	0.04
Angleton (city) Brazoria County	6	0.03
Hewitt (city) McLennan County	3	0.03
Pearland (city) Brazoria County	9	0.02
Spring (cdp) Harris County	6	0.02
Canyon Lake (cdp) Comal County	4	0.02
White Settlement (city) Tarrant County	3	0.02
Texas City (city) Galveston County	6	0.01
Killeen (city) Bell County	5	0.01

American Indian: Paiute

Top 10 Places Sorted by Number
Based on all places, regardless of population

Place	Number	%
San Antonio (city) Bexar County	22	0.00
Austin (city) Travis County	11	0.00
Houston (city) Harris County	7	0.00
Galveston (city) Galveston County	6	0.01
Carrollton (city) Denton County	5	0.00
Orange (city) Orange County	4	0.02
Pampa (city) Gray County	4	0.02
Victoria (city) Victoria County	4	0.01
El Paso (city) El Paso County	4	0.00
Plano (city) Collin County	4	0.00

Top 10 Places Sorted by Percent
Based on all places, regardless of population

Place	Number	%
Lincoln Park (town) Denton County	2	0.39
Itasca (city) Hill County	2	0.13
Whitney (town) Hill County	2	0.11
Helotes (city) Bexar County	3	0.07
Winters (city) Runnels County	2	0.07

Place	Number	%
Brazoria (city) Brazoria County	1	0.04
Anderson Mill (cdp) Williamson County	3	0.03
Orange (city) Orange County	4	0.02
Pampa (city) Gray County	4	0.02
Harker Heights (city) Bell County	3	0.02

Top 10 Places Sorted by Percent
Based on places with populations of 10,000 or more

Place	Number	%
Orange (city) Orange County	4	0.02
Pampa (city) Gray County	4	0.02
Harker Heights (city) Bell County	3	0.02
Galveston (city) Galveston County	6	0.01
Victoria (city) Victoria County	4	0.01
Fort Hood (cdp) Coryell County	2	0.01
Alamo (city) Hidalgo County	1	0.01
Burkburnett (city) Wichita County	1	0.01
Gainesville (city) Cooke County	1	0.01
San Antonio (city) Bexar County	22	0.00

American Indian: Pima

Top 10 Places Sorted by Number
Based on all places, regardless of population

Place	Number	%
San Antonio (city) Bexar County	11	0.00
Corpus Christi (city) Nueces County	9	0.00
Irving (city) Dallas County	8	0.00
Houston (city) Harris County	7	0.00
Austin (city) Travis County	5	0.00
Plano (city) Collin County	5	0.00
Seminole (city) Gaines County	4	0.07
Amarillo (city) Potter County	4	0.00
San Angelo (city) Tom Green County	4	0.00
Olton (city) Lamb County	3	0.13

Top 10 Places Sorted by Percent
Based on all places, regardless of population

Place	Number	%
Olton (city) Lamb County	3	0.13
Aurora (town) Wise County	1	0.12
Abernathy (city) Hale County	3	0.11
Seminole (city) Gaines County	4	0.07
Quitman (city) Wood County	1	0.05
Waller (city) Waller County	1	0.05
Mount Vernon (town) Franklin County	1	0.04
Alpine (city) Brewster County	1	0.02
Elgin (city) Bastrop County	1	0.02
Euless (city) Tarrant County	3	0.01

Top 10 Places Sorted by Percent
Based on places with populations of 10,000 or more

Place	Number	%
Euless (city) Tarrant County	3	0.01
Weatherford (city) Parker County	2	0.01
Levelland (city) Hockley County	1	0.01
San Antonio (city) Bexar County	11	0.00
Corpus Christi (city) Nueces County	9	0.00
Irving (city) Dallas County	8	0.00
Houston (city) Harris County	7	0.00
Austin (city) Travis County	5	0.00
Plano (city) Collin County	5	0.00
Amarillo (city) Potter County	4	0.00

American Indian: Potawatomi

Top 10 Places Sorted by Number
Based on all places, regardless of population

Place	Number	%
Dallas (city) Dallas County	81	0.01
Fort Worth (city) Tarrant County	50	0.01
Houston (city) Harris County	45	0.00

Place	Number	%
San Antonio (city) Bexar County	42	0.00
Austin (city) Travis County	41	0.01
Plano (city) Collin County	28	0.01
Mesquite (city) Dallas County	25	0.02
Arlington (city) Tarrant County	25	0.01
San Angelo (city) Tom Green County	23	0.03
Lubbock (city) Lubbock County	23	0.01

Top 10 Places Sorted by Percent
Based on all places, regardless of population

Place	Number	%
Lipscomb (cdp) Lipscomb County	1	2.27
Follett (city) Lipscomb County	5	1.21
Higgins (city) Lipscomb County	5	1.18
Pyote (town) Ward County	1	0.76
Cross Timber (town) Johnson County	2	0.72
Newcastle (city) Young County	3	0.52
Rose Hill Acres (city) Hardin County	2	0.42
Skidmore (cdp) Bee County	3	0.30
Pecan Hill (city) Ellis County	2	0.30
Fritch (city) Hutchinson County	6	0.27

Top 10 Places Sorted by Percent
Based on places with populations of 10,000 or more

Place	Number	%
Weatherford (city) Parker County	11	0.06
Borger (city) Hutchinson County	9	0.06
Katy (city) Harris County	7	0.06
San Angelo (city) Tom Green County	23	0.03
Sherman (city) Grayson County	10	0.03
Angleton (city) Brazoria County	6	0.03
Burleson (city) Johnson County	6	0.03
Balch Springs (city) Dallas County	5	0.03
Gainesville (city) Cooke County	4	0.03
Mesquite (city) Dallas County	25	0.02

American Indian: Pueblo

Top 10 Places Sorted by Number
Based on all places, regardless of population

Place	Number	%
El Paso (city) El Paso County	910	0.16
Socorro (city) El Paso County	165	0.61
San Antonio (city) Bexar County	115	0.01
Houston (city) Harris County	83	0.00
Dallas (city) Dallas County	73	0.01
Austin (city) Travis County	46	0.01
Fort Worth (city) Tarrant County	39	0.01
Amarillo (city) Potter County	36	0.02
San Elizario (cdp) El Paso County	28	0.25
Garland (city) Dallas County	20	0.01

Top 10 Places Sorted by Percent
Based on all places, regardless of population

Place	Number	%
Smyer (town) Hockley County	3	0.63
Socorro (city) El Paso County	165	0.61
Garrett (town) Ellis County	2	0.45
Kendleton (city) Fort Bend County	2	0.43
Tira (town) Hopkins County	1	0.40
Roscoe (city) Nolan County	4	0.29
Grandfalls (town) Ward County	1	0.26
San Elizario (cdp) El Paso County	28	0.25
Devers (city) Liberty County	1	0.24
Grey Forest (city) Bexar County	1	0.24

Top 10 Places Sorted by Percent
Based on places with populations of 10,000 or more

Place	Number	%
Socorro (city) El Paso County	165	0.61
San Elizario (cdp) El Paso County	28	0.25
El Paso (city) El Paso County	910	0.16

Notes: (cdp) census designated place; Refer to the User's Guide in the front of the book for more detailed information.

Place	Number	%
Stephenville (city) Erath County	7	0.05
Copperas Cove (city) Coryell County	13	0.04
Haltom City (city) Tarrant County	10	0.03
Lancaster (city) Dallas County	8	0.03
Universal City (city) Bexar County	5	0.03
Borger (city) Hutchinson County	4	0.03
Corinth (city) Denton County	3	0.03

American Indian: Puget Sound Salish

Top 10 Places Sorted by Number
Based on all places, regardless of population

Place	Number	%
Corpus Christi (city) Nueces County	11	0.00
San Antonio (city) Bexar County	8	0.00
El Paso (city) El Paso County	4	0.00
Houston (city) Harris County	4	0.00
Copperas Cove (city) Coryell County	3	0.01
Euless (city) Tarrant County	3	0.01
Fort Hood (cdp) Coryell County	3	0.01
Dallas (city) Dallas County	3	0.00
Fort Worth (city) Tarrant County	3	0.00
Eidson Road (cdp) Maverick County	2	0.02

Top 10 Places Sorted by Percent
Based on all places, regardless of population

Place	Number	%
Thompsons (town) Fort Bend County	1	0.42
Itasca (city) Hill County	1	0.07
Eidson Road (cdp) Maverick County	2	0.02
Kirby (city) Bexar County	2	0.02
Fair Oaks Ranch (city) Bexar County	1	0.02
Lago Vista (city) Travis County	1	0.02
Copperas Cove (city) Coryell County	3	0.01
Euless (city) Tarrant County	3	0.01
Fort Hood (cdp) Coryell County	3	0.01
Cedar Park (city) Williamson County	2	0.01

Top 10 Places Sorted by Percent
Based on places with populations of 10,000 or more

Place	Number	%
Copperas Cove (city) Coryell County	3	0.01
Euless (city) Tarrant County	3	0.01
Fort Hood (cdp) Coryell County	3	0.01
Cedar Park (city) Williamson County	2	0.01
Haltom City (city) Tarrant County	2	0.01
Wylie (city) Collin County	1	0.01
Corpus Christi (city) Nueces County	11	0.00
San Antonio (city) Bexar County	8	0.00
El Paso (city) El Paso County	4	0.00
Houston (city) Harris County	4	0.00

American Indian: Seminole

Top 10 Places Sorted by Number
Based on all places, regardless of population

Place	Number	%
San Antonio (city) Bexar County	104	0.01
Dallas (city) Dallas County	79	0.01
Houston (city) Harris County	61	0.00
Fort Worth (city) Tarrant County	44	0.01
Arlington (city) Tarrant County	30	0.01
Austin (city) Travis County	30	0.00
Corpus Christi (city) Nueces County	24	0.01
Garland (city) Dallas County	23	0.01
Irving (city) Dallas County	21	0.01
Kerrville (city) Kerr County	19	0.09

Top 10 Places Sorted by Percent
Based on all places, regardless of population

Place	Number	%
Elbert (cdp) Throckmorton County	3	5.36

Place	Number	%
Rocky Mound (town) Camp County	3	3.23
Grandfalls (town) Ward County	3	0.77
Sanford (town) Hutchinson County	1	0.49
New Hope (town) Collin County	3	0.45
Stagecoach (town) Montgomery County	2	0.44
Hillcrest (village) Brazoria County	3	0.42
Study Butte-Terlingua (cdp) Brewster County	1	0.37
Rosser (village) Kaufman County	1	0.26
Glen Rose (city) Somervell County	5	0.24

Top 10 Places Sorted by Percent
Based on places with populations of 10,000 or more

Place	Number	%
Kerrville (city) Kerr County	19	0.09
Taylor (city) Williamson County	7	0.05
Universal City (city) Bexar County	7	0.05
Corinth (city) Denton County	6	0.05
Del Rio (city) Val Verde County	14	0.04
Forest Hill (city) Tarrant County	5	0.04
Cedar Park (city) Williamson County	7	0.03
Cleburne (city) Johnson County	7	0.03
Alice (city) Jim Wells County	6	0.03
Orange (city) Orange County	6	0.03

American Indian: Shoshone

Top 10 Places Sorted by Number
Based on all places, regardless of population

Place	Number	%
Dallas (city) Dallas County	13	0.00
Houston (city) Harris County	13	0.00
San Antonio (city) Bexar County	12	0.00
Austin (city) Travis County	10	0.00
Fort Worth (city) Tarrant County	10	0.00
Atascocita (cdp) Harris County	8	0.02
Garland (city) Dallas County	7	0.00
Richardson (city) Dallas County	6	0.01
Arlington (city) Tarrant County	6	0.00
San Angelo (city) Tom Green County	5	0.01

Top 10 Places Sorted by Percent
Based on all places, regardless of population

Place	Number	%
Stagecoach (town) Montgomery County	4	0.88
Northlake (town) Denton County	1	0.11
Ganado (city) Jackson County	2	0.10
Onalaska (city) Polk County	1	0.09
Groesbeck (city) Limestone County	3	0.07
Cesar Chavez (cdp) Hidalgo County	1	0.07
Lumberton (city) Hardin County	4	0.05
Coleman (city) Coleman County	2	0.04
Comfort (cdp) Kendall County	1	0.04
Junction (city) Kimble County	1	0.04

Top 10 Places Sorted by Percent
Based on places with populations of 10,000 or more

Place	Number	%
Atascocita (cdp) Harris County	8	0.02
Mount Pleasant (city) Titus County	3	0.02
Richardson (city) Dallas County	6	0.01
San Angelo (city) Tom Green County	5	0.01
Baytown (city) Harris County	4	0.01
New Braunfels (city) Comal County	3	0.01
Alvin (city) Brazoria County	2	0.01
Brushy Creek (cdp) Williamson County	2	0.01
Cleburne (city) Johnson County	2	0.01
Denison (city) Grayson County	2	0.01

American Indian: Sioux

Top 10 Places Sorted by Number
Based on all places, regardless of population

Place	Number	%
San Antonio (city) Bexar County	203	0.02
Houston (city) Harris County	169	0.01
Dallas (city) Dallas County	168	0.01
Austin (city) Travis County	107	0.02
El Paso (city) El Paso County	90	0.02
Fort Worth (city) Tarrant County	84	0.02
Corpus Christi (city) Nueces County	73	0.03
Arlington (city) Tarrant County	66	0.02
Amarillo (city) Potter County	42	0.02
Grand Prairie (city) Dallas County	38	0.03

Top 10 Places Sorted by Percent
Based on all places, regardless of population

Place	Number	%
Chireno (city) Nacogdoches County	4	0.99
Stagecoach (town) Montgomery County	3	0.66
Hartley (cdp) Hartley County	2	0.45
North Cleveland (city) Liberty County	1	0.38
Robert Lee (city) Coke County	4	0.34
Venus (town) Johnson County	3	0.33
La Vernia (city) Wilson County	3	0.32
Southmayd (city) Grayson County	3	0.30
Bayside (town) Refugio County	1	0.28
Paducah (town) Cottle County	4	0.27

Top 10 Places Sorted by Percent
Based on places with populations of 10,000 or more

Place	Number	%
San Elizario (cdp) El Paso County	20	0.18
Converse (city) Bexar County	11	0.10
Fort Hood (cdp) Coryell County	29	0.09
Harker Heights (city) Bell County	15	0.09
Pampa (city) Gray County	14	0.08
Canyon (city) Randall County	9	0.07
Highland Village (city) Denton County	8	0.07
White Settlement (city) Tarrant County	9	0.06
Dumas (city) Moore County	8	0.06
Copperas Cove (city) Coryell County	14	0.05

American Indian: Tohono O'Odham

Top 10 Places Sorted by Number
Based on all places, regardless of population

Place	Number	%
El Paso (city) El Paso County	25	0.00
Dallas (city) Dallas County	17	0.00
San Antonio (city) Bexar County	15	0.00
Fort Worth (city) Tarrant County	7	0.00
Midland (city) Midland County	6	0.01
Bryan (city) Brazos County	5	0.01
Plano (city) Collin County	5	0.00
Fort Stockton (city) Pecos County	4	0.05
Pearland (city) Brazoria County	4	0.01
Texarkana (city) Bowie County	4	0.01

Top 10 Places Sorted by Percent
Based on all places, regardless of population

Place	Number	%
Aurora (town) Wise County	1	0.12
Fort Stockton (city) Pecos County	4	0.05
Camp Swift (cdp) Bastrop County	1	0.02
Lake Dallas (city) Denton County	1	0.02
Midland (city) Midland County	6	0.01
Bryan (city) Brazos County	5	0.01
Pearland (city) Brazoria County	4	0.01
Texarkana (city) Bowie County	4	0.01
Fort Hood (cdp) Coryell County	3	0.01

Notes: (cdp) census designated place; Refer to the User's Guide in the front of the book for more detailed information.

Corsicana (city) Navarro County · · · · · · · · 2 · · 0.01

Top 10 Places Sorted by Percent
Based on places with populations of 10,000 or more

Place	Number	%
Midland (city) Midland County	6	0.01
Bryan (city) Brazos County	5	0.01
Pearland (city) Brazoria County	4	0.01
Texarkana (city) Bowie County	4	0.01
Fort Hood (cdp) Coryell County	3	0.01
Corsicana (city) Navarro County	2	0.01
Beeville (city) Bee County	1	0.01
Pecan Grove (cdp) Fort Bend County	1	0.01
Vidor (city) Orange County	1	0.01
El Paso (city) El Paso County	25	0.00

American Indian: Ute

Top 10 Places Sorted by Number
Based on all places, regardless of population

Place	Number	%
Austin (city) Travis County	12	0.00
Sulphur Springs (city) Hopkins County	8	0.05
Midland (city) Midland County	7	0.01
San Angelo (city) Tom Green County	7	0.01
San Antonio (city) Bexar County	7	0.00
Abilene (city) Taylor County	6	0.01
Fort Worth (city) Tarrant County	6	0.00
Houston (city) Harris County	6	0.00
El Paso (city) El Paso County	5	0.00
Splendora (city) Montgomery County	4	0.31

Top 10 Places Sorted by Percent
Based on all places, regardless of population

Place	Number	%
Angus (city) Navarro County	2	0.60
Splendora (city) Montgomery County	4	0.31
Sadler (city) Grayson County	1	0.25
Tool (city) Henderson County	3	0.13
Bangs (city) Brown County	2	0.12
Little River-Academy (city) Bell County	1	0.06
Sulphur Springs (city) Hopkins County	8	0.05
Monahans (city) Ward County	3	0.04
Gun Barrel City (town) Henderson County	2	0.04
Odem (city) San Patricio County	1	0.04

Top 10 Places Sorted by Percent
Based on places with populations of 10,000 or more

Place	Number	%
Sulphur Springs (city) Hopkins County	8	0.05
Brushy Creek (cdp) Williamson County	3	0.02
Midland (city) Midland County	7	0.01
San Angelo (city) Tom Green County	7	0.01
Abilene (city) Taylor County	6	0.01
Fort Hood (cdp) Coryell County	3	0.01
La Porte (city) Harris County	3	0.01
San Marcos (city) Hays County	3	0.01
Waxahachie (city) Ellis County	3	0.01
Belton (city) Bell County	2	0.01

American Indian: Yakama

Top 10 Places Sorted by Number
Based on all places, regardless of population

Place	Number	%
Dallas (city) Dallas County	5	0.00
Flower Mound (town) Denton County	4	0.01
Houston (city) Harris County	4	0.00
Arlington (city) Tarrant County	2	0.00
Austin (city) Travis County	2	0.00
El Paso (city) El Paso County	2	0.00
Odessa (city) Ector County	2	0.00

West Lake Hills (city) Travis County · · · 1 · · 0.03
Bowie (city) Montague County · · · · · · · · · 1 · · 0.02
Nassau Bay (city) Harris County · · · · · · · 1 · · 0.02

Top 10 Places Sorted by Percent
Based on all places, regardless of population

Place	Number	%
West Lake Hills (city) Travis County	1	0.03
Bowie (city) Montague County	1	0.02
Nassau Bay (city) Harris County	1	0.02
Flower Mound (town) Denton County	4	0.01
Canyon (city) Randall County	1	0.01
Terrell (city) Kaufman County	1	0.01
Dallas (city) Dallas County	5	0.00
Houston (city) Harris County	4	0.00
Arlington (city) Tarrant County	2	0.00
Austin (city) Travis County	2	0.00

Top 10 Places Sorted by Percent
Based on places with populations of 10,000 or more

Place	Number	%
Flower Mound (town) Denton County	4	0.01
Canyon (city) Randall County	1	0.01
Terrell (city) Kaufman County	1	0.01
Dallas (city) Dallas County	5	0.00
Houston (city) Harris County	4	0.00
Arlington (city) Tarrant County	2	0.00
Austin (city) Travis County	2	0.00
El Paso (city) El Paso County	2	0.00
Odessa (city) Ector County	2	0.00
Allen (city) Collin County	1	0.00

American Indian: Yaqui

Top 10 Places Sorted by Number
Based on all places, regardless of population

Place	Number	%
San Antonio (city) Bexar County	61	0.01
El Paso (city) El Paso County	48	0.01
Houston (city) Harris County	31	0.00
Austin (city) Travis County	26	0.00
Lubbock (city) Lubbock County	22	0.01
Corpus Christi (city) Nueces County	12	0.00
Victoria (city) Victoria County	8	0.01
Dallas (city) Dallas County	6	0.00
Grand Prairie (city) Dallas County	6	0.00
Pasadena (city) Harris County	6	0.00

Top 10 Places Sorted by Percent
Based on all places, regardless of population

Place	Number	%
Celina (town) Collin County	3	0.16
Olton (city) Lamb County	3	0.13
Anthony (town) El Paso County	3	0.08
Stockdale (city) Wilson County	1	0.07
Briar (cdp) Tarrant County	3	0.06
Gilmer (city) Upshur County	3	0.06
Marble Falls (city) Burnet County	3	0.06
Sealy (city) Austin County	3	0.06
Honey Grove (city) Fannin County	1	0.06
Little River-Academy (city) Bell County	1	0.06

Top 10 Places Sorted by Percent
Based on places with populations of 10,000 or more

Place	Number	%
Alvin (city) Brazoria County	4	0.02
Harker Heights (city) Bell County	4	0.02
Pflugerville (city) Travis County	4	0.02
Angleton (city) Brazoria County	3	0.02
San Antonio (city) Bexar County	61	0.01
El Paso (city) El Paso County	48	0.01
Lubbock (city) Lubbock County	22	0.01

Victoria (city) Victoria County · · · · · · 8 · · 0.01
Baytown (city) Harris County · · · · · · · · · 5 · · 0.01
Lewisville (city) Denton County · · · · · · · 5 · · 0.01

American Indian: Yuman

Top 10 Places Sorted by Number
Based on all places, regardless of population

Place	Number	%
Dallas (city) Dallas County	10	0.00
Houston (city) Harris County	10	0.00
Beaumont (city) Jefferson County	7	0.01
San Antonio (city) Bexar County	5	0.00
McGregor (city) McLennan County	4	0.08
Dickinson (city) Galveston County	4	0.02
Round Rock (city) Williamson County	3	0.00
Sanford (town) Hutchinson County	2	0.99
Deer Park (city) Harris County	2	0.01
San Marcos (city) Hays County	2	0.01

Top 10 Places Sorted by Percent
Based on all places, regardless of population

Place	Number	%
Sanford (town) Hutchinson County	2	0.99
New Summerfield (city) Cherokee County	1	0.10
McGregor (city) McLennan County	4	0.08
Dickinson (city) Galveston County	4	0.02
Everman (city) Tarrant County	1	0.02
Beaumont (city) Jefferson County	7	0.01
Deer Park (city) Harris County	2	0.01
San Marcos (city) Hays County	2	0.01
Bonham (city) Fannin County	1	0.01
Ennis (city) Ellis County	1	0.01

Top 10 Places Sorted by Percent
Based on places with populations of 10,000 or more

Place	Number	%
Dickinson (city) Galveston County	4	0.02
Beaumont (city) Jefferson County	7	0.01
Deer Park (city) Harris County	2	0.01
San Marcos (city) Hays County	2	0.01
Ennis (city) Ellis County	1	0.01
Jollyville (cdp) Williamson County	1	0.01
Dallas (city) Dallas County	10	0.00
Houston (city) Harris County	10	0.00
San Antonio (city) Bexar County	5	0.00
Round Rock (city) Williamson County	3	0.00

American Indian: All other tribes

Top 10 Places Sorted by Number
Based on all places, regardless of population

Place	Number	%
Houston (city) Harris County	555	0.03
San Antonio (city) Bexar County	543	0.05
Rosita South (cdp) Maverick County	392	15.23
Dallas (city) Dallas County	383	0.04
Austin (city) Travis County	285	0.04
El Paso (city) El Paso County	194	0.03
Fort Worth (city) Tarrant County	186	0.03
Arlington (city) Tarrant County	177	0.05
Killeen (city) Bell County	110	0.13
Irving (city) Dallas County	94	0.05

Top 10 Places Sorted by Percent
Based on all places, regardless of population

Place	Number	%
Rosita South (cdp) Maverick County	392	15.23
Bryson (city) Jack County	6	1.14
Mountain City (city) Hays County	7	1.04
Rosita North (cdp) Maverick County	31	0.91
Miami (city) Roberts County	5	0.85

Notes: (cdp) census designated place; Refer to the User's Guide in the front of the book for more detailed information.

Place	Number	%
Kirvin (town) Freestone County	1	0.82
Kosse (town) Limestone County	4	0.80
Bruni (cdp) Webb County	3	0.73
Cuney (town) Cherokee County	1	0.69
Skellytown (town) Carson County	4	0.66

Top 10 Places Sorted by Percent
Based on places with populations of 10,000 or more

Place	Number	%
Killeen (city) Bell County	110	0.13
Fort Hood (cdp) Coryell County	41	0.12
Converse (city) Bexar County	13	0.11
Saginaw (city) Tarrant County	13	0.11
Hurst (city) Tarrant County	36	0.10
Eagle Pass (city) Maverick County	23	0.10
Universal City (city) Bexar County	14	0.09
Wylie (city) Collin County	14	0.09
Corinth (city) Denton County	10	0.09
Flower Mound (town) Denton County	40	0.08

American Indian tribes, not specified

Top 10 Places Sorted by Number
Based on all places, regardless of population

Place	Number	%
San Antonio (city) Bexar County	1,664	0.15
Houston (city) Harris County	1,141	0.06
Dallas (city) Dallas County	797	0.07
Austin (city) Travis County	548	0.08
El Paso (city) El Paso County	462	0.08
Fort Worth (city) Tarrant County	331	0.06
Arlington (city) Tarrant County	244	0.07
Corpus Christi (city) Nueces County	215	0.08
Lubbock (city) Lubbock County	179	0.09
Amarillo (city) Potter County	176	0.10

Top 10 Places Sorted by Percent
Based on all places, regardless of population

Place	Number	%
Corral City (town) Denton County	6	6.74
Laguna Seca (cdp) Hidalgo County	8	3.19
Study Butte-Terlingua (cdp) Brewster County	6	2.25
New Falcon (cdp) Zapata County	4	2.17
Weir (city) Williamson County	11	1.86
Morgan (city) Bosque County	7	1.44
Doyle (cdp) San Patricio County	4	1.40
Lavon (town) Collin County	5	1.29
Nordheim (city) De Witt County	4	1.24
Goldsmith (city) Ector County	3	1.19

Top 10 Places Sorted by Percent
Based on places with populations of 10,000 or more

Place	Number	%
Bay City (city) Matagorda County	46	0.25
Levelland (city) Hockley County	30	0.23
Fort Hood (cdp) Coryell County	59	0.18
Del Rio (city) Val Verde County	54	0.16
San Benito (city) Cameron County	37	0.16
Plainview (city) Hale County	35	0.16
Hereford (city) Deaf Smith County	23	0.16
Sweetwater (city) Nolan County	18	0.16
San Antonio (city) Bexar County	1,664	0.15
Mission (city) Hidalgo County	69	0.15

Arab

Top 10 Places Sorted by Number
Based on all places, regardless of population

Place	Number	%
Houston (city) Harris County	11,322	0.58
Dallas (city) Dallas County	4,137	0.35
San Antonio (city) Bexar County	3,787	0.33

Place	Number	%
Austin (city) Travis County	3,177	0.48
Arlington (city) Tarrant County	2,741	0.82
El Paso (city) El Paso County	2,105	0.37
Plano (city) Collin County	1,777	0.80
Richardson (city) Dallas County	1,506	1.64
Fort Worth (city) Tarrant County	1,475	0.28
Sugar Land (city) Fort Bend County	994	1.57

Top 10 Places Sorted by Percent
Based on all places, regardless of population

Place	Number	%
Westlake (town) Tarrant County	7	3.14
Thompsons (town) Fort Bend County	6	2.59
Four Corners (cdp) Fort Bend County	74	2.50
Piney Point Village (city) Harris County	84	2.49
Nassau Bay (city) Harris County	100	2.35
Warren City (city) Gregg County	8	2.29
Niederwald (town) Hays County	14	2.24
Chester (town) Tyler County	6	2.19
Pinehurst (city) Orange County	51	2.15
Bee Cave (village) Travis County	12	1.97

Top 10 Places Sorted by Percent
Based on places with populations of 10,000 or more

Place	Number	%
Richardson (city) Dallas County	1,506	1.64
Sugar Land (city) Fort Bend County	994	1.57
New Territory (cdp) Fort Bend County	216	1.56
Missouri City (city) Fort Bend County	570	1.09
Mission Bend (cdp) Fort Bend County	316	1.02
Stafford (city) Fort Bend County	160	1.02
Southlake (city) Tarrant County	188	0.87
Arlington (city) Tarrant County	2,741	0.82
Plano (city) Collin County	1,777	0.80
Bellaire (city) Harris County	122	0.78

Arab: Arab/Arabic

Top 10 Places Sorted by Number
Based on all places, regardless of population

Place	Number	%
Houston (city) Harris County	2,728	0.14
San Antonio (city) Bexar County	1,011	0.09
Dallas (city) Dallas County	824	0.07
Arlington (city) Tarrant County	645	0.19
Austin (city) Travis County	496	0.08
Richardson (city) Dallas County	447	0.49
Fort Worth (city) Tarrant County	431	0.08
El Paso (city) El Paso County	257	0.05
Irving (city) Dallas County	229	0.12
Mesquite (city) Dallas County	185	0.15

Top 10 Places Sorted by Percent
Based on all places, regardless of population

Place	Number	%
Thompsons (town) Fort Bend County	6	2.59
Chester (town) Tyler County	6	2.19
Oak Ridge (town) Kaufman County	8	1.91
Dalworthington Gardens (city) Tarrant County	42	1.90
Austwell (city) Refugio County	3	1.68
Rose Hill Acres (city) Hardin County	8	1.63
Piney Point Village (city) Harris County	48	1.42
Greatwood (cdp) Fort Bend County	65	0.99
Byers (city) Clay County	5	0.94
Valley View (town) Cooke County	7	0.93

Top 10 Places Sorted by Percent
Based on places with populations of 10,000 or more

Place	Number	%
New Territory (cdp) Fort Bend County	82	0.59
Richardson (city) Dallas County	447	0.49
Duncanville (city) Dallas County	152	0.42

Place	Number	%
South Houston (city) Harris County	66	0.42
Stafford (city) Fort Bend County	55	0.35
Lancaster (city) Dallas County	69	0.27
Cedar Hill (city) Dallas County	76	0.24
La Porte (city) Harris County	72	0.23
Galena Park (city) Harris County	22	0.21
Addison (town) Dallas County	28	0.20

Arab: Egyptian

Top 10 Places Sorted by Number
Based on all places, regardless of population

Place	Number	%
Houston (city) Harris County	1,286	0.07
Plano (city) Collin County	257	0.12
Dallas (city) Dallas County	218	0.02
San Antonio (city) Bexar County	203	0.02
Sugar Land (city) Fort Bend County	190	0.30
Arlington (city) Tarrant County	173	0.05
Austin (city) Travis County	136	0.02
Fort Worth (city) Tarrant County	128	0.02
Irving (city) Dallas County	104	0.05
Lubbock (city) Lubbock County	89	0.04

Top 10 Places Sorted by Percent
Based on all places, regardless of population

Place	Number	%
Sanctuary (town) Parker County	4	1.37
Premont (city) Jim Wells County	22	0.79
Bartonville (town) Denton County	9	0.75
Nassau Bay (city) Harris County	29	0.68
Eagle Mountain (cdp) Tarrant County	36	0.55
Leonard (city) Fannin County	8	0.43
Balcones Heights (city) Bexar County	11	0.35
Colleyville (city) Tarrant County	66	0.34
Sugar Land (city) Fort Bend County	190	0.30
Lackland AFB (cdp) Bexar County	21	0.29

Top 10 Places Sorted by Percent
Based on places with populations of 10,000 or more

Place	Number	%
Colleyville (city) Tarrant County	66	0.34
Sugar Land (city) Fort Bend County	190	0.30
The Colony (city) Denton County	71	0.27
Jollyville (cdp) Williamson County	38	0.25
Corsicana (city) Navarro County	48	0.20
New Territory (cdp) Fort Bend County	25	0.18
Deer Park (city) Harris County	45	0.16
Flower Mound (town) Denton County	71	0.14
Mission Bend (cdp) Fort Bend County	40	0.13
University Park (city) Dallas County	31	0.13

Arab: Iraqi

Top 10 Places Sorted by Number
Based on all places, regardless of population

Place	Number	%
Houston (city) Harris County	227	0.01
Arlington (city) Tarrant County	187	0.06
Dallas (city) Dallas County	168	0.01
Fort Worth (city) Tarrant County	79	0.01
Irving (city) Dallas County	64	0.03
McKinney (city) Collin County	62	0.11
Amarillo (city) Potter County	46	0.03
Farmers Branch (city) Dallas County	42	0.15
Austin (city) Travis County	40	0.01
Richardson (city) Dallas County	38	0.04

Top 10 Places Sorted by Percent
Based on all places, regardless of population

Place	Number	%
Yantis (town) Wood County	2	0.58

Notes: (cdp) census designated place; Refer to the User's Guide in the front of the book for more detailed information.

Place	Number	%
Hedwig Village (city) Harris County	8	0.34
Sachse (city) Dallas County	24	0.25
Ames (city) Liberty County	3	0.25
Helotes (city) Bexar County	9	0.21
Farmers Branch (city) Dallas County	42	0.15
McKinney (city) Collin County	62	0.11
Arlington (city) Tarrant County	187	0.06
New Territory (cdp) Fort Bend County	9	0.06
Richardson (city) Dallas County	38	0.04

Top 10 Places Sorted by Percent
Based on places with populations of 10,000 or more

Place	Number	%
Farmers Branch (city) Dallas County	42	0.15
McKinney (city) Collin County	62	0.11
Arlington (city) Tarrant County	187	0.06
New Territory (cdp) Fort Bend County	9	0.06
Richardson (city) Dallas County	38	0.04
Lancaster (city) Dallas County	10	0.04
Irving (city) Dallas County	64	0.03
Amarillo (city) Potter County	46	0.03
Friendswood (city) Galveston County	10	0.03
Lake Jackson (city) Brazoria County	7	0.03

Arab: Jordanian

Top 10 Places Sorted by Number
Based on all places, regardless of population

Place	Number	%
Houston (city) Harris County	567	0.03
Dallas (city) Dallas County	379	0.03
San Antonio (city) Bexar County	236	0.02
Arlington (city) Tarrant County	169	0.05
Plano (city) Collin County	136	0.06
Fort Worth (city) Tarrant County	121	0.02
Garland (city) Dallas County	107	0.05
Mesquite (city) Dallas County	102	0.08
Austin (city) Travis County	101	0.02
El Paso (city) El Paso County	89	0.02

Top 10 Places Sorted by Percent
Based on all places, regardless of population

Place	Number	%
Murphy (city) Collin County	25	0.80
Timberwood Park (cdp) Bexar County	30	0.53
Hunters Creek Village (city) Harris County	19	0.43
Seabrook (city) Harris County	26	0.29
Spring (cdp) Harris County	76	0.21
Athens (city) Henderson County	23	0.20
Honey Grove (city) Fannin County	3	0.17
Bells (town) Grayson County	2	0.17
Sugar Land (city) Fort Bend County	83	0.13
Bedford (city) Tarrant County	63	0.13

Top 10 Places Sorted by Percent
Based on places with populations of 10,000 or more

Place	Number	%
Spring (cdp) Harris County	76	0.21
Athens (city) Henderson County	23	0.20
Sugar Land (city) Fort Bend County	83	0.13
Bedford (city) Tarrant County	63	0.13
New Territory (cdp) Fort Bend County	17	0.12
Missouri City (city) Fort Bend County	55	0.10
Mesquite (city) Dallas County	102	0.08
Richardson (city) Dallas County	72	0.08
Balch Springs (city) Dallas County	15	0.08
Plano (city) Collin County	136	0.06

Arab: Lebanese

Top 10 Places Sorted by Number
Based on all places, regardless of population

Place	Number	%
Houston (city) Harris County	3,052	0.16
Austin (city) Travis County	1,748	0.27
San Antonio (city) Bexar County	1,389	0.12
Dallas (city) Dallas County	1,341	0.11
El Paso (city) El Paso County	1,142	0.20
Plano (city) Collin County	652	0.29
Arlington (city) Tarrant County	489	0.15
Carrollton (city) Denton County	478	0.44
Fort Worth (city) Tarrant County	338	0.06
Richardson (city) Dallas County	336	0.37

Top 10 Places Sorted by Percent
Based on all places, regardless of population

Place	Number	%
Four Corners (cdp) Fort Bend County	67	2.27
Niederwald (town) Hays County	14	2.24
Bee Cave (village) Travis County	12	1.97
Camp Wood (city) Real County	13	1.63
Horizon City (city) El Paso County	77	1.41
Nesbitt (town) Harrison County	4	1.37
Sachse (city) Dallas County	123	1.26
Mingus (city) Palo Pinto County	3	1.24
Wolfforth (city) Lubbock County	26	1.05
Woodbranch (city) Montgomery County	14	1.04

Top 10 Places Sorted by Percent
Based on places with populations of 10,000 or more

Place	Number	%
Southlake (city) Tarrant County	124	0.58
New Territory (cdp) Fort Bend County	77	0.55
Brushy Creek (cdp) Williamson County	84	0.53
Bellaire (city) Harris County	76	0.49
West University Place (city) Harris County	70	0.49
Carrollton (city) Denton County	478	0.44
Stafford (city) Fort Bend County	69	0.44
Sugar Land (city) Fort Bend County	271	0.43
League City (city) Galveston County	190	0.42
Coppell (city) Dallas County	151	0.42

Arab: Moroccan

Top 10 Places Sorted by Number
Based on all places, regardless of population

Place	Number	%
Houston (city) Harris County	284	0.01
Dallas (city) Dallas County	239	0.02
San Antonio (city) Bexar County	96	0.01
Austin (city) Travis County	65	0.01
Plano (city) Collin County	51	0.02
Arlington (city) Tarrant County	46	0.01
Kingsville (city) Kleberg County	29	0.11
Irving (city) Dallas County	26	0.01
Sugar Land (city) Fort Bend County	19	0.03
Crane (city) Crane County	15	0.47

Top 10 Places Sorted by Percent
Based on all places, regardless of population

Place	Number	%
Lakeshore Grdns-Hidden Acres (cdp) San Patricio Co.	9	1.33
Bardwell (city) Ellis County	3	0.51
Crane (city) Crane County	15	0.47
South Padre Island (town) Cameron County	9	0.37
Colmesneil (city) Tyler County	2	0.32
Camp Swift (cdp) Bastrop County	9	0.20
Wilmer (city) Dallas County	7	0.20
Richland Hills (city) Tarrant County	14	0.17
Kingsville (city) Kleberg County	29	0.11

Place	Number	%
Lost Creek (cdp) Travis County	4	0.09

Top 10 Places Sorted by Percent
Based on places with populations of 10,000 or more

Place	Number	%
Kingsville (city) Kleberg County	29	0.11
Harker Heights (city) Bell County	10	0.06
Seagoville (city) Dallas County	5	0.05
Sugar Land (city) Fort Bend County	19	0.03
Bellaire (city) Harris County	5	0.03
Dallas (city) Dallas County	239	0.02
Plano (city) Collin County	51	0.02
Baytown (city) Harris County	13	0.02
Galveston (city) Galveston County	10	0.02
Allen (city) Collin County	8	0.02

Arab: Palestinian

Top 10 Places Sorted by Number
Based on all places, regardless of population

Place	Number	%
Houston (city) Harris County	1,135	0.06
Arlington (city) Tarrant County	622	0.19
Pasadena (city) Harris County	200	0.14
San Antonio (city) Bexar County	184	0.02
Missouri City (city) Fort Bend County	171	0.33
Irving (city) Dallas County	160	0.08
Sugar Land (city) Fort Bend County	153	0.24
Dallas (city) Dallas County	149	0.01
Mesquite (city) Dallas County	143	0.11
El Paso (city) El Paso County	115	0.02

Top 10 Places Sorted by Percent
Based on all places, regardless of population

Place	Number	%
Bastrop (city) Bastrop County	86	1.56
Taylor Lake Village (city) Harris County	32	0.87
Murphy (city) Collin County	20	0.64
Bear Creek (village) Hays County	2	0.47
Edgecliff Village (town) Tarrant County	11	0.43
Hunters Creek Village (city) Harris County	18	0.41
Point (city) Rains County	3	0.40
Barton Creek (cdp) Travis County	6	0.38
Missouri City (city) Fort Bend County	171	0.33
Pearland (city) Brazoria County	104	0.28

Top 10 Places Sorted by Percent
Based on places with populations of 10,000 or more

Place	Number	%
Missouri City (city) Fort Bend County	171	0.33
Pearland (city) Brazoria County	104	0.28
Sugar Land (city) Fort Bend County	153	0.24
Euless (city) Tarrant County	104	0.23
Bellaire (city) Harris County	35	0.22
Duncanville (city) Dallas County	75	0.21
Arlington (city) Tarrant County	622	0.19
Pasadena (city) Harris County	200	0.14
Humble (city) Harris County	17	0.12
Mesquite (city) Dallas County	143	0.11

Arab: Syrian

Top 10 Places Sorted by Number
Based on all places, regardless of population

Place	Number	%
Houston (city) Harris County	849	0.04
Dallas (city) Dallas County	382	0.03
El Paso (city) El Paso County	352	0.06
Austin (city) Travis County	270	0.04
San Antonio (city) Bexar County	256	0.02
Arlington (city) Tarrant County	197	0.06
Richardson (city) Dallas County	162	0.18

Notes: (cdp) census designated place; Refer to the User's Guide in the front of the book for more detailed information.

Place	Number	%
Plano (city) Collin County	160	0.07
Sugar Land (city) Fort Bend County	155	0.24
Pasadena (city) Harris County	106	0.07

Top 10 Places Sorted by Percent
Based on all places, regardless of population

Place	Number	%
Westlake (town) Tarrant County	7	3.14
Warren City (city) Gregg County	8	2.29
Pinehurst (city) Orange County	51	2.15
Southside Place (city) Harris County	13	0.84
Sheldon (cdp) Harris County	14	0.78
Post (city) Garza County	27	0.73
Spring Valley (city) Harris County	24	0.66
Seabrook (city) Harris County	44	0.48
Laguna Heights (cdp) Cameron County	9	0.46
Piney Point Village (city) Harris County	14	0.41

Top 10 Places Sorted by Percent
Based on places with populations of 10,000 or more

Place	Number	%
Nederland (city) Jefferson County	45	0.26
Sugar Land (city) Fort Bend County	155	0.24
Harker Heights (city) Bell County	38	0.22
Southlake (city) Tarrant County	43	0.20
Taylor (city) Williamson County	27	0.20
Brenham (city) Washington County	26	0.19
Richardson (city) Dallas County	162	0.18
Frisco (city) Collin County	47	0.14
Victoria (city) Victoria County	79	0.13
McKinney (city) Collin County	62	0.11

Arab: Other

Top 10 Places Sorted by Number
Based on all places, regardless of population

Place	Number	%
Houston (city) Harris County	1,194	0.06
Dallas (city) Dallas County	437	0.04
San Antonio (city) Bexar County	407	0.04
Plano (city) Collin County	307	0.14
Richardson (city) Dallas County	286	0.31
Austin (city) Travis County	249	0.04
Arlington (city) Tarrant County	213	0.06
Fort Worth (city) Tarrant County	209	0.04
College Station (city) Brazos County	122	0.18
Mission Bend (cdp) Fort Bend County	112	0.36

Top 10 Places Sorted by Percent
Based on all places, regardless of population

Place	Number	%
Point Blank (city) San Jacinto County	3	0.51
Fair Oaks Ranch (city) Bexar County	24	0.50
Trophy Club (town) Denton County	32	0.49
Meadows Place (city) Fort Bend County	24	0.49
Anahuac (city) Chambers County	10	0.46
Lake Brownwood (cdp) Brown County	6	0.38
Mission Bend (cdp) Fort Bend County	112	0.36
Richardson (city) Dallas County	286	0.31
Hickory Creek (town) Denton County	6	0.29
Wells Branch (cdp) Travis County	30	0.27

Top 10 Places Sorted by Percent
Based on places with populations of 10,000 or more

Place	Number	%
Mission Bend (cdp) Fort Bend County	112	0.36
Richardson (city) Dallas County	286	0.31
Wells Branch (cdp) Travis County	30	0.27
Jollyville (cdp) Williamson County	35	0.23
Seguin (city) Guadalupe County	45	0.21
Colleyville (city) Tarrant County	41	0.21
Pflugerville (city) Travis County	34	0.21

Place	Number	%
College Station (city) Brazos County	122	0.18
Weatherford (city) Parker County	33	0.17
Harker Heights (city) Bell County	27	0.16

Armenian

Top 10 Places Sorted by Number
Based on all places, regardless of population

Place	Number	%
Houston (city) Harris County	761	0.04
San Antonio (city) Bexar County	314	0.03
Dallas (city) Dallas County	311	0.03
Austin (city) Travis County	252	0.04
Plano (city) Collin County	220	0.10
El Paso (city) El Paso County	129	0.02
Carrollton (city) Denton County	124	0.11
Fort Worth (city) Tarrant County	114	0.02
Richardson (city) Dallas County	111	0.12
The Woodlands (cdp) Montgomery County	80	0.14

Top 10 Places Sorted by Percent
Based on all places, regardless of population

Place	Number	%
Pattison (city) Waller County	5	1.18
Melissa (city) Collin County	11	0.85
Laughlin AFB (cdp) Val Verde County	15	0.68
Pittsburg (city) Camp County	28	0.65
Lakewood Village (city) Denton County	2	0.55
Scenic Oaks (cdp) Bexar County	16	0.48
West University Place (city) Harris County	54	0.38
Blossom (city) Lamar County	5	0.35
Rancho Viejo (town) Cameron County	6	0.34
Cinco Ranch (cdp) Fort Bend County	36	0.32

Top 10 Places Sorted by Percent
Based on places with populations of 10,000 or more

Place	Number	%
West University Place (city) Harris County	54	0.38
Cinco Ranch (cdp) Fort Bend County	36	0.32
Vidor (city) Orange County	21	0.18
Colleyville (city) Tarrant County	34	0.17
Burleson (city) Johnson County	34	0.16
Highland Village (city) Denton County	20	0.16
The Woodlands (cdp) Montgomery County	80	0.14
Haltom City (city) Tarrant County	54	0.14
Friendswood (city) Galveston County	40	0.14
Brushy Creek (cdp) Williamson County	23	0.14

Asian

Top 10 Places Sorted by Number
Based on all places, regardless of population

Place	Number	%
Houston (city) Harris County	116,608	5.97
Dallas (city) Dallas County	37,458	3.15
Austin (city) Travis County	35,922	5.47
Plano (city) Collin County	24,816	11.18
San Antonio (city) Bexar County	24,633	2.15
Arlington (city) Tarrant County	22,456	6.74
Garland (city) Dallas County	17,401	8.06
Irving (city) Dallas County	17,357	9.06
Fort Worth (city) Tarrant County	16,613	3.11
Sugar Land (city) Fort Bend County	16,206	25.59

Top 10 Places Sorted by Percent
Based on all places, regardless of population

Place	Number	%
New Territory (cdp) Fort Bend County	3,900	28.14
Sugar Land (city) Fort Bend County	16,206	25.59
Stafford (city) Fort Bend County	3,376	21.53
Mission Bend (cdp) Fort Bend County	5,793	18.79
Four Corners (cdp) Fort Bend County	528	17.87

Place	Number	%
Meadows Place (city) Fort Bend County	836	17.02
Hedwig Village (city) Harris County	315	13.50
Richardson (city) Dallas County	11,800	12.85
Palacios (city) Matagorda County	647	12.56
Carrollton (city) Denton County	13,140	11.99

Top 10 Places Sorted by Percent
Based on places with populations of 10,000 or more

Place	Number	%
New Territory (cdp) Fort Bend County	3,900	28.14
Sugar Land (city) Fort Bend County	16,206	25.59
Stafford (city) Fort Bend County	3,376	21.53
Mission Bend (cdp) Fort Bend County	5,793	18.79
Richardson (city) Dallas County	11,800	12.85
Carrollton (city) Denton County	13,140	11.99
Missouri City (city) Fort Bend County	6,034	11.40
Plano (city) Collin County	24,816	11.18
Wells Branch (cdp) Travis County	1,194	10.59
Coppell (city) Dallas County	3,754	10.44

Asian: Bangladeshi

Top 10 Places Sorted by Number
Based on all places, regardless of population

Place	Number	%
Houston (city) Harris County	464	0.02
Dallas (city) Dallas County	325	0.03
Irving (city) Dallas County	270	0.14
Arlington (city) Tarrant County	197	0.06
Austin (city) Travis County	157	0.02
Plano (city) Collin County	154	0.07
Richardson (city) Dallas County	111	0.12
Garland (city) Dallas County	65	0.03
College Station (city) Brazos County	64	0.09
Fort Worth (city) Tarrant County	64	0.01

Top 10 Places Sorted by Percent
Based on all places, regardless of population

Place	Number	%
Bellville (city) Austin County	9	0.24
Pine Island (town) Waller County	2	0.24
Irving (city) Dallas County	270	0.14
Richardson (city) Dallas County	111	0.12
New Territory (cdp) Fort Bend County	17	0.12
Webster (city) Harris County	9	0.10
Four Corners (cdp) Fort Bend County	3	0.10
Lucas (city) Collin County	3	0.10
Waller (city) Waller County	2	0.10
College Station (city) Brazos County	64	0.09

Top 10 Places Sorted by Percent
Based on places with populations of 10,000 or more

Place	Number	%
Irving (city) Dallas County	270	0.14
Richardson (city) Dallas County	111	0.12
New Territory (cdp) Fort Bend County	17	0.12
College Station (city) Brazos County	64	0.09
Plano (city) Collin County	154	0.07
Arlington (city) Tarrant County	197	0.06
Hurst (city) Tarrant County	22	0.06
Addison (town) Dallas County	9	0.06
Brushy Creek (cdp) Williamson County	9	0.06
Mission Bend (cdp) Fort Bend County	14	0.05

Asian: Cambodian

Top 10 Places Sorted by Number
Based on all places, regardless of population

Place	Number	%
Dallas (city) Dallas County	968	0.08
Houston (city) Harris County	907	0.05
Carrollton (city) Denton County	848	0.77

Place	Number	%
Garland (city) Dallas County	471	0.22
Fort Worth (city) Tarrant County	467	0.09
Austin (city) Travis County	214	0.03
San Antonio (city) Bexar County	143	0.01
Irving (city) Dallas County	125	0.07
Arlington (city) Tarrant County	113	0.03
Mesquite (city) Dallas County	108	0.09

Top 10 Places Sorted by Percent
Based on all places, regardless of population

Place	Number	%
Iowa Colony (village) Brazoria County	45	5.60
Bonney (village) Brazoria County	6	1.56
Angus (city) Navarro County	5	1.50
Niederwald (town) Hays County	6	1.03
Carrollton (city) Denton County	848	0.77
Payne Springs (town) Henderson County	4	0.59
Oak Grove (town) Kaufman County	4	0.56
Jones Creek (village) Brazoria County	10	0.47
Garfield (cdp) Travis County	7	0.42
Windemere (cdp) Travis County	21	0.31

Top 10 Places Sorted by Percent
Based on places with populations of 10,000 or more

Place	Number	%
Carrollton (city) Denton County	848	0.77
Pflugerville (city) Travis County	37	0.23
Garland (city) Dallas County	471	0.22
Coppell (city) Dallas County	62	0.17
Mission Bend (cdp) Fort Bend County	48	0.16
Cedar Park (city) Williamson County	37	0.14
Addison (town) Dallas County	20	0.14
Conroe (city) Montgomery County	47	0.13
Weatherford (city) Parker County	24	0.13
Richardson (city) Dallas County	106	0.12

Asian: Chinese, except Taiwanese

Top 10 Places Sorted by Number
Based on all places, regardless of population

Place	Number	%
Houston (city) Harris County	24,695	1.26
Plano (city) Collin County	9,477	4.27
Austin (city) Travis County	8,470	1.29
Dallas (city) Dallas County	6,114	0.51
Sugar Land (city) Fort Bend County	5,997	9.47
San Antonio (city) Bexar County	3,972	0.35
Richardson (city) Dallas County	3,548	3.86
Arlington (city) Tarrant County	3,008	0.90
Garland (city) Dallas County	1,984	0.92
Irving (city) Dallas County	1,680	0.88

Top 10 Places Sorted by Percent
Based on all places, regardless of population

Place	Number	%
Sugar Land (city) Fort Bend County	5,997	9.47
New Territory (cdp) Fort Bend County	873	6.30
Hebron (town) Denton County	42	4.81
Plano (city) Collin County	9,477	4.27
Meadows Place (city) Fort Bend County	202	4.11
Richardson (city) Dallas County	3,548	3.86
Stafford (city) Fort Bend County	552	3.52
Jollyville (cdp) Williamson County	519	3.28
Bellaire (city) Harris County	486	3.11
Missouri City (city) Fort Bend County	1,522	2.88

Top 10 Places Sorted by Percent
Based on places with populations of 10,000 or more

Place	Number	%
Sugar Land (city) Fort Bend County	5,997	9.47
New Territory (cdp) Fort Bend County	873	6.30
Plano (city) Collin County	9,477	4.27

Place	Number	%
Richardson (city) Dallas County	3,548	3.86
Stafford (city) Fort Bend County	552	3.52
Jollyville (cdp) Williamson County	519	3.28
Bellaire (city) Harris County	486	3.11
Missouri City (city) Fort Bend County	1,522	2.88
Mission Bend (cdp) Fort Bend County	770	2.50
College Station (city) Brazos County	1,512	2.23

Asian: Filipino

Top 10 Places Sorted by Number
Based on all places, regardless of population

Place	Number	%
Houston (city) Harris County	9,276	0.47
San Antonio (city) Bexar County	5,580	0.49
Dallas (city) Dallas County	2,680	0.23
Austin (city) Travis County	2,269	0.35
Corpus Christi (city) Nueces County	1,931	0.70
El Paso (city) El Paso County	1,741	0.31
Fort Worth (city) Tarrant County	1,359	0.25
Garland (city) Dallas County	1,338	0.62
Arlington (city) Tarrant County	1,305	0.39
Sugar Land (city) Fort Bend County	1,299	2.05

Top 10 Places Sorted by Percent
Based on all places, regardless of population

Place	Number	%
Meadows Place (city) Fort Bend County	217	4.42
Stafford (city) Fort Bend County	533	3.40
Mission Bend (cdp) Fort Bend County	1,006	3.26
Four Corners (cdp) Fort Bend County	91	3.08
New Territory (cdp) Fort Bend County	385	2.78
Laughlin AFB (cdp) Val Verde County	56	2.52
Lackland AFB (cdp) Bexar County	168	2.36
Sugar Land (city) Fort Bend County	1,299	2.05
Keene (city) Johnson County	99	1.98
Burton (town) Washington County	7	1.95

Top 10 Places Sorted by Percent
Based on places with populations of 10,000 or more

Place	Number	%
Stafford (city) Fort Bend County	533	3.40
Mission Bend (cdp) Fort Bend County	1,006	3.26
New Territory (cdp) Fort Bend County	385	2.78
Sugar Land (city) Fort Bend County	1,299	2.05
Missouri City (city) Fort Bend County	1,006	1.90
Killeen (city) Bell County	1,284	1.48
Fort Hood (cdp) Coryell County	484	1.44
Universal City (city) Bexar County	159	1.07
Converse (city) Bexar County	121	1.05
McAllen (city) Hidalgo County	1,067	1.00

Asian: Hmong

Top 10 Places Sorted by Number
Based on all places, regardless of population

Place	Number	%
Duncanville (city) Dallas County	41	0.11
Arlington (city) Tarrant County	40	0.01
Fort Worth (city) Tarrant County	39	0.01
Grand Prairie (city) Dallas County	37	0.03
Irving (city) Dallas County	32	0.02
Cedar Hill (city) Dallas County	27	0.08
Haltom City (city) Tarrant County	26	0.07
Fort Hood (cdp) Coryell County	16	0.05
Dallas (city) Dallas County	14	0.00
North Richland Hills (city) Tarrant County	8	0.01

Top 10 Places Sorted by Percent
Based on all places, regardless of population

Place	Number	%
Maypearl (city) Ellis County	5	0.67

Place	Number	%
Cactus (city) Moore County	4	0.16
Duncanville (city) Dallas County	41	0.11
El Lago (city) Harris County	3	0.10
Kempner (city) Lampasas County	1	0.10
Cedar Hill (city) Dallas County	27	0.08
Haltom City (city) Tarrant County	26	0.07
Fort Hood (cdp) Coryell County	16	0.05
Grand Prairie (city) Dallas County	37	0.03
Lackland AFB (cdp) Bexar County	2	0.03

Top 10 Places Sorted by Percent
Based on places with populations of 10,000 or more

Place	Number	%
Duncanville (city) Dallas County	41	0.11
Cedar Hill (city) Dallas County	27	0.08
Haltom City (city) Tarrant County	26	0.07
Fort Hood (cdp) Coryell County	16	0.05
Grand Prairie (city) Dallas County	37	0.03
Irving (city) Dallas County	32	0.02
Wells Branch (cdp) Travis County	2	0.02
Arlington (city) Tarrant County	40	0.01
Fort Worth (city) Tarrant County	39	0.01
North Richland Hills (city) Tarrant County	8	0.01

Asian: Indian

Top 10 Places Sorted by Number
Based on all places, regardless of population

Place	Number	%
Houston (city) Harris County	22,549	1.15
Dallas (city) Dallas County	8,625	0.73
Austin (city) Travis County	8,330	1.27
Plano (city) Collin County	6,644	2.99
Irving (city) Dallas County	6,594	3.44
Carrollton (city) Denton County	4,625	4.22
Sugar Land (city) Fort Bend County	4,573	7.22
San Antonio (city) Bexar County	3,927	0.34
Arlington (city) Tarrant County	3,439	1.03
Garland (city) Dallas County	3,321	1.54

Top 10 Places Sorted by Percent
Based on all places, regardless of population

Place	Number	%
New Territory (cdp) Fort Bend County	1,725	12.44
Stafford (city) Fort Bend County	1,219	7.77
Sugar Land (city) Fort Bend County	4,573	7.22
Four Corners (cdp) Fort Bend County	178	6.03
Mission Bend (cdp) Fort Bend County	1,537	4.99
Carrollton (city) Denton County	4,625	4.22
Wells Branch (cdp) Travis County	467	4.14
Hebron (town) Denton County	35	4.00
Missouri City (city) Fort Bend County	2,042	3.86
Meadows Place (city) Fort Bend County	177	3.60

Top 10 Places Sorted by Percent
Based on places with populations of 10,000 or more

Place	Number	%
New Territory (cdp) Fort Bend County	1,725	12.44
Stafford (city) Fort Bend County	1,219	7.77
Sugar Land (city) Fort Bend County	4,573	7.22
Mission Bend (cdp) Fort Bend County	1,537	4.99
Carrollton (city) Denton County	4,625	4.22
Wells Branch (cdp) Travis County	467	4.14
Missouri City (city) Fort Bend County	2,042	3.86
Coppell (city) Dallas County	1,281	3.56
Irving (city) Dallas County	6,594	3.44
Addison (town) Dallas County	465	3.28

Asian: Indonesian

Top 10 Places Sorted by Number
Based on all places, regardless of population

Place	Number	%
Houston (city) Harris County	709	0.04
Austin (city) Travis County	229	0.03
Dallas (city) Dallas County	176	0.01
Arlington (city) Tarrant County	135	0.04
College Station (city) Brazos County	123	0.18
Irving (city) Dallas County	111	0.06
Plano (city) Collin County	94	0.04
San Antonio (city) Bexar County	73	0.01
Sugar Land (city) Fort Bend County	59	0.09
Fort Worth (city) Tarrant County	50	0.01

Top 10 Places Sorted by Percent
Based on all places, regardless of population

Place	Number	%
Knollwood (village) Grayson County	4	1.07
Piney Point Village (city) Harris County	15	0.44
Oakhurst (city) San Jacinto County	1	0.43
Yantis (town) Wood County	1	0.31
Buffalo Gap (town) Taylor County	1	0.22
Buffalo Springs (village) Lubbock County	1	0.20
Murphy (city) Collin County	6	0.19
College Station (city) Brazos County	123	0.18
Log Cabin (city) Henderson County	1	0.14
Alvord (town) Wise County	1	0.10

Top 10 Places Sorted by Percent
Based on places with populations of 10,000 or more

Place	Number	%
College Station (city) Brazos County	123	0.18
Sugar Land (city) Fort Bend County	59	0.09
Stafford (city) Fort Bend County	14	0.09
Wells Branch (cdp) Travis County	8	0.07
Irving (city) Dallas County	111	0.06
Coppell (city) Dallas County	20	0.06
Brushy Creek (cdp) Williamson County	9	0.06
Denton (city) Denton County	40	0.05
Addison (town) Dallas County	7	0.05
Cinco Ranch (cdp) Fort Bend County	6	0.05

Asian: Japanese

Top 10 Places Sorted by Number
Based on all places, regardless of population

Place	Number	%
Houston (city) Harris County	3,277	0.17
San Antonio (city) Bexar County	2,414	0.21
Austin (city) Travis County	1,807	0.28
El Paso (city) El Paso County	1,436	0.25
Dallas (city) Dallas County	1,307	0.11
Plano (city) Collin County	804	0.36
Fort Worth (city) Tarrant County	742	0.14
Irving (city) Dallas County	718	0.37
Arlington (city) Tarrant County	538	0.16
Killeen (city) Bell County	430	0.49

Top 10 Places Sorted by Percent
Based on all places, regardless of population

Place	Number	%
Putnam (town) Callahan County	1	1.14
Cross Timber (town) Johnson County	3	1.08
La Paloma-Lost Creek (cdp) Nueces County	3	0.93
Northcliff (cdp) Guadalupe County	16	0.88
Dodson (town) Collingsworth County	1	0.87
Tioga (town) Grayson County	6	0.80
Coppell (city) Dallas County	274	0.76
Marshall Creek (town) Denton County	3	0.70
Barton Creek (cdp) Travis County	11	0.69

| **Universal City** (city) Bexar County | 92 | 0.62 |

Top 10 Places Sorted by Percent
Based on places with populations of 10,000 or more

Place	Number	%
Coppell (city) Dallas County	274	0.76
Universal City (city) Bexar County	92	0.62
Schertz (city) Guadalupe County	111	0.59
Harker Heights (city) Bell County	91	0.53
Copperas Cove (city) Coryell County	154	0.52
Killeen (city) Bell County	430	0.49
Converse (city) Bexar County	53	0.46
Jollyville (cdp) Williamson County	71	0.45
Denton (city) Denton County	309	0.38
Irving (city) Dallas County	718	0.37

Asian: Korean

Top 10 Places Sorted by Number
Based on all places, regardless of population

Place	Number	%
Houston (city) Harris County	6,172	0.32
Austin (city) Travis County	4,006	0.61
Dallas (city) Dallas County	3,578	0.30
San Antonio (city) Bexar County	2,957	0.26
Irving (city) Dallas County	2,688	1.40
Killeen (city) Bell County	2,587	2.98
El Paso (city) El Paso County	2,108	0.37
Plano (city) Collin County	1,916	0.86
Carrollton (city) Denton County	1,504	1.37
Fort Worth (city) Tarrant County	1,253	0.23

Top 10 Places Sorted by Percent
Based on all places, regardless of population

Place	Number	%
Hedwig Village (city) Harris County	104	4.46
Killeen (city) Bell County	2,587	2.98
Harker Heights (city) Bell County	391	2.26
Coppell (city) Dallas County	802	2.23
Copperas Cove (city) Coryell County	521	1.76
College Station (city) Brazos County	1,078	1.59
Lackland AFB (cdp) Bexar County	107	1.50
Latexo (city) Houston County	4	1.47
Irving (city) Dallas County	2,688	1.40
Carrollton (city) Denton County	1,504	1.37

Top 10 Places Sorted by Percent
Based on places with populations of 10,000 or more

Place	Number	%
Killeen (city) Bell County	2,587	2.98
Harker Heights (city) Bell County	391	2.26
Coppell (city) Dallas County	802	2.23
Copperas Cove (city) Coryell County	521	1.76
College Station (city) Brazos County	1,078	1.59
Irving (city) Dallas County	2,688	1.40
Carrollton (city) Denton County	1,504	1.37
Wells Branch (cdp) Travis County	148	1.31
Richardson (city) Dallas County	1,133	1.23
Addison (town) Dallas County	157	1.11

Asian: Laotian

Top 10 Places Sorted by Number
Based on all places, regardless of population

Place	Number	%
Dallas (city) Dallas County	1,169	0.10
Amarillo (city) Potter County	1,137	0.65
Haltom City (city) Tarrant County	1,017	2.61
Fort Worth (city) Tarrant County	984	0.18
Garland (city) Dallas County	629	0.29
Grand Prairie (city) Dallas County	499	0.39
Irving (city) Dallas County	480	0.25

Euless (city) Tarrant County	407	0.88
Houston (city) Harris County	346	0.02
North Richland Hills (city) Tarrant County	206	0.37

Top 10 Places Sorted by Percent
Based on all places, regardless of population

Place	Number	%
Venus (town) Johnson County	41	4.51
Haltom City (city) Tarrant County	1,017	2.61
Euless (city) Tarrant County	407	0.88
Watauga (city) Tarrant County	192	0.88
Aldine (cdp) Harris County	113	0.81
Dumas (city) Moore County	100	0.73
Farwell (city) Parmer County	10	0.73
Amarillo (city) Potter County	1,137	0.65
Kirby (city) Bexar County	56	0.65
Rockport (city) Aransas County	32	0.43

Top 10 Places Sorted by Percent
Based on places with populations of 10,000 or more

Place	Number	%
Haltom City (city) Tarrant County	1,017	2.61
Euless (city) Tarrant County	407	0.88
Watauga (city) Tarrant County	192	0.88
Aldine (cdp) Harris County	113	0.81
Dumas (city) Moore County	100	0.73
Amarillo (city) Potter County	1,137	0.65
Grand Prairie (city) Dallas County	499	0.39
North Richland Hills (city) Tarrant County	206	0.37
Garland (city) Dallas County	629	0.29
Duncanville (city) Dallas County	104	0.29

Asian: Malaysian

Top 10 Places Sorted by Number
Based on all places, regardless of population

Place	Number	%
Houston (city) Harris County	182	0.01
Dallas (city) Dallas County	96	0.01
Arlington (city) Tarrant County	70	0.02
Austin (city) Travis County	70	0.01
Fort Worth (city) Tarrant County	45	0.01
Plano (city) Collin County	34	0.02
San Antonio (city) Bexar County	28	0.00
Lubbock (city) Lubbock County	25	0.01
Richardson (city) Dallas County	24	0.03
Sugar Land (city) Fort Bend County	23	0.04

Top 10 Places Sorted by Percent
Based on all places, regardless of population

Place	Number	%
Valley View (town) Cooke County	2	0.27
Damon (cdp) Brazoria County	1	0.19
Helotes (city) Bexar County	6	0.14
Murphy (city) Collin County	3	0.10
Clute (city) Brazoria County	8	0.08
Meridian (city) Bosque County	1	0.07
Addison (town) Dallas County	9	0.06
Pottsboro (town) Grayson County	1	0.06
Southside Place (city) Harris County	1	0.06
Sugar Land (city) Fort Bend County	23	0.04

Top 10 Places Sorted by Percent
Based on places with populations of 10,000 or more

Place	Number	%
Clute (city) Brazoria County	8	0.08
Addison (town) Dallas County	9	0.06
Sugar Land (city) Fort Bend County	23	0.04
Cinco Ranch (cdp) Fort Bend County	4	0.04
Richardson (city) Dallas County	24	0.03
Euless (city) Tarrant County	14	0.03
Stafford (city) Fort Bend County	4	0.03

Notes: (cdp) census designated place; Refer to the User's Guide in the front of the book for more detailed information.

Place	Number	%
West University Place (city) Harris County	4	0.03
Arlington (city) Tarrant County	70	0.02
Plano (city) Collin County	34	0.02

Asian: Pakistani

Top 10 Places Sorted by Number
Based on all places, regardless of population

Place	Number	%
Houston (city) Harris County	6,490	0.33
Carrollton (city) Denton County	1,083	0.99
Dallas (city) Dallas County	1,062	0.09
Sugar Land (city) Fort Bend County	1,032	1.63
Austin (city) Travis County	818	0.12
Arlington (city) Tarrant County	788	0.24
Irving (city) Dallas County	681	0.36
Richardson (city) Dallas County	627	0.68
Plano (city) Collin County	578	0.26
Euless (city) Tarrant County	562	1.22

Top 10 Places Sorted by Percent
Based on all places, regardless of population

Place	Number	%
Four Corners (cdp) Fort Bend County	71	2.40
New Territory (cdp) Fort Bend County	316	2.28
Stafford (city) Fort Bend County	348	2.22
Sugar Land (city) Fort Bend County	1,032	1.63
Mission Bend (cdp) Fort Bend County	481	1.56
Euless (city) Tarrant County	562	1.22
Carrollton (city) Denton County	1,083	0.99
Hilshire Village (city) Harris County	6	0.83
Whitewright (town) Grayson County	14	0.80
Hawley (city) Jones County	5	0.77

Top 10 Places Sorted by Percent
Based on places with populations of 10,000 or more

Place	Number	%
New Territory (cdp) Fort Bend County	316	2.28
Stafford (city) Fort Bend County	348	2.22
Sugar Land (city) Fort Bend County	1,032	1.63
Mission Bend (cdp) Fort Bend County	481	1.56
Euless (city) Tarrant County	562	1.22
Carrollton (city) Denton County	1,083	0.99
Richardson (city) Dallas County	627	0.68
Missouri City (city) Fort Bend County	294	0.56
Corinth (city) Denton County	60	0.53
Wells Branch (cdp) Travis County	56	0.50

Asian: Sri Lankan

Top 10 Places Sorted by Number
Based on all places, regardless of population

Place	Number	%
Houston (city) Harris County	220	0.01
Austin (city) Travis County	156	0.02
Plano (city) Collin County	84	0.04
Dallas (city) Dallas County	59	0.00
San Antonio (city) Bexar County	47	0.00
Arlington (city) Tarrant County	46	0.01
Lubbock (city) Lubbock County	40	0.02
Irving (city) Dallas County	36	0.02
Fort Worth (city) Tarrant County	36	0.01
Coppell (city) Dallas County	33	0.09

Top 10 Places Sorted by Percent
Based on all places, regardless of population

Place	Number	%
Rancho Viejo (town) Cameron County	5	0.29
Fruitvale (city) Van Zandt County	1	0.24
Anderson Mill (cdp) Williamson County	20	0.22
Rollingwood (city) Travis County	3	0.21
Coppell (city) Dallas County	33	0.09

Place	Number	%
Robert Lee (city) Coke County	1	0.09
Shady Hollow (cdp) Travis County	4	0.08
Greatwood (cdp) Fort Bend County	4	0.06
Karnes City (city) Karnes County	2	0.06
Euless (city) Tarrant County	21	0.05

Top 10 Places Sorted by Percent
Based on places with populations of 10,000 or more

Place	Number	%
Coppell (city) Dallas County	33	0.09
Euless (city) Tarrant County	21	0.05
Friendswood (city) Galveston County	14	0.05
Brushy Creek (cdp) Williamson County	7	0.05
Plano (city) Collin County	84	0.04
College Station (city) Brazos County	25	0.04
The Woodlands (cdp) Montgomery County	21	0.04
Pearland (city) Brazoria County	14	0.04
Cedar Park (city) Williamson County	10	0.04
Jollyville (cdp) Williamson County	7	0.04

Asian: Taiwanese

Top 10 Places Sorted by Number
Based on all places, regardless of population

Place	Number	%
Houston (city) Harris County	1,846	0.09
Sugar Land (city) Fort Bend County	836	1.32
Austin (city) Travis County	760	0.12
Plano (city) Collin County	702	0.32
Dallas (city) Dallas County	407	0.03
Arlington (city) Tarrant County	365	0.11
Richardson (city) Dallas County	285	0.31
San Antonio (city) Bexar County	223	0.02
College Station (city) Brazos County	181	0.27
Port Lavaca (city) Calhoun County	142	1.18

Top 10 Places Sorted by Percent
Based on all places, regardless of population

Place	Number	%
Sugar Land (city) Fort Bend County	836	1.32
Port Lavaca (city) Calhoun County	142	1.18
Point Comfort (city) Calhoun County	9	1.15
Piney Point Village (city) Harris County	30	0.89
Bunker Hill Village (city) Harris County	27	0.74
Hedwig Village (city) Harris County	16	0.69
Bellaire (city) Harris County	96	0.61
New Territory (cdp) Fort Bend County	74	0.53
Meadows Place (city) Fort Bend County	20	0.41
Hill Country Village (city) Bexar County	4	0.39

Top 10 Places Sorted by Percent
Based on places with populations of 10,000 or more

Place	Number	%
Sugar Land (city) Fort Bend County	836	1.32
Port Lavaca (city) Calhoun County	142	1.18
Bellaire (city) Harris County	96	0.61
New Territory (cdp) Fort Bend County	74	0.53
Plano (city) Collin County	702	0.32
Richardson (city) Dallas County	285	0.31
Jollyville (cdp) Williamson County	48	0.30
College Station (city) Brazos County	181	0.27
Missouri City (city) Fort Bend County	109	0.21
Brushy Creek (cdp) Williamson County	26	0.17

Asian: Thai

Top 10 Places Sorted by Number
Based on all places, regardless of population

Place	Number	%
Houston (city) Harris County	928	0.05
San Antonio (city) Bexar County	725	0.06
Austin (city) Travis County	666	0.10

Place	Number	%
Dallas (city) Dallas County	656	0.06
Fort Worth (city) Tarrant County	349	0.07
Arlington (city) Tarrant County	306	0.09
Irving (city) Dallas County	297	0.15
Plano (city) Collin County	249	0.11
Killeen (city) Bell County	189	0.22
Garland (city) Dallas County	177	0.08

Top 10 Places Sorted by Percent
Based on all places, regardless of population

Place	Number	%
Cuney (town) Cherokee County	2	1.38
Bixby (cdp) Cameron County	4	1.12
Marion (city) Guadalupe County	11	1.00
Scottsville (city) Harrison County	2	0.76
Lowry Crossing (city) Collin County	7	0.57
Sienna Plantation (cdp) Fort Bend County	9	0.47
Bailey (city) Fannin County	1	0.47
Meadowlakes (city) Burnet County	6	0.46
Parker (city) Collin County	6	0.44
Bailey's Prairie (village) Brazoria County	3	0.43

Top 10 Places Sorted by Percent
Based on places with populations of 10,000 or more

Place	Number	%
Converse (city) Bexar County	39	0.34
Killeen (city) Bell County	189	0.22
Haltom City (city) Tarrant County	86	0.22
Copperas Cove (city) Coryell County	66	0.22
Universal City (city) Bexar County	32	0.22
Euless (city) Tarrant County	91	0.20
Jollyville (cdp) Williamson County	30	0.19
Denton (city) Denton County	148	0.18
Watauga (city) Tarrant County	39	0.18
Benbrook (city) Tarrant County	37	0.18

Asian: Vietnamese

Top 10 Places Sorted by Number
Based on all places, regardless of population

Place	Number	%
Houston (city) Harris County	33,922	1.74
Arlington (city) Tarrant County	9,954	2.99
Dallas (city) Dallas County	8,084	0.68
Garland (city) Dallas County	7,023	3.25
Austin (city) Travis County	6,426	0.98
Fort Worth (city) Tarrant County	5,666	1.06
Port Arthur (city) Jefferson County	2,869	4.97
Grand Prairie (city) Dallas County	2,589	2.03
San Antonio (city) Bexar County	2,453	0.21
Carrollton (city) Denton County	2,442	2.23

Top 10 Places Sorted by Percent
Based on all places, regardless of population

Place	Number	%
Palacios (city) Matagorda County	609	11.82
Seadrift (city) Calhoun County	132	9.76
Fulton (town) Aransas County	122	7.86
San Leon (cdp) Galveston County	302	6.92
Seven Oaks (city) Polk County	7	5.34
Port Arthur (city) Jefferson County	2,869	4.97
Mission Bend (cdp) Fort Bend County	1,468	4.76
Haltom City (city) Tarrant County	1,386	4.76
Murphy (city) Collin County	110	3.55
Four Corners (cdp) Fort Bend County	102	3.45

Top 10 Places Sorted by Percent
Based on places with populations of 10,000 or more

Place	Number	%
Port Arthur (city) Jefferson County	2,869	4.97
Mission Bend (cdp) Fort Bend County	1,468	4.76
Haltom City (city) Tarrant County	1,386	3.55

Notes: (cdp) census designated place; Refer to the User's Guide in the front of the book for more detailed information.

Place	Number	%
Garland (city) Dallas County	7,023	3.25
Stafford (city) Fort Bend County	506	3.23
Arlington (city) Tarrant County	9,954	2.99
New Territory (cdp) Fort Bend County	318	2.29
Carrollton (city) Denton County	2,442	2.23
Pflugerville (city) Travis County	362	2.22
Sugar Land (city) Fort Bend County	1,341	2.12

Asian: Other Asian, specified

Top 10 Places Sorted by Number
Based on all places, regardless of population

Place	Number	%
Houston (city) Harris County	357	0.02
Irving (city) Dallas County	222	0.12
Dallas (city) Dallas County	219	0.02
Austin (city) Travis County	147	0.02
Fort Worth (city) Tarrant County	111	0.02
San Antonio (city) Bexar County	101	0.01
Arlington (city) Tarrant County	88	0.03
Plano (city) Collin County	63	0.03
Lubbock (city) Lubbock County	35	0.02
Denton (city) Denton County	32	0.04

Top 10 Places Sorted by Percent
Based on all places, regardless of population

Place	Number	%
Warren City (city) Gregg County	6	1.75
Yantis (town) Wood County	5	1.56
Rancho Viejo (town) Cameron County	19	1.08
Rosser (village) Kaufman County	3	0.79
San Isidro (cdp) Starr County	2	0.74
Gruver (city) Hansford County	4	0.34
Buffalo (city) Leon County	6	0.33
Lytle (city) Atascosa County	7	0.29
Sunset (city) Montague County	1	0.29
Olton (city) Lamb County	6	0.26

Top 10 Places Sorted by Percent
Based on places with populations of 10,000 or more

Place	Number	%
Irving (city) Dallas County	222	0.12
Humble (city) Harris County	12	0.08
Addison (town) Dallas County	11	0.08
New Territory (cdp) Fort Bend County	11	0.08
Balch Springs (city) Dallas County	11	0.06
Vernon (city) Wilbarger County	7	0.06
Euless (city) Tarrant County	21	0.05
Haltom City (city) Tarrant County	18	0.05
Schertz (city) Guadalupe County	9	0.05
El Campo (city) Wharton County	6	0.05

Asian: Other Asian, not specified

Top 10 Places Sorted by Number
Based on all places, regardless of population

Place	Number	%
Houston (city) Harris County	4,262	0.22
Dallas (city) Dallas County	1,919	0.16
San Antonio (city) Bexar County	1,327	0.12
Austin (city) Travis County	1,266	0.19
Arlington (city) Tarrant County	911	0.27
Fort Worth (city) Tarrant County	773	0.14
Plano (city) Collin County	709	0.32
Irving (city) Dallas County	565	0.29
El Paso (city) El Paso County	450	0.08
Garland (city) Dallas County	449	0.21

Top 10 Places Sorted by Percent
Based on all places, regardless of population

Place	Number	%
Emhouse (town) Navarro County	4	2.52

Place	Number	%
Parker (city) Collin County	15	1.09
Venus (town) Johnson County	9	0.99
Lackland AFB (cdp) Bexar County	58	0.81
Hackberry (town) Denton County	4	0.74
Hartley (cdp) Hartley County	3	0.68
Lakeview (town) Hall County	1	0.66
Mission Bend (cdp) Fort Bend County	196	0.64
Iowa Colony (village) Brazoria County	5	0.62
New Territory (cdp) Fort Bend County	84	0.61

Top 10 Places Sorted by Percent
Based on places with populations of 10,000 or more

Place	Number	%
Mission Bend (cdp) Fort Bend County	196	0.64
New Territory (cdp) Fort Bend County	84	0.61
Sugar Land (city) Fort Bend County	375	0.59
Stafford (city) Fort Bend County	81	0.52
Richardson (city) Dallas County	385	0.42
Euless (city) Tarrant County	182	0.40
Carrollton (city) Denton County	379	0.35
Wells Branch (cdp) Travis County	40	0.35
Plano (city) Collin County	709	0.32
Addison (town) Dallas County	45	0.32

Assyrian/Chaldean/Syriac

Top 10 Places Sorted by Number
Based on all places, regardless of population

Place	Number	%
Houston (city) Harris County	42	0.00
Carrollton (city) Denton County	32	0.03
Mesquite (city) Dallas County	28	0.02
The Woodlands (cdp) Montgomery County	27	0.05
Fort Worth (city) Tarrant County	27	0.01
Nederland (city) Jefferson County	24	0.14
Austin (city) Travis County	20	0.00
Midland (city) Midland County	16	0.02
Highland Village (city) Denton County	14	0.12
Farmers Branch (city) Dallas County	14	0.05

Top 10 Places Sorted by Percent
Based on all places, regardless of population

Place	Number	%
Pine Island (town) Waller County	3	0.33
Port Isabel (city) Cameron County	9	0.18
Nederland (city) Jefferson County	24	0.14
Argyle (city) Denton County	3	0.13
Highland Village (city) Denton County	14	0.12
Corinth (city) Denton County	10	0.09
Jollyville (cdp) Williamson County	9	0.06
The Woodlands (cdp) Montgomery County	27	0.05
Farmers Branch (city) Dallas County	14	0.05
Colleyville (city) Tarrant County	8	0.04

Top 10 Places Sorted by Percent
Based on places with populations of 10,000 or more

Place	Number	%
Nederland (city) Jefferson County	24	0.14
Highland Village (city) Denton County	14	0.12
Corinth (city) Denton County	10	0.09
Jollyville (cdp) Williamson County	9	0.06
The Woodlands (cdp) Montgomery County	27	0.05
Farmers Branch (city) Dallas County	14	0.05
Colleyville (city) Tarrant County	8	0.04
Carrollton (city) Denton County	32	0.03
University Park (city) Dallas County	8	0.03
Mesquite (city) Dallas County	28	0.02

Australian

Top 10 Places Sorted by Number
Based on all places, regardless of population

Place	Number	%
Houston (city) Harris County	614	0.03
Dallas (city) Dallas County	312	0.03
Austin (city) Travis County	306	0.05
San Antonio (city) Bexar County	156	0.01
Plano (city) Collin County	151	0.07
Arlington (city) Tarrant County	146	0.04
Irving (city) Dallas County	105	0.05
Richardson (city) Dallas County	95	0.10
Fort Worth (city) Tarrant County	83	0.02
Corpus Christi (city) Nueces County	81	0.03

Top 10 Places Sorted by Percent
Based on all places, regardless of population

Place	Number	%
Hollywood Park (town) Bexar County	34	1.32
Nesbitt (town) Harrison County	3	1.03
Evant (town) Coryell County	3	0.74
Bunker Hill Village (city) Harris County	26	0.71
Onion Creek (cdp) Travis County	13	0.65
Sunset Valley (city) Travis County	2	0.54
Millsap (town) Parker County	2	0.52
Gladewater (city) Gregg County	28	0.46
Dripping Springs (city) Hays County	7	0.44
Sansom Park (city) Tarrant County	18	0.43

Top 10 Places Sorted by Percent
Based on places with populations of 10,000 or more

Place	Number	%
West University Place (city) Harris County	51	0.36
University Park (city) Dallas County	67	0.29
Levelland (city) Hockley County	32	0.25
Cinco Ranch (cdp) Fort Bend County	22	0.20
Addison (town) Dallas County	26	0.19
Converse (city) Bexar County	17	0.15
Alvin (city) Brazoria County	29	0.13
Bellaire (city) Harris County	20	0.13
Duncanville (city) Dallas County	42	0.12
Burleson (city) Johnson County	25	0.12

Austrian

Top 10 Places Sorted by Number
Based on all places, regardless of population

Place	Number	%
Houston (city) Harris County	2,041	0.10
Dallas (city) Dallas County	1,599	0.13
San Antonio (city) Bexar County	1,199	0.10
Austin (city) Travis County	1,198	0.18
Plano (city) Collin County	663	0.30
Arlington (city) Tarrant County	624	0.19
El Paso (city) El Paso County	591	0.10
Fort Worth (city) Tarrant County	565	0.11
Corpus Christi (city) Nueces County	352	0.13
Garland (city) Dallas County	262	0.12

Top 10 Places Sorted by Percent
Based on all places, regardless of population

Place	Number	%
Prado Verde (cdp) El Paso County	7	3.30
Falman-County Acres (cdp) San Patricio County	7	2.87
Petronila (city) Nueces County	2	2.11
Olmos Park (city) Bexar County	48	1.95
Cove (city) Chambers County	5	1.63
Cooper (city) Delta County	27	1.28
Buckholts (town) Milam County	5	1.28
Morgan's Point (city) Harris County	4	1.20
Eureka (city) Navarro County	4	1.15

Notes: (cdp) census designated place; Refer to the User's Guide in the front of the book for more detailed information.

Place	Number	%
Weir (city) Williamson County	7	1.14

Top 10 Places Sorted by Percent
Based on places with populations of 10,000 or more

Place	Number	%
West University Place (city) Harris County	91	0.64
Addison (town) Dallas County	68	0.49
Highland Village (city) Denton County	59	0.49
Bellaire (city) Harris County	74	0.47
Burkburnett (city) Wichita County	48	0.44
Grapevine (city) Tarrant County	175	0.42
Brushy Creek (cdp) Williamson County	59	0.37
Cinco Ranch (cdp) Fort Bend County	42	0.37
The Woodlands (cdp) Montgomery County	201	0.36
Frisco (city) Collin County	119	0.36

Basque

Top 10 Places Sorted by Number
Based on all places, regardless of population

Place	Number	%
San Antonio (city) Bexar County	189	0.02
Houston (city) Harris County	138	0.01
Dallas (city) Dallas County	102	0.01
Austin (city) Travis County	94	0.01
El Paso (city) El Paso County	74	0.01
Plano (city) Collin County	37	0.02
Garland (city) Dallas County	34	0.02
Laredo (city) Webb County	33	0.02
Missouri City (city) Fort Bend County	32	0.06
Hurst (city) Tarrant County	28	0.08

Top 10 Places Sorted by Percent
Based on all places, regardless of population

Place	Number	%
Sun Valley (city) Lamar County	2	3.03
Roanoke (city) Denton County	27	0.94
Buda (city) Hays County	13	0.55
Bayview (town) Cameron County	2	0.51
Lindsay (town) Cooke County	4	0.50
Rancho Viejo (town) Cameron County	7	0.40
Sanderson (cdp) Terrell County	3	0.34
Clear Lake Shores (city) Galveston County	3	0.25
Lakeside (town) Tarrant County	2	0.20
Rio Hondo (city) Cameron County	3	0.16

Top 10 Places Sorted by Percent
Based on places with populations of 10,000 or more

Place	Number	%
West University Place (city) Harris County	14	0.10
Lake Jackson (city) Brazoria County	25	0.09
Hurst (city) Tarrant County	28	0.08
Cedar Hill (city) Dallas County	26	0.08
Colleyville (city) Tarrant County	15	0.08
Stephenville (city) Erath County	11	0.07
Universal City (city) Bexar County	10	0.07
Canyon (city) Randall County	9	0.07
Missouri City (city) Fort Bend County	32	0.06
Addison (town) Dallas County	8	0.06

Belgian

Top 10 Places Sorted by Number
Based on all places, regardless of population

Place	Number	%
Houston (city) Harris County	967	0.05
San Antonio (city) Bexar County	726	0.06
Dallas (city) Dallas County	528	0.04
Austin (city) Travis County	524	0.08
Plano (city) Collin County	376	0.17
Arlington (city) Tarrant County	208	0.06
Fort Worth (city) Tarrant County	195	0.04

Place	Number	%
El Paso (city) El Paso County	188	0.03
Bedford (city) Tarrant County	161	0.34
Garland (city) Dallas County	143	0.07

Top 10 Places Sorted by Percent
Based on all places, regardless of population

Place	Number	%
Sun Valley (city) Lamar County	3	4.55
Utopia (cdp) Uvalde County	9	2.72
Wimberley (cdp) Hays County	76	2.02
Hollywood Park (town) Bexar County	52	2.01
Fayetteville (city) Fayette County	5	1.79
Bunker Hill Village (city) Harris County	65	1.78
Barton Creek (cdp) Travis County	22	1.40
Grey Forest (city) Bexar County	5	1.16
Castroville (city) Medina County	29	1.08
West Lake Hills (city) Travis County	33	1.06

Top 10 Places Sorted by Percent
Based on places with populations of 10,000 or more

Place	Number	%
Bedford (city) Tarrant County	161	0.34
Rockwall (city) Rockwall County	55	0.30
University Park (city) Dallas County	63	0.27
Bay City (city) Matagorda County	42	0.23
Pecan Grove (cdp) Fort Bend County	28	0.21
Burkburnett (city) Wichita County	23	0.21
Allen (city) Collin County	85	0.20
Jollyville (cdp) Williamson County	31	0.20
Deer Park (city) Harris County	54	0.19
College Station (city) Brazos County	125	0.18

Brazilian

Top 10 Places Sorted by Number
Based on all places, regardless of population

Place	Number	%
Houston (city) Harris County	980	0.05
Dallas (city) Dallas County	451	0.04
Austin (city) Travis County	440	0.07
Plano (city) Collin County	209	0.09
Grand Prairie (city) Dallas County	195	0.15
Irving (city) Dallas County	168	0.09
Fort Worth (city) Tarrant County	130	0.02
El Paso (city) El Paso County	122	0.02
San Antonio (city) Bexar County	110	0.01
Lewisville (city) Denton County	106	0.14

Top 10 Places Sorted by Percent
Based on all places, regardless of population

Place	Number	%
Keene (city) Johnson County	75	1.54
Bailey (city) Fannin County	2	0.81
Tehuacana (town) Limestone County	2	0.62
Trophy Club (town) Denton County	37	0.57
Hilshire Village (city) Harris County	4	0.55
Pinehurst (cdp) Montgomery County	15	0.39
Addison (town) Dallas County	52	0.38
Fair Oaks Ranch (city) Bexar County	15	0.31
Princeton (city) Collin County	9	0.27
Copper Canyon (town) Denton County	3	0.25

Top 10 Places Sorted by Percent
Based on places with populations of 10,000 or more

Place	Number	%
Addison (town) Dallas County	52	0.38
Highland Village (city) Denton County	26	0.21
Bellaire (city) Harris County	29	0.19
Grand Prairie (city) Dallas County	195	0.15
Lewisville (city) Denton County	106	0.14
The Woodlands (cdp) Montgomery County	80	0.14
Wells Branch (cdp) Travis County	16	0.14

Place	Number	%
Grapevine (city) Tarrant County	54	0.13
Haltom City (city) Tarrant County	51	0.13
College Station (city) Brazos County	84	0.12

British

Top 10 Places Sorted by Number
Based on all places, regardless of population

Place	Number	%
Houston (city) Harris County	7,483	0.38
Austin (city) Travis County	4,753	0.72
Dallas (city) Dallas County	4,278	0.36
San Antonio (city) Bexar County	2,833	0.25
Fort Worth (city) Tarrant County	1,938	0.36
Plano (city) Collin County	1,802	0.81
Arlington (city) Tarrant County	1,568	0.47
El Paso (city) El Paso County	1,018	0.18
The Woodlands (cdp) Montgomery County	857	1.54
Lubbock (city) Lubbock County	853	0.43

Top 10 Places Sorted by Percent
Based on all places, regardless of population

Place	Number	%
Murchison (city) Henderson County	28	4.45
Oak Grove (town) Kaufman County	33	4.38
Del Sol-Loma Linda (cdp) San Patricio County	27	3.75
Adrian (city) Oldham County	5	3.55
Westover Hills (town) Tarrant County	23	3.54
Todd Mission (city) Grimes County	5	3.47
Barton Creek (cdp) Travis County	44	2.80
Hilshire Village (city) Harris County	19	2.63
Cinco Ranch (cdp) Fort Bend County	290	2.58
Dalworthington Gardens (city) Tarrant County	57	2.57

Top 10 Places Sorted by Percent
Based on places with populations of 10,000 or more

Place	Number	%
Cinco Ranch (cdp) Fort Bend County	290	2.58
Highland Village (city) Denton County	237	1.95
University Park (city) Dallas County	412	1.76
The Woodlands (cdp) Montgomery County	857	1.54
West University Place (city) Harris County	214	1.51
Pecan Grove (cdp) Fort Bend County	199	1.48
Port Neches (city) Jefferson County	183	1.35
Bellaire (city) Harris County	189	1.21
Jollyville (cdp) Williamson County	182	1.18
Colleyville (city) Tarrant County	223	1.14

Bulgarian

Top 10 Places Sorted by Number
Based on all places, regardless of population

Place	Number	%
Houston (city) Harris County	295	0.02
Dallas (city) Dallas County	219	0.02
Austin (city) Travis County	149	0.02
Arlington (city) Tarrant County	125	0.04
Euless (city) Tarrant County	91	0.20
Corpus Christi (city) Nueces County	78	0.03
Plano (city) Collin County	68	0.03
Laredo (city) Webb County	54	0.03
Grapevine (city) Tarrant County	40	0.09
College Station (city) Brazos County	38	0.06

Top 10 Places Sorted by Percent
Based on all places, regardless of population

Place	Number	%
Rancho Viejo (town) Cameron County	13	0.74
Devine (city) Medina County	22	0.51
Sunnyvale (town) Dallas County	13	0.48
Highland Park (town) Dallas County	29	0.33
Tuscola (city) Taylor County	2	0.27

Notes: (cdp) census designated place; Refer to the User's Guide in the front of the book for more detailed information.

Place	Number	%
Clarendon (city) Donley County	5	0.25
Lindsay (town) Cooke County	2	0.25
Quinlan (city) Hunt County	3	0.21
Euless (city) Tarrant County	91	0.20
Meadows Place (city) Fort Bend County	10	0.20

Top 10 Places Sorted by Percent
Based on places with populations of 10,000 or more

Place	Number	%
Euless (city) Tarrant County	91	0.20
Keller (city) Tarrant County	35	0.13
University Park (city) Dallas County	28	0.12
Mission Bend (cdp) Fort Bend County	34	0.11
Watauga (city) Tarrant County	21	0.10
Grapevine (city) Tarrant County	40	0.09
Gainesville (city) Cooke County	12	0.08
College Station (city) Brazos County	38	0.06
Farmers Branch (city) Dallas County	16	0.06
Georgetown (city) Williamson County	14	0.05

Canadian

Top 10 Places Sorted by Number
Based on all places, regardless of population

Place	Number	%
Houston (city) Harris County	2,420	0.12
San Antonio (city) Bexar County	1,379	0.12
Dallas (city) Dallas County	1,377	0.12
Austin (city) Travis County	1,170	0.18
Plano (city) Collin County	1,014	0.46
Fort Worth (city) Tarrant County	606	0.11
Corpus Christi (city) Nueces County	426	0.15
Irving (city) Dallas County	421	0.22
Arlington (city) Tarrant County	415	0.12
El Paso (city) El Paso County	415	0.07

Top 10 Places Sorted by Percent
Based on all places, regardless of population

Place	Number	%
Westdale (cdp) Jim Wells County	24	6.78
Westbrook (city) Mitchell County	8	3.51
Cesar Chavez (cdp) Hidalgo County	42	3.02
Carmine (city) Fayette County	6	2.84
Coyote Acres (cdp) Jim Wells County	10	2.44
Ross (city) McLennan County	5	1.98
Windcrest (city) Bexar County	89	1.77
Garrett (town) Ellis County	7	1.71
Marshall Creek (town) Denton County	7	1.70
Serenada (cdp) Williamson County	25	1.44

Top 10 Places Sorted by Percent
Based on places with populations of 10,000 or more

Place	Number	%
Colleyville (city) Tarrant County	163	0.83
New Territory (cdp) Fort Bend County	112	0.81
Allen (city) Collin County	341	0.78
McKinney (city) Collin County	336	0.62
League City (city) Galveston County	275	0.61
The Woodlands (cdp) Montgomery County	324	0.58
Frisco (city) Collin County	193	0.58
Plano (city) Collin County	1,014	0.46
Southlake (city) Tarrant County	99	0.46
Keller (city) Tarrant County	121	0.44

Carpatho Rusyn

Top 10 Places Sorted by Number
Based on all places, regardless of population

Place	Number	%
El Paso (city) El Paso County	38	0.01
Fort Worth (city) Tarrant County	37	0.01
Dallas (city) Dallas County	27	0.00

Place	Number	%
Port Neches (city) Jefferson County	10	0.07
McAllen (city) Hidalgo County	10	0.01
Houston (city) Harris County	9	0.00
College Station (city) Brazos County	6	0.01
Pine Island (town) Waller County	3	0.33
Cockrell Hill (city) Dallas County	3	0.07
Waco (city) McLennan County	2	0.00

Top 10 Places Sorted by Percent
Based on all places, regardless of population

Place	Number	%
Pine Island (town) Waller County	3	0.33
Port Neches (city) Jefferson County	10	0.07
Cockrell Hill (city) Dallas County	3	0.07
El Paso (city) El Paso County	38	0.01
Fort Worth (city) Tarrant County	37	0.01
McAllen (city) Hidalgo County	10	0.01
College Station (city) Brazos County	6	0.01
Dallas (city) Dallas County	27	0.00
Houston (city) Harris County	9	0.00
Waco (city) McLennan County	2	0.00

Top 10 Places Sorted by Percent
Based on places with populations of 10,000 or more

Place	Number	%
Port Neches (city) Jefferson County	10	0.07
El Paso (city) El Paso County	38	0.01
Fort Worth (city) Tarrant County	37	0.01
McAllen (city) Hidalgo County	10	0.01
College Station (city) Brazos County	6	0.01
Dallas (city) Dallas County	27	0.00
Houston (city) Harris County	9	0.00
Waco (city) McLennan County	2	0.00

Celtic

Top 10 Places Sorted by Number
Based on all places, regardless of population

Place	Number	%
Austin (city) Travis County	383	0.06
San Antonio (city) Bexar County	314	0.03
Dallas (city) Dallas County	267	0.02
Houston (city) Harris County	255	0.01
El Paso (city) El Paso County	127	0.02
Fort Worth (city) Tarrant County	109	0.02
Arlington (city) Tarrant County	106	0.03
Tyler (city) Smith County	102	0.12
Beaumont (city) Jefferson County	97	0.09
Plano (city) Collin County	95	0.04

Top 10 Places Sorted by Percent
Based on all places, regardless of population

Place	Number	%
Sunset Valley (city) Travis County	8	2.17
Weston (city) Collin County	11	1.61
Goodrich (city) Polk County	4	1.54
Melissa (city) Collin County	18	1.39
Lakewood Village (city) Denton County	5	1.37
Creedmoor (city) Travis County	3	1.37
Oak Ridge (town) Cooke County	2	1.00
Pantego (town) Tarrant County	23	0.99
Pecan Gap (city) Delta County	2	0.88
Briarcliff (village) Travis County	7	0.76

Top 10 Places Sorted by Percent
Based on places with populations of 10,000 or more

Place	Number	%
Wylie (city) Collin County	52	0.35
West Odessa (cdp) Ector County	40	0.22
Watauga (city) Tarrant County	38	0.17
Portland (city) San Patricio County	23	0.15
Belton (city) Bell County	22	0.15

Place	Number	%
West University Place (city) Harris County	21	0.15
Dumas (city) Moore County	20	0.15
Athens (city) Henderson County	17	0.15
Mansfield (city) Tarrant County	41	0.14
Bedford (city) Tarrant County	59	0.13

Croatian

Top 10 Places Sorted by Number
Based on all places, regardless of population

Place	Number	%
Houston (city) Harris County	648	0.03
Dallas (city) Dallas County	479	0.04
Austin (city) Travis County	421	0.06
San Antonio (city) Bexar County	409	0.04
Plano (city) Collin County	301	0.14
Fort Worth (city) Tarrant County	175	0.03
Corpus Christi (city) Nueces County	118	0.04
Keller (city) Tarrant County	101	0.37
Richardson (city) Dallas County	99	0.11
Garland (city) Dallas County	96	0.04

Top 10 Places Sorted by Percent
Based on all places, regardless of population

Place	Number	%
Cottonwood (city) Kaufman County	4	2.33
Cove (city) Chambers County	5	1.63
Spring Valley (city) Harris County	46	1.27
Onion Creek (cdp) Travis County	22	1.10
Bayview (town) Cameron County	3	0.77
Hilshire Village (city) Harris County	5	0.69
Fritch (city) Hutchinson County	14	0.64
Westover Hills (town) Tarrant County	4	0.62
Lakeside (town) San Patricio County	2	0.54
Fulton (town) Aransas County	8	0.51

Top 10 Places Sorted by Percent
Based on places with populations of 10,000 or more

Place	Number	%
Freeport (city) Brazoria County	63	0.50
Keller (city) Tarrant County	101	0.37
Corinth (city) Denton County	41	0.36
Southlake (city) Tarrant County	76	0.35
Jollyville (cdp) Williamson County	34	0.22
Colleyville (city) Tarrant County	42	0.21
Allen (city) Collin County	74	0.17
Cinco Ranch (cdp) Fort Bend County	19	0.17
Frisco (city) Collin County	53	0.16
Rockwall (city) Rockwall County	27	0.15

Cypriot

Top 10 Places Sorted by Number
Based on all places, regardless of population

Place	Number	%
Austin (city) Travis County	46	0.01
Cinco Ranch (cdp) Fort Bend County	39	0.35
Garland (city) Dallas County	35	0.02
Houston (city) Harris County	33	0.00
Richardson (city) Dallas County	25	0.03
College Station (city) Brazos County	18	0.03
Lewisville (city) Denton County	12	0.02
Abilene (city) Taylor County	10	0.01
Highland Village (city) Denton County	7	0.06
Lake Worth (city) Tarrant County	6	0.13

Top 10 Places Sorted by Percent
Based on all places, regardless of population

Place	Number	%
Cinco Ranch (cdp) Fort Bend County	39	0.35
Lake Worth (city) Tarrant County	6	0.13
Highland Park (town) Dallas County	6	0.07

Notes: (cdp) census designated place; Refer to the User's Guide in the front of the book for more detailed information.

Place	Number	%
Highland Village (city) Denton County	7	0.06
Richardson (city) Dallas County	25	0.03
College Station (city) Brazos County	18	0.03
Garland (city) Dallas County	35	0.02
Lewisville (city) Denton County	12	0.02
Austin (city) Travis County	46	0.01
Abilene (city) Taylor County	10	0.01

Top 10 Places Sorted by Percent
Based on places with populations of 10,000 or more

Place	Number	%
Cinco Ranch (cdp) Fort Bend County	39	0.35
Highland Village (city) Denton County	7	0.06
Richardson (city) Dallas County	25	0.03
College Station (city) Brazos County	18	0.03
Garland (city) Dallas County	35	0.02
Lewisville (city) Denton County	12	0.02
Austin (city) Travis County	46	0.01
Abilene (city) Taylor County	10	0.01
The Woodlands (cdp) Montgomery County	6	0.01
Tyler (city) Smith County	6	0.01

Czech

Top 10 Places Sorted by Number
Based on all places, regardless of population

Place	Number	%
Houston (city) Harris County	9,545	0.49
Austin (city) Travis County	6,299	0.96
San Antonio (city) Bexar County	4,622	0.40
Dallas (city) Dallas County	3,598	0.30
Corpus Christi (city) Nueces County	2,337	0.84
Victoria (city) Victoria County	2,089	3.46
Arlington (city) Tarrant County	2,008	0.60
Fort Worth (city) Tarrant County	1,513	0.28
College Station (city) Brazos County	1,398	2.06
Plano (city) Collin County	1,380	0.62

Top 10 Places Sorted by Percent
Based on all places, regardless of population

Place	Number	%
Fayetteville (city) Fayette County	103	36.79
West (city) McLennan County	945	34.24
Reese Center (cdp) Lubbock County	15	32.61
Abbott (city) Hill County	95	32.31
Moulton (town) Lavaca County	275	29.01
Shiner (city) Lavaca County	584	28.16
Ross (city) McLennan County	68	26.98
East Bernard (cdp) Wharton County	401	23.77
Snook (city) Burleson County	131	23.77
Schulenburg (city) Fayette County	601	22.59

Top 10 Places Sorted by Percent
Based on places with populations of 10,000 or more

Place	Number	%
El Campo (city) Wharton County	1,176	10.87
Taylor (city) Williamson County	1,175	8.67
Ennis (city) Ellis County	942	5.88
Rosenberg (city) Fort Bend County	1,202	4.97
Pecan Grove (cdp) Fort Bend County	608	4.52
Victoria (city) Victoria County	2,089	3.46
Brenham (city) Washington County	402	2.99
Temple (city) Bell County	1,342	2.47
Bay City (city) Matagorda County	438	2.35
Lake Jackson (city) Brazoria County	618	2.33

Czechoslovakian

Top 10 Places Sorted by Number
Based on all places, regardless of population

Place	Number	%
Houston (city) Harris County	2,148	0.11
Austin (city) Travis County	1,604	0.24
Dallas (city) Dallas County	1,285	0.11
San Antonio (city) Bexar County	1,141	0.10
Fort Worth (city) Tarrant County	690	0.13
Corpus Christi (city) Nueces County	660	0.24
Arlington (city) Tarrant County	568	0.17
Plano (city) Collin County	436	0.20
Waco (city) McLennan County	340	0.30
Irving (city) Dallas County	306	0.16

Top 10 Places Sorted by Percent
Based on all places, regardless of population

Place	Number	%
East Bernard (cdp) Wharton County	170	10.08
Westdale (cdp) Jim Wells County	22	6.21
Penelope (town) Hill County	12	5.26
West (city) McLennan County	128	4.64
Zuehl (cdp) Guadalupe County	11	4.31
Hungerford (cdp) Wharton County	25	4.15
Megargel (town) Archer County	10	3.86
Ross (city) McLennan County	9	3.57
Orchard (city) Fort Bend County	14	3.36
Sandy Hollow-Escondidas (cdp) Nueces County	14	3.08

Top 10 Places Sorted by Percent
Based on places with populations of 10,000 or more

Place	Number	%
Ennis (city) Ellis County	205	1.28
El Campo (city) Wharton County	125	1.16
Taylor (city) Williamson County	148	1.09
Lake Jackson (city) Brazoria County	207	0.78
Wells Branch (cdp) Travis County	75	0.67
Richmond (city) Fort Bend County	66	0.60
Temple (city) Bell County	290	0.53
Pearland (city) Brazoria County	196	0.52
Katy (city) Harris County	59	0.50
Spring (cdp) Harris County	178	0.49

Danish

Top 10 Places Sorted by Number
Based on all places, regardless of population

Place	Number	%
Houston (city) Harris County	2,804	0.14
Austin (city) Travis County	2,590	0.39
Dallas (city) Dallas County	2,205	0.19
San Antonio (city) Bexar County	2,166	0.19
Plano (city) Collin County	1,157	0.52
Fort Worth (city) Tarrant County	984	0.18
Arlington (city) Tarrant County	848	0.25
El Paso (city) El Paso County	733	0.13
Carrollton (city) Denton County	577	0.53
Corpus Christi (city) Nueces County	498	0.18

Top 10 Places Sorted by Percent
Based on all places, regardless of population

Place	Number	%
Uncertain (city) Harrison County	6	3.97
Bee Cave (village) Travis County	20	3.28
Oakhurst (city) San Jacinto County	8	3.24
Bishop Hills (town) Potter County	7	3.23
Moran (city) Shackelford County	7	3.02
Edgewater-Paisano (cdp) San Patricio County	5	2.46
Round Top (town) Fayette County	2	2.38
Onion Creek (cdp) Travis County	47	2.34
Trophy Club (town) Denton County	144	2.22
El Campo (city) Wharton County	224	2.07

Top 10 Places Sorted by Percent
Based on places with populations of 10,000 or more

Place	Number	%
El Campo (city) Wharton County	224	2.07

Place	Number	%
Southlake (city) Tarrant County	214	1.00
Cedar Park (city) Williamson County	216	0.84
Corinth (city) Denton County	90	0.79
The Colony (city) Denton County	204	0.77
Keller (city) Tarrant County	183	0.67
Pecan Grove (cdp) Fort Bend County	88	0.65
Georgetown (city) Williamson County	178	0.63
University Park (city) Dallas County	137	0.59
Allen (city) Collin County	253	0.58

Dutch

Top 10 Places Sorted by Number
Based on all places, regardless of population

Place	Number	%
Houston (city) Harris County	9,822	0.50
Dallas (city) Dallas County	7,159	0.60
San Antonio (city) Bexar County	7,096	0.62
Austin (city) Travis County	6,591	1.00
Fort Worth (city) Tarrant County	5,231	0.98
Arlington (city) Tarrant County	4,586	1.38
Plano (city) Collin County	2,671	1.20
Amarillo (city) Potter County	2,655	1.53
Lubbock (city) Lubbock County	2,363	1.18
Corpus Christi (city) Nueces County	2,120	0.76

Top 10 Places Sorted by Percent
Based on all places, regardless of population

Place	Number	%
Santa Monica (cdp) Willacy County	24	25.00
Stagecoach (town) Montgomery County	52	10.36
Samnorwood (cdp) Collingsworth County	4	9.52
Coyanosa (cdp) Pecos County	11	7.91
Dorchester (town) Grayson County	9	7.14
Falman-County Acres (cdp) San Patricio County	16	6.56
Lake View (cdp) Val Verde County	10	6.45
Lefors (town) Gray County	32	5.65
Austwell (city) Refugio County	10	5.59
Hilltop (cdp) Frio County	18	5.42

Top 10 Places Sorted by Percent
Based on places with populations of 10,000 or more

Place	Number	%
Nederland (city) Jefferson County	524	3.03
Borger (city) Hutchinson County	419	2.93
Rockwall (city) Rockwall County	492	2.69
Vernon (city) Wilbarger County	296	2.53
Burkburnett (city) Wichita County	272	2.50
Katy (city) Harris County	281	2.40
Watauga (city) Tarrant County	484	2.22
Burleson (city) Johnson County	459	2.16
The Colony (city) Denton County	567	2.13
Sulphur Springs (city) Hopkins County	306	2.10

Eastern European

Top 10 Places Sorted by Number
Based on all places, regardless of population

Place	Number	%
Dallas (city) Dallas County	879	0.07
Houston (city) Harris County	833	0.04
Austin (city) Travis County	571	0.09
San Antonio (city) Bexar County	336	0.03
Plano (city) Collin County	319	0.14
El Paso (city) El Paso County	102	0.02
Bellaire (city) Harris County	94	0.60
Fort Worth (city) Tarrant County	81	0.02
Arlington (city) Tarrant County	69	0.02
Missouri City (city) Fort Bend County	62	0.12

Top 10 Places Sorted by Percent
Based on all places, regardless of population

Place	Number	%
Westover Hills (town) Tarrant County	14	2.16
Enchanted Oaks (town) Henderson County	10	2.05
Annetta North (town) Parker County	4	0.93
Barton Creek (cdp) Travis County	10	0.64
Bellaire (city) Harris County	94	0.60
Hill Country Village (city) Bexar County	6	0.58
Garden Ridge (city) Comal County	5	0.26
Highland Park (town) Dallas County	21	0.24
Rockwall (city) Rockwall County	43	0.23
New Territory (cdp) Fort Bend County	32	0.23

Top 10 Places Sorted by Percent
Based on places with populations of 10,000 or more

Place	Number	%
Bellaire (city) Harris County	94	0.60
Rockwall (city) Rockwall County	43	0.23
New Territory (cdp) Fort Bend County	32	0.23
West University Place (city) Harris County	28	0.20
Nederland (city) Jefferson County	28	0.16
Plano (city) Collin County	319	0.14
Missouri City (city) Fort Bend County	62	0.12
Keller (city) Tarrant County	27	0.10
Austin (city) Travis County	571	0.09
Coppell (city) Dallas County	29	0.08

English

Top 10 Places Sorted by Number
Based on all places, regardless of population

Place	Number	%
Houston (city) Harris County	98,067	5.02
Dallas (city) Dallas County	68,355	5.75
Austin (city) Travis County	57,443	8.75
San Antonio (city) Bexar County	57,099	4.99
Fort Worth (city) Tarrant County	34,747	6.49
Arlington (city) Tarrant County	28,838	8.67
Plano (city) Collin County	26,546	11.94
Lubbock (city) Lubbock County	18,417	9.23
Corpus Christi (city) Nueces County	15,884	5.72
Garland (city) Dallas County	15,829	7.33

Top 10 Places Sorted by Percent
Based on all places, regardless of population

Place	Number	%
Tulsita (cdp) Bee County	12	48.00
Bishop Hills (town) Potter County	60	27.65
Sun Valley (city) Lamar County	18	27.27
Timbercreek Canyon (village) Randall County	110	26.57
The Hills (village) Travis County	399	25.89
Hunters Creek Village (city) Harris County	1,096	25.06
Piney Point Village (city) Harris County	840	24.85
Fair Oaks Ranch (city) Bexar County	1,193	24.66
San Leanna (village) Travis County	103	24.58
Briaroaks (city) Johnson County	128	24.38

Top 10 Places Sorted by Percent
Based on places with populations of 10,000 or more

Place	Number	%
University Park (city) Dallas County	4,954	21.22
West University Place (city) Harris County	2,686	18.90
Southlake (city) Tarrant County	3,763	17.50
Highland Village (city) Denton County	2,070	17.02
Colleyville (city) Tarrant County	3,205	16.37
The Woodlands (cdp) Montgomery County	8,896	15.94
Georgetown (city) Williamson County	4,398	15.58
Cinco Ranch (cdp) Fort Bend County	1,722	15.32
Keller (city) Tarrant County	4,178	15.30
Flower Mound (town) Denton County	7,723	15.08

Estonian

Top 10 Places Sorted by Number
Based on all places, regardless of population

Place	Number	%
Houston (city) Harris County	56	0.00
Dallas (city) Dallas County	36	0.00
College Station (city) Brazos County	34	0.05
Denton (city) Denton County	27	0.03
Austin (city) Travis County	27	0.00
Irving (city) Dallas County	25	0.01
Garland (city) Dallas County	21	0.01
Cibolo (city) Guadalupe County	17	0.54
San Antonio (city) Bexar County	14	0.00
Plano (city) Collin County	13	0.01

Top 10 Places Sorted by Percent
Based on all places, regardless of population

Place	Number	%
Cibolo (city) Guadalupe County	17	0.54
Mason (city) Mason County	11	0.50
Rancho Viejo (town) Cameron County	8	0.46
Cross Mountain (cdp) Bexar County	7	0.45
Brownsboro (city) Henderson County	3	0.39
Prosper (town) Collin County	6	0.28
Clear Lake Shores (city) Galveston County	2	0.17
Marfa (city) Presidio County	3	0.14
Port Isabel (city) Cameron County	6	0.12
Whitewright (town) Grayson County	2	0.12

Top 10 Places Sorted by Percent
Based on places with populations of 10,000 or more

Place	Number	%
Southlake (city) Tarrant County	12	0.06
Forest Hill (city) Tarrant County	8	0.06
College Station (city) Brazos County	34	0.05
Frisco (city) Collin County	12	0.04
Denton (city) Denton County	27	0.03
Coppell (city) Dallas County	10	0.03
Duncanville (city) Dallas County	9	0.03
Weslaco (city) Hidalgo County	9	0.03
Irving (city) Dallas County	25	0.01
Garland (city) Dallas County	21	0.01

European

Top 10 Places Sorted by Number
Based on all places, regardless of population

Place	Number	%
Houston (city) Harris County	8,720	0.45
Austin (city) Travis County	6,347	0.97
Dallas (city) Dallas County	5,739	0.48
San Antonio (city) Bexar County	4,343	0.38
Plano (city) Collin County	2,884	1.30
Fort Worth (city) Tarrant County	2,871	0.54
Arlington (city) Tarrant County	2,084	0.63
El Paso (city) El Paso County	1,776	0.31
Garland (city) Dallas County	1,626	0.75
Corpus Christi (city) Nueces County	1,287	0.46

Top 10 Places Sorted by Percent
Based on all places, regardless of population

Place	Number	%
Dorchester (town) Grayson County	10	7.94
Hill Country Village (city) Bexar County	64	6.18
Richland Springs (town) San Saba County	18	5.86
Leona (city) Leon County	9	5.33
Murchison (city) Henderson County	33	5.25
Blackwell (city) Nolan County	19	5.21
Del Sol-Loma Linda (cdp) San Patricio County	34	4.72
Bailey (city) Fannin County	11	4.44
Kingsbury (cdp) Guadalupe County	27	4.34

| Ravenna (city) Fannin County | 9 | 3.95 |

Top 10 Places Sorted by Percent
Based on places with populations of 10,000 or more

Place	Number	%
West University Place (city) Harris County	380	2.67
Rockwall (city) Rockwall County	403	2.20
University Park (city) Dallas County	498	2.13
Colleyville (city) Tarrant County	395	2.02
The Woodlands (cdp) Montgomery County	1,073	1.92
New Territory (cdp) Fort Bend County	227	1.63
Allen (city) Collin County	684	1.57
Pecan Grove (cdp) Fort Bend County	207	1.54
Cinco Ranch (cdp) Fort Bend County	166	1.48
Brushy Creek (cdp) Williamson County	228	1.43

Finnish

Top 10 Places Sorted by Number
Based on all places, regardless of population

Place	Number	%
Houston (city) Harris County	844	0.04
Austin (city) Travis County	798	0.12
Dallas (city) Dallas County	527	0.04
San Antonio (city) Bexar County	447	0.04
Plano (city) Collin County	444	0.20
Fort Worth (city) Tarrant County	371	0.07
Arlington (city) Tarrant County	355	0.11
Irving (city) Dallas County	302	0.16
Coppell (city) Dallas County	276	0.77
Wichita Falls (city) Wichita County	265	0.26

Top 10 Places Sorted by Percent
Based on all places, regardless of population

Place	Number	%
Nesbitt (town) Harrison County	7	2.41
Iredell (city) Bosque County	9	2.39
Hudson Bend (cdp) Travis County	27	1.13
Melissa (city) Collin County	14	1.08
Sunset Valley (city) Travis County	4	1.08
Lorenzo (city) Crosby County	14	1.01
Lost Creek (cdp) Travis County	46	0.98
Lolita (cdp) Jackson County	5	0.95
Mountain City (city) Hays County	6	0.92
Oak Point (city) Denton County	15	0.87

Top 10 Places Sorted by Percent
Based on places with populations of 10,000 or more

Place	Number	%
Coppell (city) Dallas County	276	0.77
Corinth (city) Denton County	63	0.55
Southlake (city) Tarrant County	106	0.49
Weatherford (city) Parker County	63	0.33
Clute (city) Brazoria County	32	0.31
Euless (city) Tarrant County	128	0.28
Jollyville (cdp) Williamson County	43	0.28
Wichita Falls (city) Wichita County	265	0.26
Spring (cdp) Harris County	90	0.25
West University Place (city) Harris County	36	0.25

French, except Basque

Top 10 Places Sorted by Number
Based on all places, regardless of population

Place	Number	%
Houston (city) Harris County	36,790	1.88
San Antonio (city) Bexar County	19,624	1.71
Dallas (city) Dallas County	18,072	1.52
Austin (city) Travis County	17,520	2.67
Fort Worth (city) Tarrant County	9,741	1.82
Arlington (city) Tarrant County	8,434	2.54
Plano (city) Collin County	6,617	2.98

El Paso (city) El Paso County	5,608	0.99
Corpus Christi (city) Nueces County	5,327	1.92
Beaumont (city) Jefferson County	4,891	4.29

Top 10 Places Sorted by Percent
Based on all places, regardless of population

Place	Number	%
Groves (city) Jefferson County	2,864	18.08
Central Gardens (cdp) Jefferson County	716	17.08
Port Neches (city) Jefferson County	2,281	16.84
Bridge City (city) Orange County	1,419	16.62
Sour Lake (city) Hardin County	221	13.43
Nederland (city) Jefferson County	2,252	13.01
China (city) Jefferson County	128	11.26
Reese Center (cdp) Lubbock County	5	10.87
West Orange (city) Orange County	426	10.17
Winnie (cdp) Chambers County	285	9.78

Top 10 Places Sorted by Percent
Based on places with populations of 10,000 or more

Place	Number	%
Groves (city) Jefferson County	2,864	18.08
Port Neches (city) Jefferson County	2,281	16.84
Nederland (city) Jefferson County	2,252	13.01
Vidor (city) Orange County	1,017	8.94
Port Arthur (city) Jefferson County	3,416	5.91
Cinco Ranch (cdp) Fort Bend County	616	5.48
Orange (city) Orange County	1,013	5.47
Friendswood (city) Galveston County	1,570	5.46
West University Place (city) Harris County	754	5.31
Pecan Grove (cdp) Fort Bend County	710	5.28

French Canadian

Top 10 Places Sorted by Number
Based on all places, regardless of population

Place	Number	%
Houston (city) Harris County	5,419	0.28
San Antonio (city) Bexar County	3,493	0.31
Austin (city) Travis County	2,821	0.43
Dallas (city) Dallas County	2,527	0.21
Fort Worth (city) Tarrant County	1,255	0.23
Arlington (city) Tarrant County	1,233	0.37
Plano (city) Collin County	1,181	0.53
Beaumont (city) Jefferson County	1,099	0.96
Port Arthur (city) Jefferson County	1,064	1.84
Corpus Christi (city) Nueces County	976	0.35

Top 10 Places Sorted by Percent
Based on all places, regardless of population

Place	Number	%
Wixon Valley (city) Brazos County	13	5.56
Port Neches (city) Jefferson County	729	5.38
Bridge City (city) Orange County	437	5.12
Groves (city) Jefferson County	806	5.09
Nederland (city) Jefferson County	707	4.09
Pyote (town) Ward County	5	3.82
Mauriceville (cdp) Orange County	102	3.52
China (city) Jefferson County	40	3.52
Goodrich (city) Polk County	9	3.46
Vidor (city) Orange County	371	3.26

Top 10 Places Sorted by Percent
Based on places with populations of 10,000 or more

Place	Number	%
Port Neches (city) Jefferson County	729	5.38
Groves (city) Jefferson County	806	5.09
Nederland (city) Jefferson County	707	4.09
Vidor (city) Orange County	371	3.26
Orange (city) Orange County	379	2.05
Port Arthur (city) Jefferson County	1,064	1.84
Cinco Ranch (cdp) Fort Bend County	126	1.12

Corinth (city) Denton County	124	1.09
Copperas Cove (city) Coryell County	300	1.00
Cedar Park (city) Williamson County	258	1.00

German

Top 10 Places Sorted by Number
Based on all places, regardless of population

Place	Number	%
Houston (city) Harris County	118,564	6.07
San Antonio (city) Bexar County	103,366	9.03
Austin (city) Travis County	84,350	12.85
Dallas (city) Dallas County	73,062	6.15
Fort Worth (city) Tarrant County	39,403	7.36
Arlington (city) Tarrant County	37,847	11.38
Plano (city) Collin County	36,276	16.32
El Paso (city) El Paso County	25,770	4.57
Corpus Christi (city) Nueces County	24,611	8.87
Amarillo (city) Potter County	19,672	11.34

Top 10 Places Sorted by Percent
Based on all places, regardless of population

Place	Number	%
Muenster (city) Cooke County	882	58.06
Nazareth (city) Castro County	212	57.92
Lindsay (town) Cooke County	407	50.81
New Berlin (city) Guadalupe County	239	50.32
Windthorst (town) Archer County	199	46.71
Scotland (city) Archer County	201	44.77
Geronimo (cdp) Guadalupe County	264	43.49
Carmine (city) Fayette County	86	40.76
Round Top (town) Fayette County	34	40.48
Harper (cdp) Gillespie County	401	39.16

Top 10 Places Sorted by Percent
Based on places with populations of 10,000 or more

Place	Number	%
Brenham (city) Washington County	3,451	25.69
Colleyville (city) Tarrant County	4,796	24.50
Canyon Lake (cdp) Comal County	4,023	23.82
New Braunfels (city) Comal County	8,417	22.82
Pecan Grove (cdp) Fort Bend County	2,964	22.02
Pflugerville (city) Travis County	3,555	21.72
Highland Village (city) Denton County	2,642	21.72
Southlake (city) Tarrant County	4,616	21.47
The Woodlands (cdp) Montgomery County	11,653	20.87
Brushy Creek (cdp) Williamson County	3,308	20.81

German Russian

Top 10 Places Sorted by Number
Based on all places, regardless of population

Place	Number	%
El Paso (city) El Paso County	37	0.01
The Colony (city) Denton County	30	0.11
Killeen (city) Bell County	30	0.03
Dallas (city) Dallas County	27	0.00
Eagle Mountain (cdp) Tarrant County	25	0.38
Kirby (city) Bexar County	24	0.28
San Antonio (city) Bexar County	23	0.00
Copperas Cove (city) Coryell County	17	0.06
Houston (city) Harris County	17	0.00
Austin (city) Travis County	15	0.00

Top 10 Places Sorted by Percent
Based on all places, regardless of population

Place	Number	%
Eagle Mountain (cdp) Tarrant County	25	0.38
Ropesville (city) Hockley County	2	0.37
Trinidad (city) Henderson County	4	0.36
Kirby (city) Bexar County	24	0.28
Holiday Lakes (town) Brazoria County	3	0.27

Little River-Academy (city) Bell County	2	0.12
The Colony (city) Denton County	30	0.11
Alamo (city) Hidalgo County	10	0.07
Dumas (city) Moore County	10	0.07
Copperas Cove (city) Coryell County	17	0.06

Top 10 Places Sorted by Percent
Based on places with populations of 10,000 or more

Place	Number	%
The Colony (city) Denton County	30	0.11
Alamo (city) Hidalgo County	10	0.07
Dumas (city) Moore County	10	0.07
Copperas Cove (city) Coryell County	17	0.06
Killeen (city) Bell County	30	0.03
El Paso (city) El Paso County	37	0.01
Wichita Falls (city) Wichita County	14	0.01
Odessa (city) Ector County	13	0.01
Richardson (city) Dallas County	5	0.01
Dallas (city) Dallas County	27	0.00

Greek

Top 10 Places Sorted by Number
Based on all places, regardless of population

Place	Number	%
Houston (city) Harris County	3,980	0.20
Dallas (city) Dallas County	2,119	0.18
San Antonio (city) Bexar County	2,060	0.18
Austin (city) Travis County	1,437	0.22
Plano (city) Collin County	926	0.42
Arlington (city) Tarrant County	705	0.21
Fort Worth (city) Tarrant County	590	0.11
Corpus Christi (city) Nueces County	507	0.18
El Paso (city) El Paso County	456	0.08
Irving (city) Dallas County	358	0.19

Top 10 Places Sorted by Percent
Based on all places, regardless of population

Place	Number	%
Falman-County Acres (cdp) San Patricio County	30	12.30
Lavon (town) Collin County	10	2.69
Hebron (town) Denton County	19	2.30
Southside Place (city) Harris County	35	2.27
Saint Paul (cdp) San Patricio County	11	2.12
Petronila (city) Nueces County	2	2.11
Hedwig Village (city) Harris County	45	1.93
Lakeway (city) Travis County	122	1.49
Jamaica Beach (city) Galveston County	16	1.49
Bee Cave (village) Travis County	9	1.48

Top 10 Places Sorted by Percent
Based on places with populations of 10,000 or more

Place	Number	%
Cinco Ranch (cdp) Fort Bend County	110	0.98
West University Place (city) Harris County	113	0.80
Highland Village (city) Denton County	90	0.74
Benbrook (city) Tarrant County	134	0.67
Allen (city) Collin County	272	0.63
University Park (city) Dallas County	142	0.61
Jollyville (cdp) Williamson County	90	0.58
The Woodlands (cdp) Montgomery County	310	0.56
Flower Mound (town) Denton County	239	0.47
Sugar Land (city) Fort Bend County	293	0.46

Guyanese

Top 10 Places Sorted by Number
Based on all places, regardless of population

Place	Number	%
Houston (city) Harris County	202	0.01
Missouri City (city) Fort Bend County	134	0.26
San Antonio (city) Bexar County	118	0.01

Place	Number	%
Garland (city) Dallas County	90	0.04
Channelview (cdp) Harris County	68	0.23
Arlington (city) Tarrant County	66	0.02
Dallas (city) Dallas County	64	0.01
Lancaster (city) Dallas County	49	0.19
Austin (city) Travis County	38	0.01
Sugar Land (city) Fort Bend County	35	0.06

Top 10 Places Sorted by Percent
Based on all places, regardless of population

Place	Number	%
Bailey's Prairie (village) Brazoria County	2	0.29
Missouri City (city) Fort Bend County	134	0.26
Channelview (cdp) Harris County	68	0.23
Fort Bliss (cdp) El Paso County	18	0.22
Lancaster (city) Dallas County	49	0.19
Sachse (city) Dallas County	18	0.18
Stafford (city) Fort Bend County	18	0.12
Cinco Ranch (cdp) Fort Bend County	13	0.12
Frisco (city) Collin County	32	0.10
Brushy Creek (cdp) Williamson County	16	0.10

Top 10 Places Sorted by Percent
Based on places with populations of 10,000 or more

Place	Number	%
Missouri City (city) Fort Bend County	134	0.26
Channelview (cdp) Harris County	68	0.23
Lancaster (city) Dallas County	49	0.19
Stafford (city) Fort Bend County	18	0.12
Cinco Ranch (cdp) Fort Bend County	13	0.12
Frisco (city) Collin County	32	0.10
Brushy Creek (cdp) Williamson County	16	0.10
Portland (city) San Patricio County	12	0.08
Benbrook (city) Tarrant County	13	0.07
Corinth (city) Denton County	8	0.07

Hawaii Native/Pacific Islander

Top 10 Places Sorted by Number
Based on all places, regardless of population

Place	Number	%
Houston (city) Harris County	2,899	0.15
San Antonio (city) Bexar County	2,093	0.18
Dallas (city) Dallas County	1,483	0.12
Killeen (city) Bell County	1,260	1.45
Austin (city) Travis County	1,082	0.16
El Paso (city) El Paso County	1,064	0.19
Euless (city) Tarrant County	1,010	2.20
Arlington (city) Tarrant County	835	0.25
Fort Worth (city) Tarrant County	772	0.14
Fort Hood (cdp) Coryell County	480	1.42

Top 10 Places Sorted by Percent
Based on all places, regardless of population

Place	Number	%
Ranchette Estates (cdp) Willacy County	5	3.76
Keene (city) Johnson County	151	3.02
Retreat (town) Navarro County	9	2.65
Alto Bonito (cdp) Starr County	15	2.64
Euless (city) Tarrant County	1,010	2.20
Center (city) Shelby County	125	2.20
Garrett (town) Ellis County	8	1.79
Warren City (city) Gregg County	6	1.75
Yantis (town) Wood County	5	1.56
Killeen (city) Bell County	1,260	1.45

Top 10 Places Sorted by Percent
Based on places with populations of 10,000 or more

Place	Number	%
Euless (city) Tarrant County	1,010	2.20
Killeen (city) Bell County	1,260	1.45
Fort Hood (cdp) Coryell County	480	1.42

Place	Number	%
Copperas Cove (city) Coryell County	286	0.97
Harker Heights (city) Bell County	125	0.72
Corsicana (city) Navarro County	143	0.58
Hurst (city) Tarrant County	167	0.46
Universal City (city) Bexar County	63	0.42
Bedford (city) Tarrant County	184	0.39
Humble (city) Harris County	52	0.36

Hawaii Native/Pacific Islander: Melanesian

Top 10 Places Sorted by Number
Based on all places, regardless of population

Place	Number	%
Houston (city) Harris County	37	0.00
Dallas (city) Dallas County	17	0.00
Plano (city) Collin County	7	0.00
Fort Hood (cdp) Coryell County	5	0.01
Arlington (city) Tarrant County	4	0.00
Austin (city) Travis County	4	0.00
San Antonio (city) Bexar County	4	0.00
Texas City (city) Galveston County	3	0.01
Mesquite (city) Dallas County	3	0.00
Wimberley (cdp) Hays County	2	0.05

Top 10 Places Sorted by Percent
Based on all places, regardless of population

Place	Number	%
Wimberley (cdp) Hays County	2	0.05
Fifth Street (cdp) Fort Bend County	1	0.05
San Leon (cdp) Galveston County	1	0.02
Fort Hood (cdp) Coryell County	5	0.01
Texas City (city) Galveston County	3	0.01
Friendswood (city) Galveston County	2	0.01
Pearland (city) Brazoria County	2	0.01
Schertz (city) Guadalupe County	2	0.01
Belton (city) Bell County	1	0.01
Borger (city) Hutchinson County	1	0.01

Top 10 Places Sorted by Percent
Based on places with populations of 10,000 or more

Place	Number	%
Fort Hood (cdp) Coryell County	5	0.01
Texas City (city) Galveston County	3	0.01
Friendswood (city) Galveston County	2	0.01
Pearland (city) Brazoria County	2	0.01
Schertz (city) Guadalupe County	2	0.01
Belton (city) Bell County	1	0.01
Borger (city) Hutchinson County	1	0.01
Dickinson (city) Galveston County	1	0.01
Portland (city) San Patricio County	1	0.01
Universal City (city) Bexar County	1	0.01

Hawaii Native/Pacific Islander: Fijian

Top 10 Places Sorted by Number
Based on all places, regardless of population

Place	Number	%
Houston (city) Harris County	33	0.00
Dallas (city) Dallas County	16	0.00
Plano (city) Collin County	7	0.00
Texas City (city) Galveston County	3	0.01
Austin (city) Travis County	3	0.00
Mesquite (city) Dallas County	3	0.00
Wimberley (cdp) Hays County	2	0.05
Fort Hood (cdp) Coryell County	2	0.01
Friendswood (city) Galveston County	2	0.01
Pearland (city) Brazoria County	2	0.01

Top 10 Places Sorted by Percent
Based on all places, regardless of population

Place	Number	%
Wimberley (cdp) Hays County	2	0.05

Place	Number	%
Fifth Street (cdp) Fort Bend County	1	0.05
San Leon (cdp) Galveston County	1	0.02
Texas City (city) Galveston County	3	0.01
Fort Hood (cdp) Coryell County	2	0.01
Friendswood (city) Galveston County	2	0.01
Pearland (city) Brazoria County	2	0.01
Schertz (city) Guadalupe County	2	0.01
Borger (city) Hutchinson County	1	0.01
Dickinson (city) Galveston County	1	0.01

Top 10 Places Sorted by Percent
Based on places with populations of 10,000 or more

Place	Number	%
Texas City (city) Galveston County	3	0.01
Fort Hood (cdp) Coryell County	2	0.01
Friendswood (city) Galveston County	2	0.01
Pearland (city) Brazoria County	2	0.01
Schertz (city) Guadalupe County	2	0.01
Borger (city) Hutchinson County	1	0.01
Dickinson (city) Galveston County	1	0.01
Houston (city) Harris County	33	0.00
Dallas (city) Dallas County	16	0.00
Plano (city) Collin County	7	0.00

Hawaii Native/Pacific Islander: Other Melanesian

Top 10 Places Sorted by Number
Based on all places, regardless of population

Place	Number	%
Houston (city) Harris County	4	0.00
Fort Hood (cdp) Coryell County	3	0.01
Arlington (city) Tarrant County	3	0.00
Lubbock (city) Lubbock County	2	0.00
San Antonio (city) Bexar County	2	0.00
Belton (city) Bell County	1	0.01
Portland (city) San Patricio County	1	0.01
Universal City (city) Bexar County	1	0.01
Austin (city) Travis County	1	0.00
Dallas (city) Dallas County	1	0.00

Top 10 Places Sorted by Percent
Based on all places, regardless of population

Place	Number	%
Fort Hood (cdp) Coryell County	3	0.01
Belton (city) Bell County	1	0.01
Portland (city) San Patricio County	1	0.01
Universal City (city) Bexar County	1	0.01
Houston (city) Harris County	4	0.00
Arlington (city) Tarrant County	3	0.00
Lubbock (city) Lubbock County	2	0.00
San Antonio (city) Bexar County	2	0.00
Austin (city) Travis County	1	0.00
Dallas (city) Dallas County	1	0.00

Top 10 Places Sorted by Percent
Based on places with populations of 10,000 or more

Place	Number	%
Fort Hood (cdp) Coryell County	3	0.01
Belton (city) Bell County	1	0.01
Portland (city) San Patricio County	1	0.01
Universal City (city) Bexar County	1	0.01
Houston (city) Harris County	4	0.00
Arlington (city) Tarrant County	3	0.00
Lubbock (city) Lubbock County	2	0.00
San Antonio (city) Bexar County	2	0.00
Austin (city) Travis County	1	0.00
Dallas (city) Dallas County	1	0.00

Notes: (cdp) census designated place; Refer to the User's Guide in the front of the book for more detailed information.

Hawaii Native/Pacific Islander: Micronesian

Top 10 Places Sorted by Number
Based on all places, regardless of population

Place	Number	%
San Antonio (city) Bexar County	573	0.05
Killeen (city) Bell County	541	0.62
Houston (city) Harris County	475	0.02
El Paso (city) El Paso County	328	0.06
Dallas (city) Dallas County	217	0.02
Austin (city) Travis County	180	0.03
Fort Hood (cdp) Coryell County	170	0.50
Fort Worth (city) Tarrant County	156	0.03
Arlington (city) Tarrant County	150	0.05
Keene (city) Johnson County	113	2.26

Top 10 Places Sorted by Percent
Based on all places, regardless of population

Place	Number	%
Retreat (town) Navarro County	9	2.65
Alto Bonito (cdp) Starr County	15	2.64
Keene (city) Johnson County	113	2.26
Evant (town) Coryell County	3	0.76
Garrett (town) Ellis County	3	0.67
Killeen (city) Bell County	541	0.62
Angus (city) Navarro County	2	0.60
Skidmore (cdp) Bee County	6	0.59
Pelican Bay (city) Tarrant County	8	0.53
Fort Hood (cdp) Coryell County	170	0.50

Top 10 Places Sorted by Percent
Based on places with populations of 10,000 or more

Place	Number	%
Killeen (city) Bell County	541	0.62
Fort Hood (cdp) Coryell County	170	0.50
Corsicana (city) Navarro County	75	0.31
Copperas Cove (city) Coryell County	76	0.26
Harker Heights (city) Bell County	44	0.25
Portland (city) San Patricio County	32	0.22
Humble (city) Harris County	23	0.16
Universal City (city) Bexar County	22	0.15
Cleburne (city) Johnson County	37	0.14
Converse (city) Bexar County	9	0.08

Hawaii Native/Pacific Islander: Guamanian or Chamorro

Top 10 Places Sorted by Number
Based on all places, regardless of population

Place	Number	%
San Antonio (city) Bexar County	540	0.05
Killeen (city) Bell County	516	0.59
Houston (city) Harris County	442	0.02
El Paso (city) El Paso County	310	0.05
Dallas (city) Dallas County	201	0.02
Austin (city) Travis County	159	0.02
Fort Worth (city) Tarrant County	150	0.03
Fort Hood (cdp) Coryell County	126	0.37
Arlington (city) Tarrant County	117	0.04
Copperas Cove (city) Coryell County	72	0.24

Top 10 Places Sorted by Percent
Based on all places, regardless of population

Place	Number	%
Evant (town) Coryell County	3	0.76
Killeen (city) Bell County	516	0.59
Skidmore (cdp) Bee County	6	0.59
Pelican Bay (city) Tarrant County	8	0.53
Southmayd (city) Grayson County	5	0.50
Ector (city) Fannin County	3	0.50
Bovina (city) Parmer County	9	0.48

Loma Linda East (cdp) Jim Wells County	1	0.47
Bells (town) Grayson County	5	0.42
Rose Hill Acres (city) Hardin County	2	0.42

Top 10 Places Sorted by Percent
Based on places with populations of 10,000 or more

Place	Number	%
Killeen (city) Bell County	516	0.59
Fort Hood (cdp) Coryell County	126	0.37
Copperas Cove (city) Coryell County	72	0.24
Harker Heights (city) Bell County	42	0.24
Portland (city) San Patricio County	30	0.20
Humble (city) Harris County	21	0.14
Universal City (city) Bexar County	19	0.13
Converse (city) Bexar County	9	0.08
Schertz (city) Guadalupe County	14	0.07
Deer Park (city) Harris County	16	0.06

Hawaii Native/Pacific Islander: Other Micronesian

Top 10 Places Sorted by Number
Based on all places, regardless of population

Place	Number	%
Keene (city) Johnson County	113	2.26
Corsicana (city) Navarro County	75	0.31
Fort Hood (cdp) Coryell County	44	0.13
Cleburne (city) Johnson County	36	0.14
Arlington (city) Tarrant County	33	0.01
Houston (city) Harris County	33	0.02
San Antonio (city) Bexar County	33	0.00
Irving (city) Dallas County	31	0.02
Killeen (city) Bell County	25	0.03
Austin (city) Travis County	21	0.00

Top 10 Places Sorted by Percent
Based on all places, regardless of population

Place	Number	%
Retreat (town) Navarro County	9	2.65
Alto Bonito (cdp) Starr County	15	2.64
Keene (city) Johnson County	113	2.26
Garrett (town) Ellis County	3	0.67
Angus (city) Navarro County	2	0.60
Corsicana (city) Navarro County	75	0.31
Fort Bliss (cdp) El Paso County	15	0.18
Commerce (city) Hunt County	12	0.16
Cleburne (city) Johnson County	36	0.14
Fort Hood (cdp) Coryell County	44	0.13

Top 10 Places Sorted by Percent
Based on places with populations of 10,000 or more

Place	Number	%
Corsicana (city) Navarro County	75	0.31
Cleburne (city) Johnson County	36	0.14
Fort Hood (cdp) Coryell County	44	0.13
Killeen (city) Bell County	25	0.03
Alice (city) Jim Wells County	5	0.03
El Campo (city) Wharton County	3	0.03
Irving (city) Dallas County	31	0.02
Haltom City (city) Tarrant County	8	0.02
Hurst (city) Tarrant County	7	0.02
Texarkana (city) Bowie County	6	0.02

Hawaii Native/Pacific Islander: Polynesian

Top 10 Places Sorted by Number
Based on all places, regardless of population

Place	Number	%
Euless (city) Tarrant County	925	2.01
San Antonio (city) Bexar County	896	0.08
Houston (city) Harris County	877	0.04
Killeen (city) Bell County	565	0.65

El Paso (city) El Paso County	520	0.09
Dallas (city) Dallas County	511	0.04
Austin (city) Travis County	475	0.07
Arlington (city) Tarrant County	456	0.14
Fort Worth (city) Tarrant County	355	0.07
Fort Hood (cdp) Coryell County	245	0.73

Top 10 Places Sorted by Percent
Based on all places, regardless of population

Place	Number	%
Ranchette Estates (cdp) Willacy County	5	3.76
Euless (city) Tarrant County	925	2.01
Petronila (city) Nueces County	1	1.20
Garrett (town) Ellis County	5	1.12
Bloomburg (town) Cass County	3	0.80
Fort Hood (cdp) Coryell County	245	0.73
Falman-County Acres (cdp) San Patricio County	2	0.69
Killeen (city) Bell County	565	0.65
Mustang Ridge (city) Caldwell County	5	0.64
Copperas Cove (city) Coryell County	177	0.60

Top 10 Places Sorted by Percent
Based on places with populations of 10,000 or more

Place	Number	%
Euless (city) Tarrant County	925	2.01
Fort Hood (cdp) Coryell County	245	0.73
Killeen (city) Bell County	565	0.65
Copperas Cove (city) Coryell County	177	0.60
Hurst (city) Tarrant County	142	0.39
Harker Heights (city) Bell County	61	0.35
Bedford (city) Tarrant County	159	0.34
Watauga (city) Tarrant County	49	0.22
Spring (cdp) Harris County	71	0.20
North Richland Hills (city) Tarrant County	96	0.17

Hawaii Native/Pacific Islander: Native Hawaiian

Top 10 Places Sorted by Number
Based on all places, regardless of population

Place	Number	%
San Antonio (city) Bexar County	663	0.06
Houston (city) Harris County	511	0.03
Austin (city) Travis County	345	0.05
El Paso (city) El Paso County	313	0.06
Killeen (city) Bell County	302	0.35
Dallas (city) Dallas County	295	0.02
Arlington (city) Tarrant County	208	0.06
Fort Worth (city) Tarrant County	186	0.03
Corpus Christi (city) Nueces County	145	0.05
Fort Hood (cdp) Coryell County	127	0.38

Top 10 Places Sorted by Percent
Based on all places, regardless of population

Place	Number	%
Ranchette Estates (cdp) Willacy County	5	3.76
Petronila (city) Nueces County	1	1.20
Garrett (town) Ellis County	5	1.12
Bloomburg (town) Cass County	3	0.80
Falman-County Acres (cdp) San Patricio County	2	0.69
Mustang Ridge (city) Caldwell County	5	0.64
Tatum (city) Rusk County	6	0.51
Mobile City (city) Rockwall County	1	0.51
Blum (town) Hill County	2	0.50
Santa Clara (city) Guadalupe County	4	0.45

Top 10 Places Sorted by Percent
Based on places with populations of 10,000 or more

Place	Number	%
Fort Hood (cdp) Coryell County	127	0.38
Killeen (city) Bell County	302	0.35
Copperas Cove (city) Coryell County	70	0.24

Notes: (cdp) census designated place; Refer to the User's Guide in the front of the book for more detailed information.

Place	Number	%
Harker Heights (city) Bell County	41	0.24
Euless (city) Tarrant County	87	0.19
Universal City (city) Bexar County	23	0.15
Schertz (city) Guadalupe County	23	0.12
Wichita Falls (city) Wichita County	115	0.11
Spring (cdp) Harris County	39	0.11
Converse (city) Bexar County	13	0.11

Hawaii Native/Pacific Islander: Samoan

Top 10 Places Sorted by Number
Based on all places, regardless of population

Place	Number	%
Houston (city) Harris County	319	0.02
Killeen (city) Bell County	245	0.28
San Antonio (city) Bexar County	214	0.02
Dallas (city) Dallas County	192	0.02
El Paso (city) El Paso County	187	0.03
Arlington (city) Tarrant County	157	0.05
Fort Hood (cdp) Coryell County	107	0.32
Austin (city) Travis County	106	0.02
Copperas Cove (city) Coryell County	103	0.35
Fort Worth (city) Tarrant County	77	0.01

Top 10 Places Sorted by Percent
Based on all places, regardless of population

Place	Number	%
Knollwood (village) Grayson County	2	0.53
Josephine (city) Collin County	3	0.51
Manor (city) Travis County	6	0.50
Saint Paul (town) Collin County	3	0.48
Lolita (cdp) Jackson County	2	0.36
Copperas Cove (city) Coryell County	103	0.35
Fort Hood (cdp) Coryell County	107	0.32
Omaha (city) Morris County	3	0.30
Killeen (city) Bell County	245	0.28
Lakeshore Grdns-Hidden Acres (cdp) San Patricio Co.	2	0.28

Top 10 Places Sorted by Percent
Based on places with populations of 10,000 or more

Place	Number	%
Copperas Cove (city) Coryell County	103	0.35
Fort Hood (cdp) Coryell County	107	0.32
Killeen (city) Bell County	245	0.28
Euless (city) Tarrant County	70	0.15
Harker Heights (city) Bell County	20	0.12
Hurst (city) Tarrant County	28	0.08
Jacksonville (city) Cherokee County	11	0.08
Freeport (city) Brazoria County	10	0.08
Mission Bend (cdp) Fort Bend County	19	0.06
Corinth (city) Denton County	7	0.06

Hawaii Native/Pacific Islander: Tongan

Top 10 Places Sorted by Number
Based on all places, regardless of population

Place	Number	%
Euless (city) Tarrant County	710	1.54
Fort Worth (city) Tarrant County	80	0.01
Arlington (city) Tarrant County	79	0.02
Bedford (city) Tarrant County	65	0.14
North Richland Hills (city) Tarrant County	64	0.12
Hurst (city) Tarrant County	60	0.17
Houston (city) Harris County	31	0.00
Watauga (city) Tarrant County	24	0.11
Irving (city) Dallas County	24	0.01
Spring (cdp) Harris County	22	0.06

Top 10 Places Sorted by Percent
Based on all places, regardless of population

Place	Number	%
Euless (city) Tarrant County	710	1.54

Place	Number	%
Richland Hills (city) Tarrant County	19	0.23
Hurst (city) Tarrant County	60	0.17
Bedford (city) Tarrant County	65	0.14
North Richland Hills (city) Tarrant County	64	0.12
Watauga (city) Tarrant County	24	0.11
New Boston (city) Bowie County	5	0.10
Spring (cdp) Harris County	22	0.06
Lake Worth (city) Tarrant County	3	0.06
Haltom City (city) Tarrant County	21	0.05

Top 10 Places Sorted by Percent
Based on places with populations of 10,000 or more

Place	Number	%
Euless (city) Tarrant County	710	1.54
Hurst (city) Tarrant County	60	0.17
Bedford (city) Tarrant County	65	0.14
North Richland Hills (city) Tarrant County	64	0.12
Watauga (city) Tarrant County	24	0.11
Spring (cdp) Harris County	22	0.06
Haltom City (city) Tarrant County	21	0.05
Grapevine (city) Tarrant County	17	0.04
Athens (city) Henderson County	3	0.03
Arlington (city) Tarrant County	79	0.02

Hawaii Native/Pacific Islander: Other Polynesian

Top 10 Places Sorted by Number
Based on all places, regardless of population

Place	Number	%
Euless (city) Tarrant County	58	0.13
Bedford (city) Tarrant County	27	0.06
Hurst (city) Tarrant County	21	0.06
Dallas (city) Dallas County	19	0.00
Irving (city) Dallas County	17	0.01
Killeen (city) Bell County	16	0.02
Houston (city) Harris County	16	0.00
Austin (city) Travis County	14	0.00
San Antonio (city) Bexar County	14	0.00
Arlington (city) Tarrant County	12	0.00

Top 10 Places Sorted by Percent
Based on all places, regardless of population

Place	Number	%
Euless (city) Tarrant County	58	0.13
Jamaica Beach (city) Galveston County	1	0.09
Bedford (city) Tarrant County	27	0.06
Hurst (city) Tarrant County	21	0.06
Lake Worth (city) Tarrant County	2	0.04
Alpine (city) Brewster County	2	0.03
Killeen (city) Bell County	16	0.02
Flower Mound (town) Denton County	8	0.02
Georgetown (city) Williamson County	5	0.02
Schertz (city) Guadalupe County	4	0.02

Top 10 Places Sorted by Percent
Based on places with populations of 10,000 or more

Place	Number	%
Euless (city) Tarrant County	58	0.13
Bedford (city) Tarrant County	27	0.06
Hurst (city) Tarrant County	21	0.06
Killeen (city) Bell County	16	0.02
Flower Mound (town) Denton County	8	0.02
Georgetown (city) Williamson County	5	0.02
Schertz (city) Guadalupe County	4	0.02
Watauga (city) Tarrant County	4	0.02
Irving (city) Dallas County	17	0.01
Lubbock (city) Lubbock County	11	0.01

Hawaii Native/Pacific Islander: Other Pacific Islander, specified

Top 10 Places Sorted by Number
Based on all places, regardless of population

Place	Number	%
Houston (city) Harris County	172	0.01
Dallas (city) Dallas County	95	0.01
Fort Worth (city) Tarrant County	46	0.01
San Antonio (city) Bexar County	41	0.00
Austin (city) Travis County	30	0.00
Waco (city) McLennan County	18	0.02
Arlington (city) Tarrant County	18	0.01
Corpus Christi (city) Nueces County	17	0.01
Lubbock (city) Lubbock County	16	0.01
Port Arthur (city) Jefferson County	14	0.02

Top 10 Places Sorted by Percent
Based on all places, regardless of population

Place	Number	%
Warren City (city) Gregg County	6	1.75
Yantis (town) Wood County	5	1.56
Rosser (village) Kaufman County	3	0.79
San Isidro (cdp) Starr County	2	0.74
Buffalo (city) Leon County	6	0.33
Lytle (city) Atascosa County	6	0.25
Shamrock (city) Wheeler County	3	0.15
Edna (city) Jackson County	8	0.14
Hempstead (city) Waller County	6	0.13
Zapata (cdp) Zapata County	6	0.12

Top 10 Places Sorted by Percent
Based on places with populations of 10,000 or more

Place	Number	%
New Territory (cdp) Fort Bend County	7	0.05
El Campo (city) Wharton County	6	0.05
Greenville (city) Hunt County	6	0.03
Colleyville (city) Tarrant County	5	0.03
Schertz (city) Guadalupe County	5	0.03
Hereford (city) Deaf Smith County	4	0.03
Waco (city) McLennan County	18	0.02
Port Arthur (city) Jefferson County	14	0.02
Tyler (city) Smith County	14	0.02
McKinney (city) Collin County	9	0.02

Hawaii Native/Pacific Islander: Other Pacific Islander, not specified

Top 10 Places Sorted by Number
Based on all places, regardless of population

Place	Number	%
Houston (city) Harris County	1,338	0.07
Dallas (city) Dallas County	643	0.05
San Antonio (city) Bexar County	579	0.05
Austin (city) Travis County	393	0.06
Fort Worth (city) Tarrant County	213	0.04
Arlington (city) Tarrant County	207	0.06
El Paso (city) El Paso County	203	0.04
Irving (city) Dallas County	177	0.09
Corpus Christi (city) Nueces County	164	0.06
Killeen (city) Bell County	150	0.17

Top 10 Places Sorted by Percent
Based on all places, regardless of population

Place	Number	%
Center (city) Shelby County	125	2.20
Encino (cdp) Brooks County	2	1.13
Holland (town) Bell County	8	0.73
Lawn (town) Taylor County	2	0.57
Keene (city) Johnson County	28	0.56
Palm Valley (city) Cameron County	6	0.46
Oakhurst (city) San Jacinto County	1	0.43

Notes: (cdp) census designated place; Refer to the User's Guide in the front of the book for more detailed information.

Knippa (cdp) Uvalde County	3	0.41
Sanctuary (town) Parker County	1	0.39
Lakeside (town) Tarrant County	4	0.38

Top 10 Places Sorted by Percent
Based on places with populations of 10,000 or more

Place	Number	%
Fort Hood (cdp) Coryell County	59	0.18
Corsicana (city) Navarro County	45	0.18
Killeen (city) Bell County	150	0.17
Mission Bend (cdp) Fort Bend County	50	0.16
Stafford (city) Fort Bend County	25	0.16
Euless (city) Tarrant County	67	0.15
Huntsville (city) Walker County	51	0.15
New Territory (cdp) Fort Bend County	21	0.15
Wells Branch (cdp) Travis County	15	0.13
Baytown (city) Harris County	82	0.12

Hispanic or Latino

Top 10 Places Sorted by Number
Based on all places, regardless of population

Place	Number	%
Houston (city) Harris County	730,865	37.41
San Antonio (city) Bexar County	671,394	58.66
El Paso (city) El Paso County	431,875	76.62
Dallas (city) Dallas County	422,587	35.55
Austin (city) Travis County	200,579	30.55
Laredo (city) Webb County	166,216	94.13
Fort Worth (city) Tarrant County	159,368	29.81
Corpus Christi (city) Nueces County	150,737	54.33
Brownsville (city) Cameron County	127,535	91.28
McAllen (city) Hidalgo County	85,427	80.28

Top 10 Places Sorted by Percent
Based on all places, regardless of population

Place	Number	%
Roma Creek (cdp) Starr County	610	100.00
New Falcon (cdp) Zapata County	184	100.00
Concepcion (cdp) Duval County	61	100.00
Cuevitas (cdp) Hidalgo County	37	100.00
Willamar (cdp) Willacy County	15	100.00
Santa Maria (cdp) Cameron County	844	99.76
West Pearsall (cdp) Frio County	348	99.71
Santa Cruz (cdp) Starr County	628	99.68
Lago (cdp) Cameron County	245	99.59
Mila Doce (cdp) Hidalgo County	4,884	99.53

Top 10 Places Sorted by Percent
Based on places with populations of 10,000 or more

Place	Number	%
San Elizario (cdp) El Paso County	10,812	97.88
La Homa (cdp) Hidalgo County	10,196	97.73
Socorro (city) El Paso County	26,183	96.43
Rio Grande City (city) Starr County	11,433	95.89
San Juan (city) Hidalgo County	24,950	95.12
Eagle Pass (city) Maverick County	21,269	94.90
Laredo (city) Webb County	166,216	94.13
Robstown (city) Nueces County	11,848	93.09
Brownsville (city) Cameron County	127,535	91.28
Pharr (city) Hidalgo County	42,282	90.62

Hispanic: Central American

Top 10 Places Sorted by Number
Based on all places, regardless of population

Place	Number	%
Houston (city) Harris County	60,642	3.10
Dallas (city) Dallas County	14,972	1.26
Irving (city) Dallas County	6,225	3.25
Austin (city) Travis County	4,290	0.65
San Antonio (city) Bexar County	3,492	0.31

Garland (city) Dallas County	3,212	1.49
Pasadena (city) Harris County	1,900	1.34
Fort Worth (city) Tarrant County	1,581	0.30
Arlington (city) Tarrant County	1,495	0.45
Carrollton (city) Denton County	1,429	1.30

Top 10 Places Sorted by Percent
Based on all places, regardless of population

Place	Number	%
Webster (city) Harris County	500	5.50
Newton (city) Newton County	112	4.55
Farmers Branch (city) Dallas County	909	3.30
Irving (city) Dallas County	6,225	3.25
Houston (city) Harris County	60,642	3.10
Mission Bend (cdp) Fort Bend County	935	3.03
Aldine (cdp) Harris County	363	2.60
Mobile City (city) Rockwall County	5	2.55
Conroe (city) Montgomery County	882	2.40
Addison (town) Dallas County	331	2.34

Top 10 Places Sorted by Percent
Based on places with populations of 10,000 or more

Place	Number	%
Farmers Branch (city) Dallas County	909	3.30
Irving (city) Dallas County	6,225	3.25
Houston (city) Harris County	60,642	3.10
Mission Bend (cdp) Fort Bend County	935	3.03
Aldine (cdp) Harris County	363	2.60
Conroe (city) Montgomery County	882	2.40
Addison (town) Dallas County	331	2.34
South Houston (city) Harris County	364	2.30
Cloverleaf (cdp) Harris County	450	1.91
Richmond (city) Fort Bend County	200	1.80

Hispanic: Costa Rican

Top 10 Places Sorted by Number
Based on all places, regardless of population

Place	Number	%
Houston (city) Harris County	567	0.03
Dallas (city) Dallas County	418	0.04
San Antonio (city) Bexar County	143	0.01
Austin (city) Travis County	134	0.02
Arlington (city) Tarrant County	95	0.03
Garland (city) Dallas County	79	0.04
Plano (city) Collin County	68	0.03
Richardson (city) Dallas County	57	0.06
Irving (city) Dallas County	55	0.03
El Paso (city) El Paso County	54	0.01

Top 10 Places Sorted by Percent
Based on all places, regardless of population

Place	Number	%
Woodloch (town) Montgomery County	5	2.02
Rice (city) Navarro County	4	0.50
Manor (city) Travis County	5	0.42
Godley (city) Johnson County	3	0.34
Palmhurst (city) Hidalgo County	11	0.23
Addison (town) Dallas County	25	0.18
Bardwell (city) Ellis County	1	0.17
Mission Bend (cdp) Fort Bend County	47	0.15
Eagle Mountain (cdp) Tarrant County	10	0.15
Oak Ridge North (city) Montgomery County	4	0.13

Top 10 Places Sorted by Percent
Based on places with populations of 10,000 or more

Place	Number	%
Addison (town) Dallas County	25	0.18
Mission Bend (cdp) Fort Bend County	47	0.15
Richardson (city) Dallas County	57	0.06
Cloverleaf (cdp) Harris County	13	0.06
Bellaire (city) Harris County	10	0.06

College Station (city) Brazos County	33	0.05
Coppell (city) Dallas County	17	0.05
Alamo (city) Hidalgo County	8	0.05
Galena Park (city) Harris County	5	0.05
Dallas (city) Dallas County	418	0.04

Hispanic: Guatemalan

Top 10 Places Sorted by Number
Based on all places, regardless of population

Place	Number	%
Houston (city) Harris County	7,220	0.37
Dallas (city) Dallas County	1,950	0.16
Garland (city) Dallas County	813	0.38
Austin (city) Travis County	748	0.11
San Antonio (city) Bexar County	584	0.05
Fort Worth (city) Tarrant County	304	0.06
El Paso (city) El Paso County	239	0.04
Plano (city) Collin County	234	0.11
Irving (city) Dallas County	221	0.12
Arlington (city) Tarrant County	218	0.07

Top 10 Places Sorted by Percent
Based on all places, regardless of population

Place	Number	%
Milano (city) Milam County	8	2.00
Lincoln Park (town) Denton County	7	1.35
Holiday Lakes (town) Brazoria County	14	1.28
Industry (city) Austin County	3	0.99
Oak Valley (town) Navarro County	3	0.75
Thorndale (city) Milam County	8	0.63
Cumings (cdp) Fort Bend County	4	0.59
Navarro (town) Navarro County	1	0.52
Webster (city) Harris County	44	0.48
Westover Hills (town) Tarrant County	3	0.46

Top 10 Places Sorted by Percent
Based on places with populations of 10,000 or more

Place	Number	%
Garland (city) Dallas County	813	0.38
Humble (city) Harris County	56	0.38
Houston (city) Harris County	7,220	0.37
Mission Bend (cdp) Fort Bend County	114	0.37
Denton (city) Denton County	217	0.27
Farmers Branch (city) Dallas County	70	0.25
Aldine (cdp) Harris County	35	0.25
Palestine (city) Anderson County	38	0.22
Addison (town) Dallas County	31	0.22
Spring (cdp) Harris County	71	0.20

Hispanic: Honduran

Top 10 Places Sorted by Number
Based on all places, regardless of population

Place	Number	%
Houston (city) Harris County	10,284	0.53
Dallas (city) Dallas County	2,637	0.22
Austin (city) Travis County	1,065	0.16
San Antonio (city) Bexar County	641	0.06
Irving (city) Dallas County	470	0.25
Conroe (city) Montgomery County	426	1.16
Pasadena (city) Harris County	354	0.25
Fort Worth (city) Tarrant County	350	0.07
Garland (city) Dallas County	306	0.14
Plano (city) Collin County	216	0.10

Top 10 Places Sorted by Percent
Based on all places, regardless of population

Place	Number	%
Newton (city) Newton County	104	4.23
Ranchitos Las Lomas (cdp) Webb County	7	2.10
Conroe (city) Montgomery County	426	1.16

Notes: (cdp) census designated place; Refer to the User's Guide in the front of the book for more detailed information.

	Number	%
Falcon Mesa (cdp) Zapata County	5	0.99
Port Isabel (city) Cameron County	34	0.70
Bayview (town) Cameron County	2	0.62
Montgomery (city) Montgomery County	3	0.61
San Perlita (city) Willacy County	4	0.59
Hilshire Village (city) Harris County	4	0.56
Houston (city) Harris County	10,284	0.53

Top 10 Places Sorted by Percent
Based on places with populations of 10,000 or more

Place	Number	%
Conroe (city) Montgomery County	426	1.16
Houston (city) Harris County	10,284	0.53
Aldine (cdp) Harris County	70	0.50
Cloverleaf (cdp) Harris County	104	0.44
South Houston (city) Harris County	66	0.42
Humble (city) Harris County	52	0.36
Athens (city) Henderson County	39	0.35
Mission Bend (cdp) Fort Bend County	97	0.31
Galveston (city) Galveston County	165	0.29
Irving (city) Dallas County	470	0.25

Hispanic: Nicaraguan

Top 10 Places Sorted by Number
Based on all places, regardless of population

Place	Number	%
Houston (city) Harris County	2,196	0.11
Austin (city) Travis County	456	0.07
Port Arthur (city) Jefferson County	432	0.75
Dallas (city) Dallas County	407	0.03
San Antonio (city) Bexar County	395	0.03
Carrollton (city) Denton County	130	0.12
El Paso (city) El Paso County	113	0.02
Grand Prairie (city) Dallas County	97	0.08
Fort Worth (city) Tarrant County	84	0.02
Irving (city) Dallas County	79	0.04

Top 10 Places Sorted by Percent
Based on all places, regardless of population

Place	Number	%
Port Arthur (city) Jefferson County	432	0.75
Green Valley Farms (cdp) Cameron County	4	0.56
Ravenna (city) Fannin County	1	0.47
Freeport (city) Brazoria County	52	0.41
Hedwig Village (city) Harris County	7	0.30
Keene (city) Johnson County	14	0.28
Sweeny (city) Brazoria County	10	0.28
Mission Bend (cdp) Fort Bend County	77	0.25
Johnson City (city) Blanco County	3	0.25
Timbercreek Canyon (village) Randall County	1	0.25

Top 10 Places Sorted by Percent
Based on places with populations of 10,000 or more

Place	Number	%
Port Arthur (city) Jefferson County	432	0.75
Freeport (city) Brazoria County	52	0.41
Mission Bend (cdp) Fort Bend County	77	0.25
Humble (city) Harris County	23	0.16
Carrollton (city) Denton County	130	0.12
New Territory (cdp) Fort Bend County	17	0.12
Houston (city) Harris County	2,196	0.11
Farmers Branch (city) Dallas County	30	0.11
Groves (city) Jefferson County	17	0.11
Jollyville (cdp) Williamson County	17	0.11

Hispanic: Panamanian

Top 10 Places Sorted by Number
Based on all places, regardless of population

Place	Number	%
San Antonio (city) Bexar County	853	0.07

	Number	%
Houston (city) Harris County	792	0.04
Killeen (city) Bell County	596	0.69
El Paso (city) El Paso County	369	0.07
Austin (city) Travis County	345	0.05
Dallas (city) Dallas County	319	0.03
Fort Hood (cdp) Coryell County	148	0.44
Fort Worth (city) Tarrant County	143	0.03
Copperas Cove (city) Coryell County	131	0.44
Arlington (city) Tarrant County	122	0.04

Top 10 Places Sorted by Percent
Based on all places, regardless of population

Place	Number	%
Toco (city) Lamar County	1	1.12
Liverpool (city) Brazoria County	3	0.74
Killeen (city) Bell County	596	0.69
Bonney (village) Brazoria County	2	0.52
Geronimo (cdp) Guadalupe County	3	0.48
Fort Hood (cdp) Coryell County	148	0.44
Copperas Cove (city) Coryell County	131	0.44
Windcrest (city) Bexar County	18	0.35
Abbott (city) Hill County	1	0.33
Lackland AFB (cdp) Bexar County	22	0.31

Top 10 Places Sorted by Percent
Based on places with populations of 10,000 or more

Place	Number	%
Killeen (city) Bell County	596	0.69
Fort Hood (cdp) Coryell County	148	0.44
Copperas Cove (city) Coryell County	131	0.44
Harker Heights (city) Bell County	51	0.29
Converse (city) Bexar County	22	0.19
Mission Bend (cdp) Fort Bend County	39	0.13
Wells Branch (cdp) Travis County	15	0.13
Universal City (city) Bexar County	15	0.10
West University Place (city) Harris County	14	0.10
College Station (city) Brazos County	58	0.09

Hispanic: Salvadoran

Top 10 Places Sorted by Number
Based on all places, regardless of population

Place	Number	%
Houston (city) Harris County	36,799	1.88
Dallas (city) Dallas County	8,582	0.72
Irving (city) Dallas County	5,102	2.66
Garland (city) Dallas County	1,737	0.81
Austin (city) Travis County	1,331	0.20
Pasadena (city) Harris County	1,109	0.78
Carrollton (city) Denton County	885	0.81
Arlington (city) Tarrant County	755	0.23
Farmers Branch (city) Dallas County	692	2.52
San Antonio (city) Bexar County	665	0.06

Top 10 Places Sorted by Percent
Based on all places, regardless of population

Place	Number	%
Webster (city) Harris County	381	4.19
Irving (city) Dallas County	5,102	2.66
Mobile City (city) Rockwall County	5	2.55
Farmers Branch (city) Dallas County	692	2.52
Houston (city) Harris County	36,799	1.88
South Houston (city) Harris County	255	1.61
Mission Bend (cdp) Fort Bend County	489	1.59
Aldine (cdp) Harris County	218	1.56
Fifth Street (cdp) Fort Bend County	31	1.51
Pleak (village) Fort Bend County	14	1.48

Top 10 Places Sorted by Percent
Based on places with populations of 10,000 or more

Place	Number	%
Irving (city) Dallas County	5,102	2.66

	Number	%
Farmers Branch (city) Dallas County	692	2.52
Houston (city) Harris County	36,799	1.88
South Houston (city) Harris County	255	1.61
Mission Bend (cdp) Fort Bend County	489	1.59
Aldine (cdp) Harris County	218	1.56
Addison (town) Dallas County	208	1.47
Richmond (city) Fort Bend County	160	1.44
Rosenberg (city) Fort Bend County	338	1.41
Jacinto City (city) Harris County	113	1.10

Hispanic: Other Central American

Top 10 Places Sorted by Number
Based on all places, regardless of population

Place	Number	%
Houston (city) Harris County	2,784	0.14
Dallas (city) Dallas County	659	0.06
Austin (city) Travis County	211	0.03
San Antonio (city) Bexar County	211	0.02
Irving (city) Dallas County	207	0.11
Garland (city) Dallas County	168	0.08
Pasadena (city) Harris County	101	0.07
Mission Bend (cdp) Fort Bend County	72	0.23
Fort Worth (city) Tarrant County	72	0.01
Plano (city) Collin County	67	0.03

Top 10 Places Sorted by Percent
Based on all places, regardless of population

Place	Number	%
Los Angeles Subdivision (cdp) Willacy County	2	2.33
Del Mar Heights (cdp) Cameron County	2	0.77
Copper Canyon (town) Denton County	6	0.49
Santa Maria (cdp) Cameron County	4	0.47
Laguna Heights (cdp) Cameron County	8	0.40
Webster (city) Harris County	32	0.35
Bixby (cdp) Cameron County	1	0.28
Mission Bend (cdp) Fort Bend County	72	0.23
Four Corners (cdp) Fort Bend County	6	0.20
Omaha (city) Morris County	2	0.20

Top 10 Places Sorted by Percent
Based on places with populations of 10,000 or more

Place	Number	%
Mission Bend (cdp) Fort Bend County	72	0.23
Humble (city) Harris County	24	0.16
Aldine (cdp) Harris County	22	0.16
Houston (city) Harris County	2,784	0.14
Farmers Branch (city) Dallas County	37	0.13
Addison (town) Dallas County	19	0.13
Galena Park (city) Harris County	14	0.13
Richmond (city) Fort Bend County	13	0.12
Irving (city) Dallas County	207	0.11
Cloverleaf (cdp) Harris County	21	0.09

Hispanic: Cuban

Top 10 Places Sorted by Number
Based on all places, regardless of population

Place	Number	%
Houston (city) Harris County	4,970	0.25
Dallas (city) Dallas County	2,283	0.19
San Antonio (city) Bexar County	1,491	0.13
Austin (city) Travis County	1,425	0.22
Fort Worth (city) Tarrant County	608	0.11
El Paso (city) El Paso County	476	0.08
Arlington (city) Tarrant County	339	0.10
Plano (city) Collin County	334	0.15
Corpus Christi (city) Nueces County	334	0.12
Carrollton (city) Denton County	321	0.29

Notes: (cdp) census designated place; Refer to the User's Guide in the front of the book for more detailed information.

Top 10 Places Sorted by Percent
Based on all places, regardless of population

Place	Number	%
Reese Center (cdp) Lubbock County	1	2.38
Godley (city) Johnson County	11	1.25
Meadows Place (city) Fort Bend County	44	0.90
Tiki Island (village) Galveston County	9	0.89
Roaring Springs (town) Motley County	2	0.75
Mission Bend (cdp) Fort Bend County	221	0.72
Westover Hills (town) Tarrant County	4	0.61
Skidmore (cdp) Bee County	6	0.59
Bellaire (city) Harris County	81	0.52
Josephine (city) Collin County	3	0.51

Top 10 Places Sorted by Percent
Based on places with populations of 10,000 or more

Place	Number	%
Mission Bend (cdp) Fort Bend County	221	0.72
Bellaire (city) Harris County	81	0.52
New Territory (cdp) Fort Bend County	61	0.44
Sugar Land (city) Fort Bend County	254	0.40
Southlake (city) Tarrant County	74	0.34
Coppell (city) Dallas County	110	0.31
Carrollton (city) Denton County	321	0.29
Mansfield (city) Tarrant County	81	0.29
Farmers Branch (city) Dallas County	74	0.27
Houston (city) Harris County	4,970	0.25

Hispanic: Dominican Republic

Top 10 Places Sorted by Number
Based on all places, regardless of population

Place	Number	%
Houston (city) Harris County	990	0.05
San Antonio (city) Bexar County	267	0.02
Dallas (city) Dallas County	219	0.02
Killeen (city) Bell County	162	0.19
Austin (city) Travis County	129	0.02
El Paso (city) El Paso County	126	0.02
Fort Hood (cdp) Coryell County	104	0.31
Fort Worth (city) Tarrant County	104	0.02
Arlington (city) Tarrant County	87	0.03
Irving (city) Dallas County	65	0.03

Top 10 Places Sorted by Percent
Based on all places, regardless of population

Place	Number	%
Cumings (cdp) Fort Bend County	3	0.44
Lackland AFB (cdp) Bexar County	23	0.32
Vinton (village) El Paso County	6	0.32
Fort Hood (cdp) Coryell County	104	0.31
Jones Creek (village) Brazoria County	6	0.28
La Paloma (cdp) Cameron County	1	0.28
Post (city) Garza County	9	0.24
Killeen (city) Bell County	162	0.19
Nolanville (city) Bell County	4	0.19
Mission Bend (cdp) Fort Bend County	52	0.17

Top 10 Places Sorted by Percent
Based on places with populations of 10,000 or more

Place	Number	%
Fort Hood (cdp) Coryell County	104	0.31
Killeen (city) Bell County	162	0.19
Mission Bend (cdp) Fort Bend County	52	0.17
Big Spring (city) Howard County	42	0.17
Copperas Cove (city) Coryell County	32	0.11
Harker Heights (city) Bell County	17	0.10
League City (city) Galveston County	36	0.08
McAllen (city) Hidalgo County	64	0.06
Hurst (city) Tarrant County	22	0.06
Channelview (cdp) Harris County	18	0.06

Hispanic: Mexican

Top 10 Places Sorted by Number
Based on all places, regardless of population

Place	Number	%
Houston (city) Harris County	527,442	27.00
San Antonio (city) Bexar County	473,420	41.36
El Paso (city) El Paso County	359,699	63.81
Dallas (city) Dallas County	350,491	29.49
Austin (city) Travis County	153,868	23.44
Laredo (city) Webb County	133,185	75.43
Fort Worth (city) Tarrant County	132,894	24.85
Brownsville (city) Cameron County	103,297	73.93
Corpus Christi (city) Nueces County	98,146	35.37
McAllen (city) Hidalgo County	69,931	65.72

Top 10 Places Sorted by Percent
Based on all places, regardless of population

Place	Number	%
Roma Creek (cdp) Starr County	606	99.34
El Refugio (cdp) Starr County	219	99.10
Santa Cruz (cdp) Starr County	619	98.25
Las Lomas (cdp) Starr County	2,636	98.21
Granjeno (city) Hidalgo County	306	97.76
South Alamo (cdp) Hidalgo County	3,029	97.68
Lozano (cdp) Cameron County	315	97.19
Alto Bonito (cdp) Starr County	553	97.19
Sparks (cdp) El Paso County	2,888	97.11
Muniz (cdp) Hidalgo County	1,070	96.75

Top 10 Places Sorted by Percent
Based on places with populations of 10,000 or more

Place	Number	%
San Elizario (cdp) El Paso County	10,496	95.02
La Homa (cdp) Hidalgo County	9,666	92.65
San Juan (city) Hidalgo County	22,175	84.54
Socorro (city) El Paso County	22,438	82.64
Eagle Pass (city) Maverick County	17,965	80.15
Pharr (city) Hidalgo County	36,574	78.38
Rio Grande City (city) Starr County	9,241	77.51
Laredo (city) Webb County	133,185	75.43
Brownsville (city) Cameron County	103,297	73.93
Donna (city) Hidalgo County	10,596	71.75

Hispanic: Puerto Rican

Top 10 Places Sorted by Number
Based on all places, regardless of population

Place	Number	%
San Antonio (city) Bexar County	7,774	0.68
Houston (city) Harris County	6,906	0.35
Killeen (city) Bell County	4,499	5.18
El Paso (city) El Paso County	3,660	0.65
Austin (city) Travis County	2,529	0.39
Dallas (city) Dallas County	2,369	0.20
Arlington (city) Tarrant County	2,081	0.62
Fort Worth (city) Tarrant County	1,892	0.35
Fort Hood (cdp) Coryell County	1,540	4.57
Grand Prairie (city) Dallas County	812	0.64

Top 10 Places Sorted by Percent
Based on all places, regardless of population

Place	Number	%
Keene (city) Johnson County	264	5.28
Killeen (city) Bell County	4,499	5.18
Fort Bliss (cdp) El Paso County	413	5.00
Fort Hood (cdp) Coryell County	1,540	4.57
Lackland AFB (cdp) Bexar County	298	4.18
Copperas Cove (city) Coryell County	809	2.73
Harker Heights (city) Bell County	362	2.09
Kempner (city) Lampasas County	21	2.09
Westbrook (city) Mitchell County	4	1.97

Las Lomitas (cdp) Jim Hogg County | 4 | 1.50

Top 10 Places Sorted by Percent
Based on places with populations of 10,000 or more

Place	Number	%
Killeen (city) Bell County	4,499	5.18
Fort Hood (cdp) Coryell County	1,540	4.57
Copperas Cove (city) Coryell County	809	2.73
Harker Heights (city) Bell County	362	2.09
Euless (city) Tarrant County	645	1.40
Converse (city) Bexar County	128	1.11
Schertz (city) Guadalupe County	176	0.94
Universal City (city) Bexar County	139	0.94
Mission Bend (cdp) Fort Bend County	283	0.92
Bedford (city) Tarrant County	339	0.72

Hispanic: South American

Top 10 Places Sorted by Number
Based on all places, regardless of population

Place	Number	%
Houston (city) Harris County	13,214	0.68
Dallas (city) Dallas County	2,895	0.24
San Antonio (city) Bexar County	2,288	0.20
Austin (city) Travis County	2,161	0.33
Irving (city) Dallas County	1,028	0.54
Fort Worth (city) Tarrant County	904	0.17
Plano (city) Collin County	901	0.41
Arlington (city) Tarrant County	901	0.27
Mission Bend (cdp) Fort Bend County	790	2.56
El Paso (city) El Paso County	747	0.13

Top 10 Places Sorted by Percent
Based on all places, regardless of population

Place	Number	%
Corral City (town) Denton County	9	10.11
Mission Bend (cdp) Fort Bend County	790	2.56
Mobile City (city) Rockwall County	5	2.55
Grand Acres (cdp) Cameron County	4	1.97
Hill Country Village (city) Bexar County	18	1.75
Keene (city) Johnson County	83	1.66
Cinco Ranch (cdp) Fort Bend County	139	1.24
Byers (city) Clay County	5	0.97
Addison (town) Dallas County	133	0.94
Stafford (city) Fort Bend County	145	0.92

Top 10 Places Sorted by Percent
Based on places with populations of 10,000 or more

Place	Number	%
Mission Bend (cdp) Fort Bend County	790	2.56
Cinco Ranch (cdp) Fort Bend County	139	1.24
Addison (town) Dallas County	133	0.94
Stafford (city) Fort Bend County	145	0.92
Bellaire (city) Harris County	119	0.76
New Territory (cdp) Fort Bend County	101	0.73
The Woodlands (cdp) Montgomery County	390	0.70
Sugar Land (city) Fort Bend County	440	0.69
Houston (city) Harris County	13,214	0.68
College Station (city) Brazos County	412	0.61

Hispanic: Argentinean

Top 10 Places Sorted by Number
Based on all places, regardless of population

Place	Number	%
Houston (city) Harris County	1,256	0.06
Austin (city) Travis County	242	0.04
Irving (city) Dallas County	240	0.13
San Antonio (city) Bexar County	223	0.02
Dallas (city) Dallas County	222	0.02
El Paso (city) El Paso County	134	0.02
Plano (city) Collin County	90	0.04

Notes: (cdp) census designated place; Refer to the User's Guide in the front of the book for more detailed information.

Place	Number	%
The Woodlands (cdp) Montgomery County	81	0.15
McAllen (city) Hidalgo County	77	0.07
Fort Worth (city) Tarrant County	65	0.01

Top 10 Places Sorted by Percent
Based on all places, regardless of population

Place	Number	%
Hays (city) Hays County	1	0.43
Clear Lake Shores (city) Galveston County	5	0.41
Megargel (town) Archer County	1	0.40
Doyle (cdp) San Patricio County	1	0.35
Meadows Place (city) Fort Bend County	14	0.29
Highland Haven (city) Burnet County	1	0.22
Mission Bend (cdp) Fort Bend County	62	0.20
Oak Ridge North (city) Montgomery County	5	0.17
The Woodlands (cdp) Montgomery County	81	0.15
Piney Point Village (city) Harris County	5	0.15

Top 10 Places Sorted by Percent
Based on places with populations of 10,000 or more

Place	Number	%
Mission Bend (cdp) Fort Bend County	62	0.20
The Woodlands (cdp) Montgomery County	81	0.15
New Territory (cdp) Fort Bend County	20	0.14
Irving (city) Dallas County	240	0.13
Bellaire (city) Harris County	21	0.13
Cinco Ranch (cdp) Fort Bend County	14	0.13
Spring (cdp) Harris County	38	0.10
Sugar Land (city) Fort Bend County	58	0.09
Stafford (city) Fort Bend County	14	0.09
Missouri City (city) Fort Bend County	40	0.08

Hispanic: Bolivian

Top 10 Places Sorted by Number
Based on all places, regardless of population

Place	Number	%
Houston (city) Harris County	480	0.02
Dallas (city) Dallas County	119	0.01
Austin (city) Travis County	109	0.02
San Antonio (city) Bexar County	73	0.01
Garland (city) Dallas County	41	0.02
League City (city) Galveston County	37	0.08
El Paso (city) El Paso County	36	0.01
Arlington (city) Tarrant County	33	0.01
College Station (city) Brazos County	29	0.04
Sugar Land (city) Fort Bend County	28	0.04

Top 10 Places Sorted by Percent
Based on all places, regardless of population

Place	Number	%
Sienna Plantation (cdp) Fort Bend County	4	0.21
Southside Place (city) Harris County	3	0.19
Bunker Hill Village (city) Harris County	6	0.16
Spring Valley (city) Harris County	5	0.14
Taylor Lake Village (city) Harris County	5	0.14
Roanoke (city) Denton County	4	0.14
Selma (city) Bexar County	1	0.13
Hickory Creek (town) Denton County	2	0.10
Lago Vista (city) Travis County	4	0.09
Piney Point Village (city) Harris County	3	0.09

Top 10 Places Sorted by Percent
Based on places with populations of 10,000 or more

Place	Number	%
League City (city) Galveston County	37	0.08
Lake Jackson (city) Brazoria County	18	0.07
Wells Branch (cdp) Travis County	8	0.07
Mission Bend (cdp) Fort Bend County	15	0.05
Colleyville (city) Tarrant County	9	0.05
Cinco Ranch (cdp) Fort Bend County	6	0.05
Converse (city) Bexar County	6	0.05

Place	Number	%
College Station (city) Brazos County	29	0.04
Sugar Land (city) Fort Bend County	28	0.04
Katy (city) Harris County	5	0.04

Hispanic: Chilean

Top 10 Places Sorted by Number
Based on all places, regardless of population

Place	Number	%
Houston (city) Harris County	591	0.03
Dallas (city) Dallas County	170	0.01
Austin (city) Travis County	168	0.03
San Antonio (city) Bexar County	150	0.01
Fort Worth (city) Tarrant County	82	0.02
Plano (city) Collin County	70	0.03
El Paso (city) El Paso County	65	0.01
Irving (city) Dallas County	61	0.03
Corpus Christi (city) Nueces County	51	0.02
Arlington (city) Tarrant County	38	0.01

Top 10 Places Sorted by Percent
Based on all places, regardless of population

Place	Number	%
Grand Acres (cdp) Cameron County	4	1.97
Todd Mission (city) Grimes County	1	0.68
Dumas (city) Moore County	31	0.23
Shenandoah (city) Montgomery County	3	0.20
Southside Place (city) Harris County	3	0.19
Magnolia (city) Montgomery County	2	0.18
Kingsbury (cdp) Guadalupe County	1	0.15
Payne Springs (town) Henderson County	1	0.15
Westworth Village (city) Tarrant County	3	0.14
Clarksville (city) Red River County	5	0.13

Top 10 Places Sorted by Percent
Based on places with populations of 10,000 or more

Place	Number	%
Dumas (city) Moore County	31	0.23
Mission Bend (cdp) Fort Bend County	35	0.11
Cloverleaf (cdp) Harris County	13	0.06
Galena Park (city) Harris County	6	0.06
The Woodlands (cdp) Montgomery County	27	0.05
Farmers Branch (city) Dallas County	14	0.05
Bellaire (city) Harris County	8	0.05
Pecan Grove (cdp) Fort Bend County	7	0.05
Sugar Land (city) Fort Bend County	24	0.04
Euless (city) Tarrant County	20	0.04

Hispanic: Colombian

Top 10 Places Sorted by Number
Based on all places, regardless of population

Place	Number	%
Houston (city) Harris County	5,821	0.30
San Antonio (city) Bexar County	888	0.08
Dallas (city) Dallas County	862	0.07
Austin (city) Travis County	596	0.09
Mission Bend (cdp) Fort Bend County	458	1.49
Arlington (city) Tarrant County	396	0.12
Fort Worth (city) Tarrant County	359	0.07
Garland (city) Dallas County	320	0.15
Plano (city) Collin County	267	0.12
Irving (city) Dallas County	258	0.13

Top 10 Places Sorted by Percent
Based on all places, regardless of population

Place	Number	%
Mission Bend (cdp) Fort Bend County	458	1.49
Hill Country Village (city) Bexar County	13	1.26
Keene (city) Johnson County	40	0.80
Bixby (cdp) Cameron County	2	0.56
Addison (town) Dallas County	76	0.54

Place	Number	%
Pleak (village) Fort Bend County	5	0.53
Wallis (city) Austin County	6	0.51
Mobile City (city) Rockwall County	1	0.51
Blanket (town) Brown County	2	0.50
Camp Swift (cdp) Bastrop County	23	0.49

Top 10 Places Sorted by Percent
Based on places with populations of 10,000 or more

Place	Number	%
Mission Bend (cdp) Fort Bend County	458	1.49
Addison (town) Dallas County	76	0.54
Cinco Ranch (cdp) Fort Bend County	46	0.41
Big Spring (city) Howard County	98	0.39
Seagoville (city) Dallas County	36	0.33
Bellaire (city) Harris County	50	0.32
Houston (city) Harris County	5,821	0.30
Stafford (city) Fort Bend County	42	0.27
Sugar Land (city) Fort Bend County	157	0.25
Cloverleaf (cdp) Harris County	56	0.24

Hispanic: Ecuadorian

Top 10 Places Sorted by Number
Based on all places, regardless of population

Place	Number	%
Houston (city) Harris County	864	0.04
Dallas (city) Dallas County	229	0.02
Austin (city) Travis County	143	0.02
San Antonio (city) Bexar County	113	0.01
Irving (city) Dallas County	91	0.05
Carrollton (city) Denton County	76	0.07
Arlington (city) Tarrant County	72	0.02
Garland (city) Dallas County	62	0.03
Mission Bend (cdp) Fort Bend County	61	0.20
El Paso (city) El Paso County	57	0.01

Top 10 Places Sorted by Percent
Based on all places, regardless of population

Place	Number	%
Corral City (town) Denton County	9	10.11
Mobile City (city) Rockwall County	4	2.04
Mission Bend (cdp) Fort Bend County	61	0.20
Jersey Village (city) Harris County	14	0.20
Richwood (city) Brazoria County	4	0.13
Fort Bliss (cdp) El Paso County	9	0.11
Abernathy (city) Hale County	3	0.11
Gholson (city) McLennan County	1	0.11
Windemere (cdp) Travis County	7	0.10
Murphy (city) Collin County	3	0.10

Top 10 Places Sorted by Percent
Based on places with populations of 10,000 or more

Place	Number	%
Mission Bend (cdp) Fort Bend County	61	0.20
Clute (city) Brazoria County	8	0.08
Carrollton (city) Denton County	76	0.07
Sugar Land (city) Fort Bend County	43	0.07
Killeen (city) Bell County	50	0.06
College Station (city) Brazos County	39	0.06
Fort Hood (cdp) Coryell County	21	0.06
Irving (city) Dallas County	91	0.05
Euless (city) Tarrant County	23	0.05
Spring (cdp) Harris County	17	0.05

Hispanic: Paraguayan

Top 10 Places Sorted by Number
Based on all places, regardless of population

Place	Number	%
Houston (city) Harris County	48	0.00
Stafford (city) Fort Bend County	24	0.15
Austin (city) Travis County	20	0.00

Notes: (cdp) census designated place; Refer to the User's Guide in the front of the book for more detailed information.

Place	Number	%
San Antonio (city) Bexar County	19	0.00
Dallas (city) Dallas County	15	0.00
Richardson (city) Dallas County	13	0.01
Carrollton (city) Denton County	9	0.01
Pasadena (city) Harris County	9	0.01
Plano (city) Collin County	9	0.00
Brownsville (city) Cameron County	6	0.00

Top 10 Places Sorted by Percent
Based on all places, regardless of population

Place	Number	%
Cross Mountain (cdp) Bexar County	3	0.20
Hill Country Village (city) Bexar County	2	0.19
Dalworthington Gardens (city) Tarrant County	4	0.18
Stafford (city) Fort Bend County	24	0.15
Columbus (city) Colorado County	1	0.03
Canyon Lake (cdp) Comal County	4	0.02
Highland Park (town) Dallas County	2	0.02
Timberwood Park (cdp) Bexar County	1	0.02
Richardson (city) Dallas County	13	0.01
Carrollton (city) Denton County	9	0.01

Top 10 Places Sorted by Percent
Based on places with populations of 10,000 or more

Place	Number	%
Stafford (city) Fort Bend County	24	0.15
Canyon Lake (cdp) Comal County	4	0.02
Richardson (city) Dallas County	13	0.01
Carrollton (city) Denton County	9	0.01
Pasadena (city) Harris County	9	0.01
Galveston (city) Galveston County	5	0.01
Lewisville (city) Denton County	4	0.01
Mission (city) Hidalgo County	4	0.01
Sugar Land (city) Fort Bend County	4	0.01
Texarkana (city) Bowie County	4	0.01

Hispanic: Peruvian

Top 10 Places Sorted by Number
Based on all places, regardless of population

Place	Number	%
Houston (city) Harris County	1,656	0.08
Dallas (city) Dallas County	853	0.07
San Antonio (city) Bexar County	470	0.04
Austin (city) Travis County	359	0.05
Plano (city) Collin County	250	0.11
Irving (city) Dallas County	181	0.09
Arlington (city) Tarrant County	174	0.05
Carrollton (city) Denton County	164	0.15
Garland (city) Dallas County	139	0.06
Fort Worth (city) Tarrant County	115	0.02

Top 10 Places Sorted by Percent
Based on all places, regardless of population

Place	Number	%
Byers (city) Clay County	5	0.97
Hays (city) Hays County	1	0.43
Ferris (city) Ellis County	9	0.41
Lindsay (town) Cooke County	3	0.38
Hillcrest (village) Brazoria County	2	0.28
Hilshire Village (city) Harris County	2	0.28
Hedwig Village (city) Harris County	6	0.26
Southside Place (city) Harris County	4	0.26
Shamrock (city) Wheeler County	5	0.25
Lexington (town) Lee County	3	0.25

Top 10 Places Sorted by Percent
Based on places with populations of 10,000 or more

Place	Number	%
Mission Bend (cdp) Fort Bend County	70	0.23
Carrollton (city) Denton County	164	0.15
Fort Hood (cdp) Coryell County	50	0.15

Place	Number	%
Spring (cdp) Harris County	49	0.13
Plano (city) Collin County	250	0.11
Stafford (city) Fort Bend County	18	0.11
Addison (town) Dallas County	16	0.11
West University Place (city) Harris County	15	0.11
Irving (city) Dallas County	181	0.09
South Houston (city) Harris County	14	0.09

Hispanic: Uruguayan

Top 10 Places Sorted by Number
Based on all places, regardless of population

Place	Number	%
Houston (city) Harris County	230	0.01
Austin (city) Travis County	32	0.00
San Antonio (city) Bexar County	26	0.00
Dallas (city) Dallas County	22	0.00
Mission Bend (cdp) Fort Bend County	16	0.05
Arlington (city) Tarrant County	12	0.00
Pasadena (city) Harris County	11	0.01
Fort Worth (city) Tarrant County	11	0.00
Irving (city) Dallas County	9	0.00
The Woodlands (cdp) Montgomery County	8	0.01

Top 10 Places Sorted by Percent
Based on all places, regardless of population

Place	Number	%
Covington (city) Hill County	1	0.35
Roanoke (city) Denton County	3	0.11
Hollywood Park (town) Bexar County	3	0.10
Haslet (city) Tarrant County	1	0.09
Shady Hollow (cdp) Travis County	3	0.06
Mission Bend (cdp) Fort Bend County	16	0.05
Addison (town) Dallas County	7	0.05
Pinehurst (cdp) Montgomery County	2	0.05
Sheldon (cdp) Harris County	1	0.05
Cinco Ranch (cdp) Fort Bend County	5	0.04

Top 10 Places Sorted by Percent
Based on places with populations of 10,000 or more

Place	Number	%
Mission Bend (cdp) Fort Bend County	16	0.05
Addison (town) Dallas County	7	0.05
Cinco Ranch (cdp) Fort Bend County	5	0.04
Southlake (city) Tarrant County	7	0.03
Groves (city) Jefferson County	5	0.03
Katy (city) Harris County	4	0.03
Friendswood (city) Galveston County	5	0.02
University Park (city) Dallas County	4	0.02
Houston (city) Harris County	230	0.01
Pasadena (city) Harris County	11	0.01

Hispanic: Venezuelan

Top 10 Places Sorted by Number
Based on all places, regardless of population

Place	Number	%
Houston (city) Harris County	1,592	0.08
Austin (city) Travis County	390	0.06
Dallas (city) Dallas County	275	0.02
San Antonio (city) Bexar County	169	0.01
Fort Worth (city) Tarrant County	147	0.03
Irving (city) Dallas County	118	0.06
College Station (city) Brazos County	90	0.13
Plano (city) Collin County	85	0.04
Arlington (city) Tarrant County	85	0.03
The Woodlands (cdp) Montgomery County	78	0.14

Top 10 Places Sorted by Percent
Based on all places, regardless of population

Place	Number	%
Keene (city) Johnson County	23	0.46

Place	Number	%
Jamaica Beach (city) Galveston County	4	0.37
Cinco Ranch (cdp) Fort Bend County	38	0.34
Hedwig Village (city) Harris County	7	0.30
New Territory (cdp) Fort Bend County	32	0.23
Thorntonville (town) Ward County	1	0.23
Jersey Village (city) Harris County	14	0.20
Stafford (city) Fort Bend County	30	0.19
Danbury (city) Brazoria County	3	0.19
Kemah (city) Galveston County	4	0.17

Top 10 Places Sorted by Percent
Based on places with populations of 10,000 or more

Place	Number	%
Cinco Ranch (cdp) Fort Bend County	38	0.34
New Territory (cdp) Fort Bend County	32	0.23
Stafford (city) Fort Bend County	30	0.19
West University Place (city) Harris County	23	0.16
Mission Bend (cdp) Fort Bend County	46	0.15
The Woodlands (cdp) Montgomery County	78	0.14
College Station (city) Brazos County	90	0.13
Atascocita (cdp) Harris County	43	0.12
Katy (city) Harris County	14	0.12
Addison (town) Dallas County	15	0.11

Hispanic: Other South American

Top 10 Places Sorted by Number
Based on all places, regardless of population

Place	Number	%
Houston (city) Harris County	676	0.03
San Antonio (city) Bexar County	157	0.01
Dallas (city) Dallas County	128	0.01
Austin (city) Travis County	102	0.02
Plano (city) Collin County	62	0.03
Irving (city) Dallas County	43	0.02
El Paso (city) El Paso County	43	0.01
Carrollton (city) Denton County	39	0.04
Fort Worth (city) Tarrant County	39	0.01
Garland (city) Dallas County	36	0.02

Top 10 Places Sorted by Percent
Based on all places, regardless of population

Place	Number	%
Whiteface (town) Cochran County	1	0.22
Hill Country Village (city) Bexar County	2	0.19
Piney Point Village (city) Harris County	5	0.15
Bee Cave (village) Travis County	1	0.15
Normangee (town) Leon County	1	0.14
Cinco Ranch (cdp) Fort Bend County	14	0.13
Mission Bend (cdp) Fort Bend County	27	0.09
Bartonville (town) Denton County	1	0.09
Santa Anna (town) Coleman County	1	0.09
Stafford (city) Fort Bend County	12	0.08

Top 10 Places Sorted by Percent
Based on places with populations of 10,000 or more

Place	Number	%
Cinco Ranch (cdp) Fort Bend County	14	0.13
Mission Bend (cdp) Fort Bend County	27	0.09
Stafford (city) Fort Bend County	12	0.08
Humble (city) Harris County	11	0.08
Addison (town) Dallas County	9	0.06
Bellaire (city) Harris County	9	0.06
Wells Branch (cdp) Travis County	7	0.06
Sugar Land (city) Fort Bend County	33	0.05
Deer Park (city) Harris County	14	0.05
New Territory (cdp) Fort Bend County	7	0.05

Notes: (cdp) census designated place; Refer to the User's Guide in the front of the book for more detailed information.

Hispanic: Other

Top 10 Places Sorted by Number
Based on all places, regardless of population

Place	Number	%
San Antonio (city) Bexar County	182,662	15.96
Houston (city) Harris County	116,701	5.97
El Paso (city) El Paso County	65,939	11.70
Corpus Christi (city) Nueces County	50,633	18.25
Dallas (city) Dallas County	49,358	4.15
Austin (city) Travis County	36,177	5.51
Laredo (city) Webb County	32,137	18.20
Brownsville (city) Cameron County	23,296	16.67
Lubbock (city) Lubbock County	21,590	10.82
Fort Worth (city) Tarrant County	21,385	4.00

Top 10 Places Sorted by Percent
Based on all places, regardless of population

Place	Number	%
Guerra (cdp) Jim Hogg County	5	62.50
Loma Linda East (cdp) Jim Wells County	129	60.28
Hilltop (cdp) Frio County	161	53.67
Willamar (cdp) Willacy County	8	53.33
Freer (city) Duval County	1,712	52.82
San Diego (city) Duval County	2,501	52.62
Owl Ranch-Amargosa (cdp) Jim Wells County	272	51.61
Rancho Banquete (cdp) Nueces County	228	48.61
Benavides (city) Duval County	775	45.97
Pawnee (cdp) Bee County	90	44.78

Top 10 Places Sorted by Percent
Based on places with populations of 10,000 or more

Place	Number	%
Robstown (city) Nueces County	4,490	35.28
Alice (city) Jim Wells County	6,472	34.05
Beeville (city) Bee County	3,669	27.95
San Benito (city) Cameron County	5,394	23.01
Uvalde (city) Uvalde County	3,413	22.86
Mercedes (city) Hidalgo County	2,924	21.42
Kingsville (city) Kleberg County	5,141	20.10
Corpus Christi (city) Nueces County	50,633	18.25
Laredo (city) Webb County	32,137	18.20
Rio Grande City (city) Starr County	2,154	18.07

Hungarian

Top 10 Places Sorted by Number
Based on all places, regardless of population

Place	Number	%
Houston (city) Harris County	3,161	0.16
Austin (city) Travis County	1,741	0.27
Dallas (city) Dallas County	1,703	0.14
San Antonio (city) Bexar County	1,272	0.11
Plano (city) Collin County	893	0.40
Arlington (city) Tarrant County	655	0.20
El Paso (city) El Paso County	575	0.10
Fort Worth (city) Tarrant County	459	0.09
Corpus Christi (city) Nueces County	325	0.12
Richardson (city) Dallas County	313	0.34

Top 10 Places Sorted by Percent
Based on all places, regardless of population

Place	Number	%
Novice (city) Coleman County	6	3.73
Falcon Lake Estates (cdp) Zapata County	17	2.59
Hebron (town) Denton County	19	2.30
San Leanna (village) Travis County	9	2.15
Olmos Park (city) Bexar County	51	2.07
Lakewood Village (city) Denton County	7	1.92
Buffalo Gap (town) Taylor County	8	1.82
New Hope (town) Collin County	11	1.62
Grey Forest (city) Bexar County	7	1.62

Talty (city) Kaufman County	11	1.35

Top 10 Places Sorted by Percent
Based on places with populations of 10,000 or more

Place	Number	%
West University Place (city) Harris County	136	0.96
Cinco Ranch (cdp) Fort Bend County	108	0.96
Canyon Lake (cdp) Comal County	149	0.88
Colleyville (city) Tarrant County	148	0.76
Highland Village (city) Denton County	81	0.67
Corinth (city) Denton County	70	0.61
Pecan Grove (cdp) Fort Bend County	78	0.58
Bellaire (city) Harris County	87	0.56
Pearland (city) Brazoria County	207	0.55
Keller (city) Tarrant County	149	0.55

Icelander

Top 10 Places Sorted by Number
Based on all places, regardless of population

Place	Number	%
San Antonio (city) Bexar County	95	0.01
Houston (city) Harris County	87	0.00
Dallas (city) Dallas County	71	0.01
The Woodlands (cdp) Montgomery County	67	0.12
El Paso (city) El Paso County	53	0.01
Garland (city) Dallas County	37	0.02
Cleburne (city) Johnson County	32	0.12
Copperas Cove (city) Coryell County	30	0.10
Austin (city) Travis County	30	0.00
Denton (city) Denton County	29	0.04

Top 10 Places Sorted by Percent
Based on all places, regardless of population

Place	Number	%
Weston (city) Collin County	6	0.88
Van Horn (town) Culberson County	9	0.38
Dublin (city) Erath County	14	0.37
Shoreacres (city) Harris County	5	0.33
Brookshire (city) Waller County	10	0.29
Alto (town) Cherokee County	3	0.25
Hewitt (city) McLennan County	26	0.24
Kempner (city) Lampasas County	2	0.20
Palm Valley (city) Cameron County	2	0.15
Alvarado (city) Johnson County	4	0.13

Top 10 Places Sorted by Percent
Based on places with populations of 10,000 or more

Place	Number	%
Hewitt (city) McLennan County	26	0.24
The Woodlands (cdp) Montgomery County	67	0.12
Cleburne (city) Johnson County	32	0.12
Corinth (city) Denton County	14	0.12
Copperas Cove (city) Coryell County	30	0.10
Benbrook (city) Tarrant County	20	0.10
Jacinto City (city) Harris County	9	0.09
Bellaire (city) Harris County	8	0.05
White Settlement (city) Tarrant County	8	0.05
New Territory (cdp) Fort Bend County	7	0.05

Iranian

Top 10 Places Sorted by Number
Based on all places, regardless of population

Place	Number	%
Houston (city) Harris County	4,436	0.23
Plano (city) Collin County	2,152	0.97
Dallas (city) Dallas County	1,994	0.17
Austin (city) Travis County	1,369	0.21
Arlington (city) Tarrant County	1,000	0.30
San Antonio (city) Bexar County	954	0.08
Carrollton (city) Denton County	519	0.48

Sugar Land (city) Fort Bend County	423	0.67
Richardson (city) Dallas County	369	0.40
Irving (city) Dallas County	361	0.19

Top 10 Places Sorted by Percent
Based on all places, regardless of population

Place	Number	%
Lake View (cdp) Val Verde County	6	3.87
Hunters Creek Village (city) Harris County	92	2.10
Bulverde (city) Comal County	62	1.65
Stagecoach (town) Montgomery County	7	1.39
Hebron (town) Denton County	10	1.21
Meadows Place (city) Fort Bend County	54	1.09
Hedwig Village (city) Harris County	24	1.03
Plano (city) Collin County	2,152	0.97
Pantego (town) Tarrant County	21	0.91
Nassau Bay (city) Harris County	38	0.89

Top 10 Places Sorted by Percent
Based on places with populations of 10,000 or more

Place	Number	%
Plano (city) Collin County	2,152	0.97
Sugar Land (city) Fort Bend County	423	0.67
Addison (town) Dallas County	75	0.54
Carrollton (city) Denton County	519	0.48
Stafford (city) Fort Bend County	75	0.48
Mission Bend (cdp) Fort Bend County	132	0.43
Jollyville (cdp) Williamson County	64	0.41
Richardson (city) Dallas County	369	0.40
Missouri City (city) Fort Bend County	210	0.40
Coppell (city) Dallas County	137	0.38

Irish

Top 10 Places Sorted by Number
Based on all places, regardless of population

Place	Number	%
Houston (city) Harris County	83,633	4.28
San Antonio (city) Bexar County	59,637	5.21
Dallas (city) Dallas County	58,746	4.94
Austin (city) Travis County	55,063	8.39
Fort Worth (city) Tarrant County	33,209	6.20
Arlington (city) Tarrant County	28,487	8.56
Plano (city) Collin County	23,979	10.79
Corpus Christi (city) Nueces County	17,977	6.48
El Paso (city) El Paso County	16,469	2.92
Garland (city) Dallas County	16,092	7.45

Top 10 Places Sorted by Percent
Based on all places, regardless of population

Place	Number	%
Tulsita (cdp) Bee County	8	32.00
Dorchester (town) Grayson County	37	29.37
Latexo (city) Houston County	76	25.59
Post Oak Bend City (town) Kaufman County	96	23.70
Payne Springs (town) Henderson County	153	23.50
Moran (city) Shackelford County	52	22.41
Dawson (town) Navarro County	183	21.40
Union Grove (city) Upshur County	70	21.15
Byers (city) Clay County	112	21.09
Box Canyon-Amistad (cdp) Val Verde County	12	20.69

Top 10 Places Sorted by Percent
Based on places with populations of 10,000 or more

Place	Number	%
Flower Mound (town) Denton County	7,774	15.18
Keller (city) Tarrant County	4,082	14.95
Colleyville (city) Tarrant County	2,872	14.67
Canyon Lake (cdp) Comal County	2,413	14.29
Allen (city) Collin County	6,207	14.28
Highland Village (city) Denton County	1,732	14.24
Southlake (city) Tarrant County	2,992	13.92

Notes: (cdp) census designated place; Refer to the User's Guide in the front of the book for more detailed information.

	Number	%
Universal City (city) Bexar County	2,056	13.83
Pecan Grove (cdp) Fort Bend County	1,817	13.50
Bedford (city) Tarrant County	6,279	13.34

Israeli

Top 10 Places Sorted by Number
Based on all places, regardless of population

Place	Number	%
Dallas (city) Dallas County	736	0.06
Houston (city) Harris County	661	0.03
Austin (city) Travis County	226	0.03
San Antonio (city) Bexar County	188	0.02
Plano (city) Collin County	104	0.05
Garland (city) Dallas County	101	0.05
Denton (city) Denton County	44	0.05
Bellaire (city) Harris County	42	0.27
Galveston (city) Galveston County	40	0.07
Friendswood (city) Galveston County	34	0.12

Top 10 Places Sorted by Percent
Based on all places, regardless of population

Place	Number	%
Ponder (town) Denton County	7	1.54
Callisburg (city) Cooke County	3	0.88
South Padre Island (town) Cameron County	19	0.77
Lost Creek (cdp) Travis County	18	0.38
Alamo Heights (city) Bexar County	25	0.34
Winnsboro (city) Wood County	12	0.33
Bellaire (city) Harris County	42	0.27
Vidor (city) Orange County	31	0.27
West University Place (city) Harris County	32	0.23
Kempner (city) Lampasas County	2	0.20

Top 10 Places Sorted by Percent
Based on places with populations of 10,000 or more

Place	Number	%
Bellaire (city) Harris County	42	0.27
Vidor (city) Orange County	31	0.27
West University Place (city) Harris County	32	0.23
Friendswood (city) Galveston County	34	0.12
Watauga (city) Tarrant County	22	0.10
Galveston (city) Galveston County	40	0.07
Kingsville (city) Kleberg County	17	0.07
Dallas (city) Dallas County	736	0.06
Stafford (city) Fort Bend County	10	0.06
Cinco Ranch (cdp) Fort Bend County	7	0.06

Italian

Top 10 Places Sorted by Number
Based on all places, regardless of population

Place	Number	%
Houston (city) Harris County	31,899	1.63
San Antonio (city) Bexar County	21,697	1.90
Austin (city) Travis County	16,185	2.47
Dallas (city) Dallas County	16,058	1.35
Plano (city) Collin County	9,042	4.07
Fort Worth (city) Tarrant County	7,607	1.42
Arlington (city) Tarrant County	7,571	2.28
El Paso (city) El Paso County	6,800	1.21
Corpus Christi (city) Nueces County	3,932	1.42
Garland (city) Dallas County	3,609	1.67

Top 10 Places Sorted by Percent
Based on all places, regardless of population

Place	Number	%
Westdale (cdp) Jim Wells County	67	18.93
Quintana (town) Brazoria County	4	9.09
Tulsita (cdp) Bee County	2	8.00
Mingus (city) Palo Pinto County	19	7.88
Bayview (town) Cameron County	27	6.89

	Number	%
Lakewood Village (city) Denton County	25	6.87
Mobile City (city) Rockwall County	16	6.50
Bayou Vista (city) Galveston County	107	6.38
Trophy Club (town) Denton County	407	6.27
Imperial (cdp) Pecos County	27	6.21

Top 10 Places Sorted by Percent
Based on places with populations of 10,000 or more

Place	Number	%
The Woodlands (cdp) Montgomery County	3,128	5.60
Pecan Grove (cdp) Fort Bend County	742	5.51
Highland Village (city) Denton County	652	5.36
Cinco Ranch (cdp) Fort Bend County	602	5.36
Bellaire (city) Harris County	805	5.17
Southlake (city) Tarrant County	1,103	5.13
Brushy Creek (cdp) Williamson County	765	4.81
West University Place (city) Harris County	660	4.64
Allen (city) Collin County	2,012	4.63
Cedar Park (city) Williamson County	1,194	4.63

Latvian

Top 10 Places Sorted by Number
Based on all places, regardless of population

Place	Number	%
Houston (city) Harris County	255	0.01
San Antonio (city) Bexar County	158	0.01
Austin (city) Travis County	153	0.02
Dallas (city) Dallas County	111	0.01
Plano (city) Collin County	86	0.04
Burleson (city) Johnson County	48	0.23
Richardson (city) Dallas County	43	0.05
Midland (city) Midland County	40	0.04
Spring (cdp) Harris County	33	0.09
El Paso (city) El Paso County	33	0.01

Top 10 Places Sorted by Percent
Based on all places, regardless of population

Place	Number	%
Shenandoah (city) Montgomery County	9	0.61
Lakeside (town) San Patricio County	2	0.54
Rollingwood (city) Travis County	7	0.50
Shady Hollow (cdp) Travis County	27	0.49
Terrell Hills (city) Bexar County	20	0.40
Weimar (city) Colorado County	8	0.40
Highland Park (town) Dallas County	29	0.33
Hughes Springs (city) Cass County	6	0.33
Palm Valley (city) Cameron County	4	0.31
Hondo (city) Medina County	23	0.29

Top 10 Places Sorted by Percent
Based on places with populations of 10,000 or more

Place	Number	%
Burleson (city) Johnson County	48	0.23
Stafford (city) Fort Bend County	15	0.10
Spring (cdp) Harris County	33	0.09
Rockwall (city) Rockwall County	16	0.09
Southlake (city) Tarrant County	17	0.08
Dickinson (city) Galveston County	14	0.08
Jollyville (cdp) Williamson County	13	0.08
Conroe (city) Montgomery County	25	0.07
Colleyville (city) Tarrant County	13	0.07
Temple (city) Bell County	31	0.06

Lithuanian

Top 10 Places Sorted by Number
Based on all places, regardless of population

Place	Number	%
Houston (city) Harris County	1,202	0.06
San Antonio (city) Bexar County	938	0.08
Dallas (city) Dallas County	867	0.07

	Number	%
Austin (city) Travis County	791	0.12
Plano (city) Collin County	525	0.24
Fort Worth (city) Tarrant County	400	0.07
Arlington (city) Tarrant County	289	0.09
El Paso (city) El Paso County	236	0.04
Grand Prairie (city) Dallas County	117	0.09
Carrollton (city) Denton County	111	0.10

Top 10 Places Sorted by Percent
Based on all places, regardless of population

Place	Number	%
Todd Mission (city) Grimes County	6	4.17
Normanna (cdp) Bee County	2	1.82
Shavano Park (city) Bexar County	29	1.63
Bee Cave (village) Travis County	9	1.48
El Lago (city) Harris County	39	1.17
Cibolo (city) Guadalupe County	32	1.01
Shady Hollow (cdp) Travis County	54	0.99
Laughlin AFB (cdp) Val Verde County	22	0.99
Hunters Creek Village (city) Harris County	42	0.96
Point (city) Rains County	7	0.94

Top 10 Places Sorted by Percent
Based on places with populations of 10,000 or more

Place	Number	%
West University Place (city) Harris County	82	0.58
Addison (town) Dallas County	75	0.54
Highland Village (city) Denton County	65	0.53
Burleson (city) Johnson County	93	0.44
Southlake (city) Tarrant County	84	0.39
Weatherford (city) Parker County	70	0.37
Brushy Creek (cdp) Williamson County	50	0.31
Frisco (city) Collin County	97	0.29
Bellaire (city) Harris County	44	0.28
Colleyville (city) Tarrant County	50	0.26

Luxemburger

Top 10 Places Sorted by Number
Based on all places, regardless of population

Place	Number	%
Plano (city) Collin County	57	0.03
Pearland (city) Brazoria County	50	0.13
Austin (city) Travis County	50	0.01
Houston (city) Harris County	46	0.00
Arlington (city) Tarrant County	43	0.01
Fort Worth (city) Tarrant County	40	0.01
The Woodlands (cdp) Montgomery County	33	0.06
San Antonio (city) Bexar County	30	0.00
Cedar Park (city) Williamson County	28	0.11
Duncanville (city) Dallas County	26	0.07

Top 10 Places Sorted by Percent
Based on all places, regardless of population

Place	Number	%
Siesta Shores (cdp) Zapata County	7	0.74
Boyd (town) Wise County	6	0.55
Richland Hills (city) Tarrant County	23	0.29
McLean (town) Gray County	2	0.24
Port Isabel (city) Cameron County	11	0.23
Willis (city) Montgomery County	9	0.22
Johnson City (city) Blanco County	2	0.17
Pearland (city) Brazoria County	50	0.13
Southside Place (city) Harris County	2	0.13
The Hills (village) Travis County	2	0.13

Top 10 Places Sorted by Percent
Based on places with populations of 10,000 or more

Place	Number	%
Pearland (city) Brazoria County	50	0.13
Universal City (city) Bexar County	18	0.12
Cedar Park (city) Williamson County	28	0.11

Notes: (cdp) census designated place; Refer to the User's Guide in the front of the book for more detailed information.

Place	Number	%
Duncanville (city) Dallas County	26	0.07
The Woodlands (cdp) Montgomery County	33	0.06
Missouri City (city) Fort Bend County	26	0.05
Donna (city) Hidalgo County	8	0.05
Robstown (city) Nueces County	6	0.05
Bellaire (city) Harris County	6	0.04
Plano (city) Collin County	57	0.03

Macedonian

Top 10 Places Sorted by Number
Based on all places, regardless of population

Place	Number	%
Houston (city) Harris County	52	0.00
Austin (city) Travis County	43	0.01
Plano (city) Collin County	36	0.02
Arlington (city) Tarrant County	36	0.01
El Paso (city) El Paso County	26	0.00
Sugar Land (city) Fort Bend County	18	0.03
Mansfield (city) Tarrant County	17	0.06
Fort Worth (city) Tarrant County	17	0.00
Lackland AFB (cdp) Bexar County	15	0.21
Huntsville (city) Walker County	13	0.04

Top 10 Places Sorted by Percent
Based on all places, regardless of population

Place	Number	%
Hedwig Village (city) Harris County	11	0.47
Whitewright (town) Grayson County	5	0.29
Lackland AFB (cdp) Bexar County	15	0.21
Overton (city) Rusk County	5	0.21
Floresville (city) Wilson County	11	0.19
Van Alstyne (city) Grayson County	3	0.12
Commerce (city) Hunt County	7	0.09
Mansfield (city) Tarrant County	17	0.06
Huntsville (city) Walker County	13	0.04
Sugar Land (city) Fort Bend County	18	0.03

Top 10 Places Sorted by Percent
Based on places with populations of 10,000 or more

Place	Number	%
Mansfield (city) Tarrant County	17	0.06
Huntsville (city) Walker County	13	0.04
Sugar Land (city) Fort Bend County	18	0.03
League City (city) Galveston County	13	0.03
San Marcos (city) Hays County	10	0.03
Keller (city) Tarrant County	8	0.03
La Porte (city) Harris County	8	0.03
Plano (city) Collin County	36	0.02
Bryan (city) Brazos County	11	0.02
Euless (city) Tarrant County	9	0.02

Maltese

Top 10 Places Sorted by Number
Based on all places, regardless of population

Place	Number	%
Plano (city) Collin County	111	0.05
Houston (city) Harris County	81	0.00
Dallas (city) Dallas County	57	0.00
San Antonio (city) Bexar County	47	0.00
Denton (city) Denton County	26	0.03
Arlington (city) Tarrant County	24	0.01
Texas City (city) Galveston County	23	0.06
Austin (city) Travis County	23	0.00
University Park (city) Dallas County	19	0.08
Fort Worth (city) Tarrant County	17	0.00

Top 10 Places Sorted by Percent
Based on all places, regardless of population

Place	Number	%
Reklaw (city) Cherokee County	2	0.63

Place	Number	%
Lago Vista (city) Travis County	12	0.27
Forney (city) Kaufman County	8	0.15
Kingsland (cdp) Llano County	7	0.15
Lake Dallas (city) Denton County	8	0.13
University Park (city) Dallas County	19	0.08
Addison (town) Dallas County	9	0.07
Texas City (city) Galveston County	23	0.06
Plano (city) Collin County	111	0.05
San Juan (city) Hidalgo County	13	0.05

Top 10 Places Sorted by Percent
Based on places with populations of 10,000 or more

Place	Number	%
University Park (city) Dallas County	19	0.08
Addison (town) Dallas County	9	0.07
Texas City (city) Galveston County	23	0.06
Plano (city) Collin County	111	0.05
San Juan (city) Hidalgo County	13	0.05
West University Place (city) Harris County	7	0.05
Denton (city) Denton County	26	0.03
West Odessa (cdp) Ector County	6	0.03
De Soto (city) Dallas County	7	0.02
Arlington (city) Tarrant County	24	0.01

New Zealander

Top 10 Places Sorted by Number
Based on all places, regardless of population

Place	Number	%
Houston (city) Harris County	102	0.01
Austin (city) Travis County	73	0.01
Dallas (city) Dallas County	57	0.00
Arlington (city) Tarrant County	56	0.02
Plano (city) Collin County	55	0.02
Fort Worth (city) Tarrant County	52	0.01
San Antonio (city) Bexar County	39	0.00
Big Spring (city) Howard County	29	0.11
Lubbock (city) Lubbock County	28	0.01
Corpus Christi (city) Nueces County	20	0.01

Top 10 Places Sorted by Percent
Based on all places, regardless of population

Place	Number	%
Tulsita (cdp) Bee County	4	16.00
Ore City (city) Upshur County	10	0.88
Hedwig Village (city) Harris County	14	0.60
Hudson Bend (cdp) Travis County	10	0.42
Shamrock (city) Wheeler County	6	0.30
Hardin (city) Liberty County	2	0.25
White Oak (city) Gregg County	13	0.24
Rendon (cdp) Tarrant County	18	0.20
Rockport (city) Aransas County	13	0.18
Marfa (city) Presidio County	3	0.14

Top 10 Places Sorted by Percent
Based on places with populations of 10,000 or more

Place	Number	%
Big Spring (city) Howard County	29	0.11
Palestine (city) Anderson County	9	0.05
Wylie (city) Collin County	8	0.05
Pearland (city) Brazoria County	13	0.03
Harker Heights (city) Bell County	5	0.03
Arlington (city) Tarrant County	56	0.02
Plano (city) Collin County	55	0.02
Carrollton (city) Denton County	19	0.02
Allen (city) Collin County	7	0.02
Georgetown (city) Williamson County	6	0.02

Northern European

Top 10 Places Sorted by Number
Based on all places, regardless of population

Place	Number	%
Austin (city) Travis County	823	0.13
Houston (city) Harris County	582	0.03
Dallas (city) Dallas County	559	0.05
San Antonio (city) Bexar County	492	0.04
Fort Worth (city) Tarrant County	223	0.04
Coppell (city) Dallas County	147	0.41
San Angelo (city) Tom Green County	132	0.15
Abilene (city) Taylor County	132	0.11
Irving (city) Dallas County	120	0.06
El Paso (city) El Paso County	112	0.02

Top 10 Places Sorted by Percent
Based on all places, regardless of population

Place	Number	%
Trent (town) Taylor County	11	3.58
Fulshear (city) Fort Bend County	17	2.41
Plum Grove (city) Liberty County	20	2.30
Fayetteville (city) Fayette County	6	2.14
Merkel (town) Taylor County	40	1.57
Ector (city) Fannin County	7	1.10
Westover Hills (town) Tarrant County	6	0.92
Santa Anna (town) Coleman County	9	0.85
Annetta (town) Parker County	10	0.83
Lexington (town) Lee County	9	0.79

Top 10 Places Sorted by Percent
Based on places with populations of 10,000 or more

Place	Number	%
Stephenville (city) Erath County	70	0.47
Coppell (city) Dallas County	147	0.41
Burkburnett (city) Wichita County	45	0.41
University Park (city) Dallas County	88	0.38
Hewitt (city) McLennan County	40	0.37
West Odessa (cdp) Ector County	56	0.31
Rockwall (city) Rockwall County	53	0.29
Southlake (city) Tarrant County	55	0.26
San Marcos (city) Hays County	76	0.22
Mansfield (city) Tarrant County	63	0.22

Norwegian

Top 10 Places Sorted by Number
Based on all places, regardless of population

Place	Number	%
Houston (city) Harris County	7,367	0.38
Dallas (city) Dallas County	5,596	0.47
Austin (city) Travis County	5,544	0.84
San Antonio (city) Bexar County	4,914	0.43
Fort Worth (city) Tarrant County	3,050	0.57
Plano (city) Collin County	3,034	1.36
Arlington (city) Tarrant County	2,569	0.77
El Paso (city) El Paso County	1,887	0.33
Corpus Christi (city) Nueces County	1,394	0.50
Irving (city) Dallas County	1,284	0.67

Top 10 Places Sorted by Percent
Based on all places, regardless of population

Place	Number	%
Cranfills Gap (city) Bosque County	66	18.91
Clifton (city) Bosque County	286	7.97
Timbercreek Canyon (village) Randall County	26	6.28
Falman-County Acres (cdp) San Patricio County	13	5.33
Box Canyon-Amistad (cdp) Val Verde County	3	5.17
Bear Creek (village) Hays County	19	4.46
Adrian (city) Oldham County	6	4.26
Westlake (town) Tarrant County	9	4.04
Stagecoach (town) Montgomery County	20	3.98

Notes: (cdp) census designated place; Refer to the User's Guide in the front of the book for more detailed information.

Crawford (town) McLennan County | 31 | 3.92

Top 10 Places Sorted by Percent
Based on places with populations of 10,000 or more

Place	Number	%
Colleyville (city) Tarrant County	545	2.78
The Woodlands (cdp) Montgomery County	1,099	1.97
Copperas Cove (city) Coryell County	584	1.95
Coppell (city) Dallas County	695	1.93
Flower Mound (town) Denton County	966	1.89
Southlake (city) Tarrant County	393	1.83
Cedar Park (city) Williamson County	464	1.80
West University Place (city) Harris County	250	1.76
Corinth (city) Denton County	199	1.74
League City (city) Galveston County	772	1.70

Pennsylvania German

Top 10 Places Sorted by Number
Based on all places, regardless of population

Place	Number	%
Houston (city) Harris County	174	0.01
Dallas (city) Dallas County	124	0.01
San Antonio (city) Bexar County	124	0.01
Austin (city) Travis County	112	0.02
Fort Worth (city) Tarrant County	87	0.02
Arlington (city) Tarrant County	58	0.02
El Paso (city) El Paso County	53	0.01
Garland (city) Dallas County	52	0.02
Irving (city) Dallas County	50	0.03
San Angelo (city) Tom Green County	48	0.05

Top 10 Places Sorted by Percent
Based on all places, regardless of population

Place	Number	%
Meadow (town) Terry County	10	1.58
Bulverde (city) Comal County	40	1.06
Clear Lake Shores (city) Galveston County	6	0.51
Friona (city) Parmer County	19	0.49
Plains (town) Yoakum County	7	0.48
Grey Forest (city) Bexar County	2	0.46
Tatum (city) Rusk County	5	0.44
Sunrise Beach Village (city) Llano County	3	0.42
Seabrook (city) Harris County	34	0.37
Ingleside on the Bay (city) San Patricio County	2	0.30

Top 10 Places Sorted by Percent
Based on places with populations of 10,000 or more

Place	Number	%
Burkburnett (city) Wichita County	32	0.29
Katy (city) Harris County	28	0.24
Alamo (city) Hidalgo County	22	0.15
Sherman (city) Grayson County	39	0.11
Georgetown (city) Williamson County	29	0.10
Bedford (city) Tarrant County	44	0.09
Bay City (city) Matagorda County	14	0.08
Snyder (city) Scurry County	9	0.08
Huntsville (city) Walker County	26	0.07
Pampa (city) Gray County	13	0.07

Polish

Top 10 Places Sorted by Number
Based on all places, regardless of population

Place	Number	%
Houston (city) Harris County	19,297	0.99
San Antonio (city) Bexar County	14,475	1.26
Dallas (city) Dallas County	9,642	0.81
Austin (city) Travis County	9,466	1.44
Plano (city) Collin County	5,490	2.47
Fort Worth (city) Tarrant County	4,368	0.82
Arlington (city) Tarrant County	4,250	1.28

El Paso (city) El Paso County	2,964	0.53
Corpus Christi (city) Nueces County	2,522	0.91
Irving (city) Dallas County	1,928	1.01

Top 10 Places Sorted by Percent
Based on all places, regardless of population

Place	Number	%
Falls City (city) Karnes County	281	47.79
Saint Hedwig (town) Bexar County	543	28.94
Bremond (city) Robertson County	203	23.85
China Grove (town) Bexar County	212	16.77
Poth (town) Wilson County	280	15.27
Mustang (town) Navarro County	3	11.54
La Vernia (city) Wilson County	97	10.19
Dorchester (town) Grayson County	12	9.52
Cross Mountain (cdp) Bexar County	145	9.39
Stonewall (cdp) Gillespie County	40	7.86

Top 10 Places Sorted by Percent
Based on places with populations of 10,000 or more

Place	Number	%
Brenham (city) Washington County	552	4.11
Highland Village (city) Denton County	414	3.40
Pecan Grove (cdp) Fort Bend County	451	3.35
Cinco Ranch (cdp) Fort Bend County	358	3.19
Flower Mound (town) Denton County	1,583	3.09
Spring (cdp) Harris County	1,090	2.99
The Woodlands (cdp) Montgomery County	1,623	2.91
West University Place (city) Harris County	381	2.68
Wells Branch (cdp) Travis County	299	2.66
Schertz (city) Guadalupe County	490	2.65

Portuguese

Top 10 Places Sorted by Number
Based on all places, regardless of population

Place	Number	%
Houston (city) Harris County	1,466	0.07
San Antonio (city) Bexar County	1,341	0.12
Austin (city) Travis County	872	0.13
Dallas (city) Dallas County	600	0.05
Fort Worth (city) Tarrant County	481	0.09
Arlington (city) Tarrant County	340	0.10
Plano (city) Collin County	316	0.14
El Paso (city) El Paso County	292	0.05
Irving (city) Dallas County	224	0.12
Grand Prairie (city) Dallas County	211	0.17

Top 10 Places Sorted by Percent
Based on all places, regardless of population

Place	Number	%
Toyah (town) Reeves County	4	3.85
Lakeshore Grdns-Hidden Acres (cdp) San Patricio Co.	23	3.40
Oak Ridge (town) Cooke County	5	2.49
Paint Rock (town) Concho County	5	1.50
Avinger (town) Cass County	6	1.23
Buchanan Dam (cdp) Llano County	18	1.07
New Home (city) Lynn County	3	0.96
Santa Clara (city) Guadalupe County	8	0.76
Riesel (city) McLennan County	7	0.71
Blum (town) Hill County	3	0.71

Top 10 Places Sorted by Percent
Based on places with populations of 10,000 or more

Place	Number	%
Jollyville (cdp) Williamson County	93	0.60
Wells Branch (cdp) Travis County	67	0.60
Saginaw (city) Tarrant County	69	0.56
Pecan Grove (cdp) Fort Bend County	74	0.55
Port Neches (city) Jefferson County	64	0.47
Universal City (city) Bexar County	67	0.45
Harker Heights (city) Bell County	62	0.36

Cinco Ranch (cdp) Fort Bend County	38	0.34
Frisco (city) Collin County	112	0.33
Pflugerville (city) Travis County	52	0.32

Romanian

Top 10 Places Sorted by Number
Based on all places, regardless of population

Place	Number	%
Houston (city) Harris County	1,448	0.07
Dallas (city) Dallas County	954	0.08
Austin (city) Travis County	490	0.07
San Antonio (city) Bexar County	449	0.04
Plano (city) Collin County	240	0.11
El Paso (city) El Paso County	201	0.04
Fort Worth (city) Tarrant County	179	0.03
Carrollton (city) Denton County	169	0.10
Pasadena (city) Harris County	137	0.10
Garland (city) Dallas County	136	0.06

Top 10 Places Sorted by Percent
Based on all places, regardless of population

Place	Number	%
Rocky Mound (town) Camp County	3	3.37
Del Sol-Loma Linda (cdp) San Patricio County	19	2.64
Keene (city) Johnson County	125	2.56
Bear Creek (village) Hays County	7	1.64
Bailey (city) Fannin County	4	1.61
Port Mansfield (cdp) Willacy County	5	1.30
Ravenna (city) Fannin County	2	0.88
Heath (city) Rockwall County	27	0.69
Moody (city) McLennan County	9	0.64
Ingram (city) Kerr County	11	0.62

Top 10 Places Sorted by Percent
Based on places with populations of 10,000 or more

Place	Number	%
New Territory (cdp) Fort Bend County	60	0.43
Levelland (city) Hockley County	36	0.28
The Colony (city) Denton County	68	0.26
Clute (city) Brazoria County	25	0.24
University Park (city) Dallas County	54	0.23
Cloverleaf (cdp) Harris County	49	0.21
Vidor (city) Orange County	22	0.19
Balch Springs (city) Dallas County	35	0.18
Carrollton (city) Denton County	169	0.15
Bellaire (city) Harris County	23	0.15

Russian

Top 10 Places Sorted by Number
Based on all places, regardless of population

Place	Number	%
Houston (city) Harris County	8,423	0.43
Dallas (city) Dallas County	6,152	0.52
Austin (city) Travis County	4,168	0.64
San Antonio (city) Bexar County	3,126	0.27
Plano (city) Collin County	2,722	1.22
Fort Worth (city) Tarrant County	1,374	0.26
El Paso (city) El Paso County	1,350	0.24
Arlington (city) Tarrant County	1,057	0.32
Richardson (city) Dallas County	893	0.97
Sugar Land (city) Fort Bend County	608	0.96

Top 10 Places Sorted by Percent
Based on all places, regardless of population

Place	Number	%
Prado Verde (cdp) El Paso County	14	6.60
Lipscomb (city) Lipscomb County	2	4.88
Barton Creek (cdp) Travis County	67	4.26
Southside Place (city) Harris County	62	4.02
Bunker Hill Village (city) Harris County	90	2.46

Place	Number	%
Olmos Park (city) Bexar County	58	2.35
Huxley (city) Shelby County	7	2.23
West Lake Hills (city) Travis County	67	2.16
Wixon Valley (city) Brazos County	5	2.14
Piney Point Village (city) Harris County	69	2.04

Top 10 Places Sorted by Percent
Based on places with populations of 10,000 or more

Place	Number	%
Bellaire (city) Harris County	283	1.82
West University Place (city) Harris County	255	1.79
Plano (city) Collin County	2,722	1.22
Jollyville (cdp) Williamson County	173	1.12
Highland Village (city) Denton County	121	0.99
Richardson (city) Dallas County	893	0.97
University Park (city) Dallas County	226	0.97
Sugar Land (city) Fort Bend County	608	0.96
Addison (town) Dallas County	131	0.95
Southlake (city) Tarrant County	203	0.94

Scandinavian

Top 10 Places Sorted by Number
Based on all places, regardless of population

Place	Number	%
Houston (city) Harris County	1,092	0.06
Austin (city) Travis County	935	0.14
San Antonio (city) Bexar County	691	0.06
Dallas (city) Dallas County	662	0.06
Fort Worth (city) Tarrant County	458	0.09
Arlington (city) Tarrant County	416	0.13
Plano (city) Collin County	356	0.16
Garland (city) Dallas County	194	0.09
El Paso (city) El Paso County	158	0.03
Pasadena (city) Harris County	147	0.10

Top 10 Places Sorted by Percent
Based on all places, regardless of population

Place	Number	%
Broaddus (town) San Augustine County	10	5.81
Morgan's Point (city) Harris County	12	3.61
Gallatin (city) Cherokee County	11	2.77
Paint Rock (town) Concho County	9	2.69
Leakey (city) Real County	8	2.08
West Orange (city) Orange County	62	1.48
Todd Mission (city) Grimes County	2	1.39
Midway (city) Madison County	3	0.91
Riverside (city) Walker County	4	0.90
Nassau Bay (city) Harris County	38	0.89

Top 10 Places Sorted by Percent
Based on places with populations of 10,000 or more

Place	Number	%
Wylie (city) Collin County	88	0.59
Brushy Creek (cdp) Williamson County	87	0.55
Cinco Ranch (cdp) Fort Bend County	55	0.49
West University Place (city) Harris County	68	0.48
Keller (city) Tarrant County	93	0.34
University Park (city) Dallas County	72	0.31
Allen (city) Collin County	112	0.26
Belton (city) Bell County	34	0.23
Coppell (city) Dallas County	80	0.22
Round Rock (city) Williamson County	121	0.20

Scotch-Irish

Top 10 Places Sorted by Number
Based on all places, regardless of population

Place	Number	%
Houston (city) Harris County	21,553	1.10
Dallas (city) Dallas County	16,308	1.37
Austin (city) Travis County	16,024	2.44
San Antonio (city) Bexar County	14,938	1.31
Fort Worth (city) Tarrant County	8,654	1.62
Arlington (city) Tarrant County	6,023	1.81
Plano (city) Collin County	5,027	2.26
Lubbock (city) Lubbock County	4,693	2.35
Corpus Christi (city) Nueces County	4,365	1.57
El Paso (city) El Paso County	3,933	0.70

Top 10 Places Sorted by Percent
Based on all places, regardless of population

Place	Number	%
Elbert (cdp) Throckmorton County	14	20.29
South Fork Estates (cdp) Jim Hogg County	8	16.33
Falcon Village (cdp) Starr County	8	11.76
Catarina (cdp) Dimmit County	15	11.11
Ross (city) McLennan County	27	10.71
Cottonwood (city) Kaufman County	16	9.30
Mertens (town) Hill County	15	8.98
Jolly (city) Clay County	16	8.89
Leakey (city) Real County	32	8.33
Ratamosa (cdp) Cameron County	13	8.33

Top 10 Places Sorted by Percent
Based on places with populations of 10,000 or more

Place	Number	%
University Park (city) Dallas County	1,000	4.28
Kerrville (city) Kerr County	823	3.96
Highland Village (city) Denton County	457	3.76
Canyon Lake (cdp) Comal County	630	3.73
Belton (city) Bell County	537	3.65
Benbrook (city) Tarrant County	692	3.48
Bellaire (city) Harris County	536	3.44
Georgetown (city) Williamson County	914	3.24
Richardson (city) Dallas County	2,906	3.17
West University Place (city) Harris County	445	3.13

Scottish

Top 10 Places Sorted by Number
Based on all places, regardless of population

Place	Number	%
Houston (city) Harris County	20,171	1.03
Austin (city) Travis County	15,382	2.34
Dallas (city) Dallas County	14,482	1.22
San Antonio (city) Bexar County	11,915	1.04
Fort Worth (city) Tarrant County	7,923	1.48
Arlington (city) Tarrant County	6,042	1.82
Plano (city) Collin County	5,888	2.65
El Paso (city) El Paso County	3,492	0.62
Garland (city) Dallas County	3,460	1.60
Lubbock (city) Lubbock County	3,238	1.62

Top 10 Places Sorted by Percent
Based on all places, regardless of population

Place	Number	%
South Fork Estates (cdp) Jim Hogg County	18	36.73
Caney City (town) Henderson County	21	10.40
Falcon Mesa (cdp) Zapata County	38	8.21
Ranchos Penitas West (cdp) Webb County	35	7.78
Bayview (town) Cameron County	30	7.65
Novice (city) Coleman County	12	7.45
Annetta North (town) Parker County	30	6.98
San Leanna (village) Travis County	29	6.92
West Lake Hills (city) Travis County	213	6.87
Hilshire Village (city) Harris County	48	6.65

Top 10 Places Sorted by Percent
Based on places with populations of 10,000 or more

Place	Number	%
University Park (city) Dallas County	1,072	4.59
West University Place (city) Harris County	582	4.10
Southlake (city) Tarrant County	835	3.88

Place	Number	%
Cinco Ranch (cdp) Fort Bend County	432	3.84
The Woodlands (cdp) Montgomery County	1,991	3.57
Flower Mound (town) Denton County	1,764	3.45
Schertz (city) Guadalupe County	623	3.38
Grapevine (city) Tarrant County	1,366	3.24
Coppell (city) Dallas County	1,122	3.12
Allen (city) Collin County	1,319	3.04

Serbian

Top 10 Places Sorted by Number
Based on all places, regardless of population

Place	Number	%
Houston (city) Harris County	264	0.01
Austin (city) Travis County	237	0.04
Dallas (city) Dallas County	216	0.02
Fort Worth (city) Tarrant County	130	0.02
San Antonio (city) Bexar County	66	0.01
Pflugerville (city) Travis County	64	0.39
The Woodlands (cdp) Montgomery County	64	0.11
Plano (city) Collin County	60	0.03
El Paso (city) El Paso County	58	0.01
Grand Prairie (city) Dallas County	56	0.04

Top 10 Places Sorted by Percent
Based on all places, regardless of population

Place	Number	%
Springlake (town) Lamb County	2	1.40
Magnolia (city) Montgomery County	6	0.56
Oak Ridge North (city) Montgomery County	15	0.50
Kempner (city) Lampasas County	4	0.41
Pleak (village) Fort Bend County	4	0.41
Pflugerville (city) Travis County	64	0.39
Moody (city) McLennan County	5	0.36
Hedwig Village (city) Harris County	8	0.34
Fair Oaks Ranch (city) Bexar County	15	0.31
Silverton (city) Briscoe County	2	0.27

Top 10 Places Sorted by Percent
Based on places with populations of 10,000 or more

Place	Number	%
Pflugerville (city) Travis County	64	0.39
Jollyville (cdp) Williamson County	24	0.16
Harker Heights (city) Bell County	23	0.13
The Woodlands (cdp) Montgomery County	64	0.11
Lake Jackson (city) Brazoria County	26	0.10
University Park (city) Dallas County	24	0.10
Hewitt (city) McLennan County	10	0.09
College Station (city) Brazos County	55	0.08
Fort Hood (cdp) Coryell County	28	0.08
Colleyville (city) Tarrant County	15	0.08

Slavic

Top 10 Places Sorted by Number
Based on all places, regardless of population

Place	Number	%
Houston (city) Harris County	306	0.02
Austin (city) Travis County	255	0.04
San Antonio (city) Bexar County	224	0.02
Dallas (city) Dallas County	211	0.02
Arlington (city) Tarrant County	103	0.03
El Paso (city) El Paso County	86	0.02
Killeen (city) Bell County	67	0.08
San Angelo (city) Tom Green County	61	0.07
Corpus Christi (city) Nueces County	61	0.02
Wichita Falls (city) Wichita County	50	0.05

Top 10 Places Sorted by Percent
Based on all places, regardless of population

Place	Number	%
Greatwood (cdp) Fort Bend County	48	0.73

Place	Number	%
Manvel (city) Brazoria County	21	0.72
Northcliff (cdp) Guadalupe County	9	0.51
Kempner (city) Lampasas County	5	0.51
Taylor Lake Village (city) Harris County	18	0.49
Iraan (city) Pecos County	6	0.44
Timberwood Park (cdp) Bexar County	24	0.42
Hedwig Village (city) Harris County	8	0.34
El Lago (city) Harris County	11	0.33
Blue Mound (city) Tarrant County	8	0.33

Top 10 Places Sorted by Percent
Based on places with populations of 10,000 or more

Place	Number	%
Pecan Grove (cdp) Fort Bend County	25	0.19
Southlake (city) Tarrant County	32	0.15
Friendswood (city) Galveston County	41	0.14
Jollyville (cdp) Williamson County	21	0.14
Watauga (city) Tarrant County	29	0.13
Seguin (city) Guadalupe County	28	0.13
Borger (city) Hutchinson County	19	0.13
Cedar Park (city) Williamson County	29	0.11
Georgetown (city) Williamson County	28	0.10
Benbrook (city) Tarrant County	20	0.10

Slovak

Top 10 Places Sorted by Number
Based on all places, regardless of population

Place	Number	%
Houston (city) Harris County	922	0.05
Austin (city) Travis County	645	0.10
San Antonio (city) Bexar County	549	0.05
Dallas (city) Dallas County	437	0.04
Plano (city) Collin County	367	0.17
Arlington (city) Tarrant County	302	0.09
El Paso (city) El Paso County	218	0.04
The Woodlands (cdp) Montgomery County	188	0.34
Fort Worth (city) Tarrant County	170	0.03
Grapevine (city) Tarrant County	139	0.33

Top 10 Places Sorted by Percent
Based on all places, regardless of population

Place	Number	%
Todd Mission (city) Grimes County	8	5.56
Santa Clara (city) Guadalupe County	16	1.51
Northcliff (cdp) Guadalupe County	22	1.25
Serenada (cdp) Williamson County	18	1.04
Laughlin AFB (cdp) Val Verde County	22	0.99
Copper Canyon (town) Denton County	11	0.91
Parker (city) Collin County	12	0.89
Westworth Village (city) Tarrant County	18	0.84
Southside Place (city) Harris County	13	0.84
Castroville (city) Medina County	22	0.82

Top 10 Places Sorted by Percent
Based on places with populations of 10,000 or more

Place	Number	%
Addison (town) Dallas County	53	0.38
The Woodlands (cdp) Montgomery County	188	0.34
Grapevine (city) Tarrant County	139	0.33
Keller (city) Tarrant County	79	0.29
Weatherford (city) Parker County	53	0.28
Southlake (city) Tarrant County	58	0.27
Cedar Park (city) Williamson County	65	0.25
Colleyville (city) Tarrant County	48	0.25
West University Place (city) Harris County	35	0.25
The Colony (city) Denton County	55	0.21

Slovene

Top 10 Places Sorted by Number
Based on all places, regardless of population

Place	Number	%
Austin (city) Travis County	348	0.05
Houston (city) Harris County	297	0.02
San Antonio (city) Bexar County	204	0.02
Dallas (city) Dallas County	129	0.01
Arlington (city) Tarrant County	92	0.03
Plano (city) Collin County	86	0.04
The Woodlands (cdp) Montgomery County	76	0.14
Garland (city) Dallas County	74	0.03
Corpus Christi (city) Nueces County	69	0.02
Richardson (city) Dallas County	59	0.06

Top 10 Places Sorted by Percent
Based on all places, regardless of population

Place	Number	%
Thorndale (city) Milam County	21	1.65
Serenada (cdp) Williamson County	24	1.38
Hollywood Park (town) Bexar County	33	1.28
West Lake Hills (city) Travis County	20	0.64
Heath (city) Rockwall County	23	0.59
Lakehills (cdp) Bandera County	25	0.56
Giddings (city) Lee County	27	0.53
Willow Park (city) Parker County	14	0.50
Boerne (city) Kendall County	27	0.44
Hutto (city) Williamson County	5	0.39

Top 10 Places Sorted by Percent
Based on places with populations of 10,000 or more

Place	Number	%
Pflugerville (city) Travis County	36	0.22
Bellaire (city) Harris County	34	0.22
Angleton (city) Brazoria County	30	0.16
The Woodlands (cdp) Montgomery County	76	0.14
University Park (city) Dallas County	32	0.14
West University Place (city) Harris County	18	0.13
Canyon (city) Randall County	17	0.13
Benbrook (city) Tarrant County	23	0.12
Katy (city) Harris County	13	0.11
Saginaw (city) Tarrant County	12	0.10

Soviet Union

Top 10 Places Sorted by Number
Based on all places, regardless of population

Place	Number	%
Garland (city) Dallas County	15	0.01

Top 10 Places Sorted by Percent
Based on all places, regardless of population

Place	Number	%
Garland (city) Dallas County	15	0.01

Top 10 Places Sorted by Percent
Based on places with populations of 10,000 or more

Place	Number	%
Garland (city) Dallas County	15	0.01

Swedish

Top 10 Places Sorted by Number
Based on all places, regardless of population

Place	Number	%
Houston (city) Harris County	8,798	0.45
Austin (city) Travis County	7,553	1.15
Dallas (city) Dallas County	6,748	0.57
San Antonio (city) Bexar County	5,322	0.46

Place	Number	%
Plano (city) Collin County	3,201	1.44
Fort Worth (city) Tarrant County	2,971	0.55
Arlington (city) Tarrant County	2,917	0.88
El Paso (city) El Paso County	1,502	0.27
Corpus Christi (city) Nueces County	1,309	0.47
Carrollton (city) Denton County	1,305	1.19

Top 10 Places Sorted by Percent
Based on all places, regardless of population

Place	Number	%
Melvin (town) McCulloch County	16	10.00
Las Colonias (cdp) Zavala County	20	8.73
Box Canyon-Amistad (cdp) Val Verde County	4	6.90
Zuehl (cdp) Guadalupe County	16	6.27
Round Top (town) Fayette County	5	5.95
Hays (city) Hays County	16	5.37
Fayetteville (city) Fayette County	14	5.00
Lakeway (city) Travis County	362	4.43
Onion Creek (cdp) Travis County	87	4.33
Tuleta (cdp) Bee County	12	3.96

Top 10 Places Sorted by Percent
Based on places with populations of 10,000 or more

Place	Number	%
Highland Village (city) Denton County	306	2.52
Southlake (city) Tarrant County	515	2.40
Colleyville (city) Tarrant County	455	2.32
Georgetown (city) Williamson County	586	2.08
Flower Mound (town) Denton County	1,024	2.00
Corinth (city) Denton County	229	2.00
Wells Branch (cdp) Travis County	221	1.96
Grapevine (city) Tarrant County	819	1.94
Frisco (city) Collin County	611	1.82
West University Place (city) Harris County	258	1.82

Swiss

Top 10 Places Sorted by Number
Based on all places, regardless of population

Place	Number	%
Houston (city) Harris County	2,226	0.11
Dallas (city) Dallas County	1,803	0.15
Austin (city) Travis County	1,633	0.25
San Antonio (city) Bexar County	1,359	0.12
Plano (city) Collin County	804	0.36
Arlington (city) Tarrant County	559	0.17
Fort Worth (city) Tarrant County	528	0.10
Richardson (city) Dallas County	318	0.35
Corpus Christi (city) Nueces County	300	0.11
Irving (city) Dallas County	288	0.15

Top 10 Places Sorted by Percent
Based on all places, regardless of population

Place	Number	%
Estelline (town) Hall County	5	3.23
Noonday (city) Smith County	13	2.44
West Lake Hills (city) Travis County	70	2.26
Grays Prairie (village) Kaufman County	6	2.21
Lake Kiowa (cdp) Cooke County	35	1.83
Paradise (city) Wise County	8	1.82
Shavano Park (city) Bexar County	32	1.80
Smyer (town) Hockley County	8	1.67
Siesta Shores (cdp) Zapata County	15	1.59
Liberty City (cdp) Gregg County	24	1.35

Top 10 Places Sorted by Percent
Based on places with populations of 10,000 or more

Place	Number	%
University Park (city) Dallas County	211	0.90
Cinco Ranch (cdp) Fort Bend County	91	0.81
Pecan Grove (cdp) Fort Bend County	101	0.75
Bellaire (city) Harris County	102	0.65

Notes: (cdp) census designated place; Refer to the User's Guide in the front of the book for more detailed information.

Place	Number	%
Universal City (city) Bexar County	97	0.65
West University Place (city) Harris County	89	0.63
Pflugerville (city) Travis County	91	0.56
Colleyville (city) Tarrant County	105	0.54
Rockwall (city) Rockwall County	96	0.52
Lake Jackson (city) Brazoria County	124	0.47

Turkish

Top 10 Places Sorted by Number
Based on all places, regardless of population

Place	Number	%
Houston (city) Harris County	764	0.04
Austin (city) Travis County	355	0.05
Dallas (city) Dallas County	300	0.03
San Antonio (city) Bexar County	247	0.02
Arlington (city) Tarrant County	223	0.07
Plano (city) Collin County	196	0.09
College Station (city) Brazos County	187	0.28
Lubbock (city) Lubbock County	94	0.05
Richardson (city) Dallas County	65	0.07
Wichita Falls (city) Wichita County	64	0.06

Top 10 Places Sorted by Percent
Based on all places, regardless of population

Place	Number	%
McLendon-Chisholm (city) Rockwall County	8	0.86
Piney Point Village (city) Harris County	23	0.68
West Lake Hills (city) Travis County	19	0.61
Lakewood Village (city) Denton County	2	0.55
Annetta North (town) Parker County	2	0.47
Bear Creek (village) Hays County	2	0.47
Lakeside (town) Tarrant County	4	0.40
Hebron (town) Denton County	3	0.36
Southside Place (city) Harris County	5	0.32
Dayton (city) Liberty County	18	0.31

Top 10 Places Sorted by Percent
Based on places with populations of 10,000 or more

Place	Number	%
College Station (city) Brazos County	187	0.28
Paris (city) Lamar County	51	0.20
Saginaw (city) Tarrant County	19	0.15
League City (city) Galveston County	59	0.13
Keller (city) Tarrant County	35	0.13
Vidor (city) Orange County	13	0.11
Rockwall (city) Rockwall County	18	0.10
Plano (city) Collin County	196	0.09
Copperas Cove (city) Coryell County	26	0.09
Burleson (city) Johnson County	20	0.09

Ukrainian

Top 10 Places Sorted by Number
Based on all places, regardless of population

Place	Number	%
Houston (city) Harris County	1,693	0.09
Dallas (city) Dallas County	923	0.08
Austin (city) Travis County	854	0.13
San Antonio (city) Bexar County	761	0.07
Plano (city) Collin County	575	0.26
Irving (city) Dallas County	357	0.19
Arlington (city) Tarrant County	351	0.11
Fort Worth (city) Tarrant County	317	0.06
El Paso (city) El Paso County	199	0.04
The Woodlands (cdp) Montgomery County	186	0.33

Top 10 Places Sorted by Percent
Based on all places, regardless of population

Place	Number	%
Cross Timber (town) Johnson County	6	2.23
Knollwood (village) Grayson County	7	1.87

Place	Number	%
Bremond (city) Robertson County	14	1.65
Parker (city) Collin County	19	1.41
Sanctuary (town) Parker County	4	1.37
New Berlin (city) Guadalupe County	6	1.26
Lindsay (town) Cooke County	10	1.25
Scenic Oaks (cdp) Bexar County	41	1.24
Mountain City (city) Hays County	7	1.07
Beasley (city) Fort Bend County	5	0.84

Top 10 Places Sorted by Percent
Based on places with populations of 10,000 or more

Place	Number	%
West University Place (city) Harris County	86	0.61
Frisco (city) Collin County	181	0.54
Portland (city) San Patricio County	76	0.51
Port Neches (city) Jefferson County	56	0.41
The Colony (city) Denton County	102	0.38
Katy (city) Harris County	44	0.38
The Woodlands (cdp) Montgomery County	186	0.33
Bellaire (city) Harris County	47	0.30
Flower Mound (town) Denton County	151	0.29
Watauga (city) Tarrant County	63	0.29

United States or American

Top 10 Places Sorted by Number
Based on all places, regardless of population

Place	Number	%
Houston (city) Harris County	71,531	3.66
Dallas (city) Dallas County	48,183	4.06
San Antonio (city) Bexar County	36,123	3.16
Fort Worth (city) Tarrant County	34,680	6.48
Austin (city) Travis County	28,052	4.27
Arlington (city) Tarrant County	25,940	7.80
Amarillo (city) Potter County	18,352	10.58
Lubbock (city) Lubbock County	18,232	9.14
Garland (city) Dallas County	17,564	8.13
Mesquite (city) Dallas County	15,311	12.29

Top 10 Places Sorted by Percent
Based on all places, regardless of population

Place	Number	%
Aquilla (city) Hill County	79	56.03
Millican (town) Brazos County	64	55.17
Kirvin (town) Freestone County	51	42.15
Dickens (city) Dickens County	159	41.41
Alba (town) Wood County	190	41.39
Quail (cdp) Collingsworth County	11	40.74
Channing (town) Hartley County	150	40.54
Kennard (city) Houston County	115	39.79
Millsap (town) Parker County	151	39.43
Carbon (town) Eastland County	91	38.89

Top 10 Places Sorted by Percent
Based on places with populations of 10,000 or more

Place	Number	%
Vidor (city) Orange County	2,008	17.65
Sulphur Springs (city) Hopkins County	2,543	17.45
Wylie (city) Collin County	2,558	17.09
Kilgore (city) Gregg County	1,814	16.24
Pampa (city) Gray County	2,880	16.10
Burleson (city) Johnson County	3,402	16.00
Sweetwater (city) Nolan County	1,763	15.41
Watauga (city) Tarrant County	3,270	14.97
Canyon (city) Randall County	1,832	14.14
Burkburnett (city) Wichita County	1,507	13.87

Welsh

Top 10 Places Sorted by Number
Based on all places, regardless of population

Place	Number	%
Houston (city) Harris County	5,325	0.27
Austin (city) Travis County	4,261	0.65
Dallas (city) Dallas County	4,060	0.34
San Antonio (city) Bexar County	3,598	0.31
Fort Worth (city) Tarrant County	2,061	0.38
Arlington (city) Tarrant County	1,879	0.56
Plano (city) Collin County	1,643	0.74
El Paso (city) El Paso County	1,157	0.21
Lubbock (city) Lubbock County	1,099	0.55
Garland (city) Dallas County	959	0.44

Top 10 Places Sorted by Percent
Based on all places, regardless of population

Place	Number	%
Opdyke West (town) Hockley County	10	5.05
Gallatin (city) Cherokee County	20	5.04
Union Grove (city) Upshur County	16	4.83
Dorchester (town) Grayson County	6	4.76
Port Mansfield (cdp) Willacy County	16	4.16
Rosser (village) Kaufman County	15	3.71
Creedmoor (city) Travis County	8	3.65
Todd Mission (city) Grimes County	5	3.47
Thompsons (town) Fort Bend County	8	3.45
Kenefick (town) Liberty County	22	3.19

Top 10 Places Sorted by Percent
Based on places with populations of 10,000 or more

Place	Number	%
Cinco Ranch (cdp) Fort Bend County	153	1.36
Southlake (city) Tarrant County	277	1.29
Hurst (city) Tarrant County	459	1.26
Mansfield (city) Tarrant County	364	1.26
Greenville (city) Hunt County	275	1.14
Flower Mound (town) Denton County	564	1.10
University Park (city) Dallas County	242	1.04
Colleyville (city) Tarrant County	199	1.02
Richardson (city) Dallas County	928	1.01
The Woodlands (cdp) Montgomery County	557	1.00

West Indian, excluding Hispanic

Top 10 Places Sorted by Number
Based on all places, regardless of population

Place	Number	%
Houston (city) Harris County	6,543	0.33
Dallas (city) Dallas County	1,837	0.15
San Antonio (city) Bexar County	1,486	0.13
Austin (city) Travis County	1,241	0.19
Fort Worth (city) Tarrant County	1,080	0.20
Killeen (city) Bell County	851	0.98
Arlington (city) Tarrant County	833	0.25
Baytown (city) Harris County	823	1.23
Missouri City (city) Fort Bend County	806	1.54
Irving (city) Dallas County	592	0.31

Top 10 Places Sorted by Percent
Based on all places, regardless of population

Place	Number	%
South Fork Estates (cdp) Jim Hogg County	6	12.24
Industry (city) Austin County	16	5.52
Pyote (town) Ward County	7	5.34
Las Colonias (cdp) Zavala County	8	3.49
Hawk Cove (city) Hunt County	14	3.21
Barton Creek (cdp) Travis County	48	3.05
Zuehl (cdp) Guadalupe County	7	2.75
Josephine (city) Collin County	13	2.18
Blackwell (city) Nolan County	7	1.92

Notes: (cdp) census designated place; Refer to the User's Guide in the front of the book for more detailed information.

Grays Prairie (village) Kaufman County   5   1.85

Top 10 Places Sorted by Percent
Based on places with populations of 10,000 or more

Place	Number	%
Stafford (city) Fort Bend County	244	1.56
Mission Bend (cdp) Fort Bend County	478	1.55
Missouri City (city) Fort Bend County	806	1.54
Baytown (city) Harris County	823	1.23
Killeen (city) Bell County	851	0.98
New Territory (cdp) Fort Bend County	123	0.89
Fort Hood (cdp) Coryell County	253	0.75
Portland (city) San Patricio County	110	0.74
Copperas Cove (city) Coryell County	192	0.64
Humble (city) Harris County	81	0.55

West Indian: Bahamian, excluding Hispanic

Top 10 Places Sorted by Number
Based on all places, regardless of population

Place	Number	%
Houston (city) Harris County	154	0.01
Killeen (city) Bell County	56	0.06
San Antonio (city) Bexar County	33	0.00
Irving (city) Dallas County	30	0.02
Flower Mound (town) Denton County	24	0.05
Wichita Falls (city) Wichita County	23	0.02
Stafford (city) Fort Bend County	17	0.11
Lewisville (city) Denton County	14	0.02
Grand Prairie (city) Dallas County	13	0.01
Corpus Christi (city) Nueces County	13	0.00

Top 10 Places Sorted by Percent
Based on all places, regardless of population

Place	Number	%
Kemah (city) Galveston County	3	0.12
Stafford (city) Fort Bend County	17	0.11
Troup (city) Smith County	2	0.10
Killeen (city) Bell County	56	0.06
Jacksonville (city) Cherokee County	9	0.06
Highland Village (city) Denton County	7	0.06
Seagoville (city) Dallas County	6	0.06
Fort Bliss (cdp) El Paso County	5	0.06
Flower Mound (town) Denton County	24	0.05
Greenville (city) Hunt County	11	0.05

Top 10 Places Sorted by Percent
Based on places with populations of 10,000 or more

Place	Number	%
Stafford (city) Fort Bend County	17	0.11
Killeen (city) Bell County	56	0.06
Jacksonville (city) Cherokee County	9	0.06
Highland Village (city) Denton County	7	0.06
Seagoville (city) Dallas County	6	0.06
Flower Mound (town) Denton County	24	0.05
Greenville (city) Hunt County	11	0.05
Dickinson (city) Galveston County	8	0.05
Mansfield (city) Tarrant County	10	0.03
Irving (city) Dallas County	30	0.02

West Indian: Barbadian, excluding Hispanic

Top 10 Places Sorted by Number
Based on all places, regardless of population

Place	Number	%
Houston (city) Harris County	102	0.01
San Antonio (city) Bexar County	63	0.01
Dallas (city) Dallas County	49	0.00
Sugar Land (city) Fort Bend County	45	0.07
Austin (city) Travis County	39	0.01

Place	Number	%
Arlington (city) Tarrant County	34	0.01
Port Arthur (city) Jefferson County	33	0.06
Killeen (city) Bell County	27	0.03
Carrollton (city) Denton County	27	0.02
McGregor (city) McLennan County	25	0.54

Top 10 Places Sorted by Percent
Based on all places, regardless of population

Place	Number	%
McGregor (city) McLennan County	25	0.54
Keene (city) Johnson County	24	0.49
Oak Ridge North (city) Montgomery County	13	0.44
Brazoria (city) Brazoria County	3	0.11
Alpine (city) Brewster County	6	0.10
La Marque (city) Galveston County	13	0.09
Sugar Land (city) Fort Bend County	45	0.07
Port Arthur (city) Jefferson County	33	0.06
Deer Park (city) Harris County	13	0.05
Missouri City (city) Fort Bend County	21	0.04

Top 10 Places Sorted by Percent
Based on places with populations of 10,000 or more

Place	Number	%
La Marque (city) Galveston County	13	0.09
Sugar Land (city) Fort Bend County	45	0.07
Port Arthur (city) Jefferson County	33	0.06
Deer Park (city) Harris County	13	0.05
Missouri City (city) Fort Bend County	21	0.04
Farmers Branch (city) Dallas County	12	0.04
Plainview (city) Hale County	9	0.04
Killeen (city) Bell County	27	0.03
Carrollton (city) Denton County	27	0.02
Galveston (city) Galveston County	14	0.02

West Indian: Belizean, excluding Hispanic

Top 10 Places Sorted by Number
Based on all places, regardless of population

Place	Number	%
Houston (city) Harris County	379	0.02
Garland (city) Dallas County	188	0.09
Dallas (city) Dallas County	152	0.01
San Antonio (city) Bexar County	96	0.01
Irving (city) Dallas County	83	0.04
Arlington (city) Tarrant County	73	0.02
Plano (city) Collin County	66	0.03
Pleasanton (city) Atascosa County	59	0.72
Friendswood (city) Galveston County	49	0.17
Abilene (city) Taylor County	48	0.04

Top 10 Places Sorted by Percent
Based on all places, regardless of population

Place	Number	%
Industry (city) Austin County	16	5.52
Pleasanton (city) Atascosa County	59	0.72
Lexington (town) Lee County	8	0.70
Hubbard (city) Hill County	9	0.55
Fresno (cdp) Fort Bend County	20	0.30
Oak Point (city) Denton County	5	0.29
Friendswood (city) Galveston County	49	0.17
Rancho Viejo (town) Cameron County	3	0.17
Carrizo Springs (city) Dimmit County	9	0.16
Dickinson (city) Galveston County	25	0.15

Top 10 Places Sorted by Percent
Based on places with populations of 10,000 or more

Place	Number	%
Friendswood (city) Galveston County	49	0.17
Dickinson (city) Galveston County	25	0.15
Mission Bend (cdp) Fort Bend County	35	0.11
Garland (city) Dallas County	188	0.09
Conroe (city) Montgomery County	22	0.06

Place	Number	%
Burkburnett (city) Wichita County	7	0.06
Georgetown (city) Williamson County	13	0.05
Taylor (city) Williamson County	7	0.05
Irving (city) Dallas County	83	0.04
Abilene (city) Taylor County	48	0.04

West Indian: Bermudan, excluding Hispanic

Top 10 Places Sorted by Number
Based on all places, regardless of population

Place	Number	%
Corpus Christi (city) Nueces County	31	0.01
San Antonio (city) Bexar County	28	0.00
Houston (city) Harris County	17	0.00
Stafford (city) Fort Bend County	12	0.08
Plano (city) Collin County	10	0.00
Henrietta (city) Clay County	8	0.24
Benbrook (city) Tarrant County	8	0.04
Arlington (city) Tarrant County	5	0.00
Carrollton (city) Denton County	4	0.00
Port Aransas (city) Nueces County	3	0.09

Top 10 Places Sorted by Percent
Based on all places, regardless of population

Place	Number	%
Henrietta (city) Clay County	8	0.24
Port Aransas (city) Nueces County	3	0.09
Stafford (city) Fort Bend County	12	0.08
Benbrook (city) Tarrant County	8	0.04
Corpus Christi (city) Nueces County	31	0.01
San Antonio (city) Bexar County	28	0.00
Houston (city) Harris County	17	0.00
Plano (city) Collin County	10	0.00
Arlington (city) Tarrant County	5	0.00
Carrollton (city) Denton County	4	0.00

Top 10 Places Sorted by Percent
Based on places with populations of 10,000 or more

Place	Number	%
Stafford (city) Fort Bend County	12	0.08
Benbrook (city) Tarrant County	8	0.04
Corpus Christi (city) Nueces County	31	0.01
San Antonio (city) Bexar County	28	0.00
Houston (city) Harris County	17	0.00
Plano (city) Collin County	10	0.00
Arlington (city) Tarrant County	5	0.00
Carrollton (city) Denton County	4	0.00

West Indian: British West Indian, excluding Hispanic

Top 10 Places Sorted by Number
Based on all places, regardless of population

Place	Number	%
Houston (city) Harris County	450	0.02
Baytown (city) Harris County	224	0.33
Austin (city) Travis County	86	0.01
Dallas (city) Dallas County	73	0.01
Wichita Falls (city) Wichita County	67	0.06
Missouri City (city) Fort Bend County	55	0.10
Grand Prairie (city) Dallas County	55	0.04
Arlington (city) Tarrant County	51	0.02
San Antonio (city) Bexar County	51	0.00
Fort Worth (city) Tarrant County	47	0.01

Top 10 Places Sorted by Percent
Based on all places, regardless of population

Place	Number	%
South Fork Estates (cdp) Jim Hogg County	6	12.24
Baytown (city) Harris County	224	0.33
Meadows Place (city) Fort Bend County	14	0.28

Stafford (city) Fort Bend County	28	0.18
Copperas Cove (city) Coryell County	42	0.14
Dripping Springs (city) Hays County	2	0.13
Horizon City (city) El Paso County	6	0.11
Missouri City (city) Fort Bend County	55	0.10
Corsicana (city) Navarro County	25	0.10
Wells Branch (cdp) Travis County	11	0.10

Top 10 Places Sorted by Percent
Based on places with populations of 10,000 or more

Place	Number	%
Baytown (city) Harris County	224	0.33
Stafford (city) Fort Bend County	28	0.18
Copperas Cove (city) Coryell County	42	0.14
Missouri City (city) Fort Bend County	55	0.10
Corsicana (city) Navarro County	25	0.10
Wells Branch (cdp) Travis County	11	0.10
Universal City (city) Bexar County	14	0.09
Port Neches (city) Jefferson County	12	0.09
Fort Hood (cdp) Coryell County	27	0.08
Humble (city) Harris County	10	0.07

West Indian: Dutch West Indian, excluding Hispanic

Top 10 Places Sorted by Number
Based on all places, regardless of population

Place	Number	%
Amarillo (city) Potter County	259	0.15
Dallas (city) Dallas County	234	0.02
San Antonio (city) Bexar County	230	0.02
Odessa (city) Ector County	196	0.22
Fort Worth (city) Tarrant County	195	0.04
Wichita Falls (city) Wichita County	152	0.15
Lubbock (city) Lubbock County	142	0.07
Houston (city) Harris County	117	0.01
San Angelo (city) Tom Green County	113	0.13
Austin (city) Travis County	109	0.02

Top 10 Places Sorted by Percent
Based on all places, regardless of population

Place	Number	%
Pyote (town) Ward County	7	5.34
Las Colonias (cdp) Zavala County	8	3.49
Hawk Cove (city) Hunt County	14	3.21
Zuehl (cdp) Guadalupe County	7	2.75
Josephine (city) Collin County	13	2.18
Blackwell (city) Nolan County	7	1.92
Grays Prairie (village) Kaufman County	5	1.85
Moran (city) Shackelford County	4	1.72
Box Canyon-Amistad (cdp) Val Verde County	1	1.72
Wink (city) Winkler County	15	1.62

Top 10 Places Sorted by Percent
Based on places with populations of 10,000 or more

Place	Number	%
Pampa (city) Gray County	59	0.33
Vernon (city) Wilbarger County	38	0.33
Levelland (city) Hockley County	36	0.28
Gainesville (city) Cooke County	39	0.25
Snyder (city) Scurry County	27	0.25
Balch Springs (city) Dallas County	45	0.23
Odessa (city) Ector County	196	0.22
Paris (city) Lamar County	56	0.22
Burleson (city) Johnson County	46	0.22
West Odessa (cdp) Ector County	40	0.22

West Indian: Haitian, excluding Hispanic

Top 10 Places Sorted by Number
Based on all places, regardless of population

Place	Number	%
Houston (city) Harris County	592	0.03
Austin (city) Travis County	191	0.03
El Paso (city) El Paso County	171	0.03
San Antonio (city) Bexar County	152	0.01
Killeen (city) Bell County	103	0.12
Dallas (city) Dallas County	73	0.01
Missouri City (city) Fort Bend County	66	0.13
Plano (city) Collin County	56	0.03
Arlington (city) Tarrant County	45	0.01
Irving (city) Dallas County	42	0.02

Top 10 Places Sorted by Percent
Based on all places, regardless of population

Place	Number	%
Progreso Lakes (city) Hidalgo County	4	1.54
Fulshear (city) Fort Bend County	3	0.43
Keene (city) Johnson County	10	0.21
Joaquin (city) Shelby County	2	0.21
Bellmead (city) McLennan County	18	0.20
Frankston (town) Anderson County	2	0.17
Hughes Springs (city) Cass County	3	0.16
Fresno (cdp) Fort Bend County	10	0.15
Granite Shoals (city) Burnet County	3	0.15
Taylor Lake Village (city) Harris County	5	0.14

Top 10 Places Sorted by Percent
Based on places with populations of 10,000 or more

Place	Number	%
Missouri City (city) Fort Bend County	66	0.13
Killeen (city) Bell County	103	0.12
Fort Hood (cdp) Coryell County	27	0.08
Big Spring (city) Howard County	21	0.08
Mansfield (city) Tarrant County	20	0.07
Corsicana (city) Navarro County	16	0.07
Lewisville (city) Denton County	36	0.05
Beeville (city) Bee County	6	0.05
Midland (city) Midland County	34	0.04
Richardson (city) Dallas County	33	0.04

West Indian: Jamaican, excluding Hispanic

Top 10 Places Sorted by Number
Based on all places, regardless of population

Place	Number	%
Houston (city) Harris County	2,344	0.12
Dallas (city) Dallas County	865	0.07
Fort Worth (city) Tarrant County	641	0.12
Austin (city) Travis County	547	0.08
Missouri City (city) Fort Bend County	514	0.98
San Antonio (city) Bexar County	444	0.04
Killeen (city) Bell County	393	0.45
Mission Bend (cdp) Fort Bend County	371	1.20
Arlington (city) Tarrant County	301	0.09
Irving (city) Dallas County	169	0.09

Top 10 Places Sorted by Percent
Based on all places, regardless of population

Place	Number	%
Barton Creek (cdp) Travis County	48	3.05
Pleak (village) Fort Bend County	16	1.65
Mission Bend (cdp) Fort Bend County	371	1.20
Prairie View (city) Waller County	45	1.02
Missouri City (city) Fort Bend County	514	0.98
Shady Hollow (cdp) Travis County	48	0.88
Hart (city) Castro County	10	0.83
Fort Bliss (cdp) El Paso County	62	0.75

Lackland AFB (cdp) Bexar County	47	0.66
Stafford (city) Fort Bend County	98	0.63

Top 10 Places Sorted by Percent
Based on places with populations of 10,000 or more

Place	Number	%
Mission Bend (cdp) Fort Bend County	371	1.20
Missouri City (city) Fort Bend County	514	0.98
Stafford (city) Fort Bend County	98	0.63
Killeen (city) Bell County	393	0.45
Fort Hood (cdp) Coryell County	137	0.41
Atascocita (cdp) Harris County	121	0.34
Bedford (city) Tarrant County	156	0.33
Channelview (cdp) Harris County	95	0.32
Euless (city) Tarrant County	144	0.31
The Woodlands (cdp) Montgomery County	167	0.30

West Indian: Trinidadian and Tobagonian, excluding Hispanic

Top 10 Places Sorted by Number
Based on all places, regardless of population

Place	Number	%
Houston (city) Harris County	1,097	0.06
Baytown (city) Harris County	267	0.40
San Antonio (city) Bexar County	199	0.02
Austin (city) Travis County	128	0.02
Pasadena (city) Harris County	108	0.08
Garland (city) Dallas County	102	0.05
Dallas (city) Dallas County	95	0.01
New Territory (cdp) Fort Bend County	74	0.53
Plano (city) Collin County	65	0.03
Irving (city) Dallas County	60	0.03

Top 10 Places Sorted by Percent
Based on all places, regardless of population

Place	Number	%
New Territory (cdp) Fort Bend County	74	0.53
Navasota (city) Grimes County	33	0.49
Baytown (city) Harris County	267	0.40
Alto (town) Cherokee County	3	0.25
Humble (city) Harris County	31	0.21
Stafford (city) Fort Bend County	30	0.19
Jollyville (cdp) Williamson County	29	0.19
Anderson Mill (cdp) Williamson County	17	0.19
Nolanville (city) Bell County	4	0.18
Spring (cdp) Harris County	53	0.15

Top 10 Places Sorted by Percent
Based on places with populations of 10,000 or more

Place	Number	%
New Territory (cdp) Fort Bend County	74	0.53
Baytown (city) Harris County	267	0.40
Humble (city) Harris County	31	0.21
Stafford (city) Fort Bend County	30	0.19
Jollyville (cdp) Williamson County	29	0.19
Spring (cdp) Harris County	53	0.15
Corsicana (city) Navarro County	34	0.14
Converse (city) Bexar County	16	0.14
La Marque (city) Galveston County	16	0.12
Missouri City (city) Fort Bend County	58	0.11

West Indian: U.S. Virgin Islander, excluding Hispanic

Top 10 Places Sorted by Number
Based on all places, regardless of population

Place	Number	%
Houston (city) Harris County	272	0.01
Baytown (city) Harris County	71	0.11
Killeen (city) Bell County	50	0.06
Fort Worth (city) Tarrant County	45	0.01

Notes: (cdp) census designated place; Refer to the User's Guide in the front of the book for more detailed information.

Austin (city) Travis County	28	0.00
Plano (city) Collin County	25	0.01
San Antonio (city) Bexar County	24	0.00
Dallas (city) Dallas County	20	0.00
Prairie View (city) Waller County	13	0.30
Irving (city) Dallas County	12	0.01

Top 10 Places Sorted by Percent
Based on all places, regardless of population

Place	Number	%
Prairie View (city) Waller County	13	0.30
Dalworthington Gardens (city) Tarrant County	6	0.27
Collinsville (town) Grayson County	2	0.16
Baytown (city) Harris County	71	0.11
Fort Bliss (cdp) El Paso County	9	0.11
Bacliff (cdp) Galveston County	6	0.09
Killeen (city) Bell County	50	0.06
Sachse (city) Dallas County	5	0.05
Cleburne (city) Johnson County	11	0.04
Fort Hood (cdp) Coryell County	8	0.02

Top 10 Places Sorted by Percent
Based on places with populations of 10,000 or more

Place	Number	%
Baytown (city) Harris County	71	0.11
Killeen (city) Bell County	50	0.06
Cleburne (city) Johnson County	11	0.04
Fort Hood (cdp) Coryell County	8	0.02
Texas City (city) Galveston County	7	0.02
Houston (city) Harris County	272	0.01
Fort Worth (city) Tarrant County	45	0.01
Plano (city) Collin County	25	0.01
Irving (city) Dallas County	12	0.01
Wichita Falls (city) Wichita County	9	0.01

West Indian: West Indian, excluding Hispanic

Top 10 Places Sorted by Number
Based on all places, regardless of population

Place	Number	%
Houston (city) Harris County	975	0.05
Dallas (city) Dallas County	270	0.02
Baytown (city) Harris County	221	0.33
San Antonio (city) Bexar County	166	0.01
Arlington (city) Tarrant County	154	0.05
Irving (city) Dallas County	119	0.06
Killeen (city) Bell County	114	0.13
Austin (city) Travis County	90	0.01
El Paso (city) El Paso County	89	0.02
Portland (city) San Patricio County	88	0.59

Top 10 Places Sorted by Percent
Based on all places, regardless of population

Place	Number	%
Greatwood (cdp) Fort Bend County	60	0.91
Highlands (cdp) Harris County	56	0.80
Barrett (cdp) Harris County	19	0.70
Lometa (city) Lampasas County	5	0.66
Richland Hills (city) Tarrant County	50	0.62
Portland (city) San Patricio County	88	0.59
Jones Creek (village) Brazoria County	11	0.49
Shepherd (city) San Jacinto County	8	0.40
Stafford (city) Fort Bend County	59	0.38
Lackland AFB (cdp) Bexar County	24	0.34

Top 10 Places Sorted by Percent
Based on places with populations of 10,000 or more

Place	Number	%
Portland (city) San Patricio County	88	0.59
Stafford (city) Fort Bend County	59	0.38
Baytown (city) Harris County	221	0.33

Mission Bend (cdp) Fort Bend County	62	0.20
Humble (city) Harris County	29	0.20
Copperas Cove (city) Coryell County	45	0.15
Bay City (city) Matagorda County	28	0.15
Missouri City (city) Fort Bend County	75	0.14
New Territory (cdp) Fort Bend County	20	0.14
Killeen (city) Bell County	114	0.13

West Indian: Other, excluding Hispanic

Top 10 Places Sorted by Number
Based on all places, regardless of population

Place	Number	%
Houston (city) Harris County	44	0.00
Port Arthur (city) Jefferson County	34	0.06
Carrollton (city) Denton County	32	0.03
Nederland (city) Jefferson County	31	0.18
Frisco (city) Collin County	19	0.06
Corinth (city) Denton County	11	0.10
Palestine (city) Anderson County	11	0.06
Jacinto City (city) Harris County	8	0.08
Austin (city) Travis County	8	0.00
Seguin (city) Guadalupe County	7	0.03

Top 10 Places Sorted by Percent
Based on all places, regardless of population

Place	Number	%
Nederland (city) Jefferson County	31	0.18
Huntington (city) Angelina County	3	0.14
Southside Place (city) Harris County	2	0.13
Corinth (city) Denton County	11	0.10
Jacinto City (city) Harris County	8	0.08
Clear Lake Shores (city) Galveston County	1	0.08
Port Arthur (city) Jefferson County	34	0.06
Frisco (city) Collin County	19	0.06
Palestine (city) Anderson County	11	0.06
Carrollton (city) Denton County	32	0.03

Top 10 Places Sorted by Percent
Based on places with populations of 10,000 or more

Place	Number	%
Nederland (city) Jefferson County	31	0.18
Corinth (city) Denton County	11	0.10
Jacinto City (city) Harris County	8	0.08
Port Arthur (city) Jefferson County	34	0.06
Frisco (city) Collin County	19	0.06
Palestine (city) Anderson County	11	0.06
Carrollton (city) Denton County	32	0.03
Seguin (city) Guadalupe County	7	0.03
Wichita Falls (city) Wichita County	7	0.01
Galveston (city) Galveston County	5	0.01

White

Top 10 Places Sorted by Number
Based on all places, regardless of population

Place	Number	%
Houston (city) Harris County	1,012,413	51.82
San Antonio (city) Bexar County	810,913	70.84
Dallas (city) Dallas County	630,419	53.04
Austin (city) Travis County	445,388	67.84
El Paso (city) El Paso County	430,142	76.31
Fort Worth (city) Tarrant County	331,448	61.99
Arlington (city) Tarrant County	233,461	70.11
Corpus Christi (city) Nueces County	206,308	74.36
Plano (city) Collin County	178,070	80.20
Laredo (city) Webb County	149,389	84.60

Top 10 Places Sorted by Percent
Based on all places, regardless of population

Place	Number	%
Lozano (cdp) Cameron County	324	100.00

El Refugio (cdp) Starr County	221	100.00
Broaddus (town) San Augustine County	189	100.00
Jolly (city) Clay County	188	100.00
Coyanosa (cdp) Pecos County	138	100.00
Quintana (town) Brazoria County	38	100.00
Cuevitas (cdp) Hidalgo County	37	100.00
Guerra (cdp) Jim Hogg County	8	100.00
Falcon Heights (cdp) Starr County	334	99.70
Arroyo Colorado Estates (cdp) Cameron County	752	99.60

Top 10 Places Sorted by Percent
Based on places with populations of 10,000 or more

Place	Number	%
Vidor (city) Orange County	11,264	98.46
Burleson (city) Johnson County	20,337	96.95
Canyon Lake (cdp) Comal County	16,259	96.38
Port Neches (city) Jefferson County	13,030	95.80
Southlake (city) Tarrant County	20,572	95.60
Highland Village (city) Denton County	11,603	95.32
University Park (city) Dallas County	22,175	95.07
San Elizario (cdp) El Paso County	10,500	95.06
Keller (city) Tarrant County	25,987	95.03
Nederland (city) Jefferson County	16,487	94.63

White: Not Hispanic

Top 10 Places Sorted by Number
Based on all places, regardless of population

Place	Number	%
Houston (city) Harris County	618,504	31.66
Dallas (city) Dallas County	420,044	35.34
San Antonio (city) Bexar County	374,557	32.72
Austin (city) Travis County	355,695	54.18
Fort Worth (city) Tarrant County	250,412	46.83
Arlington (city) Tarrant County	203,832	61.22
Plano (city) Collin County	164,535	74.10
Lubbock (city) Lubbock County	123,822	62.05
Amarillo (city) Potter County	120,784	69.57
Garland (city) Dallas County	117,531	54.47

Top 10 Places Sorted by Percent
Based on all places, regardless of population

Place	Number	%
Jolly (city) Clay County	188	100.00
Marietta (town) Cass County	111	99.11
Dayton Lakes (city) Liberty County	100	99.01
Ravenna (city) Fannin County	212	98.60
Deweyville (cdp) Newton County	1,173	98.57
Sunrise Beach Village (city) Llano County	693	98.44
Lindsay (town) Cooke County	775	98.35
Evadale (cdp) Jasper County	1,403	98.11
Avery (town) Red River County	453	98.05
Tira (town) Hopkins County	243	97.98

Top 10 Places Sorted by Percent
Based on places with populations of 10,000 or more

Place	Number	%
Vidor (city) Orange County	10,951	95.73
Burleson (city) Johnson County	19,534	93.13
University Park (city) Dallas County	21,668	92.90
Southlake (city) Tarrant County	19,944	92.68
Highland Village (city) Denton County	11,276	92.63
Port Neches (city) Jefferson County	12,507	91.96
Colleyville (city) Tarrant County	18,016	91.75
Keller (city) Tarrant County	25,083	91.73
Nederland (city) Jefferson County	15,760	90.46
West University Place (city) Harris County	12,758	89.78

Notes: (cdp) census designated place; Refer to the User's Guide in the front of the book for more detailed information.

White: Hispanic

Top 10 Places Sorted by Number
Based on all places, regardless of population

Place	Number	%
San Antonio (city) Bexar County	436,356	38.12
Houston (city) Harris County	393,909	20.16
El Paso (city) El Paso County	323,182	57.34
Dallas (city) Dallas County	210,375	17.70
Laredo (city) Webb County	140,279	79.44
Brownsville (city) Cameron County	106,012	75.87
Corpus Christi (city) Nueces County	97,057	34.98
Austin (city) Travis County	89,693	13.66
Fort Worth (city) Tarrant County	81,036	15.16
McAllen (city) Hidalgo County	67,912	63.82

Top 10 Places Sorted by Percent
Based on all places, regardless of population

Place	Number	%
Cuevitas (cdp) Hidalgo County	37	100.00
El Refugio (cdp) Starr County	219	99.10
Roma Creek (cdp) Starr County	602	98.69
Lozano (cdp) Cameron County	319	98.46
Granjeno (city) Hidalgo County	305	97.44
Laureles (cdp) Cameron County	3,174	96.62
La Puerta (cdp) Starr County	1,578	96.45
Arroyo Colorado Estates (cdp) Cameron County	726	96.16
Westway (cdp) El Paso County	3,681	96.13
South Alamo (cdp) Hidalgo County	2,981	96.13

Top 10 Places Sorted by Percent
Based on places with populations of 10,000 or more

Place	Number	%
San Elizario (cdp) El Paso County	10,323	93.45
La Homa (cdp) Hidalgo County	8,974	86.02
Rio Grande City (city) Starr County	9,860	82.70
Laredo (city) Webb County	140,279	79.44
San Juan (city) Hidalgo County	20,551	78.35
Brownsville (city) Cameron County	106,012	75.87
Socorro (city) El Paso County	19,902	73.30
Pharr (city) Hidalgo County	33,794	72.43
Mercedes (city) Hidalgo County	9,797	71.78
Eagle Pass (city) Maverick County	16,025	71.50

Yugoslavian

Top 10 Places Sorted by Number
Based on all places, regardless of population

Place	Number	%
Houston (city) Harris County	1,789	0.09
Dallas (city) Dallas County	1,618	0.14
Fort Worth (city) Tarrant County	1,005	0.19
Austin (city) Travis County	603	0.09
San Antonio (city) Bexar County	368	0.03
Amarillo (city) Potter County	286	0.16
Arlington (city) Tarrant County	266	0.08
Plano (city) Collin County	233	0.10
Flower Mound (town) Denton County	208	0.41
Carrollton (city) Denton County	130	0.12

Top 10 Places Sorted by Percent
Based on all places, regardless of population

Place	Number	%
Liberty Hill (city) Williamson County	25	1.62
Utopia (cdp) Uvalde County	5	1.51
Angus (city) Navarro County	5	1.50
Eureka (city) Navarro County	4	1.15
Sierra Blanca (cdp) Hudspeth County	6	1.01
Cranfills Gap (city) Bosque County	3	0.86
Mingus (city) Palo Pinto County	2	0.83
Bayside (town) Refugio County	3	0.80
Goldsmith (city) Ector County	2	0.79
Newton (city) Newton County	15	0.62

Top 10 Places Sorted by Percent
Based on places with populations of 10,000 or more

Place	Number	%
Brenham (city) Washington County	59	0.44
Flower Mound (town) Denton County	208	0.41
Southlake (city) Tarrant County	80	0.37
Freeport (city) Brazoria County	38	0.30
Gainesville (city) Cooke County	43	0.28
West University Place (city) Harris County	36	0.25
Highland Village (city) Denton County	27	0.22
Galveston (city) Galveston County	117	0.20
The Woodlands (cdp) Montgomery County	113	0.20
Fort Worth (city) Tarrant County	1,005	0.19

Notes: (cdp) census designated place; Refer to the User's Guide in the front of the book for more detailed information.

Hispanic Population

Population

Total Population
Top 10 Places Sorted by Number

Place (place type) County	Number
Houston (city) Harris	1,954,848
Dallas (city) Dallas	1,188,204
San Antonio (city) Bexar	1,144,554
Austin (city) Travis	656,302
El Paso (city) El Paso	564,280
Fort Worth (city) Tarrant	535,420
Arlington (city) Tarrant	332,695
Corpus Christi (city) Nueces	277,569
Plano (city) Collin	222,301
Garland (city) Dallas	215,991

Hispanic
Top 10 Places Sorted by Number

Place (place type) County	Number
Houston (city) Harris	731,680
San Antonio (city) Bexar	671,200
El Paso (city) El Paso	432,544
Dallas (city) Dallas	423,178
Austin (city) Travis	201,040
Laredo (city) Webb	166,544
Fort Worth (city) Tarrant	159,212
Corpus Christi (city) Nueces	150,620
Brownsville (city) Cameron	128,127
McAllen (city) Hidalgo	85,064

Hispanic
Top 10 Places Sorted by Percent of Total Population

Place (place type) County	Percent
La Homa (cdp) Hidalgo	98.77
San Elizario (cdp) El Paso	98.45
Socorro (city) El Paso	96.58
Rio Grande City (city) Starr	96.03
San Juan (city) Hidalgo	95.27
Eagle Pass (city) Maverick	95.23
Laredo (city) Webb	94.20
Robstown (city) Nueces	93.02
Brownsville (city) Cameron	91.47
Pharr (city) Hidalgo	90.52

Argentinian
Top 10 Places Sorted by Number

Place (place type) County	Number
Houston (city) Harris	1,349

Argentinian
Top 10 Places Sorted by Percent of Hispanic Population

Place (place type) County	Percent
Houston (city) Harris	0.18

Argentinian
Top 10 Places Sorted by Percent of Total Population

Place (place type) County	Percent
Houston (city) Harris	0.07

Bolivian
Top 10 Places Sorted by Number

Place (place type) County	Number
Houston (city) Harris	681

Bolivian
Top 10 Places Sorted by Percent of Hispanic Population

Place (place type) County	Percent
Houston (city) Harris	0.09

Bolivian
Top 10 Places Sorted by Percent of Total Population

Place (place type) County	Percent
Houston (city) Harris	0.03

Central American
Top 10 Places Sorted by Number

Place (place type) County	Number
Houston (city) Harris	66,889
Dallas (city) Dallas	16,284
Irving (city) Dallas	7,243
Austin (city) Travis	4,627
San Antonio (city) Bexar	3,740
Garland (city) Dallas	3,641
Pasadena (city) Harris	2,053
Fort Worth (city) Tarrant	1,775
Farmers Branch (city) Dallas	1,682
Arlington (city) Tarrant	1,590

Central American
Top 10 Places Sorted by Percent of Hispanic Population

Place (place type) County	Percent
Farmers Branch (city) Dallas	15.81
Addison (town) Dallas	14.01
Irving (city) Dallas	12.09
Mission Bend (cdp) Fort Bend	9.15
Houston (city) Harris	9.14
Carrollton (city) Denton	7.12
Richardson (city) Dallas	6.95
Garland (city) Dallas	6.55
Plano (city) Collin	5.84
Conroe (city) Montgomery	5.71

Central American
Top 10 Places Sorted by Percent of Total Population

Place (place type) County	Percent
Farmers Branch (city) Dallas	5.94
Irving (city) Dallas	3.78
Houston (city) Harris	3.42
Addison (town) Dallas	3.29
Mission Bend (cdp) Fort Bend	2.47
Conroe (city) Montgomery	1.87
Garland (city) Dallas	1.69
Pasadena (city) Harris	1.45
Rosenberg (city) Fort Bend	1.45
Carrollton (city) Denton	1.38

Chilean
Top 10 Places Sorted by Number

Place (place type) County	Number
Houston (city) Harris	713

Chilean
Top 10 Places Sorted by Percent of Hispanic Population

Place (place type) County	Percent
Houston (city) Harris	0.10

Chilean
Top 10 Places Sorted by Percent of Total Population

Place (place type) County	Percent
Houston (city) Harris	0.04

Colombian
Top 10 Places Sorted by Number

Place (place type) County	Number
Houston (city) Harris	6,226
Dallas (city) Dallas	1,057
Austin (city) Travis	801
San Antonio (city) Bexar	748
Mission Bend (cdp) Fort Bend	543

Colombian
Top 10 Places Sorted by Percent of Hispanic Population

Place (place type) County	Percent
Mission Bend (cdp) Fort Bend	6.51
Houston (city) Harris	0.85
Austin (city) Travis	0.40
Dallas (city) Dallas	0.25
San Antonio (city) Bexar	0.11

Colombian
Top 10 Places Sorted by Percent of Total Population

Place (place type) County	Percent
Mission Bend (cdp) Fort Bend	1.76
Houston (city) Harris	0.32
Austin (city) Travis	0.12
Dallas (city) Dallas	0.09
San Antonio (city) Bexar	0.07

Costa Rican
Top 10 Places Sorted by Number

Place (place type) County	Number
Houston (city) Harris	862
Dallas (city) Dallas	464

Costa Rican
Top 10 Places Sorted by Percent of Hispanic Population

Place (place type) County	Percent
Houston (city) Harris	0.12
Dallas (city) Dallas	0.11

Costa Rican
Top 10 Places Sorted by Percent of Total Population

Place (place type) County	Percent
Dallas (city) Dallas	0.04
Houston (city) Harris	0.04

Cuban
Top 10 Places Sorted by Number

Place (place type) County	Number
Houston (city) Harris	5,437
Dallas (city) Dallas	2,373
San Antonio (city) Bexar	1,945
Austin (city) Travis	1,477
Fort Worth (city) Tarrant	928
El Paso (city) El Paso	489

Cuban
Top 10 Places Sorted by Percent of Hispanic Population

Place (place type) County	Percent
Houston (city) Harris	0.74
Austin (city) Travis	0.73
Fort Worth (city) Tarrant	0.58
Dallas (city) Dallas	0.56
San Antonio (city) Bexar	0.29
El Paso (city) El Paso	0.11

Cuban
Top 10 Places Sorted by Percent of Total Population

Place (place type) County	Percent
Houston (city) Harris	0.28
Austin (city) Travis	0.23
Dallas (city) Dallas	0.20
Fort Worth (city) Tarrant	0.17
San Antonio (city) Bexar	0.17
El Paso (city) El Paso	0.09

Dominican
Top 10 Places Sorted by Number

Place (place type) County	Number
Houston (city) Harris	924

Dominican
Top 10 Places Sorted by Percent of Hispanic Population

Place (place type) County	Percent
Houston (city) Harris	0.13

Dominican
Top 10 Places Sorted by Percent of Total Population

Place (place type) County	Percent
Houston (city) Harris	0.05

Ecuadorian
Top 10 Places Sorted by Number

Place (place type) County	Number
Houston (city) Harris	1,031

Ecuadorian
Top 10 Places Sorted by Percent of Hispanic Population

Place (place type) County	Percent
Houston (city) Harris	0.14

Ecuadorian
Top 10 Places Sorted by Percent of Total Population

Place (place type) County	Percent
Houston (city) Harris	0.05

Guatelmalan
Top 10 Places Sorted by Number

Place (place type) County	Number
Houston (city) Harris	7,695
Dallas (city) Dallas	2,574
Austin (city) Travis	863
Garland (city) Dallas	855
Fort Worth (city) Tarrant	433
San Antonio (city) Bexar	405

Guatelmalan
Top 10 Places Sorted by Percent of Hispanic Population

Place (place type) County	Percent
Garland (city) Dallas	1.54
Houston (city) Harris	1.05
Dallas (city) Dallas	0.61
Austin (city) Travis	0.43
Fort Worth (city) Tarrant	0.27
San Antonio (city) Bexar	0.06

Guatelmalan
Top 10 Places Sorted by Percent of Total Population

Place (place type) County	Percent
Garland (city) Dallas	0.40
Houston (city) Harris	0.39
Dallas (city) Dallas	0.22
Austin (city) Travis	0.13
Fort Worth (city) Tarrant	0.08
San Antonio (city) Bexar	0.04

Honduran
Top 10 Places Sorted by Number

Place (place type) County	Number
Houston (city) Harris	11,221
Dallas (city) Dallas	2,946
Austin (city) Travis	1,201
Irving (city) Dallas	776
San Antonio (city) Bexar	699
Garland (city) Dallas	414

Honduran
Top 10 Places Sorted by Percent of Hispanic Population

Place (place type) County	Percent
Houston (city) Harris	1.53
Irving (city) Dallas	1.29
Garland (city) Dallas	0.75
Dallas (city) Dallas	0.70
Austin (city) Travis	0.60
San Antonio (city) Bexar	0.10

Honduran
Top 10 Places Sorted by Percent of Total Population

Place (place type) County	Percent
Houston (city) Harris	0.57
Irving (city) Dallas	0.40
Dallas (city) Dallas	0.25
Garland (city) Dallas	0.19
Austin (city) Travis	0.18
San Antonio (city) Bexar	0.06

Mexican
Top 10 Places Sorted by Number

Place (place type) County	Number
Houston (city) Harris	537,834
San Antonio (city) Bexar	485,008
El Paso (city) El Paso	368,858
Dallas (city) Dallas	356,600
Austin (city) Travis	158,957
Laredo (city) Webb	138,582
Fort Worth (city) Tarrant	133,938
Brownsville (city) Cameron	107,525
Corpus Christi (city) Nueces	102,872
McAllen (city) Hidalgo	71,629

Mexican
Top 10 Places Sorted by Percent of Hispanic Population

Place (place type) County	Percent
San Elizario (cdp) El Paso	97.94
La Homa (cdp) Hidalgo	95.42
Terrell (city) Kaufman	93.89
Marshall (city) Harrison	92.31
Alamo (city) Hidalgo	90.58
Mount Pleasant (city) Titus	90.26
Gainesville (city) Cooke	89.70
Pharr (city) Hidalgo	89.19
Gatesville (city) Coryell	89.02
San Juan (city) Hidalgo	88.63

Mexican
Top 10 Places Sorted by Percent of Total Population

Place (place type) County	Percent
San Elizario (cdp) El Paso	96.42
La Homa (cdp) Hidalgo	94.25
San Juan (city) Hidalgo	84.43
Eagle Pass (city) Maverick	84.31
Socorro (city) El Paso	83.86
Pharr (city) Hidalgo	80.73
Rio Grande City (city) Starr	78.39
Laredo (city) Webb	78.38
Brownsville (city) Cameron	76.76
Edinburg (city) Hidalgo	73.27

Nicaraguan
Top 10 Places Sorted by Number

Place (place type) County	Number
Houston (city) Harris	2,390
San Antonio (city) Bexar	491
Dallas (city) Dallas	436
Austin (city) Travis	379
Port Arthur (city) Jefferson	328

Nicaraguan
Top 10 Places Sorted by Percent of Hispanic Population

Place (place type) County	Percent
Port Arthur (city) Jefferson	3.24
Houston (city) Harris	0.33

Nicaraguan
Top 10 Places Sorted by Percent of Total Population

Place (place type) County	Percent
Austin (city) Travis	0.19
Dallas (city) Dallas	0.10
San Antonio (city) Bexar	0.07

Nicaraguan
Top 10 Places Sorted by Percent of Total Population

Place (place type) County	Percent
Port Arthur (city) Jefferson	0.57
Houston (city) Harris	0.12
Austin (city) Travis	0.06
Dallas (city) Dallas	0.04
San Antonio (city) Bexar	0.04

Panamanian
Top 10 Places Sorted by Number

Place (place type) County	Number
San Antonio (city) Bexar	942
Houston (city) Harris	788
Killeen (city) Bell	491
El Paso (city) El Paso	470

Panamanian
Top 10 Places Sorted by Percent of Hispanic Population

Place (place type) County	Percent
Killeen (city) Bell	3.18
San Antonio (city) Bexar	0.14
El Paso (city) El Paso	0.11
Houston (city) Harris	0.11

Panamanian
Top 10 Places Sorted by Percent of Total Population

Place (place type) County	Percent
Killeen (city) Bell	0.57
El Paso (city) El Paso	0.08
San Antonio (city) Bexar	0.08
Houston (city) Harris	0.04

Paraguayan
Top 10 Places Sorted by Number

Place (place type) County	Number
No places met population threshold.	

Paraguayan
Top 10 Places Sorted by Percent of Hispanic Population

Place (place type) County	Percent
No places met population threshold.	

Paraguayan
Top 10 Places Sorted by Percent of Total Population

Place (place type) County	Percent
No places met population threshold.	

Peruvian
Top 10 Places Sorted by Number

Place (place type) County	Number
Houston (city) Harris	1,468
Dallas (city) Dallas	924
San Antonio (city) Bexar	446

Peruvian
Top 10 Places Sorted by Percent of Hispanic Population

Place (place type) County	Percent
Dallas (city) Dallas	0.22
Houston (city) Harris	0.20
San Antonio (city) Bexar	0.07

Notes: Please refer to the User's Guide for an explanation of data; tables include places with populations > 9,999 and reflect only those areas that meet Summary File 4 population thresholds, therefore there may be less than 10 places listed

Peruvian
Top 10 Places Sorted by Percent of Total Population

Place (place type) County	Percent
Dallas (city) Dallas	0.08
Houston (city) Harris	0.08
San Antonio (city) Bexar	0.04

Puerto Rican
Top 10 Places Sorted by Number

Place (place type) County	Number
San Antonio (city) Bexar	8,434
Houston (city) Harris	7,511
Killeen (city) Bell	4,547
El Paso (city) El Paso	4,172
Austin (city) Travis	2,683
Dallas (city) Dallas	2,381
Fort Worth (city) Tarrant	1,975
Arlington (city) Tarrant	1,862
Fort Hood (cdp) Coryell	1,377
Corpus Christi (city) Nueces	1,091

Puerto Rican
Top 10 Places Sorted by Percent of Hispanic Population

Place (place type) County	Percent
Killeen (city) Bell	29.43
Copperas Cove (city) Coryell	25.70
Fort Hood (cdp) Coryell	24.47
Euless (city) Tarrant	10.06
Temple (city) Bell	4.79
Mission Bend (cdp) Fort Bend	4.70
Plano (city) Collin	4.07
Arlington (city) Tarrant	3.05
Wichita Falls (city) Wichita	2.64
Carrollton (city) Denton	1.96

Puerto Rican
Top 10 Places Sorted by Percent of Total Population

Place (place type) County	Percent
Killeen (city) Bell	5.24
Fort Hood (cdp) Coryell	4.10
Copperas Cove (city) Coryell	2.80
Euless (city) Tarrant	1.39
Mission Bend (cdp) Fort Bend	1.27
Temple (city) Bell	0.86
El Paso (city) El Paso	0.74
San Antonio (city) Bexar	0.74
Grand Prairie (city) Dallas	0.61
Arlington (city) Tarrant	0.56

Salvadoran
Top 10 Places Sorted by Number

Place (place type) County	Number
Houston (city) Harris	41,344
Dallas (city) Dallas	9,166
Irving (city) Dallas	6,014
Garland (city) Dallas	2,045
Austin (city) Travis	1,578
Farmers Branch (city) Dallas	1,492
Pasadena (city) Harris	1,198
Carrollton (city) Denton	1,038
San Antonio (city) Bexar	759
Fort Worth (city) Tarrant	699

Salvadoran
Top 10 Places Sorted by Percent of Hispanic Population

Place (place type) County	Percent
Farmers Branch (city) Dallas	14.02
Irving (city) Dallas	10.03
Houston (city) Harris	5.65
Carrollton (city) Denton	4.91
Mission Bend (cdp) Fort Bend	4.86
Garland (city) Dallas	3.68
Conroe (city) Montgomery	3.06

Place (place type) County	Percent
Plano (city) Collin	2.56
Dallas (city) Dallas	2.17
Galveston (city) Galveston	1.88

Salvadoran
Top 10 Places Sorted by Percent of Total Population

Place (place type) County	Percent
Farmers Branch (city) Dallas	5.27
Irving (city) Dallas	3.14
Houston (city) Harris	2.11
Mission Bend (cdp) Fort Bend	1.31
Conroe (city) Montgomery	1.00
Carrollton (city) Denton	0.95
Garland (city) Dallas	0.95
Pasadena (city) Harris	0.85
Dallas (city) Dallas	0.77
Galveston (city) Galveston	0.48

South American
Top 10 Places Sorted by Number

Place (place type) County	Number
Houston (city) Harris	13,947
Dallas (city) Dallas	3,269
Austin (city) Travis	2,649
San Antonio (city) Bexar	2,340
Irving (city) Dallas	973
Fort Worth (city) Tarrant	914
Plano (city) Collin	873
Arlington (city) Tarrant	813
Mission Bend (cdp) Fort Bend	763
El Paso (city) El Paso	651

South American
Top 10 Places Sorted by Percent of Hispanic Population

Place (place type) County	Percent
The Woodlands (cdp) Montgomery	13.87
Sugar Land (city) Fort Bend	10.02
Mission Bend (cdp) Fort Bend	9.15
College Station (city) Brazos	8.56
Richardson (city) Dallas	4.90
Plano (city) Collin	3.90
Carrollton (city) Denton	2.75
Houston (city) Harris	1.91
Irving (city) Dallas	1.62
Arlington (city) Tarrant	1.33

South American
Top 10 Places Sorted by Percent of Total Population

Place (place type) County	Percent
Mission Bend (cdp) Fort Bend	2.47
The Woodlands (cdp) Montgomery	0.95
College Station (city) Brazos	0.86
Sugar Land (city) Fort Bend	0.83
Houston (city) Harris	0.71
Carrollton (city) Denton	0.53
Irving (city) Dallas	0.51
Richardson (city) Dallas	0.50
Austin (city) Travis	0.40
Plano (city) Collin	0.39

Spaniard
Top 10 Places Sorted by Number

Place (place type) County	Number
Houston (city) Harris	924
San Antonio (city) Bexar	820
Dallas (city) Dallas	475

Spaniard
Top 10 Places Sorted by Percent of Hispanic Population

Place (place type) County	Percent
Houston (city) Harris	0.13
San Antonio (city) Bexar	0.12

Place (place type) County	Percent
Dallas (city) Dallas	0.11

Spaniard
Top 10 Places Sorted by Percent of Total Population

Place (place type) County	Percent
San Antonio (city) Bexar	0.07
Houston (city) Harris	0.05
Dallas (city) Dallas	0.04

Uruguayan
Top 10 Places Sorted by Number

Place (place type) County	Number
No places met population threshold.	

Uruguayan
Top 10 Places Sorted by Percent of Hispanic Population

Place (place type) County	Percent
No places met population threshold.	

Uruguayan
Top 10 Places Sorted by Percent of Total Population

Place (place type) County	Percent
No places met population threshold.	

Venezuelan
Top 10 Places Sorted by Number

Place (place type) County	Number
Houston (city) Harris	1,674
Austin (city) Travis	503

Venezuelan
Top 10 Places Sorted by Percent of Hispanic Population

Place (place type) County	Percent
Austin (city) Travis	0.25
Houston (city) Harris	0.23

Venezuelan
Top 10 Places Sorted by Percent of Total Population

Place (place type) County	Percent
Houston (city) Harris	0.09
Austin (city) Travis	0.08

Other Hispanic
Top 10 Places Sorted by Number

Place (place type) County	Number
San Antonio (city) Bexar	168,680
Houston (city) Harris	98,214
El Paso (city) El Paso	56,430
Corpus Christi (city) Nueces	45,139
Dallas (city) Dallas	41,452
Austin (city) Travis	30,165
Laredo (city) Webb	27,003
Lubbock (city) Lubbock	21,461
Brownsville (city) Cameron	19,723
Fort Worth (city) Tarrant	19,235

Other Hispanic
Top 10 Places Sorted by Percent of Hispanic Population

Place (place type) County	Percent
Alice (city) Jim Wells	44.32
Lubbock (city) Lubbock	39.06
Beeville (city) Bee	38.50
Robstown (city) Nueces	35.55
Levelland (city) Hockley	35.01
Portland (city) San Patricio	34.63
El Campo (city) Wharton	33.19
Pflugerville (city) Travis	32.91
Plainview (city) Hale	31.97
Sweetwater (city) Nolan	31.30

Notes: Please refer to the User's Guide for an explanation of data; tables include places with populations > 9,999 and reflect only those areas that meet Summary File 4 population thresholds, therefore there may be less than 10 places listed

Other Hispanic
Top 10 Places Sorted by Percent of Total Population

Place (place type) County	Percent
Alice (city) Jim Wells	34.62
Robstown (city) Nueces	33.07
Beeville (city) Bee	26.12
Uvalde (city) Uvalde	22.90
San Benito (city) Cameron	18.83
Kingsville (city) Kleberg	18.41
Mercedes (city) Hidalgo	17.86
Rio Grande City (city) Starr	17.22
Corpus Christi (city) Nueces	16.26
Weslaco (city) Hidalgo	16.22

Median Age

Total Population
Top 10 Places Sorted by Number

Place (place type) County	Years
Kerrville (city) Kerr	44.3
Canyon Lake (cdp) Comal	42.8
Colleyville (city) Tarrant	40.2
Bellaire (city) Harris	40.0
Benbrook (city) Tarrant	39.4
Groves (city) Jefferson	39.1
West University Place (city) Harris	39.0
Denison (city) Grayson	38.9
Pampa (city) Gray	38.9
Port Neches (city) Jefferson	38.2

Hispanic
Top 10 Places Sorted by Number

Place (place type) County	Years
Cinco Ranch (cdp) Fort Bend	37.3
West University Place (city) Harris	37.1
Bellaire (city) Harris	36.7
Colleyville (city) Tarrant	35.1
Gatesville (city) Coryell	33.9
Canyon Lake (cdp) Comal	33.8
Southlake (city) Tarrant	33.8
The Woodlands (cdp) Montgomery	32.1
Eagle Pass (city) Maverick	31.1
Big Spring (city) Howard	30.9

Argentinian
Top 10 Places Sorted by Number

Place (place type) County	Years
Houston (city) Harris	36.1

Bolivian
Top 10 Places Sorted by Number

Place (place type) County	Years
Houston (city) Harris	35.3

Central American
Top 10 Places Sorted by Number

Place (place type) County	Years
El Paso (city) El Paso	32.8
Grand Prairie (city) Dallas	32.2
Corpus Christi (city) Nueces	31.7
San Antonio (city) Bexar	31.6
Mission Bend (cdp) Fort Bend	30.2
Denton (city) Denton	29.6
Galveston (city) Galveston	29.5
Brownsville (city) Cameron	29.1
Plano (city) Collin	28.9
Killeen (city) Bell	28.0

Chilean
Top 10 Places Sorted by Number

Place (place type) County	Years
Houston (city) Harris	35.4

Colombian
Top 10 Places Sorted by Number

Place (place type) County	Years
San Antonio (city) Bexar	37.4
Houston (city) Harris	34.2
Dallas (city) Dallas	32.6
Mission Bend (cdp) Fort Bend	29.1
Austin (city) Travis	28.5

Costa Rican
Top 10 Places Sorted by Number

Place (place type) County	Years
Dallas (city) Dallas	33.9
Houston (city) Harris	33.3

Cuban
Top 10 Places Sorted by Number

Place (place type) County	Years
Houston (city) Harris	39.6
Dallas (city) Dallas	38.5
El Paso (city) El Paso	38.2
San Antonio (city) Bexar	37.4
Fort Worth (city) Tarrant	35.1
Austin (city) Travis	31.5

Dominican
Top 10 Places Sorted by Number

Place (place type) County	Years
Houston (city) Harris	32.0

Ecuadorian
Top 10 Places Sorted by Number

Place (place type) County	Years
Houston (city) Harris	31.9

Guatelmalan
Top 10 Places Sorted by Number

Place (place type) County	Years
San Antonio (city) Bexar	33.7
Garland (city) Dallas	29.6
Fort Worth (city) Tarrant	28.3
Dallas (city) Dallas	27.3
Houston (city) Harris	27.3
Austin (city) Travis	27.2

Honduran
Top 10 Places Sorted by Number

Place (place type) County	Years
Houston (city) Harris	27.5
Irving (city) Dallas	26.7
Garland (city) Dallas	26.6
San Antonio (city) Bexar	26.5
Austin (city) Travis	26.2
Dallas (city) Dallas	26.2

Mexican
Top 10 Places Sorted by Number

Place (place type) County	Years
Bellaire (city) Harris	36.1
West University Place (city) Harris	35.7
Gatesville (city) Coryell	34.3
Colleyville (city) Tarrant	34.0
Canyon Lake (cdp) Comal	33.5
Alice (city) Jim Wells	32.2
Eagle Pass (city) Maverick	31.9

Place (place type) County	
The Woodlands (cdp) Montgomery	31.8
Big Spring (city) Howard	31.3
Schertz (city) Guadalupe	31.1

Nicaraguan
Top 10 Places Sorted by Number

Place (place type) County	Years
San Antonio (city) Bexar	32.8
Houston (city) Harris	29.3
Dallas (city) Dallas	27.5
Austin (city) Travis	24.0
Port Arthur (city) Jefferson	22.9

Panamanian
Top 10 Places Sorted by Number

Place (place type) County	Years
El Paso (city) El Paso	34.5
Houston (city) Harris	33.2
San Antonio (city) Bexar	33.0
Killeen (city) Bell	29.6

Paraguayan
Top 10 Places Sorted by Number

Place (place type) County	Years
No places met population threshold.	

Peruvian
Top 10 Places Sorted by Number

Place (place type) County	Years
Dallas (city) Dallas	33.8
Houston (city) Harris	33.0
San Antonio (city) Bexar	30.3

Puerto Rican
Top 10 Places Sorted by Number

Place (place type) County	Years
McAllen (city) Hidalgo	38.6
Plano (city) Collin	36.6
Carrollton (city) Denton	34.0
San Antonio (city) Bexar	33.0
Corpus Christi (city) Nueces	31.2
El Paso (city) El Paso	31.0
Dallas (city) Dallas	30.8
Irving (city) Dallas	29.5
Euless (city) Tarrant	29.2
Temple (city) Bell	28.6

Salvadoran
Top 10 Places Sorted by Number

Place (place type) County	Years
Galveston (city) Galveston	34.9
Mission Bend (cdp) Fort Bend	31.1
Grand Prairie (city) Dallas	29.8
San Antonio (city) Bexar	28.9
Houston (city) Harris	27.6
Arlington (city) Tarrant	27.4
Dallas (city) Dallas	27.4
Garland (city) Dallas	27.2
Pasadena (city) Harris	27.2
Farmers Branch (city) Dallas	25.8

South American
Top 10 Places Sorted by Number

Place (place type) County	Years
Richardson (city) Dallas	36.3
Corpus Christi (city) Nueces	36.1
Carrollton (city) Denton	35.2
Plano (city) Collin	35.2
El Paso (city) El Paso	34.5
San Antonio (city) Bexar	34.5
Arlington (city) Tarrant	34.0

Notes: Please refer to the User's Guide for an explanation of data; tables include places with populations > 9,999 and reflect only those areas that meet Summary File 4 population thresholds, therefore there may be less than 10 places listed

Place (place type) County	
Houston (city) Harris	33.9
The Woodlands (cdp) Montgomery	33.7
Mission Bend (cdp) Fort Bend	33.6

Spaniard
Top 10 Places Sorted by Number

Place (place type) County	Years
San Antonio (city) Bexar	40.2
Houston (city) Harris	34.7
Dallas (city) Dallas	30.6

Uruguayan
Top 10 Places Sorted by Number

Place (place type) County	Years
No places met population threshold.	

Venezuelan
Top 10 Places Sorted by Number

Place (place type) County	Years
Austin (city) Travis	30.3
Houston (city) Harris	28.4

Other Hispanic
Top 10 Places Sorted by Number

Place (place type) County	Years
Sugar Land (city) Fort Bend	32.1
Bedford (city) Tarrant	31.9
La Marque (city) Galveston	31.3
Universal City (city) Bexar	31.3
Richardson (city) Dallas	30.4
Allen (city) Collin	29.8
Richmond (city) Fort Bend	29.2
Texas City (city) Galveston	29.1
League City (city) Galveston	29.0
Cedar Hill (city) Dallas	28.9

Average Household Size

Total Population
Top 10 Places Sorted by Number

Place (place type) County	Number
San Elizario (cdp) El Paso	4.31
La Homa (cdp) Hidalgo	4.29
Socorro (city) El Paso	4.02
Fort Hood (cdp) Coryell	3.94
San Juan (city) Hidalgo	3.92
Laredo (city) Webb	3.70
Pharr (city) Hidalgo	3.64
Brownsville (city) Cameron	3.61
Rio Grande City (city) Starr	3.53
New Territory (cdp) Fort Bend	3.49

Hispanic
Top 10 Places Sorted by Number

Place (place type) County	Number
Farmers Branch (city) Dallas	4.71
Marshall (city) Harrison	4.66
Jacksonville (city) Cherokee	4.51
Aldine (cdp) Harris	4.47
Mount Pleasant (city) Titus	4.41
Ennis (city) Ellis	4.40
Galena Park (city) Harris	4.40
La Homa (cdp) Hidalgo	4.34
San Elizario (cdp) El Paso	4.34
Athens (city) Henderson	4.29

Argentinian
Top 10 Places Sorted by Number

Place (place type) County	Number
Houston (city) Harris	2.55

Bolivian
Top 10 Places Sorted by Number

Place (place type) County	Number
Houston (city) Harris	3.18

Central American
Top 10 Places Sorted by Number

Place (place type) County	Number
Farmers Branch (city) Dallas	5.53
Rosenberg (city) Fort Bend	4.63
Garland (city) Dallas	4.54
Carrollton (city) Denton	4.26
Mission Bend (cdp) Fort Bend	4.24
Conroe (city) Montgomery	4.18
Irving (city) Dallas	4.18
Grand Prairie (city) Dallas	3.97
Richardson (city) Dallas	3.97
Pasadena (city) Harris	3.87

Chilean
Top 10 Places Sorted by Number

Place (place type) County	Number
Houston (city) Harris	2.57

Colombian
Top 10 Places Sorted by Number

Place (place type) County	Number
Mission Bend (cdp) Fort Bend	3.76
Dallas (city) Dallas	2.87
San Antonio (city) Bexar	2.87
Houston (city) Harris	2.80
Austin (city) Travis	2.09

Costa Rican
Top 10 Places Sorted by Number

Place (place type) County	Number
Houston (city) Harris	3.50
Dallas (city) Dallas	3.04

Cuban
Top 10 Places Sorted by Number

Place (place type) County	Number
Fort Worth (city) Tarrant	3.02
El Paso (city) El Paso	2.93
San Antonio (city) Bexar	2.86
Austin (city) Travis	2.74
Dallas (city) Dallas	2.64
Houston (city) Harris	2.35

Dominican
Top 10 Places Sorted by Number

Place (place type) County	Number
Houston (city) Harris	3.11

Ecuadorian
Top 10 Places Sorted by Number

Place (place type) County	Number
Houston (city) Harris	2.70

Guatelmalan
Top 10 Places Sorted by Number

Place (place type) County	Number
Garland (city) Dallas	4.98
Fort Worth (city) Tarrant	4.03
Houston (city) Harris	3.68
Dallas (city) Dallas	3.55
Austin (city) Travis	3.29
San Antonio (city) Bexar	3.15

Honduran
Top 10 Places Sorted by Number

Place (place type) County	Number
Garland (city) Dallas	5.11
Austin (city) Travis	4.45
Dallas (city) Dallas	3.65
Irving (city) Dallas	3.64
Houston (city) Harris	3.48
San Antonio (city) Bexar	3.21

Mexican
Top 10 Places Sorted by Number

Place (place type) County	Number
Marshall (city) Harrison	4.79
Farmers Branch (city) Dallas	4.70
Aldine (cdp) Harris	4.50
Vidor (city) Orange	4.50
Jacksonville (city) Cherokee	4.49
Mount Pleasant (city) Titus	4.45
Conroe (city) Montgomery	4.43
McKinney (city) Collin	4.39
Galena Park (city) Harris	4.37
La Homa (cdp) Hidalgo	4.36

Nicaraguan
Top 10 Places Sorted by Number

Place (place type) County	Number
Port Arthur (city) Jefferson	4.23
Austin (city) Travis	3.98
Houston (city) Harris	3.64
San Antonio (city) Bexar	3.33
Dallas (city) Dallas	3.04

Panamanian
Top 10 Places Sorted by Number

Place (place type) County	Number
El Paso (city) El Paso	3.31
San Antonio (city) Bexar	2.97
Killeen (city) Bell	2.55
Houston (city) Harris	2.43

Paraguayan
Top 10 Places Sorted by Number

Place (place type) County	Number
No places met population threshold.	

Peruvian
Top 10 Places Sorted by Number

Place (place type) County	Number
Dallas (city) Dallas	3.25
San Antonio (city) Bexar	2.82
Houston (city) Harris	2.70

Puerto Rican
Top 10 Places Sorted by Number

Place (place type) County	Number
McAllen (city) Hidalgo	4.18
Fort Hood (cdp) Coryell	4.13
Mission Bend (cdp) Fort Bend	3.75
Abilene (city) Taylor	3.38
Copperas Cove (city) Coryell	3.37
Temple (city) Bell	3.35
Garland (city) Dallas	3.22
Killeen (city) Bell	3.16
El Paso (city) El Paso	3.12
Corpus Christi (city) Nueces	3.11

Salvadoran
Top 10 Places Sorted by Number

Place (place type) County	Number
Farmers Branch (city) Dallas	5.66

Notes: Please refer to the User's Guide for an explanation of data; tables include places with populations > 9,999 and reflect only those areas that meet Summary File 4 population thresholds, therefore there may be less than 10 places listed

Place (place type) County	
Plano (city) Collin	5.23
Conroe (city) Montgomery	4.57
Grand Prairie (city) Dallas	4.43
Garland (city) Dallas	4.28
Arlington (city) Tarrant	4.27
Pasadena (city) Harris	4.25
Irving (city) Dallas	4.24
Mission Bend (cdp) Fort Bend	4.24
Fort Worth (city) Tarrant	4.17

South American
Top 10 Places Sorted by Number

Place (place type) County	Number
Mission Bend (cdp) Fort Bend	4.02
Carrollton (city) Denton	3.81
Garland (city) Dallas	3.76
Sugar Land (city) Fort Bend	3.67
Corpus Christi (city) Nueces	3.48
El Paso (city) El Paso	3.34
Irving (city) Dallas	3.08
The Woodlands (cdp) Montgomery	3.04
Dallas (city) Dallas	2.76
Fort Worth (city) Tarrant	2.75

Spaniard
Top 10 Places Sorted by Number

Place (place type) County	Number
Dallas (city) Dallas	2.39
Houston (city) Harris	2.38
San Antonio (city) Bexar	2.24

Uruguayan
Top 10 Places Sorted by Number

Place (place type) County	Number
No places met population threshold.	

Venezuelan
Top 10 Places Sorted by Number

Place (place type) County	Number
Austin (city) Travis	3.03
Houston (city) Harris	2.35

Other Hispanic
Top 10 Places Sorted by Number

Place (place type) County	Number
Mansfield (city) Tarrant	5.15
Ennis (city) Ellis	4.63
San Juan (city) Hidalgo	4.54
Jacinto City (city) Harris	4.53
Corsicana (city) Navarro	4.47
Mineral Wells (city) Palo Pinto	4.42
Fort Hood (cdp) Coryell	4.40
Galena Park (city) Harris	4.40
South Houston (city) Harris	4.36
Cloverleaf (cdp) Harris	4.32

Language Spoken at Home: English Only

Total Populations 5 Years and Over Who Speak English-Only at Home
Top 10 Places Sorted by Number

Place (place type) County	Number
Houston (city) Harris	1,053,207
Dallas (city) Dallas	685,534
San Antonio (city) Bexar	560,786
Austin (city) Travis	419,884
Fort Worth (city) Tarrant	347,721
Arlington (city) Tarrant	231,505
Plano (city) Collin	158,931
Corpus Christi (city) Nueces	150,742
El Paso (city) El Paso	148,224
Lubbock (city) Lubbock	144,093

Total Populations 5 Years and Over Who Speak English-Only at Home
Top 10 Places Sorted by Percent

Place (place type) County	Percent
Texarkana (city) Bowie	95.38
Denison (city) Grayson	95.03
Paris (city) Lamar	94.99
Vidor (city) Orange	94.93
Orange (city) Orange	93.70
Burleson (city) Johnson	93.62
Burkburnett (city) Wichita	93.50
Keller (city) Tarrant	93.15
Canyon Lake (cdp) Comal	92.62
Highland Village (city) Denton	92.42

Hispanics 5 Years and Over Who Speak English-Only at Home
Top 10 Places Sorted by Number

Place (place type) County	Number
San Antonio (city) Bexar	164,373
Houston (city) Harris	84,760
El Paso (city) El Paso	49,336
Austin (city) Travis	43,424
Corpus Christi (city) Nueces	41,358
Dallas (city) Dallas	41,175
Fort Worth (city) Tarrant	25,278
Lubbock (city) Lubbock	14,407
Arlington (city) Tarrant	11,239
Pasadena (city) Harris	9,793

Hispanics 5 Years and Over Who Speak English-Only at Home
Top 10 Places Sorted by Percent

Place (place type) County	Percent
Nederland (city) Jefferson	65.84
Vidor (city) Orange	64.66
Keller (city) Tarrant	63.88
Port Neches (city) Jefferson	56.27
Orange (city) Orange	54.74
Groves (city) Jefferson	54.05
Highland Village (city) Denton	53.36
Canyon Lake (cdp) Comal	52.32
Saginaw (city) Tarrant	51.96
Brushy Creek (cdp) Williamson	50.97

Argentinians 5 Years and Over Who Speak English-Only at Home
Top 10 Places Sorted by Number

Place (place type) County	Number
Houston (city) Harris	97

Argentinians 5 Years and Over Who Speak English-Only at Home
Top 10 Places Sorted by Percent

Place (place type) County	Percent
Houston (city) Harris	7.45

Bolivians 5 Years and Over Who Speak English-Only at Home
Top 10 Places Sorted by Number

Place (place type) County	Number
Houston (city) Harris	56

Bolivians 5 Years and Over Who Speak English-Only at Home
Top 10 Places Sorted by Percent

Place (place type) County	Percent
Houston (city) Harris	8.27

Central Americans 5 Years and Over Who Speak English-Only at Home
Top 10 Places Sorted by Number

Place (place type) County	Number
Houston (city) Harris	3,389
Dallas (city) Dallas	757
San Antonio (city) Bexar	615
Austin (city) Travis	356
Irving (city) Dallas	312
Plano (city) Collin	197
El Paso (city) El Paso	195
Fort Worth (city) Tarrant	185
Arlington (city) Tarrant	174
Garland (city) Dallas	153

Central Americans 5 Years and Over Who Speak English-Only at Home
Top 10 Places Sorted by Percent

Place (place type) County	Percent
Brownsville (city) Cameron	18.08
San Antonio (city) Bexar	17.51
Corpus Christi (city) Nueces	17.23
Plano (city) Collin	16.74
Killeen (city) Bell	15.97
El Paso (city) El Paso	14.09
Fort Worth (city) Tarrant	11.69
Arlington (city) Tarrant	11.31
Port Arthur (city) Jefferson	10.26
Grand Prairie (city) Dallas	9.98

Chileans 5 Years and Over Who Speak English-Only at Home
Top 10 Places Sorted by Number

Place (place type) County	Number
Houston (city) Harris	77

Chileans 5 Years and Over Who Speak English-Only at Home
Top 10 Places Sorted by Percent

Place (place type) County	Percent
Houston (city) Harris	11.86

Colombians 5 Years and Over Who Speak English-Only at Home
Top 10 Places Sorted by Number

Place (place type) County	Number
Houston (city) Harris	454
Austin (city) Travis	292
Dallas (city) Dallas	89
San Antonio (city) Bexar	85
Mission Bend (cdp) Fort Bend	32

Colombians 5 Years and Over Who Speak English-Only at Home
Top 10 Places Sorted by Percent

Place (place type) County	Percent
Austin (city) Travis	38.17
San Antonio (city) Bexar	11.97
Dallas (city) Dallas	8.63
Houston (city) Harris	7.71
Mission Bend (cdp) Fort Bend	6.12

Costa Ricans 5 Years and Over Who Speak English-Only at Home
Top 10 Places Sorted by Number

Place (place type) County	Number
Houston (city) Harris	114
Dallas (city) Dallas	69

Notes: Please refer to the User's Guide for an explanation of data; tables include places with populations > 9,999 and reflect only those areas that meet Summary File 4 population thresholds, therefore there may be less than 10 places listed

Costa Ricans 5 Years and Over Who Speak English-Only at Home
Top 10 Places Sorted by Percent

Place (place type) County	Percent
Dallas (city) Dallas	16.55
Houston (city) Harris	13.80

Cubans 5 Years and Over Who Speak English-Only at Home
Top 10 Places Sorted by Number

Place (place type) County	Number
Houston (city) Harris	790
Dallas (city) Dallas	373
San Antonio (city) Bexar	366
Austin (city) Travis	260
Fort Worth (city) Tarrant	182
El Paso (city) El Paso	79

Cubans 5 Years and Over Who Speak English-Only at Home
Top 10 Places Sorted by Percent

Place (place type) County	Percent
Fort Worth (city) Tarrant	21.06
San Antonio (city) Bexar	20.88
El Paso (city) El Paso	18.90
Austin (city) Travis	18.41
Dallas (city) Dallas	16.66
Houston (city) Harris	15.24

Dominicans 5 Years and Over Who Speak English-Only at Home
Top 10 Places Sorted by Number

Place (place type) County	Number
Houston (city) Harris	37

Dominicans 5 Years and Over Who Speak English-Only at Home
Top 10 Places Sorted by Percent

Place (place type) County	Percent
Houston (city) Harris	4.40

Ecuadorians 5 Years and Over Who Speak English-Only at Home
Top 10 Places Sorted by Number

Place (place type) County	Number
Houston (city) Harris	112

Ecuadorians 5 Years and Over Who Speak English-Only at Home
Top 10 Places Sorted by Percent

Place (place type) County	Percent
Houston (city) Harris	12.12

Guatelmalans 5 Years and Over Who Speak English-Only at Home
Top 10 Places Sorted by Number

Place (place type) County	Number
Houston (city) Harris	337
Dallas (city) Dallas	86
San Antonio (city) Bexar	47
Austin (city) Travis	40
Fort Worth (city) Tarrant	11
Garland (city) Dallas	10

Guatelmalans 5 Years and Over Who Speak English-Only at Home
Top 10 Places Sorted by Percent

Place (place type) County	Percent
San Antonio (city) Bexar	12.11

Austin (city) Travis	4.99
Houston (city) Harris	4.76
Dallas (city) Dallas	3.63
Fort Worth (city) Tarrant	2.64
Garland (city) Dallas	1.20

Hondurans 5 Years and Over Who Speak English-Only at Home
Top 10 Places Sorted by Number

Place (place type) County	Number
Houston (city) Harris	477
Dallas (city) Dallas	154
San Antonio (city) Bexar	147
Austin (city) Travis	94
Irving (city) Dallas	70
Garland (city) Dallas	24

Hondurans 5 Years and Over Who Speak English-Only at Home
Top 10 Places Sorted by Percent

Place (place type) County	Percent
San Antonio (city) Bexar	22.62
Irving (city) Dallas	9.36
Austin (city) Travis	8.49
Garland (city) Dallas	6.19
Dallas (city) Dallas	5.64
Houston (city) Harris	4.61

Mexicans 5 Years and Over Who Speak English-Only at Home
Top 10 Places Sorted by Number

Place (place type) County	Number
San Antonio (city) Bexar	112,261
Houston (city) Harris	60,947
El Paso (city) El Paso	38,736
Dallas (city) Dallas	31,994
Austin (city) Travis	31,744
Corpus Christi (city) Nueces	27,780
Fort Worth (city) Tarrant	19,044
Arlington (city) Tarrant	8,066
Lubbock (city) Lubbock	7,852
Pasadena (city) Harris	7,305

Mexicans 5 Years and Over Who Speak English-Only at Home
Top 10 Places Sorted by Percent

Place (place type) County	Percent
Keller (city) Tarrant	63.38
Nederland (city) Jefferson	62.61
Hewitt (city) McLennan	62.10
Port Neches (city) Jefferson	58.20
Vidor (city) Orange	55.43
Groves (city) Jefferson	54.20
Canyon Lake (cdp) Comal	52.63
Saginaw (city) Tarrant	50.70
Burleson (city) Johnson	50.30
Benbrook (city) Tarrant	50.23

Nicaraguans 5 Years and Over Who Speak English-Only at Home
Top 10 Places Sorted by Number

Place (place type) County	Number
Houston (city) Harris	134
San Antonio (city) Bexar	107
Austin (city) Travis	32
Dallas (city) Dallas	13
Port Arthur (city) Jefferson	0

Nicaraguans 5 Years and Over Who Speak English-Only at Home
Top 10 Places Sorted by Percent

Place (place type) County	Percent
San Antonio (city) Bexar	23.26
Austin (city) Travis	8.67
Houston (city) Harris	6.04
Dallas (city) Dallas	3.10
Port Arthur (city) Jefferson	0.00

Panamanians 5 Years and Over Who Speak English-Only at Home
Top 10 Places Sorted by Number

Place (place type) County	Number
Houston (city) Harris	205
San Antonio (city) Bexar	162
El Paso (city) El Paso	146
Killeen (city) Bell	92

Panamanians 5 Years and Over Who Speak English-Only at Home
Top 10 Places Sorted by Percent

Place (place type) County	Percent
El Paso (city) El Paso	34.11
Houston (city) Harris	27.01
Killeen (city) Bell	20.63
San Antonio (city) Bexar	18.64

Paraguayans 5 Years and Over Who Speak English-Only at Home
Top 10 Places Sorted by Number

Place (place type) County	Number
No places met population threshold.	

Paraguayans 5 Years and Over Who Speak English-Only at Home
Top 10 Places Sorted by Percent

Place (place type) County	Percent
No places met population threshold.	

Peruvians 5 Years and Over Who Speak English-Only at Home
Top 10 Places Sorted by Number

Place (place type) County	Number
Houston (city) Harris	139
Dallas (city) Dallas	77
San Antonio (city) Bexar	58

Peruvians 5 Years and Over Who Speak English-Only at Home
Top 10 Places Sorted by Percent

Place (place type) County	Percent
San Antonio (city) Bexar	14.04
Houston (city) Harris	9.89
Dallas (city) Dallas	8.71

Puerto Ricans 5 Years and Over Who Speak English-Only at Home
Top 10 Places Sorted by Number

Place (place type) County	Number
San Antonio (city) Bexar	1,966
Houston (city) Harris	1,818
Austin (city) Travis	889
El Paso (city) El Paso	809
Dallas (city) Dallas	660
Killeen (city) Bell	642
Fort Worth (city) Tarrant	493
Arlington (city) Tarrant	358
Plano (city) Collin	322
Corpus Christi (city) Nueces	251

Notes: Please refer to the User's Guide for an explanation of data; tables include places with populations > 9,999 and reflect only those areas that meet Summary File 4 population thresholds, therefore there may be less than 10 places listed

Puerto Ricans 5 Years and Over Who Speak English-Only at Home
Top 10 Places Sorted by Percent

Place (place type) County	Percent
Abilene (city) Taylor	38.84
Plano (city) Collin	37.40
Austin (city) Travis	37.10
San Angelo (city) Tom Green	36.56
Grand Prairie (city) Dallas	35.77
Garland (city) Dallas	35.41
Temple (city) Bell	30.67
Dallas (city) Dallas	30.53
Carrollton (city) Denton	29.95
Irving (city) Dallas	29.72

Salvadorans 5 Years and Over Who Speak English-Only at Home
Top 10 Places Sorted by Number

Place (place type) County	Number
Houston (city) Harris	1,907
Dallas (city) Dallas	355
Irving (city) Dallas	210
Garland (city) Dallas	101
San Antonio (city) Bexar	82
Austin (city) Travis	60
Pasadena (city) Harris	60
Plano (city) Collin	37
Conroe (city) Montgomery	27
Grand Prairie (city) Dallas	26

Salvadorans 5 Years and Over Who Speak English-Only at Home
Top 10 Places Sorted by Percent

Place (place type) County	Percent
San Antonio (city) Bexar	11.26
Conroe (city) Montgomery	8.57
Plano (city) Collin	7.49
Mission Bend (cdp) Fort Bend	5.88
Pasadena (city) Harris	5.49
Garland (city) Dallas	5.47
Grand Prairie (city) Dallas	5.09
Houston (city) Harris	5.04
Arlington (city) Tarrant	4.61
Dallas (city) Dallas	4.26

South Americans 5 Years and Over Who Speak English-Only at Home
Top 10 Places Sorted by Number

Place (place type) County	Number
Houston (city) Harris	1,128
Austin (city) Travis	765
Dallas (city) Dallas	294
San Antonio (city) Bexar	258
Plano (city) Collin	176
Arlington (city) Tarrant	113
Fort Worth (city) Tarrant	107
Corpus Christi (city) Nueces	78
Sugar Land (city) Fort Bend	75
El Paso (city) El Paso	67

South Americans 5 Years and Over Who Speak English-Only at Home
Top 10 Places Sorted by Percent

Place (place type) County	Percent
Austin (city) Travis	30.24
Plano (city) Collin	20.83
Corpus Christi (city) Nueces	15.20
Sugar Land (city) Fort Bend	15.15
Arlington (city) Tarrant	14.91
Richardson (city) Dallas	13.69
The Woodlands (cdp) Montgomery	13.00
Fort Worth (city) Tarrant	12.46
San Antonio (city) Bexar	11.73

El Paso (city) El Paso	11.04

Spaniards 5 Years and Over Who Speak English-Only at Home
Top 10 Places Sorted by Number

Place (place type) County	Number
San Antonio (city) Bexar	372
Houston (city) Harris	287
Dallas (city) Dallas	85

Spaniards 5 Years and Over Who Speak English-Only at Home
Top 10 Places Sorted by Percent

Place (place type) County	Percent
San Antonio (city) Bexar	46.44
Houston (city) Harris	32.58
Dallas (city) Dallas	19.63

Uruguayans 5 Years and Over Who Speak English-Only at Home
Top 10 Places Sorted by Number

No places met population threshold.

Uruguayans 5 Years and Over Who Speak English-Only at Home
Top 10 Places Sorted by Percent

No places met population threshold.

Venezuelans 5 Years and Over Who Speak English-Only at Home
Top 10 Places Sorted by Number

Place (place type) County	Number
Austin (city) Travis	147
Houston (city) Harris	117

Venezuelans 5 Years and Over Who Speak English-Only at Home
Top 10 Places Sorted by Percent

Place (place type) County	Percent
Austin (city) Travis	31.01
Houston (city) Harris	7.34

Other Hispanics 5 Years and Over Who Speak English-Only at Home
Top 10 Places Sorted by Number

Place (place type) County	Number
San Antonio (city) Bexar	48,518
Houston (city) Harris	16,364
Corpus Christi (city) Nueces	13,015
El Paso (city) El Paso	9,373
Austin (city) Travis	9,237
Dallas (city) Dallas	6,919
Lubbock (city) Lubbock	6,359
Fort Worth (city) Tarrant	5,142
Amarillo (city) Potter	3,592
Victoria (city) Victoria	2,853

Other Hispanics 5 Years and Over Who Speak English-Only at Home
Top 10 Places Sorted by Percent

Place (place type) County	Percent
Canyon (city) Randall	63.66
Cedar Park (city) Williamson	56.65
Bedford (city) Tarrant	56.59
Schertz (city) Guadalupe	52.66
La Marque (city) Galveston	51.87
College Station (city) Brazos	51.61
Watauga (city) Tarrant	51.56

Nacogdoches (city) Nacogdoches	51.51
Pampa (city) Gray	50.70
DeSoto (city) Dallas	50.57

Language Spoken at Home: Spanish

Total Populations 5 Years and Over Who Speak Spanish at Home
Top 10 Places Sorted by Number

Place (place type) County	Number
Houston (city) Harris	597,000
San Antonio (city) Bexar	463,028
El Paso (city) El Paso	356,558
Dallas (city) Dallas	348,225
Austin (city) Travis	149,123
Laredo (city) Webb	144,633
Fort Worth (city) Tarrant	122,678
Brownsville (city) Cameron	109,153
Corpus Christi (city) Nueces	100,368
McAllen (city) Hidalgo	71,800

Total Populations 5 Years and Over Who Speak Spanish at Home
Top 10 Places Sorted by Percent

Place (place type) County	Percent
San Elizario (cdp) El Paso	97.29
La Homa (cdp) Hidalgo	94.81
Socorro (city) El Paso	91.63
Laredo (city) Webb	91.29
Eagle Pass (city) Maverick	90.54
San Juan (city) Hidalgo	89.94
Brownsville (city) Cameron	86.55
Rio Grande City (city) Starr	86.04
Pharr (city) Hidalgo	85.50
Mercedes (city) Hidalgo	81.22

Hispanics 5 Years and Over Who Speak Spanish at Home
Top 10 Places Sorted by Number

Place (place type) County	Number
Houston (city) Harris	562,975
San Antonio (city) Bexar	442,117
El Paso (city) El Paso	342,587
Dallas (city) Dallas	330,083
Laredo (city) Webb	140,565
Austin (city) Travis	135,728
Fort Worth (city) Tarrant	114,750
Brownsville (city) Cameron	106,083
Corpus Christi (city) Nueces	95,079
McAllen (city) Hidalgo	68,925

Hispanics 5 Years and Over Who Speak Spanish at Home
Top 10 Places Sorted by Percent

Place (place type) County	Percent
San Elizario (cdp) El Paso	97.70
La Homa (cdp) Hidalgo	95.86
Laredo (city) Webb	94.31
Socorro (city) El Paso	93.74
Pharr (city) Hidalgo	93.42
Eagle Pass (city) Maverick	93.25
San Juan (city) Hidalgo	93.10
Mount Pleasant (city) Titus	92.54
Brownsville (city) Cameron	92.35
Terrell (city) Kaufman	91.80

Argentinians 5 Years and Over Who Speak Spanish at Home
Top 10 Places Sorted by Number

Place (place type) County	Number
Houston (city) Harris	1,199

Notes: Please refer to the User's Guide for an explanation of data; tables include places with populations > 9,999 and reflect only those areas that meet Summary File 4 population thresholds, therefore there may be less than 10 places listed

Argentinians 5 Years and Over Who Speak Spanish at Home
Top 10 Places Sorted by Percent

Place (place type) County	Percent
Houston (city) Harris	92.09

Bolivians 5 Years and Over Who Speak Spanish at Home
Top 10 Places Sorted by Number

Place (place type) County	Number
Houston (city) Harris	613

Bolivians 5 Years and Over Who Speak Spanish at Home
Top 10 Places Sorted by Percent

Place (place type) County	Percent
Houston (city) Harris	90.55

Central Americans 5 Years and Over Who Speak Spanish at Home
Top 10 Places Sorted by Number

Place (place type) County	Number
Houston (city) Harris	58,050
Dallas (city) Dallas	14,153
Irving (city) Dallas	6,322
Austin (city) Travis	3,918
Garland (city) Dallas	3,211
San Antonio (city) Bexar	2,889
Pasadena (city) Harris	1,787
Farmers Branch (city) Dallas	1,499
Fort Worth (city) Tarrant	1,382
Arlington (city) Tarrant	1,350

Central Americans 5 Years and Over Who Speak Spanish at Home
Top 10 Places Sorted by Percent

Place (place type) County	Percent
Denton (city) Denton	100.00
Farmers Branch (city) Dallas	99.60
Huntsville (city) Walker	96.73
Carrollton (city) Denton	96.15
Irving (city) Dallas	95.30
Garland (city) Dallas	95.20
Lewisville (city) Denton	95.06
Dallas (city) Dallas	94.76
Houston (city) Harris	94.42
Conroe (city) Montgomery	94.29

Chileans 5 Years and Over Who Speak Spanish at Home
Top 10 Places Sorted by Number

Place (place type) County	Number
Houston (city) Harris	572

Chileans 5 Years and Over Who Speak Spanish at Home
Top 10 Places Sorted by Percent

Place (place type) County	Percent
Houston (city) Harris	88.14

Colombians 5 Years and Over Who Speak Spanish at Home
Top 10 Places Sorted by Number

Place (place type) County	Number
Houston (city) Harris	5,428
Dallas (city) Dallas	929
San Antonio (city) Bexar	614
Mission Bend (cdp) Fort Bend	491
Austin (city) Travis	473

Colombians 5 Years and Over Who Speak Spanish at Home
Top 10 Places Sorted by Percent

Place (place type) County	Percent
Mission Bend (cdp) Fort Bend	93.88
Houston (city) Harris	92.14
Dallas (city) Dallas	90.11
San Antonio (city) Bexar	86.48
Austin (city) Travis	61.83

Costa Ricans 5 Years and Over Who Speak Spanish at Home
Top 10 Places Sorted by Number

Place (place type) County	Number
Houston (city) Harris	712
Dallas (city) Dallas	348

Costa Ricans 5 Years and Over Who Speak Spanish at Home
Top 10 Places Sorted by Percent

Place (place type) County	Percent
Houston (city) Harris	86.20
Dallas (city) Dallas	83.45

Cubans 5 Years and Over Who Speak Spanish at Home
Top 10 Places Sorted by Number

Place (place type) County	Number
Houston (city) Harris	4,320
Dallas (city) Dallas	1,866
San Antonio (city) Bexar	1,375
Austin (city) Travis	1,119
Fort Worth (city) Tarrant	671
El Paso (city) El Paso	339

Cubans 5 Years and Over Who Speak Spanish at Home
Top 10 Places Sorted by Percent

Place (place type) County	Percent
Dallas (city) Dallas	83.34
Houston (city) Harris	83.33
El Paso (city) El Paso	81.10
Austin (city) Travis	79.25
San Antonio (city) Bexar	78.44
Fort Worth (city) Tarrant	77.66

Dominicans 5 Years and Over Who Speak Spanish at Home
Top 10 Places Sorted by Number

Place (place type) County	Number
Houston (city) Harris	804

Dominicans 5 Years and Over Who Speak Spanish at Home
Top 10 Places Sorted by Percent

Place (place type) County	Percent
Houston (city) Harris	95.60

Ecuadorians 5 Years and Over Who Speak Spanish at Home
Top 10 Places Sorted by Number

Place (place type) County	Number
Houston (city) Harris	812

Ecuadorians 5 Years and Over Who Speak Spanish at Home
Top 10 Places Sorted by Percent

Place (place type) County	Percent
Houston (city) Harris	87.88

Guatemalans 5 Years and Over Who Speak Spanish at Home
Top 10 Places Sorted by Number

Place (place type) County	Number
Houston (city) Harris	6,723
Dallas (city) Dallas	2,284
Garland (city) Dallas	824
Austin (city) Travis	761
Fort Worth (city) Tarrant	406
San Antonio (city) Bexar	341

Guatemalans 5 Years and Over Who Speak Spanish at Home
Top 10 Places Sorted by Percent

Place (place type) County	Percent
Garland (city) Dallas	98.80
Fort Worth (city) Tarrant	97.36
Dallas (city) Dallas	96.37
Austin (city) Travis	95.01
Houston (city) Harris	94.96
San Antonio (city) Bexar	87.89

Hondurans 5 Years and Over Who Speak Spanish at Home
Top 10 Places Sorted by Number

Place (place type) County	Number
Houston (city) Harris	9,853
Dallas (city) Dallas	2,578
Austin (city) Travis	1,013
Irving (city) Dallas	678
San Antonio (city) Bexar	495
Garland (city) Dallas	364

Hondurans 5 Years and Over Who Speak Spanish at Home
Top 10 Places Sorted by Percent

Place (place type) County	Percent
Houston (city) Harris	95.27
Dallas (city) Dallas	94.36
Garland (city) Dallas	93.81
Austin (city) Travis	91.51
Irving (city) Dallas	90.64
San Antonio (city) Bexar	76.15

Mexicans 5 Years and Over Who Speak Spanish at Home
Top 10 Places Sorted by Number

Place (place type) County	Number
Houston (city) Harris	413,963
San Antonio (city) Bexar	327,824
El Paso (city) El Paso	296,508
Dallas (city) Dallas	280,144
Laredo (city) Webb	117,685
Austin (city) Travis	109,700
Fort Worth (city) Tarrant	98,646
Brownsville (city) Cameron	89,685
Corpus Christi (city) Nueces	65,432
McAllen (city) Hidalgo	58,583

Mexicans 5 Years and Over Who Speak Spanish at Home
Top 10 Places Sorted by Percent

Place (place type) County	Percent
San Elizario (cdp) El Paso	97.72
La Homa (cdp) Hidalgo	96.20
Laredo (city) Webb	94.55
Socorro (city) El Paso	94.28
San Juan (city) Hidalgo	94.22
Pharr (city) Hidalgo	93.84
Eagle Pass (city) Maverick	93.21
Mount Pleasant (city) Titus	93.12
Brownsville (city) Cameron	92.84

Notes: Please refer to the User's Guide for an explanation of data; tables include places with populations > 9,999 and reflect only those areas that meet Summary File 4 population thresholds, therefore there may be less than 10 places listed

Addison (town) Dallas — 91.88

Nicaraguans 5 Years and Over Who Speak Spanish at Home
Top 10 Places Sorted by Number

Place (place type) County	Number
Houston (city) Harris	2,085
Dallas (city) Dallas	394
San Antonio (city) Bexar	353
Austin (city) Travis	321
Port Arthur (city) Jefferson	271

Nicaraguans 5 Years and Over Who Speak Spanish at Home
Top 10 Places Sorted by Percent

Place (place type) County	Percent
Port Arthur (city) Jefferson	98.19
Houston (city) Harris	93.96
Dallas (city) Dallas	93.81
Austin (city) Travis	86.99
San Antonio (city) Bexar	76.74

Panamanians 5 Years and Over Who Speak Spanish at Home
Top 10 Places Sorted by Number

Place (place type) County	Number
San Antonio (city) Bexar	707
Houston (city) Harris	554
Killeen (city) Bell	347
El Paso (city) El Paso	273

Panamanians 5 Years and Over Who Speak Spanish at Home
Top 10 Places Sorted by Percent

Place (place type) County	Percent
San Antonio (city) Bexar	81.36
Killeen (city) Bell	77.80
Houston (city) Harris	72.99
El Paso (city) El Paso	63.79

Paraguayans 5 Years and Over Who Speak Spanish at Home
Top 10 Places Sorted by Number

Place (place type) County	Number
No places met population threshold.

Paraguayans 5 Years and Over Who Speak Spanish at Home
Top 10 Places Sorted by Percent

Place (place type) County	Percent
No places met population threshold.

Peruvians 5 Years and Over Who Speak Spanish at Home
Top 10 Places Sorted by Number

Place (place type) County	Number
Houston (city) Harris	1,255
Dallas (city) Dallas	807
San Antonio (city) Bexar	338

Peruvians 5 Years and Over Who Speak Spanish at Home
Top 10 Places Sorted by Percent

Place (place type) County	Percent
Dallas (city) Dallas	91.29
Houston (city) Harris	89.26
San Antonio (city) Bexar	81.84

Puerto Ricans 5 Years and Over Who Speak Spanish at Home
Top 10 Places Sorted by Number

Place (place type) County	Number
San Antonio (city) Bexar	5,932
Houston (city) Harris	4,890
Killeen (city) Bell	3,492
El Paso (city) El Paso	3,006
Austin (city) Travis	1,507
Dallas (city) Dallas	1,474
Arlington (city) Tarrant	1,281
Fort Worth (city) Tarrant	1,227
Fort Hood (cdp) Coryell	951
Corpus Christi (city) Nueces	754

Puerto Ricans 5 Years and Over Who Speak Spanish at Home
Top 10 Places Sorted by Percent

Place (place type) County	Percent
Euless (city) Tarrant	87.84
Killeen (city) Bell	84.12
Fort Hood (cdp) Coryell	79.52
Copperas Cove (city) Coryell	78.37
El Paso (city) El Paso	77.77
Pasadena (city) Harris	77.18
Arlington (city) Tarrant	76.98
McAllen (city) Hidalgo	76.02
San Antonio (city) Bexar	74.83
Corpus Christi (city) Nueces	74.21

Salvadorans 5 Years and Over Who Speak Spanish at Home
Top 10 Places Sorted by Number

Place (place type) County	Number
Houston (city) Harris	35,947
Dallas (city) Dallas	7,959
Irving (city) Dallas	5,278
Garland (city) Dallas	1,736
Austin (city) Travis	1,376
Farmers Branch (city) Dallas	1,319
Pasadena (city) Harris	1,032
Carrollton (city) Denton	927
San Antonio (city) Bexar	646
Fort Worth (city) Tarrant	577

Salvadorans 5 Years and Over Who Speak Spanish at Home
Top 10 Places Sorted by Percent

Place (place type) County	Percent
Farmers Branch (city) Dallas	99.55
Carrollton (city) Denton	98.72
Fort Worth (city) Tarrant	97.47
Galveston (city) Galveston	97.05
Irving (city) Dallas	96.17
Dallas (city) Dallas	95.58
Austin (city) Travis	95.42
Arlington (city) Tarrant	95.39
Houston (city) Harris	94.96
Grand Prairie (city) Dallas	94.91

South Americans 5 Years and Over Who Speak Spanish at Home
Top 10 Places Sorted by Number

Place (place type) County	Number
Houston (city) Harris	12,013
Dallas (city) Dallas	2,753
San Antonio (city) Bexar	1,873
Austin (city) Travis	1,744
Irving (city) Dallas	862
Fort Worth (city) Tarrant	741
Mission Bend (cdp) Fort Bend	686
Plano (city) Collin	655
Arlington (city) Tarrant	624

El Paso (city) El Paso — 540

South Americans 5 Years and Over Who Speak Spanish at Home
Top 10 Places Sorted by Percent

Place (place type) County	Percent
Carrollton (city) Denton	97.24
Irving (city) Dallas	93.90
Garland (city) Dallas	93.26
Mission Bend (cdp) Fort Bend	92.33
Houston (city) Harris	90.94
Dallas (city) Dallas	89.41
El Paso (city) El Paso	88.96
College Station (city) Brazos	86.30
Fort Worth (city) Tarrant	86.26
San Antonio (city) Bexar	85.14

Spaniards 5 Years and Over Who Speak Spanish at Home
Top 10 Places Sorted by Number

Place (place type) County	Number
Houston (city) Harris	560
San Antonio (city) Bexar	429
Dallas (city) Dallas	338

Spaniards 5 Years and Over Who Speak Spanish at Home
Top 10 Places Sorted by Percent

Place (place type) County	Percent
Dallas (city) Dallas	78.06
Houston (city) Harris	63.56
San Antonio (city) Bexar	53.56

Uruguayans 5 Years and Over Who Speak Spanish at Home
Top 10 Places Sorted by Number

Place (place type) County	Number
No places met population threshold.

Uruguayans 5 Years and Over Who Speak Spanish at Home
Top 10 Places Sorted by Percent

Place (place type) County	Percent
No places met population threshold.

Venezuelans 5 Years and Over Who Speak Spanish at Home
Top 10 Places Sorted by Number

Place (place type) County	Number
Houston (city) Harris	1,459
Austin (city) Travis	327

Venezuelans 5 Years and Over Who Speak Spanish at Home
Top 10 Places Sorted by Percent

Place (place type) County	Percent
Houston (city) Harris	91.59
Austin (city) Travis	68.99

Other Hispanics 5 Years and Over Who Speak Spanish at Home
Top 10 Places Sorted by Number

Place (place type) County	Number
San Antonio (city) Bexar	101,598
Houston (city) Harris	68,375
El Paso (city) El Paso	40,733
Dallas (city) Dallas	29,109
Corpus Christi (city) Nueces	27,781
Laredo (city) Webb	22,059
Austin (city) Travis	17,466

Notes: Please refer to the User's Guide for an explanation of data; tables include places with populations > 9,999 and reflect only those areas that meet Summary File 4 population thresholds, therefore there may be less than 10 places listed

Place (place type) County	Number
Brownsville (city) Cameron	15,677
Lubbock (city) Lubbock	12,672
Fort Worth (city) Tarrant	11,831

Other Hispanics 5 Years and Over Who Speak Spanish at Home
Top 10 Places Sorted by Percent

Place (place type) County	Percent
Rio Grande City (city) Starr	94.86
Eagle Pass (city) Maverick	93.28
Alamo (city) Hidalgo	93.22
Laredo (city) Webb	93.17
Donna (city) Hidalgo	91.93
Socorro (city) El Paso	90.51
Galena Park (city) Harris	90.29
Pharr (city) Hidalgo	90.19
Brownsville (city) Cameron	89.95
Corsicana (city) Navarro	89.45

Foreign Born

Total Population
Top 10 Places Sorted by Number

Place (place type) County	Number
Houston (city) Harris	516,105
Dallas (city) Dallas	290,436
El Paso (city) El Paso	147,505
San Antonio (city) Bexar	133,675
Austin (city) Travis	109,006
Fort Worth (city) Tarrant	87,120
Arlington (city) Tarrant	50,911
Irving (city) Dallas	50,696
Laredo (city) Webb	50,233
Brownsville (city) Cameron	44,116

Total Population
Top 10 Places Sorted by Percent

Place (place type) County	Percent
La Homa (cdp) Hidalgo	46.61
San Elizario (cdp) El Paso	44.78
Socorro (city) El Paso	36.90
Eagle Pass (city) Maverick	35.69
South Houston (city) Harris	35.22
San Juan (city) Hidalgo	34.37
Galena Park (city) Harris	33.25
Pharr (city) Hidalgo	33.20
Jacinto City (city) Harris	32.95
Brownsville (city) Cameron	31.49

Hispanic
Top 10 Places Sorted by Number

Place (place type) County	Number
Houston (city) Harris	367,491
Dallas (city) Dallas	232,265
El Paso (city) El Paso	134,282
San Antonio (city) Bexar	104,843
Austin (city) Travis	70,422
Fort Worth (city) Tarrant	67,876
Laredo (city) Webb	48,946
Brownsville (city) Cameron	42,656
Irving (city) Dallas	31,486
Pasadena (city) Harris	27,367

Hispanic
Top 10 Places Sorted by Percent

Place (place type) County	Percent
Addison (town) Dallas	63.98
Athens (city) Henderson	63.33
Conroe (city) Montgomery	61.14
Mount Pleasant (city) Titus	59.27
Terrell (city) Kaufman	58.73
Henderson (city) Rusk	58.54
Jacksonville (city) Cherokee	58.46

Place (place type) County	Percent
Kilgore (city) Gregg	57.00
Dallas (city) Dallas	54.89
Corsicana (city) Navarro	54.72

Argentinian
Top 10 Places Sorted by Number

Place (place type) County	Number
Houston (city) Harris	1,019

Argentinian
Top 10 Places Sorted by Percent

Place (place type) County	Percent
Houston (city) Harris	75.54

Bolivian
Top 10 Places Sorted by Number

Place (place type) County	Number
Houston (city) Harris	588

Bolivian
Top 10 Places Sorted by Percent

Place (place type) County	Percent
Houston (city) Harris	86.34

Central American
Top 10 Places Sorted by Number

Place (place type) County	Number
Houston (city) Harris	53,103
Dallas (city) Dallas	13,227
Irving (city) Dallas	5,426
Austin (city) Travis	3,551
Garland (city) Dallas	2,909
San Antonio (city) Bexar	2,722
Pasadena (city) Harris	1,510
Fort Worth (city) Tarrant	1,310
Carrollton (city) Denton	1,234
Arlington (city) Tarrant	1,225

Central American
Top 10 Places Sorted by Percent

Place (place type) County	Percent
Brownsville (city) Cameron	90.86
Rosenberg (city) Fort Bend	86.00
Lewisville (city) Denton	82.31
Carrollton (city) Denton	81.88
Dallas (city) Dallas	81.23
Addison (town) Dallas	80.84
Garland (city) Dallas	79.90
Houston (city) Harris	79.39
Conroe (city) Montgomery	79.04
Richardson (city) Dallas	78.58

Chilean
Top 10 Places Sorted by Number

Place (place type) County	Number
Houston (city) Harris	492

Chilean
Top 10 Places Sorted by Percent

Place (place type) County	Percent
Houston (city) Harris	69.00

Colombian
Top 10 Places Sorted by Number

Place (place type) County	Number
Houston (city) Harris	4,967
Dallas (city) Dallas	854
San Antonio (city) Bexar	547
Austin (city) Travis	483

Place (place type) County	Number
Mission Bend (cdp) Fort Bend	392

Colombian
Top 10 Places Sorted by Percent

Place (place type) County	Percent
Dallas (city) Dallas	80.79
Houston (city) Harris	79.78
San Antonio (city) Bexar	73.13
Mission Bend (cdp) Fort Bend	72.19
Austin (city) Travis	60.30

Costa Rican
Top 10 Places Sorted by Number

Place (place type) County	Number
Houston (city) Harris	670
Dallas (city) Dallas	276

Costa Rican
Top 10 Places Sorted by Percent

Place (place type) County	Percent
Houston (city) Harris	77.73
Dallas (city) Dallas	59.48

Cuban
Top 10 Places Sorted by Number

Place (place type) County	Number
Houston (city) Harris	3,637
Dallas (city) Dallas	1,780
San Antonio (city) Bexar	1,081
Austin (city) Travis	904
Fort Worth (city) Tarrant	554
El Paso (city) El Paso	256

Cuban
Top 10 Places Sorted by Percent

Place (place type) County	Percent
Dallas (city) Dallas	75.01
Houston (city) Harris	66.89
Austin (city) Travis	61.21
Fort Worth (city) Tarrant	59.70
San Antonio (city) Bexar	55.58
El Paso (city) El Paso	52.35

Dominican
Top 10 Places Sorted by Number

Place (place type) County	Number
Houston (city) Harris	596

Dominican
Top 10 Places Sorted by Percent

Place (place type) County	Percent
Houston (city) Harris	64.50

Ecuadorian
Top 10 Places Sorted by Number

Place (place type) County	Number
Houston (city) Harris	753

Ecuadorian
Top 10 Places Sorted by Percent

Place (place type) County	Percent
Houston (city) Harris	73.04

Guatelmalan
Top 10 Places Sorted by Number

Place (place type) County	Number
Houston (city) Harris	6,485
Dallas (city) Dallas	2,104

Notes: Please refer to the User's Guide for an explanation of data; tables include places with populations > 9,999 and reflect only those areas that meet Summary File 4 population thresholds, therefore there may be less than 10 places listed

Place (place type) County	
Garland (city) Dallas	753
Austin (city) Travis	698
Fort Worth (city) Tarrant	371
San Antonio (city) Bexar	323

Guatelmalan
Top 10 Places Sorted by Percent

Place (place type) County	Percent
Garland (city) Dallas	88.07
Fort Worth (city) Tarrant	85.68
Houston (city) Harris	84.28
Dallas (city) Dallas	81.74
Austin (city) Travis	80.88
San Antonio (city) Bexar	79.75

Honduran
Top 10 Places Sorted by Number

Place (place type) County	Number
Houston (city) Harris	9,514
Dallas (city) Dallas	2,637
Austin (city) Travis	973
Irving (city) Dallas	717
San Antonio (city) Bexar	498
Garland (city) Dallas	343

Honduran
Top 10 Places Sorted by Percent

Place (place type) County	Percent
Irving (city) Dallas	92.40
Dallas (city) Dallas	89.51
Houston (city) Harris	84.79
Garland (city) Dallas	82.85
Austin (city) Travis	81.02
San Antonio (city) Bexar	71.24

Mexican
Top 10 Places Sorted by Number

Place (place type) County	Number
Houston (city) Harris	261,059
Dallas (city) Dallas	198,409
El Paso (city) El Paso	123,637
San Antonio (city) Bexar	88,449
Fort Worth (city) Tarrant	60,861
Austin (city) Travis	59,423
Laredo (city) Webb	44,230
Brownsville (city) Cameron	38,553
McAllen (city) Hidalgo	24,764
Pasadena (city) Harris	23,498

Mexican
Top 10 Places Sorted by Percent

Place (place type) County	Percent
Addison (town) Dallas	65.08
Kilgore (city) Gregg	64.85
Conroe (city) Montgomery	62.17
Athens (city) Henderson	61.46
Mount Pleasant (city) Titus	60.58
Jacksonville (city) Cherokee	58.97
Terrell (city) Kaufman	58.48
Greenville (city) Hunt	58.21
Henderson (city) Rusk	57.92
Corsicana (city) Navarro	57.84

Nicaraguan
Top 10 Places Sorted by Number

Place (place type) County	Number
Houston (city) Harris	1,851
San Antonio (city) Bexar	353
Dallas (city) Dallas	347
Austin (city) Travis	284
Port Arthur (city) Jefferson	233

Nicaraguan
Top 10 Places Sorted by Percent

Place (place type) County	Percent
Dallas (city) Dallas	79.59
Houston (city) Harris	77.45
Austin (city) Travis	74.93
San Antonio (city) Bexar	71.89
Port Arthur (city) Jefferson	71.04

Panamanian
Top 10 Places Sorted by Number

Place (place type) County	Number
San Antonio (city) Bexar	646
Houston (city) Harris	537
Killeen (city) Bell	350
El Paso (city) El Paso	255

Panamanian
Top 10 Places Sorted by Percent

Place (place type) County	Percent
Killeen (city) Bell	71.28
San Antonio (city) Bexar	68.58
Houston (city) Harris	68.15
El Paso (city) El Paso	54.26

Paraguayan
Top 10 Places Sorted by Number

Place (place type) County	Number
No places met population threshold.	

Paraguayan
Top 10 Places Sorted by Percent

Place (place type) County	Percent
No places met population threshold.	

Peruvian
Top 10 Places Sorted by Number

Place (place type) County	Number
Houston (city) Harris	1,171
Dallas (city) Dallas	742
San Antonio (city) Bexar	332

Peruvian
Top 10 Places Sorted by Percent

Place (place type) County	Percent
Dallas (city) Dallas	80.30
Houston (city) Harris	79.77
San Antonio (city) Bexar	74.44

Puerto Rican
Top 10 Places Sorted by Number

Place (place type) County	Number
Houston (city) Harris	276
Dallas (city) Dallas	127
San Antonio (city) Bexar	120
Fort Worth (city) Tarrant	62
Fort Hood (cdp) Coryell	54
McAllen (city) Hidalgo	40
Arlington (city) Tarrant	36
El Paso (city) El Paso	36
Austin (city) Travis	35
Copperas Cove (city) Coryell	31

Puerto Rican
Top 10 Places Sorted by Percent

Place (place type) County	Percent
McAllen (city) Hidalgo	7.34
Dallas (city) Dallas	5.33
Pasadena (city) Harris	3.96
Fort Hood (cdp) Coryell	3.92
Copperas Cove (city) Coryell	3.69
Houston (city) Harris	3.67
Plano (city) Collin	3.19
San Angelo (city) Tom Green	3.18
Fort Worth (city) Tarrant	3.14
Irving (city) Dallas	2.81

Salvadoran
Top 10 Places Sorted by Number

Place (place type) County	Number
Houston (city) Harris	32,148
Dallas (city) Dallas	7,332
Irving (city) Dallas	4,391
Garland (city) Dallas	1,580
Austin (city) Travis	1,187
Farmers Branch (city) Dallas	1,042
Pasadena (city) Harris	874
Carrollton (city) Denton	855
San Antonio (city) Bexar	623
Fort Worth (city) Tarrant	538

Salvadoran
Top 10 Places Sorted by Percent

Place (place type) County	Percent
Galveston (city) Galveston	84.48
Arlington (city) Tarrant	84.23
Carrollton (city) Denton	82.37
San Antonio (city) Bexar	82.08
Dallas (city) Dallas	79.99
Plano (city) Collin	79.02
Houston (city) Harris	77.76
Garland (city) Dallas	77.26
Fort Worth (city) Tarrant	76.97
Grand Prairie (city) Dallas	75.78

South American
Top 10 Places Sorted by Number

Place (place type) County	Number
Houston (city) Harris	10,979
Dallas (city) Dallas	2,562
San Antonio (city) Bexar	1,689
Austin (city) Travis	1,621
Irving (city) Dallas	735
Fort Worth (city) Tarrant	723
Plano (city) Collin	668
Mission Bend (cdp) Fort Bend	580
Arlington (city) Tarrant	551
Garland (city) Dallas	472

South American
Top 10 Places Sorted by Percent

Place (place type) County	Percent
Fort Worth (city) Tarrant	79.10
Garland (city) Dallas	78.93
Houston (city) Harris	78.72
Dallas (city) Dallas	78.37
Plano (city) Collin	76.52
Mission Bend (cdp) Fort Bend	76.02
Irving (city) Dallas	75.54
Carrollton (city) Denton	75.39
San Antonio (city) Bexar	72.18
El Paso (city) El Paso	70.20

Spaniard
Top 10 Places Sorted by Number

Place (place type) County	Number
Houston (city) Harris	423
Dallas (city) Dallas	229
San Antonio (city) Bexar	152

Notes: Please refer to the User's Guide for an explanation of data; tables include places with populations > 9,999 and reflect only those areas that meet Summary File 4 population thresholds, therefore there may be less than 10 places listed

Spaniard
Top 10 Places Sorted by Percent

Place (place type) County	Percent
Dallas (city) Dallas	48.21
Houston (city) Harris	45.78
San Antonio (city) Bexar	18.54

Uruguayan
Top 10 Places Sorted by Number

Place (place type) County	Number
No places met population threshold.	

Uruguayan
Top 10 Places Sorted by Percent

Place (place type) County	Percent
No places met population threshold.	

Venezuelan
Top 10 Places Sorted by Number

Place (place type) County	Number
Houston (city) Harris	1,371
Austin (city) Travis	350

Venezuelan
Top 10 Places Sorted by Percent

Place (place type) County	Percent
Houston (city) Harris	81.90
Austin (city) Travis	69.58

Other Hispanic
Top 10 Places Sorted by Number

Place (place type) County	Number
Houston (city) Harris	37,418
Dallas (city) Dallas	15,799
San Antonio (city) Bexar	10,458
El Paso (city) El Paso	8,761
Austin (city) Travis	4,736
Fort Worth (city) Tarrant	4,246
Laredo (city) Webb	4,201
Brownsville (city) Cameron	3,466
Irving (city) Dallas	3,173
Garland (city) Dallas	2,337

Other Hispanic
Top 10 Places Sorted by Percent

Place (place type) County	Percent
Ennis (city) Ellis	51.95
Conroe (city) Montgomery	48.03
Farmers Branch (city) Dallas	46.68
Mount Pleasant (city) Titus	42.26
Addison (town) Dallas	41.16
Sherman (city) Grayson	40.95
Lufkin (city) Angelina	39.90
Dallas (city) Dallas	38.11
Houston (city) Harris	38.10
Irving (city) Dallas	38.09

Foreign-Born Naturalized Citizens

Total Population
Top 10 Places Sorted by Number

Place (place type) County	Number
Houston (city) Harris	136,472
El Paso (city) El Paso	64,900
Dallas (city) Dallas	55,607
San Antonio (city) Bexar	54,322
Austin (city) Travis	26,747
Fort Worth (city) Tarrant	23,713
Laredo (city) Webb	17,120
Arlington (city) Tarrant	15,569

Place (place type) County	
Brownsville (city) Cameron	15,559
Plano (city) Collin	13,559

Total Population
Top 10 Places Sorted by Percent

Place (place type) County	Percent
Socorro (city) El Paso	16.19
Eagle Pass (city) Maverick	16.16
Mission Bend (cdp) Fort Bend	16.16
Sugar Land (city) Fort Bend	13.80
New Territory (cdp) Fort Bend	13.73
San Elizario (cdp) El Paso	12.89
El Paso (city) El Paso	11.50
Brownsville (city) Cameron	11.11
Stafford (city) Fort Bend	10.52
La Homa (cdp) Hidalgo	10.22

Hispanic
Top 10 Places Sorted by Number

Place (place type) County	Number
Houston (city) Harris	75,177
El Paso (city) El Paso	57,763
San Antonio (city) Bexar	38,149
Dallas (city) Dallas	34,919
Laredo (city) Webb	16,540
Fort Worth (city) Tarrant	15,309
Brownsville (city) Cameron	14,998
Austin (city) Travis	11,878
McAllen (city) Hidalgo	9,678
Pasadena (city) Harris	6,396

Hispanic
Top 10 Places Sorted by Percent

Place (place type) County	Percent
Bellaire (city) Harris	22.92
Mission Bend (cdp) Fort Bend	19.43
West University Place (city) Harris	19.24
Southlake (city) Tarrant	18.36
Mount Pleasant (city) Titus	16.81
Eagle Pass (city) Maverick	16.61
Socorro (city) El Paso	16.61
New Territory (cdp) Fort Bend	16.37
Missouri City (city) Fort Bend	15.38
Cinco Ranch (cdp) Fort Bend	14.39

Argentinian
Top 10 Places Sorted by Number

Place (place type) County	Number
Houston (city) Harris	352

Argentinian
Top 10 Places Sorted by Percent

Place (place type) County	Percent
Houston (city) Harris	26.09

Bolivian
Top 10 Places Sorted by Number

Place (place type) County	Number
Houston (city) Harris	242

Bolivian
Top 10 Places Sorted by Percent

Place (place type) County	Percent
Houston (city) Harris	35.54

Central American
Top 10 Places Sorted by Number

Place (place type) County	Number
Houston (city) Harris	10,417
Dallas (city) Dallas	1,702

Place (place type) County	
San Antonio (city) Bexar	1,088
Irving (city) Dallas	666
Garland (city) Dallas	621
Austin (city) Travis	615
El Paso (city) El Paso	467
Pasadena (city) Harris	338
Farmers Branch (city) Dallas	314
Fort Worth (city) Tarrant	309

Central American
Top 10 Places Sorted by Percent

Place (place type) County	Percent
Killeen (city) Bell	34.09
Mission Bend (cdp) Fort Bend	32.90
El Paso (city) El Paso	30.74
San Antonio (city) Bexar	29.09
Corpus Christi (city) Nueces	29.02
Grand Prairie (city) Dallas	19.88
Denton (city) Denton	19.07
Farmers Branch (city) Dallas	18.67
Rosenberg (city) Fort Bend	18.29
Fort Worth (city) Tarrant	17.41

Chilean
Top 10 Places Sorted by Number

Place (place type) County	Number
Houston (city) Harris	163

Chilean
Top 10 Places Sorted by Percent

Place (place type) County	Percent
Houston (city) Harris	22.86

Colombian
Top 10 Places Sorted by Number

Place (place type) County	Number
Houston (city) Harris	1,790
San Antonio (city) Bexar	326
Dallas (city) Dallas	252
Austin (city) Travis	227
Mission Bend (cdp) Fort Bend	198

Colombian
Top 10 Places Sorted by Percent

Place (place type) County	Percent
San Antonio (city) Bexar	43.58
Mission Bend (cdp) Fort Bend	36.46
Houston (city) Harris	28.75
Austin (city) Travis	28.34
Dallas (city) Dallas	23.84

Costa Rican
Top 10 Places Sorted by Number

Place (place type) County	Number
Houston (city) Harris	150
Dallas (city) Dallas	69

Costa Rican
Top 10 Places Sorted by Percent

Place (place type) County	Percent
Houston (city) Harris	17.40
Dallas (city) Dallas	14.87

Cuban
Top 10 Places Sorted by Number

Place (place type) County	Number
Houston (city) Harris	1,958
San Antonio (city) Bexar	734
Dallas (city) Dallas	546
Fort Worth (city) Tarrant	273

Notes: Please refer to the User's Guide for an explanation of data; tables include places with populations > 9,999 and reflect only those areas that meet Summary File 4 population thresholds, therefore there may be less than 10 places listed

Place (place type) County	
Austin (city) Travis	179
El Paso (city) El Paso	168

Cuban
Top 10 Places Sorted by Percent

Place (place type) County	Percent
San Antonio (city) Bexar	37.74
Houston (city) Harris	36.01
El Paso (city) El Paso	34.36
Fort Worth (city) Tarrant	29.42
Dallas (city) Dallas	23.01
Austin (city) Travis	12.12

Dominican
Top 10 Places Sorted by Number

Place (place type) County	Number
Houston (city) Harris	208

Dominican
Top 10 Places Sorted by Percent

Place (place type) County	Percent
Houston (city) Harris	22.51

Ecuadorian
Top 10 Places Sorted by Number

Place (place type) County	Number
Houston (city) Harris	302

Ecuadorian
Top 10 Places Sorted by Percent

Place (place type) County	Percent
Houston (city) Harris	29.29

Guatelmalan
Top 10 Places Sorted by Number

Place (place type) County	Number
Houston (city) Harris	863
Dallas (city) Dallas	281
Garland (city) Dallas	162
San Antonio (city) Bexar	128
Fort Worth (city) Tarrant	117
Austin (city) Travis	74

Guatelmalan
Top 10 Places Sorted by Percent

Place (place type) County	Percent
San Antonio (city) Bexar	31.60
Fort Worth (city) Tarrant	27.02
Garland (city) Dallas	18.95
Houston (city) Harris	11.22
Dallas (city) Dallas	10.92
Austin (city) Travis	8.57

Honduran
Top 10 Places Sorted by Number

Place (place type) County	Number
Houston (city) Harris	1,254
Dallas (city) Dallas	306
San Antonio (city) Bexar	169
Austin (city) Travis	130
Irving (city) Dallas	60
Garland (city) Dallas	28

Honduran
Top 10 Places Sorted by Percent

Place (place type) County	Percent
San Antonio (city) Bexar	24.18
Houston (city) Harris	11.18
Austin (city) Travis	10.82

Place (place type) County	
Dallas (city) Dallas	10.39
Irving (city) Dallas	7.73
Garland (city) Dallas	6.76

Mexican
Top 10 Places Sorted by Number

Place (place type) County	Number
El Paso (city) El Paso	52,730
Houston (city) Harris	49,872
San Antonio (city) Bexar	30,566
Dallas (city) Dallas	29,081
Laredo (city) Webb	14,678
Brownsville (city) Cameron	13,397
Fort Worth (city) Tarrant	13,343
Austin (city) Travis	9,223
McAllen (city) Hidalgo	8,683
Pasadena (city) Harris	5,296

Mexican
Top 10 Places Sorted by Percent

Place (place type) County	Percent
Eagle Pass (city) Maverick	17.26
Mount Pleasant (city) Titus	17.24
Socorro (city) El Paso	17.11
Sulphur Springs (city) Hopkins	16.95
Mission Bend (cdp) Fort Bend	15.46
Bellaire (city) Harris	14.89
West Odessa (cdp) Ector	14.67
Lufkin (city) Angelina	14.36
El Paso (city) El Paso	14.30
Watauga (city) Tarrant	13.87

Nicaraguan
Top 10 Places Sorted by Number

Place (place type) County	Number
Houston (city) Harris	500
San Antonio (city) Bexar	184
Dallas (city) Dallas	105
Austin (city) Travis	64
Port Arthur (city) Jefferson	18

Nicaraguan
Top 10 Places Sorted by Percent

Place (place type) County	Percent
San Antonio (city) Bexar	37.47
Dallas (city) Dallas	24.08
Houston (city) Harris	20.92
Austin (city) Travis	16.89
Port Arthur (city) Jefferson	5.49

Panamanian
Top 10 Places Sorted by Number

Place (place type) County	Number
San Antonio (city) Bexar	297
Houston (city) Harris	282
Killeen (city) Bell	197
El Paso (city) El Paso	186

Panamanian
Top 10 Places Sorted by Percent

Place (place type) County	Percent
Killeen (city) Bell	40.12
El Paso (city) El Paso	39.57
Houston (city) Harris	35.79
San Antonio (city) Bexar	31.53

Paraguayan
Top 10 Places Sorted by Number

Place (place type) County	Number
No places met population threshold.	

Paraguayan
Top 10 Places Sorted by Percent

Place (place type) County	Percent
No places met population threshold.	

Peruvian
Top 10 Places Sorted by Number

Place (place type) County	Number
Houston (city) Harris	432
Dallas (city) Dallas	158
San Antonio (city) Bexar	138

Peruvian
Top 10 Places Sorted by Percent

Place (place type) County	Percent
San Antonio (city) Bexar	30.94
Houston (city) Harris	29.43
Dallas (city) Dallas	17.10

Puerto Rican
Top 10 Places Sorted by Number

Place (place type) County	Number
Houston (city) Harris	96
San Antonio (city) Bexar	54
McAllen (city) Hidalgo	40
Copperas Cove (city) Coryell	31
Arlington (city) Tarrant	19
El Paso (city) El Paso	17
Pasadena (city) Harris	11
San Angelo (city) Tom Green	11
Abilene (city) Taylor	9
Garland (city) Dallas	9

Puerto Rican
Top 10 Places Sorted by Percent

Place (place type) County	Percent
McAllen (city) Hidalgo	7.34
Copperas Cove (city) Coryell	3.69
San Angelo (city) Tom Green	3.18
Pasadena (city) Harris	2.42
Abilene (city) Taylor	2.41
Garland (city) Dallas	1.95
Houston (city) Harris	1.28
Arlington (city) Tarrant	1.02
Irving (city) Dallas	0.84
San Antonio (city) Bexar	0.64

Salvadoran
Top 10 Places Sorted by Number

Place (place type) County	Number
Houston (city) Harris	6,903
Dallas (city) Dallas	777
Irving (city) Dallas	492
Garland (city) Dallas	337
Farmers Branch (city) Dallas	299
Austin (city) Travis	218
Pasadena (city) Harris	206
San Antonio (city) Bexar	171
Carrollton (city) Denton	146
Fort Worth (city) Tarrant	93

Salvadoran
Top 10 Places Sorted by Percent

Place (place type) County	Percent
San Antonio (city) Bexar	22.53
Mission Bend (cdp) Fort Bend	22.47
Farmers Branch (city) Dallas	20.04
Pasadena (city) Harris	17.20
Galveston (city) Galveston	16.97
Houston (city) Harris	16.70
Garland (city) Dallas	16.48
Carrollton (city) Denton	14.07

Notes: Please refer to the User's Guide for an explanation of data; tables include places with populations > 9,999 and reflect only those areas that meet Summary File 4 population thresholds, therefore there may be less than 10 places listed

Place (place type) County	
Austin (city) Travis	13.81
Fort Worth (city) Tarrant	13.30

South American
Top 10 Places Sorted by Number

Place (place type) County	Number
Houston (city) Harris	3,813
San Antonio (city) Bexar	812
Dallas (city) Dallas	647
Austin (city) Travis	634
Plano (city) Collin	299
Arlington (city) Tarrant	277
Mission Bend (cdp) Fort Bend	270
Fort Worth (city) Tarrant	255
El Paso (city) El Paso	251
Carrollton (city) Denton	183

South American
Top 10 Places Sorted by Percent

Place (place type) County	Percent
El Paso (city) El Paso	38.56
Mission Bend (cdp) Fort Bend	35.39
San Antonio (city) Bexar	34.70
Plano (city) Collin	34.25
Arlington (city) Tarrant	34.07
Carrollton (city) Denton	31.50
Richardson (city) Dallas	30.20
Fort Worth (city) Tarrant	27.90
Houston (city) Harris	27.34
Garland (city) Dallas	27.09

Spaniard
Top 10 Places Sorted by Number

Place (place type) County	Number
Houston (city) Harris	86
San Antonio (city) Bexar	69
Dallas (city) Dallas	67

Spaniard
Top 10 Places Sorted by Percent

Place (place type) County	Percent
Dallas (city) Dallas	14.11
Houston (city) Harris	9.31
San Antonio (city) Bexar	8.41

Uruguayan
Top 10 Places Sorted by Number

Place (place type) County	Number
No places met population threshold.	

Uruguayan
Top 10 Places Sorted by Percent

Place (place type) County	Percent
No places met population threshold.	

Venezuelan
Top 10 Places Sorted by Number

Place (place type) County	Number
Houston (city) Harris	304
Austin (city) Travis	70

Venezuelan
Top 10 Places Sorted by Percent

Place (place type) County	Percent
Houston (city) Harris	18.16
Austin (city) Travis	13.92

Other Hispanic
Top 10 Places Sorted by Number

Place (place type) County	Number
Houston (city) Harris	8,727
San Antonio (city) Bexar	4,727
El Paso (city) El Paso	4,073
Dallas (city) Dallas	2,843
Laredo (city) Webb	1,696
Brownsville (city) Cameron	1,410
Austin (city) Travis	1,129
Fort Worth (city) Tarrant	1,077
Corpus Christi (city) Nueces	708
McAllen (city) Hidalgo	704

Other Hispanic
Top 10 Places Sorted by Percent

Place (place type) County	Percent
Friendswood (city) Galveston	20.26
Galena Park (city) Harris	17.32
Mission Bend (cdp) Fort Bend	15.15
Socorro (city) El Paso	12.80
Mount Pleasant (city) Titus	12.24
Port Arthur (city) Jefferson	12.09
Eagle Pass (city) Maverick	11.98
Lufkin (city) Angelina	11.82
Farmers Branch (city) Dallas	11.51
Missouri City (city) Fort Bend	11.11

Educational Attainment: High School Graduates

Total Populations 25 Years and Over Who are High School Graduates
Top 10 Places Sorted by Number

Place (place type) County	Number
Houston (city) Harris	845,709
San Antonio (city) Bexar	522,459
Dallas (city) Dallas	516,743
Austin (city) Travis	334,626
Fort Worth (city) Tarrant	236,466
El Paso (city) El Paso	229,053
Arlington (city) Tarrant	172,717
Plano (city) Collin	135,274
Corpus Christi (city) Nueces	129,104
Garland (city) Dallas	102,825

Total Populations 25 Years and Over Who are High School Graduates
Top 10 Places Sorted by Percent

Place (place type) County	Percent
Cinco Ranch (cdp) Fort Bend	98.53
University Park (city) Dallas	98.34
West University Place (city) Harris	97.96
Flower Mound (town) Denton	97.40
Pecan Grove (cdp) Fort Bend	97.38
Highland Village (city) Denton	97.30
Colleyville (city) Tarrant	96.70
Coppell (city) Dallas	96.64
Southlake (city) Tarrant	96.61
Corinth (city) Denton	96.01

Hispanics 25 Years and Over Who are High School Graduates
Top 10 Places Sorted by Number

Place (place type) County	Number
San Antonio (city) Bexar	227,910
El Paso (city) El Paso	144,190
Houston (city) Harris	143,095
Dallas (city) Dallas	67,751
Austin (city) Travis	56,400
Corpus Christi (city) Nueces	52,374
Laredo (city) Webb	46,160
Brownsville (city) Cameron	32,084
Fort Worth (city) Tarrant	28,451
McAllen (city) Hidalgo	26,795

Hispanics 25 Years and Over Who are High School Graduates
Top 10 Places Sorted by Percent

Place (place type) County	Percent
Highland Village (city) Denton	96.69
West University Place (city) Harris	95.62
Flower Mound (town) Denton	94.55
Hewitt (city) McLennan	91.84
Cinco Ranch (cdp) Fort Bend	91.49
Fort Hood (cdp) Coryell	91.09
Colleyville (city) Tarrant	90.46
The Woodlands (cdp) Montgomery	90.07
Copperas Cove (city) Coryell	90.06
Brushy Creek (cdp) Williamson	89.94

Argentinians 25 Years and Over Who are High School Graduates
Top 10 Places Sorted by Number

Place (place type) County	Number
Houston (city) Harris	737

Argentinians 25 Years and Over Who are High School Graduates
Top 10 Places Sorted by Percent

Place (place type) County	Percent
Houston (city) Harris	80.72

Bolivians 25 Years and Over Who are High School Graduates
Top 10 Places Sorted by Number

Place (place type) County	Number
Houston (city) Harris	419

Bolivians 25 Years and Over Who are High School Graduates
Top 10 Places Sorted by Percent

Place (place type) County	Percent
Houston (city) Harris	84.82

Central Americans 25 Years and Over Who are High School Graduates
Top 10 Places Sorted by Number

Place (place type) County	Number
Houston (city) Harris	10,485
Dallas (city) Dallas	2,606
San Antonio (city) Bexar	1,561
Austin (city) Travis	1,133
Irving (city) Dallas	1,065
Garland (city) Dallas	689
El Paso (city) El Paso	676
Arlington (city) Tarrant	447
Fort Worth (city) Tarrant	447
Plano (city) Collin	395

Central Americans 25 Years and Over Who are High School Graduates
Top 10 Places Sorted by Percent

Place (place type) County	Percent
Killeen (city) Bell	90.71
El Paso (city) El Paso	70.05
San Antonio (city) Bexar	66.12
Denton (city) Denton	63.11
Mission Bend (cdp) Fort Bend	61.56
Plano (city) Collin	52.88
Addison (town) Dallas	50.46
Corpus Christi (city) Nueces	46.76
Fort Worth (city) Tarrant	45.75
Richardson (city) Dallas	45.24

Notes: Please refer to the User's Guide for an explanation of data; tables include places with populations > 9,999 and reflect only those areas that meet Summary File 4 population thresholds, therefore there may be less than 10 places listed

Chileans 25 Years and Over Who are High School Graduates
Top 10 Places Sorted by Number

Place (place type) County	Number
Houston (city) Harris	432

Chileans 25 Years and Over Who are High School Graduates
Top 10 Places Sorted by Percent

Place (place type) County	Percent
Houston (city) Harris	89.07

Colombians 25 Years and Over Who are High School Graduates
Top 10 Places Sorted by Number

Place (place type) County	Number
Houston (city) Harris	3,054
Dallas (city) Dallas	527
San Antonio (city) Bexar	462
Austin (city) Travis	458
Mission Bend (cdp) Fort Bend	270

Colombians 25 Years and Over Who are High School Graduates
Top 10 Places Sorted by Percent

Place (place type) County	Percent
Austin (city) Travis	93.09
Mission Bend (cdp) Fort Bend	90.30
San Antonio (city) Bexar	90.23
Dallas (city) Dallas	75.94
Houston (city) Harris	70.32

Costa Ricans 25 Years and Over Who are High School Graduates
Top 10 Places Sorted by Number

Place (place type) County	Number
Houston (city) Harris	414
Dallas (city) Dallas	198

Costa Ricans 25 Years and Over Who are High School Graduates
Top 10 Places Sorted by Percent

Place (place type) County	Percent
Houston (city) Harris	72.00
Dallas (city) Dallas	69.72

Cubans 25 Years and Over Who are High School Graduates
Top 10 Places Sorted by Number

Place (place type) County	Number
Houston (city) Harris	3,162
Dallas (city) Dallas	1,155
San Antonio (city) Bexar	1,063
Austin (city) Travis	817
Fort Worth (city) Tarrant	445
El Paso (city) El Paso	289

Cubans 25 Years and Over Who are High School Graduates
Top 10 Places Sorted by Percent

Place (place type) County	Percent
El Paso (city) El Paso	86.01
Austin (city) Travis	80.41
San Antonio (city) Bexar	77.59
Houston (city) Harris	75.50
Fort Worth (city) Tarrant	74.79
Dallas (city) Dallas	60.50

Dominicans 25 Years and Over Who are High School Graduates
Top 10 Places Sorted by Number

Place (place type) County	Number
Houston (city) Harris	427

Dominicans 25 Years and Over Who are High School Graduates
Top 10 Places Sorted by Percent

Place (place type) County	Percent
Houston (city) Harris	70.00

Ecuadorians 25 Years and Over Who are High School Graduates
Top 10 Places Sorted by Number

Place (place type) County	Number
Houston (city) Harris	447

Ecuadorians 25 Years and Over Who are High School Graduates
Top 10 Places Sorted by Percent

Place (place type) County	Percent
Houston (city) Harris	67.93

Guatelmalans 25 Years and Over Who are High School Graduates
Top 10 Places Sorted by Number

Place (place type) County	Number
Houston (city) Harris	1,391
Dallas (city) Dallas	618
Austin (city) Travis	226
Garland (city) Dallas	184
San Antonio (city) Bexar	167
Fort Worth (city) Tarrant	149

Guatelmalans 25 Years and Over Who are High School Graduates
Top 10 Places Sorted by Percent

Place (place type) County	Percent
San Antonio (city) Bexar	57.79
Fort Worth (city) Tarrant	52.65
Austin (city) Travis	47.58
Dallas (city) Dallas	42.74
Garland (city) Dallas	36.65
Houston (city) Harris	31.75

Hondurans 25 Years and Over Who are High School Graduates
Top 10 Places Sorted by Number

Place (place type) County	Number
Houston (city) Harris	1,644
Dallas (city) Dallas	538
Austin (city) Travis	207
San Antonio (city) Bexar	175
Irving (city) Dallas	174
Garland (city) Dallas	72

Hondurans 25 Years and Over Who are High School Graduates
Top 10 Places Sorted by Percent

Place (place type) County	Percent
San Antonio (city) Bexar	48.34
Irving (city) Dallas	38.07
Dallas (city) Dallas	32.55
Austin (city) Travis	31.99
Garland (city) Dallas	29.39
Houston (city) Harris	25.22

Mexicans 25 Years and Over Who are High School Graduates
Top 10 Places Sorted by Number

Place (place type) County	Number
San Antonio (city) Bexar	164,576
El Paso (city) El Paso	121,241
Houston (city) Harris	98,102
Dallas (city) Dallas	52,585
Austin (city) Travis	41,752
Laredo (city) Webb	37,803
Corpus Christi (city) Nueces	35,632
Brownsville (city) Cameron	26,050
McAllen (city) Hidalgo	21,732
Fort Worth (city) Tarrant	21,514

Mexicans 25 Years and Over Who are High School Graduates
Top 10 Places Sorted by Percent

Place (place type) County	Percent
University Park (city) Dallas	100.00
Flower Mound (town) Denton	94.67
West University Place (city) Harris	94.14
Hewitt (city) McLennan	91.43
Copperas Cove (city) Coryell	90.11
Coppell (city) Dallas	89.60
Brushy Creek (cdp) Williamson	89.41
The Woodlands (cdp) Montgomery	89.05
Fort Hood (cdp) Coryell	87.96
Colleyville (city) Tarrant	87.83

Nicaraguans 25 Years and Over Who are High School Graduates
Top 10 Places Sorted by Number

Place (place type) County	Number
Houston (city) Harris	727
San Antonio (city) Bexar	223
Dallas (city) Dallas	156
Austin (city) Travis	117
Port Arthur (city) Jefferson	31

Nicaraguans 25 Years and Over Who are High School Graduates
Top 10 Places Sorted by Percent

Place (place type) County	Percent
San Antonio (city) Bexar	72.40
Austin (city) Travis	63.59
Dallas (city) Dallas	56.93
Houston (city) Harris	51.63
Port Arthur (city) Jefferson	20.13

Panamanians 25 Years and Over Who are High School Graduates
Top 10 Places Sorted by Number

Place (place type) County	Number
San Antonio (city) Bexar	551
Houston (city) Harris	471
Killeen (city) Bell	291
El Paso (city) El Paso	231

Panamanians 25 Years and Over Who are High School Graduates
Top 10 Places Sorted by Percent

Place (place type) County	Percent
Houston (city) Harris	94.01
Killeen (city) Bell	90.37
San Antonio (city) Bexar	83.87
El Paso (city) El Paso	73.10

Notes: Please refer to the User's Guide for an explanation of data; tables include places with populations > 9,999 and reflect only those areas that meet Summary File 4 population thresholds, therefore there may be less than 10 places listed

Paraguayans 25 Years and Over Who are High School Graduates
Top 10 Places Sorted by Number

Place (place type) County	Number
No places met population threshold.	

Paraguayans 25 Years and Over Who are High School Graduates
Top 10 Places Sorted by Percent

Place (place type) County	Percent
No places met population threshold.	

Peruvians 25 Years and Over Who are High School Graduates
Top 10 Places Sorted by Number

Place (place type) County	Number
Houston (city) Harris	890
Dallas (city) Dallas	537
San Antonio (city) Bexar	238

Peruvians 25 Years and Over Who are High School Graduates
Top 10 Places Sorted by Percent

Place (place type) County	Percent
San Antonio (city) Bexar	91.89
Dallas (city) Dallas	87.60
Houston (city) Harris	85.00

Puerto Ricans 25 Years and Over Who are High School Graduates
Top 10 Places Sorted by Number

Place (place type) County	Number
San Antonio (city) Bexar	4,376
Houston (city) Harris	3,267
El Paso (city) El Paso	2,184
Killeen (city) Bell	1,987
Austin (city) Travis	1,291
Dallas (city) Dallas	1,216
Fort Worth (city) Tarrant	956
Arlington (city) Tarrant	943
Plano (city) Collin	549
Corpus Christi (city) Nueces	513

Puerto Ricans 25 Years and Over Who are High School Graduates
Top 10 Places Sorted by Percent

Place (place type) County	Percent
Fort Hood (cdp) Coryell	97.03
Plano (city) Collin	92.74
Copperas Cove (city) Coryell	92.16
Abilene (city) Taylor	91.67
Carrollton (city) Denton	91.60
Austin (city) Travis	91.11
Arlington (city) Tarrant	90.94
Euless (city) Tarrant	90.03
El Paso (city) El Paso	89.47
Irving (city) Dallas	88.65

Salvadorans 25 Years and Over Who are High School Graduates
Top 10 Places Sorted by Number

Place (place type) County	Number
Houston (city) Harris	5,393
Dallas (city) Dallas	820
Irving (city) Dallas	698
Garland (city) Dallas	300
San Antonio (city) Bexar	259
Austin (city) Travis	251
Farmers Branch (city) Dallas	207
Pasadena (city) Harris	184
Carrollton (city) Denton	141

Fort Worth (city) Tarrant	105

Salvadorans 25 Years and Over Who are High School Graduates
Top 10 Places Sorted by Percent

Place (place type) County	Percent
San Antonio (city) Bexar	54.07
Mission Bend (cdp) Fort Bend	38.40
Fort Worth (city) Tarrant	32.51
Austin (city) Travis	32.18
Pasadena (city) Harris	30.36
Carrollton (city) Denton	28.09
Farmers Branch (city) Dallas	26.57
Plano (city) Collin	25.90
Arlington (city) Tarrant	25.82
Garland (city) Dallas	25.27

South Americans 25 Years and Over Who are High School Graduates
Top 10 Places Sorted by Number

Place (place type) County	Number
Houston (city) Harris	7,267
Dallas (city) Dallas	1,793
Austin (city) Travis	1,641
San Antonio (city) Bexar	1,374
Arlington (city) Tarrant	564
Plano (city) Collin	548
Irving (city) Dallas	500
Fort Worth (city) Tarrant	499
El Paso (city) El Paso	413
Mission Bend (cdp) Fort Bend	383

South Americans 25 Years and Over Who are High School Graduates
Top 10 Places Sorted by Percent

Place (place type) County	Percent
Sugar Land (city) Fort Bend	97.59
College Station (city) Brazos	97.19
Carrollton (city) Denton	95.67
Plano (city) Collin	93.84
Austin (city) Travis	92.45
Arlington (city) Tarrant	91.11
Richardson (city) Dallas	90.66
San Antonio (city) Bexar	90.22
Corpus Christi (city) Nueces	90.00
El Paso (city) El Paso	89.39

Spaniards 25 Years and Over Who are High School Graduates
Top 10 Places Sorted by Number

Place (place type) County	Number
Houston (city) Harris	512
San Antonio (city) Bexar	477
Dallas (city) Dallas	179

Spaniards 25 Years and Over Who are High School Graduates
Top 10 Places Sorted by Percent

Place (place type) County	Percent
San Antonio (city) Bexar	81.54
Houston (city) Harris	77.11
Dallas (city) Dallas	61.72

Uruguayans 25 Years and Over Who are High School Graduates
Top 10 Places Sorted by Number

Place (place type) County	Number
No places met population threshold.	

Uruguayans 25 Years and Over Who are High School Graduates
Top 10 Places Sorted by Percent

Place (place type) County	Percent
No places met population threshold.	

Venezuelans 25 Years and Over Who are High School Graduates
Top 10 Places Sorted by Number

Place (place type) County	Number
Houston (city) Harris	945
Austin (city) Travis	324

Venezuelans 25 Years and Over Who are High School Graduates
Top 10 Places Sorted by Percent

Place (place type) County	Percent
Austin (city) Travis	94.74
Houston (city) Harris	91.93

Other Hispanics 25 Years and Over Who are High School Graduates
Top 10 Places Sorted by Number

Place (place type) County	Number
San Antonio (city) Bexar	54,410
Houston (city) Harris	19,873
El Paso (city) El Paso	19,199
Corpus Christi (city) Nueces	15,505
Austin (city) Travis	9,427
Dallas (city) Dallas	8,042
Laredo (city) Webb	7,956
Lubbock (city) Lubbock	5,812
Brownsville (city) Cameron	5,644
Fort Worth (city) Tarrant	4,442

Other Hispanics 25 Years and Over Who are High School Graduates
Top 10 Places Sorted by Percent

Place (place type) County	Percent
Flower Mound (town) Denton	96.90
Pflugerville (city) Travis	91.67
Fort Hood (cdp) Coryell	90.05
Cedar Park (city) Williamson	89.44
Allen (city) Collin	89.30
DeSoto (city) Dallas	88.24
Hurst (city) Tarrant	88.24
College Station (city) Brazos	87.53
Euless (city) Tarrant	87.35
Converse (city) Bexar	86.53

Educational Attainment: Four-Year College Graduates

Total Populations 25 Years and Over Who are Four-Year College Graduates
Top 10 Places Sorted by Number

Place (place type) County	Number
Houston (city) Harris	324,039
Dallas (city) Dallas	203,004
Austin (city) Travis	161,937
San Antonio (city) Bexar	150,680
Plano (city) Collin	76,706
Fort Worth (city) Tarrant	72,313
Arlington (city) Tarrant	61,837
El Paso (city) El Paso	61,217
Irving (city) Dallas	36,273
Corpus Christi (city) Nueces	33,446

Notes: Please refer to the User's Guide for an explanation of data; tables include places with populations > 9,999 and reflect only those areas that meet Summary File 4 population thresholds, therefore there may be less than 10 places listed

Total Populations 25 Years and Over Who are Four-Year College Graduates
Top 10 Places Sorted by Percent

Place (place type) County	Percent
University Park (city) Dallas	80.45
West University Place (city) Harris	79.40
Bellaire (city) Harris	66.60
Cinco Ranch (cdp) Fort Bend	65.92
Coppell (city) Dallas	62.59
Southlake (city) Tarrant	59.19
College Station (city) Brazos	58.10
Colleyville (city) Tarrant	56.56
New Territory (cdp) Fort Bend	56.13
The Woodlands (cdp) Montgomery	55.70

Hispanics 25 Years and Over Who are Four-Year College Graduates
Top 10 Places Sorted by Number

Place (place type) County	Number
San Antonio (city) Bexar	38,848
Houston (city) Harris	29,058
El Paso (city) El Paso	28,899
Austin (city) Travis	15,683
Dallas (city) Dallas	13,211
Laredo (city) Webb	11,356
Corpus Christi (city) Nueces	8,343
McAllen (city) Hidalgo	8,246
Brownsville (city) Cameron	7,249
Fort Worth (city) Tarrant	5,076

Hispanics 25 Years and Over Who are Four-Year College Graduates
Top 10 Places Sorted by Percent

Place (place type) County	Percent
West University Place (city) Harris	71.89
University Park (city) Dallas	57.30
Highland Village (city) Denton	56.61
Colleyville (city) Tarrant	54.12
Cinco Ranch (cdp) Fort Bend	52.13
Southlake (city) Tarrant	49.50
Coppell (city) Dallas	47.72
Flower Mound (town) Denton	46.70
College Station (city) Brazos	43.91
The Woodlands (cdp) Montgomery	40.05

Argentinians 25 Years and Over Who are Four-Year College Graduates
Top 10 Places Sorted by Number

Place (place type) County	Number
Houston (city) Harris	406

Argentinians 25 Years and Over Who are Four-Year College Graduates
Top 10 Places Sorted by Percent

Place (place type) County	Percent
Houston (city) Harris	44.47

Bolivians 25 Years and Over Who are Four-Year College Graduates
Top 10 Places Sorted by Number

Place (place type) County	Number
Houston (city) Harris	189

Bolivians 25 Years and Over Who are Four-Year College Graduates
Top 10 Places Sorted by Percent

Place (place type) County	Percent
Houston (city) Harris	38.26

Central Americans 25 Years and Over Who are Four-Year College Graduates
Top 10 Places Sorted by Number

Place (place type) County	Number
Houston (city) Harris	1,845
Dallas (city) Dallas	532
San Antonio (city) Bexar	509
Austin (city) Travis	404
El Paso (city) El Paso	221
Irving (city) Dallas	219
Garland (city) Dallas	198
Fort Worth (city) Tarrant	114
Plano (city) Collin	100
Arlington (city) Tarrant	94

Central Americans 25 Years and Over Who are Four-Year College Graduates
Top 10 Places Sorted by Percent

Place (place type) County	Percent
El Paso (city) El Paso	22.90
San Antonio (city) Bexar	21.56
Austin (city) Travis	15.99
Galveston (city) Galveston	15.18
Corpus Christi (city) Nueces	15.11
Plano (city) Collin	13.39
Killeen (city) Bell	12.62
Fort Worth (city) Tarrant	11.67
Brownsville (city) Cameron	9.76
Arlington (city) Tarrant	9.44

Chileans 25 Years and Over Who are Four-Year College Graduates
Top 10 Places Sorted by Number

Place (place type) County	Number
Houston (city) Harris	155

Chileans 25 Years and Over Who are Four-Year College Graduates
Top 10 Places Sorted by Percent

Place (place type) County	Percent
Houston (city) Harris	31.96

Colombians 25 Years and Over Who are Four-Year College Graduates
Top 10 Places Sorted by Number

Place (place type) County	Number
Houston (city) Harris	1,126
Austin (city) Travis	284
Dallas (city) Dallas	230
San Antonio (city) Bexar	189
Mission Bend (cdp) Fort Bend	57

Colombians 25 Years and Over Who are Four-Year College Graduates
Top 10 Places Sorted by Percent

Place (place type) County	Percent
Austin (city) Travis	57.72
San Antonio (city) Bexar	36.91
Dallas (city) Dallas	33.14
Houston (city) Harris	25.93
Mission Bend (cdp) Fort Bend	19.06

Costa Ricans 25 Years and Over Who are Four-Year College Graduates
Top 10 Places Sorted by Number

Place (place type) County	Number
Houston (city) Harris	144
Dallas (city) Dallas	39

Costa Ricans 25 Years and Over Who are Four-Year College Graduates
Top 10 Places Sorted by Percent

Place (place type) County	Percent
Houston (city) Harris	25.04
Dallas (city) Dallas	13.73

Cubans 25 Years and Over Who are Four-Year College Graduates
Top 10 Places Sorted by Number

Place (place type) County	Number
Houston (city) Harris	1,623
Dallas (city) Dallas	501
San Antonio (city) Bexar	430
Austin (city) Travis	374
El Paso (city) El Paso	188
Fort Worth (city) Tarrant	154

Cubans 25 Years and Over Who are Four-Year College Graduates
Top 10 Places Sorted by Percent

Place (place type) County	Percent
El Paso (city) El Paso	55.95
Houston (city) Harris	38.75
Austin (city) Travis	36.81
San Antonio (city) Bexar	31.39
Dallas (city) Dallas	26.24
Fort Worth (city) Tarrant	25.88

Dominicans 25 Years and Over Who are Four-Year College Graduates
Top 10 Places Sorted by Number

Place (place type) County	Number
Houston (city) Harris	121

Dominicans 25 Years and Over Who are Four-Year College Graduates
Top 10 Places Sorted by Percent

Place (place type) County	Percent
Houston (city) Harris	19.84

Ecuadorians 25 Years and Over Who are Four-Year College Graduates
Top 10 Places Sorted by Number

Place (place type) County	Number
Houston (city) Harris	106

Ecuadorians 25 Years and Over Who are Four-Year College Graduates
Top 10 Places Sorted by Percent

Place (place type) County	Percent
Houston (city) Harris	16.11

Guatelmalans 25 Years and Over Who are Four-Year College Graduates
Top 10 Places Sorted by Number

Place (place type) County	Number
Houston (city) Harris	238
Dallas (city) Dallas	86
Austin (city) Travis	85
Fort Worth (city) Tarrant	53
San Antonio (city) Bexar	40
Garland (city) Dallas	16

Guatelmalans 25 Years and Over Who are Four-Year College Graduates
Top 10 Places Sorted by Percent

Place (place type) County	Percent
Fort Worth (city) Tarrant	18.73

Notes: Please refer to the User's Guide for an explanation of data; tables include places with populations > 9,999 and reflect only those areas that meet Summary File 4 population thresholds, therefore there may be less than 10 places listed

Place (place type) County	
Austin (city) Travis	17.89
San Antonio (city) Bexar	13.84
Dallas (city) Dallas	5.95
Houston (city) Harris	5.43
Garland (city) Dallas	3.19

Hondurans 25 Years and Over Who are Four-Year College Graduates
Top 10 Places Sorted by Number

Place (place type) County	Number
Houston (city) Harris	260
Dallas (city) Dallas	109
San Antonio (city) Bexar	48
Irving (city) Dallas	29
Garland (city) Dallas	25
Austin (city) Travis	21

Hondurans 25 Years and Over Who are Four-Year College Graduates
Top 10 Places Sorted by Percent

Place (place type) County	Percent
San Antonio (city) Bexar	13.26
Garland (city) Dallas	10.20
Dallas (city) Dallas	6.59
Irving (city) Dallas	6.35
Houston (city) Harris	3.99
Austin (city) Travis	3.25

Mexicans 25 Years and Over Who are Four-Year College Graduates
Top 10 Places Sorted by Number

Place (place type) County	Number
San Antonio (city) Bexar	29,664
El Paso (city) El Paso	24,670
Houston (city) Harris	17,295
Austin (city) Travis	11,132
Laredo (city) Webb	9,832
Dallas (city) Dallas	9,250
McAllen (city) Hidalgo	6,847
Corpus Christi (city) Nueces	6,215
Brownsville (city) Cameron	6,106
Fort Worth (city) Tarrant	3,309

Mexicans 25 Years and Over Who are Four-Year College Graduates
Top 10 Places Sorted by Percent

Place (place type) County	Percent
West University Place (city) Harris	66.53
University Park (city) Dallas	54.42
Flower Mound (town) Denton	48.44
Colleyville (city) Tarrant	46.56
Coppell (city) Dallas	45.56
Brushy Creek (cdp) Williamson	40.45
Cedar Park (city) Williamson	38.86
Southlake (city) Tarrant	37.56
Wells Branch (cdp) Travis	36.24
The Woodlands (cdp) Montgomery	35.53

Nicaraguans 25 Years and Over Who are Four-Year College Graduates
Top 10 Places Sorted by Number

Place (place type) County	Number
Houston (city) Harris	223
San Antonio (city) Bexar	94
Dallas (city) Dallas	90
Austin (city) Travis	20
Port Arthur (city) Jefferson	0

Nicaraguans 25 Years and Over Who are Four-Year College Graduates
Top 10 Places Sorted by Percent

Place (place type) County	Percent
Dallas (city) Dallas	32.85
San Antonio (city) Bexar	30.52
Houston (city) Harris	15.84
Austin (city) Travis	10.87
Port Arthur (city) Jefferson	0.00

Panamanians 25 Years and Over Who are Four-Year College Graduates
Top 10 Places Sorted by Number

Place (place type) County	Number
Houston (city) Harris	244
San Antonio (city) Bexar	180
El Paso (city) El Paso	77
Killeen (city) Bell	53

Panamanians 25 Years and Over Who are Four-Year College Graduates
Top 10 Places Sorted by Percent

Place (place type) County	Percent
Houston (city) Harris	48.70
San Antonio (city) Bexar	27.40
El Paso (city) El Paso	24.37
Killeen (city) Bell	16.46

Paraguayans 25 Years and Over Who are Four-Year College Graduates
Top 10 Places Sorted by Number

Place (place type) County	Number
No places met population threshold.	

Paraguayans 25 Years and Over Who are Four-Year College Graduates
Top 10 Places Sorted by Percent

Place (place type) County	Percent
No places met population threshold.	

Peruvians 25 Years and Over Who are Four-Year College Graduates
Top 10 Places Sorted by Number

Place (place type) County	Number
Houston (city) Harris	394
Dallas (city) Dallas	151
San Antonio (city) Bexar	71

Peruvians 25 Years and Over Who are Four-Year College Graduates
Top 10 Places Sorted by Percent

Place (place type) County	Percent
Houston (city) Harris	37.63
San Antonio (city) Bexar	27.41
Dallas (city) Dallas	24.63

Puerto Ricans 25 Years and Over Who are Four-Year College Graduates
Top 10 Places Sorted by Number

Place (place type) County	Number
San Antonio (city) Bexar	1,448
Houston (city) Harris	1,253
El Paso (city) El Paso	755
Austin (city) Travis	543
Dallas (city) Dallas	435
Fort Worth (city) Tarrant	384
Killeen (city) Bell	374
Arlington (city) Tarrant	344
Plano (city) Collin	270
Corpus Christi (city) Nueces	200

Puerto Ricans 25 Years and Over Who are Four-Year College Graduates
Top 10 Places Sorted by Percent

Place (place type) County	Percent
Plano (city) Collin	45.61
Austin (city) Travis	38.32
McAllen (city) Hidalgo	37.84
Carrollton (city) Denton	36.80
Irving (city) Dallas	35.99
Fort Worth (city) Tarrant	35.16
Corpus Christi (city) Nueces	34.19
Arlington (city) Tarrant	33.17
El Paso (city) El Paso	30.93
Temple (city) Bell	30.68

Salvadorans 25 Years and Over Who are Four-Year College Graduates
Top 10 Places Sorted by Number

Place (place type) County	Number
Houston (city) Harris	620
Irving (city) Dallas	130
Dallas (city) Dallas	111
Garland (city) Dallas	107
Austin (city) Travis	85
San Antonio (city) Bexar	67
Pasadena (city) Harris	36
Carrollton (city) Denton	23
Farmers Branch (city) Dallas	15
Fort Worth (city) Tarrant	15

Salvadorans 25 Years and Over Who are Four-Year College Graduates
Top 10 Places Sorted by Percent

Place (place type) County	Percent
San Antonio (city) Bexar	13.99
Austin (city) Travis	10.90
Garland (city) Dallas	9.01
Pasadena (city) Harris	5.94
Fort Worth (city) Tarrant	4.64
Carrollton (city) Denton	4.58
Irving (city) Dallas	4.26
Mission Bend (cdp) Fort Bend	4.00
Grand Prairie (city) Dallas	3.66
Galveston (city) Galveston	2.99

South Americans 25 Years and Over Who are Four-Year College Graduates
Top 10 Places Sorted by Number

Place (place type) County	Number
Houston (city) Harris	3,130
Austin (city) Travis	1,051
Dallas (city) Dallas	682
San Antonio (city) Bexar	541
Plano (city) Collin	273
Arlington (city) Tarrant	266
Fort Worth (city) Tarrant	264
Irving (city) Dallas	251
College Station (city) Brazos	229
Sugar Land (city) Fort Bend	206

South Americans 25 Years and Over Who are Four-Year College Graduates
Top 10 Places Sorted by Percent

Place (place type) County	Percent
College Station (city) Brazos	80.35
Sugar Land (city) Fort Bend	70.79
Austin (city) Travis	59.21
The Woodlands (cdp) Montgomery	55.87
Corpus Christi (city) Nueces	50.91
Plano (city) Collin	46.75
Fort Worth (city) Tarrant	43.00
Arlington (city) Tarrant	42.97
El Paso (city) El Paso	42.21

Notes: Please refer to the User's Guide for an explanation of data; tables include places with populations > 9,999 and reflect only those areas that meet Summary File 4 population thresholds, therefore there may be less than 10 places listed

Place (place type) County	
Irving (city) Dallas	39.59

Spaniards 25 Years and Over Who are Four-Year College Graduates
Top 10 Places Sorted by Number

Place (place type) County	Number
Houston (city) Harris	249
San Antonio (city) Bexar	137
Dallas (city) Dallas	97

Spaniards 25 Years and Over Who are Four-Year College Graduates
Top 10 Places Sorted by Percent

Place (place type) County	Percent
Houston (city) Harris	37.50
Dallas (city) Dallas	33.45
San Antonio (city) Bexar	23.42

Uruguayans 25 Years and Over Who are Four-Year College Graduates
Top 10 Places Sorted by Number

Place (place type) County	Number
No places met population threshold.	

Uruguayans 25 Years and Over Who are Four-Year College Graduates
Top 10 Places Sorted by Percent

Place (place type) County	Percent
No places met population threshold.	

Venezuelans 25 Years and Over Who are Four-Year College Graduates
Top 10 Places Sorted by Number

Place (place type) County	Number
Houston (city) Harris	634
Austin (city) Travis	168

Venezuelans 25 Years and Over Who are Four-Year College Graduates
Top 10 Places Sorted by Percent

Place (place type) County	Percent
Houston (city) Harris	61.67
Austin (city) Travis	49.12

Other Hispanics 25 Years and Over Who are Four-Year College Graduates
Top 10 Places Sorted by Number

Place (place type) County	Number
San Antonio (city) Bexar	6,112
Houston (city) Harris	3,542
El Paso (city) El Paso	2,847
Austin (city) Travis	2,034
Dallas (city) Dallas	1,606
Corpus Christi (city) Nueces	1,591
Laredo (city) Webb	1,361
Brownsville (city) Cameron	958
McAllen (city) Hidalgo	916
Fort Worth (city) Tarrant	813

Other Hispanics 25 Years and Over Who are Four-Year College Graduates
Top 10 Places Sorted by Percent

Place (place type) County	Percent
Flower Mound (town) Denton	46.75
College Station (city) Brazos	40.42
Sugar Land (city) Fort Bend	36.58
Nacogdoches (city) Nacogdoches	32.77
Pflugerville (city) Travis	29.43
Plano (city) Collin	28.82
Allen (city) Collin	28.07

Place (place type) County	
Frisco (city) Collin	27.00
Addison (town) Dallas	25.56
Canyon (city) Randall	25.18

Median Household Income

Total Population
Top 10 Places Sorted by Number

Place (place type) County	Dollars
Southlake (city) Tarrant	131,549
West University Place (city) Harris	130,721
Colleyville (city) Tarrant	117,419
Cinco Ranch (cdp) Fort Bend	111,517
Highland Village (city) Denton	102,141
Coppell (city) Dallas	96,935
Flower Mound (town) Denton	95,416
New Territory (cdp) Fort Bend	93,972
University Park (city) Dallas	92,778
Bellaire (city) Harris	89,775

Hispanic
Top 10 Places Sorted by Number

Place (place type) County	Dollars
Highland Village (city) Denton	119,249
Colleyville (city) Tarrant	111,374
Southlake (city) Tarrant	109,108
West University Place (city) Harris	106,292
Cinco Ranch (cdp) Fort Bend	91,215
Corinth (city) Denton	86,383
Flower Mound (town) Denton	86,185
Keller (city) Tarrant	81,059
New Territory (cdp) Fort Bend	76,512
Brushy Creek (cdp) Williamson	75,291

Argentinian
Top 10 Places Sorted by Number

Place (place type) County	Dollars
Houston (city) Harris	36,154

Bolivian
Top 10 Places Sorted by Number

Place (place type) County	Dollars
Houston (city) Harris	39,531

Central American
Top 10 Places Sorted by Number

Place (place type) County	Dollars
Farmers Branch (city) Dallas	53,833
Mission Bend (cdp) Fort Bend	50,714
Carrollton (city) Denton	49,750
Plano (city) Collin	47,644
Grand Prairie (city) Dallas	42,891
Arlington (city) Tarrant	41,098
Lewisville (city) Denton	40,556
Garland (city) Dallas	37,321
Addison (town) Dallas	36,154
Austin (city) Travis	33,836

Chilean
Top 10 Places Sorted by Number

Place (place type) County	Dollars
Houston (city) Harris	43,438

Colombian
Top 10 Places Sorted by Number

Place (place type) County	Dollars
Mission Bend (cdp) Fort Bend	44,524
Dallas (city) Dallas	41,296
San Antonio (city) Bexar	41,042
Austin (city) Travis	27,321
Houston (city) Harris	26,694

Costa Rican
Top 10 Places Sorted by Number

Place (place type) County	Dollars
Houston (city) Harris	31,384
Dallas (city) Dallas	19,153

Cuban
Top 10 Places Sorted by Number

Place (place type) County	Dollars
El Paso (city) El Paso	51,761
San Antonio (city) Bexar	41,823
Fort Worth (city) Tarrant	37,554
Austin (city) Travis	35,256
Houston (city) Harris	33,689
Dallas (city) Dallas	28,490

Dominican
Top 10 Places Sorted by Number

Place (place type) County	Dollars
Houston (city) Harris	40,329

Ecuadorian
Top 10 Places Sorted by Number

Place (place type) County	Dollars
Houston (city) Harris	41,250

Guatelmalan
Top 10 Places Sorted by Number

Place (place type) County	Dollars
Garland (city) Dallas	42,125
Fort Worth (city) Tarrant	34,375
Dallas (city) Dallas	30,929
San Antonio (city) Bexar	30,903
Austin (city) Travis	30,197
Houston (city) Harris	29,193

Honduran
Top 10 Places Sorted by Number

Place (place type) County	Dollars
Austin (city) Travis	34,779
Garland (city) Dallas	30,313
Irving (city) Dallas	27,788
Dallas (city) Dallas	27,301
Houston (city) Harris	22,585
San Antonio (city) Bexar	22,333

Mexican
Top 10 Places Sorted by Number

Place (place type) County	Dollars
Colleyville (city) Tarrant	116,498
West University Place (city) Harris	92,694
Flower Mound (town) Denton	90,590
Southlake (city) Tarrant	88,544
Keller (city) Tarrant	85,000
New Territory (cdp) Fort Bend	77,101
Brushy Creek (cdp) Williamson	76,188
Coppell (city) Dallas	73,281
Cedar Park (city) Williamson	69,750
Bellaire (city) Harris	68,077

Nicaraguan
Top 10 Places Sorted by Number

Place (place type) County	Dollars
Dallas (city) Dallas	45,500
San Antonio (city) Bexar	42,143
Houston (city) Harris	36,101
Port Arthur (city) Jefferson	33,542
Austin (city) Travis	27,656

Notes: Please refer to the User's Guide for an explanation of data; tables include places with populations > 9,999 and reflect only those areas that meet Summary File 4 population thresholds, therefore there may be less than 10 places listed

Panamanian
Top 10 Places Sorted by Number

Place (place type) County	Dollars
San Antonio (city) Bexar	40,938
Houston (city) Harris	33,989
El Paso (city) El Paso	31,944
Killeen (city) Bell	25,083

Paraguayan
Top 10 Places Sorted by Number

Place (place type) County	Dollars
No places met population threshold.	

Peruvian
Top 10 Places Sorted by Number

Place (place type) County	Dollars
San Antonio (city) Bexar	54,375
Dallas (city) Dallas	38,854
Houston (city) Harris	36,060

Puerto Rican
Top 10 Places Sorted by Number

Place (place type) County	Dollars
Plano (city) Collin	76,262
Carrollton (city) Denton	57,375
Garland (city) Dallas	46,500
Euless (city) Tarrant	44,830
Arlington (city) Tarrant	44,013
Copperas Cove (city) Coryell	43,750
Mission Bend (cdp) Fort Bend	41,875
Fort Worth (city) Tarrant	39,821
Grand Prairie (city) Dallas	39,813
El Paso (city) El Paso	38,990

Salvadoran
Top 10 Places Sorted by Number

Place (place type) County	Dollars
Farmers Branch (city) Dallas	55,729
Carrollton (city) Denton	44,861
Arlington (city) Tarrant	42,083
Mission Bend (cdp) Fort Bend	40,714
Plano (city) Collin	37,016
San Antonio (city) Bexar	36,458
Austin (city) Travis	35,577
Garland (city) Dallas	33,971
Irving (city) Dallas	32,977
Dallas (city) Dallas	32,366

South American
Top 10 Places Sorted by Number

Place (place type) County	Dollars
The Woodlands (cdp) Montgomery	93,518
Corpus Christi (city) Nueces	71,250
Sugar Land (city) Fort Bend	64,792
Carrollton (city) Denton	57,708
Plano (city) Collin	47,292
Arlington (city) Tarrant	45,179
Mission Bend (cdp) Fort Bend	43,750
Richardson (city) Dallas	39,773
Irving (city) Dallas	37,344
Fort Worth (city) Tarrant	36,910

Spaniard
Top 10 Places Sorted by Number

Place (place type) County	Dollars
Dallas (city) Dallas	46,500
San Antonio (city) Bexar	33,233
Houston (city) Harris	27,670

Uruguayan
Top 10 Places Sorted by Number

Place (place type) County	Dollars
No places met population threshold.	

Venezuelan
Top 10 Places Sorted by Number

Place (place type) County	Dollars
Austin (city) Travis	34,107
Houston (city) Harris	34,038

Other Hispanic
Top 10 Places Sorted by Number

Place (place type) County	Dollars
Pflugerville (city) Travis	66,696
Flower Mound (town) Denton	66,071
Allen (city) Collin	62,500
Rowlett (city) Dallas	62,500
League City (city) Galveston	61,667
Atascocita (cdp) Harris	61,538
Sugar Land (city) Fort Bend	61,442
Cedar Park (city) Williamson	60,714
Friendswood (city) Galveston	60,069
Frisco (city) Collin	56,304

Per Capita Income

Total Population
Top 10 Places Sorted by Number

Place (place type) County	Dollars
West University Place (city) Harris	69,674
University Park (city) Dallas	63,414
Colleyville (city) Tarrant	50,418
Southlake (city) Tarrant	47,597
Bellaire (city) Harris	46,674
Highland Village (city) Denton	40,613
Coppell (city) Dallas	40,219
Addison (town) Dallas	38,606
Cinco Ranch (cdp) Fort Bend	37,747
The Woodlands (cdp) Montgomery	37,724

Hispanic
Top 10 Places Sorted by Number

Place (place type) County	Dollars
Colleyville (city) Tarrant	51,108
West University Place (city) Harris	44,505
Southlake (city) Tarrant	35,070
Highland Village (city) Denton	33,844
Cinco Ranch (cdp) Fort Bend	33,578
University Park (city) Dallas	33,114
Bellaire (city) Harris	30,927
The Woodlands (cdp) Montgomery	28,873
Flower Mound (town) Denton	26,992
Sugar Land (city) Fort Bend	23,931

Argentinian
Top 10 Places Sorted by Number

Place (place type) County	Dollars
Houston (city) Harris	24,778

Bolivian
Top 10 Places Sorted by Number

Place (place type) County	Dollars
Houston (city) Harris	16,969

Central American
Top 10 Places Sorted by Number

Place (place type) County	Dollars
Plano (city) Collin	19,596
Mission Bend (cdp) Fort Bend	17,203

Corpus Christi (city) Nueces	16,003
Arlington (city) Tarrant	15,851
Denton (city) Denton	15,222
Irving (city) Dallas	14,947
Lewisville (city) Denton	14,583
San Antonio (city) Bexar	14,270
El Paso (city) El Paso	14,143
Carrollton (city) Denton	13,825

Chilean
Top 10 Places Sorted by Number

Place (place type) County	Dollars
Houston (city) Harris	28,057

Colombian
Top 10 Places Sorted by Number

Place (place type) County	Dollars
San Antonio (city) Bexar	29,016
Austin (city) Travis	21,685
Houston (city) Harris	16,326
Mission Bend (cdp) Fort Bend	15,685
Dallas (city) Dallas	15,628

Costa Rican
Top 10 Places Sorted by Number

Place (place type) County	Dollars
Houston (city) Harris	14,336
Dallas (city) Dallas	13,510

Cuban
Top 10 Places Sorted by Number

Place (place type) County	Dollars
El Paso (city) El Paso	27,524
Houston (city) Harris	23,465
San Antonio (city) Bexar	23,148
Dallas (city) Dallas	20,052
Austin (city) Travis	17,887
Fort Worth (city) Tarrant	17,521

Dominican
Top 10 Places Sorted by Number

Place (place type) County	Dollars
Houston (city) Harris	16,109

Ecuadorian
Top 10 Places Sorted by Number

Place (place type) County	Dollars
Houston (city) Harris	14,051

Guatelmalan
Top 10 Places Sorted by Number

Place (place type) County	Dollars
Fort Worth (city) Tarrant	19,907
San Antonio (city) Bexar	13,422
Dallas (city) Dallas	11,189
Austin (city) Travis	10,863
Houston (city) Harris	10,829
Garland (city) Dallas	10,731

Honduran
Top 10 Places Sorted by Number

Place (place type) County	Dollars
Irving (city) Dallas	27,730
Austin (city) Travis	10,076
Dallas (city) Dallas	9,560
Houston (city) Harris	8,690
San Antonio (city) Bexar	8,095
Garland (city) Dallas	7,738

Notes: Please refer to the User's Guide for an explanation of data; tables include places with populations > 9,999 and reflect only those areas that meet Summary File 4 population thresholds, therefore there may be less than 10 places listed

Mexican
Top 10 Places Sorted by Number

Place (place type) County	Dollars
Colleyville (city) Tarrant	49,650
West University Place (city) Harris	39,670
Bellaire (city) Harris	31,057
The Woodlands (cdp) Montgomery	28,895
Flower Mound (town) Denton	26,850
Southlake (city) Tarrant	26,508
Pflugerville (city) Travis	25,308
Coppell (city) Dallas	24,831
Wells Branch (cdp) Travis	23,632
Allen (city) Collin	21,953

Nicaraguan
Top 10 Places Sorted by Number

Place (place type) County	Dollars
Dallas (city) Dallas	26,531
San Antonio (city) Bexar	23,256
Houston (city) Harris	13,975
Port Arthur (city) Jefferson	7,909
Austin (city) Travis	7,601

Panamanian
Top 10 Places Sorted by Number

Place (place type) County	Dollars
Houston (city) Harris	27,102
San Antonio (city) Bexar	15,601
El Paso (city) El Paso	12,979
Killeen (city) Bell	9,190

Paraguayan
Top 10 Places Sorted by Number

Place (place type) County	Dollars
No places met population threshold.	

Peruvian
Top 10 Places Sorted by Number

Place (place type) County	Dollars
San Antonio (city) Bexar	22,216
Houston (city) Harris	17,925
Dallas (city) Dallas	17,128

Puerto Rican
Top 10 Places Sorted by Number

Place (place type) County	Dollars
Plano (city) Collin	50,170
Temple (city) Bell	43,876
Carrollton (city) Denton	30,210
McAllen (city) Hidalgo	22,170
Corpus Christi (city) Nueces	22,080
Fort Worth (city) Tarrant	22,072
Dallas (city) Dallas	21,646
Garland (city) Dallas	19,126
Austin (city) Travis	18,514
San Antonio (city) Bexar	18,073

Salvadoran
Top 10 Places Sorted by Number

Place (place type) County	Dollars
Galveston (city) Galveston	15,453
Arlington (city) Tarrant	14,698
Mission Bend (cdp) Fort Bend	13,734
Austin (city) Travis	13,283
Irving (city) Dallas	13,213
San Antonio (city) Bexar	12,539
Carrollton (city) Denton	12,225
Farmers Branch (city) Dallas	11,869
Plano (city) Collin	11,631
Fort Worth (city) Tarrant	11,211

South American
Top 10 Places Sorted by Number

Place (place type) County	Dollars
Sugar Land (city) Fort Bend	42,262
The Woodlands (cdp) Montgomery	30,945
College Station (city) Brazos	27,157
San Antonio (city) Bexar	23,031
Corpus Christi (city) Nueces	22,106
Carrollton (city) Denton	22,096
Fort Worth (city) Tarrant	21,964
El Paso (city) El Paso	21,535
Austin (city) Travis	20,336
Arlington (city) Tarrant	20,142

Spaniard
Top 10 Places Sorted by Number

Place (place type) County	Dollars
Houston (city) Harris	22,756
San Antonio (city) Bexar	18,021
Dallas (city) Dallas	16,268

Uruguayan
Top 10 Places Sorted by Number

Place (place type) County	Dollars
No places met population threshold.	

Venezuelan
Top 10 Places Sorted by Number

Place (place type) County	Dollars
Houston (city) Harris	17,653
Austin (city) Travis	16,729

Other Hispanic
Top 10 Places Sorted by Number

Place (place type) County	Dollars
Deer Park (city) Harris	32,285
The Woodlands (cdp) Montgomery	31,951
Flower Mound (town) Denton	23,479
Sugar Land (city) Fort Bend	22,369
Atascocita (cdp) Harris	20,772
Allen (city) Collin	20,588
Friendswood (city) Galveston	19,908
League City (city) Galveston	19,566
Bedford (city) Tarrant	18,472
Plano (city) Collin	18,340

Poverty Status

Total Populations with Income Below Poverty Level
Top 10 Places Sorted by Number

Place (place type) County	Number
Houston (city) Harris	369,045
Dallas (city) Dallas	207,493
San Antonio (city) Bexar	193,731
El Paso (city) El Paso	124,281
Austin (city) Travis	92,011
Fort Worth (city) Tarrant	82,953
Laredo (city) Webb	51,493
Brownsville (city) Cameron	49,701
Corpus Christi (city) Nueces	47,842
Lubbock (city) Lubbock	35,176

Total Populations with Income Below Poverty Level
Top 10 Places Sorted by Percent

Place (place type) County	Percent
La Homa (cdp) Hidalgo	57.43
San Elizario (cdp) El Paso	44.47
Rio Grande City (city) Starr	44.10
Donna (city) Hidalgo	37.78
College Station (city) Brazos	37.39
Mercedes (city) Hidalgo	36.37

Brownsville (city) Cameron	35.97
Pharr (city) Hidalgo	35.51
San Juan (city) Hidalgo	34.39
San Benito (city) Cameron	32.70

Hispanics with Income Below Poverty Level
Top 10 Places Sorted by Number

Place (place type) County	Number
Houston (city) Harris	185,326
San Antonio (city) Bexar	148,477
El Paso (city) El Paso	112,397
Dallas (city) Dallas	101,705
Laredo (city) Webb	49,833
Brownsville (city) Cameron	47,984
Austin (city) Travis	41,203
Fort Worth (city) Tarrant	34,283
Corpus Christi (city) Nueces	33,938
McAllen (city) Hidalgo	23,413

Hispanics with Income Below Poverty Level
Top 10 Places Sorted by Percent

Place (place type) County	Percent
La Homa (cdp) Hidalgo	57.57
Texarkana (city) Bowie	46.19
Nacogdoches (city) Nacogdoches	45.87
Rio Grande City (city) Starr	45.34
San Elizario (cdp) El Paso	45.13
College Station (city) Brazos	42.28
Donna (city) Hidalgo	41.24
Alamo (city) Hidalgo	39.66
Mercedes (city) Hidalgo	38.65
Pharr (city) Hidalgo	38.40

Argentinians with Income Below Poverty Level
Top 10 Places Sorted by Number

Place (place type) County	Number
Houston (city) Harris	196

Argentinians with Income Below Poverty Level
Top 10 Places Sorted by Percent

Place (place type) County	Percent
Houston (city) Harris	14.53

Bolivians with Income Below Poverty Level
Top 10 Places Sorted by Number

Place (place type) County	Number
Houston (city) Harris	103

Bolivians with Income Below Poverty Level
Top 10 Places Sorted by Percent

Place (place type) County	Percent
Houston (city) Harris	15.12

Central Americans with Income Below Poverty Level
Top 10 Places Sorted by Number

Place (place type) County	Number
Houston (city) Harris	16,657
Dallas (city) Dallas	3,656
Irving (city) Dallas	1,686
Austin (city) Travis	1,004
Garland (city) Dallas	682
San Antonio (city) Bexar	611
Pasadena (city) Harris	559
Fort Worth (city) Tarrant	317
El Paso (city) El Paso	291
Grand Prairie (city) Dallas	234

Notes: Please refer to the User's Guide for an explanation of data; tables include places with populations > 9,999 and reflect only those areas that meet Summary File 4 population thresholds, therefore there may be less than 10 places listed

Central Americans with Income Below Poverty Level
Top 10 Places Sorted by Percent

Place (place type) County	Percent
Brownsville (city) Cameron	54.49
Corpus Christi (city) Nueces	38.46
Conroe (city) Montgomery	28.55
Pasadena (city) Harris	27.23
Grand Prairie (city) Dallas	27.21
Houston (city) Harris	25.05
Irving (city) Dallas	23.31
Huntsville (city) Walker	23.13
Dallas (city) Dallas	22.60
Austin (city) Travis	21.99

Chileans with Income Below Poverty Level
Top 10 Places Sorted by Number

Place (place type) County	Number
Houston (city) Harris	81

Chileans with Income Below Poverty Level
Top 10 Places Sorted by Percent

Place (place type) County	Percent
Houston (city) Harris	11.64

Colombians with Income Below Poverty Level
Top 10 Places Sorted by Number

Place (place type) County	Number
Houston (city) Harris	1,237
Dallas (city) Dallas	255
Austin (city) Travis	116
San Antonio (city) Bexar	54
Mission Bend (cdp) Fort Bend	30

Colombians with Income Below Poverty Level
Top 10 Places Sorted by Percent

Place (place type) County	Percent
Dallas (city) Dallas	25.02
Houston (city) Harris	19.95
Austin (city) Travis	14.91
San Antonio (city) Bexar	7.51
Mission Bend (cdp) Fort Bend	5.52

Costa Ricans with Income Below Poverty Level
Top 10 Places Sorted by Number

Place (place type) County	Number
Houston (city) Harris	166
Dallas (city) Dallas	130

Costa Ricans with Income Below Poverty Level
Top 10 Places Sorted by Percent

Place (place type) County	Percent
Dallas (city) Dallas	28.02
Houston (city) Harris	19.26

Cubans with Income Below Poverty Level
Top 10 Places Sorted by Number

Place (place type) County	Number
Houston (city) Harris	915
Dallas (city) Dallas	503
San Antonio (city) Bexar	279
Austin (city) Travis	191
Fort Worth (city) Tarrant	138
El Paso (city) El Paso	81

Cubans with Income Below Poverty Level
Top 10 Places Sorted by Percent

Place (place type) County	Percent
Dallas (city) Dallas	21.63
Houston (city) Harris	17.15
El Paso (city) El Paso	16.56

Fort Worth (city) Tarrant	15.12
San Antonio (city) Bexar	14.79
Austin (city) Travis	13.04

Dominicans with Income Below Poverty Level
Top 10 Places Sorted by Number

Place (place type) County	Number
Houston (city) Harris	150

Dominicans with Income Below Poverty Level
Top 10 Places Sorted by Percent

Place (place type) County	Percent
Houston (city) Harris	16.29

Ecuadorians with Income Below Poverty Level
Top 10 Places Sorted by Number

Place (place type) County	Number
Houston (city) Harris	230

Ecuadorians with Income Below Poverty Level
Top 10 Places Sorted by Percent

Place (place type) County	Percent
Houston (city) Harris	22.62

Guatelmalans with Income Below Poverty Level
Top 10 Places Sorted by Number

Place (place type) County	Number
Houston (city) Harris	1,845
Dallas (city) Dallas	554
Austin (city) Travis	188
San Antonio (city) Bexar	81
Garland (city) Dallas	55
Fort Worth (city) Tarrant	54

Guatelmalans with Income Below Poverty Level
Top 10 Places Sorted by Percent

Place (place type) County	Percent
Houston (city) Harris	24.20
Austin (city) Travis	22.12
Dallas (city) Dallas	21.60
San Antonio (city) Bexar	20.72
Fort Worth (city) Tarrant	12.47
Garland (city) Dallas	6.43

Hondurans with Income Below Poverty Level
Top 10 Places Sorted by Number

Place (place type) County	Number
Houston (city) Harris	4,031
Dallas (city) Dallas	757
Austin (city) Travis	375
Irving (city) Dallas	291
San Antonio (city) Bexar	237
Garland (city) Dallas	146

Hondurans with Income Below Poverty Level
Top 10 Places Sorted by Percent

Place (place type) County	Percent
Irving (city) Dallas	37.50
Houston (city) Harris	36.31
Garland (city) Dallas	35.27
San Antonio (city) Bexar	34.25
Austin (city) Travis	31.43
Dallas (city) Dallas	26.20

Mexicans with Income Below Poverty Level
Top 10 Places Sorted by Number

Place (place type) County	Number
Houston (city) Harris	139,672
San Antonio (city) Bexar	104,469

El Paso (city) El Paso	97,257
Dallas (city) Dallas	86,601
Laredo (city) Webb	41,584
Brownsville (city) Cameron	40,612
Austin (city) Travis	33,389
Fort Worth (city) Tarrant	29,369
Corpus Christi (city) Nueces	23,052
McAllen (city) Hidalgo	20,302

Mexicans with Income Below Poverty Level
Top 10 Places Sorted by Percent

Place (place type) County	Percent
La Homa (cdp) Hidalgo	57.86
Nacogdoches (city) Nacogdoches	47.37
Rio Grande City (city) Starr	46.39
College Station (city) Brazos	46.32
San Elizario (cdp) El Paso	45.68
Texarkana (city) Bowie	41.36
Alamo (city) Hidalgo	39.99
Mercedes (city) Hidalgo	39.80
Donna (city) Hidalgo	39.79
Burkburnett (city) Wichita	39.20

Nicaraguans with Income Below Poverty Level
Top 10 Places Sorted by Number

Place (place type) County	Number
Houston (city) Harris	392
Austin (city) Travis	104
Port Arthur (city) Jefferson	88
San Antonio (city) Bexar	57
Dallas (city) Dallas	42

Nicaraguans with Income Below Poverty Level
Top 10 Places Sorted by Percent

Place (place type) County	Percent
Austin (city) Travis	28.42
Port Arthur (city) Jefferson	27.24
Houston (city) Harris	16.49
San Antonio (city) Bexar	12.10
Dallas (city) Dallas	9.63

Panamanians with Income Below Poverty Level
Top 10 Places Sorted by Number

Place (place type) County	Number
El Paso (city) El Paso	90
Houston (city) Harris	61
Killeen (city) Bell	60
San Antonio (city) Bexar	34

Panamanians with Income Below Poverty Level
Top 10 Places Sorted by Percent

Place (place type) County	Percent
El Paso (city) El Paso	19.15
Killeen (city) Bell	12.22
Houston (city) Harris	7.74
San Antonio (city) Bexar	3.66

Paraguayans with Income Below Poverty Level
Top 10 Places Sorted by Number

Place (place type) County	Number
No places met population threshold.	

Paraguayans with Income Below Poverty Level
Top 10 Places Sorted by Percent

Place (place type) County	Percent
No places met population threshold.	

Notes: Please refer to the User's Guide for an explanation of data; tables include places with populations > 9,999 and reflect only those areas that meet Summary File 4 population thresholds, therefore there may be less than 10 places listed

Peruvians with Income Below Poverty Level
Top 10 Places Sorted by Number

Place (place type) County	Number
Houston (city) Harris	224
Dallas (city) Dallas	201
San Antonio (city) Bexar	51

Peruvians with Income Below Poverty Level
Top 10 Places Sorted by Percent

Place (place type) County	Percent
Dallas (city) Dallas	21.75
Houston (city) Harris	15.26
San Antonio (city) Bexar	12.32

Puerto Ricans with Income Below Poverty Level
Top 10 Places Sorted by Number

Place (place type) County	Number
Houston (city) Harris	1,073
San Antonio (city) Bexar	831
Killeen (city) Bell	617
El Paso (city) El Paso	569
Austin (city) Travis	420
Dallas (city) Dallas	367
Fort Worth (city) Tarrant	318
Arlington (city) Tarrant	204
Fort Hood (cdp) Coryell	197
Corpus Christi (city) Nueces	118

Puerto Ricans with Income Below Poverty Level
Top 10 Places Sorted by Percent

Place (place type) County	Percent
San Angelo (city) Tom Green	18.10
Fort Hood (cdp) Coryell	16.97
Wichita Falls (city) Wichita	16.73
Pasadena (city) Harris	16.52
Fort Worth (city) Tarrant	16.34
Austin (city) Travis	16.14
Dallas (city) Dallas	15.64
Abilene (city) Taylor	14.99
Irving (city) Dallas	14.81
McAllen (city) Hidalgo	14.68

Salvadorans with Income Below Poverty Level
Top 10 Places Sorted by Number

Place (place type) County	Number
Houston (city) Harris	9,418
Dallas (city) Dallas	2,070
Irving (city) Dallas	1,367
Garland (city) Dallas	459
Pasadena (city) Harris	297
Austin (city) Travis	251
Grand Prairie (city) Dallas	178
San Antonio (city) Bexar	145
Conroe (city) Montgomery	135
Farmers Branch (city) Dallas	117

Salvadorans with Income Below Poverty Level
Top 10 Places Sorted by Percent

Place (place type) County	Percent
Conroe (city) Montgomery	37.09
Grand Prairie (city) Dallas	32.66
Pasadena (city) Harris	24.79
Houston (city) Harris	22.89
Irving (city) Dallas	22.77
Dallas (city) Dallas	22.68
Garland (city) Dallas	22.62
San Antonio (city) Bexar	19.46
Fort Worth (city) Tarrant	16.17
Austin (city) Travis	15.98

South Americans with Income Below Poverty Level
Top 10 Places Sorted by Number

Place (place type) County	Number
Houston (city) Harris	2,374
Dallas (city) Dallas	656
Austin (city) Travis	432
San Antonio (city) Bexar	317
Irving (city) Dallas	157
Fort Worth (city) Tarrant	155
College Station (city) Brazos	150
El Paso (city) El Paso	83
Mission Bend (cdp) Fort Bend	78
Arlington (city) Tarrant	72

South Americans with Income Below Poverty Level
Top 10 Places Sorted by Percent

Place (place type) County	Percent
College Station (city) Brazos	28.41
Dallas (city) Dallas	20.37
Houston (city) Harris	17.11
Fort Worth (city) Tarrant	17.09
Austin (city) Travis	16.93
Irving (city) Dallas	16.72
San Antonio (city) Bexar	13.99
El Paso (city) El Paso	13.61
Mission Bend (cdp) Fort Bend	10.22
Arlington (city) Tarrant	9.11

Spaniards with Income Below Poverty Level
Top 10 Places Sorted by Number

Place (place type) County	Number
Houston (city) Harris	192
Dallas (city) Dallas	111
San Antonio (city) Bexar	109

Spaniards with Income Below Poverty Level
Top 10 Places Sorted by Percent

Place (place type) County	Percent
Dallas (city) Dallas	23.37
Houston (city) Harris	20.78
San Antonio (city) Bexar	13.71

Uruguayans with Income Below Poverty Level
Top 10 Places Sorted by Number

Place (place type) County	Number
No places met population threshold.	

Uruguayans with Income Below Poverty Level
Top 10 Places Sorted by Percent

Place (place type) County	Percent
No places met population threshold.	

Venezuelans with Income Below Poverty Level
Top 10 Places Sorted by Number

Place (place type) County	Number
Houston (city) Harris	266
Austin (city) Travis	86

Venezuelans with Income Below Poverty Level
Top 10 Places Sorted by Percent

Place (place type) County	Percent
Austin (city) Travis	17.48
Houston (city) Harris	15.89

Other Hispanics with Income Below Poverty Level
Top 10 Places Sorted by Number

Place (place type) County	Number
San Antonio (city) Bexar	41,845
Houston (city) Harris	24,293
El Paso (city) El Paso	14,071
Corpus Christi (city) Nueces	10,448
Dallas (city) Dallas	9,811
Laredo (city) Webb	8,056
Brownsville (city) Cameron	7,074
Lubbock (city) Lubbock	5,796
Austin (city) Travis	5,735
Fort Worth (city) Tarrant	3,887

Other Hispanics with Income Below Poverty Level
Top 10 Places Sorted by Percent

Place (place type) County	Percent
Huntsville (city) Walker	55.14
Mineral Wells (city) Palo Pinto	53.75
Donna (city) Hidalgo	48.74
Kerrville (city) Kerr	45.46
Rio Grande City (city) Starr	40.32
Nacogdoches (city) Nacogdoches	39.36
Cloverleaf (cdp) Harris	38.93
San Benito (city) Cameron	38.36
Beeville (city) Bee	37.72
Hereford (city) Deaf Smith	37.12

Homeownership

Total Populations Who Own Their Own Homes
Top 10 Places Sorted by Number

Place (place type) County	Number
Houston (city) Harris	329,006
San Antonio (city) Bexar	235,584
Dallas (city) Dallas	195,227
Austin (city) Travis	119,191
El Paso (city) El Paso	111,808
Fort Worth (city) Tarrant	109,152
Arlington (city) Tarrant	68,309
Corpus Christi (city) Nueces	58,918
Plano (city) Collin	55,725
Garland (city) Dallas	48,043

Total Populations Who Own Their Own Homes
Top 10 Places Sorted by Percent

Place (place type) County	Percent
Colleyville (city) Tarrant	96.80
Southlake (city) Tarrant	96.69
Highland Village (city) Denton	96.56
Corinth (city) Denton	95.74
Brushy Creek (cdp) Williamson	94.30
Keller (city) Tarrant	92.90
Cinco Ranch (cdp) Fort Bend	92.70
Flower Mound (town) Denton	92.65
Rowlett (city) Dallas	92.10
New Territory (cdp) Fort Bend	92.05

Hispanics Who Own Their Own Homes
Top 10 Places Sorted by Number

Place (place type) County	Number
San Antonio (city) Bexar	114,841
El Paso (city) El Paso	74,706
Houston (city) Harris	69,542
Dallas (city) Dallas	35,650
Laredo (city) Webb	28,053
Corpus Christi (city) Nueces	25,590
Austin (city) Travis	21,026
Fort Worth (city) Tarrant	20,459
Brownsville (city) Cameron	19,852
McAllen (city) Hidalgo	14,566

Hispanics Who Own Their Own Homes
Top 10 Places Sorted by Percent

Place (place type) County	Percent
Corinth (city) Denton	100.00
Highland Village (city) Denton	95.69
Watauga (city) Tarrant	91.56
Southlake (city) Tarrant	89.16

Notes: Please refer to the User's Guide for an explanation of data; tables include places with populations > 9,999 and reflect only those areas that meet Summary File 4 population thresholds, therefore there may be less than 10 places listed

Place (place type) County	Number
Rowlett (city) Dallas	88.85
Atascocita (cdp) Harris	88.83
West Odessa (cdp) Ector	88.42
Mission Bend (cdp) Fort Bend	87.63
Brushy Creek (cdp) Williamson	86.73
Keller (city) Tarrant	86.58

Argentinians Who Own Their Own Homes
Top 10 Places Sorted by Number

Place (place type) County	Number
Houston (city) Harris	231

Argentinians Who Own Their Own Homes
Top 10 Places Sorted by Percent

Place (place type) County	Percent
Houston (city) Harris	41.55

Bolivians Who Own Their Own Homes
Top 10 Places Sorted by Number

Place (place type) County	Number
Houston (city) Harris	97

Bolivians Who Own Their Own Homes
Top 10 Places Sorted by Percent

Place (place type) County	Percent
Houston (city) Harris	36.33

Central Americans Who Own Their Own Homes
Top 10 Places Sorted by Number

Place (place type) County	Number
Houston (city) Harris	5,183
Dallas (city) Dallas	988
Irving (city) Dallas	555
Garland (city) Dallas	496
San Antonio (city) Bexar	442
Austin (city) Travis	440
Fort Worth (city) Tarrant	300
El Paso (city) El Paso	256
Mission Bend (cdp) Fort Bend	254
Pasadena (city) Harris	243

Central Americans Who Own Their Own Homes
Top 10 Places Sorted by Percent

Place (place type) County	Percent
Mission Bend (cdp) Fort Bend	92.70
Grand Prairie (city) Dallas	71.70
Farmers Branch (city) Dallas	57.83
Fort Worth (city) Tarrant	57.69
Brownsville (city) Cameron	56.18
Port Arthur (city) Jefferson	56.17
Lewisville (city) Denton	54.63
El Paso (city) El Paso	52.35
Garland (city) Dallas	50.87
Conroe (city) Montgomery	45.21

Chileans Who Own Their Own Homes
Top 10 Places Sorted by Number

Place (place type) County	Number
Houston (city) Harris	131

Chileans Who Own Their Own Homes
Top 10 Places Sorted by Percent

Place (place type) County	Percent
Houston (city) Harris	45.49

Colombians Who Own Their Own Homes
Top 10 Places Sorted by Number

Place (place type) County	Number
Houston (city) Harris	720
San Antonio (city) Bexar	165
Dallas (city) Dallas	137
Mission Bend (cdp) Fort Bend	132
Austin (city) Travis	67

Colombians Who Own Their Own Homes
Top 10 Places Sorted by Percent

Place (place type) County	Percent
Mission Bend (cdp) Fort Bend	80.98
San Antonio (city) Bexar	52.72
Dallas (city) Dallas	35.77
Houston (city) Harris	31.82
Austin (city) Travis	23.76

Costa Ricans Who Own Their Own Homes
Top 10 Places Sorted by Number

Place (place type) County	Number
Houston (city) Harris	57
Dallas (city) Dallas	34

Costa Ricans Who Own Their Own Homes
Top 10 Places Sorted by Percent

Place (place type) County	Percent
Dallas (city) Dallas	29.57
Houston (city) Harris	27.01

Cubans Who Own Their Own Homes
Top 10 Places Sorted by Number

Place (place type) County	Number
Houston (city) Harris	1,072
San Antonio (city) Bexar	423
Dallas (city) Dallas	336
Austin (city) Travis	190
Fort Worth (city) Tarrant	167
El Paso (city) El Paso	121

Cubans Who Own Their Own Homes
Top 10 Places Sorted by Percent

Place (place type) County	Percent
San Antonio (city) Bexar	61.13
El Paso (city) El Paso	52.16
Fort Worth (city) Tarrant	50.61
Houston (city) Harris	45.17
Dallas (city) Dallas	34.15
Austin (city) Travis	33.22

Dominicans Who Own Their Own Homes
Top 10 Places Sorted by Number

Place (place type) County	Number
Houston (city) Harris	93

Dominicans Who Own Their Own Homes
Top 10 Places Sorted by Percent

Place (place type) County	Percent
Houston (city) Harris	32.40

Ecuadorians Who Own Their Own Homes
Top 10 Places Sorted by Number

Place (place type) County	Number
Houston (city) Harris	165

Ecuadorians Who Own Their Own Homes
Top 10 Places Sorted by Percent

Place (place type) County	Percent
Houston (city) Harris	39.47

Guatelmalans Who Own Their Own Homes
Top 10 Places Sorted by Number

Place (place type) County	Number
Houston (city) Harris	449
Dallas (city) Dallas	142
Garland (city) Dallas	134
Fort Worth (city) Tarrant	63
Austin (city) Travis	62
San Antonio (city) Bexar	62

Guatelmalans Who Own Their Own Homes
Top 10 Places Sorted by Percent

Place (place type) County	Percent
Garland (city) Dallas	67.68
Fort Worth (city) Tarrant	47.73
San Antonio (city) Bexar	36.26
Austin (city) Travis	21.38
Dallas (city) Dallas	19.67
Houston (city) Harris	19.01

Hondurans Who Own Their Own Homes
Top 10 Places Sorted by Number

Place (place type) County	Number
Houston (city) Harris	371
Austin (city) Travis	87
Dallas (city) Dallas	78
San Antonio (city) Bexar	64
Garland (city) Dallas	26
Irving (city) Dallas	19

Hondurans Who Own Their Own Homes
Top 10 Places Sorted by Percent

Place (place type) County	Percent
San Antonio (city) Bexar	30.48
Garland (city) Dallas	25.24
Austin (city) Travis	24.37
Houston (city) Harris	10.87
Dallas (city) Dallas	9.57
Irving (city) Dallas	7.79

Mexicans Who Own Their Own Homes
Top 10 Places Sorted by Number

Place (place type) County	Number
San Antonio (city) Bexar	84,398
El Paso (city) El Paso	64,256
Houston (city) Harris	51,560
Dallas (city) Dallas	29,665
Laredo (city) Webb	23,189
Corpus Christi (city) Nueces	17,639
Fort Worth (city) Tarrant	17,032
Brownsville (city) Cameron	16,726
Austin (city) Travis	16,221
McAllen (city) Hidalgo	12,117

Mexicans Who Own Their Own Homes
Top 10 Places Sorted by Percent

Place (place type) County	Percent
Corinth (city) Denton	100.00
Atascocita (cdp) Harris	90.51
Mission Bend (cdp) Fort Bend	90.26
Cedar Hill (city) Dallas	90.07
Colleyville (city) Tarrant	89.39
Rowlett (city) Dallas	89.22
Watauga (city) Tarrant	87.98
The Colony (city) Denton	87.85
West Odessa (cdp) Ector	87.81
Flower Mound (town) Denton	87.44

Nicaraguans Who Own Their Own Homes
Top 10 Places Sorted by Number

Place (place type) County	Number
Houston (city) Harris	235

Notes: Please refer to the User's Guide for an explanation of data; tables include places with populations > 9,999 and reflect only those areas that meet Summary File 4 population thresholds, therefore there may be less than 10 places listed

Place (place type) County	
Dallas (city) Dallas	59
Port Arthur (city) Jefferson	48
San Antonio (city) Bexar	47
Austin (city) Travis	32

Nicaraguans Who Own Their Own Homes
Top 10 Places Sorted by Percent

Place (place type) County	Percent
Port Arthur (city) Jefferson	57.14
San Antonio (city) Bexar	36.15
Dallas (city) Dallas	32.60
Houston (city) Harris	31.76
Austin (city) Travis	28.32

Panamanians Who Own Their Own Homes
Top 10 Places Sorted by Number

Place (place type) County	Number
Houston (city) Harris	131
San Antonio (city) Bexar	97
El Paso (city) El Paso	85
Killeen (city) Bell	66

Panamanians Who Own Their Own Homes
Top 10 Places Sorted by Percent

Place (place type) County	Percent
El Paso (city) El Paso	60.28
Houston (city) Harris	40.56
Killeen (city) Bell	38.15
San Antonio (city) Bexar	32.44

Paraguayans Who Own Their Own Homes
Top 10 Places Sorted by Number

Place (place type) County	Number

No places met population threshold.

Paraguayans Who Own Their Own Homes
Top 10 Places Sorted by Percent

Place (place type) County	Percent

No places met population threshold.

Peruvians Who Own Their Own Homes
Top 10 Places Sorted by Number

Place (place type) County	Number
Houston (city) Harris	178
Dallas (city) Dallas	74
San Antonio (city) Bexar	63

Peruvians Who Own Their Own Homes
Top 10 Places Sorted by Percent

Place (place type) County	Percent
San Antonio (city) Bexar	50.00
Houston (city) Harris	27.99
Dallas (city) Dallas	27.61

Puerto Ricans Who Own Their Own Homes
Top 10 Places Sorted by Number

Place (place type) County	Number
San Antonio (city) Bexar	1,787
Houston (city) Harris	915
El Paso (city) El Paso	865
Killeen (city) Bell	842
Austin (city) Travis	349
Dallas (city) Dallas	343
Fort Worth (city) Tarrant	299
Arlington (city) Tarrant	285
Plano (city) Collin	262
Copperas Cove (city) Coryell	173

Puerto Ricans Who Own Their Own Homes
Top 10 Places Sorted by Percent

Place (place type) County	Percent
Plano (city) Collin	75.72
Garland (city) Dallas	63.64
Copperas Cove (city) Coryell	61.13
Carrollton (city) Denton	60.67
El Paso (city) El Paso	56.21
San Antonio (city) Bexar	54.51
Killeen (city) Bell	53.84
Mission Bend (cdp) Fort Bend	53.61
Grand Prairie (city) Dallas	47.32
Arlington (city) Tarrant	45.67

Salvadorans Who Own Their Own Homes
Top 10 Places Sorted by Number

Place (place type) County	Number
Houston (city) Harris	3,672
Dallas (city) Dallas	596
Irving (city) Dallas	462
Garland (city) Dallas	275
Austin (city) Travis	196
Farmers Branch (city) Dallas	172
Pasadena (city) Harris	166
Grand Prairie (city) Dallas	130
San Antonio (city) Bexar	117
Mission Bend (cdp) Fort Bend	115

Salvadorans Who Own Their Own Homes
Top 10 Places Sorted by Percent

Place (place type) County	Percent
Mission Bend (cdp) Fort Bend	92.00
Grand Prairie (city) Dallas	73.45
Farmers Branch (city) Dallas	55.31
Fort Worth (city) Tarrant	54.60
Pasadena (city) Harris	50.61
Garland (city) Dallas	46.22
Carrollton (city) Denton	44.07
San Antonio (city) Bexar	42.39
Austin (city) Travis	41.97
Conroe (city) Montgomery	38.10

South Americans Who Own Their Own Homes
Top 10 Places Sorted by Number

Place (place type) County	Number
Houston (city) Harris	1,764
San Antonio (city) Bexar	439
Dallas (city) Dallas	342
Austin (city) Travis	291
Mission Bend (cdp) Fort Bend	180
El Paso (city) El Paso	147
Plano (city) Collin	140
Fort Worth (city) Tarrant	136
The Woodlands (cdp) Montgomery	127
Arlington (city) Tarrant	116

South Americans Who Own Their Own Homes
Top 10 Places Sorted by Percent

Place (place type) County	Percent
The Woodlands (cdp) Montgomery	81.94
Mission Bend (cdp) Fort Bend	81.45
Garland (city) Dallas	68.75
Corpus Christi (city) Nueces	65.49
Sugar Land (city) Fort Bend	62.60
El Paso (city) El Paso	62.55
Plano (city) Collin	59.32
San Antonio (city) Bexar	47.77
Carrollton (city) Denton	47.64
Fort Worth (city) Tarrant	45.64

Spaniards Who Own Their Own Homes
Top 10 Places Sorted by Number

Place (place type) County	Number
San Antonio (city) Bexar	186
Houston (city) Harris	141
Dallas (city) Dallas	60

Spaniards Who Own Their Own Homes
Top 10 Places Sorted by Percent

Place (place type) County	Percent
San Antonio (city) Bexar	57.06
Dallas (city) Dallas	38.71
Houston (city) Harris	30.65

Uruguayans Who Own Their Own Homes
Top 10 Places Sorted by Number

Place (place type) County	Number

No places met population threshold.

Uruguayans Who Own Their Own Homes
Top 10 Places Sorted by Percent

Place (place type) County	Percent

No places met population threshold.

Venezuelans Who Own Their Own Homes
Top 10 Places Sorted by Number

Place (place type) County	Number
Houston (city) Harris	162
Austin (city) Travis	36

Venezuelans Who Own Their Own Homes
Top 10 Places Sorted by Percent

Place (place type) County	Percent
Austin (city) Travis	26.67
Houston (city) Harris	25.35

Other Hispanics Who Own Their Own Homes
Top 10 Places Sorted by Number

Place (place type) County	Number
San Antonio (city) Bexar	27,147
El Paso (city) El Paso	8,996
Houston (city) Harris	8,814
Corpus Christi (city) Nueces	7,534
Laredo (city) Webb	4,725
Dallas (city) Dallas	3,892
Austin (city) Travis	3,437
Brownsville (city) Cameron	2,990
Lubbock (city) Lubbock	2,792
Fort Worth (city) Tarrant	2,439

Other Hispanics Who Own Their Own Homes
Top 10 Places Sorted by Percent

Place (place type) County	Percent
Watauga (city) Tarrant	94.39
Atascocita (cdp) Harris	91.49
West Odessa (cdp) Ector	90.74
Pflugerville (city) Travis	87.25
Rowlett (city) Dallas	87.03
Missouri City (city) Fort Bend	85.71
Mission Bend (cdp) Fort Bend	85.45
La Porte (city) Harris	83.78
Sugar Land (city) Fort Bend	83.62
Rio Grande City (city) Starr	80.40

Notes: Please refer to the User's Guide for an explanation of data; tables include places with populations > 9,999 and reflect only those areas that meet Summary File 4 population thresholds, therefore there may be less than 10 places listed

Median Gross Rent

All Specified Renter-Occupied Housing Units
Top 10 Places Sorted by Number

Place (place type) County	Dollars/Month
West University Place (city) Harris	1,418
Highland Village (city) Denton	1,276
Bellaire (city) Harris	1,119
Brushy Creek (cdp) Williamson	1,084
Flower Mound (town) Denton	1,050
University Park (city) Dallas	1,028
Cinco Ranch (cdp) Fort Bend	1,016
Corinth (city) Denton	1,002
The Colony (city) Denton	986
Coppell (city) Dallas	946

Specified Housing Units Rented by Hispanics
Top 10 Places Sorted by Number

Place (place type) County	Dollars/Month
Cinco Ranch (cdp) Fort Bend	1,275
Highland Village (city) Denton	1,125
Brushy Creek (cdp) Williamson	1,083
New Territory (cdp) Fort Bend	1,083
Friendswood (city) Galveston	944
Coppell (city) Dallas	940
The Colony (city) Denton	932
Cedar Park (city) Williamson	928
Bellaire (city) Harris	921
West University Place (city) Harris	894

Specified Housing Units Rented by Argentinians
Top 10 Places Sorted by Number

Place (place type) County	Dollars/Month
Houston (city) Harris	615

Specified Housing Units Rented by Bolivians
Top 10 Places Sorted by Number

Place (place type) County	Dollars/Month
Houston (city) Harris	621

Specified Housing Units Rented by Central Americans
Top 10 Places Sorted by Number

Place (place type) County	Dollars/Month
Mission Bend (cdp) Fort Bend	950
Plano (city) Collin	750
Addison (town) Dallas	710
Austin (city) Travis	661
Carrollton (city) Denton	646
Farmers Branch (city) Dallas	643
Lewisville (city) Denton	638
Richardson (city) Dallas	600
Denton (city) Denton	579
Dallas (city) Dallas	577

Specified Housing Units Rented by Chileans
Top 10 Places Sorted by Number

Place (place type) County	Dollars/Month
Houston (city) Harris	707

Specified Housing Units Rented by Colombians
Top 10 Places Sorted by Number

Place (place type) County	Dollars/Month
Mission Bend (cdp) Fort Bend	907
San Antonio (city) Bexar	719
Austin (city) Travis	670
Dallas (city) Dallas	659
Houston (city) Harris	579

Specified Housing Units Rented by Costa Ricans
Top 10 Places Sorted by Number

Place (place type) County	Dollars/Month
Dallas (city) Dallas	690
Houston (city) Harris	620

Specified Housing Units Rented by Cubans
Top 10 Places Sorted by Number

Place (place type) County	Dollars/Month
Austin (city) Travis	724
Dallas (city) Dallas	611
Fort Worth (city) Tarrant	603
El Paso (city) El Paso	601
San Antonio (city) Bexar	594
Houston (city) Harris	590

Specified Housing Units Rented by Dominicans
Top 10 Places Sorted by Number

Place (place type) County	Dollars/Month
Houston (city) Harris	613

Specified Housing Units Rented by Ecuadorians
Top 10 Places Sorted by Number

Place (place type) County	Dollars/Month
Houston (city) Harris	662

Specified Housing Units Rented by Guatelmalans
Top 10 Places Sorted by Number

Place (place type) County	Dollars/Month
Austin (city) Travis	666
Garland (city) Dallas	573
Dallas (city) Dallas	572
Houston (city) Harris	547
San Antonio (city) Bexar	488
Fort Worth (city) Tarrant	389

Specified Housing Units Rented by Hondurans
Top 10 Places Sorted by Number

Place (place type) County	Dollars/Month
Austin (city) Travis	646
Dallas (city) Dallas	578
Irving (city) Dallas	565
Garland (city) Dallas	548
Houston (city) Harris	492
San Antonio (city) Bexar	447

Specified Housing Units Rented by Mexicans
Top 10 Places Sorted by Number

Place (place type) County	Dollars/Month
Brushy Creek (cdp) Williamson	1,068
Friendswood (city) Galveston	1,011
Coppell (city) Dallas	993
The Colony (city) Denton	986
Bellaire (city) Harris	936
Allen (city) Collin	913
Cedar Park (city) Williamson	909
New Territory (cdp) Fort Bend	888
University Park (city) Dallas	868
Colleyville (city) Tarrant	850

Specified Housing Units Rented by Nicaraguans
Top 10 Places Sorted by Number

Place (place type) County	Dollars/Month
Austin (city) Travis	584
Houston (city) Harris	547
Dallas (city) Dallas	523
San Antonio (city) Bexar	495
Port Arthur (city) Jefferson	450

Specified Housing Units Rented by Panamanians
Top 10 Places Sorted by Number

Place (place type) County	Dollars/Month
El Paso (city) El Paso	708
San Antonio (city) Bexar	624
Houston (city) Harris	574
Killeen (city) Bell	489

Specified Housing Units Rented by Paraguayans
Top 10 Places Sorted by Number

Place (place type) County	Dollars/Month
No places met population threshold.	

Specified Housing Units Rented by Peruvians
Top 10 Places Sorted by Number

Place (place type) County	Dollars/Month
Dallas (city) Dallas	710
Houston (city) Harris	596
San Antonio (city) Bexar	571

Specified Housing Units Rented by Puerto Ricans
Top 10 Places Sorted by Number

Place (place type) County	Dollars/Month
Carrollton (city) Denton	961
Plano (city) Collin	850
Grand Prairie (city) Dallas	753
Mission Bend (cdp) Fort Bend	753
Austin (city) Travis	748
Irving (city) Dallas	681
Euless (city) Tarrant	680
Garland (city) Dallas	667
Houston (city) Harris	648
Corpus Christi (city) Nueces	645

Specified Housing Units Rented by Salvadorans
Top 10 Places Sorted by Number

Place (place type) County	Dollars/Month
Mission Bend (cdp) Fort Bend	850
Plano (city) Collin	762
Austin (city) Travis	649
Farmers Branch (city) Dallas	648
Carrollton (city) Denton	623
Dallas (city) Dallas	575
Conroe (city) Montgomery	562
Garland (city) Dallas	562
Irving (city) Dallas	557
San Antonio (city) Bexar	519

Specified Housing Units Rented by South Americans
Top 10 Places Sorted by Number

Place (place type) County	Dollars/Month
The Woodlands (cdp) Montgomery	1,316
Sugar Land (city) Fort Bend	1,167
Richardson (city) Dallas	1,000
Plano (city) Collin	986
Mission Bend (cdp) Fort Bend	882
Irving (city) Dallas	730
Austin (city) Travis	694
Arlington (city) Tarrant	666
Dallas (city) Dallas	651
Carrollton (city) Denton	646

Specified Housing Units Rented by Spaniards
Top 10 Places Sorted by Number

Place (place type) County	Dollars/Month
Dallas (city) Dallas	605
San Antonio (city) Bexar	590
Houston (city) Harris	531

Notes: Please refer to the User's Guide for an explanation of data; tables include places with populations > 9,999 and reflect only those areas that meet Summary File 4 population thresholds, therefore there may be less than 10 places listed

Specified Housing Units Rented by Uruguayans
Top 10 Places Sorted by Number

Place (place type) County	Dollars/Month
No places met population threshold.	

Specified Housing Units Rented by Venezuelans
Top 10 Places Sorted by Number

Place (place type) County	Dollars/Month
Austin (city) Travis	885
Houston (city) Harris	672

Specified Housing Units Rented by Other Hispanics
Top 10 Places Sorted by Number

Place (place type) County	Dollars/Month
Cedar Park (city) Williamson	1,019
Pflugerville (city) Travis	1,013
Watauga (city) Tarrant	950
Friendswood (city) Galveston	911
The Colony (city) Denton	883
Stafford (city) Fort Bend	841
Round Rock (city) Williamson	833
Sugar Land (city) Fort Bend	831
Galena Park (city) Harris	807
Plano (city) Collin	805

Median Home Value

All Specified Owner-Occupied Housing Units
Top 10 Places Sorted by Number

Place (place type) County	Dollars
University Park (city) Dallas	549,400
West University Place (city) Harris	372,800
Southlake (city) Tarrant	341,400
Colleyville (city) Tarrant	267,100
Bellaire (city) Harris	233,200
Addison (town) Dallas	222,400
Coppell (city) Dallas	210,700
Cinco Ranch (cdp) Fort Bend	199,800
Highland Village (city) Denton	188,500
Flower Mound (town) Denton	183,500

Specified Housing Units Owned and Occupied by Hispanics
Top 10 Places Sorted by Number

Place (place type) County	Dollars
University Park (city) Dallas	490,000
Southlake (city) Tarrant	311,300
West University Place (city) Harris	287,500
Colleyville (city) Tarrant	230,700
Highland Village (city) Denton	196,000
Cinco Ranch (cdp) Fort Bend	195,800
Addison (town) Dallas	185,400
Flower Mound (town) Denton	180,000
Coppell (city) Dallas	177,900
Keller (city) Tarrant	176,500

Specified Housing Units Owned and Occupied by Argentinians
Top 10 Places Sorted by Number

Place (place type) County	Dollars
Houston (city) Harris	133,100

Specified Housing Units Owned and Occupied by Bolivians
Top 10 Places Sorted by Number

Place (place type) County	Dollars
Houston (city) Harris	106,400

Specified Housing Units Owned and Occupied by Central Americans
Top 10 Places Sorted by Number

Place (place type) County	Dollars
Plano (city) Collin	159,400
Carrollton (city) Denton	99,100
Lewisville (city) Denton	91,200
Austin (city) Travis	88,000
Richardson (city) Dallas	86,700
Corpus Christi (city) Nueces	86,000
Farmers Branch (city) Dallas	83,700
El Paso (city) El Paso	79,400
Denton (city) Denton	79,200
Irving (city) Dallas	74,900

Specified Housing Units Owned and Occupied by Chileans
Top 10 Places Sorted by Number

Place (place type) County	Dollars
Houston (city) Harris	102,600

Specified Housing Units Owned and Occupied by Colombians
Top 10 Places Sorted by Number

Place (place type) County	Dollars
Austin (city) Travis	162,500
Dallas (city) Dallas	141,100
San Antonio (city) Bexar	121,700
Houston (city) Harris	84,300
Mission Bend (cdp) Fort Bend	82,200

Specified Housing Units Owned and Occupied by Costa Ricans
Top 10 Places Sorted by Number

Place (place type) County	Dollars
Houston (city) Harris	64,100
Dallas (city) Dallas	40,000

Specified Housing Units Owned and Occupied by Cubans
Top 10 Places Sorted by Number

Place (place type) County	Dollars
El Paso (city) El Paso	135,000
Austin (city) Travis	115,300
Houston (city) Harris	88,900
Dallas (city) Dallas	88,400
San Antonio (city) Bexar	85,000
Fort Worth (city) Tarrant	76,700

Specified Housing Units Owned and Occupied by Dominicans
Top 10 Places Sorted by Number

Place (place type) County	Dollars
Houston (city) Harris	85,500

Specified Housing Units Owned and Occupied by Ecuadorians
Top 10 Places Sorted by Number

Place (place type) County	Dollars
Houston (city) Harris	72,500

Specified Housing Units Owned and Occupied by Guatemalans
Top 10 Places Sorted by Number

Place (place type) County	Dollars
Austin (city) Travis	110,000
Garland (city) Dallas	68,100
Houston (city) Harris	61,300
Fort Worth (city) Tarrant	57,200
Dallas (city) Dallas	55,300

San Antonio (city) Bexar   54,500

Specified Housing Units Owned and Occupied by Hondurans
Top 10 Places Sorted by Number

Place (place type) County	Dollars
Austin (city) Travis	80,600
San Antonio (city) Bexar	80,000
Irving (city) Dallas	67,900
Dallas (city) Dallas	66,800
Houston (city) Harris	62,400
Garland (city) Dallas	57,500

Specified Housing Units Owned and Occupied by Mexicans
Top 10 Places Sorted by Number

Place (place type) County	Dollars
Colleyville (city) Tarrant	432,800
Southlake (city) Tarrant	300,000
West University Place (city) Harris	265,600
Addison (town) Dallas	211,500
Coppell (city) Dallas	181,100
Flower Mound (town) Denton	180,100
Keller (city) Tarrant	167,300
Bellaire (city) Harris	166,700
Brushy Creek (cdp) Williamson	163,300
Allen (city) Collin	144,800

Specified Housing Units Owned and Occupied by Nicaraguans
Top 10 Places Sorted by Number

Place (place type) County	Dollars
San Antonio (city) Bexar	88,500
Austin (city) Travis	84,400
Dallas (city) Dallas	77,100
Houston (city) Harris	75,800
Port Arthur (city) Jefferson	33,600

Specified Housing Units Owned and Occupied by Panamanians
Top 10 Places Sorted by Number

Place (place type) County	Dollars
El Paso (city) El Paso	84,200
Killeen (city) Bell	82,300
San Antonio (city) Bexar	78,100
Houston (city) Harris	63,800

Specified Housing Units Owned and Occupied by Paraguayans
Top 10 Places Sorted by Number

Place (place type) County	Dollars
No places met population threshold.	

Specified Housing Units Owned and Occupied by Peruvians
Top 10 Places Sorted by Number

Place (place type) County	Dollars
San Antonio (city) Bexar	93,100
Dallas (city) Dallas	85,800
Houston (city) Harris	83,600

Specified Housing Units Owned and Occupied by Puerto Ricans
Top 10 Places Sorted by Number

Place (place type) County	Dollars
Plano (city) Collin	159,600
Austin (city) Travis	108,500
Carrollton (city) Denton	102,500
Arlington (city) Tarrant	98,300
Fort Worth (city) Tarrant	95,700
Garland (city) Dallas	94,300

Notes: Please refer to the User's Guide for an explanation of data; tables include places with populations > 9,999 and reflect only those areas that meet Summary File 4 population thresholds, therefore there may be less than 10 places listed

San Antonio (city) Bexar	88,000
Euless (city) Tarrant	85,900
Dallas (city) Dallas	85,700
Corpus Christi (city) Nueces	85,300

Specified Housing Units Owned and Occupied by Salvadorans
Top 10 Places Sorted by Number

Place (place type) County	Dollars
Carrollton (city) Denton	99,800
Austin (city) Travis	89,000
Plano (city) Collin	85,900
Farmers Branch (city) Dallas	83,100
Dallas (city) Dallas	74,900
Mission Bend (cdp) Fort Bend	73,600
Irving (city) Dallas	71,800
Garland (city) Dallas	66,000
Conroe (city) Montgomery	65,000
Pasadena (city) Harris	63,500

Specified Housing Units Owned and Occupied by South Americans
Top 10 Places Sorted by Number

Place (place type) County	Dollars
Sugar Land (city) Fort Bend	234,600

The Woodlands (cdp) Montgomery	195,500
College Station (city) Brazos	155,800
Austin (city) Travis	154,200
Carrollton (city) Denton	135,900
Richardson (city) Dallas	130,000
Plano (city) Collin	125,000
Arlington (city) Tarrant	123,800
San Antonio (city) Bexar	113,000
Dallas (city) Dallas	107,600

Specified Housing Units Owned and Occupied by Spaniards
Top 10 Places Sorted by Number

Place (place type) County	Dollars
Dallas (city) Dallas	130,300
Houston (city) Harris	98,800
San Antonio (city) Bexar	90,600

Specified Housing Units Owned and Occupied by Uruguayans
Top 10 Places Sorted by Number

Place (place type) County	Dollars
No places met population threshold.	

Specified Housing Units Owned and Occupied by Venezuelans
Top 10 Places Sorted by Number

Place (place type) County	Dollars
Austin (city) Travis	160,900
Houston (city) Harris	114,200

Specified Housing Units Owned and Occupied by Other Hispanics
Top 10 Places Sorted by Number

Place (place type) County	Dollars
Frisco (city) Collin	165,800
Flower Mound (town) Denton	164,800
Addison (town) Dallas	162,500
Pflugerville (city) Travis	137,900
Cedar Park (city) Williamson	131,500
Allen (city) Collin	125,900
DeSoto (city) Dallas	114,400
Plano (city) Collin	112,700
Humble (city) Harris	112,500
Rowlett (city) Dallas	112,500

Notes: Please refer to the User's Guide for an explanation of data; tables include places with populations > 9,999 and reflect only those areas that meet Summary File 4 population thresholds, therefore there may be less than 10 places listed

Asian Population

Population

Total Population
Top 10 Places Sorted by Number

Place (place type) County	Number
Houston (city) Harris	1,954,848
Dallas (city) Dallas	1,188,204
San Antonio (city) Bexar	1,144,554
Austin (city) Travis	656,302
El Paso (city) El Paso	564,280
Fort Worth (city) Tarrant	535,420
Arlington (city) Tarrant	332,695
Corpus Christi (city) Nueces	277,569
Plano (city) Collin	222,301
Garland (city) Dallas	215,991

Asian
Top 10 Places Sorted by Number

Place (place type) County	Number
Houston (city) Harris	102,484
Dallas (city) Dallas	32,165
Austin (city) Travis	30,866
Plano (city) Collin	22,465
Arlington (city) Tarrant	19,271
San Antonio (city) Bexar	18,085
Garland (city) Dallas	15,646
Irving (city) Dallas	15,637
Sugar Land (city) Fort Bend	14,417
Fort Worth (city) Tarrant	13,838

Asian
Top 10 Places Sorted by Percent of Total Population

Place (place type) County	Percent
New Territory (cdp) Fort Bend	23.40
Sugar Land (city) Fort Bend	22.70
Stafford (city) Fort Bend	21.20
Four Corners (cdp) Fort Bend	19.11
Mission Bend (cdp) Fort Bend	16.75
Meadows Place (city) Fort Bend	15.60
Hedwig Village (city) Harris	13.64
Palacios (city) Matagorda	11.80
Richardson (city) Dallas	11.13
Missouri City (city) Fort Bend	10.95

Native Hawaiian and Other Pacific Islander
Top 10 Places Sorted by Number

Place (place type) County	Number
Killeen (city) Bell	1,046
Houston (city) Harris	876
San Antonio (city) Bexar	707
Dallas (city) Dallas	641
Fort Worth (city) Tarrant	555
El Paso (city) El Paso	515
Austin (city) Travis	445

Native Hawaiian and Other Pacific Islander
Top 10 Places Sorted by Percent of Total Population

Place (place type) County	Percent
Killeen (city) Bell	1.20
Fort Worth (city) Tarrant	0.10
El Paso (city) El Paso	0.09
Austin (city) Travis	0.07
San Antonio (city) Bexar	0.06
Dallas (city) Dallas	0.05
Houston (city) Harris	0.04

Asian Indian
Top 10 Places Sorted by Number

Place (place type) County	Number
Houston (city) Harris	20,476
Dallas (city) Dallas	7,358
Austin (city) Travis	7,336
Irving (city) Dallas	6,093
Plano (city) Collin	5,680
Carrollton (city) Denton	4,384
Sugar Land (city) Fort Bend	4,338
San Antonio (city) Bexar	3,329
Garland (city) Dallas	3,102
Arlington (city) Tarrant	3,007

Asian Indian
Top 10 Places Sorted by Percent of Asian Population

Place (place type) County	Percent
Addison (town) Dallas	54.89
Mesquite (city) Dallas	50.32
Flower Mound (town) Denton	50.00
New Territory (cdp) Fort Bend	48.28
Lewisville (city) Denton	40.22
Midland (city) Midland	39.25
Irving (city) Dallas	38.97
Stafford (city) Fort Bend	38.65
Euless (city) Tarrant	38.49
Carrollton (city) Denton	38.41

Asian Indian
Top 10 Places Sorted by Percent of Total Population

Place (place type) County	Percent
New Territory (cdp) Fort Bend	11.30
Stafford (city) Fort Bend	8.19
Sugar Land (city) Fort Bend	6.83
Addison (town) Dallas	4.39
Mission Bend (cdp) Fort Bend	4.24
Carrollton (city) Denton	4.01
Missouri City (city) Fort Bend	3.66
Irving (city) Dallas	3.18
Coppell (city) Dallas	3.17
Euless (city) Tarrant	2.70

Bangladeshi
Top 10 Places Sorted by Number

Place (place type) County	Number
No places met population threshold.	

Bangladeshi
Top 10 Places Sorted by Percent of Asian Population

Place (place type) County	Percent
No places met population threshold.	

Bangladeshi
Top 10 Places Sorted by Percent of Total Population

Place (place type) County	Percent
No places met population threshold.	

Cambodian
Top 10 Places Sorted by Number

Place (place type) County	Number
Dallas (city) Dallas	1,059
Carrollton (city) Denton	818
Houston (city) Harris	723

Cambodian
Top 10 Places Sorted by Percent of Asian Population

Place (place type) County	Percent
Carrollton (city) Denton	7.17
Dallas (city) Dallas	3.29
Houston (city) Harris	0.71

Cambodian
Top 10 Places Sorted by Percent of Total Population

Place (place type) County	Percent
Carrollton (city) Denton	0.75
Dallas (city) Dallas	0.09
Houston (city) Harris	0.04

Chinese (except Taiwanese)
Top 10 Places Sorted by Number

Place (place type) County	Number
Houston (city) Harris	21,856
Plano (city) Collin	9,305
Austin (city) Travis	8,022
Dallas (city) Dallas	6,083
Sugar Land (city) Fort Bend	5,287
San Antonio (city) Bexar	3,276
Richardson (city) Dallas	3,055
Arlington (city) Tarrant	2,763
Garland (city) Dallas	1,675
Irving (city) Dallas	1,547

Chinese (except Taiwanese)
Top 10 Places Sorted by Percent of Asian Population

Place (place type) County	Percent
Bellaire (city) Harris	43.16
Plano (city) Collin	41.42
Sugar Land (city) Fort Bend	36.67
Richardson (city) Dallas	29.96
College Station (city) Brazos	28.14
Galveston (city) Galveston	27.73
Austin (city) Travis	25.99
Missouri City (city) Fort Bend	24.10
Denton (city) Denton	23.84
Coppell (city) Dallas	22.53

Chinese (except Taiwanese)
Top 10 Places Sorted by Percent of Total Population

Place (place type) County	Percent
Sugar Land (city) Fort Bend	8.33
New Territory (cdp) Fort Bend	5.03
Plano (city) Collin	4.19
Stafford (city) Fort Bend	3.42
Richardson (city) Dallas	3.33
Bellaire (city) Harris	2.91
Missouri City (city) Fort Bend	2.64
Mission Bend (cdp) Fort Bend	2.22
Coppell (city) Dallas	2.16
College Station (city) Brazos	2.14

Fijian
Top 10 Places Sorted by Number

Place (place type) County	Number
No places met population threshold.	

Fijian
Top 10 Places Sorted by Percent of Asian Population

Place (place type) County	Percent
No places met population threshold.	

Fijian
Top 10 Places Sorted by Percent of Total Population

Place (place type) County	Percent
No places met population threshold.	

Filipino
Top 10 Places Sorted by Number

Place (place type) County	Number
Houston (city) Harris	7,686
San Antonio (city) Bexar	3,786
Austin (city) Travis	1,732
Dallas (city) Dallas	1,681
El Paso (city) El Paso	1,627
Corpus Christi (city) Nueces	1,601
Arlington (city) Tarrant	1,192
Garland (city) Dallas	1,113
Killeen (city) Bell	1,100
Missouri City (city) Fort Bend	1,035

Notes: Please refer to the User's Guide for an explanation of data; tables reflect only those areas that meet Summary File 4 population thresholds, therefore there may be less than 10 places listed

Filipino
Top 10 Places Sorted by Percent of Asian Population

Place (place type) County	Percent
McAllen (city) Hidalgo	48.79
Corpus Christi (city) Nueces	47.01
Abilene (city) Taylor	35.72
Killeen (city) Bell	28.91
Beaumont (city) Jefferson	25.19
El Paso (city) El Paso	24.70
Wichita Falls (city) Wichita	23.32
San Antonio (city) Bexar	20.93
Mesquite (city) Dallas	20.19
Missouri City (city) Fort Bend	18.01

Filipino
Top 10 Places Sorted by Percent of Total Population

Place (place type) County	Percent
Stafford (city) Fort Bend	3.32
Mission Bend (cdp) Fort Bend	2.98
Missouri City (city) Fort Bend	1.97
Sugar Land (city) Fort Bend	1.57
Killeen (city) Bell	1.27
McAllen (city) Hidalgo	0.90
Mesquite (city) Dallas	0.74
Beaumont (city) Jefferson	0.59
Corpus Christi (city) Nueces	0.58
Grand Prairie (city) Dallas	0.55

Guamanian or Chamorro
Top 10 Places Sorted by Number

Place (place type) County	Number
Killeen (city) Bell	500
Houston (city) Harris	442

Guamanian or Chamorro
Top 10 Places Sorted by Percent of Asian Population

Place (place type) County	Percent
Houston (city) Harris	50.46
Killeen (city) Bell	47.80

Guamanian or Chamorro
Top 10 Places Sorted by Percent of Total Population

Place (place type) County	Percent
Killeen (city) Bell	0.58
Houston (city) Harris	0.02

Hawaiian, Native
Top 10 Places Sorted by Number

Place (place type) County	Number
No places met population threshold.	

Hawaiian, Native
Top 10 Places Sorted by Percent of Asian Population

Place (place type) County	Percent
No places met population threshold.	

Hawaiian, Native
Top 10 Places Sorted by Percent of Total Population

Place (place type) County	Percent
No places met population threshold.	

Hmong
Top 10 Places Sorted by Number

Place (place type) County	Number
No places met population threshold.	

Hmong
Top 10 Places Sorted by Percent of Asian Population

Place (place type) County	Percent
No places met population threshold.	

Hmong
Top 10 Places Sorted by Percent of Total Population

Place (place type) County	Percent
No places met population threshold.	

Indonesian
Top 10 Places Sorted by Number

Place (place type) County	Number
Houston (city) Harris	517

Indonesian
Top 10 Places Sorted by Percent of Asian Population

Place (place type) County	Percent
Houston (city) Harris	0.50

Indonesian
Top 10 Places Sorted by Percent of Total Population

Place (place type) County	Percent
Houston (city) Harris	0.03

Japanese
Top 10 Places Sorted by Number

Place (place type) County	Number
Houston (city) Harris	2,407
San Antonio (city) Bexar	1,383
Austin (city) Travis	1,135
Dallas (city) Dallas	857
El Paso (city) El Paso	750
Irving (city) Dallas	678
Plano (city) Collin	499

Japanese
Top 10 Places Sorted by Percent of Asian Population

Place (place type) County	Percent
El Paso (city) El Paso	11.39
San Antonio (city) Bexar	7.65
Irving (city) Dallas	4.34
Austin (city) Travis	3.68
Dallas (city) Dallas	2.66
Houston (city) Harris	2.35
Plano (city) Collin	2.22

Japanese
Top 10 Places Sorted by Percent of Total Population

Place (place type) County	Percent
Irving (city) Dallas	0.35
Plano (city) Collin	0.22
Austin (city) Travis	0.17
El Paso (city) El Paso	0.13
Houston (city) Harris	0.12
San Antonio (city) Bexar	0.12
Dallas (city) Dallas	0.07

Korean
Top 10 Places Sorted by Number

Place (place type) County	Number
Houston (city) Harris	5,190
Austin (city) Travis	3,632
Dallas (city) Dallas	3,337
Irving (city) Dallas	2,480
Plano (city) Collin	2,139
San Antonio (city) Bexar	1,896
El Paso (city) El Paso	1,674
Killeen (city) Bell	1,570
Garland (city) Dallas	1,138
Fort Worth (city) Tarrant	1,105

Korean
Top 10 Places Sorted by Percent of Asian Population

Place (place type) County	Percent
Killeen (city) Bell	41.26
Hedwig Village (city) Harris	37.42
El Paso (city) El Paso	25.42
Denton (city) Denton	21.37
Coppell (city) Dallas	19.74
Irving (city) Dallas	15.86
College Station (city) Brazos	15.08
Austin (city) Travis	11.77
San Antonio (city) Bexar	10.48
Dallas (city) Dallas	10.37

Korean
Top 10 Places Sorted by Percent of Total Population

Place (place type) County	Percent
Hedwig Village (city) Harris	5.10
Coppell (city) Dallas	1.89
Killeen (city) Bell	1.81
Irving (city) Dallas	1.29
College Station (city) Brazos	1.15
Richardson (city) Dallas	1.13
Carrollton (city) Denton	0.96
Plano (city) Collin	0.96
Denton (city) Denton	0.70
Sugar Land (city) Fort Bend	0.69

Laotian
Top 10 Places Sorted by Number

Place (place type) County	Number
Amarillo (city) Potter	1,061
Dallas (city) Dallas	908
Haltom City (city) Tarrant	812
Fort Worth (city) Tarrant	530
Irving (city) Dallas	479
Grand Prairie (city) Dallas	391

Laotian
Top 10 Places Sorted by Percent of Asian Population

Place (place type) County	Percent
Amarillo (city) Potter	29.09
Haltom City (city) Tarrant	26.14
Grand Prairie (city) Dallas	7.38
Fort Worth (city) Tarrant	3.83
Irving (city) Dallas	3.06
Dallas (city) Dallas	2.82

Laotian
Top 10 Places Sorted by Percent of Total Population

Place (place type) County	Percent
Haltom City (city) Tarrant	2.07
Amarillo (city) Potter	0.61
Grand Prairie (city) Dallas	0.31
Irving (city) Dallas	0.25
Fort Worth (city) Tarrant	0.10
Dallas (city) Dallas	0.08

Malaysian
Top 10 Places Sorted by Number

Place (place type) County	Number
No places met population threshold.	

Malaysian
Top 10 Places Sorted by Percent of Asian Population

Place (place type) County	Percent
No places met population threshold.	

Malaysian
Top 10 Places Sorted by Percent of Total Population

Place (place type) County	Percent
No places met population threshold.	

Notes: Please refer to the User's Guide for an explanation of data; tables reflect only those areas that meet Summary File 4 population thresholds, therefore there may be less than 10 places listed

Pakistani
Top 10 Places Sorted by Number

Place (place type) County	Number
Houston (city) Harris	4,997
Dallas (city) Dallas	1,202
Carrollton (city) Denton	1,166
Garland (city) Dallas	831
Sugar Land (city) Fort Bend	618
Plano (city) Collin	604
Austin (city) Travis	526
Mission Bend (cdp) Fort Bend	480
Irving (city) Dallas	429
Richardson (city) Dallas	423

Pakistani
Top 10 Places Sorted by Percent of Asian Population

Place (place type) County	Percent
Carrollton (city) Denton	10.21
Mission Bend (cdp) Fort Bend	9.28
Garland (city) Dallas	5.31
Houston (city) Harris	4.88
Sugar Land (city) Fort Bend	4.29
Richardson (city) Dallas	4.15
Dallas (city) Dallas	3.74
Irving (city) Dallas	2.74
Plano (city) Collin	2.69
Austin (city) Travis	1.70

Pakistani
Top 10 Places Sorted by Percent of Total Population

Place (place type) County	Percent
Mission Bend (cdp) Fort Bend	1.55
Carrollton (city) Denton	1.07
Sugar Land (city) Fort Bend	0.97
Richardson (city) Dallas	0.46
Garland (city) Dallas	0.38
Plano (city) Collin	0.27
Houston (city) Harris	0.26
Irving (city) Dallas	0.22
Dallas (city) Dallas	0.10
Austin (city) Travis	0.08

Samoan
Top 10 Places Sorted by Number

Place (place type) County	Number
No places met population threshold.	

Samoan
Top 10 Places Sorted by Percent of Asian Population

Place (place type) County	Percent
No places met population threshold.	

Samoan
Top 10 Places Sorted by Percent of Total Population

Place (place type) County	Percent
No places met population threshold.	

Sri Lankan
Top 10 Places Sorted by Number

Place (place type) County	Number
No places met population threshold.	

Sri Lankan
Top 10 Places Sorted by Percent of Asian Population

Place (place type) County	Percent
No places met population threshold.	

Sri Lankan
Top 10 Places Sorted by Percent of Total Population

Place (place type) County	Percent
No places met population threshold.	

Taiwanese
Top 10 Places Sorted by Number

Place (place type) County	Number
Houston (city) Harris	1,492
Sugar Land (city) Fort Bend	937
Austin (city) Travis	748
Plano (city) Collin	564
Arlington (city) Tarrant	415

Taiwanese
Top 10 Places Sorted by Percent of Asian Population

Place (place type) County	Percent
Sugar Land (city) Fort Bend	6.50
Plano (city) Collin	2.51
Austin (city) Travis	2.42
Arlington (city) Tarrant	2.15
Houston (city) Harris	1.46

Taiwanese
Top 10 Places Sorted by Percent of Total Population

Place (place type) County	Percent
Sugar Land (city) Fort Bend	1.48
Plano (city) Collin	0.25
Arlington (city) Tarrant	0.12
Austin (city) Travis	0.11
Houston (city) Harris	0.08

Thai
Top 10 Places Sorted by Number

Place (place type) County	Number
Houston (city) Harris	881
San Antonio (city) Bexar	577

Thai
Top 10 Places Sorted by Percent of Asian Population

Place (place type) County	Percent
San Antonio (city) Bexar	3.19
Houston (city) Harris	0.86

Thai
Top 10 Places Sorted by Percent of Total Population

Place (place type) County	Percent
Houston (city) Harris	0.05
San Antonio (city) Bexar	0.05

Tongan
Top 10 Places Sorted by Number

Place (place type) County	Number
No places met population threshold.	

Tongan
Top 10 Places Sorted by Percent of Asian Population

Place (place type) County	Percent
No places met population threshold.	

Tongan
Top 10 Places Sorted by Percent of Total Population

Place (place type) County	Percent
No places met population threshold.	

Vietnamese
Top 10 Places Sorted by Number

Place (place type) County	Number
Houston (city) Harris	31,820
Arlington (city) Tarrant	9,023
Dallas (city) Dallas	7,070
Garland (city) Dallas	6,301
Austin (city) Travis	5,789
Fort Worth (city) Tarrant	5,374
Port Arthur (city) Jefferson	2,829
Carrollton (city) Denton	2,404
Grand Prairie (city) Dallas	2,383
San Antonio (city) Bexar	2,272

Vietnamese
Top 10 Places Sorted by Percent of Asian Population

Place (place type) County	Percent
Palacios (city) Matagorda	98.04
Seadrift (city) Calhoun	97.20
Fulton (town) Aransas	90.06
Port Arthur (city) Jefferson	83.50
San Leon (cdp) Galveston	81.87
Pearland (city) Brazoria	51.16
Haltom City (city) Tarrant	50.74
Arlington (city) Tarrant	46.82
Grand Prairie (city) Dallas	45.00
League City (city) Galveston	44.72

Vietnamese
Top 10 Places Sorted by Percent of Total Population

Place (place type) County	Percent
Palacios (city) Matagorda	11.57
Seadrift (city) Calhoun	10.41
Fulton (town) Aransas	9.23
San Leon (cdp) Galveston	7.11
Port Arthur (city) Jefferson	4.90
Mission Bend (cdp) Fort Bend	4.09
Haltom City (city) Tarrant	4.02
Stafford (city) Fort Bend	3.87
Garland (city) Dallas	2.92
Arlington (city) Tarrant	2.71

Median Age

Total Population
Top 10 Places Sorted by Number

Place (place type) County	Years
Fulton (town) Aransas	44.8
Bunker Hill Village (city) Harris	44.3
Hunters Creek Village (city) Harris	43.1
Hedwig Village (city) Harris	41.0
Colleyville (city) Tarrant	40.2
Bellaire (city) Harris	40.0
Meadows Place (city) Fort Bend	39.7
San Leon (cdp) Galveston	39.7
Benbrook (city) Tarrant	39.4
West University Place (city) Harris	39.0

Asian
Top 10 Places Sorted by Number

Place (place type) County	Years
Hunters Creek Village (city) Harris	46.1
Universal City (city) Bexar	46.1
Harker Heights (city) Bell	42.1
Temple (city) Bell	41.6
Copperas Cove (city) Coryell	40.9
Duncanville (city) Dallas	39.9
West University Place (city) Harris	38.3
Bellaire (city) Harris	37.8
Meadows Place (city) Fort Bend	37.6
Benbrook (city) Tarrant	37.0

Native Hawaiian and Other Pacific Islander
Top 10 Places Sorted by Number

Place (place type) County	Years
San Antonio (city) Bexar	29.8
Houston (city) Harris	28.8
El Paso (city) El Paso	28.4
Dallas (city) Dallas	27.7
Austin (city) Travis	26.2
Fort Worth (city) Tarrant	26.0
Killeen (city) Bell	25.4

Notes: Please refer to the User's Guide for an explanation of data; tables reflect only those areas that meet Summary File 4 population thresholds, therefore there may be less than 10 places listed

Asian Indian
Top 10 Places Sorted by Number

Place (place type) County	Years
Corpus Christi (city) Nueces	38.6
Mission Bend (cdp) Fort Bend	37.5
Missouri City (city) Fort Bend	36.8
Sugar Land (city) Fort Bend	35.3
Amarillo (city) Potter	33.6
The Woodlands (cdp) Montgomery	33.2
Grand Prairie (city) Dallas	32.4
Mesquite (city) Dallas	32.3
Pasadena (city) Harris	32.2
Carrollton (city) Denton	32.1

Bangladeshi
Top 10 Places Sorted by Number

Place (place type) County	Years
No places met population threshold.	

Cambodian
Top 10 Places Sorted by Number

Place (place type) County	Years
Houston (city) Harris	33.3
Carrollton (city) Denton	25.2
Dallas (city) Dallas	20.7

Chinese (except Taiwanese)
Top 10 Places Sorted by Number

Place (place type) County	Years
Bellaire (city) Harris	40.8
Sugar Land (city) Fort Bend	39.8
Stafford (city) Fort Bend	38.2
Mission Bend (cdp) Fort Bend	37.8
Coppell (city) Dallas	37.3
New Territory (cdp) Fort Bend	36.9
San Antonio (city) Bexar	36.2
Missouri City (city) Fort Bend	36.0
Richardson (city) Dallas	35.7
Galveston (city) Galveston	35.5

Fijian
Top 10 Places Sorted by Number

Place (place type) County	Years
No places met population threshold.	

Filipino
Top 10 Places Sorted by Number

Place (place type) County	Years
Irving (city) Dallas	40.1
Missouri City (city) Fort Bend	39.9
Garland (city) Dallas	39.4
Richardson (city) Dallas	39.3
Sugar Land (city) Fort Bend	37.5
El Paso (city) El Paso	35.8
Corpus Christi (city) Nueces	35.7
Dallas (city) Dallas	35.5
Mesquite (city) Dallas	35.5
Arlington (city) Tarrant	35.4

Guamanian or Chamorro
Top 10 Places Sorted by Number

Place (place type) County	Years
Killeen (city) Bell	39.2
Houston (city) Harris	28.9

Hawaiian, Native
Top 10 Places Sorted by Number

Place (place type) County	Years
No places met population threshold.	

Hmong
Top 10 Places Sorted by Number

Place (place type) County	Years
No places met population threshold.	

Indonesian
Top 10 Places Sorted by Number

Place (place type) County	Years
Houston (city) Harris	29.1

Japanese
Top 10 Places Sorted by Number

Place (place type) County	Years
El Paso (city) El Paso	51.3
San Antonio (city) Bexar	41.4
Dallas (city) Dallas	38.0
Plano (city) Collin	35.7
Irving (city) Dallas	33.9
Houston (city) Harris	32.9
Austin (city) Travis	31.9

Korean
Top 10 Places Sorted by Number

Place (place type) County	Years
Killeen (city) Bell	41.6
Sugar Land (city) Fort Bend	39.9
Richardson (city) Dallas	39.3
San Antonio (city) Bexar	38.7
El Paso (city) El Paso	38.5
Hedwig Village (city) Harris	37.3
Coppell (city) Dallas	35.8
Garland (city) Dallas	35.2
Carrollton (city) Denton	33.9
Dallas (city) Dallas	33.6

Laotian
Top 10 Places Sorted by Number

Place (place type) County	Years
Fort Worth (city) Tarrant	29.4
Amarillo (city) Potter	29.2
Dallas (city) Dallas	29.1
Haltom City (city) Tarrant	27.5
Irving (city) Dallas	27.2
Grand Prairie (city) Dallas	20.4

Malaysian
Top 10 Places Sorted by Number

Place (place type) County	Years
No places met population threshold.	

Pakistani
Top 10 Places Sorted by Number

Place (place type) County	Years
Richardson (city) Dallas	32.1
Mission Bend (cdp) Fort Bend	31.1
Irving (city) Dallas	29.7
Dallas (city) Dallas	29.4
Plano (city) Collin	29.1
Houston (city) Harris	29.0
Sugar Land (city) Fort Bend	28.2
Garland (city) Dallas	27.0
Austin (city) Travis	25.2
Carrollton (city) Denton	24.5

Samoan
Top 10 Places Sorted by Number

Place (place type) County	Years
No places met population threshold.	

Sri Lankan
Top 10 Places Sorted by Number

Place (place type) County	Years
No places met population threshold.	

Taiwanese
Top 10 Places Sorted by Number

Place (place type) County	Years
Sugar Land (city) Fort Bend	39.9
Houston (city) Harris	39.1
Plano (city) Collin	34.8
Arlington (city) Tarrant	30.1
Austin (city) Travis	23.8

Thai
Top 10 Places Sorted by Number

Place (place type) County	Years
San Antonio (city) Bexar	36.3
Houston (city) Harris	31.1

Tongan
Top 10 Places Sorted by Number

Place (place type) County	Years
No places met population threshold.	

Vietnamese
Top 10 Places Sorted by Number

Place (place type) County	Years
San Antonio (city) Bexar	35.6
Missouri City (city) Fort Bend	34.0
Sugar Land (city) Fort Bend	33.6
Mission Bend (cdp) Fort Bend	33.2
Wichita Falls (city) Wichita	32.6
Stafford (city) Fort Bend	32.5
San Leon (cdp) Galveston	32.4
Allen (city) Collin	32.3
Carrollton (city) Denton	31.7
Richardson (city) Dallas	31.4

Average Household Size

Total Population
Top 10 Places Sorted by Number

Place (place type) County	Number
Fort Hood (cdp) Coryell	3.94
Four Corners (cdp) Fort Bend	3.77
Laredo (city) Webb	3.70
Brownsville (city) Cameron	3.61
New Territory (cdp) Fort Bend	3.49
Mission Bend (cdp) Fort Bend	3.42
Aldine (cdp) Harris	3.37
Southlake (city) Tarrant	3.35
Cinco Ranch (cdp) Fort Bend	3.33
Channelview (cdp) Harris	3.24

Asian
Top 10 Places Sorted by Number

Place (place type) County	Number
Palacios (city) Matagorda	5.67
Bunker Hill Village (city) Harris	4.76
Brenham (city) Washington	4.64
Humble (city) Harris	4.57
Four Corners (cdp) Fort Bend	4.27
Seadrift (city) Calhoun	4.25
Nederland (city) Jefferson	4.18
San Leon (cdp) Galveston	4.14
Port Arthur (city) Jefferson	4.00
Channelview (cdp) Harris	3.97

Notes: Please refer to the User's Guide for an explanation of data; tables reflect only those areas that meet Summary File 4 population thresholds, therefore there may be less than 10 places listed

Native Hawaiian and Other Pacific Islander
Top 10 Places Sorted by Number

Place (place type) County	Number
El Paso (city) El Paso	4.40
Killeen (city) Bell	4.06
Dallas (city) Dallas	3.43
Houston (city) Harris	3.11
San Antonio (city) Bexar	3.00
Fort Worth (city) Tarrant	2.92
Austin (city) Travis	2.41

Asian Indian
Top 10 Places Sorted by Number

Place (place type) County	Number
Rowlett (city) Dallas	4.33
Grand Prairie (city) Dallas	4.20
New Territory (cdp) Fort Bend	4.09
Pasadena (city) Harris	3.83
Sugar Land (city) Fort Bend	3.81
Garland (city) Dallas	3.80
Allen (city) Collin	3.79
Mesquite (city) Dallas	3.68
Carrollton (city) Denton	3.66
Stafford (city) Fort Bend	3.63

Bangladeshi
Top 10 Places Sorted by Number

Place (place type) County	Number
No places met population threshold.	

Cambodian
Top 10 Places Sorted by Number

Place (place type) County	Number
Carrollton (city) Denton	4.57
Dallas (city) Dallas	4.13
Houston (city) Harris	3.33

Chinese (except Taiwanese)
Top 10 Places Sorted by Number

Place (place type) County	Number
Missouri City (city) Fort Bend	3.84
New Territory (cdp) Fort Bend	3.57
Bellaire (city) Harris	3.49
Sugar Land (city) Fort Bend	3.46
Mission Bend (cdp) Fort Bend	3.39
Coppell (city) Dallas	3.38
Garland (city) Dallas	3.37
Plano (city) Collin	3.28
Carrollton (city) Denton	2.99
Arlington (city) Tarrant	2.94

Fijian
Top 10 Places Sorted by Number

Place (place type) County	Number
No places met population threshold.	

Filipino
Top 10 Places Sorted by Number

Place (place type) County	Number
Mission Bend (cdp) Fort Bend	4.38
Mesquite (city) Dallas	3.89
Sugar Land (city) Fort Bend	3.68
Stafford (city) Fort Bend	3.58
Missouri City (city) Fort Bend	3.57
Beaumont (city) Jefferson	3.47
Corpus Christi (city) Nueces	3.27
Plano (city) Collin	3.17
Grand Prairie (city) Dallas	3.15
Killeen (city) Bell	3.05

Guamanian or Chamorro
Top 10 Places Sorted by Number

Place (place type) County	Number
Killeen (city) Bell	3.57
Houston (city) Harris	3.17

Hawaiian, Native
Top 10 Places Sorted by Number

Place (place type) County	Number
No places met population threshold.	

Hmong
Top 10 Places Sorted by Number

Place (place type) County	Number
No places met population threshold.	

Indonesian
Top 10 Places Sorted by Number

Place (place type) County	Number
Houston (city) Harris	2.66

Japanese
Top 10 Places Sorted by Number

Place (place type) County	Number
Plano (city) Collin	2.61
Houston (city) Harris	2.23
San Antonio (city) Bexar	2.18
Irving (city) Dallas	2.17
Austin (city) Travis	1.94
El Paso (city) El Paso	1.93
Dallas (city) Dallas	1.82

Korean
Top 10 Places Sorted by Number

Place (place type) County	Number
Coppell (city) Dallas	3.75
Carrollton (city) Denton	3.53
Plano (city) Collin	3.46
Richardson (city) Dallas	3.41
Garland (city) Dallas	3.35
Sugar Land (city) Fort Bend	3.32
Hedwig Village (city) Harris	3.05
Arlington (city) Tarrant	2.72
Killeen (city) Bell	2.71
Irving (city) Dallas	2.68

Laotian
Top 10 Places Sorted by Number

Place (place type) County	Number
Grand Prairie (city) Dallas	4.96
Haltom City (city) Tarrant	4.13
Amarillo (city) Potter	3.95
Fort Worth (city) Tarrant	3.81
Dallas (city) Dallas	3.64
Irving (city) Dallas	3.45

Malaysian
Top 10 Places Sorted by Number

Place (place type) County	Number
No places met population threshold.	

Pakistani
Top 10 Places Sorted by Number

Place (place type) County	Number
Mission Bend (cdp) Fort Bend	5.26
Sugar Land (city) Fort Bend	4.58
Carrollton (city) Denton	4.05
Garland (city) Dallas	3.89
Plano (city) Collin	3.78
Richardson (city) Dallas	3.52
Houston (city) Harris	3.50

Place (place type) County	Number
Irving (city) Dallas	3.05
Austin (city) Travis	2.94
Dallas (city) Dallas	2.83

Samoan
Top 10 Places Sorted by Number

Place (place type) County	Number
No places met population threshold.	

Sri Lankan
Top 10 Places Sorted by Number

Place (place type) County	Number
No places met population threshold.	

Taiwanese
Top 10 Places Sorted by Number

Place (place type) County	Number
Sugar Land (city) Fort Bend	3.72
Plano (city) Collin	3.22
Arlington (city) Tarrant	2.68
Austin (city) Travis	2.44
Houston (city) Harris	2.41

Thai
Top 10 Places Sorted by Number

Place (place type) County	Number
Houston (city) Harris	2.63
San Antonio (city) Bexar	2.37

Tongan
Top 10 Places Sorted by Number

Place (place type) County	Number
No places met population threshold.	

Vietnamese
Top 10 Places Sorted by Number

Place (place type) County	Number
Palacios (city) Matagorda	5.67
League City (city) Galveston	4.67
Pearland (city) Brazoria	4.49
Seadrift (city) Calhoun	4.44
Port Arthur (city) Jefferson	4.40
Lewisville (city) Denton	4.39
San Leon (cdp) Galveston	4.09
Pasadena (city) Harris	4.08
Arlington (city) Tarrant	3.92
Carrollton (city) Denton	3.92

Language Spoken at Home: English Only

Total Populations 5 Years and Over Who Speak English-Only at Home
Top 10 Places Sorted by Number

Place (place type) County	Number
Houston (city) Harris	1,053,207
Dallas (city) Dallas	685,534
San Antonio (city) Bexar	560,786
Austin (city) Travis	419,884
Fort Worth (city) Tarrant	347,721
Arlington (city) Tarrant	231,505
Plano (city) Collin	158,931
Corpus Christi (city) Nueces	150,742
El Paso (city) El Paso	148,224
Lubbock (city) Lubbock	144,093

Total Populations 5 Years and Over Who Speak English-Only at Home
Top 10 Places Sorted by Percent

Place (place type) County	Percent
Keller (city) Tarrant	93.15
Benbrook (city) Tarrant	92.14

Notes: Please refer to the User's Guide for an explanation of data; tables reflect only those areas that meet Summary File 4 population thresholds, therefore there may be less than 10 places listed

Place (place type) County	
Nederland (city) Jefferson	91.85
Southlake (city) Tarrant	91.70
Colleyville (city) Tarrant	91.55
Flower Mound (town) Denton	90.79
University Park (city) Dallas	90.47
Friendswood (city) Galveston	89.64
Longview (city) Gregg	89.49
DeSoto (city) Dallas	89.45

Asians 5 Years and Over Who Speak English-Only at Home
Top 10 Places Sorted by Number

Place (place type) County	Number
Houston (city) Harris	9,852
Austin (city) Travis	5,237
San Antonio (city) Bexar	4,415
Dallas (city) Dallas	3,911
Plano (city) Collin	2,180
Irving (city) Dallas	1,874
Arlington (city) Tarrant	1,834
Fort Worth (city) Tarrant	1,819
Sugar Land (city) Fort Bend	1,660
El Paso (city) El Paso	1,634

Asians 5 Years and Over Who Speak English-Only at Home
Top 10 Places Sorted by Percent

Place (place type) County	Percent
West University Place (city) Harris	38.03
Benbrook (city) Tarrant	35.73
Bedford (city) Tarrant	31.99
Copperas Cove (city) Coryell	31.77
Spring (cdp) Harris	31.53
San Angelo (city) Tom Green	31.50
Colleyville (city) Tarrant	31.14
Fort Hood (cdp) Coryell	30.83
Brushy Creek (cdp) Williamson	28.78
Abilene (city) Taylor	28.74

Native Hawaiian and Other Pacific Islanders 5 Years and Over Who Speak English-Only at Home
Top 10 Places Sorted by Number

Place (place type) County	Number
Killeen (city) Bell	571
San Antonio (city) Bexar	366
Houston (city) Harris	311
Austin (city) Travis	250
Dallas (city) Dallas	246
El Paso (city) El Paso	242
Fort Worth (city) Tarrant	227

Native Hawaiian and Other Pacific Islanders 5 Years and Over Who Speak English-Only at Home
Top 10 Places Sorted by Percent

Place (place type) County	Percent
Austin (city) Travis	60.83
Killeen (city) Bell	55.82
San Antonio (city) Bexar	54.14
El Paso (city) El Paso	50.31
Fort Worth (city) Tarrant	48.30
Dallas (city) Dallas	40.80
Houston (city) Harris	38.92

Asian Indians 5 Years and Over Who Speak English-Only at Home
Top 10 Places Sorted by Number

Place (place type) County	Number
Houston (city) Harris	2,670
Austin (city) Travis	1,498
Dallas (city) Dallas	1,055
Irving (city) Dallas	836
Plano (city) Collin	721
Sugar Land (city) Fort Bend	673
San Antonio (city) Bexar	598

Place (place type) County	
Carrollton (city) Denton	506
Fort Worth (city) Tarrant	375
Garland (city) Dallas	369

Asian Indians 5 Years and Over Who Speak English-Only at Home
Top 10 Places Sorted by Percent

Place (place type) County	Percent
Flower Mound (town) Denton	33.72
Lubbock (city) Lubbock	31.55
El Paso (city) El Paso	24.55
The Woodlands (cdp) Montgomery	23.63
Pasadena (city) Harris	23.59
Austin (city) Travis	22.14
Lewisville (city) Denton	21.77
Midland (city) Midland	21.33
San Antonio (city) Bexar	19.72
Allen (city) Collin	18.75

Bangladeshis 5 Years and Over Who Speak English-Only at Home
Top 10 Places Sorted by Number

Place (place type) County	Number
No places met population threshold.	

Bangladeshis 5 Years and Over Who Speak English-Only at Home
Top 10 Places Sorted by Percent

Place (place type) County	Percent
No places met population threshold.	

Cambodians 5 Years and Over Who Speak English-Only at Home
Top 10 Places Sorted by Number

Place (place type) County	Number
Carrollton (city) Denton	89
Houston (city) Harris	67
Dallas (city) Dallas	66

Cambodians 5 Years and Over Who Speak English-Only at Home
Top 10 Places Sorted by Percent

Place (place type) County	Percent
Carrollton (city) Denton	11.59
Houston (city) Harris	9.64
Dallas (city) Dallas	7.07

Chinese (except Taiwanese) 5 Years and Over Who Speak English-Only at Home
Top 10 Places Sorted by Number

Place (place type) County	Number
Houston (city) Harris	2,072
Austin (city) Travis	1,073
Dallas (city) Dallas	774
San Antonio (city) Bexar	605
Plano (city) Collin	603
Sugar Land (city) Fort Bend	446
Richardson (city) Dallas	263
Arlington (city) Tarrant	239
Fort Worth (city) Tarrant	191
Irving (city) Dallas	142

Chinese (except Taiwanese)s 5 Years and Over Who Speak English-Only at Home
Top 10 Places Sorted by Percent

Place (place type) County	Percent
Bellaire (city) Harris	28.31
San Antonio (city) Bexar	19.45
El Paso (city) El Paso	16.69
Fort Worth (city) Tarrant	14.69
Austin (city) Travis	14.19
Mission Bend (cdp) Fort Bend	14.11

Place (place type) County	
Denton (city) Denton	13.70
Dallas (city) Dallas	13.64
Carrollton (city) Denton	13.14
New Territory (cdp) Fort Bend	13.02

Fijians 5 Years and Over Who Speak English-Only at Home
Top 10 Places Sorted by Number

Place (place type) County	Number
No places met population threshold.	

Fijians 5 Years and Over Who Speak English-Only at Home
Top 10 Places Sorted by Percent

Place (place type) County	Percent
No places met population threshold.	

Filipinos 5 Years and Over Who Speak English-Only at Home
Top 10 Places Sorted by Number

Place (place type) County	Number
Houston (city) Harris	1,457
San Antonio (city) Bexar	1,321
Austin (city) Travis	723
Dallas (city) Dallas	554
El Paso (city) El Paso	530
Corpus Christi (city) Nueces	386
Arlington (city) Tarrant	381
Garland (city) Dallas	349
Killeen (city) Bell	309
Mesquite (city) Dallas	258

Filipinos 5 Years and Over Who Speak English-Only at Home
Top 10 Places Sorted by Percent

Place (place type) County	Percent
Austin (city) Travis	44.11
San Antonio (city) Bexar	36.65
Abilene (city) Taylor	36.51
El Paso (city) El Paso	34.02
Arlington (city) Tarrant	33.93
Richardson (city) Dallas	33.78
Dallas (city) Dallas	33.31
Wichita Falls (city) Wichita	31.98
Garland (city) Dallas	31.79
Killeen (city) Bell	30.09

Guamanian or Chamorros 5 Years and Over Who Speak English-Only at Home
Top 10 Places Sorted by Number

Place (place type) County	Number
Killeen (city) Bell	257
Houston (city) Harris	165

Guamanian or Chamorros 5 Years and Over Who Speak English-Only at Home
Top 10 Places Sorted by Percent

Place (place type) County	Percent
Killeen (city) Bell	51.40
Houston (city) Harris	42.20

Hawaiian, Natives 5 Years and Over Who Speak English-Only at Home
Top 10 Places Sorted by Number

Place (place type) County	Number
No places met population threshold.	

Notes: Please refer to the User's Guide for an explanation of data; tables reflect only those areas that meet Summary File 4 population thresholds, therefore there may be less than 10 places listed

Hawaiian, Natives 5 Years and Over Who Speak English-Only at Home
Top 10 Places Sorted by Percent

Place (place type) County	Percent
No places met population threshold.	

Hmongs 5 Years and Over Who Speak English-Only at Home
Top 10 Places Sorted by Number

Place (place type) County	Number
No places met population threshold.	

Hmongs 5 Years and Over Who Speak English-Only at Home
Top 10 Places Sorted by Percent

Place (place type) County	Percent
No places met population threshold.	

Indonesians 5 Years and Over Who Speak English-Only at Home
Top 10 Places Sorted by Number

Place (place type) County	Number
Houston (city) Harris	73

Indonesians 5 Years and Over Who Speak English-Only at Home
Top 10 Places Sorted by Percent

Place (place type) County	Percent
Houston (city) Harris	15.57

Japaneses 5 Years and Over Who Speak English-Only at Home
Top 10 Places Sorted by Number

Place (place type) County	Number
San Antonio (city) Bexar	670
Houston (city) Harris	598
Austin (city) Travis	300
Dallas (city) Dallas	281
El Paso (city) El Paso	184
Irving (city) Dallas	89
Plano (city) Collin	89

Japaneses 5 Years and Over Who Speak English-Only at Home
Top 10 Places Sorted by Percent

Place (place type) County	Percent
San Antonio (city) Bexar	49.78
Dallas (city) Dallas	33.61
Houston (city) Harris	27.11
Austin (city) Travis	26.93
El Paso (city) El Paso	24.90
Plano (city) Collin	18.78
Irving (city) Dallas	15.34

Koreans 5 Years and Over Who Speak English-Only at Home
Top 10 Places Sorted by Number

Place (place type) County	Number
Houston (city) Harris	652
Austin (city) Travis	606
San Antonio (city) Bexar	394
El Paso (city) El Paso	362
Dallas (city) Dallas	346
Plano (city) Collin	292
Killeen (city) Bell	248
Fort Worth (city) Tarrant	201
Irving (city) Dallas	155
Arlington (city) Tarrant	145

Koreans 5 Years and Over Who Speak English-Only at Home
Top 10 Places Sorted by Percent

Place (place type) County	Percent
El Paso (city) El Paso	22.95
San Antonio (city) Bexar	21.74
Fort Worth (city) Tarrant	20.24
Austin (city) Travis	18.27
Arlington (city) Tarrant	17.47
Killeen (city) Bell	16.60
Sugar Land (city) Fort Bend	16.59
Plano (city) Collin	15.10
Houston (city) Harris	13.04
Denton (city) Denton	11.74

Laotians 5 Years and Over Who Speak English-Only at Home
Top 10 Places Sorted by Number

Place (place type) County	Number
Irving (city) Dallas	94
Dallas (city) Dallas	92
Haltom City (city) Tarrant	48
Fort Worth (city) Tarrant	27
Grand Prairie (city) Dallas	26
Amarillo (city) Potter	14

Laotians 5 Years and Over Who Speak English-Only at Home
Top 10 Places Sorted by Percent

Place (place type) County	Percent
Irving (city) Dallas	20.80
Dallas (city) Dallas	10.76
Grand Prairie (city) Dallas	7.22
Haltom City (city) Tarrant	6.54
Fort Worth (city) Tarrant	5.39
Amarillo (city) Potter	1.44

Malaysians 5 Years and Over Who Speak English-Only at Home
Top 10 Places Sorted by Number

Place (place type) County	Number
No places met population threshold.	

Malaysians 5 Years and Over Who Speak English-Only at Home
Top 10 Places Sorted by Percent

Place (place type) County	Percent
No places met population threshold.	

Pakistanis 5 Years and Over Who Speak English-Only at Home
Top 10 Places Sorted by Number

Place (place type) County	Number
Houston (city) Harris	183
Carrollton (city) Denton	128
Dallas (city) Dallas	83
Garland (city) Dallas	71
Austin (city) Travis	30
Plano (city) Collin	30
Irving (city) Dallas	15
Richardson (city) Dallas	5
Mission Bend (cdp) Fort Bend	0
Sugar Land (city) Fort Bend	0

Pakistanis 5 Years and Over Who Speak English-Only at Home
Top 10 Places Sorted by Percent

Place (place type) County	Percent
Carrollton (city) Denton	11.87
Garland (city) Dallas	10.03
Dallas (city) Dallas	8.10
Austin (city) Travis	6.16
Plano (city) Collin	5.64
Houston (city) Harris	4.12
Irving (city) Dallas	3.77
Richardson (city) Dallas	1.23
Mission Bend (cdp) Fort Bend	0.00
Sugar Land (city) Fort Bend	0.00

Samoans 5 Years and Over Who Speak English-Only at Home
Top 10 Places Sorted by Number

Place (place type) County	Number
No places met population threshold.	

Samoans 5 Years and Over Who Speak English-Only at Home
Top 10 Places Sorted by Percent

Place (place type) County	Percent
No places met population threshold.	

Sri Lankans 5 Years and Over Who Speak English-Only at Home
Top 10 Places Sorted by Number

Place (place type) County	Number
No places met population threshold.	

Sri Lankans 5 Years and Over Who Speak English-Only at Home
Top 10 Places Sorted by Percent

Place (place type) County	Percent
No places met population threshold.	

Taiwaneses 5 Years and Over Who Speak English-Only at Home
Top 10 Places Sorted by Number

Place (place type) County	Number
Houston (city) Harris	87
Austin (city) Travis	81
Sugar Land (city) Fort Bend	76
Arlington (city) Tarrant	25
Plano (city) Collin	9

Taiwaneses 5 Years and Over Who Speak English-Only at Home
Top 10 Places Sorted by Percent

Place (place type) County	Percent
Austin (city) Travis	11.62
Sugar Land (city) Fort Bend	8.40
Arlington (city) Tarrant	6.31
Houston (city) Harris	5.92
Plano (city) Collin	1.65

Thais 5 Years and Over Who Speak English-Only at Home
Top 10 Places Sorted by Number

Place (place type) County	Number
San Antonio (city) Bexar	189
Houston (city) Harris	119

Thais 5 Years and Over Who Speak English-Only at Home
Top 10 Places Sorted by Percent

Place (place type) County	Percent
San Antonio (city) Bexar	32.76
Houston (city) Harris	14.22

Tongans 5 Years and Over Who Speak English-Only at Home
Top 10 Places Sorted by Number

Place (place type) County	Number
No places met population threshold.	

Notes: Please refer to the User's Guide for an explanation of data; tables reflect only those areas that meet Summary File 4 population thresholds, therefore there may be less than 10 places listed

Tongans 5 Years and Over Who Speak English-Only at Home
Top 10 Places Sorted by Percent

Place (place type) County	Percent
No places met population threshold.	

Vietnamese 5 Years and Over Who Speak English-Only at Home
Top 10 Places Sorted by Number

Place (place type) County	Number
Houston (city) Harris	1,222
Austin (city) Travis	429
Arlington (city) Tarrant	369
Dallas (city) Dallas	355
Fort Worth (city) Tarrant	333
Garland (city) Dallas	277
San Antonio (city) Bexar	189
Grand Prairie (city) Dallas	172
Irving (city) Dallas	143
Sugar Land (city) Fort Bend	96

Vietnamese 5 Years and Over Who Speak English-Only at Home
Top 10 Places Sorted by Percent

Place (place type) County	Percent
Lewisville (city) Denton	20.00
League City (city) Galveston	17.40
North Richland Hills (city) Tarrant	12.23
Allen (city) Collin	11.34
Palacios (city) Matagorda	10.67
Irving (city) Dallas	10.10
San Leon (cdp) Galveston	9.85
San Antonio (city) Bexar	8.90
Austin (city) Travis	7.97
Sugar Land (city) Fort Bend	7.91

Foreign Born

Total Population
Top 10 Places Sorted by Number

Place (place type) County	Number
Houston (city) Harris	516,105
Dallas (city) Dallas	290,436
El Paso (city) El Paso	147,505
San Antonio (city) Bexar	133,675
Austin (city) Travis	109,006
Fort Worth (city) Tarrant	87,120
Arlington (city) Tarrant	50,911
Irving (city) Dallas	50,696
Laredo (city) Webb	50,233
Brownsville (city) Cameron	44,116

Total Population
Top 10 Places Sorted by Percent

Place (place type) County	Percent
Four Corners (cdp) Fort Bend	33.73
Brownsville (city) Cameron	31.49
Mission Bend (cdp) Fort Bend	29.66
Laredo (city) Webb	28.41
Stafford (city) Fort Bend	27.75
McAllen (city) Hidalgo	27.70
Aldine (cdp) Harris	27.35
Addison (town) Dallas	27.15
Irving (city) Dallas	26.46
Houston (city) Harris	26.40

Asian
Top 10 Places Sorted by Number

Place (place type) County	Number
Houston (city) Harris	80,093
Dallas (city) Dallas	25,247
Austin (city) Travis	21,947
Plano (city) Collin	16,470
Arlington (city) Tarrant	14,810
San Antonio (city) Bexar	12,496
Irving (city) Dallas	12,388
Garland (city) Dallas	11,621
Sugar Land (city) Fort Bend	10,270
Fort Worth (city) Tarrant	10,052

Asian
Top 10 Places Sorted by Percent

Place (place type) County	Percent
Bryan (city) Brazos	86.86
Conroe (city) Montgomery	85.68
Anderson Mill (cdp) Williamson	81.65
Farmers Branch (city) Dallas	80.49
Galveston (city) Galveston	79.45
Brownsville (city) Cameron	79.29
Irving (city) Dallas	79.22
Lubbock (city) Lubbock	78.68
Cedar Park (city) Williamson	78.67
Richardson (city) Dallas	78.51

Native Hawaiian and Other Pacific Islander
Top 10 Places Sorted by Number

Place (place type) County	Number
Houston (city) Harris	246
Fort Worth (city) Tarrant	227
Dallas (city) Dallas	178
San Antonio (city) Bexar	139
Killeen (city) Bell	130
El Paso (city) El Paso	46
Austin (city) Travis	33

Native Hawaiian and Other Pacific Islander
Top 10 Places Sorted by Percent

Place (place type) County	Percent
Fort Worth (city) Tarrant	40.90
Houston (city) Harris	28.08
Dallas (city) Dallas	27.77
San Antonio (city) Bexar	19.66
Killeen (city) Bell	12.43
El Paso (city) El Paso	8.93
Austin (city) Travis	7.42

Asian Indian
Top 10 Places Sorted by Number

Place (place type) County	Number
Houston (city) Harris	15,810
Dallas (city) Dallas	6,040
Austin (city) Travis	5,458
Irving (city) Dallas	4,850
Plano (city) Collin	4,287
Carrollton (city) Denton	3,239
Sugar Land (city) Fort Bend	3,109
Arlington (city) Tarrant	2,399
San Antonio (city) Bexar	2,346
Garland (city) Dallas	2,342

Asian Indian
Top 10 Places Sorted by Percent

Place (place type) County	Percent
Addison (town) Dallas	86.47
Dallas (city) Dallas	82.09
The Woodlands (cdp) Montgomery	81.28
Richardson (city) Dallas	81.05
Galveston (city) Galveston	80.41
Arlington (city) Tarrant	79.78
Irving (city) Dallas	79.60
El Paso (city) El Paso	79.41
Pasadena (city) Harris	79.12
Mission Bend (cdp) Fort Bend	78.47

Bangladeshi
Top 10 Places Sorted by Number

Place (place type) County	Number
No places met population threshold.	

Bangladeshi
Top 10 Places Sorted by Percent

Place (place type) County	Percent
No places met population threshold.	

Cambodian
Top 10 Places Sorted by Number

Place (place type) County	Number
Dallas (city) Dallas	641
Houston (city) Harris	585
Carrollton (city) Denton	516

Cambodian
Top 10 Places Sorted by Percent

Place (place type) County	Percent
Houston (city) Harris	80.91
Carrollton (city) Denton	63.08
Dallas (city) Dallas	60.53

Chinese (except Taiwanese)
Top 10 Places Sorted by Number

Place (place type) County	Number
Houston (city) Harris	17,136
Plano (city) Collin	6,796
Austin (city) Travis	5,778
Dallas (city) Dallas	4,688
Sugar Land (city) Fort Bend	3,802
Richardson (city) Dallas	2,407
San Antonio (city) Bexar	2,284
Arlington (city) Tarrant	2,103
Irving (city) Dallas	1,302
Garland (city) Dallas	1,232

Chinese (except Taiwanese)
Top 10 Places Sorted by Percent

Place (place type) County	Percent
Irving (city) Dallas	84.16
Lubbock (city) Lubbock	83.51
Carrollton (city) Denton	79.14
Richardson (city) Dallas	78.79
Houston (city) Harris	78.40
Denton (city) Denton	77.55
Dallas (city) Dallas	77.07
College Station (city) Brazos	76.45
Arlington (city) Tarrant	76.11
Galveston (city) Galveston	75.69

Fijian
Top 10 Places Sorted by Number

Place (place type) County	Number
No places met population threshold.	

Fijian
Top 10 Places Sorted by Percent

Place (place type) County	Percent
No places met population threshold.	

Filipino
Top 10 Places Sorted by Number

Place (place type) County	Number
Houston (city) Harris	5,793
San Antonio (city) Bexar	2,495
Corpus Christi (city) Nueces	1,199
Dallas (city) Dallas	1,193
Austin (city) Travis	1,001
El Paso (city) El Paso	938

Notes: Please refer to the User's Guide for an explanation of data; tables reflect only those areas that meet Summary File 4 population thresholds, therefore there may be less than 10 places listed

Arlington (city) Tarrant 879
Garland (city) Dallas 794
McAllen (city) Hidalgo 783
Killeen (city) Bell 771

Filipino
Top 10 Places Sorted by Percent

Place (place type) County	Percent
McAllen (city) Hidalgo	82.33
Richardson (city) Dallas	80.53
Mission Bend (cdp) Fort Bend	78.07
Plano (city) Collin	75.90
Houston (city) Harris	75.37
Corpus Christi (city) Nueces	74.89
Mesquite (city) Dallas	74.35
Irving (city) Dallas	73.90
Arlington (city) Tarrant	73.74
Fort Worth (city) Tarrant	72.05

Guamanian or Chamorro
Top 10 Places Sorted by Number

Place (place type) County	Number
Houston (city) Harris	54
Killeen (city) Bell	18

Guamanian or Chamorro
Top 10 Places Sorted by Percent

Place (place type) County	Percent
Houston (city) Harris	12.22
Killeen (city) Bell	3.60

Hawaiian, Native
Top 10 Places Sorted by Number

Place (place type) County	Number
No places met population threshold.	

Hawaiian, Native
Top 10 Places Sorted by Percent

Place (place type) County	Percent
No places met population threshold.	

Hmong
Top 10 Places Sorted by Number

Place (place type) County	Number
No places met population threshold.	

Hmong
Top 10 Places Sorted by Percent

Place (place type) County	Percent
No places met population threshold.	

Indonesian
Top 10 Places Sorted by Number

Place (place type) County	Number
Houston (city) Harris	503

Indonesian
Top 10 Places Sorted by Percent

Place (place type) County	Percent
Houston (city) Harris	97.29

Japanese
Top 10 Places Sorted by Number

Place (place type) County	Number
Houston (city) Harris	1,745
Austin (city) Travis	797
San Antonio (city) Bexar	746
Dallas (city) Dallas	582
El Paso (city) El Paso	552
Irving (city) Dallas	527

Plano (city) Collin 377

Japanese
Top 10 Places Sorted by Percent

Place (place type) County	Percent
Irving (city) Dallas	77.73
Plano (city) Collin	75.55
El Paso (city) El Paso	73.60
Houston (city) Harris	72.50
Austin (city) Travis	70.22
Dallas (city) Dallas	67.91
San Antonio (city) Bexar	53.94

Korean
Top 10 Places Sorted by Number

Place (place type) County	Number
Houston (city) Harris	4,200
Dallas (city) Dallas	2,723
Austin (city) Travis	2,567
Irving (city) Dallas	1,939
Plano (city) Collin	1,545
San Antonio (city) Bexar	1,509
Killeen (city) Bell	1,349
El Paso (city) El Paso	1,230
Garland (city) Dallas	933
Richardson (city) Dallas	866

Korean
Top 10 Places Sorted by Percent

Place (place type) County	Percent
Hedwig Village (city) Harris	92.44
Killeen (city) Bell	85.92
Richardson (city) Dallas	84.00
Arlington (city) Tarrant	83.77
College Station (city) Brazos	82.01
Garland (city) Dallas	81.99
Dallas (city) Dallas	81.60
Houston (city) Harris	80.92
San Antonio (city) Bexar	79.59
Sugar Land (city) Fort Bend	78.86

Laotian
Top 10 Places Sorted by Number

Place (place type) County	Number
Amarillo (city) Potter	731
Dallas (city) Dallas	641
Haltom City (city) Tarrant	531
Irving (city) Dallas	375
Fort Worth (city) Tarrant	335
Grand Prairie (city) Dallas	278

Laotian
Top 10 Places Sorted by Percent

Place (place type) County	Percent
Irving (city) Dallas	78.29
Grand Prairie (city) Dallas	71.10
Dallas (city) Dallas	70.59
Amarillo (city) Potter	68.90
Haltom City (city) Tarrant	65.39
Fort Worth (city) Tarrant	63.21

Malaysian
Top 10 Places Sorted by Number

Place (place type) County	Number
No places met population threshold.	

Malaysian
Top 10 Places Sorted by Percent

Place (place type) County	Percent
No places met population threshold.	

Pakistani
Top 10 Places Sorted by Number

Place (place type) County	Number
Houston (city) Harris	4,081
Dallas (city) Dallas	932
Carrollton (city) Denton	795
Garland (city) Dallas	519
Sugar Land (city) Fort Bend	444
Austin (city) Travis	434
Mission Bend (cdp) Fort Bend	402
Plano (city) Collin	393
Richardson (city) Dallas	347
Irving (city) Dallas	327

Pakistani
Top 10 Places Sorted by Percent

Place (place type) County	Percent
Mission Bend (cdp) Fort Bend	83.75
Austin (city) Travis	82.51
Richardson (city) Dallas	82.03
Houston (city) Harris	81.67
Dallas (city) Dallas	77.54
Irving (city) Dallas	76.22
Sugar Land (city) Fort Bend	71.84
Carrollton (city) Denton	68.18
Plano (city) Collin	65.07
Garland (city) Dallas	62.45

Samoan
Top 10 Places Sorted by Number

Place (place type) County	Number
No places met population threshold.	

Samoan
Top 10 Places Sorted by Percent

Place (place type) County	Percent
No places met population threshold.	

Sri Lankan
Top 10 Places Sorted by Number

Place (place type) County	Number
No places met population threshold.	

Sri Lankan
Top 10 Places Sorted by Percent

Place (place type) County	Percent
No places met population threshold.	

Taiwanese
Top 10 Places Sorted by Number

Place (place type) County	Number
Houston (city) Harris	1,262
Sugar Land (city) Fort Bend	714
Austin (city) Travis	508
Plano (city) Collin	377
Arlington (city) Tarrant	326

Taiwanese
Top 10 Places Sorted by Percent

Place (place type) County	Percent
Houston (city) Harris	84.58
Arlington (city) Tarrant	78.55
Sugar Land (city) Fort Bend	76.20
Austin (city) Travis	67.91
Plano (city) Collin	66.84

Thai
Top 10 Places Sorted by Number

Place (place type) County	Number
Houston (city) Harris	704
San Antonio (city) Bexar	420

Notes: Please refer to the User's Guide for an explanation of data; tables reflect only those areas that meet Summary File 4 population thresholds, therefore there may be less than 10 places listed

Thai
Top 10 Places Sorted by Percent

Place (place type) County	Percent
Houston (city) Harris	79.91
San Antonio (city) Bexar	72.79

Tongan
Top 10 Places Sorted by Number

Place (place type) County	Number
No places met population threshold.	

Tongan
Top 10 Places Sorted by Percent

Place (place type) County	Percent
No places met population threshold.	

Vietnamese
Top 10 Places Sorted by Number

Place (place type) County	Number
Houston (city) Harris	25,244
Arlington (city) Tarrant	6,946
Dallas (city) Dallas	5,895
Garland (city) Dallas	4,927
Austin (city) Travis	4,159
Fort Worth (city) Tarrant	4,039
San Antonio (city) Bexar	1,814
Carrollton (city) Denton	1,811
Grand Prairie (city) Dallas	1,603
Port Arthur (city) Jefferson	1,551

Vietnamese
Top 10 Places Sorted by Percent

Place (place type) County	Percent
Lubbock (city) Lubbock	85.05
Dallas (city) Dallas	83.38
San Antonio (city) Bexar	79.84
Houston (city) Harris	79.33
Garland (city) Dallas	78.19
Amarillo (city) Potter	78.04
Arlington (city) Tarrant	76.98
Pasadena (city) Harris	76.60
Irving (city) Dallas	76.18
Carrollton (city) Denton	75.33

Foreign-Born Naturalized Citizens

Total Population
Top 10 Places Sorted by Number

Place (place type) County	Number
Houston (city) Harris	136,472
El Paso (city) El Paso	64,900
Dallas (city) Dallas	55,607
San Antonio (city) Bexar	54,322
Austin (city) Travis	26,747
Fort Worth (city) Tarrant	23,713
Laredo (city) Webb	17,120
Arlington (city) Tarrant	15,569
Brownsville (city) Cameron	15,559
Plano (city) Collin	13,559

Total Population
Top 10 Places Sorted by Percent

Place (place type) County	Percent
Mission Bend (cdp) Fort Bend	16.16
Four Corners (cdp) Fort Bend	14.41
Sugar Land (city) Fort Bend	13.80
New Territory (cdp) Fort Bend	13.73
Meadows Place (city) Fort Bend	11.66
El Paso (city) El Paso	11.50
Brownsville (city) Cameron	11.11
Stafford (city) Fort Bend	10.52
McAllen (city) Hidalgo	9.82

Missouri City (city) Fort Bend	9.74

Asian
Top 10 Places Sorted by Number

Place (place type) County	Number
Houston (city) Harris	35,425
Dallas (city) Dallas	8,886
Austin (city) Travis	8,452
San Antonio (city) Bexar	7,160
Plano (city) Collin	7,003
Sugar Land (city) Fort Bend	6,257
Arlington (city) Tarrant	6,207
Garland (city) Dallas	5,176
Fort Worth (city) Tarrant	4,568
Carrollton (city) Denton	3,755

Asian
Top 10 Places Sorted by Percent

Place (place type) County	Percent
Universal City (city) Bexar	59.50
Hunters Creek Village (city) Harris	58.64
Copperas Cove (city) Coryell	54.91
Colleyville (city) Tarrant	53.83
Aldine (cdp) Harris	53.73
Temple (city) Bell	52.30
Meadows Place (city) Fort Bend	50.97
Pflugerville (city) Travis	50.96
Duncanville (city) Dallas	49.49
Cedar Park (city) Williamson	49.47

Native Hawaiian and Other Pacific Islander
Top 10 Places Sorted by Number

Place (place type) County	Number
Fort Worth (city) Tarrant	115
Houston (city) Harris	79
San Antonio (city) Bexar	47
Killeen (city) Bell	43
Dallas (city) Dallas	39
El Paso (city) El Paso	21
Austin (city) Travis	5

Native Hawaiian and Other Pacific Islander
Top 10 Places Sorted by Percent

Place (place type) County	Percent
Fort Worth (city) Tarrant	20.72
Houston (city) Harris	9.02
San Antonio (city) Bexar	6.65
Dallas (city) Dallas	6.08
Killeen (city) Bell	4.11
El Paso (city) El Paso	4.08
Austin (city) Travis	1.12

Asian Indian
Top 10 Places Sorted by Number

Place (place type) County	Number
Houston (city) Harris	5,190
Sugar Land (city) Fort Bend	1,684
Dallas (city) Dallas	1,598
Austin (city) Travis	1,385
Plano (city) Collin	1,280
San Antonio (city) Bexar	1,236
Carrollton (city) Denton	1,193
Irving (city) Dallas	849
Missouri City (city) Fort Bend	845
Garland (city) Dallas	811

Asian Indian
Top 10 Places Sorted by Percent

Place (place type) County	Percent
Mission Bend (cdp) Fort Bend	53.44
The Woodlands (cdp) Montgomery	52.22
Corpus Christi (city) Nueces	48.56
Missouri City (city) Fort Bend	43.94

New Territory (cdp) Fort Bend	39.26
Sugar Land (city) Fort Bend	38.82
San Antonio (city) Bexar	37.13
Grand Prairie (city) Dallas	37.11
Midland (city) Midland	35.93
Rowlett (city) Dallas	32.22

Bangladeshi
Top 10 Places Sorted by Number

Place (place type) County	Number
No places met population threshold.	

Bangladeshi
Top 10 Places Sorted by Percent

Place (place type) County	Percent
No places met population threshold.	

Cambodian
Top 10 Places Sorted by Number

Place (place type) County	Number
Dallas (city) Dallas	335
Houston (city) Harris	254
Carrollton (city) Denton	244

Cambodian
Top 10 Places Sorted by Percent

Place (place type) County	Percent
Houston (city) Harris	35.13
Dallas (city) Dallas	31.63
Carrollton (city) Denton	29.83

Chinese (except Taiwanese)
Top 10 Places Sorted by Number

Place (place type) County	Number
Houston (city) Harris	7,033
Plano (city) Collin	2,882
Sugar Land (city) Fort Bend	2,270
Austin (city) Travis	2,165
Dallas (city) Dallas	1,681
Richardson (city) Dallas	1,153
San Antonio (city) Bexar	1,044
Arlington (city) Tarrant	913
Garland (city) Dallas	702
Fort Worth (city) Tarrant	602

Chinese (except Taiwanese)
Top 10 Places Sorted by Percent

Place (place type) County	Percent
Mission Bend (cdp) Fort Bend	44.83
Fort Worth (city) Tarrant	43.28
Sugar Land (city) Fort Bend	42.94
Missouri City (city) Fort Bend	42.67
Bellaire (city) Harris	42.07
Garland (city) Dallas	41.91
Stafford (city) Fort Bend	41.39
Carrollton (city) Denton	37.87
Richardson (city) Dallas	37.74
Coppell (city) Dallas	34.79

Fijian
Top 10 Places Sorted by Number

Place (place type) County	Number
No places met population threshold.	

Fijian
Top 10 Places Sorted by Percent

Place (place type) County	Percent
No places met population threshold.	

Notes: Please refer to the User's Guide for an explanation of data; tables reflect only those areas that meet Summary File 4 population thresholds, therefore there may be less than 10 places listed

Filipino
Top 10 Places Sorted by Number

Place (place type) County	Number
Houston (city) Harris	2,941
San Antonio (city) Bexar	1,545
Corpus Christi (city) Nueces	788
Dallas (city) Dallas	687
El Paso (city) El Paso	565
Austin (city) Travis	551
Arlington (city) Tarrant	547
Mission Bend (cdp) Fort Bend	542
Garland (city) Dallas	474
Killeen (city) Bell	455

Filipino
Top 10 Places Sorted by Percent

Place (place type) County	Percent
Mission Bend (cdp) Fort Bend	58.85
Corpus Christi (city) Nueces	49.22
Arlington (city) Tarrant	45.89
Irving (city) Dallas	44.06
Garland (city) Dallas	42.59
Missouri City (city) Fort Bend	41.45
Killeen (city) Bell	41.36
Sugar Land (city) Fort Bend	41.06
Dallas (city) Dallas	40.87
San Antonio (city) Bexar	40.81

Guamanian or Chamorro
Top 10 Places Sorted by Number

Place (place type) County	Number
Houston (city) Harris	10
Killeen (city) Bell	0

Guamanian or Chamorro
Top 10 Places Sorted by Percent

Place (place type) County	Percent
Houston (city) Harris	2.26
Killeen (city) Bell	0.00

Hawaiian, Native
Top 10 Places Sorted by Number

Place (place type) County	Number
No places met population threshold.	

Hawaiian, Native
Top 10 Places Sorted by Percent

Place (place type) County	Percent
No places met population threshold.	

Hmong
Top 10 Places Sorted by Number

Place (place type) County	Number
No places met population threshold.	

Hmong
Top 10 Places Sorted by Percent

Place (place type) County	Percent
No places met population threshold.	

Indonesian
Top 10 Places Sorted by Number

Place (place type) County	Number
Houston (city) Harris	14

Indonesian
Top 10 Places Sorted by Percent

Place (place type) County	Percent
Houston (city) Harris	2.71

Japanese
Top 10 Places Sorted by Number

Place (place type) County	Number
San Antonio (city) Bexar	437
El Paso (city) El Paso	336
Houston (city) Harris	225
Austin (city) Travis	151
Dallas (city) Dallas	131
Irving (city) Dallas	21
Plano (city) Collin	18

Japanese
Top 10 Places Sorted by Percent

Place (place type) County	Percent
El Paso (city) El Paso	44.80
San Antonio (city) Bexar	31.60
Dallas (city) Dallas	15.29
Austin (city) Travis	13.30
Houston (city) Harris	9.35
Plano (city) Collin	3.61
Irving (city) Dallas	3.10

Korean
Top 10 Places Sorted by Number

Place (place type) County	Number
Houston (city) Harris	1,999
Dallas (city) Dallas	1,147
San Antonio (city) Bexar	948
Plano (city) Collin	811
Austin (city) Travis	764
El Paso (city) El Paso	708
Irving (city) Dallas	705
Killeen (city) Bell	654
Carrollton (city) Denton	367
Richardson (city) Dallas	351

Korean
Top 10 Places Sorted by Percent

Place (place type) County	Percent
Sugar Land (city) Fort Bend	53.18
San Antonio (city) Bexar	50.00
El Paso (city) El Paso	42.29
Killeen (city) Bell	41.66
Houston (city) Harris	38.52
Plano (city) Collin	37.91
Carrollton (city) Denton	34.85
Dallas (city) Dallas	34.37
Coppell (city) Dallas	34.12
Richardson (city) Dallas	34.04

Laotian
Top 10 Places Sorted by Number

Place (place type) County	Number
Amarillo (city) Potter	467
Haltom City (city) Tarrant	344
Dallas (city) Dallas	288
Fort Worth (city) Tarrant	184
Grand Prairie (city) Dallas	128
Irving (city) Dallas	102

Laotian
Top 10 Places Sorted by Percent

Place (place type) County	Percent
Amarillo (city) Potter	44.02
Haltom City (city) Tarrant	42.36
Fort Worth (city) Tarrant	34.72
Grand Prairie (city) Dallas	32.74
Dallas (city) Dallas	31.72
Irving (city) Dallas	21.29

Malaysian
Top 10 Places Sorted by Number

Place (place type) County	Number
No places met population threshold.	

Malaysian
Top 10 Places Sorted by Percent

Place (place type) County	Percent
No places met population threshold.	

Pakistani
Top 10 Places Sorted by Number

Place (place type) County	Number
Houston (city) Harris	1,249
Carrollton (city) Denton	290
Sugar Land (city) Fort Bend	263
Dallas (city) Dallas	220
Garland (city) Dallas	207
Plano (city) Collin	141
Mission Bend (cdp) Fort Bend	133
Richardson (city) Dallas	125
Irving (city) Dallas	96
Austin (city) Travis	86

Pakistani
Top 10 Places Sorted by Percent

Place (place type) County	Percent
Sugar Land (city) Fort Bend	42.56
Richardson (city) Dallas	29.55
Mission Bend (cdp) Fort Bend	27.71
Houston (city) Harris	24.99
Garland (city) Dallas	24.91
Carrollton (city) Denton	24.87
Plano (city) Collin	23.34
Irving (city) Dallas	22.38
Dallas (city) Dallas	18.30
Austin (city) Travis	16.35

Samoan
Top 10 Places Sorted by Number

Place (place type) County	Number
No places met population threshold.	

Samoan
Top 10 Places Sorted by Percent

Place (place type) County	Percent
No places met population threshold.	

Sri Lankan
Top 10 Places Sorted by Number

Place (place type) County	Number
No places met population threshold.	

Sri Lankan
Top 10 Places Sorted by Percent

Place (place type) County	Percent
No places met population threshold.	

Taiwanese
Top 10 Places Sorted by Number

Place (place type) County	Number
Houston (city) Harris	762
Sugar Land (city) Fort Bend	400
Plano (city) Collin	300
Austin (city) Travis	270
Arlington (city) Tarrant	177

Notes: Please refer to the User's Guide for an explanation of data; tables reflect only those areas that meet Summary File 4 population thresholds, therefore there may be less than 10 places listed

Taiwanese
Top 10 Places Sorted by Percent

Place (place type) County	Percent
Plano (city) Collin	53.19
Houston (city) Harris	51.07
Sugar Land (city) Fort Bend	42.69
Arlington (city) Tarrant	42.65
Austin (city) Travis	36.10

Thai
Top 10 Places Sorted by Number

Place (place type) County	Number
San Antonio (city) Bexar	240
Houston (city) Harris	233

Thai
Top 10 Places Sorted by Percent

Place (place type) County	Percent
San Antonio (city) Bexar	41.59
Houston (city) Harris	26.45

Tongan
Top 10 Places Sorted by Number

Place (place type) County	Number
No places met population threshold.	

Tongan
Top 10 Places Sorted by Percent

Place (place type) County	Percent
No places met population threshold.	

Vietnamese
Top 10 Places Sorted by Number

Place (place type) County	Number
Houston (city) Harris	14,200
Arlington (city) Tarrant	3,143
Austin (city) Travis	2,614
Garland (city) Dallas	2,274
Dallas (city) Dallas	2,233
Fort Worth (city) Tarrant	2,012
San Antonio (city) Bexar	1,223
Carrollton (city) Denton	1,136
Grand Prairie (city) Dallas	944
Plano (city) Collin	941

Vietnamese
Top 10 Places Sorted by Percent

Place (place type) County	Percent
Stafford (city) Fort Bend	61.32
Missouri City (city) Fort Bend	60.51
Pearland (city) Brazoria	58.77
Lewisville (city) Denton	58.63
Sugar Land (city) Fort Bend	56.43
San Antonio (city) Bexar	53.83
Plano (city) Collin	52.16
North Richland Hills (city) Tarrant	51.25
Round Rock (city) Williamson	48.31
Mission Bend (cdp) Fort Bend	48.06

Educational Attainment: High School Graduates

Total Populations 25 Years and Over Who are High School Graduates
Top 10 Places Sorted by Number

Place (place type) County	Number
Houston (city) Harris	845,709
San Antonio (city) Bexar	522,459
Dallas (city) Dallas	516,743
Austin (city) Travis	334,626
Fort Worth (city) Tarrant	236,466

(continued next column)

Place (place type) County	Number
El Paso (city) El Paso	229,053
Arlington (city) Tarrant	172,717
Plano (city) Collin	135,274
Corpus Christi (city) Nueces	129,104
Garland (city) Dallas	102,825

Total Populations 25 Years and Over Who are High School Graduates
Top 10 Places Sorted by Percent

Place (place type) County	Percent
Cinco Ranch (cdp) Fort Bend	98.53
University Park (city) Dallas	98.34
West University Place (city) Harris	97.96
Bunker Hill Village (city) Harris	97.55
Flower Mound (town) Denton	97.40
Hunters Creek Village (city) Harris	96.94
Colleyville (city) Tarrant	96.70
Coppell (city) Dallas	96.64
Southlake (city) Tarrant	96.61
Hedwig Village (city) Harris	95.99

Asians 25 Years and Over Who are High School Graduates
Top 10 Places Sorted by Number

Place (place type) County	Number
Houston (city) Harris	54,429
Dallas (city) Dallas	17,275
Austin (city) Travis	16,212
Plano (city) Collin	13,713
San Antonio (city) Bexar	10,255
Irving (city) Dallas	9,548
Arlington (city) Tarrant	8,428
Sugar Land (city) Fort Bend	7,886
Garland (city) Dallas	6,849
Fort Worth (city) Tarrant	6,266

Asians 25 Years and Over Who are High School Graduates
Top 10 Places Sorted by Percent

Place (place type) County	Percent
Frisco (city) Collin	98.74
Harlingen (city) Cameron	98.03
Four Corners (cdp) Fort Bend	97.48
Bryan (city) Brazos	97.18
Cinco Ranch (cdp) Fort Bend	97.01
The Woodlands (cdp) Montgomery	96.34
College Station (city) Brazos	95.86
Lake Jackson (city) Brazoria	95.76
McAllen (city) Hidalgo	95.74
Bunker Hill Village (city) Harris	95.56

Native Hawaiian and Other Pacific Islanders 25 Years and Over Who are High School Graduates
Top 10 Places Sorted by Number

Place (place type) County	Number
Killeen (city) Bell	440
Houston (city) Harris	388
San Antonio (city) Bexar	370
Fort Worth (city) Tarrant	227
Dallas (city) Dallas	225
Austin (city) Travis	205
El Paso (city) El Paso	192

Native Hawaiian and Other Pacific Islanders 25 Years and Over Who are High School Graduates
Top 10 Places Sorted by Percent

Place (place type) County	Percent
Austin (city) Travis	82.66
Killeen (city) Bell	81.94
San Antonio (city) Bexar	81.32
Fort Worth (city) Tarrant	77.21
Houston (city) Harris	71.99
El Paso (city) El Paso	70.59
Dallas (city) Dallas	61.48

Asian Indians 25 Years and Over Who are High School Graduates
Top 10 Places Sorted by Number

Place (place type) County	Number
Houston (city) Harris	11,565
Dallas (city) Dallas	4,330
Austin (city) Travis	3,993
Irving (city) Dallas	3,842
Plano (city) Collin	3,600
Sugar Land (city) Fort Bend	2,338
Carrollton (city) Denton	2,289
San Antonio (city) Bexar	1,755
Arlington (city) Tarrant	1,573
Garland (city) Dallas	1,479

Asian Indians 25 Years and Over Who are High School Graduates
Top 10 Places Sorted by Percent

Place (place type) County	Percent
The Woodlands (cdp) Montgomery	100.00
Plano (city) Collin	96.23
Austin (city) Travis	95.69
Denton (city) Denton	95.65
Lewisville (city) Denton	93.83
College Station (city) Brazos	93.20
Rowlett (city) Dallas	93.02
Flower Mound (town) Denton	92.82
Irving (city) Dallas	92.60
Lubbock (city) Lubbock	92.49

Bangladeshis 25 Years and Over Who are High School Graduates
Top 10 Places Sorted by Number

Place (place type) County	Number
No places met population threshold.	

Bangladeshis 25 Years and Over Who are High School Graduates
Top 10 Places Sorted by Percent

Place (place type) County	Percent
No places met population threshold.	

Cambodians 25 Years and Over Who are High School Graduates
Top 10 Places Sorted by Number

Place (place type) County	Number
Dallas (city) Dallas	231
Carrollton (city) Denton	217
Houston (city) Harris	158

Cambodians 25 Years and Over Who are High School Graduates
Top 10 Places Sorted by Percent

Place (place type) County	Percent
Carrollton (city) Denton	52.93
Dallas (city) Dallas	51.56
Houston (city) Harris	36.83

Chinese (except Taiwanese)s 25 Years and Over Who are High School Graduates
Top 10 Places Sorted by Number

Place (place type) County	Number
Houston (city) Harris	13,722
Plano (city) Collin	5,731
Austin (city) Travis	4,719
Dallas (city) Dallas	3,970
Sugar Land (city) Fort Bend	3,150
San Antonio (city) Bexar	1,890
Richardson (city) Dallas	1,853
Arlington (city) Tarrant	1,478
Irving (city) Dallas	1,010
Missouri City (city) Fort Bend	837

Chinese (except Taiwanese)s 25 Years and Over Who are High School Graduates
Top 10 Places Sorted by Percent

Place (place type) County	Percent
Lubbock (city) Lubbock	100.00
College Station (city) Brazos	98.24
Austin (city) Travis	96.88
Coppell (city) Dallas	95.85
Plano (city) Collin	94.82
El Paso (city) El Paso	94.35
Denton (city) Denton	92.63
Missouri City (city) Fort Bend	92.38
Bellaire (city) Harris	90.91
Sugar Land (city) Fort Bend	90.03

Fijians 25 Years and Over Who are High School Graduates
Top 10 Places Sorted by Number

Place (place type) County	Number
No places met population threshold.	

Fijians 25 Years and Over Who are High School Graduates
Top 10 Places Sorted by Percent

Place (place type) County	Percent
No places met population threshold.	

Filipinos 25 Years and Over Who are High School Graduates
Top 10 Places Sorted by Number

Place (place type) County	Number
Houston (city) Harris	5,091
San Antonio (city) Bexar	2,348
Dallas (city) Dallas	1,272
Corpus Christi (city) Nueces	1,062
El Paso (city) El Paso	952
Austin (city) Travis	867
Garland (city) Dallas	792
Arlington (city) Tarrant	711
Fort Worth (city) Tarrant	639
Missouri City (city) Fort Bend	625

Filipinos 25 Years and Over Who are High School Graduates
Top 10 Places Sorted by Percent

Place (place type) County	Percent
Beaumont (city) Jefferson	100.00
McAllen (city) Hidalgo	99.49
Plano (city) Collin	98.73
Richardson (city) Dallas	97.28
Stafford (city) Fort Bend	97.02
Fort Worth (city) Tarrant	96.09
Mission Bend (cdp) Fort Bend	95.94
Garland (city) Dallas	95.54
Irving (city) Dallas	94.77
Dallas (city) Dallas	94.57

Guamanian or Chamorros 25 Years and Over Who are High School Graduates
Top 10 Places Sorted by Number

Place (place type) County	Number
Killeen (city) Bell	257
Houston (city) Harris	205

Guamanian or Chamorros 25 Years and Over Who are High School Graduates
Top 10 Places Sorted by Percent

Place (place type) County	Percent
Killeen (city) Bell	84.54
Houston (city) Harris	73.21

Hawaiian, Natives 25 Years and Over Who are High School Graduates
Top 10 Places Sorted by Number

Place (place type) County	Number
No places met population threshold.	

Hawaiian, Natives 25 Years and Over Who are High School Graduates
Top 10 Places Sorted by Percent

Place (place type) County	Percent
No places met population threshold.	

Hmongs 25 Years and Over Who are High School Graduates
Top 10 Places Sorted by Number

Place (place type) County	Number
No places met population threshold.	

Hmongs 25 Years and Over Who are High School Graduates
Top 10 Places Sorted by Percent

Place (place type) County	Percent
No places met population threshold.	

Indonesians 25 Years and Over Who are High School Graduates
Top 10 Places Sorted by Number

Place (place type) County	Number
Houston (city) Harris	325

Indonesians 25 Years and Over Who are High School Graduates
Top 10 Places Sorted by Percent

Place (place type) County	Percent
Houston (city) Harris	95.87

Japaneses 25 Years and Over Who are High School Graduates
Top 10 Places Sorted by Number

Place (place type) County	Number
Houston (city) Harris	1,621
San Antonio (city) Bexar	950
Austin (city) Travis	795
Dallas (city) Dallas	743
El Paso (city) El Paso	508
Irving (city) Dallas	497
Plano (city) Collin	386

Japaneses 25 Years and Over Who are High School Graduates
Top 10 Places Sorted by Percent

Place (place type) County	Percent
Irving (city) Dallas	100.00
Dallas (city) Dallas	98.93
Plano (city) Collin	98.72
Houston (city) Harris	96.83
Austin (city) Travis	94.64
San Antonio (city) Bexar	89.20
El Paso (city) El Paso	81.28

Koreans 25 Years and Over Who are High School Graduates
Top 10 Places Sorted by Number

Place (place type) County	Number
Houston (city) Harris	3,333
Dallas (city) Dallas	1,975
Austin (city) Travis	1,810
Irving (city) Dallas	1,383
Plano (city) Collin	1,193
San Antonio (city) Bexar	1,022
El Paso (city) El Paso	792
Killeen (city) Bell	790
Fort Worth (city) Tarrant	644
Richardson (city) Dallas	627

Koreans 25 Years and Over Who are High School Graduates
Top 10 Places Sorted by Percent

Place (place type) County	Percent
College Station (city) Brazos	100.00
Denton (city) Denton	100.00
Plano (city) Collin	94.31
Hedwig Village (city) Harris	94.20
Austin (city) Travis	93.83
Houston (city) Harris	89.91
Fort Worth (city) Tarrant	89.82
Sugar Land (city) Fort Bend	89.04
Carrollton (city) Denton	88.47
Coppell (city) Dallas	87.56

Laotians 25 Years and Over Who are High School Graduates
Top 10 Places Sorted by Number

Place (place type) County	Number
Dallas (city) Dallas	250
Amarillo (city) Potter	236
Haltom City (city) Tarrant	222
Fort Worth (city) Tarrant	220
Irving (city) Dallas	196
Grand Prairie (city) Dallas	103

Laotians 25 Years and Over Who are High School Graduates
Top 10 Places Sorted by Percent

Place (place type) County	Percent
Fort Worth (city) Tarrant	73.09
Irving (city) Dallas	70.00
Grand Prairie (city) Dallas	60.23
Haltom City (city) Tarrant	51.51
Dallas (city) Dallas	48.26
Amarillo (city) Potter	40.83

Malaysians 25 Years and Over Who are High School Graduates
Top 10 Places Sorted by Number

Place (place type) County	Number
No places met population threshold.	

Malaysians 25 Years and Over Who are High School Graduates
Top 10 Places Sorted by Percent

Place (place type) County	Percent
No places met population threshold.	

Pakistanis 25 Years and Over Who are High School Graduates
Top 10 Places Sorted by Number

Place (place type) County	Number
Houston (city) Harris	2,382
Dallas (city) Dallas	601
Carrollton (city) Denton	430
Garland (city) Dallas	333
Sugar Land (city) Fort Bend	301
Plano (city) Collin	300
Irving (city) Dallas	243
Richardson (city) Dallas	199
Austin (city) Travis	194
Mission Bend (cdp) Fort Bend	175

Notes: Please refer to the User's Guide for an explanation of data; tables reflect only those areas that meet Summary File 4 population thresholds, therefore there may be less than 10 places listed

Pakistanis 25 Years and Over Who are High School Graduates
Top 10 Places Sorted by Percent

Place (place type) County	Percent
Sugar Land (city) Fort Bend	91.49
Plano (city) Collin	87.72
Irving (city) Dallas	85.26
Houston (city) Harris	84.44
Dallas (city) Dallas	83.94
Richardson (city) Dallas	76.54
Garland (city) Dallas	75.00
Carrollton (city) Denton	74.91
Austin (city) Travis	72.93
Mission Bend (cdp) Fort Bend	68.90

Samoans 25 Years and Over Who are High School Graduates
Top 10 Places Sorted by Number

Place (place type) County	Number
No places met population threshold.	

Samoans 25 Years and Over Who are High School Graduates
Top 10 Places Sorted by Percent

Place (place type) County	Percent
No places met population threshold.	

Sri Lankans 25 Years and Over Who are High School Graduates
Top 10 Places Sorted by Number

Place (place type) County	Number
No places met population threshold.	

Sri Lankans 25 Years and Over Who are High School Graduates
Top 10 Places Sorted by Percent

Place (place type) County	Percent
No places met population threshold.	

Taiwaneses 25 Years and Over Who are High School Graduates
Top 10 Places Sorted by Number

Place (place type) County	Number
Houston (city) Harris	1,038
Sugar Land (city) Fort Bend	496
Plano (city) Collin	366
Austin (city) Travis	327
Arlington (city) Tarrant	267

Taiwaneses 25 Years and Over Who are High School Graduates
Top 10 Places Sorted by Percent

Place (place type) County	Percent
Arlington (city) Tarrant	100.00
Plano (city) Collin	96.57
Austin (city) Travis	95.34
Houston (city) Harris	93.60
Sugar Land (city) Fort Bend	88.41

Thais 25 Years and Over Who are High School Graduates
Top 10 Places Sorted by Number

Place (place type) County	Number
Houston (city) Harris	563
San Antonio (city) Bexar	386

Thais 25 Years and Over Who are High School Graduates
Top 10 Places Sorted by Percent

Place (place type) County	Percent
Houston (city) Harris	87.56
San Antonio (city) Bexar	78.30

Tongans 25 Years and Over Who are High School Graduates
Top 10 Places Sorted by Number

Place (place type) County	Number
No places met population threshold.	

Tongans 25 Years and Over Who are High School Graduates
Top 10 Places Sorted by Percent

Place (place type) County	Percent
No places met population threshold.	

Vietnamese 25 Years and Over Who are High School Graduates
Top 10 Places Sorted by Number

Place (place type) County	Number
Houston (city) Harris	12,718
Arlington (city) Tarrant	3,062
Austin (city) Travis	2,613
Dallas (city) Dallas	2,400
Garland (city) Dallas	2,392
Fort Worth (city) Tarrant	1,717
San Antonio (city) Bexar	1,164
Carrollton (city) Denton	1,096
Plano (city) Collin	963
Grand Prairie (city) Dallas	886

Vietnamese 25 Years and Over Who are High School Graduates
Top 10 Places Sorted by Percent

Place (place type) County	Percent
Stafford (city) Fort Bend	90.87
Allen (city) Collin	86.58
Missouri City (city) Fort Bend	85.40
Plano (city) Collin	83.74
Round Rock (city) Williamson	80.71
North Richland Hills (city) Tarrant	78.46
Richardson (city) Dallas	76.85
Austin (city) Travis	76.38
San Antonio (city) Bexar	72.75
Irving (city) Dallas	72.61

Educational Attainment: Four-Year College Graduates

Total Populations 25 Years and Over Who are Four-Year College Graduates
Top 10 Places Sorted by Number

Place (place type) County	Number
Houston (city) Harris	324,039
Dallas (city) Dallas	203,004
Austin (city) Travis	161,937
San Antonio (city) Bexar	150,680
Plano (city) Collin	76,706
Fort Worth (city) Tarrant	72,313
Arlington (city) Tarrant	61,837
El Paso (city) El Paso	61,217
Irving (city) Dallas	36,273
Corpus Christi (city) Nueces	33,446

Total Populations 25 Years and Over Who are Four-Year College Graduates
Top 10 Places Sorted by Percent

Place (place type) County	Percent
Bunker Hill Village (city) Harris	80.52

Place (place type) County	Percent
University Park (city) Dallas	80.45
West University Place (city) Harris	79.40
Hunters Creek Village (city) Harris	76.24
Bellaire (city) Harris	66.60
Cinco Ranch (cdp) Fort Bend	65.92
Hedwig Village (city) Harris	65.60
Coppell (city) Dallas	62.59
Southlake (city) Tarrant	59.19
College Station (city) Brazos	58.10

Asians 25 Years and Over Who are Four-Year College Graduates
Top 10 Places Sorted by Number

Place (place type) County	Number
Houston (city) Harris	32,817
Austin (city) Travis	11,966
Dallas (city) Dallas	11,125
Plano (city) Collin	10,562
Irving (city) Dallas	6,263
Sugar Land (city) Fort Bend	5,442
San Antonio (city) Bexar	5,159
Arlington (city) Tarrant	4,320
Richardson (city) Dallas	3,776
Fort Worth (city) Tarrant	3,170

Asians 25 Years and Over Who are Four-Year College Graduates
Top 10 Places Sorted by Percent

Place (place type) County	Percent
Bunker Hill Village (city) Harris	91.85
College Station (city) Brazos	82.50
Hunters Creek Village (city) Harris	82.17
West University Place (city) Harris	81.48
Port Lavaca (city) Calhoun	80.07
University Park (city) Dallas	79.55
Frisco (city) Collin	75.86
Bryan (city) Brazos	75.25
Bellaire (city) Harris	73.84
Cinco Ranch (cdp) Fort Bend	73.13

Native Hawaiian and Other Pacific Islanders 25 Years and Over Who are Four-Year College Graduates
Top 10 Places Sorted by Number

Place (place type) County	Number
Houston (city) Harris	71
Dallas (city) Dallas	64
Fort Worth (city) Tarrant	53
Austin (city) Travis	52
San Antonio (city) Bexar	45
El Paso (city) El Paso	26
Killeen (city) Bell	19

Native Hawaiian and Other Pacific Islanders 25 Years and Over Who are Four-Year College Graduates
Top 10 Places Sorted by Percent

Place (place type) County	Percent
Austin (city) Travis	20.97
Fort Worth (city) Tarrant	18.03
Dallas (city) Dallas	17.49
Houston (city) Harris	13.17
San Antonio (city) Bexar	9.89
El Paso (city) El Paso	9.56
Killeen (city) Bell	3.54

Asian Indians 25 Years and Over Who are Four-Year College Graduates
Top 10 Places Sorted by Number

Place (place type) County	Number
Houston (city) Harris	8,850
Austin (city) Travis	3,575
Dallas (city) Dallas	3,260
Plano (city) Collin	3,164
Irving (city) Dallas	3,128
Sugar Land (city) Fort Bend	1,739

Place (place type) County	Number
Carrollton (city) Denton	1,264
San Antonio (city) Bexar	1,156
Fort Worth (city) Tarrant	1,129
Arlington (city) Tarrant	1,089

Asian Indians 25 Years and Over Who are Four-Year College Graduates
Top 10 Places Sorted by Percent

Place (place type) County	Percent
Austin (city) Travis	85.67
College Station (city) Brazos	85.11
Plano (city) Collin	84.58
Flower Mound (town) Denton	83.80
The Woodlands (cdp) Montgomery	81.17
Irving (city) Dallas	75.39
Lubbock (city) Lubbock	74.47
Beaumont (city) Jefferson	73.56
Richardson (city) Dallas	72.96
Galveston (city) Galveston	71.64

Bangladeshis 25 Years and Over Who are Four-Year College Graduates
Top 10 Places Sorted by Number

Place (place type) County	Number
No places met population threshold.	

Bangladeshis 25 Years and Over Who are Four-Year College Graduates
Top 10 Places Sorted by Percent

Place (place type) County	Percent
No places met population threshold.	

Cambodians 25 Years and Over Who are Four-Year College Graduates
Top 10 Places Sorted by Number

Place (place type) County	Number
Houston (city) Harris	32
Dallas (city) Dallas	19
Carrollton (city) Denton	13

Cambodians 25 Years and Over Who are Four-Year College Graduates
Top 10 Places Sorted by Percent

Place (place type) County	Percent
Houston (city) Harris	7.46
Dallas (city) Dallas	4.24
Carrollton (city) Denton	3.17

Chinese (except Taiwanese)s 25 Years and Over Who are Four-Year College Graduates
Top 10 Places Sorted by Number

Place (place type) County	Number
Houston (city) Harris	9,532
Plano (city) Collin	4,563
Austin (city) Travis	4,004
Dallas (city) Dallas	3,117
Sugar Land (city) Fort Bend	2,228
Richardson (city) Dallas	1,287
San Antonio (city) Bexar	1,213
Arlington (city) Tarrant	1,111
Irving (city) Dallas	816
College Station (city) Brazos	720

Chinese (except Taiwanese)s 25 Years and Over Who are Four-Year College Graduates
Top 10 Places Sorted by Percent

Place (place type) County	Percent
Lubbock (city) Lubbock	95.14
College Station (city) Brazos	84.71
Bellaire (city) Harris	83.57
Austin (city) Travis	82.20
Denton (city) Denton	78.13

Place (place type) County	Percent
Galveston (city) Galveston	77.85
Plano (city) Collin	75.50
Coppell (city) Dallas	74.67
Irving (city) Dallas	72.40
Missouri City (city) Fort Bend	70.64

Fijians 25 Years and Over Who are Four-Year College Graduates
Top 10 Places Sorted by Number

Place (place type) County	Number
No places met population threshold.	

Fijians 25 Years and Over Who are Four-Year College Graduates
Top 10 Places Sorted by Percent

Place (place type) County	Percent
No places met population threshold.	

Filipinos 25 Years and Over Who are Four-Year College Graduates
Top 10 Places Sorted by Number

Place (place type) County	Number
Houston (city) Harris	3,234
San Antonio (city) Bexar	1,191
Dallas (city) Dallas	819
El Paso (city) El Paso	564
Corpus Christi (city) Nueces	544
Austin (city) Travis	534
McAllen (city) Hidalgo	489
Missouri City (city) Fort Bend	467
Garland (city) Dallas	423
Mission Bend (cdp) Fort Bend	417

Filipinos 25 Years and Over Who are Four-Year College Graduates
Top 10 Places Sorted by Percent

Place (place type) County	Percent
Beaumont (city) Jefferson	93.69
McAllen (city) Hidalgo	82.88
Stafford (city) Fort Bend	77.45
Mission Bend (cdp) Fort Bend	73.54
Sugar Land (city) Fort Bend	71.80
Missouri City (city) Fort Bend	70.23
Plano (city) Collin	68.66
Richardson (city) Dallas	64.59
Dallas (city) Dallas	60.89
Houston (city) Harris	59.62

Guamanian or Chamorros 25 Years and Over Who are Four-Year College Graduates
Top 10 Places Sorted by Number

Place (place type) County	Number
Houston (city) Harris	47
Killeen (city) Bell	10

Guamanian or Chamorros 25 Years and Over Who are Four-Year College Graduates
Top 10 Places Sorted by Percent

Place (place type) County	Percent
Houston (city) Harris	16.79
Killeen (city) Bell	3.29

Hawaiian, Natives 25 Years and Over Who are Four-Year College Graduates
Top 10 Places Sorted by Number

Place (place type) County	Number
No places met population threshold.	

Hawaiian, Natives 25 Years and Over Who are Four-Year College Graduates
Top 10 Places Sorted by Percent

Place (place type) County	Percent
No places met population threshold.	

Hmongs 25 Years and Over Who are Four-Year College Graduates
Top 10 Places Sorted by Number

Place (place type) County	Number
No places met population threshold.	

Hmongs 25 Years and Over Who are Four-Year College Graduates
Top 10 Places Sorted by Percent

Place (place type) County	Percent
No places met population threshold.	

Indonesians 25 Years and Over Who are Four-Year College Graduates
Top 10 Places Sorted by Number

Place (place type) County	Number
Houston (city) Harris	234

Indonesians 25 Years and Over Who are Four-Year College Graduates
Top 10 Places Sorted by Percent

Place (place type) County	Percent
Houston (city) Harris	69.03

Japaneses 25 Years and Over Who are Four-Year College Graduates
Top 10 Places Sorted by Number

Place (place type) County	Number
Houston (city) Harris	1,038
Austin (city) Travis	475
Dallas (city) Dallas	448
San Antonio (city) Bexar	364
Irving (city) Dallas	340
Plano (city) Collin	239
El Paso (city) El Paso	173

Japaneses 25 Years and Over Who are Four-Year College Graduates
Top 10 Places Sorted by Percent

Place (place type) County	Percent
Irving (city) Dallas	68.41
Houston (city) Harris	62.01
Plano (city) Collin	61.13
Dallas (city) Dallas	59.65
Austin (city) Travis	56.55
San Antonio (city) Bexar	34.18
El Paso (city) El Paso	27.68

Koreans 25 Years and Over Who are Four-Year College Graduates
Top 10 Places Sorted by Number

Place (place type) County	Number
Houston (city) Harris	1,654
Austin (city) Travis	1,286
Dallas (city) Dallas	955
Plano (city) Collin	752
Irving (city) Dallas	490
College Station (city) Brazos	427
San Antonio (city) Bexar	374
Fort Worth (city) Tarrant	352
Arlington (city) Tarrant	293
Richardson (city) Dallas	281

Notes: Please refer to the User's Guide for an explanation of data; tables reflect only those areas that meet Summary File 4 population thresholds, therefore there may be less than 10 places listed

Koreans 25 Years and Over Who are Four-Year College Graduates
Top 10 Places Sorted by Percent

Place (place type) County	Percent
College Station (city) Brazos	96.61
Austin (city) Travis	66.67
Denton (city) Denton	63.02
Plano (city) Collin	59.45
Arlington (city) Tarrant	51.40
Hedwig Village (city) Harris	50.72
Fort Worth (city) Tarrant	49.09
Houston (city) Harris	44.62
Coppell (city) Dallas	41.39
Carrollton (city) Denton	39.77

Laotians 25 Years and Over Who are Four-Year College Graduates
Top 10 Places Sorted by Number

Place (place type) County	Number
Dallas (city) Dallas	41
Irving (city) Dallas	27
Haltom City (city) Tarrant	21
Amarillo (city) Potter	18
Fort Worth (city) Tarrant	15
Grand Prairie (city) Dallas	13

Laotians 25 Years and Over Who are Four-Year College Graduates
Top 10 Places Sorted by Percent

Place (place type) County	Percent
Irving (city) Dallas	9.64
Dallas (city) Dallas	7.92
Grand Prairie (city) Dallas	7.60
Fort Worth (city) Tarrant	4.98
Haltom City (city) Tarrant	4.87
Amarillo (city) Potter	3.11

Malaysians 25 Years and Over Who are Four-Year College Graduates
Top 10 Places Sorted by Number

Place (place type) County	Number
No places met population threshold.	

Malaysians 25 Years and Over Who are Four-Year College Graduates
Top 10 Places Sorted by Percent

Place (place type) County	Percent
No places met population threshold.	

Pakistanis 25 Years and Over Who are Four-Year College Graduates
Top 10 Places Sorted by Number

Place (place type) County	Number
Houston (city) Harris	1,770
Dallas (city) Dallas	483
Carrollton (city) Denton	231
Plano (city) Collin	211
Garland (city) Dallas	205
Sugar Land (city) Fort Bend	203
Irving (city) Dallas	187
Richardson (city) Dallas	152
Austin (city) Travis	144
Mission Bend (cdp) Fort Bend	92

Pakistanis 25 Years and Over Who are Four-Year College Graduates
Top 10 Places Sorted by Percent

Place (place type) County	Percent
Dallas (city) Dallas	67.46
Irving (city) Dallas	65.61
Houston (city) Harris	62.74
Plano (city) Collin	61.70

Place (place type) County	Percent
Sugar Land (city) Fort Bend	61.70
Richardson (city) Dallas	58.46
Austin (city) Travis	54.14
Garland (city) Dallas	46.17
Carrollton (city) Denton	40.24
Mission Bend (cdp) Fort Bend	36.22

Samoans 25 Years and Over Who are Four-Year College Graduates
Top 10 Places Sorted by Number

Place (place type) County	Number
No places met population threshold.	

Samoans 25 Years and Over Who are Four-Year College Graduates
Top 10 Places Sorted by Percent

Place (place type) County	Percent
No places met population threshold.	

Sri Lankans 25 Years and Over Who are Four-Year College Graduates
Top 10 Places Sorted by Number

Place (place type) County	Number
No places met population threshold.	

Sri Lankans 25 Years and Over Who are Four-Year College Graduates
Top 10 Places Sorted by Percent

Place (place type) County	Percent
No places met population threshold.	

Taiwaneses 25 Years and Over Who are Four-Year College Graduates
Top 10 Places Sorted by Number

Place (place type) County	Number
Houston (city) Harris	795
Plano (city) Collin	314
Sugar Land (city) Fort Bend	308
Austin (city) Travis	275
Arlington (city) Tarrant	206

Taiwaneses 25 Years and Over Who are Four-Year College Graduates
Top 10 Places Sorted by Percent

Place (place type) County	Percent
Plano (city) Collin	82.85
Austin (city) Travis	80.17
Arlington (city) Tarrant	77.15
Houston (city) Harris	71.69
Sugar Land (city) Fort Bend	54.90

Thais 25 Years and Over Who are Four-Year College Graduates
Top 10 Places Sorted by Number

Place (place type) County	Number
Houston (city) Harris	350
San Antonio (city) Bexar	185

Thais 25 Years and Over Who are Four-Year College Graduates
Top 10 Places Sorted by Percent

Place (place type) County	Percent
Houston (city) Harris	54.43
San Antonio (city) Bexar	37.53

Tongans 25 Years and Over Who are Four-Year College Graduates
Top 10 Places Sorted by Number

Place (place type) County	Number
No places met population threshold.	

Tongans 25 Years and Over Who are Four-Year College Graduates
Top 10 Places Sorted by Percent

Place (place type) County	Percent
No places met population threshold.	

Vietnamese 25 Years and Over Who are Four-Year College Graduates
Top 10 Places Sorted by Number

Place (place type) County	Number
Houston (city) Harris	4,233
Austin (city) Travis	1,091
Dallas (city) Dallas	919
Arlington (city) Tarrant	886
Garland (city) Dallas	697
Plano (city) Collin	513
Fort Worth (city) Tarrant	477
Richardson (city) Dallas	423
Irving (city) Dallas	336
San Antonio (city) Bexar	275

Vietnamese 25 Years and Over Who are Four-Year College Graduates
Top 10 Places Sorted by Percent

Place (place type) County	Percent
Allen (city) Collin	60.61
Plano (city) Collin	44.61
Missouri City (city) Fort Bend	42.08
Richardson (city) Dallas	39.02
Stafford (city) Fort Bend	38.58
Pearland (city) Brazoria	36.39
Sugar Land (city) Fort Bend	32.50
Austin (city) Travis	31.89
North Richland Hills (city) Tarrant	30.89
Irving (city) Dallas	29.79

Median Household Income

Total Population
Top 10 Places Sorted by Number

Place (place type) County	Dollars
Bunker Hill Village (city) Harris	177,274
Hunters Creek Village (city) Harris	171,294
Southlake (city) Tarrant	131,549
West University Place (city) Harris	130,721
Colleyville (city) Tarrant	117,419
Cinco Ranch (cdp) Fort Bend	111,517
Coppell (city) Dallas	96,935
Flower Mound (town) Denton	95,416
New Territory (cdp) Fort Bend	93,972
University Park (city) Dallas	92,778

Asian
Top 10 Places Sorted by Number

Place (place type) County	Dollars
Bunker Hill Village (city) Harris	200,001
Southlake (city) Tarrant	142,113
Hunters Creek Village (city) Harris	127,715
Cinco Ranch (cdp) Fort Bend	126,858
Colleyville (city) Tarrant	124,370
West University Place (city) Harris	112,773
Bellaire (city) Harris	101,159
New Territory (cdp) Fort Bend	99,113
Flower Mound (town) Denton	97,962
Murphy (city) Collin	95,030

Native Hawaiian and Other Pacific Islander
Top 10 Places Sorted by Number

Place (place type) County	Dollars
Killeen (city) Bell	51,763
Houston (city) Harris	43,712
Dallas (city) Dallas	38,571
San Antonio (city) Bexar	34,375

Notes: Please refer to the User's Guide for an explanation of data; tables reflect only those areas that meet Summary File 4 population thresholds, therefore there may be less than 10 places listed

Place (place type) County	
Austin (city) Travis	32,222
El Paso (city) El Paso	31,591
Fort Worth (city) Tarrant	25,208

Asian Indian
Top 10 Places Sorted by Number

Place (place type) County	Dollars
Flower Mound (town) Denton	98,895
Plano (city) Collin	97,786
Sugar Land (city) Fort Bend	97,045
New Territory (cdp) Fort Bend	96,924
Missouri City (city) Fort Bend	91,862
Coppell (city) Dallas	91,374
The Woodlands (cdp) Montgomery	90,000
Rowlett (city) Dallas	84,725
Amarillo (city) Potter	76,262
Mission Bend (cdp) Fort Bend	76,025

Bangladeshi
Top 10 Places Sorted by Number

Place (place type) County	Dollars
No places met population threshold.	

Cambodian
Top 10 Places Sorted by Number

Place (place type) County	Dollars
Carrollton (city) Denton	56,667
Dallas (city) Dallas	48,393
Houston (city) Harris	33,618

Chinese (except Taiwanese)
Top 10 Places Sorted by Number

Place (place type) County	Dollars
Coppell (city) Dallas	98,517
New Territory (cdp) Fort Bend	97,586
Plano (city) Collin	87,840
Missouri City (city) Fort Bend	85,080
Sugar Land (city) Fort Bend	83,033
Bellaire (city) Harris	79,178
Mission Bend (cdp) Fort Bend	60,054
Carrollton (city) Denton	58,571
Irving (city) Dallas	51,331
Stafford (city) Fort Bend	50,139

Fijian
Top 10 Places Sorted by Number

Place (place type) County	Dollars
No places met population threshold.	

Filipino
Top 10 Places Sorted by Number

Place (place type) County	Dollars
Sugar Land (city) Fort Bend	91,286
Missouri City (city) Fort Bend	90,276
Mesquite (city) Dallas	85,848
Mission Bend (cdp) Fort Bend	82,023
Grand Prairie (city) Dallas	68,929
McAllen (city) Hidalgo	66,364
Stafford (city) Fort Bend	65,313
Plano (city) Collin	63,533
Beaumont (city) Jefferson	62,045
Fort Worth (city) Tarrant	55,875

Guamanian or Chamorro
Top 10 Places Sorted by Number

Place (place type) County	Dollars
Killeen (city) Bell	51,382
Houston (city) Harris	46,389

Hawaiian, Native
Top 10 Places Sorted by Number

Place (place type) County	Dollars
No places met population threshold.	

Hmong
Top 10 Places Sorted by Number

Place (place type) County	Dollars
No places met population threshold.	

Indonesian
Top 10 Places Sorted by Number

Place (place type) County	Dollars
Houston (city) Harris	50,000

Japanese
Top 10 Places Sorted by Number

Place (place type) County	Dollars
Plano (city) Collin	82,610
Houston (city) Harris	53,194
Austin (city) Travis	51,211
Irving (city) Dallas	49,063
Dallas (city) Dallas	41,645
San Antonio (city) Bexar	41,250
El Paso (city) El Paso	31,285

Korean
Top 10 Places Sorted by Number

Place (place type) County	Dollars
Sugar Land (city) Fort Bend	74,375
Plano (city) Collin	71,129
Coppell (city) Dallas	64,453
Carrollton (city) Denton	55,156
Richardson (city) Dallas	44,000
El Paso (city) El Paso	33,026
Hedwig Village (city) Harris	32,917
Irving (city) Dallas	32,012
Houston (city) Harris	31,257
San Antonio (city) Bexar	30,450

Laotian
Top 10 Places Sorted by Number

Place (place type) County	Dollars
Dallas (city) Dallas	47,969
Fort Worth (city) Tarrant	46,875
Amarillo (city) Potter	46,071
Grand Prairie (city) Dallas	44,531
Irving (city) Dallas	39,821
Haltom City (city) Tarrant	39,464

Malaysian
Top 10 Places Sorted by Number

Place (place type) County	Dollars
No places met population threshold.	

Pakistani
Top 10 Places Sorted by Number

Place (place type) County	Dollars
Sugar Land (city) Fort Bend	81,006
Plano (city) Collin	66,518
Richardson (city) Dallas	50,461
Carrollton (city) Denton	45,368
Irving (city) Dallas	37,500
Mission Bend (cdp) Fort Bend	36,979
Garland (city) Dallas	35,903
Dallas (city) Dallas	35,404
Houston (city) Harris	33,281
Austin (city) Travis	25,263

Samoan
Top 10 Places Sorted by Number

Place (place type) County	Dollars
No places met population threshold.	

Sri Lankan
Top 10 Places Sorted by Number

Place (place type) County	Dollars
No places met population threshold.	

Taiwanese
Top 10 Places Sorted by Number

Place (place type) County	Dollars
Plano (city) Collin	103,208
Sugar Land (city) Fort Bend	54,597
Arlington (city) Tarrant	50,875
Houston (city) Harris	40,486
Austin (city) Travis	34,464

Thai
Top 10 Places Sorted by Number

Place (place type) County	Dollars
San Antonio (city) Bexar	36,071
Houston (city) Harris	30,388

Tongan
Top 10 Places Sorted by Number

Place (place type) County	Dollars
No places met population threshold.	

Vietnamese
Top 10 Places Sorted by Number

Place (place type) County	Dollars
Allen (city) Collin	85,248
Plano (city) Collin	84,195
Round Rock (city) Williamson	72,333
Stafford (city) Fort Bend	72,250
League City (city) Galveston	70,083
Missouri City (city) Fort Bend	69,219
Sugar Land (city) Fort Bend	67,778
Richardson (city) Dallas	67,569
Mission Bend (cdp) Fort Bend	61,146
Carrollton (city) Denton	60,909

Per Capita Income

Total Population
Top 10 Places Sorted by Number

Place (place type) County	Dollars
Hunters Creek Village (city) Harris	88,821
Bunker Hill Village (city) Harris	86,434
West University Place (city) Harris	69,674
University Park (city) Dallas	63,414
Hedwig Village (city) Harris	52,153
Colleyville (city) Tarrant	50,418
Southlake (city) Tarrant	47,597
Bellaire (city) Harris	46,674
Coppell (city) Dallas	40,219
Addison (town) Dallas	38,606

Asian
Top 10 Places Sorted by Number

Place (place type) County	Dollars
Hunters Creek Village (city) Harris	65,625
West University Place (city) Harris	64,108
Bunker Hill Village (city) Harris	57,084
Harlingen (city) Cameron	45,319
The Woodlands (cdp) Montgomery	43,612
Frisco (city) Collin	43,236
Colleyville (city) Tarrant	41,171
Bellaire (city) Harris	38,716

Notes: Please refer to the User's Guide for an explanation of data; tables reflect only those areas that meet Summary File 4 population thresholds, therefore there may be less than 10 places listed

Place (place type) County	Dollars
Murphy (city) Collin	38,352
Southlake (city) Tarrant	37,775

Native Hawaiian and Other Pacific Islander
Top 10 Places Sorted by Number

Place (place type) County	Dollars
Austin (city) Travis	17,679
San Antonio (city) Bexar	17,080
Dallas (city) Dallas	17,008
Houston (city) Harris	16,088
Fort Worth (city) Tarrant	14,826
Killeen (city) Bell	14,233
El Paso (city) El Paso	12,206

Asian Indian
Top 10 Places Sorted by Number

Place (place type) County	Dollars
The Woodlands (cdp) Montgomery	65,670
Midland (city) Midland	37,397
Plano (city) Collin	36,664
Flower Mound (town) Denton	34,340
Lubbock (city) Lubbock	33,629
Amarillo (city) Potter	33,327
Coppell (city) Dallas	33,200
New Territory (cdp) Fort Bend	32,515
Beaumont (city) Jefferson	31,895
Sugar Land (city) Fort Bend	29,478

Bangladeshi
Top 10 Places Sorted by Number

Place (place type) County	Dollars
No places met population threshold.	

Cambodian
Top 10 Places Sorted by Number

Place (place type) County	Dollars
Carrollton (city) Denton	12,855
Dallas (city) Dallas	12,178
Houston (city) Harris	11,207

Chinese (except Taiwanese)
Top 10 Places Sorted by Number

Place (place type) County	Dollars
Bellaire (city) Harris	40,482
El Paso (city) El Paso	32,040
New Territory (cdp) Fort Bend	31,252
Coppell (city) Dallas	30,343
Irving (city) Dallas	29,616
Dallas (city) Dallas	29,491
Plano (city) Collin	28,651
Sugar Land (city) Fort Bend	26,383
Austin (city) Travis	24,124
Missouri City (city) Fort Bend	24,032

Fijian
Top 10 Places Sorted by Number

Place (place type) County	Dollars
No places met population threshold.	

Filipino
Top 10 Places Sorted by Number

Place (place type) County	Dollars
Plano (city) Collin	39,477
McAllen (city) Hidalgo	28,267
Dallas (city) Dallas	27,512
Irving (city) Dallas	26,582
Missouri City (city) Fort Bend	26,169
Sugar Land (city) Fort Bend	24,574
El Paso (city) El Paso	24,418
Houston (city) Harris	23,755
Richardson (city) Dallas	22,699
Mesquite (city) Dallas	21,180

Guamanian or Chamorro
Top 10 Places Sorted by Number

Place (place type) County	Dollars
Killeen (city) Bell	16,823
Houston (city) Harris	15,836

Hawaiian, Native
Top 10 Places Sorted by Number

Place (place type) County	Dollars
No places met population threshold.	

Hmong
Top 10 Places Sorted by Number

Place (place type) County	Dollars
No places met population threshold.	

Indonesian
Top 10 Places Sorted by Number

Place (place type) County	Dollars
Houston (city) Harris	18,016

Japanese
Top 10 Places Sorted by Number

Place (place type) County	Dollars
Dallas (city) Dallas	33,620
Plano (city) Collin	30,921
Houston (city) Harris	28,368
Irving (city) Dallas	25,587
Austin (city) Travis	23,832
San Antonio (city) Bexar	22,118
El Paso (city) El Paso	19,194

Korean
Top 10 Places Sorted by Number

Place (place type) County	Dollars
Sugar Land (city) Fort Bend	36,667
Plano (city) Collin	27,287
San Antonio (city) Bexar	18,380
Houston (city) Harris	18,107
Coppell (city) Dallas	17,823
Carrollton (city) Denton	17,018
Irving (city) Dallas	16,823
Hedwig Village (city) Harris	16,353
Richardson (city) Dallas	16,341
Dallas (city) Dallas	15,968

Laotian
Top 10 Places Sorted by Number

Place (place type) County	Dollars
Fort Worth (city) Tarrant	14,304
Dallas (city) Dallas	13,299
Irving (city) Dallas	13,010
Amarillo (city) Potter	11,782
Haltom City (city) Tarrant	11,773
Grand Prairie (city) Dallas	9,226

Malaysian
Top 10 Places Sorted by Number

Place (place type) County	Dollars
No places met population threshold.	

Pakistani
Top 10 Places Sorted by Number

Place (place type) County	Dollars
Plano (city) Collin	26,363
Richardson (city) Dallas	20,244
Sugar Land (city) Fort Bend	19,986
Irving (city) Dallas	18,290
Carrollton (city) Denton	17,257
Houston (city) Harris	13,157
Dallas (city) Dallas	12,507

Place (place type) County	Dollars
Austin (city) Travis	11,122
Garland (city) Dallas	9,741
Mission Bend (cdp) Fort Bend	7,655

Samoan
Top 10 Places Sorted by Number

Place (place type) County	Dollars
No places met population threshold.	

Sri Lankan
Top 10 Places Sorted by Number

Place (place type) County	Dollars
No places met population threshold.	

Taiwanese
Top 10 Places Sorted by Number

Place (place type) County	Dollars
Plano (city) Collin	31,279
Arlington (city) Tarrant	24,280
Houston (city) Harris	22,563
Sugar Land (city) Fort Bend	17,939
Austin (city) Travis	15,436

Thai
Top 10 Places Sorted by Number

Place (place type) County	Dollars
Houston (city) Harris	23,413
San Antonio (city) Bexar	20,394

Tongan
Top 10 Places Sorted by Number

Place (place type) County	Dollars
No places met population threshold.	

Vietnamese
Top 10 Places Sorted by Number

Place (place type) County	Dollars
Round Rock (city) Williamson	30,759
Missouri City (city) Fort Bend	29,181
Plano (city) Collin	26,303
Stafford (city) Fort Bend	24,298
Richardson (city) Dallas	23,390
Allen (city) Collin	22,461
Lewisville (city) Denton	22,427
Irving (city) Dallas	21,812
Sugar Land (city) Fort Bend	20,488
Austin (city) Travis	18,650

Poverty Status

Total Populations with Income Below Poverty Level
Top 10 Places Sorted by Number

Place (place type) County	Number
Houston (city) Harris	369,045
Dallas (city) Dallas	207,493
San Antonio (city) Bexar	193,731
El Paso (city) El Paso	124,281
Austin (city) Travis	92,011
Fort Worth (city) Tarrant	82,953
Laredo (city) Webb	51,493
Brownsville (city) Cameron	49,701
Corpus Christi (city) Nueces	47,842
Lubbock (city) Lubbock	35,176

Total Populations with Income Below Poverty Level
Top 10 Places Sorted by Percent

Place (place type) County	Percent
College Station (city) Brazos	37.39
Brownsville (city) Cameron	35.97
Laredo (city) Webb	29.58
Waco (city) McLennan	26.32

Notes: Please refer to the User's Guide for an explanation of data; tables reflect only those areas that meet Summary File 4 population thresholds, therefore there may be less than 10 places listed

Port Arthur (city) Jefferson	25.16
Seadrift (city) Calhoun	25.13
Harlingen (city) Cameron	24.91
Palacios (city) Matagorda	24.19
McAllen (city) Hidalgo	23.76
Galveston (city) Galveston	22.34

Asians with Income Below Poverty Level
Top 10 Places Sorted by Number

Place (place type) County	Number
Houston (city) Harris	15,952
Austin (city) Travis	5,789
Dallas (city) Dallas	4,421
Arlington (city) Tarrant	2,920
San Antonio (city) Bexar	2,033
Fort Worth (city) Tarrant	1,877
Garland (city) Dallas	1,770
College Station (city) Brazos	1,643
Irving (city) Dallas	1,332
Port Arthur (city) Jefferson	1,161

Asians with Income Below Poverty Level
Top 10 Places Sorted by Percent

Place (place type) County	Percent
Palacios (city) Matagorda	48.94
Waco (city) McLennan	48.20
Denton (city) Denton	45.42
Bryan (city) Brazos	39.24
Seadrift (city) Calhoun	37.86
College Station (city) Brazos	34.61
Port Arthur (city) Jefferson	34.27
Humble (city) Harris	33.12
University Park (city) Dallas	30.47
Fulton (town) Aransas	30.43

Native Hawaiian and Other Pacific Islanders with Income Below Poverty Level
Top 10 Places Sorted by Number

Place (place type) County	Number
Dallas (city) Dallas	244
Houston (city) Harris	151
Fort Worth (city) Tarrant	144
San Antonio (city) Bexar	129
Austin (city) Travis	75
El Paso (city) El Paso	75
Killeen (city) Bell	48

Native Hawaiian and Other Pacific Islanders with Income Below Poverty Level
Top 10 Places Sorted by Percent

Place (place type) County	Percent
Dallas (city) Dallas	39.17
Fort Worth (city) Tarrant	25.95
San Antonio (city) Bexar	18.86
Houston (city) Harris	17.40
Austin (city) Travis	16.85
El Paso (city) El Paso	14.73
Killeen (city) Bell	4.59

Asian Indians with Income Below Poverty Level
Top 10 Places Sorted by Number

Place (place type) County	Number
Houston (city) Harris	2,643
Austin (city) Travis	1,321
Dallas (city) Dallas	726
Arlington (city) Tarrant	454
Irving (city) Dallas	411
San Antonio (city) Bexar	403
Fort Worth (city) Tarrant	389
Richardson (city) Dallas	384
College Station (city) Brazos	359
Lubbock (city) Lubbock	242

Asian Indians with Income Below Poverty Level
Top 10 Places Sorted by Percent

Place (place type) County	Percent
Denton (city) Denton	36.66
Lubbock (city) Lubbock	34.67
College Station (city) Brazos	31.41
El Paso (city) El Paso	22.62
Galveston (city) Galveston	22.16
Austin (city) Travis	18.90
Fort Worth (city) Tarrant	16.98
Richardson (city) Dallas	15.94
Arlington (city) Tarrant	15.42
Stafford (city) Fort Bend	14.53

Bangladeshis with Income Below Poverty Level
Top 10 Places Sorted by Number

Place (place type) County	Number
No places met population threshold.	

Bangladeshis with Income Below Poverty Level
Top 10 Places Sorted by Percent

Place (place type) County	Percent
No places met population threshold.	

Cambodians with Income Below Poverty Level
Top 10 Places Sorted by Number

Place (place type) County	Number
Dallas (city) Dallas	196
Houston (city) Harris	115
Carrollton (city) Denton	29

Cambodians with Income Below Poverty Level
Top 10 Places Sorted by Percent

Place (place type) County	Percent
Dallas (city) Dallas	18.99
Houston (city) Harris	15.91
Carrollton (city) Denton	3.55

Chinese (except Taiwanese)s with Income Below Poverty Level
Top 10 Places Sorted by Number

Place (place type) County	Number
Houston (city) Harris	3,589
Austin (city) Travis	1,430
Dallas (city) Dallas	609
Arlington (city) Tarrant	538
Plano (city) Collin	458
San Antonio (city) Bexar	450
Richardson (city) Dallas	367
College Station (city) Brazos	327
Sugar Land (city) Fort Bend	306
Fort Worth (city) Tarrant	244

Chinese (except Taiwanese)s with Income Below Poverty Level
Top 10 Places Sorted by Percent

Place (place type) County	Percent
Denton (city) Denton	38.93
College Station (city) Brazos	23.97
Galveston (city) Galveston	23.00
Arlington (city) Tarrant	19.57
Austin (city) Travis	19.09
Fort Worth (city) Tarrant	17.84
Houston (city) Harris	16.57
Lubbock (city) Lubbock	16.33
San Antonio (city) Bexar	13.85
Carrollton (city) Denton	12.13

Fijians with Income Below Poverty Level
Top 10 Places Sorted by Number

Place (place type) County	Number
No places met population threshold.	

Fijians with Income Below Poverty Level
Top 10 Places Sorted by Percent

Place (place type) County	Percent
No places met population threshold.	

Filipinos with Income Below Poverty Level
Top 10 Places Sorted by Number

Place (place type) County	Number
Houston (city) Harris	503
San Antonio (city) Bexar	394
Austin (city) Travis	197
Garland (city) Dallas	151
Killeen (city) Bell	149
El Paso (city) El Paso	112
Arlington (city) Tarrant	110
Dallas (city) Dallas	73
Irving (city) Dallas	64
Wichita Falls (city) Wichita	52

Filipinos with Income Below Poverty Level
Top 10 Places Sorted by Percent

Place (place type) County	Percent
Garland (city) Dallas	13.57
Killeen (city) Bell	13.55
Austin (city) Travis	12.06
Wichita Falls (city) Wichita	11.18
San Antonio (city) Bexar	10.56
Arlington (city) Tarrant	9.23
Irving (city) Dallas	8.38
Abilene (city) Taylor	8.11
Stafford (city) Fort Bend	7.72
El Paso (city) El Paso	6.88

Guamanian or Chamorros with Income Below Poverty Level
Top 10 Places Sorted by Number

Place (place type) County	Number
Houston (city) Harris	84
Killeen (city) Bell	17

Guamanian or Chamorros with Income Below Poverty Level
Top 10 Places Sorted by Percent

Place (place type) County	Percent
Houston (city) Harris	19.00
Killeen (city) Bell	3.40

Hawaiian, Natives with Income Below Poverty Level
Top 10 Places Sorted by Number

Place (place type) County	Number
No places met population threshold.	

Hawaiian, Natives with Income Below Poverty Level
Top 10 Places Sorted by Percent

Place (place type) County	Percent
No places met population threshold.	

Hmongs with Income Below Poverty Level
Top 10 Places Sorted by Number

Place (place type) County	Number
No places met population threshold.	

Notes: Please refer to the User's Guide for an explanation of data; tables reflect only those areas that meet Summary File 4 population thresholds, therefore there may be less than 10 places listed

Hmongs with Income Below Poverty Level
Top 10 Places Sorted by Percent

Place (place type) County	Percent
No places met population threshold.	

Indonesians with Income Below Poverty Level
Top 10 Places Sorted by Number

Place (place type) County	Number
Houston (city) Harris	141

Indonesians with Income Below Poverty Level
Top 10 Places Sorted by Percent

Place (place type) County	Percent
Houston (city) Harris	27.27

Japaneses with Income Below Poverty Level
Top 10 Places Sorted by Number

Place (place type) County	Number
Houston (city) Harris	278
Austin (city) Travis	145
San Antonio (city) Bexar	135
Dallas (city) Dallas	75
El Paso (city) El Paso	74
Irving (city) Dallas	20
Plano (city) Collin	15

Japaneses with Income Below Poverty Level
Top 10 Places Sorted by Percent

Place (place type) County	Percent
Austin (city) Travis	13.06
Houston (city) Harris	11.76
El Paso (city) El Paso	9.87
San Antonio (city) Bexar	9.76
Dallas (city) Dallas	8.95
Plano (city) Collin	3.01
Irving (city) Dallas	2.95

Koreans with Income Below Poverty Level
Top 10 Places Sorted by Number

Place (place type) County	Number
Austin (city) Travis	1,153
Houston (city) Harris	1,052
Dallas (city) Dallas	740
College Station (city) Brazos	388
Fort Worth (city) Tarrant	334
Irving (city) Dallas	330
Arlington (city) Tarrant	327
Denton (city) Denton	280
Garland (city) Dallas	214
San Antonio (city) Bexar	161

Koreans with Income Below Poverty Level
Top 10 Places Sorted by Percent

Place (place type) County	Percent
Denton (city) Denton	57.49
College Station (city) Brazos	50.92
Arlington (city) Tarrant	36.09
Austin (city) Travis	33.28
Fort Worth (city) Tarrant	31.19
Dallas (city) Dallas	22.36
Houston (city) Harris	20.51
Garland (city) Dallas	18.80
Carrollton (city) Denton	14.81
Irving (city) Dallas	13.31

Laotians with Income Below Poverty Level
Top 10 Places Sorted by Number

Place (place type) County	Number
Dallas (city) Dallas	117
Amarillo (city) Potter	111
Fort Worth (city) Tarrant	104
Haltom City (city) Tarrant	83
Grand Prairie (city) Dallas	42
Irving (city) Dallas	26

Laotians with Income Below Poverty Level
Top 10 Places Sorted by Percent

Place (place type) County	Percent
Fort Worth (city) Tarrant	19.96
Dallas (city) Dallas	12.89
Grand Prairie (city) Dallas	10.74
Amarillo (city) Potter	10.46
Haltom City (city) Tarrant	10.22
Irving (city) Dallas	5.43

Malaysians with Income Below Poverty Level
Top 10 Places Sorted by Number

Place (place type) County	Number
No places met population threshold.	

Malaysians with Income Below Poverty Level
Top 10 Places Sorted by Percent

Place (place type) County	Percent
No places met population threshold.	

Pakistanis with Income Below Poverty Level
Top 10 Places Sorted by Number

Place (place type) County	Number
Houston (city) Harris	1,085
Garland (city) Dallas	206
Dallas (city) Dallas	203
Austin (city) Travis	132
Mission Bend (cdp) Fort Bend	77
Carrollton (city) Denton	76
Sugar Land (city) Fort Bend	60
Richardson (city) Dallas	58
Irving (city) Dallas	22
Plano (city) Collin	0

Pakistanis with Income Below Poverty Level
Top 10 Places Sorted by Percent

Place (place type) County	Percent
Austin (city) Travis	27.16
Garland (city) Dallas	24.79
Houston (city) Harris	21.71
Dallas (city) Dallas	17.20
Mission Bend (cdp) Fort Bend	16.04
Richardson (city) Dallas	13.71
Sugar Land (city) Fort Bend	9.71
Carrollton (city) Denton	6.52
Irving (city) Dallas	5.13
Plano (city) Collin	0.00

Samoans with Income Below Poverty Level
Top 10 Places Sorted by Number

Place (place type) County	Number
No places met population threshold.	

Samoans with Income Below Poverty Level
Top 10 Places Sorted by Percent

Place (place type) County	Percent
No places met population threshold.	

Sri Lankans with Income Below Poverty Level
Top 10 Places Sorted by Number

Place (place type) County	Number
No places met population threshold.	

Sri Lankans with Income Below Poverty Level
Top 10 Places Sorted by Percent

Place (place type) County	Percent
No places met population threshold.	

Taiwaneses with Income Below Poverty Level
Top 10 Places Sorted by Number

Place (place type) County	Number
Houston (city) Harris	249
Sugar Land (city) Fort Bend	157
Austin (city) Travis	144
Arlington (city) Tarrant	74
Plano (city) Collin	0

Taiwaneses with Income Below Poverty Level
Top 10 Places Sorted by Percent

Place (place type) County	Percent
Austin (city) Travis	23.57
Arlington (city) Tarrant	17.83
Houston (city) Harris	17.14
Sugar Land (city) Fort Bend	16.76
Plano (city) Collin	0.00

Thais with Income Below Poverty Level
Top 10 Places Sorted by Number

Place (place type) County	Number
Houston (city) Harris	118
San Antonio (city) Bexar	9

Thais with Income Below Poverty Level
Top 10 Places Sorted by Percent

Place (place type) County	Percent
Houston (city) Harris	13.55
San Antonio (city) Bexar	1.64

Tongans with Income Below Poverty Level
Top 10 Places Sorted by Number

Place (place type) County	Number
No places met population threshold.	

Tongans with Income Below Poverty Level
Top 10 Places Sorted by Percent

Place (place type) County	Percent
No places met population threshold.	

Vietnamese with Income Below Poverty Level
Top 10 Places Sorted by Number

Place (place type) County	Number
Houston (city) Harris	5,438
Dallas (city) Dallas	1,216
Port Arthur (city) Jefferson	1,072
Austin (city) Travis	860
Arlington (city) Tarrant	853
Garland (city) Dallas	652
Fort Worth (city) Tarrant	470
San Antonio (city) Bexar	308
Palacios (city) Matagorda	300
Haltom City (city) Tarrant	260

Vietnamese with Income Below Poverty Level
Top 10 Places Sorted by Percent

Place (place type) County	Percent
Palacios (city) Matagorda	49.92
Port Arthur (city) Jefferson	37.89
Seadrift (city) Calhoun	36.03
Fulton (town) Aransas	33.79
San Leon (cdp) Galveston	32.57
Beaumont (city) Jefferson	24.83
Allen (city) Collin	20.71
Dallas (city) Dallas	17.24
Houston (city) Harris	17.21
Haltom City (city) Tarrant	16.50

Notes: Please refer to the User's Guide for an explanation of data; tables reflect only those areas that meet Summary File 4 population thresholds, therefore there may be less than 10 places listed

Homeownership

Total Populations Who Own Their Own Homes
Top 10 Places Sorted by Number

Place (place type) County	Number
Houston (city) Harris	329,006
San Antonio (city) Bexar	235,584
Dallas (city) Dallas	195,227
Austin (city) Travis	119,191
El Paso (city) El Paso	111,808
Fort Worth (city) Tarrant	109,152
Arlington (city) Tarrant	68,309
Corpus Christi (city) Nueces	58,918
Plano (city) Collin	55,725
Garland (city) Dallas	48,043

Total Populations Who Own Their Own Homes
Top 10 Places Sorted by Percent

Place (place type) County	Percent
Bunker Hill Village (city) Harris	97.47
Hunters Creek Village (city) Harris	97.08
Colleyville (city) Tarrant	96.80
Southlake (city) Tarrant	96.69
Murphy (city) Collin	95.42
Brushy Creek (cdp) Williamson	94.30
Meadows Place (city) Fort Bend	94.15
Keller (city) Tarrant	92.90
Cinco Ranch (cdp) Fort Bend	92.70
Flower Mound (town) Denton	92.65

Asians Who Own Their Own Homes
Top 10 Places Sorted by Number

Place (place type) County	Number
Houston (city) Harris	14,784
Plano (city) Collin	4,992
Sugar Land (city) Fort Bend	3,566
Austin (city) Travis	3,508
Dallas (city) Dallas	3,365
San Antonio (city) Bexar	3,179
Arlington (city) Tarrant	2,789
Garland (city) Dallas	2,751
Carrollton (city) Denton	2,045
Fort Worth (city) Tarrant	1,971

Asians Who Own Their Own Homes
Top 10 Places Sorted by Percent

Place (place type) County	Percent
Brushy Creek (cdp) Williamson	100.00
Bunker Hill Village (city) Harris	100.00
Colleyville (city) Tarrant	100.00
Four Corners (cdp) Fort Bend	100.00
Frisco (city) Collin	100.00
Hunters Creek Village (city) Harris	100.00
Keller (city) Tarrant	100.00
Mansfield (city) Tarrant	100.00
Murphy (city) Collin	100.00
New Territory (cdp) Fort Bend	98.91

Native Hawaiian and Other Pacific Islanders Who Own Their Own Homes
Top 10 Places Sorted by Number

Place (place type) County	Number
Killeen (city) Bell	186
Houston (city) Harris	119
San Antonio (city) Bexar	117
Dallas (city) Dallas	61
Fort Worth (city) Tarrant	45
Austin (city) Travis	41
El Paso (city) El Paso	28

Native Hawaiian and Other Pacific Islanders Who Own Their Own Homes
Top 10 Places Sorted by Percent

Place (place type) County	Percent
Killeen (city) Bell	58.49
San Antonio (city) Bexar	50.00
Houston (city) Harris	38.64
Dallas (city) Dallas	33.89
El Paso (city) El Paso	31.46
Fort Worth (city) Tarrant	29.22
Austin (city) Travis	20.81

Asian Indians Who Own Their Own Homes
Top 10 Places Sorted by Number

Place (place type) County	Number
Houston (city) Harris	2,404
Plano (city) Collin	1,239
Sugar Land (city) Fort Bend	1,003
Austin (city) Travis	745
Carrollton (city) Denton	741
Dallas (city) Dallas	665
San Antonio (city) Bexar	598
Missouri City (city) Fort Bend	549
Garland (city) Dallas	537
Mesquite (city) Dallas	520

Asian Indians Who Own Their Own Homes
Top 10 Places Sorted by Percent

Place (place type) County	Percent
Rowlett (city) Dallas	100.00
New Territory (cdp) Fort Bend	97.63
Missouri City (city) Fort Bend	96.32
Mission Bend (cdp) Fort Bend	94.91
Flower Mound (town) Denton	94.62
Grand Prairie (city) Dallas	83.68
Sugar Land (city) Fort Bend	81.94
Mesquite (city) Dallas	80.75
Allen (city) Collin	80.34
Midland (city) Midland	77.88

Bangladeshis Who Own Their Own Homes
Top 10 Places Sorted by Number

Place (place type) County	Number
No places met population threshold.	

Bangladeshis Who Own Their Own Homes
Top 10 Places Sorted by Percent

Place (place type) County	Percent
No places met population threshold.	

Cambodians Who Own Their Own Homes
Top 10 Places Sorted by Number

Place (place type) County	Number
Carrollton (city) Denton	140
Houston (city) Harris	126
Dallas (city) Dallas	70

Cambodians Who Own Their Own Homes
Top 10 Places Sorted by Percent

Place (place type) County	Percent
Carrollton (city) Denton	73.68
Houston (city) Harris	54.08
Dallas (city) Dallas	30.43

Chinese (except Taiwanese)s Who Own Their Own Homes
Top 10 Places Sorted by Number

Place (place type) County	Number
Houston (city) Harris	4,008
Plano (city) Collin	2,294
Sugar Land (city) Fort Bend	1,473
Austin (city) Travis	1,128
Dallas (city) Dallas	884
San Antonio (city) Bexar	627
Richardson (city) Dallas	574
Arlington (city) Tarrant	479
Missouri City (city) Fort Bend	372
Garland (city) Dallas	358

Chinese (except Taiwanese)s Who Own Their Own Homes
Top 10 Places Sorted by Percent

Place (place type) County	Percent
Mission Bend (cdp) Fort Bend	100.00
New Territory (cdp) Fort Bend	100.00
Missouri City (city) Fort Bend	97.13
Bellaire (city) Harris	95.20
Sugar Land (city) Fort Bend	92.53
Coppell (city) Dallas	84.85
Plano (city) Collin	82.91
Carrollton (city) Denton	79.31
Garland (city) Dallas	76.66
Stafford (city) Fort Bend	71.50

Fijians Who Own Their Own Homes
Top 10 Places Sorted by Number

Place (place type) County	Number
No places met population threshold.	

Fijians Who Own Their Own Homes
Top 10 Places Sorted by Percent

Place (place type) County	Percent
No places met population threshold.	

Filipinos Who Own Their Own Homes
Top 10 Places Sorted by Number

Place (place type) County	Number
Houston (city) Harris	1,168
San Antonio (city) Bexar	602
El Paso (city) El Paso	378
Garland (city) Dallas	292
Corpus Christi (city) Nueces	274
Missouri City (city) Fort Bend	256
Sugar Land (city) Fort Bend	251
Dallas (city) Dallas	215
Killeen (city) Bell	209
Mission Bend (cdp) Fort Bend	173

Filipinos Who Own Their Own Homes
Top 10 Places Sorted by Percent

Place (place type) County	Percent
Missouri City (city) Fort Bend	100.00
Mission Bend (cdp) Fort Bend	89.64
Sugar Land (city) Fort Bend	85.96
Garland (city) Dallas	81.79
Mesquite (city) Dallas	79.10
Richardson (city) Dallas	78.20
El Paso (city) El Paso	65.28
Corpus Christi (city) Nueces	62.56
Grand Prairie (city) Dallas	60.66
Beaumont (city) Jefferson	58.02

Guamanian or Chamorros Who Own Their Own Homes
Top 10 Places Sorted by Number

Place (place type) County	Number
Killeen (city) Bell	104
Houston (city) Harris	72

Notes: Please refer to the User's Guide for an explanation of data; tables reflect only those areas that meet Summary File 4 population thresholds, therefore there may be less than 10 places listed

Guamanian or Chamorros Who Own Their Own Homes
Top 10 Places Sorted by Percent

Place (place type) County	Percent
Killeen (city) Bell	61.90
Houston (city) Harris	43.11

Hawaiian, Natives Who Own Their Own Homes
Top 10 Places Sorted by Number

Place (place type) County	Number
No places met population threshold.	

Hawaiian, Natives Who Own Their Own Homes
Top 10 Places Sorted by Percent

Place (place type) County	Percent
No places met population threshold.	

Hmongs Who Own Their Own Homes
Top 10 Places Sorted by Number

Place (place type) County	Number
No places met population threshold.	

Hmongs Who Own Their Own Homes
Top 10 Places Sorted by Percent

Place (place type) County	Percent
No places met population threshold.	

Indonesians Who Own Their Own Homes
Top 10 Places Sorted by Number

Place (place type) County	Number
Houston (city) Harris	32

Indonesians Who Own Their Own Homes
Top 10 Places Sorted by Percent

Place (place type) County	Percent
Houston (city) Harris	16.58

Japaneses Who Own Their Own Homes
Top 10 Places Sorted by Number

Place (place type) County	Number
San Antonio (city) Bexar	266
Houston (city) Harris	249
El Paso (city) El Paso	180
Austin (city) Travis	139
Dallas (city) Dallas	134
Plano (city) Collin	76
Irving (city) Dallas	43

Japaneses Who Own Their Own Homes
Top 10 Places Sorted by Percent

Place (place type) County	Percent
El Paso (city) El Paso	52.17
Plano (city) Collin	50.00
San Antonio (city) Bexar	45.63
Austin (city) Travis	30.96
Dallas (city) Dallas	29.26
Houston (city) Harris	23.29
Irving (city) Dallas	15.52

Koreans Who Own Their Own Homes
Top 10 Places Sorted by Number

Place (place type) County	Number
Houston (city) Harris	658
Plano (city) Collin	363
Dallas (city) Dallas	307
El Paso (city) El Paso	257
San Antonio (city) Bexar	240
Carrollton (city) Denton	208
Austin (city) Travis	193
Irving (city) Dallas	182
Killeen (city) Bell	176
Fort Worth (city) Tarrant	152

Koreans Who Own Their Own Homes
Top 10 Places Sorted by Percent

Place (place type) County	Percent
Sugar Land (city) Fort Bend	93.28
Carrollton (city) Denton	64.60
Coppell (city) Dallas	62.70
Plano (city) Collin	58.83
El Paso (city) El Paso	58.14
Killeen (city) Bell	48.35
Richardson (city) Dallas	47.50
Garland (city) Dallas	47.00
San Antonio (city) Bexar	44.94
Fort Worth (city) Tarrant	44.06

Laotians Who Own Their Own Homes
Top 10 Places Sorted by Number

Place (place type) County	Number
Amarillo (city) Potter	204
Haltom City (city) Tarrant	139
Dallas (city) Dallas	131
Fort Worth (city) Tarrant	93
Irving (city) Dallas	68
Grand Prairie (city) Dallas	57

Laotians Who Own Their Own Homes
Top 10 Places Sorted by Percent

Place (place type) County	Percent
Grand Prairie (city) Dallas	79.17
Amarillo (city) Potter	72.08
Haltom City (city) Tarrant	71.65
Fort Worth (city) Tarrant	65.96
Dallas (city) Dallas	52.61
Irving (city) Dallas	47.89

Malaysians Who Own Their Own Homes
Top 10 Places Sorted by Number

Place (place type) County	Number
No places met population threshold.	

Malaysians Who Own Their Own Homes
Top 10 Places Sorted by Percent

Place (place type) County	Percent
No places met population threshold.	

Pakistanis Who Own Their Own Homes
Top 10 Places Sorted by Number

Place (place type) County	Number
Houston (city) Harris	291
Carrollton (city) Denton	129
Sugar Land (city) Fort Bend	119
Garland (city) Dallas	117
Plano (city) Collin	83
Mission Bend (cdp) Fort Bend	61
Richardson (city) Dallas	53
Dallas (city) Dallas	42
Irving (city) Dallas	38
Austin (city) Travis	33

Pakistanis Who Own Their Own Homes
Top 10 Places Sorted by Percent

Place (place type) County	Percent
Sugar Land (city) Fort Bend	76.28
Mission Bend (cdp) Fort Bend	70.93
Garland (city) Dallas	65.00
Plano (city) Collin	52.53
Carrollton (city) Denton	45.10
Richardson (city) Dallas	36.81
Irving (city) Dallas	25.50
Houston (city) Harris	19.76

Austin (city) Travis	18.97
Dallas (city) Dallas	12.14

Samoans Who Own Their Own Homes
Top 10 Places Sorted by Number

Place (place type) County	Number
No places met population threshold.	

Samoans Who Own Their Own Homes
Top 10 Places Sorted by Percent

Place (place type) County	Percent
No places met population threshold.	

Sri Lankans Who Own Their Own Homes
Top 10 Places Sorted by Number

Place (place type) County	Number
No places met population threshold.	

Sri Lankans Who Own Their Own Homes
Top 10 Places Sorted by Percent

Place (place type) County	Percent
No places met population threshold.	

Taiwaneses Who Own Their Own Homes
Top 10 Places Sorted by Number

Place (place type) County	Number
Houston (city) Harris	426
Sugar Land (city) Fort Bend	220
Plano (city) Collin	146
Austin (city) Travis	104
Arlington (city) Tarrant	59

Taiwaneses Who Own Their Own Homes
Top 10 Places Sorted by Percent

Place (place type) County	Percent
Plano (city) Collin	96.05
Sugar Land (city) Fort Bend	82.09
Houston (city) Harris	67.73
Arlington (city) Tarrant	38.82
Austin (city) Travis	36.62

Thais Who Own Their Own Homes
Top 10 Places Sorted by Number

Place (place type) County	Number
Houston (city) Harris	148
San Antonio (city) Bexar	102

Thais Who Own Their Own Homes
Top 10 Places Sorted by Percent

Place (place type) County	Percent
San Antonio (city) Bexar	42.50
Houston (city) Harris	40.33

Tongans Who Own Their Own Homes
Top 10 Places Sorted by Number

Place (place type) County	Number
No places met population threshold.	

Tongans Who Own Their Own Homes
Top 10 Places Sorted by Percent

Place (place type) County	Percent
No places met population threshold.	

Vietnamese Who Own Their Own Homes
Top 10 Places Sorted by Number

Place (place type) County	Number
Houston (city) Harris	4,730
Arlington (city) Tarrant	1,453
Garland (city) Dallas	1,006

Notes: Please refer to the User's Guide for an explanation of data; tables reflect only those areas that meet Summary File 4 population thresholds, therefore there may be less than 10 places listed

Place (place type) County	
Austin (city) Travis	837
Fort Worth (city) Tarrant	733
Dallas (city) Dallas	560
San Antonio (city) Bexar	485
Grand Prairie (city) Dallas	468
Carrollton (city) Denton	461
Port Arthur (city) Jefferson	446

Vietnamese Who Own Their Own Homes
Top 10 Places Sorted by Percent

Place (place type) County	Percent
Pearland (city) Brazoria	100.00
Mission Bend (cdp) Fort Bend	95.32
League City (city) Galveston	94.70
Palacios (city) Matagorda	91.38
Missouri City (city) Fort Bend	88.55
Sugar Land (city) Fort Bend	87.50
Wichita Falls (city) Wichita	83.96
Fulton (town) Aransas	83.87
Plano (city) Collin	82.12
Round Rock (city) Williamson	80.47

Median Gross Rent

All Specified Renter-Occupied Housing Units
Top 10 Places Sorted by Number

Place (place type) County	Dollars/Month
Bunker Hill Village (city) Harris	2,001
West University Place (city) Harris	1,418
Hunters Creek Village (city) Harris	1,208
Bellaire (city) Harris	1,119
Brushy Creek (cdp) Williamson	1,084
Flower Mound (town) Denton	1,050
Meadows Place (city) Fort Bend	1,045
University Park (city) Dallas	1,028
Cinco Ranch (cdp) Fort Bend	1,016
The Colony (city) Denton	986

Specified Housing Units Rented by Asians
Top 10 Places Sorted by Number

Place (place type) County	Dollars/Month
Cinco Ranch (cdp) Fort Bend	2,001
West University Place (city) Harris	1,625
Flower Mound (town) Denton	1,375
Meadows Place (city) Fort Bend	1,375
The Colony (city) Denton	1,375
Cedar Park (city) Williamson	1,271
New Territory (cdp) Fort Bend	1,125
Coppell (city) Dallas	956
Sugar Land (city) Fort Bend	955
Watauga (city) Tarrant	950

Specified Housing Units Rented by Native Hawaiian and Other Pacific Islanders
Top 10 Places Sorted by Number

Place (place type) County	Dollars/Month
Austin (city) Travis	812
Dallas (city) Dallas	692
Houston (city) Harris	619
San Antonio (city) Bexar	600
Fort Worth (city) Tarrant	567
El Paso (city) El Paso	561
Killeen (city) Bell	484

Specified Housing Units Rented by Asian Indians
Top 10 Places Sorted by Number

Place (place type) County	Dollars/Month
New Territory (cdp) Fort Bend	1,125
Flower Mound (town) Denton	1,075
Coppell (city) Dallas	928
Sugar Land (city) Fort Bend	890
Plano (city) Collin	819
Lewisville (city) Denton	788

Place (place type) County	Dollars/Month
Allen (city) Collin	786
Irving (city) Dallas	773
Richardson (city) Dallas	771
The Woodlands (cdp) Montgomery	763

Specified Housing Units Rented by Bangladeshis
Top 10 Places Sorted by Number

Place (place type) County	Dollars/Month
No places met population threshold.	

Specified Housing Units Rented by Cambodians
Top 10 Places Sorted by Number

Place (place type) County	Dollars/Month
Carrollton (city) Denton	543
Dallas (city) Dallas	510
Houston (city) Harris	509

Specified Housing Units Rented by Chinese (except Taiwanese)s
Top 10 Places Sorted by Number

Place (place type) County	Dollars/Month
Missouri City (city) Fort Bend	1,625
Bellaire (city) Harris	1,375
Sugar Land (city) Fort Bend	992
Carrollton (city) Denton	900
Stafford (city) Fort Bend	826
Plano (city) Collin	817
Coppell (city) Dallas	738
Richardson (city) Dallas	708
Irving (city) Dallas	701
Austin (city) Travis	640

Specified Housing Units Rented by Fijians
Top 10 Places Sorted by Number

Place (place type) County	Dollars/Month
No places met population threshold.	

Specified Housing Units Rented by Filipinos
Top 10 Places Sorted by Number

Place (place type) County	Dollars/Month
Sugar Land (city) Fort Bend	911
Irving (city) Dallas	886
Stafford (city) Fort Bend	886
Mission Bend (cdp) Fort Bend	829
Plano (city) Collin	763
Austin (city) Travis	714
Mesquite (city) Dallas	667
Richardson (city) Dallas	664
Garland (city) Dallas	663
Dallas (city) Dallas	650

Specified Housing Units Rented by Guamanian or Chamorros
Top 10 Places Sorted by Number

Place (place type) County	Dollars/Month
Houston (city) Harris	672
Killeen (city) Bell	496

Specified Housing Units Rented by Hawaiian, Natives
Top 10 Places Sorted by Number

Place (place type) County	Dollars/Month
No places met population threshold.	

Specified Housing Units Rented by Hmongs
Top 10 Places Sorted by Number

Place (place type) County	Dollars/Month
No places met population threshold.	

Specified Housing Units Rented by Indonesians
Top 10 Places Sorted by Number

Place (place type) County	Dollars/Month
Houston (city) Harris	698

Specified Housing Units Rented by Japaneses
Top 10 Places Sorted by Number

Place (place type) County	Dollars/Month
Plano (city) Collin	1,129
Irving (city) Dallas	940
Houston (city) Harris	861
Austin (city) Travis	836
Dallas (city) Dallas	731
San Antonio (city) Bexar	663
El Paso (city) El Paso	655

Specified Housing Units Rented by Koreans
Top 10 Places Sorted by Number

Place (place type) County	Dollars/Month
Plano (city) Collin	998
Coppell (city) Dallas	991
Richardson (city) Dallas	906
Sugar Land (city) Fort Bend	850
Hedwig Village (city) Harris	835
Carrollton (city) Denton	785
Irving (city) Dallas	724
Austin (city) Travis	675
Houston (city) Harris	675
Dallas (city) Dallas	673

Specified Housing Units Rented by Laotians
Top 10 Places Sorted by Number

Place (place type) County	Dollars/Month
Grand Prairie (city) Dallas	753
Fort Worth (city) Tarrant	567
Irving (city) Dallas	545
Dallas (city) Dallas	523
Haltom City (city) Tarrant	468
Amarillo (city) Potter	357

Specified Housing Units Rented by Malaysians
Top 10 Places Sorted by Number

Place (place type) County	Dollars/Month
No places met population threshold.	

Specified Housing Units Rented by Pakistanis
Top 10 Places Sorted by Number

Place (place type) County	Dollars/Month
Sugar Land (city) Fort Bend	1,205
Plano (city) Collin	1,065
Mission Bend (cdp) Fort Bend	874
Carrollton (city) Denton	834
Richardson (city) Dallas	812
Austin (city) Travis	770
Irving (city) Dallas	741
Dallas (city) Dallas	709
Garland (city) Dallas	681
Houston (city) Harris	662

Specified Housing Units Rented by Samoans
Top 10 Places Sorted by Number

Place (place type) County	Dollars/Month
No places met population threshold.	

Specified Housing Units Rented by Sri Lankans
Top 10 Places Sorted by Number

Place (place type) County	Dollars/Month
No places met population threshold.	

Notes: Please refer to the User's Guide for an explanation of data; tables reflect only those areas that meet Summary File 4 population thresholds, therefore there may be less than 10 places listed

Specified Housing Units Rented by Taiwaneses
Top 10 Places Sorted by Number

Place (place type) County	Dollars/Month
Sugar Land (city) Fort Bend	1,008
Plano (city) Collin	850
Austin (city) Travis	639
Houston (city) Harris	609
Arlington (city) Tarrant	516

Specified Housing Units Rented by Thais
Top 10 Places Sorted by Number

Place (place type) County	Dollars/Month
San Antonio (city) Bexar	623
Houston (city) Harris	523

Specified Housing Units Rented by Tongans
Top 10 Places Sorted by Number

Place (place type) County	Dollars/Month

No places met population threshold.

Specified Housing Units Rented by Vietnamese
Top 10 Places Sorted by Number

Place (place type) County	Dollars/Month
Missouri City (city) Fort Bend	1,534
League City (city) Galveston	1,125
Sugar Land (city) Fort Bend	964
Stafford (city) Fort Bend	886
Plano (city) Collin	792
Grand Prairie (city) Dallas	755
Richardson (city) Dallas	720
Carrollton (city) Denton	717
Round Rock (city) Williamson	689
San Leon (cdp) Galveston	668

Median Home Value

All Specified Owner-Occupied Housing Units
Top 10 Places Sorted by Number

Place (place type) County	Dollars
Hunters Creek Village (city) Harris	567,300
Bunker Hill Village (city) Harris	566,900
University Park (city) Dallas	549,400
Hedwig Village (city) Harris	438,300
West University Place (city) Harris	372,800
Southlake (city) Tarrant	341,400
Colleyville (city) Tarrant	267,100
Bellaire (city) Harris	233,200
Addison (town) Dallas	222,400
Coppell (city) Dallas	210,700

Specified Housing Units Owned and Occupied by Asians
Top 10 Places Sorted by Number

Place (place type) County	Dollars
Hunters Creek Village (city) Harris	671,100
Bunker Hill Village (city) Harris	619,600
Hedwig Village (city) Harris	457,100
Bellaire (city) Harris	346,300
Southlake (city) Tarrant	310,500
West University Place (city) Harris	302,100
University Park (city) Dallas	290,000
Colleyville (city) Tarrant	242,000
Coppell (city) Dallas	212,000
Flower Mound (town) Denton	208,700

Specified Housing Units Owned and Occupied by Native Hawaiian and Other Pacific Islanders
Top 10 Places Sorted by Number

Place (place type) County	Dollars
El Paso (city) El Paso	93,800
Dallas (city) Dallas	87,100
Houston (city) Harris	82,800

Austin (city) Travis	79,300
Killeen (city) Bell	77,600
Fort Worth (city) Tarrant	75,000
San Antonio (city) Bexar	72,600

Specified Housing Units Owned and Occupied by Asian Indians
Top 10 Places Sorted by Number

Place (place type) County	Dollars
College Station (city) Brazos	245,500
The Woodlands (cdp) Montgomery	225,000
Lubbock (city) Lubbock	220,300
Flower Mound (town) Denton	213,800
Euless (city) Tarrant	204,500
Plano (city) Collin	203,600
Austin (city) Travis	197,500
Coppell (city) Dallas	196,800
Sugar Land (city) Fort Bend	192,900
Addison (town) Dallas	192,500

Specified Housing Units Owned and Occupied by Bangladeshis
Top 10 Places Sorted by Number

Place (place type) County	Dollars

No places met population threshold.

Specified Housing Units Owned and Occupied by Cambodians
Top 10 Places Sorted by Number

Place (place type) County	Dollars
Carrollton (city) Denton	99,300
Dallas (city) Dallas	86,300
Houston (city) Harris	60,500

Specified Housing Units Owned and Occupied by Chinese (except Taiwanese)s
Top 10 Places Sorted by Number

Place (place type) County	Dollars
Bellaire (city) Harris	350,000
Coppell (city) Dallas	212,500
Plano (city) Collin	180,500
Austin (city) Travis	177,600
Sugar Land (city) Fort Bend	173,100
New Territory (cdp) Fort Bend	160,400
Irving (city) Dallas	153,100
Dallas (city) Dallas	151,300
Missouri City (city) Fort Bend	144,300
Carrollton (city) Denton	140,000

Specified Housing Units Owned and Occupied by Fijians
Top 10 Places Sorted by Number

Place (place type) County	Dollars

No places met population threshold.

Specified Housing Units Owned and Occupied by Filipinos
Top 10 Places Sorted by Number

Place (place type) County	Dollars
Plano (city) Collin	196,400
Austin (city) Travis	153,000
Missouri City (city) Fort Bend	126,000
Grand Prairie (city) Dallas	119,300
Richardson (city) Dallas	114,800
Stafford (city) Fort Bend	114,600
Sugar Land (city) Fort Bend	112,200
Corpus Christi (city) Nueces	106,100
McAllen (city) Hidalgo	105,600
Garland (city) Dallas	97,900

Specified Housing Units Owned and Occupied by Guamanian or Chamorros
Top 10 Places Sorted by Number

Place (place type) County	Dollars
Houston (city) Harris	87,000
Killeen (city) Bell	78,800

Specified Housing Units Owned and Occupied by Hawaiian, Natives
Top 10 Places Sorted by Number

Place (place type) County	Dollars

No places met population threshold.

Specified Housing Units Owned and Occupied by Hmongs
Top 10 Places Sorted by Number

Place (place type) County	Dollars

No places met population threshold.

Specified Housing Units Owned and Occupied by Indonesians
Top 10 Places Sorted by Number

Place (place type) County	Dollars
Houston (city) Harris	121,900

Specified Housing Units Owned and Occupied by Japaneses
Top 10 Places Sorted by Number

Place (place type) County	Dollars
Irving (city) Dallas	278,800
Plano (city) Collin	177,500
Austin (city) Travis	176,000
Houston (city) Harris	155,400
Dallas (city) Dallas	154,200
San Antonio (city) Bexar	79,500
El Paso (city) El Paso	71,300

Specified Housing Units Owned and Occupied by Koreans
Top 10 Places Sorted by Number

Place (place type) County	Dollars
Hedwig Village (city) Harris	875,000
Coppell (city) Dallas	238,400
Plano (city) Collin	168,300
Sugar Land (city) Fort Bend	160,300
Austin (city) Travis	157,800
Carrollton (city) Denton	151,400
Dallas (city) Dallas	139,100
College Station (city) Brazos	137,500
Irving (city) Dallas	123,600
Richardson (city) Dallas	121,300

Specified Housing Units Owned and Occupied by Laotians
Top 10 Places Sorted by Number

Place (place type) County	Dollars
Irving (city) Dallas	86,100
Grand Prairie (city) Dallas	84,600
Haltom City (city) Tarrant	67,400
Dallas (city) Dallas	59,800
Fort Worth (city) Tarrant	53,900
Amarillo (city) Potter	48,200

Specified Housing Units Owned and Occupied by Malaysians
Top 10 Places Sorted by Number

Place (place type) County	Dollars

No places met population threshold.

Notes: Please refer to the User's Guide for an explanation of data; tables reflect only those areas that meet Summary File 4 population thresholds, therefore there may be less than 10 places listed

Specified Housing Units Owned and Occupied by Pakistanis
Top 10 Places Sorted by Number

Place (place type) County	Dollars
Irving (city) Dallas	275,000
Plano (city) Collin	221,300
Sugar Land (city) Fort Bend	208,300
Richardson (city) Dallas	204,700
Carrollton (city) Denton	203,700
Austin (city) Travis	165,000
Dallas (city) Dallas	165,000
Houston (city) Harris	93,600
Garland (city) Dallas	84,800
Mission Bend (cdp) Fort Bend	72,700

Specified Housing Units Owned and Occupied by Samoans
Top 10 Places Sorted by Number

Place (place type) County	Dollars
No places met population threshold.	

Specified Housing Units Owned and Occupied by Sri Lankans
Top 10 Places Sorted by Number

Place (place type) County	Dollars
No places met population threshold.	

Specified Housing Units Owned and Occupied by Taiwaneses
Top 10 Places Sorted by Number

Place (place type) County	Dollars
Austin (city) Travis	211,800
Plano (city) Collin	168,900
Sugar Land (city) Fort Bend	155,700
Arlington (city) Tarrant	148,800
Houston (city) Harris	122,500

Specified Housing Units Owned and Occupied by Thais
Top 10 Places Sorted by Number

Place (place type) County	Dollars
Houston (city) Harris	89,300
San Antonio (city) Bexar	86,700

Specified Housing Units Owned and Occupied by Tongans
Top 10 Places Sorted by Number

Place (place type) County	Dollars
No places met population threshold.	

Specified Housing Units Owned and Occupied by Vietnamese
Top 10 Places Sorted by Number

Place (place type) County	Dollars
Richardson (city) Dallas	177,200
Allen (city) Collin	170,400
Plano (city) Collin	162,200
Pearland (city) Brazoria	159,300
Sugar Land (city) Fort Bend	152,800
Missouri City (city) Fort Bend	144,200
Stafford (city) Fort Bend	131,800
Austin (city) Travis	120,700
Carrollton (city) Denton	119,400
Lewisville (city) Denton	117,000

Notes: Please refer to the User's Guide for an explanation of data; tables reflect only those areas that meet Summary File 4 population thresholds, therefore there may be less than 10 places listed

Climate

Texas Physical Features and Climate Narrative

PHYSICAL FEATURES. Texas has been called "the crossroads of North American geology." Within the State's boundaries four great physiographic subdivisions of the North American Continent come together. These are: the Gulf Coastal Forested Plain; Great Western Lower Plains; Great Western High Plains; and the Rocky Mountain Region. Texas may be described as a vast amphitheater, sloping upward from sea level along the coast of the Gulf of Mexico to more than 4,000 feet general elevation along the Texas-New Mexico line. While much of the State is relatively flat, there are 90 mountains a mile or more high, all of them in the Trans-Pecos region. Guadalupe Peak, at 8,751 feet, is the State's highest.

Texas contains 267,339 square miles or 7.4 percent of the Nation's total area. In straight-line distance, Texas extends 801 miles from north to south and 773 miles from east to west. The boundary of Texas extends 4,137 miles. The Rio Grande forms the longest segment of the boundary, 1,569 miles. The second longest segment, 726 miles, is formed by the Red River. The tidewater coastline extends 624 miles. Texas ranks second only to Alaska among the 50 states in volume of inland water with nearly 6,000 square miles of lakes and streams. Most Texas rivers parallel each other and flow directly into the Gulf, but the Canadian, Red, and Sulphur Rivers are part of the Mississippi River system. The Brazos is the largest river between the Rio Grande and the Red and third in size of all rivers flowing either partly or wholly in Texas. Other principal rivers are the Colorado, Trinity, Sabine, Nueces, Neches, and Guadalupe.

GENERAL CLIMATE. Wedged between the warm waters of the Gulf of Mexico and the high plateaus and mountain ranges of the North American Continent, Texas has diverse meteorological and climatological conditions. Continental, marine, and mountain types of climates are all found in Texas, the marine climate modified by surges of continental air. The High Plains, separated from the Lower Plains by the Cap Rock Escarpment, lies in a cool-temperature climatic zone. Most of the remainder of the State lies in a warm-temperature subtropical zone.

The proximity to the Gulf of Mexico, the persistent southerly and southeasterly flow of warm tropical maritime air into Texas from around the westward extension of the Azores High, and adequate rainfall combine to produce a humid subtropical climate with hot summers across the eastern third of the State. The Gulf moisture supply gradually decreases westward and is cut off more frequently during the colder months by intrusions of drier polar air from the north and west; as a result, most of Central Texas, as far north as the High Plains, has a subtropical climate with dry winters and humid summers. This region is semi-arid. As the distance from the Gulf increases westward, the summer moisture supply continues to decrease gradually, producing a subtropical steppe climate across a broad section along the middle Rio Grande Valley that extends as far west as the Pecos Valley. The area west of the Pecos is mostly arid subtropical. The mountain climates in the Trans-Pecos are cooler throughout the year than those of the adjacent lowlands.

Stretching over the largest level plain of its kind in the United States, the High Plains rise gradually from about 2,700 feet on the east to more than 4,000 feet in spots along the New Mexico border. The combination of high elevation, remoteness from moisture source regions, and frequent intrusions of dry polar airmasses, results in a dry steppe climate with relatively mild winters.

While the changes in climate across Texas are considerable, they are nevertheless gradual; no natural boundary separates the moist East from the dry West or the cool North from the warm South.

PRECIPITATION. Rainfall in Texas is not evenly distributed over the State and varies greatly from year to year. Average annual rainfall along the Louisiana border exceeds 56 inches, and in the western extremity of the State, is less than 8 inches. Except along the upper Texas coast, it is possible for one or two thunderstorms to account for the entire month's rainfall. Torrential rains of 10 to 20 inches or more may accompany a tropical storm as it moves inland across the Texas coast. Rains occur most frequently in late spring as a result of squall-line thunderstorms; consequently, most areas of the State show a peak in May. Rainfall in the Pecos Valley, most of southern Texas, the lower Rio Grande Valley, and in the coastal section, shows a peak in September, with a secondary peak in May. On the High Plains a significant percentage of the total annual precipitation occurs during the summer months (following the May

peak). Throughout the central part of the State, July and August are relatively dry months. In the mountainous Trans-Pecos area of West Texas, afternoon thundershowers during July, August, and September account for most of the annual rainfall. Throughout most of East Texas, rainfall is fairly evenly distributed throughout the year. East of about 96° W. longitude, annual rainfall exceeds average potential evapotranspiration. West of this meridian, average potential evapotranspiration exceeds annual average rainfall.

FLOOD AND DROUGHT. In most of Texas a large portion of the annual rainfall occurs within short periods of time, resulting in excessive run-off and frequently producing damaging floods. Flood stage is reached on some Texas streams nearly every year. From the early days of Texas history recorded by Spaniards exploring the Southwest, drought has been a re-occurring problem. A drought in Central Texas dried up the San Gabriel River in 1756, forcing the abandonment of a settlement of missionaries and Indians. Stephen F. Austin's first colonists also were hurt by drought. Their initial corn crop was snuffed out in 1822, forcing the once ambitious farmers into desperate hunters. In most years, some sections of the State receive less than normal rainfall, while other sections receive a greater than normal supply. Severe drought or excessively wet conditions rarely exist over the entire State at the same time.

TEMPERATURE. The vast land area of Texas experiences a wide range of temperatures. The High Plains experiences rather low temperatures in winter, while there are several separate areas within the State that experience very high temperatures in summer. Extended periods of subfreezing temperatures are rare, even on the High Plains. In South Texas, subfreezing temperatures associated with Arctic airmasses ordinarily are confined to several hours prior to sunrise, and seasons may pass with no subfreezing temperatures at all. In summer, the temperature contrast is much less pronounced from north to south with daily highs generally in the 90s. August is the hottest month.

OTHER CLIMATIC ELEMENTS. Relative humidity is highest in the coastal region, and decreases gradually inland, as the distance from the Gulf of Mexico increases. Mean annual relative humidity at noon varies from slightly more than 60 percent near the coast to around 35 percent in the El Paso area. As temperatures increase, relative humidities generally decrease.

Sunshine is abundant in the extreme southwestern section of the State, decreasing gradually eastward. On an average, the western Trans-Pecos receives 80 percent of the total possible sunshine annually, while the Upper Coast receives only 60 percent.

Significant amounts of snowfall are confined almost entirely to the mountainous Trans-Pecos region and the High Plains. Measurable snow falls south of the High Plains but usually melts almost as fast as it falls. Blizzards, characterized by subfreezing temperatures, very strong winds, and considerable blowing or drifting of snow, may occur in extreme West Texas or Northwest Texas during the winter or early spring months, but are rare.

STORMS. Tropical cyclones are a threat to all sections of the Texas coast during the summer and fall. Those tropical cyclones with sustained wind speeds of 64 knots (74 m.p.h.) or greater are known as hurricanes. Virtually all tropical cyclones which have affected the Texas coast originated in the Gulf of Mexico, the Caribbean Sea, or the southern part of the North Atlantic Ocean. The season extends from June to October; storms are most frequent in August and September, and rarely affect the Texas coast after the first days of October. The average storm frequency for the entire Texas coast is approximately one per year.

Tornadoes have occurred in Texas during all seasons; however, they have occurred with greatest frequency during April, May, and June. Approximately one-fourth of the total annual number of tornadoes occur in the month of May alone. Hailstorms occur in all parts of the State. The most frequent and most damaging of these occur in spring and early summer. Thunderstorms, from which most damaging local weather develops (tornadoes, hail, windstorms, and high intensity showers) occur on about 60 days each year in the extreme eastern section of the State. The mean annual number of thunderstorm days decreases to about 40 in extreme West Texas, and to 30 in the lower Rio Grande Valley.

Blowing dust and sand may occur occasionally in West Texas where strong winds are more frequent and vegetation is sparse.

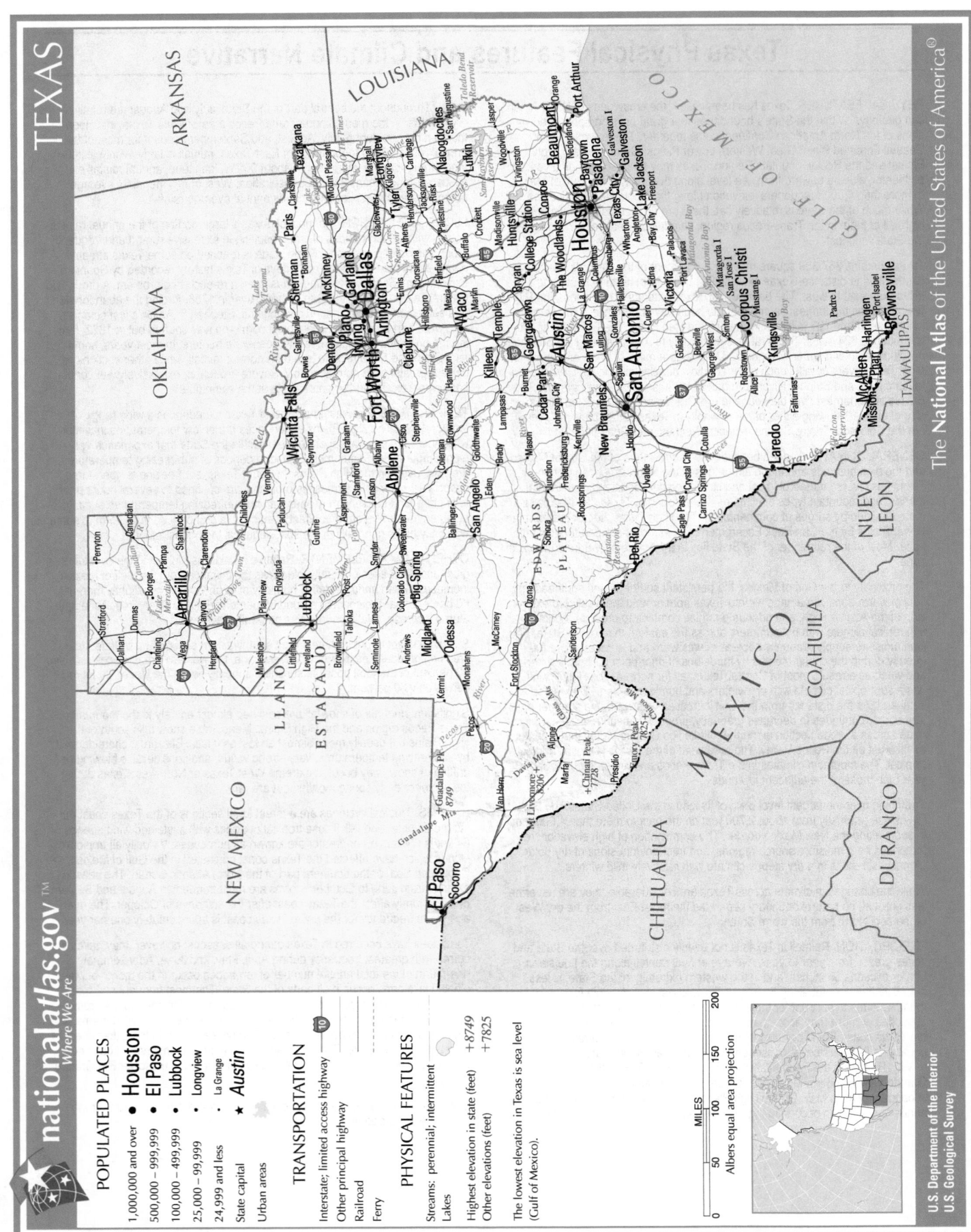

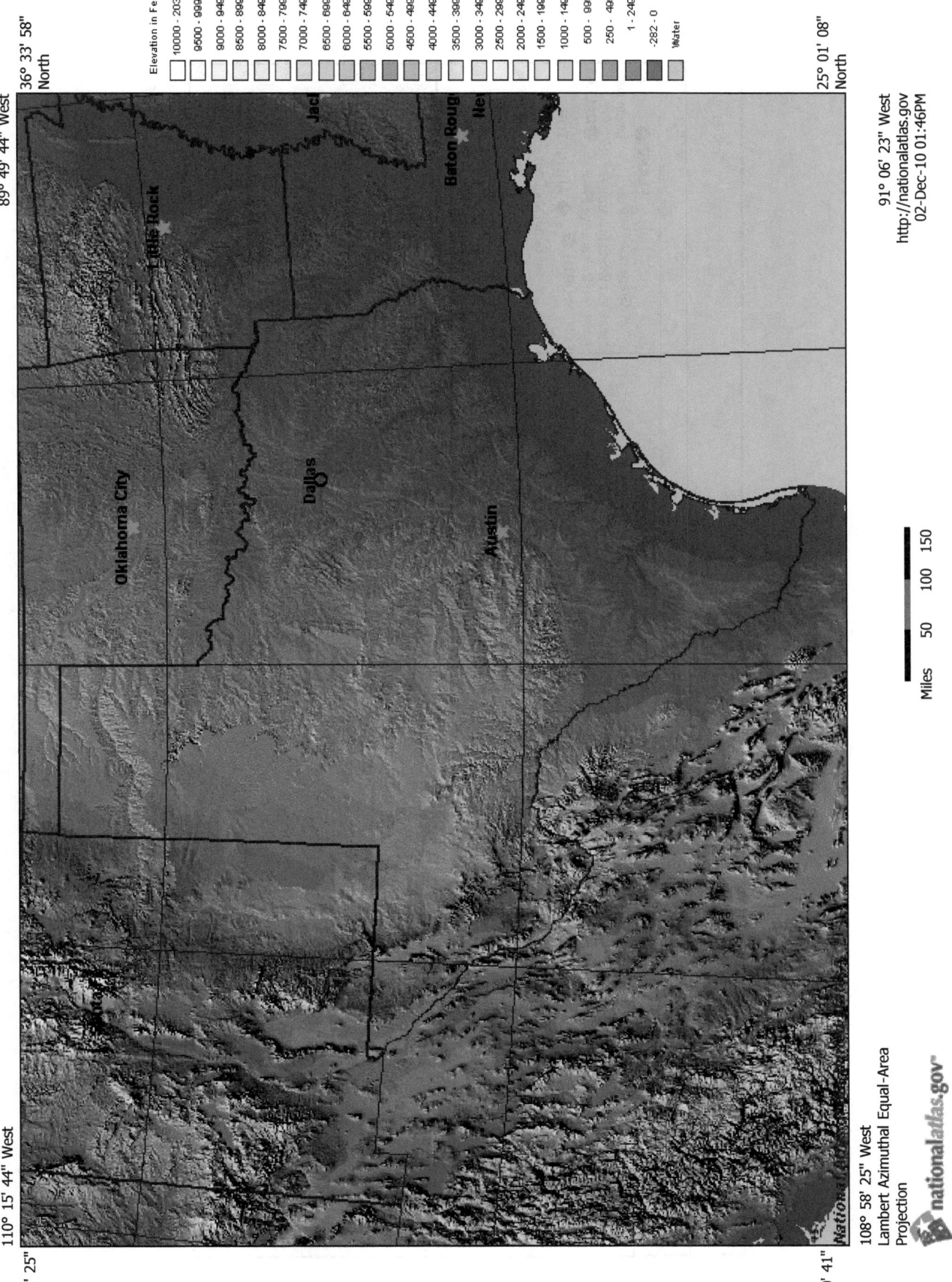

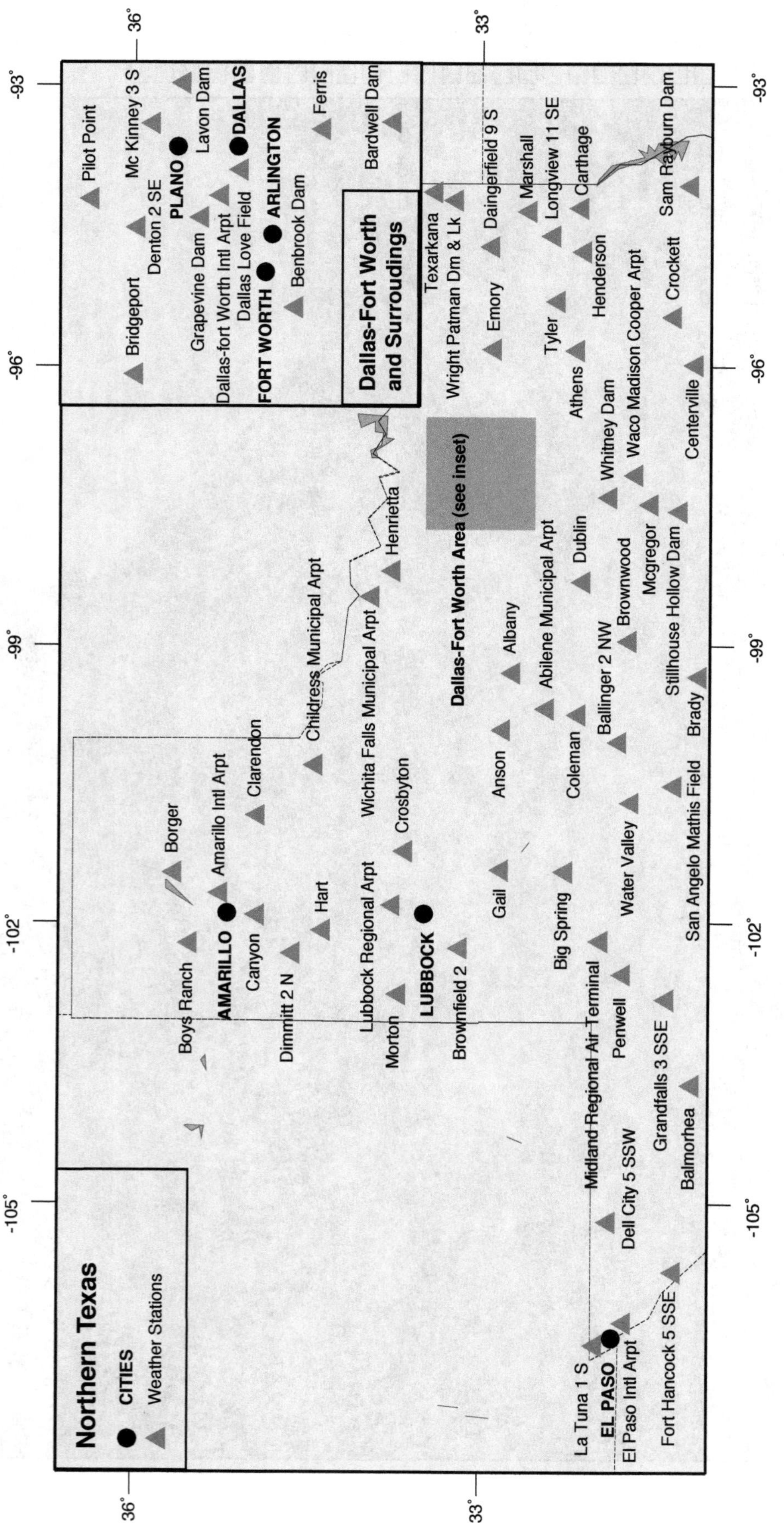

Northern Texas

CITIES ●
Weather Stations ▲

Dallas-Fort Worth and Surroudings

Pilot Point
Mc Kinney 3 S
Lavon Dam
PLANO ●
DALLAS ●
Denton 2 SE
Grapevine Dam
Dallas-fort Worth Intl Arpt
Dallas Love Field
ARLINGTON ●
FORT WORTH ●
Benbrook Dam
Ferris
Bridgeport
Bardwell Dam

Texarkana
Wright Patman Dm & Lk
Daingerfield 9 S
Marshall
Longview 11 SE
Carthage
Emory
Tyler
Athens
Henderson
Sam Rayburn Dam
Whitney Dam
Waco Madison Cooper Arpt
Crockett
Centerville

Dallas-Fort Worth Area (see inset)

Henrietta
Childress Municipal Arpt
Wichita Falls Municipal Arpt
Clarendon
Crosbyton
Hart
Borger
Amarillo Intl Arpt
Boys Ranch
AMARILLO ●
Canyon
Dimmitt 2 N
Lubbock Regional Arpt
Morton
LUBBOCK ●
Brownfield 2
Gail
Anson
Albany
Abilene Municipal Arpt
Dublin
Brownwood
Mcgregor
Stillhouse Hollow Dam
Brady
Coleman
Ballinger 2 NW
Big Spring
Water Valley
San Angelo Mathis Field
Penwell
Midland Regional Air Terminal
Grandfalls 3 SSE
Balmorhea
Dell City 5 SSW
La Tuna 1 S
EL PASO ●
El Paso Intl Arpt
Fort Hancock 5 SSE

36°
33°
-93°
-96°
-99°
-102°
-105°

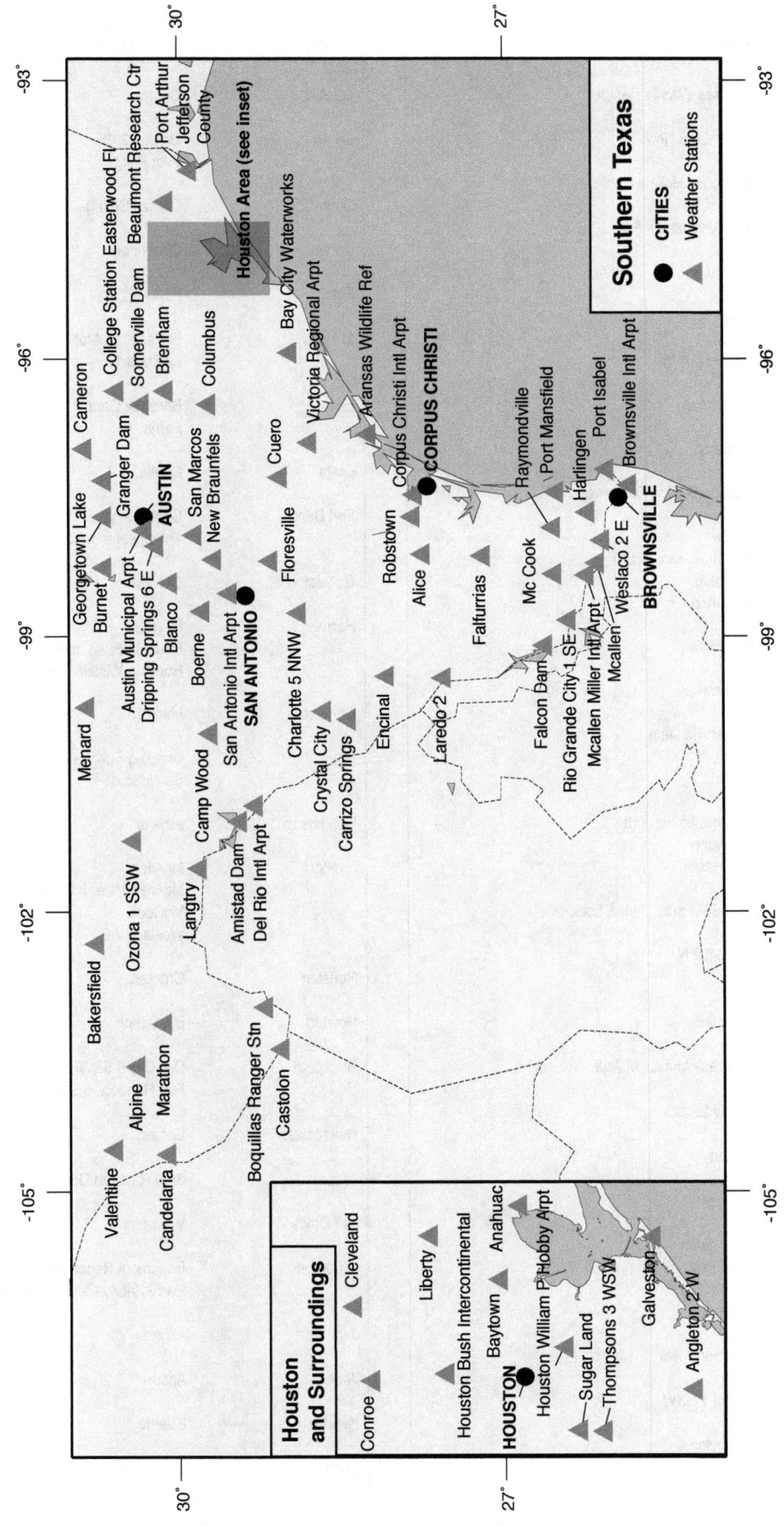

Southern Texas

CITIES
Weather Stations

Houston Area (see inset)

Houston and Surroundings

Texas Weather Stations by County

County	Station Name
Aransas	Aransas Wildlife Refuge
Atascosa	Charlotte 5 NNW
Bell	Stillhouse Hollow Dam
Bexar	San Antonio Intl Arpt
Blanco	Blanco
Borden	Gail
Bosque	Whitney Dam
Bowie	Texarkana
Brazoria	Angleton 2 W
Brazos	College Station Easterwood
Brewster	Alpine Boquillas Ranger Stn Castolon Marathon
Brooks	Falfurrias
Brown	Brownwood
Burleson	Somerville Dam
Burnet	Burnet
Cameron	Brownsville Intl Arpt Harlingen Port Isabel
Cass	Wright Patman Dam & Lock
Castro	Dimmitt 2 N Hart
Chambers	Anahuac
Childress	Childress Municipal Arpt
Clay	Henrietta
Cochran	Morton
Coleman	Coleman
Collin	Lavon Dam McKinney 3 S
Colorado	Columbus
Comal	New Braunfels
Crockett	Ozona 1 SSW
Crosby	Crosbyton
Dallas	Dallas Love Field

County	Station Name
De Witt	Cuero
Denton	Denton 2 SE Pilot Point
Dimmit	Carrizo Springs
Donley	Clarendon
Ector	Penwell
El Paso	El Paso Intl Arpt La Tuna 1 S
Ellis	Bardwell Dam Ferris
Erath	Dublin
Fort Bend	Sugar Land Thompsons 3 WSW
Galveston	Galveston
Harris	Baytown Houston Bush Intercontinental Houston William P Hobby Arpt
Harrison	Marshall
Hays	Dripping Springs 6 E San Marcos
Henderson	Athens
Hidalgo	McAllen McAllen Miller Intl Arpt McCook Weslaco 2 E
Houston	Crockett
Howard	Big Spring
Hudspeth	Dell City 5 SSW Fort Hancock 5 SSE
Hutchinson	Borger
Jasper	Sam Rayburn Dam
Jeff Davis	Valentine
Jefferson	Beaumont Research Ctr Port Arthur Jefferson County
Jim Wells	Alice
Jones	Anson
Kendall	Boerne
Leon	Centerville

See User Guide for station inclusion criteria.

County	Station Name
Liberty	Cleveland
	Liberty
Lubbock	Lubbock Regional Arpt
Matagorda	Bay City Waterworks
Mcculloch	Brady
Mclennan	McGregor
	Waco Madison Cooper Arpt
Menard	Menard
Midland	Midland Regional Air Terminal
Milam	Cameron
Montgomery	Conroe
Morris	Daingerfield 9 S
Nueces	Corpus Christi Intl Arpt
	Robstown
Oldham	Boys Ranch
Panola	Carthage
Pecos	Bakersfield
Potter	Amarillo Intl Arpt
Presidio	Candelaria
Rains	Emory
Randall	Canyon
Real	Camp Wood
Reeves	Balmorhea
Runnels	Ballinger 2 NW
Rusk	Henderson
	Longview 11 SE
Shackelford	Albany
Smith	Tyler
Starr	Falcon Dam
	Rio Grande City 1 SE
Tarrant	Benbrook Dam
	Dallas-Fort Worth Intl Arpt
	Grapevine Dam
Taylor	Abilene Municipal Arpt
Terry	Brownfield 2
Tom Green	San Angelo Mathis Field
	Water Valley

County	Station Name
Travis	Austin Municipal Arpt
Val Verde	Amistad Dam
	Del Rio Intl Arpt
	Langtry
Victoria	Victoria Regional Arpt
Ward	Grandfalls 3 SSE
Washington	Brenham
Webb	Encinal
	Laredo 2
Wichita	Wichita Falls Municipal Arpt
Willacy	Port Mansfield
	Raymondville
Williamson	Georgetown Lake
	Granger Dam
Wilson	Floresville
Wise	Bridgeport
Zavala	Crystal City

See User Guide for station inclusion criteria.

Texas Weather Stations by City

City	Station Name	Miles
Abilene	Abilene Municipal Arpt	4.4
	Anson	24.0
	Coleman	21.4
Allen	Dallas-Fort Worth Intl Arpt	24.5
	Dallas Love Field	20.1
	Grapevine Dam	24.5
	Lavon Dam	11.4
	McKinney 3 S	5.6
Amarillo	Amarillo Intl Arpt	9.0
	Canyon	15.0
Arlington	Benbrook Dam	19.5
	Dallas-Fort Worth Intl Arpt	14.8
	Dallas Love Field	18.7
	Grapevine Dam	17.5
Atascocita	Baytown	15.5
	Houston Bush Intercontinental	10.9
	Houston William P Hobby Arpt	24.3
	Liberty	23.6
Austin	Austin Municipal Arpt	2.8
	Dripping Springs 6 E	15.2
Baytown	Anahuac	18.4
	Baytown	5.9
	Houston William P Hobby Arpt	20.0
	Liberty	24.0
Beaumont	Beaumont Research Ctr	8.8
	Port Arthur Jefferson County	11.9
Brownsville	Brownsville Intl Arpt	3.3
	Harlingen	22.3
	Port Isabel	19.0
Bryan	College Station Easterwood	5.5
	Somerville Dam	25.0
Carrollton	Dallas-Fort Worth Intl Arpt	9.6
	Dallas Love Field	10.0
	Denton 2 SE	18.9
	Grapevine Dam	9.7
	Lavon Dam	23.8
	McKinney 3 S	20.0
Cedar Park	Austin Municipal Arpt	16.3
	Dripping Springs 6 E	21.8
	Georgetown Lake	14.2
College Station	College Station Easterwood	3.4
	Somerville Dam	22.8
Conroe	Cleveland	21.9
	Conroe	1.8
	Houston Bush Intercontinental	22.5
Corpus Christi	Corpus Christi Intl Arpt	7.1
	Robstown	16.2
Dallas	Dallas-Fort Worth Intl Arpt	14.8
	Dallas Love Field	4.6

City	Station Name	Miles
Dallas (cont.)	Ferris	21.8
	Grapevine Dam	18.1
	Lavon Dam	22.9
Denton	Dallas-Fort Worth Intl Arpt	22.6
	Denton 2 SE	1.8
	Grapevine Dam	18.7
	Pilot Point	15.0
Edinburg	McAllen	8.9
	McAllen Miller Intl Arpt	9.4
	McCook	18.3
	Raymondville	24.8
	Weslaco 2 E	16.3
El Paso	El Paso Intl Arpt	3.8
	La Tuna 1 S	12.6
Euless	Benbrook Dam	24.8
	Dallas-Fort Worth Intl Arpt	5.8
	Dallas Love Field	14.1
	Denton 2 SE	24.4
	Grapevine Dam	7.6
Flower Mound	Dallas-Fort Worth Intl Arpt	9.6
	Dallas Love Field	17.9
	Denton 2 SE	11.8
	Grapevine Dam	5.8
Fort Worth	Benbrook Dam	8.9
	Dallas-Fort Worth Intl Arpt	21.7
	Grapevine Dam	22.2
Frisco	Dallas-Fort Worth Intl Arpt	20.5
	Dallas Love Field	19.9
	Denton 2 SE	17.8
	Grapevine Dam	19.2
	Lavon Dam	19.7
	McKinney 3 S	10.9
	Pilot Point	19.6
Galveston	Galveston	1.6
Garland	Dallas-Fort Worth Intl Arpt	22.1
	Dallas Love Field	13.0
	Grapevine Dam	24.2
	Lavon Dam	12.5
	McKinney 3 S	18.1
Grand Prairie	Dallas-Fort Worth Intl Arpt	12.6
	Dallas Love Field	13.3
	Ferris	24.6
	Grapevine Dam	16.2
Grapevine	Dallas-Fort Worth Intl Arpt	5.1
	Dallas Love Field	15.4
	Denton 2 SE	18.8
	Grapevine Dam	3.2
Harlingen	Harlingen	1.7
	Raymondville	21.5
	Weslaco 2 E	17.2
Houston	Houston Bush Intercontinental	17.7

City	Station Name	Miles
Houston *(cont.)*	Houston William P Hobby Arpt	10.4
	Sugar Land	16.0
	Thompsons 3 WSW	22.5
Irving	Dallas-Fort Worth Intl Arpt	4.8
	Dallas Love Field	6.8
	Grapevine Dam	8.7
Killeen	Stillhouse Hollow Dam	12.2
Laredo	Laredo 2	3.1
League City	Baytown	23.1
	Galveston	22.5
	Houston William P Hobby Arpt	15.3
Lewisville	Dallas-Fort Worth Intl Arpt	9.2
	Dallas Love Field	15.7
	Denton 2 SE	12.6
	Grapevine Dam	6.2
	McKinney 3 S	24.6
	Pilot Point	24.3
Longview	Henderson	22.9
	Longview 11 SE	13.0
	Marshall	23.9
Lubbock	Lubbock Regional Arpt	8.6
Mansfield	Benbrook Dam	19.3
	Dallas-Fort Worth Intl Arpt	22.9
	Dallas Love Field	24.6
McAllen	McAllen	1.7
	McAllen Miller Intl Arpt	2.7
	McCook	20.1
	Weslaco 2 E	17.6
McKinney	Lavon Dam	14.5
	McKinney 3 S	2.5
	Pilot Point	22.6
Mesquite	Dallas-Fort Worth Intl Arpt	24.8
	Dallas Love Field	14.6
	Ferris	18.8
	Lavon Dam	18.7
Midland	Midland Regional Air Terminal	5.8
Mission	McAllen	4.5
	McAllen Miller Intl Arpt	5.9
	McCook	18.8
	Weslaco 2 E	22.4
Missouri City	Houston William P Hobby Arpt	16.0
	Sugar Land	6.0
	Thompsons 3 WSW	9.1
New Braunfels	New Braunfels	2.4
	San Antonio Intl Arpt	23.6
	San Marcos	14.7
North Richland Hills	Benbrook Dam	19.6
	Dallas-Fort Worth Intl Arpt	12.2
	Dallas Love Field	21.5

City	Station Name	Miles
North Richland Hills *(cont.)*	Denton 2 SE	24.7
	Grapevine Dam	11.8
Odessa	Midland Regional Air Terminal	12.0
	Penwell	15.9
Pasadena	Baytown	15.2
	Houston William P Hobby Arpt	6.6
Pearland	Houston William P Hobby Arpt	6.6
	Sugar Land	21.8
	Thompsons 3 WSW	21.9
Pharr	McAllen	4.2
	McAllen Miller Intl Arpt	2.9
	McCook	24.4
	Weslaco 2 E	13.8
Plano	Dallas-Fort Worth Intl Arpt	18.8
	Dallas Love Field	15.1
	Denton 2 SE	23.0
	Grapevine Dam	19.0
	Lavon Dam	15.2
	McKinney 3 S	11.0
Port Arthur	Beaumont Research Ctr	23.3
	Port Arthur Jefferson County	5.4
Richardson	Dallas-Fort Worth Intl Arpt	17.9
	Dallas Love Field	11.0
	Grapevine Dam	19.3
	Lavon Dam	14.4
	McKinney 3 S	15.2
Round Rock	Austin Municipal Arpt	14.8
	Georgetown Lake	12.1
	Granger Dam	23.9
Rowlett	Dallas Love Field	18.1
	Lavon Dam	9.4
	McKinney 3 S	18.4
San Angelo	San Angelo Mathis Field	7.3
	Water Valley	22.2
San Antonio	San Antonio Intl Arpt	5.7
Sugar Land	Houston William P Hobby Arpt	20.0
	Sugar Land	1.7
	Thompsons 3 WSW	8.2
Temple	McGregor	23.8
	Stillhouse Hollow Dam	10.5
The Woodlands	Conroe	11.1
	Houston Bush Intercontinental	14.5
Tyler	Tyler	1.7
Victoria	Victoria Regional Arpt	4.3
Waco	McGregor	16.2
	Waco Madison Cooper Arpt	6.4
	Whitney Dam	24.2

See User Guide for station inclusion criteria.

City	Station Name	Miles
Wichita Falls	Henrietta	19.6
	Wichita Falls Municipal Arpt	5.8

Note: Miles is the distance between the geographic center of the city and the weather station.

Texas Weather Stations by Elevation

Feet	Station Name		Feet	Station Name
4,529	Alpine		723	McGregor
4,430	Valentine		709	New Braunfels
4,089	Marathon		706	Stillhouse Hollow Dam
3,917	El Paso Intl Arpt		689	Pilot Point
3,904	Fort Hancock 5 SSE		629	Denton 2 SE
3,850	Dimmitt 2 N		621	Austin Municipal Arpt
3,799	La Tuna 1 S		612	Carrizo Springs
3,770	Dell City 5 SSW		611	San Marcos
3,759	Morton		595	McKinney 3 S
3,640	Hart		589	Encinal
3,589	Canyon		584	Grapevine Dam
3,585	Amarillo Intl Arpt		580	Crystal City
3,299	Brownfield 2		574	Whitney Dam
3,253	Lubbock Regional Arpt		564	Granger Dam
3,219	Balmorhea		560	Dallas-Fort Worth Intl Arpt
3,190	Boys Ranch		549	Tyler
3,140	Borger		509	Lavon Dam
3,009	Crosbyton		500	Waco Madison Cooper Arpt
2,939	Penwell		470	Ferris
2,875	Candelaria		460	Bardwell Dam
2,861	Midland Regional Air Terminal		448	Athens
2,703	Clarendon		440	Charlotte 5 NNW
2,540	Bakersfield		439	Dallas Love Field
2,528	Gail		435	Emory
2,500	Big Spring		430	Laredo 2
2,439	Grandfalls 3 SSE		419	Henderson
2,339	Ozona 1 SSW		407	Longview 11 SE
2,167	Castolon		399	Floresville
2,120	Water Valley		390	Texarkana
1,951	Childress Municipal Arpt		363	Cameron
1,951	Menard		352	Marshall
1,916	San Angelo Mathis Field		347	Crockett
1,879	Boquillas Ranger Stn		339	Carthage
1,790	Abilene Municipal Arpt		319	Centerville
1,754	Ballinger 2 NW		319	Falcon Dam
1,727	Coleman		313	College Station Easterwood
1,720	Brady		312	Brenham
1,709	Anson		299	Daingerfield 9 S
1,501	Dublin		282	Wright Patman Dam & Lock
1,470	Camp Wood		263	Somerville Dam
1,443	Boerne		245	Conroe
1,419	Albany		220	McCook
1,384	Brownwood		201	Alice
1,370	Blanco		199	Columbus
1,290	Langtry		195	Cleveland
1,274	Burnet		188	Sam Rayburn Dam
1,157	Amistad Dam		178	Cuero
1,120	Dripping Springs 6 E		171	Rio Grande City 1 SE
1,029	Wichita Falls Municipal Arpt		120	Falfurrias
999	Del Rio Intl Arpt		115	Victoria Regional Arpt
930	Henrietta		100	McAllen
839	Georgetown Lake		100	McAllen Miller Intl Arpt
809	San Antonio Intl Arpt		95	Houston Bush Intercontinental
790	Benbrook Dam		84	Robstown
745	Bridgeport		82	Sugar Land

See User Guide for station inclusion criteria.

Feet	Station Name
75	Weslaco 2 E
71	Thompsons 3 WSW
51	Bay City Waterworks
49	Houston William P Hobby Arpt
43	Corpus Christi Intl Arpt
38	Harlingen
35	Liberty
34	Baytown
30	Raymondville
26	Angleton 2 W
26	Beaumont Research Ctr
23	Anahuac
19	Brownsville Intl Arpt
17	Port Isabel
16	Port Arthur Jefferson County
15	Aransas Wildlife Refuge
15	Galveston
8	Port Mansfield

Abilene Municipal Airport

Abilene is located in north central Texas. The station elevation is 1,750 feet above sea level. Topography of the area includes rolling plains, treeless except for mesquite, broken by low hills to the south and west. The land rises gently to the east and southeast. Regional agricultural products are mainly cattle, dry-land cotton, and feed crops.

Abilene is on the boundary between the humid east Texas climate and the semi-arid west and north Texas climate. The rainfall pattern is typical of the Great Plains. Most precipitation occurs from April to October and is usually associated with thunderstorms. Severe storms are infrequent, occurring mostly in the spring.

The large range of high and low temperatures, characteristic of the Great Plains, extends south to the Abilene area. High daytime temperatures prevail in the summer, but are normally broken by thunderstorms about five times a month. Rapid cooling after sunset results in pleasant nights with low summertime temperatures in the upper 60s and low 70s. High summer temperatures are usually associated with fair skies, southwesterly winds, and low humidities.

Rapid wintertime temperature changes occur when cold, dry, arctic air replaces warm moist tropical air. Drops in temperature of 20 to 30 degrees in one hour are not unusual. However, cold weather periods are short lived. Fair, mild weather is typical.

South is the prevailing wind direction, and southerly winds are frequently high and persist for several days. Strong northerly winds often occur during the passage of cold fronts. Dusty conditions are infrequent, occurring mostly with westerly winds. Dust storm frequency and intensity depend on soil conditions in eastern New Mexico, west Texas, and the Texas Panhandle.

Based on the 1951-1980 period, the average first occurrence of 32 degrees Fahrenheit in the fall is November 13 and the average last occurrence in the spring is March 25.

Abilene Municipal Airport *Taylor County*   Elevation: 1,790 ft.   Latitude: 32° 25' N   Longitude: 99° 41' W

	JAN	FEB	MAR	APR	MAY	JUN	JUL	AUG	SEP	OCT	NOV	DEC	YEAR
Mean Maximum Temp. (°F)	56.8	60.8	68.7	77.4	84.6	90.6	94.5	94.0	86.7	77.2	66.0	56.9	76.2
Mean Temp. (°F)	45.1	48.9	56.5	64.7	73.0	79.6	83.4	82.9	75.5	65.8	54.5	45.4	64.6
Mean Minimum Temp. (°F)	33.3	36.9	44.2	51.9	61.4	68.6	72.3	71.7	64.3	54.4	43.0	33.9	53.0
Extreme Maximum Temp. (°F)	87	93	95	98	109	109	107	107	107	99	92	87	109
Extreme Minimum Temp. (°F)	5	-7	10	27	39	51	57	50	38	23	16	-7	-7
Days Maximum Temp. ≥ 90°F	0	0	1	3	9	19	26	25	12	2	0	0	97
Days Maximum Temp. ≤ 32°F	1	1	0	0	0	0	0	0	0	0	0	1	3
Days Minimum Temp. ≤ 32°F	15	9	4	0	0	0	0	0	0	0	5	14	47
Days Minimum Temp. ≤ 0°F	0	0	0	0	0	0	0	0	0	0	0	0	0
Heating Degree Days (base 65°F)	612	455	288	107	17	0	0	0	12	90	326	602	2,509
Cooling Degree Days (base 65°F)	1	6	31	104	272	445	577	561	334	122	19	1	2,473
Mean Precipitation (in.)	0.94	1.31	1.70	1.58	3.23	3.48	1.67	2.63	2.37	2.96	1.46	1.24	24.57
Maximum Precipitation (in.)*	4.3	3.6	5.2	6.8	13.2	9.6	7.1	8.2	11.0	10.7	4.6	6.3	36.8
Minimum Precipitation (in.)*	trace	trace	trace	trace	0.1	trace	trace	trace	trace	0	0	trace	9.8
Extreme Maximum Daily Precip. (in.)	1.82	1.77	1.71	2.40	4.72	3.62	5.67	4.79	2.85	3.83	1.55	2.17	5.67
Days With ≥ 0.1" Precipitation	2	3	3	3	5	5	3	4	4	4	3	3	42
Days With ≥ 0.5" Precipitation	1	1	1	1	2	3	1	2	2	2	1	1	18
Days With ≥ 1.0" Precipitation	0	0	0	0	1	1	1	0	1	1	0	0	5
Mean Snowfall (in.)	*1.8*	*0.7*	*0.4*	*0.4*	*trace*	*trace*	*trace*	*trace*	*0.0*	*trace*	*0.7*	*1.2*	*5.2*
Maximum Snowfall (in.)*	14	8	7	0	0	0	0	0	0	trace	8	8	19
Maximum 24-hr. Snowfall (in.)*	7	5	6	0	0	0	0	0	0	trace	4	4	7
Maximum Snow Depth (in.)	*5*	*5*	*5*	*6*	*trace*	*trace*	*trace*	*trace*	*0*	*trace*	*3*	*3*	*6*
Days With ≥ 1.0" Snow Depth	*1*	*1*	*0*	*0*	*0*	*0*	*0*	*0*	*0*	*0*	*0*	*1*	*3*
Thunderstorm Days*	1	1	3	5	8	6	5	5	4	3	1	1	43
Foggy Days*	7	7	4	4	4	2	1	1	5	5	5	7	52
Predominant Sky Cover*	OVR	OVR	CLR	CLR	CLR	CLR	CLR	CLR	CLR	CLR	CLR	CLR	CLR
Mean Relative Humidity 6am (%)*	73	73	69	72	80	79	73	73	78	76	74	72	74
Mean Relative Humidity 3pm (%)*	45	44	37	38	43	41	38	38	44	42	42	44	41
Mean Dewpoint (°F)*	28	32	36	45	56	62	63	62	59	49	38	30	47
Prevailing Wind Direction*	S	S	S	SSE	SSE	S	SSE	SSE	SSE	S	S	S	S
Prevailing Wind Speed (mph)*	13	13	15	15	14	14	12	10	10	12	13	13	13
Maximum Wind Gust (mph)*	51	56	74	61	71	73	78	55	59	58	62	59	78

Note: (*) Period of record is 1948-1995

Amarillo Int'l Airport

The station is located 7 statute miles east northeast of the downtown post office in a region of rather flat topography. The Canadian River flows eastward 18 miles north of the station, with its bed about 800 feet below the plains. The Prairie Dog Town Fork of the Red River flows southeastward about 15 miles south of the station where it enters the Palo Duro Canyon, which is about 1,000 feet deep. There are numerous shallow Playa lakes, often dry, over the area, and the nearly treeless grasslands slope downward to the east. The terrain gradually rises to the west and northwest.

Three-fourths of the total annual precipitation falls from April through September, occurring from thunderstorm activity. Snow usually melts within a few days after it falls. Heavier snowfalls of 10 inches or more, usually with near blizzard conditions, average once every five years and last two to three days.

The Amarillo area is subject to rapid and large temperature changes, especially during the winter months when cold fronts from the northern Rocky Mountain and Plains states sweep across the area. Temperature drops of 50 to 60 degrees within a 12-hour period are not uncommon. Temperature drops of 40 degrees have occurred within a few minutes.

Humidity averages are low, occasionally dropping below 20 percent in the spring. Low humidity moderates the effect of high summer afternoon temperatures, permits evaporative cooling systems to be very effective, and provides many pleasant evenings and nights.

Severe local storms are infrequent, although a few thunderstorms with damaging hail, lightning, and wind in a very localized area occur most years, usually in spring and summer. These storms are often accompanied by very heavy rain, which produces local flooding, particularly of roads and streets. Tornadoes are rare.

Based on the 1951-1980 period, the average first occurrence of 32 degrees Fahrenheit in the fall is October 29 and the average last occurrence in the spring is April 14.

Amarillo Int'l Airport *Potter County*   Elevation: 3,585 ft.   Latitude: 35° 13' N   Longitude: 101° 42' W

	JAN	FEB	MAR	APR	MAY	JUN	JUL	AUG	SEP	OCT	NOV	DEC	YEAR
Mean Maximum Temp. (°F)	50.3	54.5	62.4	70.9	79.3	87.7	91.6	89.2	82.1	71.6	59.8	49.9	70.8
Mean Temp. (°F)	36.9	40.5	47.8	56.1	65.5	74.4	78.5	76.7	69.3	58.1	46.1	37.0	57.2
Mean Minimum Temp. (°F)	23.5	26.5	33.1	41.3	51.7	61.0	65.3	64.2	56.3	44.5	32.5	24.0	43.7
Extreme Maximum Temp. (°F)	80	84	92	98	103	108	106	105	103	99	87	80	108
Extreme Minimum Temp. (°F)	-11	-12	4	17	31	41	51	52	30	12	3	-8	-12
Days Maximum Temp. ≥ 90°F	0	0	0	1	5	13	21	17	6	1	0	0	64
Days Maximum Temp. ≤ 32°F	3	2	1	0	0	0	0	0	0	0	1	4	11
Days Minimum Temp. ≤ 32°F	27	21	14	4	0	0	0	0	0	2	15	27	110
Days Minimum Temp. ≤ 0°F	0	0	0	0	0	0	0	0	0	0	0	1	1
Heating Degree Days (base 65°F)	863	687	529	278	84	6	0	1	43	237	560	862	4,150
Cooling Degree Days (base 65°F)	0	0	2	19	108	293	425	372	177	29	1	0	1,426
Mean Precipitation (in.)	0.71	0.53	1.38	1.31	2.31	3.17	2.59	2.89	1.91	1.64	0.73	0.72	19.89
Maximum Precipitation (in.)*	2.3	1.8	4.0	2.8	9.8	10.7	7.6	7.5	5.0	4.8	2.3	4.5	36.6
Minimum Precipitation (in.)*	0	trace	trace	trace	trace	trace	0.1	0.3	trace	0	0	trace	9.6
Extreme Maximum Daily Precip. (in.)	1.57	1.20	1.84	2.65	3.40	4.92	3.47	2.30	2.33	2.38	0.88	1.16	4.92
Days With ≥ 0.1" Precipitation	2	1	3	3	4	5	4	5	4	3	2	2	38
Days With ≥ 0.5" Precipitation	1	0	1	1	2	2	2	2	1	1	0	0	13
Days With ≥ 1.0" Precipitation	0	0	0	0	0	1	1	1	0	0	0	0	3
Mean Snowfall (in.)	4.8	2.6	2.7	0.7	0.2	trace	trace	trace	trace	0.2	2.6	4.0	17.8
Maximum Snowfall (in.)*	15	17	15	6	1	0	0	0	trace	4	14	15	47
Maximum 24-hr. Snowfall (in.)*	9	11	8	4	1	0	0	0	trace	3	8	8	11
Maximum Snow Depth (in.)	10	14	12	3	2	trace	trace	trace	trace	3	7	15	15
Days With ≥ 1.0" Snow Depth	4	3	1	0	0	0	0	0	0	0	1	3	12
Thunderstorm Days*	< 1	< 1	2	3	8	10	9	9	4	2	1	< 1	48
Foggy Days*	7	8	8	6	8	4	3	4	6	6	6	7	73
Predominant Sky Cover*	CLR	CLR	CLR	CLR	CLR	CLR	SCT	SCT	CLR	CLR	CLR	CLR	CLR
Mean Relative Humidity 6am (%)*	71	72	68	69	76	77	75	78	78	73	71	70	73
Mean Relative Humidity 3pm (%)*	42	41	34	31	37	37	36	39	40	36	38	40	38
Mean Dewpoint (°F)*	19	22	25	33	45	55	58	58	51	39	28	21	38
Prevailing Wind Direction*	SW	SW	SW	S	S	S	S	S	S	SSW	SW	SW	S
Prevailing Wind Speed (mph)*	14	14	15	16	16	16	14	13	14	14	14	13	14
Maximum Wind Gust (mph)*	64	67	76	81	70	69	69	66	60	74	73	63	81

Note: (*) Period of record is 1948-1995

Austin Municipal Airport

Austin, capital of Texas, is located on the Colorado River where the stream crosses the Balcones steep slope separating the Texas Hill Country from the Blackland Prairies to the east. Elevations within the city vary from 400 feet to nearly 1,000 feet above sea level. Native trees include cedar, oak, walnut, mesquite, and pecan.

The climate of Austin is humid subtropical with hot summers. Winters are mild, with below freezing temperatures occurring on an average of about 25 days each year. Rather strong northerly winds, accompanied by sharp drops in temperature, frequently occur during the winter months in connection with cold fronts, but cold spells are usually of short duration, seldom lasting more than two days. Daytime temperatures in summer are hot, but summer nights are usually pleasant.

Precipitation is fairly evenly distributed throughout the year, with heaviest amounts occurring in late spring. A secondary rainfall peak occurs in September, primarily because of tropical cyclones that migrate out of the Gulf of Mexico. Precipitation from April through September usually results from thunderstorms, with fairly large amounts of rain falling within short periods of time. While thunderstorms and heavy rains may occur in all months of the year, most of the winter precipitation consists of light rain. Snow is insignificant as a source of moisture, and usually melts as rapidly as it falls. The city may experience several seasons in succession with no measurable snowfall.

Prevailing winds are southerly, however in winter, northerly winds are about as frequent as those from the south. Destructive winds and damaging hailstorms are infrequent. On rare occasions dissipating tropical storms produce strong winds and heavy rains in the area. Blowing dust occurs occasionally in spring, but visibility rarely drops substantially, and then only for a few hours.

The average length of the warm season (freeze-free period) is 273 days. The average occurrence of the last temperature of 32 degrees in spring is early March and the average occurrence of the first temperature of 32 degrees is late November.

Austin Municipal Airport *Travis County*   Elevation: 621 ft.   Latitude: 30° 18' N   Longitude: 97° 42' W

	JAN	FEB	MAR	APR	MAY	JUN	JUL	AUG	SEP	OCT	NOV	DEC	YEAR
Mean Maximum Temp. (°F)	61.6	65.4	72.2	79.7	86.2	92.1	95.6	96.7	90.5	81.6	71.2	62.6	79.6
Mean Temp. (°F)	51.6	55.2	61.8	69.1	76.4	82.2	85.0	85.7	80.0	71.1	60.9	52.5	69.3
Mean Minimum Temp. (°F)	41.6	44.9	51.4	58.4	66.6	72.3	74.4	74.6	69.5	60.6	50.5	42.4	58.9
Extreme Maximum Temp. (°F)	87	99	96	99	102	108	107	110	112	98	91	86	112
Extreme Minimum Temp. (°F)	11	14	19	34	46	57	67	62	48	30	26	4	4
Days Maximum Temp. ≥ 90°F	0	0	0	2	10	22	28	29	19	6	0	0	116
Days Maximum Temp. ≤ 32°F	0	0	0	0	0	0	0	0	0	0	0	0	0
Days Minimum Temp. ≤ 32°F	5	3	1	0	0	0	0	0	0	0	1	5	15
Days Minimum Temp. ≤ 0°F	0	0	0	0	0	0	0	0	0	0	0	0	0
Heating Degree Days (base 65°F)	419	292	157	38	1	0	0	0	2	29	177	395	1,510
Cooling Degree Days (base 65°F)	11	21	65	168	363	523	627	648	460	226	60	15	3,187
Mean Precipitation (in.)	2.14	1.99	2.76	2.09	4.44	4.14	1.83	2.39	2.74	3.92	3.05	2.41	33.90
Maximum Precipitation (in.)*	9.2	6.6	6.0	9.9	10.0	15.0	10.5	8.9	7.4	12.3	7.3	14.2	52.2
Minimum Precipitation (in.)*	trace	0.3	trace	0.1	0.8	trace	0	0	0.1	trace	trace	trace	11.4
Extreme Maximum Daily Precip. (in.)	4.41	2.56	3.26	2.23	3.88	5.66	2.17	5.68	3.17	6.24	7.55	4.21	7.55
Days With ≥ 0.1" Precipitation	4	4	5	4	5	5	3	3	4	5	4	4	50
Days With ≥ 0.5" Precipitation	1	1	2	1	3	3	1	1	2	2	2	1	20
Days With ≥ 1.0" Precipitation	1	0	1	1	2	1	0	1	1	1	1	1	11
Mean Snowfall (in.)	*0.4*	*0.2*	*trace*	*trace*	*trace*	*trace*	0.0	0.0	0.0	0.0	0.1	trace	*0.7*
Maximum Snowfall (in.)*	8	6	2	0	0	0	0	0	0	0	2	trace	9
Maximum 24-hr. Snowfall (in.)*	7	5	2	0	0	0	0	0	0	0	1	trace	7
Maximum Snow Depth (in.)	4	1	trace	trace	*trace*	*trace*	0	0	*0*	0	trace	trace	*4*
Days With ≥ 1.0" Snow Depth	0	0	0	0	*0*	*0*	*0*	0	*0*	0	0	0	*0*
Thunderstorm Days*	1	2	3	5	7	5	4	5	4	3	2	1	42
Foggy Days*	13	11	12	12	12	7	4	4	9	11	11	12	118
Predominant Sky Cover*	OVR	OVR	OVR	OVR	OVR	SCT	SCT	SCT	CLR	CLR	OVR	OVR	OVR
Mean Relative Humidity 6am (%)*	80	80	80	83	89	89	89	87	86	84	81	80	84
Mean Relative Humidity 3pm (%)*	53	51	47	50	54	50	43	42	47	47	49	52	49
Mean Dewpoint (°F)*	38	41	46	55	64	69	69	68	65	56	47	40	55
Prevailing Wind Direction*	N	S	S	S	SSE	S	S	S	S	S	S	S	S
Prevailing Wind Speed (mph)*	14	9	12	10	10	10	9	8	8	8	9	9	10
Maximum Wind Gust (mph)*	54	55	56	58	63	54	69	47	81	46	58	63	81

Note: (*) Period of record is 1948-1995

Brownsville Int'l Airport

Brownsville is located at the southern tip of Texas. It is the largest city in the four county area referred to as the Lower Rio Grande Valley or just the Valley.

The Gulf of Mexico, located about 18 miles east, is the dominant influence on local weather. Prevailing southeast breezes off the Gulf provide a humid but generally mild climate. Winds are frequently strong and gusty in the spring.

Brownsville weather is generally favorable for outdoor activities and the Valley is a popular tourist area, especially for Winter Texans who come to enjoy the mild winters. High temperatures range mostly in the 70s and 80s from October through April, with lows in the 50s and 60s during the same period. For the remainder of the year highs are frequently in the 90s with lows in the 70s.

Temperature extremes are rare but do occur. Temperatures in the 90s have occurred in every month of the year, with 100 degree readings noted as early as March and as late as September. Very hot temperatures are often moderated by a cooling sea breeze from the Gulf during the afternoon hours.

Located about 150 miles north of the tropics, cold weather in Brownsville is infrequent and of short duration. Some winters pass without a single day with freezing temperatures. This climate permits year around gardening and cultivation of citrus and other cold sensitive tropical and sub-tropical plants. Damaging cold comes from frigid air masses, called northers or arctic outbreaks, plunging south from Canada or the Arctic. The worst of these can drop temperatures well below freezing for several hours, and a few have produced readings in the teens. Fortunately such events are very rare since they are disasterous to the local economy.

Rainfall is not well distributed. Heaviest rains occur in May through June and mid August through mid October. Extended periods of cool rainy weather, called overrunning, can occur in winter. Torrential rains of 10 to 20 inches or more may accompany tropical storms or hurricanes that occasionally move over the area in summer or fall. Rainy spells may be followed by long dry periods. Irrigation is required to ensure production of corps such as cotton, grains, and vegetables. Snow and freezing rain or drizzle are so rare that years may pass between occurrences.

Damaging hail or winds from heavy thunderstorms are generally limited to the spring and many years elapse between occurrences. Tornadoes are even more rare. Tropical storms and hurricanes from the Gulf are a threat each summer and fall, but damaging storms are quite rare.

Brownsville Int'l Airport *Cameron County*   Elevation: 19 ft.   Latitude: 25° 54' N   Longitude: 97° 26' W

	JAN	FEB	MAR	APR	MAY	JUN	JUL	AUG	SEP	OCT	NOV	DEC	YEAR
Mean Maximum Temp. (°F)	70.9	73.9	79.1	83.9	88.5	92.4	93.9	94.4	90.8	85.6	79.0	71.8	83.7
Mean Temp. (°F)	61.3	64.4	69.5	74.8	80.4	84.1	85.1	85.3	82.0	76.2	69.2	62.3	74.5
Mean Minimum Temp. (°F)	51.7	54.7	59.8	65.7	72.3	75.8	76.3	76.2	73.1	66.8	59.4	52.6	65.4
Extreme Maximum Temp. (°F)	91	94	106	102	102	102	104	104	105	96	97	91	106
Extreme Minimum Temp. (°F)	25	28	32	38	52	61	68	69	55	35	31	16	16
Days Maximum Temp. ≥ 90°F	0	0	1	4	14	26	29	29	21	8	1	0	133
Days Maximum Temp. ≤ 32°F	0	0	0	0	0	0	0	0	0	0	0	0	0
Days Minimum Temp. ≤ 32°F	1	0	0	0	0	0	0	0	0	0	0	1	2
Days Minimum Temp. ≤ 0°F	0	0	0	0	0	0	0	0	0	0	0	0	0
Heating Degree Days (base 65°F)	173	104	41	8	0	0	0	0	0	7	51	163	547
Cooling Degree Days (base 65°F)	66	92	186	310	485	580	631	637	515	361	184	84	4,131
Mean Precipitation (in.)	1.28	1.00	1.20	1.48	2.60	2.31	1.92	2.65	5.54	3.82	1.89	1.21	26.90
Maximum Precipitation (in.)*	4.8	10.3	3.5	10.3	9.1	8.5	9.4	9.6	20.2	17.1	7.7	4.0	47.5
Minimum Precipitation (in.)*	trace	trace	trace	trace	trace	trace	trace	trace	0.1	0.3	trace	trace	11.6
Extreme Maximum Daily Precip. (in.)	2.28	2.32	4.79	9.17	4.56	4.42	6.68	5.46	7.90	9.09	4.08	2.86	9.17
Days With ≥ 0.1" Precipitation	3	2	2	2	3	3	3	4	6	5	3	3	39
Days With ≥ 0.5" Precipitation	1	1	1	1	2	1	1	2	3	2	1	1	17
Days With ≥ 1.0" Precipitation	0	0	0	0	1	1	1	1	2	1	1	0	8
Mean Snowfall (in.)	*trace*	*0.0*	*trace*	*0.0*	*0.0*	*0.0*	*0.0*	*trace*	*0.0*	*0.0*	*trace*	*trace*	*trace*
Maximum Snowfall (in.)*	trace	trace	0	0	0	0	0	0	0	0	trace	trace	trace
Maximum 24-hr. Snowfall (in.)*	trace	trace	0	0	0	0	0	0	0	0	trace	trace	trace
Maximum Snow Depth (in.)	*trace*	*0*	*trace*	*0*	*0*	*0*	*0*	*trace*	*0*	*0*	*trace*	*trace*	*trace*
Days With ≥ 1.0" Snow Depth	*0*	*0*	*0*	*0*	*0*	*0*	*0*	*0*	*0*	*0*	*0*	*0*	*0*
Thunderstorm Days*	< 1	1	1	2	3	3	3	5	5	2	1	< 1	26
Foggy Days*	17	14	13	12	9	4	3	3	5	7	11	15	113
Predominant Sky Cover*	OVR	OVR	OVR	OVR	BRK	SCT	SCT	SCT	SCT	SCT	OVR	OVR	OVR
Mean Relative Humidity 6am (%)*	88	89	88	89	90	91	92	92	91	89	87	87	90
Mean Relative Humidity 3pm (%)*	63	60	57	58	60	59	54	55	60	58	59	62	59
Mean Dewpoint (°F)*	52	55	59	65	70	73	73	73	72	66	59	54	64
Prevailing Wind Direction*	NNW	SSE	SSE	SSE	SE	SE	SSE	SE	SE	SE	SSE	NNW	SSE
Prevailing Wind Speed (mph)*	13	15	16	17	14	13	13	12	10	10	13	12	13
Maximum Wind Gust (mph)*	53	68	59	66	81	62	51	78	109	55	53	53	109

Note: (*) Period of record is 1948-1995

Corpus Christi Int'l Airport

Corpus Christi is located on Corpus Christi Bay, an inlet of the Gulf of Mexico, in south Texas. The climatic conditions vary between the humid subtropical region to the northeast along the Texas coast and the semi-arid region to the west and southwest. Temperatures at the International Airport, which is about 7 miles west of downtown Corpus Christi, may be substantially different than those in the city during calm winter mornings and during summer afternoon sea breezes.

Peak rainfall months are May and September. Winter months have the least amounts of rainfall. The hurricane season from June to November can greatly effect the rainfall totals. Dry periods frequently occur. Several months during the years of record have had no rainfall, or only a trace. Snow falls on an average of about one day every two years.

There is little change in the day-to-day weather of the summer months, except for an occasional rainshower or a tropical storm in the area. High temperatures range in the high 80s to mid 90s, except for brief periods in the high 90s. The sea breeze during the afternoon and evening hours moderates the summer heat. Low temperatures are usually in the mid 70s. Summertime temperatures rarely reach 100 degrees near the bay, but occasionally do in most other parts of the city. In the summer season the region receives nearly 80 percent of the possible sunshine.

September and October are an extension of summer. November is a transition to the conditions of the coming winter months, with greater temperature extremes, stronger winds, and the first occurrences of northers. The winter months are relatively mild, but with temperatures sufficiently low to be stimulating. January is the coldest month with a prevailing northerly wind. Daytime highs that do not exceed 32 degrees, do not occur more than once every three or four years. The earliest occurrence of a temperature below 32 degrees is in early November and the latest occurrence in the spring is mid to late March.

Relative humidity, because of the nearness of the Gulf of Mexico, is high throughout the year. However, during the afternoons the humidity usually drops to between 50 and 60 percent.

Severe tropical storms average about one every ten years. Lesser strength storms average about one every five years. The city of Corpus Christi has a bluff that rises 30 to 40 feet above the level of the lowlands area near the bay. This serves as a natural protection from high water.

Chief hurricane months are August and September, although tropical storms have occurred as early as June and as late as October. The majority of the storms pass either to the south or east of the city.

Corpus Christi Int'l Airport *Nueces County*   Elevation: 43 ft.   Latitude: 27° 46' N   Longitude: 97° 31' W

	JAN	FEB	MAR	APR	MAY	JUN	JUL	AUG	SEP	OCT	NOV	DEC	YEAR
Mean Maximum Temp. (°F)	67.2	70.7	76.0	81.8	86.5	91.0	93.3	94.2	90.2	84.2	75.8	68.2	81.6
Mean Temp. (°F)	57.3	60.6	66.3	72.3	78.3	82.5	84.0	84.6	81.1	74.5	66.0	58.4	72.2
Mean Minimum Temp. (°F)	47.4	50.6	56.5	62.8	70.0	73.9	74.7	75.0	72.0	64.8	56.1	48.6	62.7
Extreme Maximum Temp. (°F)	90	97	102	102	103	106	103	104	109	97	98	90	109
Extreme Minimum Temp. (°F)	19	23	24	33	52	59	67	64	52	28	28	13	13
Days Maximum Temp. ≥ 90°F	0	1	1	3	7	22	27	28	19	6	0	0	114
Days Maximum Temp. ≤ 32°F	0	0	0	0	0	0	0	0	0	0	0	0	0
Days Minimum Temp. ≤ 32°F	2	1	0	0	0	0	0	0	0	0	0	2	5
Days Minimum Temp. ≤ 0°F	0	0	0	0	0	0	0	0	0	0	0	0	0
Heating Degree Days (base 65°F)	265	170	77	17	0	0	0	0	0	12	90	247	878
Cooling Degree Days (base 65°F)	34	54	124	242	419	530	596	615	490	313	126	50	3,593
Mean Precipitation (in.)	1.49	1.81	1.86	1.79	3.15	3.13	2.58	3.38	4.65	3.67	2.04	1.81	31.36
Maximum Precipitation (in.)*	10.8	8.1	4.9	8.0	9.4	13.3	11.9	14.8	20.3	11.0	5.2	9.8	48.1
Minimum Precipitation (in.)*	trace	trace	trace	trace	trace	trace	0	0.1	0.5	0	trace	trace	14.7
Extreme Maximum Daily Precip. (in.)	2.89	4.70	3.66	6.18	4.00	8.62	9.85	6.93	5.30	7.92	4.55	6.77	9.85
Days With ≥ 0.1" Precipitation	3	2	3	2	4	4	3	4	6	4	3	3	41
Days With ≥ 0.5" Precipitation	1	1	1	1	2	2	2	2	3	2	1	1	19
Days With ≥ 1.0" Precipitation	0	1	1	0	1	1	1	1	1	1	1	0	9
Mean Snowfall (in.)	*trace*	na	na	na	na	na	na	na	na	na	na	*0.2*	na
Maximum Snowfall (in.)*	1	1	trace	0	0	0	0	0	0	0	trace	trace	1
Maximum 24-hr. Snowfall (in.)*	1	1	trace	0	0	0	0	0	0	0	trace	trace	1
Maximum Snow Depth (in.)	*trace*	*trace*	na	*trace*	na	na	na	na	na	na	na	*4*	na
Days With ≥ 1.0" Snow Depth	*0*	*0*	*0*	*0*	na	na	na	*0*	na	na	na	*0*	na
Thunderstorm Days*	1	1	1	2	4	3	2	4	5	2	1	1	27
Foggy Days*	16	14	14	12	9	4	2	3	5	7	10	14	110
Predominant Sky Cover*	OVR	OVR	OVR	OVR	BRK	SCT	SCT	SCT	SCT	CLR	OVR	OVR	OVR
Mean Relative Humidity 6am (%)*	87	88	87	89	92	92	93	92	90	89	86	86	89
Mean Relative Humidity 3pm (%)*	62	60	58	61	64	62	56	56	60	57	58	60	59
Mean Dewpoint (°F)*	48	51	56	63	70	73	74	74	71	64	56	50	62
Prevailing Wind Direction*	SSE	SSE	SSE	SE	SE	SE	SE	SE	SE	SE	SSE	SSE	SE
Prevailing Wind Speed (mph)*	15	16	17	15	14	13	13	13	12	12	15	15	14
Maximum Wind Gust (mph)*	53	61	54	67	62	61	58	161	70	53	60	54	161

Note: (*) Period of record is 1948-1995

Dallas-Fort Worth Int'l Airport

The Dallas-Fort Worth Metroplex is located in North Central Texas, approximately 250 miles north of the Gulf of Mexico. It is near the headwaters of the Trinity River, which lie in the upper margins of the Coastal Plain. The rolling hills in the area range from 500 to 800 feet in elevation.

The Dallas-Fort Worth climate is humid subtropical with hot summers. It is also continental, characterized by a wide annual temperature range. Precipitation also varies considerably, ranging from less than 20 to more than 50 inches.

Winters are mild, but northers occur about three times each month, and often are accompanied by sudden drops in temperature. Periods of extreme cold that occasionally occur are short-lived, so that even in January mild weather occurs frequently.

The highest temperatures of summer are associated with fair skies, westerly winds and low humidities. Characteristically, hot spells in summer are broken into three-to-five day periods by thunderstorm activity. There are only a few nights each summer when the low temperature exceeds 80 degrees. Summer daytime temperatures frequently exceed 100 degrees. Air conditioners are recommended for maximum comfort indoors and while traveling via automobile.

Throughout the year, rainfall occurs more frequently during the night. Usually, periods of rainy weather last for only a day or two, and are followed by several days with fair skies. A large part of the annual precipitation results from thunderstorm activity, with occasional heavy rainfall over brief periods of time. Thunderstorms occur throughout the year, but are most frequent in the spring. Hail falls on about two or three days a year, ordinarily with only slight and scattered damage. Windstorms occurring during thunderstorm activity are sometimes destructive. Snowfall is rare.

The average length of the warm season (freeze-free period) in the Dallas-Fort Worth Metroplex is about 249 days. The average last occurrence of 32 degrees or below is mid March and the average first occurrence of 32 degrees or below is in late November.

Dallas-Fort Worth Int'l Airport *Tarrant County* Elevation: 560 ft. Latitude: 32° 54' N Longitude: 97° 01' W

	JAN	FEB	MAR	APR	MAY	JUN	JUL	AUG	SEP	OCT	NOV	DEC	YEAR
Mean Maximum Temp. (°F)	56.4	60.8	68.3	76.2	83.7	91.5	96.1	96.2	88.6	78.2	66.8	57.2	76.7
Mean Temp. (°F)	46.0	50.1	57.6	65.4	73.9	81.4	85.7	85.6	78.1	67.5	56.5	47.2	66.3
Mean Minimum Temp. (°F)	35.6	39.4	46.9	54.5	64.1	71.3	75.2	75.1	67.5	56.7	46.1	37.1	55.8
Extreme Maximum Temp. (°F)	84	95	96	101	103	113	110	109	111	97	89	89	113
Extreme Minimum Temp. (°F)	7	7	15	29	44	54	62	59	43	29	23	-1	-1
Days Maximum Temp. ≥ 90°F	0	0	0	1	6	21	28	27	16	3	0	0	102
Days Maximum Temp. ≤ 32°F	1	1	0	0	0	0	0	0	0	0	0	1	3
Days Minimum Temp. ≤ 32°F	12	7	2	0	0	0	0	0	0	0	2	10	33
Days Minimum Temp. ≤ 0°F	0	0	0	0	0	0	0	0	0	0	0	0	0
Heating Degree Days (base 65°F)	585	421	255	81	8	0	0	0	6	66	276	550	2,248
Cooling Degree Days (base 65°F)	3	6	33	100	291	499	648	647	406	150	28	5	2,816
Mean Precipitation (in.)	2.12	2.60	3.39	3.03	4.97	3.82	2.08	1.90	2.46	4.21	2.70	2.55	35.83
Maximum Precipitation (in.)*	5.4	6.2	6.7	12.2	13.7	8.8	11.1	6.8	9.5	14.2	6.2	8.8	53.5
Minimum Precipitation (in.)*	trace	0.1	0.1	0.1	1.0	trace	0	trace	0.1	trace	trace	trace	18.5
Extreme Maximum Daily Precip. (in.)	3.15	2.90	4.39	3.18	3.50	3.08	3.83	3.90	3.90	3.81	2.23	4.22	4.39
Days With ≥ 0.1" Precipitation	4	4	5	4	6	6	3	3	4	5	4	4	52
Days With ≥ 0.5" Precipitation	1	2	2	2	4	3	1	1	2	3	2	2	25
Days With ≥ 1.0" Precipitation	0	1	1	1	2	1	1	0	1	1	1	1	11
Mean Snowfall (in.)	na	0.6	na	trace	na	na	na	na	na	na	na	0.3	na
Maximum Snowfall (in.)*	12	14	3	0	0	0	0	0	0	trace	5	3	18
Maximum 24-hr. Snowfall (in.)*	8	8	3	0	0	0	0	0	0	trace	5	2	8
Maximum Snow Depth (in.)	2	3	na	na	na	trace	na	na	na	na	na	2	na
Days With ≥ 1.0" Snow Depth	0	1	na	na	na	0	na	na	na	na	na	0	na
Thunderstorm Days*	1	2	4	6	8	6	5	5	4	3	2	1	47
Foggy Days*	11	9	9	8	8	3	2	2	5	7	8	10	82
Predominant Sky Cover*	OVR	OVR	OVR	OVR	OVR	SCT	CLR	CLR	CLR	CLR	CLR	OVR	CLR
Mean Relative Humidity 6am (%)*	80	79	79	82	87	85	80	80	84	82	81	80	82
Mean Relative Humidity 3pm (%)*	53	51	48	50	53	48	42	41	47	47	49	52	48
Mean Dewpoint (°F)*	32	36	42	52	61	67	68	67	63	53	43	35	52
Prevailing Wind Direction*	S	S	S	S	S	S	S	S	S	S	S	S	S
Prevailing Wind Speed (mph)*	13	13	15	15	14	13	12	10	12	12	13	12	13
Maximum Wind Gust (mph)*	69	64	79	76	71	69	71	83	64	63	68	60	83

Note: (*) Period of record is 1948-1995

Del Rio Int'l Airport

Del Rio is located on the Rio Grande River, on the western tip of the Balcones escarpment, in southwest Texas. Elevation is near 1,000 feet and varies little within the city but rises to 2,300 feet in the northern part of the county. Regional agriculture is chiefly wool and mohair production to the north and west of Del Rio and garden crops to the southeast. Lake Amistad, a reservoir of 65,000 surface acres, lies 10 miles west of Del Rio.

The climate of Del Rio is semi-arid continental. Annual precipitation is insufficient for dry farming. However, San Felipe Springs and the Rio Grande provide adequate water for irrigation farming. Over 80 percent of the average annual precipitation occurs from April through October. During this period, rainfall is chiefly in the form of showers and thunderstorms, often as heavy downpours, resulting in flash flooding. The small amount of precipitation for November through March usually falls as steady light rain.

Hail occurs in the vicinity of Del Rio about once per year and reaches severe proportions about once every five years. Sleet or snow falls on an average of once a year, but frequently melts as it falls. A snowfall heavy enough to blanket the ground only occurs about once every four or five years, and seldom remains more than 24 hours.

Temperature averages indicate mild winters and quite warm summers. Cold periods in winter are ushered in by strong, dry, dusty north, and northwest winds known as northers, and temperature drops of as much as 25 degrees in a few hours are not uncommon. Cold weather periods usually do not last more than two or three days. Temperatures as low as 32 degrees have occurred as early as October and as late as March. Normal occurrences of the earliest freezing temperature in autumn and the latest in spring are early December and mid February, which results in an average growing season of 300 days. Hot weather is rather persistent from late May to mid September and temperatures above 100 degrees have been recorded as early as March and as late as October. Low humidity and fresh breezes tend to alleviate uncomfortable conditions usually associated with high temperatures. The mean early morning humidity is about 79 percent, and the mean afternoon humidity is near 44 percent.

Clear to partly cloudy skies predominate, and even in the more cloudy winter months, the mean number of cloudy days are less than the number of clear days.

Del Rio Int'l Airport *Val Verde County*   Elevation: 999 ft.   Latitude: 29° 23' N   Longitude: 100° 56' W

	JAN	FEB	MAR	APR	MAY	JUN	JUL	AUG	SEP	OCT	NOV	DEC	YEAR
Mean Maximum Temp. (°F)	64.1	69.0	76.3	83.7	89.9	94.8	96.9	96.9	90.9	82.2	71.9	63.9	81.7
Mean Temp. (°F)	52.4	57.1	64.3	71.6	78.9	84.1	86.1	86.1	80.4	71.6	60.7	52.5	70.5
Mean Minimum Temp. (°F)	40.8	45.1	52.2	59.5	68.0	73.4	75.2	75.1	69.8	61.0	49.6	41.0	59.2
Extreme Maximum Temp. (°F)	90	99	99	106	109	112	108	108	110	99	96	89	112
Extreme Minimum Temp. (°F)	15	14	21	33	49	60	65	66	43	28	25	10	10
Days Maximum Temp. ≥ 90°F	0	0	2	7	16	25	28	29	20	5	0	0	132
Days Maximum Temp. ≤ 32°F	0	0	0	0	0	0	0	0	0	0	0	0	0
Days Minimum Temp. ≤ 32°F	5	2	1	0	0	0	0	0	0	0	1	5	14
Days Minimum Temp. ≤ 0°F	0	0	0	0	0	0	0	0	0	0	0	0	0
Heating Degree Days (base 65°F)	386	238	108	25	0	0	0	0	2	23	168	385	1,335
Cooling Degree Days (base 65°F)	3	20	92	231	440	581	660	660	470	235	47	4	3,443
Mean Precipitation (in.)	0.65	0.84	1.11	1.47	2.63	2.33	1.63	1.63	2.19	2.23	0.99	0.68	18.38
Maximum Precipitation (in.)*	1.9	3.8	3.2	7.5	10.2	5.7	13.2	6.1	15.8	11.3	3.4	3.1	33.2
Minimum Precipitation (in.)*	trace	0	trace	trace	trace	trace	trace	0	trace	0	trace	trace	4.3
Extreme Maximum Daily Precip. (in.)	1.81	2.57	1.64	2.90	6.53	2.90	3.86	6.09	2.65	7.59	2.02	1.70	7.59
Days With ≥ 0.1" Precipitation	2	2	2	2	4	3	2	2	3	3	2	2	29
Days With ≥ 0.5" Precipitation	0	0	1	1	2	1	1	1	1	1	1	0	10
Days With ≥ 1.0" Precipitation	0	0	0	0	1	1	1	0	1	1	0	0	5
Mean Snowfall (in.)	na	na	na	na	na	na	na	na	na	na	na	na	na
Maximum Snowfall (in.)*	10	3	3	0	0	0	0	0	0	1	trace	trace	10
Maximum 24-hr. Snowfall (in.)*	8	3	3	0	0	0	0	0	0	1	trace	trace	8
Maximum Snow Depth (in.)	na	na	na	na	na	na	na	na	na	na	na	na	na
Days With ≥ 1.0" Snow Depth	na	na	na	na	na	na	na	na	na	na	na	na	na
Thunderstorm Days*	< 1	1	2	4	8	4	3	4	3	2	1	< 1	32
Foggy Days*	10	7	6	6	6	2	1	1	3	5	8	9	64
Predominant Sky Cover*	OVR	CLR	CLR	OVR	OVR	CLR	CLR	CLR	CLR	CLR	CLR	CLR	CLR
Mean Relative Humidity 6am (%)*	76	73	70	76	82	82	78	78	81	80	78	75	77
Mean Relative Humidity 3pm (%)*	44	40	35	40	45	42	37	38	43	43	43	42	41
Mean Dewpoint (°F)*	35	36	42	52	61	65	65	65	63	55	44	36	52
Prevailing Wind Direction*	SE	SE	SE	SE	SE	SE	SE	ESE	SE	SE	SE	SE	SE
Prevailing Wind Speed (mph)*	9	10	13	13	13	13	12	10	10	10	10	9	12
Maximum Wind Gust (mph)*	59	54	56	59	71	52	46	52	54	53	44	56	71

Note: (*) Period of record is 1951-1979

El Paso Int'l Airport

The city of El Paso is located in the extreme west point of Texas at an elevation of about 3,700 feet . The National Weather Service station is located on a mesa about 200 feet higher than the city. The climate of the region is characterized by an abundance of sunshine throughout the year, high daytime summer temperatures, very low humidity, scanty rainfall, and a relatively mild winter season. The Franklin Mountains begin within the city limits and extend northward for about 16 miles. Peaks of these mountains range from 4,687 to 7,152 feet above sea level.

Rainfall throughout the year is light, insufficient for any growth except desert vegetation. Irrigation is necessary for crops, gardens, and lawns. Dry periods lasting several months are not unusual. Almost half of the precipitation occurs in the three-month period, July through September, from brief but often heavy thunderstorms. Small amounts of snow fall nearly every winter, but snow cover rarely amounts to more than an inch and seldom remains on the ground for more than a few hours.

Daytime summer temperatures are high, frequently above 90 degrees and occasionally above 100 degrees. Summer nights are usually comfortable, with temperatures in the 60s. When temperatures are high the relative humidity is generally quite low. With temperatures above 90 degrees in April, May, and June the humidity averaged from 10 to 14 percent, while in July, August, and September it averaged 22 to 24 percent.

Winter daytime temperatures are mild. At night they drop below freezing about half the time in December and January. The flat, irrigated land of the Rio Grande Valley in the vicinity of El Paso is noticeably cooler, particularly at night, than the airport or the city proper, both in summer and winter. This results in more comfortable temperatures in summer but increases the severity of freezes in winter. The cooler air in the Valley also causes marked short-period fluctuations of temperature and dewpoint at the airport with changes in wind direction, especially during the early morning hours.

Dust and sandstorms are the most unpleasant features of the weather in El Paso. While wind velocities are not excessively high, the soil surface is dry and loose and natural vegetation is sparse, so moderately strong winds raise considerable dust and sand. Duststorms are most frequent in March and April, and comparatively rare in the period July through December. prevailing winds are from the north in winter and the south in summer.

El Paso Int'l Airport *El Paso County*   Elevation: 3,917 ft.   Latitude: 31° 49' N   Longitude: 106° 23' W

	JAN	FEB	MAR	APR	MAY	JUN	JUL	AUG	SEP	OCT	NOV	DEC	YEAR
Mean Maximum Temp. (°F)	58.4	64.0	71.0	79.2	88.4	96.3	95.6	93.0	88.1	78.6	66.7	57.7	78.1
Mean Temp. (°F)	45.3	50.3	56.7	64.6	73.9	81.9	83.0	81.1	75.4	64.9	53.0	44.9	64.6
Mean Minimum Temp. (°F)	32.1	36.6	42.3	49.9	59.3	67.3	70.3	69.0	62.6	51.1	39.3	32.0	51.0
Extreme Maximum Temp. (°F)	77	83	89	98	105	114	111	108	104	96	87	79	114
Extreme Minimum Temp. (°F)	9	8	16	23	35	46	57	57	43	26	17	6	6
Days Maximum Temp. ≥ 90°F	0	0	0	2	14	26	27	24	14	2	0	0	109
Days Maximum Temp. ≤ 32°F	0	0	0	0	0	0	0	0	0	0	0	0	0
Days Minimum Temp. ≤ 32°F	16	9	3	1	0	0	0	0	0	0	7	17	53
Days Minimum Temp. ≤ 0°F	0	0	0	0	0	0	0	0	0	0	0	0	0
Heating Degree Days (base 65°F)	604	411	262	90	7	0	0	0	3	83	356	616	2,432
Cooling Degree Days (base 65°F)	0	1	10	85	289	512	565	505	320	86	3	0	2,376
Mean Precipitation (in.)	0.39	0.43	0.27	0.24	0.47	0.90	1.52	2.06	1.52	0.64	0.51	0.77	9.72
Maximum Precipitation (in.)*	1.8	1.7	2.3	1.4	4.2	3.2	5.5	5.6	6.7	3.1	1.6	3.3	17.2
Minimum Precipitation (in.)*	0	0	0	0	0	trace	trace	trace	trace	0	0	0	4.3
Extreme Maximum Daily Precip. (in.)	0.76	0.99	0.62	0.63	1.26	1.85	1.77	2.84	2.20	1.13	0.85	1.46	2.84
Days With ≥ 0.1" Precipitation	2	1	1	1	1	2	4	4	3	2	2	2	25
Days With ≥ 0.5" Precipitation	0	0	0	0	0	1	1	1	1	0	0	0	4
Days With ≥ 1.0" Precipitation	0	0	0	0	0	0	0	0	0	0	0	0	0
Mean Snowfall (in.)	na	na	na	na	na	na	na	na	na	na	na	na	na
Maximum Snowfall (in.)*	8	9	7	17	0	0	0	0	0	1	13	26	33
Maximum 24-hr. Snowfall (in.)*	5	7	6	7	0	0	0	0	0	1	7	15	15
Maximum Snow Depth (in.)	na	na	na	na	na	na	na	na	na	na	na	na	na
Days With ≥ 1.0" Snow Depth	na	na	na	na	na	na	na	na	na	na	na	na	na
Thunderstorm Days*	< 1	< 1	1	1	3	4	10	10	4	2	< 1	< 1	35
Foggy Days*	2	1	1	< 1	< 1	< 1	< 1	< 1	1	1	1	2	9
Predominant Sky Cover*	CLR	CLR	CLR	CLR	CLR	CLR	SCT	SCT	CLR	CLR	CLR	CLR	CLR
Mean Relative Humidity 6am (%)*	68	60	50	43	44	46	63	69	72	66	63	68	59
Mean Relative Humidity 3pm (%)*	34	27	21	17	17	17	28	30	32	29	30	36	26
Mean Dewpoint (°F)*	24	24	24	26	34	42	54	56	52	40	29	26	36
Prevailing Wind Direction*	NNE	WSW	W	WSW	WSW	SE	SE	SE	SE	N	NNE	N	WSW
Prevailing Wind Speed (mph)*	7	12	15	14	13	8	8	7	7	7	7	7	9
Maximum Wind Gust (mph)*	61	73	84	74	55	69	73	67	63	59	59	74	84

Note: (*) Period of record is 1948-1995

Galveston

The city of Galveston is located on Galveston Island off the southeast coast of Texas. The island is about two and three fourths miles across at the widest point and 29 miles long. It is bounded on the southeast by the Gulf of Mexico and on the northwest by Galveston Bay, which is about three miles wide at this point. The climate of the Galveston area is predominantly marine, with periods of modified continental influence during the colder months, when cold fronts from the northwest some-times reach the coast.

Because of its coastal location and relatively low latitude, cold fronts which do reach the area are very seldom severe and temperatures below 32 degrees are re-corded on an average only four times a year. Normal monthly high temperatures range from about 60 degrees in January to nearly 88 degrees in August. Lows range from about 48 degrees in January to the upper 70s during the summer season.

High humidities prevail throughout the year. Annual precipitation averages about 42 inches. Rainfall during the summer months may vary greatly on different parts of the island, as most of the rain in this season is from local thunderstorm activity. Hail is rare because the necessary strong vertical lifting is usually absent. There have been several instances when a monthly rainfall total amounted to only a trace, but these have been offset in the means by many monthly totals in excess of 15 inches. Winter precipitation comes mainly from frontal activity and from low stratus clouds, which produce slow, steady rains.

The island has been subject at infrequent intervals to major tropical storms of hurricane force.

Galveston *Galveston County*   Elevation: 15 ft.   Latitude: 29° 18' N   Longitude: 94° 48' W

	JAN	FEB	MAR	APR	MAY	JUN	JUL	AUG	SEP	OCT	NOV	DEC	YEAR
Mean Maximum Temp. (°F)	na	63.4	68.2	74.7	81.1	86.6	89.0	89.5	86.4	79.1	na	62.8	na
Mean Temp. (°F)	na	57.2	62.6	69.6	76.6	na	84.5	84.5	80.8	73.4	na	56.5	na
Mean Minimum Temp. (°F)	na	50.9	56.9	64.4	72.1	na	79.9	79.5	75.1	67.7	na	49.9	na
Extreme Maximum Temp. (°F)	78	80	86	90	94	99	100	102	100	92	na	81	na
Extreme Minimum Temp. (°F)	20	24	26	42	56	64	69	69	54	39	na	14	na
Days Maximum Temp. ≥ 90°F	0	0	0	0	0	4	12	14	7	0	na	0	na
Days Maximum Temp. ≤ 32°F	0	0	0	0	0	0	0	0	0	0	na	0	na
Days Minimum Temp. ≤ 32°F	1	1	0	0	0	0	0	0	0	0	na	1	na
Days Minimum Temp. ≤ 0°F	0	0	0	0	0	0	0	0	0	0	na	0	na
Heating Degree Days (base 65°F)	na	223	109	20	0	na	0	0	0	13	na	278	na
Cooling Degree Days (base 65°F)	na	8	42	164	366	na	612	611	479	283	na	20	na
Mean Precipitation (in.)	4.39	2.88	3.00	2.02	3.29	5.04	2.87	3.48	5.05	3.72	na	3.65	na
Maximum Precipitation (in.)*	10.8	8.3	9.5	10.4	11.0	13.0	17.5	13.4	14.3	9.0	9.5	9.0	60.5
Minimum Precipitation (in.)*	0.2	0.2	0.1	trace	trace	0.4	0.1	0.2	0.3	0	0.6	0.5	29.3
Extreme Maximum Daily Precip. (in.)	4.10	4.51	3.60	5.00	4.04	6.90	2.86	10.86	6.59	3.81	na	na	na
Days With ≥ 0.1" Precipitation	6	4	4	3	4	5	4	4	6	5	na	5	na
Days With ≥ 0.5" Precipitation	3	2	2	1	2	3	2	2	3	2	na	2	na
Days With ≥ 1.0" Precipitation	1	1	1	1	1	2	1	1	2	1	na	1	na
Mean Snowfall (in.)	trace	trace	trace	trace	trace	0.0	0.0	0.0	0.0	0.0	na	0.0	na
Maximum Snowfall (in.)*	3	2	trace	0	0	0	0	0	0	0	0	1	4
Maximum 24-hr. Snowfall (in.)*	3	2	trace	0	0	0	0	0	0	0	0	1	3
Maximum Snow Depth (in.)	trace	trace	trace	trace	trace	0	0	0	0	0	na	1	na
Days With ≥ 1.0" Snow Depth	0	0	0	0	0	0	0	0	0	0	na	0	na
Thunderstorm Days*	1	< 1	1	3	4	2	2	4	3	2	1	< 1	23
Foggy Days*	9	6	10	10	3	3	1	2	2	6	5	8	65
Predominant Sky Cover*	na	na	na	na	na	na	na	na	na	na	na	na	na
Mean Relative Humidity 7am (%)*	na	na	na	na	na	na	na	na	na	na	na	na	na
Mean Relative Humidity 4pm (%)*	na	na	na	na	na	na	na	na	na	na	na	na	na
Mean Dewpoint (°F)*	na	na	na	na	na	na	na	na	na	na	na	na	na
Prevailing Wind Direction*	na	na	na	na	na	na	na	na	na	na	na	na	na
Prevailing Wind Speed (mph)*	na	na	na	na	na	na	na	na	na	na	na	na	na
Maximum Wind Gust (mph)*	na	na	na	na	na	na	na	na	na	na	na	na	na

Note: (*) Period of record is 1963-1995

Houston Bush Intercontinental

Houston, the largest city in Texas, is located in the flat Coastal Plains, about 50 miles from the Gulf of Mexico and about 25 miles from Galveston Bay. The climate is predominantly marine. The terrain includes numerous small streams and bayous which, together with the nearness to Galveston Bay, favor the development of both ground and advective fogs. Prevailing winds are from the southeast and south, except in January, when frequent passages of high pressure areas bring invasions of polar air and prevailing northerly winds.

Temperatures are moderated by the influence of winds from the Gulf, which result in mild winters. Another effect of the nearness of the Gulf is abundant rainfall, except for rare extended dry periods. Polar air penetrates the area frequently enough to provide variability in the weather.

Records of sky cover for daylight hours indicate about one-fourth of the days per year as clear, with a high number of clear days in October and November. Cloudy days are relatively frequent from December to May and partly cloudy days are the more frequent for June through September. Sunshine averages nearly 60 percent of the possible amount for the year ranging from 42 percent in January to 67 percent in June.

Heavy fog occurs on an average of 16 days a year and light fog occurs about 62 days a year in the city. The frequency of heavy fog is considerably higher at William P. Hobby Airport and at Intercontinental Airport.

Destructive windstorms are fairly infrequent, but both thundersqualls and tropical storms occasionally pass through the area.

Houston Bush Intercontinental *Harris County*   Elevation: 95 ft.   Latitude: 30° 00' N   Longitude: 95° 22' W

	JAN	FEB	MAR	APR	MAY	JUN	JUL	AUG	SEP	OCT	NOV	DEC	YEAR
Mean Maximum Temp. (°F)	63.0	66.4	73.0	79.5	86.1	91.4	93.9	94.3	89.7	81.6	72.3	64.2	79.6
Mean Temp. (°F)	52.9	56.2	62.4	69.1	76.6	82.0	84.2	84.2	79.5	70.9	61.7	54.1	69.5
Mean Minimum Temp. (°F)	42.7	45.9	51.9	58.6	67.0	72.5	74.4	74.0	69.2	60.1	51.2	43.9	59.3
Extreme Maximum Temp. (°F)	83	91	91	95	99	104	104	107	109	96	89	85	109
Extreme Minimum Temp. (°F)	12	20	22	31	46	53	62	60	49	29	27	7	7
Days Maximum Temp. ≥ 90°F	0	0	0	1	8	21	27	27	18	4	0	0	106
Days Maximum Temp. ≤ 32°F	0	0	0	0	0	0	0	0	0	0	0	0	0
Days Minimum Temp. ≤ 32°F	4	2	1	0	0	0	0	0	0	0	1	4	12
Days Minimum Temp. ≤ 0°F	0	0	0	0	0	0	0	0	0	0	0	0	0
Heating Degree Days (base 65°F)	384	268	143	39	0	0	0	0	1	31	161	358	1,385
Cooling Degree Days (base 65°F)	15	26	71	168	365	516	601	601	441	221	70	27	3,122
Mean Precipitation (in.)	3.50	3.16	3.53	3.28	5.15	5.84	3.41	3.78	4.16	5.83	4.32	3.68	49.64
Maximum Precipitation (in.)*	9.8	6.0	8.5	10.9	14.4	16.3	8.1	9.4	11.3	16.0	8.9	9.3	70.2
Minimum Precipitation (in.)*	0.4	0.4	0.9	0.4	0.8	0.3	0.5	0.3	0.8	0	0.4	0.6	22.9
Extreme Maximum Daily Precip. (in.)	2.58	2.22	4.56	3.52	6.87	10.34	5.40	6.69	7.73	9.25	5.19	5.64	10.34
Days With ≥ 0.1" Precipitation	5	5	5	4	5	5	5	6	5	5	5	6	63
Days With ≥ 0.5" Precipitation	2	2	2	2	3	4	2	2	2	3	3	2	29
Days With ≥ 1.0" Precipitation	1	1	1	1	2	2	1	1	1	2	1	1	15
Mean Snowfall (in.)	0.0	0.1	trace	trace	trace	trace	0.0	0.0	0.0	0.0	0.0	0.1	0.2
Maximum Snowfall (in.)*	2	3	0	0	0	0	0	0	0	0	trace	2	5
Maximum 24-hr. Snowfall (in.)*	2	1	0	0	0	0	0	0	0	0	trace	2	2
Maximum Snow Depth (in.)	trace	trace	trace	trace	trace	trace	0	0	0	0	0	trace	trace
Days With ≥ 1.0" Snow Depth	0	0	0	0	0	0	0	0	0	0	0	0	0
Thunderstorm Days*	2	2	4	4	7	8	10	11	8	4	3	2	65
Foggy Days*	18	15	18	17	19	13	11	14	16	16	15	17	189
Predominant Sky Cover*	OVR	OVR	OVR	OVR	OVR	SCT	SCT	SCT	SCT	CLR	OVR	OVR	OVR
Mean Relative Humidity 6am (%)*	86	87	88	89	92	92	93	93	93	91	89	87	90
Mean Relative Humidity 3pm (%)*	58	55	54	55	57	57	54	55	56	52	55	57	55
Mean Dewpoint (°F)*	42	45	51	58	66	71	72	72	68	60	51	46	59
Prevailing Wind Direction*	N	N	SE	SE	SE	SE	S	S	ENE	SE	N	N	SE
Prevailing Wind Speed (mph)*	9	9	12	12	10	10	8	8	7	9	8	9	9
Maximum Wind Gust (mph)*	44	61	54	59	69	68	68	98	56	58	49	56	98

Note: (*) Period of record is 1969-1995

Lubbock Regional Airport

Lubbock is located on a plateau area of Northwestern Texas that is referred to locally as the South Plains Region. The general elevation of the area is about 3,250 feet. The Region is a major part of the Llano Estacado (staked plains). The latter, which includes a large portion of Northwest Texas, is bounded on the east and southeast by an erosional escarpment that is usually referred to as the Cap Rock. The Llano Estacado extends southwestward into the upper Pecos Valley and westward into eastern New Mexico.

The South Plains are predominately flat, but contain numerous small playas (or clay lined depressions) and small stream valleys. During the rainy months the playas collect run-off water and form small lakes or ponds. The stream valleys drain into the major rivers of West Texas, but throughout most of the year these streams carry only very light flows.

Cap Rock causes a noticeable distortion of the smooth wind flow patterns across the South Plains, the most noticeable on southeasterly winds as they are deflected upward along its face.

The Lubbock area is the heart of the largest cotton-producing section of Texas. Irrigation from underground sources is often used as a supplement to natural rainfall to improve crop yields. The soils of the region are sandy clay loams.

The area is semi-arid, transitional between the desert conditions on the west and the humid climates to the east and southeast. The greatest monthly rainfall totals occur from May through September when warm moist tropical air may be carried into the area from the Gulf of Mexico. This air mass often brings moderate to heavy afternoon and evening thunderstorms, accompanied by hail. Precipitation across the area is characterized by its variability. The monthly precipitation extremes range from trace amounts in several isolated months to 14 inches.

Snow may occur from late October until April. Each snowfall is generally light and seldom remains on the ground for more than two or three days at any one period.

High winds are associated primarily with intense thunderstorms and at times may cause significant damage to structures. Winds in excess of 25 mph occasionally occur for periods of 12 hours or longer. These prolonged winds are generally associated with late winter and springtime low-pressure centers. Spring winds often bring widespread dust.

The summer heat is moderated by a variable, but usually gentle, wind. Dry air from the west often reduce any discomfort from the summer heat and lower temperatures into the 60s.

The average first occurrence of temperatures below 32 degrees Fahrenheit in the fall is the first of November and the average last occurrence in the spring is in mid April.

Lubbock Regional Airport *Lubbock County*   Elevation: 3,253 ft.   Latitude: 33° 40' N   Longitude: 101° 49' W

	JAN	FEB	MAR	APR	MAY	JUN	JUL	AUG	SEP	OCT	NOV	DEC	YEAR
Mean Maximum Temp. (°F)	54.0	59.1	66.8	75.5	83.8	90.8	93.3	91.3	84.4	75.0	63.4	54.1	74.3
Mean Temp. (°F)	40.6	44.9	52.1	60.8	70.1	77.7	80.8	79.2	71.8	61.6	49.9	40.8	60.9
Mean Minimum Temp. (°F)	27.0	30.7	37.4	46.0	56.3	64.7	68.3	67.1	59.2	48.2	36.3	27.6	47.4
Extreme Maximum Temp. (°F)	83	89	95	100	109	114	108	105	103	100	90	81	114
Extreme Minimum Temp. (°F)	0	3	8	22	37	46	54	54	33	18	7	-2	-2
Days Maximum Temp. ≥ 90°F	0	0	0	2	10	18	24	21	9	2	0	0	86
Days Maximum Temp. ≤ 32°F	2	1	0	0	0	0	0	0	0	0	0	2	5
Days Minimum Temp. ≤ 32°F	24	16	9	1	0	0	0	0	0	1	10	23	84
Days Minimum Temp. ≤ 0°F	0	0	0	0	0	0	0	0	0	0	0	0	0
Heating Degree Days (base 65°F)	751	562	400	172	37	1	0	0	21	154	449	742	3,289
Cooling Degree Days (base 65°F)	0	0	8	53	201	389	498	448	232	56	2	0	1,887
Mean Precipitation (in.)	0.62	0.70	1.01	1.30	2.37	3.01	1.67	1.92	2.60	1.85	0.92	0.77	18.74
Maximum Precipitation (in.)*	4.0	2.5	3.2	3.5	7.8	7.9	7.2	8.8	8.2	10.8	2.7	2.2	29.4
Minimum Precipitation (in.)*	0	trace	trace	trace	0.1	trace	trace	0	trace	0	0	trace	10.8
Extreme Maximum Daily Precip. (in.)	1.39	1.17	1.90	2.18	2.67	3.51	2.65	2.45	7.46	5.43	1.59	1.22	7.46
Days With ≥ 0.1" Precipitation	2	2	2	3	4	5	3	4	4	3	2	2	36
Days With ≥ 0.5" Precipitation	0	0	1	1	2	2	1	1	1	1	1	0	11
Days With ≥ 1.0" Precipitation	0	0	0	0	1	1	0	0	1	0	0	0	3
Mean Snowfall (in.)	2.6	1.5	0.5	0.3	trace	trace	trace	0.0	trace	trace	1.6	2.2	8.7
Maximum Snowfall (in.)*	25	17	14	5	0	0	0	0	0	8	21	10	36
Maximum 24-hr. Snowfall (in.)*	11	12	8	4	0	0	0	0	0	4	11	6	12
Maximum Snow Depth (in.)	17	7	3	3	trace	trace	trace	0	trace	trace	11	8	17
Days With ≥ 1.0" Snow Depth	2	1	0	0	0	0	0	0	0	0	1	2	6
Thunderstorm Days*	< 1	1	2	4	8	9	8	7	5	3	1	< 1	48
Foggy Days*	7	7	5	4	6	3	2	3	6	6	6	6	61
Predominant Sky Cover*	CLR	CLR	CLR	CLR	CLR	CLR	SCT	SCT	CLR	CLR	CLR	CLR	CLR
Mean Relative Humidity 6am (%)*	73	72	68	68	76	78	73	78	82	77	74	73	74
Mean Relative Humidity 3pm (%)*	41	39	32	29	34	36	38	42	45	38	38	41	38
Mean Dewpoint (°F)*	22	25	29	36	47	57	60	60	56	43	32	24	41
Prevailing Wind Direction*	WSW	WSW	S	S	S	S	S	S	S	S	SW	WSW	S
Prevailing Wind Speed (mph)*	12	13	14	15	15	14	13	12	12	12	12	10	13
Maximum Wind Gust (mph)*	59	66	77	71	70	85	85	59	58	64	66	64	85

Note: (*) Period of record is 1948-1995

Midland Regional Air Terminal

The Midland-Odessa region is on the southern extension of the South Plains of Texas. The terrain is level with only slight occasional undulations.

The climate is typical of a semi-arid region. The vegetation of the area consists mostly of native grasses and a few trees, mostly of the mesquite variety.

Most of the annual precipitation in the area comes as a result of very violent spring and early summer thunderstorms. These are usually accompanied by excessive rainfall, over limited areas, and sometimes hail. Due to the flat nature of the countryside, local flooding occurs, but is of short duration. Tornadoes are occasionally sighted.

During the late winter and early spring months, blowing dust occurs frequently. The flat plains of the area with only grass as vegetation offer little resistance to the strong winds. The sky is occasionally obscured by dust but in most storms visibilities range from one to three miles.

Daytime temperatures are quite hot in the summer, but there is a large diurnal range of temperature and most nights are comfortable. The temperature drops below 32 degrees in the fall about mid- November and the last temperature below 32 degrees in spring comes early in April.

Winters are characterized by frequent cold periods followed by rapid warming. Cold frontal passages are followed by chilly weather for two or three days. Cloudiness is at a minimum. Summers are hot and dry with numerous small convective showers.

The prevailing wind direction in this area is from the southeast. This, together with the upslope of the terrain from the same direction, causes occasional low cloudiness and drizzle during winter and spring months. Snow is infrequent. Maximum temperatures during the summer months frequently are from two to six degrees cooler than those at places 100 miles southeast, due to the cooling effect of the upslope winds.

Very low humidities are conducive to personal comfort, because even though summer afternoon temperatures are frequently above 90 degrees, the low humidity with resultant rapid evaporation, has a cooling effect. The climate of the area is generally quite pleasant with the most disagreeable weather concentrated in the late winter and spring months.

Midland Regional Air Terminal *Midland County*   Elevation: 2,861 ft.   Latitude: 31° 57' N   Longitude: 102° 11' W

	JAN	FEB	MAR	APR	MAY	JUN	JUL	AUG	SEP	OCT	NOV	DEC	YEAR
Mean Maximum Temp. (°F)	57.5	62.6	70.1	79.1	87.4	93.3	94.9	93.4	86.7	77.6	66.3	57.9	77.2
Mean Temp. (°F)	44.0	48.6	55.5	64.1	73.5	80.3	82.3	81.1	74.4	64.7	52.7	44.4	63.8
Mean Minimum Temp. (°F)	30.4	34.5	40.9	49.0	59.5	67.2	69.7	68.7	62.0	51.7	39.1	30.8	50.3
Extreme Maximum Temp. (°F)	83	90	95	101	108	116	112	106	104	101	90	84	116
Extreme Minimum Temp. (°F)	5	-11	9	25	39	47	58	54	36	24	11	-1	-11
Days Maximum Temp. ≥ 90°F	0	0	0	4	14	22	27	25	12	3	0	0	107
Days Maximum Temp. ≤ 32°F	1	1	0	0	0	0	0	0	0	0	0	1	3
Days Minimum Temp. ≤ 32°F	19	12	5	1	0	0	0	0	0	0	7	18	62
Days Minimum Temp. ≤ 0°F	0	0	0	0	0	0	0	0	0	0	0	0	0
Heating Degree Days (base 65°F)	645	460	302	111	15	0	0	0	12	97	367	632	2,641
Cooling Degree Days (base 65°F)	0	2	16	90	285	465	544	507	299	94	6	0	2,308
Mean Precipitation (in.)	0.52	0.66	0.58	0.61	1.75	1.72	1.76	1.86	2.11	1.73	0.72	0.64	14.66
Maximum Precipitation (in.)*	3.7	2.5	2.9	2.8	7.6	4.0	8.5	4.4	9.7	7.4	2.3	3.3	32.1
Minimum Precipitation (in.)*	0	trace	trace	0	0.1	trace	trace	0.2	0.1	0	0	0	4.6
Extreme Maximum Daily Precip. (in.)	0.96	1.13	0.72	1.33	2.72	3.07	3.59	2.72	3.29	3.59	1.55	1.05	3.59
Days With ≥ 0.1" Precipitation	1	2	2	2	3	3	3	3	3	3	2	2	29
Days With ≥ 0.5" Precipitation	0	0	0	0	1	1	1	1	2	1	0	0	7
Days With ≥ 1.0" Precipitation	0	0	0	0	0	1	0	1	1	1	0	0	4
Mean Snowfall (in.)	2.0	0.5	0.2	0.1	trace	trace	trace	trace	trace	trace	0.8	1.6	5.2
Maximum Snowfall (in.)*	9	4	6	1	0	0	0	0	0	1	7	9	12
Maximum 24-hr. Snowfall (in.)*	6	3	5	1	0	0	0	0	0	1	6	4	6
Maximum Snow Depth (in.)	6	5	3	trace	trace	trace	trace	trace	trace	1	8	5	8
Days With ≥ 1.0" Snow Depth	1	0	0	0	0	0	0	0	0	0	0	0	1
Thunderstorm Days*	< 1	1	1	3	7	6	6	6	4	3	1	< 1	38
Foggy Days*	7	7	4	3	3	1	1	1	4	5	6	7	49
Predominant Sky Cover*	CLR	CLR	CLR	CLR	CLR	CLR	CLR	CLR	CLR	CLR	CLR	CLR	CLR
Mean Relative Humidity 6am (%)*	72	72	65	67	75	76	73	74	79	78	74	71	73
Mean Relative Humidity 3pm (%)*	38	35	27	27	31	32	34	34	40	37	35	37	34
Mean Dewpoint (°F)*	25	28	30	38	48	57	59	59	56	46	34	27	43
Prevailing Wind Direction*	S	S	S	S	SSE	SSE	SSE	SSE	SSE	S	S	S	S
Prevailing Wind Speed (mph)*	9	10	13	13	14	13	12	10	10	12	10	10	12
Maximum Wind Gust (mph)*	59	63	74	76	83	71	82	66	82	69	60	69	83

Note: (*) Period of record is 1948-1995

Port Arthur Jefferson County

Port Arthur is located on the flat Coastal Plain in the extreme southeast corner of Texas. The climate is a mixture of tropical and temperate zone conditions.

Sea breezes prevent extremely high temperatures in the summer, except on rare occasions. The area lies far enough south so that cold air masses modify in severity but still provide freezing temperatures up to six times a year.

High humidity is the result of fairly evenly distributed high normal rainfall and prevailing southerly winds from the Gulf of Mexico.

Cloudy, rainy weather is most common in the winter. Only slightly more than half the winters record even a trace of sleet or snow. Heavy rainfall in summer occurs in short duration thunderstorms and in infrequent tropical storms.

Slow moving systems in the spring and fall often result in three to five days of stormy weather and heavy rain. The lightest precipitation usually occurs in March and October. Funnel clouds and waterspouts are common near the coast. The area enjoys approximately 60 percent of possible sunshine.

Fog, most frequent in midwinter and early spring, is rare in summer. It usually dissipates before noon, but occasionally under stagnant conditions lasts a day or two. Along the immediate coast, fog usually does not form until daybreak, but inland it may form before midnight.

The average wind movement is near ll mph. Except for severe storms and tropical disturbances, wind seldom exceeds 45 mph. It exceeds 30 mph on only about 40 days in any one year.

The climate is favorable for outdoor activities throughout the year. The abundant rainfall, moderate temperatures, and the short period of temperatures below freezing are particularly favorable for farming and livestock production. Heaviest rain usually falls in the summer when needed for rice. The comparatively dry harvest season simplifies the gathering of rice and feed crops. Cattle on the open range of the coastal marshes need little supplemental feeding or protection. Improved pastures are easily provided because of the moderate temperatures and abundant rainfall.

Port Arthur Jefferson County *Jefferson County* Elevation: 16 ft. Latitude: 29° 57' N Longitude: 94° 01' W

	JAN	FEB	MAR	APR	MAY	JUN	JUL	AUG	SEP	OCT	NOV	DEC	YEAR
Mean Maximum Temp. (°F)	62.3	65.6	72.0	78.2	84.6	89.7	91.8	92.1	88.3	80.5	71.6	63.8	78.4
Mean Temp. (°F)	53.0	56.2	62.4	68.7	75.9	81.3	83.1	83.2	79.2	70.6	61.7	54.4	69.1
Mean Minimum Temp. (°F)	43.7	46.9	52.7	59.1	67.2	72.8	74.4	74.1	70.0	60.6	51.8	45.0	59.9
Extreme Maximum Temp. (°F)	82	85	89	94	98	102	103	108	105	94	88	82	108
Extreme Minimum Temp. (°F)	15	20	23	32	47	56	61	60	49	30	28	12	12
Days Maximum Temp. ≥ 90°F	0	0	0	0	3	18	25	25	14	2	0	0	87
Days Maximum Temp. ≤ 32°F	0	0	0	0	0	0	0	0	0	0	0	0	0
Days Minimum Temp. ≤ 32°F	4	2	1	0	0	0	0	0	0	0	0	3	10
Days Minimum Temp. ≤ 0°F	0	0	0	0	0	0	0	0	0	0	0	0	0
Heating Degree Days (base 65°F)	376	261	137	37	1	0	0	0	1	32	157	345	1,347
Cooling Degree Days (base 65°F)	12	19	62	154	347	495	569	570	432	212	66	24	2,962
Mean Precipitation (in.)	5.32	3.46	3.66	3.23	5.46	7.01	5.57	5.28	6.53	5.78	4.43	5.19	60.92
Maximum Precipitation (in.)*	14.9	13.1	10.2	8.7	13.2	18.9	18.7	17.3	22.0	15.1	10.8	18.0	81.5
Minimum Precipitation (in.)*	0.6	0.2	0.1	0.3	0.1	0.8	0.6	1.0	0.5	0	0.1	1.3	33.1
Extreme Maximum Daily Precip. (in.)	4.30	2.97	3.84	5.75	9.89	4.87	4.99	5.79	11.80	6.58	6.32	8.04	11.80
Days With ≥ 0.1" Precipitation	7	5	5	4	5	7	7	7	7	5	6	6	71
Days With ≥ 0.5" Precipitation	3	2	2	2	3	4	4	3	3	3	3	3	35
Days With ≥ 1.0" Precipitation	1	1	1	1	2	2	2	2	2	2	1	2	19
Mean Snowfall (in.)	na	na	na	na	na	na	na	na	na	na	na	na	na
Maximum Snowfall (in.)*	3	4	1	0	0	0	0	0	0	0	trace	1	4
Maximum 24-hr. Snowfall (in.)*	3	4	1	0	0	0	0	0	0	0	trace	1	4
Maximum Snow Depth (in.)	na	na	na	na	na	na	na	na	na	na	na	na	na
Days With ≥ 1.0" Snow Depth	na	na	na	na	na	na	na	na	na	na	na	na	na
Thunderstorm Days*	3	3	4	4	6	8	14	12	7	3	3	2	69
Foggy Days*	18	16	17	13	14	10	8	11	14	16	15	17	171
Predominant Sky Cover*	OVR	OVR	OVR	OVR	SCT	SCT	SCT	SCT	SCT	CLR	OVR	OVR	OVR
Mean Relative Humidity 6am (%)*	88	88	88	90	92	93	94	94	92	91	89	89	91
Mean Relative Humidity 3pm (%)*	64	61	59	61	62	62	64	62	60	55	59	64	61
Mean Dewpoint (°F)*	45	47	52	60	67	72	74	74	70	61	52	47	60
Prevailing Wind Direction*	N	S	S	SSE	S	S	S	S	NE	N	N	N	S
Prevailing Wind Speed (mph)*	12	12	13	14	12	10	8	8	9	9	10	12	10
Maximum Wind Gust (mph)*	56	54	60	59	62	76	69	59	58	48	61	61	76

Note: (*) Period of record is 1948-1995

San Angelo Mathis Field

San Angelo is located near the center of Texas at the northern edge of the Edwards Plateau. Ground elevation ranges from about 1,700 to 2,700 feet above sea level. Topography varies from level and slightly rolling to broken. The climate is generally classified as semi-arid or steppe, but has some humid temperate characteristics. Warm, dry weather predominates, although changes may be rapid and frequent with the passage of cold fronts or northers.

High temperatures of summer are associated with fair skies, south to southwest winds and dry air. Low humidities, however, are conducive to personal comfort because of rapid evaporation. Rapid temperature drops occur after sunset, and most nights are pleasant with lows in the upper 60s and lower 70s. Rapid temperature drops occur in the winter as cold polar air invades the region. Temperature drops of 20 to 30 degrees in a short time are not uncommon. Cold polar outbreaks have produced record low temperatures of zero or below throughout the area.

The rainfall is typical of the Great Plains. Much of the rainfall occurs from thunderstorm activity, and wide variations in annual precipitation occur from year to year. Heavy rainfall occurs in April, May, June, September and October. Also, in the late summer months, heavy precipitation may occur when tropical disturbances move inland over south Texas and pass near the San Angelo area.

The prevailing wind direction is from the south, and winds are frequently high and persistent for several days. Dusty conditions are infrequent and occur in early spring when west or northwest winds predominate. The frequency and intensity of the dust storms are dependent on soil conditions in the Texas Panhandle and in New Mexico.

Agriculture in the region consists of cattle, sheep, and goat raising. Cotton, from dry-land and irrigated fields, maize, corn, melons, truck farming, and pecan production are also important crops.

San Angelo Mathis Field *Tom Green County*   Elevation: 1,916 ft.   Latitude: 31° 21' N   Longitude: 100° 30' W

	JAN	FEB	MAR	APR	MAY	JUN	JUL	AUG	SEP	OCT	NOV	DEC	YEAR
Mean Maximum Temp. (°F)	59.5	63.8	71.1	80.1	87.1	92.1	95.3	94.6	87.6	78.7	68.1	59.9	78.2
Mean Temp. (°F)	46.4	50.4	57.7	65.8	74.3	80.3	83.2	82.5	75.5	66.0	55.1	46.7	65.3
Mean Minimum Temp. (°F)	33.2	36.9	44.1	51.5	61.5	68.5	70.9	70.3	63.3	53.3	42.1	33.6	52.4
Extreme Maximum Temp. (°F)	87	97	95	101	109	110	109	109	107	99	93	88	110
Extreme Minimum Temp. (°F)	5	-1	8	26	37	49	56	54	37	26	18	-4	-4
Days Maximum Temp. ≥ 90°F	0	0	1	5	13	21	27	26	13	3	0	0	109
Days Maximum Temp. ≤ 32°F	1	1	0	0	0	0	0	0	0	0	0	1	3
Days Minimum Temp. ≤ 32°F	16	9	4	1	0	0	0	0	0	0	6	15	51
Days Minimum Temp. ≤ 0°F	0	0	0	0	0	0	0	0	0	0	0	0	0
Heating Degree Days (base 65°F)	571	413	254	89	10	0	0	0	9	81	308	560	2,295
Cooling Degree Days (base 65°F)	1	5	33	120	306	466	570	550	330	120	18	1	2,520
Mean Precipitation (in.)	0.88	1.29	1.48	1.35	2.93	2.63	1.15	2.33	2.77	2.64	1.23	0.89	21.57
Maximum Precipitation (in.)*	3.6	4.4	5.0	5.1	11.2	6.0	7.2	8.1	11.0	8.7	3.5	4.0	33.9
Minimum Precipitation (in.)*	0	trace	trace	0.1	0.3	0	trace	trace	trace	0	0	trace	7.4
Extreme Maximum Daily Precip. (in.)	1.64	3.16	2.05	2.28	2.26	2.82	2.31	4.00	6.24	3.24	2.19	1.52	6.24
Days With ≥ 0.1" Precipitation	2	3	3	2	5	4	2	3	3	4	2	2	35
Days With ≥ 0.5" Precipitation	1	1	1	1	2	2	1	1	2	2	1	0	15
Days With ≥ 1.0" Precipitation	0	0	0	0	1	1	0	1	1	1	0	0	5
Mean Snowfall (in.)	*1.4*	*0.3*	*0.1*	*0.0*	*trace*	*trace*	*trace*	*0.0*	*trace*	*trace*	*0.3*	*0.3*	*2.4*
Maximum Snowfall (in.)*	9	6	3	trace	0	0	0	0	0	trace	9	4	14
Maximum 24-hr. Snowfall (in.)*	7	3	3	trace	0	0	0	0	0	trace	6	3	7
Maximum Snow Depth (in.)	*6*	*2*	*2*	*trace*	*trace*	*trace*	*trace*	*0*	*trace*	*trace*	*3*	*3*	*6*
Days With ≥ 1.0" Snow Depth	*1*	*0*	*0*	*0*	*0*	*0*	*0*	*0*	*0*	*0*	*0*	*0*	*1*
Thunderstorm Days*	1	1	2	4	7	5	4	5	4	3	1	1	38
Foggy Days*	7	6	4	3	4	1	1	1	4	4	5	6	46
Predominant Sky Cover*	OVR	CLR	CLR	CLR	CLR	CLR	CLR	CLR	CLR	CLR	CLR	CLR	CLR
Mean Relative Humidity 6am (%)*	76	76	71	74	81	80	77	77	82	81	78	76	77
Mean Relative Humidity 3pm (%)*	44	41	35	35	40	40	36	36	44	43	41	43	40
Mean Dewpoint (°F)*	30	33	37	46	56	62	62	62	60	51	40	32	48
Prevailing Wind Direction*	SSW	SSW	S	S	S	S	S	S	S	S	SSW	SSW	S
Prevailing Wind Speed (mph)*	13	13	14	14	13	13	12	10	10	12	12	13	13
Maximum Wind Gust (mph)*	61	59	63	76	93	71	68	67	76	68	74	60	93

Note: (*) Period of record is 1948-1995

San Antonio Int'l Airport

The city of San Antonio is located in the south-central portion of Texas on the Balcones escarpment. Northwest of the city, the terrain slopes upward to the Edwards Plateau and to the southeast it slopes downward to the Gulf Coastal Plains. Soils are blackland clay and silty loam on the Plains and thin limestone soils on the Edwards Plateau.

The location of San Antonio on the edge of the Gulf Coastal Plains is influenced by a modified subtropical climate, predominantly continental during the winter months and marine during the summer months. Temperatures range from 50 degrees in January to the middle 80s in July and August. While the summer is hot, with daily temperatures above 90 degrees over 80 percent of the time, extremely high temperatures are rare. Mild weather prevails during much of the winter months, with below-freezing temperatures occurring on an average of about 20 days each year.

San Antonio is situated between a semi-arid area to the west and the coastal area of heavy precipitation to the east. Precipitation is fairly well distributed throughout the year with the heaviest amounts occurring during May and September. The precipitation from April through September usually occurs from thunderstorms. Most of the winter precipitation occurs as light rain or drizzle. Thunderstorms and heavy rains have occurred in all months of the year. Hail of damaging intensity seldom occurs but light hail is frequent with the springtime thunderstorms. Measurable snow occurs only once in three or four years.

Northerly winds prevail during most of the winter, and strong northerly winds occasionally occur during storms called northers. Southeasterly winds from the Gulf of Mexico also occur frequently during winter and are predominant in summer.

Since San Antonio is located only 140 miles from the Gulf of Mexico, tropical storms occasionally affect the city with strong winds and heavy rains. One of the fastest winds recorded, 74 mph, occurred as a tropical storm moved inland east of the city in August 1942.

Relative humidity is above 80 percent during the early morning hours most of the year, dropping to near 50 percent in the late afternoon.

San Antonio has about 50 percent of the possible amount of sunshine during the winter months and more than 70 percent during the summer months. Skies are clear to partly cloudy more than 60 percent of the time and cloudy less than 40 percent.

The first occurrence of 32 degrees Fahrenheit is in late November and the average last occurrence is in early March.

San Antonio Int'l Airport *Bexar County*   Elevation: 809 ft.   Latitude: 29° 32' N   Longitude: 98° 28' W

	JAN	FEB	MAR	APR	MAY	JUN	JUL	AUG	SEP	OCT	NOV	DEC	YEAR
Mean Maximum Temp. (°F)	63.1	67.3	73.7	80.8	87.1	92.5	95.0	96.0	90.5	82.3	72.2	64.1	80.4
Mean Temp. (°F)	51.9	55.8	62.3	69.5	77.0	82.6	84.9	85.4	79.9	71.3	61.1	53.0	69.5
Mean Minimum Temp. (°F)	40.7	44.3	50.9	58.0	66.8	72.6	74.7	74.7	69.3	60.2	49.9	41.8	58.7
Extreme Maximum Temp. (°F)	86	100	100	101	104	107	106	108	111	99	94	88	111
Extreme Minimum Temp. (°F)	13	14	19	31	43	57	64	61	46	27	23	6	6
Days Maximum Temp. ≥ 90°F	0	0	1	3	10	23	28	29	19	5	0	0	118
Days Maximum Temp. ≤ 32°F	0	0	0	0	0	0	0	0	0	0	0	0	0
Days Minimum Temp. ≤ 32°F	6	4	1	0	0	0	0	0	0	0	1	6	18
Days Minimum Temp. ≤ 0°F	0	0	0	0	0	0	0	0	0	0	0	0	0
Heating Degree Days (base 65°F)	407	276	147	38	1	0	0	0	2	31	174	382	1,458
Cooling Degree Days (base 65°F)	9	23	71	178	379	533	623	639	456	232	63	16	3,222
Mean Precipitation (in.)	1.63	1.67	2.27	2.04	4.07	4.01	2.63	2.17	2.89	4.14	2.39	1.91	31.82
Maximum Precipitation (in.)*	8.5	6.4	6.1	9.3	12.8	11.9	8.3	11.1	13.1	9.8	6.0	14.0	52.3
Minimum Precipitation (in.)*	trace	trace	trace	0.1	0.2	trace	trace	0	0.5	trace	trace	trace	13.7
Extreme Maximum Daily Precip. (in.)	2.50	2.44	2.50	3.60	6.26	5.13	9.52	5.73	3.21	11.26	3.47	5.97	11.26
Days With ≥ 0.1" Precipitation	4	3	4	3	5	5	3	3	4	5	4	3	46
Days With ≥ 0.5" Precipitation	1	1	1	1	3	3	1	1	2	2	2	1	19
Days With ≥ 1.0" Precipitation	0	0	1	1	1	1	1	1	1	1	1	0	9
Mean Snowfall (in.)	0.7	0.1	trace	trace	trace	trace	0.0	0.0	0.0	trace	trace	trace	0.8
Maximum Snowfall (in.)*	16	4	trace	0	0	0	0	0	0	trace	trace	trace	16
Maximum 24-hr. Snowfall (in.)*	13	3	trace	0	0	0	0	0	0	trace	trace	trace	13
Maximum Snow Depth (in.)	9	trace	trace	trace	trace	trace	0	0	0	trace	trace	trace	9
Days With ≥ 1.0" Snow Depth	0	0	0	0	0	0	0	0	0	0	0	0	0
Thunderstorm Days*	1	1	3	4	6	5	3	4	4	3	2	1	37
Foggy Days*	14	12	13	13	12	6	4	4	7	10	12	13	120
Predominant Sky Cover*	OVR	OVR	OVR	OVR	OVR	SCT	SCT	SCT	SCT	CLR	OVR	OVR	OVR
Mean Relative Humidity 6am (%)*	80	80	79	82	87	88	87	86	85	83	81	80	83
Mean Relative Humidity 3pm (%)*	51	48	45	48	52	49	43	42	46	46	48	50	47
Mean Dewpoint (°F)*	38	41	46	55	64	68	69	68	65	57	47	41	55
Prevailing Wind Direction*	N	N	SSE	SE	SE	SSE	SSE	SSE	SE	SSE	N	N	SSE
Prevailing Wind Speed (mph)*	10	12	12	12	12	12	10	9	9	9	10	10	10
Maximum Wind Gust (mph)*	54	56	64	74	63	58	77	49	61	54	54	48	77

Note: (*) Period of record is 1948-1995

Victoria Regional Airport

The city of Victoria is located in the south-central Texas Coastal Plain. The climate is classified as humid subtropical. Summers are hot with about 100 days with temperatures of 90 degrees or above. However, pleasant sea breezes from the nearby Gulf of Mexico make the high temperatures bearable.

Spring is characterized by mild days, brisk winds, and occasional showers and thunderstorms. Strong southeast winds begin in March, diminish in April and May, and become pleasant sea breezes in the first half of June. Thunderstorm activity increases through March and April, reaching a peak in May. Considerable cloudiness is the rule, with almost 50 percent of the days in the spring having overcast or nearly overcast skies.

The sea breeze diminishes during the summer, and at times fails altogether, and some hot nights are experienced in late June, July, and early August. High summer humidity gives way to clear, drier air in late August. Nighttime temperatures drop to pleasant levels. Thunderstorms continue, and lawns and fields remain green.

The first norther usually arrives near the beginning of fall, in late September. October and November are ideal fall months with long periods of clear days with mild temperatures and cool nights. The amount of rainfall decreases.

The winter season weather conditions alternate between clear, cold, dry periods and cloudy, mild, drizzly days as fronts move down from the north. The temperature drops below 32 degrees on an average of about a dozen mornings per year.

The normal rainfall of about 36 inches is well distributed throughout the year, with the heaviest falls coming during the growing season. Some of the smaller streams dry up in the late summer, and during occasional periods of general drought some of the larger streams may reach pool stage.

The area is subject to occasional tropical disturbances during summer and fall. Destructive winds and torrential rains may occur in these storms. Approximately 50 days per year have thunderstorms, but hail is infrequent. Destructive storms with tornados are rare.

Victoria Regional Airport *Victoria County*   Elevation: 115 ft.   Latitude: 28° 52' N   Longitude: 96° 56' W

	JAN	FEB	MAR	APR	MAY	JUN	JUL	AUG	SEP	OCT	NOV	DEC	YEAR
Mean Maximum Temp. (°F)	64.8	68.3	74.1	80.5	86.5	91.6	94.1	94.8	90.4	83.2	74.0	66.0	80.7
Mean Temp. (°F)	54.4	57.7	63.7	70.2	77.3	82.4	84.4	84.6	80.2	72.4	63.3	55.5	70.5
Mean Minimum Temp. (°F)	44.0	47.2	53.3	59.9	68.1	73.1	74.7	74.4	70.0	61.6	52.4	45.0	60.3
Extreme Maximum Temp. (°F)	85	95	97	95	99	106	103	105	111	99	93	85	111
Extreme Minimum Temp. (°F)	14	19	21	33	45	59	67	62	48	31	26	9	9
Days Maximum Temp. ≥ 90°F	0	0	0	1	8	22	28	29	20	6	0	0	114
Days Maximum Temp. ≤ 32°F	0	0	0	0	0	0	0	0	0	0	0	0	0
Days Minimum Temp. ≤ 32°F	3	2	1	0	0	0	0	0	0	0	0	3	9
Days Minimum Temp. ≤ 0°F	0	0	0	0	0	0	0	0	0	0	0	0	0
Heating Degree Days (base 65°F)	340	230	116	27	0	0	0	0	1	22	130	318	1,184
Cooling Degree Days (base 65°F)	18	32	84	191	388	528	608	616	464	259	84	31	3,303
Mean Precipitation (in.)	2.56	2.03	2.78	2.77	5.23	4.36	3.76	3.03	3.87	4.67	3.24	2.29	40.59
Maximum Precipitation (in.)*	7.8	9.1	6.9	11.1	14.7	12.7	13.6	7.7	19.0	10.5	8.7	7.0	56.7
Minimum Precipitation (in.)*	trace	0.2	trace	trace	0.7	trace	0.1	0.3	0.8	0.3	trace	0.4	14.3
Extreme Maximum Daily Precip. (in.)	3.14	2.69	4.35	9.87	7.65	3.94	7.58	4.07	3.65	6.46	6.94	3.55	9.87
Days With ≥ 0.1" Precipitation	4	4	4	3	5	5	5	5	6	5	4	4	54
Days With ≥ 0.5" Precipitation	2	1	2	1	3	3	2	2	3	3	2	1	25
Days With ≥ 1.0" Precipitation	1	1	1	1	2	2	1	1	1	2	1	1	15
Mean Snowfall (in.)	na	na	na	na	na	na	na	na	na	na	na	na	na
Maximum Snowfall (in.)*	2	3	trace	0	0	0	0	0	0	0	trace	trace	3
Maximum 24-hr. Snowfall (in.)*	2	3	trace	0	0	0	0	0	0	0	trace	trace	3
Maximum Snow Depth (in.)	na	na	na	na	na	na	na	na	na	na	na	na	na
Days With ≥ 1.0" Snow Depth	na	na	na	na	na	na	na	na	na	na	na	na	na
Thunderstorm Days*	1	2	3	4	6	6	7	9	8	4	2	1	53
Foggy Days*	18	17	19	18	19	12	10	12	15	16	16	17	189
Predominant Sky Cover*	OVR	OVR	OVR	OVR	OVR	SCT	SCT	SCT	SCT	CLR	OVR	OVR	OVR
Mean Relative Humidity 6am (%)*	87	87	86	88	91	92	92	92	91	89	87	86	89
Mean Relative Humidity 3pm (%)*	59	56	54	56	59	58	53	53	56	52	54	58	56
Mean Dewpoint (°F)*	44	47	53	61	67	72	73	73	70	61	53	47	60
Prevailing Wind Direction*	N	N	SSE	SSE	SSE	SSE	S	S	SE	N	N	N	SSE
Prevailing Wind Speed (mph)*	14	14	13	14	13	12	10	10	9	10	13	13	12
Maximum Wind Gust (mph)*	59	63	59	62	68	81	99	67	54	75	55	54	99

Note: (*) Period of record is 1953-1995

Waco Madison Cooper Airport

One of the major cities of Texas, Waco is located in the rich agricultural region of the Brazos River Valley in North Central Texas. The city lies on the edge of the gently rolling Blackland Prairies. To the west lies the rolling to hilly Grand Prairie. Waco is a commercial hub with an economy based on industry, education and agriculture. Baylor University, founded in 1845, is located here. Regional agriculture includes chiefly cattle, poultry, sorghum, cotton and corn. Soils are black waxy, loam and sandy types. Lake Waco, a reservoir of 7,260 surface acres, lies within the Waco city limits, with the north shoreline approximately 0.8 mile south of the Municipal Airport.

The climate of Waco is humid subtropical with hot summers. It is a continental type climate characterized by extreme variations in temperature. Tropical maritime air masses predominate throughout the late spring, summer and early fall months, while Polar air masses frequent the area in winter. In an average year, April and May are the wettest months, while the July-August period is the driest. Most warm season rainfall occurs from thunderstorm activity. Consequently, considerable spatial variation in amounts occur.

Winters are mild. Cold fronts moving down from the High Plains often are accompanied by strong, gusty, northerly winds and sharp drops in temperature. Cold spells are of short duration, rarely lasting longer than two or three days before a rapid warming occurs. Winter precipitation is closely associated with frontal activity, and may fall as rain, freezing rain, sleet or snow. During most years, snowfall is of little or no consequence.

Daytime temperatures are hot in summer, particularly in July and August. The highest temperatures are associated with fair skies, light winds, and comparatively low humidities. There is little variety in the day-to-day weather during July and August. Air conditioning is recommended for maximum comfort indoors or while traveling.

The spring and fall seasons are very pleasant at Waco. Temperatures are comfortable. Cloudiness and showers are more frequent in the spring than in the fall. The average first occurrence of 32 degrees Fahrenheit is late November and the average last occurrence is in mid March.

Waco Madison Cooper Airport *Mclennan County*   Elevation: 500 ft.   Latitude: 31° 37' N   Longitude: 97° 14' W

	JAN	FEB	MAR	APR	MAY	JUN	JUL	AUG	SEP	OCT	NOV	DEC	YEAR
Mean Maximum Temp. (°F)	58.7	62.4	69.8	78.0	85.3	92.3	97.0	97.4	90.3	80.2	68.9	59.5	78.3
Mean Temp. (°F)	47.7	51.3	58.6	66.4	74.7	81.7	85.7	85.8	78.6	68.6	57.8	48.7	67.1
Mean Minimum Temp. (°F)	36.6	40.1	47.4	54.7	64.0	71.0	74.4	74.1	66.8	56.8	46.7	37.8	55.9
Extreme Maximum Temp. (°F)	86	96	97	98	102	109	109	109	111	101	92	87	111
Extreme Minimum Temp. (°F)	6	4	16	26	37	54	60	53	40	25	22	-4	-4
Days Maximum Temp. ≥ 90°F	0	0	0	2	8	22	29	29	18	5	0	0	113
Days Maximum Temp. ≤ 32°F	0	0	0	0	0	0	0	0	0	0	0	1	1
Days Minimum Temp. ≤ 32°F	11	6	2	0	0	0	0	0	0	0	3	10	32
Days Minimum Temp. ≤ 0°F	0	0	0	0	0	0	0	0	0	0	0	0	0
Heating Degree Days (base 65°F)	534	391	230	73	5	0	0	0	5	56	247	506	2,047
Cooling Degree Days (base 65°F)	4	9	39	122	313	507	648	650	419	174	38	7	2,930
Mean Precipitation (in.)	2.02	2.58	3.07	2.69	4.41	3.25	1.68	1.89	2.81	3.89	2.86	2.81	33.96
Maximum Precipitation (in.)*	5.8	6.3	5.6	13.4	15.0	12.1	8.6	8.9	7.3	10.5	6.2	8.4	48.9
Minimum Precipitation (in.)*	trace	0.2	trace	0.1	0.6	0.3	0	trace	0	0	0.1	trace	14.9
Extreme Maximum Daily Precip. (in.)	3.21	3.97	3.15	5.07	4.23	3.37	4.93	3.76	3.51	3.60	2.99	7.98	7.98
Days With ≥ 0.1" Precipitation	4	4	5	4	5	5	3	3	4	5	5	4	51
Days With ≥ 0.5" Precipitation	1	2	2	2	3	2	1	1	2	3	2	2	23
Days With ≥ 1.0" Precipitation	0	1	1	1	1	1	0	1	1	1	1	1	10
Mean Snowfall (in.)	0.3	na	0.1	0.2	trace	0.0	0.0	trace	0.0	trace	0.2	trace	na
Maximum Snowfall (in.)*	7	5	1	0	0	0	0	0	0	trace	2	1	7
Maximum 24-hr. Snowfall (in.)*	7	4	1	0	0	0	0	0	0	trace	2	1	7
Maximum Snow Depth (in.)	4	na	1	1	trace	0	0	trace	0	trace	2	trace	na
Days With ≥ 1.0" Snow Depth	0	na	0	0	0	0	0	0	0	0	0	0	na
Thunderstorm Days*	1	2	4	6	8	6	4	4	4	3	2	1	45
Foggy Days*	12	11	11	11	11	5	3	4	8	10	11	12	109
Predominant Sky Cover*	OVR	OVR	OVR	OVR	OVR	CLR	CLR	SCT	CLR	CLR	CLR	OVR	CLR
Mean Relative Humidity 6am (%)*	83	83	81	84	88	86	83	82	85	84	83	82	83
Mean Relative Humidity 3pm (%)*	56	53	49	52	54	49	42	40	46	47	50	54	49
Mean Dewpoint (°F)*	36	39	45	54	63	68	69	68	64	55	45	38	54
Prevailing Wind Direction*	S	S	S	S	S	S	S	S	S	S	S	S	S
Prevailing Wind Speed (mph)*	13	13	15	15	14	14	13	12	13	12	13	13	13
Maximum Wind Gust (mph)*	54	60	75	87	61	61	49	54	60	64	58	66	87

Note: (*) Period of record is 1948-1995

Wichita Falls Municipal Airport

Wichita Falls is located in the West Cross Timbers subdivision of the North Central Plains of Texas, about 10 miles south of the Red River and 400 miles northwest of the nearest portion of the Gulf of Mexico. The topography is gently rolling mesquite plain, and the elevation of the area is about 1,000 feet.

This region lies between the humid subtropical climate of east Texas and a continental climate to the north and west. The climate of Wichita Falls is classified as continental. It is characterized by rapid changes in temperature, large daily and annual temperature extremes, and by rather erratic rainfall.

The area lies in the path of polar air masses which move down from the north during the winter season. With the passage of cold fronts or northers in the fall and winter, abrupt drops in temperature of as much as 20 to 30 degrees within an hour sometimes occur. January, the coldest month, has an average temperature around 40 degrees.

The summers in Wichita Falls are generally of the continental climate type, characterized by low humidity and windy conditions. Temperatures over 100 degrees are frequent during the common periods of hot weather. July and August, the hottest months, have average temperatures in the middle 80s.

The normal rainfall is nearly 27 inches per year, but the distribution is erratic. Several lakes in the area provide water for domestic, industrial, and irrigation purposes. The greater part of the rainfall comes in the form of showers rather than general rains. Over 75 percent of the annual moisture occurs during the period from late March to mid November, but dry periods of three to four weeks are to be expected during this time almost every year. Moderate flooding along Holliday Creek and the Wichita River, which run through the city, occur about once in each ten-year period. Snowfall, measuring an inch or more, occurs on average only two days a year.

Wind speeds average over 11 mph, and southerly winds prevail. Rather strong winds are observed in all months.

Wichita Falls Municipal Airport *Wichita County*   Elevation: 1,029 ft.   Latitude: 33° 59' N   Longitude: 98° 30' W

	JAN	FEB	MAR	APR	MAY	JUN	JUL	AUG	SEP	OCT	NOV	DEC	YEAR
Mean Maximum Temp. (°F)	54.4	58.6	67.1	75.9	83.7	91.5	97.4	96.7	88.2	77.0	65.0	54.7	75.8
Mean Temp. (°F)	42.5	46.4	54.4	62.9	72.0	80.0	85.1	84.5	76.1	64.8	53.0	43.2	63.7
Mean Minimum Temp. (°F)	30.6	34.2	41.7	49.9	60.3	68.3	72.7	72.2	64.0	52.6	41.0	31.6	51.6
Extreme Maximum Temp. (°F)	85	93	98	102	110	117	114	110	111	102	89	83	117
Extreme Minimum Temp. (°F)	2	-8	8	27	39	51	58	53	38	21	15	-7	-8
Days Maximum Temp. ≥ 90°F	0	0	1	2	8	20	28	27	15	3	0	0	104
Days Maximum Temp. ≤ 32°F	2	1	0	0	0	0	0	0	0	0	0	2	5
Days Minimum Temp. ≤ 32°F	19	12	5	1	0	0	0	0	0	0	6	17	60
Days Minimum Temp. ≤ 0°F	0	0	0	0	0	0	0	0	0	0	0	0	0
Heating Degree Days (base 65°F)	691	522	343	132	20	0	0	0	12	104	366	670	2,860
Cooling Degree Days (base 65°F)	1	2	22	75	244	456	630	610	352	106	13	1	2,512
Mean Precipitation (in.)	1.13	1.69	2.19	2.48	3.87	4.04	1.49	2.46	2.88	3.11	1.69	1.68	28.71
Maximum Precipitation (in.)*	4.5	4.5	5.4	8.5	13.2	8.6	11.9	7.6	10.2	7.9	5.7	6.9	41.6
Minimum Precipitation (in.)*	0	trace	trace	0.3	trace	0.3	trace	trace	trace	trace	0	trace	16.1
Extreme Maximum Daily Precip. (in.)	2.11	1.88	3.60	5.20	4.54	5.36	2.01	3.65	6.19	4.34	2.06	2.25	6.19
Days With ≥ 0.1" Precipitation	2	3	4	4	5	5	3	4	4	4	3	3	44
Days With ≥ 0.5" Precipitation	1	1	1	2	3	3	1	2	2	2	1	1	20
Days With ≥ 1.0" Precipitation	0	0	1	1	1	1	0	1	1	1	1	0	8
Mean Snowfall (in.)	1.7	0.8	0.5	trace	trace	trace	trace	0.0	0.0	0.0	0.2	1.0	4.2
Maximum Snowfall (in.)*	12	12	11	1	0	0	0	0	0	1	4	7	17
Maximum 24-hr. Snowfall (in.)*	8	4	10	1	0	0	0	0	0	1	4	6	10
Maximum Snow Depth (in.)	5	8	10	trace	trace	trace	trace	0	0	1	2	8	10
Days With ≥ 1.0" Snow Depth	1	1	0	0	0	0	0	0	0	0	0	0	2
Thunderstorm Days*	1	1	3	5	9	7	5	5	4	3	2	1	46
Foggy Days*	9	9	8	7	7	4	2	3	6	6	7	9	77
Predominant Sky Cover*	OVR	OVR	CLR	CLR	OVR	CLR	CLR	CLR	CLR	CLR	CLR	CLR	CLR
Mean Relative Humidity 6am (%)*	79	78	76	78	85	83	78	78	83	81	79	78	80
Mean Relative Humidity 3pm (%)*	48	47	42	42	47	44	38	38	44	43	44	47	44
Mean Dewpoint (°F)*	28	32	37	47	58	64	65	64	60	50	38	30	48
Prevailing Wind Direction*	N	N	S	S	SSE	SSE	S	S	SSE	S	S	S	S
Prevailing Wind Speed (mph)*	14	14	15	15	14	14	13	12	12	13	13	12	13
Maximum Wind Gust (mph)*	62	75	69	69	90	79	74	81	69	68	62	61	90

Note: (*) Period of record is 1948-1995

Albany *Shackelford County*   Elevation: 1,419 ft.   Latitude: 32° 44' N   Longitude: 99° 18' W

	JAN	FEB	MAR	APR	MAY	JUN	JUL	AUG	SEP	OCT	NOV	DEC	YEAR
Mean Maximum Temp. (°F)	58.2	61.6	69.7	78.1	84.7	91.0	95.3	95.4	88.0	78.9	67.9	58.6	77.3
Mean Temp. (°F)	45.4	48.6	56.2	64.1	72.3	79.2	83.0	82.7	75.1	65.5	54.9	46.0	64.4
Mean Minimum Temp. (°F)	32.5	35.6	42.6	50.1	59.7	67.3	70.8	69.9	62.2	52.0	41.9	33.4	51.5
Extreme Maximum Temp. (°F)	89	96	97	102	113	111	108	109	111	102	94	86	113
Extreme Minimum Temp. (°F)	7	3	8	27	35	49	57	55	37	19	14	-6	-6
Days Maximum Temp. ≥ 90°F	0	0	1	3	9	19	27	26	14	3	0	0	102
Days Maximum Temp. ≤ 32°F	1	1	0	0	0	0	0	0	0	0	0	1	3
Days Minimum Temp. ≤ 32°F	16	11	5	1	0	0	0	0	0	1	6	15	55
Days Minimum Temp. ≤ 0°F	0	0	0	0	0	0	0	0	0	0	0	0	0
Heating Degree Days (base 65°F)	601	462	295	111	19	1	0	0	13	92	317	584	2,495
Cooling Degree Days (base 65°F)	1	6	29	92	251	433	566	555	324	113	20	2	2,392
Mean Precipitation (in.)	1.01	1.89	2.28	2.44	3.81	4.00	1.99	2.04	2.56	2.87	1.93	1.55	28.37
Extreme Maximum Daily Precip. (in.)	1.38	1.92	2.49	5.85	4.39	3.97	2.60	3.95	2.60	3.87	2.40	2.39	5.85
Days With ≥ 0.1" Precipitation	3	3	4	3	5	5	3	3	3	4	3	2	41
Days With ≥ 0.5" Precipitation	1	1	2	2	3	3	2	1	2	2	1	1	21
Days With ≥ 1.0" Precipitation	0	1	1	1	1	1	1	1	1	1	1	0	10
Mean Snowfall (in.)	0.6	0.6	0.3	0.1	0.0	0.0	0.0	0.0	0.0	0.0	0.4	0.8	2.8
Maximum Snow Depth (in.)	1	2	7	3	0	0	0	0	0	0	3	5	7
Days With ≥ 1.0" Snow Depth	0	0	0	0	0	0	0	0	0	0	0	0	0

Alice *Jim Wells County*   Elevation: 201 ft.   Latitude: 27° 44' N   Longitude: 98° 04' W

	JAN	FEB	MAR	APR	MAY	JUN	JUL	AUG	SEP	OCT	NOV	DEC	YEAR
Mean Maximum Temp. (°F)	68.0	72.0	78.2	84.7	89.3	94.4	96.3	96.8	92.2	85.5	77.4	69.4	83.7
Mean Temp. (°F)	56.8	60.7	66.8	73.1	79.2	83.8	85.3	85.7	81.6	74.3	66.2	58.2	72.6
Mean Minimum Temp. (°F)	45.6	49.3	55.3	61.6	69.0	73.3	74.2	74.5	70.9	63.0	55.0	46.9	61.5
Extreme Maximum Temp. (°F)	91	100	102	107	108	111	106	105	110	98	97	90	111
Extreme Minimum Temp. (°F)	19	25	23	37	52	57	65	65	52	28	28	12	12
Days Maximum Temp. ≥ 90°F	0	1	2	8	16	26	29	29	22	10	1	0	144
Days Maximum Temp. ≤ 32°F	0	0	0	0	0	0	0	0	0	0	0	0	0
Days Minimum Temp. ≤ 32°F	2	1	0	0	0	0	0	0	0	0	0	2	5
Days Minimum Temp. ≤ 0°F	0	0	0	0	0	0	0	0	0	0	0	0	0
Heating Degree Days (base 65°F)	275	177	78	16	1	0	0	0	0	14	96	253	910
Cooling Degree Days (base 65°F)	28	59	139	267	448	572	635	650	505	309	138	50	3,800
Mean Precipitation (in.)	1.17	1.47	1.46	1.27	3.05	2.74	2.92	2.67	4.05	3.03	1.68	1.13	26.64
Extreme Maximum Daily Precip. (in.)	1.60	2.35	3.00	4.37	6.64	4.96	4.92	7.30	5.23	6.80	5.50	3.45	7.30
Days With ≥ 0.1" Precipitation	2	3	3	2	4	4	3	3	4	3	2	2	35
Days With ≥ 0.5" Precipitation	1	1	1	1	2	2	2	2	2	2	1	1	18
Days With ≥ 1.0" Precipitation	0	1	0	0	1	1	1	1	1	1	0	0	7
Mean Snowfall (in.)	0.0	0.0	0.0	0.0	0.0	0.0	0.0	0.0	0.0	0.0	0.0	0.3	0.3
Maximum Snow Depth (in.)	0	0	0	0	0	0	0	0	0	0	0	0	0
Days With ≥ 1.0" Snow Depth	0	0	0	0	0	0	0	0	0	0	0	0	0

Alpine *Brewster County*   Elevation: 4,529 ft.   Latitude: 30° 22' N   Longitude: 103° 40' W

	JAN	FEB	MAR	APR	MAY	JUN	JUL	AUG	SEP	OCT	NOV	DEC	YEAR
Mean Maximum Temp. (°F)	61.6	65.4	71.6	79.0	86.3	90.6	89.3	87.6	83.8	77.8	68.7	61.6	76.9
Mean Temp. (°F)	47.0	50.2	55.5	62.7	71.0	76.5	76.7	75.2	70.6	63.3	54.0	47.1	62.5
Mean Minimum Temp. (°F)	32.4	35.0	39.4	46.4	55.7	62.3	63.9	62.7	57.4	48.8	39.2	32.6	48.0
Extreme Maximum Temp. (°F)	80	84	89	96	101	106	103	100	100	97	86	79	106
Extreme Minimum Temp. (°F)	2	-1	10	20	34	45	53	51	36	21	14	-3	-3
Days Maximum Temp. ≥ 90°F	0	0	0	1	10	18	16	13	6	1	0	0	65
Days Maximum Temp. ≤ 32°F	0	0	0	0	0	0	0	0	0	0	0	0	0
Days Minimum Temp. ≤ 32°F	16	11	7	2	0	0	0	0	0	1	7	15	59
Days Minimum Temp. ≤ 0°F	0	0	0	0	0	0	0	0	0	0	0	0	0
Heating Degree Days (base 65°F)	549	412	296	121	na	0	0	0	17	105	326	546	na
Cooling Degree Days (base 65°F)	0	1	7	59	na	352	369	323	192	57	4	0	na
Mean Precipitation (in.)	0.46	0.64	0.45	0.62	1.28	2.67	2.65	3.06	2.77	1.55	0.51	0.63	17.29
Extreme Maximum Daily Precip. (in.)	0.96	2.71	1.35	1.40	1.00	3.77	2.31	3.92	2.61	1.81	1.32	1.02	3.92
Days With ≥ 0.1" Precipitation	1	1	1	1	3	5	5	6	5	3	1	1	33
Days With ≥ 0.5" Precipitation	0	0	0	0	1	2	2	2	2	1	0	0	10
Days With ≥ 1.0" Precipitation	0	0	0	0	0	1	1	1	1	0	0	0	4
Mean Snowfall (in.)	0.4	0.1	trace	trace	0.0	0.0	0.0	0.0	0.0	trace	0.4	0.3	1.2
Maximum Snow Depth (in.)	2	na	trace	trace	0	0	0	0	0	na	na	3	na
Days With ≥ 1.0" Snow Depth	0	0	0	0	0	0	0	0	0	0	0	0	0

Amistad Dam *Val Verde County*   Elevation: 1,157 ft.   Latitude: 29° 28' N   Longitude: 101° 02' W

	JAN	FEB	MAR	APR	MAY	JUN	JUL	AUG	SEP	OCT	NOV	DEC	YEAR
Mean Maximum Temp. (°F)	63.5	68.2	75.8	83.6	90.1	95.2	97.6	97.7	91.5	82.3	72.1	63.4	81.7
Mean Temp. (°F)	51.9	56.1	63.5	71.0	78.4	84.0	86.0	86.0	80.3	71.1	60.8	52.2	70.1
Mean Minimum Temp. (°F)	40.2	44.1	51.2	58.3	66.7	72.6	74.4	74.3	69.0	59.9	49.5	41.0	58.4
Extreme Maximum Temp. (°F)	88	98	99	105	109	113	114	110	110	98	95	90	114
Extreme Minimum Temp. (°F)	17	17	24	34	48	60	63	65	47	30	29	9	9
Days Maximum Temp. ≥ 90°F	0	0	2	8	18	26	29	29	21	6	0	0	139
Days Maximum Temp. ≤ 32°F	0	0	0	0	0	0	0	0	0	0	0	0	0
Days Minimum Temp. ≤ 32°F	5	2	1	0	0	0	0	0	0	0	0	4	12
Days Minimum Temp. ≤ 0°F	0	0	0	0	0	0	0	0	0	0	0	0	0
Heating Degree Days (base 65°F)	402	258	120	29	1	0	0	0	2	27	165	393	1,397
Cooling Degree Days (base 65°F)	2	14	81	215	425	575	658	658	466	224	46	3	3,367
Mean Precipitation (in.)	0.67	0.75	1.17	1.12	2.47	1.94	1.81	2.02	2.69	1.87	1.12	0.70	18.33
Extreme Maximum Daily Precip. (in.)	1.04	1.53	2.53	2.10	2.49	3.45	5.58	7.10	4.10	4.38	1.50	2.16	7.10
Days With ≥ 0.1" Precipitation	2	2	2	2	4	3	3	3	3	3	2	2	31
Days With ≥ 0.5" Precipitation	1	0	1	1	2	1	1	1	2	1	1	0	12
Days With ≥ 1.0" Precipitation	0	0	0	0	1	1	1	1	1	0	0	0	5
Mean Snowfall (in.)	0.2	0.0	0.0	0.0	0.0	0.0	0.0	0.0	0.0	0.0	0.0	0.0	0.2
Maximum Snow Depth (in.)	3	0	0	0	0	0	0	0	0	0	0	0	3
Days With ≥ 1.0" Snow Depth	0	0	0	0	0	0	0	0	0	0	0	0	0

The period of record for all cooperative weather station data is 1980 – 2009. See User Guide for detailed explanation of data.

Anahuac *Chambers County*   Elevation: 23 ft.   Latitude: 29° 47' N   Longitude: 94° 40' W

	JAN	FEB	MAR	APR	MAY	JUN	JUL	AUG	SEP	OCT	NOV	DEC	YEAR
Mean Maximum Temp. (°F)	61.8	64.7	71.0	77.2	84.0	89.3	91.5	92.1	88.4	80.7	71.8	63.4	78.0
Mean Temp. (°F)	52.2	55.3	61.4	67.9	75.3	81.0	83.1	83.1	78.7	70.1	61.6	53.7	68.6
Mean Minimum Temp. (°F)	42.6	45.8	51.7	58.5	66.6	72.6	74.7	74.0	68.9	59.4	51.4	43.9	59.2
Extreme Maximum Temp. (°F)	82	82	85	93	97	102	103	103	105	100	89	81	105
Extreme Minimum Temp. (°F)	16	21	24	36	48	56	64	60	50	33	28	8	8
Days Maximum Temp. ≥ 90°F	0	0	0	0	3	15	23	24	14	2	0	0	81
Days Maximum Temp. ≤ 32°F	0	0	0	0	0	0	0	0	0	0	0	0	0
Days Minimum Temp. ≤ 32°F	4	2	1	0	0	0	0	0	0	0	1	3	11
Days Minimum Temp. ≤ 0°F	0	0	0	0	0	0	0	0	0	0	0	0	0
Heating Degree Days (base 65°F)	397	282	152	41	1	0	0	0	1	34	157	363	1,428
Cooling Degree Days (base 65°F)	9	13	47	133	329	487	569	568	418	199	62	18	2,852
Mean Precipitation (in.)	4.65	3.00	3.56	3.63	5.28	6.45	5.18	5.12	6.38	5.13	4.10	4.46	56.94
Extreme Maximum Daily Precip. (in.)	6.26	3.50	7.55	8.06	7.20	13.20	9.80	6.10	6.00	8.20	5.50	6.55	13.20
Days With ≥ 0.1" Precipitation	6	5	5	4	5	7	7	7	7	5	5	6	69
Days With ≥ 0.5" Precipitation	3	2	2	2	3	3	3	3	3	3	3	3	33
Days With ≥ 1.0" Precipitation	1	1	1	1	2	2	2	2	2	2	1	1	18
Mean Snowfall (in.)	0.0	trace	0.0	0.0	0.0	0.0	0.0	0.0	0.0	0.0	0.0	trace	trace
Maximum Snow Depth (in.)	0	trace	0	0	0	0	0	0	0	0	0	trace	trace
Days With ≥ 1.0" Snow Depth	0	0	0	0	0	0	0	0	0	0	0	0	0

Angleton 2 W *Brazoria County*   Elevation: 26 ft.   Latitude: 29° 09' N   Longitude: 95° 27' W

	JAN	FEB	MAR	APR	MAY	JUN	JUL	AUG	SEP	OCT	NOV	DEC	YEAR
Mean Maximum Temp. (°F)	63.7	66.4	71.9	77.6	83.8	89.1	91.4	92.0	88.3	81.2	73.0	65.5	78.7
Mean Temp. (°F)	53.9	57.0	62.7	68.4	75.4	80.6	82.6	82.8	78.9	71.1	62.9	55.6	69.3
Mean Minimum Temp. (°F)	44.1	47.5	53.4	59.0	66.9	72.0	73.6	73.5	69.5	60.9	52.8	45.8	59.9
Extreme Maximum Temp. (°F)	81	86	88	93	98	98	100	101	107	95	90	88	107
Extreme Minimum Temp. (°F)	15	20	22	31	44	55	62	60	49	30	27	7	7
Days Maximum Temp. ≥ 90°F	0	0	0	0	2	14	23	25	13	2	0	0	79
Days Maximum Temp. ≤ 32°F	0	0	0	0	0	0	0	0	0	0	0	0	0
Days Minimum Temp. ≤ 32°F	3	2	1	0	0	0	0	0	0	0	1	3	10
Days Minimum Temp. ≤ 0°F	0	0	0	0	0	0	0	0	0	0	0	0	0
Heating Degree Days (base 65°F)	352	246	130	38	1	0	0	0	1	28	134	313	1,243
Cooling Degree Days (base 65°F)	14	26	66	145	330	475	551	558	426	225	79	30	2,925
Mean Precipitation (in.)	4.74	3.26	3.82	3.45	4.60	6.06	4.43	5.16	6.93	5.40	4.73	4.43	57.01
Extreme Maximum Daily Precip. (in.)	4.86	3.49	4.75	8.62	8.30	12.36	4.40	10.30	11.42	10.65	5.25	11.00	12.36
Days With ≥ 0.1" Precipitation	6	6	5	4	5	6	6	6	7	6	5	6	68
Days With ≥ 0.5" Precipitation	3	2	2	2	3	3	3	3	4	3	3	3	34
Days With ≥ 1.0" Precipitation	1	1	1	1	2	2	2	1	2	2	1	1	17
Mean Snowfall (in.)	0.0	trace	0.0	0.0	0.0	0.0	0.0	0.0	0.0	0.0	0.0	trace	trace
Maximum Snow Depth (in.)	0	trace	0	0	0	0	0	0	0	0	0	trace	trace
Days With ≥ 1.0" Snow Depth	0	0	0	0	0	0	0	0	0	0	0	0	0

Anson *Jones County*   Elevation: 1,709 ft.   Latitude: 32° 46' N   Longitude: 99° 54' W

	JAN	FEB	MAR	APR	MAY	JUN	JUL	AUG	SEP	OCT	NOV	DEC	YEAR
Mean Maximum Temp. (°F)	57.8	61.0	69.4	78.8	86.1	92.3	95.9	95.4	87.9	78.3	66.5	57.4	77.2
Mean Temp. (°F)	45.4	48.6	56.1	65.1	73.7	80.5	83.9	83.5	75.8	65.9	54.3	45.5	64.9
Mean Minimum Temp. (°F)	32.7	36.3	42.9	51.3	61.2	68.6	71.9	71.5	63.8	53.5	42.1	33.5	52.4
Extreme Maximum Temp. (°F)	88	95	98	101	113	114	109	109	109	104	92	85	114
Extreme Minimum Temp. (°F)	6	-4	9	26	38	52	58	50	32	24	16	-12	-12
Days Maximum Temp. ≥ 90°F	0	0	1	4	12	20	26	26	14	3	0	0	106
Days Maximum Temp. ≤ 32°F	1	1	0	0	0	0	0	0	0	0	0	1	3
Days Minimum Temp. ≤ 32°F	15	10	4	1	0	0	0	0	0	0	5	13	48
Days Minimum Temp. ≤ 0°F	0	0	0	0	0	0	0	0	0	0	0	0	0
Heating Degree Days (base 65°F)	604	460	296	99	16	0	0	0	13	88	331	599	2,506
Cooling Degree Days (base 65°F)	1	5	28	109	294	471	592	579	345	123	17	1	2,565
Mean Precipitation (in.)	1.04	1.70	1.64	1.85	3.34	3.80	2.02	2.68	2.82	2.53	1.69	1.47	26.58
Extreme Maximum Daily Precip. (in.)	1.87	2.70	2.00	2.30	3.10	4.63	3.50	2.73	5.60	2.51	2.10	2.67	5.60
Days With ≥ 0.1" Precipitation	2	3	3	3	5	5	3	4	4	4	3	3	42
Days With ≥ 0.5" Precipitation	1	1	1	1	2	3	1	2	2	2	1	1	18
Days With ≥ 1.0" Precipitation	0	0	0	1	1	1	1	1	1	1	0	0	7
Mean Snowfall (in.)	1.1	0.5	0.3	0.5	0.0	0.0	0.0	0.0	0.0	0.0	1.0	1.2	4.6
Maximum Snow Depth (in.)	4	4	4	8	0	0	0	0	0	0	8	4	8
Days With ≥ 1.0" Snow Depth	0	1	0	0	0	0	0	0	0	0	0	1	2

Aransas Wildlife Refuge *Aransas County*   Elevation: 15 ft.   Latitude: 28° 16' N   Longitude: 96° 48' W

	JAN	FEB	MAR	APR	MAY	JUN	JUL	AUG	SEP	OCT	NOV	DEC	YEAR
Mean Maximum Temp. (°F)	64.3	66.9	72.5	77.8	83.2	88.1	89.8	90.5	87.7	81.7	73.8	65.4	78.5
Mean Temp. (°F)	55.4	58.3	64.3	70.5	77.2	82.0	83.4	83.7	80.3	73.5	65.3	56.5	70.9
Mean Minimum Temp. (°F)	46.4	49.7	56.1	63.2	71.2	75.8	76.9	76.8	72.7	65.1	56.6	47.5	63.2
Extreme Maximum Temp. (°F)	80	86	91	94	102	97	98	99	102	99	96	82	102
Extreme Minimum Temp. (°F)	17	20	22	30	47	60	67	65	51	28	28	9	9
Days Maximum Temp. ≥ 90°F	0	0	0	0	1	8	18	22	10	1	0	0	60
Days Maximum Temp. ≤ 32°F	0	0	0	0	0	0	0	0	0	0	0	0	0
Days Minimum Temp. ≤ 32°F	2	1	1	0	0	0	0	0	0	0	0	2	6
Days Minimum Temp. ≤ 0°F	0	0	0	0	0	0	0	0	0	0	0	0	0
Heating Degree Days (base 65°F)	303	206	95	21	0	0	0	0	0	15	94	286	1,020
Cooling Degree Days (base 65°F)	14	24	81	193	387	518	578	586	464	286	111	28	3,270
Mean Precipitation (in.)	3.10	2.61	2.71	1.76	4.34	3.78	3.82	3.40	4.23	4.46	3.54	2.13	39.88
Extreme Maximum Daily Precip. (in.)	3.34	10.73	4.74	4.20	8.80	7.31	7.02	3.50	7.45	7.00	7.40	3.98	10.73
Days With ≥ 0.1" Precipitation	4	4	3	3	4	4	3	4	5	4	4	4	46
Days With ≥ 0.5" Precipitation	2	1	1	1	2	2	2	2	2	2	2	1	20
Days With ≥ 1.0" Precipitation	1	1	1	1	1	1	1	1	1	1	1	0	11
Mean Snowfall (in.)	trace	trace	trace	0.0	0.0	0.0	0.0	0.0	0.0	0.0	0.0	0.2	0.2
Maximum Snow Depth (in.)	trace	trace	trace	0	0	0	0	0	0	0	0	0	trace
Days With ≥ 1.0" Snow Depth	0	0	0	0	0	0	0	0	0	0	0	0	0

The period of record for all cooperative weather station data is 1980 – 2009. See User Guide for detailed explanation of data.

Athens *Henderson County*   Elevation: 448 ft.   Latitude: 32° 10' N   Longitude: 95° 50' W

	JAN	FEB	MAR	APR	MAY	JUN	JUL	AUG	SEP	OCT	NOV	DEC	YEAR
Mean Maximum Temp. (°F)	57.7	62.3	69.5	76.6	83.0	89.3	93.4	94.9	88.6	78.5	67.6	58.7	76.7
Mean Temp. (°F)	46.7	50.7	57.7	64.7	72.6	79.2	82.5	83.0	76.7	66.6	56.3	47.7	65.4
Mean Minimum Temp. (°F)	35.6	39.0	45.8	52.8	62.1	69.1	71.5	71.1	64.8	54.6	44.9	36.6	54.0
Extreme Maximum Temp. (°F)	84	93	90	93	97	101	106	108	109	97	88	84	109
Extreme Minimum Temp. (°F)	-5	-6	15	25	39	41	54	55	38	26	18	-2	-6
Days Maximum Temp. ≥ 90°F	0	0	0	0	3	16	26	26	15	2	0	0	88
Days Maximum Temp. ≤ 32°F	0	0	0	0	0	0	0	0	0	0	0	1	1
Days Minimum Temp. ≤ 32°F	13	8	3	0	0	0	0	0	0	0	4	12	40
Days Minimum Temp. ≤ 0°F	0	0	0	0	0	0	0	0	0	0	0	0	0
Heating Degree Days (base 65°F)	565	408	249	86	9	0	0	0	5	73	277	537	2,209
Cooling Degree Days (base 65°F)	4	8	30	85	251	433	549	565	364	130	23	7	2,449
Mean Precipitation (in.)	3.09	3.88	4.01	3.23	4.91	4.27	2.01	2.35	2.49	4.96	3.81	3.78	42.79
Extreme Maximum Daily Precip. (in.)	5.23	4.08	3.72	7.19	6.28	3.90	3.81	4.63	*3.06*	4.96	3.65	3.58	*7.19*
Days With ≥ 0.1" Precipitation	5	5	5	4	5	5	3	3	3	5	5	5	53
Days With ≥ 0.5" Precipitation	2	2	3	2	3	3	1	1	2	3	2	3	27
Days With ≥ 1.0" Precipitation	1	1	2	1	2	2	1	1	1	2	2	1	17
Mean Snowfall (in.)	0.3	0.3	trace	0.0	0.0	0.0	0.0	0.0	0.0	0.0	0.0	0.2	0.8
Maximum Snow Depth (in.)	2	2	1	0	0	0	0	0	0	0	0	3	3
Days With ≥ 1.0" Snow Depth	0	0	0	0	0	0	0	0	0	0	0	0	0

Bakersfield *Pecos County*   Elevation: 2,540 ft.   Latitude: 30° 53' N   Longitude: 102° 19' W

	JAN	FEB	MAR	APR	MAY	JUN	JUL	AUG	SEP	OCT	NOV	DEC	YEAR
Mean Maximum Temp. (°F)	60.8	65.4	73.2	81.8	89.4	94.2	95.8	94.8	89.1	79.7	69.5	61.1	79.6
Mean Temp. (°F)	47.2	51.7	59.0	67.3	75.9	81.9	83.9	83.0	76.9	67.3	56.3	47.6	66.5
Mean Minimum Temp. (°F)	33.6	37.9	44.8	52.7	62.3	69.5	71.9	71.1	64.7	54.9	43.0	34.0	53.4
Extreme Maximum Temp. (°F)	86	91	97	101	111	114	110	107	108	102	91	86	114
Extreme Minimum Temp. (°F)	10	3	12	26	40	51	60	57	39	24	14	5	3
Days Maximum Temp. ≥ 90°F	0	0	1	7	16	23	28	27	16	4	0	0	122
Days Maximum Temp. ≤ 32°F	1	0	0	0	0	0	0	0	0	0	0	1	2
Days Minimum Temp. ≤ 32°F	14	8	3	0	0	0	0	0	0	0	5	14	44
Days Minimum Temp. ≤ 0°F	0	0	0	0	0	0	0	0	0	0	0	0	0
Heating Degree Days (base 65°F)	544	374	216	71	7	0	0	0	7	65	274	533	2,091
Cooling Degree Days (base 65°F)	0	4	38	145	352	513	592	564	371	144	18	0	2,741
Mean Precipitation (in.)	0.61	0.68	0.62	1.12	1.61	1.69	1.18	1.57	2.32	2.09	0.72	0.63	14.84
Extreme Maximum Daily Precip. (in.)	1.90	2.51	1.40	7.10	2.24	2.44	2.77	1.93	4.28	4.46	2.76	1.35	7.10
Days With ≥ 0.1" Precipitation	2	2	2	2	3	3	2	3	3	3	2	2	29
Days With ≥ 0.5" Precipitation	0	0	0	1	1	1	1	1	2	1	1	0	9
Days With ≥ 1.0" Precipitation	0	0	0	0	1	0	0	0	1	1	0	0	3
Mean Snowfall (in.)	0.7	trace	trace	0.0	0.0	0.0	0.0	0.0	0.0	trace	0.6	0.3	1.6
Maximum Snow Depth (in.)	5	1	trace	0	0	0	0	0	0	1	5	5	5
Days With ≥ 1.0" Snow Depth	0	0	0	0	0	0	0	0	0	0	0	0	0

Ballinger 2 NW *Runnels County*   Elevation: 1,754 ft.   Latitude: 31° 44' N   Longitude: 99° 59' W

	JAN	FEB	MAR	APR	MAY	JUN	JUL	AUG	SEP	OCT	NOV	DEC	YEAR
Mean Maximum Temp. (°F)	60.0	64.7	72.1	80.9	87.3	92.3	95.3	94.8	88.3	79.8	68.9	60.1	78.7
Mean Temp. (°F)	46.2	50.5	58.0	66.3	74.4	80.4	83.2	82.8	75.9	66.7	55.7	46.7	65.6
Mean Minimum Temp. (°F)	32.4	36.3	43.9	51.5	61.5	68.5	71.0	70.7	63.5	53.4	42.5	33.1	52.4
Extreme Maximum Temp. (°F)	90	98	97	101	110	110	110	107	107	100	92	88	110
Extreme Minimum Temp. (°F)	3	-3	8	26	40	48	56	51	38	22	16	-3	-3
Days Maximum Temp. ≥ 90°F	0	0	1	6	13	21	27	26	14	4	0	0	112
Days Maximum Temp. ≤ 32°F	1	0	0	0	0	0	0	0	0	0	0	1	2
Days Minimum Temp. ≤ 32°F	16	10	4	1	0	0	0	0	0	0	5	15	51
Days Minimum Temp. ≤ 0°F	0	0	0	0	0	0	0	0	0	0	0	0	0
Heating Degree Days (base 65°F)	577	407	244	80	9	0	0	0	8	73	293	562	2,253
Cooling Degree Days (base 65°F)	1	5	34	124	308	469	570	559	342	131	20	1	2,564
Mean Precipitation (in.)	0.94	1.51	1.94	1.36	3.38	3.37	1.46	2.37	2.73	2.48	1.44	1.14	24.12
Extreme Maximum Daily Precip. (in.)	1.02	2.15	2.98	2.47	3.52	6.78	2.76	3.36	6.19	4.04	2.94	2.90	6.78
Days With ≥ 0.1" Precipitation	2	3	4	3	4	5	3	3	4	4	3	2	40
Days With ≥ 0.5" Precipitation	1	1	1	1	2	2	1	2	2	2	1	1	17
Days With ≥ 1.0" Precipitation	0	0	0	1	1	1	0	1	1	1	0	0	5
Mean Snowfall (in.)	*0.2*	0.1	trace	0.0	0.0	0.0	0.0	0.0	0.0	0.0	0.1	0.1	*0.5*
Maximum Snow Depth (in.)	4	2	trace	0	0	0	0	0	0	0	trace	2	4
Days With ≥ 1.0" Snow Depth	0	0	0	0	0	0	0	0	0	0	0	0	0

Balmorhea *Reeves County*   Elevation: 3,219 ft.   Latitude: 30° 59' N   Longitude: 103° 44' W

	JAN	FEB	MAR	APR	MAY	JUN	JUL	AUG	SEP	OCT	NOV	DEC	YEAR
Mean Maximum Temp. (°F)	61.2	66.2	73.2	81.1	89.2	94.9	95.1	93.3	87.2	79.6	69.9	60.9	79.3
Mean Temp. (°F)	46.0	50.1	56.3	64.2	73.0	79.7	81.0	79.6	73.3	64.5	54.1	45.4	63.9
Mean Minimum Temp. (°F)	30.7	33.9	39.4	47.3	56.8	64.4	66.8	65.8	59.3	49.4	38.3	30.0	48.5
Extreme Maximum Temp. (°F)	86	90	96	99	106	111	108	106	105	101	90	87	111
Extreme Minimum Temp. (°F)	8	2	13	27	38	45	59	55	40	26	15	2	2
Days Maximum Temp. ≥ 90°F	0	0	1	6	17	24	26	25	13	4	0	0	116
Days Maximum Temp. ≤ 32°F	1	0	0	0	0	0	0	0	0	0	0	1	2
Days Minimum Temp. ≤ 32°F	19	12	6	1	0	0	0	0	0	0	7	20	65
Days Minimum Temp. ≤ 0°F	0	0	0	0	0	0	0	0	0	0	0	0	0
Heating Degree Days (base 65°F)	583	417	279	105	14	1	0	0	13	94	328	600	2,434
Cooling Degree Days (base 65°F)	0	3	17	90	269	449	502	459	268	85	8	0	2,150
Mean Precipitation (in.)	0.59	0.70	0.26	0.68	1.20	1.25	1.56	2.14	2.64	1.25	0.59	0.59	13.45
Extreme Maximum Daily Precip. (in.)	0.75	1.71	0.73	2.34	2.40	2.20	1.46	*2.24*	3.23	2.00	1.48	*2.00*	*3.23*
Days With ≥ 0.1" Precipitation	2	1	1	1	3	3	4	4	4	3	1	1	28
Days With ≥ 0.5" Precipitation	0	0	0	1	1	1	1	1	2	1	0	1	8
Days With ≥ 1.0" Precipitation	0	0	0	0	1	1	0	1	1	0	0	0	2
Mean Snowfall (in.)	1.2	0.2	trace	trace	0.0	0.0	0.0	0.0	0.0	0.0	trace	0.3	1.7
Maximum Snow Depth (in.)	8	*2*	trace	1	0	0	0	*0*	0	0	trace	*4*	*8*
Days With ≥ 1.0" Snow Depth	0	*0*	0	0	0	0	0	0	0	0	0	0	*0*

The period of record for all cooperative weather station data is 1980 – 2009. See User Guide for detailed explanation of data.

Bardwell Dam *Ellis County*   Elevation: 460 ft.   Latitude: 32° 16' N   Longitude: 96° 38' W

	JAN	FEB	MAR	APR	MAY	JUN	JUL	AUG	SEP	OCT	NOV	DEC	YEAR
Mean Maximum Temp. (°F)	57.3	61.3	68.2	75.9	83.4	90.5	95.3	96.0	89.3	79.4	67.8	58.4	76.9
Mean Temp. (°F)	45.0	49.2	56.4	64.1	72.7	79.6	83.6	83.7	76.6	66.1	55.5	46.4	64.9
Mean Minimum Temp. (°F)	32.7	37.0	44.6	52.5	62.0	68.8	72.0	71.5	64.0	52.7	43.1	34.3	52.9
Extreme Maximum Temp. (°F)	84	95	90	97	100	108	108	108	110	99	89	83	110
Extreme Minimum Temp. (°F)	2	8	11	25	43	49	57	53	37	26	21	-7	-7
Days Maximum Temp. ≥ 90°F	0	0	0	1	5	19	27	27	16	4	0	0	99
Days Maximum Temp. ≤ 32°F	1	1	0	0	0	0	0	0	0	0	0	1	3
Days Minimum Temp. ≤ 32°F	16	8	3	0	0	0	0	0	0	0	4	13	44
Days Minimum Temp. ≤ 0°F	0	0	0	0	0	0	0	0	0	0	0	0	0
Heating Degree Days (base 65°F)	614	447	281	98	11	0	0	0	10	81	301	574	2,417
Cooling Degree Days (base 65°F)	1	5	22	79	257	447	585	589	364	123	22	3	2,497
Mean Precipitation (in.)	2.65	2.91	3.60	2.98	4.50	4.04	1.82	2.19	2.93	4.23	3.23	3.23	38.31
Extreme Maximum Daily Precip. (in.)	4.51	2.53	3.95	3.53	3.15	4.90	1.40	3.10	3.74	7.87	5.27	6.40	7.87
Days With ≥ 0.1" Precipitation	4	5	5	4	6	5	3	4	4	5	5	4	54
Days With ≥ 0.5" Precipitation	2	2	2	2	3	3	1	1	2	2	2	2	24
Days With ≥ 1.0" Precipitation	1	1	1	1	2	1	1	0	1	1	1	1	12
Mean Snowfall (in.)	0.1	trace	0.0	0.0	0.0	0.0	0.0	0.0	0.0	0.0	0.0	0.1	0.2
Maximum Snow Depth (in.)	0	0	0	0	0	0	0	0	0	0	0	trace	trace
Days With ≥ 1.0" Snow Depth	0	0	0	0	0	0	0	0	0	0	0	0	0

Bay City Waterworks *Matagorda County*   Elevation: 51 ft.   Latitude: 28° 59' N   Longitude: 95° 59' W

	JAN	FEB	MAR	APR	MAY	JUN	JUL	AUG	SEP	OCT	NOV	DEC	YEAR
Mean Maximum Temp. (°F)	64.0	67.0	72.6	78.6	84.3	89.6	91.9	92.5	89.2	82.1	73.5	65.7	79.2
Mean Temp. (°F)	54.5	57.7	63.5	69.8	76.2	81.6	83.4	83.6	79.8	72.3	63.7	56.0	70.2
Mean Minimum Temp. (°F)	45.0	48.2	54.4	60.9	68.0	73.5	74.9	74.6	70.4	62.5	53.9	46.4	61.1
Extreme Maximum Temp. (°F)	86	84	90	93	97	100	107	103	109	96	88	83	109
Extreme Minimum Temp. (°F)	14	20	22	36	43	58	65	61	50	29	28	7	7
Days Maximum Temp. ≥ 90°F	0	0	0	0	2	16	25	26	16	3	0	0	88
Days Maximum Temp. ≤ 32°F	0	0	0	0	0	0	0	0	0	0	0	0	0
Days Minimum Temp. ≤ 32°F	3	1	1	0	0	0	0	0	0	0	0	2	7
Days Minimum Temp. ≤ 0°F	0	0	0	0	0	0	0	0	0	0	0	0	0
Heating Degree Days (base 65°F)	335	226	115	27	2	0	0	0	1	22	122	302	1,152
Cooling Degree Days (base 65°F)	17	25	75	177	355	503	577	582	453	255	90	31	3,140
Mean Precipitation (in.)	4.00	2.90	3.17	3.09	4.94	4.72	4.47	3.78	4.84	6.70	4.14	3.54	50.29
Extreme Maximum Daily Precip. (in.)	6.24	3.86	2.60	6.31	7.18	5.76	4.24	3.79	7.48	20.85	3.84	6.20	20.85
Days With ≥ 0.1" Precipitation	6	5	4	3	5	6	5	6	6	6	5	5	62
Days With ≥ 0.5" Precipitation	2	2	2	2	3	3	3	2	2	3	2	2	28
Days With ≥ 1.0" Precipitation	1	1	1	1	2	1	2	1	1	2	1	1	15
Mean Snowfall (in.)	0.0	0.0	0.0	0.0	0.0	0.0	0.0	0.0	0.0	0.0	0.0	0.0	0.0
Maximum Snow Depth (in.)	0	0	0	0	0	0	0	0	0	0	0	8	8
Days With ≥ 1.0" Snow Depth	0	0	0	0	0	0	0	0	0	0	0	0	0

Baytown *Harris County*   Elevation: 34 ft.   Latitude: 29° 50' N   Longitude: 95° 00' W

	JAN	FEB	MAR	APR	MAY	JUN	JUL	AUG	SEP	OCT	NOV	DEC	YEAR
Mean Maximum Temp. (°F)	62.5	66.1	71.7	77.7	84.0	89.3	91.7	92.5	88.5	81.1	72.0	63.8	78.4
Mean Temp. (°F)	52.8	56.5	62.5	68.8	76.2	81.6	83.9	84.0	79.1	70.9	62.2	54.1	69.4
Mean Minimum Temp. (°F)	43.1	46.8	53.3	59.9	68.3	73.9	76.0	75.4	69.8	60.6	52.3	44.4	60.3
Extreme Maximum Temp. (°F)	82	86	90	93	96	100	102	103	109	96	88	84	109
Extreme Minimum Temp. (°F)	17	20	25	35	47	59	64	61	48	30	27	7	7
Days Maximum Temp. ≥ 90°F	0	0	0	0	3	16	24	25	14	2	0	0	84
Days Maximum Temp. ≤ 32°F	0	0	0	0	0	0	0	0	0	0	0	0	0
Days Minimum Temp. ≤ 32°F	4	2	1	0	0	0	0	0	0	0	1	3	11
Days Minimum Temp. ≤ 0°F	0	0	0	0	0	0	0	0	0	0	0	0	0
Heating Degree Days (base 65°F)	383	254	133	36	1	0	0	0	1	28	149	350	1,335
Cooling Degree Days (base 65°F)	13	20	64	158	354	506	593	595	432	217	71	21	3,044
Mean Precipitation (in.)	4.68	3.85	3.70	3.68	5.52	7.07	4.81	4.94	5.68	6.11	5.24	4.73	60.01
Extreme Maximum Daily Precip. (in.)	8.29	3.97	6.23	6.33	4.53	9.50	5.98	5.55	6.19	15.74	4.81	4.68	15.74
Days With ≥ 0.1" Precipitation	6	5	5	4	5	7	7	7	7	6	6	7	72
Days With ≥ 0.5" Precipitation	3	2	2	2	4	4	3	3	3	3	3	3	35
Days With ≥ 1.0" Precipitation	1	1	1	1	2	2	2	1	2	1	2	1	17
Mean Snowfall (in.)	0.0	0.0	0.0	0.0	0.0	0.0	0.0	0.0	0.0	0.0	0.0	0.0	0.0
Maximum Snow Depth (in.)	0	0	0	0	0	0	0	0	0	0	0	0	0
Days With ≥ 1.0" Snow Depth	0	0	0	0	0	0	0	0	0	0	0	0	0

Beaumont Research Ctr *Jefferson County*   Elevation: 26 ft.   Latitude: 30° 04' N   Longitude: 94° 17' W

	JAN	FEB	MAR	APR	MAY	JUN	JUL	AUG	SEP	OCT	NOV	DEC	YEAR
Mean Maximum Temp. (°F)	61.9	65.1	71.7	78.2	85.0	90.0	92.2	92.7	88.5	80.8	71.8	63.6	78.5
Mean Temp. (°F)	51.8	55.0	61.4	68.0	75.5	80.8	82.8	82.7	78.2	69.7	61.1	53.4	68.4
Mean Minimum Temp. (°F)	41.6	44.8	51.1	57.8	65.9	71.6	73.4	72.7	67.9	58.6	50.3	43.1	58.2
Extreme Maximum Temp. (°F)	82	86	87	94	98	99	103	104	107	96	88	83	107
Extreme Minimum Temp. (°F)	13	19	23	30	46	52	61	58	48	27	26	8	8
Days Maximum Temp. ≥ 90°F	0	0	0	0	5	20	26	26	15	2	0	0	94
Days Maximum Temp. ≤ 32°F	0	0	0	0	0	0	0	0	0	0	0	0	0
Days Minimum Temp. ≤ 32°F	6	3	1	0	0	0	0	0	0	0	1	5	16
Days Minimum Temp. ≤ 0°F	0	0	0	0	0	0	0	0	0	0	0	0	0
Heating Degree Days (base 65°F)	414	294	160	47	2	0	0	0	2	40	171	373	1,503
Cooling Degree Days (base 65°F)	10	16	56	145	334	482	560	557	406	194	59	20	2,839
Mean Precipitation (in.)	4.56	3.93	3.64	2.96	5.51	8.05	4.80	4.92	5.64	5.93	4.60	4.78	59.32
Extreme Maximum Daily Precip. (in.)	3.55	6.56	3.34	4.32	6.02	15.21	4.09	4.80	10.28	9.15	6.57	6.14	15.21
Days With ≥ 0.1" Precipitation	6	6	5	4	5	8	7	7	7	5	5	6	71
Days With ≥ 0.5" Precipitation	3	2	2	2	3	4	3	3	3	3	3	3	34
Days With ≥ 1.0" Precipitation	2	1	1	1	2	2	1	2	2	2	2	1	19
Mean Snowfall (in.)	trace	0.0	0.0	0.0	0.0	0.0	0.0	0.0	0.0	0.0	0.0	0.0	trace
Maximum Snow Depth (in.)	trace	0	0	0	0	0	0	0	0	0	0	0	3	3
Days With ≥ 1.0" Snow Depth	0	0	0	0	0	0	0	0	0	0	0	0	0

The period of record for all cooperative weather station data is 1980 – 2009. See User Guide for detailed explanation of data.

Benbrook Dam *Tarrant County* Elevation: 790 ft. Latitude: 32° 39' N Longitude: 97° 27' W

	JAN	FEB	MAR	APR	MAY	JUN	JUL	AUG	SEP	OCT	NOV	DEC	YEAR
Mean Maximum Temp. (°F)	57.0	60.8	67.8	76.0	83.3	90.8	95.9	96.2	88.4	78.6	67.4	57.6	76.6
Mean Temp. (°F)	45.0	48.9	56.0	64.2	72.4	80.0	84.2	84.3	76.6	66.5	55.9	46.1	65.0
Mean Minimum Temp. (°F)	32.9	36.9	44.2	52.4	61.5	69.2	72.5	72.3	64.8	54.3	44.4	34.6	53.3
Extreme Maximum Temp. (°F)	88	94	94	99	99	110	110	107	110	98	89	87	110
Extreme Minimum Temp. (°F)	4	5	12	29	38	53	59	54	40	22	20	-6	-6
Days Maximum Temp. ≥ 90°F	0	0	0	1	6	19	28	27	15	3	0	0	99
Days Maximum Temp. ≤ 32°F	1	1	0	0	0	0	0	0	0	0	0	1	3
Days Minimum Temp. ≤ 32°F	15	9	3	0	0	0	0	0	0	0	4	12	43
Days Minimum Temp. ≤ 0°F	0	0	0	0	0	0	0	0	0	0	0	0	0
Heating Degree Days (base 65°F)	615	453	295	102	13	0	0	0	9	79	291	580	2,437
Cooling Degree Days (base 65°F)	1	5	23	84	250	457	602	605	363	131	25	2	2,548
Mean Precipitation (in.)	1.85	2.40	3.25	2.84	4.59	3.88	1.81	2.09	3.15	3.97	2.57	2.35	34.75
Extreme Maximum Daily Precip. (in.)	3.02	3.65	3.83	2.80	4.38	5.35	2.20	3.50	2.88	6.36	3.20	4.00	6.36
Days With ≥ 0.1" Precipitation	4	4	5	4	6	6	4	3	4	5	4	4	53
Days With ≥ 0.5" Precipitation	1	1	2	2	3	3	1	1	2	2	2	2	22
Days With ≥ 1.0" Precipitation	0	1	1	1	2	1	0	1	1	1	1	0	10
Mean Snowfall (in.)	trace	0.1	trace	0.0	0.0	0.0	0.0	0.0	0.0	0.0	trace	0.1	0.2
Maximum Snow Depth (in.)	1	2	trace	0	0	0	0	0	0	0	0	trace	2
Days With ≥ 1.0" Snow Depth	0	0	0	0	0	0	0	0	0	0	0	0	0

Big Spring *Howard County* Elevation: 2,500 ft. Latitude: 32° 15' N Longitude: 101° 27' W

	JAN	FEB	MAR	APR	MAY	JUN	JUL	AUG	SEP	OCT	NOV	DEC	YEAR
Mean Maximum Temp. (°F)	57.0	61.1	69.2	78.5	86.7	92.0	94.9	93.4	87.3	77.9	66.9	57.3	76.9
Mean Temp. (°F)	44.5	48.1	55.6	64.3	73.4	79.8	83.1	82.0	75.6	65.5	53.9	44.8	64.2
Mean Minimum Temp. (°F)	31.6	35.2	41.8	50.2	60.1	67.5	71.3	70.6	63.7	53.0	40.9	32.2	51.5
Extreme Maximum Temp. (°F)	85	90	95	100	109	114	108	106	108	101	92	82	114
Extreme Minimum Temp. (°F)	4	-5	13	27	40	49	51	50	39	27	16	1	-5
Days Maximum Temp. ≥ 90°F	0	0	0	4	13	20	26	24	13	3	0	0	103
Days Maximum Temp. ≤ 32°F	1	1	0	0	0	0	0	0	0	0	0	2	4
Days Minimum Temp. ≤ 32°F	18	10	4	0	0	0	0	0	0	0	6	16	54
Days Minimum Temp. ≤ 0°F	0	0	0	0	0	0	0	0	0	0	0	0	0
Heating Degree Days (base 65°F)	630	472	306	112	17	1	0	0	12	91	336	620	2,597
Cooling Degree Days (base 65°F)	0	2	21	98	286	451	568	535	337	113	11	0	2,422
Mean Precipitation (in.)	0.67	0.85	0.98	1.21	2.49	2.69	1.42	2.74	2.98	1.86	0.92	0.65	19.46
Extreme Maximum Daily Precip. (in.)	1.10	2.30	4.20	2.90	4.84	2.10	2.20	5.09	3.79	2.90	2.10	1.60	5.09
Days With ≥ 0.1" Precipitation	1	2	2	2	4	4	2	4	3	3	2	2	31
Days With ≥ 0.5" Precipitation	1	1	1	1	1	2	1	2	2	1	1	0	14
Days With ≥ 1.0" Precipitation	0	0	0	0	1	1	0	1	1	1	0	0	5
Mean Snowfall (in.)	0.4	0.3	0.1	trace	0.0	0.0	0.0	0.0	0.0	0.0	0.6	0.7	2.1
Maximum Snow Depth (in.)	4	4	trace	trace	0	0	0	0	0	0	6	7	7
Days With ≥ 1.0" Snow Depth	0	0	0	0	0	0	0	0	0	0	0	0	0

Blanco *Blanco County* Elevation: 1,370 ft. Latitude: 30° 06' N Longitude: 98° 25' W

	JAN	FEB	MAR	APR	MAY	JUN	JUL	AUG	SEP	OCT	NOV	DEC	YEAR
Mean Maximum Temp. (°F)	59.9	63.7	70.2	77.8	84.1	89.9	93.4	94.6	88.6	79.3	69.1	60.8	77.6
Mean Temp. (°F)	47.3	50.8	57.8	65.0	72.9	78.9	81.7	82.1	76.1	66.9	56.9	48.6	65.4
Mean Minimum Temp. (°F)	34.7	37.9	45.3	52.1	61.6	67.8	70.0	69.5	63.6	54.5	44.7	36.4	53.2
Extreme Maximum Temp. (°F)	87	98	93	100	101	106	105	106	110	96	89	87	110
Extreme Minimum Temp. (°F)	6	2	14	27	34	46	58	53	38	22	18	0	0
Days Maximum Temp. ≥ 90°F	0	0	0	1	6	17	25	27	14	2	0	0	92
Days Maximum Temp. ≤ 32°F	0	0	0	0	0	0	0	0	0	0	0	0	0
Days Minimum Temp. ≤ 32°F	14	9	4	1	0	0	0	0	0	0	5	12	45
Days Minimum Temp. ≤ 0°F	0	0	0	0	0	0	0	0	0	0	0	0	0
Heating Degree Days (base 65°F)	542	401	249	92	9	0	0	0	7	74	265	507	2,146
Cooling Degree Days (base 65°F)	2	7	33	98	259	422	525	537	348	141	30	5	2,407
Mean Precipitation (in.)	1.94	1.96	2.93	2.32	4.18	4.20	2.29	2.00	3.11	4.39	2.93	2.32	34.57
Extreme Maximum Daily Precip. (in.)	2.65	2.95	3.14	2.90	3.34	5.10	4.50	3.14	6.75	5.53	6.33	3.60	6.75
Days With ≥ 0.1" Precipitation	4	4	5	4	6	5	3	3	4	5	4	4	51
Days With ≥ 0.5" Precipitation	1	1	2	2	3	3	1	1	2	3	2	1	22
Days With ≥ 1.0" Precipitation	0	1	1	1	2	1	1	1	1	1	1	1	12
Mean Snowfall (in.)	0.3	0.1	trace	0.0	0.0	0.0	0.0	0.0	0.0	0.0	trace	trace	0.4
Maximum Snow Depth (in.)	10	0	trace	0	0	0	0	0	0	0	trace	trace	10
Days With ≥ 1.0" Snow Depth	0	0	0	0	0	0	0	0	0	0	0	0	0

Boerne *Kendall County* Elevation: 1,443 ft. Latitude: 29° 48' N Longitude: 98° 44' W

	JAN	FEB	MAR	APR	MAY	JUN	JUL	AUG	SEP	OCT	NOV	DEC	YEAR
Mean Maximum Temp. (°F)	61.0	64.9	71.3	78.5	84.2	89.7	92.8	93.9	88.6	80.0	70.1	61.7	78.0
Mean Temp. (°F)	48.4	51.8	58.4	65.6	73.0	78.8	81.3	81.6	76.2	67.4	57.5	49.2	65.8
Mean Minimum Temp. (°F)	35.6	38.7	45.5	52.6	61.8	67.8	69.7	69.2	63.8	54.7	44.9	36.6	53.4
Extreme Maximum Temp. (°F)	86	98	95	100	99	105	103	105	109	97	90	85	109
Extreme Minimum Temp. (°F)	8	5	14	27	34	45	56	55	37	21	17	2	2
Days Maximum Temp. ≥ 90°F	0	0	0	2	6	16	24	27	14	2	0	0	91
Days Maximum Temp. ≤ 32°F	0	0	0	0	0	0	0	0	0	0	0	0	0
Days Minimum Temp. ≤ 32°F	13	8	4	1	0	0	0	0	0	0	5	12	43
Days Minimum Temp. ≤ 0°F	0	0	0	0	0	0	0	0	0	0	0	0	0
Heating Degree Days (base 65°F)	512	374	233	82	7	0	0	0	6	67	249	488	2,018
Cooling Degree Days (base 65°F)	3	8	36	106	264	420	512	520	348	148	32	5	2,402
Mean Precipitation (in.)	1.97	2.23	2.98	2.24	4.64	4.57	3.02	2.80	3.34	4.27	3.23	2.21	37.50
Extreme Maximum Daily Precip. (in.)	1.74	3.39	4.48	2.89	4.95	8.93	6.76	7.33	4.38	5.80	4.75	5.68	8.93
Days With ≥ 0.1" Precipitation	5	4	5	4	6	5	3	3	5	5	4	4	53
Days With ≥ 0.5" Precipitation	1	1	2	1	3	3	1	1	2	2	2	1	20
Days With ≥ 1.0" Precipitation	0	1	1	1	2	2	1	1	1	2	1	1	14
Mean Snowfall (in.)	0.3	trace	0.0	0.0	0.0	0.0	0.0	0.0	0.0	0.0	trace	trace	0.3
Maximum Snow Depth (in.)	11	2	0	0	0	0	0	0	0	0	trace	trace	11
Days With ≥ 1.0" Snow Depth	0	0	0	0	0	0	0	0	0	0	0	0	0

The period of record for all cooperative weather station data is 1980 – 2009. See User Guide for detailed explanation of data.

Boquillas Ranger Stn *Brewster County*   Elevation: 1,879 ft.   Latitude: 29° 11' N   Longitude: 102° 58' W

	JAN	FEB	MAR	APR	MAY	JUN	JUL	AUG	SEP	OCT	NOV	DEC	YEAR
Mean Maximum Temp. (°F)	69.6	74.6	82.7	91.7	99.5	103.6	103.0	101.3	97.0	88.4	77.7	68.6	88.1
Mean Temp. (°F)	50.5	55.3	63.2	71.9	81.6	87.3	87.5	86.1	81.3	71.3	59.2	50.1	70.4
Mean Minimum Temp. (°F)	31.3	36.1	43.6	52.1	63.6	71.0	72.0	70.9	65.6	54.0	40.7	31.6	52.7
Extreme Maximum Temp. (°F)	92	99	103	112	116	117	116	112	110	105	97	90	117
Extreme Minimum Temp. (°F)	13	13	14	29	44	59	59	61	40	24	16	4	4
Days Maximum Temp. ≥ 90°F	0	2	9	20	28	28	30	30	26	16	3	0	192
Days Maximum Temp. ≤ 32°F	0	0	0	0	0	0	0	0	0	0	0	0	0
Days Minimum Temp. ≤ 32°F	18	9	3	0	0	0	0	0	0	0	5	18	53
Days Minimum Temp. ≤ 0°F	0	0	0	0	0	0	0	0	0	0	0	0	0
Heating Degree Days (base 65°F)	444	275	121	27	0	0	0	0	2	27	197	455	1,548
Cooling Degree Days (base 65°F)	0	8	71	241	521	676	705	661	499	228	30	1	3,641
Mean Precipitation (in.)	0.41	0.42	0.25	0.44	1.20	1.32	1.07	1.22	0.99	1.37	0.60	0.39	9.68
Extreme Maximum Daily Precip. (in.)	1.02	1.01	0.55	1.76	1.83	1.75	1.84	2.06	1.53	2.14	1.75	1.16	2.14
Days With ≥ 0.1" Precipitation	1	1	1	1	3	3	2	3	2	3	2	1	23
Days With ≥ 0.5" Precipitation	0	0	0	0	1	1	1	1	1	1	0	0	6
Days With ≥ 1.0" Precipitation	0	0	0	0	0	0	0	0	0	0	0	0	0
Mean Snowfall (in.)	trace	0.0	0.0	0.0	0.0	0.0	0.0	0.0	0.0	0.0	0.0	trace	trace
Maximum Snow Depth (in.)	3	0	0	0	0	0	0	0	0	0	0	trace	3
Days With ≥ 1.0" Snow Depth	0	0	0	0	0	0	0	0	0	0	0	0	0

Borger *Hutchinson County*   Elevation: 3,140 ft.   Latitude: 35° 39' N   Longitude: 101° 27' W

	JAN	FEB	MAR	APR	MAY	JUN	JUL	AUG	SEP	OCT	NOV	DEC	YEAR
Mean Maximum Temp. (°F)	50.9	55.6	63.7	72.2	80.6	88.6	93.1	91.1	84.0	73.4	60.7	50.3	72.0
Mean Temp. (°F)	38.1	41.9	49.4	57.7	66.9	75.2	79.9	78.3	70.9	59.7	47.6	38.1	58.6
Mean Minimum Temp. (°F)	25.3	28.2	35.0	43.1	53.1	61.8	66.6	65.5	57.7	46.0	34.5	25.8	45.2
Extreme Maximum Temp. (°F)	81	84	92	97	103	108	107	107	105	99	88	79	108
Extreme Minimum Temp. (°F)	-4	-5	4	16	29	45	51	51	29	13	7	-7	-7
Days Maximum Temp. ≥ 90°F	0	0	0	1	6	14	23	20	8	1	0	0	73
Days Maximum Temp. ≤ 32°F	3	2	0	0	0	0	0	0	0	0	1	3	9
Days Minimum Temp. ≤ 32°F	25	18	12	3	0	0	0	0	0	2	12	24	96
Days Minimum Temp. ≤ 0°F	0	0	0	0	0	0	0	0	0	0	0	1	1
Heating Degree Days (base 65°F)	826	646	481	241	67	5	1	1	30	196	518	828	3,840
Cooling Degree Days (base 65°F)	0	0	4	27	131	319	468	420	214	40	2	0	1,625
Mean Precipitation (in.)	0.75	0.70	1.68	1.80	2.84	3.28	2.65	3.59	2.13	1.89	0.99	0.84	23.14
Extreme Maximum Daily Precip. (in.)	1.67	1.12	3.32	2.50	3.82	2.87	3.66	2.51	6.27	2.87	1.77	1.40	6.27
Days With ≥ 0.1" Precipitation	2	2	3	3	5	5	5	6	3	3	2	2	41
Days With ≥ 0.5" Precipitation	1	0	1	1	2	3	2	2	1	1	1	1	16
Days With ≥ 1.0" Precipitation	0	0	0	0	1	1	1	1	0	0	0	0	4
Mean Snowfall (in.)	5.3	4.0	3.5	0.9	trace	trace	0.0	trace	trace	0.2	2.4	5.3	21.6
Maximum Snow Depth (in.)	13	15	13	3	trace	trace	0	trace	0	4	8	17	17
Days With ≥ 1.0" Snow Depth	3	2	1	0	0	0	0	0	0	0	1	3	10

Boys Ranch *Oldham County*   Elevation: 3,190 ft.   Latitude: 35° 32' N   Longitude: 102° 15' W

	JAN	FEB	MAR	APR	MAY	JUN	JUL	AUG	SEP	OCT	NOV	DEC	YEAR
Mean Maximum Temp. (°F)	52.6	56.8	64.5	72.9	81.0	89.0	92.7	90.4	83.8	73.5	62.2	52.2	72.6
Mean Temp. (°F)	36.9	41.0	48.3	56.9	66.4	75.2	79.3	77.4	69.8	57.9	46.0	36.8	57.7
Mean Minimum Temp. (°F)	21.1	25.2	32.1	40.9	51.8	61.4	65.8	64.4	55.8	42.4	29.7	21.2	42.7
Extreme Maximum Temp. (°F)	80	85	95	96	103	109	110	104	104	96	89	80	110
Extreme Minimum Temp. (°F)	-8	-7	3	19	29	44	49	51	28	13	-2	-11	-11
Days Maximum Temp. ≥ 90°F	0	0	0	1	6	15	23	20	8	1	0	0	74
Days Maximum Temp. ≤ 32°F	2	2	0	0	0	0	0	0	0	0	1	3	8
Days Minimum Temp. ≤ 32°F	29	23	16	5	0	0	0	0	0	4	19	28	124
Days Minimum Temp. ≤ 0°F	0	0	0	0	0	0	0	0	0	0	0	1	1
Heating Degree Days (base 65°F)	863	672	511	261	70	5	0	1	37	238	564	875	4,097
Cooling Degree Days (base 65°F)	0	0	2	20	122	317	450	393	188	26	0	0	1,518
Mean Precipitation (in.)	0.52	0.36	1.12	1.33	2.11	2.55	2.69	3.46	1.96	1.59	0.69	0.62	19.00
Extreme Maximum Daily Precip. (in.)	1.61	0.67	1.54	2.10	4.20	2.78	3.00	3.13	4.50	2.99	1.29	1.06	4.50
Days With ≥ 0.1" Precipitation	1	1	3	2	4	5	5	5	3	2	2	2	35
Days With ≥ 0.5" Precipitation	0	0	1	1	2	2	2	2	1	1	0	0	12
Days With ≥ 1.0" Precipitation	0	0	0	0	0	1	1	1	1	1	0	0	5
Mean Snowfall (in.)	3.3	1.4	1.1	0.3	0.1	0.0	0.0	0.0	0.0	0.0	1.6	2.7	10.5
Maximum Snow Depth (in.)	10	2	5	3	0	0	0	0	0	3	8	14	14
Days With ≥ 1.0" Snow Depth	1	0	0	0	0	0	0	0	0	0	0	1	2

Brady *Mcculloch County*   Elevation: 1,720 ft.   Latitude: 31° 07' N   Longitude: 99° 20' W

	JAN	FEB	MAR	APR	MAY	JUN	JUL	AUG	SEP	OCT	NOV	DEC	YEAR
Mean Maximum Temp. (°F)	59.5	63.3	70.3	78.9	85.4	91.1	94.7	95.1	88.6	79.5	68.9	60.0	77.9
Mean Temp. (°F)	46.7	50.5	57.4	65.2	73.2	79.3	82.4	82.5	76.0	66.6	56.3	47.4	65.3
Mean Minimum Temp. (°F)	33.9	37.6	44.5	51.4	60.9	67.5	70.1	69.9	63.4	53.6	43.6	34.8	52.6
Extreme Maximum Temp. (°F)	89	99	95	101	107	110	109	108	109	98	92	88	110
Extreme Minimum Temp. (°F)	5	3	11	27	38	51	59	51	40	24	19	-2	-2
Days Maximum Temp. ≥ 90°F	0	0	1	3	9	20	27	27	15	3	0	0	105
Days Maximum Temp. ≤ 32°F	1	1	0	0	0	0	0	0	0	0	0	1	3
Days Minimum Temp. ≤ 32°F	15	8	4	1	0	0	0	0	0	0	4	13	45
Days Minimum Temp. ≤ 0°F	0	0	0	0	0	0	0	0	0	0	0	0	0
Heating Degree Days (base 65°F)	561	411	259	90	11	1	0	0	8	75	279	540	2,235
Cooling Degree Days (base 65°F)	2	6	31	103	270	437	547	551	345	130	23	3	2,448
Mean Precipitation (in.)	1.14	1.74	2.18	1.87	3.68	3.34	2.14	2.10	3.02	2.74	1.92	1.56	27.43
Extreme Maximum Daily Precip. (in.)	2.12	2.15	2.77	4.55	5.94	3.78	3.74	3.32	5.03	2.28	4.25	4.42	5.94
Days With ≥ 0.1" Precipitation	3	4	4	3	5	5	3	3	4	4	3	3	44
Days With ≥ 0.5" Precipitation	1	1	2	1	3	2	1	2	2	2	1	1	19
Days With ≥ 1.0" Precipitation	0	0	0	0	1	1	1	1	1	1	1	0	7
Mean Snowfall (in.)	0.0	0.0	0.0	0.0	0.0	0.0	0.0	0.0	0.0	0.0	trace	0.1	0.1
Maximum Snow Depth (in.)	0	0	0	0	0	0	0	0	0	0	0	1	1
Days With ≥ 1.0" Snow Depth	0	0	0	0	0	0	0	0	0	0	0	0	0

The period of record for all cooperative weather station data is 1980 – 2009. See User Guide for detailed explanation of data.

Brenham *Washington County* Elevation: 312 ft.   Latitude: 30° 10' N   Longitude: 96° 24' W

	JAN	FEB	MAR	APR	MAY	JUN	JUL	AUG	SEP	OCT	NOV	DEC	YEAR
Mean Maximum Temp. (°F)	61.8	65.5	72.4	79.6	86.2	92.0	95.3	96.5	91.2	82.0	71.5	62.7	79.7
Mean Temp. (°F)	51.3	54.6	61.2	68.5	75.9	81.8	84.7	85.1	79.7	70.5	60.6	52.2	68.8
Mean Minimum Temp. (°F)	40.7	43.7	50.0	57.2	65.5	71.6	73.7	73.6	68.1	58.8	49.6	41.5	57.8
Extreme Maximum Temp. (°F)	83	94	92	94	101	105	106	107	113	97	89	85	113
Extreme Minimum Temp. (°F)	7	15	19	33	44	53	64	61	46	29	24	4	4
Days Maximum Temp. ≥ 90°F	0	0	0	1	9	22	28	29	20	6	0	0	115
Days Maximum Temp. ≤ 32°F	0	0	0	0	0	0	0	0	0	0	0	0	0
Days Minimum Temp. ≤ 32°F	6	3	1	0	0	0	0	0	0	0	1	6	17
Days Minimum Temp. ≤ 0°F	0	0	0	0	0	0	0	0	0	0	0	0	0
Heating Degree Days (base 65°F)	429	305	172	44	2	0	0	0	1	37	185	408	1,583
Cooling Degree Days (base 65°F)	11	18	61	154	346	511	616	628	448	213	60	17	3,083
Mean Precipitation (in.)	3.53	2.94	3.40	2.90	4.66	4.80	2.54	2.87	4.49	5.20	4.34	3.41	45.08
Extreme Maximum Daily Precip. (in.)	5.65	3.03	3.64	4.12	3.43	5.37	5.44	5.81	5.87	10.38	5.39	3.34	10.38
Days With ≥ 0.1" Precipitation	6	5	5	4	6	6	4	4	5	6	5	6	62
Days With ≥ 0.5" Precipitation	2	2	2	2	3	3	2	2	3	3	3	2	29
Days With ≥ 1.0" Precipitation	1	1	1	1	2	2	1	1	1	2	1	1	15
Mean Snowfall (in.)	0.1	trace	trace	0.0	0.0	0.0	0.0	0.0	0.0	0.0	0.0	trace	0.1
Maximum Snow Depth (in.)	1	1	trace	0	0	0	0	0	0	0	0	trace	1
Days With ≥ 1.0" Snow Depth	0	0	0	0	0	0	0	0	0	0	0	0	0

Bridgeport *Wise County* Elevation: 745 ft.   Latitude: 33° 12' N   Longitude: 97° 46' W

	JAN	FEB	MAR	APR	MAY	JUN	JUL	AUG	SEP	OCT	NOV	DEC	YEAR
Mean Maximum Temp. (°F)	57.1	60.8	68.2	77.2	83.8	90.8	96.7	96.7	88.9	78.6	67.0	57.7	77.0
Mean Temp. (°F)	44.3	48.0	55.2	63.7	71.9	79.1	83.7	83.1	75.5	65.0	54.4	45.1	64.1
Mean Minimum Temp. (°F)	31.5	35.2	42.1	50.2	60.0	67.5	70.7	69.5	62.1	51.4	41.7	32.4	51.2
Extreme Maximum Temp. (°F)	85	96	94	97	102	115	113	110	111	98	92	86	115
Extreme Minimum Temp. (°F)	2	3	9	24	35	48	56	52	33	21	19	-8	-8
Days Maximum Temp. ≥ 90°F	0	0	0	1	6	18	28	27	15	3	0	0	98
Days Maximum Temp. ≤ 32°F	1	0	0	0	0	0	0	0	0	0	0	1	2
Days Minimum Temp. ≤ 32°F	18	11	6	1	0	0	0	0	0	0	7	16	59
Days Minimum Temp. ≤ 0°F	0	0	0	0	0	0	0	0	0	0	0	0	0
Heating Degree Days (base 65°F)	636	478	319	113	19	1	0	0	13	98	329	612	2,618
Cooling Degree Days (base 65°F)	1	3	23	81	240	431	587	570	336	106	17	2	2,397
Mean Precipitation (in.)	1.55	2.40	2.85	2.74	5.21	4.12	1.95	1.90	3.07	4.57	2.34	2.13	34.83
Extreme Maximum Daily Precip. (in.)	1.70	2.44	2.85	3.38	6.00	3.74	4.75	2.90	4.43	8.09	2.72	3.08	8.09
Days With ≥ 0.1" Precipitation	3	4	4	4	6	5	3	3	4	5	4	4	49
Days With ≥ 0.5" Precipitation	1	2	2	2	3	3	1	1	2	3	2	1	23
Days With ≥ 1.0" Precipitation	0	1	1	1	2	2	1	1	1	1	1	1	13
Mean Snowfall (in.)	0.3	0.8	0.1	0.1	0.0	0.0	0.0	0.0	0.0	0.0	0.2	0.3	1.8
Maximum Snow Depth (in.)	2	5	6	2	0	0	0	0	0	0	1	1	6
Days With ≥ 1.0" Snow Depth	0	0	0	0	0	0	0	0	0	0	0	0	0

Brownfield 2 *Terry County* Elevation: 3,299 ft.   Latitude: 33° 11' N   Longitude: 102° 16' W

	JAN	FEB	MAR	APR	MAY	JUN	JUL	AUG	SEP	OCT	NOV	DEC	YEAR
Mean Maximum Temp. (°F)	55.0	59.9	67.3	76.0	84.2	90.9	92.8	91.3	84.9	76.2	64.5	55.2	74.8
Mean Temp. (°F)	41.1	45.0	51.7	60.0	69.4	77.0	79.6	78.3	71.4	61.7	50.1	41.5	60.6
Mean Minimum Temp. (°F)	27.1	30.1	36.1	43.9	54.5	63.0	66.3	65.2	57.8	47.1	35.7	27.7	46.2
Extreme Maximum Temp. (°F)	81	86	95	98	110	111	108	106	103	101	88	82	111
Extreme Minimum Temp. (°F)	5	2	9	23	36	45	56	52	36	19	9	-1	-1
Days Maximum Temp. ≥ 90°F	0	0	0	2	10	19	24	21	9	2	0	0	87
Days Maximum Temp. ≤ 32°F	2	1	0	0	0	0	0	0	0	0	0	2	5
Days Minimum Temp. ≤ 32°F	25	17	10	2	0	0	0	0	0	1	10	23	88
Days Minimum Temp. ≤ 0°F	0	0	0	0	0	0	0	0	0	0	0	0	0
Heating Degree Days (base 65°F)	734	559	409	184	40	2	0	0	22	150	442	721	3,263
Cooling Degree Days (base 65°F)	0	1	5	40	183	367	460	418	221	54	2	0	1,751
Mean Precipitation (in.)	0.64	0.68	0.96	1.08	2.81	2.98	2.09	1.89	2.54	1.60	0.94	0.79	19.00
Extreme Maximum Daily Precip. (in.)	1.90	1.21	2.04	2.09	4.37	2.62	2.63	3.38	4.53	5.05	2.57	1.24	5.05
Days With ≥ 0.1" Precipitation	2	2	2	2	4	4	4	4	3	2	2	2	35
Days With ≥ 0.5" Precipitation	0	0	1	1	2	2	1	1	2	1	1	1	13
Days With ≥ 1.0" Precipitation	0	0	0	0	1	1	1	1	1	0	0	0	5
Mean Snowfall (in.)	2.1	1.5	0.2	0.2	0.0	0.0	0.0	0.0	0.0	trace	0.6	1.6	6.2
Maximum Snow Depth (in.)	12	3	4	trace	0	0	0	0	0	trace	4	6	12
Days With ≥ 1.0" Snow Depth	1	0	0	0	0	0	0	0	0	0	0	1	2

Brownwood *Brown County* Elevation: 1,384 ft.   Latitude: 31° 41' N   Longitude: 98° 58' W

	JAN	FEB	MAR	APR	MAY	JUN	JUL	AUG	SEP	OCT	NOV	DEC	YEAR
Mean Maximum Temp. (°F)	60.3	64.0	71.2	79.5	85.9	91.7	96.0	96.6	89.6	80.4	69.4	60.9	78.8
Mean Temp. (°F)	46.1	50.0	57.3	65.1	73.2	79.5	83.1	83.4	76.2	66.2	55.8	46.7	65.2
Mean Minimum Temp. (°F)	31.9	35.9	43.1	50.7	60.5	67.3	70.2	70.1	62.7	51.9	42.1	32.5	51.6
Extreme Maximum Temp. (°F)	90	98	95	102	105	106	109	110	109	100	91	89	110
Extreme Minimum Temp. (°F)	2	6	10	26	39	51	53	51	37	21	16	-6	-6
Days Maximum Temp. ≥ 90°F	0	0	1	4	10	21	28	27	17	4	0	0	112
Days Maximum Temp. ≤ 32°F	0	0	0	0	0	0	0	0	0	0	0	1	1
Days Minimum Temp. ≤ 32°F	18	10	5	1	0	0	0	0	0	1	6	16	57
Days Minimum Temp. ≤ 0°F	0	0	0	0	0	0	0	0	0	0	0	0	0
Heating Degree Days (base 65°F)	579	423	259	92	10	1	0	0	6	81	291	561	2,303
Cooling Degree Days (base 65°F)	1	4	27	103	273	444	570	576	348	124	21	1	2,492
Mean Precipitation (in.)	1.32	2.36	2.62	2.24	3.97	4.66	1.84	2.36	2.97	2.96	1.79	1.61	30.70
Extreme Maximum Daily Precip. (in.)	1.85	3.49	3.62	2.26	2.88	6.60	2.57	5.73	3.32	3.20	2.07	2.80	6.60
Days With ≥ 0.1" Precipitation	3	3	4	3	5	5	3	3	4	4	3	3	43
Days With ≥ 0.5" Precipitation	1	2	2	1	3	3	1	2	2	2	1	1	21
Days With ≥ 1.0" Precipitation	0	1	1	0	1	2	1	1	1	1	1	0	10
Mean Snowfall (in.)	0.4	trace	trace	0.1	0.0	0.0	0.0	0.0	0.0	0.0	0.1	0.3	0.9
Maximum Snow Depth (in.)	6	trace	0	3	0	0	0	0	0	0	trace	3	6
Days With ≥ 1.0" Snow Depth	0	0	0	0	0	0	0	0	0	0	0	0	0

The period of record for all cooperative weather station data is 1980 – 2009. See User Guide for detailed explanation of data.

Burnet *Burnet County*   Elevation: 1,274 ft.   Latitude: 30° 44' N   Longitude: 98° 14' W

	JAN	FEB	MAR	APR	MAY	JUN	JUL	AUG	SEP	OCT	NOV	DEC	YEAR
Mean Maximum Temp. (°F)	59.6	62.7	69.5	77.6	83.6	89.5	93.3	94.2	87.9	79.0	68.6	59.6	77.1
Mean Temp. (°F)	47.3	50.4	57.4	65.4	72.9	78.7	82.2	82.4	76.3	66.8	56.8	47.8	65.4
Mean Minimum Temp. (°F)	35.0	38.1	45.3	53.2	62.2	68.2	71.1	70.6	64.5	55.0	45.0	35.9	53.7
Extreme Maximum Temp. (°F)	87	97	95	100	101	106	103	105	108	96	92	84	108
Extreme Minimum Temp. (°F)	5	-1	12	27	38	50	58	50	38	22	17	-4	-4
Days Max. Temp. ≥ 90°F	0	0	0	1	6	16	25	26	13	2	0	0	89
Days Maximum Temp. ≤ 32°F	0	0	0	0	0	0	0	0	0	0	0	1	1
Days Minimum Temp. ≤ 32°F	13	8	3	0	0	0	0	0	0	0	4	11	39
Days Minimum Temp. ≤ 0°F	0	0	0	0	0	0	0	0	0	0	0	0	0
Heating Degree Days (base 65°F)	542	411	253	82	9	0	0	0	7	71	263	529	2,167
Cooling Degree Days (base 65°F)	2	6	26	103	261	419	541	547	352	134	25	3	2,419
Mean Precipitation (in.)	1.65	2.05	2.76	2.14	4.25	4.58	2.00	1.75	3.38	3.71	2.75	2.06	33.08
Extreme Maximum Daily Precip. (in.)	1.95	1.98	2.80	3.30	4.02	5.65	3.00	3.01	6.10	6.10	3.85	4.52	6.10
Days With ≥ 0.1" Precipitation	4	4	5	3	5	5	3	3	4	5	4	4	49
Days With ≥ 0.5" Precipitation	1	2	2	2	3	3	1	1	2	2	2	1	22
Days With ≥ 1.0" Precipitation	0	1	1	1	1	2	1	1	1	1	1	1	12
Mean Snowfall (in.)	trace	trace	0.0	0.0	0.0	0.0	0.0	0.0	0.0	0.0	0.1	0.0	0.1
Maximum Snow Depth (in.)	0	0	0	0	0	0	0	0	0	0	0	0	0
Days With ≥ 1.0" Snow Depth	0	0	0	0	0	0	0	0	0	0	0	0	0

Cameron *Milam County*   Elevation: 363 ft.   Latitude: 30° 51' N   Longitude: 96° 58' W

	JAN	FEB	MAR	APR	MAY	JUN	JUL	AUG	SEP	OCT	NOV	DEC	YEAR
Mean Maximum Temp. (°F)	61.3	64.8	71.6	78.8	84.6	90.0	93.9	94.9	89.5	80.7	70.7	62.4	78.6
Mean Temp. (°F)	50.2	53.7	60.6	67.7	74.8	80.4	83.4	83.8	78.4	69.4	59.8	51.2	67.8
Mean Minimum Temp. (°F)	39.1	42.5	49.4	56.5	65.0	70.8	72.9	72.7	67.2	58.1	48.8	40.0	56.9
Extreme Maximum Temp. (°F)	85	98	96	95	100	105	104	107	110	96	89	85	110
Extreme Minimum Temp. (°F)	8	10	17	28	40	56	61	58	44	27	17	2	2
Days Max. Temp. ≥ 90°F	0	0	0	1	6	18	25	26	16	3	0	0	95
Days Maximum Temp. ≤ 32°F	0	0	0	0	0	0	0	0	0	0	0	0	0
Days Minimum Temp. ≤ 32°F	9	5	2	0	0	0	0	0	0	0	2	8	26
Days Minimum Temp. ≤ 0°F	0	0	0	0	0	0	0	0	0	0	0	0	0
Heating Degree Days (base 65°F)	460	331	186	55	4	0	0	0	3	45	204	437	1,725
Cooling Degree Days (base 65°F)	9	18	56	143	316	469	578	591	410	189	54	15	2,848
Mean Precipitation (in.)	2.31	2.64	2.69	2.39	5.26	3.65	1.95	2.14	2.92	4.00	3.33	2.88	36.16
Extreme Maximum Daily Precip. (in.)	2.66	3.03	2.73	6.90	6.00	3.40	4.67	2.86	4.00	7.00	3.34	6.08	7.00
Days With ≥ 0.1" Precipitation	5	4	5	4	6	6	3	3	4	5	5	5	55
Days With ≥ 0.5" Precipitation	1	2	2	2	3	2	1	1	2	2	2	2	22
Days With ≥ 1.0" Precipitation	1	1	1	1	2	1	1	1	1	1	1	1	13
Mean Snowfall (in.)	trace	trace	trace	0.0	0.0	0.0	0.0	0.0	0.0	0.0	0.0	0.0	trace
Maximum Snow Depth (in.)	0	trace	trace	0	0	0	0	0	0	0	0	0	trace
Days With ≥ 1.0" Snow Depth	0	0	0	0	0	0	0	0	0	0	0	0	0

Camp Wood *Real County*   Elevation: 1,470 ft.   Latitude: 29° 41' N   Longitude: 100° 01' W

	JAN	FEB	MAR	APR	MAY	JUN	JUL	AUG	SEP	OCT	NOV	DEC	YEAR
Mean Maximum Temp. (°F)	62.1	65.7	72.5	79.7	86.0	90.8	93.7	94.1	*89.4*	*80.3*	70.6	62.6	*79.0*
Mean Temp. (°F)	48.1	51.6	58.8	66.2	74.2	79.5	81.8	81.8	*76.8*	*67.7*	57.1	48.7	*66.0*
Mean Minimum Temp. (°F)	34.0	37.3	45.0	52.6	62.3	68.1	69.9	69.4	*64.2*	*55.0*	43.6	34.8	*53.0*
Extreme Maximum Temp. (°F)	89	96	96	101	105	108	106	109	109	*96*	93	87	*109*
Extreme Minimum Temp. (°F)	11	5	12	26	40	49	55	59	42	*26*	20	5	*5*
Days Max. Temp. ≥ 90°F	0	0	1	3	9	19	25	26	16	*3*	0	0	*102*
Days Maximum Temp. ≤ 32°F	0	0	0	0	0	0	0	0	0	*0*	0	0	*0*
Days Minimum Temp. ≤ 32°F	15	9	4	1	0	0	0	0	0	*0*	5	14	*48*
Days Minimum Temp. ≤ 0°F	0	0	0	0	0	0	0	0	0	*0*	0	0	*0*
Heating Degree Days (base 65°F)	518	376	217	73	4	0	0	0	*5*	*53*	255	500	*2,001*
Cooling Degree Days (base 65°F)	1	3	32	115	296	442	528	527	*365*	*143*	24	2	*2,478*
Mean Precipitation (in.)	1.22	1.40	2.05	1.96	3.10	3.73	2.30	2.45	3.35	3.35	2.49	1.45	28.85
Extreme Maximum Daily Precip. (in.)	1.89	3.10	4.08	5.57	3.02	5.10	4.46	4.75	*3.95*	4.50	8.37	3.76	*8.37*
Days With ≥ 0.1" Precipitation	3	3	3	3	5	5	4	3	4	4	3	3	43
Days With ≥ 0.5" Precipitation	1	1	1	1	2	2	1	1	2	2	1	1	16
Days With ≥ 1.0" Precipitation	0	0	1	0	1	1	1	1	1	1	1	0	8
Mean Snowfall (in.)	0.1	0.1	0.0	0.0	0.0	0.0	0.0	0.0	0.0	0.0	0.1	0.0	0.3
Maximum Snow Depth (in.)	10	4	0	0	0	0	0	0	0	*0*	0	1	*10*
Days With ≥ 1.0" Snow Depth	0	0	0	0	0	0	0	0	0	*0*	0	0	*0*

Candelaria *Presidio County*   Elevation: 2,875 ft.   Latitude: 30° 08' N   Longitude: 104° 41' W

	JAN	FEB	MAR	APR	MAY	JUN	JUL	AUG	SEP	OCT	NOV	DEC	YEAR
Mean Maximum Temp. (°F)	66.7	72.8	80.6	88.9	96.4	101.4	99.9	97.7	93.4	85.8	74.4	66.6	85.4
Mean Temp. (°F)	49.1	54.3	60.7	68.6	76.8	83.7	84.4	82.6	77.8	68.5	56.3	49.1	67.6
Mean Minimum Temp. (°F)	31.5	35.7	40.8	48.3	57.2	65.9	68.8	67.4	62.2	51.2	38.2	31.5	49.9
Extreme Maximum Temp. (°F)	85	92	99	103	109	115	114	110	109	103	93	86	115
Extreme Minimum Temp. (°F)	9	14	16	21	35	49	56	50	37	22	15	6	6
Days Max. Temp. ≥ 90°F	0	0	3	16	27	29	30	27	23	10	0	0	165
Days Maximum Temp. ≤ 32°F	0	0	0	0	0	0	0	0	0	0	0	0	0
Days Minimum Temp. ≤ 32°F	17	10	5	1	0	0	0	0	0	0	7	17	57
Days Minimum Temp. ≤ 0°F	0	0	0	0	0	0	0	0	0	0	0	0	0
Heating Degree Days (base 65°F)	486	299	154	33	1	0	0	0	1	34	261	487	1,756
Cooling Degree Days (base 65°F)	0	4	29	147	373	566	607	551	391	151	6	0	2,825
Mean Precipitation (in.)	0.51	0.47	0.36	0.53	0.72	1.95	2.12	2.56	2.02	1.47	0.46	0.58	13.75
Extreme Maximum Daily Precip. (in.)	0.90	1.12	1.25	1.42	1.83	2.50	1.80	2.62	2.21	3.43	2.05	1.27	3.43
Days With ≥ 0.1" Precipitation	1	1	1	1	2	4	5	5	4	3	1	1	29
Days With ≥ 0.5" Precipitation	0	0	0	0	1	2	2	1	1	1	0	0	7
Days With ≥ 1.0" Precipitation	0	0	0	0	0	0	0	0	0	0	0	0	0
Mean Snowfall (in.)	0.1	0.0	0.0	trace	0.0	0.0	0.0	0.0	0.0	0.0	trace	0.0	0.1
Maximum Snow Depth (in.)	0	0	0	trace	0	0	0	0	0	0	0	0	trace
Days With ≥ 1.0" Snow Depth	0	0	0	0	0	0	0	0	0	0	0	0	0

The period of record for all cooperative weather station data is 1980 – 2009. See User Guide for detailed explanation of data.

Canyon *Randall County*   Elevation: 3,589 ft.   Latitude: 34° 59' N   Longitude: 101° 56' W

	JAN	FEB	MAR	APR	MAY	JUN	JUL	AUG	SEP	OCT	NOV	DEC	YEAR
Mean Maximum Temp. (°F)	52.8	57.3	65.2	73.8	82.2	90.0	92.7	90.5	84.5	74.6	62.2	52.6	73.2
Mean Temp. (°F)	38.7	42.4	49.8	58.2	67.6	75.9	79.6	77.8	70.7	60.1	47.9	38.8	59.0
Mean Minimum Temp. (°F)	24.6	27.4	34.3	42.5	52.9	61.8	66.3	65.0	57.0	45.5	33.6	25.2	44.7
Extreme Maximum Temp. (°F)	79	82	93	97	103	109	106	104	103	98	87	82	109
Extreme Minimum Temp. (°F)	-3	-11	5	19	27	44	51	51	29	15	5	-6	-11
Days Maximum Temp. ≥ 90°F	0	0	0	1	7	17	23	20	9	1	0	0	78
Days Maximum Temp. ≤ 32°F	2	2	0	0	0	0	0	0	0	0	0	2	6
Days Minimum Temp. ≤ 32°F	26	19	12	3	0	0	0	0	0	2	13	24	99
Days Minimum Temp. ≤ 0°F	0	0	0	0	0	0	0	0	0	0	0	0	0
Heating Degree Days (base 65°F)	808	633	469	226	57	2	0	0	30	184	506	805	3,720
Cooling Degree Days (base 65°F)	0	0	4	28	145	337	458	403	209	38	1	0	1,623
Mean Precipitation (in.)	0.56	0.48	1.10	1.05	2.50	3.33	2.11	3.13	2.23	1.88	0.72	0.65	19.74
Extreme Maximum Daily Precip. (in.)	1.15	1.22	2.10	2.11	3.80	4.57	2.50	3.20	7.18	2.58	1.10	1.28	7.18
Days With ≥ 0.1" Precipitation	1	1	2	2	4	5	4	5	3	3	2	2	34
Days With ≥ 0.5" Precipitation	0	0	1	1	2	2	1	2	1	1	0	0	11
Days With ≥ 1.0" Precipitation	0	0	0	0	1	1	1	1	1	1	0	0	6
Mean Snowfall (in.)	2.6	1.9	1.1	0.4	0.1	0.0	0.0	0.0	0.0	trace	1.4	3.0	10.5
Maximum Snow Depth (in.)	11	16	4	1	0	0	0	0	0	trace	6	14	16
Days With ≥ 1.0" Snow Depth	1	1	0	0	0	0	0	0	0	0	0	1	3

Carrizo Springs *Dimmit County*   Elevation: 612 ft.   Latitude: 28° 29' N   Longitude: 99° 52' W

	JAN	FEB	MAR	APR	MAY	JUN	JUL	AUG	SEP	OCT	NOV	DEC	YEAR
Mean Maximum Temp. (°F)	66.6	71.0	78.1	85.7	91.6	96.6	98.6	98.9	93.2	85.0	75.1	66.1	83.9
Mean Temp. (°F)	53.7	57.7	65.0	72.7	79.7	84.8	86.5	86.7	81.4	72.8	62.4	53.3	71.4
Mean Minimum Temp. (°F)	40.7	44.6	51.8	59.6	67.7	73.1	74.5	74.6	69.5	60.5	49.7	40.6	58.9
Extreme Maximum Temp. (°F)	90	101	105	111	109	111	110	109	111	103	96	92	111
Extreme Minimum Temp. (°F)	18	16	21	34	47	61	66	62	49	31	25	10	10
Days Maximum Temp. ≥ 90°F	0	1	3	11	19	26	27	29	23	10	1	0	150
Days Maximum Temp. ≤ 32°F	0	0	0	0	0	0	0	0	0	0	0	0	0
Days Minimum Temp. ≤ 32°F	6	3	1	0	0	0	0	0	0	0	1	8	19
Days Minimum Temp. ≤ 0°F	0	0	0	0	0	0	0	0	0	0	0	0	0
Heating Degree Days (base 65°F)	355	230	104	22	1	0	0	0	1	24	141	367	1,245
Cooling Degree Days (base 65°F)	11	30	111	259	463	602	674	681	499	273	73	12	3,688
Mean Precipitation (in.)	1.06	0.98	1.15	1.36	2.89	2.12	1.86	1.68	2.26	2.13	1.27	0.77	19.53
Extreme Maximum Daily Precip. (in.)	1.30	3.40	2.18	1.96	5.17	3.40	8.78	4.38	3.59	4.35	1.94	0.92	8.78
Days With ≥ 0.1" Precipitation	2	2	2	2	3	3	3	2	4	3	2	2	30
Days With ≥ 0.5" Precipitation	1	0	1	1	2	1	1	1	1	1	1	0	11
Days With ≥ 1.0" Precipitation	0	0	0	0	1	1	0	0	1	1	0	0	4
Mean Snowfall (in.)	0.0	0.0	0.0	0.0	0.0	0.0	0.0	0.0	0.0	0.0	0.0	0.0	0.0
Maximum Snow Depth (in.)	0	0	0	0	0	0	0	0	0	0	trace	0	trace
Days With ≥ 1.0" Snow Depth	0	0	0	0	0	0	0	0	0	0	0	0	0

Carthage *Panola County*   Elevation: 339 ft.   Latitude: 32° 08' N   Longitude: 94° 21' W

	JAN	FEB	MAR	APR	MAY	JUN	JUL	AUG	SEP	OCT	NOV	DEC	YEAR
Mean Maximum Temp. (°F)	56.8	61.8	69.5	76.1	83.0	89.6	93.6	94.0	87.9	78.0	67.4	58.5	76.4
Mean Temp. (°F)	45.9	50.0	57.4	63.8	72.0	78.9	82.4	82.2	75.6	65.3	55.5	47.2	64.7
Mean Minimum Temp. (°F)	34.9	38.2	45.2	51.5	60.9	68.2	71.2	70.3	63.3	52.5	43.6	36.0	53.0
Extreme Maximum Temp. (°F)	81	90	89	93	98	101	106	108	109	95	86	82	109
Extreme Minimum Temp. (°F)	5	10	18	28	40	45	56	50	38	26	19	1	1
Days Maximum Temp. ≥ 90°F	0	0	0	0	4	17	26	26	13	2	0	0	88
Days Maximum Temp. ≤ 32°F	1	0	0	0	0	0	0	0	0	0	0	1	2
Days Minimum Temp. ≤ 32°F	14	9	3	0	0	0	0	0	0	0	4	13	43
Days Minimum Temp. ≤ 0°F	0	0	0	0	0	0	0	0	0	0	0	0	0
Heating Degree Days (base 65°F)	589	425	260	110	12	0	0	0	9	93	297	549	2,344
Cooling Degree Days (base 65°F)	3	7	31	82	236	426	547	539	334	109	20	6	2,340
Mean Precipitation (in.)	4.28	4.44	4.16	3.97	4.77	4.91	3.12	3.09	3.61	5.09	4.79	5.13	51.36
Extreme Maximum Daily Precip. (in.)	6.31	3.45	5.54	9.25	3.73	6.72	4.78	5.87	4.10	6.82	7.14	4.65	9.25
Days With ≥ 0.1" Precipitation	6	6	6	4	6	5	4	4	5	5	6	6	63
Days With ≥ 0.5" Precipitation	3	3	3	2	3	3	2	2	2	3	3	3	32
Days With ≥ 1.0" Precipitation	1	2	1	1	2	1	1	1	1	2	2	2	17
Mean Snowfall (in.)	0.4	0.2	0.1	trace	0.0	0.0	0.0	0.0	0.0	0.0	trace	0.2	0.9
Maximum Snow Depth (in.)	3	3	2	trace	0	0	0	0	0	0	0	trace	3
Days With ≥ 1.0" Snow Depth	0	0	0	0	0	0	0	0	0	0	0	0	0

Castolon *Brewster County*   Elevation: 2,167 ft.   Latitude: 29° 08' N   Longitude: 103° 30' W

	JAN	FEB	MAR	APR	MAY	JUN	JUL	AUG	SEP	OCT	NOV	DEC	YEAR
Mean Maximum Temp. (°F)	68.1	74.4	82.8	91.4	99.6	103.6	102.3	100.6	96.2	88.0	77.3	68.1	87.7
Mean Temp. (°F)	51.4	57.4	65.3	73.7	83.0	88.4	88.3	86.9	82.1	72.8	60.8	51.8	71.8
Mean Minimum Temp. (°F)	34.6	40.4	47.8	56.2	66.4	73.1	74.3	73.2	68.2	57.5	44.3	35.4	55.9
Extreme Maximum Temp. (°F)	90	97	105	109	114	117	115	114	110	105	99	90	117
Extreme Minimum Temp. (°F)	15	15	23	29	44	58	60	64	47	29	21	7	7
Days Maximum Temp. ≥ 90°F	0	1	8	19	28	29	30	29	25	15	2	0	186
Days Maximum Temp. ≤ 32°F	0	0	0	0	0	0	0	0	0	0	0	0	0
Days Minimum Temp. ≤ 32°F	12	3	1	0	0	0	0	0	0	0	2	11	29
Days Minimum Temp. ≤ 0°F	0	0	0	0	0	0	0	0	0	0	0	0	0
Heating Degree Days (base 65°F)	414	224	88	18	0	0	0	0	1	20	161	405	1,331
Cooling Degree Days (base 65°F)	0	17	105	287	566	708	730	687	522	268	42	1	3,933
Mean Precipitation (in.)	0.42	0.32	0.27	0.42	0.97	1.46	1.67	1.73	1.44	1.24	0.42	0.32	10.68
Extreme Maximum Daily Precip. (in.)	0.68	1.14	0.64	1.61	1.66	1.92	1.49	1.90	1.65	3.95	1.33	0.63	3.95
Days With ≥ 0.1" Precipitation	1	1	1	1	2	3	3	4	3	2	1	1	23
Days With ≥ 0.5" Precipitation	0	0	0	0	1	1	1	1	1	1	0	0	6
Days With ≥ 1.0" Precipitation	0	0	0	0	0	0	0	0	0	0	0	0	0
Mean Snowfall (in.)	0.1	trace	trace	0.0	0.0	0.0	0.0	0.0	0.0	0.0	trace	trace	0.1
Maximum Snow Depth (in.)	3	trace	trace	0	0	0	0	0	0	0	trace	trace	3
Days With ≥ 1.0" Snow Depth	0	0	0	0	0	0	0	0	0	0	0	0	0

The period of record for all cooperative weather station data is 1980 – 2009. See User Guide for detailed explanation of data.

Centerville *Leon County* Elevation: 319 ft. Latitude: 31° 15' N Longitude: 95° 58' W

	JAN	FEB	MAR	APR	MAY	JUN	JUL	AUG	SEP	OCT	NOV	DEC	YEAR
Mean Maximum Temp. (°F)	59.0	62.8	70.0	77.3	84.0	90.3	94.1	95.0	89.1	79.4	69.2	60.2	77.5
Mean Temp. (°F)	47.3	50.9	57.9	65.1	73.1	79.5	82.8	82.9	76.7	66.5	57.1	48.5	65.7
Mean Minimum Temp. (°F)	35.6	39.0	45.7	52.8	62.1	68.7	71.4	70.8	64.3	53.5	45.0	36.7	53.8
Extreme Maximum Temp. (°F)	83	94	91	94	98	106	105	107	110	96	88	84	110
Extreme Minimum Temp. (°F)	5	12	15	26	39	49	56	52	42	27	18	1	1
Days Maximum Temp. ≥ 90°F	0	0	0	1	5	18	27	27	16	3	0	0	97
Days Maximum Temp. ≤ 32°F	0	0	0	0	0	0	0	0	0	0	0	1	1
Days Minimum Temp. ≤ 32°F	13	8	3	1	0	0	0	0	0	0	4	13	42
Days Minimum Temp. ≤ 0°F	0	0	0	0	0	0	0	0	0	0	0	0	0
Heating Degree Days (base 65°F)	546	401	248	93	10	0	0	0	6	78	264	515	2,161
Cooling Degree Days (base 65°F)	5	8	34	101	267	442	559	562	365	130	33	9	2,515
Mean Precipitation (in.)	3.27	3.44	3.77	2.83	4.84	4.06	2.50	2.65	2.82	4.98	3.85	3.66	42.67
Extreme Maximum Daily Precip. (in.)	3.77	3.00	2.87	3.01	5.21	4.14	3.75	7.25	3.60	6.00	3.40	3.55	7.25
Days With ≥ 0.1" Precipitation	5	5	5	4	5	6	4	4	5	5	5	5	58
Days With ≥ 0.5" Precipitation	2	2	3	2	3	2	2	2	2	3	3	3	29
Days With ≥ 1.0" Precipitation	1	1	1	1	2	1	1	1	1	2	1	1	14
Mean Snowfall (in.)	0.2	0.2	trace	0.1	0.0	0.0	0.0	0.0	0.0	0.0	0.0	0.0	0.5
Maximum Snow Depth (in.)	0	trace	0	0	0	0	0	0	0	0	0	0	trace
Days With ≥ 1.0" Snow Depth	0	0	0	0	0	0	0	0	0	0	0	0	0

Charlotte 5 NNW *Atascosa County* Elevation: 440 ft. Latitude: 28° 56' N Longitude: 98° 45' W

	JAN	FEB	MAR	APR	MAY	JUN	JUL	AUG	SEP	OCT	NOV	DEC	YEAR
Mean Maximum Temp. (°F)	67.7	71.7	77.9	84.7	89.9	94.5	96.8	97.5	92.5	85.3	76.1	68.0	83.6
Mean Temp. (°F)	54.9	58.7	65.0	71.8	78.5	83.1	84.9	85.1	80.7	73.1	63.8	55.7	71.3
Mean Minimum Temp. (°F)	42.1	45.6	52.0	58.7	67.1	71.7	72.9	72.7	68.9	60.8	51.4	43.5	58.9
Extreme Maximum Temp. (°F)	88	100	99	107	104	109	106	105	110	99	97	89	110
Extreme Minimum Temp. (°F)	15	14	17	28	44	54	59	60	46	27	23	6	6
Days Maximum Temp. ≥ 90°F	0	1	2	7	17	25	29	30	22	10	1	0	144
Days Maximum Temp. ≤ 32°F	0	0	0	0	0	0	0	0	0	0	0	0	0
Days Minimum Temp. ≤ 32°F	6	3	1	0	0	0	0	0	0	0	1	6	17
Days Minimum Temp. ≤ 0°F	0	0	0	0	0	0	0	0	0	0	0	0	0
Heating Degree Days (base 65°F)	325	212	103	24	1	0	0	0	1	19	125	308	1,118
Cooling Degree Days (base 65°F)	18	40	109	233	427	551	624	631	478	277	96	29	3,513
Mean Precipitation (in.)	1.32	1.63	1.96	1.86	3.03	3.28	2.20	2.18	2.82	3.13	1.88	1.52	26.81
Extreme Maximum Daily Precip. (in.)	2.25	4.48	3.27	3.52	6.70	4.15	5.50	4.60	5.04	4.31	5.35	4.27	6.70
Days With ≥ 0.1" Precipitation	3	3	3	3	4	4	3	3	4	4	3	3	40
Days With ≥ 0.5" Precipitation	1	1	1	1	2	2	1	1	2	2	1	1	16
Days With ≥ 1.0" Precipitation	0	0	1	1	1	1	1	1	1	1	1	0	9
Mean Snowfall (in.)	0.0	0.0	0.0	0.0	0.0	0.0	0.0	0.0	0.0	trace	0.0	trace	trace
Maximum Snow Depth (in.)	7	0	0	0	0	0	0	0	0	trace	0	trace	7
Days With ≥ 1.0" Snow Depth	0	0	0	0	0	0	0	0	0	0	0	0	0

Childress Municipal Arpt *Childress County* Elevation: 1,951 ft. Latitude: 34° 26' N Longitude: 100° 17' W

	JAN	FEB	MAR	APR	MAY	JUN	JUL	AUG	SEP	OCT	NOV	DEC	YEAR
Mean Maximum Temp. (°F)	53.7	57.6	66.4	76.1	83.2	90.5	95.1	94.3	86.1	75.6	64.0	53.6	74.7
Mean Temp. (°F)	40.8	44.4	52.8	62.1	70.7	78.4	82.8	81.9	73.6	62.6	51.1	41.3	61.9
Mean Minimum Temp. (°F)	27.8	31.3	39.2	48.0	58.1	66.2	70.5	69.4	61.0	49.5	38.2	29.0	49.0
Extreme Maximum Temp. (°F)	87	93	100	100	111	117	110	107	107	103	93	84	117
Extreme Minimum Temp. (°F)	3	-5	10	25	37	50	55	55	34	21	9	-5	-5
Days Maximum Temp. ≥ 90°F	0	0	1	4	8	18	26	24	12	2	0	0	95
Days Maximum Temp. ≤ 32°F	2	2	0	0	0	0	0	0	0	0	0	2	6
Days Minimum Temp. ≤ 32°F	23	16	7	1	0	0	0	0	0	1	8	20	76
Days Minimum Temp. ≤ 0°F	0	0	0	0	0	0	0	0	0	0	0	0	0
Heating Degree Days (base 65°F)	744	576	385	150	32	1	0	0	19	140	417	728	3,192
Cooling Degree Days (base 65°F)	0	1	16	69	214	409	560	534	284	71	7	0	2,165
Mean Precipitation (in.)	0.66	0.89	1.56	1.78	3.17	4.08	1.90	2.47	2.41	2.14	1.30	0.93	23.29
Extreme Maximum Daily Precip. (in.)	1.41	1.07	2.92	1.64	2.79	4.46	2.97	4.53	5.16	5.32	2.28	2.03	5.32
Days With ≥ 0.1" Precipitation	2	2	3	4	5	6	4	4	4	3	3	2	42
Days With ≥ 0.5" Precipitation	0	1	1	1	2	3	1	2	1	1	1	0	14
Days With ≥ 1.0" Precipitation	0	0	0	0	1	1	0	1	1	1	0	0	5
Mean Snowfall (in.)	na	na	na	na	na	na	na	na	na	na	na	na	na
Maximum Snow Depth (in.)	na	na	na	na	na	na	na	na	na	na	na	na	na
Days With ≥ 1.0" Snow Depth	na	na	na	na	na	na	na	na	na	na	na	na	na

Clarendon *Donley County* Elevation: 2,703 ft. Latitude: 34° 56' N Longitude: 100° 53' W

	JAN	FEB	MAR	APR	MAY	JUN	JUL	AUG	SEP	OCT	NOV	DEC	YEAR
Mean Maximum Temp. (°F)	52.8	56.6	64.4	73.3	81.3	89.1	94.7	93.0	85.2	74.5	62.8	52.7	73.4
Mean Temp. (°F)	38.4	41.9	49.4	58.1	67.3	75.6	80.5	79.1	71.0	59.7	48.2	38.7	59.0
Mean Minimum Temp. (°F)	24.0	27.2	34.3	42.8	53.2	62.2	66.3	65.1	56.9	44.9	33.5	24.8	44.6
Extreme Maximum Temp. (°F)	84	89	98	100	109	112	110	107	108	104	92	83	112
Extreme Minimum Temp. (°F)	-3	-7	2	21	31	42	48	48	30	17	10	-11	-11
Days Maximum Temp. ≥ 90°F	0	0	0	2	7	15	25	23	10	2	0	0	84
Days Maximum Temp. ≤ 32°F	3	2	1	0	0	0	0	0	0	0	1	3	10
Days Minimum Temp. ≤ 32°F	27	20	13	3	0	0	0	0	0	2	14	26	105
Days Minimum Temp. ≤ 0°F	0	0	0	0	0	0	0	0	0	0	0	0	0
Heating Degree Days (base 65°F)	818	645	482	235	63	4	0	0	33	200	502	807	3,789
Cooling Degree Days (base 65°F)	0	0	5	33	141	330	487	444	221	42	4	0	1,707
Mean Precipitation (in.)	0.72	0.77	1.48	2.17	3.30	3.56	2.02	3.06	2.46	2.12	1.05	1.01	23.72
Extreme Maximum Daily Precip. (in.)	1.29	1.28	2.14	8.71	9.25	4.46	3.08	3.23	2.28	3.47	2.58	1.72	9.25
Days With ≥ 0.1" Precipitation	2	2	3	3	5	5	3	5	4	3	2	2	39
Days With ≥ 0.5" Precipitation	0	0	1	1	2	2	1	2	2	1	1	1	14
Days With ≥ 1.0" Precipitation	0	0	0	1	1	1	1	1	1	1	0	0	7
Mean Snowfall (in.)	1.7	0.6	0.7	0.3	0.0	0.0	0.0	0.0	0.0	0.0	0.7	2.3	6.3
Maximum Snow Depth (in.)	6	14	9	0	0	0	0	0	0	0	0	12	14
Days With ≥ 1.0" Snow Depth	1	1	0	0	0	0	0	0	0	0	0	1	3

The period of record for all cooperative weather station data is 1980 – 2009. See User Guide for detailed explanation of data.

Cleveland *Liberty County*   Elevation: 195 ft.   Latitude: 30° 22' N   Longitude: 95° 06' W

	JAN	FEB	MAR	APR	MAY	JUN	JUL	AUG	SEP	OCT	NOV	DEC	YEAR
Mean Maximum Temp. (°F)	60.8	64.6	71.6	77.6	84.0	89.3	92.2	93.2	88.3	79.5	69.6	61.8	77.7
Mean Temp. (°F)	49.8	53.2	60.0	66.3	73.9	79.5	82.1	82.3	77.3	68.1	58.6	50.8	66.8
Mean Minimum Temp. (°F)	38.8	41.7	48.4	54.9	63.8	69.6	71.9	71.3	66.1	56.6	47.5	39.9	55.9
Extreme Maximum Temp. (°F)	83	90	91	92	98	101	105	107	110	95	87	84	110
Extreme Minimum Temp. (°F)	11	16	20	29	44	51	59	54	46	28	25	5	5
Days Maximum Temp. ≥ 90°F	0	0	0	0	4	16	24	26	14	2	0	0	86
Days Maximum Temp. ≤ 32°F	0	0	0	0	0	0	0	0	0	0	0	0	0
Days Minimum Temp. ≤ 32°F	10	5	2	0	0	0	0	0	0	0	3	10	30
Days Minimum Temp. ≤ 0°F	0	0	0	0	0	0	0	0	0	0	0	0	0
Heating Degree Days (base 65°F)	472	343	195	67	4	0	0	0	3	58	226	446	1,814
Cooling Degree Days (base 65°F)	8	15	47	112	288	441	537	542	377	160	41	14	2,582
Mean Precipitation (in.)	4.12	4.11	3.92	3.43	5.53	5.57	3.27	3.45	4.48	6.28	5.55	4.57	54.28
Extreme Maximum Daily Precip. (in.)	3.65	6.74	2.74	3.26	9.06	5.58	5.55	4.99	6.90	13.17	9.00	5.08	13.17
Days With ≥ 0.1" Precipitation	6	6	6	4	5	8	6	5	6	6	6	7	71
Days With ≥ 0.5" Precipitation	3	3	3	3	3	3	2	2	2	3	3	3	33
Days With ≥ 1.0" Precipitation	1	1	1	1	2	2	1	1	1	2	2	1	16
Mean Snowfall (in.)	0.1	0.2	0.0	0.0	0.0	0.0	0.0	0.0	0.0	0.0	0.0	trace	0.3
Maximum Snow Depth (in.)	1	2	0	0	0	0	0	0	0	0	0	2	2
Days With ≥ 1.0" Snow Depth	0	0	0	0	0	0	0	0	0	0	0	0	0

Coleman *Coleman County*   Elevation: 1,727 ft.   Latitude: 32° 08' N   Longitude: 99° 45' W

	JAN	FEB	MAR	APR	MAY	JUN	JUL	AUG	SEP	OCT	NOV	DEC	YEAR
Mean Maximum Temp. (°F)	59.4	62.9	70.6	79.2	85.6	91.1	95.1	95.2	88.3	79.2	68.2	59.3	77.9
Mean Temp. (°F)	46.9	50.3	57.6	65.4	73.2	79.2	82.6	82.5	75.7	66.4	55.9	47.1	65.2
Mean Minimum Temp. (°F)	34.3	37.6	44.5	51.6	60.8	67.3	70.1	69.8	63.1	53.6	43.4	34.9	52.6
Extreme Maximum Temp. (°F)	89	99	97	100	110	107	108	110	109	99	91	88	110
Extreme Minimum Temp. (°F)	3	8	9	25	40	52	58	55	36	25	19	-4	-4
Days Maximum Temp. ≥ 90°F	0	0	1	3	10	19	27	26	15	4	0	0	105
Days Maximum Temp. ≤ 32°F	1	1	0	0	0	0	0	0	0	0	0	1	3
Days Minimum Temp. ≤ 32°F	14	8	3	0	0	0	0	0	0	0	4	12	41
Days Minimum Temp. ≤ 0°F	0	0	0	0	0	0	0	0	0	0	0	0	0
Heating Degree Days (base 65°F)	556	415	255	86	11	0	0	0	8	74	287	549	2,241
Cooling Degree Days (base 65°F)	1	6	32	106	273	434	553	549	338	126	19	1	2,438
Mean Precipitation (in.)	1.10	2.02	2.44	1.86	3.84	4.46	1.81	2.48	2.91	2.95	1.92	1.38	29.17
Extreme Maximum Daily Precip. (in.)	1.70	3.25	2.85	4.30	2.95	4.04	4.72	3.08	5.35	4.00	2.43	5.25	5.35
Days With ≥ 0.1" Precipitation	3	3	4	3	6	5	2	4	4	4	3	3	44
Days With ≥ 0.5" Precipitation	1	1	2	1	3	3	1	1	2	2	1	1	19
Days With ≥ 1.0" Precipitation	0	1	1	1	1	2	1	1	1	1	1	0	11
Mean Snowfall (in.)	0.6	0.5	0.2	0.1	0.0	0.0	0.0	0.0	0.0	trace	0.2	0.5	2.1
Maximum Snow Depth (in.)	2	3	trace	3	0	0	0	0	0	0	1	4	4
Days With ≥ 1.0" Snow Depth	0	0	0	0	0	0	0	0	0	0	0	0	0

College Station Easterwood *Brazos County*   Elevation: 313 ft.   Latitude: 30° 35' N   Longitude: 96° 22' W

	JAN	FEB	MAR	APR	MAY	JUN	JUL	AUG	SEP	OCT	NOV	DEC	YEAR
Mean Maximum Temp. (°F)	60.9	*64.8*	71.8	79.1	85.5	91.7	94.9	96.1	90.5	81.4	71.2	62.3	*79.2*
Mean Temp. (°F)	50.7	*54.2*	61.2	68.4	75.8	81.9	84.4	85.0	79.6	70.5	60.5	52.0	*68.7*
Mean Minimum Temp. (°F)	40.5	*43.6*	50.5	57.6	66.0	72.0	73.9	73.9	68.6	59.5	49.8	41.6	*58.1*
Extreme Maximum Temp. (°F)	83	*99*	91	94	100	106	105	109	112	96	89	86	*112*
Extreme Minimum Temp. (°F)	9	*14*	17	30	45	57	63	60	44	29	20	2	*2*
Days Maximum Temp. ≥ 90°F	0	*0*	0	1	8	22	28	29	19	4	0	0	*111*
Days Maximum Temp. ≤ 32°F	0	*0*	0	0	0	0	0	0	0	0	0	0	*0*
Days Minimum Temp. ≤ 32°F	6	*4*	1	0	0	0	0	0	0	0	1	6	*18*
Days Minimum Temp. ≤ 0°F	0	*0*	0	0	0	0	0	0	0	0	0	0	*0*
Heating Degree Days (base 65°F)	446	*319*	171	48	2	0	0	0	2	37	187	414	*1,626*
Cooling Degree Days (base 65°F)	11	*20*	60	156	343	513	609	627	447	213	60	17	*3,076*
Mean Precipitation (in.)	3.18	*2.77*	3.31	2.45	4.64	4.25	2.18	2.65	3.27	4.48	3.21	3.23	*39.62*
Extreme Maximum Daily Precip. (in.)	5.63	*4.76*	4.20	3.62	6.23	3.58	3.18	3.47	4.86	5.28	4.56	5.79	*6.23*
Days With ≥ 0.1" Precipitation	5	*4*	5	4	6	6	4	4	4	5	5	5	*57*
Days With ≥ 0.5" Precipitation	2	*2*	2	2	3	3	2	2	2	3	2	2	*27*
Days With ≥ 1.0" Precipitation	1	*1*	1	1	1	1	1	1	1	1	1	1	*12*
Mean Snowfall (in.)	na	na	na	na	na	na	na	na	na	na	na	na	na
Maximum Snow Depth (in.)	na	na	na	na	na	na	na	na	na	na	na	na	na
Days With ≥ 1.0" Snow Depth	na	na	na	na	na	na	na	na	na	na	na	na	na

Columbus *Colorado County*   Elevation: 199 ft.   Latitude: 29° 43' N   Longitude: 96° 32' W

	JAN	FEB	MAR	APR	MAY	JUN	JUL	AUG	SEP	OCT	NOV	DEC	YEAR
Mean Maximum Temp. (°F)	64.6	67.7	74.5	80.9	87.1	92.7	95.6	97.6	93.1	84.6	74.4	65.6	81.5
Mean Temp. (°F)	51.1	54.3	61.1	67.8	75.2	80.6	82.5	83.2	78.4	69.5	60.4	52.0	68.0
Mean Minimum Temp. (°F)	37.6	40.9	47.7	54.6	63.3	68.4	69.4	68.8	63.6	54.5	46.4	38.5	54.5
Extreme Maximum Temp. (°F)	88	97	93	95	102	106	108	109	116	102	93	88	116
Extreme Minimum Temp. (°F)	10	8	8	28	40	49	59	46	40	25	18	4	4
Days Maximum Temp. ≥ 90°F	0	0	0	2	11	24	29	29	23	9	0	0	127
Days Maximum Temp. ≤ 32°F	0	0	0	0	0	0	0	0	0	0	0	0	0
Days Minimum Temp. ≤ 32°F	10	6	3	0	0	0	0	0	0	0	4	10	33
Days Minimum Temp. ≤ 0°F	0	0	0	0	0	0	0	0	0	0	0	0	0
Heating Degree Days (base 65°F)	435	315	176	53	3	0	0	0	3	45	191	413	1,634
Cooling Degree Days (base 65°F)	11	19	63	143	327	473	551	571	411	192	61	18	2,840
Mean Precipitation (in.)	3.63	2.81	3.17	3.12	4.83	4.92	3.05	2.89	3.07	4.78	4.51	3.23	44.01
Extreme Maximum Daily Precip. (in.)	3.35	2.90	2.80	5.10	3.80	5.90	2.50	3.31	3.30	8.50	5.33	3.15	8.50
Days With ≥ 0.1" Precipitation	6	5	5	4	6	6	4	5	5	6	6	6	64
Days With ≥ 0.5" Precipitation	2	2	2	2	3	3	2	2	2	3	3	2	28
Days With ≥ 1.0" Precipitation	1	1	1	1	2	2	1	1	1	2	1	1	15
Mean Snowfall (in.)	0.0	0.0	trace	0.0	0.0	0.0	0.0	0.0	0.0	0.0	0.0	trace	trace
Maximum Snow Depth (in.)	0	0	trace	0	0	0	0	0	0	0	0	trace	trace
Days With ≥ 1.0" Snow Depth	0	0	0	0	0	0	0	0	0	0	0	0	0

The period of record for all cooperative weather station data is 1980 – 2009. See User Guide for detailed explanation of data.

Conroe *Montgomery County* Elevation: 245 ft. Latitude: 30° 20' N Longitude: 95° 29' W

	JAN	FEB	MAR	APR	MAY	JUN	JUL	AUG	SEP	OCT	NOV	DEC	YEAR
Mean Maximum Temp. (°F)	61.6	64.8	72.1	78.6	85.3	91.0	94.1	94.5	89.3	80.7	71.1	62.2	78.8
Mean Temp. (°F)	51.0	54.1	61.1	67.8	75.2	81.1	83.6	83.7	78.5	69.5	60.4	51.7	68.1
Mean Minimum Temp. (°F)	40.4	43.4	50.1	57.0	65.1	71.0	73.1	72.8	67.7	58.2	49.6	41.2	57.5
Extreme Maximum Temp. (°F)	82	91	89	93	100	104	105	106	109	96	89	83	109
Extreme Minimum Temp. (°F)	11	13	18	33	46	52	60	58	44	26	24	3	3
Days Maximum Temp. ≥ 90°F	0	0	0	1	7	20	27	27	17	3	0	0	102
Days Maximum Temp. ≤ 32°F	0	0	0	0	0	0	0	0	0	0	0	0	0
Days Minimum Temp. ≤ 32°F	7	3	1	0	0	0	0	0	0	0	1	6	18
Days Minimum Temp. ≤ 0°F	0	0	0	0	0	0	0	0	0	0	0	0	0
Heating Degree Days (base 65°F)	439	317	171	51	3	0	0	0	2	44	185	420	1,632
Cooling Degree Days (base 65°F)	10	16	57	144	327	489	584	586	415	190	53	14	2,885
Mean Precipitation (in.)	3.90	3.38	3.24	2.91	5.15	5.15	2.87	3.70	3.63	5.84	5.02	3.84	48.63
Extreme Maximum Daily Precip. (in.)	4.20	2.77	2.50	2.90	6.20	3.53	2.68	4.16	3.50	7.95	6.01	3.50	7.95
Days With ≥ 0.1" Precipitation	6	5	5	4	5	6	5	5	5	5	5	6	62
Days With ≥ 0.5" Precipitation	2	2	2	2	3	3	2	2	2	3	3	3	29
Days With ≥ 1.0" Precipitation	1	1	1	1	2	1	1	1	1	2	2	1	15
Mean Snowfall (in.)	trace	trace	0.0	0.0	0.0	0.0	0.0	0.0	0.0	0.0	0.0	trace	trace
Maximum Snow Depth (in.)	1	trace	0	0	0	0	0	0	0	0	0	trace	1
Days With ≥ 1.0" Snow Depth	0	0	0	0	0	0	0	0	0	0	0	0	0

Crockett *Houston County* Elevation: 347 ft. Latitude: 31° 18' N Longitude: 95° 27' W

	JAN	FEB	MAR	APR	MAY	JUN	JUL	AUG	SEP	OCT	NOV	DEC	YEAR
Mean Maximum Temp. (°F)	58.9	63.2	70.0	77.3	84.0	90.3	93.9	94.8	89.2	80.0	69.0	60.2	77.6
Mean Temp. (°F)	48.0	51.7	58.4	65.4	73.6	80.2	83.2	83.5	77.7	67.8	57.6	49.1	66.3
Mean Minimum Temp. (°F)	37.1	40.2	46.8	53.5	63.1	69.9	72.4	72.1	66.2	55.5	46.1	38.0	55.1
Extreme Maximum Temp. (°F)	83	95	90	95	100	106	109	107	110	99	90	84	110
Extreme Minimum Temp. (°F)	6	13	18	28	40	50	59	55	41	27	21	0	0
Days Maximum Temp. ≥ 90°F	0	0	0	1	4	17	25	26	15	4	0	0	92
Days Maximum Temp. ≤ 32°F	0	0	0	0	0	0	0	0	0	0	0	0	0
Days Minimum Temp. ≤ 32°F	11	6	2	0	0	0	0	0	0	0	3	10	32
Days Minimum Temp. ≤ 0°F	0	0	0	0	0	0	0	0	0	0	0	0	0
Heating Degree Days (base 65°F)	525	378	235	81	6	0	0	0	4	61	252	494	2,036
Cooling Degree Days (base 65°F)	6	9	37	101	279	461	570	580	393	156	36	9	2,637
Mean Precipitation (in.)	3.94	3.49	3.65	3.19	4.70	4.63	2.98	2.99	3.31	4.69	3.88	3.86	45.31
Extreme Maximum Daily Precip. (in.)	5.83	3.56	6.27	3.67	3.22	9.11	4.49	3.21	6.83	5.14	3.20	4.40	9.11
Days With ≥ 0.1" Precipitation	6	5	6	4	5	6	4	4	5	5	5	6	61
Days With ≥ 0.5" Precipitation	2	2	3	2	3	2	2	2	2	3	3	3	29
Days With ≥ 1.0" Precipitation	1	1	1	1	2	1	1	1	1	2	1	1	14
Mean Snowfall (in.)	0.2	trace	0.0	0.0	0.0	0.0	0.0	0.0	0.0	0.0	trace	trace	0.2
Maximum Snow Depth (in.)	trace	trace	0	0	0	0	0	0	0	0	trace	trace	trace
Days With ≥ 1.0" Snow Depth	0	0	0	0	0	0	0	0	0	0	0	0	0

Crosbyton *Crosby County* Elevation: 3,009 ft. Latitude: 33° 39' N Longitude: 101° 15' W

	JAN	FEB	MAR	APR	MAY	JUN	JUL	AUG	SEP	OCT	NOV	DEC	YEAR
Mean Maximum Temp. (°F)	53.9	58.4	66.2	75.2	82.5	89.1	92.8	91.4	84.3	75.1	63.7	53.9	73.9
Mean Temp. (°F)	40.1	43.8	51.1	59.8	68.7	76.3	79.8	78.7	71.4	61.4	49.9	40.6	60.1
Mean Minimum Temp. (°F)	26.3	29.3	36.0	44.4	54.9	63.5	66.7	65.9	58.4	47.7	36.0	27.3	46.4
Extreme Maximum Temp. (°F)	85	89	96	99	111	113	108	106	104	101	92	81	113
Extreme Minimum Temp. (°F)	3	-3	10	21	36	45	53	55	32	19	10	-6	-6
Days Maximum Temp. ≥ 90°F	0	0	0	2	8	15	23	22	9	2	0	0	81
Days Maximum Temp. ≤ 32°F	2	2	0	0	0	0	0	0	0	0	0	2	6
Days Minimum Temp. ≤ 32°F	25	18	10	2	0	0	0	0	0	1	10	23	89
Days Minimum Temp. ≤ 0°F	0	0	0	0	0	0	0	0	0	0	0	0	0
Heating Degree Days (base 65°F)	764	592	430	194	47	2	0	0	26	159	450	749	3,413
Cooling Degree Days (base 65°F)	0	0	6	45	169	348	465	432	224	55	3	0	1,747
Mean Precipitation (in.)	0.81	0.91	1.34	1.86	2.83	3.11	2.05	2.57	3.03	2.12	1.14	0.99	22.76
Extreme Maximum Daily Precip. (in.)	1.98	1.25	2.35	3.25	2.95	2.66	3.27	5.02	5.75	4.98	2.05	1.49	5.75
Days With ≥ 0.1" Precipitation	2	2	3	3	5	5	3	4	4	3	2	2	38
Days With ≥ 0.5" Precipitation	0	1	1	1	2	2	1	2	2	1	1	1	15
Days With ≥ 1.0" Precipitation	0	0	0	1	1	1	1	1	1	1	0	0	7
Mean Snowfall (in.)	2.2	1.3	0.6	0.1	0.0	0.0	0.0	0.0	0.0	trace	1.2	1.6	7.0
Maximum Snow Depth (in.)	trace	3	trace	trace	0	0	0	0	0	trace	trace	3	3
Days With ≥ 1.0" Snow Depth	0	0	0	0	0	0	0	0	0	0	0	0	0

Crystal City *Zavala County* Elevation: 580 ft. Latitude: 28° 41' N Longitude: 99° 50' W

	JAN	FEB	MAR	APR	MAY	JUN	JUL	AUG	SEP	OCT	NOV	DEC	YEAR
Mean Maximum Temp. (°F)	67.4	72.1	79.0	85.5	90.9	95.6	97.3	97.8	92.9	85.0	75.0	67.7	83.9
Mean Temp. (°F)	55.8	60.1	66.8	73.7	80.3	85.1	86.5	86.8	82.2	74.2	64.2	56.3	72.7
Mean Minimum Temp. (°F)	44.1	48.0	54.6	61.8	69.7	74.5	75.6	75.8	71.5	63.4	53.2	44.9	61.4
Extreme Maximum Temp. (°F)	89	100	102	107	106	109	109	108	115	100	95	90	115
Extreme Minimum Temp. (°F)	19	17	22	36	50	62	67	65	47	29	26	11	11
Days Maximum Temp. ≥ 90°F	0	1	3	9	18	27	29	30	23	9	0	0	149
Days Maximum Temp. ≤ 32°F	0	0	0	0	0	0	0	0	0	0	0	0	0
Days Minimum Temp. ≤ 32°F	3	1	1	0	0	0	0	0	0	0	0	3	8
Days Minimum Temp. ≤ 0°F	0	0	0	0	0	0	0	0	0	0	0	0	0
Heating Degree Days (base 65°F)	297	178	75	15	0	0	0	0	0	15	113	284	977
Cooling Degree Days (base 65°F)	17	46	138	282	481	608	673	684	523	307	94	22	3,875
Mean Precipitation (in.)	1.04	1.01	1.40	1.46	2.27	2.62	2.15	1.67	1.91	2.09	1.22	0.75	19.59
Extreme Maximum Daily Precip. (in.)	1.44	2.15	2.97	2.15	2.37	3.81	4.44	3.54	2.70	2.23	2.28	1.52	4.44
Days With ≥ 0.1" Precipitation	2	2	2	2	4	4	3	3	3	3	2	2	32
Days With ≥ 0.5" Precipitation	1	1	1	1	2	2	1	1	1	1	1	0	13
Days With ≥ 1.0" Precipitation	0	0	0	0	1	1	1	0	0	1	0	0	4
Mean Snowfall (in.)	0.2	trace	0.0	0.0	0.0	0.0	0.0	0.0	0.0	trace	0.0	0.0	0.2
Maximum Snow Depth (in.)	3	trace	0	0	0	0	0	0	0	trace	0	0	3
Days With ≥ 1.0" Snow Depth	0	0	0	0	0	0	0	0	0	0	0	0	0

The period of record for all cooperative weather station data is 1980 – 2009. See User Guide for detailed explanation of data.

Cuero *De Witt County*   Elevation: 178 ft.   Latitude: 29° 05' N   Longitude: 97° 19' W

	JAN	FEB	MAR	APR	MAY	JUN	JUL	AUG	SEP	OCT	NOV	DEC	YEAR
Mean Maximum Temp. (°F)	66.5	69.7	75.4	81.5	87.8	92.9	95.4	96.6	92.3	84.8	75.6	67.2	82.1
Mean Temp. (°F)	54.3	57.5	63.4	69.5	76.9	81.9	83.9	84.4	79.9	71.8	62.8	54.9	70.1
Mean Minimum Temp. (°F)	42.1	45.3	51.4	57.5	66.0	70.9	72.3	72.2	67.5	58.7	49.9	42.8	58.0
Extreme Maximum Temp. (°F)	89	98	96	98	100	108	106	106	113	99	98	87	113
Extreme Minimum Temp. (°F)	13	17	18	31	41	50	61	54	44	24	21	7	7
Days Maximum Temp. ≥ 90°F	0	0	1	2	11	24	29	30	22	9	1	0	129
Days Maximum Temp. ≤ 32°F	0	0	0	0	0	0	0	0	0	0	0	0	0
Days Minimum Temp. ≤ 32°F	7	4	2	0	0	0	0	0	0	0	2	6	21
Days Minimum Temp. ≤ 0°F	0	0	0	0	0	0	0	0	0	0	0	0	0
Heating Degree Days (base 65°F)	345	239	126	36	1	0	0	0	0	27	145	336	1,255
Cooling Degree Days (base 65°F)	20	33	83	179	377	514	591	609	454	244	83	29	3,216
Mean Precipitation (in.)	2.18	1.83	2.61	2.84	3.54	4.32	2.66	2.39	3.37	3.39	2.77	2.21	34.11
Extreme Maximum Daily Precip. (in.)	3.20	2.30	3.57	7.50	4.20	7.50	3.60	3.80	7.00	5.00	5.30	4.38	7.50
Days With ≥ 0.1" Precipitation	3	3	4	3	4	5	3	3	4	4	3	4	43
Days With ≥ 0.5" Precipitation	2	1	2	1	2	3	2	2	2	2	2	2	23
Days With ≥ 1.0" Precipitation	1	1	1	1	1	1	1	1	1	1	1	1	12
Mean Snowfall (in.)	0.0	trace	0.0	0.0	0.0	0.0	0.0	0.0	0.0	0.0	0.0	0.1	0.1
Maximum Snow Depth (in.)	6	trace	0	0	0	0	0	0	0	0	0	0	6
Days With ≥ 1.0" Snow Depth	0	0	0	0	0	0	0	0	0	0	0	0	0

Daingerfield 9 S *Morris County*   Elevation: 299 ft.   Latitude: 32° 55' N   Longitude: 94° 43' W

	JAN	FEB	MAR	APR	MAY	JUN	JUL	AUG	SEP	OCT	NOV	DEC	YEAR
Mean Maximum Temp. (°F)	57.3	61.7	69.4	77.0	83.9	90.6	94.5	95.5	88.6	78.4	68.0	58.5	77.0
Mean Temp. (°F)	46.8	50.6	58.1	65.7	73.8	80.7	84.3	84.6	77.7	67.2	57.2	48.1	66.2
Mean Minimum Temp. (°F)	36.2	39.5	46.7	54.4	63.6	70.7	74.1	73.7	66.8	55.9	46.5	37.7	55.5
Extreme Maximum Temp. (°F)	81	91	92	96	100	104	107	112	111	97	95	83	112
Extreme Minimum Temp. (°F)	10	9	17	33	43	55	60	56	44	26	22	5	5
Days Maximum Temp. ≥ 90°F	0	0	0	1	6	19	27	27	15	2	0	0	97
Days Maximum Temp. ≤ 32°F	0	0	0	0	0	0	0	0	0	0	0	1	1
Days Minimum Temp. ≤ 32°F	12	7	2	0	0	0	0	0	0	0	2	10	33
Days Minimum Temp. ≤ 0°F	0	0	0	0	0	0	0	0	0	0	0	0	0
Heating Degree Days (base 65°F)	561	407	242	81	6	0	0	0	6	67	256	521	2,147
Cooling Degree Days (base 65°F)	4	8	34	109	286	477	606	615	394	141	30	6	2,710
Mean Precipitation (in.)	3.22	3.82	4.58	3.62	4.82	4.14	3.07	2.66	3.38	4.59	4.31	4.38	46.59
Extreme Maximum Daily Precip. (in.)	2.43	4.83	3.20	2.84	5.42	5.98	7.50	2.94	5.19	3.85	3.42	3.89	7.50
Days With ≥ 0.1" Precipitation	5	6	6	5	6	6	4	4	4	5	5	6	62
Days With ≥ 0.5" Precipitation	2	3	3	2	3	3	2	2	2	3	3	3	31
Days With ≥ 1.0" Precipitation	1	1	1	1	1	1	1	1	1	2	2	2	15
Mean Snowfall (in.)	0.3	0.1	trace	0.0	trace	0.0	0.0	0.0	0.0	0.0	trace	0.2	0.6
Maximum Snow Depth (in.)	4	trace	trace	0	trace	0	0	0	0	0	trace	trace	4
Days With ≥ 1.0" Snow Depth	0	0	0	0	0	0	0	0	0	0	0	0	0

Dallas Love Field *Dallas County*   Elevation: 439 ft.   Latitude: 32° 51' N   Longitude: 96° 51' W

	JAN	FEB	MAR	APR	MAY	JUN	JUL	AUG	SEP	OCT	NOV	DEC	YEAR
Mean Maximum Temp. (°F)	56.7	60.9	69.0	76.8	83.9	91.5	96.0	96.3	88.7	78.4	67.3	57.5	76.9
Mean Temp. (°F)	46.9	51.0	58.8	66.5	74.6	82.1	86.3	86.5	78.8	68.2	57.4	48.0	67.1
Mean Minimum Temp. (°F)	37.1	40.9	48.5	56.1	65.1	72.6	76.6	76.7	68.8	58.0	47.4	38.4	57.2
Extreme Maximum Temp. (°F)	83	95	95	100	103	112	108	109	110	97	89	88	112
Extreme Minimum Temp. (°F)	7	10	16	33	45	53	60	60	43	27	23	1	1
Days Maximum Temp. ≥ 90°F	0	0	0	1	7	21	28	27	15	3	0	0	102
Days Maximum Temp. ≤ 32°F	1	1	0	0	0	0	0	0	0	0	0	1	3
Days Minimum Temp. ≤ 32°F	10	6	2	0	0	0	0	0	0	0	2	8	28
Days Minimum Temp. ≤ 0°F	0	0	0	0	0	0	0	0	0	0	0	0	0
Heating Degree Days (base 65°F)	557	400	228	71	6	0	0	0	5	59	256	525	2,107
Cooling Degree Days (base 65°F)	4	10	41	122	310	518	668	674	426	166	35	5	2,979
Mean Precipitation (in.)	1.99	2.60	3.43	3.14	5.06	4.14	2.21	1.90	2.68	4.72	2.80	2.49	37.16
Extreme Maximum Daily Precip. (in.)	3.23	3.35	6.89	2.84	3.37	5.28	4.12	3.41	4.68	3.91	3.06	3.98	6.89
Days With ≥ 0.1" Precipitation	3	4	4	4	6	5	3	3	4	5	4	4	49
Days With ≥ 0.5" Precipitation	1	2	2	2	3	3	1	1	2	3	2	2	24
Days With ≥ 1.0" Precipitation	0	1	1	1	2	1	1	1	1	2	1	1	13
Mean Snowfall (in.)	*0.5*	*0.3*	*trace*	*trace*	*trace*	*trace*	*0.0*	*0.0*	*0.0*	*trace*	*0.1*	*0.3*	*1.2*
Maximum Snow Depth (in.)	*3*	*2*	*1*	*trace*	*trace*	*trace*	*0*	*0*	*0*	*trace*	*1*	*2*	*3*
Days With ≥ 1.0" Snow Depth	*0*	*0*	*0*	*0*	*0*	*0*	*0*	*0*	*0*	*0*	*0*	*0*	*0*

Dell City 5 SSW *Hudspeth County*   Elevation: 3,770 ft.   Latitude: 31° 54' N   Longitude: 105° 13' W

	JAN	FEB	MAR	APR	MAY	JUN	JUL	AUG	SEP	OCT	NOV	DEC	YEAR
Mean Maximum Temp. (°F)	59.7	64.7	72.2	80.2	89.2	97.1	97.1	94.3	88.8	79.9	67.9	59.2	79.2
Mean Temp. (°F)	42.7	47.7	54.0	61.5	71.0	79.0	80.9	78.9	72.6	62.2	50.2	42.5	61.9
Mean Minimum Temp. (°F)	25.7	30.6	35.8	42.7	52.8	60.8	64.8	63.4	56.3	44.5	32.5	25.8	44.6
Extreme Maximum Temp. (°F)	81	87	92	100	108	115	112	108	105	101	90	79	115
Extreme Minimum Temp. (°F)	6	6	11	20	32	44	53	50	34	21	9	-5	-5
Days Maximum Temp. ≥ 90°F	0	0	0	4	16	27	28	26	16	4	0	0	121
Days Maximum Temp. ≤ 32°F	0	0	0	0	0	0	0	0	0	0	0	0	0
Days Minimum Temp. ≤ 32°F	26	17	10	3	0	0	0	0	0	2	15	26	99
Days Minimum Temp. ≤ 0°F	0	0	0	0	0	0	0	0	0	0	0	0	0
Heating Degree Days (base 65°F)	684	484	338	144	16	0	0	0	11	127	440	691	2,935
Cooling Degree Days (base 65°F)	0	0	4	45	209	427	502	437	246	49	1	0	1,920
Mean Precipitation (in.)	0.42	0.46	0.30	0.24	0.96	0.97	1.48	1.91	1.75	1.05	0.54	0.54	10.62
Extreme Maximum Daily Precip. (in.)	0.90	0.95	0.76	0.90	2.44	1.76	2.00	1.62	1.80	1.49	2.00	1.15	2.44
Days With ≥ 0.1" Precipitation	1	1	1	1	2	2	3	4	3	3	1	1	23
Days With ≥ 0.5" Precipitation	0	0	0	0	0	0	1	1	1	1	0	0	4
Days With ≥ 1.0" Precipitation	0	0	0	0	0	0	0	0	0	0	0	0	0
Mean Snowfall (in.)	0.3	0.1	0.0	0.0	0.0	0.0	0.0	0.0	0.0	0.0	0.1	0.1	0.6
Maximum Snow Depth (in.)	0	0	0	0	0	0	0	0	0	0	0	0	0
Days With ≥ 1.0" Snow Depth	0	0	0	0	0	0	0	0	0	0	0	0	0

The period of record for all cooperative weather station data is 1980 – 2009. See User Guide for detailed explanation of data.

Denton 2 SE *Denton County*   Elevation: 629 ft.   Latitude: 33° 12' N   Longitude: 97° 06' W

	JAN	FEB	MAR	APR	MAY	JUN	JUL	AUG	SEP	OCT	NOV	DEC	YEAR
Mean Maximum Temp. (°F)	55.8	59.7	67.8	75.7	82.6	90.1	95.1	95.2	87.4	77.2	65.8	56.2	75.7
Mean Temp. (°F)	45.3	48.7	56.7	64.4	72.6	80.0	84.5	84.2	76.6	66.2	55.3	46.4	65.1
Mean Minimum Temp. (°F)	34.6	37.9	45.5	53.1	62.4	69.9	73.8	73.2	65.7	55.1	44.7	36.1	54.3
Extreme Maximum Temp. (°F)	83	92	94	100	104	108	108	109	111	95	88	86	111
Extreme Minimum Temp. (°F)	4	6	13	30	40	51	59	58	40	24	20	0	0
Days Maximum Temp. ≥ 90°F	0	0	0	1	4	18	27	26	13	2	0	0	91
Days Maximum Temp. ≤ 32°F	1	1	0	0	0	0	0	0	0	0	0	1	3
Days Minimum Temp. ≤ 32°F	14	8	3	0	0	0	0	0	0	0	3	11	39
Days Minimum Temp. ≤ 0°F	0	0	0	0	0	0	0	0	0	0	0	0	0
Heating Degree Days (base 65°F)	606	458	276	98	13	0	0	0	9	80	303	573	2,416
Cooling Degree Days (base 65°F)	2	5	26	86	255	457	611	602	363	123	19	3	2,552
Mean Precipitation (in.)	2.08	2.81	3.16	3.20	5.37	3.66	2.29	2.14	3.07	4.79	2.94	2.51	38.02
Extreme Maximum Daily Precip. (in.)	2.31	7.11	5.00	8.08	7.30	3.75	4.20	4.04	4.88	6.25	4.54	2.38	8.08
Days With ≥ 0.1" Precipitation	4	4	4	4	6	5	3	3	4	5	4	4	50
Days With ≥ 0.5" Precipitation	1	1	2	2	3	3	2	1	2	3	2	1	25
Days With ≥ 1.0" Precipitation	1	1	1	1	2	1	1	1	1	1	1	1	13
Mean Snowfall (in.)	0.1	0.2	0.1	0.0	0.0	0.0	0.0	0.0	0.0	0.0	trace	0.2	0.6
Maximum Snow Depth (in.)	5	2	0	0	0	0	0	0	0	0	trace	4	5
Days With ≥ 1.0" Snow Depth	0	0	0	0	0	0	0	0	0	0	0	0	0

Dimmitt 2 N *Castro County*   Elevation: 3,850 ft.   Latitude: 34° 36' N   Longitude: 102° 19' W

	JAN	FEB	MAR	APR	MAY	JUN	JUL	AUG	SEP	OCT	NOV	DEC	YEAR
Mean Maximum Temp. (°F)	50.8	55.4	63.0	71.5	80.5	88.1	91.3	89.1	82.6	72.2	60.2	50.3	71.2
Mean Temp. (°F)	36.1	39.7	46.6	54.7	64.5	73.1	76.5	75.0	67.8	56.8	44.9	36.0	56.0
Mean Minimum Temp. (°F)	21.4	23.9	30.1	37.8	48.5	58.0	61.8	60.8	53.0	41.5	29.5	21.7	40.7
Extreme Maximum Temp. (°F)	78	83	92	98	104	108	111	105	102	97	87	78	111
Extreme Minimum Temp. (°F)	-7	-9	0	18	28	40	47	49	29	14	-2	-8	-9
Days Maximum Temp. ≥ 90°F	0	0	0	1	6	14	20	16	7	1	0	0	65
Days Maximum Temp. ≤ 32°F	4	2	1	0	0	0	0	0	0	0	1	3	11
Days Minimum Temp. ≤ 32°F	29	24	19	8	0	0	0	0	0	4	19	28	131
Days Minimum Temp. ≤ 0°F	0	0	0	0	0	0	0	0	0	0	0	1	1
Heating Degree Days (base 65°F)	888	709	565	314	100	8	1	2	50	264	596	892	4,389
Cooling Degree Days (base 65°F)	0	0	0	11	91	258	364	318	142	17	0	0	1,201
Mean Precipitation (in.)	0.59	0.53	1.03	1.01	2.84	3.80	2.13	3.32	2.58	1.79	0.74	0.78	21.14
Extreme Maximum Daily Precip. (in.)	1.40	1.11	1.59	1.57	3.90	2.67	2.67	3.16	4.15	4.38	1.23	1.33	4.38
Days With ≥ 0.1" Precipitation	1	2	3	3	4	6	4	5	4	3	2	2	39
Days With ≥ 0.5" Precipitation	0	0	1	1	2	3	1	2	2	1	0	0	13
Days With ≥ 1.0" Precipitation	0	0	0	0	1	1	0	1	1	1	0	0	5
Mean Snowfall (in.)	3.2	1.5	1.0	0.4	0.0	0.0	0.0	0.0	0.0	0.1	1.3	3.4	10.9
Maximum Snow Depth (in.)	17	3	7	3	0	0	0	0	0	2	6	5	17
Days With ≥ 1.0" Snow Depth	2	1	1	0	0	0	0	0	0	0	1	2	7

Dripping Springs 6 E *Hays County*   Elevation: 1,120 ft.   Latitude: 30° 13' N   Longitude: 97° 59' W

	JAN	FEB	MAR	APR	MAY	JUN	JUL	AUG	SEP	OCT	NOV	DEC	YEAR
Mean Maximum Temp. (°F)	61.2	65.2	72.1	79.6	85.6	91.1	94.4	95.8	89.6	80.5	69.8	61.8	78.9
Mean Temp. (°F)	50.0	53.9	60.2	67.6	74.8	80.2	83.0	83.5	77.5	68.8	58.7	50.8	67.4
Mean Minimum Temp. (°F)	38.7	42.5	48.3	55.6	63.9	69.3	71.5	71.2	65.4	57.1	47.6	39.8	55.9
Extreme Maximum Temp. (°F)	86	99	95	100	101	106	106	109	111	98	89	84	111
Extreme Minimum Temp. (°F)	10	4	16	25	38	51	59	52	38	22	18	-2	-2
Days Maximum Temp. ≥ 90°F	0	0	0	2	8	20	26	28	17	3	0	0	104
Days Maximum Temp. ≤ 32°F	0	0	0	0	0	0	0	0	0	0	0	0	0
Days Minimum Temp. ≤ 32°F	10	5	3	0	0	0	0	0	0	0	3	9	30
Days Minimum Temp. ≤ 0°F	0	0	0	0	0	0	0	0	0	0	0	0	0
Heating Degree Days (base 65°F)	465	326	192	55	4	0	0	0	4	53	223	443	1,765
Cooling Degree Days (base 65°F)	5	18	51	141	314	463	564	581	387	178	40	10	2,752
Mean Precipitation (in.)	2.42	2.30	2.90	2.36	4.04	4.70	2.24	1.80	2.78	3.99	3.39	2.82	35.74
Extreme Maximum Daily Precip. (in.)	4.36	3.66	3.09	2.52	3.13	6.59	4.46	3.20	4.06	6.66	4.26	5.65	6.66
Days With ≥ 0.1" Precipitation	4	4	5	4	5	5	4	3	4	5	4	4	51
Days With ≥ 0.5" Precipitation	1	2	2	2	2	3	1	1	2	3	2	2	23
Days With ≥ 1.0" Precipitation	1	1	1	1	2	2	1	1	1	1	1	1	14
Mean Snowfall (in.)	0.5	0.2	trace	trace	0.0	0.0	0.0	0.0	0.0	0.0	trace	0.1	0.8
Maximum Snow Depth (in.)	8	2	trace	trace	0	0	0	0	0	0	trace	1	8
Days With ≥ 1.0" Snow Depth	0	0	0	0	0	0	0	0	0	0	0	0	0

Dublin *Erath County*   Elevation: 1,501 ft.   Latitude: 32° 06' N   Longitude: 98° 20' W

	JAN	FEB	MAR	APR	MAY	JUN	JUL	AUG	SEP	OCT	NOV	DEC	YEAR
Mean Maximum Temp. (°F)	55.4	59.6	67.0	75.6	82.3	88.7	93.5	94.2	86.6	76.6	65.3	56.1	75.1
Mean Temp. (°F)	44.1	47.9	55.0	63.1	71.3	77.9	81.9	82.2	74.9	65.2	54.4	45.2	63.6
Mean Minimum Temp. (°F)	32.7	36.3	43.0	50.6	60.2	67.0	70.3	70.2	63.1	53.8	43.5	34.2	52.1
Extreme Maximum Temp. (°F)	84	96	93	99	104	107	106	107	109	96	92	82	109
Extreme Minimum Temp. (°F)	3	2	9	12	41	51	57	56	39	25	18	-7	-7
Days Maximum Temp. ≥ 90°F	0	0	0	1	5	14	24	24	12	2	0	0	82
Days Maximum Temp. ≤ 32°F	1	1	0	0	0	0	0	0	0	0	0	1	3
Days Minimum Temp. ≤ 32°F	16	9	4	1	0	0	0	0	0	0	4	13	47
Days Minimum Temp. ≤ 0°F	0	0	0	0	0	0	0	0	0	0	0	0	0
Heating Degree Days (base 65°F)	643	480	323	122	18	1	0	0	12	92	327	608	2,626
Cooling Degree Days (base 65°F)	1	4	20	73	219	394	532	540	316	105	15	1	2,220
Mean Precipitation (in.)	1.61	2.65	2.97	2.81	5.08	5.10	1.91	2.88	3.47	3.63	2.59	2.22	36.92
Extreme Maximum Daily Precip. (in.)	1.50	4.00	3.80	6.09	6.50	4.72	2.52	4.50	3.01	3.24	4.00	3.75	6.50
Days With ≥ 0.1" Precipitation	3	4	5	4	6	6	3	4	4	5	4	4	52
Days With ≥ 0.5" Precipitation	1	2	2	2	3	3	1	2	2	3	2	1	24
Days With ≥ 1.0" Precipitation	0	1	1	1	2	2	1	1	1	1	1	1	13
Mean Snowfall (in.)	0.3	0.2	trace	0.1	0.0	0.0	0.0	0.0	0.0	trace	0.1	0.4	1.1
Maximum Snow Depth (in.)	6	4	2	2	0	0	0	0	0	trace	0	3	6
Days With ≥ 1.0" Snow Depth	0	0	0	0	0	0	0	0	0	0	0	0	0

The period of record for all cooperative weather station data is 1980 – 2009. See User Guide for detailed explanation of data.

Emory *Rains County*   Elevation: 435 ft.   Latitude: 32° 52' N   Longitude: 95° 46' W

	JAN	FEB	MAR	APR	MAY	JUN	JUL	AUG	SEP	OCT	NOV	DEC	YEAR
Mean Maximum Temp. (°F)	55.2	59.2	66.9	74.4	81.2	87.9	92.5	93.4	86.7	76.7	66.0	56.5	74.7
Mean Temp. (°F)	44.0	47.6	55.4	62.9	70.9	78.3	81.9	81.9	75.1	64.7	54.5	45.3	63.5
Mean Minimum Temp. (°F)	32.8	35.9	43.9	51.1	60.6	68.6	71.3	70.4	63.4	52.2	42.9	34.0	52.3
Extreme Maximum Temp. (°F)	80	91	88	93	96	101	105	107	108	96	85	82	108
Extreme Minimum Temp. (°F)	3	4	15	28	39	50	57	53	39	23	18	-5	-5
Days Maximum Temp. ≥ 90°F	0	0	0	0	1	11	23	25	12	2	0	0	74
Days Maximum Temp. ≤ 32°F	1	1	0	0	0	0	0	0	0	0	0	1	3
Days Minimum Temp. ≤ 32°F	17	11	4	0	0	0	0	0	0	0	5	15	52
Days Minimum Temp. ≤ 0°F	0	0	0	0	0	0	0	0	0	0	0	0	0
Heating Degree Days (base 65°F)	647	489	307	122	19	1	0	0	13	100	326	608	2,632
Cooling Degree Days (base 65°F)	2	3	18	65	208	405	532	532	323	97	17	3	2,205
Mean Precipitation (in.)	2.98	3.52	4.37	3.28	5.17	4.09	2.73	2.21	3.12	5.15	3.78	3.80	44.20
Extreme Maximum Daily Precip. (in.)	4.55	4.25	4.85	3.05	5.41	5.65	4.00	2.60	3.94	5.60	4.10	4.55	5.65
Days With ≥ 0.1" Precipitation	5	5	6	5	6	5	3	3	4	5	4	5	56
Days With ≥ 0.5" Precipitation	2	2	3	2	3	3	2	2	2	3	3	3	30
Days With ≥ 1.0" Precipitation	1	1	1	1	2	1	1	1	1	2	2	1	15
Mean Snowfall (in.)	0.2	0.3	trace	0.0	0.0	0.0	0.0	0.0	0.0	0.0	0.0	0.3	0.8
Maximum Snow Depth (in.)	2	1	trace	0	0	0	0	0	0	0	0	trace	2
Days With ≥ 1.0" Snow Depth	0	0	0	0	0	0	0	0	0	0	0	0	0

Encinal *Webb County*   Elevation: 589 ft.   Latitude: 28° 03' N   Longitude: 99° 26' W

	JAN	FEB	MAR	APR	MAY	JUN	JUL	AUG	SEP	OCT	NOV	DEC	YEAR
Mean Maximum Temp. (°F)	67.1	71.5	79.7	87.2	92.5	97.9	98.9	99.5	93.7	85.9	76.3	67.8	84.8
Mean Temp. (°F)	54.5	58.7	65.7	73.3	79.7	85.1	86.1	86.5	81.6	73.2	63.7	55.6	72.0
Mean Minimum Temp. (°F)	42.0	45.8	51.6	59.4	66.9	72.4	73.2	73.5	69.4	60.5	51.0	43.4	59.1
Extreme Maximum Temp. (°F)	93	101	103	109	110	116	109	109	111	102	98	93	116
Extreme Minimum Temp. (°F)	20	19	24	36	45	57	64	60	50	31	30	12	12
Days Maximum Temp. ≥ 90°F	0	1	5	13	21	26	28	30	24	11	2	0	161
Days Maximum Temp. ≤ 32°F	0	0	0	0	0	0	0	0	0	0	0	0	0
Days Minimum Temp. ≤ 32°F	4	2	1	0	0	0	0	0	0	0	0	3	10
Days Minimum Temp. ≤ 0°F	0	0	0	0	0	0	0	0	0	0	0	0	0
Heating Degree Days (base 65°F)	330	214	96	16	1	0	0	0	1	21	124	309	1,112
Cooling Degree Days (base 65°F)	13	41	123	271	464	611	660	675	504	284	90	23	3,759
Mean Precipitation (in.)	0.89	0.74	1.33	1.15	2.92	2.35	2.02	2.06	2.63	2.05	1.15	0.84	20.13
Extreme Maximum Daily Precip. (in.)	1.80	2.00	4.10	2.15	4.20	na	2.66	5.50	2.98	3.35	na	na	na
Days With ≥ 0.1" Precipitation	1	1	2	2	4	2	2	2	3	2	2	1	24
Days With ≥ 0.5" Precipitation	1	0	1	1	2	1	1	1	2	1	1	0	12
Days With ≥ 1.0" Precipitation	0	0	1	0	1	1	1	1	1	1	0	0	7
Mean Snowfall (in.)	trace	0.0	0.0	0.0	0.0	0.0	0.0	0.0	0.0	0.0	0.0	0.2	0.2
Maximum Snow Depth (in.)	trace	0	0	0	0	0	0	0	0	0	0	na	5	na
Days With ≥ 1.0" Snow Depth	0	0	0	0	0	0	0	0	0	0	0	0	0

Falcon Dam *Starr County*   Elevation: 319 ft.   Latitude: 26° 33' N   Longitude: 99° 08' W

	JAN	FEB	MAR	APR	MAY	JUN	JUL	AUG	SEP	OCT	NOV	DEC	YEAR
Mean Maximum Temp. (°F)	69.1	74.2	82.1	88.6	94.4	98.9	100.3	100.3	94.4	87.6	78.5	69.6	86.5
Mean Temp. (°F)	57.9	62.4	69.4	75.7	82.3	86.6	87.6	87.5	83.0	76.0	67.2	58.7	74.5
Mean Minimum Temp. (°F)	46.6	50.5	56.7	62.7	70.2	74.3	74.8	74.8	71.5	64.5	55.8	47.6	62.5
Extreme Maximum Temp. (°F)	97	102	105	109	114	116	110	109	112	101	97	94	116
Extreme Minimum Temp. (°F)	23	24	27	30	49	59	63	64	51	31	32	15	15
Days Maximum Temp. ≥ 90°F	0	2	7	15	24	28	30	30	24	14	4	0	178
Days Maximum Temp. ≤ 32°F	0	0	0	0	0	0	0	0	0	0	0	0	0
Days Minimum Temp. ≤ 32°F	1	1	0	0	0	0	0	0	0	0	0	1	3
Days Minimum Temp. ≤ 0°F	0	0	0	0	0	0	0	0	0	0	0	0	0
Heating Degree Days (base 65°F)	249	146	55	13	1	0	0	0	1	12	82	237	796
Cooling Degree Days (base 65°F)	36	78	200	341	545	656	707	705	547	362	154	47	4,378
Mean Precipitation (in.)	0.91	0.98	0.64	1.42	2.35	1.95	1.83	2.19	3.88	1.83	1.24	0.94	20.16
Extreme Maximum Daily Precip. (in.)	1.32	2.75	1.66	2.61	4.42	2.99	5.25	3.41	7.70	3.40	3.20	2.00	7.70
Days With ≥ 0.1" Precipitation	3	2	1	2	3	3	3	3	5	3	2	2	32
Days With ≥ 0.5" Precipitation	0	0	0	1	1	1	1	1	2	1	1	0	9
Days With ≥ 1.0" Precipitation	0	0	0	0	1	1	1	1	1	0	0	0	5
Mean Snowfall (in.)	0.0	0.0	0.0	0.0	0.0	0.0	0.0	0.0	0.0	0.0	0.0	0.0	0.0
Maximum Snow Depth (in.)	0	0	0	0	0	0	0	0	0	0	0	0	0
Days With ≥ 1.0" Snow Depth	0	0	0	0	0	0	0	0	0	0	0	0	0

Falfurrias *Brooks County*   Elevation: 120 ft.   Latitude: 27° 13' N   Longitude: 98° 08' W

	JAN	FEB	MAR	APR	MAY	JUN	JUL	AUG	SEP	OCT	NOV	DEC	YEAR
Mean Maximum Temp. (°F)	68.5	72.3	78.7	85.5	90.9	95.5	97.3	97.5	92.2	85.9	77.3	69.4	84.3
Mean Temp. (°F)	56.7	60.2	66.4	73.4	79.9	84.4	85.7	85.6	81.3	74.1	65.5	57.9	72.6
Mean Minimum Temp. (°F)	44.8	48.0	54.0	61.2	68.8	73.2	74.0	73.7	70.3	62.3	53.6	46.4	60.9
Extreme Maximum Temp. (°F)	95	99	104	108	109	115	107	107	111	100	96	93	115
Extreme Minimum Temp. (°F)	21	25	23	34	48	55	66	65	50	28	25	13	13
Days Maximum Temp. ≥ 90°F	0	1	3	10	19	25	26	27	20	11	2	0	144
Days Maximum Temp. ≤ 32°F	0	0	0	0	0	0	0	0	0	0	0	0	0
Days Minimum Temp. ≤ 32°F	3	2	1	0	0	0	0	0	0	0	1	3	10
Days Minimum Temp. ≤ 0°F	0	0	0	0	0	0	0	0	0	0	0	0	0
Heating Degree Days (base 65°F)	285	185	90	21	0	0	0	0	0	18	105	267	971
Cooling Degree Days (base 65°F)	34	56	140	279	468	587	649	647	497	308	125	54	3,844
Mean Precipitation (in.)	1.05	1.45	1.15	1.12	2.74	2.73	2.40	2.74	3.66	3.38	1.36	1.26	25.04
Extreme Maximum Daily Precip. (in.)	1.30	3.78	1.72	1.78	5.01	3.67	6.90	7.36	4.35	4.60	2.20	3.21	7.36
Days With ≥ 0.1" Precipitation	3	3	2	2	4	4	3	3	5	3	2	2	36
Days With ≥ 0.5" Precipitation	1	1	1	1	2	2	1	1	2	2	1	1	16
Days With ≥ 1.0" Precipitation	0	0	0	0	1	1	1	1	1	1	0	0	6
Mean Snowfall (in.)	0.0	0.0	0.0	0.0	0.0	0.0	0.0	0.0	0.0	0.0	0.0	0.0	0.0
Maximum Snow Depth (in.)	0	0	0	0	0	0	0	0	0	0	0	0	0
Days With ≥ 1.0" Snow Depth	0	0	0	0	0	0	0	0	0	0	0	0	0

The period of record for all cooperative weather station data is 1980 – 2009. See User Guide for detailed explanation of data.

Ferris *Ellis County*   Elevation: 470 ft.   Latitude: 32° 31' N   Longitude: 96° 40' W

	JAN	FEB	MAR	APR	MAY	JUN	JUL	AUG	SEP	OCT	NOV	DEC	YEAR
Mean Maximum Temp. (°F)	57.3	61.9	68.6	76.8	83.6	90.8	96.2	96.6	89.7	79.2	68.0	57.8	77.2
Mean Temp. (°F)	46.0	50.3	57.0	64.7	73.0	80.1	84.3	84.4	77.5	67.1	56.6	46.8	65.6
Mean Minimum Temp. (°F)	34.7	38.6	45.3	52.5	62.3	69.3	72.5	72.2	65.4	54.9	45.1	35.8	54.0
Extreme Maximum Temp. (°F)	84	96	93	99	102	110	109	111	111	97	91	87	111
Extreme Minimum Temp. (°F)	7	7	14	29	42	53	57	56	42	26	23	-1	-1
Days Maximum Temp. ≥ 90°F	0	0	0	1	5	20	28	27	17	3	0	0	101
Days Maximum Temp. ≤ 32°F	0	1	0	0	0	0	0	0	0	0	0	1	2
Days Minimum Temp. ≤ 32°F	14	8	3	0	0	0	0	0	0	0	3	12	40
Days Minimum Temp. ≤ 0°F	0	0	0	0	0	0	0	0	0	0	0	0	0
Heating Degree Days (base 65°F)	585	415	267	93	9	0	0	0	6	68	273	561	2,277
Cooling Degree Days (base 65°F)	3	6	26	90	264	459	606	609	389	139	27	5	2,623
Mean Precipitation (in.)	2.86	2.95	3.90	3.13	4.60	3.97	1.86	2.44	2.58	4.59	3.00	3.38	39.26
Extreme Maximum Daily Precip. (in.)	6.15	2.50	5.21	2.26	4.70	3.86	3.50	3.23	3.68	4.88	2.73	5.20	6.15
Days With ≥ 0.1" Precipitation	4	4	5	4	6	5	3	3	4	5	4	4	51
Days With ≥ 0.5" Precipitation	2	2	3	2	3	3	1	2	2	3	2	2	27
Days With ≥ 1.0" Precipitation	1	1	1	1	2	1	1	1	1	1	1	1	13
Mean Snowfall (in.)	0.1	0.3	trace	0.0	0.0	0.0	0.0	0.0	0.0	0.0	trace	0.3	0.7
Maximum Snow Depth (in.)	3	2	3	0	0	0	0	0	0	0	trace	3	3
Days With ≥ 1.0" Snow Depth	0	0	0	0	0	0	0	0	0	0	0	0	0

Floresville *Wilson County*   Elevation: 399 ft.   Latitude: 29° 08' N   Longitude: 98° 10' W

	JAN	FEB	MAR	APR	MAY	JUN	JUL	AUG	SEP	OCT	NOV	DEC	YEAR
Mean Maximum Temp. (°F)	64.8	68.9	75.0	82.1	88.2	93.5	96.3	97.2	91.9	83.9	74.5	66.0	81.9
Mean Temp. (°F)	51.7	55.7	62.5	69.4	77.2	82.5	84.9	85.1	79.7	71.1	61.6	52.8	69.5
Mean Minimum Temp. (°F)	38.6	42.3	49.9	56.7	66.1	71.3	73.4	73.0	67.5	58.2	48.6	39.5	57.1
Extreme Maximum Temp. (°F)	87	99	97	100	109	109	107	110	111	99	95	89	111
Extreme Minimum Temp. (°F)	5	10	16	30	37	46	62	58	43	26	20	7	5
Days Maximum Temp. ≥ 90°F	0	0	1	4	14	25	28	29	21	8	0	0	130
Days Maximum Temp. ≤ 32°F	0	0	0	0	0	0	0	0	0	0	0	0	0
Days Minimum Temp. ≤ 32°F	10	5	2	0	0	0	0	0	0	0	2	9	28
Days Minimum Temp. ≤ 0°F	0	0	0	0	0	0	0	0	0	0	0	0	0
Heating Degree Days (base 65°F)	416	280	144	41	2	0	0	0	2	36	167	388	1,476
Cooling Degree Days (base 65°F)	11	22	75	180	385	530	622	632	449	233	71	18	3,228
Mean Precipitation (in.)	1.42	1.66	2.06	2.03	3.22	2.92	2.31	2.39	2.85	2.89	2.27	1.46	27.48
Extreme Maximum Daily Precip. (in.)	2.14	3.45	*4.50*	4.04	4.00	3.15	3.05	*5.07*	6.36	3.75	8.82	*3.01*	8.82
Days With ≥ 0.1" Precipitation	3	3	3	3	4	4	3	3	4	4	3	3	40
Days With ≥ 0.5" Precipitation	1	1	1	1	2	2	1	1	2	2	1	1	16
Days With ≥ 1.0" Precipitation	0	0	1	1	1	1	1	1	1	1	1	0	9
Mean Snowfall (in.)	0.4	0.0	0.0	0.0	0.0	0.0	0.0	0.0	0.0	trace	0.0	0.0	0.4
Maximum Snow Depth (in.)	0	0	0	0	0	0	0	0	0	trace	0	0	trace
Days With ≥ 1.0" Snow Depth	0	0	0	0	0	0	0	0	0	0	0	0	0

Fort Hancock 5 SSE *Hudspeth County*   Elevation: 3,904 ft.   Latitude: 31° 13' N   Longitude: 105° 47' W

	JAN	FEB	MAR	APR	MAY	JUN	JUL	AUG	SEP	OCT	NOV	DEC	YEAR
Mean Maximum Temp. (°F)	61.2	66.8	73.8	82.0	91.3	97.8	96.2	93.1	89.1	81.0	70.0	60.4	80.2
Mean Temp. (°F)	43.5	48.5	*55.3*	62.8	72.3	80.4	81.3	79.0	73.6	63.5	51.9	43.1	*62.9*
Mean Minimum Temp. (°F)	25.6	30.2	*36.6*	43.4	53.3	62.8	66.4	64.9	57.9	45.7	33.4	26.0	*45.5*
Extreme Maximum Temp. (°F)	83	87	92	98	107	113	111	106	104	100	89	81	113
Extreme Minimum Temp. (°F)	7	9	15	23	34	42	53	53	40	*24*	12	-1	*-1*
Days Maximum Temp. ≥ 90°F	0	0	0	4	20	27	27	24	16	4	0	0	122
Days Maximum Temp. ≤ 32°F	0	0	0	0	0	0	0	0	0	0	0	0	0
Days Minimum Temp. ≤ 32°F	26	17	9	2	0	0	0	0	0	2	14	26	96
Days Minimum Temp. ≤ 0°F	0	0	0	0	0	0	0	0	0	0	0	0	0
Heating Degree Days (base 65°F)	660	460	*296*	110	7	0	0	0	5	101	388	671	*2,698*
Cooling Degree Days (base 65°F)	0	0	*3*	49	243	466	512	441	268	61	2	0	*2,045*
Mean Precipitation (in.)	0.49	0.33	0.24	0.28	0.45	0.89	1.56	1.52	1.55	0.95	0.40	0.59	9.25
Extreme Maximum Daily Precip. (in.)	2.01	0.78	0.70	1.65	1.27	1.27	2.60	1.12	3.70	2.70	0.97	1.06	3.70
Days With ≥ 0.1" Precipitation	1	1	1	1	1	2	4	5	3	2	1	2	24
Days With ≥ 0.5" Precipitation	0	0	0	0	0	0	1	1	1	0	0	0	3
Days With ≥ 1.0" Precipitation	0	0	0	0	0	0	0	0	0	0	0	0	0
Mean Snowfall (in.)	0.1	trace	0.0	0.0	0.0	0.0	0.0	0.0	0.0	0.0	trace	0.3	0.4
Maximum Snow Depth (in.)	trace	0	0	0	0	0	0	0	0	0	*0*	*trace*	3	*3*
Days With ≥ 1.0" Snow Depth	0	0	0	0	0	0	0	0	0	0	0	0	0

Gail *Borden County*   Elevation: 2,528 ft.   Latitude: 32° 46' N   Longitude: 101° 27' W

	JAN	FEB	MAR	APR	MAY	JUN	JUL	AUG	SEP	OCT	NOV	DEC	YEAR
Mean Maximum Temp. (°F)	58.0	62.6	70.7	79.7	86.8	*92.2*	94.9	*93.6*	86.5	77.7	66.5	57.9	*77.3*
Mean Temp. (°F)	45.0	49.0	56.3	64.8	73.0	*79.3*	82.3	*81.2*	74.2	64.9	53.3	45.1	*64.0*
Mean Minimum Temp. (°F)	32.1	35.3	41.9	49.8	59.2	*66.3*	69.6	*68.8*	61.8	52.0	40.1	32.3	*50.8*
Extreme Maximum Temp. (°F)	87	91	96	101	111	116	113	107	106	103	91	84	116
Extreme Minimum Temp. (°F)	4	0	9	25	38	45	57	55	36	21	8	-1	-1
Days Maximum Temp. ≥ 90°F	0	0	1	4	13	18	25	23	12	3	0	0	99
Days Maximum Temp. ≤ 32°F	1	1	0	0	0	0	0	0	0	0	0	1	3
Days Minimum Temp. ≤ 32°F	15	11	5	1	0	0	0	0	0	0	6	15	53
Days Minimum Temp. ≤ 0°F	0	0	0	0	0	0	0	0	0	0	0	0	0
Heating Degree Days (base 65°F)	613	451	287	100	17	*0*	0	*0*	13	98	354	610	*2,543*
Cooling Degree Days (base 65°F)	0	3	24	102	272	*435*	542	*511*	296	101	8	0	*2,294*
Mean Precipitation (in.)	0.63	0.72	0.95	1.29	2.77	2.67	1.78	2.25	2.71	1.96	0.90	0.80	19.43
Extreme Maximum Daily Precip. (in.)	1.30	1.56	1.70	2.85	3.52	3.35	2.93	4.25	4.52	2.95	2.40	1.56	4.52
Days With ≥ 0.1" Precipitation	2	2	2	2	4	4	3	3	4	3	2	2	33
Days With ≥ 0.5" Precipitation	0	0	1	1	2	2	1	1	2	1	1	1	13
Days With ≥ 1.0" Precipitation	0	0	0	0	1	1	1	1	1	1	0	0	6
Mean Snowfall (in.)	0.1	0.2	trace	trace	0.0	0.0	0.0	0.0	0.0	0.0	0.1	0.3	0.7
Maximum Snow Depth (in.)	trace	trace	trace	0	0	0	0	0	0	0	trace	3	3
Days With ≥ 1.0" Snow Depth	0	0	0	0	0	0	0	0	0	0	0	0	0

The period of record for all cooperative weather station data is 1980 – 2009. See User Guide for detailed explanation of data.

Georgetown Lake *Williamson County*   Elevation: 839 ft.   Latitude: 30° 41' N   Longitude: 97° 43' W

	JAN	FEB	MAR	APR	MAY	JUN	JUL	AUG	SEP	OCT	NOV	DEC	YEAR
Mean Maximum Temp. (°F)	59.9	63.7	70.5	78.3	85.4	90.8	95.1	96.1	89.5	80.5	69.7	60.5	78.3
Mean Temp. (°F)	48.0	51.8	59.1	66.4	74.7	80.0	83.5	83.9	77.6	68.5	58.3	49.2	66.8
Mean Minimum Temp. (°F)	36.0	39.9	47.6	54.5	63.9	69.2	71.8	71.7	65.7	56.5	47.0	37.8	55.1
Extreme Maximum Temp. (°F)	88	98	97	99	100	105	108	109	111	98	93	84	111
Extreme Minimum Temp. (°F)	6	6	20	31	42	50	59	57	34	28	23	-2	-2
Days Maximum Temp. ≥ 90°F	0	0	0	2	8	19	27	28	17	4	0	0	105
Days Maximum Temp. ≤ 32°F	0	1	0	0	0	0	0	0	0	0	0	1	2
Days Minimum Temp. ≤ 32°F	10	6	2	0	0	0	0	0	0	0	2	9	29
Days Minimum Temp. ≤ 0°F	0	0	0	0	0	0	0	0	0	0	0	0	0
Heating Degree Days (base 65°F)	523	376	220	70	5	0	0	0	5	53	227	489	1,968
Cooling Degree Days (base 65°F)	3	9	44	120	312	459	580	593	390	171	34	5	2,720
Mean Precipitation (in.)	2.14	2.51	3.06	2.74	4.48	4.33	2.02	2.25	3.26	4.37	3.21	2.58	36.95
Extreme Maximum Daily Precip. (in.)	2.50	4.19	2.85	5.50	3.30	3.56	3.40	3.98	4.79	3.50	3.72	4.17	5.50
Days With ≥ 0.1" Precipitation	5	4	5	4	6	5	3	3	4	5	4	4	52
Days With ≥ 0.5" Precipitation	1	2	2	2	3	3	1	1	2	3	2	2	24
Days With ≥ 1.0" Precipitation	1	0	1	1	2	2	1	1	1	2	1	1	14
Mean Snowfall (in.)	0.0	0.0	0.0	0.0	0.0	0.0	0.0	0.0	0.0	0.0	0.0	trace	trace
Maximum Snow Depth (in.)	7	0	0	0	0	0	0	0	0	0	0	trace	7
Days With ≥ 1.0" Snow Depth	0	0	0	0	0	0	0	0	0	0	0	0	0

Grandfalls 3 SSE *Ward County*   Elevation: 2,439 ft.   Latitude: 31° 18' N   Longitude: 102° 50' W

	JAN	FEB	MAR	APR	MAY	JUN	JUL	AUG	SEP	OCT	NOV	DEC	YEAR
Mean Maximum Temp. (°F)	61.8	66.9	75.1	83.3	91.3	97.8	98.4	97.0	90.6	82.2	70.9	61.1	81.4
Mean Temp. (°F)	44.7	49.4	57.3	65.3	74.4	82.7	83.9	82.5	75.9	66.2	53.8	44.7	65.1
Mean Minimum Temp. (°F)	27.7	32.0	39.4	47.1	57.5	67.3	69.3	68.0	61.0	50.0	36.6	28.2	48.7
Extreme Maximum Temp. (°F)	86	94	97	104	110	117	116	112	107	100	94	85	117
Extreme Minimum Temp. (°F)	8	-9	12	24	37	51	55	52	36	22	7	0	-9
Days Maximum Temp. ≥ 90°F	0	0	2	10	18	25	29	28	na	7	0	0	na
Days Maximum Temp. ≤ 32°F	1	0	0	0	0	0	0	0	0	0	0	1	2
Days Minimum Temp. ≤ 32°F	23	15	6	1	0	0	0	0	0	1	10	22	78
Days Minimum Temp. ≤ 0°F	0	0	0	0	0	0	0	0	0	0	0	0	0
Heating Degree Days (base 65°F)	622	436	258	95	12	0	0	0	10	77	339	622	2,471
Cooling Degree Days (base 65°F)	0	2	24	109	312	537	591	551	343	120	9	0	2,598
Mean Precipitation (in.)	0.48	0.69	0.48	0.90	1.70	1.50	1.42	1.74	2.50	1.55	0.59	0.83	14.38
Extreme Maximum Daily Precip. (in.)	1.31	1.35	1.30	3.00	2.30	2.34	2.20	2.82	na	2.45	1.63	na	na
Days With ≥ 0.1" Precipitation	2	2	1	2	3	3	3	3	3	3	2	2	29
Days With ≥ 0.5" Precipitation	0	0	0	1	1	1	1	1	1	1	0	1	8
Days With ≥ 1.0" Precipitation	0	0	0	0	0	1	0	0	1	1	0	0	3
Mean Snowfall (in.)	1.0	0.1	0.1	0.0	0.0	0.0	0.0	0.0	0.0	0.0	0.3	0.4	1.9
Maximum Snow Depth (in.)	5	4	2	1	0	0	0	0	na	0	0	4	na
Days With ≥ 1.0" Snow Depth	0	0	0	0	0	0	0	0	0	0	0	0	0

Granger Dam *Williamson County*   Elevation: 564 ft.   Latitude: 30° 42' N   Longitude: 97° 20' W

	JAN	FEB	MAR	APR	MAY	JUN	JUL	AUG	SEP	OCT	NOV	DEC	YEAR
Mean Maximum Temp. (°F)	59.7	63.9	70.0	78.0	84.5	90.7	94.6	95.5	89.8	80.0	69.8	60.4	78.1
Mean Temp. (°F)	48.3	52.5	59.3	66.8	74.3	80.4	83.5	84.0	78.3	68.6	58.7	49.7	67.0
Mean Minimum Temp. (°F)	36.8	41.0	48.5	55.6	64.0	70.1	72.3	72.5	66.7	57.2	47.5	39.0	55.9
Extreme Maximum Temp. (°F)	86	98	94	97	100	105	104	107	110	98	89	84	110
Extreme Minimum Temp. (°F)	7	3	19	31	42	51	58	57	44	27	21	2	2
Days Maximum Temp. ≥ 90°F	0	0	0	1	7	20	27	28	17	4	0	0	104
Days Maximum Temp. ≤ 32°F	0	0	0	0	0	0	0	0	0	0	0	1	1
Days Minimum Temp. ≤ 32°F	10	5	2	0	0	0	0	0	0	0	2	8	27
Days Minimum Temp. ≤ 0°F	0	0	0	0	0	0	0	0	0	0	0	0	0
Heating Degree Days (base 65°F)	516	358	214	64	6	0	0	0	4	53	222	474	1,911
Cooling Degree Days (base 65°F)	4	12	44	126	300	468	581	596	410	174	41	8	2,764
Mean Precipitation (in.)	2.20	2.22	2.71	2.00	5.01	4.24	1.62	2.02	3.00	3.68	2.69	2.89	34.28
Extreme Maximum Daily Precip. (in.)	2.88	2.07	2.80	2.80	3.80	5.40	3.53	3.33	4.12	6.05	3.50	7.84	7.84
Days With ≥ 0.1" Precipitation	4	4	5	4	6	5	3	3	4	5	4	4	51
Days With ≥ 0.5" Precipitation	1	2	2	1	3	3	1	1	2	2	2	2	22
Days With ≥ 1.0" Precipitation	1	0	1	0	2	2	0	1	1	1	1	1	11
Mean Snowfall (in.)	0.0	0.0	0.0	0.0	0.0	0.0	0.0	0.0	0.0	0.0	0.0	trace	trace
Maximum Snow Depth (in.)	0	0	0	0	0	0	0	0	0	0	0	trace	trace
Days With ≥ 1.0" Snow Depth	0	0	0	0	0	0	0	0	0	0	0	0	0

Grapevine Dam *Tarrant County*   Elevation: 584 ft.   Latitude: 32° 57' N   Longitude: 97° 03' W

	JAN	FEB	MAR	APR	MAY	JUN	JUL	AUG	SEP	OCT	NOV	DEC	YEAR
Mean Maximum Temp. (°F)	56.3	60.5	67.5	75.8	83.3	91.0	96.0	96.4	88.7	78.6	66.9	56.9	76.5
Mean Temp. (°F)	44.3	48.6	55.8	63.7	72.4	80.0	84.4	84.4	76.6	65.9	55.2	45.3	64.7
Mean Minimum Temp. (°F)	32.1	36.4	43.9	51.6	61.4	68.9	72.7	72.4	64.4	53.2	43.3	33.8	52.8
Extreme Maximum Temp. (°F)	85	95	96	101	101	109	110	108	109	100	89	83	110
Extreme Minimum Temp. (°F)	6	4	13	29	41	50	57	55	38	22	19	-1	-1
Days Maximum Temp. ≥ 90°F	0	0	0	1	6	20	27	27	15	4	0	0	100
Days Maximum Temp. ≤ 32°F	1	1	0	0	0	0	0	0	0	0	0	1	3
Days Minimum Temp. ≤ 32°F	17	9	3	0	0	0	0	0	0	0	4	13	46
Days Minimum Temp. ≤ 0°F	0	0	0	0	0	0	0	0	0	0	0	0	0
Heating Degree Days (base 65°F)	637	461	303	108	14	1	0	0	10	88	308	603	2,533
Cooling Degree Days (base 65°F)	1	5	24	77	250	456	607	609	363	123	20	2	2,537
Mean Precipitation (in.)	2.17	2.77	3.48	3.13	4.81	3.89	2.26	1.82	3.12	4.00	2.94	2.69	37.08
Extreme Maximum Daily Precip. (in.)	3.93	3.92	3.78	2.80	6.47	8.30	7.50	1.94	4.67	5.01	3.40	3.67	8.30
Days With ≥ 0.1" Precipitation	4	4	5	4	6	5	3	3	4	5	4	5	52
Days With ≥ 0.5" Precipitation	1	2	2	2	3	3	1	1	2	3	2	2	24
Days With ≥ 1.0" Precipitation	0	1	1	1	2	1	1	0	1	1	1	1	11
Mean Snowfall (in.)	0.0	0.2	0.0	0.0	0.0	0.0	0.0	0.0	0.0	0.0	0.0	0.1	0.3
Maximum Snow Depth (in.)	trace	2	0	0	0	0	0	0	0	0	0	3	3
Days With ≥ 1.0" Snow Depth	0	0	0	0	0	0	0	0	0	0	0	0	0

The period of record for all cooperative weather station data is 1980 – 2009. See User Guide for detailed explanation of data.

Harlingen *Cameron County*   Elevation: 38 ft.   Latitude: 26° 12' N   Longitude: 97° 40' W

	JAN	FEB	MAR	APR	MAY	JUN	JUL	AUG	SEP	OCT	NOV	DEC	YEAR
Mean Maximum Temp. (°F)	69.8	73.6	79.4	84.4	89.2	93.7	95.1	95.6	91.6	85.7	78.6	70.6	83.9
Mean Temp. (°F)	59.9	63.2	68.8	74.3	80.0	84.1	85.2	85.4	82.0	75.6	68.3	60.7	74.0
Mean Minimum Temp. (°F)	49.8	52.7	58.1	64.2	70.7	74.6	75.3	75.3	72.3	65.6	57.9	50.8	63.9
Extreme Maximum Temp. (°F)	93	95	104	103	102	104	102	104	106	97	97	89	106
Extreme Minimum Temp. (°F)	26	28	29	37	49	57	67	67	56	33	33	15	15
Days Maximum Temp. ≥ 90°F	0	1	2	7	17	26	29	29	22	8	1	0	142
Days Maximum Temp. ≤ 32°F	0	0	0	0	0	0	0	0	0	0	0	0	0
Days Minimum Temp. ≤ 32°F	1	0	0	0	0	0	0	0	0	0	0	1	2
Days Minimum Temp. ≤ 0°F	0	0	0	0	0	0	0	0	0	0	0	0	0
Heating Degree Days (base 65°F)	208	129	53	12	0	0	0	0	0	9	64	198	673
Cooling Degree Days (base 65°F)	56	83	177	298	471	580	633	641	517	345	169	72	4,042
Mean Precipitation (in.)	1.26	1.62	1.44	1.92	3.11	2.25	2.08	2.49	5.06	3.25	1.49	1.62	27.59
Extreme Maximum Daily Precip. (in.)	1.73	7.95	2.32	9.79	6.09	3.46	5.77	5.77	5.05	4.66	2.88	3.19	9.79
Days With ≥ 0.1" Precipitation	3	2	3	2	3	3	3	4	6	4	3	3	39
Days With ≥ 0.5" Precipitation	1	1	1	1	2	1	1	2	3	2	1	1	17
Days With ≥ 1.0" Precipitation	0	0	1	0	1	1	1	1	1	1	0	0	7
Mean Snowfall (in.)	0.0	0.0	0.0	0.0	0.0	0.0	0.0	0.0	0.0	0.0	0.0	0.1	0.1
Maximum Snow Depth (in.)	0	0	0	0	0	0	0	0	0	0	0	2	2
Days With ≥ 1.0" Snow Depth	0	0	0	0	0	0	0	0	0	0	0	0	0

Hart *Castro County*   Elevation: 3,640 ft.   Latitude: 34° 22' N   Longitude: 102° 05' W

	JAN	FEB	MAR	APR	MAY	JUN	JUL	AUG	SEP	OCT	NOV	DEC	YEAR
Mean Maximum Temp. (°F)	51.6	56.7	63.5	72.2	80.7	88.0	90.0	88.2	82.0	73.4	61.2	51.4	71.6
Mean Temp. (°F)	37.0	41.0	47.6	56.1	66.0	73.9	76.5	75.1	68.1	58.0	46.1	37.0	56.9
Mean Minimum Temp. (°F)	22.3	25.3	31.7	39.9	51.2	59.9	63.0	62.0	54.1	42.7	30.8	22.6	42.1
Extreme Maximum Temp. (°F)	81	85	91	98	108	110	103	104	107	98	91	80	110
Extreme Minimum Temp. (°F)	2	-1	3	20	32	44	52	50	34	16	-2	-11	-11
Days Maximum Temp. ≥ 90°F	0	0	0	1	6	14	18	15	5	1	0	0	60
Days Maximum Temp. ≤ 32°F	3	1	1	0	0	0	0	0	0	0	1	3	9
Days Minimum Temp. ≤ 32°F	29	23	16	5	0	0	0	0	0	3	18	28	122
Days Minimum Temp. ≤ 0°F	0	0	0	0	0	0	0	0	0	0	0	1	1
Heating Degree Days (base 65°F)	861	671	533	277	78	4	1	2	43	229	562	861	4,122
Cooling Degree Days (base 65°F)	0	0	1	16	115	279	366	322	142	20	0	0	1,261
Mean Precipitation (in.)	0.54	0.56	1.03	1.16	2.61	2.85	1.77	2.74	1.95	1.34	0.84	0.70	18.09
Extreme Maximum Daily Precip. (in.)	1.02	1.14	1.18	2.10	3.66	3.75	1.91	2.41	2.73	2.62	1.10	1.10	3.75
Days With ≥ 0.1" Precipitation	1	1	3	3	4	5	4	5	3	3	2	2	36
Days With ≥ 0.5" Precipitation	0	0	1	1	2	2	1	2	1	1	1	0	12
Days With ≥ 1.0" Precipitation	0	0	0	0	1	1	0	1	1	0	0	0	4
Mean Snowfall (in.)	0.5	0.8	0.5	trace	0.0	0.0	0.0	0.0	0.0	0.0	0.9	1.0	3.7
Maximum Snow Depth (in.)	7	na	na	trace	0	0	0	0	0	0	na	na	na
Days With ≥ 1.0" Snow Depth	0	0	0	0	0	0	0	0	0	0	0	0	0

Henderson *Rusk County*   Elevation: 419 ft.   Latitude: 32° 11' N   Longitude: 94° 48' W

	JAN	FEB	MAR	APR	MAY	JUN	JUL	AUG	SEP	OCT	NOV	DEC	YEAR
Mean Maximum Temp. (°F)	57.0	61.3	68.4	75.8	82.6	89.2	93.0	93.9	87.7	77.8	67.4	58.6	76.0
Mean Temp. (°F)	46.0	49.7	56.5	63.8	71.9	78.7	82.2	82.4	75.9	65.6	55.9	47.4	64.7
Mean Minimum Temp. (°F)	35.0	38.2	44.6	51.7	61.2	68.2	71.4	70.8	64.1	53.4	44.4	36.2	53.2
Extreme Maximum Temp. (°F)	83	93	88	93	101	104	108	110	111	96	86	82	111
Extreme Minimum Temp. (°F)	4	11	16	25	38	51	55	54	40	24	20	-1	-1
Days Maximum Temp. ≥ 90°F	0	0	0	0	3	16	25	25	14	2	0	0	85
Days Maximum Temp. ≤ 32°F	1	1	0	0	0	0	0	0	0	0	0	1	3
Days Minimum Temp. ≤ 32°F	14	9	4	0	0	0	0	0	0	0	4	12	43
Days Minimum Temp. ≤ 0°F	0	0	0	0	0	0	0	0	0	0	0	0	0
Heating Degree Days (base 65°F)	586	432	282	111	13	0	0	0	9	90	291	545	2,359
Cooling Degree Days (base 65°F)	4	7	25	80	234	418	540	545	342	116	24	6	2,341
Mean Precipitation (in.)	3.78	4.17	4.26	3.74	4.80	5.05	2.96	2.76	3.57	4.80	4.74	4.44	49.07
Extreme Maximum Daily Precip. (in.)	3.00	2.71	11.05	4.26	4.73	6.33	4.57	3.72	6.25	4.27	5.50	3.30	11.05
Days With ≥ 0.1" Precipitation	6	6	6	5	6	6	5	4	5	5	6	6	66
Days With ≥ 0.5" Precipitation	2	3	3	3	3	3	2	2	2	3	3	3	32
Days With ≥ 1.0" Precipitation	1	1	1	1	2	1	1	1	1	2	2	2	16
Mean Snowfall (in.)	0.4	0.3	trace	trace	0.0	0.0	0.0	0.0	0.0	0.0	trace	0.2	0.9
Maximum Snow Depth (in.)	2	2	trace	0	0	0	0	0	0	0	trace	trace	2
Days With ≥ 1.0" Snow Depth	0	0	0	0	0	0	0	0	0	0	0	0	0

Henrietta *Clay County*   Elevation: 930 ft.   Latitude: 33° 49' N   Longitude: 98° 12' W

	JAN	FEB	MAR	APR	MAY	JUN	JUL	AUG	SEP	OCT	NOV	DEC	YEAR
Mean Maximum Temp. (°F)	54.3	58.2	66.2	75.5	83.0	90.2	96.6	96.6	88.6	77.4	65.1	55.3	75.6
Mean Temp. (°F)	41.3	45.2	53.0	61.9	70.8	78.3	83.7	83.2	75.3	64.0	52.1	42.7	62.6
Mean Minimum Temp. (°F)	28.4	32.1	39.6	48.2	58.5	66.4	70.6	69.8	62.0	50.5	39.1	30.1	49.6
Extreme Maximum Temp. (°F)	86	95	98	100	103	115	113	111	107	100	90	84	115
Extreme Minimum Temp. (°F)	3	-7	6	27	38	48	57	51	37	20	16	-8	-8
Days Maximum Temp. ≥ 90°F	0	0	0	1	7	17	27	27	15	3	0	0	97
Days Maximum Temp. ≤ 32°F	2	1	0	0	0	0	0	0	0	0	0	2	5
Days Minimum Temp. ≤ 32°F	22	14	7	1	0	0	0	0	0	1	8	19	72
Days Minimum Temp. ≤ 0°F	0	0	0	0	0	0	0	0	0	0	0	0	0
Heating Degree Days (base 65°F)	727	554	380	152	25	1	0	0	17	117	390	684	3,047
Cooling Degree Days (base 65°F)	0	1	13	65	212	408	585	571	334	91	10	1	2,291
Mean Precipitation (in.)	1.56	2.20	2.60	2.70	4.31	3.95	1.73	2.51	2.82	3.50	2.00	2.29	32.17
Extreme Maximum Daily Precip. (in.)	2.04	4.56	2.12	3.76	3.75	3.12	4.17	3.93	4.46	4.56	2.47	5.39	5.39
Days With ≥ 0.1" Precipitation	3	4	5	4	5	5	3	4	4	5	3	4	49
Days With ≥ 0.5" Precipitation	1	1	2	2	3	3	1	2	2	2	1	2	22
Days With ≥ 1.0" Precipitation	0	1	1	1	1	2	0	1	1	1	1	1	11
Mean Snowfall (in.)	0.2	0.1	trace	0.0	0.0	0.0	0.0	0.0	0.0	trace	0.1	0.2	0.6
Maximum Snow Depth (in.)	2	1	7	0	0	0	0	0	0	0	trace	1	7
Days With ≥ 1.0" Snow Depth	0	0	0	0	0	0	0	0	0	0	0	0	0

The period of record for all cooperative weather station data is 1980 – 2009. See User Guide for detailed explanation of data.

Houston William P Hobby Arpt *Harris County*　Elevation: 49 ft.　Latitude: 29° 39' N　Longitude: 95° 17' W

	JAN	FEB	MAR	APR	MAY	JUN	JUL	AUG	SEP	OCT	NOV	DEC	YEAR
Mean Maximum Temp. (°F)	62.8	65.9	72.4	78.8	85.3	90.2	92.3	92.6	88.4	81.0	72.3	64.5	78.9
Mean Temp. (°F)	53.9	57.2	63.4	69.7	77.0	82.0	83.9	84.1	80.1	71.9	63.0	55.6	70.2
Mean Minimum Temp. (°F)	45.1	48.4	54.4	60.6	68.7	73.8	75.5	75.6	71.6	62.8	53.6	46.6	61.4
Extreme Maximum Temp. (°F)	82	87	90	92	100	102	103	104	108	94	88	84	108
Extreme Minimum Temp. (°F)	15	20	24	22	49	56	45	65	53	33	28	9	9
Days Maximum Temp. ≥ 90°F	0	0	0	1	5	18	25	25	14	2	0	0	90
Days Maximum Temp. ≤ 32°F	0	0	0	0	0	0	0	0	0	0	0	0	0
Days Minimum Temp. ≤ 32°F	2	1	1	0	0	0	0	0	0	0	0	2	6
Days Minimum Temp. ≤ 0°F	0	0	0	0	0	0	0	0	0	0	0	0	0
Heating Degree Days (base 65°F)	351	242	117	28	0	0	0	0	0	22	134	316	1,210
Cooling Degree Days (base 65°F)	16	27	75	177	379	517	593	600	459	245	80	30	3,198
Mean Precipitation (in.)	4.01	3.24	3.28	3.28	4.94	6.99	4.31	4.81	4.93	5.79	4.24	3.84	53.66
Extreme Maximum Daily Precip. (in.)	4.10	3.54	3.09	5.38	9.48	9.28	3.47	8.58	8.08	7.86	4.28	4.18	9.48
Days With ≥ 0.1" Precipitation	6	5	5	4	5	7	6	6	6	6	5	5	66
Days With ≥ 0.5" Precipitation	3	2	2	2	3	4	3	3	3	3	3	2	33
Days With ≥ 1.0" Precipitation	1	1	1	1	2	2	1	1	2	2	1	1	16
Mean Snowfall (in.)	na	na	na	na	na	na	na	na	na	na	na	na	na
Maximum Snow Depth (in.)	na	na	na	na	na	na	na	na	na	na	na	na	na
Days With ≥ 1.0" Snow Depth	na	na	na	na	na	na	na	na	na	na	na	na	na

La Tuna 1 S *El Paso County*　Elevation: 3,799 ft.　Latitude: 31° 58' N　Longitude: 106° 36' W

	JAN	FEB	MAR	APR	MAY	JUN	JUL	AUG	SEP	OCT	NOV	DEC	YEAR
Mean Maximum Temp. (°F)	58.7	64.8	71.9	80.4	89.0	96.6	96.3	93.5	89.0	79.9	67.5	57.7	78.8
Mean Temp. (°F)	44.4	49.8	56.1	64.1	73.0	81.0	82.6	80.4	75.1	64.6	52.5	43.9	63.9
Mean Minimum Temp. (°F)	30.1	34.7	40.3	47.6	57.0	65.4	69.0	67.3	61.2	49.2	37.4	30.0	49.1
Extreme Maximum Temp. (°F)	77	83	*91*	98	105	112	109	106	102	95	86	75	*112*
Extreme Minimum Temp. (°F)	6	12	18	27	36	48	53	51	40	24	17	9	6
Days Maximum Temp. ≥ 90°F	0	0	0	2	14	26	28	25	15	2	0	0	112
Days Maximum Temp. ≤ 32°F	0	0	0	0	0	0	0	0	0	0	0	0	0
Days Minimum Temp. ≤ 32°F	20	11	4	0	0	0	0	0	0	1	8	21	65
Days Minimum Temp. ≤ 0°F	0	0	0	0	0	0	0	0	0	0	0	0	0
Heating Degree Days (base 65°F)	631	424	275	86	6	0	0	0	3	81	370	649	2,525
Cooling Degree Days (base 65°F)	0	0	7	64	261	487	552	486	312	75	1	0	2,245
Mean Precipitation (in.)	0.54	0.35	0.19	0.08	0.38	0.93	1.67	2.05	1.20	0.70	0.42	0.69	9.20
Extreme Maximum Daily Precip. (in.)	2.08	0.93	0.48	0.36	1.83	4.25	2.00	2.65	*2.00*	*1.08*	0.90	1.80	*4.25*
Days With ≥ 0.1" Precipitation	1	1	1	0	1	1	3	4	3	2	1	2	20
Days With ≥ 0.5" Precipitation	0	0	0	0	0	1	1	1	1	0	0	0	5
Days With ≥ 1.0" Precipitation	0	0	0	0	0	0	0	0	0	0	0	0	0
Mean Snowfall (in.)	0.0	trace	0.0	0.0	0.0	0.0	0.0	0.0	0.0	0.0	trace	0.0	trace
Maximum Snow Depth (in.)	0	trace	*0*	0	0	0	0	0	*0*	0	*trace*	*0*	trace
Days With ≥ 1.0" Snow Depth	0	0	0	0	0	0	0	0	0	0	0	0	*0*

Langtry *Val Verde County*　Elevation: 1,290 ft.　Latitude: 29° 48' N　Longitude: 101° 34' W

	JAN	FEB	MAR	APR	MAY	JUN	JUL	AUG	SEP	OCT	NOV	DEC	YEAR
Mean Maximum Temp. (°F)	63.6	68.5	76.2	84.9	91.6	96.2	98.3	98.2	92.5	82.9	72.2	63.6	82.4
Mean Temp. (°F)	49.6	54.5	62.7	71.1	79.6	85.0	87.2	86.9	80.9	70.8	59.3	49.9	69.8
Mean Minimum Temp. (°F)	35.6	40.3	49.1	57.3	67.4	73.8	76.0	75.7	69.3	58.7	46.3	36.2	57.1
Extreme Maximum Temp. (°F)	93	100	98	110	110	113	111	112	112	100	97	89	113
Extreme Minimum Temp. (°F)	16	11	21	31	47	58	57	62	46	26	21	9	9
Days Maximum Temp. ≥ 90°F	0	1	2	9	20	26	29	29	22	7	1	0	146
Days Maximum Temp. ≤ 32°F	0	0	0	0	0	0	0	0	0	0	0	0	0
Days Minimum Temp. ≤ 32°F	12	5	2	0	0	0	0	0	0	0	2	11	32
Days Minimum Temp. ≤ 0°F	0	0	0	0	0	0	0	0	0	0	0	0	0
Heating Degree Days (base 65°F)	470	300	138	32	1	0	0	0	2	33	201	461	1,638
Cooling Degree Days (base 65°F)	0	9	72	222	459	608	694	687	485	220	37	1	3,494
Mean Precipitation (in.)	0.61	0.69	0.88	0.98	1.87	1.62	1.12	1.80	1.90	1.86	0.77	0.46	14.56
Extreme Maximum Daily Precip. (in.)	1.01	1.95	2.92	4.32	2.11	2.10	2.12	6.04	4.19	3.20	1.50	1.78	6.04
Days With ≥ 0.1" Precipitation	2	2	2	2	3	3	2	2	3	3	2	1	27
Days With ≥ 0.5" Precipitation	0	0	1	1	1	1	1	1	1	1	1	0	9
Days With ≥ 1.0" Precipitation	0	0	0	0	1	0	0	1	1	1	0	0	4
Mean Snowfall (in.)	0.3	0.0	0.0	0.0	0.0	0.0	0.0	0.0	0.0	0.0	0.0	0.0	0.3
Maximum Snow Depth (in.)	trace	0	0	0	0	0	0	0	0	0	0	0	trace
Days With ≥ 1.0" Snow Depth	0	0	0	0	0	0	0	0	0	0	0	0	0

Laredo 2 *Webb County*　Elevation: 430 ft.　Latitude: 27° 34' N　Longitude: 99° 30' W

	JAN	FEB	MAR	APR	MAY	JUN	JUL	AUG	SEP	OCT	NOV	DEC	YEAR
Mean Maximum Temp. (°F)	68.1	73.1	80.7	88.5	94.4	99.1	100.4	100.6	94.4	86.8	76.9	68.4	85.9
Mean Temp. (°F)	56.8	61.4	68.5	76.0	82.6	87.2	88.3	88.4	83.2	75.7	65.7	57.3	74.3
Mean Minimum Temp. (°F)	45.5	49.8	56.4	63.5	70.8	75.2	76.1	76.2	72.0	64.5	54.4	46.1	62.5
Extreme Maximum Temp. (°F)	93	103	105	110	114	114	113	111	110	103	99	92	114
Extreme Minimum Temp. (°F)	21	21	27	32	45	61	66	67	50	28	27	11	11
Days Maximum Temp. ≥ 90°F	0	2	6	15	24	29	30	30	24	13	2	0	175
Days Maximum Temp. ≤ 32°F	0	0	0	0	0	0	0	0	0	0	0	0	0
Days Minimum Temp. ≤ 32°F	3	1	0	0	0	0	0	0	0	0	0	3	7
Days Minimum Temp. ≤ 0°F	0	0	0	0	0	0	0	0	0	0	0	0	0
Heating Degree Days (base 65°F)	278	163	65	13	0	0	0	0	0	14	102	270	906
Cooling Degree Days (base 65°F)	30	69	181	349	554	672	729	733	554	352	129	37	4,389
Mean Precipitation (in.)	0.84	0.91	1.13	1.31	2.45	2.15	2.06	2.01	2.79	2.24	1.20	0.89	19.98
Extreme Maximum Daily Precip. (in.)	1.20	2.25	2.71	2.12	4.43	4.29	6.65	3.92	4.60	4.75	2.84	2.41	6.65
Days With ≥ 0.1" Precipitation	2	2	2	2	3	3	3	3	4	3	2	2	31
Days With ≥ 0.5" Precipitation	0	1	1	1	2	1	1	1	2	1	1	1	13
Days With ≥ 1.0" Precipitation	0	0	0	0	1	1	1	1	1	1	0	0	6
Mean Snowfall (in.)	trace	trace	0.0	0.0	0.0	0.0	0.0	0.0	0.0	trace	0.0	trace	trace
Maximum Snow Depth (in.)	trace	trace	0	0	0	0	0	0	0	trace	0	1	1
Days With ≥ 1.0" Snow Depth	0	0	0	0	0	0	0	0	0	0	0	0	0

The period of record for all cooperative weather station data is 1980 – 2009. See User Guide for detailed explanation of data.

Lavon Dam *Collin County*   Elevation: 509 ft.   Latitude: 33° 02' N   Longitude: 96° 29' W

	JAN	FEB	MAR	APR	MAY	JUN	JUL	AUG	SEP	OCT	NOV	DEC	YEAR
Mean Maximum Temp. (°F)	55.5	59.8	66.6	75.0	82.4	90.0	94.5	95.5	88.6	78.5	67.0	56.8	75.9
Mean Temp. (°F)	43.7	48.4	55.5	63.8	72.1	79.5	83.3	83.6	76.4	65.8	55.5	45.6	64.4
Mean Minimum Temp. (°F)	32.4	36.8	44.3	52.5	61.7	68.8	72.1	71.5	64.2	53.0	43.8	34.6	53.0
Extreme Maximum Temp. (°F)	82	96	93	97	99	107	109	107	111	100	88	85	111
Extreme Minimum Temp. (°F)	5	7	12	28	39	49	58	54	36	26	19	-3	-3
Days Maximum Temp. ≥ 90°F	0	0	0	0	4	18	27	27	15	3	0	0	94
Days Maximum Temp. ≤ 32°F	1	1	0	0	0	0	0	0	0	0	0	1	3
Days Minimum Temp. ≤ 32°F	16	9	3	0	0	0	0	0	0	0	4	12	44
Days Minimum Temp. ≤ 0°F	0	0	0	0	0	0	0	0	0	0	0	0	0
Heating Degree Days (base 65°F)	653	465	307	105	12	0	0	0	8	82	302	596	2,530
Cooling Degree Days (base 65°F)	1	3	18	74	238	440	574	582	358	112	21	2	2,423
Mean Precipitation (in.)	2.55	2.91	3.63	3.46	5.19	4.53	2.02	1.84	3.19	4.41	3.61	3.21	40.55
Extreme Maximum Daily Precip. (in.)	3.11	3.45	4.79	3.90	6.08	4.00	3.10	2.68	3.91	4.76	2.92	4.03	6.08
Days With ≥ 0.1" Precipitation	4	5	5	5	6	6	3	3	5	5	5	5	57
Days With ≥ 0.5" Precipitation	2	2	3	2	3	3	1	1	2	2	3	2	26
Days With ≥ 1.0" Precipitation	1	1	1	1	2	1	1	1	1	1	1	1	13
Mean Snowfall (in.)	0.0	0.1	0.0	0.0	0.0	0.0	0.0	0.0	0.0	0.0	0.0	0.1	0.2
Maximum Snow Depth (in.)	0	3	0	0	0	0	0	0	0	0	0	3	3
Days With ≥ 1.0" Snow Depth	0	0	0	0	0	0	0	0	0	0	0	0	0

Liberty *Liberty County*   Elevation: 35 ft.   Latitude: 30° 04' N   Longitude: 94° 48' W

	JAN	FEB	MAR	APR	MAY	JUN	JUL	AUG	SEP	OCT	NOV	DEC	YEAR
Mean Maximum Temp. (°F)	62.7	65.8	72.6	78.4	85.0	90.4	92.9	93.4	88.9	81.2	71.9	63.8	78.9
Mean Temp. (°F)	52.3	55.5	62.0	68.1	75.6	81.2	83.5	83.6	78.8	70.4	61.0	53.5	68.8
Mean Minimum Temp. (°F)	41.7	45.1	51.3	57.8	66.1	71.9	74.1	73.8	68.6	59.4	50.1	43.2	58.6
Extreme Maximum Temp. (°F)	82	87	93	93	97	102	103	107	107	95	90	86	107
Extreme Minimum Temp. (°F)	14	19	22	31	45	54	62	60	48	31	26	7	7
Days Maximum Temp. ≥ 90°F	0	0	0	1	4	20	26	26	15	3	0	0	95
Days Maximum Temp. ≤ 32°F	0	0	0	0	0	0	0	0	0	0	0	0	0
Days Minimum Temp. ≤ 32°F	5	2	1	0	0	0	0	0	0	0	1	5	14
Days Minimum Temp. ≤ 0°F	0	0	0	0	0	0	0	0	0	0	0	0	0
Heating Degree Days (base 65°F)	399	282	149	45	1	0	0	0	1	34	174	369	1,454
Cooling Degree Days (base 65°F)	11	19	63	145	336	491	581	583	420	208	62	22	2,941
Mean Precipitation (in.)	4.47	4.05	4.00	3.80	5.51	7.11	4.84	4.59	6.00	7.18	5.32	4.95	61.82
Extreme Maximum Daily Precip. (in.)	7.02	3.60	4.90	4.20	10.60	11.79	6.50	5.40	7.40	18.50	7.00	4.20	18.50
Days With ≥ 0.1" Precipitation	6	6	5	4	5	8	7	6	7	6	5	6	71
Days With ≥ 0.5" Precipitation	3	2	3	2	3	4	3	3	3	3	3	3	35
Days With ≥ 1.0" Precipitation	1	1	1	1	2	2	1	1	2	2	2	2	18
Mean Snowfall (in.)	0.1	trace	0.0	0.0	0.0	0.0	0.0	0.0	0.0	0.0	0.0	0.1	0.2
Maximum Snow Depth (in.)	trace	trace	0	0	0	0	0	0	0	0	0	0	trace
Days With ≥ 1.0" Snow Depth	0	0	0	0	0	0	0	0	0	0	0	0	0

Longview 11 SE *Rusk County*   Elevation: 407 ft.   Latitude: 32° 21' N   Longitude: 94° 39' W

	JAN	FEB	MAR	APR	MAY	JUN	JUL	AUG	SEP	OCT	NOV	DEC	YEAR
Mean Maximum Temp. (°F)	57.7	61.6	69.0	76.2	83.1	89.5	93.5	94.2	87.7	77.8	67.5	58.8	76.4
Mean Temp. (°F)	47.7	51.4	58.3	65.3	73.3	79.6	83.2	83.3	76.9	66.9	57.3	48.8	66.0
Mean Minimum Temp. (°F)	37.7	41.0	47.6	54.4	63.4	69.7	73.0	72.4	66.0	55.8	47.0	38.7	55.6
Extreme Maximum Temp. (°F)	83	90	88	93	98	102	106	109	111	96	86	83	111
Extreme Minimum Temp. (°F)	4	10	17	30	45	54	62	56	41	27	23	2	2
Days Maximum Temp. ≥ 90°F	0	0	0	0	4	17	25	26	13	2	0	0	87
Days Maximum Temp. ≤ 32°F	0	0	0	0	0	0	0	0	0	0	0	1	1
Days Minimum Temp. ≤ 32°F	10	6	2	0	0	0	0	0	0	0	2	9	29
Days Minimum Temp. ≤ 0°F	0	0	0	0	0	0	0	0	0	0	0	0	0
Heating Degree Days (base 65°F)	533	388	235	81	6	0	0	0	5	72	257	503	2,080
Cooling Degree Days (base 65°F)	5	10	34	98	270	446	573	575	369	137	30	8	2,555
Mean Precipitation (in.)	3.76	4.19	4.43	3.67	5.18	5.21	2.99	2.87	3.44	4.65	4.69	4.80	49.88
Extreme Maximum Daily Precip. (in.)	3.70	2.80	7.80	5.06	3.86	8.69	4.30	3.80	3.46	5.15	4.26	4.87	8.69
Days With ≥ 0.1" Precipitation	6	6	6	5	6	6	4	4	5	6	6	6	66
Days With ≥ 0.5" Precipitation	3	3	3	2	3	3	2	2	2	3	3	3	32
Days With ≥ 1.0" Precipitation	1	1	2	1	2	2	1	1	1	2	2	2	18
Mean Snowfall (in.)	0.5	0.4	trace	trace	0.0	0.0	0.0	0.0	0.0	0.0	trace	0.2	1.1
Maximum Snow Depth (in.)	8	6	1	trace	0	0	0	0	0	0	trace	3	8
Days With ≥ 1.0" Snow Depth	1	0	0	0	0	0	0	0	0	0	0	0	1

Marathon *Brewster County*   Elevation: 4,089 ft.   Latitude: 30° 13' N   Longitude: 103° 14' W

	JAN	FEB	MAR	APR	MAY	JUN	JUL	AUG	SEP	OCT	NOV	DEC	YEAR
Mean Maximum Temp. (°F)	62.4	66.1	73.1	80.5	87.7	91.4	90.7	89.7	85.0	78.9	69.9	63.7	78.2
Mean Temp. (°F)	46.3	49.6	55.9	63.1	71.2	76.4	76.9	76.1	71.3	63.4	53.5	47.4	62.6
Mean Minimum Temp. (°F)	30.0	33.1	38.7	45.6	54.8	61.4	63.0	62.4	57.6	47.9	37.2	31.1	46.9
Extreme Maximum Temp. (°F)	82	88	90	100	105	108	105	103	100	96	89	81	108
Extreme Minimum Temp. (°F)	9	7	11	19	35	48	50	51	36	17	9	0	0
Days Maximum Temp. ≥ 90°F	0	0	0	3	14	18	19	17	8	2	0	0	81
Days Maximum Temp. ≤ 32°F	0	0	0	0	0	0	0	0	0	0	0	0	0
Days Minimum Temp. ≤ 32°F	19	13	6	2	0	0	0	0	0	1	9	18	68
Days Minimum Temp. ≤ 0°F	0	0	0	0	0	0	0	0	0	0	0	0	0
Heating Degree Days (base 65°F)	574	431	282	105	10	0	0	0	14	97	340	540	2,393
Cooling Degree Days (base 65°F)	0	1	8	53	211	350	375	350	210	55	3	0	1,616
Mean Precipitation (in.)	0.48	0.35	0.35	0.65	1.54	2.08	2.36	2.19	1.99	1.81	0.39	0.47	14.66
Extreme Maximum Daily Precip. (in.)	1.20	1.37	1.30	1.53	2.96	1.91	2.15	2.60	2.00	2.96	1.60	1.57	2.96
Days With ≥ 0.1" Precipitation	1	1	1	1	3	4	4	4	4	3	1	1	28
Days With ≥ 0.5" Precipitation	0	0	0	0	1	1	2	1	1	1	0	0	7
Days With ≥ 1.0" Precipitation	0	0	0	0	0	1	1	1	1	1	0	0	4
Mean Snowfall (in.)	0.6	trace	trace	trace	0.0	0.0	0.0	0.0	0.0	trace	0.2	0.1	0.9
Maximum Snow Depth (in.)	trace	trace	0	0	0	0	0	0	0	trace	trace	2	2
Days With ≥ 1.0" Snow Depth	0	0	0	0	0	0	0	0	0	0	0	0	0

The period of record for all cooperative weather station data is 1980 – 2009. See User Guide for detailed explanation of data.

Marshall *Harrison County*　Elevation: 352 ft.　Latitude: 32° 32' N　Longitude: 94° 21' W

	JAN	FEB	MAR	APR	MAY	JUN	JUL	AUG	SEP	OCT	NOV	DEC	YEAR
Mean Maximum Temp. (°F)	55.8	60.1	67.4	75.1	82.1	88.7	92.7	93.1	86.9	76.6	66.6	57.3	75.2
Mean Temp. (°F)	45.4	49.4	56.7	64.0	72.0	78.9	82.5	82.5	75.9	65.1	55.9	47.0	64.6
Mean Minimum Temp. (°F)	34.9	38.6	45.9	52.8	61.9	69.1	72.3	71.9	64.8	53.4	45.1	36.7	54.0
Extreme Maximum Temp. (°F)	81	90	87	94	97	104	105	107	105	96	88	82	107
Extreme Minimum Temp. (°F)	0	10	16	30	42	48	52	55	35	27	22	3	0
Days Maximum Temp. ≥ 90°F	0	0	0	0	3	14	24	24	12	1	0	0	78
Days Maximum Temp. ≤ 32°F	1	0	0	0	0	0	0	0	0	0	0	1	2
Days Minimum Temp. ≤ 32°F	14	8	3	0	0	0	0	0	0	0	3	11	39
Days Minimum Temp. ≤ 0°F	0	0	0	0	0	0	0	0	0	0	0	0	0
Heating Degree Days (base 65°F)	605	442	280	105	13	0	0	0	9	93	288	554	2,389
Cooling Degree Days (base 65°F)	4	6	29	82	238	423	550	550	342	106	23	5	2,358
Mean Precipitation (in.)	3.77	4.28	4.50	3.83	5.01	5.11	3.24	2.63	3.39	4.88	4.60	5.04	50.28
Extreme Maximum Daily Precip. (in.)	4.15	2.60	8.58	4.23	5.10	6.84	5.55	2.90	4.08	4.35	3.40	6.95	8.58
Days With ≥ 0.1" Precipitation	6	6	6	5	6	6	5	4	5	6	6	6	67
Days With ≥ 0.5" Precipitation	3	3	3	3	3	3	2	2	2	3	3	3	33
Days With ≥ 1.0" Precipitation	1	2	1	1	2	2	1	1	1	2	2	2	18
Mean Snowfall (in.)	0.3	0.1	0.0	0.0	0.0	0.0	0.0	0.0	0.0	0.0	0.0	trace	0.4
Maximum Snow Depth (in.)	4	2	1	0	0	0	0	0	0	0	0	0	4
Days With ≥ 1.0" Snow Depth	0	0	0	0	0	0	0	0	0	0	0	0	0

McAllen *Hidalgo County*　Elevation: 100 ft.　Latitude: 26° 12' N　Longitude: 98° 15' W

	JAN	FEB	MAR	APR	MAY	JUN	JUL	AUG	SEP	OCT	NOV	DEC	YEAR
Mean Maximum Temp. (°F)	69.8	73.9	80.4	85.7	90.3	95.1	96.3	97.1	92.8	*87.0*	78.8	70.7	*84.8*
Mean Temp. (°F)	59.6	63.4	69.5	75.3	80.8	85.2	86.2	86.8	82.8	*76.4*	68.2	60.4	*74.5*
Mean Minimum Temp. (°F)	49.3	52.8	58.4	64.8	71.3	75.3	76.1	76.5	72.8	*65.8*	57.6	50.0	*64.2*
Extreme Maximum Temp. (°F)	92	100	104	105	109	108	107	106	108	*99*	97	92	*109*
Extreme Minimum Temp. (°F)	24	29	31	39	40	59	68	66	54	*44*	33	18	*18*
Days Maximum Temp. ≥ 90°F	0	1	4	9	19	27	29	29	23	*12*	2	0	*155*
Days Maximum Temp. ≤ 32°F	0	0	0	0	0	0	0	0	0	*0*	0	0	*0*
Days Minimum Temp. ≤ 32°F	1	0	0	0	0	0	0	0	0	*0*	0	1	*2*
Days Minimum Temp. ≤ 0°F	0	0	0	0	0	0	0	0	0	*0*	0	0	*0*
Heating Degree Days (base 65°F)	214	129	50	10	0	0	0	0	0	*4*	65	201	*673*
Cooling Degree Days (base 65°F)	52	89	195	325	498	613	664	684	542	*367*	170	65	*4,264*
Mean Precipitation (in.)	0.96	1.15	0.87	1.29	2.22	2.10	1.92	2.02	3.72	*2.18*	0.97	0.95	*20.35*
Extreme Maximum Daily Precip. (in.)	2.36	5.25	2.41	2.97	4.48	3.50	7.78	7.81	3.20	*2.50*	2.03	1.84	*7.81*
Days With ≥ 0.1" Precipitation	2	2	2	2	3	3	2	3	5	*4*	2	2	*32*
Days With ≥ 0.5" Precipitation	0	1	0	1	1	1	1	1	2	*2*	1	1	*12*
Days With ≥ 1.0" Precipitation	0	0	0	0	1	1	1	1	1	*1*	0	0	*6*
Mean Snowfall (in.)	trace	0.0	0.0	0.0	0.0	0.0	0.0	0.0	0.0	*0.0*	0.0	0.1	*0.1*
Maximum Snow Depth (in.)	trace	0	0	0	0	0	0	0	0	*0*	0	2	*2*
Days With ≥ 1.0" Snow Depth	0	0	0	0	0	0	0	0	0	*0*	0	0	*0*

McAllen Miller Intl Arpt *Hidalgo County*　Elevation: 100 ft.　Latitude: 26° 11' N　Longitude: 98° 14' W

	JAN	FEB	MAR	APR	MAY	JUN	JUL	AUG	SEP	OCT	NOV	DEC	YEAR
Mean Maximum Temp. (°F)	*70.7*	*74.9*	82.0	87.5	91.7	95.9	97.4	97.9	93.2	*87.7*	*79.9*	71.8	*85.9*
Mean Temp. (°F)	*60.7*	*64.5*	71.1	76.9	82.0	85.8	86.9	87.3	83.4	*77.3*	*69.3*	61.9	*75.6*
Mean Minimum Temp. (°F)	*50.6*	*54.1*	60.1	66.2	72.3	75.6	76.4	76.6	73.5	*66.9*	*58.6*	51.9	*65.2*
Extreme Maximum Temp. (°F)	*93*	*101*	105	107	110	107	109	108	*107*	103	102	92	*110*
Extreme Minimum Temp. (°F)	*26*	*24*	31	40	51	61	69	57	*37*	44	32	18	*18*
Days Maximum Temp. ≥ 90°F	*0*	*2*	5	13	22	28	29	30	24	14	3	1	*171*
Days Maximum Temp. ≤ 32°F	*0*	*0*	0	0	0	0	0	0	0	*0*	0	0	*0*
Days Minimum Temp. ≤ 32°F	*0*	*0*	0	0	0	0	0	0	0	*0*	0	1	*1*
Days Minimum Temp. ≤ 0°F	*0*	*0*	0	0	0	0	0	0	0	*0*	0	0	*0*
Heating Degree Days (base 65°F)	*189*	*114*	36	7	0	0	0	0	0	*7*	56	175	*584*
Cooling Degree Days (base 65°F)	*63*	*107*	230	370	534	631	686	698	559	*396*	190	85	*4,549*
Mean Precipitation (in.)	*1.05*	*1.11*	0.77	1.14	2.40	2.25	2.09	2.46	4.15	*2.03*	0.98	1.29	*21.72*
Extreme Maximum Daily Precip. (in.)	*1.51*	*4.00*	2.92	3.24	4.30	3.89	4.25	9.42	6.89	*2.74*	4.08	2.93	*9.42*
Days With ≥ 0.1" Precipitation	*3*	*2*	1	2	3	3	3	3	5	*4*	2	3	*34*
Days With ≥ 0.5" Precipitation	*1*	*1*	0	1	1	1	1	1	2	*1*	1	1	*12*
Days With ≥ 1.0" Precipitation	*0*	*0*	0	0	1	1	1	1	1	*1*	0	0	*6*
Mean Snowfall (in.)	na	na	na	na	na	na	na	na	na	na	na	na	na
Maximum Snow Depth (in.)	na	na	na	na	na	na	na	na	na	na	na	na	na
Days With ≥ 1.0" Snow Depth	na	na	na	na	na	na	na	na	na	na	na	na	na

McCook *Hidalgo County*　Elevation: 220 ft.　Latitude: 26° 29' N　Longitude: 98° 23' W

	JAN	FEB	MAR	APR	MAY	JUN	JUL	AUG	SEP	OCT	NOV	DEC	YEAR
Mean Maximum Temp. (°F)	69.7	74.1	80.9	86.8	91.1	96.1	97.8	98.6	93.4	87.0	78.7	70.4	85.4
Mean Temp. (°F)	58.9	62.9	69.2	75.1	80.7	84.9	86.2	86.4	82.1	75.6	67.8	59.8	74.1
Mean Minimum Temp. (°F)	48.1	51.6	57.4	63.4	70.2	73.7	74.5	74.2	70.8	64.1	56.7	49.2	62.8
Extreme Maximum Temp. (°F)	95	100	105	108	110	113	110	109	110	101	97	92	113
Extreme Minimum Temp. (°F)	22	25	28	36	49	56	65	65	53	39	33	14	14
Days Maximum Temp. ≥ 90°F	0	1	5	12	20	27	29	30	23	13	3	0	163
Days Maximum Temp. ≤ 32°F	0	0	0	0	0	0	0	0	0	0	0	0	0
Days Minimum Temp. ≤ 32°F	1	1	0	0	0	0	0	0	0	0	0	1	3
Days Minimum Temp. ≤ 0°F	0	0	0	0	0	0	0	0	0	0	0	0	0
Heating Degree Days (base 65°F)	232	143	55	13	0	0	0	0	1	13	78	222	757
Cooling Degree Days (base 65°F)	51	87	192	323	493	605	663	672	521	349	169	68	4,193
Mean Precipitation (in.)	0.94	1.07	0.80	1.06	2.50	2.36	2.13	1.48	3.59	2.69	1.04	1.12	20.78
Extreme Maximum Daily Precip. (in.)	1.55	2.98	3.20	3.49	5.65	4.04	8.28	2.98	4.55	7.44	3.78	2.17	8.28
Days With ≥ 0.1" Precipitation	2	2	2	2	3	3	3	2	5	3	2	3	32
Days With ≥ 0.5" Precipitation	0	1	0	1	2	1	1	1	2	1	0	1	11
Days With ≥ 1.0" Precipitation	0	0	0	0	1	1	1	0	0	1	1	0	4
Mean Snowfall (in.)	0.0	0.0	trace	0.0	0.0	0.0	0.0	0.0	0.0	0.0	0.0	0.1	0.1
Maximum Snow Depth (in.)	0	0	trace	0	0	0	0	0	0	0	0	2	2
Days With ≥ 1.0" Snow Depth	0	0	0	0	0	0	0	0	0	0	0	0	0

The period of record for all cooperative weather station data is 1980 – 2009. See User Guide for detailed explanation of data.

McGregor *Mclennan County*   Elevation: 723 ft.   Latitude: 31° 26' N   Longitude: 97° 24' W

	JAN	FEB	MAR	APR	MAY	JUN	JUL	AUG	SEP	OCT	NOV	DEC	YEAR
Mean Maximum Temp. (°F)	57.4	61.1	68.1	76.3	83.3	89.9	95.0	95.4	88.8	78.5	67.3	58.4	76.6
Mean Temp. (°F)	46.2	49.9	57.0	64.8	72.9	79.6	83.7	84.0	77.3	67.1	56.7	47.7	65.6
Mean Minimum Temp. (°F)	35.0	38.7	45.8	53.3	62.5	69.3	72.4	72.4	65.7	55.7	46.0	37.0	54.5
Extreme Maximum Temp. (°F)	90	95	95	96	100	109	106	107	108	98	89	82	109
Extreme Minimum Temp. (°F)	5	10	14	29	37	52	58	53	40	27	21	-1	-1
Days Maximum Temp. ≥ 90°F	0	0	0	1	4	17	27	27	15	3	0	0	94
Days Maximum Temp. ≤ 32°F	1	1	0	0	0	0	0	0	0	0	0	1	3
Days Minimum Temp. ≤ 32°F	13	7	3	0	0	0	0	0	0	0	2	9	34
Days Minimum Temp. ≤ 0°F	0	0	0	0	0	0	0	0	0	0	0	0	0
Heating Degree Days (base 65°F)	577	426	270	90	10	0	0	0	6	67	268	537	2,251
Cooling Degree Days (base 65°F)	2	6	29	92	262	446	587	594	381	141	25	5	2,570
Mean Precipitation (in.)	2.20	2.63	3.31	2.79	4.58	3.74	1.72	2.33	2.59	4.26	2.98	2.86	35.99
Extreme Maximum Daily Precip. (in.)	3.20	2.95	3.50	3.07	3.80	3.45	2.90	4.78	3.30	6.00	2.62	6.45	6.45
Days With ≥ 0.1" Precipitation	4	4	5	4	6	5	3	3	4	5	5	4	52
Days With ≥ 0.5" Precipitation	1	2	2	2	3	2	1	2	2	3	2	2	24
Days With ≥ 1.0" Precipitation	1	1	1	1	1	1	0	1	1	2	1	1	12
Mean Snowfall (in.)	0.2	trace	0.0	0.0	0.0	0.0	0.0	0.0	0.0	0.0	trace	0.0	0.2
Maximum Snow Depth (in.)	0	0	0	0	0	0	0	0	0	0	0	0	0
Days With ≥ 1.0" Snow Depth	0	0	0	0	0	0	0	0	0	0	0	0	0

McKinney 3 S *Collin County*   Elevation: 595 ft.   Latitude: 33° 10' N   Longitude: 96° 37' W

	JAN	FEB	MAR	APR	MAY	JUN	JUL	AUG	SEP	OCT	NOV	DEC	YEAR
Mean Maximum Temp. (°F)	56.0	59.9	68.0	76.3	83.0	89.7	94.8	95.6	88.3	78.0	66.3	56.7	76.1
Mean Temp. (°F)	45.1	48.5	56.4	64.3	72.4	79.3	83.8	83.9	76.3	65.9	55.3	46.2	64.8
Mean Minimum Temp. (°F)	34.1	37.1	44.8	52.3	61.7	68.9	72.6	71.7	64.3	53.8	44.3	35.7	53.4
Extreme Maximum Temp. (°F)	81	86	92	100	99	108	109	107	109	96	89	88	109
Extreme Minimum Temp. (°F)	5	6	13	28	40	52	58	54	39	24	21	-4	-4
Days Maximum Temp. ≥ 90°F	0	0	0	1	4	16	27	27	14	2	0	0	91
Days Maximum Temp. ≤ 32°F	1	1	0	0	0	0	0	0	0	0	0	1	3
Days Minimum Temp. ≤ 32°F	14	9	3	0	0	0	0	0	0	0	5	12	43
Days Minimum Temp. ≤ 0°F	0	0	0	0	0	0	0	0	0	0	0	0	0
Heating Degree Days (base 65°F)	612	462	282	99	10	0	0	0	11	83	305	577	2,441
Cooling Degree Days (base 65°F)	1	3	24	84	247	437	590	593	358	116	22	3	2,478
Mean Precipitation (in.)	2.76	3.15	3.72	3.54	5.85	4.27	2.25	1.94	2.90	4.20	3.78	3.35	41.71
Extreme Maximum Daily Precip. (in.)	4.14	3.93	4.70	4.25	7.75	4.30	4.65	3.95	3.09	4.70	4.01	3.39	7.75
Days With ≥ 0.1" Precipitation	4	4	5	5	6	6	3	3	4	4	4	4	52
Days With ≥ 0.5" Precipitation	2	2	2	3	3	3	1	1	2	2	2	2	25
Days With ≥ 1.0" Precipitation	1	1	1	1	2	1	1	1	1	1	1	1	13
Mean Snowfall (in.)	0.3	0.5	0.2	0.0	0.0	0.0	0.0	0.0	0.0	0.0	0.1	0.2	1.3
Maximum Snow Depth (in.)	3	4	3	0	0	0	0	0	0	0	1	4	4
Days With ≥ 1.0" Snow Depth	1	1	0	0	0	0	0	0	0	0	0	1	2

Menard *Menard County*   Elevation: 1,951 ft.   Latitude: 30° 55' N   Longitude: 99° 47' W

	JAN	FEB	MAR	APR	MAY	JUN	JUL	AUG	SEP	OCT	NOV	DEC	YEAR
Mean Maximum Temp. (°F)	60.6	64.7	71.9	80.6	86.4	91.2	94.8	94.3	88.2	79.4	68.8	60.7	78.5
Mean Temp. (°F)	46.1	50.1	57.5	65.2	73.2	78.8	81.6	81.1	74.7	65.5	54.8	46.5	64.6
Mean Minimum Temp. (°F)	31.6	35.5	43.0	49.9	60.0	66.3	68.5	67.7	61.1	51.6	40.8	32.3	50.7
Extreme Maximum Temp. (°F)	89	97	95	102	108	108	107	109	108	98	91	87	109
Extreme Minimum Temp. (°F)	3	-1	7	21	34	48	53	50	33	21	12	-2	-2
Days Maximum Temp. ≥ 90°F	0	0	1	4	11	20	25	25	13	2	0	0	101
Days Maximum Temp. ≤ 32°F	1	1	0	0	0	0	0	0	0	0	0	1	3
Days Minimum Temp. ≤ 32°F	18	11	6	2	0	0	0	0	0	1	8	16	62
Days Minimum Temp. ≤ 0°F	0	0	0	0	0	0	0	0	0	0	0	0	0
Heating Degree Days (base 65°F)	579	420	255	94	11	0	0	0	10	90	315	567	2,341
Cooling Degree Days (base 65°F)	1	5	29	107	274	421	523	505	306	114	16	1	2,302
Mean Precipitation (in.)	1.04	1.52	1.88	1.49	3.25	3.26	1.94	1.99	2.31	2.45	1.65	1.18	23.96
Extreme Maximum Daily Precip. (in.)	1.78	2.39	3.03	2.20	4.35	2.96	3.65	4.00	4.12	3.92	3.12	3.22	4.35
Days With ≥ 0.1" Precipitation	2	3	4	2	5	5	3	3	3	4	3	2	39
Days With ≥ 0.5" Precipitation	1	1	1	1	2	2	1	1	2	2	1	1	16
Days With ≥ 1.0" Precipitation	0	0	0	0	1	1	1	1	1	1	1	0	7
Mean Snowfall (in.)	0.8	0.2	trace	0.0	0.0	0.0	0.0	0.0	0.0	0.0	trace	0.2	1.2
Maximum Snow Depth (in.)	2	trace	trace	0	0	0	0	0	0	0	0	4	6	6
Days With ≥ 1.0" Snow Depth	0	0	0	0	0	0	0	0	0	0	0	0	0

Morton *Cochran County*   Elevation: 3,759 ft.   Latitude: 33° 43' N   Longitude: 102° 46' W

	JAN	FEB	MAR	APR	MAY	JUN	JUL	AUG	SEP	OCT	NOV	DEC	YEAR
Mean Maximum Temp. (°F)	53.8	58.6	65.6	74.3	82.9	90.4	92.0	90.0	83.5	74.3	63.1	53.7	73.5
Mean Temp. (°F)	39.1	43.1	49.5	57.8	67.5	75.8	78.3	76.6	69.6	59.6	48.3	39.5	58.7
Mean Minimum Temp. (°F)	24.5	27.4	33.3	41.2	52.1	61.0	64.5	63.1	55.7	44.7	33.4	25.2	43.8
Extreme Maximum Temp. (°F)	80	85	92	98	107	110	107	105	102	99	87	80	110
Extreme Minimum Temp. (°F)	-4	0	7	21	34	43	52	53	32	16	7	-6	-6
Days Maximum Temp. ≥ 90°F	0	0	0	1	8	18	22	18	8	1	0	0	76
Days Maximum Temp. ≤ 32°F	2	1	0	0	0	0	0	0	0	0	1	2	6
Days Minimum Temp. ≤ 32°F	27	21	14	4	0	0	0	0	0	2	14	25	107
Days Minimum Temp. ≤ 0°F	0	0	0	0	0	0	0	0	0	0	0	0	0
Heating Degree Days (base 65°F)	794	614	477	233	56	3	0	1	32	194	495	784	3,683
Cooling Degree Days (base 65°F)	0	0	2	22	141	333	419	367	178	33	1	0	1,496
Mean Precipitation (in.)	0.63	0.64	1.06	0.86	2.20	2.53	2.57	2.67	2.50	1.77	0.89	0.79	19.11
Extreme Maximum Daily Precip. (in.)	1.77	1.60	1.93	2.10	2.65	3.85	3.30	4.10	3.59	3.00	1.31	1.22	4.10
Days With ≥ 0.1" Precipitation	2	2	2	2	4	5	4	5	4	3	2	2	37
Days With ≥ 0.5" Precipitation	0	0	1	0	1	2	2	1	2	1	1	0	11
Days With ≥ 1.0" Precipitation	0	0	0	0	0	1	1	1	1	1	0	0	5
Mean Snowfall (in.)	2.2	1.3	0.4	0.3	0.0	0.0	0.0	0.0	0.0	0.1	1.4	2.9	8.6
Maximum Snow Depth (in.)	5	2	5	1	0	0	0	0	0	trace	7	4	7
Days With ≥ 1.0" Snow Depth	0	0	0	0	0	0	0	0	0	0	0	0	0

The period of record for all cooperative weather station data is 1980 – 2009. See User Guide for detailed explanation of data.

New Braunfels *Comal County*   Elevation: 709 ft.   Latitude: 29° 44' N   Longitude: 98° 07' W

	JAN	FEB	MAR	APR	MAY	JUN	JUL	AUG	SEP	OCT	NOV	DEC	YEAR
Mean Maximum Temp. (°F)	62.6	65.8	73.0	80.1	86.3	91.6	94.7	95.9	90.2	81.6	72.0	62.9	79.7
Mean Temp. (°F)	50.3	53.2	60.4	67.5	75.3	80.8	83.6	83.9	78.3	69.3	60.0	50.9	67.8
Mean Minimum Temp. (°F)	38.0	40.5	47.8	55.0	64.2	69.9	72.4	71.9	66.3	56.8	47.9	38.8	55.8
Extreme Maximum Temp. (°F)	84	98	97	100	100	110	105	107	112	97	94	84	112
Extreme Minimum Temp. (°F)	9	11	17	29	37	46	61	58	43	24	24	2	2
Days Maximum Temp. ≥ 90°F	0	0	0	2	10	22	27	29	19	5	0	0	114
Days Maximum Temp. ≤ 32°F	0	0	0	0	0	0	0	0	0	0	0	0	0
Days Minimum Temp. ≤ 32°F	10	6	3	0	0	0	0	0	0	0	2	9	30
Days Minimum Temp. ≤ 0°F	0	0	0	0	0	0	0	0	0	0	0	0	0
Heating Degree Days (base 65°F)	456	337	188	56	3	0	0	0	3	48	195	440	1,726
Cooling Degree Days (base 65°F)	7	11	53	139	329	479	583	592	410	187	51	10	2,851
Mean Precipitation (in.)	1.93	1.89	2.40	2.10	4.00	4.74	2.47	2.25	2.98	4.35	2.52	2.43	34.06
Extreme Maximum Daily Precip. (in.)	2.25	2.24	3.36	2.49	4.51	4.25	5.89	4.50	4.00	18.35	3.91	4.81	18.35
Days With ≥ 0.1" Precipitation	4	4	4	3	5	5	3	3	4	4	4	3	46
Days With ≥ 0.5" Precipitation	1	1	1	1	3	3	1	1	2	2	2	1	19
Days With ≥ 1.0" Precipitation	0	0	1	1	1	2	1	1	1	1	1	1	11
Mean Snowfall (in.)	0.3	0.0	0.0	0.0	0.0	0.0	0.0	0.0	0.0	0.0	0.0	0.0	0.3
Maximum Snow Depth (in.)	trace	0	0	0	0	0	0	0	0	0	0	0	trace
Days With ≥ 1.0" Snow Depth	0	0	0	0	0	0	0	0	0	0	0	0	0

Ozona 1 SSW *Crockett County*   Elevation: 2,339 ft.   Latitude: 30° 41' N   Longitude: 101° 12' W

	JAN	FEB	MAR	APR	MAY	JUN	JUL	AUG	SEP	OCT	NOV	DEC	YEAR
Mean Maximum Temp. (°F)	59.2	63.5	71.1	79.2	86.7	91.1	93.2	93.1	87.2	78.4	67.6	59.5	77.5
Mean Temp. (°F)	44.7	48.9	56.4	64.4	73.5	79.1	81.0	80.7	74.3	64.9	53.7	45.1	63.9
Mean Minimum Temp. (°F)	30.2	34.2	41.7	49.5	60.3	67.0	68.8	68.2	61.4	51.4	39.7	30.6	50.3
Extreme Maximum Temp. (°F)	86	93	94	102	106	107	107	107	107	96	89	85	107
Extreme Minimum Temp. (°F)	0	9	8	22	36	49	50	51	34	20	13	-2	-2
Days Maximum Temp. ≥ 90°F	0	0	0	3	11	18	24	24	12	1	0	0	93
Days Maximum Temp. ≤ 32°F	1	0	0	0	0	0	0	0	0	0	0	1	2
Days Minimum Temp. ≤ 32°F	19	13	6	1	0	0	0	0	0	1	8	18	66
Days Minimum Temp. ≤ 0°F	0	0	0	0	0	0	0	0	0	0	0	0	0
Heating Degree Days (base 65°F)	622	450	277	100	9	0	0	0	12	94	340	609	2,513
Cooling Degree Days (base 65°F)	0	1	17	88	280	429	503	492	299	96	9	0	2,214
Mean Precipitation (in.)	0.91	0.95	1.58	1.29	2.33	2.11	0.98	2.10	2.21	2.32	1.06	0.71	18.55
Extreme Maximum Daily Precip. (in.)	1.50	2.10	3.50	2.55	3.50	2.38	2.82	3.10	4.72	4.00	2.60	1.51	4.72
Days With ≥ 0.1" Precipitation	2	2	3	3	3	4	2	3	3	3	2	2	32
Days With ≥ 0.5" Precipitation	1	1	1	1	2	1	1	1	2	1	1	0	13
Days With ≥ 1.0" Precipitation	0	0	0	0	1	1	0	1	1	1	0	0	5
Mean Snowfall (in.)	0.1	0.0	trace	0.0	0.0	0.0	0.0	0.0	0.0	0.1	0.3	trace	0.5
Maximum Snow Depth (in.)	0	0	trace	0	0	0	0	0	0	0	3	trace	3
Days With ≥ 1.0" Snow Depth	0	0	0	0	0	0	0	0	0	0	0	0	0

Penwell *Ector County*   Elevation: 2,939 ft.   Latitude: 31° 44' N   Longitude: 102° 35' W

	JAN	FEB	MAR	APR	MAY	JUN	JUL	AUG	SEP	OCT	NOV	DEC	YEAR
Mean Maximum Temp. (°F)	58.9	63.4	70.9	79.4	88.2	94.3	95.5	94.5	88.1	79.0	68.0	58.5	78.2
Mean Temp. (°F)	44.4	48.9	56.0	64.1	73.6	80.8	82.6	81.6	75.1	65.2	53.7	44.4	64.2
Mean Minimum Temp. (°F)	29.8	34.3	41.0	48.7	59.0	67.2	69.6	68.6	62.1	51.3	39.4	30.3	50.1
Extreme Maximum Temp. (°F)	83	90	94	101	110	116	111	108	105	102	91	82	116
Extreme Minimum Temp. (°F)	6	-12	8	24	39	49	56	57	38	22	10	1	-12
Days Maximum Temp. ≥ 90°F	0	0	0	5	15	23	27	26	14	4	0	0	114
Days Maximum Temp. ≤ 32°F	1	1	0	0	0	0	0	0	0	0	0	1	3
Days Minimum Temp. ≤ 32°F	20	11	5	1	0	0	0	0	0	1	7	18	63
Days Minimum Temp. ≤ 0°F	0	0	0	0	0	0	0	0	0	0	0	0	0
Heating Degree Days (base 65°F)	633	450	290	109	14	1	0	0	12	90	339	632	2,570
Cooling Degree Days (base 65°F)	0	1	16	88	289	480	553	521	321	103	8	0	2,380
Mean Precipitation (in.)	0.57	0.69	0.60	0.62	2.20	1.57	1.18	1.52	2.12	1.41	0.74	0.61	13.83
Extreme Maximum Daily Precip. (in.)	2.00	1.78	1.04	2.23	2.97	2.10	2.00	3.00	3.63	2.50	3.40	1.38	3.63
Days With ≥ 0.1" Precipitation	1	2	1	1	3	3	2	2	3	2	1	1	22
Days With ≥ 0.5" Precipitation	0	0	0	0	1	1	1	1	1	1	0	0	6
Days With ≥ 1.0" Precipitation	0	0	0	0	1	0	0	0	1	0	0	0	2
Mean Snowfall (in.)	0.6	0.3	0.1	0.0	0.0	0.0	0.0	0.0	0.0	0.0	trace	0.5	1.5
Maximum Snow Depth (in.)	0	0	0	0	0	0	0	0	0	0	0	6	6
Days With ≥ 1.0" Snow Depth	0	0	0	0	0	0	0	0	0	0	0	0	0

Pilot Point *Denton County*   Elevation: 689 ft.   Latitude: 33° 23' N   Longitude: 96° 58' W

	JAN	FEB	MAR	APR	MAY	JUN	JUL	AUG	SEP	OCT	NOV	DEC	YEAR
Mean Maximum Temp. (°F)	54.2	58.9	66.6	75.5	83.3	90.3	96.6	96.5	89.3	77.7	65.3	55.8	75.8
Mean Temp. (°F)	42.7	47.0	54.1	62.9	71.9	79.6	85.2	84.9	77.4	66.0	53.6	44.7	64.2
Mean Minimum Temp. (°F)	31.2	35.0	41.6	50.2	60.3	68.9	74.0	73.2	65.5	54.2	41.8	33.5	52.5
Extreme Maximum Temp. (°F)	81	93	94	98	103	102	111	109	112	97	89	82	112
Extreme Minimum Temp. (°F)	1	1	10	28	39	49	50	57	40	24	17	-2	-2
Days Maximum Temp. ≥ 90°F	0	0	0	1	6	19	28	27	16	3	0	0	100
Days Maximum Temp. ≤ 32°F	1	1	0	0	0	0	0	0	0	0	0	1	3
Days Minimum Temp. ≤ 32°F	17	10	4	1	0	0	0	0	0	0	5	13	50
Days Minimum Temp. ≤ 0°F	0	0	0	0	0	0	0	0	0	0	0	0	0
Heating Degree Days (base 65°F)	683	504	343	124	16	1	0	0	11	86	350	624	2,742
Cooling Degree Days (base 65°F)	0	3	14	67	236	446	634	625	391	121	13	1	2,551
Mean Precipitation (in.)	2.45	3.57	3.89	3.19	6.71	4.28	2.32	2.69	3.64	5.21	3.74	3.57	45.26
Extreme Maximum Daily Precip. (in.)	2.20	5.60	4.10	2.50	13.00	5.10	5.40	3.20	na	na	4.46	3.60	na
Days With ≥ 0.1" Precipitation	5	5	6	6	8	6	4	4	5	6	5	5	65
Days With ≥ 0.5" Precipitation	2	2	3	3	4	3	1	2	2	3	3	2	30
Days With ≥ 1.0" Precipitation	1	1	1	1	3	1	1	1	1	2	1	1	15
Mean Snowfall (in.)	0.1	0.5	trace	0.0	0.0	0.0	0.0	0.0	0.0	0.0	trace	0.1	0.7
Maximum Snow Depth (in.)	trace	2	trace	0	0	0	0	0	0	na	0	trace	na
Days With ≥ 1.0" Snow Depth	0	0	0	0	0	0	0	0	0	na	0	0	na

The period of record for all cooperative weather station data is 1980 – 2009. See User Guide for detailed explanation of data.

Port Isabel *Cameron County*   Elevation: 17 ft.   Latitude: 26° 04' N   Longitude: 97° 13' W

	JAN	FEB	MAR	APR	MAY	JUN	JUL	AUG	SEP	OCT	NOV	DEC	YEAR
Mean Maximum Temp. (°F)	68.5	71.0	75.6	80.2	85.2	89.3	90.5	91.2	88.6	84.1	77.4	70.0	81.0
Mean Temp. (°F)	60.9	63.6	68.5	73.8	79.4	83.3	84.1	84.5	81.9	77.1	70.0	62.2	74.1
Mean Minimum Temp. (°F)	53.2	56.2	61.3	67.4	73.6	77.2	77.6	77.8	75.1	70.1	62.5	54.4	67.2
Extreme Maximum Temp. (°F)	87	91	98	96	98	96	99	99	103	95	95	87	103
Extreme Minimum Temp. (°F)	28	28	34	42	52	68	69	70	55	37	37	17	17
Days Maximum Temp. ≥ 90°F	0	0	0	1	3	15	21	25	14	4	0	0	83
Days Maximum Temp. ≤ 32°F	0	0	0	0	0	0	0	0	0	0	0	0	0
Days Minimum Temp. ≤ 32°F	0	0	0	0	0	0	0	0	0	0	0	0	0
Days Minimum Temp. ≤ 0°F	0	0	0	0	0	0	0	0	0	0	0	0	0
Heating Degree Days (base 65°F)	171	107	44	8	0	0	0	0	0	6	45	158	539
Cooling Degree Days (base 65°F)	53	75	159	280	454	556	598	612	513	389	201	79	3,969
Mean Precipitation (in.)	1.82	1.48	1.43	1.44	2.21	2.14	1.70	1.87	5.78	4.11	2.55	1.53	28.06
Extreme Maximum Daily Precip. (in.)	3.70	2.65	5.00	6.37	3.45	4.30	4.87	3.35	4.89	5.62	7.80	2.86	7.80
Days With ≥ 0.1" Precipitation	4	3	2	2	3	3	3	3	6	5	4	3	41
Days With ≥ 0.5" Precipitation	1	1	1	1	2	1	1	1	3	2	1	1	16
Days With ≥ 1.0" Precipitation	0	0	0	0	1	1	0	1	2	1	1	0	7
Mean Snowfall (in.)	0.0	0.0	0.0	0.0	0.0	0.0	0.0	0.0	0.0	0.0	0.0	0.1	0.1
Maximum Snow Depth (in.)	0	0	0	0	0	0	0	0	0	0	0	3	3
Days With ≥ 1.0" Snow Depth	0	0	0	0	0	0	0	0	0	0	0	0	0

Port Mansfield *Willacy County*   Elevation: 8 ft.   Latitude: 26° 33' N   Longitude: 97° 26' W

	JAN	FEB	MAR	APR	MAY	JUN	JUL	AUG	SEP	OCT	NOV	DEC	YEAR
Mean Maximum Temp. (°F)	65.6	68.7	73.6	78.4	83.0	87.5	88.8	89.2	86.6	81.6	74.9	67.5	78.8
Mean Temp. (°F)	57.8	61.2	66.9	72.3	78.0	82.2	83.2	83.2	80.0	74.7	67.5	59.6	72.2
Mean Minimum Temp. (°F)	49.9	53.7	60.1	66.2	73.0	76.8	77.5	77.2	73.4	67.8	60.0	51.7	65.6
Extreme Maximum Temp. (°F)	86	90	101	98	104	101	113	99	102	96	98	88	113
Extreme Minimum Temp. (°F)	23	26	29	41	37	60	65	67	55	32	34	15	15
Days Maximum Temp. ≥ 90°F	0	0	0	1	1	7	11	13	6	2	0	0	41
Days Maximum Temp. ≤ 32°F	0	0	0	0	0	0	0	0	0	0	0	0	0
Days Minimum Temp. ≤ 32°F	1	1	0	0	0	0	0	0	0	0	0	1	3
Days Minimum Temp. ≤ 0°F	0	0	0	0	0	0	0	0	0	0	0	0	0
Heating Degree Days (base 65°F)	251	157	65	14	0	0	*0*	*0*	0	12	71	215	*785*
Cooling Degree Days (base 65°F)	33	55	131	241	411	523	*569*	*571*	457	321	152	57	*3,521*
Mean Precipitation (in.)	1.32	1.72	1.36	1.26	2.55	2.15	1.94	1.62	4.99	3.22	1.79	1.33	25.25
Extreme Maximum Daily Precip. (in.)	2.50	4.50	4.00	2.05	2.68	4.40	8.48	*2.08*	6.11	3.50	6.73	2.80	*8.48*
Days With ≥ 0.1" Precipitation	3	3	2	2	3	3	2	3	6	4	3	3	37
Days With ≥ 0.5" Precipitation	1	1	1	1	2	1	1	1	3	2	1	1	16
Days With ≥ 1.0" Precipitation	0	0	0	1	1	1	0	0	2	1	1	0	7
Mean Snowfall (in.)	trace	0.0	0.0	0.0	0.0	0.0	0.0	0.0	0.0	0.0	0.0	0.1	0.1
Maximum Snow Depth (in.)	trace	0	0	0	0	0	0	0	0	0	0	2	2
Days With ≥ 1.0" Snow Depth	0	0	0	0	0	0	0	0	0	0	0	0	0

Raymondville *Willacy County*   Elevation: 30 ft.   Latitude: 26° 29' N   Longitude: 97° 49' W

	JAN	FEB	MAR	APR	MAY	JUN	JUL	AUG	SEP	OCT	NOV	DEC	YEAR
Mean Maximum Temp. (°F)	70.6	74.3	80.4	86.0	90.2	94.6	97.0	97.2	92.7	87.1	79.4	71.5	85.1
Mean Temp. (°F)	59.4	62.8	68.5	74.5	79.9	84.1	85.7	85.7	81.9	75.7	67.7	60.2	73.8
Mean Minimum Temp. (°F)	48.1	51.2	56.6	62.9	69.7	73.5	74.3	74.3	71.0	64.3	56.1	48.8	62.5
Extreme Maximum Temp. (°F)	91	97	104	106	107	108	107	107	107	100	99	92	108
Extreme Minimum Temp. (°F)	22	24	28	33	46	57	63	65	45	33	31	15	15
Days Maximum Temp. ≥ 90°F	0	1	4	10	18	27	28	28	23	13	3	0	155
Days Maximum Temp. ≤ 32°F	0	0	0	0	0	0	0	0	0	0	0	0	0
Days Minimum Temp. ≤ 32°F	1	1	0	0	0	0	0	0	0	0	0	2	4
Days Minimum Temp. ≤ 0°F	0	0	0	0	0	0	0	0	0	0	0	0	0
Heating Degree Days (base 65°F)	220	139	63	13	0	0	0	0	1	11	76	213	736
Cooling Degree Days (base 65°F)	52	82	178	303	470	578	647	650	514	350	164	70	4,058
Mean Precipitation (in.)	1.16	1.44	1.48	1.28	3.00	2.26	2.17	2.47	5.08	3.38	1.30	1.17	26.19
Extreme Maximum Daily Precip. (in.)	1.72	2.84	3.70	4.00	4.65	6.23	5.74	3.07	4.53	4.36	1.66	2.37	6.23
Days With ≥ 0.1" Precipitation	3	3	2	2	3	3	3	4	6	4	2	2	37
Days With ≥ 0.5" Precipitation	1	1	1	1	2	1	1	1	3	2	1	1	16
Days With ≥ 1.0" Precipitation	0	0	0	0	1	1	1	1	2	1	0	0	7
Mean Snowfall (in.)	0.0	0.0	0.0	0.0	0.0	0.0	0.0	0.0	0.0	0.0	0.0	0.1	0.1
Maximum Snow Depth (in.)	0	0	0	0	0	0	0	0	0	0	0	4	4
Days With ≥ 1.0" Snow Depth	0	0	0	0	0	0	0	0	0	0	0	0	0

Rio Grande City 1 SE *Starr County*   Elevation: 171 ft.   Latitude: 26° 23' N   Longitude: 98° 49' W

	JAN	FEB	MAR	APR	MAY	JUN	JUL	AUG	SEP	OCT	NOV	DEC	YEAR
Mean Maximum Temp. (°F)	70.3	75.0	82.1	88.6	93.3	97.7	99.4	99.6	94.3	87.6	79.0	70.4	86.4
Mean Temp. (°F)	58.1	62.3	69.0	75.6	81.8	86.1	87.3	87.4	82.8	75.7	67.0	58.5	74.3
Mean Minimum Temp. (°F)	45.9	49.5	55.9	62.6	70.3	74.5	75.1	75.1	71.2	63.7	55.0	46.5	62.1
Extreme Maximum Temp. (°F)	97	100	105	108	111	116	111	110	111	101	97	93	116
Extreme Minimum Temp. (°F)	22	24	25	34	50	55	59	66	51	29	26	16	16
Days Maximum Temp. ≥ 90°F	1	3	7	15	23	29	30	30	24	14	3	0	179
Days Maximum Temp. ≤ 32°F	0	0	0	0	0	0	0	0	0	0	0	0	0
Days Minimum Temp. ≤ 32°F	2	1	0	0	0	0	0	0	0	0	1	3	7
Days Minimum Temp. ≤ 0°F	0	0	0	0	0	0	0	0	0	0	0	0	0
Heating Degree Days (base 65°F)	249	150	61	12	0	0	0	0	1	13	88	247	821
Cooling Degree Days (base 65°F)	42	79	192	338	529	640	698	701	542	350	155	52	4,318
Mean Precipitation (in.)	0.98	1.09	0.80	1.15	2.35	2.86	1.84	1.94	4.12	2.55	1.18	0.97	21.83
Extreme Maximum Daily Precip. (in.)	2.23	3.17	2.66	2.30	4.97	6.13	3.80	4.97	5.50	5.00	2.21	2.09	6.13
Days With ≥ 0.1" Precipitation	3	2	2	2	3	3	3	3	5	3	2	2	33
Days With ≥ 0.5" Precipitation	1	1	1	1	2	2	1	1	3	1	1	0	12
Days With ≥ 1.0" Precipitation	0	0	0	0	1	1	1	1	2	1	0	0	7
Mean Snowfall (in.)	trace	0.0	0.0	0.0	0.0	0.0	0.0	0.0	0.0	0.0	0.0	0.1	0.1
Maximum Snow Depth (in.)	trace	0	0	0	0	0	0	0	0	0	0	3	3
Days With ≥ 1.0" Snow Depth	0	0	0	0	0	0	0	0	0	0	0	0	0

The period of record for all cooperative weather station data is 1980 – 2009. See User Guide for detailed explanation of data.

Robstown *Nueces County*   Elevation: 84 ft.   Latitude: 27° 47' N   Longitude: 97° 40' W

	JAN	FEB	MAR	APR	MAY	JUN	JUL	AUG	SEP	OCT	NOV	DEC	YEAR
Mean Maximum Temp. (°F)	66.8	70.1	76.0	82.4	87.3	92.4	94.4	95.4	91.2	84.5	76.1	68.0	82.1
Mean Temp. (°F)	56.6	59.8	66.0	72.5	78.6	83.2	84.9	85.5	81.5	74.4	66.0	57.9	72.2
Mean Minimum Temp. (°F)	46.4	49.5	56.0	62.5	69.9	74.0	75.2	75.5	71.8	64.3	55.8	47.7	62.4
Extreme Maximum Temp. (°F)	90	95	104	104	104	108	103	113	109	98	98	91	113
Extreme Minimum Temp. (°F)	19	20	23	37	52	60	63	66	53	32	29	12	12
Days Maximum Temp. ≥ 90°F	0	0	1	4	11	25	28	29	20	7	1	0	126
Days Maximum Temp. ≤ 32°F	0	0	0	0	0	0	0	0	0	0	0	0	0
Days Minimum Temp. ≤ 32°F	2	1	0	0	0	0	0	0	0	0	0	2	5
Days Minimum Temp. ≤ 0°F	0	0	0	0	0	0	0	0	0	0	0	0	0
Heating Degree Days (base 65°F)	282	185	84	16	0	0	0	0	0	13	90	259	929
Cooling Degree Days (base 65°F)	29	45	122	246	429	554	622	641	503	312	128	44	3,675
Mean Precipitation (in.)	1.74	1.94	1.94	1.56	3.07	2.76	3.24	3.33	4.28	3.59	2.26	1.62	31.33
Extreme Maximum Daily Precip. (in.)	5.00	3.63	3.15	4.35	4.52	3.05	5.24	5.36	6.08	5.15	6.80	5.10	6.80
Days With ≥ 0.1" Precipitation	4	3	3	2	4	4	4	4	5	4	3	3	43
Days With ≥ 0.5" Precipitation	1	1	1	1	2	2	2	2	2	2	1	1	18
Days With ≥ 1.0" Precipitation	0	1	1	0	1	1	1	1	1	1	1	0	9
Mean Snowfall (in.)	0.0	trace	0.0	0.0	0.0	0.0	0.0	0.0	0.0	0.0	0.0	0.2	0.2
Maximum Snow Depth (in.)	0	trace	0	0	0	0	0	0	0	0	0	5	5
Days With ≥ 1.0" Snow Depth	0	0	0	0	0	0	0	0	0	0	0	0	0

Sam Rayburn Dam *Jasper County*   Elevation: 188 ft.   Latitude: 31° 04' N   Longitude: 94° 06' W

	JAN	FEB	MAR	APR	MAY	JUN	JUL	AUG	SEP	OCT	NOV	DEC	YEAR
Mean Maximum Temp. (°F)	58.4	62.2	69.6	76.9	84.3	90.3	93.2	93.7	88.6	79.0	68.8	60.3	77.1
Mean Temp. (°F)	47.6	51.1	58.3	65.2	73.4	79.5	81.9	81.9	76.9	66.8	57.6	49.4	65.8
Mean Minimum Temp. (°F)	36.8	39.9	47.0	53.4	62.5	68.6	70.6	70.0	65.1	54.6	46.4	38.5	54.5
Extreme Maximum Temp. (°F)	83	88	91	93	101	103	107	107	109	95	87	84	109
Extreme Minimum Temp. (°F)	11	14	19	24	38	50	59	52	39	20	18	7	7
Days Maximum Temp. ≥ 90°F	0	0	0	1	6	19	25	26	14	2	0	0	93
Days Maximum Temp. ≤ 32°F	0	0	0	0	0	0	0	0	0	0	0	0	0
Days Minimum Temp. ≤ 32°F	12	7	3	0	0	0	0	0	0	0	3	10	35
Days Minimum Temp. ≤ 0°F	0	0	0	0	0	0	0	0	0	0	0	0	0
Heating Degree Days (base 65°F)	538	396	238	89	8	0	0	0	4	74	249	484	2,080
Cooling Degree Days (base 65°F)	6	10	38	102	276	440	532	530	367	136	35	9	2,481
Mean Precipitation (in.)	5.30	4.69	5.18	4.09	4.86	6.16	3.97	4.00	4.30	5.63	6.23	6.11	60.52
Extreme Maximum Daily Precip. (in.)	4.32	7.85	9.04	4.26	3.45	6.38	3.95	3.75	14.00	10.10	7.36	5.66	14.00
Days With ≥ 0.1" Precipitation	7	6	6	5	6	7	6	6	6	5	6	7	73
Days With ≥ 0.5" Precipitation	4	3	3	3	3	4	3	3	2	3	4	4	39
Days With ≥ 1.0" Precipitation	2	1	2	1	2	2	1	1	1	2	2	2	19
Mean Snowfall (in.)	trace	0.0	0.0	0.0	0.0	0.0	0.0	0.0	0.0	0.0	0.0	trace	trace
Maximum Snow Depth (in.)	1	0	0	0	0	0	0	0	0	0	0	trace	1
Days With ≥ 1.0" Snow Depth	0	0	0	0	0	0	0	0	0	0	0	0	0

San Marcos *Hays County*   Elevation: 611 ft.   Latitude: 29° 51' N   Longitude: 97° 57' W

	JAN	FEB	MAR	APR	MAY	JUN	JUL	AUG	SEP	OCT	NOV	DEC	YEAR
Mean Maximum Temp. (°F)	62.9	66.3	72.9	80.1	86.2	92.2	95.2	96.3	90.8	82.4	72.1	63.3	80.1
Mean Temp. (°F)	51.4	54.3	61.1	68.2	75.8	81.9	84.3	84.9	79.4	70.4	60.5	51.7	68.7
Mean Minimum Temp. (°F)	39.7	42.3	49.2	56.3	65.4	71.4	73.4	73.5	67.9	58.3	48.9	40.1	57.2
Extreme Maximum Temp. (°F)	85	99	97	98	100	109	104	107	111	97	91	85	111
Extreme Minimum Temp. (°F)	11	17	17	32	44	52	62	60	42	28	24	4	4
Days Maximum Temp. ≥ 90°F	0	0	0	2	10	23	28	29	20	5	0	0	117
Days Maximum Temp. ≤ 32°F	0	0	0	0	0	0	0	0	0	0	0	0	0
Days Minimum Temp. ≤ 32°F	7	4	1	0	0	0	0	0	0	0	1	7	20
Days Minimum Temp. ≤ 0°F	0	0	0	0	0	0	0	0	0	0	0	0	0
Heating Degree Days (base 65°F)	422	311	170	46	2	0	0	0	2	35	178	416	1,582
Cooling Degree Days (base 65°F)	8	15	55	149	345	512	605	624	439	208	51	11	3,022
Mean Precipitation (in.)	2.08	1.93	2.40	2.40	4.62	4.87	2.34	2.19	3.41	4.22	3.05	2.29	35.80
Extreme Maximum Daily Precip. (in.)	2.27	2.65	2.50	2.48	3.30	13.98	4.53	4.41	4.70	15.78	3.48	5.98	15.78
Days With ≥ 0.1" Precipitation	4	4	5	4	6	6	3	3	4	5	4	3	51
Days With ≥ 0.5" Precipitation	1	1	2	2	3	3	1	1	2	2	2	1	21
Days With ≥ 1.0" Precipitation	1	0	1	1	2	1	1	1	1	1	1	1	12
Mean Snowfall (in.)	trace	0.1	0.0	0.0	0.0	0.0	0.0	0.0	0.0	0.0	trace	trace	0.1
Maximum Snow Depth (in.)	trace	trace	0	0	0	0	0	0	0	0	0	trace	trace
Days With ≥ 1.0" Snow Depth	0	0	0	0	0	0	0	0	0	0	0	0	0

Somerville Dam *Burleson County*   Elevation: 263 ft.   Latitude: 30° 20' N   Longitude: 96° 32' W

	JAN	FEB	MAR	APR	MAY	JUN	JUL	AUG	SEP	OCT	NOV	DEC	YEAR
Mean Maximum Temp. (°F)	61.0	64.4	71.1	78.4	85.2	91.9	95.4	96.4	91.1	81.6	71.3	62.5	79.2
Mean Temp. (°F)	49.1	52.8	59.8	66.9	74.7	81.2	84.2	84.4	78.5	68.9	59.3	50.4	67.5
Mean Minimum Temp. (°F)	37.2	41.1	48.4	55.4	64.2	70.6	72.9	72.3	65.9	56.1	47.3	38.3	55.8
Extreme Maximum Temp. (°F)	83	96	90	96	100	109	107	108	114	98	90	84	114
Extreme Minimum Temp. (°F)	8	13	16	29	44	54	57	59	42	28	18	3	3
Days Maximum Temp. ≥ 90°F	0	0	0	1	7	22	29	29	20	5	0	0	113
Days Maximum Temp. ≤ 32°F	0	0	0	0	0	0	0	0	0	0	0	0	0
Days Minimum Temp. ≤ 32°F	10	5	2	0	0	0	0	0	0	0	2	10	29
Days Minimum Temp. ≤ 0°F	0	0	0	0	0	0	0	0	0	0	0	0	0
Heating Degree Days (base 65°F)	489	348	200	61	4	0	0	0	4	52	210	455	1,823
Cooling Degree Days (base 65°F)	4	9	46	126	312	494	601	608	415	180	47	10	2,852
Mean Precipitation (in.)	2.92	2.86	3.10	2.80	4.24	4.31	1.81	2.48	3.23	4.64	3.61	3.09	39.09
Extreme Maximum Daily Precip. (in.)	2.50	3.78	2.11	2.65	2.90	4.75	2.43	3.32	3.85	15.25	3.82	3.16	15.25
Days With ≥ 0.1" Precipitation	5	5	5	4	6	6	4	4	4	6	5	5	59
Days With ≥ 0.5" Precipitation	2	2	2	2	3	2	1	2	2	3	2	2	25
Days With ≥ 1.0" Precipitation	1	1	1	1	1	1	0	1	1	2	1	1	12
Mean Snowfall (in.)	0.0	trace	0.0	0.0	0.0	0.0	0.0	0.0	0.0	0.0	0.0	0.0	trace
Maximum Snow Depth (in.)	0	trace	0	0	0	0	0	0	0	0	0	0	trace
Days With ≥ 1.0" Snow Depth	0	0	0	0	0	0	0	0	0	0	0	0	0

The period of record for all cooperative weather station data is 1980 – 2009. See User Guide for detailed explanation of data.

Stillhouse Hollow Dam *Bell County*   Elevation: 706 ft.   Latitude: 31° 02' N   Longitude: 97° 32' W

	JAN	FEB	MAR	APR	MAY	JUN	JUL	AUG	SEP	OCT	NOV	DEC	YEAR
Mean Maximum Temp. (°F)	59.7	64.7	70.7	78.5	85.0	91.4	95.6	96.4	90.2	80.7	70.3	60.8	78.7
Mean Temp. (°F)	47.4	52.0	58.4	66.2	74.0	80.4	83.8	84.1	78.0	68.2	58.2	49.0	66.7
Mean Minimum Temp. (°F)	35.1	39.3	46.1	53.8	63.0	69.3	72.0	71.8	65.6	55.7	46.0	37.2	54.6
Extreme Maximum Temp. (°F)	88	98	93	99	100	106	108	109	110	99	92	86	110
Extreme Minimum Temp. (°F)	6	12	15	31	41	52	57	57	39	22	19	-5	-5
Days Maximum Temp. ≥ 90°F	0	0	0	2	7	20	28	28	18	5	0	0	108
Days Maximum Temp. ≤ 32°F	0	0	0	0	0	0	0	0	0	0	0	1	1
Days Minimum Temp. ≤ 32°F	12	6	2	0	0	0	0	0	0	0	2	9	31
Days Minimum Temp. ≤ 0°F	0	0	0	0	0	0	0	0	0	0	0	0	0
Heating Degree Days (base 65°F)	540	372	232	70	5	0	0	0	5	57	233	496	2,010
Cooling Degree Days (base 65°F)	3	11	35	112	293	469	590	600	402	163	36	8	2,722
Mean Precipitation (in.)	2.22	2.54	3.06	2.62	4.88	4.03	1.79	2.27	3.49	3.82	3.02	2.59	36.33
Extreme Maximum Daily Precip. (in.)	2.10	4.17	3.63	3.30	3.97	6.51	2.70	6.04	5.38	4.82	3.05	5.68	6.51
Days With ≥ 0.1" Precipitation	4	4	5	4	6	5	3	3	5	5	5	4	53
Days With ≥ 0.5" Precipitation	1	2	2	2	3	3	1	1	2	2	2	1	22
Days With ≥ 1.0" Precipitation	1	1	1	1	2	1	1	1	1	1	1	1	13
Mean Snowfall (in.)	0.0	0.0	trace	0.0	0.0	0.0	0.0	0.0	0.0	0.0	trace	trace	trace
Maximum Snow Depth (in.)	0	0	trace	0	0	0	0	0	0	0	trace	trace	trace
Days With ≥ 1.0" Snow Depth	0	0	0	0	0	0	0	0	0	0	0	0	0

Sugar Land *Fort Bend County*   Elevation: 82 ft.   Latitude: 29° 37' N   Longitude: 95° 38' W

	JAN	FEB	MAR	APR	MAY	JUN	JUL	AUG	SEP	OCT	NOV	DEC	YEAR
Mean Maximum Temp. (°F)	62.5	66.5	72.7	79.5	86.0	91.1	93.8	94.1	89.8	82.0	72.3	64.5	79.6
Mean Temp. (°F)	52.7	56.3	62.6	69.1	76.7	82.1	84.4	84.4	79.8	71.3	61.8	54.3	69.6
Mean Minimum Temp. (°F)	42.9	46.1	52.3	58.8	67.4	73.0	75.1	74.6	69.8	60.5	51.3	44.0	59.6
Extreme Maximum Temp. (°F)	84	89	92	94	99	104	103	104	108	95	90	85	108
Extreme Minimum Temp. (°F)	12	19	21	32	47	59	63	64	47	30	26	6	6
Days Maximum Temp. ≥ 90°F	0	0	0	1	7	20	26	25	17	4	0	0	100
Days Maximum Temp. ≤ 32°F	0	0	0	0	0	0	0	0	0	0	0	0	0
Days Minimum Temp. ≤ 32°F	3	2	1	0	0	0	0	0	0	0	1	3	10
Days Minimum Temp. ≤ 0°F	0	0	0	0	0	0	0	0	0	0	0	0	0
Heating Degree Days (base 65°F)	387	263	142	36	1	0	0	0	1	28	160	347	1,365
Cooling Degree Days (base 65°F)	15	24	72	167	371	520	609	609	451	230	70	22	3,160
Mean Precipitation (in.)	3.75	2.97	3.55	3.37	4.50	5.62	3.68	4.33	4.82	5.02	4.35	3.21	49.17
Extreme Maximum Daily Precip. (in.)	3.00	2.92	3.55	4.46	3.27	10.60	4.04	8.29	7.02	7.10	7.69	3.85	10.60
Days With ≥ 0.1" Precipitation	5	4	5	3	5	6	5	5	5	5	4	5	57
Days With ≥ 0.5" Precipitation	2	2	2	2	3	4	2	2	2	3	2	2	28
Days With ≥ 1.0" Precipitation	1	1	1	1	2	2	1	1	1	2	1	1	15
Mean Snowfall (in.)	trace	trace	trace	0.0	0.0	0.0	0.0	0.0	0.0	0.0	0.0	trace	trace
Maximum Snow Depth (in.)	1	trace	trace	0	0	0	0	0	0	0	0	trace	1
Days With ≥ 1.0" Snow Depth	0	0	0	0	0	0	0	0	0	0	0	0	0

Texarkana *Bowie County*   Elevation: 390 ft.   Latitude: 33° 25' N   Longitude: 94° 05' W

	JAN	FEB	MAR	APR	MAY	JUN	JUL	AUG	SEP	OCT	NOV	DEC	YEAR
Mean Maximum Temp. (°F)	54.4	58.8	66.8	75.0	81.7	88.9	93.1	93.6	86.6	76.3	65.2	56.0	74.7
Mean Temp. (°F)	43.9	47.6	55.4	63.3	71.7	79.1	83.0	82.8	75.6	64.7	54.3	45.7	63.9
Mean Minimum Temp. (°F)	33.4	36.4	43.9	51.6	61.6	69.3	72.8	72.0	64.5	53.2	43.4	35.4	53.1
Extreme Maximum Temp. (°F)	81	90	89	95	98	101	105	106	108	95	85	83	108
Extreme Minimum Temp. (°F)	3	8	15	29	42	53	59	55	38	27	23	-6	-6
Days Maximum Temp. ≥ 90°F	0	0	0	0	3	15	24	24	12	1	0	0	79
Days Maximum Temp. ≤ 32°F	1	1	0	0	0	0	0	0	0	0	0	1	3
Days Minimum Temp. ≤ 32°F	17	10	3	0	0	0	0	0	0	0	4	13	47
Days Minimum Temp. ≤ 0°F	0	0	0	0	0	0	0	0	0	0	0	0	0
Heating Degree Days (base 65°F)	650	491	312	118	15	0	0	0	10	102	329	594	2,621
Cooling Degree Days (base 65°F)	2	3	21	74	229	431	565	560	336	101	16	4	2,342
Mean Precipitation (in.)	4.02	4.20	4.81	4.27	5.21	4.81	3.60	2.20	3.74	5.24	5.00	5.07	52.17
Extreme Maximum Daily Precip. (in.)	2.98	4.02	5.45	3.86	3.96	6.35	4.57	2.73	3.63	4.95	5.30	5.15	6.35
Days With ≥ 0.1" Precipitation	6	6	7	6	7	6	4	4	4	6	6	6	68
Days With ≥ 0.5" Precipitation	3	3	3	3	4	3	2	2	3	3	3	3	35
Days With ≥ 1.0" Precipitation	1	1	1	1	2	2	1	1	1	2	2	2	17
Mean Snowfall (in.)	0.5	0.5	trace	0.0	0.0	0.0	0.0	0.0	0.0	0.0	0.0	0.1	1.1
Maximum Snow Depth (in.)	8	5	trace	0	0	0	0	0	0	0	0	2	8
Days With ≥ 1.0" Snow Depth	1	0	0	0	0	0	0	0	0	0	0	0	1

Thompsons 3 WSW *Fort Bend County*   Elevation: 71 ft.   Latitude: 29° 29' N   Longitude: 95° 38' W

	JAN	FEB	MAR	APR	MAY	JUN	JUL	AUG	SEP	OCT	NOV	DEC	YEAR
Mean Maximum Temp. (°F)	63.7	66.7	73.0	79.9	86.6	91.9	93.7	94.7	90.4	82.9	73.5	65.3	80.2
Mean Temp. (°F)	53.7	56.6	62.8	69.3	76.7	82.0	83.9	84.3	79.9	71.6	63.1	55.1	69.9
Mean Minimum Temp. (°F)	43.9	46.5	52.7	58.7	66.5	72.1	74.0	74.0	69.3	60.4	52.7	45.0	59.7
Extreme Maximum Temp. (°F)	85	88	92	94	99	105	106	106	106	97	91	87	106
Extreme Minimum Temp. (°F)	14	20	21	35	46	45	64	60	51	32	27	8	8
Days Maximum Temp. ≥ 90°F	0	0	0	1	9	23	26	28	19	5	0	0	111
Days Maximum Temp. ≤ 32°F	0	0	0	0	0	0	0	0	0	0	0	0	0
Days Minimum Temp. ≤ 32°F	3	2	1	0	0	0	0	0	0	0	0	3	9
Days Minimum Temp. ≤ 0°F	0	0	0	0	0	0	0	0	0	0	0	0	0
Heating Degree Days (base 65°F)	360	257	133	33	1	0	0	0	1	26	140	327	1,278
Cooling Degree Days (base 65°F)	17	25	73	168	369	516	592	607	454	239	90	28	3,178
Mean Precipitation (in.)	3.99	2.82	3.37	3.38	3.95	4.77	3.92	4.36	4.48	4.80	4.30	3.57	47.71
Extreme Maximum Daily Precip. (in.)	3.37	3.04	2.79	8.65	3.75	4.00	5.70	8.80	9.53	5.40	7.81	3.20	9.53
Days With ≥ 0.1" Precipitation	6	4	4	3	4	6	6	6	6	5	5	5	60
Days With ≥ 0.5" Precipitation	3	2	2	2	2	3	2	3	2	3	2	2	28
Days With ≥ 1.0" Precipitation	1	1	1	1	1	2	1	1	1	2	1	1	14
Mean Snowfall (in.)	trace	trace	0.0	0.0	0.0	0.0	0.0	0.0	0.0	0.0	0.0	0.1	0.1
Maximum Snow Depth (in.)	trace	0	0	0	0	0	0	0	0	0	0	0	trace
Days With ≥ 1.0" Snow Depth	0	0	0	0	0	0	0	0	0	0	0	0	0

The period of record for all cooperative weather station data is 1980 – 2009. See User Guide for detailed explanation of data.

Tyler *Smith County*   Elevation: 549 ft.   Latitude: 32° 18' N   Longitude: 95° 18' W

	JAN	FEB	MAR	APR	MAY	JUN	JUL	AUG	SEP	OCT	NOV	DEC	YEAR
Mean Maximum Temp. (°F)	58.5	63.1	70.7	77.8	84.1	90.0	93.4	94.1	87.9	78.5	67.5	58.9	77.0
Mean Temp. (°F)	48.0	52.2	59.3	66.4	73.9	80.0	83.3	83.3	77.1	67.4	57.3	48.9	66.4
Mean Minimum Temp. (°F)	37.6	41.3	47.8	55.0	63.6	69.9	73.1	72.5	66.2	56.3	47.1	38.9	55.8
Extreme Maximum Temp. (°F)	83	90	92	94	101	102	105	107	107	97	86	83	107
Extreme Minimum Temp. (°F)	9	11	19	30	43	52	61	55	43	27	23	0	0
Days Maximum Temp. ≥ 90°F	0	0	0	1	5	19	26	26	14	2	0	0	93
Days Maximum Temp. ≤ 32°F	0	0	0	0	0	0	0	0	0	0	0	1	1
Days Minimum Temp. ≤ 32°F	10	6	2	0	0	0	0	0	0	0	2	9	29
Days Minimum Temp. ≤ 0°F	0	0	0	0	0	0	0	0	0	0	0	0	0
Heating Degree Days (base 65°F)	524	367	215	67	6	0	0	0	5	60	254	500	1,998
Cooling Degree Days (base 65°F)	6	12	44	117	288	456	574	575	374	142	29	8	2,625
Mean Precipitation (in.)	3.66	4.22	4.27	3.44	4.45	4.76	2.66	2.83	3.20	5.02	4.45	4.70	47.66
Extreme Maximum Daily Precip. (in.)	3.71	5.48	3.67	3.99	3.06	4.19	4.68	6.47	3.24	8.02	4.54	3.36	8.02
Days With ≥ 0.1" Precipitation	6	6	6	5	6	7	4	4	4	5	6	6	65
Days With ≥ 0.5" Precipitation	2	2	3	2	3	3	2	2	2	3	3	3	30
Days With ≥ 1.0" Precipitation	1	1	2	1	1	1	1	1	1	2	1	2	15
Mean Snowfall (in.)	0.2	0.6	0.1	trace	0.0	0.0	0.0	0.0	0.0	0.0	trace	trace	0.9
Maximum Snow Depth (in.)	3	5	1	trace	0	0	0	0	0	0	trace	trace	5
Days With ≥ 1.0" Snow Depth	0	0	0	0	0	0	0	0	0	0	0	0	0

Valentine *Jeff Davis County*   Elevation: 4,430 ft.   Latitude: 30° 35' N   Longitude: 104° 30' W

	JAN	FEB	MAR	APR	MAY	JUN	JUL	AUG	SEP	OCT	NOV	DEC	YEAR
Mean Maximum Temp. (°F)	60.0	65.0	71.6	79.7	87.7	93.6	92.2	90.2	86.1	78.7	68.4	60.3	77.8
Mean Temp. (°F)	43.7	48.0	53.9	61.6	70.2	77.2	77.6	76.0	71.3	62.8	51.9	44.0	61.5
Mean Minimum Temp. (°F)	27.2	30.9	36.0	43.4	52.6	60.8	63.0	61.7	56.4	46.9	35.3	27.6	45.2
Extreme Maximum Temp. (°F)	83	84	89	97	101	108	106	103	100	96	86	77	108
Extreme Minimum Temp. (°F)	3	7	12	21	32	46	51	50	39	17	8	0	0
Days Maximum Temp. ≥ 90°F	0	0	0	2	12	24	21	18	9	1	0	0	87
Days Maximum Temp. ≤ 32°F	0	0	0	0	0	0	0	0	0	0	0	0	0
Days Minimum Temp. ≤ 32°F	23	16	10	3	0	0	0	0	0	1	10	23	86
Days Minimum Temp. ≤ 0°F	0	0	0	0	0	0	0	0	0	0	0	0	0
Heating Degree Days (base 65°F)	651	475	341	132	15	0	0	0	10	111	388	642	2,765
Cooling Degree Days (base 65°F)	0	0	2	37	183	373	398	347	206	51	2	0	1,599
Mean Precipitation (in.)	0.42	0.48	0.27	0.41	0.76	2.14	2.30	2.17	2.11	1.44	0.47	0.51	13.48
Extreme Maximum Daily Precip. (in.)	0.86	1.60	1.12	1.30	1.40	3.06	2.80	2.40	2.22	2.93	2.10	1.10	3.06
Days With ≥ 0.1" Precipitation	1	1	1	1	2	4	5	5	4	3	1	1	29
Days With ≥ 0.5" Precipitation	0	0	0	0	0	1	1	1	2	1	0	0	6
Days With ≥ 1.0" Precipitation	0	0	0	0	0	1	1	0	0	0	0	0	2
Mean Snowfall (in.)	0.7	trace	trace	0.1	0.0	0.0	0.0	0.0	0.0	trace	0.1	0.8	1.7
Maximum Snow Depth (in.)	trace	1	trace	0	0	0	0	0	0	trace	trace	8	8
Days With ≥ 1.0" Snow Depth	0	0	0	0	0	0	0	0	0	0	0	0	0

Water Valley *Tom Green County*   Elevation: 2,120 ft.   Latitude: 31° 40' N   Longitude: 100° 44' W

	JAN	FEB	MAR	APR	MAY	JUN	JUL	AUG	SEP	OCT	NOV	DEC	YEAR
Mean Maximum Temp. (°F)	59.6	63.3	70.7	79.6	87.0	92.0	95.2	94.4	87.7	79.0	68.3	59.1	78.0
Mean Temp. (°F)	44.6	48.1	55.7	63.9	73.0	79.4	82.3	81.4	74.4	64.7	53.4	44.4	63.8
Mean Minimum Temp. (°F)	29.5	32.8	40.8	48.1	59.0	66.6	69.3	68.4	61.0	50.4	38.6	29.7	49.5
Extreme Maximum Temp. (°F)	88	97	96	102	112	112	109	107	108	103	93	86	112
Extreme Minimum Temp. (°F)	3	5	5	23	38	48	54	51	33	23	12	-4	-4
Days Maximum Temp. ≥ 90°F	0	0	1	5	13	19	26	26	13	4	0	0	107
Days Maximum Temp. ≤ 32°F	1	1	0	0	0	0	0	0	0	0	0	1	3
Days Minimum Temp. ≤ 32°F	21	14	6	2	0	0	0	0	0	1	9	20	73
Days Minimum Temp. ≤ 0°F	0	0	0	0	0	0	0	0	0	0	0	0	0
Heating Degree Days (base 65°F)	627	475	301	119	17	0	0	0	14	101	351	632	2,637
Cooling Degree Days (base 65°F)	0	3	20	91	272	438	544	516	302	99	10	0	2,295
Mean Precipitation (in.)	0.75	1.23	1.50	1.45	2.86	3.06	1.67	2.80	2.63	2.81	1.10	0.98	22.84
Extreme Maximum Daily Precip. (in.)	1.65	3.13	3.30	2.61	2.35	3.06	3.30	5.35	5.32	4.43	2.60	2.15	5.35
Days With ≥ 0.1" Precipitation	2	2	3	2	5	4	3	4	3	3	2	2	35
Days With ≥ 0.5" Precipitation	0	1	1	1	2	2	1	2	1	2	1	1	15
Days With ≥ 1.0" Precipitation	0	0	0	0	1	1	1	1	1	1	0	0	6
Mean Snowfall (in.)	0.7	0.1	0.0	0.2	0.0	0.0	0.0	0.0	0.0	0.0	0.6	0.2	1.8
Maximum Snow Depth (in.)	5	trace	trace	3	0	0	0	0	0	0	4	2	5
Days With ≥ 1.0" Snow Depth	0	0	0	0	0	0	0	0	0	0	0	0	0

Weslaco 2 E *Hidalgo County*   Elevation: 75 ft.   Latitude: 26° 09' N   Longitude: 97° 58' W

	JAN	FEB	MAR	APR	MAY	JUN	JUL	AUG	SEP	OCT	NOV	DEC	YEAR
Mean Maximum Temp. (°F)	70.5	74.7	80.6	85.6	90.1	94.2	96.1	96.5	92.1	86.9	79.4	71.9	84.9
Mean Temp. (°F)	60.1	64.0	69.7	75.1	80.6	84.5	85.7	85.9	82.1	76.1	68.9	61.3	74.5
Mean Minimum Temp. (°F)	49.6	53.2	58.8	64.4	71.0	74.7	75.3	75.3	72.1	65.4	58.3	50.8	64.1
Extreme Maximum Temp. (°F)	91	98	104	102	105	105	104	104	107	100	99	91	107
Extreme Minimum Temp. (°F)	25	28	30	36	50	61	66	64	56	33	34	16	16
Days Maximum Temp. ≥ 90°F	0	1	3	8	18	27	28	29	22	12	2	0	150
Days Maximum Temp. ≤ 32°F	0	0	0	0	0	0	0	0	0	0	0	0	0
Days Minimum Temp. ≤ 32°F	0	0	0	0	0	0	0	0	0	0	0	1	1
Days Minimum Temp. ≤ 0°F	0	0	0	0	0	0	0	0	0	0	0	0	0
Heating Degree Days (base 65°F)	198	114	45	10	0	0	0	0	0	8	59	185	619
Cooling Degree Days (base 65°F)	54	91	198	319	490	591	649	656	521	360	183	81	4,193
Mean Precipitation (in.)	1.13	1.31	1.11	1.36	2.71	2.49	2.15	2.33	4.95	2.43	1.42	1.25	24.64
Extreme Maximum Daily Precip. (in.)	1.56	2.65	2.93	2.80	3.64	4.35	7.20	4.81	8.50	4.26	3.80	2.38	8.50
Days With ≥ 0.1" Precipitation	3	3	2	2	3	3	3	3	6	4	3	3	38
Days With ≥ 0.5" Precipitation	1	1	1	1	2	1	1	1	3	2	1	1	15
Days With ≥ 1.0" Precipitation	0	0	0	1	1	1	0	1	2	1	0	0	6
Mean Snowfall (in.)	0.0	0.0	0.0	0.0	0.0	0.0	0.0	0.0	0.0	0.0	0.0	0.0	0.0
Maximum Snow Depth (in.)	0	0	0	0	0	0	0	0	0	0	0	0	0
Days With ≥ 1.0" Snow Depth	0	0	0	0	0	0	0	0	0	0	0	0	0

The period of record for all cooperative weather station data is 1980 – 2009. See User Guide for detailed explanation of data.

Whitney Dam *Bosque County*   Elevation: 574 ft.   Latitude: 31° 51' N   Longitude: 97° 22' W

	JAN	FEB	MAR	APR	MAY	JUN	JUL	AUG	SEP	OCT	NOV	DEC	YEAR
Mean Maximum Temp. (°F)	58.7	62.1	69.3	77.3	84.9	91.6	96.7	97.1	90.3	79.9	68.7	59.0	78.0
Mean Temp. (°F)	46.7	49.8	57.4	65.1	73.8	80.3	84.2	84.2	77.7	67.2	56.8	47.3	65.9
Mean Minimum Temp. (°F)	34.7	37.5	45.5	52.9	62.6	69.0	71.6	71.3	65.0	54.4	44.8	35.5	53.7
Extreme Maximum Temp. (°F)	87	97	97	103	101	110	109	111	113	99	90	91	113
Extreme Minimum Temp. (°F)	4	7	15	28	42	52	59	56	38	26	21	-3	-3
Days Maximum Temp. ≥ 90°F	0	0	0	1	8	21	29	28	18	5	0	0	110
Days Maximum Temp. ≤ 32°F	0	1	0	0	0	0	0	0	0	0	0	1	2
Days Minimum Temp. ≤ 32°F	14	8	3	0	0	0	0	0	0	0	4	12	41
Days Minimum Temp. ≤ 0°F	0	0	0	0	0	0	0	0	0	0	0	0	0
Heating Degree Days (base 65°F)	565	427	256	90	7	0	0	0	6	67	267	547	2,232
Cooling Degree Days (base 65°F)	3	6	30	100	285	466	602	602	393	141	28	4	2,660
Mean Precipitation (in.)	2.03	2.38	3.52	2.82	4.20	4.52	1.63	2.06	2.67	4.00	2.78	2.77	35.38
Extreme Maximum Daily Precip. (in.)	3.58	2.70	6.87	5.75	6.50	5.76	2.71	3.55	5.66	3.18	3.38	5.15	6.87
Days With ≥ 0.1" Precipitation	4	4	5	4	6	6	3	3	4	5	4	4	52
Days With ≥ 0.5" Precipitation	1	2	2	2	3	3	1	1	2	3	2	2	24
Days With ≥ 1.0" Precipitation	0	1	1	1	1	1	1	1	1	1	1	1	11
Mean Snowfall (in.)	0.0	trace	0.0	0.0	0.0	0.0	0.0	0.0	0.0	0.0	0.0	0.1	0.1
Maximum Snow Depth (in.)	12	trace	0	0	0	0	0	0	0	0	0	2	12
Days With ≥ 1.0" Snow Depth	0	0	0	0	0	0	0	0	0	0	0	0	0

Wright Patman Dam & Lock *Cass County*   Elevation: 282 ft.   Latitude: 33° 18' N   Longitude: 94° 10' W

	JAN	FEB	MAR	APR	MAY	JUN	JUL	AUG	SEP	OCT	NOV	DEC	YEAR
Mean Maximum Temp. (°F)	54.3	58.9	66.8	74.5	82.0	88.9	92.9	93.4	86.4	76.0	65.3	55.6	74.6
Mean Temp. (°F)	43.6	47.8	55.8	63.0	71.6	78.5	82.3	81.9	74.7	63.8	54.2	45.2	63.5
Mean Minimum Temp. (°F)	32.8	36.7	44.7	51.5	61.1	68.1	71.6	70.4	62.9	51.5	43.0	34.8	52.4
Extreme Maximum Temp. (°F)	82	88	90	93	95	103	107	108	109	93	86	84	109
Extreme Minimum Temp. (°F)	4	5	14	28	40	52	56	51	39	27	19	-1	-1
Days Maximum Temp. ≥ 90°F	0	0	0	0	3	16	24	24	11	1	0	0	79
Days Maximum Temp. ≤ 32°F	1	1	0	0	0	0	0	0	0	0	0	1	3
Days Minimum Temp. ≤ 32°F	17	9	3	0	0	0	0	0	0	0	5	13	47
Days Minimum Temp. ≤ 0°F	0	0	0	0	0	0	0	0	0	0	0	0	0
Heating Degree Days (base 65°F)	660	482	302	121	14	0	0	0	12	115	332	608	2,646
Cooling Degree Days (base 65°F)	3	3	23	69	225	413	542	532	309	84	14	4	2,221
Mean Precipitation (in.)	3.74	3.97	4.52	3.91	4.66	4.56	3.23	2.50	3.18	5.09	4.56	4.59	48.51
Extreme Maximum Daily Precip. (in.)	3.43	4.35	5.25	3.75	4.00	4.15	3.94	2.73	3.56	5.42	3.67	5.85	5.85
Days With ≥ 0.1" Precipitation	5	6	6	6	6	6	5	4	5	6	6	6	67
Days With ≥ 0.5" Precipitation	2	3	3	3	4	3	2	2	2	3	3	3	33
Days With ≥ 1.0" Precipitation	1	1	1	1	1	2	1	1	1	2	2	1	15
Mean Snowfall (in.)	0.1	0.4	0.0	0.0	0.0	0.0	0.0	0.0	0.0	0.0	trace	0.1	0.6
Maximum Snow Depth (in.)	4	3	0	0	0	0	0	0	0	0	trace	1	4
Days With ≥ 1.0" Snow Depth	0	0	0	0	0	0	0	0	0	0	0	0	0

Texas Weather Station Rankings

Annual Extreme Maximum Temperature

Highest				Lowest		
Rank	Station Name	°F		Rank	Station Name	°F
1	Boquillas Ranger Stn	117		1	Aransas Wildlife Refuge	102
1	Castolon	117		2	Port Isabel	103
1	Childress Municipal Arpt	117		3	Anahuac	105
1	Grandfalls 3 SSE	117		4	Alpine	106
1	Wichita Falls Municipal Arpt	117		4	Brownsville Intl Arpt	106
6	Columbus	116		4	Harlingen	106
6	Encinal	116		4	Thompsons 3 WSW	106
6	Falcon Dam	116		8	Angleton 2 W	107
6	Gail	116		8	Beaumont Research Ctr	107
6	Midland Regional Air Terminal	116		8	Liberty	107
6	Penwell	116		8	Marshall	107
6	Rio Grande City 1 SE	116		8	Ozona 1 SSW	107
13	Bridgeport	115		8	Tyler	107
13	Candelaria	115		8	Weslaco 2 E	107
13	Crystal City	115		15	Amarillo Intl Arpt	108
13	Dell City 5 SSW	115		15	Borger	108
13	Falfurrias	115		15	Burnet	108
13	Henrietta	115		15	Emory	108
19	Amistad Dam	114		15	Houston William P Hobby Arpt	108
19	Anson	114		15	Marathon	108
19	Bakersfield	114		15	Port Arthur Jefferson County	108
19	Big Spring	114		15	Raymondville	108
19	El Paso Intl Arpt	114		15	Sugar Land	108
19	Laredo 2	114		15	Texarkana	108
19	Lubbock Regional Arpt	114		15	Valentine	108

Annual Mean Maximum Temperature

Highest				Lowest		
Rank	Station Name	°F		Rank	Station Name	°F
1	Boquillas Ranger Stn	88.1		1	Amarillo Intl Arpt	70.8
2	Castolon	87.7		2	Dimmitt 2 N	71.3
3	Falcon Dam	86.5		3	Hart	71.6
4	Rio Grande City 1 SE	86.4		4	Borger	72.0
5	Laredo 2	85.9		5	Boys Ranch	72.6
5	McAllen Miller Intl Arpt	85.9		6	Canyon	73.2
7	Candelaria	85.4		7	Clarendon	73.4
7	McCook	85.4		8	Morton	73.5
9	Raymondville	85.1		9	Crosbyton	73.9
10	Weslaco 2 E	84.9		10	Lubbock Regional Arpt	74.3
11	Encinal	84.8		11	Wright Patman Dam & Lock	74.6
11	McAllen	84.8		12	Childress Municipal Arpt	74.7
13	Falfurrias	84.3		12	Emory	74.7
14	Carrizo Springs	83.9		12	Texarkana	74.7
14	Crystal City	83.9		15	Brownfield 2	74.9
14	Harlingen	83.9		16	Dublin	75.1
17	Alice	83.7		17	Marshall	75.2
17	Brownsville Intl Arpt	83.7		18	Henrietta	75.6
19	Charlotte 5 NNW	83.6		19	Denton 2 SE	75.7
20	Langtry	82.4		20	Pilot Point	75.8
21	Cuero	82.1		20	Wichita Falls Municipal Arpt	75.8
21	Robstown	82.1		22	Lavon Dam	75.9
23	Floresville	81.9		23	Henderson	76.0
24	Amistad Dam	81.8		24	McKinney 3 S	76.1
25	Del Rio Intl Arpt	81.7		25	Abilene Municipal Arpt	76.2

Rankings include 25 highest/lowest stations. If state has less than 25 stations, all stations are included. The period of record is 1980–2009. See User Guide for detailed explanation of data.

Annual Mean Temperature

	Highest			Lowest	
Rank	Station Name	°F	Rank	Station Name	°F
1	McAllen Miller Intl Arpt	75.6	1	Dimmitt 2 N	56.0
2	Brownsville Intl Arpt	74.6	2	Hart	56.9
2	McAllen	74.6	3	Amarillo Intl Arpt	57.2
4	Falcon Dam	74.5	4	Boys Ranch	57.7
4	Weslaco 2 E	74.5	5	Borger	58.6
6	Laredo 2	74.3	6	Morton	58.7
6	Rio Grande City 1 SE	74.3	7	Canyon	59.0
8	McCook	74.1	7	Clarendon	59.0
8	Port Isabel	74.1	9	Crosbyton	60.1
10	Harlingen	74.0	10	Brownfield 2	60.6
11	Raymondville	73.8	11	Lubbock Regional Arpt	60.9
12	Crystal City	72.7	12	Valentine	61.5
13	Alice	72.6	13	Childress Municipal Arpt	61.9
13	Falfurrias	72.6	13	Dell City 5 SSW	61.9
15	Robstown	72.3	15	Alpine	62.5
16	Corpus Christi Intl Arpt	72.2	16	Henrietta	62.6
16	Port Mansfield	72.2	16	Marathon	62.6
18	Encinal	72.0	18	Fort Hancock 5 SSE	62.9
19	Castolon	71.8	19	Emory	63.5
20	Carrizo Springs	71.4	19	Wright Patman Dam & Lock	63.5
21	Charlotte 5 NNW	71.3	21	Dublin	63.6
22	Aransas Wildlife Refuge	70.9	22	Wichita Falls Municipal Arpt	63.7
23	Del Rio Intl Arpt	70.5	23	Midland Regional Air Terminal	63.8
23	Victoria Regional Arpt	70.5	23	Water Valley	63.8
25	Boquillas Ranger Stn	70.4	25	Balmorhea	63.9

Annual Mean Minimum Temperature

	Highest			Lowest	
Rank	Station Name	°F	Rank	Station Name	°F
1	Port Isabel	67.2	1	Dimmitt 2 N	40.7
2	Port Mansfield	65.6	2	Hart	42.1
3	Brownsville Intl Arpt	65.4	3	Boys Ranch	42.7
4	McAllen Miller Intl Arpt	65.2	4	Amarillo Intl Arpt	43.7
5	McAllen	64.2	5	Morton	43.8
6	Weslaco 2 E	64.1	6	Clarendon	44.6
7	Harlingen	63.9	6	Dell City 5 SSW	44.6
8	Aransas Wildlife Refuge	63.2	8	Canyon	44.7
9	McCook	62.8	9	Borger	45.2
10	Corpus Christi Intl Arpt	62.7	9	Valentine	45.2
11	Raymondville	62.6	11	Fort Hancock 5 SSE	45.5
12	Falcon Dam	62.5	12	Brownfield 2	46.2
12	Laredo 2	62.5	13	Crosbyton	46.4
14	Robstown	62.4	14	Marathon	46.9
15	Rio Grande City 1 SE	62.1	15	Lubbock Regional Arpt	47.4
16	Alice	61.5	16	Alpine	48.0
17	Crystal City	61.4	17	Balmorhea	48.5
17	Houston William P Hobby Arpt	61.4	18	Grandfalls 3 SSE	48.7
19	Bay City Waterworks	61.1	19	Childress Municipal Arpt	49.0
20	Falfurrias	60.9	20	La Tuna 1 S	49.1
21	Baytown	60.3	21	Water Valley	49.5
21	Victoria Regional Arpt	60.3	22	Henrietta	49.6
23	Angleton 2 W	59.9	23	Candelaria	49.9
23	Port Arthur Jefferson County	59.9	24	Penwell	50.1
25	Sugar Land	59.7	25	Midland Regional Air Terminal	50.3

Rankings include 25 highest/lowest stations. If state has less than 25 stations, all stations are included. The period of record is 1980–2009. See User Guide for detailed explanation of data.

Annual Extreme Minimum Temperature

	Highest				Lowest	
Rank	Station Name	°F		Rank	Station Name	°F
1	McAllen	*18*		1	Amarillo Intl Arpt	-12
1	McAllen Miller Intl Arpt	*18*		1	Anson	*-12*
3	Port Isabel	17		1	Penwell	-12
4	Brownsville Intl Arpt	16		4	Boys Ranch	-11
4	Rio Grande City 1 SE	16		4	Canyon	-11
4	Weslaco 2 E	16		4	Clarendon	-11
7	Falcon Dam	15		4	Hart	*-11*
7	Harlingen	15		4	Midland Regional Air Terminal	-11
7	Port Mansfield	15		9	Dimmitt 2 N	-9
7	Raymondville	15		9	Grandfalls 3 SSE	*-9*
11	McCook	14		11	Bridgeport	*-8*
12	Corpus Christi Intl Arpt	13		11	Henrietta	*-8*
12	Falfurrias	13		11	Wichita Falls Municipal Arpt	-8
14	Alice	*12*		14	Abilene Municipal Arpt	-7
14	Encinal	*12*		14	Bardwell Dam	-7
14	Port Arthur Jefferson County	12		14	Borger	-7
14	Robstown	12		14	Dublin	-7
18	Crystal City	11		18	Albany	*-6*
18	Laredo 2	11		18	Athens	-6
20	Carrizo Springs	*10*		18	Benbrook Dam	-6
20	Del Rio Intl Arpt	10		18	Brownwood	-6
22	Amistad Dam	9		18	Crosbyton	-6
22	Aransas Wildlife Refuge	9		18	Morton	-6
22	Houston William P Hobby Arpt	9		18	Texarkana	-6
22	Langtry	9		25	Big Spring	*-5*

July Mean Maximum Temperature

	Highest				Lowest	
Rank	Station Name	°F		Rank	Station Name	°F
1	Boquillas Ranger Stn	*103.0*		1	Port Mansfield	88.8
2	Castolon	102.3		2	Galveston	*89.0*
3	Laredo 2	100.4		3	Alpine	89.3
4	Falcon Dam	100.3		4	Aransas Wildlife Refuge	89.8
5	Candelaria	99.9		5	Hart	*90.0*
6	Rio Grande City 1 SE	99.4		6	Port Isabel	90.5
7	Encinal	*98.9*		7	Marathon	90.7
8	Carrizo Springs	98.6		8	Dimmitt 2 N	91.3
9	Grandfalls 3 SSE	98.4		9	Angleton 2 W	91.4
10	Langtry	98.3		10	Anahuac	91.5
11	McCook	97.8		11	Amarillo Intl Arpt	91.6
12	Amistad Dam	97.6		12	Baytown	91.7
13	McAllen Miller Intl Arpt	97.4		13	Port Arthur Jefferson County	91.8
13	Wichita Falls Municipal Arpt	97.4		14	Bay City Waterworks	91.9
15	Crystal City	97.3		15	Morton	92.0
15	Falfurrias	97.3		16	Beaumont Research Ctr	92.2
17	Dell City 5 SSW	97.1		16	Cleveland	92.2
18	Raymondville	97.0		16	Valentine	92.2
18	Waco Madison Cooper Arpt	97.0		19	Houston William P Hobby Arpt	92.3
20	Del Rio Intl Arpt	96.9		20	Emory	*92.5*
21	Charlotte 5 NNW	96.8		21	Boys Ranch	92.7
22	Bridgeport	96.7		21	Canyon	92.7
22	Whitney Dam	96.7		21	Marshall	92.7
24	Henrietta	*96.6*		24	Boerne	92.8
24	Pilot Point	*96.6*		24	Brownfield 2	92.8

Rankings include 25 highest/lowest stations. If state has less than 25 stations, all stations are included. The period of record is 1980–2009. See User Guide for detailed explanation of data.

January Mean Minimum Temperature

	Highest				Lowest	
Rank	**Station Name**	**°F**		**Rank**	**Station Name**	**°F**
1	Port Isabel	53.2		1	Boys Ranch	21.1
2	Brownsville Intl Arpt	51.7		2	Dimmitt 2 N	21.4
3	McAllen Miller Intl Arpt	*50.6*		3	Hart	*22.3*
4	Port Mansfield	49.9		4	Amarillo Intl Arpt	23.5
5	Harlingen	49.8		5	Clarendon	24.0
6	Weslaco 2 E	49.6		6	Morton	24.5
7	McAllen	49.3		7	Canyon	24.6
8	McCook	48.1		8	Borger	25.3
8	Raymondville	48.1		9	Fort Hancock 5 SSE	25.6
10	Corpus Christi Intl Arpt	47.4		10	Dell City 5 SSW	25.7
11	Falcon Dam	46.7		11	Crosbyton	26.3
12	Aransas Wildlife Refuge	46.4		12	Lubbock Regional Arpt	27.0
12	Robstown	46.4		13	Brownfield 2	27.1
14	Rio Grande City 1 SE	45.9		14	Valentine	27.2
15	Alice	*45.6*		15	Grandfalls 3 SSE	*27.7*
16	Laredo 2	45.5		16	Childress Municipal Arpt	27.8
17	Houston William P Hobby Arpt	45.1		17	Henrietta	*28.4*
18	Bay City Waterworks	45.0		18	Water Valley	29.5
19	Falfurrias	44.8		19	Penwell	29.8
20	Angleton 2 W	44.1		20	Marathon	30.0
20	Crystal City	44.1		21	La Tuna 1 S	30.1
22	Victoria Regional Arpt	44.0		22	Ozona 1 SSW	30.2
23	Thompsons 3 WSW	43.9		23	Midland Regional Air Terminal	30.4
24	Port Arthur Jefferson County	43.7		24	Wichita Falls Municipal Arpt	30.6
25	Baytown	43.1		25	Balmorhea	30.7

Number of Days Annually Maximum Temperature ≥ 90°F

	Highest				Lowest	
Rank	**Station Name**	**Days**		**Rank**	**Station Name**	**Days**
1	Boquillas Ranger Stn	*192*		1	Port Mansfield	41
2	Castolon	186		2	Aransas Wildlife Refuge	60
3	Rio Grande City 1 SE	179		2	Hart	*60*
4	Falcon Dam	178		4	Amarillo Intl Arpt	64
5	Laredo 2	175		5	Alpine	*65*
6	McAllen Miller Intl Arpt	*171*		5	Dimmitt 2 N	65
7	Candelaria	165		7	Borger	73
8	McCook	163		8	Boys Ranch	74
9	Encinal	*161*		8	Emory	*74*
10	McAllen	*155*		10	Morton	76
10	Raymondville	155		11	Canyon	78
12	Carrizo Springs	150		11	Marshall	78
12	Weslaco 2 E	150		13	Angleton 2 W	79
14	Crystal City	149		13	Texarkana	79
15	Langtry	146		13	Wright Patman Dam & Lock	79
16	Alice	144		16	Anahuac	81
16	Charlotte 5 NNW	144		16	Crosbyton	81
16	Falfurrias	144		16	Marathon	81
19	Harlingen	142		19	Dublin	82
20	Amistad Dam	139		20	Port Isabel	83
21	Brownsville Intl Arpt	133		21	Baytown	84
22	Del Rio Intl Arpt	132		21	Clarendon	84
23	Floresville	130		23	Henderson	85
24	Cuero	129		24	Cleveland	86
25	Columbus	127		24	Lubbock Regional Arpt	86

Rankings include 25 highest/lowest stations. If state has less than 25 stations, all stations are included. The period of record is 1980–2009. See User Guide for detailed explanation of data.

Number of Days Annually Maximum Temperature ≤ 32°F

	Highest			Lowest	
Rank	Station Name	Days	Rank	Station Name	Days
1	Amarillo Intl Arpt	11	1	Alice	0
1	Dimmitt 2 N	11	1	Alpine	0
3	Clarendon	10	1	Amistad Dam	0
4	Borger	9	1	Anahuac	0
4	Hart	9	1	Angleton 2 W	0
6	Boys Ranch	8	1	Aransas Wildlife Refuge	0
7	Canyon	6	1	Austin Municipal Arpt	0
7	Childress Municipal Arpt	6	1	Bay City Waterworks	0
7	Crosbyton	6	1	Baytown	0
7	Morton	6	1	Beaumont Research Ctr	0
11	Brownfield 2	5	1	Blanco	0
11	Henrietta	5	1	Boerne	0
11	Lubbock Regional Arpt	5	1	Boquillas Ranger Stn	0
11	Wichita Falls Municipal Arpt	5	1	Brenham	0
15	Big Spring	4	1	Brownsville Intl Arpt	0
16	Abilene Municipal Arpt	3	1	Cameron	0
16	Albany	3	1	Camp Wood	0
16	Anson	3	1	Candelaria	0
16	Bardwell Dam	3	1	Carrizo Springs	0
16	Benbrook Dam	3	1	Castolon	0
16	Brady	3	1	Charlotte 5 NNW	0
16	Coleman	3	1	Cleveland	0
16	Dallas-Fort Worth Intl Arpt	3	1	College Station Easterwood	0
16	Dallas Love Field	3	1	Columbus	0
16	Denton 2 SE	3	1	Conroe	0

Number of Days Annually Minimum Temperature ≤ 32°F

	Highest			Lowest	
Rank	Station Name	Days	Rank	Station Name	Days
1	Dimmitt 2 N	131	1	Port Isabel	0
2	Boys Ranch	124	2	McAllen Miller Intl Arpt	1
3	Hart	122	2	Weslaco 2 E	1
4	Amarillo Intl Arpt	110	4	Brownsville Intl Arpt	2
5	Morton	107	4	Harlingen	2
6	Clarendon	105	4	McAllen	2
7	Canyon	99	7	Falcon Dam	3
7	Dell City 5 SSW	99	7	McCook	3
9	Borger	96	7	Port Mansfield	3
9	Fort Hancock 5 SSE	96	10	Raymondville	4
11	Crosbyton	89	11	Alice	5
12	Brownfield 2	88	11	Corpus Christi Intl Arpt	5
13	Valentine	86	11	Robstown	5
14	Lubbock Regional Arpt	84	14	Aransas Wildlife Refuge	6
15	Grandfalls 3 SSE	78	14	Houston William P Hobby Arpt	6
16	Childress Municipal Arpt	76	16	Bay City Waterworks	7
17	Water Valley	73	16	Laredo 2	7
18	Henrietta	72	16	Rio Grande City 1 SE	7
19	Marathon	68	19	Crystal City	8
20	Ozona 1 SSW	66	20	Thompsons 3 WSW	9
21	Balmorhea	65	20	Victoria Regional Arpt	9
21	La Tuna 1 S	65	22	Angleton 2 W	10
23	Penwell	63	22	Encinal	10
24	Menard	62	22	Falfurrias	10
24	Midland Regional Air Terminal	62	22	Port Arthur Jefferson County	10

Rankings include 25 highest/lowest stations. If state has less than 25 stations, all stations are included. The period of record is 1980–2009. See User Guide for detailed explanation of data.

Number of Days Annually Minimum Temperature ≤ 0°F

	Highest			Lowest	
Rank	Station Name	Days	Rank	Station Name	Days
1	Amarillo Intl Arpt	1	1	Abilene Municipal Arpt	0
1	Borger	1	1	Albany	0
1	Boys Ranch	1	1	Alice	0
1	Dimmitt 2 N	1	1	Alpine	0
1	Hart	1	1	Amistad Dam	0
6	Abilene Municipal Arpt	0	1	Anahuac	0
6	Albany	0	1	Angleton 2 W	0
6	Alice	0	1	Anson	0
6	Alpine	0	1	Aransas Wildlife Refuge	0
6	Amistad Dam	0	1	Athens	0
6	Anahuac	0	1	Austin Municipal Arpt	0
6	Angleton 2 W	0	1	Bakersfield	0
6	Anson	0	1	Ballinger 2 NW	0
6	Aransas Wildlife Refuge	0	1	Balmorhea	0
6	Athens	0	1	Bardwell Dam	0
6	Austin Municipal Arpt	0	1	Bay City Waterworks	0
6	Bakersfield	0	1	Baytown	0
6	Ballinger 2 NW	0	1	Beaumont Research Ctr	0
6	Balmorhea	0	1	Benbrook Dam	0
6	Bardwell Dam	0	1	Big Spring	0
6	Bay City Waterworks	0	1	Blanco	0
6	Baytown	0	1	Boerne	0
6	Beaumont Research Ctr	0	1	Boquillas Ranger Stn	0
6	Benbrook Dam	0	1	Brady	0
6	Big Spring	0	1	Brenham	0

Number of Annual Heating Degree Days

	Highest			Lowest	
Rank	Station Name	Num.	Rank	Station Name	Num.
1	Dimmitt 2 N	4,389	1	Port Isabel	539
2	Amarillo Intl Arpt	4,150	2	Brownsville Intl Arpt	547
3	Hart	4,122	3	McAllen Miller Intl Arpt	584
4	Boys Ranch	4,097	4	Weslaco 2 E	619
5	Borger	3,840	5	Harlingen	673
6	Clarendon	3,789	5	McAllen	673
7	Canyon	3,720	7	Raymondville	736
8	Morton	3,683	8	McCook	757
9	Crosbyton	3,413	9	Port Mansfield	785
10	Lubbock Regional Arpt	3,289	10	Falcon Dam	796
11	Brownfield 2	3,263	11	Rio Grande City 1 SE	821
12	Childress Municipal Arpt	3,192	12	Corpus Christi Intl Arpt	878
13	Henrietta	3,047	13	Laredo 2	906
14	Dell City 5 SSW	2,935	14	Alice	910
15	Wichita Falls Municipal Arpt	2,860	15	Robstown	929
16	Valentine	2,765	16	Falfurrias	971
17	Pilot Point	2,742	17	Crystal City	977
18	Fort Hancock 5 SSE	2,698	18	Aransas Wildlife Refuge	1,020
19	Wright Patman Dam & Lock	2,646	19	Encinal	1,112
20	Midland Regional Air Terminal	2,641	20	Charlotte 5 NNW	1,118
21	Water Valley	2,637	21	Bay City Waterworks	1,152
22	Emory	2,632	22	Victoria Regional Arpt	1,184
23	Dublin	2,626	23	Houston William P Hobby Arpt	1,210
24	Texarkana	2,621	24	Angleton 2 W	1,243
25	Bridgeport	2,618	25	Carrizo Springs	1,245

Rankings include 25 highest/lowest stations. If state has less than 25 stations, all stations are included. The period of record is 1980–2009. See User Guide for detailed explanation of data.

Number of Annual Cooling Degree Days

	Highest			Lowest	
Rank	Station Name	Num.	Rank	Station Name	Num.
1	McAllen Miller Intl Arpt	*4,549*	1	Dimmitt 2 N	1,201
2	Laredo 2	4,389	2	Hart	*1,261*
3	Falcon Dam	4,378	3	Amarillo Intl Arpt	1,426
4	Rio Grande City 1 SE	4,318	4	Morton	1,496
5	McAllen	*4,264*	5	Boys Ranch	1,518
6	McCook	4,193	6	Valentine	1,599
6	Weslaco 2 E	4,193	7	Marathon	*1,616*
8	Brownsville Intl Arpt	4,131	8	Canyon	1,623
9	Raymondville	4,058	9	Borger	1,625
10	Harlingen	4,042	10	Clarendon	1,707
11	Port Isabel	3,969	11	Crosbyton	1,747
12	Castolon	3,933	12	Brownfield 2	1,751
13	Crystal City	3,875	13	Lubbock Regional Arpt	1,887
14	Falfurrias	3,844	14	Dell City 5 SSW	1,920
15	Alice	*3,800*	15	Fort Hancock 5 SSE	*2,045*
16	Encinal	*3,759*	16	Balmorhea	2,150
17	Carrizo Springs	3,688	17	Childress Municipal Arpt	2,165
18	Robstown	3,675	18	Emory	*2,205*
19	Boquillas Ranger Stn	*3,641*	19	Ozona 1 SSW	2,214
20	Corpus Christi Intl Arpt	3,593	20	Dublin	2,220
21	Port Mansfield	*3,521*	21	Wright Patman Dam & Lock	2,221
22	Charlotte 5 NNW	3,513	22	La Tuna 1 S	2,245
23	Langtry	3,494	23	Henrietta	*2,291*
24	Del Rio Intl Arpt	3,443	24	Gail	*2,294*
25	Amistad Dam	3,367	25	Water Valley	2,295

Annual Precipitation

	Highest			Lowest	
Rank	Station Name	Inches	Rank	Station Name	Inches
1	Liberty	61.82	1	La Tuna 1 S	9.20
2	Port Arthur Jefferson County	60.92	2	Fort Hancock 5 SSE	9.25
3	Sam Rayburn Dam	60.52	3	Boquillas Ranger Stn	*9.68*
4	Baytown	60.01	4	El Paso Intl Arpt	9.72
5	Beaumont Research Ctr	59.32	5	Dell City 5 SSW	10.62
6	Angleton 2 W	57.01	6	Castolon	10.68
7	Anahuac	56.94	7	Balmorhea	13.45
8	Cleveland	54.28	8	Valentine	13.48
9	Houston William P Hobby Arpt	53.66	9	Candelaria	13.75
10	Texarkana	52.17	10	Penwell	13.83
11	Carthage	51.36	11	Grandfalls 3 SSE	*14.38*
12	Bay City Waterworks	50.29	12	Langtry	14.56
13	Marshall	50.28	13	Marathon	14.66
14	Longview 11 SE	49.88	13	Midland Regional Air Terminal	14.66
15	Houston Bush Intercontinental	49.64	15	Bakersfield	14.84
16	Sugar Land	49.17	16	Alpine	*17.29*
17	Henderson	49.07	17	Hart	*18.09*
18	Conroe	48.63	18	Amistad Dam	18.33
19	Wright Patman Dam & Lock	48.51	19	Del Rio Intl Arpt	18.38
20	Thompsons 3 WSW	47.71	20	Ozona 1 SSW	18.55
21	Tyler	*47.66*	21	Lubbock Regional Arpt	18.74
22	Daingerfield 9 S	46.59	22	Boys Ranch	19.00
23	Crockett	45.31	22	Brownfield 2	19.00
24	Pilot Point	*45.26*	24	Morton	19.11
25	Brenham	45.08	25	Gail	19.43

Rankings include 25 highest/lowest stations. If state has less than 25 stations, all stations are included. The period of record is 1980–2009. See User Guide for detailed explanation of data.

Annual Extreme Maximum Daily Precipitation

	Highest			Lowest	
Rank	Station Name	Inches	Rank	Station Name	Inches
1	Bay City Waterworks	20.85	1	Boquillas Ranger Stn	*2.14*
2	Liberty	18.50	2	Dell City 5 SSW	2.44
3	New Braunfels	*18.35*	3	El Paso Intl Arpt	2.84
4	San Marcos	15.78	4	Marathon	2.96
5	Baytown	15.74	5	Valentine	3.06
6	Somerville Dam	15.25	6	Balmorhea	*3.23*
7	Beaumont Research Ctr	15.21	7	Candelaria	3.43
8	Sam Rayburn Dam	14.00	8	Midland Regional Air Terminal	3.59
9	Anahuac	13.20	9	Penwell	*3.63*
10	Cleveland	13.17	10	Fort Hancock 5 SSE	3.70
11	Angleton 2 W	12.36	11	Hart	*3.75*
12	Port Arthur Jefferson County	11.80	12	Alpine	*3.92*
13	San Antonio Intl Arpt	11.26	13	Castolon	3.95
14	Henderson	11.05	14	Morton	4.10
15	Aransas Wildlife Refuge	10.73	15	La Tuna 1 S	*4.25*
16	Sugar Land	*10.60*	16	Menard	4.35
17	Brenham	10.38	17	Dimmitt 2 N	4.38
18	Houston Bush Intercontinental	10.34	18	Dallas-Fort Worth Intl Arpt	4.39
19	Victoria Regional Arpt	9.87	19	Crystal City	4.44
20	Corpus Christi Intl Arpt	9.85	20	Boys Ranch	4.50
21	Harlingen	9.79	21	Gail	4.52
22	Thompsons 3 WSW	*9.53*	22	Ozona 1 SSW	4.72
23	Houston William P Hobby Arpt	9.48	23	Amarillo Intl Arpt	4.92
24	McAllen Miller Intl Arpt	*9.42*	24	Brownfield 2	5.05
25	Carthage	9.25	25	Big Spring	*5.09*

Number of Days Annually With ≥ 0.1 Inches of Precipitation

	Highest			Lowest	
Rank	Station Name	Days	Rank	Station Name	Days
1	Sam Rayburn Dam	73	1	La Tuna 1 S	20
2	Baytown	72	2	Penwell	22
3	Beaumont Research Ctr	71	3	Boquillas Ranger Stn	*23*
3	Cleveland	71	3	Castolon	23
3	Liberty	71	3	Dell City 5 SSW	23
3	Port Arthur Jefferson County	71	6	Encinal	*24*
7	Anahuac	69	6	Fort Hancock 5 SSE	24
8	Angleton 2 W	68	8	El Paso Intl Arpt	25
8	Texarkana	68	9	Langtry	27
10	Marshall	67	10	Balmorhea	28
10	Wright Patman Dam & Lock	67	10	Marathon	28
12	Henderson	66	12	Bakersfield	29
12	Houston William P Hobby Arpt	66	12	Candelaria	29
12	Longview 11 SE	66	12	Del Rio Intl Arpt	29
15	Pilot Point	*65*	12	Grandfalls 3 SSE	*29*
15	Tyler	*65*	12	Midland Regional Air Terminal	29
17	Columbus	64	12	Valentine	29
18	Carthage	63	18	Carrizo Springs	30
18	Houston Bush Intercontinental	63	19	Amistad Dam	31
20	Bay City Waterworks	62	19	Big Spring	31
20	Brenham	62	19	Laredo 2	31
20	Conroe	62	22	Crystal City	32
20	Daingerfield 9 S	62	22	Falcon Dam	32
24	Crockett	61	22	McAllen	*32*
25	Thompsons 3 WSW	60	22	McCook	32

Rankings include 25 highest/lowest stations. If state has less than 25 stations, all stations are included. The period of record is 1980–2009. See User Guide for detailed explanation of data.

Number of Days Annually With ≥ 0.5 Inches of Precipitation

Highest			Lowest		
Rank	Station Name	Days	Rank	Station Name	Days
1	Sam Rayburn Dam	39	1	Fort Hancock 5 SSE	3
2	Baytown	35	2	Dell City 5 SSW	4
2	Liberty	35	2	El Paso Intl Arpt	4
2	Port Arthur Jefferson County	35	4	La Tuna 1 S	5
2	Texarkana	35	5	Boquillas Ranger Stn	6
6	Angleton 2 W	34	5	Castolon	6
6	Beaumont Research Ctr	34	5	Penwell	6
8	Anahuac	33	5	Valentine	6
8	Cleveland	33	9	Candelaria	7
8	Houston William P Hobby Arpt	33	9	Marathon	7
8	Marshall	33	9	Midland Regional Air Terminal	7
8	Wright Patman Dam & Lock	33	12	Balmorhea	8
13	Carthage	32	12	Grandfalls 3 SSE	8
13	Henderson	32	14	Bakersfield	9
13	Longview 11 SE	32	14	Falcon Dam	9
16	Daingerfield 9 S	31	14	Langtry	9
17	Emory	30	17	Alpine	10
17	Pilot Point	30	17	Del Rio Intl Arpt	10
17	Tyler	30	19	Canyon	11
20	Brenham	29	19	Carrizo Springs	11
20	Centerville	29	19	Lubbock Regional Arpt	11
20	Conroe	29	19	McCook	11
20	Crockett	29	19	Morton	11
20	Houston Bush Intercontinental	29	24	Amistad Dam	12
25	Bay City Waterworks	28	24	Boys Ranch	12

Number of Days Annually With ≥ 1.0 Inches of Precipitation

Highest			Lowest		
Rank	Station Name	Days	Rank	Station Name	Days
1	Beaumont Research Ctr	19	1	Boquillas Ranger Stn	0
1	Port Arthur Jefferson County	19	1	Candelaria	0
1	Sam Rayburn Dam	19	1	Castolon	0
4	Anahuac	18	1	Dell City 5 SSW	0
4	Liberty	18	1	El Paso Intl Arpt	0
4	Longview 11 SE	18	1	Fort Hancock 5 SSE	0
4	Marshall	18	1	La Tuna 1 S	0
8	Angleton 2 W	17	8	Balmorhea	2
8	Athens	17	8	Penwell	2
8	Baytown	17	8	Valentine	2
8	Carthage	17	11	Amarillo Intl Arpt	3
8	Texarkana	17	11	Bakersfield	3
13	Cleveland	16	11	Grandfalls 3 SSE	3
13	Henderson	16	11	Lubbock Regional Arpt	3
13	Houston William P Hobby Arpt	16	15	Alpine	4
16	Bay City Waterworks	15	15	Borger	4
16	Brenham	15	15	Carrizo Springs	4
16	Columbus	15	15	Crystal City	4
16	Conroe	15	15	Hart	4
16	Daingerfield 9 S	15	15	Langtry	4
16	Emory	15	15	Marathon	4
16	Houston Bush Intercontinental	15	15	McCook	4
16	Pilot Point	15	15	Midland Regional Air Terminal	4
16	Sugar Land	15	24	Abilene Municipal Arpt	5
16	Tyler	15	24	Amistad Dam	5

Rankings include 25 highest/lowest stations. If state has less than 25 stations, all stations are included. The period of record is 1980–2009. See User Guide for detailed explanation of data.

Annual Snowfall

	Highest			Lowest	
Rank	Station Name	Inches	Rank	Station Name	Inches
1	Borger	21.6	1	Bay City Waterworks	0.0
2	Amarillo Intl Arpt	17.8	1	Baytown	0.0
3	Dimmitt 2 N	10.9	1	Carrizo Springs	0.0
4	Boys Ranch	10.5	1	Falcon Dam	0.0
4	Canyon	10.5	1	Falfurrias	0.0
6	Lubbock Regional Arpt	8.7	1	Weslaco 2 E	0.0
7	Morton	8.6	7	Anahuac	Trace
8	Crosbyton	7.0	7	Angleton 2 W	Trace
9	Clarendon	6.3	7	Beaumont Research Ctr	Trace
10	Brownfield 2	6.2	7	Boquillas Ranger Stn	*Trace*
11	Abilene Municipal Arpt	*5.2*	7	Brownsville Intl Arpt	*Trace*
11	Midland Regional Air Terminal	5.2	7	Cameron	Trace
13	Anson	*4.6*	7	Charlotte 5 NNW	Trace
14	Wichita Falls Municipal Arpt	*4.2*	7	Columbus	Trace
15	Hart	*3.7*	7	Conroe	Trace
16	Albany	*2.8*	7	Georgetown Lake	Trace
17	San Angelo Mathis Field	*2.4*	7	Granger Dam	Trace
18	Big Spring	*2.1*	7	La Tuna 1 S	Trace
18	Coleman	2.1	7	Laredo 2	Trace
20	Grandfalls 3 SSE	*1.9*	7	Sam Rayburn Dam	Trace
21	Bridgeport	1.8	7	Somerville Dam	Trace
21	Water Valley	1.8	7	Stillhouse Hollow Dam	Trace
23	Balmorhea	1.7	7	Sugar Land	Trace
23	Valentine	1.7	24	Brady	0.1
25	Bakersfield	1.6	24	Brenham	0.1

Annual Maximum Snow Depth

	Highest			Lowest	
Rank	Station Name	Inches	Rank	Station Name	Inches
1	Borger	17	1	Alice	*0*
1	Dimmitt 2 N	17	1	Baytown	0
1	Lubbock Regional Arpt	17	1	Burnet	0
4	Canyon	16	1	Dell City 5 SSW	0
5	Amarillo Intl Arpt	15	1	Falcon Dam	0
6	Boys Ranch	14	1	Falfurrias	0
6	Clarendon	14	1	McGregor	0
8	Brownfield 2	*12*	1	Weslaco 2 E	0
8	Whitney Dam	12	9	Anahuac	Trace
10	Boerne	11	9	Angleton 2 W	Trace
11	Blanco	10	9	Aransas Wildlife Refuge	Trace
11	Camp Wood	*10*	9	Bardwell Dam	Trace
11	Wichita Falls Municipal Arpt	*10*	9	Brownsville Intl Arpt	Trace
14	San Antonio Intl Arpt	9	9	Cameron	Trace
15	Anson	*8*	9	Candelaria	Trace
15	Balmorhea	*8*	9	Carrizo Springs	Trace
15	Bay City Waterworks	8	9	Centerville	Trace
15	Dripping Springs 6 E	*8*	9	Columbus	Trace
15	Longview 11 SE	8	9	Crockett	Trace
15	Midland Regional Air Terminal	8	9	Floresville	Trace
15	Texarkana	8	9	Granger Dam	Trace
15	Valentine	8	9	Houston Bush Intercontinental	Trace
23	Albany	*7*	9	La Tuna 1 S	Trace
23	Big Spring	*7*	9	Langtry	Trace
23	Charlotte 5 NNW	7	9	Liberty	Trace

Rankings include 25 highest/lowest stations. If state has less than 25 stations, all stations are included. The period of record is 1980–2009. See User Guide for detailed explanation of data.

Number of Days Annually With ≥ 1.0 Inch Snow Depth

	Highest			Lowest	
Rank	Station Name	Days	Rank	Station Name	Days
1	Amarillo Intl Arpt	12	1	Albany	0
2	Borger	10	1	Alice	0
3	Dimmitt 2 N	7	1	Alpine	0
4	Lubbock Regional Arpt	6	1	Amistad Dam	0
5	Abilene Municipal Arpt	3	1	Anahuac	0
5	Canyon	3	1	Angleton 2 W	0
5	Clarendon	3	1	Aransas Wildlife Refuge	0
8	Anson	2	1	Athens	0
8	Boys Ranch	2	1	Austin Municipal Arpt	0
8	Brownfield 2	2	1	Bakersfield	0
8	McKinney 3 S	2	1	Ballinger 2 NW	0
8	Wichita Falls Municipal Arpt	2	1	Balmorhea	0
13	Longview 11 SE	1	1	Bardwell Dam	0
13	Midland Regional Air Terminal	1	1	Bay City Waterworks	0
13	San Angelo Mathis Field	1	1	Baytown	0
13	Texarkana	1	1	Beaumont Research Ctr	0
17	Albany	0	1	Benbrook Dam	0
17	Alice	0	1	Big Spring	0
17	Alpine	0	1	Blanco	0
17	Amistad Dam	0	1	Boerne	0
17	Anahuac	0	1	Boquillas Ranger Stn	0
17	Angleton 2 W	0	1	Brady	0
17	Aransas Wildlife Refuge	0	1	Brenham	0
17	Athens	0	1	Bridgeport	0
17	Austin Municipal Arpt	0	1	Brownsville Intl Arpt	0

Significant Storm Events in Texas: 2000 – 2009

Location or County	Date	Type	Mag.	Deaths	Injuries	Property Damage ($mil.)	Crop Damage ($mil.)
Tarrant	03/28/00	Tornado	F3	2	80	0.0	0.0
North Texas	07/01/00	Excessive Heat	na	8	0	0.0	0.0
Southeast Texas	07/06/00	Excessive Heat	na	19	0	0.0	0.0
North Texas	08/01/00	Excessive Heat	na	5	0	0.0	0.0
North Texas	09/01/00	Excessive Heat	na	5	0	0.0	0.0
Southeast Texas	09/01/00	Excessive Heat	na	5	0	0.0	0.0
Northeast Texas	12/12/00	Ice Storm	na	0	0	123.0	0.0
Bexar	05/06/01	Hail	4.00 in.	0	0	120.0	30.0
Travis	05/20/01	Thunderstorm Wind	na	0	10	2.0	0.1
Galveston Island	06/05/01	Tropical Storm	na	22	0	5,150.0	0.0
Medina	10/12/01	Tornado	F2	0	25	20.0	0.0
Travis	11/15/01	Flash Flood	na	2	50	0.5	0.0
Williamson	11/15/01	Flash Flood	na	2	10	0.5	0.0
Blanco	11/15/01	Flash Flood	na	1	10	0.1	0.0
Llano	11/15/01	Flash Flood	na	1	20	0.1	0.0
Bexar	03/19/02	Tornado	F2	0	30	2.0	0.0
Bexar	03/19/02	Thunderstorm Wind	na	0	10	2.0	0.1
Nueces	10/24/02	Tornado	F2	1	20	75.0	0.0
Cameron	04/08/03	Hail	2.75 in.	0	5	50.0	0.0
Hidalgo	04/30/03	Tornado	F1	0	11	1.5	0.0
Houston	09/14/04	Lightning	na	1	40	0.0	0.0
Travis	03/25/05	Hail	2.00 in.	0	0	100.0	0.0
Chambers, Harris, Houston, and Montgomery Counties	09/21/05	Excessive Heat	na	49	0	0.0	0.0
Southeast Texas	09/23/05	Hurricane Rita	na	1	0	2,090.0	0.0
Extreme Southeast Texas	09/23/05	Hurricane Rita	na	3	3	159.5	0.0
Central Texas	12/01/05	Drought	na	0	0	50.0	0.0
Texas Panhandle Region	12/17/05	Winter Weather/Mix	na	5	15	0.1	0.0
Cross Plains	12/27/05	Wildfire	na	2	16	11.0	0.0
Cooke, Hood and Tarrant Counties	12/27/05	Wildfire	na	1	10	5.8	0.0
Carson and Gray County	03/12/06	Wildfire	na	12	8	49.9	45.4
Northwest Texas	04/01/06	Drought	na	0	0	100.0	0.0
Hays	04/20/06	Hail	4.25 in.	0	1	100.0	0.0
El Paso	08/01/06	Flash Flood	na	0	0	180.0	0.0
Johnson	12/29/06	Tornado	F2	0	12	2.0	0.0
Limestone	12/29/06	Tornado	F2	1	20	1.0	0.0
Moore	04/21/07	Tornado	F2	0	14	1.3	0.0
Maverick	04/24/07	Tornado	F3	7	0	80.0	0.0
Burnet	06/26/07	Flash Flood	na	2	0	137.0	0.0
Southwestern Jefferson County	09/13/07	Hurricane Humberto	na	0	12	25.0	0.0
Potter County	12/22/07	Winter Weather	na	1	137	1.2	0.0
Gray County	12/22/07	Winter Weather	na	1	13	0.4	0.0
Bowie	03/31/08	Hail	2.75 in.	0	0	120.0	0.0
Travis	05/14/08	Thunderstorm Wind	81 mph	0	0	50.0	0.0
Texas Gulf Coast near Galveston	09/12/08	Storm Surge/Tide	na	11	0	4,000.0	0.0
Harris and Matagorda Co.	09/12/08	Hurricane Ike	na	0	0	1,000.0	0.0
Southeast Texas	09/12/08	Hurricane Ike	na	0	0	500.0	0.0
Jefferson and Orange County	09/12/08	Storm Surge/Tide	na	0	0	500.0	0.0
Jefferson and Newton Co.	09/12/08	Hurricane Ike	na	0	0	100.0	0.0
Orange County	09/12/08	Hurricane Ike	na	0	0	75.0	0.0
Hardin County	09/12/08	Hurricane Ike	na	0	0	70.0	0.0
Southern Jasper County	09/12/08	Hurricane Ike	na	0	0	53.0	0.0
Travis	03/25/09	Hail	3.00 in.	0	0	160.0	0.0
Midland	04/11/09	Hail	2.00 in.	0	1	161.2	0.0
Harris	04/18/09	Flash Flood	na	5	0	3.5	0.0

Location or County	Date	Type	Mag.	Deaths	Injuries	Property Damage ($mil.)	Crop Damage ($mil.)
Dallas	05/02/09	Thunderstorm Wind	70 mph	0	12	5.0	0.0
Jefferson	08/18/09	Tornado	F1	0	10	20.0	0.0
El Paso	09/16/09	Hail	1.75 in.	0	10	100.0	0.0

Note: Deaths, injuries, and damages are date and location specific.

Demographic and Reference Maps

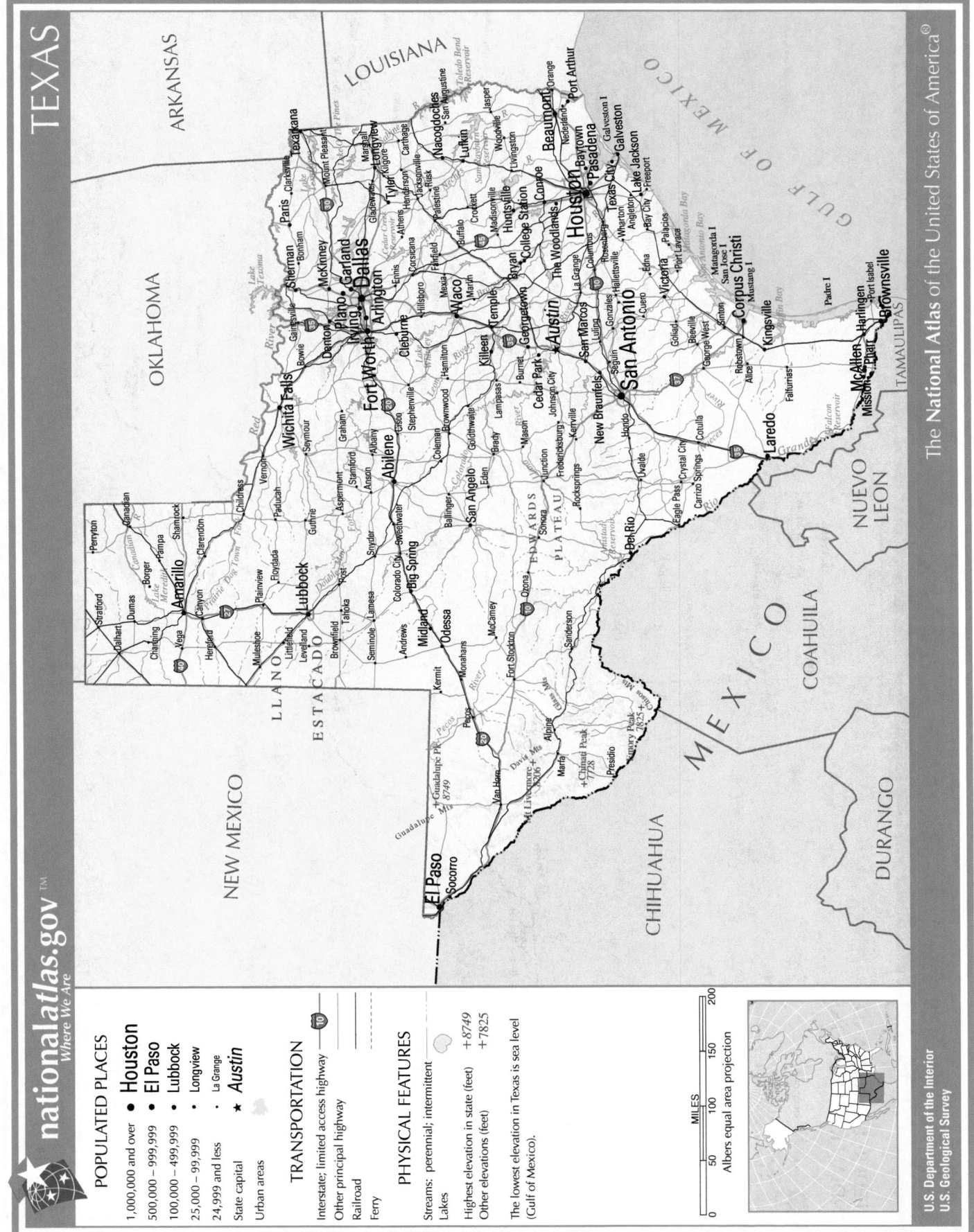

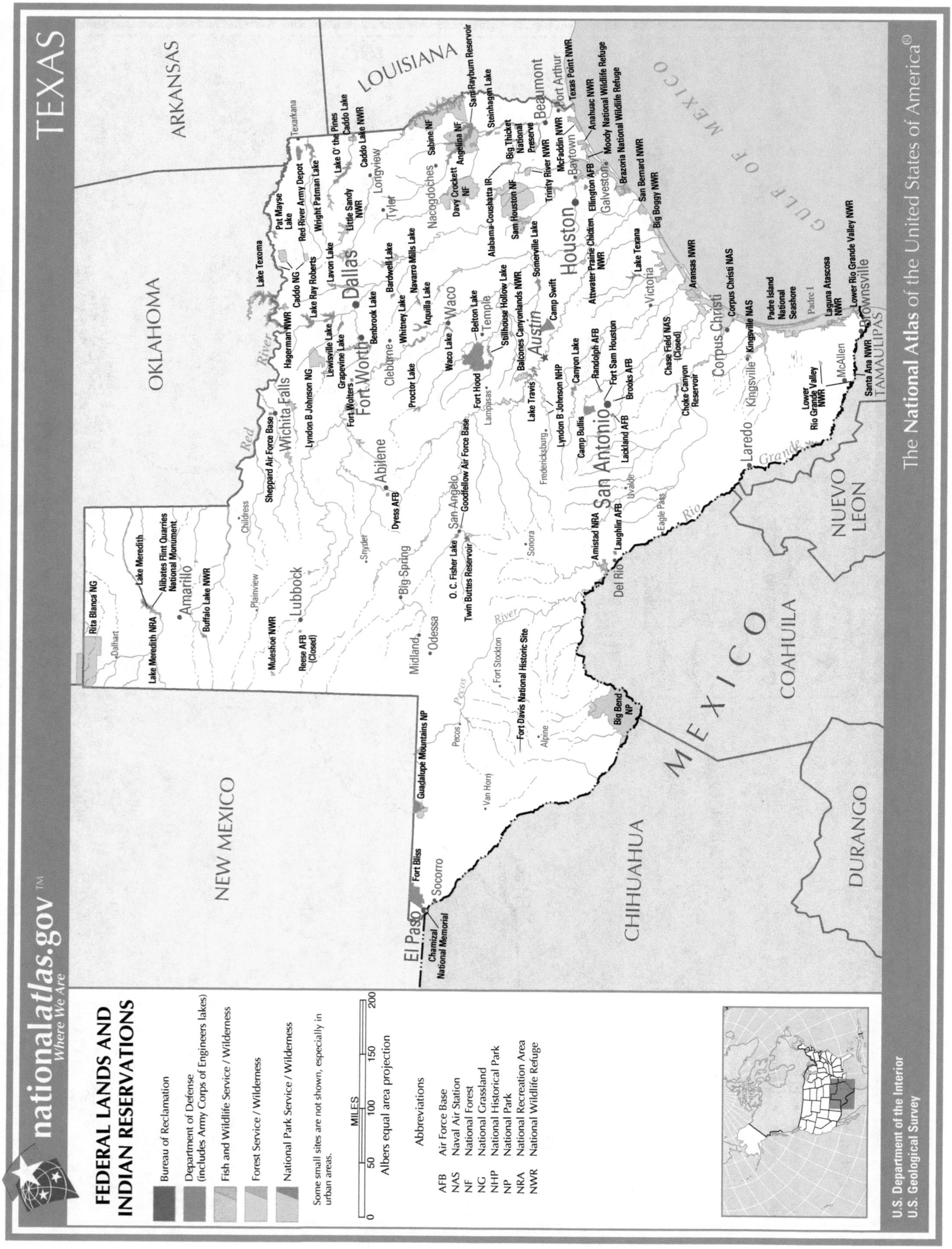

TEXAS

nationalatlas.gov ™
Where We Are

FEDERAL LANDS AND INDIAN RESERVATIONS

- Bureau of Reclamation
- Department of Defense (includes Army Corps of Engineers lakes)
- Fish and Wildlife Service / Wilderness
- Forest Service / Wilderness
- National Park Service / Wilderness

Some small sites are not shown, especially in urban areas.

MILES
0   50   100   150   200
Albers equal area projection

Abbreviations
AFB	Air Force Base
NAS	Naval Air Station
NF	National Forest
NG	National Grassland
NHP	National Historical Park
NP	National Park
NRA	National Recreation Area
NWR	National Wildlife Refuge

The **National Atlas** of the United States of America®

U.S. Department of the Interior
U.S. Geological Survey

ARKANSAS
LOUISIANA
OKLAHOMA
NEW MEXICO
MEXICO
CHIHUAHUA
COAHUILA
DURANGO
NUEVO LEON
TAMAULIPAS
GULF OF MEXICO

Dallas, Fort Worth, Houston, San Antonio, Austin, El Paso, Waco, Abilene, Lubbock, Amarillo, Odessa, Midland, Corpus Christi, Brownsville, Laredo, Beaumont, Galveston, Wichita Falls, Temple

Red River, Rio Grande, Pecos River

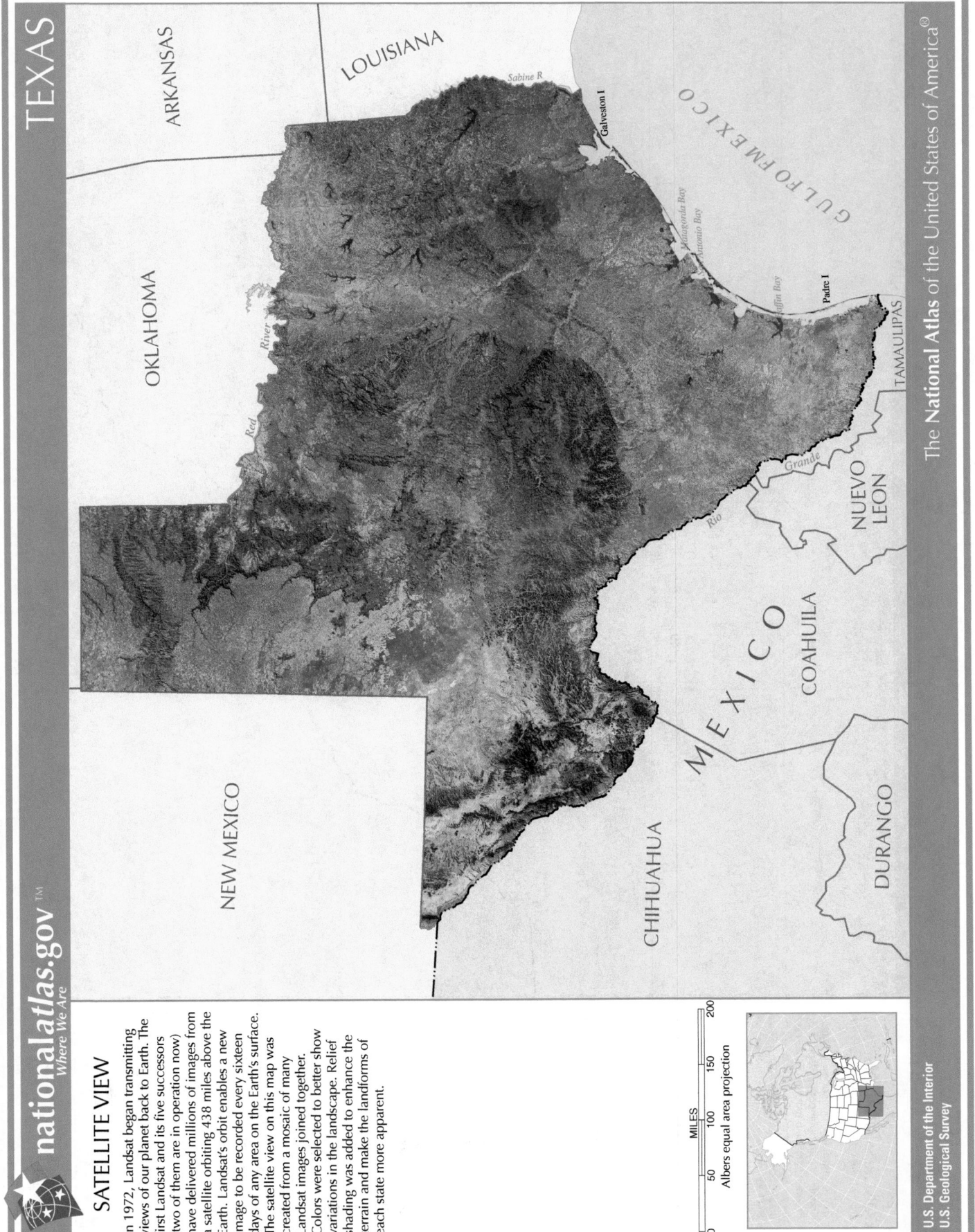

TEXAS

nationalatlas.gov ™
Where We Are

SATELLITE VIEW

In 1972, Landsat began transmitting views of our planet back to Earth. The first Landsat and its five successors (two of them are in operation now) have delivered millions of images from a satellite orbiting 438 miles above the Earth. Landsat's orbit enables a new image to be recorded every sixteen days of any area on the Earth's surface. The satellite view on this map was created from a mosaic of many Landsat images joined together. Colors were selected to better show variations in the landscape. Relief shading was added to enhance the terrain and make the landforms of each state more apparent.

MILES

0   50   100   150   200

Albers equal area projection

U.S. Department of the Interior
U.S. Geological Survey

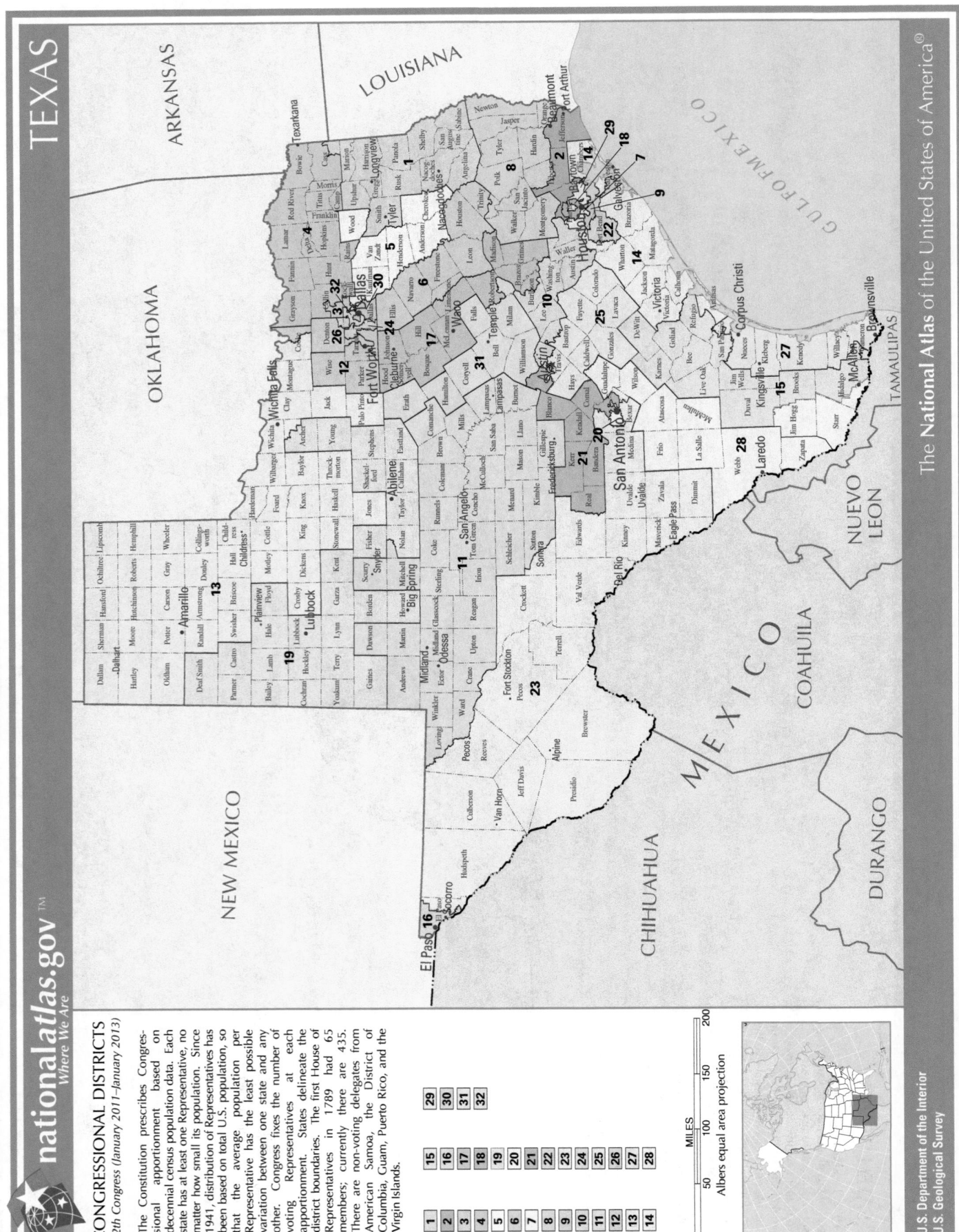

U.S. Department of the Interior
U.S. Geological Survey

The **National Atlas** of the United States of America®

TEXAS

CONGRESSIONAL DISTRICTS
112th Congress (January 2011–January 2013)

The Constitution prescribes Congressional apportionment based on decennial census population data. Each state has at least one Representative, no matter how small its population. Since 1941, distribution of Representatives has been based on total U.S. population, so that the average population per Representative has the least possible variation between one state and any other. Congress fixes the number of voting Representatives at each apportionment. States delineate the district boundaries. The first House of Representatives in 1789 had 65 members; currently there are 435. There are non-voting delegates from American Samoa, the District of Columbia, Guam, Puerto Rico, and the Virgin Islands.

nationalatlas.gov™
Where We Are

Albers equal area projection

TEXAS - Core Based Statistical Areas and Counties

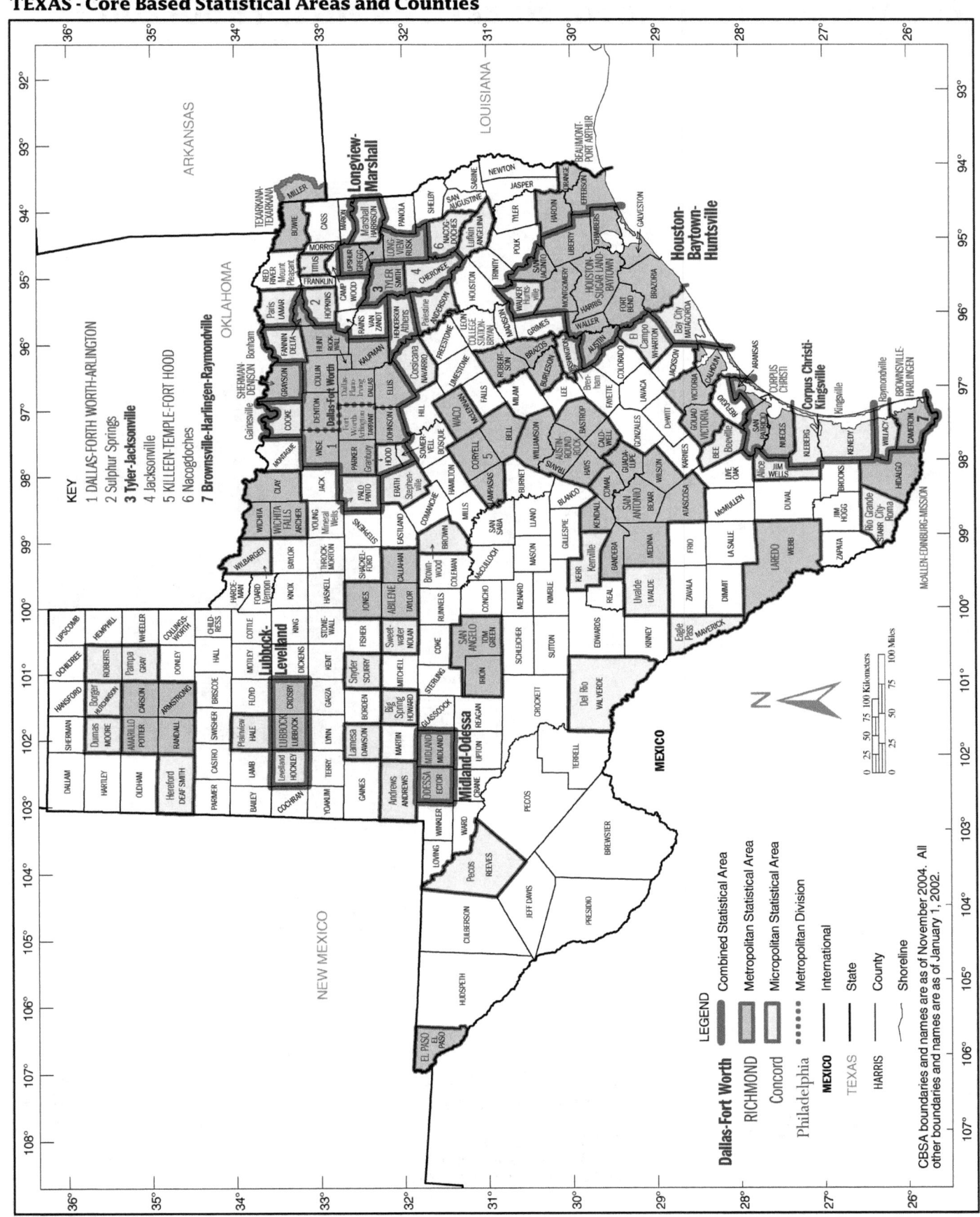

Economic Losses from Hazard Events, 1960-2009

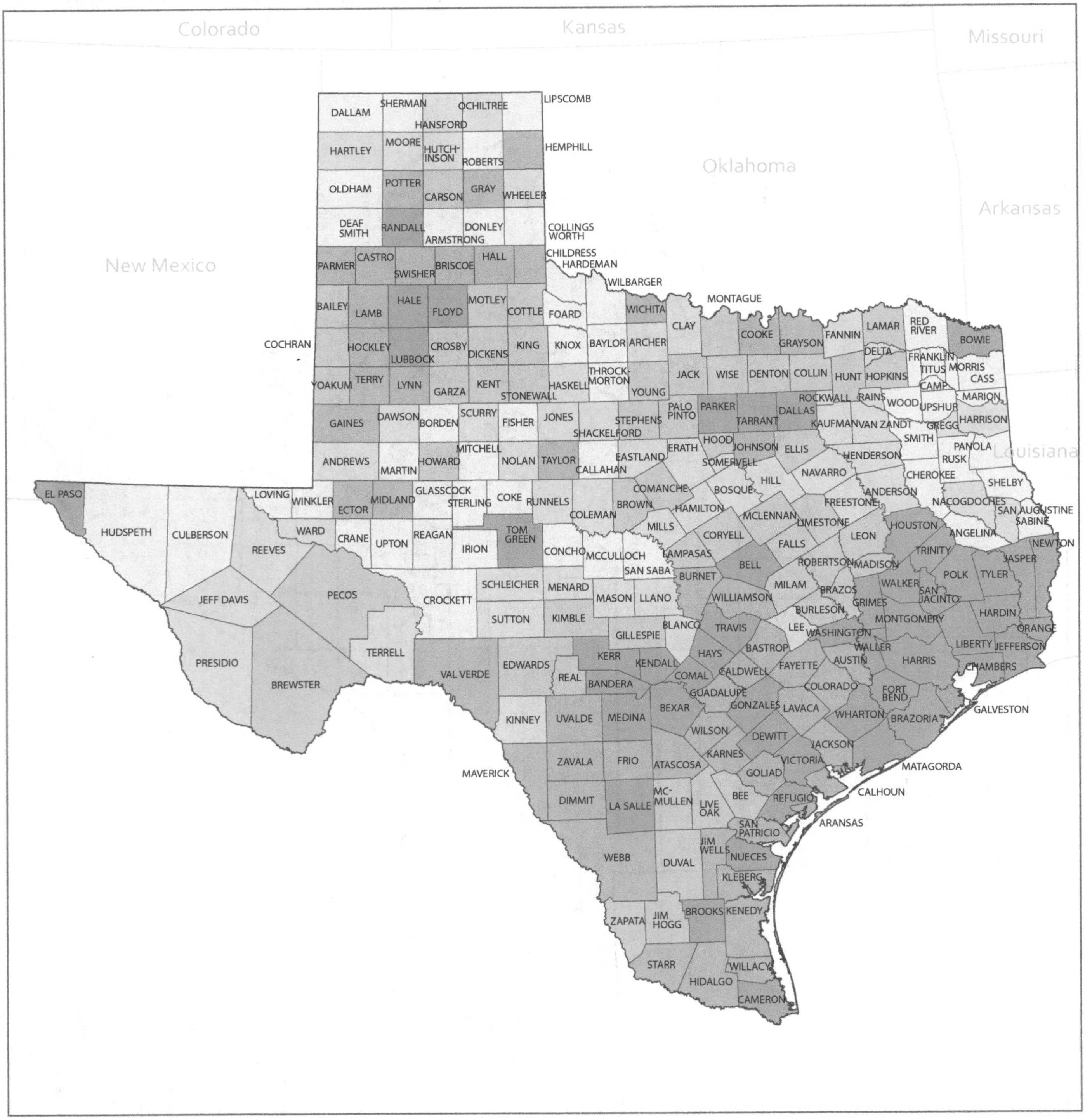

Colorado

Kansas

Missouri

Oklahoma

Arkansas

New Mexico

Louisiana

DALLAM SHERMAN OCHILTREE LIPSCOMB
HANSFORD
HARTLEY MOORE HUTCH-INSON ROBERTS HEMPHILL
OLDHAM POTTER CARSON GRAY WHEELER
DEAF SMITH RANDALL ARMSTRONG DONLEY COLLINGS WORTH
PARMER CASTRO SWISHER BRISCOE HALL CHILDRESS HARDEMAN
BAILEY LAMB HALE FLOYD MOTLEY COTTLE FOARD WILBARGER WICHITA MONTAGUE
COCHRAN HOCKLEY LUBBOCK CROSBY DICKENS KING KNOX BAYLOR ARCHER CLAY COOKE GRAYSON FANNIN LAMAR RED RIVER BOWIE
YOAKUM TERRY LYNN GARZA KENT STONEWALL HASKELL THROCK-MORTON YOUNG JACK WISE DENTON COLLIN HUNT HOPKINS DELTA FRANKLIN TITUS MORRIS CAMP CASS
GAINES DAWSON BORDEN SCURRY FISHER JONES SHACKELFORD STEPHENS PALO PINTO PARKER TARRANT DALLAS ROCKWALL KAUFMAN VAN ZANDT RAINS WOOD UPSHUR SMITH GREGG HARRISON MARION PANOLA
ANDREWS MARTIN HOWARD MITCHELL NOLAN TAYLOR CALLAHAN EASTLAND ERATH HOOD SOMERVELL JOHNSON ELLIS NAVARRO HENDERSON ANDERSON CHEROKEE RUSK SHELBY
EL PASO HUDSPETH CULBERSON LOVING WINKLER ECTOR MIDLAND GLASSCOCK STERLING COKE RUNNELS COLEMAN BROWN COMANCHE HAMILTON MILLS BOSQUE HILL MCLENNAN LIMESTONE FREESTONE LEON HOUSTON TRINITY ANGELINA NACOGDOCHES SAN AUGUSTINE SABINE NEWTON
REEVES WARD CRANE UPTON REAGAN IRION TOM GREEN CONCHO MCCULLOCH SAN SABA CORYELL FALLS ROBERTSON MADISON WALKER POLK TYLER JASPER
JEFF DAVIS PECOS CROCKETT SCHLEICHER MENARD MASON LLANO LAMPASAS BURNET BELL MILAM BRAZOS GRIMES SAN JACINTO HARDIN ORANGE
PRESIDIO TERRELL VAL VERDE EDWARDS SUTTON KIMBLE GILLESPIE BLANCO HAYS TRAVIS WILLIAMSON BURLESON LEE WASHINGTON MONTGOMERY WALLER LIBERTY JEFFERSON
BREWSTER KERR KENDALL COMAL CALDWELL BASTROP AUSTIN HARRIS CHAMBERS
REAL BANDERA GUADALUPE FAYETTE COLORADO FORT BEND GALVESTON
KINNEY UVALDE MEDINA BEXAR GONZALES LAVACA WHARTON BRAZORIA
MAVERICK ZAVALA FRIO ATASCOSA WILSON KARNES DEWITT JACKSON VICTORIA MATAGORDA
DIMMIT LA SALLE MC-MULLEN LIVE OAK BEE GOLIAD REFUGIO CALHOUN ARANSAS
WEBB DUVAL SAN PATRICIO JIM WELLS NUECES KLEBERG
ZAPATA JIM HOGG BROOKS KENEDY
STARR HIDALGO WILLACY CAMERON

TEXAS

Total Losses (Property and Crop)

- 11,881,027 - 51,015,282
- 51,015,283 - 80,607,107
- 80,607,108 - 136,887,521
- 136,887,522 - 246,224,973
- 246,224,974 - 1,799,912,260

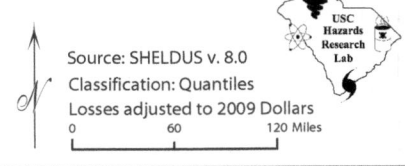

Source: SHELDUS v. 8.0
Classification: Quantiles
Losses adjusted to 2009 Dollars

0   60   120 Miles

TEXAS
Hazard Losses
1960-2009

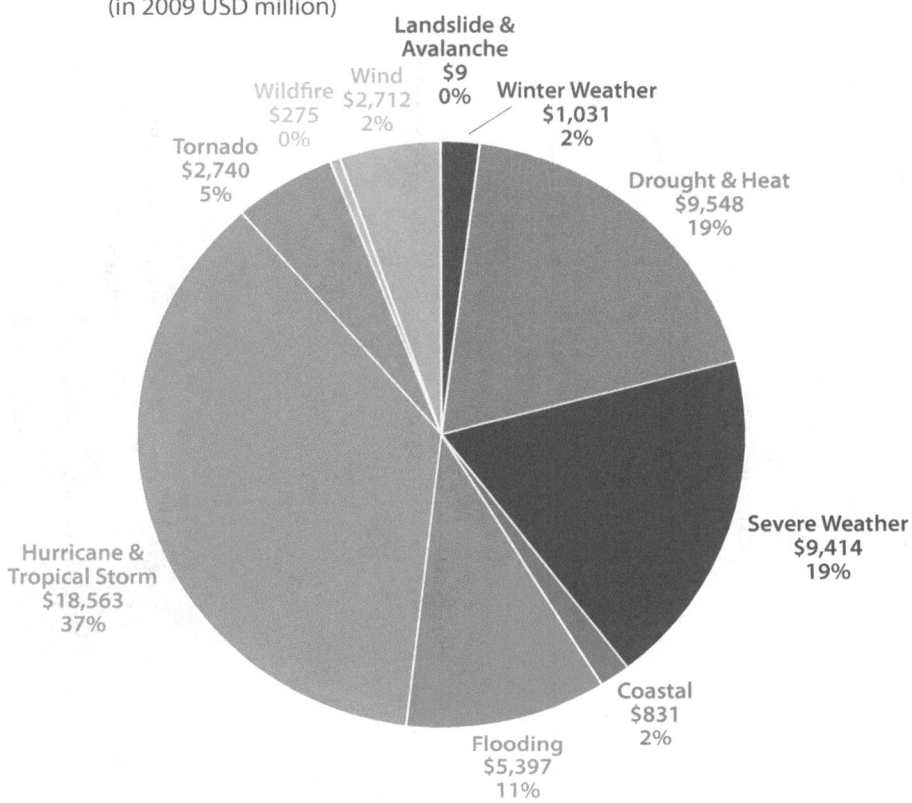

Distribution of Losses by Hazard Type
(in 2009 USD million)

- Landslide & Avalanche $9 0%
- Wind $2,712 2%
- Wildfire $275 0%
- Winter Weather $1,031 2%
- Tornado $2,740 5%
- Drought & Heat $9,548 19%
- Severe Weather $9,414 19%
- Coastal $831 2%
- Flooding $5,397 11%
- Hurricane & Tropical Storm $18,563 37%

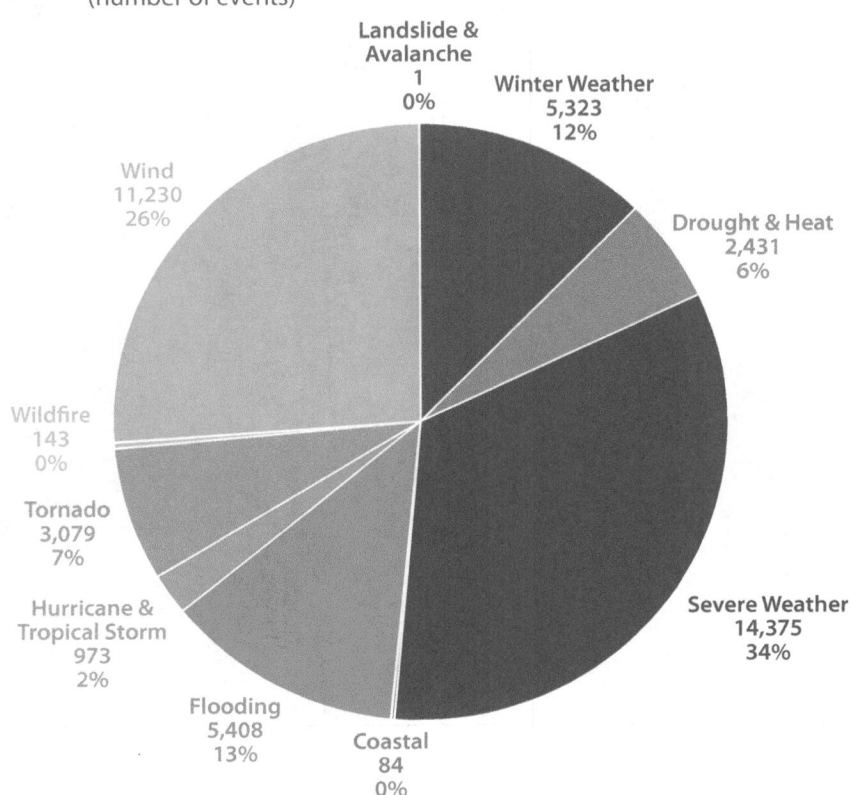

Distribution of Hazard Events
(number of events)

- Landslide & Avalanche 1 0%
- Winter Weather 5,323 12%
- Wind 11,230 26%
- Drought & Heat 2,431 6%
- Wildfire 143 0%
- Tornado 3,079 7%
- Severe Weather 14,375 34%
- Hurricane & Tropical Storm 973 2%
- Flooding 5,408 13%
- Coastal 84 0%

Population (2010)

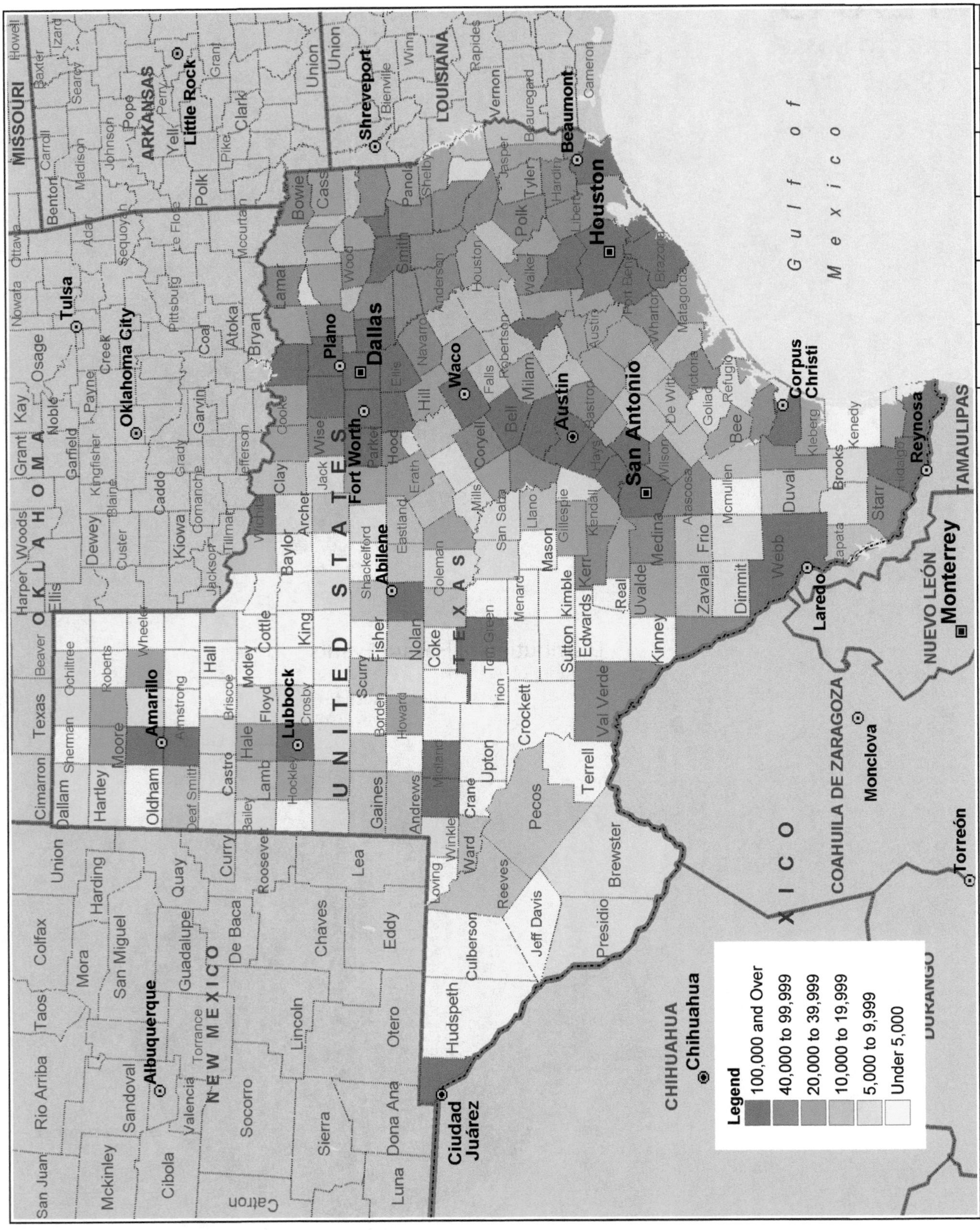

Legend
- 100,000 and Over
- 40,000 to 99,999
- 20,000 to 39,999
- 10,000 to 19,999
- 5,000 to 9,999
- Under 5,000

Percent White (2010)

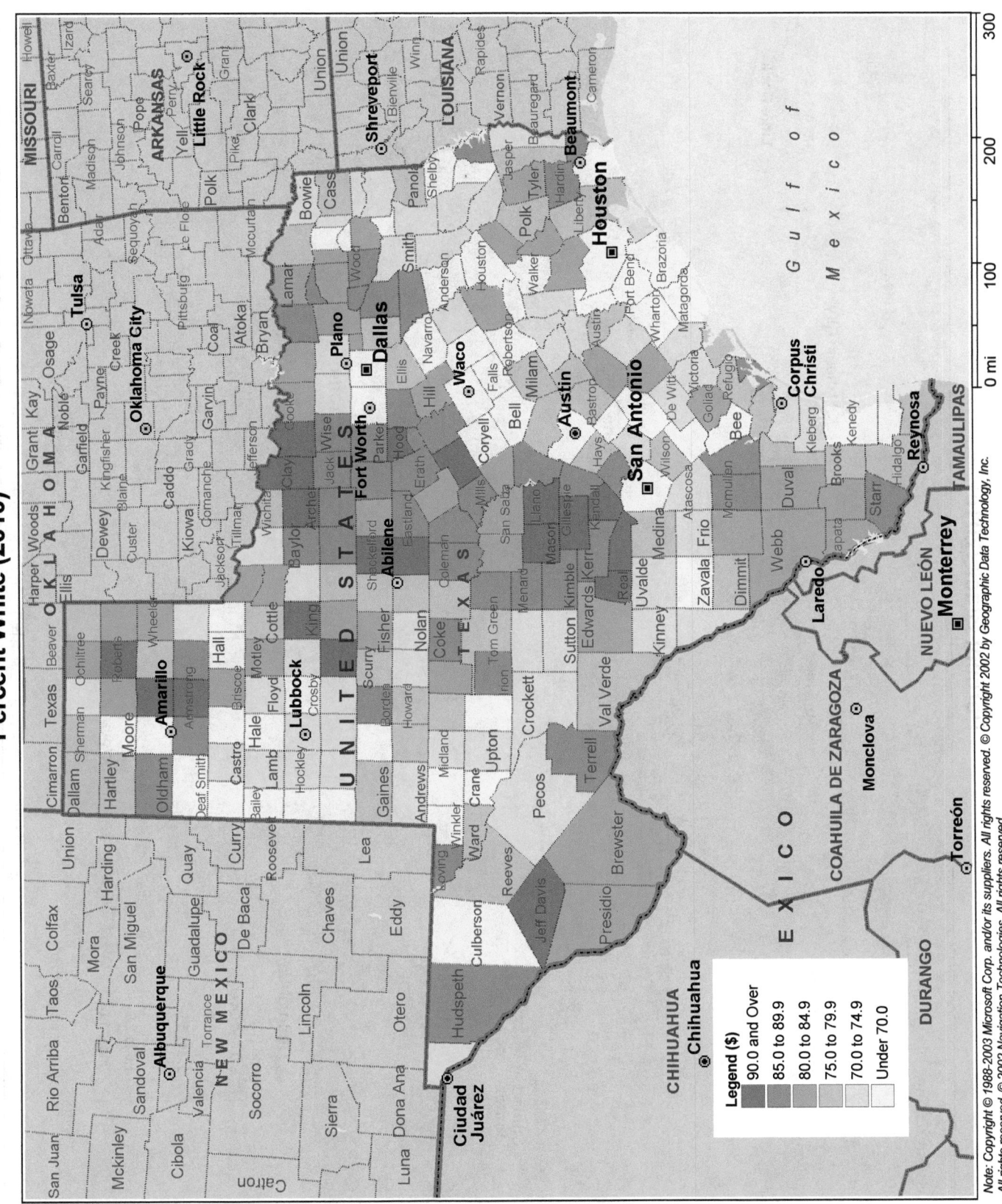

Legend ($)

- 90.0 and Over
- 85.0 to 89.9
- 80.0 to 84.9
- 75.0 to 79.9
- 70.0 to 74.9
- Under 70.0

Percent Black (2010)

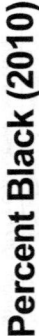

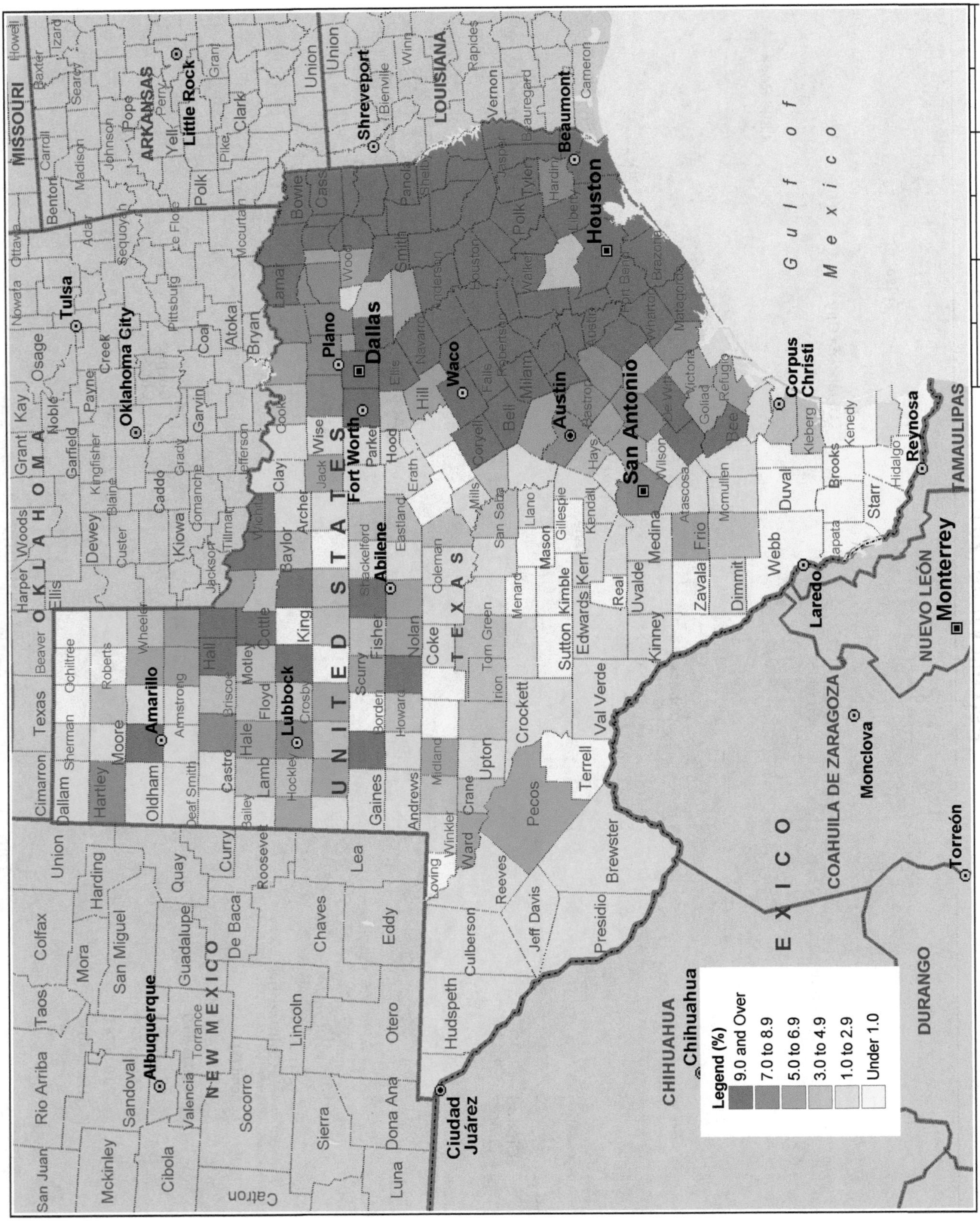

Legend (%)
- 9.0 and Over
- 7.0 to 8.9
- 5.0 to 6.9
- 3.0 to 4.9
- 1.0 to 2.9
- Under 1.0

Percent Asian (2010)

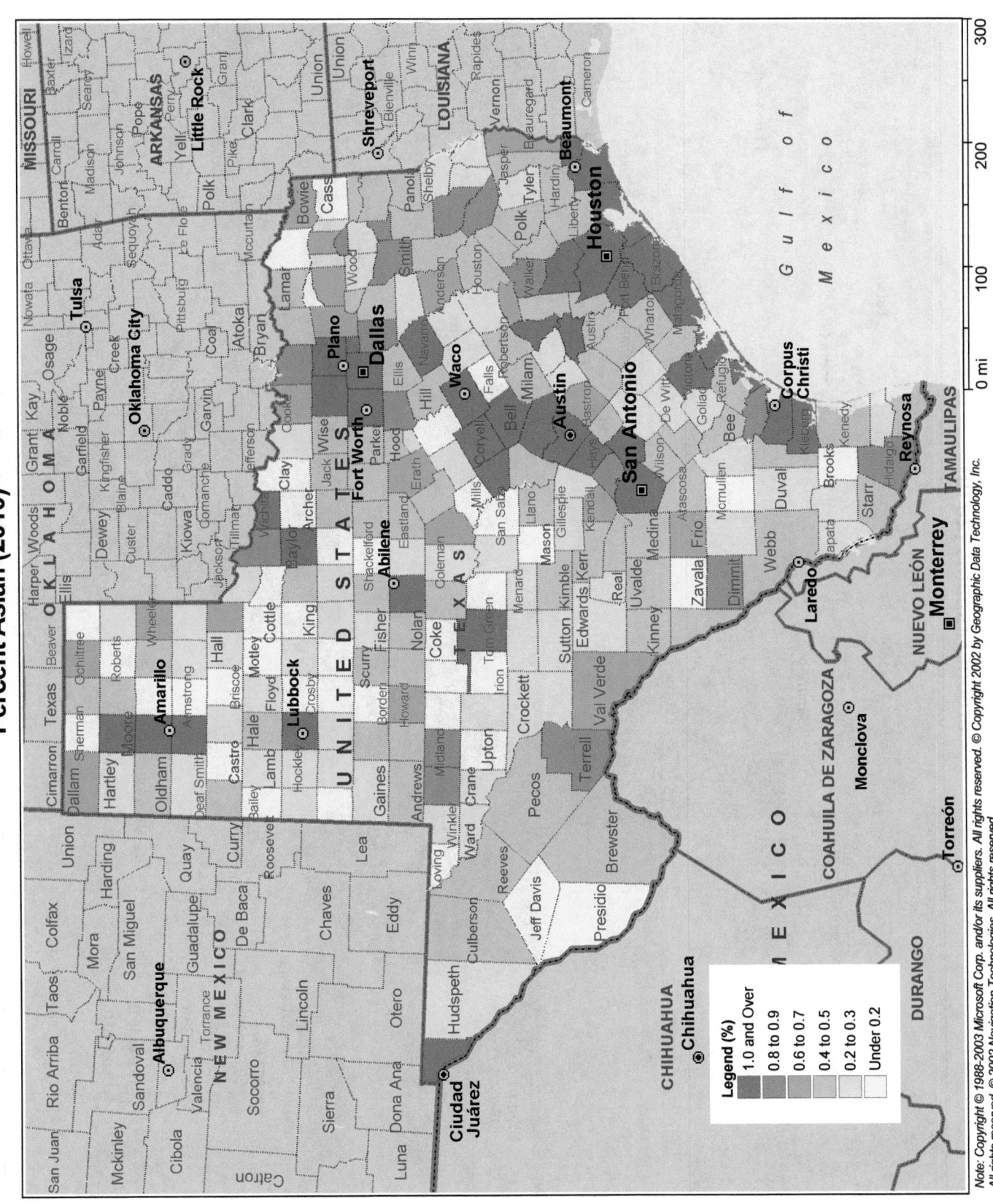

Legend (%)
- 1.0 and Over
- 0.8 to 0.9
- 0.6 to 0.7
- 0.4 to 0.5
- 0.2 to 0.3
- Under 0.2

Percent Hispanic (2010)

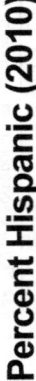

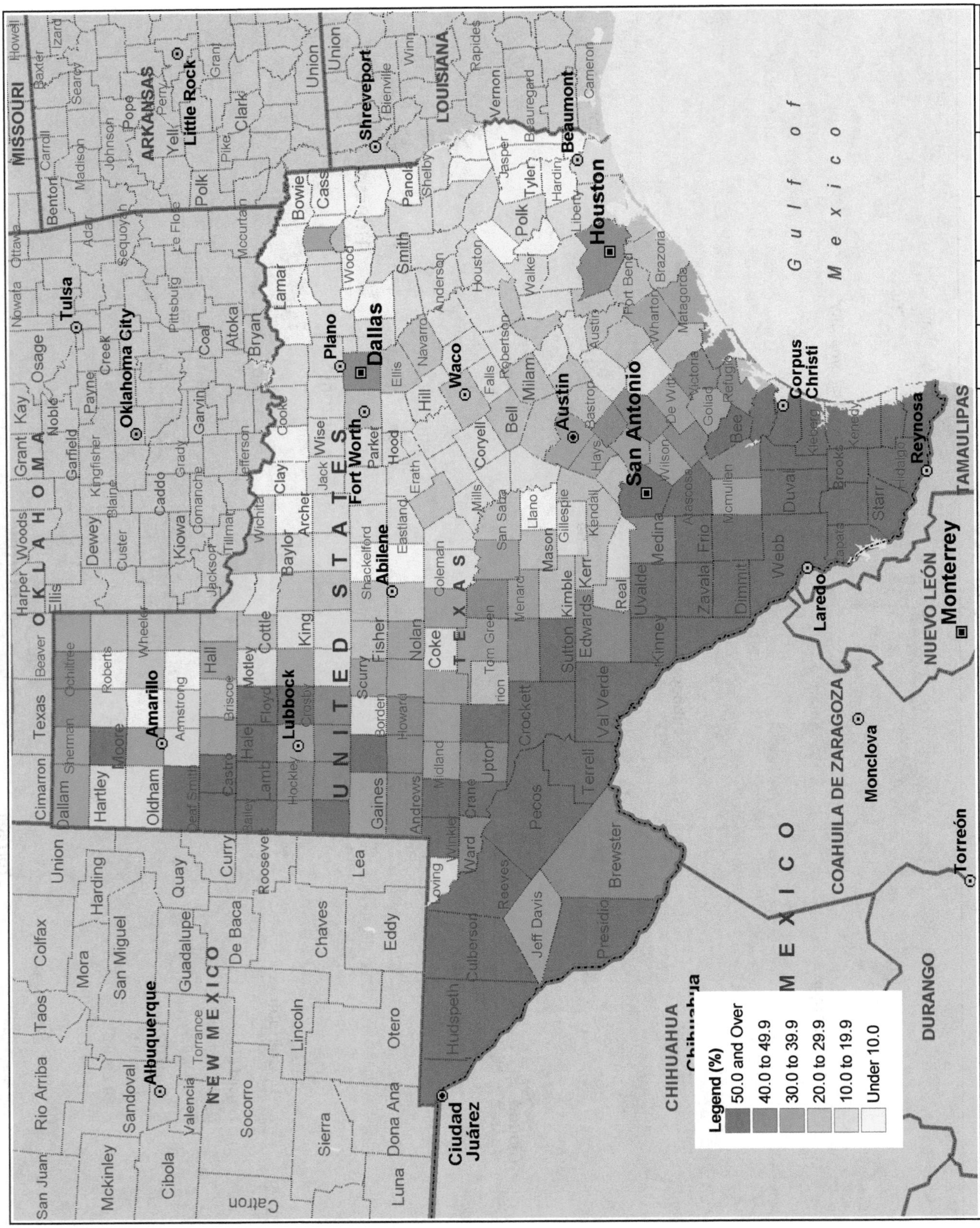

Legend (%)
- 50.0 and Over
- 40.0 to 49.9
- 30.0 to 39.9
- 20.0 to 29.9
- 10.0 to 19.9
- Under 10.0

0 mi   100   200   300

Median Age (2010)

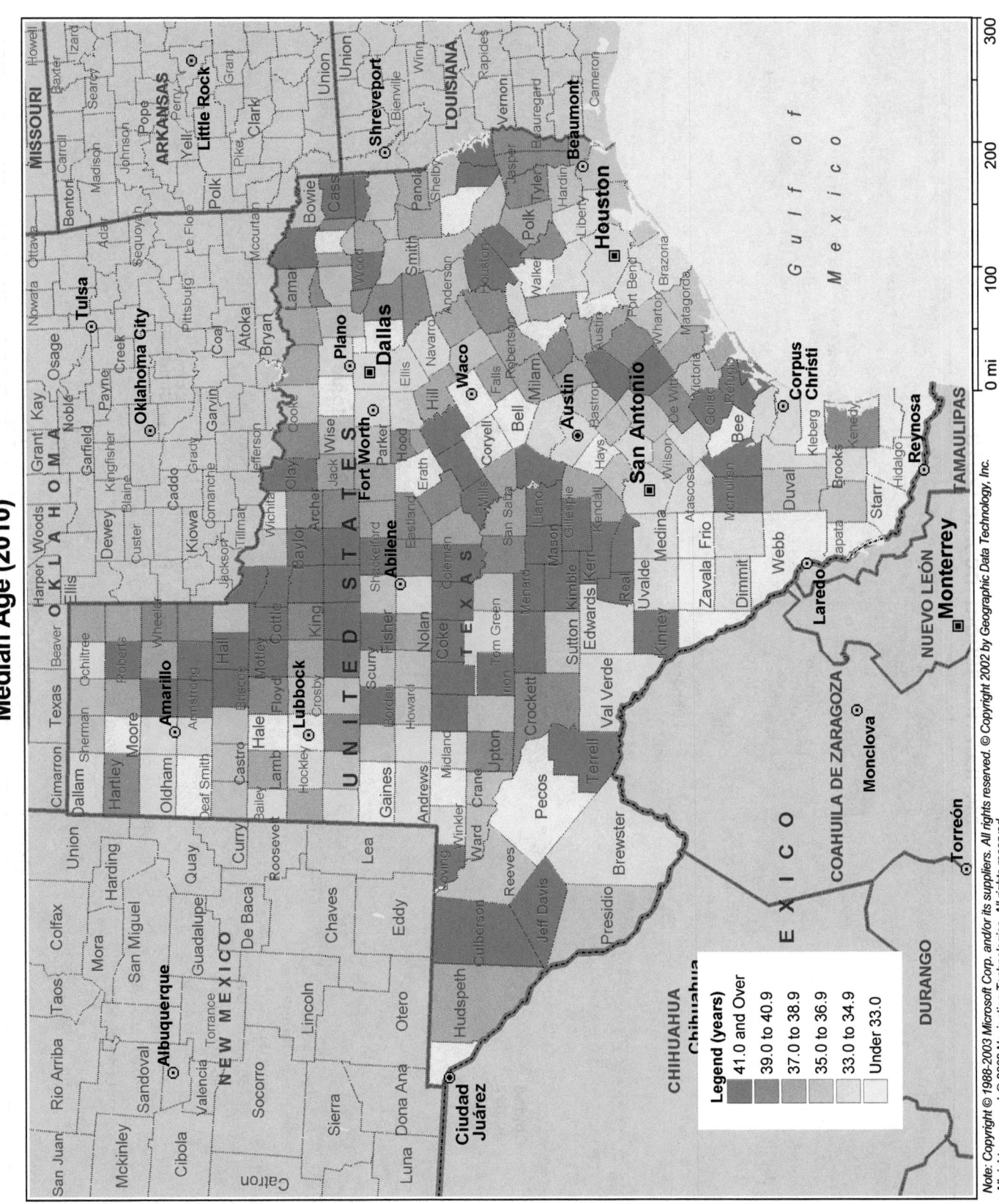

Legend (years)
- 41.0 and Over
- 39.0 to 40.9
- 37.0 to 38.9
- 35.0 to 36.9
- 33.0 to 34.9
- Under 33.0

Median Household Income (2010)

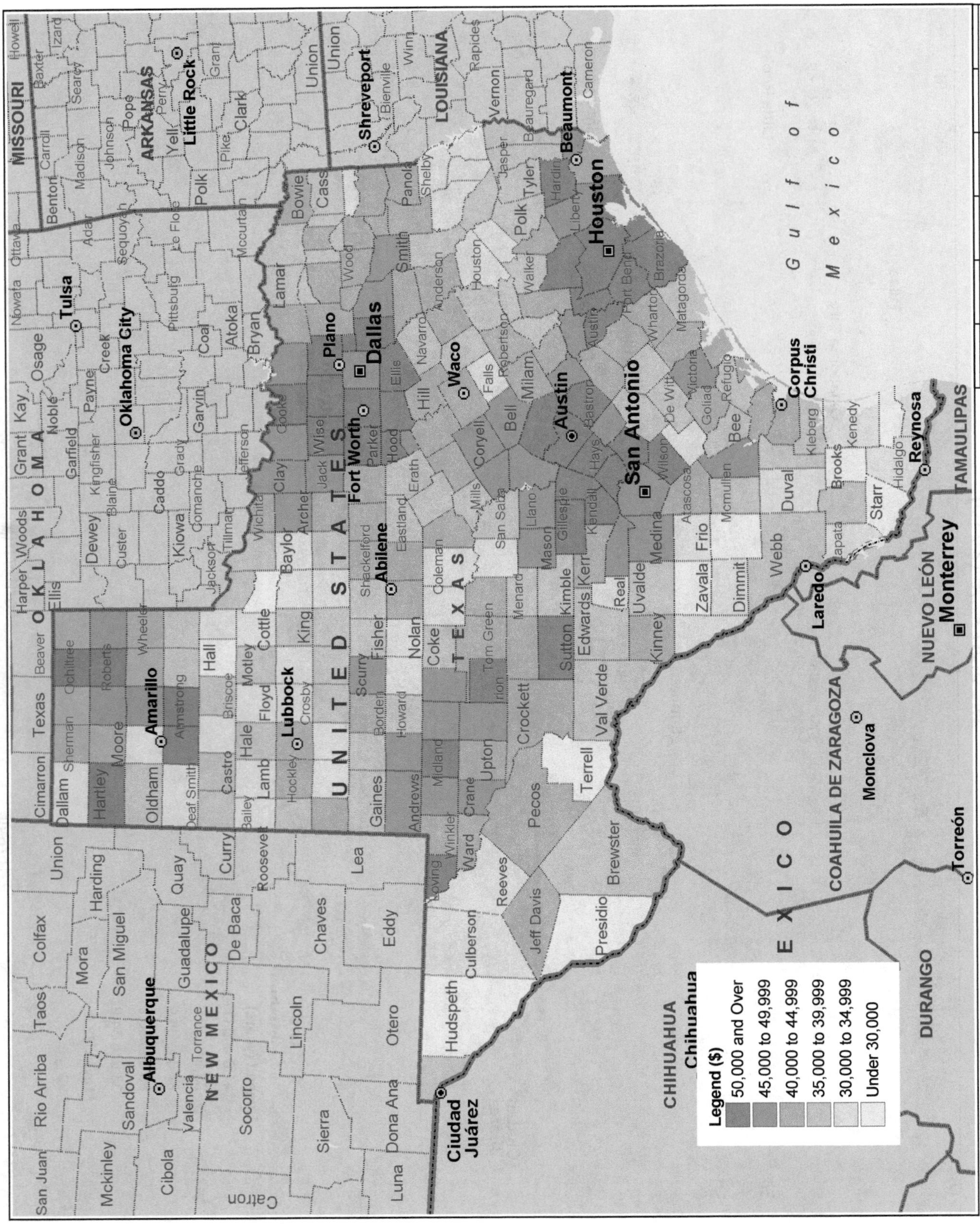

Legend ($)

- 50,000 and Over
- 45,000 to 49,999
- 40,000 to 44,999
- 35,000 to 39,999
- 30,000 to 34,999
- Under 30,000